ST/ESA/STAT/SER.G/46

DEPARTMENT OF ECONOMIC AND SOCIAL AFFAIRS
STATISTICS DIVISION

DÉPARTEMENT DES AFFAIRES ÉCONOMIQUES ET SOCIALES
DIVISION DE STATISTIQUE

1997
INTERNATIONAL TRADE STATISTICS YEARBOOK
ANNUAIRE STATISTIQUE DU COMMERCE INTERNATIONAL

VOLUME I

TRADE BY COUNTRY

COMMERCE PAR PAYS

UNITED NATIONS/NATIONS UNIES
New York, 1999

NOTE

Symbols of United Nations documents are composed of capital letters combined with figures.

General disclaimer

The designations employed and the presentation of material in this publication do not imply the expression of any opinion whatsoever on the part of the Secretariat of the United Nations concerning the legal status of any country, territory, city or area, or of its authorities, or concerning the delimitation of its frontiers or boundaries.

Where the designation "country or area" appears in this publication, it covers countries, territories, cities or areas. In previous issues of this publication, where the designation "country" appears in the headings of tables, it should be interpreted to cover countries, territories, cities or areas.

In some tables, the designation "developed" or "developing" economies is intended for statistical convenience and does not necessarily express a judgement about the stage reached by a particular country or area in the development process.

NOTE

Les cotes des documents de l'Organisation des Nations Unies se composent de lettres majuscules et de chiffres.

Déni de responsabilité

Les appellations employées dans cette publication et la présentation des données qui y figurent n'impliquent de la part du Secrétariat de l'Organisation des Nations Unies aucune prise de position quant au statut juridique des pays, territoires, villes ou zones, ou de leurs autorités, ni quant au tracé de leurs frontières ou limites.

L'appellation "pays ou zone", figurant dans cette publication, désigne des pays, des territoires, des villes ou des zones. L'appellation "pays" figurant dans certaines rubriques des tableaux de numéros antérieurs de cette publication doit être interprétée comme désignant des pays, des territoires, des villes ou des zones.

L'appellation économie "développée" ou économie "en voie de développement" qui figure dans certains tableaux est utilisée pour plus de commodité dans la présentation des statistiques et n'implique pas nécessairement un jugement quant au stade de développement auquel est parvenu un pays ou une zone donnée.

ST/ESA/STAT/SER.G/46

UNITED NATIONS PUBLICATION
Sales No. E/F.99.XVII.2, vol. I

PUBLICATION DES NATIONS UNIES
Numéro de vente : E/F.99.XVII.2, vol. I

ISBN 92-1-061177-2

Inquiries should be directed to:
PUBLISHING DIVISION
UNITED NATIONS
NEW YORK, NY 10017

Adresser toutes demandes de renseignements à la :
DIVISION DES PUBLICATIONS
NATIONS UNIES
NEW YORK, NY 10017

Printed by the United Nations Reproduction Section, New York
Imprimé par la Section de la reproduction des Nations Unies, New York

TABLE OF CONTENTS

Volume I

COUNTRY TABLES

TABLE DES MATIERES

Volume I

TABLEAUX PAR PAYS

ABBREVIATIONS AND COUNTRY NOMENCLATURE

Names of some countries or groups of countries and of some commodities or groups of commodities have been abbreviated. Exact titles and the composition of groups of countries will be found in the following publications referred to in the introduction:

(i) United Nations Standard Country Code (Annex II, Country classification for international trade statistics)

(ii) United Nations Standard Country or Area Code for Statistical Use, (Revision 1)

(iii) Standard Country or Area Codes for Statistical Use, (Revision 2)

(iv) Standard Country or Area Codes for Statistical Use, (Revision 3)

(v) Standard International Trade Classification, Revised (SITC, Revised)

(vi) Standard International Trade Classification, Revision 2, (SITC, Revision 2)

(vii) Classification by Broad Economic Categories (BEC)

(viii) Classification of Commodities by Industrial Origin

(ix) International Standard Industrial Classification of all Economic Activities (ISIC)

1. Data relating to the People's Republic of China generally include those for Taiwan Province in the field of statistics relating to population, area, natural resources, natural conditions such as climate, etc. In other fields of statistics, they do not include Taiwan Province unless otherwise stated. Therefore, in this publication the data published under the heading China exclude those for Taiwan Province. Figures representing the trade with Taiwan Province which may have been reported by any reporting country or area are included in the grouping Asia. Pursuant to a Joint Declaration signed on 19 December 1984, the United Kingdom restored Hong Kong to the People's Republic of China with effect from 1 July 1997; the People's Republic of China resumed the exercise of sovereignty over the territory with effect from that date. For statistical purposes, the data for China do not include those for Hong Kong Special Administrative Region.

2. On 22 May 1990 Democratic Yemen and Yemen merged to form a single State. Since that date they have been represented as one Member with the name "Yemen". All data shown in this publication relating to the period prior to 1990 refer to the former Democratic Yemen and the former Yemen.

3. Through accession of the German Democratic Republic to the Federal Republic of Germany with effect from 3 October 1990, the two German States have united to form one sovereign State. As from the date of unification, the Federal Republic of Germany acts in the United Nations under

the designation of "Germany": All data shown which pertain to Germany prior to 3 October 1990 are indicated separately for the Federal Republic of Germany and the former German Democratic Republic based on their respective territories at the time indicated. Where data for united Germany (subsequent to 3 October 1990) are not available, they are shown separately and pertain to the territorial boundaries prior to 3 October 1990.

4. In 1991, the Union of Soviet Socialist Republics formally dissolved into fifteen independent countries (Armenia, Azerbaijan, Belarus, Estonia, Georgia, Kazakhstan, Kyrgyzstan, Latvia, Lithuania, Republic of Moldova, Russian Federation, Tajikistan, Turkmenistan, Ukraine and Uzbekistan). From 1992 onwards data are shown for the individual countries. Prior to 1992 data are shown for the former USSR.

5. Unless otherwise indicated, data provided for Yugoslavia prior to 1 January 1992 refer to the Socialist Federal Republic of Yugoslavia which was composed of six republics, whereas data provided for Yugoslavia after that date refer to the Federal Republic of Yugoslavia which is composed of two republics (Serbia and Montenegro).

6. Data for the Czech Republic and Slovakia, where available, are shown separately under the appropriate country name. For periods prior to 1 January 1993, where no separate data are available for the Czech Republic and Slovakia, unless otherwise indicated, data for the former Czechoslovakia are shown under the country name "former Czechoslovakia".

7. Beginning 1 January 1997, the overseas departments of France were included in the statistical territory of France for the purposes of international trade statistics. Values on this basis have been provided by France for 1996 also, and values are published on that basis in this publication.

ABREVIATIONS ET CODES DES PAYS.

Les noms de certains pays ou groupes de pays et de certains produits ou groupes de produits ont dû être abrégés. On trouvera les intitulés exacts de ces noms dans les publications suivantes qui figurent dans l'Introduction:

(i) United Nations Standard Country Code (Annex V, 'Standardized Abbreviated French Country Names')

(ii) United Nations Standard Country or Area Code for Statistical Use, (Révision 1)

(iii) Standard Country or Area Codes for Statistical Use, (Révision 2)

(iv) Codes standard des pays et des zones à usage statistique, (Révision 3)

(v) Classification type pour le commerce international révisée, (CTCI révisée)

(vi) Classification type pour le commerce international (deuxième version révisée), (CTCI, Révision 2)

(vii) Classification par grandes catégories économiques (CGCE)

(viii) Classification des marchandises par origine industrielle

(ix) Classification internationale type, par industrie, de toutes les branches d'activité économique (CITI)

1. Les données relatives à la République populaire de Chine comprennent en général les données relatives à la province de Taïwan lorsqu'il s'agit de statistiques concernant la population, la superficie, les ressources naturelles, les conditions naturelles tel que le climat, etc. Dans les statistiques relevant d'autres domaines, la province de Taïwan n'est pas comprise, sauf indication contraire. C'est le cas dans cet Annuaire où les données pour la Chine ne comprennent pas celles de la province de Taïwan. Lorsque des pays partenaires ont déclaré des échanges avec Taïwan ceux-ci sont inclus dans Asie. Conformément à une Déclaration commune signée le 19 décembre 1984, le Royaume-Uni a rétrocédé Hong-kong à la République populaire de Chine, avec effet au ler juillet 1997; la souveraineté de la République populaire de Chine s'exerce à nouveau sur le territoire à compter de cette date. Pour les statistiques, les données de la Chine ne comprennent pas celles de la région administrative spéciale de Hong Kong.

2. Le Yémen et le Yémen démocratique ont fusionné le 22 mai 1990 pour ne plus former qu'un seul Etat, qui est depuis lors représenté comme tel à l'Organisation, sous le nom 'Yémen'. Toutes les données présentées dans cet Annuaire qui se rapportent à la période antérieure à l'année 1990 se réfèrent aux anciens Yémen démocratique et Yémen.

3. En vertu de l'adhésion de la République démocratique allemande à la République fédérale d'Allemagne, prenant effet le 3 octobre 1990, les deux Etats allemands se sont unis pour former un seul Etat souverain. A compter de la date de l'unification, la République fédérale d'Allemagne est désignée à l'ONU sous le nom 'Allemagne'. Toutes les données se rapportant à l'Allemagne avant le 3 octobre 1990 figurent dans deux rubriques séparées, basées sur les territoires respectifs de la République fédérale d'Allemagne et l'ancienne République démocratique allemande selon la période indiquée. En l'absence de données pour l'Allemagne unifiée (à compter du 3 octobre 1990), les données sont fournies séparément sous les rubriques Allemagne (République fédérale d') et Allemagne (ancienne République démocratique) et se rapportent aux limites territoriales antérieures au 3 octobre 1990 lorsqu'elles sont disponibles.

4. En 1991, l'ex Union Soviétique a été scindée officiellement en quinze républiques indépendantes (Arménie, Azerbaïdjan, Bélarus, Estonie, Fédération de Russie, Géorgie, Kazakstan, Kirghizistan, Lettonie, Lituanie, Ouzbékistan, République de Moldova, Tadjikistan, Turkménistan et Ukraine). A partir de 1992 les données sont indiquées pour chaque république individuellement. Avant 1992, les données sont indiquées pour l'ancienne URSS.

5. Sauf indication contraire, les données fournies pour la Yougoslavie avant le 1er janvier 1992 se rapportent à la République fédérative socialiste de Yougoslavie, qui était composée de six républiques; les données fournies pour la Yougoslavie après cette date se rapportent à la République fédérative de Yougoslavie, qui est composée de deux républiques (Serbie et Monténégro).

6. Les données relatives à la République tchèque, et à la Slovaquie, lorsqu'elles sont disponibles, sont présentées séparément sous le nom de chacun des pays. En ce qui concerne la période antérieure au 1er janvier 1993, pour laquelle on ne possède pas de données séparées pour les deux Républiques, les données relatives à l'ancienne Tchécoslovaquie sont, sauf indication contraire, présentées sous le titre 'ancienne Tchécoslovaquie'.

7. A partir de ler janvier 1997, pour les statistiques du commerce international, le territoire statistique de la France comprend les départements d'outre-mer. Les valeurs ont été fournies aussi sur cette base par la France pour 1996, et sont publiées dans cet annuaire.

EXPLANATION OF SYMBOLS
EXPLICATION DES SIGNES

Category not applicable .... Ne s'applique pas	. or ..
Not available.. Aucune donnée disponible	blank or ...
Magnitude of less than half the unit used.. Grandeur inférieure à la moitié de l'unité utilisée	0 or 0.0
Provisional or estimated figures.. Donnée provisoire ou estimation	X
Area (1,000 square metres).. Superficie (1,000 mètres carrés)	A
1,000 kilowatt-hours.. 1,000 kilowatts-heures	H
Weight (kilograms).. Poids (kilogrammes)	K
Length (1,000 metres).. Longueur (1,000 mètres)	L
1,000 times unit shown.. 1,000 fois l'unité indiquée	M
Number.. Nombre	N
Other.. Autres	O
Number of pairs.. Paires	P
Volume (cubic metres).. Volume (mètre cube)	V
Weight (metric tons).. Poids (tonnes métriques)	W
1,000,000 times unit shown.. 1 million de fois l'unité indiquée	Y
Decimal figures are always preceded by a period except for the Country Notes in French where they are preceded by a comma.. Les décimales sont toujours précédées d'un point, à l'exception des notes de pays en français où elles sont précédées par une virgule.	(.)

TRADE DATA IN ELECTRONIC FORM

External trade data, for the majority of countries from 1962 to the latest year, are available in electronic form and can be transmitted on magnetic tape, diskette, CD-ROM or by electronic mail. Detailed information on coverage and price is available, on request, from the United Nations Statistics Division, New York, N.Y. 10017, USA; tel. (212) 963-6170; fax (212) 963-9851 and e-mail tradestat@un.org.

DONNEES DU COMMERCE EXTERIEUR SOUS FORME ELECTRONIQUE

Les données du commerce extérieur pour la majorité des pays de 1962 à la dernière année écoulée sont disponibles sous forme électronique et peuvent être envoyées sur bande magnétique, sur disquette, sur CD-ROM, ou par message électronique. Les informations détaillées sur la nature, le volume, les dates et les prix de ces supports magnétiques peuvent être obtenues auprès de la Division de Statistique des Nations Unies, New York, N.Y. 10017, Etats Unis; tel. (212) 963-6170; fax (212) 963-9851 and e-mail tradestat@un.org.

INTRODUCTION

1. The forty-sixth edition of the International Trade Statistics Yearbook provides the basic information for individual countries' external trade performances in terms of the overall trends in current value, as well as in volume and price, the importance of trading partners and the significance of individual commodities imported and exported. This edition shows annual statistics for 168 countries or reporting customs areas. It is published in two volumes.

VOLUME I

2. Volume I contains detailed data for individual countries. For each country the following tables usually appear:

(a) Table 1, showing ten series, five for imports and five for exports. The five are: total merchandise trade and trade in gold (generally in national currency, but in US dollars for some countries), conversion factors for converting total merchandise trade from national currency into United States dollars, quantum index numbers and unit value index numbers for total imports and exports.

(b) Table 2, showing up to the most recent seven years available, percentage breakdowns of imports by broad economic categories and of exports by industrial origin. Data for earlier years generally were shown in previous issues of this Yearbook. The analysis for imports is based on the Classification by Broad Economic Categories[1/] and for exports on the Classification of Commodities by Industrial Origin[2/]. Reclassification of foreign trade according to broad economic categories or industrial origin requires statistical information at the five-digit level of the Standard International Trade Classification, Revised. (For history and background of the SITC, see pages xx-xxii). When such details are not available, approximate allocations are made, using the three-digit level of the SITC Revised. In comparing statistics of international trade with statistics of production, problems of limitation exist in addition to those of classification. Exports of products which are obviously not produced in the reporting countries (e.g., exports of tea and cocoa from the Netherlands or the United Kingdom) have been allocated to the industrial origin in which they would have been classified in the producing countries; in the case of tea and cocoa: Agriculture. The industrial origin in the reporting country of these exports is, in fact, the wholesale trade. In the Classification of Commodities by Industrial Origin, SITC, Revised headings are subdivided to correspond, roughly, to groups of the International Standard Industrial Classification of All Economic Activities, (Revision 1)[3/]. The breakdown of exports by industrial origin is derived as much as possible from national or special exports.

(c) Table 3, showing up to the most recent five years available, the value in United States dollars of import and export trade analyzed by the principal countries or areas and regions of provenance and destination. The analysis is made according to the United Nations Standard Country or Area Codes for Statistical Use[4/]. In some instances, owing to the nature of the national country classification, the conversion to the United Nations country classification could not be done precisely. A maximum of 40 trading partners are shown, in order of magnitude, based on the sum of the values over the years included in the table, with imports and exports ranked separately. Below the value table is a listing showing the percentage breakdown of trade by regions and the percent of trade accounted for by each of the first ten trading partners for the latest available ten years. The line for the European Union (EU) is calculated for all years on the basis of the current membership (fifteen countries). The lines for the Asian part of the former USSR (Armenia, Azerbaijan, Georgia, Kazakhstan, Kyrgyzstan, Tajikistan, Turkmenistan, and Uzbekistan) and the European part of the former USSR (Belarus, Estonia, Latvia, Lithuania, Republic of Moldova, Russian Federation and Ukraine) are calculated as the sum of the appropriate independent countries from 1992 to date. For years prior to 1992 this was not possible and the line for the European part of the former USSR includes the entire former USSR for those years. Eastern Europe comprises Albania, Bulgaria, Czech Republic, Hungary, Poland, Romania and Slovakia. Regional totals are calculated only if the available partner detail exceeds 80% of the reported total imports or exports.

(d) Tables 4 and 5, showing up to the most recent four years available, the quantity and the value in United States dollars of imports and exports analyzed by commodities. Data for a commodity will appear if the value in any year is greater than or equal to 0.3 per cent of the total trade for that year. The commodities are shown in terms of SITC headings (abbreviated). An asterisk (*) preceding the description indicates that these are the only codes belonging to the next higher level of the SITC, and the next higher level is, therefore, not shown.

3. In some instances the figures shown in United States dollars in the tables indicated under (c) and (d) above may not correspond to those in United States dollars in the table described under (a) above or to those in national currency in that table after the application of the currency conversion factors. These discrepancies arise in part from revisions to the more recent data at the total level and these revisions were not broken down for the more detailed data by commodity and partner. In some cases the differences may be due to differences in coverage/definitions of the data. It was felt, however, that a partial revision of the tables referred to under (c) and (d) above to make the totals consistent with those in (a) should not be made.

4. For all countries, the data in Tables 4 and 5 are presented according to the Standard International Trade Classification (SITC)[5/] Revision 2. Many countries report data according to the SITC, Revision 3 or the Harmonized Commodity Description and Coding System (HS). The data so reported for these countries, were converted to SITC Revision 2. This is a difficult conversion and results in data for some SITC Revision 2 codes which are not comparable with data reported in terms of SITC, Revision 2 to a very significant extent. In a few cases, countries reported data using a national commodity classification related to SITC Revision 1; conversion to SITC Revision 2 could not be done precisely and,

therefore, in these cases some of the SITC Revision 2 codes are not exact in their coverage (Bahamas 1988 and 1991; Bahrain 1989 to 1993; Belize 1988 to 1990; Bermuda 1988 to 1993; Malta 1988 and 1989; Myanmar 1991; Netherlands Antilles 1988 to 1992 and 1995; Sudan 1992 to 1994; United Republic of Tanzania 1987; and Tonga 1987 to 1995).

5. When available, more detailed data by commodity and partner country according to the HS96, HS88, SITC Revision 3, Revision 2 or Revised are published in the Commodity Trade Statistics[6/] on microfiches.

6. Detailed descriptions of the current concepts and definitions applied by countries are available in the United Nations mimeograph "National Reporting Practices in International Merchandise Trade Statistics" (ST/ESA/STAT/112), issued February 1996 and available from the United Nations Statistics Division.

VOLUME II

7. Volume II contains commodity tables showing the total trade of certain commodities analyzed by regions and countries. The regional structure is identical to that which is used in Volume I.

8. Commodity tables. These tables show imports and exports of commodities at the group (3-digit) level of the SITC, Revision 2. All groups are covered except for 286, Ores and concentrates of uranium and thorium; the exports of 333, Petroleum oils, crude, and crude oils obtained from bituminous minerals; 351, Electric current; 675, Hoops and strip, of iron or steel, hot-rolled or cold-rolled; 688, Uranium depleted in U235 and thorium, and their alloys, unwrought or wrought, and articles thereof; n.e.s.; waste and scrap of uranium depleted in U235 and of thorium; 911, Postal packages not classified according to kind; 961, Coin (other than gold coin), not being legal tender (for an explanation, see paragraph 9 below) and 971, Gold, non-monetary (excluding gold ores and concentrates). The years covered are the five years 1993 to 1997. The values are in U.S. dollars and both imports and exports are analyzed by regions and principal trading countries. A maximum of 40 countries are shown in order of magnitude, based on the sum of the values over the years 1994, 1995 and 1996 included in the table, with imports and exports ranked separately. No quantity data are shown.

9. In preparing these tables, in many cases estimates were made for countries whose data were not yet available and these are shown with an 'x'. In some cases, estimates were made for particular countries, and they were considered adequate to include in regional and world totals but not sufficiently explained to be published separately for the country; consequently, they have been suppressed and only an 'x' appears in the table. The commodity groups mentioned in paragraph 8 above, (286, the exports of 333, 351, 675, 688, 911, 961 and 971) are suppressed from publication because they were poorly reported and contain many estimates which are not sufficiently explainable. Strictly speaking, an 'x' should appear against a regional or world total that contains estimates. However, virtually

all the regional and world totals include estimates and the 'x's have been omitted for cosmetic purposes.

10. The procedure for estimating trade data for a given year and a given country takes some reported ('true') data as a starting point. The minimum of required reported input data are the import and export totals of a country. Sometimes other aggregated commodity information is also available and is taken into account; this may include some 3-digit or other commodity totals reported by the country. The estimation procedure then takes the available reported data and initial estimates which may be either (1) the 3-digit commodity totals of the country for an adjacent (reported) year or (2) the 3-digit commodity totals for the country as reported by all its trading partners combined, for the given year. Thereafter, these initial estimates are scaled in such a way that at every level of the commodity classification the total of the commodity estimates and any reported data add up to the reported ("true") totals at the higher level and ultimately to the totals of the imports and exports.

11. Volume II also contains special tables showing, inter alia, (a) the contribution of the trade of each country to the trade of its region and of the world, (b) the flow of trade between countries and regions and (c) the fluctuations of the prices at which goods moved internationally. The special tables are:

A. Total imports and exports by regions and countries and areas;
B. World exports by commodity classes and by regions;
C. Growth of world exports by commodity classes and by regions;
D. Structure of world exports by commodity classes and by regions;
E. Total imports and exports: index numbers by countries or areas, terms of trade, and purchasing power of exports;
F. Total exports and imports: index numbers of quantum, unit value and terms of trade by regions;
G. Manufactured goods exports;
H. Fuel imports: developed economies;
I. Some indicators on fuel imports: developed economies;
J. Export price index numbers of primary commodities and non-ferrous base metals.

Special Tables

12. The economic and geographic groupings in all the special tables are in accordance with those of Special Table A in this issue, although Special Table A sometimes includes more detailed geographic sub-groups. (See Special Table A for the details.)

(A) Total imports and exports by regions and countries or areas. The regional, economic and world totals have been adjusted: (a) to include estimates for countries or areas for which full data are not available; (b) to include insurance and freight for imports valued f.o.b.; (c) to include countries or areas not listed separately; (d) to approximate special trade; (e) to approximate calendar years; and (f) where possible, to eliminate incomparabilities owing to geographical changes, by adjusting the figures for periods before the change to be comparable to those for periods after the change, for example, the European Union and the European Free Trade Association. The figures shown for individual countries correspond to the figures which appear and are described in table 1 of the country tables. For footnotes see the end of the table.

Monthly and quarterly data appear in the Monthly Bulletin of Statistics.

(B) World exports by commodity classes and by regions. For the general note and footnotes, see the end of the table.

(C) Growth of world exports by commodity classes and by regions. The annual average rates of change in percentage terms given in this table have been uniformly calculated by the use of the compound interest formula:

$$r = \left(\sqrt[t]{\frac{Vn}{Vo}} - 1 \right) 100$$

r = Annual average rate of change in percentage terms.
Vn = Value of exports during the last year of the period.
Vo = Value of exports during the first year of the period.
t = Number of years in period.

For the general note and footnotes, see the end of Special Table D.

(D) Structure of world exports by commodity classes and by regions. The figures shown under the heading 'Origin of Exports' refer to the exports of the region or country appearing in the 'Area' column; those shown under the heading 'Destination of Exports' refer to the exports of the world to the region or country appearing in the 'Area' column. For the general note and footnotes, see the end of the table.

(E) Total imports and exports: index numbers by countries or areas, terms of trade, and purchasing power of exports. Unless otherwise stated in the footnotes, the unit value indices are in terms of national currencies. For the general note and footnotes, see the end of the table.

Monthly and quarterly data appear in the Monthly Bulletin of Statistics for the quantum and unit value indexes.

(F) Total exports and imports: index numbers of quantum, unit value and terms of trade by regions. For the footnotes, see the end of the table.

Quarterly data appear in the Monthly Bulletin of Statistics.

(G) Manufactured goods exports. For the general note and footnotes, see the end of Table I.

Quarterly data appear in the Monthly Bulletin of Statistics.

(H) Fuel imports: developed economies. For the general note and footnotes, see the end of Table I.

Quarterly data appear in the Monthly Bulletin of Statistics.

(I) Some indicators on fuel imports: developed economies. This table shows the share of fuel imports in the total value of imports and in the total value of exports, and the ratio of unit value indices of manufactured goods exports to those of fuel imports. For the general note and footnotes, see the end of the table.

Quarterly data appear in the Monthly Bulletin of Statistics.

(J) Export price index numbers of primary commodities and non-ferrous base metals. For the general note and footnote, see the end of the table.

Monthly and quarterly data appear in the Monthly Bulletin of Statistics.

SOURCES AND PRESENTATION

13. The figures for Volumes I and II are obtained from national published sources, from data supplied by the Governments for use in this publication, and the United Nations publications: Monthly Bulletin of Statistics, and Statistical Yearbook. Estimates for some missing data are made by the United Nations Statistics Division.

14. The country and regional names used by various countries are not uniform for their trade statistics. Also, where former geographical entities commonly referred to in national statistics have changed, countries may introduce the corresponding changes in their statistics at different times. Wherever possible, however, parts of the world have been designated by the names they currently bear. To satisfy the needs of some users for analytical data over time, the ability to reconstruct some former geographic/political entities has been maintained e.g. data relating to the former USSR.

15. The regional aggregates shown throughout this publication are based on those set forth in the United Nations Standard Country or Area Codes for Statistical Use[4/], except where indicated.

16. Generally, data refer to calendar years; however, for those countries which report according to some other reference year, the data are presented in the year which covers the majority of the reference year used by the country.

NATIONAL INDEX NUMBERS

17. National index numbers of unit value in national currencies or United States dollars and of quantum are shown in Table 1. They are the official indices which show the changes in the volume, (quantum index) and the average price (unit value index) of the aggregate merchandise imports or exports. Each index number represents a change between the period to which the number refers, called the current period, and a fixed period, called the publication base, in which the index is represented by the percentage 100. In order to facilitate comparison, the indices shown have been adjusted, where possible, so that the calendar year 1990 is the publication base. When changes are made in the coverage, formula or base period of an index, the two series are linked together if they have an overlapping period and are sufficiently comparable.

18. Quarterly and monthly figures for these index series appear in the United Nations Monthly Bulletin of Statistics and a more detailed description of their compilation is given in the 1977 Supplement to the Statistical Yearbook and the Monthly Bulletin of Statistics[7/].

TRANSITION COUNTRIES

19. For the period covered by this Yearbook, countries formerly classified for statistical purposes as centrally planned economies had systems of official rates between their currencies and other currencies, all consistent with rates of 0.90 new roubles to the United States dollar prior to 24 December 1971 and 0.829 new roubles to the United States dollar until February 1973; since then these rates have been fluctuating. They generally used these rates when it was necessary to convert foreign into domestic currencies for the purpose of compiling external trade statistics. The resulting data are for comparison with the external transactions of the rest of the world rather than with domestic monetary transactions.

20. The trade statistics of these countries had definitions somewhat different from those which exist in other countries. Differences in definition contribute to the discrepancies which can be observed between statistical records referring to the same flow of goods but kept by two trading partners having different economic systems. The trade among these countries was carried out on a basis not comparable to that governing trade with other countries. The concept of transaction value, for instance, as applied outside those countries is based on the existence of a market between exporters and importers in which the interaction of supply and demand has more effect than it can be assumed to have had in those countries; in the absence of data on the unit values of specific commodities entering the trade of those countries with one another, it is difficult to assess the possible effects on the trade statistics of this kind of incomparability. Increasingly since 1992, the transition countries have adopted similar concepts and definitions for international trade statistics as are in effect in other countries.

GENERAL STATEMENTS

21. The statistics in this Yearbook have been compiled by national statistical authorities largely consistent with the United Nations recommended International Trade Statistics

Concepts and Definitions, Revision 1.[8/] In 1998 the United Nations issued a further revision of this publication; [8/] countries have been requested to commence introduction of the new concepts and definitions with data for 1999. The main elements of the concepts and definitions (Revision 1) are:

1. Territory. The statistics reported by a country generally refer to the customs area of the country. In most cases this coincides with the geographical area of the country. Unless otherwise stated, the combination of two territories, formerly separate, results in the elimination from the statistics of their trade with each other. The separation of two territories, formerly together, results in the appearance of their trade with each other in the statistics for each territory.

2. System of trade. Two systems of recording trade are in common use, differing mainly in the way warehoused and re-exported goods are recorded:

(a) Special trade: special imports are the combined total of imports declared directly from abroad for home use or inward processing and withdrawals from bonded warehouses or free zones for home use. Special exports comprise exports of goods of national origin, namely, goods wholly or partly produced or manufactured in the country, including goods exported after inward processing, and re-exports of imported goods that have been in free circulation.

(b) General trade: general imports are the combined total of imports declared directly from abroad for home use or inward processing, and imports into bonded warehouses or free zones. General exports comprise exports of goods of national origin, including goods exported after inward processing, re-exports of imported goods that have been in free circulation and re-exports of goods from bonded warehouses or free zones.

Direct transit trade, i.e., goods merely being trans-shipped or moving through the country for purposes of transport only, is excluded from the statistics of both special and general trade.

Each of the tables indicates in its heading the system of trade to which the figures relate.

3. Valuation. At its fifteenth session, in 1953, the Economic and Social Council, taking the view that trade statistics must reflect economic realities, recommended that the Governments of Member States of the United Nations, wherever possible, use transaction values in the compilation of their national statistics of external trade or, when national practices are based on other values, endeavour to provide supplementary statistical data based on transaction values (Economic and Social Council resolution 469 B (XV)). In the case of imports, the transaction value is the value at which the goods were purchased by the importer plus the cost of transportation and insurance to the frontier of the importing country (a c.i.f. valuation). In the case of exports, the transaction value is the value at which the goods were sold by the exporter, including the cost of transportation and insurance, to

bring the goods onto the transporting vehicle at the frontier of the exporting country (a f.o.b. valuation).

4. Currency conversion. For data in this publication, conversion of values from national currencies into United States dollars is done by means of currency conversion factors based on official exchange rates. Values in currencies subject to fluctuation (such currencies increased in number beginning December 1971) are converted into United States dollars using weighted average exchange rates specially calculated for this purpose. The weighted average exchange rate for a given currency for a given year is the component monthly factors, mostly furnished by the International Monetary Fund, weighted by the value of the relevant trade in each month; a monthly factor is the exchange rate (or the simple average rate) in effect during that month. These factors are applicable to total imports and exports respectively, but not necessarily to trade in individual commodities or with individual countries.

5. Merchandise. In order that external trade statistics shall be suited to the measurement of the influence of national economies upon one another, merchandise trade is defined to include, as far as possible, all goods which add to or subtract from the material resources of a country as a result of their movements into or out of the country. Unless, therefore, statements to the contrary are made in footnotes to the country tables, the treatment of the classes of goods listed below is as indicated:

(a) Gold. Gold traded internationally is usually defined as encompassing the three following types:

i) Gold coins (issued and unissued) and bullion, including banking and monetary gold;
ii) Unrefined gold, including gold ores and concentrates;
iii) Partly-worked gold in which the value of the gold is 80 per cent or more of the total value, including scrap, jewellers' sweepings, dust, primary shapes (such as rods, wire and gold leaf) and gold alloys (crude or in primary shapes).

Of the types of gold listed above, those belonging to the category of monetary gold are excluded from merchandise trade, and those classified as non-monetary gold are included, except as indicated below. Any gold shipment received by the central monetary authority of a country is treated as monetary gold. All other gold shipments (whether to commercial banks or to individuals), on the other hand, are considered non-monetary.

(b) Silver ore, concentrates, bullion, unissued coin (as noted below), scrap and partly-worked and manufactured silver are all included in merchandise trade statistics.

(c) Currency and titles of ownership which have been issued into circulation, e.g., issued silver and base metal coins, bank notes, other paper currency and securities, are excluded from merchandise trade statistics. Unissued currency and titles of ownership are included at their intrinsic value as stamped metal or printed paper rather than at face value.

(d) Trade on government account is included as merchandise trade. Movements under government foreign aid programmes (civil and military), war reparations and restitutions and military goods[9/] moving internationally are therefore included. When goods are destined for use of national agencies (including embassies and military forces) stationed abroad they are, however, not considered to have moved in external trade and are excluded.

(e) Temporary imports and exports. Goods for exhibitions or study, animals admitted to a country temporarily, merely for racing or breeding, returnable containers, etc., the movements of all of which are expected to be reversed within a limited time, are excluded.

(f) Improvement and repair trade. Countries sending goods abroad for improvement or repair and later returned are said to be engaging in the passive improvement and repair trade; countries receiving goods from other countries for improvement or repair and eventual return engage in the active improvement and repair trade. Inward and outward movement in this trade are generally excluded from imports and exports.

(g) Postal trade is included in merchandise trade.

(h) Trade in fish, etc. Fish and salvage sold abroad or to foreign vessels off national vessels, and fish and salvage landed from foreign vessels in national ports are excluded from merchandise trade statistics.

(i) Trade in ships and aircraft. Ships and aircraft bought and sold should be included.

(j) Bunkers and stores for ships and aircraft. In general, bunkers and stores should be included in aggregate merchandise exports.

6. Partner country. The following terms describe methods that may be used by reporting countries in determining, for each shipment of goods, the partner country under whose name it should be recorded: (a) for imports: country of origin or production, country of consignment, country of purchase or country of provenance; (b) for exports: country of consumption or consignment, or country of sale.

7. Trade analyzed by commodity. Analysis is according to the Standard International Trade Classification.

THE STANDARD INTERNATIONAL TRADE CLASSIFICATION (SITC) AND THE HARMONIZED COMMODITY DESCRIPTION AND CODING SYSTEM (HS)

22. In July 1950, the United Nations Economic and Social Council, on the advice of its Statistical Commission, recommended that Governments compile trade by commodity

statistics according to the original SITC[5/] in order to have available data in internationally comparable categories suitable for the economic analysis of trade. The original SITC had been prepared by the United Nations Secretariat with the assistance of expert consultants and in co-operation with Member Governments and interested international organizations.

23. In May 1960, the Statistical Commission approved a revision, similarly prepared, of the original SITC, known as the SITC, Revised, designed to take account of the changes in the pattern of trade since 1950 and to simplify the relation between the SITC and internationally agreed customs tariff nomenclatures. The SITC, Revised, is a rearrangement into statistical order of the items of the 1955 Tariff Nomenclature (CCCN) of the Customs Co-operation Council.

24. The SITC, Revised, is based on 625 subgroups (identified by code numbers of four digits), most of which correspond to items of the original SITC. A number of subgroups are further subdivided either to distinguish commodities of statistical importance or to permit exact correspondence with the CCCN; this results in a basic (5-digit code) level for the SITC, Revised, consisting of 1,312 items. The subgroups are combined, progressively, into 177 groups, 56 divisions and 10 sections.

25. The headings of the SITC, Revised, are fully determined by their code numbers. The precise composition of each number is defined in the SITC, Revised, itself. In comparing data according to the SITC, Revised, with data according to a national commodity classification it must be remembered that the same brief description may refer to aggregates differing somewhat in composition.

26. Although the SITC, Revised, of 1960 represented a great improvement on the original SITC, basically the same reasons which led to the creation of the SITC and its first revision were found, in the late nineteen-sixties, to be once more valid. Since 1960 the volume of trade had increased rapidly and its geographic and commodity patterns had changed fundamentally. Consequently, a second revision of the SITC was undertaken. In October 1974 the Statistical Commission approved of this revision, known as SITC, Revision 2[5/], and in May 1975 the Economic and Social Council recommended that Member States of the United Nations should report data on external trade according to the SITC, Revision 2, as far and as soon as possible. Starting with data for 1976, some countries began reporting trade statistics based on the SITC, Revision 2.

27. The basic headings of the SITC, Revision 2 had a one-to-one correspondence with the subdivisions of the Customs Co-operation Council Nomenclature (CCCN). However, there were a number of users who found the subdivisions of CCCN (and thus SITC, Revision 2) insufficient for their needs[10/]. There was also an expressed need for the harmonization of economic classifications[11/]. Partly to satisfy these needs, the Customs Co-operation Council in May 1973 undertook responsibility for the development and completion of the Harmonized Commodity Description and Coding System (HS)[12/].

28. At its twenty-first session, in January 1981, the Statistical Commission had taken note of the fact that a third revision of SITC would have to be made available when both the

revised CCCN and HS came into force[13/]. Accordingly, later that year, the United Nations Secretariat commenced work on the revision of SITC, Revision 2, based on the principle that every effort should be made to maintain its general character and structure but taking into account the need for its harmonization with the revised CCCN, the International Standard Industrial Classification (ISIC) Revision 3[14/] and a Central Product Classification[15/] which was developed jointly by the United Nations Statistics Division and the Statistical Office of the European Communities.

29. The final draft was revised and approved by the Statistical Commission at its twenty-third session, in February 1985,[16/] and a resolution was adopted by the Economic and Social Council on 28 May 1985 which, inter alia, recommended that Member States should report internationally external trade statistics according to the Standard International Trade Classification, Revision 3 (resolution 1985/7).

30. The Harmonized System was adopted by the Customs Cooperation Council in June 1983, and the International Convention on the Harmonized System (HS Convention) entered into force 1 January 1988 (HS88). As of 29 October 1998 there were 95 Contracting Parties, and another 76 countries or territories which were not contracting parties but were using the HS for customs/statistical purposes.

31. The United Nations Statistical Commission, at its twenty-seventh session, held from 22 February to 3 March 1993, recommended that countries "adopt the HS for compilation and dissemination of their international trade statistics"[17/].

32. In accordance with the preamble of the HS Convention, which recognized the importance of ensuring that the HS be kept up-to-date in the light of changes in technology or in patterns of international trade, the HS is regularly reviewed and revised. The United Nations Statistical Commission at its twenty-seventh session "recommended that the Customs Cooperation Council take fully into account the statistical implications of any changes proposed for HS and the statistical needs and capacities of developing countries"[18/]. Some minor revisions to the HS88, which also resulted in the deletion of one six-digit code, were made in 1992 (HS92). A more comprehensive set of amendments was adopted in 1993 and these amendments entered into force 1 January 1996 (HS96).

33. The Statistical Commission, at its twenty-eighth session, 27 February - 3 March 1995 considered changes that would be required to the SITC, Rev. 3 to bring it into correlation with HS96; the Commission decided that the changes required in SITC, Rev. 3 to make it fully correlated with HS96 were minor in scale. The Commission therefore decided that it would not be necessary to issue a fourth revision of the SITC[19/].

1/ Classification by Broad Economic Categories (in terms of the SITC Revised), Statistical Papers, Series M No.53, (United Nations publication, Sales No. 71.XVII.12).

2/ Classification of Commodities by Industrial Origin (Relationship of the Standard International Trade Classification Revised to the International Standard Industrial Classification of All Economic Activities, Revision 1), Statistical Papers, Series M No.43, (United Nations publication, Sales No. 66.XVII.7).

3/ International Standard Industrial Classification of All Economic Activities (Revision 1), Statistical Papers, Series M No. 4, Rev. 1, (United Nations publication, Sales No. 58.XVII.7).

4/ United Nations Standard Country Codes, Statistical Papers, Series M No. 49, (United Nations publication, Sales No. E.70.XVII.13).

United Nations Standard Country or Area Codes for Statistical Use, Statistical Papers, Series M No. 49, Rev. 1, (United Nations publication, Sales No. E.75.XVII.8).

Standard Country or Area Codes for Statistical Use, Statistical Papers, Series M No. 49, Rev.2, (United Nations publication, Sales No. E.82.XVII.8).

Standard Country or Area Codes for Statistical Use, Series M No. 49, Rev. 3.

5/ Standard International Trade Classification Revision 2, Statistical Papers, Series M No.34/Rev.2, (United Nations publication, Sales No. E.75.XVII.6).

Standard International Trade Classification Revision 3, Statistical Papers, Series M No.34/Rev.3, (United Nations publication, Sales No. E.86.XVII.12).

6/ Commodity Trade Statistics, on microfiche (CTS SER.DCOM), carries annual figures showing the provenance and destination of trade for a large number of commodity headings of the HS and SITC classifications.

7/ 1977 Supplement to the Statistical Yearbook and Monthly Bulletin of Statistics, ST/ESA/STAT/SER.S/SUPPL.2, ST/ESA/STAT/SER.Q/SUPPL.2, (United Nations publication, Sales No. E.78.XVII.10).

8/ Statistical Papers, Series M No. 52, Rev.1, (United Nations publication, Sales No. E.82.XVII.14).

Statistical Papers, Series M No. 52, Rev.2, (United Nations publication, Sales No. E.98.XVII.16).

9/ Countries excluding military goods from imports or exports use varying definitions of this category of merchandise, but for most countries concerned, weapons and their ammunition constitute a major part of the military goods excluded.

10/ United Nations Statistics Division and Statistical Office of the European Communities Joint Working Group on World Level Classifications, "A Harmonized Commodity Description and Coding System for Use in International Trade" (UNSO/SOEC/1/2).

11/ United Nations Secretariat, "The Harmonization of Statistical Classifications: report of an expert group meeting". (ST/ESA/STAT/78).

12/ Customs Co-operation Council, "The Harmonized Commodity Description and Coding System", Brussels, 1985.

13/ Official Records of the Economic and Social Council, 1981, Supplement No. 2, (E/1981/12), para. 41.

14/ International Standard Industrial Classification of All Economic Activities, Statistical Papers, Series M No.4, Rev.3, (United Nations publication, Sales No.E.90.XVII.11).

15/ Provisional Central Product Classification, Statistical Papers, Series M No.77, (United Nations publication, Sales No.E.91.XVII.7).

16/ Official Records of the Economic and Social Council, 1985, Supplement No. 6, (E/1985/26), para. 57 (d).

17/ Official Records of the Economic and Social Council, 1993, Supplement No. 6, (E/1993/26), para. 162 (d).

18/ Official Records of the Economic and Social Council, 1993, Supplement No. 6, (E/1993/26), para. 162 (e).

19/ Official Records of the Economic and Social Council, 1995, Supplement No. 8, (E/CN.3/1995/28), para. 19 (e).

INTRODUCTION

1. La quarante sixième édition de l' annuaire statistique du commerce international présente les informations nécessaires à l'étude des échanges de chaque pays, en termes de valeur courante, de volume et de prix ainsi que l'importance des différents pays partenaires et des principaux produits importés et exportés. Cette édition présente des données annuelles pour 168 pays ou zones douanières déclarants. L'annuaire est publié en deux volumes.

VOLUME I

2. Le Volume I fournit des renseignements détaillés sur chaque pays au sujet duquel on trouvera généralement les tableaux suivants:

a) Tableau 1, donnant 10 séries, 5 à l'importation, 5 à l'exportation. Ces cinq séries sont: échanges de marchandises et échanges portant sur l'or (généralement en monnaie nationale mais pour quelques pays, en dollars des Etats-Unis), facteurs pour convertir les monnaies nationales en dollars des Etats-Unis, indices du quantum et de la valeur unitaire pour les importations et exportations totales.

b) Tableau 2, présentant jusqu'aux sept années les plus récentes disponible, les pourcentages par rapport au commerce total des importations par grandes catégories économiques et les exportations par branches d'origine. Les pourcentages pour des années moins récentes ont été publiés dans les éditions précédentes de cet Annuaire. L'analyse pour les importations est basée sur la Classification par grandes catégories économiques;[1/] pour les exportations sur la Classification des marchandises par origine industrielle[2/]. Toute reclassification du commerce extérieur par grandes catégories économiques ou par origine industrielle nécessite le détail au niveau des 5 chiffres de la CTCI, révisée. (Se référer aux pages xxxv à xxxvii pour l'histoire et le fond de la CTCI). Lorsque les statistiques n'étaient pas disponibles à ce niveau on a utilisé les données au niveau des trois chiffres de la CTCI, révisée. En comparant des statistiques du commerce extérieur avec des statistiques de production on se heurte à certaines incohérences qui s'ajoutent aux problèmes de classification. Les exportations de marchandises qui de toute évidence n'ont pas été produites dans les pays exportateurs (exportation de thé et de cacao des Pays-Bas ou du Royaume-Uni) ont été classées dans la branche où elles auraient été classées dans le pays d'origine; dans le cas du thé et du cacao: l'agriculture. La branche dans le pays déclarant est en fait dans ce cas le commerce de gros. Pour obtenir la Classification des marchandises par origine industrielle, les postes de la CTCI, révisée sont regroupés afin de correspondre approximativement aux groupes de la Classification international type, par industrie, de toutes les branches d'activité économique (révisée) (CITI, Révision 1)[3/]. Dans toute la mesure du possible les exportations nationales ou spéciales ont été utilisées.

c) Tableau 3, présentant jusqu'aux cinq années les plus récentes la valeur en dollars des Etats-Unis des importations et des exportations selon les principaux pays ou zones et régions d'originé et de destination. La distribution géographique est faite selon le Standard Country or Area Codes for Statistical Use[4/] des Nations Unies. Parfois, étant donné la nature des codes géographiques nationaux, la conversion des données selon le code des Nations Unies n'a pu être effectuée que moyennant quelques imprécisions. Dans ces tableaux figurent les 40 pays partenaires les plus importants classés par ordre d'importance selon la somme des valeurs sur les années comprises dans le tableau. Une classification est effectuée séparément pour les importations et les exportations. La ventilation en pourcentage est également indiquée pour les zones d'origine et de destination et pour les 10 premiers pays partenaires pour les dix plus récentes années. Les totaux pour l'union européenne (UE) sont calculés pour toutes les années sur la base des pays membres actuels. Les totaux pour la partie asiatique de l'ancienne URSS (Arménie, Azerbaïdjan, Géorgie, Kazakhstan, Kirghizistan, Tajikistan, Turkménistan, and Ouzbékistan) et pour la partie européenne de l'ancienne URSS (Bélarus, Estonie, Lettonie, Lituanie, République de Moldova, Fédération de Russie and Ukraine) sont calculés sur la base des pays indiqués à partir de l'année 1992. Pour les années avant 1992 cette division n'était pas possible et par consequence les totaux pour la partie européenne de l'ancienne URSS incluent la totalité de l'ancienne URSS pour ces années. L'Europe de l'Est comprend l'Albanie, la Bulgarie, la République tchéque, l'Hongrie, la Pologne, la Roumanie et la Slovaquie. Les totaux régionaux sont calculés seulement si la ventilation des partenaires disponibles dépasse 80% du total rapporté pour les importations et également pour les exportations.

d) Tableaux 4 et 5, présentant les quantités et les valeurs en dollars des Etats-Unis des importations et des exportations par marchandises jusqu'aux quatre plus récentes années. Les chiffres sont publiés pour une marchandise donnée si sa valeur pour une année donnée est égale ou supérieure à 0,3 pour cent de la valeur totale pour ladite année. Les marchandises sont présentées selon les titres de la CTCI (en abrégé); lorsque les descriptions sont précédées d'un astérisque (*) cela indique que les chiffres donnés sont égaux à ceux du niveau de la CTCI immédiatement supérieur qui dans ce cas n'est pas publié.

3. Parfois les données en dollars des tableaux décrits en (c) et (d) ci-dessus peuvent ne pas correspondre à celles en dollars des Etats Unis du tableau décrit en (a) ou à celles en monnaies nationales de ce tableau après l'application des facteurs de conversion. Les différences sont dues pour la plupart à des révisions au niveau du total du commerce qui parfois ne sont pas disponibles à un plus grand niveau de détail par produit et partenaire et qui n'ont donc pas été apportées aux tableaux décrits en (c) et (d).

4. Pour tous les pays, les données présentées aux tableaux 4 et 5 sont fondées sur la Classification type du commerce international (CTCI)[5/], Révision 2. De nombreux pays déclarent leurs données fondées sur la CTCI, Révision 3 ou le Système harmonisé de désignation et de codification des marchandises (SH). Les données ainsi déclarées ont été converties en CTCI, Révision 2. C'est une conversion difficile qui, pour certains codes de la CTCI, Révision 2 produit des données qui ne sont pas comparables avec celles déclarées en termes de CTCI, Révision 2, de façon très substantielle. Dans quelques cas, les données etaient déclarées à partir des nomenclatures nationales rélatives à la CTCI, Révisée; dans ces

cas la conversion en CTCI, Révision 2, est inexacte et certains codes de la CTCI ne couvrent pas exactement les échanges qui devraient leur être imputables. (Les Bahamas 1988 et 1991; Bahreïn 1989 jusqu'a 1993; Belize 1988 jusqu'à 1990; les Bermudes 1988 jusqu'à 1993; Malte 1988 et 1989; Myanmar 1991; les Antilles néerlandaises de 1988 à 1992 et 1995; Soudan 1992 jusqu'à 1994; République-Unie de Tanzanie 1987; et Tonga 1987 jusqu'à 1995).

5. Lorsqu'elles sont disponibles, des données plus détaillées par produit et pays partenaire du commerce extérieur, en SH96, en SH88, en CTCI, Révision 3, en CTCI, Révision 2, ou en CTCI, Révisée sont publiées dans Commodity Trade Statistics[6/] sous forme de microfiches.

6. Des descriptions détaillées des concepts et définitions actuels appliqués par les pays sont disponibles dans le document miméographé des Nations Unies "Pratiques nationales en matière de statistiques du commerce international des marchandises (ST/ESA/STAT/112), publié en février 1996 et disponible auprès de la Division de statistique des Nations Unies.

VOLUME II

7. Le volume II contient des tableaux présentant le commerce total de certains produits de base, analysé par régions et pays. Les régions aux noms identiques ont la même composition que celles du Volume I.

8. Tableaux par produits. Ces tableaux comprennent les importations et les exportations au niveau du groupe à 3 chiffres de la CTCI, Révision 2. Tous les groupes sont y compris à l'exception de 286, Minerais et concentrés d'uranium et de thorium; les exportations de 333, Huiles brutes de pétrole ou de minéraux bitumineux; 351, Energie électrique; 675, Feuillards en fer ou en acier; 688, Uranium et thorium et leurs alliages; 911, Colis postaux, non classés par catégorie; 961, Monnaies (autres que les pièces d'or) n'ayant pas cours légal et 971, Or, non monétaire (à l'exclusion des minerais et concentrés d'or). Les années couvertes sont les cinq années de 1993 à 1997. Les valeurs sont exprimées en dollars des Etats-Unis et les échanges sont analysés par pays et régions. Dans ces tableaux figurent les 40 pays les plus importants classés selon la somme des valeurs sur les années 1994, 1995 et 1996 inclus dans le tableau. Les quantités ne figurent pas dans ces tableaux.

9. Lors de la préparation de ces tableaux, on a eu recours à des estimations pour les pays dont les données n'étaient pas encore disponibles et ces estimations sont signalées par la lettre 'x'. Dans quelques cas, des estimations ont été faites pour certains pays qui ont été jugées adéquates pour être incluses dans les totaux régionaux et du monde mais non suffisamment élaborées pour être publiées séparément pour ces pays. Elles ont de ce fait été éliminées et remplacées par un 'x' dans les tableaux. Les groupes des produits mentionnés dans paragraphe 8 au-dessus, (286, les exportations de 333, 351, 675, 688, 911, 961 et 971) sont supprimés de la publication parce que ils étaient rapportés insuffisamment et portaient beaucoup d'estimations qui n'étaient pas assez expliquées. A vrai dire, un 'x' devrait signaler que les totaux régionaux et du monde comprennent des estimations.

Cependant, et en général, pratiquement tous les totaux régionaux et du monde comprennent des estimations. La lettre 'x' a été omise pour des raisons d'esthétique.

10. La procédure pour estimer les données du commerce extérieur pour une certaine année et un certain pays attend au départ quelques données declarées ('vraies'). Au moins il faut les totaux pour les importations et les exportations. Parfois des autres informations sur la ventilation des produits sont disponibles et sont utilisées; ça pourrait être des valeurs au niveau de 1-, 2- ou 3- chiffre de la classification des produits, qui sont déclarés par le pays. Ensuite la procédure d'estimation prend les données déclarées disponibles et les estimations initiales, qui comprennent soit (1) les valeurs des produits au niveau 3-chiffre qui étaient declarées par le pays pour une année adjointe, soit (2) les totaux des valeurs au niveau 3- chiffre sur la base des données declarées par les partenaires du pays concerné. Ensuite ces estimations initiales sont récalculées dans la façon que sur tous les niveaux de la classification des produits le total des valeurs estimés plus les valeurs déclarés est égale au valeur déclaré au niveau au-dessus et finalement est égale au valeur total pour les importations et les exportations.

11. Le Volume II aussi fournit des tableaux spéciaux où sont indiqués, entre autres, (a) la contribution des échanges de chaque pays par rapport à sa région et par rapport au monde; (b) le flux du commerce entre pays et régions et (c) les fluctuations des prix sur la base desquels les produits bouchaient au niveau international. Les titres des tableaux spéciaux sont:

A. Importations et exportations totales par régions et pays ou zones;
B. Exportations mondiales p ar classes de marchandises et par régions;
C. Croissance des exportations mondiales par catégories de marchandises et par régions;
D. Structure des exportations mondiales par catégories de marchandises et par régions;
E. Importations et exportations totales: indices par pays ou zones;
F. Exportations et importations totales: indices du quantum, de la valeur unitaire et des termes de l'échange par régions;
G. Exportations des produits manufacturés;
H. Importations des produits énergétiques: pays à économies développées;
I. Quelques indicateurs sur les importations des produits énergétiques: pays à économies développées;
J. Indices des prix des exportations des matières premières et des métaux non-ferreux.

Tableaux spéciaux.

12. Les groupes économiques et géographiques dans tous les tableaux spéciaux sont conformes aux groupes de pays ou zones sont présentés dans le Tableau Spécial A de ce numéro, bien que le Tableau Spécial A comprend quelquefois plus de détails en ce qui concerne les sous-groupes géographiques. (Voir le Tableau Spécial A pour les détails).

(A) Importations et exportations totales par régions et pays ou zones. Les totaux régionaux, économiques et mondiaux, ont été ajustés: a) pour y inclure des estimations pour les données non disponibles; b) pour transformer le cas échéant les importations f.o.b. en importations c.a.f.; c) pour y inclure les pays ou zones pour lesquels il n'existe pas de liste séparée; d) pour ramener les données au commerce spécial; e) pour ramener les données à l'année civile; et f) autant que possible, éliminer les incompatibilités dues à des modifications géographiques pour obtenir des séries comparables par exemple, la union européenne et l'Association européenne de libre-échange. Les données pour chaque pays correspondent aux données en monnaie nationale sont présentés dans le tableau 1 des tableaux par pays. Voir la fin du tableau pour les notes.

Le Bulletin Mensuel de Statistique présente des données mensuelles et trimestrielles.

(B) Exportations mondiales par classes de marchandises et par régions. Voir la fin du tableau pour la remarque générale et les notes.

(C) Croissance des exportations mondiales par catégories de marchandises et par régions. Les taux annuels de croissance ont tous été calculés à l'aide de la formule des intérêts composés:

$$r = \left(\sqrt[t]{\frac{Vn}{Vo}} - 1 \right) 100$$

r = Le taux annuel de croissance en pourcentage.
Vn = La valeur des exportations durant la dernière année de la période.
Vo = La valeur des exportations durant la première année de la période.
t = Le nombre d'années.

Voir la fin du Tableau Spécial D pour la remarque générale et les notes.

(D) Structure des exportations mondiales par catégories de marchandises et par régions. Les chiffres publiés sous le titre 'Origine des exportations' se réfèrent aux exportations de la région ou du pays indiqués dans la colonne zone. Il en est de même pour les 'Destinations des exportations'. Voir la fin du tableau pour la remarque générale et les notes.

(E) Importations et exportations totales: indices par pays ou zones. Sauf indication contraire, les indices de la valeur unitaire sont exprimés en monnaie nationale. Voir la fin du tableau pour la remarque générale et les notes.

Le Bulletin Mensuel de Statistique présente des données mensuelles et trimestrielles.

(F) Exportations et importations totales: indices du quantum, de la valeur unitaire et des termes de l'échange par régions. Voir la fin du tableau pour les notes.

Le Bulletin Mensuel de Statistique présente des données trimestrielles.

(G) Exportations des produits manufacturés. Voir la fin du tableau pour la remarque générale et les notes.

Le Bulletin Mensuel de Statistique présente des données trimestrielles.

(H) Importations des produits énergétiques: pays à économies développées. Voir la fin du tableau pour la remarque générale et les notes.

Le Bulletin Mensuel de Statistique présente des données trimestrielles.

(I) Quelques indicateurs sur les importations des produits énergétiques: pays à économies développées. Ce tableau indique la part des importations de combustibles dans la valeur totale des importations et des exportations ainsi que le rapport de l'indice de la valeur unitaire des produits manufacturés qu'ils exportent et de l'indice de la valeur unitaire des combustibles qu'ils importent. Voir la fin du tableau pour la remarque générale et les notes.

Le Bulletin Mensuel de Statistique présente des données trimestrielles.

(J) Indices des prix des exportations des matières et des métaux non-ferreux: économies de marché. Voir la fin du tableau pour la remarque générale et les notes.

Le Bulletin Mensuel de Statistique présente des données mensuelles et trimestrielles.

SOURCE ET PRESENTATION

13. Les données pour les Volumes I et II sont obtenues à partir de publications nationales, d'états soumis par les gouvernements pour cet ouvrage, et d'autres publications des Nations Unies telles que: Bulletin Mensuel de Statistique, et Annuaire Statistique. Des estimations pour quelques données faisant défaut sont préparées par la Division de Statistique des Nations Unies.

14. Les noms de pays et régions utilisés par divers pays pour leurs statistiques du commerce extérieur ne sont pas uniformes. Aussi, lorsque d'anciennes entités géographiques généralement indiquées dans les statistiques nationales ont changé, les pays peuvent avoir introduit les changements correspondants dans leurs statistiques à différentes époques. Dans la mesure du possible toutefois, les pays ou zones ont été désignés par leur nom actuel. Pour satisfaire les demandes des certains utilisateurs d'avoir des données d'un serie des années consécutives la possibilité de reconstruire des anciennes entités géographiques ou politiques était gardée pour, par exemple, les données relatives à l'ancienne URSS.

15. Sauf indication contraire, les groupements de pays sont conformes à ceux du Standard Country or Area Code for Statistical Use[4/] des Nations Unies.

16. En général, les données se réfèrent aux années selon le calendrier; cependant, pour les pays, qui déclarent leurs données selon l'année fiscale, les données sont présentées dans l'année qui couvre la plupart de l'année en référence.

INDICES NATIONAUX

17. Les indices nationaux, exprimés en monnaies nationales, ou en dollars des Etat Unis sont présentés dans le tableau 1. Ils indiquent les modifications dans le quantum et dans les prix (valeur unitaire) des agrégats des importations et des exportations. Chaque indice représente une modification entre la période à laquelle l'indice se réfère, la période courante, et une période fixe, la base de publication pour laquelle l'indice est représenté par 100. Pour faciliter les comparaisons, chaque fois qu'il était possible de le faire, les indices ont été ramenés à la base de publication 1990. Lorsque des modifications sont faites dans la couverture, la formule ou la période de base d'un indice, si cela est techniquement possible les deux séries s'enchaînent.

18. Les indices mensuels et trimestriels sont publiés dans le Bulletin Mensuel de Statistique des Nations Unies. On trouvera également dans le Supplément de 1977 à l'Annuaire Statistique et au Bulletin Mensuel de Statistique[7/] des notes plus détaillées sur les méthodes de calcul des indices nationaux.

PAYS EN TRANSITION

19. Pour la période couverte par l'Annuaire les pays classifiés antérieurement pour des raisons statistiques à économies planifiées centralement avaient un système de taux de change officiel entre leurs monnaies et celles des pays extérieurs consistant avec le taux de 0,90 nouveau roubles pour 1 dollar des Etats-Unis avant le 24 décembre 1971 et 0,829 jusqu'à février 1973; depuis cette date le taux a fluctué. Les pays d'Europe orientale utilisaient généralement ces taux lorsqu'il était nécessaire de convertir des devises en monnaie nationale pour préparer les statistiques du commerce extérieur. Les données qui en résultent permettent davantage une comparaison avec les transactions des autres pays qu'une comparaison avec les transactions monétaires intérieures.

20. Les statistiques du commerce extérieur de ces pays ont des définitions différentes de celles qui peuvent exister dans les autres pays. Les différentes définitions peuvent être la source des divergences observées pour le même flux de marchandise enregistré par deux pays partenaires ayant un système économique différent. Les échanges entre ces pays peuvent être conduits sur une base différente de celle qui régit les échanges entre autres pays. Le concept de la valeur de transaction, par exemple, est basé sur l'existence d'un prix de marché entre l'importateur et l'exportateur sur lequel les variations de l'offre et de la demande ont plus d'influence qu'ils ne peuvent en avoir dans les échanges de ces pays. Faute de données précises sur les valeurs unitaires des produits de base échangés entre ces pays,

il est difficile de connaître les effets possibles de ces différences sur les statistiques du commerce extérieur. De plus en plus, depuis 1992, les pays en transition ont adopté les concepts et définitions pour la statistique du commerce international comparables à celles qui sont en vigueur dans les autres pays.

NOTE GENERALE[8/]

21. Les statistiques dans cet Annuaire ont été compilées par les autorités nationales des statistiques principalement conforme aux recommandations des Nations Unies publiées dans les Statistiques du Commerce international concepts et définitions, révision 1.[8/] En 1998 les Nations Unies ont fait paraître une révision de suite de cette publication; les pays étaient demandées d'introduire ces nouveaux concepts et définitions à partir des données pour l'année 1999. Les éléments principaux de ces concepts et définitions (Révision 1) sont:

1. Territoire. Les statistiques rapportées par un pays s'appliquent en général au territoire douanier de cet état. Généralement territoire douanier et territoire géographique coïncident, le cas contraire étant indiqué dans les notes par pays. Les modifications dans le territoire douanier sont également indiquées dans les notes par pays. Sauf information contraire, l'unification de deux territoires séparés auparavant donne lieu à l'élimination des échanges entre ces deux territoires. Dans le cas d'une séparation d'un territoire en deux, les échanges entre ces deux territoires viennent à apparaître.

2. Système du commerce. Deux systèmes sont généralement utilisés ne différant que par la façon dont le commerce d'entrepôt et les réexportations sont enregistrés.

a) Commerce spécial. Les importations spéciales comprennent les marchandises entrées directement pour la consommation (y compris les transformations et réparations) et les marchandises sorties des entrepôts douaniers ou des zones franches pour être mises à la consommation. Les exportations spéciales comprennent les exportations de produits nationaux, c'est-à-dire les marchandises entièrement ou partiellement produites ou fabriquées dans le pays, ainsi que les exportations nationalisées (ces dernières sont des biens qui ayant été inclus dans les importations spéciales sont réexportés en l'état.)

b) Commerce général. Les importations générales comprennent les importations pour la consommation et les importations en entrepôt douanier ou en zone franche. Les exportations générales comprennent les exportations de produits nationaux et les réexportations. Ces dernières, dans le système du commerce général, comprennent les exportations nationalisées et les marchandises exportées des entrepôts douaniers et des zones franches sans avoir été transformées depuis leur importation.

Le transit direct, c'est-à-dire les marchandises uniquement transbordées ou traversant le pays pour des raisons de transport, est exclu du commerce général aussi bien que du commerce spécial.

Les titres de chaque tableau indiquent le système du commerce auquel se réfèrent les données.

3. Evaluation. Lors de sa quinzième session en 1953, le Conseil Economique et Social, tenant compte du fait que les statistiques du commerce extérieur doivent refléter la réalité économique, a recommandé que les gouvernements des pays membres des Nations Unies utilisent, dans la mesure du possible, les valeurs de transaction en préparant leurs statistiques du commerce international ou qu'ils fournissent des informations supplémentaires basées sur les valeurs de transaction quand les politiques nationales font état d'autres valeurs (Résolution 469 B (XV) du Conseil Economique et Social). La valeur de transaction à l'importation est la valeur à laquelle les marchandises ont été achetées par l'importateur plus le coût de l'assurance et du fret jusqu'à la frontière des pays importateurs (valeur c.a.f.). A l'exportation, la valeur de transaction représente la valeur à laquelle les marchandises ont été vendues par l'exportateur y compris le coût de l'assurance du transport pour amener les marchandises à la frontière des pays exportateurs (valeur f.o.b.).

4. Conversion des monnaies. Pour les données dans cet Annuaire la conversion des valeurs nationales en dollars des Etats-Unis est effectuée au moyen de taux de conversion basés sur les taux de change officiels. Pour les monnaies sujettes à de larges marges de fluctuations par rapport au dollar, dont le nombre s'est accru considérablement depuis 1971, on utilise des moyennes pondérées des taux de change calculées spécialement dans ce but. La moyenne pondérée est le résultat des taux de change mensuels, généralement fournis par le Fonds Monétaire International, pondérés par les valeurs des importations et des exportations correspondantes. Les facteurs de conversion s'appliquent aux totaux des échanges mais pas nécessairement aux importations ou à l'exportation d'une marchandise donnée.

5. Marchandises. Dans la définition du commerce extérieur on entend par marchandises tous les biens dont l'importation ou l'exportation contribue à l'accroissement ou à la diminution du stock des ressources matérielles dans un pays. Sauf information contraire dans les notes par pays, le traitement des catégories de marchandises suit les règles énoncées ci-dessous:

a) Or. L'or dans le commerce international se présente sous trois formes:

i) Pièces d'or et lingots y compris l'or monétaire;
ii) Or non raffiné y compris les minerais et les concentrés;
iii) Or semi-ouvré dont la valeur de l'or représente au moins 80% de la valeur totale, y compris la limaille et les poussières et les formes primaires telles que feuilles et barres et les alliages d'or.

De ces différents types d'or, l'or monétaire est exclu du commerce des marchandises tandis que les autres types sont inclus, à l'exception de ceux indiqués ci-dessous. Tout transfert d'or entre les autorités monétaires doit être traité comme échange d'or monétaire, les autres échanges portant sur l'or sont classés comme or non-monétaire.

b) Minerai d'argent. Concentrés, lingots, pièces non émises, limailles et argent ouvré ou semi-ouvré sont tous inclus dans les échanges de marchandises.

c) Monnaie et titres de propriété. Pièces de monnaie d'argent et de métal, billets de banque et titres en circulation sont exclus du commerce. Les pièces, billets et titres non en circulation sont inclus à la valeur intrinsèque du papier ou du métal frappé.

d) Le commerce pour le compte de l'Etat. Il est inclus dans le commerce des marchandises. Les échanges au titre des programmes d'aide civile et militaire, les réparations de guerre et les équipements militaires[9/] sont donc inclus. Quand les marchandises sont destinées à des institutions nationales (ambassades ou forces armées) stationnées à l'étranger, elles ne sont pas comprises dans les statistiques.

e) Importations et exportations temporaires. Les effets des touristes et des voyageurs (y compris les véhicules) qui n'ont pas été acquis à l'étranger, les objets pour expositions ou études, les animaux pour la course ou la reproduction, les échantillons et les emballages en retour qui sont considérés comme devant être retournés dans un intervalle de temps assez court sont exclus.

f) Trafic de perfectionnement et de réparation. Les pays qui envoient à l'étranger temporairement des marchandises pour réparation ou complément d'ouvraison effectuent un trafic passif de réparation. Les pays recevant des marchandises dans les mêmes conditions effectuent un trafic actif de réparation. Les mouvements d'entrée et de sortie sont généralement exclus des importations et des exportations.

g) Commerce par poste. Il est inclus dans le commerce des marchandises.

h) Poisson. Le poisson et les épaves débarqués dans des ports étrangers par des navires nationaux et ceux débarqués dans des ports du pays par des navires étrangers sont exclus des statistiques.

i) Vente et achat de navires et d'aéronefs. La vente et l'achat de navires et d'aéronefs neufs sont inclus. Les navires et les aéronefs d'occasion inscrits sur le registre d'immatriculation du pays ou radiés de ce registre sont exclus du commerce quand ces mouvements sont dûs à un transfert de propriété.

j) Avitaillement des navires et des avions. Ils doivent être généralement inclus dans les exportations de marchandises.

6. Pays Partenaire. Les pays partenaires peuvent être distingués: a) à l'importation, suivant: l'origine ou la production, la consignation ou la provenance ou il'achat; b) à l'exportation, suivant: la consommation, la dernière destination connue ou la vente.

7. Echanges par produits. L'analyse est selon la Classification Type pour le Commerce International.

CLASSIFICATION TYPE POUR LE COMMERCE INTERNATIONAL (CTCI) ET UN SYSTEME HARMONISE DE DESIGNATION ET DE CODIFICATION DES MARCHANDISES (SH)

22. En juillet 1950, le Conseil Economique et Social des Nations Unies, sur avis de la Commission de Statistique, a recommandé aux pays de rassembler leurs statistiques des échanges par produits selon la CTCI originale[5/] afin de disposer au niveau mondial de données comparables pour l'analyse du commerce extérieur. La CTCI originale a été préparée par le Secrétariat des Nations Unies avec l'aide d'experts et en coopération avec les gouvernements et les organisations internationales concernées.

23. En mai 1960 la Commission de Statistique a approuvé une révision de la CTCI appelée la CTCI, révisée, qui tenait compte des modifications dans les courants commerciaux intervenus depuis 1950 et qui permettait un passage plus facile entre la CTCI et les nomenclatures internationales. La CTCI, révisée présentait selon une classification statistique les positions de la nomenclature tarifaire NCCD du Conseil de Coopération Douanière.

24. La CTCI, révisée comprend 625 sous-groupes (identifiés par un code à quatre chiffres) qui correspondent pour l'essentiel aux postes de la CTCI originale. Un certain nombre de sous-groupes ont été subdivisés soit pour obtenir des détails supplémentaires soit pour assurer une concordance exacte avec la NCCD. La CTCI, révisée comporte donc 1312 rubriques de base (niveau des 5 chiffres de la CTCI). Les sous-groupes sont rassemblés en 177 groupes, 56 divisions et 10 sections.

25. Les positions de la CTCI sont individualisées par leur numéro de code. Le contenu précis de chaque code est défini dans la CTCI, révisée. Si l'on compare les données selon la CTCI, révisée avec des données classées selon une nomenclature nationale, il faut tenir compte de ce que la même description, généralement abrégée, peut s'appliquer à des groupes de marchandises légèrement différents.

26. La révision de 1960 représentait par rapport à la CTCI initiale une amélioration considérable. Néanmoins vers la fin des années 1960 on a constaté que, pour l'essentiel, les raisons qui avaient conduit à l'établissement de la CTCI puis à sa première révision, se retrouvaient à nouveau valables. Depuis 1960 le volume des échanges commerciaux s'est accru rapidement tandis que leur répartition géographique et leur composition par produits se modifiaient radicalement. Une nouvelle révision de la CTCI fut donc entreprise. En octobre 1974, la Commission Statistique a approuvé cette révision, la désignation de la nouvelle révision est CTCI, Révision 2[5/]. En mai 1975 le Conseil Economique et Social a recommandé aux Etats membres des Nations Unies de communiquer les données sur les statistiques du commerce extérieur en se conformant autant que possible et le plus tôt possible à la CTCI, Révision 2. A partir des données pour 1976, certains pays ont commencé à communiquer leurs données selon la CTCI, Révision 2.

27. Il y avait entre les titres de base de la <u>Classification type pour le commerce international, Révision 2</u> et les subdivisions de la Nomenclature du Conseil de Coopération

Douanière une correspondance biunivoque. Toutefois, un certain nombre d'utilisateurs ont estimé que les subdivisions des positions de la NCCD (et par conséquent celles de la CTCI, Révision 2) ne suffisaient pas à leurs besoins[10/]. La nécessité d'une harmonisation des classifications économiques a également été signalée[11/]. En partie pour répondre à ces besoins, le Conseil de coopération douanière a assumé en mai 1973 la responsabilité d'élaborer et de mettre au point un système harmonisé de désignation et de codification des marchandises (SH)[12/].

28. A sa vingt et unième session, en janvier 1981, la Commission de statistique a pris note du fait qu'une troisième révision de la CTCI devait être disponible lorsque la NCCD révisée et le SH entreraient tous deux en vigueur[13/]. En conséquence, dans le courant de la même année, le Secrétariat de l'ONU a commencé à travailler à la révision de la CTCI, Révision 2 en partant du principe que le maximum devait être fait pour en conserver le caractère général et la structure, tout en tenant compte de la nécessité de son harmonisation avec la NCCD révisée, avec la Classification internationale type, par industrie, de toutes les branches d'activité économique (CITI), Révision 3[14/] et avec une Classification des produits centrale (CPC)[15/] dont l'élaboration était menée conjointement par la Division de statistique des Nations Unies et l'Office statistique des Communautés européennes.

29. Le projet final a été révisé et approuvé par la Commission de statistique à sa vingt-troisième session, en février 1985[16/], et une résolution a été adoptée par le Conseil économique et social le 28 mai 1985 (résolution 1985/7) qui, inter-alia, a recommandé aux Etats Membres de communiquer des données sur les statistiques du commerce extérieur aux institutions internationales en se conformant autant que possible et le plus rapidement possible à la Classification type pour le commerce international (troisième version révisée).

30. Le système harmonisé de désignation et de codification des marchandises (appelé système harmonisé) (SH) a été adopté par le Conseil de coopération douanière en juin 1983, tandis que la Convention internationale sur le système harmonisé de désignation et de codification des marchandises (Convention SH) est entré en vigueur le ler janvier 1988 (SH88). Au ler 18 avril 1997, les parties contractantes étaient au nombre de 88 et 64 autres pays ou territoires ne figuraient pas parmi les parties contractantes, mais utilisaient le système harmonisé à des fins douanières/statistiques.

31. Lors de la vingt-septième session, qui s'est tenue à New York du 22 février au 3 mars 1993, la Commission de statistique des Nations Unies a recommandé "que les pays adoptent le SH pour l'établissement et la diffusion de leurs statistiques du commerce international"[17/].

32. Conformément au préambule à la Convention SH, qui reconnaissait l'importance d'une actualisation effective du système harmonisé compte tenu de l'évolution de la technologie ou des courants commerciaux internationaux, le système harmonisé est régulièrement passé en revue et corrigé. Lors de sa vingt-septième session, la Commission de statistique des Nations Unies a "recommendé que le Conseil de coopération douanière tienne pleinement compte des effets que les modifications proposées pourraient avoir sur

le plan statistique et de prendre dûment en considération les besoins et les capacités des pays en développement"[18/]. Quelques corrections mineures du système harmonisé de 1988, résultant par ailleurs de la suppression d'un code à 6 chiffres, ont été introduites en 1992 (SH92). Une série plus complète de modifications a été adoptée en 1993 et celles-ci sont entrées en vigueur le ler janvier 1996 (SH96).

33. A sa vingt-huitième session (27 février - 3 mars 1995), la Commission de statistique a examiné les changements qu'il faudrait apporter à la troisième version révisée de la CTCI pour l'adapter au SH96. La Commission a décidé que les changements à apporter à la troisième version révisée de la CTCI pour préserver une parfaite correspondance avec le système harmonisé étaient simplement des modifications mineures. La Commission a donc décidé qu'il serait inutile de publier une quatrième version révisée de la CTCI[19/].

1/ Classification par grandes catégories économiques, (selon les définitions de la CTCI, révisée), Etudes statistiques, Série M N° 53, (publication des Nations Unies, numéro de vente 71.XVII.12).

2/ Classification des marchandises par origine industrielle (Relation entre la Classification type pour le commerce international et la Classification internationale type, par industrie, de toutes les branches d'activité économique), Etudes statistiques, Série M N° 43, (publication des Nations Unies, numéro de vente 66.XVII.7).

3/ Classification internationale type, par industrie, de toutes les branches d'activité économique (révisée), Etudes statistiques, Série M N° 4, Rev. 1. (publication des Nations Unies, numéro de vente 58.XVII.7).

4/ United Nations Standard Country Code, Statistical Papers, Series M N° 49, (United Nations publication, Sales No. E.70.XVII.13).

United Nations Standard Country or Area Code for Statistical Use, Statistical Papers, Series M N° 49, Rev. 1, (United Nations publication, Sales No. E.75.XVII.8).

Standard Country or Area Codes for Statistical Use, Statistical Papers Series M N° 49, Rev.2, (United Nations publication, Sales No. E.82.XVII.8).

Codes standard des pays et des zones à usage statistique, Documents statistiques, Series M N° 49, Rev. 3.

5/ Classification type pour le commerce international, (deuxième version révisée), Etudes statistiques, Série M N° 34/Rev. 2, (publication des Nations Unies, numéro de vente F.75.XVII.6).

Classification type pour le commerce international (troisième version révisée), Etudes statistiques, Série M N° 34/Rev. 3, (publication des Nations Unies, numéro de vente F.86.XVII.12).

6/ Commodity Trade Statistics, Sous forme de microfiches (CTS SER.D COM), présentent annuellement les échanges par origine et destination pour un grand nombre de positions des classifications SH et CTCI.

7/ Supplément de 1977 à l'Annuaire Statistique et au Bulletin mensuel de statistique, ST/ESA/STAT/SER.S/SUPPL.2, ST/ESA/STAT/SER.Q/SUPPL.2, (publication des Nations Unies, numéro de vente F.78.XVII.10).

8/ Statistiques du commerce international concepts et définitions, Etudes statistiques, Série M N° 52 Révision 1, (publication des Nations Unies, numéro de vente F.82.XVII.14).

Statistiques du commerce international concepts et définitions, Etudes statistiques, Série M N° 52 Révision 2, (publication des Nations Unies, numéro de vente F.98.XVII.16).

9/ Les pays qui excluent l'équipement militaire utilisent des définitions différentes pour cette catégorie de marchandise, pour la majorité des pays cependant, armes et munitions constituent la plupart de l'équipement militaire exclu des statistiques.

10/ Groupe de travail commun Division de statistique de l'ONU - Office statistique des communautés européennes sur les nomenclatures au niveau mondial, "Système harmonisé de désignation et de codification des marchandises pour les besoins du commerce international" (UNSO/SOEC/1/2).

11/ Secrétariat de l'ONU, "L'harmonisation des classifications statistiques: compte rendu d'une réunion d'un groupe d'experts" (ST/ESA/STAT/78).

12/ Conseil de coopération douanière, "Système harmonisé de désignation et de codification des marchandises", 1985.

13/ Documents officiels du Conseil économique et social, 1981, Supplément N° 2. (E/1981/12).

14/ Classification International Type, par industrie, de toutes les branches d'activité économique, Etudes statistiques, Série M N° 4, Révision 3 (publication des Nations Unies, numéro de vente F.90.XVII.11).

15/ Classification centrale de produits (CPC) provisoire, Etudes statistiques, Série M N° 77 (publication des Nations Unies, numéro de vente F.91.XVII.7).

16/ Documents officiels du Conseil économique et social, 1985, Supplément N° 6 (E/1985/26), para. 57 (d).

17/ Documents officiels du Conseil économique et social, 1993, Supplément N° 6 (E/1993/26), para. 162 (d).

18/ Documents officiels du Conseil économique et social, 1993, Supplément N° 6 (E/1993/26), para. 162 (e).

19/ Documents officiels du Conseil économique et social, 1995, Supplément N° 8 (E/CN.3/1995/28), para. 19 (e).

1997 INTERNATIONAL TRADE STATISTICS YEARBOOK

VOLUME I

COUNTRY TABLES

ANNUAIRE DE STATISTIQUE DU COMMERCE INTERNATIONAL 1997

VOLUME I

TABLEAUX PAR PAYS

FOOTNOTES

Footnotes relating to each set of country tables are located at the bottom of Table 5.

NOTES

Les notes relatives à chaque ensemble de tableau par pays sont situées à la fin du tableau 5.

1. HISTORICAL SERIES, 1958–1997 GENERAL TRADE, IMPORTS C.I.F., EXPORTS F.O.B.
SERIES HISTORIQUES, 1958–1997 COMMERCE GENERAL, IMPORTATIONS C.A.F., EXPORTATIONS F.O.B

YEAR ANNEE	VALUE IN MILLION U.S. DOLLARS VALEUR EN MILLION U.S. DOLLARS MERCHANDISE –MARCHANDISE		GOLD –OR		CONVERSION FACTORS FACTEURS DE CONVERSION CENTS E.U. PAR		INDEX NUMBERS –INDICES QUANTUM		UNIT VALUE VALEUR UNITAIRE	
	IMPORTS	EXPORTS	IMPORTS	EXPORTS	IMPORTS	EXPORTS	IMPORTS	EXPORTS	IMPORTS	EXPORTS
1958	79.00	29.00								
1960	81.00	49.00								
1963	71.00	48.00								
1965	90.00	60.00								
1967	105.00	66.00								
1968	115.00	70.00								
1969	125.00	75.00								
1970	135.00	76.00								
1971	146.00	77.00								
1972	154.00	85.00								
1973	175.00	100.90								
1974	197.00	142.20								
1975	222.00	175.00								
1976	245.00	200.00								
1977	280.00	235.00								
1978	325.00	260.00								
1979	370.00	350.00								
1985	360.14	300.14								
1986	380.86	355.71								
1987	378.57	355.71								
1988	536.17	424.83								
1989	592.50	473.28								
1990	253.00	151.53								
1995	650.01	201.96								
1996	938.49	211.14								
1997	628.98	137.68								

2. IMPORTS BY BROAD ECONOMIC CATEGORY AND EXPORTS BY INDUSTRIAL ORIGIN. (PERCENTAGE OF TOTAL VALUE)
IMPORTATIONS PAR CATEGORIES ECONOMIQUES ET EXPORTATIONS PAR BRANCHE D'ACTIVITE.(EN POURCENTAGE DE LA VALEUR TOTALE)

IMPORTS – IMPORTATIONS

	1991	1992	1993	1994	1995	1996	1997
TOTAL IMPORTS–IMPORTATIONS TOTALES						100.	100.
1 FOOD BEV–ALIMENTATION BOISSONS						33.0	26.4
11 PRIMARY–PRODUITS DE BASE						12.9	9.4
111 FOR INDUSTRY–POUR L'INDUSTRIE						6.6	3.4
112 FOR HOUSEHOLDS–POUR LES MENAGES						6.2	6.0
12 PROCESSED–PRODUITS ELABORES						20.1	17.0
121 FOR INDUSTRY–POUR L'INDUSTRIE						11.7	9.4
122 FOR HOUSEHOLDS–POUR LES MENAGES						8.5	7.5
2 IND SUPPLIES–APPROV INDUSTRIELS						30.0	36.4
21 PRIMARY–PRODUITS DE BASE						1.3	1.8
22 PROCESSED–PRODUITS ELABORES						28.7	34.7
3 FUELS–COMBUSTIBLES						2.4	2.9
31 PRIMARY–PRODUITS DE BASE						0.5	1.0
32 PROCESSED–PRODUITS ELABORES						2.0	1.9
321 MOTOR SPIRIT–ESSENCE							
322 OTHER–AUTRES						2.0	1.9
4 MACHINERY–EQUIPEMENT						14.8	13.4
41 CAPITAL EQUIPMENT–MACHINES						14.3	12.7
42 PARTS–PIECES ACCESSOIRES						0.5	0.7
5 TRANSPORT–TRANSPORT						6.9	5.6
51 PASSENGER CARS–AUTOMOBILES						2.3	2.1
52 OTHER–AUTRES						3.1	2.3
521 INDUSTRIAL–INDUSTRIELS						3.0	2.3
522 NON INDUSTRIAL–NON INDUSTRIEL						0.2	0.0
53 PARTS–PIECES ACCESSOIRES						1.5	1.2
6 CONSUM GOODS–BIENS CONSOMMATION						12.5	14.8
61 DURABLE–DURABLES						2.5	3.9
62 SEMI DURABLE–SEMI DURABLES						6.8	8.4
63 NON DURABLE–NON DURABLES						3.3	2.6
7 GOODS NES–BIENS NDA						0.3	0.4

EXPORTS – EXPORTATIONS

	1991	1992	1993	1994	1995	1996	1997
TOTAL EXPORTS–EXPORTATIONS TOTALES						100.	100.
1 AGRICULTURE						10.3	15.1
2 MINING QUARRY–INDUS EXTRACTIVES						7.2	4.0
3 MANUFACTURING–IND MANUFACTUR						82.4	80.9
31 FOOD BEV TOBACCO–ALIM BOISS TAB						8.9	8.7
32 TEXTILES–INDUSTRIES TEXTILES						50.9	45.4
33 WOOD & PRODUCTS–BOIS & PRODUITS						2.3	2.6
34 PAPER & PRODUCTS–PAPIER & PRODT						1.5	2.9
35 CHEMICALS–INDUSTRIES CHIMIQUES						4.2	2.6
36 NON METAL MIN–MIN NON METAL						0.2	0.5
37 BASIC METAL–IND METAL BASE						9.5	5.5
38 METAL MANUF–MANUF METAL						4.1	11.8
39 OTH MANUF IND–AUTRES MANUF						0.7	1.0

3. TRADE BY PRINCIPAL COUNTRIES OF ORIGIN AND DESTINATION (VALUE IN MILLION U.S. DOLLARS)
ECHANGES SELON LES PRINCIPAUX PAYS D'ORIGINE ET DE DESTINATION (VALEUR EN MILLIONS DE DOLLARS EU)

COUNTRIES–PAYS	GENERAL IMPORTS C.I.F. IMPORTATIONS GENERALES C.A.F				
	1993	1994	1995	1996	1997
World				979.7	950.1
Africa				9.0	2.5
Americas				21.6	3.0
– Northern America				16.0	2.8
– LAIA				5.4	0.1
– CACM					0.0
– Caribbean				0.1	0.1
– Rest of America				0.2	
Asia excl fmr USSR				52.3	47.8
– Middle East				45.3	45.9
Asia former USSR				0.0	0.0
Europe excl fmr USSR				890.8	890.8
– European Union				744.9	792.3
– Eastern Europe				74.2	41.4
– Rest of Europe				71.8	57.2
Europe former USSR				6.0	5.1
Oceania				0.0	0.9
Other				0.0	
Italy/Italie				394.9	435.7
Greece/Grèce				198.9	247.5
Germany/Allemagne				57.0	40.7
Turkey/Turquie				41.2	41.6
Bulgaria/Bulgarie				37.2	25.2
TFYR Macedonia				19.6	19.4
France, Monaco				26.7	11.8
Switzerland, Liechtenst.				19.4	15.2
Belgium–Luxembourg				23.5	10.2
Romania/Roumanie				23.8	2.8
Austria/Autriche				10.8	15.6
Slovenia/Slovénie				11.4	14.3
United Kingdom				13.3	9.8
Croatia/Croatie				13.9	4.2
USA/Etats–Unis d'Amer				15.7	2.0
Hungary/Hongrie				7.5	9.8
Netherlands/Pays–Bas				9.1	7.6
Denmark/Danemark				5.5	6.0
Egypt/Egypte				8.9	1.9
Yugoslavia/Yougoslavie				7.0	1.4
Czech Republic				4.7	3.0
Ukraine				3.4	3.8
Spain/Espagne				0.8	6.3
Cyprus/Chypre				2.7	3.4
Brazil/Brésil				5.3	0.0
India/Inde				3.6	0.1
Sweden/Suède				3.5	0.2
Russian Federation				2.2	0.6
China/Chine				1.4	1.0
Malta/Malte				0.0	2.3
Poland/Pologne				1.0	0.6
Ireland/Irlande				0.5	0.9
Canada				0.3	0.8
Republic of Moldova				0.3	0.7
Japan/Japon				0.6	0.3
Australia/Australie				0.0	0.7
Lebanon/Liban				0.2	0.5
Norway, Svalbard and JM				0.4	0.3
Other Asia n.e.s.				0.7	0.0
Syrian Arab Republic				0.4	0.3

COUNTRIES–PAYS	GENERAL EXPORTS F.O.B. EXPORTATIONS GENERALES F.O.B.				
	1993	1994	1995	1996	1997
Monde				220.0	210.4
Afrique				0.0	0.0
Amériques				2.9	3.2
– Amérique du Nord				2.6	3.1
– ALAI				0.3	0.1
– MCAC					
– Caraïbes					
– Autre Amérique					
Asie anc. URSS exclus				7.5	2.1
– Moyen–Orient				6.9	2.0
Asie ancienne URSS					
Europe anc. URSS exclus				205.9	205.1
– Union Européenne				189.2	184.1
– Europe de l'Est				1.0	1.3
– Autre de l'Europe				15.7	19.7
Europe ancienne URSS				0.1	0.0
Océanie				3.5	0.0
Autre				0.0	
Italy/Italie				127.3	104.0
Greece/Grèce				28.6	43.1
Germany/Allemagne				15.2	14.4
Netherlands/Pays–Bas				6.4	11.7
TFYR Macedonia				6.8	5.5
Croatia/Croatie				1.5	8.8
Turkey/Turquie				6.8	1.9
France, Monaco				4.4	4.0
USA/Etats–Unis d'Amer				2.6	3.1
Austria/Autriche				2.4	3.1
Slovenia/Slovénie				2.8	2.6
Yugoslavia/Yougoslavie				3.2	0.8
Belgium–Luxembourg				3.0	1.0
New Zealand				3.5	0.0
Switzerland, Liechtenst.				1.3	0.9
Denmark/Danemark				0.6	0.7
Sweden/Suède					1.2
Malta/Malte				0.2	0.9
United Kingdom				0.6	0.2
Japan/Japon				0.6	0.1
Poland/Pologne				0.2	0.5
Hungary/Hongrie				0.3	0.4
Ireland/Irlande				0.0	0.7
Czech Republic				0.4	0.3
Spain/Espagne				0.6	0.0
Brazil/Brésil				0.3	
Romania/Roumanie				0.2	0.1
Venezuela				0.1	0.1
Bulgaria/Bulgarie				0.0	0.0
Iran (Islamic Rep of)				0.1	
Russian Federation				0.1	0.0
Canada				0.0	0.0
Australia/Australie				0.0	
Jordan/Jordanie					0.0
Cyprus/Chypre				0.0	
Republic of Moldova				0.0	
Egypt/Egypte					0.0
Lebanon/Liban					0.0
Areas n.e.s.				0.0	

(VALUE AS PERCENTAGE OF WORLD TOTAL)(VALEURS EN POURCENTAGE DU TOTAL MONDIAL)

	1988	1989	1990	1991	1992	1993	1994	1995	1996	1997
Africa	1.8	1.2	1.2						0.9	0.3
Americas									2.2	0.3
– Northern America									1.6	0.3
– LAIA									0.5	0.0
– CACM										0.0
– Caribbean									0.0	0.0
– Rest of America									0.0	
Asia excl fmr USSR	9.5	5.6	7.7						5.3	5.0
– Middle East	0.6	1.0	1.4						4.6	4.8
Asia former USSR									0.0	0.0
Europe excl fmr USSR	79.5	82.9	80.2						90.9	93.8
– European Union	24.5	33.4	34.9						76.0	83.4
– Eastern Europe	50.7	44.8	40.1						7.6	4.4
– Rest of Europe	4.3	4.8	5.2						7.3	6.0
Europe former USSR									0.6	0.5
Oceania									0.0	0.1
Other	9.3	10.3	10.9						0.0	
Italy/Italie	7.2	8.7	9.8						40.3	45.9
Greece/Grèce	4.9	7.3	5.5						20.3	26.0
Germany/Allemagne									5.8	4.3
Turkey/Turquie	0.6	1.0	1.4						4.2	4.4
Bulgaria/Bulgarie	9.3	7.3	6.3						3.8	2.7
TFYR Macedonia									2.0	2.0
France, Monaco	1.4	1.7	2.6						2.7	1.2
Switzerland, Liechtenst.									2.0	1.6
Belgium–Luxembourg									2.4	1.1
Romania/Roumanie	8.1	7.0	4.8						2.4	0.3

	1988	1989	1990	1991	1992	1993	1994	1995	1996	1997
Afrique	1.2	1.1	1.7						0.0	0.0
Amériques									1.3	1.5
– Amérique du Nord									1.2	1.5
– ALAI									0.1	0.1
– MCAC										
– Caraïbes										
– Autre Amérique										
Asie anc. URSS exclus	7.1	7.6	7.5						3.4	1.0
– Moyen–Orient	0.2	0.2	0.4						3.2	0.9
Asie ancienne URSS										
Europe anc. URSS exclus	80.9	80.9	76.8						93.6	97.5
– Union Européenne	19.5	21.5	23.4						86.0	87.5
– Europe de l'Est	54.3	54.5	46.6						0.5	0.6
– Autre de l'Europe	7.1	4.9	6.9						7.2	9.4
Europe ancienne URSS									0.0	0.0
Océanie									1.6	0.0
Autre	10.7	10.3	14.0						0.0	
Italy/Italie	6.3	7.9	9.0						57.8	49.4
Greece/Grèce	1.8	3.0	2.9						13.0	20.5
Germany/Allemagne									6.9	6.9
Netherlands/Pays–Bas									2.9	5.5
TFYR Macedonia									3.1	2.6
Croatia/Croatie									0.7	4.2
Turkey/Turquie	0.2	0.2	0.4						3.1	0.9
France, Monaco	1.6	1.7	1.4						2.0	1.9
USA/Etats–Unis d'Amer									1.2	1.5
Austria/Autriche	5.4	4.1	4.8						1.1	1.5

4. General Imports C.I.F. by Commodities according to the S.I.T.C. (Rev. 2) in million U.S. Dollars
Importations Générales C.A.F. par Produits d'après la C.T.C.I. (Rév. 2) en millions de Dollars E.U.

SITC CTCI	COMMODITY	1994 QUANTITY QUANTITE	1994 VALUE VALEUR	1995 QUANTITY QUANTITE	1995 VALUE VALEUR	1996 QUANTITY QUANTITE	1996 VALUE VALEUR	1997 QUANTITY QUANTITE	1997 VALUE VALEUR	PRODUIT
	ALL COMMODITIES						979.8		950.2	TOUS PRODUITS
0	FOOD AND LIVE ANIMALS						288.1		220.5	ALIMENTS,ANIMAUX VIVANTS
01	MEAT AND PREPARATIONS						35.7		28.6	VIANDES ET PREPARATIONS
011	MEAT FRESH,CHILLD,FROZEN					W 28595	33.0	W 14632	26.3	VIANDES FRAICHES,REF,CONGE
0111	BOVINE MEAT FRESH,FROZEN					W 6083	8.6	W 2557	5.7	VIANDES BOVIN FRAI,REF
01111	BOVINE MEAT WITH BONE IN					W 2546	3.6	W 663	1.5	VIANDES BOVIN NON DESOSS
01112	BOVINE MEAT BONELESS					W 3537	5.1	W 1893	4.3	VIANDES BOVIN DESOSSEES
0113	PIG MEAT FRESH,CHLD,FRZN					W 2473	3.6	W 821	1.8	VIANDE DE PORC
0114	POULTRY FRESH CHLLD,FRZN					W 18674	18.6	W 9830	16.3	VOLAILLES MORTES
02	DAIRY PRODCTS,BIRDS'EGGS						11.2		6.7	PRODUITS LAITIERS,OEUFS
023	BUTTER					W 1735	3.2	W 651	2.3	BEURRE
024	CHEESE AND CURD					W 3169	4.1	W 500	1.4	FROMAGE ET CAILLEBOTTE
03	FISH AND PREPARATIONS						2.0		3.9	POISSONS ET PREPARATIONS
04	CEREALS AND PREPARATIONS						158.9		115.3	CEREALES ET PRODUITS
041	WHEAT ETC UNMILLED					W 242739	51.8	W 74799	22.3	FROMENT,EPEAUTRE
0411	DURUM WHEAT UNMILLED					W 198840	43.7	W 34289	11.2	FROMENT DUR NON MOULU
0412	OTHER WHEAT ETC UNMILLED					W 43900	8.1	W 40510	11.1	AUTRE FROMENT NON MOULU
042	RICE					W 25459	8.9	W 13727	7.5	RIZ
0421	RICE IN HUSK OR HUSKED					W 25390	8.9	W 13706	7.5	RIZ SANS AUTRE PREPARATION
04212	RICE HUSKED					W 23095	8.0	W 13545	7.5	RIZ CARGO
046	WHEAT ETC MEAL OR FLOUR					W 227889	76.2	W 141263	60.2	SEMOULE FARINE,FROMENT
04601	FLOUR OF WHEAT OR MESLIN					W 227767	76.1	W 140456	59.8	FARINE DE FROMENT
048	CEREAL ETC PREPARATIONS					W 29705	19.4	W 20751	23.0	PREPTNS A BASE CEREALES
0481	PREPD BREAKFAST FOOD ETC					W 1898	0.7	W 3075	3.9	CEREALES TRAVAILLEES
04811	CEREAL FLAKED,ROLLED,ETC					W 1382	0.4	W 2745	3.5	GRAINS GERMES DE CEREALES
0483	MACARONI,SPAGHETTI ETC					W 16561	8.1	W 9339	7.5	PATES ALMENTAIRES
0484	BAKERY PRODUCTS					W 7271	8.6	W 6467	10.0	PRODUITS DE BOULANGERIE
04841	BREAD,BISCUIT,COM WAFERS					W 2760	2.5	W 1923	4.5	PAINS,BISCUITS DE MER
04842	PASTRY, CAKES ETC					W 4511	6.1	W 4545	5.5	PATISSERIE ETC.
05	VEGETABLES AND FRUIT						27.9		32.6	LEGUMES ET FRUITS
054	VEG ETC FRSH,SMPLY PRSVD					W 35292	7.8	W 19407	7.6	LEGUMES FRAIS,CONG,SECS
057	FRUIT,NUTS,FRESH,DRIED					W 70579	17.5	W 33284	20.3	FRUITS FRAIS OU SECS
0571	ORANGES, MANDARINS ETC					W 14599	2.8	W 10705	5.5	ORANGES,MAND,CLEMENTINES
05711	ORANGES,FRESH OR DRIED					W 12100	1.9	W 8004	4.0	ORANGES FRAICHES,SECHEES
0573	BANANA,PLANTAIN,FRSH,DRY					W 11734	5.2	W 4163	3.2	BANANES FRAICHES,SECHEES
0574	APPLES FRESH					W 25431	4.3	W 12360	7.0	POMMES FRAICHES
058	FRUIT PRESERVED,PREPARED					W 4363	1.9	W 4966	3.9	CONSERVES DE FRUITS
0585	FRUIT OR VEGETABLE JUICE					W 3471	1.6	W 4440	3.3	JUS DE FRUITS
06	SUGAR AND PREPS,HONEY						39.4		21.8	SUCRES ET PRODUITS
061	SUGAR AND HONEY					W 103695	37.6	W 39476	20.9	SUCRES ET MIEL
0611	RAW BEET AND CANE SUGAR					W 85040	29.3	W 37197	19.5	SUCRES BRUTS
0612	REFINED SUGAR ETC					W 16230	6.2	W 1423	0.8	SUCRES RAFFINES
07	COFFEE,TEA,COCOA,SPICES						5.0		3.4	CAFE,THE,CACAO,EPICES
09	MISC EDIBLE PRODUCTS						5.6		5.5	PREP ALIMENTAIRES DIVERSES
098	EDIBLE PRODCTS,PREPS NES						3.9		2.8	PREP ALIMENTAIRES NDA
1	BEVERAGES AND TOBACCO						20.0		7.9	BOISSONS ET TABACS
11	BEVERAGES						10.6		5.8	BOISSONS
111	NON-ALCOHL BEVERAGES NES					W 14874	4.0	W 4737	2.0	BOISSONS NON ALCOOLIQUES
112	ALCOHOLIC BEVERAGES					W 14449	6.6	W 5084	3.9	BOISSONS ALCOOLIQUES
1123	BEER,ALE,STOUT,PORTER					W 12072	5.3	W 4754	3.4	BIERES
12	TOBACCO AND MANUFACTURES						9.4		2.1	TABACS BRUTS FABRIQUES
122	TOBACCO,MANUFACTURED					W 1374	9.0	W 246	1.8	TABACS FABRIQUES
1222	CIGARETTES					W 969	8.4	W 117	1.3	CIGARETTES
2	CRUDE MATERLS,EXCL FUELS						14.6		16.8	MAT BRUTES NON COMESTIBLES
26	TEXTILE FIBRES AND WASTE						6.3		8.4	FIBRES TEXTILES
269	WASTE OF TEXTILE FABRICS					W 9265	5.6	W 6820	7.5	FRIPERIE DRILLES,CHIFFONS
26901	BULK TEXT WSTE,OLD CLTHG					W 8694	5.3	W 6232	7.3	ART ET ACCESS D'HABILLEMENT
27	CRUDE FERTLZR,MINRLS NES						4.1		4.5	ENGRAIS MINERAUX BRUTS
278	OTHER CRUDE MINERALS					W 7154	1.1	W 14100	2.9	AUTRES MINERAUX BRUTS
3	MINERAL FUELS ETC						25.1		30.2	COMBUSTIBLES MINERAUX LUB
32	COAL,COKE AND BRIQUETTES						3.2		1.6	HOUILLES,COKES,BRIQUETTES
33	PETROLEUM AND PRODUCTS						20.0		25.6	PETROLE ET DERIVES
333	CRUDE PETROLEUM					W 3815	1.0	W 16720	5.3	HUILES BRUTES DE PETROLE
334	PETROLEUM PRODUCTS,REFIN					W 78094	16.7	W 54258	17.4	PRODUITS RAFFINES
335	RESIDUAL PETRLM PROD NES					W 17245	2.4	W 11571	3.0	PRODUITS RESIDUELS NDA
341	*GAS,NATURAL AND MANUFCT					W 8742	2.0	W 6509	3.1	GAZ NATUREL,GAZ MANUFACT
4	ANIMAL,VEGETABLE OIL,FAT						26.7		29.0	HUILES,GRAISSES ANIM,VEG
42	FIXED VEGETABLE OIL,FAT						24.4		26.0	HUILES VEGETALES FIXES
423	FIXED VEG OILS,SOFT					W 37515	24.3	W 22268	24.5	HUILES VEGET DOUCES FIXES
4236	SUNFLOWER SEED OIL					W 36040	22.8	W 17612	19.1	HUILE DE TOURNESOL
5	CHEMCLS,RELATED PROD NES						55.1		65.8	PRODUITS CHIMIQUES
51	ORGANIC CHEMICALS						4.6		4.5	PROD CHIMIQ ORGANIQUES
512	ALCOHOLS,PHENOLS ETC						3.1		2.3	PHENOLS,PHENOLS-ALCOOLS
5121	ACYCLIC ALCOHOLS,DERIVS						3.0		2.1	ALCOOLS ACYCLIQUES
52	INORGANIC CHEMICALS						7.8		7.8	PROD CHIM INORGANIQUES
522	INORG ELEMNTS,OXIDES,ETC					W 26241	3.0	W 14442	3.0	ELEMENTS INORGANIQUES
523	OTHR INORG CHEMICALS ETC					W 24546	4.8	W 10078	4.8	AUT PRODUITS CHIMIQUES INORG
5231	METAL CMPD OF INORG ACID					W 8909	2.2	W 2655	3.5	SELS METALLIQUES
52313	HYPOCHLORITES ETC					W 513	0.1	W 1994	3.0	CHLORITES,HYPOCHLORITES
541	*MEDICINAL,PHARM PRODUCT					K 1675477	18.7	K 1044726	17.5	PROD MEDICINAUX PHARMACEUT
5416	GLYCOSIDES,GLANDS,SERA					K 222699	4.7	K 247111	3.1	HETEROSIDES
54164	ANTISERA,MICROB VACCINES					K 77469	4.2	K 71495	2.8	SERUMS,VACCINS
5417	MEDICAMENTS					K 1243482	13.1	K 607225	13.1	MEDICAMENTS
54171	— CONTAINNG ANTIBIOTICS					K 236803	4.1	K 141970	5.0	MED CONTN ANTIBIOTIQUES
54179	— CONTNG OTH SUBSTANCES					K 928298	8.3	K 362591	6.9	MED CONT AUT SUBSTANCES
55	PERFUME,CLEANING ETC PRD						8.0		11.0	PROD POUR PARFUM,TOILETTE
554	SOAP,CLEANSING ETC PREPS					W 10297	6.8	W 5841	7.1	SAVONS,PRODUITS DETERSIFS
5541	SOAPS					W 5001	3.3	W 2396	3.1	SAVONS,PROD TENSIO-ACTIFS
5542	WASHING PREPARATIONS ETC					W 3664	2.6	W 3351	3.9	PROD ORG TENSIO-ACT NDA
562	*FERTILIZERS,MANUFACTURE					W 42497	5.6	W 37246	8.9	ENGRAIS MANUFACTURES
5621	CHEM NITROGENOUS FERTLZR					W 38971	5.1	W 27335	7.0	ENGRAIS AZOTES
56211	AMMONIUM NITRATE					W 26401	3.4	W 18684	4.4	NITRATE D'AMMONIUM
58	PLASTIC MATERIALS ETC						6.0		8.7	MAT PLAST ARTIFICIELLES
583	POLYMERIZATION ETC PRODS					W 5459	3.7	W 5660	5.7	PROD POLYMERISATION
59	CHEMICAL MATERIALS NES						2.7		5.4	MAT PROD CHIMIQUES NDA
598	MISCEL CHEM PRODUCTS NES					W 1950	1.3	W 4626	3.0	PROD DIV INDUST CHIM NDA
6	BASIC MANUFACTURES						236.7		276.1	ART MANUFACTURES
61	LEATHER,DRESSED FUR,ETC						73.4		68.6	CUIRS,PELLETERIES
611	LEATHER					W 1274	18.7	W 817	20.0	CUIRS,PEAUX PREPARES
6114	LEATHR BOVINE NES,EQUINE					W 1057	16.9	W 711	17.2	CUIRS DE BOVINS
612	LEATHER ETC MANUFACTURES					W 4909	54.7	W 3839	48.6	OUVRAGES EN CUIRS NDA

4. General Imports C.I.F. by Commodities according to the S.I.T.C. (Rev. 2) in million U.S. Dollars
Importations Générales C.A.F. par Produits d'après la C.T.C.I. (Rév. 2) en millions de Dollars E.U.

SITC CTCI	COMMODITY	1994 QUANTITY QUANTITE	1994 VALUE VALEUR	1995 QUANTITY QUANTITE	1995 VALUE VALEUR	1996 QUANTITY QUANTITE	1996 VALUE VALEUR	1997 QUANTITY QUANTITE	1997 VALUE VALEUR	PRODUIT
6123	PREPRD PARTS OF FOOTWEAR					W 4899	54.5	W 3835	48.5	PARTIES DE CHAUSSURES
62	RUBBER MANUFACTURES NES						5.1		5.1	CAOUTCHOUC MANUFACTURE
625	RUBBER TYRES, TUBES ETC					N 298660	3.7	N 238990	3.6	PNEUS CAOUTCHOUC VULCANISE
63	WOOD,CORK MANUFACTRS NES						6.9		8.9	OUVRAGES LIEGE ET BOIS
634	VENEERS,PLYWOOD,ETC						4.8		6.5	PLACAGES,CONTRE–PLAQUES
6343	IMPROVED,RECONSTIT WOOD					W 6305	3.5	W 6459	5.6	BOIS AMELIORES,RECONST
63432	RECONSTITUTED WOOD					W 5538	3.0	W 6414	5.5	BOIS RECONSTITUES
64	PAPER,PAPERBOARD AND MFR						11.6		13.3	PAPIERS,CARTONS & OUVRAGES
641	PAPER AND PAPERBOARD					W 11996	8.2	W 9632	9.3	PAPIERS ET CARTONS
6411	NEWSPRINT					W 2400	2.0	W 2790	3.0	PAPIER JOURNAL
642	PAPER,ETC,PRECUT,ARTS OF					W 3246	3.4	W 2133	4.0	PAP,CARTONS DECOUPES
65	TEXTILE YARN,FABRICS,ETC						45.4		46.7	FILS,TISSUS,ARTICLES TEXTILE
651	TEXTILE YARN					W 896	3.4	W 768	3.4	FILS TEXTILES
652	COTTON FABRICS,WOVEN					W 2924	12.1	W 1900	13.0	TISSUS DE COTON
6522	WOVEN COTTON BLEACHD,ETC					W 2436	9.4	W 1509	11.1	TISSUS COTON BLANCHIS ETC
65224	BLCHED COTTON FABRIC NES					W 1597	7.5	W 974	7.4	AUT TIS PLUS 85% COT BLANCHI
65225	BLCHD COTN BLEND FAB NES					W 177	0.7	W 458	3.3	AUT TIS MOINS 85% COT BLANCH
653	WOVN MAN–MADE FIB FABRIC					W 1630	15.8	W 1362	17.5	TISSUS FIBRES SYNTH,ARTIF
6531	CONT SYNT WEAVES NONPILE					W 379	2.9	W 193	4.9	TISSUS FIBRES SYNTH CONTINUE
65315	CONT SYN TXTL FABRC NES					W 289	2.0	W 161	4.1	TIS PLUS 85% TEXT SYNT CONT
6534	DISC SYN BLEND FABRC NES					W 377	3.5	W 266	3.5	TISSUS FIBRES SYNTH DISCONT
65341	DISC SYN FIB–COTTN FABRC					W 298	3.3	W 254	3.4	TISSUS FIB SYNT DIS MEL COTO
6535	CONT REGN WEAVES NONPILE					W 411	7.4	W 171	2.5	TISSUS FIB TEXT ART CONTINU
65355	CONT REGN TXTL FABRC NES					W 328	5.5	W 43	1.1	TISSUS 85% TEXT ART CONT
6536	DISC REGN TXTL FABRC NES					W 81	0.7	W 256	4.6	TISSUS 85% TEXT ART DISC
655	KNITTED,ETC FABRICS					W 456	3.3	W 179	1.7	ETOF BONNETERIE PIECES ETC
6552	OTHER KNIT ETC FAB NONEL					W 456	3.3	W 179	1.7	ETOF BON NON ELAS NON SYNT
657	SPECIAL TXTL FABRC,PRODS					W 1024	3.5	W 1238	4.2	TISSUS SPECIAUX
658	TEXTILE ARTICLES NES					W 1477	2.6	W 1148	3.0	ART FACONNES MAT TEXTILES
66	NONMETAL MINERAL MFS NES						46.9		72.2	ART MIN NON METALLIQUES
661	LIME,CEMENT,BLDG PRODS					W 481477	24.5	W 574063	42.2	CHAUX,CIMENTS MAT CONSTR
6612	CEMENT					W 473515	23.3	W 570826	41.1	CIMENTS HYDRAULIQUES
662	CLAY,REFRACTORY BLDG PRD						12.8		20.5	MAT CONST REFRACTAIRES
6624	BRICKS ETC NONREFRACTORY						11.3		19.5	BRIQUES ETC CERAM NON REFR
66242	ROOFNG TILES ETC,CERAMIC					W 32452	2.3	W 38092	4.0	TUILES,ORNEMENTS ARCH
66244	UNGLAZD CERAMC SETTS ETC						2.6	A 758	4.0	CARREAUX, NON VERNIS
66245	GLAZED CERAMIC SETTS ETC					A 1842	5.2	A 1766	10.7	AUT CARREAUX CERAMIQUE
664	GLASS						4.0		4.7	VERRE
67	IRON AND STEEL						21.5		31.6	FER ET ACIER
673	IRON,STEEL SHAPES ETC					W 17594	7.3	W 35265	18.7	BARRES,PROFIL FER,ACIER
6731	IRON,STEEL WIRE ROD					W 4539	1.8	W 24806	12.8	FIL MACHINE FER,ACIER
67311	IRON,SIMPLE STL WIRE ROD					W 3116	1.3	W 17629	9.0	FIL MACH AUT ACIER FIN
67312	HIGH CARBON STL WIRE ROD					W 176	0.1	W 7175	3.9	FIL MACH ACIER FIN CARBONE
6732	IRON,STEEL BARS ETC					W 8295	3.3	W 9255	5.1	BARRES FER,ACIER
67326	IRN,OTH STL BARS HOTROLD					W 2363	1.0	W 8073	4.4	BARRES PLEINES FER,ACIER
674	IRN,STL UNIV,PLATE,SHEET					W 2931	1.5		3.1	LARGES PLATS,TOLES
678	IRON,STL TUBES,PIPES,ETC					W 10446	9.9	W 5109	6.5	TUBES,TUYAUX EN FONTE,FER
6783	IRON,STL TUBES,PIPES NES					W 5608	4.8	W 2960	2.8	AUT TUBES,TUYAUX FER,ACIER
68	NON–FERROUS METALS						5.7		9.4	METAUX NON FERREUX
684	ALUMINIUM					W 2447	3.7	W 1569	8.1	ALUMINIUM
6842	ALUMINIUM,ALLOYS WORKED					W 2442	3.7	W 1563	8.1	ALUMINIUM,ALLIAGES OUVRE
68421	ALUMINIUM BARS,WIRE,ETC					W 2252	3.3	W 1119	6.0	BARRES,PROFILES FILS ALU
69	METAL MANUFACTURES NES						20.5		20.8	ART MANUFACT EN METAL NDA
691	STRUCTURES AND PARTS NES					W 7127	6.1	W 1298	2.7	CONSTRUCT FER,ACIER,ALU
6911	STRUCTURES,PARTS IRN,STL					W 6898	5.6	W 1244	2.5	CONSTRUCT FER,ACIER,FONTE
697	BASE MTL HOUSEHOLD EQUIP						5.2		3.2	ART MENAGE MET COMMUNS
6973	DMSTC HEATG,COOKG APPARA					N 4020413	3.7	N 181870	1.7	APPS CHAUF NON ELECTRIQ
69731	IRN,STL DOM COOKG APPARA					N 209167	3.1	N 29011	1.1	APPS CUISSON FER,ACIER
699	BASE METAL MFRS NES					W 4267	4.2	W 3582	6.4	ART MANUFACTURES MET NDA
7	MACHINES,TRANSPORT EQUIP						221.8		202.6	MACHINES MATERIEL TRANSPORT
71	POWER GENERATING EQUIPMT						5.8		4.9	MACHINES GENERATRICES
716	ROTATING ELECTRIC PLANT						4.3		2.2	APP ELECTR ROTATIFS,PIECES
7162	AC MTRS,GENRTRS,GEN SETS					N 9783	3.4		1.6	MOTEURS ELECTRIQUES
72	MACHS FOR SPCL INDUSTRYS						37.5		57.7	MAC SPECIALES POUR INDUST
721	AGRIC MACHY,EXC TRACTORS						5.1		9.2	MACHINES AGRICOLES
7219	AGRICULTURE MACHINES NES						2.5		8.3	ENGINS AGRICOLES NDA
72191	WINE–MAKING ETC MACHNERY					N 13	0.2	N 175	8.1	APPAREILS DE VINIFICATION
723	CIVIL ENGNEERG EQUIP ETC						11.9		5.4	APPAREILS DE GENIE CIVIL
7234	CONST,MINING MACHNRY NES					N 49538	7.9	N 3045	4.9	MACH POUR LA CONST, MINES
72342	SLFPRP SHOVELS,EXCAVATRS					N 639	2.8	N 614	3.4	PELLES MECANIQUES
72344	BORING,SINKING MACHINERY					N 33316	3.5	N 566	0.3	MACHINES DE FORAGE
7239	CONSTR ETC MACHY PTS NES					W 157	3.9	W 110	0.3	PIECES 723.41–723.46
724	TEXTILE,LEATHER MACHNRY						6.2		8.3	MACH POUR INDUSTRIE TEXTILE
7243	SEWING MACHS,NEEDLES ETC						2.5		4.8	MACHINES A COUDRE,PIECES
72431	SEWING MACHINES					N 22787	2.2	N 5349	4.4	MACHINES A COUDRE
727	FOOD MACHRY NON–DOMESTIC						5.6		6.8	MACH INDUSTRIES ALIMENT
7272	OTH FOOD PROC MCHY,PARTS					N 13152	4.7	N 1494	6.1	AUT MACH IND ALIMENTAIRE
72722	INDUS FOOD PROC MACH NES					N 12938	4.6	N 1478	5.8	MACHINES BOULANGERIE
728	OTH MACHY FOR SPCL INDUS						6.8		24.7	AUT MACH IND PARTICULIERES
7281	MACH–TOOLS FR SPCL INDUS						2.7		9.2	MACH–OUTILS SPEC IND PART
72812	MACH–TOOLS TO WORK WOOD					N 23435	2.4	N 4038	8.7	MACH–OUT POUR TRAVAIL BOIS
7283	OTHR MINERAL WORKG MACHY						2.1		5.8	MACH TRIER,CRIBLER,BROYER
72833	MNRL MIXING,KNEADING MCH					N 516	0.7	N 6867	3.9	MACH MELANGER MAT MINER
7284	MACHY FOR SPCL INDUS NES						2.0		9.7	MACH SPEC IND PARTICUL.
72842	RUBBER,PLASTICS WRKG MCH					N 9884	0.5	N 10639	5.9	MACH IND CAOUT MAT PLAST
74	GENRL INDUSTRL MACHY NES						42.5		19.2	MACH APP INDUSTRIE
741	HEATING,COOLING EQUIPMNT						5.1		3.0	MACH CHAUFFAGE,PIECES
742	PUMPS FOR LIQUIDS ETC						24.7		3.9	POMPES MOTO–POMPES
7428	OTHER PUMPS FOR LIQUIDS					N 36430	23.7	N 23810	3.2	AUTRES POMPES POUR LIQ
74288	PUMPS FR LIQUIDS NES ETC					N 35840	23.6	N 23693	3.1	POMPES POUR LIQUIDES NDA
744	MECHANICAL HANDLING EQU						7.3		2.3	EQUIP MANUTENTION PIECES
7442	LIFTING,LOADING MACH NES					N 55468	5.3	N 4580	1.3	APP LEVAGE,MANUTENTION
74422	SHIP DERRICKS,CRANES ETC					N 8690	3.3	N 111	0.3	GRUES,PONTS ROULANTS
745	NONELEC MACHY,TOOLS NES						2.5		4.3	AUT MACH NON ELEC,PIECES
7452	OTH NONELEC MCHS,PTS NES						2.4		4.2	AUT MACH NON ELEC,PIECES
749	NONELEC MACH PTS,ACC NES						1.4		3.8	PIECES MACH NON ELEC NDA
75	OFFICE MACHNES,ADP EQUIP						6.9		7.8	MACH BUREAU TRAIT AUTOM
752	AUTOMTIC DATA PROC EQUIP					N 13366	3.2	N 10185	4.9	MACH TRAIT INFORMATION
76	TELECOMM,SOUND EQUIPMENT						23.3		20.0	EQUIPMENT DE TELECOM
761	TELEVISION RECEIVERS					N 12117	1.1	N 36902	3.6	RECEPTEURS DE TELEVISION
7611	COLOUR TV RECEIVERS					N 12117	1.1	N 13149	3.5	RECEPTEURS COULEUR

4. General Imports C.I.F. by Commodities according to the S.I.T.C. (Rev. 2) in million U.S. Dollars
Importations Générales C.A.F. par Produits d'après la C.T.C.I. (Rév. 2) en millions de Dollars E.U.

SITC CTCI	COMMODITY	1994		1995		1996		1997		PRODUIT
		QUANTITY QUANTITE	VALUE VALEUR	QUANTITY QUANTITE	VALUE VALEUR	QUANTITY QUANTITE	VALUE VALEUR	QUANTITY QUANTITE	VALUE VALEUR	
764	TELECOM EQPT,PTS,ACC NES						21.2		15.4	EQUIP TELECOM,PIECES
7641	LINE TELEPHONE,ETC EQUIP					N 58854	7.3	N 11916	1.9	APP TELEPHON PAR FIL
7643	TV,RADIO TRANSMITTRS ETC					N 8713	7.0	N 3037	3.7	APP EMET TELE RADIO
7649	PTS NES OF EQUIPMT OF 76					W 669	4.5	W 315	9.1	PIECES DE LA DIV 76
76491	PTS NES OF APPAR OF 7641					W 54	2.9	W 78	8.2	PIECES POUR 764.1
77	ELECTRIC MACHNRY NES ETC						45.1		47.1	MACH APP ELECT NDA
771	ELECTRIC POWER MACHY NES						4.8		2.4	MACH PROD,TRANS ELECTR
7711	TRANSFORMERS,ELECTRICAL					N 16035	4.3	N 12756	2.1	TRANSFO ELECTRIQUES
772	SWITCHGEAR ETC,PARTS NES					W 1611	11.2	W 1533	10.2	APP COUPURE,SECT ETC
7721	SWITCHGEAR ETC					W 1601	11.0	W 1528	10.1	APP COUPURE,SECTIONMNT
773	ELECTR DISTRIBUTNG EQUIP					W 2358	12.0	W 1366	8.7	EQUIPMT DISTRIBUTION ELECT
7731	INSULATED WIRE,CABLE ETC					W 2311	11.8	W 1323	8.4	FILS,CABLES ISOLES ELECT
774	ELECTRO-MEDCL,XRAY EQUIP						4.3		5.4	APPAREILS MEDICAUX
7741	ELECTRO-MEDICAL EQUIPMNT					N 170562	3.3	N 16820	2.5	APP ELECTRICITE MEDICALE
7742	X-RAY APPARATUS ETC						1.1	W 22	3.0	APPAREILS A RAYONS X
775	HOUSEHOLD TYPE EQUIP NES						5.9		16.3	MACH,APP USAGE DOMESTQUE
7751	HOUSEHOLD LDRY EQUIP NES					N 11152	0.8	N 57262	8.2	MACH A LAVER ET SECHOIRS
77511	DOMESTIC WASHING MACHNES					N 11150	0.8	N 56741	8.1	MACH LAVER LINGE MOINS 6 KG
7758	ELECTRO-THERMIC APPL NES						2.1		4.9	APP ELECTROTHERMIQ NDA
778	ELECTRICAL MACHINERY NES						6.6		3.8	AUTRES MACH ELECT NDA
7781	BATTERIES,ACCUMULATORS						5.0		2.1	PILES ET ACCUMULATEURS
77812	ELECTRIC ACCUMULATORS					W 341	4.0	N 310559	1.5	ACCUMULATEURS ELECTRIQ
78	ROAD VEHICLES						56.4		44.5	VEHICULES ROUTIERS
781	PASS MOTOR VEH EXC BUSES					N 11179	22.2	N 6118	19.9	AUTO TRANSPORT PERSONNES
782	LORRIES,SPCL MTR VEH NES					N 4910	22.5	N 1828	17.2	VEHICULES SPECIAUX,MARCH
7821	LORRIES,TRUCKS					N 4236	18.3	N 1520	12.6	VEHICULES TRANSP MARCHAND
7822	SPECIAL MOTOR VEHCLS NES					N 674	4.3	N 308	4.7	VEHICULES USAGES SPECIAUX
785	CYCLES,ETC MOTRZD OR NOT						4.6		0.6	MOTOCYCLES SCOOTERS
7853	INVAL CARR, PTS OF 785						3.3		0.2	FAUTEUILS INVALIDES,PIECES
79	OTHR TRANSPORT EQUIPMENT						3.5		0.9	AUTRE MATERIEL TRANSPORT
8	MISC MANUFACTURED GOODS						91.4		101.5	ART MANUFACTURES DIVERS
812	*PLUMBG,HEATNG,LGHTNG EQ						3.7		4.6	APPAR SANITAIRES CHAUFFAGE
821	*FURNITURE,PARTS THEREOF						11.0		8.3	MEUBLES ET PIECES
8212	MED FURN,STUFFD FURNSHGS						3.1		1.4	MOB MEDICO-CHIRUR,PIECES
8219	FURNITURE AND PARTS NES						6.9		6.1	AUTRES MEUBLES ET PIECES
82192	WOOD FURNITURE NES					N 154485	5.0	N 71469	5.1	MEUBLES NDA EN BOIS
84	CLOTHING AND ACCESSORIES						37.2		42.6	VETEMENTS
842	MENS OUTERWEAR NOT KNIT						10.5		8.5	VET DESSUS POUR HOMMES
8423	— TROUSERS,BREECHES ETC					N 2549047	4.4	N 1355812	5.5	PANTALONS HOMMES MAT TEX
8429	— OTHER OUTER GARMENTS						5.4	W 181	2.4	AUT VET DES HOM MAT TEX
843	WOMENS OUTERWEAR NONKNIT						6.0		7.0	VET DESSUS FEMMES MAT TEX
8439	— OTHER OUTER GARMENTS						3.6	W 260	4.4	AUT VET DES FEM MAT TEXT
844	UNDER GARMENTS NOT KNIT						5.0		6.5	VETEMENT DESSOUS MAT TEX
8441	— MENS SHIRTS						3.5		5.7	CHEMISES HOMMES MAT TEXT
84411	—— OF COTTON					N 722093	2.1	N 1739556	3.8	CHEMISES HOMMES DE COTON
845	OUTERWEAR KNIT NONELASTC						8.3		7.8	VET DESSOUS,ACCES BONNET
8459	— OTHER,CLTHG ACCESRYS						6.9		6.7	AUT VET DESSUS DE BONNE
846	UNDER GARMENTS KNITTED						6.6		12.4	SOUS VETS DE BONNETERIE
8462	— OF COTTON NON ELASTIC					MN 9231	6.1	N 8116788	11.7	SOUS-VET BONNET COTON
84629	—— OTHER					MN 9231	6.1	N 8116788	11.7	AUT SOUS-VET BONNET COTON
851	*FOOTWEAR					P 4243762	6.3	P 2150717	3.9	CHAUSSURES
85102	FOOTWEAR LEATHER					P 1963098	3.4	P 1013717	1.8	CHAUS SEMELLES EN CUIR
87	PRECISION INSTRUMNTS NES						5.9		5.3	INSTRUM,APPAR SCIENT NDA
89	MISC MANUFCTRD GOODS NES						25.3		35.0	ART MANUFACTURES DIVERS
892	PRINTED MATTER					W 978	4.6		5.9	IMPRIMES
8928	PRINTED MATTER NES					W 375	2.8	W 290	5.1	IMPRIMES NDA
89283	UNISSUED BANKNOTES ETC					W 76	2.0	W 21	4.1	TIMBRES-POSTE FISCAUX
893	ARTICLES OF PLASTIC NES						10.9		14.9	OUVRAGES EN MAT DIVIS 58
8931	PLSTC PACKG CONTNRS,LIDS					W 3267	4.5	W 3894	7.7	ART TRANSP EMBALLAGE ETC
8939	MISC PLASTIC ARTICLES					W 6373	6.2	W 3358	6.7	ART DIVERS EN MAT DIV 58
89399	OTHR PLASTC ARTICLES NES					W 5696	5.5	W 3053	6.3	AUT OUV MAT DIV 58
894	TOYS,SPORTING GOODS,ETC						3.0		5.1	VOITURES ENFANTS,JOUETS
8942	TOYS,INDOOR GAMES ETC						2.3		4.5	JOUETS,JEUX ETC
89423	TOYS NES					MN 77839	1.3	MN 133199	3.6	JOUETS,MODELES REDUITS
899	OTHER MANUFACTURED GOODS						5.2		7.8	AUT ART MANUF DIVERS NDA
8998	SMALLWARES,TOILETRYS ETC						4.1		5.8	ART MERCERIE,TOILETTE
89983	BUTTONS,STUDS,ETC					W 359	3.5	W 401	4.9	BOUTONS,BOUTONS-PRESSION

5. General Exports F.O.B. by Commodities according to the S.I.T.C. (Rev. 2) in million U.S. Dollars
Exportations Générales F.O.B. par Produits d'après la C.T.C.I. (Rév. 2) en millions de Dollars E.U.

SITC CTCI	COMMODITY	1994		1995		1996		1997		PRODUIT
		QUANTITY QUANTITE	VALUE VALEUR	QUANTITY QUANTITE	VALUE VALEUR	QUANTITY QUANTITE	VALUE VALEUR	QUANTITY QUANTITE	VALUE VALEUR	
	ALL COMMODITIES						220.1		210.5	TOUS PRODUITS
0	FOOD AND LIVE ANIMALS						10.2		13.4	ALIMENTS,ANIMAUX VIVANTS
01	MEAT AND PREPARATIONS						1.5		0.9	VIANDES ET PREPARATIONS
011	MEAT FRESH,CHILLD,FROZEN					W 241	1.5	W 256	0.9	VIANDES FRAICHES,REF,CONGE
0118	MEAT NES FRESH,CHLD,FRZN					W 241	1.5	W 206	0.7	AUTRES VIANDES,ABATS
01189	OTHER MEAT NES FRESH,ETC					W 241	1.5	W 206	0.7	VIANDE,ABATS COMESTIBLES
03	FISH AND PREPARATIONS						5.3		7.9	POISSONS ET PREPARATIONS
034	FISH,FRESH,CHILLED,FROZN					W 1025	2.0	W 519	1.6	POISSON FRAIS, REFRIG,CONG
0341	FISH FRSH,CHLLD,EX FILLT					W 969	1.8	W 497	1.6	POISSON FRAIS,REFRIGERE
036	SHELL FISH FRESH,FROZEN					W 611	3.0	W 535	3.2	CRUSTACES,MOLLUSQUES
037	FISH ETC PREPD,PRSVD NES					W 113	0.2	W 672	3.1	POIS,CRUST,MOL PREPARES
0371	FISH PREPARD,PRESRVD NES					W 113	0.2	W 672	3.1	CONSERVES DE POISSONS
05	VEGETABLES AND FRUIT						2.6		3.4	LEGUMES ET FRUITS
054	VEG ETC FRSH,SMPLY PRSVD					W 2925	2.2	W 2308	2.8	LEGUMES FRAIS,CONG,SECS
0545	OTHER FRESH VEGETABLES					W 1913	1.3	W 1704	2.1	AUTRES LEGUMES FRAIS,REF
05459	FRESH VEGETABLES NES					W 1887	1.3	W 1704	2.1	LEGUMES FRAIS,REFRI NDA
1	BEVERAGES AND TOBACCO						9.3		9.9	BOISSONS ET TABACS
12	TOBACCO AND MANUFACTURES						9.3		9.9	TABACS BRUTS FABRIQUES
121	TOBACCO UNMNFCTRD,REFUSE					W 610	1.4	W 503	1.2	TABACS BRUTS,DECHETS
1211	TOBACCO,NOT STRIPPED					W 414	1.1	W 245	0.5	TABACS NON ECOTES
1212	TOBACCO STRIPPED OR PART					W 196	0.3	W 259	0.7	TABACS PART ECOTES
122	TOBACCO,MANUFACTURED					W 3743	8.0	W 2606	8.7	TABACS FABRIQUES
1223	OTH MANUFACTURED TOBACCO					W 3723	7.9	W 2606	8.7	TABACS FUMER,CHIQUER,PRISER
2	CRUDE MATERLS,EXCL FUELS						39.7		46.1	MAT BRUTES NON COMESTIBLES
21	HIDES,SKINS,FURS UNDRSSD						4.5		5.3	CUIRS,PEAUX BRUTS
211	HIDES,SKINS,EXC FURS,RAW					W 2272	4.5	W 1853	5.2	CUIRS ET PEAUX
2111	BOVINE,EQUINE HIDES,RAW					W 464	1.1	W 231	0.7	PEAUX DE BOVINS
2112	CALF AND KIP SKINS,RAW					W 1281	2.6	W 714	2.1	PEAUX DE VEAUX
2117	SHEEP SKIN WITHOUT WOOL					W 127	0.2	W 206	0.8	PEAUX EPILEES D'OVINS
2119	SKIN NES,WASTE,USED LTHR					W 34	0.1	W 249	0.8	CUIRS ET PEAUX NDA
21199	HIDES AND SKINS NES,RAW					W 34	0.1	W 245	0.8	CUIRS,PEAUX NDA
24	CORK AND WOOD						2.2		4.9	LIEGE ET BOIS
245	FUEL WOOD NES, CHARCOAL					W 2043	0.4	W 3725	1.9	BOIS DE CHAUFFAGE
24502	WOOD CHARCOAL					W 2030	0.4	W 3572	1.8	CHARBON DE BOIS
248	WOOD SHAPED,SLEEPERS					W 2550	1.9	W 6432	2.9	BOIS SIMPLEMENT TRAVAILLES
2483	LUMBER SHAPED NON-CONIFR					W 2204	1.8	W 6239	2.7	NON CONIFERES SCIES,RABOTES
24831	LUMBER SAWN ETC NON-CON					W 968	1.3	W 6161	2.6	SCIES LONGITUDINALEMENT
26	TEXTILE FIBRES AND WASTE						0.3		0.9	FIBRES TEXTILES
263	COTTON					W 8	0.1	W 282	0.8	COTON
2631	RAW COTTON,EXCL LINTERS							W 265	0.8	COTON EN MASSE
27	CRUDE FERTLZR,MINRLS NES						1.1		1.0	ENGRAIS MINERAUX BRUTS
278	OTHER CRUDE MINERALS					W 30964	1.1	W 6322	0.9	AUTRES MINERAUX BRUTS
2789	MINERALS CRUDE NES					W 228	0.1	W 4269	0.8	MINERAUX BRUTS NDA
27896	NATURAL ASPHALT,BITUMEN					W 228	0.1	W 4269	0.8	BITUMES,ASPHALTES NATURELS
28	METALLIFEROUS ORES,SCRAP						18.8		15.5	MINERAIS METAL,DECHETS
281	IRON ORE,CONCENTRATES					W 39780	4.5	W 1243	0.3	MINERAIS DE FER
2815	IRON ORE,CONC,NOT AGGLOM					W 36319	4.3	W 1243	0.3	MINERAIS NON AGGLOMERES
282	IRON AND STEEL SCRAP					W 3406	1.1	W 11684	7.9	FERRAILLES
28201	— OF PIG OR CAST IRON					W 1250	0.7	W 8381	5.6	FERRAILLES DE FONTE
28202	— OF ALLOY STEEL					W 2155	0.5	W 3302	2.4	FERRAILLES D'ACIERS ALLIES
287	BASE METAL ORES,CONC NES					W 29168	12.8	W 55569	7.0	MINERAIS METAUX COMMUNS
2871	CPR ORE ETC,CEMENT COPPR					W 973	2.7			MINERAIS DE CUIVRE,MATTES
28712	COPPER MATTE,CEMENT COPR					W 973	2.7			MATTES DE CUIVRE
2872	NICKEL ORES,CONCENTRATES					W 303	1.0			MINERAIS DE NICKEL
28722	NICKEL MATTE,SINTERS,ETC					W 303	1.0			MATTES,SINTERS
2879	OTH NONFER ORE,CONCNTRTE					W 27892	9.2	W 55569	7.0	MINERAIS D'AUTRES METAUX
28791	CHROMIUM ORE,CONCENTRATE					W 27892	9.2	W 55569	7.0	MINERAIS DE CHROME
29	CRUDE ANIMAL,VEG MAT NES						13.0		18.8	MATIERES BRUTES ANIM,VEGET
292	CRUDE VEG MATERIALS NES						12.5		18.6	MAT BRUTES VEGETALES NDA
2924	VEG USED IN PHARMACY ETC					W 6874	11.8	W 6298	17.9	PLANTES MEDICINALES
3	MINERAL FUELS ETC						6.7		3.7	COMBUSTIBLES MINERAUX LUB
33	PETROLEUM AND PRODUCTS						6.4		3.4	PETROLE ET DERIVES
333	CRUDE PETROLEUM					W 5486	1.3			HUILES BRUTES DE PETROLE
334	PETROLEUM PRODUCTS,REFIN					W 13489	2.8	W 1419	0.5	PRODUITS RAFFINES
335	RESIDUAL PETRLM PROD NES					W 41352	2.5	W 17063	3.0	PRODUITS RESIDUELS NDA
3352	MINERAL TARS AND PRODCTS					W 2492	0.4	W 10196	2.0	GOUDRONS MINERAUX
33522	BENZOLE							W 10166	2.0	BENZOLS
3354	PETROLM BITUMEN,COKE ETC					W 34860	2.0	W 4838	0.9	BITUME,COKE DE PETROLE
33541	PETROLEUM BITUMEN, ETC					W 9438	1.5	W 2903	0.6	BITUME DE PETROLE
4	ANIMAL,VEGETABLE OIL,FAT						4.9		0.1	HUILES,GRAISSES ANIM,VEG
42	FIXED VEGETABLE OIL,FAT						4.9		0.1	HUILES VEGETALES FIXES
423	FIXED VEG OILS,SOFT					W 1942	4.8	W 15	0.1	HUILES VEGET DOUCES FIXES
4235	OLIVE OIL					W 1876	4.7	W 15	0.1	HUILE D'OLIVE
5	CHEMCLS,RELATED PROD NES						3.1		1.7	PRODUITS CHIMIQUES
562	*FERTILIZERS,MANUFACTURE					W 20408	1.2	W 5658	0.6	ENGRAIS MANUFACTURES
5622	CHEM PHOSPHATIC FERTILZR					W 20408	1.2	W 5614	0.6	ENGRAIS PHOSPHATES
56222	SUPERPHOSPHATES					W 20408	1.2	W 5614	0.6	SUPERPHOSPHATES
58	PLASTIC MATERIALS ETC						0.8		0.3	MAT PLAST ARTIFICIELLES
6	BASIC MANUFACTURES						70.9		58.4	ART MANUFACTURES
61	LEATHER,DRESSED FUR,ETC						44.4		39.1	CUIRS,PELLETERIES
611	LEATHER					W 1143	3.9	W 1010	5.9	CUIRS,PEAUX PREPARES
6113	CALF LEATHER					W 408	1.1	W 432	2.5	CUIRS,PEAUX DE VEAUX
6114	LEATHR BOVINE NES,EQUINE					W 111	0.7	W 182	1.7	CUIRS DE BOVINS
6115	LEATHER FROM SHEEP,LAMBS					W 579	1.8	W 273	1.5	PEAUX D'OVINS PREPAREES
612	LEATHER ETC MANUFACTURES					W 4450	40.6	W 3697	33.1	OUVRAGES EN CUIRS NDA
6123	PREPRD PARTS OF FOOTWEAR					W 4448	40.6	W 3697	33.1	PARTIES DE CHAUSSURES
63	WOOD,CORK MANUFACTRS NES						3.4		2.6	OUVRAGES LIEGE ET BOIS
634	VENEERS,PLYWOOD,ETC						1.5	W 485	0.7	PLACAGES,CONTRE-PLAQUES
635	WOOD MANUFACTURES NES					W 3619	2.0	W 3533	1.9	ART MANUF EN BOIS NDA
6359	OTHER WOOD MANUFACTURES					W 1588	1.2	W 979	0.9	OUVRAGES EN BOIS NDA
63591	TOOLS,HANDLES ETC WOOD					W 638	0.6	W 744	0.8	OUTILS MANCHES D'OUTILS
64	PAPER,PAPERBOARD AND MFR						1.0		1.2	PAPIERS,CARTONS & OUVRAGES
642	PAPER,ETC,PRECUT,ARTS OF					W 881	0.8	W 762	0.9	PAP,CARTONS DECOUPES
6421	PAPER ETC CONTAINERS					W 749	0.7	W 680	0.7	BOITES,SACS EMBALLAGES
65	TEXTILE YARN,FABRICS,ETC						2.5		1.7	FILS,TISSUS,ARTICLES TEXTILE
658	TEXTILE ARTICLES NES					W 117	1.2	W 115	0.7	ART FACONNES MAT TEXTILES
6581	BAGS,SACKS OF TEXTILES					W 88	1.0	W 30	0.4	SACS EMBALLAGE TEXTILES
67	IRON AND STEEL						11.3		8.1	FER ET ACIER
671	PIG IRON ETC					W 32838	9.2	W 13397	7.5	FONTE,SPIEGEL,POUDRES
6713	IRON,STL POWDER,SHOT,ETC					W 11470	3.7	W 7	0.1	POUDRES,GREN FER,ACIER
67133	SPONGE IRON OR STEEL					W 11470	3.7			FER,ACIER SPONGIEUX AUT POUD

5. General Exports F.O.B. by Commodities according to the S.I.T.C. (Rev. 2) in million U.S. Dollars
Exportations Générales F.O.B. par Produits d'après la C.T.C.I. (Rév. 2) en millions de Dollars E.U.

SITC CTCI	COMMODITY	1994		1995		1996		1997		PRODUIT
		QUANTITY QUANTITE	VALUE VALEUR	QUANTITY QUANTITE	VALUE VALEUR	QUANTITY QUANTITE	VALUE VALEUR	QUANTITY QUANTITE	VALUE VALEUR	
6716	FERRO–ALLOYS					W 18016	5.2	W 13390	7.5	FERRO–ALLIAGES
67169	OTHER FERRO–ALLOYS					W 18016	5.2	W 13390	7.5	AUTRES FERRO–ALLIAGES
677	IRN,STL WIRE(EXCL W ROD)					W 4427	1.8			FILS EN FER,ACIER
67705	OTHER ALLOY STEEL WIRE					W 4426	1.8			FILS ACIER AUT ACIERS ALLIES
68	NON–FERROUS METALS						5.8		3.3	METAUX NON FERREUX
682	COPPER EXC CEMENT COPPER					W 2112	3.6	W 138	0.3	CUIVRE
6821	COPPER NES,ALLOYS,UNWRT					W 908	1.6	W 82	0.2	CUIVRE BRUT
68212	COPPER REFINED,UNWROUGHT					W 908	1.6	W 82	0.2	CUIVRE AFFINE BRUT
6822	COPPER,ALLOYS WORKED					W 1204	2.0	W 56	0.1	CUIVRE,ALLIAGES OUVRES
68222	COPPER PLATE,SHEET,STRIP					W 1010	1.8	W 56	0.1	TOLES DE PLUS 0.15 MM
684	ALUMINIUM					W 1645	2.0	W 1624	2.9	ALUMINIUM
6841	ALUMINIUM,ALLOYS,UNWRGHT					W 111	0.2	W 598	1.0	ALUMINIUM,ALLIAGES BRUTS
6842	ALUMINIUM,ALLOYS WORKED					W 1533	1.9	W 1027	1.9	ALUMINIUM,ALLIAGES OUVRE
68421	ALUMINIUM BARS,WIRE,ETC					W 1130	1.4	W 799	1.5	BARRES,PROFILES FILS ALU
69	METAL MANUFACTURES NES						2.4		2.2	ART MANUFACT EN METAL NDA
699	BASE METAL MFRS NES					W 636	1.5	W 331	1.1	ART MANUFACTURES MET NDA
6993	PINS,HOOKS,EYES,ETC					W 202	1.0	W 143	1.0	EPINGLES,AIGUILLES FER,AC
69933	BASE METL HOOKS,EYES ETC					W 202	1.0	W 143	1.0	FERMOIRS,BOUCLES,AGRAFES
7	MACHINES,TRANSPORT EQUIP						3.8		12.0	MACHINES MATERIEL TRANSPORT
72	MACHS FOR SPCL INDUSTRYS						0.4		7.8	MAC SPECIALES POUR INDUST
723	CIVIL ENGNEERG EQUIP ETC						0.1	N 214	6.6	APPAREILS DE GENIE CIVIL
7234	CONST,MINING MACHNRY NES					N 1287	0.1	N 185	6.6	MACH POUR LA CONST, MINES
72346	OTH CONST,MINING MCH NES							N 165	6.1	AUT MACH EXTRACTION,EXCAV ET
724	TEXTILE,LEATHER MACHNRY						0.2		1.0	MACH POUR INDUSTRIE TEXTILE
7243	SEWING MACHS,NEEDLES ETC						0.1		0.8	MACHINES A COUDRE,PIECES
72431	SEWING MACHINES					N 64	0.1	N 646	0.8	MACHINES A COUDRE
74	GENRL INDUSTRL MACHY NES						1.2		1.4	MACH APP INDUSTRIE
744	MECHANICAL HANDLING EQU						1.2		1.0	EQUIP MANUTENTION PIECES
7442	LIFTING,LOADING MACH NES					N 37	1.0	N 13	1.0	APP LEVAGE,MANUTENTION
74421	PULLEY TACKLE,WINCHS ETC					N 2	0.1	N 1	0.7	PALANS,TREUILS
74428	OTH HANDLING ETC MCH NES					N 32	1.0	N 7	0.1	AUT APP LEVAGE ETC
77	ELECTRIC MACHNRY NES ETC						1.7		1.5	MACH APP ELECT NDA
771	ELECTRIC POWER MACHY NES					W 3	0.2		1.0	MACH PROD,TRANS ELECTR
773	ELECTR DISTRIBUTNG EQUIP					W 75	0.7			EQUIPMT DISTRIBUTION ELECT
7731	INSULATED WIRE,CABLE ETC					W 61	0.7			FILS,CABLES ISOLES ELECT
79	OTHR TRANSPORT EQUIPMENT						0.1		0.8	AUTRE MATERIEL TRANSPORT
793	SHIPS AND BOATS ETC					N 110	0.1	N 1118	0.8	NAVIRES BATEAUX,ETC
7932	SHIPS AND BOATS NES					N 100	0.1	N 18	0.8	NAVIRES ET BATEAUX
79323	OTHER CARGO VESSELS							N 13	0.8	AUT BATEAUX TRANS MARCH
8	MISC MANUFACTURED GOODS						71.8		65.4	ART MANUFACTURES DIVERS
821	*FURNITURE,PARTS THEREOF						1.5		2.6	MEUBLES ET PIECES
8211	CHAIRS,SEATS AND PARTS						0.5		1.9	SIEGES ET PIECES
82119	PTS NES OF CHAIRS ETC					W 61	0.5	W 198	1.7	PIECES DU 821.11
8219	FURNITURE AND PARTS NES						0.9		0.5	AUTRES MEUBLES ET PIECES
84	CLOTHING AND ACCESSORIES						52.5		49.8	VETEMENTS
842	MENS OUTERWEAR NOT KNIT						15.7		9.6	VET DESSUS POUR HOMMES
8423	— TROUSERS,BREECHES ETC					N 4656963	10.6	N 2351726	6.3	PANTALONS HOMMES MAT TEX
8424	— JACKETS,BLAZERS ETC					N 195550	0.8	N 142512	1.0	VESTES HOMMES MAT TEXTIL
8429	— OTHER OUTER GARMENTS						3.6		1.9	AUT VET DES HOM MAT TEX
843	WOMENS OUTERWEAR NONKNIT						10.4		7.0	VET DESSUS FEMMES MAT TEX
8431	— COATS AND JACKETS					N 100168	0.6	N 109192	0.8	MANT,VEST FEM MAT TEXTIL
8432	— SUITS AND COSTUMES					N 154691	1.1	N 91343	0.5	COSTUMES–TAIL MAT TEXIL
8435	— BLOUSES					N 1569262	4.0	N 1020626	2.4	BLOUSES FEM MAT TEXTILES
8439	— OTHER OUTER GARMENTS						4.0		2.8	AUT VET DES FEM MAT TEXT
844	UNDER GARMENTS NOT KNIT					N 3342247	7.2	N 3948854	11.6	VETEMENT DESSOUS MAT TEX
8441	— MENS SHIRTS					N 1473020	4.0	N 2112648	9.0	CHEMISES HOMMES MAT TEXT
84411	—— OF COTTON					N 426678	1.4	N 899268	3.4	CHEMISES HOMMES DE COTON
84412	—— OF SYNTHETIC FIBRES					N 1046342	2.6	N 1213380	5.7	CHEMISES HOMMES FIB SYNT
8442	— MENS,OTHR THAN SHIRTS					N 1489339	1.5	N 1095649	1.2	SOUS–VET HOMMES MAT TEXT
8443	— WOMENS					N 379888	1.8	N 740557	1.5	VET DESSOUS FEM MAT TEXT
845	OUTERWEAR KNIT NONELASTC						13.9		11.4	VET DESSOUS,ACCES BONNET
8451	— JERSEYS,PULLOVERS ETC					N 248298	0.7	N 237819	2.8	CHANDAILS,PULL–OVERS ETC
8452	— WOMENS DRESSES ETC					N 755228	4.4	N 59856	0.1	ROBES,JUPES BONNETERIE
8459	— OTHER,CLTHG ACCESRYS						9.0		8.6	AUT VET DESSUS DE BONNE
846	UNDER GARMENTS KNITTED						5.4		10.1	SOUS VETS DE BONNETERIE
8462	— OF COTTON NON ELASTIC					MN 16187	4.9	N 5985539	9.4	SOUS–VET BONNET COTON
84629	—— OTHER					MN 16187	4.9	N 5985539	9.4	AUT SOUS–VET BONNET COTON
851	*FOOTWEAR					P 2120153	12.5	P 690301	5.0	CHAUSSURES
85102	FOOTWEAR LEATHER					P 2069439	12.1	P 662991	4.9	CHAUS SEMELLES EN CUIR
89	MISC MANUFCTRD GOODS NES						4.7		7.4	ART MANUFACTURES DIVERS
892	PRINTED MATTER					W 86	2.4	W 65	5.0	IMPRIMES
8928	PRINTED MATTER NES					W 50	2.0	W 40	4.9	IMPRIMES NDA
89283	UNISSUED BANKNOTES ETC					W 33	2.0	W 34	4.8	TIMBRES–POSTE FISCAUX
894	TOYS,SPORTING GOODS,ETC						1.2		0.9	VOITURES ENFANTS,JOUETS
8942	TOYS,INDOOR GAMES ETC						0.5		0.9	JOUETS,JEUX ETC
89423	TOYS NES					MN 31271	0.5	W 269	0.8	JOUETS,MODELES REDUITS
899	OTHER MANUFACTURED GOODS						0.8		1.1	AUT ART MANUF DIVERS NDA
8993	COMBUSTIBLE PRODUCTS ETC						0.6		0.7	BOUGIES,ALLUMETTES ETC
89935	SMOKING PIPES AND PARTS						0.6		0.7	PIPES,FUME–CIGARETTE ETC

1. HISTORICAL SERIES, 1961–1996 SPECIAL TRADE, IMPORTS C.I.F., EXPORTS F.O.B.
SERIES HISTORIQUES, 1961–1996 COMMERCE SPECIAL, IMPORTATIONS C.A.F., EXPORTATIONS F.O.B

YEAR ANNEE	VALUE IN MILLION ALGERIAN DINARS / VALEUR EN MILLION ALGERIAN DINARS: MERCHANDISE –MARCHANDISE		GOLD –OR		CONVERSION FACTORS U.S. CENTS PER ALGERIAN DINAR FACTEURS DE CONVERSION CENTS E.U. PAR ALGERIAN DINAR		INDEX NUMBERS –INDICES: QUANTUM		UNIT VALUE VALEUR UNITAIRE	
	IMPORTS	EXPORTS	IMPORTS	EXPORTS	IMPORTS	EXPORTS	IMPORTS	EXPORTS	IMPORTS	EXPORTS
1961	5054.50	1814.00	2.50	6.40	20.2600	20.2600				
1962	1938.30	948.70	0.50		20.2600	20.2600				
1963	3371.70	3746.20			20.2600	20.2600				
1964	3471.20	3588.80	0.20		20.2600	20.2600				
1965	3309.40	3145.80			20.2600	20.2600				
1966	3152.90	3067.20			20.2600	20.2600				
1967	3154.10	3571.80			20.2600	20.2600				
1968	4022.60	4097.90			20.2600	20.2600				
1969	4981.10	4610.70			20.2600	20.2600				
1970	6204.80	4980.40			20.2600	20.2600				
1971	6027.90	4207.60			20.3615	20.3615				
1972	6693.60	5853.80			22.3062	22.3080				
1973	9535.00	7478.60			25.4507	25.4863				
1974	17754.00	19584.00			23.9914	23.9273				
1975	23755.10	18563.00			25.2517	25.3113				
1976	22226.70	22205.00			24.0283	24.0259				
1977	29534.50	25356.00			24.1245	24.1339				
1978	34437.00	25125.00			25.2102	25.2497				
1979	32376.10	36870.00			26.0332	26.2131				
1980	40519.00	59952.80			26.0221	26.0512				
1981	48636.60	57383.50			23.2238	23.2127				
1982	49311.60	52699.50			21.7621	21.6594				
1983	49781.60	53457.10			20.8857	20.9086				
1984	51257.10	59106.50			20.0731	20.1089				
1985	49491.40	51027.70			19.8847	19.8884				
1986	43393.34	36828.02			21.2804	21.2625				
1987	34152.99	41736.00			20.5768	20.5203				
1988	43426.99	45420.99			17.0384	16.9678				
1989	70072.00	71936.99			13.1423	13.1423				
1990	87018.00	114392.00			11.0017	11.0804				
1991	139241.00	233589.00			5.3416	5.4186				
1992	188406.00	243087.00			4.5903	4.5815				
1993	181389.50	238817.80			4.2836	4.2836				
1994	328402.90	306820.30			2.8532	2.8942				
1995	487585.70	488517.80			2.1022	2.0961				
1996	475275.00	691486.90			1.8285	1.8251				

2. IMPORTS BY BROAD ECONOMIC CATEGORY AND EXPORTS BY INDUSTRIAL ORIGIN. (PERCENTAGE OF TOTAL VALUE)
IMPORTATIONS PAR CATEGORIES ECONOMIQUES ET EXPORTATIONS PAR BRANCHE D'ACTIVITE.(EN POURCENTAGE DE LA VALEUR TOTALE)

IMPORTS – IMPORTATIONS

	1990	1991	1992	1993	1994	1995	1996
TOTAL IMPORTS–IMPORTATIONS TOTALES	100.	100.	100.	100.	100.	100.	100.
1 FOOD BEV–ALIMENTATION BOISSONS	19.4	21.7	25.5	23.9	29.1	26.6	28.2
11 PRIMARY–PRODUITS DE BASE	8.1	8.1	9.5	7.4	13.4	11.4	11.7
111 FOR INDUSTRY–POUR L'INDUSTRIE	6.0	5.6	5.3	6.5	11.3	9.0	7.5
112 FOR HOUSEHOLDS–POUR LES MENAGES	2.1	2.5	4.2	0.9	2.1	2.3	4.2
12 PROCESSED–PRODUITS ELABORES	11.3	13.6	16.0	16.5	15.7	15.3	16.5
121 FOR INDUSTRY–POUR L'INDUSTRIE	2.4	3.0	7.0	7.7	6.5	5.6	6.8
122 FOR HOUSEHOLDS–POUR LES MENAGES	9.0	10.6	9.0	8.7	9.2	9.7	9.7
2 IND SUPPLIES–APPROV INDUSTRIELS	30.8	35.0	33.1	34.0	33.5	31.1	30.8
21 PRIMARY–PRODUITS DE BASE	3.5	3.6	3.8	3.7	4.0	2.6	2.9
22 PROCESSED–PRODUITS ELABORES	27.4	31.3	29.3	30.3	29.4	28.5	27.9
3 FUELS–COMBUSTIBLES	1.0	2.4	1.3	1.3	0.5	1.0	1.1
31 PRIMARY–PRODUITS DE BASE	0.7	0.8	0.6	0.8	0.2	0.4	0.3
32 PROCESSED–PRODUITS ELABORES	0.3	1.5	0.7	0.5	0.3	0.6	0.8
321 MOTOR SPIRIT–ESSENCE	0.0	0.0	0.0	0.0	0.0	0.0	0.0
322 OTHER–AUTRES	0.3	1.5	0.7	0.5	0.3	0.6	0.8
4 MACHINERY–EQUIPEMENT	29.0	28.7	24.7	25.8	22.3	25.2	21.8
41 CAPITAL EQUIPMENT–MACHINES	25.1	24.9	21.1	22.0	18.3	19.9	17.9
42 PARTS–PIECES ACCESSOIRES	3.9	3.8	3.6	3.8	4.0	5.3	3.9
5 TRANSPORT–TRANSPORT	14.9	7.9	7.3	7.3	6.7	7.3	10.7
51 PASSENGER CARS–AUTOMOBILES	0.6	0.5	1.2	1.2	0.7	1.4	2.6
52 OTHER–AUTRES	5.9	2.6	2.2	1.9	1.8	1.5	3.3
521 INDUSTRIAL–INDUSTRIELS	5.9	2.6	2.2	1.8	1.8	1.4	3.3
522 NON INDUSTRIAL–NON INDUSTRIEL	0.0	0.0	0.0	0.1	0.0	0.0	0.0
53 PARTS–PIECES ACCESSOIRES	8.4	4.8	3.9	4.3	4.2	4.4	4.8
6 CONSUM GOODS–BIENS CONSOMMATION	4.8	4.3	8.0	7.6	7.9	8.7	7.3
61 DURABLE–DURABLES	0.6	0.6	1.7	1.7	1.0	1.3	1.0
62 SEMI DURABLE–SEMI DURABLES	0.5	0.7	1.0	1.5	1.2	1.6	2.1
63 NON DURABLE–NON DURABLES	3.8	2.9	5.3	4.5	5.6	5.7	4.1
7 GOODS NES–BIENS NDA	0.0	0.0	0.1	0.0	0.1	0.1	0.1

EXPORTS – EXPORTATIONS

	1990	1991	1992	1993	1994	1995	1996
TOTAL EXPORTS–EXPORTATIONS TOTALES	100.	100.	100.	100.	100.	100.	100.
1 AGRICULTURE	0.2	0.2	0.6	0.6	0.2	0.9	0.7
2 MINING QUARRY–INDUS EXTRACTIVES	75.8	77.2	76.1	77.2	77.0	76.6	80.5
3 MANUFACTURING–IND MANUFACTUR	24.0	22.6	23.3	22.2	22.8	22.5	18.8
31 FOOD BEV TOBACCO–ALIM BOISS TAB	0.3	0.3	0.1	0.4	0.2	0.3	0.6
32 TEXTILES–INDUSTRIES TEXTILES	0.4	0.3	0.1	0.3	0.1	0.4	0.6
33 WOOD & PRODUCTS–BOIS & PRODUITS	0.1	0.1	0.1	0.0	0.0	0.0	0.0
34 PAPER & PRODUCTS–PAPIER & PRODT	0.0	0.0	0.0	0.0	0.0	0.0	0.0
35 CHEMICALS–INDUSTRIES CHIMIQUES	21.4	20.6	20.8	20.3	20.5	19.9	15.9
36 NON METAL MIN–MIN NON METAL	0.0	0.0	0.0	0.0	0.0	0.0	0.0
37 BASIC METAL–IND METAL BASE	0.8	0.5	0.6	0.7	0.7	1.0	0.9
38 METAL MANUF–MANUF METAL	1.0	0.8	0.9	0.3	0.3	0.6	0.7
39 OTH MANUF IND–AUTRES MANUF	0.0	0.0	0.6	0.1	0.9	0.1	0.1

3. TRADE BY PRINCIPAL COUNTRIES OF ORIGIN AND DESTINATION (VALUE IN MILLION U.S. DOLLARS)
ECHANGES SELON LES PRINCIPAUX PAYS D'ORIGINE ET DE DESTINATION (VALEUR EN MILLIONS DE DOLLARS EU)

COUNTRIES–PAYS	SPECIAL IMPORTS C.I.F. IMPORTATIONS SPECIALES C.A.F				
	1992	1993	1994	1995	1996
World	8647.8	8785.3	9598.7	10782.4	9105.6
Africa	296.6	303.9	375.3	302.7	238.5
Americas	1319.2	1719.3	1976.2	2238.8	1643.9
– Northern America	1133.7	1559.6	1755.0	1870.7	1287.0
– LAIA	117.2	110.6	181.8	290.1	325.9
– CACM	3.9	0.1	4.7	11.6	4.4
– Caribbean	63.5	48.8	30.9	64.5	19.4
– Rest of America	0.8	0.1	3.8	1.9	7.3
Asia excl fmr USSR	929.6	1036.0	1144.6	1310.3	1144.2
– Middle East	184.2	147.1	318.0	380.8	412.0
Asia former USSR				12.7	6.5
Europe excl fmr USSR	5991.3	5588.9	5962.6	6727.5	5921.4
– European Union	5752.6	5397.1	5730.8	6394.3	5692.8
– Eastern Europe	89.1	87.9	107.3	186.9	130.5
– Rest of Europe	149.6	103.9	124.5	146.3	98.0
Europe former USSR	12.5	8.7	53.2	79.6	79.8
Oceania	98.7	128.6	87.0	110.8	71.2
Other					0.0
France, Monaco	2097.0	2240.6	2376.3	2686.9	2227.2
USA/Etats–Unis d'Amer	954.2	1311.5	1371.9	1418.0	931.3
Italy/Italie	1242.4	952.1	931.4	1039.1	835.1
Spain/Espagne	832.2	926.2	901.3	923.4	1116.0
Germany/Allemagne	752.1	469.1	517.1	737.3	597.2
Japan/Japon	385.0	375.9	254.0	365.8	239.8
Canada	179.5	248.0	383.1	452.7	355.7
Turkey/Turquie	131.0	108.5	250.4	305.0	318.4
Belgium–Luxembourg	256.7	164.6	214.7	247.8	215.4
Austria/Autriche	174.7	172.5	286.6	219.6	120.4
China/Chine	157.1	120.0	156.5	252.8	202.9
Indonesia/Indonésie	55.2	216.5	240.2	116.7	86.2
United Kingdom	96.9	119.1	132.0	155.6	202.0
Netherlands/Pays–Bas	121.1	159.5	109.6	144.6	149.3
Tunisia/Tunisie	123.7	122.5	138.5	142.8	79.5
Brazil/Brésil	41.0	79.4	126.4	136.0	169.7
Switzerland,Liechtenst.	87.5	69.8	91.8	87.2	76.1
Morocco/Maroc	96.9	84.8	120.6	51.5	41.3
New Zealand	59.1	96.7	76.9	77.9	57.1
Sweden/Suède	85.1	71.5	67.5	81.6	53.3
Korea, Republic of	48.8	42.6	38.4	46.8	86.3
Egypt/Egypte	51.5	48.2	62.4	58.8	39.0
Argentina/Argentine	21.7	7.5	36.7	66.7	91.8
Russian Federation	12.5	8.7	53.2	75.7	62.4
Cuba	54.3	48.7	30.6	49.8	18.9
Finland/Finlande	19.4	30.9	21.4	59.6	65.5
Poland/Pologne	27.6	37.3	48.1	43.4	32.0
Greece/Grèce	13.9	19.8	69.1	30.9	22.8
Portugal	13.0	38.5	48.4	30.6	20.0
Romania/Roumanie	5.1	5.8	20.4	64.4	48.2
Viet Nam	14.9	13.1	39.1	45.0	26.4
Mexico/Mexique	10.6	5.9	16.0	60.5	40.1
Denmark/Danemark	38.4	21.4	22.2	18.9	25.2
Australia/Australie	37.9	31.8	9.7	31.9	14.0
Syrian Arab Republic	18.1	11.2	27.2	31.1	35.7
Other Asia n.e.s.	10.1	26.7	28.3	31.6	24.8
Norway,Svalbard and JM	30.7	22.7	26.3	32.4	9.1
Ireland/Irlande	9.6	11.2	33.3	18.4	43.6
India/Inde	13.9	20.3	28.5	16.2	23.2
Malaysia/Malaisie	21.1	36.5	10.5	14.8	14.3

COUNTRIES–PAYS	SPECIAL EXPORTS F.O.B. EXPORTATIONS SPECIALES F.O.B.				
	1992	1993	1994	1995	1996
Monde	11136.8	10097.7	8593.8	9356.7	11099.2
Afrique	247.2	192.0	260.1	233.6	223.7
Amériques	1973.5	2283.9	1819.9	2049.2	2718.0
– Amérique du Nord	1586.6	1766.9	1588.1	1783.8	2106.0
– ALAI	386.0	506.5	228.8	264.1	599.9
– MCAC	0.8	0.0	0.0		0.0
– Caraïbes	0.1	10.4	3.0	1.3	11.0
– Autre Amérique	0.0	0.1	0.0	0.0	1.1
Asie anc. URSS exclus	302.4	312.0	267.5	578.2	803.4
– Moyen–Orient	50.1	29.3	66.1	329.1	585.7
Asie ancienne URSS					0.7
Europe anc. URSS exclus	8487.5	7180.6	6203.5	6363.2	6872.1
– Union Européenne	8386.1	7117.9	6104.9	6067.0	6658.7
– Europe de l'Est	72.9	36.1	61.2	104.7	86.7
– Autre de l'Europe	28.4	26.6	37.5	191.4	126.7
Europe ancienne URSS	126.2	126.3	42.2	132.6	479.1
Océanie		2.9	0.7		2.2
Autre					
Italy/Italie	2414.6	2219.7	1535.1	2098.7	2208.8
USA/Etats–Unis d'Amer	1553.4	1608.7	1414.0	1563.2	1701.8
France, Monaco	2037.8	1688.6	1326.2	1315.6	1457.8
Netherlands/Pays–Bas	896.0	784.5	885.0	972.4	965.6
Spain/Espagne	846.1	679.2	650.2	625.1	846.2
Belgium–Luxembourg	796.0	627.8	528.4	367.1	328.2
Germany/Allemagne	524.0	504.2	524.8	171.5	275.8
Brazil/Brésil	351.0	443.8	195.2	225.2	565.9
United Kingdom	377.4	192.4	140.0	204.0	258.1
Portugal	157.8	284.7	285.0	142.4	131.2
Canada	33.2	158.2	174.1	220.5	404.2
Turkey/Turquie	27.3	7.2	49.5	314.4	575.4
Russian Federation	126.2	126.3	40.0	132.4	479.1
Austria/Autriche	206.9	67.2	161.2	116.3	159.7
Morocco/Maroc	136.5	70.7	101.3	81.2	82.8
Tunisia/Tunisie	78.3	62.2	113.1	108.3	101.9
Korea, Republic of	49.5	34.2	20.7	121.9	116.2
Japan/Japon	80.1	48.2	79.5	66.6	59.0
Singapore/Singapour	58.1	154.2	59.9	46.0	15.0
Bulgaria/Bulgarie	54.6	33.4	40.2	62.8	15.2
Switzerland,Liechtenst.	2.0	3.1	4.3	110.1	71.2
Greece/Grèce	52.4	45.5	24.6	35.6	21.0
Paraguay	22.9	47.2	27.3	13.3	20.2
Sweden/Suède	70.9	19.8	23.3	4.5	5.5
Poland/Pologne	1.1	1.8	15.1	32.8	71.5
Mauritania/Mauritanie	16.2	31.3	15.8	19.8	23.2
Yugoslavia/Yougoslavie	8.1	13.6	24.3	8.9	31.9
Malta/Malte	3.8	4.2	2.5	45.0	19.3
Thailand/Thaïlande	23.0	16.6	0.0		15.7
Cyprus/Chypre	22.1	9.4	14.4	3.4	0.1
Liberia/Libéria	10.1	10.5	10.1	13.8	1.8
Norway,Svalbard and JM	13.5	5.6	6.3	16.0	4.4
Ecuador/Equateur	1.8	14.6	4.6	10.2	4.4
India/Inde	1.7	1.6	26.8	2.9	1.0
Indonesia/Indonésie	23.8	2.9	1.1	0.9	0.0
Egypt/Egypte	1.5	13.6	5.3	5.4	2.8
Finland/Finlande	0.0		11.3	13.8	0.0
Argentina/Argentine	10.2			14.8	
China/Chine	2.0	11.3	3.5	8.0	0.0
Korea Dem People's Rp	14.0		6.7		3.7

(VALUE AS PERCENTAGE OF WORLD TOTAL)(VALEURS EN POURCENTAGE DU TOTAL MONDIAL)

	1987	1988	1989	1990	1991	1992	1993	1994	1995	1996
Africa	2.8	2.1	2.6	2.1	3.1	3.4	3.5	3.9	2.8	2.6
Americas	14.0	16.9	19.3	17.6	15.3	15.3	19.6	20.6	20.8	18.1
– Northern America	8.9	13.2	15.5	14.8	12.5	13.1	17.8	18.3	17.3	14.1
– LAIA	4.9	3.0	2.8	2.0	2.0	1.4	1.3	1.9	2.7	3.6
– CACM	0.0		0.0	0.1	0.0	0.0	0.0	0.0	0.1	0.0
– Caribbean	0.1	0.7	0.9	0.7	0.7	0.7	0.6	0.3	0.6	0.2
– Rest of America	0.1	0.0	0.0	0.0	0.0	0.0	0.0	0.0	0.0	0.1
Asia excl fmr USSR	10.4	9.1	10.3	8.7	9.7	10.7	11.8	11.9	12.2	12.6
– Middle East	3.1	3.3	3.6	2.5	2.9	2.1	1.7	3.3	3.5	4.5
Asia former USSR									0.1	0.1
Europe excl fmr USSR	71.4	70.3	65.5	69.5	69.8	69.3	63.6	62.1	62.4	65.0
– European Union	65.1	63.5	58.5	64.3	65.3	66.5	61.4	59.7	59.3	62.5
– Eastern Europe	3.3	3.1	4.0	2.7	1.8	1.0	1.0	1.1	1.7	1.4
– Rest of Europe	3.1	3.6	3.0	2.4	2.6	1.7	1.2	1.3	1.4	1.1
Europe former USSR	0.4	0.8	1.8	1.0	0.3	0.1	0.1	0.6	0.7	0.9
Oceania	1.0	0.9	0.4	1.1	1.8	1.1	1.5	0.9	1.0	0.8
Other		0.0		0.0						0.0
France, Monaco	22.9	18.9	17.4	23.1	20.6	24.2	25.5	24.8	24.9	24.5
USA/Etats–Unis d'Amer	7.0	10.8	12.0	11.5	9.9	11.0	14.9	14.3	13.2	10.2
Italy/Italie	11.2	10.0	13.3	12.3	15.4	14.4	10.8	9.7	9.6	9.2
Spain/Espagne	4.6	4.6	4.0	6.2	8.4	9.6	10.5	9.4	8.6	12.3
Germany/Allemagne					9.8	8.7	5.3	5.4	6.8	6.6
Japan/Japon	3.9	4.3	3.8	4.6	4.8	4.5	4.3	2.6	3.4	2.6
Canada	1.9	2.4	3.5	3.3	2.6	2.1	2.8	4.0	4.2	3.9
Turkey/Turquie	2.3	2.9	2.9	2.1	2.5	1.5	1.2	2.6	2.8	3.5
Belgium–Luxembourg	4.5	4.5	3.2	3.7	3.3	3.0	1.9	2.2	2.3	2.4
Austria/Autriche	2.2	3.1	2.1	1.5	1.6	2.0	2.0	3.0	2.0	1.3

	1987	1988	1989	1990	1991	1992	1993	1994	1995	1996
Afrique	1.7	2.4	1.9	2.6	1.8	2.2	1.9	3.0	2.5	2.0
Amériques	21.3	20.2	21.3	21.6	19.7	17.7	22.6	21.2	21.9	24.5
– Amérique du Nord	19.4	18.8	19.2	19.6	17.3	14.2	17.5	18.5	19.1	19.0
– ALAI	1.8	1.4	2.1	2.0	2.3	3.5	5.0	2.7	2.8	5.4
– MCAC		0.0			0.0	0.0	0.0	0.0		0.0
– Caraïbes	0.1		0.0		0.1	0.0	0.1	0.0	0.0	0.1
– Autre Amérique	0.0	0.0	0.0	0.1	0.0	0.0	0.0	0.0	0.0	0.0
Asie anc. URSS exclus	3.2	5.1	4.7	3.6	2.5	2.7	3.1	3.1	6.2	7.2
– Moyen–Orient	1.5	1.5	1.8	2.1	1.4	0.5	0.3	0.8	3.5	5.3
Asie ancienne URSS										0.0
Europe anc. URSS exclus	73.4	70.9	70.7	70.9	74.9	76.2	71.1	72.2	68.0	61.9
– Union Européenne	72.3	69.7	69.6	69.7	74.1	75.3	70.5	71.0	64.8	60.0
– Europe de l'Est	0.3	1.0	0.6	0.3	0.2	0.7	0.4	0.7	1.1	0.8
– Autre de l'Europe	0.9	0.2	0.5	0.8	0.6	0.3	0.3	0.4	2.0	1.1
Europe ancienne URSS	0.3	1.4	1.4	1.3	1.1	1.1	1.3	0.5	1.4	4.3
Océanie	0.0	0.0	0.0	0.0	0.0		0.0	0.0		0.0
Autre										
Italy/Italie	15.3	17.1	20.5	20.5	23.7	21.7	22.0	17.9	22.4	19.9
USA/Etats–Unis d'Amer	19.2	18.7	19.1	19.2	17.3	13.9	15.9	16.5	16.7	15.3
France, Monaco	22.1	19.6	18.6	17.3	18.8	18.3	16.7	15.4	14.1	13.1
Netherlands/Pays–Bas	15.1	10.5	8.9	9.3	8.4	8.0	7.8	10.3	10.4	8.7
Spain/Espagne	4.4	6.2	5.5	6.0	6.8	7.6	6.7	7.6	6.7	7.6
Belgium–Luxembourg	6.4	7.1	7.0	6.9	6.2	7.1	6.2	6.1	3.9	3.0
Germany/Allemagne					2.3	4.7	5.0	6.1	1.8	2.5
Brazil/Brésil	1.3	0.9	1.7	1.5	2.0	3.2	4.4	2.3	2.4	5.1
United Kingdom	1.6	2.1	1.3	2.2	2.6	3.4	1.9	1.6	2.2	2.3
Portugal	1.0	1.2	1.6	2.0	2.0	1.4	2.8	3.3	1.5	1.2

4. Special Imports C.I.F. by Commodities according to the S.I.T.C. (Rev. 2) in million U.S. Dollars
Importations Spéciales C.A.F. par Produits d'après la C.T.C.I. (Rév. 2) en millions de Dollars E.U.

SITC CTCI	COMMODITY	1993 QUANTITY QUANTITE	1993 VALUE VALEUR	1994 QUANTITY QUANTITE	1994 VALUE VALEUR	1995 QUANTITY QUANTITE	1995 VALUE VALEUR	1996 QUANTITY QUANTITE	1996 VALUE VALEUR	PRODUIT
	ALL COMMODITIES		8785.3		9598.7		10782.5		9105.7	TOUS PRODUITS
0	FOOD AND LIVE ANIMALS		2155.6		2848.9		2700.9		2501.0	ALIMENTS,ANIMAUX VIVANTS
01	MEAT AND PREPARATIONS		25.6		41.3		62.9		48.8	VIANDES ET PREPARATIONS
011	MEAT FRESH,CHILLD,FROZEN	W 20933	25.4	W 20306	41.0	W 30361	62.5	W 24140	47.8	VIANDES FRAICHES,REF,CONGE
0111	BOVINE MEAT FRESH,FROZEN	W 20921	25.3	W 20256	41.0	W 28138	57.2	W 22389	44.1	VIANDES BOVIN FRAI,REF
01112	BOVINE MEAT BONELESS	W 16868	18.7	W 16457	33.1	W 17545	35.9	W 19524	38.5	VIANDES BOVIN DESOSSEES
02	DAIRY PRODCTS,BIRDS'EGGS		654.1		540.9		476.9		400.7	PRODUITS LAITIERS,OEUFS
022	MILK AND CREAM	W 264174	569.5	W 227923	493.7	W 185762	411.3	W 137964	338.6	LAIT ET CREME
0224	MILK,CREAM PRESERVED ETC	W 259839	557.9	W 223226	485.1	W 184089	409.6	W 130152	325.2	LAIT,CREME CONS,CONC
02242	MILK DRY,1.5% FAT OR LES	W 139265	282.8	W 110766	197.2	W 108108	231.0	W 55382	138.5	LAIT POUDRE INF 1.5%
02243	MILK DRY,OVER 1.5% FAT	W 118835	273.0	W 112296	287.6	W 74719	177.0	W 67865	176.4	LAIT POUDRE SUP 1.5%
023	BUTTER	W 38447	74.1	W 22188	37.4	W 21584	40.7	W 14394	35.4	BEURRE
03	FISH AND PREPARATIONS		0.3		1.4		20.5		111.3	POISSONS ET PREPARATIONS
034	FISH,FRESH,CHILLED,FROZN	W 23	0.2	W 241	0.5	W 2660	4.8	W 103895	107.7	POISSON FRAIS, REFRIG,CONG
0341	FISH FRSH,CHLLD,EX FILLT			W 7	0.1	W 49	0.3	W 102747	105.2	POISSON FRAIS,REFRIGERE
04	CEREALS AND PREPARATIONS		904.2		1324.1		1252.9		1115.4	CEREALES ET PRODUITS
041	WHEAT ETC UNMILLED	W 2588227	353.8	W 3511937	602.4	W 3504679	726.9	W 1971633	495.3	FROMENT,EPEAUTRE
0411	DURUM WHEAT UNMILLED	W 2380941	327.2	W 3297721	577.1	W 3271708	677.8	W 1365580	351.1	FROMENT DUR NON MOULU
0412	OTHER WHEAT ETC UNMILLED	W 207286	26.7	W 214216	25.4	W 232971	49.2	W 606053	144.3	AUTRE FROMENT NON MOULU
043	BARLEY UNMILLED	W 500169	70.3	W 666566	113.6	W 154986	17.0	W 470	0.2	ORGE NON MONDEE
044	MAIZE UNMILLED	W 1154617	142.5	W 1378024	186.1	W 895146	133.3	W 730507	145.4	MAIS NON MOULU
046	WHEAT ETC MEAL OR FLOUR	W 1130789	281.3	W 1224556	323.2	W 1116301	335.7	W 883435	416.0	SEMOULE FARINE,FROMENT
04601	FLOUR OF WHEAT OR MESLIN	W 385363	84.0	W 585956	133.1	W 762417	213.5	W 831660	398.3	FARINE DE FROMENT
04602	MEAL,GROATS OF WHEAT ETC	W 745426	197.3	W 638599	190.2	W 353885	122.2	W 51775	17.8	GRUAUX,SEMOULES FROMENT
048	CEREAL ETC PREPARATIONS	W 14677	16.7	W 40272	36.1	W 35990	28.8	W 48044	35.9	PREPTNS A BASE CEREALES
05	VEGETABLES AND FRUIT		38.6		136.7		211.5		192.2	LEGUMES ET FRUITS
054	VEG ETC FRSH,SMPLY PRSVD		37.4	W 315610	133.6	W 254984	161.4	W 312065	172.2	LEGUMES FRAIS,CONG,SECS
0541	POTATOES FRSH EXCL SWEET	W 50579	13.4	W 150778	55.1	W 91324	38.9	W 47860	22.3	POMMES DE TERRE
0542	LEGUMINOUS VEGETBLES DRY	W 49510	22.7	W 160089	74.2	W 129824	84.4	W 250378	142.1	LEGUMES A COSSE SECS
0546	VEGETABLES SIMPLY PRESVD		0.6	W 3683	3.7	W 33087	37.4	W 9932	5.1	LEGUMES CONG,CONSER
05461	VEGETABLES FROZEN		0.6	W 3683	3.7	W 33072	37.4	W 9930	5.1	LEGUMES CONGELES
057	FRUIT,NUTS,FRESH,DRIED	W 1015	1.2	W 3274	3.0	W 43858	39.8	W 9986	15.5	FRUITS FRAIS OU SECS
06	SUGAR AND PREPS,HONEY		253.4		298.2		324.5		267.5	SUCRES ET PRODUITS
061	SUGAR AND HONEY	W 780922	253.3	W 836921	297.3	W 701550	318.7	W 652651	266.0	SUCRES ET MIEL
0611	RAW BEET AND CANE SUGAR	W 659798	216.3	W 393884	107.4	W 214688	95.8	W 224665	71.9	SUCRES BRUTS
0612	REFINED SUGAR ETC	W 93610	33.5	W 415089	182.4	W 472545	218.4	W 424094	192.2	SUCRES RAFFINES
07	COFFEE,TEA,COCOA,SPICES		114.0		336.8		203.3		174.4	CAFE,THE,CACAO,EPICES
071	COFFEE AND SUBSTITUTES	W 88203	105.9	W 104446	308.2	W 53673	173.5	W 73463	136.5	CAFE ET SUCCEDANES
0711	COFFEE GREEN,ROASTED,SUB	W 88203	105.9	W 104391	307.5	W 53624	173.2	W 73462	136.5	CAFE TORREFIE OU DECAFEINE
07111	COFFEE GREEN,HUSKS,SKINS	W 88195	105.8	W 103722	306.1	W 52273	168.0	W 71874	132.4	CAFE NON TORREFIE
081	*FEEDING STUFF FOR ANIML	W 286990	89.4	W 204138	65.4	W 238157	59.8	W 198392	67.1	NOURRITURE POUR ANIMAUX
0813	OILCAKE AND OTH RESIDUES	W 284202	84.0	W 200358	59.4	W 234914	56.1	W 197584	66.0	TOURTEAUX
08131	— OF SOYA BEANS	W 284003	84.0	W 200358	59.4	W 234914	56.1	W 197584	66.0	TOURTEAUX DE SOJA
09	MISC EDIBLE PRODUCTS		54.3		77.9		73.0		105.1	PREP ALIMENTAIRES DIVERSES
091	MARGARINE AND SHORTENING	W 24123	26.0	W 39392	39.8	W 32623	37.1	W 43111	47.1	MARGARINE ET GRAISSES
0914	MARGARINE,EDIBLE FAT NES	W 24118	26.0	W 39392	39.8	W 32623	37.1	W 43097	47.1	MARGARINES,SIMILI SAINDOUX
09141	MARGARINE	W 24111	26.0	W 34407	34.0	W 31866	36.1	W 42033	45.9	MARGARINE
098	EDIBLE PRODCTS,PREPS NES	W 12369	28.4	W 18453	38.2	W 26964	36.0	W 22802	58.0	PREP ALIMENTAIRES NDA
09806	YEASTS,BAKING POWDERS	W 12074	26.8	W 17666	35.2	W 16852	32.5	W 19771	46.9	LEVURES
1	BEVERAGES AND TOBACCO		45.4		75.9		84.5		40.8	BOISSONS ET TABACS
12	TOBACCO AND MANUFACTURES		44.9		75.4		70.1		28.9	TABACS BRUTS FABRIQUES
121	TOBACCO UNMNFCTRD,REFUSE	W 23784	44.9	W 29459	69.4	W 22406	44.9	W 8153	14.7	TABACS BRUTS,DECHETS
1211	TOBACCO,NOT STRIPPED	W 23784	44.9	W 29459	69.4	W 22022	43.8	W 8153	14.7	TABACS NON ECOTES
2	CRUDE MATERLS,EXCL FUELS		386.1		378.7		415.3		312.2	MAT BRUTES NON COMESTIBLES
22	OIL SEEDS,OLEAGINOUS FRT		18.4		23.5		38.8		23.6	GRAINES,FRUITS OLEAGINEUX
222	SEEDS FOR'SOFT'FIXED OIL	W 22560	18.1	W 25172	23.1	W 33381	38.6	W 20259	23.4	GRAINES HUILES FIXES
2221	GROUNDNUTS,GREEN	W 21876	17.2	W 24206	21.3	W 32907	38.0	W 19128	22.0	ARACHIDES NON GRILLEES
24	CORK AND WOOD		172.5		169.0		218.8		139.6	LIEGE ET BOIS
248	WOOD SHAPED,SLEEPERS	W 375254	157.5	W 335492	154.6	W 384017	203.2	W 290083	134.3	BOIS SIMPLEMENT TRAVAILLES
2482	LUMBER SHAPED CONIFER	W 320546	136.4	W 300218	137.2	W 306973	158.4	W 190539	87.5	CONIFERES SCIES,RABOTES
24821	LUMBER SAWN ETC CONIFER	W 320510	136.4	W 300204	137.2	W 306869	158.3	W 190453	87.4	CONIFERES SCIES LONGITUD
2483	LUMBER SHAPED NON–CONIFR	W 54041	20.7	W 34442	16.9	W 76173	44.2	W 99529	46.9	NON CONIFERES SCIES,RABOTES
24831	LUMBER SAWN ETC NON–CON	W 53975	20.6	W 34345	16.8	W 76128	44.2	W 99408	46.8	SCIES LONGITUDINALEMENT
251	*PULP AND WASTE PAPER	W 54614	30.2	W 57843	50.1	W 38969	35.7	W 65564	37.3	PATES A PAPIER,DECHETS
2517	SODA,SULPHATE WOOD PULP	W 53244	29.0	W 56638	49.2	W 37577	34.2	W 60865	33.7	PATES CHIMIQUES AU SULFATE
25172	— BLEACHED,NONDISSOLVNG	W 33221	18.9	W 31020	40.6	W 30709	28.7	W 49432	27.3	PATES BLANCHIES
26	TEXTILE FIBRES AND WASTE		100.7		75.8		59.8		74.9	FIBRES TEXTILES
263	COTTON	W 27789	59.7	W 24467	35.7	W 14457	36.0	W 23072	53.5	COTON
2631	RAW COTTON,EXCL LINTERS	W 26233	57.3	W 23170	34.2	W 13346	28.7	W 22146	52.0	COTON EN MASSE
266	SYNTHETIC FIBRES TO SPIN	W 21798	36.1	W 19722	38.0	W 8007	19.5	W 9199	14.7	FIBRES SYNTHETIQUES
2665	DISCN SYNTH FIBRE UNCMBD	W 19186	30.7	W 14327	27.1	W 7164	16.8	W 6640	8.0	DISCONTINUES EN MASSE
3	MINERAL FUELS ETC		126.6		58.6		118.6		111.6	COMBUSTIBLES MINERAUX LUB
32	COAL,COKE AND BRIQUETTES		70.8		23.2		47.1		36.3	HOUILLES,COKES,BRIQUETTES
322	COAL,LIGNITE AND PEAT	W 1092054	70.6	W 425326	23.1	W 711526	47.0	W 318684	22.4	HOUILLES,LIGNITES,TOURBE
3222	OTH COAL,NOT AGGLOMERATD	W 1091555	70.4	W 424543	22.8	W 710364	46.5	W 317793	22.1	AUTRES HOUILLES
33	PETROLEUM AND PRODUCTS		55.8		35.4		71.4		75.1	PETROLE ET DERIVES
334	PETROLEUM PRODUCTS,REFIN	W 420963	44.0	W 255135	26.7	W 400561	61.1	W 310309	56.3	PRODUITS RAFFINES
3345	LUBS,PETROLEUM OILS NES	W 146444	19.8	W 136913	16.4	W 126016	32.4	W 139933	38.5	HUILES LUBRIFIANTES
33451	LUBS(HIGH PETR CONT) ETC	W 145306	16.4	W 135206	13.7	W 124964	29.5	W 138718	35.7	HUILES LUBRIF,H LOURDES
4	ANIMAL,VEGETABLE OIL,FAT		184.3		222.9		351.9		280.8	HUILES,GRAISSES ANIM,VEG
411	*ANIMAL OILS AND FATS	W 48030	23.3	W 51555	27.4	W 74045	48.1	W 39003	19.5	HUILES,GRAISSES ANIMALES
4113	ANIML OIL,FAT,GREASE NES	W 42004	18.7	W 43515	20.7	W 59835	35.8	W 37704	18.4	HUILES,GRAISSES ANIMALES NDA
41132	FATS OF BOVINE,SHEEP,ETC	W 41980	18.5	W 43401	20.5	W 56750	34.2	W 26705	13.8	SUIFS BRUTS FONDUS
42	FIXED VEGETABLE OIL,FAT		153.1		188.7		294.9		234.7	HUILES VEGETALES FIXES
423	FIXED VEG OILS,SOFT	W 246521	115.2	W 281951	177.0	W 390525	278.7	W 281578	228.4	HUILES VEGET DOUCES FIXES
4232	SOYA BEAN OIL	W 177089	75.7	W 177509	103.7	W 116551	76.7	W 1830	16.4	HUILE DE SOJA
4233	COTTON SEED OIL	W 1	0.1			W 97	0.2	W 1123	28.4	HUILE DE COTON
4236	SUNFLOWER SEED OIL	W 69415	39.6	W 98642	69.4	W 262077	192.1	W 264614	172.2	HUILE DE TOURNESOL
424	FIXED VEG OIL NONSOFT	W 76631	37.9	W 21479	11.8	W 28289	16.3	W 9448	6.4	AUTRES HUILES VEG FIXES
4242	PALM OIL	W 68519	34.1	W 16757	8.7	W 9668	8.6	W 4704	2.8	HUILE DE PALME
5	CHEMCLS,RELATED PROD NES		895.5		1027.1		1200.6		771.1	PRODUITS CHIMIQUES
51	ORGANIC CHEMICALS		68.0		67.1		87.7		59.9	PROD CHIMIQ ORGANIQUES
513	CARBOXYLIC ACIDS ETC	W 17552	21.5	W 15048	17.6	W 20284	37.6	W 16911	20.9	ACIDES CARBOXYLIQUES
52	INORGANIC CHEMICALS		92.1		79.7		95.4		68.0	PROD CHIM INORGANIQUES
522	INORG ELEMNTS,OXIDES,ETC	W 27421	30.2	W 30441	26.3	W 28834	34.9	W 16714	30.2	ELEMENTS INORGANIQUES
523	OTHR INORG CHEMICALS ETC	W 173223	60.8	W 165297	52.0	W 166583	59.2	W 86631	35.6	AUT PRODUITS CHIMIQUES INORG
5232	OTH MTL CMPD OF INRG ACD	W 95907	38.3	W 92549	33.2	W 94624	39.9	W 42378	18.4	SELS METALLIQUES
52322	PHOSPHITES,PHOSPHATES	W 42674	26.8	W 38407	21.0	W 43401	26.7	W 17715	11.1	PHOSPHITES,PHOSPHATES
53	DYES,TANNING,COLOUR PROD		40.9		40.7		44.9		31.1	PROD TEINTURE,COLORANTS
541	*MEDICINAL,PHARM PRODUCT	MK 27466	366.8	MK 31804	509.8	MK 37728	567.7	MK 20593	324.3	PROD MEDICINAUX PHARMACEUT
5417	MEDICAMENTS	MK 26470	334.7	MK 30314	474.0	MK 36106	504.6	MK 18529	293.2	MEDICAMENTS

4. Special Imports C.I.F. by Commodities according to the S.I.T.C. (Rev. 2) in million U.S. Dollars
Importations Spéciales C.A.F. par Produits d'après la C.T.C.I. (Rév. 2) en millions de Dollars E.U.

SITC CTCI	COMMODITY	1993 QUANTITY QUANTITE	1993 VALUE VALEUR	1994 QUANTITY QUANTITE	1994 VALUE VALEUR	1995 QUANTITY QUANTITE	1995 VALUE VALEUR	1996 QUANTITY QUANTITE	1996 VALUE VALEUR	PRODUIT
54171	— CONTAINNG ANTIBIOTICS	K 977054	23.9	K 2947719	81.8	K 4512954	105.4	K 1659509	52.9	MED CONTN ANTIBIOTIQUES
54179	— CONTNG OTH SUBSTANCES	MK 24404	303.4	MK 25642	367.2	MK 30551	382.0	MK 16085	225.2	MED CONT AUT SUBSTANCES
55	PERFUME,CLEANING ETC PRD		24.3		25.7		37.4		26.7	PROD POUR PARFUM,TOILETTE
562	*FERTILIZERS,MANUFACTURE	W 64673	14.5	W 84194	17.3	W 135852	34.9	W 114371	27.2	ENGRAIS MANUFACTURES
58	PLASTIC MATERIALS ETC		134.8		160.1		189.5		121.0	MAT PLAST ARTIFICIELLES
583	POLYMERIZATION ETC PRODS		97.7	W 248360	120.1	W 89660	142.7	W 59472	87.1	PROD POLYMERISATION
5831	POLYETHYLENE	W 44322	41.5	W 32143	28.0	W 45783	62.8	W 22878	25.5	POLYETHYLENE
58311	— IN PRIMARY FORMS	W 41916	36.0	W 30670	24.8	W 38781	45.1	W 22128	23.6	POLYETHYLENE PRIMAIRES
5833	POLYSTYRENE,ITS COPOLYMR	W 6669	8.7	W 11598	30.3	W 7399	14.1	W 9300	13.0	POLYPROPYLENE COPOLYMERES
5839	OTH POLYMRZTION ETC PROD	W 38385	22.7	W 184454	35.1	W 15011	31.8	W 10434	22.3	AUT PROD POLYMER COPOLYM
59	CHEMICAL MATERIALS NES		144.0		126.2		139.3		109.3	MAT PROD CHIMIQUES NDA
598	MISCEL CHEM PRODUCTS NES		107.5	W 53552	95.1	W 35686	109.1	W 37430	88.5	PROD DIV INDUST CHIM NDA
5982	ANTI-KNOCK PREPARTNS ETC	W 7809	26.1	W 8329	29.3	W 5125	29.6	W 10177	39.0	PREPARAT ANTIDETONANTES
5989	CHEM PRODUCTS,PREPS NES		75.7	W 42414	61.4	W 28558	75.8	W 25706	47.0	PROD PREP CHIMIQUES NDA
59899	OTH CHEM PRODS,PREPS,NES		57.7	W 37955	51.4	W 24889	60.6	W 21692	36.4	AUT PRODUITS CHIMIQUES NDA
6	BASIC MANUFACTURES		1905.6		2087.5		2235.5		1887.7	ART MANUFACTURES
62	RUBBER MANUFACTURES NES		180.3		140.9		180.8		126.1	CAOUTCHOUC MANUFACTURE
625	RUBBER TYRES, TUBES ETC	W 43318	119.3	W 51984	92.3	W 56023	130.8	W 34028	89.9	PNEUS CAOUTCHOUC VULCANISE
6252	TYRES,NEW,BUS OR LORRY	W 25159	74.1	W 13583	45.4	W 29808	74.1	W 11847	44.7	PNEUS POUR AUTOBUS,CAMIONS
6259	OTH TYRES,TYRE CASES,ETC	W 12710	22.8	W 31775	26.1	W 17777	32.5	W 19755	34.5	AUTRES PNEUS RECHAPES FLAPS
628	RUBBER ARTICLES NES	W 2994	38.0	W 3144	34.9	W 3109	33.7	W 2098	25.3	OUVRAGES CAOUTCHOUC NDA
63	WOOD,CORK MANUFACTRS NES		164.6		78.0		45.6		47.9	OUVRAGES LIEGE ET BOIS
634	VENEERS,PLYWOOD,ETC		156.3		48.3	W 35313	31.6	W 26036	25.4	PLACAGES,CONTRE-PLAQUES
6342	PLYWOOD OF WOOD SHEETS	W 53135	152.0	W 63267	46.9	W 30183	25.3	W 17677	15.5	BOIS CONTRE-PLAQUES
635	WOOD MANUFACTURES NES	W 1800	8.3	W 7088	29.8	W 1999	14.1	W 7348	22.4	ART MANUF EN BOIS NDA
64	PAPER,PAPERBOARD AND MFR		148.0		157.7		165.0		245.6	PAPIERS,CARTONS & OUVRAGES
641	PAPER AND PAPERBOARD	W 145149	105.9	W 143492	143.5	W 237802	131.7	W 124283	222.4	PAPIERS ET CARTONS
6413	KRAFT PAPER,PAPERBOARD	W 33517	19.3	W 45078	28.7	W 32698	30.7	W 41574	145.1	PAPIER ET CARTON KRAFT
64132	SACK KRAFT PAPER IN BULK	W 19530	12.0	W 25294	14.6	W 21519	21.0	W 24650	131.7	PAPIER KRAFT POUR SACS
6415	PAPER,PAPERBRD,BULK,NES	W 21396	15.7	W 31400	53.4	W 39986	31.9	W 22131	17.4	PAPIERS,CARTONS ROULEAUX
64159	OTHER PAPER ETC,BULK,NES	W 18186	13.8	W 27934	51.1	W 34167	27.6	W 15450	13.6	AUT PAPIER ROULEAUX FEUILLES
6418	COATED ETC PAPER NES BLK	W 25719	27.6	W 16661	22.4	W 18711	25.4	W 13852	21.1	PAP,CARTONS COUCHES,ENDUITS
642	PAPER,ETC,PRECUT,ARTS OF	W 25536	42.2	W 7222	14.2	W 14193	33.4	W 13448	23.3	PAP,CARTONS DECOUPES
65	TEXTILE YARN,FABRICS,ETC		96.8		170.0		175.9		155.9	FILS,TISSUS,ARTICLES TEXTILE
651	TEXTILE YARN		60.6	W 27737	81.3	W 11563	57.6	W 13965	50.9	FILS TEXTILES
6514	SYN FIB YRN,BULK,MONOFIL	W 10067	14.0	W 11885	30.3	W 4887	19.8	W 6450	20.0	FILS CONT 85% FIB TEXT SYNTH
6516	DISCON SYN FIB BLEND YRN		27.0	W 12140	33.8	W 4068	19.5	W 3565	11.5	FILS FIBR TEX SYNT DIS MOINS
653	WOVN MAN-MADE FIB FABRIC		3.5	W 11753	44.3	W 11821	51.2	W 16420	43.4	TISSUS FIBRES SYNTH,ARTIF
66	NONMETAL MINERAL MFS NES		194.7		246.1		248.3		213.4	ART MIN NON METALLIQUES
661	LIME,CEMENT,BLDG PRODS	W 1429056	82.8	W 2175234	119.4	W 2030104	115.8	W 1498497	94.7	CHAUX,CIMENTS MAT CONSTR
6612	CEMENT	W 1426559	78.8	W 2174887	119.1	W 2026918	112.5	W 1491676	90.2	CIMENTS HYDRAULIQUES
662	CLAY,REFRACTORY BLDG PRD	W 399668	21.6	W 64552	43.2	W 81062	47.4	W 88351	44.5	MAT CONST REFRACTAIRES
6623	REFRACTORY BUILDING PROD	W 395781	19.9	W 43127	36.8	W 27457	28.3	W 27174	26.4	BRIQUES REFRACTAIRES
663	MINERAL MANUFCTURES NES	W 22423	28.8	W 13812	30.5	W 7841	25.7	W 6405	17.2	ART MIN MANUF NDA
664	GLASS	W 27562	43.8	W 42239	37.9	W 39873	36.6	W 40483	35.5	VERRE
6649	GLASS NES	W 6244	28.5	W 4002	8.4	W 5323	9.0	W 3591	5.8	VERRE NDA
67	IRON AND STEEL		740.3		913.7		899.7		742.6	FER ET ACIER
672	IRON,STEEL PRIMARY FORMS	W 126237	53.6	W 136970	44.6	W 44790	24.0	W 117628	71.7	LINGOTS FER,ACIER
6727	IRN,STL COIL FR REROLLNG	W 119779	50.8	W 97730	34.4	W 43388	22.1	W 115928	69.9	EBAUCHES POUR TOLES FER
67271	IRON,SIMPLE STEEL COILS	W 119698	50.6	W 97688	34.2	W 41955	20.7	W 115847	69.5	EBAUCHES NON EN ACIER
673	IRON,STEEL SHAPES ETC	W 699129	254.1	W 1299641	418.2	W 969568	283.3	W 619176	214.0	BARRES,PROFIL FER,ACIER
6731	IRON,STEEL WIRE ROD	W 178999	68.2	W 165002	58.5	W 129401	44.6	W 225041	70.3	FIL MACHINE FER,ACIER
67311	IRON,SIMPLE STL WIRE ROD	W 147755	55.4	W 138796	50.5	W 115894	40.3	W 205587	64.6	FIL MACH AUT ACIER FIN
6732	IRON,STEEL BARS ETC	W 462499	161.1	W 1086364	336.0	W 671103	197.9	W 256863	86.7	BARRES FER,ACIER
67322	HIGH CARBON STL BARS ETC	W 182044	64.7	W 174814	55.2	W 81485	22.3	W 5132	2.3	BARRES ACIER FIN CARBONE
67326	IRN,OTH STL BARS HOTROLD	W 240991	81.3	W 854121	258.6	W 531481	154.2	W 221959	71.5	BARRES PLEINES FER,ACIER
6733	IRON,STEEL PROFILES ETC	W 57630	25.0	W 48276	23.9	W 169065	40.9	W 137271	57.1	PROFILES,PALPLAN FER,ACIER
67332	LARGE U,I,H SECTIONS ETC	W 28037	11.2	W 18894	10.5	W 45758	17.7	W 76475	34.5	PROFILES PLUS 80MM
674	IRN,STL UNIV,PLATE,SHEET	W 174055	142.2	W 100924	102.3	W 120516	115.8	W 82926	62.8	LARGES PLATS,TOLES
6746	IRN,STL THIN PLATE,ROLLD	W 60598	62.1	W 32897	37.7	W 25640	25.6	W 14882	13.1	TOLES LAM MOINS 3MM
67461	— OF IRON OR SIMPLE STL	W 58985	57.8	W 31155	33.3	W 24555	21.8	W 12856	7.1	TOL NON AC FIN MOINS 3 MM
6747	TINNED PLATES,SHEETS	W 18965	23.2	W 27012	34.3	W 31947	37.1	W 12636	13.2	TOLES ETAMEES EN ACIER
676	RAILWY RAILS ETC IRN,STL	W 32453	28.4	W 5729	3.7	W 3275	4.1	W 2900	5.0	RAILS,ELEMENTS VOIES FERREE
678	IRON,STL TUBES,PIPES,ETC	W 114283	224.9	W 238704	325.4	W 375411	447.7	W 288061	365.3	TUBES,TUYAUX EN FONTE,FER
6782	IRON,STL SEAMLESS TUBES	W 94447	157.8	W 91091	176.5	W 142993	176.9	W 130120	190.1	TUBES,TUYAUX SANS SOUDURE
6783	IRON,STL TUBES,PIPES NES	W 13030	23.8	W 120990	100.3	W 227542	239.5	W 149823	142.6	AUT TUBES,TUYAUX FER,ACIER
6785	IRON,STEEL TUBE FITTINGS	W 5907	42.3	W 5878	32.4	W 4174	30.7	W 5420	30.4	ACCESSOIRES DE TUYAUTERIE
68	NON-FERROUS METALS		110.9		105.4		135.4		105.3	METAUX NON FERREUX
682	COPPER EXC CEMENT COPPER	W 11665	37.8	W 16660	50.5	W 80803	62.5	W 13888	47.4	CUIVRE
6822	COPPER,ALLOYS WORKED	W 10870	35.5	W 15443	47.5	W 75583	57.6	W 11832	44.9	CUIVRE,ALLIAGES OUVRES
68221	COPPER BARS,WIRE,ETC	W 7903	21.7	W 11705	31.7	W 10443	33.7	W 5496	17.0	BARRES,PROFILES ET FILS
684	ALUMINIUM	W 44423	52.2	W 17390	46.4	W 20481	63.2	W 21494	48.4	ALUMINIUM
6842	ALUMINIUM,ALLOYS WORKED	W 37379	41.0	W 11405	34.2	W 14136	48.6	W 15920	34.0	ALUMINIUM,ALLIAGES OUVRE
69	METAL MANUFACTURES NES		262.8		270.7		376.3		246.6	ART MANUFACT EN METAL NDA
691	STRUCTURES AND PARTS NES	W 16078	42.8	W 17809	63.2	W 49841	127.6	W 16319	57.4	CONSTRUCT FER,ACIER,ALU
6911	STRUCTURES,PARTS IRN,STL	W 10118	42.3	W 17638	62.3	W 48782	126.3	W 15375	52.9	CONSTRUCT FER,ACIER,FONTE
692	METAL TANKS,BOXES,ETC	W 11198	22.3	W 8720	46.8	W 8276	53.2	W 4639	19.1	RECIPIENTS METALLIQUES
6924	MTL TRANSPORT BOXES ETC	W 6239	10.9	W 6185	38.1	W 7819	48.8	W 4346	16.8	FUTS,TAMBOURS,BIDONS
69243	IRN,STL COMP GAS CYLINDR	W 674	4.5	W 3407	28.5	W 3599	38.7	W 979	6.2	RECIP FER,ACIER GAZ COMP
694	STL,COPPR NAILS,NUTS,ETC	W 37281	35.4	W 3389	19.7	W 5064	25.1	W 3928	21.7	CLOUS,VIS,ECROUS
69402	IRN,STL NUTS,BOLTS,ETC	W 4334	32.5	W 2538	18.3	W 3233	22.7	W 3170	20.4	BOULONS,VIS,ECROUS FER,AC
695	TOOLS	W 3547	53.0	W 3531	51.8	W 5279	61.7	W 4814	55.5	OUTILS A MAIN
6954	BLADES,TIPS,ETC FR TOOLS	W 1038	32.1	W 985	33.4	W 836	35.0	W 615	34.0	OUTILS POUR MACHINE-OUTIL
69541	PARTS TO INSERT IN TOOLS	W 909	26.5	W 899	30.0	W 684	29.9	W 562	30.6	OUTILS DE FORAGE
699	BASE METAL MFRS NES		56.6		53.4	W 17490	67.3	W 11467	55.5	ART MANUFACTURES MET NDA
7	MACHINES,TRANSPORT EQUIP		2784.2		2572.3		3279.9		2793.5	MACHINES MATERIEL TRANSPORT
71	POWER GENERATING EQUIPMT		355.6		398.6		299.6		306.5	MACHINES GENERATRICES
711	STEAM BOILERS & AUX PLNT	W 11061	117.9	W 1613	17.0	W 500	6.6	W 326	5.5	GENERATEURS VAPEUR EAU ETC
7111	STEAM BOILERS ETC	W 6727	88.4	W 534	6.1	W 361	4.0	W 251	2.1	GENERATEURS VAPEUR EAU
712	STEAM ENGINES,TURBINES	W 600	32.1	W 922	16.2	W 64	5.2	W 68	8.4	MACHINES A VAPEUR D'EAU PIEC
713	INTRNL COMBUS PSTN ENGIN	W 6868	90.9	W 6487	106.9	W 7371	114.2	W 3944	155.2	MOTEURS EXPL COMB INT, PIECE
7139	PISTON ENGINE PARTS NES	W 4342	56.1	W 3680	69.5	W 5007	75.9	W 2810	136.7	PIECES POUR 713.2,3,8
714	ENGINES AND MOTORS NES	W 1096	56.8	W 4069	196.3	W 3502	126.6	W 842	82.0	MOTEURS NON ELECTRIQUES
7148	GAS TURBINES NES	W 950	24.1	W 2444	100.4	W 676	30.4	W 295	25.2	TURBINES A GAZ
71488	OTHER GAS TURBINES NES	W 948	24.1	W 2266	95.5	W 672	29.8	W 288	8.2	AUTRES TURBINES A GAZ
7149	ENGINE & MOTOR PARTS NES	W 129	31.0	W 1618	93.7	W 2800	91.2	W 506	47.2	PIECES 714 ET 718.88
71499	PARTS NES,OF 71488,71888	W 128	30.6	W 1607	92.9	W 2524	88.4	W 496	41.0	PIECES 714.88 ET 718.88
716	ROTATING ELECTRIC PLANT	W 3137	52.4	W 3208	60.0	W 2348	39.9	W 3316	51.7	APP ELECTR ROTATIFS,PIECES
7162	AC MTRS,GENRTRS,GEN SETS	W 1981	31.6	W 2252	41.3	W 1697	26.9	W 2565	36.3	MOTEURS ELECTRIQUES
72	MACHS FOR SPCL INDUSTRYS		241.2		233.0		262.6		258.6	MAC SPECIALES POUR INDUST
723	CIVIL ENGNEERG EQUIP ETC	W 6135	57.1	W 5984	58.4	W 6258	49.9	W 14687	79.9	APPAREILS DE GENIE CIVIL

4. Special Imports C.I.F. by Commodities according to the S.I.T.C. (Rev. 2) in million U.S. Dollars
Importations Spéciales C.A.F. par Produits d'après la C.T.C.I. (Rév. 2) en millions de Dollars E.U.

SITC CTCI	COMMODITY	1993		1994		1995		1996		PRODUIT
		QUANTITY QUANTITE	VALUE VALEUR	QUANTITY QUANTITE	VALUE VALEUR	QUANTITY QUANTITE	VALUE VALEUR	QUANTITY QUANTITE	VALUE VALEUR	
7234	CONST,MINING MACHNRY NES	W 5046	37.5	W 4719	38.9	W 5253	29.7	W 13216	51.3	MACH POUR LA CONST, MINES
7239	CONSTR ETC MACHY PTS NES	W 1064	19.6	W 935	17.1	W 978	20.1	W 1300	28.3	PIECES 723.41–723.46
724	TEXTILE,LEATHER MACHNRY	W 8925	31.0	W 10548	42.6	W 7570	34.2	W 4816	21.4	MACH POUR INDUSTRIE TEXTILE
727	FOOD MACHRY NON–DOMESTIC	W 2723	29.0	W 1926	22.7	W 2692	29.1	W 3051	30.5	MACH INDUSTRIES ALIMENT
728	OTH MACHY FOR SPCL INDUS	W 10141	95.5	W 7723	89.3	W 10662	110.3	W 11594	93.2	AUT MACH IND PARTICULIERES
7283	OTHR MINERAL WORKG MACHY	W 4766	38.0	W 3609	35.1	W 3712	35.4	W 4675	42.4	MACH TRIER,CRIBLER,BROYER
7284	MACHY FOR SPCL INDUS NES	W 4343	43.4	W 3503	46.6	W 5845	63.8	W 5935	43.9	MACH SPEC IND PARTICUL.
73	METALWORKING MACHINERY		80.9		42.3		66.4		53.4	MACH TRAVAIL DES METAUX
736	METALWORKING MACH–TOOLS	W 4684	60.3	W 2062	23.4	W 2178	34.2	W 2286	25.3	MACH–OUTILS TRAVAIL METAUX
7361	METAL CUTTING MACH–TOOLS	W 2872	32.8	W 939	8.9	W 756	8.2	W 1317	11.1	MACH–OUT ENLEVEMENT METAL
737	METALWORKING MACHNRY NES	W 1158	20.6	W 2590	18.9	W 3634	32.3	W 2149	28.1	MACH TRAV METAUX PIECES
74	GENRL INDUSTRL MACHY NES		974.2		739.6		1076.1		795.6	MACH APP INDUSTRIE
741	HEATING,COOLING EQUIPMNT	W 35288	251.4	W 14167	158.2	W 22048	159.2	W 24395	187.4	MACH CHAUFFAGE,PIECES
7413	INDUS FURNACES ETC,PARTS	W 10813	56.1	W 4672	26.3	W 5625	37.6	W 11897	74.1	FOURS IND,LABOR,PIECES
74132	INDUST FURNACES NONELECT	W 10421	52.7	W 3776	22.6	W 5271	33.2	W 11536	65.4	FOURS NON ELECTRIQUES
7416	HEATING,COOLING EQU NES	W 19490	168.2	W 6202	93.0	W 7836	71.8	W 7684	74.0	APP CHANGEMENT TEMP
742	PUMPS FOR LIQUIDS ETC	W 5643	92.5	W 5150	83.6	W 6049	86.1	W 5659	99.9	POMPES MOTO–POMPES
7428	OTHER PUMPS FOR LIQUIDS	W 3798	50.4	W 3771	53.0	W 4660	52.4	W 3657	48.8	AUTRES POMPES POUR LIQ
74288	PUMPS FR LIQUIDS NES ETC	W 3793	50.3	W 3721	52.2	W 4621	51.9	W 3637	48.7	POMPES POUR LIQUIDES NDA
7429	PTS NES OF PUMPS OF 742	W 968	19.7	W 377	17.1	W 478	18.2	W 803	31.5	PIECES POUR GROUPE 742
743	PUMPS NES,CENTRFUGES ETC	W 9630	219.2	W 17744	125.2	W 12424	258.0	W 10538	172.3	POMPES COMPRES,VENT ETC
7431	PUMPS FOR GASES ETC	W 4801	104.9	W 3066	24.9	W 6127	156.1	W 5323	82.9	POMPES AIR A VIDE,COMPRES
7436	GAS,LIQUID FILTERS ETC	W 3239	52.4	W 3067	36.6	W 4263	48.4	W 4074	53.9	APP POUR FILT DES LIQUIDES
7439	PTS NES OF APP OF 7435,6	W 1000	54.4	W 11424	60.7	W 1554	42.6	W 813	24.5	PIECES 743.5 ET 743.6
744	MECHANICAL HANDLING EQU	W 13890	98.4	W 9895	74.8	W 7956	88.5	W 7503	63.0	EQUIP MANUTENTION PIECES
7442	LIFTING,LOADING MACH NES	W 6255	48.7	W 4122	37.1	W 5601	65.0	W 3359	30.5	APP LEVAGE,MANUTENTION
74428	OTH HANDLING ETC MCH NES	W 4343	34.4	W 2976	25.7	W 4431	53.9	W 2762	25.3	AUT APP LEVAGE ETC
745	NONELEC MACHY,TOOLS NES		104.9	W 2878	55.0	W 4260	52.6	W 3196	58.8	AUT MACH NON ELEC,PIECES
7452	OTH NONELEC MCHS,PTS NES		102.1	W 2761	51.8	W 4069	47.8	W 3059	55.9	AUT MACH NON ELEC,PIECES
74527	SPRAYING MACHINERY		75.0	W 1834	31.0	W 2745	18.4	W 1335	21.5	APP PROJETER ETC LIQUID
749	NONELEC MACH PTS,ACC NES	W 13213	208.0	W 14517	242.9	W 53597	432.0	W 14217	214.6	PIECES MACH NON ELEC NDA
7492	COCKS,VALVES ETC NES	W 6823	103.8	W 8905	141.8	W 47360	304.1	W 9680	110.8	ART ROB,SIM POUR TUYAUX
7493	SHAFT,CRANK,PULLEY ETC	W 2799	57.7	W 2456	50.8	W 2362	64.2	W 1782	53.3	ARBRES TRANS,VILEBREQUINS
7499	OTH NONELEC MCHY PTS NES	W 2280	25.6	W 1812	29.4	W 1333	32.4	W 1193	24.0	PIECES NON ELECT NDA
75	OFFICE MACHNES,ADP EQUIP		90.1		102.8		219.8		115.8	MACH BUREAU TRAIT AUTOM
752	AUTOMTIC DATA PROC EQUIP	W 1296	55.7	W 1046	64.0	W 2577	171.7	W 1681	85.7	MACH TRAIT INFORMATION
7522	DIGITAL COMPUTERS	W 360	29.5	W 373	30.9	W 1231	106.3	W 495	32.4	MACH DIGITALES COMPLETES
7528	OFF–LINE DATA PROC EQUIP	W 76	5.5	W 345	9.5	W 883	35.1	W 511	20.8	MACH AUXIL TRAIT INFORM
76	TELECOMM,SOUND EQUIPMENT		136.0		134.1		323.7		165.8	EQUIPMENT DE TELECOM
761	TELEVISION RECEIVERS	W 3903	32.3	W 8580	20.8	W 4467	40.4	W 2502	14.3	RECEPTEURS DE TELEVISION
7611	COLOUR TV RECEIVERS	W 3517	30.2	W 5544	18.6	W 3118	34.1	W 1634	11.4	RECEPTEURS COULEUR
764	TELECOM EQPT,PTS,ACC NES	W 4001	93.4	W 1928	103.4	W 4745	265.7	W 82833	137.9	EQUIP TELECOM,PIECES
7641	LINE TELEPHONE,ETC EQUIP	W 469	40.7	W 584	57.0	W 894	74.0	W 77008	50.7	APP TELEPHON PAR FIL
7643	TV,RADIO TRANSMITTRS ETC	W 2258	24.1	W 93	22.3	W 316	31.5	W 181	29.2	APP EMET TELE RADIO
7649	PTS NES OF EQUIPMT OF 76	W 1089	22.6	W 1071	20.8	W 3286	151.1	W 4953	48.9	PIECES DE LA DIV 76
76493	TELECOMM EQUIPMT PTS NES	W 995	15.5	W 955	12.4	W 3229	144.9	W 4714	35.5	PIECES 761,762,764.3,8
77	ELECTRIC MACHNRY NES ETC		508.5		508.0		528.1		433.8	MACH APP ELECT NDA
771	ELECTRIC POWER MACHY NES	W 3927	57.3	W 3228	51.9	W 2992	38.3	W 1859	23.8	MACH PROD,TRANS ELECTR
7711	TRANSFORMERS,ELECTRICAL	W 2419	35.6	W 1949	35.3	W 1406	17.9	W 641	9.0	TRANSFO ELECTRIQUES
772	SWITCHGEAR ETC,PARTS NES	W 12607	164.1		217.3	W 8346	226.3	W 6955	141.5	APP COUPURE,SECT ETC
7721	SWITCHGEAR ETC	W 12397	158.0		210.7	W 8183	218.7	W 6638	131.7	APP COUPURE,SECTIONMNT
773	ELECTR DISTRIBUTNG EQUIP	W 19488	81.3	W 12010	73.4	W 8992	51.1	W 19789	76.4	EQUIPMT DISTRIBUTION ELECT
7731	INSULATED WIRE,CABLE ETC	W 18238	75.3	W 8533	66.2	W 7385	44.4	W 18066	69.4	FILS,CABLES ISOLES ELECT
774	ELECTRO–MEDCL,XRAY EQUIP	W 111	7.9	W 279	17.1	W 214	13.4	W 263	29.5	APPAREILS MEDICAUX
775	HOUSEHOLD TYPE EQUIP NES	W 8717	57.3	W 8871	24.1	W 10148	41.4	W 9005	24.5	MACH,APP USAGE DOMESTQUE
7757	DOMESTIC ELECTRC EQU NES	W 2483	31.5	W 861	8.2	W 1710	8.6	W 2155	6.7	APP ELECTR DOMEST NDA
77572	DOM ELEC ROOM FANS ETC	W 1863	26.7	W 594	3.1	W 1283	5.8	W 1406	4.6	HOTTES ASPIRANTES,VENTIL
776	TRANSISTORS,VALVES,ETC	W 3016	38.4	W 1901	33.0	W 2456	42.5	W 3614	58.5	LAMPES,TUBES,VALVES
7761	TV PICTURE TUBES	W 2536	16.7	W 1642	11.3	W 2154	19.5	W 3062	30.3	TUBES CATHODIQUES
778	ELECTRICAL MACHINERY NES	W 18433	102.5	W 16938	91.4	W 14304	115.4	W 10472	79.9	AUTRES MACH ELECT NDA
7783	AUTOMOTIVE ELECTR EQUIP	W 8891	35.2	W 8306	26.1	W 2571	33.9	W 2106	23.2	EQUIP ELECT MOTEURS EXPL
7788	OTH ELEC MACHY,EQUIP NES	W 1487	31.0	W 1840	33.0	W 1438	37.9	W 1067	31.2	AUT MACH APP ELEC NDA
78	ROAD VEHICLES		351.8		348.3		448.5		554.4	VEHICULES ROUTIERS
781	PASS MOTOR VEH EXC BUSES	W 11448	105.4	W 4700	69.0	W 10799	154.2	W 21972	232.7	AUTO TRANSPORT PERSONNES
782	LORRIES,SPCL MTR VEH NES	W 7610	64.8	W 7904	83.4	W 8359	86.3	W 15839	153.1	VEHICULES SPECIAUX,MARCH
7821	LORRIES,TRUCKS	W 6362	48.4	W 5590	39.5	W 5281	41.5	W 11668	76.5	VEHICULES TRANSP MARCHAND
7822	SPECIAL MOTOR VEHCLS NES	W 1248	16.4	W 2314	43.9	W 3079	44.9	W 4171	76.7	VEHICULES USAGES SPECIAUX
783	ROAD MOTOR VEHICLES NES	W 10731	41.1	W 12477	48.3	W 9971	29.7	W 27874	49.9	VEHICULES ROUTIERS NDA
7831	BUSES	W 2066	23.1	W 2713	37.5	W 1709	22.6	W 2296	12.0	VOITURES TRANSPORT COMMUN
7832	TRACTORS FOR TR–TRAILERS	W 8665	18.0	W 9763	10.8	W 8262	7.1	W 25578	38.0	TRACTEURS ROUTIERS
784	MOTOR VEH PRTS,ACCES NES	W 42099	102.1	W 25749	129.7	W 15531	149.0	W 11406	92.5	PIECES 722,781,782,783
7849	OTHER MOTOR VEHCL PARTS	W 42060	101.6	W 25710	129.4	W 15465	148.4	W 11301	91.7	PIECES 722,781,782,783
786	TRAILERS,NONMOTR VEH,NES	W 60112	31.2	W 15419	15.2	W 42876	21.3	W 30935	21.1	REMORQUES,CADRES,CONTAIN
79	OTHR TRANSPORT EQUIPMENT		46.3		66.1		55.5		110.0	AUTRE MATERIEL TRANSPORT
791	RAILWAY VEHICLES	W 6919	32.5	W 10087	54.9	W 3214	25.0	W 3643	80.6	VEHIC MAT CHEMINS DE FER
7911	ELEC LOCOS NON–SELF–GEN	W 11	0.2					W 1536	63.5	LOCOMOTIVES ELECTRIQUES
7919	RY TRACK FIXT,ETC,PARTS	W 5912	14.3	W 8848	32.7	W 3172	24.9	W 1729	9.6	MATER FIXE VOIES FERREES
8	MISC MANUFACTURED GOODS		300.0		321.9		387.9		399.8	ART MANUFACTURES DIVERS
84	CLOTHING AND ACCESSORIES		7.9		5.8		25.9		55.0	VETEMENTS
87	PRECISION INSTRUMNTS NES		139.0		154.2		150.0		147.6	INSTRUM,APPAR SCIENT NDA
872	MEDICAL INSTRUMENTS NES		27.8	W 1115	23.2	W 978	30.5	W 1773	25.7	INSTR,APP MEDIC–CHIR NDA
874	MEASURNG,CONTROLNG INSTR		99.2		120.5	W 3728	111.5	W 2548	114.7	INSTRUMENTS DE MESURE
8743	GAS,LIQUID CONTROL INSTR	W 680	29.1	W 1138	37.0	W 2077	43.4	W 659	34.8	APP,INSTR MESURE FLUIDES
8748	ELEC MEAS,CONTRL EQU NES	W 140	17.3		29.6	W 224	20.0	W 261	25.3	APP ELEC ELECTRO MESURE
88	PHOTO EQU,OPTICL GDS ETC		20.9		29.4		32.0		22.9	APP,FOURN PHOTO,OP,MONTR
89	MISC MANUFCTRD GOODS NES		111.8		114.4		127.6		120.8	ART MANUFACTURES DIVERS
893	ARTICLES OF PLASTIC NES		61.0		52.2		44.0		52.0	OUVRAGES EN MAT DIVIS 58
8939	MISC PLASTIC ARTICLES		54.2	W 9599	44.0	W 8428	35.1	W 7310	36.0	ART DIVERS EN MAT DIV 58
89399	OTHR PLASTC ARTICLES NES	W 10276	53.2	W 9498	43.7	W 8008	34.1	W 6647	34.4	AUT OUV MAT DIV 58

5. Special Exports F.O.B. by Commodities according to the S.I.T.C. (Rev. 2) in million U.S. Dollars
Exportations Spéciales F.O.B. par Produits d'après la C.T.C.I. (Rév. 2) en millions de Dollars E.U.

SITC CTCI	COMMODITY	1993 QUANTITY QUANTITE	1993 VALUE VALEUR	1994 QUANTITY QUANTITE	1994 VALUE VALEUR	1995 QUANTITY QUANTITE	1995 VALUE VALEUR	1996 QUANTITY QUANTITE	1996 VALUE VALEUR	PRODUIT
	ALL COMMODITIES		10097.7		8593.9		9356.7		11099.3	TOUS PRODUITS
0	FOOD AND LIVE ANIMALS		94.1		32.7		99.9		114.2	ALIMENTS,ANIMAUX VIVANTS
05	VEGETABLES AND FRUIT		88.5		28.4		80.9		89.2	LEGUMES ET FRUITS
057	FRUIT,NUTS,FRESH,DRIED	W 19876	55.4	W 3916	12.1	W 21964	78.9	W 20654	66.4	FRUITS FRAIS OU SECS
0579	FRUIT FRESH OR DRIED NES	W 19820	55.4	W 3763	12.0	W 21856	78.7	W 20600	66.3	FRUITS FRAIS,SECS NDA
05796	DATES,FRESH OR DRIED	W 19809	55.4	W 3763	12.0	W 21852	78.7	W 20598	66.3	DATTES FRAICHES OU SECHES
2	CRUDE MATERLS,EXCL FUELS		26.0		23.0		40.4		53.8	MAT BRUTES NON COMESTIBLES
3	MINERAL FUELS ETC		9679.3		8342.0		8909.1		10312.7	COMBUSTIBLES MINERAUX LUB
33	PETROLEUM AND PRODUCTS		6339.7		5585.6		6056.0		6719.8	PETROLE ET DERIVES
333	CRUDE PETROLEUM	MW 39108	4448.8	MW 31492	3924.5	MW 32287	4309.8	MW 33934	5329.1	HUILES BRUTES DE PETROLE
334	PETROLEUM PRODUCTS,REFIN	MW 13588	1828.8	MW 12648	1617.1	MW 12592	1684.6	W 7873446	1295.1	PRODUITS RAFFINES
3341	GASOLINE,OTH LIGHT OILS	W 3496501	539.9	W 3849867	564.3	W 3539241	545.1	W 2423858	441.9	ESSENCES POUR MOTEURS
33411	MOTOR,AVIATION SPIRIT	W 31942	5.5	W 372650	64.6	W 231830	41.4	W 230429	41.7	ESSENCES MOTEURS D'AVIONS
33412	SPIRIT TYPE JET FUEL	W 98313	13.5	W 708507	106.7	W 425470	78.5	W 266519	51.8	CARBUREACTEURS
33419	OTH LIGHT PETROLEUM OILS	W 3366246	521.0	W 2768709	393.2	W 2881941	425.3	W 1926911	348.5	AUTRES HUILES LEGERES
3342	KEROSENE,OTH MEDIUM OILS	W 129568	18.9	W 434227	63.5	W 353005	55.3	W 129055	25.8	PETR LAMPANTS,AUT HUIL
33421	KEROSENE INCL JET FUEL	W 129568	18.9	W 434227	63.5	W 353005	55.3	W 129055	25.8	PETROLES LAMPANTS
3343	GAS OILS	W 4057442	677.0	W 3436500	494.2	W 3384114	522.7	W 2012997	378.1	GAS OILS
3344	FUEL OILS,NES	W 5879350	587.9	W 4886914	485.2	W 5287350	552.2	W 3295975	447.1	FUEL OILS
335	RESIDUAL PETRLM PROD NES	W 403057	62.2	W 366601	44.1	W 408972	61.7	W 560108	95.8	PRODUITS RESIDUELS NDA
3352	MINERAL TARS AND PRODCTS	W 403057	62.2	W 366601	44.1	W 408972	61.7	W 560108	95.8	GOUDRONS MINERAUX
33525	MINERAL TAR OILS ETC NES	W 378319	60.4	W 351990	42.4	W 398752	60.7	W 551730	95.0	AUTRES PRODUITS NDA
341	*GAS,NATURAL AND MANUFCT		3329.9		2677.6		2840.7	MW 37204	3580.9	GAZ NATUREL,GAZ MANUFACT
3413	PETROLM GASES,LIQUEFIED	MW 18348	2198.9	MW 18378	1773.9	MW 13709	1536.2	MW 18935	2336.2	GAZ DE PETROLE LIQUEFIE
34131	LIQUEFIED PROPANE,BUTANE	W 3377424	508.9	W 3757483	459.4	W 2866824	439.6	W 3863933	711.3	PROPANE,BUTANE LIQUEFIES
34139	OTH HYDROCARBON GAS LQFD	MW 14971	1690.0	MW 14621	1314.6	MW 10843	1096.7	MW 15071	1624.9	HYDROCARBURES GAZEUX NDA
3414	PETROLEUM GASES, GASEOUS		1131.1		903.7		1304.5	MW 18269	1244.7	GAZ DE PETROLE GAZEUX
351	*ELECTRIC CURRENT		9.7		78.2		12.5		12.1	ENERGIE ELECTRIQUE
5	CHEMCLS,RELATED PROD NES		148.1		95.6		114.0		284.5	PRODUITS CHIMIQUES
51	ORGANIC CHEMICALS		19.8		44.1		46.6		26.2	PROD CHIMIQ ORGANIQUES
511	HYDROCARBONS NES,DERIVS	W 44393	11.0	W 85502	28.6	W 76514	27.7	W 47138	15.1	HYDROCARBURES NDA
52	INORGANIC CHEMICALS		112.8		27.7		43.7		41.7	PROD CHIM INORGANIQUES
522	INORG ELEMNTS,OXIDES,ETC	W 296307	112.8	W 193314	27.6	W 181096	43.7	W 157516	41.6	ELEMENTS INORGANIQUES
5225	INORGANIC BASES ETC NES	W 275867	111.4	W 167893	25.3	W 167032	31.2	W 129821	28.8	AUTRES BASES OXYDES METAL
52251	AMMONIA,ANHYDROUS ETC	W 275867	111.4	W 167893	25.3	W 167032	31.2	W 129821	28.8	AMMONIAC LIQUEFIE
55	PERFUME,CLEANING ETC PRD		6.8		9.1		10.2		198.4	PROD POUR PARFUM,TOILETTE
551	ESSENTL OILS,PERFUME,ETC					W 39	0.2	W 14911	187.5	HUILES ESSENTIELLES
5514	MIXED PERFUME SUBSTANCES					W 39	0.2	W 14911	187.5	MELANGES SUBSTAN ODORIFER
6	BASIC MANUFACTURES		101.1		77.3		136.0		155.2	ART MANUFACTURES
67	IRON AND STEEL		63.2		56.1		73.7		70.8	FER ET ACIER
671	PIG IRON ETC	W 133565	14.9	W 105474	13.9	W 107022	15.7	W 298285	43.4	FONTE,SPIEGEL,POUDRES
6712	PIG IRN,SPIEGELEISEN ETC	W 133565	14.9	W 105474	13.9	W 107022	15.7	W 298285	43.4	FONTES BRUTES
672	IRON,STEEL PRIMARY FORMS	W 125817	28.8	W 114180	30.0	W 117672	30.2	W 30767	6.8	LINGOTS FER,ACIER
6727	IRN,STL COIL FR REROLLNG	W 125817	28.8	W 114005	30.0	W 53404	13.9	W 11660	2.5	EBAUCHES POUR TOLES FER
67271	IRON,SIMPLE STEEL COILS	W 95317	22.2	W 113359	29.8	W 51504	13.5	W 11660	2.5	EBAUCHES NON EN ACIER
7	MACHINES,TRANSPORT EQUIP		19.9		14.1		35.3		43.4	MACHINES MATERIEL TRANSPORT
8	MISC MANUFACTURED GOODS		24.8		7.7		11.8		114.2	ART MANUFACTURES DIVERS
89	MISC MANUFCTRD GOODS NES		10.6		1.2		4.2		94.9	ART MANUFACTURES DIVERS
893	ARTICLES OF PLASTIC NES	W 962	6.6	W 10	0.1		0.2		91.8	OUVRAGES EN MAT DIVIS 58
8932	PLSTC SANITRY,TOILET ART	W 739	3.9					W 20030	91.7	OBJETS HYGIEN MAT DU 58

1. HISTORICAL SERIES, 1962–1997 SPECIAL TRADE, IMPORTS C.I.F., EXPORTS F.O.B.
SERIES HISTORIQUES, 1962–1997 COMMERCE SPECIAL, IMPORTATIONS C.A.F., EXPORTATIONS F.O.B

YEAR ANNEE	VALUE IN MILLION U.S. DOLLARS / VALEUR EN MILLION U.S. DOLLARS — MERCHANDISE –MARCHANDISE		GOLD –OR		CONVERSION FACTORS FACTEURS DE CONVERSION CENTS E.U. PAR		INDEX NUMBERS –INDICES — QUANTUM		UNIT VALUE VALEUR UNITAIRE	
	IMPORTS	EXPORTS	IMPORTS	EXPORTS	IMPORTS	EXPORTS	IMPORTS	EXPORTS	IMPORTS	EXPORTS
1962	1357.00	1216.00								
1963	981.00	1365.00								
1964	1077.00	1410.00								
1965	1199.00	1493.00								
1966	1124.00	1593.00								
1967	1096.00	1465.00								
1968	1169.00	1368.00								
1969	1576.00	1612.00								
1970	1694.00	1773.20								
1971	1868.00	1740.40								
1972	1905.00	1941.20								
1973	2230.00	3266.00								
1974	3635.00	3930.70								
1975	3947.00	2961.30								
1976	3034.00	3916.00								
1977	4165.00	5655.00								
1978	3834.00	6399.00								
1979	6711.00	7813.00								
1980	10541.00	8020.00								
1981	9430.00	9143.00								
1982	5337.00	7626.00								
1983	4501.00	7835.00								
1984	4584.70	8107.40								
1985	3814.10	8396.00								
1986	4724.10	6852.20					136	68	86	81
1987	5817.80	6360.20					161	61	89	84
1988	5321.60	9134.80					138	76	95	98
1989	4203.20	9579.30					104	78	99	99
1990	4076.70	12352.50					100	100	100	100
1991	8275.30	11977.80					213	98	96	98
1992	14871.80	12235.00					387	97	94	102
1993	16783.50	13117.80					448	104	92	102
1994	21527.30	15659.30					569	122	93	105
1995	20121.70	20967.41					503	152	98	111
1996	23761.81	23810.70					601	162	97	119
1997	30349.01	25516.00								

2. IMPORTS BY BROAD ECONOMIC CATEGORY AND EXPORTS BY INDUSTRIAL ORIGIN. (PERCENTAGE OF TOTAL VALUE)
IMPORTATIONS PAR CATEGORIES ECONOMIQUES ET EXPORTATIONS PAR BRANCHE D'ACTIVITE.(EN POURCENTAGE DE LA VALEUR TOTALE)

IMPORTS – IMPORTATIONS

	1991	1992	1993	1994	1995	1996	1997
TOTAL IMPORTS–IMPORTATIONS TOTALES	100.	100.	100.	100.	100.	100.	100.
1 FOOD BEV–ALIMENTATION BOISSONS	5.1	5.8	5.2	5.0	5.2	4.5	4.9
11 PRIMARY–PRODUITS DE BASE	2.4	2.4	2.2	1.9	1.9	1.9	2.5
111 FOR INDUSTRY–POUR L'INDUSTRIE	0.8	0.6	0.4	0.5	0.7	0.5	1.3
112 FOR HOUSEHOLDS–POUR LES MENAGES	1.6	1.8	1.8	1.4	1.2	1.4	1.2
12 PROCESSED–PRODUITS ELABORES	2.7	3.4	3.0	3.1	3.2	2.6	2.4
121 FOR INDUSTRY–POUR L'INDUSTRIE	0.5	0.4	0.4	0.4	0.5	0.4	0.4
122 FOR HOUSEHOLDS–POUR LES MENAGES	2.2	3.0	2.6	2.7	2.7	2.1	2.0
2 IND SUPPLIES–APPROV INDUSTRIELS	40.0	30.7	28.9	27.3	33.6	33.5	30.5
21 PRIMARY–PRODUITS DE BASE	3.3	2.2	1.8	1.6	2.1	2.1	1.7
22 PROCESSED–PRODUITS ELABORES	36.7	28.5	27.1	25.7	31.5	31.4	28.8
3 FUELS–COMBUSTIBLES	5.5	2.8	2.3	2.8	4.0	3.6	2.9
31 PRIMARY–PRODUITS DE BASE	3.8	1.4	0.9	1.0	1.3	1.2	1.1
32 PROCESSED–PRODUITS ELABORES	1.7	1.4	1.4	1.8	2.7	2.3	1.8
321 MOTOR SPIRIT–ESSENCE	0.0				0.5	0.4	0.2
322 OTHER–AUTRES	1.7	1.4	1.4	1.8	2.2	1.9	1.6
4 MACHINERY–EQUIPEMENT	24.4	26.0	28.3	30.5	29.1	28.5	29.1
41 CAPITAL EQUIPMENT–MACHINES	19.3	21.2	24.2	26.4	24.9	24.4	24.8
42 PARTS–PIECES ACCESSOIRES	5.1	4.7	4.1	4.0	4.3	4.1	4.3
5 TRANSPORT–TRANSPORT	10.7	18.1	18.8	20.1	15.3	17.5	19.8
51 PASSENGER CARS–AUTOMOBILES	2.4	5.3	5.0	6.5	3.8	5.0	5.1
52 OTHER–AUTRES	2.2	4.8	5.4	6.2	3.8	4.3	5.2
521 INDUSTRIAL–INDUSTRIELS	1.1	3.1	3.9	5.3	3.4	4.0	4.9
522 NON INDUSTRIAL–NON INDUSTRIEL	1.1	1.7	1.5	0.9	0.4	0.3	0.3
53 PARTS–PIECES ACCESSOIRES	6.0	8.0	8.3	7.5	7.7	8.2	9.5
6 CONSUM GOODS–BIENS CONSOMMATION	14.1	16.5	16.4	14.2	12.6	12.3	12.5
61 DURABLE–DURABLES	5.5	6.5	6.0	4.7	3.1	3.3	3.5
62 SEMI DURABLE–SEMI DURABLES	5.8	7.6	7.6	6.6	6.2	5.8	5.7
63 NON DURABLE–NON DURABLES	2.7	2.4	2.8	2.9	3.4	3.3	3.3
7 GOODS NES–BIENS NDA	0.3	0.1	0.1	0.1	0.1	0.0	0.3

EXPORTS – EXPORTATIONS

	1991	1992	1993	1994	1995	1996	1997
TOTAL EXPORTS–EXPORTATIONS TOTALES	100.	100.	100.	100.	100.	100.	
1 AGRICULTURE	29.5	30.3	26.7	25.1	24.3	25.5	
2 MINING QUARRY–INDUS EXTRACTIVES	1.7	3.4	4.7	7.7	8.1	10.4	
3 MANUFACTURING–IND MANUFACTUR	68.8	66.3	68.7	67.2	67.6	64.1	
31 FOOD BEV TOBACCO–ALIM BOISS TAB	33.2	32.2	29.5	28.9	28.5	29.1	
32 TEXTILES–INDUSTRIES TEXTILES	7.3	6.6	8.2	8.3	7.9	6.3	
33 WOOD & PRODUCTS–BOIS & PRODUITS	0.1	0.0	0.1	0.1	0.2	0.3	
34 PAPER & PRODUCTS–PAPIER & PRODT	1.0	1.1	1.2	1.3	2.0	1.7	
35 CHEMICALS–INDUSTRIES CHIMIQUES	11.5	12.3	11.4	9.8	9.9	9.5	
36 NON METAL MIN–MIN NON METAL	0.7	0.6	0.7	0.5	0.6	0.5	
37 BASIC METAL–IND METAL BASE	6.8	4.6	4.3	4.1	4.9	4.3	
38 METAL MANUF–MANUF METAL	8.1	8.7	12.8	12.5	13.0	12.3	
39 OTH MANUF IND–AUTRES MANUF	0.1	0.2	0.5	1.6	0.7	0.2	

3. TRADE BY PRINCIPAL COUNTRIES OF ORIGIN AND DESTINATION (VALUE IN MILLION U.S. DOLLARS)
ECHANGES SELON LES PRINCIPAUX PAYS D'ORIGINE ET DE DESTINATION (VALEUR EN MILLIONS DE DOLLARS EU)

COUNTRIES–PAYS	SPECIAL IMPORTS C.I.F. IMPORTATIONS SPECIALES C.A.F				
	1993	1994	1995	1996	1997
World	16772.9	21581.1	20121.7	23761.6	30349.4
Africa	131.5	189.2	255.9	281.4	330.5
Americas	9556.2	11871.7	10369.2	12454.0	15907.6
– Northern America	3946.6	5061.0	4480.2	5024.6	6527.8
– LAIA	5427.1	6604.3	5859.9	7352.3	9326.6
– CACM	9.7	19.1	5.5	15.3	10.5
– Caribbean	18.6	71.7	21.2	33.6	41.3
– Rest of America	154.2	115.5	2.4	28.2	1.4
Asia excl fmr USSR	2358.4	2591.5	2506.7	2959.9	4211.1
– Middle East	8.2	40.4	28.5	38.1	60.1
Asia former USSR		0.2	0.3	0.2	0.6
Europe excl fmr USSR	4586.4	6763.9	6429.8	7388.5	8797.5
– European Union	4327.2	6476.6	6024.7	6901.7	8303.8
– Eastern Europe	69.7	83.1	110.9	147.9	180.4
– Rest of Europe	189.6	204.2	294.2	338.9	313.2
Europe former USSR	45.3	69.5	104.2	128.5	164.0
Oceania	95.1	95.1	150.9	122.3	142.3
Other		0.1	304.7	426.9	795.9
Brazil/Brésil	3568.5	4285.9	4176.0	5327.1	6894.6
USA/Etats–Unis d'Amer	3858.6	4928.3	4206.6	4749.2	6085.3
Italy/Italie	980.9	1431.2	1259.0	1503.5	1737.5
Germany/Allemagne	1023.5	1382.4	1250.7	1427.3	1653.4
France, Monaco	738.7	1072.2	1040.0	1181.3	1373.1
Spain/Espagne	509.8	865.8	929.7	1063.6	1253.8
Japan/Japon	668.5	619.8	710.8	725.3	1124.9
Chile/Chili	702.0	828.9	513.8	559.4	682.9
China/Chine	214.8	217.1	607.9	697.9	1005.2
Korea, Republic of	525.6	503.3	362.1	428.1	639.6
United Kingdom	258.3	351.8	412.9	563.0	802.1
Uruguay	570.8	789.1	286.9	299.8	373.7
Mexico/Mexique	235.5	260.7	376.4	541.0	608.9
Belgium–Luxembourg	331.6	591.8	231.4	226.6	297.7
Areas n.e.s.		0.1	304.7	426.9	795.9
Other Asia n.e.s.	187.8	232.3	228.9	387.2	395.7
Netherlands/Pays–Bas	224.8	352.1	210.8	223.2	256.4
Sweden/Suède	116.1	168.3	252.6	304.4	403.4
Canada	87.9	132.7	273.5	275.4	442.5
Switzerland,Liechtenst.	164.1	177.9	236.1	269.4	282.7
China, Hong Kong SAR	387.0	489.7	75.9	89.3	71.4
Singapore/Singapour	200.9	265.8	109.1	103.1	147.4
Paraguay	72.9	71.6	139.8	182.1	319.5
Bolivia/Bolivie	107.9	145.0	135.1	136.3	135.5
So. African Customs Un	95.6	99.6	124.5	105.0	109.2
Ecuador/Equateur	63.2	92.4	100.8	108.7	111.0
Australia/Australie	73.6	66.1	121.8	96.4	103.5
Finland/Finlande	43.8	67.9	110.4	110.4	120.0
Malaysia/Malaisie	13.3	19.7	98.8	117.9	188.0
Russian Federation	45.3	59.5	85.6	96.7	128.6
Austria/Autriche	26.7	33.8	91.5	100.6	143.5
Israel/Israël	37.1	54.5	62.2	91.3	146.1
Denmark/Danemark	31.1	47.6	97.7	84.5	110.8
India/Inde	35.5	50.9	62.4	81.6	127.9
Indonesia/Indonésie	26.3	40.8	68.9	78.6	119.0
Venezuela	40.1	46.3	46.3	111.9	62.3
Colombia/Colombie	41.9	60.4	50.9	49.0	88.5
Thailand/Thaïlande	22.5	24.7	51.8	71.5	117.8
Ireland/Irlande	19.3	35.3	71.2	69.0	85.9
Panama	154.2	115.5	2.4	3.2	1.4

COUNTRIES–PAYS	SPECIAL EXPORTS F.O.B. EXPORTATIONS SPECIALES F.O.B.				
	1993	1994	1995	1996	1997
Monde	13117.8	15838.7	20962.6	23809.6	
Afrique	394.2	533.0	873.0	1099.3	
Amériques	6928.8	9026.0	11783.4	13525.9	
– Amérique du Nord	1343.5	1815.5	1885.9	2079.1	
– ALAI	5287.3	6956.6	9624.9	11097.7	
– MCAC	39.9	46.2	73.8	79.1	
– Caraïbes	215.5	187.6	163.6	227.1	
– Autre Amérique	42.6	20.1	35.2	42.9	
Asie anc. URSS exclus	1800.4	2096.1	3342.7	4026.7	
– Moyen–Orient	511.0	420.1	862.6	1086.6	
Asie ancienne URSS		4.3	1.1	7.1	
Europe anc. URSS exclus	3816.7	4076.9	4793.3	4863.0	
– Union Européenne	3684.7	3930.5	4484.1	4590.2	
– Europe de l'Est	75.5	36.0	40.6	134.5	
– Autre de l'Europe	56.6	110.4	268.7	138.2	
Europe ancienne URSS	109.5	42.9	98.9	171.6	
Océanie	68.1	59.4	58.3	73.0	
Autre			12.0	43.1	
Brazil/Brésil	2814.2	3654.8	5484.1	6614.8	
USA/Etats–Unis d'Amer	1278.7	1736.9	1803.4	1974.4	
Netherlands/Pays–Bas	1270.1	1179.6	1191.3	1225.4	
Chile/Chili	591.9	998.8	1475.1	1765.8	
Italy/Italie	505.1	654.4	736.5	721.6	
Uruguay	512.0	649.8	662.8	725.2	
Spain/Espagne	504.4	592.4	714.0	736.7	
Germany/Allemagne	625.1	605.5	649.9	565.5	
Paraguay	357.8	498.5	631.4	584.2	
Japan/Japon	466.8	445.2	457.3	512.5	
Iran (Islamic Rep of)	248.2	228.8	509.6	637.3	
China/Chine	163.3	224.7	285.7	607.4	
Venezuela	229.1	211.2	377.7	351.3	
France, Monaco	208.3	215.6	318.5	311.5	
United Kingdom	162.0	222.4	310.1	355.1	
Peru/Pérou	222.2	288.6	275.6	254.2	
Bolivia/Bolivie	178.0	192.4	254.0	291.6	
Mexico/Mexique	219.4	273.7	144.4	248.2	
China, Hong Kong SAR	155.8	204.8	289.0	215.9	
So. African Customs Un	80.5	184.8	340.0	251.0	
Egypt/Egypte	135.4	151.5	228.5	323.3	
Belgium–Luxembourg	165.4	153.3	237.5	269.5	
Malaysia/Malaisie	73.4	132.6	259.3	303.2	
Other Asia n.e.s.	77.1	237.0	207.7	227.7	
Colombia/Colombie	112.8	123.2	233.4	182.6	
Indonesia/Indonésie	74.0	105.1	167.1	222.4	
Denmark/Danemark	91.4	140.6	107.5	180.6	
Turkey/Turquie	118.2	35.7	155.4	139.0	
Korea, Republic of	49.1	48.9	133.1	204.0	
India/Inde	37.9	51.8	153.2	183.3	
Russian Federation	109.5	41.3	90.2	152.2	
Switzerland,Liechtenst.	32.5	65.4	190.5	56.1	
Thailand/Thaïlande	29.0	28.5	124.4	144.8	
Canada	64.4	72.9	81.7	104.7	
Greece/Grèce	61.0	74.3	79.9	95.9	
Cuba	71.6	48.2	65.2	124.9	
Singapore/Singapour	38.4	70.3	143.6	43.6	
Ecuador/Equateur	49.9	65.5	86.3	79.6	
Morocco/Maroc	30.0	56.1	45.1	147.1	
Portugal	60.9	53.2	85.6	65.4	

(VALUE AS PERCENTAGE OF WORLD TOTAL)(VALEURS EN POURCENTAGE DU TOTAL MONDIAL)

	1988	1989	1990	1991	1992	1993	1994	1995	1996	1997
Africa	1.4	0.6	0.6	1.4	0.7	0.8	0.9	1.3	1.2	1.1
Americas	50.6	55.4	54.0	50.1	56.9	57.0	55.0	51.5	52.4	52.4
– Northern America	17.4	21.8	20.9	18.9	22.2	23.5	23.5	22.3	21.1	21.5
– LAIA	32.7	33.1	33.0	30.6	33.5	32.4	30.6	29.1	30.9	30.7
– CACM	0.0	0.1	0.0	0.0	0.0	0.1	0.1	0.0	0.1	0.0
– Caribbean	0.5	0.1	0.1	0.4	0.2	0.1	0.3	0.1	0.1	0.1
– Rest of America	0.0	0.3	0.0	0.0	1.1	0.9	0.5	0.0	0.1	0.0
Asia excl fmr USSR	11.8	8.5	10.3	17.0	14.3	14.1	12.0	12.5	12.5	13.9
– Middle East	0.6	0.2	0.3	0.1	0.2	0.0	0.2	0.1	0.2	0.2
Asia former USSR							0.0	0.0	0.0	0.0
Europe excl fmr USSR	34.0	32.2	31.4	26.6	27.2	27.3	31.3	32.0	31.1	29.0
– European Union	29.4	28.9	27.5	24.2	25.6	25.8	30.0	29.9	29.0	27.4
– Eastern Europe	2.1	1.2	1.0	0.8	0.4	0.4	0.4	0.6	0.6	0.6
– Rest of Europe	2.5	2.1	3.0	1.6	1.2	1.1	0.9	1.5	1.4	1.0
Europe former USSR	0.4	0.6	0.4	0.3	0.2	0.3	0.3	0.5	0.5	0.5
Oceania	1.1	2.7	2.2	1.4	0.8	0.6	0.4	0.7	0.5	0.5
Other	0.6		1.1	3.3	0.0		0.0	1.5	1.8	2.6
Brazil/Brésil	18.2	17.2	17.5	18.5	22.5	21.3	19.9	20.8	22.4	22.7
USA/Etats–Unis d'Amer	16.7	21.2	20.1	18.1	21.7	23.0	22.8	20.9	20.0	20.1
Italy/Italie	6.0	5.8	5.2	4.5	5.1	5.8	6.6	6.3	6.3	5.7
Germany/Allemagne				7.9	7.3	6.1	6.4	6.2	6.0	5.4
France, Monaco	5.6	4.5	4.3	3.6	3.9	4.4	5.0	5.2	5.0	4.5
Spain/Espagne	1.9	2.2	2.7	2.4	2.7	3.0	4.0	4.6	4.5	4.1
Japan/Japon	7.3	4.3	4.4	7.3	4.7	4.0	2.9	3.5	3.1	3.7
Chile/Chili	2.7	2.6	2.3	2.8	4.3	4.2	3.8	2.6	2.4	2.3
China/Chine	0.4	0.4	0.8	2.3	1.1	1.3	1.0	3.0	2.9	3.3
Korea, Republic of	1.6	1.6	2.2	3.3	3.1	3.1	2.3	1.8	1.8	2.1

	1988	1989	1990	1991	1992	1993	1994	1995	1996	1997
Afrique	3.6	2.5	3.2	3.2	5.5	3.0	3.4	4.2	4.6	
Amériques	36.9	41.2	42.0	42.1	46.1	52.8	57.0	56.2	56.8	
– Amérique du Nord	14.2	13.2	14.4	11.0	11.5	10.2	11.5	9.0	8.7	
– ALAI	19.3	25.0	25.3	28.1	32.0	40.3	43.9	45.9	46.6	
– MCAC	0.5	0.4	0.3	0.3	0.3	0.3	0.3	0.4	0.3	
– Caraïbes	2.7	2.5	1.8	2.4	2.0	1.6	1.2	0.8	1.0	
– Autre Amérique	0.2	0.1	0.1	0.2	0.2	0.3	0.1	0.2	0.2	
Asie anc. URSS exclus	15.8	16.5	16.9	16.6	14.7	13.7	13.2	15.9	16.9	
– Moyen–Orient	2.7	4.5	6.1	5.0	5.0	3.9	2.7	4.1	4.6	
Asie ancienne URSS							0.0	0.0	0.0	
Europe anc. URSS exclus	33.6	29.6	33.3	35.7	32.5	29.1	25.7	22.9	20.4	
– Union Européenne	30.4	26.8	30.8	33.6	31.1	28.1	24.8	21.4	19.3	
– Europe de l'Est	2.3	2.2	1.7	1.2	0.9	0.6	0.2	0.2	0.6	
– Autre de l'Europe	0.9	0.6	0.8	0.9	0.6	0.4	0.7	1.3	0.6	
Europe ancienne URSS	9.4	8.7	4.0	1.9	0.9	0.8	0.3	0.5	0.7	
Océanie	0.8	1.5	0.6	0.5	0.3	0.5	0.4	0.3	0.3	
Autre	0.0		0.0	0.0	0.0			0.1	0.2	
Brazil/Brésil	6.7	11.8	11.5	12.4	13.7	21.5	23.1	26.2	27.8	
USA/Etats–Unis d'Amer	13.3	12.4	13.8	10.4	11.0	9.7	11.0	8.6	8.3	
Netherlands/Pays–Bas	11.9	10.3	11.1	11.1	9.9	9.7	7.4	5.7	5.1	
Chile/Chili	2.8	3.7	3.7	4.1	4.7	4.5	6.3	7.0	7.4	
Italy/Italie	3.7	3.0	4.3	4.8	4.3	3.9	4.1	3.5	3.0	
Uruguay	2.1	2.2	2.1	2.6	3.1	3.9	4.1	3.2	3.0	
Spain/Espagne	2.2	2.1	2.7	4.0	4.1	3.8	3.7	3.4	3.1	
Germany/Allemagne				6.1	6.0	4.8	3.8	3.1	2.4	
Paraguay	0.9	1.0	1.2	1.5	2.2	2.7	3.1	3.0	2.5	
Japan/Japon	3.6	2.8	3.2	3.8	3.1	3.6	2.8	2.2	2.2	

4. Special Imports C.I.F. by Commodities according to the S.I.T.C. (Rev. 2) in million U.S. Dollars
Importations Spéciales C.A.F. par Produits d'après la C.T.C.I. (Rév. 2) en millions de Dollars E.U.

SITC CTCI	COMMODITY	1994		1995		1996		1997		PRODUIT
		QUANTITY QUANTITE	VALUE VALEUR	QUANTITY QUANTITE	VALUE VALEUR	QUANTITY QUANTITE	VALUE VALEUR	QUANTITY QUANTITE	VALUE VALEUR	
	ALL COMMODITIES		21581.1		20121.7		23761.6		30349.5	TOUS PRODUITS
0	FOOD AND LIVE ANIMALS		992.7		969.8		1025.7		1212.0	ALIMENTS,ANIMAUX VIVANTS
01	MEAT AND PREPARATIONS		157.3		125.5		169.0		212.8	VIANDES ET PREPARATIONS
011	MEAT FRESH,CHILLD,FROZEN	W 86533	125.1	W 42384	82.6	W 67469	123.9	W 92245	162.9	VIANDES FRAICHES,REF,CONGE
02	DAIRY PRODCTS,BIRDS'EGGS		66.3		53.5		56.5		63.4	PRODUITS LAITIERS,OEUFS
03	FISH AND PREPARATIONS		65.2		70.1		71.0		87.5	POISSONS ET PREPARATIONS
04	CEREALS AND PREPARATIONS		54.9		73.3		90.7		150.4	CEREALES ET PRODUITS
05	VEGETABLES AND FRUIT		236.0		249.5		289.4		285.6	LEGUMES ET FRUITS
057	FRUIT,NUTS,FRESH,DRIED	W 320500	121.1	W 270539	108.5	W 332014	138.4	W 322220	137.4	FRUITS FRAIS OU SECS
0573	BANANA,PLANTAIN,FRSH,DRY	W 247101	63.6	W 201864	56.1	W 248376	72.6	W 250679	77.9	BANANES FRAICHES,SECHEES
058	FRUIT PRESERVED,PREPARED	W 67966	62.7	W 65641	77.2	W 65287	78.8	W 57539	75.2	CONSERVES DE FRUITS
06	SUGAR AND PREPS,HONEY		109.6		82.2		23.9		48.4	SUCRES ET PRODUITS
061	SUGAR AND HONEY	W 281370	91.6	W 184922	64.6	W 16203	7.5	W 64191	21.6	SUCRES ET MIEL
0612	REFINED SUGAR ETC	W 253372	81.3	W 177667	60.5	W 9802	2.9	W 52137	15.1	SUCRES RAFFINES
07	COFFEE,TEA,COCOA,SPICES		210.2		224.8		210.5		228.9	CAFE,THE,CACAO,EPICES
071	COFFEE AND SUBSTITUTES	W 36796	95.6	W 36295	118.4	W 41164	106.2	W 43053	114.1	CAFE ET SUCCEDANES
0711	COFFEE GREEN,ROASTED,SUB	W 35484	87.7	W 35105	109.9	W 40203	100.5	W 41595	106.2	CAFE TORREFIE OU DECAFEINE
07111	COFFEE GREEN,HUSKS,SKINS	W 35449	87.5	W 35057	109.6	W 40170	100.1	W 41537	105.8	CAFE NON TORREFIE
09	MISC EDIBLE PRODUCTS		64.6		60.0		75.1		78.5	PREP ALIMENTAIRES DIVERSES
098	EDIBLE PRODCTS,PREPS NES	W 17144	63.1	W 16543	58.2	W 21991	73.2	W 24617	75.9	PREP ALIMENTAIRES NDA
1	BEVERAGES AND TOBACCO		97.1		92.3		89.1		111.2	BOISSONS ET TABACS
11	BEVERAGES		87.9		70.7		64.2		84.7	BOISSONS
112	ALCOHOLIC BEVERAGES	W 91359	76.0	W 60581	59.1	W 46553	58.2	W 63910	79.2	BOISSONS ALCOOLIQUES
2	CRUDE MATERLS,EXCL FUELS		591.7		714.1		787.4		1023.4	MAT BRUTES NON COMESTIBLES
22	OIL SEEDS,OLEAGINOUS FRT		5.0		6.7		9.2		227.7	GRAINES,FRUITS OLEAGINEUX
222	SEEDS FOR'SOFT'FIXED OIL	W 3909	4.6	W 3916	6.2	W 4652	8.6	W 763921	226.7	GRAINES HUILES FIXES
2222	SOYA BEANS	W 257	0.4	W 116	0.2	W 536	1.2	W 744087	215.7	FEVES DE SOJA
23	RUBBER, CRUDE		64.9		86.2		89.1		91.4	CAOUTCHOUC BRUT
24	CORK AND WOOD		70.3		56.1		63.6		83.4	LIEGE ET BOIS
251	*PULP AND WASTE PAPER	W 112750	54.4	W 115639	86.8	W 152619	80.1	W 170848	87.3	PATES A PAPIER,DECHETS
2517	SODA,SULPHATE WOOD PULP	W 93447	50.2	W 87729	78.2	W 128842	74.1	W 158371	82.2	PATES CHIMIQUES AU SULFATE
25172	— BLEACHED,NONDISSOLVNG	W 92834	49.9	W 87492	78.0	W 128599	74.0	W 158008	82.0	PATES BLANCHIES
26	TEXTILE FIBRES AND WASTE		63.4		80.5		77.1		64.8	FIBRES TEXTILES
28	METALLIFEROUS ORES,SCRAP		194.0		248.5		277.1		273.4	MINERAIS METAL,DECHETS
281	IRON ORE,CONCENTRATES	W 3819660	117.6	W 4361701	146.4	W 4947040	174.7	W 5054185	178.2	MINERAIS DE FER
2815	IRON ORE,CONC,NOT AGGLOM	W 1869726	48.1	W 2333398	64.7	W 2363846	70.1	W 2262635	63.2	MINERAIS NON AGGLOMERES
2816	IRON ORE AGGLOMERATES	W 1949935	69.6	W 2028303	81.7	W 2583194	104.6	W 2791550	115.0	MINERAIS AGGLOMERES
287	BASE METAL ORES,CONC NES		75.7	W 551216	101.5	W 529721	100.9	W 540410	94.7	MINERAIS METAUX COMMUNS
2873	ALUMINIUM ORES,ALUMINA	W 370834	63.2	W 410927	88.1	W 407930	85.8	W 405546	77.4	MINERAIS D'ALUMINIUM
28732	ALUMINA(ALUMINIUM OXIDE)	W 330666	59.2	W 367947	84.3	W 371768	81.6	W 371254	73.2	ALUMINE (OXYDE ALUMINIUM)
29	CRUDE ANIMAL,VEG MAT NES		93.8		97.2		133.7		134.5	MATIERES BRUTES ANIM,VEGET
292	CRUDE VEG MATERIALS NES	W 21053	82.7	W 21332	83.0	W 28686	110.4	W 26899	109.7	MAT BRUTES VEGETALES NDA
3	MINERAL FUELS ETC		645.7		859.1		885.8		927.1	COMBUSTIBLES MINERAUX LUB
32	COAL,COKE AND BRIQUETTES		65.3		69.6		67.4		66.0	HOUILLES,COKES,BRIQUETTES
322	COAL,LIGNITE AND PEAT	W 1278798	63.9	W 1156134	69.6	W 1030023	66.6	W 1052833	65.9	HOUILLES,LIGNITES,TOURBE
3222	OTH COAL,NOT AGGLOMERATD	W 1278076	63.5	W 1154762	68.9	W 1028682	66.0	W 1050738	64.9	AUTRES HOUILLES
33	PETROLEUM AND PRODUCTS		487.2		624.0		616.7		617.7	PETROLE ET DERIVES
333	CRUDE PETROLEUM	W 493402	65.5	W 699756	98.6	W 780149	127.0	W 1227139	192.1	HUILES BRUTES DE PETROLE
334	PETROLEUM PRODUCTS,REFIN	W 2153296	382.4	W 2464062	475.9	W 2040490	448.6	W 1628000	383.2	PRODUITS RAFFINES
3341	GASOLINE,OTH LIGHT OILS			W 812996	170.9	W 424860	96.6	W 214121	53.9	ESSENCES POUR MOTEURS
33411	MOTOR,AVIATION SPIRIT			W 465735	93.7	W 340879	78.3	W 167021	42.7	ESSENCES MOTEURS D'AVIONS
33412	SPIRIT TYPE JET FUEL			W 282671	65.0					CARBUREACTEURS
3342	KEROSENE,OTH MEDIUM OILS			W 1548038	243.6	W 218569	48.4	W 266145	54.8	PETR LAMPANTS,AUT HUIL
33421	KEROSENE INCL JET FUEL			W 1548038	243.6	W 218569	48.4	W 266145	54.8	PETROLES LAMPANTS
3343	GAS OILS			W 80934	37.3	W 1241945	212.8	W 983430	179.7	GAS OILS
3345	LUBS,PETROLEUM OILS NES	W 4400	12.8	W 21268	23.9	W 155099	90.8	W 164298	94.9	HUILES LUBRIFIANTES
341	*GAS,NATURAL AND MANUFCT	W 48102	92.4	W 24857	97.9	W 208463	97.1	W 36701	73.5	GAZ NATUREL,GAZ MANUFACT
3414	PETROLEUM GASES, GASEOUS	W 47393	92.1	W 17499	95.3	W 205005	95.6	W 24296	70.8	GAZ DE PETROLE GAZEUX
351	*ELECTRIC CURRENT		1.0		67.7		104.8		170.1	ENERGIE ELECTRIQUE
5	CHEMCLS,RELATED PROD NES		2933.1		3482.4		4264.1		4724.3	PRODUITS CHIMIQUES
51	ORGANIC CHEMICALS		867.0		1053.4		1226.9		1397.6	PROD CHIMIQ ORGANIQUES
511	HYDROCARBONS NES,DERIVS		76.0		110.6	W 194717	107.4	W 269720	149.1	HYDROCARBURES NDA
512	ALCOHOLS,PHENOLS ETC	W 63377	53.0	W 62335	67.4	W 110120	83.5	W 136252	98.1	PHENOLS,PHENOLS–ALCOOLS
513	CARBOXYLIC ACIDS ETC	W 111475	134.8	W 105834	161.9	W 118134	185.4	W 136927	195.0	ACIDES CARBOXYLIQUES
5137	MONOACIDS AND DERIVATIVS	W 55270	62.6	W 46762	74.3	W 50456	85.0	W 64230	94.3	ACIDES MONOCARBOXYLIQUES
514	NITROGEN–FNCTN COMPOUNDS	W 52124	251.4	W 55270	292.0	W 70281	337.0	W 86895	379.2	COMPOSES FONCT AZOTEES
5148	OTH NITROGN–FNCTN CMPNDS	W 17253	138.9	W 17790	154.9	W 22884	166.2	W 37858	213.7	AUTRES COMPOSES AZOTES
51482	IMIDE–,IMIDE–FNCT CMPNDS	W 5498	89.5	W 6758	99.5	W 7948	102.7	W 10491	135.9	COMPOSES A FONCTION IMIDE
515	ORG–INORG COMPOUNDS ETC	W 20795	267.0	W 23244	305.4	W 30596	375.5	W 39322	445.4	COMPOSES ORGANO–MINERAUX
5155	OTH ORG–INORG COMPOUNDS	W 6148	37.5	W 8752	53.7	W 11082	69.0	W 18540	103.0	AUTR COMP ORG–MINERAUX
5156	HETEROCYCLIC CMPDS ETC	W 7446	178.0	W 7631	202.2	W 10969	245.9	W 11030	270.7	COMPOSES HETEROCYCLIQUES
51569	OTH HETEROCYC CMPDS,ETC	W 4237	173.2	W 4845	196.8	W 5691	234.5	W 7159	263.1	AUT COMP HETEROCYCLIQUES
516	OTHER ORGANIC CHEMICALS	W 89587	85.0	W 129034	116.4	W 153021	138.4	W 111599	131.1	AUTRES PROD ORGANIQUES
5161	ETHERS,EPOXIDES,ACETALS	W 81326	44.1	W 120314	64.3	W 142456	74.2	W 99426	64.0	ETHERS–OXYDES,ALCOOLS
52	INORGANIC CHEMICALS		153.2		168.2		203.3		209.0	PROD CHIM INORGANIQUES
522	INORG ELEMNTS,OXIDES,ETC	W 186163	63.0	W 139195	62.7	W 203288	81.7	W 195037	80.2	ELEMENTS INORGANIQUES
523	OTHR INORG CHEMICALS ETC	W 301670	85.8		100.5	W 363539	115.5	W 371222	122.1	AUT PRODUITS CHIMIQUES INORG
5232	OTH MTL CMPD OF INRG ACD	W 240958	54.6	W 250054	60.9	W 284805	75.2	W 281151	78.3	SELS METALLIQUES
53	DYES,TANNING,COLOUR PROD		185.7		191.3		248.1		281.3	PROD TEINTURE,COLORANTS
533	PIGMENTS,PAINTS,ETC	W 52430	128.7	W 44244	131.7	W 57695	170.3	W 71099	193.6	PIGMENTS,PEINTURES,VERNIS
541	*MEDICINAL,PHARM PRODUCT	K 5513668	495.1		488.9	K 8462090	582.6		663.6	PROD MEDICINAUX PHARMACEUT
5413	ANTIBIOTICS IN BULK	K 690165	79.5	K 596632	74.8	K 692529	90.0	K 795374	93.7	ANTIBIOTIQUES NDA
5416	GLYCOSIDES,GLANDS,SERA	K 485299	134.7	K 969473	93.7	K 432066	103.1	K 478311	95.1	HETEROSIDES
54164	ANTISERA,MICROB VACCINES	K 237365	93.1	K 215910	51.4	K 223980	75.6	K 234875	76.0	SERUMS,VACCINS
5417	MEDICAMENTS	K 2399771	181.5	K 4154774	224.1	K 4860096	273.5	K 8097614	350.8	MEDICAMENTS
54179	— CONTNG OTH SUBSTANCES	K 1802162	101.9	K 3466004	123.7	K 3997950	166.6	K 6811854	219.0	MED CONT AUT SUBSTANCES
55	PERFUME,CLEANING ETC PRD		175.8		191.7		229.5		293.7	PROD POUR PARFUM,TOILETTE
553	PERFUMERY,COSMETICS,ETC	W 8958	61.1	W 10609	63.1	W 14190	89.2	W 17677	122.1	PRODUITS DE PARFUMERIE
554	SOAP,CLEANSING ETC PREPS	W 51300	85.4	W 50840	91.6	W 60110	103.4	W 71776	122.6	SAVONS,PRODUITS DETERSIFS
5542	WASHING PREPARATIONS ETC	W 42904	67.9	W 46132	80.8	W 54413	90.6	W 61472	103.7	PROD ORG TENSIO–ACT NDA
562	*FERTILIZERS,MANUFACTURE	W 773682	123.1	W 1055705	226.7	W 1970285	429.2	W 1265574	243.9	ENGRAIS MANUFACTURES
5621	CHEM NITROGENOUS FERTLZR	W 407806	53.8	W 527589	107.4	W 1007812	205.7	W 577716	91.8	ENGRAIS AZOTES
56216	UREA	W 365735	48.1	W 417071	90.7	W 838590	175.7	W 397211	64.6	UREE
5629	FERTILIZERS NES	W 313600	61.7	W 433212	102.7	W 854233	203.1	W 597010	135.9	ENGRAIS NDA
56292	NITROG–PHOS FERTILZR NES	W 289522	56.2	W 409956	95.6	W 830516	195.0	W 566315	126.5	ENGRAIS NDA CONT N P
58	PLASTIC MATERIALS ETC		535.5		679.3		770.9		961.2	MAT PLAST ARTIFICIELLES
582	PROD OF CONDENSATION ETC	W 74537	152.4	W 83661	203.2	W 113533	239.5	W 157716	274.2	PROD CONDENS,POLYCOND
5823	ALKYDS,OTHER POLYESTERS	W 46820	87.7	W 58043	135.0	W 80643	151.8	W 113294	161.4	ALKYDES ET AUT POLYESTERS
58231	— IN PRIMARY FORMS	W 41128	60.6	W 53347	112.9	W 76496	130.2	W 107712	134.6	SOUS FORMES PRIMAIRES
583	POLYMERIZATION ETC PRODS	W 275714	337.6	W 255970	427.0	W 337945	479.6	W 460287	632.8	PROD POLYMERISATION
5831	POLYETHYLENE	W 145473	113.3	W 128106	150.8	W 172817	176.8	W 253698	270.1	POLYETHYLENE

4. Special Imports C.I.F. by Commodities according to the S.I.T.C. (Rev. 2) in million U.S. Dollars
Importations Spéciales C.A.F. par Produits d'après la C.T.C.I. (Rév. 2) en millions de Dollars E.U.

SITC CTCI	COMMODITY	1994 QUANTITY QUANTITE	1994 VALUE VALEUR	1995 QUANTITY QUANTITE	1995 VALUE VALEUR	1996 QUANTITY QUANTITE	1996 VALUE VALEUR	1997 QUANTITY QUANTITE	1997 VALUE VALEUR	PRODUIT
58311	— IN PRIMARY FORMS	W 141003	101.6	W 122725	134.8	W 165281	156.6	W 243476	245.5	POLYETHYLENE PRIMAIRES
5839	OTH POLYMRZTION ETC PROD	W 25652	73.7	W 32218	100.0	W 38772	105.5	W 45745	121.6	AUT PROD POLYMER COPOLYM
59	CHEMICAL MATERIALS NES		387.4		474.0		562.2		661.0	MAT PROD CHIMIQUES NDA
591	PESTICIDES,DISINFECTANTS	W 24430	154.2	W 31044	207.2	W 39085	240.4	W 48409	314.4	DESINF,INSECT,FONG,HERB
5913	HERBICIDES,FOR RETAIL	W 13808	97.1	W 18748	137.8	W 25169	155.2	W 28817	195.0	HERBICIDES VENTE AU DET
598	MISCEL CHEM PRODUCTS NES	W 91189	201.5	W 98785	231.1	W 116929	280.9	W 135426	296.7	PROD DIV INDUST CHIM NDA
5989	CHEM PRODUCTS,PREPS NES	W 52877	130.6	W 62285	161.5	W 72650	201.8	W 88420	214.9	PROD PREP CHIMIQUES NDA
59899	OTH CHEM PRODS,PREPS,NES	W 36407	90.9	W 42782	111.4	W 48120	130.7	W 58291	143.9	AUT PRODUITS CHIMIQUES NDA
6	BASIC MANUFACTURES		2854.7		3023.7		3544.8		4615.4	ART MANUFACTURES
62	RUBBER MANUFACTURES NES		207.1		212.4		307.7		426.3	CAOUTCHOUC MANUFACTURE
625	RUBBER TYRES, TUBES ETC	W 36532	115.1	W 35211	116.8	W 50976	176.2	W 69886	235.6	PNEUS CAOUTCHOUC VULCANISE
6252	TYRES,NEW,BUS OR LORRY	W 16019	49.5	W 16236	55.3	W 23074	81.7	W 30709	105.2	PNEUS POUR AUTOBUS,CAMIONS
628	RUBBER ARTICLES NES	W 6672	65.2	W 6640	66.6	W 8408	88.4	W 13006	123.6	OUVRAGES CAOUTCHOUC NDA
6289	OTH RUBBER ARTICLES NES	W 4655	47.3	W 4618	47.2	W 5775	61.1	W 9577	91.3	AUT OUVR CAOUTCHOUC NDA
63	WOOD,CORK MANUFACTRS NES		80.8		117.1		144.5		107.2	OUVRAGES LIEGE ET BOIS
635	WOOD MANUFACTURES NES	W 20587	37.8	W 39983	80.3	W 35733	101.6	W 24592	55.0	ART MANUF EN BOIS NDA
6353	BUILDERS WOODWRK,PREFABS	W 14792	27.5	W 32559	71.2	W 29705	90.5	W 14378	37.0	OUVRAGES DE MENUISERIE
64	PAPER,PAPERBOARD AND MFR		524.5		665.7		721.8		865.8	PAPIERS,CARTONS & OUVRAGES
641	PAPER AND PAPERBOARD	W 534720	410.9	W 521473	544.4	W 569517	583.1	W 795338	693.3	PAPIERS ET CARTONS
6411	NEWSPRINT	W 117077	59.0	W 105298	81.8	W 64419	50.5	W 138436	76.1	PAPIER JOURNAL
6412	PRINTG,WRITING PAPER NES	W 129485	109.7	W 130228	150.8	W 156471	166.2	W 235608	220.2	PAPIERS POUR L'IMPRESSION
64122	— COATED,IMPREGNATD ETC	W 114588	96.3	W 113297	127.2	W 128521	135.0	W 196695	184.1	PAPIERS IMPRESSION COUCHES
6413	KRAFT PAPER,PAPERBOARD	W 108782	64.6	W 119184	95.2	W 148877	106.0	W 201776	128.1	PAPIER ET CARTON KRAFT
6415	PAPER,PAPERBRD,BULK,NES	W 111775	86.7	W 86555	97.2	W 103688	113.2	W 122121	107.9	PAPIERS,CARTONS ROULEAUX
64159	OTHER PAPER ETC,BULK,NES	W 82581	70.0	W 75019	84.4	W 85787	96.3	W 99898	89.7	AUT PAPIER ROULEAUX FEUILLES
6418	COATED ETC PAPER NES BLK	W 29231	55.9	W 57006	94.9	W 73862	123.1	W 73336	133.9	PAP,CARTONS COUCHES,ENDUITS
64181	PLASTIC COATED PAPER ETC	W 13891	31.2	W 37254	63.8	W 47695	84.9	W 48695	94.1	PAP,CARTONS ENDUITS,RESINES
642	PAPER,ETC,PRECUT,ARTS OF	W 57829	113.7	W 57847	121.3	W 67004	138.8	W 89987	172.5	PAP,CARTONS DECOUPES
65	TEXTILE YARN,FABRICS,ETC		485.6		428.7		609.7		792.5	FILS,TISSUS,ARTICLES TEXTILE
651	TEXTILE YARN	W 21344	87.3	W 21376	90.0	W 35173	144.5	W 44762	174.8	FILS TEXTILES
652	COTTON FABRICS,WOVEN	W 10798	60.3	W 8998	54.2	W 13801	86.1	W 17200	111.0	TISSUS DE COTON
6522	WOVEN COTTON BLEACHD,ETC	W 9714	55.7	W 7812	49.1	W 11268	74.9	W 14633	99.2	TISSUS COTON BLANCHIS ETC
653	WOVN MAN–MADE FIB FABRIC	W 17386	121.6	W 12910	90.9	W 18239	125.2	W 25262	162.2	TISSUS FIBRES SYNTH,ARTIF
657	SPECIAL TXTL FABRC,PRODS	W 11987	71.9	W 13112	76.3	W 16198	96.9	W 21424	123.7	TISSUS SPECIAUX
658	TEXTILE ARTICLES NES	W 10471	63.6	W 9583	60.4	W 10894	73.8	W 11944	89.4	ART FACONNES MAT TEXTILES
66	NONMETAL MINERAL MFS NES		262.1		231.9		269.1		333.7	ART MIN NON METALLIQUES
664	GLASS	W 28801	76.2	W 17003	59.8	W 21499	66.7	W 68960	77.4	VERRE
67	IRON AND STEEL		487.6		514.3		525.0		845.0	FER ET ACIER
672	IRON,STEEL PRIMARY FORMS	W 624673	163.8	W 485402	152.6	W 363846	114.8	W 602763	174.1	LINGOTS FER,ACIER
6725	IRN,STL BLOOMS,SLABS,ETC	W 497456	120.7	W 396136	112.9	W 270454	76.5	W 528306	143.8	BLOOMS,BILLETTES FER ACIER
67251	IRN,SMPLE STL BLOOMS,ETC	W 481335	113.4	W 372293	99.9	W 263849	72.2	W 519109	138.0	BLOOMS ETC NON ACIER FIN
673	IRON,STEEL SHAPES ETC	W 116435	57.2	W 87335	48.9	W 142271	75.3	W 322965	135.6	BARRES,PROFIL FER,ACIER
674	IRN,STL UNIV,PLATE,SHEET	W 246253	166.1	W 232661	178.9	W 258133	192.6	W 343132	239.4	LARGES PLATS,TOLES
6746	IRN,STL THIN PLATE,ROLLD	W 105175	73.3	W 78034	72.0	W 112971	90.5	W 120523	94.7	TOLES LAM MOINS 3MM
678	IRON,STL TUBES,PIPES,ETC	W 41659	64.8	W 54628	92.4	W 39239	89.4	W 151378	211.6	TUBES,TUYAUX EN FONTE,FER
6783	IRON,STL TUBES,PIPES NES	W 16112	17.3	W 9093	12.9	W 9285	19.8	W 114510	113.6	AUT TUBES,TUYAUX FER,ACIER
68	NON–FERROUS METALS		214.9		247.4		285.2		323.3	METAUX NON FERREUX
682	COPPER EXC CEMENT COPPER	W 51757	125.6	W 42832	139.5	W 48938	134.4	W 56578	151.9	CUIVRE
6821	COPPER NES,ALLOYS,UNWRT	W 40640	92.1	W 31804	97.0	W 33900	86.1	W 36183	89.4	CUIVRE BRUT
68212	COPPER REFINED,UNWROUGHT	W 40601	92.0	W 31787	96.9	W 33864	86.0	W 36149	89.2	CUIVRE AFFINE BRUT
684	ALUMINIUM	W 20521	58.5	W 22538	73.7	W 36541	114.8	W 39165	122.4	ALUMINIUM
6842	ALUMINIUM,ALLOYS WORKED	W 19789	57.6	W 21196	70.3	W 35382	112.4	W 37912	119.8	ALUMINIUM,ALLIAGES OUVRE
69	METAL MANUFACTURES NES		575.6		591.9		647.4		874.0	ART MANUFACT EN METAL NDA
691	STRUCTURES AND PARTS NES	W 15212	29.6	W 24810	67.4	W 27536	67.3	W 34354	83.3	CONSTRUCT FER,ACIER,ALU
692	METAL TANKS,BOXES,ETC	W 23711	88.6	W 26438	87.3	W 23950	63.5	W 23395	76.2	RECIPIENTS METALLIQUES
6924	MTL TRANSPORT BOXES ETC	W 18804	70.5	W 24900	80.5	W 18505	49.0	W 19522	57.8	FUTS,TAMBOURS,BIDONS
694	STL,COPPR NAILS,NUTS,ETC	W 13660	50.7	W 10912	48.3	W 15329	63.1	W 26096	92.8	CLOUS,VIS,ECROUS
695	TOOLS	W 17686	120.3	W 11306	107.2	W 11935	119.9	W 19899	207.2	OUTILS A MAIN
6954	BLADES,TIPS,ETC FR TOOLS	W 6688	71.5	W 3033	68.4	W 2960	73.8	W 8046	147.8	OUTILS POUR MACHINE–OUTIL
69541	PARTS TO INSERT IN TOOLS	W 6324	55.6	W 2636	51.7	W 2420	56.1	W 7374	126.0	OUTILS DE FORAGE
699	BASE METAL MFRS NES	W 34486	156.7	W 32425	170.9	W 35531	190.9		251.2	ART MANUFACTURES MET NDA
7	MACHINES,TRANSPORT EQUIP		11188.2		8930.6		10902.0		14794.2	MACHINES MATERIEL TRANSPORT
71	POWER GENERATING EQUIPMT		660.8		767.3		887.5		1115.4	MACHINES GENERATRICES
713	INTRNL COMBUS PSTN ENGIN	W 39610	359.7	W 37750	402.4	W 45787	506.9	W 70744	719.8	MOTEURS EXPL COMB INT, PIECE
7132	MOTOR VEHCL PSTN ENGINS	W 14890	147.5	W 22130	228.8	W 28538	302.5	W 48722	472.4	MOTEURS EXPL POUR VEHICULES
7139	PISTON ENGINE PARTS NES	W 22266	176.6	W 13881	145.4	W 15061	170.7	W 19738	212.2	PIECES POUR 713.2,3,8
716	ROTATING ELECTRIC PLANT	W 18960	233.5	W 19379	288.4	W 23398	295.7	W 27257	293.4	APP ELECTR ROTATIFS,PIECES
7161	DC MOTORS AND GENERATORS	W 4728	98.3	W 4859	147.3	W 2436	55.8	W 3684	62.6	MOTEURS COURANT CONTINU
7162	AC MTRS,GENRTRS,GEN SETS	W 12495	84.4	W 11662	91.5	W 13702	98.9	W 17057	116.2	MOTEURS ELECTRIQUES
7169	PTS NES OF ROT ELEC PLNT	W 1730	50.7	W 2847	49.7	W 7257	141.0	W 6513	114.6	PIECES MAC APP ROTATIFS
72	MACHS FOR SPCL INDUSTRYS		1132.2		814.6		1091.0		1435.0	MAC SPECIALES POUR INDUST
721	AGRIC MACHY,EXC TRACTORS	W 22570	129.1	W 18386	119.1	W 28665	186.1	W 33222	228.6	MACHINES AGRICOLES
7212	HARVESTING ETC MACHINES	W 15084	89.6	W 13816	91.5	W 21803	149.9	W 23880	178.1	ENGINS POUR LA RECOLTE
72122	COMBINE HARVESTR–THRESHR	W 8832	50.7	W 6018	35.1	W 11354	73.3	W 11310	78.8	MOISSONNEUSES–BATTEUSES
722	TRACTORS NON–ROAD	W 11870	55.8	W 7795	42.9	W 16826	102.5	W 18536	112.0	TRACTEURS
7224	WHEELED TRACTORS NES	W 11440	52.2	W 6961	35.7	W 14898	85.8	W 16612	96.2	TRACTEURS A ROUES
723	CIVIL ENGNEERG EQUIP ETC	W 43971	211.6	W 18462	112.9	W 15504	119.4	W 32905	220.5	APPAREILS DE GENIE CIVIL
7234	CONST,MINING MACHNRY NES	W 39598	181.5	W 15809	87.5	W 13318	97.8	W 29660	189.6	MACH POUR LA CONST, MINES
72342	SLFPRP SHOVELS,EXCAVATRS	W 23053	102.9	W 9397	49.9	W 8371	53.2	W 19399	111.7	PELLES MECANIQUES
724	TEXTILE,LEATHER MACHNRY	W 12220	166.0	W 9076	93.1	W 13409	154.4	W 15256	203.1	MACH POUR INDUSTRIE TEXTILE
726	PRINTG,BKBINDG MACHY,PTS	W 6484	129.9	W 2970	79.3	W 3458	80.7	W 6973	144.9	MACHINES POUR IMPRIMERIE
7264	PRINTING PRESSES	W 4960	80.0	W 2072	44.5	W 2713	48.5	W 5754	100.3	MACHINES A IMPRIMER
72641	ROTARY PRINTING PRESSES	W 4960	80.0	W 2072	44.5	W 2713	48.5	W 5754	100.3	MACH IMPRIMER ROTATIVES
727	FOOD MACHRY NON–DOMESTIC	W 3738	73.4	W 2709	64.3	W 2605	52.5	W 2996	64.1	MACH INDUSTRIES ALIMENT
7272	OTH FOOD PROC MCHY,PARTS	W 3310	68.6	W 2346	58.5	W 1914	43.9	W 2038	50.9	AUT MACH IND ALIMENTAIRE
728	OTH MACHY FOR SPCL INDUS	W 22402	319.5	W 20218	266.1	W 31067	356.4	W 36806	405.5	AUT MACH IND PARTICULIERES
7284	MACHY FOR SPCL INDUS NES	W 12877	247.8	W 14606	220.1	W 18673	268.2	W 25991	326.6	MACH SPEC IND PARTICUL.
72842	RUBBER,PLASTICS WRKG MCH	W 6093	114.8	W 3413	67.3	W 4212	64.3	W 8681	139.2	MACH IND CAOUT MAT PLAST
72848	OTH MCHY WITH INDIV FNCT	W 4263	83.4	W 8472	102.5	W 12540	167.9	W 15031	133.3	AUTRES MACHINES NDA
73	METALWORKING MACHINERY		177.1		145.3		231.6		215.9	MACH TRAVAIL DES METAUX
736	METALWORKING MACH–TOOLS	W 13952	131.3	W 8406	97.9	W 13698	161.4	W 16149	135.8	MACH–OUTILS TRAVAIL METAUX
7361	METAL CUTTING MACH–TOOLS	W 7533	65.6	W 4191	34.5	W 4554	56.2	W 5326	50.3	MACH–OUT ENLEVEMENT METAL
74	GENRL INDUSTRL MACHY NES		1559.9		1691.8		1867.0		2247.4	MACH APP INDUSTRIE
741	HEATING,COOLING EQUIPMNT	W 35744	315.0	W 33887	346.5	W 35072	346.9	W 48945	461.6	MACH CHAUFFAGE,PIECES
7414	NONDOM REFRIG EQUIPT,PTS	W 11600	97.0	W 10098	92.6	W 11528	99.8	W 14072	119.2	MAT PRODUCTION DU FROID
74141	REFRIG EQUIP NONDOMESTIC	W 10338	86.7	W 8978	81.9	W 10285	89.3	W 12108	105.6	REFIG INDUSTRIELS
7415	AIR–CONDITIONING MACHNRY	W 5946	58.7	W 6943	65.6	W 10078	96.3	W 15537	138.0	GROUPES CONDITION AIR
7416	HEATING,COOLING EQU NES	W 11791	113.3	W 13032	145.6	W 10147	118.3	W 13780	159.8	APP CHANGEMENT TEMP
742	PUMPS FOR LIQUIDS ETC	W 10092	124.3	W 9058	128.1	W 11374	172.7	W 13314	186.7	POMPES MOTO–POMPES
7428	OTHER PUMPS FOR LIQUIDS	W 2962	57.9	W 3152	58.3	W 4272	83.6	W 4380	77.5	AUTRES POMPES POUR LIQ
743	PUMPS NES,CENTRFUGES ETC	W 25293	270.4	W 25624	277.3	W 27200	292.4	W 38483	406.0	POMPES COMPRES,VENT ETC

4. Special Imports C.I.F. by Commodities according to the S.I.T.C. (Rev. 2) in million U.S. Dollars
Importations Spéciales C.A.F. par Produits d'après la C.T.C.I. (Rév. 2) en millions de Dollars E.U.

SITC CTCI	COMMODITY	1994 QUANTITY QUANTITE	1994 VALUE VALEUR	1995 QUANTITY QUANTITE	1995 VALUE VALEUR	1996 QUANTITY QUANTITE	1996 VALUE VALEUR	1997 QUANTITY QUANTITE	1997 VALUE VALEUR	PRODUIT
7431	PUMPS FOR GASES ETC	W 16763	160.3	W 15482	132.6	W 14979	123.3	W 23293	194.3	POMPES AIR A VIDE,COMPRES
7436	GAS,LIQUID FILTERS ETC	W 4630	58.3	W 4980	69.2	W 7220	91.9	W 8468	118.9	APP POUR FILT DES LIQUIDES
744	MECHANICAL HANDLING EQU	W 37579	225.1	W 36761	307.9	W 36981	294.5	W 46341	331.9	EQUIP MANUTENTION PIECES
7441	FORK LIFT TRCKS,ETC,PTS	W 16426	76.6	W 12687	70.6	W 12104	62.3	W 17799	82.0	CHARIOTS POUR USINES ETC
74411	FORK LIFT TRUCKS ETC	W 16412	76.5	W 12681	70.5	W 12096	62.3	W 17787	81.9	CHARIOTS POUR LES GARES
7442	LIFTING,LOADING MACH NES	W 17093	127.9	W 19010	193.0	W 17425	175.7	W 20496	188.8	APP LEVAGE,MANUTENTION
74428	OTH HANDLING ETC MCH NES	W 12902	100.1	W 14246	152.0	W 12252	126.4	W 14332	138.8	AUT APP LEVAGE ETC
745	NONELEC MACHY,TOOLS NES	W 15626	288.4	W 17617	268.2	W 29628	331.5	W 30405	361.5	AUT MACH NON ELEC,PIECES
7452	OTH NONELEC MCHS,PTS NES	W 14612	263.9	W 16784	251.7	W 28664	306.3	W 29029	330.1	AUT MACH NON ELEC,PIECES
74522	PACKAGNG,BOTTLNG,ETC MCH	W 4093	147.9	W 3354	118.5	W 2938	119.5	W 3589	128.3	MACH NETT BOUTEILLES,ETC
74527	SPRAYING MACHINERY	W 8008	63.6	W 11525	86.1	W 24120	146.5	W 22527	143.5	APP PROJETER ETC LIQUID
749	NONELEC MACH PTS,ACC NES	W 32011	336.9	W 35978	364.1	W 41288	429.1	W 43574	500.1	PIECES MACH NON ELEC NDA
7491	BALL,ROLLER,ETC BEARINGS	W 7398	92.9	W 7876	100.9	W 9217	115.4	W 11322	128.9	ROULEMENTS BILLES ETC
7492	COCKS,VALVES ETC NES	W 7344	99.4	W 8217	110.5	W 8840	130.7	W 11097	158.7	ART ROB,SIM POUR TUYAUX
7493	SHAFT,CRANK,PULLEY ETC	W 14952	91.4	W 17989	105.6	W 20551	114.3	W 18293	126.7	ARBRES TRANS,VILEBREQUINS
75	OFFICE MACHNES,ADP EQUIP		927.5		707.7		815.3		1125.0	MACH BUREAU TRAIT AUTOM
751	OFFICE MACHINES	W 5127	134.1	W 3484	86.9	W 4575	103.9	W 6416	148.3	MACH,APPAREILS DE BUREAU
7518	OFFICE MACHINES NES	W 3110	63.7	W 2048	49.5	W 3130	67.9	W 4741	103.3	MACH,APP DE BUREAU NDA
752	AUTOMTIC DATA PROC EQUIP	W 14927	670.6	W 9819	469.1	W 13444	543.1	W 18406	746.2	MACH TRAIT INFORMATION
7523	DIGITL CENTRL PROCESSORS	W 4121	229.0	W 1850	145.1	W 2109	162.2	W 2758	231.4	UNITES CENTRALES
7524	DIGITL CENTRL STOR UNITS	W 662	50.5	W 945	57.7	W 939	69.2	W 1507	114.6	UNITES MEMOIRE CENTRALES
7525	ADP PERIPHERAL UNITS	W 9200	277.9	W 6511	186.6	W 9888	215.9	W 13530	281.8	UNITES PERIPHERIQUES
759	OFFICE,ADP MCH PTS,ACCES	W 2100	122.9	W 3888	151.8	W 6701	168.4	W 7774	230.6	PIECES DU 751 ET 752
7599	ACCTG,ETC,ADP MCH PTS,AC	W 1719	108.7	W 3470	136.6	W 6226	150.3	W 7118	205.7	PIECES DU 751 ET 752
76	TELECOMM,SOUND EQUIPMENT		1495.1		1028.7		1083.1		1720.7	EQUIPMENT DE TELECOM
761	TELEVISION RECEIVERS	W 8563	122.3	W 1699	27.4	W 1547	29.4	W 1691	39.3	RECEPTEURS DE TELEVISION
7611	COLOUR TV RECEIVERS	W 8036	119.2	W 1507	26.1	W 1376	28.3	W 1463	37.9	RECEPTEURS COULEUR
762	RADIO BROADCAST RECEIVRS	W 15654	214.2	W 8809	121.6	W 11285	131.4	W 15144	217.2	RECEPTEURS RADIODIFFUSION
7628	OTHER RADIO RECEIVERS	W 12616	175.7	W 5715	78.7	W 6323	69.6	W 9571	128.2	AUTRES RECEPT RADIO
764	TELECOM EQPT,PTS,ACC NES	W 24597	1102.1	W 13729	850.4	W 15446	883.3	W 21044	1407.1	EQUIP TELECOM,PIECES
7641	LINE TELEPHONE,ETC EQUIP	W 4813	278.6	W 3559	261.2	W 4033	265.1	W 4544	316.7	APP TELEPHON PAR FIL
7643	TV,RADIO TRANSMITTRS ETC	W 5145	363.7	W 1387	248.7	W 1638	281.4	W 3202	653.4	APP EMET TELE RADIO
7649	PTS NES OF EQUIPMT OF 76	W 10631	370.9	W 6100	285.7	W 6513	272.7	W 8307	357.3	PIECES DE LA DIV 76
76491	PTS NES OF APPAR OF 7641	W 610	65.7	W 626	88.6	W 430	79.4	W 464	121.3	PIECES POUR 764.1
76493	TELECOMM EQUIPMT PTS NES	W 8561	260.2	W 4841	177.0	W 5385	173.7	W 6637	197.4	PIECES 761,762,764.3,8
77	ELECTRIC MACHNRY NES ETC		1504.8		1338.3		1604.3		2112.6	MACH APP ELECT NDA
771	ELECTRIC POWER MACHY NES	W 12506	122.0	W 7311	102.4	W 11814	132.7	W 13438	168.3	MACH PROD,TRANS ELECTR
7712	OTH ELEC POWER MACHY NES	W 4645	72.0	W 3682	68.7	W 4889	77.6	W 6575	105.3	AUT APP PROD TRANSF ELEC
772	SWITCHGEAR ETC,PARTS NES	W 10351	227.1	W 9168	232.7	W 11525	289.1	W 16680	373.3	APP COUPURE,SECT ETC
7721	SWITCHGEAR ETC	W 9273	192.9	W 8332	205.5	W 10600	265.5	W 15298	341.4	APP COUPURE,SECTIONMNT
773	ELECTR DISTRIBUTNG EQUIP	W 29389	138.5	W 27152	150.0	W 18751	144.4	W 21153	176.9	EQUIPMT DISTRIBUTION ELECT
7731	INSULATED WIRE,CABLE ETC	W 27043	127.8	W 24852	137.7	W 16533	129.7	W 18682	153.3	FILS,CABLES ISOLES ELECT
774	ELECTRO-MEDCL,XRAY EQUIP	W 1123	70.0	W 661	64.5	W 598	61.8	W 955	91.8	APPAREILS MEDICAUX
775	HOUSEHOLD TYPE EQUIP NES	W 66091	311.5	W 47848	221.2	W 64809	296.1	W 77661	356.6	MACH,APP USAGE DOMESTQUE
7751	HOUSEHOLD LDRY EQUIP NES	W 25965	93.3	W 16190	60.6	W 27537	101.9	W 29710	106.1	MACH A LAVER ET SECHOIRS
77511	DOMESTIC WASHING MACHNES	W 25703	91.8	W 16084	60.0	W 27419	101.2	W 29575	105.4	MACH LAVER LINGE MOINS 6 KG
7758	ELECTRO-THERMIC APPL NES	W 12960	88.1	W 8107	51.9	W 9959	64.6	W 14496	89.8	APP ELECTROTHERMIQ NDA
776	TRANSISTORS,VALVES,ETC	W 21764	250.5	W 13276	182.8	W 15772	202.3	W 24869	304.1	LAMPES,TUBES,VALVES
7761	TV PICTURE TUBES	W 18916	125.2	W 11156	76.3	W 12832	92.0	W 20102	145.2	TUBES CATHODIQUES
7764	ELECTRONIC MICROCIRCUITS	W 1680	84.5	W 1321	77.4	W 1737	78.3	W 2684	116.6	MICROSTRUCTURES ELECTRON
778	ELECTRICAL MACHINERY NES	W 48627	385.5	W 46703	385.1	W 53775	478.3	W 70942	641.8	AUTRES MACH ELECT NDA
7781	BATTERIES,ACCUMULATORS	W 19433	75.3	W 19744	77.5	W 24073	93.5	W 29884	118.2	PILES ET ACCUMULATEURS
7783	AUTOMOTIVE ELECTR EQUIP	W 9123	104.5	W 7836	93.7	W 9054	109.8	W 15055	159.4	EQUIP ELECT MOTEURS EXPL
77831	IGNITION,STARTING EQUIP	W 5264	67.9	W 4838	63.0	W 5049	65.9	W 8643	97.2	APP ELEC ALLUM,DEMARRAGE
7788	OTH ELEC MACHY,EQUIP NES	W 12735	116.9	W 12419	136.2	W 12720	186.3	W 16575	252.8	AUT MACH APP ELEC NDA
77886	OTH ELEC MACHINERY NES	W 1475	36.0	W 2500	62.5	W 2952	100.3	W 3929	138.2	AUT MACH APP ELECTRIQUES
78	ROAD VEHICLES		3330.6		2119.0		2983.7		4383.9	VEHICULES ROUTIERS
781	PASS MOTOR VEH EXC BUSES	W 141497	1394.5	W 79048	773.3	W 127638	1198.4	W 169928	1561.3	AUTO TRANSPORT PERSONNES
782	LORRIES,SPCL MTR VEH NES	W 75889	558.7	W 40974	311.0	W 69430	532.9	W 123426	866.5	VEHICULES SPECIAUX,MARCH
7821	LORRIES,TRUCKS	W 69133	519.8	W 35753	284.4	W 65972	509.4	W 115484	839.8	VEHICULES TRANSP MARCHAND
783	ROAD MOTOR VEHICLES NES	W 16867	137.7	W 4541	35.5	W 5035	39.6	W 15194	124.1	VEHICULES ROUTIERS NDA
7831	BUSES	W 10340	93.5	W 2570	21.1	W 3061	24.1	W 7406	62.3	VOITURES TRANSPORT COMMUN
784	MOTOR VEH PRTS,ACCES NES	W 166620	968.1	W 134310	867.8	W 153894	1061.4	W 245901	1620.3	PIECES 722,781,782,783
7849	OTHER MOTOR VEHCL PARTS	W 160022	919.6	W 128939	826.2	W 146219	999.1	W 239151	1554.5	PIECES 722,781,782,783
785	CYCLES,ETC MOTRZD OR NOT	W 30983	225.9	W 15687	104.7	W 18098	111.7	W 25462	152.3	MOTOCYCLES SCOOTERS
7851	MOTORCYCLES ETC	W 15558	164.5	W 6171	62.7	W 4685	53.8	W 6970	79.9	MOTO VELO MOTEUR AUXIL
79	OTHR TRANSPORT EQUIPMENT		400.6		318.2		339.0		438.6	AUTRE MATERIEL TRANSPORT
792	AIRCRAFT ETC	W 1043	329.4	W 561	175.3	W 1088	205.0	W 958	332.5	APP NAVIGATION AERIENNE
7923	AIRCRFT NES2000-15000KG	W 196	74.7	W 142	49.9	W 158	87.0	W 279	171.9	AERODYNES 2000 A 15000 KG
7924	AIRCRFT NES OVER 15000KG	W 736	236.2	W 186	98.4	W 867	104.7	W 557	135.6	AERODYNES PLUS 15000 KG
793	SHIPS AND BOATS ETC	W 23225	64.7	W 25329	104.2	W 47550	114.5	W 47888	68.4	NAVIRES BATEAUX,ETC
7932	SHIPS AND BOATS NES	W 22933	62.3	W 24877	102.3	W 46390	109.8	W 45314	64.2	NAVIRES ET BATEAUX
79324	FISHING VESSELS ETC	W 18606	42.4	W 18914	68.8	W 19157	73.2	W 9679	19.6	BATEAUX DE PECHE
8	MISC MANUFACTURED GOODS		2236.3		1996.9		2209.7		2779.2	ART MANUFACTURES DIVERS
821	*FURNITURE,PARTS THEREOF	W 40835	115.3	W 28630	94.6	W 34961	124.4	W 52582	178.7	MEUBLES ET PIECES
84	CLOTHING AND ACCESSORIES		315.5		229.2		232.3		256.6	VETEMENTS
842	MENS OUTERWEAR NOT KNIT	W 5483	81.9	W 2457	49.2	W 1896	46.2	W 1991	49.6	VET DESSUS POUR HOMMES
851	*FOOTWEAR	W 11204	141.5	W 8719	114.3	W 8142	116.7	W 11003	156.5	CHAUSSURES
85102	FOOTWEAR LEATHER	W 6142	96.5	W 4588	72.8	W 4505	70.0	W 5597	86.0	CHAUS SEMELLES EN CUIR
87	PRECISION INSTRUMNTS NES		403.4		367.4		439.1		519.0	INSTRUM,APPAR SCIENT NDA
872	MEDICAL INSTRUMENTS NES	W 2640	110.4	W 2278	60.6	W 2400	73.7	W 3095	90.6	INSTR,APP MEDIC-CHIR NDA
87202	OTH MEDICAL INSTRUMENTS	W 2375	102.5	W 1980	54.7	W 2106	67.3	W 2739	78.9	INSTRUM,APP MEDECINE
874	MEASURNG,CONTROLNG INSTR	W 6159	251.3	W 6534	270.8	W 8055	332.3	W 9791	369.2	INSTRUMENTS DE MESURE
8742	MEASUR,DRAW ETC INST,PTS	W 1520	54.0	W 1691	54.8	W 2387	87.6	W 2579	78.4	INST DESSIN,TRACAGE,PCS
87421	MEASURNG,DRAWNG ETC INST	W 1445	48.8	W 1615	48.8	W 2295	81.5	W 2424	71.1	INSTRUM DESSIN,TRACAGE
8743	GAS,LIQUID CONTROL INSTR	W 2128	64.1	W 2142	77.6	W 3166	97.1	W 4460	133.3	APP,INSTR MESURE FLUIDES
8748	ELEC MEAS,CONTRL EQU NES	W 920	78.4	W 640	83.4	W 634	83.9	W 762	93.1	APP ELEC ELECTRO MESURE
87483	OTH ELCTRNC MEAS ETC EQU	W 798	74.6	W 511	77.3	W 547	79.4	W 691	88.5	AUT APP ELECTRO DE MESURE
88	PHOTO EQU,OPTICL GDS ETC		232.1		199.6		219.4		268.3	APP,FOURN PHOTO,OP,MONTR
882	PHOTO,CINEMA SUPPLIES	W 7833	115.1	W 7147	118.6	W 7466	120.9	W 9057	146.0	PRODUITS PHOTO,CINEMA
8822	PHOTO FILM EXC DEV CINMA	W 5343	90.5	W 4837	93.1	W 4865	95.6	W 5882	119.6	PLAQUES,PELLICULES,FILMS
89	MISC MANUFCTRD GOODS NES		951.4		916.6		994.5		1286.0	ART MANUFACTURES DIVERS
892	PRINTED MATTER	W 22924	121.5	W 24147	148.4	W 21431	137.5	W 30477	186.0	IMPRIMES
8921	PRINTED BOOKS,GLOBES,ETC	W 9604	54.9	W 13016	82.0	W 10911	68.5	W 16006	95.2	LIVRES,BROCHURES,CARTES
89211	PRINTED BOOKS,PAMPHLETS	W 9052	52.2	W 12110	78.0	W 10271	66.1	W 15174	91.9	LIVRES,BROCHURES
893	ARTICLES OF PLASTIC NES		294.4		324.2		332.6		425.3	OUVRAGES EN MAT DIVIS 58
8931	PLSTC PACKG CONTNRS,LIDS	W 36913	97.2	W 36467	116.7	W 25805	83.4	W 36781	102.4	ART TRANSP EMBALLAGE ETC
8939	MISC PLASTIC ARTICLES	W 34619	194.6	W 36462	202.8	W 44320	244.1	W 59578	316.8	ART DIVERS EN MAT DIV 58
89399	OTHR PLASTC ARTICLES NES	W 32572	186.3	W 33964	194.3	W 40769	233.2	W 54922	303.4	AUT OUV MAT DIV 58
894	TOYS,SPORTING GOODS,ETC	W 43797	225.0	W 37100	176.7	W 43231	188.3	W 57237	255.2	VOITURES ENFANTS,JOUETS
8942	TOYS,INDOOR GAMES ETC	W 34765	169.0	W 27409	124.4	W 34687	140.2	W 44907	199.3	JOUETS,JEUX ETC

4. Special Imports C.I.F. by Commodities according to the S.I.T.C. (Rev. 2) in million U.S. Dollars
Importations Spéciales C.A.F. par Produits d'après la C.T.C.I. (Rév. 2) en millions de Dollars E.U.

SITC CTCI	COMMODITY	1994			1995			1996			1997			PRODUIT
		QUANTITY QUANTITE		VALUE VALEUR	QUANTITY QUANTITE		VALUE VALEUR	QUANTITY QUANTITE		VALUE VALEUR	QUANTITY QUANTITE		VALUE VALEUR	
89423	TOYS NES	W	19417	99.4	W	15409	68.9	W	19279	81.0	W	24542	115.0	JOUETS,MODELES REDUITS
898	MUSICAL INSTRUMENTS,PTS	W	10135	151.5	W	8054	135.9			183.9	W	9947	232.9	INSTRUMENTS DE MUSIQUE
8983	SOUND RECRDNG TAPE,DISCS	W	8778	130.1	W	7182	123.2			166.9	W	8516	213.5	SUPPORTS SON POUR 763
89832	RECORDED DISCS,TAPES ETC	W	2353	72.0	W	2179	79.5			118.1	W	2986	157.1	DISQUES,PHONO,BANDES
899	OTHER MANUFACTURED GOODS			98.6			79.1			91.9			112.7	AUT ART MANUF DIVERS NDA
9	GOODS NOT CLASSD BY KIND			17.0			22.2			7.5			100.4	ART TRANSACT NON CLASSES
931	*SPECIAL TRANSACTIONS	W	10884	1.8	W	242	1.1	W	248	1.0			95.1	TRANS.SPECIALES

5. Special Exports F.O.B. by Commodities according to the S.I.T.C. (Rev. 2) in million U.S. Dollars
Exportations Spéciales F.O.B. par Produits d'après la C.T.C.I. (Rév. 2) en millions de Dollars E.U.

SITC CTCI	COMMODITY	1994 QUANTITY QUANTITE	1994 VALUE VALEUR	1995 QUANTITY QUANTITE	1995 VALUE VALEUR	1996 QUANTITY QUANTITE	1996 VALUE VALEUR	1997 QUANTITY QUANTITE	1997 VALUE VALEUR	PRODUIT
	ALL COMMODITIES		15838.7		20962.6		23809.7			TOUS PRODUITS
0	FOOD AND LIVE ANIMALS		5584.5		7214.6		9241.6			ALIMENTS,ANIMAUX VIVANTS
001	*LIVE ANIMALS FOR FOOD	W 71563	50.7	W 140998	97.4	W 60764	44.4			ANIMAUX VIVANTS
0011	BOVINE SPECIES,LIVE	W 70062	43.8	W 138724	87.0	W 58810	33.2			ESPECE BOVINE
00119	— OTHR THAN FR BREEDING	W 69104	41.7	W 137490	85.3	W 58084	32.3			BOVINS NON REPRODUCTEURS
01	MEAT AND PREPARATIONS		918.1		1229.2		1073.9			VIANDES ET PREPARATIONS
011	MEAT FRESH,CHILLD,FROZEN	W 217192	628.0	W 303463	848.1	W 303822	781.0			VIANDES FRAICHES,REF,CONGE
0111	BOVINE MEAT FRESH,FROZEN	W 140423	494.4	W 217585	695.2	W 216948	627.1			VIANDES BOVIN FRAI,REF
01112	BOVINE MEAT BONELESS	W 116601	470.5	W 174873	653.4	W 174293	583.6			VIANDES BOVIN DESOSSEES
0115	HORSE MEAT FRSH,CHLD,FRN	W 31826	66.1	W 30979	68.2	W 35298	81.8			VIANDES DE CHEVAL
014	MEAT PREPD,PRSVD,NES ETC	W 106156	290.0	W 129128	381.1	W 109165	292.8			CONSERVES DE VIANDES
0149	OTH PREPARD,PRESRVD MEAT	W 104668	280.4	W 127545	371.1	W 106899	283.8			AUTRES PREP DE VIANDES
02	DAIRY PRODCTS,BIRDS'EGGS		135.4		260.1		280.6			PRODUITS LAITIERS,OEUFS
022	MILK AND CREAM	W 45900	87.3	W 111896	195.3	W 124303	215.1			LAIT ET CREME
0224	MILK,CREAM PRESERVED ETC	W 38791	83.8	W 75621	175.3	W 77954	186.2			LAIT,CREME CONS,CONC
02243	MILK DRY,OVER 1.5% FAT	W 26334	62.3	W 57267	136.0	W 56437	138.7			LAIT POUDRE SUP 1.5%
03	FISH AND PREPARATIONS		725.2		914.3		1003.9			POISSONS ET PREPARATIONS
034	FISH,FRESH,CHILLED,FROZN	W 299925	365.7	W 351369	501.6	W 365829	494.9			POISSON FRAIS, REFRIG,CONG
0342	FISH FROZEN,EXCL FILLETS	W 160113	144.5	W 166304	174.8	W 168032	168.4			POISSONS CONGELES
0344	FISH FILLETS,FROZEN	W 128674	209.2	W 171129	311.5	W 179085	299.7			FILETS CONGELES
036	SHELL FISH FRESH,FROZEN	W 201577	292.0	W 196825	320.0	W 258825	432.7			CRUSTACES,MOLLUSQUES
037	FISH ETC PREPD,PRSVD NES	W 23925	52.8	W 27432	75.7	W 27529	58.8			POIS,CRUST,MOL PREPARES
0371	FISH PREPARD,PRESRVD NES	W 23408	50.2	W 26866	71.5	W 26280	53.8			CONSERVES DE POISSONS
04	CEREALS AND PREPARATIONS		1456.4		2017.8		2802.9			CEREALES ET PRODUITS
041	WHEAT ETC UNMILLED	W 5172297	670.0	W 6913286	1005.4	W 5921995	1065.7			FROMENT,EPEAUTRE
0412	OTHER WHEAT ETC UNMILLED	W 5142921	666.1	W 6837418	994.7	W 5914223	1064.5			AUTRE FROMENT NON MOULU
042	RICE	W 221386	79.9	W 403205	138.1	W 379591	139.4			RIZ
0422	RICE SEMI-MILLED,MILLED	W 198278	74.2	W 355630	128.2	W 310170	120.9			RIZ POLI,GLACE INCL BRISURES
04221	RICE MILLED UNBROKEN	W 180075	70.7	W 311014	118.9	W 281826	114.6			RIZ POLI,GLACE EXCL BRISURES
044	MAIZE UNMILLED	W 4153740	491.9	W 6000872	682.3	W 7079801	1239.4			MAIS NON MOULU
045	CEREALS NES UNMILLED	W 544784	78.7	W 242169	33.2	W 728209	114.1			AUTRES CEREALES NON MOULUES
0459	OTHER CEREALS UNMILLED	W 524794	76.2	W 234172	32.1	W 727889	114.0			SARRASIN,MILLET,SORGHO
04592	SORGHUM UNMILLED	W 428896	42.7	W 188620	17.9	W 672064	99.3			SORGHO NON MOULU
046	WHEAT ETC MEAL OR FLOUR	W 287723	59.2	W 227604	57.7	W 328532	107.3			SEMOULE FARINE,FROMENT
04601	FLOUR OF WHEAT OR MESLIN	W 283642	57.9	W 223926	56.4	W 323929	105.2			FARINE DE FROMENT
048	CEREAL ETC PREPARATIONS	W 140648	64.0	W 134064	96.8	W 183774	134.4			PREPTNS A BASE CEREALES
05	VEGETABLES AND FRUIT		699.3		1035.0		1180.5			LEGUMES ET FRUITS
054	VEG ETC FRSH,SMPLY PRSVD	W 589573	262.7	W 490821	267.0	W 586906	291.6			LEGUMES FRAIS,CONG,SECS
0542	LEGUMINOUS VEGETBLES DRY	W 214715	139.8	W 201058	140.2	W 203956	147.8			LEGUMES A COSSE SECS
0545	OTHER FRESH VEGETABLES	W 195533	93.5	W 234889	113.7	W 331587	113.5			AUTRES LEGUMES FRAIS,REF
05451	ALLIACEOUS VEGTBLS,FRESH	W 194053	92.0	W 232206	110.6	W 326238	110.6			OIGNONS,ECHALOTES,AULX
056	VEGTBLES ETC PRSVD,PREPD	W 41655	49.7	W 45421	77.7	W 43170	78.9			CONSERVES DE LEGUMES
0565	VEGTBLES PRSVD,PREPD NES	W 40424	45.6	W 43325	70.7	W 41308	73.1			LEGUMES PREPARES CONSERVE
05659	OTH VEG PRESVD,PREPD NES	W 38438	44.0	W 41180	69.0	W 39665	71.6			LEGUM PREPAP,CONSERV NDA
057	FRUIT,NUTS,FRESH,DRIED	W 548792	275.8	W 763295	444.9	W 818528	508.7			FRUITS FRAIS OU SECS
0572	LEMONS,GRAPEFRUIT ETC	W 120568	50.9	W 147279	77.6	W 195687	109.2			AUTRES AGRUMES FRAIS,SECS
05721	LEMONS,LIMES,FRESH,DRIED	W 93022	41.7	W 110785	61.6	W 161253	93.1			CITRONS ET LIMES
0574	APPLES FRESH	W 146800	70.8	W 243320	137.2	W 209534	126.1			POMMES FRAICHES
0579	FRUIT FRESH OR DRIED NES	W 161849	101.9	W 245359	164.8	W 262097	184.3			FRUITS FRAIS,SECS NDA
05792	PEARS, QUINCES FRESH	W 142568	71.3	W 222403	132.1	W 237787	148.5			POIRES ET COINGS FRAIS
058	FRUIT PRESERVED,PREPARED	W 132248	111.3	W 254855	245.6	W 263764	301.5			CONSERVES DE FRUITS
0585	FRUIT OR VEGETABLE JUICE	W 104700	83.2	W 223606	214.5	W 219839	255.9			JUS DE FRUITS
05857	JUICE OF OTHER FRUIT,VEG	W 85443	66.4	W 187525	172.5	W 194729	219.6			JUS AUTRES FRUITS,LEGUMES
06	SUGAR AND PREPS,HONEY		112.5		192.5		235.2			SUCRES ET PRODUITS
061	SUGAR AND HONEY	W 128269	76.5	W 238306	132.1	W 263685	169.3			SUCRES ET MIEL
0616	NATURAL HONEY	W 62437	53.8	W 63511	70.5	W 53559	90.7			MIEL NATUREL
07	COFFEE,TEA,COCOA,SPICES		80.5		122.1		145.6			CAFE,THE,CACAO,EPICES
074	TEA AND MATE	W 64743	60.0	W 81804	66.0	W 84259	63.3			THE ET MATE
081	*FEEDING STUFF FOR ANIML	W 8546943	1349.0	MW 9538	1254.7	MW 11204	2367.0			NOURRITURE POUR ANIMAUX
0813	OILCAKE AND OTH RESIDUES	W 8236372	1301.8	MW 9228	1196.2	MW 10868	2293.4			TOURTEAUX
08131	— OF SOYA BEANS	W 6670928	1145.9	W 6887996	1022.3	W 8345207	1984.1			TOURTEAUX DE SOJA
08135	— OF SUNFLOWER SEEDS	W 1285949	120.0	W 1910256	125.9	W 2096781	245.5			TOURTEAUX DE TOURNESOL
09	MISC EDIBLE PRODUCTS		57.8		92.0		108.2			PREP ALIMENTAIRES DIVERSES
098	EDIBLE PRODCTS,PREPS NES	W 15539	43.9	W 22680	74.2	W 29365	88.8			PREP ALIMENTAIRES NDA
1	BEVERAGES AND TOBACCO		159.7		269.4		283.5			BOISSONS ET TABACS
11	BEVERAGES		60.0		147.1		121.1			BOISSONS
112	ALCOHOLIC BEVERAGES	W 46522	47.5	W 254641	97.2	W 166310	104.3			BOISSONS ALCOOLIQUES
1121	WINE OF FRESH GRAPES ETC	W 33966	35.3	W 231575	78.6	W 141339	83.8			VINS DE RAISINS FRAIS
11212	WINE OF FRESH GRAPES	W 33093	34.2	W 217967	73.9	W 138137	81.8			VINS DE MOUTS DE RAISINS
12	TOBACCO AND MANUFACTURES		99.8		122.4		162.5			TABACS BRUTS FABRIQUES
121	TOBACCO UNMNFCTRD,REFUSE	W 37995	87.5	W 43440	100.8	W 55781	146.0			TABACS BRUTS,DECHETS
1212	TOBACCO STRIPPED OR PART	W 25337	77.0	W 29644	87.4	W 35133	130.2			TABACS PART ECOTES
2	CRUDE MATERLS,EXCL FUELS		1446.9		1768.0		1869.2			MAT BRUTES NON COMESTIBLES
22	OIL SEEDS,OLEAGINOUS FRT		943.7		875.1		955.1			GRAINES,FRUITS OLEAGINEUX
222	SEEDS FOR'SOFT'FIXED OIL	W 3610218	943.2	W 3593880	874.3	W 2962635	954.4			GRAINES HUILES FIXES
2221	GROUNDNUTS,GREEN	W 104432	84.8	W 165126	123.4	W 264575	203.3			ARACHIDES NON GRILLEES
2222	SOYA BEANS	W 2909527	690.5	W 2549840	536.0	W 2055882	588.2			FEVES DE SOJA
2224	SUNFLOWER SEEDS	W 585214	163.3	W 845095	208.3	W 586106	152.9			GRAINES DE TOURNESOL
24	CORK AND WOOD		39.4		73.5		67.8			LIEGE ET BOIS
251	*PULP AND WASTE PAPER	W 177583	63.5	W 162808	121.0	W 192801	83.5			PATES A PAPIER,DECHETS
2517	SODA,SULPHATE WOOD PULP	W 177126	63.4	W 152266	115.4	W 181415	79.3			PATES CHIMIQUES AU SULFATE
25172	— BLEACHED,NONDISSOLVNG	W 176926	63.3	W 151816	115.1	W 180515	78.9			PATES BLANCHIES
26	TEXTILE FIBRES AND WASTE		319.0		582.2		625.5			FIBRES TEXTILES
263	COTTON	W 127168	179.2	W 249012	437.5	W 363344	500.8			COTON
2631	RAW COTTON,EXCL LINTERS	W 124081	176.4	W 243474	432.8	W 357447	497.1			COTON EN MASSE
268	WOOL(EXC TOPS),ANML HAIR	W 57282	132.4	W 42502	135.0	W 41709	114.7			LAINES ET POILS
2681	WOOL GREASY,FLEECE-WSHED	W 35717	74.7	W 26584	86.2	W 24810	64.7			LAINE EN SUINT
3	MINERAL FUELS ETC		1657.2		2175.4		3096.2			COMBUSTIBLES MINERAUX LUB
33	PETROLEUM AND PRODUCTS		1581.0		2088.7		2973.4			PETROLE ET DERIVES
333	CRUDE PETROLEUM	MW 10526	1125.6	MW 14010	1591.9	MW 16473	2320.0			HUILES BRUTES DE PETROLE
334	PETROLEUM PRODUCTS,REFIN	W 3249097	413.6	W 2915078	435.6	W 3135450	584.9			PRODUITS RAFFINES
3341	GASOLINE,OTH LIGHT OILS			W 1240712	185.7	W 1614807	301.8			ESSENCES POUR MOTEURS
33411	MOTOR,AVIATION SPIRIT			W 1174978	174.4	W 796375	151.8			ESSENCES MOTEURS D'AVIONS
33419	OTH LIGHT PETROLEUM OILS			W 28318	5.4	W 818432	150.0			AUTRES HUILES LEGERES
3342	KEROSENE,OTH MEDIUM OILS			W 980367	131.5	W 28510	6.6			PETR LAMPANTS,AUT HUIL
33421	KEROSENE INCL JET FUEL			W 980367	131.5	W 28510	6.6			PETROLES LAMPANTS
3343	GAS OILS			W 61442	28.0	W 1046435	179.1			GAS OILS
3345	LUBS,PETROLEUM OILS NES	W 2717	6.6	W 627824	89.0	W 236072	65.2			HUILES LUBRIFIANTES
33451	LUBS(HIGH PETR CONT) ETC			W 624551	81.1	W 232427	57.0			HUILES LUBRIF,H LOURDES
341	*GAS,NATURAL AND MANUFCT	W 502313	71.9	W 461261	75.8	W 550749	109.7			GAZ NATUREL,GAZ MANUFACT
3413	PETROLM GASES,LIQUEFIED	W 502313	71.9	W 461261	75.8	W 548350	109.5			GAZ DE PETROLE LIQUEFIE

5. Special Exports F.O.B. by Commodities according to the S.I.T.C. (Rev. 2) in million U.S. Dollars
Exportations Spéciales F.O.B. par Produits d'après la C.T.C.I. (Rév. 2) en millions de Dollars E.U.

SITC CTCI	COMMODITY	1994 QUANTITY QUANTITE	1994 VALUE VALEUR	1995 QUANTITY QUANTITE	1995 VALUE VALEUR	1996 QUANTITY QUANTITE	1996 VALUE VALEUR	1997 QUANTITY QUANTITE	1997 VALUE VALEUR	PRODUIT
34131	LIQUEFIED PROPANE,BUTANE	W 430498	61.7	W 282048	44.9	W 278330	55.6			PROPANE,BUTANE LIQUEFIES
4	ANIMAL,VEGETABLE OIL,FAT		1519.0		2077.4		1882.6			HUILES,GRAISSES ANIM,VEG
42	FIXED VEGETABLE OIL,FAT		1498.6		2043.9		1857.2			HUILES VEGETALES FIXES
423	FIXED VEG OILS,SOFT	W 2523463	1481.2	W 3234164	2007.7	W 3287955	1828.9			HUILES VEGET DOUCES FIXES
4232	SOYA BEAN OIL	W 1502120	859.5	W 1546358	943.0	W 1694060	900.8			HUILE DE SOJA
4236	SUNFLOWER SEED OIL	W 927690	546.9	W 1578502	973.7	W 1482974	832.1			HUILE DE TOURNESOL
5	CHEMCLS,RELATED PROD NES		919.0		1314.8		1320.1			PRODUITS CHIMIQUES
51	ORGANIC CHEMICALS		225.5		335.8		335.6			PROD CHIMIQ ORGANIQUES
511	HYDROCARBONS NES,DERIVS	W 94562	56.3	W 117301	87.9	W 150828	64.4			HYDROCARBURES NDA
5112	CYCLIC HYDROCARBONS	W 75255	42.9	W 94489	71.5	W 94085	39.2			HYDROCARBURES CYCLIQUES
513	CARBOXYLIC ACIDS ETC	W 30139	38.5	W 38384	63.4	W 37601	53.9			ACIDES CARBOXYLIQUES
514	NITROGEN–FNCTN COMPOUNDS	W 20596	47.5	W 20235	61.8	W 22168	72.6			COMPOSES FONCT AZOTEES
52	INORGANIC CHEMICALS		98.0		124.5		77.2			PROD CHIM INORGANIQUES
523	OTHR INORG CHEMICALS ETC		70.9	W 70481	82.4	W 80643	42.0			AUT PRODUITS CHIMIQUES INORG
5233	METALLIC ACID SALTS ETC	W 11137	48.7	W 13890	55.9	W 13788	12.3			SELS ACIDES D'OXYDES METAL E
53	DYES,TANNING,COLOUR PROD		95.6		104.4		123.2			PROD TEINTURE,COLORANTS
541	*MEDICINAL,PHARM PRODUCT	K 2667599	112.0		140.9	K 4522979	198.9			PROD MEDICINAUX PHARMACEUT
5417	MEDICAMENTS	K 2092046	76.0	K 3155362	107.2	K 3471319	152.1			MEDICAMENTS
54179	— CONTNG OTH SUBSTANCES	K 1728091	46.4	K 2712126	71.6	K 2775292	97.0			MED CONT AUT SUBSTANCES
55	PERFUME,CLEANING ETC PRD		130.1		172.5		138.5			PROD POUR PARFUM,TOILETTE
553	PERFUMERY,COSMETICS,ETC	W 9218	71.8	W 12239	92.0	W 13823	54.4			PRODUITS DE PARFUMERIE
58	PLASTIC MATERIALS ETC		136.0		272.7		254.2			MAT PLAST ARTIFICIELLES
583	POLYMERIZATION ETC PRODS	W 138413	118.2	W 209394	239.1	W 199710	207.3			PROD POLYMERISATION
5832	POLYPROPYLENE	W 61066	43.7	W 80961	93.6	W 61239	64.1			POLYPROPYLENE
58321	— IN PRIMARY FORMS	W 56911	32.3	W 75023	71.5	W 53333	42.4			POLYPROPYLENE PRIMAIRES
59	CHEMICAL MATERIALS NES		119.6		161.8		189.2			MAT PROD CHIMIQUES NDA
598	MISCEL CHEM PRODUCTS NES	W 41261	52.1	W 48558	65.0	W 58430	78.6			PROD DIV INDUST CHIM NDA
6	BASIC MANUFACTURES		2095.5		2972.5		2852.0			ART MANUFACTURES
61	LEATHER,DRESSED FUR,ETC		876.4		989.2		926.5			CUIRS,PELLETERIES
611	LEATHER	W 88050	733.5	W 106001	893.8	W 107663	823.8			CUIRS,PEAUX PREPARES
6114	LEATHR BOVINE NES,EQUINE	W 87810	726.7	W 105606	884.4	W 107340	818.3			CUIRS DE BOVINS
612	LEATHER ETC MANUFACTURES	W 5273	122.3	W 5575	63.1	W 4934	44.7			OUVRAGES EN CUIRS NDA
6123	PREPRD PARTS OF FOOTWEAR	W 2739	53.1	W 3493	31.9	W 2208	22.2			PARTIES DE CHAUSSURES
6129	LEATHER MANUFACTURES NES	W 2295	63.2	W 1848	22.5	W 2464	11.9			AUT OUV CUIR NAT,ARTIF
62	RUBBER MANUFACTURES NES		66.9		100.8		98.0			CAOUTCHOUC MANUFACTURE
625	RUBBER TYRES, TUBES ETC	W 20237	56.3	W 28873	85.3	W 27226	81.9			PNEUS CAOUTCHOUC VULCANISE
64	PAPER,PAPERBOARD AND MFR		69.0		188.8		177.5			PAPIERS,CARTONS & OUVRAGES
641	PAPER AND PAPERBOARD	W 45808	35.5	W 135143	112.9	W 123748	85.5			PAPIERS ET CARTONS
6415	PAPER,PAPERBRD,BULK,NES	W 12379	10.9	W 76756	65.7	W 45778	30.4			PAPIERS,CARTONS ROULEAUX
642	PAPER,ETC,PRECUT,ARTS OF	W 24998	33.6	W 32858	76.0	W 35659	92.0			PAP,CARTONS DECOUPES
65	TEXTILE YARN,FABRICS,ETC		238.5		359.4		329.5			FILS,TISSUS,ARTICLES TEXTILE
651	TEXTILE YARN	W 33556	140.8	W 42397	200.8	W 38928	178.0			FILS TEXTILES
6512	WOOL,HAIR YARN,INCL TOPS	W 13435	60.3	W 11690	69.5	W 14190	73.6			FILS DE LAINE,DE POILS
65121	WOOL TOPS	W 13089	56.1	W 11566	67.2	W 14093	71.6			RUBANS LAINE PEIGN,TOPS
6514	SYN FIB YRN,BULK,MONOFIL	W 13353	52.1	W 16930	73.5	W 16602	71.3			FILS CONT 85% FIB TEXT SYNTH
652	COTTON FABRICS,WOVEN	W 12827	51.1	W 16620	75.7	W 12540	63.2			TISSUS DE COTON
6522	WOVEN COTTON BLEACHD,ETC	W 11203	45.3	W 14303	65.8	W 11144	56.4			TISSUS COTON BLANCHIS ETC
66	NONMETAL MINERAL MFS NES		77.1		119.6		115.9			ART MIN NON METALLIQUES
67	IRON AND STEEL		468.0		732.0		797.8			FER ET ACIER
673	IRON,STEEL SHAPES ETC	W 152609	52.6	W 242366	89.4	W 209821	76.5			BARRES,PROFIL FER,ACIER
674	IRN,STL UNIV,PLATE,SHEET	W 264761	115.1	W 527311	256.1	W 438631	185.4			LARGES PLATS,TOLES
6746	IRN,STL THIN PLATE,ROLLD	W 193317	78.5	W 388948	177.6	W 324021	124.9			TOLES LAM MOINS 3MM
67461	— OF IRON OR SIMPLE STL	W 192977	77.7	W 388662	176.9	W 323826	124.3			TOL NON AC FIN MOINS 3 MM
678	IRON,STL TUBES,PIPES,ETC	W 440563	273.4	W 509292	334.5	W 616593	457.9			TUBES,TUYAUX EN FONTE,FER
6782	IRON,STL SEAMLESS TUBES	W 424766	261.6	W 483330	315.1	W 570013	417.2			TUBES,TUYAUX SANS SOUDURE
68	NON–FERROUS METALS		179.6		293.9		214.0			METAUX NON FERREUX
684	ALUMINIUM	W 103707	161.0	W 130754	260.5	W 115272	189.7			ALUMINIUM
6841	ALUMINIUM,ALLOYS,UNWRGHT	W 81423	118.9	W 100765	186.8	W 93852	145.2			ALUMINIUM,ALLIAGES BRUTS
6842	ALUMINIUM,ALLOYS WORKED	W 22284	42.1	W 29989	73.8	W 21420	44.6			ALUMINIUM,ALLIAGES OUVRE
69	METAL MANUFACTURES NES		105.9		169.2		153.2			ART MANUFACT EN METAL NDA
7	MACHINES,TRANSPORT EQUIP		1770.8		2275.3		2592.5			MACHINES MATERIEL TRANSPORT
71	POWER GENERATING EQUIPMT		165.3		223.2		289.5			MACHINES GENERATRICES
713	INTRNL COMBUS PSTN ENGIN	W 23019	148.9	W 22356	187.7	W 23735	253.1			MOTEURS EXPL COMB INT, PIECE
7132	MOTOR VEHCL PISTN ENGINS	W 9284	99.8	W 9635	129.4	W 11877	173.9			MOTEURS EXPL POUR VEHICULES
7139	PISTON ENGINE PARTS NES	W 13675	48.1	W 12594	56.5	W 11712	76.6			PIECES POUR 713.2,3,8
72	MACHS FOR SPCL INDUSTRYS		52.1		70.1		77.1			MAC SPECIALES POUR INDUST
74	GENRL INDUSTRL MACHY NES		214.0		331.5		332.5			MACH APP INDUSTRIE
744	MECHANICAL HANDLING EQU	W 1674	19.1	W 4888	64.4	W 4149	54.5			EQUIP MANUTENTION PIECES
749	NONELEC MACH PTS,ACC NES	W 8833	73.8	W 12115	105.6	W 9793	105.8			PIECES MACH NON ELEC NDA
75	OFFICE MACHNES,ADP EQUIP		83.0		68.9		45.4			MACH BUREAU TRAIT AUTOM
76	TELECOMM,SOUND EQUIPMENT		47.3		84.6		57.7			EQUIPMENT DE TELECOM
77	ELECTRIC MACHNRY NES ETC		284.9		167.7		133.0			MACH APP ELECT NDA
772	SWITCHGEAR ETC,PARTS NES	W 1974	204.5	W 903	53.5	W 900	25.7			APP COUPURE,SECT ETC
7721	SWITCHGEAR ETC	W 1958	203.7	W 897	52.9	W 894	24.9			APP COUPURE,SECTIONMNT
78	ROAD VEHICLES		863.4		1233.2		1514.6			VEHICULES ROUTIERS
781	PASS MOTOR VEH EXC BUSES	W 25011	180.9	W 24552	238.8	W 89744	803.9			AUTO TRANSPORT PERSONNES
782	LORRIES,SPCL MTR VEH NES	W 26004	207.0	W 54429	427.0	W 31437	253.1			VEHICULES SPECIAUX,MARCH
7821	LORRIES,TRUCKS	W 25936	206.7	W 54377	426.5	W 31245	250.6			VEHICULES TRANSP MARCHAND
784	MOTOR VEH PRTS,ACCES NES	W 70871	456.8	W 83691	546.2	W 65287	440.8			PIECES 722,781,782,783
7841	MOTOR VEHICLE CHASSIS	W 9595	53.8	W 13432	83.6	W 13318	84.6			CHASSIS 722,781,782,783
7849	OTHER MOTOR VEHCL PARTS	W 61245	402.7	W 70084	460.9	W 51620	354.3			PIECES 722,781,782,783
79	OTHR TRANSPORT EQUIPMENT		51.3		70.1		123.1			AUTRE MATERIEL TRANSPORT
792	AIRCRAFT ETC	W 31	2.6	W 108	23.7	W 1106	97.5			APP NAVIGATION AERIENNE
7924	AIRCRFT NES OVER 15000KG				9.4	W 997	79.9			AERODYNES PLUS 15000 KG
8	MISC MANUFACTURED GOODS		642.4		890.0		667.0			ART MANUFACTURES DIVERS
821	*FURNITURE,PARTS THEREOF	W 4019	20.3	W 8799	56.3	W 9800	85.2			MEUBLES ET PIECES
84	CLOTHING AND ACCESSORIES		101.2		188.8		157.3			VETEMENTS
848	HEADGEAR,NONTXTL CLOTHNG	W 1276	80.8	W 1380	106.6	W 1615	120.7			VET ACCES MAT AUT QUE TEX
8483	FUR ETC,CLOTHES,PRODUCTS	W 255	37.0	W 395	62.4	W 534	85.1			VETEMENTS DE FOURRURE
84831	ARTICLES OF FURSKIN,NES	W 255	37.0	W 395	62.4	W 534	85.1			PELLETERIES OUVREES NDA
851	*FOOTWEAR	W 2667	33.7	W 3205	70.6	W 2506	50.6			CHAUSSURES
85102	FOOTWEAR LEATHER	W 2148	27.2	W 2768	65.9	W 2220	48.0			CHAUS SEMELLES EN CUIR
88	PHOTO EQU,OPTICL GDS ETC		51.2		169.9		40.1			APP,FOURN PHOTO,OP,MONTR
885	WATCHES AND CLOCKS		10.8		125.1		2.8			HORLOGERIE
8851	WATCHES,MOVEMENTS,CASES		9.4		123.6		0.6			MONTRES,MOUVEMENTS,BOITES
88514	WATCH CASES,CASE PARTS		9.4		111.2					BOITES DU 885.11,PIECES
89	MISC MANUFCTRD GOODS NES		397.2		362.4		284.6			ART MANUFACTURES DIVERS
892	PRINTED MATTER	W 8839	78.5	W 16171	116.0	W 21712	138.3			IMPRIMES
893	ARTICLES OF PLASTIC NES		44.6		68.1		85.5			OUVRAGES EN MAT DIVIS 58
897	GOLD,SILVER WARE,JEWELRY		236.6		109.7		3.5			BIJOUTERIE,ORFEVRERIE
8973	PREC JEWLRY,GLD–SILVWARE		148.7		104.8		1.6			BIJOUX OR,ARGENT ORFEVRE

5. Special Exports F.O.B. by Commodities according to the S.I.T.C. (Rev. 2) in million U.S. Dollars
Exportations Spéciales F.O.B. par Produits d'après la C.T.C.I. (Rév. 2) en millions de Dollars E.U.

SITC CTCI	COMMODITY	1994		1995		1996		1997		PRODUIT
		QUANTITY QUANTITE	VALUE VALEUR	QUANTITY QUANTITE	VALUE VALEUR	QUANTITY QUANTITE	VALUE VALEUR	QUANTITY QUANTITE	VALUE VALEUR	
89731	PRECIOUS METAL JEWELLERY		132.8		87.7		0.9			ART BIJOUTERIE,JOAILLER

1. HISTORICAL SERIES, 1992–1996 SPECIAL TRADE, IMPORTS C.I.F., EXPORTS F.O.B.
SERIES HISTORIQUES, 1992–1996 COMMERCE SPECIAL, IMPORTATIONS C.A.F., EXPORTATIONS F.O.B

YEAR ANNEE	VALUE IN MILLION U.S. DOLLARS VALEUR EN MILLION U.S. DOLLARS MERCHANDISE –MARCHANDISE IMPORTS	EXPORTS	GOLD –OR IMPORTS	EXPORTS	CONVERSION FACTORS FACTEURS DE CONVERSION CENTS E.U. PAR IMPORTS	EXPORTS	INDEX NUMBERS –INDICES QUANTUM IMPORTS	EXPORTS	UNIT VALUE VALEUR UNITAIRE IMPORTS	EXPORTS
1992	50.00	26.00								
1993	86.00	30.00								
1994	415.00	232.00								
1995	661.00	248.00								
1996	855.80	290.31								

2. IMPORTS BY BROAD ECONOMIC CATEGORY AND EXPORTS BY INDUSTRIAL ORIGIN. (PERCENTAGE OF TOTAL VALUE)
IMPORTATIONS PAR CATEGORIES ECONOMIQUES ET EXPORTATIONS PAR BRANCHE D'ACTIVITE.(EN POURCENTAGE DE LA VALEUR TOTALE)

IMPORTS – IMPORTATIONS

	1990	1991	1992	1993	1994	1995	1996
TOTAL IMPORTS–IMPORTATIONS TOTALES							
1 FOOD BEV–ALIMENTATION BOISSONS							
11 PRIMARY–PRODUITS DE BASE							
111 FOR INDUSTRY–POUR L'INDUSTRIE							
112 FOR HOUSEHOLDS–POUR LES MENAGES							
12 PROCESSED–PRODUITS ELABORES							
121 FOR INDUSTRY–POUR L'INDUSTRIE							
122 FOR HOUSEHOLDS–POUR LES MENAGES							
2 IND SUPPLIES–APPROV INDUSTRIELS							
21 PRIMARY–PRODUITS DE BASE							
22 PROCESSED–PRODUITS ELABORES							
3 FUELS–COMBUSTIBLES							
31 PRIMARY–PRODUITS DE BASE							
32 PROCESSED–PRODUITS ELABORES							
321 MOTOR SPIRIT–ESSENCE							
322 OTHER–AUTRES							
4 MACHINERY–EQUIPEMENT							
41 CAPITAL EQUIPMENT–MACHINES							
42 PARTS–PIECES ACCESSOIRES							
5 TRANSPORT–TRANSPORT							
51 PASSENGER CARS–AUTOMOBILES							
52 OTHER–AUTRES							
521 INDUSTRIAL–INDUSTRIELS							
522 NON INDUSTRIAL–NON INDUSTRIEL							
53 PARTS–PIECES ACCESSOIRES							
6 CONSUM GOODS–BIENS CONSOMMATION							
61 DURABLE–DURABLES							
62 SEMI DURABLE–SEMI DURABLES							
63 NON DURABLE–NON DURABLES							
7 GOODS NES–BIENS NDA							

EXPORTS – EXPORTATIONS

	1990	1991	1992	1993	1994	1995	1996
TOTAL EXPORTS–EXPORTATIONS TOTALES							
1 AGRICULTURE							
2 MINING QUARRY–INDUS EXTRACTIVES							
3 MANUFACTURING–IND MANUFACTUR							
31 FOOD BEV TOBACCO–ALIM BOISS TAB							
32 TEXTILES–INDUSTRIES TEXTILES							
33 WOOD & PRODUCTS–BOIS & PRODUITS							
34 PAPER & PRODUCTS–PAPIER & PRODT							
35 CHEMICALS–INDUSTRIES CHIMIQUES							
36 NON METAL MIN–MIN NON METAL							
37 BASIC METAL–IND METAL BASE							
38 METAL MANUF–MANUF METAL							
39 OTH MANUF IND–AUTRES MANUF							

3. TRADE BY PRINCIPAL COUNTRIES OF CONSIGNMENT AND DESTINATION (VALUE IN MILLION U.S. DOLLARS)
ECHANGES SELON LES PRINCIPAUX PAYS DE CONSIGNATION ET DE DESTINATION (VALEUR EN MILLIONS DE DOLLARS EU)

COUNTRIES–PAYS	GENERAL IMPORTS C.I.F. IMPORTATIONS GENERALES C.A.F				
	1992	1993	1994	1995	1996
World		254.1	393.8	673.9	855.8
Africa				3.0	42.6
Americas		26.9	96.3	114.6	104.8
– Northern America		26.9	96.3	114.6	104.8
– LAIA					
– CACM					
– Caribbean					
– Rest of America					
Asia excl fmr USSR		0.2	49.2	110.3	194.0
– Middle East		0.1	44.4	109.5	191.6
Asia former USSR		85.0	87.6	191.4	138.0
Europe excl fmr USSR		38.2	40.9	109.4	176.5
– European Union		35.8	37.1	88.8	132.6
– Eastern Europe		2.0	1.2	12.9	21.9
– Rest of Europe		0.4	2.6	7.7	22.0
Europe former USSR		80.2	119.4	144.7	144.0
Oceania					0.3
Other					
Russian Federation		77.9	112.1	135.1	125.5
Turkmenistan/Turkménistn		64.1	69.6	129.3	86.5
USA/Etats–Unis d'Amer		26.9	96.1	114.4	103.6
Iran (Islamic Rep of)			42.5	89.8	149.8
Georgia/Géorgie		19.5	17.8	61.9	51.2
Italy/Italie		31.1	8.9	22.4	26.2
Belgium–Luxembourg		2.9	1.4	15.6	49.5
United Arab Emirates			1.1	13.8	33.4
So. African Customs Un				3.0	42.0
France, Monaco		0.9	10.7	16.3	12.0
Germany/Allemagne		0.3	6.9	11.3	17.4
Switzerland,Liechtenst.		0.3	2.4	6.4	17.9
Ukraine		0.1	5.3	5.4	12.0
Netherlands/Pays–Bas		0.3	8.3	6.0	5.7
Bulgaria/Bulgarie		0.2	0.9	4.6	14.3
Greece/Grèce				5.6	5.3
United Kingdom		0.2	0.5	2.2	7.1
Turkey/Turquie			0.5	2.6	6.3
Czech Republic		1.0	0.1	6.3	0.8
Denmark/Danemark				4.9	2.7
Lithuania/Lituanie		0.3	0.7	2.1	3.5
Romania/Roumanie				1.4	4.8
Belarus/Bélarus		1.2	0.4	1.9	2.2
Norway,Svalbard and JM				1.1	3.7
Ireland/Irlande				1.7	2.4
Austria/Autriche				2.1	1.9
Lebanon/Liban			0.1	2.6	1.2
China/Chine			1.6	0.4	0.8
India/Inde		0.1	1.8	0.2	0.7
Poland/Pologne		0.8	0.2	0.4	0.8
Finland/Finlande			0.4	0.7	1.0
Korea, Republic of			1.4	0.2	0.1
Canada			0.2	0.2	1.2
Kazakhstan		1.2	0.1	0.1	0.1
Hungary/Hongrie				0.2	1.2
Sweden/Suède					1.4
Estonia/Estonie		0.4	0.3	0.1	0.5
Syrian Arab Republic		0.1		0.6	0.4
Latvia/Lettonie		0.2	0.5		0.2
Yugoslavia/Yougoslavie		0.1	0.2	0.2	0.4

COUNTRIES–PAYS	GENERAL EXPORTS F.O.B. EXPORTATIONS GENERALES F.O.B.				
	1992	1993	1994	1995	1996
Monde		156.1	215.5	270.9	290.3
Afrique		0.2		8.8	36.5
Amériques		0.2	0.4	0.6	4.5
– Amérique du Nord		0.2	0.4	0.6	4.4
– ALAI					0.1
– MCAC					
– Caraïbes					
– Autre Amérique					
Asie anc. URSS exclus		1.2	15.2	39.6	52.5
– Moyen–Orient		1.2	15.2	39.5	52.2
Asie ancienne URSS		61.7	69.6	73.3	25.8
Europe anc. URSS exclus		18.3	37.9	51.6	62.6
– Union Européenne		16.6	35.4	48.4	61.9
– Europe de l'Est		1.3		0.1	0.3
– Autre de l'Europe		0.4	2.5	3.1	0.4
Europe ancienne URSS		61.1	88.6	94.0	102.8
Océanie					
Autre					
Russian Federation		58.5	83.9	88.5	96.1
Turkmenistan/Turkménistn		57.0	65.7	68.7	17.5
Belgium–Luxembourg		14.9	26.0	30.8	44.8
Iran (Islamic Rep of)			14.6	35.0	43.9
So. African Customs Un				8.5	36.4
Germany/Allemagne		0.3	6.6	10.1	3.7
Georgia/Géorgie		3.2	2.9	2.7	6.9
Netherlands/Pays–Bas		0.1	0.7	5.3	8.7
Ukraine		0.3	3.7	4.5	4.9
Turkey/Turquie		0.3	0.2	2.6	6.0
Switzerland,Liechtenst.		0.4	2.5	3.1	0.3
USA/Etats–Unis d'Amer		0.2	0.4	0.6	4.4
United Kingdom			0.5	1.3	3.2
Kazakhstan		1.4	0.9	1.6	1.0
Belarus/Bélarus		1.9	0.7	0.9	1.2
United Arab Emirates			0.1	0.4	1.9
France, Monaco		1.3	0.4	0.2	0.4
Ireland/Irlande			1.2	0.5	0.2
Syrian Arab Republic		0.9	0.2	0.3	0.2
Lebanon/Liban			0.1	1.2	0.2
Bulgaria/Bulgarie		1.0		0.1	0.2
Uzbekistan/Ouzbékistan			0.1	0.3	0.4
Greece/Grèce				0.1	0.5
Lithuania/Lituanie		0.1	0.2	0.1	0.1
Latvia/Lettonie		0.1	0.1		0.2
Egypt/Egypte				0.3	0.1
Poland/Pologne		0.3			
Pakistan					0.3
Estonia/Estonie		0.1			0.2
Spain/Espagne					0.3
Libyan Arab Jamahiriya		0.2			
Italy/Italie				0.1	0.1
Romania/Roumanie					0.1
Yugoslavia/Yougoslavie					0.1
India/Inde				0.1	
Tajikistan/Tadjikistan		0.1			

(VALUE AS PERCENTAGE OF WORLD TOTAL)(VALEURS EN POURCENTAGE DU TOTAL MONDIAL)

	1987	1988	1989	1990	1991	1992	1993	1994	1995	1996
Africa									0.4	5.0
Americas							10.6	24.5	17.0	12.2
– Northern America							10.6	24.5	17.0	12.2
– LAIA										
– CACM										
– Caribbean										
– Rest of America										
Asia excl fmr USSR							0.1	12.5	16.4	22.7
– Middle East							0.0	11.3	16.2	22.4
Asia former USSR							33.5	22.2	28.4	16.1
Europe excl fmr USSR							15.0	10.4	16.2	20.6
– European Union							14.1	9.4	13.2	15.5
– Eastern Europe							0.8	0.3	1.9	2.6
– Rest of Europe							0.2	0.7	1.1	2.6
Europe former USSR							31.6	30.3	21.5	16.8
Oceania										0.0
Other										
Russian Federation							30.7	28.5	20.0	14.7
Turkmenistan/Turkménistn							25.2	17.7	19.2	10.1
USA/Etats–Unis d'Amer							10.6	24.4	17.0	12.1
Iran (Islamic Rep of)								10.8	13.3	17.5
Georgia/Géorgie							7.7	4.5	9.2	6.0
Italy/Italie							12.2	2.3	3.3	3.1
Belgium–Luxembourg							1.1	0.4	2.3	5.8
United Arab Emirates								0.3	2.0	3.9
So. African Customs Un									0.4	4.9
France, Monaco							0.4	2.7	2.4	1.4

	1987	1988	1989	1990	1991	1992	1993	1994	1995	1996
Afrique							0.1		3.2	12.6
Amériques							0.1	0.2	0.2	1.6
– Amérique du Nord							0.1	0.2	0.2	1.5
– ALAI										0.0
– MCAC										
– Caraïbes										
– Autre Amérique										
Asie anc. URSS exclus							0.8	7.1	14.6	18.1
– Moyen–Orient							0.8	7.1	14.6	18.0
Asie ancienne URSS							39.5	32.3	27.1	8.9
Europe anc. URSS exclus							11.7	17.6	19.0	21.6
– Union Européenne							10.6	16.4	17.9	21.3
– Europe de l'Est							0.8		0.0	0.1
– Autre de l'Europe							0.3	1.2	1.1	0.1
Europe ancienne URSS							39.1	41.1	34.7	35.4
Océanie										
Autre										
Russian Federation							37.5	38.9	32.7	33.1
Turkmenistan/Turkménistn							36.5	30.5	25.4	6.0
Belgium–Luxembourg							9.5	12.1	11.4	15.4
Iran (Islamic Rep of)								6.8	12.9	15.1
So. African Customs Un									3.1	12.5
Germany/Allemagne							0.2	3.1	3.7	1.3
Georgia/Géorgie							2.0	1.3	1.0	2.4
Netherlands/Pays–Bas							0.1	0.3	2.0	3.0
Ukraine							0.2	1.7	1.7	1.7
Turkey/Turquie							0.2	0.1	1.0	2.1

4. General Imports C.I.F. by Commodities according to the S.I.T.C. (Rev. 2) in million U.S. Dollars
Importations Générales C.A.F. par Produits d'après la C.T.C.I. (Rév. 2) en millions de Dollars E.U.

SITC CTCI	COMMODITY	1993		1994		1995		1996		PRODUIT
		QUANTITY QUANTITE	VALUE VALEUR	QUANTITY QUANTITE	VALUE VALEUR	QUANTITY QUANTITE	VALUE VALEUR	QUANTITY QUANTITE	VALUE VALEUR	
	ALL COMMODITIES				393.8		673.9		855.8	TOUS PRODUITS
0	FOOD AND LIVE ANIMALS				110.5					ALIMENTS,ANIMAUX VIVANTS
01	MEAT AND PREPARATIONS						18.1		34.1	VIANDES ET PREPARATIONS
02	DAIRY PRODCTS,BIRDS'EGGS						45.1		33.1	PRODUITS LAITIERS,OEUFS
054	VEG ETC FRSH,SMPLY PRSVD						6.1		4.1	LEGUMES FRAIS,CONG,SECS
057	FRUIT,NUTS,FRESH,DRIED						3.1		7.1	FRUITS FRAIS OU SECS
11	BEVERAGES						3.1		10.1	BOISSONS
3	MINERAL FUELS ETC				161.0		224.0		185.0	COMBUSTIBLES MINERAUX LUB
4	ANIMAL,VEGETABLE OIL,FAT				12.0					HUILES,GRAISSES ANIM,VEG
5	CHEMCLS,RELATED PROD NES				9.2					PRODUITS CHIMIQUES
51	ORGANIC CHEMICALS						1.1		3.1	PROD CHIMIQ ORGANIQUES
52	INORGANIC CHEMICALS						3.1		3.1	PROD CHIM INORGANIQUES
53	DYES,TANNING,COLOUR PROD						1.1		3.1	PROD TEINTURE,COLORANTS
541	*MEDICINAL,PHARM PRODUCT						40.1		34.1	PROD MEDICINAUX PHARMACEUT
572	*EXPLOSIVES,PYROTECH PRO						2.1		8.1	EXPLOSIFS
6	BASIC MANUFACTURES				4.5					ART MANUFACTURES
62	RUBBER MANUFACTURES NES						2.1		6.1	CAOUTCHOUC MANUFACTURE
64	PAPER,PAPERBOARD AND MFR						7.1		8.1	PAPIERS,CARTONS & OUVRAGES
66	NONMETAL MINERAL MFS NES						64.1		137.0	ART MIN NON METALLIQUES
67	IRON AND STEEL						1.1		3.1	FER ET ACIER
684	ALUMINIUM						6.1		1.1	ALUMINIUM
69	METAL MANUFACTURES NES						7.1		4.1	ART MANUFACT EN METAL NDA
7	MACHINES,TRANSPORT EQUIP				10.1		56.1		92.1	MACHINES MATERIEL TRANSPORT
78	ROAD VEHICLES						6.1		10.1	VEHICULES ROUTIERS
8	MISC MANUFACTURED GOODS				7.1					ART MANUFACTURES DIVERS
821	*FURNITURE,PARTS THEREOF						2.1		9.1	MEUBLES ET PIECES
84	CLOTHING AND ACCESSORIES						2.1		10.1	VETEMENTS
851	*FOOTWEAR						1.1		5.1	CHAUSSURES
892	PRINTED MATTER						1.1		4.1	IMPRIMES

5. General Exports F.O.B. by Commodities according to the S.I.T.C. (Rev. 2) in million U.S. Dollars
Exportations Générales F.O.B. par Produits d'après la C.T.C.I. (Rév. 2) en millions de Dollars E.U.

SITC CTCI	COMMODITY	1993		1994		1995		1996		PRODUIT
		QUANTITY QUANTITE	VALUE VALEUR	QUANTITY QUANTITE	VALUE VALEUR	QUANTITY QUANTITE	VALUE VALEUR	QUANTITY QUANTITE	VALUE VALEUR	
	ALL COMMODITIES						270.9		290.3	TOUS PRODUITS
057	FRUIT,NUTS,FRESH,DRIED								1.1	FRUITS FRAIS OU SECS
11	BEVERAGES						12.1		10.1	BOISSONS
51	ORGANIC CHEMICALS						2.1		2.1	PROD CHIMIQ ORGANIQUES
52	INORGANIC CHEMICALS								2.1	PROD CHIM INORGANIQUES
541	*MEDICINAL,PHARM PRODUCT						3.1		1.1	PROD MEDICINAUX PHARMACEUT
572	*EXPLOSIVES,PYROTECH PRO						3.1		2.1	EXPLOSIFS
62	RUBBER MANUFACTURES NES						9.1		3.1	CAOUTCHOUC MANUFACTURE
65	TEXTILE YARN,FABRICS,ETC						1.1		1.1	FILS,TISSUS,ARTICLES TEXTILE
66	NONMETAL MINERAL MFS NES						93.1		141.0	ART MIN NON METALLIQUES
67	IRON AND STEEL						9.1		10.1	FER ET ACIER
682	COPPER EXC CEMENT COPPER						6.1		17.1	CUIVRE
684	ALUMINIUM						8.1		14.1	ALUMINIUM
69	METAL MANUFACTURES NES						3.1		5.1	ART MANUFACT EN METAL NDA
7	MACHINES,TRANSPORT EQUIP						45.1		37.1	MACHINES MATERIEL TRANSPORT
78	ROAD VEHICLES						7.1		2.1	VEHICULES ROUTIERS
821	*FURNITURE,PARTS THEREOF						4.1		1.1	MEUBLES ET PIECES
84	CLOTHING AND ACCESSORIES						16.1		8.1	VETEMENTS
851	*FOOTWEAR						4.1		2.1	CHAUSSURES
892	PRINTED MATTER						1.1		1.1	IMPRIMES

1. HISTORICAL SERIES, 1962–1997 GENERAL TRADE, IMPORTS F.O.B., EXPORTS F.O.B.
SERIES HISTORIQUES, 1962–1997 COMMERCE GENERAL, IMPORTATIONS F.O.B., EXPORTATIONS F.O.B

YEAR ANNEE	VALUE IN MILLION ASTL. DOLLARS / VALEUR EN MILLION ASTL. DOLLARS — MERCHANDISE – MARCHANDISE		GOLD – OR		CONVERSION FACTORS U.S. CENTS PER ASTL. DOLLAR / FACTEURS DE CONVERSION CENTS E.U. PAR ASTL. DOLLAR		INDEX NUMBERS – INDICES — QUANTUM		UNIT VALUE / VALEUR UNITAIRE	
	IMPORTS	EXPORTS	IMPORTS	EXPORTS	IMPORTS	EXPORTS	IMPORTS	EXPORTS	IMPORTS	EXPORTS
1962	1738.80	2100.20	4.30	18.00	112.0000	112.0000				
1963	2128.30	2102.40	5.00	12.00	112.0000	112.0000				
1964	2329.60	2725.60	4.60	14.00	112.0000	112.0000				
1965	2841.30	2579.20	4.10	18.00	112.0000	112.0000				
1966	2853.90	2742.30	4.20	24.00	112.0000	112.0000				
1967	3083.30	3001.80	4.20	18.00	112.0000	112.0000				
1968	3444.40	3037.20	4.40	15.00	112.0000	112.0000				
1969	3573.80	3610.20	4.00	22.00	112.0000	112.0000				
1970	4056.00	4259.00	6.90	29.00	112.0000	112.0000				
1971	4139.00	4599.00	3.80	20.00	113.3598	113.3800				
1972	3876.00	5419.00	4.60	19.00	119.0998	119.0998				
1973	4781.00	6590.00	5.80	24.00	142.2887	141.7039				
1974	7769.00	7684.00	8.70	34.00	143.8411	143.8174				
1975	7637.00	9118.00			130.8722	131.0039				
1976	9134.00	10743.00			122.4246	122.4827				
1977	11036.00	12036.00			110.8736	110.9228				
1978	12329.00	12591.00			114.5297	114.4904				
1979	14801.00	16715.00			111.7402	111.6801				
1980	17826.00	19341.00			114.0842	113.9083	58	64	60	62
1981	20693.00	18938.00			114.8582	114.9408	66	60	61	63
1982	23775.10	21718.10			101.7311	101.4743	70	64	65	65
1983	21539.90	22927.60			90.0350	90.2287	61	62	71	70
1984	26711.00	27374.00			87.6945	87.6682	80	72	72	71
1985	33631.00	32865.00			69.7270	69.6287	77	81	86	79
1986	39033.01	33716.00			66.8895	66.9509	74	84	94	80
1987	41816.00	37947.01			70.1184	70.1614	76	94	99	84
1988	45925.01	42369.01			78.6084	78.4488	89	89	97	94
1989	56801.01	47005.01			79.1259	79.0011	108	94	96	98
1990	53785.01	50892.00			78.1337	78.1257	100	100	100	100
1991	53427.01	53728.00			77.9592	77.9015	99	115	101	91
1992	59732.00	58383.01			73.3416	73.3766	107	121	106	93
1993	66910.00	62840.00			67.9686	67.9575	115	128	114	94
1994	72881.01	64899.01			73.3049	73.2297	133	139	111	92
1995	81370.00	71637.01			74.1266	74.1191	148	141	115	99
1996	83544.00	76978.00			78.3164	78.3336	162	157	109	95
1997	88910.00	84773.01			74.1316	74.1994	192	183	109	96

2. IMPORTS BY BROAD ECONOMIC CATEGORY AND EXPORTS BY INDUSTRIAL ORIGIN. (PERCENTAGE OF TOTAL VALUE)
IMPORTATIONS PAR CATEGORIES ECONOMIQUES ET EXPORTATIONS PAR BRANCHE D'ACTIVITE. (EN POURCENTAGE DE LA VALEUR TOTALE)

IMPORTS – IMPORTATIONS

	1991	1992	1993	1994	1995	1996	1997
TOTAL IMPORTS–IMPORTATIONS TOTALES	100.	100.	100.	100.	100.	100.	100.
1 FOOD BEV–ALIMENTATION BOISSONS	4.5	4.4	4.6	4.5	4.5	4.4	4.4
11 PRIMARY–PRODUITS DE BASE	1.2	1.1	1.2	1.2	1.3	1.2	1.2
111 FOR INDUSTRY–POUR L'INDUSTRIE	0.3	0.2	0.2	0.3	0.4	0.3	0.3
112 FOR HOUSEHOLDS–POUR LES MENAGES	0.9	0.8	0.9	0.9	0.9	0.9	0.9
12 PROCESSED–PRODUITS ELABORES	3.3	3.3	3.4	3.3	3.2	3.2	3.2
121 FOR INDUSTRY–POUR L'INDUSTRIE	0.4	0.4	0.5	0.5	0.6	0.5	0.5
122 FOR HOUSEHOLDS–POUR LES MENAGES	2.9	2.9	2.9	2.7	2.6	2.7	2.7
2 IND SUPPLIES–APPROV INDUSTRIELS	22.4	22.3	24.5	24.1	24.2	22.9	22.6
21 PRIMARY–PRODUITS DE BASE	1.3	1.3	1.2	1.3	1.3	1.3	1.3
22 PROCESSED–PRODUITS ELABORES	21.1	21.0	23.3	22.8	22.9	21.6	21.3
3 FUELS–COMBUSTIBLES	5.7	5.7	6.2	4.9	5.1	6.3	6.1
31 PRIMARY–PRODUITS DE BASE	3.0	3.3	3.9	3.2	3.4	4.6	4.7
32 PROCESSED–PRODUITS ELABORES	2.6	2.4	2.3	1.6	1.7	1.7	1.4
321 MOTOR SPIRIT–ESSENCE							
322 OTHER–AUTRES	2.6	2.4	2.3	1.6	1.7	1.7	1.4
4 MACHINERY–EQUIPEMENT	26.3	25.7	29.0	30.4	31.6	31.3	30.8
41 CAPITAL EQUIPMENT–MACHINES	20.8	20.2	22.7	23.8	24.9	24.9	24.6
42 PARTS–PIECES ACCESSOIRES	5.5	5.5	6.3	6.6	6.7	6.4	6.3
5 TRANSPORT–TRANSPORT	17.3	15.9	16.6	17.1	16.5	16.6	16.7
51 PASSENGER CARS–AUTOMOBILES	4.4	5.1	5.5	5.7	5.6	5.4	6.4
52 OTHER–AUTRES	7.0	4.9	4.5	4.6	4.7	4.9	4.2
521 INDUSTRIAL–INDUSTRIELS	6.7	4.6	4.1	4.2	4.3	4.5	3.8
522 NON INDUSTRIAL–NON INDUSTRIEL	0.3	0.3	0.4	0.4	0.4	0.4	0.4
53 PARTS–PIECES ACCESSOIRES	5.8	5.9	6.6	6.8	6.1	6.2	6.1
6 CONSUM GOODS–BIENS CONSOMMATION	16.8	17.5	18.5	18.4	17.4	17.9	18.7
61 DURABLE–DURABLES	4.2	4.1	4.6	4.6	4.5	4.7	4.8
62 SEMI DURABLE–SEMI DURABLES	8.3	8.8	9.2	9.1	8.5	8.5	8.9
63 NON DURABLE–NON DURABLES	4.3	4.6	4.7	4.7	4.5	4.7	5.0
7 GOODS NES–BIENS NDA	7.1	8.4	0.4	0.6	0.7	0.6	0.6

EXPORTS – EXPORTATIONS

	1991	1992	1993	1994	1995	1996	1997
TOTAL EXPORTS–EXPORTATIONS TOTALES	100.	100.	100.	100.	100.	100.	100.
1 AGRICULTURE	13.2	12.6	13.1	14.2	12.0	15.7	15.8
2 MINING QUARRY–INDUS EXTRACTIVES	23.7	23.5	26.5	23.4	23.9	23.5	24.6
3 MANUFACTURING–IND MANUFACTUR	63.1	63.9	60.4	62.4	64.1	60.8	59.6
31 FOOD BEV TOBACCO–ALIM BOISS TAB	11.3	11.9	15.6	16.4	15.1	13.6	13.8
32 TEXTILES–INDUSTRIES TEXTILES	2.7	3.1	3.5	4.0	4.2	3.8	3.8
33 WOOD & PRODUCTS–BOIS & PRODUITS	0.1	0.2	1.0	1.0	1.1	1.0	0.9
34 PAPER & PRODUCTS–PAPIER & PRODT	0.8	0.7	0.9	0.9	0.9	0.9	1.0
35 CHEMICALS–INDUSTRIES CHIMIQUES	6.2	6.2	11.1	10.7	11.2	11.2	10.5
36 NON METAL MIN–MIN NON METAL	0.4	0.4	0.5	0.5	0.6	0.6	0.5
37 BASIC METAL–IND METAL BASE	9.0	9.0	9.7	9.8	11.0	9.3	8.7
38 METAL MANUF–MANUF METAL	11.9	12.3	14.8	15.6	16.6	16.7	17.0
39 OTH MANUF IND–AUTRES MANUF	20.9	20.1	3.3	3.5	3.4	3.6	3.4

3. TRADE BY PRINCIPAL COUNTRIES OF ORIGIN AND DESTINATION (VALUE IN MILLION U.S. DOLLARS)
ECHANGES SELON LES PRINCIPAUX PAYS D'ORIGINE ET DE DESTINATION (VALEUR EN MILLIONS DE DOLLARS EU)

COUNTRIES–PAYS	GENERAL IMPORTS F.O.B. IMPORTATIONS GENERALES F.O.B.					COUNTRIES–PAYS	EXPORTS EXPORTATIONS ES F.O.B.				
	1993	1994	1995	1996	1997		1993	1994	1995	1996	1997
World	42412.5	49918.1	57422.8	61400.2	61832.4	Monde	42484.9	47253.8	53000.6	60203.9	62566.4
Africa	219.5	272.4	361.0	496.3	518.5	Afrique	666.2	688.3	764.2	1377.8	1521.5
Americas	10269.3	12380.3	14361.7	16113.2	15186.7	Amériques	4823.9	4802.8	4907.6	5645.3	6314.8
– Northern America	9819.4	11857.5	13683.4	15465.5	14569.6	– Amérique du Nord	4258.8	4184.8	4326.4	4915.0	5550.0
– LAIA	427.3	493.2	641.3	618.8	589.7	– ALAI	549.8	601.3	552.5	706.4	720.9
– CACM	3.4	6.3	9.1	7.9	9.7	– MCAC	3.0	1.6	2.0	2.1	9.6
– Caribbean	18.0	22.3	25.9	20.0	16.9	– Caraïbes	10.7	11.5	24.0	18.9	31.8
– Rest of America	1.3	1.0	2.0	1.2	0.9	– Autre Amérique	1.6	3.6	2.7	2.9	2.5
Asia excl fmr USSR	18600.5	21026.7	23385.7	24246.4	26054.6	Asie anc. URSS exclus	27021.4	30628.0	34745.5	38846.0	40440.4
– Middle East	1171.4	1083.8	1355.6	1500.1	1447.1	– Moyen–Orient	1252.7	1332.1	1374.9	2110.9	2669.8
Asia former USSR	0.4	1.6	1.7	1.3	0.4	Asie ancienne URSS	3.3	2.8	16.3	6.2	3.8
Europe excl fmr USSR	10084.5	12630.1	15417.4	16255.9	16015.5	Europe anc. URSS exclus	5407.8	5497.3	6396.0	7145.5	7042.6
– European Union	9391.8	11747.3	14407.0	15256.4	15040.6	– Union Européenne	5038.1	5253.6	5885.1	6536.1	6398.0
– Eastern Europe	78.4	98.5	106.2	100.0	145.6	– Europe de l'Est	74.5	87.9	137.8	156.4	194.5
– Rest of Europe	614.3	784.3	904.2	899.4	829.3	– Autre de l'Europe	295.1	155.8	373.1	453.0	450.1
Europe former USSR	16.9	18.2	30.0	18.3	19.3	Europe ancienne URSS	136.1	212.0	133.3	73.6	136.8
Oceania	3160.8	3519.8	3791.8	4116.6	3769.9	Océanie	3734.6	4586.4	5377.0	6317.1	6275.9
Other	60.6	69.1	73.5	152.2	267.5	Autre	691.6	836.1	660.7	792.4	830.8
USA/Etats–Unis d'Amer	9115.1	11049.2	12577.2	14327.6	13642.7	Japan/Japon	10597.9	11701.3	12260.9	12184.3	12463.5
Japan/Japon	8078.0	8869.6	8869.1	7998.4	8457.8	Korea, Republic of	2962.3	3447.3	4488.8	5721.6	4996.1
United Kingdom	2417.0	2974.2	3451.3	3939.7	3944.8	USA/Etats–Unis d'Amer	3418.4	3375.9	3427.5	3896.8	4690.1
Germany/Allemagne	2448.9	2988.8	3828.9	3681.8	3459.9	New Zealand	2508.4	3214.4	3929.5	4432.4	4512.2
China/Chine	1987.7	2472.6	2862.4	3228.2	3513.3	Singapore/Singapour	2219.0	2494.8	2839.6	2479.0	2846.0
New Zealand	2062.8	2479.3	2672.6	2874.1	2743.6	Other Asia n.e.s.	1881.2	2072.8	2433.3	2672.6	2992.5
Other Asia n.e.s.	1557.2	1799.8	1912.7	1992.1	1966.6	China/Chine	1561.0	2061.5	2321.0	3037.2	2949.8
Singapore/Singapour	1089.4	1513.8	1855.0	2092.1	1845.1	China, Hong Kong SAR	1826.8	1894.9	2132.5	2359.3	2774.0
Korea, Republic of	1268.1	1294.8	1672.8	1820.6	2198.9	United Kingdom	1938.1	1732.3	1851.1	2160.0	1803.2
Italy/Italie	970.5	1345.4	1604.3	1808.1	1756.2	Indonesia/Indonésie	1231.9	1447.9	1773.6	2468.8	2512.9
France, Monaco	997.2	1200.4	1403.5	1530.9	1411.6	Malaysia/Malaisie	1068.9	1426.5	1650.6	1733.1	1738.7
Malaysia/Malaisie	704.5	894.1	1158.6	1335.4	1557.5	Thailand/Thaïlande	850.3	1001.0	1287.4	1314.8	1207.4
Indonesia/Indonésie	826.4	760.9	995.9	1340.6	1680.0	Italy/Italie	622.9	838.6	966.0	977.2	1221.7
Sweden/Suède	675.8	898.4	1173.6	1205.6	1139.7	Canada	840.2	808.5	898.7	1018.0	856.2
Canada	704.0	808.2	1106.2	1137.9	926.9	India/Inde	626.3	640.1	816.1	959.0	1255.2
Papua New Guinea	902.2	822.1	865.2	925.7	711.0	Papua New Guinea	625.2	709.0	688.1	971.1	893.1
Thailand/Thaïlande	521.2	642.6	752.0	847.0	987.4	Germany/Allemagne	606.8	712.5	800.2	806.0	788.5
China, Hong Kong SAR	518.7	616.8	752.9	710.2	737.3	Philippines	437.6	530.4	740.8	888.0	975.9
Switzerland,Liechtenst.	503.2	639.9	760.0	730.8	665.2	Areas n.e.s.	691.6	621.6	460.1	535.1	621.6
Saudi Arabia	485.4	411.6	659.6	669.4	599.3	France, Monaco	531.4	558.7	564.9	540.4	672.6
Netherlands/Pays–Bas	445.4	507.8	510.1	579.1	634.1	So. African Customs Un	236.0	320.1	492.8	748.1	762.8
Belgium–Luxembourg	350.9	427.4	573.0	580.6	544.3	Netherlands/Pays–Bas	506.4	539.4	504.3	519.3	445.9
United Arab Emirates	502.1	403.1	414.1	514.7	471.2	Belgium–Luxembourg	363.7	318.5	406.9	646.5	685.4
Finland/Finlande	308.4	371.7	552.4	454.6	509.4	United Arab Emirates	287.2	290.5	317.6	449.6	658.2
India/Inde	276.6	349.0	410.1	441.8	471.8	Iran (Islamic Rep of)	296.3	306.5	258.6	509.8	515.3
Ireland/Irlande	194.2	243.4	346.8	341.7	494.4	Fiji/Fidji	225.2	257.0	312.6	399.0	392.8
Spain/Espagne	151.7	289.5	374.2	394.6	397.2	Saudi Arabia	206.3	229.1	277.9	366.5	342.4
Brazil/Brésil	238.6	285.6	356.8	300.8	276.8	Brazil/Brésil	255.0	201.0	243.1	310.2	279.5
So. African Customs Un	159.9	212.6	274.8	359.6	356.6	Turkey/Turquie	170.6	166.0	210.1	298.4	381.8
Viet Nam	170.8	212.1	212.6	307.6	434.2	Egypt/Egypte	253.8	196.4	90.6	341.0	336.8
Denmark/Danemark	198.5	237.0	245.8	282.3	288.7	Switzerland,Liechtenst.	200.4	92.8	291.5	330.7	299.0
Austria/Autriche	155.0	171.4	225.7	308.3	311.4	Spain/Espagne	190.6	208.5	221.6	216.7	277.4
Israel/Israël	126.0	170.1	222.1	221.2	257.9	Pakistan	195.3	147.2	142.8	204.2	387.0
Philippines	126.1	169.5	171.9	222.0	279.6	Finland/Finlande	64.1	118.8	235.1	251.1	214.4
Fiji/Fidji	107.5	121.2	142.3	211.6	210.2	Special Categories	0.0	214.5	200.6	257.3	209.2
Norway,Svalbard and JM	83.3	111.9	108.4	132.2	125.5	New Caledonia	115.1	110.0	136.9	166.5	143.2
Mexico/Mexique	67.8	86.8	116.0	128.3	141.0	Sweden/Suède	95.5	98.6	132.8	202.9	107.3
Pakistan	97.4	107.4	92.5	113.8	115.9	Viet Nam	72.9	82.8	139.8	159.5	175.3
Qatar	57.3	132.1	126.9	112.5	85.5	Russian Federation	130.8	201.0	108.4	58.4	116.6
Free zones/Zone franches	29.7	39.6	46.8	117.7	226.1	Bangladesh	53.1	88.4	89.9	175.8	188.1

(VALUE AS PERCENTAGE OF WORLD TOTAL)(VALEURS EN POURCENTAGE DU TOTAL MONDIAL)

	1988	1989	1990	1991	1992	1993	1994	1995	1996	1997		1988	1989	1990	1991	1992	1993	1994	1995	1996	1997
Africa	0.5	0.4	0.4	0.3	0.3	0.5	0.5	0.6	0.8	0.8	Afrique	1.4	1.6	1.4	1.2	1.0	1.6	1.5	1.4	2.3	2.4
Americas	25.3	26.7	27.7	26.9	25.4	24.2	24.8	25.0	26.2	24.6	Amériques	13.5	13.0	14.0	12.9	13.0	11.4	10.2	9.3	9.4	10.1
– Northern America	23.9	25.1	26.5	25.8	24.3	23.2	23.8	23.8	25.2	23.6	– Amérique du Nord	12.5	12.1	13.0	11.9	12.0	10.0	8.9	8.2	8.2	8.9
– LAIA	1.3	1.5	1.2	1.1	0.9	1.0	1.0	1.1	1.0	1.0	– ALAI	0.9	0.8	1.0	0.9	0.9	1.3	1.3	1.0	1.2	1.2
– CACM	0.0	0.0	0.0	0.0	0.0	0.0	0.0	0.0	0.0	0.0	– MCAC	0.0	0.0	0.0	0.0	0.0	0.0	0.0	0.0	0.0	0.0
– Caribbean	0.0	0.0	0.0	0.0	0.1	0.0	0.0	0.0	0.0	0.0	– Caraïbes	0.1	0.0	0.0	0.1	0.0	0.0	0.0	0.0	0.0	0.1
– Rest of America	0.0	0.0	0.0	0.0	0.1	0.0	0.0	0.0	0.0	0.0	– Autre Amérique	0.0	0.0	0.0	0.0	0.0	0.0	0.0	0.0	0.0	0.0
Asia excl fmr USSR	40.3	41.2	38.3	39.2	40.7	43.9	42.1	40.7	39.5	42.1	Asie anc. URSS exclus	56.9	57.2	57.3	61.0	59.0	63.6	64.8	65.6	64.5	64.6
– Middle East	2.1	2.7	2.9	2.6	2.5	2.8	2.2	2.4	2.4	2.3	– Moyen–Orient	3.5	3.6	4.0	2.8	2.6	2.9	2.8	2.6	3.5	4.3
Asia former USSR					0.0	0.0	0.0	0.0	0.0	0.0	Asie ancienne URSS					0.0	0.0	0.0	0.0	0.0	0.0
Europe excl fmr USSR	28.7	26.8	27.4	25.3	25.5	23.8	25.3	26.8	26.5	25.9	Europe anc. URSS exclus	17.0	16.7	16.5	14.4	14.8	12.7	11.6	12.1	11.9	11.3
– European Union	26.5	24.8	25.3	23.5	23.6	22.1	23.5	25.1	24.8	24.3	– Union Européenne	15.0	14.5	13.8	12.5	13.6	11.9	11.1	11.1	10.9	10.2
– Eastern Europe	0.4	0.3	0.2	0.2	0.2	0.2	0.2	0.2	0.2	0.2	– Europe de l'Est	1.1	0.8	0.5	0.2	0.3	0.2	0.2	0.3	0.3	0.3
– Rest of Europe	1.7	1.6	1.8	1.6	1.7	1.4	1.6	1.6	1.5	1.3	– Autre de l'Europe	0.9	1.4	2.2	1.7	1.0	0.7	0.3	0.7	0.8	0.7
Europe former USSR	0.1	0.1	0.1	0.1	0.3	0.0	0.0	0.1	0.0	0.0	Europe ancienne URSS	1.7	2.2	0.8	0.9	0.2	0.3	0.4	0.3	0.1	0.2
Oceania	5.1	4.9	6.1	7.0	7.7	7.5	7.1	6.6	6.7	6.1	Océanie	8.1	8.0	8.2	8.0	7.9	8.8	9.7	10.1	10.5	10.0
Other	0.0	0.0	0.1	1.3	0.1	0.1	0.1	0.1	0.2	0.4	Autre	1.4	1.3	1.8	1.6	4.1	1.6	1.8	1.2	1.3	1.3
USA/Etats–Unis d'Amer	21.7	22.7	24.4	24.1	22.7	21.5	22.1	21.9	23.3	22.1	Japan/Japon	27.1	26.7	25.2	27.1	23.5	24.9	24.8	23.1	20.2	19.9
Japan/Japon	20.1	20.3	18.3	16.9	17.3	19.0	17.8	15.4	13.0	13.7	Korea, Republic of	4.7	5.2	5.6	6.1	5.6	7.0	7.3	8.5	9.5	8.0
United Kingdom	7.5	6.8	6.9	6.2	6.2	5.7	6.0	6.0	6.4	6.4	USA/Etats–Unis d'Amer	10.7	10.8	11.4	10.4	10.1	8.0	7.1	6.5	6.5	7.5
Germany/Allemagne				6.0	5.6	5.8	6.0	6.7	6.0	5.6	New Zealand	5.0	5.2	5.2	5.1	5.2	5.9	6.8	7.4	7.4	7.2
China/Chine	2.1	2.4	2.6	3.4	4.0	4.7	5.0	5.0	5.3	5.7	Singapore/Singapour	3.2	3.6	5.0	5.8	7.0	5.2	5.3	5.4	4.1	4.5
New Zealand	4.4	4.1	4.3	4.4	4.4	4.9	5.0	4.7	4.7	4.4	Other Asia n.e.s.	3.5	3.6	3.4	4.2	4.2	4.4	4.4	4.6	4.4	4.8
Other Asia n.e.s.	4.2	4.0	3.4	3.6	3.6	3.7	3.6	3.3	3.2	3.2	China/Chine	2.6	2.5	2.5	2.8	2.9	3.7	4.4	4.4	5.0	4.7
Singapore/Singapour	2.3	2.5	2.4	2.6	2.6	2.6	3.0	3.2	3.4	3.0	China, Hong Kong SAR	5.2	3.5	2.5	3.5	3.9	4.3	4.0	4.0	3.9	4.4
Korea, Republic of	2.6	2.6	2.3	2.4	2.6	3.0	2.6	2.9	3.0	3.6	United Kingdom	3.6	3.6	3.7	3.3	4.1	4.6	3.7	3.5	3.6	2.9
Italy/Italie	3.1	3.0	2.9	2.5	2.2	2.3	2.7	2.8	2.9	2.8	Indonesia/Indonésie	1.5	2.0	2.6	2.6	2.4	2.9	3.1	3.3	4.1	4.0

4. General Imports F.O.B. by Commodities according to the S.I.T.C. (Rev. 2) in million U.S. Dollars
Importations Générales F.O.B. par Produits d'après la C.T.C.I. (Rév. 2) en millions de Dollars E.U.

SITC CTCI	COMMODITY	1994 QUANTITY QUANTITE	1994 VALUE VALEUR	1995 QUANTITY QUANTITE	1995 VALUE VALEUR	1996 QUANTITY QUANTITE	1996 VALUE VALEUR	1997 QUANTITY QUANTITE	1997 VALUE VALEUR	PRODUIT
	ALL COMMODITIES		49918.1		57422.9		61400.2		61832.5	TOUS PRODUITS
0	FOOD AND LIVE ANIMALS		1888.0		2159.0		2276.8		2345.0	ALIMENTS,ANIMAUX VIVANTS
03	FISH AND PREPARATIONS		427.4		444.0		473.6		467.1	POISSONS ET PREPARATIONS
037	FISH ETC PREPD,PRSVD NES	W 43239	165.7	W 40506	162.5	W 43540	174.8	W 40030	160.1	POIS,CRUST,MOL PREPARES
04	CEREALS AND PREPARATIONS		128.5		190.7		165.0		185.2	CEREALES ET PRODUITS
05	VEGETABLES AND FRUIT		364.2		419.5		459.6		430.4	LEGUMES ET FRUITS
07	COFFEE,TEA,COCOA,SPICES		318.4		387.3		379.4		429.2	CAFE,THE,CACAO,EPICES
071	COFFEE AND SUBSTITUTES	W 47286	138.1		200.2		159.0		182.7	CAFE ET SUCCEDANES
09	MISC EDIBLE PRODUCTS		320.8		351.7		398.6		411.8	PREP ALIMENTAIRES DIVERSES
098	EDIBLE PRODCTS,PREPS NES		316.3		348.0		394.2		408.1	PREP ALIMENTAIRES NDA
09809	MISC FOOD PREPRTIONS NES		237.5		258.4		296.0		306.2	PREP ALIMENTAIRES NDA
1	BEVERAGES AND TOBACCO		366.2		373.7		399.8		402.3	BOISSONS ET TABACS
11	BEVERAGES		247.3		252.7		266.9		297.3	BOISSONS
112	ALCOHOLIC BEVERAGES	W 40329	234.9	W 53087	241.9	W 49889	258.5	W 44246	286.4	BOISSONS ALCOOLIQUES
1124	DISTILLED ALCOHOLIC BEVS	W 17294	177.6	W 17613	174.0	W 18731	188.6	W 20078	193.2	ALCOOLS,EAUX-DE-VIE
2	CRUDE MATERLS,EXCL FUELS		1208.3		1296.7		1183.2		1155.1	MAT BRUTES NON COMESTIBLES
24	CORK AND WOOD		442.9		387.5		328.7		342.8	LIEGE ET BOIS
248	WOOD SHAPED,SLEEPERS		441.6	W 597178	385.8	W 513169	326.4	W 525440	341.0	BOIS SIMPLEMENT TRAVAILLES
2482	LUMBER SHAPED CONIFER	W 523405	300.2	W 467301	261.5	W 403478	225.9	W 409700	239.0	CONIFERES SCIES,RABOTES
24821	LUMBER SAWN ETC CONIFER	W 497979	271.4	W 444221	237.1	W 380334	203.7	W 387369	215.2	CONIFERES SCIES LONGITUD
3	MINERAL FUELS ETC		2425.8		2915.9		3871.9		3764.6	COMBUSTIBLES MINERAUX LUB
33	PETROLEUM AND PRODUCTS		2386.9		2867.3		3793.3		3683.4	PETROLE ET DERIVES
333	CRUDE PETROLEUM	MW 13434	1567.8	MW 14842	1882.2	MW 18226	2749.5	MW 19258	2788.4	HUILES BRUTES DE PETROLE
334	PETROLEUM PRODUCTS,REFIN	W 5464289	703.2	W 6509980	876.6	W 5259825	869.0	W 4729381	745.9	PRODUITS RAFFINES
4	ANIMAL,VEGETABLE OIL,FAT		160.6		193.4		213.6		200.6	HUILES,GRAISSES ANIM,VEG
42	FIXED VEGETABLE OIL,FAT		137.3		167.6		185.6		177.8	HUILES VEGETALES FIXES
5	CHEMCLS,RELATED PROD NES		5152.2		6112.2		6840.1		6693.1	PRODUITS CHIMIQUES
51	ORGANIC CHEMICALS		1212.7		1332.4		1517.6		1480.2	PROD CHIMIQ ORGANIQUES
513	CARBOXYLIC ACIDS ETC		166.8	W 124019	228.0		244.3		255.2	ACIDES CARBOXYLIQUES
514	NITROGEN-FNCTN COMPOUNDS	W 89772	371.1	W 89955	395.4	W 95528	497.3	W 98750	484.3	COMPOSES FONCT AZOTEES
5148	OTH NITROGN-FNCTN CMPNDS	W 55699	259.0	W 58196	270.2	W 54465	335.7	W 56643	318.5	AUTRES COMPOSES AZOTES
51482	IMIDE-,IMIDE-FNCT CMPNDS	W 28741	180.1	W 29042	187.6	W 27301	237.6	W 30476	240.1	COMPOSES A FONCTION IMIDE
515	ORG-INORG COMPOUNDS ETC	W 34324	355.6	W 35119	390.2	W 67882	469.0	W 42513	438.2	COMPOSES ORGANO-MINERAUX
5156	HETEROCYCLIC CMPDS ETC	W 7668	154.9	W 6317	162.0	W 7246	189.9	W 6469	212.8	COMPOSES HETEROCYCLIQUES
51569	OTH HETEROCYC CMPDS,ETC	W 6916	152.1	W 5692	159.6	W 6508	185.3	W 5649	207.1	AUT COMP HETEROCYCLIQUES
52	INORGANIC CHEMICALS		324.7		590.0		622.9		470.3	PROD CHIM INORGANIQUES
522	INORG ELEMNTS,OXIDES,ETC	W 1260514	163.4	W 1618562	398.6	W 1613861	410.1	W 1557280	272.1	ELEMENTS INORGANIQUES
5225	INORGANIC BASES ETC NES	W 1105822	79.8	W 1265418	304.3	W 1298032	309.6	W 1228897	173.6	AUTRES BASES OXYDES METAL
52253	SODIUM HYDROXIDE, OTHER	W 1010023	50.8	W 1174153	266.9	W 1127558	260.6	W 1009589	119.3	HYDROXYDE SODIUM AQUEUX
523	OTHR INORG CHEMICALS ETC		151.2		181.7		202.3		187.3	AUT PRODUITS CHIMIQUES INORG
53	DYES,TANNING,COLOUR PROD		257.6		271.9		314.2		311.0	PROD TEINTURE,COLORANTS
533	PIGMENTS,PAINTS,ETC		128.3		146.9		177.8		185.9	PIGMENTS,PEINTURES,VERNIS
541	*MEDICINAL,PHARM PRODUCT		1100.7		1252.3		1516.5		1642.1	PROD MEDICINAUX PHARMACEUT
5417	MEDICAMENTS		802.2		934.9		1164.9		1251.3	MEDICAMENTS
54179	— CONTNG OTH SUBSTANCES		686.8		781.2		954.8		1047.2	MED CONT AUT SUBSTANCES
55	PERFUME,CLEANING ETC PRD		403.1		443.1		486.3		498.7	PROD POUR PARFUM,TOILETTE
553	PERFUMERY,COSMETICS,ETC		248.9		259.5		279.9		298.2	PRODUITS DE PARFUMERIE
562	*FERTILIZERS,MANUFACTURE	W 2123129	323.3	W 2257960	432.3	W 2806650	584.3	W 2757491	489.8	ENGRAIS MANUFACTURES
5621	CHEM NITROGENOUS FERTLZR	W 740990	109.2	W 678586	143.5	W 966724	202.0	W 1058523	175.8	ENGRAIS AZOTES
5629	FERTILIZERS NES	W 776796	137.0	W 869868	188.5	W 1190756	279.1	W 978526	207.5	ENGRAIS NDA
56292	NITROG-PHOS FERTILZR NES	W 743454	124.4	W 833279	173.7	W 1162472	262.3	W 943899	189.0	ENGRAIS NDA CONT N P
58	PLASTIC MATERIALS ETC		921.5		1120.6		1062.8		1066.1	MAT PLAST ARTIFICIELLES
582	PROD OF CONDENSATION ETC	W 124682	283.3	W 143325	374.5	W 142250	344.9	W 159141	327.3	PROD CONDENS,POLYCOND
5823	ALKYDS,OTHER POLYESTERS	W 68125	137.3	W 85661	213.3	W 84855	183.3	W 93846	163.2	ALKYDES ET AUT POLYESTERS
583	POLYMERIZATION ETC PRODS		574.4	W 353706	685.8		659.7		686.9	PROD POLYMERISATION
5839	OTH POLYMRZTION ETC PROD		219.7	W 75352	243.6	W 78428	242.7	W 87911	245.4	AUT PROD POLYMER COPOLYM
59	CHEMICAL MATERIALS NES		588.0		649.1		706.3		712.1	MAT PROD CHIMIQUES NDA
598	MISCEL CHEM PRODUCTS NES		430.7		457.0		473.4		453.3	PROD DIV INDUST CHIM NDA
5989	CHEM PRODUCTS,PREPS NES		270.7		315.2		324.6		318.4	PROD PREP CHIMIQUES NDA
59899	OTH CHEM PRODS,PREPS,NES		188.8		222.0		235.8		230.1	AUT PRODUITS CHIMIQUES NDA
6	BASIC MANUFACTURES		7406.7		8495.2		8414.5		8641.6	ART MANUFACTURES
62	RUBBER MANUFACTURES NES		732.9		806.5		877.0		848.0	CAOUTCHOUC MANUFACTURE
625	RUBBER TYRES, TUBES ETC	MN 17772	457.1	MN 17741	517.0	MN 17988	565.5	MN 17151	536.4	PNEUS CAOUTCHOUC VULCANISE
6259	OTH TYRES,TYRE CASES,ETC	MN 10302	159.4	MN 9958	177.0	MN 10326	209.6	MN 9484	202.0	AUTRES PNEUS RECHAPES FLAPS
62599	TYRES NES,TYRE CASES,ETC	N 4921581	146.1	N 4789688	164.7	N 5132324	195.8	N 4675744	189.8	PNEUS,FLAPS
628	RUBBER ARTICLES NES		183.5		193.3		212.7		212.8	OUVRAGES CAOUTCHOUC NDA
63	WOOD,CORK MANUFACTRS NES		192.9		206.0		217.7		242.4	OUVRAGES LIEGE ET BOIS
64	PAPER,PAPERBOARD AND MFR		1236.2		1558.3		1423.4		1394.8	PAPIERS,CARTONS & OUVRAGES
641	PAPER AND PAPERBOARD		1023.5		1323.5		1182.0		1152.0	PAPIERS ET CARTONS
6411	NEWSPRINT	W 234042	119.5	W 288677	193.4	W 266785	205.6	W 237752	141.0	PAPIER JOURNAL
6412	PRINTG,WRITING PAPER NES	W 440910	375.2	W 488219	522.9	W 395354	403.5	W 496733	437.6	PAPIERS POUR L'IMPRESSION
64122	— COATED,IMPREGNATD ETC	W 394630	334.4	W 422955	449.5	W 328086	335.2	W 414818	357.6	PAPIERS IMPRESSION COUCHES
6415	PAPER,PAPERBRD,BULK,NES	W 210453	173.2	W 231627	224.1	W 190232	200.2	W 210823	183.8	PAPIERS,CARTONS ROULEAUX
64159	OTHER PAPER ETC,BULK,NES	W 189329	148.2	W 196499	196.7	W 168299	171.8	W 186199	157.0	AUT PAPIER ROULEAUX FEUILLES
6418	COATED ETC PAPER NES BLK	W 166473	199.4		217.0	W 125537	204.1	W 171219	230.1	PAP,CARTONS COUCHES,ENDUITS
64189	COATED PAPER ETC NES	W 127254	152.5	W 87493	155.4	W 82327	144.8	W 105597	158.0	PAPIERS,CARTONS COUCHES
642	PAPER,ETC,PRECUT,ARTS OF		212.7		234.9		241.5		242.9	PAP,CARTONS DECOUPES
65	TEXTILE YARN,FABRICS,ETC		1736.0		1791.5		1819.6		1771.5	FILS,TISSUS,ARTICLES TEXTILE
651	TEXTILE YARN	W 122096	474.7	W 95010	420.3	W 93897	395.0	W 93418	377.7	FILS TEXTILES
6514	SYN FIB YRN,BULK,MONOFIL	W 41160	171.3	W 36710	162.2	W 37525	152.2	W 38011	143.7	FILS CONT 85% FIB TEXT SYNTH
652	COTTON FABRICS,WOVEN	A 212315	223.2	A 184368	217.0	A 211896	240.9	A 182037	211.2	TISSUS DE COTON
6522	WOVEN COTTON BLEACHD,ETC	A 175803	197.7	A 146912	187.0	A 169829	207.7	A 145056	182.7	TISSUS COTON BLANCHIS ETC
65224	BLCHED COTTON FABRIC NES	A 167251	180.4	A 134916	163.2	A 154245	177.1	A 130456	153.3	AUT TIS PLUS 85% COT BLANCHI
653	WOVN MAN-MADE FIB FABRIC	A 232366	336.3	A 250224	365.3		326.0		310.8	TISSUS FIBRES SYNTH,ARTIF
6531	CONT SYNT WEAVES NONPILE	A 109719	157.9	A 120766	170.3	A 113908	151.8	A 108020	140.7	TISSUS FIBRES SYNTH CONTINUE
657	SPECIAL TXTL FABRC,PRODS		173.2		198.9		205.7		202.8	TISSUS SPECIAUX
658	TEXTILE ARTICLES NES		199.7		220.8		245.8		269.1	ART FACONNES MAT TEXTILES
66	NONMETAL MINERAL MFS NES		842.7		910.1		970.5		999.3	ART MIN NON METALLIQUES
662	CLAY,REFRACTORY BLDG PRD		200.6		213.3		199.2		194.5	MAT CONST REFRACTAIRES
6624	BRICKS ETC NONREFRACTORY		161.7		167.8		152.0		156.2	BRIQUES ETC CERAM NON REFR
66245	GLAZED CERAMIC SETTS ETC	A 20336	151.9	A 20623	154.7	A 18641	139.4	A 21682	146.3	AUT CARREAUX CERAMIQUE
667	PEARL,PREC-,SEMI-P STONE		105.1		112.8		155.5		203.2	PERLES, PIERRES GEMMES
67	IRON AND STEEL		820.8		1097.9		1008.7		1116.0	FER ET ACIER
674	IRN,STL UNIV,PLATE,SHEET	W 704792	298.3	W 420627	344.9	W 385544	347.8	W 483795	417.5	LARGES PLATS,TOLES
678	IRON,STL TUBES,PIPES,ETC		211.8		318.3		312.1		319.5	TUBES,TUYAUX EN FONTE,FER
68	NON-FERROUS METALS		430.7		510.3		471.7		513.0	METAUX NON FERREUX
682	COPPER EXC CEMENT COPPER		143.6		211.4		151.1		136.3	CUIVRE
684	ALUMINIUM	W 48159	157.8	W 54089	196.7	W 68413	228.1	W 73512	240.3	ALUMINIUM
6842	ALUMINIUM,ALLOYS WORKED	W 44561	151.0	W 47188	181.3	W 55327	199.3	W 69351	230.8	ALUMINIUM,ALLIAGES OUVRE
69	METAL MANUFACTURES NES		1273.5		1454.7		1456.9		1591.0	ART MANUFACT EN METAL NDA
694	STL,COPPR NAILS,NUTS,ETC		159.5		182.7		169.9		179.1	CLOUS,VIS,ECROUS

4. General Imports F.O.B. by Commodities according to the S.I.T.C. (Rev. 2) in million U.S. Dollars
Importations Générales F.O.B. par Produits d'après la C.T.C.I. (Rév. 2) en millions de Dollars E.U.

SITC CTCI	COMMODITY	1994		1995		1996		1997		PRODUIT
		QUANTITY QUANTITE	VALUE VALEUR	QUANTITY QUANTITE	VALUE VALEUR	QUANTITY QUANTITE	VALUE VALEUR	QUANTITY QUANTITE	VALUE VALEUR	
695	TOOLS		261.9		315.3		312.9		327.1	OUTILS A MAIN
699	BASE METAL MFRS NES		536.7		598.1		582.3		635.1	ART MANUFACTURES MET NDA
6991	LOCKSMITHS WARES,ETC		203.9		213.4		201.7		204.9	ARTICLES DE SERRURERIE
7	MACHINES,TRANSPORT EQUIP		23008.3		26938.7		28777.4		28652.9	MACHINES MATERIEL TRANSPORT
71	POWER GENERATING EQUIPMT		1289.2		1368.6		1595.2		1448.0	MACHINES GENERATRICES
713	INTRNL COMBUS PSTN ENGIN		685.7		695.0		771.2		736.5	MOTEURS EXPL COMB INT, PIECE
7138	PISTON ENGINES NES	N 320036	138.1	N 301831	132.2	N 320031	190.4	N 299961	202.4	MOTEURS A PISTONS NDA
7139	PISTON ENGINE PARTS NES		279.2		314.0		314.7		288.0	PIECES POUR 713.2,3,8
714	ENGINES AND MOTORS NES		186.2		218.2		276.2		237.3	MOTEURS NON ELECTRIQUES
716	ROTATING ELECTRIC PLANT		294.3		363.9		416.0		356.1	APP ELECTR ROTATIFS,PIECES
7162	AC MTRS,GENRTRS,GEN SETS		218.4	N 8438164	219.6	MN 17953	217.0	MN 18750	221.0	MOTEURS ELECTRIQUES
72	MACHS FOR SPCL INDUSTRYS		2375.2		2801.5		3085.1		2844.6	MAC SPECIALES POUR INDUST
721	AGRIC MACHY,EXC TRACTORS		233.3		241.5		397.7		383.3	MACHINES AGRICOLES
7212	HARVESTING ETC MACHINES		163.7		160.0		290.0		270.4	ENGINS POUR LA RECOLTE
722	TRACTORS NON–ROAD	N 25118	222.4	N 10680	248.2	N 13095	353.2	N 14342	379.2	TRACTEURS
7224	WHEELED TRACTORS NES	N 25063	218.8	N 10608	241.9	N 12941	336.4	N 14138	358.2	TRACTEURS A ROUES
723	CIVIL ENGNEERG EQUIP ETC		663.4		690.4		762.4		662.8	APPAREILS DE GENIE CIVIL
7234	CONST,MINING MACHNRY NES	N 163772	612.9	N 195336	635.0	N 35019	687.6	N 13812	583.0	MACH POUR LA CONST, MINES
72342	SLFPRP SHOVELS,EXCAVATRS	N 5379	394.0	N 4976	412.5	N 4736	368.1	N 6267	365.1	PELLES MECANIQUES
724	TEXTILE,LEATHER MACHNRY		237.8		230.7		188.6		164.6	MACH POUR INDUSTRIE TEXTILE
726	PRINTG,BKBINDG MACHY,PTS		290.5		455.7		279.2		215.0	MACHINES POUR IMPRIMERIE
7264	PRINTING PRESSES	N 17594	139.7	N 81858	207.4	N 6717	128.7	N 616	90.2	MACHINES A IMPRIMER
72641	ROTARY PRINTING PRESSES	N 17594	139.7	N 81858	207.4	N 6717	128.7	N 616	90.2	MACH IMPRIMER ROTATIVES
728	OTH MACHY FOR SPCL INDUS		544.3		698.2		900.3		831.5	AUT MACH IND PARTICULIERES
7284	MACHY FOR SPCL INDUS NES		401.8		531.7		705.9		644.6	MACH SPEC IND PARTICUL.
72848	OTH MCHY WITH INDIV FNCT	N 1064612	215.3	N 1369773	279.7		443.9		316.6	AUTRES MACHINES NDA
73	METALWORKING MACHINERY		315.6		406.9		462.7		432.3	MACH TRAVAIL DES METAUX
736	METALWORKING MACH–TOOLS	N 1789566	218.7	N 1718326	300.0	N 2036860	357.8	N 2140992	344.4	MACH–OUTILS TRAVAIL METAUX
74	GENRL INDUSTRL MACHY NES		2884.7		3295.4		3669.3		3838.9	MACH APP INDUSTRIE
741	HEATING,COOLING EQUIPMNT		438.2		469.7		527.0		646.6	MACH CHAUFFAGE,PIECES
7415	AIR–CONDITIONING MACHNRY	N 344306	157.7	N 431858	190.6		178.1	N 597007	239.9	GROUPES CONDITION AIR
7416	HEATING,COOLING EQU NES		151.6		151.6		214.4		226.3	APP CHANGEMENT TEMP
742	PUMPS FOR LIQUIDS ETC		219.3		249.4		271.5		251.6	POMPES MOTO–POMPES
743	PUMPS NES,CENTRFUGES ETC		540.1		596.7		645.3		654.4	POMPES COMPRES,VENT ETC
7431	PUMPS FOR GASES ETC	N 3086763	255.7	N 3172215	284.3	N 3379538	306.5	N 3608753	291.6	POMPES AIR A VIDE,COMPRES
7436	GAS,LIQUID FILTERS ETC	MN 24898	147.0	MN 30897	159.5	MN 45196	183.0	MN 33696	194.4	APP POUR FILT DES LIQUIDES
744	MECHANICAL HANDLING EQU		421.2		559.5		685.9		723.7	EQUIP MANUTENTION PIECES
7441	FORK LIFT TRCKS,ETC,PTS		134.1		188.6		190.9		206.8	CHARIOTS POUR USINES ETC
74411	FORK LIFT TRUCKS ETC	N 7858	133.9	N 9189	188.4	N 9316	190.6	N 10448	206.5	CHARIOTS POUR LES GARES
7442	LIFTING,LOADING MACH NES	N 688090	160.9	N 610230	190.8	N 625582	280.8	N 690189	287.8	APP LEVAGE,MANUTENTION
74428	OTH HANDLING ETC MCH NES	N 496726	118.0	N 408927	137.9	N 417308	203.8	N 463770	206.8	AUT APP LEVAGE ETC
7449	PTS NES OF MACHY OF 7442		126.3		180.2		214.3		229.2	PIECES DU 744.2
745	NONELEC MACHY,TOOLS NES		374.1		424.8		445.6		469.6	AUT MACH NON ELEC,PIECES
7452	OTH NONELEC MCHS,PTS NES		291.6		350.4		355.8		385.9	AUT MACH NON ELEC,PIECES
749	NONELEC MACH PTS,ACC NES		892.2		995.6		1094.2		1093.2	PIECES MACH NON ELEC NDA
7491	BALL,ROLLER,ETC BEARINGS	MN 43118	164.2	MN 51682	179.1	MN 60507	196.0	MN 58786	178.0	ROULEMENTS BILLES ETC
7492	COCKS,VALVES ETC NES	MN 67649	353.0	MN 87800	376.0	MN 104266	402.6	MN 117393	434.2	ART ROB,SIM POUR TUYAUX
7493	SHAFT,CRANK,PULLEY ETC	MN 18748	258.7	MN 29573	299.9	MN 28874	348.0		319.3	ARBRES TRANS,VILEBREQUINS
75	OFFICE MACHNES,ADP EQUIP		3813.0		4424.6		4587.2		4784.5	MACH BUREAU TRAIT AUTOM
751	OFFICE MACHINES	N 7077236	281.5	N 7077293	303.8	N 8079831	265.4	N 7917574	259.1	MACH,APPAREILS DE BUREAU
7518	OFFICE MACHINES NES	N 3579859	232.4	N 3527860	251.1	N 4051497	206.9	N 3963175	216.3	MACH,APP DE BUREAU NDA
75182	PHOTO,THERMOCOPY APPARAT	N 82399	176.5	N 117524	194.5	N 71836	159.1	N 75648	158.1	APPAREILS DE PHOTOCOPIE
752	AUTOMTIC DATA PROC EQUIP	N 5781916	2094.1	N 7096906	2578.3	N 8648220	2791.5	MN 9812	2999.2	MACH TRAIT INFORMATION
7522	DIGITAL COMPUTERS	N 444811	701.9	N 459949	801.3	N 4387058	1757.3	N 500430	778.9	MACH DIGITALES COMPLETES
7523	DIGITL CENTRL PROCESSORS	N 243865	290.9	N 342604	411.5	N 409800	250.1	N 224912	434.6	UNITES CENTRALES
7524	DIGITL CENTRL STOR UNITS	N 2696014	473.8	N 3190185	587.7	N 1466769	273.0	N 3202778	615.7	UNITES MEMOIRE CENTRALES
7525	ADP PERIPHERAL UNITS	N 1855174	511.6	N 2553951	634.9	N 1632528	356.5	N 4073291	782.5	UNITES PERIPHERIQUES
7528	OFF–LINE DATA PROC EQUIP	N 541966	115.8	N 550213	142.7	N 751978	154.4	N 1809983	384.0	MACH AUXIL TRAIT INFORM
759	OFFICE,ADP MCH PTS,ACCES		1437.6		1542.5		1530.3		1526.2	PIECES DU 751 ET 752
7599	ACCTG,ETC,ADP MCH PTS,AC		1310.2		1403.5		1399.2		1382.3	PIECES DU 751 ET 752
76	TELECOMM,SOUND EQUIPMENT		2106.4		2731.4		2916.5		2791.5	EQUIPMENT DE TELECOM
761	TELEVISION RECEIVERS	N 936631	221.4	N 1341436	285.3	N 1697571	376.3	N 1299575	318.9	RECEPTEURS DE TELEVISION
7611	COLOUR TV RECEIVERS	N 916078	218.7	N 1313917	282.6	N 1672607	373.6	N 1271633	315.8	RECEPTEURS COULEUR
762	RADIO BROADCAST RECEIVRS	N 5227619	297.6	N 4934476	296.4	N 5401623	320.0	N 5162885	296.7	RECEPTEURS RADIODIFFUSION
763	SOUND RECORDRS,PHONOGRPH	N 1872970	258.6	N 2176817	284.4	N 2421520	346.9	N 2578744	358.6	PHONO,APP ENREGISTREMENT
7638	OTHR SOUND APPARATUS ETC	N 1838510	257.2	N 2154568	283.0	N 2388417	345.2	N 2544747	356.9	AUT APP D'ENREGIS,REPROD
76381	TV IMAGE,SND RECRDRS ETC	N 773386	176.2	N 857379	192.3	N 1088890	248.1	N 1172702	269.0	APP ENREG,REPRO IMAG,SON
764	TELECOM EQPT,PTS,ACC NES		1329.0		1865.5		1873.4		1817.6	EQUIP TELECOM,PIECES
7641	LINE TELEPHONE,ETC EQUIP		326.1		368.4		401.0		462.5	APP TELEPHON PAR FIL
7643	TV,RADIO TRANSMITTRS ETC		431.2		745.8		692.5	N 2982274	680.7	APP EMET TELE RADIO
7648	TELECOMM EQUIPMENT NES		182.8		216.3		181.8		87.0	APP TELECOM NDA
7649	PTS NES OF EQUIPMT OF 76		312.2		446.1		498.7		484.1	PIECES DE LA DIV 76
76491	PTS NES OF APPAR OF 7641		125.4		234.2		240.7		262.1	PIECES POUR 764.1
76493	TELECOMM EQUIPMT PTS NES		167.8		191.1		236.3		203.9	PIECES 761,762,764.3,8
77	ELECTRIC MACHNRY NES ETC		3237.1		3944.6		4012.3		3817.8	MACH APP ELECT NDA
771	ELECTRIC POWER MACHY NES		151.2		201.7		246.7		223.3	MACH PROD,TRANS ELECTR
7712	OTH ELEC POWER MACHY NES		120.0		161.2		207.3		181.2	AUT APP PROD TRANSF ELEC
772	SWITCHGEAR ETC,PARTS NES		601.6	MN 1453125	626.8		653.5		642.4	APP COUPURE,SECT ETC
7721	SWITCHGEAR ETC		525.8	MN 580170	539.9		576.8		568.5	APP COUPURE,SECTIONMNT
773	ELECTR DISTRIBUTNG EQUIP		236.2		313.8		297.4		290.9	EQUIPMT DISTRIBUTION ELECT
7731	INSULATED WIRE,CABLE ETC		217.6		293.7		276.8		273.5	FILS,CABLES ISOLES ELECT
774	ELECTRO–MEDCL,XRAY EQUIP		212.0		230.2		235.2		212.6	APPAREILS MEDICAUX
775	HOUSEHOLD TYPE EQUIP NES		478.5		524.2		570.6		618.4	MACH,APP USAGE DOMESTQUE
7758	ELECTRO–THERMIC APPL NES		202.3		232.1		239.0		272.7	APP ELECTROTHERMIQ NDA
77586	ELECTROTHERM DOM APP NES	N 4947228	142.7	N 4735296	167.1	N 5604430	170.5	N 6084977	197.8	APP ELECTRO THERMIQUES
776	TRANSISTORS,VALVES,ETC	MN 445988	678.8		967.6		887.1		823.2	LAMPES,TUBES,VALVES
7764	ELECTRONIC MICROCIRCUITS	MN 150867	578.6	MN 168280	854.0	MN 146322	783.7	MN 182180	727.4	MICROSTRUCTURES ELECTRON
778	ELECTRICAL MACHINERY NES		879.1		1080.5		1122.0		1007.4	AUTRES MACH ELECT NDA
7781	BATTERIES,ACCUMULATORS		143.7		170.6		191.2		190.9	PILES ET ACCUMULATEURS
7783	AUTOMOTIVE ELECTR EQUIP	MN 47223	149.9	MN 43905	152.8		156.7	MN 55683	144.6	EQUIP ELECT MOTEURS EXPL
7788	OTH ELEC MACHY,EQUIP NES		381.6		528.2		547.3		453.8	AUT MACH APP ELEC NDA
77886	OTH ELEC MACHINERY NES	N 6906729	201.8	MN 20580	326.4	MN 34921	322.0	MN 22924	259.0	AUT MACH APP ELECTRIQUES
78	ROAD VEHICLES		5839.0		6252.0		6455.3		7108.8	VEHICULES ROUTIERS
781	PASS MOTOR VEH EXC BUSES	N 247018	2802.5	N 283542	3208.6	N 305869	3312.1	N 367750	3930.1	AUTO TRANSPORT PERSONNES
782	LORRIES,SPCL MTR VEH NES	N 128026	1336.8	N 119853	1383.8	N 112214	1392.3	N 112117	1383.0	VEHICULES SPECIAUX,MARCH
7821	LORRIES,TRUCKS	N 127926	1322.6	N 119671	1355.4	N 111990	1353.2	N 111847	1331.5	VEHICULES TRANSP MARCHAND
783	ROAD MOTOR VEHICLES NES		162.0		154.5		144.4		135.9	VEHICULES ROUTIERS NDA
784	MOTOR VEH PRTS,ACCES NES		1244.3		1168.6		1239.4		1290.0	PIECES 722,781,782,783
7849	OTHER MOTOR VEHCL PARTS		1195.9		1118.0		1187.9		1237.2	PIECES 722,781,782,783
785	CYCLES,ETC MOTRZD OR NOT		238.2		282.0		302.4		301.7	MOTOCYCLES SCOOTERS
7851	MOTORCYCLES ETC	N 47895	152.7	N 48652	188.1	N 51050	189.3	N 59780	190.8	MOTO VELO MOTEUR AUXIL

4. General Imports F.O.B. by Commodities according to the S.I.T.C. (Rev. 2) in million U.S. Dollars
Importations Générales F.O.B. par Produits d'après la C.T.C.I. (Rév. 2) en millions de Dollars E.U.

SITC CTCI	COMMODITY	1994 QUANTITY QUANTITE	1994 VALUE VALEUR	1995 QUANTITY QUANTITE	1995 VALUE VALEUR	1996 QUANTITY QUANTITE	1996 VALUE VALEUR	1997 QUANTITY QUANTITE	1997 VALUE VALEUR	PRODUIT
79	OTHR TRANSPORT EQUIPMENT		1148.5		1714.2		1994.2		1586.9	AUTRE MATERIEL TRANSPORT
792	AIRCRAFT ETC		981.2		1111.3		1709.0		1167.3	APP NAVIGATION AERIENNE
7923	AIRCRFT NES2000–15000KG	N 91	88.8	N 90	123.6	N 110	208.1	N 100	126.3	AERODYNES 2000 A 15000 KG
7924	AIRCRFT NES OVER 15000KG	N 17	279.4	N 13	285.5	N 25	796.0	N 12	322.3	AERODYNES PLUS 15000 KG
7929	AIRCRAFT PARTS NES		542.6		629.5		665.3		668.2	PIECES DU 792
793	SHIPS AND BOATS ETC	N 63597	86.8	N 81087	524.7	N 80412	240.4	N 87707	380.0	NAVIRES BATEAUX,ETC
7932	SHIPS AND BOATS NES	N 35368	34.6	N 65510	311.6	N 63996	78.9	N 76442	239.9	NAVIRES ET BATEAUX
79322	TANKERS OF ALL KINDS			N 1	268.4			N 1	40.1	BATEAUX–CITERNES
7938	TUGS,SPECIAL VESSELS ETC	N 27326	27.3	N 15398	189.0	N 16239	125.3	N 10844	117.1	REMORQUEURS,BATEAUX SPEC
79382	SPECL PURPOSE VESSLS ETC	N 18621	21.2	N 12993	180.9	N 15	120.9	N 6477	106.7	BAT–PHARES,–POMPES,DRAGUES
8	MISC MANUFACTURED GOODS		7513.6		8096.5		8657.8		9143.5	ART MANUFACTURES DIVERS
821	*FURNITURE,PARTS THEREOF		345.8		369.7		423.1		496.9	MEUBLES ET PIECES
8211	CHAIRS,SEATS AND PARTS		141.1		150.2		171.6		200.1	SIEGES ET PIECES
8219	FURNITURE AND PARTS NES		146.8		168.9		195.4		231.4	AUTRES MEUBLES ET PIECES
831	*TRAVEL GOODS,HANDBAGS		230.1		265.6		267.9		265.0	ARTICLES DE VOYAGE ETC
83109	OTHER TRAVEL BAGS,CASES		150.5		177.1		177.6		183.0	AUT CONTENANTS SIMILAIRES
84	CLOTHING AND ACCESSORIES		1140.3		1268.5		1418.6		1525.6	VETEMENTS
842	MENS OUTERWEAR NOT KNIT	MN 25653	165.5		194.5	MN 29060	223.7	MN 32143	238.3	VET DESSUS POUR HOMMES
843	WOMENS OUTERWEAR NONKNIT		187.7		220.6	MN 48214	279.0	MN 52591	283.3	VET DESSUS FEMMES MAT TEX
845	OUTERWEAR KNIT NONELASTC		267.8	MN 72068	277.6	MN 68608	302.2	MN 80777	359.9	VET DESSOUS,ACCES BONNET
8451	— JERSEYS,PULLOVERS ETC	MN 23730	154.6	MN 24306	157.2	MN 23148	165.8	MN 26793	184.6	CHANDAILS,PULL–OVERS ETC
846	UNDER GARMENTS KNITTED		196.1		211.5		231.1		278.8	SOUS VETS DE BONNETERIE
851	*FOOTWEAR	MP 58881	382.1	MP 53434	384.2	MP 51717	431.8	MP 56182	440.2	CHAUSSURES
85102	FOOTWEAR LEATHER	MP 35638	295.8	MP 31566	292.0	MP 31429	339.1	MP 33410	344.3	CHAUS SEMELLES EN CUIR
87	PRECISION INSTRUMNTS NES		1292.5		1408.3		1489.8		1588.6	INSTRUM,APPAR SCIENT NDA
872	MEDICAL INSTRUMENTS NES		277.6		310.2		356.3		384.5	INSTR,APP MEDIC–CHIR NDA
87202	OTH MEDICAL INSTRUMENTS		243.9		266.4		311.2		342.6	INSTRUM,APP MEDECINE
874	MEASURNG,CONTROLNG INSTR		904.0		978.3		1008.9		1074.0	INSTRUMENTS DE MESURE
8743	GAS,LIQUID CONTROL INSTR	MN 11700	310.2	MN 13126	323.2	MN 15134	342.0	MN 12864	327.2	APP,INSTR MESURE FLUIDES
8748	ELEC MEAS,CONTRL EQU NES	N 3107897	211.1	N 3244316	225.8	N 3628332	235.9	N 4859354	238.7	APP ELEC ELECTRO MESURE
87483	OTH ELCTRNC MEAS ETC EQU	N 2625727	194.8	N 2719295	206.1	N 3190616	215.1	N 4394529	218.5	AUT APP ELECTRO DE MESURE
88	PHOTO EQU,OPTICL GDS ETC		796.8		867.1		922.9		925.8	APP,FOURN PHOTO,OP,MONTR
882	PHOTO,CINEMA SUPPLIES		365.6		392.4		436.3		436.6	PRODUITS PHOTO,CINEMA
8822	PHOTO FILM EXC DEV CINMA		294.1		314.5		359.8		376.9	PLAQUES,PELLICULES,FILMS
88222	PHOTO FILM ROLL UNEXPOSD	A 25071	155.6	A 23244	178.8	A 24671	216.0	A 25454	237.8	PEL SENSIB PERF OU NON
885	WATCHES AND CLOCKS		166.0		181.5		167.9		168.2	HORLOGERIE
89	MISC MANUFCTRD GOODS NES		3181.5		3378.1		3538.0		3720.8	ART MANUFACTURES DIVERS
892	PRINTED MATTER		657.0		662.1		666.5		676.9	IMPRIMES
8921	PRINTED BOOKS,GLOBES,ETC	MN 157313	379.1	MN 181478	390.8	MN 186878	401.5	MN 163866	407.2	LIVRES,BROCHURES,CARTES
89211	PRINTED BOOKS,PAMPHLETS	MN 152262	371.3	MN 176198	383.4	MN 181308	393.1	MN 156827	399.7	LIVRES,BROCHURES
8922	NEWSPAPERS,PERIODICALS	MN 107447	162.3	MN 100997	158.2	MN 98441	148.6	MN 101497	158.6	JOURNAUX ET PERIODIQUES
893	ARTICLES OF PLASTIC NES		670.6		768.8		783.8		810.2	OUVRAGES EN MAT DIVIS 58
8931	PLSTC PACKG CONTNRS,LIDS		152.9		189.3		192.7		198.6	ART TRANSP EMBALLAGE ETC
8939	MISC PLASTIC ARTICLES		503.5		563.5		575.3		596.6	ART DIVERS EN MAT DIV 58
89399	OTHR PLASTC ARTICLES NES		429.4		483.4		497.6		513.5	AUT OUV MAT DIV 58
894	TOYS,SPORTING GOODS,ETC		554.6		618.6		736.4		799.0	VOITURES ENFANTS,JOUETS
8942	TOYS,INDOOR GAMES ETC		380.8		429.8		503.3		553.0	JOUETS,JEUX ETC
89423	TOYS NES	MN 301477	192.2	MN 360268	199.1		233.8		257.7	JOUETS,MODELES REDUITS
89424	INDOOR GAME EQUIPMENT		132.9		168.3		200.6		226.9	ART,JEUX DE SOCIETE
8947	OTH SPORT GDS,FAIR AMUSM		144.1		155.3		181.4		190.8	AUT ART DE SPORT
898	MUSICAL INSTRUMENTS,PTS		706.7		677.3		643.5		669.2	INSTRUMENTS DE MUSIQUE
8983	SOUND RECRDNG TAPE,DISCS	MN 214691	649.6	MN 214611	612.6	MN 198776	576.3	MN 223918	599.4	SUPPORTS SON POUR 763
89832	RECORDED DISCS,TAPES ETC	MN 55340	520.1	MN 50603	478.8	MN 40455	436.1	MN 41520	455.6	DISQUES,PHONO,BANDES
899	OTHER MANUFACTURED GOODS		270.2		313.2		335.8		371.3	AUT ART MANUF DIVERS NDA
8996	HEARING,ORTHOPAEDIC AIDS		124.3		151.2		167.5		198.2	APPAREILS D'ORTHOPEDIE
89962	ORTHOPAEDIC ETC GOODS		118.0		145.4		162.3		192.4	APPAREILS D'ORTHOPEDIE
9	GOODS NOT CLASSD BY KIND		788.9		841.9		765.5		834.4	ART TRANSACT NON CLASSES
971	*GOLD,NON MONETARY NES		566.8		542.4		503.4		589.5	OR NON MONETAIRE
97101	NONMON GLD UNWRT,SEMIMFD		565.6		538.8		501.2		589.4	OR,ALLIAGES D'OR BRUTS

5. General Exports F.O.B. by Commodities according to the S.I.T.C. (Rev. 2) in million U.S. Dollars
Exportations Générales F.O.B. par Produits d'après la C.T.C.I. (Rév. 2) en millions de Dollars E.U.

SITC CTCI	COMMODITY	1994 QUANTITY QUANTITE	1994 VALUE VALEUR	1995 QUANTITY QUANTITE	1995 VALUE VALEUR	1996 QUANTITY QUANTITE	1996 VALUE VALEUR	1997 QUANTITY QUANTITE	1997 VALUE VALEUR	PRODUIT
	ALL COMMODITIES		47253.9		53000.6		60203.9		62566.5	TOUS PRODUITS
0	FOOD AND LIVE ANIMALS		9801.3		9678.1		12365.7		12751.9	ALIMENTS,ANIMAUX VIVANTS
001	*LIVE ANIMALS FOR FOOD	W 391625	256.3	W 481207	417.2	W 558625	503.4	W 616434	541.2	ANIMAUX VIVANTS
0011	BOVINE SPECIES,LIVE	W 102615	111.4	W 181920	216.7	W 264920	306.7	W 348973	352.1	ESPECE BOVINE
00119	— OTHR THAN FR BREEDING	W 99508	105.7	W 169089	198.2	W 258525	294.5	W 336692	337.5	BOVINS NON REPRODUCTEURS
0012	SHEEP AND GOATS,LIVE	W 287762	120.2	W 297892	164.1	W 292477	164.2	W 265932	147.2	ESPECES OVINE ET CAPRINE
00121	SHEEP,LIVE	W 286735	119.2	W 297352	163.4	W 291078	162.4	W 263358	144.8	ESPECE OVINE
01	MEAT AND PREPARATIONS		2783.1		2622.9		2264.5		2554.6	VIANDES ET PREPARATIONS
011	MEAT FRESH,CHILLD,FROZEN	W 1182681	2749.6	W 1114350	2578.3	W 1059243	2219.0	W 1218240	2512.4	VIANDES FRAICHES,REF,CONGE
0111	BOVINE MEAT FRESH,FROZEN	W 823141	2184.1	W 796621	2019.2	W 737681	1621.2	W 852161	1842.2	VIANDES BOVIN FRAI,REF
01112	BOVINE MEAT BONELESS	W 764411	2061.7	W 739010	1901.6	W 685059	1520.4	W 795306	1738.7	VIANDES BOVIN DESOSSEES
0112	MUTTON ETC FRSH,CHLD,FRN	W 253902	396.4	W 215333	375.4	W 216687	413.1	W 241651	475.2	VIANDE DE MOUTON
02	DAIRY PRODCTS,BIRDS'EGGS		1013.3		1077.5		1344.3		1325.3	PRODUITS LAITIERS,OEUFS
022	MILK AND CREAM	W 441676	597.6	W 398375	624.8	W 481697	810.2	W 486147	751.7	LAIT ET CREME
0224	MILK,CREAM PRESERVED ETC	W 353213	527.2	W 303359	542.9	W 377956	709.2	W 369736	649.9	LAIT,CREME CONS,CONC
02242	MILK DRY,1.5% FAT OR LES	W 202000	309.1	W 152901	295.9	W 198174	403.7	W 183499	327.6	LAIT POUDRE INF 1.5%
02243	MILK DRY,OVER 1.5% FAT	W 109134	186.7	W 97693	200.1	W 110500	242.1	W 130487	273.1	LAIT POUDRE SUP 1.5%
024	CHEESE AND CURD	W 123176	282.9	W 133950	329.6	W 135257	368.4	W 149974	388.5	FROMAGE ET CAILLEBOTTE
03	FISH AND PREPARATIONS		799.4		859.1		821.8		893.8	POISSONS ET PREPARATIONS
036	SHELL FISH FRESH,FROZEN	W 36875	623.6	W 41562	659.3	W 38523	622.3	W 37746	630.4	CRUSTACES,MOLLUSQUES
04	CEREALS AND PREPARATIONS		2479.2		2022.2		4547.3		4527.0	CEREALES ET PRODUITS
041	WHEAT ETC UNMILLED	MW 12931	1670.8		1308.3	W 30	0.1		3270.3	FROMENT,EPEAUTRE
0412	OTHER WHEAT ETC UNMILLED	MW 12927	1669.8		1308.2		3118.7		3249.6	AUTRE FROMENT NON MOULU
042	RICE	W 627660	268.0	W 513479	203.2	W 566669	244.1	W 656032	280.9	RIZ
0422	RICE SEMI–MILLED,MILLED	W 390554	153.0	W 408574	159.9	W 432488	183.1	W 576487	251.1	RIZ POLI,GLACE INCL BRISURES
04221	RICE MILLED UNBROKEN	W 390554	153.0	W 408574	159.9	W 432488	183.1	W 576487	251.1	RIZ POLI,GLACE EXCL BRISURES
043	BARLEY UNMILLED	W 2520450	249.1	W 1345006	213.0	W 3712270	669.7	W 3564574	559.7	ORGE NON MONDEE
048	CEREAL ETC PREPARATIONS	W 433231	210.1	W 440566	240.9	W 476578	292.4	W 510142	310.9	PREPTNS A BASE CEREALES
05	VEGETABLES AND FRUIT		682.3		690.3		856.2		863.9	LEGUMES ET FRUITS
054	VEG ETC FRSH,SMPLY PRSVD	W 846601	296.6	W 481254	253.5	W 889777	361.4	W 1003726	382.4	LEGUMES FRAIS,CONG,SECS
0542	LEGUMINOUS VEGETBLES DRY	W 634937	145.0	W 249801	77.7	W 660007	181.8	W 796023	220.4	LEGUMES A COSSE SECS
057	FRUIT,NUTS,FRESH,DRIED	W 241766	240.3	W 253301	278.5	W 1171	2.3	W 290764	334.0	FRUITS FRAIS OU SECS
06	SUGAR AND PREPS,HONEY		1217.7		1383.7		1284.5		1271.8	SUCRES ET PRODUITS
061	SUGAR AND HONEY	W 4756777	1189.9	W 45	0.1	W 4	0.1	W 20	0.1	SUCRES ET MIEL
0611	RAW BEET AND CANE SUGAR	W 4197341	1124.7	W 21	0.1		1084.3		1122.6	SUCRES BRUTS
081	*FEEDING STUFF FOR ANIML	W 805889	295.0	W 769315	305.6	W 945800	390.6	W 1045175	413.9	NOURRITURE POUR ANIMAUX
0819	FOOD WASTE AND FEED NES	W 266655	188.2	W 243299	190.4	W 280067	236.6	W 302198	240.2	DECHETS,ALIMENTS NDA
08199	FODDER NES,INCL SWEETNED	W 266535	188.1	W 243206	190.3	W 279889	236.4	W 302062	240.0	PREPARATIONS FOURRAGERES
09	MISC EDIBLE PRODUCTS		149.2		167.2		202.1		218.1	PREP ALIMENTAIRES DIVERSES
1	BEVERAGES AND TOBACCO		390.0		431.4		577.4		661.6	BOISSONS ET TABACS
11	BEVERAGES		361.8		400.6		528.2		618.9	BOISSONS
112	ALCOHOLIC BEVERAGES	W 266507	345.5	W 272005	374.3	W 307702	496.6	W 337776	600.8	BOISSONS ALCOOLIQUES
1121	WINE OF FRESH GRAPES ETC	W 185401	281.1	W 185286	307.4	W 235205	433.1	W 270696	536.2	VINS DE RAISINS FRAIS
11212	WINE OF FRESH GRAPES	W 185000	280.6	W 184607	306.2	W 234177	430.5	W 270236	534.4	VINS DE MOUTS DE RAISINS
2	CRUDE MATERLS,EXCL FUELS		9023.8		10130.7		10955.4		11905.2	MAT BRUTES NON COMESTIBLES
21	HIDES,SKINS,FURS UNDRSSD		330.3		364.5		388.1		404.3	CUIRS,PEAUX BRUTS
211	HIDES,SKINS,EXC FURS,RAW	W 211273	328.9	W 195158	364.1	W 206650	386.3	W 216858	403.7	CUIRS ET PEAUX
2111	BOVINE,EQUINE HIDES,RAW	W 93099	156.0	W 82632	145.8	W 79437	128.8	W 87099	146.3	PEAUX DE BOVINS
2116	SHEEP SKIN WITH WOOL	W 104568	125.8	W 101078	165.7	W 110701	204.3	W 111116	203.8	PEAUX LAINEES D'OVINS
22	OIL SEEDS,OLEAGINOUS FRT		93.9		89.5		170.3		188.4	GRAINES,FRUITS OLEAGINEUX
24	CORK AND WOOD		390.0		479.2		485.7		506.1	LIEGE ET BOIS
246	PULPWOOD,CHIPS,WOODWASTE	W 6270803	345.7	W 7216591	421.2	W 6676480	418.2	W 7417985	430.3	BOIS DE TRITURATION
24602	PULPWOOD CHIPS,PARTICLES	W 6270757	345.7	W 7216579	421.1	W 6676277	418.2	W 7417881	430.2	EN FORME DE PLAQUETTES
26	TEXTILE FIBRES AND WASTE		2924.5		2914.9		2995.9		3475.8	FIBRES TEXTILES
263	COTTON	W 317720	491.4	W 307873	570.6	W 400940	680.5	W 588869	954.6	COTON
2631	RAW COTTON,EXCL LINTERS	W 316823	489.9	W 307097	569.0	W 400541	678.7	W 587577	953.8	COTON EN MASSE
268	WOOL(EXC TOPS),ANML HAIR	W 689828	2411.7	W 544815	2319.0	W 639335	2283.5	W 638403	2474.2	LAINES ET POILS
2681	WOOL GREASY,FLEECE–WSHED	W 541119	1753.2	W 419893	1662.7	W 506814	1651.9	W 507999	1814.8	LAINE EN SUINT
2682	WOOL DEGREASED,UNCOMBED	W 134823	604.7	W 113686	607.2	W 119157	587.6	W 117846	616.4	LAINE DEGRAISSEE
27	CRUDE FERTLZR,MINRLS NES		257.5		316.9		301.3		285.0	ENGRAIS MINERAUX BRUTS
278	OTHER CRUDE MINERALS	W 7778500	202.3	W 8320590	226.8	W 8484196	224.0	W 8801683	209.5	AUTRES MINERAUX BRUTS
28	METALLIFEROUS ORES,SCRAP		4844.4		5757.0		6421.4		6858.5	MINERAIS METAL,DECHETS
281	IRON ORE,CONCENTRATES	MW 125018	1898.4	MW 137075	2173.5	MW 135502	2278.7	MW 155486	2645.0	MINERAIS DE FER
2815	IRON ORE,CONC,NOT AGGLOM	MW 124615	1888.0	MW 136581	2159.7	MW 135096	2266.1	MW 155342	2640.1	MINERAIS NON AGGLOMERES
286	URANIUM,THORIUM ORE,CONC		124.8		130.6		194.5		213.0	MINERAIS URANIUM,THORIUM
287	BASE METAL ORES,CONC NES	MW 14188	2616.0	MW 14222	3173.4	MW 14740	3666.2	MW 15435	3746.3	MINERAIS METAUX COMMUNS
2871	CPR ORE ETC,CEMENT COPPR	W 463291	221.6	W 406523	282.2	W 796545	500.5	W 1002084	551.8	MINERAIS DE CUIVRE,MATTES
28711	COPPER ORES,EXCL MATTE	W 460277	220.2	W 406283	282.1	W 796513	500.5	W 1002084	551.8	MINERAIS DE CUIVRE
2872	NICKEL ORES,CONCENTRATES	W 100288	196.4	W 158818	343.3	W 189025	331.5	W 216397	316.8	MINERAIS DE NICKEL
28722	NICKEL MATTE,SINTERS,ETC	W 32082	169.7	W 32452	233.2	W 28145	193.6	W 28294	178.0	MATTES,SINTERS
2873	ALUMINIUM ORES,ALUMINA	MW 10235	1578.4	MW 10269	1809.7	MW 10367	1994.5	MW 10535	1982.7	MINERAIS D'ALUMINIUM
28732	ALUMINA(ALUMINIUM OXIDE)	MW 10235	1578.4	MW 10269	1809.7	MW 10367	1994.5	MW 10535	1982.7	ALUMINE (OXYDE ALUMINIUM)
2875	ZINC ORES,CONCENTRATES	W 1400297	296.6	W 1386492	318.3	W 1512334	348.6	W 1508140	405.9	MINERAIS DE ZINC
2879	OTH NONFER ORE,CONCNTRTE	W 1819881	257.8	W 1832959	340.1	W 1688078	405.0	W 1953785	404.3	MINERAIS D'AUTRES METAUX
28793	MOLYBD, NIOBIUM ETC ORES	W 1818004	256.5	W 1830717	336.7	W 1685584	402.3	W 1935119	399.0	MINERAIS DE MOLYBDENE,TITANE
288	NONFERR METAL SCRAP NES	W 164807	133.0	W 171580	162.8	W 180419	176.0	W 111134	130.5	DECHETS NON FERREUX
29	CRUDE ANIMAL,VEG MAT NES		155.8		167.2		173.9		168.9	MATIERES BRUTES ANIM,VEGET
3	MINERAL FUELS ETC		7820.0		8881.6		10189.0		11108.9	COMBUSTIBLES MINERAUX LUB
32	COAL,COKE AND BRIQUETTES		4944.0		5509.3		6123.6		6544.9	HOUILLES,COKES,BRIQUETTES
322	COAL,LIGNITE AND PEAT	MW 131160	4903.0	MW 136480	5472.8	MW 140839	6081.2	MW 157739	6515.9	HOUILLES,LIGNITES,TOURBE
3222	OTH COAL,NOT AGGLOMERATD	MW 130888	4893.9	MW 136078	5456.5	MW 140436	6063.7	MW 157254	6497.2	AUTRES HOUILLES
33	PETROLEUM AND PRODUCTS		1985.1		2248.6		2752.4		3049.0	PETROLE ET DERIVES
333	CRUDE PETROLEUM	W 8146753	1058.1	W 8542001	1202.7	W 8283699	1337.0	MW 10111	1586.5	HUILES BRUTES DE PETROLE
334	PETROLEUM PRODUCTS,REFIN	W 4273811	911.6	W 4651717	1022.7	W 5670863	1382.2	W 5846812	1423.1	PRODUITS RAFFINES
341	*GAS,NATURAL AND MANUFCT		891.0	W 92	0.1	W 237	0.3	W 382	0.2	GAZ NATUREL,GAZ MANUFACT
3413	PETROLM GASES,LIQUEFIED		890.9	W 92	0.1	W 191	0.1	W 380	0.2	GAZ DE PETROLE LIQUEFIE
34131	LIQUEFIED PROPANE,BUTANE	W 708300	99.3	W 625633	115.1	W 1177566	223.3	W 1483321	311.5	PROPANE,BUTANE LIQUEFIES
34139	OTH HYDROCARBON GAS LQFD		791.6	W 2	0.1		1089.2		1202.8	HYDROCARBURES GAZEUX NDA
4	ANIMAL,VEGETABLE OIL,FAT		164.0		190.1		186.5		200.0	HUILES,GRAISSES ANIM,VEG
411	*ANIMAL OILS AND FATS	W 349265	134.8	W 312294	160.4	W 348496	151.3	W 333003	145.2	HUILES,GRAISSES ANIMALES
4113	ANIML OIL,FAT,GREASE NES	W 348550	133.8	W 311947	159.2	W 348150	149.6	W 332769	143.4	HUILES,GRAISSES ANIMALES NDA
5	CHEMCLS,RELATED PROD NES		1756.6		2093.5		2286.7		2262.8	PRODUITS CHIMIQUES
52	INORGANIC CHEMICALS		201.6		263.6		260.4		244.4	PROD CHIM INORGANIQUES
522	INORG ELEMNTS,OXIDES,ETC	W 2512	1.0		166.5	W 557	0.9	W 1307	1.1	ELEMENTS INORGANIQUES
53	DYES,TANNING,COLOUR PROD		271.1		313.1		327.1		325.6	PROD TEINTURE,COLORANTS
533	PIGMENTS,PAINTS,ETC	W 140643	251.2	W 145245	289.8	W 156796	295.5	W 164295	292.5	PIGMENTS,PEINTURES,VERNIS
5331	COLOURING MATERIAL NES	W 121560	191.9	W 127498	237.5	W 136157	229.3	W 137991	208.6	AUT MATIERES COLORANTES
541	*MEDICINAL,PHARM PRODUCT	MK 17912	534.4	MK 19008	618.9	MK 21304	737.7	MK 24183	784.3	PROD MEDICINAUX PHARMACEUT
5417	MEDICAMENTS	MK 13991	379.9	MK 14754	453.1	MK 15919	567.1	MK 17011	585.7	MEDICAMENTS
54179	— CONTNG OTH SUBSTANCES	MK 11349	295.0	MK 12097	344.4	MK 13273	434.2	MK 14286	466.9	MED CONT AUT SUBSTANCES
55	PERFUME,CLEANING ETC PRD		172.3		207.1		234.9		198.5	PROD POUR PARFUM,TOILETTE

5. General Exports F.O.B. by Commodities according to the S.I.T.C. (Rev. 2) in million U.S. Dollars
Exportations Générales F.O.B. par Produits d'après la C.T.C.I. (Rév. 2) en millions de Dollars E.U.

SITC CTCI	COMMODITY	1994 QUANTITY QUANTITE	1994 VALUE VALEUR	1995 QUANTITY QUANTITE	1995 VALUE VALEUR	1996 QUANTITY QUANTITE	1996 VALUE VALEUR	1997 QUANTITY QUANTITE	1997 VALUE VALEUR	PRODUIT
58	PLASTIC MATERIALS ETC		196.4		311.9		295.1		287.1	MAT PLAST ARTIFICIELLES
583	POLYMERIZATION ETC PRODS	W 150759	144.8	W 173146	208.6	W 180892	204.1	W 213589	208.7	PROD POLYMERISATION
59	CHEMICAL MATERIALS NES		283.6		276.4		323.6		282.3	MAT PROD CHIMIQUES NDA
6	BASIC MANUFACTURES		6316.4		7651.1		7816.6		7842.9	ART MANUFACTURES
61	LEATHER,DRESSED FUR,ETC		316.1		377.6		374.3		380.1	CUIRS,PELLETERIES
611	LEATHER	W 74775	289.6	W 85427	344.7	W 85623	331.7	W 89066	341.7	CUIRS,PEAUX PREPARES
6114	LEATHR BOVINE NES,EQUINE	W 71902	256.0	W 84003	318.2	W 84355	306.7	W 85894	312.1	CUIRS DE BOVINS
64	PAPER,PAPERBOARD AND MFR		214.3		230.3		284.5		331.9	PAPIERS,CARTONS & OUVRAGES
641	PAPER AND PAPERBOARD		147.5		156.8	W 380431	193.7	W 496527	235.3	PAPIERS ET CARTONS
65	TEXTILE YARN,FABRICS,ETC		521.9		732.6		802.8		864.4	FILS,TISSUS,ARTICLES TEXTILE
651	TEXTILE YARN	W 210	1.5	W 231	1.8	W 237	1.6	W 1392	4.0	FILS TEXTILES
6512	WOOL,HAIR YARN,INCL TOPS	W 37066	226.2	W 44613	358.3	W 51619	367.4	W 54086	411.0	FILS DE LAINE,DE POILS
65121	WOOL TOPS	W 35479	216.0	W 43399	350.0	W 50713	360.2	W 52583	400.0	RUBANS LAINE PEIGN,TOPS
66	NONMETAL MINERAL MFS NES		589.6		524.6		633.3		624.0	ART MIN NON METALLIQUES
667	PEARL,PREC-,SEMI-P STONE		361.0		256.0		319.7		322.7	PERLES, PIERRES GEMMES
6671	PEARLS UNSET,UNSTRUNG		152.6		115.6		174.2		199.3	PERLES FINES NON SERTIES
67	IRON AND STEEL		1142.0		1358.6		1335.1		1289.5	FER ET ACIER
672	IRON,STEEL PRIMARY FORMS	W 2236601	532.8	W 2006387	613.8	W 2015124	497.9	W 1823487	460.6	LINGOTS FER,ACIER
6725	IRN,STL BLOOMS,SLABS,ETC	W 1412600	309.2	W 999981	262.2	W 1024114	229.5	W 1082402	255.9	BLOOMS,BILLETTES FER ACIER
67251	IRN,SMPLE STL BLOOMS,ETC	W 1412485	308.6	W 999822	261.5	W 1023088	227.7	W 1081567	254.3	BLOOMS ETC NON ACIER FIN
6727	IRN,STL COIL FR REROLLNG	W 823668	223.3	W 857159	308.1	W 729282	202.9	W 364175	99.2	EBAUCHES POUR TOLES FER
67271	IRON,SIMPLE STEEL COILS	W 823558	223.2	W 856292	306.8	W 728426	201.9	W 363045	98.1	EBAUCHES NON EN ACIER
674	IRN,STL UNIV,PLATE,SHEET	W 523063	290.6	W 562221	353.4	W 707423	390.0	W 865141	420.5	LARGES PLATS,TOLES
6749	OTH IRN,STL PLATES,SHEET	W 310421	186.9	W 328639	220.0	W 406104	249.5	W 439293	259.0	AUTRES TOLES FER,ACIER
67491	— OF IRON OR SIMPLE STL	W 308807	183.9	W 326073	214.9	W 400622	239.2	W 435968	252.3	AUT TOLES AUTRES ACIER FIN
68	NON-FERROUS METALS		2924.7		3775.4		3618.9		3648.3	METAUX NON FERREUX
682	COPPER EXC CEMENT COPPER	W 271780	602.2	W 219967	680.3	W 250247	644.3	W 192789	477.8	CUIVRE
6821	COPPER NES,ALLOYS,UNWRT	W 183279	389.3	W 107748	316.4	W 118507	279.4	W 117112	264.8	CUIVRE BRUT
68212	COPPER REFINED,UNWROUGHT	W 178550	380.0	W 107728	316.3	W 118463	279.3	W 117056	264.6	CUIVRE AFFINE BRUT
6822	COPPER,ALLOYS WORKED	W 88500	212.9	W 112219	364.0	W 131741	365.0	W 75678	213.1	CUIVRE,ALLIAGES OUVRES
68221	COPPER BARS,WIRE,ETC	W 74489	166.0	W 93914	292.0	W 113015	292.4	W 58936	153.1	BARRES,PROFILES ET FILS
683	NICKEL	W 39123	234.6	W 50448	410.9	W 53828	390.3	W 49960	343.2	NICKEL
6831	NICKEL,ALLOYS UNWROUGHT	W 36024	216.0	W 46195	376.0	W 49992	361.3	W 45707	315.0	NICKEL ET ALLIAGES BRUTS
684	ALUMINIUM	W 1067439	1555.1	W 1075693	2101.9	W 1159247	1910.1	W 1265676	2149.8	ALUMINIUM
6841	ALUMINIUM,ALLOYS,UNWRGHT	W 952339	1321.2	W 960700	1801.7	W 1071174	1676.9	W 1158782	1875.3	ALUMINIUM,ALLIAGES BRUTS
6842	ALUMINIUM,ALLOYS WORKED	W 115100	233.9	W 114993	300.3	W 88073	233.3	W 106893	274.6	ALUMINIUM,ALLIAGES OUVRE
68422	ALUMNM PLATE,SHEET,STRIP	W 89188	175.0	W 97456	248.6	W 70515	184.3	W 88905	219.0	TOLES, PLANCHES EN ALU
685	LEAD	W 359426	203.5	W 368224	253.3	W 356637	307.7	W 359642	276.9	PLOMB
6851	LEAD,ALLOYS UNWROUGHT	W 358471	202.7	W 367530	252.3	W 355169	306.0	W 358582	275.2	PLOMB,ALLIAGES BRUTS
686	ZINC	W 259677	281.0	W 227382	274.6	W 241803	286.3	W 219384	302.6	ZINC
6861	ZINC,ALLOYS UNWROUGHT	W 257052	278.6	W 224754	272.4	W 239722	284.1	W 218430	300.9	ZINC ET ALLIAGES BRUTS
69	METAL MANUFACTURES NES		463.3		468.2		553.3		506.8	ART MANUFACT EN METAL NDA
691	STRUCTURES AND PARTS NES	W 138311	144.2	W 131794	122.8	W 124596	147.2	W 62567	104.0	CONSTRUCT FER,ACIER,ALU
699	BASE METAL MFRS NES	W 32931	145.4	W 34725	152.5	W 43480	192.1	W 49388	202.4	ART MANUFACTURES MET NDA
7	MACHINES,TRANSPORT EQUIP		5552.8		6769.0		7769.4		8329.6	MACHINES MATERIEL TRANSPORT
71	POWER GENERATING EQUIPMT		439.6		592.1		688.4		768.8	MACHINES GENERATRICES
713	INTRNL COMBUS PSTN ENGIN	W 43872	328.4	W 55628	446.4	W 54554	442.4	W 64984	516.7	MOTEURS EXPL COMB INT, PIECE
7132	MOTOR VEHCL PSTN ENGINS	W 23220	166.5	W 36440	238.8	W 28334	215.5	W 36695	296.0	MOTEURS EXPL POUR VEHICULES
72	MACHS FOR SPCL INDUSTRYS		535.0		737.8		800.6		830.8	MAC SPECIALES POUR INDUST
728	OTH MACHY FOR SPCL INDUS	W 23603	245.3	W 40085	363.9	W 38726	413.6	W 39020	425.7	AUT MACH IND PARTICULIERES
7284	MACHY FOR SPCL INDUS NES	W 12803	167.3	W 25634	238.9	W 24078	278.5	W 23549	289.8	MACH SPEC IND PARTICUL.
74	GENRL INDUSTRL MACHY NES		747.7		816.0		1037.5		933.8	MACH APP INDUSTRIE
741	HEATING,COOLING EQUIPMNT	W 21282	182.2	W 24072	199.2	W 30513	254.5	W 25329	203.2	MACH CHAUFFAGE,PIECES
744	MECHANICAL HANDLING EQU	W 27080	165.9	W 42369	183.0	W 39904	248.0	W 31419	231.6	EQUIP MANUTENTION PIECES
749	NONELEC MACH PTS,ACC NES	W 15253	165.0	W 17283	173.2	W 21108	206.2	W 18795	194.2	PIECES MACH NON ELEC NDA
75	OFFICE MACHNES,ADP EQUIP		1105.9		1299.8		1394.6		1243.3	MACH BUREAU TRAIT AUTOM
752	AUTOMTIC DATA PROC EQUIP	W 3110	304.2	W 3169	295.9	W 3478	301.5	W 3364	269.5	MACH TRAIT INFORMATION
7523	DIGITL CENTRL PROCESSORS	W 1806	145.9	W 681	82.4	W 1259	87.9	W 1478	132.1	UNITES CENTRALES
759	OFFICE,ADP MCH PTS,ACCES	W 6788	783.9	W 8150	985.8	W 8862	1066.2	W 9630	950.0	PIECES DU 751 ET 752
7599	ACCTG,ETC,ADP MCH PTS,AC	W 5848	743.5	W 7007	913.0	W 7475	989.3	W 8060	859.9	PIECES DU 751 ET 752
76	TELECOMM,SOUND EQUIPMENT		504.1		510.5		512.7		706.4	EQUIPMENT DE TELECOM
764	TELECOM EQPT,PTS,ACC NES	W 10490	480.9	W 15422	489.4	W 17092	488.1	W 8456	673.9	EQUIP TELECOM,PIECES
7641	LINE TELEPHONE,ETC EQUIP	W 7988	268.9	W 12111	226.7	W 11815	164.3	W 2249	169.7	APP TELEPHON PAR FIL
7649	PTS NES OF EQUIPMT OF 76	W 1483	108.9	W 2102	149.7	W 4239	224.5	W 4153	291.2	PIECES DE LA DIV 76
77	ELECTRIC MACHNRY NES ETC		787.2		990.3		1028.4		892.9	MACH APP ELECT NDA
772	SWITCHGEAR ETC,PARTS NES	W 7291	214.4	W 8963	297.0	W 11894	302.3	W 11919	254.3	APP COUPURE,SECT ETC
7721	SWITCHGEAR ETC	W 7257	180.7	W 8924	263.5	W 11832	297.1	W 11875	246.3	APP COUPURE,SECTIONMNT
778	ELECTRICAL MACHINERY NES	W 1596	56.4	W 1622	80.9	W 23538	274.5	W 21412	243.8	AUTRES MACH ELECT NDA
7788	OTH ELEC MACHY,EQUIP NES	W 5816	173.8	W 10323	224.9	W 5361	212.8	W 3663	176.9	AUT MACH APP ELEC NDA
78	ROAD VEHICLES		742.2		835.0		1208.3		1389.6	VEHICULES ROUTIERS
781	PASS MOTOR VEH EXC BUSES	W 38350	361.3	W 41248	389.9	W 68309	690.3	W 76375	812.6	AUTO TRANSPORT PERSONNES
784	MOTOR VEH PRTS,ACCES NES	W 34777	278.8	W 38504	302.1	W 47278	383.2	W 52769	425.7	PIECES 722,781,782,783
7849	OTHER MOTOR VEHCL PARTS	W 34555	277.5	W 37935	297.6	W 46087	374.0	W 51788	412.3	PIECES 722,781,782,783
79	OTHR TRANSPORT EQUIPMENT		617.2		902.4		978.1		1434.6	AUTRE MATERIEL TRANSPORT
792	AIRCRAFT ETC	W 1559	388.7	W 1840	483.0	W 2238	498.4	W 2295	488.9	APP NAVIGATION AERIENNE
7929	AIRCRAFT PARTS NES	W 1222	358.7	W 1482	405.7	W 1721	427.7	W 1786	380.1	PIECES DU 792
793	SHIPS AND BOATS ETC	W 26781	206.4	W 99236	286.5	W 90285	416.3	W 102596	803.1	NAVIRES BATEAUX,ETC
7931	WARSHIPS	W 212	4.8	W 208	4.6	W 203	4.9	W 5522	381.3	NAVIRES DE GUERRE
7932	SHIPS AND BOATS NES	W 22264	194.8	W 95841	245.1	W 88632	404.1	W 86254	379.4	NAVIRES ET BATEAUX
79323	OTHER CARGO VESSELS	W 17484	142.2	W 74200	173.0	W 27328	317.6	W 26937	289.5	AUT BATEAUX TRANS MARCH
8	MISC MANUFACTURED GOODS		1661.6		1880.9		2220.3		2128.8	ART MANUFACTURES DIVERS
84	CLOTHING AND ACCESSORIES		211.1		224.2		266.4		276.2	VETEMENTS
87	PRECISION INSTRUMNTS NES		365.3		393.5		502.0		558.6	INSTRUM,APPAR SCIENT NDA
872	MEDICAL INSTRUMENTS NES	W 1355	96.0	W 1529	115.5	W 1796	145.6	W 2718	205.7	INSTR,APP MEDIC-CHIR NDA
874	MEASURNG,CONTROLNG INSTR	W 2135	205.0	W 2012	207.1	W 2817	272.6	W 3202	290.4	INSTRUMENTS DE MESURE
88	PHOTO EQU,OPTICL GDS ETC		307.2		337.5		393.8		305.1	APP,FOURN PHOTO,OP,MONTR
882	PHOTO,CINEMA SUPPLIES	W 20632	234.4	W 23253	260.6	W 29675	310.2	W 33777	211.3	PRODUITS PHOTO,CINEMA
8822	PHOTO FILM EXC DEV CINMA	W 9372	208.6	W 11388	229.4	W 13789	259.7	W 15746	163.7	PLAQUES,PELLICULES,FILMS
88222	PHOTO FILM ROLL UNEXPOSD	W 4245	153.4	W 4375	152.9	W 5227	180.9	W 1942	61.1	PEL SENSIB PERF OU NON
89	MISC MANUFCTRD GOODS NES		651.0		772.8		858.9		805.8	ART MANUFACTURES DIVERS
892	PRINTED MATTER	W 22804	177.5	W 22268	187.8	W 23613	226.8	W 22900	218.0	IMPRIMES
893	ARTICLES OF PLASTIC NES		158.4		192.1		206.8		171.5	OUVRAGES EN MAT DIVIS 58
9	GOODS NOT CLASSD BY KIND		4767.8		5294.7		5837.3		5375.3	ART TRANSACT NON CLASSES
931	*SPECIAL TRANSACTIONS	MW 10503	1335.8	W 11941	93.2		1709.0		1704.0	TRANS.SPECIALES
971	*GOLD,NON MONETARY NES	K 281641	3421.9	K 337164	3900.9	K 337737	4101.3	K 347948	3653.3	OR NON MONETAIRE
97101	NONMON GLD UNWRT,SEMIMFD	K 281139	3421.7	K 320910	3898.4	K 331185	4098.9	K 347658	3651.2	OR,ALLIAGES D'OR BRUTS

1. HISTORICAL SERIES, 1961–1996 SPECIAL TRADE, IMPORTS C.I.F., EXPORTS F.O.B.
SERIES HISTORIQUES, 1961–1996 COMMERCE SPECIAL, IMPORTATIONS C.A.F., EXPORTATIONS F.O.B

YEAR ANNEE	VALUE IN MILLION SCHILLINGS / VALEUR EN MILLION SCHILLINGS — MERCHANDISE –MARCHANDISE		GOLD –OR		CONVERSION FACTORS U.S. CENTS PER SCHILLING FACTEURS DE CONVERSION CENTS E.U. PAR SCHILLING		INDEX NUMBERS –INDICES — QUANTUM		UNIT VALUE VALEUR UNITAIRE	
	IMPORTS	EXPORTS	IMPORTS	EXPORTS	IMPORTS	EXPORTS	IMPORTS	EXPORTS	IMPORTS	EXPORTS
1961	38604.00	31262.00	677.40	579.90	3.8460	3.8460				
1962	40348.00	32851.00	873.00	746.00	3.8460	3.8460				
1963	43557.00	34475.00	686.70	479.40	3.8460	3.8460				
1964	48433.00	37601.00	619.40	293.10	3.8460	3.8460				
1965	54614.00	41600.00	904.60	275.60	3.8460	3.8460				
1966	60519.00	43773.00	1060.10	366.20	3.8460	3.8460				
1967	60046.00	47029.00	1480.60	316.60	3.8460	3.8460				
1968	64896.00	51707.00	961.10	163.80	3.8460	3.8460				
1969	73460.00	62723.00	648.90	67.00	3.8460	3.8460				
1970	92266.00	74270.00	864.70	73.50	3.8460	3.8460				
1971	104476.00	78997.00	1306.20	89.00	4.0110	4.0120				
1972	120576.00	89747.00	1191.60	105.10	4.3261	4.3270				
1973	137863.00	101977.00	482.00	89.00	5.1650	5.1820				
1974	168281.00	133356.00			5.3616	5.3701				
1975	163376.00	130884.00			5.7488	5.7441				
1976	206081.00	152114.00			5.5910	5.5924				
1977	234841.00	161781.00			6.0670	6.0623				
1978	231888.00	176112.00			6.9093	6.9139				
1979	269862.00	206253.00			7.5055	7.5064				
1980	315846.00	226169.00			7.7410	7.7344	59	53	96	92
1981	334510.10	251769.00			6.2921	6.2933	57	55	107	98
1982	332550.90	266860.00			5.8808	5.8776	56	56	107	102
1983	348338.90	277139.70			5.5591	5.5670	60	59	106	102
1984	392094.00	314504.40			5.0067	5.0050	65	64	110	106
1985	430969.10	353962.00			4.8581	4.8667	69	70	113	109
1986	407954.90	342479.10			6.5821	6.5782	71	71	103	105
1987	411852.00	342432.00			7.9357	7.9360	75	72	99	103
1988	451440.10	383219.90			8.0995	8.1055	82	80	100	103
1989	514692.10	429312.00			7.5648	7.5668	90	90	103	100
1990	556233.90	466066.90			8.8258	8.8267	100	100	100	100
1991	591898.10	479028.90			8.5833	8.5852	101	106	100	97
1992	593924.10	487556.10			9.1127	9.1019	107	111	99	95
1993	565556.90	467655.90			8.5962	8.5960	106	108	96	91
1994	629421.00	511888.10			8.7922	8.7971	119	119	94	85
1995	668030.90	580014.00			9.9304	9.9300				
1996	712760.00	612189.90			9.4455	9.4455				

2. IMPORTS BY BROAD ECONOMIC CATEGORY AND EXPORTS BY INDUSTRIAL ORIGIN. (PERCENTAGE OF TOTAL VALUE)
IMPORTATIONS PAR CATEGORIES ECONOMIQUES ET EXPORTATIONS PAR BRANCHE D'ACTIVITE.(EN POURCENTAGE DE LA VALEUR TOTALE)

IMPORTS – IMPORTATIONS

	1990	1991	1992	1993	1994	1995	1996
TOTAL IMPORTS–IMPORTATIONS TOTALES	100.	100.	100.	100.	100.	100.	100.
1 FOOD BEV–ALIMENTATION BOISSONS	4.6	4.6	4.5	4.8	4.9	5.2	5.5
11 PRIMARY–PRODUITS DE BASE	2.3	2.3	2.1	2.1	2.2	2.4	2.4
111 FOR INDUSTRY–POUR L'INDUSTRIE	0.5	0.5	0.4	0.4	0.5	0.6	0.5
112 FOR HOUSEHOLDS–POUR LES MENAGES	1.8	1.8	1.7	1.7	1.6	1.8	1.9
12 PROCESSED–PRODUITS ELABORES	2.3	2.4	2.4	2.7	2.7	2.8	3.1
121 FOR INDUSTRY–POUR L'INDUSTRIE	0.3	0.3	0.3	0.3	0.4	0.4	0.4
122 FOR HOUSEHOLDS–POUR LES MENAGES	2.0	2.0	2.1	2.3	2.4	2.4	2.7
2 IND SUPPLIES–APPROV INDUSTRIELS	30.7	29.2	29.2	29.3	30.3	30.8	28.8
21 PRIMARY–PRODUITS DE BASE	3.0	2.9	2.8	2.6	2.8	3.0	2.5
22 PROCESSED–PRODUITS ELABORES	27.7	26.2	26.4	26.7	27.5	27.8	26.3
3 FUELS–COMBUSTIBLES	6.2	5.9	5.1	5.0	4.4	4.4	5.3
31 PRIMARY–PRODUITS DE BASE	4.3	4.0	3.6	3.6	3.0	3.0	3.4
32 PROCESSED–PRODUITS ELABORES	1.9	1.9	1.5	1.4	1.4	1.4	1.9
321 MOTOR SPIRIT–ESSENCE	0.3	0.3	0.3	0.3	0.0	0.3	0.3
322 OTHER–AUTRES	1.6	1.6	1.2	1.1	1.4	1.2	1.7
4 MACHINERY–EQUIPEMENT	24.1	24.3	23.6	23.4	23.8	22.0	22.4
41 CAPITAL EQUIPMENT–MACHINES	18.5	18.7	18.3	18.0	18.1	16.9	17.4
42 PARTS–PIECES ACCESSOIRES	5.6	5.6	5.3	5.4	5.6	5.1	5.0
5 TRANSPORT–TRANSPORT	14.1	15.1	16.6	15.0	14.9	15.6	16.1
51 PASSENGER CARS–AUTOMOBILES	7.0	7.6	7.9	7.0	6.6	6.5	7.0
52 OTHER–AUTRES	3.0	3.0	3.5	2.8	2.9	3.2	3.1
521 INDUSTRIAL–INDUSTRIELS	2.7	2.6	3.1	2.4	2.4	2.9	2.7
522 NON INDUSTRIAL–NON INDUSTRIEL	0.3	0.4	0.4	0.4	0.5	0.3	0.3
53 PARTS–PIECES ACCESSOIRES	4.1	4.6	5.2	5.2	5.3	5.9	6.1
6 CONSUM GOODS–BIENS CONSOMMATION	20.3	20.8	20.8	22.4	21.5	21.2	21.2
61 DURABLE–DURABLES	5.6	5.6	5.3	5.7	5.5	5.5	5.6
62 SEMI DURABLE–SEMI DURABLES	10.5	10.9	11.1	11.9	11.2	11.0	10.9
63 NON DURABLE–NON DURABLES	4.2	4.3	4.4	4.8	4.8	4.7	4.7
7 GOODS NES–BIENS NDA	0.1	0.1	0.2	0.2	0.4	0.8	0.7

EXPORTS – EXPORTATIONS

	1990	1991	1992	1993	1994	1995	1996
TOTAL EXPORTS–EXPORTATIONS TOTALES	100.	100.	100.	100.	100.	100.	100.
1 AGRICULTURE	1.2	1.0	1.1	0.9	1.0	1.1	1.0
2 MINING QUARRY–INDUS EXTRACTIVES	0.5	0.4	0.4	0.5	0.4	0.4	0.4
3 MANUFACTURING–IND MANUFACTUR	98.4	98.5	98.5	98.6	98.5	98.5	98.6
31 FOOD BEV TOBACCO–ALIM BOISS TAB	2.6	2.6	2.6	2.9	3.1	3.1	3.8
32 TEXTILES–INDUSTRIES TEXTILES	9.2	8.8	8.8	8.4	7.7	7.1	7.2
33 WOOD & PRODUCTS–BOIS & PRODUITS	4.4	3.9	3.7	3.6	3.8	3.7	3.4
34 PAPER & PRODUCTS–PAPIER & PRODT	7.2	7.4	7.1	6.9	7.1	7.3	6.8
35 CHEMICALS–INDUSTRIES CHIMIQUES	12.4	12.8	12.6	13.1	13.3	9.6	13.3
36 NON METAL MIN–MIN NON METAL	3.3	3.2	3.2	3.1	3.1	3.0	2.8
37 BASIC METAL–IND METAL BASE	9.4	8.3	7.8	7.5	7.8	8.3	7.6
38 METAL MANUF–MANUF METAL	47.2	48.7	49.7	50.0	49.7	45.9	50.9
39 OTH MANUF IND–AUTRES MANUF	2.7	2.8	3.0	3.1	3.0	10.5	2.8

3. TRADE BY PRINCIPAL COUNTRIES OF ORIGIN AND DESTINATION (VALUE IN MILLION U.S. DOLLARS)
ECHANGES SELON LES PRINCIPAUX PAYS D'ORIGINE ET DE DESTINATION (VALEUR EN MILLIONS DE DOLLARS EU)

COUNTRIES–PAYS	SPECIAL IMPORTS C.I.F. IMPORTATIONS SPECIALES C.A.F				
	1992	1993	1994	1995	1996
World	54115.6	48561.3	55290.4	66405.7	67283.8
Africa	1003.6	972.4	909.0	892.6	1183.0
Americas	2907.4	2740.2	3354.0	3559.3	3899.6
– Northern America	2412.3	2327.8	2815.8	3085.7	3443.9
– LAIA	405.6	322.3	429.8	340.0	323.4
– CACM	70.6	73.1	91.2	114.9	111.8
– Caribbean	6.5	4.7	6.5	5.2	5.8
– Rest of America	12.4	12.2	10.8	13.6	14.7
Asia excl fmr USSR	5731.2	5290.2	6036.0	5089.5	5195.7
– Middle East	670.4	593.6	675.3	679.7	716.1
Asia former USSR	7.7	13.1	19.7	22.0	35.4
Europe excl fmr USSR	43621.8	38739.9	43870.1	54782.8	55622.5
– European Union	38097.4	33657.2	37803.7	47506.1	47654.4
– Eastern Europe	2710.4	2512.4	3115.4	3822.7	4564.9
– Rest of Europe	2814.0	2570.2	2951.0	3453.9	3403.2
Europe former USSR	781.8	749.5	1033.5	563.9	1294.1
Oceania	62.1	55.9	68.1	55.0	53.3
Other				1440.5	0.0
Germany/Allemagne	23201.0	20132.2	22133.2	28631.2	28844.5
Italy/Italie	4668.0	4379.6	4881.8	5788.4	5923.9
France, Monaco	2402.9	2132.4	2604.8	3239.3	3230.3
USA/Etats–Unis d'Amer	2136.3	2141.9	2418.6	2792.5	3000.1
Switzerland,Liechtenst.	2166.9	1983.6	2253.4	2569.8	2442.2
Japan/Japon	2557.3	2131.2	2366.5	1631.8	1624.7
Netherlands/Pays–Bas	1461.9	1405.2	1667.8	2266.8	2160.7
United Kingdom	1472.4	1326.9	1602.5	1955.6	2027.5
Belgium–Luxembourg	1631.1	1386.9	1599.4	1755.7	1541.3
Hungary/Hongrie	1089.7	930.6	1128.1	1234.8	1807.9
Sweden/Suède	975.2	809.0	969.8	1099.6	1036.4
Czech Republic		784.9	992.6	1240.5	1355.9
Spain/Espagne	679.6	660.9	745.6	867.5	968.4
Russian Federation	682.5	658.9	895.1	465.9	1064.1
China/Chine	543.8	668.8	851.2	806.1	848.7
Poland/Pologne	456.5	402.2	454.1	617.3	534.6
Other Asia n.e.s.	528.6	478.8	527.4	462.6	462.8
Denmark/Danemark	429.0	390.5	444.1	505.6	505.2
Slovenia/Slovénie	273.0	290.1	356.8	520.5	561.0
Finland/Finlande	379.0	311.9	378.2	450.9	447.7
Slovakia/Slovaquie		270.2	362.8	521.0	617.3
Portugal	323.8	285.4	310.5	376.4	432.7
Canada	275.9	185.9	397.1	293.1	443.6
Turkey/Turquie	238.1	248.8	293.1	349.7	374.7
Ireland/Irlande	259.3	247.3	270.9	363.2	357.5
Korea, Republic of	306.2	288.9	271.9	280.1	240.6
Nigeria/Nigéria	280.7	334.7	164.4	258.2	275.9
China, Hong Kong SAR	259.6	234.8	257.8	251.5	216.9
Special Categories				1156.5	
Algeria/Algérie	244.9	205.1	236.6	117.5	269.9
Former Czechoslovakia	1009.3				
Greece/Grèce	214.2	189.1	195.1	206.0	178.3
Saudi Arabia	143.1	182.1	196.6	169.0	172.2
Singapore/Singapour	183.2	158.9	202.8	145.5	153.5
So. African Customs Un	177.6	158.0	166.8	148.4	176.8
India/Inde	132.3	146.0	178.6	171.6	180.3
Libyan Arab Jamahiriya	138.4	101.9	164.6	196.9	190.6
Brazil/Brésil	157.0	141.4	207.0	127.0	141.1
Malaysia/Malaisie	110.0	127.3	156.8	184.9	185.0
Croatia/Croatie	85.4	118.7	132.4	190.6	236.6

COUNTRIES–PAYS	SPECIAL EXPORTS F.O.B. EXPORTATIONS SPECIALES F.O.B.				
	1992	1993	1994	1995	1996
Monde	44434.8	40159.1	45072.2	57583.0	57830.5
Afrique	586.1	554.5	691.9	612.8	595.0
Amériques	1824.1	1971.5	2337.0	2445.7	2911.9
– Amérique du Nord	1430.4	1583.7	1869.0	1935.0	2254.5
– ALAI	343.1	340.0	419.4	455.7	614.7
– MCAC	20.6	15.6	19.0	15.1	17.6
– Caraïbes	24.0	21.8	25.1	34.4	22.3
– Autre Amérique	5.9	10.3	4.5	5.5	2.8
Asie anc. URSS exclus	3456.0	3330.5	3353.8	3815.4	4433.5
– Moyen–Orient	1227.3	993.6	820.0	884.5	1197.7
Asie ancienne URSS	17.1	50.1	63.7	60.9	42.2
Europe anc. URSS exclus	37634.1	33468.9	37659.0	47005.2	48393.0
– Union Européenne	30275.8	26316.4	29218.4	36578.6	37102.4
– Europe de l'Est	3560.0	3536.7	4123.9	5284.4	6012.2
– Autre de l'Europe	3798.3	3615.8	4316.6	5142.2	5278.3
Europe ancienne URSS	722.3	620.6	767.9	1030.0	1089.4
Océanie	195.2	163.0	198.7	274.4	365.6
Autre			0.2	2338.5	0.0
Germany/Allemagne	17693.2	15666.4	17177.4	21523.4	21636.4
Italy/Italie	3911.2	3171.1	3657.9	4939.7	4819.2
Switzerland,Liechtenst.	2636.3	2476.0	2869.0	3289.5	3144.9
France, Monaco	1947.2	1779.7	2051.4	2393.7	2477.0
Hungary/Hongrie	1417.8	1422.6	1763.7	2057.8	2299.1
United Kingdom	1587.4	1312.3	1427.1	1797.5	2045.1
USA/Etats–Unis d'Amer	1172.6	1327.3	1568.6	1598.8	1840.9
Netherlands/Pays–Bas	1295.9	1189.8	1343.9	1593.2	1495.8
Czech Republic		975.2	1181.1	1535.4	1676.9
Spain/Espagne	1053.2	836.4	965.8	1142.8	1291.9
Belgium–Luxembourg	876.6	762.2	849.1	948.6	1115.3
Slovenia/Slovénie	514.1	585.3	703.7	939.0	931.8
Japan/Japon	682.8	616.4	696.0	707.9	893.4
Russian Federation	625.8	533.7	657.3	822.7	750.6
Sweden/Suède	658.7	559.4	628.6	772.2	763.5
Poland/Pologne	643.2	553.1	529.6	744.7	855.6
Special Categories				2106.2	
Denmark/Danemark	400.2	352.4	385.5	463.0	461.8
Slovakia/Slovaquie		351.8	395.3	552.7	731.0
Croatia/Croatie	174.6	243.6	367.8	511.7	577.9
China/Chine	236.4	315.3	327.6	430.7	342.0
Canada	252.6	256.3	298.9	335.7	413.5
Turkey/Turquie	286.2	259.8	173.6	242.6	483.2
Finland/Finlande	257.9	209.6	234.0	353.7	353.5
Norway,Svalbard and JM	277.1	226.4	250.1	256.1	343.5
Greece/Grèce	282.9	202.4	206.8	310.5	276.1
China, Hong Kong SAR	212.4	222.8	247.2	308.4	283.5
Former Czechoslovakia	1259.0				
Iran (Islamic Rep of)	384.1	289.4	240.6	133.5	206.0
Korea, Republic of	136.5	192.9	231.9	302.7	307.1
Portugal	227.0	194.3	194.2	219.4	241.4
Saudi Arabia	308.9	218.6	173.9	185.4	182.3
Australia/Australie	165.7	140.1	169.8	230.1	321.2
Indonesia/Indonésie	180.3	211.0	138.8	207.4	268.3
Romania/Roumanie	109.0	111.2	131.4	235.3	308.6
Singapore/Singapour	110.5	111.0	198.3	234.9	191.8
Other Asia n.e.s.	135.8	136.6	169.4	187.7	202.6
Brazil/Brésil	62.5	74.1	127.4	234.2	281.8
So. African Customs Un	102.6	110.0	163.7	159.5	177.0
Thailand/Thaïlande	122.5	160.8	80.9	122.2	182.9

(VALUE AS PERCENTAGE OF WORLD TOTAL)(VALEURS EN POURCENTAGE DU TOTAL MONDIAL)

	1987	1988	1989	1990	1991	1992	1993	1994	1995	1996
Africa	2.2	1.7	2.2	2.4	2.1	1.9	2.0	1.6	1.3	1.8
Americas	5.2	5.1	5.4	5.2	5.4	5.4	5.6	6.1	5.4	5.8
– Northern America	3.8	3.8	4.1	4.1	4.4	4.5	4.8	5.1	4.6	5.1
– LAIA	1.1	1.0	1.0	0.8	0.8	0.7	0.7	0.8	0.5	0.5
– CACM	0.2	0.2	0.2	0.2	0.2	0.1	0.2	0.2	0.2	0.2
– Caribbean	0.0	0.0	0.0	0.0	0.0	0.0	0.0	0.0	0.0	0.0
– Rest of America	0.1	0.1	0.0	0.1	0.0	0.0	0.0	0.0	0.0	0.0
Asia excl fmr USSR	8.8	10.1	10.0	9.7	10.6	10.6	10.9	10.9	7.7	7.7
– Middle East	1.1	1.0	1.1	1.0	1.1	1.2	1.2	1.2	1.0	1.1
Asia former USSR						0.0	0.0	0.0	0.0	0.1
Europe excl fmr USSR	81.5	81.0	80.6	80.7	80.1	80.6	79.8	79.3	82.5	82.7
– European Union	70.6	70.6	70.4	71.1	70.2	70.4	69.3	68.4	71.5	70.8
– Eastern Europe	4.7	4.5	4.4	3.9	4.4	5.0	5.2	5.6	5.8	6.8
– Rest of Europe	6.3	5.9	5.7	5.8	5.5	5.2	5.3	5.3	5.2	5.1
Europe former USSR	2.1	1.9	1.7	1.8	1.6	1.4	1.5	1.9	0.8	1.9
Oceania	0.2	0.2	0.1	0.1	0.1	0.1	0.1	0.1	0.1	0.1
Other		0.0							2.2	0.0
Germany/Allemagne					43.0	42.9	41.5	40.0	43.1	42.9
Italy/Italie	9.4	8.9	9.0	9.1	8.8	8.6	9.0	8.8	8.7	8.8
France, Monaco	4.1	3.9	4.4	4.2	4.4	4.4	4.4	4.7	4.9	4.8
USA/Etats–Unis d'Amer	3.5	3.4	3.6	3.6	4.0	3.9	4.4	4.4	4.2	4.5
Switzerland,Liechtenst.	4.7	4.4	4.1	4.3	4.2	4.0	4.1	4.1	3.9	3.6
Japan/Japon	4.4	5.1	4.9	4.5	4.8	4.7	4.4	4.3	2.5	2.4
Netherlands/Pays–Bas	2.8	2.8	2.8	2.8	2.7	2.7	2.9	3.0	3.4	3.2
United Kingdom	2.4	2.5	2.5	2.6	2.7	2.7	2.7	2.9	2.9	3.0
Belgium–Luxembourg	2.4	2.7	2.7	2.9	3.0	3.0	2.9	2.9	2.6	2.3
Hungary/Hongrie	1.5	1.4	1.5	1.6	1.9	2.0	1.9	2.0	1.9	2.7

	1987	1988	1989	1990	1991	1992	1993	1994	1995	1996
Afrique	2.1	1.9	1.8	1.6	1.6	1.3	1.4	1.5	1.1	1.0
Amériques	5.3	5.0	5.2	4.7	4.2	4.1	4.9	5.2	4.2	5.0
– Amérique du Nord	4.3	4.2	4.5	4.0	3.4	3.2	3.9	4.1	3.4	3.9
– ALAI	0.8	0.6	0.6	0.6	0.7	0.8	0.8	0.9	0.8	1.1
– MCAC	0.1	0.0	0.0	0.0	0.0	0.0	0.0	0.0	0.0	0.0
– Caraïbes	0.1	0.1	0.1	0.1	0.0	0.1	0.1	0.1	0.1	0.0
– Autre Amérique	0.0	0.0	0.0	0.0	0.0	0.0	0.0	0.0	0.0	0.0
Asie anc. URSS exclus	6.5	6.9	6.9	7.4	7.8	7.8	8.3	7.4	6.6	7.7
– Moyen–Orient	2.7	2.9	2.5	2.5	2.7	2.8	2.5	1.8	1.5	2.1
Asie ancienne URSS						0.0	0.1	0.1	0.1	0.1
Europe anc. URSS exclus	83.1	82.9	83.0	83.7	84.1	84.7	83.3	83.6	81.6	83.7
– Union Européenne	66.2	66.7	66.6	67.9	68.0	68.1	65.5	64.8	63.5	64.2
– Europe de l'Est	6.5	6.3	6.4	5.6	7.0	8.0	8.8	9.1	9.2	10.4
– Autre de l'Europe	10.4	10.0	10.1	10.2	9.0	8.5	9.0	9.6	8.9	9.1
Europe ancienne URSS	2.5	2.9	2.7	2.2	1.9	1.6	1.5	1.7	1.8	1.9
Océanie	0.5	0.5	0.5	0.5	0.4	0.4	0.4	0.4	0.5	0.6
Autre		0.0						0.0	4.1	0.0
Germany/Allemagne					39.0	39.8	39.0	38.1	37.4	37.4
Italy/Italie	10.4	10.4	10.5	9.8	9.4	8.8	7.9	8.1	8.6	8.3
Switzerland,Liechtenst.	7.4	7.2	7.3	6.9	6.4	5.9	6.2	6.4	5.7	5.4
France, Monaco	4.5	4.6	4.7	4.8	4.3	4.4	4.4	4.6	4.2	4.3
Hungary/Hongrie	1.9	1.8	2.0	2.2	3.0	3.2	3.5	3.9	3.6	4.0
United Kingdom	4.6	4.7	4.5	3.9	3.6	3.6	3.3	3.2	3.1	3.5
USA/Etats–Unis d'Amer	3.6	3.5	3.5	3.2	2.8	2.6	3.3	3.5	2.8	3.2
Netherlands/Pays–Bas	2.7	2.6	3.0	2.9	3.0	2.9	3.0	3.0	2.8	2.6
Czech Republic							2.4	2.6	2.7	2.9
Spain/Espagne	1.8	1.9	2.2	2.2	2.2	2.4	2.1	2.1	2.0	2.2

4. Special Imports C.I.F. by Commodities according to the S.I.T.C. (Rev. 2) in million U.S. Dollars
Importations Spéciales C.A.F. par Produits d'après la C.T.C.I. (Rév. 2) en millions de Dollars E.U.

SITC CTCI	COMMODITY	1993		1994		1995		1996		PRODUIT
		QUANTITY QUANTITE	VALUE VALEUR	QUANTITY QUANTITE	VALUE VALEUR	QUANTITY QUANTITE	VALUE VALEUR	QUANTITY QUANTITE	VALUE VALEUR	
	ALL COMMODITIES		48561.3		55290.5		66405.8		67283.8	TOUS PRODUITS
0	FOOD AND LIVE ANIMALS		2324.3		2663.6		3345.9		3639.6	ALIMENTS,ANIMAUX VIVANTS
01	MEAT AND PREPARATIONS		108.0		115.6		350.8		381.4	VIANDES ET PREPARATIONS
011	MEAT FRESH,CHILLD,FROZEN	W 24617	91.1	W 25115	94.4	W 80380	277.8	W 88388	297.8	VIANDES FRAICHES,REF,CONGE
02	DAIRY PRODCTS,BIRDS'EGGS		156.2		170.4		217.7		290.9	PRODUITS LAITIERS,OEUFS
03	FISH AND PREPARATIONS		145.9		182.6		175.1		190.6	POISSONS ET PREPARATIONS
04	CEREALS AND PREPARATIONS		246.4		302.6		319.7		467.9	CEREALES ET PRODUITS
048	CEREAL ETC PREPARATIONS	W 98673	185.7	W 91298	214.9	W 112330	254.1	W 145436	342.1	PREPTNS A BASE CEREALES
0484	BAKERY PRODUCTS	W 41382	123.5	W 48230	145.4	W 52735	147.4	W 78560	234.6	PRODUITS DE BOULANGERIE
05	VEGETABLES AND FRUIT		875.3		958.4		1105.2		1108.0	LEGUMES ET FRUITS
054	VEG ETC FRSH,SMPLY PRSVD	W 232023	235.2	W 241894	245.6	W 390004	358.0	W 362909	334.1	LEGUMES FRAIS,CONG,SECS
057	FRUIT,NUTS,FRESH,DRIED	W 784090	446.3		477.1	W 639003	481.4	W 628091	507.3	FRUITS FRAIS OU SECS
0579	FRUIT FRESH OR DRIED NES	W 148424	144.1	W 164545	166.8	W 163903	159.6	W 160742	166.3	FRUITS FRAIS,SECS NDA
058	FRUIT PRESERVED,PREPARED	W 141263	152.4	W 169793	193.2	W 128612	203.0	W 155589	207.3	CONSERVES DE FRUITS
07	COFFEE,TEA,COCOA,SPICES		333.0		434.7		523.9		502.3	CAFE,THE,CACAO,EPICES
071	COFFEE AND SUBSTITUTES	W 105071	158.9	W 82091	238.0	W 70074	282.0	W 69777	211.4	CAFE ET SUCCEDANES
0711	COFFEE GREEN,ROASTED,SUB	W 101300	135.2	W 79050	208.4	W 67610	251.9	W 67456	187.0	CAFE TORREFIE OU DECAFEINE
07111	COFFEE GREEN,HUSKS,SKINS	W 99236	127.0	W 76222	197.4	W 65568	240.8	W 63818	169.1	CAFE NON TORREFIE
081	*FEEDING STUFF FOR ANIML	W 658984	187.4	W 647336	189.3	W 617119	212.1	W 560794	217.3	NOURRITURE POUR ANIMAUX
09	MISC EDIBLE PRODUCTS		174.6		198.0		276.4		247.3	PREP ALIMENTAIRES DIVERSES
098	EDIBLE PRODCTS,PREPS NES	W 43403	168.1	W 44738	190.3	W 58416	263.6	W 56630	234.6	PREP ALIMENTAIRES NDA
09809	MISC FOOD PREPRTIONS NES	W 29375	136.3	W 29793	153.2	W 41086	218.2	W 35317	180.0	PREP ALIMENTAIRES NDA
1	BEVERAGES AND TOBACCO		187.1		217.0		266.6		261.4	BOISSONS ET TABACS
2	CRUDE MATERLS,EXCL FUELS		1875.2		2323.2		3060.2		2513.6	MAT BRUTES NON COMESTIBLES
24	CORK AND WOOD		526.2		655.5		786.5		650.9	LIEGE ET BOIS
247	OTH WOOD ROUGH,SQUARED	W 3611196	247.6	W 3849815	303.5	W 3943364	394.9	W 3684318	322.7	BOIS BRUTS EQUARRIS
2471	SAW-,VENEER-LOGS CONIFER	W 2755158	197.0	W 3105946	254.9	W 3100864	325.6	W 2850943	265.9	CONIFERES POUR SCIAGE,PLACAG
24711	— IN THE ROUGH	W 2755158	197.0	W 3105946	254.9	W 3100864	325.6	W 2850943	265.9	ECORCES OU DEGROSSIS
248	WOOD SHAPED,SLEEPERS	W 550631	239.1	W 689997	297.6	W 710607	329.9	W 626448	270.9	BOIS SIMPLEMENT TRAVAILLES
2482	LUMBER SHAPED CONIFER	W 421078	158.8	W 518990	197.4	W 529085	220.1	W 468647	176.0	CONIFERES SCIES,RABOTES
24821	LUMBER SAWN ETC CONIFER	W 399380	134.1	W 500617	174.4	W 513519	200.0	W 452591	156.8	CONIFERES SCIES LONGITUD
251	*PULP AND WASTE PAPER	W 953359	244.7	W 1067044	348.7	W 1128995	583.5	W 1131185	347.7	PATES A PAPIER,DECHETS
2517	SODA,SULPHATE WOOD PULP	W 383607	155.2	W 425385	217.4	W 413980	351.0	W 437786	234.7	PATES CHIMIQUES AU SULFATE
25172	— BLEACHED,NONDISSOLVNG	W 383132	155.0	W 421823	216.0	W 407126	346.4	W 437252	234.4	PATES BLANCHIES
27	CRUDE FERTLZR,MINRLS NES		202.3		223.1		290.3		263.1	ENGRAIS MINERAUX BRUTS
278	OTHER CRUDE MINERALS	W 723571	142.5		165.0	W 1038326	212.3	W 1087990	180.9	AUTRES MINERAUX BRUTS
28	METALLIFEROUS ORES,SCRAP		327.4		432.8		628.6		508.7	MINERAIS METAL,DECHETS
288	NONFERR METAL SCRAP NES	W 122027	111.9	W 145302	173.7	W 175367	286.0	W 165497	216.0	DECHETS NON FERREUX
2882	OTHER BASE MTL SCRAP NES	W 95128	102.1	W 119748	163.4	W 156415	274.6	W 63859	107.2	AUTRES DECHETS
29	CRUDE ANIMAL,VEG MAT NES		293.0		325.6		358.9		367.7	MATIERES BRUTES ANIM,VEGET
292	CRUDE VEG MATERIALS NES	W 67650	244.1		271.1	W 81311	296.1	W 69579	303.5	MAT BRUTES VEGETALES NDA
3	MINERAL FUELS ETC		2474.5		2469.6		2982.2		3638.3	COMBUSTIBLES MINERAUX LUB
32	COAL,COKE AND BRIQUETTES		299.4		276.6		329.5		366.9	HOUILLES,COKES,BRIQUETTES
322	COAL,LIGNITE AND PEAT	W 3282634	203.0	W 3123076	186.2	W 3093174	214.0	W 3830131	262.5	HOUILLES,LIGNITES,TOURBE
3222	OTH COAL,NOT AGGLOMERATD	W 3173276	189.1	W 2996596	171.0	W 2976433	198.3	W 3659783	241.6	AUTRES HOUILLES
33	PETROLEUM AND PRODUCTS		1567.5		1588.4		1787.8		2227.8	PETROLE ET DERIVES
333	CRUDE PETROLEUM	W 7453315	979.9	W 7789848	970.4	W 7599330	1030.5	W 7728454	1245.7	HUILES BRUTES DE PETROLE
334	PETROLEUM PRODUCTS,REFIN	W 2690760	533.4	W 2903390	562.5	W 3293622	686.7	W 3723206	905.6	PRODUITS RAFFINES
3343	GAS OILS	W 1275309	240.5	W 432431	84.1	W 267	0.4	W 2244270	521.4	GAS OILS
3344	FUEL OILS,NES	W 541992	46.2			W 2237526	365.6	W 439122	49.5	FUEL OILS
3345	LUBS,PETROLEUM OILS NES	W 184134	92.4	W 2008793	436.7	W 164072	135.2	W 193066	141.5	HUILES LUBRIFIANTES
33451	LUBS(HIGH PETR CONT) ETC	W 174440	65.0	W 1997286	403.6	W 148288	89.9	W 178059	97.8	HUILES LUBRIF,H LOURDES
341	*GAS,NATURAL AND MANUFCT	W 4090941	514.8	W 3769158	469.9	W 4823165	687.6	W 4963103	725.3	GAZ NATUREL,GAZ MANUFACT
3413	PETROLM GASES,LIQUEFIED	W 166212	33.0	W 135308	27.9	W 165233	38.6	W 4963013	725.1	GAZ DE PETROLE LIQUEFIE
34139	OTH HYDROCARBON GAS LQFD	W 22336	3.1	W 17526	3.6	W 13850	2.1	W 4807312	682.9	HYDROCARBURES GAZEUX NDA
3414	PETROLEUM GASES, GASEOUS	W 3924729	481.9	W 3633850	442.0	W 4657898	649.0	W 7	0.1	GAZ DE PETROLE GAZEUX
351	*ELECTRIC CURRENT		92.9		134.9		177.4		318.5	ENERGIE ELECTRIQUE
5	CHEMCLS,RELATED PROD NES		4843.7		5495.5		6773.2		6658.3	PRODUITS CHIMIQUES
51	ORGANIC CHEMICALS		492.8		577.0		746.6		693.9	PROD CHIMIQ ORGANIQUES
52	INORGANIC CHEMICALS		286.3		336.0		406.3		406.8	PROD CHIM INORGANIQUES
522	INORG ELEMNTS,OXIDES,ETC	W 400392	164.2		204.3		251.0	W 472427	249.4	ELEMENTS INORGANIQUES
53	DYES,TANNING,COLOUR PROD		424.9		483.6		548.8		538.3	PROD TEINTURE,COLORANTS
533	PIGMENTS,PAINTS,ETC	W 158937	334.2	W 181709	386.5	W 169979	435.3	W 173708	428.2	PIGMENTS,PEINTURES,VERNIS
5334	VARNISHES,DISTEMPERS ETC	W 49029	157.7	W 55243	182.4	W 51410	199.6	W 51635	199.3	PEINTURES A L'EAU
541	*MEDICINAL,PHARM PRODUCT		1228.8		1341.1		1733.8		1842.2	PROD MEDICINAUX PHARMACEUT
5416	GLYCOSIDES,GLANDS,SERA	K 1742100	214.3		211.1		271.8	K 2755917	285.2	HETEROSIDES
54164	ANTISERA,MICROB VACCINES	K 1538700	189.4		188.3	K 1578730	235.2	K 1453858	241.6	SERUMS,VACCINS
5417	MEDICAMENTS	MK 15440	787.7		892.4	MK 16435	1132.5	MK 15913	1121.9	MEDICAMENTS
54179	— CONTNG OTH SUBSTANCES	MK 13803	630.4		715.5	MK 14509	867.4	MK 14283	892.3	MED CONT AUT SUBSTANCES
55	PERFUME,CLEANING ETC PRD		511.3		580.6		671.4		684.5	PROD POUR PARFUM,TOILETTE
553	PERFUMERY,COSMETICS,ETC	W 32497	284.7		335.1	W 43428	380.9	W 47474	413.5	PRODUITS DE PARFUMERIE
554	SOAP,CLEANSING ETC PREPS	W 124476	187.0		198.5	W 141401	232.5	W 145021	216.1	SAVONS,PRODUITS DETERSIFS
5542	WASHING PREPARATIONS ETC	W 108498	151.9	W 113595	163.1	W 125966	196.9	W 130245	182.6	PROD ORG TENSIO-ACT NDA
58	PLASTIC MATERIALS ETC		1236.0		1468.8		1776.5		1620.6	MAT PLAST ARTIFICIELLES
582	PROD OF CONDENSATION ETC	W 231155	375.2	W 276212	456.3	W 272407	565.2	W 315448	520.6	PROD CONDENS,POLYCOND
5823	ALKYDS,OTHER POLYESTERS	W 66281	144.7	W 88385	179.6	W 83377	223.4	W 75873	188.4	ALKYDES ET AUT POLYESTERS
583	POLYMERIZATION ETC PRODS	W 577851	825.4	W 678678	974.0	W 676846	1162.6	W 1070858	1051.0	PROD POLYMERISATION
5831	POLYETHYLENE	W 188524	179.3	W 188535	186.5	W 153038	204.0	W 307389	193.8	POLYETHYLENE
5839	OTH POLYMRZTION ETC PROD	W 49949	192.5	W 94422	269.9	W 120275	304.5	W 178938	308.0	AUT PROD POLYMER COPOLYM
59	CHEMICAL MATERIALS NES		589.3		625.0		798.2		774.9	MAT PROD CHIMIQUES NDA
598	MISCEL CHEM PRODUCTS NES	W 332088	439.5		461.5	W 530508	589.0	W 460340	552.5	PROD DIV INDUST CHIM NDA
5989	CHEM PRODUCTS,PREPS NES	W 278455	383.0		396.1	W 467997	513.5	W 398572	480.7	PROD PREP CHIMIQUES NDA
59899	OTH CHEM PRODS,PREPS,NES	W 210189	298.3	W 218853	319.4	W 423098	417.5	W 204052	383.4	AUT PRODUITS CHIMIQUES NDA
6	BASIC MANUFACTURES		9191.6		10807.1		13060.5		12483.0	ART MANUFACTURES
61	LEATHER,DRESSED FUR,ETC		232.2		267.6		304.4		326.8	CUIRS,PELLETERIES
62	RUBBER MANUFACTURES NES		599.2		624.7		787.0		755.5	CAOUTCHOUC MANUFACTURE
625	RUBBER TYRES, TUBES ETC	W 75580	351.7	W 76833	342.9	W 98345	445.8	W 90583	416.2	PNEUS CAOUTCHOUC VULCANISE
6251	TYRES NEW FOR MOTOR CARS	W 39505	215.7	W 37889	197.8	W 46182	242.7	W 47307	242.3	PNEUS POUR VOITURES
63	WOOD,CORK MANUFACTRS NES		478.3		568.3		683.0		659.7	OUVRAGES LIEGE ET BOIS
634	VENEERS,PLYWOOD,ETC	W 157276	145.3	W 183050	174.0	W 175225	215.3	W 169706	197.1	PLACAGES,CONTRE-PLAQUES
635	WOOD MANUFACTURES NES	W 179938	310.3	W 212633	371.5	W 240962	434.0	W 243774	431.3	ART MANUF EN BOIS NDA
6353	BUILDERS WOODWRK,PREFABS	W 95295	232.5	W 109181	279.8	W 111138	321.8	W 125300	320.1	OUVRAGES DE MENUISERIE
64	PAPER,PAPERBOARD AND MFR		1032.9		1202.9		1497.7		1467.3	PAPIERS,CARTONS & OUVRAGES
641	PAPER AND PAPERBOARD	W 677626	637.9		751.5	W 775056	1000.6	W 875227	980.7	PAPIERS ET CARTONS
6412	PRINTG,WRITING PAPER NES	W 165139	154.4	W 195489	187.4	W 215246	274.4	W 233452	254.8	PAPIERS POUR L'IMPRESSION
64122	— COATED,IMPREGNATD ETC	W 155043	142.1	W 179847	169.5	W 192409	240.6	W 208907	221.9	PAPIERS IMPRESSION COUCHES
6415	PAPER,PAPERBRD,BULK,NES	W 255149	195.6		215.3	W 252256	270.2	W 279417	256.3	PAPIERS,CARTONS ROULEAUX
64159	OTHER PAPER ETC,BULK,NES	W 236049	179.3		194.4	W 234832	249.2	W 265038	238.6	AUT PAPIER ROULEAUX FEUILLES
6418	COATED ETC PAPER NES BLK	W 91161	165.1		204.0	W 109694	251.0	W 121132	255.1	PAP,CARTONS COUCHES,ENDUITS
642	PAPER,ETC,PRECUT,ARTS OF	W 174051	395.0		451.5	W 191749	497.1	W 204933	486.7	PAP,CARTONS DECOUPES
6428	PAPER ETC ARTICLES NES	W 79831	185.6		203.4	W 86980	235.5	W 88186	211.9	OUVRAGES EN PATE A PAPIER

4. Special Imports C.I.F. by Commodities according to the S.I.T.C. (Rev. 2) in million U.S. Dollars
Importations Spéciales C.A.F. par Produits d'après la C.T.C.I. (Rév. 2) en millions de Dollars E.U.

SITC CTCI	COMMODITY	1993		1994		1995		1996		PRODUIT
		QUANTITY QUANTITE	VALUE VALEUR	QUANTITY QUANTITE	VALUE VALEUR	QUANTITY QUANTITE	VALUE VALEUR	QUANTITY QUANTITE	VALUE VALEUR	
65	TEXTILE YARN,FABRICS,ETC		1709.7		1818.0		2062.5		1910.9	FILS,TISSUS,ARTICLES TEXTILE
651	TEXTILE YARN	W 69509	411.7	W 73148	446.5	W 74546	531.7	W 65997	457.9	FILS TEXTILES
6514	SYN FIB YRN,BULK,MONOFIL	W 21385	142.7	W 22603	150.3	W 27620	205.4	W 25157	183.3	FILS CONT 85% FIB TEXT SYNTH
652	COTTON FABRICS,WOVEN	W 13049	177.2	W 14356	181.8	W 12619	195.6		190.9	TISSUS DE COTON
653	WOVN MAN-MADE FIB FABRIC	W 11431	192.6	W 12295	202.0	W 12987	230.2	W 14340	203.6	TISSUS FIBRES SYNTH,ARTIF
657	SPECIAL TXTL FABRC,PRODS	W 21347	182.8		203.0	W 25106	226.6	W 23539	224.1	TISSUS SPECIAUX
658	TEXTILE ARTICLES NES	W 17873	179.9		209.5	W 22694	259.8	W 23032	277.0	ART FACONNES MAT TEXTILES
659	FLOOR COVERINGS,ETC	W 32300	218.5	W 33678	218.1	W 33513	230.9	W 33540	213.8	COUVRE-PARQUETS,TAPIS ETC
66	NONMETAL MINERAL MFS NES		1029.2		1172.5		1386.6		1363.3	ART MIN NON METALLIQUES
661	LIME,CEMENT,BLDG PRODS	W 726598	138.7		178.3	W 1522737	204.6	W 1561476	195.2	CHAUX,CIMENTS MAT CONSTR
662	CLAY,REFRACTORY BLDG PRD	W 473427	239.7		268.7	W 501947	293.7	W 492915	272.1	MAT CONST REFRACTAIRES
6624	BRICKS ETC NONREFRACTORY	W 430487	206.2	W 513323	232.0	W 435713	237.3	W 427655	227.2	BRIQUES ETC CERAM NON REFR
66245	GLAZED CERAMIC SETTS ETC	W 233668	156.5	W 248923	171.5	W 217787	172.3	W 224798	159.6	AUT CARREAUX CERAMIQUE
663	MINERAL MANUFCTURES NES	W 326555	221.8		252.5	W 373287	307.0	W 386190	284.4	ART MIN MANUF NDA
664	GLASS	W 141629	186.3		196.8	W 163556	248.0	W 184677	277.8	VERRE
67	IRON AND STEEL		1191.1		1492.6		2029.7		1743.9	FER ET ACIER
673	IRON,STEEL SHAPES ETC	W 522674	254.0	W 575756	294.4	W 555881	387.9	W 560702	335.1	BARRES,PROFIL FER,ACIER
6732	IRON,STEEL BARS ETC	W 258005	129.9	W 280335	154.7	W 292760	231.8	W 322139	211.9	BARRES FER,ACIER
674	IRN,STL UNIV,PLATE,SHEET	W 576947	407.2	W 727562	533.0	W 746322	727.1	W 678308	551.3	LARGES PLATS,TOLES
6746	IRN,STL THIN PLATE,ROLLD	W 138140	120.2	W 178185	156.8	W 195473	244.2	W 166516	155.5	TOLES LAM MOINS 3MM
6749	OTH IRN,STL PLATES,SHEET	W 184398	123.2	W 253706	176.3	W 236874	196.5	W 228090	164.6	AUTRES TOLES FER,ACIER
678	IRON,STL TUBES,PIPES,ETC	W 237545	290.4	W 277690	346.6	W 287477	466.7	W 260307	406.9	TUBES,TUYAUX EN FONTE,FER
6783	IRON,STL TUBES,PIPES NES	W 137643	120.1	W 155455	141.1	W 167869	207.8	W 148951	164.2	AUT TUBES,TUYAUX FER,ACIER
68	NON-FERROUS METALS		1041.4		1485.8		1661.8		1486.9	METAUX NON FERREUX
682	COPPER EXC CEMENT COPPER	W 122451	342.1		421.0	W 173517	615.7	W 158652	494.5	CUIVRE
6822	COPPER,ALLOYS WORKED	W 100543	299.2		338.5	W 128471	486.8	W 110257	379.6	CUIVRE,ALLIAGES OUVRES
68221	COPPER BARS,WIRE,ETC	W 70731	165.9		192.9	W 94235	283.7	W 74620	193.7	BARRES,PROFILES ET FILS
684	ALUMINIUM	W 270161	521.3	W 417575	833.5	W 278919	788.3	W 312487	725.9	ALUMINIUM
6841	ALUMINIUM,ALLOYS,UNWRGHT	W 178783	224.8	W 299027	456.2	W 159557	330.8	W 195481	335.0	ALUMINIUM,ALLIAGES BRUTS
6842	ALUMINIUM,ALLOYS WORKED	W 91378	296.6	W 118548	377.3	W 119362	457.6	W 117006	390.9	ALUMINIUM,ALLIAGES OUVRE
69	METAL MANUFACTURES NES		1878.0		2175.3		2648.2		2769.0	ART MANUFACT EN METAL NDA
691	STRUCTURES AND PARTS NES	W 116796	317.4	W 130863	352.7	W 139433	430.7	W 153043	442.3	CONSTRUCT FER,ACIER,ALU
6911	STRUCTURES,PARTS IRN,STL	W 105253	227.7	W 118214	255.8	W 122676	304.1	W 134256	312.3	CONSTRUCT FER,ACIER,FONTE
694	STL,COPPR NAILS,NUTS,ETC	W 45054	179.6		217.8	W 63171	278.7	W 62062	269.3	CLOUS,VIS,ECROUS
69402	IRN,STL NUTS,BOLTS,ETC	W 37253	159.1		194.1	W 53313	250.6	W 53174	242.8	BOULONS,VIS,ECROUS FER,AC
695	TOOLS	W 15138	266.0		295.9	W 20618	394.5	W 20492	387.3	OUTILS A MAIN
6954	BLADES,TIPS,ETC FR TOOLS	W 4830	165.9		174.4	W 6556	232.7	W 6055	223.5	OUTILS POUR MACHINE-OUTIL
697	BASE MTL HOUSEHOLD EQUIP	W 29490	176.4	W 30925	201.7	W 29785	209.6	W 38026	227.1	ART MENAGE MET COMMUNS
699	BASE METAL MFRS NES	W 117819	681.9		799.2		979.1	W 187977	1079.4	ART MANUFACTURES MET NDA
6991	LOCKSMITHS WARES,ETC	W 29638	249.2		288.1	W 46522	371.7	W 46090	373.0	ARTICLES DE SERRURERIE
69913	BASE MTL DOOR,ETC FITTNG	W 24341	205.4		240.9	W 40880	315.1	W 39844	310.9	GARNITURES POUR MEUBLES
6997	IRON,STEEL ARTICLES NES	W 56164	202.4		224.8	W 71190	256.2	W 93864	369.5	OUV FONTE,FER,ACIER NDA
69979	IRN,STL MANUFACTURES NES	W 56144	202.3		224.7	W 71156	256.0	W 93850	369.4	AUT OUVRAGES EN FER NDA
7	MACHINES,TRANSPORT EQUIP		18290.7		20979.5		24399.5		25438.6	MACHINES MATERIEL TRANSPORT
71	POWER GENERATING EQUIPMT		1149.9		1326.9		1576.9		1617.2	MACHINES GENERATRICES
713	INTRNL COMBUS PSTN ENGIN	W 82873	753.5		859.5	W 110152	1059.1	W 120815	1129.5	MOTEURS EXPL COMB INT, PIECE
7132	MOTOR VEHCL PSTN ENGINS	W 13786	243.2	W 15728	222.4	W 18167	278.7	W 25282	320.4	MOTEURS EXPL POUR VEHICULES
7139	PISTON ENGINE PARTS NES	W 65846	466.3		589.3	W 87984	720.2	W 91419	755.6	PIECES POUR 713.2,3,8
716	ROTATING ELECTRIC PLANT	W 17606	237.7	W 21372	268.7	W 19977	256.0	W 18938	251.0	APP ELECTR ROTATIFS,PIECES
7162	AC MTRS,GENRTRS,GEN SETS	W 11860	151.2	W 14654	184.2	W 12325	174.9	W 12014	165.5	MOTEURS ELECTRIQUES
72	MACHS FOR SPCL INDUSTRYS		1645.5		1825.2		2067.6		2117.2	MAC SPECIALES POUR INDUST
721	AGRIC MACHY,EXC TRACTORS	W 26626	162.9		187.9	W 37187	278.2	W 40896	281.7	MACHINES AGRICOLES
723	CIVIL ENGNEERG EQUIP ETC	W 32777	211.8	W 41060	262.3	W 35454	272.9	W 39809	277.3	APPAREILS DE GENIE CIVIL
7234	CONST,MINING MACHNRY NES	W 28762	188.3	W 35480	232.7	W 30260	230.4	W 34687	241.2	MACH POUR LA CONST, MINES
72342	SLFPRP SHOVELS,EXCAVATRS	W 23818	142.0	W 29455	181.1	W 24654	176.5	W 28323	177.6	PELLES MECANIQUES
726	PRINTG,BKBINDG MACHY,PTS	W 8529	185.0	W 6401	163.9	W 10285	182.0	W 6837	199.0	MACHINES POUR IMPRIMERIE
728	OTH MACHY FOR SPCL INDUS	W 48111	644.1	W 57109	721.9	W 47992	795.7	W 54418	793.2	AUT MACH IND PARTICULIERES
7281	MACH-TOOLS FR SPCL INDUS	W 12354	141.2	W 15089	174.0	W 13424	187.1	W 13984	182.2	MACH-OUTILS SPEC IND PART
7284	MACHY FOR SPCL INDUS NES	W 24998	427.8	W 29019	465.0	W 20656	491.8	W 28393	509.5	MACH SPEC IND PARTICUL.
72848	OTH MCHY WITH INDIV FNCT	W 9904	202.1	W 10308	225.0	W 8874	215.1	W 7983	189.9	AUTRES MACHINES NDA
73	METALWORKING MACHINERY		451.1		454.9		511.2		694.8	MACH TRAVAIL DES METAUX
736	METALWORKING MACH-TOOLS	W 21436	374.4	W 24765	364.4	W 21671	406.2	W 22408	551.8	MACH-OUTILS TRAVAIL METAUX
74	GENRL INDUSTRL MACHY NES		2873.9		3309.9		3893.3		3921.0	MACH APP INDUSTRIE
741	HEATING,COOLING EQUIPMNT	W 33980	421.2		444.8	W 42435	517.4	W 47472	563.9	MACH CHAUFFAGE,PIECES
7416	HEATING,COOLING EQU NES	W 13549	193.1		196.7	W 11665	192.8	W 15251	213.1	APP CHANGEMENT TEMP
742	PUMPS FOR LIQUIDS ETC	W 13121	271.8	W 15533	336.5	W 17081	396.1	W 16479	375.6	POMPES MOTO-POMPES
7428	OTHER PUMPS FOR LIQUIDS	W 6149	151.1	W 7354	195.7	W 5976	170.3	W 5911	167.0	AUTRES POMPES POUR LIQ
74288	PUMPS FR LIQUIDS NES ETC	W 5718	137.6	W 6670	173.8	W 5778	162.4	W 5502	150.0	POMPES POUR LIQUIDES NDA
743	PUMPS NES,CENTRFUGES ETC	W 32695	384.2		438.6	W 46127	506.6	W 45248	527.2	POMPES COMPRES,VENT ETC
744	MECHANICAL HANDLING EQU	W 65692	439.8	W 86730	512.8	W 91547	629.0	W 91761	620.2	EQUIP MANUTENTION PIECES
7442	LIFTING,LOADING MACH NES	W 26409	210.7	W 30233	233.1	W 28815	239.0	W 31390	261.5	APP LEVAGE,MANUTENTION
7449	PTS NES OF MACHY OF 7442	W 29361	162.5	W 44861	204.4	W 50716	290.9	W 48984	270.5	PIECES DU 744.2
745	NONELEC MACHY,TOOLS NES	W 21435	375.9		445.7	W 29479	532.1	W 30447	518.1	AUT MACH NON ELEC,PIECES
7452	OTH NONELEC MCHS,PTS NES	W 20277	347.6		407.7	W 27538	480.9	W 28517	464.7	AUT MACH NON ELEC,PIECES
749	NONELEC MACH PTS,ACC NES	W 72201	981.3		1131.9	W 100377	1312.3	W 105584	1316.2	PIECES MACH NON ELEC NDA
7491	BALL,ROLLER,ETC BEARINGS	W 10564	126.8		168.5	W 18808	212.1	W 21625	210.6	ROULEMENTS BILLES ETC
7492	COCKS,VALVES ETC NES	W 17765	359.2		407.6	W 24660	504.4	W 24772	496.2	ART ROB,SIM POUR TUYAUX
7493	SHAFT,CRANK,PULLEY ETC	W 37451	325.2		370.1	W 48954	408.1	W 50840	417.4	ARBRES TRANS,VILEBREQUINS
7499	OTH NONELEC MCHY PTS NES	W 6420	170.3		185.8	W 7956	187.8	W 8347	192.1	PIECES NON ELECT NDA
75	OFFICE MACHNES,ADP EQUIP		1683.7		1979.1		2114.8		2029.3	MACH BUREAU TRAIT AUTOM
751	OFFICE MACHINES	W 4453	146.9	W 5910	196.4	W 4858	175.3	W 4999	166.0	MACH,APPAREILS DE BUREAU
752	AUTOMTIC DATA PROC EQUIP	W 12251	916.9	W 14332	1083.9	W 14090	1256.4	W 13740	1192.2	MACH TRAIT INFORMATION
7523	DIGITL CENTRL PROCESSORS	W 2764	321.5	W 3291	390.8	W 3339	426.5	W 2884	358.9	UNITES CENTRALES
7525	ADP PERIPHERAL UNITS	W 7736	343.1	W 9081	387.5	W 8516	365.4	W 8415	332.2	UNITES PERIPHERIQUES
759	OFFICE,ADP MCH PTS,ACCES	W 5822	620.0		698.9	W 8766	683.3	W 7677	671.2	PIECES DU 751 ET 752
7599	ACCTG,ETC,ADP MCH PTS,AC	W 4676	563.7		629.2	W 7465	627.4	W 6554	607.8	PIECES DU 751 ET 752
76	TELECOMM,SOUND EQUIPMENT		1294.9		1450.5		1518.0		1649.7	EQUIPMENT DE TELECOM
761	TELEVISION RECEIVERS	W 11792	189.0	W 13090	203.4	W 13366	239.3	W 14478	232.5	RECEPTEURS DE TELEVISION
7611	COLOUR TV RECEIVERS	W 11706	185.5	W 13021	201.3	W 13235	234.1	W 14389	230.0	RECEPTEURS COULEUR
764	TELECOM EQPT,PTS,ACC NES	W 22181	876.2		1001.9	W 17581	951.3	W 20449	1051.8	EQUIP TELECOM,PIECES
7641	LINE TELEPHONE,ETC EQUIP	W 1521	135.5	W 1683	156.0	W 1915	208.5	W 2013	203.5	APP TELEPHON PAR FIL
7649	PTS NES OF EQUIPMT OF 76	W 15299	518.0		606.7	W 10016	492.9	W 11949	539.1	PIECES DE LA DIV 76
76493	TELECOMM EQUIPMT PTS NES	W 5552	189.9	W 6638	239.1	W 6150	252.6	W 6280	239.7	PIECES 761,762,764.3,8
76499	PARTS ETC OF SOUND EQUIP	W 7918	213.2		221.6	W 2479	71.9	W 3786	115.7	PIECES NDA POUR 763
77	ELECTRIC MACHNRY NES ETC		3290.6		3901.9		4363.8		4574.1	MACH APP ELECT NDA
771	ELECTRIC POWER MACHY NES	W 10799	224.1		283.5	W 12559	292.3	W 15248	280.6	MACH PROD,TRANS ELECTR
7712	OTH ELEC POWER MACHY NES	W 6285	159.2		207.4	W 7896	212.3	W 10393	199.0	AUT APP PROD TRANSF ELEC
772	SWITCHGEAR ETC,PARTS NES	W 22779	687.0		810.0	W 35702	922.7	W 35302	926.5	APP COUPURE,SECT ETC
7721	SWITCHGEAR ETC	W 21606	608.3		718.9	W 34179	823.1	W 33428	817.8	APP COUPURE,SECTIONMNT
773	ELECTR DISTRIBUTNG EQUIP	W 44481	272.2		303.7	W 58030	439.7	W 66498	580.7	EQUIPMT DISTRIBUTION ELECT
7731	INSULATED WIRE,CABLE ETC	W 42129	239.3		267.8	W 55607	392.8	W 63684	532.0	FILS,CABLES ISOLES ELECT

4. Special Imports C.I.F. by Commodities according to the S.I.T.C. (Rev. 2) in million U.S. Dollars
Importations Spéciales C.A.F. par Produits d'après la C.T.C.I. (Rév. 2) en millions de Dollars E.U.

SITC CTCI	COMMODITY	1993		1994		1995		1996		PRODUIT
		QUANTITY QUANTITE	VALUE VALEUR	QUANTITY QUANTITE	VALUE VALEUR	QUANTITY QUANTITE	VALUE VALEUR	QUANTITY QUANTITE	VALUE VALEUR	
775	HOUSEHOLD TYPE EQUIP NES	W 78452	617.0		672.2	W 85620	806.0	W 92934	823.4	MACH,APP USAGE DOMESTQUE
7758	ELECTRO–THERMIC APPL NES	W 26893	254.1		280.4	W 30790	331.9	W 32608	345.0	APP ELECTROTHERMIQ NDA
77586	ELECTROTHERM DOM APP NES	W 15569	145.8	W 16677	168.5	W 18229	212.3	W 19408	217.7	APP ELECTRO THERMIQUES
776	TRANSISTORS,VALVES,ETC	W 29565	627.8		860.1	W 24824	797.3	W 25559	759.5	LAMPES,TUBES,VALVES
7761	TV PICTURE TUBES	W 16716	110.8		193.8	W 19461	148.0	W 19751	147.4	TUBES CATHODIQUES
7764	ELECTRONIC MICROCIRCUITS	W 542	329.3		427.5	W 1090	415.9	W 666	358.7	MICROSTRUCTURES ELECTRON
778	ELECTRICAL MACHINERY NES	W 42544	719.5		816.1	W 57913	968.2	W 66366	1049.3	AUTRES MACH ELECT NDA
7783	AUTOMOTIVE ELECTR EQUIP	W 9662	184.5		197.9	W 13287	259.5	W 12691	246.8	EQUIP ELECT MOTEURS EXPL
7788	OTH ELEC MACHY,EQUIP NES	W 8924	281.0		330.7	W 9969	362.4	W 15437	464.2	AUT MACH APP ELEC NDA
78	ROAD VEHICLES		5610.4		6326.9		7565.7		8134.3	VEHICULES ROUTIERS
781	PASS MOTOR VEH EXC BUSES	W 305858	3388.4	W 318639	3670.5	W 324165	4287.6	W 373374	4673.6	AUTO TRANSPORT PERSONNES
782	LORRIES,SPCL MTR VEH NES	W 60618	577.2	W 67523	663.9	W 69242	705.5	W 66384	679.5	VEHICULES SPECIAUX,MARCH
7821	LORRIES,TRUCKS	W 54233	502.2	W 60726	580.1	W 64851	651.2	W 61552	632.4	VEHICULES TRANSP MARCHAND
783	ROAD MOTOR VEHICLES NES	W 14443	194.1	W 16809	219.8	W 21567	321.2	W 31152	368.7	VEHICULES ROUTIERS NDA
7832	TRACTORS FOR TR–TRAILERS	W 9389	87.2	W 12204	124.7	W 14134	176.0	W 25313	266.0	TRACTEURS ROUTIERS
784	MOTOR VEH PRTS,ACCES NES	W 149322	1048.0		1263.7	W 202872	1692.9	W 229408	1847.8	PIECES 722,781,782,783
7849	OTHER MOTOR VEHCL PARTS	W 143212	976.7		1194.4	W 196284	1598.8	W 223544	1768.9	PIECES 722,781,782,783
785	CYCLES,ETC MOTRZD OR NOT	W 15894	246.0		309.9	W 15528	282.7	W 17707	315.9	MOTOCYCLES SCOOTERS
786	TRAILERS,NONMOTR VEH,NES	W 45858	157.0		199.4	W 66923	276.1	W 63251	249.1	REMORQUES,CADRES,CONTAIN
79	OTHR TRANSPORT EQUIPMENT		291.0		404.5		788.6		701.5	AUTRE MATERIEL TRANSPORT
792	AIRCRAFT ETC	W 360	135.1	W 441	213.9	W 1106	600.2	W 882	557.4	APP NAVIGATION AERIENNE
7924	AIRCRFT NES OVER 15000KG	W 74	68.9	W 29	42.1	W 575	463.2	W 351	368.3	AERODYNES PLUS 15000 KG
8	MISC MANUFACTURED GOODS		9181.0		10021.1		11607.9		11957.0	ART MANUFACTURES DIVERS
812	*PLUMBG,HEATNG,LGHTNG EQ	W 51683	354.4	W 58385	404.5	W 70817	472.9	W 72584	486.3	APPAR SANITAIRES CHAUFFAGE
8124	LIGHTING EQUIPMENT NES	W 19558	219.7	W 21523	246.6	W 29407	299.0	W 28569	299.6	APPAREILS ECLAIRAGE ETC
81242	LAMPS,FITTINGS BASE METL	W 12667	165.1	W 15359	193.8	W 18559	230.7	W 18178	220.7	APPAREILS D'ECLAIRAGE
821	*FURNITURE,PARTS THEREOF	W 238948	1100.1		1245.0	W 311786	1479.0	W 354729	1596.4	MEUBLES ET PIECES
8211	CHAIRS,SEATS AND PARTS	W 46138	308.0		350.2	W 60284	402.7	W 67616	450.6	SIEGES ET PIECES
82111	CHAIRS AND OTHER SEATS	W 40504	279.7	W 46426	313.2	W 51547	344.0	W 54302	354.8	SIEGES
8219	FURNITURE AND PARTS NES	W 181254	658.2	W 208572	751.2	W 238753	936.5	W 270021	984.3	AUTRES MEUBLES ET PIECES
82192	WOOD FURNITURE NES	W 133757	473.0	W 152604	536.6	W 175013	665.3	W 199682	701.0	MEUBLES NDA EN BOIS
84	CLOTHING AND ACCESSORIES		2525.8		2666.7		3091.4		3186.3	VETEMENTS
842	MENS OUTERWEAR NOT KNIT	W 10266	377.8	W 10783	387.6	W 11587	466.7	W 12800	498.9	VET DESSUS POUR HOMMES
8423	— TROUSERS,BREECHES ETC	W 5091	160.7	W 5569	167.7	W 6139	208.4	W 6909	224.5	PANTALONS HOMMES MAT TEX
843	WOMENS OUTERWEAR NONKNIT	W 14296	751.1	W 16079	802.6	W 17305	936.8	W 18200	897.2	VET DESSUS FEMMES MAT TEX
8431	— COATS AND JACKETS	W 2167	152.8	W 2172	150.2	W 2622	189.3	W 2771	176.4	MANT,VEST FEM MAT TEXTIL
8439	— OTHER OUTER GARMENTS	W 8193	319.6	W 9283	352.1	W 9037	358.5	W 9605	362.5	AUT VET DES FEM MAT TEXT
845	OUTERWEAR KNIT NONELASTC	W 17543	623.4		641.2	W 17283	700.1	W 20787	744.6	VET DESSOUS,ACCES BONNET
8451	— JERSEYS,PULLOVERS ETC	W 10364	371.2		384.4	W 9052	370.9	W 10998	415.9	CHANDAILS,PULL–OVERS ETC
8459	— OTHER,CLTHG ACCESRYS	W 6486	214.0		218.2	W 7060	268.0	W 8564	268.4	AUT VET DESSUS DE BONNE
846	UNDER GARMENTS KNITTED	W 12987	354.0		383.1	W 14769	472.3	W 17308	515.4	SOUS VETS DE BONNETERIE
8462	— OF COTTON NON ELASTIC	W 9629	233.1		250.6	W 10612	303.4	W 12623	319.5	SOUS–VET BONNET COTON
84629	—— OTHER	W 9629	233.1		250.6	W 10612	303.4	W 12623	319.5	AUT SOUS–VET BONNET COTON
848	HEADGEAR,NONTXTL CLOTHNG	W 6992	185.8		210.4	W 8409	212.1	W 10295	230.3	VET ACCES MAT AUT QUE TEX
851	*FOOTWEAR	W 28040	540.3		568.5	W 28889	684.5	W 27709	696.2	CHAUSSURES
85102	FOOTWEAR LEATHER	W 20990	465.8	W 21917	490.3	W 21441	584.7	W 20986	599.7	CHAUS SEMELLES EN CUIR
87	PRECISION INSTRUMNTS NES		914.7		1047.8		1199.0		1225.7	INSTRUM,APPAR SCIENT NDA
872	MEDICAL INSTRUMENTS NES	W 4581	241.2		263.7	W 6225	285.3	W 6339	296.0	INSTR,APP MEDIC–CHIR NDA
87202	OTH MEDICAL INSTRUMENTS	W 3908	214.5		237.4	W 5208	245.6	W 5349	253.4	INSTRUM,APP MEDECINE
874	MEASURNG,CONTROLNG INSTR		572.1		657.4	W 12210	778.7	W 13397	791.9	INSTRUMENTS DE MESURE
8743	GAS,LIQUID CONTROL INSTR	W 3691	190.0		227.8	W 4578	236.5	W 5724	260.8	APP,INSTR MESURE FLUIDES
88	PHOTO EQU,OPTICL GDS ETC		574.2		607.3		583.6		625.7	APP,FOURN PHOTO,OP,MONTR
882	PHOTO,CINEMA SUPPLIES	W 12340	201.3		211.1	W 13148	190.6	W 14441	231.0	PRODUITS PHOTO,CINEMA
8822	PHOTO FILM EXC DEV CINMA	W 7920	161.2		167.7	W 8469	148.9	W 8493	177.8	PLAQUES,PELLICULES,FILMS
885	WATCHES AND CLOCKS		158.4		172.7		171.5		172.2	HORLOGERIE
89	MISC MANUFCTRD GOODS NES		3035.1		3338.1		3933.4		3984.0	ART MANUFACTURES DIVERS
892	PRINTED MATTER	W 111846	758.2		842.8		938.8	W 107360	964.6	IMPRIMES
8921	PRINTED BOOKS,GLOBES,ETC	W 24644	279.7	W 25260	315.4	W 23739	361.5	W 29105	370.3	LIVRES,BROCHURES,CARTES
89211	PRINTED BOOKS,PAMPHLETS	W 23621	269.1	W 24194	305.0	W 22579	349.3	W 27914	356.4	LIVRES,BROCHURES
8922	NEWSPAPERS,PERIODICALS	W 41690	230.6	W 45590	250.9	W 43416	299.5	W 38073	255.9	JOURNAUX ET PERIODIQUES
8928	PRINTED MATTER NES	W 44244	226.0		256.1		260.4	W 39082	319.8	IMPRIMES NDA
893	ARTICLES OF PLASTIC NES		836.4		937.8		1157.3		1180.4	OUVRAGES EN MAT DIVIS 58
8931	PLSTC PACKG CONTNRS,LIDS	W 37823	147.3	W 45756	165.2	W 56561	183.1	W 57429	192.1	ART TRANSP EMBALLAGE ETC
8939	MISC PLASTIC ARTICLES	W 111536	640.1		716.4	W 200078	905.8	W 191613	903.8	ART DIVERS EN MAT DIV 58
89399	OTHR PLASTC ARTICLES NES	W 98322	586.0		656.1	W 183318	836.5	W 174708	840.5	AUT OUV MAT DIV 58
894	TOYS,SPORTING GOODS,ETC	W 36681	422.9		495.3	W 45101	562.7	W 53440	624.5	VOITURES ENFANTS,JOUETS
8942	TOYS,INDOOR GAMES ETC	W 24394	280.4		311.3	W 29069	350.9	W 33948	381.1	JOUETS,JEUX ETC
8947	OTH SPORT GDS,FAIR AMUSM	W 11123	133.6	W 14086	140.4	W 13564	179.7	W 17285	211.4	AUT ART DE SPORT
897	GOLD,SILVER WARE,JEWELRY		209.4		209.6		272.8		260.4	BIJOUTERIE,ORFEVRERIE
8973	PREC JEWLRY,GLD–SILVWARE		167.2		162.2		217.4		211.3	BIJOUX OR,ARGENT ORFEVRE
89731	PRECIOUS METAL JEWELLERY		153.9		147.5		189.7		180.5	ART BIJOUTERIE,JOAILLER
898	MUSICAL INSTRUMENTS,PTS	W 17318	463.8		469.2	W 15723	441.6	W 15221	413.7	INSTRUMENTS DE MUSIQUE
8983	SOUND RECRDNG TAPE,DISCS	W 15834	419.1		419.2	W 14207	386.5	W 13620	358.8	SUPPORTS SON POUR 763
89832	RECORDED DISCS,TAPES ETC	W 5878	302.5		322.8	W 7015	300.4	W 5947	266.0	DISQUES,PHONO,BANDES
899	OTHER MANUFACTURED GOODS		235.1		268.3		328.2		333.7	AUT ART MANUF DIVERS NDA
9	GOODS NOT CLASSD BY KIND		107.1		214.4		790.0		563.8	ART TRANSACT NON CLASSES
911	*MAIL NOT CLASSED BY KIN								348.0	COLIS POSTAUX
931	*SPECIAL TRANSACTIONS		0.6				532.0			TRANS.SPECIALES
951	*WAR FIREARMS,AMMUNITION	W 1909	72.3	W 2794	184.2	W 129	7.4		69.6	VEHIC BLINDES ARMES
971	*GOLD,NON MONETARY NES		28.7		25.4		245.8		141.4	OR NON MONETAIRE
97101	NONMON GLD UNWRT,SEMIMFD	K 1800	28.5		25.3	K 36853	244.9	K 23933	139.7	OR,ALLIAGES D'OR BRUTS

5. Special Exports F.O.B. by Commodities according to the S.I.T.C. (Rev. 2) in million U.S. Dollars
Exportations Spéciales F.O.B. par Produits d'après la C.T.C.I. (Rév. 2) en millions de Dollars E.U.

SITC CTCI	COMMODITY	1993 QUANTITY QUANTITE	1993 VALUE VALEUR	1994 QUANTITY QUANTITE	1994 VALUE VALEUR	1995 QUANTITY QUANTITE	1995 VALUE VALEUR	1996 QUANTITY QUANTITE	1996 VALUE VALEUR	PRODUIT
	ALL COMMODITIES		40159.2		45072.3		57583.0		57830.6	TOUS PRODUITS
0	FOOD AND LIVE ANIMALS		1148.1		1316.4		1695.6		2166.1	ALIMENTS,ANIMAUX VIVANTS
01	MEAT AND PREPARATIONS		169.4		189.6		332.9		393.1	VIANDES ET PREPARATIONS
011	MEAT FRESH,CHILLD,FROZEN	W 47543	141.3	W 45308	134.3	W 92675	273.0	W 113132	322.0	VIANDES FRAICHES,REF,CONGE
0111	BOVINE MEAT FRESH,FROZEN	W 36857	107.8	W 32274	98.3	W 44655	179.5	W 53114	166.1	VIANDES BOVIN FRAI,REF
02	DAIRY PRODCTS,BIRDS'EGGS		169.4		171.4		252.9		285.8	PRODUITS LAITIERS,OEUFS
04	CEREALS AND PREPARATIONS		189.5		241.1		218.4		352.6	CEREALES ET PRODUITS
048	CEREAL ETC PREPARATIONS	W 72389	112.9	W 83970	125.9	W 51178	77.9	W 96084	198.8	PREPTNS A BASE CEREALES
05	VEGETABLES AND FRUIT		169.6		230.7		330.2		395.3	LEGUMES ET FRUITS
058	FRUIT PRESERVED,PREPARED	W 82485	108.9	W 134284	152.7	W 128588	191.0	W 133483	227.8	CONSERVES DE FRUITS
07	COFFEE,TEA,COCOA,SPICES		156.2		174.6		160.3		232.1	CAFE,THE,CACAO,EPICES
073	CHOCOLATE AND PRODUCTS	W 31307	97.0	W 30103	107.4	W 24935	95.2	W 50413	186.6	CHOCOLAT
1	BEVERAGES AND TOBACCO		219.3		312.0		393.7		367.9	BOISSONS ET TABACS
11	BEVERAGES		181.8		270.3		337.2		309.1	BOISSONS
111	NON–ALCOHL BEVERAGES NES	W 210889	94.2	W 301237	144.7	W 284299	212.2	W 281281	209.9	BOISSONS NON ALCOOLIQUES
11102	FLAVORED WATERS NON–ALCO	W 203921	92.5	W 290739	142.1	W 275968	209.5	W 272325	207.3	LIMONADES,EAUX GAZEUSES
2	CRUDE MATERLS,EXCL FUELS		1581.4		1933.2		2124.7		2100.2	MAT BRUTES NON COMESTIBLES
24	CORK AND WOOD		820.5		1050.4		1267.2		1080.1	LIEGE ET BOIS
248	WOOD SHAPED,SLEEPERS	W 2338046	748.3	W 2662823	961.5	W 2707288	1147.7	W 2475249	986.3	BOIS SIMPLEMENT TRAVAILLES
2482	LUMBER SHAPED CONIFER	W 2247175	703.2	W 2565037	907.3	W 2611241	1082.7	W 2391698	933.0	CONIFERES SCIES,RABOTES
24821	LUMBER SAWN ETC CONIFER	W 2190451	649.9	W 2489262	831.8	W 2545013	1005.3	W 2327218	863.5	CONIFERES SCIES LONGITUD
251	*PULP AND WASTE PAPER		88.5	W 318502	137.3	W 330677	212.0	W 372127	144.8	PATES A PAPIER,DECHETS
26	TEXTILE FIBRES AND WASTE		283.7		294.8		77.6		315.4	FIBRES TEXTILES
267	OTHER MAN–MADE FIBRES	W 101687	216.0	W 95652	213.0	W 2487	3.4	W 103830	221.1	AUTR FIBR TEXT ARTIF SYNTH
2671	REGENERATD FIBRE TO SPIN	W 99229	214.8	W 93080	211.6	W 347	1.6	W 101820	219.6	FIBRES TEXT ARTIFIC
26711	DISCN REGEN FIBRE UNCMBD	W 99226	214.8	W 93049	211.5	W 245	1.2	W 101685	219.1	FIBRES TEX ARTIF DISCONT
27	CRUDE FERTLZR,MINRLS NES		168.7		188.2		247.9		239.0	ENGRAIS MINERAUX BRUTS
28	METALLIFEROUS ORES,SCRAP		128.0		150.8		169.0		186.3	MINERAIS METAL,DECHETS
3	MINERAL FUELS ETC		463.9		603.4		602.5		736.7	COMBUSTIBLES MINERAUX LUB
33	PETROLEUM AND PRODUCTS		170.4		233.6		258.8		340.0	PETROLE ET DERIVES
334	PETROLEUM PRODUCTS,REFIN	W 601919	146.8		206.7	W 849934	229.7	W 1101102	306.0	PRODUITS RAFFINES
3341	GASOLINE,OTH LIGHT OILS	W 311932	64.8	W 639722	122.5	W 617013	123.6	W 830011	182.2	ESSENCES POUR MOTEURS
33411	MOTOR,AVIATION SPIRIT	W 300142	62.6	W 158	0.1	W 616652	123.2	W 829889	181.9	ESSENCES MOTEURS D'AVIONS
351	*ELECTRIC CURRENT		292.6		366.5		337.8		392.3	ENERGIE ELECTRIQUE
5	CHEMCLS,RELATED PROD NES		3464.4		3948.1		3762.0		5157.4	PRODUITS CHIMIQUES
51	ORGANIC CHEMICALS		487.6		531.2		400.7		710.3	PROD CHIMIQ ORGANIQUES
513	CARBOXYLIC ACIDS ETC		220.0	W 140251	217.5	W 35918	80.6	W 203032	272.4	ACIDES CARBOXYLIQUES
5139	OXY–FNCT ACIDS,DERIVATVS	W 106120	166.6	W 97742	167.4	W 12084	48.0	W 115013	156.6	ACIDES CARBOXYLIQUES
514	NITROGEN–FNCTN COMPOUNDS	W 34722	97.1		107.3		90.9		174.4	COMPOSES FONCT AZOTEES
515	ORG–INORG COMPOUNDS ETC	W 7869	114.2	W 8563	136.6	W 10081	149.8	W 9434	168.2	COMPOSES ORGANO–MINERAUX
52	INORGANIC CHEMICALS		216.6		260.0		114.2		306.8	PROD CHIM INORGANIQUES
522	INORG ELEMNTS,OXIDES,ETC	W 281245	113.9	W 278495	139.1	W 100885	59.9		148.8	ELEMENTS INORGANIQUES
53	DYES,TANNING,COLOUR PROD		192.2		219.3		285.0		278.4	PROD TEINTURE,COLORANTS
533	PIGMENTS,PAINTS,ETC	W 232502	175.1		199.8	W 264212	240.1	W 234635	230.3	PIGMENTS,PEINTURES,VERNIS
541	*MEDICINAL,PHARM PRODUCT		890.4		1054.0		1333.7		1374.6	PROD MEDICINAUX PHARMACEUT
5413	ANTIBIOTICS IN BULK	K 1958200	149.3	K 2267915	162.8	K 2330536	167.9	K 2658608	179.3	ANTIBIOTIQUES NDA
5416	GLYCOSIDES,GLANDS,SERA	K 867300	309.5		339.3	K 1248311	483.2	K 2095014	481.4	HETEROSIDES
54164	ANTISERA,MICROB VACCINES	K 615500	289.3	K 648599	312.5	K 789297	448.3	K 944317	454.1	SERUMS,VACCINS
5417	MEDICAMENTS	MK 16924	364.3		472.7	MK 22522	606.8		634.7	MEDICAMENTS
54171	— CONTAINNG ANTIBIOTICS	K 4693000	137.5	K 5199242	157.3	K 6240609	196.4	K 5233895	146.6	MED CONTN ANTIBIOTIQUES
54179	— CONTNG OTH SUBSTANCES	MK 12148	194.1		207.0	MK 15392	292.6	MK 17278	339.7	MED CONT AUT SUBSTANCES
55	PERFUME,CLEANING ETC PRD		189.9		195.7		250.4		234.9	PROD POUR PARFUM,TOILETTE
58	PLASTIC MATERIALS ETC		1056.1		1237.1		1001.9		1580.0	MAT PLAST ARTIFICIELLES
582	PROD OF CONDENSATION ETC	W 226437	194.6		240.5	W 63319	212.4	W 240536	295.1	PROD CONDENS,POLYCOND
583	POLYMERIZATION ETC PRODS	W 695561	841.1		970.8	W 234020	758.2	W 817976	1251.8	PROD POLYMERISATION
5831	POLYETHYLENE	W 307281	246.1	W 333360	291.1	W 46477	107.5	W 52404	103.7	POLYETHYLENE
58311	— IN PRIMARY FORMS			W 284632	204.1					POLYETHYLENE PRIMAIRES
5832	POLYPROPYLENE	W 201296	152.4	W 119396	115.3	W 15621	48.5	W 14255	41.6	POLYPROPYLENE
5839	OTH POLYMRZTION ETC PROD	W 57791	208.8		328.7	W 86029	333.2	W 640610	851.2	AUT PROD POLYMER COPOLYM
59	CHEMICAL MATERIALS NES		314.8		321.8		362.7		489.1	MAT PROD CHIMIQUES NDA
598	MISCEL CHEM PRODUCTS NES	W 156130	212.7		230.9	W 192587	313.8	W 193557	321.0	PROD DIV INDUST CHIM NDA
5989	CHEM PRODUCTS,PREPS NES	W 142670	199.2		216.9	W 175925	294.9	W 175642	300.8	PROD PREP CHIMIQUES NDA
59899	OTH CHEM PRODS,PREPS,NES	W 110992	162.9		180.1	W 136761	247.0	W 135797	256.4	AUT PRODUITS CHIMIQUES NDA
6	BASIC MANUFACTURES		11669.4		13112.8		16068.4		15832.4	ART MANUFACTURES
61	LEATHER,DRESSED FUR,ETC		210.4		234.9		359.5		370.7	CUIRS,PELLETERIES
611	LEATHER	W 8651	146.0	W 8392	163.0	W 14317	242.5	W 12533	246.3	CUIRS,PEAUX PREPARES
6114	LEATHR BOVINE NES,EQUINE	W 8312	138.7	W 7845	155.1	W 13250	213.2	W 11624	219.5	CUIRS DE BOVINS
62	RUBBER MANUFACTURES NES		545.1		561.9		283.0		687.4	CAOUTCHOUC MANUFACTURE
625	RUBBER TYRES, TUBES ETC	W 71520	324.3		322.0			W 92466	396.5	PNEUS CAOUTCHOUC VULCANISE
6251	TYRES NEW FOR MOTOR CARS	W 34076	203.1	W 32281	184.8					PNEUS POUR VOITURES
6259	OTH TYRES,TYRE CASES,ETC	W 11342	20.9		22.0			W 92466	396.5	AUTRES PNEUS RECHAPES FLAPS
62599	TYRES NES,TYRE CASES,ETC	W 11132	19.6	W 13947	21.0			W 90838	388.0	PNEUS,FLAPS
63	WOOD,CORK MANUFACTRS NES		672.6		762.4		961.7		953.5	OUVRAGES LIEGE ET BOIS
634	VENEERS,PLYWOOD,ETC	W 706035	347.7	W 721284	388.2	W 842616	509.0	W 859095	469.3	PLACAGES,CONTRE–PLAQUES
6343	IMPROVED,RECONSTIT WOOD	W 630765	228.6	W 638838	247.4	W 767490	360.6	W 773815	326.1	BOIS AMELIORES,RECONST
63432	RECONSTITUTED WOOD	W 630604	228.3	W 638271	246.8	W 766940	359.8	W 772971	324.8	BOIS RECONSTITUES
635	WOOD MANUFACTURES NES	W 156379	322.5		370.9	W 212913	444.9	W 266796	474.3	ART MANUF EN BOIS NDA
6353	BUILDERS WOODWRK,PREFABS	W 117752	265.2	W 139684	305.1	W 166566	367.2	W 193649	385.0	OUVRAGES DE MENUISERIE
64	PAPER,PAPERBOARD AND MFR		2300.0		2656.5		3509.3		3337.5	PAPIERS,CARTONS & OUVRAGES
641	PAPER AND PAPERBOARD	W 2625272	1746.8		2067.0	W 2883264	2912.6	W 3052018	2771.4	PAPIERS ET CARTONS
6412	PRINTG,WRITING PAPER NES	W 1218913	948.4	W 1311102	1087.3	W 1317073	1546.0	W 1364981	1414.9	PAPIERS POUR L'IMPRESSION
64121	— UNCOATED	W 201226	184.8	W 175544	175.3	W 158857	218.7	W 241769	376.4	PAPIERS IMPRES NON COUCHES
64122	— COATED,IMPREGNATD ETC	W 1017687	763.6	W 1135558	912.1	W 1158216	1327.4	W 1123212	1038.5	PAPIERS IMPRESSION COUCHES
6413	KRAFT PAPER,PAPERBOARD	W 313539	172.1	W 348301	197.0	W 289299	242.5	W 352394	242.8	PAPIER ET CARTON KRAFT
6415	PAPER,PAPERBRD,BULK,NES	W 981727	508.2	W 1128139	626.8	W 1109795	930.1	W 1148010	896.3	PAPIERS,CARTONS ROULEAUX
64159	OTHER PAPER ETC,BULK,NES	W 914583	486.6	W 1078028	608.1	W 1080421	912.2	W 1089667	872.6	AUT PAPIER ROULEAUX FEUILLES
642	PAPER,ETC,PRECUT,ARTS OF	W 277473	553.3		589.5	W 273402	596.8	W 276314	566.2	PAP,CARTONS DECOUPES
6421	PAPER ETC CONTAINERS	W 165389	280.7		309.4	W 177613	390.6	W 194465	387.3	BOITES,SACS EMBALLAGES
6424	PAPER ETC CT TO SIZE NES	W 56827	145.3		149.2	W 34541	49.6	W 28221	40.4	PAP,CARTONS DECOUPES
65	TEXTILE YARN,FABRICS,ETC		1781.7		1836.8		1980.6		1996.8	FILS,TISSUS,ARTICLES TEXTILE
651	TEXTILE YARN	W 80173	370.4		411.9		346.9	W 86964	424.0	FILS TEXTILES
6517	REGEN FIBRE YARN,MONOFIL	W 38507	159.6	W 42011	174.8	W 135377	142.6	W 35194	137.6	FILS TEXT ART NON VENTE DT
652	COTTON FABRICS,WOVEN	W 15436	272.5		243.0		302.7	W 16630	285.4	TISSUS DE COTON
6522	WOVEN COTTON BLEACHD,ETC	W 9435	236.8		204.9		256.9	W 9579	244.5	TISSUS COTON BLANCHIS ETC
65224	BLCHED COTTON FABRIC NES	W 6414	163.5		144.8	W 6961	188.2	W 6986	187.5	AUT TIS PLUS 85% COT BLANCHI
653	WOVN MAN–MADE FIB FABRIC	W 14791	253.8		255.1	W 14058	300.7	W 14167	283.7	TISSUS FIBRES SYNTH,ARTIF
655	KNITTED,ETC FABRICS	W 13922	228.9		242.2	W 11303	239.0	W 13331	257.8	ETOF BONNETERIE PIECES ETC
6552	OTHER KNIT ETC FAB NONEL	W 13922	228.9		242.2	W 11303	239.0	W 13331	257.8	ETOF BON NON ELAS NON SYNT
656	LACE,RIBBONS,TULLE,ETC	W 3578	202.1		196.6	W 4118	228.4	W 3979	193.1	TULLES,BRODERIE
65606	EMBROIDERY	W 2047	158.9		151.9	W 2158	167.1	W 1707	128.3	BRODERIES PIECES,BANDES
657	SPECIAL TXTL FABRC,PRODS		164.0		181.8		254.0		276.4	TISSUS SPECIAUX

5. Special Exports F.O.B. by Commodities according to the S.I.T.C. (Rev. 2) in million U.S. Dollars
Exportations Spéciales F.O.B. par Produits d'après la C.T.C.I. (Rév. 2) en millions de Dollars E.U.

SITC CTCI	COMMODITY	1993 QUANTITY QUANTITE	1993 VALUE VALEUR	1994 QUANTITY QUANTITE	1994 VALUE VALEUR	1995 QUANTITY QUANTITE	1995 VALUE VALEUR	1996 QUANTITY QUANTITE	1996 VALUE VALEUR	PRODUIT
66	NONMETAL MINERAL MFS NES		1179.5		1317.6		1611.9		1533.0	ART MIN NON METALLIQUES
662	CLAY,REFRACTORY BLDG PRD	W 388122	253.7	W 487068	296.9	W 430618	384.8	W 385708	343.1	MAT CONST REFRACTAIRES
6623	REFRACTORY BUILDING PROD	W 307043	235.1	W 413612	280.3	W 380190	370.9	W 350350	334.3	BRIQUES REFRACTAIRES
66232	REFRACTRY BRICKS ETC NES	W 156166	155.1	W 183143	183.6	W 185579	236.9	W 181934	224.9	BRIQUES ETC REFRACTAIRES
663	MINERAL MANUFCTURES NES	W 472114	379.4		421.8	W 579078	530.5	W 550547	472.0	ART MIN MANUF NDA
6633	MINRL MFS NES NONCERAMIC	W 372650	188.9		205.0	W 465086	260.3	W 459536	231.7	OUVR MAT MINERALE NDA
66339	OTH MINRL MFS NONCERAMIC	W 80983	121.3		136.3	W 97632	168.9	W 82802	139.3	OUVRAGES EN PIERRES
665	GLASSWARE	W 114269	351.3		394.9	W 142417	448.5		450.8	OUVRAGES EN VERRE
6658	GLASS ARTICLES NES	W 8701	168.8		195.5	W 8358	224.9	W 7933	216.2	ARTICLES FAB EN VERRE NDA
66582	GLASS ORNAMENTS NES	W 6022	154.5	W 5732	180.4	W 7056	214.0	W 6668	204.8	PERLES DE VERRE
67	IRON AND STEEL		2120.5		2420.6		3374.9		2858.7	FER ET ACIER
671	PIG IRON ETC	W 28422	73.1	W 30036	93.1	W 32666	180.4	W 25779	119.7	FONTE,SPIEGEL,POUDRES
6716	FERRO–ALLOYS	W 20084	71.6	W 19077	91.1	W 30462	178.2	W 20802	116.6	FERRO–ALLIAGES
672	IRON,STEEL PRIMARY FORMS	W 316270	117.9		158.3	W 599565	271.2	W 436648	172.8	LINGOTS FER,ACIER
673	IRON,STEEL SHAPES ETC	W 299921	294.6		355.9	W 344449	464.8	W 303925	456.7	BARRES,PROFIL FER,ACIER
6732	IRON,STEEL BARS ETC	W 125806	191.1		223.1	W 98688	276.6	W 108508	308.9	BARRES FER,ACIER
67325	OTH ALLOY STEEL BARS ETC	W 64610	134.3		148.6	W 71284	208.8	W 74468	219.9	BARRES NON ACIERS ALLIES
674	IRN,STL UNIV,PLATE,SHEET	W 1691885	934.8	W 1861637	1091.0	W 2034648	1458.9	W 1579910	1101.5	LARGES PLATS,TOLES
6744	IRN,STL HVY PLATE,ROLLED	W 209064	130.9	W 268852	166.2	W 334991	271.1	W 220121	183.3	TOLES LAMINEES PLUS 4.75 MM
67441	— OF IRON OR SIMPLE STL	W 199094	84.3	W 258943	119.2	W 321450	199.2	W 205661	112.9	TOLES NON ACIER FIN CARB
6745	IRN,STL MED PLATE,ROLLED	W 229105	109.3	W 289666	144.9	W 347369	219.9	W 244382	147.8	TOLES 3 A 4.75 MM
6746	IRN,STL THIN PLATE,ROLLD	W 622492	294.5	W 629892	333.7	W 628245	411.7	W 409610	281.5	TOLES LAM MOINS 3MM
67461	— OF IRON OR SIMPLE STL	W 537477	224.4	W 554466	256.3	W 560089	317.0	W 352480	187.1	TOL NON AC FIN MOINS 3 MM
6749	OTH IRN,STL PLATES,SHEET	W 629974	398.9	W 672145	445.2	W 723093	554.6	W 704581	487.6	AUTRES TOLES FER,ACIER
67491	— OF IRON OR SIMPLE STL	W 623862	373.7	W 663688	419.2	W 720437	549.8	W 701614	482.6	AUT TOLES AUTRES ACIER FIN
676	RAILWY RAILS ETC IRN,STL	W 219267	166.9	W 249707	170.7	W 226294	183.7	W 196034	148.2	RAILS,ELEMENTS VOIES FERREE
67601	RAILWAY RAILS IRN,STL	W 200807	138.4	W 237782	153.6	W 218924	164.8	W 187639	131.7	RAILS,ELEMENTS FER,ACIER
678	IRON,STL TUBES,PIPES,ETC	W 441914	436.9		444.4	W 486798	644.5	W 554596	705.6	TUBES,TUYAUX EN FONTE,FER
6782	IRON,STL SEAMLESS TUBES	W 202423	187.7	W 165316	151.5	W 190643	240.7	W 263500	298.8	TUBES,TUYAUX SANS SOUDURE
6783	IRON,STL TUBES,PIPES NES	W 204675	141.2		172.3	W 267004	261.0	W 248508	223.7	AUT TUBES,TUYAUX FER,ACIER
68	NON–FERROUS METALS		773.0		938.6		1318.4		1293.7	METAUX NON FERREUX
682	COPPER EXC CEMENT COPPER	W 85562	242.2		294.7	W 121942	470.0	W 121294	390.4	CUIVRE
6821	COPPER NES,ALLOYS,UNWRT	W 61036	123.0	W 64992	148.4	W 83386	249.0	W 79834	191.2	CUIVRE BRUT
68212	COPPER REFINED,UNWROUGHT	W 61033	123.0	W 64991	148.4	W 83326	248.8	W 79817	191.2	CUIVRE AFFINE BRUT
6822	COPPER,ALLOYS WORKED	W 24527	119.3		146.3	W 38556	221.0	W 41460	199.2	CUIVRE,ALLIAGES OUVRES
684	ALUMINIUM	W 172452	483.1		590.3	W 208742	777.8	W 219130	728.0	ALUMINIUM
6842	ALUMINIUM,ALLOYS WORKED	W 115957	411.0		484.6	W 134066	611.8	W 143719	595.3	ALUMINIUM,ALLIAGES OUVRE
68421	ALUMINIUM BARS,WIRE,ETC	W 40829	131.1	W 53940	172.7	W 56182	239.4	W 59606	225.8	BARRES,PROFILES FILS ALU
68422	ALUMNM PLATE,SHEET,STRIP	W 42365	112.1	W 45595	135.7	W 44105	167.6	W 47298	162.3	TOLES, PLANCHES EN ALU
68423	ALUMINIUM FOIL	W 25208	147.2	W 26163	152.2	W 24647	173.4			FEUILLES,BANDES MINCES AL
69	METAL MANUFACTURES NES		2086.9		2383.9		2669.5		2801.4	ART MANUFACT EN METAL NDA
691	STRUCTURES AND PARTS NES	W 166557	459.9		475.7	W 177669	593.0	W 187028	581.5	CONSTRUCT FER,ACIER,ALU
6911	STRUCTURES,PARTS IRN,STL	W 154210	340.7		359.8	W 165117	449.1	W 174401	439.9	CONSTRUCT FER,ACIER,FONTE
692	METAL TANKS,BOXES,ETC	W 26015	107.3	W 34185	141.0	W 40090	180.7	W 43445	186.6	RECIPIENTS METALLIQUES
695	TOOLS	W 17782	332.9		395.8	W 18964	486.3	W 21160	455.3	OUTILS A MAIN
6954	BLADES,TIPS,ETC FR TOOLS	W 11686	253.7		293.5	W 11146	315.4	W 12787	300.9	OUTILS POUR MACHINE–OUTIL
69541	PARTS TO INSERT IN TOOLS	W 4897	151.7		177.4	W 3451	156.9	W 4752	148.5	OUTILS DE FORAGE
699	BASE METAL MFRS NES	W 178289	961.1		1128.0		1090.1		1282.8	ART MANUFACTURES MET NDA
6991	LOCKSMITHS WARES,ETC	W 82047	471.8		545.8	W 85330	539.4	W 81365	523.3	ARTICLES DE SERRURERIE
69913	BASE MTL DOOR,ETC FITTNG	W 79983	437.5		508.1	W 83510	500.7	W 79396	477.0	GARNITURES POUR MEUBLES
6997	IRON,STEEL ARTICLES NES	W 49742	159.1		163.2	W 39428	162.3	W 59076	204.7	OUV FONTE,FER,ACIER NDA
69979	IRN,STL MANUFACTURES NES	W 49723	159.0		163.1	W 39416	162.2	W 59073	204.7	AUT OUVRAGES EN FER NDA
6998	MFRS NES OF CPR,NIKL,ETC	W 21185	135.6		167.9	W 23550	180.2	W 27036	205.1	OUVRAGES EN CU,NI,AL,PB,ZN
6999	OTHR BASE METAL MFRS ETC	W 3606	94.2		128.1		64.4		210.5	OUVRAGES EN TUNGST,MOLYB
69999	BASE MTLS NES WRGHT,MFRS	W 135	2.9		4.3	W 2216	20.1	W 9048	210.5	MET COMMUNS OUVRES NDA
7	MACHINES,TRANSPORT EQUIP		15666.7		17544.9		20738.3		23474.1	MACHINES MATERIEL TRANSPORT
71	POWER GENERATING EQUIPMT		2387.2		2758.7		3324.1		3624.5	MACHINES GENERATRICES
713	INTRNL COMBUS PSTN ENGIN	W 154037	1883.2		2220.6	W 161332	2562.4	W 187797	2939.4	MOTEURS EXPL COMB INT, PIECE
7132	MOTOR VEHCL PISTN ENGINS	W 124594	1489.4	W 137207	1726.9	W 116297	1817.9	W 136187	2104.1	MOTEURS EXPL POUR VEHICULES
7139	PISTON ENGINE PARTS NES	W 26645	330.0		409.4	W 39568	615.1	W 45135	679.4	PIECES POUR 713.2,3,8
716	ROTATING ELECTRIC PLANT	W 25252	281.7		337.4	W 29996	371.6	W 33582	412.1	APP ELECTR ROTATIFS,PIECES
7162	AC MTRS,GENRTRS,GEN SETS	W 14837	187.6		211.2	W 19375	276.5	W 21574	311.2	MOTEURS ELECTRIQUES
72	MACHS FOR SPCL INDUSTRYS		2355.5		2579.1		3150.4		3106.8	MAC SPECIALES POUR INDUST
721	AGRIC MACHY,EXC TRACTORS	W 25538	165.6	W 28767	185.1	W 31635	229.7	W 30671	232.6	MACHINES AGRICOLES
723	CIVIL ENGNEERG EQUIP ETC	W 40986	303.4	W 54439	390.0	W 52843	462.3	W 47726	364.6	APPAREILS DE GENIE CIVIL
7234	CONST,MINING MACHNRY NES	W 36641	265.8	W 49210	359.3	W 47957	420.6	W 42291	320.2	MACH POUR LA CONST, MINES
72342	SLFPRP SHOVELS,EXCAVATRS	W 25992	160.7	W 35745	235.1	W 33576	260.9	W 30750	206.5	PELLES MECANIQUES
724	TEXTILE,LEATHER MACHNRY	W 15288	184.7		158.7	W 13178	177.4	W 15554	215.8	MACH POUR INDUSTRIE TEXTILE
725	PAPER ETC MILL MACHINERY	W 10973	184.2		201.7	W 14619	250.7	W 13301	202.0	MACHINES FABR PATE PAPIER
7259	PTS NES OF MACHS OF 725	W 8857	155.4		169.2	W 8665	147.8	W 9537	142.2	PIECES GROUPE 725
72591	PTS NES OF MACHS OF 7251	W 8714	152.2	W 9040	162.9	W 8492	143.2	W 9333	137.8	PIECES DU 725.1
726	PRINTG,BKBINDG MACHY,PTS	W 9107	185.2		201.0	W 9118	206.1	W 8587	205.2	MACHINES POUR IMPRIMERIE
727	FOOD MACHRY NON–DOMESTIC	W 5594	120.5	W 5276	128.6	W 5403	172.9		192.0	MACH INDUSTRIES ALIMENT
7272	OTH FOOD PROC MCHY,PARTS	W 5155	117.3	W 4994	125.6	W 5140	169.5		187.8	AUT MACH IND ALIMENTAIRE
72722	INDUS FOOD PROC MACH NES	W 5125	117.1	W 4983	125.5	W 5139	169.5	W 5880	187.8	MACHINES BOULANGERIE
728	OTH MACHY FOR SPCL INDUS	W 80117	1139.8		1228.2	W 74949	1552.3	W 198107	1548.5	AUT MACH IND PARTICULIERES
7281	MACH–TOOLS FR SPCL INDUS	W 17744	205.8		229.8	W 16159	250.9	W 15761	216.6	MACH–OUTILS SPEC IND PART
72812	MACH–TOOLS TO WORK WOOD	W 13285	154.7	W 16727	173.0	W 12311	183.2	W 12485	162.6	MACH–OUT POUR TRAVAIL BOIS
7284	MACHY FOR SPCL INDUS NES	W 43455	827.2		899.9	W 44934	1178.1	W 168523	1194.1	MACH SPEC IND PARTICUL.
72842	RUBBER,PLASTICS WRKG MCH	W 22015	369.4	W 20488	367.1	W 21534	496.1	W 27802	492.8	MACH IND CAOUT MAT PLAST
72848	OTH MCHY WITH INDIV FNCT	W 9487	234.8	W 17138	271.5	W 9589	294.7	W 8586	305.8	AUTRES MACHINES NDA
72849	PTS OF MACHS OF 7284 ETC	W 11071	210.6		243.5	W 12757	361.0	W 130765	349.5	PIECES DU 728.4 ETC
73	METALWORKING MACHINERY		536.8		463.8		634.7		573.2	MACH TRAVAIL DES METAUX
736	METALWORKING MACH–TOOLS		337.6		279.6	W 18083	374.1	W 19138	359.0	MACH–OUTILS TRAVAIL METAUX
737	METALWORKING MACHNRY NES	W 18646	199.2		184.3	W 17531	260.6	W 19165	214.2	MACH TRAV METAUX PIECES
74	GENRL INDUSTRL MACHY NES		2589.0		2914.5		3796.5		3840.1	MACH APP INDUSTRIE
741	HEATING,COOLING EQUIPMNT	W 38421	397.0		418.4	W 40413	559.4	W 50381	609.7	MACH CHAUFFAGE,PIECES
7416	HEATING,COOLING EQU NES	W 12833	128.9	W 12716	141.8	W 18162	214.4	W 19914	203.0	APP CHANGEMENT TEMP
742	PUMPS FOR LIQUIDS ETC	W 13144	199.1		242.6	W 13024	299.1	W 14365	295.1	POMPES MOTO–POMPES
743	PUMPS NES,CENTRFUGES ETC	W 43451	353.0		388.3	W 51651	537.2	W 52288	515.2	POMPES COMPRES,VENT ETC
7436	GAS,LIQUID FILTERS ETC	W 13263	128.4		153.7	W 17562	251.1	W 16909	242.4	APP POUR FILT DES LIQUIDES
744	MECHANICAL HANDLING EQU	W 79928	659.0		730.1	W 88721	861.4	W 87868	878.9	EQUIP MANUTENTION PIECES
7442	LIFTING,LOADING MACH NES	W 39302	316.7	W 44961	349.4	W 44109	445.6	W 45183	455.9	APP LEVAGE,MANUTENTION
74428	OTH HANDLING ETC MCH NES	W 17964	191.1	W 24688	213.1	W 22825	298.4	W 27539	322.5	AUT APP LEVAGE ETC
7449	PTS NES OF MACHY OF 7442	W 32709	288.3		310.2	W 37228	354.6	W 32400	342.7	PIECES DU 744.2
745	NONELEC MACHY,TOOLS NES	W 14978	214.0		279.4	W 22192	368.2	W 24139	362.8	AUT MACH NON ELEC,PIECES
7452	OTH NONELEC MCHS,PTS NES	W 14770	204.6		266.7	W 21826	351.1	W 23634	347.8	AUT MACH NON ELEC,PIECES
749	NONELEC MACH PTS,ACC NES	W 44092	767.1		856.1	W 62309	1171.4	W 66989	1178.7	PIECES MACH NON ELEC NDA
7491	BALL,ROLLER,ETC BEARINGS	W 10234	136.9		163.5	W 20053	258.2	W 20776	208.5	ROULEMENTS BILLES ETC
7492	COCKS,VALVES ETC NES	W 12104	247.1		260.3	W 14637	370.9	W 16139	395.0	ART ROB,SIM POUR TUYAUX
7493	SHAFT,CRANK,PULLEY ETC	W 15243	216.2		243.4	W 19164	315.5	W 20506	340.7	ARBRES TRANS,VILEBREQUINS

5. Special Exports F.O.B. by Commodities according to the S.I.T.C. (Rev. 2) in million U.S. Dollars
Exportations Spéciales F.O.B. par Produits d'après la C.T.C.I. (Rév. 2) en millions de Dollars E.U.

SITC CTCI	COMMODITY	1993 QUANTITY QUANTITE	1993 VALUE VALEUR	1994 QUANTITY QUANTITE	1994 VALUE VALEUR	1995 QUANTITY QUANTITE	1995 VALUE VALEUR	1996 QUANTITY QUANTITE	1996 VALUE VALEUR	PRODUIT
7499	OTH NONELEC MCHY PTS NES	W 6510	167.0		189.0	W 8456	226.9	W 9569	234.6	PIECES NON ELECT NDA
74991	FOUNDRY MOULDS ETC NES	W 5563	137.8	W 6363	155.5	W 7360	187.0	W 8424	194.7	MOULES POUR METAUX
75	OFFICE MACHNES,ADP EQUIP		520.8		501.9		683.4		603.8	MACH BUREAU TRAIT AUTOM
752	AUTOMTIC DATA PROC EQUIP	W 3695	195.0		189.3	W 2355	338.0	W 2038	295.5	MACH TRAIT INFORMATION
759	OFFICE,ADP MCH PTS,ACCES	W 2487	297.5		282.6	W 2611	311.1	W 2789	257.1	PIECES DU 751 ET 752
7599	ACCTG,ETC,ADP MCH PTS,AC	W 2191	285.0		266.9	W 2047	292.6	W 2110	237.3	PIECES DU 751 ET 752
76	TELECOMM,SOUND EQUIPMENT		1406.2		1549.7		557.8		1764.7	EQUIPMENT DE TELECOM
761	TELEVISION RECEIVERS	W 25246	408.9	W 30509	484.0	W 774	19.3	W 35117	572.5	RECEPTEURS DE TELEVISION
7611	COLOUR TV RECEIVERS	W 25238	408.4	W 30493	483.4	W 674	17.5	W 35102	572.2	RECEPTEURS COULEUR
763	SOUND RECORDRS,PHONOGRPH	W 11921	456.1		438.9	W 219	26.1	W 7987	302.7	PHONO,APP ENREGISTREMENT
7638	OTHR SOUND APPARATUS ETC	W 11910	455.8		438.7	W 202	25.4	W 7931	301.8	AUT APP D'ENREGIS,REPROD
76381	TV IMAGE,SND RECRDRS ETC				390.4	W 47	3.5	W 7720	269.5	APP ENREG,REPRO IMAG,SON
764	TELECOM EQPT,PTS,ACC NES	W 7005	483.0		603.2		502.4	W 11338	876.2	EQUIP TELECOM,PIECES
7641	LINE TELEPHONE,ETC EQUIP	W 1500	169.6		233.9	W 572	106.5	W 1766	229.1	APP TELEPHON PAR FIL
7649	PTS NES OF EQUIPMT OF 76	W 4333	247.4		301.6	W 6573	353.7	W 7817	506.2	PIECES DE LA DIV 76
76491	PTS NES OF APPAR OF 7641	W 858	70.8		110.1	W 808	135.0	W 886	202.3	PIECES POUR 764.1
76499	PARTS ETC OF SOUND EQUIP	W 2502	103.2		109.0	W 3689	112.0	W 5249	176.7	PIECES NDA POUR 763
77	ELECTRIC MACHNRY NES ETC		2909.4		3440.2		3799.3		4319.0	MACH APP ELECT NDA
771	ELECTRIC POWER MACHY NES	W 21929	277.9		332.5	W 27474	394.6	W 30329	467.7	MACH PROD,TRANS ELECTR
7712	OTH ELEC POWER MACHY NES	W 14228	208.5		255.6	W 16509	259.9	W 17428	336.2	AUT APP PROD TRANSF ELEC
772	SWITCHGEAR ETC,PARTS NES	W 16167	716.7		855.1	W 19241	1008.3	W 74378	1055.9	APP COUPURE,SECT ETC
7721	SWITCHGEAR ETC	W 13394	506.3		595.2	W 15732	670.3	W 18199	706.4	APP COUPURE,SECTIONMNT
7723	FIXED,VARIABLE RESISTORS	W 1286	120.6		132.9	W 1497	169.1	W 53553	177.4	POTENTIOMETRES PIECES
773	ELECTR DISTRIBUTNG EQUIP	W 54292	420.9		502.5	W 54637	517.0	W 76473	644.3	EQUIPMT DISTRIBUTION ELECT
7731	INSULATED WIRE,CABLE ETC	W 48394	369.2		443.1	W 47301	433.7	W 68713	553.5	FILS,CABLES ISOLES ELECT
775	HOUSEHOLD TYPE EQUIP NES	W 254674	413.6		429.2	W 24137	341.6	W 45747	533.2	MACH,APP USAGE DOMESTQUE
7758	ELECTRO–THERMIC APPL NES	W 26984	212.1		213.3	W 16848	160.0	W 19795	230.2	APP ELECTROTHERMIQ NDA
776	TRANSISTORS,VALVES,ETC	W 10702	511.6		634.8	W 2387	771.4	W 14600	807.1	LAMPES,TUBES,VALVES
7763	DIODES,TRANSISTORS,ETC	W 727	93.1		98.3	W 1251	225.8	W 3188	204.6	DIODES,TRANSISTORS
7764	ELECTRONIC MICROCIRCUITS	W 186	307.8		397.6	W 464	502.2	W 421	431.8	MICROSTRUCTURES ELECTRON
778	ELECTRICAL MACHINERY NES		506.7		622.4	W 71309	676.6		719.0	AUTRES MACH ELECT NDA
7788	OTH ELEC MACHY,EQUIP NES		259.5		353.1	W 16242	347.4		366.1	AUT MACH APP ELEC NDA
78	ROAD VEHICLES		2558.4		2866.6		4187.0		5115.9	VEHICULES ROUTIERS
781	PASS MOTOR VEH EXC BUSES	W 78898	892.3	W 83339	993.3	W 210194	1668.6	W 264291	2435.9	AUTO TRANSPORT PERSONNES
782	LORRIES,SPCL MTR VEH NES	W 62121	595.6	W 57268	514.0	W 66597	682.5	W 69058	647.9	VEHICULES SPECIAUX,MARCH
7821	LORRIES,TRUCKS	W 55649	474.1	W 50998	416.0	W 60978	596.9	W 63161	568.8	VEHICULES TRANSP MARCHAND
7822	SPECIAL MOTOR VEHCLS NES	W 6471	121.6	W 6269	98.1	W 5619	85.7	W 5896	79.2	VEHICULES USAGES SPECIAUX
783	ROAD MOTOR VEHICLES NES	W 10402	80.2	W 13484	91.6	W 16899	152.6	W 72856	338.8	VEHICULES ROUTIERS NDA
7832	TRACTORS FOR TR–TRAILERS	W 5793	38.5	W 7129	41.9	W 10176	97.2	W 63441	268.7	TRACTEURS ROUTIERS
784	MOTOR VEH PRTS,ACCES NES	W 83683	803.0		1042.6	W 122949	1354.5	W 112739	1341.4	PIECES 722,781,782,783
7849	OTHER MOTOR VEHCL PARTS	W 80823	771.8		953.8	W 116620	1243.3	W 107598	1261.5	PIECES 722,781,782,783
786	TRAILERS,NONMOTR VEH,NES	W 32999	122.4		154.8	W 40858	213.0	W 58266	226.1	REMORQUES,CADRES,CONTAIN
79	OTHR TRANSPORT EQUIPMENT		403.8		470.6		605.4		526.4	AUTRE MATERIEL TRANSPORT
791	RAILWAY VEHICLES	W 21864	337.1	W 23984	366.8	W 21208	488.6	W 21650	399.5	VEHIC MAT CHEMINS DE FER
7915	FRT,MAINT CARS NOT POWRD	W 9399	220.1	W 7991	178.6	W 9586	212.6	W 9834	214.9	WAGONS DE SERVICE
79151	RY SERV CARS NOT POWERED	W 9266	219.0	W 7186	176.8	W 7814	205.2	W 8146	210.7	WAGONS–ATELIERS,–GRUES
7919	RY TRACK FIXT,ETC,PARTS	W 11718	107.6	W 12920	101.1	W 8164	133.6	W 11270	179.4	MATER FIXE VOIES FERREES
8	MISC MANUFACTURED GOODS		5743.4		6144.6		7561.3		7706.0	ART MANUFACTURES DIVERS
812	*PLUMBG,HEATNG,LGHTNG EQ	W 58958	371.3		410.0	W 66417	486.5	W 69774	484.2	APPAR SANITAIRES CHAUFFAGE
8124	LIGHTING EQUIPMENT NES	W 23749	271.5		300.9	W 26132	354.3	W 29227	357.5	APPAREILS ECLAIRAGE ETC
81242	LAMPS,FITTINGS BASE METL	W 13113	178.2		207.1	W 13000	229.5	W 16869	248.9	APPAREILS D'ECLAIRAGE
821	*FURNITURE,PARTS THEREOF	W 85655	650.7		714.9	W 115322	903.4	W 143905	1040.7	MEUBLES ET PIECES
8211	CHAIRS,SEATS AND PARTS	W 21821	161.7	W 24769	196.3	W 24580	211.8	W 30747	304.0	SIEGES ET PIECES
82111	CHAIRS AND OTHER SEATS	W 20347	149.5	W 23448	183.9	W 22292	175.8	W 25175	182.8	SIEGES
8212	MED FURN,STUFFD FURNSHGS	W 10228	124.6		120.2	W 8016	133.0	W 7884	135.5	MOB MEDICO–CHIRUR,PIECES
8219	FURNITURE AND PARTS NES	W 53606	364.5	W 63715	398.5	W 82726	558.7	W 105274	601.3	AUTRES MEUBLES ET PIECES
82192	WOOD FURNITURE NES	W 32254	258.7	W 41463	292.0	W 36889	356.0	W 41138	355.3	MEUBLES NDA EN BOIS
84	CLOTHING AND ACCESSORIES		1058.9		1063.8		1287.1		1390.5	VETEMENTS
842	MENS OUTERWEAR NOT KNIT	W 2004	135.5		135.4	W 2055	143.9	W 2899	155.9	VET DESSUS POUR HOMMES
843	WOMENS OUTERWEAR NONKNIT	W 2555	202.2		184.1	W 3002	236.9	W 3585	248.1	VET DESSUS FEMMES MAT TEX
845	OUTERWEAR KNIT NONELASTC	W 3691	242.0		238.7	W 3752	293.0	W 4805	308.8	VET DESSOUS,ACCES BONNET
8451	— JERSEYS,PULLOVERS ETC	W 1821	121.2		108.4	W 1671	119.9	W 1978	108.9	CHANDAILS,PULL–OVERS ETC
846	UNDER GARMENTS KNITTED	W 5373	333.6		337.6	W 5017	411.1	W 5568	463.5	SOUS VETS DE BONNETERIE
8462	— OF COTTON NON ELASTIC	W 2962	164.3		174.8	W 2966	195.4	W 3395	216.6	SOUS–VET BONNET COTON
84629	—— OTHER	W 2962	164.3		174.8	W 2966	195.4	W 3395	216.6	AUT SOUS–VET BONNET COTON
851	*FOOTWEAR	W 9910	362.7	W 10144	389.3	W 12757	537.2	W 11974	482.0	CHAUSSURES
85102	FOOTWEAR LEATHER	W 6989	288.2	W 7013	309.1	W 9637	446.7	W 9031	409.1	CHAUS SEMELLES EN CUIR
87	PRECISION INSTRUMNTS NES		573.8		618.1		888.3		836.8	INSTRUM,APPAR SCIENT NDA
872	MEDICAL INSTRUMENTS NES	W 634	44.6		57.7	W 1468	192.0	W 1322	104.9	INSTR,APP MEDIC–CHIR NDA
874	MEASURNG,CONTROLNG INSTR		444.6		454.6		595.8	W 5430	612.2	INSTRUMENTS DE MESURE
8742	MEASUR,DRAW ETC INST,PTS	W 1893	154.1		149.8	W 2161	183.0	W 2197	195.2	INST DESSIN,TRACAGE,PCS
87421	MEASURNG,DRAWNG ETC INST	W 1714	132.9		120.3	W 1840	139.9	W 1850	146.6	INSTRUM DESSIN,TRACAGE
8743	GAS,LIQUID CONTROL INSTR	W 1629	110.5		118.0	W 2131	190.3	W 1650	152.1	APP,INSTR MESURE FLUIDES
88	PHOTO EQU,OPTICL GDS ETC		259.7		224.0		321.8		283.5	APP,FOURN PHOTO,OP,MONTR
884	OPTICAL GOODS NES	W 2054	152.2		107.5		176.1		137.9	ELEMENTS OPTIQ,ART LUNET
8842	SPECTACLES AND FRAMES	W 2033	143.8		99.1	W 436	165.3	W 369	129.3	LUNETTES ET MONTURES
89	MISC MANUFCTRD GOODS NES		2452.0		2707.8		3116.9		3168.3	ART MANUFACTURES DIVERS
892	PRINTED MATTER	W 96578	393.0		393.8		458.2	W 87445	446.7	IMPRIMES
8928	PRINTED MATTER NES	W 37970	178.4		191.5		207.0	W 34428	198.1	IMPRIMES NDA
893	ARTICLES OF PLASTIC NES		714.1		836.2		986.7		1011.0	OUVRAGES EN MAT DIVIS 58
8931	PLSTC PACKG CONTNRS,LIDS	W 54207	183.6		226.5	W 73326	289.2	W 84382	297.3	ART TRANSP EMBALLAGE ETC
8939	MISC PLASTIC ARTICLES	W 76993	470.3		537.7	W 117787	615.2	W 111930	651.7	ART DIVERS EN MAT DIV 58
89399	OTHR PLASTC ARTICLES NES	W 71227	441.2		508.2	W 111846	581.8	W 106306	622.9	AUT OUV MAT DIV 58
894	TOYS,SPORTING GOODS,ETC	W 24471	577.9		653.4	W 26566	764.4	W 26542	659.9	VOITURES ENFANTS,JOUETS
8942	TOYS,INDOOR GAMES ETC	W 6339	123.8		126.9	W 6455	172.7	W 7695	139.9	JOUETS,JEUX ETC
8947	OTH SPORT GDS,FAIR AMUSM	W 17823	451.0		491.3	W 19519	566.0	W 17879	483.5	AUT ART DE SPORT
89472	OTH OUTDOOR SPORT GOODS	W 17392	447.6		486.8	W 19251	562.1	W 17563	479.0	ART POUR JEUX PLEIN AIR
895	OFFICE SUPPLIES NES	W 22352	128.7		138.3		153.5		159.8	ART PAPET NDA
897	GOLD,SILVER WARE,JEWELRY		145.6		151.5		188.7		187.8	BIJOUTERIE,ORFEVRERIE
898	MUSICAL INSTRUMENTS,PTS	W 18031	372.6		413.5		410.4		540.3	INSTRUMENTS DE MUSIQUE
8983	SOUND RECRDNG TAPE,DISCS	W 17772	347.9		388.8	W 11562	390.7	W 11769	447.2	SUPPORTS SON POUR 763
89832	RECORDED DISCS,TAPES ETC	W 7254	235.8		283.1	W 10868	368.9	W 10791	423.0	DISQUES,PHONO,BANDES
9	GOODS NOT CLASSD BY KIND		181.0		127.3		4588.6		254.1	ART TRANSACT NON CLASSES
931	*SPECIAL TRANSACTIONS		1.2				4570.9			TRANS.SPECIALES
951	*WAR FIREARMS,AMMUNITION	W 2458	143.4		113.5	W 135	9.2	W 1019	88.3	VEHIC BLINDES ARMES
95101	ARMORED FIGHTNG VEHICLES	W 2458	143.4	W 410	17.7					CHARS DE COMBAT

1. HISTORICAL SERIES, 1992–1997 GENERAL TRADE, IMPORTS C.I.F., EXPORTS F.O.B.
SERIES HISTORIQUES, 1992–1997 COMMERCE GENERAL, IMPORTATIONS C.A.F., EXPORTATIONS F.O.B

YEAR ANNEE	VALUE IN MILLION U.S. DOLLARS VALEUR EN MILLION U.S. DOLLARS MERCHANDISE –MARCHANDISE		GOLD –OR		CONVERSION FACTORS FACTEURS DE CONVERSION CENTS E.U. PAR		INDEX NUMBERS –INDICES QUANTUM		UNIT VALUE VALEUR UNITAIRE	
	IMPORTS	EXPORTS	IMPORTS	EXPORTS	IMPORTS	EXPORTS	IMPORTS	EXPORTS	IMPORTS	EXPORTS
1992	332.53	754.15								
1993	241.00	350.90								
1994	726.77	625.09								
1995	681.00	550.00								
1996	960.63	631.25								
1997	794.34	781.31								

2. IMPORTS BY BROAD ECONOMIC CATEGORY AND EXPORTS BY INDUSTRIAL ORIGIN. (PERCENTAGE OF TOTAL VALUE)
IMPORTATIONS PAR CATEGORIES ECONOMIQUES ET EXPORTATIONS PAR BRANCHE D'ACTIVITE.(EN POURCENTAGE DE LA VALEUR TOTALE)

IMPORTS – IMPORTATIONS

	1990	1991	1992	1993	1994	1995	1996
TOTAL IMPORTS–IMPORTATIONS TOTALES							
1 FOOD BEV–ALIMENTATION BOISSONS							
11 PRIMARY–PRODUITS DE BASE							
111 FOR INDUSTRY–POUR L'INDUSTRIE							
112 FOR HOUSEHOLDS–POUR LES MENAGES							
12 PROCESSED–PRODUITS ELABORES							
121 FOR INDUSTRY–POUR L'INDUSTRIE							
122 FOR HOUSEHOLDS–POUR LES MENAGES							
2 IND SUPPLIES–APPROV INDUSTRIELS							
21 PRIMARY–PRODUITS DE BASE							
22 PROCESSED–PRODUITS ELABORES							
3 FUELS–COMBUSTIBLES							
31 PRIMARY–PRODUITS DE BASE							
32 PROCESSED–PRODUITS ELABORES							
321 MOTOR SPIRIT–ESSENCE							
322 OTHER–AUTRES							
4 MACHINERY–EQUIPEMENT							
41 CAPITAL EQUIPMENT–MACHINES							
42 PARTS–PIECES ACCESSOIRES							
5 TRANSPORT–TRANSPORT							
51 PASSENGER CARS–AUTOMOBILES							
52 OTHER–AUTRES							
521 INDUSTRIAL–INDUSTRIELS							
522 NON INDUSTRIAL–NON INDUSTRIEL							
53 PARTS–PIECES ACCESSOIRES							
6 CONSUM GOODS–BIENS CONSOMMATION							
61 DURABLE–DURABLES							
62 SEMI DURABLE–SEMI DURABLES							
63 NON DURABLE–NON DURABLES							
7 GOODS NES–BIENS NDA							

EXPORTS – EXPORTATIONS

	1990	1991	1992	1993	1994	1995	1996
TOTAL EXPORTS–EXPORTATIONS TOTALES							
1 AGRICULTURE							
2 MINING QUARRY–INDUS EXTRACTIVES							
3 MANUFACTURING–IND MANUFACTUR							
31 FOOD BEV TOBACCO–ALIM BOISS TAB							
32 TEXTILES–INDUSTRIES TEXTILES							
33 WOOD & PRODUCTS–BOIS & PRODUITS							
34 PAPER & PRODUCTS–PAPIER & PRODT							
35 CHEMICALS–INDUSTRIES CHIMIQUES							
36 NON METAL MIN–MIN NON METAL							
37 BASIC METAL–IND METAL BASE							
38 METAL MANUF–MANUF METAL							
39 OTH MANUF IND–AUTRES MANUF							

3. TRADE BY PRINCIPAL COUNTRIES OF ORIGIN AND DESTINATION (VALUE IN MILLION U.S. DOLLARS)
ECHANGES SELON LES PRINCIPAUX PAYS D'ORIGINE ET DE DESTINATION (VALEUR EN MILLIONS DE DOLLARS EU)

COUNTRIES–PAYS	SPECIAL IMPORTS C.I.F. IMPORTATIONS SPECIALES C.A.F				
	1992	1993	1994	1995	1996
World	939.8	549.9	777.9	667.6	960.6
Africa		0.1			
Americas		10.9	10.0	13.4	25.3
– Northern America		10.9	10.0	13.3	16.8
– LAIA					7.5
– CACM					
– Caribbean				0.1	1.0
– Rest of America					
Asia excl fmr USSR		70.1	182.9	300.9	415.6
– Middle East		63.6	158.1	290.4	394.2
Asia former USSR		110.2	260.6	97.4	73.4
Europe excl fmr USSR		68.3	80.9	107.7	161.1
– European Union		48.0	69.7	84.5	136.0
– Eastern Europe		10.3	8.8	19.9	9.9
– Rest of Europe		10.0	2.4	3.3	15.2
Europe former USSR		211.1	237.4	143.2	271.3
Oceania			0.3		11.7
Other					
Turkey/Turquie	87.1	63.6	76.0	140.5	216.3
Russian Federation	25.5	127.0	117.5	88.3	158.4
Ukraine	214.2	53.6	86.3	33.5	94.4
Turkmenistan/Turkménistn	26.6	54.6	195.6	51.4	14.7
Iran (Islamic Rep of)			66.8	80.3	66.0
United Arab Emirates			9.0	68.7	108.6
Germany/Allemagne	9.6	18.8	31.9	43.8	77.2
Kazakhstan	42.5	35.1	51.9	17.5	19.3
Georgia/Géorgie	18.4	18.4	7.9	18.9	28.3
United Kingdom	41.4	5.3	6.9	9.3	14.9
USA/Etats–Unis d'Amer	23.6	10.8	10.0	13.3	16.8
Belarus/Bélarus	34.7	8.2	7.9	4.7	5.0
France, Monaco	26.8	1.4	5.6	5.7	12.3
Poland/Pologne	24.6	6.1	2.5	7.7	1.2
Republic of Moldova	5.3	9.5	13.5	4.4	8.6
Belgium–Luxembourg	5.8	0.1	8.9	8.8	8.3
Switzerland,Liechtenst.	0.7	9.7	2.4	3.3	15.2
Uzbekistan/Ouzbékistan	6.7	1.4	2.6	7.7	7.2
Austria/Autriche	8.3	7.5	0.9	3.6	2.7
Italy/Italie	4.8	8.7	3.9	2.5	2.6
Korea, Republic of			14.2	2.4	5.5
Lithuania/Lituanie	1.8	5.0	4.6	4.5	2.2
Netherlands/Pays–Bas	3.0	1.2	1.3	3.2	7.9
Bulgaria/Bulgarie	2.7	1.7	1.3	7.0	3.4
Israel/Israël			7.0	2.8	5.7
Estonia/Estonie	1.4	5.4	2.7	3.8	2.0
Hungary/Hongrie	4.4	1.3	4.1	1.6	2.0
Ireland/Irlande	4.8	4.6	1.4	0.3	2.2
Latvia/Lettonie	0.2	2.4	4.9	4.0	0.7
Finland/Finlande			7.3	1.5	2.9
China/Chine	0.1	2.9	2.5	2.8	2.8
Cyprus/Chypre			6.3	0.7	2.1
Kyrgyzstan/Kirghizistan	0.8	0.6	2.4	1.8	3.5
Czech Republic		1.2	0.7	3.3	2.6
New Zealand					7.5
Mexico/Mexique					7.5
Tajikistan/Tadjikistan	6.5	0.1	0.2	0.1	0.4
Former Czechoslovakia	6.8				
Denmark/Danemark			0.5	3.8	2.3
Afghanistan	2.3	2.4			

COUNTRIES–PAYS	SPECIAL EXPORTS F.O.B. EXPORTATIONS SPECIALES F.O.B.				
	1992	1993	1994	1995	1996
Monde	1483.9	724.6	652.7	637.2	631.2
Afrique					
Amériques				1.1	5.0
– Amérique du Nord				1.1	2.2
– ALAI					
– MCAC					
– Caraïbes					2.8
– Autre Amérique					
Asie anc. URSS exclus			276.2	218.1	268.9
– Moyen–Orient			274.8	215.5	268.3
Asie ancienne URSS			56.3	144.5	149.7
Europe anc. URSS exclus			88.7	123.4	62.8
– Union Européenne			79.8	93.6	58.7
– Europe de l'Est			4.9	1.5	2.2
– Autre de l'Europe			4.0	28.3	1.9
Europe ancienne URSS			225.8	147.7	144.4
Océanie			0.7	0.8	0.2
Autre					
Russian Federation	347.6	185.2	139.7	100.2	111.4
Iran (Islamic Rep of)			257.4	186.1	226.1
Ukraine	136.7	48.3	58.6	33.6	21.9
United Kingdom	144.9	2.9	61.7	48.6	13.0
Turkey/Turquie	125.6	60.6	16.5	26.4	39.0
Georgia/Géorgie	61.1	30.6	16.6	45.3	91.6
Turkmenistan/Turkménistn	55.1	39.3	17.1	70.6	34.3
Kazakhstan	38.7	30.5	16.5	20.5	15.4
Italy/Italie	19.0	13.3	0.1	26.4	10.1
Belarus/Bélarus	29.3	14.9	7.6	2.7	3.3
Austria/Autriche	33.6	5.6	9.5	3.5	3.9
Republic of Moldova	14.7	13.2	12.6	3.7	3.8
Tajikistan/Tadjikistan	35.0	6.3	1.1	3.3	1.7
USA/Etats–Unis d'Amer	39.5	3.4		1.1	2.2
Switzerland,Liechtenst.	2.4	3.2	4.0	28.3	1.9
Germany/Allemagne	12.9	4.3	4.1	3.9	3.1
Uzbekistan/Ouzbékistan	8.7	4.1	2.8	4.0	5.6
Lithuania/Lituanie	5.2	6.2	3.7	6.4	3.2
Greece/Grèce			1.2	10.0	9.8
Sweden/Suède			0.1		18.0
Poland/Pologne	6.0	5.7	4.3	0.4	1.6
Latvia/Lettonie	8.1	4.2	3.4	1.0	0.7
Former Czechoslovakia	14.8				
Bulgaria/Bulgarie	5.4	2.2	0.3	0.8	0.5
Estonia/Estonie	3.3	4.6	0.2	0.1	0.1
Kyrgyzstan/Kirghizistan	2.7	1.3	2.2	0.8	1.1
Hungary/Hongrie	5.7	0.8	0.3	0.3	0.1
Finland/Finlande	1.0	5.5			
Belgium–Luxembourg	3.7	0.3	0.9	0.6	0.4
United Arab Emirates			0.9	1.6	3.1
France, Monaco	1.5	2.0	1.0	0.1	0.4
Denmark/Danemark	4.8				
Afghanistan	0.4	2.5	1.1	0.4	0.1
Australia/Australie	1.9	0.5	0.7	0.8	0.2
Czech Republic		3.5			
China/Chine	0.3		0.3	1.8	0.5
British Virgin Islds					2.8
Ireland/Irlande			1.2		
Oman				1.1	
Yugoslavia/Yougoslavie	0.9				

(VALUE AS PERCENTAGE OF WORLD TOTAL)(VALEURS EN POURCENTAGE DU TOTAL MONDIAL)

	1987	1988	1989	1990	1991	1992	1993	1994	1995	1996
Africa							0.0			
Americas							2.0	1.3	2.0	2.6
– Northern America							2.0	1.3	2.0	1.7
– LAIA										0.8
– CACM										
– Caribbean									0.0	0.1
– Rest of America										
Asia excl fmr USSR							12.7	23.5	45.1	43.3
– Middle East							11.6	20.3	43.5	41.0
Asia former USSR							20.0	33.5	14.6	7.6
Europe excl fmr USSR							12.4	10.4	16.1	16.8
– European Union							8.7	9.0	12.7	14.2
– Eastern Europe							1.9	1.1	3.0	1.0
– Rest of Europe							1.8	0.3	0.5	1.6
Europe former USSR							38.4	30.5	21.4	28.2
Oceania								0.0		1.2
Other										
Turkey/Turquie						9.3	11.6	9.8	21.0	22.5
Russian Federation						2.7	23.1	15.1	13.2	16.5
Ukraine						22.8	9.7	11.1	5.0	9.8
Turkmenistan/Turkménistn						2.8	9.9	25.1	7.7	1.5
Iran (Islamic Rep of)								8.6	12.0	6.9
United Arab Emirates								1.2	10.3	11.3
Germany/Allemagne						1.0	3.4	4.1	6.6	8.0
Kazakhstan						4.5	6.4	6.7	2.6	2.0
Georgia/Géorgie						2.0	3.3	1.0	2.8	2.9
United Kingdom						4.4	1.0	0.9	1.4	1.6

	1987	1988	1989	1990	1991	1992	1993	1994	1995	1996
Afrique										
Amériques									0.2	0.8
– Amérique du Nord									0.2	0.3
– ALAI										
– MCAC										
– Caraïbes										0.4
– Autre Amérique										
Asie anc. URSS exclus								42.3	34.2	42.6
– Moyen–Orient								42.1	33.8	42.5
Asie ancienne URSS								8.6	22.7	23.7
Europe anc. URSS exclus								13.6	19.4	9.9
– Union Européenne								12.2	14.7	9.3
– Europe de l'Est								0.8	0.2	0.3
– Autre de l'Europe								0.6	4.4	0.3
Europe ancienne URSS								34.6	23.2	22.9
Océanie								0.1	0.1	0.0
Autre										
Russian Federation						23.4	25.6	21.4	15.7	17.6
Iran (Islamic Rep of)								39.4	29.2	35.8
Ukraine						9.2	6.7	9.0	5.3	3.5
United Kingdom						9.8	0.4	9.5	7.6	2.1
Turkey/Turquie						8.5	8.4	2.5	4.1	6.2
Georgia/Géorgie						4.1	4.2	2.5	7.1	14.5
Turkmenistan/Turkménistn						3.7	5.4	2.6	11.1	5.4
Kazakhstan						2.6	4.2	2.5	3.2	2.4
Italy/Italie						1.3	1.8	0.0	4.1	1.6
Belarus/Bélarus						2.0	2.1	1.2	0.4	0.5

4. Special Imports C.I.F. by Commodities according to the S.I.T.C. (Rev. 2) in million U.S. Dollars
Importations Spéciales C.A.F. par Produits d'après la C.T.C.I. (Rév. 2) en millions de Dollars E.U.

SITC CTCI	COMMODITY	1993 QUANTITY QUANTITE	1993 VALUE VALEUR	1994 QUANTITY QUANTITE	1994 VALUE VALEUR	1995 QUANTITY QUANTITE	1995 VALUE VALEUR	1996 QUANTITY QUANTITE	1996 VALUE VALEUR	PRODUIT
	ALL COMMODITIES				778.0		667.6		960.6	TOUS PRODUITS
01	MEAT AND PREPARATIONS				16.6		32.1		45.1	VIANDES ET PREPARATIONS
02	DAIRY PRODCTS,BIRDS'EGGS						42.1		58.1	PRODUITS LAITIERS,OEUFS
023	BUTTER			W 5700	6.7					BEURRE
04	CEREALS AND PREPARATIONS						40.1		109.1	CEREALES ET PRODUITS
044	MAIZE UNMILLED			W 124840	10.2					MAIS NON MOULU
04601	FLOUR OF WHEAT OR MESLIN			W 246544	31.9					FARINE DE FROMENT
054	VEG ETC FRSH,SMPLY PRSVD						4.1		9.1	LEGUMES FRAIS,CONG,SECS
057	FRUIT,NUTS,FRESH,DRIED						4.1		5.1	FRUITS FRAIS OU SECS
06	SUGAR AND PREPS,HONEY						51.1		72.1	SUCRES ET PRODUITS
061	SUGAR AND HONEY			W 46459	14.5					SUCRES ET MIEL
07	COFFEE,TEA,COCOA,SPICES						4.1			CAFE,THE,CACAO,EPICES
11	BEVERAGES						10.1		15.1	BOISSONS
12	TOBACCO AND MANUFACTURES				12.9					TABACS BRUTS FABRIQUES
24	CORK AND WOOD				5.5		5.1		17.1	LIEGE ET BOIS
263	COTTON						1.1		4.1	COTON
3	MINERAL FUELS ETC						88.1		43.1	COMBUSTIBLES MINERAUX LUB
333	CRUDE PETROLEUM			W 852600	31.5					HUILES BRUTES DE PETROLE
341	*GAS,NATURAL AND MANUFCT			MV 2478300	192.6					GAZ NATUREL,GAZ MANUFACT
4	ANIMAL,VEGETABLE OIL,FAT				31.5					HUILES,GRAISSES ANIM,VEG
51	ORGANIC CHEMICALS						3.1		6.1	PROD CHIMIQ ORGANIQUES
51216	ETHYL ALC,DENATRD SPIRIT			V 2259	2.7					ALCOOL ETHYLIQUE NON DENAT
52	INORGANIC CHEMICALS						3.1		4.1	PROD CHIM INORGANIQUES
53	DYES,TANNING,COLOUR PROD				2.1		3.1		10.1	PROD TEINTURE,COLORANTS
541	*MEDICINAL,PHARM PRODUCT						27.1		10.1	PROD MEDICINAUX PHARMACEUT
55	PERFUME,CLEANING ETC PRD						1.1		3.1	PROD POUR PARFUM,TOILETTE
572	*EXPLOSIVES,PYROTECH PRO						5.1		12.1	EXPLOSIFS
62	RUBBER MANUFACTURES NES						7.1		18.1	CAOUTCHOUC MANUFACTURE
6252	TYRES,NEW,BUS OR LORRY			N 37800	4.1					PNEUS POUR AUTOBUS,CAMIONS
64	PAPER,PAPERBOARD AND MFR						13.1		18.1	PAPIERS,CARTONS & OUVRAGES
65	TEXTILE YARN,FABRICS,ETC				0.3		2.1		5.1	FILS,TISSUS,ARTICLES TEXTILE
657	SPECIAL TXTL FABRC,PRODS						1.1		3.1	TISSUS SPECIAUX
66	NONMETAL MINERAL MFS NES				4.8		5.1		11.1	ART MIN NON METALLIQUES
67	IRON AND STEEL						14.1		34.1	FER ET ACIER
682	COPPER EXC CEMENT COPPER						2.1		4.1	CUIVRE
684	ALUMINIUM				1.6		2.1		12.1	ALUMINIUM
69	METAL MANUFACTURES NES						22.1		32.1	ART MANUFACT EN METAL NDA
7	MACHINES,TRANSPORT EQUIP						118.0		224.0	MACHINES MATERIEL TRANSPORT
761	TELEVISION RECEIVERS				3.0					RECEPTEURS DE TELEVISION
78	ROAD VEHICLES						35.1		39.1	VEHICULES ROUTIERS
781	PASS MOTOR VEH EXC BUSES			N 1091	9.1					AUTO TRANSPORT PERSONNES
782	LORRIES,SPCL MTR VEH NES			N 348	3.0					VEHICULES SPECIAUX,MARCH
821	*FURNITURE,PARTS THEREOF				5.9		6.1		8.1	MEUBLES ET PIECES
84	CLOTHING AND ACCESSORIES						3.1		3.1	VETEMENTS
892	PRINTED MATTER						2.1		16.1	IMPRIMES

5. Special Exports F.O.B. by Commodities according to the S.I.T.C. (Rev. 2) in million U.S. Dollars
Exportations Spéciales F.O.B. par Produits d'après la C.T.C.I. (Rév. 2) en millions de Dollars E.U.

SITC CTCI	COMMODITY	1993		1994		1995		1996		PRODUIT
		QUANTITY QUANTITE	VALUE VALEUR	QUANTITY QUANTITE	VALUE VALEUR	QUANTITY QUANTITE	VALUE VALEUR	QUANTITY QUANTITE	VALUE VALEUR	
	ALL COMMODITIES				652.7		637.2		631.2	TOUS PRODUITS
054	VEG ETC FRSH,SMPLY PRSVD			W 29700	10.0		1.1		1.1	LEGUMES FRAIS,CONG,SECS
0565	VEGTBLES PRSVD,PREPD NES			W 1000	5.6					LEGUMES PREPARES CONSERVE
057	FRUIT,NUTS,FRESH,DRIED						10.1		3.1	FRUITS FRAIS OU SECS
11	BEVERAGES						11.1		7.1	BOISSONS
1121	WINE OF FRESH GRAPES ETC				16.1					VINS DE RAISINS FRAIS
11242	DISTILLD WINE,GRAPE MARC				9.4					EAUX–DE–VIE NATURELLES
1223	OTH MANUFACTURED TOBACCO			W 12900	10.9					TABACS FUMER,CHIQUER,PRISER
263	COTTON						117.0		59.1	COTON
2631	RAW COTTON,EXCL LINTERS			W 74800	98.6					COTON EN MASSE
3	MINERAL FUELS ETC						372.0		419.0	COMBUSTIBLES MINERAUX LUB
334	PETROLEUM PRODUCTS,REFIN			W 1804000	207.1					PRODUITS RAFFINES
51	ORGANIC CHEMICALS						8.1		11.1	PROD CHIMIQ ORGANIQUES
5157	SULPHONAMIDES,ETC			W 4500	3.1					SULFAMIDES,SULTONES ETC
52	INORGANIC CHEMICALS						6.1		6.1	PROD CHIM INORGANIQUES
5542	WASHING PREPARATIONS ETC			W 172100	3.7					PROD ORG TENSIO–ACT NDA
572	*EXPLOSIVES,PYROTECH PRO						11.1		23.1	EXPLOSIFS
62	RUBBER MANUFACTURES NES						3.1		3.1	CAOUTCHOUC MANUFACTURE
659	FLOOR COVERINGS,ETC				2.6					COUVRE–PARQUETS,TAPIS ETC
67	IRON AND STEEL						8.1		3.1	FER ET ACIER
678	IRON,STL TUBES,PIPES,ETC			W 5900	2.0					TUBES,TUYAUX EN FONTE,FER
684	ALUMINIUM				10.4		4.1		1.1	ALUMINIUM
69	METAL MANUFACTURES NES						4.1		2.1	ART MANUFACT EN METAL NDA
69781	DOMSTC FOOD MACH NONELEC				2.3					MOULINS A CAFE ETC
7	MACHINES,TRANSPORT EQUIP						42.1		48.1	MACHINES MATERIEL TRANSPORT
716	ROTATING ELECTRIC PLANT				11.2					APP ELECTR ROTATIFS,PIECES
72343	SLFPRP CONST ETC MCH NES				25.3					AUT MACH EXTR,TERRASSEM
7415	AIR–CONDITIONING MACHNRY			N 112536	20.6					GROUPES CONDITION AIR
77521	DOMESTIC REFRIGERATORS			N 59255	9.2					REFRIGERATEURS
78	ROAD VEHICLES						3.1		4.1	VEHICULES ROUTIERS
84	CLOTHING AND ACCESSORIES						4.1		4.1	VETEMENTS

Bahamas

1. HISTORICAL SERIES, 1961–1996 GENERAL TRADE, IMPORTS C.I.F., EXPORTS F.O.B.
SERIES HISTORIQUES, 1961–1996 COMMERCE GENERAL, IMPORTATIONS C.A.F., EXPORTATIONS F.O.B

YEAR ANNEE	VALUE IN MILLION BAHAMIAN DOLLARS VALEUR EN MILLION BAHAMIAN DOLLARS MERCHANDISE –MARCHANDISE		GOLD –OR		CONVERSION FACTORS U.S. CENTS PER BAHAMIAN DOLLAR FACTEURS DE CONVERSION CENTS E.U. PAR BAHAMIAN DOLLAR		INDEX NUMBERS –INDICES QUANTUM		UNIT VALUE VALEUR UNITAIRE	
	IMPORTS	EXPORTS	IMPORTS	EXPORTS	IMPORTS	EXPORTS	IMPORTS	EXPORTS	IMPORTS	EXPORTS
1961	86.90	8.50			98.0000	98.0000				
1962	70.10	9.20			98.0000	98.0000				
1963	80.80	9.90			98.0000	98.0000				
1964	102.00	16.00			98.0000	98.0000				
1965	107.00	19.00			98.0000	98.0000				
1966	141.60	22.80			98.0000	98.0000				
1967	165.50	32.30			98.0000	98.0000				
1968	180.00	51.80			98.0000	98.0000				
1969	302.30	54.30			98.0000	98.0000				
1970	337.50	89.60			100.0000	100.0000				
1971	511.30	266.60			100.0000	100.0000				
1972	484.90	343.40			100.0000	100.0000				
1973	764.30	529.80			100.0000	100.0000				
1974	1908.40	1443.60			100.0000	100.0000				
1975	2696.90	2508.30			100.0000	100.0000				
1976	3124.50	2992.30			100.0000	100.0000				
1977	3568.20	3260.70			100.0000	100.0000				
1978	3149.60	3058.40			100.0000	100.0000				
1979	3513.90	3786.00			100.0000	100.0000				
1980	7545.60	5009.40			100.0000	100.0000				
1981	7284.50	6189.20			100.0000	100.0000				
1982	6348.80	4534.40			100.0000	100.0000				
1983	4616.30	3970.30			100.0000	100.0000				
1984	4097.90	3392.70			100.0000	100.0000				
1985	3077.90	2629.50			100.0000	100.0000				
1986	3288.90	2701.00			100.0000	100.0000				
1987	3041.00	2727.70			100.0000	100.0000				
1988	2263.50	2163.80			100.0000	100.0000				
1989	3001.00	2786.00			100.0000	100.0000				
1990	2919.90	2678.00			100.0000	100.0000				
1991	1091.10	225.10			100.0000	100.0000				
1992	1037.50	192.30			100.0000	100.0000				
1993	953.90	162.30			100.0000	100.0000				
1994	1055.90	167.00			100.0000	100.0000				
1995	1243.10	175.90			100.0000	100.0000				
1996	1261.60	201.70			100.0000	100.0000				

2. IMPORTS BY BROAD ECONOMIC CATEGORY AND EXPORTS BY INDUSTRIAL ORIGIN. (PERCENTAGE OF TOTAL VALUE)
IMPORTATIONS PAR CATEGORIES ECONOMIQUES ET EXPORTATIONS PAR BRANCHE D'ACTIVITE.(EN POURCENTAGE DE LA VALEUR TOTALE)

IMPORTS – IMPORTATIONS

	1989	1990	1991	1992	1993	1994	1995
TOTAL IMPORTS–IMPORTATIONS TOTALES							
1 FOOD BEV–ALIMENTATION BOISSONS							
11 PRIMARY–PRODUITS DE BASE							
111 FOR INDUSTRY–POUR L'INDUSTRIE							
112 FOR HOUSEHOLDS–POUR LES MENAGES							
12 PROCESSED–PRODUITS ELABORES							
121 FOR INDUSTRY–POUR L'INDUSTRIE							
122 FOR HOUSEHOLDS–POUR LES MENAGES							
2 IND SUPPLIES–APPROV INDUSTRIELS							
21 PRIMARY–PRODUITS DE BASE							
22 PROCESSED–PRODUITS ELABORES							
3 FUELS–COMBUSTIBLES							
31 PRIMARY–PRODUITS DE BASE							
32 PROCESSED–PRODUITS ELABORES							
321 MOTOR SPIRIT–ESSENCE							
322 OTHER–AUTRES							
4 MACHINERY–EQUIPEMENT							
41 CAPITAL EQUIPMENT–MACHINES							
42 PARTS–PIECES ACCESSOIRES							
5 TRANSPORT–TRANSPORT							
51 PASSENGER CARS–AUTOMOBILES							
52 OTHER–AUTRES							
521 INDUSTRIAL–INDUSTRIELS							
522 NON INDUSTRIAL–NON INDUSTRIEL							
53 PARTS–PIECES ACCESSOIRES							
6 CONSUM GOODS–BIENS CONSOMMATION							
61 DURABLE–DURABLES							
62 SEMI DURABLE–SEMI DURABLES							
63 NON DURABLE–NON DURABLES							
7 GOODS NES–BIENS NDA							

EXPORTS – EXPORTATIONS

	1989	1990	1991	1992	1993	1994	1995
TOTAL EXPORTS–EXPORTATIONS TOTALES							
1 AGRICULTURE							
2 MINING QUARRY–INDUS EXTRACTIVES							
3 MANUFACTURING–IND MANUFACTUR							
31 FOOD BEV TOBACCO–ALIM BOISS TAB							
32 TEXTILES–INDUSTRIES TEXTILES							
33 WOOD & PRODUCTS–BOIS & PRODUITS							
34 PAPER & PRODUCTS–PAPIER & PRODT							
35 CHEMICALS–INDUSTRIES CHIMIQUES							
36 NON METAL MIN–MIN NON METAL							
37 BASIC METAL–IND METAL BASE							
38 METAL MANUF–MANUF METAL							
39 OTH MANUF IND–AUTRES MANUF							

 Bahamas

3. TRADE BY PRINCIPAL COUNTRIES OF ORIGIN AND DESTINATION (VALUE IN MILLION U.S. DOLLARS)
ECHANGES SELON LES PRINCIPAUX PAYS D'ORIGINE ET DE DESTINATION (VALEUR EN MILLIONS DE DOLLARS EU)

COUNTRIES–PAYS	GENERAL IMPORTS C.I.F. IMPORTATIONS GENERALES C.A.F				
	1991	1992	1993	1994	1995
World	1091.2	1037.5	953.9	1071.1	1243.1
Africa	0.1				
Americas	964.8		772.0	907.5	1020.0
– Northern America	887.4		772.0	907.5	1020.0
– LAIA	13.3				
– CACM	2.8				
– Caribbean	55.5				
– Rest of America	5.8				
Asia excl fmr USSR	20.6				
– Middle East	0.0				
Asia former USSR					
Europe excl fmr USSR	104.0		15.1	7.3	8.7
– European Union	91.0		15.1	7.3	8.7
– Eastern Europe	0.5				
– Rest of Europe	12.6				
Europe former USSR	0.1				
Oceania	1.2				
Other	0.4				
USA/Etats–Unis d'Amer	866.0	759.9	757.3	901.4	1008.7
United Kingdom	23.9	22.2	15.1	7.3	8.7
Canada	21.2	20.2	14.7	6.2	11.3
Aruba	52.2				
Denmark/Danemark	23.7				
France, Monaco	20.8				
Japan/Japon	14.6				
Switzerland,Liechtenst.	12.5				
Panama	5.8				
Germany/Allemagne	5.6				
Netherlands/Pays–Bas	5.0				
Argentina/Argentine	4.4				
Austria/Autriche	3.7				
Spain/Espagne	3.5				
Italy/Italie	3.3				
China, Hong Kong SAR	3.1				
Venezuela	2.9				
Brazil/Brésil	2.3				
Mexico/Mexique	1.7				
Guatemala	1.5				
Peru/Pérou	1.3				
Trinidad and Tobago	1.2				
El Salvador	1.0				
Barbados/Barbade	0.9				
Australia/Australie	0.8				
Colombia/Colombie	0.7				
Other Asia n.e.s.	0.6				
Jamaica/Jamaïque	0.6				
Korea, Republic of	0.6				
Belgium–Luxembourg	0.5				
China/Chine	0.5				
New Zealand	0.4				
Areas n.e.s.	0.4				
Costa Rica	0.4				
Sweden/Suède	0.4				
Ireland/Irlande	0.3				
Thailand/Thaïlande	0.3				
Former Czechoslovakia	0.3				
Bermuda/Bermudes	0.3				
Philippines	0.2				

COUNTRIES–PAYS	GENERAL EXPORTS F.O.B. EXPORTATIONS GENERALES F.O.B.				
	1991	1992	1993	1994	1995
Monde	225.1	192.4	162.3	167.0	175.9
Afrique					
Amériques	174.1			126.3	146.0
– Amérique du Nord	149.8			126.3	146.0
– ALAI	8.3				
– MCAC	1.0				
– Caraïbes	12.3				
– Autre Amérique	2.7				
Asie anc. URSS exclus	0.1				
– Moyen–Orient	0.0				
Asie ancienne URSS					
Europe anc. URSS exclus	50.8			10.5	4.0
– Union Européenne	50.5			10.5	4.0
– Europe de l'Est	0.0				
– Autre de l'Europe	0.3				
Europe ancienne URSS					
Océanie	0.0				
Autre	0.1				
USA/Etats–Unis d'Amer	142.5	105.1	105.6	122.6	142.6
United Kingdom	27.2	9.3	5.8	10.5	4.0
Canada	6.7	8.4	4.8	3.7	3.4
France, Monaco	14.5				
Germany/Allemagne	6.2				
Mexico/Mexique	4.0				
Grenada/Grenade	2.9				
Aruba	2.6				
Panama	2.6				
Brazil/Brésil	2.3				
Netherlands Antilles	1.6				
Jamaica/Jamaïque	1.4				
Haiti/Haïti	1.0				
Italy/Italie	1.0				
Dominican Republic	0.7				
Netherlands/Pays–Bas	0.6				
Venezuela	0.6				
Bermuda/Bermudes	0.6				
Cayman Is/Is Caïmans	0.5				
Belgium–Luxembourg	0.5				
Uruguay	0.4				
Barbados/Barbade	0.3				
Switzerland,Liechtenst.	0.3				
Honduras	0.3				
Guatemala	0.3				
Trinidad and Tobago	0.3				
Antigua and Barbuda	0.3				
Ireland/Irlande	0.2				
Costa Rica	0.2				
Paraguay	0.2				
Bolivia/Bolivie	0.2				
Turks and Caicos Isls	0.2				
Colombia/Colombie	0.2				
Spain/Espagne	0.2				
Argentina/Argentine	0.1				
Chile/Chili	0.1				
Peru/Pérou	0.1				
Saint Lucia/Ste–Lucie	0.1				
Nicaragua	0.1				
British Antarctic Ter	0.1				

(VALUE AS PERCENTAGE OF WORLD TOTAL)(VALEURS EN POURCENTAGE DU TOTAL MONDIAL)

	1986	1987	1988	1989	1990	1991	1992	1993	1994	1995
Africa			17.1		4.8	0.0				
Americas			46.6		47.0	88.4		80.9	84.7	82.1
– Northern America			41.0		36.7	81.3		80.9	84.7	82.1
– LAIA			4.8		7.5	1.2				
– CACM			0.1		0.1	0.3				
– Caribbean			0.5		2.5	5.1				
– Rest of America			0.2		0.2	0.5				
Asia excl fmr USSR			26.5		40.9	1.9				
– Middle East			22.7		39.7	0.0				
Asia former USSR										
Europe excl fmr USSR			8.6		7.0	9.5		1.6	0.7	0.7
– European Union			8.0		5.9	8.3		1.6	0.7	0.7
– Eastern Europe			0.0		0.0	0.0				
– Rest of Europe			0.6		1.1	1.2				
Europe former USSR			0.0		0.3	0.0				
Oceania			0.0		0.0	0.1				
Other			1.1		0.0	0.0				
USA/Etats–Unis d'Amer			40.1		36.2	79.4	73.2	79.4	84.2	81.1
United Kingdom			5.0		3.7	2.2	2.1	1.6	0.7	0.7
Canada			0.9		0.6	1.9	2.0	1.5	0.6	0.9
Aruba			0.0		0.4	4.8				
Denmark/Danemark			0.1		0.1	2.2				
France, Monaco			0.7		0.6	1.9				
Japan/Japon			0.6		0.5	1.3				
Switzerland,Liechtenst.			0.6		0.4	1.1				
Panama			0.2		0.2	0.5				
Germany/Allemagne						0.5				

	1986	1987	1988	1989	1990	1991	1992	1993	1994	1995
Afrique			0.1		0.0					
Amériques			95.2		96.0	77.4			75.6	83.0
– Amérique du Nord			92.9		94.7	66.6			75.6	83.0
– ALAI			0.5		0.3	3.7				
– MCAC			0.0		0.0	0.4				
– Caraïbes			0.8		0.6	5.4				
– Autre Amérique			0.9		0.3	1.2				
Asie anc. URSS exclus			2.2		1.0	0.0				
– Moyen–Orient			0.0		0.0	0.0				
Asie ancienne URSS										
Europe anc. URSS exclus			2.3		2.9	22.6			6.3	2.3
– Union Européenne			2.2		2.6	22.4			6.3	2.3
– Europe de l'Est			0.0		0.3	0.0				
– Autre de l'Europe			0.1		0.0	0.1				
Europe ancienne URSS					0.0					
Océanie			0.2		0.1	0.0				
Autre			0.0		0.0	0.0				
USA/Etats–Unis d'Amer			90.9		93.8	63.3	54.7	65.1	73.4	81.1
United Kingdom			0.8		0.8	12.1	4.8	3.6	6.3	2.3
Canada			1.9		0.9	3.0	4.4	2.9	2.2	1.9
France, Monaco			0.2		0.4	6.5				
Germany/Allemagne						2.8				
Mexico/Mexique			0.1		0.2	1.8				
Grenada/Grenade			0.0		0.0	1.3				
Aruba			0.1		0.0	1.2				
Panama			0.9		0.3	1.2				
Brazil/Brésil			0.3		0.1	1.0				

Bahamas

4. General Imports C.I.F. by Commodities according to the S.I.T.C. (Rev. 2) in million U.S. Dollars
Importations Générales C.A.F. par Produits d'après la C.T.C.I. (Rév. 2) en millions de Dollars E.U.

SITC CTCI	COMMODITY	1992		1993		1994		1995		PRODUIT
		QUANTITY QUANTITE	VALUE VALEUR	QUANTITY QUANTITE	VALUE VALEUR	QUANTITY QUANTITE	VALUE VALEUR	QUANTITY QUANTITE	VALUE VALEUR	
	ALL COMMODITIES		1037.6		954.0		1071.1		1243.1	TOUS PRODUITS
0	FOOD AND LIVE ANIMALS		184.3		190.0		196.9		209.0	ALIMENTS,ANIMAUX VIVANTS
1	BEVERAGES AND TOBACCO		24.8		22.1		19.6		20.4	BOISSONS ET TABACS
2	CRUDE MATERLS,EXCL FUELS		18.2		19.5		23.1		26.2	MAT BRUTES NON COMESTIBLES
3	MINERAL FUELS ETC		116.8		76.3		87.7		156.5	COMBUSTIBLES MINERAUX LUB
334	PETROLEUM PRODUCTS,REFIN		83.6		69.0		72.1		81.7	PRODUITS RAFFINES
33411	MOTOR,AVIATION SPIRIT		42.4		37.5		36.2		40.8	ESSENCES MOTEURS D'AVIONS
33421	KEROSENE INCL JET FUEL		3.1		3.1		3.3		3.7	PETROLES LAMPANTS
3343	GAS OILS		35.2		25.6		29.1		33.0	GAS OILS
3345	LUBS,PETROLEUM OILS NES		2.9		2.9		3.6		4.4	HUILES LUBRIFIANTES
341	*GAS,NATURAL AND MANUFCT		4.9							GAZ NATUREL,GAZ MANUFACT
4	ANIMAL,VEGETABLE OIL,FAT		2.3		2.9		3.5		3.8	HUILES,GRAISSES ANIM,VEG
5	CHEMCLS,RELATED PROD NES		100.4		94.3		104.5		100.7	PRODUITS CHIMIQUES
6	BASIC MANUFACTURES		170.9		154.4		177.8		194.1	ART MANUFACTURES
7	MACHINES,TRANSPORT EQUIP		223.8		198.9		245.9		308.7	MACHINES MATERIEL TRANSPORT
8	MISC MANUFACTURED GOODS		172.6		174.0		188.6		203.0	ART MANUFACTURES DIVERS
9	GOODS NOT CLASSD BY KIND		24.0		22.0		12.9		21.1	ART TRANSACT NON CLASSES

Bahamas

5. General Exports F.O.B. by Commodities according to the S.I.T.C. (Rev. 2) in million U.S. Dollars
Exportations Générales F.O.B. par Produits d'après la C.T.C.I. (Rév. 2) en millions de Dollars E.U.

SITC CTCI	COMMODITY	1992		1993		1994		1995		PRODUIT
		QUANTITY QUANTITE	VALUE VALEUR	QUANTITY QUANTITE	VALUE VALEUR	QUANTITY QUANTITE	VALUE VALEUR	QUANTITY QUANTITE	VALUE VALEUR	
	ALL COMMODITIES		192.4		162.4		167.1		176.0	TOUS PRODUITS
0	FOOD AND LIVE ANIMALS		63.1		48.6		66.1		64.9	ALIMENTS,ANIMAUX VIVANTS
034	FISH,FRESH,CHILLED,FROZN		5.7		4.5		3.0			POISSON FRAIS, REFRIG,CONG
036	SHELL FISH FRESH,FROZEN		51.8						56.2	CRUSTACES,MOLLUSQUES
05	VEGETABLES AND FRUIT		5.7		4.4		3.2		2.9	LEGUMES ET FRUITS
1	BEVERAGES AND TOBACCO		21.9		12.1		9.0		3.5	BOISSONS ET TABACS
112	ALCOHOLIC BEVERAGES		21.2				8.6		3.3	BOISSONS ALCOOLIQUES
11249	OTH ALCOHOLC BEVS,CMPNDS				12.0					BOISSONS ALCOOLIQUES NDA
2	CRUDE MATERLS,EXCL FUELS		18.9		26.4		33.1		31.3	MAT BRUTES NON COMESTIBLES
278	OTHER CRUDE MINERALS		9.3							AUTRES MINERAUX BRUTS
2783	COMMON SALT,ETC		8.2		14.8		15.6		13.5	SEL
27899	MINERAL SUBSTANCES NES		1.1		1.3		0.9		0.4	MATIERES MINERALES NDA
3	MINERAL FUELS ETC		5.1		0.1		3.4		0.1	COMBUSTIBLES MINERAUX LUB
5	CHEMCLS,RELATED PROD NES		37.3		44.5		22.1		16.8	PRODUITS CHIMIQUES
553	PERFUMERY,COSMETICS,ETC		1.5		0.1					PRODUITS DE PARFUMERIE
6	BASIC MANUFACTURES		9.6		8.7		4.2		7.5	ART MANUFACTURES
7	MACHINES,TRANSPORT EQUIP		29.5		14.6		22.8		46.0	MACHINES MATERIEL TRANSPORT
8	MISC MANUFACTURED GOODS		6.9		7.3		6.7		6.0	ART MANUFACTURES DIVERS

1. HISTORICAL SERIES, 1961–1996 GENERAL TRADE, IMPORTS C.I.F., EXPORTS F.O.B. # 1
SERIES HISTORIQUES, 1961–1996 COMMERCE GENERAL, IMPORTATIONS C.A.F., EXPORTATIONS F.O.B

YEAR ANNEE	VALUE IN MILLION BAHRAINI DINARS VALEUR EN MILLION BAHRAINI DINARS MERCHANDISE –MARCHANDISE		GOLD –OR		CONVERSION FACTORS U.S. CENTS PER BAHRAINI DINAR FACTEURS DE CONVERSION CENTS E.U. PAR BAHRAINI DINAR		INDEX NUMBERS –INDICES QUANTUM		UNIT VALUE VALEUR UNITAIRE	
	IMPORTS	EXPORTS	IMPORTS	EXPORTS	IMPORTS	EXPORTS	IMPORTS	EXPORTS	IMPORTS	EXPORTS
1961		9.40				210.0000				
1962	31.20	11.00			210.0000	210.0000				
1963	33.00	10.60			210.0000	210.0000				
1964	37.90	10.50			210.0000	210.0000				
1965	38.80	10.70			210.0000	210.0000				
1966	42.00	12.60			210.0000	210.0000				
1967	45.50	14.70			210.0000	210.0000				
1968	52.00	18.50			210.0000	210.0000				
1969	99.50	121.30			210.0000	210.0000				
1970	117.70	130.60			210.0000	210.0000				
1971	148.00	151.60			210.0000	210.0000				
1972	165.60	141.70			228.0000	228.0000				
1973	212.60	162.40			250.7580	250.7620				
1974	473.30	459.00			253.3320	253.3320				
1975	458.10	453.70			252.8400	252.8400				
1976	660.50	548.50			252.7750	252.7750				
1977	802.80	730.10			252.7500	252.7500				
1978	792.30	733.10			258.2230	258.1640				
1979	945.30	948.00			262.4090	262.4520				
1980	1313.10	1355.90			265.3140	265.3320				
1981	1550.60	1634.60			265.9598	265.9595				
1982	1358.90	1424.80			265.9598	265.9596				
1983	1256.60	1202.80			265.9599	265.9598				
1984	1308.30	1204.70			265.9465	265.9597				
1985	1168.10	1089.20			265.9598	265.9597				
1986	904.30	827.00			265.9597	265.9596				
1987	1020.30	913.50			265.9596	265.9597				
1988	975.10	906.70			265.9597	265.9596				
1989	1178.20	1064.50			265.9597	265.9597				
1990	1395.60	1414.00			265.9597	265.9597				
1991	1547.30	1320.00			265.9597	265.9597				
1992	1602.90	1302.60			265.9596	265.9598				
1993	1450.60	1400.00			265.9591	265.9591				
1994	1409.20	1359.90			265.9578	265.9577				
1995	1397.10	1546.40			265.9579	265.9579				
1996	1538.80	1730.50			265.9576	265.9576				

2. IMPORTS BY BROAD ECONOMIC CATEGORY AND EXPORTS BY INDUSTRIAL ORIGIN. (PERCENTAGE OF TOTAL VALUE)
IMPORTATIONS PAR CATEGORIES ECONOMIQUES ET EXPORTATIONS PAR BRANCHE D'ACTIVITE.(EN POURCENTAGE DE LA VALEUR TOTALE)

IMPORTS – IMPORTATIONS

	1990	1991	1992	1993	1994	1995	1996
TOTAL IMPORTS–IMPORTATIONS TOTALES	100.	100.	100.	100.	100.	100.	100.
1 FOOD BEV–ALIMENTATION BOISSONS	7.6	7.3	7.6	8.9	9.6	10.6	10.2
11 PRIMARY–PRODUITS DE BASE	3.5	3.3	3.4	4.1	4.9	5.3	5.1
111 FOR INDUSTRY–POUR L'INDUSTRIE	0.9	0.7	0.8	0.8	1.4	1.5	1.8
112 FOR HOUSEHOLDS–POUR LES MENAGES	2.6	2.6	2.7	3.3	3.5	3.8	3.3
12 PROCESSED–PRODUITS ELABORES	4.1	4.1	4.2	4.9	4.7	5.3	5.1
121 FOR INDUSTRY–POUR L'INDUSTRIE	0.6	0.7	0.7	0.7	0.8	1.1	1.0
122 FOR HOUSEHOLDS–POUR LES MENAGES	3.5	3.4	3.5	4.1	3.9	4.3	4.1
2 IND SUPPLIES–APPROV INDUSTRIELS	18.6	18.4	18.6	23.0	22.1	23.5	22.4
21 PRIMARY–PRODUITS DE BASE	1.0	1.0	0.8	1.1	1.3	1.3	1.1
22 PROCESSED–PRODUITS ELABORES	17.6	17.4	17.8	22.0	20.8	22.2	21.3
3 FUELS–COMBUSTIBLES	49.2	42.6	36.4	37.1	33.2	37.4	41.0
31 PRIMARY–PRODUITS DE BASE	49.2	42.6	36.4	37.1	33.2	37.4	41.0
32 PROCESSED–PRODUITS ELABORES	0.0	0.0	0.0	0.0	0.0	0.0	0.0
321 MOTOR SPIRIT–ESSENCE							
322 OTHER–AUTRES	0.0	0.0	0.0	0.0	0.0	0.0	0.0
4 MACHINERY–EQUIPEMENT	6.8	13.8	16.5	10.0	11.8	10.5	10.3
41 CAPITAL EQUIPMENT–MACHINES	5.1	8.9	7.4	7.4	10.4	9.0	8.6
42 PARTS–PIECES ACCESSOIRES	1.7	4.9	9.1	2.6	1.5	1.5	1.7
5 TRANSPORT–TRANSPORT	7.2	6.4	9.4	8.8	10.1	6.0	5.3
51 PASSENGER CARS–AUTOMOBILES	2.5	2.3	3.4	3.7	3.4	2.6	2.6
52 OTHER–AUTRES	0.9	1.1	1.4	1.0	3.2	0.6	0.5
521 INDUSTRIAL–INDUSTRIELS	0.9	1.0	1.4	1.0	3.2	0.6	0.5
522 NON INDUSTRIAL–NON INDUSTRIEL	0.0	0.0	0.0	0.0	0.0	0.0	0.0
53 PARTS–PIECES ACCESSOIRES	3.8	3.0	4.5	4.1	3.5	2.8	2.3
6 CONSUM GOODS–BIENS CONSOMMATION	8.5	8.9	10.5	11.8	11.2	11.4	9.9
61 DURABLE–DURABLES	3.2	3.3	4.3	4.8	3.4	3.1	2.7
62 SEMI DURABLE–SEMI DURABLES	3.9	4.0	4.5	5.0	5.4	5.7	4.7
63 NON DURABLE–NON DURABLES	1.5	1.6	1.7	2.0	2.5	2.7	2.5
7 GOODS NES–BIENS NDA	2.1	2.6	1.0	0.4	1.9	0.5	0.8

EXPORTS – EXPORTATIONS

	1990	1991	1992	1993	1994	1995	1996
TOTAL EXPORTS–EXPORTATIONS TOTALES	100.	100.	100.	100.	100.	100.	100.
1 AGRICULTURE	0.1	0.3	0.3	0.5	0.5	0.4	0.4
2 MINING QUARRY–INDUS EXTRACTIVES	78.2	77.6	75.2	65.8	59.5	60.1	66.5
3 MANUFACTURING–IND MANUFACTUR	21.7	22.1	24.5	33.8	39.9	39.5	33.1
31 FOOD BEV TOBACCO–ALIM BOISS TAB	0.6	1.1	1.6	1.9	1.8	2.0	1.8
32 TEXTILES–INDUSTRIES TEXTILES	0.6	0.7	1.3	1.8	2.4	2.6	2.4
33 WOOD & PRODUCTS–BOIS & PRODUITS	0.0	0.0	0.0	0.0	0.0	0.0	0.0
34 PAPER & PRODUCTS–PAPIER & PRODT	0.2	0.2	0.1	0.4	0.5	0.6	0.6
35 CHEMICALS–INDUSTRIES CHIMIQUES	3.7	4.7	3.0	3.2	6.0	6.0	3.8
36 NON METAL MIN–MIN NON METAL	0.3	0.2	0.1	0.1	0.1	0.1	0.2
37 BASIC METAL–IND METAL BASE	12.5	12.4	15.2	21.9	25.5	25.0	21.6
38 METAL MANUF–MANUF METAL	3.7	2.6	3.0	4.1	3.5	3.0	2.6
39 OTH MANUF IND–AUTRES MANUF	0.2	0.2	0.2	0.3	0.1	0.2	0.1

3. TRADE BY PRINCIPAL COUNTRIES OF ORIGIN AND DESTINATION (VALUE IN MILLION U.S. DOLLARS)
ECHANGES SELON LES PRINCIPAUX PAYS D'ORIGINE ET DE DESTINATION (VALEUR EN MILLIONS DE DOLLARS EU)

COUNTRIES–PAYS	GENERAL IMPORTS C.I.F. IMPORTATIONS GENERALES C.A.F				
	1992	1993	1994	1995	1996
World	4272.1	3858.0	3761.8	3715.7	4092.6
Africa	18.6	27.4	27.9	23.4	31.2
Americas	420.6	415.9	485.4	399.9	374.4
– Northern America	368.9	357.7	416.6	320.8	293.1
– LAIA	49.6	57.2	67.1	77.8	80.0
– CACM	1.3	0.7	1.2	0.9	0.8
– Caribbean	0.8	0.3	0.5	0.4	0.5
– Rest of America	0.0	0.0	0.0	0.0	0.0
Asia excl fmr USSR	997.6	934.1	2175.0	2243.6	2491.7
– Middle East	313.1	313.3	1559.0	1713.9	1966.3
Asia former USSR			0.0	0.0	1.4
Europe excl fmr USSR	1102.8	794.9	842.7	778.9	841.4
– European Union	1017.9	747.5	767.6	718.4	771.9
– Eastern Europe	15.0	3.5	3.6	6.3	5.8
– Rest of Europe	69.9	43.8	71.5	54.2	63.7
Europe former USSR	0.6	0.8	1.3	4.5	1.6
Oceania	172.6	250.3	191.9	190.2	278.0
Other	1559.2	1434.6	37.7	75.3	72.9
Saudi Arabia	148.0	133.3	1353.8	1515.0	1780.8
Areas n.e.s.	1512.0	1370.5	0.0	0.0	0.1
USA/Etats–Unis d'Amer	355.1	349.7	407.7	302.8	272.6
United Kingdom	287.6	235.0	233.5	213.3	221.7
Japan/Japon	275.2	244.7	209.6	148.2	151.2
Australia/Australie	160.2	241.6	181.7	179.5	265.5
Germany/Allemagne	269.8	159.7	137.5	145.5	169.8
France, Monaco	146.1	92.9	125.4	85.1	117.2
Italy/Italie	112.1	96.5	97.8	79.5	87.5
United Arab Emirates	78.7	81.2	97.5	97.8	93.8
India/Inde	72.6	87.4	98.0	89.4	96.0
Bunkers, ship stores	47.2	64.1	37.7	75.2	72.8
Brazil/Brésil	45.6	51.2	60.9	72.9	65.4
Netherlands/Pays–Bas	61.8	50.7	56.9	52.5	49.0
China/Chine	35.8	46.7	54.1	51.6	49.3
Switzerland,Liechtenst.	55.2	35.5	39.8	45.4	44.2
Korea, Republic of	32.0	39.7	53.6	39.9	43.5
Malaysia/Malaisie	40.1	35.7	46.6	41.2	32.2
China, Hong Kong SAR	83.8	21.3	22.8	18.0	17.4
Other Asia n.e.s.	36.9	34.8	32.9	27.0	26.8
Thailand/Thaïlande	32.8	31.6	26.0	31.9	27.0
Pakistan	22.7	23.8	21.5	34.6	33.2
Belgium–Luxembourg	37.4	18.9	23.0	22.9	22.6
Spain/Espagne	28.7	20.6	20.0	22.8	24.1
Indonesia/Indonésie	20.1	21.4	25.0	22.8	24.1
Sweden/Suède	22.5	19.5	17.9	30.8	22.1
Denmark/Danemark	23.2	21.4	18.8	24.2	25.2
Iran (Islamic Rep of)	19.4	20.4	25.9	17.6	14.7
Singapore/Singapour	22.4	22.2	13.4	12.5	12.0
Turkey/Turquie	14.2	16.2	21.8	16.8	12.7
Jordan/Jordanie	12.3	17.3	15.7	18.0	15.4
Canada	13.8	8.0	8.9	18.0	20.4
Norway,Svalbard and JM	12.4	6.1	29.5	6.5	12.6
Kuwait/ Koweït	8.5	12.7	11.3	14.9	13.5
Ireland/Irlande	7.7	10.7	13.2	12.8	13.5
Austria/Autriche	10.3	8.6	9.4	19.0	9.8
New Zealand	12.3	8.7	10.1	10.7	12.4
Tunisia/Tunisie	7.5	10.1	9.4	6.4	11.1
Qatar	8.2	8.8	9.3	9.6	8.3
Egypt/Egypte	8.0	9.3	8.9	7.8	9.0

COUNTRIES–PAYS	EXPORTS EXPORTATIONS ES F.O.B.				
	1992	1993	1994	1995	1996
Monde	3464.4	3710.1	3452.1	4160.6	4602.0
Afrique	5.9	12.1	16.0	17.1	25.2
Amériques	72.3	104.8	152.5	134.5	110.5
– Amérique du Nord	72.2	104.4	152.1	131.6	107.8
– ALAI	0.1	0.4	0.4	2.9	2.6
– MCAC					
– Caraïbes	0.1		0.0	0.0	0.0
– Autre Amérique					
Asie anc. URSS exclus	609.6	970.5	1090.7	1280.9	1231.0
– Moyen–Orient	297.8	423.9	450.2	524.5	512.4
Asie ancienne URSS			0.1	0.0	0.2
Europe anc. URSS exclus	104.4	100.6	85.4	132.3	77.0
– Union Européenne	100.8	98.6	81.2	125.8	73.6
– Europe de l'Est	0.1	0.0	0.1	0.1	0.1
– Autre de l'Europe	3.5	2.0	4.1	6.4	3.3
Europe ancienne URSS		0.1	0.1	1.1	0.9
Océanie	6.0	6.3	2.5	5.9	15.0
Autre	2666.1	2515.7	2104.8	2588.8	3142.2
Special Categories			2054.7	2501.4	3059.3
Areas n.e.s.	2651.7	2503.2	37.7	75.2	72.8
Saudi Arabia	142.6	200.6	219.5	251.2	247.6
Japan/Japon	76.1	192.1	193.1	142.3	195.7
Korea, Republic of	100.5	115.9	119.7	157.6	119.1
USA/Etats–Unis d'Amer	69.1	102.6	150.4	130.8	106.6
Other Asia n.e.s.	21.0	76.5	92.1	136.5	124.3
India/Inde	32.8	62.3	101.9	103.6	85.9
United Arab Emirates	36.2	70.0	58.5	74.2	83.0
Kuwait/ Koweït	41.7	45.5	42.1	58.3	48.2
Iran (Islamic Rep of)	20.9	49.4	55.8	48.2	40.4
Netherlands/Pays–Bas	43.7	18.4	34.6	46.9	13.5
Qatar	25.9	24.0	27.9	31.6	42.4
Singapore/Singapour	20.1	20.1	32.3	30.1	26.8
Indonesia/Indonésie	16.1	14.6	27.0	35.8	25.8
Malaysia/Malaisie	12.3	24.8	18.4	42.4	20.7
United Kingdom	18.2	40.7	16.7	23.6	17.8
Jordan/Jordanie	11.5	14.0	21.7	36.3	20.2
Pakistan	17.4	8.7	12.1	14.6	28.9
China, Hong Kong SAR	4.0	10.9	13.3	19.4	21.2
Oman	4.2	12.0	20.7	11.0	17.3
China/Chine	1.0	4.6	13.5	22.3	23.7
Italy/Italie	16.7	10.7	9.1	16.9	11.4
Bunkers, ship stores	14.4	12.6	12.4	12.2	10.1
Thailand/Thaïlande	4.2	6.4	8.2	21.9	18.9
Philippines	3.9	7.5	6.4	20.2	18.1
Belgium–Luxembourg	3.3	2.7	2.9	12.8	20.0
Turkey/Turquie	13.2	6.5	0.3	8.9	6.6
Germany/Allemagne	5.3	8.6	7.0	5.4	4.3
Tunisia/Tunisie	3.2	6.1	4.8	6.8	6.6
Australia/Australie	4.7	5.0	1.1	4.0	10.9
Sweden/Suède	7.7	12.7	3.3	0.4	0.1
France, Monaco	4.0	3.5	4.8	8.2	1.9
Egypt/Egypte	0.9	2.5	2.7	1.8	7.0
Spain/Espagne	1.2	0.9	2.2	7.2	3.4
Bangladesh	0.8	0.7	0.1	5.0	4.9
Norway,Svalbard and JM	1.2	0.5	2.2	5.6	1.3
Sri Lanka	1.6	0.9	1.2	3.0	3.1
New Zealand	1.2	1.2	1.3	1.8	4.2
Lebanon/Liban	0.6	1.3	1.6	2.1	3.5

(VALUE AS PERCENTAGE OF WORLD TOTAL)(VALEURS EN POURCENTAGE DU TOTAL MONDIAL)

	1987	1988	1989	1990	1991	1992	1993	1994	1995	1996
Africa	0.3	0.3	0.2	0.3	0.2	0.4	0.7	0.7	0.6	0.8
Americas	13.5	26.5	8.8	8.4	9.4	9.8	10.8	12.9	10.8	9.1
– Northern America	12.0	25.4	7.7	7.2	8.7	8.6	9.3	11.1	8.6	7.2
– LAIA	1.3	1.1	1.1	1.1	0.7	1.2	1.5	1.8	2.1	2.0
– CACM	0.2		0.0	0.0	0.0	0.0	0.0	0.0	0.0	0.0
– Caribbean	0.0	0.0	0.0	0.0	0.0	0.0	0.0	0.0	0.0	0.0
– Rest of America			0.0	0.0	0.0	0.0	0.0	0.0	0.0	0.0
Asia excl fmr USSR	28.3	23.0	21.4	17.8	19.4	23.4	24.2	57.8	60.4	60.9
– Middle East	1.6	1.6	7.0	6.3	7.2	7.3	8.1	41.4	46.1	48.0
Asia former USSR								0.0	0.0	0.0
Europe excl fmr USSR	55.4	48.0	24.0	18.5	24.7	25.8	20.6	22.4	21.0	20.6
– European Union	49.2	42.7	23.0	17.6	23.2	23.8	19.4	20.4	19.3	18.9
– Eastern Europe	0.1	0.0	0.2	0.1	0.2	0.4	0.1	0.1	0.2	0.1
– Rest of Europe	6.1	5.3	0.9	0.7	1.3	1.6	1.1	1.9	1.5	1.6
Europe former USSR			0.0	0.1	0.1	0.0	0.0	0.0	0.1	0.0
Oceania	2.5	2.1	4.4	5.4	3.4	4.0	6.5	5.1	5.1	6.8
Other	0.0	0.0	41.1	49.6	42.9	36.5	37.2	1.0	2.0	1.8
Saudi Arabia			2.8	2.7	3.3	3.5	3.5	36.0	40.8	43.5
Areas n.e.s.	0.0	0.0	39.6	48.2	41.7	35.4	35.5	0.0	0.0	0.0
USA/Etats–Unis d'Amer	11.1	24.6	7.5	7.1	8.4	8.3	9.1	10.8	8.1	6.7
United Kingdom	21.3	18.5	9.8	5.7	6.2	6.7	6.1	6.2	5.7	5.4
Japan/Japon	12.3	10.7	6.4	5.0	4.9	6.4	6.3	5.6	4.0	3.7
Australia/Australie	2.0	1.7	4.2	5.1	3.2	3.8	6.3	4.8	4.8	6.5
Germany/Allemagne					5.1	6.3	4.1	3.7	3.9	4.1
France, Monaco	4.2	3.6	1.8	1.9	3.5	3.4	2.4	3.3	2.3	2.9
Italy/Italie	6.0	5.2	2.8	1.7	2.6	2.6	2.5	2.6	2.1	2.1
United Arab Emirates			1.8	1.6	2.2	1.8	2.1	2.6	2.6	2.3

	1987	1988	1989	1990	1991	1992	1993	1994	1995	1996
Afrique	5.9	5.0	0.6	0.5	0.2	0.2	0.3	0.5	0.4	0.5
Amériques	6.0	10.5	1.8	2.0	2.0	2.1	2.8	4.4	3.2	2.4
– Amérique du Nord	6.0	10.4	1.8	1.9	2.0	2.1	2.8	4.4	3.2	2.3
– ALAI	0.0	0.1	0.0	0.0	0.0	0.0	0.0	0.0	0.1	0.1
– MCAC	0.0									
– Caraïbes			0.0		0.0	0.0		0.0	0.0	0.0
– Autre Amérique										
Asie anc. URSS exclus	70.7	65.8	17.6	15.3	15.9	17.6	26.2	31.6	30.8	26.7
– Moyen–Orient	7.3	8.6	11.4	8.7	7.4	8.6	11.4	13.0	12.6	11.1
Asie ancienne URSS								0.0	0.0	0.0
Europe anc. URSS exclus	16.2	17.5	2.5	2.2	2.5	3.0	2.7	2.5	3.2	1.7
– Union Européenne	12.8	13.8	2.5	2.2	2.4	2.9	2.7	2.4	3.0	1.6
– Europe de l'Est			0.0		0.0	0.0	0.0	0.0	0.0	0.0
– Autre de l'Europe	3.4	3.7	0.0	0.0	0.1	0.1	0.1	0.1	0.2	0.1
Europe ancienne URSS							0.0	0.0	0.0	0.0
Océanie	1.2	1.3	0.1	0.0	0.0	0.2	0.2	0.1	0.1	0.3
Autre	0.0	0.0	77.4	80.0	79.3	77.0	67.8	61.0	62.2	68.3
Special Categories								59.5	60.1	66.5
Areas n.e.s.	0.0	0.0	76.9	79.7	78.9	76.5	67.5	1.1	1.8	1.6
Saudi Arabia	5.4	5.8	4.5	2.9	3.4	4.1	5.4	6.4	6.0	5.4
Japan/Japon	26.3	28.5	1.5	1.9	2.4	2.2	5.2	5.6	3.4	4.3
Korea, Republic of	2.7	2.9	1.0	1.4	1.8	2.9	3.1	3.5	3.8	2.6
USA/Etats–Unis d'Amer	5.9	10.3	1.8	1.9	1.9	2.0	2.8	4.4	3.1	2.3
Other Asia n.e.s.			0.9	0.6	0.8	0.6	2.1	2.7	3.3	2.7
India/Inde	9.9		1.1	1.1	1.4	0.9	1.7	3.0	2.5	1.9
United Arab Emirates			1.7	0.7	0.7	1.0	1.9	1.7	1.8	1.8
Kuwait/ Koweït			1.1	0.4	1.4	1.2	1.2	1.2	1.4	1.0

4. General Imports C.I.F. by Commodities according to the S.I.T.C. (Rev. 2) in million U.S. Dollars
Importations Générales C.A.F. par Produits d'après la C.T.C.I. (Rév. 2) en millions de Dollars E.U.

SITC CTCI	COMMODITY	1993		1994		1995		1996		PRODUIT
		QUANTITY QUANTITE	VALUE VALEUR	QUANTITY QUANTITE	VALUE VALEUR	QUANTITY QUANTITE	VALUE VALEUR	QUANTITY QUANTITE	VALUE VALEUR	
	ALL COMMODITIES		3858.1		3761.8		3715.7		4092.6	TOUS PRODUITS
0	FOOD AND LIVE ANIMALS		308.5		308.4		343.9		372.3	ALIMENTS,ANIMAUX VIVANTS
001	*LIVE ANIMALS FOR FOOD		17.3		20.6		23.9	W 35860	39.6	ANIMAUX VIVANTS
0011	BOVINE SPECIES,LIVE	W 1084	1.9	W 742	1.2	W 20	0.1	W 18282	23.5	ESPECE BOVINE
00119	— OTHR THAN FR BREEDING			W 742	1.2	W 20	0.1	W 18282	23.5	BOVINS NON REPRODUCTEURS
0012	SHEEP AND GOATS,LIVE	W 15313	15.1	W 19651	19.3	W 28959	23.6	W 17181	15.8	ESPECES OVINE ET CAPRINE
00121	SHEEP,LIVE			W 8837	8.5	W 24213	18.8	W 14238	12.7	ESPECE OVINE
01	MEAT AND PREPARATIONS		37.6		40.2		47.9		39.8	VIANDES ET PREPARATIONS
011	MEAT FRESH,CHILLD,FROZEN	W 21533	36.1	W 22215	35.3	W 24132	41.5	W 18152	33.5	VIANDES FRAICHES,REF,CONGE
0111	BOVINE MEAT FRESH,FROZEN	W 6388	11.7	W 5082	9.2	W 4738	9.3	W 4332	8.2	VIANDES BOVIN FRAI,REF
0114	POULTRY FRESH CHLLD,FRZN	W 12686	18.3	W 14873	20.5	W 17226	26.1	W 12001	19.6	VOLAILLES MORTES
02	DAIRY PRODCTS,BIRDS'EGGS		42.9		48.8		54.3		57.7	PRODUITS LAITIERS,OEUFS
022	MILK AND CREAM	W 13954	24.8	W 117299	27.7	W 18169	32.1	W 19873	34.7	LAIT ET CREME
0223	MILK AND CREAM FRESH	W 5943	6.6	W 109288	10.0	W 10589	13.6	W 11902	15.0	LAIT,CREME FRAIS
0224	MILK,CREAM PRESERVED ETC	W 8011	18.2	W 8011	17.7	W 7580	18.5	W 7971	19.8	LAIT,CREME CONS,CONC
02242	MILK DRY,1.5% FAT OR LES	W 4705	13.7	W 7824	17.4	W 7396	18.2	W 7867	19.6	LAIT POUDRE INF 1.5%
024	CHEESE AND CURD	W 3638	11.3	W 655986	12.2	W 4091	14.3	W 3535	13.8	FROMAGE ET CAILLEBOTTE
04	CEREALS AND PREPARATIONS		61.1		45.9		59.8		64.9	CEREALES ET PRODUITS
041	WHEAT ETC UNMILLED	W 66154	10.2	W 66117	9.8	W 60773	12.1	W 43669	10.2	FROMENT,EPEAUTRE
0411	DURUM WHEAT UNMILLED			W 66001	9.8	W 59799	11.8	W 43053	9.9	FROMENT DUR NON MOULU
042	RICE	W 39616	20.2	W 35470	18.7	W 29432	16.0	W 36003	20.5	RIZ
0421	RICE IN HUSK OR HUSKED	W 22	0.1	W 34747	18.3	W 28030	15.5	W 35564	20.4	RIZ SANS AUTRE PREPARATION
04212	RICE HUSKED			W 34074	17.9	W 27966	15.5	W 35499	20.3	RIZ CARGO
0422	RICE SEMI–MILLED,MILLED	W 39594	20.2	W 723	0.4	W 1402	0.6	W 439	0.2	RIZ POLI,GLACE INCL BRISURES
046	WHEAT ETC MEAL OR FLOUR	W 31080	10.8	W 800	0.5	W 56261	14.6	W 46280	13.4	SEMOULE FARINE,FROMENT
04601	FLOUR OF WHEAT OR MESLIN	W 30578	10.6	W 750	0.5	W 56223	14.6	W 46189	13.3	FARINE DE FROMENT
048	CEREAL ETC PREPARATIONS	W 6421	15.1	W 5312	11.9	W 6030	13.8	W 6178	14.1	PREPTNS A BASE CEREALES
05	VEGETABLES AND FRUIT		88.3		86.8		88.8		94.7	LEGUMES ET FRUITS
054	VEG ETC FRSH,SMPLY PRSVD	W 105236	36.9	W 95614	34.2	W 100785	36.2	W 94994	34.4	LEGUMES FRAIS,CONG,SECS
0545	OTHER FRESH VEGETABLES	W 47432	17.8	W 48290	17.4	W 53848	18.4	W 55265	19.4	AUTRES LEGUMES FRAIS,REF
05451	ALLIACEOUS VEGTBLS,FRESH	W 47432	17.8	W 16340	4.7	W 17786	4.8	W 21808	5.6	OIGNONS,ECHALOTES,AULX
05459	FRESH VEGETABLES NES			W 31950	12.7	W 36062	13.6	W 33457	13.8	LEGUMES FRAIS,REFRI NDA
057	FRUIT,NUTS,FRESH,DRIED	W 78226	31.6	W 91005	34.7	W 86197	34.1	W 88725	38.1	FRUITS FRAIS OU SECS
0579	FRUIT FRESH OR DRIED NES	W 34924	12.1	W 41512	12.6	W 35771	13.4	W 40693	17.3	FRUITS FRAIS,SECS NDA
06	SUGAR AND PREPS,HONEY		16.1		16.5		13.6		15.4	SUCRES ET PRODUITS
07	COFFEE,TEA,COCOA,SPICES		19.0		22.0		22.3		22.7	CAFE,THE,CACAO,EPICES
09	MISC EDIBLE PRODUCTS		14.9		18.6		20.7		22.1	PREP ALIMENTAIRES DIVERSES
098	EDIBLE PRODCTS,PREPS NES	W 4311	12.9	W 7514	18.0	W 7986	19.9	W 7946	21.5	PREP ALIMENTAIRES NDA
09809	MISC FOOD PREPRTIONS NES	W 2119	9.2	W 3261	11.6	W 3282	11.8	W 3459	13.7	PREP ALIMENTAIRES NDA
1	BEVERAGES AND TOBACCO		57.3		60.5		64.2		66.3	BOISSONS ET TABACS
11	BEVERAGES		38.0		42.1		46.0		46.4	BOISSONS
111	NON–ALCOHL BEVERAGES NES	W 18412	6.9	W 22533	11.7	W 21034	11.4	W 22156	10.8	BOISSONS NON ALCOOLIQUES
112	ALCOHOLIC BEVERAGES	W 33015	31.2	W 26853	30.4	W 22811	34.7	W 21379	35.7	BOISSONS ALCOOLIQUES
1123	BEER,ALE,STOUT,PORTER	W 19121	15.8	W 22718	15.1	W 18343	14.8	W 16843	13.6	BIERES
1124	DISTILLED ALCOHOLIC BEVS	W 12462	10.8	W 2712	11.2	W 2767	13.3	W 3260	17.2	ALCOOLS,EAUX–DE–VIE
12	TOBACCO AND MANUFACTURES		19.3		18.4		18.2		19.9	TABACS BRUTS FABRIQUES
122	TOBACCO,MANUFACTURED	W 1074	18.7	W 1176	17.9	W 1050	17.8	W 1131	19.0	TABACS FABRIQUES
1222	CIGARETTES	W 991	17.9	W 1140	17.3	W 1023	17.0	W 1109	18.2	CIGARETTES
2	CRUDE MATERLS,EXCL FUELS		240.7		190.2		183.7		242.3	MAT BRUTES NON COMESTIBLES
24	CORK AND WOOD		22.7		22.9		20.6		15.6	LIEGE ET BOIS
247	OTH WOOD ROUGH,SQUARED	W 64324	18.5	W 49007	22.1	W 42481	19.6	W 29038	14.2	BOIS BRUTS EQUARRIS
2472	SAW–,VENEER–LOGS NON–CON			W 29122	16.3	W 28190	14.7	W 15619	9.1	NON CONIFERES SCIAGE,PLAC
24721	— IN THE ROUGH			W 29122	16.3	W 28190	14.7	W 15619	9.1	BRUTS ECORCES DEGROSSIS
2479	PTPROPS,POLES,PILING,ETC	W 64324	18.5							POTEAUX DE MINES
27	CRUDE FERTLZR,MINRLS NES		8.5		13.9		14.1		11.1	ENGRAIS MINERAUX BRUTS
28	METALLIFEROUS ORES,SCRAP		202.6		143.8		133.4		203.0	MINERAIS METAL,DECHETS
287	BASE METAL ORES,CONC NES	W 955740	200.6	W 865069	141.1	W 900290	129.4	W 844938	200.3	MINERAIS METAUX COMMUNS
2873	ALUMINIUM ORES,ALUMINA	W 943696	200.0	W 864560	140.1	W 900029	128.6	W 844630	199.2	MINERAIS D'ALUMINIUM
28732	ALUMINA(ALUMINIUM OXIDE)	W 943653	199.9	W 864412	139.6	W 899833	128.0	W 844618	199.2	ALUMINE (OXYDE ALUMINIUM)
3	MINERAL FUELS ETC		1429.4		1247.1		1386.0		1675.4	COMBUSTIBLES MINERAUX LUB
33	PETROLEUM AND PRODUCTS		1429.3		54.9		55.9		71.5	PETROLE ET DERIVES
333	CRUDE PETROLEUM		1370.6							HUILES BRUTES DE PETROLE
334	PETROLEUM PRODUCTS,REFIN	W 9744	10.5	W 30455	17.3	W 28882	13.1	W 10081	10.6	PRODUITS RAFFINES
3345	LUBS,PETROLEUM OILS NES	W 9676	10.4	W 30180	17.0	W 28839	13.0	W 9760	10.4	HUILES LUBRIFIANTES
33451	LUBS(HIGH PETR CONT) ETC	W 9544	10.2	W 30121	16.9	W 28580	12.4	W 9627	10.0	HUILES LUBRIF,H LOURDES
335	RESIDUAL PETRLM PROD NES	W 255195	48.4	W 172681	37.7	W 218468	42.8	W 230489	60.9	PRODUITS RESIDUELS NDA
3353	MIN TAR PITCH,PITCH COKE	W 255193	48.4	W 44304	12.1	W 121415	25.9	W 76037	21.0	BRAI,COKE DE BRAI
33532	PITCH COKE	W 253463	46.9	W 36302	9.9	W 121415	25.9	W 76037	21.0	COKE DE BRAI
3354	PETROLM BITUMEN,COKE ETC			W 128307	25.5	W 96985	16.8	W 154398	39.9	BITUME,COKE DE PETROLE
33542	PETROLEUM COKE			W 127404	24.9	W 96504	16.4	W 153749	39.3	COKE DE PETROLE
4	ANIMAL,VEGETABLE OIL,FAT		34.0		31.3		42.7		37.1	HUILES,GRAISSES ANIM,VEG
42	FIXED VEGETABLE OIL,FAT		33.9		31.2		42.6		37.1	HUILES VEGETALES FIXES
424	FIXED VEG OIL NONSOFT	W 45915	31.5	W 41258	28.3	W 48641	39.0	W 39999	31.1	AUTRES HUILES VEG FIXES
4242	PALM OIL	W 4408	2.1	W 21045	12.0	W 10554	7.5	W 10234	6.2	HUILE DE PALME
4249	FIXED VEGETABLE OILS NES	W 41366	29.2	W 19966	16.1	W 35806	29.8	W 27566	23.5	HUILES VEGET FIXES NDA
5	CHEMCLS,RELATED PROD NES		164.8		173.6		196.9		200.7	PRODUITS CHIMIQUES
52	INORGANIC CHEMICALS		22.1		19.2		22.4		27.6	PROD CHIM INORGANIQUES
522	INORG ELEMNTS,OXIDES,ETC	W 11010	4.6	W 15005	7.8	W 19509	12.4	W 20578	13.1	ELEMENTS INORGANIQUES
523	OTHR INORG CHEMICALS ETC	W 21698	17.5	W 19132	11.3	W 20953	10.0	W 23538	14.6	AUT PRODUITS CHIMIQUES INORG
5231	METAL CMPD OF INORG ACID	W 14836	12.4	W 13606	9.2	W 9006	6.2	W 12402	11.1	SELS METALLIQUES
52311	FLUORIDES ETC	W 14836	12.4	W 12521	8.9	W 8000	5.7	W 10044	10.4	FLUORURES
53	DYES,TANNING,COLOUR PROD		24.6		21.6		33.7		34.2	PROD TEINTURE,COLORANTS
531	SYNT DYE,NAT INDGO,LAKES			W 8695	15.7	W 15708	28.6	W 31291	29.0	MAT COLOR ORGAN,LAQUES
5311	SYNTHIC ORGNIC DYESTUFFS			W 8695	15.7	W 15708	28.6	W 31291	29.0	MAT COLOR ORGAN SYNTHET
533	PIGMENTS,PAINTS,ETC	W 15990	24.6	W 2742	5.9	W 1591	5.2	W 1617	5.3	PIGMENTS,PEINTURES,VERNIS
5334	VARNISHES,DISTEMPERS ETC	W 14457	21.7	W 1189	2.3	W 289	0.7	W 287	0.9	PEINTURES A L'EAU
541	*MEDICINAL,PHARM PRODUCT	K 1474866	22.6	K 1615042	27.2	K 1386749	30.0	K 1437788	28.3	PROD MEDICINAUX PHARMACEUT
5417	MEDICAMENTS			K 720439	19.0	K 1126482	24.7	K 1164965	24.2	MEDICAMENTS
54171	— CONTAINNG ANTIBIOTICS			K 641788	17.3	K 786031	20.7	K 515030	17.7	MED CONTN ANTIBIOTIQUES
5419	PHARMACEUTICAL GOODS NES	K 1450856	22.3	K 810057	6.8	K 188311	4.5	K 209518	3.5	PREP,ART PHARMACEUTIQUES
54199	OTH PHARMACEUTICAL GOODS	K 1344741	21.0	K 734255	5.9	K 127347	3.6	K 112386	2.1	AUT PREP PHARMACEUTIQUES
55	PERFUME,CLEANING ETC PRD		49.4		49.1		49.2		50.8	PROD POUR PARFUM,TOILETTE
553	PERFUMERY,COSMETICS,ETC	W 4159	31.2	W 3567	30.5	W 2833	30.7	W 2975	31.8	PRODUITS DE PARFUMERIE
554	SOAP,CLEANSING ETC PREPS	W 12356	17.2	W 11242	17.0	W 11356	16.6	W 11279	16.6	SAVONS,PRODUITS DETERSIFS
5542	WASHING PREPARATIONS ETC	W 10170	12.0	W 9527	11.7	W 9805	12.1	W 9710	11.7	PROD ORG TENSIO–ACT NDA
58	PLASTIC MATERIALS ETC		6.7		8.0		10.8		16.7	MAT PLAST ARTIFICIELLES
583	POLYMERIZATION ETC PRODS			W 8529	7.9	W 9193	10.3	W 16798	16.1	PROD POLYMERISATION
59	CHEMICAL MATERIALS NES		38.1		46.1		46.1		37.0	MAT PROD CHIMIQUES NDA
598	MISCEL CHEM PRODUCTS NES	W 25930	33.7	W 31524	41.1	W 26498	41.0	W 21035	32.3	PROD DIV INDUST CHIM NDA
5981	CHEMCLS FROM WOOD,RESIN	W 7	0.1	W 14365	14.5	W 7329	9.1	W 827	0.9	PROD CHIM BASE BOIS RESIN
59814	ROSIN,RESIN ACIDS,ETC			W 14365	14.5	W 7328	9.1	W 681	0.8	COLOPHANES RESINIQUES

4. General Imports C.I.F. by Commodities according to the S.I.T.C. (Rev. 2) in million U.S. Dollars
Importations Générales C.A.F. par Produits d'après la C.T.C.I. (Rév. 2) en millions de Dollars E.U.

SITC CTCI	COMMODITY	1993 QUANTITY QUANTITE	1993 VALUE VALEUR	1994 QUANTITY QUANTITE	1994 VALUE VALEUR	1995 QUANTITY QUANTITE	1995 VALUE VALEUR	1996 QUANTITY QUANTITE	1996 VALUE VALEUR	PRODUIT
5989	CHEM PRODUCTS,PREPS NES	W 25913	33.7	W 17042	26.2	W 17232	29.2	W 17429	26.0	PROD PREP CHIMIQUES NDA
59899	OTH CHEM PRODS,PREPS,NES	W 25151	32.8	W 15546	24.4	W 16115	27.4	W 16002	24.4	AUT PRODUITS CHIMIQUES NDA
6	BASIC MANUFACTURES		521.5		555.5		565.1		546.1	ART MANUFACTURES
62	RUBBER MANUFACTURES NES		19.2		20.4		16.2		17.9	CAOUTCHOUC MANUFACTURE
625	RUBBER TYRES, TUBES ETC	W 5601	16.2	W 6418	17.5		13.0	W 3749	13.7	PNEUS CAOUTCHOUC VULCANISE
63	WOOD,CORK MANUFACTRS NES		23.6		29.3		24.3		21.2	OUVRAGES LIEGE ET BOIS
634	VENEERS,PLYWOOD,ETC	W 27381	20.1	W 29704	23.3	W 31064	17.3	W 18635	14.7	PLACAGES,CONTRE–PLAQUES
6342	PLYWOOD OF WOOD SHEETS	W 26663	19.4	W 28921	22.8	W 30562	16.7	W 18078	13.8	BOIS CONTRE–PLAQUES
64	PAPER,PAPERBOARD AND MFR		60.0		67.9		66.7		64.1	PAPIERS,CARTONS & OUVRAGES
641	PAPER AND PAPERBOARD	W 16865	17.0	W 24056	24.6	W 25782	32.4	W 29763	29.5	PAPIERS ET CARTONS
6412	PRINTG,WRITING PAPER NES	W 5883	6.1	W 8122	9.2	W 7921	13.0	W 7649	10.4	PAPIERS POUR L'IMPRESSION
642	PAPER,ETC,PRECUT,ARTS OF	W 20216	43.0	W 20372	43.4	W 12964	34.3	W 12952	34.7	PAP,CARTONS DECOUPES
6421	PAPER ETC CONTAINERS	W 7124	11.9	W 8150	11.5	W 4810	8.0	W 5076	8.5	BOITES,SACS EMBALLAGES
6428	PAPER ETC ARTICLES NES	W 8570	22.3	W 9264	24.0	W 6337	18.9	W 5787	18.7	OUVRAGES EN PATE A PAPIER
64282	PUNCHED CARD MACH CARDS	W 8570	22.3	W 9	0.3	W 40	0.4	W 8	0.4	CARTES POUR MACHINES
65	TEXTILE YARN,FABRICS,ETC		109.1		111.8		116.1		115.1	FILS,TISSUS,ARTICLES TEXTILE
651	TEXTILE YARN	W 370	2.3	W 796	4.0	W 4536	15.2	W 4870	14.8	FILS TEXTILES
6513	COTTON YARN			W 228	1.0	W 3891	12.3	W 4421	12.4	FILS DE COTON
652	COTTON FABRICS,WOVEN	W 3889	28.1	W 7029	35.0	W 6672	38.1	W 7270	42.3	TISSUS DE COTON
6521	GREY WOVEN COTTON FABRIC	W 3889	28.1	W 2232	12.7	W 677	3.2	W 268	2.1	TISSUS COT ECRUS NON MERCER
65214	GREY WOVEN COTTON NES	W 3889	28.1	W 2232	12.7	W 677	3.2	W 268	2.1	AUT TISSUS 85% COTON ECRUS
65215	GREY WOVN COTN BLEND NES									AUT TIS MOINS 85% COT ECRUS
6522	WOVEN COTTON BLEACHD,ETC			W 4798	22.4	W 5995	35.0	W 7002	40.2	TISSUS COTON BLANCHIS ETC
65224	BLCHED COTTON FABRIC NES			W 4571	22.2	W 5968	34.8	W 6976	40.2	AUT TIS PLUS 85% COT BLANCHI
653	WOVN MAN–MADE FIB FABRIC	W 3044	35.7	W 4420	36.2	W 3015	29.7	W 2467	26.4	TISSUS FIBRES SYNTH,ARTIF
6531	CONT SYNT WEAVES NONPILE			W 4340	35.7	W 2973	29.3	W 2441	25.9	TISSUS FIBRES SYNTH CONTINUE
65315	CONT SYN TXTL FABRIC NES			W 4340	35.7	W 2973	29.3	W 2441	25.9	TIS PLUS 85% TEXT SYNT CONT
658	TEXTILE ARTICLES NES	W 3577	15.6	W 6848	10.3	W 1345	10.6	W 1647	10.8	ART FACONNES MAT TEXTILES
659	FLOOR COVERINGS,ETC	W 4786	19.1		18.1		14.4	W 3912	14.2	COUVRE–PARQUETS,TAPIS ETC
66	NONMETAL MINERAL MFS NES		90.9		104.6		101.7		102.6	ART MIN NON METALLIQUES
661	LIME,CEMENT,BLDG PRODS	W 719274	48.2	W 733377	55.9	W 679886	54.6	W 584872	44.9	CHAUX,CIMENTS MAT CONSTR
6612	CEMENT	W 708259	38.4	W 703284	44.0	W 652362	43.5	W 561515	37.2	CIMENTS HYDRAULIQUES
6613	BUILDING STONE ETC WORKD	W 8191	8.0	W 27520	11.7	W 26609	11.0	W 22361	7.7	PIERRES A BATIR
66132	BUILDING STONE WORKED	W 8118	7.9	W 27507	11.7	W 26461	11.0	W 22063	7.7	OUVR EN PIERRES DE TAILLE
662	CLAY,REFRACTORY BLDG PRD	W 36850	18.6	W 40895	24.2	W 41181	21.7	W 54887	35.0	MAT CONST REFRACTAIRES
6623	REFRACTORY BUILDING PROD	W 7051	5.7	W 9037	9.6	W 10894	7.8	W 27440	23.2	BRIQUES REFRACTAIRES
66232	REFRACTRY BRICKS ETC NES			W 5944	5.2	W 7992	5.6	W 18815	16.2	BRIQUES ETC REFRACTAIRES
6624	BRICKS ETC NONREFRACTORY	W 29799	12.9	W 31858	14.6	W 30287	13.9	W 27447	11.8	BRIQUES ETC CERAM NON REFR
66245	GLAZED CERAMIC SETTS ETC	W 20510	11.0	W 23841	12.3	W 25791	12.8	W 23057	10.7	AUT CARREAUX CERAMIQUE
67	IRON AND STEEL		112.9		119.5		128.9		127.2	FER ET ACIER
671	PIG IRON ETC	W 1827782	41.9	W 2586881	52.7	W 3246268	62.2	W 2931313	57.3	FONTE,SPIEGEL,POUDRES
6713	IRON,STL POWDER,SHOT,ETC	W 420	0.3	W 2586301	52.4	W 3245116	61.5	W 2929181	56.4	POUDRES,GREN FER,ACIER
672	IRON,STEEL PRIMARY FORMS	W 74681	28.6	W 147	0.2	W 72	0.3	W 1136	0.9	LINGOTS FER,ACIER
6725	IRN,STL BLOOMS,SLABS,ETC	W 74681	28.6	W 125	0.2			W 130	0.3	BLOOMS,BILLETTES FER ACIER
67251	IRN,SMPLE STL BLOOMS,ETC	W 74681	28.6							BLOOMS ETC NON ACIER FIN
673	IRON,STEEL SHAPES ETC			W 86557	33.3	W 80530	31.8	W 53676	22.3	BARRES,PROFIL FER,ACIER
6732	IRON,STEEL BARS ETC			W 55950	20.6	W 73505	27.2	W 45298	16.8	BARRES FER,ACIER
67324	STNLESS STL ETC BARS ETC			W 55950	20.6	W 73505	27.2	W 45298	16.8	BARRES ACIER INOXYDABLE
674	IRN,STL UNIV,PLATE,SHEET	W 20428	11.2	W 15337	9.1	W 15071	11.0	W 147881	19.1	LARGES PLATS,TOLES
6745	IRN,STL MED PLATE,ROLLED			W 13907	8.0	W 14403	10.3	W 145143	17.1	TOLES 3 A 4.75 MM
67451	— OF IRON OR SIMPLE STL			W 13907	8.0	W 14403	10.3	W 145143	17.1	TOLES AUT NON ACIER FIN
678	IRON,STL TUBES,PIPES,ETC	W 18083	26.5	W 13193	19.5	W 12300	19.7	W 14596	23.5	TUBES,TUYAUX EN FONTE,FER
68	NON–FERROUS METALS		24.5		21.0		25.1		28.2	METAUX NON FERREUX
684	ALUMINIUM	W 2482	8.2	W 3357	11.4	W 3805	13.9	W 5955	15.2	ALUMINIUM
6842	ALUMINIUM,ALLOYS WORKED	W 2459	8.1	W 3151	11.0	W 3701	13.4	W 5062	13.5	ALUMINIUM,ALLIAGES OUVRE
69	METAL MANUFACTURES NES		80.8		80.2		85.1		69.4	ART MANUFACT EN METAL NDA
691	STRUCTURES AND PARTS NES	W 23457	16.7	W 12967	13.9	W 15737	18.2	W 7960	11.6	CONSTRUCT FER,ACIER,ALU
6911	STRUCTURES,PARTS IRN,STL	W 23353	16.2	W 12359	11.8	W 14849	13.0	W 7517	9.4	CONSTRUCT FER,ACIER,FONTE
692	METAL TANKS,BOXES,ETC	W 3113	7.0		12.1	W 2646	12.4	W 2768	11.2	RECIPIENTS METALLIQUES
6924	MTL TRANSPORT BOXES ETC	W 2257	6.3		12.1	W 2646	12.4	W 2768	11.2	FUTS,TAMBOURS,BIDONS
69242	ALUMNM TRNSPRT BOXES ETC			W 2446	9.1	W 2115	11.4	W 2382	10.0	FUTS,TAMBOURS,BIDONS ALU
697	BASE MTL HOUSEHOLD EQUIP	W 1850	13.0	W 1763	11.1	W 1390	9.2	W 1200	7.9	ART MENAGE MET COMMUNS
699	BASE METAL MFRS NES	W 11124	28.5	W 11479	25.9	W 9697	28.6	W 7365	24.8	ART MANUFACTURES MET NDA
6997	IRON,STEEL ARTICLES NES	W 7238	11.7	W 5998	6.7	W 5447	7.4	W 4146	8.3	OUV FONTE,FER,ACIER NDA
7	MACHINES,TRANSPORT EQUIP		792.5		835.4		619.7		640.5	MACHINES MATERIEL TRANSPORT
71	POWER GENERATING EQUIPMT		29.8		21.7		18.2		53.9	MACHINES GENERATRICES
714	ENGINES AND MOTORS NES	W 149	5.9	W 131	6.6	W 109	7.3	W 1308	42.8	MOTEURS NON ELECTRIQUES
7148	GAS TURBINES NES	W 149	5.9	W 84	5.2	W 79	6.6	W 1188	41.6	TURBINES A GAZ
716	ROTATING ELECTRIC PLANT	W 1898	14.3	W 274	3.3	W 396	4.2	W 474	4.6	APP ELECTR ROTATIFS,PIECES
72	MACHS FOR SPCL INDUSTRYS		62.8		77.4		47.1		46.4	MAC SPECIALES POUR INDUST
723	CIVIL ENGNEERG EQUIP ETC	W 2751	21.6	W 1726	24.3	W 808	13.4	W 587	12.3	APPAREILS DE GENIE CIVIL
7234	CONST,MINING MACHNRY NES	W 2745	21.6	W 1713	24.1	W 804	13.3	W 577	12.2	MACH POUR LA CONST, MINES
724	TEXTILE,LEATHER MACHNRY	W 299	2.3	W 2458	16.8		5.9	W 151	1.8	MACH POUR INDUSTRIE TEXTILE
728	OTH MACHY FOR SPCL INDUS	W 1436	26.6	W 1485	12.9	W 1123	18.2	W 1335	23.5	AUT MACH IND PARTICULIERES
7284	MACHY FOR SPCL INDUS NES	W 663	19.9	W 348	4.3	W 606	9.8	W 695	15.0	MACH SPEC IND PARTICUL.
73	METALWORKING MACHINERY		14.4		17.7		50.6		27.3	MACH TRAVAIL DES METAUX
736	METALWORKING MACH–TOOLS	W 945	12.6	W 1236	12.0	W 846	14.3	W 2376	20.4	MACH–OUTILS TRAVAIL METAUX
737	METALWORKING MACHNRY NES	W 186	1.8	W 695	5.8	W 4485	36.4	W 487	6.9	MACH TRAV METAUX PIECES
7372	ROLLING MILLS AND ROLLS			W 220	2.2	W 3854	29.3	W 139	2.0	LAMINOIRS CYLINDRES PIEC
73721	ROLLING MILLS			W 52	0.8	W 3041	19.0	W 34	0.1	LAMINOIRS ET TRAINS
74	GENRL INDUSTRL MACHY NES		103.7		107.0		113.6		108.9	MACH APP INDUSTRIE
741	HEATING,COOLING EQUIPMNT	W 1954	26.3	W 6141	52.3	W 7026	56.1	W 4831	44.2	MACH CHAUFFAGE,PIECES
7414	NONDOM REFRIG EQUIPT,PTS	W 1084	12.1	W 656	5.0	W 1004	7.9	W 440	3.5	MAT PRODUCTION DU FROID
74141	REFRIG EQUIP NONDOMESTIC	W 1084	12.1	W 557	3.9	W 939	7.2	W 404	3.0	REFIG INDUSTRIELS
7415	AIR–CONDITIONING MACHNRY	W 566	4.6	W 4925	37.1	W 4933	34.9	W 3791	29.5	GROUPES CONDITION AIR
743	PUMPS NES,CENTRFUGES ETC	W 528	5.5		12.6		15.2	W 2764	22.6	POMPES COMPRES,VENT ETC
744	MECHANICAL HANDLING EQU	W 3231	16.8	W 3124	20.9	W 3032	21.0	W 2924	22.5	EQUIP MANUTENTION PIECES
7442	LIFTING,LOADING MACH NES	W 2913	14.9	W 2191	12.2	W 1765	11.4	W 1940	11.1	APP LEVAGE,MANUTENTION
745	NONELEC MACHY,TOOLS NES	W 295	6.8		10.2	W 843	11.9	W 908	10.7	AUT MACH NON ELEC,PIECES
7452	OTH NONELEC MCHS,PTS NES	W 276	6.6	W 1091	10.0	W 805	11.5	W 894	10.4	AUT MACH NON ELEC,PIECES
749	NONELEC MACH PTS,ACC NES	W 1872	39.6	W 35	0.4	W 6	0.2	W 143	2.6	PIECES MACH NON ELEC NDA
7499	OTH NONELEC MCHY PTS NES	W 1872	39.6	W 35	0.4	W 6	0.2	W 143	2.6	PIECES NON ELECT NDA
75	OFFICE MACHNES,ADP EQUIP		40.2		42.8		42.5		40.0	MACH BUREAU TRAIT AUTOM
759	OFFICE,ADP MCH PTS,ACCES	W 508	32.4	W 423	30.3	W 443	31.3	W 400	29.0	PIECES DU 751 ET 752
7591	OFFICE MACHINE PARTS NES	W 508	32.4							PIECES DU 7511,7518
75911	TYPEWRTR PARTS,ACCES NES	W 508	32.4							PIECES DU 7511
7599	ACCTG,ETC,ADP MCH PTS,AC			W 423	30.3	W 443	31.3	W 400	29.0	PIECES DU 751 ET 752
76	TELECOMM,SOUND EQUIPMENT		73.4		67.9		56.7		55.1	EQUIPMENT DE TELECOM
764	TELECOM EQPT,PTS,ACC NES	W 3057	53.6		49.2		39.3	W 606	38.3	EQUIP TELECOM,PIECES
7643	TV,RADIO TRANSMITTRS ETC	W 710	50.4	W 188	11.9		2.1	W 21	5.4	APP EMET TELE RADIO
7649	PTS NES OF EQUIPMT OF 76	W 16	0.6	W 274	26.2	W 275	24.5	W 354	25.1	PIECES DE LA DIV 76

4. General Imports C.I.F. by Commodities according to the S.I.T.C. (Rev. 2) in million U.S. Dollars
Importations Générales C.A.F. par Produits d'après la C.T.C.I. (Rév. 2) en millions de Dollars E.U.

SITC CTCI	COMMODITY	1993 QUANTITY QUANTITE	1993 VALUE VALEUR	1994 QUANTITY QUANTITE	1994 VALUE VALEUR	1995 QUANTITY QUANTITE	1995 VALUE VALEUR	1996 QUANTITY QUANTITE	1996 VALUE VALEUR	PRODUIT
76491	PTS NES OF APPAR OF 7641			W 194	20.2	W 194	19.8	W 284	22.0	PIECES POUR 764.1
77	ELECTRIC MACHNRY NES ETC		149.5		151.8		95.2		111.5	MACH APP ELECT NDA
771	ELECTRIC POWER MACHY NES			W 3238	46.3	W 1142	8.5	W 2620	15.4	MACH PROD,TRANS ELECTR
7711	TRANSFORMERS,ELECTRICAL			W 2697	25.5	W 1047	5.2	W 2484	10.2	TRANSFO ELECTRIQUES
77118	OTHER ELEC TRANSFORMERS			W 2697	25.5	W 1047	5.2	W 2484	10.2	AUTRES TRANSFO ELECTRIQ
7712	OTH ELEC POWER MACHY NES			W 541	20.9	W 95	3.4	W 135	5.2	AUT APP PROD TRANSF ELEC
77129	PTS NES OF MACHY OF 771			W 541	20.9	W 95	3.4	W 135	5.2	PIECES MACH DU 771
772	SWITCHGEAR ETC,PARTS NES	W 979	21.3	W 1199	28.9		23.7	W 961	19.9	APP COUPURE,SECT ETC
7721	SWITCHGEAR ETC			W 1173	27.4	W 1045	22.4	W 953	19.6	APP COUPURE,SECTIONMNT
773	ELECTR DISTRIBUTNG EQUIP	W 18856	30.3	W 6477	22.4	W 5978	18.1	W 6644	23.9	EQUIPMT DISTRIBUTION ELECT
7731	INSULATED WIRE,CABLE ETC	W 17048	23.8	W 6298	20.6	W 5885	17.3	W 6545	22.2	FILS,CABLES ISOLES ELECT
775	HOUSEHOLD TYPE EQUIP NES	W 10576	56.9		21.2		18.7	W 2713	16.7	MACH,APP USAGE DOMESTQUE
7757	DOMESTIC ELECTRC EQU NES	W 6078	33.7	W 234	3.2	W 243	2.9	W 232	2.5	APP ELECTR DOMEST NDA
778	ELECTRICAL MACHINERY NES	W 2705	39.8		31.2		23.3	W 8957	31.7	AUTRES MACH ELECT NDA
7788	OTH ELEC MACHY,EQUIP NES	W 1010	31.6	W 2141	21.2		13.6	W 6651	22.0	AUT MACH APP ELEC NDA
77887	ELECTRICAL CARBONS			W 1250	4.5	W 2823	6.5	W 6446	12.7	PIECES CHARBON,GRAPHITE
77889	ELEC PARTS OF MACHY NES	W 579	27.7	W 65	2.7	W 29	2.4	W 67	4.9	PIECES ELEC DE MACH NDA
78	ROAD VEHICLES		215.9		212.7		164.4		163.6	VEHICULES ROUTIERS
781	PASS MOTOR VEH EXC BUSES	W 18049	141.5	W 10799	127.8	W 8365	98.0	W 9078	104.8	AUTO TRANSPORT PERSONNES
782	LORRIES,SPCL MTR VEH NES	W 5070	21.3	W 1653	15.1	W 1030	6.5	W 774	7.7	VEHICULES SPECIAUX,MARCH
7821	LORRIES,TRUCKS	W 3577	15.1	W 1115	7.4	W 656	3.2	W 350	2.7	VEHICULES TRANSP MARCHAND
784	MOTOR VEH PRTS,ACCES NES	W 3524	44.1	W 7760	57.1	W 5435	49.8	W 4633	42.4	PIECES 722,781,782,783
7849	OTHER MOTOR VEHCL PARTS	W 3451	43.9	W 7640	56.5	W 5399	49.6	W 4631	42.4	PIECES 722,781,782,783
79	OTHR TRANSPORT EQUIPMENT		103.3		136.8		31.8		34.1	AUTRE MATERIEL TRANSPORT
792	AIRCRAFT ETC		86.2	W 331	98.8	W 219	23.2	W 159	19.5	APP NAVIGATION AERIENNE
7921	HELICOPTERS		0.1	W 64	61.2	W 2	0.2			HELICOPTERES
7929	AIRCRAFT PARTS NES	W 416	86.2	W 265	37.5	W 217	23.1	W 159	19.5	PIECES DU 792
793	SHIPS AND BOATS ETC	W 5473	17.2	W 100432	37.9	W 1521	8.7	W 11563	14.5	NAVIRES BATEAUX,ETC
7932	SHIPS AND BOATS NES	W 1096	9.0	W 3535	28.6	W 1132	5.1	W 719	4.2	NAVIRES ET BATEAUX
79323	OTHER CARGO VESSELS			W 2603	24.9	W 135	0.3	W 18	0.1	AUT BATEAUX TRANS MARCH
8	MISC MANUFACTURED GOODS		293.6		286.3		288.9		279.9	ART MANUFACTURES DIVERS
812	*PLUMBG,HEATNG,LGHTNG EQ	W 3407	21.9	W 4264	26.1	W 3971	24.9	W 3928	23.3	APPAR SANITAIRES CHAUFFAGE
8124	LIGHTING EQUIPMENT NES	W 1805	16.5	W 2203	18.6	W 1967	18.0	W 2403	18.6	APPAREILS ECLAIRAGE ETC
81242	LAMPS,FITTINGS BASE METL	W 1761	16.2	W 892	10.6	W 906	9.8	W 1241	10.2	APPAREILS D'ECLAIRAGE
821	*FURNITURE,PARTS THEREOF	W 12019	53.6	W 10622	44.8	W 9102	37.2	W 8009	34.1	MEUBLES ET PIECES
8211	CHAIRS,SEATS AND PARTS	W 9557	42.9	W 349	2.0	W 391	2.0	W 582	3.4	SIEGES ET PIECES
8219	FURNITURE AND PARTS NES	W 1475	7.2	W 9532	39.6	W 7847	31.3	W 6852	27.6	AUTRES MEUBLES ET PIECES
82192	WOOD FURNITURE NES			W 7124	31.0	W 5282	22.2	W 4602	19.8	MEUBLES NDA EN BOIS
84	CLOTHING AND ACCESSORIES		60.3		60.8		68.7		57.9	VETEMENTS
842	MENS OUTERWEAR NOT KNIT	W 1843	21.8		12.0		11.9	W 902	9.8	VET DESSUS POUR HOMMES
843	WOMENS OUTERWEAR NONKNIT	W 1612	24.3		26.0		30.7	W 1628	27.1	VET DESSUS FEMMES MAT TEX
8439	— OTHER OUTER GARMENTS				11.8		13.6	W 991	14.0	AUT VET DES FEM MAT TEXT
844	UNDER GARMENTS NOT KNIT	W 489	6.5	W 1500	15.4		17.8	W 1757	14.8	VETEMENT DESSOUS MAT TEX
8441	— MENS SHIRTS	W 251	3.2	W 1110	11.8		14.2	W 1302	10.5	CHEMISES HOMMES MAT TEXT
851	*FOOTWEAR	W 1622	14.3		14.9		14.7	W 1435	14.6	CHAUSSURES
87	PRECISION INSTRUMNTS NES		15.9		16.9		14.8		25.0	INSTRUM,APPAR SCIENT NDA
872	MEDICAL INSTRUMENTS NES	W 153	8.0	W 141	7.3	W 181	7.7	W 237	15.0	INSTR,APP MEDIC–CHIR NDA
87202	OTH MEDICAL INSTRUMENTS			W 135	7.2	W 176	7.6	W 231	14.8	INSTRUM,APP MEDECINE
88	PHOTO EQU,OPTICL GDS ETC		34.0		31.5		30.9		30.3	APP,FOURN PHOTO,OP,MONTR
885	WATCHES AND CLOCKS		19.4		17.6		18.6		17.9	HORLOGERIE
8851	WATCHES,MOVEMENTS,CASES		19.0		16.4		17.5		16.8	MONTRES,MOUVEMENTS,BOITES
88511	WATCHES		18.1		16.1		17.4		16.8	MONTRES POCHE,BRACELET
89	MISC MANUFCTRD GOODS NES		89.1		86.3		92.3		89.5	ART MANUFACTURES DIVERS
893	ARTICLES OF PLASTIC NES	W 14282	38.0		41.2		44.0		43.5	OUVRAGES EN MAT DIVIS 58
8939	MISC PLASTIC ARTICLES			W 11635	32.0	W 10926	30.8	W 10387	30.8	ART DIVERS EN MAT DIV 58
89399	OTHR PLASTC ARTICLES NES			W 9573	29.3	W 9646	28.5	W 9538	29.1	AUT OUV MAT DIV 58
894	TOYS,SPORTING GOODS,ETC	W 2847	12.2	W 1928	13.1		13.6	W 1368	10.6	VOITURES ENFANTS,JOUETS
9	GOODS NOT CLASSD BY KIND		16.2		73.9		25.2		32.3	ART TRANSACT NON CLASSES
931	*SPECIAL TRANSACTIONS	W 2301	15.8	W 763	7.1	W 774	8.5	W 469	3.9	TRANS.SPECIALES
951	*WAR FIREARMS,AMMUNITION	W 6	0.2	W 2423	62.5	W 386	8.0	W 1689	26.8	VEHIC BLINDES ARMES
95106	AMMUNITION NES			W 2423	62.5	W 386	8.0	W 1689	26.8	PROJECTILES,MUNITIONS

5. General Exports F.O.B. by Commodities according to the S.I.T.C. (Rev. 2) in million U.S. Dollars
Exportations Générales F.O.B. par Produits d'après la C.T.C.I. (Rév. 2) en millions de Dollars E.U.

SITC CTCI	COMMODITY	1993		1994		1995		1996		PRODUIT
		QUANTITY QUANTITE	VALUE VALEUR	QUANTITY QUANTITE	VALUE VALEUR	QUANTITY QUANTITE	VALUE VALEUR	QUANTITY QUANTITE	VALUE VALEUR	
	ALL COMMODITIES		3710.1		3452.2		4160.7		4602.0	TOUS PRODUITS
0	FOOD AND LIVE ANIMALS		43.0		28.7		42.0		48.5	ALIMENTS,ANIMAUX VIVANTS
04	CEREALS AND PREPARATIONS		14.9		1.9		15.1		14.2	CEREALES ET PRODUITS
046	WHEAT ETC MEAL OR FLOUR	W 32834	10.9	W 6278	1.7	W 56928	14.6	W 45371	12.8	SEMOULE FARINE,FROMENT
04601	FLOUR OF WHEAT OR MESLIN	W 32815	10.9	W 6271	1.7	W 56925	14.6	W 45371	12.8	FARINE DE FROMENT
05	VEGETABLES AND FRUIT		15.3		15.7		13.1		11.6	LEGUMES ET FRUITS
2	CRUDE MATERLS,EXCL FUELS		12.4		15.4		20.3		16.8	MAT BRUTES NON COMESTIBLES
28	METALLIFEROUS ORES,SCRAP		10.8		13.1		18.3		13.7	MINERAIS METAL,DECHETS
3	MINERAL FUELS ETC		2439.6		2055.4		2502.6		3059.8	COMBUSTIBLES MINERAUX LUB
33	PETROLEUM AND PRODUCTS		2439.6		0.7		1.2		0.4	PETROLE ET DERIVES
333	CRUDE PETROLEUM		2439.1							HUILES BRUTES DE PETROLE
4	ANIMAL,VEGETABLE OIL,FAT		37.1		42.3		47.0		40.1	HUILES,GRAISSES ANIM,VEG
42	FIXED VEGETABLE OIL,FAT		36.9		42.2		46.8		40.0	HUILES VEGETALES FIXES
424	FIXED VEG OIL NONSOFT	W 37467	36.9	W 39757	41.9	W 38732	46.1	W 33367	38.8	AUTRES HUILES VEG FIXES
4249	FIXED VEGETABLE OILS NES	W 31862	31.7	W 31607	36.2	W 35281	41.9	W 30034	34.7	HUILES VEGET FIXES NDA
5	CHEMCLS,RELATED PROD NES		89.8		174.6		212.4		139.2	PRODUITS CHIMIQUES
51	ORGANIC CHEMICALS		35.9		99.1		88.8		50.3	PROD CHIMIQ ORGANIQUES
512	ALCOHOLS,PHENOLS ETC	W 412848	35.9	W 429352	99.1	W 546727	88.8	W 505204	50.2	PHENOLS,PHENOLS–ALCOOLS
5121	ACYCLIC ALCOHOLS,DERIVS	W 412848	35.9	W 429352	99.1	W 546727	88.8	W 505204	50.2	ALCOOLS ACYCLIQUES
51211	METHYL ALCOHOL(METHANOL)	W 412848	35.9	W 429352	99.1	W 545527	87.8	W 505204	50.2	ALCOOLS METHYLIQUES
52	INORGANIC CHEMICALS		41.4		66.8		100.9		63.8	PROD CHIM INORGANIQUES
522	INORG ELEMNTS,OXIDES,ETC	W 459087	41.1	W 435638	65.2	W 600756	99.9	W 522588	62.4	ELEMENTS INORGANIQUES
5225	INORGANIC BASES ETC NES	W 425253	37.9	W 402764	61.5	W 554416	95.7	W 425212	57.7	AUTRES BASES OXYDES METAL
52251	AMMONIA,ANHYDROUS ETC	W 425253	37.9	W 402684	61.5	W 554204	95.6	W 425194	57.6	AMMONIAC LIQUEFIE
53	DYES,TANNING,COLOUR PROD		3.9		2.5		14.8		15.0	PROD TEINTURE,COLORANTS
531	SYNT DYE,NAT INDGO,LAKES			W 1423	2.3	W 8974	14.7	W 25789	15.0	MAT COLOR ORGAN,LAQUES
5311	SYNTHIC ORGNIC DYESTUFFS			W 1423	2.3	W 8974	14.7	W 25789	15.0	MAT COLOR ORGAN SYNTHET
6	BASIC MANUFACTURES		854.7		938.7		1121.2		1085.7	ART MANUFACTURES
64	PAPER,PAPERBOARD AND MFR		14.2		16.3		26.2		26.3	PAPIERS,CARTONS & OUVRAGES
641	PAPER AND PAPERBOARD	W 611	1.2	W 1035	2.2	W 9737	16.1	W 9614	16.3	PAPIERS ET CARTONS
6417	CORRUGATED PAPER ETC,BLK			W 795	1.8	W 9035	14.4	W 8787	14.2	PAPIERS,CARTONS ONDULES
64172	CREPED HSHOLD PAPER ETC			W 795	1.8	W 9035	14.4	W 8787	14.2	PAPIER NON KRAFT CREPE
642	PAPER,ETC,PRECUT,ARTS OF	W 6486	13.0	W 7604	14.1	W 5664	10.0	W 6442	10.0	PAP,CARTONS DECOUPES
6428	PAPER ETC ARTICLES NES	W 4830	9.4	W 5963	11.9	W 3843	7.7	W 3393	6.7	OUVRAGES EN PATE A PAPIER
65	TEXTILE YARN,FABRICS,ETC		1.4		3.2		17.2		21.6	FILS,TISSUS,ARTICLES TEXTILE
652	COTTON FABRICS,WOVEN	W 29	0.3	W 160	0.9	W 3772	14.0	W 5349	19.4	TISSUS DE COTON
6522	WOVEN COTTON BLEACHD,ETC			W 89	0.4	W 3741	13.8	W 5329	19.2	TISSUS COTON BLANCHIS ETC
65224	BLCHED COTTON FABRIC NES			W 54	0.3	W 3741	13.8	W 5329	19.2	AUT TIS PLUS 85% COT BLANCHI
67	IRON AND STEEL		112.3		141.5		157.5		156.7	FER ET ACIER
671	PIG IRON ETC	W 1822850	106.3	W 2801220	128.9	W 2919225	150.8	W 2746755	141.3	FONTE,SPIEGEL,POUDRES
6713	IRON,STL POWDER,SHOT,ETC			W 2801220	128.9	W 2919225	150.8	W 2746755	141.3	POUDRES,GREN FER,ACIER
68	NON–FERROUS METALS		701.4		739.4		881.1		838.7	METAUX NON FERREUX
684	ALUMINIUM	W 469151	701.3	W 443176	739.0	W 504578	880.9	W 453194	838.0	ALUMINIUM
6841	ALUMINIUM,ALLOYS,UNWRGHT	W 333449	411.4	W 307925	455.1	W 363600	560.1	W 330646	570.4	ALUMINIUM,ALLIAGES BRUTS
6842	ALUMINIUM,ALLOYS WORKED	W 135702	290.0	W 135250	284.0	W 140978	320.8	W 122549	267.7	ALUMINIUM,ALLIAGES OUVRE
68421	ALUMINIUM BARS,WIRE,ETC	W 67991	129.0	W 63665	115.2	W 70527	149.9	W 70505	150.4	BARRES,PROFILES FILS ALU
68422	ALUMNM PLATE,SHEET,STRIP	W 63751	149.7	W 65438	152.8	W 62596	151.7	W 46935	107.3	TOLES, PLANCHES EN ALU
68424	ALUMINIUM POWDERS,FLAKES	W 3815	10.2	W 5035	11.9	W 6152	12.8	W 4790	8.6	POUDRES ET PAILLETTES ALU
69	METAL MANUFACTURES NES		17.9		27.6		30.8		30.7	ART MANUFACT EN METAL NDA
691	STRUCTURES AND PARTS NES	W 3828	4.2	W 5567	12.6	W 5840	7.2	W 945	1.4	CONSTRUCT FER,ACIER,ALU
6911	STRUCTURES,PARTS IRN,STL	W 3720	3.8	W 5407	12.1	W 5455	4.2	W 758	0.7	CONSTRUCT FER,ACIER,FONTE
699	BASE METAL MFRS NES	W 1618	4.5	W 2020	6.7	W 4664	15.1	W 7664	22.2	ART MANUFACTURES MET NDA
6998	MFRS NES OF CPR,NIKL,ETC	W 200	0.5	W 1572	5.6	W 3699	11.8	W 7318	19.5	OUVRAGES EN CU,NI,AL,PB,ZN
69983	ALUMINIUM MANUFACTS NES	W 200	0.5	W 1572	5.6	W 3699	11.8	W 7318	19.5	OUVRAGES EN ALUMINIUM
7	MACHINES,TRANSPORT EQUIP		97.0		57.4		57.9		48.1	MACHINES MATERIEL TRANSPORT
72	MACHS FOR SPCL INDUSTRYS		17.7		7.3		8.5		2.6	MAC SPECIALES POUR INDUST
723	CIVIL ENGNEERG EQUIP ETC	W 2739	16.6	W 1197	5.6	W 2964	7.0	W 1999	1.8	APPAREILS DE GENIE CIVIL
7234	CONST,MINING MACHNRY NES	W 2722	16.6	W 1184	5.6	W 2964	7.0	W 1989	1.8	MACH POUR LA CONST, MINES
74	GENRL INDUSTRL MACHY NES		3.2		6.7		13.6		16.3	MACH APP INDUSTRIE
78	ROAD VEHICLES		20.5		19.6		9.3		7.2	VEHICULES ROUTIERS
79	OTHR TRANSPORT EQUIPMENT		34.0		10.5		9.8		6.1	AUTRE MATERIEL TRANSPORT
792	AIRCRAFT ETC	W 116	29.3		0.1	W 13	1.0	W 9	2.0	APP NAVIGATION AERIENNE
7929	AIRCRAFT PARTS NES	W 116	29.3		0.1	W 13	1.0	W 9	2.0	PIECES DU 792
793	SHIPS AND BOATS ETC	W 4870	4.8	W 3220	10.5	W 10631	8.8	W 523	4.1	NAVIRES BATEAUX,ETC
8	MISC MANUFACTURED GOODS		126.9		131.2		147.9		155.0	ART MANUFACTURES DIVERS
812	*PLUMBG,HEATNG,LGHTNG EQ	W 1863	9.5	W 1858	11.1	W 1702	9.1	W 1850	10.6	APPAR SANITAIRES CHAUFFAGE
8124	LIGHTING EQUIPMENT NES	W 1852	9.4	W 1856	11.1	W 1693	9.1	W 1826	10.6	APPAREILS ECLAIRAGE ETC
81242	LAMPS,FITTINGS BASE METL	W 1850	9.4	W 1853	11.1	W 1624	8.8	W 1755	10.2	APPAREILS D'ECLAIRAGE
84	CLOTHING AND ACCESSORIES		66.9		79.9		89.8		90.7	VETEMENTS
842	MENS OUTERWEAR NOT KNIT	W 2400	31.4	W 631	6.5	W 238	3.8	W 412	4.7	VET DESSUS POUR HOMMES
843	WOMENS OUTERWEAR NONKNIT	W 2927	34.7	W 3441	47.7	W 3483	51.0	W 3193	46.1	VET DESSUS FEMMES MAT TEX
8435	— BLOUSES			W 1601	21.1	W 1432	18.6	W 1298	19.5	BLOUSES FEM MAT TEXTILES
8439	— OTHER OUTER GARMENTS			W 1661	24.2	W 1781	29.3	W 1529	22.2	AUT VET DES FEM MAT TEXT
844	UNDER GARMENTS NOT KNIT	W 29	0.5	W 1744	21.8	W 2756	31.5	W 2903	36.9	VETEMENT DESSOUS MAT TEX
8441	— MENS SHIRTS	W 10	0.2	W 1552	19.9	W 2586	29.7	W 2856	36.2	CHEMISES HOMMES MAT TEXT
89	MISC MANUFCTRD GOODS NES		34.7		28.1		40.1		35.9	ART MANUFACTURES DIVERS
893	ARTICLES OF PLASTIC NES	W 14954	27.7		26.4	W 15288	33.3	W 15467	33.9	OUVRAGES EN MAT DIVIS 58
8939	MISC PLASTIC ARTICLES			W 11563	17.2	W 9973	22.7	W 9949	17.9	ART DIVERS EN MAT DIV 58
89399	OTHR PLASTC ARTICLES NES			W 8805	15.5	W 9348	21.1	W 9286	16.3	AUT OUV MAT DIV 58

FOOT NOTES – NOTES

TABLE 1 –
1 Prior to 1979, special trade.
TABLEAU 1 –
1 Avant 1979, commerce spécial.

1. HISTORICAL SERIES, 1974–1996 GENERAL TRADE, IMPORTS C.I.F., EXPORTS F.O.B.
SERIES HISTORIQUES, 1974–1996 COMMERCE GENERAL, IMPORTATIONS C.A.F., EXPORTATIONS F.O.B

YEAR ANNEE	VALUE IN MILLION TAKA VALEUR EN MILLION TAKA MERCHANDISE –MARCHANDISE		GOLD –OR		CONVERSION FACTORS U.S. CENTS PER TAKA FACTEURS DE CONVERSION CENTS E.U. PAR TAKA		INDEX NUMBERS –INDICES QUANTUM		UNIT VALUE VALEUR UNITAIRE	
	IMPORTS	EXPORTS	IMPORTS	EXPORTS	IMPORTS	EXPORTS	IMPORTS	EXPORTS	IMPORTS	EXPORTS
1974	6190.50	3083.40			12.3699	12.3213				
1975	10377.40	3595.30			8.4187	8.4246				
1976	11913.50	6586.60			6.6131	6.5592				
1977	18156.40	6916.30			6.5149	6.5223				
1978	20222.00	8295.30			6.6750	6.6490				
1979	23844.00	10000.00			6.4197	6.4092				
1980	30439.30	11413.80			6.4823	6.4667			43	58
1981	32487.60	11889.70			5.5798	5.5692			48	55
1982	38359.90	14868.50			4.5281	4.4858			54	53
1983	39051.80	16982.60			4.0632	4.0603			67	60
1984	51760.00	23690.30			3.9442	3.9442			68	72
1985	59666.00	25906.30			3.6374	3.5798			77	
1986	77471.01	26761.01			3.2862	3.2879			86	89
1987	84087.01	33030.00			3.2287	3.2307			95	83
1988	96558.00	40967.01			3.1501	3.1514			89	97
1989	117797.00	42108.00			3.0990	3.0990			90	96
1990	124880.00	57885.01			2.8968	2.8873			100	100
1991	124857.00	61866.00			2.7325	2.7297			121	105
1992	145328.00	81724.00			2.5676	2.5669				
1993	158123.00	90183.01			2.5259	2.5258				
1994	185098.00	107013.00			2.4865	2.4863				
1995	261878.00	127782.00			2.4826	2.4832				
1996	276837.80	137944.00			2.3918	2.3903				

2. IMPORTS BY BROAD ECONOMIC CATEGORY AND EXPORTS BY INDUSTRIAL ORIGIN. (PERCENTAGE OF TOTAL VALUE)
IMPORTATIONS PAR CATEGORIES ECONOMIQUES ET EXPORTATIONS PAR BRANCHE D'ACTIVITE.(EN POURCENTAGE DE LA VALEUR TOTALE)

IMPORTS – IMPORTATIONS

	1990	1991	1992	1993	1994	1995	1996
TOTAL IMPORTS–IMPORTATIONS TOTALES	100.	100.	100.	100.		100.	100.
1 FOOD BEV–ALIMENTATION BOISSONS	18.7	17.1	17.7	15.3		16.6	16.2
11 PRIMARY–PRODUITS DE BASE	8.1	9.6	9.4	8.2		8.6	7.4
111 FOR INDUSTRY–POUR L'INDUSTRIE	5.3	7.3	6.7	6.0		7.5	6.3
112 FOR HOUSEHOLDS–POUR LES MENAGES	2.9	2.4	2.7	2.1		1.1	1.1
12 PROCESSED–PRODUITS ELABORES	10.6	7.5	8.2	7.1		8.0	8.8
121 FOR INDUSTRY–POUR L'INDUSTRIE	4.3	4.3	5.7	4.2		4.5	5.7
122 FOR HOUSEHOLDS–POUR LES MENAGES	6.3	3.2	2.6	2.9		3.4	3.1
2 IND SUPPLIES–APPROV INDUSTRIELS	43.1	47.0	48.9	52.6		56.6	52.7
21 PRIMARY–PRODUITS DE BASE	7.0	5.7	4.8	5.4		5.5	6.0
22 PROCESSED–PRODUITS ELABORES	36.1	41.4	44.1	47.1		51.1	46.8
3 FUELS–COMBUSTIBLES	16.4	11.4	12.1	10.9		7.6	7.1
31 PRIMARY–PRODUITS DE BASE	10.1	6.8	5.7	5.3		3.7	2.9
32 PROCESSED–PRODUITS ELABORES	6.3	4.5	6.5	5.6		3.9	4.3
321 MOTOR SPIRIT–ESSENCE	0.0	0.0	0.0	0.0		0.2	0.2
322 OTHER–AUTRES	6.3	4.5	6.5	5.6		3.7	4.1
4 MACHINERY–EQUIPEMENT	12.4	15.2	14.4	12.5		8.3	11.8
41 CAPITAL EQUIPMENT–MACHINES	11.4	13.5	13.1	11.5		7.4	10.9
42 PARTS–PIECES ACCESSOIRES	1.1	1.7	1.3	1.0		0.9	0.9
5 TRANSPORT–TRANSPORT	5.5	4.9	2.9	4.0		4.5	6.0
51 PASSENGER CARS–AUTOMOBILES	0.8	0.7	0.4	0.8		1.1	1.0
52 OTHER–AUTRES	0.9	1.6	0.7	1.0		1.8	2.5
521 INDUSTRIAL–INDUSTRIELS	0.5	1.2	0.4	0.7		1.3	1.9
522 NON INDUSTRIAL–NON INDUSTRIEL	0.3	0.4	0.3	0.3		0.4	0.6
53 PARTS–PIECES ACCESSOIRES	3.8	2.5	1.8	2.3		1.7	2.4
6 CONSUM GOODS–BIENS CONSOMMATION	3.6	4.1	3.8	4.5		6.1	5.9
61 DURABLE–DURABLES	0.6	0.9	1.1	1.2		0.6	0.7
62 SEMI DURABLE–SEMI DURABLES	2.1	2.2	1.8	2.2		4.4	4.3
63 NON DURABLE–NON DURABLES	0.9	0.9	0.9	1.1		1.1	0.9
7 GOODS NES–BIENS NDA	0.2	0.3	0.2	0.2		0.3	0.3

EXPORTS – EXPORTATIONS

	1990	1991	1992	1993	1994	1995	1996
TOTAL EXPORTS–EXPORTATIONS TOTALES	100.	100.	100.	100.	100.	100.	100.
1 AGRICULTURE	20.6	17.8	15.6	15.0	15.5	12.9	12.1
2 MINING QUARRY–INDUS EXTRACTIVES				0.1	0.0		0.0
3 MANUFACTURING–IND MANUFACTUR	79.4	82.2	84.4	84.9	84.5	87.1	87.9
31 FOOD BEV TOBACCO–ALIM BOISS TAB	0.5	0.2	0.2	0.1	0.1	0.2	0.1
32 TEXTILES–INDUSTRIES TEXTILES	75.0	75.3	77.4	79.2	80.0	76.8	80.3
33 WOOD & PRODUCTS–BOIS & PRODUITS	0.0	0.0	0.1	0.2	0.5	0.4	0.6
34 PAPER & PRODUCTS–PAPIER & PRODT	0.0	0.0	0.0	0.0	0.0	0.0	0.0
35 CHEMICALS–INDUSTRIES CHIMIQUES	2.4	4.2	2.0	3.5	2.2	3.6	3.5
36 NON METAL MIN–MIN NON METAL	0.1	0.2	0.2	0.2	0.3	1.0	0.3
37 BASIC METAL–IND METAL BASE	0.0		0.0	0.0	0.0	0.0	0.0
38 METAL MANUF–MANUF METAL	1.1	2.0	4.1	1.2	1.1	2.2	1.3
39 OTH MANUF IND–AUTRES MANUF	0.2	0.2	0.3	0.4	0.3	3.0	1.8

3. TRADE BY PRINCIPAL COUNTRIES OF CONSIGNMENT AND DESTINATION (VALUE IN MILLION U.S. DOLLARS)
ECHANGES SELON LES PRINCIPAUX PAYS DE CONSIGNATION ET DE DESTINATION (VALEUR EN MILLIONS DE DOLLARS EU)

COUNTRIES–PAYS	GENERAL IMPORTS C.I.F. IMPORTATIONS GENERALES C.A.F				
	1992	1993	1994	1995	1996
World	3467.1	3525.7		5438.4	6225.3
Africa	52.2	22.1		22.6	17.0
Americas	418.9	330.2		353.0	985.0
– Northern America	277.6	249.1		339.3	329.5
– LAIA	135.5	76.0		13.5	614.2
– CACM	2.3	4.9		0.1	1.6
– Caribbean	0.2	0.1		0.0	38.0
– Rest of America	3.4	0.0			1.7
Asia excl fmr USSR	2300.7	2498.6		3699.9	3872.4
– Middle East	252.6	242.1		45.9	103.1
Asia former USSR					
Europe excl fmr USSR	572.1	568.2		504.7	709.1
– European Union	488.0	518.3		476.2	683.4
– Eastern Europe	42.7	17.5		0.0	15.8
– Rest of Europe	41.4	32.5		28.5	9.8
Europe former USSR	42.4	36.6		47.5	49.3
Oceania	80.6	70.0		98.8	160.7
Other				711.9	431.9
India/Inde	228.3	258.7		615.2	1082.7
China, Hong Kong SAR	255.7	289.1		619.3	417.2
Korea, Republic of	309.0	357.1		462.4	475.7
Singapore/Singapour	256.9	289.8		423.4	449.9
Japan/Japon	250.7	277.6		336.1	433.8
China/Chine	251.5	236.3		472.0	186.6
Areas n.e.s.				711.9	431.9
USA/Etats–Unis d'Amer	217.6	203.3		291.4	248.5
Other Asia n.e.s.	165.9	149.6		245.0	289.6
Pakistan	113.3	121.3		215.3	113.5
Germany/Allemagne	119.9	108.6		133.0	135.6
United Kingdom	111.4	106.6		82.5	116.3
Indonesia/Indonésie	104.2	132.8		91.7	71.5
Chile/Chili	0.1	0.1			424.8
Australia/Australie	75.1	60.5		82.8	135.1
Malaysia/Malaisie	62.4	80.7		43.8	121.7
United Arab Emirates	160.7	119.1		2.1	8.4
France, Monaco	32.5	95.5		68.9	73.1
Italy/Italie	36.6	52.5		77.6	110.6
Canada	60.0	45.8		48.0	80.9
Thailand/Thaïlande	33.9	45.1		88.8	75.4
Saudi Arabia	45.3	89.3		36.1	87.2
Brazil/Brésil	37.4	46.3		13.5	102.7
Netherlands/Pays–Bas	70.4	51.0		28.7	62.4
Argentina/Argentine	90.6	28.9		0.0	83.2
Denmark/Danemark	58.5	47.7		22.6	45.3
Russian Federation	42.4	36.6		47.5	48.2
Sweden/Suède	4.1	14.7		14.6	72.2
Switzerland,Liechtenst.	28.2	26.9		23.6	2.5
Belgium–Luxembourg	20.2	19.6		21.4	21.5
Spain/Espagne	11.8	6.6		18.1	24.5
New Zealand	4.7	8.3		16.0	14.3
Tunisia/Tunisie	17.8	7.7		20.1	0.0
Myanmar	0.3	3.7		25.7	4.7
Jamaica/Jamaïque	0.0	0.0			37.1
Sri Lanka	7.8	6.3		6.2	9.4
Poland/Pologne	15.8	4.8			11.1
Iran (Islamic Rep of)	8.8	11.7		5.5	
Austria/Autriche	3.9	4.9		8.2	7.4
Korea Dem People's Rp				0.4	23.7

COUNTRIES–PAYS	GENERAL EXPORTS F.O.B. EXPORTATIONS GENERALES F.O.B.				
	1992	1993	1994	1995	1996
Monde	1941.6	2253.1	2483.3	3407.2	3538.5
Afrique	59.9	83.6	55.9	88.6	67.4
Amériques	713.2	889.9	942.9	1295.4	1250.3
– Amérique du Nord	685.4	857.8	911.6	1269.6	1229.9
– ALAI	27.1	30.5	29.9	24.3	17.2
– MCAC	0.3	1.2	0.8	1.2	2.1
– Caraïbes	0.2	0.2	0.2	0.1	0.4
– Autre Amérique	0.3	0.2	0.3	0.2	0.6
Asie anc. URSS exclus	410.3	415.6	408.6	619.2	540.2
– Moyen–Orient	129.5	107.9	114.7	99.5	122.8
Asie ancienne URSS					
Europe anc. URSS exclus	717.5	818.5	1018.2	1355.6	1644.8
– Union Européenne	689.8	790.1	989.3	1317.4	1603.5
– Europe de l'Est	9.5	15.7	16.1	13.9	21.2
– Autre de l'Europe	18.1	12.7	12.8	24.3	20.1
Europe ancienne URSS	18.8	26.9	23.7	29.3	7.6
Océanie	21.9	18.5	34.1	19.2	24.9
Autre			0.1		3.3
USA/Etats–Unis d'Amer	659.2	819.8	861.5	1204.8	1165.5
Germany/Allemagne	160.3	185.7	228.1	258.5	290.2
United Kingdom	113.7	161.6	211.6	279.9	340.8
France, Monaco	109.8	115.2	160.1	200.1	281.2
Italy/Italie	118.5	111.1	125.1	193.1	193.1
Belgium–Luxembourg	79.2	81.4	101.5	125.1	167.5
Netherlands/Pays–Bas	60.9	71.9	80.5	115.1	163.7
Japan/Japon	54.8	60.2	66.1	111.1	149.2
China, Hong Kong SAR	37.4	51.6	66.0	117.4	79.8
Singapore/Singapour	80.1	64.7	41.9	60.4	23.0
Canada	26.1	38.0	50.1	64.7	64.5
Iran (Islamic Rep of)	55.3	35.0	35.7	29.8	41.2
Spain/Espagne	16.7	21.7	29.4	43.1	48.2
Pakistan	32.7	28.1	20.7	35.3	37.2
Denmark/Danemark	8.9	14.5	24.1	37.0	47.9
Sweden/Suède	14.0	13.8	13.3	39.8	42.4
China/Chine	18.1	9.9	12.0	47.6	24.3
Russian Federation	18.8	26.9	23.7	29.3	7.6
Syrian Arab Republic	16.7	15.4	18.9	26.9	26.6
Turkey/Turquie	18.9	23.7	15.8	15.5	26.0
Sudan/Soudan	6.6	30.5	7.6	30.1	8.8
Australia/Australie	17.4	13.9	15.0	15.1	19.9
United Arab Emirates	24.1	12.1	9.2	16.7	14.7
India/Inde	1.3	2.4	13.3	27.0	32.1
Brazil/Brésil	21.3	15.4	14.9	11.5	7.9
Egypt/Egypte	16.5	11.1	7.0	17.9	17.3
Thailand/Thaïlande	11.1	14.5	10.2	12.7	16.9
Poland/Pologne	6.2	13.0	14.2	7.9	18.3
Korea, Republic of	8.1	5.7	7.9	26.0	10.9
Norway,Svalbard and JM	10.4	8.5	8.6	15.2	10.0
Viet Nam	2.1	14.0	2.8	25.6	1.9
Indonesia/Indonésie	8.9	13.8	11.3	5.0	3.1
Sri Lanka	9.7	8.1	5.5	14.0	3.9
Other Asia n.e.s.	5.7	6.6	7.3	12.0	6.0
Philippines	2.1	8.4	6.6	8.9	10.9
Malaysia/Malaisie	6.9	8.3	8.5	7.0	5.5
Saudi Arabia	3.9	4.5	19.9	3.5	3.9
Uruguay	2.3	11.1	7.6	5.6	3.2
New Zealand	2.8	3.0	17.6	2.5	3.1
Switzerland,Liechtenst.	4.2	4.0	3.8	6.7	7.1

(VALUE AS PERCENTAGE OF WORLD TOTAL)(VALEURS EN POURCENTAGE DU TOTAL MONDIAL)

	1987	1988	1989	1990	1991	1992	1993	1994	1995	1996
Africa	1.6	0.3	1.0	1.5	0.8	1.5	0.6		0.4	0.3
Americas	15.6	5.1	17.5	10.3	12.8	12.1	9.4		6.5	15.8
– Northern America	14.8	4.9	14.6	8.2	9.7	8.0	7.1		6.2	5.3
– LAIA	0.8	0.2	2.9	2.0	3.0	3.9	2.2		0.2	9.9
– CACM	0.0	0.0	0.0	0.1	0.1	0.1	0.1		0.0	0.0
– Caribbean	0.0		0.0	0.0	0.0	0.0	0.0		0.0	0.6
– Rest of America	0.0		0.0	0.0	0.0	0.1	0.0			0.0
Asia excl fmr USSR	61.2	70.3	59.6	66.5	64.6	66.4	70.9		68.0	62.2
– Middle East	12.3	11.8	12.0	14.6	8.4	7.3	6.9		0.8	1.7
Asia former USSR										
Europe excl fmr USSR	18.7	18.8	18.0	18.0	17.2	16.5	16.1		9.3	11.4
– European Union	15.7	13.7	15.6	15.8	15.1	14.1	14.7		8.8	11.0
– Eastern Europe	1.6	3.3	1.4	1.1	0.9	1.2	0.5		0.0	0.3
– Rest of Europe	1.4	1.8	1.0	1.2	1.1	1.2	0.9		0.5	0.2
Europe former USSR	1.2	1.9	1.2	0.8	2.2	1.2	1.0		0.9	0.8
Oceania	1.7	3.6	2.8	2.9	2.4	2.3	2.0		1.8	2.6
Other									13.1	6.9
India/Inde	4.9	4.8	5.7	6.2	6.4	6.6	7.3		11.3	17.4
China, Hong Kong SAR	3.3	6.7	3.7	5.0	6.8	7.4	8.2		11.4	6.7
Korea, Republic of	5.0	4.9	5.9	6.6	9.4	8.9	10.1		8.5	7.6
Singapore/Singapour	7.4	8.7	5.4	5.9	6.5	7.4	8.2		7.8	7.2
Japan/Japon	12.0	10.4	10.7	9.2	10.5	7.2	7.9		6.2	7.0
China/Chine	3.7	4.9	4.1	4.4	5.8	7.3	6.7		8.7	3.0
Areas n.e.s.									13.1	6.9
USA/Etats–Unis d'Amer	9.1	3.8	11.8	5.7	6.9	6.3	5.8		5.4	4.0
Other Asia n.e.s.	2.0	3.1	2.5	3.5	3.7	4.8	4.2		4.5	4.7
Pakistan	3.3	3.9	2.5	2.5	2.3	3.3	3.4		4.0	1.8

	1987	1988	1989	1990	1991	1992	1993	1994	1995	1996
Afrique	5.7	5.0	7.0	3.7	3.7	3.1	3.7	2.2	2.6	1.9
Amériques	35.0	30.4	29.1	34.9	31.9	36.7	39.5	38.0	38.0	35.3
– Amérique du Nord	34.0	29.5	27.4	33.2	30.6	35.3	38.1	36.7	37.3	34.8
– ALAI	0.9	0.9	1.3	1.5	1.2	1.4	1.4	1.2	0.7	0.5
– MCAC	0.0	0.0	0.0	0.1	0.0	0.0	0.1	0.0	0.0	0.1
– Caraïbes	0.0	0.0	0.0	0.0	0.1	0.0	0.0	0.0	0.0	0.0
– Autre Amérique	0.0		0.4	0.1	0.0	0.0	0.0	0.0	0.0	0.0
Asie anc. URSS exclus	24.7	24.9	25.4	20.3	19.1	21.1	18.4	16.5	18.2	15.3
– Moyen–Orient	7.4	6.2	4.7	6.7	4.6	6.7	4.8	4.6	2.9	3.5
Asie ancienne URSS										
Europe anc. URSS exclus	30.0	34.0	34.5	36.1	41.9	37.0	36.3	41.0	39.8	46.5
– Union Européenne	27.3	28.7	30.3	32.3	38.9	35.5	35.1	39.8	38.7	45.3
– Europe de l'Est	1.7	3.5	3.0	3.0	1.9	0.5	0.7	0.6	0.4	0.6
– Autre de l'Europe	0.9	1.8	1.1	0.8	1.0	0.9	0.6	0.5	0.7	0.6
Europe ancienne URSS	3.1	3.0	2.4	3.5	1.7	1.0	1.2	1.0	0.9	0.2
Océanie	1.6	2.7	1.6	1.5	1.7	1.1	0.8	1.4	0.6	0.7
Autre	0.0							0.0		0.1
USA/Etats–Unis d'Amer	31.9	27.9	26.2	31.7	28.9	34.0	36.4	34.7	35.4	32.9
Germany/Allemagne					9.6	8.3	8.2	9.2	7.6	8.2
United Kingdom	5.4	5.4	6.2	6.2	7.7	5.9	7.2	8.5	8.2	9.6
France, Monaco	1.5	1.5	2.8	4.0	5.4	5.7	5.1	6.4	5.9	7.9
Italy/Italie	8.6	10.2	7.7	8.1	5.5	6.1	4.9	5.0	5.7	5.5
Belgium–Luxembourg	3.1	2.9	4.2	4.1	4.5	4.1	3.6	4.1	3.7	4.7
Netherlands/Pays–Bas	.8	1.8	1.9	2.1	3.2	3.1	3.2	3.2	3.4	4.6
Japan/Japon	5.5	5.9	5.0	4.2	3.4	2.8	2.7	2.7	3.3	4.2
China, Hong Kong SAR	0.7	1.3	1.0	0.9	1.1	1.9	2.3	2.7	3.4	2.3
Singapore/Singapour	4.3	3.0	6.3	4.2	3.8	4.1	2.9	1.7	1.8	0.6

4. General Imports C.I.F. by Commodities according to the S.I.T.C. (Rev. 2) in million U.S. Dollars
Importations Générales C.A.F. par Produits d'après la C.T.C.I. (Rév. 2) en millions de Dollars E.U.

SITC CTCI	COMMODITY	1993 QUANTITY QUANTITE	1993 VALUE VALEUR	1994 QUANTITY QUANTITE	1994 VALUE VALEUR	1995 QUANTITY QUANTITE	1995 VALUE VALEUR	1996 QUANTITY QUANTITE	1996 VALUE VALEUR	PRODUIT
	ALL COMMODITIES		3525.8				5438.5		6225.4	TOUS PRODUITS
0	FOOD AND LIVE ANIMALS		352.8				630.1		607.1	ALIMENTS,ANIMAUX VIVANTS
02	DAIRY PRODCTS,BIRDS'EGGS		78.6				45.3		53.8	PRODUITS LAITIERS,OEUFS
022	MILK AND CREAM	W 37620	73.3				42.1	W 23396	52.5	LAIT ET CREME
0224	MILK,CREAM PRESERVED ETC	W 37618	73.3				42.0	W 23380	52.4	LAIT,CREME CONS,CONC
02242	MILK DRY,1.5% FAT OR LES	W 9541	21.4				25.1	W 14030	31.5	LAIT POUDRE INF 1.5%
02243	MILK DRY,OVER 1.5% FAT	W 16616	41.1				16.6	W 9324	20.9	LAIT POUDRE SUP 1.5%
02249	MILK(EX DRY) PRSVD,SWEET	W 11461	10.9				0.3	W 13	0.1	LAIT CONS,CONC SUCRE
04	CEREALS AND PREPARATIONS		167.2				453.6		447.6	CEREALES ET PRODUITS
041	WHEAT ETC UNMILLED	W 1033520	152.6			W 1384363	215.1	W 1199270	171.5	FROMENT,EPEAUTRE
0411	DURUM WHEAT UNMILLED	W 244144	38.0			W 576360	99.0	W 136122	19.4	FROMENT DUR NON MOULU
0412	OTHER WHEAT ETC UNMILLED	W 789376	114.6			W 808002	116.2	W 1063148	152.2	AUTRE FROMENT NON MOULU
042	RICE	W 20930	3.6			W 1221750	217.3	W 1238755	258.6	RIZ
0421	RICE IN HUSK OR HUSKED	W 186	0.1			W 696725	96.5	W 649966	136.1	RIZ SANS AUTRE PREPARATION
04211	RICE IN THE HUSK	W 186	0.1			W 579901	75.1	W 573016	120.0	RIZ PADDY
04212	RICE HUSKED					W 116824	21.5	W 76950	16.2	RIZ CARGO
0422	RICE SEMI–MILLED,MILLED	W 20744	3.6			W 525026	120.9	W 588790	122.6	RIZ POLI,GLACE INCL BRISURES
04221	RICE MILLED UNBROKEN	W 20744	3.6			W 518080	120.7	W 586590	122.2	RIZ POLI,GLACE EXCL BRISURES
048	CEREAL ETC PREPARATIONS	W 3403	9.4				8.4	W 3576	8.3	PREPTNS A BASE CEREALES
0488	OTH CEREAL PREPS,MALT EX	W 2854	8.6				7.9	W 2638	7.0	EXTRAITS DE MALT
05	VEGETABLES AND FRUIT		47.5				40.2		48.0	LEGUMES ET FRUITS
054	VEG ETC FRSH,SMPLY PRSVD	W 130759	26.8				15.2		23.5	LEGUMES FRAIS,CONG,SECS
0542	LEGUMINOUS VEGETBLES DRY	W 63521	16.0				10.6	W 48327	16.1	LEGUMES A COSSE SECS
0545	OTHER FRESH VEGETABLES	W 65823	10.3				4.1		7.1	AUTRES LEGUMES FRAIS,REF
05451	ALLIACEOUS VEGTBLS,FRESH	W 65335	10.1				4.0	W 43372	7.1	OIGNONS,ECHALOTES,AULX
057	FRUIT,NUTS,FRESH,DRIED	W 30741	19.2				22.6	W 100352	21.9	FRUITS FRAIS OU SECS
0577	NUTS EDIBLE,FRESH,DRIED	W 7828	8.0				3.0	W 2585	2.2	FRUITS A COQUES
05779	NUTS EDIBLE,FRSH,DRY,NES	W 7790	7.8				2.8	W 2568	2.1	FRUITS A COQUES NDA
0579	FRUIT FRESH OR DRIED NES	W 13729	6.4				3.8	W 18766	6.6	FRUITS FRAIS,SECS NDA
06	SUGAR AND PREPS,HONEY		26.2				52.5		13.9	SUCRES ET PRODUITS
061	SUGAR AND HONEY	W 75405	26.2				52.4	W 32943	13.2	SUCRES ET MIEL
0611	RAW BEET AND CANE SUGAR	W 48030	15.9			W 144630	47.1	W 26202	10.3	SUCRES BRUTS
07	COFFEE,TEA,COCOA,SPICES		26.1				17.3		23.4	CAFE,THE,CACAO,EPICES
075	SPICES	W 13943	26.0				16.4	W 20250	22.3	EPICES
0751	PEPPER AND PIMENTO	W 2502	2.6				1.2	W 10489	10.1	POIVRE,PIMENTS
0752	SPICES,EX PEPPER,PIMENTO	W 11441	23.5				15.3	W 9761	12.3	AUTRES EPICES
07525	SEEDS OF ANISE,CUMIN,ETC	W 5839	12.5				5.8	W 3797	5.6	GRAINES ANIS,FENOUIL
09	MISC EDIBLE PRODUCTS		4.0				5.7		5.5	PREP ALIMENTAIRES DIVERSES
098	EDIBLE PRODCTS,PREPS NES		4.0				5.7		5.4	PREP ALIMENTAIRES NDA
1	BEVERAGES AND TOBACCO		14.3				10.7		17.4	BOISSONS ET TABACS
12	TOBACCO AND MANUFACTURES		10.2				7.0		14.1	TABACS BRUTS FABRIQUES
121	TOBACCO UNMNFCTRD,REFUSE	W 1680	8.4				5.4	W 2854	13.2	TABACS BRUTS,DECHETS
2	CRUDE MATERLS,EXCL FUELS		247.2				312.0		404.3	MAT BRUTES NON COMESTIBLES
22	OIL SEEDS,OLEAGINOUS FRT		57.8				85.6		74.3	GRAINES,FRUITS OLEAGINEUX
222	SEEDS FOR'SOFT'FIXED OIL	W 72255	21.2				27.4	W 127225	37.4	GRAINES HUILES FIXES
2226	RAPE AND COLZA SEEDS	W 72255	21.2				27.1	W 127224	37.4	GRAINES DE NAVETTE,COLZA
223	SEEDS FOR OTH FIXED OILS	W 102916	36.7				58.2	W 112323	36.9	GRAINES AUTRES HUILES FIXES
2231	COPRA	W 73808	28.8				25.9	W 32042	13.4	COPRAH
2238	OIL SEEDS AND FRUITS NES	W 29108	7.9				31.9	W 80185	23.6	GRAINES D'OLEAGINEUX NDA
24	CORK AND WOOD		27.3				21.1		31.9	LIEGE ET BOIS
247	OTH WOOD ROUGH,SQUARED	W 2970085	25.8				17.3	W 5185050	30.4	BOIS BRUTS EQUARRIS
2471	SAW–,VENEER–LOGS CONIFER	W 2372258	21.3				14.3	W 5020966	25.6	CONIFERES POUR SCIAGE,PLACAG
24711	— IN THE ROUGH	W 2372258	21.3				14.3	W 5020966	25.6	ECORCES OU DEGROSSIS
251	*PULP AND WASTE PAPER	W 21897	11.3				4.8	W 12323	4.3	PATES A PAPIER,DECHETS
26	TEXTILE FIBRES AND WASTE		122.6				149.4		223.1	FIBRES TEXTILES
261	SILK	W 118	3.0			W 1443	10.1	W 1893	32.6	SOIE
2613	RAW SILK NOT THROWN	W 118	2.9			W 1224	9.7	W 1888	32.5	SOIE GREGE
263	COTTON	W 72459	95.4				104.3	W 105705	154.7	COTON
2631	RAW COTTON,EXCL LINTERS	W 72447	95.4				103.4	W 105497	153.9	COTON EN MASSE
266	SYNTHETIC FIBRES TO SPIN	W 14771	17.6			W 18726	28.4		29.0	FIBRES SYNTHETIQUES
2665	DISCN SYNTH FIBRE UNCMBD	W 14439	16.4			W 17894	26.0		23.7	DISCONTINUES EN MASSE
26652	— POLYESTER	W 14414	16.3			W 17095	24.8	W 13439	23.3	FIBRES EN POLYESTERS
27	CRUDE FERTLZR,MINRLS NES		18.9				41.7		62.0	ENGRAIS MINERAUX BRUTS
273	STONE,SAND AND GRAVEL	W 235538	3.2				14.6	W 909435	28.0	PIERRES,SABLES,GRAVIERS
2731	BLDG,DIMENSION STONE	W 161341	1.8				7.9	W 538375	20.6	PIERRES DE TAILLE
27313	GRANITE,SANDSTONE,ETC	W 145000	0.9			W 271018	7.2	W 516496	20.1	GYPSE,BASALTE,GRES
278	OTHER CRUDE MINERALS	W 78231	6.5				13.4	W 82454	24.5	AUTRES MINERAUX BRUTS
2783	COMMON SALT,ETC	W 42592	1.4			W 63650	2.7	W 516	0.1	SEL
3	MINERAL FUELS ETC		391.6				421.9		448.1	COMBUSTIBLES MINERAUX LUB
32	COAL,COKE AND BRIQUETTES		4.0				28.2		20.0	HOUILLES,COKES,BRIQUETTES
322	COAL,LIGNITE AND PEAT	W 55946	2.9				26.6	W 344919	18.0	HOUILLES,LIGNITES,TOURBE
3222	OTH COAL,NOT AGGLOMERATD	W 55946	2.9			W 595550	25.8	W 344131	18.0	AUTRES HOUILLES
33	PETROLEUM AND PRODUCTS		387.3				393.6		428.1	PETROLE ET DERIVES
333	CRUDE PETROLEUM	W 1221286	183.5				173.7	W 1241197	158.9	HUILES BRUTES DE PETROLE
334	PETROLEUM PRODUCTS,REFIN		195.5				209.0	W 1415628	263.1	PRODUITS RAFFINES
3342	KEROSENE,OTH MEDIUM OILS	V 82377	17.1			W 151236	28.4	W 204189	40.0	PETR LAMPANTS,AUT HUIL
33421	KEROSENE INCL JET FUEL	V 20443	4.1			W 146516	27.5	W 203848	40.0	PETROLES LAMPANTS
33429	OTH MEDIUM PETROLEUM OIL	V 61934	13.0			W 4719	0.9	W 342	0.1	AUTRES HUILES MOYENNES
3343	GAS OILS	V 776675	154.8			W 848390	153.4	W 1012406	182.3	GAS OILS
3345	LUBS,PETROLEUM OILS NES		23.7				17.8	W 114516	26.6	HUILES LUBRIFIANTES
33451	LUBS(HIGH PETR CONT) ETC	V 40867	13.1				17.0	W 113151	23.7	HUILES LUBRIF,H LOURDES
33452	LUBS (LOW PETRLM CONTNT)	W 5327	10.7				0.9	W 1365	2.9	PREPARATIONS LUBRIFIANTES
4	ANIMAL,VEGETABLE OIL,FAT		136.9				214.9		361.6	HUILES,GRAISSES ANIM,VEG
411	*ANIMAL OILS AND FATS	W 34769	11.2				22.4	W 97292	28.7	HUILES,GRAISSES ANIMALES
4113	ANIML OIL,FAT,GREASE NES	W 34767	11.2				22.3	W 97276	28.7	HUILES,GRAISSES ANIMALES NDA
41132	FATS OF BOVINE,SHEEP,ETC	W 33635	10.7				20.9	W 96607	28.4	SUIFS BRUTS FONDUS
42	FIXED VEGETABLE OIL,FAT		124.4				189.4		328.6	HUILES VEGETALES FIXES
423	FIXED VEG OILS,SOFT	W 195051	87.1				170.5	W 539587	264.1	HUILES VEGET DOUCES FIXES
4232	SOYA BEAN OIL	W 195044	87.1				168.8	W 539542	264.1	HUILE DE SOJA
424	FIXED VEG OIL NONSOFT	W 83464	37.4				18.9	W 122235	64.6	AUTRES HUILES VEG FIXES
4242	PALM OIL	W 79880	34.8				14.3	W 117220	60.4	HUILE DE PALME
5	CHEMCLS,RELATED PROD NES		369.5				533.9		462.8	PRODUITS CHIMIQUES
51	ORGANIC CHEMICALS		59.7				70.4		66.3	PROD CHIMIQ ORGANIQUES
514	NITROGEN–FNCTN COMPOUNDS	W 1147	9.9				21.9		21.6	COMPOSES FONCT AZOTEES
515	ORG–INORG COMPOUNDS ETC	W 3457	33.5			W 794	21.9	W 757	18.9	COMPOSES ORGANO–MINERAUX
5155	OTH ORG–INORG COMPOUNDS	W 3066	25.3			W 47	0.3	W 4	0.1	AUTR COMP ORG–MINERAUX
5156	HETEROCYCLIC CMPDS ETC	W 256	6.1			W 472	18.0	W 497	15.2	COMPOSES HETEROCYCLIQUES
51569	OTH HETEROCYC CMPDS,ETC	W 222	5.8			W 472	17.2	W 497	14.5	AUT COMP HETEROCYCLIQUES
52	INORGANIC CHEMICALS		37.8				47.9		44.6	PROD CHIM INORGANIQUES
522	INORG ELEMNTS,OXIDES,ETC		18.8				22.0		19.2	ELEMENTS INORGANIQUES
523	OTHR INORG CHEMICALS ETC		19.1				25.6	W 96955	25.3	AUT PRODUITS CHIMIQUES INORG

4. General Imports C.I.F. by Commodities according to the S.I.T.C. (Rev. 2) in million U.S. Dollars
Importations Générales C.A.F. par Produits d'après la C.T.C.I. (Rév. 2) en millions de Dollars E.U.

SITC CTCI	COMMODITY	1993 QUANTITY QUANTITE	1993 VALUE VALEUR	1994 QUANTITY QUANTITE	1994 VALUE VALEUR	1995 QUANTITY QUANTITE	1995 VALUE VALEUR	1996 QUANTITY QUANTITE	1996 VALUE VALEUR	PRODUIT
53	DYES,TANNING,COLOUR PROD		38.9				50.3		50.6	PROD TEINTURE,COLORANTS
531	SYNT DYE,NAT INDGO,LAKES	W 5446	21.6			W 8921	26.7	W 6410	29.4	MAT COLOR ORGAN,LAQUES
5311	SYNTHIC ORGNIC DYESTUFFS	W 4770	19.7			W 6390	22.6	W 5514	27.0	MAT COLOR ORGAN SYNTHET
541	*MEDICINAL,PHARM PRODUCT	K 3489554	76.9				78.1		62.3	PROD MEDICINAUX PHARMACEUT
5413	ANTIBIOTICS IN BULK	K 353354	20.2			K 248926	15.0		14.7	ANTIBIOTIQUES NDA
54131	PENICILLINS AND DERIVTVS	K 158290	10.0			K 138188	6.0		5.4	PENICILLINES ET DERIVES
5417	MEDICAMENTS	K 1856793	20.7				20.8	K 4668302	16.0	MEDICAMENTS
54179	— CONTNG OTH SUBSTANCES	K 1726416	17.9			K 1305624	9.2	K 3937401	10.9	MED CONT AUT SUBSTANCES
5419	PHARMACEUTICAL GOODS NES	K 898884	26.3				23.0	K 1565623	10.5	PREP,ART PHARMACEUTIQUES
54199	OTH PHARMACEUTICAL GOODS	K 810534	25.8				21.8	K 1300731	9.8	AUT PREP PHARMACEUTIQUES
562	*FERTILIZERS,MANUFACTURE	W 342879	55.4			W 1574204	134.9	W 456450	61.0	ENGRAIS MANUFACTURES
5622	CHEM PHOSPHATIC FERTILZR	W 262523	44.9			W 1303901	97.5	W 361693	49.8	ENGRAIS PHOSPHATES
56222	SUPERPHOSPHATES	W 252773	43.2			W 1296736	96.7	W 347166	47.6	SUPERPHOSPHATES
5623	CHEM POTASSIC FERTILIZER	W 68001	8.7			W 263180	36.6	W 88038	10.2	ENGRAIS POTASSIQUES
56232	POTASSIUM SULPHATE NES	W 65926	8.4			W 213010	25.3	W 38359	4.7	SULFATE DE POTASSIUM
58	PLASTIC MATERIALS ETC		62.4				104.8		122.5	MAT PLAST ARTIFICIELLES
582	PROD OF CONDENSATION ETC	W 5906	8.6				17.7	W 10677	21.2	PROD CONDENS,POLYCOND
583	POLYMERIZATION ETC PRODS	W 49162	38.8				83.3	W 122834	98.9	PROD POLYMERISATION
5831	POLYETHYLENE	W 17624	12.6				24.4	W 39927	27.5	POLYETHYLENE
58311	— IN PRIMARY FORMS	W 17525	12.5				23.9	W 38920	26.6	POLYETHYLENE PRIMAIRES
5834	POLYVINYL CHLORIDE	W 13182	8.9				21.0	W 37892	25.1	CHLORURE DE POLYVINYLE
58341	— IN PRIMARY FORMS	W 13078	8.6				20.0	W 36268	22.5	SOUS FORMES PRIMAIRES
5839	OTH POLYMRZTION ETC PROD	W 5982	7.8				16.6	W 10720	16.2	AUT PROD POLYMER COPOLYM
585	PLASTIC MATERIAL NES	W 19194	13.8			W 1279	1.9	W 52	0.2	RESINES ARTIFICIELLES
5852	OTH ART PLASTIC MTLS NES	W 19194	13.8			W 1279	1.9	W 52	0.2	AUT MAT PLAST ARTIFICIEL
58521	HARDENED PROTEINS	W 19188	13.8			W 1215	1.7	W 2	0.1	MAT ALBUMINOIDES DURCIES
59	CHEMICAL MATERIALS NES		33.9				37.2		40.8	MAT PROD CHIMIQUES NDA
591	PESTICIDES,DISINFECTANTS	W 3727	14.6				11.0	W 3541	14.2	DESINF,INSECT,FONG,HERB
5911	INSECTICIDES,FOR RETAIL	W 2591	9.7				9.3	W 2714	11.3	INSECTICIDES VENTE DET
598	MISCEL CHEM PRODUCTS NES	W 16490	16.1				22.6	W 13949	21.4	PROD DIV INDUST CHIM NDA
5989	CHEM PRODUCTS,PREPS NES	W 12911	12.0				15.9	W 9703	16.6	PROD PREP CHIMIQUES NDA
6	BASIC MANUFACTURES		1205.5				2167.0		2330.3	ART MANUFACTURES
62	RUBBER MANUFACTURES NES		24.9				28.2		43.4	CAOUTCHOUC MANUFACTURE
625	RUBBER TYRES, TUBES ETC	N 1774566	21.8				18.9	N 3563203	32.5	PNEUS CAOUTCHOUC VULCANISE
6252	TYRES,NEW,BUS OR LORRY	N 204059	12.7				12.0	N 352297	22.9	PNEUS POUR AUTOBUS,CAMIONS
64	PAPER,PAPERBOARD AND MFR		41.8				78.8		95.3	PAPIERS,CARTONS & OUVRAGES
641	PAPER AND PAPERBOARD	W 55884	37.5				67.1	W 102929	86.5	PAPIERS ET CARTONS
6412	PRINTG,WRITING PAPER NES	W 1909	3.0				8.0	W 4866	5.4	PAPIERS POUR L'IMPRESSION
6415	PAPER,PAPERBRD,BULK,NES	W 30512	19.0				25.3	W 59401	45.2	PAPIERS,CARTONS ROULEAUX
64151	SEMI-CHEM FLUTING PAPER	W 14240	5.2			W 9192	4.8	W 6246	7.3	PAPIER FLUTING
64159	OTHER PAPER ETC,BULK,NES	W 15812	13.5				20.2	W 51763	37.0	AUT PAPIER ROULEAUX FEUILLES
6417	CORRUGATED PAPER ETC,BLK	W 9676	7.2				12.6	W 14667	10.5	PAPIERS,CARTONS ONDULES
64172	CREPED HSHOLD PAPER ETC	W 9367	7.1			W 13428	12.3	W 12397	10.1	PAPIER NON KRAFT CREPE
642	PAPER,ETC,PRECUT,ARTS OF	W 4587	4.4				11.8		8.9	PAP,CARTONS DECOUPES
65	TEXTILE YARN,FABRICS,ETC		675.6				1479.1		1376.5	FILS,TISSUS,ARTICLES TEXTILE
651	TEXTILE YARN	W 37476	115.1				222.9	W 107827	398.1	FILS TEXTILES
6513	COTTON YARN	W 7572	35.0			W 30369	121.0	W 66742	265.9	FILS DE COTON
6514	SYN FIB YRN,BULK,MONOFIL	W 23941	59.4			W 21305	47.9	W 18950	47.3	FILS CONT 85% FIB TEXT SYNTH
65141	— TEXTRD,CONT POLYAMIDE	W 4068	14.7			W 5776	23.0	W 5453	24.0	FILS TEXT FIB CONT POLYAMID
65142	— NONTXT ETC CONT PAMID	W 7802	16.0			W 9983	12.6	W 4654	10.2	FILS NON TEX FI CON POLYAMID
65144	— TEXTRD,CONT POLYESTER	W 11590	27.3			W 4202	8.6	W 8230	11.6	FILS TEX FI CONT POLYESTERS
6516	DISCON SYN FIB BLEND YRN	W 5135	18.1			W 14929	49.5	W 19284	79.3	FILS FIBR TEX SYNT DIS MOINS
65168	OTH DISC SYN BLEND YARN	W 4719	17.2			W 13368	45.5	W 18454	76.3	FILS TEXT SYNT MELANGE AUT F
652	COTTON FABRICS,WOVEN		232.6				725.4		457.0	TISSUS DE COTON
6521	GREY WOVEN COTTON FABRIC	L 18893	22.5				109.5		95.5	TISSUS COT ECRUS NON MERCER
65214	GREY WOVEN COTTON NES	L 14485	18.9				80.1	L 60815	76.2	AUT TISSUS 85% COTON ECRUS
65215	GREY WOVN COTN BLEND NES	L 4408	3.7			L 28051	29.4	L 18202	19.4	AUT TIS MOINS 85% COT ECRUS
6522	WOVEN COTTON BLEACHD,ETC		210.1				616.0	L 288814	361.6	TISSUS COTON BLANCHIS ETC
65224	BLCHED COTTON FABRIC NES		104.4				211.7	L 130047	187.2	AUT TIS PLUS 85% COT BLANCHI
65225	BLCHD COTN BLEND FAB NES	L 115290	104.4			L 397622	398.9	L 154410	168.4	AUT TIS MOINS 85% COT BLANCH
653	WOVN MAN-MADE FIB FABRIC	L 250975	229.0				347.8	L 258316	318.1	TISSUS FIBRES SYNTH,ARTIF
6531	CONT SYNT WEAVES NONPILE	L 56653	68.1			L 69911	103.3	L 80218	114.3	TISSUS FIBRES SYNTH CONTINUE
65314	CONT SYN TYRE CORD FABRC	L 35428	42.4			L 20023	25.9	L 20443	26.4	TIS ARMATURE PNEUMATIQUES
65315	CONT SYN TXTL FABRIC NES	L 21226	25.7			L 49888	77.5	L 59774	87.9	TIS PLUS 85% TEXT SYNT CONT
6532	DISC SYN TXTL FABRIC NES	L 10816	10.0			L 35653	35.3	L 34705	41.9	TIS DISC MOINS 85% FIBR TEXT
6534	DISC SYN BLEND FABRC NES	L 176783	143.2				178.0	L 123488	134.8	TISSUS FIBRES SYNTH DISCONT
65341	DISC SYN FIB-COTTN FABRC	L 171342	137.6			L 145708	172.7	L 119277	128.4	TISSUS FIB SYNT DIS MEL COTO
6535	CONT REGN WEAVES NONPILE	L 5780	6.8			L 15056	20.1	L 12086	17.4	TISSUS FIB TEXT ART CONTINU
65355	CONT REGN TXTL FABRC NES	L 5652	6.6			L 12431	16.5	L 10272	15.0	TISSUS 85% TEXT ART CONT
655	KNITTED,ETC FABRICS	L 41178	42.6			L 71252	89.4	L 86979	118.9	ETOF BONNETERIE PIECES ETC
6552	OTHER KNIT ETC FAB NONEL	L 41178	42.6			L 71252	89.4	L 86979	118.9	ETOF BON NON ELAS NON SYNT
656	LACE,RIBBONS,TULLE,ETC		30.0				40.4		36.8	TULLES,BRODERIE
65602	WOVEN LABELS ETC NES	W 20058	29.3			W 31606	38.0	W 39893	34.8	ECUSSONS,ART SIMIL TISSES
657	SPECIAL TXTL FABRC,PRODS		21.5				36.0		35.1	TISSUS SPECIAUX
6573	COATED ETC TEXTILES NES		19.5				26.3		25.9	TISSUS,ART MATIERE TEXT NDA
65732	PLASTIC COATED TEXTILES	L 20180	17.0			L 23964	22.2	L 19041	19.9	TISSUS IMPREGNES
6575	CORDAGE AND MANUFACTURES		0.4				2.6		1.9	FICELLES,CORDES,CORDAGES
65751	CORDAGE,CABLE,ROPE,TWINE	W 116	0.3			W 2656	2.2	W 1989	1.7	CORDAGES TRESSES OU NON
66	NONMETAL MINERAL MFS NES		156.4				155.9		222.5	ART MIN NON METALLIQUES
661	LIME,CEMENT,BLDG PRODS	W 2159669	141.0				124.6	W 2982856	193.0	CHAUX,CIMENTS MAT CONSTR
6612	CEMENT	W 2159036	140.8			W 3167370	123.7	W 2957948	192.2	CIMENTS HYDRAULIQUES
664	GLASS		7.7				10.3		12.6	VERRE
67	IRON AND STEEL		152.9				233.6		343.0	FER ET ACIER
672	IRON,STEEL PRIMARY FORMS	W 29881	10.4				17.4	W 25503	13.5	LINGOTS FER,ACIER
673	IRON,STEEL SHAPES ETC	W 9781	3.8				5.6	W 32450	53.7	BARRES,PROFIL FER,ACIER
6733	IRON,STEEL PROFILES ETC	W 928	0.4				1.0	W 24373	48.2	PROFILES,PALPLAN FER,ACIER
67336	IRN,SMPL STL SHEET PILNG	W 377	0.2			W 229	0.5	W 19465	44.7	PALPLANCHES EN FER,ACIER
674	IRN,STL UNIV,PLATE,SHEET	W 415418	119.1				189.7		216.4	LARGES PLATS,TOLES
6746	IRN,STL THIN PLATE,ROLLD	W 368004	92.0			MW 14701	163.3	W 399988	187.5	TOLES LAM MOINS 3MM
67461	— OF IRON OR SIMPLE STL	W 367409	91.0			MW 14690	162.4	W 399222	186.3	TOL NON AC FIN MOINS 3 MM
6749	OTH IRN,STL PLATES,SHEET	W 25594	16.0				12.0		17.2	AUTRES TOLES FER,ACIER
67491	— OF IRON OR SIMPLE STL	W 25505	15.8			W 206032	11.2	W 34001	16.4	AUT TOLES AUTRES ACIER FIN
678	IRON,STL TUBES,PIPES,ETC	W 14671	10.6				9.4	W 153781	44.3	TUBES,TUYAUX EN FONTE,FER
6783	IRON,STL TUBES,PIPES NES	W 8577	5.9				4.5	W 107754	30.5	AUT TUBES,TUYAUX FER,ACIER
68	NON-FERROUS METALS		63.7				80.6		106.5	METAUX NON FERREUX
684	ALUMINIUM	W 14742	25.9				25.4	W 16243	38.9	ALUMINIUM
6841	ALUMINIUM,ALLOYS,UNWRGHT	W 10310	14.1				8.2	W 10391	15.3	ALUMINIUM,ALLIAGES BRUTS
6842	ALUMINIUM,ALLOYS WORKED	W 4431	11.8				17.3	W 5852	23.6	ALUMINIUM,ALLIAGES OUVRE
686	ZINC	W 18525	23.9				38.6	W 36442	37.4	ZINC
6861	ZINC,ALLOYS UNWROUGHT	W 18521	23.9				38.6	W 36376	37.4	ZINC ET ALLIAGES BRUTS
69	METAL MANUFACTURES NES		88.7				98.9		129.3	ART MANUFACT EN METAL NDA

4. General Imports C.I.F. by Commodities according to the S.I.T.C. (Rev. 2) in million U.S. Dollars
Importations Générales C.A.F. par Produits d'après la C.T.C.I. (Rév. 2) en millions de Dollars E.U.

SITC CTCI	COMMODITY	1993		1994		1995		1996		PRODUIT
		QUANTITY QUANTITE	VALUE VALEUR	QUANTITY QUANTITE	VALUE VALEUR	QUANTITY QUANTITE	VALUE VALEUR	QUANTITY QUANTITE	VALUE VALEUR	
691	STRUCTURES AND PARTS NES	W 20703	53.5				48.3	W 47333	47.4	CONSTRUCT FER,ACIER,ALU
6911	STRUCTURES,PARTS IRN,STL	W 20341	52.2				45.6	W 46647	45.0	CONSTRUCT FER,ACIER,FONTE
693	WIRE PRODUCTS NON ELECTR	W 6625	10.6				8.2	W 17405	19.9	OUVRAGES FILS METALLIQUES
694	STL,COPPR NAILS,NUTS,ETC	W 1056	2.4			W 9900	2.4		18.9	CLOUS,VIS,ECROUS
699	BASE METAL MFRS NES		15.1				25.9		30.6	ART MANUFACTURES MET NDA
7	MACHINES,TRANSPORT EQUIP		639.3				796.4		1191.6	MACHINES MATERIEL TRANSPORT
71	POWER GENERATING EQUIPMT		80.4				75.3		122.3	MACHINES GENERATRICES
712	STEAM ENGINES,TURBINES		4.7				3.9		19.4	MACHINES A VAPEUR D'EAU PIEC
713	INTRNL COMBUS PSTN ENGIN		29.3				41.2		53.0	MOTEURS EXPL COMB INT, PIECE
7138	PISTON ENGINES NES	N 65063	21.0				21.4	N 350448	37.0	MOTEURS A PISTONS NDA
714	ENGINES AND MOTORS NES		25.5				12.6		8.7	MOTEURS NON ELECTRIQUES
7149	ENGINE & MOTOR PARTS NES		22.3				6.4		8.2	PIECES 714 ET 718.88
71499	PARTS NES,OF 71488,71888		22.3				6.3		7.1	PIECES 714.88 ET 718.88
716	ROTATING ELECTRIC PLANT		14.5				14.0		29.0	APP ELECTR ROTATIFS,PIECES
7162	AC MTRS,GENRTRS,GEN SETS	N 26131	11.1				10.0		18.0	MOTEURS ELECTRIQUES
72	MACHS FOR SPCL INDUSTRYS		179.3				137.6		293.0	MAC SPECIALES POUR INDUST
721	AGRIC MACHY,EXC TRACTORS		8.6				18.1		26.7	MACHINES AGRICOLES
7211	CULTIVATING MACHINERY		6.8				15.0		21.5	MACH PREPARATION DU SOL
72118	OTH AGRIC,HORTIC MACHNRY	N 8297	6.3				2.3	N 94362	21.0	AUT MACHINES AGRICOLES
724	TEXTILE,LEATHER MACHNRY		85.3				73.4		174.2	MACH POUR INDUSTRIE TEXTILE
7243	SEWING MACHS,NEEDLES ETC	MN 9436	32.6				12.3		17.4	MACHINES A COUDRE,PIECES
72431	SEWING MACHINES	N 83277	30.6				10.4	N 159765	15.5	MACHINES A COUDRE
7244	SPINNING,EXTRDNG,ETC MCH		25.4				21.6		61.6	MACH POUR LE FILAGE
72443	SPINNING,REELING,ETC MCH	N 663	12.3				7.5		38.9	MACH POUR LA FILATURE
7245	WEAVING,FELT MFG,ETC MCH	N 6830	11.7				15.3		50.7	METIERS A TISSER,PIECES
72451	WEAVING MACHINES (LOOMS)	N 962	2.3				4.4	N 37072	26.5	METIERS A TISSER
7247	TEXTILE MACHINERY NES		5.8				19.4		35.4	MACH LAVAGE,TEINTURE TEX
72474	OTH TEXTILE MACHNERY NES	N 1323	3.8				15.0	N 160220	31.7	MACH LAVAGE ETC MAT TEXT
725	PAPER ETC MILL MACHINERY		6.2				4.9		20.7	MACHINES FABR PATE PAPIER
728	OTH MACHY FOR SPCL INDUS		61.8				22.1		40.1	AUT MACH IND PARTICULIERES
7284	MACHY FOR SPCL INDUS NES		56.7				15.9		27.3	MACH SPEC IND PARTICUL.
72848	OTH MCHY WITH INDIV FNCT	N 1041	46.2				6.4		14.4	AUTRES MACHINES NDA
73	METALWORKING MACHINERY		4.3				10.5		25.2	MACH TRAVAIL DES METAUX
736	METALWORKING MACH–TOOLS		3.1				9.4		21.3	MACH–OUTILS TRAVAIL METAUX
74	GENRL INDUSTRL MACHY NES		60.9				126.6		168,0	MACH APP INDUSTRIE
741	HEATING,COOLING EQUIPMNT		12.2				40.0		67.3	MACH CHAUFFAGE,PIECES
7411	GAS GENERATORS,PARTS NES	N 59209	3.7				5.6		30.8	GAZOGENES
7413	INDUS FURNACES ETC,PARTS	N 594	1.1				20.5		1.9	FOURS IND,LABOR,PIECES
74132	INDUST FURNACES NONELECT	N 440	0.9				20.3		1.5	FOURS NON ELECTRIQUES
742	PUMPS FOR LIQUIDS ETC		5.2				4.9		31.8	POMPES MOTO–POMPES
7428	OTHER PUMPS FOR LIQUIDS	N 2214	2.1				2.9		26.0	AUTRES POMPES POUR LIQ
74288	PUMPS FR LIQUIDS NES ETC	N 2132	2.0				2.4		24.8	POMPES POUR LIQUIDES NDA
743	PUMPS NES,CENTRFUGES ETC		8.3				35.8		15.5	POMPES COMPRES,VENT ETC
7439	PTS NES OF APP OF 7435,6		4.3				21.0		3.9	PIECES 743.5 ET 743.6
744	MECHANICAL HANDLING EQU		7.6				12.8		20.7	EQUIP MANUTENTION PIECES
749	NONELEC MACH PTS,ACC NES		21.2				22.6		23.2	PIECES MACH NON ELEC NDA
75	OFFICE MACHNES,ADP EQUIP		13.1				16.4		25.1	MACH BUREAU TRAIT AUTOM
76	TELECOMM,SOUND EQUIPMENT		31.1				40.7		34.2	EQUIPMENT DE TELECOM
764	TELECOM EQPT,PTS,ACC NES		27.8				37.9		28.9	EQUIP TELECOM,PIECES
7643	TV,RADIO TRANSMITTRS ETC	N 90	15.2				5.5		5.8	APP EMET TELE RADIO
77	ELECTRIC MACHNRY NES ETC		150.3				99.2		128.4	MACH APP ELECT NDA
771	ELECTRIC POWER MACHY NES		68.6				25.7		29.8	MACH PROD,TRANS ELECTR
7711	TRANSFORMERS,ELECTRICAL	N 19656	28.8				18.2		24.4	TRANSFO ELECTRIQUES
77118	OTHER ELEC TRANSFORMERS	N 18288	19.4				15.7	N 35600	22.7	AUTRES TRANSFO ELECTRIQ
7712	OTH ELEC POWER MACHY NES		39.8				7.6		5.5	AUT APP PROD TRANSF ELEC
77129	PTS NES OF MACHY OF 771		34.8				4.8		2.5	PIECES MACH DU 771
772	SWITCHGEAR ETC,PARTS NES	N 2502132	27.7				21.0	N 3746093	24.9	APP COUPURE,SECT ETC
7721	SWITCHGEAR ETC	N 2492015	27.6				19.6	N 3624015	22.6	APP COUPURE,SECTIONMNT
773	ELECTR DISTRIBUTNG EQUIP	W 8242	36.3				13.4		20.5	EQUIPMT DISTRIBUTION ELECT
7731	INSULATED WIRE,CABLE ETC	W 5898	30.5				9.3		16.8	FILS,CABLES ISOLES ELECT
78	ROAD VEHICLES		74.3				150.9		199.0	VEHICULES ROUTIERS
781	PASS MOTOR VEH EXC BUSES	N 5109	27.4			N 129669	58.8	N 8041	61.8	AUTO TRANSPORT PERSONNES
782	LORRIES,SPCL MTR VEH NES	N 633	7.2				31.0	N 27487	59.2	VEHICULES SPECIAUX,MARCH
7821	LORRIES,TRUCKS	N 594	5.9			N 286899	29.6	N 27229	54.3	VEHICULES TRANSP MARCHAND
783	ROAD MOTOR VEHICLES NES	N 1431	11.1			N 180448	24.0	N 1988	21.0	VEHICULES ROUTIERS NDA
7831	BUSES	N 1430	11.1			N 180430	23.4	N 1808	20.5	VOITURES TRANSPORT COMMUN
784	MOTOR VEH PRTS,ACCES NES		11.4				5.7		11.4	PIECES 722,781,782,783
785	CYCLES,ETC MOTRZD OR NOT		16.8				30.5		43.2	MOTOCYCLES SCOOTERS
7851	MOTORCYCLES ETC	N 10198	9.5			N 78214	18.5	N 39922	33.1	MOTO VELO MOTEUR AUXIL
79	OTHR TRANSPORT EQUIPMENT		46.0				139.6		196.8	AUTRE MATERIEL TRANSPORT
791	RAILWAY VEHICLES		10.7				13.9		3.5	VEHIC MAT CHEMINS DE FER
792	AIRCRAFT ETC		0.1				11.0		46.0	APP NAVIGATION AERIENNE
7929	AIRCRAFT PARTS NES		0.1				7.0		40.1	PIECES DU 792
793	SHIPS AND BOATS ETC		35.3				114.8		147.5	NAVIRES BATEAUX,ETC
7932	SHIPS AND BOATS NES	N 71833	3.2				1.0		26.0	NAVIRES ET BATEAUX
79323	OTHER CARGO VESSELS	N 1	3.0				0.4	N 3154	24.3	AUT BATEAUX TRANS MARCH
7933	VESSELS FOR BREAKING UP	W 190516	32.0				113.7	W 715851	99.5	BATEAUX A DEPECER
7938	TUGS,SPECIAL VESSELS ETC	N 622	0.2			N 60	0.1		22.0	REMORQUEURS,BATEAUX SPEC
8	MISC MANUFACTURED GOODS		165.2				342.4		390.1	ART MANUFACTURES DIVERS
84	CLOTHING AND ACCESSORIES		6.5				101.9		155.5	VETEMENTS
844	UNDER GARMENTS NOT KNIT	N 17292	1.0				34.8		46.5	VETEMENT DESSOUS MAT TEX
8441	— MENS SHIRTS	N 17256	1.0				34.8		46.5	CHEMISES HOMMES MAT TEXT
84412	—— OF SYNTHETIC FIBRES	N 17220	1.0				34.7		46.4	CHEMISES HOMMES FIB SYNT
845	OUTERWEAR KNIT NONELASTC	N 4067088	2.3			MN 86507	55.6	MN 84327	94.7	VET DESSOUS,ACCES BONNET
8451	— JERSEYS,PULLOVERS ETC	N 3786192	2.1			MN 62538	37.1	MN 56483	66.0	CHANDAILS,PULL–OVERS ETC
8459	— OTHER,CLTHG ACCESRYS	N 280896	0.2			MN 23962	18.6	MN 27666	28.7	AUT VET DESSUS DE BONNE
87	PRECISION INSTRUMNTS NES		26.3				31.5		34.5	INSTRUM,APPAR SCIENT NDA
874	MEASURNG,CONTROLNG INSTR		13.0				18.1		18.2	INSTRUMENTS DE MESURE
88	PHOTO EQU,OPTICL GDS ETC		11.7				17.0		16.4	APP,FOURN PHOTO,OP,MONTR
89	MISC MANUFCTRD GOODS NES		117.7				187.7		177.7	ART MANUFACTURES DIVERS
892	PRINTED MATTER		16.1				26.1		28.5	IMPRIMES
8928	PRINTED MATTER NES		9.9				19.3		21.1	IMPRIMES NDA
89281	LABELS PAPER,PAPERBOARD	MN 1011157	6.3			MN 5851611	12.5	MN 7247141	14.8	ETIQUETTES TOUS GENRES
89283	UNISSUED BANKNOTES ETC	W 401	2.4			W 1504	5.1	W 743	3.5	TIMBRES–POSTE FISCAUX
893	ARTICLES OF PLASTIC NES		60.1				59.5		49.5	OUVRAGES EN MAT DIVIS 58
8931	PLSTC PACKG CONTNRS,LIDS	W 20949	39.1			W 23078	23.4	W 16447	23.0	ART TRANSP EMBALLAGE ETC
8939	MISC PLASTIC ARTICLES		21.0				36.1		26.4	ART DIVERS EN MAT DIV 58
89399	OTHR PLASTC ARTICLES NES		20.9				35.6		26.1	AUT OUV MAT DIV 58
894	TOYS,SPORTING GOODS,ETC		4.3				47.6		43.0	VOITURES ENFANTS,JOUETS
8947	OTH SPORT GDS,FAIR AMUSM		3.8				46.5		38.0	AUT ART DE SPORT
89471	FISHNG,HUNTNG EQUIP NES		1.8				43.4		35.6	HAMECONS ET EPUISETTES

4. General Imports C.I.F. by Commodities according to the S.I.T.C. (Rev. 2) in million U.S. Dollars
Importations Générales C.A.F. par Produits d'après la C.T.C.I. (Rév. 2) en millions de Dollars E.U.

SITC CTCI	COMMODITY	1993 QUANTITY QUANTITE	1993 VALUE VALEUR	1994 QUANTITY QUANTITE	1994 VALUE VALEUR	1995 QUANTITY QUANTITE	1995 VALUE VALEUR	1996 QUANTITY QUANTITE	1996 VALUE VALEUR	PRODUIT
899	OTHER MANUFACTURED GOODS		33.0				49.3		49.8	AUT ART MANUF DIVERS NDA
8998	SMALLWARES,TOILETRYS ETC		30.7				46.1		45.9	ART MERCERIE,TOILETTE
89983	BUTTONS,STUDS,ETC	MN 1586775	20.8			MN 3166553	29.4	MN 3686380	27.3	BOUTONS,BOUTONS–PRESSION
89984	SLIDE FASTENERS,PARTS	MN 351832	9.9			MN 259603	16.6	MN 1133106	18.5	FERMETURES A GLISSIERE

5. General Exports F.O.B. by Commodities according to the S.I.T.C. (Rev. 2) in million U.S. Dollars
Exportations Générales F.O.B. par Produits d'après la C.T.C.I. (Rév. 2) en millions de Dollars E.U.

SITC CTCI	COMMODITY	1993 QUANTITY QUANTITE	1993 VALUE VALEUR	1994 QUANTITY QUANTITE	1994 VALUE VALEUR	1995 QUANTITY QUANTITE	1995 VALUE VALEUR	1996 QUANTITY QUANTITE	1996 VALUE VALEUR	PRODUIT
	ALL COMMODITIES		2253.1		2483.4		3407.3		3538.6	TOUS PRODUITS
0	FOOD AND LIVE ANIMALS		264.0		335.8		354.8		354.6	ALIMENTS,ANIMAUX VIVANTS
03	FISH AND PREPARATIONS		211.4		269.1		321.3		323.7	POISSONS ET PREPARATIONS
034	FISH,FRESH,CHILLED,FROZN	W 6418	18.0	W 7587	20.0	W 10233	25.4	W 10096	23.7	POISSON FRAIS, REFRIG,CONG
0342	FISH FROZEN,EXCL FILLETS	W 6418	18.0	W 7561	19.9	W 10091	25.0	W 10074	23.7	POISSONS CONGELES
035	FISH SALTED,DRIED,SMOKED	W 1260	9.0	W 1497	10.1	W 1333	12.8	W 1413	8.7	POISSON SECHE,SALE,FUME
03503	FISH(EX COD)DRIED,SALTED	W 960	5.5	W 1317	7.6	W 1054	7.9	W 1148	6.9	POISSONS SECHES,SALES
036	SHELL FISH FRESH,FROZEN	W 27574	184.4	W 31518	239.2	W 28716	283.1	W 28293	291.4	CRUSTACES,MOLLUSQUES
05	VEGETABLES AND FRUIT		10.8		24.3		0.2		0.1	LEGUMES ET FRUITS
054	VEG ETC FRSH,SMPLY PRSVD		9.5		23.4		0.1		0.1	LEGUMES FRAIS,CONG,SECS
0545	OTHER FRESH VEGETABLES		8.0		7.0		0.1		0.1	AUTRES LEGUMES FRAIS,REF
05459	FRESH VEGETABLES NES		8.0		7.0		0.1		0.1	LEGUMES FRAIS,REFRI NDA
0548	EDIBLE VEG NES FRESH,DRY	W 1122	1.5	W 2755	16.5					RACINES,TUBERCULES
05488	VEG PRODTS NES FRESH,DRY	W 1122	1.5	W 2755	16.5					PROD VEGET ALIM HUMAINE
07	COFFEE,TEA,COCOA,SPICES		41.6		41.9		33.0		30.8	CAFE,THE,CACAO,EPICES
074	TEA AND MATE	W 29620	39.8	W 29040	41.8	W 26577	32.9	W 20981	30.8	THE ET MATE
0741	TEA	W 29620	39.8	W 29040	41.8	W 26430	32.7	W 20981	30.8	THE
2	CRUDE MATERLS,EXCL FUELS		74.6		49.4		90.4		74.8	MAT BRUTES NON COMESTIBLES
26	TEXTILE FIBRES AND WASTE		71.5		47.9		79.5		73.7	FIBRES TEXTILES
264	JUTE,OTH TEX BAST FIBRES	W 266115	71.4	W 183530	47.5	W 315696	79.2	W 318571	72.7	JUTE
3	MINERAL FUELS ETC		19.3		11.9		15.4		9.5	COMBUSTIBLES MINERAUX LUB
33	PETROLEUM AND PRODUCTS		19.3		11.9		15.4		9.5	PETROLE ET DERIVES
334	PETROLEUM PRODUCTS,REFIN	V 146542	19.3		11.9	V 145854	15.4	V 98192	9.5	PRODUITS RAFFINES
3341	GASOLINE,OTH LIGHT OILS	V 67108	11.5	V 18224	2.2	V 44076	6.3	V 9908	2.8	ESSENCES POUR MOTEURS
33419	OTH LIGHT PETROLEUM OILS	V 67108	11.5	V 18211	2.2	V 44076	6.3	V 9908	2.8	AUTRES HUILES LEGERES
3344	FUEL OILS,NES	V 72082	6.4	V 134302	8.9	V 101760	9.1	V 87474	6.6	FUEL OILS
5	CHEMCLS,RELATED PROD NES		59.1		43.5		103.4		104.4	PRODUITS CHIMIQUES
562	*FERTILIZERS,MANUFACTURE	W 423969	56.0	W 353001	41.5	W 613367	99.0	W 526542	101.5	ENGRAIS MANUFACTURES
5621	CHEM NITROGENOUS FERTLZR	W 423969	56.0	W 353001	41.5	W 512813	80.2	W 357740	71.3	ENGRAIS AZOTES
56216	UREA	W 423969	56.0	W 351801	41.3	W 512813	80.2	W 354940	70.9	UREE
5629	FERTILIZERS NES					W 100500	18.9	W 150602	26.7	ENGRAIS NDA
56299	OTHER FERTILIZERS NES					W 100500	18.9	W 140602	25.2	AUTRES ENGRAIS NDA
6	BASIC MANUFACTURES		483.3		513.4		673.4		635.8	ART MANUFACTURES
61	LEATHER,DRESSED FUR,ETC		136.7		153.5		193.0		150.5	CUIRS,PELLETERIES
611	LEATHER	W 12105	134.7	W 14463	152.7	W 18724	192.6	W 15033	149.6	CUIRS,PEAUX PREPARES
6113	CALF LEATHER	W 1037	15.5	W 1036	16.8	W 725	12.5	W 379	6.2	CUIRS,PEAUX DE VEAUX
6114	LEATHR BOVINE NES,EQUINE	W 9313	93.0	W 11521	109.0	W 16481	153.8	W 13608	124.4	CUIRS DE BOVINS
6116	LEATHER OF OTH HIDE,SKIN	W 1625	24.9	W 1848	26.2	W 1266	23.1	W 989	18.4	PEAUX PREP D'AUTRES ANIMAUX
61161	LEATHER FROM GOAT,KID	W 1616	24.8	W 1848	26.2	W 1266	23.1	W 989	18.4	PEAUX DE CAPRINS PREPAREES
63	WOOD,CORK MANUFACTRS NES		5.4		12.3		12.1		19.9	OUVRAGES LIEGE ET BOIS
634	VENEERS,PLYWOOD,ETC	W 99	5.4	W 209	12.3	W 222	12.1	W 387	19.9	PLACAGES,CONTRE–PLAQUES
6349	WOOD SIMPLY SHAPED NES	W 99	5.4	W 204	12.3	W 215	12.1	W 378	19.8	BOIS SIMPL TRAVAILLES NDA
63491	HOOPWOOD,SPLIT POLES ETC	W 99	5.4	W 204	12.3	W 215	12.1	W 378	19.8	BOIS ETC
65	TEXTILE YARN,FABRICS,ETC		333.8		337.2		432.3		444.9	FILS,TISSUS,ARTICLES TEXTILE
651	TEXTILE YARN	W 33076	27.0	W 45849	34.8	W 61491	49.8	W 69944	59.1	FILS TEXTILES
6519	TEXTILE FIBRE YARN NES	W 32982	26.8	W 45795	34.7	W 59575	47.1	W 69855	58.9	FILS TEXT NDA FILE FIB VER
65196	FLAX,RAMIE YARN IN BULK	W 32982	26.8	W 45795	34.7	W 59541	47.1	W 69855	58.9	FILS LIN,RAMIE NON POUR DET
652	COTTON FABRICS,WOVEN		13.1		19.0		49.2		47.1	TISSUS DE COTON
6522	WOVEN COTTON BLEACHD,ETC		12.9		18.9		49.2		46.4	TISSUS COTON BLANCHIS ETC
65222	BLCHD COTTON TERRY FABRC	L 26060	12.5	L 39552	18.7	L 84606	40.0	L 84948	38.1	TISSUS COT BOUCLES BLANCHIS
653	WOVN MAN–MADE FIB FABRIC	L 186	0.3	L 718	0.8	L 6815	5.7	L 27326	26.9	TISSUS FIBRES SYNTH,ARTIF
6534	DISC SYN BLEND FABRC NES	L 107	0.1	L 718	0.8	L 6657	5.5	L 27277	26.9	TISSUS FIBRES SYNTH DISCONT
65343	DISC SYN–CONT MAN–MD FAB	L 99	0.1	L 228	0.3	L 2648	2.8	L 23368	24.1	TISSUS FIB SYNT MEL TEXT SY
654	OTH WOVEN TEXTILE FABRIC		84.1		106.4		98.7		88.1	TISSUS AUT COTON SYNT,ARTIF
6545	WEAVES OF FIBRES OF 2640	W 133162	83.6	W 160453	106.0	W 138201	95.9	W 152217	88.0	TISSUS DE JUTE
657	SPECIAL TXTL FABRC,PRODS		57.2		52.4		68.7		54.6	TISSUS SPECIAUX
6575	CORDAGE AND MANUFACTURES		56.4		51.8		68.6		54.5	FICELLES,CORDES,CORDAGES
65751	CORDAGE,CABLE,ROPE,TWINE	W 65817	54.1	W 65852	49.6	W 69645	66.5	W 71211	52.5	CORDAGES TRESSES OU NON
658	TEXTILE ARTICLES NES		146.3		104.2		151.0		160.5	ART FACONNES MAT TEXTILES
6581	BAGS,SACKS OF TEXTILES	W 5310520	122.8	W 180672	90.6	W 237934	118.0	W 2459090	110.2	SACS EMBALLAGE TEXTILES
6582	MADE–UP CANVAS GOODS	W 1498	10.9	W 1184	7.6	W 4013	26.3	W 5829	38.3	BACHES,TENTES ETC
6584	LINENS ETC	MN 28119	12.0	N 5852496	5.9		6.6		9.4	LINGE DE MAISON
65841	BED LINEN OF COTTON	N 3308976	7.5	N 1016844	3.9	N 62028	0.3	N 188976	0.7	LINGE DE LIT DE COTON
659	FLOOR COVERINGS,ETC		6.0		19.9		4.1		5.6	COUVRE–PARQUETS,TAPIS ETC
6596	OTH TXTL CARPETS ETC NES	A 10963	5.9	A 10041	19.8		4.1	A 6511	5.5	TAPIS AUT MAT TEXT NDA
65961	— TUFTED	A 9661	5.2	A 8980	19.1		3.5	A 5625	4.5	TAPIS AUT MAT TEXT TOUFF
66	NONMETAL MINERAL MFS NES		5.3		7.7		30.2		10.9	ART MIN NON METALLIQUES
666	POTTERY		5.3		7.6		22.7		10.8	POTERIE
6664	PORCELN,CHINA HOUSE WARE	N 9950	5.3		7.6		22.7		10.8	VAISSELLE,ARTS MEN PORC
7	MACHINES,TRANSPORT EQUIP		23.1		19.0		54.7		20.1	MACHINES MATERIEL TRANSPORT
72	MACHS FOR SPCL INDUSTRYS		7.3		10.7		26.7		4.2	MAC SPECIALES POUR INDUST
728	OTH MACHY FOR SPCL INDUS		5.9		10.1		21.7		3.0	AUT MACH IND PARTICULIERES
7284	MACHY FOR SPCL INDUS NES		5.9		10.1		21.7		3.0	MACH SPEC IND PARTICUL.
72848	OTH MCHY WITH INDIV FNCT		3.8		9.7		15.4		2.6	AUTRES MACHINES NDA
74	GENRL INDUSTRL MACHY NES		10.1		2.3		9.8		0.9	MACH APP INDUSTRIE
744	MECHANICAL HANDLING EQU		9.9		2.2		1.1			EQUIP MANUTENTION PIECES
8	MISC MANUFACTURED GOODS		1326.6		1507.7		2070.1		2326.3	ART MANUFACTURES DIVERS
812	*PLUMBG,HEATNG,LGHTNG EQ	N 4749136	2.2	N 6756024	2.3		13.5		10.6	APPAR SANITAIRES CHAUFFAGE
84	CLOTHING AND ACCESSORIES		1307.4		1478.8		1969.3		2218.5	VETEMENTS
842	MENS OUTERWEAR NOT KNIT	MN 79382	431.8		451.2		517.8		592.3	VET DESSUS POUR HOMMES
8421	— OVERCOATS,OTHER COATS	MN 30701	28.8	MN 39727	40.5	MN 59270	61.1	MN 88289	94.0	MANTEAUX HOMMES MAT TEXT
84219	—— OF OTHER FIBRES	MN 30701	28.8	MN 39547	40.3	MN 57803	59.8	MN 86537	91.5	MANTEAUX HOMMES AUT FIBR
8422	— SUITS	N 3828000	25.0	N 3299604	22.9	N 3817032	21.5	N 4008888	25.2	COMPLETS HOMMES MAT TEXT
84223	—— OF MAN–MADE FIBRES	N 3828000	25.0	N 3299604	22.9	N 3812052	21.4	N 4008888	25.2	COMPLETS HOMMES FIB SYNT
8423	— TROUSERS,BREECHES ETC	MN 28413	105.3	MN 31012	113.4	MN 53914	206.6	MN 63312	226.5	PANTALONS HOMMES MAT TEX
8424	— JACKETS,BLAZERS ETC	MN 9489	78.5	MN 9742	77.7	MN 13966	117.6	MN 24892	146.1	VESTES HOMMES MAT TEXTIL
8429	— OTHER OUTER GARMENTS	N 6951180	194.4		196.9		111.3		100.8	AUT VET DES HOM MAT TEX
843	WOMENS OUTERWEAR NONKNIT	MN 71910	244.4		261.2		364.2		324.6	VET DESSUS FEMMES MAT TEX
8431	— COATS AND JACKETS	N 4679280	32.9	N 4442148	35.0	N 6386988	43.8	N 7952664	47.9	MANT,VEST FEM MAT TEXTIL
8433	— DRESSES	N 2396496	8.5	N 2091660	7.8	N 2871660	12.1	N 3694656	16.1	ROBES EN MAT–TEXTILES
8435	— BLOUSES	MN 35531	104.8	MN 33673	102.5	MN 39034	123.7	MN 31422	95.3	BLOUSES FEM MAT TEXTILES
8439	— OTHER OUTER GARMENTS	MN 26616	87.1		104.9		169.9		147.3	AUT VET DES FEM MAT TEXT
844	UNDER GARMENTS NOT KNIT	MN 143763	400.2	MN 184198	499.2	MN 234049	677.3	MN 256065	737.4	VETEMENT DESSOUS MAT TEX
8441	— MENS SHIRTS	MN 133049	376.7	MN 169942	473.8	MN 217229	644.0	MN 228108	695.4	CHEMISES HOMMES MAT TEXT
84411	—— OF COTTON	MN 53093	174.5	MN 70620	224.5	MN 91768	311.2	MN 91516	322.7	CHEMISES HOMMES DE COTON
84412	—— OF SYNTHETIC FIBRES	MN 79955	202.2	MN 99322	249.4	MN 125461	332.9	MN 136593	372.7	CHEMISES HOMMES FIB SYNT
8442	— MENS,OTHR THAN SHIRTS	N 6538176	12.3	MN 10179	14.1	MN 13364	20.8	MN 15333	28.3	SOUS–VET HOMMES MAT TEXT
8443	— WOMENS	N 4175964	11.4	N 4077336	11.5	N 3455892	12.6	MN 12624	13.8	VET DESSOUS FEM MAT TEXT
845	OUTERWEAR KNIT NONELASTC	MN 31465	76.5	MN 28636	87.4	MN 60250	173.0	MN 69890	231.5	VET DESSOUS,ACCES BONNET
8451	— JERSEYS,PULLOVERS ETC	MN 14967	39.6	MN 16183	50.1	MN 33807	103.2	MN 47659	154.7	CHANDAILS,PULL–OVERS ETC
8459	— OTHER,CLTHG ACCESRYS	MN 15459	31.5	MN 11956	35.2	MN 25535	64.5	MN 20784	68.3	AUT VET DESSUS DE BONNE

5. General Exports F.O.B. by Commodities according to the S.I.T.C. (Rev. 2) in million U.S. Dollars
Exportations Générales F.O.B. par Produits d'après la C.T.C.I. (Rév. 2) en millions de Dollars E.U.

SITC CTCI	COMMODITY	1993 QUANTITY QUANTITE		1993 VALUE VALEUR	1994 QUANTITY QUANTITE		1994 VALUE VALEUR	1995 QUANTITY QUANTITE		1995 VALUE VALEUR	1996 QUANTITY QUANTITE		1996 VALUE VALEUR	PRODUIT
846	UNDER GARMENTS KNITTED	MN	153523	150.2	MN	168624	175.5	MN	194452	233.7	MN	248597	328.4	SOUS VETS DE BONNETERIE
8462	— OF COTTON NON ELASTIC	MN	143677	125.8	MN	162592	161.5	MN	184320	210.0	MN	234804	301.2	SOUS–VET BONNET COTON
84629	—— OTHER	MN	143677	125.8	MN	162592	161.5	MN	184320	210.0	MN	234804	301.2	AUT SOUS–VET BONNET COTON
8463	— OF SYNTH FBR NONELAST	MN	9846	24.5	N	6032436	14.1	MN	9433	23.2	MN	11312	25.9	SOUS–VET BONNET FIB SYNT
84632	—— MENS SHIRTS	MN	9846	24.5	N	6032436	14.1	MN	9403	23.2	MN	11228	25.8	CHEMISES DE BON FIB SYNMT
851	*FOOTWEAR	N	444912	6.4			16.5			21.5			28.2	CHAUSSURES
85102	FOOTWEAR LEATHER	N	444912	6.4			15.9			21.5			27.9	CHAUS SEMELLES EN CUIR
89	MISC MANUFCTRD GOODS NES			9.6			6.7			61.6			63.2	ART MANUFACTURES DIVERS
894	TOYS,SPORTING GOODS,ETC			5.4			3.0			53.2			51.1	VOITURES ENFANTS,JOUETS
8947	OTH SPORT GDS,FAIR AMUSM			5.4			2.9			52.9			51.1	AUT ART DE SPORT
89471	FISHNG,HUNTNG EQUIP NES			5.4			2.9			52.9			51.1	HAMECONS ET EPUISETTES
9	GOODS NOT CLASSD BY KIND			1.7			2.0			44.2			11.0	ART TRANSACT NON CLASSES
931	*SPECIAL TRANSACTIONS			1.0			0.9			44.2			10.8	TRANS.SPECIALES

1. HISTORICAL SERIES, 1962–1997 GENERAL TRADE, IMPORTS C.I.F., EXPORTS F.O.B.
SERIES HISTORIQUES, 1962–1997 COMMERCE GENERAL, IMPORTATIONS C.A.F., EXPORTATIONS F.O.B

YEAR ANNEE	VALUE IN MILLION BARBADOS DOLLARS / VALEUR EN MILLION BARBADOS DOLLARS — MERCHANDISE –MARCHANDISE IMPORTS	EXPORTS	GOLD –OR IMPORTS	EXPORTS	CONVERSION FACTORS U.S. CENTS PER BARBADOS DOLLAR FACTEURS DE CONVERSION CENTS E.U. PAR BARBADOS DOLLAR IMPORTS	EXPORTS	INDEX NUMBERS –INDICES — QUANTUM IMPORTS	EXPORTS	UNIT VALUE / VALEUR UNITAIRE IMPORTS	EXPORTS
1962	89.10	50.30			58.3300	58.3300				
1963	98.90	69.80			58.3300	58.3300				
1964	108.90	60.30			58.3300	58.3300				
1965	116.30	64.30			58.3300	58.3300				
1966	131.10	70.00			58.3300	58.3300				
1967	134.10	71.60			57.3100	57.7800				
1968	168.00	80.20			50.0000	50.0000				
1969	194.60	74.30			50.0000	50.0000				
1970	236.00	79.20			50.0000	50.0000				
1971	243.70	80.40			50.0000	50.0000				
1972	270.40	84.50			52.1438	52.9137				
1973	328.60	103.70			51.0097	51.5789				
1974	417.70	172.40			48.7561	49.1835				
1975	437.20	216.50			49.4897	49.2208				
1976	473.30	173.60			49.9052	49.9052				
1977	545.10	193.00			49.8273	49.8360				
1978	628.20	261.10			49.7199	49.7200				
1979	852.50	306.00			49.7199	49.7200				
1980	1049.10	455.40			49.7199	49.7200				
1981	1165.90	448.60			49.7200	49.7200				
1982	1106.60	519.60			49.7199	49.7200				
1983	1258.00	717.40			49.7191	49.7191				
1984	1324.60	787.40			49.7191	49.7191				
1985	1221.60	707.80			49.7191	49.7191				
1986	1181.10	552.30			49.7200	49.7200				
1987	1035.90	313.50			49.7200	49.7200				
1988	1163.90	354.20			49.7200	49.7200				
1989	1354.30	375.50			49.7200	49.7200				
1990	1407.90	430.20			49.7200	49.7200				
1991	1397.70	414.70			49.7200	49.7200				
1992	1048.50	380.30			49.7200	49.7200				
1993	1154.10	374.00			49.7200	49.7200				
1994	1228.60	363.10			49.7200	49.7200				
1995	1541.20	477.80			49.7200	49.7200				
1996	1667.30	561.20			50.0000	50.0000				
1997	1973.80	562.80			50.0000	50.0000				

2. IMPORTS BY BROAD ECONOMIC CATEGORY AND EXPORTS BY INDUSTRIAL ORIGIN. (PERCENTAGE OF TOTAL VALUE)
IMPORTATIONS PAR CATEGORIES ECONOMIQUES ET EXPORTATIONS PAR BRANCHE D'ACTIVITE.(EN POURCENTAGE DE LA VALEUR TOTALE)

IMPORTS – IMPORTATIONS

	1991	1992	1993	1994	1995	1996	1997
TOTAL IMPORTS–IMPORTATIONS TOTALES	100.	100.	100.	100.	100.	100.	100.
1 FOOD BEV–ALIMENTATION BOISSONS	16.3	19.1	18.0	19.0	17.0	15.9	16.7
11 PRIMARY–PRODUITS DE BASE	5.8	6.2	6.1	6.9	6.3	5.9	5.9
111 FOR INDUSTRY–POUR L'INDUSTRIE	1.5	0.8	1.4	1.9	1.9	1.8	2.1
112 FOR HOUSEHOLDS–POUR LES MENAGES	4.3	5.4	4.7	5.0	4.4	4.0	3.9
12 PROCESSED–PRODUITS ELABORES	10.5	12.9	11.9	12.1	10.6	10.1	10.8
121 FOR INDUSTRY–POUR L'INDUSTRIE	1.6	2.8	2.3	1.8	1.6	1.9	2.5
122 FOR HOUSEHOLDS–POUR LES MENAGES	8.8	10.1	9.6	10.4	9.0	8.1	8.3
2 IND SUPPLIES–APPROV INDUSTRIELS	28.3	27.9	27.3	27.3	27.1	27.5	26.0
21 PRIMARY–PRODUITS DE BASE	1.9	2.1	1.5	1.6	1.5	2.3	1.1
22 PROCESSED–PRODUITS ELABORES	26.4	25.8	25.8	25.7	25.7	25.2	24.9
3 FUELS–COMBUSTIBLES	13.2	11.2	9.7	8.7	8.5	9.9	8.3
31 PRIMARY–PRODUITS DE BASE	0.9	0.7	0.8	0.6	0.5	0.6	0.5
32 PROCESSED–PRODUITS ELABORES	12.4	10.6	8.9	8.1	7.9	9.3	7.8
321 MOTOR SPIRIT–ESSENCE	0.1	0.2	0.0	0.1	0.1	0.1	0.1
322 OTHER–AUTRES	12.3	10.4	8.9	8.0	7.8	9.2	7.8
4 MACHINERY–EQUIPEMENT	15.1	14.4	15.6	16.2	15.4	17.3	17.2
41 CAPITAL EQUIPMENT–MACHINES	13.0	11.5	12.7	12.6	12.5	14.5	14.5
42 PARTS–PIECES ACCESSOIRES	2.1	3.0	2.9	3.5	3.0	2.8	2.7
5 TRANSPORT–TRANSPORT	7.6	4.9	6.3	6.7	10.2	9.6	10.5
51 PASSENGER CARS–AUTOMOBILES	3.5	1.5	2.4	2.6	4.8	4.9	4.8
52 OTHER–AUTRES	2.1	1.1	1.7	1.7	2.3	2.4	3.1
521 INDUSTRIAL–INDUSTRIELS	2.0	1.0	1.6	1.6	2.2	2.3	3.0
522 NON INDUSTRIAL–NON INDUSTRIEL	0.1	0.1	0.1	0.1	0.1	0.1	0.1
53 PARTS–PIECES ACCESSOIRES	2.1	2.3	2.2	2.3	3.1	2.4	2.6
6 CONSUM GOODS–BIENS CONSOMMATION	16.9	21.9	22.4	21.1	20.9	19.3	20.9
61 DURABLE–DURABLES	3.2	4.5	5.8	5.1	6.0	5.5	6.6
62 SEMI DURABLE–SEMI DURABLES	7.5	9.6	8.7	8.4	8.1	7.4	7.9
63 NON DURABLE–NON DURABLES	6.1	7.7	7.8	7.5	6.9	6.3	6.4
7 GOODS NES–BIENS NDA	2.6	0.6	0.6	1.1	0.8	0.5	0.3

EXPORTS – EXPORTATIONS

	1991	1992	1993	1994	1995	1996	1997
TOTAL EXPORTS–EXPORTATIONS TOTALES	100.	100.	100.	100.	100.	100.	100.
1 AGRICULTURE	1.2	1.9	1.6	1.8	2.2	1.5	1.8
2 MINING QUARRY–INDUS EXTRACTIVES	0.1	0.3	0.3	0.3	1.6	1.0	0.2
3 MANUFACTURING–IND MANUFACTUR	98.7	97.8	98.1	97.9	96.2	97.5	98.0
31 FOOD BEV TOBACCO–ALIM BOISS TAB	24.8	31.2	27.5	27.9	27.4	35.9	33.2
32 TEXTILES–INDUSTRIES TEXTILES	4.7	3.8	3.7	2.9	2.4	2.2	1.9
33 WOOD & PRODUCTS–BOIS & PRODUITS	0.5	0.5	0.4	0.3	0.6	0.6	0.3
34 PAPER & PRODUCTS–PAPIER & PRODT	3.8	4.4	4.6	5.2	7.6	8.1	7.2
35 CHEMICALS–INDUSTRIES CHIMIQUES	41.8	32.1	31.5	30.1	29.1	26.8	30.3
36 NON METAL MIN–MIN NON METAL	1.5	0.5	0.8	0.7	0.7	1.2	2.8
37 BASIC METAL–IND METAL BASE	0.5	0.2	0.5	0.4	0.2	0.4	0.7
38 METAL MANUF–MANUF METAL	19.3	23.5	28.2	28.8	28.0	21.4	21.2
39 OTH MANUF IND–AUTRES MANUF	1.8	1.6	0.8	1.4	0.3	0.9	0.5

3. TRADE BY PRINCIPAL COUNTRIES OF ORIGIN AND DESTINATION (VALUE IN MILLION U.S. DOLLARS)
ECHANGES SELON LES PRINCIPAUX PAYS D'ORIGINE ET DE DESTINATION (VALEUR EN MILLIONS DE DOLLARS EU)

COUNTRIES–PAYS	GENERAL IMPORTS C.I.F. IMPORTATIONS GENERALES C.A.F				
	1993	1994	1995	1996	1997
World	574.0	614.4	766.0	829.0	995.2
Africa	0.2	0.3	0.9	0.5	3.3
Americas	402.7	442.9	528.1	591.4	691.2
– Northern America	248.0	284.8	350.7	403.3	490.8
– LAIA	31.5	31.6	43.2	56.2	63.2
– CACM	7.2	5.2	6.1	5.7	7.6
– Caribbean	107.7	110.6	117.3	115.9	118.2
– Rest of America	8.3	10.8	10.8	10.3	11.4
Asia excl fmr USSR	53.9	52.1	82.0	74.1	113.6
– Middle East	0.5	0.4	0.7	0.7	1.2
Asia former USSR	0.0	0.0	0.0		0.0
Europe excl fmr USSR	106.2	109.1	143.3	149.6	169.8
– European Union	97.3	99.2	130.8	135.3	148.1
– Eastern Europe	0.5	0.6	1.5	2.6	1.2
– Rest of Europe	8.3	9.3	11.0	11.8	20.5
Europe former USSR	0.1	0.1	0.1	0.0	0.1
Oceania	10.8	9.9	11.6	13.3	17.3
Other	0.2	0.0	0.0	0.0	0.0
USA/Etats–Unis d'Amer	219.4	247.0	312.0	360.8	451.8
Trinidad and Tobago	76.0	78.7	82.7	89.3	90.6
United Kingdom	53.6	56.3	73.1	69.4	80.6
Japan/Japon	31.0	29.8	51.6	41.9	68.0
Canada	28.5	37.8	38.6	42.5	38.9
Venezuela	20.9	19.3	30.9	37.4	30.4
Jamaica/Jamaïque	15.0	18.0	16.6	13.6	12.0
Germany/Allemagne	10.7	10.5	17.9	17.4	18.5
New Zealand	9.0	8.6	10.2	11.1	13.1
Brazil/Brésil	6.9	7.5	7.6	6.7	17.3
France, Monaco	8.5	7.7	10.8	8.0	9.7
Guyana	6.9	7.9	9.2	7.5	9.5
Korea, Republic of	5.5	5.4	9.6	13.2	6.8
China/Chine	5.0	6.4	8.5	6.1	12.4
Netherlands/Pays–Bas	8.1	6.8	6.1	6.5	7.3
Italy/Italie	4.1	3.8	5.8	7.5	8.2
Switzerland,Liechtenst.	5.0	5.5	7.4	4.8	5.5
Belgium–Luxembourg	2.5	4.4	5.0	5.1	7.2
St Vincent & Grenadines	3.0	5.6	5.8	4.9	3.9
Other Asia n.e.s.	4.5	3.6	3.9	3.9	6.6
Guatemala	4.2	3.0	3.7	4.5	4.0
Mexico/Mexique	0.8	1.2	1.3	5.4	9.9
TFYR Macedonia		1.6	0.9	3.2	10.3
Norway,Svalbard and JM	3.1	2.0	2.5	3.8	4.6
Sweden/Suède	1.1	1.5	1.0	9.6	2.3
China, Hong Kong SAR	1.6	1.4	1.6	1.7	9.1
Denmark/Danemark	1.7	2.0	2.8	3.5	4.6
Spain/Espagne	1.8	1.8	3.3	3.9	3.7
Saint Lucia/Ste–Lucie	2.4	1.8	2.1	2.5	2.4
Dominica/Dominique	3.4	1.7	1.9	1.6	2.5
Colombia/Colombie	1.4	1.7	0.6	4.5	2.7
Australia/Australie	1.8	1.3	1.4	2.2	4.2
Ireland/Irlande	2.5	2.1	2.3	1.4	1.8
Finland/Finlande	2.0	1.5	1.6	2.2	2.5
Dominican Republic		1.7	2.0	1.6	4.4
Netherlands Antilles	5.5	0.6	2.3	0.1	0.2
Grenada/Grenade	1.4	1.9	2.4	1.5	1.5
Thailand/Thaïlande	1.1	1.2	1.3	1.4	2.0
Indonesia/Indonésie	0.8	1.0	0.9	1.3	2.6
Honduras	1.9	1.4	1.4	0.2	1.0

COUNTRIES–PAYS	EXPORTS EXPORTATIONS ES F.O.B.				
	1993	1994	1995	1996	1997
Monde	181.0	181.8	237.5	279.0	282.9
Afrique	0.0	0.1	0.1	0.1	0.3
Amériques	115.6	112.7	149.4	183.9	176.2
– Amérique du Nord	39.9	43.3	51.1	51.9	52.0
– ALAI	0.2	0.2	3.4	24.5	16.6
– MCAC	0.1	0.2	0.5	0.2	0.5
– Caraïbes	70.2	63.4	85.1	93.3	91.4
– Autre Amérique	5.3	5.5	9.3	14.0	15.7
Asie anc. URSS exclus	2.1	1.2	3.4	2.2	2.1
– Moyen–Orient	0.0	0.0	0.2	0.1	0.0
Asie ancienne URSS		0.0			0.1
Europe anc. URSS exclus	33.3	39.7	50.5	55.3	59.4
– Union Européenne	33.0	38.7	48.8	53.6	57.2
– Europe de l'Est	0.0	0.0	0.0	0.0	0.0
– Autre de l'Europe	0.3	1.0	1.7	1.7	2.2
Europe ancienne URSS	0.0	0.0			0.0
Océanie	0.2	0.2	0.3	0.3	0.7
Autre	29.7	28.0	34.0	37.2	44.1
United Kingdom	29.5	35.4	38.9	46.4	48.4
USA/Etats–Unis d'Amer	33.7	34.7	38.1	39.2	41.5
Bunkers, ship stores		26.8	34.0	37.2	44.1
Trinidad and Tobago	20.7	17.1	21.7	20.5	19.0
Jamaica/Jamaïque	13.2	11.3	17.5	25.0	20.4
Saint Lucia/Ste–Lucie	10.1	9.2	11.9	12.4	12.8
Canada	5.9	8.0	12.6	12.2	10.0
Venezuela	0.1	0.1	3.1	24.2	16.3
St Vincent & Grenadines	5.8	5.5	7.4	8.3	8.8
Guyana	3.5	3.8	7.2	8.5	8.2
Areas n.e.s.	29.7	1.3		0.0	
Antigua and Barbuda	3.9	4.2	7.4	6.0	8.8
Grenada/Grenade	4.0	4.0	4.6	5.4	6.2
Dominica/Dominique	3.9	3.1	5.4	4.9	5.1
Saint Kitts and Nevis	3.1	3.6	3.8	4.0	4.0
Belize/Bélize	1.5	1.4	1.3	1.8	1.9
Suriname/Surinam	0.1	0.0	0.2	2.9	4.5
France, Monaco	0.7	0.6	1.7	1.7	2.5
Germany/Allemagne	0.5	0.7	1.8	1.5	1.8
Bahamas	0.8	1.1	1.3	1.5	1.4
Netherlands Antilles	1.7	1.0	0.7	1.7	0.9
Netherlands/Pays–Bas	0.9	0.4	1.1	0.8	1.9
British Virgin Islds	0.7	1.2	0.9	1.0	1.1
Japan/Japon	1.1	0.4	1.5	0.4	1.0
TFYR Macedonia		0.5	1.0	1.2	1.6
Denmark/Danemark	0.6	0.4	0.9	1.1	1.0
Spain/Espagne	0.2	0.2	2.2	0.5	0.2
Panama	0.1	0.3	0.6	0.8	1.2
Montserrat	0.5	0.5	0.5	0.4	0.5
Bermuda/Bermudes	0.3	0.6	0.4	0.4	0.5
Anguilla	0.2	0.4	0.3	0.6	0.6
Haiti/Haïti	0.2	0.1	0.4	0.9	0.4
Switzerland,Liechtenst.	0.3	0.4	0.6	0.4	0.3
Belgium–Luxembourg	0.2	0.2	0.6	0.4	0.5
Sweden/Suède	0.2	0.4	0.4	0.4	0.3
Singapore/Singapour	0.2	0.3	0.4	0.5	0.5
Aruba	0.2	0.2	0.2	0.3	0.9
Korea, Republic of	0.2	0.3	0.5	0.5	0.3
Italy/Italie	0.1	0.3	0.4	0.4	0.3
Martinique	0.4	0.5	0.5		

(VALUE AS PERCENTAGE OF WORLD TOTAL)(VALEURS EN POURCENTAGE DU TOTAL MONDIAL)

	1988	1989	1990	1991	1992	1993	1994	1995	1996	1997
Africa	0.0	0.0	0.0	0.0	0.0	0.0	0.0	0.1	0.1	0.3
Americas	65.0	67.3	67.3	68.8	72.8	70.2	72.1	68.9	71.3	69.4
– Northern America	41.7	42.9	39.6	42.0	43.9	43.2	46.4	45.8	48.7	49.3
– LAIA	5.9	6.8	5.9	5.9	6.0	5.5	5.1	5.6	6.8	6.3
– CACM	1.0	0.7	1.0	0.6	1.1	1.3	0.8	0.8	0.7	0.8
– Caribbean	15.6	16.2	20.2	19.3	20.5	18.8	18.0	15.3	14.0	11.9
– Rest of America	0.7	0.7	0.7	1.0	1.3	1.5	1.8	1.4	1.2	1.1
Asia excl fmr USSR	10.4	9.7	8.6	9.8	7.8	9.4	8.5	10.7	8.9	11.4
– Middle East	0.0	0.0	0.0	0.0	0.0	0.1	0.1	0.1	0.1	0.1
Asia former USSR						0.0	0.0	0.0		0.0
Europe excl fmr USSR	22.2	21.0	22.2	19.5	17.4	18.5	17.8	18.7	18.0	17.1
– European Union	20.7	19.8	20.9	18.3	16.1	17.0	16.1	17.1	16.3	14.9
– Eastern Europe	0.1	0.1	0.1	0.1	0.1	0.1	0.1	0.2	0.3	0.1
– Rest of Europe	1.4	1.1	1.2	1.1	1.1	1.4	1.5	1.4	1.4	2.1
Europe former USSR	0.1	0.1	0.0	0.0	0.0	0.0	0.0	0.0	0.0	0.0
Oceania	2.2	1.9	1.8	1.7	2.0	1.9	1.6	1.5	1.6	1.7
Other	0.1	0.0	0.1	0.1	0.0	0.0	0.0	0.0	0.0	0.0
USA/Etats–Unis d'Amer	34.5	35.3	33.8	36.1	38.2	38.2	40.2	40.7	43.5	45.4
Trinidad and Tobago	8.7	9.2	10.8	10.4	12.2	13.2	12.8	10.8	10.8	9.1
United Kingdom	11.8	11.0	10.6	11.2	8.8	9.3	9.2	9.5	8.4	8.1
Japan/Japon	5.4	5.8	5.3	6.0	3.9	5.4	4.8	6.7	5.1	6.8
Canada	7.1	7.5	5.7	5.9	5.7	5.0	6.2	5.0	5.1	3.9
Venezuela	3.4	4.2	4.0	4.0	4.0	3.6	3.1	4.0	4.5	3.1
Jamaica/Jamaïque	2.6	2.3	2.4	2.3	2.6	2.6	2.9	2.2	1.6	1.2
Germany/Allemagne				1.7	2.2	1.9	1.7	2.3	2.1	1.9
New Zealand	1.7	1.5	1.5	1.4	1.6	1.6	1.4	1.3	1.3	1.3
Brazil/Brésil	1.8	2.1	1.1	1.2	1.2	1.2	1.2	1.0	0.8	1.7

	1988	1989	1990	1991	1992	1993	1994	1995	1996	1997
Afrique	0.0	0.0	0.0	0.1	0.0	0.0	0.0	0.0	0.0	0.1
Amériques	60.0	62.0	50.2	52.6	56.9	63.9	62.0	62.9	65.9	62.3
– Amérique du Nord	28.5	25.6	16.3	16.9	19.9	22.1	23.8	21.5	18.6	18.4
– ALAI	0.1	0.2	0.3	0.1	0.1	0.1	0.1	1.4	8.8	5.9
– MCAC	0.0	0.0	0.0	0.0	0.1	0.0	0.1	0.2	0.1	0.2
– Caraïbes	29.8	34.8	32.3	33.8	34.0	38.8	34.9	35.8	33.4	32.3
– Autre Amérique	1.6	1.5	1.2	1.8	2.7	2.9	3.0	3.9	5.0	5.6
Asie anc. URSS exclus	0.8	0.9	0.3	0.4	1.1	1.2	0.7	1.4	0.8	0.7
– Moyen–Orient	0.0	0.0	0.0	0.0	0.0	0.0	0.0	0.1	0.0	0.0
Asie ancienne URSS							0.0			0.0
Europe anc. URSS exclus	21.3	16.3	20.3	17.7	23.8	18.4	21.8	21.2	19.8	21.0
– Union Européenne	21.0	16.1	20.1	17.5	23.6	18.2	21.3	20.5	19.2	20.2
– Europe de l'Est	0.0	0.0			0.0	0.0	0.0	0.0	0.0	0.0
– Autre de l'Europe	0.3	0.2	0.1	0.2	0.2	0.2	0.5	0.7	0.6	0.8
Europe ancienne URSS					0.0	0.0	0.0			0.0
Océanie	0.0	0.1	0.1	0.0	0.1	0.1	0.1	0.1	0.1	0.3
Autre	17.8	20.6	29.1	29.2	18.0	16.4	15.4	14.3	13.3	15.6
United Kingdom	17.8	13.0	18.3	10.5	20.1	16.3	19.5	16.4	16.6	17.1
USA/Etats–Unis d'Amer	24.8	22.4	13.2	13.6	16.9	18.6	19.1	16.0	14.1	14.7
Bunkers, ship stores	17.8	20.6	29.1	29.2	17.4		14.7	14.3	13.3	15.6
Trinidad and Tobago	7.2	10.4	8.6	10.8	10.9	11.4	9.4	9.1	7.3	6.7
Jamaica/Jamaïque	2.9	4.8	6.0	4.1	2.9	7.3	6.2	7.3	9.0	7.2
Saint Lucia/Ste–Lucie	4.2	4.3	4.6	5.0	5.3	5.6	5.1	5.0	4.4	4.5
Canada	3.5	2.9	2.9	3.1	2.7	3.3	4.4	5.3	4.4	3.5
Venezuela	0.0	0.1	0.3	0.1	0.0	0.0	0.1	1.3	8.7	5.8
St Vincent & Grenadines	3.0	3.1	2.9	3.4	3.4	3.2	3.0	3.1	3.0	3.1
Guyana	1.1	1.0	0.8	1.2	2.0	2.0	2.1	3.0	3.0	2.9

4. General Imports C.I.F. by Commodities according to the S.I.T.C. (Rev. 2) in million U.S. Dollars
Importations Générales C.A.F. par Produits d'après la C.T.C.I. (Rév. 2) en millions de Dollars E.U.

SITC CTCI	COMMODITY	1994 QUANTITY QUANTITE	1994 VALUE VALEUR	1995 QUANTITY QUANTITE	1995 VALUE VALEUR	1996 QUANTITY QUANTITE	1996 VALUE VALEUR	1997 QUANTITY QUANTITE	1997 VALUE VALEUR	PRODUIT
	ALL COMMODITIES		614.5		766.1		829.0		995.3	TOUS PRODUITS
0	FOOD AND LIVE ANIMALS		103.9		112.5		120.9		138.9	ALIMENTS,ANIMAUX VIVANTS
01	MEAT AND PREPARATIONS		15.2		16.9		14.1		18.1	VIANDES ET PREPARATIONS
011	MEAT FRESH,CHILLD,FROZEN	W 6135	10.6	W 6146	11.3	W 4912	10.3	W 6448	12.9	VIANDES FRAICHES,REF,CONGE
0111	BOVINE MEAT FRESH,FROZEN	W 1237	3.4	W 1183	3.2	W 1083	3.1	W 1696	4.4	VIANDES BOVIN FRAI,REF
01112	BOVINE MEAT BONELESS	W 1087	2.8	W 1057	2.8	W 992	2.8	W 1414	3.6	VIANDES BOVIN DESOSSEES
0112	MUTTON ETC FRSH,CHLD,FRN	W 2276	3.6	W 2009	3.7	W 1822	3.7	W 2353	4.6	VIANDE DE MOUTON
014	MEAT PREPD,PRSVD,NES ETC	W 1898	3.5	W 2181	4.1	W 1688	2.8	W 2127	3.8	CONSERVES DE VIANDES
0149	OTH PREPARD,PRESRVD MEAT	W 1764	2.9	W 2059	3.8	W 1571	2.5	W 1999	3.4	AUTRES PREP DE VIANDES
02	DAIRY PRODCTS,BIRDS'EGGS		10.2		12.8		13.6		16.3	PRODUITS LAITIERS,OEUFS
022	MILK AND CREAM	W 1737	3.1	W 2031	3.7	W 2936	4.7	W 2798	5.4	LAIT ET CREME
0224	MILK,CREAM PRESERVED ETC	W 1718	3.0	W 2010	3.7	W 2635	4.3	W 2436	4.9	LAIT,CREME CONS,CONC
024	CHEESE AND CURD	W 1587	4.2	W 1834	5.5	W 1709	5.1	W 2565	7.2	FROMAGE ET CAILLEBOTTE
025	EGGS,BIRDS,FRESH,PRSRVD	W 649	1.9	W 726	2.6	W 754	3.0	W 811	2.8	OEUFS
0251	— IN SHELL	W 649	1.9	W 726	2.6	W 754	3.0	W 809	2.8	OEUFS EN COQUILLE
03	FISH AND PREPARATIONS		6.6		7.8		7.5		9.5	POISSONS ET PREPARATIONS
037	FISH ETC PREPD,PRSVD NES	W 1068	2.2	W 1466	2.8	W 1149	2.3	W 1584	3.5	POIS,CRUST,MOL PREPARES
0371	FISH PREPARD,PRESRVD NES	W 1059	2.2	W 1455	2.7	W 1139	2.3	W 1572	3.5	CONSERVES DE POISSONS
04	CEREALS AND PREPARATIONS		24.1		24.8		32.0		33.7	CEREALES ET PRODUITS
041	WHEAT ETC UNMILLED	W 40358	4.4	W 9780	3.4	W 18251	4.8	W 4636	4.2	FROMENT,EPEAUTRE
0412	OTHER WHEAT ETC UNMILLED	W 40358	4.4	W 9780	3.4	W 18251	4.8	W 4636	4.2	AUTRE FROMENT NON MOULU
042	RICE	W 3813	3.1	W 7883	3.8	W 10284	4.8	W 7739	4.2	RIZ
0421	RICE IN HUSK OR HUSKED	W 2129	1.7	W 6391	2.7	W 8632	3.5	W 5596	2.7	RIZ SANS AUTRE PREPARATION
04212	RICE HUSKED	W 2129	1.7	W 6390	2.7	W 8632	3.5	W 5596	2.7	RIZ CARGO
044	MAIZE UNMILLED	W 39817	4.5	W 68125	4.2	W 33427	7.7	W 7189	1.4	MAIS NON MOULU
046	WHEAT ETC MEAL OR FLOUR	W 1809	1.2	W 2389	1.4	W 7083	2.6	W 7148	2.7	SEMOULE FARINE,FROMENT
047	OTHER CEREAL MEALS,FLOUR	W 493	0.3	W 782	0.4	W 1262	0.7	W 8545	6.6	AUTRES SEMOULES,FARINES
04702	MEAL OR GROATS NON-WHEAT	W 474	0.3	W 774	0.4	W 1191	0.6	W 8380	6.4	GRUAUX,SEMOULES DE CEREALES
048	CEREAL ETC PREPARATIONS	W 5308	10.7	W 6244	11.7	W 5715	11.4	W 6309	14.6	PREPTNS A BASE CEREALES
0481	PREPD BREAKFAST FOOD ETC	W 883	3.1	W 1257	3.5	W 1281	3.5	W 1274	4.2	CEREALES TRAVAILLEES
04812	CEREAL ROASTED, PUFFED	W 480	2.1	W 609	2.3	W 613	2.2	W 891	3.1	PRODTS BASE CEREALES
0484	BAKERY PRODUCTS	W 894	2.5	W 1001	2.6	W 950	2.8	W 1099	3.4	PRODUITS DE BOULANGERIE
0488	OTH CEREAL PREPS,MALT EX	W 946	3.5	W 1000	3.3	W 958	3.6	W 1246	4.2	EXTRAITS DE MALT
05	VEGETABLES AND FRUIT		19.2		21.0		21.3		24.1	LEGUMES ET FRUITS
054	VEG ETC FRSH,SMPLY PRSVD	W 13038	6.8	W 13380	7.6	W 14471	7.8	W 16295	9.2	LEGUMES FRAIS,CONG,SECS
0541	POTATOES FRSH EXCL SWEET	W 9031	3.7	W 9177	3.7	W 9438	3.4	W 10067	3.6	POMMES DE TERRE
057	FRUIT,NUTS,FRESH,DRIED	W 8647	6.3	W 9905	7.2	W 9282	7.0	W 9447	7.2	FRUITS FRAIS OU SECS
058	FRUIT PRESERVED,PREPARED	W 2808	4.4	W 2965	4.9	W 2783	4.9	W 3932	6.2	CONSERVES DE FRUITS
0585	FRUIT OR VEGETABLE JUICE	W 1738	2.3	W 1846	2.9	W 1666	2.9	W 2530	3.6	JUS DE FRUITS
06	SUGAR AND PREPS,HONEY		9.9		10.5		12.6		13.1	SUCRES ET PRODUITS
061	SUGAR AND HONEY	W 34314	8.9	W 32344	9.6	W 32806	11.7	W 44040	12.0	SUCRES ET MIEL
0611	RAW BEET AND CANE SUGAR	W 7519	2.8	W 5593	2.3	W 4881	2.2	W 4235	2.2	SUCRES BRUTS
0612	REFINED SUGAR ETC	W 6511	3.6	W 8240	4.4	W 8294	4.6	W 9768	4.6	SUCRES RAFFINES
0619	SUGARS AND SYRUPS NES	W 282	1.0	W 464	1.2	W 586	2.8	W 560	2.4	AUTRES SUCRES SIROPS
07	COFFEE,TEA,COCOA,SPICES		5.1		5.2		4.7		6.6	CAFE,THE,CACAO,EPICES
073	CHOCOLATE AND PRODUCTS	W 418	2.5	W 458	2.3	W 434	2.1	W 650	2.9	CHOCOLAT
081	*FEEDING STUFF FOR ANIML	W 6070	2.8	W 5157	2.5	W 7783	3.1	W 8130	3.9	NOURRITURE POUR ANIMAUX
09	MISC EDIBLE PRODUCTS		10.7		11.0		12.0		14.0	PREP ALIMENTAIRES DIVERSES
098	EDIBLE PRODCTS,PREPS NES	W 4787	10.4	W 5818	10.7	W 5756	11.8	W 6581	13.8	PREP ALIMENTAIRES NDA
09804	SAUCES,MIXED SEASONINGS	W 2362	4.3	W 2879	4.1	W 2769	4.2	W 2778	4.4	SAUCES,ASSAISONNEMENTS
09809	MISC FOOD PREPRTIONS NES	W 1941	5.3	W 2482	5.7	W 2547	6.8	W 3078	8.3	PREP ALIMENTAIRES NDA
1	BEVERAGES AND TOBACCO		14.0		14.8		14.1		16.7	BOISSONS ET TABACS
11	BEVERAGES		12.9		13.1		11.7		13.8	BOISSONS
111	NON-ALCOHL BEVERAGES NES	W 1913	3.4	W 2394	3.1	W 2361	2.7	W 2994	3.5	BOISSONS NON ALCOOLIQUES
11102	FLAVORED WATERS NON-ALCO	W 1579	3.2	W 1969	2.8	W 1686	2.3	W 2439	3.1	LIMONADES,EAUX GAZEUSES
112	ALCOHOLIC BEVERAGES	W 4104	9.5	W 5511	10.1	W 4920	9.1	W 5220	10.4	BOISSONS ALCOOLIQUES
1121	WINE OF FRESH GRAPES ETC	W 1223	3.5	W 1225	3.9	W 1484	3.7	W 1367	4.4	VINS DE RAISINS FRAIS
11212	WINE OF FRESH GRAPES	W 1119	3.3	W 1145	3.8	W 1399	3.5	W 1313	4.3	VINS DE MOUTS DE RAISINS
1123	BEER,ALE,STOUT,PORTER	W 1988	2.2	W 3036	2.5	W 2310	2.2	W 3012	2.9	BIERES
1124	DISTILLED ALCOHOLIC BEVS	W 662	3.6	W 956	3.3	W 748	2.7	W 645	2.9	ALCOOLS,EAUX-DE-VIE
2	CRUDE MATERLS,EXCL FUELS		24.9		29.6		32.0		44.3	MAT BRUTES NON COMESTIBLES
22	OIL SEEDS,OLEAGINOUS FRT		5.3		8.2		6.0		13.7	GRAINES,FRUITS OLEAGINEUX
222	SEEDS FOR'SOFT'FIXED OIL	W 12427	5.2	W 9847	8.2	W 16626	6.0	W 11139	13.0	GRAINES HUILES FIXES
2222	SOYA BEANS	W 11915	4.5	W 9402	7.7	W 16240	5.4	W 10650	12.4	FEVES DE SOJA
24	CORK AND WOOD		14.3		14.5		15.0		22.0	LIEGE ET BOIS
248	WOOD SHAPED,SLEEPERS	W 19920	14.2	W 19488	13.9	W 19680	14.0	W 27382	21.2	BOIS SIMPLEMENT TRAVAILLES
2482	LUMBER SHAPED CONIFER	W 15962	11.8	W 14950	10.9	W 13971	10.5	W 21565	16.6	CONIFERES SCIES,RABOTES
24821	LUMBER SAWN ETC CONIFER	W 1157	0.8	W 1521	1.1	W 1648	1.5	W 3940	3.2	CONIFERES SCIES LONGITUD
24822	LUMBER PLANED ETC CONIFR	W 14805	11.0	W 13429	9.8	W 12324	9.1	W 17625	13.5	CONIFER RABOTES,RAINES
2483	LUMBER SHAPED NON-CONIFR	W 3958	2.5	W 4538	3.1	W 5709	3.5	W 5817	4.6	NON CONIFERES SCIES,RABOTES
24832	LUMBER PLANED ETC NONCON	W 1874	1.5	W 1338	1.6	W 2334	2.1	W 2910	3.1	RABOTES,RAINES,LANGUETES
27	CRUDE FERTLZR,MINRLS NES		2.4		3.3		3.9		3.6	ENGRAIS MINERAUX BRUTS
277	NATURAL ABRASIVES NES		1.3		2.2		2.6		0.1	ABRASIFS NATURELS NDA
2771	INDUSTRIAL DIAMONDS		1.3		2.2		2.6		0.1	DIAMANTS INDUSTRIELS
29	CRUDE ANIMAL,VEG MAT NES		2.1		2.4		5.6		4.0	MATIERES BRUTES ANIM,VEGET
292	CRUDE VEG MATERIALS NES		2.0		2.1		5.3		3.8	MAT BRUTES VEGETALES NDA
2929	OTH CRUDE VEG MATERIALS	W 33	0.5	W 56	0.9	W 301	3.8	W 157	2.0	MATIERES VEGETALES NDA
29291	VEGETABLE SAPS,EXTRACTS	W 32	0.5	W 55	0.9	W 298	3.8	W 146	2.0	SUCS,EXTRAITS VEGETAUX
3	MINERAL FUELS ETC		53.5		65.2		82.1		82.8	COMBUSTIBLES MINERAUX LUB
33	PETROLEUM AND PRODUCTS		49.9		61.0		77.0		78.0	PETROLE ET DERIVES
334	PETROLEUM PRODUCTS,REFIN	W 275894	49.8	W 386264	60.9	W 402478	76.9	W 430317	77.9	PRODUITS RAFFINES
3342	KEROSENE,OTH MEDIUM OILS	W 99965	20.8	W 121103	23.2	W 133634	31.6	W 159483	34.0	PETR LAMPANTS,AUT HUIL
33421	KEROSENE INCL JET FUEL	W 99965	20.8	W 121102	23.2	W 133634	31.6	W 159483	34.0	PETROLES LAMPANTS
3343	GAS OILS	W 20754	3.2	W 12401	2.4	W 13332	2.4	W 22251	4.1	GAS OILS
3344	FUEL OILS,NES	W 149918	20.8	W 244912	30.9	W 243357	37.0	W 240917	35.1	FUEL OILS
3345	LUBS,PETROLEUM OILS NES	W 2414	4.6	W 2755	3.6	W 8329	5.3	W 3245	4.2	HUILES LUBRIFIANTES
33451	LUBS(HIGH PETR CONT) ETC	W 2400	4.6	W 2749	3.6	W 8316	5.2	W 3226	4.1	HUILES LUBRIF,H LOURDES
341	*GAS,NATURAL AND MANUFCT	W 8018	3.5	W 9403	4.1	W 9634	5.0	W 8719	4.7	GAZ NATUREL,GAZ MANUFACT
3413	PETROLM GASES,LIQUEFIED	W 7914	3.5	W 9403	4.1	W 9631	5.0	W 8716	4.6	GAZ DE PETROLE LIQUEFIE
34131	LIQUEFIED PROPANE,BUTANE	W 3693	1.6	W 4269	2.1	W 4438	2.7	W 1989	1.3	PROPANE,BUTANE LIQUEFIES
34139	OTH HYDROCARBON GAS LQFD	W 4222	1.9	W 5134	2.1	W 5193	2.3	W 6727	3.4	HYDROCARBURES GAZEUX NDA
4	ANIMAL,VEGETABLE OIL,FAT		3.4		4.6		5.6		6.9	HUILES,GRAISSES ANIM,VEG
431	*PROCESD ANML VEG OIL,ET	W 2002	2.1	W 3599	2.6	W 4194	4.0	W 5909	5.2	HUILES,GRAISSES PREPAREES
4312	HYDROGENATED OIL,FAT	W 1958	2.0	W 3546	2.6	W 4087	3.9	W 5861	5.2	HUILES HYDROGENEES
5	CHEMCLS,RELATED PROD NES		73.6		90.4		97.4		104.1	PRODUITS CHIMIQUES
51	ORGANIC CHEMICALS		5.7		9.3		9.2		9.0	PROD CHIMIQ ORGANIQUES
511	HYDROCARBONS NES,DERIVS	W 1800	2.2	W 1935	2.3	W 2220	2.3	W 2358	2.7	HYDROCARBURES NDA
516	OTHER ORGANIC CHEMICALS	W 691	2.4	W 1330	5.6	W 1394	4.9	W 1335	4.9	AUTRES PROD ORGANIQUES
5169	ORGANIC CHEMICALS,NES	W 437	2.2	W 595	5.0	W 486	4.1	W 444	3.7	PROD CHIM ORGANIQUES NDA
51699	OTHER ORGANIC COMPOUNDS	W 362	2.0	W 542	4.9	W 479	4.1	W 437	3.6	AUTRES COMPOS ORGANIQUES
52	INORGANIC CHEMICALS		6.2		6.7		7.0		7.0	PROD CHIM INORGANIQUES

4. General Imports C.I.F. by Commodities according to the S.I.T.C. (Rev. 2) in million U.S. Dollars
Importations Générales C.A.F. par Produits d'après la C.T.C.I. (Rév. 2) en millions de Dollars E.U.

SITC CTCI	COMMODITY	1994 QUANTITY QUANTITE	1994 VALUE VALEUR	1995 QUANTITY QUANTITE	1995 VALUE VALEUR	1996 QUANTITY QUANTITE	1996 VALUE VALEUR	1997 QUANTITY QUANTITE	1997 VALUE VALEUR	PRODUIT
522	INORG ELEMNTS,OXIDES,ETC	W 1688	2.5	W 2095	3.0	W 1771	2.6	W 4482	3.5	ELEMENTS INORGANIQUES
523	OTHR INORG CHEMICALS ETC	W 6248	3.7	W 5743	3.3	W 8221	4.4	W 6216	3.5	AUT PRODUITS CHIMIQUES INORG
5232	OTH MTL CMPD OF INRG ACD	W 3822	2.3	W 3210	2.1	W 3626	2.3	W 2674	1.7	SELS METALLIQUES
53	DYES,TANNING,COLOUR PROD		4.0		4.3		5.3		5.0	PROD TEINTURE,COLORANTS
533	PIGMENTS,PAINTS,ETC	W 1452	3.8	W 1467	4.1	W 1585	5.0	W 2036	4.7	PIGMENTS,PEINTURES,VERNIS
5334	VARNISHES,DISTEMPERS ETC	W 613	2.3	W 678	2.5	W 553	3.2	W 537	2.6	PEINTURES A L'EAU
53344	DISTEMPERS,DYES NES ETC	W 295	1.5	W 382	2.0	W 373	2.7	W 384	2.0	PEINTURES A L'EAU
541	*MEDICINAL,PHARM PRODUCT	K 878061	18.2		20.7		22.3	K 1222085	24.8	PROD MEDICINAUX PHARMACEUT
5417	MEDICAMENTS	K 756971	16.8	K 786884	18.6	K 1267655	20.5	K 1097557	22.8	MEDICAMENTS
54179	— CONTNG OTH SUBSTANCES	K 717690	14.5	K 738232	16.1	K 1208081	17.7	K 1016344	19.3	MED CONT AUT SUBSTANCES
55	PERFUME,CLEANING ETC PRD		17.9		23.1		24.1		27.4	PROD POUR PARFUM,TOILETTE
551	ESSENTL OILS,PERFUME,ETC	W 175	2.4	W 260	4.0	W 492	8.7	W 536	7.1	HUILES ESSENTIELLES
5514	MIXED PERFUME SUBSTANCES	W 154	2.2	W 233	3.8	W 464	8.5	W 506	7.0	MELANGES SUBSTAN ODORIFER
553	PERFUMERY,COSMETICS,ETC	W 1117	8.6	W 1408	11.9	W 1169	9.4	W 1553	12.8	PRODUITS DE PARFUMERIE
554	SOAP,CLEANSING ETC PREPS	W 4278	7.1	W 4591	7.3	W 3863	6.0	W 4977	7.5	SAVONS,PRODUITS DETERSIFS
5541	SOAPS	W 991	3.1	W 948	2.8	W 725	2.1	W 844	2.5	SAVONS,PROD TENSIO-ACTIFS
5542	WASHING PREPARATIONS ETC	W 3107	3.6	W 3435	4.1	W 2972	3.6	W 3884	4.5	PROD ORG TENSIO-ACT NDA
58	PLASTIC MATERIALS ETC		9.1		11.6		11.4		11.7	MAT PLAST ARTIFICIELLES
582	PROD OF CONDENSATION ETC	W 1055	2.0	W 1529	2.6	W 1370	2.5	W 1445	2.6	PROD CONDENS,POLYCOND
583	POLYMERIZATION ETC PRODS	W 4007	7.1	W 4414	8.9	W 4982	8.9	W 4235	9.0	PROD POLYMERISATION
5839	OTH POLYMRZTION ETC PROD	W 2922	5.0	W 3031	6.1	W 3810	6.6	W 3994	8.5	AUT PROD POLYMER COPOLYM
59	CHEMICAL MATERIALS NES		11.3		12.6		16.7		16.7	MAT PROD CHIMIQUES NDA
591	PESTICIDES,DISINFECTANTS	W 1359	5.0	W 1400	5.5	W 1172	5.0	W 1510	5.7	DESINF,INSECT,FONG,HERB
5913	HERBICIDES,FOR RETAIL	W 358	1.8	W 512	2.4	W 339	1.8	W 469	1.9	HERBICIDES VENTE AU DET
598	MISCEL CHEM PRODUCTS NES	W 1235	5.3	W 1205	6.0	W 1461	10.7	W 1812	9.6	PROD DIV INDUST CHIM NDA
5989	CHEM PRODUCTS,PREPS NES	W 882	3.6	W 954	4.4	W 1257	9.3	W 1483	7.9	PROD PREP CHIMIQUES NDA
59899	OTH CHEM PRODS,PREPS,NES	W 702	3.1	W 776	3.7	W 1093	8.9	W 1250	7.3	AUT PRODUITS CHIMIQUES NDA
6	BASIC MANUFACTURES		105.2		132.2		132.2		170.4	ART MANUFACTURES
62	RUBBER MANUFACTURES NES		6.3		6.8		7.0		10.8	CAOUTCHOUC MANUFACTURE
625	RUBBER TYRES, TUBES ETC	W 861	3.8	W 882	3.7	W 847	3.9	W 1121	5.0	PNEUS CAOUTCHOUC VULCANISE
6251	TYRES NEW FOR MOTOR CARS	W 376	2.0	W 319	1.6	W 299	1.4	W 367	1.8	PNEUS POUR VOITURES
628	RUBBER ARTICLES NES	W 279	1.8	W 166	2.1	W 188	1.9	W 309	4.2	OUVRAGES CAOUTCHOUC NDA
6289	OTH RUBBER ARTICLES NES	W 224	1.3	W 136	1.6	W 163	1.3	W 262	3.3	AUT OUVR CAOUTCHOUC NDA
62898	UNHARD RUBBER PRODS NES	W 217	1.2	W 128	1.5	W 153	1.3	W 253	3.3	OUV CAOUT VULC NON DURCI
63	WOOD,CORK MANUFACTRS NES		8.8		9.7		9.8		16.3	OUVRAGES LIEGE ET BOIS
634	VENEERS,PLYWOOD,ETC	W 5797	5.0	W 7329	5.2	W 5307	4.9	W 8311	7.6	PLACAGES,CONTRE-PLAQUES
6342	PLYWOOD OF WOOD SHEETS	W 5008	4.3	W 6661	4.6	W 4491	4.1	W 5950	5.4	BOIS CONTRE-PLAQUES
635	WOOD MANUFACTURES NES	W 1205	3.7	W 1350	4.4	W 1550	4.8	W 2541	8.6	ART MANUF EN BOIS NDA
6353	BUILDERS WOODWRK,PREFABS	W 649	2.6	W 703	3.0	W 790	3.2	W 1532	6.6	OUVRAGES DE MENUISERIE
64	PAPER,PAPERBOARD AND MFR		19.3		26.6		25.1		30.8	PAPIERS,CARTONS & OUVRAGES
641	PAPER AND PAPERBOARD	W 8010	10.9	W 30444	15.9	W 19488	14.8	W 11633	17.5	PAPIERS ET CARTONS
6412	PRINTG,WRITING PAPER NES	W 2760	4.5	W 2884	6.9	W 3452	5.9	W 4099	7.1	PAPIERS POUR L'IMPRESSION
64121	— UNCOATED	W 2423	3.9	W 2475	4.6	W 2940	4.9	W 3820	6.5	PAPIERS IMPRES NON COUCHES
64122	— COATED,IMPREGNATD ETC	W 338	0.6	W 409	2.4	W 512	1.0	W 280	0.6	PAPIERS IMPRESSION COUCHES
6418	COATED ETC PAPER NES BLK	W 908	1.3	W 1407	2.4	W 1662	3.5	W 2067	4.3	PAP,CARTONS COUCHES,ENDUITS
642	PAPER,ETC,PRECUT,ARTS OF	W 4003	8.5	W 4672	10.8	W 4677	10.3	W 5932	13.3	PAP,CARTONS DECOUPES
6421	PAPER ETC CONTAINERS	W 2412	3.5	W 2793	4.6	W 2944	4.9	W 3587	5.9	BOITES,SACS EMBALLAGES
6428	PAPER ETC ARTICLES NES	W 907	2.8	W 1073	3.6	W 1003	3.1	W 1350	4.3	OUVRAGES EN PATE A PAPIER
65	TEXTILE YARN,FABRICS,ETC		15.3		17.6		16.7		21.8	FILS,TISSUS,ARTICLES TEXTILE
652	COTTON FABRICS,WOVEN	W 494	3.9	W 842	4.8	W 467	3.5	W 452	3.6	TISSUS DE COTON
6521	GREY WOVEN COTTON FABRIC	W 150	1.2	W 498	2.4	W 131	0.9	W 109	0.8	TISSUS COT ECRUS NON MERCER
6522	WOVEN COTTON BLEACHD,ETC	W 344	2.8	W 345	2.4	W 336	2.7	W 343	2.9	TISSUS COTON BLANCHIS ETC
653	WOVN MAN-MADE FIB FABRIC	W 645	5.5	W 724	6.4	W 702	5.6	W 1039	9.1	TISSUS FIBRES SYNTH,ARTIF
6534	DISC SYN BLEND FABRC NES	W 253	2.0	W 260	2.4	W 248	1.7	W 417	3.1	TISSUS FIBRES SYNTH DISCONT
658	TEXTILE ARTICLES NES	W 284	2.2	W 267	2.2	W 358	2.7	W 868	4.0	ART FACONNES MAT TEXTILES
66	NONMETAL MINERAL MFS NES		16.0		19.2		22.3		25.6	ART MIN NON METALLIQUES
661	LIME,CEMENT,BLDG PRODS	W 54011	3.6	W 57321	4.6	W 96310	6.1	W 33053	3.6	CHAUX,CIMENTS MAT CONSTR
6612	CEMENT	W 53280	2.9	W 56040	3.5	W 95355	5.1	W 31545	2.2	CIMENTS HYDRAULIQUES
662	CLAY,REFRACTORY BLDG PRD	W 3772	3.3	W 4004	2.8	W 4031	4.2	W 7865	7.1	MAT CONST REFRACTAIRES
6624	BRICKS ETC NONREFRACTORY	W 3737	3.2	W 3952	2.8	W 3780	3.9	W 7531	6.8	BRIQUES ETC CERAM NON REFR
66245	GLAZED CERAMIC SETTS ETC	W 3328	3.0	W 3542	2.5	W 3009	2.6	W 5874	5.4	AUT CARREAUX CERAMIQUE
663	MINERAL MANUFCTURES NES	W 1152	1.1	W 3421	1.6	W 1333	1.2	W 2756	3.6	ART MIN MANUF NDA
664	GLASS	W 994	1.8	W 906	2.4	W 1420	2.4	W 1596	3.0	VERRE
665	GLASSWARE	W 4952	5.1	W 4407	5.3	W 4914	7.2	W 5581	6.6	OUVRAGES EN VERRE
6651	BOTTLES ETC OF GLASS	W 4573	3.5	W 4029	3.2	W 4606	5.5	W 5092	4.4	RECIPIENTS EN VERRE
66511	GLASS BOTTLES ETC NONVAC	W 4572	3.5	W 4029	3.2	W 4606	5.5	W 5092	4.4	BONBONNES,BOUTEILLES,ETC
666	POTTERY	W 218	1.4	W 239	2.5	W 170	1.4	W 380	2.0	POTERIE
67	IRON AND STEEL		12.3		18.1		17.1		22.7	FER ET ACIER
673	IRON,STEEL SHAPES ETC	W 6991	3.8	W 8448	6.0	W 8835	5.1	W 10825	5.9	BARRES,PROFIL FER,ACIER
6731	IRON,STEEL WIRE ROD	W 4057	1.6	W 1984	0.8	W 5738	2.3	W 7323	3.1	FIL MACHINE FER,ACIER
6732	IRON,STEEL BARS ETC	W 2211	1.7	W 5682	4.4	W 1944	1.9	W 1979	1.5	BARRES FER,ACIER
67322	HIGH CARBON STL BARS ETC	W 1893	0.9	W 5331	3.5	W 1581	0.9	W 1625	0.9	BARRES ACIER FIN CARBONE
674	IRN,STL UNIV,PLATE,SHEET	W 5135	6.2	W 7978	8.3	W 6140	7.5	W 8964	9.3	LARGES PLATS,TOLES
6747	TINNED PLATES,SHEETS	W 2029	3.1	W 2024	2.0	W 1744	2.4	W 2798	3.6	TOLES ETAMEES EN ACIER
6749	OTH IRN,STL PLATES,SHEET	W 2833	2.9	W 5670	6.2	W 3890	4.7	W 5752	5.4	AUTRES TOLES FER,ACIER
67491	— OF IRON OR SIMPLE STL	W 2826	2.9	W 5669	6.2	W 3865	4.6	W 5706	5.3	AUT TOLES AUTRES ACIER FIN
678	IRON,STL TUBES,PIPES,ETC	W 2420	2.0	W 1279	3.3	W 1565	3.8	W 3825	6.1	TUBES,TUYAUX EN FONTE,FER
6783	IRON,STL TUBES,PIPES NES	W 1737	0.7	W 764	1.0	W 1280	2.3	W 2463	3.2	AUT TUBES,TUYAUX FER,ACIER
68	NON-FERROUS METALS		3.4		5.5		5.6		6.0	METAUX NON FERREUX
684	ALUMINIUM	W 654	2.5	W 880	4.0	W 3001	4.4	W 1307	4.6	ALUMINIUM
69	METAL MANUFACTURES NES		24.0		28.7		28.7		36.4	ART MANUFACT EN METAL NDA
691	STRUCTURES AND PARTS NES	W 662	2.3	W 1001	4.9	W 1268	3.4	W 1140	3.8	CONSTRUCT FER,ACIER,ALU
6912	STRUCTURES,PARTS ALUMNM	W 239	1.1	W 326	3.1	W 177	1.1	W 237	1.0	CONSTRUCT ALUMINIUM
692	METAL TANKS,BOXES,ETC	W 859	2.9	W 1079	3.5	W 923	4.0	W 1403	3.8	RECIPIENTS METALLIQUES
6924	MTL TRANSPORT BOXES ETC	W 798	2.8	W 1004	2.7	W 724	3.2	W 1129	2.9	FUTS,TAMBOURS,BIDONS
694	STL,COPPR NAILS,NUTS,ETC	W 530	2.9	W 597	3.1	W 663	3.3	W 949	4.5	CLOUS,VIS,ECROUS
69402	IRN,STL NUTS,BOLTS,ETC	W 195	2.4	W 241	2.5	W 306	2.7	W 349	2.9	BOULONS,VIS,ECROUS FER,AC
695	TOOLS	W 209	1.7	W 234	2.2	W 213	2.1	W 881	3.2	OUTILS A MAIN
697	BASE MTL HOUSEHOLD EQUIP	W 701	4.1	W 742	4.3	W 653	3.6	W 1092	6.0	ART MENAGE MET COMMUNS
6973	DMSTC HEATG,COOKG APPARA	W 340	2.1	W 382	2.4	W 401	2.0	W 611	3.3	APPS CHAUF NON ELECTRIQ
69731	IRN,STL DOM COOKG APPARA	W 325	2.0	W 365	2.2	W 380	1.9	W 596	3.1	APPS CUISSON FER,ACIER
699	BASE METAL MFRS NES	W 1857	8.9		9.6	W 2223	10.6		12.8	ART MANUFACTURES MET NDA
6991	LOCKSMITHS WARES,ETC	W 332	2.5	W 363	2.5	W 504	3.1	W 771	4.4	ARTICLES DE SERRURERIE
6997	IRON,STEEL ARTICLES NES	W 755	2.8	W 672	2.6	W 743	3.3	W 735	3.4	OUV FONTE,FER,ACIER NDA
69979	IRN,STL MANUFACTURES NES	W 729	2.8	W 661	2.6	W 719	3.2	W 730	3.4	AUT OUVRAGES EN FER NDA
7	MACHINES,TRANSPORT EQUIP		144.3		205.0		229.4		290.6	MACHINES MATERIEL TRANSPORT
71	POWER GENERATING EQUIPMT		4.7		10.0		16.7		9.9	MACHINES GENERATRICES
713	INTRNL COMBUS PSTN ENGIN	W 215	3.1	W 325	7.0	W 299	4.9	W 437	6.6	MOTEURS EXPL COMB INT, PIECE
7139	PISTON ENGINE PARTS NES	W 93	2.5	W 108	3.1	W 109	2.6	W 137	4.7	PIECES POUR 713.2,3,8
716	ROTATING ELECTRIC PLANT	W 92	1.2	W 143	1.8	W 306	9.7	W 181	2.3	APP ELECTR ROTATIFS,PIECES
7162	AC MTRS,GENRTRS,GEN SETS	W 65	0.9	W 86	1.0	W 240	8.6	W 102	1.4	MOTEURS ELECTRIQUES

4. General Imports C.I.F. by Commodities according to the S.I.T.C. (Rev. 2) in million U.S. Dollars
Importations Générales C.A.F. par Produits d'après la C.T.C.I. (Rév. 2) en millions de Dollars E.U.

SITC CTCI	COMMODITY	1994 QUANTITY QUANTITE	1994 VALUE VALEUR	1995 QUANTITY QUANTITE	1995 VALUE VALEUR	1996 QUANTITY QUANTITE	1996 VALUE VALEUR	1997 QUANTITY QUANTITE	1997 VALUE VALEUR	PRODUIT
71623	GEN SETS WITH PISTN ENGN	W 32	0.4	W 47	0.4	W 199	8.1	W 33	0.5	GROUPES MOTEUR EXPLOSION
72	MACHS FOR SPCL INDUSTRYS		11.8		16.9		22.1		28.1	MAC SPECIALES POUR INDUST
721	AGRIC MACHY,EXC TRACTORS	W 246	1.8	W 262	1.6	W 316	2.9	W 316	3.0	MACHINES AGRICOLES
723	CIVIL ENGNEERG EQUIP ETC	W 252	2.0	W 178	1.7	W 831	5.3	W 1159	11.2	APPAREILS DE GENIE CIVIL
7234	CONST,MINING MACHNRY NES	W 230	1.7	W 153	1.4	W 717	4.5	W 973	9.1	MACH POUR LA CONST, MINES
72342	SLFPRP SHOVELS,EXCAVATRS	W 141	1.1	W 125	1.0	W 457	2.8	W 596	3.9	PELLES MECANIQUES
72343	SLFPRP CONST ETC MCH NES	W 28	0.4	W 7	0.3	W 52	1.0	W 207	3.3	AUT MACH EXTR,TERRASSEM
726	PRINTG,BKBINDG MACHY,PTS	W 125	2.1	W 99	3.9	W 130	3.7		4.8	MACHINES POUR IMPRIMERIE
727	FOOD MACHRY NON–DOMESTIC	W 99	1.1	W 222	2.6	W 278	3.2	W 301	2.4	MACH INDUSTRIES ALIMENT
7272	OTH FOOD PROC MCHY,PARTS	W 96	1.1	W 217	2.5	W 274	3.2	W 291	2.2	AUT MACH IND ALIMENTAIRE
72722	INDUS FOOD PROC MACH NES	W 94	1.1	W 217	2.5	W 274	3.2	W 291	2.2	MACHINES BOULANGERIE
728	OTH MACHY FOR SPCL INDUS	W 202	2.8	W 246	4.2	W 269	4.0		4.3	AUT MACH IND PARTICULIERES
7284	MACHY FOR SPCL INDUS NES	W 151	2.2	W 130	2.4	W 128	2.4		2.3	MACH SPEC IND PARTICUL.
74	GENRL INDUSTRL MACHY NES		22.8		26.7		31.6		40.3	MACH APP INDUSTRIE
741	HEATING,COOLING EQUIPMNT	W 1197	5.8	W 992	7.1	W 766	7.7	W 1528	10.9	MACH CHAUFFAGE,PIECES
7415	AIR–CONDITIONING MACHNRY	W 201	1.7	W 214	2.2	W 267	2.2	W 375	3.7	GROUPES CONDITION AIR
7416	HEATING,COOLING EQU NES	W 168	1.9	W 356	2.4	W 257	3.1	W 654	3.6	APP CHANGEMENT TEMP
742	PUMPS FOR LIQUIDS ETC	W 84	1.9	W 197	2.1	W 153	2.6	W 211	3.4	POMPES MOTO–POMPES
743	PUMPS NES,CENTRFUGES ETC	W 209	2.5	W 289	4.0	W 295	4.1	W 975	5.0	POMPES COMPRES,VENT ETC
744	MECHANICAL HANDLING EQU	W 441	4.0	W 377	2.8	W 755	5.3	W 909	6.2	EQUIP MANUTENTION PIECES
7442	LIFTING,LOADING MACH NES	W 312	2.9	W 162	1.3	W 273	2.2	W 392	2.3	APP LEVAGE,MANUTENTION
7449	PTS NES OF MACHY OF 7442	W 55	0.9	W 42	0.8	W 411	2.6	W 124	1.8	PIECES DU 744.2
745	NONELEC MACHY,TOOLS NES	W 270	3.3	W 318	4.3	W 291	5.4	W 483	6.5	AUT MACH NON ELEC,PIECES
7452	OTH NONELEC MCHS,PTS NES	W 238	3.0	W 278	3.8	W 234	4.8	W 407	5.8	AUT MACH NON ELEC,PIECES
74522	PACKAGNG,BOTTLNG,ETC MCH	W 101	1.2	W 145	1.6	W 85	2.1	W 212	3.2	MACH NETT BOUTEILLES,ETC
749	NONELEC MACH PTS,ACC NES	W 375	5.5	W 427	6.7	W 468	6.8	W 760	8.6	PIECES MACH NON ELEC NDA
7492	COCKS,VALVES ETC NES	W 226	2.7	W 300	3.3	W 278	3.3	W 506	4.2	ART ROB,SIM POUR TUYAUX
75	OFFICE MACHNES,ADP EQUIP		18.9		23.3		26.3		34.9	MACH BUREAU TRAIT AUTOM
751	OFFICE MACHINES	W 70	1.7	W 87	2.6	W 64	1.9	W 125	3.1	MACH,APPAREILS DE BUREAU
752	AUTOMTIC DATA PROC EQUIP	W 261	10.9	W 243	13.9	W 470	16.8	W 491	22.6	MACH TRAIT INFORMATION
7522	DIGITAL COMPUTERS	W 116	6.1	W 134	7.6	W 248	8.8	W 222	11.0	MACH DIGITALES COMPLETES
7523	DIGITL CENTRL PROCESSORS	W 21	1.4	W 19	1.4	W 61	2.3	W 60	3.9	UNITES CENTRALES
7525	ADP PERIPHERAL UNITS	W 114	2.8	W 77	3.9	W 146	4.3	W 152	5.5	UNITES PERIPHERIQUES
759	OFFICE,ADP MCH PTS,ACCES	W 104	6.3	W 119	6.9	W 153	7.7	W 178	9.3	PIECES DU 751 ET 752
7599	ACCTG,ETC,ADP MCH PTS,AC	W 82	5.6	W 96	6.1	W 130	6.7	W 151	7.9	PIECES DU 751 ET 752
76	TELECOMM,SOUND EQUIPMENT		20.0		20.4		21.1		33.8	EQUIPMENT DE TELECOM
761	TELEVISION RECEIVERS	W 181	2.0	W 250	2.8	W 218	2.7	W 489	5.3	RECEPTEURS DE TELEVISION
7611	COLOUR TV RECEIVERS	W 174	1.8	W 246	2.7	W 214	2.6	W 486	5.3	RECEPTEURS COULEUR
763	SOUND RECORDRS,PHONOGRPH	W 112	1.8	W 156	2.2	W 130	1.8	W 228	3.2	PHONO,APP ENREGISTREMENT
7638	OTHR SOUND APPARATUS ETC	W 110	1.8	W 154	2.1	W 129	1.8	W 224	3.2	AUT APP D'ENREGIS,REPROD
764	TELECOM EQPT,PTS,ACC NES	W 369	15.0	W 250	14.5	W 328	15.7	W 663	22.5	EQUIP TELECOM,PIECES
7641	LINE TELEPHONE,ETC EQUIP	W 161	6.4	W 122	9.2	W 157	9.0	W 199	8.0	APP TELEPHON PAR FIL
7643	TV,RADIO TRANSMITTRS ETC	W 23	1.8	W 18	1.5	W 22	2.0	W 57	4.4	APP EMET TELE RADIO
7649	PTS NES OF EQUIPMT OF 76	W 118	6.0	W 76	2.9	W 112	3.9	W 254	7.5	PIECES DE LA DIV 76
76491	PTS NES OF APPAR OF 7641	W 41	4.2	W 24	1.6	W 40	2.6	W 75	3.2	PIECES POUR 764.1
76493	TELECOMM EQUIPMT PTS NES	W 68	1.7	W 44	1.2	W 65	1.2	W 153	4.1	PIECES 761,762,764.3,8
77	ELECTRIC MACHNRY NES ETC		33.4		40.4		40.1		50.8	MACH APP ELECT NDA
771	ELECTRIC POWER MACHY NES	W 133	1.6	W 274	2.7	W 178	2.8	W 493	3.5	MACH PROD,TRANS ELECTR
772	SWITCHGEAR ETC,PARTS NES	W 269	7.1	W 411	9.3	W 496	9.6	W 687	10.9	APP COUPURE,SECT ETC
7721	SWITCHGEAR ETC	W 202	4.0	W 338	5.5	W 419	6.2	W 447	6.5	APP COUPURE,SECTIONMNT
7723	FIXED,VARIABLE RESISTORS	W 55	1.7	W 63	2.5	W 65	1.7	W 218	2.9	POTENTIOMETRES PIECES
773	ELECTR DISTRIBUTNG EQUIP	W 1038	4.6		6.4	W 1396	7.9	W 1829	8.2	EQUIPMT DISTRIBUTION ELECT
7731	INSULATED WIRE,CABLE ETC	W 993	4.1	W 936	5.7	W 1312	7.3	W 1528	7.5	FILS,CABLES ISOLES ELECT
775	HOUSEHOLD TYPE EQUIP NES	W 917	5.8	W 1391	7.9	W 1036	6.5	W 2179	12.6	MACH,APP USAGE DOMESTQUE
7752	DOM REFRIGERATRS,FREEZRS	W 470	2.8	W 706	3.9	W 496	3.1	W 1100	6.2	REFRIG,CONGEL MENAGER
77521	DOMESTIC REFRIGERATORS	W 407	2.5	W 603	3.4	W 430	2.7	W 924	5.2	REFRIGERATEURS
776	TRANSISTORS,VALVES,ETC	W 115	9.0	W 151	8.1	W 160	7.6	W 164	7.3	LAMPES,TUBES,VALVES
7763	DIODES,TRANSISTORS,ETC	W 13	1.1	W 15	2.0	W 21	1.4	W 40	3.3	DIODES,TRANSISTORS
7768	ELCTRNC COMP PTS,CRYSTLS	W 98	7.6	W 133	5.9	W 137	5.9	W 123	3.8	CRIST PIEZO–ELEC,PCS 776
77689	ELECTRNIC COMPON PTS NES	W 98	7.6	W 133	5.9	W 137	5.9	W 123	3.8	PIECES DU GROUPE 776
778	ELECTRICAL MACHINERY NES	W 789	5.2	W 594	5.9	W 570	5.7	W 981	7.6	AUTRES MACH ELECT NDA
78	ROAD VEHICLES		31.2		59.5		62.6		88.0	VEHICULES ROUTIERS
781	PASS MOTOR VEH EXC BUSES	W 1908	16.0	W 4081	37.0	W 4764	40.5	W 6410	48.1	AUTO TRANSPORT PERSONNES
782	LORRIES,SPCL MTR VEH NES	W 994	7.6	W 1875	13.1	W 1852	12.2	W 2648	16.3	VEHICULES SPECIAUX,MARCH
7821	LORRIES,TRUCKS	W 954	7.4	W 1839	12.3	W 1651	11.3	W 2205	14.5	VEHICULES TRANSP MARCHAND
783	ROAD MOTOR VEHICLES NES	W 121	1.1	W 136	1.1	W 212	1.3	W 1754	9.3	VEHICULES ROUTIERS NDA
7831	BUSES	W 95	1.0	W 104	1.0	W 102	0.9	W 1668	8.8	VOITURES TRANSPORT COMMUN
784	MOTOR VEH PRTS,ACCES NES	W 489	5.0	W 488	6.5		6.8	W 1877	11.2	PIECES 722,781,782,783
7849	OTHER MOTOR VEHCL PARTS	W 482	4.9	W 461	6.0	W 702	6.3	W 1795	10.3	PIECES 722,781,782,783
79	OTHR TRANSPORT EQUIPMENT		1.2		7.4		7.8		2.7	AUTRE MATERIEL TRANSPORT
792	AIRCRAFT ETC	W 4	0.4	W 16	4.4	W 9	2.3	W 10	0.8	APP NAVIGATION AERIENNE
7929	AIRCRAFT PARTS NES	W 4	0.4	W 16	4.4	W 9	2.3	W 9	0.8	PIECES DU 792
793	SHIPS AND BOATS ETC	W 110	0.8	W 200	3.0	W 673	5.6	W 390	1.8	NAVIRES BATEAUX,ETC
7932	SHIPS AND BOATS NES	W 105	0.8	W 194	2.0	W 644	4.5	W 375	1.7	NAVIRES ET BATEAUX
79323	OTHER CARGO VESSELS	W 28	0.4	W 92	1.2	W 320	3.3	W 14	0.2	AUT BATEAUX TRANS MARCH
8	MISC MANUFACTURED GOODS		89.5		110.3		113.0		139.2	ART MANUFACTURES DIVERS
812	*PLUMBG,HEATNG,LGHTNG EQ	W 792	3.3	W 652	3.8	W 690	4.1	W 892	5.6	APPAR SANITAIRES CHAUFFAGE
8124	LIGHTING EQUIPMENT NES	W 498	2.3	W 332	2.7	W 333	2.8	W 436	3.9	APPAREILS ECLAIRAGE ETC
81242	LAMPS,FITTINGS BASE METL	W 479	2.1	W 315	2.6	W 313	2.6	W 412	3.6	APPAREILS D'ECLAIRAGE
821	*FURNITURE,PARTS THEREOF	W 1424	6.3	W 1602	5.9	W 1691	7.1	W 2499	12.7	MEUBLES ET PIECES
8211	CHAIRS,SEATS AND PARTS	W 459	2.0	W 483	1.8	W 478	2.1	W 782	4.0	SIEGES ET PIECES
82111	CHAIRS AND OTHER SEATS	W 399	1.7	W 405	1.5	W 431	1.8	W 704	3.5	SIEGES
8219	FURNITURE AND PARTS NES	W 745	3.9	W 867	3.5	W 1016	4.4	W 1532	7.7	AUTRES MEUBLES ET PIECES
82192	WOOD FURNITURE NES	W 371	1.9	W 392	1.3	W 350	1.5	W 679	3.8	MEUBLES NDA EN BOIS
84	CLOTHING AND ACCESSORIES		12.1		13.6		12.9		15.8	VETEMENTS
843	WOMENS OUTERWEAR NONKNIT	W 85	2.2	W 92	2.9	W 150	3.1	W 104	3.3	VET DESSUS FEMMES MAT TEX
846	UNDER GARMENTS KNITTED	W 235	5.1	W 243	5.0	W 207	4.2	W 234	5.1	SOUS VETS DE BONNETERIE
8462	— OF COTTON NON ELASTIC	W 136	2.1	W 116	1.6	W 105	1.4	W 102	1.6	SOUS–VET BONNET COTON
84629	—— OTHER	W 136	2.1	W 116	1.6	W 105	1.4	W 102	1.6	AUT SOUS–VET BONNET COTON
8465	CORSETS,GARTERS,ETC	W 29	2.1	W 51	2.3	W 47	2.0	W 53	2.4	CORSETS,GAINES ART SIM
851	*FOOTWEAR	W 372	4.9	W 581	6.1	W 585	7.0	W 728	9.4	CHAUSSURES
85102	FOOTWEAR LEATHER	W 224	3.4	W 412	4.3	W 451	5.9	W 531	7.9	CHAUS SEMELLES EN CUIR
87	PRECISION INSTRUMNTS NES		5.1		6.1		6.4		8.7	INSTRUM,APPAR SCIENT NDA
872	MEDICAL INSTRUMENTS NES	W 65	2.0	W 83	1.7	W 78	1.9	W 101	2.4	INSTR,APP MEDIC–CHIR NDA
87202	OTH MEDICAL INSTRUMENTS	W 61	1.9	W 78	1.6	W 71	1.8	W 84	2.1	INSTRUM,APP MEDECINE
874	MEASURNG,CONTROLNG INSTR	W 81	2.8	W 130	3.9	W 106	4.0	W 207	5.9	INSTRUMENTS DE MESURE
88	PHOTO EQU,OPTICL GDS ETC		8.8		13.2		12.2		13.3	APP,FOURN PHOTO,OP,MONTR
882	PHOTO,CINEMA SUPPLIES	W 210	2.9	W 215	3.3	W 399	3.1	W 913	3.0	PRODUITS PHOTO,CINEMA
8822	PHOTO FILM EXC DEV CINMA	W 148	2.3	W 147	2.6	W 95	2.3	W 124	1.8	PLAQUES,PELLICULES,FILMS
885	WATCHES AND CLOCKS		4.0		7.8		6.9		7.5	HORLOGERIE
8851	WATCHES,MOVEMENTS,CASES		3.6		7.1		6.3		7.0	MONTRES,MOUVEMENTS,BOITES

4. General Imports C.I.F. by Commodities according to the S.I.T.C. (Rev. 2) in million U.S. Dollars
Importations Générales C.A.F. par Produits d'après la C.T.C.I. (Rév. 2) en millions de Dollars E.U.

SITC CTCI	COMMODITY	1994 QUANTITY QUANTITE	1994 VALUE VALEUR	1995 QUANTITY QUANTITE	1995 VALUE VALEUR	1996 QUANTITY QUANTITE	1996 VALUE VALEUR	1997 QUANTITY QUANTITE	1997 VALUE VALEUR	PRODUIT
88511	WATCHES		3.5		7.0		6.3		6.9	MONTRES POCHE,BRACELET
89	MISC MANUFCTRD GOODS NES		48.0		60.1		61.9		71.4	ART MANUFACTURES DIVERS
892	PRINTED MATTER	W 1929	14.7	W 1822	14.0	W 1991	12.2	W 2038	13.9	IMPRIMES
8921	PRINTED BOOKS,GLOBES,ETC	W 1059	6.1	W 1285	6.3	W 1393	7.4	W 1333	7.7	LIVRES,BROCHURES,CARTES
89211	PRINTED BOOKS,PAMPHLETS	W 1027	5.9	W 1251	6.1	W 1357	7.2	W 1301	7.4	LIVRES,BROCHURES
8928	PRINTED MATTER NES	W 551	6.6	W 235	5.4	W 305	2.6	W 309	3.8	IMPRIMES NDA
89283	UNISSUED BANKNOTES ETC	W 13	4.1	W 14	3.1	W 8	0.6	W 15	1.3	TIMBRES–POSTE FISCAUX
893	ARTICLES OF PLASTIC NES		16.3		19.7		21.2		25.0	OUVRAGES EN MAT DIVIS 58
8931	PLSTC PACKG CONTNRS,LIDS	W 2305	7.3	W 3613	10.1	W 3068	9.9	W 3725	10.9	ART TRANSP EMBALLAGE ETC
8939	MISC PLASTIC ARTICLES	W 3709	8.8	W 3196	9.3	W 3026	11.1	W 4404	13.7	ART DIVERS EN MAT DIV 58
89399	OTHR PLASTC ARTICLES NES	W 3103	7.9	W 2215	8.3	W 2461	10.1	W 3666	12.5	AUT OUV MAT DIV 58
894	TOYS,SPORTING GOODS,ETC	W 408	3.0	W 670	3.8	W 705	4.1	W 754	4.8	VOITURES ENFANTS,JOUETS
897	GOLD,SILVER WARE,JEWELRY		6.7		14.0		16.8		16.8	BIJOUTERIE,ORFEVRERIE
8973	PREC JEWLRY,GLD–SILVWARE		6.5		13.6		16.5		16.4	BIJOUX OR,ARGENT ORFEVRE
89731	PRECIOUS METAL JEWELLERY		6.3		13.4		16.4		16.3	ART BIJOUTERIE,JOAILLER
898	MUSICAL INSTRUMENTS,PTS	W 169	3.7	W 212	4.6	W 202	3.5	W 150	4.9	INSTRUMENTS DE MUSIQUE
8983	SOUND RECRDNG TAPE,DISCS	W 128	3.3	W 189	4.0	W 172	3.1	W 115	4.4	SUPPORTS SON POUR 763
89832	RECORDED DISCS,TAPES ETC	W 65	2.6	W 152	3.5	W 105	2.7	W 57	3.7	DISQUES,PHONO,BANDES
899	OTHER MANUFACTURED GOODS		2.5		2.9		2.6		3.9	AUT ART MANUF DIVERS NDA
9	GOODS NOT CLASSD BY KIND		2.6		2.1		2.6		1.8	ART TRANSACT NON CLASSES

5. General Exports F.O.B. by Commodities according to the S.I.T.C. (Rev. 2) in million U.S. Dollars
Exportations Générales F.O.B. par Produits d'après la C.T.C.I. (Rév. 2) en millions de Dollars E.U.

SITC CTCI	COMMODITY	1994 QUANTITY QUANTITE	1994 VALUE VALEUR	1995 QUANTITY QUANTITE	1995 VALUE VALEUR	1996 QUANTITY QUANTITE	1996 VALUE VALEUR	1997 QUANTITY QUANTITE	1997 VALUE VALEUR	PRODUIT
	ALL COMMODITIES		181.9		237.6		279.1		283.0	TOUS PRODUITS
0	FOOD AND LIVE ANIMALS		45.1		54.1		87.3		79.1	ALIMENTS,ANIMAUX VIVANTS
01	MEAT AND PREPARATIONS		1.2		2.0		2.4		2.7	VIANDES ET PREPARATIONS
014	MEAT PREPD,PRSVD,NES ETC	W 939	1.2	W 580	1.5	W 904	2.3	W 917	2.5	CONSERVES DE VIANDES
0142	SAUSAGES INCLDING TINNED	W 821	0.8	W 499	1.2	W 740	1.7	W 799	2.0	SAUCISSES,SAUCISSONS
03	FISH AND PREPARATIONS		0.4		0.9		0.6		1.6	POISSONS ET PREPARATIONS
034	FISH,FRESH,CHILLED,FROZN	W 84	0.4	W 208	0.9	W 114	0.5	W 258	1.5	POISSON FRAIS, REFRIG,CONG
0341	FISH FRSH,CHLLD,EX FILLT	W 7	0.1	W 90	0.4	W 31	0.2	W 211	1.4	POISSON FRAIS,REFRIGERE
04	CEREALS AND PREPARATIONS		2.8		4.5		6.1		6.2	CEREALES ET PRODUITS
042	RICE	W 30	0.1	W 690	0.3	W 1983	1.0	W 1715	0.9	RIZ
0422	RICE SEMI-MILLED,MILLED	W 28	0.1	W 689	0.3	W 1945	1.0	W 1520	0.8	RIZ POLI,GLACE INCL BRISURES
04221	RICE MILLED UNBROKEN	W 28	0.1	W 689	0.3	W 1945	1.0	W 1520	0.8	RIZ POLI,GLACE EXCL BRISURES
046	WHEAT ETC MEAL OR FLOUR	W 248	0.2	W 665	0.4	W 727	0.5	W 2707	1.3	SEMOULE FARINE,FROMENT
04601	FLOUR OF WHEAT OR MESLIN	W 248	0.2	W 660	0.4	W 720	0.5	W 2706	1.3	FARINE DE FROMENT
048	CEREAL ETC PREPARATIONS	W 1208	2.3	W 1716	3.5	W 2101	4.4	W 1767	3.8	PREPTNS A BASE CEREALES
0481	PREPD BREAKFAST FOOD ETC	W 378	0.5	W 293	0.8	W 240	0.6	W 268	0.7	CEREALES TRAVAILLEES
0484	BAKERY PRODUCTS	W 757	1.5	W 1021	2.0	W 1406	2.9	W 1455	3.0	PRODUITS DE BOULANGERIE
05	VEGETABLES AND FRUIT		2.4		3.2		3.1		2.5	LEGUMES ET FRUITS
054	VEG ETC FRSH,SMPLY PRSVD	W 1383	0.9	W 1396	1.2	W 1217	1.3	W 103	0.2	LEGUMES FRAIS,CONG,SECS
058	FRUIT PRESERVED,PREPARED	W 238	0.6	W 448	1.0	W 418	0.8	W 368	0.8	CONSERVES DE FRUITS
06	SUGAR AND PREPS,HONEY		30.0		28.8		36.0		36.1	SUCRES ET PRODUITS
061	SUGAR AND HONEY	W 30865	29.9	W 37345	28.7	W 53542	35.9	W 54370	35.9	SUCRES ET MIEL
0611	RAW BEET AND CANE SUGAR	W 30863	29.9	W 37343	28.7	W 53523	35.9	W 54360	35.9	SUCRES BRUTS
081	*FEEDING STUFF FOR ANIML	W 1365	0.5	W 2183	0.6	W 1386	0.5	W 7069	2.2	NOURRITURE POUR ANIMAUX
0813	OILCAKE AND OTH RESIDUES	W 532	0.3	W 1038	0.3			W 5150	1.6	TOURTEAUX
08131	— OF SOYA BEANS	W 532	0.3	W 1038	0.3			W 5150	1.6	TOURTEAUX DE SOJA
09	MISC EDIBLE PRODUCTS		7.4		13.4		37.7		26.6	PREP ALIMENTAIRES DIVERSES
091	MARGARINE AND SHORTENING	W 2279	3.0	W 2982	4.7	W 3422	5.8	W 3399	5.6	MARGARINE ET GRAISSES
0914	MARGARINE,EDIBLE FAT NES	W 2279	3.0	W 2982	4.7	W 3421	5.8	W 3399	5.6	MARGARINES,SIMILI SAINDOUX
09141	MARGARINE	W 1996	2.5	W 2546	4.0	W 2941	4.6	W 2828	4.7	MARGARINE
09149	OTH PREPARED EDIBLE FATS	W 283	0.5	W 436	0.7	W 479	1.2	W 571	1.0	SIMILI-SAINDOUX
098	EDIBLE PRODCTS,PREPS NES	W 487	4.5	W 906	8.7	W 3254	31.9	W 2168	21.0	PREP ALIMENTAIRES NDA
09809	MISC FOOD PREPRTIONS NES	W 390	4.3	W 724	8.4	W 2525	31.5	W 2040	20.7	PREP ALIMENTAIRES NDA
1	BEVERAGES AND TOBACCO		8.2		14.2		15.6		18.1	BOISSONS ET TABACS
11	BEVERAGES		7.3		13.1		15.1		17.2	BOISSONS
111	NON-ALCOHL BEVERAGES NES	W 1410	1.5	W 1930	2.1	W 2204	2.6	W 1628	1.7	BOISSONS NON ALCOOLIQUES
11102	FLAVORED WATERS NON-ALCO	W 1218	1.5	W 1751	2.0	W 2069	2.5	W 1503	1.6	LIMONADES,EAUX GAZEUSES
112	ALCOHOLIC BEVERAGES	W 2151	5.8	W 4464	11.0	W 5543	12.6	W 8156	15.5	BOISSONS ALCOOLIQUES
1124	DISTILLED ALCOHOLIC BEVS	W 1756	5.1	W 4234	10.2	W 5256	12.3	W 7927	15.2	ALCOOLS,EAUX-DE-VIE
11249	OTH ALCOHOLC BEVS,CMPNDS	W 1716	4.8	W 4213	10.1	W 5197	12.0	W 7875	14.9	BOISSONS ALCOOLIQUES NDA
12	TOBACCO AND MANUFACTURES		1.0		1.2		0.6		0.9	TABACS BRUTS FABRIQUES
122	TOBACCO,MANUFACTURED	W 69	1.0	W 39	1.1	W 15	0.6	W 36	0.9	TABACS FABRIQUES
1222	CIGARETTES	W 62	0.9	W 37	1.0	W 13	0.5	W 31	0.7	CIGARETTES
2	CRUDE MATERLS,EXCL FUELS		1.5		5.8		2.5		2.6	MAT BRUTES NON COMESTIBLES
26	TEXTILE FIBRES AND WASTE		0.3		1.3		0.4		0.7	FIBRES TEXTILES
263	COTTON	W 37	0.3	W 268	1.3	W 50	0.4	W 84	0.6	COTON
2631	RAW COTTON,EXCL LINTERS	W 37	0.3	W 268	1.3	W 50	0.4	W 84	0.6	COTON EN MASSE
27	CRUDE FERTLZR,MINRLS NES		0.7		3.2		0.4		0.7	ENGRAIS MINERAUX BRUTS
277	NATURAL ABRASIVES NES		0.3							ABRASIFS NATURELS NDA
2771	INDUSTRIAL DIAMONDS		0.3		2.8					DIAMANTS INDUSTRIELS
3	MINERAL FUELS ETC		26.3		34.2		37.0		45.5	COMBUSTIBLES MINERAUX LUB
33	PETROLEUM AND PRODUCTS		26.3		34.2		37.0		45.5	PETROLE ET DERIVES
334	PETROLEUM PRODUCTS,REFIN	W 127018	26.3	W 161244	34.2	W 161099	37.0	W 203220	45.5	PRODUITS RAFFINES
3341	GASOLINE,OTH LIGHT OILS	W 1072	0.4	W 22713	4.9	W 708	0.3	W 537	0.2	ESSENCES POUR MOTEURS
33411	MOTOR,AVIATION SPIRIT	W 1072	0.4	W 22713	4.9	W 708	0.3	W 537	0.2	ESSENCES MOTEURS D'AVIONS
3342	KEROSENE,OTH MEDIUM OILS	W 106774	21.5	W 114973	25.3	W 138119	31.4	W 164642	37.8	PETR LAMPANTS,AUT HUIL
33421	KEROSENE INCL JET FUEL	W 106774	21.5	W 114973	25.3	W 138119	31.4	W 164642	37.8	PETROLES LAMPANTS
3343	GAS OILS	W 13924	3.5	W 10398	1.7	W 8902	2.5	W 10228	2.8	GAS OILS
3344	FUEL OILS,NES	W 5235	0.9	W 13031	2.2	W 13271	2.7	W 27772	4.7	FUEL OILS
5	CHEMCLS,RELATED PROD NES		25.8		32.1		34.0		36.9	PRODUITS CHIMIQUES
51	ORGANIC CHEMICALS		3.0		1.7		0.2		0.3	PROD CHIMIQ ORGANIQUES
512	ALCOHOLS,PHENOLS ETC	W 2452	3.0	W 1167	1.6	W 59	0.1	W 162	0.3	PHENOLS,PHENOLS-ALCOOLS
5121	ACYCLIC ALCOHOLS,DERIVS	W 2452	3.0	W 1166	1.6	W 59	0.1	W 153	0.3	ALCOOLS ACYCLIQUES
51216	ETHYL ALC,DENATRD SPIRIT	W 2451	2.9	W 1166	1.5	W 59	0.1	W 153	0.3	ALCOOL ETHYLIQUE NON DENAT
53	DYES,TANNING,COLOUR PROD		4.6		5.3		5.2		4.7	PROD TEINTURE,COLORANTS
533	PIGMENTS,PAINTS,ETC	W 1386	4.4	W 1592	5.3	W 61	0.2	W 1268	4.6	PIGMENTS,PEINTURES,VERNIS
5334	VARNISHES,DISTEMPERS ETC	W 1235	4.2	W 1451	4.9	W 1282	4.8	W 1118	4.3	PEINTURES A L'EAU
53341	WATER-THINNED PAINTS	W 310	1.4	W 321	1.0	W 239	0.9	W 182	0.7	PEINTURES DILUEES
53342	OTH PAINTS,VARNISHES ETC	W 918	2.7	W 1122	3.8	W 1035	4.0	W 933	3.6	AUTRES PEINTURES,VERNIS
541	*MEDICINAL,PHARM PRODUCT	K 293046	5.5	K 356963	7.2	K 257072	2.6	K 297032	4.4	PROD MEDICINAUX PHARMACEUT
5417	MEDICAMENTS	K 283393	5.2	K 339465	7.0	K 578135	7.9	K 296962	4.4	MEDICAMENTS
54171	— CONTAINNG ANTIBIOTICS	K 10833	0.6	K 7052	0.6	K 7804	0.7	K 14801	0.9	MED CONTN ANTIBIOTIQUES
54179	— CONTNG OTH SUBSTANCES	K 272080	4.6	K 331310	6.2	K 569170	7.0	K 720408	10.0	MED CONT AUT SUBSTANCES
55	PERFUME,CLEANING ETC PRD		7.8		9.2		10.9		10.6	PROD POUR PARFUM,TOILETTE
553	PERFUMERY,COSMETICS,ETC	W 112	1.0	W 95	0.9	W 132	1.1	W 111	0.8	PRODUITS DE PARFUMERIE
554	SOAP,CLEANSING ETC PREPS	W 5550	6.8	W 6923	8.3	W 8312	9.6	W 7921	9.7	SAVONS,PRODUITS DETERSIFS
5542	WASHING PREPARATIONS ETC	W 5541	6.7	W 6916	8.3	W 8308	9.6	W 7910	9.7	PROD ORG TENSIO-ACT NDA
59	CHEMICAL MATERIALS NES		4.6		8.2		9.1		9.3	MAT PROD CHIMIQUES NDA
591	PESTICIDES,DISINFECTANTS	W 868	4.1	W 1440	7.4	W 1704	8.2	W 1815	8.1	DESINF,INSECT,FONG,HERB
5911	INSECTICIDES,FOR RETAIL	W 774	3.9	W 1336	7.1	W 1547	7.8	W 1653	7.8	!INSECTICIDES VENTE DET
598	MISCEL CHEM PRODUCTS NES	W 174	0.5	W 292	0.8	W 201	1.0	W 594	1.2	PROD DIV INDUST CHIM NDA
5989	CHEM PRODUCTS,PREPS NES	W 170	0.5	W 288	0.8	W 195	1.0	W 578	1.1	PROD PREP CHIMIQUES NDA
6	BASIC MANUFACTURES		26.1		33.9		39.7		37.8	ART MANUFACTURES
63	WOOD,CORK MANUFACTRS NES		0.7		1.4		1.6		0.9	OUVRAGES LIEGE ET BOIS
635	WOOD MANUFACTURES NES	W 230	0.6	W 443	1.1	W 597	1.5	W 251	0.9	ART MANUF EN BOIS NDA
6353	BUILDERS WOODWRK,PREFABS	W 221	0.6	W 426	1.1	W 577	1.5	W 229	0.8	OUVRAGES DE MENUISERIE
64	PAPER,PAPERBOARD AND MFR		5.6		10.9		14.2		11.7	PAPIERS,CARTONS & OUVRAGES
642	PAPER,ETC,PRECUT,ARTS OF	W 1424	5.5	W 2526	10.8	W 51	0.3	W 3204	11.6	PAP,CARTONS DECOUPES
6421	PAPER ETC CONTAINERS	W 724	2.1	W 1250	4.3	W 1647	4.7	W 1571	5.4	BOITES,SACS EMBALLAGES
6428	PAPER ETC ARTICLES NES	W 624	2.8	W 1197	5.6	W 1	0.1	W 1553	5.4	OUVRAGES EN PATE A PAPIER
64285	PAPER ETC DIAPERS ETC	W 531	2.3	W 975	4.8	W 1552	7.5	W 1457	4.7	SERVIETTES HYGIENIQUES
65	TEXTILE YARN,FABRICS,ETC		1.9		2.2		2.1		1.6	FILS,TISSUS,ARTICLES TEXTILE
658	TEXTILE ARTICLES NES	W 31	0.1	W 2	0.1	W 2	0.1	W 23	1.5	ART FACONNES MAT TEXTILES
6582	MADE-UP CANVAS GOODS	W 67	1.5	W 23	1.7	W 25	1.9	W 21	1.4	BACHES,TENTES ETC
66	NONMETAL MINERAL MFS NES		1.3		2.1		5.7		8.0	ART MIN NON METALLIQUES
661	LIME,CEMENT,BLDG PRODS	W 4082	0.4	W 2582	0.3	W 5603	2.1	W 24187	6.5	CHAUX,CIMENTS MAT CONSTR
6611	LIME,QUICK,SLKD,HYDRAULC	W 4046	0.3	W 2469	0.3	W 1924	1.0	W 4059	0.9	CHAUX ORDINAIRE,HYDRAUL
6612	CEMENT	W 1	0.1			W 3559	1.1	W 20106	5.7	CIMENTS HYDRAULIQUES
665	GLASSWARE	W 1333	0.8	W 1764	1.2	W 50	0.1	W 2013	1.2	OUVRAGES EN VERRE
6651	BOTTLES ETC OF GLASS	W 1329	0.8	W 1762	1.2	W 1856	1.1	W 2009	1.2	RECIPIENTS EN VERRE
66511	GLASS BOTTLES ETC NONVAC	W 1329	0.8	W 1762	1.2	W 1856	1.1	W 2009	1.2	BONBONNES,BOUTEILLES,ETC

5. General Exports F.O.B. by Commodities according to the S.I.T.C. (Rev. 2) in million U.S. Dollars
Exportations Générales F.O.B. par Produits d'après la C.T.C.I. (Rév. 2) en millions de Dollars E.U.

SITC CTCI	COMMODITY	1994 QUANTITY QUANTITE	1994 VALUE VALEUR	1995 QUANTITY QUANTITE	1995 VALUE VALEUR	1996 QUANTITY QUANTITE	1996 VALUE VALEUR	1997 QUANTITY QUANTITE	1997 VALUE VALEUR	PRODUIT
667	PEARL,PREC–,SEMI–P STONE				0.6		2.4		0.1	PERLES, PIERRES GEMMES
6672	DIAMONDS NONINDUST,UNSET				0.6		2.4			DIAMANTS BRUTS
66721	— ROUGH,UNSORTED				0.6		2.4			DIAMANTS BRUTS NON TRIES
67	IRON AND STEEL		0.7		0.6		1.0		1.9	FER ET ACIER
673	IRON,STEEL SHAPES ETC	W 253	0.2	W 266	0.2	W 1613	0.3	W 1283	1.7	BARRES,PROFIL FER,ACIER
6732	IRON,STEEL BARS ETC	W 232	0.2	W 181	0.1	W 313	0.2	W 1275	1.6	BARRES FER,ACIER
67322	HIGH CARBON STL BARS ETC	W 219	0.2	W 181	0.1	W 287	0.2	W 1275	1.6	BARRES ACIER FIN CARBONE
69	METAL MANUFACTURES NES		16.0		16.8		14.8		13.7	ART MANUFACT EN METAL NDA
691	STRUCTURES AND PARTS NES	W 508	2.7	W 625	3.1	W 816	3.5	W 542	3.1	CONSTRUCT FER,ACIER,ALU
6912	STRUCTURES,PARTS ALUMNM	W 283	2.2	W 503	2.7	W 578	3.1	W 418	2.9	CONSTRUCT ALUMINIUM
692	METAL TANKS,BOXES,ETC	W 4428	7.5	W 2996	6.3	W 1976	5.7	W 127	0.2	RECIPIENTS METALLIQUES
6924	MTL TRANSPORT BOXES ETC	W 4427	7.5	W 2978	6.2	W 2190	5.9	W 127	0.2	FUTS,TAMBOURS,BIDONS
69241	STL TRANSPORT BOXES ETC	W 4335	7.2	W 2856	6.0	W 2015	5.7	W 1043	4.7	FUTS,TAMBOURS,BIDONS FER
695	TOOLS	W 318	3.2	W 300	6.0	W 358	4.1	W 340	4.1	OUTILS A MAIN
6953	OTHER HAND TOOLS	W 317	3.2	W 299	6.0	W 353	4.0	W 338	4.1	AUTRES OUTILS A MAIN
69539	HAND TOOLS ETC NES	W 315	3.2	W 299	6.0	W 352	4.0	W 332	4.1	OUTILLAGE A MAIN NDA
699	BASE METAL MFRS NES	W 73	0.2	W 86	0.3		1.0	W 57	1.1	ART MANUFACTURES MET NDA
6994	SPRINGS AND LEAVES	W 67	2.2	W 11	0.9	W 7	0.8	W 29	1.1	RESSORTS FER,ACIER
69942	COPPER SPRINGS,LEAVES	W 65	2.2	W 6	0.9	W 7	0.8	W 29	1.1	RESSORTS,LAMES EN CUIVRE
7	MACHINES,TRANSPORT EQUIP		34.0		47.0		39.0		39.5	MACHINES MATERIEL TRANSPORT
71	POWER GENERATING EQUIPMT		0.2		0.5		0.9		0.9	MACHINES GENERATRICES
72	MACHS FOR SPCL INDUSTRYS		1.5		6.4		2.1		2.3	MAC SPECIALES POUR INDUST
722	TRACTORS NON–ROAD			W 53	2.6			W 3	0.1	TRACTEURS
7224	WHEELED TRACTORS NES			W 53	2.6			W 3	0.1	TRACTEURS A ROUES
723	CIVIL ENGNEERG EQUIP ETC	W 68	0.5	W 86	0.8	W 64	0.6	W 201	1.2	APPAREILS DE GENIE CIVIL
7234	CONST,MINING MACHNRY NES	W 58	0.4	W 82	0.8	W 46	0.5	W 132	1.1	MACH POUR LA CONST, MINES
72342	SLFPRP SHOVELS,EXCAVATRS	W 44	0.3	W 11	0.1	W 36	0.4	W 123	0.9	PELLES MECANIQUES
726	PRINTG,BKBINDG MACHY,PTS	W 32	0.4	W 66	2.4	W 34	0.4	W 35	0.4	MACHINES POUR IMPRIMERIE
7263	TYPESET ETC MCH,TYPE ETC	W 8	0.2	W 35	1.0	W 31	0.3	W 21	0.3	MACH COMPOSER,CLICHER
7267	OTH PRINTG & ANCILL MACH	W 22	0.2	W 22	1.0	W 1	0.1	W 12	0.1	AUT MACH IMPRIMERIE,PIEC
72671	PRINTING MACHINERY NES	W 22	0.2	W 22	1.0	W 1	0.1	W 12	0.1	AUT MACH IMPRIMERIE
74	GENRL INDUSTRL MACHY NES		0.4		1.0		3.4		2.7	MACH APP INDUSTRIE
744	MECHANICAL HANDLING EQU	W 16	0.1	W 37	0.2	W 125	0.6	W 87	1.8	EQUIP MANUTENTION PIECES
7442	LIFTING,LOADING MACH NES	W 11	0.1	W 23	0.2	W 72	0.4	W 62	1.7	APP LEVAGE,MANUTENTION
74422	SHIP DERRICKS,CRANES ETC			W 19	0.1	W 31	0.3	W 47	1.7	GRUES,PONTS ROULANTS
745	NONELEC MACHY,TOOLS NES	W 23	0.1	W 66	0.5	W 196	2.4	W 12	0.1	AUT MACH NON ELEC,PIECES
7452	OTH NONELEC MCHS,PTS NES	W 23	0.1	W 64	0.5	W 193	2.4	W 11	0.1	AUT MACH NON ELEC,PIECES
74522	PACKAGNG,BOTTLNG,ETC MCH	W 20	0.1	W 60	0.4	W 177	2.1	W 9	0.1	MACH NETT BOUTEILLES,ETC
75	OFFICE MACHNES,ADP EQUIP		2.8		1.4		1.4		1.8	MACH BUREAU TRAIT AUTOM
759	OFFICE,ADP MCH PTS,ACCES	W 28	2.4	W 26	0.8	W 20	0.8	W 27	1.1	PIECES DU 751 ET 752
7599	ACCTG,ETC,ADP MCH PTS,AC	W 28	2.4	W 26	0.8	W 20	0.8	W 26	1.1	PIECES DU 751 ET 752
76	TELECOMM,SOUND EQUIPMENT		0.8		6.1		0.5		1.5	EQUIPMENT DE TELECOM
764	TELECOM EQPT,PTS,ACC NES	W 57	0.6		0.1	W 5	0.4	W 35	1.5	EQUIP TELECOM,PIECES
7641	LINE TELEPHONE,ETC EQUIP	W 2	0.2	W 43	1.0	W 4	0.2	W 2	0.1	APP TELEPHON PAR FIL
7643	TV,RADIO TRANSMITTRS ETC		0.1	W 21	4.8	W 2	0.1	W 2	0.3	APP EMET TELE RADIO
7648	TELECOMM EQUIPMENT NES		0.1		0.1		0.1	W 5	1.1	APP TELECOM NDA
76483	RADAR APPARATUS ETC						0.1	W 5	1.1	APP DE RADIOGUIDAGE ETC
77	ELECTRIC MACHNRY NES ETC		25.8		28.4		27.3		26.7	MACH APP ELECT NDA
772	SWITCHGEAR ETC,PARTS NES	W 189	15.1	W 229	17.5	W 232	18.8	W 296	19.0	APP COUPURE,SECT ETC
7722	PRINTED CIRCUITS,PTS NES	W 58	3.2	W 77	3.7	W 82	4.0	W 119	6.1	CIRCUITS ET PIECES
7723	FIXED,VARIABLE RESISTORS	W 111	11.4	W 123	13.3	W 142	14.5	W 173	12.7	POTENTIOMETRES PIECES
776	TRANSISTORS,VALVES,ETC	W 134	7.2	W 135	6.8	W 111	4.5	W 103	3.4	LAMPES,TUBES,VALVES
7764	ELECTRONIC MICROCIRCUITS	W 128	6.5	W 130	6.3	W 106	4.3	W 83	3.0	MICROSTRUCTURES ELECTRON
778	ELECTRICAL MACHINERY NES	W 255	3.5	W 399	3.7	W 430	3.9	W 54	0.2	AUTRES MACH ELECT NDA
7788	OTH ELEC MACHY,EQUIP NES	W 6	3.1	W 9	3.2	W 5	3.3	W 3	0.1	AUT MACH APP ELEC NDA
77884	ELECTRICAL CONDENSERS	W 4	3.0	W 4	3.1	W 2	3.2	W 4	3.0	CONDENSATEURS ELECTRIQUES
78	ROAD VEHICLES		2.3		2.4		2.1		2.3	VEHICULES ROUTIERS
781	PASS MOTOR VEH EXC BUSES	W 46	0.7	W 77	1.0	W 83	1.3	W 93	1.4	AUTO TRANSPORT PERSONNES
782	LORRIES,SPCL MTR VEH NES	W 285	1.1	W 55	0.2	W 156	0.4	W 54	0.4	VEHICULES SPECIAUX,MARCH
7821	LORRIES,TRUCKS	W 285	1.1	W 51	0.2	W 147	0.4	W 21	0.2	VEHICULES TRANSP MARCHAND
79	OTHR TRANSPORT EQUIPMENT		0.6		1.0		1.6		1.5	AUTRE MATERIEL TRANSPORT
792	AIRCRAFT ETC	W 12	0.6	W 18	1.0	W 11	1.2	W 8	0.8	APP NAVIGATION AERIENNE
7929	AIRCRAFT PARTS NES	W 12	0.6	W 18	1.0	W 11	1.2	W 8	0.8	PIECES DU 792
8	MISC MANUFACTURED GOODS		12.8		15.7		22.5		22.1	ART MANUFACTURES DIVERS
821	*FURNITURE,PARTS THEREOF	W 177	0.7	W 162	0.7	W 260	1.0	W 269	1.0	MEUBLES ET PIECES
84	CLOTHING AND ACCESSORIES		3.5		3.5		4.0		3.6	VETEMENTS
842	MENS OUTERWEAR NOT KNIT	W 13	0.5	W 17	0.9	W 22	0.7	W 19	0.6	VET DESSUS POUR HOMMES
8423	— TROUSERS,BREECHES ETC	W 11	0.4	W 15	0.9	W 20	0.6	W 18	0.5	PANTALONS HOMMES MAT TEX
845	OUTERWEAR KNIT NONELASTC	W 7	0.8	W 5	0.4	W 6	0.4	W 4	0.3	VET DESSOUS,ACCES BONNET
846	UNDER GARMENTS KNITTED	W 57	2.1	W 56	2.0	W 62	2.6	W 59	2.4	SOUS VETS DE BONNETERIE
8462	— OF COTTON NON ELASTIC	W 38	1.1	W 40	1.1	W 37	0.9	W 31	0.9	SOUS–VET BONNET COTON
84629	—— OTHER	W 38	1.1	W 40	1.1	W 37	0.9	W 31	0.9	AUT SOUS–VET BONNET COTON
8465	CORSETS,GARTERS,ETC	W 19	1.1	W 15	0.9	W 25	1.7	W 28	1.6	CORSETS,GAINES ART SIM
84651	BRASSIERES	W 18	1.1	W 13	0.8	W 22	1.5	W 27	1.5	SOUTIENS–GORGE,BUSTIERS
87	PRECISION INSTRUMNTS NES		0.4		1.1		0.8		1.4	INSTRUM,APPAR SCIENT NDA
874	MEASURNG,CONTROLNG INSTR	W 13	0.3	W 5	0.8		0.4	W 5	0.9	INSTRUMENTS DE MESURE
88	PHOTO EQU,OPTICL GDS ETC		0.9		0.5		3.8		3.6	APP,FOURN PHOTO,OP,MONTR
882	PHOTO,CINEMA SUPPLIES	W 61	0.6	W 8	0.2	W 52	0.4	W 10	0.2	PRODUITS PHOTO,CINEMA
885	WATCHES AND CLOCKS		0.3		0.2		3.2		3.4	HORLOGERIE
8852	CLOCKS,CLOCK,WATCH PARTS		0.1		0.1		3.1		3.2	HORLOGES,MOUV,PARTIES
88523	TIME–CLOCKS ETC		0.1		0.1		2.7		3.2	COMPTEURS DE TEMPS,MINUT
89	MISC MANUFCTRD GOODS NES		7.3		10.1		13.0		12.5	ART MANUFACTURES DIVERS
892	PRINTED MATTER	W 495	3.9	W 494	6.2	W 531	7.8	W 516	8.4	IMPRIMES
8921	PRINTED BOOKS,GLOBES,ETC	W 108	0.7	W 74	0.4	W 91	0.7	W 90	0.6	LIVRES,BROCHURES,CARTES
89211	PRINTED BOOKS,PAMPHLETS	W 100	0.7	W 80	0.5	W 82	0.7	W 84	0.5	LIVRES,BROCHURES
8928	PRINTED MATTER NES	W 185	2.9	W 342	5.5	W 343	6.6	W 307	7.1	IMPRIMES NDA
89281	LABELS PAPER,PAPERBOARD	W 91	1.0	W 162	1.8	W 178	2.5	W 185	2.2	ETIQUETTES TOUS GENRES
89283	UNISSUED BANKNOTES ETC	W 7	1.5	W 15	3.0	W 16	3.4	W 16	4.3	TIMBRES–POSTE FISCAUX
893	ARTICLES OF PLASTIC NES		2.2	W 260	0.5	W 252	0.5	W 242	0.5	OUVRAGES EN MAT DIVIS 58
8931	PLSTC PACKG CONTNRS,LIDS	W 454	1.0	W 494	1.8	W 587	2.0	W 633	2.3	ART TRANSP EMBALLAGE ETC
8939	MISC PLASTIC ARTICLES	W 356	1.2	W 587	1.2	W 573	1.4	W 303	1.1	ART DIVERS EN MAT DIV 58
89399	OTHR PLASTC ARTICLES NES	W 354	1.2	W 585	1.2	W 570	1.4	W 282	1.0	AUT OUV MAT DIV 58
897	GOLD,SILVER WARE,JEWELRY		0.7		0.2		1.5		0.6	BIJOUTERIE,ORFEVRERIE
8973	PREC JEWLRY,GLD–SILVWARE		0.7		0.1		1.5		0.6	BIJOUX OR,ARGENT ORFEVRE
89731	PRECIOUS METAL JEWELLERY		0.7		0.1		1.5		0.6	ART BIJOUTERIE,JOAILLER
9	GOODS NOT CLASSD BY KIND		2.5		0.7		1.3		1.2	ART TRANSACT NON CLASSES
931	*SPECIAL TRANSACTIONS		1.6		0.3		0.8		0.6	TRANS.SPECIALES

1. HISTORICAL SERIES, 1992–1997 GENERAL TRADE, IMPORTS C.I.F., EXPORTS F.O.B.
SERIES HISTORIQUES, 1992–1997 COMMERCE GENERAL, IMPORTATIONS C.A.F., EXPORTATIONS F.O.B

YEAR ANNEE	VALUE IN MILLION U.S. DOLLARS / VALEUR EN MILLION U.S. DOLLARS — MERCHANDISE –MARCHANDISE		GOLD –OR		CONVERSION FACTORS FACTEURS DE CONVERSION CENTS E.U. PAR		INDEX NUMBERS –INDICES — QUANTUM		UNIT VALUE VALEUR UNITAIRE	
	IMPORTS	EXPORTS	IMPORTS	EXPORTS	IMPORTS	EXPORTS	IMPORTS	EXPORTS	IMPORTS	EXPORTS
1992	750.90	1060.90								
1993	779.00	758.00								
1994	4746.00	2509.00								
1995	4644.00	4156.00								
1996	6939.30	5462.70								
1997	8643.80	7146.60								

2. IMPORTS BY BROAD ECONOMIC CATEGORY AND EXPORTS BY INDUSTRIAL ORIGIN. (PERCENTAGE OF TOTAL VALUE)
IMPORTATIONS PAR CATEGORIES ECONOMIQUES ET EXPORTATIONS PAR BRANCHE D'ACTIVITE.(EN POURCENTAGE DE LA VALEUR TOTALE)

IMPORTS – IMPORTATIONS

	1991	1992	1993	1994	1995	1996	1997
TOTAL IMPORTS–IMPORTATIONS TOTALES							
1 FOOD BEV–ALIMENTATION BOISSONS							
11 PRIMARY–PRODUITS DE BASE							
111 FOR INDUSTRY–POUR L'INDUSTRIE							
112 FOR HOUSEHOLDS–POUR LES MENAGES							
12 PROCESSED–PRODUITS ELABORES							
121 FOR INDUSTRY–POUR L'INDUSTRIE							
122 FOR HOUSEHOLDS–POUR LES MENAGES							
2 IND SUPPLIES–APPROV INDUSTRIELS							
21 PRIMARY–PRODUITS DE BASE							
22 PROCESSED–PRODUITS ELABORES							
3 FUELS–COMBUSTIBLES							
31 PRIMARY–PRODUITS DE BASE							
32 PROCESSED–PRODUITS ELABORES							
321 MOTOR SPIRIT–ESSENCE							
322 OTHER–AUTRES							
4 MACHINERY–EQUIPEMENT							
41 CAPITAL EQUIPMENT–MACHINES							
42 PARTS–PIECES ACCESSOIRES							
5 TRANSPORT–TRANSPORT							
51 PASSENGER CARS–AUTOMOBILES							
52 OTHER–AUTRES							
521 INDUSTRIAL–INDUSTRIELS							
522 NON INDUSTRIAL–NON INDUSTRIEL							
53 PARTS–PIECES ACCESSOIRES							
6 CONSUM GOODS–BIENS CONSOMMATION							
61 DURABLE–DURABLES							
62 SEMI DURABLE–SEMI DURABLES							
63 NON DURABLE–NON DURABLES							
7 GOODS NES–BIENS NDA							

EXPORTS – EXPORTATIONS

	1991	1992	1993	1994	1995	1996	1997
TOTAL EXPORTS–EXPORTATIONS TOTALES							
1 AGRICULTURE							
2 MINING QUARRY–INDUS EXTRACTIVES							
3 MANUFACTURING–IND MANUFACTUR							
31 FOOD BEV TOBACCO–ALIM BOISS TAB							
32 TEXTILES–INDUSTRIES TEXTILES							
33 WOOD & PRODUCTS–BOIS & PRODUITS							
34 PAPER & PRODUCTS–PAPIER & PRODT							
35 CHEMICALS–INDUSTRIES CHIMIQUES							
36 NON METAL MIN–MIN NON METAL							
37 BASIC METAL–IND METAL BASE							
38 METAL MANUF–MANUF METAL							
39 OTH MANUF IND–AUTRES MANUF							

3. TRADE BY PRINCIPAL COUNTRIES OF ORIGIN AND DESTINATION (VALUE IN MILLION U.S. DOLLARS)
ECHANGES SELON LES PRINCIPAUX PAYS D'ORIGINE ET DE DESTINATION (VALEUR EN MILLIONS DE DOLLARS EU)

COUNTRIES–PAYS	GENERAL IMPORTS C.I.F. IMPORTATIONS GENERALES C.A.F					COUNTRIES–PAYS	GENERAL EXPORTS F.O.B. EXPORTATIONS GENERALES F.O.B.				
	1993	1994	1995	1996	1997		1993	1994	1995	1996	1997
World		3066.3	5563.7	6939.3	8643.8	Monde		2510.0	4706.8	5462.7	7146.6
Africa			10.1	16.0	24.8	Afrique		27.4	95.2	105.1	116.4
Americas		57.4	135.8	225.3	317.4	Amériques		58.6	66.0	130.4	321.8
– Northern America		52.8	102.1	159.5	146.6	– Amérique du Nord		58.6	63.9	66.9	97.8
– LAIA		3.6	27.2	31.9	76.3	– ALAI			0.5	58.4	207.2
– CACM					7.1	– MCAC					5.6
– Caribbean		1.0	6.5	33.9	87.4	– Caraïbes			1.6	5.1	11.2
– Rest of America					0.0	– Autre Amérique					
Asia excl fmr USSR		28.5	99.7	150.6	257.6	Asie anc. URSS exclus		127.2	144.3	151.5	300.2
– Middle East		10.2	7.6	16.9	28.1	– Moyen–Orient		31.8	43.3	50.6	57.7
Asia former USSR		47.1	92.7	95.3	116.7	Asie ancienne URSS		44.9	151.8	182.7	112.3
Europe excl fmr USSR		759.1	1380.1	1720.8	1995.0	Europe anc. URSS exclus		560.4	989.7	957.3	949.1
– European Union		509.9	928.1	1248.8	1431.4	– Union Européenne		309.8	572.9	439.9	492.5
– Eastern Europe		213.1	399.4	359.3	447.0	– Europe de l'Est		196.2	404.9	480.8	391.3
– Rest of Europe		36.1	52.6	112.7	116.5	– Autre de l'Europe		54.4	11.9	36.6	65.3
Europe former USSR		2059.9	3760.4	4672.1	5929.3	Europe ancienne URSS		1494.4	3128.1	3877.8	5339.4
Oceania					2.9	Océanie					3.3
Other						Autre					
Russian Federation		1873.8	2965.0	3522.1	4631.3	Russian Federation		1157.6	2088.9	2907.6	4626.2
Ukraine		149.2	569.0	889.4	967.5	Ukraine		243.9	607.2	478.1	425.4
Germany/Allemagne		315.5	424.1	600.6	713.6	Poland/Pologne		103.7	271.4	324.6	245.4
Poland/Pologne		125.6	197.4	195.0	250.0	Germany/Allemagne		154.8	267.8	198.2	224.2
Lithuania/Lituanie		12.2	117.8	153.4	191.8	Latvia/Lettonie		24.5	195.7	241.0	72.5
USA/Etats–Unis d'Amer		51.3	97.2	151.5	138.1	Lithuania/Lituanie		34.0	146.4	167.1	137.8
Italy/Italie		18.7	82.7	111.0	157.8	USA/Etats–Unis d'Amer		54.5	57.7	60.9	93.4
Netherlands/Pays–Bas		24.2	86.8	116.6	85.1	Netherlands/Pays–Bas		24.3	76.2	64.0	83.2
France, Monaco		71.5	62.0	47.7	97.0	Kazakhstan		25.3	76.5	84.8	53.4
United Kingdom		14.2	57.2	98.7	99.1	Republic of Moldova		28.0	70.9	68.9	61.0
Hungary/Hongrie		64.0	88.0	48.4	63.6	Italy/Italie		32.1	60.8	57.4	64.2
Kazakhstan		32.7	56.0	58.8	59.1	Egypt/Egypte		12.8	70.4	74.7	52.4
Austria/Autriche		35.8	45.3	54.5	62.6	Peru/Pérou			0.5	58.4	126.1
Czech Republic		7.4	53.7	57.0	70.3	Uzbekistan/Ouzbékistan		12.1	60.0	77.5	30.0
Latvia/Lettonie		14.0	57.8	49.0	67.1	Hungary/Hongrie		43.3	37.9	57.0	38.9
Belgium–Luxembourg		3.9	43.6	66.3	70.2	China/Chine		39.7	16.0	21.3	70.2
Republic of Moldova		9.1	35.0	48.1	59.7	Slovakia/Slovaquie		24.2	40.0	36.6	31.8
Finland/Finlande		16.8	38.3	33.3	36.8	Belgium–Luxembourg		29.7	53.4	22.1	24.2
Switzerland,Liechtenst.		23.2	16.7	37.8	43.2	Turkey/Turquie		28.5	33.6	30.1	32.9
Uzbekistan/Ouzbékistan		14.4	36.7	36.5	31.1	United Kingdom		19.3	42.5	32.1	30.2
Cuba		1.0	5.3	27.2	84.3	Romania/Roumanie		8.4	24.3	29.9	31.4
Denmark/Danemark		2.3	24.2	39.8	46.8	China, Hong Kong SAR		14.6	15.2	18.4	45.6
Slovakia/Slovaquie		7.1	32.7	34.1	37.6	Switzerland,Liechtenst.		40.1	7.5	19.8	21.8
Sweden/Suède		4.7	41.6	28.2	28.8	Pakistan		5.2	39.4	20.6	9.3
Japan/Japon		8.0	20.8	25.3	46.2	Algeria/Algérie		6.2	19.5	11.1	35.4
Slovenia/Slovénie		5.3	16.8	37.1	31.5	France, Monaco		8.0	22.8	17.0	20.0
China/Chine		3.3	16.7	25.2	31.9	Austria/Autriche		16.8	18.4	15.4	16.4
Bulgaria/Bulgarie		6.9	22.6	19.0	22.4	Czech Republic		4.7	15.4	20.0	26.5
Brazil/Brésil			5.7	13.8	50.6	Other Asia n.e.s.		7.8	10.3	17.6	29.3
Croatia/Croatie		7.5	8.7	23.6	15.2	Brazil/Brésil					60.6
Ireland/Irlande		0.9	4.5	24.9	24.4	Bulgaria/Bulgarie		11.9	15.9	12.7	17.4
Turkey/Turquie		10.2	7.6	16.9	19.9	Estonia/Estonie		6.4	19.0	15.1	16.4
Israel/Israël		1.2	13.6	13.4	25.4	Viet Nam		13.2	12.9	14.3	9.7
India/Inde		3.5	11.8	14.6	22.0	Iran (Islamic Rep of)		1.6	8.5	16.1	20.1
Korea, Republic of		0.4	7.3	13.7	25.5	Finland/Finlande		7.3	18.2	10.4	4.5
Singapore/Singapour		0.9	12.1	19.6	13.7	Croatia/Croatie		12.3	1.3	11.0	12.0
Other Asia n.e.s.		0.2	7.6	10.7	25.3	Denmark/Danemark		3.9	5.8	7.5	16.3
Norway,Svalbard and JM		0.1	10.4	14.2	17.2	India/Inde		10.7	4.0	4.0	13.7
Estonia/Estonie		1.6	15.8	10.1	11.8	Morocco/Maroc		6.8	5.0	8.2	8.5
Ecuador/Equateur			16.1	11.8	10.6	Korea, Republic of		4.2	3.2	4.7	16.1

(VALUE AS PERCENTAGE OF WORLD TOTAL)(VALEURS EN POURCENTAGE DU TOTAL MONDIAL)

	1988	1989	1990	1991	1992	1993	1994	1995	1996	1997		1988	1989	1990	1991	1992	1993	1994	1995	1996	1997
Africa								0.2	0.2	0.3	Afrique							1.1	2.0	1.9	1.6
Americas							1.9	2.4	3.2	3.7	Amériques							2.3	1.4	2.4	4.5
– Northern America							1.7	1.8	2.3	1.7	– Amérique du Nord							2.3	1.4	1.2	1.4
– LAIA							0.1	0.5	0.5	0.9	– ALAI								0.0	1.1	2.9
– CACM										0.1	– MCAC										0.1
– Caribbean							0.0	0.1	0.5	1.0	– Caraïbes								0.0	0.1	0.2
– Rest of America										0.0	– Autre Amérique										
Asia excl fmr USSR							0.9	1.8	2.2	3.0	Asie anc. URSS exclus							5.1	3.1	2.8	4.2
– Middle East							0.3	0.1	0.2	0.3	– Moyen–Orient							1.3	0.9	0.9	0.8
Asia former USSR							1.5	1.7	1.4	1.3	Asie ancienne URSS							1.8	3.2	3.3	1.6
Europe excl fmr USSR							24.8	24.8	24.8	23.1	Europe anc. URSS exclus							22.3	21.0	17.5	13.3
– European Union							16.6	16.7	18.0	16.6	– Union Européenne							12.3	12.2	8.1	6.9
– Eastern Europe							6.9	7.2	5.2	5.2	– Europe de l'Est							7.8	8.6	8.8	5.5
– Rest of Europe							1.2	0.9	1.6	1.3	– Autre de l'Europe							2.2	0.3	0.7	0.9
Europe former USSR							67.2	67.6	67.3	68.6	Europe ancienne URSS							59.5	66.5	71.0	74.7
Oceania										0.0	Océanie										0.0
Other											Autre										
Russian Federation							61.1	53.3	50.8	53.6	Russian Federation							46.1	44.4	53.2	64.7
Ukraine							4.9	10.2	12.8	11.2	Ukraine							9.7	12.9	8.8	6.0
Germany/Allemagne							10.3	7.6	8.7	8.3	Poland/Pologne							4.1	5.8	5.9	3.4
Poland/Pologne							4.1	3.5	2.8	2.9	Germany/Allemagne							6.2	5.7	3.6	3.1
Lithuania/Lituanie							0.4	2.1	2.2	2.2	Latvia/Lettonie							1.0	4.2	4.4	1.0
USA/Etats–Unis d'Amer							1.7	1.7	2.2	1.6	Lithuania/Lituanie							1.4	3.1	3.1	1.9
Italy/Italie							0.6	1.5	1.6	1.8	USA/Etats–Unis d'Amer							2.2	1.2	1.1	1.3
Netherlands/Pays–Bas							0.8	1.6	1.7	1.0	Netherlands/Pays–Bas							1.0	1.6	1.2	1.2
France, Monaco							2.3	1.1	0.7	1.1	Kazakhstan							1.0	1.6	1.6	0.7
United Kingdom							0.5	1.0	1.4	1.1	Republic of Moldova							1.1	1.5	1.3	0.9

4. General Imports C.I.F. by Commodities according to the S.I.T.C. (Rev. 2) in million U.S. Dollars
Importations Générales C.A.F. par Produits d'après la C.T.C.I. (Rév. 2) en millions de Dollars E.U.

SITC CTCI	COMMODITY	1994 QUANTITY QUANTITE	1994 VALUE VALEUR	1995 QUANTITY QUANTITE	1995 VALUE VALEUR	1996 QUANTITY QUANTITE	1996 VALUE VALEUR	1997 QUANTITY QUANTITE	1997 VALUE VALEUR	PRODUIT
	ALL COMMODITIES				5563.7		6939.3			TOUS PRODUITS
04	CEREALS AND PREPARATIONS				110.1		284.0			CEREALES ET PRODUITS
057	FRUIT,NUTS,FRESH,DRIED				46.1		46.1			FRUITS FRAIS OU SECS
06	SUGAR AND PREPS,HONEY				138.0		85.1			SUCRES ET PRODUITS
081	*FEEDING STUFF FOR ANIML				35.1		73.1			NOURRITURE POUR ANIMAUX
11	BEVERAGES				41.1		129.0			BOISSONS
263	COTTON				44.1		53.1			COTON
268	WOOL(EXC TOPS),ANML HAIR				27.1		48.1			LAINES ET POILS
3	MINERAL FUELS ETC				1947.0		2088.0			COMBUSTIBLES MINERAUX LUB
4	ANIMAL,VEGETABLE OIL,FAT				65.1		62.1			HUILES,GRAISSES ANIM,VEG
51	ORGANIC CHEMICALS				251.0		256.0			PROD CHIMIQ ORGANIQUES
52	INORGANIC CHEMICALS				73.1		123.0			PROD CHIM INORGANIQUES
53	DYES,TANNING,COLOUR PROD				48.1		67.1			PROD TEINTURE,COLORANTS
541	*MEDICINAL,PHARM PRODUCT				73.1		95.1			PROD MEDICINAUX PHARMACEUT
55	PERFUME,CLEANING ETC PRD				19.1		16.1			PROD POUR PARFUM,TOILETTE
572	*EXPLOSIVES,PYROTECH PRO				141.0		146.0			EXPLOSIFS
62	RUBBER MANUFACTURES NES				131.0		201.0			CAOUTCHOUC MANUFACTURE
64	PAPER,PAPERBOARD AND MFR				69.1		110.1			PAPIERS,CARTONS & OUVRAGES
65	TEXTILE YARN,FABRICS,ETC				97.1		119.0			FILS,TISSUS,ARTICLES TEXTILE
66	NONMETAL MINERAL MFS NES				59.1		72.1			ART MIN NON METALLIQUES
67	IRON AND STEEL				303.0		429.0			FER ET ACIER
682	COPPER EXC CEMENT COPPER				42.1		55.1			CUIVRE
684	ALUMINIUM				47.1		46.1			ALUMINIUM
69	METAL MANUFACTURES NES				113.0		233.0			ART MANUFACT EN METAL NDA
7	MACHINES,TRANSPORT EQUIP				905.0		1148.0			MACHINES MATERIEL TRANSPORT
78	ROAD VEHICLES				275.0		230.0			VEHICULES ROUTIERS
821	*FURNITURE,PARTS THEREOF				27.1		24.1			MEUBLES ET PIECES
84	CLOTHING AND ACCESSORIES				35.1		37.1			VETEMENTS
851	*FOOTWEAR				20.1		20.1			CHAUSSURES

5. General Exports F.O.B. by Commodities according to the S.I.T.C. (Rev. 2) in million U.S. Dollars
Exportations Générales F.O.B. par Produits d'après la C.T.C.I. (Rév. 2) en millions de Dollars E.U.

SITC CTCI	COMMODITY	1994		1995		1996		1997		PRODUIT
		QUANTITY QUANTITE	VALUE VALEUR	QUANTITY QUANTITE	VALUE VALEUR	QUANTITY QUANTITE	VALUE VALEUR	QUANTITY QUANTITE	VALUE VALEUR	
	ALL COMMODITIES				4706.8		5462.7			TOUS PRODUITS
01	MEAT AND PREPARATIONS				41.1		24.1			VIANDES ET PREPARATIONS
02	DAIRY PRODCTS,BIRDS'EGGS				90.1		121.0			PRODUITS LAITIERS,OEUFS
04	CEREALS AND PREPARATIONS				23.1		19.1			CEREALES ET PRODUITS
054	VEG ETC FRSH,SMPLY PRSVD				26.1		34.1			LEGUMES FRAIS,CONG,SECS
06	SUGAR AND PREPS,HONEY				15.1		27.1			SUCRES ET PRODUITS
11	BEVERAGES				44.1		165.0			BOISSONS
24	CORK AND WOOD				99.1		103.1			LIEGE ET BOIS
263	COTTON				14.1		26.1			COTON
268	WOOL(EXC TOPS),ANML HAIR				15.1		16.1			LAINES ET POILS
3	MINERAL FUELS ETC				548.0		670.0			COMBUSTIBLES MINERAUX LUB
51	ORGANIC CHEMICALS				163.0		136.0			PROD CHIMIQ ORGANIQUES
52	INORGANIC CHEMICALS				21.1		18.1			PROD CHIM INORGANIQUES
53	DYES,TANNING,COLOUR PROD				31.1		36.1			PROD TEINTURE,COLORANTS
541	*MEDICINAL,PHARM PRODUCT				22.1		34.1			PROD MEDICINAUX PHARMACEUT
572	*EXPLOSIVES,PYROTECH PRO				141.0		105.1			EXPLOSIFS
62	RUBBER MANUFACTURES NES				112.0		179.0			CAOUTCHOUC MANUFACTURE
64	PAPER,PAPERBOARD AND MFR				52.1		72.1			PAPIERS,CARTONS & OUVRAGES
65	TEXTILE YARN,FABRICS,ETC				382.0		287.0			FILS,TISSUS,ARTICLES TEXTILE
66	NONMETAL MINERAL MFS NES				121.0		141.0			ART MIN NON METALLIQUES
67	IRON AND STEEL				146.0		181.0			FER ET ACIER
69	METAL MANUFACTURES NES				123.0		173.0			ART MANUFACT EN METAL NDA
7	MACHINES,TRANSPORT EQUIP				1376.0		1634.0			MACHINES MATERIEL TRANSPORT
78	ROAD VEHICLES				720.0		820.0			VEHICULES ROUTIERS
792	AIRCRAFT ETC				23.1		67.1			APP NAVIGATION AERIENNE
821	*FURNITURE,PARTS THEREOF				127.0		131.0			MEUBLES ET PIECES
84	CLOTHING AND ACCESSORIES				126.0		188.0			VETEMENTS
851	*FOOTWEAR				49.1		41.1			CHAUSSURES

1. HISTORICAL SERIES, 1962–1997 SPECIAL TRADE, IMPORTS C.I.F., EXPORTS F.O.B.
SERIES HISTORIQUES, 1962–1997 COMMERCE SPECIAL, IMPORTATIONS C.A.F., EXPORTATIONS F.O.B

YEAR ANNEE	VALUE IN MILLION BELGIAN FRANCS / VALEUR EN MILLION BELGIAN FRANCS — MERCHANDISE –MARCHANDISE: IMPORTS	EXPORTS	GOLD –OR: IMPORTS	EXPORTS	CONVERSION FACTORS U.S. CENTS PER BELGIAN FRANC FACTEURS DE CONVERSION CENTS E.U. PAR BELGIAN FRANC: IMPORTS	EXPORTS	INDEX NUMBERS –INDICES — QUANTUM: IMPORTS	EXPORTS	UNIT VALUE / VALEUR UNITAIRE: IMPORTS	EXPORTS
1962	228435.00	216613.00	1030.00	650.00	2.0000	2.0000				
1963	256421.00	242012.00	1139.00	741.00	2.0000	2.0000				
1964	296511.00	280028.00	1372.00	369.00	2.0000	2.0000				
1965	325074.00	319684.00	3087.00	290.00	2.0000	2.0000				
1966	359104.00	341578.00	2367.00	407.00	2.0000	2.0000				
1967	364337.00	354132.00	3237.00	362.00	2.0000	2.0000				
1968	419758.00	408559.00	2723.00	1358.00	2.0000	2.0000				
1969	501053.00	504466.00	3881.00	1806.00	2.0000	2.0000				
1970	570647.00	579981.00	1176.00	615.00	2.0000	2.0000				
1971	629063.00	620238.00	1235.00	1131.00	2.0505	2.0525				
1972	681773.00	710980.00	779.00	1633.00	2.2719	2.2717				
1973	856129.00	870245.00	2310.00	2305.00	2.5785	2.5804				
1974	1160685.00	1099825.00	10030.00	5280.00	2.5740	2.5758				
1975	1130945.00	1056879.00			2.7225	2.7254				
1976	1368961.00	1266457.00			2.5940	2.5969				
1977	1447981.00	1344704.00			2.7913	2.7918				
1978	1526044.00	1410258.00			3.1855	3.1882				
1979	1784353.00	1661224.00			3.4140	3.4135				
1980	2100807.00	1890359.00			3.4213	3.4207	70	67	74	73
1981	2309761.00	2062316.00			2.7044	2.7011	67	67	85	80
1982	2653362.00	2393153.00			2.1949	2.1881	68	68	96	91
1983	2820865.00	2651341.00			1.9609	1.9590	67	71	104	97
1984	3195769.00	2992116.00			1.7305	1.7305	71	74	112	104
1985	3317812.00	3167691.00			1.6942	1.6971	73	77	112	106
1986	3065200.00	3070299.00			2.2422	2.2460	80	83	94	96
1987	3110099.00	3100100.00			2.6864	2.6873	88	89	88	90
1988	3393600.00	3382299.00			2.7243	2.7245	88	90	94	98
1989	3883899.00	3943099.00			2.5386	2.5385	94	94	102	106
1990	4011600.00	3944499.00			2.9994	2.9998	100	100	100	100
1991	4116300.00	4023399.00			2.9410	2.9417	104	104	99	98
1992	4023300.00	3969799.00			3.1107	3.1126	105	104	95	97
1993	3875000.00	4128999.00			2.8968	2.8947	106	111	91	95
1994	4192000.00	4579000.00			2.9971	2.9979	115	123	91	94
1995	4568399.00	4996100.00			3.3953	3.3951				
1996	4729098.00	5133099.00			3.2305	3.2300	135	138	96	97
1997	5554401.00	5916200.00			2.7996	2.7989	141	148	102	101

2. IMPORTS BY BROAD ECONOMIC CATEGORY AND EXPORTS BY INDUSTRIAL ORIGIN. (PERCENTAGE OF TOTAL VALUE)
IMPORTATIONS PAR CATEGORIES ECONOMIQUES ET EXPORTATIONS PAR BRANCHE D'ACTIVITE.(EN POURCENTAGE DE LA VALEUR TOTALE)

IMPORTS – IMPORTATIONS

	1991	1992	1993	1994	1995	1996	1997
TOTAL IMPORTS–IMPORTATIONS TOTALES	100.	100.	100.	100.	100.	100.	100.
1 FOOD BEV–ALIMENTATION BOISSONS	9.0	9.4	9.5	9.6	9.7	9.2	9.0
11 PRIMARY–PRODUITS DE BASE	4.4	4.4	4.3	4.4	4.2	4.2	4.3
111 FOR INDUSTRY–POUR L'INDUSTRIE	2.2	2.1	1.9	1.9	1.9	1.6	1.6
112 FOR HOUSEHOLDS–POUR LES MENAGES	2.3	2.3	2.4	2.5	2.4	2.6	2.7
12 PROCESSED–PRODUITS ELABORES	4.6	5.0	5.2	5.1	5.4	5.0	4.7
121 FOR INDUSTRY–POUR L'INDUSTRIE	0.5	0.5	0.6	0.6	0.6	0.6	0.6
122 FOR HOUSEHOLDS–POUR LES MENAGES	4.1	4.5	4.6	4.5	4.8	4.4	4.1
2 IND SUPPLIES–APPROV INDUSTRIELS	36.8	36.5	37.8	38.8	39.3	38.0	39.0
21 PRIMARY–PRODUITS DE BASE	10.0	9.7	11.0	11.1	10.6	10.6	10.5
22 PROCESSED–PRODUITS ELABORES	26.8	26.8	26.9	27.7	28.8	27.4	28.5
3 FUELS–COMBUSTIBLES	8.3	7.6	7.4	6.8	6.1	7.0	7.0
31 PRIMARY–PRODUITS DE BASE	5.5	5.0	4.6	4.0	3.6	4.3	4.6
32 PROCESSED–PRODUITS ELABORES	2.9	2.6	2.8	2.8	2.5	2.6	2.4
321 MOTOR SPIRIT–ESSENCE	0.6	0.6	0.6	0.6	0.7	0.8	0.8
322 OTHER–AUTRES	2.3	2.0	2.2	2.2	1.8	1.8	1.6
4 MACHINERY–EQUIPEMENT	13.9	14.3	12.5	12.9	13.4	14.4	14.7
41 CAPITAL EQUIPMENT–MACHINES	11.3	11.6	10.3	10.5	10.8	11.4	11.4
42 PARTS–PIECES ACCESSOIRES	2.6	2.7	2.1	2.4	2.6	3.0	3.3
5 TRANSPORT–TRANSPORT	12.8	12.1	12.9	12.9	13.3	14.4	15.3
51 PASSENGER CARS–AUTOMOBILES	5.4	5.0	5.3	5.4	5.0	5.9	6.0
52 OTHER–AUTRES	2.4	1.7	1.8	1.4	1.6	1.7	1.9
521 INDUSTRIAL–INDUSTRIELS	2.2	1.5	1.6	1.2	1.4	1.6	1.8
522 NON INDUSTRIAL–NON INDUSTRIEL	0.2	0.2	0.2	0.2	0.2	0.2	0.2
53 PARTS–PIECES ACCESSOIRES	4.9	5.4	5.9	6.1	6.7	6.8	7.4
6 CONSUM GOODS–BIENS CONSOMMATION	13.4	14.1	14.6	13.9	13.0	13.3	13.6
61 DURABLE–DURABLES	3.4	3.5	3.5	3.3	3.1	3.1	3.2
62 SEMI DURABLE–SEMI DURABLES	7.1	7.6	7.8	7.2	6.8	7.0	7.1
63 NON DURABLE–NON DURABLES	2.9	3.1	3.3	3.4	3.1	3.1	3.3
7 GOODS NES–BIENS NDA	5.7	6.0	5.3	5.2	5.1	3.7	1.3

EXPORTS – EXPORTATIONS

	1991	1992	1993	1994	1995	1996	1997
TOTAL EXPORTS–EXPORTATIONS TOTALES	100.	100.	100.	100.	100.	100.	100.
1 AGRICULTURE	2.6	2.6	2.6	2.8	2.3	2.1	2.5
2 MINING QUARRY–INDUS EXTRACTIVES	7.1	6.8	7.7	7.5	7.1	7.6	7.8
3 MANUFACTURING–IND MANUFACTUR	90.3	90.6	89.7	89.7	90.6	90.3	89.7
31 FOOD BEV TOBACCO–ALIM BOISS TAB	8.5	9.1	9.0	8.6	8.7	8.6	8.3
32 TEXTILES–INDUSTRIES TEXTILES	7.5	7.5	7.3	6.8	6.6	6.8	6.9
33 WOOD & PRODUCTS–BOIS & PRODUITS	0.9	0.9	0.8	0.8	0.8	0.8	0.8
34 PAPER & PRODUCTS–PAPIER & PRODT	2.7	2.6	2.4	2.5	2.8	2.6	2.4
35 CHEMICALS–INDUSTRIES CHIMIQUES	21.0	21.4	22.0	23.1	22.0	22.3	22.6
36 NON METAL MIN–MIN NON METAL	2.2	2.4	2.3	2.3	2.2	2.1	1.9
37 BASIC METAL–IND METAL BASE	10.3	9.2	8.2	8.6	8.9	7.6	7.6
38 METAL MANUF–MANUF METAL	32.0	32.4	32.6	33.1	32.4	33.6	33.0
39 OTH MANUF IND–AUTRES MANUF	5.0	5.1	5.1	4.0	6.3	6.0	6.2

3. TRADE BY PRINCIPAL COUNTRIES OF ORIGIN AND DESTINATION (VALUE IN MILLION U.S. DOLLARS)
ECHANGES SELON LES PRINCIPAUX PAYS D'ORIGINE ET DE DESTINATION (VALEUR EN MILLIONS DE DOLLARS EU)

COUNTRIES–PAYS	SPECIAL IMPORTS C.I.F. IMPORTATIONS SPECIALES C.A.F				
	1993	1994	1995	1996	1997
World	111305.9	125615.6	153388.4	157996.2	152106.1
Africa	3878.2	4066.8	5304.4	5514.8	5084.9
Americas	7948.0	9331.0	11890.2	12964.1	15166.1
– Northern America	6435.8	7381.3	9603.5	10417.3	12413.2
– LAIA	1265.4	1676.9	1966.0	1999.7	2257.6
– CACM	48.0	67.8	70.7	234.6	237.8
– Caribbean	153.2	167.7	228.5	279.3	189.3
– Rest of America	45.7	37.3	21.5	33.3	68.3
Asia excl fmr USSR	9113.3	10388.7	11834.5	12324.7	13612.0
– Middle East	507.1	693.9	727.7	772.3	816.1
Asia former USSR	35.2	73.3	136.0	111.2	197.0
Europe excl fmr USSR	88479.1	98490.0	120382.2	123616.1	114763.1
– European Union	84740.4	94256.0	115229.1	118571.7	109850.6
– Eastern Europe	707.1	1174.6	1594.5	1614.0	1745.5
– Rest of Europe	3031.5	3059.4	3558.7	3430.4	3166.9
Europe former USSR	1248.9	1652.8	1589.5	1552.8	1712.3
Oceania	406.1	457.6	515.8	643.0	876.3
Other	197.1	1155.4	1735.6	1269.5	694.4
Germany/Allemagne	23962.8	25331.7	32001.8	31281.3	28270.7
Netherlands/Pays–Bas	19780.4	22146.9	27160.4	29210.5	27097.4
France, Monaco	17958.0	20178.0	23486.8	23825.7	21375.8
United Kingdom	10330.3	11806.4	13540.8	14347.5	13836.6
USA/Etats–Unis d'Amer	5973.4	6639.7	8576.9	9564.0	11483.0
Italy/Italie	4899.5	5381.2	6544.4	6645.0	5920.4
Japan/Japon	3064.5	3383.0	3945.5	3750.6	3593.9
Sweden/Suède	2049.9	2877.1	4043.4	4129.3	3866.4
Spain/Espagne	1847.5	2094.8	2694.1	2904.8	2663.2
Switzerland,Liechtenst.	2161.1	1977.5	2154.6	1972.5	1751.2
Ireland/Irlande	1177.2	1292.3	1745.9	2289.0	2610.5
Russian Federation	1127.6	1431.3	1346.6	1263.3	1397.2
China/Chine	429.3	1199.6	1325.5	1545.7	1971.7
Israel/Israël	918.5	929.4	1085.8	1255.7	1426.4
India/Inde	787.4	940.6	1117.1	1202.8	1181.9
Norway,Svalbard and JM	709.1	889.6	1134.6	1191.8	1128.0
Finland/Finlande	573.5	801.2	1243.1	999.8	968.5
Denmark/Danemark	686.8	789.0	997.2	943.5	862.2
Austria/Autriche	741.6	755.6	870.5	960.2	911.3
Canada	462.3	741.4	1026.4	853.1	930.1
So. African Customs Un	653.2	626.0	819.1	857.1	882.9
Special Categories	126.2	197.2	1563.7	1198.8	627.3
Portugal	578.8	645.6	708.1	836.4	846.6
Brazil/Brésil	486.5	623.7	762.2	763.6	892.4
Thailand/Thaïlande	587.2	654.9	681.1	725.4	838.8
Dem Rep of the Congo	419.1	651.5	692.2	706.6	569.6
Algeria/Algérie	474.4	387.3	475.5	473.1	605.1
Poland/Pologne	270.6	434.3	571.6	512.1	517.4
Indonesia/Indonésie	269.4	400.1	407.4	538.6	672.4
Liberia/Libéria	291.4	317.0	759.4	531.3	329.8
China, Hong Kong SAR	847.5	274.7	344.2	314.9	434.8
Malaysia/Malaisie	274.0	375.1	495.8	450.5	510.2
Congo	326.8	248.7	436.2	617.0	460.9
Other Asia n.e.s.	352.3	357.4	393.9	427.6	505.2
Australia/Australie	298.3	316.4	349.5	453.2	576.6
Turkey/Turquie	238.8	310.1	381.3	413.1	473.1
Korea, Republic of	235.3	293.3	352.2	377.2	441.9
Hungary/Hongrie	181.9	264.4	397.0	414.8	432.9
Tunisia/Tunisie	225.6	251.2	365.5	422.9	374.6
Czech Republic	124.6	230.9	298.1	374.5	424.1

COUNTRIES–PAYS	SPECIAL EXPORTS F.O.B. EXPORTATIONS SPECIALES F.O.B.				
	1993	1994	1995	1996	1997
Monde	120861.9	137269.9	168153.7	168343.6	166040.9
Afrique	2639.7	2829.3	3433.4	3273.3	3426.2
Amériques	7441.7	9042.0	8983.4	9176.6	10681.4
– Amérique du Nord	6166.0	7456.1	6734.6	7440.0	8623.5
– ALAI	1014.5	1355.7	1928.3	1530.5	1789.7
– MCAC	64.6	63.0	60.9	58.4	59.4
– Caraïbes	153.7	117.8	204.3	109.2	148.0
– Autre Amérique	43.0	49.4	55.4	38.5	60.7
Asie anc. URSS exclus	12950.1	14299.0	16209.5	15876.9	16320.0
– Moyen–Orient	2687.5	2365.1	2758.0	2820.4	3158.6
Asie ancienne URSS	43.1	48.9	62.1	162.7	146.4
Europe anc. URSS exclus	96020.2	108822.9	127174.0	127960.7	128363.3
– Union Européenne	91342.0	103341.4	120830.9	121376.9	121467.3
– Europe de l'Est	1333.9	1697.6	2313.6	2614.9	3021.2
– Autre de l'Europe	3344.3	3783.9	4029.5	3968.9	3874.9
Europe ancienne URSS	713.1	984.5	1388.3	1696.9	2109.2
Océanie	470.6	597.4	722.6	690.2	736.2
Autre	583.4	645.9	10180.3	9506.4	4258.2
Germany/Allemagne	25358.5	28773.4	34715.8	33014.7	30808.3
France, Monaco	23024.2	26068.3	29229.9	28964.0	26825.0
Netherlands/Pays–Bas	15852.3	18069.5	21499.4	21841.8	20079.4
United Kingdom	10238.5	11605.1	13179.8	14873.8	16393.8
Italy/Italie	6608.6	7084.2	8532.2	8520.8	8517.7
USA/Etats–Unis d'Amer	5708.0	6887.6	6248.8	6964.4	8075.2
Spain/Espagne	3484.0	4148.4	4680.8	4915.0	4975.7
Special Categories	113.3	110.4	9544.7	8765.8	3606.5
Switzerland,Liechtenst.	2549.3	2838.2	2973.0	2841.0	2775.0
Israel/Israël	2344.8	2647.9	2838.7	2942.3	3141.1
India/Inde	1837.9	1863.0	2580.6	2461.7	2826.7
Sweden/Suède	1509.5	1820.6	2297.2	2265.9	2365.2
Japan/Japon	1360.7	1805.7	2178.9	2132.6	1737.2
Austria/Autriche	1396.2	1427.3	1671.2	1700.6	1740.1
Denmark/Danemark	1124.9	1276.9	1535.2	1455.2	1440.8
China, Hong Kong SAR	1008.4	1204.0	1179.1	1230.3	1375.2
Portugal	1071.1	1115.3	1178.1	1237.7	1191.7
Russian Federation	579.5	752.9	1041.8	1272.0	1537.6
Poland/Pologne	554.9	656.0	926.6	1119.5	1336.3
Turkey/Turquie	686.0	546.3	922.4	1144.3	1291.1
European Union n.e.s.					4584.7
Greece/Grèce	717.4	810.4	872.6	967.7	880.7
China/Chine	711.6	929.1	903.1	702.6	700.9
Finland/Finlande	518.6	574.4	826.5	958.3	969.1
Thailand/Thaïlande	586.7	651.2	824.1	827.2	540.6
Other Asia n.e.s.	578.9	772.7	723.0	522.0	535.0
Norway,Svalbard and JM	556.5	632.0	663.4	630.2	628.1
Saudi Arabia	766.1	649.9	555.7	512.2	517.2
Ireland/Irlande	438.1	567.6	612.2	661.4	694.9
Bunkers, ship stores	450.1	443.8	629.1	735.9	649.7
Brazil/Brésil	223.0	375.6	969.4	584.2	728.7
Singapore/Singapour	465.0	558.6	581.9	532.2	655.3
Australia/Australie	382.2	477.2	596.0	556.8	588.6
So. African Customs Un	385.5	545.5	549.5	554.5	551.1
Canada	452.9	565.5	483.0	474.2	547.6
Czech Republic	283.1	429.3	553.8	641.0	614.4
Korea, Republic of	425.5	521.0	493.6	516.2	494.0
Hungary/Hongrie	319.2	383.9	421.8	450.0	650.2
Tunisia/Tunisie	283.0	293.6	373.9	362.1	353.5
Algeria/Algérie	277.3	314.8	313.6	266.9	328.5

(VALUE AS PERCENTAGE OF WORLD TOTAL)(VALEURS EN POURCENTAGE DU TOTAL MONDIAL)

	1988	1989	1990	1991	1992	1993	1994	1995	1996	1997
Africa	4.1	4.7	4.0	3.8	3.9	3.5	3.2	3.5	3.5	3.3
Americas	6.7	7.1	6.7	6.9	6.3	7.1	7.4	7.8	8.2	10.0
– Northern America	5.0	5.3	5.0	5.3	4.9	5.8	5.9	6.3	6.6	8.2
– LAIA	1.6	1.6	1.5	1.4	1.3	1.1	1.3	1.3	1.3	1.5
– CACM	0.0	0.0	0.0	0.0	0.0	0.0	0.1	0.0	0.1	0.2
– Caribbean	0.1	0.1	0.1	0.1	0.1	0.1	0.1	0.1	0.2	0.1
– Rest of America	0.0	0.0	0.0	0.0	0.0	0.0	0.0	0.0	0.0	0.0
Asia excl fmr USSR	7.5	8.2	7.3	7.8	7.8	8.2	8.3	7.7	7.8	8.9
– Middle East	1.8	2.3	1.7	2.0	1.9	0.5	0.6	0.5	0.5	0.5
Asia former USSR					0.0	0.0	0.1	0.1	0.1	0.1
Europe excl fmr USSR	79.7	78.0	80.2	80.0	80.5	79.5	78.4	78.5	78.2	75.4
– European Union	76.4	74.8	76.8	76.5	76.8	76.1	75.0	75.1	75.0	72.2
– Eastern Europe	0.7	0.6	0.6	0.6	0.6	0.6	0.9	1.0	1.0	1.1
– Rest of Europe	2.6	2.6	2.8	3.0	3.1	2.7	2.4	2.3	2.2	2.1
Europe former USSR	1.4	1.2	1.2	1.1	1.0	1.1	1.3	1.0	1.0	1.1
Oceania	0.6	0.7	0.5	0.4	0.4	0.4	0.4	0.3	0.4	0.6
Other	0.1	0.1	0.1	0.1	0.1	0.2	0.9	1.1	0.8	0.5
Germany/Allemagne				23.5	23.9	21.5	20.2	20.9	19.8	18.6
Netherlands/Pays–Bas	17.8	17.6	17.6	17.2	17.5	17.8	17.6	17.7	18.5	17.8
France, Monaco	15.1	14.9	15.9	15.8	16.5	16.1	16.1	15.3	15.1	14.1
United Kingdom	7.7	7.9	8.3	8.4	7.7	9.3	9.4	8.8	9.1	9.1
USA/Etats–Unis d'Amer	4.3	4.6	4.5	4.8	4.4	5.4	5.3	5.6	6.1	7.5
Italy/Italie	4.3	4.2	4.5	4.5	4.5	4.4	4.3	4.3	4.2	3.9
Japan/Japon	2.3	2.3	2.1	2.2	2.2	2.8	2.7	2.6	2.4	2.4
Sweden/Suède	2.2	2.1	2.2	2.4	2.0	1.8	2.3	2.6	2.6	2.5
Spain/Espagne	1.5	1.4	1.3	1.5	1.6	1.7	1.7	1.8	1.8	1.8
Switzerland,Liechtenst.	1.8	1.6	1.6	1.5	1.7	1.9	1.6	1.4	1.2	1.2

	1988	1989	1990	1991	1992	1993	1994	1995	1996	1997
Afrique	2.4	2.5	2.5	2.4	2.3	2.2	2.1	2.0	1.9	2.1
Amériques	6.2	6.1	5.5	5.0	5.1	6.2	6.6	5.3	5.5	6.4
– Amérique du Nord	5.4	5.3	4.8	4.1	4.2	5.1	5.4	4.0	4.4	5.2
– ALAI	0.6	0.6	0.6	0.7	0.8	0.8	1.0	1.1	0.9	1.1
– MCAC	0.0	0.0	0.0	0.0	0.0	0.1	0.0	0.0	0.0	0.0
– Caraïbes	0.1	0.1	0.1	0.1	0.1	0.1	0.1	0.1	0.1	0.1
– Autre Amérique	0.0	0.0	0.0	0.0	0.0	0.0	0.0	0.0	0.0	0.0
Asie anc. URSS exclus	8.6	9.0	8.5	9.1	9.2	10.7	10.4	9.6	9.4	9.8
– Moyen–Orient	1.6	1.6	1.7	2.1	2.2	2.2	1.7	1.6	1.7	1.9
Asie ancienne URSS					0.0	0.0	0.0	0.0	0.1	0.1
Europe anc. URSS exclus	81.4	80.7	81.9	82.0	82.0	79.4	79.3	75.6	76.0	77.3
– Union Européenne	77.6	76.9	78.5	78.3	78.1	75.6	75.3	71.9	72.1	73.2
– Europe de l'Est	0.7	0.7	0.6	0.8	1.0	1.1	1.2	1.4	1.6	1.8
– Autre de l'Europe	3.1	3.1	2.9	2.9	2.9	2.8	2.8	2.4	2.4	2.3
Europe ancienne URSS	0.5	0.5	0.4	0.4	0.4	0.6	0.7	0.8	1.0	1.3
Océanie	0.4	0.4	0.4	0.3	0.3	0.4	0.4	0.4	0.4	0.4
Autre	0.7	0.7	0.8	0.8	0.7	0.5	0.5	6.1	5.6	2.6
Germany/Allemagne				23.7	22.8	21.0	21.0	20.6	19.6	18.6
France, Monaco	19.9	20.4	20.2	19.1	19.3	19.1	19.0	17.4	17.2	16.2
Netherlands/Pays–Bas	14.9	13.7	13.6	13.7	13.7	13.1	13.2	12.8	13.0	12.1
United Kingdom	9.4	9.4	8.7	7.7	7.8	8.5	8.5	7.8	8.8	9.9
Italy/Italie	6.1	6.4	6.6	6.0	5.9	5.5	5.2	5.1	5.1	5.1
USA/Etats–Unis d'Amer	4.9	4.8	4.3	3.8	3.9	4.7	5.0	3.7	4.1	4.9
Spain/Espagne	2.2	2.4	2.4	2.6	2.8	2.9	3.0	2.8	2.9	3.0
Special Categories	0.1	0.2	0.2	0.2	0.1	0.1	0.1	5.7	5.2	2.2
Switzerland,Liechtenst.	2.3	2.3	2.1	2.2	2.2	2.1	2.1	1.8	1.7	1.7
Israel/Israël	1.6	1.5	1.5	1.6	1.9	1.9	1.9	1.7	1.7	1.9

4. Special Imports C.I.F. by Commodities according to the S.I.T.C. (Rev. 2) in million U.S. Dollars
Importations Spéciales C.A.F. par Produits d'après la C.T.C.I. (Rév. 2) en millions de Dollars E.U.

SITC CTCI	COMMODITY	1994 QUANTITY QUANTITE	1994 VALUE VALEUR	1995 QUANTITY QUANTITE	1995 VALUE VALEUR	1996 QUANTITY QUANTITE	1996 VALUE VALEUR	1997 QUANTITY QUANTITE	1997 VALUE VALEUR	PRODUIT
	ALL COMMODITIES		125615.7		153388.4		157996.3		152106.2	TOUS PRODUITS
0	FOOD AND LIVE ANIMALS		11082.0		13756.1		13478.8		12559.1	ALIMENTS,ANIMAUX VIVANTS
001	*LIVE ANIMALS FOR FOOD	W 248812	407.2	W 230362	385.5	W 227317	374.3		296.9	ANIMAUX VIVANTS
01	MEAT AND PREPARATIONS		941.6		1057.4		1137.7		1090.9	VIANDES ET PREPARATIONS
011	MEAT FRESH,CHILLD,FROZEN	W 287689	746.4	W 281973	809.2	W 307784	862.5	W 375927	836.8	VIANDES FRAICHES,REF,CONGE
02	DAIRY PRODCTS,BIRDS'EGGS		1988.1		2835.4		2267.5		1946.2	PRODUITS LAITIERS,OEUFS
022	MILK AND CREAM	W 687728	805.0	W 951946	1456.8	W 828270	991.5	W 863582	776.3	LAIT ET CREME
0223	MILK AND CREAM FRESH	W 496381	442.8	W 616318	582.8	W 599878	562.0	W 665338	480.1	LAIT,CREME FRAIS
0224	MILK,CREAM PRESERVED ETC	W 191347	362.3	W 335628	874.1	W 228392	429.6	W 198245	296.2	LAIT,CREME CONS,CONC
02243	MILK DRY,OVER 1.5% FAT	W 66043	200.2	W 135334	484.6	W 71735	218.2	W 53776	135.7	LAIT POUDRE SUP 1.5%
023	BUTTER	W 113839	362.5	W 108655	476.7	W 97770	388.9	W 103729	378.6	BEURRE
024	CHEESE AND CURD	W 174573	756.5	W 176035	842.1	W 181067	818.9	W 186598	718.0	FROMAGE ET CAILLEBOTTE
03	FISH AND PREPARATIONS		808.3		925.1		890.8		802.6	POISSONS ET PREPARATIONS
04	CEREALS AND PREPARATIONS		1763.1		2286.6		2296.3		1876.9	CEREALES ET PRODUITS
041	WHEAT ETC UNMILLED	W 1895057	365.9	W 2818671	583.5	W 2733877	553.1	W 2838614	499.3	FROMENT,EPEAUTRE
0412	OTHER WHEAT ETC UNMILLED	W 1558647	292.8	W 2395145	475.4	W 2287337	445.1	W 2271165	367.4	AUTRE FROMENT NON MOULU
048	CEREAL ETC PREPARATIONS	W 489835	609.4	W 515546	728.7	W 519022	770.8	W 565855	692.9	PREPTNS A BASE CEREALES
05	VEGETABLES AND FRUIT		2217.8		2556.5		2978.7		3140.2	LEGUMES ET FRUITS
054	VEG ETC FRSH,SMPLY PRSVD	W 2879218	812.3	W 2609575	963.6	W 2748252	904.4	W 2927636	777.0	LEGUMES FRAIS,CONG,SECS
057	FRUIT,NUTS,FRESH,DRIED	W 928239	825.1	W 808501	885.7	W 1390203	1302.1	W 1993919	1627.6	FRUITS FRAIS OU SECS
0573	BANANA,PLANTAIN,FRSH,DRY	W 243962	156.1	W 165832	140.8	W 374355	329.5	W 800037	487.1	BANANES FRAICHES,SECHEES
058	FRUIT PRESERVED,PREPARED	W 365389	372.4	W 420952	467.8	W 528534	562.9	W 598020	542.3	CONSERVES DE FRUITS
06	SUGAR AND PREPS,HONEY		419.0		685.9		669.7		714.9	SUCRES ET PRODUITS
061	SUGAR AND HONEY	W 644097	329.3	W 900411	568.4	W 873743	550.3	W 1126442	614.6	SUCRES ET MIEL
0612	REFINED SUGAR ETC	W 323437	239.0	W 515590	437.8	W 540266	434.9	W 769169	510.8	SUCRES RAFFINES
07	COFFEE,TEA,COCOA,SPICES		967.4		1293.0		1114.0		1073.7	CAFE,THE,CACAO,EPICES
071	COFFEE AND SUBSTITUTES	W 129305	421.8	W 138173	610.8	W 148255	469.2	W 146758	505.4	CAFE ET SUCCEDANES
0711	COFFEE GREEN,ROASTED,SUB	W 121508	381.5	W 130862	561.0	W 140588	423.0	W 139587	461.8	CAFE TORREFIE OU DECAFEINE
081	*FEEDING STUFF FOR ANIML	W 4092173	983.3	W 4161698	1088.3	W 4185674	1120.1	W 4084160	1063.3	NOURRITURE POUR ANIMAUX
0819	FOOD WASTE AND FEED NES	W 1615326	532.5	W 1720562	638.5	W 1864837	628.5	W 1823847	566.0	DECHETS,ALIMENTS NDA
08199	FODDER NES,INCL SWEETNED	W 793922	435.1	W 825818	517.1	W 933179	514.0	W 995592	481.2	PREPARATIONS FOURRAGERES
09	MISC EDIBLE PRODUCTS		586.8		642.6		630.1		553.8	PREP ALIMENTAIRES DIVERSES
098	EDIBLE PRODCTS,PREPS NES	W 206931	507.2	W 217820	570.3	W 225530	554.0	W 225100	481.0	PREP ALIMENTAIRES NDA
1	BEVERAGES AND TOBACCO		1629.3		1912.8		1883.3		1732.7	BOISSONS ET TABACS
11	BEVERAGES		1236.7		1459.9		1417.6		1232.9	BOISSONS
112	ALCOHOLIC BEVERAGES	W 357609	899.8	W 364458	1054.1	W 403894	1047.9	W 396082	948.8	BOISSONS ALCOOLIQUES
1121	WINE OF FRESH GRAPES ETC	W 254743	648.4	W 255792	772.8	W 262177	750.0	W 252875	665.1	VINS DE RAISINS FRAIS
11212	WINE OF FRESH GRAPES	W 232578	619.7	W 231868	736.7	W 235349	708.9	W 228162	629.9	VINS DE MOUTS DE RAISINS
12	TOBACCO AND MANUFACTURES		392.7		452.9		465.8		499.9	TABACS BRUTS FABRIQUES
2	CRUDE MATERLS,EXCL FUELS		6434.6		7758.6		7046.4		6957.3	MAT BRUTES NON COMESTIBLES
22	OIL SEEDS,OLEAGINOUS FRT		649.9		694.7		713.2		724.0	GRAINES,FRUITS OLEAGINEUX
222	SEEDS FOR'SOFT'FIXED OIL		587.3	W 2221086	622.9	W 2111353	623.2	W 2183584	630.2	GRAINES HUILES FIXES
23	RUBBER, CRUDE		383.7		540.1		494.9		520.9	CAOUTCHOUC BRUT
233	RUBBER,SYNTHTIC,RECLAIMD	W 265080	320.0	W 306487	455.8	W 304691	433.9	W 374416	461.4	LATEX CAOUTCH SYNTH REGEN
2331	SYNTHETIC RUBBER ETC	W 244521	314.3	W 281651	448.6	W 286169	427.6	W 360482	458.0	LATEX CAOUTCH SYNTHETIQUE
24	CORK AND WOOD		819.3		916.3		797.9		764.9	LIEGE ET BOIS
248	WOOD SHAPED,SLEEPERS	W 1118779	601.2	W 1143306	669.2	W 1237500	593.6	W 1322985	570.2	BOIS SIMPLEMENT TRAVAILLES
251	*PULP AND WASTE PAPER	W 647982	295.6	W 703054	476.7	W 783192	328.2	W 781066	285.7	PATES A PAPIER,DECHETS
26	TEXTILE FIBRES AND WASTE		662.0		692.0		616.5		590.3	FIBRES TEXTILES
27	CRUDE FERTLZR,MINRLS NES		864.9		893.5		900.2		863.0	ENGRAIS MINERAUX BRUTS
28	METALLIFEROUS ORES,SCRAP		2259.4		2985.1		2625.5		2646.8	MINERAIS METAL,DECHETS
281	IRON ORE,CONCENTRATES	MW 17011	395.4	MW 15331	398.4	MW 12996	333.7	MW 11161	275.2	MINERAIS DE FER
282	IRON AND STEEL SCRAP	W 2990241	520.6	W 3741418	835.9	W 3960126	658.0	W 4001848	668.1	FERRAILLES
287	BASE METAL ORES,CONC NES	W 974448	469.6	W 956678	645.2	W 1817490	639.1	W 1939905	781.6	MINERAIS METAUX COMMUNS
2875	ZINC ORES,CONCENTRATES	W 520721	149.6	W 553969	177.0	W 1393376	381.1	W 1605860	566.0	MINERAIS DE ZINC
288	NONFERR METAL SCRAP NES	W 746757	672.3	W 724133	881.3	W 702677	736.9	W 753436	716.2	DECHETS NON FERREUX
2882	OTHER BASE MTL SCRAP NES	W 466608	470.6	W 431614	632.2	W 375383	475.5	W 388704	502.3	AUTRES DECHETS
29	CRUDE ANIMAL,VEG MAT NES		407.8		469.2		479.0		477.2	MATIERES BRUTES ANIM,VEGET
3	MINERAL FUELS ETC		8641.3		9489.6		11222.1		10858.2	COMBUSTIBLES MINERAUX LUB
32	COAL,COKE AND BRIQUETTES		965.5		993.7		873.9		799.3	HOUILLES,COKES,BRIQUETTES
322	COAL,LIGNITE AND PEAT	MW 13870	742.4	MW 13745	777.9	MW 12946	737.0	MW 13395	730.1	HOUILLES,LIGNITES,TOURBE
3222	OTH COAL,NOT AGGLOMERATD	MW 12392	608.2	MW 12036	627.6	MW 11371	590.6	MW 11863	608.7	AUTRES HOUILLES
33	PETROLEUM AND PRODUCTS		5999.5		6577.8		8271.1		7763.3	PETROLE ET DERIVES
333	CRUDE PETROLEUM	MW 26349	3032.3	MW 25797	3286.0	MW 29308	4387.2	MW 32327	4317.6	HUILES BRUTES DE PETROLE
334	PETROLEUM PRODUCTS,REFIN	MW 18863	2793.5	MW 18463	3102.2	MW 19414	3671.8	MW 18122	3253.5	PRODUITS RAFFINES
3341	GASOLINE,OTH LIGHT OILS	W 4559186	759.3	W 6015786	1088.4	W 6494276	1334.2	W 6040985	1220.1	ESSENCES POUR MOTEURS
33419	OTH LIGHT PETROLEUM OILS	W 3250352	534.7	W 4682058	841.6	W 5195501	1054.8	W 4945394	985.5	AUTRES HUILES LEGERES
3343	GAS OILS	W 6640029	996.7	W 6510560	1042.3	W 15048	2.4	W 56304	11.0	GAS OILS
3344	FUEL OILS,NES	W 6595288	635.9	W 4743855	505.2	MW 11839	1884.4	MW 10857	1551.3	FUEL OILS
341	*GAS,NATURAL AND MANUFCT	MW 10762	1232.0	MW 11505	1468.3	MW 12591	1726.0	MW 13019	1928.8	GAZ NATUREL,GAZ MANUFACT
3413	PETROLM GASES,LIQUEFIED	W 4111044	522.1	W 4439551	629.2	W 4207498	691.7	W 4970610	925.0	GAZ DE PETROLE LIQUEFIE
34139	OTH HYDROCARBON GAS LQFD	W 3540722	438.3	W 3954384	533.2	W 3664763	576.7	W 4295223	781.9	HYDROCARBURES GAZEUX NDA
3414	PETROLEUM GASES, GASEOUS	W 6626042	705.5	W 7058438	832.4	W 8371417	1028.5	W 7972716	999.4	GAZ DE PETROLE GAZEUX
351	*ELECTRIC CURRENT	MH 11817	444.4		450.1		351.3		367.0	ENERGIE ELECTRIQUE
4	ANIMAL,VEGETABLE OIL,FAT		606.5		742.3		707.7		762.7	HUILES,GRAISSES ANIM,VEG
42	FIXED VEGETABLE OIL,FAT		370.3		423.0		438.6		503.3	HUILES VEGETALES FIXES
5	CHEMCLS,RELATED PROD NES		16283.0		20597.0		21447.1		22230.2	PRODUITS CHIMIQUES
51	ORGANIC CHEMICALS		4999.6		6295.7		6782.8		7155.0	PROD CHIMIQ ORGANIQUES
511	HYDROCARBONS NES,DERIVS	W 3926201	1640.1	W 3290840	1727.2	W 3778599	1642.6	W 4327686	1987.6	HYDROCARBURES NDA
5111	ACYCLIC HYDROCARBONS	W 1662623	587.5	W 1520920	766.1	W 1560671	700.1	W 1710387	838.5	HYDROCARBURES ACYCLIQUES
51111	ETHYLENE	W 1065813	388.8	W 958558	490.3	W 989450	463.2	W 1034410	529.9	ETHYLENE
5112	CYCLIC HYDROCARBONS	W 1530354	640.0	W 1623805	784.3	W 2014517	744.3	W 2470531	974.6	HYDROCARBURES CYCLIQUES
512	ALCOHOLS,PHENOLS ETC	W 772100	523.4	W 666154	573.6	W 868722	614.3	W 873307	650.9	PHENOLS,PHENOLS–ALCOOLS
5121	ACYCLIC ALCOHOLS,DERIVS	W 576295	350.9	W 555360	428.1	W 727858	465.6	W 736025	509.6	ALCOOLS ACYCLIQUES
513	CARBOXYLIC ACIDS ETC	W 749774	737.7	W 748049	1029.7	W 894598	1061.7	W 1059366	1111.6	ACIDES CARBOXYLIQUES
5137	MONOACIDS AND DERIVATIVS	W 444465	377.0	W 509456	587.6	W 561575	578.4	W 694893	681.0	ACIDES MONOCARBOXYLIQUES
514	NITROGEN–FNCTN COMPOUNDS	W 270312	764.3	W 316090	1076.6	W 359193	1227.5	W 407682	1319.6	COMPOSES FONCT AZOTEES
5148	OTH NITROGN–FNCTN CMPNDS	W 113129	369.7	W 122252	580.9	W 129140	587.8	W 137356	655.0	AUTRES COMPOSES AZOTES
515	ORG–INORG COMPOUNDS ETC	W 128348	762.4	W 185779	1209.7	W 207077	1574.6	W 188172	1430.5	COMPOSES ORGANO–MINERAUX
5156	HETEROCYCLIC CMPDS ETC	W 65648	567.4	W 125106	966.2	W 118787	1230.1	W 127251	1250.8	COMPOSES HETEROCYCLIQUES
51569	OTH HETEROCYC CMPDS,ETC	W 26221	492.6	W 61317	827.3	W 61614	1106.6	W 63522	1116.5	AUT COMP HETEROCYCLIQUES
516	OTHER ORGANIC CHEMICALS	W 652790	572.0	W 606502	679.1	W 592261	662.3	W 598488	654.9	AUTRES PROD ORGANIQUES
52	INORGANIC CHEMICALS		955.6		1198.3		1202.3		1474.8	PROD CHIM INORGANIQUES
522	INORG ELEMNTS,OXIDES,ETC	W 2452325	493.3	W 2423947	635.6	W 3247189	651.3	W 3128316	604.7	ELEMENTS INORGANIQUES
523	OTHR INORG CHEMICALS ETC	W 959275	424.9	W 1222161	522.3	W 1428966	507.4	W 1186816	483.8	AUT PRODUITS CHIMIQUES INORG
53	DYES,TANNING,COLOUR PROD		860.8		1098.3		1108.8		1189.0	PROD TEINTURE,COLORANTS
533	PIGMENTS,PAINTS,ETC	W 243182	567.9	W 270190	752.2	W 283917	764.9	W 405618	841.4	PIGMENTS,PEINTURES,VERNIS
541	*MEDICINAL,PHARM PRODUCT		2569.1	MK 60938	3128.4		3453.4	MK 79652	3541.0	PROD MEDICINAUX PHARMACEUT
5416	GLYCOSIDES,GLANDS,SERA	K 2398400	334.1	K 2097062	404.1	K 1785264	484.2	K 2084959	412.9	HETEROSIDES
5417	MEDICAMENTS	MK 36435	1673.7	MK 46545	1987.1	MK 50185	2096.9	MK 62144	2279.7	MEDICAMENTS
54179	— CONTNG OTH SUBSTANCES	MK 31387	1269.5	MK 42047	1555.2	MK 44688	1571.7	MK 56434	1758.1	MED CONT AUT SUBSTANCES

4. Special Imports C.I.F. by Commodities according to the S.I.T.C. (Rev. 2) in million U.S. Dollars
Importations Spéciales C.A.F. par Produits d'après la C.T.C.I. (Rév. 2) en millions de Dollars E.U.

SITC CTCI	COMMODITY	1994 QUANTITY QUANTITE	1994 VALUE VALEUR	1995 QUANTITY QUANTITE	1995 VALUE VALEUR	1996 QUANTITY QUANTITE	1996 VALUE VALEUR	1997 QUANTITY QUANTITE	1997 VALUE VALEUR	PRODUIT
55	PERFUME,CLEANING ETC PRD		1171.3		1285.2		1285.9		1129.3	PROD POUR PARFUM,TOILETTE
553	PERFUMERY,COSMETICS,ETC	W 74030	559.5	W 73703	578.6	W 74751	567.7	W 78178	501.1	PRODUITS DE PARFUMERIE
554	SOAP,CLEANSING ETC PREPS	W 421859	519.5	W 424180	604.4	W 423907	598.1	W 408774	521.8	SAVONS,PRODUITS DETERSIFS
5542	WASHING PREPARATIONS ETC	W 387558	451.1	W 385500	521.0	W 383151	513.5	W 370242	453.2	PROD ORG TENSIO–ACT NDA
562	*FERTILIZERS,MANUFACTURE	W 3371643	416.9	W 3509985	516.9	W 3526910	532.2	W 3431738	430.6	ENGRAIS MANUFACTURES
58	PLASTIC MATERIALS ETC		3641.6		5039.5		4972.1		5353.1	MAT PLAST ARTIFICIELLES
582	PROD OF CONDENSATION ETC	W 652760	1046.7	W 714844	1565.3	W 756683	1526.7	W 975722	1607.2	PROD CONDENS,POLYCOND
5823	ALKYDS,OTHER POLYESTERS	W 161835	338.3	W 195253	552.4	W 206351	475.7	W 279222	483.3	ALKYDES ET AUT POLYESTERS
583	POLYMERIZATION ETC PRODS	W 2147179	2466.6	W 2200854	3303.8	W 2441662	3274.0	W 2792638	3587.9	PROD POLYMERISATION
5831	POLYETHYLENE	W 759853	600.6	W 751346	811.6	W 800762	750.5	W 913533	848.4	POLYETHYLENE
58311	— IN PRIMARY FORMS	W 680828	488.0	W 653815	649.0	W 685287	576.8	W 790083	675.7	POLYETHYLENE PRIMAIRES
5832	POLYPROPYLENE	W 453779	451.7	W 473087	655.2	W 509240	606.5	W 525651	577.3	POLYPROPYLENE
58321	— IN PRIMARY FORMS	W 400397	297.4	W 425534	466.5	W 456067	414.0	W 472888	400.1	POLYPROPYLENE PRIMAIRES
5839	OTH POLYMRZTION ETC PROD	W 352920	687.8	W 420730	887.7	W 486218	998.1	W 660007	1245.9	AUT PROD POLYMER COPOLYM
59	CHEMICAL MATERIALS NES		1656.5		2021.6		2090.8		1944.7	MAT PROD CHIMIQUES NDA
598	MISCEL CHEM PRODUCTS NES	W 825516	1115.3	W 876795	1411.7	W 942249	1487.0	W 1051449	1370.4	PROD DIV INDUST CHIM NDA
5989	CHEM PRODUCTS,PREPS NES	W 638805	837.2	W 635225	1044.2	W 672610	1066.8	W 797746	1013.5	PROD PREP CHIMIQUES NDA
59899	OTH CHEM PRODS,PREPS,NES	W 517540	570.4	W 517974	732.5	W 532293	753.0	W 640608	739.9	AUT PRODUITS CHIMIQUES NDA
6	BASIC MANUFACTURES		28464.1		34790.6		34525.1		33089.3	ART MANUFACTURES
62	RUBBER MANUFACTURES NES		1108.9		1297.7		1365.5		1258.5	CAOUTCHOUC MANUFACTURE
625	RUBBER TYRES, TUBES ETC	W 166180	711.4	W 165388	772.6	W 167499	763.3	W 166222	669.0	PNEUS CAOUTCHOUC VULCANISE
6251	TYRES NEW FOR MOTOR CARS	W 81608	407.7	W 73478	402.3	W 84589	440.8	W 86289	396.9	PNEUS POUR VOITURES
63	WOOD,CORK MANUFACTRS NES		655.0		762.0		757.7		740.3	OUVRAGES LIEGE ET BOIS
635	WOOD MANUFACTURES NES	W 281560	361.8	W 276688	432.2	W 306856	447.5	W 374711	458.4	ART MANUF EN BOIS NDA
64	PAPER,PAPERBOARD AND MFR		3027.2		4116.4		3676.9		3286.4	PAPIERS,CARTONS & OUVRAGES
641	PAPER AND PAPERBOARD	W 2606002	2156.5	W 2765422	3016.1	W 2786626	2657.7	W 3040657	2404.0	PAPIERS ET CARTONS
6412	PRINTG,WRITING PAPER NES	W 689227	616.6	W 694229	854.7	W 631102	684.0	W 878747	735.6	PAPIERS POUR L'IMPRESSION
64122	— COATED,IMPREGNATD ETC	W 576618	499.2	W 566915	676.1	W 504315	528.1	W 714839	580.3	PAPIERS IMPRESSION COUCHES
6415	PAPER,PAPERBRD,BULK,NES	W 892312	604.6	W 1029202	942.4	W 1043169	769.4	W 1067519	654.1	PAPIERS,CARTONS ROULEAUX
64159	OTHER PAPER ETC,BULK,NES	W 849841	573.6	W 969037	890.2	W 977249	725.4	W 1001834	612.8	AUT PAPIER ROULEAUX FEUILLES
6418	COATED ETC PAPER NES BLK	W 269986	441.3	W 286953	557.4	W 311693	572.7	W 302320	502.2	PAP,CARTONS COUCHES,ENDUITS
642	PAPER,ETC,PRECUT,ARTS OF	W 476888	870.7	W 454533	1100.4	W 449488	1019.2	W 512037	882.5	PAP,CARTONS DECOUPES
6428	PAPER ETC ARTICLES NES	W 165923	414.4	W 157791	506.2	W 156705	447.7	W 145525	361.1	OUVRAGES EN PATE A PAPIER
65	TEXTILE YARN,FABRICS,ETC		3637.4		4168.1		3949.4		4001.7	FILS,TISSUS,ARTICLES TEXTILE
651	TEXTILE YARN	W 467280	1431.2	W 455342	1625.7	W 411372	1421.3	W 561691	1469.5	FILS TEXTILES
6514	SYN FIB YRN,BULK,MONOFIL	W 176368	646.7	W 158681	718.5	W 160561	655.4	W 174270	653.8	FILS CONT 85% FIB TEXT SYNTH
652	COTTON FABRICS,WOVEN	W 66952	435.9	W 58328	486.5	W 75070	557.7	W 91493	584.3	TISSUS DE COTON
653	WOVN MAN–MADE FIB FABRIC	W 63434	434.6	W 57695	496.0	W 57921	456.5	W 69319	450.8	TISSUS FIBRES SYNTH,ARTIF
657	SPECIAL TXTL FABRC,PRODS	W 74558	393.5	W 72842	468.2	W 73356	460.8	W 88625	491.2	TISSUS SPECIAUX
66	NONMETAL MINERAL MFS NES		10776.9		12449.6		13435.8		12727.6	ART MIN NON METALLIQUES
662	CLAY,REFRACTORY BLDG PRD	W 821096	404.7	W 843153	465.1	W 764098	397.6	W 723434	334.6	MAT CONST REFRACTAIRES
663	MINERAL MANUFCTURES NES	W 1077508	394.8	W 1168195	495.9	W 1208664	480.9	W 1192468	430.0	ART MIN MANUF NDA
664	GLASS	W 318975	307.2	W 316226	395.0	W 370017	442.8	W 384077	469.7	VERRE
667	PEARL,PREC–,SEMI–P STONE		8994.2		10304.1		11384.7		10842.0	PERLES, PIERRES GEMMES
6672	DIAMONDS NONINDUST,UNSET		8955.5		10261.5		11340.2		10792.7	DIAMANTS BRUTS
66721	— ROUGH,UNSORTED		628.7		665.0		604.6		205.1	DIAMANTS BRUTS NON TRIES
66722	— SRTD,ROUGH,SIMPLY WKD		4808.1		5701.3		6400.8		6476.1	DIAMANTS TRIES BRUTS
66729	— CUT ETC NOT SET		3518.7		3895.3		4334.9		4111.6	DIAMANTS TAILLES
67	IRON AND STEEL		3674.3		4956.2		4557.8		4402.0	FER ET ACIER
672	IRON,STEEL PRIMARY FORMS	W 1960253	934.5	W 2361730	1338.5	W 2460213	1463.2	W 3841012	1531.7	LINGOTS FER,ACIER
6725	IRN,STL BLOOMS,SLABS,ETC	W 1391541	521.9	W 1664329	727.4	W 1743034	783.6	W 2853428	919.9	BLOOMS,BILLETTES FER ACIER
67251	IRN,SMPLE STL BLOOMS,ETC	W 1171834	310.2	W 1421286	454.9	W 1475995	440.4	W 2613955	654.4	BLOOMS ETC NON ACIER FIN
6727	IRN,STL COIL FR REROLLNG	W 555374	394.8	W 669667	585.0	W 692712	653.7	W 959789	603.2	EBAUCHES POUR TOLES FER
67274	STNLESS STEEL ETC COILS	W 220021	270.2	W 295932	414.6	W 282257	507.6	W 293194	388.6	EBAUCHES ACIER INOXYDBLE
673	IRON,STEEL SHAPES ETC	W 1515126	665.6	W 1604877	863.2	W 1471718	676.7	W 1549587	638.8	BARRES,PROFIL FER,ACIER
674	IRN,STL UNIV,PLATE,SHEET	W 1860227	1153.1	W 2021455	1546.5	W 1948488	1345.1	W 2120840	1234.2	LARGES PLATS,TOLES
6746	IRN,STL THIN PLATE,ROLLD	W 692245	399.1	W 574440	454.0	W 577354	386.1	W 636965	366.2	TOLES LAM MOINS 3MM
6749	OTH IRN,STL PLATES,SHEET	W 512688	378.5	W 623874	519.2	W 682248	496.9	W 751892	463.1	AUTRES TOLES FER,ACIER
67491	— OF IRON OR SIMPLE STL	W 496522	354.1	W 619133	501.2	W 672161	474.0	W 737367	443.0	AUT TOLES AUTRES ACIER FIN
678	IRON,STL TUBES,PIPES,ETC	W 350240	408.8	W 396397	554.4	W 437201	522.3	W 491881	522.2	TUBES,TUYAUX EN FONTE,FER
68	NON–FERROUS METALS		2686.5		3496.9		3130.6		3188.7	METAUX NON FERREUX
682	COPPER EXC CEMENT COPPER	W 406887	993.5	W 320817	1039.8	W 285488	795.1	W 277474	757.9	CUIVRE
6821	COPPER NES,ALLOYS,UNWRT	W 326902	721.9	W 243879	704.2	W 209590	504.8	W 208096	502.8	CUIVRE BRUT
68212	COPPER REFINED,UNWROUGHT	W 179237	390.5	W 113298	320.7	W 86557	195.9	W 106920	244.2	CUIVRE AFFINE BRUT
684	ALUMINIUM	W 550196	1098.3	W 547459	1473.7	W 539626	1284.7	W 578626	1289.6	ALUMINIUM
6841	ALUMINIUM,ALLOYS,UNWRGHT	W 370417	564.7	W 364208	760.5	W 365425	635.2	W 388334	664.3	ALUMINIUM,ALLIAGES BRUTS
6842	ALUMINIUM,ALLOYS WORKED	W 179779	533.7	W 183251	713.2	W 174200	649.6	W 190292	625.3	ALUMINIUM,ALLIAGES OUVRE
69	METAL MANUFACTURES NES		2719.1		3354.2		3466.4		3315.7	ART MANUFACT EN METAL NDA
691	STRUCTURES AND PARTS NES	W 210668	388.6	W 197510	425.6	W 220925	469.8	W 216711	362.8	CONSTRUCT FER,ACIER,ALU
695	TOOLS	W 25088	351.1	W 27300	466.1	W 25223	502.0	W 25806	471.8	OUTILS A MAIN
699	BASE METAL MFRS NES	W 298249	971.3	W 224853	1215.0	W 225532	1246.6	W 259781	1290.9	ART MANUFACTURES MET NDA
7	MACHINES,TRANSPORT EQUIP		32056.5		40259.8		44881.5		45223.9	MACHINES MATERIEL TRANSPORT
71	POWER GENERATING EQUIPMT		2138.2		2786.8		3094.2		3533.1	MACHINES GENERATRICES
713	INTRNL COMBUS PSTN ENGIN	W 134367	1520.7	W 146291	2063.1	W 166843	2350.3	W 209074	2623.4	MOTEURS EXPL COMB INT, PIECE
7132	MOTOR VEHCL PSTN ENGINS	W 99821	1108.9	W 107999	1543.8	W 123532	1794.5	W 145910	1826.8	MOTEURS EXPL POUR VEHICULES
7139	PISTON ENGINE PARTS NES	W 22707	279.9	W 26373	341.6	W 29506	363.4	W 43284	528.2	PIECES POUR 713.2,3,8
72	MACHS FOR SPCL INDUSTRYS		2409.2		2935.1		3025.6		2568.9	MAC SPECIALES POUR INDUST
724	TEXTILE,LEATHER MACHNRY	W 26853	437.6	W 28280	441.2	W 22771	409.6	W 26833	400.8	MACH POUR INDUSTRIE TEXTILE
728	OTH MACHY FOR SPCL INDUS	W 70381	722.6	W 87524	929.6	W 60797	1000.6	W 48504	757.7	AUT MACH IND PARTICULIERES
7284	MACHY FOR SPCL INDUS NES	W 34785	495.7	W 62201	624.0	W 34704	690.6	W 27114	537.2	MACH SPEC IND PARTICUL.
73	METALWORKING MACHINERY		608.6		620.5		731.2		741.0	MACH TRAVAIL DES METAUX
74	GENRL INDUSTRL MACHY NES		4102.3		5210.0		5988.1		5791.5	MACH APP INDUSTRIE
741	HEATING,COOLING EQUIPMNT	W 56295	641.2	W 71452	797.6	W 83970	1084.1	W 87543	941.6	MACH CHAUFFAGE,PIECES
743	PUMPS NES,CENTRFUGES ETC	W 60168	570.1	W 70782	740.7	W 84244	949.7	W 104066	911.1	POMPES COMPRES,VENT ETC
744	MECHANICAL HANDLING EQU	W 181517	814.4	W 189552	1018.6	W 199488	1060.9	W 217909	1024.7	EQUIP MANUTENTION PIECES
7449	PTS NES OF MACHY OF 7442	W 111979	408.6	W 114526	514.7	W 114809	503.8	W 120485	509.4	PIECES DU 744.2
745	NONELEC MACHY,TOOLS NES	W 27623	595.5	W 28013	703.4	W 27767	706.4	W 27604	662.5	AUT MACH NON ELEC,PIECES
7452	OTH NONELEC MCHS,PTS NES	W 23806	434.1	W 25601	526.5	W 24014	500.0	W 24003	469.6	AUT MACH NON ELEC,PIECES
749	NONELEC MACH PTS,ACC NES	W 143603	1192.5	W 183918	1590.4	W 173143	1821.6	W 158808	1877.7	PIECES MACH NON ELEC NDA
7491	BALL,ROLLER,ETC BEARINGS	W 16092	200.1	W 35558	382.0	W 48323	547.0	W 54094	630.7	ROULEMENTS BILLES ETC
7492	COCKS,VALVES ETC NES	W 32269	464.7	W 29461	540.7	W 37836	581.1	W 32632	576.5	ART ROB,SIM POUR TUYAUX
75	OFFICE MACHNES,ADP EQUIP		2513.0		3493.9		4018.9		3794.1	MACH BUREAU TRAIT AUTOM
752	AUTOMTIC DATA PROC EQUIP	W 20607	1699.3	W 27401	2377.8	W 37714	2835.2	W 32858	2459.6	MACH TRAIT INFORMATION
7523	DIGITL CENTRL PROCESSORS	W 3259	423.8	W 3416	568.1	W 5387	620.6	W 7055	789.6	UNITES CENTRALES
7524	DIGITL CENTRL STOR UNITS	W 2415	316.6	W 3014	413.4	W 2804	557.2	W 2898	440.1	UNITES MEMOIRE CENTRALES
7525	ADP PERIPHERAL UNITS	W 10628	484.6	W 14427	647.6	W 20735	751.5	W 17687	639.2	UNITES PERIPHERIQUES
759	OFFICE,ADP MCH PTS,ACCES	W 9578	645.1	W 20194	875.1	W 14722	924.5	W 11386	1047.4	PIECES DU 751 ET 752
7599	ACCTG,ETC,ADP MCH PTS,AC	W 6007	544.6	W 6604	704.9	W 6764	777.5	W 7298	906.1	PIECES DU 751 ET 752
76	TELECOMM,SOUND EQUIPMENT		2127.8		2632.4		2790.4		3017.7	EQUIPMENT DE TELECOM
762	RADIO BROADCAST RECEIVRS	W 14742	414.2	W 15519	491.0	W 17529	546.4	W 24476	654.9	RECEPTEURS RADIODIFFUSION
764	TELECOM EQPT,PTS,ACC NES	W 31445	1158.8	W 31860	1583.1	W 33288	1609.4		1714.3	EQUIP TELECOM,PIECES

4. Special Imports C.I.F. by Commodities according to the S.I.T.C. (Rev. 2) in million U.S. Dollars
Importations Spéciales C.A.F. par Produits d'après la C.T.C.I. (Rév. 2) en millions de Dollars E.U.

SITC CTCI	COMMODITY	1994 QUANTITY QUANTITE	1994 VALUE VALEUR	1995 QUANTITY QUANTITE	1995 VALUE VALEUR	1996 QUANTITY QUANTITE	1996 VALUE VALEUR	1997 QUANTITY QUANTITE	1997 VALUE VALEUR	PRODUIT
7641	LINE TELEPHONE,ETC EQUIP	W 3319	278.2	W 4713	460.6	W 4252	446.2	W 6071	545.9	APP TELEPHON PAR FIL
7649	PTS NES OF EQUIPMT OF 76	W 11423	490.6	W 11078	640.7	W 10144	615.2	W 9646	646.3	PIECES DE LA DIV 76
77	ELECTRIC MACHNRY NES ETC		4673.0		5617.3		6311.4		6675.8	MACH APP ELECT NDA
772	SWITCHGEAR ETC,PARTS NES	W 30863	938.7	W 32948	1134.6	W 34235	1184.9	W 38827	1276.4	APP COUPURE,SECT ETC
7721	SWITCHGEAR ETC	W 29203	809.4	W 31022	994.5	W 31239	1040.5	W 35129	1034.2	APP COUPURE,SECTIONMNT
773	ELECTR DISTRIBUTNG EQUIP	W 65719	570.1	W 69410	652.9	W 77169	712.5	W 84045	765.1	EQUIPMT DISTRIBUTION ELECT
7731	INSULATED WIRE,CABLE ETC	W 59960	503.6	W 64924	588.6	W 73313	650.1	W 80244	711.6	FILS,CABLES ISOLES ELECT
775	HOUSEHOLD TYPE EQUIP NES	W 106716	825.4	W 114185	950.0	W 118888	939.0	W 110940	799.1	MACH,APP USAGE DOMESTQUE
776	TRANSISTORS,VALVES,ETC	W 22371	702.5	W 24506	882.8	W 21260	1334.9		1466.8	LAMPES,TUBES,VALVES
7764	ELECTRONIC MICROCIRCUITS	W 895	444.0	W 1711	516.9	W 1135	947.7		1128.9	MICROSTRUCTURES ELECTRON
778	ELECTRICAL MACHINERY NES	W 106395	1268.2	W 119570	1532.3	W 155322	1625.1	W 215796	1852.8	AUTRES MACH ELECT NDA
7783	AUTOMOTIVE ELECTR EQUIP	W 19776	294.6	W 19432	338.3	W 24818	417.9	W 40627	465.1	EQUIP ELECT MOTEURS EXPL
7788	OTH ELEC MACHY,EQUIP NES	W 19181	372.4	W 23146	483.9	W 23551	472.1	W 27785	572.0	AUT MACH APP ELEC NDA
78	ROAD VEHICLES		12748.8		16115.4		17652.7		17730.2	VEHICULES ROUTIERS
781	PASS MOTOR VEH EXC BUSES	W 622180	6799.1	W 612612	7631.8	W 757110	9259.1	W 804558	9114.1	AUTO TRANSPORT PERSONNES
782	LORRIES,SPCL MTR VEH NES	W 112887	619.3	W 137814	891.1	W 149646	986.4	W 174014	1150.8	VEHICULES SPECIAUX,MARCH
7821	LORRIES,TRUCKS	W 107400	590.1	W 129690	845.1	W 140019	913.3	W 161542	1078.0	VEHICULES TRANSP MARCHAND
783	ROAD MOTOR VEHICLES NES	W 55292	430.4	W 65490	628.6	W 60006	567.1	W 68971	447.7	VEHICULES ROUTIERS NDA
784	MOTOR VEH PRTS,ACCES NES	W 703202	4330.9	W 826158	6230.4	W 983658	6130.2	W 1218885	6330.1	PIECES 722,781,782,783
7849	OTHER MOTOR VEHCL PARTS	W 681541	4107.5	W 801319	5944.9	W 959235	5856.6	W 1202449	6195.2	PIECES 722,781,782,783
79	OTHR TRANSPORT EQUIPMENT		736.0		848.9		1269.5		1372.0	AUTRE MATERIEL TRANSPORT
792	AIRCRAFT ETC	W 1110	341.5	W 2194	682.1	W 2832	1046.0	W 2304	875.8	APP NAVIGATION AERIENNE
7929	AIRCRAFT PARTS NES	W 928	329.4	W 1310	408.5	W 1548	533.0	W 1556	484.3	PIECES DU 792
8	MISC MANUFACTURED GOODS		13780.7		16041.5		16921.1		16600.8	ART MANUFACTURES DIVERS
812	*PLUMBG,HEATNG,LGHTNG EQ	W 131712	509.6	W 83784	588.5	W 86658	601.0	W 96545	575.9	APPAR SANITAIRES CHAUFFAGE
821	*FURNITURE,PARTS THEREOF	W 372545	1544.3	W 347054	1886.4	W 368755	1985.1	W 404885	1883.0	MEUBLES ET PIECES
8211	CHAIRS,SEATS AND PARTS	W 121274	598.8	W 99071	756.3	W 102762	788.4	W 115101	815.0	SIEGES ET PIECES
82111	CHAIRS AND OTHER SEATS	W 54855	381.0	W 52705	434.2	W 61043	471.1	W 64505	422.6	SIEGES
8219	FURNITURE AND PARTS NES	W 237570	830.5	W 234119	989.7	W 253002	1060.3	W 276085	943.8	AUTRES MEUBLES ET PIECES
82192	WOOD FURNITURE NES	W 150188	557.2	W 152768	665.4	W 160558	699.7	W 182158	634.4	MEUBLES NDA EN BOIS
84	CLOTHING AND ACCESSORIES		3844.0		4379.4		4585.8		4480.2	VETEMENTS
842	MENS OUTERWEAR NOT KNIT	W 37950	915.7	W 37534	990.1	W 42627	1046.2	W 40179	915.6	VET DESSUS POUR HOMMES
8423	— TROUSERS,BREECHES ETC	W 26240	555.5	W 24585	558.7	W 29499	621.9	W 25782	515.8	PANTALONS HOMMES MAT TEX
843	WOMENS OUTERWEAR NONKNIT	W 24156	988.3	W 25010	1150.0	W 29484	1155.1	W 33531	1086.3	VET DESSUS FEMMES MAT TEX
8439	— OTHER OUTER GARMENTS	W 12670	398.1	W 12280	434.9	W 15966	482.4	W 19652	500.8	AUT VET DES FEM MAT TEXT
845	OUTERWEAR KNIT NONELASTC	W 149277	771.8	W 26301	842.1	W 31507	937.8	W 96467	993.9	VET DESSOUS,ACCES BONNET
8451	— JERSEYS,PULLOVERS ETC	W 74116	401.3	W 12605	423.5	W 15468	487.5	W 47028	502.3	CHANDAILS,PULL–OVERS ETC
846	UNDER GARMENTS KNITTED	W 23844	563.7	W 27046	707.5	W 31191	763.5	W 142435	787.9	SOUS VETS DE BONNETERIE
8462	— OF COTTON NON ELASTIC	W 19353	386.7	W 22037	483.6	W 25666	526.6	W 112412	529.6	SOUS–VET BONNET COTON
84629	—— OTHER	W 19353	386.7	W 22037	483.6	W 25666	526.6	W 112412	529.6	AUT SOUS–VET BONNET COTON
851	*FOOTWEAR	W 41921	757.2	W 42965	855.9	W 57977	1073.6	W 71923	1203.6	CHAUSSURES
85102	FOOTWEAR LEATHER	W 31385	653.9	W 32882	742.3	W 44289	907.5	W 56328	1013.4	CHAUS SEMELLES EN CUIR
87	PRECISION INSTRUMNTS NES		1382.7		1741.6		1885.8		1943.2	INSTRUM,APPAR SCIENT NDA
872	MEDICAL INSTRUMENTS NES	W 19780	539.2	W 21326	702.0	W 24581	854.0	W 29569	765.0	INSTR,APP MEDIC–CHIR NDA
87202	OTH MEDICAL INSTRUMENTS	W 18824	515.6	W 20315	671.5	W 23166	813.4	W 27973	723.2	INSTRUM,APP MEDECINE
874	MEASURNG,CONTROLNG INSTR	W 11733	712.2	W 15839	874.1	W 11884	827.3	W 15140	943.0	INSTRUMENTS DE MESURE
88	PHOTO EQU,OPTICL GDS ETC		779.0		1021.8		948.5		1058.0	APP,FOURN PHOTO,OP,MONTR
882	PHOTO,CINEMA SUPPLIES	W 30123	375.0	W 38244	519.6	W 33946	475.4	W 41617	489.9	PRODUITS PHOTO,CINEMA
89	MISC MANUFCTRD GOODS NES		4743.8		5302.8		5567.4		5171.5	ART MANUFACTURES DIVERS
892	PRINTED MATTER	W 207118	976.2	W 138599	953.4	W 136596	1012.0	W 139048	888.7	IMPRIMES
893	ARTICLES OF PLASTIC NES		1652.2		2004.4		2107.1		1950.1	OUVRAGES EN MAT DIVIS 58
8931	PLSTC PACKG CONTNRS,LIDS	W 171676	527.8	W 232408	652.7	W 200723	641.8	W 218254	635.2	ART TRANSP EMBALLAGE ETC
8939	MISC PLASTIC ARTICLES	W 206436	1033.6	W 216094	1237.4	W 243930	1365.7	W 234150	1230.5	ART DIVERS EN MAT DIV 58
89399	OTHR PLASTC ARTICLES NES	W 182584	937.7	W 194170	1129.6	W 221519	1257.1	W 212793	1137.9	AUT OUV MAT DIV 58
894	TOYS,SPORTING GOODS,ETC	W 100321	745.3	W 82434	770.0	W 86026	880.5	W 100966	886.3	VOITURES ENFANTS,JOUETS
8942	TOYS,INDOOR GAMES ETC	W 77314	604.1	W 62848	623.3	W 66920	687.7	W 79439	691.1	JOUETS,JEUX ETC
898	MUSICAL INSTRUMENTS,PTS	W 141220	606.8	W 30310	759.3	W 30649	743.1		693.7	INSTRUMENTS DE MUSIQUE
8983	SOUND RECRDNG TAPE,DISCS	W 139751	565.7	W 28632	710.0	W 28965	697.9	W 25257	656.2	SUPPORTS SON POUR 763
89832	RECORDED DISCS,TAPES ETC	W 8938	366.4	W 13008	470.1	W 10360	474.1	W 8980	439.5	DISQUES,PHONO,BANDES
899	OTHER MANUFACTURED GOODS		395.8		426.5		455.9		416.1	AUT ART MANUF DIVERS NDA
9	GOODS NOT CLASSD BY KIND		6637.9		8040.7		5883.5		2092.5	ART TRANSACT NON CLASSES
931	*SPECIAL TRANSACTIONS	W 2087686	6415.8	W 2537103	7811.5	W 1558976	5713.4	W 1155883	1932.0	TRANS.SPECIALES

5. Special Exports F.O.B. by Commodities according to the S.I.T.C. (Rev. 2) in million U.S. Dollars
Exportations Spéciales F.O.B. par Produits d'après la C.T.C.I. (Rév. 2) en millions de Dollars E.U.

SITC CTCI	COMMODITY	1994 QUANTITY QUANTITE	1994 VALUE VALEUR	1995 QUANTITY QUANTITE	1995 VALUE VALEUR	1996 QUANTITY QUANTITE	1996 VALUE VALEUR	1997 QUANTITY QUANTITE	1997 VALUE VALEUR	PRODUIT
	ALL COMMODITIES		137269.9		168153.7		168343.7		166041.0	TOUS PRODUITS
0	FOOD AND LIVE ANIMALS		12512.6		15113.2		14934.4		14741.5	ALIMENTS,ANIMAUX VIVANTS
001	*LIVE ANIMALS FOR FOOD	W 208709	458.7	W 221086	524.1	W 213397	485.1		375.7	ANIMAUX VIVANTS
01	MEAT AND PREPARATIONS		2546.6		2946.7		3142.1		2986.6	VIANDES ET PREPARATIONS
011	MEAT FRESH,CHILLD,FROZEN	W 812264	1937.0	W 884576	2253.5	W 952179	2386.9	W 1000255	2213.1	VIANDES FRAICHES,REF,CONGE
0111	BOVINE MEAT FRESH,FROZEN	W 140898	548.4	W 140824	551.7	W 145379	458.9	W 139402	428.3	VIANDES BOVIN FRAI,REF
01111	BOVINE MEAT WITH BONE IN	W 95785	427.8	W 87947	401.5	W 88639	314.9	W 88370	292.7	VIANDES BOVIN NON DESOSS
0113	PIG MEAT FRESH,CHLD,FRZN	W 433130	969.4	W 480227	1233.6	W 491305	1355.5	W 475401	1191.6	VIANDE DE PORC
014	MEAT PREPD,PRSVD,NES ETC	W 148382	506.1	W 150618	582.9	W 181471	633.2	W 237647	661.2	CONSERVES DE VIANDES
0149	OTH PREPARD,PRESRVD MEAT	W 113944	420.7	W 114724	479.0	W 132015	511.8	W 146827	496.7	AUTRES PREP DE VIANDES
02	DAIRY PRODCTS,BIRDS'EGGS		1918.9		2459.8		2196.6		1890.7	PRODUITS LAITIERS,OEUFS
022	MILK AND CREAM	W 1414592	1019.9	W 1581686	1438.1	W 1471399	1207.6	W 1325038	985.8	LAIT ET CREME
0223	MILK AND CREAM FRESH	W 1060657	529.2	W 1100199	631.3	W 1108321	624.8	W 994308	541.9	LAIT,CREME FRAIS
0224	MILK,CREAM PRESERVED ETC	W 353935	490.8	W 481487	806.8	W 363078	582.9	W 330729	443.9	LAIT,CREME CONS,CONC
024	CHEESE AND CURD	W 107516	428.8	W 114834	455.5	W 116128	462.2	W 109668	400.0	FROMAGE ET CAILLEBOTTE
04	CEREALS AND PREPARATIONS		1625.2		2042.0		2116.0		1945.0	CEREALES ET PRODUITS
048	CEREAL ETC PREPARATIONS	W 823882	998.9	W 1077484	1316.5	W 1104419	1370.7	W 1168249	1354.2	PREPTNS A BASE CEREALES
0484	BAKERY PRODUCTS	W 185417	544.3	W 209473	678.3	W 226745	697.4	W 268600	738.9	PRODUITS DE BOULANGERIE
04842	PASTRY, CAKES ETC	W 142984	449.1	W 160189	557.2	W 163480	542.7	W 167221	485.6	PATISSERIE ETC.
05	VEGETABLES AND FRUIT		2412.3		2596.2		2694.8		3339.9	LEGUMES ET FRUITS
054	VEG ETC FRSH,SMPLY PRSVD	W 2443801	1245.6	W 2362141	1414.6	W 2321518	1342.2	W 2480810	1176.3	LEGUMES FRAIS,CONG,SECS
0546	VEGETABLES SIMPLY PRESVD	W 754140	579.2	W 744426	700.4	W 817879	677.1	W 882249	612.4	LEGUMES CONG,CONSER
05461	VEGETABLES FROZEN	W 745858	569.7	W 740174	696.4	W 812529	670.6	W 877360	606.0	LEGUMES CONGELES
057	FRUIT,NUTS,FRESH,DRIED	W 671962	591.1	W 507039	484.3	W 522892	512.5	W 1398255	1319.0	FRUITS FRAIS OU SECS
058	FRUIT PRESERVED,PREPARED	W 249657	279.6	W 313228	377.8	W 406711	477.9	W 527530	540.6	CONSERVES DE FRUITS
06	SUGAR AND PREPS,HONEY		669.6		955.7		713.0		729.4	SUCRES ET PRODUITS
061	SUGAR AND HONEY	W 1138712	437.5	W 1630147	686.8	W 952104	455.9	W 1272096	507.2	SUCRES ET MIEL
0612	REFINED SUGAR ETC	W 1029061	388.6	W 1468016	591.8	W 812580	365.2	W 1155809	449.7	SUCRES RAFFINES
07	COFFEE,TEA,COCOA,SPICES		1182.9		1491.3		1455.7		1301.0	CAFE,THE,CACAO,EPICES
073	CHOCOLATE AND PRODUCTS	W 194257	827.9	W 212465	1035.6	W 237104	1080.9	W 241795	916.8	CHOCOLAT
081	*FEEDING STUFF FOR ANIML	W 2413657	682.6	W 3137095	878.8	W 3006179	913.3	W 3359863	1031.5	NOURRITURE POUR ANIMAUX
0819	FOOD WASTE AND FEED NES	W 1091941	417.8	W 1346324	527.9	W 1288282	524.1	W 1529052	603.3	DECHETS,ALIMENTS NDA
08199	FODDER NES,INCL SWEETNED	W 791794	400.0	W 1055660	510.7	W 990687	504.4	W 1151176	584.5	PREPARATIONS FOURRAGERES
09	MISC EDIBLE PRODUCTS		756.7		927.6		891.0		836.9	PREP ALIMENTAIRES DIVERSES
098	EDIBLE PRODCTS,PREPS NES	W 266643	558.8	W 309461	635.4	W 276736	621.2	W 295088	593.7	PREP ALIMENTAIRES NDA
1	BEVERAGES AND TOBACCO		1230.3		1339.9		1359.9		1307.6	BOISSONS ET TABACS
11	BEVERAGES		764.3		958.2		928.2		835.5	BOISSONS
112	ALCOHOLIC BEVERAGES	W 638255	460.7	W 692989	593.8	W 594672	560.8	W 561022	481.3	BOISSONS ALCOOLIQUES
12	TOBACCO AND MANUFACTURES		466.1		381.7		431.7		472.1	TABACS BRUTS FABRIQUES
2	CRUDE MATERLS,EXCL FUELS		3158.3		3679.1		3433.6		3578.0	MAT BRUTES NON COMESTIBLES
23	RUBBER, CRUDE		469.0		238.1		234.4		249.1	CAOUTCHOUC BRUT
233	RUBBER,SYNTHTIC,RECLAIMD	W 288957	467.2	W 99190	236.6	W 110885	232.1	W 138923	246.2	LATEX CAOUTCH SYNTH REGEN
26	TEXTILE FIBRES AND WASTE		563.3		609.8		496.1		474.9	FIBRES TEXTILES
27	CRUDE FERTLZR,MINRLS NES		552.2		625.4		605.9		608.8	ENGRAIS MINERAUX BRUTS
28	METALLIFEROUS ORES,SCRAP		550.4		890.7		915.3		1104.3	MINERAIS METAL,DECHETS
287	BASE METAL ORES,CONC NES		134.0	W 477105	308.2	W 1166309	422.5	W 1266467	554.4	MINERAIS METAUX COMMUNS
29	CRUDE ANIMAL,VEG MAT NES		413.3		487.2		484.5		486.8	MATIERES BRUTES ANIM,VEGET
3	MINERAL FUELS ETC		4210.2		4467.4		5463.8		5125.6	COMBUSTIBLES MINERAUX LUB
33	PETROLEUM AND PRODUCTS		3837.8		4011.5		4996.2		4519.8	PETROLE ET DERIVES
334	PETROLEUM PRODUCTS,REFIN	MW 22545	3526.3	MW 20840	3665.6	MW 23944	4651.5	MW 22768	4112.4	PRODUITS RAFFINES
3341	GASOLINE,OTH LIGHT OILS	W 6270784	1121.5	W 5548732	1054.5	W 6138377	1316.9	W 5762323	1222.0	ESSENCES POUR MOTEURS
33411	MOTOR,AVIATION SPIRIT	W 4337809	762.0	W 3663349	659.6	W 4499420	928.5	W 4193002	835.9	ESSENCES MOTEURS D'AVIONS
3343	GAS OILS	W 5004383	792.0	W 5508327	911.2	W 602	0.2	W 73597	13.1	GAS OILS
3344	FUEL OILS,NES	MW 9637	920.0	W 8403836	937.9	MW 16099	2457.7	MW 15404	2070.2	FUEL OILS
3345	LUBS,PETROLEUM OILS NES	W 578933	481.4	W 554303	585.6	W 571215	597.2	W 608375	581.2	HUILES LUBRIFIANTES
33451	LUBS(HIGH PETR CONT) ETC	W 556918	428.2	W 534458	514.3	W 546647	513.0	W 572490	473.5	HUILES LUBRIF,H LOURDES
4	ANIMAL,VEGETABLE OIL,FAT		528.7		739.4		684.0		772.0	HUILES,GRAISSES ANIM,VEG
42	FIXED VEGETABLE OIL,FAT		412.7		594.6		546.7		619.6	HUILES VEGETALES FIXES
5	CHEMCLS,RELATED PROD NES		22934.0		26781.9		26428.9		27353.6	PRODUITS CHIMIQUES
51	ORGANIC CHEMICALS		5297.1		4795.7		4853.2		5714.5	PROD CHIMIQ ORGANIQUES
511	HYDROCARBONS NES,DERIVS	W 2023982	883.5	W 1959035	1142.8	W 1975864	898.9	W 1740045	878.6	HYDROCARBURES NDA
512	ALCOHOLS,PHENOLS ETC	W 563906	347.4	W 683158	543.8	W 712704	492.2	W 955317	632.9	PHENOLS,PHENOLS-ALCOOLS
513	CARBOXYLIC ACIDS ETC		1147.2	W 380146	646.6	W 735626	970.0	W 959379	1021.4	ACIDES CARBOXYLIQUES
5137	MONOACIDS AND DERIVATIVS	W 308703	359.7	W 347770	507.3	W 526584	677.8	W 640669	694.0	ACIDES MONOCARBOXYLIQUES
5139	OXY–FNCT ACIDS,DERIVATVS	W 793527	744.0	W 10652	97.0	W 8686	139.5	W 12694	98.4	ACIDES CARBOXYLIQUES
514	NITROGEN–FNCTN COMPOUNDS	W 436065	1013.3	W 375226	1091.5	W 402144	1077.3	W 499651	1514.8	COMPOSES FONCT AZOTEES
5148	OTH NITROGN–FNCTN CMPNDS	W 162707	528.[illegible]	W 153735	695.2	W 179752	641.2	W 192896	874.4	AUTRES COMPOSES AZOTES
51482	IMIDE–,IMIDE–FNCT CMPNDS	W 36229	281.1	W 36246	419.3	W 35044	318.9	W 40538	574.2	COMPOSES A FONCTION IMIDE
515	ORG–INORG COMPOUNDS ETC		1493.6	W 124807	826.7	W 127252	886.7	W 178544	1080.5	COMPOSES ORGANO–MINERAUX
5156	HETEROCYCLIC CMPDS ETC		481.5	W 74734	621.2	W 78514	665.6	W 96253	750.4	COMPOSES HETEROCYCLIQUES
51569	OTH HETEROCYC CMPDS,ETC		452.1	W 71414	584.6	W 75512	629.8	W 84933	701.5	AUT COMP HETEROCYCLIQUES
516	OTHER ORGANIC CHEMICALS	W 554979	412.5	W 535106	544.5	W 631522	528.3	W 772269	586.6	AUTRES PROD ORGANIQUES
52	INORGANIC CHEMICALS		1298.6		943.6		749.4		748.8	PROD CHIM INORGANIQUES
522	INORG ELEMNTS,OXIDES,ETC	W 4010462	717.0	W 3418092	625.4	W 3348074	468.4	W 3406602	455.6	ELEMENTS INORGANIQUES
523	OTHR INORG CHEMICALS ETC	W 1558265	534.8	W 510674	263.1	W 543953	227.3	W 715874	244.2	AUT PRODUITS CHIMIQUES INORG
53	DYES,TANNING,COLOUR PROD		1373.3		1616.0		1690.4		1670.6	PROD TEINTURE,COLORANTS
533	PIGMENTS,PAINTS,ETC	W 429808	1057.1	W 442554	1259.2	W 455194	1299.2	W 522831	1304.3	PIGMENTS,PEINTURES,VERNIS
5331	COLOURING MATERIAL NES	W 225354	432.3	W 241154	549.5	W 246048	523.1	W 286860	521.3	AUT MATIERES COLORANTES
541	*MEDICINAL,PHARM PRODUCT		3333.1	MK 70788	4120.6		4301.6	MK 79787	4809.7	PROD MEDICINAUX PHARMACEUT
5416	GLYCOSIDES,GLANDS,SERA	K 1854200	786.3	K 4479819	958.1	K 2367997	834.2	K 3144277	961.5	HETEROSIDES
54164	ANTISERA,MICROB VACCINES	K 1606300	780.2	K 3934356	944.0	K 2024889	736.7	K 2102782	850.1	SERUMS,VACCINS
5417	MEDICAMENTS	MK 44210	2248.8	MK 60187	2776.7	MK 49178	2997.9	MK 68629	3220.2	MEDICAMENTS
54171	— CONTAINNG ANTIBIOTICS	K 6112100	459.6	K 7401778	564.9	K 7348747	611.4	K 7891722	671.1	MED CONTN ANTIBIOTIQUES
54179	— CONTNG OTH SUBSTANCES	MK 35135	1539.0	MK 49572	1957.1	MK 38918	2123.7	MK 57218	2262.0	MED CONT AUT SUBSTANCES
55	PERFUME,CLEANING ETC PRD		1458.9		1771.8		1776.6		1704.8	PROD POUR PARFUM,TOILETTE
553	PERFUMERY,COSMETICS,ETC	W 107242	656.9	W 104534	698.8	W 100352	680.3	W 104823	596.3	PRODUITS DE PARFUMERIE
554	SOAP,CLEANSING ETC PREPS	W 567276	753.7	W 617409	987.8	W 696938	1006.0	W 798838	1012.3	SAVONS,PRODUITS DETERSIFS
5542	WASHING PREPARATIONS ETC	W 520170	685.3	W 578741	910.9	W 655703	937.2	W 755779	949.6	PROD ORG TENSIO–ACT NDA
562	*FERTILIZERS,MANUFACTURE	W 5783359	634.0	W 5727278	799.5	W 5949203	853.8	W 6046739	749.2	ENGRAIS MANUFACTURES
58	PLASTIC MATERIALS ETC		6959.1		9484.5		8914.4		9436.4	MAT PLAST ARTIFICIELLES
582	PROD OF CONDENSATION ETC	W 832237	1786.1	W 893897	2482.8	W 888292	2375.5	W 987170	2284.8	PROD CONDENS,POLYCOND
5823	ALKYDS,OTHER POLYESTERS	W 163044	535.7	W 187845	778.4	W 172439	670.6	W 198682	657.9	ALKYDES ET AUT POLYESTERS
5829	OTH CONDNSATION,ETC PROD	W 356517	490.8	W 372187	693.9	W 373459	695.7	W 426926	684.3	AUT PROD CONDENSATION
583	POLYMERIZATION ETC PRODS	W 4811992	5062.4	W 4691015	6835.5	W 5113400	6370.3	W 5860988	6988.8	PROD POLYMERISATION
5831	POLYETHYLENE	W 1770442	1524.4	W 1675184	2038.7	W 1803278	1808.2	W 2043964	2025.8	POLYETHYLENE
58311	— IN PRIMARY FORMS	W 1581138	1246.8	W 1488456	1682.7	W 1601079	1493.3	W 1818371	1719.5	POLYETHYLENE PRIMAIRES
5832	POLYPROPYLENE	W 1038512	1036.5	W 1028364	1476.1	W 1061813	1255.6	W 1156043	1281.9	POLYPROPYLENE
58321	— IN PRIMARY FORMS	W 907731	661.8	W 891607	937.8	W 921498	783.2	W 1014347	850.2	POLYPROPYLENE PRIMAIRES
58322	— PLATES,FILM,STRIP,ETC	W 130782	374.7	W 136757	538.4	W 140316	472.4	W 141696	431.7	POLYPROPYLENE PLAQUES
5833	POLYSTYRENE,ITS COPOLYMR	W 671545	695.8	W 651417	923.9	W 732894	821.9	W 890267	909.8	POLYPROPYLENE COPOLYMERES
58331	— IN PRIMARY FORMS	W 627101	611.7	W 614921	816.2	W 697665	731.2	W 857621	835.6	SOUS FORMES PRIMAIRES

5. Special Exports F.O.B. by Commodities according to the S.I.T.C. (Rev. 2) in million U.S. Dollars
Exportations Spéciales F.O.B. par Produits d'après la C.T.C.I. (Rév. 2) en millions de Dollars E.U.

SITC CTCI	COMMODITY	1994 QUANTITY QUANTITE	1994 VALUE VALEUR	1995 QUANTITY QUANTITE	1995 VALUE VALEUR	1996 QUANTITY QUANTITE	1996 VALUE VALEUR	1997 QUANTITY QUANTITE	1997 VALUE VALEUR	PRODUIT
5834	POLYVINYL CHLORIDE	W 398692	402.5	W 390678	513.4	W 470234	450.8	W 525890	499.1	CHLORURE DE POLYVINYLE
5839	OTH POLYMRZTION ETC PROD	W 883364	1269.2	W 887729	1687.4	W 972449	1803.8	W 1163683	2020.3	AUT PROD POLYMER COPOLYM
59	CHEMICAL MATERIALS NES		2557.3		3227.6		3271.7		2499.4	MAT PROD CHIMIQUES NDA
591	PESTICIDES,DISINFECTANTS	W 112374	698.3	W 143215	935.2	W 152586	1010.8	W 78158	380.1	DESINF,INSECT,FONG,HERB
5913	HERBICIDES,FOR RETAIL	W 69720	522.0	W 96980	708.5	W 105836	766.9	W 32692	145.0	HERBICIDES VENTE AU DET
598	MISCEL CHEM PRODUCTS NES	W 2425112	1605.2	W 2269542	1970.3	W 1639660	1937.4	W 1612459	1798.7	PROD DIV INDUST CHIM NDA
5989	CHEM PRODUCTS,PREPS NES	W 2152260	1153.7	W 1980114	1428.5	W 1347844	1387.4	W 1302549	1247.3	PROD PREP CHIMIQUES NDA
59899	OTH CHEM PRODS,PREPS,NES	W 2056362	835.6	W 1846567	1082.5	W 1234996	1050.2	W 1170722	947.3	AUT PRODUITS CHIMIQUES NDA
6	BASIC MANUFACTURES		37561.2		45807.8		43520.9		41913.6	ART MANUFACTURES
62	RUBBER MANUFACTURES NES		1117.8		1401.4		1335.5		1252.4	CAOUTCHOUC MANUFACTURE
625	RUBBER TYRES, TUBES ETC	W 170765	626.5	W 197552	806.6	W 185219	733.8	W 192879	671.9	PNEUS CAOUTCHOUC VULCANISE
63	WOOD,CORK MANUFACTRS NES		918.7		1153.0		1102.5		1077.3	OUVRAGES LIEGE ET BOIS
634	VENEERS,PLYWOOD,ETC	W 1338680	524.0	W 1297492	629.5	W 1436262	596.6	W 1429228	533.8	PLACAGES,CONTRE-PLAQUES
635	WOOD MANUFACTURES NES	W 305451	391.7	W 313701	518.3	W 325057	501.9	W 398474	540.5	ART MANUF EN BOIS NDA
64	PAPER,PAPERBOARD AND MFR		2255.8		3286.0		3109.5		2904.2	PAPIERS,CARTONS & OUVRAGES
641	PAPER AND PAPERBOARD	W 1323388	1383.4	W 1559961	2089.4	W 1684396	1947.6	W 2118267	1923.6	PAPIERS ET CARTONS
6412	PRINTG,WRITING PAPER NES	W 646548	571.4	W 794027	953.3	W 801090	800.8	W 1068719	894.0	PAPIERS POUR L'IMPRESSION
64122	— COATED,IMPREGNATD ETC	W 623305	536.6	W 733829	855.8	W 741407	718.1	W 978825	806.2	PAPIERS IMPRESSION COUCHES
642	PAPER,ETC,PRECUT,ARTS OF	W 476781	872.5	W 538212	1196.7	W 566671	1162.0	W 540566	980.6	PAP,CARTONS DECOUPES
65	TEXTILE YARN,FABRICS,ETC		6816.7		7887.6		7439.9		7008.0	FILS,TISSUS,ARTICLES TEXTILE
651	TEXTILE YARN	W 327475	1205.0	W 332985	1371.4	W 273632	1122.9	W 307744	1055.5	FILS TEXTILES
652	COTTON FABRICS,WOVEN	W 72946	588.7	W 74272	737.1	W 83270	800.6	W 108502	854.4	TISSUS DE COTON
6522	WOVEN COTTON BLEACHD,ETC	W 58113	509.1	W 58111	643.5	W 61769	676.1	W 66063	631.0	TISSUS COTON BLANCHIS ETC
653	WOVN MAN-MADE FIB FABRIC	W 98047	1013.0	W 99258	1129.6	W 110560	1122.6	W 121108	1061.1	TISSUS FIBRES SYNTH,ARTIF
657	SPECIAL TXTL FABRC,PRODS		924.1	W 148644	1177.6	W 140661	1087.1	W 134254	946.1	TISSUS SPECIAUX
6573	COATED ETC TEXTILES NES	W 60571	483.1	W 66490	587.2	W 67995	578.8	W 55891	470.5	TISSUS,ART MATIERE TEXT NDA
659	FLOOR COVERINGS,ETC	W 788754	2417.3	W 778036	2680.3	W 802137	2552.8	W 543766	2340.6	COUVRE-PARQUETS,TAPIS ETC
6595	MAN-MADE TXTL CARPTS NES	W 604671	1870.3	W 599059	2059.3	W 615161	1954.5	W 399288	1824.1	TAPIS MAT TEXT SYNT ARTIF
65951	— TUFTED	W 455708	1329.6	W 456927	1486.9	W 468782	1405.7	W 309396	1292.7	TAPIS MAT TEXT SYNT TOUFFT
65952	— WOVEN	W 148963	540.8	W 142132	572.5	W 146379	548.8	W 89892	531.4	TAPIS MAT TEXT SYNT TISSES
66	NONMETAL MINERAL MFS NES		12354.9		14224.0		14721.3		14396.3	ART MIN NON METALLIQUES
661	LIME,CEMENT,BLDG PRODS	W 5217687	524.7	W 4119926	517.1	W 4205099	485.3	W 4143379	455.8	CHAUX,CIMENTS MAT CONSTR
663	MINERAL MANUFCTURES NES	W 1671998	558.4	W 1748202	704.2	W 1808611	646.9	W 1820366	602.6	ART MIN MANUF NDA
664	GLASS	W 1686266	1274.5	W 1710615	1502.8	W 1780509	1464.0	W 1601404	1333.8	VERRE
6644	GLASS SURFACE-GROUND ETC	W 982264	436.6	W 973126	520.4	W 1000813	446.8	W 815982	333.1	VERRE COULE,LAMINE
667	PEARL,PREC-,SEMI-P STONE		9361.4		10735.1		11405.4		11336.9	PERLES, PIERRES GEMMES
6672	DIAMONDS NONINDUST,UNSET		9325.5		10698.3		11366.1		11287.5	DIAMANTS BRUTS
66722	— SRTD,ROUGH,SIMPLY WKD		4916.5		5819.2		6220.4		6191.5	DIAMANTS TRIES BRUTS
66729	— CUT ETC NOT SET		4408.9		4878.6		5144.4		5082.8	DIAMANTS TAILLES
67	IRON AND STEEL		8177.4		10218.1		8914.5		8786.1	FER ET ACIER
672	IRON,STEEL PRIMARY FORMS	W 4872102	2169.2	W 4627977	2644.3	W 5174701	2432.7	W 5470843	2418.1	LINGOTS FER,ACIER
6725	IRN,STL BLOOMS,SLABS,ETC	W 1183523	520.2	W 968974	597.3	W 1056634	531.8	W 823557	524.3	BLOOMS,BILLETTES FER ACIER
6727	IRN,STL COIL FR REROLLNG	W 3670553	1634.4	W 3611548	2028.3	W 4003926	1832.8	W 4514263	1840.4	EBAUCHES POUR TOLES FER
67271	IRON,SIMPLE STEEL COILS	W 3344118	1204.2	W 3275111	1487.2	W 3660748	1340.7	W 4146314	1377.1	EBAUCHES NON EN ACIER
67274	STNLESS STEEL ETC COILS	W 315237	426.1	W 322051	534.5	W 325991	485.2	W 346724	456.4	EBAUCHES ACIER INOXYDBLE
673	IRON,STEEL SHAPES ETC	W 3489390	1384.3	W 3218509	1591.7	W 3157915	1374.4	W 3393795	1386.7	BARRES,PROFIL FER,ACIER
6733	IRON,STEEL PROFILES ETC	W 1974023	850.0	W 1840531	997.2	W 1758056	858.5	W 1860372	848.2	PROFILES,PALPLAN FER,ACIER
67332	LARGE U,I,H SECTIONS ETC	W 1311960	516.3	W 1123715	563.6	W 1094650	486.8	W 1156838	479.3	PROFILES PLUS 80MM
674	IRN,STL UNIV,PLATE,SHEET	W 5877585	3530.6	W 6273128	4995.2	W 6089743	4202.1	W 6748977	4076.8	LARGES PLATS,TOLES
6744	IRN,STL HVY PLATE,ROLLED	W 1105236	652.8	W 1174528	995.0	W 932851	709.7	W 711350	498.5	TOLES LAMINEES PLUS 4.75 MM
67441	— OF IRON OR SIMPLE STL	W 988846	419.5	W 1009611	543.1	W 810566	379.5	W 591275	244.3	TOLES NON ACIER FIN CARB
6746	IRN,STL THIN PLATE,ROLLD	W 1811949	1077.2	W 1884636	1507.4	W 1951225	1269.0	W 2201344	1246.0	TOLES LAM MOINS 3MM
67461	— OF IRON OR SIMPLE STL	W 1605222	745.7	W 1619949	915.3	W 1720392	834.1	W 1932895	833.7	TOL NON AC FIN MOINS 3 MM
67463	— OF STAINLESS ETC STL	W 145349	274.2	W 182602	506.3	W 164363	363.0	W 178102	327.5	TOL ACIER INOX MOINS 3 MM
6749	OTH IRN,STL PLATES,SHEET	W 2270377	1353.5	W 2455211	1846.2	W 2409788	1634.7	W 2951487	1775.2	AUTRES TOLES FER,ACIER
67491	— OF IRON OR SIMPLE STL	W 2254743	1330.9	W 2430105	1793.4	W 2391640	1592.6	W 2928026	1735.9	AUT TOLES AUTRES ACIER FIN
677	IRN,STL WIRE(EXCL W ROD)	W 517254	491.9	W 298760	266.2	W 306875	243.3	W 372931	247.2	FILS EN FER,ACIER
68	NON-FERROUS METALS		3451.6		4510.1		3779.8		3685.5	METAUX NON FERREUX
682	COPPER EXC CEMENT COPPER	W 544532	1453.2	W 538165	1865.3	W 476031	1367.2	W 463197	1286.8	CUIVRE
6821	COPPER NES,ALLOYS,UNWRT	W 182420	438.9	W 210921	647.7	W 155832	382.2	W 157020	377.0	CUIVRE BRUT
68212	COPPER REFINED,UNWROUGHT	W 152751	363.3	W 173527	529.2	W 130737	312.7	W 146761	345.7	CUIVRE AFFINE BRUT
6822	COPPER,ALLOYS WORKED	W 361709	1011.1	W 327244	1217.7	W 320199	985.0	W 306177	909.9	CUIVRE,ALLIAGES OUVRES
68221	COPPER BARS,WIRE,ETC	W 297413	729.4	W 258432	833.2	W 251846	637.7	W 237019	585.9	BARRES,PROFILES ET FILS
684	ALUMINIUM	W 463530	1125.2	W 482329	1564.2	W 434338	1284.9	W 495591	1366.0	ALUMINIUM
6842	ALUMINIUM,ALLOYS WORKED	W 356257	973.2	W 368155	1327.7	W 350706	1147.4	W 420390	1239.1	ALUMINIUM,ALLIAGES OUVRE
68422	ALUMNM PLATE,SHEET,STRIP	W 196492	457.6	W 191717	591.1	W 182183	493.8	W 228518	580.5	TOLES, PLANCHES EN ALU
69	METAL MANUFACTURES NES		2310.1		2957.7		2950.4		2668.4	ART MANUFACT EN METAL NDA
691	STRUCTURES AND PARTS NES	W 313985	514.6	W 366219	656.8	W 340876	650.8	W 329950	529.7	CONSTRUCT FER,ACIER,ALU
6911	STRUCTURES,PARTS IRN,STL	W 298101	420.7	W 351737	546.5	W 327181	546.9	W 318460	450.0	CONSTRUCT FER,ACIER,FONTE
699	BASE METAL MFRS NES	W 137437	618.4	W 184280	830.9	W 213944	852.0	W 239795	862.6	ART MANUFACTURES MET NDA
7	MACHINES,TRANSPORT EQUIP		38548.5		45924.5		47848.1		46914.0	MACHINES MATERIEL TRANSPORT
71	POWER GENERATING EQUIPMT		914.8		1254.0		1129.3		1427.3	MACHINES GENERATRICES
713	INTRNL COMBUS PSTN ENGIN	W 34218	431.4	W 43194	642.5	W 35474	567.7	W 44212	628.8	MOTEURS EXPL COMB INT, PIECE
72	MACHS FOR SPCL INDUSTRYS		3053.7		3675.8		3480.6		3145.2	MAC SPECIALES POUR INDUST
721	AGRIC MACHY,EXC TRACTORS	W 50014	438.0	W 57470	491.2	W 69600	595.6	W 71644	541.8	MACHINES AGRICOLES
723	CIVIL ENGNEERG EQUIP ETC	W 205456	1251.2	W 209888	1437.1	W 181761	1138.1	W 196595	1073.2	APPAREILS DE GENIE CIVIL
7234	CONST,MINING MACHNRY NES	W 202466	1235.2	W 206014	1414.0	W 177602	1109.8	W 187371	1006.0	MACH POUR LA CONST, MINES
72342	SLFPRP SHOVELS,EXCAVATRS	W 196228	1209.9	W 199028	1374.8	W 169506	1070.5	W 181200	982.8	PELLES MECANIQUES
728	OTH MACHY FOR SPCL INDUS	W 49037	616.3	W 59185	774.3	W 101553	842.1	W 67331	690.4	AUT MACH IND PARTICULIERES
7284	MACHY FOR SPCL INDUS NES	W 23189	433.7	W 25874	526.1	W 30625	574.3	W 29754	459.7	MACH SPEC IND PARTICUL.
73	METALWORKING MACHINERY		516.4		658.4		688.9		632.5	MACH TRAVAIL DES METAUX
74	GENRL INDUSTRL MACHY NES		3484.2		4562.5		5053.1		5096.8	MACH APP INDUSTRIE
741	HEATING,COOLING EQUIPMNT	W 72118	696.8	W 81851	859.4	W 90057	916.1	W 93519	901.4	MACH CHAUFFAGE,PIECES
743	PUMPS NES,CENTRFUGES ETC	W 44021	754.4	W 53350	935.6	W 57565	989.5	W 68512	985.1	POMPES COMPRES,VENT ETC
744	MECHANICAL HANDLING EQU	W 103131	707.3	W 115821	830.1	W 123094	890.4	W 150548	810.5	EQUIP MANUTENTION PIECES
7449	PTS NES OF MACHY OF 7442	W 60469	446.2	W 66579	527.3	W 61658	517.5	W 59965	460.2	PIECES DU 744.2
749	NONELEC MACH PTS,ACC NES	W 48688	831.8	W 65253	1288.4	W 81933	1567.6	W 95617	1697.3	PIECES MACH NON ELEC NDA
7491	BALL,ROLLER,ETC BEARINGS	W 5279	96.5	W 12297	231.3	W 22923	415.4	W 30083	500.5	ROULEMENTS BILLES ETC
75	OFFICE MACHNES,ADP EQUIP		1580.9		2342.8		2749.4		2611.8	MACH BUREAU TRAIT AUTOM
752	AUTOMTIC DATA PROC EQUIP	W 11629	1015.8	W 22602	1484.7	W 21100	1922.0	W 18293	1685.3	MACH TRAIT INFORMATION
7525	ADP PERIPHERAL UNITS	W 5543	357.5	W 9585	581.1	W 12916	697.3	W 9524	508.3	UNITES PERIPHERIQUES
759	OFFICE,ADP MCH PTS,ACCES	W 7392	429.9	W 11628	592.7	W 9858	615.0	W 10631	724.1	PIECES DU 751 ET 752
7599	ACCTG,ETC,ADP MCH PTS,AC	W 3689	374.8	W 4230	493.9	W 4374	490.5	W 6825	603.4	PIECES DU 751 ET 752
76	TELECOMM,SOUND EQUIPMENT		2895.6		3374.0		3442.0		3379.1	EQUIPMENT DE TELECOM
761	TELEVISION RECEIVERS	W 31673	522.5	W 31555	607.0	W 34147	772.4	W 25868	675.0	RECEPTEURS DE TELEVISION
7611	COLOUR TV RECEIVERS	W 31582	519.3	W 31393	602.9	W 33831	765.1	W 25731	671.4	RECEPTEURS COULEUR
762	RADIO BROADCAST RECEIVRS	W 9183	392.1	W 11089	526.8	W 13682	562.3	W 17321	563.0	RECEPTEURS RADIODIFFUSION
764	TELECOM EQPT,PTS,ACC NES	W 35579	1637.7	W 35851	1873.3	W 35131	1751.6		1850.8	EQUIP TELECOM,PIECES
7649	PTS NES OF EQUIPMT OF 76	W 15521	1154.5	W 15988	1191.2	W 15245	1052.7	W 16084	1101.9	PIECES DE LA DIV 76
76491	PTS NES OF APPAR OF 7641	W 5054	849.1	W 4780	772.1	W 3706	635.1	W 3027	520.1	PIECES POUR 764.1
77	ELECTRIC MACHNRY NES ETC		3782.2		4840.9		5413.0		5622.3	MACH APP ELECT NDA

5. Special Exports F.O.B. by Commodities according to the S.I.T.C. (Rev. 2) in million U.S. Dollars
Exportations Spéciales F.O.B. par Produits d'après la C.T.C.I. (Rév. 2) en millions de Dollars E.U.

SITC CTCI	COMMODITY	1994 QUANTITY QUANTITE	1994 VALUE VALEUR	1995 QUANTITY QUANTITE	1995 VALUE VALEUR	1996 QUANTITY QUANTITE	1996 VALUE VALEUR	1997 QUANTITY QUANTITE	1997 VALUE VALEUR	PRODUIT
772	SWITCHGEAR ETC,PARTS NES	W 17810	683.5	W 21046	1029.4	W 20858	963.4	W 23588	1061.1	APP COUPURE,SECT ETC
7721	SWITCHGEAR ETC	W 15194	521.8	W 18211	830.0	W 18148	771.3	W 19606	777.8	APP COUPURE,SECTIONMNT
773	ELECTR DISTRIBUTNG EQUIP	W 73071	465.8	W 79584	682.0	W 80540	611.8	W 84696	616.3	EQUIPMT DISTRIBUTION ELECT
7731	INSULATED WIRE,CABLE ETC	W 65245	328.8	W 71400	536.0	W 72310	460.6	W 76170	484.6	FILS,CABLES ISOLES ELECT
776	TRANSISTORS,VALVES,ETC	W 7737	423.6	W 8540	486.5	W 8726	1018.2		1044.7	LAMPES,TUBES,VALVES
7764	ELECTRONIC MICROCIRCUITS	W 552	327.0	W 602	338.2	W 559	817.1		821.2	MICROSTRUCTURES ELECTRON
778	ELECTRICAL MACHINERY NES	W 133257	1560.6	W 146961	1908.6	W 179138	2050.9	W 187091	2147.6	AUTRES MACH ELECT NDA
7781	BATTERIES,ACCUMULATORS	W 93095	564.2	W 99640	631.7	W 132873	676.5	W 105368	639.1	PILES ET ACCUMULATEURS
77811	PRIMARY BATTERIES,CELLS	W 51856	417.4	W 55578	468.7	W 57594	500.6	W 59194	434.0	PILES ELECTRIQUES,PIECES
7788	OTH ELEC MACHY,EQUIP NES	W 7455	283.1	W 6875	323.4	W 8689	394.3	W 13663	518.1	AUT MACH APP ELEC NDA
78	ROAD VEHICLES		21695.1		24503.9		25180.1		24045.2	VEHICULES ROUTIERS
781	PASS MOTOR VEH EXC BUSES	W 1546352	16900.9	W 1507210	18023.5	W 1579661	18740.4	W 1620957	17585.2	AUTO TRANSPORT PERSONNES
782	LORRIES,SPCL MTR VEH NES	W 180637	1380.2	W 194595	1658.6	W 194419	1502.5	W 237437	1670.4	VEHICULES SPECIAUX,MARCH
7821	LORRIES,TRUCKS	W 176536	1363.6	W 189393	1627.6	W 187773	1472.3	W 228666	1627.3	VEHICULES TRANSP MARCHAND
783	ROAD MOTOR VEHICLES NES	W 98206	998.6	W 115338	1299.5	W 118190	1285.1	W 126269	1166.3	VEHICULES ROUTIERS NDA
7831	BUSES	W 34288	474.2	W 32846	489.4	W 33733	510.8	W 34530	446.8	VOITURES TRANSPORT COMMUN
7832	TRACTORS FOR TR–TRAILERS	W 63918	524.4	W 82492	810.1	W 84457	774.3	W 91739	719.6	TRACTEURS ROUTIERS
784	MOTOR VEH PRTS,ACCES NES	W 305773	2039.5	W 371362	3074.7	W 456480	3140.2	W 466459	3082.4	PIECES 722,781,782,783
7849	OTHER MOTOR VEHCL PARTS	W 288294	1865.2	W 348086	2805.6	W 428822	2852.6	W 433612	2769.3	PIECES 722,781,782,783
79	OTHR TRANSPORT EQUIPMENT		625.9		712.7		712.0		954.2	AUTRE MATERIEL TRANSPORT
792	AIRCRAFT ETC	W 709	272.9	W 876	402.3	W 879	429.4	W 1060	507.0	APP NAVIGATION AERIENNE
8	MISC MANUFACTURED GOODS		11657.3		14471.2		15419.5		14901.2	ART MANUFACTURES DIVERS
812	*PLUMBG,HEATNG,LGHTNG EQ	W 162065	598.2	W 153960	713.7	W 166589	736.6	W 178030	671.3	APPAR SANITAIRES CHAUFFAGE
821	*FURNITURE,PARTS THEREOF	W 304996	1497.4	W 308847	1706.1	W 322279	1713.1	W 361454	1595.3	MEUBLES ET PIECES
8211	CHAIRS,SEATS AND PARTS	W 55373	464.0	W 53051	496.0	W 54717	496.8	W 60411	471.9	SIEGES ET PIECES
8219	FURNITURE AND PARTS NES	W 190551	746.6	W 198422	885.2	W 205991	878.1	W 237248	822.2	AUTRES MEUBLES ET PIECES
82192	WOOD FURNITURE NES	W 134235	576.0	W 140978	671.6	W 138077	637.5	W 161264	590.0	MEUBLES NDA EN BOIS
84	CLOTHING AND ACCESSORIES		2161.2		2722.9		3017.5		3007.9	VETEMENTS
842	MENS OUTERWEAR NOT KNIT	W 33023	766.0	W 31607	945.5	W 36546	1037.6	W 35499	863.9	VET DESSUS POUR HOMMES
8423	— TROUSERS,BREECHES ETC	W 25551	586.4	W 22494	677.6	W 26932	740.7	W 25642	623.7	PANTALONS HOMMES MAT TEX
843	WOMENS OUTERWEAR NONKNIT	W 12896	512.3	W 12849	577.8	W 13907	574.6	W 16607	579.1	VET DESSUS FEMMES MAT TEX
845	OUTERWEAR KNIT NONELASTC	W 10514	302.5	W 11883	421.7	W 15274	531.9	W 45572	620.7	VET DESSOUS,ACCES BONNET
851	*FOOTWEAR		165.7	W 12451	174.4	W 28207	814.1	W 44479	1231.5	CHAUSSURES
85102	FOOTWEAR LEATHER	W 9730	124.7	W 8783	131.9	W 20903	638.0	W 34465	1007.2	CHAUS SEMELLES EN CUIR
87	PRECISION INSTRUMNTS NES		1085.5		1498.4		1633.3		1388.0	INSTRUM,APPAR SCIENT NDA
872	MEDICAL INSTRUMENTS NES	W 18309	477.1	W 26276	759.6	W 23814	953.3	W 28302	710.5	INSTR,APP MEDIC–CHIR NDA
87202	OTH MEDICAL INSTRUMENTS	W 17792	465.3	W 25594	744.3	W 22855	935.1	W 27032	691.3	INSTRUM,APP MEDECINE
874	MEASURNG,CONTROLNG INSTR		539.4	W 16999	655.4	W 13242	597.9	W 15365	576.5	INSTRUMENTS DE MESURE
88	PHOTO EQU,OPTICL GDS ETC		1551.0		2105.0		1934.7		1735.2	APP,FOURN PHOTO,OP,MONTR
882	PHOTO,CINEMA SUPPLIES	W 123132	1292.2	W 152453	1677.9	W 133670	1475.4	W 135098	1305.1	PRODUITS PHOTO,CINEMA
8822	PHOTO FILM EXC DEV CINMA	W 59829	1122.8	W 76326	1436.4	W 61783	1236.5	W 64186	1098.7	PLAQUES,PELLICULES,FILMS
88221	PHOTO FILM FLAT UNEXPOSD	W 20923	445.3	W 26093	608.9	W 20466	516.6	W 19664	436.6	PLAQUES PHOTO,FILMS SENS
88222	PHOTO FILM ROLL UNEXPOSD	W 25055	519.9	W 30052	621.2	W 28369	574.6	W 29133	523.2	PEL SENSIB PERF OU NON
89	MISC MANUFCTRD GOODS NES		4367.2		5242.2		5251.4		4919.7	ART MANUFACTURES DIVERS
892	PRINTED MATTER		991.7	W 270899	1164.7	W 268980	1102.7	W 283228	978.6	IMPRIMES
8928	PRINTED MATTER NES	W 145211	494.3	W 136595	528.0	W 133518	528.8	W 150425	477.0	IMPRIMES NDA
893	ARTICLES OF PLASTIC NES		1878.5		2400.6		2417.4		2324.3	OUVRAGES EN MAT DIVIS 58
8931	PLSTC PACKG CONTNRS,LIDS	W 172335	420.4	W 174033	584.3	W 189927	568.9	W 212655	541.0	ART TRANSP EMBALLAGE ETC
8939	MISC PLASTIC ARTICLES	W 315057	1368.5	W 295339	1707.7	W 302416	1742.9	W 318883	1693.0	ART DIVERS EN MAT DIV 58
89399	OTHR PLASTC ARTICLES NES	W 188193	1088.4	W 198955	1375.4	W 200453	1414.4	W 217681	1399.1	AUT OUV MAT DIV 58
894	TOYS,SPORTING GOODS,ETC	W 47689	447.3	W 33825	370.9	W 38307	429.1	W 45625	434.8	VOITURES ENFANTS,JOUETS
898	MUSICAL INSTRUMENTS,PTS		552.6	W 44356	632.0	W 46966	648.8		577.6	INSTRUMENTS DE MUSIQUE
8983	SOUND RECRDNG TAPE,DISCS	W 38964	537.0	W 43926	612.4	W 46322	629.0	W 40627	560.2	SUPPORTS SON POUR 763
9	GOODS NOT CLASSD BY KIND		4929.3		9829.8		9251.1		9434.3	ART TRANSACT NON CLASSES
931	*SPECIAL TRANSACTIONS	W 3120230	4457.0	W 7718048	9468.0	W 7815338	8865.1	W 8499699	9076.5	TRANS.SPECIALES
971	*GOLD,NON MONETARY NES		436.9		312.7	K 34773	333.7	K 48415	316.4	OR NON MONETAIRE
97101	NONMON GLD UNWRT,SEMIMFD	K 48600	436.8	K 25173	311.9	K 27176	331.1	K 29746	312.9	OR,ALLIAGES D'OR BRUTS

Belize

1. HISTORICAL SERIES, 1962–1997 GENERAL TRADE, IMPORTS C.I.F., EXPORTS F.O.B.
SERIES HISTORIQUES, 1962–1997 COMMERCE GENERAL, IMPORTATIONS C.A.F., EXPORTATIONS F.O.B

YEAR ANNEE	VALUE IN MILLION BELIZE DOLLARS / VALEUR EN MILLION BELIZE DOLLARS — MERCHANDISE –MARCHANDISE		GOLD –OR		CONVERSION FACTORS U.S. CENTS PER BELIZE DOLLAR / FACTEURS DE CONVERSION CENTS E.U. PAR BELIZE DOLLAR		INDEX NUMBERS –INDICES — QUANTUM		UNIT VALUE / VALEUR UNITAIRE	
	IMPORTS	EXPORTS	IMPORTS	EXPORTS	IMPORTS	EXPORTS	IMPORTS	EXPORTS	IMPORTS	EXPORTS
1962	31.20	12.40			70.0000	70.0000				
1963	27.60	18.60			70.0000	70.0000				
1964	31.30	19.20			70.0000	70.0000				
1965	35.00	17.50			70.0000	70.0000				
1966	38.80	19.20			70.0000	70.0000				
1967	37.00	20.50			69.1500	69.1500				
1968	44.20	25.20			60.0000	60.0000				
1969	49.40	28.10			60.0000	60.0000				
1970	55.60	31.30			60.0000	60.0000				
1971	58.60	31.70			60.8600	60.8600				
1972	69.30	40.20			62.6000	62.6000				
1973	72.30	52.70			61.3042	61.3042				
1974	109.20	76.90			58.4761	58.4761				
1975	159.20	120.40			55.5952	55.5952				
1976	161.50	94.00			45.1552	45.1552				
1977	180.20	124.20			43.6378	43.6378				
1978	213.00	159.60			47.9874	47.9875				
1979	263.70	173.50			53.0379	53.0380				
1980	300.00	221.30			50.0000	50.0000				
1981	323.90	238.00			50.0000	50.0000				
1982	256.00	182.00			50.0000	50.0000				
1983	223.60	155.50			50.0000	50.0000				
1984	260.30	186.40			50.0000	50.0000				
1985	227.60	173.20			50.0000	50.0000				
1986	243.93	185.21			50.0000	50.0000				
1987	285.89	205.66			50.0000	50.0000				
1988	361.95	232.51			50.0000	50.0000				
1989	431.39	249.07			50.0000	50.0000				
1990	422.59	265.92			50.0000	50.0000				
1991	512.49	243.44			50.0000	50.0000				
1992	548.06	281.01			50.0000	50.0000				
1993	561.92	272.97			50.0000	50.0000				
1994	519.86	301.97			50.0000	50.0000				
1995	511.11	323.25			50.0000	50.0000				
1996	510.97	335.27			50.0000	50.0000				
1997	572.43	354.15			50.0000	50.0000				

2. IMPORTS BY BROAD ECONOMIC CATEGORY AND EXPORTS BY INDUSTRIAL ORIGIN. (PERCENTAGE OF TOTAL VALUE)
IMPORTATIONS PAR CATEGORIES ECONOMIQUES ET EXPORTATIONS PAR BRANCHE D'ACTIVITE.(EN POURCENTAGE DE LA VALEUR TOTALE)

IMPORTS – IMPORTATIONS

	1991	1992	1993	1994	1995	1996	1997
TOTAL IMPORTS–IMPORTATIONS TOTALES		100.	100.	100.	100.	100.	100.
1 FOOD BEV–ALIMENTATION BOISSONS		18.6	15.6	15.1	16.2	16.5	16.0
11 PRIMARY–PRODUITS DE BASE		4.0	2.6	3.2	3.4	4.3	3.6
111 FOR INDUSTRY–POUR L'INDUSTRIE		1.4	1.2	1.7	1.6	2.3	1.4
112 FOR HOUSEHOLDS–POUR LES MENAGES		2.7	1.4	1.5	1.8	2.0	2.2
12 PROCESSED–PRODUITS ELABORES		14.5	12.9	11.9	12.8	12.3	12.4
121 FOR INDUSTRY–POUR L'INDUSTRIE		0.7	0.7	0.7	0.7	0.7	0.6
122 FOR HOUSEHOLDS–POUR LES MENAGES		13.9	12.2	11.3	12.1	11.6	11.8
2 IND SUPPLIES–APPROV INDUSTRIELS		29.4	30.1	30.8	28.7	28.5	27.7
21 PRIMARY–PRODUITS DE BASE		1.6	0.8	1.1	0.8	0.7	0.7
22 PROCESSED–PRODUITS ELABORES		27.8	29.3	29.7	27.9	27.9	27.0
3 FUELS–COMBUSTIBLES		11.8	11.1	11.3	11.5	11.4	12.9
31 PRIMARY–PRODUITS DE BASE		0.8	0.7	0.8	0.9	1.2	1.0
32 PROCESSED–PRODUITS ELABORES		11.0	10.3	10.5	10.5	10.2	11.9
321 MOTOR SPIRIT–ESSENCE		3.2	3.2	3.5	2.9	3.3	4.0
322 OTHER–AUTRES		7.8	7.1	7.0	7.7	6.9	7.9
4 MACHINERY–EQUIPEMENT		14.5	16.2	16.9	16.2	14.7	16.6
41 CAPITAL EQUIPMENT–MACHINES		13.0	14.4	14.9	14.3	13.0	14.9
42 PARTS–PIECES ACCESSOIRES		1.5	1.8	2.0	1.9	1.6	1.7
5 TRANSPORT–TRANSPORT		9.8	9.8	8.9	10.0	10.4	9.3
51 PASSENGER CARS–AUTOMOBILES		2.4	1.9	1.7	2.2	2.1	1.7
52 OTHER–AUTRES		4.1	4.5	3.9	4.6	5.1	4.2
521 INDUSTRIAL–INDUSTRIELS		3.8	4.1	3.6	4.3	4.8	3.9
522 NON INDUSTRIAL–NON INDUSTRIEL		0.2	0.4	0.3	0.3	0.3	0.3
53 PARTS–PIECES ACCESSOIRES		3.4	3.4	3.3	3.2	3.2	3.5
6 CONSUM GOODS–BIENS CONSOMMATION		15.3	17.1	16.8	17.2	17.6	16.8
61 DURABLE–DURABLES		2.5	2.6	2.8	3.5	3.1	2.7
62 SEMI DURABLE–SEMI DURABLES		8.8	10.3	8.5	8.8	9.1	8.8
63 NON DURABLE–NON DURABLES		4.0	4.2	5.4	4.9	5.4	5.3
7 GOODS NES–BIENS NDA		0.6	0.2	0.2	0.2	1.0	0.7

EXPORTS – EXPORTATIONS

	1991	1992	1993	1994	1995	1996	1997
TOTAL EXPORTS–EXPORTATIONS TOTALES		100.	100.	100.	100.	100.	100.
1 AGRICULTURE		14.3	18.9	22.2	25.5	27.1	28.7
2 MINING QUARRY–INDUS EXTRACTIVES		0.1	0.0	0.2	0.1	0.1	0.1
3 MANUFACTURING–IND MANUFACTUR		85.6	81.1	77.6	74.4	72.8	71.2
31 FOOD BEV TOBACCO–ALIM BOISS TAB		58.8	53.7	48.5	54.4	54.7	52.4
32 TEXTILES–INDUSTRIES TEXTILES		14.4	16.3	13.0	9.7	10.7	10.5
33 WOOD & PRODUCTS–BOIS & PRODUITS		2.9	2.8	3.7	1.5	1.2	1.7
34 PAPER & PRODUCTS–PAPIER & PRODT		0.0	0.2	0.0	0.0	0.0	0.1
35 CHEMICALS–INDUSTRIES CHIMIQUES		4.0	3.1	3.8	4.4	2.8	2.8
36 NON METAL MIN–MIN NON METAL		0.0	0.0	0.0	0.0	0.0	0.1
37 BASIC METAL–IND METAL BASE		0.0	0.0	0.0	0.0	0.0	0.0
38 METAL MANUF–MANUF METAL		5.4	4.8	7.1	3.8	2.9	2.9
39 OTH MANUF IND–AUTRES MANUF		0.0	0.1	1.6	0.4	0.5	0.6

3. TRADE BY PRINCIPAL COUNTRIES OF ORIGIN AND DESTINATION (VALUE IN MILLION U.S. DOLLARS)
ECHANGES SELON LES PRINCIPAUX PAYS D'ORIGINE ET DE DESTINATION (VALEUR EN MILLIONS DE DOLLARS EU)

COUNTRIES–PAYS	GENERAL IMPORTS C.I.F. IMPORTATIONS GENERALES C.A.F				
	1993	1994	1995	1996	1997
World	280.9	259.9	258.5	255.6	286.1
Africa	0.1	0.1	0.1	0.2	0.1
Americas	243.5	198.3	219.8	222.7	248.8
– Northern America	185.4	144.5	147.8	145.0	155.8
– LAIA	35.0	28.6	31.1	33.6	43.1
– CACM	11.3	12.8	10.0	11.5	11.2
– Caribbean	10.9	11.3	29.9	31.7	37.4
– Rest of America	0.8	1.1	0.9	0.9	1.3
Asia excl fmr USSR	16.1	13.7	9.8	9.2	10.0
– Middle East	0.0	0.0	0.1	0.0	0.0
Asia former USSR					
Europe excl fmr USSR	20.3	47.3	28.4	23.2	26.8
– European Union	19.7	44.9	27.6	22.4	26.3
– Eastern Europe	0.2	0.1	0.0	0.0	0.0
– Rest of Europe	0.5	2.2	0.8	0.7	0.5
Europe former USSR	0.1	0.0	0.1	0.0	0.0
Oceania	0.7	0.6	0.4	0.3	0.2
Other	0.1			0.0	0.0
USA/Etats–Unis d'Amer	179.6	138.5	139.9	141.0	148.0
Mexico/Mexique	26.9	25.0	28.5	31.3	36.2
United Kingdom		18.9	16.2	11.9	15.3
Netherlands Antilles			12.6		26.4
Netherlands/Pays–Bas	11.2	17.1	2.5	4.5	3.4
Guatemala	7.7	8.9	7.0	7.5	7.5
Canada	5.8	6.0	7.9	4.0	7.8
Cuba	0.0		4.6	20.7	0.0
Jamaica/Jamaïque	4.6	4.0	4.6	4.4	4.1
China/Chine	8.4	8.3	2.0	1.4	1.5
Trinidad and Tobago	3.0	4.4	5.6	4.0	4.4
Japan/Japon	3.5	3.0	3.4	4.1	4.8
Barbados/Barbade	2.2	2.4	2.2	2.0	2.1
El Salvador	2.0	1.9	1.8	2.4	2.6
Denmark/Danemark	1.7	1.8	1.8	1.6	2.0
Venezuela	5.7	0.5	0.3	0.6	1.6
Germany/Allemagne	2.3	1.2	2.8	1.0	1.0
Ireland/Irlande	1.2	1.2	1.6	1.4	2.2
Brazil/Brésil	1.8	1.9	1.4	1.1	1.0
Other Asia n.e.s.			1.8	1.4	1.7
Panama	0.8	1.1	0.9	0.9	1.2
Costa Rica	1.0	1.0	0.8	1.1	0.7
France, Monaco	0.9	1.5	0.8	0.4	1.0
Switzerland,Liechtenst.	0.4	2.2	0.7	0.7	0.5
China, Hong Kong SAR	1.3	0.7	0.7	0.9	0.5
Colombia/Colombie	0.6	0.9	0.7	0.3	1.3
Italy/Italie	0.5	0.4	0.7	1.0	0.8
Argentina/Argentine	0.0	0.1	0.0	0.1	2.7
Spain/Espagne	0.4	2.0	0.5	0.1	0.1
Honduras	0.6	1.1	0.4	0.4	0.5
Korea, Republic of	1.2		0.2	0.4	0.9
Sweden/Suède	0.4	0.5	0.4	0.4	0.3
Thailand/Thaïlande	0.4	0.3	0.3	0.4	0.2
Singapore/Singapour	0.4	0.5	0.4	0.0	0.0
Dominica/Dominique	0.8	0.1	0.0	0.2	0.2
India/Inde	0.4	0.4	0.3	0.1	0.1
New Zealand	0.4	0.2	0.3	0.2	0.2
Austria/Autriche	0.8	0.2	0.1	0.1	0.1
Saint Lucia/Ste–Lucie	0.3	0.2	0.2	0.2	0.2
Australia/Australie	0.4	0.4	0.1	0.2	0.1

COUNTRIES–PAYS	EXPORTS EXPORTATIONS ES F.O.B.				
	1993	1994	1995	1996	1997
Monde	126.6	142.9	161.7	167.6	176.2
Afrique	0.0		0.0	0.0	
Amériques	121.6	91.5	77.8	87.5	104.9
– Amérique du Nord	103.9	73.6	66.1	75.2	88.1
– ALAI	12.0	12.0	4.6	5.9	5.9
– MCAC	0.7	0.8	0.6	1.5	2.9
– Caraïbes	4.9	5.1	6.4	4.5	7.2
– Autre Amérique	0.2	0.0	0.1	0.4	0.7
Asie anc. URSS exclus	0.8	0.6	0.3	0.1	0.2
– Moyen–Orient	0.0				0.0
Asie ancienne URSS					
Europe anc. URSS exclus	4.1	50.8	83.5	79.8	70.6
– Union Européenne	4.1	50.6	82.9	79.6	70.5
– Europe de l'Est	0.0		0.0		
– Autre de l'Europe	0.0	0.2	0.5	0.1	0.1
Europe ancienne URSS					
Océanie	0.0	0.0	0.0		0.0
Autre		0.0		0.3	0.4
USA/Etats–Unis d'Amer	95.6	63.4	59.1	70.8	82.3
United Kingdom		43.4	68.5	70.3	53.0
Mexico/Mexique	11.9	11.9	4.5	5.9	5.9
Canada	8.3	10.2	6.9	4.4	5.8
Germany/Allemagne	2.8	3.1	8.4	3.9	1.3
Netherlands/Pays–Bas	0.2	0.1	0.5	3.5	12.4
France, Monaco	1.0	3.8	3.3	1.2	3.6
Jamaica/Jamaïque	2.5	2.0	2.0	1.4	3.9
Trinidad and Tobago	1.5	2.0	2.1	2.2	2.2
Guatemala	0.3	0.5	0.4	1.4	2.0
Barbados/Barbade	0.7	0.8	1.1	0.5	0.5
Italy/Italie		0.0	2.0	0.2	0.0
Honduras	0.3	0.2	0.1	0.1	0.8
Japan/Japon	0.6	0.1	0.2	0.0	0.1
Switzerland,Liechtenst.	0.0	0.2	0.5	0.1	0.1
Netherlands Antilles			0.9		0.0
Guyana	0.0	0.0	0.0	0.2	0.5
Panama	0.2	0.0	0.1	0.2	0.2
Antigua and Barbuda	0.1	0.1	0.1	0.1	0.1
Dominica/Dominique	0.1	0.1	0.1	0.2	0.1
Spain/Espagne	0.0	0.0	0.1	0.1	0.2
Ireland/Irlande	0.0			0.3	0.1
Free zones/Zone franches					0.4
Areas n.e.s.		0.0		0.3	
Singapore/Singapour		0.3			
El Salvador	0.0	0.0	0.0	0.0	0.1
Turks and Caicos Isls				0.0	0.2
Costa Rica	0.0	0.1	0.1	0.0	0.0
St Vincent & Grenadines		0.0		0.0	0.1
Venezuela		0.1	0.1		0.0
Other Asia n.e.s.			0.0	0.0	0.1
Saint Lucia/Ste–Lucie	0.0	0.0	0.0	0.0	0.0
China/Chine	0.1	0.1	0.0		
Denmark/Danemark		0.1			
China, Hong Kong SAR	0.1	0.0			
Belgium–Luxembourg	0.0		0.0	0.1	0.0
India/Inde		0.0		0.0	0.0
Nicaragua	0.0	0.0		0.0	0.1
Malaysia/Malaisie			0.1		
Israel/Israël			0.1		

(VALUE AS PERCENTAGE OF WORLD TOTAL)(VALEURS EN POURCENTAGE DU TOTAL MONDIAL)

	1988	1989	1990	1991	1992	1993	1994	1995	1996	1997
Africa	0.0	0.0	0.0		0.0	0.0	0.0	0.0	0.1	0.0
Americas	75.3	75.9	78.7		78.1	86.7	76.3	85.0	87.1	87.0
– Northern America	57.7	59.4	60.1		58.9	66.0	55.6	57.2	56.7	54.5
– LAIA	7.6	7.7	7.8		11.0	12.5	11.0	12.0	13.2	15.1
– CACM	4.0	3.5	3.2		3.9	4.0	4.9	3.9	4.5	3.9
– Caribbean	5.6	5.1	7.7		4.0	3.9	4.3	11.6	12.4	13.1
– Rest of America	0.3	0.1	0.0		0.2	0.3	0.4	0.4	0.3	0.4
Asia excl fmr USSR	6.0	4.7	5.0		5.4	5.7	5.3	3.8	3.6	3.5
– Middle East	0.0	0.0	0.0		0.0	0.0	0.0	0.0	0.0	0.0
Asia former USSR										
Europe excl fmr USSR	18.4	19.0	15.9		16.3	7.2	18.2	11.0	9.1	9.4
– European Union	17.7	18.5	15.5		15.9	7.0	17.3	10.7	8.8	9.2
– Eastern Europe	0.4	0.2	0.2		0.0	0.1	0.0	0.0	0.0	0.0
– Rest of Europe	0.3	0.2	0.2		0.3	0.2	0.9	0.3	0.3	0.2
Europe former USSR	0.0	0.0	0.0			0.0	0.0	0.0	0.0	0.0
Oceania	0.3	0.3	0.3		0.2	0.3	0.2	0.1	0.1	0.1
Other	0.0	0.0			0.0	0.0			0.0	0.0
USA/Etats–Unis d'Amer	53.6	57.2	57.8		57.0	63.9	53.3	54.1	55.2	51.7
Mexico/Mexique	6.9	6.9	6.8		8.8	9.6	9.6	11.0	12.2	12.7
United Kingdom	8.9	9.2	8.2		8.5		7.3	6.3	4.7	5.3
Netherlands Antilles	0.8	0.2	1.5					4.9		9.2
Netherlands/Pays–Bas	4.4	5.2	3.7		3.1	4.0	6.6	1.0	1.8	1.2
Guatemala	1.2	1.5	1.6		2.3	2.7	3.4	2.7	3.0	2.6
Canada	4.1	2.2	2.3		2.0	2.1	2.3	3.1	1.6	2.7
Cuba						0.0		1.8	8.1	0.0
Jamaica/Jamaïque	3.5	3.6	4.8		1.7	1.6	1.6	1.8	1.7	1.4
China/Chine	0.0	0.1	0.7		0.7	3.0	3.2	0.8	0.6	0.5

	1988	1989	1990	1991	1992	1993	1994	1995	1996	1997
Afrique	0.0	0.0	0.0		2.2	0.0		0.0	0.0	
Amériques	66.8	70.2	69.7		69.1	96.1	64.0	48.1	52.2	59.6
– Amérique du Nord	45.1	45.3	50.1		51.6	82.1	51.5	40.9	44.8	50.0
– ALAI	13.8	17.2	11.8		12.5	9.4	8.4	2.9	3.5	3.4
– MCAC	0.7	0.6	1.1		0.5	0.5	0.6	0.4	0.9	1.6
– Caraïbes	7.1	7.2	6.7		4.6	3.8	3.5	4.0	2.7	4.1
– Autre Amérique	0.0	0.0	0.0		0.0	0.2	0.0	0.1	0.3	0.4
Asie anc. URSS exclus	0.5	0.6	1.9		0.9	0.6	0.4	0.2	0.1	0.1
– Moyen–Orient	0.0	0.0	1.2			0.0				0.0
Asie ancienne URSS										
Europe anc. URSS exclus	32.7	29.1	28.3		27.7	3.3	35.6	51.6	47.6	40.1
– Union Européenne	32.4	29.1	28.2		27.6	3.2	35.4	51.3	47.5	40.0
– Europe de l'Est						0.0		0.0		
– Autre de l'Europe	0.3	0.1	0.0		0.0	0.0	0.2	0.3	0.1	0.0
Europe ancienne URSS										
Océanie		0.0	0.0		0.0	0.0	0.0	0.0		0.0
Autre		0.0					0.0		0.2	0.2
USA/Etats–Unis d'Amer	41.6	42.4	45.6		47.2	75.5	44.3	36.6	42.2	46.7
United Kingdom	30.2	26.3	27.1		23.6		30.4	42.4	41.9	30.1
Mexico/Mexique	13.8	17.1	11.7		12.5	9.4	8.3	2.8	3.5	3.3
Canada	3.5	2.9	4.4		4.4	6.6	7.2	4.3	2.6	3.3
Germany/Allemagne					2.5	2.2	2.1	5.2	2.3	0.7
Netherlands/Pays–Bas	0.1	0.3	0.0		0.4	0.2	0.1	0.3	2.1	7.0
France, Monaco	0.9	0.6	0.4		0.9	0.8	2.7	2.0	0.7	2.0
Jamaica/Jamaïque	2.8	4.4	3.0		0.8	2.0	1.4	1.3	0.8	2.2
Trinidad and Tobago	3.3	1.8	2.8		2.8	1.2	1.4	1.3	1.3	1.2
Guatemala	0.3	0.1	0.8		0.3	0.2	0.3	0.3	0.8	1.1

4. General Imports C.I.F. by Commodities according to the S.I.T.C. (Rev. 2) in million U.S. Dollars
Importations Générales C.A.F. par Produits d'après la C.T.C.I. (Rév. 2) en millions de Dollars E.U.

SITC CTCI	COMMODITY	1994		1995		1996		1997		PRODUIT
		QUANTITY QUANTITE	VALUE VALEUR	QUANTITY QUANTITE	VALUE VALEUR	QUANTITY QUANTITE	VALUE VALEUR	QUANTITY QUANTITE	VALUE VALEUR	
	ALL COMMODITIES		260.0		258.6		255.6		286.1	TOUS PRODUITS
0	FOOD AND LIVE ANIMALS		39.3		41.4		44.2		46.2	ALIMENTS,ANIMAUX VIVANTS
01	MEAT AND PREPARATIONS		3.4		3.7		3.2		3.9	VIANDES ET PREPARATIONS
012	MEAT DRIED,SALTED,SMOKED	W 686	0.8	W 703	0.8	W 555	0.8	W 475	0.9	VIANDE,ABATS SALES,SECHES
014	MEAT PREPD,PRSVD,NES ETC	W 1196	2.5	W 1254	2.7	W 1009	2.4	W 1166	3.0	CONSERVES DE VIANDES
0142	SAUSAGES INCLDING TINNED	W 514	1.1	W 547	1.1	W 500	1.2	W 500	1.3	SAUCISSES,SAUCISSONS
0149	OTH PREPARD,PRESRVD MEAT	W 681	1.4	W 707	1.6	W 509	1.3	W 667	1.7	AUTRES PREP DE VIANDES
02	DAIRY PRODCTS,BIRDS'EGGS		9.3		10.0		10.3		10.2	PRODUITS LAITIERS,OEUFS
022	MILK AND CREAM	W 3859	6.0	W 4024	6.6	W 3730	7.2	W 3468	6.8	LAIT ET CREME
0224	MILK,CREAM PRESERVED ETC	W 3706	5.8	W 3948	6.5	W 3658	7.1	W 3380	6.7	LAIT,CREME CONS,CONC
02243	MILK DRY,OVER 1.5% FAT	W 1152	3.1	W 1005	3.1	W 892	3.0	W 1228	3.8	LAIT POUDRE SUP 1.5%
02249	MILK(EX DRY) PRSVD,SWEET	W 2541	2.7	W 2900	3.4	W 2705	4.0	W 2091	2.7	LAIT CONS,CONC SUCRE
024	CHEESE AND CURD	W 1071	2.9	W 893	2.9	W 866	2.5	W 817	2.7	FROMAGE ET CAILLEBOTTE
03	FISH AND PREPARATIONS		0.8		1.0		0.8		0.8	POISSONS ET PREPARATIONS
04	CEREALS AND PREPARATIONS		8.3		8.0		9.8		8.3	CEREALES ET PRODUITS
041	WHEAT ETC UNMILLED	W 12524	3.4	W 3771	3.3	W 17327	5.0	W 10565	3.5	FROMENT,EPEAUTRE
0411	DURUM WHEAT UNMILLED	W 12524	3.4	W 3771	3.3	W 17327	5.0	W 10565	3.5	FROMENT DUR NON MOULU
048	CEREAL ETC PREPARATIONS	W 2915	4.1	W 3123	3.6	W 2830	4.1	W 2434	3.8	PREPTNS A BASE CEREALES
0484	BAKERY PRODUCTS	W 755	1.1	W 719	0.8	W 628	0.8	W 625	1.0	PRODUITS DE BOULANGERIE
0488	OTH CEREAL PREPS,MALT EX	W 703	1.9	W 620	1.5	W 706	2.0	W 596	1.6	EXTRAITS DE MALT
05	VEGETABLES AND FRUIT		3.8		4.6		5.1		6.6	LEGUMES ET FRUITS
054	VEG ETC FRSH,SMPLY PRSVD		2.5	W 4932	2.8	W 6398	3.6	W 7113	4.0	LEGUMES FRAIS,CONG,SECS
0541	POTATOES FRSH EXCL SWEET	W 2289	1.3	W 2236	1.5	W 2791	1.8	W 3068	2.1	POMMES DE TERRE
0545	OTHER FRESH VEGETABLES		0.9	W 2364	1.1	W 3232	1.4	W 3662	1.6	AUTRES LEGUMES FRAIS,REF
05459	FRESH VEGETABLES NES		0.3	W 898	0.5	W 1768	0.8	W 2126	1.0	LEGUMES FRAIS,REFRI NDA
058	FRUIT PRESERVED,PREPARED	W 683	0.5	W 637	0.7	W 543	0.6	W 1429	1.1	CONSERVES DE FRUITS
07	COFFEE,TEA,COCOA,SPICES		1.8		1.8		1.8		2.2	CAFE,THE,CACAO,EPICES
071	COFFEE AND SUBSTITUTES	W 262	1.0	W 227	0.9	W 406	1.0	W 378	1.1	CAFE ET SUCCEDANES
0711	COFFEE GREEN,ROASTED,SUB	W 236	0.9	W 143	0.6	W 339	0.6	W 55	0.4	CAFE TORREFIE OU DECAFEINE
07112	COFFEE ROASTED	W 236	0.9	W 143	0.6	W 339	0.6	W 55	0.4	CAFE TORREFIE
081	*FEEDING STUFF FOR ANIML	W 11668	5.1	W 10045	4.2	W 11813	5.6	W 10576	6.0	NOURRITURE POUR ANIMAUX
0813	OILCAKE AND OTH RESIDUES					W 3107	1.1	W 2685	1.5	TOURTEAUX
08131	— OF SOYA BEANS					W 3107	1.1	W 2685	1.5	TOURTEAUX DE SOJA
0819	FOOD WASTE AND FEED NES	W 11380	5.0	W 9831	4.2	W 8079	4.3	W 7038	4.2	DECHETS,ALIMENTS NDA
08199	FODDER NES,INCL SWEETNED	W 11379	5.0	W 9831	4.2	W 8079	4.3	W 7038	4.2	PREPARATIONS FOURRAGERES
09	MISC EDIBLE PRODUCTS		6.6		7.4		7.3		7.8	PREP ALIMENTAIRES DIVERSES
091	MARGARINE AND SHORTENING	W 2807	2.7	W 3060	3.1	W 3029	3.2	W 2804	3.1	MARGARINE ET GRAISSES
0913	PIG,POULTRY FAT RENDERED	W 1296	1.1	W 1310	1.2	W 1283	1.2	W 1022	1.0	SAINDOUX
0914	MARGARINE,EDIBLE FAT NES	W 1511	1.6	W 1750	1.9	W 1746	2.0	W 1782	2.1	MARGARINES,SIMILI SAINDOUX
09141	MARGARINE	W 514	0.7	W 685	0.8	W 546	0.8	W 494	0.8	MARGARINE
09149	OTH PREPARED EDIBLE FATS	W 996	1.0	W 1065	1.1	W 1200	1.3	W 1289	1.4	SIMILI–SAINDOUX
098	EDIBLE PRODCTS,PREPS NES		4.0		4.4		4.2		4.7	PREP ALIMENTAIRES NDA
09804	SAUCES,MIXED SEASONINGS	W 930	1.1	W 967	1.2	W 947	1.2	W 1069	1.4	SAUCES,ASSAISONNEMENTS
09809	MISC FOOD PREPRTIONS NES	W 549	2.0	W 621	2.4	W 576	2.2	W 688	2.5	PREP ALIMENTAIRES NDA
1	BEVERAGES AND TOBACCO		7.8		7.2		7.0		9.3	BOISSONS ET TABACS
11	BEVERAGES		5.0		4.2		3.4		5.3	BOISSONS
112	ALCOHOLIC BEVERAGES	W 829	4.5	W 735	3.7	W 621	2.9	W 747	4.8	BOISSONS ALCOOLIQUES
1124	DISTILLED ALCOHOLIC BEVS	W 302	3.4	W 278	2.9	W 233	2.2	W 374	3.9	ALCOOLS,EAUX–DE–VIE
11241	WHISKY	W 206	2.7	W 180	2.2	W 136	1.6	W 230	3.0	WHISKY
12	TOBACCO AND MANUFACTURES		2.8		3.0		3.7		4.0	TABACS BRUTS FABRIQUES
122	TOBACCO,MANUFACTURED	W 97	2.2	W 466	2.5	W 149	3.2	W 103	3.5	TABACS FABRIQUES
1222	CIGARETTES	W 96	2.2	W 465	2.5	W 148	3.1	W 100	3.5	CIGARETTES
2	CRUDE MATERLS,EXCL FUELS		2.4		1.8		1.2		1.4	MAT BRUTES NON COMESTIBLES
27	CRUDE FERTLZR,MINRLS NES		1.1		0.7		0.5		0.5	ENGRAIS MINERAUX BRUTS
278	OTHER CRUDE MINERALS	W 301811	1.0	W 1723	0.7		0.4	W 1841	0.5	AUTRES MINERAUX BRUTS
2789	MINERALS CRUDE NES	W 300963	0.9	W 851	0.6		0.3	W 762	0.3	MINERAUX BRUTS NDA
27896	NATURAL ASPHALT,BITUMEN	W 300936	0.8	W 819	0.5	W 500	0.3	W 746	0.3	BITUMES,ASPHALTES NATURELS
3	MINERAL FUELS ETC		29.4		29.8		29.1		37.0	COMBUSTIBLES MINERAUX LUB
33	PETROLEUM AND PRODUCTS		27.3		27.3		26.1		34.1	PETROLE ET DERIVES
334	PETROLEUM PRODUCTS,REFIN	W 126089	27.3	W 128397	27.3	W 102714	26.1	W 139369	34.1	PRODUITS RAFFINES
3341	GASOLINE,OTH LIGHT OILS	W 42964	9.2	W 36506	7.5	W 33208	8.6	W 47306	11.4	ESSENCES POUR MOTEURS
33411	MOTOR,AVIATION SPIRIT	W 42964	9.2	W 36505	7.5	W 33208	8.6	W 47305	11.4	ESSENCES MOTEURS D'AVIONS
3342	KEROSENE,OTH MEDIUM OILS	W 18639	3.8	W 17283	3.4	W 14579	3.6	W 15954	3.6	PETR LAMPANTS,AUT HUIL
33421	KEROSENE INCL JET FUEL	W 18638	3.8	W 17283	3.4	W 14578	3.6	W 15954	3.6	PETROLES LAMPANTS
3343	GAS OILS	W 59893	11.3	W 69750	13.2	W 47070	10.7	W 71056	15.8	GAS OILS
3345	LUBS,PETROLEUM OILS NES	W 2967	2.9	W 2589	2.9	W 7858	3.5	W 2737	2.9	HUILES LUBRIFIANTES
33451	LUBS(HIGH PETR CONT) ETC	W 2946	2.8	W 2577	2.9	W 7844	3.4	W 2711	2.9	HUILES LUBRIF,H LOURDES
341	*GAS,NATURAL AND MANUFCT	W 9013	2.1	W 9761	2.5	W 9973	3.0	W 9839	2.9	GAZ NATUREL,GAZ MANUFACT
3413	PETROLM GASES,LIQUEFIED	W 9013	2.1	W 9761	2.5	W 9973	3.0	W 9839	2.9	GAZ DE PETROLE LIQUEFIE
34131	LIQUEFIED PROPANE,BUTANE	W 8755	2.1	W 9760	2.5	W 9973	3.0	W 9839	2.9	PROPANE,BUTANE LIQUEFIES
4	ANIMAL,VEGETABLE OIL,FAT		0.6		0.6		0.8		1.0	HUILES,GRAISSES ANIM,VEG
5	CHEMCLS,RELATED PROD NES		26.4		25.1		27.2		28.9	PRODUITS CHIMIQUES
52	INORGANIC CHEMICALS		0.9		1.0		1.1		1.5	PROD CHIM INORGANIQUES
522	INORG ELEMNTS,OXIDES,ETC	W 820	0.5	W 622	0.5	W 692	0.5	W 981	1.0	ELEMENTS INORGANIQUES
53	DYES,TANNING,COLOUR PROD		3.2		3.3		3.2		3.1	PROD TEINTURE,COLORANTS
533	PIGMENTS,PAINTS,ETC		3.2	W 1269	3.3	W 1512	3.2	W 1598	3.1	PIGMENTS,PEINTURES,VERNIS
5334	VARNISHES,DISTEMPERS ETC	W 1228	2.7	W 953	2.8	W 1184	2.8	W 1290	2.6	PEINTURES A L'EAU
53341	WATER–THINNED PAINTS	W 543	1.3	W 387	1.0	W 507	1.3	W 782	1.3	PEINTURES DILUEES
53342	OTH PAINTS,VARNISHES ETC	W 678	1.5	W 544	1.7	W 611	1.4	W 491	1.2	AUTRES PEINTURES,VERNIS
541	*MEDICINAL,PHARM PRODUCT	K 547873	4.4	K 485042	4.2	K 547111	4.4		4.9	PROD MEDICINAUX PHARMACEUT
5417	MEDICAMENTS	K 529018	3.9	K 452168	3.8	K 532885	4.1	K 502291	4.5	MEDICAMENTS
54179	— CONTNG OTH SUBSTANCES	K 495381	3.2	K 422559	3.1	K 498278	3.3	K 461253	3.5	MED CONT AUT SUBSTANCES
55	PERFUME,CLEANING ETC PRD		5.6		3.9		3.8		4.8	PROD POUR PARFUM,TOILETTE
553	PERFUMERY,COSMETICS,ETC		3.1	W 684	1.7	W 527	1.4	W 726	1.8	PRODUITS DE PARFUMERIE
554	SOAP,CLEANSING ETC PREPS	W 2517	2.5	W 2421	2.1	W 2517	2.4	W 3113	3.0	SAVONS,PRODUITS DETERSIFS
5542	WASHING PREPARATIONS ETC	W 2042	1.8	W 2086	1.6	W 2095	1.8	W 2593	2.3	PROD ORG TENSIO–ACT NDA
562	*FERTILIZERS,MANUFACTURE		4.0		4.8		5.2		5.2	ENGRAIS MANUFACTURES
5621	CHEM NITROGENOUS FERTLZR	W 6113	1.2	W 6978	1.7	W 6670	1.8	W 6384	1.4	ENGRAIS AZOTES
56216	UREA	W 4806	1.0	W 4788	1.2	W 4498	1.2	W 5079	1.1	UREE
5623	CHEM POTASSIC FERTILIZER	W 4584	0.8		0.6	W 962	0.2		0.1	ENGRAIS POTASSIQUES
56239	CHEM POTASS FERTILZR NES	W 4584	0.8	W 2036	0.4	W 788	0.2	W 310	0.1	ENGRAIS POTASSIQUES NDA
5629	FERTILIZERS NES		2.1	W 10024	2.6	W 13877	3.3	W 16614	3.7	ENGRAIS NDA
56291	NIT–PHOS–POT FERTLZR NES	W 16550	1.0	W 4403	1.1	W 6142	1.4	W 4677	1.2	ENGRAIS CONT N P K
56292	NITROG–PHOS FERTILZR NES		1.0	W 4153	1.0	W 4388	1.2	W 8657	1.9	ENGRAIS NDA CONT N P
58	PLASTIC MATERIALS ETC		1.3		1.7		1.4		1.5	MAT PLAST ARTIFICIELLES
583	POLYMERIZATION ETC PRODS	W 690	1.0	W 471	1.4	W 562	1.1	W 530	1.1	PROD POLYMERISATION
5839	OTH POLYMRZTION ETC PROD	W 68	0.2	W 420	1.3	W 244	0.7	W 493	1.1	AUT PROD POLYMER COPOLYM
59	CHEMICAL MATERIALS NES		6.8		6.3		7.8		7.7	MAT PROD CHIMIQUES NDA
591	PESTICIDES,DISINFECTANTS	W 1532	5.4	W 1536	4.9	W 1596	6.2	W 1583	5.9	DESINF,INSECT,FONG,HERB
5911	INSECTICIDES,FOR RETAIL	W 601	1.9	W 610	2.0	W 667	2.5	W 696	2.3	INSECTICIDES VENTE DET
5912	FUNGICIDES,FOR RETAIL	W 313	1.4	W 330	1.2	W 206	1.6	W 228	1.6	FONGICIDES VENTE AU DET

4. General Imports C.I.F. by Commodities according to the S.I.T.C. (Rev. 2) in million U.S. Dollars
Importations Générales C.A.F. par Produits d'après la C.T.C.I. (Rév. 2) en millions de Dollars E.U.

SITC CTCI	COMMODITY	1994 QUANTITY QUANTITE	1994 VALUE VALEUR	1995 QUANTITY QUANTITE	1995 VALUE VALEUR	1996 QUANTITY QUANTITE	1996 VALUE VALEUR	1997 QUANTITY QUANTITE	1997 VALUE VALEUR	PRODUIT
5913	HERBICIDES,FOR RETAIL	W 370	1.6	W 337	1.5	W 466	1.8	W 443	1.8	HERBICIDES VENTE AU DET
598	MISCEL CHEM PRODUCTS NES		1.1		1.1		1.3		1.3	PROD DIV INDUST CHIM NDA
5989	CHEM PRODUCTS,PREPS NES	W 663	0.9	W 688	0.9	W 980	1.1	W 1221	1.2	PROD PREP CHIMIQUES NDA
6	BASIC MANUFACTURES		53.3		51.8		48.5		54.1	ART MANUFACTURES
62	RUBBER MANUFACTURES NES		4.2		4.2		4.0		5.1	CAOUTCHOUC MANUFACTURE
625	RUBBER TYRES, TUBES ETC	N 208772	3.1	N 162796	3.3	N 153473	3.2	N 187595	4.1	PNEUS CAOUTCHOUC VULCANISE
6252	TYRES,NEW,BUS OR LORRY	N 24734	1.6	N 18704	1.9	N 15691	1.7	N 22455	2.4	PNEUS POUR AUTOBUS,CAMIONS
6259	OTH TYRES,TYRE CASES,ETC	N 136047	1.0	N 106019	0.9	N 98870	0.9	N 123008	1.1	AUTRES PNEUS RECHAPES FLAPS
62599	TYRES NES,TYRE CASES,ETC	N 71363	0.8	N 27640	0.7	N 29511	0.7	N 37552	1.0	PNEUS,FLAPS
63	WOOD,CORK MANUFACTRS NES		2.6		6.9		2.7		1.9	OUVRAGES LIEGE ET BOIS
634	VENEERS,PLYWOOD,ETC		1.9		1.2		1.0		1.0	PLACAGES,CONTRE–PLAQUES
6342	PLYWOOD OF WOOD SHEETS	V 4718	1.2	V 6404	1.1	V 13996	0.9	V 3096	0.9	BOIS CONTRE–PLAQUES
635	WOOD MANUFACTURES NES	W 5965	0.8	W 1431	5.7	W 412	1.8	W 1932	1.0	ART MANUF EN BOIS NDA
6353	BUILDERS WOODWRK,PREFABS	W 5933	0.7	W 914	5.4	W 370	1.7	W 501	0.8	OUVRAGES DE MENUISERIE
64	PAPER,PAPERBOARD AND MFR		7.6		7.6		9.2		11.2	PAPIERS,CARTONS & OUVRAGES
641	PAPER AND PAPERBOARD	W 2323	2.4	W 2093	2.4	W 2607	3.0	W 2392	2.6	PAPIERS ET CARTONS
6412	PRINTG,WRITING PAPER NES	W 411	0.7	W 150	0.3	W 581	1.1	W 124	0.3	PAPIERS POUR L'IMPRESSION
64121	— UNCOATED	W 411	0.7	W 150	0.3	W 580	1.1	W 124	0.3	PAPIERS IMPRES NON COUCHES
642	PAPER,ETC,PRECUT,ARTS OF	W 4418	5.3	W 3817	5.3	W 5085	6.3		8.6	PAP,CARTONS DECOUPES
6421	PAPER ETC CONTAINERS	W 3235	3.2	W 2787	3.3	W 3791	4.0	W 6246	5.8	BOITES,SACS EMBALLAGES
6428	PAPER ETC ARTICLES NES	W 619	1.2	W 636	1.1	W 776	1.3		1.6	OUVRAGES EN PATE A PAPIER
64285	PAPER ETC DIAPERS ETC	W 383	0.9	W 352	0.7	W 501	0.9	W 586	1.1	SERVIETTES HYGIENIQUES
65	TEXTILE YARN,FABRICS,ETC		5.1		5.2		3.7		4.2	FILS,TISSUS,ARTICLES TEXTILE
653	WOVN MAN–MADE FIB FABRIC		1.1		0.9		0.7		1.0	TISSUS FIBRES SYNTH,ARTIF
655	KNITTED,ETC FABRICS	A 96	1.2	A 47	0.5	A 204	0.4	A 16	0.1	ETOF BONNETERIE PIECES ETC
6552	OTHER KNIT ETC FAB NONEL	A 96	1.2	A 47	0.5	A 204	0.4	A 16	0.1	ETOF BON NON ELAS NON SYNT
657	SPECIAL TXTL FABRC,PRODS		0.7		1.5		0.8		0.7	TISSUS SPECIAUX
6577	TEXTILES FOR MACHINERY	W 106	0.3	W 177	1.2	W 49	0.2	W 75	0.4	OUATES,MECHES ART TEXT
65773	TEXTLS FOR MACHINES NES	W 2	0.1	W 48	0.9	W 5	0.1	W 4	0.1	TISSUS USAGE TECH MAT TEX
658	TEXTILE ARTICLES NES		0.8		1.0		0.7		1.0	ART FACONNES MAT TEXTILES
66	NONMETAL MINERAL MFS NES		11.3		8.9		9.6		9.7	ART MIN NON METALLIQUES
661	LIME,CEMENT,BLDG PRODS	W 98308	6.7	W 78256	5.5	W 71946	5.9	W 71567	6.0	CHAUX,CIMENTS MAT CONSTR
6612	CEMENT	W 96875	6.2	W 76761	5.1	W 70129	5.5	W 69951	5.6	CIMENTS HYDRAULIQUES
662	CLAY,REFRACTORY BLDG PRD		1.4		1.2		1.0		0.9	MAT CONST REFRACTAIRES
6624	BRICKS ETC NONREFRACTORY		1.3		1.1		0.9		0.8	BRIQUES ETC CERAM NON REFR
66245	GLAZED CERAMIC SETTS ETC		1.1	N 3444807	1.0	N 1306899	0.8	N 1364308	0.7	AUT CARREAUX CERAMIQUE
663	MINERAL MANUFCTURES NES	W 1798	0.7		0.6	W 2144	0.9	W 2011	0.9	ART MIN MANUF NDA
664	GLASS		0.8		0.6		0.6		1.0	VERRE
665	GLASSWARE		1.7		1.0		1.2		1.0	OUVRAGES EN VERRE
6651	BOTTLES ETC OF GLASS		1.4		0.7	N 3963362	0.8		0.7	RECIPIENTS EN VERRE
66511	GLASS BOTTLES ETC NONVAC		1.4	N 3425424	0.7	N 3963362	0.8	N 2465647	0.7	BONBONNES,BOUTEILLES,ETC
67	IRON AND STEEL		8.1		5.0		6.5		6.2	FER ET ACIER
673	IRON,STEEL SHAPES ETC		3.1	W 8437	2.6		3.3	W 7584	2.4	BARRES,PROFIL FER,ACIER
6732	IRON,STEEL BARS ETC		2.7	W 5942	2.3	W 6483	2.4	W 5381	1.7	BARRES FER,ACIER
67322	HIGH CARBON STL BARS ETC	W 6159	1.3	W 5850	2.3	W 328	0.2	W 5288	1.7	BARRES ACIER FIN CARBONE
67326	IRN,OTH STL BARS HOTROLD	W 112772	1.4			W 6084	2.2			BARRES PLEINES FER,ACIER
674	IRN,STL UNIV,PLATE,SHEET		1.5	W 1823	1.5		1.8	W 2405	2.3	LARGES PLATS,TOLES
6749	OTH IRN,STL PLATES,SHEET		1.3	W 1200	1.0	W 1925	1.7	W 1816	1.9	AUTRES TOLES FER,ACIER
67491	— OF IRON OR SIMPLE STL		1.3	W 1125	1.0	W 1881	1.6	W 1810	1.9	AUT TOLES AUTRES ACIER FIN
678	IRON,STL TUBES,PIPES,ETC		3.3	W 722	0.9	W 1741	1.1	W 957	1.3	TUBES,TUYAUX EN FONTE,FER
6783	IRON,STL TUBES,PIPES NES		1.4	W 377	0.5	W 536	0.5	W 435	0.5	AUT TUBES,TUYAUX FER,ACIER
6785	IRON,STEEL TUBE FITTINGS		1.4	W 141	0.3	W 889	0.3	W 154	0.4	ACCESSOIRES DE TUYAUTERIE
68	NON–FERROUS METALS		1.2		1.1		1.2		0.8	METAUX NON FERREUX
69	METAL MANUFACTURES NES		13.5		13.3		11.9		15.3	ART MANUFACT EN METAL NDA
691	STRUCTURES AND PARTS NES	W 22013	3.8	W 2474	3.3	W 1160	2.8	W 3176	2.9	CONSTRUCT FER,ACIER,ALU
6911	STRUCTURES,PARTS IRN,STL	W 20172	2.6	W 2196	2.0	W 889	1.3	W 2882	2.1	CONSTRUCT FER,ACIER,FONTE
6912	STRUCTURES,PARTS ALUMNM	W 1841	1.3	W 278	1.3	W 271	1.5	W 294	0.8	CONSTRUCT ALUMINIUM
692	METAL TANKS,BOXES,ETC	W 4537	1.1	W 1310	2.0		2.1	W 2338	2.7	RECIPIENTS METALLIQUES
6924	MTL TRANSPORT BOXES ETC	W 4397	1.0	W 1227	1.6	W 1575	1.9	W 2284	2.5	FUTS,TAMBOURS,BIDONS
69241	STL TRANSPORT BOXES ETC	W 4081	0.8	W 1063	1.4	W 1411	1.6	W 1952	2.1	FUTS,TAMBOURS,BIDONS FER
693	WIRE PRODUCTS NON ELECTR		0.8	W 1529	0.7	W 894	0.8	W 1021	1.0	OUVRAGES FILS METALLIQUES
694	STL,COPPR NAILS,NUTS,ETC	W 2331	1.5	W 599	1.3		1.3	W 685	1.5	CLOUS,VIS,ECROUS
69402	IRN,STL NUTS,BOLTS,ETC	W 1377	1.0	W 219	0.8	W 216	0.7	W 264	0.9	BOULONS,VIS,ECROUS FER,AC
695	TOOLS		1.8	W 720	1.3	W 243	1.1	W 239	1.6	OUTILS A MAIN
6953	OTHER HAND TOOLS	W 867	1.0	W 154	0.9	W 131	0.7	W 151	1.0	AUTRES OUTILS A MAIN
697	BASE MTL HOUSEHOLD EQUIP	W 696	1.5	W 422	1.6	W 457	1.6	W 461	1.4	ART MENAGE MET COMMUNS
6973	DMSTC HEATG,COOKG APPARA	W 533	0.9	W 287	1.0	W 305	1.1	W 327	0.9	APPS CHAUF NON ELECTRIQ
69731	IRN,STL DOM COOKG APPARA	W 475	0.9	W 278	0.9	W 300	1.0	W 316	0.8	APPS CUISSON FER,ACIER
699	BASE METAL MFRS NES	W 1736	3.1	W 1276	3.2	W 618	2.4		4.5	ART MANUFACTURES MET NDA
6991	LOCKSMITHS WARES,ETC	W 697	1.1	W 194	0.9	W 154	0.7	W 223	1.3	ARTICLES DE SERRURERIE
6997	IRON,STEEL ARTICLES NES	W 403	0.8	W 676	1.0	W 155	0.6	W 299	1.7	OUV FONTE,FER,ACIER NDA
69979	IRN,STL MANUFACTURES NES	W 389	0.8	W 673	1.0	W 153	0.6	W 256	1.5	AUT OUVRAGES EN FER NDA
7	MACHINES,TRANSPORT EQUIP		66.4		66.5		63.8		73.1	MACHINES MATERIEL TRANSPORT
71	POWER GENERATING EQUIPMT		5.8		4.4		4.2		5.4	MACHINES GENERATRICES
713	INTRNL COMBUS PSTN ENGIN		3.0	W 564	2.6		2.9	W 220	3.1	MOTEURS EXPL COMB INT, PIECE
7133	MARINE PISTON ENGINES		1.2	W 67	1.3	W 75	1.3	W 83	1.7	MOTEURS EXPL POUR BATEAUX
71331	—— OUTBOARD	W 158	1.0	W 55	1.1	W 59	1.1	W 73	1.5	MOTEURS BATEAUX HORSBORD
7139	PISTON ENGINE PARTS NES		1.5	W 453	1.1	W 58	1.3	W 94	1.2	PIECES POUR 713.2,3,8
716	ROTATING ELECTRIC PLANT	W 236	1.5	W 241	1.7	W 181	1.2	W 373	2.0	APP ELECTR ROTATIFS,PIECES
7162	AC MTRS,GENRTRS,GEN SETS	W 211	0.8	W 224	1.5	W 168	1.0	W 355	1.7	MOTEURS ELECTRIQUES
71623	GEN SETS WITH PISTN ENGN	W 136	0.6	W 192	1.3	W 142	0.8	W 313	1.5	GROUPES MOTEUR EXPLOSION
718	OTH POWER GENERATG MACHY		1.1	W 5	0.1	W 1	0.1	W 2	0.1	AUTRES MOTEURS PARTIES
7188	WIND,WATER,ETC ENGINES	W 214	1.1	W 5	0.1	W 1	0.1	W 2	0.1	MOT MACHINES MOTRICES NDA
71889	PARTS NES OF 71881,71882	W 178	1.0		0.1					PARTIES DES POS 718.81,82
72	MACHS FOR SPCL INDUSTRYS		9.2		8.2		11.0		10.3	MAC SPECIALES POUR INDUST
721	AGRIC MACHY,EXC TRACTORS	W 1286	1.0	W 418	1.4	W 671	2.1	W 536	1.3	MACHINES AGRICOLES
7212	HARVESTING ETC MACHINES	W 1089	0.5	W 300	0.8	W 397	1.1	W 339	0.7	ENGINS POUR LA RECOLTE
722	TRACTORS NON–ROAD	N 1160	1.3	N 92	1.3	N 141	1.5	N 129	2.2	TRACTEURS
7224	WHEELED TRACTORS NES	N 907	1.2	N 80	1.0	N 134	1.4	N 122	2.1	TRACTEURS A ROUES
723	CIVIL ENGNEERG EQUIP ETC		2.4	W 753	2.4	W 690	3.8	W 1486	4.1	APPAREILS DE GENIE CIVIL
7234	CONST,MINING MACHNRY NES		2.4	W 720	2.3	W 658	3.8	W 1477	4.0	MACH POUR LA CONST, MINES
72341	SELF–PROPELLD DOZERS,ETC	W 2645	1.2	W 329	1.6	W 306	1.8	W 133	0.4	BULLDOZERS
72342	SLFPRP SHOVELS,EXCAVATRS	W 421	0.8	W 305	0.7	W 266	1.7	W 221	0.6	PELLES MECANIQUES
72346	OTH CONST,MINING MCH NES	W 9	0.1	W 43	0.1			W 1018	2.7	AUT MACH EXTRACTION,EXCAV ET
724	TEXTILE,LEATHER MACHNRY		0.3		0.5		0.9		0.8	MACH POUR INDUSTRIE TEXTILE
727	FOOD MACHRY NON–DOMESTIC	W 825	2.0	W 358	1.1	W 398	1.3	W 137	0.6	MACH INDUSTRIES ALIMENT
7272	OTH FOOD PROC MCHY,PARTS	W 412	1.4	W 342	0.9	W 270	1.1	W 130	0.5	AUT MACH IND ALIMENTAIRE
72722	INDUS FOOD PROC MACH NES	W 412	1.4	W 342	0.9	W 270	1.1	W 130	0.5	MACHINES BOULANGERIE
728	OTH MACHY FOR SPCL INDUS		2.1	W 439	1.6	W 283	1.5	W 214	1.4	AUT MACH IND PARTICULIERES
7283	OTHR MINERAL WORKG MACHY	W 483	1.3	W 273	0.9	W 126	0.8	W 62	0.7	MACH TRIER,CRIBLER,BROYER
74	GENRL INDUSTRL MACHY NES		13.9		13.7		10.9		12.7	MACH APP INDUSTRIE

4. General Imports C.I.F. by Commodities according to the S.I.T.C. (Rev. 2) in million U.S. Dollars
Importations Générales C.A.F. par Produits d'après la C.T.C.I. (Rév. 2) en millions de Dollars E.U.

SITC CTCI	COMMODITY	1994 QUANTITY QUANTITE	1994 VALUE VALEUR	1995 QUANTITY QUANTITE	1995 VALUE VALEUR	1996 QUANTITY QUANTITE	1996 VALUE VALEUR	1997 QUANTITY QUANTITE	1997 VALUE VALEUR	PRODUIT
741	HEATING,COOLING EQUIPMNT		3.5	W 591	2.7	W 491	1.8	W 526	2.6	MACH CHAUFFAGE,PIECES
7414	NONDOM REFRIG EQUIPT,PTS	W 431	1.0	W 166	1.4	W 275	0.6	W 126	0.7	MAT PRODUCTION DU FROID
74141	REFRIG EQUIP NONDOMESTIC	W 420	0.9	W 153	1.3	W 271	0.6	W 90	0.6	REFIG INDUSTRIELS
7415	AIR–CONDITIONING MACHNRY	W 312	1.2	W 174	1.0	W 103	0.7	W 121	0.9	GROUPES CONDITION AIR
7416	HEATING,COOLING EQU NES		1.3	W 242	0.4	W 93	0.5	W 262	1.0	APP CHANGEMENT TEMP
742	PUMPS FOR LIQUIDS ETC	W 267	1.6	W 243	1.8	W 167	2.1	W 138	1.7	POMPES MOTO–POMPES
7428	OTHER PUMPS FOR LIQUIDS	W 109	0.9	W 111	0.9	W 116	1.3	W 69	0.8	AUTRES POMPES POUR LIQ
74288	PUMPS FR LIQUIDS NES ETC	W 103	0.7	W 107	0.8	W 98	1.0	W 56	0.7	POMPES POUR LIQUIDES NDA
743	PUMPS NES,CENTRFUGES ETC		1.7		1.8		2.2		1.8	POMPES COMPRES,VENT ETC
7436	GAS,LIQUID FILTERS ETC	W 103	0.8	W 62	0.8	W 112	1.2	W 79	0.9	APP POUR FILT DES LIQUIDES
744	MECHANICAL HANDLING EQU		2.3	W 460	1.6	W 403	1.1	W 371	2.0	EQUIP MANUTENTION PIECES
7441	FORK LIFT TRCKS,ETC,PTS	W 175	0.9	W 112	0.3	W 177	0.2	W 121	0.4	CHARIOTS POUR USINES ETC
74411	FORK LIFT TRUCKS ETC	W 174	0.9	W 112	0.3	W 177	0.2	W 121	0.4	CHARIOTS POUR LES GARES
7449	PTS NES OF MACHY OF 7442	W 185	0.7	W 154	0.6	W 82	0.5	W 117	1.0	PIECES DU 744.2
745	NONELEC MACHY,TOOLS NES		1.4	W 233	3.3		1.4	W 231	2.0	AUT MACH NON ELEC,PIECES
7451	POWER TOOLS NONELEC, PTS	W 17	0.3	W 19	0.2	W 37	0.3	W 129	1.1	OUT MACH PNEUM A MOTEUR
74511	POWER HAND TOOLS NONELEC	W 16	0.2	W 18	0.2	W 35	0.3	W 126	1.1	OUT MACH PNEUM A MOTEUR
7452	OTH NONELEC MCHS,PTS NES		1.2	W 214	3.1		1.2	W 102	0.9	AUT MACH NON ELEC,PIECES
74522	PACKAGNG,BOTTLNG,ETC MCH	W 48	0.7	W 68	2.3	W 62	0.3	W 19	0.2	MACH NETT BOUTEILLES,ETC
749	NONELEC MACH PTS,ACC NES	W 2496	3.6	W 363	2.8	W 216	2.6	W 341	3.0	PIECES MACH NON ELEC NDA
7492	COCKS,VALVES ETC NES	W 2134	1.2	W 157	0.9	W 104	0.8	W 144	1.1	ART ROB,SIM POUR TUYAUX
7493	SHAFT,CRANK,PULLEY ETC	W 245	1.2	W 53	0.9	W 45	0.8	W 114	0.9	ARBRES TRANS,VILEBREQUINS
75	OFFICE MACHNES,ADP EQUIP		3.0		2.7		3.6		4.4	MACH BUREAU TRAIT AUTOM
752	AUTOMTIC DATA PROC EQUIP		1.7		1.4	N 3693	1.9	N 6137	2.5	MACH TRAIT INFORMATION
7522	DIGITAL COMPUTERS	N 1501	1.0	N 593	0.9	N 773	1.0	N 1372	1.3	MACH DIGITALES COMPLETES
759	OFFICE,ADP MCH PTS,ACCES	W 22	0.7	W 25	0.8	W 25	0.9	W 42	1.2	PIECES DU 751 ET 752
7599	ACCTG,ETC,ADP MCH PTS,AC	W 17	0.6	W 16	0.6	W 21	0.8	W 32	0.9	PIECES DU 751 ET 752
76	TELECOMM,SOUND EQUIPMENT		4.1		6.2		4.1		4.7	EQUIPMENT DE TELECOM
764	TELECOM EQPT,PTS,ACC NES		3.1		4.8		2.9		3.5	EQUIP TELECOM,PIECES
7641	LINE TELEPHONE,ETC EQUIP	W 31	1.3	W 52	3.6	W 32	1.7	W 30	1.9	APP TELEPHON PAR FIL
7643	TV,RADIO TRANSMITTRS ETC		1.0	N 1997	0.4	N 1188	0.5	N 838	0.9	APP EMET TELE RADIO
77	ELECTRIC MACHNRY NES ETC		14.0		11.3		10.2		17.0	MACH APP ELECT NDA
771	ELECTRIC POWER MACHY NES	W 4978	2.0	W 155	0.9	W 104	0.9	W 338	2.3	MACH PROD,TRANS ELECTR
7711	TRANSFORMERS,ELECTRICAL	W 4931	1.7	W 128	0.6	W 82	0.4	W 312	1.8	TRANSFO ELECTRIQUES
77111	LIQUID DIELEC TRANSFRMRS	W 72	0.6	W 46	0.2	W 33	0.2	W 281	1.6	TRANSFO DIELEC LIQUIDE
77118	OTHER ELEC TRANSFORMERS	W 4859	1.2	W 82	0.4	W 49	0.3	W 31	0.3	AUTRES TRANSFO ELECTRIQ
772	SWITCHGEAR ETC,PARTS NES	W 265	3.4	W 163	1.9	W 176	1.7	W 1505	4.6	APP COUPURE,SECT ETC
7721	SWITCHGEAR ETC	W 264	3.3	W 163	1.9	W 176	1.6	W 1503	4.6	APP COUPURE,SECTIONMNT
773	ELECTR DISTRIBUTNG EQUIP	W 624	2.3	W 537	2.2	W 448	1.9	W 1213	4.1	EQUIPMT DISTRIBUTION ELECT
7731	INSULATED WIRE,CABLE ETC	W 584	2.1	W 529	2.1	W 421	1.8	W 1084	3.5	FILS,CABLES ISOLES ELECT
774	ELECTRO–MEDCL,XRAY EQUIP	W 8	1.0	W 10	0.7	W 7	0.1	W 20	0.4	APPAREILS MEDICAUX
7741	ELECTRO–MEDICAL EQUIPMNT	W 7	1.0		0.1	W 4	0.1	W 16	0.3	APP ELECTRICITE MEDICALE
775	HOUSEHOLD TYPE EQUIP NES		3.1		3.4		3.2		3.2	MACH,APP USAGE DOMESTQUE
7752	DOM REFRIGERATRS,FREEZRS		1.9		1.9		1.9		1.7	REFRIG,CONGEL MENAGER
77521	DOMESTIC REFRIGERATORS		1.7	N 4967	1.7		1.6		1.4	REFRIGERATEURS
778	ELECTRICAL MACHINERY NES		2.4		2.4		2.2		2.5	AUTRES MACH ELECT NDA
7788	OTH ELEC MACHY,EQUIP NES		0.9	W 1835	0.8		0.9	W 909	0.9	AUT MACH APP ELEC NDA
78	ROAD VEHICLES		15.0		15.6		16.0		15.1	VEHICULES ROUTIERS
781	PASS MOTOR VEH EXC BUSES	N 34308	4.5	N 6670	5.8	N 2102	5.4	N 8742	4.8	AUTO TRANSPORT PERSONNES
782	LORRIES,SPCL MTR VEH NES	N 161835	5.0	N 1871	6.0	N 1966	6.6	N 2057	6.3	VEHICULES SPECIAUX,MARCH
7821	LORRIES,TRUCKS	N 161825	4.6	N 1861	5.7	N 1952	6.3	N 2047	6.1	VEHICULES TRANSP MARCHAND
783	ROAD MOTOR VEHICLES NES	N 27717	1.1	N 243	1.5	N 271	1.4	N 279	1.3	VEHICULES ROUTIERS NDA
7831	BUSES	N 27655	0.7	N 193	1.2	N 183	0.9	N 196	0.9	VOITURES TRANSPORT COMMUN
784	MOTOR VEH PRTS,ACCES NES		1.4	W 214	1.2		1.2		1.5	PIECES 722,781,782,783
7849	OTHER MOTOR VEHCL PARTS	W 572	1.3	W 200	1.2	W 166	1.2	W 200	1.5	PIECES 722,781,782,783
785	CYCLES,ETC MOTRZD OR NOT		1.0		0.9		0.9		1.0	MOTOCYCLES SCOOTERS
786	TRAILERS,NONMOTR VEH,NES		2.3		0.5		0.8		0.5	REMORQUES,CADRES,CONTAIN
7861	TRAILERS,TRANSP CONTAINR		2.0		0.3		0.5		0.3	REMORQUES TOUS VEHICULES
78611	HOUSING,CAMPING TRAILERS	W 705	1.8	W 26	0.1	W 35	0.2	W 22	0.1	REMORQUES POUR CAMPING
79	OTHR TRANSPORT EQUIPMENT		1.4		4.0		4.1		3.6	AUTRE MATERIEL TRANSPORT
792	AIRCRAFT ETC		0.4		2.4		3.0		2.6	APP NAVIGATION AERIENNE
7923	AIRCRFT NES2000–15000KG	W 16	0.1	N 13	2.1	N 7	2.8	N 3	1.2	AERODYNES 2000 A 15000 KG
7924	AIRCRFT NES OVER 15000KG	N 1	0.1						1.3	AERODYNES PLUS 15000 KG
793	SHIPS AND BOATS ETC		1.0		1.7	N 462	1.1	N 1976	1.1	NAVIRES BATEAUX,ETC
7932	SHIPS AND BOATS NES		0.9		1.2	N 306	0.7	N 187	0.8	NAVIRES ET BATEAUX
8	MISC MANUFACTURED GOODS		34.6		34.7		32.0		33.9	ART MANUFACTURES DIVERS
812	*PLUMBG,HEATNG,LGHTNG EQ		1.2		1.1		1.1		1.3	APPAR SANITAIRES CHAUFFAGE
8124	LIGHTING EQUIPMENT NES	W 458	0.8	W 139	0.9	W 114	0.8	W 169	1.1	APPAREILS ECLAIRAGE ETC
821	*FURNITURE,PARTS THEREOF		2.4	W 660	2.6	W 560	1.8	W 559	1.5	MEUBLES ET PIECES
8212	MED FURN,STUFFD FURNSHGS	W 405	0.9	W 200	0.7	W 191	0.5	W 226	0.4	MOB MEDICO–CHIRUR,PIECES
8219	FURNITURE AND PARTS NES	W 838	1.2	W 358	1.6	W 286	1.0	W 263	0.9	AUTRES MEUBLES ET PIECES
82191	METAL FURNITURE NES	W 453	0.9	W 219	1.0	W 136	0.5	W 152	0.5	MEUBLES NDA EN METAL
84	CLOTHING AND ACCESSORIES		11.6		10.6		11.6		12.1	VETEMENTS
842	MENS OUTERWEAR NOT KNIT	N 2082600	9.9	N 2928418	9.6	N 2934355	10.8	N 1949799	11.2	VET DESSUS POUR HOMMES
8423	— TROUSERS,BREECHES ETC	N 1480656	6.1	N 1822185	5.3	N 2040205	6.7	N 1041463	5.1	PANTALONS HOMMES MAT TEX
8429	— OTHER OUTER GARMENTS	N 546000	3.8	N 1085008	4.2	N 883135	4.1	N 897849	6.1	AUT VET DES HOM MAT TEX
851	*FOOTWEAR		1.7		1.3	P 540188	1.4	P 570863	1.8	CHAUSSURES
85103	SHOES WOOD–,CORK–SOLED	P 220020	0.9	P 137671	0.6	P 138185	0.7	P 161028	0.6	CHAUS SEMELLES BOIS,LIEGE
87	PRECISION INSTRUMNTS NES		1.7		2.1		1.5		2.0	INSTRUM,APPAR SCIENT NDA
872	MEDICAL INSTRUMENTS NES	W 11	0.4	W 18	0.9	W 18	0.3	W 17	0.4	INSTR,APP MEDIC–CHIR NDA
874	MEASURNG,CONTROLNG INSTR	W 44	1.0	W 54	1.1	W 54	0.9		1.3	INSTRUMENTS DE MESURE
88	PHOTO EQU,OPTICL GDS ETC		1.2		1.2		1.1		1.1	APP,FOURN PHOTO,OP,MONTR
89	MISC MANUFCTRD GOODS NES		14.9		15.7		13.6		14.0	ART MANUFACTURES DIVERS
892	PRINTED MATTER	W 357	3.3	W 406	3.4	W 387	3.7		3.4	IMPRIMES
8921	PRINTED BOOKS,GLOBES,ETC	W 179	1.6	W 190	1.6	W 234	2.2	W 244	1.8	LIVRES,BROCHURES,CARTES
89211	PRINTED BOOKS,PAMPHLETS	W 174	1.6	W 180	1.6	W 221	2.1	W 229	1.8	LIVRES,BROCHURES
8928	PRINTED MATTER NES	W 138	1.2	W 164	1.4	W 112	1.3		1.2	IMPRIMES NDA
893	ARTICLES OF PLASTIC NES		5.1		6.7		6.6		7.1	OUVRAGES EN MAT DIVIS 58
8931	PLSTC PACKG CONTNRS,LIDS		1.8	W 809	1.9	W 1016	2.1	W 1183	2.6	ART TRANSP EMBALLAGE ETC
8939	MISC PLASTIC ARTICLES		3.2	W 2035	4.8	W 2201	4.5	W 2137	4.4	ART DIVERS EN MAT DIV 58
89399	OTHR PLASTC ARTICLES NES		2.9	W 1716	4.4	W 1780	3.9	W 1873	4.0	AUT OUV MAT DIV 58
894	TOYS,SPORTING GOODS,ETC		1.0		1.3		1.0		1.3	VOITURES ENFANTS,JOUETS
8942	TOYS,INDOOR GAMES ETC		0.7	W 252	1.0	W 179	0.7	W 253	0.9	JOUETS,JEUX ETC
899	OTHER MANUFACTURED GOODS		4.8		3.7		1.2		1.4	AUT ART MANUF DIVERS NDA
8998	SMALLWARES,TOILETRYS ETC	W 693	2.3	W 1111	2.9	W 63	0.6	W 65	0.7	ART MERCERIE,TOILETTE
89981	HAND SIEVES AND RIDDLES			W 1057	2.3		0.1	W 1	0.1	TAMIS ET CRIBLES
8999	OTHER MANUF GOODS NES	W 129	2.0	W 24	0.3	W 9	0.1		0.1	OUVRAGES DIVERS NDA

Belize

4. General Imports C.I.F. by Commodities according to the S.I.T.C. (Rev. 2) in million U.S. Dollars
Importations Générales C.A.F. par Produits d'après la C.T.C.I. (Rév. 2) en millions de Dollars E.U.

SITC CTCI	COMMODITY	1994 QUANTITY QUANTITE	1994 VALUE VALEUR	1995 QUANTITY QUANTITE	1995 VALUE VALEUR	1996 QUANTITY QUANTITE	1996 VALUE VALEUR	1997 QUANTITY QUANTITE	1997 VALUE VALEUR	PRODUIT
89991	ARTICLES OF GUT,ETC	W 117	1.9	W 13	0.2				0.1	OUVRAGES EN BOYAUX
9	GOODS NOT CLASSD BY KIND		0.3		0.2		2.1		1.7	ART TRANSACT NON CLASSES
931	*SPECIAL TRANSACTIONS					W 804	1.9	W 699	1.6	TRANS.SPECIALES

5. General Exports F.O.B. by Commodities according to the S.I.T.C. (Rev. 2) in million U.S. Dollars
Exportations Générales F.O.B. par Produits d'après la C.T.C.I. (Rév. 2) en millions de Dollars E.U.

SITC CTCI	COMMODITY	1994 QUANTITY QUANTITE	1994 VALUE VALEUR	1995 QUANTITY QUANTITE	1995 VALUE VALEUR	1996 QUANTITY QUANTITE	1996 VALUE VALEUR	1997 QUANTITY QUANTITE	1997 VALUE VALEUR	PRODUIT
	ALL COMMODITIES		143.0		161.7		167.7		176.2	TOUS PRODUITS
0	FOOD AND LIVE ANIMALS		96.8		124.0		132.3		136.7	ALIMENTS,ANIMAUX VIVANTS
02	DAIRY PRODCTS,BIRDS'EGGS		1.3		0.4		0.4		0.5	PRODUITS LAITIERS,OEUFS
024	CHEESE AND CURD	W 336	1.0	W 89	0.3	W 195	0.4	W 130	0.4	FROMAGE ET CAILLEBOTTE
03	FISH AND PREPARATIONS		13.3		15.8		12.5		18.0	POISSONS ET PREPARATIONS
036	SHELL FISH FRESH,FROZEN	W 915	13.1	W 1139	15.6	W 960	12.1	W 1328	17.7	CRUSTACES,MOLLUSQUES
05	VEGETABLES AND FRUIT		35.9		57.0		66.2		67.8	LEGUMES ET FRUITS
054	VEG ETC FRSH,SMPLY PRSVD	W 2240	2.0	W 2871	2.3	W 2243	1.7	W 3910	3.2	LEGUMES FRAIS,CONG,SECS
0542	LEGUMINOUS VEGETBLES DRY	W 2230	2.0	W 2835	2.2	W 2212	1.7	W 3888	3.2	LEGUMES A COSSE SECS
057	FRUIT,NUTS,FRESH,DRIED	W 17	0.1	W 50605	22.9	W 1	0.1	W 63995	28.6	FRUITS FRAIS OU SECS
0573	BANANA,PLANTAIN,FRSH,DRY		14.9	W 49565	22.1		28.8	W 59975	26.2	BANANES FRAICHES,SECHEES
0579	FRUIT FRESH OR DRIED NES	W 2161	1.4	W 904	0.7	W 2875	2.0	W 3637	2.2	FRUITS FRAIS,SECS NDA
05798	OTHER FRESH FRUIT	W 2104	1.1	W 808	0.5	W 2490	1.5	W 3558	2.2	AUTRES FRUITS FRAIS
058	FRUIT PRESERVED,PREPARED	W 11154	17.7	W 20937	32.0	W 22039	33.7	W 41208	36.1	CONSERVES DE FRUITS
0585	FRUIT OR VEGETABLE JUICE	W 11147	17.7	W 20936	32.0	W 22031	33.7	W 41149	36.0	JUS DE FRUITS
05851	ORANGE JUICE	W 8400	12.4	W 16923	24.8	W 16975	26.7	W 33800	30.6	JUS D'ORANGE
05852	GRAPEFRUIT JUICE	W 2708	5.3	W 3913	7.0	W 4966	6.8	W 7298	5.3	JUS DE PAMPLEMOUSSE
06	SUGAR AND PREPS,HONEY		45.6		50.7		52.8		49.4	SUCRES ET PRODUITS
061	SUGAR AND HONEY		45.6		50.6		52.8		49.4	SUCRES ET MIEL
0611	RAW BEET AND CANE SUGAR	W 94335	40.4	W 93799	47.8	W 96350	47.2	W 110708	46.0	SUCRES BRUTS
0615	MOLASSES	V 41726	5.3	V 29284	2.9	V 43584	5.6	V 34082	3.4	MELASSES
1	BEVERAGES AND TOBACCO		4.1		4.8		4.7		6.1	BOISSONS ET TABACS
11	BEVERAGES		2.5		2.0		2.1		3.2	BOISSONS
112	ALCOHOLIC BEVERAGES	W 656	2.4	W 217	2.0	W 193	2.1	W 308	3.2	BOISSONS ALCOOLIQUES
1124	DISTILLED ALCOHOLIC BEVS	W 594	2.3	W 178	1.9	W 181	2.0	W 266	3.0	ALCOOLS,EAUX–DE–VIE
11241	WHISKY	W 552	2.0	W 124	1.6	W 134	1.6	W 178	2.4	WHISKY
12	TOBACCO AND MANUFACTURES		1.7		2.9		2.6		2.9	TABACS BRUTS FABRIQUES
122	TOBACCO,MANUFACTURED	W 37	1.7	W 272	2.9	W 137	2.6	W 95	2.9	TABACS FABRIQUES
1222	CIGARETTES	W 37	1.7	W 272	2.9	W 137	2.6	W 94	2.9	CIGARETTES
2	CRUDE MATERLS,EXCL FUELS		4.3		2.4		2.0		2.9	MAT BRUTES NON COMESTIBLES
24	CORK AND WOOD		3.9		2.0		1.4		2.6	LIEGE ET BOIS
248	WOOD SHAPED,SLEEPERS	W 7275	3.8	W 2904	1.8	W 2546	1.4	W 4831	2.4	BOIS SIMPLEMENT TRAVAILLES
2483	LUMBER SHAPED NON–CONIFR	W 7260	3.8	W 2659	1.7	W 2395	1.4	W 4687	2.3	NON CONIFERES SCIES,RABOTES
24831	LUMBER SAWN ETC NON–CON	W 7235	3.8	W 2652	1.7	W 2341	1.4	W 4619	2.3	SCIES LONGITUDINALEMENT
3	MINERAL FUELS ETC		3.5		5.2		3.2		3.8	COMBUSTIBLES MINERAUX LUB
33	PETROLEUM AND PRODUCTS		3.4		5.1		3.2		3.7	PETROLE ET DERIVES
334	PETROLEUM PRODUCTS,REFIN	W 15857	3.4	W 11878	5.1	W 12968	3.2	W 15551	3.7	PRODUITS RAFFINES
3342	KEROSENE,OTH MEDIUM OILS	W 14155	3.0	W 11516	5.0	W 7844	1.9	W 5819	1.5	PETR LAMPANTS,AUT HUIL
33421	KEROSENE INCL JET FUEL	W 14155	3.0	W 11516	5.0	W 7844	1.9	W 5819	1.5	PETROLES LAMPANTS
3343	GAS OILS	W 88	0.1	W 178	0.1	W 4892	1.2	W 8772	1.9	GAS OILS
5	CHEMCLS,RELATED PROD NES		2.0		1.9		1.4		0.9	PRODUITS CHIMIQUES
55	PERFUME,CLEANING ETC PRD		1.8		1.9		1.3		0.9	PROD POUR PARFUM,TOILETTE
551	ESSENTL OILS,PERFUME,ETC	W 227	0.4	W 435	1.6	W 249	1.2	W 263	0.7	HUILES ESSENTIELLES
5513	ESSENTL OIL,RESINOID,ETC	W 227	0.4	W 435	1.6	W 249	1.2	W 263	0.7	HUILES ESSENTIELLES,RESIN
553	PERFUMERY,COSMETICS,ETC		1.5			W 2	0.1		0.2	PRODUITS DE PARFUMERIE
6	BASIC MANUFACTURES		2.3		2.0		1.0		1.1	ART MANUFACTURES
63	WOOD,CORK MANUFACTRS NES		1.6		0.7		0.7		0.7	OUVRAGES LIEGE ET BOIS
634	VENEERS,PLYWOOD,ETC		1.5		0.3	V 1	0.1		0.5	PLACAGES,CONTRE–PLAQUES
6342	PLYWOOD OF WOOD SHEETS	V 1594	1.2	V 411	0.3	V 476	0.3	V 286	0.2	BOIS CONTRE–PLAQUES
65	TEXTILE YARN,FABRICS,ETC		0.2		1.0		0.1		0.1	FILS,TISSUS,ARTICLES TEXTILE
658	TEXTILE ARTICLES NES	W 10	0.1	W 44	0.8		0.1	W 1	0.1	ART FACONNES MAT TEXTILES
6582	MADE–UP CANVAS GOODS			W 44	0.8		0.1			BACHES,TENTES ETC
69	METAL MANUFACTURES NES		0.6		0.2		0.2		0.1	ART MANUFACT EN METAL NDA
7	MACHINES,TRANSPORT EQUIP		8.4		4.9		4.3		4.6	MACHINES MATERIEL TRANSPORT
71	POWER GENERATING EQUIPMT		0.3		1.3		0.9		1.2	MACHINES GENERATRICES
716	ROTATING ELECTRIC PLANT		0.1	W 62	1.1		0.7	W 64	1.0	APP ELECTR ROTATIFS,PIECES
7162	AC MTRS,GENRTRS,GEN SETS		0.1	W 62	1.1		0.7	W 64	1.0	MOTEURS ELECTRIQUES
71623	GEN SETS WITH PISTN ENGN	W 18	0.1	W 62	1.1	W 40	0.7	W 64	1.0	GROUPES MOTEUR EXPLOSION
72	MACHS FOR SPCL INDUSTRYS		0.9		0.4		1.8		1.9	MAC SPECIALES POUR INDUST
723	CIVIL ENGNEERG EQUIP ETC		0.4	W 14	0.1		1.3	W 861	1.7	APPAREILS DE GENIE CIVIL
7234	CONST,MINING MACHNRY NES		0.4	W 14	0.1		1.3	W 861	1.7	MACH POUR LA CONST, MINES
72341	SELF–PROPELLD DOZERS,ETC	W 21	0.2	W 14	0.1	W 78	0.7	W 34	0.2	BULLDOZERS
72344	BORING,SINKING MACHINERY					W 120	0.3	W 774	1.3	MACHINES DE FORAGE
74	GENRL INDUSTRL MACHY NES		1.1		0.2		0.8		0.6	MACH APP INDUSTRIE
744	MECHANICAL HANDLING EQU	W 178	0.9	W 3	0.1	W 69	0.3	W 116	0.4	EQUIP MANUTENTION PIECES
7441	FORK LIFT TRCKS,ETC,PTS	W 87	0.6	W 1	0.1	W 33	0.1	W 11	0.1	CHARIOTS POUR USINES ETC
74411	FORK LIFT TRUCKS ETC	W 87	0.6	W 1	0.1	W 33	0.1	W 11	0.1	CHARIOTS POUR LES GARES
76	TELECOMM,SOUND EQUIPMENT		4.0		0.2		0.3		0.1	EQUIPMENT DE TELECOM
764	TELECOM EQPT,PTS,ACC NES		3.9		0.1		0.3		0.1	EQUIP TELECOM,PIECES
7643	TV,RADIO TRANSMITTRS ETC		2.2	N 10	0.1	N 5	0.1			APP EMET TELE RADIO
7648	TELECOMM EQUIPMENT NES	N 11	1.7	N 2	0.1			N 1	0.1	APP TELECOM NDA
76482	TELEVISION CAMERAS	N 9	1.7	N 2	0.1					APP PRISE DE VUES TELE
78	ROAD VEHICLES		1.5		1.9		0.5		0.5	VEHICULES ROUTIERS
781	PASS MOTOR VEH EXC BUSES	N 30	0.6	N 63	1.4	N 25	0.2	N 20	0.3	AUTO TRANSPORT PERSONNES
782	LORRIES,SPCL MTR VEH NES	N 21998	0.8	N 12	0.2	N 23	0.3	N 11	0.2	VEHICULES SPECIAUX,MARCH
7821	LORRIES,TRUCKS	N 21997	0.8	N 9	0.1	N 21	0.2	N 10	0.2	VEHICULES TRANSP MARCHAND
79	OTHR TRANSPORT EQUIPMENT		0.4		1.1		0.1		0.4	AUTRE MATERIEL TRANSPORT
792	AIRCRAFT ETC		0.2		0.9		0.1		0.3	APP NAVIGATION AERIENNE
7924	AIRCRFT NES OVER 15000KG				0.9					AERODYNES PLUS 15000 KG
8	MISC MANUFACTURED GOODS		22.0		16.8		18.4		19.7	ART MANUFACTURES DIVERS
84	CLOTHING AND ACCESSORIES		18.4		14.8		17.9		18.6	VETEMENTS
842	MENS OUTERWEAR NOT KNIT	N 2482620	16.5	N 1736886	14.6	N 1913628	17.6	N 1891053	18.5	VET DESSUS POUR HOMMES
8423	— TROUSERS,BREECHES ETC	N 1823652	10.0	N 1090236	8.0	N 1309488	10.7	N 998100	8.2	PANTALONS HOMMES MAT TEX
8429	— OTHER OUTER GARMENTS	N 639756	6.5	N 646650	6.7	N 604140	6.9	N 892953	10.3	AUT VET DES HOM MAT TEX
846	UNDER GARMENTS KNITTED	N 872616	1.7	N 72738	0.2	N 93012	0.4	N 77763	0.1	SOUS VETS DE BONNETERIE
8462	— OF COTTON NON ELASTIC	N 872616	1.7	N 22080	0.1	N 93012	0.4	N 77763	0.1	SOUS–VET BONNET COTON
84629	—— OTHER	N 872616	1.7	N 22080	0.1	N 93012	0.4	N 77763	0.1	AUT SOUS–VET BONNET COTON
89	MISC MANUFCTRD GOODS NES		2.9		1.5		0.3		0.8	ART MANUFACTURES DIVERS
899	OTHER MANUFACTURED GOODS		2.8	W 198	1.0		0.1	W 82	0.3	AUT ART MANUF DIVERS NDA
8998	SMALLWARES,TOILETRYS ETC	W 81	0.6	W 120	0.7		0.1	W 13	0.2	ART MERCERIE,TOILETTE
89981	HAND SIEVES AND RIDDLES			W 117	0.6			W 2	0.1	TAMIS ET CRIBLES
8999	OTHER MANUF GOODS NES	W 203	2.2	W 105	0.7			W 69	0.2	OUVRAGES DIVERS NDA
89991	ARTICLES OF GUT,ETC	W 202	2.2	W 105	0.7			W 69	0.2	OUVRAGES EN BOYAUX
9	GOODS NOT CLASSD BY KIND		0.1				0.8		0.8	ART TRANSACT NON CLASSES
931	*SPECIAL TRANSACTIONS					W 159	0.8	W 153	0.8	TRANS.SPECIALES

1. HISTORICAL SERIES, 1961–1996 SPECIAL TRADE, IMPORTS C.I.F., EXPORTS F.O.B.
SERIES HISTORIQUES, 1961–1996 COMMERCE SPECIAL, IMPORTATIONS C.A.F., EXPORTATIONS F.O.B

YEAR ANNEE	VALUE IN MILLION C.F.A. FRANCS VALEUR EN MILLION C.F.A. FRANCS — MERCHANDISE –MARCHANDISE		GOLD –OR		CONVERSION FACTORS U.S. CENTS PER C.F.A. FRANC FACTEURS DE CONVERSION CENTS E.U. PAR C.F.A. FRANC		INDEX NUMBERS –INDICES — QUANTUM		UNIT VALUE VALEUR UNITAIRE	
	IMPORTS	EXPORTS	IMPORTS	EXPORTS	IMPORTS	EXPORTS	IMPORTS	EXPORTS	IMPORTS	EXPORTS
1961	6275.00	3579.00			0.4051	0.4051				
1962	6627.00	2699.00			0.4051	0.4051				
1963	8249.00	3155.00			0.4051	0.4051				
1964	7762.00	3254.00			0.4051	0.4051				
1965	8491.00	3367.00			0.4051	0.4051				
1966	8264.00	2585.00			0.4051	0.4051				
1967	10745.00	3750.00			0.4051	0.4051				
1968	12208.00	5508.00			0.4051	0.4051				
1969	14124.00	7067.00			0.3916	0.3909				
1970	17660.00	9062.00			0.3601	0.3601				
1971	21202.00	11648.00			0.3601	0.3601				
1972	23510.00	9189.00			0.3967	0.3969				
1973	24859.00	9794.00			0.4500	0.4453				
1974	35530.00	10240.00			0.4158	0.4158				
1975	42080.00	6791.00			0.4672	0.4672				
1976	50500.00	9053.00			0.4191	0.4191				
1977	60400.00	10120.00			0.4080	0.4080				
1978	70197.00	6140.00			0.4440	0.4440				
1979	68100.00	9770.00			0.4701	0.4701				
1980	69970.00	13270.00			0.4733	0.4733				
1981	147499.00	9141.00			0.3680	0.3680				
1982	152553.00	7837.00			0.3043	0.3043				
1983	112032.00	25351.00			0.2624	0.2624				
1984	125900.00	72820.00			0.2289	0.2289				
1985	148780.00	67350.00			0.2243	0.2243				
1986	133850.00	36012.99			0.2885	0.2897				
1987	104980.00	34270.00			0.3317	0.3326				
1988	97000.00	21000.00			0.3359	0.3368				
1989	66130.00	24580.00			0.3135	0.3135				
1990	72190.00	33250.00			0.3683	0.3683				
1991	68050.00	94262.53			0.3573	0.3573				
1992	153020.00	88800.00			0.3783	0.3783				
1993	161780.00	108600.00			0.3534	0.3534				
1994	239350.00	217200.00			0.1803	0.1803				
1995	345299.90	206500.00			0.2005	0.1976				
1996	324800.00	216700.00			0.1955	0.1956				

2. IMPORTS BY BROAD ECONOMIC CATEGORY AND EXPORTS BY INDUSTRIAL ORIGIN. (PERCENTAGE OF TOTAL VALUE)
IMPORTATIONS PAR CATEGORIES ECONOMIQUES ET EXPORTATIONS PAR BRANCHE D'ACTIVITE.(EN POURCENTAGE DE LA VALEUR TOTALE)

IMPORTS – IMPORTATIONS

	1989	1990	1991	1992	1993	1994	1995
TOTAL IMPORTS–IMPORTATIONS TOTALES							
1 FOOD BEV–ALIMENTATION BOISSONS							
11 PRIMARY–PRODUITS DE BASE							
111 FOR INDUSTRY–POUR L'INDUSTRIE							
112 FOR HOUSEHOLDS–POUR LES MENAGES							
12 PROCESSED–PRODUITS ELABORES							
121 FOR INDUSTRY–POUR L'INDUSTRIE							
122 FOR HOUSEHOLDS–POUR LES MENAGES							
2 IND SUPPLIES–APPROV INDUSTRIELS							
21 PRIMARY–PRODUITS DE BASE							
22 PROCESSED–PRODUITS ELABORES							
3 FUELS–COMBUSTIBLES							
31 PRIMARY–PRODUITS DE BASE							
32 PROCESSED–PRODUITS ELABORES							
321 MOTOR SPIRIT–ESSENCE							
322 OTHER–AUTRES							
4 MACHINERY–EQUIPEMENT							
41 CAPITAL EQUIPMENT–MACHINES							
42 PARTS–PIECES ACCESSOIRES							
5 TRANSPORT–TRANSPORT							
51 PASSENGER CARS–AUTOMOBILES							
52 OTHER–AUTRES							
521 INDUSTRIAL–INDUSTRIELS							
522 NON INDUSTRIAL–NON INDUSTRIEL							
53 PARTS–PIECES ACCESSOIRES							
6 CONSUM GOODS–BIENS CONSOMMATION							
61 DURABLE–DURABLES							
62 SEMI DURABLE–SEMI DURABLES							
63 NON DURABLE–NON DURABLES							
7 GOODS NES–BIENS NDA							

EXPORTS – EXPORTATIONS

	1989	1990	1991	1992	1993	1994	1995
TOTAL EXPORTS–EXPORTATIONS TOTALES							
1 AGRICULTURE							
2 MINING QUARRY–INDUS EXTRACTIVES							
3 MANUFACTURING–IND MANUFACTUR							
31 FOOD BEV TOBACCO–ALIM BOISS TAB							
32 TEXTILES–INDUSTRIES TEXTILES							
33 WOOD & PRODUCTS–BOIS & PRODUITS							
34 PAPER & PRODUCTS–PAPIER & PRODT							
35 CHEMICALS–INDUSTRIES CHIMIQUES							
36 NON METAL MIN–MIN NON METAL							
37 BASIC METAL–IND METAL BASE							
38 METAL MANUF–MANUF METAL							
39 OTH MANUF IND–AUTRES MANUF							

3. TRADE BY PRINCIPAL COUNTRIES OF ORIGIN AND DESTINATION (VALUE IN MILLION U.S. DOLLARS)
ECHANGES SELON LES PRINCIPAUX PAYS D'ORIGINE ET DE DESTINATION (VALEUR EN MILLIONS DE DOLLARS EU)

COUNTRIES–PAYS	SPECIAL IMPORTS C.I.F. IMPORTATIONS SPECIALES C.A.F 1991	1992	1993	1994	1995
World		578.9	571.7	431.6	647.1
Africa		57.3	33.5	28.1	62.4
Americas		42.0	31.8	24.5	43.0
– Northern America		35.8	25.4	21.6	35.3
– LAIA		5.8	6.0	2.8	6.5
– CACM			0.0		0.1
– Caribbean		0.3	0.1	0.1	1.0
– Rest of America		0.1	0.3		0.0
Asia excl fmr USSR		207.7	220.1	158.1	176.7
– Middle East		1.1	1.4	3.8	10.2
Asia former USSR					
Europe excl fmr USSR		270.4	284.9	220.3	363.2
– European Union		256.9	274.8	210.5	351.1
– Eastern Europe		6.2	4.0	4.5	7.4
– Rest of Europe		7.4	6.1	5.4	4.7
Europe former USSR		1.0	0.4	0.3	0.1
Oceania		0.2	0.9	0.1	1.7
Other		0.3	0.2	0.1	0.1
France, Monaco		134.3	148.5	111.5	225.3
Thailand/Thaïlande		102.5	99.2	69.6	64.5
Netherlands/Pays–Bas		42.9	52.0	22.7	31.1
Japan/Japon		32.1	33.8	24.8	28.6
USA/Etats–Unis d'Amer		34.6	24.2	18.5	31.8
China/Chine		24.2	33.2	17.7	20.4
Germany/Allemagne		19.0	16.8	21.6	22.8
United Kingdom		20.9	15.5	14.3	21.8
Pakistan		25.6	13.2	15.9	5.6
Cote d'Ivoire		8.9	10.1	12.5	23.4
Spain/Espagne		8.3	11.5	13.6	17.7
Senegal/Sénégal		12.0	9.0	5.7	21.6
Belgium–Luxembourg		14.0	9.0	10.8	11.6
Italy/Italie		9.2	12.3	9.6	12.3
India/Inde		6.8	6.2	6.1	12.2
Nigeria/Nigéria		25.5	0.2	0.4	0.1
Korea, Republic of		2.6	3.8	5.8	11.9
Brazil/Brésil		5.7	5.9	2.2	6.5
China, Hong Kong SAR		0.8	5.5	4.1	8.5
Norway,Svalbard and JM		5.7	5.2	4.1	3.2
Mauritania/Mauritanie		4.5	6.2	3.2	3.9
Denmark/Danemark		4.9	3.8	2.5	3.6
Korea Dem People's Rp		1.1	3.1	3.1	5.4
Turkey/Turquie		1.0	0.8	1.2	9.3
Malaysia/Malaisie		1.1	7.6	0.8	1.6
Tunisia/Tunisie		2.3	2.5	2.8	3.0
Viet Nam		4.4	3.4	0.2	1.4
Canada		1.2	1.2	3.1	3.6
Singapore/Singapour		1.5	4.4	1.1	1.4
Other Asia n.e.s.		2.2	2.9	1.4	1.8
Czech Republic			3.7	2.2	2.2
Indonesia/Indonésie		0.7	1.7	3.0	1.2
Romania/Roumanie		0.5	0.1	1.4	4.6
Morocco/Maroc		1.5	1.7	0.7	2.1
Former Czechoslovakia		5.4			
Austria/Autriche		1.6	1.5	1.0	1.3
Switzerland,Liechtenst.		1.7	0.8	1.3	1.5
Togo		0.4	0.4	0.3	4.0
Ireland/Irlande		0.6	1.8	1.1	1.4
Bangladesh		0.9	0.8	0.7	1.7

COUNTRIES–PAYS	SPECIAL EXPORTS F.O.B. EXPORTATIONS SPECIALES F.O.B. 1991	1992	1993	1994	1995
Monde		335.9	383.8	391.6	408.0
Afrique		115.9	190.6	109.1	86.2
Amériques		15.8	29.0	84.6	87.5
– Amérique du Nord		2.5	5.8	6.5	3.4
– ALAI		12.7	22.5	77.9	81.9
– MCAC		0.5			0.1
– Caraïbes			0.4	0.0	0.0
– Autre Amérique		0.1	0.4	0.2	2.1
Asie anc. URSS exclus		73.5	80.2	64.8	104.8
– Moyen–Orient		1.3	0.1	2.3	6.7
Asie ancienne URSS					
Europe anc. URSS exclus		130.2	83.9	128.8	128.4
– Union Européenne		128.5	83.5	125.9	121.6
– Europe de l'Est			0.2		
– Autre de l'Europe		1.6	0.2	2.9	6.9
Europe ancienne URSS		0.0		3.1	
Océanie		0.5		0.8	1.0
Autre			0.1	0.4	0.1
Morocco/Maroc		42.4	135.1	36.2	41.6
Brazil/Brésil		12.7	22.5	74.7	81.4
Portugal		20.6	19.5	42.9	60.0
Italy/Italie		26.7	28.5	17.1	17.5
Nigeria/Nigéria		19.6	12.4	28.0	10.7
Belgium–Luxembourg		49.6	8.1	6.6	5.9
France, Monaco		6.1	12.6	27.8	11.3
India/Inde		4.4	15.2	8.7	26.2
Indonesia/Indonésie		12.7	5.5	17.1	18.0
Thailand/Thaïlande		13.6	7.2	11.5	20.8
China/Chine		3.0	28.1	2.3	10.3
Niger		6.5	6.0	21.6	5.2
Spain/Espagne		7.9	1.8	14.8	10.2
So. African Customs Un		5.9	11.0	6.0	10.6
Togo		8.2	3.3	5.3	4.0
United Kingdom		7.3	2.9	5.2	5.0
Cote d'Ivoire		9.2	7.1	2.4	1.4
Pakistan		12.8	3.9	0.2	2.2
USA/Etats–Unis d'Amer		1.9	5.3	6.5	3.4
Singapore/Singapour		8.6	2.1	3.1	1.1
Other Asia n.e.s.		3.7	0.5	1.1	8.6
Netherlands/Pays–Bas		3.8	1.3	4.7	3.9
Germany/Allemagne		1.5	4.8	2.6	4.6
Burkina Faso		6.9	4.5	0.7	0.4
Switzerland,Liechtenst.		1.5	0.2	2.9	6.9
China, Hong Kong SAR		2.9	5.0	1.0	2.0
Japan/Japon		4.2	3.0	1.9	0.9
Denmark/Danemark		3.2	1.2	2.6	2.3
Viet Nam			3.3	5.2	0.0
Bangladesh		0.5	1.0	2.3	4.5
Cape Verde/Cap–Vert		4.2			4.0
Saudi Arabia		0.6	0.0	2.3	3.8
Korea, Republic of		2.4	0.5	2.6	0.5
Senegal/Sénégal		2.7	1.4	0.5	1.1
Malaysia/Malaisie		0.2	1.7	0.8	2.9
Congo		3.3	0.8	0.6	0.6
Cameroon/Cameroun		0.3	0.1	4.1	0.7
Gabon		0.8	1.5	1.3	1.4
Mali		2.7	0.8	0.1	0.7
Philippines		0.9	0.7	1.8	

(VALUE AS PERCENTAGE OF WORLD TOTAL)(VALEURS EN POURCENTAGE DU TOTAL MONDIAL)

	1986	1987	1988	1989	1990	1991	1992	1993	1994	1995
Africa	8.2	10.2	18.8	23.0			9.9	5.9	6.5	9.6
Americas	7.4	4.9	6.6	8.3			7.3	5.6	5.7	6.6
– Northern America	5.0	4.2	5.5	7.6			6.2	4.4	5.0	5.5
– LAIA	2.4	0.8	1.1	0.7			1.0	1.0	0.6	1.0
– CACM								0.0		0.0
– Caribbean							0.1	0.0	0.0	0.2
– Rest of America							0.0	0.1		0.0
Asia excl fmr USSR	12.1	23.7	18.1	12.5			35.9	38.5	36.6	27.3
– Middle East							0.2	0.2	0.9	1.6
Asia former USSR										
Europe excl fmr USSR	52.3	43.0	40.4	43.9			46.7	49.8	51.1	56.1
– European Union	50.1	41.7	36.9	41.1			44.4	48.1	48.8	54.3
– Eastern Europe	1.3	1.0	2.5	2.4			1.1	0.7	1.0	1.1
– Rest of Europe	0.9	0.4	1.0	0.5			1.3	1.1	1.2	0.7
Europe former USSR	0.6	0.5	2.4	0.3			0.2	0.1	0.1	0.0
Oceania	0.3	0.0	0.0	0.0			0.0	0.2	0.0	0.3
Other	1.4	0.7					0.0	0.0	0.0	0.0
France, Monaco	23.1	17.6	19.3	18.7			23.2	26.0	25.8	34.8
Thailand/Thaïlande	1.4	14.1	12.0	6.0			17.7	17.4	16.1	10.0
Netherlands/Pays–Bas	6.0	7.1	5.4	8.9			7.4	9.1	5.3	4.8
Japan/Japon	5.1	5.6	2.3	2.7			5.5	5.9	5.7	4.4
USA/Etats–Unis d'Amer	4.7	3.9	5.3	7.3			6.0	4.2	4.3	4.9
China/Chine	5.5	4.1	3.8	3.8			4.2	5.8	4.1	3.2
Germany/Allemagne							3.3	2.9	5.0	3.5
United Kingdom	7.1	4.7	4.1	4.4			3.6	2.7	3.3	3.4
Pakistan							4.4	2.3	3.7	0.9
Cote d'Ivoire	1.7	2.4	4.6	5.8			1.5	1.8	2.9	3.6

	1986	1987	1988	1989	1990	1991	1992	1993	1994	1995
Afrique	7.2	10.1	22.1	16.5			34.5	49.7	27.9	21.1
Amériques	0.0	16.8	30.1	21.3			4.7	7.6	21.6	21.4
– Amérique du Nord	0.0	16.8	30.1	21.3			0.7	1.5	1.7	0.8
– ALAI							3.8	5.9	19.9	20.1
– MCAC							0.1			0.0
– Caraïbes								0.1	0.0	0.0
– Autre Amérique							0.0	0.1	0.1	0.5
Asie anc. URSS exclus	7.1	12.2	1.0	14.5			21.9	20.9	16.5	25.7
– Moyen–Orient							0.4	0.0	0.6	1.7
Asie ancienne URSS										
Europe anc. URSS exclus	82.9	51.2	34.6	28.5			38.7	21.9	32.9	31.5
– Union Européenne	80.3	50.4	33.0	27.3			38.3	21.8	32.2	29.8
– Europe de l'Est	0.2							0.1		
– Autre de l'Europe	2.5	0.8	1.6	1.2			0.5	0.1	0.7	1.7
Europe ancienne URSS		0.1					0.0		0.8	
Océanie							0.2		0.2	0.2
Autre	0.3	0.1						0.0	0.1	0.0
Morocco/Maroc	0.1	0.9	0.5	2.1			12.6	35.2	9.2	10.2
Brazil/Brésil							3.8	5.9	19.1	20.0
Portugal	9.1	21.0	13.8	12.2			6.1	5.1	10.9	14.7
Italy/Italie	16.7	13.8	2.1	5.7			8.0	7.4	4.4	4.3
Nigeria/Nigéria	1.9	7.3	12.8	6.2			5.8	3.2	7.1	2.6
Belgium–Luxembourg	0.7	1.1	0.6	1.8			14.8	2.1	1.7	1.4
France, Monaco	10.4	3.8	9.0	2.4			1.8	3.3	7.1	2.8
India/Inde							1.3	4.0	2.2	6.4
Indonesia/Indonésie							3.8	1.4	4.4	4.4
Thailand/Thaïlande							4.0	1.9	2.9	5.1

4. Special Imports C.I.F. by Commodities according to the S.I.T.C. (Rev. 2) in million U.S. Dollars
Importations Spéciales C.A.F. par Produits d'après la C.T.C.I. (Rév. 2) en millions de Dollars E.U.

SITC CTCI	COMMODITY	1992		1993		1994		1995		PRODUIT
		QUANTITY QUANTITE	VALUE VALEUR	QUANTITY QUANTITE	VALUE VALEUR	QUANTITY QUANTITE	VALUE VALEUR	QUANTITY QUANTITE	VALUE VALEUR	
	ALL COMMODITIES									TOUS PRODUITS

5. Special Exports F.O.B. by Commodities according to the S.I.T.C. (Rev. 2) in million U.S. Dollars
Exportations Spéciales F.O.B. par Produits d'après la C.T.C.I. (Rév. 2) en millions de Dollars E.U.

SITC CTCI	COMMODITY	1992		1993		1994		1995		PRODUIT
		QUANTITY QUANTITE	VALUE VALEUR	QUANTITY QUANTITE	VALUE VALEUR	QUANTITY QUANTITE	VALUE VALEUR	QUANTITY QUANTITE	VALUE VALEUR	
	ALL COMMODITIES									TOUS PRODUITS

1. HISTORICAL SERIES, 1962–1997 GENERAL TRADE, IMPORTS C.I.F., EXPORTS F.O.B.
SERIES HISTORIQUES, 1962–1997 COMMERCE GENERAL, IMPORTATIONS C.A.F., EXPORTATIONS F.O.B

YEAR ANNEE	VALUE IN MILLION BERMUDA DOLLARS / VALEUR EN MILLION BERMUDA DOLLARS — MERCHANDISE –MARCHANDISE: IMPORTS	MERCHANDISE –MARCHANDISE: EXPORTS	GOLD –OR: IMPORTS	GOLD –OR: EXPORTS	CONVERSION FACTORS U.S. CENTS PER BERMUDA DOLLAR / FACTEURS DE CONVERSION CENTS E.U. PAR BERMUDA DOLLAR: IMPORTS	EXPORTS	INDEX NUMBERS –INDICES — QUANTUM: IMPORTS	QUANTUM: EXPORTS	UNIT VALUE / VALEUR UNITAIRE: IMPORTS	UNIT VALUE / VALEUR UNITAIRE: EXPORTS
1962	48.70	22.50			116.6660	116.6660				
1963	47.30	33.00			116.6660	116.6660				
1964	50.40	31.70			116.6660	116.6660				
1965	50.20	46.70			116.6660	116.6660				
1966	56.80	46.10			116.6660	116.6660				
1967	59.10	52.10			114.5820	114.5820				
1968	72.70	66.10			98.0000	98.0000				
1969	85.00	78.80			98.0000	98.0000				
1970	105.10	97.10			100.0000	100.0000				
1971	108.50	91.60			100.0000	100.0000				
1972	109.40	34.10			100.0000	100.0000				
1973	122.90	29.80			100.0000	100.0000				
1974	149.80	34.30			100.0000	100.0000				
1975	162.40	36.20			100.0000	100.0000				
1976	165.50	46.30			100.0000	100.0000				
1977	185.60	38.60			100.0000	100.0000				
1978	211.60	41.20			100.0000	100.0000				
1979	234.00	31.30			100.0000	100.0000				
1980	311.50	36.70			100.0000	100.0000				
1981	322.70	29.40			100.0000	100.0000				
1982	351.00	16.90			100.0000	100.0000				
1983	377.70	22.80			100.0000	100.0000				
1984	414.10	40.50			100.0000	100.0000				
1985	402.50	23.10			100.0000	100.0000				
1986	492.00	65.00			100.0000	100.0000				
1987	420.00	29.00			100.0000	100.0000				
1988	488.00	30.81			100.0000	100.0000				
1989	535.00	50.40			100.0000	100.0000				
1990	594.69	59.81			100.0000	100.0000				
1991	510.12	54.53			100.0000	100.0000				
1992	562.25	84.98			100.0000	100.0000				
1993	534.00	35.89			100.0000	100.0000				
1994	550.00	65.54			100.0000	100.0000				
1995	629.88	52.78			100.0000	100.0000				
1996		67.75				100.0000				
1997	631.92				100.0000					

2. IMPORTS BY BROAD ECONOMIC CATEGORY AND EXPORTS BY INDUSTRIAL ORIGIN. (PERCENTAGE OF TOTAL VALUE)
IMPORTATIONS PAR CATEGORIES ECONOMIQUES ET EXPORTATIONS PAR BRANCHE D'ACTIVITE.(EN POURCENTAGE DE LA VALEUR TOTALE)

IMPORTS – IMPORTATIONS

	1991	1992	1993	1994	1995	1996	1997
TOTAL IMPORTS–IMPORTATIONS TOTALES	100.	100.	100.		100.		100.
1 FOOD BEV–ALIMENTATION BOISSONS	23.0	20.4	18.5		18.8		18.6
11 PRIMARY–PRODUITS DE BASE	8.3	7.9	7.4		8.8		8.5
111 FOR INDUSTRY–POUR L'INDUSTRIE	0.1	0.1	0.1		0.8		0.8
112 FOR HOUSEHOLDS–POUR LES MENAGES	8.2	7.8	7.3		8.0		7.7
12 PROCESSED–PRODUITS ELABORES	14.7	12.6	11.1		10.0		10.1
121 FOR INDUSTRY–POUR L'INDUSTRIE	0.4	0.4	0.4		0.4		0.3
122 FOR HOUSEHOLDS–POUR LES MENAGES	14.3	12.2	10.7		9.7		9.7
2 IND SUPPLIES–APPROV INDUSTRIELS	16.6	16.5	16.2		16.4		16.6
21 PRIMARY–PRODUITS DE BASE	0.9	0.9	0.8		3.3		3.4
22 PROCESSED–PRODUITS ELABORES	15.7	15.6	15.4		13.1		13.2
3 FUELS–COMBUSTIBLES	9.2	6.6	5.6		6.0		7.2
31 PRIMARY–PRODUITS DE BASE	0.2	0.2	0.2		0.2		0.2
32 PROCESSED–PRODUITS ELABORES	9.0	6.4	5.4		5.8		7.0
321 MOTOR SPIRIT–ESSENCE	1.4	1.3	0.8		0.8		1.2
322 OTHER–AUTRES	7.6	5.2	4.6		5.0		5.7
4 MACHINERY–EQUIPEMENT	11.8	14.3	15.1		20.2		19.2
41 CAPITAL EQUIPMENT–MACHINES	10.8	13.4	14.1		20.2		19.2
42 PARTS–PIECES ACCESSOIRES	1.0	0.9	1.0		0.0		0.0
5 TRANSPORT–TRANSPORT	4.8	4.3	5.2		6.5		5.4
51 PASSENGER CARS–AUTOMOBILES	1.7	1.4	2.0		2.0		1.8
52 OTHER–AUTRES	1.6	1.4	1.8		2.5		2.1
521 INDUSTRIAL–INDUSTRIELS	1.1	1.1	1.3		1.4		1.3
522 NON INDUSTRIAL–NON INDUSTRIEL	0.5	0.4	0.5		1.1		0.8
53 PARTS–PIECES ACCESSOIRES	1.5	1.5	1.4		2.0		1.4
6 CONSUM GOODS–BIENS CONSOMMATION	33.0	36.3	38.1		27.5		28.7
61 DURABLE–DURABLES	7.7	8.4	10.1		6.2		6.4
62 SEMI DURABLE–SEMI DURABLES	13.8	13.8	13.6		13.1		13.9
63 NON DURABLE–NON DURABLES	11.5	14.0	14.4		8.2		8.5
7 GOODS NES–BIENS NDA	1.6	1.7	1.4		4.5		4.3

EXPORTS – EXPORTATIONS

	1991	1992	1993	1994	1995	1996	1997
TOTAL EXPORTS–EXPORTATIONS TOTALES	100.	100.	100.	100.	100.		
1 AGRICULTURE	0.0	0.0	0.1	0.0			
2 MINING QUARRY–INDUS EXTRACTIVES							
3 MANUFACTURING–IND MANUFACTUR	100.	100.	99.9	100.	100.		
31 FOOD BEV TOBACCO–ALIM BOISS TAB	2.1	1.2	2.4	0.7	1.5		
32 TEXTILES–INDUSTRIES TEXTILES	0.1	0.0	0.1				
33 WOOD & PRODUCTS–BOIS & PRODUITS							
34 PAPER & PRODUCTS–PAPIER & PRODT	1.6	0.1	0.8				
35 CHEMICALS–INDUSTRIES CHIMIQUES	80.4	90.0	70.0				
36 NON METAL MIN–MIN NON METAL	0.2	0.2	0.1				
37 BASIC METAL–IND METAL BASE							
38 METAL MANUF–MANUF METAL	7.2	3.9	15.7				
39 OTH MANUF IND–AUTRES MANUF	8.3	4.6	10.9	99.3	98.5		

3. TRADE BY PRINCIPAL COUNTRIES OF ORIGIN AND DESTINATION (VALUE IN MILLION U.S. DOLLARS) ECHANGES SELON LES PRINCIPAUX PAYS D'ORIGINE ET DE DESTINATION (VALEUR EN MILLIONS DE DOLLARS EU)

COUNTRIES–PAYS	GENERAL IMPORTS C.I.F. IMPORTATIONS GENERALES C.A.F				
	1993	1994	1995	1996	1997
World	530.8		680.2		631.9
Africa	0.3		0.9		0.4
Americas	418.4		562.4		536.1
– Northern America	392.1		519.6		514.5
– LAIA	2.5		12.5		3.3
– CACM	0.1		0.2		0.3
– Caribbean	23.3		29.8		17.7
– Rest of America	0.5		0.4		0.2
Asia excl fmr USSR	38.9		37.2		30.0
– Middle East	0.1		0.2		0.4
Asia former USSR					
Europe excl fmr USSR	72.1		77.9		63.6
– European Union	64.1		73.7		59.7
– Eastern Europe	1.1		0.6		0.5
– Rest of Europe	6.8		3.6		3.4
Europe former USSR	0.0		0.2		0.1
Oceania	0.7		1.0		1.4
Other	0.4		0.7		0.4
USA/Etats–Unis d'Amer	371.0		489.5		480.0
United Kingdom	39.2		33.6		30.8
Canada	21.1		30.0		34.5
Japan/Japon	27.7		25.7		20.0
Aruba	21.3		20.4		5.7
France, Monaco	5.7		8.1		7.5
China, Hong Kong SAR	5.2		5.0		6.1
Germany/Allemagne	4.8		4.4		4.8
Venezuela	1.1		10.8		1.6
Italy/Italie	2.7		5.4		5.4
Switzerland,Liechtenst.	6.4		3.4		2.8
Netherlands/Pays–Bas	3.1		5.2		3.2
Sweden/Suède	0.4		8.6		1.3
Netherlands Antilles			4.8		3.4
Ireland/Irlande	2.9		2.7		2.5
Trinidad and Tobago	0.1		0.1		6.9
Denmark/Danemark	2.6		2.6		1.8
Spain/Espagne	1.4		2.0		1.5
Korea, Republic of	1.5		2.0		0.5
Other Asia n.e.s.	1.0		1.1		1.0
Jamaica/Jamaïque	1.1		0.9		0.4
China/Chine	0.7		1.0		0.4
Hungary/Hongrie	0.8		0.4		0.5
Antigua and Barbuda	0.0		1.7		
Australia/Australie	0.3		0.3		1.0
Areas n.e.s.	0.4		0.7		0.4
Malaysia/Malaisie	1.3		0.2		0.0
Indonesia/Indonésie	0.3		0.5		0.7
Bahamas	0.4		0.7		0.3
Peru/Pérou	0.3		0.6		0.5
Portugal	0.5		0.4		0.4
Brazil/Brésil	0.3		0.4		0.5
New Zealand	0.4		0.6		0.2
Mexico/Mexique	0.5		0.4		0.2
Austria/Autriche	0.3		0.4		0.3
Panama	0.4		0.3		0.2
Barbados/Barbade	0.2		0.4		0.3
Thailand/Thaïlande	0.4		0.4		0.2
Dominica/Dominique	0.0		0.5		0.4
Norway,Svalbard and JM	0.2		0.1		0.5

COUNTRIES–PAYS	GENERAL EXPORTS F.O.B. EXPORTATIONS GENERALES F.O.B.				
	1993	1994	1995	1996	1997
Monde	35.9	65.5	62.9		
Afrique					
Amériques	33.8	55.7	31.3		
– Amérique du Nord	33.4	54.8	31.3		
– ALAI	0.4	0.3	0.0		
– MCAC					
– Caraïbes	0.1	0.6	0.0		
– Autre Amérique					
Asie anc. URSS exclus	0.0	0.0	0.0		
– Moyen–Orient	0.0		0.0		
Asie ancienne URSS					
Europe anc. URSS exclus	1.4	9.4	3.9		
– Union Européenne	1.4	9.4	3.9		
– Europe de l'Est	0.0				
– Autre de l'Europe					
Europe ancienne URSS					
Océanie					
Autre	0.7	0.4	27.7		
USA/Etats–Unis d'Amer	33.1	52.7	31.3		
Areas n.e.s.	0.1	0.4	27.7		
United Kingdom	1.3	9.4	3.9		
Canada	0.2	2.2	0.0		
Bunkers, ship stores	0.6				
Mexico/Mexique	0.4	0.2	0.0		
Bahamas		0.1	0.0		
Brazil/Brésil		0.2			
Trinidad and Tobago		0.1			
Jamaica/Jamaïque	0.0	0.0	0.0		
Netherlands Antilles		0.1	0.0		
Aruba	0.0	0.1	0.0		
Netherlands/Pays–Bas	0.0				
Hungary/Hongrie	0.0				
Turkey/Turquie	0.0		0.0		
Barbados/Barbade	0.0	0.0	0.0		
Venezuela	0.0	0.0			
Spain/Espagne	0.0				
Germany/Allemagne	0.0	0.0	0.0		
China, Hong Kong SAR		0.0			
Denmark/Danemark	0.0				
France, Monaco		0.0	0.0		
Japan/Japon	0.0				
Malaysia/Malaisie	0.0				
Antigua and Barbuda			0.0		
Ecuador/Equateur			0.0		
Dominica/Dominique			0.0		
Colombia/Colombie		0.0			

(VALUE AS PERCENTAGE OF WORLD TOTAL)(VALEURS EN POURCENTAGE DU TOTAL MONDIAL)

	1988	1989	1990	1991	1992	1993	1994	1995	1996	1997
Africa	0.1		0.0	0.0	0.0	0.0		0.1		0.1
Americas	72.4		73.9	78.1	75.9	78.8		82.7		84.8
– Northern America	68.6		66.7	68.8	69.5	73.9		76.4		81.4
– LAIA	0.8		5.4	7.2	4.6	0.5		1.8		0.5
– CACM	0.2		0.0	0.0	0.0	0.0		0.0		0.1
– Caribbean	2.8		1.7	1.9	1.7	4.4		4.4		2.8
– Rest of America	0.1		0.1	0.1	0.2	0.1		0.1		0.0
Asia excl fmr USSR	8.1		7.9	7.1	7.6	7.3		5.5		4.7
– Middle East	0.0		0.0	0.0	0.0	0.0		0.0		0.1
Asia former USSR										
Europe excl fmr USSR	18.7		17.7	14.2	16.2	13.6		11.4		10.1
– European Union	17.3		16.2	13.4	12.8	12.1		10.8		9.5
– Eastern Europe	0.2		0.2	0.1	0.1	0.2		0.1		0.1
– Rest of Europe	1.2		1.3	0.7	3.3	1.3		0.5		0.5
Europe former USSR	0.0		0.0	0.0	0.0	0.0		0.0		0.0
Oceania	0.4		0.3	0.4	0.2	0.1		0.1		0.2
Other	0.3		0.2	0.2	0.2	0.1		0.1		0.1
USA/Etats–Unis d'Amer	62.2		61.8	64.4	65.6	69.9		72.0		76.0
United Kingdom	10.0		8.7	7.3	6.6	7.4		4.9		4.9
Canada	6.4		4.9	4.4	3.9	4.0		4.4		5.5
Japan/Japon	5.8		5.3	5.0	5.4	5.2		3.8		3.2
Aruba	1.9		1.3	1.4	1.3	4.0		3.0		0.9
France, Monaco	2.0		2.0	2.0	1.7	1.1		1.2		1.2
China, Hong Kong SAR	1.4		1.5	1.2	1.1	1.0		0.7		1.0
Germany/Allemagne				1.1	1.0	0.9		0.6		0.8
Venezuela	0.6		5.0	6.8	4.2	0.2		1.6		0.2
Italy/Italie	0.8		1.0	0.8	1.1	0.5		0.8		0.9

	1988	1989	1990	1991	1992	1993	1994	1995	1996	1997
Afrique	0.0									
Amériques	73.6	84.7	65.4	76.1	69.8	94.1	85.0	49.8		
– Amérique du Nord	72.7	83.8	65.0	75.4	66.3	92.9	83.7	49.7		
– ALAI	0.6		0.0	0.1	2.7	1.0	0.5	0.0		
– MCAC		0.0			0.1					
– Caraïbes	0.4	0.9	0.3	0.7	0.7	0.2	0.8	0.0		
– Autre Amérique			0.1		0.0					
Asie anc. URSS exclus	0.0	0.0	0.0	0.0	1.6	0.1	0.0	0.0		
– Moyen–Orient					1.1	0.1		0.0		
Asie ancienne URSS										
Europe anc. URSS exclus	23.6	13.6	33.7	21.8	27.5	4.0	14.3	6.2		
– Union Européenne	23.4	13.6	33.7	21.8	27.5	3.9	14.3	6.2		
– Europe de l'Est						0.1				
– Autre de l'Europe	0.1	0.0								
Europe ancienne URSS										
Océanie		0.0								
Autre	2.8	1.7	0.9	2.0	1.1	1.8	0.7	44.0		
USA/Etats–Unis d'Amer	57.6	79.1	54.1	74.3	62.3	92.3	80.4	49.7		
Areas n.e.s.	1.8	1.3	0.8	1.8	0.7	0.1	0.7	44.0		
United Kingdom	23.0	13.5	33.7	21.5	20.8	3.8	14.3	6.2		
Canada	15.1	4.7	10.8	1.2	4.0	0.7	3.3	0.1		
Bunkers, ship stores	0.9	0.4	0.1	0.2	0.5	1.7				
Mexico/Mexique	0.6				1.4	1.0	0.3	0.0		
Bahamas	0.1	0.1	0.2	0.1	0.1		0.2	0.0		
Brazil/Brésil					0.7		0.3			
Trinidad and Tobago			0.0		0.1		0.2			
Jamaica/Jamaïque	0.2	0.7	0.0	0.3	0.1	0.1	0.1	0.0		

4. General Imports C.I.F. by Commodities according to the S.I.T.C. (Rev. 2) in million U.S. Dollars
Importations Générales C.A.F. par Produits d'après la C.T.C.I. (Rév. 2) en millions de Dollars E.U.

SITC CTCI	COMMODITY	1994 QUANTITY QUANTITE	1994 VALUE VALEUR	1995 QUANTITY QUANTITE	1995 VALUE VALEUR	1996 QUANTITY QUANTITE	1996 VALUE VALEUR	1997 QUANTITY QUANTITE	1997 VALUE VALEUR	PRODUIT
	ALL COMMODITIES				680.2				632.0	TOUS PRODUITS
0	FOOD AND LIVE ANIMALS				108.9				98.0	ALIMENTS,ANIMAUX VIVANTS
01	MEAT AND PREPARATIONS				26.0				24.6	VIANDES ET PREPARATIONS
011	MEAT FRESH,CHILLD,FROZEN				23.2				21.2	VIANDES FRAICHES,REF,CONGE
0118	MEAT NES FRESH,CHLD,FRZN				23.2				21.2	AUTRES VIANDES,ABATS
01189	OTHER MEAT NES FRESH,ETC				23.2				21.2	VIANDE,ABATS COMESTIBLES
014	MEAT PREPD,PRSVD,NES ETC				2.9				3.4	CONSERVES DE VIANDES
0149	OTH PREPARD,PRESRVD MEAT				2.9				3.4	AUTRES PREP DE VIANDES
03	FISH AND PREPARATIONS				10.7				9.3	POISSONS ET PREPARATIONS
036	SHELL FISH FRESH,FROZEN				10.6				9.1	CRUSTACES,MOLLUSQUES
04	CEREALS AND PREPARATIONS				13.9				13.6	CEREALES ET PRODUITS
048	CEREAL ETC PREPARATIONS				11.1				11.7	PREPTNS A BASE CEREALES
0481	PREPD BREAKFAST FOOD ETC				2.0				2.1	CEREALES TRAVAILLEES
04811	CEREAL FLAKED,ROLLED,ETC				2.0				2.1	GRAINS GERMES DE CEREALES
0488	OTH CEREAL PREPS,MALT EX				9.1				9.6	EXTRAITS DE MALT
05	VEGETABLES AND FRUIT				25.2				22.0	LEGUMES ET FRUITS
054	VEG ETC FRSH,SMPLY PRSVD				7.9				6.7	LEGUMES FRAIS,CONG,SECS
0545	OTHER FRESH VEGETABLES				7.9				6.7	AUTRES LEGUMES FRAIS,REF
05459	FRESH VEGETABLES NES				7.9				6.7	LEGUMES FRAIS,REFRI NDA
057	FRUIT,NUTS,FRESH,DRIED				6.9				6.4	FRUITS FRAIS OU SECS
0579	FRUIT FRESH OR DRIED NES				6.9				6.4	FRUITS FRAIS,SECS NDA
05798	OTHER FRESH FRUIT				6.9				6.4	AUTRES FRUITS FRAIS
058	FRUIT PRESERVED,PREPARED				10.5				9.0	CONSERVES DE FRUITS
0585	FRUIT OR VEGETABLE JUICE				4.1				3.2	JUS DE FRUITS
05858	MIXTURES OF DIFF JUICES				4.1				3.2	MELANGES JUS FRUITS,LEGUMES
0589	FRUIT PREPRD,PRESRVD,NES				6.4				5.8	FRUITS PREPARES CONSERV
05899	FRUIT,NUTS NES,PRESERVED				6.4				5.8	FRUITS PREP CONSERV NDA
06	SUGAR AND PREPS,HONEY				5.0				3.6	SUCRES ET PRODUITS
062	SUGAR CANDY NON-CHOCLATE				3.3				2.3	SUCRERIES
07	COFFEE,TEA,COCOA,SPICES				3.9				4.5	CAFE,THE,CACAO,EPICES
081	*FEEDING STUFF FOR ANIML				3.8				3.4	NOURRITURE POUR ANIMAUX
0819	FOOD WASTE AND FEED NES				3.8				3.4	DECHETS,ALIMENTS NDA
08199	FODDER NES,INCL SWEETNED				3.8				3.4	PREPARATIONS FOURRAGERES
09	MISC EDIBLE PRODUCTS				18.8				15.6	PREP ALIMENTAIRES DIVERSES
098	EDIBLE PRODCTS,PREPS NES				17.3				14.7	PREP ALIMENTAIRES NDA
09808	EDIBLE ANIML PRODCTS NES				6.2				5.8	PRODUITS ORIGINE ANIM NDA
09809	MISC FOOD PREPRTIONS NES				11.1				8.9	PREP ALIMENTAIRES NDA
1	BEVERAGES AND TOBACCO				26.3				26.4	BOISSONS ET TABACS
11	BEVERAGES				23.0				22.9	BOISSONS
111	NON-ALCOHL BEVERAGES NES				4.7				5.2	BOISSONS NON ALCOOLIQUES
11102	FLAVORED WATERS NON-ALCO				4.0				4.5	LIMONADES,EAUX GAZEUSES
112	ALCOHOLIC BEVERAGES				18.3				17.8	BOISSONS ALCOOLIQUES
1121	WINE OF FRESH GRAPES ETC				7.3				9.2	VINS DE RAISINS FRAIS
11212	WINE OF FRESH GRAPES				7.2				9.0	VINS DE MOUTS DE RAISINS
1123	BEER,ALE,STOUT,PORTER				7.1				4.9	BIERES
1124	DISTILLED ALCOHOLIC BEVS				3.9				3.6	ALCOOLS,EAUX-DE-VIE
11249	OTH ALCOHOLC BEVS,CMPNDS				2.9				2.5	BOISSONS ALCOOLIQUES NDA
12	TOBACCO AND MANUFACTURES				3.4				3.6	TABACS BRUTS FABRIQUES
122	TOBACCO,MANUFACTURED				3.4				3.6	TABACS FABRIQUES
1222	CIGARETTES				2.8				2.2	CIGARETTES
2	CRUDE MATERLS,EXCL FUELS				10.6				9.0	MAT BRUTES NON COMESTIBLES
24	CORK AND WOOD				7.0				6.0	LIEGE ET BOIS
247	OTH WOOD ROUGH,SQUARED				6.8				6.0	BOIS BRUTS EQUARRIS
2472	SAW-,VENEER-LOGS NON-CON				6.8				6.0	NON CONIFERES SCIAGE,PLAC
24721	— IN THE ROUGH				6.8				6.0	BRUTS ECORCES DEGROSSIS
3	MINERAL FUELS ETC				40.8				45.3	COMBUSTIBLES MINERAUX LUB
33	PETROLEUM AND PRODUCTS				39.4				44.2	PETROLE ET DERIVES
334	PETROLEUM PRODUCTS,REFIN				39.4				44.2	PRODUITS RAFFINES
3341	GASOLINE,OTH LIGHT OILS				5.5				7.9	ESSENCES POUR MOTEURS
33411	MOTOR,AVIATION SPIRIT				5.5				7.9	ESSENCES MOTEURS D'AVIONS
3342	KEROSENE,OTH MEDIUM OILS				3.2				5.9	PETR LAMPANTS,AUT HUIL
33421	KEROSENE INCL JET FUEL				3.2				5.9	PETROLES LAMPANTS
3343	GAS OILS				20.9				20.5	GAS OILS
3344	FUEL OILS,NES				8.2				8.6	FUEL OILS
5	CHEMCLS,RELATED PROD NES				53.4				49.0	PRODUITS CHIMIQUES
53	DYES,TANNING,COLOUR PROD				4.9				4.6	PROD TEINTURE,COLORANTS
533	PIGMENTS,PAINTS,ETC				3.6				3.9	PIGMENTS,PEINTURES,VERNIS
5334	VARNISHES,DISTEMPERS ETC				3.6				3.9	PEINTURES A L'EAU
53342	OTH PAINTS,VARNISHES ETC				2.2				2.8	AUTRES PEINTURES,VERNIS
541	*MEDICINAL,PHARM PRODUCT				26.1				24.6	PROD MEDICINAUX PHARMACEUT
5417	MEDICAMENTS				21.7				19.7	MEDICAMENTS
54179	— CONTNG OTH SUBSTANCES				21.7				19.7	MED CONT AUT SUBSTANCES
5419	PHARMACEUTICAL GOODS NES				4.5				5.0	PREP,ART PHARMACEUTIQUES
54191	BANDAGES PREPARED ETC				4.1				4.7	OUATES,GAZES,BANDES
55	PERFUME,CLEANING ETC PRD				15.9				14.8	PROD POUR PARFUM,TOILETTE
551	ESSENTL OILS,PERFUME,ETC				6.7				6.2	HUILES ESSENTIELLES
5513	ESSENTL OIL,RESINOID,ETC				6.7				6.2	HUILES ESSENTIELLES,RESIN
553	PERFUMERY,COSMETICS,ETC				2.8				2.5	PRODUITS DE PARFUMERIE
554	SOAP,CLEANSING ETC PREPS				6.6				6.2	SAVONS,PRODUITS DETERSIFS
5541	SOAPS				6.6				6.2	SAVONS,PROD TENSIO-ACTIFS
59	CHEMICAL MATERIALS NES				4.5				3.7	MAT PROD CHIMIQUES NDA
598	MISCEL CHEM PRODUCTS NES				2.4				2.1	PROD DIV INDUST CHIM NDA
5989	CHEM PRODUCTS,PREPS NES				2.4				2.1	PROD PREP CHIMIQUES NDA
59899	OTH CHEM PRODS,PREPS,NES				2.4				2.1	AUT PRODUITS CHIMIQUES NDA
6	BASIC MANUFACTURES				102.8				98.5	ART MANUFACTURES
62	RUBBER MANUFACTURES NES				2.3				1.9	CAOUTCHOUC MANUFACTURE
63	WOOD,CORK MANUFACTRS NES				5.2				3.6	OUVRAGES LIEGE ET BOIS
635	WOOD MANUFACTURES NES				3.4				2.3	ART MANUF EN BOIS NDA
6353	BUILDERS WOODWRK,PREFABS				3.4				2.3	OUVRAGES DE MENUISERIE
64	PAPER,PAPERBOARD AND MFR				16.3				12.8	PAPIERS,CARTONS & OUVRAGES
641	PAPER AND PAPERBOARD				3.4				2.3	PAPIERS ET CARTONS
642	PAPER,ETC,PRECUT,ARTS OF				12.9				10.6	PAP,CARTONS DECOUPES
6428	PAPER ETC ARTICLES NES				11.5				9.6	OUVRAGES EN PATE A PAPIER
64289	OTHER ARTICLES OF PAPER				11.5				9.6	ARTICLES,OUVRAGES EN PAPIER
65	TEXTILE YARN,FABRICS,ETC				12.6				11.7	FILS,TISSUS,ARTICLES TEXTILE
658	TEXTILE ARTICLES NES				6.0				6.0	ART FACONNES MAT TEXTILES
6589	OTH TEXTILE ARTICLES NES				6.0				6.0	AUT ART EN TEXTILES NDA
65898	KNITTED ETC ARTICLES NES				6.0				6.0	ART BONNET NON ELASTIQUE
659	FLOOR COVERINGS,ETC				4.4				3.7	COUVRE-PARQUETS,TAPIS ETC
6596	OTH TXTL CARPETS ETC NES				4.3				3.6	TAPIS AUT MAT TEXT NDA
65962	— OTHR THAN KNOTTED ETC				4.3				3.6	TAPIS AUT QUE NOUES TOUF

4. General Imports C.I.F. by Commodities according to the S.I.T.C. (Rev. 2) in million U.S. Dollars
Importations Générales C.A.F. par Produits d'après la C.T.C.I. (Rév. 2) en millions de Dollars E.U.

SITC CTCI	COMMODITY	1994 QUANTITY QUANTITE	1994 VALUE VALEUR	1995 QUANTITY QUANTITE	1995 VALUE VALEUR	1996 QUANTITY QUANTITE	1996 VALUE VALEUR	1997 QUANTITY QUANTITE	1997 VALUE VALEUR	PRODUIT
66	NONMETAL MINERAL MFS NES				35.8				36.7	ART MIN NON METALLIQUES
663	MINERAL MANUFCTURES NES				11.2				12.8	ART MIN MANUF NDA
6633	MINRL MFS NES NONCERAMIC				9.2				11.2	OUVR MAT MINERALE NDA
66339	OTH MINRL MFS NONCERAMIC				9.2				11.2	OUVRAGES EN PIERRES
665	GLASSWARE				3.5				3.0	OUVRAGES EN VERRE
6652	HOUSEHLD,HOTEL ETC GLASS				2.3				2.2	OBJETS VERRE TABLE,CUISINE
666	POTTERY				5.3				4.4	POTERIE
6664	PORCELN,CHINA HOUSE WARE				3.2				2.3	VAISSELLE,ARTS MEN PORC
6666	CERAMIC ORNAMENTS ETC				2.2				2.2	OBJETS PORCELAINE,CERAM
667	PEARL,PREC-,SEMI-P STONE				13.6				14.0	PERLES, PIERRES GEMMES
69	METAL MANUFACTURES NES				28.8				30.4	ART MANUFACT EN METAL NDA
691	STRUCTURES AND PARTS NES				4.8				6.0	CONSTRUCT FER,ACIER,ALU
6912	STRUCTURES,PARTS ALUMNM				4.8				6.0	CONSTRUCT ALUMINIUM
695	TOOLS				3.9				3.8	OUTILS A MAIN
6953	OTHER HAND TOOLS				3.9				3.8	AUTRES OUTILS A MAIN
69539	HAND TOOLS ETC NES				3.9				3.8	OUTILLAGE A MAIN NDA
699	BASE METAL MFRS NES				17.9				18.0	ART MANUFACTURES MET NDA
6996	BASE MTL MISC ARTICLES				9.0				9.2	ART DIVERS METAUX COMMUNS
69965	BASE MTL SOLDERING RODS				9.0				9.2	FILS,BAGUETTES POUR SOUDURE
6997	IRON,STEEL ARTICLES NES				6.9				7.1	OUV FONTE,FER,ACIER NDA
69979	IRN,STL MANUFACTURES NES				6.9				7.1	AUT OUVRAGES EN FER NDA
7	MACHINES,TRANSPORT EQUIP				172.3				151.0	MACHINES MATERIEL TRANSPORT
71	POWER GENERATING EQUIPMT				22.3				3.5	MACHINES GENERATRICES
713	INTRNL COMBUS PSTN ENGIN				5.4				3.2	MOTEURS EXPL COMB INT, PIECE
7138	PISTON ENGINES NES				5.4				3.2	MOTEURS A PISTONS NDA
716	ROTATING ELECTRIC PLANT				17.0				0.3	APP ELECTR ROTATIFS,PIECES
7161	DC MOTORS AND GENERATORS				17.0				0.3	MOTEURS COURANT CONTINU
74	GENRL INDUSTRL MACHY NES				17.5				17.5	MACH APP INDUSTRIE
741	HEATING,COOLING EQUIPMNT				13.8				14.4	MACH CHAUFFAGE,PIECES
7414	NONDOM REFRIG EQUIPT,PTS				8.3				9.0	MAT PRODUCTION DU FROID
74141	REFRIG EQUIP NONDOMESTIC				8.3				9.0	REFIG INDUSTRIELS
7415	AIR-CONDITIONING MACHNRY				5.5				5.5	GROUPES CONDITION AIR
744	MECHANICAL HANDLING EQU				3.5				2.9	EQUIP MANUTENTION PIECES
7442	LIFTING,LOADING MACH NES				3.5				2.9	APP LEVAGE,MANUTENTION
74428	OTH HANDLING ETC MCH NES				3.5				2.9	AUT APP LEVAGE ETC
75	OFFICE MACHNES,ADP EQUIP				43.9				43.9	MACH BUREAU TRAIT AUTOM
751	OFFICE MACHINES				8.0				7.2	MACH,APPAREILS DE BUREAU
7518	OFFICE MACHINES NES				8.0				7.2	MACH,APP DE BUREAU NDA
75188	OTHR OFFICE MACHINES NES				8.0				7.2	AUTRES MACH DE BUREAU
752	AUTOMTIC DATA PROC EQUIP				36.0				36.8	MACH TRAIT INFORMATION
7528	OFF-LINE DATA PROC EQUIP				36.0				36.8	MACH AUXIL TRAIT INFORM
76	TELECOMM,SOUND EQUIPMENT				23.3				27.1	EQUIPMENT DE TELECOM
761	TELEVISION RECEIVERS				2.7				2.4	RECEPTEURS DE TELEVISION
7611	COLOUR TV RECEIVERS				2.7				2.4	RECEPTEURS COULEUR
764	TELECOM EQPT,PTS,ACC NES				18.9				23.8	EQUIP TELECOM,PIECES
7641	LINE TELEPHONE,ETC EQUIP				11.3				22.0	APP TELEPHON PAR FIL
7648	TELECOMM EQUIPMENT NES				6.7				1.1	APP TELECOM NDA
76481	RADIOTELEPHONE ETC RCVRS				2.4				1.0	RECEP RADIOTELEPHONIE
76483	RADAR APPARATUS ETC				4.4				0.1	APP DE RADIOGUIDAGE ETC
77	ELECTRIC MACHNRY NES ETC				20.3				20.2	MACH APP ELECT NDA
778	ELECTRICAL MACHINERY NES				20.3				20.2	AUTRES MACH ELECT NDA
7788	OTH ELEC MACHY,EQUIP NES				19.1				19.0	AUT MACH APP ELEC NDA
77886	OTH ELEC MACHINERY NES				19.1				19.0	AUT MACH APP ELECTRIQUES
78	ROAD VEHICLES				35.5				27.9	VEHICULES ROUTIERS
781	PASS MOTOR VEH EXC BUSES				13.9				11.7	AUTO TRANSPORT PERSONNES
782	LORRIES,SPCL MTR VEH NES				7.2				5.1	VEHICULES SPECIAUX,MARCH
7821	LORRIES,TRUCKS				7.2				5.1	VEHICULES TRANSP MARCHAND
784	MOTOR VEH PRTS,ACCES NES				6.5				4.7	PIECES 722,781,782,783
7849	OTHER MOTOR VEHCL PARTS				6.5				4.7	PIECES 722,781,782,783
785	CYCLES,ETC MOTRZD OR NOT				7.6				5.4	MOTOCYCLES SCOOTERS
7851	MOTORCYCLES ETC				6.5				4.6	MOTO VELO MOTEUR AUXIL
79	OTHR TRANSPORT EQUIPMENT				9.9				10.2	AUTRE MATERIEL TRANSPORT
793	SHIPS AND BOATS ETC				8.5				9.6	NAVIRES BATEAUX,ETC
7931	WARSHIPS				4.0				4.2	NAVIRES DE GUERRE
7938	TUGS,SPECIAL VESSELS ETC				4.0				4.2	REMORQUEURS,BATEAUX SPEC
79382	SPECL PURPOSE VESSLS ETC				4.0				4.2	BAT-PHARES,-POMPES,DRAGUES
8	MISC MANUFACTURED GOODS				137.7				131.4	ART MANUFACTURES DIVERS
812	*PLUMBG,HEATNG,LGHTNG EQ				10.6				5.5	APPAR SANITAIRES CHAUFFAGE
8121	CENTRAL HEATING EQUIPMNT				10.6				5.5	CHAUDIERES,RADIATEURS
821	*FURNITURE,PARTS THEREOF				25.2				24.5	MEUBLES ET PIECES
84	CLOTHING AND ACCESSORIES				43.0				44.0	VETEMENTS
845	OUTERWEAR KNIT NONELASTC				41.8				42.9	VET DESSOUS,ACCES BONNET
8459	— OTHER,CLTHG ACCESRYS				41.8				42.9	AUT VET DESSUS DE BONNE
851	*FOOTWEAR				7.1				8.0	CHAUSSURES
85102	FOOTWEAR LEATHER				7.1				8.0	CHAUS SEMELLES EN CUIR
87	PRECISION INSTRUMNTS NES				6.1				5.7	INSTRUM,APPAR SCIENT NDA
871	OPTICAL INSTRUMENTS				6.1				5.7	APPAR,INSTRUM D'OPTIQUE
87109	OPTICAL INSTRUMENTS NES				6.1				5.7	APP,INSTRUM OPTIQUE NDA
88	PHOTO EQU,OPTICL GDS ETC				7.9				7.9	APP,FOURN PHOTO,OP,MONTR
885	WATCHES AND CLOCKS				4.8				5.0	HORLOGERIE
8851	WATCHES,MOVEMENTS,CASES				4.8				5.0	MONTRES,MOUVEMENTS,BOITES
88511	WATCHES				4.8				5.0	MONTRES POCHE,BRACELET
89	MISC MANUFCTRD GOODS NES				38.2				36.1	ART MANUFACTURES DIVERS
892	PRINTED MATTER				13.4				13.4	IMPRIMES
8921	PRINTED BOOKS,GLOBES,ETC				9.1				9.4	LIVRES,BROCHURES,CARTES
89211	PRINTED BOOKS,PAMPHLETS				9.1				9.4	LIVRES,BROCHURES
8928	PRINTED MATTER NES				4.4				4.0	IMPRIMES NDA
89289	OTHER PRINTED MATTER				4.4				4.0	GRAVURES,PHOTO AUT IMPR
893	ARTICLES OF PLASTIC NES				13.4				11.2	OUVRAGES EN MAT DIVIS 58
8933	PLASTIC ORNAMENTS				2.8				1.2	OBJETS ORNEMENT MAT 58
8939	MISC PLASTIC ARTICLES				10.4				9.5	ART DIVERS EN MAT DIV 58
89399	OTHR PLASTC ARTICLES NES				10.4				9.5	AUT OUV MAT DIV 58
894	TOYS,SPORTING GOODS,ETC				6.8				6.7	VOITURES ENFANTS,JOUETS
8942	TOYS,INDOOR GAMES ETC				6.6				6.5	JOUETS,JEUX ETC
89423	TOYS NES				6.6				6.5	JOUETS,MODELES REDUITS
898	MUSICAL INSTRUMENTS,PTS				3.7				4.0	INSTRUMENTS DE MUSIQUE
8983	SOUND RECRDNG TAPE,DISCS				2.8				3.2	SUPPORTS SON POUR 763
89832	RECORDED DISCS,TAPES ETC				2.8				3.2	DISQUES,PHONO,BANDES

4. General Imports C.I.F. by Commodities according to the S.I.T.C. (Rev. 2) in million U.S. Dollars
Importations Générales C.A.F. par Produits d'après la C.T.C.I. (Rév. 2) en millions de Dollars E.U.

SITC CTCI	COMMODITY	1994		1995		1996		1997		PRODUIT
		QUANTITY QUANTITE	VALUE VALEUR	QUANTITY QUANTITE	VALUE VALEUR	QUANTITY QUANTITE	VALUE VALEUR	QUANTITY QUANTITE	VALUE VALEUR	
9	GOODS NOT CLASSD BY KIND				26.8				23.0	ART TRANSACT NON CLASSES
931	*SPECIAL TRANSACTIONS				26.7				22.8	TRANS.SPECIALES

5. General Exports F.O.B. by Commodities according to the S.I.T.C. (Rev. 2) in million U.S. Dollars
Exportations Générales F.O.B. par Produits d'après la C.T.C.I. (Rév. 2) en millions de Dollars E.U.

SITC CTCI	COMMODITY	1994			1995			1996		1997		PRODUIT
		QUANTITY QUANTITE		VALUE VALEUR	QUANTITY QUANTITE		VALUE VALEUR	QUANTITY QUANTITE	VALUE VALEUR	QUANTITY QUANTITE	VALUE VALEUR	
	ALL COMMODITIES			65.6			63.0					TOUS PRODUITS
1	BEVERAGES AND TOBACCO			0.5			1.0					BOISSONS ET TABACS
11	BEVERAGES			0.5			1.0					BOISSONS
112	ALCOHOLIC BEVERAGES	W	112	0.5	W	339	1.0					BOISSONS ALCOOLIQUES
1124	DISTILLED ALCOHOLIC BEVS	W	105	0.4	W	242	0.8					ALCOOLS,EAUX-DE-VIE
11249	OTH ALCOHOLC BEVS,CMPNDS	W	105	0.4	W	241	0.8					BOISSONS ALCOOLIQUES NDA
9	GOODS NOT CLASSD BY KIND			65.1			62.0					ART TRANSACT NON CLASSES
931	*SPECIAL TRANSACTIONS			65.1			62.0					TRANS.SPECIALES

1. HISTORICAL SERIES, 1985–1994 GENERAL TRADE, IMPORTS C.I.F., EXPORTS F.O.B.
SERIES HISTORIQUES, 1985–1994 COMMERCE GENERAL, IMPORTATIONS C.A.F., EXPORTATIONS F.O.B

YEAR ANNEE	VALUE IN MILLION NGULTRUMS VALEUR EN MILLION NGULTRUMS MERCHANDISE –MARCHANDISE IMPORTS	EXPORTS	GOLD –OR IMPORTS	EXPORTS	CONVERSION FACTORS U.S. CENTS PER NGULTRUM FACTEURS DE CONVERSION CENTS E.U. PAR NGULTRUM IMPORTS	EXPORTS	INDEX NUMBERS –INDICES QUANTUM IMPORTS	EXPORTS	UNIT VALUE VALEUR UNITAIRE IMPORTS	EXPORTS
1985	1041.60	272.00			8.0847	8.0847				
1986	1168.03	387.26			7.9296	7.9296				
1987	1124.16	714.99			7.7149	7.7149				
1988	1874.50	1041.30			7.1855	7.1855				
1989	1613.90	1132.30			6.1629	6.1629				
1990	1889.80	1306.40			5.7127	5.7127				
1991	2148.50	1631.90			4.5072	4.5072				
1992	3470.90	1837.30			3.8608	3.8608				
1993	3064.10	2097.90			3.3072	3.3070				
1994	3562.40	2225.00			3.1874	3.1874				

2. IMPORTS BY BROAD ECONOMIC CATEGORY AND EXPORTS BY INDUSTRIAL ORIGIN. (PERCENTAGE OF TOTAL VALUE)
IMPORTATIONS PAR CATEGORIES ECONOMIQUES ET EXPORTATIONS PAR BRANCHE D'ACTIVITE.(EN POURCENTAGE DE LA VALEUR TOTALE)

IMPORTS – IMPORTATIONS

	1988	1989	1990	1991	1992	1993	1994
TOTAL IMPORTS–IMPORTATIONS TOTALES				100.	100.	100.	100.
1 FOOD BEV–ALIMENTATION BOISSONS				23.3	11.9	17.6	19.3
11 PRIMARY–PRODUITS DE BASE				3.1	3.7	9.5	11.4
111 FOR INDUSTRY–POUR L'INDUSTRIE				1.0	2.1	7.4	9.0
112 FOR HOUSEHOLDS–POUR LES MENAGES				2.1	1.6	2.1	2.4
12 PROCESSED–PRODUITS ELABORES				20.2	8.2	8.1	7.9
121 FOR INDUSTRY–POUR L'INDUSTRIE				6.5	0.8	4.1	3.7
122 FOR HOUSEHOLDS–POUR LES MENAGES				13.7	7.4	4.0	4.2
2 IND SUPPLIES–APPROV INDUSTRIELS				20.7	22.0	26.6	25.5
21 PRIMARY–PRODUITS DE BASE				1.3	1.4	3.4	1.2
22 PROCESSED–PRODUITS ELABORES				19.5	20.6	23.2	24.3
3 FUELS–COMBUSTIBLES				11.9	8.2	10.1	11.8
31 PRIMARY–PRODUITS DE BASE				1.2	1.0	1.7	1.2
32 PROCESSED–PRODUITS ELABORES				10.7	7.1	8.4	10.7
321 MOTOR SPIRIT–ESSENCE				3.1	1.5	2.1	2.6
322 OTHER–AUTRES				7.6	5.6	6.4	8.1
4 MACHINERY–EQUIPEMENT				20.4	17.8	24.5	19.7
41 CAPITAL EQUIPMENT–MACHINES				19.0	16.0	24.1	19.3
42 PARTS–PIECES ACCESSOIRES				1.4	1.8	0.5	0.4
5 TRANSPORT–TRANSPORT				16.7	12.3	10.4	11.7
51 PASSENGER CARS–AUTOMOBILES				4.6	2.5	2.3	4.6
52 OTHER–AUTRES				4.7	5.1	0.7	1.4
521 INDUSTRIAL–INDUSTRIELS				3.1	4.4	0.2	1.2
522 NON INDUSTRIAL–NON INDUSTRIEL				1.6	0.7	0.5	0.2
53 PARTS–PIECES ACCESSOIRES				7.4	4.7	7.5	5.7
6 CONSUM GOODS–BIENS CONSOMMATION				6.4	5.4	9.3	10.9
61 DURABLE–DURABLES				1.4	1.9	1.1	1.3
62 SEMI DURABLE–SEMI DURABLES				2.6	1.9	4.8	5.1
63 NON DURABLE–NON DURABLES				2.4	1.6	3.5	4.5
7 GOODS NES–BIENS NDA				0.6	22.6	1.3	1.0

EXPORTS – EXPORTATIONS

	1988	1989	1990	1991	1992	1993	1994
TOTAL EXPORTS–EXPORTATIONS TOTALES				100.	100.	100.	100.
1 AGRICULTURE				19.0	27.0	20.4	15.3
2 MINING QUARRY–INDUS EXTRACTIVES				4.5	4.8	2.8	4.2
3 MANUFACTURING–IND MANUFACTUR				76.4	68.2	76.8	80.5
31 FOOD BEV TOBACCO–ALIM BOISS TAB				7.3	7.1	8.9	12.3
32 TEXTILES–INDUSTRIES TEXTILES				0.0	0.0	0.0	0.0
33 WOOD & PRODUCTS–BOIS & PRODUITS				11.4	10.6	10.6	8.9
34 PAPER & PRODUCTS–PAPIER & PRODT				0.2	0.5	0.4	0.3
35 CHEMICALS–INDUSTRIES CHIMIQUES				20.5	21.6	18.7	20.9
36 NON METAL MIN–MIN NON METAL				10.1	8.0	11.0	13.0
37 BASIC METAL–IND METAL BASE						0.0	0.0
38 METAL MANUF–MANUF METAL				0.0	0.0	0.1	0.0
39 OTH MANUF IND–AUTRES MANUF				26.9	20.4	27.0	25.0

3. TRADE BY PRINCIPAL COUNTRIES OF ORIGIN AND DESTINATION (VALUE IN MILLION U.S. DOLLARS)
ECHANGES SELON LES PRINCIPAUX PAYS D'ORIGINE ET DE DESTINATION (VALEUR EN MILLIONS DE DOLLARS EU)

COUNTRIES–PAYS	GENERAL IMPORTS C.I.F. IMPORTATIONS GENERALES C.A.F				
	1990	1991	1992	1993	1994
World		96.6	128.0	90.8	91.1
Africa		0.0	0.0		
Americas		1.5	1.2	0.4	1.4
– Northern America		1.4	1.2	0.4	1.3
– LAIA		0.1	0.0	0.0	0.2
– CACM					
– Caribbean					
– Rest of America					
Asia excl fmr USSR		88.7	82.4	78.1	80.1
– Middle East		0.0	0.0	0.1	0.0
Asia former USSR					
Europe excl fmr USSR		5.6	43.5	12.2	9.4
– European Union		4.7	33.3	6.1	8.6
– Eastern Europe					0.0
– Rest of Europe		0.9	10.2	6.1	0.8
Europe former USSR					
Oceania		0.5	0.2	0.0	0.1
Other		0.3	0.6		
India/Inde		72.6	67.3	63.8	65.4
Japan/Japon		14.2	13.8	11.9	12.7
United Kingdom		0.4	26.4	2.4	1.9
Norway,Svalbard and JM		0.7	10.1	6.1	0.4
Germany/Allemagne		3.0	3.6	1.4	2.0
Denmark/Danemark		0.8	2.2	0.7	2.7
Singapore/Singapour		0.6	0.8	1.2	1.2
USA/Etats–Unis d'Amer		0.5	1.1	0.3	1.2
Netherlands/Pays–Bas		0.1	0.7	0.5	0.6
Austria/Autriche		0.3	0.2	0.5	0.8
Canada		0.9	0.1	0.1	0.1
Korea, Republic of		0.5	0.0	0.2	0.2
Malaysia/Malaisie		0.2	0.1	0.5	0.1
Areas n.e.s.		0.3	0.6		
Switzerland,Liechtenst.		0.2	0.2	0.1	0.4
China, Hong Kong SAR		0.2	0.2	0.1	0.3
Australia/Australie		0.5	0.1	0.0	0.0
Bangladesh		0.1	0.2	0.2	0.1
Italy/Italie		0.0	0.1	0.2	0.2
France, Monaco		0.1	0.0	0.1	0.3
Sweden/Suède		0.1		0.1	0.2
Brazil/Brésil			0.0		0.2
Belgium–Luxembourg		0.0		0.1	0.0
New Zealand		0.0	0.1	0.0	0.0
Thailand/Thaïlande		0.1	0.0	0.0	0.0
Indonesia/Indonésie					0.1
Saudi Arabia		0.0	0.0		

COUNTRIES–PAYS	GENERAL EXPORTS F.O.B. EXPORTATIONS GENERALES F.O.B.				
	1990	1991	1992	1993	1994
Monde		65.0	67.1	65.8	66.4
Afrique					
Amériques					0.0
– Amérique du Nord					0.0
– ALAI					
– MCAC					
– Caraïbes					
– Autre Amérique					
Asie anc. URSS exclus		64.8	66.7	65.5	66.1
– Moyen–Orient					
Asie ancienne URSS					
Europe anc. URSS exclus		0.1	0.1	0.1	0.0
– Union Européenne		0.1	0.1	0.1	0.0
– Europe de l'Est					
– Autre de l'Europe					
Europe ancienne URSS				0.0	
Océanie					
Autre		0.1	0.3	0.3	0.2
India/Inde		58.8	56.2	59.1	62.0
Bangladesh		5.3	10.4	6.3	4.1
Areas n.e.s.		0.1	0.3	0.3	0.2
Singapore/Singapour		0.6			
Netherlands/Pays–Bas		0.1	0.0	0.0	
Germany/Allemagne		0.0	0.0	0.0	
Japan/Japon			0.0	0.0	0.0
USA/Etats–Unis d'Amer					0.0
Thailand/Thaïlande		0.0	0.0	0.0	
Austria/Autriche					0.0
United Kingdom				0.0	

(VALUE AS PERCENTAGE OF WORLD TOTAL)(VALEURS EN POURCENTAGE DU TOTAL MONDIAL)

	1985	1986	1987	1988	1989	1990	1991	1992	1993	1994
Africa		0.0					0.0	0.0		
Americas		2.8	2.7	0.0			1.5	0.9	0.5	1.6
– Northern America		2.8	2.7	0.0			1.5	0.9	0.5	1.4
– LAIA							0.1	0.0	0.0	0.2
– CACM										
– Caribbean										
– Rest of America										
Asia excl fmr USSR	86.3	88.9	83.6	69.5			91.8	64.4	86.0	88.0
– Middle East		0.0	0.3	0.0			0.0	0.0	0.1	0.0
Asia former USSR										
Europe excl fmr USSR		6.0	8.9	26.5			5.8	34.0	13.4	10.3
– European Union		4.9	4.4	26.2			4.8	26.0	6.7	9.4
– Eastern Europe										0.0
– Rest of Europe		1.1	4.5	0.3			0.9	8.0	6.8	0.9
Europe former USSR										
Oceania		1.0	0.5	0.0			0.5	0.2	0.1	0.1
Other		1.3	4.4	3.9			0.3	0.5		
India/Inde	86.3	69.7	80.0	62.6			75.2	52.6	70.3	71.8
Japan/Japon		18.0	2.3	5.8			14.7	10.8	13.1	13.9
United Kingdom		1.1	0.4	24.2			0.4	20.6	2.6	2.0
Norway,Svalbard and JM		0.9	4.1	0.0			0.7	7.9	6.7	0.5
Germany/Allemagne							3.1	2.8	1.6	2.1
Denmark/Danemark		0.1	0.7	0.0			0.8	1.7	0.8	3.0
Singapore/Singapour		0.9	0.2	0.6			0.6	0.6	1.3	1.4
USA/Etats–Unis d'Amer		2.5	2.1	0.0			0.6	0.8	0.4	1.3
Netherlands/Pays–Bas				0.1			0.1	0.5	0.6	0.7
Austria/Autriche		0.6	0.6	0.0			0.3	0.2	0.5	0.8

	1985	1986	1987	1988	1989	1990	1991	1992	1993	1994
Afrique										
Amériques										0.1
– Amérique du Nord										0.1
– ALAI										
– MCAC										
– Caraïbes										
– Autre Amérique										
Asie anc. URSS exclus	99.3	98.1	98.2	95.0			99.7	99.4	99.5	99.6
– Moyen–Orient										
Asie ancienne URSS										
Europe anc. URSS exclus							0.1	0.1	0.1	0.0
– Union Européenne							0.1	0.1	0.1	0.0
– Europe de l'Est										
– Autre de l'Europe										
Europe ancienne URSS									0.0	
Océanie										
Autre							0.2	0.5	0.4	0.3
India/Inde	99.3	98.1	98.2	95.0			90.5	83.8	89.7	93.4
Bangladesh							8.2	15.6	9.6	6.1
Areas n.e.s.							0.2	0.5	0.4	0.3
Singapore/Singapour							1.0			
Netherlands/Pays–Bas							0.1	0.1	0.1	
Germany/Allemagne							0.0	0.1	0.0	
Japan/Japon								0.0	0.1	0.0
USA/Etats–Unis d'Amer										0.1
Thailand/Thaïlande							0.0	0.0	0.0	
Austria/Autriche										0.0

4. General Imports C.I.F. by Commodities according to the S.I.T.C. (Rev. 2) in million U.S. Dollars
Importations Générales C.A.F. par Produits d'après la C.T.C.I. (Rév. 2) en millions de Dollars E.U.

SITC CTCI	COMMODITY	1991 QUANTITY QUANTITE	1991 VALUE VALEUR	1992 QUANTITY QUANTITE	1992 VALUE VALEUR	1993 QUANTITY QUANTITE	1993 VALUE VALEUR	1994 QUANTITY QUANTITE	1994 VALUE VALEUR	PRODUIT
	ALL COMMODITIES		96.7		128.0		90.8		91.1	TOUS PRODUITS
0	FOOD AND LIVE ANIMALS		16.8		13.6		13.1		14.9	ALIMENTS,ANIMAUX VIVANTS
001	*LIVE ANIMALS FOR FOOD	N 56013	0.3	N 34185	0.6	N 33043	0.2	N 90460	0.4	ANIMAUX VIVANTS
0011	BOVINE SPECIES,LIVE	N 7022	0.3	N 18286	0.5	N 20796	0.2	N 16089	0.3	ESPECE BOVINE
00111	— PURE BRED FR BREEDING	N 7012	0.3	N 18286	0.5	N 5422	0.2	N 42	0.1	BOVINS REPRODUCTEURS
02	DAIRY PRODCTS,BIRDS'EGGS		1.4		2.2		1.8		1.6	PRODUITS LAITIERS,OEUFS
022	MILK AND CREAM		0.8		1.4		1.1	W 377	0.9	LAIT ET CREME
0224	MILK,CREAM PRESERVED ETC		0.7		1.4		1.1	W 372	0.9	LAIT,CREME CONS,CONC
02242	MILK DRY,1.5% FAT OR LES		0.6		0.6		0.9	W 319	0.8	LAIT POUDRE INF 1.5%
02243	MILK DRY,OVER 1.5% FAT				0.6					LAIT POUDRE SUP 1.5%
023	BUTTER	W 132	0.5	W 187	0.6	W 212	0.5	W 151	0.4	BEURRE
025	EGGS,BIRDS,FRESH,PRSRVD	N 8218644	0.3	N 8456988	0.3	W 729	0.3	W 604	0.4	OEUFS
0251	— IN SHELL	N 8218644	0.3	N 8456988	0.3	W 729	0.3	W 604	0.4	OEUFS EN COQUILLE
03	FISH AND PREPARATIONS		0.9		0.8		0.4		0.3	POISSONS ET PREPARATIONS
035	FISH SALTED,DRIED,SMOKED		0.9		0.8		0.4	W 436	0.3	POISSON SECHE,SALE,FUME
03503	FISH(EX COD)DRIED,SALTED		0.9		0.8		0.4	W 436	0.3	POISSONS SECHES,SALES
04	CEREALS AND PREPARATIONS		10.7		7.7		6.8		8.9	CEREALES ET PRODUITS
041	WHEAT ETC UNMILLED			W 15915	2.1	W 14694	1.5	W 10389	1.5	FROMENT,EPEAUTRE
0411	DURUM WHEAT UNMILLED					W 380	0.1	W 5380	0.8	FROMENT DUR NON MOULU
0412	OTHER WHEAT ETC UNMILLED			W 15915	2.1	W 14313	1.5	W 5009	0.7	AUTRE FROMENT NON MOULU
042	RICE		5.7		3.8	W 22250	4.2	W 26976	6.1	RIZ
0421	RICE IN HUSK OR HUSKED		0.1		0.1	W 22247	4.2	W 26913	6.1	RIZ SANS AUTRE PREPARATION
04212	RICE HUSKED					W 22226	4.2	W 26908	6.1	RIZ CARGO
0422	RICE SEMI–MILLED,MILLED	W 23800	5.7	W 19568	3.8			W 62	0.1	RIZ POLI,GLACE INCL BRISURES
04221	RICE MILLED UNBROKEN	W 23800	5.7	W 19568	3.8					RIZ POLI,GLACE EXCL BRISURES
046	WHEAT ETC MEAL OR FLOUR	W 25611	3.8	W 1651	0.3		0.5	W 2558	0.5	SEMOULE FARINE,FROMENT
04601	FLOUR OF WHEAT OR MESLIN	W 1109	0.3	W 1618	0.3	W 2216	0.3	W 2558	0.5	FARINE DE FROMENT
04602	MEAL,GROATS OF WHEAT ETC	W 24502	3.6	W 33	0.1		0.2			GRUAUX,SEMOULES FROMENT
048	CEREAL ETC PREPARATIONS		0.8		1.0	W 665	0.5	W 698	0.6	PREPTNS A BASE CEREALES
0488	OTH CEREAL PREPS,MALT EX		0.3		0.6	W 58	0.1	W 12	0.1	EXTRAITS DE MALT
05	VEGETABLES AND FRUIT		1.4		0.9		2.4		1.8	LEGUMES ET FRUITS
054	VEG ETC FRSH,SMPLY PRSVD		1.1		0.5	W 7456	1.6	W 4584	1.1	LEGUMES FRAIS,CONG,SECS
0542	LEGUMINOUS VEGETBLES DRY	W 447	0.2	W 550	0.2	W 1024	0.3	W 511	0.5	LEGUMES A COSSE SECS
0545	OTHER FRESH VEGETABLES	W 850	0.2	W 1875	0.3	W 3227	0.5	W 3013	0.5	AUTRES LEGUMES FRAIS,REF
05459	FRESH VEGETABLES NES	W 653	0.2	W 1676	0.2	W 3070	0.5	W 2753	0.4	LEGUMES FRAIS,REFRI NDA
0548	EDIBLE VEG NES FRESH,DRY		0.7		0.1	W 3028	0.8	W 589	0.2	RACINES,TUBERCULES
05482	SUGAR BEET FRSH DRY,CANE		0.7		0.1	W 3028	0.8	W 589	0.2	BETTERAVES,CANNES A SUCRE
057	FRUIT,NUTS,FRESH,DRIED		0.3		0.3	W 1244	0.3	W 1723	0.4	FRUITS FRAIS OU SECS
058	FRUIT PRESERVED,PREPARED		0.1		0.2	W 1341	0.2	W 1111	0.4	CONSERVES DE FRUITS
06	SUGAR AND PREPS,HONEY		1.9		1.0		1.3		1.5	SUCRES ET PRODUITS
061	SUGAR AND HONEY	W 4731	1.9	W 3184	0.9	W 4664	1.2	W 3767	1.4	SUCRES ET MIEL
0611	RAW BEET AND CANE SUGAR					W 4532	1.2	W 3486	1.3	SUCRES BRUTS
0612	REFINED SUGAR ETC	W 4725	1.9	W 3130	0.9	W 110	0.1	W 233	0.1	SUCRES RAFFINES
07	COFFEE,TEA,COCOA,SPICES		0.3		0.3		0.2		0.4	CAFE,THE,CACAO,EPICES
1	BEVERAGES AND TOBACCO		4.0		1.8		1.4		1.6	BOISSONS ET TABACS
11	BEVERAGES		3.8		1.7		1.4		1.5	BOISSONS
112	ALCOHOLIC BEVERAGES		3.7		1.7		1.4	W 3813	1.5	BOISSONS ALCOOLIQUES
1123	BEER,ALE,STOUT,PORTER	V 685	2.3	V 292	1.0	W 1427	0.9	W 3736	1.2	BIERES
1124	DISTILLED ALCOHOLIC BEVS		1.5		0.7		0.4	W 36	0.2	ALCOOLS,EAUX–DE–VIE
11241	WHISKY		0.2		0.2		0.4	W 26	0.2	WHISKY
11249	OTH ALCOHOLC BEVS,CMPNDS	W 2479	1.3		0.6	W 6	0.1	W 10	0.1	BOISSONS ALCOOLIQUES NDA
2	CRUDE MATERLS,EXCL FUELS		1.5		2.2		3.6		1.8	MAT BRUTES NON COMESTIBLES
24	CORK AND WOOD		0.7		1.2		0.9		1.0	LIEGE ET BOIS
245	FUEL WOOD NES, CHARCOAL		0.4		0.7	W 4041	0.7	W 4423	1.0	BOIS DE CHAUFFAGE
24502	WOOD CHARCOAL	W 3168	0.4	W 69	0.7	W 4040	0.7	W 4423	1.0	CHARBON DE BOIS
27	CRUDE FERTLZR,MINRLS NES		0.8		0.9		2.4		0.5	ENGRAIS MINERAUX BRUTS
271	FERTILIZERS,CRUDE						2.1	W 571	0.1	ENGRAIS BRUTS
2711	ANIMAL,VEG FERTLZR,CRUDE						2.1	W 571	0.1	GUANO,ENGRAIS NATURELS
273	STONE,SAND AND GRAVEL		0.7		0.8	W 12467	0.3	W 17660	0.3	PIERRES,SABLES,GRAVIERS
2732	CALCAREOUS STONE		0.6		0.7	W 11855	0.3	W 17264	0.2	GYPSE,PLATRES,CASTINES
27322	CALCAREOUS STONE NES	V 181682	0.6	V 142052	0.7	W 11854	0.3	W 17260	0.2	PIERRES A CHAUX
29	CRUDE ANIMAL,VEG MAT NES		0.1		0.2		0.3		0.2	MATIERES BRUTES ANIM,VEGET
292	CRUDE VEG MATERIALS NES		0.1		0.2		0.3	W 281	0.2	MAT BRUTES VEGETALES NDA
3	MINERAL FUELS ETC		11.6		10.4		9.0		10.5	COMBUSTIBLES MINERAUX LUB
32	COAL,COKE AND BRIQUETTES		1.9		1.8		1.6		1.5	HOUILLES,COKES,BRIQUETTES
322	COAL,LIGNITE AND PEAT	W 20891	0.9	W 30014	1.1	W 26124	1.3	W 11283	0.7	HOUILLES,LIGNITES,TOURBE
3222	OTH COAL,NOT AGGLOMERATD	W 20891	0.9	W 30014	1.1	W 26124	1.3	W 11283	0.7	AUTRES HOUILLES
323	BRIQUETS,COKE,SEMI–COKE	W 10140	1.0	W 10865	0.8	W 8628	0.4	W 8718	0.8	BRIQUETTES
3232	COKE,SEMI–COKE,RTRT CRBN	W 10140	1.0	W 10865	0.8	W 8628	0.4	W 8699	0.8	COKES ET SEMI–COKES
32321	COKE OF COAL,RETORT CRBN	W 10140	1.0	W 10865	0.8					COKES,SEMI–COKES HOUILLE
33	PETROLEUM AND PRODUCTS		9.3		8.2		6.8		8.6	PETROLE ET DERIVES
334	PETROLEUM PRODUCTS,REFIN		8.9		7.6	W 24912	6.4	W 28260	8.1	PRODUITS RAFFINES
3341	GASOLINE,OTH LIGHT OILS	V 5478	3.0	V 4557	2.3	W 3499	1.9	W 3568	2.4	ESSENCES POUR MOTEURS
33411	MOTOR,AVIATION SPIRIT	V 5451	3.0	V 3583	1.9	W 3499	1.9	W 3568	2.4	ESSENCES MOTEURS D'AVIONS
3342	KEROSENE,OTH MEDIUM OILS	V 6245	0.7	V 6969	0.7	W 6956	0.7	W 5643	0.6	PETR LAMPANTS,AUT HUIL
33421	KEROSENE INCL JET FUEL	V 6245	0.7	V 6969	0.7					PETROLES LAMPANTS
33429	OTH MEDIUM PETROLEUM OIL					W 6956	0.7	W 5643	0.6	AUTRES HUILES MOYENNES
3343	GAS OILS	V 17478	3.6	V 18553	3.5	W 13856	3.0	W 13464	3.3	GAS OILS
3344	FUEL OILS,NES	V 2419	0.5	V 2595	0.5	W 193	0.4	W 4601	1.0	FUEL OILS
3345	LUBS,PETROLEUM OILS NES		1.3		0.7	W 407	0.6	W 984	1.0	HUILES LUBRIFIANTES
33451	LUBS(HIGH PETR CONT) ETC	W 34	0.1	W 26	0.1	W 392	0.6	W 920	0.9	HUILES LUBRIF,H LOURDES
33452	LUBS (LOW PETRLM CONTNT)	V 711	1.3	V 636	0.7	W 15	0.1	W 64	0.1	PREPARATIONS LUBRIFIANTES
335	RESIDUAL PETRLM PROD NES		0.5		0.7	W 2225	0.4	W 2039	0.6	PRODUITS RESIDUELS NDA
3354	PETROLM BITUMEN,COKE ETC		0.5		0.6	W 2174	0.4	W 1973	0.6	BITUME,COKE DE PETROLE
33541	PETROLEUM BITUMEN, ETC					W 2104	0.4	W 1725	0.5	BITUME DE PETROLE
33543	BITUMINOUS MIXTURES ETC		0.3		0.5	W 60	0.1	W 190	0.1	MELANGES BITUMINEUX
341	*GAS,NATURAL AND MANUFCT		0.3		0.3	W 1945	0.3	W 3607	0.5	GAZ NATUREL,GAZ MANUFACT
3413	PETROLM GASES,LIQUEFIED		0.3		0.3	W 1945	0.3	W 3607	0.5	GAZ DE PETROLE LIQUEFIE
34131	LIQUEFIED PROPANE,BUTANE		0.3		0.3	W 1945	0.3	W 3340	0.4	PROPANE,BUTANE LIQUEFIES
351	*ELECTRIC CURRENT		0.3		0.3		0.4			ENERGIE ELECTRIQUE
4	ANIMAL,VEGETABLE OIL,FAT		3.7		2.7		3.3		3.2	HUILES,GRAISSES ANIM,VEG
42	FIXED VEGETABLE OIL,FAT		3.7		2.7		3.2		3.2	HUILES VEGETALES FIXES
423	FIXED VEG OILS,SOFT		2.2		1.5	W 1477	1.4	W 1710	1.6	HUILES VEGET DOUCES FIXES
4232	SOYA BEAN OIL	W 8	0.7			W 19	0.1	W 17	0.1	HUILE DE SOJA
4239	OTH FIXED VEG OILS,SOFT	W 936	1.3	W 994	1.2	W 1434	1.4	W 1596	1.6	AUTRES HUILES FIXES
42391	RAPE,COLZA,MUSTARD OILS	W 936	1.3	W 114	0.2	W 1434	1.4	W 1596	1.6	H NAVETTE COLZA MOUTARDE
42392	SESAME OIL			W 880	1.0					HUILE DE SESAME
424	FIXED VEG OIL NONSOFT	W 674	1.6	W 852	1.3		1.8	W 1236	1.6	AUTRES HUILES VEG FIXES
4242	PALM OIL	W 65	0.1	W 13	0.1		0.6			HUILE DE PALME
4249	FIXED VEGETABLE OILS NES	W 593	1.5	W 822	1.2	W 1089	1.2	W 1169	1.5	HUILES VEGET FIXES NDA
5	CHEMCLS,RELATED PROD NES		5.2		6.3		7.3		7.7	PRODUITS CHIMIQUES

4. General Imports C.I.F. by Commodities according to the S.I.T.C. (Rev. 2) in million U.S. Dollars
Importations Générales C.A.F. par Produits d'après la C.T.C.I. (Rév. 2) en millions de Dollars E.U.

SITC CTCI	COMMODITY	1991		1992		1993		1994		PRODUIT
		QUANTITY QUANTITE	VALUE VALEUR	QUANTITY QUANTITE	VALUE VALEUR	QUANTITY QUANTITE	VALUE VALEUR	QUANTITY QUANTITE	VALUE VALEUR	
51	ORGANIC CHEMICALS		0.5		0.3		3.1		3.3	PROD CHIMIQ ORGANIQUES
511	HYDROCARBONS NES,DERIVS	V 690	0.4	V 386	0.3	W 1895	1.0	W 2058	1.1	HYDROCARBURES NDA
5111	ACYCLIC HYDROCARBONS	V 690	0.4	V 386	0.3	W 1895	1.0	W 2058	1.1	HYDROCARBURES ACYCLIQUES
51111	ETHYLENE	V 690	0.4	V 386	0.3					ETHYLENE
51119	OTH ACYCLIC HYDROCARBONS					W 1895	1.0	W 2058	1.1	AUT HYDROCARBURES ACYCL
512	ALCOHOLS,PHENOLS ETC		0.1		0.1	V 4817	2.0		2.0	PHENOLS,PHENOLS–ALCOOLS
5121	ACYCLIC ALCOHOLS,DERIVS					V 4817	2.0	V 3244	2.0	ALCOOLS ACYCLIQUES
51216	ETHYL ALC,DENATRD SPIRIT					V 4817	2.0	V 3244	2.0	ALCOOL ETHYLIQUE NON DENAT
52	INORGANIC CHEMICALS		0.7		1.2		0.9		0.7	PROD CHIM INORGANIQUES
522	INORG ELEMNTS,OXIDES,ETC		0.1		0.1		0.6	W 545	0.3	ELEMENTS INORGANIQUES
5221	CHEMICAL ELEMENTS		0.1		0.1		0.5	W 509	0.3	ELEMENTS CHIMIQUES
52217	ALKALI,RARE EARTH METALS					W 791	0.5	W 97	0.2	METAUX ALCALINS
523	OTHR INORG CHEMICALS ETC		0.1		0.1		0.4	W 756	0.4	AUT PRODUITS CHIMIQUES INORG
5232	OTH MTL CMPD OF INRG ACD					W 532	0.3	W 698	0.4	SELS METALLIQUES
52324	CARBONATE NES,PERCBONATE					W 532	0.3	W 698	0.4	CARBONATES,PERCARBONATES
524	RADIOACTIVE ETC MATERIAL	W 1110	0.5	W 2354	1.1					MATIERES RADIOACTIVES
5241	RADIOACTIVE ELEMENTS ETC	W 1110	0.5	W 2354	1.1					RADIOELEMENTS,ISOTOPES
53	DYES,TANNING,COLOUR PROD		0.4		0.4		0.4		0.5	PROD TEINTURE,COLORANTS
533	PIGMENTS,PAINTS,ETC		0.4		0.4	W 284	0.4		0.5	PIGMENTS,PEINTURES,VERNIS
5334	VARNISHES,DISTEMPERS ETC	W 219	0.4	W 263	0.4	W 276	0.4	W 305	0.4	PEINTURES A L'EAU
53342	OTH PAINTS,VARNISHES ETC			W 190	0.4	W 276	0.4	W 305	0.4	AUTRES PEINTURES,VERNIS
53343	PIGMNTS IN PAINT ETC MED	W 209	0.4							PIGMENTS BROYES
541	*MEDICINAL,PHARM PRODUCT		1.4		1.4		1.2	K 264	1.6	PROD MEDICINAUX PHARMACEUT
5415	HORMONES,NAT,SYN IN BULK		1.0		1.0					HORMONES
54151	INSULIN		1.0		1.0					INSULINE
5417	MEDICAMENTS		0.2		0.1		1.1	K 186	1.1	MEDICAMENTS
54171	— CONTAINNG ANTIBIOTICS		0.1		0.1	K 329881	0.8	K 186	1.1	MED CONTN ANTIBIOTIQUES
54179	— CONTNG OTH SUBSTANCES		0.2		0.1		0.3			MED CONT AUT SUBSTANCES
5419	PHARMACEUTICAL GOODS NES		0.2		0.3		0.1	K 71	0.5	PREP,ART PHARMACEUTIQUES
54199	OTH PHARMACEUTICAL GOODS		0.2		0.3		0.1	K 53	0.4	AUT PREP PHARMACEUTIQUES
55	PERFUME,CLEANING ETC PRD		0.9		1.0		1.0		1.0	PROD POUR PARFUM,TOILETTE
554	SOAP,CLEANSING ETC PREPS		0.7		0.8	W 773	0.9	W 671	0.8	SAVONS,PRODUITS DETERSIFS
5541	SOAPS		0.6		0.7	W 750	0.8	W 652	0.8	SAVONS,PROD TENSIO–ACTIFS
562	*FERTILIZERS,MANUFACTURE	W 2408	0.3	W 2869	0.4		0.4		0.3	ENGRAIS MANUFACTURES
5621	CHEM NITROGENOUS FERTLZR	W 15	0.1	W 551	0.1		0.4	W 1412	0.3	ENGRAIS AZOTES
56216	UREA						0.4	W 1386	0.3	UREE
572	*EXPLOSIVES,PYROTECH PRO		0.5		0.2	W 583	0.2	W 125	0.2	EXPLOSIFS
5721	PREPARED EXPLOSIVES		0.4		0.1	W 518	0.2	W 53	0.1	POUDRES,EXPLOSIFS
57211	PROPELLENT POWDERS		0.4		0.1	W 168	0.1			POUDRES A TIRER
59	CHEMICAL MATERIALS NES		0.9		1.6		0.3		0.3	MAT PROD CHIMIQUES NDA
598	MISCEL CHEM PRODUCTS NES		0.6		1.3		0.1	W 16	0.1	PROD DIV INDUST CHIM NDA
5989	CHEM PRODUCTS,PREPS NES		0.6		1.3		0.1			PROD PREP CHIMIQUES NDA
59899	OTH CHEM PRODS,PREPS,NES		0.5		1.2					AUT PRODUITS CHIMIQUES NDA
6	BASIC MANUFACTURES		16.0		21.0		16.1		16.4	ART MANUFACTURES
62	RUBBER MANUFACTURES NES		2.3		2.3		1.5		1.8	CAOUTCHOUC MANUFACTURE
625	RUBBER TYRES, TUBES ETC		2.2		2.2		1.4	N 61530	1.6	PNEUS CAOUTCHOUC VULCANISE
6251	TYRES NEW FOR MOTOR CARS		0.5		0.6	N 5653	0.3	N 6440	0.4	PNEUS POUR VOITURES
6252	TYRES,NEW,BUS OR LORRY	N 10190	1.5		1.3	N 6173	0.8	N 40290	1.1	PNEUS POUR AUTOBUS,CAMIONS
6259	OTH TYRES,TYRE CASES,ETC	N 15940	0.2	N 25964	0.3		0.3	N 13972	0.3	AUTRES PNEUS RECHAPES FLAPS
63	WOOD,CORK MANUFACTRS NES		0.6		0.8		0.6		0.8	OUVRAGES LIEGE ET BOIS
634	VENEERS,PLYWOOD,ETC		0.5		0.5		0.2		0.3	PLACAGES,CONTRE–PLAQUES
6341	VENEER SHEETS ETC		0.5		0.4	V 83742	0.1	V 350359	0.2	BOIS SIMPLEMENT SCIES
64	PAPER,PAPERBOARD AND MFR		1.8		2.1		1.8		1.6	PAPIERS,CARTONS & OUVRAGES
641	PAPER AND PAPERBOARD		1.1		1.3		1.1		0.8	PAPIERS ET CARTONS
6411	NEWSPRINT		0.4		0.6					PAPIER JOURNAL
6412	PRINTG,WRITING PAPER NES		0.7		0.8	W 32	0.1	W 2	0.1	PAPIERS POUR L'IMPRESSION
64121	— UNCOATED		0.7		0.8	W 32	0.1	W 2	0.1	PAPIERS IMPRES NON COUCHES
6413	KRAFT PAPER,PAPERBOARD					W 848	0.6	W 939	0.8	PAPIER ET CARTON KRAFT
64131	KRAFT LINER IN BULK					W 504	0.3	W 669	0.5	PAP KRAFT POUR COUVERTURES
64139	KRAFT PAPER PAPERBD,NES					W 343	0.4	W 270	0.3	PAPIER,CARTON KRAFT NDA
6419	CONVERTED PAPER ETC NES	N 82626	0.1	N 11190	0.1		0.5			PAP,CART TRANSFORMES NDA
64197	WALLPAPER,LINCRUSTA,ETC						0.5			PAPIERS DE TENTURE
642	PAPER,ETC,PRECUT,ARTS OF		0.8		0.8	W 1028	0.7	W 817	0.8	PAP,CARTONS DECOUPES
6423	EXERCISE BOOKS ETC		0.4		0.5	W 440	0.5	W 466	0.7	REGISTRES,CAHIERS,CARNETS
65	TEXTILE YARN,FABRICS,ETC		3.2		3.2		2.0		2.1	FILS,TISSUS,ARTICLES TEXTILE
651	TEXTILE YARN		0.7		0.8	W 266	0.7	W 282	0.6	FILS TEXTILES
6513	COTTON YARN		0.4		0.2	W 156	0.2	W 24	0.1	FILS DE COTON
65131	— 14 KM PER KG OR LESS		0.4		0.2					FILS COT MOINS 14000 M KG
6514	SYN FIB YRN,BULK,MONOFIL				0.1	W 88	0.4	W 13	0.1	FILS CONT 85% FIB TEXT SYNTH
65142	— NONTXT ETC CONT PAMID					W 79	0.4	W 7	0.1	FILS NON TEX FI CON POLYAMID
652	COTTON FABRICS,WOVEN		1.4		1.3	A 1260	1.0	A 1847	1.1	TISSUS DE COTON
6521	GREY WOVEN COTTON FABRIC		1.4		1.3	A 1236	1.0	A 1815	1.1	TISSUS COT ECRUS NON MERCER
65211	GREY COTTON GAUZE		1.4		1.3					TISSUS COT POINT GAZE ECRUS
65214	GREY WOVEN COTTON NES				0.1	A 1236	1.0	A 1815	1.1	AUT TISSUS 85% COTON ECRUS
658	TEXTILE ARTICLES NES		1.1		1.0		0.2		0.3	ART FACONNES MAT TEXTILES
6581	BAGS,SACKS OF TEXTILES		0.5		0.6	W 24	0.1	W 31	0.1	SACS EMBALLAGE TEXTILES
6582	MADE–UP CANVAS GOODS		0.4		0.2		0.1	N 63804	0.2	BACHES,TENTES ETC
66	NONMETAL MINERAL MFS NES		1.7		1.8		3.0		3.2	ART MIN NON METALLIQUES
661	LIME,CEMENT,BLDG PRODS		0.1		0.1	W 3642	0.9	W 2589	1.0	CHAUX,CIMENTS MAT CONSTR
6618	MNRL BLDG PRD UNFIRD NES					W 679	0.8	W 729	0.9	MAT CONST AMIANTE–CIMENT
66183	ASBESTOS–,FIBRE–CMNT PRD					W 674	0.8	W 728	0.9	OUVRAGES AMIANTE–CIMENT
662	CLAY,REFRACTORY BLDG PRD		0.3		0.6	W 20808	0.5	W 17356	0.4	MAT CONST REFRACTAIRES
6624	BRICKS ETC NONREFRACTORY		0.3		0.6	W 8120	0.3	W 12834	0.3	BRIQUES ETC CERAM NON REFR
664	GLASS		0.5		0.3	W 293	0.3	W 243	0.3	VERRE
6649	GLASS NES		0.4	N 218286	0.2	W 292	0.3	W 236	0.3	VERRE NDA
66491	GLASS IN SHAPES		0.3			W 216	0.2	W 172	0.2	VERRE A VITRES DECOUPES
665	GLASSWARE	MN 9909	0.7	MN 12053	0.8	W 8601	1.3	W 8724	1.4	OUVRAGES EN VERRE
6651	BOTTLES ETC OF GLASS	MN 9845	0.7	MN 11986	0.8	W 8559	1.2	W 8697	1.4	RECIPIENTS EN VERRE
66511	GLASS BOTTLES ETC NONVAC	MN 9845	0.7	MN 11986	0.8	W 8559	1.2	W 8697	1.4	BONBONNES,BOUTEILLES,ETC
67	IRON AND STEEL		3.8		7.2		4.8		4.1	FER ET ACIER
673	IRON,STEEL SHAPES ETC		1.1		3.3	W 345101	2.2	W 814049	1.8	BARRES,PROFIL FER,ACIER
6732	IRON,STEEL BARS ETC		0.7		1.4	W 2822	1.2	W 1733	0.8	BARRES FER,ACIER
67325	OTH ALLOY STEEL BARS ETC					W 2822	1.2	W 1733	0.8	BARRES NON ACIERS ALLIES
67326	IRN,OTH STL BARS HOTROLD	W 1424	0.7	W 2600	1.3					BARRES PLEINES FER,ACIER
6733	IRON,STEEL PROFILES ETC	N 315977	0.4	N 584632	2.0	W 342247	1.1	W 811957	0.8	PROFILES,PALPLAN FER,ACIER
67333	OTH PRFILES HOTROLLD ETC	N 292007	0.4	N 562793	2.0	W 1659	0.9	W 705	0.3	AUT PROFILES LAMINES,FILES
67339	OTHER ALLOY STL PROFILES					W 168339	0.2	W 581053	0.4	PROFILES NON ACIERS ALLIES
674	IRN,STL UNIV,PLATE,SHEET		1.2		2.7		1.6	W 857	1.0	LARGES PLATS,TOLES
6741	IRON OR STEEL UNIVERSALS		0.2	N 306367	0.7					LARGES PLATS FER,ACIER
67414	IRN,SMPL STL UNIVERSALS		0.2	N 306180	0.7					PLATS NON ACIER FIN
6747	TINNED PLATES,SHEETS	N 492185	1.0	N 190318	1.5	W 8	0.1	W 6	0.1	TOLES ETAMEES EN ACIER

4. General Imports C.I.F. by Commodities according to the S.I.T.C. (Rev. 2) in million U.S. Dollars
Importations Générales C.A.F. par Produits d'après la C.T.C.I. (Rév. 2) en millions de Dollars E.U.

SITC CTCI	COMMODITY	1991		1992		1993		1994		PRODUIT
		QUANTITY QUANTITE	VALUE VALEUR	QUANTITY QUANTITE	VALUE VALEUR	QUANTITY QUANTITE	VALUE VALEUR	QUANTITY QUANTITE	VALUE VALEUR	
6749	OTH IRN,STL PLATES,SHEET				0.7		1.5	W 852	1.0	AUTRES TOLES FER,ACIER
67491	— OF IRON OR SIMPLE STL				0.7		1.5	W 852	1.0	AUT TOLES AUTRES ACIER FIN
675	IRON,STEEL HOOP,STRIP		0.9							FEUILLARDS LAMINES
67501	IRN,SMPLE STL HOOP,STRIP		0.9							FEUILLARDS NON ACIER FIN
677	IRN,STL WIRE(EXCL W ROD)	W 208	0.2	W 60	0.1	W 12576	0.1	W 547266	0.5	FILS EN FER,ACIER
67701	IRON, SIMPLE STEEL WIRE	W 208	0.2	W 60	0.1	W 7402	0.1	W 444072	0.4	FILS NON ACIER FIN CARBONE
678	IRON,STL TUBES,PIPES,ETC		0.7		1.1	W 218259	1.0	W 578001	1.0	TUBES,TUYAUX EN FONTE,FER
6782	IRON,STL SEAMLESS TUBES		0.1		0.2	W 155671	1.0	W 339839	0.9	TUBES,TUYAUX SANS SOUDURE
6783	IRON,STL TUBES,PIPES NES	N 145861	0.4	N 180609	0.5					AUT TUBES,TUYAUX FER,ACIER
68	NON-FERROUS METALS		0.1		0.1		0.3		0.4	METAUX NON FERREUX
69	METAL MANUFACTURES NES		2.8		3.8		2.5		2.8	ART MANUFACT EN METAL NDA
691	STRUCTURES AND PARTS NES	N 39327	0.2	N 73631	1.0		0.6	W 1452	0.9	CONSTRUCT FER,ACIER,ALU
6911	STRUCTURES,PARTS IRN,STL	N 33074	0.2	N 57490	0.7	W 1078	0.6	W 1435	0.9	CONSTRUCT FER,ACIER,FONTE
692	METAL TANKS,BOXES,ETC	N 1474779	0.5	N 736958	0.2		0.4	W 189	0.2	RECIPIENTS METALLIQUES
6924	MTL TRANSPORT BOXES ETC	N 1474476	0.5	N 736678	0.2		0.3	W 175	0.1	FUTS,TAMBOURS,BIDONS
69241	STL TRANSPORT BOXES ETC	N 1452664	0.4	N 730016	0.2	W 9	0.1	W 40	0.1	FUTS,TAMBOURS,BIDONS FER
693	WIRE PRODUCTS NON ELECTR		0.4		0.4	W 644	0.5	W 794	0.7	OUVRAGES FILS METALLIQUES
6932	IRON,STEEL FENCING WIRE	W 146	0.1	W 284	0.2	W 561	0.4	W 466	0.5	RONCES DE FER OU ACIER
694	STL,COPPR NAILS,NUTS,ETC	W 603	0.3	W 249	0.2	W 378	0.3	W 277	0.2	CLOUS,VIS,ECROUS
697	BASE MTL HOUSEHOLD EQUIP		0.5		0.8	W 376	0.4	W 191	0.3	ART MENAGE MET COMMUNS
6978	BASE MTL HOUSE EQUIP NES	N 112630	0.2	N 130263	0.5					ART MENAGE MET COMMUNS
69781	DOMSTC FOOD MACH NONELEC	N 112630	0.2	N 130263	0.5					MOULINS A CAFE ETC
699	BASE METAL MFRS NES		0.6		1.1	W 385	0.4	W 577	0.5	ART MANUFACTURES MET NDA
6997	IRON,STEEL ARTICLES NES	N 121661	0.3	N 719380	0.7	W 5	0.1	W 1	0.1	OUV FONTE,FER,ACIER NDA
69979	IRN,STL MANUFACTURES NES	N 121661	0.3	N 719380	0.7	W 5	0.1	W 1	0.1	AUT OUVRAGES EN FER NDA
6998	MFRS NES OF CPR,NIKL,ETC		0.1		0.1	W 332	0.3	W 166	0.3	OUVRAGES EN CU,NI,AL,PB,ZN
69986	TIN MANUFACTURES NES				0.1	W 332	0.3	W 165	0.3	OUVRAGES EN ETAIN
7	MACHINES,TRANSPORT EQUIP		33.7		59.2		30.7		27.6	MACHINES MATERIEL TRANSPORT
71	POWER GENERATING EQUIPMT		0.2		0.2		2.4		0.3	MACHINES GENERATRICES
713	INTRNL COMBUS PSTN ENGIN				0.1		1.3	N 465	0.1	MOTEURS EXPL COMB INT, PIECE
7131	AIRCRAFT PSTN ENGINS,PTS						1.2			MOTEURS EXPL P.AVIATION, PIE
71311	AIRCRAFT PISTON ENGINES						1.2			MOTEURS EXPL P.AVIATION
716	ROTATING ELECTRIC PLANT		0.2		0.2		1.1	W 81	0.3	APP ELECTR ROTATIFS,PIECES
7162	AC MTRS,GENRTRS,GEN SETS		0.2		0.2		1.1	W 80	0.3	MOTEURS ELECTRIQUES
71622	AC GENERATORS		0.1		0.1	W 47	1.0	W 38	0.2	GENER COURANT ALTERNATIF
72	MACHS FOR SPCL INDUSTRYS		9.2		5.4		1.4		7.6	MAC SPECIALES POUR INDUST
721	AGRIC MACHY,EXC TRACTORS		7.3		3.1		0.6	W 108	3.5	MACHINES AGRICOLES
7219	AGRICULTURE MACHINES NES		7.2		3.0		0.5	W 78	3.4	ENGINS AGRICOLES NDA
72191	WINE-MAKING ETC MACHNERY		7.2		3.0	W 3	0.1	W 3	0.1	APPAREILS DE VINIFICATION
72199	PTS NES OF MCHY OF 72197				0.1		0.5	W 53	3.4	PIECES DES APP 721.97
723	CIVIL ENGNEERG EQUIP ETC		0.8		0.8		0.4		1.9	APPAREILS DE GENIE CIVIL
7234	CONST,MINING MACHNRY NES		0.1		0.2		0.3		0.7	MACH POUR LA CONST, MINES
72341	SELF-PROPELLD DOZERS,ETC		0.1		0.1	N 4	0.3	N 406	0.4	BULLDOZERS
72348	PUBLIC WORKS MACHNRY NES				0.1	W 36	0.1	W 53	0.4	MACHINES TRAVAUX PUBLICS
7239	CONSTR ETC MACHY PTS NES		0.6		0.5	W 18	0.1	W 132	1.2	PIECES 723.41–723.46
728	OTH MACHY FOR SPCL INDUS		1.1		1.1		0.3	W 149	2.0	AUT MACH IND PARTICULIERES
7281	MACH-TOOLS FR SPCL INDUS		0.5		0.2		0.1	W 20	0.2	MACH-OUTILS SPEC IND PART
7284	MACHY FOR SPCL INDUS NES		0.3		0.8	W 24	0.1	W 107	1.7	MACH SPEC IND PARTICUL.
72844	WOOD TREATING MACHNS NES	N 603	0.3	N 54	0.1	W 4	0.1	W 73	1.6	MACH TRAITEMENT DU BOIS
72848	OTH MCHY WITH INDIV FNCT		0.1		0.5	W 18	0.1	W 2	0.1	AUTRES MACHINES NDA
73	METALWORKING MACHINERY		0.2		0.2		0.2		0.4	MACH TRAVAIL DES METAUX
74	GENRL INDUSTRL MACHY NES		2.6		8.1		9.8		2.3	MACH APP INDUSTRIE
741	HEATING,COOLING EQUIPMNT		0.7		3.7		8.0	W 802	1.6	MACH CHAUFFAGE,PIECES
7412	BURNERS,MECH STOKERS,ETC						6.0	W 1	0.1	BRULEURS POUR FOYERS
7413	INDUS FURNACES ETC,PARTS		0.1		3.6		0.1	W 13	0.1	FOURS IND,LABOR,PIECES
74131	INDUS FURNACES ETC ELCTR		0.1		3.6		0.1	W 6	0.1	FOURS ELECTRIQUES
7414	NONDOM REFRIG EQUIPT,PTS		0.6		0.1		0.1	W 18	0.1	MAT PRODUCTION DU FROID
74149	PTS NES OF REFRIG EQUIPT		0.6		0.1				0.1	PIECES POUR MACH FROID
7416	HEATING,COOLING EQU NES		0.1		0.1	W 1095	1.9	W 754	1.4	APP CHANGEMENT TEMP
744	MECHANICAL HANDLING EQU		0.4		1.0		1.4	W 31	0.2	EQUIP MANUTENTION PIECES
7441	FORK LIFT TRCKS,ETC,PTS	N 1	0.1		0.2		0.3	W 7	0.1	CHARIOTS POUR USINES ETC
74411	FORK LIFT TRUCKS ETC	N 1	0.1	N 1	0.1	N 109	0.3	W 6	0.1	CHARIOTS POUR LES GARES
7442	LIFTING,LOADING MACH NES		0.1		0.8		0.8	W 22	0.1	APP LEVAGE,MANUTENTION
74422	SHIP DERRICKS,CRANES ETC					N 3	0.5			GRUES,PONTS ROULANTS
74428	OTH HANDLING ETC MCH NES		0.1		0.8	W 70	0.3	W 3	0.1	AUT APP LEVAGE ETC
7449	PTS NES OF MACHY OF 7442		0.3	N 106	0.1		0.4	W 3	0.1	PIECES DU 744.2
745	NONELEC MACHY,TOOLS NES		0.2		1.4		0.2	W 138	0.2	AUT MACH NON ELEC,PIECES
7452	OTH NONELEC MCHS,PTS NES		0.2		1.4	W 71	0.1	W 135	0.2	AUT MACH NON ELEC,PIECES
74522	PACKAGNG,BOTTLNG,ETC MCH		0.1		0.5	W 5	0.1		0.1	MACH NETT BOUTEILLES,ETC
74527	SPRAYING MACHINERY		0.1		0.9	W 55	0.1	W 23	0.1	APP PROJETER ETC LIQUID
749	NONELEC MACH PTS,ACC NES		1.1		1.9		0.3	W 77	0.2	PIECES MACH NON ELEC NDA
7492	COCKS,VALVES ETC NES		1.1		0.1		0.1	W 9	0.1	ART ROB,SIM POUR TUYAUX
7493	SHAFT,CRANK,PULLEY ETC		0.1		1.8	W 126	0.2	W 68	0.2	ARBRES TRANS,VILEBREQUINS
75	OFFICE MACHNES,ADP EQUIP		0.5		0.5		0.4		0.7	MACH BUREAU TRAIT AUTOM
751	OFFICE MACHINES		0.4		0.3		0.2	W 15	0.3	MACH,APPAREILS DE BUREAU
76	TELECOMM,SOUND EQUIPMENT		0.7		6.4		7.3		4.9	EQUIPMENT DE TELECOM
764	TELECOM EQPT,PTS,ACC NES		0.6		6.2		7.2	W 291	4.6	EQUIP TELECOM,PIECES
7648	TELECOMM EQUIPMENT NES		0.2		6.0	W 12	0.1	W 114	4.4	APP TELECOM NDA
76481	RADIOTELEPHONE ETC RCVRS		0.2		6.0	W 12	0.1	W 114	4.4	RECEP RADIOTELEPHONIE
7649	PTS NES OF EQUIPMT OF 76		0.1		0.1		7.2	W 6	0.1	PIECES DE LA DIV 76
76491	PTS NES OF APPAR OF 7641		0.1		0.1		7.2	W 3	0.1	PIECES POUR 764.1
77	ELECTRIC MACHNRY NES ETC		6.6		3.0		2.5		2.6	MACH APP ELECT NDA
771	ELECTRIC POWER MACHY NES		3.9		0.3		0.2	W 48	0.2	MACH PROD,TRANS ELECTR
7711	TRANSFORMERS,ELECTRICAL		3.6		0.1	W 25	0.1	W 14	0.1	TRANSFO ELECTRIQUES
77111	LIQUID DIELEC TRANSFRMRS		3.1							TRANSFO DIELEC LIQUIDE
77118	OTHER ELEC TRANSFORMERS		0.6		0.1	W 25	0.1	W 14	0.1	AUTRES TRANSFO ELECTRIQ
772	SWITCHGEAR ETC,PARTS NES		0.9		0.7		1.0	W 222	0.5	APP COUPURE,SECT ETC
7721	SWITCHGEAR ETC		0.9		0.7	W 612	1.0	W 222	0.5	APP COUPURE,SECTIONMNT
773	ELECTR DISTRIBUTNG EQUIP		0.5		0.4	W 171	0.4	W 416	0.8	EQUIPMT DISTRIBUTION ELECT
7731	INSULATED WIRE,CABLE ETC	L 564	0.5	L 449	0.3	W 164	0.4	W 177	0.4	FILS,CABLES ISOLES ELECT
7732	ELECTRC INSULATING EQUIP	N 14863	0.1	N 62197	0.2	W 7	0.1	W 239	0.5	EQUIP ISOL ELECTRIQUE
77324	OTHER ELECTRC INSULATORS	N 4164	0.1	N 4408	0.1	W 6	0.1	W 227	0.4	ISOLATEURS AUTRES MATIERES
774	ELECTRO-MEDCL,XRAY EQUIP		0.4		0.2		0.3	W 11	0.2	APPAREILS MEDICAUX
7742	X-RAY APPARATUS ETC		0.4		0.2		0.2	W 11	0.2	APPAREILS A RAYONS X
775	HOUSEHOLD TYPE EQUIP NES		0.4		0.7		0.3	W 58	0.3	MACH,APP USAGE DOMESTQUE
778	ELECTRICAL MACHINERY NES		0.7		0.9		0.4	W 163	0.7	AUTRES MACH ELECT NDA
7781	BATTERIES,ACCUMULATORS		0.5		0.5	W 172	0.4	W 99	0.4	PILES ET ACCUMULATEURS
77811	PRIMARY BATTERIES,CELLS		0.5		0.5	W 171	0.4	W 98	0.4	PILES ELECTRIQUES,PIECES
78	ROAD VEHICLES		12.8		10.0		6.8		7.1	VEHICULES ROUTIERS
781	PASS MOTOR VEH EXC BUSES	N 428	4.5	N 388	3.2	N 185	2.1	N 311	4.3	AUTO TRANSPORT PERSONNES
782	LORRIES,SPCL MTR VEH NES		1.5		1.4			N 3974	1.1	VEHICULES SPECIAUX,MARCH

4. General Imports C.I.F. by Commodities according to the S.I.T.C. (Rev. 2) in million U.S. Dollars
Importations Générales C.A.F. par Produits d'après la C.T.C.I. (Rév. 2) en millions de Dollars E.U.

SITC CTCI	COMMODITY	1991 QUANTITY QUANTITE		1991 VALUE VALEUR	1992 QUANTITY QUANTITE		1992 VALUE VALEUR	1993 QUANTITY QUANTITE		1993 VALUE VALEUR	1994 QUANTITY QUANTITE		1994 VALUE VALEUR	PRODUIT
7821	LORRIES,TRUCKS	N	67	1.0	N	21230	1.1				N	3972	1.0	VEHICULES TRANSP MARCHAND
7822	SPECIAL MOTOR VEHCLS NES			0.6			0.4				N	2	0.2	VEHICULES USAGES SPECIAUX
783	ROAD MOTOR VEHICLES NES			0.2			0.8	N	7	0.1				VEHICULES ROUTIERS NDA
7831	BUSES	N	46	0.2	N	3994	0.6	N	7	0.1				VOITURES TRANSPORT COMMUN
784	MOTOR VEH PRTS,ACCES NES			5.1			3.7			4.1			1.6	PIECES 722,781,782,783
7841	MOTOR VEHICLE CHASSIS			3.9			2.5	N	39	0.5	N	5	0.1	CHASSIS 722,781,782,783
7842	MOTOR VEHICLE BODIES							N	50599	1.6	N	716	0.1	CARROS 722,781,782,783
7849	OTHER MOTOR VEHCL PARTS			1.2			1.3			2.2	W	313	1.5	PIECES 722,781,782,783
785	CYCLES,ETC MOTRZD OR NOT			1.6			1.0			0.5			0.3	MOTOCYCLES SCOOTERS
7851	MOTORCYCLES ETC			1.6			0.9	N	656	0.5	N	334	0.2	MOTO VELO MOTEUR AUXIL
79	OTHR TRANSPORT EQUIPMENT			1.3			25.7			0.1			2.1	AUTRE MATERIEL TRANSPORT
792	AIRCRAFT ETC			1.3			3.5			0.1	W	2	2.1	APP NAVIGATION AERIENNE
7922	AIRCRFT NES 2000KG OR LS			0.4										AERODYNES MOINS 2000 KG
7924	AIRCRFT NES OVER 15000KG			0.9			3.5							AERODYNES PLUS 15000 KG
7929	AIRCRAFT PARTS NES										W	2	2.1	PIECES DU 792
793	SHIPS AND BOATS ETC				N	1	22.2							NAVIRES BATEAUX,ETC
7931	WARSHIPS				N	1	22.2							NAVIRES DE GUERRE
8	MISC MANUFACTURED GOODS			3.8			4.6			6.1			6.9	ART MANUFACTURES DIVERS
821	*FURNITURE,PARTS THEREOF			0.4			0.8	W	296	0.5			0.7	MEUBLES ET PIECES
8212	MED FURN,STUFFD FURNSHGS			0.1			0.3	W	73	0.2			0.3	MOB MEDICO–CHIRUR,PIECES
8219	FURNITURE AND PARTS NES			0.3			0.5	W	223	0.4	W	112	0.4	AUTRES MEUBLES ET PIECES
84	CLOTHING AND ACCESSORIES			0.7			0.6			1.0			0.9	VETEMENTS
842	MENS OUTERWEAR NOT KNIT	N	77351	0.3	N	128500	0.3			0.5	N	138965	0.3	VET DESSUS POUR HOMMES
8429	— OTHER OUTER GARMENTS									0.4	N	136113	0.2	AUT VET DES HOM MAT TEX
847	TEXTILE CLTHNG ACCES NES									0.4	N	419255	0.5	ACCES VET MAT TEXT NDA
8471	— NOT KNITTED							N	298016	0.4	N	378555	0.4	ACCES VET MAT TEX NON BON
84712	SHAWLS,VEILS ETC,NOT KNT							N	298016	0.4	N	377491	0.4	ECHARPES ETC MAT TEXT
851	*FOOTWEAR			0.6			0.7			1.0	N	368633	0.8	CHAUSSURES
85101	FOOTWEAR RUBBER,PLASTIC	P	183726	0.4	P	187840	0.4			0.1				CHAUS SEMELLES CAOUTCH
85102	FOOTWEAR LEATHER			0.2			0.4	P	524374	1.0	N	368633	0.8	CHAUS SEMELLES EN CUIR
87	PRECISION INSTRUMNTS NES			0.8			0.8			0.5			0.8	INSTRUM,APPAR SCIENT NDA
874	MEASURNG,CONTROLNG INSTR			0.6			0.3			0.4	W	159	0.6	INSTRUMENTS DE MESURE
8741	SURVEYING INSTRUMENTS			0.6			0.1	W	10	0.1	W	3	0.1	INST GEODESIE,TOPO ETC
87412	SURVEY INSTR ETC NONELEC			0.5			0.1	W	10	0.1	W	3	0.1	INSTR GEODESIE,TOPO ETC
8742	MEASUR,DRAW ETC INST,PTS			0.1			0.1			0.2	W	135	0.5	INST DESSIN,TRACAGE,PCS
87421	MEASURNG,DRAWNG ETC INST			0.1			0.1	W	54	0.2	W	135	0.5	INSTRUM DESSIN,TRACAGE
89	MISC MANUFCTRD GOODS NES			1.0			1.4			3.0			3.7	ART MANUFACTURES DIVERS
892	PRINTED MATTER			0.4			0.7			1.2	W	2203	1.4	IMPRIMES
8921	PRINTED BOOKS,GLOBES,ETC			0.3			0.4	W	329	0.5	W	272	0.5	LIVRES,BROCHURES,CARTES
89211	PRINTED BOOKS,PAMPHLETS			0.3			0.4	W	329	0.5	W	220	0.5	LIVRES,BROCHURES
8928	PRINTED MATTER NES			0.2			0.3			0.7	W	1916	1.0	IMPRIMES NDA
89283	UNISSUED BANKNOTES ETC									0.4				TIMBRES–POSTE FISCAUX
89289	OTHER PRINTED MATTER									0.1	W	87	0.8	GRAVURES,PHOTO AUT IMPR
893	ARTICLES OF PLASTIC NES			0.2			0.3	W	2307	1.4	W	4534	1.9	OUVRAGES EN MAT DIVIS 58
8931	PLSTC PACKG CONTNRS,LIDS	N	70921	0.1	N	27502	0.1	W	1144	0.5	W	3634	0.7	ART TRANSP EMBALLAGE ETC
8935	PLASTC ELEC LIGHT ARTICL	N	2678	0.1	N	1682	0.1	W	49	0.1	W	127	0.4	ART ECLAIRAG ELEC MAT 58
8939	MISC PLASTIC ARTICLES			0.2			0.2	W	1023	0.8	W	743	0.9	ART DIVERS EN MAT DIV 58
89399	OTHR PLASTC ARTICLES NES			0.1				W	1013	0.8	W	736	0.9	AUT OUV MAT DIV 58
9	GOODS NOT CLASSD BY KIND			0.6			6.7			0.9			0.9	ART TRANSACT NON CLASSES
931	*SPECIAL TRANSACTIONS			0.6			6.6			0.9	W	65	0.9	TRANS.SPECIALES

5. General Exports F.O.B. by Commodities according to the S.I.T.C. (Rev. 2) in million U.S. Dollars
Exportations Générales F.O.B. par Produits d'après la C.T.C.I. (Rév. 2) en millions de Dollars E.U.

SITC CTCI	COMMODITY	1991 QUANTITY QUANTITE	1991 VALUE VALEUR	1992 QUANTITY QUANTITE	1992 VALUE VALEUR	1993 QUANTITY QUANTITE	1993 VALUE VALEUR	1994 QUANTITY QUANTITE	1994 VALUE VALEUR	PRODUIT
	ALL COMMODITIES		65.1		67.1		65.9		66.4	TOUS PRODUITS
0	FOOD AND LIVE ANIMALS		12.3		16.6		13.0		10.5	ALIMENTS,ANIMAUX VIVANTS
04	CEREALS AND PREPARATIONS		1.5		1.8		1.3		0.5	CEREALES ET PRODUITS
046	WHEAT ETC MEAL OR FLOUR	W 8947	1.5	W 7909	1.3	W 7257	1.0	W 2080	0.4	SEMOULE FARINE,FROMENT
04601	FLOUR OF WHEAT OR MESLIN	W 8818	1.5	W 7753	1.3	W 7257	1.0	W 2080	0.4	FARINE DE FROMENT
048	CEREAL ETC PREPARATIONS				0.4	W 487	0.2	W 59	0.1	PREPTNS A BASE CEREALES
0484	BAKERY PRODUCTS				0.4	W 487	0.2	W 59	0.1	PRODUITS DE BOULANGERIE
04842	PASTRY, CAKES ETC				0.4	W 475	0.2	W 59	0.1	PATISSERIE ETC.
05	VEGETABLES AND FRUIT		7.2		12.0		10.3		7.6	LEGUMES ET FRUITS
054	VEG ETC FRSH,SMPLY PRSVD	W 6244	0.9	W 8984	1.0	W 11292	1.4	W 8447	0.9	LEGUMES FRAIS,CONG,SECS
0541	POTATOES FRSH EXCL SWEET	W 5808	0.8	W 8271	0.9	W 10829	1.3	W 7743	0.8	POMMES DE TERRE
057	FRUIT,NUTS,FRESH,DRIED		4.0		9.3	W 23571	6.5	W 11832	4.0	FRUITS FRAIS OU SECS
0571	ORANGES, MANDARINS ETC		2.3		7.6	W 1564	0.3	W 1791	0.3	ORANGES,MAND,CLEMENTINES
05711	ORANGES,FRESH OR DRIED		2.3		7.6	W 1564	0.3	W 1791	0.3	ORANGES FRAICHES,SECHEES
0574	APPLES FRESH	W 3203	1.7	W 4012	1.7	W 2473	1.1	W 3538	1.8	POMMES FRAICHES
0579	FRUIT FRESH OR DRIED NES	W 5	0.1	W 25	0.1	W 19367	5.0	W 6247	1.9	FRUITS FRAIS,SECS NDA
05797	OTH TROP FRUIT,FRESH,DRY					W 19310	5.0	W 6237	1.9	AVOCATS,MANGUES,GOYAVES
058	FRUIT PRESERVED,PREPARED		2.4		1.8	W 4603	2.4	W 5059	2.8	CONSERVES DE FRUITS
0583	FRUIT JAMS,JELLIES ETC		0.4		0.3	W 505	0.4	W 273	0.2	PATES DE FRUITS CONFITURES
0585	FRUIT OR VEGETABLE JUICE		2.0		1.4	W 4098	2.0	W 4786	2.6	JUS DE FRUITS
05851	ORANGE JUICE		0.2		0.1	W 558	0.2	W 2355	0.9	JUS D'ORANGE
05858	MIXTURES OF DIFF JUICES		1.9		1.4	W 3517	1.8	W 2391	1.7	MELANGES JUS FRUITS,LEGUMES
07	COFFEE,TEA,COCOA,SPICES		3.3		2.7		1.6		2.5	CAFE,THE,CACAO,EPICES
075	SPICES	W 2373	3.3	W 1739	2.7	W 1602	1.6	W 2385	2.5	EPICES
0752	SPICES,EX PEPPER,PIMENTO	W 2328	3.3	W 1697	2.7	W 1548	1.5	W 2268	2.4	AUTRES EPICES
07524	NUTMEG,MACE,CARDAMOMS	W 590	1.6	W 858	2.1	W 1099	1.4	W 1410	2.2	NOIX MUSCADES
07525	SEEDS OF ANISE,CUMIN,ETC	W 511	1.4	W 173	0.6					GRAINES ANIS,FENOUIL
07526	GINGER (EXCPT SWEETENED)	W 1227	0.4	W 666	0.1	W 448	0.1	W 858	0.3	GINGEMBRE
081	*FEEDING STUFF FOR ANIML	W 2320	0.2	W 1423	0.2			W 200	0.1	NOURRITURE POUR ANIMAUX
1	BEVERAGES AND TOBACCO		0.6		1.1		2.2		5.0	BOISSONS ET TABACS
11	BEVERAGES		0.6		1.1		2.2		5.0	BOISSONS
111	NON-ALCOHL BEVERAGES NES		0.5		0.4	W 668	0.5	W 558	0.6	BOISSONS NON ALCOOLIQUES
11102	FLAVORED WATERS NON-ALCO		0.5		0.4	W 668	0.5	W 558	0.6	LIMONADES,EAUX GAZEUSES
112	ALCOHOLIC BEVERAGES		0.2		0.8	W 2824	1.8	W 5270	4.4	BOISSONS ALCOOLIQUES
1124	DISTILLED ALCOHOLIC BEVS		0.2		0.7	W 2812	1.7	W 5269	4.4	ALCOOLS,EAUX-DE-VIE
11249	OTH ALCOHOLC BEVS,CMPNDS	W 21	0.2	W 113	0.7	W 2778	1.7	W 5131	4.3	BOISSONS ALCOOLIQUES NDA
2	CRUDE MATERLS,EXCL FUELS		6.7		7.6		6.0		7.4	MAT BRUTES NON COMESTIBLES
24	CORK AND WOOD		4.4		5.2		4.6		4.9	LIEGE ET BOIS
245	FUEL WOOD NES, CHARCOAL		0.2		0.3	W 8690	1.2	W 7450	0.4	BOIS DE CHAUFFAGE
24501	FUEL WOOD IN LOGS,ETC		0.1		0.3	W 7760	1.2	W 7450	0.4	RONDINS,BUCHES ETC.
247	OTH WOOD ROUGH,SQUARED		4.0		4.9	MW 11331	2.8	W 8172958	2.4	BOIS BRUTS EQUARRIS
2471	SAW-,VENEER-LOGS CONIFER		2.7		1.9	MW 11331	2.8	W 3886227	0.7	CONIFERES POUR SCIAGE,PLACAG
24711	— IN THE ROUGH		0.7		0.8	MW 11331	2.8	W 3886227	0.7	ECORCES OU DEGROSSIS
24712	— RGHLY OR HALF SQUARED	V 12951	2.1	V 9901	1.2					BOIS SIMPLEMENT EQUARRIS
2472	SAW-,VENEER-LOGS NON-CON	V 8835	1.3	V 26672	2.8			W 4286731	1.8	NON CONIFERES SCIAGE,PLAC
24721	— IN THE ROUGH	V 4070	0.7	V 17647	1.9			W 4286731	1.8	BRUTS ECORCES DEGROSSIS
24722	— RGHLY OR HALF SQUARED	V 4765	0.7	V 9024	1.0					BOIS SIMPLEMENT EQUARRIS
248	WOOD SHAPED,SLEEPERS		0.3		0.2	W 2759016	0.7	W 3617399	2.1	BOIS SIMPLEMENT TRAVAILLES
2482	LUMBER SHAPED CONIFER	V 592	0.1	V 752	0.1	W 481704	0.2	W 623232	0.4	CONIFERES SCIES,RABOTES
24821	LUMBER SAWN ETC CONIFER	V 43	0.1	V 448	0.1	W 480338	0.1	W 623170	0.4	CONIFERES SCIES LONGITUD
2483	LUMBER SHAPED NON-CONIFR		0.2		0.1	W 2277312	0.6	W 2994167	1.8	NON CONIFERES SCIES,RABOTES
24831	LUMBER SAWN ETC NON-CON				0.1	W 2276903	0.4	W 2994124	1.8	SCIES LONGITUDINALEMENT
27	CRUDE FERTLZR,MINRLS NES		2.2		2.2		1.2		2.4	ENGRAIS MINERAUX BRUTS
273	STONE,SAND AND GRAVEL		1.0		1.1		0.6	W 55951	1.1	PIERRES,SABLES,GRAVIERS
2732	CALCAREOUS STONE		0.9		0.8	W 17877	0.5	W 35617	0.9	GYPSE,PLATRES,CASTINES
27323	GYPSUM AND ANHYDRITE		0.7		0.6	W 17209	0.5	W 31345	0.7	GYPSE ANHYDRITE
278	OTHER CRUDE MINERALS	V 1788603	1.2		1.1	W 190502	0.6	W 342139	1.3	AUTRES MINERAUX BRUTS
2782	REFRACTORY MINERALS NES	V 1788603	1.2	V 1418315	1.1	W 190300	0.6	W 342139	1.3	ARGILE MINERAUX REFRACTAIRES
27823	DOLOMITE	V 1788603	1.2	V 1418315	1.1	W 190300	0.6	W 342139	1.3	DOLOMIE BRUTE
3	MINERAL FUELS ETC		18.3		14.8		18.5		17.1	COMBUSTIBLES MINERAUX LUB
32	COAL,COKE AND BRIQUETTES		0.8		1.1		0.8		0.5	HOUILLES,COKES,BRIQUETTES
322	COAL,LIGNITE AND PEAT	W 43008	0.8	W 58825	1.1	W 55361	0.8	W 39963	0.5	HOUILLES,LIGNITES,TOURBE
3222	OTH COAL,NOT AGGLOMERATD	W 43008	0.8	W 58825	1.1	W 55361	0.8	W 39963	0.5	AUTRES HOUILLES
351	*ELECTRIC CURRENT		17.5		13.8	H 1	17.8	H 1	16.6	ENERGIE ELECTRIQUE
5	CHEMCLS,RELATED PROD NES		13.4		14.5		12.2		13.6	PRODUITS CHIMIQUES
52	INORGANIC CHEMICALS		12.8		13.7		11.8		13.3	PROD CHIM INORGANIQUES
523	OTHR INORG CHEMICALS ETC	W 25638	12.8	W 26816	13.7	W 25390	11.8	W 26304	13.3	AUT PRODUITS CHIMIQUES INORG
5239	INORG CHEM PRODUCTS NES	W 25638	12.8	W 26816	13.7	W 25390	11.8	W 26304	13.3	PROD CHIM INORGANIQ NDA
52393	CALCIUM CARBIDE	W 25638	12.8	W 26816	13.7	W 25390	11.8	W 26304	13.3	CARBURES DE CALCIUM
59	CHEMICAL MATERIALS NES		0.5		0.7		0.4		0.3	MAT PROD CHIMIQUES NDA
598	MISCEL CHEM PRODUCTS NES		0.5		0.7	W 304	0.4	W 301	0.3	PROD DIV INDUST CHIM NDA
5981	CHEMCLS FROM WOOD,RESIN		0.2		0.4	W 304	0.4	W 301	0.3	PROD CHIM BASE BOIS RESIN
59814	ROSIN,RESIN ACIDS,ETC	W 118	0.2	W 247	0.3	W 210	0.3	W 230	0.2	COLOPHANES RESINIQUES
5989	CHEM PRODUCTS,PREPS NES	W 342	0.3		0.4					PROD PREP CHIMIQUES NDA
59892	ACTIVTED NAT MINRL PROD	W 342	0.3	W 430	0.4					CHARBONS ACTIVES
6	BASIC MANUFACTURES		13.9		12.4		13.7		12.5	ART MANUFACTURES
63	WOOD,CORK MANUFACTRS NES		7.3		7.0		6.4		3.9	OUVRAGES LIEGE ET BOIS
634	VENEERS,PLYWOOD,ETC		7.3		7.0		6.4		3.9	PLACAGES,CONTRE-PLAQUES
6342	PLYWOOD OF WOOD SHEETS	A 544	3.2	A 1043	5.5	A 1107	0.5	A 636	0.7	BOIS CONTRE-PLAQUES
6343	IMPROVED,RECONSTIT WOOD					W 8003	5.6	W 2875	2.6	BOIS AMELIORES,RECONST
63432	RECONSTITUTED WOOD					W 7898	5.5	W 2875	2.6	BOIS RECONSTITUES
6344	WOOD-BASED PANELS NES		3.9		1.5					PANNEAUX SUPPORT BOIS NDA
63441	BLOCKBOARD,LAMINBRD, ETC		3.9		1.5					BOIS CONTRE-PLAQUES
6349	WOOD SIMPLY SHAPED NES		0.2		0.1	W 2770	0.4	W 4731	0.6	BOIS SIMPL TRAVAILLES NDA
63491	HOOPWOOD,SPLIT POLES ETC	N 167475	0.1	N 67625	0.1	W 2770	0.4	W 4731	0.6	BOIS ETC
66	NONMETAL MINERAL MFS NES		6.6		5.4		7.3		8.7	ART MIN NON METALLIQUES
661	LIME,CEMENT,BLDG PRODS		6.6		5.4	W 108047	7.3	W 133837	8.7	CHAUX,CIMENTS MAT CONSTR
6612	CEMENT		6.4		5.3	W 106671	7.2	W 133837	8.7	CIMENTS HYDRAULIQUES
8	MISC MANUFACTURED GOODS		0.2		0.4		0.5		0.7	ART MANUFACTURES DIVERS
89	MISC MANUFCTRD GOODS NES		0.2		0.4		0.5		0.7	ART MANUFACTURES DIVERS
892	PRINTED MATTER		0.2		0.4		0.3		0.3	IMPRIMES
8928	PRINTED MATTER NES		0.2		0.4		0.3		0.3	IMPRIMES NDA
89283	UNISSUED BANKNOTES ETC						0.3		0.3	TIMBRES-POSTE FISCAUX
89289	OTHER PRINTED MATTER		0.2		0.4					GRAVURES,PHOTO AUT IMPR
893	ARTICLES OF PLASTIC NES					W 224	0.3	W 230	0.4	OUVRAGES EN MAT DIVIS 58
8939	MISC PLASTIC ARTICLES					W 222	0.3	W 222	0.4	ART DIVERS EN MAT DIV 58
89399	OTHR PLASTC ARTICLES NES					W 222	0.3	W 222	0.4	AUT OUV MAT DIV 58

1. HISTORICAL SERIES, 1962–1997 SPECIAL TRADE, IMPORTS C.I.F., EXPORTS F.O.B.
SERIES HISTORIQUES, 1962–1997 COMMERCE SPECIAL, IMPORTATIONS C.A.F., EXPORTATIONS F.O.B

YEAR ANNEE	VALUE IN MILLION U.S. DOLLARS VALEUR EN MILLION U.S. DOLLARS MERCHANDISE –MARCHANDISE IMPORTS	EXPORTS	GOLD –OR IMPORTS	EXPORTS	CONVERSION FACTORS FACTEURS DE CONVERSION CENTS E.U. PAR IMPORTS	EXPORTS	INDEX NUMBERS –INDICES QUANTUM IMPORTS	EXPORTS	UNIT VALUE VALEUR UNITAIRE IMPORTS	EXPORTS
1962	96.90	74.90		1.22						
1963	103.30	81.00		5.36						
1964	102.70	112.10		1.75						
1965	133.80	128.90		2.94						
1966	138.70	127.40		0.55						
1967	151.70	149.90		0.04						
1968	152.80	152.10		0.03						
1969	165.00	172.30		1.50						
1970	159.20	190.20		0.17						
1971	169.60	181.10		0.02						
1972	185.40	202.20								
1973	229.40	260.50								
1974	390.00	556.40								
1975	557.90	444.70								
1976	587.60	566.10								
1977	665.90	634.30								
1978	768.70	635.10								
1979	894.70	857.20								
1980	665.40	1037.20						113		176
1981	917.10	984.00						122		171
1982	554.10	898.50						112		162
1983	578.70	818.10						97		166
1984	488.50	781.50						100		164
1985	692.90	672.80						84		156
1986	674.00	637.80						94		131
1987	766.30	569.50						81		104
1988	590.50	600.20						82		99
1989	610.90	821.80						94		110
1990	687.20	926.10						100		64
1991	969.50	848.60						102		96
1992	1090.30	710.10						99		76
1993	1205.90	727.50						93		64
1994	1209.00	1032.40						95		66
1995	1423.80	1100.70						91		73
1996	1635.00	1137.10						92		71
1997	1810.40	1128.10						100		48

2. IMPORTS BY BROAD ECONOMIC CATEGORY AND EXPORTS BY INDUSTRIAL ORIGIN. (PERCENTAGE OF TOTAL VALUE)
IMPORTATIONS PAR CATEGORIES ECONOMIQUES ET EXPORTATIONS PAR BRANCHE D'ACTIVITE.(EN POURCENTAGE DE LA VALEUR TOTALE)

IMPORTS – IMPORTATIONS

	1991	1992	1993	1994	1995	1996	1997
TOTAL IMPORTS–IMPORTATIONS TOTALES	100.	100.	100.	100.	100.	100.	100.
1 FOOD BEV–ALIMENTATION BOISSONS	10.3	10.7	8.9	9.6	9.0	9.9	8.3
11 PRIMARY–PRODUITS DE BASE	4.0	4.0	3.6	4.3	3.8	4.4	3.3
111 FOR INDUSTRY–POUR L'INDUSTRIE	3.5	3.5	3.1	3.8	3.4	4.0	2.8
112 FOR HOUSEHOLDS–POUR LES MENAGES	0.5	0.5	0.5	0.5	0.4	0.4	0.5
12 PROCESSED–PRODUITS ELABORES	6.4	6.7	5.4	5.3	5.2	5.5	5.0
121 FOR INDUSTRY–POUR L'INDUSTRIE	2.9	3.5	1.9	1.3	1.2	1.2	0.8
122 FOR HOUSEHOLDS–POUR LES MENAGES	3.5	3.2	3.4	4.0	4.0	4.4	4.2
2 IND SUPPLIES–APPROV INDUSTRIELS	30.5	27.5	27.8	29.7	29.8	27.1	25.8
21 PRIMARY–PRODUITS DE BASE	1.4	1.4	2.5	2.9	2.8	2.4	1.5
22 PROCESSED–PRODUITS ELABORES	29.1	26.1	25.4	26.8	27.0	24.7	24.3
3 FUELS–COMBUSTIBLES	0.7	2.9	4.6	4.9	4.2	2.5	7.3
31 PRIMARY–PRODUITS DE BASE	0.0	0.0	0.0	0.0	0.0	0.0	0.0
32 PROCESSED–PRODUITS ELABORES	0.7	2.9	4.6	4.9	4.2	2.5	7.3
321 MOTOR SPIRIT–ESSENCE	0.0	0.1	0.0	0.0	0.0	0.0	0.0
322 OTHER–AUTRES	0.7	2.8	4.6	4.9	4.2	2.5	7.3
4 MACHINERY–EQUIPEMENT	29.6	28.5	24.7	20.7	23.5	24.4	26.5
41 CAPITAL EQUIPMENT–MACHINES	27.3	26.3	22.7	18.8	21.7	22.8	24.6
42 PARTS–PIECES ACCESSOIRES	2.3	2.1	2.1	1.9	1.8	1.7	1.9
5 TRANSPORT–TRANSPORT	19.3	21.2	24.8	24.3	24.0	25.7	23.3
51 PASSENGER CARS–AUTOMOBILES	7.7	7.5	6.9	9.3	7.2	6.7	8.0
52 OTHER–AUTRES	8.2	10.1	14.0	11.2	13.3	16.4	13.4
521 INDUSTRIAL–INDUSTRIELS	7.9	9.8	13.6	10.7	12.9	16.0	13.1
522 NON INDUSTRIAL–NON INDUSTRIEL	0.3	0.4	0.4	0.5	0.4	0.4	0.3
53 PARTS–PIECES ACCESSOIRES	3.3	3.6	3.8	3.8	3.5	2.6	1.9
6 CONSUM GOODS–BIENS CONSOMMATION	9.4	8.9	8.9	10.4	9.4	10.3	8.7
61 DURABLE–DURABLES	1.9	1.7	1.5	1.8	1.8	2.2	1.8
62 SEMI DURABLE–SEMI DURABLES	3.7	4.1	3.8	4.2	3.8	3.3	2.9
63 NON DURABLE–NON DURABLES	3.8	3.1	3.6	4.3	3.9	4.7	4.0
7 GOODS NES–BIENS NDA	0.2	0.3	0.2	0.4	0.2	0.0	0.0

EXPORTS – EXPORTATIONS

	1991	1992	1993	1994	1995	1996	1997
TOTAL EXPORTS–EXPORTATIONS TOTALES	100.	100.	100.	100.	100.	100.	100.
1 AGRICULTURE	9.8	6.1	7.1	10.6	13.9	15.7	16.2
2 MINING QUARRY–INDUS EXTRACTIVES	53.7	52.5	39.4	28.2	36.6	34.1	32.5
3 MANUFACTURING–IND MANUFACTUR	36.5	41.4	53.5	61.2	49.6	50.2	51.3
31 FOOD BEV TOBACCO–ALIM BOISS TAB	9.5	9.4	11.3	14.0	11.0	16.1	19.7
32 TEXTILES–INDUSTRIES TEXTILES	2.8	3.3	4.2	3.2	2.9	4.0	4.0
33 WOOD & PRODUCTS–BOIS & PRODUITS	5.4	6.6	7.2	8.6	7.2	7.5	7.4
34 PAPER & PRODUCTS–PAPIER & PRODT	0.0	0.2	0.4	0.3	0.3	0.5	0.6
35 CHEMICALS–INDUSTRIES CHIMIQUES	0.6	0.6	1.7	1.5	2.4	2.4	2.1
36 NON METAL MIN–MIN NON METAL	0.0	0.1	0.1	0.1	0.2	0.3	0.2
37 BASIC METAL–IND METAL BASE	12.6	13.2	15.7	13.3	12.2	10.5	8.8
38 METAL MANUF–MANUF METAL	0.1	3.7	2.9	3.4	4.2	7.6	1.9
39 OTH MANUF IND–AUTRES MANUF	5.6	4.3	10.1	16.6	9.0	1.3	6.6

3. TRADE BY PRINCIPAL COUNTRIES OF ORIGIN AND DESTINATION (VALUE IN MILLION U.S. DOLLARS)
ECHANGES SELON LES PRINCIPAUX PAYS D'ORIGINE ET DE DESTINATION (VALEUR EN MILLIONS DE DOLLARS EU)

COUNTRIES–PAYS	SPECIAL IMPORTS C.I.F. IMPORTATIONS SPECIALES C.A.F				
	1993	1994	1995	1996	1997
World	1176.9	1196.3	1396.3	1643.1	1909.2
Africa	2.0	1.3	2.4	1.5	2.7
Americas	733.6	774.0	877.1	1108.6	1316.2
– Northern America	271.9	245.7	335.1	498.5	479.6
– LAIA	448.8	514.9	532.9	601.4	823.4
– CACM	0.6	2.0	1.7	0.7	1.7
– Caribbean	0.4	0.4	1.0	3.0	3.0
– Rest of America	11.9	10.9	6.4	5.0	8.5
Asia excl fmr USSR	157.7	228.8	221.1	256.8	289.3
– Middle East	0.6	0.2	0.3	0.5	0.4
Asia former USSR	0.0	0.0	0.0	0.0	0.0
Europe excl fmr USSR	277.6	185.1	286.8	269.9	293.0
– European Union	256.0	173.2	273.5	254.0	280.6
– Eastern Europe	10.9	1.7	2.4	4.0	1.9
– Rest of Europe	10.7	10.3	10.9	11.9	10.6
Europe former USSR	4.1	3.3	4.0	1.5	0.7
Oceania	1.9	3.5	4.5	4.7	6.0
Other	0.0	0.4	0.4	0.1	1.3
USA/Etats–Unis d'Amer	265.2	235.1	312.6	455.7	443.5
Japan/Japon	128.9	181.8	171.7	199.1	236.2
Brazil/Brésil	149.9	178.6	174.2	181.6	227.6
Argentina/Argentine	114.7	117.5	117.4	136.6	259.4
Chile/Chili	88.5	94.0	104.8	110.6	122.5
Peru/Pérou	54.1	65.1	73.0	89.1	97.5
Germany/Allemagne	66.5	59.3	69.9	60.9	58.7
Sweden/Suède	26.6	32.4	38.8	48.2	89.4
Italy/Italie	23.9	17.2	36.9	55.6	43.2
United Kingdom	67.2	13.1	26.3	12.4	23.3
Colombia/Colombie	15.8	22.7	22.9	33.8	40.0
Spain/Espagne	36.6	16.9	19.3	35.0	25.2
Canada	6.7	10.6	22.4	42.7	36.1
Mexico/Mexique	12.8	16.7	19.5	25.5	37.2
Belgium–Luxembourg	4.6	6.7	54.7	9.6	7.7
Korea, Republic of	9.0	14.5	18.1	20.4	20.4
France, Monaco	15.9	9.7	13.5	11.4	16.0
Venezuela	6.0	12.6	10.9	13.2	23.2
Other Asia n.e.s.	7.7	15.7	9.8	9.1	9.9
China/Chine	4.0	10.0	14.5	12.4	9.3
Switzerland,Liechtenst.	8.8	9.7	9.4	9.4	9.3
Panama	11.9	10.9	6.4	5.0	8.5
Netherlands/Pays–Bas	5.0	4.7	6.1	8.8	5.5
Denmark/Danemark	4.2	8.2	1.9	4.4	3.2
Uruguay	2.7	3.8	4.7	4.9	5.2
Ecuador/Equateur	1.6	2.5	4.1	4.9	7.6
New Zealand	1.5	2.6	2.7	4.1	4.5
Czech Republic	10.0	1.2	1.5	1.3	1.0
Ireland/Irlande	2.2	2.2	2.4	3.3	3.7
Russian Federation	4.0	3.3	4.0	1.4	0.6
Israel/Israël	1.5	1.4	1.4	3.8	5.0
Austria/Autriche	2.5	1.9	1.4	2.6	3.1
Paraguay	2.7	1.5	1.3	1.1	3.2
India/Inde	0.9	1.9	1.6	2.3	1.8
So. African Customs Un	0.7	1.0	2.0	1.3	2.3
China, Hong Kong SAR	1.5	1.0	1.1	1.8	1.7
Finland/Finlande	0.7	1.0	1.9	1.6	1.3
Australia/Australie	0.3	0.9	1.7	0.6	1.5
Cuba	0.2	0.2	0.4	1.9	2.2
Malaysia/Malaisie	1.0	0.7	0.3	1.5	1.1

COUNTRIES–PAYS	SPECIAL EXPORTS F.O.B. EXPORTATIONS SPECIALES F.O.B.				
	1993	1994	1995	1996	1997
Monde	808.9	1124.2	1181.2	1086.9	1272.1
Afrique	0.1	0.7	0.2	0.2	0.5
Amériques	523.2	802.2	776.7	769.0	819.4
– Amérique du Nord	220.9	364.2	341.5	246.2	271.0
– ALAI	301.8	436.5	422.1	510.1	546.5
– MCAC	0.1	0.2	0.1	0.2	0.4
– Caraïbes	0.3	0.7	8.2	1.8	1.4
– Autre Amérique	0.2	0.6	4.8	10.8	0.1
Asie anc. URSS exclus	9.2	11.7	10.9	7.9	7.8
– Moyen–Orient	0.9	1.5	3.0	0.8	0.2
Asie ancienne URSS					
Europe anc. URSS exclus	274.9	305.8	388.2	300.2	430.2
– Union Européenne	271.8	291.3	306.3	247.4	313.2
– Europe de l'Est	0.2	0.0	0.9	0.7	1.5
– Autre de l'Europe	2.9	14.5	81.1	52.1	115.5
Europe ancienne URSS	0.1	0.1	0.1	0.5	0.3
Océanie	0.1	0.4	0.6	1.0	2.3
Autre	1.3	3.3	4.5	8.1	11.7
USA/Etats–Unis d'Amer	214.8	360.9	331.7	237.4	264.1
United Kingdom	154.2	150.6	153.3	155.6	154.7
Argentina/Argentine	126.8	160.1	142.7	143.4	183.0
Peru/Pérou	79.2	122.9	144.4	138.7	158.5
Colombia/Colombie	36.9	63.9	64.4	116.0	87.6
Switzerland,Liechtenst.	2.8	14.5	81.0	52.0	115.5
Belgium–Luxembourg	48.8	26.6	40.4	49.3	70.4
Germany/Allemagne	32.0	54.0	57.1	24.4	56.9
Chile/Chili	14.9	19.2	25.8	43.5	59.3
Brazil/Brésil	22.2	35.4	23.4	36.3	37.4
France, Monaco	20.6	47.4	41.2	2.1	2.4
Mexico/Mexique	7.7	13.1	1.4	11.8	11.2
Ecuador/Equateur	6.9	14.6	7.3	7.8	3.7
Netherlands/Pays–Bas	8.0	7.4	4.1	6.2	9.0
Areas n.e.s.	1.3	3.3	4.5	8.1	11.7
Italy/Italie	1.1	3.1	6.8	6.2	9.7
Canada	2.1	3.3	5.7	8.8	6.9
Spain/Espagne	6.6	1.5	2.5	2.8	9.3
Uruguay	1.5	4.8	2.0	8.5	2.8
Panama	0.2	0.6	4.8	10.8	0.1
Japan/Japon	2.3	2.1	3.7	3.8	4.1
Paraguay	3.8	1.0	5.0	2.7	1.6
Venezuela	1.9	1.5	5.7	1.3	1.5
Malaysia/Malaisie	2.7	1.1	2.5	2.2	1.7
Korea, Republic of	2.1	4.8	0.7	0.5	0.5
Bermuda/Bermudes	4.0		4.1		
Bahamas			7.7		
Australia/Australie	0.1	0.4	0.6	0.7	1.8
Dominican Republic	0.0	0.4	0.3	1.6	1.3
Saudi Arabia	0.5	0.8	1.4	0.5	0.1
Syrian Arab Republic	0.2	0.3	1.0	0.0	
Poland/Pologne	0.0		0.4	0.1	0.8
Czech Republic	0.0	0.0	0.4	0.1	0.7
China, Hong Kong SAR	0.2	0.5	0.1	0.0	0.3
Other Asia n.e.s.	0.1	0.2	0.3	0.2	0.3
Korea Dem People's Rp	0.3	0.6	0.0	0.0	0.1
Russian Federation	0.1	0.0	0.1	0.5	0.3
Portugal	0.2	0.1	0.3	0.2	0.2
Denmark/Danemark	0.2	0.3	0.1	0.1	0.2
Turkey/Turquie		0.4	0.4	0.0	0.0

(VALUE AS PERCENTAGE OF WORLD TOTAL)(VALEURS EN POURCENTAGE DU TOTAL MONDIAL)

	1988	1989	1990	1991	1992	1993	1994	1995	1996	1997
Africa	0.1	0.2	0.1	0.4	0.1	0.2	0.1	0.2	0.1	0.1
Americas	68.8	69.6	70.2	64.7	62.1	62.3	64.7	62.8	67.5	68.9
– Northern America	22.2	25.3	23.1	26.6	25.3	23.1	20.5	24.0	30.3	25.1
– LAIA	45.3	43.2	46.0	37.0	35.7	38.1	43.0	38.2	36.6	43.1
– CACM	0.0	0.1	0.0	0.0	0.1	0.1	0.2	0.1	0.0	0.1
– Caribbean	0.0	0.0	0.1	0.0	0.0	0.0	0.0	0.1	0.2	0.2
– Rest of America	1.3	0.9	1.0	1.0	1.0	1.0	0.9	0.5	0.3	0.4
Asia excl fmr USSR	15.0	12.3	11.8	14.4	14.6	13.4	19.1	15.8	15.6	15.2
– Middle East	0.0	0.0	0.0	0.0	0.0	0.1	0.0	0.0	0.0	0.0
Asia former USSR						0.0	0.0	0.0	0.0	0.0
Europe excl fmr USSR	15.7	17.8	17.3	19.7	22.7	23.6	15.5	20.5	16.4	15.3
– European Union	14.4	16.5	16.3	18.4	21.4	21.8	14.5	19.6	15.5	14.7
– Eastern Europe	0.5	0.5	0.3	0.4	0.6	0.9	0.1	0.2	0.2	0.1
– Rest of Europe	0.7	0.8	0.7	1.0	0.8	0.9	0.9	0.8	0.7	0.6
Europe former USSR	0.3	0.2	0.3	0.5	0.2	0.3	0.3	0.3	0.1	0.0
Oceania	0.0	0.0	0.0	0.1	0.1	0.2	0.3	0.3	0.3	0.3
Other	0.0	0.0	0.3	0.2	0.2	0.0	0.0	0.0	0.0	0.1
USA/Etats–Unis d'Amer	21.8	24.4	22.2	25.9	24.4	22.5	19.6	22.4	27.7	23.2
Japan/Japon	11.9	10.0	9.9	12.3	12.0	10.9	15.2	12.3	12.1	12.4
Brazil/Brésil	19.1	20.7	16.8	14.3	14.5	12.7	14.9	12.5	11.1	11.9
Argentina/Argentine	15.2	11.0	10.5	11.2	9.1	9.7	9.8	8.4	8.3	13.6
Chile/Chili	6.2	6.6	12.5	6.4	6.9	7.5	7.9	7.5	6.7	6.4
Peru/Pérou	2.3	2.7	3.2	2.1	2.4	4.6	5.4	5.2	5.4	5.1
Germany/Allemagne				8.4	7.6	5.6	5.0	5.0	3.7	3.1
Sweden/Suède	1.6	1.3	1.3	1.8	2.3	2.3	2.7	2.8	2.9	4.7
Italy/Italie	1.7	1.5	1.7	2.4	3.3	2.0	1.4	2.6	3.4	2.3
United Kingdom	1.5	1.3	1.3	0.9	2.4	5.7	1.1	1.9	0.8	1.2

	1988	1989	1990	1991	1992	1993	1994	1995	1996	1997
Afrique	0.0	0.0	0.0	0.0	0.0	0.0	0.1	0.0	0.0	0.0
Amériques	68.1	62.8	65.6	70.8	60.0	64.7	71.4	65.8	70.7	64.4
– Amérique du Nord	20.7	19.3	20.5	22.3	21.3	27.3	32.4	28.9	22.6	21.3
– ALAI	47.1	42.8	44.8	48.4	38.6	37.3	38.8	35.7	46.9	43.0
– MCAC	0.0	0.2	0.0	0.0	0.0	0.0	0.0	0.0	0.0	0.0
– Caraïbes	0.2	0.5	0.3	0.0	0.0	0.0	0.1	0.7	0.2	0.1
– Autre Amérique	0.1	0.1	0.0	0.0	0.0	0.0	0.1	0.4	1.0	0.0
Asie anc. URSS exclus	1.2	1.4	0.9	1.4	1.6	1.1	1.0	0.9	0.7	0.6
– Moyen–Orient	0.0	0.1	0.1	0.1	0.3	0.1	0.1	0.3	0.1	0.0
Asie ancienne URSS										
Europe anc. URSS exclus	30.7	35.8	33.4	27.8	38.0	34.0	27.2	32.9	27.6	33.8
– Union Européenne	27.7	30.9	29.0	26.5	37.3	33.6	25.9	25.9	22.8	24.6
– Europe de l'Est	1.6	2.6	2.2	0.0	0.0	0.0	0.0	0.1	0.1	0.1
– Autre de l'Europe	1.3	2.2	2.2	1.3	0.7	0.4	1.3	6.9	4.8	9.1
Europe ancienne URSS				0.0	0.0	0.0	0.0	0.0	0.0	0.0
Océanie	0.0	0.0	0.0	0.0	0.0	0.0	0.0	0.1	0.1	0.2
Autre				0.0	0.4	0.2	0.3	0.4	0.7	0.9
USA/Etats–Unis d'Amer	20.7	19.2	20.0	21.9	20.1	26.6	32.1	28.1	21.8	20.8
United Kingdom	12.1	13.5	12.3	11.6	16.7	19.1	13.4	13.0	14.3	12.2
Argentina/Argentine	38.1	27.9	25.6	29.2	20.1	15.7	14.2	12.1	13.2	14.4
Peru/Pérou	3.8	5.5	5.7	6.0	7.9	9.8	10.9	12.2	12.8	12.5
Colombia/Colombie	0.7	0.5	0.4	3.4	3.3	4.6	5.7	5.4	10.7	6.9
Switzerland,Liechtenst.	1.3	2.2	2.2	1.3	0.7	0.3	1.3	6.9	4.8	9.1
Belgium–Luxembourg	5.[illegible]	7.7	7.3	9.1	10.8	6.0	2.4	3.4	4.5	5.5
Germany/Allemagne				3.1	4.1	4.0	4.8	4.8	2.2	4.5
Chile/Chili	2.4	2.7	3.7	3.7	2.4	1.8	1.7	2.2	4.0	4.7
Brazil/Brésil	1.8	5.6	8.4	4.6	2.0	2.7	3.1	2.0	3.3	2.9

4. Special Imports C.I.F. by Commodities according to the S.I.T.C. (Rev. 2) in million U.S. Dollars
Importations Spéciales C.A.F. par Produits d'après la C.T.C.I. (Rév. 2) en millions de Dollars E.U.

SITC CTCI	COMMODITY	1994 QUANTITY QUANTITE	1994 VALUE VALEUR	1995 QUANTITY QUANTITE	1995 VALUE VALEUR	1996 QUANTITY QUANTITE	1996 VALUE VALEUR	1997 QUANTITY QUANTITE	1997 VALUE VALEUR	PRODUIT
	ALL COMMODITIES		1196.4		1396.3		1643.1		1909.2	TOUS PRODUITS
0	FOOD AND LIVE ANIMALS		112.4		124.6		156.7		142.2	ALIMENTS,ANIMAUX VIVANTS
02	DAIRY PRODCTS,BIRDS'EGGS		11.7		13.5		19.5		18.8	PRODUITS LAITIERS,OEUFS
022	MILK AND CREAM	W 6981	10.5	W 6993	11.8	W 10557	18.8	W 10689	17.6	LAIT ET CREME
0224	MILK,CREAM PRESERVED ETC	W 6202	10.1	W 6304	11.5	W 9391	18.1	W 9894	17.1	LAIT,CREME CONS,CONC
02243	MILK DRY,OVER 1.5% FAT	W 3077	6.3	W 4199	8.8	W 6360	14.4	W 5845	12.5	LAIT POUDRE SUP 1.5%
04	CEREALS AND PREPARATIONS		63.9		70.3		86.4		65.9	CEREALES ET PRODUITS
041	WHEAT ETC UNMILLED	W 202443	42.4	W 183358	43.0	W 200263	60.3	W 174188	38.4	FROMENT,EPEAUTRE
0411	DURUM WHEAT UNMILLED	W 162411	32.8	W 97585	26.2	W 91480	29.3	W 69592	16.9	FROMENT DUR NON MOULU
0412	OTHER WHEAT ETC UNMILLED	W 40032	9.7	W 85773	16.8	W 108784	31.1	W 104596	21.6	AUTRE FROMENT NON MOULU
046	WHEAT ETC MEAL OR FLOUR	W 25853	8.1	W 12988	7.8	W 26635	10.2	W 12909	6.1	SEMOULE FARINE,FROMENT
04601	FLOUR OF WHEAT OR MESLIN	W 25502	7.9	W 12345	7.4	W 26633	10.2	W 12884	6.0	FARINE DE FROMENT
048	CEREAL ETC PREPARATIONS	W 18369	11.0	W 21244	13.4	W 18997	13.8	W 27206	19.0	PREPTNS A BASE CEREALES
0482	MALT INCLUDING FLOUR	W 12619	4.7	W 10077	3.9	W 12430	5.8	W 15134	6.8	MALT MEME TORREFIE
0484	BAKERY PRODUCTS	W 3259	3.6	W 3851	4.7	W 3734	4.3	W 4647	5.4	PRODUITS DE BOULANGERIE
05	VEGETABLES AND FRUIT		5.5		7.1		7.5		8.5	LEGUMES ET FRUITS
06	SUGAR AND PREPS,HONEY		5.6		7.6		9.6		10.3	SUCRES ET PRODUITS
062	SUGAR CANDY NON–CHOCLATE	W 3508	5.0	W 4053	6.7	W 5282	8.7	W 6735	9.8	SUCRERIES
07	COFFEE,TEA,COCOA,SPICES		4.7		4.6		6.1		7.2	CAFE,THE,CACAO,EPICES
09	MISC EDIBLE PRODUCTS		13.1		16.2		19.1		22.3	PREP ALIMENTAIRES DIVERSES
098	EDIBLE PRODCTS,PREPS NES	W 5767	12.3	W 5249	15.2	W 6117	17.3	W 7278	19.9	PREP ALIMENTAIRES NDA
09809	MISC FOOD PREPRTIONS NES	W 2827	8.6	W 2326	11.0	W 3088	12.9	W 3411	15.0	PREP ALIMENTAIRES NDA
1	BEVERAGES AND TOBACCO		5.4		6.5		8.8		7.8	BOISSONS ET TABACS
12	TOBACCO AND MANUFACTURES		3.6		4.0		5.8		3.3	TABACS BRUTS FABRIQUES
121	TOBACCO UNMNFCTRD,REFUSE	W 1230	3.3	W 1506	3.5	W 1694	5.7	W 857	3.2	TABACS BRUTS,DECHETS
1212	TOBACCO STRIPPED OR PART	W 1223	3.2	W 1506	3.5	W 1668	5.7	W 756	3.1	TABACS PART ECOTES
2	CRUDE MATERLS,EXCL FUELS		43.5		51.2		52.0		52.4	MAT BRUTES NON COMESTIBLES
22	OIL SEEDS,OLEAGINOUS FRT		0.8		1.4		1.8		12.0	GRAINES,FRUITS OLEAGINEUX
222	SEEDS FOR'SOFT'FIXED OIL	W 488	0.6	W 574	1.0	W 812	1.3	W 37711	11.8	GRAINES HUILES FIXES
2222	SOYA BEANS	W 224	0.1	W 23	0.1	W 1	0.1	W 36999	10.4	FEVES DE SOJA
26	TEXTILE FIBRES AND WASTE		15.9		19.7		20.0		18.3	FIBRES TEXTILES
266	SYNTHETIC FIBRES TO SPIN	W 6709	10.6	W 7498	14.1	W 9107	14.9	W 8920	14.5	FIBRES SYNTHETIQUES
2666	CONTIN FILAMNT TOW SYNTH	W 3356	5.7	W 3153	6.6	W 3912	6.9	W 3601	6.8	CABLES POUR DISCONTINUS
26663	— OF ACRYLIC FIBRES	W 3275	5.6	W 3130	6.6	W 3912	6.9	W 3557	6.7	DE FIBRES ACRYLIQUES
27	CRUDE FERTLZR,MINRLS NES		5.3		4.7		3.7		2.5	ENGRAIS MINERAUX BRUTS
278	OTHER CRUDE MINERALS	W 16846	4.9	W 6919	3.8	W 12120	3.2	W 4442	2.0	AUTRES MINERAUX BRUTS
2789	MINERALS CRUDE NES	W 15465	4.1	W 5046	2.8	W 10192	2.1	W 1632	0.5	MINERAUX BRUTS NDA
27896	NATURAL ASPHALT,BITUMEN	W 15243	3.9	W 4478	2.4	W 9966	1.9	W 1196	0.3	BITUMES,ASPHALTES NATURELS
28	METALLIFEROUS ORES,SCRAP		19.0		22.0		23.7		15.2	MINERAIS METAL,DECHETS
287	BASE METAL ORES,CONC NES	W 11370	18.9	W 11076	22.0	W 11509	23.6	W 8663	15.1	MINERAIS METAUX COMMUNS
2876	TIN ORES,CONCENTRATES	W 11340	18.9	W 11011	21.9	W 11479	23.6	W 8550	15.0	MINERAIS D'ETAIN
3	MINERAL FUELS ETC		60.5		63.8		48.0		144.2	COMBUSTIBLES MINERAUX LUB
33	PETROLEUM AND PRODUCTS		60.0		63.8		48.0		144.2	PETROLE ET DERIVES
334	PETROLEUM PRODUCTS,REFIN	W 185534	57.0	W 202355	58.4	W 112723	39.8	W 472095	136.5	PRODUITS RAFFINES
3343	GAS OILS	W 103195	30.1	W 133069	36.1	W 103427	30.9	W 390911	109.4	GAS OILS
3344	FUEL OILS,NES	W 69345	16.3	W 59191	13.2			W 69929	17.4	FUEL OILS
3345	LUBS,PETROLEUM OILS NES	W 12747	10.6	W 9929	9.0	W 8882	8.7	W 10822	9.6	HUILES LUBRIFIANTES
33451	LUBS(HIGH PETR CONT) ETC	W 12254	9.7	W 9367	8.1	W 8171	7.6	W 10174	8.6	HUILES LUBRIF,H LOURDES
335	RESIDUAL PETRLM PROD NES	W 8170	3.0	W 18356	5.5	W 26488	8.2	W 25498	7.7	PRODUITS RESIDUELS NDA
3354	PETROLM BITUMEN,COKE ETC	W 6918	1.8	W 17160	4.2	W 24580	6.4	W 23459	5.8	BITUME,COKE DE PETROLE
33543	BITUMINOUS MIXTURES ETC	W 5864	1.4	W 17160	4.2	W 24575	6.4	W 23141	5.7	MELANGES BITUMINEUX
5	CHEMCLS,RELATED PROD NES		152.8		185.5		202.7		232.2	PRODUITS CHIMIQUES
51	ORGANIC CHEMICALS		10.2		12.7		13.5		16.1	PROD CHIMIQ ORGANIQUES
52	INORGANIC CHEMICALS		21.2		26.4		29.3		28.8	PROD CHIM INORGANIQUES
522	INORG ELEMNTS,OXIDES,ETC	W 5675	2.7	W 6887	3.6	W 8078	4.0	W 14201	5.8	ELEMENTS INORGANIQUES
523	OTHR INORG CHEMICALS ETC	W 29891	18.5	W 33939	22.8	W 35901	25.3	W 37286	23.0	AUT PRODUITS CHIMIQUES INORG
5232	OTH MTL CMPD OF INRG ACD	W 21398	13.8	W 23863	17.5	W 25404	19.4	W 26370	18.1	SELS METALLIQUES
52325	CYANIDES,COMPLEX CYANIDE	W 10516	10.3	W 10484	12.5	W 9062	12.9	W 7756	10.6	CYANURES SIMPLES,COMPLEXES
53	DYES,TANNING,COLOUR PROD		11.4		12.7		12.9		15.0	PROD TEINTURE,COLORANTS
533	PIGMENTS,PAINTS,ETC	W 4491	6.4	W 3499	7.1	W 5073	7.1	W 7216	8.8	PIGMENTS,PEINTURES,VERNIS
541	*MEDICINAL,PHARM PRODUCT	K 1723240	23.5	K 1958007	28.6	K 2251354	28.3	K 2827938	26.6	PROD MEDICINAUX PHARMACEUT
5417	MEDICAMENTS	K 1234185	17.3	K 1394768	20.1	K 1597505	20.9	K 2253440	20.1	MEDICAMENTS
54179	— CONTNG OTH SUBSTANCES	K 1016286	13.6	K 1078998	15.2	K 1338486	16.9	K 2010203	15.6	MED CONT AUT SUBSTANCES
55	PERFUME,CLEANING ETC PRD		28.6		23.7		31.3		35.9	PROD POUR PARFUM,TOILETTE
553	PERFUMERY,COSMETICS,ETC	W 5424	10.7	W 3876	9.3	W 4509	14.2	W 7383	18.7	PRODUITS DE PARFUMERIE
554	SOAP,CLEANSING ETC PREPS	W 17637	15.4	W 12855	11.6	W 14033	14.0	W 12548	14.4	SAVONS,PRODUITS DETERSIFS
5541	SOAPS	W 8604	3.7	W 6534	3.5	W 6433	4.3	W 5779	5.1	SAVONS,PROD TENSIO–ACTIFS
5542	WASHING PREPARATIONS ETC	W 8868	11.4	W 6020	7.4	W 7339	9.1	W 6521	8.9	PROD ORG TENSIO–ACT NDA
562	*FERTILIZERS,MANUFACTURE	W 5504	2.0	W 14032	9.6	W 18121	9.1	W 24847	8.4	ENGRAIS MANUFACTURES
5629	FERTILIZERS NES	W 1156	0.5	W 4723	3.9	W 12200	6.8	W 16193	5.0	ENGRAIS NDA
58	PLASTIC MATERIALS ETC		29.6		41.6		42.7		48.3	MAT PLAST ARTIFICIELLES
582	PROD OF CONDENSATION ETC	W 3014	3.1	W 3167	4.2	W 4646	5.4	W 6182	7.4	PROD CONDENS,POLYCOND
583	POLYMERIZATION ETC PRODS	W 27306	24.6	W 25692	33.7	W 32535	34.2	W 35671	39.6	PROD POLYMERISATION
5831	POLYETHYLENE	W 11842	8.2	W 9608	11.2	W 12717	12.6	W 13813	15.1	POLYETHYLENE
58311	— IN PRIMARY FORMS	W 11721	8.0	W 9456	10.8	W 12449	12.0	W 13358	14.1	POLYETHYLENE PRIMAIRES
5832	POLYPROPYLENE	W 2849	2.6	W 3035	4.4	W 3423	3.8	W 4204	5.1	POLYPROPYLENE
5834	POLYVINYL CHLORIDE	W 5534	5.7	W 6585	8.5	W 9467	9.4	W 10682	10.7	CHLORURE DE POLYVINYLE
58341	— IN PRIMARY FORMS	W 5209	5.4	W 6437	8.3	W 9285	9.0	W 10483	10.1	SOUS FORMES PRIMAIRES
5839	OTH POLYMRZTION ETC PROD	W 3265	4.1	W 3599	5.9	W 2642	3.7	W 2471	3.3	AUT PROD POLYMER COPOLYM
59	CHEMICAL MATERIALS NES		24.5		28.2		32.9		48.4	MAT PROD CHIMIQUES NDA
591	PESTICIDES,DISINFECTANTS	W 3553	10.5	W 3267	12.2	W 4122	18.2	W 7114	29.8	DESINF,INSECT,FONG,HERB
5911	INSECTICIDES,FOR RETAIL	W 978	3.2	W 1046	4.4	W 1162	5.5	W 1889	8.1	INSECTICIDES VENTE DET
5913	HERBICIDES,FOR RETAIL	W 1732	4.9	W 1666	5.7	W 2367	10.3	W 4169	17.4	HERBICIDES VENTE AU DET
598	MISCEL CHEM PRODUCTS NES	W 7975	11.1	W 9020	13.4	W 7494	11.5	W 11087	15.0	PROD DIV INDUST CHIM NDA
5982	ANTI–KNOCK PREPARTNS ETC	W 1618	3.9	W 1248	2.7	W 682	1.7	W 1791	3.2	PREPARAT ANTIDETONANTES
5989	CHEM PRODUCTS,PREPS NES	W 6116	6.8	W 7476	10.2	W 6681	9.5	W 9050	11.6	PROD PREP CHIMIQUES NDA
59899	OTH CHEM PRODS,PREPS,NES	W 4040	4.7	W 5246	7.8	W 4381	6.5	W 6476	8.7	AUT PRODUITS CHIMIQUES NDA
6	BASIC MANUFACTURES		203.3		216.9		230.0		251.0	ART MANUFACTURES
62	RUBBER MANUFACTURES NES		17.7		16.6		16.8		14.1	CAOUTCHOUC MANUFACTURE
625	RUBBER TYRES, TUBES ETC	W 7846	14.9	W 7637	12.7	W 7808	12.4	W 7458	10.3	PNEUS CAOUTCHOUC VULCANISE
6251	TYRES NEW FOR MOTOR CARS	W 3361	6.0	W 3998	5.9	W 3555	4.8	W 3218	4.7	PNEUS POUR VOITURES
6252	TYRES,NEW,BUS OR LORRY	W 2604	5.8	W 1440	3.5	W 1490	4.0	W 2131	2.6	PNEUS POUR AUTOBUS,CAMIONS
64	PAPER,PAPERBOARD AND MFR		26.4		38.7		35.9		45.2	PAPIERS,CARTONS & OUVRAGES
641	PAPER AND PAPERBOARD	W 32004	21.0	W 34227	30.5	W 33361	25.9	W 47094	32.1	PAPIERS ET CARTONS
6411	NEWSPRINT	W 10048	6.5	W 11267	9.5	W 8395	7.7	W 13675	9.6	PAPIER JOURNAL
6413	KRAFT PAPER,PAPERBOARD	W 7192	4.0	W 8179	6.2	W 8859	5.9	W 8453	4.9	PAPIER ET CARTON KRAFT
6415	PAPER,PAPERBRD,BULK,NES	W 9366	5.6	W 8653	7.7	W 9741	6.6	W 17331	9.7	PAPIERS,CARTONS ROULEAUX
64159	OTHER PAPER ETC,BULK,NES	W 8898	5.2	W 8411	7.4	W 8580	5.9	W 15018	8.5	AUT PAPIER ROULEAUX FEUILLES
642	PAPER,ETC,PRECUT,ARTS OF	W 3552	5.5	W 4517	8.3	W 5305	10.0	W 7373	13.1	PAP,CARTONS DECOUPES
6428	PAPER ETC ARTICLES NES	W 1598	2.4	W 1845	3.6	W 2135	4.5	W 3429	7.1	OUVRAGES EN PATE A PAPIER
64285	PAPER ETC DIAPERS ETC	W 764	1.4	W 1182	2.6	W 1403	3.3	W 2640	5.8	SERVIETTES HYGIENIQUES

4. Special Imports C.I.F. by Commodities according to the S.I.T.C. (Rev. 2) in million U.S. Dollars
Importations Spéciales C.A.F. par Produits d'après la C.T.C.I. (Rév. 2) en millions de Dollars E.U.

SITC CTCI	COMMODITY	1994		1995		1996		1997		PRODUIT
		QUANTITY QUANTITE	VALUE VALEUR	QUANTITY QUANTITE	VALUE VALEUR	QUANTITY QUANTITE	VALUE VALEUR	QUANTITY QUANTITE	VALUE VALEUR	
65	TEXTILE YARN,FABRICS,ETC		28.4		28.8		29.7		28.9	FILS,TISSUS,ARTICLES TEXTILE
651	TEXTILE YARN	W 2618	8.2	W 3033	10.0	W 3203	10.9	W 4399	12.2	FILS TEXTILES
6514	SYN FIB YRN,BULK,MONOFIL	W 1129	3.3	W 1678	4.9	W 1545	4.4	W 1512	4.5	FILS CONT 85% FIB TEXT SYNTH
652	COTTON FABRICS,WOVEN	W 1107	3.7	W 1220	4.8	W 1386	6.0	W 1215	4.3	TISSUS DE COTON
6522	WOVEN COTTON BLEACHD,ETC	W 1049	3.6	W 1112	4.6	W 1315	5.7	W 1189	4.3	TISSUS COTON BLANCHIS ETC
653	WOVN MAN–MADE FIB FABRIC	W 3368	6.8	W 3451	6.3	W 3285	4.7	W 4787	4.8	TISSUS FIBRES SYNTH,ARTIF
66	NONMETAL MINERAL MFS NES		19.5		20.5		26.6		26.7	ART MIN NON METALLIQUES
661	LIME,CEMENT,BLDG PRODS	W 51624	3.9	W 57435	4.5	W 77181	5.5	W 72642	5.8	CHAUX,CIMENTS MAT CONSTR
662	CLAY,REFRACTORY BLDG PRD	W 14131	4.9	W 10516	3.7	W 12318	5.4	W 17866	6.4	MAT CONST REFRACTAIRES
664	GLASS	W 11293	6.1	W 11029	6.3	W 12674	9.7	W 13901	8.9	VERRE
67	IRON AND STEEL		59.8		61.0		68.9		78.8	FER ET ACIER
672	IRON,STEEL PRIMARY FORMS	W 8532	2.6	W 14756	4.4	W 11323	3.8	W 12244	3.9	LINGOTS FER,ACIER
673	IRON,STEEL SHAPES ETC	W 38941	14.7	W 58397	21.6	W 46820	18.8	W 51708	22.7	BARRES,PROFIL FER,ACIER
6732	IRON,STEEL BARS ETC	W 29882	11.1	W 48595	17.3	W 34706	13.8	W 40184	17.5	BARRES FER,ACIER
67326	IRN,OTH STL BARS HOTROLD	W 25826	9.4	W 42333	14.9	W 28949	11.3	W 35975	16.1	BARRES PLEINES FER,ACIER
674	IRN,STL UNIV,PLATE,SHEET	W 22337	11.7	W 22247	14.1	W 33836	20.3	W 28895	16.9	LARGES PLATS,TOLES
6746	IRN,STL THIN PLATE,ROLLD	W 7081	3.6	W 4112	2.9	W 8241	5.1	W 5673	3.5	TOLES LAM MOINS 3MM
6749	OTH IRN,STL PLATES,SHEET	W 9405	5.6	W 9344	6.6	W 13263	10.1	W 12369	8.0	AUTRES TOLES FER,ACIER
67491	— OF IRON OR SIMPLE STL	W 8764	5.2	W 8791	6.3	W 13108	9.8	W 11852	7.7	AUT TOLES AUTRES ACIER FIN
678	IRON,STL TUBES,PIPES,ETC	W 29623	24.2	W 15756	15.2	W 16593	18.3	W 24835	26.7	TUBES,TUYAUX EN FONTE,FER
6782	IRON,STL SEAMLESS TUBES	W 23450	18.7	W 7819	6.9	W 7635	8.4	W 13568	16.7	TUBES,TUYAUX SANS SOUDURE
6783	IRON,STL TUBES,PIPES NES	W 5656	4.4	W 7422	7.3	W 7054	7.9	W 9475	7.0	AUT TUBES,TUYAUX FER,ACIER
679	IRN,STL CASTINGS UNWORKD	W 8602	5.8	W 6924	4.7	W 8120	6.3	W 9163	6.4	OUVRAGES EN FONTE,FER,ACIER
68	NON–FERROUS METALS		5.9		9.4		6.9		10.9	METAUX NON FERREUX
684	ALUMINIUM	W 1456	3.3	W 1583	5.9	W 1406	4.1	W 2920	7.6	ALUMINIUM
6842	ALUMINIUM,ALLOYS WORKED	W 1446	3.3	W 1553	5.7	W 1303	3.8	W 2460	6.6	ALUMINIUM,ALLIAGES OUVRE
69	METAL MANUFACTURES NES		43.0		39.4		42.4		43.5	ART MANUFACT EN METAL NDA
691	STRUCTURES AND PARTS NES	W 18140	9.4	W 4876	6.1	W 3333	4.5	W 4165	5.9	CONSTRUCT FER,ACIER,ALU
6911	STRUCTURES,PARTS IRN,STL	W 18000	9.0	W 4836	5.9	W 3290	4.3	W 4109	5.6	CONSTRUCT FER,ACIER,FONTE
692	METAL TANKS,BOXES,ETC	W 4703	8.4	W 3981	8.4	W 4442	8.4	W 3459	5.2	RECIPIENTS METALLIQUES
6924	MTL TRANSPORT BOXES ETC	W 2809	5.0	W 2550	5.6	W 2311	3.9	W 2554	3.5	FUTS,TAMBOURS,BIDONS
695	TOOLS	W 1366	6.2	W 1148	6.4	W 1210	7.1	W 2215	7.7	OUTILS A MAIN
697	BASE MTL HOUSEHOLD EQUIP	W 1602	3.2	W 1245	2.8	W 2398	5.7	W 1993	4.5	ART MENAGE MET COMMUNS
699	BASE METAL MFRS NES	W 3103	6.7	W 3732	7.0	W 4192	7.2	W 3873	7.9	ART MANUFACTURES MET NDA
7	MACHINES,TRANSPORT EQUIP		516.0		645.5		788.8		931.0	MACHINES MATERIEL TRANSPORT
71	POWER GENERATING EQUIPMT		18.8		50.3		47.3		22.6	MACHINES GENERATRICES
713	INTRNL COMBUS PSTN ENGIN	W 2288	9.0	W 2199	10.0	W 3566	9.1	W 2364	6.8	MOTEURS EXPL COMB INT, PIECE
7139	PISTON ENGINE PARTS NES	W 466	5.1	W 326	4.8	W 1594	3.7	W 264	3.4	PIECES POUR 713.2,3,8
714	ENGINES AND MOTORS NES	W 88	2.7	W 652	16.8	W 251	6.7	W 17	1.4	MOTEURS NON ELECTRIQUES
7148	GAS TURBINES NES	W 7	0.8	W 187	6.9	W 11	1.1	W 3	0.2	TURBINES A GAZ
71488	OTHER GAS TURBINES NES	W 7	0.8	W 185	6.5	W 9	1.1		0.1	AUTRES TURBINES A GAZ
7149	ENGINE & MOTOR PARTS NES	W 78	1.7	W 463	9.8	W 233	3.4	W 13	1.2	PIECES 714 ET 718.88
71499	PARTS NES,OF 71488,71888	W 78	1.7	W 456	8.7	W 232	3.4	W 13	1.2	PIECES 714.88 ET 718.88
716	ROTATING ELECTRIC PLANT	W 896	5.3	W 1636	21.4	W 1714	23.6	W 1080	7.5	APP ELECTR ROTATIFS,PIECES
7161	DC MOTORS AND GENERATORS	W 200	2.2	W 690	12.3	W 217	2.5	W 71	0.5	MOTEURS COURANT CONTINU
7162	AC MTRS,GENRTRS,GEN SETS	W 679	2.7	W 911	8.5	W 1430	20.7	W 935	6.4	MOTEURS ELECTRIQUES
71622	AC GENERATORS	W 50	0.3	W 74	1.6	W 382	5.1	W 188	2.6	GENER COURANT ALTERNATIF
71623	GEN SETS WITH PISTN ENGN	W 172	0.9	W 397	5.8	W 623	14.7	W 218	2.2	GROUPES MOTEUR EXPLOSION
718	OTH POWER GENERATG MACHY	W 43	1.3	W 49	1.6	W 264	6.6	W 292	5.0	AUTRES MOTEURS PARTIES
7188	WIND,WATER,ETC ENGINES	W 43	1.3	W 49	1.6	W 264	6.6	W 292	5.0	MOT MACHINES MOTRICES NDA
71882	OTH HYDRAULIC ENGNS,MTRS	W 12	0.5	W 34	1.2	W 246	6.4	W 257	4.5	MACH MOTRICES HYDRAULQUES
72	MACHS FOR SPCL INDUSTRYS		90.8		107.4		101.5		122.4	MAC SPECIALES POUR INDUST
721	AGRIC MACHY,EXC TRACTORS	W 3312	6.9	W 2746	5.7	W 3351	6.6	W 3482	9.4	MACHINES AGRICOLES
722	TRACTORS NON–ROAD	W 2698	11.2	W 2551	10.2	W 2774	12.0	W 1956	6.9	TRACTEURS
7223	TRACK–LAYING TRACTORS	W 1163	5.0	W 622	2.3	W 921	4.5	W 310	0.3	TRACTEURS A CHENILLES
7224	WHEELED TRACTORS NES	W 1535	6.2	W 1929	7.9	W 1853	7.5	W 1645	6.6	TRACTEURS A ROUES
723	CIVIL ENGNEERG EQUIP ETC	W 6216	28.6	W 8233	43.9	W 7117	35.3	W 9921	56.1	APPAREILS DE GENIE CIVIL
7234	CONST,MINING MACHNRY NES	W 5611	23.4	W 6617	34.6	W 4962	24.5	W 7285	30.0	MACH POUR LA CONST, MINES
72341	SELF–PROPELLD DOZERS,ETC	W 2682	10.9	W 2110	9.9	W 1531	7.3	W 1630	6.8	BULLDOZERS
72342	SLFPRP SHOVELS,EXCAVATRS	W 1355	5.7	W 2556	11.8	W 1861	9.6	W 2095	8.5	PELLES MECANIQUES
72343	SLFPRP CONST ETC MCH NES	W 195	1.0	W 1229	8.5	W 271	1.9	W 709	4.6	AUT MACH EXTR,TERRASSEM
72344	BORING,SINKING MACHINERY	W 1040	3.5	W 233	1.7	W 1090	3.5	W 2503	9.1	MACHINES DE FORAGE
7239	CONSTR ETC MACHY PTS NES	W 374	4.1	W 1295	8.2	W 1899	9.5	W 2388	25.3	PIECES 723.41–723.46
724	TEXTILE,LEATHER MACHNRY	W 2613	13.7	W 1933	11.9	W 2505	12.3	W 2955	13.4	MACH POUR INDUSTRIE TEXTILE
7244	SPINNING,EXTRDNG,ETC MCH	W 1152	4.7	W 334	1.6	W 1051	4.2	W 1494	4.3	MACH POUR LE FILAGE
7245	WEAVING,FELT MFG,ETC MCH	W 491	4.0	W 484	4.7	W 697	3.6	W 615	3.3	METIERS A TISSER,PIECES
727	FOOD MACHRY NON–DOMESTIC	W 1594	6.4	W 590	3.8	W 2116	10.7	W 1396	11.6	MACH INDUSTRIES ALIMENT
7272	OTH FOOD PROC MCHY,PARTS	W 1458	5.8	W 550	3.4	W 2080	10.2	W 1367	11.3	AUT MACH IND ALIMENTAIRE
72722	INDUS FOOD PROC MACH NES	W 928	4.9	W 268	2.2	W 603	7.8	W 933	7.5	MACHINES BOULANGERIE
728	OTH MACHY FOR SPCL INDUS	W 4308	19.7	W 5170	28.3	W 4186	18.9	W 2892	19.1	AUT MACH IND PARTICULIERES
7283	OTHR MINERAL WORKG MACHY	W 2625	10.5	W 3077	17.5	W 2547	8.6	W 1488	6.0	MACH TRIER,CRIBLER,BROYER
72832	MINRL CRUSHING ETC MACHY	W 1166	4.0	W 1486	9.3	W 1032	1.9	W 705	2.0	MACH CONCASSER MAT MINER
7284	MACHY FOR SPCL INDUS NES	W 1256	8.1	W 853	7.7	W 1089	7.7	W 1054	11.4	MACH SPEC IND PARTICUL.
72842	RUBBER,PLASTICS WRKG MCH	W 473	3.9	W 421	5.1	W 647	5.1	W 714	6.9	MACH IND CAOUT MAT PLAST
73	METALWORKING MACHINERY		4.3		4.4		3.8		4.0	MACH TRAVAIL DES METAUX
74	GENRL INDUSTRL MACHY NES		62.6		64.9		68.0		92.5	MACH APP INDUSTRIE
741	HEATING,COOLING EQUIPMNT	W 2049	9.0	W 3218	10.6	W 2221	11.6	W 3503	25.0	MACH CHAUFFAGE,PIECES
7411	GAS GENERATORS,PARTS NES	W 45	0.4	W 240	2.2	W 323	2.4	W 872	11.2	GAZOGENES
7416	HEATING,COOLING EQU NES	W 1062	4.1	W 568	3.3	W 671	2.9	W 759	5.2	APP CHANGEMENT TEMP
742	PUMPS FOR LIQUIDS ETC	W 930	8.2	W 991	7.2	W 1640	7.5	W 993	11.7	POMPES MOTO–POMPES
743	PUMPS NES,CENTRFUGES ETC	W 1555	9.6	W 1618	11.1	W 3613	12.7	W 1624	13.2	POMPES COMPRES,VENT ETC
7431	PUMPS FOR GASES ETC	W 638	4.6	W 496	4.5	W 624	6.3	W 775	7.1	POMPES AIR A VIDE,COMPRES
7436	GAS,LIQUID FILTERS ETC	W 622	2.5	W 859	4.4	W 1593	3.5	W 537	2.9	APP POUR FILT DES LIQUIDES
744	MECHANICAL HANDLING EQU	W 2687	11.2	W 2491	11.4	W 2161	10.7	W 2233	12.3	EQUIP MANUTENTION PIECES
7442	LIFTING,LOADING MACH NES	W 1906	7.4	W 1840	6.7	W 1434	6.1	W 1642	7.5	APP LEVAGE,MANUTENTION
745	NONELEC MACHY,TOOLS NES	W 1483	12.2	W 1724	10.9	W 1341	9.7	W 1496	15.5	AUT MACH NON ELEC,PIECES
7452	OTH NONELEC MCHS,PTS NES	W 1178	9.4	W 936	7.5	W 1213	6.6	W 1319	13.4	AUT MACH NON ELEC,PIECES
74522	PACKAGNG,BOTTLNG,ETC MCH	W 657	7.0	W 329	3.7	W 303	2.8	W 648	9.3	MACH NETT BOUTEILLES,ETC
749	NONELEC MACH PTS,ACC NES	W 1473	12.7	W 1500	13.9	W 2235	16.1	W 2279	15.1	PIECES MACH NON ELEC NDA
7491	BALL,ROLLER,ETC BEARINGS	W 354	4.1	W 314	4.4	W 461	4.8	W 1299	5.0	ROULEMENTS BILLES ETC
7492	COCKS,VALVES ETC NES	W 696	4.5	W 704	5.1	W 1365	7.5	W 746	7.1	ART ROB,SIM POUR TUYAUX
75	OFFICE MACHNES,ADP EQUIP		16.4		15.5		17.9		28.3	MACH BUREAU TRAIT AUTOM
751	OFFICE MACHINES	W 525	3.6	W 1256	2.7	W 626	3.7	W 819	5.1	MACH,APPAREILS DE BUREAU
752	AUTOMTIC DATA PROC EQUIP	W 451	8.3	W 305	10.2	W 249	10.0	W 578	11.8	MACH TRAIT INFORMATION
7522	DIGITAL COMPUTERS	W 268	4.6	W 116	5.4	W 130	5.6	W 44	1.4	MACH DIGITALES COMPLETES
759	OFFICE,ADP MCH PTS,ACCES	W 513	4.5	W 319	2.8	W 239	4.2	W 362	11.5	PIECES DU 751 ET 752
7599	ACCTG,ETC,ADP MCH PTS,AC	W 436	3.9	W 292	2.4	W 190	3.5	W 316	10.9	PIECES DU 751 ET 752
76	TELECOMM,SOUND EQUIPMENT		26.9		48.4		117.3		180.9	EQUIPMENT DE TELECOM
764	TELECOM EQPT,PTS,ACC NES	W 760	22.1	W 1431	43.7	W 2088	109.9	W 2955	176.9	EQUIP TELECOM,PIECES
7641	LINE TELEPHONE,ETC EQUIP	W 293	12.9	W 474	22.1	W 536	49.6	W 877	86.5	APP TELEPHON PAR FIL
7643	TV,RADIO TRANSMITTRS ETC	W 106	3.7	W 86	5.2	W 79	12.8	W 197	22.1	APP EMET TELE RADIO

4. Special Imports C.I.F. by Commodities according to the S.I.T.C. (Rev. 2) in million U.S. Dollars
Importations Spéciales C.A.F. par Produits d'après la C.T.C.I. (Rév. 2) en millions de Dollars E.U.

SITC CTCI	COMMODITY	1994 QUANTITY QUANTITE	1994 VALUE VALEUR	1995 QUANTITY QUANTITE	1995 VALUE VALEUR	1996 QUANTITY QUANTITE	1996 VALUE VALEUR	1997 QUANTITY QUANTITE	1997 VALUE VALEUR	PRODUIT
7648	TELECOMM EQUIPMENT NES	W 23	0.7	W 10	0.1	W 84	9.1	W 6	0.3	APP TELECOM NDA
76483	RADAR APPARATUS ETC	W 2	0.4		0.1	W 63	8.8	W 1	0.2	APP DE RADIOGUIDAGE ETC
7649	PTS NES OF EQUIPMT OF 76	W 215	4.4	W 687	15.9	W 1118	37.9	W 1663	67.6	PIECES DE LA DIV 76
76491	PTS NES OF APPAR OF 7641	W 54	2.4	W 494	12.8	W 905	34.7	W 1354	57.8	PIECES POUR 764.1
76493	TELECOMM EQUIPMT PTS NES	W 108	1.9	W 143	3.0	W 181	3.1	W 271	9.8	PIECES 761,762,764.3,8
77	ELECTRIC MACHNRY NES ETC		36.1		50.9		49.8		66.5	MACH APP ELECT NDA
771	ELECTRIC POWER MACHY NES	W 791	2.1	W 1274	6.8	W 1260	5.4	W 2033	9.6	MACH PROD,TRANS ELECTR
7711	TRANSFORMERS,ELECTRICAL	W 685	1.5	W 1200	6.3	W 1211	5.1	W 1876	8.3	TRANSFO ELECTRIQUES
77111	LIQUID DIELEC TRANSFRMRS	W 260	1.0	W 975	4.5	W 924	3.2	W 707	4.1	TRANSFO DIELEC LIQUIDE
772	SWITCHGEAR ETC,PARTS NES	W 668	7.1	W 1003	9.6	W 620	8.2	W 978	10.8	APP COUPURE,SECT ETC
7721	SWITCHGEAR ETC	W 664	6.9	W 998	9.5	W 614	8.1	W 972	10.7	APP COUPURE,SECTIONMNT
773	ELECTR DISTRIBUTNG EQUIP	W 2216	8.5	W 2815	10.7	W 2638	7.7	W 5757	16.1	EQUIPMT DISTRIBUTION ELECT
7731	INSULATED WIRE,CABLE ETC	W 2081	8.2	W 2393	10.0	W 2306	7.0	W 4971	15.2	FILS,CABLES ISOLES ELECT
775	HOUSEHOLD TYPE EQUIP NES	W 2083	4.9	W 2647	4.6	W 3055	9.8	W 4163	10.6	MACH,APP USAGE DOMESTQUE
7752	DOM REFRIGERATRS,FREEZRS	W 1197	2.2	W 848	2.1	W 2280	6.4	W 2893	7.4	REFRIG,CONGEL MENAGER
77521	DOMESTIC REFRIGERATORS	W 950	1.6	W 698	1.7	W 1928	5.5	W 1954	5.2	REFRIGERATEURS
778	ELECTRICAL MACHINERY NES	W 6169	11.7	W 6458	16.9	W 6637	14.4	W 6657	15.6	AUTRES MACH ELECT NDA
7781	BATTERIES,ACCUMULATORS	W 4931	6.0	W 5172	7.2	W 5382	8.1	W 4865	10.0	PILES ET ACCUMULATEURS
77811	PRIMARY BATTERIES,CELLS	W 3469	3.6	W 3674	4.2	W 3813	5.1	W 3564	6.8	PILES ELECTRIQUES,PIECES
78	ROAD VEHICLES		249.4		234.2		233.3		352.4	VEHICULES ROUTIERS
781	PASS MOTOR VEH EXC BUSES	W 18108	109.8	W 26612	100.1	W 18420	107.4	W 21414	148.7	AUTO TRANSPORT PERSONNES
782	LORRIES,SPCL MTR VEH NES	W 17778	82.8	W 16782	82.3	W 15594	75.7	W 23257	126.9	VEHICULES SPECIAUX,MARCH
7821	LORRIES,TRUCKS	W 17247	78.9	W 15777	75.9	W 14643	69.3	W 22182	118.9	VEHICULES TRANSP MARCHAND
7822	SPECIAL MOTOR VEHCLS NES	W 532	3.9	W 1005	6.4	W 951	6.5	W 1075	8.1	VEHICULES USAGES SPECIAUX
783	ROAD MOTOR VEHICLES NES	W 6987	31.3	W 6273	26.3	W 10141	32.2	W 12036	56.2	VEHICULES ROUTIERS NDA
7831	BUSES	W 4819	22.4	W 4593	18.7	W 9176	27.6	W 10487	47.7	VOITURES TRANSPORT COMMUN
7832	TRACTORS FOR TR–TRAILERS	W 2168	9.0	W 1680	7.6	W 965	4.6	W 1550	8.6	TRACTEURS ROUTIERS
784	MOTOR VEH PRTS,ACCES NES	W 3682	15.9	W 4682	15.8	W 3823	10.5	W 4035	11.2	PIECES 722,781,782,783
7841	MOTOR VEHICLE CHASSIS	W 999	5.3	W 797	4.9	W 474	3.0	W 411	2.3	CHASSIS 722,781,782,783
7849	OTHER MOTOR VEHCL PARTS	W 2588	10.3	W 3769	10.7	W 3318	7.4	W 3431	8.6	PIECES 722,781,782,783
785	CYCLES,ETC MOTRZD OR NOT	W 2643	7.0	W 2153	6.7	W 1683	6.7	W 3455	6.3	MOTOCYCLES SCOOTERS
7851	MOTORCYCLES ETC	W 560	3.8	W 418	4.0	W 655	5.2	W 1381	5.3	MOTO VELO MOTEUR AUXIL
79	OTHR TRANSPORT EQUIPMENT		11.1		69.9		150.5		61.7	AUTRE MATERIEL TRANSPORT
792	AIRCRAFT ETC	W 118	8.7	W 479	68.5	W 402	150.0	W 423	60.0	APP NAVIGATION AERIENNE
7921	HELICOPTERS	W 6	2.2	W 30	10.0	W 5	0.5	W 18	3.8	HELICOPTERES
7923	AIRCRFT NES2000–15000KG	W 7	1.0	W 34	2.2	W 15	21.7	W 97	4.3	AERODYNES 2000 A 15000 KG
7924	AIRCRFT NES OVER 15000KG	W 60	4.1	W 363	54.8	W 320	125.1	W 229	48.6	AERODYNES PLUS 15000 KG
8	MISC MANUFACTURED GOODS		83.5		92.5		113.1		103.8	ART MANUFACTURES DIVERS
812	*PLUMBG,HEATNG,LGHTNG EQ	W 3307	3.8	W 2724	5.5	W 3376	7.3	W 2669	4.7	APPAR SANITAIRES CHAUFFAGE
821	*FURNITURE,PARTS THEREOF	W 2350	5.2	W 2448	6.0	W 3243	7.2	W 3730	6.8	MEUBLES ET PIECES
84	CLOTHING AND ACCESSORIES		10.2		6.9		7.0		7.1	VETEMENTS
851	*FOOTWEAR	W 2354	6.4	W 4792	6.8	W 1968	7.6	W 1995	3.9	CHAUSSURES
85102	FOOTWEAR LEATHER	W 1771	4.8	W 1894	4.2	W 1183	3.5	W 1707	2.1	CHAUS SEMELLES EN CUIR
87	PRECISION INSTRUMNTS NES		13.4		14.9		19.9		16.6	INSTRUM,APPAR SCIENT NDA
872	MEDICAL INSTRUMENTS NES	W 237	3.3	W 512	2.7	W 1923	6.2	W 391	3.1	INSTR,APP MEDIC–CHIR NDA
87202	OTH MEDICAL INSTRUMENTS	W 210	2.9	W 474	2.4	W 1898	5.8	W 345	2.5	INSTRUM,APP MEDECINE
874	MEASURNG,CONTROLNG INSTR	W 429	8.4	W 751	9.9	W 586	11.5	W 519	10.7	INSTRUMENTS DE MESURE
88	PHOTO EQU,OPTICL GDS ETC		6.8		6.3		5.9		6.5	APP,FOURN PHOTO,OP,MONTR
882	PHOTO,CINEMA SUPPLIES	W 623	4.0	W 647	4.3	W 897	4.2	W 878	4.6	PRODUITS PHOTO,CINEMA
89	MISC MANUFCTRD GOODS NES		37.2		46.0		57.8		57.9	ART MANUFACTURES DIVERS
892	PRINTED MATTER	W 2081	8.4	W 2958	10.3	W 4837	22.5	W 3670	15.6	IMPRIMES
8921	PRINTED BOOKS,GLOBES,ETC	W 1454	6.1	W 2033	6.0	W 4165	20.0	W 2753	11.7	LIVRES,BROCHURES,CARTES
89211	PRINTED BOOKS,PAMPHLETS	W 1441	6.1	W 2012	5.9	W 4146	19.6	W 2736	11.6	LIVRES,BROCHURES
893	ARTICLES OF PLASTIC NES		12.3		16.7		15.9		18.3	OUVRAGES EN MAT DIVIS 58
8931	PLSTC PACKG CONTNRS,LIDS	W 1933	4.7	W 2306	6.3	W 2783	8.2	W 3676	8.9	ART TRANSP EMBALLAGE ETC
8939	MISC PLASTIC ARTICLES	W 3259	7.4	W 4331	10.1	W 3186	7.4	W 3105	9.4	ART DIVERS EN MAT DIV 58
89399	OTHR PLASTC ARTICLES NES	W 2653	6.4	W 3058	8.8	W 2342	6.3	W 2390	8.4	AUT OUV MAT DIV 58
894	TOYS,SPORTING GOODS,ETC	W 3265	7.6	W 3190	6.5	W 3890	6.4	W 2654	5.5	VOITURES ENFANTS,JOUETS
8942	TOYS,INDOOR GAMES ETC	W 2547	5.6	W 2159	4.3	W 2029	4.1	W 2234	3.9	JOUETS,JEUX ETC
897	GOLD,SILVER WARE,JEWELRY		0.9		3.1		5.4		6.7	BIJOUTERIE,ORFEVRERIE
8973	PREC JEWLRY,GLD–SILVWARE		0.5		2.5		4.9		6.2	BIJOUX OR,ARGENT ORFEVRE
89731	PRECIOUS METAL JEWELLERY		0.2		1.4		4.9		6.1	ART BIJOUTERIE,JOAILLER
898	MUSICAL INSTRUMENTS,PTS	W 302	2.3	W 496	3.0	W 421	2.2	W 901	7.0	INSTRUMENTS DE MUSIQUE
8983	SOUND RECRDNG TAPE,DISCS	W 269	2.2	W 423	2.2	W 377	2.0	W 821	6.9	SUPPORTS SON POUR 763
89832	RECORDED DISCS,TAPES ETC	W 86	1.3	W 125	1.6	W 203	1.6	W 610	6.0	DISQUES,PHONO,BANDES
9	GOODS NOT CLASSD BY KIND		18.4		9.4		42.2		44.0	ART TRANSACT NON CLASSES
951	*WAR FIREARMS,AMMUNITION	W 618	4.3	W 18	0.3	W 8	0.2	W 50	0.4	VEHIC BLINDES ARMES
95102	MILITARY FIREARMS NES	W 580	4.1				0.1		0.1	ARMES DE GUERRE
971	*GOLD,NON MONETARY NES	K 14583	14.0	K 7085	9.1	K 3486	42.0	K 3916	43.7	OR NON MONETAIRE
97101	NONMON GLD UNWRT,SEMIMFD	K 14583	14.0	K 7085	9.1	K 3486	42.0	K 3916	43.7	OR,ALLIAGES D'OR BRUTS

5. Special Exports F.O.B. by Commodities according to the S.I.T.C. (Rev. 2) in million U.S. Dollars
Exportations Spéciales F.O.B. par Produits d'après la C.T.C.I. (Rév. 2) en millions de Dollars E.U.

SITC CTCI	COMMODITY	1994 QUANTITY QUANTITE	1994 VALUE VALEUR	1995 QUANTITY QUANTITE	1995 VALUE VALEUR	1996 QUANTITY QUANTITE	1996 VALUE VALEUR	1997 QUANTITY QUANTITE	1997 VALUE VALEUR	PRODUIT
	ALL COMMODITIES		1124.3		1181.3		1087.0		1272.1	TOUS PRODUITS
0	FOOD AND LIVE ANIMALS		157.7		113.7		179.2		230.7	ALIMENTS,ANIMAUX VIVANTS
001	*LIVE ANIMALS FOR FOOD	W 5186	4.4	W 5	0.1	W 699	0.6	W 926	0.7	ANIMAUX VIVANTS
0011	BOVINE SPECIES,LIVE	W 5183	4.3			W 699	0.6	W 923	0.7	ESPECE BOVINE
01	MEAT AND PREPARATIONS		2.6		3.2		4.1		3.3	VIANDES ET PREPARATIONS
011	MEAT FRESH,CHILLD,FROZEN	W 1567	2.3	W 2764	3.1	W 3260	4.0	W 2849	3.3	VIANDES FRAICHES,REF,CONGE
04	CEREALS AND PREPARATIONS		28.8		4.8		4.7		5.7	CEREALES ET PRODUITS
047	OTHER CEREAL MEALS,FLOUR	W 104364	24.0	W 495	0.1	W 2	0.1	W 2	0.1	AUTRES SEMOULES,FARINES
04701	CEREAL FLOUR(NON–WHEAT)	W 104364	24.0	W 495	0.1	W 2	0.1	W 1	0.1	FARINES DE CEREALES
05	VEGETABLES AND FRUIT		28.9		29.9		42.3		53.0	LEGUMES ET FRUITS
054	VEG ETC FRSH,SMPLY PRSVD	W 9707	5.3	W 3713	3.2	W 4196	3.3	W 12916	9.1	LEGUMES FRAIS,CONG,SECS
0542	LEGUMINOUS VEGETBLES DRY	W 9628	5.2	W 3490	3.1	W 4010	3.1	W 12567	8.9	LEGUMES A COSSE SECS
057	FRUIT,NUTS,FRESH,DRIED	W 11305	17.3	W 9159	19.1	W 13327	29.4	W 11720	31.5	FRUITS FRAIS OU SECS
0577	NUTS EDIBLE,FRESH,DRIED	W 7488	15.8	W 7666	18.8	W 9961	28.7	W 9962	31.1	FRUITS A COQUES
05772	BRAZIL NUTS,FRESH,DRIED	W 1422	3.2	W 869	2.3	W 9679	27.8	W 9834	30.8	NOIX DU BRESIL
05779	NUTS EDIBLE,FRSH,DRY,NES	W 6065	12.7	W 6797	16.5	W 282	0.9	W 128	0.4	FRUITS A COQUES NDA
058	FRUIT PRESERVED,PREPARED	W 2019	6.4	W 1960	7.7	W 3309	9.7	W 3876	12.5	CONSERVES DE FRUITS
0589	FRUIT PREPRD,PRESRVD,NES	W 1947	6.4	W 1834	7.6	W 3161	9.6	W 3786	12.5	FRUITS PREPARES CONSERV
05899	FRUIT,NUTS NES,PRESERVED	W 1947	6.4	W 1834	7.6	W 3161	9.6	W 3786	12.5	FRUITS PREP CONSERV NDA
06	SUGAR AND PREPS,HONEY		45.6		17.0		28.2		22.3	SUCRES ET PRODUITS
061	SUGAR AND HONEY	W 107318	45.5	W 44159	16.8	W 72328	27.9	W 65669	22.1	SUCRES ET MIEL
0611	RAW BEET AND CANE SUGAR	W 36	0.1	W 368	0.3	W 18998	8.4	W 10817	4.6	SUCRES BRUTS
0612	REFINED SUGAR ETC	W 107265	45.5	W 43785	16.6	W 53329	19.5	W 54852	17.6	SUCRES RAFFINES
07	COFFEE,TEA,COCOA,SPICES		16.1		17.5		17.1		27.0	CAFE,THE,CACAO,EPICES
071	COFFEE AND SUBSTITUTES	W 4995	15.3	W 5781	16.9	W 7390	16.5	W 6727	26.1	CAFE ET SUCCEDANES
0711	COFFEE GREEN,ROASTED,SUB	W 4995	15.3	W 5781	16.9	W 7390	16.5	W 6727	26.1	CAFE TORREFIE OU DECAFEINE
07111	COFFEE GREEN,HUSKS,SKINS	W 4932	15.1	W 5738	16.8	W 7389	16.5	W 6725	26.1	CAFE NON TORREFIE
081	*FEEDING STUFF FOR ANIML	W 130426	31.1	W 203940	39.4	W 354338	81.8	W 466561	117.7	NOURRITURE POUR ANIMAUX
0813	OILCAKE AND OTH RESIDUES	W 130323	31.0	W 203473	39.3	W 351168	81.2	W 465986	117.7	TOURTEAUX
08131	— OF SOYA BEANS	W 129645	30.9	W 198447	38.6	W 335240	78.2	W 435805	112.2	TOURTEAUX DE SOJA
08135	— OF SUNFLOWER-SEEDS	W 670	0.2	W 4945	0.8	W 12608	2.6	W 24623	4.7	TOURTEAUX DE TOURNESOL
1	BEVERAGES AND TOBACCO		3.8		7.0		7.0		7.4	BOISSONS ET TABACS
11	BEVERAGES		2.0		3.8		3.2		3.8	BOISSONS
112	ALCOHOLIC BEVERAGES	W 1868	1.7	W 4076	3.7	W 2939	2.7	W 3675	3.3	BOISSONS ALCOOLIQUES
12	TOBACCO AND MANUFACTURES		1.8		3.2		3.8		3.7	TABACS BRUTS FABRIQUES
122	TOBACCO,MANUFACTURED	W 342	1.8	W 527	3.2	W 626	3.8	W 581	3.7	TABACS FABRIQUES
1222	CIGARETTES	W 342	1.8	W 527	3.2	W 626	3.8	W 581	3.7	CIGARETTES
2	CRUDE MATERLS,EXCL FUELS		329.9		415.3		428.8		468.5	MAT BRUTES NON COMESTIBLES
22	OIL SEEDS,OLEAGINOUS FRT		44.3		69.6		84.7		75.8	GRAINES,FRUITS OLEAGINEUX
222	SEEDS FOR'SOFT'FIXED OIL	W 191472	44.0	W 209400	47.2	W 272332	66.4	W 227106	62.1	GRAINES HUILES FIXES
2222	SOYA BEANS	W 189858	43.2	W 208827	46.8	W 265515	64.8	W 225462	61.6	FEVES DE SOJA
223	SEEDS FOR OTH FIXED OILS	W 1741	0.3	W 117748	22.4	W 69951	18.4	W 45946	13.8	GRAINES AUTRES HUILES FIXES
2239	OIL SEED FLOUR AND MEAL	W 1241	0.3	W 117748	22.4	W 69926	18.4	W 45943	13.8	FARINES GRAINES OLEAG
24	CORK AND WOOD		78.6		66.2		69.0		67.2	LIEGE ET BOIS
248	WOOD SHAPED,SLEEPERS	W 129243	78.6	W 93312	66.1	W 96183	69.0	W 92701	67.1	BOIS SIMPLEMENT TRAVAILLES
2481	RAILWAY SLEEPERS,TIES	W 12725	3.7	W 1808	0.5	W 2980	0.9	W 3443	0.9	TRAVERSES VOIES FERREES
2482	LUMBER SHAPED CONIFER	W 3842	4.2	W 1564	1.7	W 163	0.4	W 923	0.4	CONIFERES SCIES,RABOTES
24822	LUMBER PLANED ETC CONIFR	W 3723	4.2	W 1483	1.6	W 138	0.4	W 56	0.2	CONIFER RABOTES,RAINES
2483	LUMBER SHAPED NON–CONIFR	W 112677	70.8	W 89941	64.0	W 93041	67.8	W 88335	66.0	NON CONIFERES SCIES,RABOTES
24831	LUMBER SAWN ETC NON–CON	W 112532	70.6	W 89244	63.3	W 90209	64.6	W 84370	61.8	SCIES LONGITUDINALEMENT
24832	LUMBER PLANED ETC NONCON	W 144	0.2	W 697	0.8	W 2833	3.2	W 3965	4.2	RABOTES,RAINES,LANGUETES
26	TEXTILE FIBRES AND WASTE		15.4		31.1		32.4		40.5	FIBRES TEXTILES
263	COTTON	W 8428	14.0	W 13902	30.0	W 18188	31.3	W 22371	39.3	COTON
2631	RAW COTTON,EXCL LINTERS	W 8368	13.9	W 13902	30.0	W 18188	31.3	W 22281	39.3	COTON EN MASSE
27	CRUDE FERTLZR,MINRLS NES		4.3		3.4		2.5		4.1	ENGRAIS MINERAUX BRUTS
278	OTHER CRUDE MINERALS	W 23488	3.7	W 28183	2.9	W 17843	2.1	W 23001	3.6	AUTRES MINERAUX BRUTS
2789	MINERALS CRUDE NES	W 22196	3.5	W 22161	2.7	W 17461	2.0	W 22075	3.5	MINERAUX BRUTS NDA
28	METALLIFEROUS ORES,SCRAP		180.9		240.2		235.1		275.3	MINERAIS METAL,DECHETS
287	BASE METAL ORES,CONC NES	W 256889	132.8	W 334937	182.8	W 334425	182.5	W 354116	226.8	MINERAIS METAUX COMMUNS
2874	LEAD ORES,CONCENTRATES	W 38220	12.1	W 35076	12.6	W 29417	11.9	W 35812	11.0	MINERAIS DE PLOMB
2875	ZINC ORES,CONCENTRATES	W 210031	105.4	W 292812	151.4	W 297973	151.8	W 311324	200.1	MINERAIS DE ZINC
2876	TIN ORES,CONCENTRATES	W 2533	7.8	W 2440	8.3	W 3769	12.6	W 3553	11.0	MINERAIS D'ETAIN
2879	OTH NONFER ORE,CONCNTRTE	W 5959	7.5	W 4316	10.4	W 2984	6.2	W 2304	4.4	MINERAIS D'AUTRES METAUX
28792	TUNGSTEN ORE,CONCENTRATE	W 836	2.5	W 1174	4.9	W 1031	3.5	W 917	2.8	MINERAIS DE TUNGSTENE
28799	OTH BASE MTL ORE,CON NES	W 5119	5.0	W 3142	5.6	W 1953	2.8	W 1384	1.6	AUTRES MINERAIS
289	PREC MTAL ORES,WASTE NES	K 2204298	48.1	K 2627666	57.4	K 3742531	52.2	K 2307449	48.0	MINERAIS,DECHETS MET PREC
28901	PRECIOUS METAL ORES,CONC	K 2204298	48.1	K 2627666	57.4	K 3742531	52.2	K 2307449	48.0	MINERAIS METAUX PRECIEUX
3	MINERAL FUELS ETC		107.1		152.9		142.2		107.1	COMBUSTIBLES MINERAUX LUB
33	PETROLEUM AND PRODUCTS		15.2		60.2		47.4		37.0	PETROLE ET DERIVES
333	CRUDE PETROLEUM	W 64020	6.6	W 338819	48.2	W 218032	38.5	W 222708	28.2	HUILES BRUTES DE PETROLE
334	PETROLEUM PRODUCTS,REFIN	W 22578	8.6	W 40293	12.1	W 28592	8.9	W 30859	8.9	PRODUITS RAFFINES
3344	FUEL OILS,NES	W 22578	8.6	W 34997	10.8	W 28590	8.9	W 30120	8.7	FUEL OILS
341	*GAS,NATURAL AND MANUFCT	W 2883107	91.7	W 2729966	92.5	W 2733123	94.6	W 2154106	70.1	GAZ NATUREL,GAZ MANUFACT
3414	PETROLEUM GASES, GASEOUS	W 2883107	91.7	W 2729966	92.5	W 2733123	94.6	W 2153314	69.9	GAZ DE PETROLE GAZEUX
4	ANIMAL,VEGETABLE OIL,FAT		21.7		35.6		40.6		59.3	HUILES,GRAISSES ANIM,VEG
42	FIXED VEGETABLE OIL,FAT		21.6		35.5		40.6		59.3	HUILES VEGETALES FIXES
423	FIXED VEG OILS,SOFT	W 31780	21.6	W 51455	35.5	W 62153	40.5	W 89476	59.2	HUILES VEGET DOUCES FIXES
4232	SOYA BEAN OIL	W 30476	20.5	W 50507	34.7	W 61169	39.5	W 83114	55.1	HUILE DE SOJA
4236	SUNFLOWER SEED OIL	W 1305	1.2	W 947	0.8	W 984	1.1	W 6363	4.2	HUILE DE TOURNESOL
5	CHEMCLS,RELATED PROD NES		6.4		12.9		16.6		14.1	PRODUITS CHIMIQUES
51	ORGANIC CHEMICALS		3.6		3.7		6.3		3.3	PROD CHIMIQ ORGANIQUES
512	ALCOHOLS,PHENOLS ETC	W 10089	3.5	W 10887	3.7	W 22227	6.3	W 11592	3.3	PHENOLS,PHENOLS–ALCOOLS
5121	ACYCLIC ALCOHOLS,DERIVS	W 10089	3.5	W 10887	3.7	W 22227	6.3	W 11592	3.3	ALCOOLS ACYCLIQUES
51216	ETHYL ALC,DENATRD SPIRIT	W 10089	3.5	W 10887	3.7	W 22227	6.3	W 11592	3.3	ALCOOL ETHYLIQUE NON DENAT
52	INORGANIC CHEMICALS		2.1		8.0		8.7		9.6	PROD CHIM INORGANIQUES
522	INORG ELEMNTS,OXIDES,ETC	W 4192	1.8	W 9098	7.9	W 11484	8.5	W 12766	9.5	ELEMENTS INORGANIQUES
5225	INORGANIC BASES ETC NES			W 5497	6.3	W 5508	6.5	W 5948	7.1	AUTRES BASES OXYDES METAL
52259	OTH OXIDES,BASES ETC NES			W 5497	6.3	W 5508	6.5	W 5948	7.1	HYDRAZINE,HYDROXYLAMINE
6	BASIC MANUFACTURES		157.9		154.2		145.0		142.9	ART MANUFACTURES
61	LEATHER,DRESSED FUR,ETC		8.2		8.2		7.8		9.8	CUIRS,PELLETERIES
611	LEATHER	W 2189	8.2	W 1820	8.0	W 1660	7.7	W 2985	9.7	CUIRS,PEAUX PREPARES
6114	LEATHR BOVINE NES,EQUINE	W 1865	5.2	W 1399	4.5	W 1279	4.1	W 2718	6.9	CUIRS DE BOVINS
63	WOOD,CORK MANUFACTRS NES		8.0		9.8		12.2		19.1	OUVRAGES LIEGE ET BOIS
635	WOOD MANUFACTURES NES	W 3504	5.8	W 3297	7.9	W 4673	10.8	W 7482	16.9	ART MANUF EN BOIS NDA
6353	BUILDERS WOODWRK,PREFABS	W 3404	5.6	W 3264	7.8	W 4497	10.2	W 7301	16.4	OUVRAGES DE MENUISERIE
64	PAPER,PAPERBOARD AND MFR		1.7		2.5		3.5		4.0	PAPIERS,CARTONS & OUVRAGES
65	TEXTILE YARN,FABRICS,ETC		3.6		1.8		2.9		5.2	FILS,TISSUS,ARTICLES TEXTILE
658	TEXTILE ARTICLES NES	W 265	1.2	W 218	0.9	W 461	1.8	W 1260	4.5	ART FACONNES MAT TEXTILES
66	NONMETAL MINERAL MFS NES		1.9		2.9		3.4		2.3	ART MIN NON METALLIQUES
68	NON–FERROUS METALS		133.2		128.1		113.9		102.1	METAUX NON FERREUX
681	SILVER,PLATINUM,ETC		14.7		13.5		11.9		11.3	ARGENT ET PLATINE

5. Special Exports F.O.B. by Commodities according to the S.I.T.C. (Rev. 2) in million U.S. Dollars
Exportations Spéciales F.O.B. par Produits d'après la C.T.C.I. (Rév. 2) en millions de Dollars E.U.

SITC CTCI	COMMODITY	1994 QUANTITY QUANTITE	1994 VALUE VALEUR	1995 QUANTITY QUANTITE	1995 VALUE VALEUR	1996 QUANTITY QUANTITE	1996 VALUE VALEUR	1997 QUANTITY QUANTITE	1997 VALUE VALEUR	PRODUIT
6811	SILVER UNWKD,PARTLY WRKD		14.7		13.5		11.9		11.3	ARGENT BRUT MI-OUVRE
68113	SILVER UNWROUGHT		14.7		13.5		11.9		11.3	ARGENT ET ALLIAGES BRUTS
687	TIN	W 20444	110.1	W 18214	113.0	W 16471	101.3	W 16027	90.4	ETAIN
6871	TIN,ALLOYS UNWROUGHT	W 20309	109.7	W 18098	112.4	W 16255	100.3	W 15954	90.0	ETAIN ET ALLIAGES BRUTS
689	NON-FER BASE METALS NES	W 6926	8.4	W 464	1.6	W 192	0.6	W 159	0.3	AUT METAUX NON FERREUX
6899	BASE METALS NES,CERMETS	W 6926	8.4	W 464	1.6	W 192	0.6	W 159	0.3	METAUX COMMUNS NDA
68999	BASE MTL NES UNWRT,WASTE	W 6926	8.4	W 464	1.6	W 192	0.6	W 159	0.3	AUT METAUX COM BRUTS NDA
7	MACHINES,TRANSPORT EQUIP		28.8		38.2		76.8		14.8	MACHINES MATERIEL TRANSPORT
72	MACHS FOR SPCL INDUSTRYS		13.1		12.5		9.3		3.9	MAC SPECIALES POUR INDUST
723	CIVIL ENGNEERG EQUIP ETC	W 4683	11.8	W 2252	8.9	W 1084	6.7	W 432	2.9	APPAREILS DE GENIE CIVIL
7234	CONST,MINING MACHNRY NES	W 3805	9.5	W 1835	6.7	W 655	3.9	W 317	1.7	MACH POUR LA CONST, MINES
72344	BORING,SINKING MACHINERY	W 3240	6.6	W 604	1.6	W 129	0.6	W 72	0.9	MACHINES DE FORAGE
78	ROAD VEHICLES		3.1		4.1		2.8		1.6	VEHICULES ROUTIERS
79	OTHR TRANSPORT EQUIPMENT		8.9		18.6		59.4		4.0	AUTRE MATERIEL TRANSPORT
792	AIRCRAFT ETC	W 85	8.8	W 102	18.6	W 230	59.4	W 64	4.0	APP NAVIGATION AERIENNE
7921	HELICOPTERS	W 11	4.3			W 21	8.0			HELICOPTERES
7924	AIRCRFT NES OVER 15000KG	W 60	4.1	W 31	16.7	W 195	48.6			AERODYNES PLUS 15000 KG
8	MISC MANUFACTURED GOODS		190.4		117.9		49.7		115.1	ART MANUFACTURES DIVERS
821	*FURNITURE,PARTS THEREOF	W 1044	2.5	W 876	3.1	W 988	3.4	W 1235	4.8	MEUBLES ET PIECES
84	CLOTHING AND ACCESSORIES		18.4		18.0		28.6		26.6	VETEMENTS
844	UNDER GARMENTS NOT KNIT	W 230	4.4	W 215	4.4	W 288	8.5	W 210	7.3	VETEMENT DESSOUS MAT TEX
8441	— MENS SHIRTS	W 230	4.4	W 211	4.4	W 277	8.4	W 164	7.0	CHEMISES HOMMES MAT TEXT
84411	—— OF COTTON	W 156	3.4	W 198	4.3	W 254	7.2	W 149	6.3	CHEMISES HOMMES DE COTON
845	OUTERWEAR KNIT NONELASTC	W 3084	11.3	W 1209	8.1	W 646	12.5	W 897	13.9	VET DESSOUS,ACCES BONNET
8451	— JERSEYS,PULLOVERS ETC	W 2280	10.2	W 1149	6.7	W 487	9.5	W 495	8.1	CHANDAILS,PULL-OVERS ETC
8459	— OTHER,CLTHG ACCESRYS	W 797	1.0	W 45	1.0	W 149	2.4	W 398	5.4	AUT VET DESSUS DE BONNE
846	UNDER GARMENTS KNITTED	W 157	2.0	W 134	3.6	W 164	2.8	W 99	2.3	SOUS VETS DE BONNETERIE
89	MISC MANUFCTRD GOODS NES		165.5		92.3		13.3		78.2	ART MANUFACTURES DIVERS
897	GOLD,SILVER WARE,JEWELRY		164.4		91.0		11.4		74.6	BIJOUTERIE,ORFEVRERIE
8973	PREC JEWLRY,GLD-SILVWARE		164.3		90.7		0.1		74.6	BIJOUX OR,ARGENT ORFEVRE
89731	PRECIOUS METAL JEWELLERY		164.2		90.4		0.1		74.6	ART BIJOUTERIE,JOAILLER
8974	PREC MTL INDUS,LAB EQUIP				0.3		11.3			AUT OUV METAUX PRECIEUX
9	GOODS NOT CLASSD BY KIND		121.0		134.0		1.7		112.6	ART TRANSACT NON CLASSES
971	*GOLD,NON MONETARY NES	K 10182	119.1	K 10781	130.9			K 10497	110.6	OR NON MONETAIRE
97101	NONMON GLD UNWRT,SEMIMFD	K 10182	119.1	K 10781	130.9			K 10497	110.6	OR,ALLIAGES D'OR BRUTS

1. HISTORICAL SERIES, 1962–1997 SPECIAL TRADE, IMPORTS C.I.F., EXPORTS F.O.B.
SERIES HISTORIQUES, 1962–1997 COMMERCE SPECIAL, IMPORTATIONS C.A.F., EXPORTATIONS F.O.B

YEAR / ANNEE	VALUE IN MILLION U.S. DOLLARS / VALEUR EN MILLION U.S. DOLLARS — MERCHANDISE – MARCHANDISE		GOLD – OR		CONVERSION FACTORS FACTEURS DE CONVERSION CENTS E.U. PAR		INDEX NUMBERS – INDICES — QUANTUM		UNIT VALUE / VALEUR UNITAIRE	
	IMPORTS	EXPORTS	IMPORTS	EXPORTS	IMPORTS	EXPORTS	IMPORTS	EXPORTS	IMPORTS	EXPORTS
1962	1475.00	1214.00								
1963	1487.00	1406.00								
1964	1263.00	1430.00								
1965	1096.00	1595.00	0.01							
1966	1496.00	1741.00	0.01							
1967	1667.00	1654.00	0.78							
1968	2129.00	1881.00	3.17	0.01						
1969	2265.00	2311.00	1.63							
1970	2849.00	2739.00	4.59							
1971	3701.00	2904.00	5.62							
1972	4783.00	3990.00	7.68							
1973	6999.00	6198.00	6.91	0.01						
1974	14168.00	7951.00		0.11						
1975	12210.00	8670.00								
1976	13532.00	10128.00								
1977	13069.00	12054.00								
1978	14538.00	12527.00								
1979	19372.00	15244.00								
1980	24961.00	20132.00					115	61	97	111
1981	24079.00	23680.00					100	73	108	104
1982	21069.00	20213.00					91	66	104	98
1983	16801.00	21899.00					76	76	99	93
1984	13916.00	27005.00					73	93	94	95
1985	13153.00	25639.00					68	96	90	87
1986	15557.00	22349.01					92	79	70	93
1987	16581.00	26224.00					90	92	82	93
1988	16055.00	33494.00					80	109	89	102
1989	19875.01	34383.01					92	109	96	101
1990	22524.00	31414.00					100	100	111	100
1991	22950.00	31620.00					110	104	93	96
1992	23068.00	35793.01								
1993	27740.00	38597.01								
1994	35997.01	43558.00								
1995	53783.01	46506.00								
1996	56947.01	47762.00								
1997	65007.01	52987.01								

2. IMPORTS BY BROAD ECONOMIC CATEGORY AND EXPORTS BY INDUSTRIAL ORIGIN. (PERCENTAGE OF TOTAL VALUE)
IMPORTATIONS PAR CATEGORIES ECONOMIQUES ET EXPORTATIONS PAR BRANCHE D'ACTIVITE.(EN POURCENTAGE DE LA VALEUR TOTALE)

IMPORTS – IMPORTATIONS

	1991	1992	1993	1994	1995	1996	1997
TOTAL IMPORTS–IMPORTATIONS TOTALES	100.	100.	100.	100.	100.	100.	100.
1 FOOD BEV–ALIMENTATION BOISSONS	10.4	8.8	8.6	10.0	10.0	10.2	8.5
11 PRIMARY–PRODUITS DE BASE	5.3	5.0	2.6	3.8	3.6	5.3	4.8
111 FOR INDUSTRY–POUR L'INDUSTRIE	2.7	3.0	0.9	1.4	1.2	2.9	2.6
112 FOR HOUSEHOLDS–POUR LES MENAGES	2.6	2.0	1.7	2.3	2.4	2.4	2.2
12 PROCESSED–PRODUITS ELABORES	5.1	3.8	6.0	6.2	6.4	4.9	3.7
121 FOR INDUSTRY–POUR L'INDUSTRIE	1.2	1.1	1.0	1.2	1.0	1.1	1.0
122 FOR HOUSEHOLDS–POUR LES MENAGES	3.9	2.7	5.0	5.0	5.4	3.8	2.7
2 IND SUPPLIES–APPROV INDUSTRIELS	31.8	30.3	32.4	30.9	30.1	29.3	28.6
21 PRIMARY–PRODUITS DE BASE	4.7	4.5	5.7	4.5	3.6	3.5	3.1
22 PROCESSED–PRODUITS ELABORES	27.0	25.8	26.8	26.3	26.5	25.8	25.5
3 FUELS–COMBUSTIBLES	23.6	24.5	20.5	14.7	12.0	13.0	11.5
31 PRIMARY–PRODUITS DE BASE	20.6	20.0	12.2	9.7	7.3	8.6	7.3
32 PROCESSED–PRODUITS ELABORES	3.0	4.4	8.3	5.0	4.7	4.4	4.2
321 MOTOR SPIRIT–ESSENCE	0.5	1.7	4.1	2.2	2.6	2.0	1.9
322 OTHER–AUTRES	2.5	2.7	4.2	2.8	2.1	2.5	2.3
4 MACHINERY–EQUIPEMENT	22.6	23.8	23.6	26.0	25.5	27.8	29.9
41 CAPITAL EQUIPMENT–MACHINES	16.8	18.1	18.0	20.6	19.9	21.6	23.9
42 PARTS–PIECES ACCESSOIRES	5.8	5.8	5.6	5.4	5.6	6.2	6.0
5 TRANSPORT–TRANSPORT	6.6	8.3	9.9	12.3	13.8	11.0	13.4
51 PASSENGER CARS–AUTOMOBILES	0.5	1.3	2.6	4.3	5.8	2.8	3.9
52 OTHER–AUTRES	1.4	1.7	1.2	1.7	2.1	1.7	2.8
521 INDUSTRIAL–INDUSTRIELS	1.3	1.6	1.1	1.5	2.0	1.6	2.7
522 NON INDUSTRIAL–NON INDUSTRIEL	0.1	0.1	0.2	0.2	0.1	0.1	0.1
53 PARTS–PIECES ACCESSOIRES	4.7	5.4	6.0	6.3	5.8	6.5	6.7
6 CONSUM GOODS–BIENS CONSOMMATION	4.9	4.2	4.9	6.1	8.5	8.2	8.1
61 DURABLE–DURABLES	1.5	1.3	1.5	1.8	2.1	1.8	1.9
62 SEMI DURABLE–SEMI DURABLES	1.6	1.2	1.6	2.1	3.5	3.3	3.0
63 NON DURABLE–NON DURABLES	1.9	1.7	1.8	2.2	3.0	3.0	3.2
7 GOODS NES–BIENS NDA	0.1	0.1	0.0	0.1	0.0	0.5	0.0

EXPORTS – EXPORTATIONS

	1991	1992	1993	1994	1995	1996	1997
TOTAL EXPORTS–EXPORTATIONS TOTALES	100.	100.	100.	100.	100.	100.	100.
1 AGRICULTURE	10.6	9.3	9.1	11.6	9.6	9.8	13.5
2 MINING QUARRY–INDUS EXTRACTIVES	9.8	7.5	7.0	6.3	6.6	6.7	6.3
3 MANUFACTURING–IND MANUFACTUR	79.6	83.1	84.0	82.1	83.8	83.5	80.2
31 FOOD BEV TOBACCO–ALIM BOISS TAB	15.2	16.5	16.6	17.9	19.9	20.9	18.2
32 TEXTILES–INDUSTRIES TEXTILES	8.6	9.1	9.6	8.0	7.3	7.5	6.7
33 WOOD & PRODUCTS–BOIS & PRODUITS	1.2	1.3	1.9	2.2	2.1	2.1	2.1
34 PAPER & PRODUCTS–PAPIER & PRODT	4.2	4.4	4.4	4.4	6.1	4.3	4.0
35 CHEMICALS–INDUSTRIES CHIMIQUES	9.4	9.8	10.1	10.1	9.9	10.1	9.7
36 NON METAL MIN–MIN NON METAL	0.9	1.1	1.4	1.3	1.3	1.3	1.3
37 BASIC METAL–IND METAL BASE	17.9	16.1	14.7	13.1	13.4	12.5	10.7
38 METAL MANUF–MANUF METAL	20.8	23.6	24.2	23.7	22.0	22.9	25.5
39 OTH MANUF IND–AUTRES MANUF	1.4	1.2	1.1	1.4	1.7	1.7	1.9

3. TRADE BY PRINCIPAL COUNTRIES OF ORIGIN AND DESTINATION (VALUE IN MILLION U.S. DOLLARS)
ECHANGES SELON LES PRINCIPAUX PAYS D'ORIGINE ET DE DESTINATION (VALEUR EN MILLIONS DE DOLLARS EU)

COUNTRIES–PAYS	SPECIAL IMPORTS C.I.F. IMPORTATIONS SPECIALES C.A.F				
	1993	1994	1995	1996	1997
World	27300.2	35510.4	53736.7	56732.2	65074.6
Africa	1079.2	994.1	1459.9	1804.2	2182.3
Americas	12424.0	16506.1	25377.8	26425.9	31144.9
– Northern America	7119.5	9225.4	14051.6	14031.0	16837.4
– LAIA	4986.2	6769.6	10605.7	12210.7	14129.7
– CACM	7.1	8.4	11.5	6.6	9.1
– Caribbean	128.9	257.9	326.2	119.6	135.3
– Rest of America	182.3	244.9	382.8	57.9	33.4
Asia excl fmr USSR	5921.4	6605.0	9518.7	10322.8	12013.0
– Middle East	2525.1	2187.7	2020.5	1952.6	1839.2
Asia former USSR	6.1	38.0	46.7	164.6	107.9
Europe excl fmr USSR	7343.7	10861.5	16613.3	16358.1	18619.8
– European Union	6458.9	9760.4	14981.7	14901.2	17061.3
– Eastern Europe	172.7	188.3	293.3	350.9	306.7
– Rest of Europe	712.2	912.7	1338.3	1106.0	1251.7
Europe former USSR	234.1	241.5	259.3	419.0	379.4
Oceania	280.8	242.9	329.4	443.1	383.5
Other	10.8	21.3	131.7	794.5	243.9
USA/Etats–Unis d'Amer	6270.4	8202.8	12752.1	12631.8	15243.9
Argentina/Argentine	2816.1	3828.5	5749.9	7101.9	8576.1
Germany/Allemagne	2422.0	3613.7	5422.7	5031.5	5348.8
Japan/Japon	1663.9	1937.9	2726.4	2917.5	3809.7
Italy/Italie	1005.0	2066.5	3159.5	3070.9	3625.6
Saudi Arabia	1666.6	1416.4	1266.7	1290.4	1138.3
France, Monaco	735.6	932.7	1411.7	1420.7	1731.8
Canada	747.2	894.9	1220.0	1386.8	1592.3
United Kingdom	564.7	780.8	987.6	1327.6	1560.2
Korea, Republic of	355.4	588.4	1291.4	1251.2	1487.1
Chile/Chili	470.6	635.5	1183.3	998.2	1082.0
Switzerland,Liechtenst.	593.1	762.1	1089.9	789.6	914.4
Uruguay	439.8	697.2	999.6	960.3	1012.2
Venezuela	402.0	580.6	894.9	1056.2	1138.0
Mexico/Mexique	329.7	360.3	840.6	1018.3	1273.4
Spain/Espagne	258.1	326.0	818.2	967.9	1198.7
China/Chine	157.0	196.8	417.9	1252.1	1316.8
Netherlands/Pays–Bas	452.6	571.3	822.8	600.2	619.9
Other Asia n.e.s.	243.5	386.8	673.1	772.5	880.8
Belgium–Luxembourg	305.5	514.9	772.9	585.9	747.4
Sweden/Suède	240.1	390.4	600.5	714.1	909.3
Algeria/Algérie	548.9	278.8	253.5	707.9	818.5
China, Hong Kong SAR	269.5	458.5	907.2	363.3	458.2
Paraguay	282.0	374.6	530.9	567.4	551.7
Singapore/Singapour	354.1	312.1	594.6	412.9	340.8
Nigeria/Nigéria	140.9	246.1	570.6	261.2	577.3
Iran (Islamic Rep of)	339.0	298.7	255.0	536.8	344.6
So. African Customs Un	122.7	245.4	296.2	442.6	392.6
Malaysia/Malaisie	84.0	119.3	256.2	406.6	615.6
Australia/Australie	266.4	229.9	271.6	365.8	310.4
Russian Federation	186.0	180.4	184.4	411.7	371.6
Areas n.e.s.	10.8	21.3	131.7	794.5	243.9
Peru/Pérou	132.6	196.2	218.0	273.2	297.8
Finland/Finlande	121.3	155.3	234.5	250.3	279.9
Norway,Svalbard and JM	108.5	136.6	227.9	255.5	263.8
Austria/Autriche	58.9	98.1	178.6	285.4	360.0
Kuwait/ Koweït	321.1	338.9	300.0		
Israel/Israël	88.6	122.2	128.1	200.7	285.0
Portugal	62.6	91.1	188.9	234.4	242.8
Panama	127.7	225.2	353.3	40.2	33.4

COUNTRIES–PAYS	SPECIAL EXPORTS F.O.B. EXPORTATIONS SPECIALES F.O.B.				
	1993	1994	1995	1996	1997
Monde	38700.9	43558.0	46505.4	47746.5	52985.8
Afrique	1110.0	1349.6	1585.8	1521.5	1517.0
Amériques	18274.9	20099.9	20040.4	21475.6	24659.3
– Amérique du Nord	8490.6	9471.4	9262.1	9820.8	9992.6
– ALAI	9144.5	9745.0	9974.4	10927.8	13596.5
– MCAC	235.6	241.9	216.4	161.6	199.2
– Caraïbes	296.7	529.1	460.1	435.9	567.3
– Autre Amérique	107.5	112.5	127.4	129.5	303.7
Asie anc. URSS exclus	7566.8	8287.0	9669.7	9349.0	9405.0
– Moyen–Orient	1381.7	1148.7	1424.3	1482.4	1626.5
Asie ancienne URSS		0.4	6.5	7.2	11.7
Europe anc. URSS exclus	10755.3	12949.4	13827.8	14019.2	15484.8
– Union Européenne	10201.1	12202.1	12912.0	12882.6	14551.3
– Europe de l'Est	232.6	330.2	360.3	476.4	492.5
– Autre de l'Europe	321.6	417.0	555.5	660.2	440.9
Europe ancienne URSS	246.8	231.6	636.3	572.9	767.9
Océanie	255.6	291.4	350.4	296.3	295.4
Autre	491.4	348.7	388.3	504.9	844.8
USA/Etats–Unis d'Amer	8030.2	8969.0	8799.2	9312.4	9407.9
Argentina/Argentine	3658.2	4135.7	4041.1	5170.0	6767.2
Netherlands/Pays–Bas	2488.0	3077.1	2917.8	3548.7	3998.5
Japan/Japon	2313.0	2586.1	3101.6	3047.1	3068.1
Germany/Allemagne	1823.7	2048.9	2158.2	2082.7	2607.8
Italy/Italie	1312.1	1646.5	1713.1	1530.7	1709.2
Belgium–Luxembourg	1130.5	1355.4	1610.3	1431.6	1483.1
United Kingdom	1139.6	1228.8	1325.6	1323.7	1258.8
Paraguay	960.6	1053.6	1300.7	1324.6	1406.5
Chile/Chili	1110.3	998.9	1210.5	1055.3	1195.9
China/Chine	779.4	822.4	1203.8	1113.8	1088.2
France, Monaco	791.4	900.6	1038.4	958.9	1151.5
Spain/Espagne	675.9	709.4	876.9	937.5	1056.7
Mexico/Mexique	995.4	1050.0	496.1	679.3	828.4
Uruguay	774.8	731.8	811.1	810.5	870.0
Korea, Republic of	537.6	634.3	827.5	838.4	736.8
Bolivia/Bolivie	430.6	470.0	530.1	531.7	719.1
Areas n.e.s.	491.4	348.7	388.3	504.9	844.8
Canada	455.5	500.5	460.9	505.8	583.8
Venezuela	393.0	281.6	480.9	454.4	768.1
Other Asia n.e.s.	587.6	410.6	406.5	401.0	469.9
Russian Federation	228.5	173.3	569.3	465.7	760.6
Colombia/Colombie	377.3	400.9	457.2	431.9	507.9
China, Hong Kong SAR	331.1	376.5	405.1	432.7	465.2
Saudi Arabia	420.9	357.1	360.1	409.5	398.4
Thailand/Thaïlande	289.6	384.1	419.4	395.6	361.9
Peru/Pérou	273.9	349.7	438.3	298.0	361.8
Portugal	270.1	302.0	412.9	324.3	410.2
Switzerland,Liechtenst.	218.8	303.5	388.7	445.5	267.6
Indonesia/Indonésie	256.9	218.8	365.9	290.8	347.8
Singapore/Singapour	267.1	308.1	293.7	333.1	216.0
India/Inde	124.8	621.2	320.0	184.9	166.3
So. African Customs Un	194.7	226.8	261.9	297.0	331.8
Malaysia/Malaisie	243.7	211.0	244.3	233.2	343.1
Australia/Australie	197.7	251.9	299.1	257.2	253.3
Philippines	204.9	217.3	275.1	322.1	214.3
Egypt/Egypte	175.7	179.4	369.7	224.4	269.7
Nigeria/Nigéria	239.9	149.3	243.3	274.5	249.2
Iran (Islamic Rep of)	257.9	184.0	256.3	184.1	244.8
Turkey/Turquie	209.3	149.4	197.6	237.1	275.7

(VALUE AS PERCENTAGE OF WORLD TOTAL)(VALEURS EN POURCENTAGE DU TOTAL MONDIAL)

	1988	1989	1990	1991	1992	1993	1994	1995	1996	1997
Africa	4.7	3.1	2.9	4.0	2.7	4.0	2.8	2.7	3.2	3.4
Americas	36.1	41.1	40.0	45.0	45.5	45.5	46.5	47.2	46.6	47.9
– Northern America	23.3	23.0	22.2	26.1	26.6	26.1	26.0	26.1	24.7	25.9
– LAIA	12.2	17.5	16.9	17.2	17.3	18.3	19.1	19.7	21.5	21.7
– CACM	0.0	0.0	0.0	0.0	0.0	0.0	0.0	0.0	0.0	0.0
– Caribbean	0.3	0.3	0.7	1.0	1.1	0.5	0.7	0.6	0.2	0.2
– Rest of America	0.3	0.2	0.1	0.7	0.5	0.7	0.7	0.7	0.1	0.1
Asia excl fmr USSR	29.9	28.6	30.2	22.2	22.8	21.7	18.6	17.7	18.2	18.5
– Middle East	19.9	17.7	19.4	12.5	13.9	9.2	6.2	3.8	3.4	2.8
Asia former USSR						0.0	0.1	0.1	0.3	0.2
Europe excl fmr USSR	28.3	26.2	25.7	27.4	26.9	26.9	30.6	30.9	28.8	28.6
– European Union	23.4	21.6	21.7	23.5	23.6	23.7	27.5	27.9	26.3	26.2
– Eastern Europe	2.2	1.7	1.7	1.1	0.8	0.6	0.5	0.5	0.6	0.5
– Rest of Europe	2.8	2.8	2.3	2.8	2.6	2.6	2.6	2.5	1.9	1.9
Europe former USSR	0.3	0.4	0.6	0.6	0.9	0.9	0.7	0.5	0.7	0.6
Oceania	0.7	0.5	0.6	0.7	0.9	1.0	0.7	0.6	0.8	0.6
Other	0.0	0.1	0.0	0.1	0.2	0.0	0.1	0.2	1.4	0.4
USA/Etats–Unis d'Amer	20.1	20.3	20.1	23.5	24.1	23.0	23.1	23.7	22.3	23.4
Argentina/Argentine	4.6	6.5	6.7	7.6	8.2	10.3	10.8	10.7	12.5	13.2
Germany/Allemagne				8.8	9.0	8.9	10.2	10.1	8.9	8.2
Japan/Japon	7.1	7.6	7.2	5.9	5.6	6.1	5.5	5.1	5.1	5.9
Italy/Italie	2.0	2.5	3.3	3.7	3.9	3.7	5.8	5.9	5.4	5.6
Saudi Arabia	6.8	3.7	7.4	6.4	7.4	6.1	4.0	2.4	2.3	1.7
France, Monaco	3.9	3.0	2.8	2.8	2.8	2.7	2.6	2.6	2.5	2.7
Canada	3.1	2.7	2.2	2.5	2.4	2.7	2.5	2.3	2.4	2.4
United Kingdom	2.8	2.3	2.0	2.1	1.9	2.1	2.2	1.8	2.3	2.4
Korea, Republic of	0.2	0.4	0.4	0.6	0.7	1.3	1.7	2.4	2.2	2.3

	1988	1989	1990	1991	1992	1993	1994	1995	1996	1997
Afrique	3.8	3.8	3.2	3.3	3.2	2.9	3.1	3.4	3.2	2.9
Amériques	40.4	39.6	38.1	38.5	43.5	47.2	46.1	43.1	45.0	46.5
– Amérique du Nord	27.4	25.0	26.3	21.7	20.8	21.9	21.7	19.9	20.6	18.9
– ALAI	11.1	11.0	10.2	15.6	21.1	23.6	22.4	21.4	22.9	25.7
– MCAC	0.5	0.9	0.4	0.4	0.6	0.6	0.6	0.5	0.3	0.4
– Caraïbes	1.0	2.4	1.1	0.7	0.8	0.8	1.2	1.0	0.9	1.1
– Autre Amérique	0.3	0.4	0.2	0.2	0.2	0.3	0.3	0.3	0.3	0.6
Asie anc. URSS exclus	18.8	20.0	20.7	22.0	19.8	19.6	19.0	20.8	19.6	17.7
– Moyen–Orient	3.7	3.4	3.8	3.9	4.0	3.6	2.6	3.1	3.1	3.1
Asie ancienne URSS							0.0	0.0	0.0	0.0
Europe anc. URSS exclus	34.4	33.8	35.4	34.0	31.6	27.8	29.7	29.7	29.4	29.2
– Union Européenne	29.8	30.4	32.4	32.1	30.2	26.4	28.0	27.8	27.0	27.5
– Europe de l'Est	2.1	2.1	1.6	0.9	0.7	0.6	0.8	0.8	1.0	0.9
– Autre de l'Europe	2.4	1.4	1.4	1.0	0.7	0.8	1.0	1.2	1.4	0.8
Europe ancienne URSS	0.5	0.6	0.7	0.3	0.4	0.6	0.5	1.4	1.2	1.4
Océanie	1.4	1.2	0.7	0.8	0.7	0.7	0.7	0.8	0.6	0.6
Autre	0.8	1.0	1.2	1.1	1.0	1.3	0.8	0.8	1.1	1.6
USA/Etats–Unis d'Amer	24.9	22.5	24.6	20.2	19.7	20.7	20.6	18.9	19.5	17.8
Argentina/Argentine	2.2	1.7	2.1	4.7	8.5	9.5	9.5	8.7	10.8	12.8
Netherlands/Pays–Bas	7.5	7.6	7.9	6.8	6.5	6.4	7.1	6.3	7.4	7.5
Japan/Japon	6.7	7.0	7.5	8.1	6.4	6.0	5.9	6.7	6.4	5.8
Germany/Allemagne				6.8	5.8	4.7	4.7	4.6	4.4	4.9
Italy/Italie	4.2	3.6	5.1	4.3	4.4	3.4	3.8	3.7	3.2	3.2
Belgium–Luxembourg	2.7	2.9	3.1	3.4	3.3	2.9	3.1	3.5	3.0	2.8
United Kingdom	3.1	2.9	3.0	3.3	3.6	2.9	2.8	2.9	2.8	2.4
Paraguay	1.0	1.2	1.2	1.6	1.5	2.5	2.4	2.8	2.8	2.7
Chile/Chili	1.8	2.0	1.5	2.1	2.6	2.9	2.3	2.6	2.2	2.3

4. Special Imports C.I.F. by Commodities according to the S.I.T.C. (Rev. 2) in million U.S. Dollars
Importations Spéciales C.A.F. par Produits d'après la C.T.C.I. (Rév. 2) en millions de Dollars E.U.

SITC CTCI	COMMODITY	1994 QUANTITY QUANTITE	1994 VALUE VALEUR	1995 QUANTITY QUANTITE	1995 VALUE VALEUR	1996 QUANTITY QUANTITE	1996 VALUE VALEUR	1997 QUANTITY QUANTITE	1997 VALUE VALEUR	PRODUIT
	ALL COMMODITIES		35510.5		53736.8		56732.2		65074.7	TOUS PRODUITS
0	FOOD AND LIVE ANIMALS		3198.0		4795.5		5160.7		4828.7	ALIMENTS,ANIMAUX VIVANTS
001	*LIVE ANIMALS FOR FOOD	W 113007	124.8	W 135341	154.6	W 49836	67.4	W 62450	82.6	ANIMAUX VIVANTS
0011	BOVINE SPECIES,LIVE	W 108077	108.2	W 132760	130.2	W 43650	45.3	W 52903	58.3	ESPECE BOVINE
01	MEAT AND PREPARATIONS		146.6		231.5		228.0		255.7	VIANDES ET PREPARATIONS
011	MEAT FRESH,CHILLD,FROZEN	W 103486	144.7	W 148427	226.8	W 160430	219.4	W 137155	243.5	VIANDES FRAICHES,REF,CONGE
0111	BOVINE MEAT FRESH,FROZEN	W 76602	116.8	W 111148	178.7	W 131894	188.6	W 104506	203.5	VIANDES BOVIN FRAI,REF
02	DAIRY PRODCTS,BIRDS'EGGS		273.8		648.0		543.4		485.4	PRODUITS LAITIERS,OEUFS
022	MILK AND CREAM	W 106591	157.5	W 350755	433.2	W 510855	403.1	W 284527	377.1	LAIT ET CREME
0224	MILK,CREAM PRESERVED ETC	W 94668	151.4	W 291555	400.5	W 417894	350.0	W 159273	313.9	LAIT,CREME CONS,CONC
02243	MILK DRY,OVER 1.5% FAT	W 55076	91.3	W 216913	276.1	W 315492	228.6	W 101169	209.6	LAIT POUDRE SUP 1.5%
024	CHEESE AND CURD	W 31650	90.7	W 89345	168.8	W 33866	107.4	W 28704	88.8	FROMAGE ET CAILLEBOTTE
03	FISH AND PREPARATIONS		261.0		440.1		512.2		482.5	POISSONS ET PREPARATIONS
034	FISH,FRESH,CHILLED,FROZN	W 132455	117.3	W 174500	192.8	W 235197	229.7	W 150077	224.8	POISSON FRAIS, REFRIG,CONG
035	FISH SALTED,DRIED,SMOKED	W 22860	123.6	W 31341	198.0	W 34383	210.8	W 36377	193.9	POISSON SECHE,SALE,FUME
04	CEREALS AND PREPARATIONS		1604.5		1927.7		2382.9		1943.6	CEREALES ET PRODUITS
041	WHEAT ETC UNMILLED	W 32412	4.4	W 34789	6.2	W 6561100	1029.1	W 4850161	974.5	FROMENT,EPEAUTRE
0412	OTHER WHEAT ETC UNMILLED	W 7251	0.9	W 34789	6.2	W 6313254	965.3	W 4734201	956.2	AUTRE FROMENT NON MOULU
042	RICE	W 1077981	323.9	W 995686	293.6	W 849685	314.2	W 888897	323.4	RIZ
0422	RICE SEMI-MILLED,MILLED	W 746727	245.1	W 562824	214.6	W 561840	233.4	W 541367	224.9	RIZ POLI,GLACE INCL BRISURES
04221	RICE MILLED UNBROKEN	W 711285	237.9	W 551713	212.2	W 550232	230.6	W 531192	222.3	RIZ POLI,GLACE EXCL BRISURES
044	MAIZE UNMILLED	W 1409985	199.1	W 1309332	180.9	W 322584	81.0	W 534695	92.6	MAIS NON MOULU
048	CEREAL ETC PREPARATIONS	W 6604925	995.1	W 6857100	1340.7	W 2806457	805.6	W 768367	390.9	PREPTNS A BASE CEREALES
0481	PREPD BREAKFAST FOOD ETC	W 6109729	859.1	W 6131439	1034.1	W 1543818	400.3	W 64486	30.1	CEREALES TRAVAILLEES
04811	CEREAL FLAKED,ROLLED,ETC	W 6109434	858.5	W 6116319	1027.4	W 1539574	389.0	W 59542	16.7	GRAINS GERMES DE CEREALES
0482	MALT INCLUDING FLOUR	W 478020	114.9	W 688226	230.3	W 1207494	308.1	W 643551	258.7	MALT MEME TORREFIE
05	VEGETABLES AND FRUIT		647.3		1001.0		992.0		1040.9	LEGUMES ET FRUITS
054	VEG ETC FRSH,SMPLY PRSVD	W 755959	348.4	W 1430394	435.8	W 4702242	403.8	W 770797	504.5	LEGUMES FRAIS,CONG,SECS
0542	LEGUMINOUS VEGETBLES DRY	W 258599	118.2	W 205941	98.5	W 122820	72.6	W 196469	114.0	LEGUMES A COSSE SECS
0546	VEGETABLES SIMPLY PRESVD	W 95327	107.3	W 159973	165.7	W 129124	163.6	W 173697	180.6	LEGUMES CONG,CONSER
057	FRUIT,NUTS,FRESH,DRIED	W 254283	224.0	W 581066	414.8	W 1036392	445.9	W 428470	383.6	FRUITS FRAIS OU SECS
0579	FRUIT FRESH OR DRIED NES	W 106784	95.2	W 227695	204.3	W 572033	236.5	W 238491	198.8	FRUITS FRAIS,SECS NDA
07	COFFEE,TEA,COCOA,SPICES		40.7		172.3		152.3		146.4	CAFE,THE,CACAO,EPICES
1	BEVERAGES AND TOBACCO		141.1		357.0		280.9		314.2	BOISSONS ET TABACS
11	BEVERAGES		105.6		295.7		211.4		218.1	BOISSONS
112	ALCOHOLIC BEVERAGES	W 68383	96.7	W 291371	208.3	W 228422	201.3	W 142518	208.2	BOISSONS ALCOOLIQUES
2	CRUDE MATERLS,EXCL FUELS		2003.7		2501.3		2610.8		2753.2	MAT BRUTES NON COMESTIBLES
22	OIL SEEDS,OLEAGINOUS FRT		196.8		208.7		264.8		406.2	GRAINES,FRUITS OLEAGINEUX
222	SEEDS FOR'SOFT'FIXED OIL	W 813186	194.2	W 887152	206.4	W 959334	262.9	W 1466579	404.2	GRAINES HUILES FIXES
2222	SOYA BEANS	W 801784	187.4	W 878664	200.8	W 944273	252.7	W 1449860	393.0	FEVES DE SOJA
23	RUBBER, CRUDE		249.6		345.3		333.2		298.8	CAOUTCHOUC BRUT
232	NATURAL RUBBER,GUMS	W 99900	112.6	W 110155	190.8	W 92916	147.6	W 105539	128.8	LATEX CAOUTCHOUC NATUREL
233	RUBBER,SYNTHTIC,RECLAIMD	W 74007	137.0	W 375681	154.6	W 141009	185.7	W 98155	170.0	LATEX CAOUTCH SYNTH REGEN
2331	SYNTHETIC RUBBER ETC	W 73988	137.0	W 375663	154.5	W 140844	185.5	W 97756	169.8	LATEX CAOUTCH SYNTHETIQUE
251	*PULP AND WASTE PAPER	W 151519	83.4	W 237306	189.9		160.5		174.7	PATES A PAPIER,DECHETS
26	TEXTILE FIBRES AND WASTE		696.6		747.7		1032.5		1005.1	FIBRES TEXTILES
263	COTTON	W 393103	593.1	W 294844	575.8	W 582937	899.4	W 494368	862.1	COTON
2631	RAW COTTON,EXCL LINTERS	W 365729	585.0	W 279027	563.6	W 567211	891.0	W 472612	852.1	COTON EN MASSE
27	CRUDE FERTLZR,MINRLS NES		166.6		214.7		194.6		241.0	ENGRAIS MINERAUX BRUTS
28	METALLIFEROUS ORES,SCRAP		491.6		628.3		456.0		445.9	MINERAIS METAL,DECHETS
287	BASE METAL ORES,CONC NES	W 1290190	438.6		571.4		436.0	W 707982	433.8	MINERAIS METAUX COMMUNS
2871	CPR ORE ETC,CEMENT COPPR	W 433968	233.9	W 394034	346.2		307.6	W 422600	294.0	MINERAIS DE CUIVRE,MATTES
28711	COPPER ORES,EXCL MATTE	W 433968	233.9	W 394034	346.2	W 379668	307.6	W 422600	294.0	MINERAIS DE CUIVRE
2873	ALUMINIUM ORES,ALUMINA	W 688425	136.7	W 444200	131.3	W 91434	30.1	W 45292	11.0	MINERAIS D'ALUMINIUM
28732	ALUMINA(ALUMINIUM OXIDE)	W 683293	136.1	W 443974	131.2	W 90293	29.8	W 5482	9.3	ALUMINE (OXYDE ALUMINIUM)
3	MINERAL FUELS ETC		5294.8		6519.1		7477.5		7605.9	COMBUSTIBLES MINERAUX LUB
32	COAL,COKE AND BRIQUETTES		783.6		941.3		882.6		921.0	HOUILLES,COKES,BRIQUETTES
322	COAL,LIGNITE AND PEAT	MW 12379	618.7	MW 12542	722.6	MW 12847	716.6	MW 12299	753.6	HOUILLES,LIGNITES,TOURBE
3222	OTH COAL,NOT AGGLOMERATD	MW 11475	576.5	MW 12082	696.9	MW 12118	681.6	MW 11650	724.0	AUTRES HOUILLES
323	BRIQUETS,COKE,SEMI-COKE	W 1731627	165.0	W 1830747	218.7	W 1853234	166.0	W 1707704	167.5	BRIQUETTES
3232	COKE,SEMI-COKE,RTRT CRBN	W 1731627	165.0	W 1830747	218.7	W 1853234	166.0	W 1707682	167.4	COKES ET SEMI-COKES
33	PETROLEUM AND PRODUCTS		4250.9		5141.0		6093.8		6071.5	PETROLE ET DERIVES
333	CRUDE PETROLEUM	MW 23098	2562.7	MW 22483	2756.4	MW 24887	3640.5	MW 24433	3380.0	HUILES BRUTES DE PETROLE
334	PETROLEUM PRODUCTS,REFIN	MW 12382	1616.4	MW 11790	2299.0	MW 19580	2357.0	MW 12962	2580.7	PRODUITS RAFFINES
3341	GASOLINE,OTH LIGHT OILS	W 5580171	783.9	W 6615998	1386.2	MW 11917	1116.3	W 6272810	1255.0	ESSENCES POUR MOTEURS
33419	OTH LIGHT PETROLEUM OILS	W 5542389	777.8	W 5988132	1259.7	MW 11133	982.8	W 6035897	1204.2	AUTRES HUILES LEGERES
3343	GAS OILS	W 2824829	432.2	W 3655856	622.0	W 4157785	815.7	W 4939831	931.2	GAS OILS
3344	FUEL OILS,NES	W 3523069	293.7	W 804353	92.0	W 2603139	185.7	W 59628	9.2	FUEL OILS
3345	LUBS,PETROLEUM OILS NES	W 210010	63.7	W 194423	100.8	W 313214	95.6	W 1124202	229.7	HUILES LUBRIFIANTES
341	*GAS,NATURAL AND MANUFCT	W 1592270	260.3	W 2129834	436.9	W 2179602	501.2	W 1626721	613.4	GAZ NATUREL,GAZ MANUFACT
3413	PETROLM GASES,LIQUEFIED	W 1576083	257.6	W 2084647	428.2	W 2030458	467.0	W 1625596	613.0	GAZ DE PETROLE LIQUEFIE
34131	LIQUEFIED PROPANE,BUTANE	W 1313057	214.0	W 1818732	369.5	W 1738408	399.9	W 1409441	555.7	PROPANE,BUTANE LIQUEFIES
4	ANIMAL,VEGETABLE OIL,FAT		347.0		396.4		400.1		355.2	HUILES,GRAISSES ANIM,VEG
42	FIXED VEGETABLE OIL,FAT		284.9		318.3		333.6		320.5	HUILES VEGETALES FIXES
423	FIXED VEG OILS,SOFT	W 296125	223.6		251.2	W 254361	263.8	W 264673	253.9	HUILES VEGET DOUCES FIXES
4232	SOYA BEAN OIL	W 254522	156.0	W 204520	136.1	W 167480	94.3	W 151137	85.0	HUILE DE SOJA
5	CHEMCLS,RELATED PROD NES		5803.9		8042.4		8806.3		9815.7	PRODUITS CHIMIQUES
51	ORGANIC CHEMICALS		2409.9		3227.8		3248.6		3497.8	PROD CHIMIQ ORGANIQUES
511	HYDROCARBONS NES,DERIVS	W 193432	132.4	W 287255	231.5	W 352324	241.3	W 319324	230.6	HYDROCARBURES NDA
512	ALCOHOLS,PHENOLS ETC	W 1580605	661.7	W 1801334	814.4	W 1455232	589.9	W 1196494	511.7	PHENOLS,PHENOLS-ALCOOLS
5121	ACYCLIC ALCOHOLS,DERIVS	W 1549891	596.7	W 1774907	738.2	W 1400988	507.4	W 1167786	437.9	ALCOOLS ACYCLIQUES
51211	METHYL ALCOHOL(METHANOL)	W 493009	149.7	W 573674	148.2	W 555370	78.5	W 609243	114.8	ALCOOLS METHYLIQUES
51216	ETHYL ALC,DENATRD SPIRIT	W 1003697	400.3	W 1130649	496.6	W 738786	340.4	W 424033	188.9	ALCOOL ETHYLIQUE NON DENAT
513	CARBOXYLIC ACIDS ETC	W 176138	209.8	W 308623	362.5	W 596165	365.8	W 321937	419.3	ACIDES CARBOXYLIQUES
5137	MONOACIDS AND DERIVATIVS	W 124100	133.2	W 156144	229.1	W 230672	235.6	W 233518	278.9	ACIDES MONOCARBOXYLIQUES
514	NITROGEN-FNCTN COMPOUNDS	W 119827	645.2	W 163158	778.3	W 197384	890.3	W 178853	993.9	COMPOSES FONCT AZOTEES
5148	OTH NITROGN-FNCTN CMPNDS	W 65725	360.9	W 75979	448.1	W 86387	519.6	W 107082	593.4	AUTRES COMPOSES AZOTES
51482	IMIDE-,IMIDE-FNCT CMPNDS	W 21123	221.7	W 23167	269.6	W 22928	305.3	W 29049	356.5	COMPOSES A FONCTION IMIDE
515	ORG-INORG COMPOUNDS ETC	W 58519	609.3	W 77770	819.6	W 84810	911.6	W 96733	1108.2	COMPOSES ORGANO-MINERAUX
5154	ORGANO-SULPHUR CMPNDS	W 27644	114.1	W 36470	152.8	W 38178	159.6	W 42524	167.6	THIOCOMPOSES ORGANIQUES
5156	HETEROCYCLIC CMPDS ETC	W 18965	368.6	W 22458	470.5	W 23081	526.4	W 24029	664.7	COMPOSES HETEROCYCLIQUES
51569	OTH HETEROCYC CMPDS,ETC	W 15576	359.0	W 17256	454.5	W 22233	518.9	W 23280	656.0	AUT COMP HETEROCYCLIQUES
516	OTHER ORGANIC CHEMICALS		151.8		221.7		249.9	W 76691	234.5	AUTRES PROD ORGANIQUES
52	INORGANIC CHEMICALS		417.3		578.2		603.5		612.6	PROD CHIM INORGANIQUES
522	INORG ELEMNTS,OXIDES,ETC	W 1023471	236.3	W 1040104	313.5	W 1008646	314.8	W 1200734	313.7	ELEMENTS INORGANIQUES
5222	INORGANIC ACIDS ETC	W 643744	109.4	W 618553	129.2	W 545110	117.0	W 546587	124.7	ACIDES INORGANIQUES
523	OTHR INORG CHEMICALS ETC	W 545744	169.1	W 3955628	245.9	W 926759	273.8	W 847008	281.2	AUT PRODUITS CHIMIQUES INORG
53	DYES,TANNING,COLOUR PROD		290.0		447.6		470.9		526.6	PROD TEINTURE,COLORANTS
531	SYNT DYE,NAT INDGO,LAKES	W 8626	124.4	W 12588	155.4	W 12697	160.3	W 17526	170.4	MAT COLOR ORGAN,LAQUES
5311	SYNTHIC ORGNIC DYESTUFFS	W 8115	117.5	W 11562	144.1	W 12172	150.3	W 16130	158.9	MAT COLOR ORGAN SYNTHET
533	PIGMENTS,PAINTS,ETC	W 71121	157.8	W 116125	279.2	W 129822	295.2	W 134993	333.2	PIGMENTS,PEINTURES,VERNIS

4. Special Imports C.I.F. by Commodities according to the S.I.T.C. (Rev. 2) in million U.S. Dollars
Importations Spéciales C.A.F. par Produits d'après la C.T.C.I. (Rév. 2) en millions de Dollars E.U.

SITC CTCI	COMMODITY	1994 QUANTITY QUANTITE	1994 VALUE VALEUR	1995 QUANTITY QUANTITE	1995 VALUE VALEUR	1996 QUANTITY QUANTITE	1996 VALUE VALEUR	1997 QUANTITY QUANTITE	1997 VALUE VALEUR	PRODUIT
541	*MEDICINAL,PHARM PRODUCT	MK 9465	734.7		978.9		1299.7		1461.5	PROD MEDICINAUX PHARMACEUT
5413	ANTIBIOTICS IN BULK	K 2608147	126.3	K 3688480	168.4	K 3535879	165.0	K 4700280	168.9	ANTIBIOTIQUES NDA
5416	GLYCOSIDES,GLANDS,SERA	K 377042	159.7	K 620611	150.0	K 2437679	214.3	K 1022783	192.0	HETEROSIDES
54164	ANTISERA,MICROB VACCINES	K 258125	124.0	K 321422	90.3	K 669120	155.3	K 586251	160.7	SERUMS,VACCINS
5417	MEDICAMENTS	K 1835088	267.7	K 5179929	397.3	K 8198085	617.0	MK 10740	788.6	MEDICAMENTS
54179	— CONTNG OTH SUBSTANCES	K 955891	148.2	K 3688490	224.9	K 6001229	379.4	K 8212184	520.7	MED CONT AUT SUBSTANCES
55	PERFUME,CLEANING ETC PRD		144.3		243.7		256.3		325.6	PROD POUR PARFUM,TOILETTE
562	*FERTILIZERS,MANUFACTURE	W 5434972	711.5	W 4658660	730.0		939.9	W 7204902	1113.8	ENGRAIS MANUFACTURES
5621	CHEM NITROGENOUS FERTLZR	W 1378541	151.3	W 1260981	167.3		217.7	W 1950188	230.6	ENGRAIS AZOTES
5623	CHEM POTASSIC FERTILIZER	W 2792178	335.9	W 2534869	383.2	W 3061691	453.0	W 3619071	528.4	ENGRAIS POTASSIQUES
56231	POTASSIUM CHLORIDE	W 2752089	326.9	W 2484865	371.4	W 3015769	441.6	W 3558954	514.2	CHLORURE DE POTASSIUM
5629	FERTILIZERS NES	W 822842	162.1	W 568433	133.9	W 839440	200.3	W 1107908	262.2	ENGRAIS NDA
56292	NITROG–PHOS FERTILZR NES	W 726216	143.1	W 464475	111.6	W 731938	172.4	W 978862	230.6	ENGRAIS NDA CONT N P
58	PLASTIC MATERIALS ETC		672.4		1285.6		1338.3		1438.9	MAT PLAST ARTIFICIELLES
582	PROD OF CONDENSATION ETC	W 114050	276.0	W 211120	489.1	W 297062	515.4	W 288324	542.0	PROD CONDENS,POLYCOND
5823	ALKYDS,OTHER POLYESTERS	W 50182	107.4	W 126220	276.8	W 134045	254.4	W 175592	254.1	ALKYDES ET AUT POLYESTERS
58231	— IN PRIMARY FORMS	W 45111	77.3	W 120173	241.7	W 128375	220.5	W 170002	219.6	SOUS FORMES PRIMAIRES
583	POLYMERIZATION ETC PRODS	W 227685	360.8	W 1821391	747.9	W 1934913	761.7	W 533044	828.7	PROD POLYMERISATION
5839	OTH POLYMRZTION ETC PROD	W 31951	133.4	W 48211	193.5	W 60953	206.1	W 62379	230.8	AUT PROD POLYMER COPOLYM
59	CHEMICAL MATERIALS NES		421.6		549.1		647.5		835.4	MAT PROD CHIMIQUES NDA
591	PESTICIDES,DISINFECTANTS	W 11544	86.8	W 84026	105.1	W 51759	118.9	W 31705	212.0	DESINF,INSECT,FONG,HERB
598	MISCEL CHEM PRODUCTS NES	W 108172	299.4	W 141716	378.2	W 331838	454.0	W 190323	525.9	PROD DIV INDUST CHIM NDA
5989	CHEM PRODUCTS,PREPS NES	W 62788	214.2	W 80518	284.0	W 184319	341.6	W 129787	409.4	PROD PREP CHIMIQUES NDA
59899	OTH CHEM PRODS,PREPS,NES	W 38229	152.5	W 42013	204.5	W 104970	243.2	W 62033	277.0	AUT PRODUITS CHIMIQUES NDA
6	BASIC MANUFACTURES		3176.1		6169.7		5894.9		6991.2	ART MANUFACTURES
61	LEATHER,DRESSED FUR,ETC		200.6		188.4		169.9		177.6	CUIRS,PELLETERIES
611	LEATHER	W 16724	184.0	W 108347	171.8	W 20796	148.5	W 14688	161.5	CUIRS,PEAUX PREPARES
6114	LEATHR BOVINE NES,EQUINE	W 13837	146.3	W 19855	143.6	W 18162	123.7	W 10474	120.0	CUIRS DE BOVINS
62	RUBBER MANUFACTURES NES		323.0		802.3		540.1		667.4	CAOUTCHOUC MANUFACTURE
625	RUBBER TYRES, TUBES ETC	W 67747	131.2	W 203868	285.5	W 113102	240.7	W 140440	322.0	PNEUS CAOUTCHOUC VULCANISE
628	RUBBER ARTICLES NES	W 5005	127.2	W 27480	428.8	W 20388	190.6	W 15371	218.6	OUVRAGES CAOUTCHOUC NDA
6289	OTH RUBBER ARTICLES NES	W 3384	107.8	W 6570	398.6	W 10753	149.3	W 11490	172.7	AUT OUVR CAOUTCHOUC NDA
62898	UNHARD RUBBER PRODS NES	W 3369	106.9	W 6471	397.8	W 10700	148.4	W 11369	171.8	OUV CAOUT VULC NON DURCI
64	PAPER,PAPERBOARD AND MFR		433.9		1003.6		926.0		1018.8	PAPIERS,CARTONS & OUVRAGES
641	PAPER AND PAPERBOARD	W 467306	388.3	W 848666	874.1	W 1850189	792.9	W 996520	843.8	PAPIERS ET CARTONS
6411	NEWSPRINT	W 287588	155.8	W 377537	398.8	W 384242	298.7	W 473197	268.7	PAPIER JOURNAL
6412	PRINTG,WRITING PAPER NES	W 70934	75.5	W 162340	217.1	W 175100	199.0	W 243330	268.9	PAPIERS POUR L'IMPRESSION
64122	— COATED,IMPREGNATD ETC	W 70807	74.7	W 161654	215.0	W 173923	195.8	W 241860	264.0	PAPIERS IMPRESSION COUCHES
65	TEXTILE YARN,FABRICS,ETC		629.9		1371.8		1118.5		1212.7	FILS,TISSUS,ARTICLES TEXTILE
651	TEXTILE YARN	W 44949	212.1	W 386450	482.5	W 307937	450.8	W 127342	486.7	FILS TEXTILES
6514	SYN FIB YRN,BULK,MONOFIL	W 22752	116.5	W 136841	287.7	W 225671	306.7	W 90554	335.3	FILS CONT 85% FIB TEXT SYNTH
65142	— NONTXT ETC CONT PAMID	W 12775	71.3	W 38139	158.3	W 51082	182.6	W 44820	195.0	FILS NON TEX FI CON POLYAMID
653	WOVN MAN–MADE FIB FABRIC	W 32289	198.0	W 85647	419.4	W 45275	169.4	W 39116	175.0	TISSUS FIBRES SYNTH,ARTIF
6531	CONT SYNT WEAVES NONPILE	W 17020	103.2	W 48967	203.7	W 23931	78.7	W 13211	76.3	TISSUS FIBRES SYNTH CONTINUE
65315	CONT SYN TXTL FABRIC NES	W 15848	99.2	W 45427	188.4	W 16405	55.5	W 5422	50.6	TIS PLUS 85% TEXT SYNT CONT
657	SPECIAL TXTL FABRC,PRODS	W 9216	93.4	W 18910	147.2	W 22731	200.8	W 30189	223.5	TISSUS SPECIAUX
66	NONMETAL MINERAL MFS NES		296.1		483.5		578.4		635.8	ART MIN NON METALLIQUES
664	GLASS	W 49105	93.2	W 102017	143.3	W 121597	214.7	W 156900	218.3	VERRE
67	IRON AND STEEL		284.5		503.1		527.7		866.6	FER ET ACIER
674	IRN,STL UNIV,PLATE,SHEET	W 80259	115.6	W 153438	232.2	W 450043	197.2	W 324162	290.0	LARGES PLATS,TOLES
678	IRON,STL TUBES,PIPES,ETC	W 68498	82.0	W 62289	112.8	W 76998	127.6	W 186172	318.7	TUBES,TUYAUX EN FONTE,FER
68	NON–FERROUS METALS		546.1		996.3		852.6		1106.8	METAUX NON FERREUX
682	COPPER EXC CEMENT COPPER	W 97673	255.4	W 130609	456.2		395.7	W 148719	434.4	CUIVRE
6821	COPPER NES,ALLOYS,UNWRT	W 67313	153.5	W 91814	288.7		251.6	W 117127	310.0	CUIVRE BRUT
68212	COPPER REFINED,UNWROUGHT	W 64330	144.7	W 90805	285.4	W 102872	251.4	W 117068	309.7	CUIVRE AFFINE BRUT
6822	COPPER,ALLOYS WORKED	W 30360	102.0	W 38795	167.5	W 45006	144.2	W 31592	124.4	CUIVRE,ALLIAGES OUVRES
684	ALUMINIUM	W 43826	125.2	W 81091	274.9	W 65366	240.7	W 128427	411.1	ALUMINIUM
6842	ALUMINIUM,ALLOYS WORKED	W 36535	114.0	W 65841	241.7	W 56773	224.6	W 122719	399.8	ALUMINIUM,ALLIAGES OUVRE
68422	ALUMNM PLATE,SHEET,STRIP	W 24150	59.9	W 46414	150.7	W 41156	138.8	W 100113	293.7	TOLES, PLANCHES EN ALU
69	METAL MANUFACTURES NES		446.1		782.8		1117.1		1231.8	ART MANUFACT EN METAL NDA
695	TOOLS	W 5541	84.9	W 19739	180.4	W 25160	361.6	W 25203	253.1	OUTILS A MAIN
6954	BLADES,TIPS,ETC FR TOOLS	W 1933	62.0	W 7029	123.1	W 12641	305.9	W 6505	189.2	OUTILS POUR MACHINE–OUTIL
69541	PARTS TO INSERT IN TOOLS	W 1629	39.4	W 5561	87.2	W 12023	271.9	W 5710	141.9	OUTILS DE FORAGE
699	BASE METAL MFRS NES	W 20260	165.5		253.1	W 84012	317.7	W 77822	496.1	ART MANUFACTURES MET NDA
7	MACHINES,TRANSPORT EQUIP		13516.6		21020.5		21481.7		27659.2	MACHINES MATERIEL TRANSPORT
71	POWER GENERATING EQUIPMT		1186.8		1133.2		1470.6		2034.0	MACHINES GENERATRICES
712	STEAM ENGINES,TURBINES	W 9223	431.3	W 1510	26.0	W 1111	58.1	W 1157	42.5	MACHINES A VAPEUR D'EAU PIEC
7129	STM ENGINE ETC PARTS NES	W 9210	430.3	W 1508	25.9	W 993	57.4	W 86	10.2	PARTIES,PIECES DU 712.6
713	INTRNL COMBUS PSTN ENGIN	W 45753	491.7	W 75824	699.4	W 171184	849.2	W 92278	1192.1	MOTEURS EXPL COMB INT, PIECE
7132	MOTOR VEHCL PISTN ENGINS	W 22787	227.5	W 26976	287.2	W 28696	366.9	W 41389	520.1	MOTEURS EXPL POUR VEHICULES
7139	PISTON ENGINE PARTS NES	W 17951	187.5	W 41526	291.5	W 137639	406.1	W 41107	537.5	PIECES POUR 713.2,3,8
714	ENGINES AND MOTORS NES	W 175	87.9	W 558	170.9	W 1622	209.8	W 1272	296.4	MOTEURS NON ELECTRIQUES
716	ROTATING ELECTRIC PLANT	W 6593	112.8	W 19608	186.9	W 19945	222.3	W 28086	385.8	APP ELECTR ROTATIFS,PIECES
7162	AC MTRS,GENRTRS,GEN SETS	W 4858	72.5	W 12629	108.6	W 15464	141.1	W 22667	277.5	MOTEURS ELECTRIQUES
72	MACHS FOR SPCL INDUSTRYS		1729.4		2831.3		2703.8		3717.9	MAC SPECIALES POUR INDUST
723	CIVIL ENGNEERG EQUIP ETC	W 7461	72.1	W 15086	128.3	W 16931	127.7	W 32195	246.6	APPAREILS DE GENIE CIVIL
7234	CONST,MINING MACHNRY NES	W 6875	60.7	W 13441	111.2	W 15185	112.5	W 28701	218.2	MACH POUR LA CONST, MINES
724	TEXTILE,LEATHER MACHNRY	W 31672	557.1	W 44767	780.0	W 33036	542.9	W 33123	613.2	MACH POUR INDUSTRIE TEXTILE
7243	SEWING MACHS,NEEDLES ETC	W 10255	107.5	W 15133	158.5	W 9166	97.5	W 7097	102.2	MACHINES A COUDRE,PIECES
7244	SPINNING,EXTRDNG,ETC MCH	W 6735	135.3	W 8906	173.3	W 9324	177.0	W 9695	186.6	MACH POUR LE FILAGE
7245	WEAVING,FELT MFG,ETC MCH	W 9425	207.6	W 13020	304.2	W 6888	147.7	W 8979	185.4	METIERS A TISSER,PIECES
726	PRINTG,BKBINDG MACHY,PTS	W 7826	292.1	W 16999	561.9	W 13279	418.9	W 20116	645.5	MACHINES POUR IMPRIMERIE
7264	PRINTING PRESSES	W 5452	170.1	W 12074	339.9	W 8337	246.5	W 14816	446.8	MACHINES A IMPRIMER
72641	ROTARY PRINTING PRESSES	W 5452	170.1	W 12074	339.9	W 8337	246.5	W 14816	446.8	MACH IMPRIMER ROTATIVES
728	OTH MACHY FOR SPCL INDUS	W 25746	623.5	W 47880	1043.1	W 51106	1213.6	W 102488	1756.7	AUT MACH IND PARTICULIERES
7284	MACHY FOR SPCL INDUS NES	W 17098	499.1	W 35353	871.6	W 40232	1067.1	W 78528	1514.8	MACH SPEC IND PARTICUL.
72842	RUBBER,PLASTICS WRKG MCH	W 6753	148.5	W 15210	273.1	W 15343	280.6	W 21671	396.1	MACH IND CAOUT MAT PLAST
72848	OTH MCHY WITH INDIV FNCT	W 6978	245.9	W 17092	456.7	W 19612	636.1	W 48466	859.3	AUTRES MACHINES NDA
73	METALWORKING MACHINERY		418.2		758.1		834.7		970.9	MACH TRAVAIL DES METAUX
736	METALWORKING MACH–TOOLS	W 16430	275.1	W 32622	499.1	W 26730	606.4	W 37415	570.6	MACH–OUTILS TRAVAIL METAUX
7361	METAL CUTTING MACH–TOOLS	W 5815	109.7	W 11834	209.5	W 9037	241.1	W 10061	198.5	MACH–OUT ENLEVEMENT METAL
7362	METAL FORMING MACH–TOOLS	W 7554	89.0	W 13843	118.0	W 11221	155.0	W 21591	204.4	MACH–OUTILS DEFORM METAL
737	METALWORKING MACHNRY NES	W 10254	143.2	W 30203	259.1	W 12618	228.4	W 150104	400.3	MACH TRAV METAUX PIECES
7373	WELDING,BRAZING,ETC MCHS	W 1838	60.0	W 4453	175.8	W 2652	131.6	W 3566	148.9	MACH SOUDAGE ETC PIECES
73732	ELECTRIC WELDERS,ETC	W 1772	56.5	W 4365	171.6	W 2573	128.5	W 3366	146.1	MACH ELECT POUR SOUDER
74	GENRL INDUSTRL MACHY NES		1609.0		2656.4		2955.3		3935.0	MACH APP INDUSTRIE
741	HEATING,COOLING EQUIPMNT	W 15871	228.2	W 48074	398.1	W 46312	480.4	W 63711	722.6	MACH CHAUFFAGE,PIECES
7416	HEATING,COOLING EQU NES	W 5704	82.1	W 11071	153.2	W 20860	166.6	W 22142	297.6	APP CHANGEMENT TEMP
742	PUMPS FOR LIQUIDS ETC	W 5595	141.3	W 16223	210.4	W 13618	220.8	W 14198	285.0	POMPES MOTO–POMPES
743	PUMPS NES,CENTRFUGES ETC	W 16161	242.3	W 39990	402.4	W 45867	473.9	W 45492	583.8	POMPES COMPRES,VENT ETC
7431	PUMPS FOR GASES ETC	W 8709	94.8	W 18146	173.3	W 24524	216.4	W 22744	232.7	POMPES AIR A VIDE,COMPRES

4. Special Imports C.I.F. by Commodities according to the S.I.T.C. (Rev. 2) in million U.S. Dollars
Importations Spéciales C.A.F. par Produits d'après la C.T.C.I. (Rév. 2) en millions de Dollars E.U.

SITC CTCI	COMMODITY	1994 QUANTITY QUANTITE	1994 VALUE VALEUR	1995 QUANTITY QUANTITE	1995 VALUE VALEUR	1996 QUANTITY QUANTITE	1996 VALUE VALEUR	1997 QUANTITY QUANTITE	1997 VALUE VALEUR	PRODUIT
744	MECHANICAL HANDLING EQU	W 14755	135.4	W 39308	297.6	W 39908	346.1	W 66879	524.2	EQUIP MANUTENTION PIECES
7442	LIFTING,LOADING MACH NES	W 6644	76.5	W 13329	162.9	W 17865	199.7	W 21934	233.6	APP LEVAGE,MANUTENTION
745	NONELEC MACHY,TOOLS NES	W 9155	263.9	W 21468	455.6	W 28227	507.7	W 24081	590.6	AUT MACH NON ELEC,PIECES
7452	OTH NONELEC MCHS,PTS NES	W 8778	247.3	W 20734	429.6	W 27683	484.7	W 23276	559.8	AUT MACH NON ELEC,PIECES
74522	PACKAGNG,BOTTLNG,ETC MCH	W 3605	156.0	W 6362	246.9	W 5670	242.8	W 6884	330.3	MACH NETT BOUTEILLES,ETC
749	NONELEC MACH PTS,ACC NES	W 33748	598.1	W 68074	892.6	W 86707	926.6	W 79350	1229.1	PIECES MACH NON ELEC NDA
7491	BALL,ROLLER,ETC BEARINGS	W 15052	199.0	W 22354	273.9	W 19543	251.9	W 24659	308.0	ROULEMENTS BILLES ETC
7492	COCKS,VALVES ETC NES	W 4703	141.2	W 14164	224.7	W 26443	225.8	W 13463	301.5	ART ROB,SIM POUR TUYAUX
7493	SHAFT,CRANK,PULLEY ETC	W 12124	171.4	W 25342	269.5	W 34138	267.6	W 33744	430.1	ARBRES TRANS,VILEBREQUINS
7499	OTH NONELEC MCHY PTS NES	W 1869	86.7	W 6215	124.6	W 6583	181.4	W 7484	189.7	PIECES NON ELECT NDA
75	OFFICE MACHNES,ADP EQUIP		1234.4		1684.4		1776.9		1821.0	MACH BUREAU TRAIT AUTOM
751	OFFICE MACHINES	W 3696	113.8	W 6925	209.6	W 6636	162.6	W 6316	158.5	MACH,APPAREILS DE BUREAU
7518	OFFICE MACHINES NES	W 2970	94.0	W 5623	180.2	W 4926	134.1	W 4772	132.6	MACH,APP DE BUREAU NDA
75182	PHOTO,THERMOCOPY APPARAT	W 1554	60.3	W 5317	169.9	W 4126	123.3	W 4333	123.7	APPAREILS DE PHOTOCOPIE
752	AUTOMTIC DATA PROC EQUIP	W 9452	743.3	W 17651	892.1	W 22213	1040.5	W 21619	1100.9	MACH TRAIT INFORMATION
7522	DIGITAL COMPUTERS	W 1142	139.2	W 972	102.7	W 491	67.6	W 411	68.0	MACH DIGITALES COMPLETES
7523	DIGITL CENTRL PROCESSORS	W 1152	176.6	W 1390	165.8	W 1450	209.6	W 1581	240.1	UNITES CENTRALES
7524	DIGITL CENTRL STOR UNITS	W 733	116.9	W 2487	205.0	W 2757	282.1	W 2941	309.7	UNITES MEMOIRE CENTRALES
7525	ADP PERIPHERAL UNITS	W 5607	166.1	W 11789	279.8	W 16150	324.5	W 15225	285.2	UNITES PERIPHERIQUES
7528	OFF-LINE DATA PROC EQUIP	W 775	141.0	W 858	132.5	W 1331	152.8	W 1421	194.2	MACH AUXIL TRAIT INFORM
759	OFFICE,ADP MCH PTS,ACCES	W 8267	377.5	W 15201	582.8	W 29388	574.0	W 29184	561.7	PIECES DU 751 ET 752
7591	OFFICE MACHINE PARTS NES	W 2782	109.3	W 4522	144.5	W 3864	122.9	W 3805	132.5	PIECES DU 7511,7518
7599	ACCTG,ETC,ADP MCH PTS,AC	W 5485	268.2	W 10679	438.3	W 25525	451.1	W 25379	429.2	PIECES DU 751 ET 752
76	TELECOMM,SOUND EQUIPMENT		1360.6		2215.7		2699.2		3456.0	EQUIPMENT DE TELECOM
762	RADIO BROADCAST RECEIVRS	W 9086	111.5	W 15106	179.7	W 9880	118.2	W 13522	140.2	RECEPTEURS RADIODIFFUSION
764	TELECOM EQPT,PTS,ACC NES	W 20453	1114.8	W 36591	1799.4	W 52368	2394.9	W 60352	3016.7	EQUIP TELECOM,PIECES
7641	LINE TELEPHONE,ETC EQUIP	W 1500	128.0	W 2493	214.6	W 3046	326.7	W 4821	581.9	APP TELEPHON PAR FIL
7643	TV,RADIO TRANSMITTRS ETC	W 1486	276.7	W 2236	373.3	W 3456	641.2	W 5396	907.8	APP EMET TELE RADIO
7649	PTS NES OF EQUIPMT OF 76	W 15478	627.0	W 25725	1069.6	W 32485	1203.0	W 40309	1285.1	PIECES DE LA DIV 76
76491	PTS NES OF APPAR OF 7641	W 816	89.1	W 1597	165.6	W 2797	176.8	W 2911	255.1	PIECES POUR 764.1
76493	TELECOMM EQUIPMT PTS NES	W 6359	256.0	W 11143	445.1	W 15527	516.5	W 21806	655.0	PIECES 761,762,764.3,8
76499	PARTS ETC OF SOUND EQUIP	W 7994	278.7	W 12047	452.9	W 13163	500.6	W 12935	355.7	PIECES NDA POUR 763
77	ELECTRIC MACHNRY NES ETC		2449.8		3594.3		4343.6		5149.5	MACH APP ELECT NDA
771	ELECTRIC POWER MACHY NES	W 7720	165.6	W 14757	263.8	W 21674	324.3	W 30159	404.4	MACH PROD,TRANS ELECTR
7712	OTH ELEC POWER MACHY NES	W 2895	93.9	W 6402	156.4	W 10258	183.0	W 12482	230.4	AUT APP PROD TRANSF ELEC
772	SWITCHGEAR ETC,PARTS NES	W 8746	621.5	W 15815	596.6	W 17148	657.9	W 25565	873.6	APP COUPURE,SECT ETC
7721	SWITCHGEAR ETC	W 6538	509.3	W 12252	442.8	W 13467	490.2	W 20589	669.0	APP COUPURE,SECTIONMNT
773	ELECTR DISTRIBUTNG EQUIP	W 7407	97.4	W 14443	165.7	W 64456	242.8	W 39570	328.1	EQUIPMT DISTRIBUTION ELECT
7731	INSULATED WIRE,CABLE ETC	W 6550	81.3	W 13470	142.4	W 62881	208.9	W 37654	300.6	FILS,CABLES ISOLES ELECT
774	ELECTRO-MEDCL,XRAY EQUIP	W 1001	115.8	W 1324	186.5	W 2383	318.2	W 2726	356.7	APPAREILS MEDICAUX
7742	X-RAY APPARATUS ETC	W 859	108.7	W 1100	152.8	W 1504	200.2	W 1609	197.6	APPAREILS A RAYONS X
775	HOUSEHOLD TYPE EQUIP NES	W 17400	116.6	W 32876	203.5	W 39051	228.7	W 61190	245.5	MACH,APP USAGE DOMESTQUE
776	TRANSISTORS,VALVES,ETC	W 31396	807.7	W 52315	1329.5	W 73964	1579.6	W 74270	1723.8	LAMPES,TUBES,VALVES
7761	TV PICTURE TUBES	W 27096	198.5	W 44967	329.2	W 57530	403.8	W 58684	384.2	TUBES CATHODIQUES
7764	ELECTRONIC MICROCIRCUITS	W 844	448.5	W 1293	743.0	W 2077	813.5	W 1630	949.4	MICROSTRUCTURES ELECTRON
778	ELECTRICAL MACHINERY NES	W 39776	525.6	W 184091	848.9	W 156844	992.3	W 113843	1217.8	AUTRES MACH ELECT NDA
7783	AUTOMOTIVE ELECTR EQUIP	W 6530	138.6	W 27789	179.6	W 14499	239.7	W 19850	290.7	EQUIP ELECT MOTEURS EXPL
77831	IGNITION,STARTING EQUIP	W 4522	111.7	W 8490	134.2	W 8816	160.9	W 13190	204.9	APP ELEC ALLUM,DEMARRAGE
7788	OTH ELEC MACHY,EQUIP NES	W 21713	268.3	W 124203	432.1	W 41557	502.9	W 36612	604.1	AUT MACH APP ELEC NDA
77886	OTH ELEC MACHINERY NES	W 2008	98.3	W 4164	194.5	W 5071	213.9	W 6372	300.4	AUT MACH APP ELECTRIQUES
78	ROAD VEHICLES		3295.0		5784.1		4160.5		5548.1	VEHICULES ROUTIERS
781	PASS MOTOR VEH EXC BUSES	W 179221	1524.1	W 359097	3143.3	W 170913	1603.4	W 273760	2534.6	AUTO TRANSPORT PERSONNES
782	LORRIES,SPCL MTR VEH NES	W 37306	328.0	W 94334	736.2	W 58306	454.8	W 98504	758.7	VEHICULES SPECIAUX,MARCH
7821	LORRIES,TRUCKS	W 35358	268.1	W 93874	724.3	W 57766	440.1	W 97816	742.5	VEHICULES TRANSP MARCHAND
783	ROAD MOTOR VEHICLES NES	W 13670	79.7	W 24413	142.2	W 17183	96.8	W 41803	250.5	VEHICULES ROUTIERS NDA
7831	BUSES	W 11108	61.2	W 22377	125.6	W 16375	89.6	W 40369	237.3	VOITURES TRANSPORT COMMUN
784	MOTOR VEH PRTS,ACCES NES	W 132681	1166.3	W 302388	1486.1	W 356972	1826.3	W 232018	1756.7	PIECES 722,781,782,783
7849	OTHER MOTOR VEHCL PARTS	W 118955	1080.9	W 286757	1389.3	W 341562	1723.5	W 227930	1725.5	PIECES 722,781,782,783
785	CYCLES,ETC MOTRZD OR NOT	W 36388	194.6	W 57883	269.5	W 71672	169.8	W 43253	232.8	MOTOCYCLES SCOOTERS
7853	INVAL CARR, PTS OF 785	W 25262	117.1	W 49437	202.3	W 55358	140.6	W 37222	192.7	FAUTEUILS INVALIDES,PIECES
78539	PARTS,ACCES NES OF 785	W 25243	116.8	W 49389	201.6	W 55256	139.6	W 37138	191.2	PIECES DU 785
79	OTHR TRANSPORT EQUIPMENT		233.7		363.4		537.4		1027.1	AUTRE MATERIEL TRANSPORT
792	AIRCRAFT ETC	W 842	200.9	W 2094	271.3	W 2221	498.8	W 1895	935.2	APP NAVIGATION AERIENNE
7924	AIRCRFT NES OVER 15000KG	W 77	13.2	W 350	28.2	W 483	267.3	W 812	413.0	AERODYNES PLUS 15000 KG
7929	AIRCRAFT PARTS NES	W 345	65.5	W 361	95.6	W 1381	154.1	W 694	269.0	PIECES DU 792
8	MISC MANUFACTURED GOODS		2023.1		3924.3		4352.3		4743.3	ART MANUFACTURES DIVERS
821	*FURNITURE,PARTS THEREOF	W 11864	54.7	W 31747	125.3	W 38877	158.8	W 49586	224.2	MEUBLES ET PIECES
84	CLOTHING AND ACCESSORIES		118.5		372.4		372.0		451.5	VETEMENTS
851	*FOOTWEAR	W 5073	84.3	W 14790	213.9	W 14860	211.1	W 14958	207.4	CHAUSSURES
87	PRECISION INSTRUMNTS NES		700.6		1035.4		1237.4		1342.2	INSTRUM,APPAR SCIENT NDA
872	MEDICAL INSTRUMENTS NES	W 3077	160.1	W 6186	225.8	W 7149	228.3	W 10551	201.6	INSTR,APP MEDIC-CHIR NDA
87202	OTH MEDICAL INSTRUMENTS	W 2544	145.9	W 3696	195.6	W 3825	198.8	W 6493	172.5	INSTRUM,APP MEDECINE
874	MEASURNG,CONTROLNG INSTR	W 6665	472.7	W 12778	693.2	W 10406	866.7	W 10416	957.2	INSTRUMENTS DE MESURE
8742	MEASUR,DRAW ETC INST,PTS	W 1388	99.6	W 2443	153.9	W 3623	243.9	W 4059	225.4	INST DESSIN,TRACAGE,PCS
87421	MEASURNG,DRAWNG ETC INST	W 1319	90.0	W 2360	142.1	W 3475	225.1	W 3914	209.3	INSTRUM DESSIN,TRACAGE
8743	GAS,LIQUID CONTROL INSTR	W 3694	105.8	W 5961	160.1	W 3262	209.7	W 2944	247.4	APP,INSTR MESURE FLUIDES
8748	ELEC MEAS,CONTRL EQU NES	W 947	175.8	W 3091	235.9	W 1477	274.0	W 1499	318.6	APP ELEC ELECTRO MESURE
87483	OTH ELCTRNC MEAS ETC EQU	W 827	162.7	W 2694	221.4	W 1307	262.7	W 1412	308.9	AUT APP ELECTRO DE MESURE
88	PHOTO EQU,OPTICL GDS ETC		336.1		533.5		563.4		560.3	APP,FOURN PHOTO,OP,MONTR
882	PHOTO,CINEMA SUPPLIES	W 12158	187.9	W 18675	261.6	W 19896	300.2	W 16966	296.4	PRODUITS PHOTO,CINEMA
8822	PHOTO FILM EXC DEV CINMA	W 10405	155.4	W 14795	209.3	W 16177	256.8	W 13631	256.2	PLAQUES,PELLICULES,FILMS
89	MISC MANUFCTRD GOODS NES		704.4		1558.1		1717.2		1845.7	ART MANUFACTURES DIVERS
892	PRINTED MATTER	W 12389	134.0	W 45293	327.5	W 142978	437.5	W 87374	486.5	IMPRIMES
8921	PRINTED BOOKS,GLOBES,ETC	W 6666	62.1	W 23477	174.7	W 54533	219.4	W 35193	257.6	LIVRES,BROCHURES,CARTES
89211	PRINTED BOOKS,PAMPHLETS	W 6354	60.7	W 23024	172.4	W 54114	217.7	W 33722	247.5	LIVRES,BROCHURES
893	ARTICLES OF PLASTIC NES		204.5		454.3		502.1		540.9	OUVRAGES EN MAT DIVIS 58
8931	PLSTC PACKG CONTNRS,LIDS	W 16270	59.0	W 54045	192.1	W 48209	146.3	W 59382	158.0	ART TRANSP EMBALLAGE ETC
8939	MISC PLASTIC ARTICLES	W 18366	145.1	W 60526	260.0	W 99209	353.1	W 73252	379.3	ART DIVERS EN MAT DIV 58
89399	OTHR PLASTC ARTICLES NES	W 14450	139.2	W 52035	246.8	W 91598	338.4	W 61616	357.5	AUT OUV MAT DIV 58
894	TOYS,SPORTING GOODS,ETC	W 17142	125.8	W 65392	353.7	W 73165	325.5	W 71385	343.3	VOITURES ENFANTS,JOUETS
8942	TOYS,INDOOR GAMES ETC	W 12648	105.9	W 45820	263.9	W 50725	229.1	W 55489	233.0	JOUETS,JEUX ETC
898	MUSICAL INSTRUMENTS,PTS	W 8984	132.9	W 16773	193.4	W 19021	198.3	W 19312	196.4	INSTRUMENTS DE MUSIQUE
9	GOODS NOT CLASSD BY KIND		6.6		11.2		267.4		8.6	ART TRANSACT NON CLASSES
931	*SPECIAL TRANSACTIONS			W 24515	8.2	W 194548	264.3			TRANS.SPECIALES

5. Special Exports F.O.B. by Commodities according to the S.I.T.C. (Rev. 2) in million U.S. Dollars
Exportations Spéciales F.O.B. par Produits d'après la C.T.C.I. (Rév. 2) en millions de Dollars E.U.

SITC CTCI	COMMODITY	1994 QUANTITY QUANTITE	1994 VALUE VALEUR	1995 QUANTITY QUANTITE	1995 VALUE VALEUR	1996 QUANTITY QUANTITE	1996 VALUE VALEUR	1997 QUANTITY QUANTITE	1997 VALUE VALEUR	PRODUIT
	ALL COMMODITIES		43558.0		46505.4		47746.6		52985.9	TOUS PRODUITS
0	FOOD AND LIVE ANIMALS		9203.6		9975.4		10737.8		11434.8	ALIMENTS,ANIMAUX VIVANTS
01	MEAT AND PREPARATIONS		1333.0		1295.7		1503.2		1556.7	VIANDES ET PREPARATIONS
011	MEAT FRESH,CHILLD,FROZEN	W 636436	1008.7	W 532796	962.3	W 706647	1228.9	W 804946	1285.9	VIANDES FRAICHES,REF,CONGE
0111	BOVINE MEAT FRESH,FROZEN	W 78718	268.1	W 37505	180.8	W 46656	194.4	W 52441	196.3	VIANDES BOVIN FRAI,REF
01112	BOVINE MEAT BONELESS	W 78457	267.7	W 37499	180.8	W 46651	194.3	W 52412	196.3	VIANDES BOVIN DESOSSEES
0114	POULTRY FRESH CHLLD,FRZN	W 499482	647.0	W 440825	667.6	W 571646	876.3	W 672751	918.4	VOLAILLES MORTES
014	MEAT PREPD,PRSVD,NES ETC	W 119826	319.2	W 106542	328.1	W 100274	269.2	W 101843	268.5	CONSERVES DE VIANDES
0149	OTH PREPARD,PRESRVD MEAT	W 114832	301.4	W 101468	311.4	W 94537	254.0	W 96050	253.2	AUTRES PREP DE VIANDES
03	FISH AND PREPARATIONS		178.6		159.9		133.4		125.7	POISSONS ET PREPARATIONS
05	VEGETABLES AND FRUIT		1366.7		1487.4		1824.6		1426.8	LEGUMES ET FRUITS
057	FRUIT,NUTS,FRESH,DRIED	W 399839	266.7	W 275935	276.5	W 294268	291.2	W 316199	294.1	FRUITS FRAIS OU SECS
0577	NUTS EDIBLE,FRESH,DRIED	W 41362	138.8	W 47877	173.4	W 46798	185.6	W 51744	185.0	FRUITS A COQUES
05773	CASHEW NUTS,FRESH,DRIED	W 23079	109.3	W 31877	147.3	W 36222	167.6	W 36349	157.0	NOIX DE CAJOU
058	FRUIT PRESERVED,PREPARED	W 1222853	1070.8	W 1012281	1174.4	W 1247446	1496.8	W 1247989	1101.5	CONSERVES DE FRUITS
0585	FRUIT OR VEGETABLE JUICE	W 1189556	1019.4	W 990193	1131.9	W 1224518	1453.7	W 1224275	1057.6	JUS DE FRUITS
05851	ORANGE JUICE	W 1154379	987.8	W 968936	1108.4	W 1189072	1396.9	W 1186486	1006.7	JUS D'ORANGE
06	SUGAR AND PREPS,HONEY		1067.7		2001.9		1689.8		1860.1	SUCRES ET PRODUITS
061	SUGAR AND HONEY	W 3414237	997.0	W 6246198	1926.3	W 5388845	1619.8	W 6401762	1782.0	SUCRES ET MIEL
0611	RAW BEET AND CANE SUGAR	W 2716975	787.9	W 4800099	1450.7	W 4090398	1190.8	W 3844224	1045.4	SUCRES BRUTS
0612	REFINED SUGAR ETC	W 689936	204.4	W 1439072	468.9	W 1288496	420.8	W 2527746	726.0	SUCRES RAFFINES
07	COFFEE,TEA,COCOA,SPICES		3018.9		2748.9		2461.4		3425.1	CAFE,THE,CACAO,EPICES
071	COFFEE AND SUBSTITUTES	W 938968	2585.5	W 787595	2462.4	W 842337	2135.2	W 932618	3133.1	CAFE ET SUCCEDANES
0711	COFFEE GREEN,ROASTED,SUB	W 871427	2220.4	W 722150	1973.6	W 778702	1722.3	W 869058	2748.2	CAFE TORREFIE OU DECAFEINE
07111	COFFEE GREEN,HUSKS,SKINS	W 871018	2218.7	W 721313	1969.9	W 777909	1718.6	W 868439	2745.3	CAFE NON TORREFIE
0712	COFFEE EXTRACTS,ESSENCES	W 67541	365.1	W 65445	488.9	W 63634	413.0	W 63560	384.9	EXTRAITS DE CAFE
072	COCOA	W 187362	295.3	W 77685	131.3	W 95958	173.6	W 56450	126.9	CACAO
0723	COCOA BUTTER AND PASTE	W 78940	172.9	W 40312	92.2	W 46218	115.3	W 36607	107.8	BEURRE ET PATE DE CACAO
081	*FEEDING STUFF FOR ANIML		2152.2		2184.2		2930.2	MW 11773	2842.1	NOURRITURE POUR ANIMAUX
0813	OILCAKE AND OTH RESIDUES	MW 11068	2029.4	MW 12001	2044.3	MW 11613	2771.2	MW 10228	2703.3	TOURTEAUX
08131	— OF SOYA BEANS	MW 10644	1982.8	MW 11597	2000.2	MW 11262	2731.0	MW 10013	2680.9	TOURTEAUX DE SOJA
1	BEVERAGES AND TOBACCO		1123.9		1272.6		1636.2		1755.5	BOISSONS ET TABACS
12	TOBACCO AND MANUFACTURES		1030.8		1175.0		1515.4		1664.9	TABACS BRUTS FABRIQUES
121	TOBACCO UNMNFCTRD,REFUSE	W 275543	693.9	W 256270	768.6	W 282364	1028.6	W 318983	1091.4	TABACS BRUTS,DECHETS
1212	TOBACCO STRIPPED OR PART	W 190497	600.0	W 170984	666.2	W 190332	918.0	W 220073	962.8	TABACS PART ECOTES
122	TOBACCO,MANUFACTURED	W 60024	336.9	W 65027	406.4	W 82889	486.9	W 90935	573.5	TABACS FABRIQUES
1222	CIGARETTES	W 57818	327.7	W 63417	402.2	W 80262	481.2	W 87313	566.1	CIGARETTES
2	CRUDE MATERLS,EXCL FUELS		5447.4		6091.3		5938.2		7683.8	MAT BRUTES NON COMESTIBLES
22	OIL SEEDS,OLEAGINOUS FRT		1320.9		775.5		1020.2		2453.6	GRAINES,FRUITS OLEAGINEUX
222	SEEDS FOR'SOFT'FIXED OIL	W 5402858	1320.2	W 3496290	774.1	W 3648537	1019.6	W 8340058	2453.0	GRAINES HUILES FIXES
2222	SOYA BEANS	W 5397589	1316.0	W 3492525	770.5	W 3646933	1018.0	W 8339590	2452.5	FEVES DE SOJA
24	CORK AND WOOD		380.3		480.5		435.1		523.4	LIEGE ET BOIS
248	WOOD SHAPED,SLEEPERS	W 928695	353.5	W 884787	417.6	W 883040	381.5	W 950429	460.8	BOIS SIMPLEMENT TRAVAILLES
2483	LUMBER SHAPED NON-CONIFR	W 730513	291.8	W 689173	328.5	W 653171	272.1	W 645037	311.5	NON CONIFERES SCIES,RABOTES
24831	LUMBER SAWN ETC NON-CON	W 715957	266.2	W 673395	293.8	W 633522	238.4	W 618999	265.4	SCIES LONGITUDINALEMENT
251	*PULP AND WASTE PAPER	W 2074513	851.4	W 1983775	1475.5	W 2240084	999.5	W 2505057	1024.3	PATES A PAPIER,DECHETS
2517	SODA,SULPHATE WOOD PULP	W 2044427	839.8	W 1942495	1446.7	W 2153709	954.4	W 2381515	958.1	PATES CHIMIQUES AU SULFATE
25172	— BLEACHED,NONDISSOLVNG	W 2021832	833.5	W 1922000	1436.1	W 2133993	947.1	W 2351788	947.4	PATES BLANCHIES
26	TEXTILE FIBRES AND WASTE		62.2		172.4		65.3		60.7	FIBRES TEXTILES
27	CRUDE FERTLZR,MINRLS NES		126.3		135.8		141.1		160.1	ENGRAIS MINERAUX BRUTS
28	METALLIFEROUS ORES,SCRAP		2544.3		2793.7		3017.7		3190.6	MINERAIS METAL,DECHETS
281	IRON ORE,CONCENTRATES	MW 122801	2294.0	MW 130178	2547.8	MW 128990	2695.3	MW 134093	2846.2	MINERAIS DE FER
2815	IRON ORE,CONC,NOT AGGLOM	MW 96357	1532.6	MW 103336	1701.4	MW 100827	1740.8	MW 105319	1853.6	MINERAIS NON AGGLOMERES
2816	IRON ORE AGGLOMERATES	MW 26445	761.5	MW 26842	846.4	MW 28163	954.5	MW 28773	992.7	MINERAIS AGGLOMERES
287	BASE METAL ORES,CONC NES		226.6	W 6576406	241.2	W 6102365	278.6	W 6059857	299.2	MINERAIS METAUX COMMUNS
2873	ALUMINIUM ORES,ALUMINA	W 4704836	158.7	W 5293342	168.5	W 4996673	211.8	W 4979649	236.7	MINERAIS D'ALUMINIUM
3	MINERAL FUELS ETC		793.2		413.4		429.1		329.7	COMBUSTIBLES MINERAUX LUB
33	PETROLEUM AND PRODUCTS		792.4		413.2		425.1		328.8	PETROLE ET DERIVES
334	PETROLEUM PRODUCTS,REFIN	W 5693229	743.0	W 2299816	316.2	W 2538855	379.1	W 1909400	298.7	PRODUITS RAFFINES
3341	GASOLINE,OTH LIGHT OILS	W 2806113	422.6	W 624244	100.4	W 781468	138.6	W 464476	93.6	ESSENCES POUR MOTEURS
33411	MOTOR,AVIATION SPIRIT	W 2806090	422.5	W 624235	100.4	W 781452	138.5	W 464291	93.4	ESSENCES MOTEURS D'AVIONS
3343	GAS OILS	W 848356	111.4	W 1005068	127.3	W 261017	45.3	W 1385791	171.4	GAS OILS
3344	FUEL OILS,NES	W 1832755	155.1	W 578651	55.1	W 1422018	160.5	W 24	0.1	FUEL OILS
4	ANIMAL,VEGETABLE OIL,FAT		957.1		1234.3		880.5		763.5	HUILES,GRAISSES ANIM,VEG
42	FIXED VEGETABLE OIL,FAT		882.3		1107.8		749.1		632.6	HUILES VEGETALES FIXES
423	FIXED VEG OILS,SOFT	W 1577264	867.9	W 1811722	1084.7	W 1352988	726.3	W 1132699	602.3	HUILES VEGET DOUCES FIXES
4232	SOYA BEAN OIL	W 1533302	839.1	W 1763959	1053.1	W 1332257	713.3	W 1125891	596.7	HUILE DE SOJA
5	CHEMCLS,RELATED PROD NES		2543.2		3031.0		3127.8		3357.2	PRODUITS CHIMIQUES
51	ORGANIC CHEMICALS		893.0		1078.3		1064.2		1155.2	PROD CHIMIQ ORGANIQUES
511	HYDROCARBONS NES,DERIVS	W 771814	253.3	W 794790	283.3	W 765659	241.8	W 888294	316.3	HYDROCARBURES NDA
5112	CYCLIC HYDROCARBONS	W 338758	109.5	W 431991	143.0	W 395661	104.1	W 477334	140.7	HYDROCARBURES CYCLIQUES
512	ALCOHOLS,PHENOLS ETC	W 364861	181.2	W 395558	244.2	W 344666	210.0	W 263100	171.0	PHENOLS,PHENOLS-ALCOOLS
5121	ACYCLIC ALCOHOLS,DERIVS	W 348547	168.3	W 381535	229.5	W 332410	196.4	W 253381	154.8	ALCOOLS ACYCLIQUES
514	NITROGEN-FNCTN COMPOUNDS	W 148474	186.7	W 139774	213.5	W 164771	276.1	W 173721	301.0	COMPOSES FONCT AZOTEES
52	INORGANIC CHEMICALS		221.3		309.4		389.0		339.2	PROD CHIM INORGANIQUES
522	INORG ELEMNTS,OXIDES,ETC	W 357200	172.8		246.7	W 437447	297.9	W 331280	289.6	ELEMENTS INORGANIQUES
5221	CHEMICAL ELEMENTS	W 100778	90.3	W 134291	144.8	W 142746	188.1	W 139669	191.6	ELEMENTS CHIMIQUES
52212	NON-METALS NES	W 85158	84.1	W 115287	139.6	W 121011	181.0	W 127016	186.1	SELENIUM,PHOSPHORE
53	DYES,TANNING,COLOUR PROD		133.2		160.1		184.5		230.9	PROD TEINTURE,COLORANTS
541	*MEDICINAL,PHARM PRODUCT	K 6224320	132.9	MK 9112	167.6	MK 10083	189.2		217.3	PROD MEDICINAUX PHARMACEUT
55	PERFUME,CLEANING ETC PRD		161.7		198.9		212.7		192.0	PROD POUR PARFUM,TOILETTE
58	PLASTIC MATERIALS ETC		662.2		693.2		612.3		680.4	MAT PLAST ARTIFICIELLES
583	POLYMERIZATION ETC PRODS	W 741284	533.5	W 534683	535.0	W 517722	460.2	W 521025	505.7	PROD POLYMERISATION
5831	POLYETHYLENE	W 362900	220.6	W 236613	223.7	W 222977	188.8	W 301724	266.1	POLYETHYLENE
58311	— IN PRIMARY FORMS	W 356824	210.2	W 231279	212.4	W 218413	178.6	W 297661	257.2	POLYETHYLENE PRIMAIRES
59	CHEMICAL MATERIALS NES		296.2		353.3		404.9		470.4	MAT PROD CHIMIQUES NDA
591	PESTICIDES,DISINFECTANTS	W 19294	102.2	W 22351	127.6	W 23893	146.1	W 29653	191.3	DESINF,INSECT,FONG,HERB
598	MISCEL CHEM PRODUCTS NES	W 106731	120.9	W 120474	151.6	W 113296	163.4	W 133666	176.7	PROD DIV INDUST CHIM NDA
6	BASIC MANUFACTURES		10751.7		11741.5		11283.5		11326.5	ART MANUFACTURES
61	LEATHER,DRESSED FUR,ETC		558.1		667.3		770.9		838.4	CUIRS,PELLETERIES
611	LEATHER	W 84914	457.4	W 133106	560.2	W 178473	658.9	W 194731	726.0	CUIRS,PEAUX PREPARES
6114	LEATHR BOVINE NES,EQUINE	W 79779	421.9	W 129718	522.4	W 174127	620.4	W 190593	696.6	CUIRS DE BOVINS
62	RUBBER MANUFACTURES NES		550.4		578.0		615.4		652.2	CAOUTCHOUC MANUFACTURE
625	RUBBER TYRES, TUBES ETC	W 168804	465.5	W 158362	481.7	W 161471	512.0	W 166030	521.4	PNEUS CAOUTCHOUC VULCANISE
6251	TYRES NEW FOR MOTOR CARS	W 69083	172.3	W 59740	167.4	W 62390	183.5	W 62030	181.3	PNEUS POUR VOITURES
6252	TYRES,NEW,BUS OR LORRY	W 68459	203.6	W 63576	207.8	W 63869	217.3	W 65500	218.8	PNEUS POUR AUTOBUS,CAMIONS
63	WOOD,CORK MANUFACTRS NES		594.0		565.6		599.7		627.3	OUVRAGES LIEGE ET BOIS
634	VENEERS,PLYWOOD,ETC	W 891639	391.4	W 701825	368.5	W 1174101	403.2	W 947009	410.5	PLACAGES,CONTRE-PLAQUES
6342	PLYWOOD OF WOOD SHEETS	W 471638	293.2	W 393281	260.0	W 359637	247.7	W 379045	264.3	BOIS CONTRE-PLAQUES
635	WOOD MANUFACTURES NES	W 313266	201.6	W 251899	195.1	W 221019	194.7	W 208688	214.9	ART MANUF EN BOIS NDA
64	PAPER,PAPERBOARD AND MFR		1040.5		1326.2		1017.0		1044.0	PAPIERS,CARTONS & OUVRAGES

5. Special Exports F.O.B. by Commodities according to the S.I.T.C. (Rev. 2) in million U.S. Dollars
Exportations Spéciales F.O.B. par Produits d'après la C.T.C.I. (Rév. 2) en millions de Dollars E.U.

SITC CTCI	COMMODITY	1994 QUANTITY QUANTITE	1994 VALUE VALEUR	1995 QUANTITY QUANTITE	1995 VALUE VALEUR	1996 QUANTITY QUANTITE	1996 VALUE VALEUR	1997 QUANTITY QUANTITE	1997 VALUE VALEUR	PRODUIT
641	PAPER AND PAPERBOARD	W 1782094	969.0	W 1475787	1249.4	W 1439186	929.1	W 1522383	940.4	PAPIERS ET CARTONS
6412	PRINTG,WRITING PAPER NES	W 348921	241.2	W 327522	360.6	W 321916	264.4	W 323528	245.5	PAPIERS POUR L'IMPRESSION
64121	— UNCOATED	W 200566	146.0	W 220222	252.2	W 209871	173.8	W 229478	175.2	PAPIERS IMPRES NON COUCHES
6413	KRAFT PAPER,PAPERBOARD	W 391095	148.9	W 290535	179.3	W 334634	161.3	W 312567	147.8	PAPIER ET CARTON KRAFT
64131	KRAFT LINER IN BULK	W 341980	120.7	W 255869	148.9	W 272329	110.4	W 241688	92.8	PAP KRAFT POUR COUVERTURES
6415	PAPER,PAPERBRD,BULK,NES	W 670904	425.0	W 500476	544.6	W 466902	354.8	W 582818	413.3	PAPIERS,CARTONS ROULEAUX
64159	OTHER PAPER ETC,BULK,NES	W 630964	402.3	W 473748	519.6	W 447018	333.4	W 568351	396.6	AUT PAPIER ROULEAUX FEUILLES
65	TEXTILE YARN,FABRICS,ETC		1006.8		1026.0		1021.8		1038.7	FILS,TISSUS,ARTICLES TEXTILE
651	TEXTILE YARN	W 81534	304.7	W 68446	302.4	W 61005	290.7	W 62037	265.8	FILS TEXTILES
652	COTTON FABRICS,WOVEN	W 50999	207.6	W 49132	230.8		238.0	W 42202	231.4	TISSUS DE COTON
6522	WOVEN COTTON BLEACHD,ETC	W 36384	162.1	W 41264	201.9	W 41155	214.2	W 38438	215.6	TISSUS COTON BLANCHIS ETC
65224	BLCHED COTTON FABRIC NES	W 33333	139.1	W 38274	176.4	W 36704	177.7	W 33504	173.5	AUT TIS PLUS 85% COT BLANCHI
657	SPECIAL TXTL FABRC,PRODS	W 97717	149.3	W 103734	161.9	W 77959	143.3	W 103711	171.5	TISSUS SPECIAUX
658	TEXTILE ARTICLES NES	W 29519	248.0	W 26519	245.3	W 26291	242.7	W 27034	246.1	ART FACONNES MAT TEXTILES
6584	LINENS ETC	W 23062	211.1	W 20288	206.8	W 19286	202.0	W 20508	208.1	LINGE DE MAISON
65845	OTHER LINEN OF COTTON	W 15256	134.2	W 14512	142.0	W 14032	141.7	W 15002	147.4	LINGE DE TOILETTE COTON
66	NONMETAL MINERAL MFS NES		651.4		714.4		727.1		784.9	ART MIN NON METALLIQUES
661	LIME,CEMENT,BLDG PRODS	W 784732	132.8	W 879067	152.6	W 964035	173.3	W 1177067	216.5	CHAUX,CIMENTS MAT CONSTR
6613	BUILDING STONE ETC WORKD	W 603549	119.9	W 685148	136.5	W 749450	153.7	W 907366	192.5	PIERRES A BATIR
66132	BUILDING STONE WORKED	W 578283	109.9	W 654094	122.8	W 714617	139.4	W 857573	174.3	OUVR EN PIERRES DE TAILLE
662	CLAY,REFRACTORY BLDG PRD	W 491891	173.2	W 461955	177.9	W 463612	175.2	W 505524	192.0	MAT CONST REFRACTAIRES
6624	BRICKS ETC NONREFRACTORY	W 460011	151.1	W 423128	149.5	W 424980	146.2	W 466426	161.4	BRIQUES ETC CERAM NON REFR
66245	GLAZED CERAMIC SETTS ETC	W 413984	148.0	W 382267	145.6	W 390817	142.1	W 434015	157.7	AUT CARREAUX CERAMIQUE
67	IRON AND STEEL		4119.8		4329.4		4226.0		3919.2	FER ET ACIER
671	PIG IRON ETC	W 3045727	735.6	W 3012439	839.9	W 2983284	873.2	W 2973186	878.4	FONTE,SPIEGEL,POUDRES
6712	PIG IRN,SPIEGELEISEN ETC	W 2632021	362.7	W 2670446	427.6	W 2538099	390.1	W 2563147	384.0	FONTES BRUTES
6716	FERRO-ALLOYS	W 410869	371.4	W 339106	410.7	W 441783	481.3	W 405586	492.0	FERRO-ALLIAGES
67162	FERRO-SILICON	W 183907	108.5	W 181093	141.8	W 185794	163.2	W 159798	126.0	FERRO-SILICIUM
67169	OTHER FERRO-ALLOYS	W 147351	226.2	W 127822	254.8	W 150805	268.1	W 175718	334.7	AUTRES FERRO-ALLIAGES
672	IRON,STEEL PRIMARY FORMS	W 6416410	1567.0	W 6103076	1740.4	W 6907320	1690.9	W 6668677	1725.9	LINGOTS FER,ACIER
6725	IRN,STL BLOOMS,SLABS,ETC	W 4824860	1103.0	W 5129999	1395.5	W 5684277	1329.7	W 5524305	1384.3	BLOOMS,BILLETTES FER ACIER
67251	IRN,SMPLE STL BLOOMS,ETC	W 4741565	1072.0	W 5081209	1368.6	W 5607878	1294.3	W 5469907	1358.8	BLOOMS ETC NON ACIER FIN
6727	IRN,STL COIL FR REROLLNG	W 1589264	463.4	W 972743	344.8	W 1222861	361.1	W 1144028	341.4	EBAUCHES POUR TOLES FER
67271	IRON,SIMPLE STEEL COILS	W 1571769	454.4	W 941147	327.9	W 1213741	352.0	W 1139378	336.2	EBAUCHES NON EN ACIER
673	IRON,STEEL SHAPES ETC	W 1977050	613.9	W 1041257	401.3	W 761665	295.3	W 656520	268.3	BARRES,PROFIL FER,ACIER
6731	IRON,STEEL WIRE ROD	W 852081	240.4	W 568496	175.2	W 479866	143.0	W 311181	95.2	FIL MACHINE FER,ACIER
67311	IRON,SIMPLE STL WIRE ROD	W 724471	201.0	W 501587	149.2	W 411904	118.7	W 303971	90.5	FIL MACH AUT ACIER FIN
6732	IRON,STEEL BARS ETC	W 1040174	341.9	W 419596	202.6	W 231818	130.7	W 304949	151.3	BARRES FER,ACIER
67326	IRN,OTH STL BARS HOTROLD	W 892879	241.8	W 311620	96.3	W 137923	47.0	W 221650	74.4	BARRES PLEINES FER,ACIER
674	IRN,STL UNIV,PLATE,SHEET	W 2292660	934.3	W 2131606	1052.2	W 2205886	1049.9	W 1406293	669.8	LARGES PLATS,TOLES
6744	IRN,STL HVY PLATE,ROLLED	W 1019468	313.8	W 989581	397.7	W 983169	365.1	W 686646	262.6	TOLES LAMINEES PLUS 4.75 MM
67441	— OF IRON OR SIMPLE STL	W 1016941	309.9	W 985805	389.9	W 974196	347.2	W 678477	248.9	TOLES NON ACIER FIN CARB
6746	IRN,STL THIN PLATE,ROLLD	W 643232	291.3	W 510312	272.2	W 603059	308.1	W 280556	152.6	TOLES LAM MOINS 3MM
67461	— OF IRON OR SIMPLE STL	W 581812	244.2	W 467578	222.8	W 533137	232.3	W 223624	106.5	TOL NON AC FIN MOINS 3 MM
6747	TINNED PLATES,SHEETS	W 240127	140.0	W 218194	140.5	W 219387	152.7	W 201211	122.9	TOLES ETAMEES EN ACIER
6749	OTH IRN,STL PLATES,SHEET	W 264691	132.2	W 332965	198.3	W 309742	177.9	W 143956	85.1	AUTRES TOLES FER,ACIER
67491	— OF IRON OR SIMPLE STL	W 264427	131.5	W 324188	193.2	W 294410	170.2	W 127147	76.2	AUT TOLES AUTRES ACIER FIN
678	IRON,STL TUBES,PIPES,ETC	W 320277	211.2	W 313451	231.1	W 323422	254.7	W 353200	312.6	TUBES,TUYAUX EN FONTE,FER
6783	IRON,STL TUBES,PIPES NES	W 154245	101.5	W 180379	129.3	W 133364	111.7	W 201108	187.2	AUT TUBES,TUYAUX FER,ACIER
68	NON-FERROUS METALS		1536.1		1854.0		1636.8		1668.1	METAUX NON FERREUX
682	COPPER EXC CEMENT COPPER	W 67045	155.3	W 72974	224.8	W 61337	160.5	W 67616	174.7	CUIVRE
6821	COPPER NES,ALLOYS,UNWRT	W 55946	121.5	W 58423	167.7	W 41842	98.6	W 36884	85.7	CUIVRE BRUT
68212	COPPER REFINED,UNWROUGHT	W 55946	121.5	W 58423	167.6	W 41837	98.6	W 36877	85.6	CUIVRE AFFINE BRUT
684	ALUMINIUM	W 864563	1189.8	W 788682	1461.7	W 800327	1296.4	W 796443	1332.5	ALUMINIUM
6841	ALUMINIUM,ALLOYS,UNWRGHT	W 777840	1024.9	W 703009	1255.8	W 708973	1102.9	W 716174	1148.6	ALUMINIUM,ALLIAGES BRUTS
6842	ALUMINIUM,ALLOYS WORKED	W 86723	164.9	W 85673	206.0	W 91354	193.6	W 80269	184.0	ALUMINIUM,ALLIAGES OUVRE
69	METAL MANUFACTURES NES		695.0		680.9		669.2		754.0	ART MANUFACT EN METAL NDA
699	BASE METAL MFRS NES	W 83354	143.2	W 55910	142.0		152.8		192.9	ART MANUFACTURES MET NDA
7	MACHINES,TRANSPORT EQUIP		8973.9		8836.8		9508.1		11983.1	MACHINES MATERIEL TRANSPORT
71	POWER GENERATING EQUIPMT		1278.7		1305.3		1403.3		1488.6	MACHINES GENERATRICES
713	INTRNL COMBUS PSTN ENGIN	W 217794	854.0	W 205720	922.9	W 207498	1029.4	W 233279	1138.2	MOTEURS EXPL COMB INT, PIECE
7132	MOTOR VEHCL PSTN ENGINS	W 52237	254.8	W 26614	260.5	W 31114	332.4	W 36861	378.4	MOTEURS EXPL POUR VEHICULES
7139	PISTON ENGINE PARTS NES	W 157592	526.3	W 175864	628.2	W 172419	657.1	W 192337	717.7	PIECES POUR 713.2,3,8
714	ENGINES AND MOTORS NES	W 562	198.3	W 666	128.5	W 167	92.7	W 197	86.9	MOTEURS NON ELECTRIQUES
716	ROTATING ELECTRIC PLANT	W 41811	194.2	W 50892	224.8	W 50060	238.9	W 52344	233.1	APP ELECTR ROTATIFS,PIECES
7162	AC MTRS,GENRTRS,GEN SETS	W 29218	128.4	W 35947	152.7	W 33426	152.5	W 40920	173.3	MOTEURS ELECTRIQUES
71621	AC MTRS,INC UNIVRSL MTRS	W 26758	102.9	W 33906	134.6	W 31746	136.4	W 39874	159.9	MOT ELEC NON COUR CONTINU
72	MACHS FOR SPCL INDUSTRYS		976.5		901.0		1011.3		1237.1	MAC SPECIALES POUR INDUST
721	AGRIC MACHY,EXC TRACTORS	W 46112	126.2	W 46371	133.4	W 56837	190.5	W 62275	227.7	MACHINES AGRICOLES
722	TRACTORS NON-ROAD	W 14481	62.2	W 17073	76.3	W 26833	131.5	W 32441	166.1	TRACTEURS
7224	WHEELED TRACTORS NES	W 13585	58.2	W 15933	70.7	W 26056	128.9	W 30910	160.6	TRACTEURS A ROUES
723	CIVIL ENGNEERG EQUIP ETC	W 69715	458.4	W 54243	337.1	W 57521	338.9	W 69918	464.7	APPAREILS DE GENIE CIVIL
7234	CONST,MINING MACHNRY NES	W 56087	393.9	W 47718	310.3	W 50149	309.7	W 64426	440.8	MACH POUR LA CONST, MINES
72341	SELF-PROPELLD DOZERS,ETC	W 25828	179.0	W 25936	181.0	W 28846	192.6	W 37522	275.3	BULLDOZERS
73	METALWORKING MACHINERY		104.3		177.6		183.0		182.2	MACH TRAVAIL DES METAUX
736	METALWORKING MACH-TOOLS	W 12575	75.0	W 20526	142.3	W 18530	148.9	W 16453	132.9	MACH-OUTILS TRAVAIL METAUX
74	GENRL INDUSTRL MACHY NES		1369.3		1583.5		1551.3		1637.9	MACH APP INDUSTRIE
741	HEATING,COOLING EQUIPMNT	W 27561	146.8	W 29132	170.3	W 29172	181.7	W 30290	187.4	MACH CHAUFFAGE,PIECES
742	PUMPS FOR LIQUIDS ETC	W 10857	216.1	W 12369	271.1	W 11781	281.9	W 11540	277.5	POMPES MOTO-POMPES
7428	OTHER PUMPS FOR LIQUIDS	W 4945	161.2	W 5477	192.4	W 5425	198.8	W 4873	177.1	AUTRES POMPES POUR LIQ
74288	PUMPS FR LIQUIDS NES ETC	W 4325	155.0	W 4856	186.0	W 5044	194.1	W 4316	168.5	POMPES POUR LIQUIDES NDA
743	PUMPS NES,CENTRFUGES ETC	W 111566	443.6	W 118930	522.3	W 101740	469.5	W 110169	497.9	POMPES COMPRES,VENT ETC
7431	PUMPS FOR GASES ETC	W 93369	348.0	W 106108	429.1	W 91545	386.7	W 99613	415.1	POMPES AIR A VIDE,COMPRES
744	MECHANICAL HANDLING EQU	W 29348	116.2	W 34216	141.5	W 34567	147.6	W 35665	139.5	EQUIP MANUTENTION PIECES
745	NONELEC MACHY,TOOLS NES	W 9928	137.9	W 7828	125.2	W 7632	113.3	W 9431	151.4	AUT MACH NON ELEC,PIECES
749	NONELEC MACH PTS,ACC NES	W 48674	309.0	W 58145	353.4	W 62105	357.5	W 69390	384.5	PIECES MACH NON ELEC NDA
7493	SHAFT,CRANK,PULLEY ETC	W 35339	148.5	W 45374	185.7	W 50530	192.1	W 58821	217.9	ARBRES TRANS,VILEBREQUINS
75	OFFICE MACHNES,ADP EQUIP		217.5		261.5		353.7		343.0	MACH BUREAU TRAIT AUTOM
752	AUTOMTIC DATA PROC EQUIP	W 905	93.7	W 1775	132.8	W 3049	197.5	W 3484	231.1	MACH TRAIT INFORMATION
7523	DIGITL CENTRL PROCESSORS	W 118	28.4	W 912	62.8	W 2406	163.4	W 3129	204.8	UNITES CENTRALES
76	TELECOMM,SOUND EQUIPMENT		409.3		400.2		452.7		609.7	EQUIPMENT DE TELECOM
762	RADIO BROADCAST RECEIVRS	W 4017	339.1	W 3844	343.3	W 3830	357.9	W 4291	378.2	RECEPTEURS RADIODIFFUSION
7621	MTR VEHC RADIO RECEIVERS	W 3939	338.3	W 3758	341.7	W 3802	357.2	W 4286	378.0	RECEPTEURS RADIO AUTO
764	TELECOM EQPT,PTS,ACC NES	W 2373	67.3	W 2130	52.9	W 2421	92.9	W 4135	224.3	EQUIP TELECOM,PIECES
77	ELECTRIC MACHNRY NES ETC		875.2		948.2		964.0		1031.4	MACH APP ELECT NDA
772	SWITCHGEAR ETC,PARTS NES	W 9137	151.5	W 8135	181.3	W 8385	192.7	W 10834	206.9	APP COUPURE,SECT ETC
7721	SWITCHGEAR ETC	W 8029	125.8	W 6852	147.1	W 7092	151.9	W 9459	162.0	APP COUPURE,SECTIONMNT
775	HOUSEHOLD TYPE EQUIP NES	W 61508	145.8	W 31627	147.6	W 29283	150.7	W 33148	168.1	MACH,APP USAGE DOMESTQUE
778	ELECTRICAL MACHINERY NES	W 54858	284.8	W 56785	306.0	W 59381	317.7	W 65338	362.8	AUTRES MACH ELECT NDA
78	ROAD VEHICLES		2992.8		2663.4		2929.4		4453.3	VEHICULES ROUTIERS
781	PASS MOTOR VEH EXC BUSES	W 81668	534.0	W 67549	455.4	W 83550	619.3	W 191629	1463.0	AUTO TRANSPORT PERSONNES

5. Special Exports F.O.B. by Commodities according to the S.I.T.C. (Rev. 2) in million U.S. Dollars
Exportations Spéciales F.O.B. par Produits d'après la C.T.C.I. (Rév. 2) en millions de Dollars E.U.

SITC CTCI	COMMODITY	1994		1995		1996		1997		PRODUIT
		QUANTITY QUANTITE	VALUE VALEUR	QUANTITY QUANTITE	VALUE VALEUR	QUANTITY QUANTITE	VALUE VALEUR	QUANTITY QUANTITE	VALUE VALEUR	
782	LORRIES,SPCL MTR VEH NES	W 102463	617.7	W 81994	519.1	W 83403	559.0	W 133566	900.1	VEHICULES SPECIAUX,MARCH
7821	LORRIES,TRUCKS	W 102032	612.7	W 81757	517.4	W 83325	558.2	W 133029	894.9	VEHICULES TRANSP MARCHAND
783	ROAD MOTOR VEHICLES NES	W 40655	327.5	W 16890	147.8	W 12404	108.0	W 25397	218.6	VEHICULES ROUTIERS NDA
7831	BUSES	W 31663	262.2	W 10753	100.8	W 7925	70.8	W 14319	130.8	VOITURES TRANSPORT COMMUN
784	MOTOR VEH PRTS,ACCES NES	W 375286	1423.9	W 350364	1470.9	W 333249	1562.4	W 383226	1778.5	PIECES 722,781,782,783
7841	MOTOR VEHICLE CHASSIS	W 27638	185.5	W 20248	153.4	W 18789	143.9	W 25816	216.9	CHASSIS 722,781,782,783
7842	MOTOR VEHICLE BODIES	W 21546	144.6	W 12897	105.8	W 11984	112.9	W 17402	161.5	CARROS 722,781,782,783
7849	OTHER MOTOR VEHCL PARTS	W 326101	1093.9	W 317218	1211.9	W 302477	1305.7	W 340008	1400.3	PIECES 722,781,782,783
79	OTHR TRANSPORT EQUIPMENT		750.9		596.4		659.8		1000.2	AUTRE MATERIEL TRANSPORT
792	AIRCRAFT ETC	W 794	309.9	W 413	276.9	W 1216	457.9	W 878	789.1	APP NAVIGATION AERIENNE
7923	AIRCRFT NES2000–15000KG	W 103	92.6	W 199	171.4	W 204	226.7	W 578	647.3	AERODYNES 2000 A 15000 KG
793	SHIPS AND BOATS ETC	W 135868	412.0	W 215190	274.5	W 304618	186.1	W 92512	193.2	NAVIRES BATEAUX,ETC
7932	SHIPS AND BOATS NES	W 100555	183.1	W 163569	122.3	W 295274	154.3	W 52214	15.3	NAVIRES ET BATEAUX
79322	TANKERS OF ALL KINDS	W 50800	148.8	W 60035	57.8	W 181593	38.1	W 17348	2.8	BATEAUX–CITERNES
7938	TUGS,SPECIAL VESSELS ETC	W 35296	228.9	W 34197	151.2	W 9265	31.5	W 40252	177.8	REMORQUEURS,BATEAUX SPEC
79382	SPECL PURPOSE VESSLS ETC	W 31194	222.8	W 10807	79.5	W 6935	25.2	W 40002	176.2	BAT–PHARES,–POMPES,DRAGUES
8	MISC MANUFACTURED GOODS		3111.1		2923.7		2979.3		3034.9	ART MANUFACTURES DIVERS
821	*FURNITURE,PARTS THEREOF	W 138675	287.0	W 140692	331.4	W 146947	347.7	W 162709	383.6	MEUBLES ET PIECES
8219	FURNITURE AND PARTS NES	W 118851	215.1	W 124703	267.2	W 131450	278.2	W 144964	299.3	AUTRES MEUBLES ET PIECES
82192	WOOD FURNITURE NES	W 101783	184.6	W 110320	237.6	W 115539	244.6	W 127853	271.7	MEUBLES NDA EN BOIS
84	CLOTHING AND ACCESSORIES		381.2		298.4		248.3		210.7	VETEMENTS
851	*FOOTWEAR	W 92401	1537.3	W 78815	1413.7	W 84216	1567.3	W 87074	1523.0	CHAUSSURES
85102	FOOTWEAR LEATHER	W 85003	1489.0	W 71402	1356.5	W 74931	1480.5	W 75812	1415.5	CHAUS SEMELLES EN CUIR
87	PRECISION INSTRUMNTS NES		185.3		149.4		134.6		167.5	INSTRUM,APPAR SCIENT NDA
88	PHOTO EQU,OPTICL GDS ETC		234.5		280.9		235.5		243.5	APP,FOURN PHOTO,OP,MONTR
882	PHOTO,CINEMA SUPPLIES	W 20969	213.9	W 24344	259.2	W 22096	219.0	W 25482	226.4	PRODUITS PHOTO,CINEMA
8822	PHOTO FILM EXC DEV CINMA	W 18299	202.3	W 20422	244.2	W 18701	205.2	W 21561	210.7	PLAQUES,PELLICULES,FILMS
88223	PHOTO SENSITZD CLOTH ETC	W 13863	132.8	W 14813	145.2	W 13729	136.1	W 16691	142.6	PAPIERS SENSIB NON DEVEL
89	MISC MANUFCTRD GOODS NES		450.0		415.1		419.1		478.7	ART MANUFACTURES DIVERS
9	GOODS NOT CLASSD BY KIND		653.4		985.9		1226.6		1317.5	ART TRANSACT NON CLASSES
931	*SPECIAL TRANSACTIONS	W 2411022	442.8	W 3428593	620.2	W 3265132	637.5		807.0	TRANS.SPECIALES
971	*GOLD,NON MONETARY NES	K 16427	202.9		359.6		583.1	K 48264	507.9	OR NON MONETAIRE
97101	NONMON GLD UNWRT,SEMIMFD	K 16422	202.9	K 34777	359.6	K 46970	583.1	K 48248	507.9	OR,ALLIAGES D'OR BRUTS

1. HISTORICAL SERIES, 1960–1995 GENERAL TRADE, IMPORTS C.I.F., EXPORTS F.O.B.
SERIES HISTORIQUES, 1960–1995 COMMERCE GENERAL, IMPORTATIONS C.A.F., EXPORTATIONS F.O.B

YEAR ANNEE	VALUE IN MILLION BRUNEI DOLLARS / VALEUR EN MILLION BRUNEI DOLLARS: MERCHANDISE –MARCHANDISE IMPORTS	EXPORTS	GOLD –OR IMPORTS	EXPORTS	CONVERSION FACTORS U.S. CENTS PER BRUNEI DOLLAR / FACTEURS DE CONVERSION CENTS E.U. PAR BRUNEI DOLLAR: IMPORTS	EXPORTS	INDEX NUMBERS –INDICES: QUANTUM IMPORTS	EXPORTS	UNIT VALUE / VALEUR UNITAIRE IMPORTS	EXPORTS
1960	53.50	254.70	0.07		32.6667	32.6667				
1961	49.10	235.60	0.56		32.6667	32.6667				
1962	48.70	199.30	0.39		32.6667	32.6667				
1963	63.40	182.60	2.56		32.6667	32.6667				
1964	96.30	187.40	5.87		32.6667	32.6667				
1965	109.80	199.80	4.25		32.6667	32.6667				
1966	150.00	225.50	6.54		32.6667	32.6667				
1967	130.90	248.30	6.76		32.6667	32.6667				
1968	206.60	281.40	3.12		32.6667	32.6667				
1969	218.70	270.10	3.30		32.6667	32.6667				
1970	256.10	281.90	3.39		32.6667	32.6667				
1971	456.60	310.70	2.79		32.6667	32.6667				
1972	300.20	469.70	1.85		35.4667	35.4667				
1973	323.20	852.10	0.10		41.0779	41.0779				
1974	450.90	2388.30			41.5581	41.5581				
1975	648.90	2494.80	0.22		41.5286	41.4834				
1976	642.50	3293.20	1.06		39.3513	39.3558				
1977	680.40	3996.00			40.6289	40.7006				
1978	639.20	4195.20			43.2205	43.2206				
1979	862.10	5796.50			45.7002	45.7002				
1980	1331.50	9852.50			45.8693	45.8693				
1981	1265.00	8591.70			47.3267	47.3267				
1982	1571.70	8153.30			46.7020	46.7020				
1983	1542.20	7170.70			47.2156	47.2156				
1984	1331.50	6813.90			47.0157	47.0157				
1985	1348.40	6532.90			45.5731	45.4886				
1986	1456.96	3990.10			45.0425	45.0425				
1987	1350.18	4005.61			47.4834	47.4834				
1988	1497.30	3436.45			49.6919	49.6919				
1989	1675.01	3672.61			51.2742	51.2742				
1990	1813.16	4010.15			55.1930	55.1930				
1991	1922.38	4266.97			62.8580	62.8580				
1992	1916.80	3863.20			61.3490	61.3490				
1993	2012.60	3684.50			59.6595	59.6595				
1994	2497.00	3383.20			67.8795	67.8795				
1995	2853.67	3387.98								

2. IMPORTS BY BROAD ECONOMIC CATEGORY AND EXPORTS BY INDUSTRIAL ORIGIN. (PERCENTAGE OF TOTAL VALUE)
IMPORTATIONS PAR CATEGORIES ECONOMIQUES ET EXPORTATIONS PAR BRANCHE D'ACTIVITE.(EN POURCENTAGE DE LA VALEUR TOTALE)

IMPORTS – IMPORTATIONS

	1988	1989	1990	1991	1992	1993	1994
TOTAL IMPORTS–IMPORTATIONS TOTALES	100.	100.	100.	100.	100.	100.	100.
1 FOOD BEV–ALIMENTATION BOISSONS	19.1	16.8	17.2	13.7	11.0	8.2	12.8
11 PRIMARY–PRODUITS DE BASE	7.1	6.6	6.3	5.3	4.2	3.4	5.1
111 FOR INDUSTRY–POUR L'INDUSTRIE	1.1	0.9	0.8	0.7	0.4	0.4	0.4
112 FOR HOUSEHOLDS–POUR LES MENAGES	5.9	5.6	5.5	4.6	3.7	2.9	4.7
12 PROCESSED–PRODUITS ELABORES	12.1	10.2	10.9	8.3	6.8	4.9	7.7
121 FOR INDUSTRY–POUR L'INDUSTRIE	0.6	0.6	0.4	0.3	0.5	0.4	0.6
122 FOR HOUSEHOLDS–POUR LES MENAGES	11.5	9.6	10.5	8.0	6.3	4.5	7.1
2 IND SUPPLIES–APPROV INDUSTRIELS	27.9	30.3	31.1	30.2	28.7	23.2	32.7
21 PRIMARY–PRODUITS DE BASE	1.2	1.1	1.3	1.0	1.3	0.7	2.0
22 PROCESSED–PRODUITS ELABORES	26.7	29.2	29.8	29.1	27.4	22.5	30.8
3 FUELS–COMBUSTIBLES	0.9	0.9	0.9	0.6	0.6	1.1	0.4
31 PRIMARY–PRODUITS DE BASE	0.0	0.0	0.0	0.0	0.0	0.0	0.0
32 PROCESSED–PRODUITS ELABORES	0.9	0.9	0.9	0.6	0.6	1.1	0.4
321 MOTOR SPIRIT–ESSENCE	0.3	0.3	0.4	0.1	0.1	0.5	0.0
322 OTHER–AUTRES	0.6	0.5	0.5	0.5	0.5	0.6	0.4
4 MACHINERY–EQUIPEMENT	19.5	22.3	20.9	24.6	22.3	27.7	21.4
41 CAPITAL EQUIPMENT–MACHINES	14.5	15.9	14.2	17.6	16.0	17.6	18.8
42 PARTS–PIECES ACCESSOIRES	5.0	6.4	6.6	7.0	6.4	10.1	2.6
5 TRANSPORT–TRANSPORT	14.7	14.9	15.7	14.9	19.6	25.6	14.6
51 PASSENGER CARS–AUTOMOBILES	7.5	8.2	8.3	7.4	7.6	5.6	4.3
52 OTHER–AUTRES	1.1	1.0	1.0	1.5	8.1	16.4	5.5
521 INDUSTRIAL–INDUSTRIELS	1.0	0.9	0.9	1.4	7.9	16.3	5.5
522 NON INDUSTRIAL–NON INDUSTRIEL	0.1	0.0	0.0	0.1	0.2	0.1	0.1
53 PARTS–PIECES ACCESSOIRES	6.1	5.7	6.4	6.0	4.0	3.6	4.7
6 CONSUM GOODS–BIENS CONSOMMATION	15.4	13.9	13.8	15.5	17.5	13.9	17.8
61 DURABLE–DURABLES	3.4	2.9	3.1	3.2	6.7	6.1	3.4
62 SEMI DURABLE–SEMI DURABLES	6.7	6.5	6.4	8.3	6.8	4.7	6.7
63 NON DURABLE–NON DURABLES	5.3	4.5	4.4	4.0	4.1	3.1	7.7
7 GOODS NES–BIENS NDA	2.4	0.9	0.4	0.5	0.3	0.3	0.3

EXPORTS – EXPORTATIONS

	1988	1989	1990	1991	1992	1993	1994
TOTAL EXPORTS–EXPORTATIONS TOTALES	100.	100.	100.	100.	100.	100.	100.
1 AGRICULTURE	0.2	0.1	0.1	0.1			
2 MINING QUARRY–INDUS EXTRACTIVES	92.5	91.6	90.9	91.9	95.9	96.2	95.3
3 MANUFACTURING–IND MANUFACTUR	7.3	8.3	9.0	8.0	4.1	3.8	4.7
31 FOOD BEV TOBACCO–ALIM BOISS TAB	0.6	0.5	0.6	0.5	0.0	0.0	0.0
32 TEXTILES–INDUSTRIES TEXTILES	0.2	0.3	0.5	0.6	0.7	0.3	1.3
33 WOOD & PRODUCTS–BOIS & PRODUITS	0.0	0.0	0.0	0.0	0.0		
34 PAPER & PRODUCTS–PAPIER & PRODT	0.0	0.0	0.0	0.0	0.0	0.0	0.0
35 CHEMICALS–INDUSTRIES CHIMIQUES	5.1	5.4	5.7	4.9	3.3	3.5	3.4
36 NON METAL MIN–MIN NON METAL	0.0	0.0	0.1	0.0	0.0	0.0	
37 BASIC METAL–IND METAL BASE	0.1	0.1	0.1	0.0			
38 METAL MANUF–MANUF METAL	1.2	1.9	1.9	1.8	0.0	0.0	0.0
39 OTH MANUF IND–AUTRES MANUF	0.0	0.1	0.1	0.1	0.0		0.0

3. TRADE BY PRINCIPAL COUNTRIES OF ORIGIN AND DESTINATION (VALUE IN MILLION U.S. DOLLARS)
ECHANGES SELON LES PRINCIPAUX PAYS D'ORIGINE ET DE DESTINATION (VALEUR EN MILLIONS DE DOLLARS EU)

COUNTRIES–PAYS	GENERAL IMPORTS C.I.F. IMPORTATIONS GENERALES C.A.F					COUNTRIES–PAYS	GENERAL EXPORTS F.O.B. EXPORTATIONS GENERALES F.O.B.				
	1990	1991	1992	1993	1994		1990	1991	1992	1993	1994
World	1000.7	1208.4	1475.7	1820.5	1873.6	Monde	2213.3	2682.1	2301.2	2093.9	2110.3
Africa	0.3	1.2	37.5	51.4	101.3	Afrique	0.1	0.1	88.6	48.7	34.5
Americas	157.3	173.2	275.4	459.4	216.9	Amériques	75.9	29.2	20.8	8.7	46.6
– Northern America	154.1	169.7	274.4	458.5	215.6	– Amérique du Nord	75.9	29.2	19.9	8.6	23.6
– LAIA	3.0	3.3	0.2	0.3	0.5	– ALAI		0.0			
– CACM			0.0	0.0	0.0	– MCAC					
– Caribbean	0.0	0.0	0.3	0.2	0.4	– Caraïbes			1.0	0.0	23.0
– Rest of America	0.2	0.1	0.4	0.3	0.4	– Autre Amérique	0.0				
Asia excl fmr USSR	627.1	711.1	514.1	497.2	668.6	Asie anc. URSS exclus	2102.6	2562.1	2137.9	2019.3	2028.3
– Middle East	0.3	1.3	3.2	2.4	4.7	– Moyen–Orient	0.1	0.1			0.0
Asia former USSR						Asie ancienne URSS					
Europe excl fmr USSR	185.7	291.1	635.5	779.7	864.9	Europe anc. URSS exclus	5.5	14.1	0.7	0.1	0.7
– European Union	181.1	288.2	306.0	468.3	336.0	– Union Européenne	5.3	13.7	0.4	0.1	0.7
– Eastern Europe	0.2	0.5	329.0	311.2	522.3	– Europe de l'Est		0.0			
– Rest of Europe	4.5	2.4	0.5	0.2	6.7	– Autre de l'Europe	0.1	0.5	0.2		0.0
Europe former USSR	0.0	0.0	0.0	0.1	0.0	Europe ancienne URSS					
Oceania	29.1	29.8	13.2	32.8	21.9	Océanie	29.3	76.6	53.2	17.2	0.1
Other	1.1	1.9				Autre	0.0		0.0		0.0
USA/Etats–Unis d'Amer	152.9	165.2	272.4	457.1	212.4	Japan/Japon	1285.9	1678.6	1613.0	1567.0	1526.5
Romania/Roumanie	0.0	0.1	328.6	310.8	521.4	Thailand/Thaïlande	170.7	220.3	214.8	214.7	245.2
Japan/Japon	145.8	190.6	229.3	170.5	189.1	Viet Nam			235.2	173.7	196.8
Malaysia/Malaisie	102.8	116.2	135.1	150.8	244.6	Korea, Republic of	274.0	276.2			
Singapore/Singapour	259.0	266.7				Other Asia n.e.s.	74.6	71.5	68.7	63.5	59.5
United Kingdom	65.4	85.1	90.6	77.4	130.1	Singapore/Singapour	156.5	179.4			
Germany/Allemagne		51.3	59.9	216.9	77.1	Philippines	108.3	104.0			
Italy/Italie	21.5	53.7	82.7	94.6	37.6	Guinea–Bissau			88.6	48.7	34.5
Indonesia/Indonésie	18.7	20.0	25.5	54.8	67.2	Australia/Australie	29.2	71.0	53.2	17.2	0.1
Thailand/Thaïlande	37.2	32.4	27.8	29.3	58.5	USA/Etats–Unis d'Amer	75.6	28.4	19.6	8.6	23.3
Netherlands/Pays–Bas	20.4	31.6	21.4	52.0	41.5	Malaysia/Malaisie	27.4	27.4	1.6	0.4	0.2
China/Chine	27.1	34.8	30.7	22.7	33.4	Antigua and Barbuda			1.0	0.0	23.0
Angola			29.5	45.6	65.1	United Kingdom	2.7	8.8	0.4	0.1	0.7
China, Hong Kong SAR	15.7	21.4	27.5	29.9	19.5	China/Chine	3.2	3.8	4.6		
France, Monaco	14.4	12.5	38.3	12.0	16.2	New Zealand	0.0	5.6			
Other Asia n.e.s.	11.2	16.2	18.9	16.5	29.4	France, Monaco	1.1	1.6		0.0	
Denmark/Danemark	7.8	32.6	6.4	5.7	17.3	Netherlands/Pays–Bas	0.6	1.6	0.0	0.0	0.0
Korea, Republic of	6.2	7.6	12.5	15.8	17.7	Canada	0.3	0.8	0.3	0.0	0.3
Australia/Australie	25.8	26.4	0.0	0.0	0.0	Germany/Allemagne		1.3	0.0		
Former Fed Rep Germany	39.4					Pakistan	1.2	0.0			
New Zealand	3.4	3.4	6.1	7.2	17.2	Norway,Svalbard and JM	0.1	0.5	0.2		
So. African Customs Un			2.3	1.5	29.7	Indonesia/Indonésie	0.4	0.3			
Kiribati			5.4	22.6	3.7	Former Fed Rep Germany	0.6				
Sweden/Suède	4.2	5.9	4.4	3.7	12.2	China, Hong Kong SAR	0.1	0.3	0.1		0.0
Canada	1.2	4.5	2.0	1.5	3.2	Nepal/Népal	0.3	0.1			
India/Inde	1.3	1.8	2.3	2.8	3.9	United Arab Emirates	0.1	0.1			
Belgium–Luxembourg	2.7	4.6	0.0	3.4	0.1	Belgium–Luxembourg	0.2				
Spain/Espagne	1.6	1.7	1.3	1.7	2.6	Spain/Espagne		0.1			
Finland/Finlande	1.1	6.1	0.4	0.3	0.5	Italy/Italie	0.0	0.1			
Norway,Svalbard and JM	0.6	0.4	0.5	0.2	6.3	Other Africa n.e.s.	0.0	0.1			
Guinea–Bissau			3.0	2.3	2.6	Denmark/Danemark	0.0	0.0	0.0		0.0
United Arab Emirates	0.1	0.8	1.5	1.5	3.6	Austria/Autriche		0.1			
Gambia/Gambie			1.4	1.6	3.0	India/Inde	0.0	0.0			
Switzerland,Liechtenst.	3.7	2.0	0.0	0.0	0.2	Sweden/Suède	0.0				
Austria/Autriche	1.7	2.7				Nigeria/Nigéria	0.0				
Micronesia/Micronésie			1.5	1.3	0.6	Mexico/Mexique		0.0			
Philippines	1.6	1.6				Finland/Finlande	0.0				0.0
Areas n.e.s.	1.1	1.9				Areas n.e.s.	0.0		0.0		0.0
Brazil/Brésil	1.2	1.6				Oman	0.0	0.0			
Ireland/Irlande	0.8	0.2	0.5	0.5	0.5	So. African Customs Un					0.0

(VALUE AS PERCENTAGE OF WORLD TOTAL)(VALEURS EN POURCENTAGE DU TOTAL MONDIAL)

	1985	1986	1987	1988	1989	1990	1991	1992	1993	1994
Africa		0.0	0.0	0.0	0.0	0.0	0.1	2.5	2.8	5.4
Americas	7.8	12.5	12.5	13.1	13.2	15.7	14.3	18.7	25.2	11.6
– Northern America	7.8	12.3	12.2	12.7	12.9	15.4	14.0	18.6	25.2	11.5
– LAIA	0.0	0.1	0.2	0.3	0.3	0.3	0.3	0.0	0.0	0.0
– CACM			0.0					0.0	0.0	0.0
– Caribbean		0.0	0.0	0.0	0.0	0.0	0.0	0.0	0.0	0.0
– Rest of America		0.0	0.0	0.0		0.0	0.0	0.0	0.0	0.0
Asia excl fmr USSR	70.0	60.1	60.1	63.1	62.7	62.7	58.9	34.8	27.3	35.7
– Middle East	0.0	0.0	0.0	0.0	0.1	0.0	0.1	0.2	0.1	0.2
Asia former USSR										
Europe excl fmr USSR	21.0	24.6	23.0	19.8	21.4	18.6	24.1	43.1	42.8	46.2
– European Union	18.7	24.2	22.7	19.3	20.9	18.1	23.9	20.7	25.7	17.9
– Eastern Europe		0.0	0.0	0.0	0.1	0.0	0.0	22.3	17.1	27.9
– Rest of Europe	2.4	0.4	0.3	0.4	0.5	0.4	0.2	0.0	0.0	0.4
Europe former USSR	1.1	0.0	0.0	0.0	0.0	0.0	0.0	0.0	0.0	0.0
Oceania	0.1	2.8	3.9	3.7	2.4	2.9	2.5	0.9	1.8	1.2
Other	0.0	0.0	0.5	0.4	0.2	0.1	0.2			
USA/Etats–Unis d'Amer	7.8	12.2	12.1	12.6	12.7	15.3	13.7	18.5	25.1	11.3
Romania/Roumanie		0.0	0.0	0.0	0.0	0.0	0.0	22.3	17.1	27.8
Japan/Japon	13.8	17.7	14.4	16.0	14.7	14.6	15.8	15.5	9.4	10.1
Malaysia/Malaisie	6.3	5.9	8.2	7.9	9.1	10.3	9.6	9.2	8.3	13.1
Singapore/Singapour	44.7	25.8	24.1	26.5	26.9	25.9	22.1			
United Kingdom	13.7	7.9	8.3	7.8	8.8	6.5	7.0	6.1	4.2	6.9
Germany/Allemagne							4.2	4.1	11.9	4.1
Italy/Italie	0.8	2.2	2.7	1.6	1.8	2.1	4.4	5.6	5.2	2.0
Indonesia/Indonésie		0.7	0.9	1.3	1.7	1.9	1.7	1.7	3.0	3.6
Thailand/Thaïlande	1.5	3.1	4.4	4.0	3.8	3.7	2.7	1.9	1.6	3.1

	1985	1986	1987	1988	1989	1990	1991	1992	1993	1994
Afrique		0.0	0.0	0.0	0.0	0.0	0.0	3.9	2.3	1.6
Amériques	0.1	6.1	1.6	2.1	4.9	3.4	1.1	0.9	0.4	2.2
– Amérique du Nord	0.1	6.1	1.6	2.1	4.9	3.4	1.1	0.9	0.4	1.1
– ALAI		0.0		0.0	0.0		0.0			
– MCAC										
– Caraïbes	0.0							0.0	0.0	1.1
– Autre Amérique				0.0		0.0				
Asie anc. URSS exclus	98.7	92.9	97.1	96.5	94.0	95.0	95.5	92.9	96.4	96.1
– Moyen–Orient	0.0	0.0	0.0	0.0	0.0	0.0	0.0			0.0
Asie ancienne URSS										
Europe anc. URSS exclus	1.2	0.2	0.2	0.1	0.2	0.2	0.5	0.0	0.0	0.0
– Union Européenne	1.2	0.2	0.2	0.1	0.1	0.2	0.5	0.0	0.0	0.0
– Europe de l'Est					0.0		0.0			
– Autre de l'Europe	0.0	0.0	0.0	0.0	0.0	0.0	0.0	0.0		0.0
Europe ancienne URSS				0.0						
Océanie		0.9	1.1	1.3	0.9	1.3	2.9	2.3	0.8	0.0
Autre	0.0					0.0		0.0		0.0
Japan/Japon	70.7	66.8	61.7	65.0	58.1	58.1	62.6	70.1	74.8	72.3
Thailand/Thaïlande	8.3	8.1	11.7	8.8	10.3	7.7	8.2	9.3	10.3	11.6
Viet Nam				0.0	0.0			10.2	8.3	9.3
Korea, Republic of	8.4	7.4	9.7	10.4	13.1	12.4	10.3			
Other Asia n.e.s.		1.7	2.8	2.9	3.4	3.4	2.7	3.0	3.0	2.8
Singapore/Singapour	9.1	6.7	6.7	5.7	4.8	7.1	6.7			
Philippines	2.2	0.7	3.2	2.0	2.6	4.9	3.9			
Guinea–Bissau								3.9	2.3	1.6
Australia/Australie		0.8	1.1	1.3	0.9	1.3	2.6	2.3	0.8	0.0
USA/Etats–Unis d'Amer	0.1	6.1	1.6	2.1	4.9	3.4	1.1	0.8	0.4	1.1

4. General Imports C.I.F. by Commodities according to the S.I.T.C. (Rev. 2) in million U.S. Dollars
Importations Générales C.A.F. par Produits d'après la C.T.C.I. (Rév. 2) en millions de Dollars E.U.

SITC CTCI	COMMODITY	1991		1992		1993		1994		PRODUIT
		QUANTITY QUANTITE	VALUE VALEUR	QUANTITY QUANTITE	VALUE VALEUR	QUANTITY QUANTITE	VALUE VALEUR	QUANTITY QUANTITE	VALUE VALEUR	
	ALL COMMODITIES		1208.4		1475.7		1820.6		1873.7	TOUS PRODUITS
0	FOOD AND LIVE ANIMALS		155.5		146.7		136.5		221.6	ALIMENTS,ANIMAUX VIVANTS
001	*LIVE ANIMALS FOR FOOD	N 2441700	7.2	W 6446	4.8	W 7450	6.7	W 5801	6.1	ANIMAUX VIVANTS
0011	BOVINE SPECIES,LIVE	N 8178	5.4	W 6441	4.2	W 7446	6.1	W 5794	5.4	ESPECE BOVINE
00111	— PURE BRED FR BREEDING	N 690	0.5	W 4546	3.0	W 7177	5.9	W 5649	5.3	BOVINS REPRODUCTEURS
00119	— OTHR THAN FR BREEDING	N 7488	4.9	W 1895	1.2	W 269	0.2	W 145	0.2	BOVINS NON REPRODUCTEURS
01	MEAT AND PREPARATIONS		26.2		25.4		25.0		44.1	VIANDES ET PREPARATIONS
011	MEAT FRESH,CHILLD,FROZEN	W 11307	22.0	W 10240	21.8	W 7732	21.0	W 16156	37.4	VIANDES FRAICHES,REF,CONGE
0111	BOVINE MEAT FRESH,FROZEN	W 1441	4.3	W 1159	4.3	W 1001	3.9	W 1957	6.7	VIANDES BOVIN FRAI,REF
01111	BOVINE MEAT WITH BONE IN			W 1159	4.3	W 1001	3.9	W 1957	6.7	VIANDES BOVIN NON DESOSS
0114	POULTRY FRESH CHLLD,FRZN	W 8512	15.3	W 7876	14.1	W 5044	12.7	W 10361	20.0	VOLAILLES MORTES
0118	MEAT NES FRESH,CHLD,FRZN	W 103	0.3	W 394	1.2	W 948	2.6	W 2144	6.2	AUTRES VIANDES,ABATS
014	MEAT PREPD,PRSVD,NES ETC	W 1184	3.9	W 974	3.5	W 1106	3.2	W 1340	4.1	CONSERVES DE VIANDES
02	DAIRY PRODCTS,BIRDS'EGGS		14.7		14.3		11.3		12.8	PRODUITS LAITIERS,OEUFS
022	MILK AND CREAM	W 5160	12.1	W 4486	10.8	W 3855	8.3	W 3418	8.7	LAIT ET CREME
0224	MILK,CREAM PRESERVED ETC	W 5111	12.0	W 4313	10.4	W 3556	7.8	W 2699	7.8	LAIT,CREME CONS,CONC
02243	MILK DRY,OVER 1.5% FAT	W 1595	7.1	W 1578	5.6	W 1500	3.8	W 1417	3.6	LAIT POUDRE SUP 1.5%
02249	MILK(EX DRY) PRSVD,SWEET	W 3260	4.4	W 2528	4.4	W 1873	3.4	W 1072	3.3	LAIT CONS,CONC SUCRE
03	FISH AND PREPARATIONS		12.8		13.5		13.0		32.6	POISSONS ET PREPARATIONS
034	FISH,FRESH,CHILLED,FROZN		4.4	W 399	5.1	W 959	4.9	W 2052	8.8	POISSON FRAIS, REFRIG,CONG
036	SHELL FISH FRESH,FROZEN	W 759	3.7	W 966	3.6	W 1854	3.9	W 1920	6.4	CRUSTACES,MOLLUSQUES
037	FISH ETC PREPD,PRSVD NES	W 804	3.5	W 866	3.7	W 771	3.1	W 7979	15.6	POIS,CRUST,MOL PREPARES
0371	FISH PREPARD,PRESRVD NES	W 493	1.7	W 489	1.8	W 506	1.6	W 7454	13.2	CONSERVES DE POISSONS
04	CEREALS AND PREPARATIONS		28.3		28.3		23.4		41.2	CEREALES ET PRODUITS
042	RICE	W 21324	9.2	W 17069	8.0	W 13058	4.1	W 19334	9.9	RIZ
0422	RICE SEMI–MILLED,MILLED	W 21324	9.2	W 17069	8.0	W 13058	4.1	W 19334	9.9	RIZ POLI,GLACE INCL BRISURES
04221	RICE MILLED UNBROKEN	W 21301	9.2	W 17069	8.0	W 13058	4.1	W 19334	9.9	RIZ POLI,GLACE EXCL BRISURES
048	CEREAL ETC PREPARATIONS	W 8408	15.9	W 8177	17.7	W 10456	16.7	W 11317	27.7	PREPTNS A BASE CEREALES
0483	MACARONI,SPAGHETTI ETC	W 1502	1.8	W 2954	5.4	W 5146	4.6	W 2843	6.7	PATES ALMENTAIRES
0484	BAKERY PRODUCTS	W 2422	7.8	W 2702	7.1	W 2259	6.2	W 3379	10.4	PRODUITS DE BOULANGERIE
04841	BREAD,BISCUIT,COM WAFERS	W 19	0.1	W 1673	4.7	W 1467	4.3	W 1920	6.6	PAINS,BISCUITS DE MER
04842	PASTRY, CAKES ETC	W 2403	7.8	W 1029	2.4	W 792	1.9	W 1458	3.8	PATISSERIE ETC.
0488	OTH CEREAL PREPS,MALT EX	W 1166	3.5	W 1210	3.0	W 2069	3.9	W 3202	7.8	EXTRAITS DE MALT
05	VEGETABLES AND FRUIT		31.2		29.9		27.9		41.9	LEGUMES ET FRUITS
054	VEG ETC FRSH,SMPLY PRSVD		7.7		7.9		7.6		10.7	LEGUMES FRAIS,CONG,SECS
0545	OTHER FRESH VEGETABLES	W 5554	5.5	W 3949	5.0	W 5440	4.5	W 34652	6.6	AUTRES LEGUMES FRAIS,REF
05459	FRESH VEGETABLES NES	W 2897	3.8	W 2670	3.7	W 3564	3.3	W 32550	4.9	LEGUMES FRAIS,REFRI NDA
057	FRUIT,NUTS,FRESH,DRIED		14.1	W 11031	12.9	W 15326	12.6	W 13064	19.5	FRUITS FRAIS OU SECS
0579	FRUIT FRESH OR DRIED NES	W 5870	6.2	W 2661	5.4	W 4610	5.4	W 3786	8.3	FRUITS FRAIS,SECS NDA
05798	OTHER FRESH FRUIT	W 3907	4.1	W 1477	2.9	W 2842	3.1	W 2242	4.8	AUTRES FRUITS FRAIS
058	FRUIT PRESERVED,PREPARED	W 2985	6.1		5.8		4.9		7.1	CONSERVES DE FRUITS
0589	FRUIT PREPRD,PRESRVD,NES	W 1602	4.0		3.6		2.6		3.1	FRUITS PREPARES CONSERV
06	SUGAR AND PREPS,HONEY		6.5		4.5		4.5		5.1	SUCRES ET PRODUITS
061	SUGAR AND HONEY		3.9	W 1327	1.7	W 1754	1.4	W 587	1.7	SUCRES ET MIEL
0612	REFINED SUGAR ETC	W 6643	3.8	W 1193	1.4	W 1697	1.2	W 461	0.9	SUCRES RAFFINES
07	COFFEE,TEA,COCOA,SPICES		7.8		8.4		8.5		13.1	CAFE,THE,CACAO,EPICES
073	CHOCOLATE AND PRODUCTS	W 500	3.2	W 1034	4.0	W 1170	4.7	W 2937	8.4	CHOCOLAT
081	*FEEDING STUFF FOR ANIML	W 14429	8.3	W 7664	7.4	W 5749	6.0	W 11409	8.8	NOURRITURE POUR ANIMAUX
0819	FOOD WASTE AND FEED NES	W 7958	5.5	W 2372	4.7	W 2912	3.8	W 6820	6.2	DECHETS,ALIMENTS NDA
08199	FODDER NES,INCL SWEETNED	W 7958	5.5	W 2372	4.7	W 2912	3.8	W 6819	6.2	PREPARATIONS FOURRAGERES
09	MISC EDIBLE PRODUCTS		13.1		10.8		10.6		16.5	PREP ALIMENTAIRES DIVERSES
098	EDIBLE PRODCTS,PREPS NES		12.4	W 15792	10.1		10.2		15.5	PREP ALIMENTAIRES NDA
09804	SAUCES,MIXED SEASONINGS	W 2302	3.4	W 13267	3.7	W 15420	3.2	W 25365	7.3	SAUCES,ASSAISONNEMENTS
09809	MISC FOOD PREPRTIONS NES	W 3329	7.9	W 2027	5.4		5.0		5.9	PREP ALIMENTAIRES NDA
1	BEVERAGES AND TOBACCO		28.9		33.5		32.0		40.9	BOISSONS ET TABACS
11	BEVERAGES		17.6		19.2		16.9		21.6	BOISSONS
111	NON–ALCOHL BEVERAGES NES	W 19846	17.1	W 21821	17.1	W 22567	15.0	W 25941	19.7	BOISSONS NON ALCOOLIQUES
11102	FLAVORED WATERS NON–ALCO	W 16328	14.9	W 16444	14.3	W 15503	12.6	W 18236	15.8	LIMONADES,EAUX GAZEUSES
12	TOBACCO AND MANUFACTURES		11.4		14.3		15.1		19.4	TABACS BRUTS FABRIQUES
122	TOBACCO,MANUFACTURED	W 420	11.4	W 409	14.3	W 424	15.1	W 481	19.4	TABACS FABRIQUES
1222	CIGARETTES	W 419	11.4	W 125	3.9	W 139	4.5	W 184	6.9	CIGARETTES
1223	OTH MANUFACTURED TOBACCO			W 281	10.4	W 284	10.6	W 293	12.3	TABACS FUMER,CHIQUER,PRISER
2	CRUDE MATERLS,EXCL FUELS		14.9		24.6		17.0		46.9	MAT BRUTES NON COMESTIBLES
24	CORK AND WOOD		3.1		4.9		5.0		10.8	LIEGE ET BOIS
248	WOOD SHAPED,SLEEPERS		2.9	W 33600	4.5	W 14707	4.7	W 29743	10.3	BOIS SIMPLEMENT TRAVAILLES
2483	LUMBER SHAPED NON–CONIFR		2.9	W 33599	4.4	W 14707	4.6	W 29741	9.8	NON CONIFERES SCIES,RABOTES
24831	LUMBER SAWN ETC NON–CON	W 19536	2.7	W 30797	4.1	W 13357	4.2	W 26716	8.6	SCIES LONGITUDINALEMENT
27	CRUDE FERTLZR,MINRLS NES		7.9		15.0		9.6		31.7	ENGRAIS MINERAUX BRUTS
273	STONE,SAND AND GRAVEL	W 94945	4.9		12.5		7.4		29.0	PIERRES,SABLES,GRAVIERS
2731	BLDG,DIMENSION STONE	W 4230	3.7	W 4331	9.3	W 2301	4.3	W 19970	16.3	PIERRES DE TAILLE
27312	MARBLE,ETC BLDG STONE	W 863	2.0	W 2270	7.2	W 1387	3.3	W 13551	11.7	MARBRES,TRAVERTINS
2734	GRAVEL,CRUSHED STONE,ETC	W 83779	0.8	W 145949	2.6	W 147945	2.7	W 813504	11.9	PIERRES CONCASSEES
3	MINERAL FUELS ETC		7.4		8.8		19.8		7.6	COMBUSTIBLES MINERAUX LUB
33	PETROLEUM AND PRODUCTS		7.4		8.7		19.5		7.4	PETROLE ET DERIVES
334	PETROLEUM PRODUCTS,REFIN	W 20276	7.2	W 18306	8.2	W 40728	19.1	W 5215	6.6	PRODUITS RAFFINES
3341	GASOLINE,OTH LIGHT OILS	W 13284	1.3	W 13176	1.2	W 32916	9.0	W 156	0.1	ESSENCES POUR MOTEURS
33411	MOTOR,AVIATION SPIRIT	W 13253	1.2	W 13173	1.2	W 32915	9.0	W 147	0.1	ESSENCES MOTEURS D'AVIONS
3345	LUBS,PETROLEUM OILS NES	W 6134	5.4	W 2558	5.9	W 6337	7.8	W 4964	6.5	HUILES LUBRIFIANTES
33451	LUBS(HIGH PETR CONT) ETC	W 5790	4.9	W 1613	4.2	W 1996	3.2	W 2113	2.4	HUILES LUBRIF,H LOURDES
4	ANIMAL,VEGETABLE OIL,FAT		4.2		5.0		4.2		6.3	HUILES,GRAISSES ANIM,VEG
42	FIXED VEGETABLE OIL,FAT		4.1		3.9		3.2		3.7	HUILES VEGETALES FIXES
424	FIXED VEG OIL NONSOFT	W 1619	3.7	W 496	3.5		2.5	W 240	2.8	AUTRES HUILES VEG FIXES
5	CHEMCLS,RELATED PROD NES		75.9		77.9		70.0		86.8	PRODUITS CHIMIQUES
52	INORGANIC CHEMICALS		7.4		6.7		6.3		7.2	PROD CHIM INORGANIQUES
522	INORG ELEMNTS,OXIDES,ETC		4.2		4.5		2.7		2.6	ELEMENTS INORGANIQUES
53	DYES,TANNING,COLOUR PROD		13.4		17.0		13.6		16.0	PROD TEINTURE,COLORANTS
533	PIGMENTS,PAINTS,ETC		13.2		16.8		13.4		15.9	PIGMENTS,PEINTURES,VERNIS
5334	VARNISHES,DISTEMPERS ETC		12.1	W 5809	15.5	W 4474	12.7	W 4832	15.1	PEINTURES A L'EAU
53342	OTH PAINTS,VARNISHES ETC	V 3143	10.6	W 5779	15.5	W 4464	12.7	W 4634	14.7	AUTRES PEINTURES,VERNIS
541	*MEDICINAL,PHARM PRODUCT		14.1		16.3		13.0		20.5	PROD MEDICINAUX PHARMACEUT
5417	MEDICAMENTS		10.8		12.6		9.1		13.2	MEDICAMENTS
54179	— CONTNG OTH SUBSTANCES		10.8		8.4		8.0		9.6	MED CONT AUT SUBSTANCES
55	PERFUME,CLEANING ETC PRD		12.9		13.3		13.5		15.4	PROD POUR PARFUM,TOILETTE
553	PERFUMERY,COSMETICS,ETC		5.6		6.3		5.8		7.4	PRODUITS DE PARFUMERIE
554	SOAP,CLEANSING ETC PREPS	W 5821	7.0		6.9		7.6		7.9	SAVONS,PRODUITS DETERSIFS
5542	WASHING PREPARATIONS ETC	W 5020	5.1	W 3007	4.2	W 3196	4.6	W 2549	4.2	PROD ORG TENSIO–ACT NDA
58	PLASTIC MATERIALS ETC		4.8		2.9		4.3		5.2	MAT PLAST ARTIFICIELLES
583	POLYMERIZATION ETC PRODS	W 2292	3.9		2.2		3.5		3.8	PROD POLYMERISATION
59	CHEMICAL MATERIALS NES		18.7		16.9		15.6		18.1	MAT PROD CHIMIQUES NDA
598	MISCEL CHEM PRODUCTS NES		15.3		12.8		11.8		12.8	PROD DIV INDUST CHIM NDA
5989	CHEM PRODUCTS,PREPS NES		13.6		10.7		10.3		11.4	PROD PREP CHIMIQUES NDA

4. General Imports C.I.F. by Commodities according to the S.I.T.C. (Rev. 2) in million U.S. Dollars
Importations Générales C.A.F. par Produits d'après la C.T.C.I. (Rév. 2) en millions de Dollars E.U.

SITC CTCI	COMMODITY	1991 QUANTITY QUANTITE	1991 VALUE VALEUR	1992 QUANTITY QUANTITE	1992 VALUE VALEUR	1993 QUANTITY QUANTITE	1993 VALUE VALEUR	1994 QUANTITY QUANTITE	1994 VALUE VALEUR	PRODUIT
59899	OTH CHEM PRODS,PREPS,NES	W 4942	12.6	W 3443	8.2	W 7658	9.0	W 3233	9.3	AUT PRODUITS CHIMIQUES NDA
6	BASIC MANUFACTURES		331.2		335.8		360.7		430.0	ART MANUFACTURES
62	RUBBER MANUFACTURES NES		7.7		11.9		9.3		11.0	CAOUTCHOUC MANUFACTURE
621	MATERIALS OF RUBBER	W 375	2.6	W 862	4.7	W 331	2.0	W 577	2.5	PRODUITS EN CAOUTCHOUC
625	RUBBER TYRES, TUBES ETC	N 324782	4.1	N 365182	4.7	N 369033	4.1	N 398572	5.2	PNEUS CAOUTCHOUC VULCANISE
63	WOOD,CORK MANUFACTRS NES		8.2		11.5		9.4		12.4	OUVRAGES LIEGE ET BOIS
634	VENEERS,PLYWOOD,ETC		5.3		6.7		5.8		7.3	PLACAGES,CONTRE–PLAQUES
6342	PLYWOOD OF WOOD SHEETS	V 23138	4.3	W 30	6.0	W 26	5.3	W 48	6.7	BOIS CONTRE–PLAQUES
635	WOOD MANUFACTURES NES		2.9		4.8		3.7		5.1	ART MANUF EN BOIS NDA
64	PAPER,PAPERBOARD AND MFR		15.7		15.9		19.1		27.8	PAPIERS,CARTONS & OUVRAGES
641	PAPER AND PAPERBOARD		6.7		4.8		6.2		8.2	PAPIERS ET CARTONS
6412	PRINTG,WRITING PAPER NES	W 2257	3.8		1.0		0.8		1.1	PAPIERS POUR L'IMPRESSION
642	PAPER,ETC,PRECUT,ARTS OF		9.0		11.2		12.9		19.7	PAP,CARTONS DECOUPES
6428	PAPER ETC ARTICLES NES		2.9		5.3		6.4		10.2	OUVRAGES EN PATE A PAPIER
65	TEXTILE YARN,FABRICS,ETC		31.0		38.9		41.2		43.3	FILS,TISSUS,ARTICLES TEXTILE
652	COTTON FABRICS,WOVEN	A 1829	2.2	A 1931	2.9	A 3309	6.3	A 11414	7.6	TISSUS DE COTON
6522	WOVEN COTTON BLEACHD,ETC	A 1774	2.2	A 1644	2.6	A 2684	4.9	A 9634	6.0	TISSUS COTON BLANCHIS ETC
65224	BLCHED COTTON FABRIC NES	A 1707	2.1	A 1429	2.5	A 2544	4.7	A 9342	5.8	AUT TIS PLUS 85% COT BLANCHI
653	WOVN MAN–MADE FIB FABRIC		3.1	W 2431	4.7		3.7	W 1300	3.9	TISSUS FIBRES SYNTH,ARTIF
655	KNITTED,ETC FABRICS	A 3829	8.5	A 2813	5.5	A 2814	0.9	A 1227	1.5	ETOF BONNETERIE PIECES ETC
6552	OTHER KNIT ETC FAB NONEL	A 1988	4.6	A 2813	5.5	A 2814	0.9	A 1227	1.5	ETOF BON NON ELAS NON SYNT
65522	KNIT ETC COTTN FAB NONEL	A 1293	3.7							ETOF BON NON ELAS COTON
656	LACE,RIBBONS,TULLE,ETC		0.6		4.0		7.3		9.4	TULLES,BRODERIE
65601	NARROW FABRICS NES	L 905	0.2	L 29460	2.7	L 60035	4.7	L 63781	7.2	RUBANS SANS TRAME EN FILS
657	SPECIAL TXTL FABRC,PRODS		6.3		8.4		11.5		6.3	TISSUS SPECIAUX
6571	FELT AND ARTICLES NES		0.1		2.6	W 2	8.1	W 178	2.8	FEUTRES,ART EN FEUTRE
6577	TEXTILES FOR MACHINERY		4.1		3.3		1.3		1.1	OUATES,MECHES ART TEXT
65771	TEXTILE WADDING NES ETC		4.0		3.3		1.3		0.9	OUATES,ARTICLES EN OUATE
658	TEXTILE ARTICLES NES		4.4		5.1		3.9		4.6	ART FACONNES MAT TEXTILES
659	FLOOR COVERINGS,ETC		5.3		7.1		5.1	W 537	6.9	COUVRE–PARQUETS,TAPIS ETC
66	NONMETAL MINERAL MFS NES		71.7		70.6		70.9		97.1	ART MIN NON METALLIQUES
661	LIME,CEMENT,BLDG PRODS	W 198607	33.4	W 188812	23.9	W 338982	28.1	W 536632	39.2	CHAUX,CIMENTS MAT CONSTR
6612	CEMENT	W 186295	18.1	W 185058	18.0	W 332625	24.1	W 528923	32.6	CIMENTS HYDRAULIQUES
6613	BUILDING STONE ETC WORKD	W 11415	14.5	W 1792	4.1	W 4536	2.2	W 1050	1.8	PIERRES A BATIR
66132	BUILDING STONE WORKED	W 11415	14.5	W 1792	4.1	W 4536	2.2	W 1050	1.7	OUVR EN PIERRES DE TAILLE
662	CLAY,REFRACTORY BLDG PRD		18.7	W 22949	22.9	W 46434	19.6	W 30333	23.5	MAT CONST REFRACTAIRES
6623	REFRACTORY BUILDING PROD	W 449	0.5	W 2712	3.9	W 7229	4.7	W 9093	5.8	BRIQUES REFRACTAIRES
6624	BRICKS ETC NONREFRACTORY		18.2	W 20238	19.0	W 39205	14.9	W 21240	17.8	BRIQUES ETC CERAM NON REFR
66244	UNGLAZD CERAMC SETTS ETC	W 6051	5.0	W 2839	2.1	W 2140	2.1	W 3646	4.2	CARREAUX, NON VERNIS
66245	GLAZED CERAMIC SETTS ETC	W 16587	10.6	W 12647	11.5	W 14108	6.6	W 6947	5.8	AUT CARREAUX CERAMIQUE
663	MINERAL MANUFCTURES NES		6.9		7.4		11.5		19.0	ART MIN MANUF NDA
6633	MINRL MFS NES NONCERAMIC		5.2		6.1		9.8		17.1	OUVR MAT MINERALE NDA
66332	CEMENT,ARTFCL STONE PROD	W 9672	2.2	W 14686	4.5	W 44294	8.6	W 90957	16.1	OUVRAGES EN CIMENT
664	GLASS		4.7		8.0		5.7		7.9	VERRE
665	GLASSWARE		4.9		4.6		3.4		4.9	OUVRAGES EN VERRE
6652	HOUSEHLD,HOTEL ETC GLASS		3.7		3.3		2.6		3.7	OBJETS VERRE TABLE,CUISINE
67	IRON AND STEEL		77.8		86.3		64.9		124.5	FER ET ACIER
673	IRON,STEEL SHAPES ETC		21.0	W 37338	22.9	W 20557	26.2	W 34339	43.9	BARRES,PROFIL FER,ACIER
6731	IRON,STEEL WIRE ROD		0.8	W 2025	4.6	W 183	4.5	W 15	7.2	FIL MACHINE FER,ACIER
67314	STNLESS STL ETC WIRE ROD			W 2	1.6	W 5	2.9	W 12	6.8	FIL MACH ACIER INOXYDABLE
6732	IRON,STEEL BARS ETC	W 33369	15.0	W 17355	7.8	W 12444	6.2	W 14055	10.1	BARRES FER,ACIER
67322	HIGH CARBON STL BARS ETC	W 76	0.1	W 11477	5.2	W 2744	1.8	W 2407	1.3	BARRES ACIER FIN CARBONE
67325	OTH ALLOY STEEL BARS ETC	W 53	0.1	W 5878	2.6	W 9700	4.3	W 11648	8.8	BARRES NON ACIERS ALLIES
67326	IRN,OTH STL BARS HOTROLD	W 30392	13.5							BARRES PLEINES FER,ACIER
6733	IRON,STEEL PROFILES ETC	W 6275	5.2	W 17958	10.6	W 7930	15.6	W 20269	26.7	PROFILES,PALPLAN FER,ACIER
67338	STNLESS STL ETC PROFILES	W 17	0.1	W 10777	5.0	W 2558	10.6	W 2510	19.1	PROFILES ACIER INOXYDABLE
674	IRN,STL UNIV,PLATE,SHEET		6.1		7.4		3.8		11.3	LARGES PLATS,TOLES
6744	IRN,STL HVY PLATE,ROLLED	W 196	0.2		4.4		1.6		8.3	TOLES LAMINEES PLUS 4.75 MM
67443	— OF STAINLESS ETC STL	W 4	0.1		1.8		1.1		6.4	TOLES ACIER INOXYDABLE
6749	OTH IRN,STL PLATES,SHEET		5.0	W 1334	2.1	W 430	1.4	W 497	1.7	AUTRES TOLES FER,ACIER
67491	— OF IRON OR SIMPLE STL	W 4102	5.0	W 1334	1.4	W 428	0.6	W 495	0.6	AUT TOLES AUTRES ACIER FIN
678	IRON,STL TUBES,PIPES,ETC	W 53792	48.6	W 47828	51.5	W 33943	29.9	W 95525	63.6	TUBES,TUYAUX EN FONTE,FER
6781	CAST IRON TUBES,PIPES	W 1036	1.1	W 876	1.0	W 2542	1.8	W 7959	11.4	TUBES,TUYAUX EN FONTE
6782	IRON,STL SEAMLESS TUBES	W 33599	20.3	W 17668	21.6	W 9195	6.5	W 58240	19.6	TUBES,TUYAUX SANS SOUDURE
6783	IRON,STL TUBES,PIPES NES	W 13395	14.4	W 10725	10.2	W 8735	8.6	W 9712	12.9	AUT TUBES,TUYAUX FER,ACIER
6785	IRON,STEEL TUBE FITTINGS	W 5526	12.6	W 18560	18.9	W 13472	13.1	W 19613	19.9	ACCESSOIRES DE TUYAUTERIE
68	NON–FERROUS METALS		4.4		6.3		8.0		10.6	METAUX NON FERREUX
69	METAL MANUFACTURES NES		114.6		94.3		137.5		102.0	ART MANUFACT EN METAL NDA
691	STRUCTURES AND PARTS NES	W 12994	21.2	W 17908	31.8	W 15338	65.5	W 17106	32.3	CONSTRUCT FER,ACIER,ALU
6911	STRUCTURES,PARTS IRN,STL	W 12457	18.4	W 13772	27.2	W 13734	62.7	W 10736	24.4	CONSTRUCT FER,ACIER,FONTE
6912	STRUCTURES,PARTS ALUMNM	W 537	2.9	W 4137	4.6	W 1604	2.8	W 6370	7.9	CONSTRUCT ALUMINIUM
692	METAL TANKS,BOXES,ETC		3.2		4.5		24.3		3.9	RECIPIENTS METALLIQUES
6924	MTL TRANSPORT BOXES ETC		2.3		3.9		23.9		2.6	FUTS,TAMBOURS,BIDONS
69242	ALUMNM TRNSPRT BOXES ETC		1.8		1.6		20.4		0.3	FUTS,TAMBOURS,BIDONS ALU
693	WIRE PRODUCTS NON ELECTR		6.0	W 3984	6.6	W 2138	5.4	W 2749	7.3	OUVRAGES FILS METALLIQUES
694	STL,COPPR NAILS,NUTS,ETC	W 3893	4.2	W 3554	5.0	W 3239	5.0	W 3768	7.5	CLOUS,VIS,ECROUS
695	TOOLS		25.6		15.9		10.1		11.2	OUTILS A MAIN
6953	OTHER HAND TOOLS		3.5		6.2		5.0		6.2	AUTRES OUTILS A MAIN
6954	BLADES,TIPS,ETC FR TOOLS		21.9		9.5		4.9		4.6	OUTILS POUR MACHINE–OUTIL
69541	PARTS TO INSERT IN TOOLS		21.9		9.2		4.7		4.3	OUTILS DE FORAGE
697	BASE MTL HOUSEHOLD EQUIP		26.6		6.6		6.0		9.1	ART MENAGE MET COMMUNS
6978	BASE MTL HOUSE EQUIP NES		21.0		1.0		0.9		0.8	ART MENAGE MET COMMUNS
69782	BASE MTL DECOR ARTICLES		20.9		1.0		0.8		0.7	AUT OBJETS ORNEM INTERIEUR
699	BASE METAL MFRS NES		26.4		22.7		20.1		28.5	ART MANUFACTURES MET NDA
6991	LOCKSMITHS WARES,ETC		4.7		5.5		5.1		5.7	ARTICLES DE SERRURERIE
6997	IRON,STEEL ARTICLES NES		15.5	W 6822	9.2	W 2829	7.5	W 3589	12.7	OUV FONTE,FER,ACIER NDA
69979	IRN,STL MANUFACTURES NES		15.0	W 6822	8.8	W 2829	7.1	W 3589	12.5	AUT OUVRAGES EN FER NDA
6998	MFRS NES OF CPR,NIKL,ETC		3.7		5.1		5.0		7.8	OUVRAGES EN CU,NI,AL,PB,ZN
7	MACHINES,TRANSPORT EQUIP		462.7		650.5		902.4		793.0	MACHINES MATERIEL TRANSPORT
71	POWER GENERATING EQUIPMT		28.7		49.5		18.2		106.4	MACHINES GENERATRICES
712	STEAM ENGINES,TURBINES		8.7		1.0		1.5		12.3	MACHINES A VAPEUR D'EAU PIEC
7126	STEAM POWR UNITS,ENGINES	N 583	0.8		0.2		0.1		10.3	MACHINES A VAPEUR D EAU
7129	STM ENGINE ETC PARTS NES		8.0		0.9		1.4		2.1	PARTIES,PIECES DU 712.6
713	INTRNL COMBUS PSTN ENGIN		7.8		6.4		4.7		6.0	MOTEURS EXPL COMB INT, PIECE
714	ENGINES AND MOTORS NES		0.3	W 84	2.9	W 16	1.2	W 300	8.1	MOTEURS NON ELECTRIQUES
7149	ENGINE & MOTOR PARTS NES		0.3	W 84	2.7	W 14	1.1	W 300	7.5	PIECES 714 ET 718.88
71499	PARTS NES,OF 71488,71888			W 84	2.7	W 13	1.1	W 300	7.4	PIECES 714.88 ET 718.88
716	ROTATING ELECTRIC PLANT		9.5		38.2		9.7		78.5	APP ELECTR ROTATIFS,PIECES
7161	DC MOTORS AND GENERATORS	N 885	1.8	N 1297	2.2	N 2270	1.2	N 8350	36.8	MOTEURS COURANT CONTINU
7162	AC MTRS,GENRTRS,GEN SETS	N 1027	7.3	N 4478	29.9	N 2240	2.1		2.5	MOTEURS ELECTRIQUES
71622	AC GENERATORS	N 111	0.9	N 1766	28.2	N 91	0.4		1.2	GENER COURANT ALTERNATIF

4. General Imports C.I.F. by Commodities according to the S.I.T.C. (Rev. 2) in million U.S. Dollars
Importations Générales C.A.F. par Produits d'après la C.T.C.I. (Rév. 2) en millions de Dollars E.U.

SITC CTCI	COMMODITY	1991		1992		1993		1994		PRODUIT
		QUANTITY QUANTITE	VALUE VALEUR	QUANTITY QUANTITE	VALUE VALEUR	QUANTITY QUANTITE	VALUE VALEUR	QUANTITY QUANTITE	VALUE VALEUR	
71623	GEN SETS WITH PISTN ENGN	N 291	6.2	N 150	0.9	N 154	1.1	N 54	0.3	GROUPES MOTEUR EXPLOSION
7169	PTS NES OF ROT ELEC PLNT		0.5		6.2		6.5		39.3	PIECES MAC APP ROTATIFS
72	MACHS FOR SPCL INDUSTRYS		21.5		15.8		14.7		18.1	MAC SPECIALES POUR INDUST
723	CIVIL ENGNEERG EQUIP ETC		14.4		5.6		4.5		8.0	APPAREILS DE GENIE CIVIL
7234	CONST,MINING MACHNRY NES	N 98	3.1		4.3		3.0		5.9	MACH POUR LA CONST, MINES
7239	CONSTR ETC MACHY PTS NES		11.1		1.0		1.4		1.6	PIECES 723.41–723.46
728	OTH MACHY FOR SPCL INDUS		4.7		6.2		4.8		3.5	AUT MACH IND PARTICULIERES
74	GENRL INDUSTRL MACHY NES		94.9		123.7		218.8		87.8	MACH APP INDUSTRIE
741	HEATING,COOLING EQUIPMNT		11.3		16.2		17.5		21.1	MACH CHAUFFAGE,PIECES
7415	AIR–CONDITIONING MACHNRY		7.0		11.1		9.9		15.7	GROUPES CONDITION AIR
742	PUMPS FOR LIQUIDS ETC		2.4		6.0		6.3		5.3	POMPES MOTO–POMPES
743	PUMPS NES,CENTRFUGES ETC		12.7		16.3		8.0		9.0	POMPES COMPRES,VENT ETC
7431	PUMPS FOR GASES ETC	N 10781	6.1	N 7448	10.3	N 10686	3.3	N 11165	2.8	POMPES AIR A VIDE,COMPRES
7433	FREE–PSTN GEN FR GAS TUR		3.9							GENERATEURS A PISTONS LIBRES
744	MECHANICAL HANDLING EQU		17.8		22.1		18.6		26.1	EQUIP MANUTENTION PIECES
7441	FORK LIFT TRCKS,ETC,PTS		1.8		2.5		4.6		7.4	CHARIOTS POUR USINES ETC
74411	FORK LIFT TRUCKS ETC	N 69	1.6		2.4		4.2		7.4	CHARIOTS POUR LES GARES
7442	LIFTING,LOADING MACH NES	N 1063	11.5	N 6972	6.5	N 5300	7.2	N 1988	9.3	APP LEVAGE,MANUTENTION
74421	PULLEY TACKLE,WINCHS ETC	N 141	4.2	N 296	0.7	N 629	0.4	N 349	0.3	PALANS,TREUILS
74422	SHIP DERRICKS,CRANES ETC	N 31	3.7	N 169	3.1	N 964	2.4	N 127	4.7	GRUES,PONTS ROULANTS
7449	PTS NES OF MACHY OF 7442		4.6		13.3		6.9		9.4	PIECES DU 744.2
745	NONELEC MACHY,TOOLS NES		4.7		4.2		3.4		4.1	AUT MACH NON ELEC,PIECES
749	NONELEC MACH PTS,ACC NES		46.2		59.1		165.3		22.6	PIECES MACH NON ELEC NDA
7491	BALL,ROLLER,ETC BEARINGS		1.0		24.2		1.3		1.8	ROULEMENTS BILLES ETC
7492	COCKS,VALVES ETC NES		20.1		23.2		11.3		12.4	ART ROB,SIM POUR TUYAUX
7499	OTH NONELEC MCHY PTS NES		22.1		9.5		151.8		7.0	PIECES NON ELECT NDA
74999	MACH PARTS NONELEC NES		20.7	W 649	7.4	W 9003	150.3	W 567	5.8	PIECES MACHINES NDA
75	OFFICE MACHNES,ADP EQUIP		26.7		23.5		22.1		30.1	MACH BUREAU TRAIT AUTOM
751	OFFICE MACHINES	N 69641	3.8	W 36	2.3	W 30	2.0	W 40	2.7	MACH,APPAREILS DE BUREAU
752	AUTOMTIC DATA PROC EQUIP	N 9156	10.1		9.4		10.0		17.9	MACH TRAIT INFORMATION
7522	DIGITAL COMPUTERS	N 39	0.1	N 2989	4.9	N 2587	2.4	N 1958	4.2	MACH DIGITALES COMPLETES
7528	OFF–LINE DATA PROC EQUIP	N 4447	6.5	N 1508	1.4	N 5444	2.8	N 3285	5.6	MACH AUXIL TRAIT INFORM
759	OFFICE,ADP MCH PTS,ACCES		13.0		11.9		10.3		9.7	PIECES DU 751 ET 752
7599	ACCTG,ETC,ADP MCH PTS,AC		12.2		11.2		9.4		7.7	PIECES DU 751 ET 752
76	TELECOMM,SOUND EQUIPMENT		30.1		40.5		60.0		77.8	EQUIPMENT DE TELECOM
761	TELEVISION RECEIVERS	N 12685	2.6	N 20634	2.1	N 19650	2.2	N 119580	12.9	RECEPTEURS DE TELEVISION
7611	COLOUR TV RECEIVERS	N 12212	2.6	N 14014	2.0	N 16670	2.2	N 118710	12.9	RECEPTEURS COULEUR
763	SOUND RECORDRS,PHONOGRPH	N 30593	2.1	N 54223	3.4	N 137191	3.3	N 143891	7.5	PHONO,APP ENREGISTREMENT
7638	OTHR SOUND APPARATUS ETC	N 30567	2.1	N 50686	2.6	N 130307	2.1	N 124050	6.7	AUT APP D'ENREGIS,REPROD
764	TELECOM EQPT,PTS,ACC NES		23.7		33.2		52.5		55.7	EQUIP TELECOM,PIECES
7641	LINE TELEPHONE,ETC EQUIP		9.2	N 32311	13.5	N 136621	29.1	N 51133	17.8	APP TELEPHON PAR FIL
7643	TV,RADIO TRANSMITTRS ETC	N 1083	0.3	N 2550	1.1	N 3028	1.6	N 68080	13.3	APP EMET TELE RADIO
7649	PTS NES OF EQUIPMT OF 76		11.7		15.0		18.8		18.8	PIECES DE LA DIV 76
76491	PTS NES OF APPAR OF 7641		9.3		9.6		7.5		11.1	PIECES POUR 764.1
76493	TELECOMM EQUIPMT PTS NES		2.3		5.1		11.1		7.3	PIECES 761,762,764.3,8
77	ELECTRIC MACHNRY NES ETC		67.9		117.7		110.7		204.0	MACH APP ELECT NDA
771	ELECTRIC POWER MACHY NES		5.8		13.7		18.5		24.0	MACH PROD,TRANS ELECTR
7711	TRANSFORMERS,ELECTRICAL	N 19576	4.2	N 20480	10.7	N 10121	17.4	N 16089	10.0	TRANSFO ELECTRIQUES
77111	LIQUID DIELEC TRANSFRMRS			N 2452	5.1	N 3204	14.5	N 4626	7.5	TRANSFO DIELEC LIQUIDE
77118	OTHER ELEC TRANSFORMERS	N 19576	4.2	N 18028	5.6	N 6917	2.9	N 11463	2.5	AUTRES TRANSFO ELECTRIQ
7712	OTH ELEC POWER MACHY NES		1.6		3.1		1.1		14.1	AUT APP PROD TRANSF ELEC
77122	INDUCTORS	N 16652	0.1	N 246100	1.5	N 68595	0.4	N 2006000	12.6	BOBINES REACTANCE,SELFS
772	SWITCHGEAR ETC,PARTS NES		17.5		21.4		22.7		34.1	APP COUPURE,SECT ETC
7721	SWITCHGEAR ETC		16.3		21.2		22.5		30.8	APP COUPURE,SECTIONMNT
773	ELECTR DISTRIBUTNG EQUIP		20.6		42.7		40.9		107.9	EQUIPMT DISTRIBUTION ELECT
7731	INSULATED WIRE,CABLE ETC		18.8	W 29789	42.2	W 23293	39.8	W 46280	103.5	FILS,CABLES ISOLES ELECT
775	HOUSEHOLD TYPE EQUIP NES		7.8		9.5		8.3		9.2	MACH,APP USAGE DOMESTQUE
778	ELECTRICAL MACHINERY NES		16.1		27.2		18.1		22.6	AUTRES MACH ELECT NDA
7788	OTH ELEC MACHY,EQUIP NES		10.4		19.4		9.2		11.8	AUT MACH APP ELEC NDA
77886	OTH ELEC MACHINERY NES		8.5	W 1	8.4		6.2	W 3	3.7	AUT MACH APP ELECTRIQUES
77889	ELEC PARTS OF MACHY NES		1.4		10.2		1.6		6.8	PIECES ELEC DE MACH NDA
78	ROAD VEHICLES		123.8		144.5		176.1		164.2	VEHICULES ROUTIERS
781	PASS MOTOR VEH EXC BUSES	N 6902	89.6	N 7976	112.1	N 6128	102.2	N 5041	81.4	AUTO TRANSPORT PERSONNES
782	LORRIES,SPCL MTR VEH NES	N 138	6.9	N 314	9.3	N 649	17.3	N 1022	20.6	VEHICULES SPECIAUX,MARCH
7821	LORRIES,TRUCKS	N 119	2.6	N 265	5.5	N 536	11.1	N 916	15.9	VEHICULES TRANSP MARCHAND
7822	SPECIAL MOTOR VEHCLS NES	N 19	4.4	N 49	3.9	N 113	6.2	N 106	4.7	VEHICULES USAGES SPECIAUX
783	ROAD MOTOR VEHICLES NES	N 174	3.6	N 147	9.5	N 1943	32.4	N 522	47.8	VEHICULES ROUTIERS NDA
7831	BUSES	N 174	3.6	N 147	9.5	N 1936	32.2	N 521	47.7	VOITURES TRANSPORT COMMUN
784	MOTOR VEH PRTS,ACCES NES		22.0		9.7		10.0		11.3	PIECES 722,781,782,783
7849	OTHER MOTOR VEHCL PARTS		21.9		9.5		9.6		10.5	PIECES 722,781,782,783
786	TRAILERS,NONMOTR VEH,NES		0.9		1.5		12.2		1.9	REMORQUES,CADRES,CONTAIN
7861	TRAILERS,TRANSP CONTAINR	N 56	0.6		0.7		10.8		0.9	REMORQUES TOUS VEHICULES
78613	CONTAINERS INC ROAD–RAIL	N 38	0.3		0.2		9.8		0.4	CADRES ET CONTAINERS
79	OTHR TRANSPORT EQUIPMENT		66.7		133.0		279.6		101.6	AUTRE MATERIEL TRANSPORT
792	AIRCRAFT ETC		37.6		121.0		270.3		91.0	APP NAVIGATION AERIENNE
7923	AIRCRFT NES2000–15000KG								26.7	AERODYNES 2000 A 15000 KG
7924	AIRCRFT NES OVER 15000KG				86.3		227.3		0.1	AERODYNES PLUS 15000 KG
7929	AIRCRAFT PARTS NES		34.5		34.7		43.0		63.8	PIECES DU 792
793	SHIPS AND BOATS ETC	N 1410	29.1		12.1		9.4		10.6	NAVIRES BATEAUX,ETC
7932	SHIPS AND BOATS NES	N 1376	2.5	N 1553	10.3	N 1106	8.2	N 888	5.8	NAVIRES ET BATEAUX
79323	OTHER CARGO VESSELS			N 13	7.2	N 7	6.0	N 40	2.4	AUT BATEAUX TRANS MARCH
7938	TUGS,SPECIAL VESSELS ETC	N 29	26.6	W 2	1.3	W 3	0.9	W 1	4.5	REMORQUEURS,BATEAUX SPEC
79382	SPECL PURPOSE VESSLS ETC	N 5	24.5		0.9		0.6		3.4	BAT–PHARES,–POMPES,DRAGUES
8	MISC MANUFACTURED GOODS		122.2		190.1		273.2		236.5	ART MANUFACTURES DIVERS
812	*PLUMBG,HEATNG,LGHTNG EQ		9.2		18.4		14.1		26.7	APPAR SANITAIRES CHAUFFAGE
8124	LIGHTING EQUIPMENT NES		6.9		16.0		12.3		24.2	APPAREILS ECLAIRAGE ETC
81242	LAMPS,FITTINGS BASE METL		5.2	W 96	15.3	W 618	10.9	W 732	23.0	APPAREILS D'ECLAIRAGE
821	*FURNITURE,PARTS THEREOF		16.4		70.6		79.5		21.5	MEUBLES ET PIECES
8219	FURNITURE AND PARTS NES		12.4		64.7		74.7		13.2	AUTRES MEUBLES ET PIECES
82191	METAL FURNITURE NES		2.3		11.2		46.0		3.2	MEUBLES NDA EN METAL
82192	WOOD FURNITURE NES		3.7		51.6		7.4		8.2	MEUBLES NDA EN BOIS
82199	OTHR FURN,FURN PARTS NES		6.6		2.0		21.3		1.9	MEUBLES NDA AUTRES MATIERES
84	CLOTHING AND ACCESSORIES		19.2		16.8		14.9		17.8	VETEMENTS
842	MENS OUTERWEAR NOT KNIT		8.0		2.6		1.3		1.6	VET DESSUS POUR HOMMES
8423	— TROUSERS,BREECHES ETC	N 731508	7.1	N 656504	1.8	N 484061	0.9	N 431762	1.0	PANTALONS HOMMES MAT TEX
84232	—— OF COTTON	N 720720	7.1							PANTALONS HOMMES COTON
851	*FOOTWEAR		5.8	W 266	6.6	W 363	5.6	W 272	7.8	CHAUSSURES
87	PRECISION INSTRUMNTS NES		20.4		12.7		95.2		12.8	INSTRUM,APPAR SCIENT NDA
872	MEDICAL INSTRUMENTS NES		1.7		2.2		14.5		1.7	INSTR,APP MEDIC–CHIR NDA
87203	MECHANO–THERAPY APPARAT		0.3		1.4		13.7		0.3	APP DE MECANOTHERAPIE
874	MEASURNG,CONTROLNG INSTR		18.4		9.6		79.9		9.4	INSTRUMENTS DE MESURE

4. General Imports C.I.F. by Commodities according to the S.I.T.C. (Rev. 2) in million U.S. Dollars
Importations Générales C.A.F. par Produits d'après la C.T.C.I. (Rév. 2) en millions de Dollars E.U.

SITC CTCI	COMMODITY	1991		1992		1993		1994		PRODUIT
		QUANTITY QUANTITE	VALUE VALEUR	QUANTITY QUANTITE	VALUE VALEUR	QUANTITY QUANTITE	VALUE VALEUR	QUANTITY QUANTITE	VALUE VALEUR	
8743	GAS,LIQUID CONTROL INSTR		7.6		3.0		1.7		1.4	APP,INSTR MESURE FLUIDES
8745	MEAS,CONTRL,SCI INST NES		1.0		0.5		74.7		2.8	APP SCIENT MESURE NDA
87452	INSTRMNTS ETC FR DEMONST		0.3		0.1		74.1		0.1	INSTR POUR DEMONSTRATION
8748	ELEC MEAS,CONTRL EQU NES		4.7		2.6		1.3		1.8	APP ELEC ELECTRO MESURE
88	PHOTO EQU,OPTICL GDS ETC		3.8		6.2		4.3		5.2	APP,FOURN PHOTO,OP,MONTR
89	MISC MANUFCTRD GOODS NES		44.6		55.8		57.0		140.9	ART MANUFACTURES DIVERS
892	PRINTED MATTER		11.3		13.6		11.4		83.5	IMPRIMES
8921	PRINTED BOOKS,GLOBES,ETC		4.8		5.7		4.5		6.4	LIVRES,BROCHURES,CARTES
89211	PRINTED BOOKS,PAMPHLETS		4.7		5.5		4.4	N 707153	6.2	LIVRES,BROCHURES
8922	NEWSPAPERS,PERIODICALS		4.3		4.6		3.6		3.4	JOURNAUX ET PERIODIQUES
8928	PRINTED MATTER NES		1.8		3.0		3.0		72.9	IMPRIMES NDA
89289	OTHER PRINTED MATTER		0.9		1.5		1.7		70.6	GRAVURES,PHOTO AUT IMPR
893	ARTICLES OF PLASTIC NES		15.3		24.4		20.6		29.0	OUVRAGES EN MAT DIVIS 58
8931	PLSTC PACKG CONTNRS,LIDS		1.6	W 552	3.8		4.4	W 14428	6.4	ART TRANSP EMBALLAGE ETC
8939	MISC PLASTIC ARTICLES		13.0		19.6		14.9	W 2809	21.3	ART DIVERS EN MAT DIV 58
89399	OTHR PLASTC ARTICLES NES		12.3	W 1	18.6		14.2	W 2600	20.1	AUT OUV MAT DIV 58
894	TOYS,SPORTING GOODS,ETC		8.9		7.1		7.2		13.6	VOITURES ENFANTS,JOUETS
8942	TOYS,INDOOR GAMES ETC		4.6		5.0		5.6	W 519	8.9	JOUETS,JEUX ETC
896	WORKS OF ART ETC		0.6		0.8		8.7		1.2	OBJETS D'ART
89601	HAND PAINTINGS ETC NES		0.5		0.4		8.6		0.9	TABLEAUX,PEINTURES
9	GOODS NOT CLASSD BY KIND		5.9		3.2		5.3		4.6	ART TRANSACT NON CLASSES

5. General Exports F.O.B. by Commodities according to the S.I.T.C. (Rev. 2) in million U.S. Dollars
Exportations Générales F.O.B. par Produits d'après la C.T.C.I. (Rév. 2) en millions de Dollars E.U.

SITC CTCI	COMMODITY	1991		1992		1993		1994		PRODUIT
		QUANTITY QUANTITE	VALUE VALEUR	QUANTITY QUANTITE	VALUE VALEUR	QUANTITY QUANTITE	VALUE VALEUR	QUANTITY QUANTITE	VALUE VALEUR	
	ALL COMMODITIES		2682.2		2301.3		2094.0		2110.4	TOUS PRODUITS
0	FOOD AND LIVE ANIMALS		9.8		0.1		0.1			ALIMENTS,ANIMAUX VIVANTS
3	MINERAL FUELS ETC		2594.6		2284.2		2087.9		2082.8	COMBUSTIBLES MINERAUX LUB
33	PETROLEUM AND PRODUCTS		1402.3		1325.8		1138.5		1123.9	PETROLE ET DERIVES
333	CRUDE PETROLEUM	W 7443295	1272.7	W 8124210	1249.3	W 7896040	1065.3	W 8043467	1052.1	HUILES BRUTES DE PETROLE
334	PETROLEUM PRODUCTS,REFIN	W 649444	129.7	W 414135	76.6	W 485242	73.2	W 489710	71.9	PRODUITS RAFFINES
3341	GASOLINE,OTH LIGHT OILS	W 649438	129.7							ESSENCES POUR MOTEURS
33411	MOTOR,AVIATION SPIRIT	W 645108	128.2							ESSENCES MOTEURS D'AVIONS
3345	LUBS,PETROLEUM OILS NES	W 6	0.1	W 414135	76.6	W 485242	73.2	W 489350	71.7	HUILES LUBRIFIANTES
33451	LUBS(HIGH PETR CONT) ETC	W 6	0.1	W 414135	76.6	W 485242	73.2	W 489350	71.7	HUILES LUBRIF,H LOURDES
341	*GAS,NATURAL AND MANUFCT	W 5446911	1192.4	W 5514125	958.4	W 5639411	949.5	W 5904588	959.0	GAZ NATUREL,GAZ MANUFACT
3413	PETROLM GASES,LIQUEFIED	W 5446911	1192.4	W 5514125	958.4	W 5639411	949.5	W 5904588	959.0	GAZ DE PETROLE LIQUEFIE
34131	LIQUEFIED PROPANE,BUTANE	W 5446911	1192.4							PROPANE,BUTANE LIQUEFIES
34139	OTH HYDROCARBON GAS LQFD			W 5514125	958.4	W 5639411	949.5	W 5904588	959.0	HYDROCARBURES GAZEUX NDA
6	BASIC MANUFACTURES		11.3		0.1		0.1			ART MANUFACTURES
69	METAL MANUFACTURES NES		8.5		0.1					ART MANUFACT EN METAL NDA
7	MACHINES,TRANSPORT EQUIP		35.3							MACHINES MATERIEL TRANSPORT
71	POWER GENERATING EQUIPMT		9.4							MACHINES GENERATRICES
713	INTRNL COMBUS PSTN ENGIN		8.9							MOTEURS EXPL COMB INT, PIECE
8	MISC MANUFACTURED GOODS		24.4		16.6		6.0		27.5	ART MANUFACTURES DIVERS
84	CLOTHING AND ACCESSORIES		16.7		16.6		6.0		27.4	VETEMENTS
845	OUTERWEAR KNIT NONELASTC	N 1668132	5.5	N 2436991	8.6	N 778837	2.8	N 7260410	17.3	VET DESSOUS,ACCES BONNET
8459	— OTHER,CLTHG ACCESRYS	N 143232	0.9	N 2325401	8.2	N 359567	1.2	N 3900525	11.8	AUT VET DESSUS DE BONNE
846	UNDER GARMENTS KNITTED	N 849420	2.4	W 150	6.2	W 72	3.1		7.8	SOUS VETS DE BONNETERIE
8462	— OF COTTON NON ELASTIC	N 693564	2.0	W 125	4.1	W 55	1.8	W 166	6.8	SOUS–VET BONNET COTON
84629	—— OTHER			W 125	4.1	W 55	1.8	W 166	6.8	AUT SOUS–VET BONNET COTON

1. HISTORICAL SERIES, 1962–1997 GENERAL TRADE, IMPORTS C.I.F., EXPORTS F.O.B.
SERIES HISTORIQUES, 1962–1997 COMMERCE GENERAL, IMPORTATIONS C.A.F., EXPORTATIONS F.O.B

YEAR ANNEE	VALUE IN MILLION LEVA / VALEUR EN MILLION LEVA — MERCHANDISE –MARCHANDISE		GOLD –OR		CONVERSION FACTORS U.S. CENTS PER LEV / FACTEURS DE CONVERSION CENTS E.U. PAR LEV		INDEX NUMBERS –INDICES — QUANTUM		UNIT VALUE / VALEUR UNITAIRE	
	IMPORTS	EXPORTS	IMPORTS	EXPORTS	IMPORTS	EXPORTS	IMPORTS	EXPORTS	IMPORTS	EXPORTS
1962	918.10	903.90			85.4700	85.4700				
1963	1091.90	975.80			85.4700	85.4700				
1964	1243.00	1145.20			85.4700	85.4700				
1965	1377.90	1375.70			85.4700	85.4700				
1966	1729.60	1526.90			85.4700	85.4700				
1967	1839.10	1706.10			85.4700	85.4700				
1968	2085.30	1889.70			85.4700	85.4700				
1969	2046.70	2099.50			85.4700	85.4700				
1970	2142.30	2344.50			85.4700	85.4700				
1971	2480.00	2553.30			85.4700	85.4700				
1972	2772.20	2837.00			92.5900	92.5900				
1973	3171.70	3200.70			102.9856	103.1319				
1974	4195.80	3720.80			103.0926	103.0926				
1975	5235.60	4541.40			103.2929	103.3023				
1976	5436.00	5199.80			103.5011	103.5118				
1977	6061.70	6022.00			105.4628	105.4628				
1978	6800.90	6649.60			112.5013	112.4564				
1979	7363.40	7666.80			115.6286	115.6793				
1980	8282.90	8901.50			116.5039	116.5207	94	94		
1981	9957.90	9860.30			108.4716	108.4071	104	102		
1982	10975.90	10880.00			105.0243	105.0383	107	113		
1983	11966.00	11817.50			102.6506	102.6344	112	118		
1984	12842.30	12987.30			98.9998	98.9402	115	124		
1985	14066.50	13739.40			97.0834	97.1548	127	133		
1986	14353.30	13350.50			106.2375	106.3017	132	128		
1987	14067.30	13802.00			115.2415	115.2361	130	130		
1988	13820.40	14353.60			119.9853	119.9877	137	133		
1989	12551.70	13506.30			118.5546	118.5591	130	130		
1990	10160.30	10496.00			126.8922	127.1617	100	100		
1991	45132.42	57368.29			6.6845	6.6845				
1992	104281.20	91532.90			5.0423	4.9817				
1993	131523.10	102877.40			3.6169	3.6169				
1994	227010.30	216194.40			1.8435	1.8435				
1995	380012.00	359663.60			1.4897	1.4909				
1996	892101.10	859796.40			0.5910	0.5888				
1997	7778641.00	7829633.00			0.0612	0.0608				

2. IMPORTS BY BROAD ECONOMIC CATEGORY AND EXPORTS BY INDUSTRIAL ORIGIN. (PERCENTAGE OF TOTAL VALUE)
IMPORTATIONS PAR CATEGORIES ECONOMIQUES ET EXPORTATIONS PAR BRANCHE D'ACTIVITE.(EN POURCENTAGE DE LA VALEUR TOTALE)

IMPORTS – IMPORTATIONS

	1991	1992	1993	1994	1995	1996	1997
TOTAL IMPORTS–IMPORTATIONS TOTALES		100.					
1 FOOD BEV–ALIMENTATION BOISSONS		5.1					
11 PRIMARY–PRODUITS DE BASE		1.3					
111 FOR INDUSTRY–POUR L'INDUSTRIE		0.6					
112 FOR HOUSEHOLDS–POUR LES MENAGES		0.6					
12 PROCESSED–PRODUITS ELABORES		3.8					
121 FOR INDUSTRY–POUR L'INDUSTRIE		1.4					
122 FOR HOUSEHOLDS–POUR LES MENAGES		2.4					
2 IND SUPPLIES–APPROV INDUSTRIELS		27.8					
21 PRIMARY–PRODUITS DE BASE		4.2					
22 PROCESSED–PRODUITS ELABORES		23.6					
3 FUELS–COMBUSTIBLES		36.0					
31 PRIMARY–PRODUITS DE BASE		23.5					
32 PROCESSED–PRODUITS ELABORES		12.5					
321 MOTOR SPIRIT–ESSENCE							
322 OTHER–AUTRES		12.5					
4 MACHINERY–EQUIPEMENT		12.1					
41 CAPITAL EQUIPMENT–MACHINES		10.3					
42 PARTS–PIECES ACCESSOIRES		1.8					
5 TRANSPORT–TRANSPORT		9.2					
51 PASSENGER CARS–AUTOMOBILES		4.5					
52 OTHER–AUTRES		2.1					
521 INDUSTRIAL–INDUSTRIELS		2.0					
522 NON INDUSTRIAL–NON INDUSTRIEL		0.1					
53 PARTS–PIECES ACCESSOIRES		2.6					
6 CONSUM GOODS–BIENS CONSOMMATION		9.7					
61 DURABLE–DURABLES		3.5					
62 SEMI DURABLE–SEMI DURABLES		3.2					
63 NON DURABLE–NON DURABLES		3.0					
7 GOODS NES–BIENS NDA		0.2					

EXPORTS – EXPORTATIONS

	1991	1992	1993	1994	1995	1996	1997
TOTAL EXPORTS–EXPORTATIONS TOTALES							
1 AGRICULTURE							
2 MINING QUARRY–INDUS EXTRACTIVES							
3 MANUFACTURING–IND MANUFACTUR							
31 FOOD BEV TOBACCO–ALIM BOISS TAB							
32 TEXTILES–INDUSTRIES TEXTILES							
33 WOOD & PRODUCTS–BOIS & PRODUITS							
34 PAPER & PRODUCTS–PAPIER & PRODT							
35 CHEMICALS–INDUSTRIES CHIMIQUES							
36 NON METAL MIN–MIN NON METAL							
37 BASIC METAL–IND METAL BASE							
38 METAL MANUF–MANUF METAL							
39 OTH MANUF IND–AUTRES MANUF							

3. TRADE BY PRINCIPAL COUNTRIES OF ORIGIN AND SALE (VALUE IN MILLION U.S. DOLLARS)
ECHANGES SELON LES PRINCIPAUX PAYS D'ORIGINE ET DE VENTE (VALEUR EN MILLIONS DE DOLLARS EU)

COUNTRIES–PAYS	GENERAL IMPORTS C.I.F. IMPORTATIONS GENERALES C.A.F				
	1993	1994	1995	1996	1997
World	5111.9	4097.0	5469.5	4891.5	4760.5
Africa	156.6	88.5	122.7	52.0	77.6
Americas	287.1	282.5	320.1	272.5	386.3
– Northern America	188.4	141.0	129.7	120.5	190.9
– LAIA	83.1	87.2	124.0	97.6	175.6
– CACM	2.6	3.5	8.5	3.7	0.2
– Caribbean	8.7	50.2	56.4	50.4	19.4
– Rest of America	4.3	0.7	1.5	0.3	0.3
Asia excl fmr USSR	630.6	375.7	482.6	341.5	415.0
– Middle East	416.6	225.9	287.3	162.2	219.2
Asia former USSR	38.1	17.4	53.6	20.9	28.9
Europe excl fmr USSR	2246.9	2006.9	2625.6	2190.2	2237.1
– European Union	1715.3	1584.8	2097.8	1780.3	1823.3
– Eastern Europe	217.7	223.1	227.8	222.3	241.3
– Rest of Europe	313.9	199.0	300.0	187.6	172.6
Europe former USSR	1732.4	1309.3	1815.7	1845.4	1579.3
Oceania	15 7	11.6	38.8	23.8	14.8
Other	4.7	5.1	10.5	145.2	21.5
Russian Federation	1429.6	1100.7	1583.9	1694.2	1374.8
Germany/Allemagne	556.1	537.3	697.0	575.1	563.2
Italy/Italie	222.1	222.7	326.6	318.8	347.2
Greece/Grèce	171.2	196.9	248.7	196.1	206.4
Ukraine	255.7	174.6	188.1	122.4	176.6
United Kingdom	281.6	135.1	147.4	105.1	126.9
USA/Etats–Unis d'Amer	183.1	134.6	119.1	111.7	181.3
France, Monaco	118.1	114.7	157.3	162.7	156.5
Austria/Autriche	128.6	121.4	156.9	123.2	118.0
Iran (Islamic Rep of)	238.2	134.8	170.1	47.6	52.8
Switzerland,Liechtenst.	211.3	56.6	99.6	79.7	78.3
Netherlands/Pays–Bas	83.0	80.7	111.0	91.4	91.0
Turkey/Turquie	77.5	78.3	99.8	96.0	101.6
TFYR Macedonia	78.7	125.6	176.3	31.6	26.3
Romania/Roumanie	102.8	80.5	60.8	70.5	57.6
Czech Republic	63.8	55.5	75.5	65.9	63.0
Belgium–Luxembourg	47.2	49.0	75.2	60.6	62.7
Brazil/Brésil	28.8	44.9	55.1	34.4	65.5
Japan/Japon	66.5	38.9	43.6	35.3	36.6
Finland/Finlande	24.6	45.0	56.8	39.5	32.1
Poland/Pologne	25.9	48.6	30.7	33.4	57.0
Sweden/Suède	37.4	29.3	50.1	40.1	37.5
Cuba	8.6	49.9	56.2	50.1	18.0
Algeria/Algérie	38.3	42.8	76.3	12.2	2.4
Hungary/Hongrie	20.6	27.9	41.6	33.2	42.7
Denmark/Danemark	24.0	22.2	31.5	28.6	39.6
China/Chine	26.5	20.6	24.5	28.6	40.4
Areas n.e.s.	4.7			132.3	0.0
Korea, Republic of	28.3	22.4	42.6	21.0	20.8
Spain/Espagne	14.5	22.1	27.1	25.1	25.3
Australia/Australie	15.4	11.1	38.4	23.2	14.4
Yugoslavia/Yougoslavie	4.0	0.9	2.9	55.7	37.5
Argentina/Argentine	25.7	9.5	20.5	12.7	21.2
Syrian Arab Republic	74.7	1.8	2.9	4.0	1.1
Belarus/Bélarus	17.0	17.0	14.6	11.2	14.9
Slovakia/Slovaquie	4.2	9.9	18.9	19.1	20.9
Chile/Chili	0.3	0.0	23.0	31.6	15.3
Peru/Pérou	7.9	8.7	6.2	10.2	36.9
Republic of Moldova	16.4	11.0	20.0	11.7	9.5
Other Asia n.e.s.	13.1	13.7	17.0	11.4	13.4

COUNTRIES–PAYS	GENERAL EXPORTS F.O.B. EXPORTATIONS GENERALES F.O.B.				
	1993	1994	1995	1996	1997
Monde	3679.1	3781.2	5220.4	4781.7	4760.4
Afrique	78.4	87.1	179.6	169.3	102.4
Amériques	187.6	313.5	281.4	217.8	241.1
– Amérique du Nord	146.1	214.1	185.1	140.3	175.0
– ALAI	26.2	50.2	66.4	43.2	48.6
– MCAC	3.1	1.9	3.3	1.8	4.6
– Caraïbes	9.3	16.9	10.1	13.5	12.0
– Autre Amérique	2.8	30.4	16.6	19.0	0.8
Asie anc. URSS exclus	872.6	584.5	885.8	815.1	835.1
– Moyen–Orient	547.0	345.9	621.6	570.9	578.5
Asie ancienne URSS	53.0	38.1	114.7	176.7	202.5
Europe anc. URSS exclus	1788.8	2098.0	2901.8	2574.4	2625.1
– Union Européenne	1114.9	1362.0	2012.4	1912.5	2130.1
– Europe de l'Est	205.2	163.1	231.5	209.0	174.2
– Autre de l'Europe	468.7	572.8	657.9	453.0	320.8
Europe ancienne URSS	678.3	641.8	808.1	773.0	678.4
Océanie	2.9	4.0	4.2	3.7	4.9
Autre	17.6	14.4	44.7	51.7	70.8
Russian Federation	515.9	479.4	536.1	480.0	391.8
Italy/Italie	225.7	272.7	436.5	493.1	575.1
Germany/Allemagne	249.4	320.1	457.8	442.0	468.1
Turkey/Turquie	288.6	180.9	385.1	384.3	442.3
Greece/Grèce	212.1	289.6	367.7	347.6	405.9
TFYR Macedonia	233.2	362.1	436.2	148.6	98.2
Ukraine	120.4	117.2	190.7	166.3	146.5
USA/Etats–Unis d'Amer	128.2	189.2	162.3	113.1	128.8
Yugoslavia/Yougoslavie	123.1	134.2	85.5	231.5	124.6
United Kingdom	116.8	97.0	167.2	140.9	130.6
France, Monaco	96.9	97.3	152.9	127.0	133.6
Spain/Espagne	18.3	33.6	133.8	111.3	129.4
Netherlands/Pays–Bas	55.8	80.7	102.5	79.7	75.4
Romania/Roumanie	93.3	55.4	95.6	75.4	65.9
Belgium–Luxembourg	49.9	80.4	83.5	72.7	78.0
Syrian Arab Republic	104.1	65.5	69.9	74.4	30.5
China/Chine	109.6	65.9	19.8	43.3	30.4
Republic of Moldova	12.1	14.8	43.1	90.7	99.9
Georgia/Géorgie	10.1	4.9	39.0	78.6	122.7
Austria/Autriche	43.3	50.0	45.8	50.3	54.0
Lebanon/Liban	60.5	35.6	53.1	44.8	31.0
Switzerland,Liechtenst.	45.2	19.6	75.8	41.6	33.4
Albania/Albanie	38.5	44.3	60.6	42.9	22.6
Egypt/Egypte	28.1	27.3	43.0	55.0	43.3
Free zones/Zone franches		14.4	44.7	51.7	70.8
Israel/Israël	19.2	21.2	58.2	32.0	25.8
Canada	18.0	24.8	22.8	27.3	46.2
Thailand/Thaïlande	39.0	28.3	16.8	22.0	24.0
India/Inde	22.0	16.5	32.8	38.5	17.7
Poland/Pologne	25.1	16.6	24.1	31.1	29.6
Japan/Japon	16.7	16.3	18.0	25.5	39.6
Hungary/Hongrie	23.0	20.3	23.3	24.8	23.1
Czech Republic	21.9	15.7	18.5	23.3	18.6
Jordan/Jordanie	25.7	20.9	24.7	13.5	11.8
Sweden/Suède	15.9	14.5	17.9	16.0	28.3
Cyprus/Chypre	15.2	7.6	21.1	15.3	30.9
Belarus/Bélarus	20.8	18.6	22.4	13.3	14.3
Slovenia/Slovénie	8.7	30.8	21.9	4.1	13.9
Denmark/Danemark	12.4	11.8	16.6	18.2	19.0
Malaysia/Malaisie	14.0	9.7	21.1	16.5	16.5

(VALUE AS PERCENTAGE OF WORLD TOTAL)(VALEURS EN POURCENTAGE DU TOTAL MONDIAL)

	1988	1989	1990	1991	1992	1993	1994	1995	1996	1997
Africa		1.8	2.0	4.1	4.8	3.1	2.2	2.2	1.1	1.6
Americas		4.0	2.3	4.0	6.5	5.6	6.9	5.9	5.6	8.1
– Northern America		1.5	0.6	2.9	3.4	3.7	3.4	2.4	2.5	4.0
– LAIA		0.8	0.6	0.9	2.3	1.6	2.1	2.3	2.0	3.7
– CACM					0.3	0.1	0.1	0.2	0.1	0.0
– Caribbean		1.7	1.1	0.2	0.5	0.2	1.2	1.0	1.0	0.4
– Rest of America					0.0	0.1	0.0	0.0	0.0	0.0
Asia excl fmr USSR		2.3	2.7	3.3	14.9	12.3	9.2	8.8	7.0	8.7
– Middle East		0.1	0.1	0.4	10.0	8.2	5.5	5.3	3.3	4.6
Asia former USSR					0.2	0.7	0.4	1.0	0.4	0.6
Europe excl fmr USSR		33.8	32.0	33.4	44.9	44.0	49.0	48.0	44.8	47.0
– European Union		12.3	11.3	26.1	35.6	33.6	38.7	38.4	36.4	38.3
– Eastern Europe		18.9	18.5	3.3	5.4	4.3	5.4	4.2	4.5	5.1
– Rest of Europe		2.6	2.2	4.1	3.9	6.1	4.9	5.5	3.8	3.6
Europe former USSR		52.9	56.5	43.2	28.4	33.9	32.0	33.2	37.7	33.2
Oceania		0.0	0.1	0.0	0.1	0.3	0.3	0.7	0.5	0.3
Other					0.2	0.1	0.1	0.2	3.0	0.5
Russian Federation					22.8	28.0	26.9	29.0	34.6	28.9
Germany/Allemagne				7.0	12.0	10.9	13.1	12.7	11.8	11.8
Italy/Italie		1.4	1.9	4.2	4.9	4.3	5.4	6.0	6.5	7.3
Greece/Grèce		0.4	0.3	0.9	5.6	3.3	4.8	4.5	4.0	4.3
Ukraine					4.9	5.0	4.3	3.4	2.5	3.7
United Kingdom		1.1	1.7	3.6	2.5	5.5	3.3	2.7	2.1	2.7
USA/Etats–Unis d'Amer		1.5	0.6	2.9	3.3	3.6	3.3	2.2	2.3	3.8
France, Monaco		1.0	0.7	2.1	2.4	2.3	2.8	2.9	3.3	3.3
Austria/Autriche		1.5	1.6	4.7	3.1	2.5	3.0	2.9	2.5	2.5
Iran (Islamic Rep of)					4.2	4.7	3.3	3.1	1.0	1.1

	1988	1989	1990	1991	1992	1993	1994	1995	1996	1997
Afrique		2.2	5.1	5.2	3.1	2.1	2.3	3.4	3.5	2.2
Amériques		2.1	2.8	3.7	3.5	5.1	8.3	5.4	4.6	5.1
– Amérique du Nord		0.7	1.8	3.5	2.3	4.0	5.7	3.5	2.9	3.7
– ALAI		0.1	0.0	0.1	0.8	0.7	1.3	1.3	0.9	1.0
– MCAC					0.0	0.1	0.1	0.1	0.0	0.1
– Caraïbes		1.4	1.0	0.0	0.3	0.3	0.4	0.2	0.3	0.3
– Autre Amérique					0.1	0.1	0.8	0.3	0.4	0.0
Asie anc. URSS exclus		3.9	4.1	8.6	20.2	23.7	15.5	17.0	17.0	17.5
– Moyen–Orient		2.5	1.6	4.4	14.9	14.9	9.1	11.9	11.9	12.2
Asie ancienne URSS					0.8	1.4	1.0	2.2	3.7	4.3
Europe anc. URSS exclus		25.3	22.6	26.9	50.4	48.6	55.5	55.6	53.8	55.1
– Union Européenne		6.0	5.6	17.4	31.8	30.3	36.0	38.5	40.0	44.7
– Europe de l'Est		17.3	15.2	5.2	6.5	5.6	4.3	4.4	4.4	3.7
– Autre de l'Europe		2.0	1.9	4.3	12.1	12.7	15.1	12.6	9.5	6.7
Europe ancienne URSS		65.2	64.0	49.8	21.7	18.4	17.0	15.5	16.2	14.3
Océanie		0.0	0.0	0.1	0.1	0.1	0.1	0.1	0.1	0.1
Autre					0.1	0.5	0.4	0.9	1.1	1.5
Russian Federation					17.2	14.0	12.7	10.3	10.0	8.2
Italy/Italie		0.7	0.8	2.7	5.9	6.1	7.2	8.4	10.3	12.1
Germany/Allemagne				4.8	7.7	6.8	8.5	8.8	9.2	9.8
Turkey/Turquie					6.4	7.8	4.8	7.4	8.0	9.3
Greece/Grèce		1.3	0.8	2.2	4.6	5.8	7.7	7.0	7.3	8.5
TFYR Macedonia						6.3	9.6	8.4	3.1	2.1
Ukraine					3.7	3.3	3.1	3.7	3.5	3.1
USA/Etats–Unis d'Amer		0.6	1.7	3.4	2.1	3.5	5.0	3.1	2.4	2.7
Yugoslavia/Yougoslavie					8.5	3.3	3.5	1.6	4.8	2.6
United Kingdom		0.9	0.6	1.9	3.1	3.2	2.6	3.2	2.9	2.7

4. General Imports C.I.F. by Commodities according to the S.I.T.C. (Rev. 2) in million U.S. Dollars
Importations Générales C.A.F. par Produits d'après la C.T.C.I. (Rév. 2) en millions de Dollars E.U.

SITC CTCI	COMMODITY	1994 QUANTITY QUANTITE	1994 VALUE VALEUR	1995 QUANTITY QUANTITE	1995 VALUE VALEUR	1996 QUANTITY QUANTITE	1996 VALUE VALEUR	1997 QUANTITY QUANTITE	1997 VALUE VALEUR	PRODUIT
	ALL COMMODITIES		4097.0		5469.5		4891.6		4760.6	TOUS PRODUITS
0	FOOD AND LIVE ANIMALS		342.9		357.4		306.6		358.3	ALIMENTS,ANIMAUX VIVANTS
01	MEAT AND PREPARATIONS		30.6		32.0		14.2		39.1	VIANDES ET PREPARATIONS
02	DAIRY PRODCTS,BIRDS'EGGS		21.1		17.2		8.6		11.2	PRODUITS LAITIERS,OEUFS
03	FISH AND PREPARATIONS		8.0		10.2		8.3		15.3	POISSONS ET PREPARATIONS
04	CEREALS AND PREPARATIONS		35.8		14.9		99.3		101.1	CEREALES ET PRODUITS
05	VEGETABLES AND FRUIT		58.5		45.5		21.2		21.7	LEGUMES ET FRUITS
06	SUGAR AND PREPS,HONEY		110.6		140.3		100.0		100.9	SUCRES ET PRODUITS
07	COFFEE,TEA,COCOA,SPICES		33.2		35.7		20.8		19.6	CAFE,THE,CACAO,EPICES
081	*FEEDING STUFF FOR ANIML		18.7		39.1		19.0		22.5	NOURRITURE POUR ANIMAUX
1	BEVERAGES AND TOBACCO		82.1		66.9		67.1		46.9	BOISSONS ET TABACS
11	BEVERAGES		30.1		37.4		24.9		13.3	BOISSONS
12	TOBACCO AND MANUFACTURES		52.0		29.5		42.3		33.6	TABACS BRUTS FABRIQUES
2	CRUDE MATERLS,EXCL FUELS		251.3		379.0		342.6		431.7	MAT BRUTES NON COMESTIBLES
24	CORK AND WOOD		23.6		25.4		21.8		22.9	LIEGE ET BOIS
251	*PULP AND WASTE PAPER		11.0		26.4		15.3		16.5	PATES A PAPIER,DECHETS
26	TEXTILE FIBRES AND WASTE		117.3		164.6		147.2		190.7	FIBRES TEXTILES
263	COTTON		80.4		114.5		93.5		124.1	COTON
268	WOOL(EXC TOPS),ANML HAIR		29.8		38.3		45.2		58.9	LAINES ET POILS
27	CRUDE FERTLZR,MINRLS NES		28.3		28.3		35.0		39.8	ENGRAIS MINERAUX BRUTS
28	METALLIFEROUS ORES,SCRAP		63.3		124.6		115.5		156.2	MINERAIS METAL,DECHETS
3	MINERAL FUELS ETC		1213.9		1525.4		1711.4		1492.3	COMBUSTIBLES MINERAUX LUB
4	ANIMAL,VEGETABLE OIL,FAT		20.9		21.5		21.2		17.7	HUILES,GRAISSES ANIM,VEG
5	CHEMCLS,RELATED PROD NES		436.7		729.1		573.8		535.7	PRODUITS CHIMIQUES
51	ORGANIC CHEMICALS		107.6		139.4		100.2		95.8	PROD CHIMIQ ORGANIQUES
52	INORGANIC CHEMICALS		26.0		143.1		80.3		89.1	PROD CHIM INORGANIQUES
53	DYES,TANNING,COLOUR PROD		37.3		47.5		36.6		35.2	PROD TEINTURE,COLORANTS
541	*MEDICINAL,PHARM PRODUCT		47.7		83.8		73.3		79.2	PROD MEDICINAUX PHARMACEUT
55	PERFUME,CLEANING ETC PRD		41.0		64.3		63.8		48.5	PROD POUR PARFUM,TOILETTE
58	PLASTIC MATERIALS ETC		94.2		142.6		115.3		103.5	MAT PLAST ARTIFICIELLES
59	CHEMICAL MATERIALS NES		76.9		100.9		96.3		77.2	MAT PROD CHIMIQUES NDA
6	BASIC MANUFACTURES		674.7		1010.2		792.6		829.3	ART MANUFACTURES
61	LEATHER,DRESSED FUR,ETC		34.5		50.5		61.9		67.9	CUIRS,PELLETERIES
611	LEATHER		28.2		43.0		53.4		59.9	CUIRS,PEAUX PREPARES
62	RUBBER MANUFACTURES NES		39.2		63.9		55.5		53.5	CAOUTCHOUC MANUFACTURE
64	PAPER,PAPERBOARD AND MFR		100.3		179.6		120.6		99.7	PAPIERS,CARTONS & OUVRAGES
65	TEXTILE YARN,FABRICS,ETC		172.7		250.7		222.9		251.6	FILS,TISSUS,ARTICLES TEXTILE
655	KNITTED,ETC FABRICS		11.0		16.1		17.6		19.6	ETOF BONNETERIE PIECES ETC
66	NONMETAL MINERAL MFS NES		46.2		68.7		59.0		57.7	ART MIN NON METALLIQUES
67	IRON AND STEEL		138.2		141.1		97.9		103.8	FER ET ACIER
68	NON-FERROUS METALS		89.4		185.3		102.7		107.1	METAUX NON FERREUX
682	COPPER EXC CEMENT COPPER		39.0		81.9		32.2		33.4	CUIVRE
684	ALUMINIUM		43.7		89.4		63.4		67.6	ALUMINIUM
69	METAL MANUFACTURES NES		54.6		70.8		72.4		88.5	ART MANUFACT EN METAL NDA
7	MACHINES,TRANSPORT EQUIP		860.8		1067.9		799.7		762.3	MACHINES MATERIEL TRANSPORT
78	ROAD VEHICLES		221.0		250.1		159.0		120.5	VEHICULES ROUTIERS
79	OTHR TRANSPORT EQUIPMENT		25.3		22.0		17.8		20.5	AUTRE MATERIEL TRANSPORT
791	RAILWAY VEHICLES		16.5		10.8		5.4		12.9	VEHIC MAT CHEMINS DE FER
8	MISC MANUFACTURED GOODS		212.3		308.3		274.7		284.9	ART MANUFACTURES DIVERS
821	*FURNITURE,PARTS THEREOF		21.2		34.0		22.5		16.8	MEUBLES ET PIECES
84	CLOTHING AND ACCESSORIES		43.2		58.0		63.9		91.8	VETEMENTS
851	*FOOTWEAR		35.9		48.2		49.4		49.3	CHAUSSURES
89	MISC MANUFCTRD GOODS NES		28.0		43.4		40.1		44.6	ART MANUFACTURES DIVERS
894	TOYS,SPORTING GOODS,ETC		8.7		13.4		11.4		16.6	VOITURES ENFANTS,JOUETS

5. General Exports F.O.B. by Commodities according to the S.I.T.C. (Rev. 2) in million U.S. Dollars
Exportations Générales F.O.B. par Produits d'après la C.T.C.I. (Rév. 2) en millions de Dollars E.U.

SITC CTCI	COMMODITY	1994 QUANTITY QUANTITE	1994 VALUE VALEUR	1995 QUANTITY QUANTITE	1995 VALUE VALEUR	1996 QUANTITY QUANTITE	1996 VALUE VALEUR	1997 QUANTITY QUANTITE	1997 VALUE VALEUR	PRODUIT
	ALL COMMODITIES		3781.2		5220.5		4781.8		4760.5	TOUS PRODUITS
0	FOOD AND LIVE ANIMALS		384.7		561.7		412.9		325.7	ALIMENTS,ANIMAUX VIVANTS
001	*LIVE ANIMALS FOR FOOD		45.1		22.9		18.8		2.3	ANIMAUX VIVANTS
01	MEAT AND PREPARATIONS		33.2		39.9		55.7		49.7	VIANDES ET PREPARATIONS
02	DAIRY PRODCTS,BIRDS'EGGS		49.1		39.2		32.7		31.1	PRODUITS LAITIERS,OEUFS
03	FISH AND PREPARATIONS		16.9		33.3		39.4		22.3	POISSONS ET PREPARATIONS
04	CEREALS AND PREPARATIONS		10.7		161.5		18.1		27.8	CEREALES ET PRODUITS
05	VEGETABLES AND FRUIT		107.9		75.7		60.2		44.7	LEGUMES ET FRUITS
06	SUGAR AND PREPS,HONEY		22.0		53.2		57.5		24.9	SUCRES ET PRODUITS
07	COFFEE,TEA,COCOA,SPICES		12.6		18.6		13.9		19.7	CAFE,THE,CACAO,EPICES
081	*FEEDING STUFF FOR ANIML		9.6		33.8		5.4		3.7	NOURRITURE POUR ANIMAUX
1	BEVERAGES AND TOBACCO		372.4		500.9		438.8		309.6	BOISSONS ET TABACS
11	BEVERAGES		151.2		195.0		182.6		145.1	BOISSONS
12	TOBACCO AND MANUFACTURES		221.3		306.0		256.2		164.6	TABACS BRUTS FABRIQUES
2	CRUDE MATERLS,EXCL FUELS		257.4		336.5		313.7		330.3	MAT BRUTES NON COMESTIBLES
22	OIL SEEDS,OLEAGINOUS FRT		30.4		56.2		40.8		37.7	GRAINES,FRUITS OLEAGINEUX
24	CORK AND WOOD		70.6		77.7		79.9		84.8	LIEGE ET BOIS
251	*PULP AND WASTE PAPER		20.0		24.4		15.2		15.7	PATES A PAPIER,DECHETS
26	TEXTILE FIBRES AND WASTE		52.1		62.5		57.5		67.4	FIBRES TEXTILES
263	COTTON		33.0		39.9		35.1		41.1	COTON
268	WOOL(EXC TOPS),ANML HAIR		15.7		20.4		20.4		24.7	LAINES ET POILS
27	CRUDE FERTLZR,MINRLS NES		50.4		74.6		73.5		75.0	ENGRAIS MINERAUX BRUTS
28	METALLIFEROUS ORES,SCRAP		31.6		37.6		42.3		45.4	MINERAIS METAL,DECHETS
3	MINERAL FUELS ETC		288.7		325.0		318.2		374.8	COMBUSTIBLES MINERAUX LUB
4	ANIMAL,VEGETABLE OIL,FAT		19.8		48.4		18.8		21.9	HUILES,GRAISSES ANIM,VEG
5	CHEMCLS,RELATED PROD NES		569.1		921.4		911.7		856.8	PRODUITS CHIMIQUES
51	ORGANIC CHEMICALS		127.1		185.4		145.0		185.7	PROD CHIMIQ ORGANIQUES
52	INORGANIC CHEMICALS		74.8		121.5		128.9		117.2	PROD CHIM INORGANIQUES
53	DYES,TANNING,COLOUR PROD		9.0		10.6		11.7		15.2	PROD TEINTURE,COLORANTS
541	*MEDICINAL,PHARM PRODUCT		73.9		91.9		99.7		121.0	PROD MEDICINAUX PHARMACEUT
55	PERFUME,CLEANING ETC PRD		44.3		88.1		106.8		100.4	PROD POUR PARFUM,TOILETTE
562	*FERTILIZERS,MANUFACTURE		113.6		243.9		272.3		172.4	ENGRAIS MANUFACTURES
58	PLASTIC MATERIALS ETC		104.4		151.2		123.3		124.0	MAT PLAST ARTIFICIELLES
59	CHEMICAL MATERIALS NES		18.7		23.2		18.0		15.1	MAT PROD CHIMIQUES NDA
6	BASIC MANUFACTURES		1052.5		1476.2		1259.7		1422.9	ART MANUFACTURES
61	LEATHER,DRESSED FUR,ETC		27.9		41.1		38.7		35.7	CUIRS,PELLETERIES
611	LEATHER		19.0		21.9		21.3		18.9	CUIRS,PEAUX PREPARES
612	LEATHER ETC MANUFACTURES		6.8		15.5		15.5		13.2	OUVRAGES EN CUIRS NDA
62	RUBBER MANUFACTURES NES		40.8		60.9		59.7		48.2	CAOUTCHOUC MANUFACTURE
64	PAPER,PAPERBOARD AND MFR		44.2		69.1		47.0		46.5	PAPIERS,CARTONS & OUVRAGES
65	TEXTILE YARN,FABRICS,ETC		97.7		148.9		148.9		145.7	FILS,TISSUS,ARTICLES TEXTILE
658	TEXTILE ARTICLES NES		15.5		28.6		33.4		33.6	ART FACONNES MAT TEXTILES
66	NONMETAL MINERAL MFS NES		61.4		108.9		98.6		100.8	ART MIN NON METALLIQUES
67	IRON AND STEEL		452.3		552.2		365.7		503.7	FER ET ACIER
68	NON–FERROUS METALS		271.7		409.8		410.3		462.1	METAUX NON FERREUX
682	COPPER EXC CEMENT COPPER		183.6		280.4		262.8		284.2	CUIVRE
684	ALUMINIUM		27.3		38.1		32.2		41.6	ALUMINIUM
685	LEAD		18.8		33.2		47.3		42.8	PLOMB
686	ZINC		40.2		56.5		65.8		79.7	ZINC
69	METAL MANUFACTURES NES		56.9		85.7		91.2		80.5	ART MANUFACT EN METAL NDA
7	MACHINES,TRANSPORT EQUIP		508.2		614.1		621.1		551.1	MACHINES MATERIEL TRANSPORT
78	ROAD VEHICLES		36.3		43.7		44.9		24.9	VEHICULES ROUTIERS
79	OTHR TRANSPORT EQUIPMENT		50.8		81.5		89.6		85.5	AUTRE MATERIEL TRANSPORT
793	SHIPS AND BOATS ETC		46.2		77.2		81.7		75.9	NAVIRES BATEAUX,ETC
8	MISC MANUFACTURED GOODS		327.7		435.9		486.9		567.4	ART MANUFACTURES DIVERS
821	*FURNITURE,PARTS THEREOF		34.1		46.7		42.4		42.5	MEUBLES ET PIECES
84	CLOTHING AND ACCESSORIES		169.4		239.8		279.3		350.1	VETEMENTS
851	*FOOTWEAR		85.2		96.8		111.9		120.8	CHAUSSURES
89	MISC MANUFCTRD GOODS NES		25.8		30.3		29.5		28.7	ART MANUFACTURES DIVERS
894	TOYS,SPORTING GOODS,ETC		13.1		17.9		17.5		17.0	VOITURES ENFANTS,JOUETS

1. HISTORICAL SERIES, 1966–1997 SPECIAL TRADE, IMPORTS C.I.F., EXPORTS F.O.B.
SERIES HISTORIQUES, 1966–1997 COMMERCE SPECIAL, IMPORTATIONS C.A.F., EXPORTATIONS F.O.B

YEAR ANNEE	VALUE IN MILLION BURUNDI FRANCS VALEUR EN MILLION BURUNDI FRANCS MERCHANDISE –MARCHANDISE		GOLD –OR		CONVERSION FACTORS U.S. CENTS PER BURUNDI FRANC FACTEURS DE CONVERSION CENTS E.U. PAR BURUNDI FRANC		INDEX NUMBERS –INDICES QUANTUM		UNIT VALUE VALEUR UNITAIRE	
	IMPORTS	EXPORTS	IMPORTS	EXPORTS	IMPORTS	EXPORTS	IMPORTS	EXPORTS	IMPORTS	EXPORTS
1966	1698.00	1247.20			1.1429	1.1429				
1967	1693.50	1469.10			1.1429	1.1429				
1968	1993.90	1322.00			1.1429	1.1429				
1969	1880.10	1064.20			1.1429	1.1429				
1970	1956.10	2131.60			1.1429	1.1429				
1971	2617.80	1619.60			1.1429	1.1429				
1972	2736.40	2275.20			1.1429	1.1429				
1973	2495.10	2379.90			1.2613	1.2686				
1974	3395.60	2323.80			1.2698	1.2698				
1975	4855.60	2514.70			1.2698	1.2698				
1976	5027.10	5420.00			1.1524	1.1169				
1977	6678.00	8011.00			1.1111	1.1111				
1978	8841.70	6243.00			1.1111	1.1111				
1979	13721.00	9361.00			1.1111	1.1111				
1980	15109.00	5861.00			1.1111	1.1111				
1981	14509.00	6423.30			1.1111	1.1111				
1982	19280.00	7883.00			1.1111	1.1111				
1983	17074.90	7505.70			1.0737	1.0662				
1984	22233.50	11779.30			0.8352	0.8357				
1985	22433.00	13462.00			0.8284	0.8245				
1986	23195.01	17674.00			0.8724	0.8686				
1987	25465.01	11117.00			0.8094	0.8071				
1988	28885.01	18589.01			0.7132	0.7141				
1989	29910.00	12304.00			0.6294	0.6333				
1990	40179.01	12784.00			0.5860	0.5856				
1991	46154.00	16698.00			0.5516	0.5424				
1992	46106.00	15355.00			0.4801	0.4749				
1993	49702.00	15019.00			0.4129	0.4116				
1994	56468.00	30034.00			0.3958	0.4021				
1995	58200.00	25982.00			0.4026	0.4067				
1996	37332.00	11293.00			0.3408	0.3510				
1997	43249.01	29811.01			0.2808	0.2814				

2. IMPORTS BY BROAD ECONOMIC CATEGORY AND EXPORTS BY INDUSTRIAL ORIGIN. (PERCENTAGE OF TOTAL VALUE)
IMPORTATIONS PAR CATEGORIES ECONOMIQUES ET EXPORTATIONS PAR BRANCHE D'ACTIVITE.(EN POURCENTAGE DE LA VALEUR TOTALE)

IMPORTS – IMPORTATIONS

	1987	1988	1989	1990	1991	1992	1993
TOTAL IMPORTS–IMPORTATIONS TOTALES							
1 FOOD BEV–ALIMENTATION BOISSONS							
11 PRIMARY–PRODUITS DE BASE							
111 FOR INDUSTRY–POUR L'INDUSTRIE							
112 FOR HOUSEHOLDS–POUR LES MENAGES							
12 PROCESSED–PRODUITS ELABORES							
121 FOR INDUSTRY–POUR L'INDUSTRIE							
122 FOR HOUSEHOLDS–POUR LES MENAGES							
2 IND SUPPLIES–APPROV INDUSTRIELS							
21 PRIMARY–PRODUITS DE BASE							
22 PROCESSED–PRODUITS ELABORES							
3 FUELS–COMBUSTIBLES							
31 PRIMARY–PRODUITS DE BASE							
32 PROCESSED–PRODUITS ELABORES							
321 MOTOR SPIRIT–ESSENCE							
322 OTHER–AUTRES							
4 MACHINERY–EQUIPEMENT							
41 CAPITAL EQUIPMENT–MACHINES							
42 PARTS–PIECES ACCESSOIRES							
5 TRANSPORT–TRANSPORT							
51 PASSENGER CARS–AUTOMOBILES							
52 OTHER–AUTRES							
521 INDUSTRIAL–INDUSTRIELS							
522 NON INDUSTRIAL–NON INDUSTRIEL							
53 PARTS–PIECES ACCESSOIRES							
6 CONSUM GOODS–BIENS CONSOMMATION							
61 DURABLE–DURABLES							
62 SEMI DURABLE–SEMI DURABLES							
63 NON DURABLE–NON DURABLES							
7 GOODS NES–BIENS NDA							

EXPORTS – EXPORTATIONS

	1987	1988	1989	1990	1991	1992	1993
TOTAL EXPORTS–EXPORTATIONS TOTALES							
1 AGRICULTURE							
2 MINING QUARRY–INDUS EXTRACTIVES							
3 MANUFACTURING–IND MANUFACTUR							
31 FOOD BEV TOBACCO–ALIM BOISS TAB							
32 TEXTILES–INDUSTRIES TEXTILES							
33 WOOD & PRODUCTS–BOIS & PRODUITS							
34 PAPER & PRODUCTS–PAPIER & PRODT							
35 CHEMICALS–INDUSTRIES CHIMIQUES							
36 NON METAL MIN–MIN NON METAL							
37 BASIC METAL–IND METAL BASE							
38 METAL MANUF–MANUF METAL							
39 OTH MANUF IND–AUTRES MANUF							

3. TRADE BY PRINCIPAL COUNTRIES OF ORIGIN AND DESTINATION (VALUE IN MILLION U.S. DOLLARS)
ECHANGES SELON LES PRINCIPAUX PAYS D'ORIGINE ET DE DESTINATION (VALEUR EN MILLIONS DE DOLLARS EU)

COUNTRIES–PAYS	SPECIAL IMPORTS C.I.F. IMPORTATIONS SPECIALES C.A.F					COUNTRIES–PAYS	SPECIAL EXPORTS F.O.B. EXPORTATIONS SPECIALES F.O.B.				
	1989	1990	1991	1992	1993		1989	1990	1991	1992	1993
World	188.1	235.7	247.1	229.5	204.5	Monde					
Africa	25.0	28.4	35.7	45.9	46.3	Afrique					
Americas	7.0	3.4	6.1	11.6	5.2	Amériques					
– Northern America	2.7	2.7	4.9	10.3	4.1	– Amérique du Nord					
– LAIA			1.2			– ALAI					
– CACM						– MCAC					
– Caribbean						– Caraïbes					
– Rest of America	4.3	0.7		1.3	1.0	– Autre Amérique					
Asia excl fmr USSR	48.4	64.2	74.3	46.6	53.4	Asie anc. URSS exclus					
– Middle East	19.9	33.0	28.7	10.6	14.6	– Moyen–Orient					
Asia former USSR						Asie ancienne URSS					
Europe excl fmr USSR	102.8	126.3	115.8	113.2	98.2	Europe anc. URSS exclus					
– European Union	91.1	108.2	101.5	109.9	93.2	– Union Européenne					
– Eastern Europe	1.5	2.4	0.7	1.0	0.8	– Europe de l'Est					
– Rest of Europe	10.2	15.7	13.5	2.3	4.3	– Autre de l'Europe					
Europe former USSR	0.3	0.1	0.1	0.1	0.1	Europe ancienne URSS					
Oceania	0.0	0.1	0.0	0.4	0.4	Océanie					
Other	4.6	13.0	13.5	11.7		Autre					
Belgium–Luxembourg	29.1	34.2	35.8	34.1	33.8						
France, Monaco	19.1	23.3	24.1	25.5	23.7						
Japan/Japon	15.3	17.2	20.9	18.6	18.8						
Iran (Islamic Rep of)	18.1	29.5		7.5	12.6						
Former Fed Rep Germany	25.5	30.3									
Germany/Allemagne			18.7	17.6	13.9						
China/Chine	5.8	8.2	14.6	8.4	8.2						
Areas n.e.s.	4.6	13.0	13.5	11.7							
Italy/Italie	7.5	8.6	8.8	8.1	9.2						
United Rep of Tanzania	2.2	2.9	4.0	20.5	11.8						
Other Africa n.e.s.	3.0	3.2	6.2	7.2	18.3						
Other Europe n.e.s.	8.4	13.0	11.5	1.1	2.6						
Kenya	5.6	5.9	7.0	7.5	6.6						
Zambia/Zambie	4.5	6.7	7.7	6.6	5.0						
Cyprus/Chypre			27.1								
Netherlands/Pays–Bas	3.1	2.8	5.7	6.3	6.3						
USA/Etats–Unis d'Amer	2.3	2.4	4.3	9.8	3.6						
United Kingdom	3.8	3.8	4.1	5.3	3.5						
Other Asia n.e.s.	3.3	0.8	4.6	4.3	6.5						
Zimbabwe	4.1	5.9	4.8	2.2	2.2						
United Arab Emirates	1.8	2.0	1.6	3.1	2.1						
Korea, Republic of	1.1	1.8	2.7	1.8	1.9						
Switzerland,Liechtenst.	1.8	2.5	1.9	1.2	1.7						
Dem Rep of the Congo	2.0	1.6	2.1	1.3	1.5						
European Union n.e.s.				7.9							
Denmark/Danemark	1.2	1.7	1.8	1.5	1.6						
Rest of America n.e.s.	4.3	0.7		1.3	1.0						
Malawi	2.8	1.2	2.9	0.1	0.0						
India/Inde	1.3	0.8	1.7	1.3	1.7						
China, Hong Kong SAR	1.2	1.8	1.2	1.1	1.1						
Former Czechoslovakia	1.3	0.5	0.7	0.9							
Austria/Autriche	0.2	2.1	0.4	0.3	0.1						
Spain/Espagne	0.4	0.6	0.5	0.8	0.3						
Sweden/Suède	0.4	0.3	0.9	0.6	0.3						
Canada	0.4	0.3	0.6	0.5	0.5						
Djibouti	0.5	0.6	0.1	0.2	0.6						
Greece/Grèce	0.3	0.2	0.2	1.1	0.3						
Rwanda	0.2	0.4	0.8	0.2	0.3						
Bangladesh		0.6	0.1	0.4	0.7						
Middle East n.e.s.		1.5									

(VALUE AS PERCENTAGE OF WORLD TOTAL)(VALEURS EN POURCENTAGE DU TOTAL MONDIAL)

	1984	1985	1986	1987	1988	1989	1990	1991	1992	1993		1984	1985	1986	1987	1988	1989	1990	1991	1992	1993
Africa		10.7	12.3	13.2	13.2	13.3	12.0	14.4	20.0	22.6	Afrique			6.9	18.2	7.9					
Americas		6.0	2.6	1.9	2.7	3.7	1.5	2.5	5.0	2.5	Amériques			6.8	6.9	0.6					
– Northern America		6.0	2.6	1.8	2.0	1.4	1.2	2.0	4.5	2.0	– Amérique du Nord			6.8	6.9	0.6					
– LAIA								0.5			– ALAI										
– CACM											– MCAC										
– Caribbean											– Caraïbes										
– Rest of America		0.0	0.0	0.1	0.7	2.3	0.3		0.6	0.5	– Autre Amérique										
Asia excl fmr USSR		27.1	22.8	26.0	27.3	25.7	27.3	30.1	20.3	26.1	Asie anc. URSS exclus			2.3	4.0	5.4					
– Middle East		16.1	11.1	11.8	10.7	10.6	14.0	11.6	4.6	7.2	– Moyen–Orient				1.1						
Asia former USSR											Asie ancienne URSS										
Europe excl fmr USSR		53.7	59.8	56.1	54.2	54.6	53.6	46.9	49.3	48.0	Europe anc. URSS exclus			81.7	64.2	83.6					
– European Union		49.4	56.1	52.8	49.0	48.4	45.9	41.1	47.9	45.5	– Union Européenne			81.6	63.6	62.7					
– Eastern Europe		0.1	0.2	0.7	0.9	0.8	1.0	0.3	0.5	0.4	– Europe de l'Est										
– Rest of Europe		4.2	3.5	2.6	4.3	5.4	6.7	5.5	1.0	2.1	– Autre de l'Europe			0.1	0.6	20.9					
Europe former USSR		0.0	0.3	0.5	0.5	0.2	0.1	0.0	0.0	0.0	Europe ancienne URSS										
Oceania		0.1	0.1	0.0	0.0	0.0	0.1	0.0	0.2	0.2	Océanie					0.2					
Other		2.3	2.1	2.3	2.0	2.4	5.5	5.5	5.1		Autre			2.2	6.1	2.0					
Belgium–Luxembourg		15.6	19.1	18.1	16.7	15.5	14.5	14.5	14.9	16.5											
France, Monaco		12.3	9.8	8.3	12.4	10.2	9.9	9.8	11.1	11.6											
Japan/Japon		6.4	6.7	8.1	9.9	8.1	7.3	8.4	8.1	9.2											
Iran (Islamic Rep of)		16.1	11.1	11.8	10.7	9.6	12.5		3.3	6.1											
Former Fed Rep Germany		11.7	11.8	12.5	9.6	13.6	12.9														
Germany/Allemagne								7.6	7.7	6.8											
China/Chine		2.6	1.7	2.3	3.0	3.1	3.5	5.9	3.6	4.0											
Areas n.e.s.		2.3	2.1	2.3	2.0	2.4	5.5	5.5	5.1												
Italy/Italie		5.0	5.0	3.5	4.2	4.0	3.6	3.6	3.5	4.5											
United Rep of Tanzania		1.1	0.9	0.7	0.7	1.2	1.2	1.6	8.9	5.7											

4. Special Imports C.I.F. by Commodities according to the S.I.T.C. (Rev. 2) in million U.S. Dollars
Importations Spéciales C.A.F. par Produits d'après la C.T.C.I. (Rév. 2) en millions de Dollars E.U.

SITC CTCI	COMMODITY	1990 QUANTITY QUANTITE	1990 VALUE VALEUR	1991 QUANTITY QUANTITE	1991 VALUE VALEUR	1992 QUANTITY QUANTITE	1992 VALUE VALEUR	1993 QUANTITY QUANTITE	1993 VALUE VALEUR	PRODUIT
	ALL COMMODITIES		235.7		247.1		229.6		204.6	TOUS PRODUITS
0	FOOD AND LIVE ANIMALS		20.4		22.7		19.8		20.4	ALIMENTS,ANIMAUX VIVANTS
02	DAIRY PRODCTS,BIRDS'EGGS		2.6		2.6		3.2		2.0	PRODUITS LAITIERS,OEUFS
03	FISH AND PREPARATIONS		0.1		0.1		0.1		0.8	POISSONS ET PREPARATIONS
04	CEREALS AND PREPARATIONS		11.7		14.5		12.6		13.4	CEREALES ET PRODUITS
041	WHEAT ETC UNMILLED	W 198	0.1	W 3714	1.3	W 2881	1.1	W 3728	1.3	FROMENT,EPEAUTRE
042	RICE	W 8	0.1	W 1058	0.3	W 1672	0.5	W 2434	0.8	RIZ
046	WHEAT ETC MEAL OR FLOUR	W 12952	5.6	W 18786	6.5	W 10305	4.0			SEMOULE FARINE,FROMENT
04601	FLOUR OF WHEAT OR MESLIN	W 12952	5.6	W 18741	6.5	W 10233	3.9	W 11331	3.9	FARINE DE FROMENT
048	CEREAL ETC PREPARATIONS	W 9456	6.1	W 10081	6.5	W 8669	7.2			PREPTNS A BASE CEREALES
0482	MALT INCLUDING FLOUR	W 9422	5.9	W 9979	6.3	W 8645	7.0	W 10745	7.4	MALT MEME TORREFIE
06	SUGAR AND PREPS,HONEY		3.2		2.8		0.4		0.9	SUCRES ET PRODUITS
061	SUGAR AND HONEY	W 5347	3.2	W 2	2.8	W 752	0.4			SUCRES ET MIEL
0612	REFINED SUGAR ETC							W 1590	0.8	SUCRES RAFFINES
09	MISC EDIBLE PRODUCTS		2.8		2.5		3.4		2.9	PREP ALIMENTAIRES DIVERSES
098	EDIBLE PRODCTS,PREPS NES	W 544	2.7	W 462	2.4	W 617	3.3	W 308	2.9	PREP ALIMENTAIRES NDA
1	BEVERAGES AND TOBACCO		1.3		1.2		1.2		1.0	BOISSONS ET TABACS
11	BEVERAGES		1.3		1.2		1.2		1.0	BOISSONS
112	ALCOHOLIC BEVERAGES	W 435	1.3	W 366	1.2	W 370	1.2			BOISSONS ALCOOLIQUES
2	CRUDE MATERLS,EXCL FUELS		5.4		8.1		5.0		5.5	MAT BRUTES NON COMESTIBLES
26	TEXTILE FIBRES AND WASTE		3.6		3.7		3.1		2.7	FIBRES TEXTILES
269	WASTE OF TEXTILE FABRICS	W 3228	3.3	W 2945	3.1	W 3007	2.8	W 2767	2.2	FRIPERIE DRILLES,CHIFFONS
27	CRUDE FERTLZR,MINRLS NES		1.2		3.6		1.1		1.3	ENGRAIS MINERAUX BRUTS
278	OTHER CRUDE MINERALS	W 7911	1.2	W 17746	3.6		1.1			AUTRES MINERAUX BRUTS
2783	COMMON SALT,ETC	W 7843	1.2	W 17363	3.3		0.9	W 8344	1.2	SEL
29	CRUDE ANIMAL,VEG MAT NES		0.6		0.8		0.8		1.7	MATIERES BRUTES ANIM,VEGET
292	CRUDE VEG MATERIALS NES	W 40	0.6	W 46	0.8	W 37	0.8			MAT BRUTES VEGETALES NDA
2929	OTH CRUDE VEG MATERIALS	W 40	0.6	W 46	0.8	W 37	0.8			MATIERES VEGETALES NDA
29291	VEGETABLE SAPS,EXTRACTS	W 40	0.6	W 46	0.8	W 37	0.8	W 72	1.7	SUCS,EXTRAITS VEGETAUX
3	MINERAL FUELS ETC		32.7		31.2		28.0		25.4	COMBUSTIBLES MINERAUX LUB
33	PETROLEUM AND PRODUCTS		32.6		31.1		27.9		25.4	PETROLE ET DERIVES
334	PETROLEUM PRODUCTS,REFIN	W 66054	32.1	W 56474	29.7	W 62187	27.3			PRODUITS RAFFINES
3341	GASOLINE,OTH LIGHT OILS	W 25326	13.9	W 21475	12.6	W 22893	10.6	W 19548	8.7	ESSENCES POUR MOTEURS
3342	KEROSENE,OTH MEDIUM OILS	W 3399	1.8	W 4046	2.4	W 8333	4.1	W 9817	4.0	PETR LAMPANTS,AUT HUIL
3343	GAS OILS	W 28646	12.6	W 20729	9.9	W 22420	9.0	W 21218	8.0	GAS OILS
3344	FUEL OILS,NES	W 7246	2.3	W 8558	3.0	W 6905	2.2	W 5468	1.6	FUEL OILS
3345	LUBS,PETROLEUM OILS NES	W 1437	1.6	W 1666	2.0	W 1636	1.5	W 3138	2.4	HUILES LUBRIFIANTES
335	RESIDUAL PETRLM PROD NES	W 1617	0.6	W 2854	1.5	W 1675	0.7	W 2588	0.9	PRODUITS RESIDUELS NDA
3354	PETROLM BITUMEN,COKE ETC	W 1617	0.6	W 2854	1.5	W 1675	0.7	W 2588	0.9	BITUME,COKE DE PETROLE
4	ANIMAL,VEGETABLE OIL,FAT		0.6		1.2		0.9		1.1	HUILES,GRAISSES ANIM,VEG
42	FIXED VEGETABLE OIL,FAT		0.4		1.0		0.9		0.8	HUILES VEGETALES FIXES
5	CHEMCLS,RELATED PROD NES		29.2		33.9		32.5		28.9	PRODUITS CHIMIQUES
51	ORGANIC CHEMICALS		1.2		1.6		1.3		1.6	PROD CHIMIQ ORGANIQUES
52	INORGANIC CHEMICALS		1.9		3.3		3.1		2.5	PROD CHIM INORGANIQUES
53	DYES,TANNING,COLOUR PROD		3.4		2.7		1.8		1.7	PROD TEINTURE,COLORANTS
531	SYNT DYE,NAT INDGO,LAKES	W 345	3.4	W 261	2.7	W 248	1.8	W 210	1.7	MAT COLOR ORGAN,LAQUES
541	*MEDICINAL,PHARM PRODUCT	K 607000	9.0	K 566000	10.3	K 555000	11.6	K 465000	8.6	PROD MEDICINAUX PHARMACEUT
55	PERFUME,CLEANING ETC PRD		1.5		2.0		1.3		1.8	PROD POUR PARFUM,TOILETTE
553	PERFUMERY,COSMETICS,ETC	W 105	0.5	W 71	0.7	W 113	0.7	W 125	0.9	PRODUITS DE PARFUMERIE
554	SOAP,CLEANSING ETC PREPS	W 667	1.1	W 833	1.3	W 272	0.6	W 594	0.9	SAVONS,PRODUITS DETERSIFS
562	*FERTILIZERS,MANUFACTURE	W 5029	2.2	W 7888	3.3	W 16660	4.9	W 12959	4.6	ENGRAIS MANUFACTURES
58	PLASTIC MATERIALS ETC		5.6		4.8		4.8		5.5	MAT PLAST ARTIFICIELLES
59	CHEMICAL MATERIALS NES		4.8		6.4		4.2		3.1	MAT PROD CHIMIQUES NDA
591	PESTICIDES,DISINFECTANTS	W 430	4.1	W 440	5.9	W 347	3.6			DESINF,INSECT,FONG,HERB
5911	INSECTICIDES,FOR RETAIL	W 402	4.0	W 406	5.8	W 306	3.5	W 193	2.7	INSECTICIDES VENTE DET
6	BASIC MANUFACTURES		53.7		52.5		49.0		42.9	ART MANUFACTURES
62	RUBBER MANUFACTURES NES		3.9		6.7		5.4		7.1	CAOUTCHOUC MANUFACTURE
625	RUBBER TYRES, TUBES ETC	W 521	2.6	W 1095	5.4	W 1030	4.1			PNEUS CAOUTCHOUC VULCANISE
62591	INNER TUBES	W 50	0.3	W 155	0.7	W 128	0.5	W 1354	5.3	CHAMBRES A AIR
628	RUBBER ARTICLES NES	W 284	1.3	W 336	1.4	W 313	1.4	W 334	1.9	OUVRAGES CAOUTCHOUC NDA
64	PAPER,PAPERBOARD AND MFR		6.1		6.1		5.8		5.6	PAPIERS,CARTONS & OUVRAGES
65	TEXTILE YARN,FABRICS,ETC		2.8		2.4		2.2		1.2	FILS,TISSUS,ARTICLES TEXTILE
658	TEXTILE ARTICLES NES	W 1496	1.6	W 303	0.8	W 894	1.2			ART FACONNES MAT TEXTILES
6581	BAGS,SACKS OF TEXTILES	W 1318	1.0	W 174	0.3	W 740	0.6			SACS EMBALLAGE TEXTILES
66	NONMETAL MINERAL MFS NES		11.0		13.6		12.9		9.5	ART MIN NON METALLIQUES
661	LIME,CEMENT,BLDG PRODS	W 65719	8.8	W 80046	11.1	W 70586	10.9			CHAUX,CIMENTS MAT CONSTR
6612	CEMENT	W 65633	8.3	W 79788	10.5	W 70260	10.3	W 52275	6.9	CIMENTS HYDRAULIQUES
663	MINERAL MANUFCTURES NES	W 414	0.8	W 612	1.1	W 501	1.0			ART MIN MANUF NDA
6639	CERAMIC ARTICLES NES	W 414	0.8	W 612	1.1	W 501	1.0	W 834	1.3	ARTICLES EN CERAMIQUE NDA
665	GLASSWARE	W 729	1.4	W 638	1.5	W 489	1.1			OUVRAGES EN VERRE
68	NON-FERROUS METALS		1.5		0.8		1.2		1.3	METAUX NON FERREUX
684	ALUMINIUM	W 466	1.5	W 232	0.8	W 425	1.2	W 537	1.3	ALUMINIUM
69	METAL MANUFACTURES NES		27.7		22.2		21.0		17.7	ART MANUFACT EN METAL NDA
695	TOOLS	W 1130	2.1	W 1880	3.0		2.5		2.0	OUTILS A MAIN
699	BASE METAL MFRS NES	W 460	1.4	W 543	1.7	W 569	1.8			ART MANUFACTURES MET NDA
6991	LOCKSMITHS WARES,ETC	W 218	0.8	W 305	1.0	W 292	1.0			ARTICLES DE SERRURERIE
69911	LOCKS,KEYS AND PARTS	W 218	0.8	W 305	1.0	W 292	1.0	W 196	0.7	SERRURES,VERROUS,CADENAS
7	MACHINES,TRANSPORT EQUIP		70.8		70.2		63.3		51.7	MACHINES MATERIEL TRANSPORT
71	POWER GENERATING EQUIPMT		1.3		1.2		1.3		0.8	MACHINES GENERATRICES
716	ROTATING ELECTRIC PLANT	W 204	1.3	W 89	1.2	W 54	1.3	W 59	0.8	APP ELECTR ROTATIFS,PIECES
74	GENRL INDUSTRL MACHY NES		22.9		30.0		23.2		20.5	MACH APP INDUSTRIE
76	TELECOMM,SOUND EQUIPMENT		2.3		1.7		2.1		2.3	EQUIPMENT DE TELECOM
77	ELECTRIC MACHNRY NES ETC		19.5		10.7		12.4		9.8	MACH APP ELECT NDA
778	ELECTRICAL MACHINERY NES	W 170	0.5	W 443	1.2	W 392	1.1			AUTRES MACH ELECT NDA
7781	BATTERIES,ACCUMULATORS	W 170	0.5	W 443	1.2	W 392	1.1	W 342	0.8	PILES ET ACCUMULATEURS
78	ROAD VEHICLES		24.8		26.4		24.0		18.3	VEHICULES ROUTIERS
781	PASS MOTOR VEH EXC BUSES	W 1487	8.1	W 1600	9.7	W 1358	8.3	W 991	5.4	AUTO TRANSPORT PERSONNES
782	LORRIES,SPCL MTR VEH NES	W 1232	8.8	W 1762	9.6	W 1368	7.6			VEHICULES SPECIAUX,MARCH
7821	LORRIES,TRUCKS	W 1232	8.8	W 1762	9.6	W 1368	7.6	W 836	6.0	VEHICULES TRANSP MARCHAND
784	MOTOR VEH PRTS,ACCES NES	W 483	5.4	W 246	4.4	W 346	5.6			PIECES 722,781,782,783
7849	OTHER MOTOR VEHCL PARTS	W 483	5.4	W 246	4.4	W 346	5.6	W 199	4.2	PIECES 722,781,782,783
785	CYCLES,ETC MOTRZD OR NOT	W 239	1.4	W 281	1.1	W 410	1.5	W 319	1.2	MOTOCYCLES SCOOTERS
8	MISC MANUFACTURED GOODS		12.9		12.2		16.8		8.2	ART MANUFACTURES DIVERS
821	*FURNITURE,PARTS THEREOF	W 145	0.8	W 157	1.1	W 125	1.3	W 88	1.0	MEUBLES ET PIECES
84	CLOTHING AND ACCESSORIES		0.8		0.8		0.7		0.6	VETEMENTS
851	*FOOTWEAR	W 228	1.9	W 190	0.9	W 260	1.1	W 201	0.6	CHAUSSURES
88	PHOTO EQU,OPTICL GDS ETC		4.9		6.8		10.2		4.2	APP,FOURN PHOTO,OP,MONTR
882	PHOTO,CINEMA SUPPLIES	W 41	0.7	W 33	0.7	W 38	0.8	W 34	0.5	PRODUITS PHOTO,CINEMA
89	MISC MANUFCTRD GOODS NES		4.4		2.4		3.2		1.9	ART MANUFACTURES DIVERS
892	PRINTED MATTER	W 214	2.8	W 102	1.3	W 138	1.8	W 86	1.1	IMPRIMES
898	MUSICAL INSTRUMENTS,PTS	W 17	0.7	W 10	0.3	W 15	0.8	W 3	0.1	INSTRUMENTS DE MUSIQUE

Burundi

4. Special Imports C.I.F. by Commodities according to the S.I.T.C. (Rev. 2) in million U.S. Dollars
Importations Spéciales C.A.F. par Produits d'après la C.T.C.I. (Rév. 2) en millions de Dollars E.U.

SITC CTCI	COMMODITY	1990		1991		1992		1993		PRODUIT
		QUANTITY QUANTITE	VALUE VALEUR	QUANTITY QUANTITE	VALUE VALEUR	QUANTITY QUANTITE	VALUE VALEUR	QUANTITY QUANTITE	VALUE VALEUR	
9	GOODS NOT CLASSD BY KIND		8.6		14.3		13.5		19.9	ART TRANSACT NON CLASSES
931	*SPECIAL TRANSACTIONS	W 9426	8.6	W 9325	14.3		13.5		19.9	TRANS.SPECIALES

5. Special Exports F.O.B. by Commodities according to the S.I.T.C. (Rev. 2) in million U.S. Dollars
Exportations Spéciales F.O.B. par Produits d'après la C.T.C.I. (Rév. 2) en millions de Dollars E.U.

SITC CTCI	COMMODITY	1990		1991		1992		1993		PRODUIT
		QUANTITY QUANTITE	VALUE VALEUR	QUANTITY QUANTITE	VALUE VALEUR	QUANTITY QUANTITE	VALUE VALEUR	QUANTITY QUANTITE	VALUE VALEUR	
	ALL COMMODITIES		75.0		91.6		74.8		68.8	TOUS PRODUITS
0	FOOD AND LIVE ANIMALS		63.9		82.5		59.1		52.4	ALIMENTS,ANIMAUX VIVANTS
03	FISH AND PREPARATIONS								0.3	POISSONS ET PREPARATIONS
0341	FISH FRSH,CHLLD,EX FILLT							W 1	0.3	POISSON FRAIS,REFRIGERE
07	COFFEE,TEA,COCOA,SPICES		63.9		82.5		59.1		52.0	CAFE,THE,CACAO,EPICES
071	COFFEE AND SUBSTITUTES	W 33501	56.1		74.2	W 39991	49.7	W 27666	43.3	CAFE ET SUCCEDANES
0711	COFFEE GREEN,ROASTED,SUB	W 33501	56.1		74.2	W 39991	49.7	W 27666	43.3	CAFE TORREFIE OU DECAFEINE
074	TEA AND MATE	W 3920	7.9		8.4	W 5696	9.5	W 5216	8.7	THE ET MATE
0741	TEA	W 3920	7.9			W 5696	9.5	W 5216	8.7	THE
1	BEVERAGES AND TOBACCO		0.1		0.1		0.8		2.1	BOISSONS ET TABACS
11	BEVERAGES		0.1		0.1		0.2		0.4	BOISSONS
112	ALCOHOLIC BEVERAGES	W 226	0.1		0.1	W 497	0.2	W 1205	0.4	BOISSONS ALCOOLIQUES
1123	BEER,ALE,STOUT,PORTER	W 226	0.1		0.1	W 497	0.2	W 1205	0.4	BIERES
12	TOBACCO AND MANUFACTURES						0.6		1.8	TABACS BRUTS FABRIQUES
122	TOBACCO,MANUFACTURED					W 86	0.6			TABACS FABRIQUES
1222	CIGARETTES					W 86	0.6	W 244	1.8	CIGARETTES
2	CRUDE MATERLS,EXCL FUELS		3.6		2.4		1.7		4.1	MAT BRUTES NON COMESTIBLES
21	HIDES,SKINS,FURS UNDRSSD		3.4		2.4		1.7		0.9	CUIRS,PEAUX BRUTS
211	HIDES,SKINS,EXC FURS,RAW	W 1036	3.4		2.4	W 950	1.7	W 563	0.9	CUIRS ET PEAUX
26	TEXTILE FIBRES AND WASTE		0.2						3.3	FIBRES TEXTILES
263	COTTON	W 100	0.2					W 2445	3.3	COTON
2631	RAW COTTON,EXCL LINTERS	W 100	0.2					W 2445	3.3	COTON EN MASSE
5	CHEMCLS,RELATED PROD NES								1.0	PRODUITS CHIMIQUES
55	PERFUME,CLEANING ETC PRD								1.0	PROD POUR PARFUM,TOILETTE
5541	SOAPS							W 856	1.0	SAVONS,PROD TENSIO–ACTIFS
6	BASIC MANUFACTURES		2.0		2.5		4.5		4.5	ART MANUFACTURES
65	TEXTILE YARN,FABRICS,ETC		0.2		1.4		1.7		2.5	FILS,TISSUS,ARTICLES TEXTILE
652	COTTON FABRICS,WOVEN	W 12	0.2		1.4	W 198	1.7	W 451	2.5	TISSUS DE COTON
66	NONMETAL MINERAL MFS NES		1.8		1.1		2.5		2.0	ART MIN NON METALLIQUES
665	GLASSWARE	W 1788	1.8		1.1	W 3761	2.4		1.9	OUVRAGES EN VERRE
6651	BOTTLES ETC OF GLASS	W 1788	1.8		1.1	W 3761	2.4	W 3370	1.8	RECIPIENTS EN VERRE
69	METAL MANUFACTURES NES		0.1		0.1		0.4		0.1	ART MANUFACT EN METAL NDA
9	GOODS NOT CLASSD BY KIND		5.6		4.2		8.8		4.9	ART TRANSACT NON CLASSES
931	*SPECIAL TRANSACTIONS	W 3914	5.6		4.2		8.8		4.9	TRANS.SPECIALES

1. HISTORICAL SERIES, 1961–1996 SPECIAL TRADE, IMPORTS C.I.F., EXPORTS F.O.B.
SERIES HISTORIQUES, 1961–1996 COMMERCE SPECIAL, IMPORTATIONS C.A.F., EXPORTATIONS F.O.B

YEAR ANNEE	VALUE IN MILLION C.F.A. FRANCS / VALEUR EN MILLION C.F.A. FRANCS — MERCHANDISE – MARCHANDISE		GOLD – OR		CONVERSION FACTORS U.S. CENTS PER C.F.A. FRANC FACTEURS DE CONVERSION CENTS E.U. PAR C.F.A. FRANC		INDEX NUMBERS – INDICES — QUANTUM		UNIT VALUE VALEUR UNITAIRE	
	IMPORTS	EXPORTS	IMPORTS	EXPORTS	IMPORTS	EXPORTS	IMPORTS	EXPORTS	IMPORTS	EXPORTS
1961	23716.30	24197.70		4.90	0.4051	0.4051				
1962	25141.40	25478.20		38.10	0.4051	0.4051				
1963	31562.90	33277.50			0.4051	0.4051				
1964	32835.70	34516.20		6.30	0.4051	0.4051				
1965	37396.00	34362.50		7.10	0.4051	0.4051				
1966	36114.00	35882.60		6.80	0.4051	0.4051				
1967	46419.00	39100.00	0.70	6.10	0.4051	0.4051				
1968	46220.00	46722.60	1.30	2.20	0.4051	0.4051				
1969	53000.00	58573.50	0.30		0.3866	0.3855				
1970	67241.40	64359.20			0.3601	0.3601				
1971	69351.60	57282.80	1.70		0.3601	0.3601				
1972	76382.50	55699.20	1.90		0.3912	0.3912				
1973	74487.00	78321.40			0.4494	0.4502				
1974	104825.20	114815.00			0.4168	0.4162				
1975	128104.00	96130.00			0.4676	0.4657				
1976	145963.00	122028.00			0.4175	0.4186				
1977	192401.00	172851.00			0.4073	0.4073				
1978	237247.00	181697.00			0.4455	0.4419				
1979	271160.00	238700.00			0.4686	0.4691				
1980	337607.00	290615.00			0.4745	0.4761				
1981	386089.00	303307.00			0.3700	0.3700				
1982	394574.80	326891.30			0.3069	0.3060				
1983	463888.60	358880.80			0.2624	0.2616				
1984	484431.10	381334.00			0.2284	0.2313				
1985	508730.40	321730.80			0.2263	0.2243				
1986	590449.90	271630.00			0.2886	0.2880				
1987	517280.00	241920.00			0.3332	0.3331				
1988	378729.90	275120.10			0.3357	0.3357				
1989	402240.00	405989.80			0.3135	0.3135				
1990	381149.90	545110.00			0.3673	0.3673				
1991	330960.10	517390.00			0.3545	0.3545				
1992	307790.00	487130.10			0.3778	0.3778				
1993	311960.00	533250.00			0.3545	0.3565				
1994	601499.90	825200.10			0.1812	0.1813				
1995	619399.90	1018200.00			0.2010	0.2011				
1996	616142.40	899455.70			0.1955	0.1954				

2. IMPORTS BY BROAD ECONOMIC CATEGORY AND EXPORTS BY INDUSTRIAL ORIGIN. (PERCENTAGE OF TOTAL VALUE)
IMPORTATIONS PAR CATEGORIES ECONOMIQUES ET EXPORTATIONS PAR BRANCHE D'ACTIVITE.(EN POURCENTAGE DE LA VALEUR TOTALE)

IMPORTS – IMPORTATIONS

	1990	1991	1992	1993	1994	1995	1996
TOTAL IMPORTS–IMPORTATIONS TOTALES	100.					100.	100.
1 FOOD BEV–ALIMENTATION BOISSONS	16.5					16.2	12.7
11 PRIMARY–PRODUITS DE BASE	3.7					3.8	2.8
111 FOR INDUSTRY–POUR L'INDUSTRIE	0.4					1.4	0.8
112 FOR HOUSEHOLDS–POUR LES MENAGES	3.4					2.4	2.0
12 PROCESSED–PRODUITS ELABORES	12.8					12.4	9.9
121 FOR INDUSTRY–POUR L'INDUSTRIE	6.3					4.7	3.4
122 FOR HOUSEHOLDS–POUR LES MENAGES	6.5					7.8	6.5
2 IND SUPPLIES–APPROV INDUSTRIELS	34.8					41.5	34.2
21 PRIMARY–PRODUITS DE BASE	1.5					3.5	3.5
22 PROCESSED–PRODUITS ELABORES	33.4					38.0	30.8
3 FUELS–COMBUSTIBLES	0.7					1.5	14.3
31 PRIMARY–PRODUITS DE BASE	0.1					0.0	12.5
32 PROCESSED–PRODUITS ELABORES	0.6					1.5	1.8
321 MOTOR SPIRIT–ESSENCE	0.6					0.1	0.0
322 OTHER–AUTRES	0.0					1.5	1.8
4 MACHINERY–EQUIPEMENT	19.5					17.4	17.5
41 CAPITAL EQUIPMENT–MACHINES	17.2					15.1	15.3
42 PARTS–PIECES ACCESSOIRES	2.3					2.3	2.2
5 TRANSPORT–TRANSPORT	10.3					13.8	12.1
51 PASSENGER CARS–AUTOMOBILES	3.1					3.5	3.8
52 OTHER–AUTRES	3.7					6.5	4.8
521 INDUSTRIAL–INDUSTRIELS	3.6					6.3	4.6
522 NON INDUSTRIAL–NON INDUSTRIEL	0.0					0.1	0.3
53 PARTS–PIECES ACCESSOIRES	3.5					3.8	3.6
6 CONSUM GOODS–BIENS CONSOMMATION	18.1					9.4	9.1
61 DURABLE–DURABLES	1.3					0.8	1.0
62 SEMI DURABLE–SEMI DURABLES	3.5					2.6	2.6
63 NON DURABLE–NON DURABLES	13.3					6.0	5.5
7 GOODS NES–BIENS NDA	0.0					0.1	0.0

EXPORTS – EXPORTATIONS

	1990	1991	1992	1993	1994	1995	1996
TOTAL EXPORTS–EXPORTATIONS TOTALES	100.					100.	100.
1 AGRICULTURE	28.8					43.3	40.0
2 MINING QUARRY–INDUS EXTRACTIVES	49.8					29.0	35.8
3 MANUFACTURING–IND MANUFACTUR	21.5					27.7	24.3
31 FOOD BEV TOBACCO–ALIM BOISS TAB	3.2					4.0	4.6
32 TEXTILES–INDUSTRIES TEXTILES	1.0					0.8	0.7
33 WOOD & PRODUCTS–BOIS & PRODUITS	4.0					9.1	6.3
34 PAPER & PRODUCTS–PAPIER & PRODT	0.1					0.3	0.3
35 CHEMICALS–INDUSTRIES CHIMIQUES	1.9					1.6	1.9
36 NON METAL MIN–MIN NON METAL	1.6					1.5	2.2
37 BASIC METAL–IND METAL BASE	6.8					8.6	6.4
38 METAL MANUF–MANUF METAL	2.8					1.9	1.7
39 OTH MANUF IND–AUTRES MANUF	0.0					0.0	0.0

3. TRADE BY PRINCIPAL COUNTRIES OF ORIGIN AND DESTINATION (VALUE IN MILLION U.S. DOLLARS)
ECHANGES SELON LES PRINCIPAUX PAYS D'ORIGINE ET DE DESTINATION (VALEUR EN MILLIONS DE DOLLARS EU)

COUNTRIES–PAYS	SPECIAL IMPORTS C.I.F. IMPORTATIONS SPECIALES C.A.F				
	1992	1993	1994	1995	1996
World		1106.0	1090.0	1078.5	1204.3
Africa				123.0	253.4
Americas				125.7	135.7
– Northern America				106.3	112.7
– LAIA				17.1	15.0
– CACM				0.5	2.5
– Caribbean				1.9	5.6
– Rest of America				0.0	0.0
Asia excl fmr USSR				138.9	139.3
– Middle East				6.8	6.2
Asia former USSR					
Europe excl fmr USSR				655.4	665.8
– European Union				633.2	643.5
– Eastern Europe				11.8	15.3
– Rest of Europe				10.4	7.0
Europe former USSR				6.0	5.8
Oceania				0.3	1.3
Other				29.3	3.0
France, Monaco				337.1	325.1
USA/Etats–Unis d'Amer				83.5	102.3
Germany/Allemagne				78.4	87.7
Nigeria/Nigéria		10.0	11.0	1.8	116.6
Guinea/Guinée		32.0	32.0	40.7	30.0
Senegal/Sénégal		42.0	54.0	11.9	13.1
Japan/Japon				58.9	60.0
Belgium–Luxembourg				59.0	58.0
Italy/Italie				38.7	44.3
Netherlands/Pays–Bas				37.1	33.1
United Kingdom				33.3	35.5
Mauritania/Mauritanie		17.0	21.0	16.9	
Tunisia/Tunisie		9.0	8.0	13.2	10.4
Spain/Espagne				16.5	21.4
Equatorial Guinea				0.1	36.7
Canada				22.8	10.4
Areas n.e.s.				29.3	2.1
Cote d'Ivoire				14.1	14.9
Pakistan			6.0	13.5	8.8
Brazil/Brésil				15.2	11.8
China/Chine				11.8	14.9
India/Inde				9.1	14.8
So. African Customs Un				11.5	11.2
Finland/Finlande				12.7	9.4
Romania/Roumanie				7.4	12.1
Korea, Republic of				8.4	9.9
Malaysia/Malaisie		8.0	3.0	3.1	2.0
Indonesia/Indonésie		4.0	5.0	3.2	3.9
Morocco/Maroc		3.0	3.0	5.2	5.0
Ireland/Irlande				8.4	6.7
Switzerland,Liechtenst.				8.0	6.3
European Union n.e.s.					11.7
Russian Federation				5.5	5.7
Viet Nam				4.6	4.8
Thailand/Thaïlande				5.2	3.7
Sweden/Suède				5.3	3.4
Mauritius/Maurice				0.0	7.7
Dominican Republic				1.9	5.6
Turkey/Turquie				4.0	3.2
Bangladesh		1.0	1.0	3.4	1.6

COUNTRIES–PAYS	SPECIAL EXPORTS F.O.B. EXPORTATIONS SPECIALES F.O.B.				
	1992	1993	1994	1995	1996
Monde		1901.0	1496.0	1538.7	1757.9
Afrique				144.3	179.8
Amériques				51.1	49.8
– Amérique du Nord				36.3	41.8
– ALAI				14.6	7.5
– MCAC					
– Caraïbes				0.2	0.6
– Autre Amérique					
Asie anc. URSS exclus				151.3	164.5
– Moyen–Orient				6.4	6.6
Asie ancienne URSS					
Europe anc. URSS exclus				1191.9	1363.6
– Union Européenne				1185.7	1360.7
– Europe de l'Est				5.9	2.8
– Autre de l'Europe				0.3	0.1
Europe ancienne URSS					0.1
Océanie				0.2	0.1
Autre					
France, Monaco				407.3	311.8
Italy/Italie				237.1	358.2
Spain/Espagne				187.2	371.9
Netherlands/Pays–Bas				206.8	180.3
Senegal/Sénégal		131.0	196.0	7.6	5.5
Nigeria/Nigéria		62.0	75.0	8.4	17.7
Gabon		39.0	41.0	24.5	32.2
Morocco/Maroc		37.0	37.0	5.0	4.2
Chad/Tchad		26.0	33.0	5.7	9.7
Belgium–Luxembourg				34.5	38.9
USA/Etats–Unis d'Amer				29.0	40.9
Germany/Allemagne				37.2	31.2
China/Chine				32.8	30.8
Portugal				35.3	27.7
Korea, Republic of				43.6	17.9
United Kingdom				26.4	30.5
Equatorial Guinea				24.6	31.6
Other Asia n.e.s.				20.3	20.7
Thailand/Thaïlande				16.1	23.0
Congo				17.6	21.0
Central African Rep				12.8	16.3
Japan/Japon				12.1	14.0
China, Hong Kong SAR				8.4	11.1
Singapore/Singapour				3.4	14.0
Cote d'Ivoire				9.1	8.1
Tunisia/Tunisie		3.0	5.0	1.6	7.5
Brazil/Brésil				9.5	5.2
Greece/Grèce				8.7	5.4
Malaysia/Malaisie		2.0	2.0	1.0	8.7
Turkey/Turquie			3.0	5.1	4.9
Philippines				2.6	9.3
Algeria/Algérie		4.0	4.0	0.2	3.2
So. African Customs Un				3.7	6.1
Ireland/Irlande				5.0	4.7
Poland/Pologne				5.5	2.8
Canada				7.3	0.9
Indonesia/Indonésie			1.0	1.1	4.9
Mexico/Mexique				4.8	2.1
Dem Rep of the Congo				3.2	3.0
Guinea/Guinée		1.0	1.0	1.2	2.8

(VALUE AS PERCENTAGE OF WORLD TOTAL)(VALEURS EN POURCENTAGE DU TOTAL MONDIAL)

	1987	1988	1989	1990	1991	1992	1993	1994	1995	1996
Africa	5.8		7.7	7.0					11.4	21.0
Americas	6.6		11.5	9.4					11.7	11.3
– Northern America	3.8		8.9	5.4					9.9	9.4
– LAIA	1.3		2.2	2.4					1.6	1.2
– CACM	0.0		0.0	0.0					0.0	0.2
– Caribbean	0.0		0.0	0.0					0.2	0.5
– Rest of America	1.5		0.4	1.6					0.0	0.0
Asia excl fmr USSR	15.5		12.8	12.4					12.9	11.6
– Middle East	0.7		1.3	1.3					0.6	0.5
Asia former USSR										
Europe excl fmr USSR	69.7		65.0	70.3					60.8	55.3
– European Union	66.0		62.3	68.0					58.7	53.4
– Eastern Europe	1.0		0.8	0.7					1.1	1.3
– Rest of Europe	2.8		1.9	1.5					1.0	0.6
Europe former USSR	0.4		0.2	0.9					0.6	0.5
Oceania	0.1		0.1	0.0					0.0	0.1
Other	1.9		2.7						2.7	0.2
France, Monaco	37.5		36.5	37.7					31.3	27.0
USA/Etats–Unis d'Amer	3.5		5.1	4.4					7.7	8.5
Germany/Allemagne									7.3	7.3
Nigeria/Nigéria	0.2		0.4	0.3			0.9	1.0	0.2	9.7
Guinea/Guinée	1.6		2.7	2.5			2.9	2.9	3.8	2.5
Senegal/Sénégal	1.0		1.2	1.5			3.8	5.0	1.1	1.1
Japan/Japon	8.2		5.7	4.7					5.5	5.0
Belgium–Luxembourg	4.1		3.1	4.7					5.5	4.8
Italy/Italie	4.3		3.0	4.4					3.6	3.7
Netherlands/Pays–Bas	2.3		9.1	3.2					3.4	2.7

	1987	1988	1989	1990	1991	1992	1993	1994	1995	1996
Afrique	17.6		15.8	8.7					9.4	10.2
Amériques	9.1		11.4	8.2					3.3	2.8
– Amérique du Nord	7.4		10.3	7.6					2.4	2.4
– ALAI	1.8		1.2	0.6					0.9	0.4
– MCAC										
– Caraïbes	0.0		0.0	0.0					0.0	0.0
– Autre Amérique										
Asie anc. URSS exclus	3.2		4.4	4.9					9.8	9.4
– Moyen–Orient	0.2		0.5	0.6					0.4	0.4
Asie ancienne URSS										
Europe anc. URSS exclus	68.5		67.8	78.0					77.5	77.6
– Union Européenne	68.4		66.4	76.6					77.1	77.4
– Europe de l'Est	0.0		1.4	0.0					0.4	0.2
– Autre de l'Europe	0.0		0.0	1.3					0.0	0.0
Europe ancienne URSS	1.6		0.5	0.3						0.0
Océanie	0.0		0.0	0.0					0.0	0.0
Autre	0.0		0.0							
France, Monaco	17.5		23.5	40.6					26.5	17.7
Italy/Italie	13.8		1.4	7.0					15.4	20.4
Spain/Espagne	2.7		5.0	6.9					12.2	21.2
Netherlands/Pays–Bas	23.1		6.4	15.1					13.4	10.3
Senegal/Sénégal	0.3		1.0	0.2			6.9	13.1	0.5	0.3
Nigeria/Nigéria	3.1		2.4	1.7			3.3	5.0	0.5	1.0
Gabon	5.7		2.3	1.5			2.1	2.7	1.6	1.8
Morocco/Maroc	0.0		0.2	0.1			1.9	2.5	0.3	0.2
Chad/Tchad	2.2		0.5	0.6			1.4	2.2	0.4	0.6
Belgium–Luxembourg	3.2		19.3	1.5					2.2	2.2

4. Special Imports C.I.F. by Commodities according to the S.I.T.C. (Rev. 2) in million U.S. Dollars
Importations Spéciales C.A.F. par Produits d'après la C.T.C.I. (Rév. 2) en millions de Dollars E.U.

SITC CTCI	COMMODITY	1993		1994		1995		1996		PRODUIT
		QUANTITY QUANTITE	VALUE VALEUR	QUANTITY QUANTITE	VALUE VALEUR	QUANTITY QUANTITE	VALUE VALEUR	QUANTITY QUANTITE	VALUE VALEUR	
	ALL COMMODITIES						1078.6		1204.4	TOUS PRODUITS
0	FOOD AND LIVE ANIMALS						174.1		153.1	ALIMENTS,ANIMAUX VIVANTS
02	DAIRY PRODCTS,BIRDS'EGGS						11.6		12.7	PRODUITS LAITIERS,OEUFS
022	MILK AND CREAM					W 5702	9.8	W 6665	10.9	LAIT ET CREME
0224	MILK,CREAM PRESERVED ETC					W 4815	9.1	W 5767	10.2	LAIT,CREME CONS,CONC
02243	MILK DRY,OVER 1.5% FAT					W 1700	4.1	W 2071	4.9	LAIT POUDRE SUP 1.5%
02249	MILK(EX DRY) PRSVD,SWEET					W 2875	4.5	W 3382	4.6	LAIT CONS,CONC SUCRE
03	FISH AND PREPARATIONS						27.3		22.1	POISSONS ET PREPARATIONS
034	FISH,FRESH,CHILLED,FROZN					W 46005	24.3	W 41104	20.8	POISSON FRAIS, REFRIG,CONG
0342	FISH FROZEN,EXCL FILLETS					W 45040	23.8	W 41102	20.8	POISSONS CONGELES
04	CEREALS AND PREPARATIONS						90.5		77.7	CEREALES ET PRODUITS
041	WHEAT ETC UNMILLED					W 65969	13.0	W 34996	9.5	FROMENT,EPEAUTRE
0411	DURUM WHEAT UNMILLED					W 18769	5.1	W 10500	3.0	FROMENT DUR NON MOULU
0412	OTHER WHEAT ETC UNMILLED					W 47200	8.0	W 24496	6.6	AUTRE FROMENT NON MOULU
042	RICE					W 124946	27.0	W 81559	24.4	RIZ
0422	RICE SEMI–MILLED,MILLED					W 124943	27.0	W 81558	24.4	RIZ POLI,GLACE INCL BRISURES
04221	RICE MILLED UNBROKEN					W 124943	27.0	W 81557	24.4	RIZ POLI,GLACE EXCL BRISURES
046	WHEAT ETC MEAL OR FLOUR					W 26985	8.0	W 12500	4.4	SEMOULE FARINE,FROMENT
04601	FLOUR OF WHEAT OR MESLIN					W 24921	7.0	W 8335	2.5	FARINE DE FROMENT
047	OTHER CEREAL MEALS,FLOUR					W 10297	4.6	W 8836	4.1	AUTRES SEMOULES,FARINES
04702	MEAL OR GROATS NON–WHEAT					W 10268	4.6	W 8750	4.1	GRUAUX,SEMOULES DE CEREALES
048	CEREAL ETC PREPARATIONS					W 58874	36.7	W 46990	35.4	PREPTNS A BASE CEREALES
0482	MALT INCLUDING FLOUR					W 56985	32.0	W 44454	28.8	MALT MEME TORREFIE
0488	OTH CEREAL PREPS,MALT EX					W 868	3.5	W 1144	4.9	EXTRAITS DE MALT
05	VEGETABLES AND FRUIT						6.2		6.0	LEGUMES ET FRUITS
054	VEG ETC FRSH,SMPLY PRSVD					W 2555	3.9	W 3338	4.0	LEGUMES FRAIS,CONG,SECS
06	SUGAR AND PREPS,HONEY						11.7		12.8	SUCRES ET PRODUITS
061	SUGAR AND HONEY					W 20549	11.2	W 23407	12.0	SUCRES ET MIEL
0612	REFINED SUGAR ETC					W 18636	10.0	W 21881	11.0	SUCRES RAFFINES
081	*FEEDING STUFF FOR ANIML					W 8773	4.5	W 7800	4.9	NOURRITURE POUR ANIMAUX
09	MISC EDIBLE PRODUCTS						19.9		14.1	PREP ALIMENTAIRES DIVERSES
098	EDIBLE PRODCTS,PREPS NES					W 6904	17.1	W 5855	11.6	PREP ALIMENTAIRES NDA
09806	YEASTS,BAKING POWDERS					W 1025	3.4	W 932	2.6	LEVURES
09809	MISC FOOD PREPRTIONS NES					W 5334	10.9	W 4145	7.7	PREP ALIMENTAIRES NDA
1	BEVERAGES AND TOBACCO						11.6		11.5	BOISSONS ET TABACS
11	BEVERAGES						5.3		4.2	BOISSONS
112	ALCOHOLIC BEVERAGES					W 4849	5.1	W 3825	4.0	BOISSONS ALCOOLIQUES
1121	WINE OF FRESH GRAPES ETC					W 4150	3.5	W 3319	2.8	VINS DE RAISINS FRAIS
11212	WINE OF FRESH GRAPES					W 4137	3.4	W 3309	2.8	VINS DE MOUTS DE RAISINS
12	TOBACCO AND MANUFACTURES						6.4		7.4	TABACS BRUTS FABRIQUES
121	TOBACCO UNMNFCTRD,REFUSE					W 325	1.6	W 1204	5.6	TABACS BRUTS,DECHETS
1212	TOBACCO STRIPPED OR PART					W 221	1.1	W 1036	5.0	TABACS PART ECOTES
122	TOBACCO,MANUFACTURED					W 512	4.9	W 923	1.9	TABACS FABRIQUES
1223	OTH MANUFACTURED TOBACCO					W 394	3.8	W 134	1.1	TABACS FUMER,CHIQUER,PRISER
2	CRUDE MATERLS,EXCL FUELS						77.9		67.9	MAT BRUTES NON COMESTIBLES
26	TEXTILE FIBRES AND WASTE						22.6		25.5	FIBRES TEXTILES
269	WASTE OF TEXTILE FABRICS					W 15917	20.9	W 20180	24.0	FRIPERIE DRILLES,CHIFFONS
26901	BULK TEXT WSTE,OLD CLTHG					W 15830	20.8	W 20059	23.8	ART ET ACCESS D'HABILLEMENT
27	CRUDE FERTLZR,MINRLS NES						8.9		7.5	ENGRAIS MINERAUX BRUTS
278	OTHER CRUDE MINERALS					W 60709	6.7	W 52226	5.5	AUTRES MINERAUX BRUTS
2783	COMMON SALT,ETC					W 47767	3.4	W 38756	2.5	SEL
28	METALLIFEROUS ORES,SCRAP						41.6		30.9	MINERAIS METAL,DECHETS
287	BASE METAL ORES,CONC NES					W 197952	41.6	W 130563	30.8	MINERAIS METAUX COMMUNS
2873	ALUMINIUM ORES,ALUMINA					W 196411	40.8	W 128667	29.9	MINERAIS D'ALUMINIUM
28732	ALUMINA(ALUMINIUM OXIDE)					W 196411	40.8	W 128667	29.9	ALUMINE (OXYDE ALUMINIUM)
29	CRUDE ANIMAL,VEG MAT NES						4.2		3.5	MATIERES BRUTES ANIM,VEGET
292	CRUDE VEG MATERIALS NES					W 153	4.2	W 179	3.5	MAT BRUTES VEGETALES NDA
2929	OTH CRUDE VEG MATERIALS					W 101	3.7	W 100	2.7	MATIERES VEGETALES NDA
29291	VEGETABLE SAPS,EXTRACTS					W 98	3.7	W 99	2.7	SUCS,EXTRAITS VEGETAUX
3	MINERAL FUELS ETC						27.5		189.6	COMBUSTIBLES MINERAUX LUB
33	PETROLEUM AND PRODUCTS						27.3		188.3	PETROLE ET DERIVES
333	CRUDE PETROLEUM							W 895366	149.3	HUILES BRUTES DE PETROLE
334	PETROLEUM PRODUCTS,REFIN					W 29543	16.6	W 38542	22.0	PRODUITS RAFFINES
3345	LUBS,PETROLEUM OILS NES					W 23717	13.9	W 20741	17.4	HUILES LUBRIFIANTES
33451	LUBS(HIGH PETR CONT) ETC					W 22968	12.8	W 20615	16.9	HUILES LUBRIF,H LOURDES
335	RESIDUAL PETRLM PROD NES					W 50159	10.7	W 66612	17.1	PRODUITS RESIDUELS NDA
3353	MIN TAR PITCH,PITCH COKE					W 16233	3.9	W 9439	2.8	BRAI,COKE DE BRAI
3354	PETROLM BITUMEN,COKE ETC					W 33245	6.2	W 56146	13.4	BITUME,COKE DE PETROLE
33542	PETROLEUM COKE					W 22400	4.4	W 51631	12.3	COKE DE PETROLE
5	CHEMCLS,RELATED PROD NES						175.1		174.0	PRODUITS CHIMIQUES
51	ORGANIC CHEMICALS						9.0		8.4	PROD CHIMIQ ORGANIQUES
52	INORGANIC CHEMICALS						17.5		17.9	PROD CHIM INORGANIQUES
522	INORG ELEMNTS,OXIDES,ETC					W 19327	8.4	W 14134	6.5	ELEMENTS INORGANIQUES
5225	INORGANIC BASES ETC NES					W 17818	6.3	W 12030	3.7	AUTRES BASES OXYDES METAL
52252	SODIUM HYDROXIDE, SOLID					W 6835	3.5	W 1701	1.0	HYDROXYDE DE SODIUM
523	OTHR INORG CHEMICALS ETC					W 13156	9.1	W 19563	11.2	AUT PRODUITS CHIMIQUES INORG
5231	METAL CMPD OF INORG ACID					W 7975	6.5	W 11187	7.5	SELS METALLIQUES
52311	FLUORIDES ETC					W 4187	3.6	W 2400	2.2	FLUORURES
53	DYES,TANNING,COLOUR PROD						7.1		8.7	PROD TEINTURE,COLORANTS
533	PIGMENTS,PAINTS,ETC					W 1980	4.7	W 2849	5.8	PIGMENTS,PEINTURES,VERNIS
541	*MEDICINAL,PHARM PRODUCT					K 1838803	45.4	K 1846422	45.5	PROD MEDICINAUX PHARMACEUT
5417	MEDICAMENTS					K 1674770	42.0	K 1648274	42.2	MEDICAMENTS
54171	— CONTAINNG ANTIBIOTICS					K 278370	8.8	K 226916	6.6	MED CONTN ANTIBIOTIQUES
54179	— CONTNG OTH SUBSTANCES					K 1274415	28.8	K 1313427	31.9	MED CONT AUT SUBSTANCES
55	PERFUME,CLEANING ETC PRD						13.9		14.7	PROD POUR PARFUM,TOILETTE
551	ESSENTL OILS,PERFUME,ETC					W 1136	9.0	W 1070	9.5	HUILES ESSENTIELLES
5514	MIXED PERFUME SUBSTANCES					W 1103	8.9	W 1046	9.4	MELANGES SUBSTAN ODORIFER
554	SOAP,CLEANSING ETC PREPS					W 2056	3.9	W 2788	4.0	SAVONS,PRODUITS DETERSIFS
562	*FERTILIZERS,MANUFACTURE					W 74990	19.7	W 79258	22.8	ENGRAIS MANUFACTURES
5621	CHEM NITROGENOUS FERTLZR					W 17480	4.1	W 22084	6.8	ENGRAIS AZOTES
56216	UREA					W 13771	3.3	W 18687	6.0	UREE
5623	CHEM POTASSIC FERTILIZER					W 20014	4.8	W 9830	2.1	ENGRAIS POTASSIQUES
5629	FERTILIZERS NES					W 35542	10.4	W 45848	13.7	ENGRAIS NDA
56291	NIT–PHOS–POT FERTLZR NES					W 33780	10.0	W 39759	12.1	ENGRAIS CONT N P K
58	PLASTIC MATERIALS ETC						24.4		25.0	MAT PLAST ARTIFICIELLES
582	PROD OF CONDENSATION ETC					W 3468	5.6	W 3679	6.0	PROD CONDENS,POLYCOND
583	POLYMERIZATION ETC PRODS					W 9297	17.8	W 12031	17.8	PROD POLYMERISATION
5831	POLYETHYLENE					W 3736	5.7	W 4778	6.1	POLYETHYLENE
58311	— IN PRIMARY FORMS					W 3579	4.9	W 4516	4.8	POLYETHYLENE PRIMAIRES
5834	POLYVINYL CHLORIDE					W 3576	6.2	W 4912	6.7	CHLORURE DE POLYVINYLE
58341	— IN PRIMARY FORMS					W 3405	5.8	W 4703	6.2	SOUS FORMES PRIMAIRES

4. Special Imports C.I.F. by Commodities according to the S.I.T.C. (Rev. 2) in million U.S. Dollars
Importations Spéciales C.A.F. par Produits d'après la C.T.C.I. (Rév. 2) en millions de Dollars E.U.

SITC CTCI	COMMODITY	1993 QUANTITY QUANTITE	1993 VALUE VALEUR	1994 QUANTITY QUANTITE	1994 VALUE VALEUR	1995 QUANTITY QUANTITE	1995 VALUE VALEUR	1996 QUANTITY QUANTITE	1996 VALUE VALEUR	PRODUIT
59	CHEMICAL MATERIALS NES						37.6		30.6	MAT PROD CHIMIQUES NDA
591	PESTICIDES,DISINFECTANTS					W 4343	23.2	W 3514	14.9	DESINF,INSECT,FONG,HERB
5911	INSECTICIDES,FOR RETAIL					W 932	5.5	W 949	4.6	INSECTICIDES VENTE DET
5912	FUNGICIDES,FOR RETAIL					W 1747	10.1	W 1471	5.9	FONGICIDES VENTE AU DET
5913	HERBICIDES,FOR RETAIL					W 793	4.2	W 618	3.2	HERBICIDES VENTE AU DET
5914	DISINFECTANTS,ETC,FR RET					W 870	3.6	W 477	1.3	DESINFECTANTS VENTE DET
598	MISCEL CHEM PRODUCTS NES					W 4318	11.2	W 4526	12.8	PROD DIV INDUST CHIM NDA
5982	ANTI-KNOCK PREPARTNS ETC					W 987	3.3	W 985	4.4	PREPARAT ANTIDETONANTES
5989	CHEM PRODUCTS,PREPS NES					W 2782	7.3	W 3338	8.2	PROD PREP CHIMIQUES NDA
59899	OTH CHEM PRODS,PREPS,NES					W 1624	5.1	W 1788	5.3	AUT PRODUITS CHIMIQUES NDA
6	BASIC MANUFACTURES						229.1		216.3	ART MANUFACTURES
62	RUBBER MANUFACTURES NES						23.2		26.5	CAOUTCHOUC MANUFACTURE
625	RUBBER TYRES, TUBES ETC					W 6727	17.6	W 7278	21.1	PNEUS CAOUTCHOUC VULCANISE
6252	TYRES,NEW,BUS OR LORRY					W 2440	10.8	W 3224	14.1	PNEUS POUR AUTOBUS,CAMIONS
6259	OTH TYRES,TYRE CASES,ETC					W 4023	5.7	W 3655	5.4	AUTRES PNEUS RECHAPES FLAPS
62599	TYRES NES,TYRE CASES,ETC					W 3660	4.8	W 3182	4.2	PNEUS,FLAPS
628	RUBBER ARTICLES NES					W 238	3.4	W 227	3.5	OUVRAGES CAOUTCHOUC NDA
64	PAPER,PAPERBOARD AND MFR						51.4		45.9	PAPIERS,CARTONS & OUVRAGES
641	PAPER AND PAPERBOARD					W 44373	44.3	W 40711	37.8	PAPIERS ET CARTONS
6411	NEWSPRINT					W 3682	3.6	W 4004	3.6	PAPIER JOURNAL
6412	PRINTG,WRITING PAPER NES					W 3521	5.1	W 3676	5.0	PAPIERS POUR L'IMPRESSION
64122	— COATED,IMPREGNATD ETC					W 3028	4.1	W 2885	3.8	PAPIERS IMPRESSION COUCHES
6413	KRAFT PAPER,PAPERBOARD					W 20463	16.8	W 15983	12.0	PAPIER ET CARTON KRAFT
64131	KRAFT LINER IN BULK					W 15610	12.6	W 11131	7.3	PAP KRAFT POUR COUVERTURES
64139	KRAFT PAPER PAPERBD,NES					W 4716	4.2	W 4773	4.7	PAPIER,CARTON KRAFT NDA
6415	PAPER,PAPERBRD,BULK,NES					W 14523	14.9	W 14524	12.7	PAPIERS,CARTONS ROULEAUX
64151	SEMI-CHEM FLUTING PAPER					W 7166	5.0	W 7551	4.5	PAPIER FLUTING
64159	OTHER PAPER ETC,BULK,NES					W 7295	9.8	W 6941	8.1	AUT PAPIER ROULEAUX FEUILLES
642	PAPER,ETC,PRECUT,ARTS OF					W 3462	7.2	W 3378	8.1	PAP,CARTONS DECOUPES
65	TEXTILE YARN,FABRICS,ETC						17.7		15.7	FILS,TISSUS,ARTICLES TEXTILE
652	COTTON FABRICS,WOVEN						3.5	W 673	2.3	TISSUS DE COTON
658	TEXTILE ARTICLES NES					W 7006	5.9	W 3247	4.2	ART FACONNES MAT TEXTILES
6581	BAGS,SACKS OF TEXTILES					W 6689	5.0	W 2882	2.7	SACS EMBALLAGE TEXTILES
66	NONMETAL MINERAL MFS NES						36.7		34.1	ART MIN NON METALLIQUES
661	LIME,CEMENT,BLDG PRODS					W 364778	23.2	W 319109	20.8	CHAUX,CIMENTS MAT CONSTR
6612	CEMENT					W 360824	21.7	W 315118	19.2	CIMENTS HYDRAULIQUES
662	CLAY,REFRACTORY BLDG PRD					W 10786	5.2	W 10664	5.0	MAT CONST REFRACTAIRES
6624	BRICKS ETC NONREFRACTORY					W 8782	3.5	W 8336	2.9	BRIQUES ETC CERAM NON REFR
665	GLASSWARE					W 2726	3.5	W 2418	3.5	OUVRAGES EN VERRE
67	IRON AND STEEL						41.0		41.8	FER ET ACIER
672	IRON,STEEL PRIMARY FORMS					W 10728	4.3	W 7157	2.7	LINGOTS FER,ACIER
6725	IRN,STL BLOOMS,SLABS,ETC					W 9506	3.6	W 6545	2.3	BLOOMS,BILLETTES FER ACIER
67251	IRN,SMPLE STL BLOOMS,ETC					W 9253	3.5	W 6527	2.3	BLOOMS ETC NON ACIER FIN
673	IRON,STEEL SHAPES ETC					W 22742	9.7	W 15365	7.0	BARRES,PROFIL FER,ACIER
6732	IRON,STEEL BARS ETC					W 16441	6.0	W 6736	3.0	BARRES FER,ACIER
67326	IRN,OTH STL BARS HOTROLD					W 9237	3.8	W 5553	2.5	BARRES PLEINES FER,ACIER
6733	IRON,STEEL PROFILES ETC					W 5774	3.5	W 6019	3.3	PROFILES,PALPLAN FER,ACIER
674	IRN,STL UNIV,PLATE,SHEET					W 11784	9.4	W 11807	7.9	LARGES PLATS,TOLES
676	RAILWY RAILS ETC IRN,STL					W 1312	3.5	W 3752	3.8	RAILS,ELEMENTS VOIES FERREE
677	IRN,STL WIRE(EXCL W ROD)					W 6783	3.5	W 1905	2.0	FILS EN FER,ACIER
678	IRON,STL TUBES,PIPES,ETC					W 4629	10.1	W 12095	17.4	TUBES,TUYAUX EN FONTE,FER
6782	IRON,STL SEAMLESS TUBES					W 2640	6.2	W 8425	12.3	TUBES,TUYAUX SANS SOUDURE
68	NON-FERROUS METALS						10.5		7.7	METAUX NON FERREUX
684	ALUMINIUM					W 771	9.0	W 625	6.9	ALUMINIUM
6842	ALUMINIUM,ALLOYS WORKED					W 756	8.9	W 620	6.9	ALUMINIUM,ALLIAGES OUVRE
68423	ALUMINIUM FOIL					W 374	7.6	W 331	6.0	FEUILLES,BANDES MINCES AL
69	METAL MANUFACTURES NES						46.8		42.9	ART MANUFACT EN METAL NDA
691	STRUCTURES AND PARTS NES					W 1439	3.9	W 1875	6.0	CONSTRUCT FER,ACIER,ALU
6911	STRUCTURES,PARTS IRN,STL					W 1324	2.6	W 1831	5.8	CONSTRUCT FER,ACIER,FONTE
694	STL,COPPR NAILS,NUTS,ETC					W 1446	7.8	W 970	2.8	CLOUS,VIS,ECROUS
69402	IRN,STL NUTS,BOLTS,ETC					W 770	7.2	W 478	2.4	BOULONS,VIS,ECROUS FER,AC
695	TOOLS					W 1078	5.6	W 759	5.9	OUTILS A MAIN
6953	OTHER HAND TOOLS					W 450	3.5	W 409	3.2	AUTRES OUTILS A MAIN
699	BASE METAL MFRS NES					W 6627	20.2	W 6526	19.0	ART MANUFACTURES MET NDA
6996	BASE MTL MISC ARTICLES					W 2864	8.9	W 2259	6.9	ART DIVERS METAUX COMMUNS
69963	BASE METAL STOPPERS,ETC					W 2352	7.4	W 1833	5.5	BOUCHONS METALLIQUES
6998	MFRS NES OF CPR,NIKL,ETC					W 1625	4.4	W 1669	4.5	OUVRAGES EN CU,NI,AL,PB,ZN
69985	ZINC MANUFACTURES NES					W 1473	3.8	W 1605	3.9	OUVRAGES EN ZINC
7	MACHINES,TRANSPORT EQUIP						328.6		331.1	MACHINES MATERIEL TRANSPORT
71	POWER GENERATING EQUIPMT						14.6		12.5	MACHINES GENERATRICES
713	INTRNL COMBUS PSTN ENGIN					W 1061	6.3	W 1167	6.1	MOTEURS EXPL COMB INT, PIECE
7139	PISTON ENGINE PARTS NES					W 172	4.5	W 181	4.1	PIECES POUR 713.2,3,8
716	ROTATING ELECTRIC PLANT					W 310	5.4	W 316	3.7	APP ELECTR ROTATIFS,PIECES
72	MACHS FOR SPCL INDUSTRYS						55.6		59.7	MAC SPECIALES POUR INDUST
722	TRACTORS NON-ROAD					W 649	4.0	W 1001	5.4	TRACTEURS
7224	WHEELED TRACTORS NES					W 473	3.7	W 808	5.1	TRACTEURS A ROUES
723	CIVIL ENGNEERG EQUIP ETC					W 4777	30.1	W 4120	31.8	APPAREILS DE GENIE CIVIL
7234	CONST,MINING MACHNRY NES					W 4074	23.3	W 2730	14.3	MACH POUR LA CONST, MINES
72341	SELF-PROPELLD DOZERS,ETC					W 2042	11.0	W 1461	8.8	BULLDOZERS
72342	SLFPRP SHOVELS,EXCAVATRS					W 1995	12.1	W 1092	4.9	PELLES MECANIQUES
7239	CONSTR ETC MACHY PTS NES					W 364	4.4	W 1179	17.2	PIECES 723.41-723.46
728	OTH MACHY FOR SPCL INDUS					W 1546	11.7	W 1575	11.5	AUT MACH IND PARTICULIERES
7281	MACH-TOOLS FR SPCL INDUS					W 900	4.9	W 833	4.6	MACH-OUTILS SPEC IND PART
72812	MACH-TOOLS TO WORK WOOD					W 788	4.0	W 628	3.1	MACH-OUT POUR TRAVAIL BOIS
7284	MACHY FOR SPCL INDUS NES					W 515	6.1	W 379	4.8	MACH SPEC IND PARTICUL.
74	GENRL INDUSTRL MACHY NES						56.9		67.4	MACH APP INDUSTRIE
741	HEATING,COOLING EQUIPMNT					W 650	5.9	W 1009	8.9	MACH CHAUFFAGE,PIECES
7416	HEATING,COOLING EQU NES					W 217	1.9	W 488	4.0	APP CHANGEMENT TEMP
742	PUMPS FOR LIQUIDS ETC					W 292	6.4	W 302	5.5	POMPES MOTO-POMPES
7428	OTHER PUMPS FOR LIQUIDS					W 190	4.1	W 186	3.5	AUTRES POMPES POUR LIQ
743	PUMPS NES,CENTRFUGES ETC					W 623	8.5	W 1130	14.6	POMPES COMPRES,VENT ETC
7431	PUMPS FOR GASES ETC					W 302	2.1	W 645	7.1	POMPES AIR A VIDE,COMPRES
7436	GAS,LIQUID FILTERS ETC					W 189	3.9	W 281	3.0	APP POUR FILT DES LIQUIDES
7439	PTS NES OF APP OF 7435,6					W 83	2.0	W 165	3.7	PIECES 743.5 ET 743.6
744	MECHANICAL HANDLING EQU					W 2337	16.9	W 2870	15.4	EQUIP MANUTENTION PIECES
7441	FORK LIFT TRCKS,ETC,PTS					W 755	3.8	W 622	3.7	CHARIOTS POUR USINES ETC
74411	FORK LIFT TRUCKS ETC					W 749	3.7	W 617	3.6	CHARIOTS POUR LES GARES
7442	LIFTING,LOADING MACH NES					W 674	4.2	W 605	4.9	APP LEVAGE,MANUTENTION
7449	PTS NES OF MACHY OF 7442					W 908	9.0	W 1643	6.9	PIECES DU 744.2
745	NONELEC MACHY,TOOLS NES					W 378	5.2	W 926	7.5	AUT MACH NON ELEC,PIECES
7452	OTH NONELEC MCHS,PTS NES					W 316	4.2	W 876	6.2	AUT MACH NON ELEC,PIECES

4. Special Imports C.I.F. by Commodities according to the S.I.T.C. (Rev. 2) in million U.S. Dollars
Importations Spéciales C.A.F. par Produits d'après la C.T.C.I. (Rév. 2) en millions de Dollars E.U.

SITC CTCI	COMMODITY	1993 QUANTITY QUANTITE	1993 VALUE VALEUR	1994 QUANTITY QUANTITE	1994 VALUE VALEUR	1995 QUANTITY QUANTITE	1995 VALUE VALEUR	1996 QUANTITY QUANTITE	1996 VALUE VALEUR	PRODUIT
749	NONELEC MACH PTS,ACC NES					W 685	14.2	W 738	15.7	PIECES MACH NON ELEC NDA
7492	COCKS,VALVES ETC NES					W 327	4.8	W 346	5.9	ART ROB,SIM POUR TUYAUX
7493	SHAFT,CRANK,PULLEY ETC					W 152	4.2	W 169	4.6	ARBRES TRANS,VILEBREQUINS
75	OFFICE MACHNES,ADP EQUIP						11.6		10.2	MACH BUREAU TRAIT AUTOM
752	AUTOMTIC DATA PROC EQUIP					W 128	7.4	W 142	6.3	MACH TRAIT INFORMATION
76	TELECOMM,SOUND EQUIPMENT						9.6		16.6	EQUIPMENT DE TELECOM
764	TELECOM EQPT,PTS,ACC NES					W 198	7.9	W 215	13.2	EQUIP TELECOM,PIECES
7643	TV,RADIO TRANSMITTRS ETC					W 13	1.6	W 21	4.5	APP EMET TELE RADIO
7649	PTS NES OF EQUIPMT OF 76					W 115	3.0	W 106	4.5	PIECES DE LA DIV 76
77	ELECTRIC MACHNRY NES ETC						57.2		38.8	MACH APP ELECT NDA
771	ELECTRIC POWER MACHY NES					W 574	6.9	W 463	4.9	MACH PROD,TRANS ELECTR
7711	TRANSFORMERS,ELECTRICAL					W 408	4.4	W 374	3.6	TRANSFO ELECTRIQUES
77111	LIQUID DIELEC TRANSFRMRS					W 343	3.7	W 281	2.9	TRANSFO DIELEC LIQUIDE
772	SWITCHGEAR ETC,PARTS NES					W 729	14.3	W 583	13.8	APP COUPURE,SECT ETC
7721	SWITCHGEAR ETC					W 715	13.9	W 578	13.5	APP COUPURE,SECTIONMNT
773	ELECTR DISTRIBUTNG EQUIP					W 3240	20.9	W 1189	5.6	EQUIPMT DISTRIBUTION ELECT
7731	INSULATED WIRE,CABLE ETC					W 3041	20.0	W 1056	4.6	FILS,CABLES ISOLES ELECT
778	ELECTRICAL MACHINERY NES					W 3179	12.4	W 2374	9.8	AUTRES MACH ELECT NDA
7781	BATTERIES,ACCUMULATORS					W 1142	3.6	W 752	2.9	PILES ET ACCUMULATEURS
7788	OTH ELEC MACHY,EQUIP NES					W 1585	5.8	W 1234	3.8	AUT MACH APP ELEC NDA
77887	ELECTRICAL CARBONS					W 1511	3.7	W 1184	2.8	PIECES CHARBON,GRAPHITE
78	ROAD VEHICLES						108.0		109.7	VEHICULES ROUTIERS
781	PASS MOTOR VEH EXC BUSES					W 7237	37.4	W 10492	45.3	AUTO TRANSPORT PERSONNES
782	LORRIES,SPCL MTR VEH NES					W 4298	24.1	W 5020	18.3	VEHICULES SPECIAUX,MARCH
7821	LORRIES,TRUCKS					W 3474	17.0	W 4646	17.1	VEHICULES TRANSP MARCHAND
7822	SPECIAL MOTOR VEHCLS NES					W 824	7.1	W 374	1.3	VEHICULES USAGES SPECIAUX
783	ROAD MOTOR VEHICLES NES					W 3762	28.0	W 4469	26.7	VEHICULES ROUTIERS NDA
7831	BUSES					W 1304	8.0	W 2091	9.6	VOITURES TRANSPORT COMMUN
7832	TRACTORS FOR TR–TRAILERS					W 2458	20.0	W 2378	17.1	TRACTEURS ROUTIERS
784	MOTOR VEH PRTS,ACCES NES					W 1302	10.5	W 1247	9.3	PIECES 722,781,782,783
7849	OTHER MOTOR VEHCL PARTS					W 1282	10.3	W 1205	9.1	PIECES 722,781,782,783
785	CYCLES,ETC MOTRZD OR NOT					W 476	1.8	W 990	4.4	MOTOCYCLES SCOOTERS
786	TRAILERS,NONMOTR VEH,NES					W 2340	6.5	W 2161	5.9	REMORQUES,CADRES,CONTAIN
7868	OTH NONMOTR VEHICLES ETC					W 1271	5.1	W 996	3.5	AUT VEHIC NON AUTO,PIECES
78689	PTS NES OF TRAILERS ETC					W 882	4.2	W 795	3.2	PIECES 786.11,12,786.81
79	OTHR TRANSPORT EQUIPMENT						12.6		14.7	AUTRE MATERIEL TRANSPORT
792	AIRCRAFT ETC					W 136	9.1	W 11	1.2	APP NAVIGATION AERIENNE
7923	AIRCRFT NES2000–15000KG					W 125	7.6			AERODYNES 2000 A 15000 KG
793	SHIPS AND BOATS ETC					W 254	1.8	W 2414	11.7	NAVIRES BATEAUX,ETC
7938	TUGS,SPECIAL VESSELS ETC					W 226	1.6	W 1378	9.3	REMORQUEURS,BATEAUX SPEC
79382	SPECL PURPOSE VESSLS ETC							W 1170	7.7	BAT–PHARES,–POMPES,DRAGUES
8	MISC MANUFACTURED GOODS						52.8		60.2	ART MANUFACTURES DIVERS
812	*PLUMBG,HEATNG,LGHTNG EQ					W 1312	3.6	W 1182	3.8	APPAR SANITAIRES CHAUFFAGE
87	PRECISION INSTRUMNTS NES						11.2		12.2	INSTRUM,APPAR SCIENT NDA
874	MEASURNG,CONTROLNG INSTR					W 279	6.4	W 355	8.0	INSTRUMENTS DE MESURE
89	MISC MANUFCTRD GOODS NES						28.6		32.1	ART MANUFACTURES DIVERS
892	PRINTED MATTER					W 1244	10.4	W 1565	13.8	IMPRIMES
8921	PRINTED BOOKS,GLOBES,ETC					W 590	3.7	W 936	8.7	LIVRES,BROCHURES,CARTES
89211	PRINTED BOOKS,PAMPHLETS					W 589	3.7	W 929	8.7	LIVRES,BROCHURES
8928	PRINTED MATTER NES					W 309	3.5	W 231	2.0	IMPRIMES NDA
893	ARTICLES OF PLASTIC NES						10.8	W 3670	11.1	OUVRAGES EN MAT DIVIS 58
8931	PLSTC PACKG CONTNRS,LIDS					W 1467	5.1	W 1750	5.5	ART TRANSP EMBALLAGE ETC
8939	MISC PLASTIC ARTICLES					W 1630	5.5	W 1855	5.5	ART DIVERS EN MAT DIV 58
89399	OTHR PLASTC ARTICLES NES					W 1481	5.1	W 1483	4.9	AUT OUV MAT DIV 58

5. Special Exports F.O.B. by Commodities according to the S.I.T.C. (Rev. 2) in million U.S. Dollars
Exportations Spéciales F.O.B. par Produits d'après la C.T.C.I. (Rév. 2) en millions de Dollars E.U.

SITC CTCI	COMMODITY	1993		1994		1995		1996		PRODUIT
		QUANTITY QUANTITE	VALUE VALEUR	QUANTITY QUANTITE	VALUE VALEUR	QUANTITY QUANTITE	VALUE VALEUR	QUANTITY QUANTITE	VALUE VALEUR	
	ALL COMMODITIES						1538.8		1757.9	TOUS PRODUITS
0	FOOD AND LIVE ANIMALS						400.1		393.5	ALIMENTS,ANIMAUX VIVANTS
05	VEGETABLES AND FRUIT						80.4		66.5	LEGUMES ET FRUITS
057	FRUIT,NUTS,FRESH,DRIED					W 188422	77.4	W 163265	63.6	FRUITS FRAIS OU SECS
0573	BANANA,PLANTAIN,FRSH,DRY					W 187211	77.0	W 160192	62.9	BANANES FRAICHES,SECHEES
07	COFFEE,TEA,COCOA,SPICES						303.9		310.3	CAFE,THE,CACAO,EPICES
071	COFFEE AND SUBSTITUTES					W 63167	142.5	W 74121	127.1	CAFE ET SUCCEDANES
0711	COFFEE GREEN,ROASTED,SUB					W 63167	142.5	W 74121	127.1	CAFE TORREFIE OU DECAFEINE
07111	COFFEE GREEN,HUSKS,SKINS					W 62713	141.3	W 74039	126.9	CAFE NON TORREFIE
072	COCOA					W 119992	160.7	W 141493	182.1	CACAO
0721	COCOA BEANS,RAW,ROASTED					W 105636	133.3	W 122217	151.3	CACAO EN FEVES
0723	COCOA BUTTER AND PASTE					W 14356	27.4	W 19277	30.9	BEURRE ET PATE DE CACAO
07231	COCOA PASTE					W 10653	14.7	W 15768	20.5	CACAO EN MASSE
07232	COCOA BUTTER					W 3703	12.8	W 3509	10.4	BEURRE DE CACAO
09	MISC EDIBLE PRODUCTS						8.0		8.4	PREP ALIMENTAIRES DIVERSES
098	EDIBLE PRODCTS,PREPS NES					W 2660	8.0	W 3078	8.4	PREP ALIMENTAIRES NDA
09805	SOUPS AND BROTHS					W 1858	5.9	W 1728	5.5	SOUPES,POTAGES,BOUILLONS
1	BEVERAGES AND TOBACCO						9.0		9.8	BOISSONS ET TABACS
11	BEVERAGES						6.2		6.8	BOISSONS
112	ALCOHOLIC BEVERAGES					W 6422	5.0	W 9074	5.3	BOISSONS ALCOOLIQUES
2	CRUDE MATERLS,EXCL FUELS						424.6		445.1	MAT BRUTES NON COMESTIBLES
23	RUBBER, CRUDE						53.3		78.1	CAOUTCHOUC BRUT
232	NATURAL RUBBER,GUMS					W 33448	53.3	W 62405	78.1	LATEX CAOUTCHOUC NATUREL
23202	OTHER NATURAL RUBBER					W 27018	43.1	W 39387	51.3	CAOUTCHOUC NATUREL
23203	BALATA,GUTTA–PERCHA, ETC					W 3159	6.9	W 18701	22.8	BALATA,GUTTA–PERCHA
24	CORK AND WOOD						285.7		249.0	LIEGE ET BOIS
247	OTH WOOD ROUGH,SQUARED					W 821953	174.6	W 925063	162.9	BOIS BRUTS EQUARRIS
2472	SAW–,VENEER–LOGS NON–CON					W 821953	174.6	W 924284	162.6	NON CONIFERES SCIAGE,PLAC
24721	— IN THE ROUGH					W 821953	174.6	W 924284	162.6	BRUTS ECORCES DEGROSSIS
248	WOOD SHAPED,SLEEPERS					W 176283	111.2	W 203561	86.1	BOIS SIMPLEMENT TRAVAILLES
2483	LUMBER SHAPED NON–CONIFR					W 172600	110.2	W 197705	84.6	NON CONIFERES SCIES,RABOTES
24831	LUMBER SAWN ETC NON–CON					W 172288	109.9	W 195667	82.8	SCIES LONGITUDINALEMENT
26	TEXTILE FIBRES AND WASTE						78.3		109.8	FIBRES TEXTILES
263	COTTON					W 54300	78.3	W 65834	109.8	COTON
2631	RAW COTTON,EXCL LINTERS					W 54130	78.2	W 65834	109.8	COTON EN MASSE
29	CRUDE ANIMAL,VEG MAT NES						4.5		5.5	MATIERES BRUTES ANIM,VEGET
292	CRUDE VEG MATERIALS NES					W 1228	4.4	W 2003	5.5	MAT BRUTES VEGETALES NDA
3	MINERAL FUELS ETC						448.8		635.6	COMBUSTIBLES MINERAUX LUB
33	PETROLEUM AND PRODUCTS						448.6		635.3	PETROLE ET DERIVES
333	CRUDE PETROLEUM					W 3727760	445.3	W 4982805	628.0	HUILES BRUTES DE PETROLE
334	PETROLEUM PRODUCTS,REFIN					W 6858	3.3	W 14656	7.1	PRODUITS RAFFINES
4	ANIMAL,VEGETABLE OIL,FAT						7.0		22.6	HUILES,GRAISSES ANIM,VEG
42	FIXED VEGETABLE OIL,FAT						7.0		22.6	HUILES VEGETALES FIXES
424	FIXED VEG OIL NONSOFT					W 9118	7.0	W 35897	22.5	AUTRES HUILES VEG FIXES
4242	PALM OIL					W 8103	6.3	W 35897	22.5	HUILE DE PALME
5	CHEMCLS,RELATED PROD NES						14.9		19.6	PRODUITS CHIMIQUES
55	PERFUME,CLEANING ETC PRD						7.3		13.1	PROD POUR PARFUM,TOILETTE
554	SOAP,CLEANSING ETC PREPS					W 4325	4.1	W 8522	9.3	SAVONS,PRODUITS DETERSIFS
5541	SOAPS					W 4187	3.8	W 7988	8.2	SAVONS,PROD TENSIO–ACTIFS
6	BASIC MANUFACTURES						209.6		203.5	ART MANUFACTURES
63	WOOD,CORK MANUFACTRS NES						28.6		24.9	OUVRAGES LIEGE ET BOIS
634	VENEERS,PLYWOOD,ETC					W 27617	28.0	W 27485	24.2	PLACAGES,CONTRE–PLAQUES
6341	VENEER SHEETS ETC					W 20718	22.3	W 19552	19.1	BOIS SIMPLEMENT SCIES
6342	PLYWOOD OF WOOD SHEETS					W 6036	5.6	W 5962	4.7	BOIS CONTRE–PLAQUES
65	TEXTILE YARN,FABRICS,ETC						10.2		9.2	FILS,TISSUS,ARTICLES TEXTILE
652	COTTON FABRICS,WOVEN					W 1714	9.7	W 1823	8.6	TISSUS DE COTON
6521	GREY WOVEN COTTON FABRIC					W 1590	8.3	W 1681	7.2	TISSUS COT ECRUS NON MERCER
65214	GREY WOVEN COTTON NES					W 1489	7.7	W 1634	7.0	AUT TISSUS 85% COTON ECRUS
66	NONMETAL MINERAL MFS NES						22.5		39.3	ART MIN NON METALLIQUES
661	LIME,CEMENT,BLDG PRODS					W 141936	14.9	W 255469	28.4	CHAUX,CIMENTS MAT CONSTR
6612	CEMENT					W 141936	14.9	W 255462	28.4	CIMENTS HYDRAULIQUES
665	GLASSWARE					W 15513	7.6	W 23264	10.9	OUVRAGES EN VERRE
6651	BOTTLES ETC OF GLASS					W 15388	7.6	W 23259	10.9	RECIPIENTS EN VERRE
66511	GLASS BOTTLES ETC NONVAC					W 15388	7.6	W 23259	10.9	BONBONNES,BOUTEILLES,ETC
68	NON–FERROUS METALS						127.6		110.8	METAUX NON FERREUX
684	ALUMINIUM					W 63776	127.6	W 68604	110.8	ALUMINIUM
6841	ALUMINIUM,ALLOYS,UNWRGHT					W 59032	116.3	W 64500	101.1	ALUMINIUM,ALLIAGES BRUTS
6842	ALUMINIUM,ALLOYS WORKED					W 4744	11.3	W 4104	9.8	ALUMINIUM,ALLIAGES OUVRE
68422	ALUMNM PLATE,SHEET,STRIP					W 4743	11.3	W 4104	9.8	TOLES, PLANCHES EN ALU
69	METAL MANUFACTURES NES						10.2		9.0	ART MANUFACT EN METAL NDA
699	BASE METAL MFRS NES					W 2771	8.0	W 6776	5.4	ART MANUFACTURES MET NDA
6998	MFRS NES OF CPR,NIKL,ETC					W 2764	8.0	W 1821	4.9	OUVRAGES EN CU,NI,AL,PB,ZN
69983	ALUMINIUM MANUFACTS NES					W 2764	8.0	W 1821	4.9	OUVRAGES EN ALUMINIUM
7	MACHINES,TRANSPORT EQUIP						17.3		19.2	MACHINES MATERIEL TRANSPORT
72	MACHS FOR SPCL INDUSTRYS						2.9		6.3	MAC SPECIALES POUR INDUST
723	CIVIL ENGNEERG EQUIP ETC					W 557	2.1	W 1971	5.3	APPAREILS DE GENIE CIVIL
77	ELECTRIC MACHNRY NES ETC						7.8		7.2	MACH APP ELECT NDA
778	ELECTRICAL MACHINERY NES					W 2674	7.3	W 2634	6.9	AUTRES MACH ELECT NDA
7781	BATTERIES,ACCUMULATORS					W 2671	7.3	W 2630	6.9	PILES ET ACCUMULATEURS
77811	PRIMARY BATTERIES,CELLS					W 2670	7.3	W 2630	6.9	PILES ELECTRIQUES,PIECES
8	MISC MANUFACTURED GOODS						7.8		9.5	ART MANUFACTURES DIVERS
89	MISC MANUFCTRD GOODS NES						6.3		7.2	ART MANUFACTURES DIVERS

1. HISTORICAL SERIES, 1962–1997 GENERAL TRADE, IMPORTS F.O.B., EXPORTS F.O.B.
SERIES HISTORIQUES, 1962–1997 COMMERCE GENERAL, IMPORTATIONS F.O.B., EXPORTATIONS F.O.B

YEAR ANNEE	VALUE IN MILLION CANADIAN DOLLARS VALEUR EN MILLION CANADIAN DOLLARS MERCHANDISE –MARCHANDISE		GOLD # 1 –OR		CONVERSION FACTORS U.S. CENTS PER CANADIAN DOLLAR FACTEURS DE CONVERSION CENTS E.U. PAR CANADIAN DOLLAR		INDEX NUMBERS –INDICES QUANTUM		UNIT VALUE VALEUR UNITAIRE	
	IMPORTS	EXPORTS	IMPORTS	EXPORTS	IMPORTS	EXPORTS	IMPORTS	EXPORTS	IMPORTS	EXPORTS
1962	6294.00	6357.00		155.00	93.4100	93.3500				
1963	6578.00	6990.00		154.00	92.5000	92.5000				
1964	7488.00	8303.00		145.00	92.5000	92.5000				
1965	8633.00	8767.00		138.00	92.5000	92.5000				
1966	10072.00	10325.00		127.00	92.5000	92.5000				
1967	10872.00	11420.00		112.00	92.5000	92.5000				
1968	12358.00	13624.00		120.00	92.5000	92.5000				
1969	14130.00	14890.00		109.00	92.5000	92.5000				
1970	13952.00	16820.00			95.7600	95.8300				
1971	15617.00	17820.00			99.0400	99.0300				
1972	18669.00	20150.00			100.9960	101.0040				
1973	23324.00	25420.00			99.9960	100.0000				
1974	31692.00	32441.00			102.2730	102.2830				
1975	34691.00	32246.00			98.3110	98.3050				
1976	37444.00	38397.00			101.4600	101.4590				
1977	42332.00	44554.00			94.0370	93.9890				
1978	50102.00	53183.00			87.5590	87.5600				
1979	62871.00	65641.00			85.3900	85.3920				
1980	69274.00	76159.00			85.4970	85.5100	61	58	83	88
1981	79481.70	83811.50			83.4196	83.5425	63	60	92	93
1982	67855.70	84530.30			81.1053	81.0310	53	60	94	94
1983	75608.40	90612.50			81.1319	81.1297	61	66	90	93
1984	95460.00	112383.60			77.2100	77.1726	73	80	95	94
1985	104355.20	119474.50			73.2242	73.2194	72	80	101	98
1986	118785.00	125497.00			71.9738	71.9738	80	84	101	95
1987	122718.00	130089.00			75.4542	75.4642	89	93	97	94
1988	138802.00	144038.00			81.2077	81.3062	95	94	98	98
1989	141866.00	144248.00			84.4429	84.4625	100	96	98	101
1990	143837.00	148912.00			85.6854	85.7107	100	100	100	100
1991	142913.00	145658.00			87.3136	87.3025	102	101	99	97
1992	156246.00	162596.00			82.7334	82.6838	110	110	103	99
1993	179425.00	187346.00			77.4913	77.4943	120	123	108	103
1994	211792.00	225908.00			73.2207	73.2069	133	138	115	111
1995	230602.00	263697.00			72.8757	72.8882	143	152	120	119
1996	238489.00	274884.10			73.3625	73.3531	151	162	119	120
1997	278208.00	296928.00			72.2049	72.2153	179	175	120	120

2. IMPORTS BY BROAD ECONOMIC CATEGORY AND EXPORTS BY INDUSTRIAL ORIGIN. (PERCENTAGE OF TOTAL VALUE)
IMPORTATIONS PAR CATEGORIES ECONOMIQUES ET EXPORTATIONS PAR BRANCHE D'ACTIVITE.(EN POURCENTAGE DE LA VALEUR TOTALE)

IMPORTS – IMPORTATIONS

	1991	1992	1993	1994	1995	1996	1997
TOTAL IMPORTS–IMPORTATIONS TOTALES	100.	100.	100.	100.	100.	100.	100.
1 FOOD BEV–ALIMENTATION BOISSONS	5.9	5.8	5.7	5.5	5.2	5.3	5.0
11 PRIMARY–PRODUITS DE BASE	3.1	2.9	2.9	2.7	2.6	2.6	2.4
111 FOR INDUSTRY–POUR L'INDUSTRIE	0.5	0.4	0.4	0.5	0.5	0.5	0.5
112 FOR HOUSEHOLDS–POUR LES MENAGES	2.7	2.5	2.5	2.2	2.1	2.1	1.9
12 PROCESSED–PRODUITS ELABORES	2.8	2.9	2.8	2.8	2.6	2.7	2.6
121 FOR INDUSTRY–POUR L'INDUSTRIE	0.4	0.4	0.4	0.4	0.4	0.5	0.4
122 FOR HOUSEHOLDS–POUR LES MENAGES	2.4	2.5	2.4	2.4	2.2	2.2	2.2
2 IND SUPPLIES–APPROV INDUSTRIELS	20.8	21.1	21.6	22.2	23.0	22.4	22.2
21 PRIMARY–PRODUITS DE BASE	2.0	2.1	2.0	2.1	2.5	2.2	2.1
22 PROCESSED–PRODUITS ELABORES	18.8	18.9	19.6	20.1	20.5	20.2	20.1
3 FUELS–COMBUSTIBLES	4.8	4.3	3.9	3.4	3.5	4.2	4.4
31 PRIMARY–PRODUITS DE BASE	3.8	3.3	3.0	2.7	2.8	3.5	3.6
32 PROCESSED–PRODUITS ELABORES	1.0	1.0	0.9	0.7	0.7	0.8	0.8
321 MOTOR SPIRIT–ESSENCE	0.2	0.1	0.2	0.2	0.2	0.2	0.2
322 OTHER–AUTRES	0.8	0.8	0.7	0.5	0.5	0.5	0.6
4 MACHINERY–EQUIPEMENT	24.8	24.8	25.3	26.6	27.5	27.2	27.3
41 CAPITAL EQUIPMENT–MACHINES	18.7	18.3	18.6	19.1	19.5	19.5	20.1
42 PARTS–PIECES ACCESSOIRES	6.1	6.5	6.7	7.4	8.1	7.7	7.2
5 TRANSPORT–TRANSPORT	27.0	26.5	26.3	26.1	25.1	25.0	25.8
51 PASSENGER CARS–AUTOMOBILES	8.8	8.1	7.2	6.9	6.0	6.1	6.6
52 OTHER–AUTRES	4.1	3.9	3.3	3.6	3.8	3.8	4.4
521 INDUSTRIAL–INDUSTRIELS	4.0	3.8	3.2	3.4	3.7	3.6	4.3
522 NON INDUSTRIAL–NON INDUSTRIEL	0.1	0.1	0.1	0.1	0.1	0.1	0.1
53 PARTS–PIECES ACCESSOIRES	14.1	14.6	15.9	15.7	15.3	15.2	14.7
6 CONSUM GOODS–BIENS CONSOMMATION	13.4	14.2	14.1	13.4	12.9	12.3	12.5
61 DURABLE–DURABLES	3.8	4.0	4.0	3.8	3.6	3.3	3.4
62 SEMI DURABLE–SEMI DURABLES	6.4	6.7	6.6	6.3	6.0	5.7	5.8
63 NON DURABLE–NON DURABLES	3.2	3.4	3.4	3.3	3.3	3.3	3.3
7 GOODS NES–BIENS NDA	3.3	3.3	2.9	2.8	2.8	3.5	2.8

EXPORTS – EXPORTATIONS

	1991	1992	1993	1994	1995	1996	1997
TOTAL EXPORTS–EXPORTATIONS TOTALES	100.	100.	100.	100.	100.	100.	100.
1 AGRICULTURE	6.5	6.7	5.2	5.3	5.0	4.9	4.8
2 MINING QUARRY–INDUS EXTRACTIVES	11.2	10.7	10.2	9.4	9.0	9.7	9.9
3 MANUFACTURING–IND MANUFACTUR	82.3	82.6	84.6	85.3	85.9	85.4	85.3
31 FOOD BEV TOBACCO–ALIM BOISS TAB	3.1	3.4	3.6	3.1	3.0	3.3	3.5
32 TEXTILES–INDUSTRIES TEXTILES	1.0	1.1	1.2	1.3	1.4	1.6	1.7
33 WOOD & PRODUCTS–BOIS & PRODUITS	4.6	5.2	6.4	6.4	5.5	6.0	6.0
34 PAPER & PRODUCTS–PAPIER & PRODT	10.2	9.4	8.5	8.5	10.7	8.5	7.8
35 CHEMICALS–INDUSTRIES CHIMIQUES	9.0	8.8	8.6	8.6	8.8	9.2	9.4
36 NON METAL MIN–MIN NON METAL	0.7	0.7	0.7	0.8	0.8	0.8	0.8
37 BASIC METAL–IND METAL BASE	6.7	6.6	6.1	5.9	6.4	6.0	5.8
38 METAL MANUF–MANUF METAL	41.6	42.1	44.2	45.2	44.1	44.4	44.7
39 OTH MANUF IND–AUTRES MANUF	5.4	5.2	5.3	5.6	5.3	5.4	5.6

3. TRADE BY PRINCIPAL COUNTRIES OF ORIGIN AND DESTINATION (VALUE IN MILLION U.S. DOLLARS)
ECHANGES SELON LES PRINCIPAUX PAYS D'ORIGINE ET DE DESTINATION (VALEUR EN MILLIONS DE DOLLARS EU)

COUNTRIES–PAYS	GENERAL IMPORTS F.O.B. IMPORTATIONS GENERALES F.O.B.				
	1993	1994	1995	1996	1997
World	131331.1	148185.5	164326.9	171007.2	196029.1
Africa	1147.9	1145.7	1297.1	1518.8	1512.9
Americas	92958.4	106045.3	116696.0	123240.3	141087.7
– Northern America	88049.6	100237.7	109831.2	115542.4	132445.9
– LAIA	4229.6	5001.8	5926.0	6623.2	7555.8
– CACM	175.8	228.9	262.7	248.3	307.0
– Caribbean	369.8	405.6	526.2	634.2	571.8
– Rest of America	133.7	171.3	149.8	192.2	207.2
Asia excl fmr USSR	19265.3	20398.6	22685.4	21687.8	25625.0
– Middle East	716.6	593.3	595.6	813.4	1137.4
Asia former USSR	3.8	40.0	14.4	17.8	15.1
Europe excl fmr USSR	14096.4	16547.4	19204.7	19892.9	22912.7
– European Union	12544.2	14395.0	16449.7	16675.0	19336.0
– Eastern Europe	167.0	259.5	279.8	299.3	383.6
– Rest of Europe	1385.2	1892.9	2475.2	2918.6	3193.0
Europe former USSR	355.0	292.0	419.8	369.0	498.5
Oceania	1043.5	1085.0	1186.4	1204.2	1138.0
Other	2460.8	2631.6	2823.0	3076.4	3239.2
USA/Etats–Unis d'Amer	88041.7	100226.3	109826.1	115537.9	132437.5
Japan/Japon	8284.6	8320.7	8820.0	7661.8	9031.4
United Kingdom	3432.4	3660.7	3986.1	4334.9	4639.1
Mexico/Mexique	2785.2	3274.3	3892.0	4426.5	5032.6
Germany/Allemagne	2715.9	3216.5	3498.8	3536.7	3888.9
China/Chine	2393.0	2826.6	3380.4	3613.7	4548.4
Special Categories	2460.8	2631.6	2823.0	3076.4	3239.2
France, Monaco	1751.6	1891.8	2277.2	2494.4	3709.0
Other Asia n.e.s.	2029.4	2039.0	2034.4	2100.7	2502.8
Italy/Italie	1498.8	1896.0	2383.3	1994.8	2206.6
Korea, Republic of	1701.7	1836.7	2335.0	2001.1	2037.4
Norway,Svalbard and JM	795.5	1218.2	1686.5	2037.8	2362.5
Malaysia/Malaisie	674.6	890.2	1128.8	1159.2	1433.6
China, Hong Kong SAR	925.2	873.5	950.8	838.6	906.7
Australia/Australie	825.5	822.2	934.9	947.2	850.4
Sweden/Suède	664.7	828.0	951.4	881.1	946.4
Singapore/Singapour	617.3	845.1	946.7	873.7	845.4
Brazil/Brésil	610.6	704.0	756.4	831.6	947.7
Thailand/Thaïlande	590.9	657.2	738.8	765.4	845.4
Netherlands/Pays–Bas	516.1	629.1	697.0	683.3	761.8
Switzerland,Liechtenst.	516.1	559.9	657.4	687.9	670.6
Belgium–Luxembourg	410.8	469.2	558.0	626.4	648.5
Spain/Espagne	388.1	467.3	513.9	498.7	565.3
Venezuela	272.0	371.7	472.0	532.5	700.3
Indonesia/Indonésie	341.0	383.0	435.1	459.1	583.9
Saudi Arabia	413.0	396.8	365.7	477.4	467.7
Ireland/Irlande	334.2	342.3	411.9	433.4	551.9
Nigeria/Nigéria	533.8	463.4	426.3	228.2	375.9
India/Inde	274.7	336.7	394.5	443.1	534.5
Philippines	298.8	344.1	362.5	405.4	522.3
Austria/Autriche	270.2	334.3	390.9	445.5	435.8
Russian Federation	334.6	265.6	363.0	329.5	451.8
Algeria/Algérie	174.6	186.4	253.1	541.5	440.9
Finland/Finlande	197.4	234.9	331.6	306.4	467.1
So. African Customs Un	125.0	259.0	340.0	364.9	379.7
Denmark/Danemark	180.7	232.5	244.1	259.8	301.9
New Zealand	196.6	235.4	217.2	236.4	264.2
Cuba	132.9	142.6	233.9	294.3	255.0
Colombia/Colombie	133.0	188.8	271.1	217.9	213.4
Chile/Chili	161.4	172.9	203.2	251.1	234.6

COUNTRIES–PAYS	GENERAL EXPORTS F.O.B. EXPORTATIONS GENERALES F.O.B.				
	1993	1994	1995	1996	1997
Monde	144631.7	166254.6	192160.6	201573.7	214333.3
Afrique	808.8	890.3	1229.5	1151.5	1438.6
Amériques	119550.6	139209.1	156852.7	168470.7	181450.7
– Amérique du Nord	116756.0	135924.2	152884.5	164628.5	176825.3
– ALAI	2294.6	2808.8	3281.4	3189.4	3881.2
– MCAC	99.4	83.9	101.9	99.5	128.2
– Caraïbes	360.9	358.5	535.0	505.5	568.7
– Autre Amérique	39.7	33.7	49.8	47.8	47.4
Asie anc. URSS exclus	13135.4	14895.4	19562.1	17631.1	18136.1
– Moyen–Orient	919.5	1041.4	1222.8	1243.0	1344.6
Asie ancienne URSS	69.4	15.5	11.1	36.1	36.5
Europe anc. URSS exclus	9939.6	10286.6	13281.8	13075.9	12075.3
– Union Européenne	8588.5	8990.7	12025.9	11400.6	10842.4
– Europe de l'Est	169.3	141.6	241.7	308.1	311.9
– Autre de l'Europe	1181.8	1154.3	1014.2	1367.2	921.0
Europe ancienne URSS	393.4	153.0	199.3	288.3	292.8
Océanie	734.4	804.7	1024.0	915.6	899.1
Autre			0.1	4.4	4.3
USA/Etats–Unis d'Amer	116696.4	135879.6	152827.8	164575.4	176758.7
Japan/Japon	6555.1	7082.0	8738.9	7711.3	7861.7
United Kingdom	2266.4	2399.0	2820.1	2932.0	2756.7
Germany/Allemagne	1925.0	1669.9	2400.8	2428.8	1969.6
China/Chine	1300.4	1681.8	2465.7	2090.9	1604.1
Korea, Republic of	1329.1	1608.2	1988.6	1993.3	2115.1
France, Monaco	995.2	998.9	1422.0	1282.6	1087.4
Netherlands/Pays–Bas	1048.9	893.5	1207.5	1197.3	1222.8
Belgium–Luxembourg	712.5	985.5	1351.1	1120.7	1112.8
Other Asia n.e.s.	780.1	891.9	1252.6	1034.9	1168.2
Italy/Italie	737.8	960.8	1333.4	993.8	1071.3
China, Hong Kong SAR	588.9	853.2	1279.0	879.4	1226.4
Brazil/Brésil	594.0	713.2	943.5	1009.0	1163.3
Mexico/Mexique	633.2	769.2	829.2	888.4	919.0
Australia/Australie	625.0	695.2	880.9	741.2	700.0
Switzerland,Liechtenst.	700.2	657.1	401.1	684.3	302.1
Norway,Svalbard and JM	443.9	467.5	562.8	618.1	553.7
Venezuela	448.9	445.8	582.2	400.6	648.5
Indonesia/Indonésie	347.7	348.6	472.1	638.8	568.8
Saudi Arabia	382.4	416.6	379.6	354.4	354.9
Spain/Espagne	259.3	270.4	453.3	375.6	416.3
Thailand/Thaïlande	286.5	299.7	418.7	411.9	334.7
Singapore/Singapour	259.3	276.7	361.8	414.9	388.8
Iran (Islamic Rep of)	210.5	329.0	307.9	378.6	454.7
Malaysia/Malaisie	172.3	212.0	416.3	386.0	490.8
Algeria/Algérie	179.5	335.9	386.4	299.8	421.2
Colombia/Colombie	187.0	331.9	273.6	307.5	304.3
India/Inde	208.9	193.1	316.2	254.9	331.8
Chile/Chili	164.0	229.1	281.4	242.7	273.6
Russian Federation	351.0	138.5	151.4	234.1	253.7
Sweden/Suède	145.1	174.9	249.7	201.3	283.8
Austria/Autriche	109.8	198.0	214.8	306.2	194.4
So. African Customs Un	127.7	177.1	247.2	181.9	286.4
Philippines	151.0	135.8	233.6	192.8	291.7
Argentina/Argentine	107.5	146.2	171.9	148.6	285.0
Cuba	108.1	84.3	199.9	197.3	259.7
Turkey/Turquie	121.8	102.0	208.8	193.2	216.6
Ireland/Irlande	71.9	130.3	145.6	169.4	247.2
Israel/Israël	120.3	120.1	171.5	171.2	174.9
Finland/Finlande	73.2	101.5	168.1	146.8	174.2

(VALUE AS PERCENTAGE OF WORLD TOTAL)(VALEURS EN POURCENTAGE DU TOTAL MONDIAL)

	1988	1989	1990	1991	1992	1993	1994	1995	1996	1997
Africa	0.7	0.9	0.8	0.8	0.7	0.9	0.8	0.8	0.9	0.8
Americas	69.4	69.0	67.9	67.6	68.8	70.8	71.6	71.0	72.1	72.0
– Northern America	66.1	65.4	64.6	63.7	65.2	67.0	67.6	66.8	67.6	67.6
– LAIA	2.8	3.1	2.9	3.3	3.0	3.2	3.4	3.6	3.9	3.9
– CACM	0.2	0.2	0.1	0.2	0.2	0.1	0.2	0.2	0.1	0.2
– Caribbean	0.3	0.3	0.3	0.4	0.4	0.3	0.3	0.3	0.4	0.3
– Rest of America	0.0	0.0	0.0	0.0	0.0	0.1	0.1	0.1	0.1	0.1
Asia excl fmr USSR	14.0	14.5	14.4	15.4	15.4	14.7	13.8	13.8	12.7	13.1
– Middle East	0.2	0.5	0.7	0.6	0.5	0.5	0.4	0.4	0.5	0.6
Asia former USSR						0.0	0.0	0.0	0.0	0.0
Europe excl fmr USSR	14.8	13.7	14.7	13.7	12.3	10.7	11.2	11.7	11.6	11.7
– European Union	13.5	12.3	12.7	11.8	10.7	9.6	9.7	10.0	9.8	9.9
– Eastern Europe	0.3	0.2	0.2	0.1	0.1	0.1	0.2	0.2	0.2	0.2
– Rest of Europe	1.1	1.1	1.8	1.7	1.5	1.1	1.3	1.5	1.7	1.6
Europe former USSR	0.1	0.1	0.2	0.2	0.2	0.3	0.2	0.3	0.2	0.3
Oceania	0.7	0.6	0.7	0.6	0.7	0.8	0.7	0.7	0.7	0.6
Other	0.3	1.3	1.3	1.8	1.9	1.9	1.8	1.7	1.8	1.7
USA/Etats–Unis d'Amer	66.1	65.4	64.6	63.7	65.2	67.0	67.6	66.8	67.6	67.6
Japan/Japon	7.1	7.1	7.0	7.6	7.3	6.3	5.6	5.4	4.5	4.6
United Kingdom	3.5	3.4	3.6	3.1	2.8	2.6	2.5	2.4	2.5	2.4
Mexico/Mexique	1.0	1.3	1.3	1.9	1.9	2.1	2.2	2.4	2.6	2.6
Germany/Allemagne				2.8	2.4	2.1	2.2	2.1	2.1	2.0
China/Chine	0.7	0.9	1.0	1.4	1.7	1.8	1.9	2.1	2.1	2.3
Special Categories	0.3	1.3	1.3	1.8	1.9	1.9	1.8	1.7	1.8	1.7
France, Monaco	2.2	1.5	1.8	2.0	1.8	1.3	1.3	1.4	1.5	1.9
Other Asia n.e.s.	1.7	1.7	1.6	1.6	1.7	1.5	1.4	1.2	1.2	1.3
Italy/Italie	1.5	1.5	1.4	1.3	1.2	1.1	1.3	1.5	1.2	1.1

	1988	1989	1990	1991	1992	1993	1994	1995	1996	1997
Afrique	0.9	0.8	0.8	0.7	0.6	0.6	0.5	0.6	0.6	0.7
Amériques	75.4	75.5	76.9	77.2	79.4	82.7	83.7	81.6	83.6	84.7
– Amérique du Nord	73.4	73.6	75.1	75.4	77.4	80.7	81.8	79.6	81.7	82.5
– ALAI	1.4	1.3	1.3	1.4	1.6	1.6	1.7	1.7	1.6	1.8
– MCAC	0.1	0.1	0.1	0.0	0.1	0.1	0.1	0.1	0.0	0.1
– Caraïbes	0.5	0.4	0.4	0.3	0.3	0.2	0.2	0.3	0.3	0.3
– Autre Amérique	0.0	0.0	0.0	0.0	0.0	0.0	0.0	0.0	0.0	0.0
Asie anc. URSS exclus	12.6	12.2	11.1	11.2	10.1	9.1	9.0	10.2	8.7	8.5
– Moyen–Orient	0.6	0.9	0.8	0.8	0.6	0.6	0.6	0.6	0.6	0.6
Asie ancienne URSS						0.0	0.0	0.0	0.0	0.0
Europe anc. URSS exclus	9.5	10.1	9.8	9.4	8.6	6.9	6.2	6.9	6.5	5.6
– Union Européenne	8.4	9.0	8.5	8.4	7.4	5.9	5.4	6.3	5.7	5.1
– Europe de l'Est	0.1	0.1	0.1	0.1	0.1	0.1	0.1	0.1	0.2	0.1
– Autre de l'Europe	0.9	1.1	1.1	0.9	1.1	0.8	0.7	0.5	0.7	0.4
Europe ancienne URSS	0.8	0.5	0.8	1.0	0.8	0.3	0.1	0.1	0.1	0.1
Océanie	0.8	1.0	0.7	0.5	0.5	0.5	0.5	0.5	0.5	0.4
Autre								0.0	0.0	0.0
USA/Etats–Unis d'Amer	73.3	73.6	75.0	75.3	77.4	80.7	81.7	79.5	81.6	82.5
Japan/Japon	6.3	6.4	5.5	4.9	4.6	4.5	4.3	4.5	3.8	3.7
United Kingdom	2.6	2.6	2.4	2.1	1.9	1.6	1.4	1.5	1.5	1.3
Germany/Allemagne				1.7	1.4	1.3	1.0	1.2	1.2	0.9
China/Chine	1.9	0.8	1.1	1.3	1.4	0.9	1.0	1.3	1.0	0.7
Korea, Republic of	0.9	1.2	1.1	1.3	0.9	0.9	1.0	1.0	1.0	1.0
France, Monaco	0.9	1.0	0.9	1.0	0.9	0.7	0.6	0.7	0.6	0.5
Netherlands/Pays–Bas	1.0	1.2	1.0	1.2	0.9	0.7	0.5	0.6	0.6	0.6
Belgium–Luxembourg	0.9	0.9	0.8	0.8	0.7	0.5	0.6	0.7	0.6	0.5
Other Asia n.e.s.	0.7	0.7	0.5	0.7	0.6	0.5	0.5	0.7	0.5	0.5

4. General Imports F.O.B. by Commodities according to the S.I.T.C. (Rev. 2) in million U.S. Dollars
Importations Générales F.O.B. par Produits d'après la C.T.C.I. (Rév. 2) en millions de Dollars E.U.

SITC CTCI	COMMODITY	1994 QUANTITY QUANTITE	1994 VALUE VALEUR	1995 QUANTITY QUANTITE	1995 VALUE VALEUR	1996 QUANTITY QUANTITE	1996 VALUE VALEUR	1997 QUANTITY QUANTITE	1997 VALUE VALEUR	PRODUIT
	ALL COMMODITIES		148185.5		164326.9		171007.2		196029.2	TOUS PRODUITS
0	FOOD AND LIVE ANIMALS		7905.9		8228.5		8621.7		9279.5	ALIMENTS,ANIMAUX VIVANTS
01	MEAT AND PREPARATIONS		878.6		838.4		797.5		904.7	VIANDES ET PREPARATIONS
011	MEAT FRESH,CHILLD,FROZEN	W 301779	726.6	W 274016	681.8	W 272032	625.6	W 307832	702.6	VIANDES FRAICHES,REF,CONGE
0111	BOVINE MEAT FRESH,FROZEN	W 201362	529.2	W 178154	489.2	W 163863	416.9	W 173456	432.7	VIANDES BOVIN FRAI,REF
01112	BOVINE MEAT BONELESS	W 192508	493.4	W 171838	464.6	W 157816	394.9	W 167028	407.9	VIANDES BOVIN DESOSSEES
03	FISH AND PREPARATIONS		882.4		994.9		1105.9		1062.9	POISSONS ET PREPARATIONS
04	CEREALS AND PREPARATIONS		777.9		852.9		940.3		1018.8	CEREALES ET PRODUITS
048	CEREAL ETC PREPARATIONS	W 351150	562.3	W 367621	592.1	W 361067	614.2	W 407269	683.5	PREPTNS A BASE CEREALES
05	VEGETABLES AND FRUIT		2601.2		2762.2		2867.8		3068.3	LEGUMES ET FRUITS
054	VEG ETC FRSH,SMPLY PRSVD	W 1551312	839.1	W 1557492	919.1	W 1605597	877.5	W 1689460	970.0	LEGUMES FRAIS,CONG,SECS
0545	OTHER FRESH VEGETABLES	W 932533	501.5	W 960413	573.2	W 982310	521.0	W 1013424	588.1	AUTRES LEGUMES FRAIS,REF
05459	FRESH VEGETABLES NES	W 805796	450.1	W 827200	516.8	W 855108	470.8	W 876513	532.4	LEGUMES FRAIS,REFRI NDA
057	FRUIT,NUTS,FRESH,DRIED	W 1588124	1159.5	W 1588274	1204.0	W 1630647	1257.9	W 1730893	1295.2	FRUITS FRAIS OU SECS
058	FRUIT PRESERVED,PREPARED		439.1		470.0	W 1632225	554.6	W 1643147	592.2	CONSERVES DE FRUITS
06	SUGAR AND PREPS,HONEY		482.8		489.5		546.9		534.2	SUCRES ET PRODUITS
07	COFFEE,TEA,COCOA,SPICES		889.6		1000.6		962.2		1134.6	CAFE,THE,CACAO,EPICES
071	COFFEE AND SUBSTITUTES	W 155694	460.5	W 138018	543.4	W 154048	463.4	W 157847	570.7	CAFE ET SUCCEDANES
081	*FEEDING STUFF FOR ANIML	W 1243683	514.4	W 1492821	535.0	W 1558476	582.9	W 1493105	635.3	NOURRITURE POUR ANIMAUX
09	MISC EDIBLE PRODUCTS		567.4		466.9		510.0		604.1	PREP ALIMENTAIRES DIVERSES
098	EDIBLE PRODCTS,PREPS NES	W 240191	552.2	W 259844	451.6	W 268838	492.6	W 299958	585.1	PREP ALIMENTAIRES NDA
1	BEVERAGES AND TOBACCO		686.6		750.6		816.9		962.3	BOISSONS ET TABACS
11	BEVERAGES		634.9		696.6		745.8		874.0	BOISSONS
112	ALCOHOLIC BEVERAGES	W 243334	542.1	W 256354	591.3	W 263817	649.0	W 291843	727.9	BOISSONS ALCOOLIQUES
2	CRUDE MATERLS,EXCL FUELS		4686.4		5856.5		5548.5		5988.5	MAT BRUTES NON COMESTIBLES
23	RUBBER, CRUDE		379.1		502.1		506.2		533.5	CAOUTCHOUC BRUT
24	CORK AND WOOD		810.7		911.3		863.7		1067.5	LIEGE ET BOIS
248	WOOD SHAPED,SLEEPERS		508.3		499.3		539.5		671.5	BOIS SIMPLEMENT TRAVAILLES
251	*PULP AND WASTE PAPER	W 1940240	368.2	W 2451104	615.7	W 1516836	301.6	W 2043734	328.7	PATES A PAPIER,DECHETS
28	METALLIFEROUS ORES,SCRAP		1947.2		2489.3		2455.5		2464.2	MINERAIS METAL,DECHETS
287	BASE METAL ORES,CONC NES	W 6748823	1171.8	W 6321787	1453.8	W 6921763	1464.8	W 7035761	1381.8	MINERAIS METAUX COMMUNS
2873	ALUMINIUM ORES,ALUMINA	W 6262394	635.9	W 5782154	705.1	W 6146775	776.8	W 6346868	727.0	MINERAIS D'ALUMINIUM
28732	ALUMINA(ALUMINIUM OXIDE)	W 3332986	554.3	W 3158540	628.5	W 3572570	698.4	W 3211921	647.3	ALUMINE (OXYDE ALUMINIUM)
288	NONFERR METAL SCRAP NES	W 369791	326.0	W 497822	503.8	W 465601	464.0	W 537601	536.6	DECHETS NON FERREUX
3	MINERAL FUELS ETC		5218.7		6004.2		7502.8		8856.2	COMBUSTIBLES MINERAUX LUB
32	COAL,COKE AND BRIQUETTES		383.3		459.9		517.2		578.7	HOUILLES,COKES,BRIQUETTES
33	PETROLEUM AND PRODUCTS		4663.6		5348.1		6725.3		7921.0	PETROLE ET DERIVES
333	CRUDE PETROLEUM	MW 31164	3491.3	MW 34285	4159.7	MW 37184	5332.6	MW 44591	6226.8	HUILES BRUTES DE PETROLE
334	PETROLEUM PRODUCTS,REFIN	W 6090874	1004.2	W 5069098	913.5	W 5133484	1106.7	W 6578659	1387.7	PRODUITS RAFFINES
5	CHEMCLS,RELATED PROD NES		11315.6		12858.0		14005.9		15501.6	PRODUITS CHIMIQUES
51	ORGANIC CHEMICALS		2107.9		2433.5		2627.8		2926.5	PROD CHIMIQ ORGANIQUES
514	NITROGEN-FNCTN COMPOUNDS	W 245534	682.8	W 237244	798.3	W 229983	803.7	W 251848	793.8	COMPOSES FONCT AZOTEES
52	INORGANIC CHEMICALS		793.9		943.8		1035.7		1112.2	PROD CHIM INORGANIQUES
53	DYES,TANNING,COLOUR PROD		872.2		930.9		971.7		1127.9	PROD TEINTURE,COLORANTS
533	PIGMENTS,PAINTS,ETC		676.5		724.1		761.2		888.8	PIGMENTS,PEINTURES,VERNIS
541	*MEDICINAL,PHARM PRODUCT		1608.9		1807.6		2024.2		2248.5	PROD MEDICINAUX PHARMACEUT
5417	MEDICAMENTS		1052.9		1203.1		1364.2		1557.9	MEDICAMENTS
54179	— CONTNG OTH SUBSTANCES		781.9		897.3		1054.8		1243.0	MED CONT AUT SUBSTANCES
55	PERFUME,CLEANING ETC PRD		1004.4		1137.4		1284.9		1405.3	PROD POUR PARFUM,TOILETTE
553	PERFUMERY,COSMETICS,ETC		513.9		592.8		694.2		754.3	PRODUITS DE PARFUMERIE
58	PLASTIC MATERIALS ETC		2944.8		3358.1		3705.9		4117.0	MAT PLAST ARTIFICIELLES
582	PROD OF CONDENSATION ETC	W 439981	892.7	W 487037	1038.7	W 505259	1100.6	W 597080	1203.6	PROD CONDENS,POLYCOND
583	POLYMERIZATION ETC PRODS		1935.4		2202.3	W 1722601	2490.1	W 2009666	2785.4	PROD POLYMERISATION
5839	OTH POLYMRZTION ETC PROD		612.0		699.7	W 391128	770.5	W 400305	805.3	AUT PROD POLYMER COPOLYM
59	CHEMICAL MATERIALS NES		1710.5		1937.6		1995.9		2232.2	MAT PROD CHIMIQUES NDA
591	PESTICIDES,DISINFECTANTS	W 91757	421.3	W 108985	506.5	W 110989	506.3	W 118150	592.3	DESINF,INSECT,FONG,HERB
598	MISCEL CHEM PRODUCTS NES		1088.0		1208.6		1226.8		1340.2	PROD DIV INDUST CHIM NDA
5989	CHEM PRODUCTS,PREPS NES		835.4		947.1		986.9		1056.4	PROD PREP CHIMIQUES NDA
59899	OTH CHEM PRODS,PREPS,NES		556.4		607.8	W 465620	648.9	W 527953	709.2	AUT PRODUITS CHIMIQUES NDA
6	BASIC MANUFACTURES		19295.7		21760.8		21588.0		25530.0	ART MANUFACTURES
62	RUBBER MANUFACTURES NES		1819.3		2025.2		2023.9		2347.4	CAOUTCHOUC MANUFACTURE
625	RUBBER TYRES, TUBES ETC	MN 29758	931.3	MN 29517	1056.2	MN 28386	1017.4	MN 31069	1134.6	PNEUS CAOUTCHOUC VULCANISE
6251	TYRES NEW FOR MOTOR CARS	MN 15648	446.5	MN 15496	477.9	MN 14710	459.1	MN 16958	520.7	PNEUS POUR VOITURES
628	RUBBER ARTICLES NES		487.5		535.3		535.2		688.8	OUVRAGES CAOUTCHOUC NDA
63	WOOD,CORK MANUFACTRS NES		497.3		613.3		522.4		672.6	OUVRAGES LIEGE ET BOIS
64	PAPER,PAPERBOARD AND MFR		2256.6		2794.6		2913.1		3212.9	PAPIERS,CARTONS & OUVRAGES
641	PAPER AND PAPERBOARD	W 1596771	1427.4	W 1773422	1780.4	W 1955389	1827.0	W 2284088	2064.5	PAPIERS ET CARTONS
6412	PRINTG,WRITING PAPER NES	W 384284	380.9	W 429474	522.4	W 447657	509.7	W 542823	587.4	PAPIERS POUR L'IMPRESSION
642	PAPER,ETC,PRECUT,ARTS OF		829.2		1014.2		1086.1		1148.5	PAP,CARTONS DECOUPES
65	TEXTILE YARN,FABRICS,ETC		2925.5		3216.6		3326.0		3875.0	FILS,TISSUS,ARTICLES TEXTILE
651	TEXTILE YARN	W 160734	552.4	W 170113	637.7		674.5		771.3	FILS TEXTILES
653	WOVN MAN-MADE FIB FABRIC	W 56945	466.2	W 59037	493.8	W 55467	482.1	W 65306	560.5	TISSUS FIBRES SYNTH,ARTIF
657	SPECIAL TXTL FABRC,PRODS		535.3		616.2		650.6		734.9	TISSUS SPECIAUX
66	NONMETAL MINERAL MFS NES		2122.5		2115.1		2192.4		2453.4	ART MIN NON METALLIQUES
664	GLASS		821.8		824.2		879.5		951.0	VERRE
67	IRON AND STEEL		3194.2		3636.2		3424.1		4573.4	FER ET ACIER
672	IRON,STEEL PRIMARY FORMS	W 2157096	641.3	W 2148135	726.3	W 1735850	525.5	W 2084323	684.7	LINGOTS FER,ACIER
673	IRON,STEEL SHAPES ETC	W 1007625	486.7	W 1183840	630.6	W 1074944	582.9	W 1633981	796.6	BARRES,PROFIL FER,ACIER
674	IRN,STL UNIV,PLATE,SHEET	W 1319443	964.7	W 1271311	1049.7	W 1202297	1020.2	W 1732343	1305.1	LARGES PLATS,TOLES
678	IRON,STL TUBES,PIPES,ETC		709.2		784.4		798.7		1198.4	TUBES,TUYAUX EN FONTE,FER
68	NON-FERROUS METALS		2017.4		2517.0		2273.5		2643.2	METAUX NON FERREUX
682	COPPER EXC CEMENT COPPER	W 135807	422.0	W 167297	566.0	W 143930	456.1	W 172684	531.4	CUIVRE
684	ALUMINIUM		1199.6		1475.3		1310.7		1528.3	ALUMINIUM
6842	ALUMINIUM,ALLOYS WORKED		986.4		1254.2		1116.1		1267.8	ALUMINIUM,ALLIAGES OUVRE
68422	ALUMNM PLATE,SHEET,STRIP	W 368220	786.0	W 375154	994.2	W 342532	844.8	W 374173	944.2	TOLES, PLANCHES EN ALU
69	METAL MANUFACTURES NES		4180.5		4572.4		4646.3		5438.7	ART MANUFACT EN METAL NDA
694	STL,COPPR NAILS,NUTS,ETC		588.4		637.0		674.8		795.9	CLOUS,VIS,ECROUS
69402	IRN,STL NUTS,BOLTS,ETC		549.0		598.1		632.2		741.1	BOULONS,VIS,ECROUS FER,AC
695	TOOLS		771.9		870.0		860.9		1177.8	OUTILS A MAIN
6954	BLADES,TIPS,ETC FR TOOLS		469.4		554.3		547.5		795.4	OUTILS POUR MACHINE-OUTIL
69541	PARTS TO INSERT IN TOOLS		378.6		448.9		439.9	MN 49883	670.5	OUTILS DE FORAGE
699	BASE METAL MFRS NES		1843.8		1994.1		2037.1		2232.3	ART MANUFACTURES MET NDA
6991	LOCKSMITHS WARES,ETC		789.1		844.7		899.8		1010.3	ARTICLES DE SERRURERIE
69913	BASE MTL DOOR,ETC FITTNG		581.4		623.7		672.0		761.6	GARNITURES POUR MEUBLES
6997	IRON,STEEL ARTICLES NES		469.7		490.3		380.4		410.2	OUV FONTE,FER,ACIER NDA
69979	IRN,STL MANUFACTURES NES		468.5		489.3		379.3		408.6	AUT OUVRAGES EN FER NDA
7	MACHINES,TRANSPORT EQUIP		76310.5		84550.7		87181.6		101408.8	MACHINES MATERIEL TRANSPORT
71	POWER GENERATING EQUIPMT		6945.3		7895.8		8263.5		9302.5	MACHINES GENERATRICES
713	INTRNL COMBUS PSTN ENGIN		5204.6		5561.4		5714.9		6251.9	MOTEURS EXPL COMB INT, PIECE
7132	MOTOR VEHCL PSTN ENGINS	N 1882972	3337.8	N 1985553	3719.5	N 1938913	3560.3	N 1976049	3761.0	MOTEURS EXPL POUR VEHICULES
7139	PISTON ENGINE PARTS NES		1384.1		1314.0		1670.1		1903.4	PIECES POUR 713.2,3,8

4. General Imports F.O.B. by Commodities according to the S.I.T.C. (Rev. 2) in million U.S. Dollars
Importations Générales F.O.B. par Produits d'après la C.T.C.I. (Rév. 2) en millions de Dollars E.U.

SITC CTCI	COMMODITY	1994		1995		1996		1997		PRODUIT
		QUANTITY QUANTITE	VALUE VALEUR	QUANTITY QUANTITE	VALUE VALEUR	QUANTITY QUANTITE	VALUE VALEUR	QUANTITY QUANTITE	VALUE VALEUR	
714	ENGINES AND MOTORS NES		816.7		1101.9		1514.7		1851.8	MOTEURS NON ELECTRIQUES
7149	ENGINE & MOTOR PARTS NES		590.9		815.3		1045.3		1262.9	PIECES 714 ET 718.88
71491	PARTS NES OF 7144,71481		414.0		588.6		744.6		852.5	PIECES DES PROPULSEURS
716	ROTATING ELECTRIC PLANT		685.9		967.6		780.8		882.2	APP ELECTR ROTATIFS,PIECES
72	MACHS FOR SPCL INDUSTRYS		5091.7		5593.1		5501.9		7229.1	MAC SPECIALES POUR INDUST
721	AGRIC MACHY,EXC TRACTORS		853.3		853.3		905.5		1123.2	MACHINES AGRICOLES
7212	HARVESTING ETC MACHINES		578.6		576.4		612.9		764.6	ENGINS POUR LA RECOLTE
722	TRACTORS NON-ROAD	N 63262	474.6	N 25210	489.2	N 25771	539.2	N 34458	730.0	TRACTEURS
7224	WHEELED TRACTORS NES	N 63040	456.6	N 24968	471.0	N 25558	516.0	N 34019	690.0	TRACTEURS A ROUES
723	CIVIL ENGNEERG EQUIP ETC		1223.7		1237.0		1131.6		1658.3	APPAREILS DE GENIE CIVIL
7234	CONST,MINING MACHNRY NES	N 56957	1105.2	N 49863	1100.6	N 45797	991.3	N 89076	1471.8	MACH POUR LA CONST, MINES
72342	SLFPRP SHOVELS,EXCAVATRS	N 11541	754.3	N 11080	754.4	N 9496	646.4	N 13940	933.9	PELLES MECANIQUES
728	OTH MACHY FOR SPCL INDUS		1552.0		1818.5		1784.7		2346.4	AUT MACH IND PARTICULIERES
7284	MACHY FOR SPCL INDUS NES		1208.6		1424.8		1403.0		1895.4	MACH SPEC IND PARTICUL.
72848	OTH MCHY WITH INDIV FNCT	N 689549	583.8	N 606870	695.2	N 629141	699.4	N 629587	1117.3	AUTRES MACHINES NDA
73	METALWORKING MACHINERY		1214.6		1262.7		1307.7		1697.8	MACH TRAVAIL DES METAUX
736	METALWORKING MACH-TOOLS		970.8		966.0		983.1		1198.5	MACH-OUTILS TRAVAIL METAUX
74	GENRL INDUSTRL MACHY NES		8066.5		9149.5		9360.2		10795.7	MACH APP INDUSTRIE
741	HEATING,COOLING EQUIPMNT		1496.5		1660.3		1785.2		1909.6	MACH CHAUFFAGE,PIECES
7415	AIR-CONDITIONING MACHNRY		876.6		924.9		1015.6		1023.7	GROUPES CONDITION AIR
742	PUMPS FOR LIQUIDS ETC		776.1		822.2		871.8		1008.4	POMPES MOTO-POMPES
743	PUMPS NES,CENTRFUGES ETC		1444.7		1800.7		1630.5		1968.2	POMPES COMPRES,VENT ETC
7431	PUMPS FOR GASES ETC	N 4222871	438.0	N 5047657	456.2	N 5072334	433.3	N 6268541	600.8	POMPES AIR A VIDE,COMPRES
7436	GAS,LIQUID FILTERS ETC	MN 38876	602.9	MN 40069	846.7	MN 44540	698.3	MN 43525	801.8	APP POUR FILT DES LIQUIDES
744	MECHANICAL HANDLING EQU		1081.0		1271.2		1331.5		1574.0	EQUIP MANUTENTION PIECES
7449	PTS NES OF MACHY OF 7442		495.2		556.6		579.7		679.7	PIECES DU 744.2
745	NONELEC MACHY,TOOLS NES		756.7		761.9		794.7		943.0	AUT MACH NON ELEC,PIECES
7452	OTH NONELEC MCHS,PTS NES		596.1		595.1		645.8		761.9	AUT MACH NON ELEC,PIECES
749	NONELEC MACH PTS,ACC NES		2511.8		2833.5		2946.8		3392.7	PIECES MACH NON ELEC NDA
7491	BALL,ROLLER,ETC BEARINGS		462.0		562.7		534.7		609.3	ROULEMENTS BILLES ETC
7492	COCKS,VALVES ETC NES		907.6		1004.5		1068.0		1297.5	ART ROB,SIM POUR TUYAUX
7493	SHAFT,CRANK,PULLEY ETC		773.5		852.2		881.8		981.8	ARBRES TRANS,VILEBREQUINS
75	OFFICE MACHNES,ADP EQUIP		7784.8		8722.7		9177.9		10224.8	MACH BUREAU TRAIT AUTOM
752	AUTOMTIC DATA PROC EQUIP		4711.7		5422.5		5995.3		6919.2	MACH TRAIT INFORMATION
7522	DIGITAL COMPUTERS		480.7		542.8		977.4		1047.3	MACH DIGITALES COMPLETES
7523	DIGITL CENTRL PROCESSORS		1665.8		2050.2		2225.7		2562.5	UNITES CENTRALES
7524	DIGITL CENTRL STOR UNITS	N 4226231	972.7	N 4553078	1080.2	N 5145875	1153.7	N 5569459	1416.8	UNITES MEMOIRE CENTRALES
7525	ADP PERIPHERAL UNITS	N 5695977	1336.9	N 5746240	1422.0	N 4856112	1164.2	N 5050490	1313.0	UNITES PERIPHERIQUES
759	OFFICE,ADP MCH PTS,ACCES		2636.0		2846.0		2709.8		2837.2	PIECES DU 751 ET 752
7599	ACCTG,ETC,ADP MCH PTS,AC		2345.5		2533.9		2384.7		2452.7	PIECES DU 751 ET 752
76	TELECOMM,SOUND EQUIPMENT		4216.7		4815.9		5247.5		6086.8	EQUIPMENT DE TELECOM
762	RADIO BROADCAST RECEIVRS	MN 9067	701.5	MN 9637	789.6	N 8299136	685.8	N 8610530	731.2	RECEPTEURS RADIODIFFUSION
763	SOUND RECORDRS,PHONOGRPH	N 4438129	518.1	N 4534614	518.8	N 4147963	492.7	N 4736751	637.5	PHONO,APP ENREGISTREMENT
7638	OTHR SOUND APPARATUS ETC	N 4418292	514.1	N 4510207	515.5	N 4127870	490.0	N 4721588	635.8	AUT APP D'ENREGIS,REPROD
764	TELECOM EQPT,PTS,ACC NES		2648.8		3118.8		3691.5		4168.6	EQUIP TELECOM,PIECES
7641	LINE TELEPHONE,ETC EQUIP		797.6		953.4		1099.6		1192.1	APP TELEPHON PAR FIL
7643	TV,RADIO TRANSMITTRS ETC	N 2251340	414.8	N 2550191	541.1	N 3266419	631.4	N 3579231	1015.1	APP EMET TELE RADIO
7649	PTS NES OF EQUIPMT OF 76		911.0		1047.1		1354.4		1437.5	PIECES DE LA DIV 76
76491	PTS NES OF APPAR OF 7641		356.3		435.1		646.3		618.6	PIECES POUR 764.1
76493	TELECOMM EQUIPMT PTS NES		479.9		520.3		617.7		724.1	PIECES 761,762,764.3,8
77	ELECTRIC MACHNRY NES ETC		12671.9		14816.0		15003.5		16054.1	MACH APP ELECT NDA
771	ELECTRIC POWER MACHY NES		503.4		577.6		624.2		801.0	MACH PROD,TRANS ELECTR
7712	OTH ELEC POWER MACHY NES		388.4		470.1		512.4		677.0	AUT APP PROD TRANSF ELEC
772	SWITCHGEAR ETC,PARTS NES		2423.1		2639.4		2754.1		2865.6	APP COUPURE,SECT ETC
7721	SWITCHGEAR ETC		1672.2		1867.3		2035.0		2026.0	APP COUPURE,SECTIONMNT
7722	PRINTED CIRCUITS,PTS NES		679.1		691.5		637.7		751.8	CIRCUITS ET PIECES
773	ELECTR DISTRIBUTNG EQUIP		1160.2		1303.1		1371.0		1647.5	EQUIPMT DISTRIBUTION ELECT
7731	INSULATED WIRE,CABLE ETC		1102.5		1238.9		1306.4		1585.2	FILS,CABLES ISOLES ELECT
775	HOUSEHOLD TYPE EQUIP NES		1039.3		1043.2		1067.8		1214.8	MACH,APP USAGE DOMESTQUE
776	TRANSISTORS,VALVES,ETC		4587.8		6269.6		6089.2		6208.5	LAMPES,TUBES,VALVES
7764	ELECTRONIC MICROCIRCUITS	MN 792526	4184.3	MN 961431	5745.0	MN 959748	5616.2	MN 1007350	5688.5	MICROSTRUCTURES ELECTRON
778	ELECTRICAL MACHINERY NES		2679.4		2725.3		2806.5		3026.6	AUTRES MACH ELECT NDA
7783	AUTOMOTIVE ELECTR EQUIP		1208.5		1107.6		1174.4		1206.5	EQUIP ELECT MOTEURS EXPL
77831	IGNITION,STARTING EQUIP		707.9	MN 88440	602.2	MN 84693	625.2	MN 178074	604.9	APP ELEC ALLUM,DEMARRAGE
77832	ELECT VEHICLE LGHTNG EQU		500.6		505.5		549.2		601.7	APP ELEC ECLAIR,SIGNAL AUTO
7788	OTH ELEC MACHY,EQUIP NES		783.1		913.6		893.0		965.9	AUT MACH APP ELEC NDA
78	ROAD VEHICLES		28405.9		29588.4		30338.0		35534.1	VEHICULES ROUTIERS
781	PASS MOTOR VEH EXC BUSES	N 832800	10113.2	N 739278	9795.0	N 732784	10347.4	N 937876	12936.8	AUTO TRANSPORT PERSONNES
782	LORRIES,SPCL MTR VEH NES	N 234254	2820.2	N 232519	3100.8	N 241888	3443.3	N 271333	4032.3	VEHICULES SPECIAUX,MARCH
7821	LORRIES,TRUCKS	N 233422	2746.0	N 231577	3006.1	N 239304	3341.3	N 269939	3901.2	VEHICULES TRANSP MARCHAND
783	ROAD MOTOR VEHICLES NES	N 18996	1069.4	N 18623	1099.9	N 15670	971.2	N 19479	1202.0	VEHICULES ROUTIERS NDA
7832	TRACTORS FOR TR-TRAILERS	N 16713	994.7	N 15828	981.5	N 12443	763.3	N 16569	1033.6	TRACTEURS ROUTIERS
784	MOTOR VEH PRTS,ACCES NES		13645.6		14714.4		14716.5		16348.2	PIECES 722,781,782,783
7849	OTHER MOTOR VEHCL PARTS		13385.4		14369.6		14351.3		15925.5	PIECES 722,781,782,783
786	TRAILERS,NONMOTR VEH,NES		483.4		573.8		535.1		672.1	REMORQUES,CADRES,CONTAIN
79	OTHR TRANSPORT EQUIPMENT		1913.3		2707.2		2981.8		4484.2	AUTRE MATERIEL TRANSPORT
791	RAILWAY VEHICLES		309.2		551.3		429.6		739.7	VEHIC MAT CHEMINS DE FER
792	AIRCRAFT ETC		1441.6		1978.3		2392.3		3544.0	APP NAVIGATION AERIENNE
7924	AIRCRFT NES OVER 15000KG	N 27	309.1	N 20	686.6	N 39	803.4	N 81	1629.8	AERODYNES PLUS 15000 KG
7929	AIRCRAFT PARTS NES		901.3		1040.2		1290.8		1508.6	PIECES DU 792
8	MISC MANUFACTURED GOODS		17889.9		19050.9		18860.8		21812.6	ART MANUFACTURES DIVERS
812	*PLUMBG,HEATNG,LGHTNG EQ		487.2		481.7		515.3		594.1	APPAR SANITAIRES CHAUFFAGE
821	*FURNITURE,PARTS THEREOF		1912.2		1985.3		1951.2		2297.0	MEUBLES ET PIECES
8211	CHAIRS,SEATS AND PARTS		1053.8		1178.1		1138.0		1302.0	SIEGES ET PIECES
82119	PTS NES OF CHAIRS ETC		620.3		838.2		802.8		911.5	PIECES DU 821.11
8219	FURNITURE AND PARTS NES		719.4		674.9		681.6		823.2	AUTRES MEUBLES ET PIECES
84	CLOTHING AND ACCESSORIES		2543.6		2713.6		2561.0		3011.6	VETEMENTS
843	WOMENS OUTERWEAR NONKNIT	MN 66264	648.1	MN 64826	666.3	MN 61338	621.5	MN 64144	681.2	VET DESSUS FEMMES MAT TEX
845	OUTERWEAR KNIT NONELASTC	MN 83165	497.0	MN 92547	533.0	MN 78967	498.0	MN 88393	619.4	VET DESSOUS,ACCES BONNET
851	*FOOTWEAR	MP 87286	752.1	MP 93891	821.4	MP 84752	774.5	MP 95721	918.3	CHAUSSURES
85102	FOOTWEAR LEATHER	MP 62893	617.8	MP 67472	671.0	MP 57305	613.8	MP 64339	726.7	CHAUS SEMELLES EN CUIR
87	PRECISION INSTRUMNTS NES		3374.7		3656.7		3744.2		4441.7	INSTRUM,APPAR SCIENT NDA
872	MEDICAL INSTRUMENTS NES		511.7		540.7		561.9		644.7	INSTR,APP MEDIC-CHIR NDA
874	MEASURNG,CONTROLNG INSTR		2467.7		2709.1		2734.9		3309.7	INSTRUMENTS DE MESURE
8743	GAS,LIQUID CONTROL INSTR		1091.9		1304.6		1200.2		1570.8	APP,INSTR MESURE FLUIDES
88	PHOTO EQU,OPTICL GDS ETC		1195.0		1258.2		1266.4		1383.7	APP,FOURN PHOTO,OP,MONTR
882	PHOTO,CINEMA SUPPLIES		582.5		610.4		617.0		662.2	PRODUITS PHOTO,CINEMA
8822	PHOTO FILM EXC DEV CINMA		468.2		475.7		478.4		534.9	PLAQUES,PELLICULES,FILMS
89	MISC MANUFCTRD GOODS NES		7380.0		7848.6		7765.0		8838.4	ART MANUFACTURES DIVERS
892	PRINTED MATTER		1973.1		2144.5		2093.0		2275.5	IMPRIMES
8921	PRINTED BOOKS,GLOBES,ETC		939.2		1006.6		972.9		1058.0	LIVRES,BROCHURES,CARTES

4. General Imports F.O.B. by Commodities according to the S.I.T.C. (Rev. 2) in million U.S. Dollars
Importations Générales F.O.B. par Produits d'après la C.T.C.I. (Rév. 2) en millions de Dollars E.U.

SITC CTCI	COMMODITY	1994 QUANTITY QUANTITE	1994 VALUE VALEUR	1995 QUANTITY QUANTITE	1995 VALUE VALEUR	1996 QUANTITY QUANTITE	1996 VALUE VALEUR	1997 QUANTITY QUANTITE	1997 VALUE VALEUR	PRODUIT
89211	PRINTED BOOKS,PAMPHLETS		922.8		990.7		955.1		1040.9	LIVRES,BROCHURES
8922	NEWSPAPERS,PERIODICALS		615.7		638.8		645.4		683.4	JOURNAUX ET PERIODIQUES
893	ARTICLES OF PLASTIC NES		1534.1		1639.9		1691.3		2015.7	OUVRAGES EN MAT DIVIS 58
8939	MISC PLASTIC ARTICLES		1158.8		1208.5		1248.8		1506.2	ART DIVERS EN MAT DIV 58
89399	OTHR PLASTC ARTICLES NES		1021.9		1086.4		1126.1		1367.2	AUT OUV MAT DIV 58
894	TOYS,SPORTING GOODS,ETC		1541.1		1614.2		1627.2		1888.9	VOITURES ENFANTS,JOUETS
8942	TOYS,INDOOR GAMES ETC		1088.4		1084.8		1174.5		1394.8	JOUETS,JEUX ETC
89424	INDOOR GAME EQUIPMENT		525.4		449.3		495.9		598.3	ART,JEUX DE SOCIETE
898	MUSICAL INSTRUMENTS,PTS		1357.6		1400.5		1299.9		1470.2	INSTRUMENTS DE MUSIQUE
8983	SOUND RECRDNG TAPE,DISCS		1254.7		1293.5		1201.8		1359.7	SUPPORTS SON POUR 763
89832	RECORDED DISCS,TAPES ETC		1037.5		1088.0		997.9		1146.9	DISQUES,PHONO,BANDES
899	OTHER MANUFACTURED GOODS		499.6		547.3		556.7		616.7	AUT ART MANUF DIVERS NDA
9	GOODS NOT CLASSD BY KIND		4679.2		5034.7		6615.7		6377.8	ART TRANSACT NON CLASSES
931	*SPECIAL TRANSACTIONS		3800.8		4220.8		5474.0		5115.7	TRANS.SPECIALES
971	*GOLD,NON MONETARY NES	K 3179163	606.0	K 1474256	511.8	K 1416954	742.2	K 575315	990.7	OR NON MONETAIRE
97101	NONMON GLD UNWRT,SEMIMFD	K 36486	315.4	K 23774	237.9	K 229315	472.3	K 83372	771.1	OR,ALLIAGES D'OR BRUTS

5. General Exports F.O.B. by Commodities according to the S.I.T.C. (Rev. 2) in million U.S. Dollars
Exportations Générales F.O.B. par Produits d'après la C.T.C.I. (Rév. 2) en millions de Dollars E.U.

SITC CTCI	COMMODITY	1994 QUANTITY QUANTITE	1994 VALUE VALEUR	1995 QUANTITY QUANTITE	1995 VALUE VALEUR	1996 QUANTITY QUANTITE	1996 VALUE VALEUR	1997 QUANTITY QUANTITE	1997 VALUE VALEUR	PRODUIT
	ALL COMMODITIES		166254.6		192160.7		201573.8		214333.4	TOUS PRODUITS
0	FOOD AND LIVE ANIMALS		10173.9		11474.0		12663.3		13671.9	ALIMENTS,ANIMAUX VIVANTS
001	*LIVE ANIMALS FOR FOOD		955.9		1082.7		1371.5		1352.5	ANIMAUX VIVANTS
0011	BOVINE SPECIES,LIVE	N 1017257	830.0	N 1135555	884.6	N 1514244	1027.3	N 1383009	966.0	ESPECE BOVINE
00119	— OTHR THAN FR BREEDING	N 1010573	817.9	N 1132234	878.1	N 1509658	1018.4	N 1378455	957.7	BOVINS NON REPRODUCTEURS
01	MEAT AND PREPARATIONS		1112.1		1274.8		1518.2		1831.4	VIANDES ET PREPARATIONS
011	MEAT FRESH,CHILLD,FROZEN	W 472797	985.7	W 554669	1116.6	W 623680	1320.2	W 737309	1637.2	VIANDES FRAICHES,REF,CONGE
0111	BOVINE MEAT FRESH,FROZEN	W 182683	400.9	W 184838	401.5	W 240885	495.5	W 288851	671.9	VIANDES BOVIN FRAI,REF
0113	PIG MEAT FRESH,CHLD,FRZN	W 204478	459.0	W 238391	548.2	W 242854	626.4	W 277109	734.6	VIANDE DE PORC
03	FISH AND PREPARATIONS		2156.5		2299.0		2269.1		2258.0	POISSONS ET PREPARATIONS
034	FISH,FRESH,CHILLED,FROZN	W 245507	829.7	W 225693	757.7	W 247626	784.1	W 248989	856.8	POISSON FRAIS, REFRIG,CONG
036	SHELL FISH FRESH,FROZEN	W 110238	888.3	W 120027	1063.5	W 120202	936.0	W 123401	918.6	CRUSTACES,MOLLUSQUES
04	CEREALS AND PREPARATIONS		3714.6		4110.8		4391.4		4737.7	CEREALES ET PRODUITS
041	WHEAT ETC UNMILLED	MW 21290	2578.0	MW 16503	2866.4	MW 13781	2840.3	MW 18858	3157.7	FROMENT,EPEAUTRE
0411	DURUM WHEAT UNMILLED	W 2904004	496.6	W 3773923	812.9	W 3191761	709.4	W 3742882	748.3	FROMENT DUR NON MOULU
0412	OTHER WHEAT ETC UNMILLED	MW 18386	2081.5	MW 12729	2053.5	MW 10590	2131.0	MW 15115	2409.4	AUTRE FROMENT NON MOULU
048	CEREAL ETC PREPARATIONS	W 617300	471.1	W 692478	567.2	W 797048	714.4	W 920475	793.0	PREPTNS A BASE CEREALES
05	VEGETABLES AND FRUIT		828.5		1044.8		1136.6		1262.4	LEGUMES ET FRUITS
054	VEG ETC FRSH,SMPLY PRSVD		600.9		793.1	W 2312956	853.3	W 2527567	949.3	LEGUMES FRAIS,CONG,SECS
081	*FEEDING STUFF FOR ANIML	W 2981454	500.1	W 3273514	576.5	W 3259131	720.0	W 3184959	781.9	NOURRITURE POUR ANIMAUX
1	BEVERAGES AND TOBACCO		896.3		869.9		985.6		1037.0	BOISSONS ET TABACS
11	BEVERAGES		752.2		734.9		825.4		875.1	BOISSONS
112	ALCOHOLIC BEVERAGES	W 441301	593.9	W 421681	562.4	W 397675	613.2	W 387126	595.1	BOISSONS ALCOOLIQUES
2	CRUDE MATERLS,EXCL FUELS		19572.3		23687.7		21638.6		22281.0	MAT BRUTES NON COMESTIBLES
22	OIL SEEDS,OLEAGINOUS FRT		1352.1		1504.7		1188.6		1375.1	GRAINES,FRUITS OLEAGINEUX
222	SEEDS FOR'SOFT'FIXED OIL	W 4165847	1151.8	W 4151923	1233.2	W 2896540	915.3	W 3379149	1063.2	GRAINES HUILES FIXES
2226	RAPE AND COLZA SEEDS	W 3670423	1025.9	W 3436976	1043.9	W 2416103	759.9	W 2837272	892.2	GRAINES DE NAVETTE,COLZA
24	CORK AND WOOD		8843.3		8446.7		9674.6		9918.1	LIEGE ET BOIS
248	WOOD SHAPED,SLEEPERS		8587.4		8178.7		9407.6		9664.1	BOIS SIMPLEMENT TRAVAILLES
2482	LUMBER SHAPED CONIFER		8249.7		7817.7	MW 47535	9015.8	MW 47092	9189.1	CONIFERES SCIES,RABOTES
24821	LUMBER SAWN ETC CONIFER	MW 28091	8101.1	MW 29722	7667.1	MW 31034	8869.3	MW 29793	9001.3	CONIFERES SCIES LONGITUD
251	*PULP AND WASTE PAPER	MW 10777	4976.3	MW 11302	8074.4	MW 10900	5141.8	MW 11777	5067.4	PATES A PAPIER,DECHETS
2517	SODA,SULPHATE WOOD PULP	W 8333448	4022.1	W 8546417	6552.8	W 8237548	4202.9	W 8863486	4134.5	PATES CHIMIQUES AU SULFATE
25172	— BLEACHED,NONDISSOLVNG	W 8152745	3935.2	W 8444154	6484.1	W 8145514	4163.3	W 8733540	4077.2	PATES BLANCHIES
2519	OTHER CELLULOSIC PULPS	W 1188832	463.6	W 1285574	801.4	W 1284231	470.6	W 1406691	498.5	AUTRES PATES CELLULOSE
25191	SEMI–CHEMICAL WOOD PULP	W 1185108	461.9	W 1281692	799.7	W 1266086	463.6	W 1354355	482.1	PATES MI CHIMIQUES
27	CRUDE FERTLZR,MINRLS NES		749.5		868.8		870.2		800.9	ENGRAIS MINERAUX BRUTS
28	METALLIFEROUS ORES,SCRAP		2663.7		3658.0		3514.5		3696.9	MINERAIS METAL,DECHETS
281	IRON ORE,CONCENTRATES	MW 30126	689.3	MW 28967	677.7	MW 28880	724.0	MW 33142	921.6	MINERAIS DE FER
2816	IRON ORE AGGLOMERATES	MW 16028	474.9	MW 17299	499.4	MW 17373	540.9	MW 20489	693.1	MINERAIS AGGLOMERES
287	BASE METAL ORES,CONC NES	MW 88912	1164.9	MW 799460	1911.5	MW 890832	1872.4	MW 607530	1708.1	MINERAIS METAUX COMMUNS
2871	CPR ORE ETC,CEMENT COPPR	W 238628	402.4	W 270133	668.7	W 466800	472.3	W 526648	444.1	MINERAIS DE CUIVRE,MATTES
28711	COPPER ORES,EXCL MATTE	W 219423	370.6	W 256654	634.3	W 448485	430.0	W 509466	406.4	MINERAIS DE CUIVRE
2872	NICKEL ORES,CONCENTRATES	W 71778	409.4	W 78707	675.9	W 96242	790.5	W 86733	636.6	MINERAIS DE NICKEL
28722	NICKEL MATTE,SINTERS,ETC	W 71778	409.4	W 78707	675.9	W 96242	790.5	W 86714	636.5	MATTES,SINTERS
288	NONFERR METAL SCRAP NES	W 558574	527.4	W 503662	657.4	W 513018	542.8	W 584935	634.5	DECHETS NON FERREUX
2882	OTHER BASE MTL SCRAP NES	W 411490	497.5	W 425427	612.6	W 400942	514.1	W 442211	596.6	AUTRES DECHETS
3	MINERAL FUELS ETC		16112.1		17271.0		20513.9		21952.6	COMBUSTIBLES MINERAUX LUB
32	COAL,COKE AND BRIQUETTES		1676.8		1789.1		1741.1		2048.7	HOUILLES,COKES,BRIQUETTES
322	COAL,LIGNITE AND PEAT	MW 32037	1656.7	MW 34543	1766.6	MW 32262	1716.4	MW 36508	2022.8	HOUILLES,LIGNITES,TOURBE
3222	OTH COAL,NOT AGGLOMERATD	MW 31090	1493.8	MW 33720	1609.1	MW 31371	1567.3	MW 35614	1858.5	AUTRES HOUILLES
33	PETROLEUM AND PRODUCTS		7397.1		9138.8		11034.5		11093.0	PETROLE ET DERIVES
333	CRUDE PETROLEUM	MW 49007	5443.3	MW 56312	7081.8	MW 56733	8099.2	MW 61140	8237.1	HUILES BRUTES DE PETROLE
334	PETROLEUM PRODUCTS,REFIN	MW 11981	1794.6	MW 11612	1879.5	MW 14237	2731.5	MW 13652	2599.4	PRODUITS RAFFINES
3341	GASOLINE,OTH LIGHT OILS	W 3692983	567.8	W 3968711	682.1	W 5198030	1010.6	W 4385540	980.8	ESSENCES POUR MOTEURS
33411	MOTOR,AVIATION SPIRIT	W 3692983	567.8	W 3968711	682.1	W 5198030	1010.6	W 4385540	980.8	ESSENCES MOTEURS D'AVIONS
3343	GAS OILS	W 4604102	691.4	W 4418686	677.7	W 5243056	997.0	W 2515685	468.2	GAS OILS
341	*GAS,NATURAL AND MANUFCT		6076.1		5486.7		6848.3		7831.7	GAZ NATUREL,GAZ MANUFACT
3413	PETROLM GASES,LIQUEFIED	W 5569436	1049.6	MW 10497	1466.4	MW 9877	1790.1	W 7892014	1646.5	GAZ DE PETROLE LIQUEFIE
34131	LIQUEFIED PROPANE,BUTANE	W 4204215	555.0	W 4914735	638.5	W 4445215	846.3	W 4124802	838.8	PROPANE,BUTANE LIQUEFIES
34139	OTH HYDROCARBON GAS LQFD	W 1365221	494.6	W 5581886	828.0	W 5431590	943.9	W 3767212	807.7	HYDROCARBURES GAZEUX NDA
3414	PETROLEUM GASES, GASEOUS	MV 72362572	5026.6	MV 79264963	4020.3	MV 80974561	5058.2	MV 82345038	6185.3	GAZ DE PETROLE GAZEUX
351	*ELECTRIC CURRENT	MH 44308	962.2	MH 40378	856.4	MH 41583	890.2	MH 42718	979.3	ENERGIE ELECTRIQUE
5	CHEMCLS,RELATED PROD NES		8801.2		10902.0		11119.5		12318.0	PRODUITS CHIMIQUES
51	ORGANIC CHEMICALS		1651.5		2263.4		1987.7		1990.2	PROD CHIMIQ ORGANIQUES
511	HYDROCARBONS NES,DERIVS	W 1427134	615.7	W 1705491	940.4	W 2115994	857.4	W 2284512	825.0	HYDROCARBURES NDA
5112	CYCLIC HYDROCARBONS	W 966446	468.8	W 1080648	728.2	W 1096510	573.6	W 1070073	495.4	HYDROCARBURES CYCLIQUES
512	ALCOHOLS,PHENOLS ETC		516.9		720.2		560.9		537.3	PHENOLS,PHENOLS–ALCOOLS
5121	ACYCLIC ALCOHOLS,DERIVS		506.2		709.5		549.7		525.6	ALCOOLS ACYCLIQUES
52	INORGANIC CHEMICALS		1550.2		1720.3		1950.6		2030.8	PROD CHIM INORGANIQUES
522	INORG ELEMNTS,OXIDES,ETC	W 4186558	659.5	W 4130104	774.5	W 4165459	800.0	W 4359326	834.0	ELEMENTS INORGANIQUES
524	RADIOACTIVE ETC MATERIAL		475.4		510.2		702.5		750.3	MATIERES RADIOACTIVES
5241	RADIOACTIVE ELEMENTS ETC		452.3		498.9		613.8		626.8	RADIOELEMENTS,ISOTOPES
541	*MEDICINAL,PHARM PRODUCT		504.7		611.1		683.4		957.8	PROD MEDICINAUX PHARMACEUT
5417	MEDICAMENTS		305.0		375.4		466.0		702.2	MEDICAMENTS
55	PERFUME,CLEANING ETC PRD		478.3		581.0		659.3		697.2	PROD POUR PARFUM,TOILETTE
562	*FERTILIZERS,MANUFACTURE	MW 15865	1567.2	MW 16587	1685.6	MW 15683	1559.1	MW 17596	1757.2	ENGRAIS MANUFACTURES
5623	CHEM POTASSIC FERTILIZER	MW 12996	1196.7	MW 13803	1285.6	MW 12942	1132.1	MW 14564	1261.7	ENGRAIS POTASSIQUES
56231	POTASSIUM CHLORIDE	MW 12961	1189.1	MW 13795	1283.3	MW 12927	1129.1	MW 14544	1257.6	CHLORURE DE POTASSIUM
58	PLASTIC MATERIALS ETC		2223.9		2993.4		3064.6		3555.7	MAT PLAST ARTIFICIELLES
583	POLYMERIZATION ETC PRODS		1902.8		2624.8	W 2578188	2620.5	W 2748487	2956.2	PROD POLYMERISATION
5831	POLYETHYLENE	W 1289365	923.4	W 1404696	1336.6	W 1642439	1334.3	W 1615270	1478.4	POLYETHYLENE
58311	— IN PRIMARY FORMS	W 1225653	800.8	W 1335628	1185.2	W 1563317	1170.8	W 1527365	1294.0	POLYETHYLENE PRIMAIRES
59	CHEMICAL MATERIALS NES		468.7		613.0		721.3		743.2	MAT PROD CHIMIQUES NDA
6	BASIC MANUFACTURES		25485.1		32273.2		32789.1		34122.8	ART MANUFACTURES
62	RUBBER MANUFACTURES NES		1463.4		1580.1		1709.0		1901.3	CAOUTCHOUC MANUFACTURE
625	RUBBER TYRES, TUBES ETC	MN 24415	939.1	MN 23258	949.0	MN 23863	1039.6	MN 25482	1178.0	PNEUS CAOUTCHOUC VULCANISE
6251	TYRES NEW FOR MOTOR CARS	MN 19746	594.9	MN 18009	594.2	MN 18864	642.3	MN 20454	721.3	PNEUS POUR VOITURES
63	WOOD,CORK MANUFACTRS NES		1785.5		2221.6		2503.1		2913.6	OUVRAGES LIEGE ET BOIS
634	VENEERS,PLYWOOD,ETC		1103.3		1368.3		1427.5		1474.6	PLACAGES,CONTRE–PLAQUES
6343	IMPROVED,RECONSTIT WOOD		721.1		828.7		882.8		877.4	BOIS AMELIORES,RECONST
63432	RECONSTITUTED WOOD	W 2240529	721.0	W 2796108	828.6	W 3377162	881.8	W 3946810	875.9	BOIS RECONSTITUES
635	WOOD MANUFACTURES NES		681.3		852.6		1074.9		1438.0	ART MANUF EN BOIS NDA
6353	BUILDERS WOODWRK,PREFABS		315.5		434.3		631.5		869.7	OUVRAGES DE MENUISERIE
64	PAPER,PAPERBOARD AND MFR		8297.7		11463.6		10922.8		10441.0	PAPIERS,CARTONS & OUVRAGES
641	PAPER AND PAPERBOARD	MW 14025	7742.6	MW 14234	10654.2	MW 13955	10002.7	MW 14988	9478.8	PAPIERS ET CARTONS
6411	NEWSPRINT	MW 9387	4592.6	MW 9166	6061.3	W 8593681	5633.1	W 8906106	4886.5	PAPIER JOURNAL
6412	PRINTG,WRITING PAPER NES	W 699757	592.3	W 790876	932.9	W 936307	940.3	W 1143296	1030.9	PAPIERS POUR L'IMPRESSION
64122	— COATED,IMPREGNATD ETC	W 569403	492.0	W 615116	729.3	W 667438	698.7	W 836571	778.9	PAPIERS IMPRESSION COUCHES
6413	KRAFT PAPER,PAPERBOARD	W 914187	444.5	W 932530	641.3	W 949326	553.3	W 1000597	560.6	PAPIER ET CARTON KRAFT
6415	PAPER,PAPERBRD,BULK,NES	W 2412181	1430.6	W 2713143	2220.0	W 2761262	2052.5	W 3131806	2120.2	PAPIERS,CARTONS ROULEAUX

5. General Exports F.O.B. by Commodities according to the S.I.T.C. (Rev. 2) in million U.S. Dollars
Exportations Générales F.O.B. par Produits d'après la C.T.C.I. (Rév. 2) en millions de Dollars E.U.

SITC CTCI	COMMODITY	1994 QUANTITY QUANTITE	1994 VALUE VALEUR	1995 QUANTITY QUANTITE	1995 VALUE VALEUR	1996 QUANTITY QUANTITE	1996 VALUE VALEUR	1997 QUANTITY QUANTITE	1997 VALUE VALEUR	PRODUIT
64159	OTHER PAPER ETC,BULK,NES	W 2070746	1309.7	W 2413198	2061.2	W 2429621	1939.1	W 2744207	2006.7	AUT PAPIER ROULEAUX FEUILLES
642	PAPER,ETC,PRECUT,ARTS OF		555.2		809.5		920.2		962.2	PAP,CARTONS DECOUPES
65	TEXTILE YARN,FABRICS,ETC		1171.5		1375.8		1653.0		1845.7	FILS,TISSUS,ARTICLES TEXTILE
66	NONMETAL MINERAL MFS NES		1231.3		1450.5		1641.0		1775.0	ART MIN NON METALLIQUES
67	IRON AND STEEL		2777.0		3129.4		3201.5		3181.2	FER ET ACIER
673	IRON,STEEL SHAPES ETC	W 1354097	664.6	W 1437704	755.3	W 1675659	841.5	W 1649252	838.9	BARRES,PROFIL FER,ACIER
674	IRN,STL UNIV,PLATE,SHEET	W 1373203	836.7	W 1299183	827.2	W 1369944	836.1	W 1313069	796.6	LARGES PLATS,TOLES
678	IRON,STL TUBES,PIPES,ETC		488.4		566.3		605.8		632.6	TUBES,TUYAUX EN FONTE,FER
68	NON-FERROUS METALS		6377.9		8211.1		7897.0		8298.0	METAUX NON FERREUX
682	COPPER EXC CEMENT COPPER		1121.7		1718.3		1532.5		1425.7	CUIVRE
6821	COPPER NES,ALLOYS,UNWRT	W 388843	906.7	W 471895	1407.2	W 465743	1202.9	W 457172	1105.3	CUIVRE BRUT
68212	COPPER REFINED,UNWROUGHT	W 388787	906.6	W 430666	1288.3	W 460838	1190.2	W 381968	885.0	CUIVRE AFFINE BRUT
683	NICKEL	W 94336	602.5	W 98833	844.1		889.3	W 116610	860.8	NICKEL
6831	NICKEL,ALLOYS UNWROUGHT	W 82467	492.5	W 86234	711.1	W 97155	758.0	W 101022	709.2	NICKEL ET ALLIAGES BRUTS
684	ALUMINIUM		3500.2		4264.0		3939.1		4350.8	ALUMINIUM
6841	ALUMINIUM,ALLOYS,UNWRGHT	W 1877362	2766.1	W 1718805	3283.8	W 1820450	2987.9	W 1884608	3244.4	ALUMINIUM,ALLIAGES BRUTS
6842	ALUMINIUM,ALLOYS WORKED		734.1		980.3		951.2		1106.5	ALUMINIUM,ALLIAGES OUVRE
68422	ALUMNM PLATE,SHEET,STRIP	W 227494	454.7	W 251442	600.7	W 257137	552.1	W 263700	596.6	TOLES, PLANCHES EN ALU
686	ZINC	W 568445	575.1	W 546810	608.3	W 588932	656.4	W 557063	766.1	ZINC
6861	ZINC,ALLOYS UNWROUGHT	W 560237	561.1	W 538783	591.4	W 581770	641.8	W 547644	744.1	ZINC ET ALLIAGES BRUTS
69	METAL MANUFACTURES NES		2297.6		2745.0		3156.2		3651.4	ART MANUFACT EN METAL NDA
699	BASE METAL MFRS NES		1076.2		1252.1		1480.9		1749.2	ART MANUFACTURES MET NDA
6991	LOCKSMITHS WARES,ETC		368.2		433.1		615.4		802.1	ARTICLES DE SERRURERIE
69913	BASE MTL DOOR,ETC FITTING		262.1		326.1		533.3		733.4	GARNITURES POUR MEUBLES
7	MACHINES,TRANSPORT EQUIP		66531.3		75081.1		78636.9		83679.1	MACHINES MATERIEL TRANSPORT
71	POWER GENERATING EQUIPMT		3664.1		4122.2		5272.3		5231.7	MACHINES GENERATRICES
713	INTRNL COMBUS PSTN ENGIN		1841.9		1766.5		2526.0		2721.5	MOTEURS EXPL COMB INT, PIECE
7132	MOTOR VEHCL PISTN ENGINS	N 749163	1124.2	N 628386	1005.0	N 896794	1741.6	N 1040570	1999.7	MOTEURS EXPL POUR VEHICULES
7139	PISTON ENGINE PARTS NES		689.6		723.2		692.7		683.5	PIECES POUR 713.2,3,8
714	ENGINES AND MOTORS NES		1190.4		1496.1		1795.8		1723.5	MOTEURS NON ELECTRIQUES
7149	ENGINE & MOTOR PARTS NES		632.1		766.0		886.8		830.7	PIECES 714 ET 718.88
71491	PARTS NES OF 7144,71481		501.1		602.7		672.5		657.6	PIECES DES PROPULSEURS
72	MACHS FOR SPCL INDUSTRYS		2521.9		3134.9		3242.6		3726.1	MAC SPECIALES POUR INDUST
721	AGRIC MACHY,EXC TRACTORS		442.0		484.2		587.2		652.7	MACHINES AGRICOLES
728	OTH MACHY FOR SPCL INDUS		1006.8		1253.6		1195.2		1499.7	AUT MACH IND PARTICULIERES
7284	MACHY FOR SPCL INDUS NES		864.8		1090.1		997.7		1276.0	MACH SPEC IND PARTICUL.
73	METALWORKING MACHINERY		459.3		553.3		632.6		781.5	MACH TRAVAIL DES METAUX
74	GENRL INDUSTRL MACHY NES		4466.9		5100.8		5415.6		5630.5	MACH APP INDUSTRIE
741	HEATING,COOLING EQUIPMNT		506.2		533.2		636.4		713.2	MACH CHAUFFAGE,PIECES
743	PUMPS NES,CENTRFUGES ETC		458.9		601.2		829.0		787.2	POMPES COMPRES,VENT ETC
744	MECHANICAL HANDLING EQU		826.7		1004.6		1114.2		1273.5	EQUIP MANUTENTION PIECES
749	NONELEC MACH PTS,ACC NES		2175.2		2357.7		2119.2		2076.7	PIECES MACH NON ELEC NDA
7499	OTH NONELEC MCHY PTS NES		1214.2		1271.0		945.2		812.7	PIECES NON ELECT NDA
74991	FOUNDRY MOULDS ETC NES		1175.6		1224.6		901.6		771.5	MOULES POUR METAUX
75	OFFICE MACHNES,ADP EQUIP		4643.1		5901.6		5178.2		5108.3	MACH BUREAU TRAIT AUTOM
752	AUTOMTIC DATA PROC EQUIP		1647.7		1937.1		1691.8		1825.4	MACH TRAIT INFORMATION
7523	DIGITL CENTRL PROCESSORS		835.6		899.7		773.1		864.7	UNITES CENTRALES
759	OFFICE,ADP MCH PTS,ACCES		2925.5		3875.8		3374.8		3112.3	PIECES DU 751 ET 752
7599	ACCTG,ETC,ADP MCH PTS,AC		2763.7		3751.1		3242.2		2965.6	PIECES DU 751 ET 752
76	TELECOMM,SOUND EQUIPMENT		2701.1		3245.6		4136.8		4603.0	EQUIPMENT DE TELECOM
764	TELECOM EQPT,PTS,ACC NES		2584.5		3103.2		3980.8		4480.2	EQUIP TELECOM,PIECES
7641	LINE TELEPHONE,ETC EQUIP		537.8		744.0		943.4		1095.9	APP TELEPHON PAR FIL
7643	TV,RADIO TRANSMITTRS ETC		517.6		592.4		781.0		987.1	APP EMET TELE RADIO
7649	PTS NES OF EQUIPMT OF 76		1357.9		1545.8		1941.1		2057.5	PIECES DE LA DIV 76
76491	PTS NES OF APPAR OF 7641		1170.7		1316.6		1597.2		1669.0	PIECES POUR 764.1
77	ELECTRIC MACHNRY NES ETC		4605.2		5535.9		6565.4		7510.9	MACH APP ELECT NDA
772	SWITCHGEAR ETC,PARTS NES		1032.8		1069.7		1103.2		1241.7	APP COUPURE,SECT ETC
7721	SWITCHGEAR ETC		571.2		598.8		681.5		821.7	APP COUPURE,SECTIONMNT
776	TRANSISTORS,VALVES,ETC		1891.2		2405.5		3018.5		3537.1	LAMPES,TUBES,VALVES
7764	ELECTRONIC MICROCIRCUITS	MN 289313	1726.0	MN 287879	2206.4	MN 298598	2797.2	MN 328792	3377.1	MICROSTRUCTURES ELECTRON
778	ELECTRICAL MACHINERY NES		696.5		794.1		954.6		1067.1	AUTRES MACH ELECT NDA
7788	OTH ELEC MACHY,EQUIP NES		391.6		444.1		536.5		653.2	AUT MACH APP ELEC NDA
78	ROAD VEHICLES		39877.0		42967.0		42978.3		45906.9	VEHICULES ROUTIERS
781	PASS MOTOR VEH EXC BUSES	N 1627162	23459.1	N 1748876	26000.5	N 1723845	26168.2	N 1752956	26802.0	AUTO TRANSPORT PERSONNES
782	LORRIES,SPCL MTR VEH NES	N 502127	7029.3	N 467285	6952.2	N 437994	6710.8	N 466392	7741.4	VEHICULES SPECIAUX,MARCH
7821	LORRIES,TRUCKS	N 501630	6984.0	N 466569	6897.2	N 437283	6654.2	N 465790	7683.0	VEHICULES TRANSP MARCHAND
783	ROAD MOTOR VEHICLES NES	N 43678	1724.8	N 41284	2133.5	N 45321	2099.4	N 48349	2482.8	VEHICULES ROUTIERS NDA
7831	BUSES	N 23535	583.4	N 14012	537.4	N 22655	740.5	N 20651	782.6	VOITURES TRANSPORT COMMUN
7832	TRACTORS FOR TR-TRAILERS	N 20143	1141.4	N 27272	1596.2	N 22666	1359.0	N 27698	1700.3	TRACTEURS ROUTIERS
784	MOTOR VEH PRTS,ACCES NES		7519.0		7683.3		7801.6		8649.4	PIECES 722,781,782,783
7849	OTHER MOTOR VEHCL PARTS		7384.5		7542.5		7655.6		8457.4	PIECES 722,781,782,783
79	OTHR TRANSPORT EQUIPMENT		3593.1		4520.3		5215.4		5180.6	AUTRE MATERIEL TRANSPORT
791	RAILWAY VEHICLES		955.4		966.0		1014.1		1082.2	VEHIC MAT CHEMINS DE FER
792	AIRCRAFT ETC		2292.8		3005.6		3478.8		3560.8	APP NAVIGATION AERIENNE
7923	AIRCRFT NES2000-15000KG	N 82	921.3	N 108	1396.3	N 137	1811.2	N 134	1607.8	AERODYNES 2000 A 15000 KG
7929	AIRCRAFT PARTS NES		764.5		852.4		1013.6		1271.5	PIECES DU 792
793	SHIPS AND BOATS ETC		345.0		548.8		722.6		537.7	NAVIRES BATEAUX,ETC
7932	SHIPS AND BOATS NES	N 90927	329.2	N 139565	540.1	N 160664	707.1	N 123881	522.9	NAVIRES ET BATEAUX
79321	YACHTS,SPORTS VESSLS ETC	N 89449	308.7	N 138947	532.4	N 160584	704.8	N 123813	518.4	BATEAUX DE PLAISANCE
8	MISC MANUFACTURED GOODS		8058.3		9614.7		11209.0		12595.1	ART MANUFACTURES DIVERS
821	*FURNITURE,PARTS THEREOF		2180.0		2620.0		3112.4		3682.8	MEUBLES ET PIECES
8211	CHAIRS,SEATS AND PARTS		1057.9		1223.6		1395.8		1548.7	SIEGES ET PIECES
82111	CHAIRS AND OTHER SEATS		589.4		570.8		648.4		699.6	SIEGES
82119	PTS NES OF CHAIRS ETC		468.5		652.9		747.4		849.2	PIECES DU 821.11
8219	FURNITURE AND PARTS NES		1061.1		1311.1		1635.5		2035.0	AUTRES MEUBLES ET PIECES
82192	WOOD FURNITURE NES		636.9		746.4		964.5		1221.0	MEUBLES NDA EN BOIS
84	CLOTHING AND ACCESSORIES		830.8		1019.9		1242.4		1490.5	VETEMENTS
87	PRECISION INSTRUMNTS NES		1301.5		1395.6		1608.6		1803.7	INSTRUM,APPAR SCIENT NDA
874	MEASURNG,CONTROLNG INSTR		979.4		1084.7		1210.6		1342.8	INSTRUMENTS DE MESURE
89	MISC MANUFCTRD GOODS NES		3043.3		3774.6		4330.7		4659.4	ART MANUFACTURES DIVERS
892	PRINTED MATTER		663.0		814.1		895.2		1047.1	IMPRIMES
893	ARTICLES OF PLASTIC NES		1176.7		1448.2		1671.7		1900.5	OUVRAGES EN MAT DIVIS 58
8939	MISC PLASTIC ARTICLES		794.5		955.4		1126.9		1279.2	ART DIVERS EN MAT DIV 58
89399	OTHR PLASTC ARTICLES NES		718.4		851.8		1007.9		1155.2	AUT OUV MAT DIV 58
894	TOYS,SPORTING GOODS,ETC		507.9		694.6		823.8		803.9	VOITURES ENFANTS,JOUETS
9	GOODS NOT CLASSD BY KIND		10214.0		10496.7		11442.9		12123.4	ART TRANSACT NON CLASSES
931	*SPECIAL TRANSACTIONS		7285.1		8043.1		8659.8		9560.2	TRANS.SPECIALES
971	*GOLD,NON MONETARY NES	K 229942	2599.0	K 172590	2076.2	K 201749	2502.9	K 221194	2372.3	OR NON MONETAIRE
97101	NONMON GLD UNWRT,SEMIMFD	K 210476	2572.4	K 170976	2060.4	K 197288	2460.2	K 218139	2351.8	OR,ALLIAGES D'OR BRUTS

FOOT NOTES – NOTES

Foot Notes (Continued) – Notes (Suite)

TABLE 1 –
1 Gold exports refer to new gold production available for export.

TABLEAU 1 –
1 Les exportations d'or se réfèrent à l'or nouvellement produit pour l'exportation.

1. HISTORICAL SERIES, 1960–1995 SPECIAL TRADE, IMPORTS C.I.F., EXPORTS F.O.B.
SERIES HISTORIQUES, 1960–1995 COMMERCE SPECIAL, IMPORTATIONS C.A.F., EXPORTATIONS F.O.B

YEAR ANNEE	VALUE IN MILLION C. VERDE ESCUDOS / VALEUR EN MILLION C. VERDE ESCUDOS — MERCHANDISE –MARCHANDISE: IMPORTS	MERCHANDISE –MARCHANDISE: EXPORTS	GOLD –OR: IMPORTS	GOLD –OR: EXPORTS	CONVERSION FACTORS U.S. CENTS PER C. VERDE ESCUDO / FACTEURS DE CONVERSION CENTS E.U. PAR C. VERDE ESCUDO: IMPORTS	CONVERSION FACTORS: EXPORTS	INDEX NUMBERS –INDICES — QUANTUM: IMPORTS	QUANTUM: EXPORTS	UNIT VALUE / VALEUR UNITAIRE: IMPORTS	UNIT VALUE / VALEUR UNITAIRE: EXPORTS
1960	348.80	306.50			3.4780	3.4780				
1961	185.50	27.80			3.4780	3.4780				
1962	197.20	22.20			3.4780	3.4780				
1963	170.20	24.10			3.4780	3.4780				
1964	200.70	27.50			3.4780	3.4780				
1965	228.30	28.00			3.4780	3.4780				
1966	244.20	32.90			3.4780	3.4780				
1967	258.80	30.90			3.4780	3.4780				
1968	281.90	40.80			3.4780	3.4780				
1969	418.80	44.60			3.4780	3.4780				
1970	469.40	47.70			3.4780	3.4780				
1971	573.50	45.60			3.4780	3.4780				
1972	656.90	48.00			3.6700	3.6700				
1973	833.10	47.80			4.0636	4.0750				
1974	869.30	52.70			3.9381	3.9328				
1975	1010.90	61.30			3.9220	3.9220				
1976	913.60	48.50			3.3170	3.3170				
1977	1284.80	74.50			3.4190	3.3600				
1978	1908.20	75.10			2.2472	2.2700				
1979	1986.90	92.10			2.0408	2.0354				
1980	2742.30	170.50			2.4724	2.4764				
1981	3446.60	140.80			2.0563	2.0600				
1982	5086.00	191.00			1.7265	1.7265				
1983	6217.00	246.00			1.4018	1.4018				
1984	7011.00	212.00			1.1825	1.1825				
1985	7605.00	524.00			1.0926	1.0926				
1986	8601.00	355.00			1.2483	1.2483				
1987	8596.00	567.00			1.3777	1.3781				
1988	8626.00	237.00			1.3916	1.3557				
1989	8706.00	527.00			1.2857	1.3014				
1990	9495.00	398.00			1.4330	1.4734				
1991	10468.67	438.00			1.4043	1.4473				
1992	12233.62	327.00			1.4704	1.4538				
1993	12387.06	312.00			1.2440	1.2488				
1994	17110.91	407.87			1.2279	1.2266				
1995	19394.08	686.00			1.3015	1.3018				

2. IMPORTS BY BROAD ECONOMIC CATEGORY AND EXPORTS BY INDUSTRIAL ORIGIN. (PERCENTAGE OF TOTAL VALUE)
IMPORTATIONS PAR CATEGORIES ECONOMIQUES ET EXPORTATIONS PAR BRANCHE D'ACTIVITE.(EN POURCENTAGE DE LA VALEUR TOTALE)

IMPORTS – IMPORTATIONS

	1989	1990	1991	1992	1993	1994	1995
TOTAL IMPORTS–IMPORTATIONS TOTALES							
1 FOOD BEV–ALIMENTATION BOISSONS							
11 PRIMARY–PRODUITS DE BASE							
111 FOR INDUSTRY–POUR L'INDUSTRIE							
112 FOR HOUSEHOLDS–POUR LES MENAGES							
12 PROCESSED–PRODUITS ELABORES							
121 FOR INDUSTRY–POUR L'INDUSTRIE							
122 FOR HOUSEHOLDS–POUR LES MENAGES							
2 IND SUPPLIES–APPROV INDUSTRIELS							
21 PRIMARY–PRODUITS DE BASE							
22 PROCESSED–PRODUITS ELABORES							
3 FUELS–COMBUSTIBLES							
31 PRIMARY–PRODUITS DE BASE							
32 PROCESSED–PRODUITS ELABORES							
321 MOTOR SPIRIT–ESSENCE							
322 OTHER–AUTRES							
4 MACHINERY–EQUIPEMENT							
41 CAPITAL EQUIPMENT–MACHINES							
42 PARTS–PIECES ACCESSOIRES							
5 TRANSPORT–TRANSPORT							
51 PASSENGER CARS–AUTOMOBILES							
52 OTHER–AUTRES							
521 INDUSTRIAL–INDUSTRIELS							
522 NON INDUSTRIAL–NON INDUSTRIEL							
53 PARTS–PIECES ACCESSOIRES							
6 CONSUM GOODS–BIENS CONSOMMATION							
61 DURABLE–DURABLES							
62 SEMI DURABLE–SEMI DURABLES							
63 NON DURABLE–NON DURABLES							
7 GOODS NES–BIENS NDA							

EXPORTS – EXPORTATIONS

	1989	1990	1991	1992	1993	1994	1995
TOTAL EXPORTS–EXPORTATIONS TOTALES							
1 AGRICULTURE							
2 MINING QUARRY–INDUS EXTRACTIVES							
3 MANUFACTURING–IND MANUFACTUR							
31 FOOD BEV TOBACCO–ALIM BOISS TAB							
32 TEXTILES–INDUSTRIES TEXTILES							
33 WOOD & PRODUCTS–BOIS & PRODUITS							
34 PAPER & PRODUCTS–PAPIER & PRODT							
35 CHEMICALS–INDUSTRIES CHIMIQUES							
36 NON METAL MIN–MIN NON METAL							
37 BASIC METAL–IND METAL BASE							
38 METAL MANUF–MANUF METAL							
39 OTH MANUF IND–AUTRES MANUF							

3. TRADE BY PRINCIPAL COUNTRIES OF ORIGIN AND DESTINATION (VALUE IN MILLION U.S. DOLLARS)
ECHANGES SELON LES PRINCIPAUX PAYS D'ORIGINE ET DE DESTINATION (VALEUR EN MILLIONS DE DOLLARS EU)

COUNTRIES–PAYS	SPECIAL IMPORTS C.I.F. IMPORTATIONS SPECIALES C.A.F 1991	1992	1993	1994	1995
World	146.6	179.9	154.7	210.1	252.4
Africa	8.3	15.2	8.7	6.5	10.4
Americas	11.2	26.0	19.5	13.4	22.9
– Northern America	2.1	10.4	5.7	5.2	8.4
– LAIA	5.4	13.3	11.3	8.1	13.5
– CACM	0.8	0.3		0.0	0.6
– Caribbean	2.8	2.0	2.5	0.0	0.5
– Rest of America		0.0	0.0	0.0	0.0
Asia excl fmr USSR	16.8	10.5	15.3	18.7	24.5
– Middle East	1.4	0.1	0.5	1.6	1.1
Asia former USSR					
Europe excl fmr USSR	107.4	125.1	105.9	164.1	190.4
– European Union	100.9	116.7	100.4	159.5	186.0
– Eastern Europe	5.2	5.3	3.2	1.5	3.3
– Rest of Europe	1.4	3.1	2.3	3.1	1.1
Europe former USSR			3.6	3.6	0.4
Oceania	0.0	0.0	0.0	0.4	0.3
Other	2.9	3.1	1.8	3.4	
Portugal	50.1	57.9	52.0	72.6	100.4
Netherlands/Pays–Bas	14.3	18.7	13.2	16.8	20.0
France, Monaco	3.1	6.4	6.8	29.0	10.0
Japan/Japon	7.5	9.0	9.3	10.4	12.8
Belgium–Luxembourg	6.0	4.7	5.6	6.6	21.1
Brazil/Brésil	5.4	10.3	9.2	7.2	10.9
Germany/Allemagne	9.3	6.6	7.7	8.5	10.2
USA/Etats–Unis d'Amer	2.1	10.1	5.4	4.8	8.2
Sweden/Suède	3.8	4.0	3.6	8.8	5.9
Cote d'Ivoire	5.5	4.8	4.1	2.2	3.4
Spain/Espagne	7.9	3.7	1.2	2.0	4.4
Denmark/Danemark	2.6	3.1	2.2	8.1	2.7
United Kingdom	2.2	3.3	3.2	2.9	5.3
Italy/Italie	0.9	7.7	2.3	2.2	3.5
Romania/Roumanie	3.8	4.9	3.1	1.4	3.2
Areas n.e.s.	2.9	3.1	1.8	3.4	
Switzerland,Liechtenst.	0.4	3.0	2.1	1.9	1.0
Pakistan	2.2	0.7		3.3	1.7
Israel/Israël	1.6		0.3	2.0	3.9
Russian Federation			3.6	3.6	0.4
Viet Nam			2.8		2.7
Argentina/Argentine	0.0	2.8	1.6	0.0	1.0
So. African Customs Un	0.5	2.2	1.1	1.2	
Ireland/Irlande	0.3	0.0	2.6		1.4
Nigeria/Nigéria	0.7	1.6	0.5	1.0	0.4
Cuba	1.8	1.7	0.4		0.1
Senegal/Sénégal	0.5	0.8	1.1	0.1	1.4
Thailand/Thaïlande	0.5		2.1	0.7	0.4
China/Chine	2.7	0.2	0.1	0.1	0.2
Turkey/Turquie	0.0	0.0	0.5	1.6	1.1
Austria/Autriche	0.2		0.1	1.9	0.9
Bahamas	0.3	0.3	2.1	0.0	0.0
United Rep of Tanzania	0.4	0.9	0.4	0.8	0.0
Togo	0.2	0.9	0.3	0.3	0.7
Gambia/Gambie	0.1	0.3	0.7	0.5	0.8
Kenya	0.2	1.4	0.0		
Mexico/Mexique		0.0	0.1	0.1	1.3
Honduras	0.8			0.0	0.6
Colombia/Colombie		0.1	0.4	0.7	0.3
Guinea–Bissau	0.1	0.4	0.5	0.2	0.2

COUNTRIES–PAYS	SPECIAL EXPORTS F.O.B. EXPORTATIONS SPECIALES F.O.B. 1991	1992	1993	1994	1995
Monde	6.1	4.8	3.8	5.0	8.9
Afrique	0.0	0.0	0.7	0.0	0.5
Amériques	0.1			0.0	0.1
– Amérique du Nord	0.1			0.0	0.1
– ALAI	0.0			0.0	0.0
– MCAC					
– Caraïbes					
– Autre Amérique					0.0
Asie anc. URSS exclus	0.0		0.0	0.0	0.0
– Moyen–Orient	0.0			0.0	
Asie ancienne URSS					
Europe anc. URSS exclus	5.9	4.8	3.1	4.9	8.3
– Union Européenne	5.9	4.8	3.1	4.9	8.3
– Europe de l'Est	0.0				0.0
– Autre de l'Europe	0.0				0.0
Europe ancienne URSS				0.0	
Océanie					
Autre		0.0	0.0		
Portugal	2.5	3.9	1.9	2.9	7.4
Netherlands/Pays–Bas	2.6	0.5	0.1	0.1	0.1
Spain/Espagne	0.1	0.3	0.8	0.7	0.6
United Kingdom	0.0		0.0	0.7	0.0
France, Monaco	0.1		0.2	0.3	0.2
Angola	0.0		0.6		
Seychelles					0.5
Italy/Italie	0.3		0.1	0.0	
Belgium–Luxembourg	0.2	0.0	0.0	0.0	0.0
Germany/Allemagne	0.1	0.0	0.0	0.1	0.0
USA/Etats–Unis d'Amer	0.0			0.0	0.1
So. African Customs Un			0.1	0.0	
Guinea/Guinée			0.0	0.0	0.0
China, Hong Kong SAR			0.0	0.0	0.0
Guinea–Bissau		0.0		0.0	0.0
Canada	0.0			0.0	
Brazil/Brésil	0.0			0.0	0.0
Japan/Japon	0.0				
Areas n.e.s.		0.0	0.0		
Denmark/Danemark			0.0	0.0	
Senegal/Sénégal			0.0	0.0	
Argentina/Argentine	0.0				
Romania/Roumanie	0.0				0.0
Greece/Grèce	0.0			0.0	
Cyprus/Chypre	0.0			0.0	
Sweden/Suède	0.0				
India/Inde	0.0				
Russian Federation				0.0	
Norway,Svalbard and JM					0.0
Iceland/Islande	0.0				

(VALUE AS PERCENTAGE OF WORLD TOTAL)(VALEURS EN POURCENTAGE DU TOTAL MONDIAL)

	1986	1987	1988	1989	1990	1991	1992	1993	1994	1995
Africa	4.7	5.1	2.0	2.3	4.4	5.7	8.5	5.6	3.1	4.1
Americas	8.8	12.9	8.7	14.6	15.9	7.6	14.5	12.6	6.4	9.1
– Northern America	2.7	5.9	2.0	4.4	2.5	1.4	5.8	3.7	2.5	3.3
– LAIA	3.9	5.3	6.1	6.7	11.4	3.7	7.4	7.3	3.9	5.3
– CACM	0.0		0.0	1.2	0.2	0.6	0.2		0.0	0.2
– Caribbean	2.2	1.6	0.7	2.3	1.8	1.9	1.1	1.6	0.0	0.2
– Rest of America		0.0					0.0	0.0	0.0	0.0
Asia excl fmr USSR	2.8	4.6	6.8	7.2	5.3	11.4	5.8	9.9	8.9	9.7
– Middle East	0.0	0.0	0.4	0.2	0.0	0.9	0.1	0.3	0.8	0.5
Asia former USSR										
Europe excl fmr USSR	80.4	71.1	77.8	71.3	71.2	73.3	69.5	68.4	78.1	75.4
– European Union	77.9	69.9	74.0	66.5	67.5	68.8	64.9	64.9	75.9	73.7
– Eastern Europe	1.4	0.9	3.5	4.7	2.8	3.5	2.9	2.0	0.7	1.3
– Rest of Europe	1.1	0.3	0.3	0.1	0.8	0.9	1.7	1.5	1.5	0.4
Europe former USSR	0.8	0.5	1.4	1.4	0.4			2.3	1.7	0.2
Oceania	0.1	0.0		0.1	0.0	0.0	0.0	0.0	0.2	0.1
Other	2.3	5.7	3.3	3.1	2.7	2.0	1.7	1.2	1.6	
Portugal	34.4	30.3	33.7	30.7	32.7	34.2	32.2	33.6	34.5	39.8
Netherlands/Pays–Bas	15.7	12.9	10.8	8.8	11.1	9.8	10.4	8.5	8.0	7.9
France, Monaco	5.9	2.7	2.9	3.2	3.1	2.1	3.6	4.4	13.8	4.0
Japan/Japon	2.0	3.1	5.8	6.2	3.8	5.1	5.0	6.0	5.0	5.1
Belgium–Luxembourg	1.9	3.0	1.8	2.6	3.2	4.1	2.6	3.6	3.1	8.4
Brazil/Brésil	2.4	3.2	5.0	5.0	10.5	3.7	5.7	6.0	3.4	4.3
Germany/Allemagne						6.4	3.7	4.9	4.0	4.1
USA/Etats–Unis d'Amer	2.5	5.8	1.9	4.2	2.4	1.4	5.6	3.5	2.3	3.3
Sweden/Suède	3.9	3.8	4.9	4.9	2.5	2.6	2.2	2.3	4.2	2.3
Cote d'Ivoire	2.7	1.4	1.3	1.8	1.7	3.7	2.6	2.6	1.1	1.4

	1986	1987	1988	1989	1990	1991	1992	1993	1994	1995
Afrique	5.2	24.4	0.9	13.5	6.7	0.5	0.6	18.6	0.9	6.0
Amériques		0.0	0.1	0.2	1.3	2.0			0.3	0.9
– Amérique du Nord		0.0	0.1	0.2	1.1	1.6			0.2	0.8
– ALAI				0.0	0.2	0.4			0.1	0.1
– MCAC					0.0					
– Caraïbes					0.0					
– Autre Amérique					0.0					0.0
Asie anc. URSS exclus			0.0	0.2	0.0	0.6		1.0	0.4	0.0
– Moyen–Orient					0.0	0.0			0.0	
Asie ancienne URSS										
Europe anc. URSS exclus	8.1	7.1	15.3	10.2	11.5	96.8	99.2	80.2	98.3	92.7
– Union Européenne	8.1	7.1	15.3	10.2	11.5	96.8	99.2	80.2	98.3	92.7
– Europe de l'Est					0.0	0.0				0.0
– Autre de l'Europe		0.0			0.0	0.0				0.0
Europe ancienne URSS					0.0				0.0	
Océanie										
Autre	86.7	68.4	83.7	75.9	80.5		0.2	0.1		
Portugal	4.8	4.3	6.8	6.3	8.3	41.5	81.3	48.8	58.8	82.9
Netherlands/Pays–Bas	0.2	0.3	0.8	0.9	0.2	42.7	9.6	3.4	2.1	0.8
Spain/Espagne	0.1	0.2	5.0	0.1	0.0	2.0	6.8	19.7	14.4	6.7
United Kingdom	0.0	0.0	0.2	0.1	1.5	0.3		0.1	14.6	0.0
France, Monaco	0.9	1.2	1.2	0.8	0.6	1.3		5.8	5.1	2.0
Angola	0.7	9.4	0.4	0.1	0.2	0.4		16.1		
Seychelles										5.7
Italy/Italie	1.9	0.7	0.7	1.2	0.5	4.8		1.3	0.9	
Belgium–Luxembourg	0.1	0.2	0.3	0.3		3.2	0.7	0.4	0.0	0.1
Germany/Allemagne						1.0	0.8	0.7	2.3	0.1

4. Special Imports C.I.F. by Commodities according to the S.I.T.C. (Rev. 2) in million U.S. Dollars
Importations Spéciales C.A.F. par Produits d'après la C.T.C.I. (Rév. 2) en millions de Dollars E.U.

SITC CTCI	COMMODITY	1992 QUANTITY QUANTITE	1992 VALUE VALEUR	1993 QUANTITY QUANTITE	1993 VALUE VALEUR	1994 QUANTITY QUANTITE	1994 VALUE VALEUR	1995 QUANTITY QUANTITE	1995 VALUE VALEUR	PRODUIT
	ALL COMMODITIES		179.9		154.8		210.2			TOUS PRODUITS
0	FOOD AND LIVE ANIMALS		59.2		43.4		49.0			ALIMENTS,ANIMAUX VIVANTS
01	MEAT AND PREPARATIONS		3.2		2.6		2.4			VIANDES ET PREPARATIONS
011	MEAT FRESH,CHILLD,FROZEN		0.6		0.7		0.7			VIANDES FRAICHES,REF,CONGE
014	MEAT PREPD,PRSVD,NES ETC		2.6		1.9		1.7			CONSERVES DE VIANDES
0142	SAUSAGES INCLDING TINNED		0.4		0.6		0.8			SAUCISSES,SAUCISSONS
0149	OTH PREPARD,PRESRVD MEAT		2.2		1.4		1.0			AUTRES PREP DE VIANDES
02	DAIRY PRODCTS,BIRDS'EGGS		6.4		6.5		7.4			PRODUITS LAITIERS,OEUFS
022	MILK AND CREAM		5.9		5.8		6.6			LAIT ET CREME
0224	MILK,CREAM PRESERVED ETC		5.8		5.7		6.4			LAIT,CREME CONS,CONC
02242	MILK DRY,1.5% FAT OR LES		0.4		1.6		1.5			LAIT POUDRE INF 1.5%
02243	MILK DRY,OVER 1.5% FAT		5.2		3.6		4.5			LAIT POUDRE SUP 1.5%
02249	MILK(EX DRY) PRSVD,SWEET		0.3		0.5		0.6			LAIT CONS,CONC SUCRE
04	CEREALS AND PREPARATIONS		25.7		13.7		14.6			CEREALES ET PRODUITS
041	WHEAT ETC UNMILLED		2.1		2.3		2.1			FROMENT,EPEAUTRE
0411	DURUM WHEAT UNMILLED		2.1		2.3		2.1			FROMENT DUR NON MOULU
042	RICE		6.5		5.2		4.9			RIZ
0422	RICE SEMI–MILLED,MILLED		6.5		5.2		4.9			RIZ POLI,GLACE INCL BRISURES
04221	RICE MILLED UNBROKEN		5.4		4.7		4.9			RIZ POLI,GLACE EXCL BRISURES
04222	RICE BROKEN		1.1		0.5					BRISURES DE RIZ
044	MAIZE UNMILLED		14.5		4.2		5.3			MAIS NON MOULU
047	OTHER CEREAL MEALS,FLOUR		1.0		0.1		0.3			AUTRES SEMOULES,FARINES
04701	CEREAL FLOUR(NON–WHEAT)		1.0		0.1		0.3			FARINES DE CEREALES
048	CEREAL ETC PREPARATIONS		1.8		2.1		2.2			PREPTNS A BASE CEREALES
0483	MACARONI,SPAGHETTI ETC		0.5		0.7		0.5			PATES ALIMENTAIRES
0484	BAKERY PRODUCTS		0.6		0.8		0.8			PRODUITS DE BOULANGERIE
04842	PASTRY, CAKES ETC		0.6		0.8		0.8			PATISSERIE ETC.
05	VEGETABLES AND FRUIT		8.3		7.1		8.4			LEGUMES ET FRUITS
054	VEG ETC FRSH,SMPLY PRSVD		4.6		3.3		3.6			LEGUMES FRAIS,CONG,SECS
0541	POTATOES FRSH EXCL SWEET		1.4		1.4		1.8			POMMES DE TERRE
0542	LEGUMINOUS VEGETBLES DRY		2.9		1.6		1.5			LEGUMES A COSSE SECS
056	VEGTBLES ETC PRSVD,PREPD		1.3		1.1		1.2			CONSERVES DE LEGUMES
0565	VEGTBLES PRSVD,PREPD NES		1.2		1.0		1.2			LEGUMES PREPARES CONSERVE
05659	OTH VEG PRESVD,PREPD NES		1.2		1.0		1.2			LEGUM PREPAP,CONSERV NDA
057	FRUIT,NUTS,FRESH,DRIED		1.2		1.4		1.7			FRUITS FRAIS OU SECS
0574	APPLES FRESH		0.3		0.5		0.8			POMMES FRAICHES
0579	FRUIT FRESH OR DRIED NES		0.7		0.4		0.4			FRUITS FRAIS,SECS NDA
058	FRUIT PRESERVED,PREPARED		1.5		1.6		2.0			CONSERVES DE FRUITS
0585	FRUIT OR VEGETABLE JUICE		1.1		1.2		1.6			JUS DE FRUITS
05857	JUICE OF OTHER FRUIT,VEG		0.9		1.0		1.2			JUS AUTRES FRUITS,LEGUMES
06	SUGAR AND PREPS,HONEY		5.2		6.3		5.8			SUCRES ET PRODUITS
061	SUGAR AND HONEY		4.4		5.3		4.6			SUCRES ET MIEL
0612	REFINED SUGAR ETC		4.4		5.2		4.6			SUCRES RAFFINES
062	SUGAR CANDY NON–CHOCLATE		0.8		1.1		1.3			SUCRERIES
07	COFFEE,TEA,COCOA,SPICES		2.0		1.7		2.0			CAFE,THE,CACAO,EPICES
071	COFFEE AND SUBSTITUTES		1.6		1.2		1.4			CAFE ET SUCCEDANES
0711	COFFEE GREEN,ROASTED,SUB		1.3		1.1		1.2			CAFE TORREFIE OU DECAFEINE
07111	COFFEE GREEN,HUSKS,SKINS		0.7		0.9		1.2			CAFE NON TORREFIE
081	*FEEDING STUFF FOR ANIML		1.6		1.3		1.4			NOURRITURE POUR ANIMAUX
0813	OILCAKE AND OTH RESIDUES		0.7		0.5		0.6			TOURTEAUX
08131	— OF SOYA BEANS		0.6		0.5		0.5			TOURTEAUX DE SOJA
0819	FOOD WASTE AND FEED NES		0.7		0.5		0.6			DECHETS,ALIMENTS NDA
08199	FODDER NES,INCL SWEETNED		0.7		0.5		0.6			PREPARATIONS FOURRAGERES
09	MISC EDIBLE PRODUCTS		6.9		4.1		6.6			PREP ALIMENTAIRES DIVERSES
091	MARGARINE AND SHORTENING		3.4		1.6		2.8			MARGARINE ET GRAISSES
0913	PIG,POULTRY FAT RENDERED		1.3		0.8		1.2			SAINDOUX
0914	MARGARINE,EDIBLE FAT NES		2.2		0.8		1.7			MARGARINES,SIMILI SAINDOUX
09141	MARGARINE		2.2		0.8		1.7			MARGARINE
098	EDIBLE PRODCTS,PREPS NES		3.5		2.6		3.9			PREP ALIMENTAIRES NDA
09805	SOUPS AND BROTHS		1.2		1.0		1.4			SOUPES,POTAGES,BOUILLONS
09809	MISC FOOD PREPRTIONS NES		1.7		1.2		2.0			PREP ALIMENTAIRES NDA
1	BEVERAGES AND TOBACCO		6.2		7.1		6.8			BOISSONS ET TABACS
11	BEVERAGES		5.3		6.4		6.0			BOISSONS
111	NON–ALCOHL BEVERAGES NES		1.7		2.0		2.0			BOISSONS NON ALCOOLIQUES
11101	WATERS,ICE AND SNOW		0.3		0.5		0.5			EAU,EAUX MINERALES
11102	FLAVORED WATERS NON–ALCO		1.4		1.6		1.6			LIMONADES,EAUX GAZEUSES
112	ALCOHOLIC BEVERAGES		3.7		4.4		4.0			BOISSONS ALCOOLIQUES
1121	WINE OF FRESH GRAPES ETC		2.5		2.9		2.8			VINS DE RAISINS FRAIS
11212	WINE OF FRESH GRAPES		2.2		2.6		2.6			VINS DE MOUTS DE RAISINS
1123	BEER,ALE,STOUT,PORTER		0.6		0.7		0.7			BIERES
1124	DISTILLED ALCOHOLIC BEVS		0.7		0.9		0.6			ALCOOLS,EAUX–DE–VIE
11241	WHISKY		0.6		0.7		0.6			WHISKY
12	TOBACCO AND MANUFACTURES		1.0		0.8		0.8			TABACS BRUTS FABRIQUES
121	TOBACCO UNMNFCTRD,REFUSE		1.0		0.8		0.8			TABACS BRUTS,DECHETS
1212	TOBACCO STRIPPED OR PART		1.0		0.8		0.8			TABACS PART ECOTES
12129	— OTHER TYPES		1.0		0.8		0.8			AUTRES SECHES AIR CHAUD
2	CRUDE MATERLS,EXCL FUELS		4.0		3.7		4.3			MAT BRUTES NON COMESTIBLES
24	CORK AND WOOD		3.1		3.3		3.7			LIEGE ET BOIS
247	OTH WOOD ROUGH,SQUARED		0.2		0.2		0.9			BOIS BRUTS EQUARRIS
248	WOOD SHAPED,SLEEPERS		3.0		3.1		2.9			BOIS SIMPLEMENT TRAVAILLES
2482	LUMBER SHAPED CONIFER		1.5		0.9		1.0			CONIFERES SCIES,RABOTES
24821	LUMBER SAWN ETC CONIFER		1.5		0.9		1.0			CONIFERES SCIES LONGITUD
2483	LUMBER SHAPED NON–CONIFR		1.6		2.3		2.0			NON CONIFERES SCIES,RABOTES
24831	LUMBER SAWN ETC NON–CON		1.6		2.3		1.9			SCIES LONGITUDINALEMENT
3	MINERAL FUELS ETC		12.8		8.5		7.6			COMBUSTIBLES MINERAUX LUB
33	PETROLEUM AND PRODUCTS		10.3		7.0		6.1			PETROLE ET DERIVES
334	PETROLEUM PRODUCTS,REFIN		10.1		7.0		6.0			PRODUITS RAFFINES
3341	GASOLINE,OTH LIGHT OILS		2.8		1.2		1.2			ESSENCES POUR MOTEURS
33411	MOTOR,AVIATION SPIRIT		2.8		1.2		1.2			ESSENCES MOTEURS D'AVIONS
3342	KEROSENE,OTH MEDIUM OILS		1.4		0.5		0.6			PETR LAMPANTS,AUT HUIL
33421	KEROSENE INCL JET FUEL		1.4		0.5		0.6			PETROLES LAMPANTS
3343	GAS OILS		4.6		4.4		3.2			GAS OILS
3345	LUBS,PETROLEUM OILS NES		1.1		0.8		1.1			HUILES LUBRIFIANTES
33451	LUBS(HIGH PETR CONT) ETC		1.1		0.8		1.1			HUILES LUBRIF,H LOURDES
341	*GAS,NATURAL AND MANUFCT		2.6		1.5		1.5			GAZ NATUREL,GAZ MANUFACT
3413	PETROLM GASES,LIQUEFIED		2.6		1.5		1.5			GAZ DE PETROLE LIQUEFIE
34131	LIQUEFIED PROPANE,BUTANE		2.6		1.5		1.5			PROPANE,BUTANE LIQUEFIES
4	ANIMAL,VEGETABLE OIL,FAT		8.6		3.0		9.0			HUILES,GRAISSES ANIM,VEG
42	FIXED VEGETABLE OIL,FAT		8.4		2.8		8.4			HUILES VEGETALES FIXES
423	FIXED VEG OILS,SOFT		5.0		1.6		4.5			HUILES VEGET DOUCES FIXES
4232	SOYA BEAN OIL		0.5		0.1		1.8			HUILE DE SOJA

4. Special Imports C.I.F. by Commodities according to the S.I.T.C. (Rev. 2) in million U.S. Dollars
Importations Spéciales C.A.F. par Produits d'après la C.T.C.I. (Rév. 2) en millions de Dollars E.U.

SITC CTCI	COMMODITY	1992		1993		1994		1995		PRODUIT
		QUANTITY QUANTITE	VALUE VALEUR	QUANTITY QUANTITE	VALUE VALEUR	QUANTITY QUANTITE	VALUE VALEUR	QUANTITY QUANTITE	VALUE VALEUR	
4235	OLIVE OIL		2.2		1.0		1.8			HUILE D'OLIVE
4239	OTH FIXED VEG OILS,SOFT		2.4		0.6		1.0			AUTRES HUILES FIXES
42391	RAPE,COLZA,MUSTARD OILS		2.4				1.0			H NAVETTE COLZA MOUTARDE
424	FIXED VEG OIL NONSOFT		3.4		1.2		4.0			AUTRES HUILES VEG FIXES
4249	FIXED VEGETABLE OILS NES		3.4		1.2		4.0			HUILES VEGET FIXES NDA
5	CHEMCLS,RELATED PROD NES		10.9		10.3		10.9			PRODUITS CHIMIQUES
53	DYES,TANNING,COLOUR PROD		0.9		0.9		0.9			PROD TEINTURE,COLORANTS
533	PIGMENTS,PAINTS,ETC		0.9		0.9		0.8			PIGMENTS,PEINTURES,VERNIS
5334	VARNISHES,DISTEMPERS ETC		0.7		0.7		0.6			PEINTURES A L'EAU
53342	OTH PAINTS,VARNISHES ETC		0.6		0.5		0.3			AUTRES PEINTURES,VERNIS
541	*MEDICINAL,PHARM PRODUCT		2.5		2.8		2.9			PROD MEDICINAUX PHARMACEUT
5417	MEDICAMENTS		0.4		0.6		0.6			MEDICAMENTS
5419	PHARMACEUTICAL GOODS NES		1.8		2.1		1.9			PREP,ART PHARMACEUTIQUES
54191	BANDAGES PREPARED ETC		1.6		1.9		1.7			OUATES,GAZES,BANDES
55	PERFUME,CLEANING ETC PRD		2.7		2.4		2.7			PROD POUR PARFUM,TOILETTE
553	PERFUMERY,COSMETICS,ETC		0.7		0.7		0.9			PRODUITS DE PARFUMERIE
554	SOAP,CLEANSING ETC PREPS		2.0		1.7		1.8			SAVONS,PRODUITS DETERSIFS
5541	SOAPS		0.8		0.5		0.5			SAVONS,PROD TENSIO–ACTIFS
5542	WASHING PREPARATIONS ETC		1.1		1.2		1.2			PROD ORG TENSIO–ACT NDA
58	PLASTIC MATERIALS ETC		3.5		2.0		1.9			MAT PLAST ARTIFICIELLES
582	PROD OF CONDENSATION ETC		1.0		0.7		0.2			PROD CONDENS,POLYCOND
5825	POLYURETHANES		0.9		0.6		0.1			POLYURETHANES
58259	— OTHER FORMS,INC WASTE		0.9		0.6		0.1			POLYURETHAN AUT FORMES
583	POLYMERIZATION ETC PRODS		2.5		1.3		1.7			PROD POLYMERISATION
5834	POLYVINYL CHLORIDE		2.2		0.9		1.2			CHLORURE DE POLYVINYLE
58342	— MONOFIL,TUBES,ETC		2.1		0.9		1.0			SOUS FORME DE MONOFILS
59	CHEMICAL MATERIALS NES		1.1		1.4		2.0			MAT PROD CHIMIQUES NDA
591	PESTICIDES,DISINFECTANTS		0.4		0.5		0.6			DESINF,INSECT,FONG,HERB
592	STARCH,INULIN,GLUTEN,ETC		0.2		0.3		0.7			AMIDONS,INUL,GLUT FROM
5922	ALBUMINOID SUBSTAN,GLUES		0.2		0.3		0.7			MAT ALBUMIN,COLLES
59229	PREPARED GLUES NES,ETC		0.2		0.3		0.7			COLLES PREPAREES NDA
598	MISCEL CHEM PRODUCTS NES		0.5		0.7		0.8			PROD DIV INDUST CHIM NDA
5989	CHEM PRODUCTS,PREPS NES		0.4		0.6		0.7			PROD PREP CHIMIQUES NDA
6	BASIC MANUFACTURES		28.4		29.0		32.8			ART MANUFACTURES
62	RUBBER MANUFACTURES NES		2.0		1.8		1.7			CAOUTCHOUC MANUFACTURE
625	RUBBER TYRES, TUBES ETC		1.4		1.3		1.2			PNEUS CAOUTCHOUC VULCANISE
6251	TYRES NEW FOR MOTOR CARS		0.6		0.6		0.7			PNEUS POUR VOITURES
6252	TYRES,NEW,BUS OR LORRY		0.6		0.5		0.3			PNEUS POUR AUTOBUS,CAMIONS
63	WOOD,CORK MANUFACTRS NES		1.1		0.8		1.1			OUVRAGES LIEGE ET BOIS
634	VENEERS,PLYWOOD,ETC		0.9		0.6		0.8			PLACAGES,CONTRE–PLAQUES
64	PAPER,PAPERBOARD AND MFR		3.2		2.5		2.5			PAPIERS,CARTONS & OUVRAGES
641	PAPER AND PAPERBOARD		0.8		0.6		0.5			PAPIERS ET CARTONS
642	PAPER,ETC,PRECUT,ARTS OF		2.5		1.9		2.0			PAP,CARTONS DECOUPES
6421	PAPER ETC CONTAINERS		0.6		0.4		0.4			BOITES,SACS EMBALLAGES
6423	EXERCISE BOOKS ETC		0.5		0.6		0.5			REGISTRES,CAHIERS,CARNETS
6424	PAPER ETC CT TO SIZE NES		0.8		0.6		0.7			PAP,CARTONS DECOUPES
65	TEXTILE YARN,FABRICS,ETC		2.3		2.5		2.2			FILS,TISSUS,ARTICLES TEXTILE
652	COTTON FABRICS,WOVEN		0.5		0.6		0.4			TISSUS DE COTON
6522	WOVEN COTTON BLEACHD,ETC		0.4		0.6		0.4			TISSUS COTON BLANCHIS ETC
657	SPECIAL TXTL FABRC,PRODS		0.5		0.7		0.4			TISSUS SPECIAUX
658	TEXTILE ARTICLES NES		0.7		0.7		0.8			ART FACONNES MAT TEXTILES
66	NONMETAL MINERAL MFS NES		9.8		10.6		12.8			ART MIN NON METALLIQUES
661	LIME,CEMENT,BLDG PRODS		6.1		7.7		9.0			CHAUX,CIMENTS MAT CONSTR
6612	CEMENT		5.7		7.4		8.6			CIMENTS HYDRAULIQUES
662	CLAY,REFRACTORY BLDG PRD		2.4		1.6		1.9			MAT CONST REFRACTAIRES
6624	BRICKS ETC NONREFRACTORY		2.4		1.6		1.9			BRIQUES ETC CERAM NON REFR
66245	GLAZED CERAMIC SETTS ETC		1.9		1.3		1.6			AUT CARREAUX CERAMIQUE
664	GLASS		0.5		0.5		0.7			VERRE
67	IRON AND STEEL		3.4		4.0		3.6			FER ET ACIER
673	IRON,STEEL SHAPES ETC		2.1		2.7		2.0			BARRES,PROFIL FER,ACIER
6732	IRON,STEEL BARS ETC		1.9		2.5		1.7			BARRES FER,ACIER
67327	IRN, OTH STL BARS FORGED		1.9		2.4		1.6			BARRES FORGEES CREUSES
674	IRN,STL UNIV,PLATE,SHEET		0.4		0.5		0.7			LARGES PLATS,TOLES
678	IRON,STL TUBES,PIPES,ETC		0.6		0.5		0.9			TUBES,TUYAUX EN FONTE,FER
69	METAL MANUFACTURES NES		6.7		6.7		8.8			ART MANUFACT EN METAL NDA
691	STRUCTURES AND PARTS NES		1.7		1.2		2.4			CONSTRUCT FER,ACIER,ALU
6911	STRUCTURES,PARTS IRN,STL		1.2		0.7		1.7			CONSTRUCT FER,ACIER,FONTE
6912	STRUCTURES,PARTS ALUMNM		0.5		0.6		0.8			CONSTRUCT ALUMINIUM
692	METAL TANKS,BOXES,ETC		0.7		1.1		1.2			RECIPIENTS METALLIQUES
6924	MTL TRANSPORT BOXES ETC		0.7		1.0		1.0			FUTS,TAMBOURS,BIDONS
69243	IRN,STL COMP GAS CYLINDR		0.3		0.6		0.6			RECIP FER,ACIER GAZ COMP
694	STL,COPPR NAILS,NUTS,ETC		0.5		0.5		0.7			CLOUS,VIS,ECROUS
695	TOOLS		0.5		0.6		0.6			OUTILS A MAIN
697	BASE MTL HOUSEHOLD EQUIP		1.3		1.5		1.6			ART MENAGE MET COMMUNS
6973	DMSTC HEATG,COOKG APPARA		0.8		0.8		0.8			APPS CHAUF NON ELECTRIQ
69731	IRN,STL DOM COOKG APPARA		0.7		0.7		0.8			APPS CUISSON FER,ACIER
6974	BASE MTL DMSTC ARTIC NES		0.4		0.5		0.6			ARTICLES NDA FONTE,FER,ETC
699	BASE METAL MFRS NES		2.0		1.8		2.2			ART MANUFACTURES MET NDA
6991	LOCKSMITHS WARES,ETC		1.1		1.0		1.2			ARTICLES DE SERRURERIE
7	MACHINES,TRANSPORT EQUIP		37.7		38.7		75.7			MACHINES MATERIEL TRANSPORT
71	POWER GENERATING EQUIPMT		1.7		2.3		7.7			MACHINES GENERATRICES
711	STEAM BOILERS & AUX PLNT		0.1		0.2		1.9			GENERATEURS VAPEUR EAU ETC
7111	STEAM BOILERS ETC		0.1		0.2		1.8			GENERATEURS VAPEUR EAU
713	INTRNL COMBUS PSTN ENGIN		1.0		1.0		1.1			MOTEURS EXPL COMB INT, PIECE
7139	PISTON ENGINE PARTS NES		0.7		0.8		0.9			PIECES POUR 713.2,3,8
716	ROTATING ELECTRIC PLANT		0.7		1.2		4.8			APP ELECTR ROTATIFS,PIECES
7162	AC MTRS,GENRTRS,GEN SETS		0.5		0.8		4.0			MOTEURS ELECTRIQUES
71622	AC GENERATORS		0.3		0.5		1.8			GENER COURANT ALTERNATIF
71623	GEN SETS WITH PISTN ENGN		0.3		0.3		2.2			GROUPES MOTEUR EXPLOSION
72	MACHS FOR SPCL INDUSTRYS		1.9		1.2		2.8			MAC SPECIALES POUR INDUST
723	CIVIL ENGNEERG EQUIP ETC		0.6		0.2		0.3			APPAREILS DE GENIE CIVIL
7234	CONST,MINING MACHNRY NES		0.6		0.1		0.2			MACH POUR LA CONST, MINES
724	TEXTILE,LEATHER MACHNRY		0.1		0.1		0.7			MACH POUR INDUSTRIE TEXTILE
728	OTH MACHY FOR SPCL INDUS		0.5		0.6		0.8			AUT MACH IND PARTICULIERES
74	GENRL INDUSTRL MACHY NES		6.4		3.9		9.1			MACH APP INDUSTRIE
741	HEATING,COOLING EQUIPMNT		2.9		1.0		1.9			MACH CHAUFFAGE,PIECES
7414	NONDOM REFRIG EQUIPT,PTS		0.7		0.3		0.9			MAT PRODUCTION DU FROID
74149	PTS NES OF REFRIG EQUIPT		0.6		0.1		0.5			PIECES POUR MACH FROID
7415	AIR–CONDITIONING MACHNRY		0.5		0.5		0.6			GROUPES CONDITION AIR
7416	HEATING,COOLING EQU NES		1.8		0.2		0.3			APP CHANGEMENT TEMP
742	PUMPS FOR LIQUIDS ETC		0.9		0.5		1.4			POMPES MOTO–POMPES

4. Special Imports C.I.F. by Commodities according to the S.I.T.C. (Rev. 2) in million U.S. Dollars
Importations Spéciales C.A.F. par Produits d'après la C.T.C.I. (Rév. 2) en millions de Dollars E.U.

SITC CTCI	COMMODITY	1992		1993		1994		1995		PRODUIT
		QUANTITY QUANTITE	VALUE VALEUR	QUANTITY QUANTITE	VALUE VALEUR	QUANTITY QUANTITE	VALUE VALEUR	QUANTITY QUANTITE	VALUE VALEUR	
7428	OTHER PUMPS FOR LIQUIDS		0.4		0.3		0.8			AUTRES POMPES POUR LIQ
74288	PUMPS FR LIQUIDS NES ETC		0.4		0.3		0.8			POMPES POUR LIQUIDES NDA
743	PUMPS NES,CENTRFUGES ETC		0.6		0.5		1.0			POMPES COMPRES,VENT ETC
744	MECHANICAL HANDLING EQU		0.4		0.9		3.2			EQUIP MANUTENTION PIECES
7441	FORK LIFT TRCKS,ETC,PTS		0.2		0.3		0.8			CHARIOTS POUR USINES ETC
74411	FORK LIFT TRUCKS ETC		0.1		0.2		0.8			CHARIOTS POUR LES GARES
7442	LIFTING,LOADING MACH NES		0.2		0.6		2.4			APP LEVAGE,MANUTENTION
74422	SHIP DERRICKS,CRANES ETC				0.2		0.7			GRUES,PONTS ROULANTS
74428	OTH HANDLING ETC MCH NES		0.2		0.2		1.4			AUT APP LEVAGE ETC
745	NONELEC MACHY,TOOLS NES		0.6		0.4		0.8			AUT MACH NON ELEC,PIECES
7452	OTH NONELEC MCHS,PTS NES		0.6		0.3		0.7			AUT MACH NON ELEC,PIECES
749	NONELEC MACH PTS,ACC NES		1.2		0.9		1.1			PIECES MACH NON ELEC NDA
7492	COCKS,VALVES ETC NES		0.6		0.5		0.7			ART ROB,SIM POUR TUYAUX
75	OFFICE MACHNES,ADP EQUIP		2.5		2.1		2.7			MACH BUREAU TRAIT AUTOM
752	AUTOMTIC DATA PROC EQUIP		2.0		1.5		2.0			MACH TRAIT INFORMATION
7522	DIGITAL COMPUTERS		0.6		0.5		0.7			MACH DIGITALES COMPLETES
7528	OFF–LINE DATA PROC EQUIP		0.6		0.4		0.4			MACH AUXIL TRAIT INFORM
76	TELECOMM,SOUND EQUIPMENT		4.4		3.8		3.2			EQUIPMENT DE TELECOM
764	TELECOM EQPT,PTS,ACC NES		3.9		3.4		2.5			EQUIP TELECOM,PIECES
7641	LINE TELEPHONE,ETC EQUIP		0.9		1.8		1.2			APP TELEPHON PAR FIL
7643	TV,RADIO TRANSMITTRS ETC		0.6		0.7		0.5			APP EMET TELE RADIO
7649	PTS NES OF EQUIPMT OF 76		2.4		0.8		0.8			PIECES DE LA DIV 76
76491	PTS NES OF APPAR OF 7641		2.2		0.5		0.4			PIECES POUR 764.1
77	ELECTRIC MACHNRY NES ETC		5.9		5.3		9.2			MACH APP ELECT NDA
772	SWITCHGEAR ETC,PARTS NES		1.4		0.8		2.5			APP COUPURE,SECT ETC
7721	SWITCHGEAR ETC		1.4		0.8		2.5			APP COUPURE,SECTIONMNT
773	ELECTR DISTRIBUTNG EQUIP		0.8		0.6		0.8			EQUIPMT DISTRIBUTION ELECT
7731	INSULATED WIRE,CABLE ETC		0.8		0.6		0.7			FILS,CABLES ISOLES ELECT
775	HOUSEHOLD TYPE EQUIP NES		1.3		1.5		1.6			MACH,APP USAGE DOMESTQUE
7752	DOM REFRIGERATRS,FREEZRS		1.1		1.1		1.1			REFRIG,CONGEL MENAGER
77521	DOMESTIC REFRIGERATORS		0.9		0.9		0.8			REFRIGERATEURS
776	TRANSISTORS,VALVES,ETC		1.2		0.4		2.6			LAMPES,TUBES,VALVES
7761	TV PICTURE TUBES		1.1		0.3		1.9			TUBES CATHODIQUES
778	ELECTRICAL MACHINERY NES		1.0		1.9		1.6			AUTRES MACH ELECT NDA
7781	BATTERIES,ACCUMULATORS		0.6		0.8		1.0			PILES ET ACCUMULATEURS
77811	PRIMARY BATTERIES,CELLS		0.6		0.5		0.6			PILES ELECTRIQUES,PIECES
7788	OTH ELEC MACHY,EQUIP NES		0.2		0.8		0.2			AUT MACH APP ELEC NDA
77886	OTH ELEC MACHINERY NES		0.1		0.7		0.1			AUT MACH APP ELECTRIQUES
78	ROAD VEHICLES		14.1		14.1		15.9			VEHICULES ROUTIERS
781	PASS MOTOR VEH EXC BUSES		5.7		5.0		5.9			AUTO TRANSPORT PERSONNES
782	LORRIES,SPCL MTR VEH NES		5.9		7.2		6.9			VEHICULES SPECIAUX,MARCH
7821	LORRIES,TRUCKS		5.9		6.9		6.7			VEHICULES TRANSP MARCHAND
783	ROAD MOTOR VEHICLES NES		1.6		1.1		1.5			VEHICULES ROUTIERS NDA
7831	BUSES		1.6		1.1		1.5			VOITURES TRANSPORT COMMUN
784	MOTOR VEH PRTS,ACCES NES		0.6		0.5		0.6			PIECES 722,781,782,783
786	TRAILERS,NONMOTR VEH,NES		0.3		0.2		0.7			REMORQUES,CADRES,CONTAIN
79	OTHR TRANSPORT EQUIPMENT		1.0		6.2		25.3			AUTRE MATERIEL TRANSPORT
792	AIRCRAFT ETC		0.3		3.5		21.7			APP NAVIGATION AERIENNE
7923	AIRCRFT NES2000–15000KG				2.9					AERODYNES 2000 A 15000 KG
7924	AIRCRFT NES OVER 15000KG						21.4			AERODYNES PLUS 15000 KG
7929	AIRCRAFT PARTS NES		0.3		0.6		0.3			PIECES DU 792
793	SHIPS AND BOATS ETC		0.7		2.8		3.7			NAVIRES BATEAUX,ETC
7932	SHIPS AND BOATS NES		0.7		2.8		3.7			NAVIRES ET BATEAUX
79322	TANKERS OF ALL KINDS				2.1					BATEAUX–CITERNES
79324	FISHING VESSELS ETC		0.6		0.6		3.5			BATEAUX DE PECHE
8	MISC MANUFACTURED GOODS		12.3		11.4		14.5			ART MANUFACTURES DIVERS
812	*PLUMBG,HEATNG,LGHTNG EQ		1.1		0.9		1.2			APPAR SANITAIRES CHAUFFAGE
8124	LIGHTING EQUIPMENT NES		0.6		0.6		0.7			APPAREILS ECLAIRAGE ETC
821	*FURNITURE,PARTS THEREOF		1.7		1.5		2.1			MEUBLES ET PIECES
8219	FURNITURE AND PARTS NES		0.9		0.9		1.3			AUTRES MEUBLES ET PIECES
82191	METAL FURNITURE NES		0.7		0.6		1.0			MEUBLES NDA EN METAL
84	CLOTHING AND ACCESSORIES		1.5		1.5		1.3			VETEMENTS
851	*FOOTWEAR		1.0		1.0		1.4			CHAUSSURES
85102	FOOTWEAR LEATHER		0.6		0.7		0.9			CHAUS SEMELLES EN CUIR
87	PRECISION INSTRUMNTS NES		1.2		1.5		2.0			INSTRUM,APPAR SCIENT NDA
874	MEASURNG,CONTROLNG INSTR		0.8		1.1		1.0			INSTRUMENTS DE MESURE
8748	ELEC MEAS,CONTRL EQU NES		0.4		0.6		0.4			APP ELEC ELECTRO MESURE
87483	OTH ELCTRNC MEAS ETC EQU		0.2		0.5		0.3			AUT APP ELECTRO DE MESURE
88	PHOTO EQU,OPTICL GDS ETC		0.6		0.5		0.7			APP,FOURN PHOTO,OP,MONTR
89	MISC MANUFCTRD GOODS NES		5.3		4.6		5.7			ART MANUFACTURES DIVERS
892	PRINTED MATTER		0.9		1.0		1.1			IMPRIMES
8928	PRINTED MATTER NES		0.5		0.5		0.5			IMPRIMES NDA
893	ARTICLES OF PLASTIC NES		2.5		2.0		2.6			OUVRAGES EN MAT DIVIS 58
8939	MISC PLASTIC ARTICLES		1.8		1.5		1.7			ART DIVERS EN MAT DIV 58
89399	OTHR PLASTC ARTICLES NES		1.6		1.3		1.5			AUT OUV MAT DIV 58
899	OTHER MANUFACTURED GOODS		1.1		0.9		0.9			AUT ART MANUF DIVERS NDA

5. Special Exports F.O.B. by Commodities according to the S.I.T.C. (Rev. 2) in million U.S. Dollars
Exportations Spéciales F.O.B. par Produits d'après la C.T.C.I. (Rév. 2) en millions de Dollars E.U.

SITC CTCI	COMMODITY	1992		1993		1994		1995		PRODUIT
		QUANTITY QUANTITE	VALUE VALEUR	QUANTITY QUANTITE	VALUE VALEUR	QUANTITY QUANTITE	VALUE VALEUR	QUANTITY QUANTITE	VALUE VALEUR	
	ALL COMMODITIES		4.9		3.9		5.1			TOUS PRODUITS
0	FOOD AND LIVE ANIMALS		0.8		2.9		2.5			ALIMENTS,ANIMAUX VIVANTS
03	FISH AND PREPARATIONS		0.8		2.4		2.5			POISSONS ET PREPARATIONS
034	FISH,FRESH,CHILLED,FROZN		0.6		1.0		0.8			POISSON FRAIS, REFRIG,CONG
0341	FISH FRSH,CHLLD,EX FILLT		0.5		0.2		0.1			POISSON FRAIS,REFRIGERE
0342	FISH FROZEN,EXCL FILLETS		0.2		0.8		0.8			POISSONS CONGELES
036	SHELL FISH FRESH,FROZEN		0.2		1.5		1.6			CRUSTACES,MOLLUSQUES
037	FISH ETC PREPD,PRSVD NES		0.1		0.1		0.1			POIS,CRUST,MOL PREPARES
0371	FISH PREPARD,PRESRVD NES		0.1		0.1		0.1			CONSERVES DE POISSONS
05	VEGETABLES AND FRUIT		0.1		0.5		0.1			LEGUMES ET FRUITS
057	FRUIT,NUTS,FRESH,DRIED		0.1		0.5		0.1			FRUITS FRAIS OU SECS
0573	BANANA,PLANTAIN,FRSH,DRY		0.1		0.5		0.1			BANANES FRAICHES,SECHEES
07	COFFEE,TEA,COCOA,SPICES				0.1					CAFE,THE,CACAO,EPICES
071	COFFEE AND SUBSTITUTES				0.1					CAFE ET SUCCEDANES
0711	COFFEE GREEN,ROASTED,SUB				0.1					CAFE TORREFIE OU DECAFEINE
07111	COFFEE GREEN,HUSKS,SKINS				0.1					CAFE NON TORREFIE
2	CRUDE MATERLS,EXCL FUELS		0.1		0.1		0.1			MAT BRUTES NON COMESTIBLES
21	HIDES,SKINS,FURS UNDRSSD				0.1		0.1			CUIRS,PEAUX BRUTS
211	HIDES,SKINS,EXC FURS,RAW				0.1		0.1			CUIRS ET PEAUX
2111	BOVINE,EQUINE HIDES,RAW				0.1		0.1			PEAUX DE BOVINS
27	CRUDE FERTLZR,MINRLS NES		0.1				0.1			ENGRAIS MINERAUX BRUTS
278	OTHER CRUDE MINERALS						0.1			AUTRES MINERAUX BRUTS
2783	COMMON SALT,ETC						0.1			SEL
28	METALLIFEROUS ORES,SCRAP		0.1		0.1					MINERAIS METAL,DECHETS
288	NONFERR METAL SCRAP NES		0.1		0.1					DECHETS NON FERREUX
2882	OTHER BASE MTL SCRAP NES		0.1		0.1					AUTRES DECHETS
28821	COPPER WASTE AND SCRAP		0.1		0.1					DECHETS DE CUIVRE
29	CRUDE ANIMAL,VEG MAT NES		0.1		0.1		0.1			MATIERES BRUTES ANIM,VEGET
291	CRUDE ANIMAL MTRIALS NES		0.1		0.1		0.1			MATIERES BRUTES ANIMALES
2911	BONES,IVORY,HORNS,ETC		0.1		0.1		0.1			OS,CORNES,SABOTS
29116	IVORY,TORTOISE–SHELL ETC		0.1		0.1		0.1			IVOIRE ECAILLE
4	ANIMAL,VEGETABLE OIL,FAT				0.1					HUILES,GRAISSES ANIM,VEG
411	*ANIMAL OILS AND FATS				0.1					HUILES,GRAISSES ANIMALES
4111	OILS OF FISH,WHALES ETC				0.1					GRAISSES,HUILES DE POISSONS
41111	FISH LIVER OIL				0.1					HUILES DE FOIES
5	CHEMCLS,RELATED PROD NES				0.7		0.1			PRODUITS CHIMIQUES
541	*MEDICINAL,PHARM PRODUCT				0.7					PROD MEDICINAUX PHARMACEUT
5417	MEDICAMENTS				0.7					MEDICAMENTS
6	BASIC MANUFACTURES		0.1		0.2		1.1			ART MANUFACTURES
61	LEATHER,DRESSED FUR,ETC				0.2		1.1			CUIRS,PELLETERIES
612	LEATHER ETC MANUFACTURES				0.2		1.1			OUVRAGES EN CUIRS NDA
6123	PREPRD PARTS OF FOOTWEAR				0.2		1.1			PARTIES DE CHAUSSURES
69	METAL MANUFACTURES NES		0.1		0.1		0.1			ART MANUFACT EN METAL NDA
7	MACHINES,TRANSPORT EQUIP		0.2		0.1		0.2			MACHINES MATERIEL TRANSPORT
74	GENRL INDUSTRL MACHY NES		0.1		0.1		0.1			MACH APP INDUSTRIE
749	NONELEC MACH PTS,ACC NES		0.1		0.1		0.1			PIECES MACH NON ELEC NDA
7492	COCKS,VALVES ETC NES		0.1		0.1		0.1			ART ROB,SIM POUR TUYAUX
78	ROAD VEHICLES		0.1				0.1			VEHICULES ROUTIERS
781	PASS MOTOR VEH EXC BUSES		0.1				0.1			AUTO TRANSPORT PERSONNES
782	LORRIES,SPCL MTR VEH NES		0.1							VEHICULES SPECIAUX,MARCH
7821	LORRIES,TRUCKS		0.1							VEHICULES TRANSP MARCHAND
79	OTHR TRANSPORT EQUIPMENT		0.1		0.1		0.1			AUTRE MATERIEL TRANSPORT
792	AIRCRAFT ETC		0.1		0.1					APP NAVIGATION AERIENNE
7929	AIRCRAFT PARTS NES		0.1		0.1					PIECES DU 792
793	SHIPS AND BOATS ETC				0.1		0.1			NAVIRES BATEAUX,ETC
7932	SHIPS AND BOATS NES				0.1		0.1			NAVIRES ET BATEAUX
79321	YACHTS,SPORTS VESSLS ETC						0.1			BATEAUX DE PLAISANCE
79324	FISHING VESSELS ETC				0.1					BATEAUX DE PECHE
8	MISC MANUFACTURED GOODS		0.1		0.1		1.3			ART MANUFACTURES DIVERS
851	*FOOTWEAR						1.3			CHAUSSURES
85102	FOOTWEAR LEATHER						1.3			CHAUS SEMELLES EN CUIR
89	MISC MANUFCTRD GOODS NES		0.1		0.1		0.1			ART MANUFACTURES DIVERS
896	WORKS OF ART ETC		0.1		0.1		0.1			OBJETS D'ART
89605	COINS,NATURE COLLECTIONS		0.1		0.1		0.1			COLLECTIONS ZOOLOG,BOTAN
9	GOODS NOT CLASSD BY KIND		3.9							ART TRANSACT NON CLASSES

1. HISTORICAL SERIES, 1971–1996 GENERAL TRADE, IMPORTS C.I.F., EXPORTS F.O.B. SERIES HISTORIQUES, 1971–1996 COMMERCE GENERAL, IMPORTATIONS C.A.F., EXPORTATIONS F.O.B

YEAR ANNEE	VALUE IN MILLION C.I. DOLLARS VALEUR EN MILLION C.I. DOLLARS MERCHANDISE –MARCHANDISE		GOLD –OR		CONVERSION FACTORS U.S. CENTS PER C.I. DOLLAR FACTEURS DE CONVERSION CENTS E.U. PAR C.I. DOLLAR		INDEX NUMBERS –INDICES QUANTUM		UNIT VALUE VALEUR UNITAIRE	
	IMPORTS	EXPORTS	IMPORTS	EXPORTS	IMPORTS	EXPORTS	IMPORTS	EXPORTS	IMPORTS	EXPORTS
1971	8.90	0.50			128.2050	117.6470				
1972	12.50	0.50			117.6470	117.6470				
1973	16.50	0.70			117.6470	117.6470				
1974	21.90	0.30			117.6470	117.6470				
1975	25.70	0.20			117.6470	117.6470				
1976	29.80	0.60			117.6470	117.6470				
1977	35.70	1.30			117.6470	117.6470				
1978	41.70	2.90			117.6470	117.6470				
1979	51.00	2.50			117.6470	117.6470				
1980	85.80	2.20			117.6470	117.6470				
1981	100.42	0.65			117.6470	117.6470				
1982	107.00	1.00			117.6470	117.6470				
1983	110.00	1.00			117.6470	117.6470				
1984	118.00	1.00			117.6470	117.6470				
1985	122.71	1.50			117.6470	117.6470				
1986	134.00	2.20			120.0000	120.0000				
1987	162.60	1.80			120.0000	120.0000				
1988	192.60	1.90			120.0000	120.0000				
1989	215.60	2.10			120.0000	120.0000				
1990	239.70	3.07			120.0000	120.0000				
1991	222.90	2.45			120.0000	120.0000				
1992	278.40	3.70			120.0000	120.0000				
1993	266.10	1.76			120.0000	120.0000				
1994	272.90	2.17			120.0000	120.0000				
1995	332.50	3.43			120.0000	120.0000				
1996	314.90	2.20								

2. IMPORTS BY BROAD ECONOMIC CATEGORY AND EXPORTS BY INDUSTRIAL ORIGIN. (PERCENTAGE OF TOTAL VALUE) IMPORTATIONS PAR CATEGORIES ECONOMIQUES ET EXPORTATIONS PAR BRANCHE D'ACTIVITE.(EN POURCENTAGE DE LA VALEUR TOTALE)

IMPORTS – IMPORTATIONS

	1990	1991	1992	1993	1994	1995	1996
TOTAL IMPORTS–IMPORTATIONS TOTALES							
1 FOOD BEV–ALIMENTATION BOISSONS							
11 PRIMARY–PRODUITS DE BASE							
111 FOR INDUSTRY–POUR L'INDUSTRIE							
112 FOR HOUSEHOLDS–POUR LES MENAGES							
12 PROCESSED–PRODUITS ELABORES							
121 FOR INDUSTRY–POUR L'INDUSTRIE							
122 FOR HOUSEHOLDS–POUR LES MENAGES							
2 IND SUPPLIES–APPROV INDUSTRIELS							
21 PRIMARY–PRODUITS DE BASE							
22 PROCESSED–PRODUITS ELABORES							
3 FUELS–COMBUSTIBLES							
31 PRIMARY–PRODUITS DE BASE							
32 PROCESSED–PRODUITS ELABORES							
321 MOTOR SPIRIT–ESSENCE							
322 OTHER–AUTRES							
4 MACHINERY–EQUIPEMENT							
41 CAPITAL EQUIPMENT–MACHINES							
42 PARTS–PIECES ACCESSOIRES							
5 TRANSPORT–TRANSPORT							
51 PASSENGER CARS–AUTOMOBILES							
52 OTHER–AUTRES							
521 INDUSTRIAL–INDUSTRIELS							
522 NON INDUSTRIAL–NON INDUSTRIEL							
53 PARTS–PIECES ACCESSOIRES							
6 CONSUM GOODS–BIENS CONSOMMATION							
61 DURABLE–DURABLES							
62 SEMI DURABLE–SEMI DURABLES							
63 NON DURABLE–NON DURABLES							
7 GOODS NES–BIENS NDA							

EXPORTS – EXPORTATIONS

	1990	1991	1992	1993	1994	1995	1996
TOTAL EXPORTS–EXPORTATIONS TOTALES							
1 AGRICULTURE							
2 MINING QUARRY–INDUS EXTRACTIVES							
3 MANUFACTURING–IND MANUFACTUR							
31 FOOD BEV TOBACCO–ALIM BOISS TAB							
32 TEXTILES–INDUSTRIES TEXTILES							
33 WOOD & PRODUCTS–BOIS & PRODUITS							
34 PAPER & PRODUCTS–PAPIER & PRODT							
35 CHEMICALS–INDUSTRIES CHIMIQUES							
36 NON METAL MIN–MIN NON METAL							
37 BASIC METAL–IND METAL BASE							
38 METAL MANUF–MANUF METAL							
39 OTH MANUF IND–AUTRES MANUF							

3. TRADE BY PRINCIPAL COUNTRIES OF ORIGIN AND DESTINATION (VALUE IN MILLION U.S. DOLLARS)
ECHANGES SELON LES PRINCIPAUX PAYS D'ORIGINE ET DE DESTINATION (VALEUR EN MILLIONS DE DOLLARS EU)

COUNTRIES–PAYS	GENERAL IMPORTS C.I.F. IMPORTATIONS GENERALES C.A.F				
	1992	1993	1994	1995	1996
World	334.1	313.3	327.4	399.0	377.9
Africa					
Americas	288.0	277.8	298.8	363.7	338.2
– Northern America	261.5	241.8	259.4	319.3	292.6
– LAIA		1.8	2.3	2.6	1.1
– CACM		0.2	1.2		
– Caribbean	26.5	33.0	34.7	39.6	43.4
– Rest of America		1.0	1.2	2.2	1.1
Asia excl fmr USSR	10.2	10.6	10.9	7.9	10.0
– Middle East					
Asia former USSR					
Europe excl fmr USSR	16.7	19.7	15.4	22.0	20.0
– European Union	14.2	16.2	12.6	17.8	17.4
– Eastern Europe					
– Rest of Europe	2.5	3.5	2.8	4.2	2.6
Europe former USSR					
Oceania					
Other	19.2	5.3	2.3	5.4	9.8
USA/Etats–Unis d'Amer	255.1	240.1	256.9	314.8	289.7
Netherlands Antilles	22.4	29.4	30.2	36.4	40.1
Japan/Japon	10.2	9.8	9.4	6.5	8.2
Areas n.e.s.	19.2	5.3	2.3	5.4	9.8
United Kingdom	8.9	8.9	6.1	10.0	6.8
Canada	6.4	1.7	2.5	4.6	2.9
Jamaica/Jamaïque	4.1	3.0	4.2	3.0	2.8
Switzerland,Liechtenst.	2.5	3.5	2.8	4.2	2.6
Netherlands/Pays–Bas	1.9	2.1	2.0	2.5	2.3
France, Monaco	1.2	1.1	0.7	2.2	2.6
Mexico/Mexique		1.8	2.3	2.6	1.1
Italy/Italie		1.9	1.7	1.6	1.1
Sweden/Suède	2.2	0.6	0.4	0.6	2.2
Korea, Republic of		0.7	1.6	1.4	1.8
Panama		1.0	1.2	2.2	1.1
Ireland/Irlande		1.1	0.7	0.4	1.2
Germany/Allemagne		0.2	0.7	0.5	0.6
Barbados/Barbade		0.6	0.2	0.2	0.6
Costa Rica		0.2	1.2		
Spain/Espagne		0.4	0.2	0.1	0.6

COUNTRIES–PAYS	GENERAL EXPORTS F.O.B. EXPORTATIONS GENERALES F.O.B.				
	1992	1993	1994	1995	1996
Monde	4.4	2.1	2.6		
Afrique					
Amériques	0.6	1.6	0.9		
– Amérique du Nord	0.6	1.6	0.9		
– ALAI					
– MCAC					
– Caraïbes					
– Autre Amérique					
Asie anc. URSS exclus					
– Moyen–Orient					
Asie ancienne URSS					
Europe anc. URSS exclus					
– Union Européenne					
– Europe de l'Est					
– Autre de l'Europe					
Europe ancienne URSS					
Océanie					
Autre	3.8	0.5	1.7		
Areas n.e.s.	3.8	0.5	1.7		
USA/Etats–Unis d'Amer	0.6	1.6	0.9		

(VALUE AS PERCENTAGE OF WORLD TOTAL)(VALEURS EN POURCENTAGE DU TOTAL MONDIAL)

	1987	1988	1989	1990	1991	1992	1993	1994	1995	1996
Africa										
Americas	82.1	84.6	90.9	86.5	87.9	86.2	88.6	91.3	91.2	89.5
– Northern America	75.6	75.2	81.3	75.5	76.1	78.3	77.2	79.2	80.0	77.4
– LAIA	0.7	1.2	0.8	0.4	0.1		0.6	0.7	0.7	0.3
– CACM	0.5	0.4	0.8	0.9	0.4		0.1	0.4		
– Caribbean	5.1	7.5	7.9	9.5	11.2	7.9	10.5	10.6	9.9	11.5
– Rest of America	0.2	0.2	0.2	0.2	0.1		0.3	0.4	0.5	0.3
Asia excl fmr USSR	6.6	3.8	3.0	3.5	3.2	3.1	3.4	3.3	2.0	2.6
– Middle East										
Asia former USSR										
Europe excl fmr USSR	10.3	9.6	5.1	7.8	7.8	5.0	6.3	4.7	5.5	5.3
– European Union	9.2	8.4	4.5	6.6	6.8	4.2	5.2	3.8	4.5	4.6
– Eastern Europe										
– Rest of Europe	1.0	1.1	0.6	1.2	1.0	0.8	1.1	0.9	1.1	0.7
Europe former USSR										
Oceania										
Other	1.0	2.0	0.9	2.2	1.1	5.7	1.7	0.7	1.3	2.6
USA/Etats–Unis d'Amer	74.4	73.8	80.4	74.8	75.3	76.4	76.6	78.5	78.9	76.7
Netherlands Antilles		6.4	7.0	8.7	10.1	6.7	9.4	9.2	9.1	10.6
Japan/Japon	4.3	3.2	2.6	3.1	3.1	3.1	3.1	2.9	1.6	2.2
Areas n.e.s.	1.0	2.0	0.9	2.2	1.1	5.7	1.7	0.7	1.3	2.6
United Kingdom	3.1	3.4	2.3	3.5	3.9	2.7	2.8	1.9	2.5	1.8
Canada	1.2	1.3	0.8	0.7	0.8	1.9	0.5	0.8	1.1	0.8
Jamaica/Jamaïque	1.1	1.1	0.9	0.8	0.9	1.2	0.9	1.3	0.8	0.7
Switzerland,Liechtenst.	1.0	1.1	0.6	1.2	1.0	0.8	1.1	0.9	1.1	0.7
Netherlands/Pays–Bas	3.6	2.8	0.6	1.0	1.2	0.6	0.7	0.6	0.6	0.6
France, Monaco	1.0	1.4	0.6	0.9	0.7	0.4	0.3	0.2	0.5	0.7

	1987	1988	1989	1990	1991	1992	1993	1994	1995	1996
Afrique										
Amériques		78.2	84.7	56.8	21.7	14.4	77.7	34.5		
– Amérique du Nord		78.2	84.7	56.8	21.7	14.4	77.7	34.5		
– ALAI										
– MCAC										
– Caraïbes										
– Autre Amérique										
Asie anc. URSS exclus										
– Moyen–Orient										
Asie ancienne URSS										
Europe anc. URSS exclus										
– Union Européenne										
– Europe de l'Est										
– Autre de l'Europe										
Europe ancienne URSS										
Océanie										
Autre		21.8	15.3	43.2	78.3	85.6	22.3	65.5		
Areas n.e.s.		21.8	15.3	43.2	78.3	85.6	22.3	65.5		
USA/Etats–Unis d'Amer		78.2	84.7	56.8	21.7	14.4	77.7	34.5		

4. General Imports C.I.F. by Commodities according to the S.I.T.C. (Rev. 2) in million U.S. Dollars
Importations Générales C.A.F. par Produits d'après la C.T.C.I. (Rév. 2) en millions de Dollars E.U.

SITC CTCI	COMMODITY	1993 QUANTITY QUANTITE	1993 VALUE VALEUR	1994 QUANTITY QUANTITE	1994 VALUE VALEUR	1995 QUANTITY QUANTITE	1995 VALUE VALEUR	1996 QUANTITY QUANTITE	1996 VALUE VALEUR	PRODUIT
	ALL COMMODITIES		313.4		327.5		399.0			TOUS PRODUITS
0	FOOD AND LIVE ANIMALS		42.6		49.3		60.2			ALIMENTS,ANIMAUX VIVANTS
01	MEAT AND PREPARATIONS		8.9		11.2		15.0			VIANDES ET PREPARATIONS
011	MEAT FRESH,CHILLD,FROZEN		7.4		9.1		13.1			VIANDES FRAICHES,REF,CONGE
0111	BOVINE MEAT FRESH,FROZEN		2.8		2.4		2.5			VIANDES BOVIN FRAI,REF
0114	POULTRY FRESH CHLLD,FRZN		2.3		3.4		4.6			VOLAILLES MORTES
0118	MEAT NES FRESH,CHLD,FRZN		2.3		3.4		6.0			AUTRES VIANDES,ABATS
014	MEAT PREPD,PRSVD,NES ETC		1.5		2.1		2.0			CONSERVES DE VIANDES
0149	OTH PREPARD,PRESRVD MEAT		1.5		2.1		2.0			AUTRES PREP DE VIANDES
02	DAIRY PRODCTS,BIRDS'EGGS		4.6		5.2		6.2			PRODUITS LAITIERS,OEUFS
022	MILK AND CREAM		2.8		3.0		2.6			LAIT ET CREME
024	CHEESE AND CURD		1.5		1.9		2.0			FROMAGE ET CAILLEBOTTE
03	FISH AND PREPARATIONS		3.0		3.2		3.3			POISSONS ET PREPARATIONS
035	FISH SALTED,DRIED,SMOKED		1.5		1.5					POISSON SECHE,SALE,FUME
036	SHELL FISH FRESH,FROZEN						1.6			CRUSTACES,MOLLUSQUES
04	CEREALS AND PREPARATIONS		5.7		5.6		6.7			CEREALES ET PRODUITS
044	MAIZE UNMILLED						3.0			MAIS NON MOULU
048	CEREAL ETC PREPARATIONS		4.9		4.7		2.3			PREPTNS A BASE CEREALES
0481	PREPD BREAKFAST FOOD ETC		1.5		1.6		1.8			CEREALES TRAVAILLEES
04812	CEREAL ROASTED, PUFFED						1.8			PRODTS BASE CEREALES
0484	BAKERY PRODUCTS		3.0		2.6					PRODUITS DE BOULANGERIE
05	VEGETABLES AND FRUIT		9.4		9.0		11.9			LEGUMES ET FRUITS
054	VEG ETC FRSH,SMPLY PRSVD		3.3		3.0		3.5			LEGUMES FRAIS,CONG,SECS
0545	OTHER FRESH VEGETABLES		3.2		2.8		2.1			AUTRES LEGUMES FRAIS,REF
056	VEGTBLES ETC PRSVD,PREPD		1.8		2.0		2.6			CONSERVES DE LEGUMES
057	FRUIT,NUTS,FRESH,DRIED		1.0		0.9		2.0			FRUITS FRAIS OU SECS
058	FRUIT PRESERVED,PREPARED		3.4		3.2		4.0			CONSERVES DE FRUITS
0585	FRUIT OR VEGETABLE JUICE		2.7		2.6		3.4			JUS DE FRUITS
06	SUGAR AND PREPS,HONEY		1.4		1.7		1.9			SUCRES ET PRODUITS
07	COFFEE,TEA,COCOA,SPICES		1.9		2.5		2.5			CAFE,THE,CACAO,EPICES
081	*FEEDING STUFF FOR ANIML		2.0		1.2		1.5			NOURRITURE POUR ANIMAUX
09	MISC EDIBLE PRODUCTS		6.0		10.2		11.5			PREP ALIMENTAIRES DIVERSES
098	EDIBLE PRODCTS,PREPS NES		5.7		9.9		11.1			PREP ALIMENTAIRES NDA
09809	MISC FOOD PREPRTIONS NES		5.6		9.8					PREP ALIMENTAIRES NDA
1	BEVERAGES AND TOBACCO		13.0		12.1		15.4			BOISSONS ET TABACS
11	BEVERAGES		11.7		10.7		13.5			BOISSONS
111	NON-ALCOHL BEVERAGES NES		4.6		3.3		4.9			BOISSONS NON ALCOOLIQUES
11102	FLAVORED WATERS NON-ALCO		4.2		2.8		4.4			LIMONADES,EAUX GAZEUSES
112	ALCOHOLIC BEVERAGES		7.2		7.5		8.7			BOISSONS ALCOOLIQUES
1121	WINE OF FRESH GRAPES ETC		1.4		1.2		2.1			VINS DE RAISINS FRAIS
1123	BEER,ALE,STOUT,PORTER		3.5		3.9		3.9			BIERES
1124	DISTILLED ALCOHOLIC BEVS		2.4		2.4		2.8			ALCOOLS,EAUX-DE-VIE
12	TOBACCO AND MANUFACTURES		1.4		1.5		1.9			TABACS BRUTS FABRIQUES
122	TOBACCO,MANUFACTURED		1.4		1.5		1.9			TABACS FABRIQUES
1222	CIGARETTES		1.2		1.2		1.5			CIGARETTES
2	CRUDE MATERLS,EXCL FUELS		5.0		8.0		6.4			MAT BRUTES NON COMESTIBLES
24	CORK AND WOOD		3.2		5.0		3.1			LIEGE ET BOIS
248	WOOD SHAPED,SLEEPERS		2.9		5.0		3.1			BOIS SIMPLEMENT TRAVAILLES
27	CRUDE FERTLZR,MINRLS NES		0.3		1.3		0.9			ENGRAIS MINERAUX BRUTS
29	CRUDE ANIMAL,VEG MAT NES		1.6		1.5		2.5			MATIERES BRUTES ANIM,VEGET
292	CRUDE VEG MATERIALS NES		1.5		1.5		2.4			MAT BRUTES VEGETALES NDA
2926	LIVE PLANTS,BULBS,ETC		1.2		1.2		1.8			BULBES,TUBERCULES
3	MINERAL FUELS ETC		31.0		32.4		38.2			COMBUSTIBLES MINERAUX LUB
33	PETROLEUM AND PRODUCTS		30.1		31.0		37.3			PETROLE ET DERIVES
334	PETROLEUM PRODUCTS,REFIN		28.6		30.1		36.3			PRODUITS RAFFINES
3341	GASOLINE,OTH LIGHT OILS		7.2		6.8		9.3			ESSENCES POUR MOTEURS
3342	KEROSENE,OTH MEDIUM OILS		2.6		2.7		2.4			PETR LAMPANTS,AUT HUIL
3343	GAS OILS		18.9		20.7		24.7			GAS OILS
335	RESIDUAL PETRLM PROD NES		1.6		1.0		1.0			PRODUITS RESIDUELS NDA
5	CHEMCLS,RELATED PROD NES		17.9		17.1		20.4			PRODUITS CHIMIQUES
53	DYES,TANNING,COLOUR PROD		2.3		2.2		1.4			PROD TEINTURE,COLORANTS
533	PIGMENTS,PAINTS,ETC		2.1		1.9		1.2			PIGMENTS,PEINTURES,VERNIS
541	*MEDICINAL,PHARM PRODUCT		3.1		3.0		5.2			PROD MEDICINAUX PHARMACEUT
55	PERFUME,CLEANING ETC PRD		9.5		8.2		10.1			PROD POUR PARFUM,TOILETTE
553	PERFUMERY,COSMETICS,ETC		5.2		4.7		5.6			PRODUITS DE PARFUMERIE
554	SOAP,CLEANSING ETC PREPS		4.4		3.5		4.6			SAVONS,PRODUITS DETERSIFS
5541	SOAPS		1.5		1.4		1.7			SAVONS,PROD TENSIO-ACTIFS
5542	WASHING PREPARATIONS ETC		2.9		2.2		2.9			PROD ORG TENSIO-ACT NDA
59	CHEMICAL MATERIALS NES		2.4		2.9		2.9			MAT PROD CHIMIQUES NDA
591	PESTICIDES,DISINFECTANTS		0.8		1.1		0.9			DESINF,INSECT,FONG,HERB
598	MISCEL CHEM PRODUCTS NES		1.6		1.8		2.1			PROD DIV INDUST CHIM NDA
6	BASIC MANUFACTURES		42.7		45.4		54.3			ART MANUFACTURES
61	LEATHER,DRESSED FUR,ETC		1.0		0.5		2.1			CUIRS,PELLETERIES
62	RUBBER MANUFACTURES NES		1.6		2.1		1.9			CAOUTCHOUC MANUFACTURE
63	WOOD,CORK MANUFACTRS NES		4.9		7.1		6.8			OUVRAGES LIEGE ET BOIS
634	VENEERS,PLYWOOD,ETC		2.5		3.2		2.8			PLACAGES,CONTRE-PLAQUES
64	PAPER,PAPERBOARD AND MFR		5.6		4.7		5.9			PAPIERS,CARTONS & OUVRAGES
65	TEXTILE YARN,FABRICS,ETC		6.4		5.1		5.5			FILS,TISSUS,ARTICLES TEXTILE
658	TEXTILE ARTICLES NES		3.1		2.6		3.1			ART FACONNES MAT TEXTILES
6584	LINENS ETC		2.4		2.1		2.1			LINGE DE MAISON
659	FLOOR COVERINGS,ETC		2.3		1.7		2.5			COUVRE-PARQUETS,TAPIS ETC
66	NONMETAL MINERAL MFS NES		15.4		11.7		15.3			ART MIN NON METALLIQUES
661	LIME,CEMENT,BLDG PRODS		1.3		1.5		2.1			CHAUX,CIMENTS MAT CONSTR
6612	CEMENT		1.3		1.5		2.1			CIMENTS HYDRAULIQUES
662	CLAY,REFRACTORY BLDG PRD		9.4		7.2		10.5			MAT CONST REFRACTAIRES
665	GLASSWARE		1.3		1.5		1.3			OUVRAGES EN VERRE
666	POTTERY		3.4		1.6		1.5			POTERIE
6664	PORCELN,CHINA HOUSE WARE		1.3		0.9		0.8			VAISSELLE,ARTS MEN PORC
6666	CERAMIC ORNAMENTS ETC		1.9		0.7		0.6			OBJETS PORCELAINE,CERAM
67	IRON AND STEEL		4.2		5.8		2.2			FER ET ACIER
673	IRON,STEEL SHAPES ETC		1.6		3.2		2.2			BARRES,PROFIL FER,ACIER
69	METAL MANUFACTURES NES		3.9		8.7		14.9			ART MANUFACT EN METAL NDA
691	STRUCTURES AND PARTS NES						7.2			CONSTRUCT FER,ACIER,ALU
695	TOOLS		1.0		1.3		1.6			OUTILS A MAIN
699	BASE METAL MFRS NES		2.7		6.2		4.9			ART MANUFACTURES MET NDA
7	MACHINES,TRANSPORT EQUIP		82.0		85.6		110.8			MACHINES MATERIEL TRANSPORT
71	POWER GENERATING EQUIPMT		5.4		3.9		16.5			MACHINES GENERATRICES
718	OTH POWER GENERATG MACHY		4.8		3.8		15.9			AUTRES MOTEURS PARTIES
72	MACHS FOR SPCL INDUSTRYS		1.9		1.3		1.1			MAC SPECIALES POUR INDUST
723	CIVIL ENGNEERG EQUIP ETC		1.5		0.6		0.3			APPAREILS DE GENIE CIVIL
7234	CONST,MINING MACHNRY NES		1.5		0.6		0.3			MACH POUR LA CONST, MINES

4. General Imports C.I.F. by Commodities according to the S.I.T.C. (Rev. 2) in million U.S. Dollars
Importations Générales C.A.F. par Produits d'après la C.T.C.I. (Rév. 2) en millions de Dollars E.U.

SITC CTCI	COMMODITY	1993 QUANTITY QUANTITE	1993 VALUE VALEUR	1994 QUANTITY QUANTITE	1994 VALUE VALEUR	1995 QUANTITY QUANTITE	1995 VALUE VALEUR	1996 QUANTITY QUANTITE	1996 VALUE VALEUR	PRODUIT
74	GENRL INDUSTRL MACHY NES		7.4		7.2		9.8			MACH APP INDUSTRIE
75	OFFICE MACHNES,ADP EQUIP		6.4		6.7		11.9			MACH BUREAU TRAIT AUTOM
751	OFFICE MACHINES		0.8		0.8		3.2			MACH,APPAREILS DE BUREAU
752	AUTOMTIC DATA PROC EQUIP		5.7		5.9		8.7			MACH TRAIT INFORMATION
76	TELECOMM,SOUND EQUIPMENT		5.0		7.0		11.6			EQUIPMENT DE TELECOM
764	TELECOM EQPT,PTS,ACC NES		2.1		3.4		7.9			EQUIP TELECOM,PIECES
77	ELECTRIC MACHNRY NES ETC		14.0		12.3		15.2			MACH APP ELECT NDA
775	HOUSEHOLD TYPE EQUIP NES		14.0		12.3		15.2			MACH,APP USAGE DOMESTQUE
7752	DOM REFRIGERATRS,FREEZRS		0.9		1.5		1.0			REFRIG,CONGEL MENAGER
7757	DOMESTIC ELECTRC EQU NES		13.1		10.9		14.2			APP ELECTR DOMEST NDA
78	ROAD VEHICLES		35.0		41.1		37.4			VEHICULES ROUTIERS
781	PASS MOTOR VEH EXC BUSES		22.9		31.4		25.5			AUTO TRANSPORT PERSONNES
782	LORRIES,SPCL MTR VEH NES		2.9		2.3		1.7			VEHICULES SPECIAUX,MARCH
784	MOTOR VEH PRTS,ACCES NES		7.7		6.7		9.9			PIECES 722,781,782,783
7849	OTHER MOTOR VEHCL PARTS		7.7		6.7		9.9			PIECES 722,781,782,783
79	OTHR TRANSPORT EQUIPMENT		7.2		6.4		7.7			AUTRE MATERIEL TRANSPORT
8	MISC MANUFACTURED GOODS		74.9		72.4		90.4			ART MANUFACTURES DIVERS
812	*PLUMBG,HEATNG,LGHTNG EQ		3.2		2.2		2.4			APPAR SANITAIRES CHAUFFAGE
8124	LIGHTING EQUIPMENT NES		3.2		2.2		1.3			APPAREILS ECLAIRAGE ETC
821	*FURNITURE,PARTS THEREOF		16.8		13.2		0.5			MEUBLES ET PIECES
8211	CHAIRS,SEATS AND PARTS		1.0		0.9		0.5			SIEGES ET PIECES
8219	FURNITURE AND PARTS NES		15.9		12.3					AUTRES MEUBLES ET PIECES
82191	METAL FURNITURE NES		4.2		3.5					MEUBLES NDA EN METAL
84	CLOTHING AND ACCESSORIES		18.0		15.5		13.4			VETEMENTS
851	*FOOTWEAR		1.8		2.4		1.7			CHAUSSURES
87	PRECISION INSTRUMNTS NES		1.7		1.6		1.7			INSTRUM,APPAR SCIENT NDA
874	MEASURNG,CONTROLNG INSTR		1.7		1.6		1.6			INSTRUMENTS DE MESURE
88	PHOTO EQU,OPTICL GDS ETC		7.1		6.1		8.1			APP,FOURN PHOTO,OP,MONTR
881	PHOTO APPARAT,EQUIPT NES		2.3		1.3		1.5			APP,EQUIP PHOTO NDA
885	WATCHES AND CLOCKS		4.6		4.5		6.3			HORLOGERIE
89	MISC MANUFCTRD GOODS NES		26.2		31.4		46.6			ART MANUFACTURES DIVERS
892	PRINTED MATTER		4.9		5.0		6.5			IMPRIMES
893	ARTICLES OF PLASTIC NES		4.4		4.2		3.8			OUVRAGES EN MAT DIVIS 58
894	TOYS,SPORTING GOODS,ETC		3.7		3.9		5.1			VOITURES ENFANTS,JOUETS
8947	OTH SPORT GDS,FAIR AMUSM		3.7		3.9					AUT ART DE SPORT
895	OFFICE SUPPLIES NES						3.6			ART PAPET NDA
897	GOLD,SILVER WARE,JEWELRY		3.9		4.8		9.2			BIJOUTERIE,ORFEVRERIE
8973	PREC JEWLRY,GLD–SILVWARE		3.5		4.7		8.9			BIJOUX OR,ARGENT ORFEVRE
898	MUSICAL INSTRUMENTS,PTS		1.3		1.0		1.1			INSTRUMENTS DE MUSIQUE
8983	SOUND RECRDNG TAPE,DISCS		1.3		1.0					SUPPORTS SON POUR 763
899	OTHER MANUFACTURED GOODS		7.9		12.4		17.1			AUT ART MANUF DIVERS NDA
8999	OTHER MANUF GOODS NES		7.7		12.3					OUVRAGES DIVERS NDA
9	GOODS NOT CLASSD BY KIND		4.0		5.1		2.9			ART TRANSACT NON CLASSES
911	*MAIL NOT CLASSED BY KIN		1.2		0.9		0.8			COLIS POSTAUX
931	*SPECIAL TRANSACTIONS		2.5		4.2		2.2			TRANS.SPECIALES

5. General Exports F.O.B. by Commodities according to the S.I.T.C. (Rev. 2) in million U.S. Dollars
Exportations Générales F.O.B. par Produits d'après la C.T.C.I. (Rév. 2) en millions de Dollars E.U.

SITC CTCI	COMMODITY	1993 QUANTITY QUANTITE	1993 VALUE VALEUR	1994 QUANTITY QUANTITE	1994 VALUE VALEUR	1995 QUANTITY QUANTITE	1995 VALUE VALEUR	1996 QUANTITY QUANTITE	1996 VALUE VALEUR	PRODUIT
	ALL COMMODITIES		2.2		2.7					TOUS PRODUITS
5	CHEMCLS,RELATED PROD NES		0.2		0.1					PRODUITS CHIMIQUES
9	GOODS NOT CLASSD BY KIND		2.0		2.7					ART TRANSACT NON CLASSES
931	*SPECIAL TRANSACTIONS		2.0		2.7					TRANS.SPECIALES

1. HISTORICAL SERIES, 1961–1996 SPECIAL TRADE, IMPORTS C.I.F., EXPORTS F.O.B.
SERIES HISTORIQUES, 1961–1996 COMMERCE SPECIAL, IMPORTATIONS C.A.F., EXPORTATIONS F.O.B

YEAR ANNEE	VALUE IN MILLION C.F.A. FRANCS VALEUR EN MILLION C.F.A. FRANCS MERCHANDISE –MARCHANDISE		GOLD –OR		CONVERSION FACTORS U.S. CENTS PER C.F.A. FRANC FACTEURS DE CONVERSION CENTS E.U. PAR C.F.A. FRANC		INDEX NUMBERS –INDICES QUANTUM		UNIT VALUE VALEUR UNITAIRE	
	IMPORTS	EXPORTS	IMPORTS	EXPORTS	IMPORTS	EXPORTS	IMPORTS	EXPORTS	IMPORTS	EXPORTS
1961	5479.00	3389.00	1.20	1.10	0.4051	0.4051				
1962	6134.00	3641.00	0.10	0.70	0.4051	0.4051				
1963	6502.00	5430.00		0.50	0.4051	0.4051				
1964	7368.00	7139.00	0.10		0.4051	0.4051				
1965	6770.00	6507.00	0.30		0.4051	0.4051				
1966	7581.00	7591.00			0.4051	0.4051				
1967	9895.00	7166.00			0.4051	0.4051				
1968	8816.00	8816.00			0.4051	0.4051				
1969	9193.00	9196.00			0.3860	0.3871				
1970	9491.00	8494.00			0.3601	0.3601				
1971	9053.00	8939.00			0.3601	0.3601				
1972	8547.00	9930.00			0.3960	0.3966				
1973	11496.00	8328.00			0.4490	0.4490				
1974	11090.00	11622.00			0.4151	0.4153				
1975	14615.00	10112.00			0.4733	0.4701				
1976	13154.00	13997.00			0.4132	0.4157				
1977	15540.00	19764.00			0.4123	0.4130				
1978	12372.00	16182.00			0.4448	0.4428				
1979	14816.00	16937.00			0.4698	0.4693				
1980	17010.00	24384.00			0.4733	0.4733				
1981	25646.00	21323.00			0.3686	0.3686				
1982	41307.00	35454.00			0.3040	0.3040				
1983	32456.00	28402.00			0.2624	0.2624				
1984	38193.00	37482.00			0.2290	0.2290				
1985	50685.00	41216.00			0.2230	0.2230				
1986	57841.01	22975.01			0.2888	0.2888				
1987	61370.00	39180.00			0.3327	0.3327				
1988	42002.00	19769.01			0.3357	0.3357				
1989	47994.00	42866.00			0.3135	0.3135				
1990	42050.00	32770.00			0.3673	0.3673				
1991	26186.00	13209.00			0.3550	0.3550				
1992	38469.01	28328.00			0.3796	0.3796				
1993	35559.01	31079.01			0.3530	0.3530				
1994	77300.00	83900.00			0.1805	0.1805				
1995	86900.00	85300.00			0.2010	0.2010				
1996	92058.49	58907.80			0.1955	0.1954				

2. IMPORTS BY BROAD ECONOMIC CATEGORY AND EXPORTS BY INDUSTRIAL ORIGIN. (PERCENTAGE OF TOTAL VALUE)
IMPORTATIONS PAR CATEGORIES ECONOMIQUES ET EXPORTATIONS PAR BRANCHE D'ACTIVITE.(EN POURCENTAGE DE LA VALEUR TOTALE)

IMPORTS – IMPORTATIONS

	1990	1991	1992	1993	1994	1995	1996
TOTAL IMPORTS–IMPORTATIONS TOTALES				100.	100.	100.	100.
1 FOOD BEV–ALIMENTATION BOISSONS				14.4	18.4	12.1	8.6
11 PRIMARY–PRODUITS DE BASE				1.8	1.2	1.8	1.1
111 FOR INDUSTRY–POUR L'INDUSTRIE				0.1	0.2	1.6	0.9
112 FOR HOUSEHOLDS–POUR LES MENAGES				1.7	1.0	0.2	0.3
12 PROCESSED–PRODUITS ELABORES				12.6	17.2	10.3	7.4
121 FOR INDUSTRY–POUR L'INDUSTRIE				5.9	11.9	5.9	3.3
122 FOR HOUSEHOLDS–POUR LES MENAGES				6.7	5.3	4.4	4.1
2 IND SUPPLIES–APPROV INDUSTRIELS				19.8	27.4	27.0	29.4
21 PRIMARY–PRODUITS DE BASE				4.4	9.5	13.2	15.7
22 PROCESSED–PRODUITS ELABORES				15.4	17.8	13.8	13.6
3 FUELS–COMBUSTIBLES				16.9	7.4	8.7	8.1
31 PRIMARY–PRODUITS DE BASE				0.2	0.1	0.1	0.0
32 PROCESSED–PRODUITS ELABORES				16.7	7.3	8.6	8.0
321 MOTOR SPIRIT–ESSENCE				5.4	2.1	3.1	2.6
322 OTHER–AUTRES				11.3	5.2	5.4	5.4
4 MACHINERY–EQUIPEMENT				14.5	11.4	22.2	13.9
41 CAPITAL EQUIPMENT–MACHINES				12.4	8.7	20.4	12.6
42 PARTS–PIECES ACCESSOIRES				2.1	2.7	1.7	1.3
5 TRANSPORT–TRANSPORT				20.3	13.4	21.8	24.8
51 PASSENGER CARS–AUTOMOBILES				5.1	1.9	3.4	3.0
52 OTHER–AUTRES				7.8	5.9	11.7	11.6
521 INDUSTRIAL–INDUSTRIELS				7.4	5.1	11.1	10.9
522 NON INDUSTRIAL–NON INDUSTRIEL				0.4	0.8	0.5	0.8
53 PARTS–PIECES ACCESSOIRES				7.4	5.6	6.8	10.1
6 CONSUM GOODS–BIENS CONSOMMATION				13.9	21.7	8.3	10.6
61 DURABLE–DURABLES				1.3	0.6	0.7	1.2
62 SEMI DURABLE–SEMI DURABLES				2.7	2.7	1.5	1.8
63 NON DURABLE–NON DURABLES				9.9	18.3	6.0	7.6
7 GOODS NES–BIENS NDA				0.2	0.3	0.0	4.8

EXPORTS – EXPORTATIONS

	1990	1991	1992	1993	1994	1995	1996
TOTAL EXPORTS–EXPORTATIONS TOTALES				100.	100.	100.	100.
1 AGRICULTURE				17.0	13.2	22.6	24.6
2 MINING QUARRY–INDUS EXTRACTIVES				74.2	79.6	63.9	60.2
3 MANUFACTURING–IND MANUFACTUR				8.8	7.1	13.5	15.2
31 FOOD BEV TOBACCO–ALIM BOISS TAB				1.0	0.7	0.7	0.1
32 TEXTILES–INDUSTRIES TEXTILES				0.0	0.0	0.1	0.1
33 WOOD & PRODUCTS–BOIS & PRODUITS				0.6	1.5	0.9	1.0
34 PAPER & PRODUCTS–PAPIER & PRODT				0.2	0.4	0.1	0.1
35 CHEMICALS–INDUSTRIES CHIMIQUES				0.5	0.7	1.5	0.2
36 NON METAL MIN–MIN NON METAL				0.0	0.0	0.0	0.0
37 BASIC METAL–IND METAL BASE				2.9	0.2	0.0	0.0
38 METAL MANUF–MANUF METAL				3.4	3.7	10.3	13.7
39 OTH MANUF IND–AUTRES MANUF					0.0	0.0	

3. TRADE BY PRINCIPAL COUNTRIES OF ORIGIN AND DESTINATION (VALUE IN MILLION U.S. DOLLARS)
ECHANGES SELON LES PRINCIPAUX PAYS D'ORIGINE ET DE DESTINATION (VALEUR EN MILLIONS DE DOLLARS EU)

COUNTRIES–PAYS	SPECIAL IMPORTS C.I.F. IMPORTATIONS SPECIALES C.A.F				
	1992	1993	1994	1995	1996
World		143.5	154.2	265.5	179.9
Africa		14.2	31.5	25.9	16.5
Americas		2.5	3.2	6.0	4.1
– Northern America		2.2	3.0	5.2	3.8
– LAIA		0.3	0.2	0.4	0.1
– CACM		0.0		0.1	
– Caribbean		0.1	0.0	0.3	0.3
– Rest of America					
Asia excl fmr USSR		16.9	10.2	56.1	18.6
– Middle East		0.4	0.5	0.7	0.3
Asia former USSR					
Europe excl fmr USSR		85.3	71.6	116.1	88.0
– European Union		84.4	71.3	115.5	87.4
– Eastern Europe		0.0	0.1	0.0	0.0
– Rest of Europe		0.9	0.2	0.5	0.6
Europe former USSR			0.0	0.1	0.0
Oceania		0.0		0.0	0.0
Other		24.5	37.6	61.3	52.6
France, Monaco		70.6	59.1	90.7	71.1
Areas n.e.s.		24.5	37.6	61.3	52.6
Japan/Japon		15.1	8.6	52.3	15.7
Cameroon/Cameroun		7.1	8.4	12.9	7.1
Congo		1.2	18.0	4.7	3.4
Germany/Allemagne		4.4	3.2	7.6	2.8
Belgium–Luxembourg		3.0	2.7	6.6	2.8
USA/Etats–Unis d'Amer		1.9	2.4	4.9	3.0
Netherlands/Pays–Bas		2.0	1.7	2.8	1.8
United Kingdom		1.4	1.4	1.6	3.1
Italy/Italie		1.1	1.3	2.9	1.7
Dem Rep of the Congo		1.4	1.4	1.8	1.9
Chad/Tchad		0.7	1.4	1.4	1.5
Spain/Espagne		0.7	0.9	1.4	1.2
Senegal/Sénégal		0.8	0.8	1.9	0.2
Cote d'Ivoire		0.9	0.5	0.5	0.6
So. African Customs Un		0.3	0.2	1.0	1.0
China/Chine		0.6	0.3	0.6	0.5
Canada		0.2	0.5	0.3	0.8
Sweden/Suède		0.2	0.0	0.1	1.6
Nigeria/Nigéria		0.8	0.3	0.7	0.0
Denmark/Danemark		0.3	0.4	0.6	0.3
Switzerland,Liechtenst.		0.4	0.2	0.5	0.3
Ireland/Irlande		0.2	0.3	0.6	0.4
Korea, Republic of		0.1	0.1	0.6	0.4
Korea Dem People's Rp		0.0	0.3	0.5	0.3
Portugal		0.3	0.1	0.4	0.3
Lebanon/Liban		0.2	0.3	0.4	0.1
Malaysia/Malaisie		0.0	0.0		0.9
Morocco/Maroc		0.4	0.1	0.3	0.2
Brazil/Brésil		0.3	0.2	0.4	0.1
Other Africa n.e.s.		0.2	0.2	0.2	0.3
China, Hong Kong SAR		0.1	0.1	0.4	0.3
Norway,Svalbard and JM		0.5	0.0	0.0	0.3
British Virgin Islds		0.1	0.0	0.3	0.3
Turkey/Turquie		0.2	0.2	0.1	0.1
Thailand/Thaïlande		0.2	0.0	0.2	0.1
Afghanistan			0.1	0.2	0.1
Austria/Autriche		0.0	0.0	0.2	0.1
Finland/Finlande		0.3	0.1		0.0

COUNTRIES–PAYS	SPECIAL EXPORTS F.O.B. EXPORTATIONS SPECIALES F.O.B.				
	1992	1993	1994	1995	1996
Monde		91.7	81.5	119.5	115.1
Afrique		4.5	3.5	6.7	5.5
Amériques		0.1	0.1	0.6	0.0
– Amérique du Nord		0.1	0.1	0.6	0.0
– ALAI					
– MCAC					
– Caraïbes				0.0	
– Autre Amérique		0.0			
Asie anc. URSS exclus		0.2	0.8	2.0	0.0
– Moyen–Orient					
Asie ancienne URSS					
Europe anc. URSS exclus		86.9	76.6	108.7	109.6
– Union Européenne		86.8	76.6	108.4	109.5
– Europe de l'Est					0.0
– Autre de l'Europe		0.1	0.1	0.3	0.1
Europe ancienne URSS					
Océanie					
Autre		0.0	0.5	1.5	0.0
Belgium–Luxembourg		71.1	64.9	75.5	69.2
France, Monaco		13.9	9.9	30.2	35.6
United Kingdom		0.3	0.3	2.1	4.0
Dem Rep of the Congo		1.3	0.4	1.9	1.9
Sudan/Soudan		2.5	0.8	0.4	0.2
Cameroon/Cameroun		0.3	0.2	1.8	1.2
Congo		0.0	1.0	1.4	0.9
Areas n.e.s.		0.0	0.5	1.5	0.0
Germany/Allemagne		0.8	0.2	0.4	0.7
Chad/Tchad		0.0	0.7	0.5	0.4
Japan/Japon		0.2	0.6	0.9	
Spain/Espagne		0.0	1.2	0.0	
Italy/Italie		0.4	0.0	0.1	0.1
So. African Customs Un		0.0	0.0	0.3	0.4
Nigeria/Nigéria		0.2	0.2	0.2	0.0
China, Hong Kong SAR				0.6	0.0
Israel/Israël			0.1	0.4	
Netherlands/Pays–Bas		0.2	0.1	0.2	0.0
USA/Etats–Unis d'Amer		0.1	0.0	0.3	0.0
Switzerland,Liechtenst.		0.1	0.1	0.2	0.0
Togo		0.0		0.0	0.4
Canada		0.0	0.0	0.3	
Senegal/Sénégal		0.0	0.0	0.0	0.2
Benin/Bénin		0.1		0.0	0.0
Cote d'Ivoire		0.0	0.0	0.0	
China/Chine			0.0	0.0	0.0
Norway,Svalbard and JM				0.0	
India/Inde		0.0	0.0		
Gabon			0.0	0.0	0.0
Morocco/Maroc		0.0		0.0	
Portugal			0.0	0.0	
Greece/Grèce					0.0
British Virgin Islds				0.0	
Panama		0.0			
Korea Dem People's Rp				0.0	
Denmark/Danemark				0.0	
Finland/Finlande				0.0	

(VALUE AS PERCENTAGE OF WORLD TOTAL)(VALEURS EN POURCENTAGE DU TOTAL MONDIAL)

	1987	1988	1989	1990	1991	1992	1993	1994	1995	1996
Africa			20.9				9.9	20.5	9.8	9.2
Americas			1.8				1.8	2.1	2.3	2.3
– Northern America			1.5				1.5	1.9	1.9	2.1
– LAIA			0.3				0.2	0.1	0.2	0.0
– CACM			0.0				0.0		0.0	
– Caribbean			0.0				0.1	0.0	0.1	0.1
– Rest of America										
Asia excl fmr USSR			12.0				11.8	6.6	21.1	10.4
– Middle East			0.1				0.3	0.3	0.3	0.1
Asia former USSR										
Europe excl fmr USSR			57.9				59.5	46.5	43.7	48.9
– European Union			57.0				58.8	46.2	43.5	48.6
– Eastern Europe			0.3				0.0	0.1	0.0	0.0
– Rest of Europe			0.7				0.6	0.2	0.2	0.3
Europe former USSR			0.0					0.0	0.0	0.0
Oceania			0.2				0.0		0.0	0.0
Other			7.1				17.1	24.4	23.1	29.2
France, Monaco			42.5				49.2	38.4	34.2	39.5
Areas n.e.s.			7.1				17.1	24.4	23.1	29.2
Japan/Japon			7.6				10.5	5.6	19.7	8.7
Cameroon/Cameroun			9.1				5.0	5.5	4.9	3.9
Congo			3.2				0.8	11.7	1.8	1.9
Germany/Allemagne							3.1	2.1	2.9	1.6
Belgium–Luxembourg			2.5				2.1	1.7	2.5	1.6
USA/Etats–Unis d'Amer			1.3				1.3	1.6	1.8	1.7
Netherlands/Pays–Bas			2.1				1.4	1.1	1.1	1.0
United Kingdom			1.2				1.0	0.9	0.6	1.7

	1987	1988	1989	1990	1991	1992	1993	1994	1995	1996
Afrique			4.3				5.0	4.3	5.6	4.8
Amériques			1.2				0.1	0.1	0.5	0.0
– Amérique du Nord			0.6				0.1	0.1	0.5	0.0
– ALAI										
– MCAC										
– Caraïbes									0.0	
– Autre Amérique			0.6				0.0			
Asie anc. URSS exclus			0.0				0.2	1.0	1.6	0.0
– Moyen–Orient										
Asie ancienne URSS										
Europe anc. URSS exclus			94.4				94.7	94.1	91.0	95.2
– Union Européenne			89.4				94.7	94.0	90.7	95.1
– Europe de l'Est										0.0
– Autre de l'Europe			5.0				0.1	0.1	0.2	0.0
Europe ancienne URSS										
Océanie										
Autre			0.0				0.0	0.6	1.3	0.0
Belgium–Luxembourg			50.9				77.6	79.7	63.2	60.1
France, Monaco			34.4				15.2	12.1	25.3	30.9
United Kingdom			0.3				0.3	0.3	1.7	3.5
Dem Rep of the Congo			0.7				1.4	0.5	1.6	1.7
Sudan/Soudan			2.4				2.8	1.0	0.4	0.1
Cameroon/Cameroun			0.2				0.3	0.3	1.5	1.0
Congo			0.5				0.0	1.2	1.1	0.7
Areas n.e.s.			0.0				0.0	0.6	1.3	0.0
Germany/Allemagne							0.8	0.2	0.3	0.6
Chad/Tchad			0.1				0.0	0.9	0.4	0.4

4. Special Imports C.I.F. by Commodities according to the S.I.T.C. (Rev. 2) in million U.S. Dollars
Importations Spéciales C.A.F. par Produits d'après la C.T.C.I. (Rév. 2) en millions de Dollars E.U.

SITC CTCI	COMMODITY	1993 QUANTITY QUANTITE	1993 VALUE VALEUR	1994 QUANTITY QUANTITE	1994 VALUE VALEUR	1995 QUANTITY QUANTITE	1995 VALUE VALEUR	1996 QUANTITY QUANTITE	1996 VALUE VALEUR	PRODUIT
	ALL COMMODITIES		143.6		154.2		265.5		180.0	TOUS PRODUITS
0	FOOD AND LIVE ANIMALS		17.8		24.7		27.6		12.6	ALIMENTS,ANIMAUX VIVANTS
01	MEAT AND PREPARATIONS		2.0		0.6		0.4		0.2	VIANDES ET PREPARATIONS
011	MEAT FRESH,CHILLD,FROZEN	W 238	1.2	W 95	0.2	W 15	0.1	W 13	0.1	VIANDES FRAICHES,REF,CONGE
0111	BOVINE MEAT FRESH,FROZEN	W 85	0.6	W 29	0.1	W 1	0.1	W 3	0.1	VIANDES BOVIN FRAI,REF
01112	BOVINE MEAT BONELESS	W 81	0.6	W 28	0.1		0.1	W 2	0.1	VIANDES BOVIN DESOSSEES
0114	POULTRY FRESH CHLLD,FRZN	W 144	0.6	W 29	0.1	W 3	0.1	W 4	0.1	VOLAILLES MORTES
014	MEAT PREPD,PRSVD,NES ETC	W 269	0.8	W 151	0.4	W 124	0.3	W 47	0.2	CONSERVES DE VIANDES
0149	OTH PREPARD,PRESRVD MEAT	W 226	0.6	W 96	0.2	W 116	0.3	W 47	0.2	AUTRES PREP DE VIANDES
02	DAIRY PRODCTS,BIRDS'EGGS		2.5		2.3		1.6		0.8	PRODUITS LAITIERS,OEUFS
022	MILK AND CREAM	W 1597	2.0	W 1387	2.0	W 829	1.4	W 426	0.7	LAIT ET CREME
0223	MILK AND CREAM FRESH	W 223	0.4	W 601	1.1	W 211	0.2	W 169	0.2	LAIT,CREME FRAIS
0224	MILK,CREAM PRESERVED ETC	W 1373	1.7	W 786	1.0	W 618	1.2	W 257	0.5	LAIT,CREME CONS,CONC
02243	MILK DRY,OVER 1.5% FAT	W 533	0.7	W 187	0.4	W 32	0.2	W 49	0.2	LAIT POUDRE SUP 1.5%
02249	MILK(EX DRY) PRSVD,SWEET	W 837	1.1	W 598	0.6	W 585	1.1	W 208	0.4	LAIT CONS,CONC SUCRE
03	FISH AND PREPARATIONS		1.2		0.6		0.4		0.2	POISSONS ET PREPARATIONS
037	FISH ETC PREPD,PRSVD NES	W 403	0.8	W 245	0.4	W 203	0.4	W 24	0.1	POIS,CRUST,MOL PREPARES
0371	FISH PREPARD,PRESRVD NES	W 399	0.8	W 245	0.4	W 203	0.4	W 24	0.1	CONSERVES DE POISSONS
04	CEREALS AND PREPARATIONS		8.9		17.2		15.1		6.0	CEREALES ET PRODUITS
046	WHEAT ETC MEAL OR FLOUR	W 22393	5.7	W 33624	14.1	W 20892	8.0	W 10190	3.5	SEMOULE FARINE,FROMENT
04601	FLOUR OF WHEAT OR MESLIN	W 22392	5.7	W 33616	14.0	W 20892	8.0	W 10190	3.5	FARINE DE FROMENT
047	OTHER CEREAL MEALS,FLOUR	W 2510	0.7	W 1662	0.7	W 2546	2.1	W 416	0.4	AUTRES SEMOULES,FARINES
04702	MEAL OR GROATS NON–WHEAT	W 1080	0.4	W 1150	0.5	W 2229	1.5	W 416	0.4	GRUAUX,SEMOULES DE CEREALES
048	CEREAL ETC PREPARATIONS	W 3221	2.3	W 3546	2.3	W 3122	4.4	W 1540	1.8	PREPTNS A BASE CEREALES
0482	MALT INCLUDING FLOUR	W 2941	1.6	W 3224	1.8	W 2877	3.8	W 1356	1.4	MALT MEME TORREFIE
05	VEGETABLES AND FRUIT		1.3		1.9		2.2		2.3	LEGUMES ET FRUITS
054	VEG ETC FRSH,SMPLY PRSVD	W 676	0.8	W 608	1.5	W 616	1.9	W 439	1.9	LEGUMES FRAIS,CONG,SECS
0546	VEGETABLES SIMPLY PRESVD	W 372	0.5	W 322	1.4	W 487	1.8	W 404	1.8	LEGUMES CONG,CONSER
05461	VEGETABLES FROZEN	W 372	0.5	W 322	1.4	W 463	1.8	W 404	1.8	LEGUMES CONGELES
06	SUGAR AND PREPS,HONEY		0.9		1.4		2.3		0.5	SUCRES ET PRODUITS
061	SUGAR AND HONEY	W 1791	0.9	W 2452	1.4	W 3013	2.2	W 611	0.4	SUCRES ET MIEL
0612	REFINED SUGAR ETC	W 1790	0.9	W 2450	1.3	W 2997	2.2	W 587	0.4	SUCRES RAFFINES
07	COFFEE,TEA,COCOA,SPICES		0.3		0.3		4.0		1.7	CAFE,THE,CACAO,EPICES
071	COFFEE AND SUBSTITUTES	W 4	0.1	W 1406	0.2	W 18919	3.9	W 10160	1.6	CAFE ET SUCCEDANES
0711	COFFEE GREEN,ROASTED,SUB	W 1	0.1	W 1386	0.2	W 18916	3.9	W 10152	1.6	CAFE TORREFIE OU DECAFEINE
07111	COFFEE GREEN,HUSKS,SKINS			W 1360	0.2	W 18894	3.8	W 10147	1.6	CAFE NON TORREFIE
09	MISC EDIBLE PRODUCTS		0.9		0.7		2.0		1.3	PREP ALIMENTAIRES DIVERSES
098	EDIBLE PRODCTS,PREPS NES	W 261	0.7	W 244	0.7	W 483	1.8	W 242	1.1	PREP ALIMENTAIRES NDA
09806	YEASTS,BAKING POWDERS	W 190	0.6	W 112	0.3	W 246	0.6	W 86	0.3	LEVURES
09809	MISC FOOD PREPRTIONS NES	W 48	0.1	W 94	0.4	W 138	1.0	W 121	0.7	PREP ALIMENTAIRES NDA
1	BEVERAGES AND TOBACCO		8.1		14.3		12.2		9.0	BOISSONS ET TABACS
11	BEVERAGES		2.9		2.1		2.9		2.3	BOISSONS
111	NON–ALCOHL BEVERAGES NES	W 866	0.7	W 937	0.4	W 737	0.4	W 1066	0.6	BOISSONS NON ALCOOLIQUES
112	ALCOHOLIC BEVERAGES	W 1339	2.2	W 1275	1.7	W 2605	2.6	W 959	1.8	BOISSONS ALCOOLIQUES
1121	WINE OF FRESH GRAPES ETC	W 1032	1.1	W 955	0.9	W 2254	1.4	W 685	1.0	VINS DE RAISINS FRAIS
11212	WINE OF FRESH GRAPES	W 1025	1.1	W 951	0.9	W 2254	1.4	W 676	0.9	VINS DE MOUTS DE RAISINS
1124	DISTILLED ALCOHOLIC BEVS	W 204	1.0	W 182	0.7	W 304	1.2	W 198	0.8	ALCOOLS,EAUX–DE–VIE
11241	WHISKY	W 115	0.6	W 155	0.7	W 204	0.8	W 124	0.5	WHISKY
12	TOBACCO AND MANUFACTURES		5.3		12.3		9.3		6.8	TABACS BRUTS FABRIQUES
121	TOBACCO UNMNFCTRD,REFUSE	W 845	4.7	W 801	4.5	W 1074	8.6	W 438	3.7	TABACS BRUTS,DECHETS
1212	TOBACCO STRIPPED OR PART	W 827	4.6	W 767	4.2	W 1065	8.5	W 420	3.7	TABACS PART ECOTES
122	TOBACCO,MANUFACTURED	W 35	0.6	W 375	7.8	W 43	0.8	W 187	3.1	TABACS FABRIQUES
1222	CIGARETTES	W 35	0.6	W 375	7.8	W 43	0.8	W 187	3.1	CIGARETTES
2	CRUDE MATERLS,EXCL FUELS		1.7		10.4		27.2		25.2	MAT BRUTES NON COMESTIBLES
24	CORK AND WOOD				0.1		2.5		4.4	LIEGE ET BOIS
247	OTH WOOD ROUGH,SQUARED			W 17	0.1	W 13773	2.1	W 12034	4.0	BOIS BRUTS EQUARRIS
2471	SAW–,VENEER–LOGS CONIFER			W 17	0.1	W 12997	2.0	W 11995	4.0	CONIFERES POUR SCIAGE,PLACAG
24711	— IN THE ROUGH			W 17	0.1	W 12997	2.0	W 11995	4.0	ECORCES OU DEGROSSIS
26	TEXTILE FIBRES AND WASTE		1.2		9.4		22.5		19.2	FIBRES TEXTILES
263	COTTON			W 4346	8.0	W 12522	20.6	W 6008	17.6	COTON
2631	RAW COTTON,EXCL LINTERS			W 4346	8.0	W 12522	20.6	W 6008	17.6	COTON EN MASSE
269	WASTE OF TEXTILE FABRICS	W 700	1.2	W 1074	1.5	W 1493	1.9	W 1416	1.7	FRIPERIE DRILLES,CHIFFONS
26901	BULK TEXT WSTE,OLD CLTHG	W 697	1.2	W 1049	1.4	W 1484	1.9	W 1407	1.7	ART ET ACCESS D'HABILLEMENT
27	CRUDE FERTLZR,MINRLS NES		0.4		0.7		0.8		0.8	ENGRAIS MINERAUX BRUTS
278	OTHER CRUDE MINERALS	W 3067	0.4	W 5350	0.7	W 4979	0.8	W 3365	0.6	AUTRES MINERAUX BRUTS
2783	COMMON SALT,ETC	W 3009	0.3	W 5083	0.6	W 4764	0.6	W 3288	0.5	SEL
29	CRUDE ANIMAL,VEG MAT NES		0.2		0.2		1.2		0.9	MATIERES BRUTES ANIM,VEGET
292	CRUDE VEG MATERIALS NES	W 10	0.2	W 14	0.2	W 1194	1.2	W 1961	0.9	MAT BRUTES VEGETALES NDA
2922	NAT GUMS,RESINS,LACS,ETC					W 1139	0.5	W 1910	0.7	GOMME LAQUE
3	MINERAL FUELS ETC		24.6		11.7		23.1		14.6	COMBUSTIBLES MINERAUX LUB
33	PETROLEUM AND PRODUCTS		24.3		11.4		22.8		14.6	PETROLE ET DERIVES
334	PETROLEUM PRODUCTS,REFIN	W 91470	24.0	W 73333	11.3	W 135842	22.8	W 95975	14.5	PRODUITS RAFFINES
3341	GASOLINE,OTH LIGHT OILS	W 30002	7.9	W 23368	3.3	W 48858	8.4	W 34827	4.8	ESSENCES POUR MOTEURS
33411	MOTOR,AVIATION SPIRIT	W 19002	5.1	W 12962	1.9	W 27642	5.0	W 20366	2.8	ESSENCES MOTEURS D'AVIONS
33419	OTH LIGHT PETROLEUM OILS	W 11000	2.8	W 10406	1.4	W 21215	3.4	W 14461	2.0	AUTRES HUILES LEGERES
3342	KEROSENE,OTH MEDIUM OILS	W 28658	7.3	W 29499	4.0	W 30299	4.3	W 21568	3.0	PETR LAMPANTS,AUT HUIL
33421	KEROSENE INCL JET FUEL	W 28658	7.3	W 29499	4.0	W 30299	4.3	W 21568	3.0	PETROLES LAMPANTS
3343	GAS OILS	W 28960	6.9	W 17663	2.3	W 51362	7.7	W 35999	4.9	GAS OILS
3344	FUEL OILS,NES	W 3380	1.4	W 1814	0.4	W 4581	1.2	W 2859	0.7	FUEL OILS
3345	LUBS,PETROLEUM OILS NES	W 471	0.8	W 989	1.5	W 743	1.4	W 722	1.3	HUILES LUBRIFIANTES
33451	LUBS(HIGH PETR CONT) ETC	W 470	0.8	W 989	1.5	W 727	1.3	W 722	1.3	HUILES LUBRIF,H LOURDES
4	ANIMAL,VEGETABLE OIL,FAT		0.6		2.9		1.5		0.7	HUILES,GRAISSES ANIM,VEG
42	FIXED VEGETABLE OIL,FAT		0.6		2.9		1.4		0.6	HUILES VEGETALES FIXES
423	FIXED VEG OILS,SOFT	W 133	0.2	W 1612	1.3	W 721	0.7	W 449	0.6	HUILES VEGET DOUCES FIXES
4233	COTTON SEED OIL	W 23	0.1	W 1076	0.9	W 662	0.6	W 208	0.2	HUILE DE COTON
424	FIXED VEG OIL NONSOFT	W 249	0.4	W 2207	1.6	W 456	0.8	W 35	0.1	AUTRES HUILES VEG FIXES
4242	PALM OIL			W 490	0.5	W 400	0.7	W 23	0.1	HUILE DE PALME
4249	FIXED VEGETABLE OILS NES	W 234	0.4	W 1697	1.1	W 56	0.1	W 12	0.1	HUILES VEGET FIXES NDA
5	CHEMCLS,RELATED PROD NES		15.4		25.1		20.8		14.1	PRODUITS CHIMIQUES
52	INORGANIC CHEMICALS		0.9		0.7		1.6		0.6	PROD CHIM INORGANIQUES
522	INORG ELEMNTS,OXIDES,ETC	W 620	0.6	W 514	0.6	W 886	0.9	W 215	0.3	ELEMENTS INORGANIQUES
53	DYES,TANNING,COLOUR PROD		0.4		1.3		1.2		0.7	PROD TEINTURE,COLORANTS
533	PIGMENTS,PAINTS,ETC	W 115	0.4	W 465	1.3	W 136	1.1	W 119	0.6	PIGMENTS,PEINTURES,VERNIS
5334	VARNISHES,DISTEMPERS ETC	W 13	0.1	W 398	1.1	W 80	0.8	W 15	0.3	PEINTURES A L'EAU
53341	WATER–THINNED PAINTS	W 11	0.1	W 381	0.9	W 54	0.8	W 10	0.1	PEINTURES DILUEES
541	*MEDICINAL,PHARM PRODUCT	K 504009	9.1	K 921638	16.8	K 375609	9.6	K 325783	6.5	PROD MEDICINAUX PHARMACEUT
5416	GLYCOSIDES,GLANDS,SERA	K 43413	0.8	K 55550	0.6	K 34348	0.8	K 8010	0.3	HETEROSIDES
54164	ANTISERA,MICROB VACCINES	K 43413	0.8	K 55550	0.6	K 32786	0.8	K 2754	0.2	SERUMS,VACCINS
5417	MEDICAMENTS	K 436121	8.0	K 847721	16.0	K 320603	8.4	K 299334	6.0	MEDICAMENTS
54179	— CONTNG OTH SUBSTANCES	K 389753	7.9	K 801329	15.8	K 307173	7.7	K 294306	5.6	MED CONT AUT SUBSTANCES
55	PERFUME,CLEANING ETC PRD		1.3		1.0		1.0		0.7	PROD POUR PARFUM,TOILETTE

4. Special Imports C.I.F. by Commodities according to the S.I.T.C. (Rev. 2) in million U.S. Dollars
Importations Spéciales C.A.F. par Produits d'après la C.T.C.I. (Rév. 2) en millions de Dollars E.U.

SITC CTCI	COMMODITY	1993 QUANTITY QUANTITE	1993 VALUE VALEUR	1994 QUANTITY QUANTITE	1994 VALUE VALEUR	1995 QUANTITY QUANTITE	1995 VALUE VALEUR	1996 QUANTITY QUANTITE	1996 VALUE VALEUR	PRODUIT
554	SOAP,CLEANSING ETC PREPS	W 396	0.8	W 690	0.7	W 513	0.8	W 185	0.5	SAVONS,PRODUITS DETERSIFS
562	*FERTILIZERS,MANUFACTURE	W 1534	1.2	W 2546	0.6	W 3165	1.2	W 61	0.3	ENGRAIS MANUFACTURES
5629	FERTILIZERS NES	W 830	0.7	W 1591	0.4	W 2585	0.9	W 21	0.1	ENGRAIS NDA
56291	NIT-PHOS-POT FERTLZR NES	W 830	0.7	W 1591	0.4	W 2500	0.9	W 21	0.1	ENGRAIS CONT N P K
58	PLASTIC MATERIALS ETC		0.6		1.0		0.8		0.8	MAT PLAST ARTIFICIELLES
583	POLYMERIZATION ETC PRODS	W 88	0.4	W 229	0.8	W 195	0.7	W 324	0.6	PROD POLYMERISATION
5839	OTH POLYMRZTION ETC PROD	W 34	0.2	W 120	0.5	W 78	0.3	W 44	0.1	AUT PROD POLYMER COPOLYM
59	CHEMICAL MATERIALS NES		1.9		3.6		5.2		4.6	MAT PROD CHIMIQUES NDA
591	PESTICIDES,DISINFECTANTS	W 105	0.6	W 285	2.9	W 390	3.8	W 344	4.1	DESINF,INSECT,FONG,HERB
5911	INSECTICIDES,FOR RETAIL	W 79	0.6	W 279	2.9	W 358	3.7	W 261	2.7	INSECTICIDES VENTE DET
5914	DISINFECTANTS,ETC,FR RET	W 25	0.1	W 6	0.1	W 11	0.1	W 67	1.2	DESINFECTANTS VENTE DET
59149	RAT POISONS ETC FR RTAIL	W 25	0.1	W 3	0.1	W 7	0.1	W 63	1.2	ANTIPARASITES VENTE DET
598	MISCEL CHEM PRODUCTS NES	W 208	1.1	W 218	0.6	W 111	1.0	W 78	0.5	PROD DIV INDUST CHIM NDA
5989	CHEM PRODUCTS,PREPS NES	W 194	1.1	W 198	0.5	W 66	0.7	W 67	0.4	PROD PREP CHIMIQUES NDA
59899	OTH CHEM PRODS,PREPS,NES	W 116	0.9	W 152	0.4	W 35	0.5	W 46	0.4	AUT PRODUITS CHIMIQUES NDA
6	BASIC MANUFACTURES		16.6		21.5		29.3		19.2	ART MANUFACTURES
62	RUBBER MANUFACTURES NES		1.6		2.5		3.8		3.0	CAOUTCHOUC MANUFACTURE
625	RUBBER TYRES, TUBES ETC	W 346	1.3	W 491	2.1	W 561	3.3	W 404	2.7	PNEUS CAOUTCHOUC VULCANISE
6252	TYRES,NEW,BUS OR LORRY	W 145	0.7	W 229	1.6	W 363	2.3	W 215	2.0	PNEUS POUR AUTOBUS,CAMIONS
63	WOOD,CORK MANUFACTRS NES		0.1		0.7		0.4		0.3	OUVRAGES LIEGE ET BOIS
634	VENEERS,PLYWOOD,ETC	W 74	0.1	W 970	0.7	W 380	0.2	W 287	0.2	PLACAGES,CONTRE-PLAQUES
6342	PLYWOOD OF WOOD SHEETS	W 66	0.1	W 967	0.7	W 338	0.1	W 267	0.2	BOIS CONTRE-PLAQUES
64	PAPER,PAPERBOARD AND MFR		3.6		3.5		4.2		4.0	PAPIERS,CARTONS & OUVRAGES
641	PAPER AND PAPERBOARD	W 628	1.4	W 649	1.1	W 709	1.4	W 540	2.9	PAPIERS ET CARTONS
6412	PRINTG,WRITING PAPER NES	W 143	0.3	W 346	0.4	W 457	0.7	W 292	2.4	PAPIERS POUR L'IMPRESSION
64121	— UNCOATED	W 142	0.3	W 337	0.3	W 337	0.6	W 85	2.2	PAPIERS IMPRES NON COUCHES
6415	PAPER,PAPERBRD,BULK,NES	W 452	1.0	W 289	0.7	W 213	0.5	W 150	0.3	PAPIERS,CARTONS ROULEAUX
64159	OTHER PAPER ETC,BULK,NES	W 450	1.0	W 288	0.7	W 212	0.4	W 145	0.3	AUT PAPIER ROULEAUX FEUILLES
642	PAPER,ETC,PRECUT,ARTS OF	W 648	2.2	W 1258	2.5	W 754	2.8	W 333	1.2	PAP,CARTONS DECOUPES
6421	PAPER ETC CONTAINERS	W 455	1.4	W 813	1.5	W 538	1.8	W 174	0.6	BOITES,SACS EMBALLAGES
6423	EXERCISE BOOKS ETC	W 98	0.5	W 256	0.6	W 114	0.6	W 87	0.4	REGISTRES,CAHIERS,CARNETS
65	TEXTILE YARN,FABRICS,ETC		1.3		1.2		2.7		1.5	FILS,TISSUS,ARTICLES TEXTILE
652	COTTON FABRICS,WOVEN	W 32	0.4	W 67	0.5	W 185	0.9	W 85	0.9	TISSUS DE COTON
6522	WOVEN COTTON BLEACHD,ETC	W 31	0.4	W 60	0.4	W 86	0.9	W 71	0.8	TISSUS COTON BLANCHIS ETC
65224	BLCHED COTTON FABRIC NES	W 30	0.4	W 55	0.4	W 71	0.8	W 54	0.7	AUT TIS PLUS 85% COT BLANCHI
658	TEXTILE ARTICLES NES	W 134	0.6	W 85	0.5	W 372	0.8	W 183	0.4	ART FACONNES MAT TEXTILES
66	NONMETAL MINERAL MFS NES		3.3		2.2		2.9		2.7	ART MIN NON METALLIQUES
661	LIME,CEMENT,BLDG PRODS	W 15818	2.5	W 17511	1.5	W 14245	1.4	W 10489	1.0	CHAUX,CIMENTS MAT CONSTR
6612	CEMENT	W 15727	2.5	W 17414	1.4	W 14033	1.3	W 10357	1.0	CIMENTS HYDRAULIQUES
664	GLASS	W 66	0.3	W 112	0.3	W 98	0.5	W 91	1.0	VERRE
6647	SAFETY GLASS CUT OR NOT	W 6	0.1	W 21	0.2	W 30	0.3	W 25	0.9	GLACES DE SECURITE
67	IRON AND STEEL		1.4		1.5		1.8		1.4	FER ET ACIER
673	IRON,STEEL SHAPES ETC	W 921	0.6	W 1917	0.9	W 821	0.4	W 567	0.4	BARRES,PROFIL FER,ACIER
6732	IRON,STEEL BARS ETC	W 581	0.4	W 1598	0.8	W 672	0.4	W 324	0.2	BARRES FER,ACIER
67326	IRN,OTH STL BARS HOTROLD	W 301	0.2	W 1232	0.6	W 165	0.1	W 150	0.1	BARRES PLEINES FER,ACIER
674	IRN,STL UNIV,PLATE,SHEET	W 452	0.4	W 403	0.4	W 792	0.8	W 594	0.6	LARGES PLATS,TOLES
68	NON-FERROUS METALS		1.2		4.7		3.6		1.9	METAUX NON FERREUX
684	ALUMINIUM	W 295	1.1	W 2003	4.4	W 988	3.3	W 437	1.3	ALUMINIUM
6842	ALUMINIUM,ALLOYS WORKED	W 295	1.1	W 2003	4.4	W 988	3.3	W 437	1.3	ALUMINIUM,ALLIAGES OUVRE
68422	ALUMNM PLATE,SHEET,STRIP	W 166	0.6	W 1955	4.0	W 941	2.6	W 430	1.1	TOLES, PLANCHES EN ALU
68423	ALUMINIUM FOIL	W 129	0.6	W 41	0.5	W 46	0.7	W 7	0.2	FEUILLES,BANDES MINCES AL
686	ZINC	W 4	0.1	W 133	0.3	W 210	0.4	W 6947	0.6	ZINC
6863	ZINC,ALLOYS WKD,INC DUST	W 4	0.1	W 133	0.3	W 210	0.4	W 6947	0.6	ZINC ET ALLIAGES OUVRES
68632	ZINC SHEETS,STRIP,FOIL	W 2	0.1	W 133	0.3	W 210	0.4	W 6947	0.6	PLANCHES,FEUILLES EN ZINC
69	METAL MANUFACTURES NES		4.4		5.5		10.2		4.8	ART MANUFACT EN METAL NDA
693	WIRE PRODUCTS NON ELECTR	W 96	0.4	W 163	0.4	W 76	1.4	W 25	0.2	OUVRAGES FILS METALLIQUES
6935	METAL FENCING,GAUZE,ETC	W 70	0.2	W 52	0.2	W 49	1.4	W 22	0.1	TOILES EN FER,ACIER,CUIVRE
69351	IRN,STL FENCNG,GAUZE ETC	W 70	0.2	W 52	0.2	W 49	1.4	W 22	0.1	TOILES EN FER,ACIER
695	TOOLS	W 214	1.1	W 187	1.2	W 422	4.5	W 145	1.4	OUTILS A MAIN
6951	HAND TOOLS,AGRIC,FOREST	W 134	0.5	W 97	0.3	W 241	0.9	W 64	0.2	BECHES,PELLES,PIOCHES
6953	OTHER HAND TOOLS	W 71	0.6	W 85	0.8	W 127	2.0	W 75	1.1	AUTRES OUTILS A MAIN
69539	HAND TOOLS ETC NES	W 44	0.3	W 58	0.6	W 97	1.7	W 59	0.9	OUTILLAGE A MAIN NDA
6954	BLADES,TIPS,ETC FR TOOLS	W 9	0.1	W 4	0.2	W 54	1.7	W 6	0.1	OUTILS POUR MACHINE-OUTIL
69541	PARTS TO INSERT IN TOOLS	W 7	0.1	W 3	0.1	W 52	1.7	W 1	0.1	OUTILS DE FORAGE
696	CUTLERY	W 5	0.5	W 13	0.1	W 2	0.1	W 14	0.1	COUTELLERIE
69606	BASE METAL TABLEWARE NES	W 1	0.5	W 11	0.1		0.1	W 4	0.1	CUILLERS,FOURCHETTES
697	BASE MTL HOUSEHOLD EQUIP	W 66	0.3	W 436	1.5	W 93	0.5	W 18894	0.8	ART MENAGE MET COMMUNS
6974	BASE MTL DMSTC ARTIC NES	W 55	0.2	W 417	1.4	W 60	0.3	W 18849	0.6	ARTICLES NDA FONTE,FER,ETC
69743	— OF ALUMINIUM	W 17	0.1	W 363	1.2	W 4	0.1	W 18810	0.5	ARTICLES NDA EN ALUMINIUM
699	BASE METAL MFRS NES	W 245	1.4	W 599	1.6	W 786	2.7	W 395	1.6	ART MANUFACTURES MET NDA
6991	LOCKSMITHS WARES,ETC	W 36	0.5	W 29	0.2	W 92	0.5	W 39	0.3	ARTICLES DE SERRURERIE
6996	BASE MTL MISC ARTICLES	W 134	0.5	W 156	0.5	W 206	0.9	W 100	0.4	ART DIVERS METAUX COMMUNS
6998	MFRS NES OF CPR,NIKL,ETC	W 3	0.1	W 392	0.9	W 448	1.3	W 211	0.6	OUVRAGES EN CU,NI,AL,PB,ZN
69983	ALUMINIUM MANUFACTS NES	W 3	0.1	W 392	0.8	W 448	1.3	W 210	0.6	OUVRAGES EN ALUMINIUM
7	MACHINES,TRANSPORT EQUIP		48.8		36.7		112.2		67.3	MACHINES MATERIEL TRANSPORT
71	POWER GENERATING EQUIPMT		1.5		1.5		3.9		3.8	MACHINES GENERATRICES
713	INTRNL COMBUS PSTN ENGIN	W 21	0.4	W 72	0.8	W 91	2.3	W 96	2.9	MOTEURS EXPL COMB INT, PIECE
7138	PISTON ENGINES NES	W 2	0.1	W 21	0.2	W 55	1.3	W 75	2.3	MOTEURS A PISTONS NDA
7139	PISTON ENGINE PARTS NES	W 9	0.3	W 45	0.5	W 28	1.0	W 17	0.5	PIECES POUR 713.2,3,8
716	ROTATING ELECTRIC PLANT	W 54	0.9	W 37	0.6	W 98	1.5	W 68	0.9	APP ELECTR ROTATIFS,PIECES
7162	AC MTRS,GENRTRS,GEN SETS	W 43	0.6	W 21	0.3	W 55	0.7	W 45	0.6	MOTEURS ELECTRIQUES
71623	GEN SETS WITH PISTN ENGN	W 40	0.5	W 13	0.2	W 40	0.5	W 40	0.4	GROUPES MOTEUR EXPLOSION
72	MACHS FOR SPCL INDUSTRYS		3.1		2.9		26.3		8.0	MAC SPECIALES POUR INDUST
722	TRACTORS NON-ROAD	W 116	0.7	W 209	1.0	W 57	0.5	W 52	0.8	TRACTEURS
7224	WHEELED TRACTORS NES	W 116	0.7	W 166	0.9	W 37	0.4	W 52	0.8	TRACTEURS A ROUES
723	CIVIL ENGNEERG EQUIP ETC	W 179	0.3	W 166	0.9	W 1897	23.8	W 322	5.0	APPAREILS DE GENIE CIVIL
7233	MECHANICAL ROAD ROLLERS	W 44	0.1	W 56	0.3	W 281	3.3	W 49	1.1	ROULEAUX COMPRESSEURS
7234	CONST,MINING MACHNRY NES	W 101	0.2	W 98	0.5	W 1602	20.5	W 265	3.7	MACH POUR LA CONST, MINES
72341	SELF-PROPELLD DOZERS,ETC	W 48	0.1	W 76	0.4	W 1287	14.9	W 70	0.5	BULLDOZERS
72342	SLFPRP SHOVELS,EXCAVATRS	W 52	0.1	W 22	0.1	W 186	1.5	W 118	0.9	PELLES MECANIQUES
72343	SLFPRP CONST ETC MCH NES							W 30	0.9	AUT MACH EXTR,TERRASSEM
72344	BORING,SINKING MACHINERY					W 108	4.1	W 40	1.4	MACHINES DE FORAGE
728	OTH MACHY FOR SPCL INDUS	W 52	1.1	W 46	0.6	W 106	0.8	W 595	1.4	AUT MACH IND PARTICULIERES
7281	MACH-TOOLS FR SPCL INDUS	W 13	0.3	W 16	0.2	W 25	0.3	W 545	1.2	MACH-OUTILS SPEC IND PART
72812	MACH-TOOLS TO WORK WOOD	W 7	0.2	W 6	0.1	W 16	0.2	W 489	1.1	MACH-OUT POUR TRAVAIL BOIS
7284	MACHY FOR SPCL INDUS NES	W 18	0.8	W 24	0.5	W 57	0.5	W 15	0.1	MACH SPEC IND PARTICUL.
72843	TOBACCO WORKING MACH NES	W 4	0.7	W 12	0.4	W 10	0.3	W 4	0.1	MACH POUR IND DU TABAC
74	GENRL INDUSTRL MACHY NES		6.2		6.0		9.5		5.1	MACH APP INDUSTRIE
741	HEATING,COOLING EQUIPMNT	W 111	1.1	W 80	0.9	W 220	3.1	W 97	1.3	MACH CHAUFFAGE,PIECES
7415	AIR-CONDITIONING MACHNRY	W 51	0.6	W 42	0.4	W 96	1.1	W 46	0.5	GROUPES CONDITION AIR
7416	HEATING,COOLING EQU NES	W 4	0.1	W 21	0.3	W 70	1.3	W 18	0.3	APP CHANGEMENT TEMP

4. Special Imports C.I.F. by Commodities according to the S.I.T.C. (Rev. 2) in million U.S. Dollars
Importations Spéciales C.A.F. par Produits d'après la C.T.C.I. (Rév. 2) en millions de Dollars E.U.

SITC CTCI	COMMODITY	1993 QUANTITY QUANTITE	1993 VALUE VALEUR	1994 QUANTITY QUANTITE	1994 VALUE VALEUR	1995 QUANTITY QUANTITE	1995 VALUE VALEUR	1996 QUANTITY QUANTITE	1996 VALUE VALEUR	PRODUIT
742	PUMPS FOR LIQUIDS ETC	W 60	1.4	W 20	0.4	W 63	1.1	W 41	0.7	POMPES MOTO–POMPES
7428	OTHER PUMPS FOR LIQUIDS	W 56	1.3	W 15	0.3	W 57	1.0	W 39	0.6	AUTRES POMPES POUR LIQ
74288	PUMPS FR LIQUIDS NES ETC	W 54	1.2	W 12	0.3	W 57	1.0	W 32	0.5	POMPES POUR LIQUIDES NDA
743	PUMPS NES,CENTRFUGES ETC	W 33	0.6	W 36	0.4	W 96	1.1	W 55	0.6	POMPES COMPRES,VENT ETC
744	MECHANICAL HANDLING EQU	W 164	0.9	W 54	0.5	W 132	1.3	W 82	0.8	EQUIP MANUTENTION PIECES
7441	FORK LIFT TRCKS,ETC,PTS	W 127	0.5	W 2	0.1	W 43	0.2	W 14	0.1	CHARIOTS POUR USINES ETC
74411	FORK LIFT TRUCKS ETC	W 127	0.5			W 43	0.2	W 13	0.1	CHARIOTS POUR LES GARES
7449	PTS NES OF MACHY OF 7442	W 19	0.2	W 34	0.4	W 59	1.1	W 39	0.6	PIECES DU 744.2
745	NONELEC MACHY,TOOLS NES	W 42	0.4	W 35	0.5	W 46	0.8	W 34	0.7	AUT MACH NON ELEC,PIECES
749	NONELEC MACH PTS,ACC NES	W 137	2.0	W 266	3.7	W 159	2.3	W 46	1.3	PIECES MACH NON ELEC NDA
7492	COCKS,VALVES ETC NES	W 55	0.6	W 194	2.7	W 57	0.7	W 6	0.2	ART ROB,SIM POUR TUYAUX
7499	OTH NONELEC MCHY PTS NES	W 67	1.0	W 22	0.5	W 76	0.7	W 12	0.6	PIECES NON ELECT NDA
74992	METAL–PLASTIC GASKETS	W 22	0.7	W 21	0.4	W 26	0.6	W 8	0.4	JOINTS METALLOPLASTIQUES
75	OFFICE MACHNES,ADP EQUIP		2.4		2.2		3.1		2.8	MACH BUREAU TRAIT AUTOM
751	OFFICE MACHINES	W 21	0.7	W 26	0.8	W 24	1.0	W 44	0.8	MACH,APPAREILS DE BUREAU
7518	OFFICE MACHINES NES	W 18	0.6	W 17	0.6	W 15	0.7	W 38	0.7	MACH,APP DE BUREAU NDA
75182	PHOTO,THERMOCOPY APPARAT	W 9	0.5	W 11	0.5	W 13	0.6	W 17	0.4	APPAREILS DE PHOTOCOPIE
752	AUTOMTIC DATA PROC EQUIP	W 14	1.4	W 21	1.3	W 36	1.9	W 30	1.6	MACH TRAIT INFORMATION
7523	DIGITL CENTRL PROCESSORS	W 6	0.5	W 4	0.4	W 5	0.4	W 9	0.6	UNITES CENTRALES
759	OFFICE,ADP MCH PTS,ACCES	W 24	0.5	W 5	0.3	W 6	0.4	W 9	0.5	PIECES DU 751 ET 752
76	TELECOMM,SOUND EQUIPMENT		3.9		3.2		12.2		4.8	EQUIPMENT DE TELECOM
764	TELECOM EQPT,PTS,ACC NES	W 51	3.7	W 45	3.1	W 94	11.8	W 42	4.5	EQUIP TELECOM,PIECES
7641	LINE TELEPHONE,ETC EQUIP	W 11	1.7	W 6	0.5	W 31	1.9	W 15	1.2	APP TELEPHON PAR FIL
7643	TV,RADIO TRANSMITTRS ETC	W 16	0.8	W 8	1.0	W 18	6.2	W 13	2.5	APP EMET TELE RADIO
7648	TELECOMM EQUIPMENT NES	W 1	0.1	W 11	1.0	W 25	2.3		0.2	APP TELECOM NDA
76483	RADAR APPARATUS ETC		0.1	W 11	0.9	W 20	1.5		0.2	APP DE RADIOGUIDAGE ETC
7649	PTS NES OF EQUIPMT OF 76	W 23	1.2	W 16	0.5	W 19	1.5	W 8	0.6	PIECES DE LA DIV 76
76491	PTS NES OF APPAR OF 7641	W 7	0.9	W 3	0.1	W 4	0.3	W 2	0.3	PIECES POUR 764.1
76493	TELECOMM EQUIPMT PTS NES	W 16	0.4	W 14	0.4	W 15	1.3	W 5	0.4	PIECES 761,762,764.3,8
77	ELECTRIC MACHNRY NES ETC		4.6		4.2		5.5		4.2	MACH APP ELECT NDA
772	SWITCHGEAR ETC,PARTS NES	W 48	1.4	W 120	1.2	W 55	1.6	W 103	1.1	APP COUPURE,SECT ETC
7721	SWITCHGEAR ETC	W 48	1.4	W 119	1.2	W 55	1.6	W 103	1.1	APP COUPURE,SECTIONMNT
773	ELECTR DISTRIBUTNG EQUIP	W 171	0.9	W 183	0.5	W 150	0.8	W 163	0.9	EQUIPMT DISTRIBUTION ELECT
7731	INSULATED WIRE,CABLE ETC	W 171	0.9	W 182	0.5	W 148	0.8	W 150	0.8	FILS,CABLES ISOLES ELECT
775	HOUSEHOLD TYPE EQUIP NES	W 81	0.6	W 110	0.5	W 146	1.0	W 139	0.8	MACH,APP USAGE DOMESTQUE
778	ELECTRICAL MACHINERY NES	W 425	1.7	W 527	1.8	W 522	2.0	W 216	1.0	AUTRES MACH ELECT NDA
7781	BATTERIES,ACCUMULATORS	W 381	1.3	W 504	1.5	W 492	1.4	W 190	0.6	PILES ET ACCUMULATEURS
77811	PRIMARY BATTERIES,CELLS	W 268	0.7	W 325	0.7	W 322	0.9	W 126	0.4	PILES ELECTRIQUES,PIECES
77812	ELECTRIC ACCUMULATORS	W 107	0.6	W 179	0.8	W 159	0.5	W 64	0.3	ACCUMULATEURS ELECTRIQ
78	ROAD VEHICLES		25.7		16.5		49.8		33.1	VEHICULES ROUTIERS
781	PASS MOTOR VEH EXC BUSES	W 1031	7.3	W 793	3.0	W 1434	9.0	W 1098	5.5	AUTO TRANSPORT PERSONNES
782	LORRIES,SPCL MTR VEH NES	W 1208	7.1	W 1435	4.9	W 2693	17.2	W 2147	13.4	VEHICULES SPECIAUX,MARCH
7821	LORRIES,TRUCKS	W 1094	6.4	W 1358	4.5	W 2162	11.1	W 1774	11.4	VEHICULES TRANSP MARCHAND
7822	SPECIAL MOTOR VEHCLS NES	W 114	0.7	W 77	0.4	W 532	6.2	W 373	2.0	VEHICULES USAGES SPECIAUX
783	ROAD MOTOR VEHICLES NES	W 446	2.9	W 518	1.8	W 1191	9.1	W 778	3.9	VEHICULES ROUTIERS NDA
7831	BUSES	W 246	2.0	W 213	1.1	W 611	6.0	W 386	2.9	VOITURES TRANSPORT COMMUN
7832	TRACTORS FOR TR–TRAILERS	W 200	0.9	W 305	0.8	W 581	3.2	W 392	1.0	TRACTEURS ROUTIERS
784	MOTOR VEH PRTS,ACCES NES	W 565	6.4	W 244	4.3	W 980	9.9	W 543	7.1	PIECES 722,781,782,783
7849	OTHER MOTOR VEHCL PARTS	W 540	6.4	W 244	4.3	W 979	9.9	W 539	7.1	PIECES 722,781,782,783
785	CYCLES,ETC MOTRZD OR NOT	W 205	1.4	W 169	1.6	W 147	2.0	W 127	1.6	MOTOCYCLES SCOOTERS
7851	MOTORCYCLES ETC	W 123	0.7	W 96	1.1	W 80	1.4	W 95	1.3	MOTO VELO MOTEUR AUXIL
7853	INVAL CARR, PTS OF 785	W 65	0.8	W 46	0.4	W 33	0.6	W 23	0.2	FAUTEUILS INVALIDES,PIECES
78539	PARTS,ACCES NES OF 785	W 64	0.8	W 44	0.4	W 33	0.6	W 23	0.2	PIECES DU 785
786	TRAILERS,NONMOTR VEH,NES	W 434	0.7	W 310	1.2	W 741	2.8	W 465	1.9	REMORQUES,CADRES,CONTAIN
7861	TRAILERS,TRANSP CONTAINR	W 387	0.5	W 241	0.9	W 550	2.1	W 415	1.8	REMORQUES TOUS VEHICULES
78612	OTHER TRAILERS	W 371	0.4	W 151	0.6	W 532	1.8	W 401	1.7	REMORQUES TRANSP MARCH
79	OTHR TRANSPORT EQUIPMENT		1.3		0.6		2.0		5.8	AUTRE MATERIEL TRANSPORT
792	AIRCRAFT ETC	W 11	1.3	W 7	0.6	W 33	1.8	W 18	5.8	APP NAVIGATION AERIENNE
7922	AIRCRFT NES 2000KG OR LS					W 2	0.1	W 2	0.6	AERODYNES MOINS 2000 KG
7929	AIRCRAFT PARTS NES	W 3	1.2	W 2	0.4	W 17	1.5	W 15	5.2	PIECES DU 792
8	MISC MANUFACTURED GOODS		10.5		7.1		12.1		10.4	ART MANUFACTURES DIVERS
821	*FURNITURE,PARTS THEREOF	W 122	1.0	W 134	0.5	W 64	0.4	W 89	0.9	MEUBLES ET PIECES
8219	FURNITURE AND PARTS NES	W 111	0.8	W 97	0.3	W 41	0.3	W 68	0.6	AUTRES MEUBLES ET PIECES
82191	METAL FURNITURE NES	W 98	0.8	W 62	0.3	W 28	0.2	W 35	0.4	MEUBLES NDA EN METAL
84	CLOTHING AND ACCESSORIES		0.5		0.5		0.5		0.3	VETEMENTS
851	*FOOTWEAR	W 260	0.4	W 228	0.4	W 57	0.3	W 30	0.6	CHAUSSURES
87	PRECISION INSTRUMNTS NES		2.2		0.9		2.5		1.6	INSTRUM,APPAR SCIENT NDA
872	MEDICAL INSTRUMENTS NES	W 57	0.9	W 27	0.5	W 24	0.9	W 20	0.6	INSTR,APP MEDIC–CHIR NDA
87202	OTH MEDICAL INSTRUMENTS	W 56	0.9	W 27	0.5	W 23	0.9	W 19	0.6	INSTRUM,APP MEDECINE
874	MEASURNG,CONTROLNG INSTR	W 10	1.2	W 10	0.5	W 14	1.2	W 17	0.6	INSTRUMENTS DE MESURE
89	MISC MANUFCTRD GOODS NES		6.1		4.3		7.8		6.8	ART MANUFACTURES DIVERS
892	PRINTED MATTER	W 329	2.8	W 391	1.6	W 232	2.6	W 281	3.9	IMPRIMES
8921	PRINTED BOOKS,GLOBES,ETC	W 193	0.9	W 282	0.8	W 81	1.3	W 112	1.5	LIVRES,BROCHURES,CARTES
89211	PRINTED BOOKS,PAMPHLETS	W 192	0.9	W 282	0.8	W 81	1.3	W 111	1.5	LIVRES,BROCHURES
8922	NEWSPAPERS,PERIODICALS	W 56	1.0	W 43	0.4	W 55	0.6	W 50	0.4	JOURNAUX ET PERIODIQUES
8928	PRINTED MATTER NES	W 81	0.9	W 66	0.4	W 95	0.8	W 119	2.2	IMPRIMES NDA
89283	UNISSUED BANKNOTES ETC	W 29	0.2	W 21	0.1	W 22	0.1	W 63	1.5	TIMBRES–POSTE FISCAUX
893	ARTICLES OF PLASTIC NES	W 432	1.2	W 249	0.9	W 237	1.2	W 192	0.8	OUVRAGES EN MAT DIVIS 58
8939	MISC PLASTIC ARTICLES	W 408	1.1	W 189	0.6	W 178	0.9	W 124	0.6	ART DIVERS EN MAT DIV 58
89399	OTHR PLASTC ARTICLES NES	W 362	1.0	W 169	0.5	W 163	0.8	W 70	0.4	AUT OUV MAT DIV 58
894	TOYS,SPORTING GOODS,ETC	W 156	1.4	W 269	1.2	W 289	3.0	W 224	1.4	VOITURES ENFANTS,JOUETS
8946	NON–MILITARY ARMS,AMMO	W 115	1.2	W 250	1.1	W 245	2.7	W 197	1.3	ARMES NON MILITAIRES
89463	HUNTNG,SPORTNG AMMUNTION	W 115	1.2	W 249	1.1	W 244	2.7	W 196	1.3	MUNITIONS
899	OTHER MANUFACTURED GOODS		0.5		0.4		0.5		0.2	AUT ART MANUF DIVERS NDA
9	GOODS NOT CLASSD BY KIND		0.1		0.4		0.1		7.2	ART TRANSACT NON CLASSES
951	*WAR FIREARMS,AMMUNITION	W 1	0.1	W 9	0.1	W 1	0.1	W 232	7.2	VEHIC BLINDES ARMES
95101	ARMORED FIGHTNG VEHICLES							W 195	6.9	CHARS DE COMBAT

5. Special Exports F.O.B. by Commodities according to the S.I.T.C. (Rev. 2) in million U.S. Dollars
Exportations Spéciales F.O.B. par Produits d'après la C.T.C.I. (Rév. 2) en millions de Dollars E.U.

SITC CTCI	COMMODITY	1993 QUANTITY QUANTITE	1993 VALUE VALEUR	1994 QUANTITY QUANTITE	1994 VALUE VALEUR	1995 QUANTITY QUANTITE	1995 VALUE VALEUR	1996 QUANTITY QUANTITE	1996 VALUE VALEUR	PRODUIT
	ALL COMMODITIES		91.7		81.5		119.6		115.2	TOUS PRODUITS
0	FOOD AND LIVE ANIMALS		4.0		2.7		4.2		1.3	ALIMENTS,ANIMAUX VIVANTS
001	*LIVE ANIMALS FOR FOOD			W 894	0.5	W 643	0.9	W 1695	0.4	ANIMAUX VIVANTS
0011	BOVINE SPECIES,LIVE			W 890	0.5	W 635	0.9	W 1287	0.4	ESPECE BOVINE
00119	— OTHR THAN FR BREEDING			W 890	0.5	W 632	0.9	W 1287	0.4	BOVINS NON REPRODUCTEURS
07	COFFEE,TEA,COCOA,SPICES		4.0		2.1		3.2		0.9	CAFE,THE,CACAO,EPICES
071	COFFEE AND SUBSTITUTES	W 8281	4.0	W 8215	2.1	W 13674	3.2	W 5023	0.9	CAFE ET SUCCEDANES
0711	COFFEE GREEN,ROASTED,SUB	W 8281	4.0	W 8215	2.1	W 13674	3.2	W 5023	0.9	CAFE TORREFIE OU DECAFEINE
07111	COFFEE GREEN,HUSKS,SKINS	W 8281	4.0	W 8215	2.1	W 13674	3.2	W 5023	0.9	CAFE NON TORREFIE
1	BEVERAGES AND TOBACCO		0.9		0.5		0.7		0.1	BOISSONS ET TABACS
12	TOBACCO AND MANUFACTURES		0.8		0.4		0.7		0.1	TABACS BRUTS FABRIQUES
122	TOBACCO,MANUFACTURED	W 26	0.8	W 22	0.4	W 29	0.7	W 4	0.1	TABACS FABRIQUES
1222	CIGARETTES	W 26	0.8	W 22	0.4	W 29	0.7	W 4	0.1	CIGARETTES
2	CRUDE MATERLS,EXCL FUELS		49.5		42.9		59.9		57.4	MAT BRUTES NON COMESTIBLES
22	OIL SEEDS,OLEAGINOUS FRT		0.1		0.4		0.2		0.1	GRAINES,FRUITS OLEAGINEUX
222	SEEDS FOR'SOFT'FIXED OIL	W 31	0.1	W 791	0.4	W 904	0.2	W 206	0.1	GRAINES HUILES FIXES
2221	GROUNDNUTS,GREEN			W 781	0.4	W 879	0.2	W 191	0.1	ARACHIDES NON GRILLEES
24	CORK AND WOOD		0.8		1.3		2.8		4.8	LIEGE ET BOIS
247	OTH WOOD ROUGH,SQUARED	W 11316	0.3	W 15409	0.2	W 15204	1.9	W 12390	3.9	BOIS BRUTS EQUARRIS
2471	SAW–,VENEER–LOGS CONIFER	W 11258	0.3	W 13325	0.2	W 14227	1.8	W 12390	3.9	CONIFERES POUR SCIAGE,PLACAG
24711	— IN THE ROUGH	W 11258	0.3	W 13325	0.2	W 14227	1.8	W 12390	3.9	ECORCES OU DEGROSSIS
248	WOOD SHAPED,SLEEPERS	W 9740	0.6	W 9701	1.2	W 6674	1.0	W 4416	0.9	BOIS SIMPLEMENT TRAVAILLES
2483	LUMBER SHAPED NON–CONIFR	W 9740	0.6	W 9701	1.2	W 6674	1.0	W 4416	0.9	NON CONIFERES SCIES,RABOTES
24831	LUMBER SAWN ETC NON–CON	W 9740	0.6	W 9701	1.2	W 6674	1.0	W 4416	0.9	SCIES LONGITUDINALEMENT
26	TEXTILE FIBRES AND WASTE		10.6		7.6		20.4		22.4	FIBRES TEXTILES
263	COTTON	W 7633	10.6	W 5468	7.6	W 11879	20.4	W 12410	22.4	COTON
2631	RAW COTTON,EXCL LINTERS	W 7633	10.6	W 5468	7.6	W 11879	20.4	W 12410	22.4	COTON EN MASSE
27	CRUDE FERTLZR,MINRLS NES		37.5		33.6		36.0		29.5	ENGRAIS MINERAUX BRUTS
277	NATURAL ABRASIVES NES		37.5		33.6		36.0		29.5	ABRASIFS NATURELS NDA
2771	INDUSTRIAL DIAMONDS		37.5		33.6		36.0		29.5	DIAMANTS INDUSTRIELS
29	CRUDE ANIMAL,VEG MAT NES		0.6		0.2		0.5		0.7	MATIERES BRUTES ANIM,VEGET
292	CRUDE VEG MATERIALS NES	W 346	0.6	W 313	0.2	W 1201	0.5	W 1930	0.7	MAT BRUTES VEGETALES NDA
2922	NAT GUMS,RESINS,LACS,ETC	W 164	0.1	W 300	0.1	W 1163	0.5	W 1900	0.7	GOMME LAQUE
2924	VEG USED IN PHARMACY ETC	W 182	0.5	W 12	0.1	W 36	0.1	W 29	0.1	PLANTES MEDICINALES
3	MINERAL FUELS ETC		0.2		0.4		1.0		0.3	COMBUSTIBLES MINERAUX LUB
33	PETROLEUM AND PRODUCTS		0.2		0.4		1.0		0.3	PETROLE ET DERIVES
334	PETROLEUM PRODUCTS,REFIN	W 134	0.2	W 2251	0.4	W 4620	1.0	W 337	0.3	PRODUITS RAFFINES
3343	GAS OILS	W 132	0.2	W 148	0.1	W 2584	0.7	W 290	0.2	GAS OILS
5	CHEMCLS,RELATED PROD NES		0.3		0.2		0.5		0.1	PRODUITS CHIMIQUES
6	BASIC MANUFACTURES		32.6		31.2		41.8		40.2	ART MANUFACTURES
66	NONMETAL MINERAL MFS NES		29.9		30.9		39.9		39.8	ART MIN NON METALLIQUES
667	PEARL,PREC–,SEMI–P STONE		29.8		30.9		39.9		39.8	PERLES, PIERRES GEMMES
6672	DIAMONDS NONINDUST,UNSET		29.8		30.9		39.9		39.8	DIAMANTS BRUTS
66722	— SRTD,ROUGH,SIMPLY WKD		13.6		29.9		39.9		39.7	DIAMANTS TRIES BRUTS
66729	— CUT ETC NOT SET		16.3		1.0		0.1		0.1	DIAMANTS TAILLES
67	IRON AND STEEL		2.7		0.2		0.1		0.1	FER ET ACIER
671	PIG IRON ETC	W 9506	2.7							FONTE,SPIEGEL,POUDRES
6716	FERRO–ALLOYS	W 9506	2.7							FERRO–ALLIAGES
67162	FERRO–SILICON	W 9506	2.7							FERRO–SILICIUM
69	METAL MANUFACTURES NES		0.1		0.1		1.6		0.1	ART MANUFACT EN METAL NDA
693	WIRE PRODUCTS NON ELECTR	W 4	0.1			W 5	1.3			OUVRAGES FILS METALLIQUES
6935	METAL FENCING,GAUZE,ETC	W 1	0.1			W 5	1.3			TOILES EN FER,ACIER,CUIVRE
69351	IRN,STL FENCNG,GAUZE ETC	W 1	0.1			W 5	1.3			TOILES EN FER,ACIER
7	MACHINES,TRANSPORT EQUIP		1.7		2.3		10.6		8.7	MACHINES MATERIEL TRANSPORT
71	POWER GENERATING EQUIPMT		0.5		0.1		0.3		0.1	MACHINES GENERATRICES
713	INTRNL COMBUS PSTN ENGIN	W 36	0.4	W 8	0.1	W 3	0.1	W 6	0.1	MOTEURS EXPL COMB INT, PIECE
72	MACHS FOR SPCL INDUSTRYS		0.2		0.1		0.7		0.5	MAC SPECIALES POUR INDUST
723	CIVIL ENGNEERG EQUIP ETC	W 2	0.1	W 13	0.1	W 75	0.6	W 11	0.2	APPAREILS DE GENIE CIVIL
7234	CONST,MINING MACHNRY NES	W 2	0.1			W 65	0.5	W 11	0.2	MACH POUR LA CONST, MINES
74	GENRL INDUSTRL MACHY NES		0.1		0.1		0.1		0.9	MACH APP INDUSTRIE
741	HEATING,COOLING EQUIPMNT		0.1				0.1	W 60	0.9	MACH CHAUFFAGE,PIECES
7416	HEATING,COOLING EQU NES							W 60	0.9	APP CHANGEMENT TEMP
78	ROAD VEHICLES		0.9		2.1		9.3		7.2	VEHICULES ROUTIERS
782	LORRIES,SPCL MTR VEH NES	W 75	0.4	W 105	0.6	W 344	2.0	W 57	1.6	VEHICULES SPECIAUX,MARCH
7821	LORRIES,TRUCKS	W 75	0.4	W 105	0.6	W 252	1.0	W 57	1.2	VEHICULES TRANSP MARCHAND
7822	SPECIAL MOTOR VEHCLS NES					W 92	1.0		0.4	VEHICULES USAGES SPECIAUX
783	ROAD MOTOR VEHICLES NES	W 2	0.1	W 9	0.1	W 186	3.4	W 325	1.2	VEHICULES ROUTIERS NDA
7831	BUSES	W 2	0.1	W 9	0.1	W 171	3.3	W 46	0.9	VOITURES TRANSPORT COMMUN
7832	TRACTORS FOR TR–TRAILERS					W 15	0.2	W 278	0.4	TRACTEURS ROUTIERS
784	MOTOR VEH PRTS,ACCES NES	W 76	0.4	W 128	1.3	W 125	3.4	W 175	4.2	PIECES 722,781,782,783
7849	OTHER MOTOR VEHCL PARTS	W 76	0.4	W 118	1.3	W 125	3.4	W 170	4.1	PIECES 722,781,782,783
8	MISC MANUFACTURED GOODS		0.5		0.5		0.4		0.2	ART MANUFACTURES DIVERS
89	MISC MANUFCTRD GOODS NES		0.3		0.3		0.2		0.2	ART MANUFACTURES DIVERS
892	PRINTED MATTER	W 30	0.3	W 31	0.3	W 11	0.2	W 12	0.2	IMPRIMES
8921	PRINTED BOOKS,GLOBES,ETC	W 29	0.2	W 31	0.3	W 11	0.2	W 12	0.2	LIVRES,BROCHURES,CARTES
89211	PRINTED BOOKS,PAMPHLETS	W 29	0.2	W 31	0.3	W 11	0.2	W 12	0.2	LIVRES,BROCHURES
9	GOODS NOT CLASSD BY KIND		2.4		1.4		0.7		7.3	ART TRANSACT NON CLASSES
951	*WAR FIREARMS,AMMUNITION	W 9	1.2	W 44	0.7			W 196	7.0	VEHIC BLINDES ARMES
95101	ARMORED FIGHTNG VEHICLES							W 195	6.9	CHARS DE COMBAT
95106	AMMUNITION NES			W 44	0.7					PROJECTILES,MUNITIONS
95109	PARTS OF ARMS NES	W 9	1.2							PIECES POUR ARMES
971	*GOLD,NON MONETARY NES	K 153	1.2	K 78	0.7	K 66	0.7	K 24	0.3	OR NON MONETAIRE
97101	NONMON GLD UNWRT,SEMIMFD	K 153	1.2	K 78	0.7	K 66	0.7	K 24	0.3	OR,ALLIAGES D'OR BRUTS

1. HISTORICAL SERIES, 1960–1995 SPECIAL TRADE, IMPORTS C.I.F., EXPORTS F.O.B.
SERIES HISTORIQUES, 1960–1995 COMMERCE SPECIAL, IMPORTATIONS C.A.F., EXPORTATIONS F.O.B

YEAR ANNEE	VALUE IN MILLION C.F.A. FRANCS / VALEUR EN MILLION C.F.A. FRANCS — MERCHANDISE –MARCHANDISE		GOLD –OR		CONVERSION FACTORS U.S. CENTS PER C.F.A. FRANC / FACTEURS DE CONVERSION CENTS E.U. PAR C.F.A. FRANC		INDEX NUMBERS –INDICES — QUANTUM		UNIT VALUE / VALEUR UNITAIRE	
	IMPORTS	EXPORTS	IMPORTS	EXPORTS	IMPORTS	EXPORTS	IMPORTS	EXPORTS	IMPORTS	EXPORTS
1960	6231.00	3271.00			0.4051	0.4051				
1961	6250.00	5293.00			0.4051	0.4051				
1962	7508.00	4178.00			0.4051	0.4051				
1963	7167.00	5605.00			0.4051	0.4051				
1964	8537.00	6544.00			0.4051	0.4051				
1965	7700.00	6722.00			0.4051	0.4051				
1966	7338.00	5848.00			0.4051	0.4051				
1967	9248.00	6635.00			0.4051	0.4051				
1968	8262.00	6824.00			0.4051	0.4051				
1969	13797.00	8020.00			0.3942	0.3938				
1970	17058.99	8205.00			0.3601	0.3601				
1971	17117.39	7786.00			0.3601	0.3601				
1972	15475.51	9028.30			0.3969	0.3969				
1973	18213.44	8483.22			0.4490	0.4490				
1974	20858.99	9052.65			0.4178	0.4128				
1975	28324.99	10183.00			0.4670	0.4670				
1976	27592.99	14861.00			0.4193	0.4261				
1977	46464.99	26176.99			0.4071	0.4071				
1978	49034.00	22328.99			0.4432	0.4432				
1979	18132.00	18776.00			0.4701	0.4701				
1980	15533.00	14999.00			0.4733	0.4733				
1981	29349.01	22665.01			0.3680	0.3680				
1982	35701.01	18968.00			0.3040	0.3040				
1983	59707.01	39824.00			0.2624	0.2624				
1984	79272.00	57384.00			0.2290	0.2290				
1985	74708.00	27781.01			0.2226	0.2226				
1986	73437.01	34145.01			0.2888	0.2888				
1987	67894.00	32892.00			0.3327	0.3327				
1988	68000.00	42900.00			0.3707	0.3707				
1989	75100.00	49570.00			0.3135	0.3135				
1990	77742.00	51202.00			0.3673	0.3673				
1991	70500.00	54600.00			0.3570	0.3570				
1992	64320.00	48250.00			0.3777	0.3777				
1993	56910.00	37330.00			0.3541	0.3541				
1994	98310.00	82160.00			0.1800	0.1800				
1995	109720.00	125600.00			0.2002	0.2002				

2. IMPORTS BY BROAD ECONOMIC CATEGORY AND EXPORTS BY INDUSTRIAL ORIGIN. (PERCENTAGE OF TOTAL VALUE)
IMPORTATIONS PAR CATEGORIES ECONOMIQUES ET EXPORTATIONS PAR BRANCHE D'ACTIVITE.(EN POURCENTAGE DE LA VALEUR TOTALE)

IMPORTS – IMPORTATIONS

	1989	1990	1991	1992	1993	1994	1995
TOTAL IMPORTS–IMPORTATIONS TOTALES							100.
1 FOOD BEV–ALIMENTATION BOISSONS							21.2
11 PRIMARY–PRODUITS DE BASE							1.1
111 FOR INDUSTRY–POUR L'INDUSTRIE							0.1
112 FOR HOUSEHOLDS–POUR LES MENAGES							1.0
12 PROCESSED–PRODUITS ELABORES							20.1
121 FOR INDUSTRY–POUR L'INDUSTRIE							5.2
122 FOR HOUSEHOLDS–POUR LES MENAGES							14.8
2 IND SUPPLIES–APPROV INDUSTRIELS							17.3
21 PRIMARY–PRODUITS DE BASE							0.9
22 PROCESSED–PRODUITS ELABORES							16.4
3 FUELS–COMBUSTIBLES							17.9
31 PRIMARY–PRODUITS DE BASE							0.0
32 PROCESSED–PRODUITS ELABORES							17.9
321 MOTOR SPIRIT–ESSENCE							3.0
322 OTHER–AUTRES							14.9
4 MACHINERY–EQUIPEMENT							15.5
41 CAPITAL EQUIPMENT–MACHINES							13.2
42 PARTS–PIECES ACCESSOIRES							2.3
5 TRANSPORT–TRANSPORT							11.5
51 PASSENGER CARS–AUTOMOBILES							0.7
52 OTHER–AUTRES							3.7
521 INDUSTRIAL–INDUSTRIELS							3.3
522 NON INDUSTRIAL–NON INDUSTRIEL							0.4
53 PARTS–PIECES ACCESSOIRES							7.1
6 CONSUM GOODS–BIENS CONSOMMATION							10.0
61 DURABLE–DURABLES							1.2
62 SEMI DURABLE–SEMI DURABLES							3.0
63 NON DURABLE–NON DURABLES							5.8
7 GOODS NES–BIENS NDA							6.5

EXPORTS – EXPORTATIONS

	1989	1990	1991	1992	1993	1994	1995
TOTAL EXPORTS–EXPORTATIONS TOTALES							
1 AGRICULTURE							
2 MINING QUARRY–INDUS EXTRACTIVES							
3 MANUFACTURING–IND MANUFACTUR							
31 FOOD BEV TOBACCO–ALIM BOISS TAB							
32 TEXTILES–INDUSTRIES TEXTILES							
33 WOOD & PRODUCTS–BOIS & PRODUITS							
34 PAPER & PRODUCTS–PAPIER & PRODT							
35 CHEMICALS–INDUSTRIES CHIMIQUES							
36 NON METAL MIN–MIN NON METAL							
37 BASIC METAL–IND METAL BASE							
38 METAL MANUF–MANUF METAL							
39 OTH MANUF IND–AUTRES MANUF							

3. TRADE BY PRINCIPAL COUNTRIES OF ORIGIN AND DESTINATION (VALUE IN MILLION U.S. DOLLARS)
ECHANGES SELON LES PRINCIPAUX PAYS D'ORIGINE ET DE DESTINATION (VALEUR EN MILLIONS DE DOLLARS EU)

COUNTRIES–PAYS	SPECIAL IMPORTS C.I.F. IMPORTATIONS SPECIALES C.A.F					COUNTRIES–PAYS	SPECIAL EXPORTS F.O.B. EXPORTATIONS SPECIALES F.O.B.				
	1991	1992	1993	1994	1995		1991	1992	1993	1994	1995
World					215.2	Monde					
Africa					64.8	Afrique					
Americas					14.2	Amériques					
– Northern America					14.0	– Amérique du Nord					
– LAIA					0.1	– ALAI					
– CACM						– MCAC					
– Caribbean					0.0	– Caraïbes					
– Rest of America						– Autre Amérique					
Asia excl fmr USSR					14.6	Asie anc. URSS exclus					
– Middle East					0.2	– Moyen–Orient					
Asia former USSR						Asie ancienne URSS					
Europe excl fmr USSR					111.7	Europe anc. URSS exclus					
– European Union					110.3	– Union Européenne					
– Eastern Europe					0.0	– Europe de l'Est					
– Rest of Europe					1.3	– Autre de l'Europe					
Europe former USSR					0.9	Europe ancienne URSS					
Oceania					0.0	Océanie					
Other					9.0	Autre					
France, Monaco					88.9						
Cameroon/Cameroun					33.9						
Nigeria/Nigéria					25.3						
USA/Etats–Unis d'Amer					14.0						
Areas n.e.s.					9.0						
Italy/Italie					6.5						
China/Chine					6.3						
Japan/Japon					5.1						
Belgium–Luxembourg					4.8						
Spain/Espagne					3.4						
Central African Rep					3.0						
Germany/Allemagne					3.0						
Netherlands/Pays–Bas					2.8						
Malaysia/Malaisie					2.2						
Russian Federation					0.9						
Cote d'Ivoire					0.8						
Switzerland,Liechtenst.					0.8						
Denmark/Danemark					0.6						
So. African Customs Un					0.6						
Norway,Svalbard and JM					0.5						
Sudan/Soudan					0.5						
Indonesia/Indonésie					0.4						
Sweden/Suède					0.2						
Congo					0.2						
Afghanistan					0.2						
Ethiopia/Ethiopie					0.1						
Benin/Bénin					0.1						
Saudi Arabia					0.1						
India/Inde					0.1						

(VALUE AS PERCENTAGE OF WORLD TOTAL)(VALEURS EN POURCENTAGE DU TOTAL MONDIAL)

	1986	1987	1988	1989	1990	1991	1992	1993	1994	1995		1986	1987	1988	1989	1990	1991	1992	1993	1994	1995
Africa										30.1	Afrique										
Americas										6.6	Amériques										
– Northern America										6.5	– Amérique du Nord										
– LAIA										0.1	– ALAI										
– CACM											– MCAC										
– Caribbean										0.0	– Caraïbes										
– Rest of America											– Autre Amérique										
Asia excl fmr USSR										6.8	Asie anc. URSS exclus										
– Middle East										0.1	– Moyen–Orient										
Asia former USSR											Asie ancienne URSS										
Europe excl fmr USSR										51.9	Europe anc. URSS exclus										
– European Union										51.3	– Union Européenne										
– Eastern Europe										0.0	– Europe de l'Est										
– Rest of Europe										0.6	– Autre de l'Europe										
Europe former USSR										0.4	Europe ancienne URSS										
Oceania										0.0	Océanie										
Other										4.2	Autre										
France, Monaco										41.3											
Cameroon/Cameroun										15.8											
Nigeria/Nigéria										11.7											
USA/Etats–Unis d'Amer										6.5											
Areas n.e.s.										4.2											
Italy/Italie										3.0											
China/Chine										2.9											
Japan/Japon										2.4											
Belgium–Luxembourg										2.2											
Spain/Espagne										1.6											

4. Special Imports C.I.F. by Commodities according to the S.I.T.C. (Rev. 2) in million U.S. Dollars
Importations Spéciales C.A.F. par Produits d'après la C.T.C.I. (Rév. 2) en millions de Dollars E.U.

SITC CTCI	COMMODITY	1992 QUANTITY QUANTITE	1992 VALUE VALEUR	1993 QUANTITY QUANTITE	1993 VALUE VALEUR	1994 QUANTITY QUANTITE	1994 VALUE VALEUR	1995 QUANTITY QUANTITE	1995 VALUE VALEUR	PRODUIT
	ALL COMMODITIES								215.2	TOUS PRODUITS
0	FOOD AND LIVE ANIMALS								41.2	ALIMENTS,ANIMAUX VIVANTS
01	MEAT AND PREPARATIONS								0.9	VIANDES ET PREPARATIONS
02	DAIRY PRODCTS,BIRDS'EGGS								2.6	PRODUITS LAITIERS,OEUFS
022	MILK AND CREAM							W 712	1.6	LAIT ET CREME
0224	MILK,CREAM PRESERVED ETC							W 690	1.4	LAIT,CREME CONS,CONC
02243	MILK DRY,OVER 1.5% FAT							W 667	1.4	LAIT POUDRE SUP 1.5%
024	CHEESE AND CURD							W 103	0.8	FROMAGE ET CAILLEBOTTE
03	FISH AND PREPARATIONS								1.0	POISSONS ET PREPARATIONS
037	FISH ETC PREPD,PRSVD NES							W 348	0.9	POIS,CRUST,MOL PREPARES
0371	FISH PREPARD,PRESRVD NES							W 345	0.9	CONSERVES DE POISSONS
04	CEREALS AND PREPARATIONS								16.1	CEREALES ET PRODUITS
042	RICE							W 6208	4.6	RIZ
0422	RICE SEMI-MILLED,MILLED							W 6208	4.6	RIZ POLI,GLACE INCL BRISURES
04221	RICE MILLED UNBROKEN							W 6208	4.6	RIZ POLI,GLACE EXCL BRISURES
046	WHEAT ETC MEAL OR FLOUR							W 22717	9.0	SEMOULE FARINE,FROMENT
04601	FLOUR OF WHEAT OR MESLIN							W 22717	9.0	FARINE DE FROMENT
047	OTHER CEREAL MEALS,FLOUR							W 4294	1.4	AUTRES SEMOULES,FARINES
04701	CEREAL FLOUR(NON-WHEAT)							W 4190	1.3	FARINES DE CEREALES
048	CEREAL ETC PREPARATIONS							W 699	0.8	PREPTNS A BASE CEREALES
05	VEGETABLES AND FRUIT								1.0	LEGUMES ET FRUITS
06	SUGAR AND PREPS,HONEY								17.1	SUCRES ET PRODUITS
061	SUGAR AND HONEY							W 24203	17.0	SUCRES ET MIEL
0612	REFINED SUGAR ETC							W 23970	16.9	SUCRES RAFFINES
07	COFFEE,TEA,COCOA,SPICES								1.2	CAFE,THE,CACAO,EPICES
074	TEA AND MATE							W 813	0.9	THE ET MATE
0741	TEA							W 813	0.9	THE
09	MISC EDIBLE PRODUCTS								1.7	PREP ALIMENTAIRES DIVERSES
098	EDIBLE PRODCTS,PREPS NES							W 813	1.7	PREP ALIMENTAIRES NDA
09809	MISC FOOD PREPRTIONS NES							W 444	1.2	PREP ALIMENTAIRES NDA
1	BEVERAGES AND TOBACCO								7.2	BOISSONS ET TABACS
11	BEVERAGES								4.6	BOISSONS
111	NON-ALCOHL BEVERAGES NES							W 2518	1.1	BOISSONS NON ALCOOLIQUES
11101	WATERS,ICE AND SNOW							W 2328	0.8	EAU,EAUX MINERALES
112	ALCOHOLIC BEVERAGES							W 4444	3.5	BOISSONS ALCOOLIQUES
1123	BEER,ALE,STOUT,PORTER							W 4166	3.0	BIERES
12	TOBACCO AND MANUFACTURES								2.7	TABACS BRUTS FABRIQUES
122	TOBACCO,MANUFACTURED							W 224	2.5	TABACS FABRIQUES
1223	OTH MANUFACTURED TOBACCO							W 217	2.3	TABACS FUMER,CHIQUER,PRISER
2	CRUDE MATERLS,EXCL FUELS								2.3	MAT BRUTES NON COMESTIBLES
27	CRUDE FERTLZR,MINRLS NES								1.0	ENGRAIS MINERAUX BRUTS
278	OTHER CRUDE MINERALS							W 4904	0.9	AUTRES MINERAUX BRUTS
2783	COMMON SALT,ETC							W 4801	0.8	SEL
3	MINERAL FUELS ETC								38.6	COMBUSTIBLES MINERAUX LUB
33	PETROLEUM AND PRODUCTS								38.6	PETROLE ET DERIVES
334	PETROLEUM PRODUCTS,REFIN							W 94019	38.6	PRODUITS RAFFINES
3341	GASOLINE,OTH LIGHT OILS							W 15815	6.5	ESSENCES POUR MOTEURS
33411	MOTOR,AVIATION SPIRIT							W 8817	3.8	ESSENCES MOTEURS D'AVIONS
33419	OTH LIGHT PETROLEUM OILS							W 6998	2.8	AUTRES HUILES LEGERES
3342	KEROSENE,OTH MEDIUM OILS							W 21658	8.5	PETR LAMPANTS,AUT HUIL
33421	KEROSENE INCL JET FUEL							W 21595	8.5	PETROLES LAMPANTS
3343	GAS OILS							W 56338	23.4	GAS OILS
4	ANIMAL,VEGETABLE OIL,FAT								3.4	HUILES,GRAISSES ANIM,VEG
42	FIXED VEGETABLE OIL,FAT								0.7	HUILES VEGETALES FIXES
431	*PROCESD ANML VEG OIL,ET							W 3596	2.7	HUILES,GRAISSES PREPAREES
4313	FATTY ACIDS ETC,RESIDUES							W 3596	2.7	ACIDES GRAS INDUST,RESIDUS
43131	FATTY ACIDS,ACID OILS							W 3596	2.7	ACIDES GRAS INDUSTRIELS
5	CHEMCLS,RELATED PROD NES								15.6	PRODUITS CHIMIQUES
541	*MEDICINAL,PHARM PRODUCT							K 617692	7.8	PROD MEDICINAUX PHARMACEUT
5416	GLYCOSIDES,GLANDS,SERA							K 13301	0.7	HETEROSIDES
54164	ANTISERA,MICROB VACCINES							K 12216	0.7	SERUMS,VACCINS
5417	MEDICAMENTS							K 551938	6.4	MEDICAMENTS
54179	— CONTNG OTH SUBSTANCES							K 499550	5.9	MED CONT AUT SUBSTANCES
55	PERFUME,CLEANING ETC PRD								0.9	PROD POUR PARFUM,TOILETTE
562	*FERTILIZERS,MANUFACTURE							W 5031	2.5	ENGRAIS MANUFACTURES
5621	CHEM NITROGENOUS FERTLZR							W 1391	0.9	ENGRAIS AZOTES
56213	AMMONIUM SULPHATE							W 1032	0.8	SULFATE D'AMMONIUM
5629	FERTILIZERS NES							W 2328	1.4	ENGRAIS NDA
56299	OTHER FERTILIZERS NES							W 1418	0.8	AUTRES ENGRAIS NDA
58	PLASTIC MATERIALS ETC								1.2	MAT PLAST ARTIFICIELLES
584	CELLULOSE DERIVATIVS ETC							W 109	0.8	CEL REGEN NIT ACETATE
5843	CELLULOSE ACETATES							W 109	0.8	ACETATES DE CELLULOSE
58431	— NON-PLASTICIZED							W 109	0.8	ACETAT CELLULOSE NON PLAST
59	CHEMICAL MATERIALS NES								2.3	MAT PROD CHIMIQUES NDA
591	PESTICIDES,DISINFECTANTS							W 168	1.6	DESINF,INSECT,FONG,HERB
5911	INSECTICIDES,FOR RETAIL							W 106	1.0	INSECTICIDES VENTE DET
6	BASIC MANUFACTURES								26.2	ART MANUFACTURES
62	RUBBER MANUFACTURES NES								3.1	CAOUTCHOUC MANUFACTURE
625	RUBBER TYRES, TUBES ETC							W 364	2.5	PNEUS CAOUTCHOUC VULCANISE
6252	TYRES,NEW,BUS OR LORRY							W 184	1.5	PNEUS POUR AUTOBUS,CAMIONS
6259	OTH TYRES,TYRE CASES,ETC							W 129	0.7	AUTRES PNEUS RECHAPES FLAPS
64	PAPER,PAPERBOARD AND MFR								3.6	PAPIERS,CARTONS & OUVRAGES
641	PAPER AND PAPERBOARD							W 429	1.3	PAPIERS ET CARTONS
642	PAPER,ETC,PRECUT,ARTS OF							W 1137	2.4	PAP,CARTONS DECOUPES
6421	PAPER ETC CONTAINERS							W 930	1.5	BOITES,SACS EMBALLAGES
65	TEXTILE YARN,FABRICS,ETC								2.6	FILS,TISSUS,ARTICLES TEXTILE
653	WOVN MAN-MADE FIB FABRIC							W 206	1.0	TISSUS FIBRES SYNTH,ARTIF
658	TEXTILE ARTICLES NES							W 392	0.8	ART FACONNES MAT TEXTILES
66	NONMETAL MINERAL MFS NES								7.7	ART MIN NON METALLIQUES
661	LIME,CEMENT,BLDG PRODS							W 52158	6.4	CHAUX,CIMENTS MAT CONSTR
6612	CEMENT							W 51546	6.3	CIMENTS HYDRAULIQUES
67	IRON AND STEEL								2.8	FER ET ACIER
672	IRON,STEEL PRIMARY FORMS							W 1248	1.3	LINGOTS FER,ACIER
6727	IRN,STL COIL FR REROLLNG							W 1247	1.3	EBAUCHES POUR TOLES FER
67271	IRON,SIMPLE STEEL COILS							W 1049	1.1	EBAUCHES NON EN ACIER
673	IRON,STEEL SHAPES ETC							W 2574	0.9	BARRES,PROFIL FER,ACIER
69	METAL MANUFACTURES NES								6.1	ART MANUFACT EN METAL NDA
691	STRUCTURES AND PARTS NES							W 727	1.0	CONSTRUCT FER,ACIER,ALU
6911	STRUCTURES,PARTS IRN,STL							W 621	0.7	CONSTRUCT FER,ACIER,FONTE
694	STL,COPPR NAILS,NUTS,ETC							W 147	1.1	CLOUS,VIS,ECROUS
695	TOOLS							W 102	1.2	OUTILS A MAIN

4. Special Imports C.I.F. by Commodities according to the S.I.T.C. (Rev. 2) in million U.S. Dollars
Importations Spéciales C.A.F. par Produits d'après la C.T.C.I. (Rév. 2) en millions de Dollars E.U.

SITC CTCI	COMMODITY	1992 QUANTITY QUANTITE	1992 VALUE VALEUR	1993 QUANTITY QUANTITE	1993 VALUE VALEUR	1994 QUANTITY QUANTITE	1994 VALUE VALEUR	1995 QUANTITY QUANTITE	1995 VALUE VALEUR	PRODUIT
6953	OTHER HAND TOOLS							W 77	0.9	AUTRES OUTILS A MAIN
699	BASE METAL MFRS NES							W 199	1.7	ART MANUFACTURES MET NDA
6996	BASE MTL MISC ARTICLES							W 101	0.8	ART DIVERS METAUX COMMUNS
7	MACHINES,TRANSPORT EQUIP								51.3	MACHINES MATERIEL TRANSPORT
71	POWER GENERATING EQUIPMT								3.9	MACHINES GENERATRICES
713	INTRNL COMBUS PSTN ENGIN							W 59	1.9	MOTEURS EXPL COMB INT, PIECE
7139	PISTON ENGINE PARTS NES							W 29	1.3	PIECES POUR 713.2,3,8
716	ROTATING ELECTRIC PLANT							W 127	1.5	APP ELECTR ROTATIFS,PIECES
7162	AC MTRS,GENRTRS,GEN SETS							W 104	1.1	MOTEURS ELECTRIQUES
72	MACHS FOR SPCL INDUSTRYS								4.0	MAC SPECIALES POUR INDUST
724	TEXTILE,LEATHER MACHNRY							W 176	2.0	MACH POUR INDUSTRIE TEXTILE
7244	SPINNING,EXTRDNG,ETC MCH							W 172	2.0	MACH POUR LE FILAGE
72442	FIBRE PROCESSNG MACH NES							W 145	1.4	MACH PREP MAT TEXTILES
727	FOOD MACHRY NON-DOMESTIC							W 182	0.8	MACH INDUSTRIES ALIMENT
74	GENRL INDUSTRL MACHY NES								8.2	MACH APP INDUSTRIE
741	HEATING,COOLING EQUIPMNT							W 55	1.0	MACH CHAUFFAGE,PIECES
742	PUMPS FOR LIQUIDS ETC							W 116	1.8	POMPES MOTO-POMPES
7428	OTHER PUMPS FOR LIQUIDS							W 102	1.4	AUTRES POMPES POUR LIQ
74288	PUMPS FR LIQUIDS NES ETC							W 101	1.4	POMPES POUR LIQUIDES NDA
743	PUMPS NES,CENTRFUGES ETC							W 84	1.1	POMPES COMPRES,VENT ETC
744	MECHANICAL HANDLING EQU							W 61	0.8	EQUIP MANUTENTION PIECES
745	NONELEC MACHY,TOOLS NES							W 58	0.8	AUT MACH NON ELEC,PIECES
7452	OTH NONELEC MCHS,PTS NES							W 58	0.8	AUT MACH NON ELEC,PIECES
749	NONELEC MACH PTS,ACC NES							W 94	2.9	PIECES MACH NON ELEC NDA
7493	SHAFT,CRANK,PULLEY ETC							W 53	1.4	ARBRES TRANS,VILEBREQUINS
75	OFFICE MACHNES,ADP EQUIP								3.7	MACH BUREAU TRAIT AUTOM
751	OFFICE MACHINES							W 28	0.8	MACH,APPAREILS DE BUREAU
752	AUTOMTIC DATA PROC EQUIP							W 23	2.2	MACH TRAIT INFORMATION
7522	DIGITAL COMPUTERS							W 11	1.3	MACH DIGITALES COMPLETES
759	OFFICE,ADP MCH PTS,ACCES							W 11	0.8	PIECES DU 751 ET 752
7599	ACCTG,ETC,ADP MCH PTS,AC							W 8	0.7	PIECES DU 751 ET 752
76	TELECOMM,SOUND EQUIPMENT								4.6	EQUIPMENT DE TELECOM
764	TELECOM EQPT,PTS,ACC NES							W 68	4.4	EQUIP TELECOM,PIECES
7641	LINE TELEPHONE,ETC EQUIP							W 23	2.0	APP TELEPHON PAR FIL
7643	TV,RADIO TRANSMITTRS ETC							W 5	0.7	APP EMET TELE RADIO
7649	PTS NES OF EQUIPMT OF 76							W 40	1.7	PIECES DE LA DIV 76
76493	TELECOMM EQUIPMT PTS NES							W 36	1.4	PIECES 761,762,764.3,8
77	ELECTRIC MACHNRY NES ETC								8.1	MACH APP ELECT NDA
771	ELECTRIC POWER MACHY NES							W 18	2.7	MACH PROD,TRANS ELECTR
7711	TRANSFORMERS,ELECTRICAL							W 12	2.4	TRANSFO ELECTRIQUES
77118	OTHER ELEC TRANSFORMERS							W 12	2.4	AUTRES TRANSFO ELECTRIQ
772	SWITCHGEAR ETC,PARTS NES							W 90	1.0	APP COUPURE,SECT ETC
7721	SWITCHGEAR ETC							W 90	1.0	APP COUPURE,SECTIONMNT
773	ELECTR DISTRIBUTNG EQUIP							W 218	0.9	EQUIPMT DISTRIBUTION ELECT
778	ELECTRICAL MACHINERY NES							W 343	2.8	AUTRES MACH ELECT NDA
7781	BATTERIES,ACCUMULATORS							W 268	0.9	PILES ET ACCUMULATEURS
7783	AUTOMOTIVE ELECTR EQUIP							W 32	1.2	EQUIP ELECT MOTEURS EXPL
78	ROAD VEHICLES								17.9	VEHICULES ROUTIERS
781	PASS MOTOR VEH EXC BUSES							W 529	1.6	AUTO TRANSPORT PERSONNES
782	LORRIES,SPCL MTR VEH NES							W 2232	4.5	VEHICULES SPECIAUX,MARCH
7821	LORRIES,TRUCKS							W 2185	4.4	VEHICULES TRANSP MARCHAND
783	ROAD MOTOR VEHICLES NES							W 537	1.8	VEHICULES ROUTIERS NDA
7831	BUSES							W 255	1.7	VOITURES TRANSPORT COMMUN
784	MOTOR VEH PRTS,ACCES NES							W 522	8.3	PIECES 722,781,782,783
7849	OTHER MOTOR VEHCL PARTS							W 476	8.2	PIECES 722,781,782,783
785	CYCLES,ETC MOTRZD OR NOT							W 200	1.0	MOTOCYCLES SCOOTERS
786	TRAILERS,NONMOTR VEH,NES							W 352	0.9	REMORQUES,CADRES,CONTAIN
79	OTHR TRANSPORT EQUIPMENT								0.9	AUTRE MATERIEL TRANSPORT
792	AIRCRAFT ETC							W 5	0.9	APP NAVIGATION AERIENNE
7929	AIRCRAFT PARTS NES							W 4	0.9	PIECES DU 792
8	MISC MANUFACTURED GOODS								27.4	ART MANUFACTURES DIVERS
821	*FURNITURE,PARTS THEREOF							W 177	2.1	MEUBLES ET PIECES
8211	CHAIRS,SEATS AND PARTS							W 84	1.3	SIEGES ET PIECES
82111	CHAIRS AND OTHER SEATS							W 84	1.3	SIEGES
84	CLOTHING AND ACCESSORIES								2.1	VETEMENTS
842	MENS OUTERWEAR NOT KNIT							W 64	1.0	VET DESSUS POUR HOMMES
87	PRECISION INSTRUMNTS NES								5.1	INSTRUM,APPAR SCIENT NDA
872	MEDICAL INSTRUMENTS NES							W 149	1.9	INSTR,APP MEDIC-CHIR NDA
87202	OTH MEDICAL INSTRUMENTS							W 63	1.9	INSTRUM,APP MEDECINE
874	MEASURNG,CONTROLNG INSTR							W 41	3.0	INSTRUMENTS DE MESURE
8741	SURVEYING INSTRUMENTS							W 16	1.9	INST GEODESIE,TOPO ETC
87412	SURVEY INSTR ETC NONELEC							W 15	1.8	INSTR GEODESIE,TOPO ETC
89	MISC MANUFCTRD GOODS NES								17.0	ART MANUFACTURES DIVERS
892	PRINTED MATTER							W 219	13.6	IMPRIMES
8921	PRINTED BOOKS,GLOBES,ETC							W 129	1.1	LIVRES,BROCHURES,CARTES
89211	PRINTED BOOKS,PAMPHLETS							W 127	1.0	LIVRES,BROCHURES
8928	PRINTED MATTER NES							W 68	12.1	IMPRIMES NDA
89283	UNISSUED BANKNOTES ETC							W 37	11.7	TIMBRES-POSTE FISCAUX
893	ARTICLES OF PLASTIC NES							W 374	1.8	OUVRAGES EN MAT DIVIS 58
8939	MISC PLASTIC ARTICLES							W 244	1.4	ART DIVERS EN MAT DIV 58
89399	OTHR PLASTC ARTICLES NES							W 212	1.3	AUT OUV MAT DIV 58
894	TOYS,SPORTING GOODS,ETC							W 35	1.0	VOITURES ENFANTS,JOUETS
9	GOODS NOT CLASSD BY KIND								2.5	ART TRANSACT NON CLASSES
931	*SPECIAL TRANSACTIONS								1.5	TRANS.SPECIALES
951	*WAR FIREARMS,AMMUNITION							W 22	1.0	VEHIC BLINDES ARMES
95106	AMMUNITION NES							W 14	0.8	PROJECTILES,MUNITIONS

5. Special Exports F.O.B. by Commodities according to the S.I.T.C. (Rev. 2) in million U.S. Dollars
Exportations Spéciales F.O.B. par Produits d'après la C.T.C.I. (Rév. 2) en millions de Dollars E.U.

SITC CTCI	COMMODITY	1992		1993		1994		1995		PRODUIT
		QUANTITY QUANTITE	VALUE VALEUR	QUANTITY QUANTITE	VALUE VALEUR	QUANTITY QUANTITE	VALUE VALEUR	QUANTITY QUANTITE	VALUE VALEUR	
	ALL COMMODITIES									TOUS PRODUITS

1. HISTORICAL SERIES, 1962–1997 SPECIAL TRADE, IMPORTS C.I.F., EXPORTS F.O.B.
SERIES HISTORIQUES, 1962–1997 COMMERCE SPECIAL, IMPORTATIONS C.A.F., EXPORTATIONS F.O.B

YEAR ANNEE	VALUE IN MILLION U.S. DOLLARS VALEUR EN MILLION U.S. DOLLARS MERCHANDISE –MARCHANDISE		GOLD –OR		CONVERSION FACTORS FACTEURS DE CONVERSION CENTS E.U. PAR		INDEX NUMBERS –INDICES QUANTUM		UNIT VALUE VALEUR UNITAIRE	
	IMPORTS	EXPORTS	IMPORTS	EXPORTS	IMPORTS	EXPORTS	IMPORTS	EXPORTS	IMPORTS	EXPORTS
1962	511.70	532.10								
1963	637.30	542.00								
1964	607.20	625.80								
1965	603.60	687.90								
1966	749.20	875.50								
1967	722.50	907.70								
1968	743.60	935.90								
1969	907.90	1067.90								
1970	930.10	1233.60								
1971	979.80	961.20								
1972	941.20	855.40								
1973	1097.90	1230.50								
1974	1681.40	1247.50								
1975	1338.20	1552.10								
1976	1683.80	2082.60								
1977	2414.00	2190.30								
1978	3002.40	2477.70								
1979	4217.60	3894.20								
1980	5123.70	4670.70								
1981	6363.80	3906.30								
1982	3830.90	3709.50								
1983	2968.80	3835.50								
1984	3480.50	3657.20								
1985	3006.60	3822.90								
1986	3436.30	4191.20								
1987	4396.40	5223.70								
1988	5291.80	7051.80								
1989	7144.20	8080.00								
1990	7677.60	8372.70								
1991	8093.70	8941.50								
1992	10128.60	10007.40								
1993	11125.40	9198.70								
1994	11824.60	11604.10								
1995	15914.10	16136.50								
1996	17827.50	15353.00								
1997	19859.81	16875.41								

2. IMPORTS BY BROAD ECONOMIC CATEGORY AND EXPORTS BY INDUSTRIAL ORIGIN. (PERCENTAGE OF TOTAL VALUE)
IMPORTATIONS PAR CATEGORIES ECONOMIQUES ET EXPORTATIONS PAR BRANCHE D'ACTIVITE.(EN POURCENTAGE DE LA VALEUR TOTALE)

IMPORTS – IMPORTATIONS

	1991	1992	1993	1994	1995	1996	1997
TOTAL IMPORTS–IMPORTATIONS TOTALES	100.	100.	100.	100.	100.	100.	100.
1 FOOD BEV–ALIMENTATION BOISSONS	4.7	5.1	5.0	5.7	5.6	5.8	5.2
11 PRIMARY–PRODUITS DE BASE	1.6	2.5	2.5	2.9	2.7	3.0	2.3
111 FOR INDUSTRY–POUR L'INDUSTRIE	0.5	1.1	1.1	1.3	1.2	1.5	0.7
112 FOR HOUSEHOLDS–POUR LES MENAGES	1.1	1.4	1.5	1.6	1.5	1.5	1.6
12 PROCESSED–PRODUITS ELABORES	3.2	2.6	2.5	2.8	2.8	2.9	2.9
121 FOR INDUSTRY–POUR L'INDUSTRIE	0.6	0.7	0.7	0.8	0.7	0.6	0.5
122 FOR HOUSEHOLDS–POUR LES MENAGES	2.5	1.9	1.8	2.0	2.2	2.2	2.4
2 IND SUPPLIES–APPROV INDUSTRIELS	30.7	28.8	27.8	27.7	29.5	26.5	26.2
21 PRIMARY–PRODUITS DE BASE	2.5	2.1	2.0	2.5	2.9	2.0	2.0
22 PROCESSED–PRODUITS ELABORES	28.2	26.7	25.8	25.2	26.6	24.5	24.2
3 FUELS–COMBUSTIBLES	14.8	11.5	9.9	9.7	8.8	10.8	9.9
31 PRIMARY–PRODUITS DE BASE	12.7	9.8	8.6	8.0	7.5	8.7	8.0
32 PROCESSED–PRODUITS ELABORES	2.1	1.6	1.3	1.7	1.4	2.1	1.9
321 MOTOR SPIRIT–ESSENCE	2.1	1.6	0.1	0.4	0.2	0.4	0.4
322 OTHER–AUTRES	0.1	0.0	1.2	1.3	1.2	1.6	1.5
4 MACHINERY–EQUIPEMENT	24.9	25.0	28.1	28.7	26.6	26.5	28.5
41 CAPITAL EQUIPMENT–MACHINES	21.5	21.8	24.7	25.4	23.5	23.7	25.6
42 PARTS–PIECES ACCESSOIRES	3.4	3.2	3.3	3.3	3.1	2.9	2.9
5 TRANSPORT–TRANSPORT	12.7	16.2	14.9	13.8	15.1	15.5	14.6
51 PASSENGER CARS–AUTOMOBILES	3.8	5.6	4.6	4.0	5.0	5.1	5.1
52 OTHER–AUTRES	5.4	7.0	6.7	6.6	7.1	7.4	6.6
521 INDUSTRIAL–INDUSTRIELS	5.3	6.9	6.5	6.4	7.0	7.3	6.5
522 NON INDUSTRIAL–NON INDUSTRIEL	0.1	0.2	0.2	0.2	0.1	0.2	0.1
53 PARTS–PIECES ACCESSOIRES	3.6	3.6	3.7	3.3	3.0	2.9	2.9
6 CONSUM GOODS–BIENS CONSOMMATION	10.6	11.7	12.6	12.8	13.2	13.6	14.4
61 DURABLE–DURABLES	3.6	4.1	4.1	4.0	4.1	3.9	4.2
62 SEMI DURABLE–SEMI DURABLES	4.9	5.5	6.2	6.4	6.7	7.2	7.6
63 NON DURABLE–NON DURABLES	2.1	2.2	2.3	2.4	2.4	2.5	2.5
7 GOODS NES–BIENS NDA	1.6	1.6	1.7	1.5	1.3	1.3	1.3

EXPORTS – EXPORTATIONS

	1991	1992	1993	1994	1995	1996	1997
TOTAL EXPORTS–EXPORTATIONS TOTALES	100.	100.	100.	100.	100.	100.	100.
1 AGRICULTURE	17.1	17.2	18.4	17.0	14.4	16.1	15.2
2 MINING QUARRY–INDUS EXTRACTIVES	14.4	14.3	13.0	13.7	16.5	15.7	15.6
3 MANUFACTURING–IND MANUFACTUR	68.5	68.4	68.7	69.3	69.2	68.2	69.3
31 FOOD BEV TOBACCO–ALIM BOISS TAB	12.3	13.2	12.6	12.2	12.0	13.5	12.1
32 TEXTILES–INDUSTRIES TEXTILES	1.7	1.6	2.0	1.8	1.3	1.4	1.5
33 WOOD & PRODUCTS–BOIS & PRODUITS	4.3	3.8	4.4	4.3	4.0	4.1	4.3
34 PAPER & PRODUCTS–PAPIER & PRODT	5.5	7.3	7.5	8.9	10.5	7.4	6.5
35 CHEMICALS–INDUSTRIES CHIMIQUES	4.9	4.5	5.1	5.7	4.4	4.6	5.8
36 NON METAL MIN–MIN NON METAL	0.2	0.2	0.2	0.2	0.2	0.2	0.3
37 BASIC METAL–IND METAL BASE	35.7	33.2	30.7	30.2	32.4	31.1	33.1
38 METAL MANUF–MANUF METAL	2.1	2.7	3.7	4.0	2.7	3.8	3.8
39 OTH MANUF IND–AUTRES MANUF	1.9	2.0	2.3	2.1	1.5	2.0	1.9

3. TRADE BY PRINCIPAL COUNTRIES OF PURCHASE AND SALE (VALUE IN MILLION U.S. DOLLARS)
ECHANGES SELON LES PRINCIPAUX PAYS D'ACHAT ET DE VENTE (VALEUR EN MILLIONS DE DOLLARS EU)

COUNTRIES–PAYS	SPECIAL IMPORTS C.I.F. IMPORTATIONS SPECIALES C.A.F 1993	1994	1995	1996	1997	COUNTRIES–PAYS	SPECIAL EXPORTS F.O.B. EXPORTATIONS SPECIALES F.O.B. 1993	1994	1995	1996	1997
World	10541.9	11149.1	14903.1	16810.0	18110.8	Monde	9308.3	11368.7	15901.1	15406.8	16678.2
Africa	596.1	315.2	315.3	438.0	359.5	Afrique	40.6	102.4	129.6	120.4	106.2
Americas	5151.0	5885.3	8258.4	9331.5	10088.7	Amériques	3457.7	4374.3	5320.6	5572.2	6082.4
– Northern America	2680.1	2902.7	4108.0	4517.6	4764.4	– Amérique du Nord	1587.5	1931.7	2233.2	2515.4	2573.1
– LAIA	2424.3	2883.4	4035.5	4655.6	5183.5	– ALAI	1798.2	2337.5	2984.6	2928.5	3361.0
– CACM	11.2	25.2	42.0	41.6	71.1	– MCAC	32.0	37.0	41.1	52.1	67.0
– Caribbean	26.0	68.4	63.2	109.7	59.7	– Caraïbes	18.6	29.8	37.9	51.0	51.3
– Rest of America	9.4	5.5	9.7	7.1	10.0	– Autre Amérique	21.5	38.2	23.8	25.2	29.9
Asia excl fmr USSR	1941.6	2097.1	2640.8	2817.9	3101.2	Asie anc. URSS exclus	2952.6	3796.8	5581.0	5369.2	5909.5
– Middle East	124.4	10.5	27.0	33.6	35.5	– Moyen–Orient	132.1	92.4	134.6	154.9	168.0
Asia former USSR			0.7	0.4	0.0	Asie ancienne URSS			0.0	3.8	0.8
Europe excl fmr USSR	2507.4	2532.5	3346.1	3813.0	4169.7	Europe anc. URSS exclus	2578.9	2763.7	4461.5	3909.2	4222.0
– European Union	2312.4	2347.7	3155.6	3538.0	3957.8	– Union Européenne	2532.7	2705.5	4241.4	3731.9	4079.8
– Eastern Europe	32.5	44.0	31.7	49.4	39.6	– Europe de l'Est	7.0	5.0	73.9	57.9	34.7
– Rest of Europe	162.5	140.8	158.8	225.6	172.4	– Autre de l'Europe	39.2	53.1	146.2	119.4	107.4
Europe former USSR	58.9	38.2	43.7	46.7	35.7	Europe ancienne URSS	22.5	51.7	146.7	136.0	48.5
Oceania	113.8	133.2	173.5	215.0	194.8	Océanie	39.6	50.2	87.3	108.7	86.7
Other	173.1	147.7	124.7	147.5	161.0	Autre	216.4	229.6	174.3	187.3	222.1
USA/Etats–Unis d'Amer	2477.1	2637.9	3792.9	4109.5	4332.2	Japan/Japon	1542.9	1972.1	2840.2	2530.6	2681.9
Argentina/Argentine	580.2	954.7	1384.5	1634.2	1837.2	USA/Etats–Unis d'Amer	1525.8	1861.2	2138.3	2372.6	2439.1
Brazil/Brésil	1059.9	999.8	1194.6	1065.7	1242.8	United Kingdom	551.9	505.1	1044.2	916.6	1040.2
Japan/Japon	882.6	1007.1	1012.9	949.7	1054.7	Brazil/Brésil	424.2	616.7	1063.9	946.8	974.5
Germany/Allemagne	620.0	506.5	789.7	729.9	843.6	Korea, Republic of	421.4	594.5	891.2	892.2	991.1
Mexico/Mexique	209.6	263.7	600.6	927.2	1076.2	Germany/Allemagne	493.1	547.9	808.2	758.3	750.2
Italy/Italie	335.5	350.4	508.7	550.8	699.5	Argentina/Argentine	588.5	635.6	584.1	699.9	778.0
Korea, Republic of	343.2	333.4	527.4	556.8	588.7	Other Asia n.e.s.	413.2	535.0	691.6	652.6	773.3
France, Monaco	345.6	362.5	445.9	582.0	502.2	Italy/Italie	330.5	351.5	596.3	490.5	497.5
Spain/Espagne	278.3	340.8	445.0	530.3	621.1	France, Monaco	375.6	394.1	500.9	404.2	450.2
China/Chine	212.5	280.7	390.3	515.1	659.1	Peru/Pérou	206.2	328.3	432.3	324.9	343.4
Canada	203.0	264.8	315.1	408.1	432.2	Netherlands/Pays–Bas	227.7	293.4	358.9	345.2	389.4
United Kingdom	214.7	243.1	247.0	281.7	320.2	China/Chine	183.3	133.3	287.2	372.9	435.2
Venezuela	141.6	139.9	226.8	313.2	273.4	Spain/Espagne	243.4	220.7	304.0	274.9	334.4
Sweden/Suède	112.9	119.1	193.2	271.3	352.0	Belgium–Luxembourg	141.2	203.9	370.3	283.5	274.4
Ecuador/Equateur	129.4	187.1	209.1	224.9	258.6	Areas n.e.s.	216.4	229.6	174.3	187.3	222.1
Other Asia n.e.s.	185.4	161.2	201.8	220.9	225.1	Mexico/Mexique	124.4	202.9	127.4	146.2	371.2
Nigeria/Nigéria	397.3	134.4	166.6	154.2	140.7	Bolivia/Bolivie	162.2	171.6	196.9	207.8	228.4
Colombia/Colombie	98.2	118.9	149.9	222.4	201.2	Colombia/Colombie	71.7	116.8	188.4	194.1	226.0
Areas n.e.s.	173.1	147.7	124.7	147.5	161.0	Indonesia/Indonésie	49.7	88.7	158.8	147.5	154.3
Belgium–Luxembourg	105.3	115.0	125.5	143.3	138.7	Venezuela	73.9	72.7	135.1	141.0	156.7
Australia/Australie	86.1	95.5	119.1	153.3	138.9	Thailand/Thaïlande	65.2	112.4	149.7	119.0	132.8
Switzerland,Liechtenst.	107.7	117.1	124.5	120.6	114.3	Ecuador/Equateur	54.6	82.8	124.2	143.8	156.1
Peru/Pérou	72.3	94.5	147.4	117.9	118.5	Canada	61.7	70.5	94.9	142.9	134.0
Netherlands/Pays–Bas	87.7	91.2	106.4	123.9	108.6	Sweden/Suède	62.8	64.9	82.6	71.6	104.6
Finland/Finlande	77.0	71.4	90.3	103.7	140.4	China, Hong Kong SAR		34.0	81.7	105.4	159.8
Angola	29.0	69.9	70.5	116.2	102.8	Singapore/Singapour	38.9	54.9	78.6	88.1	115.8
Denmark/Danemark	56.5	56.3	87.3	94.4	79.9	So. African Customs Un	31.9	84.0	96.3	67.9	84.6
Indonesia/Indonésie	27.9	42.4	82.7	97.1	109.0	Russian Federation	22.5	51.7	116.7	120.1	42.2
China, Hong Kong SAR		63.5	108.1	120.8	62.2	India/Inde	19.6	58.0	89.0	99.2	73.9
So. African Customs Un	69.8	51.6	72.0	70.1	85.7	Philippines	44.1	54.9	59.2	103.2	73.8
Malaysia/Malaisie	42.4	44.5	76.4	80.8	95.7	Malaysia/Malaisie	29.8	40.5	87.4	69.6	107.5
Paraguay	68.1	55.6	58.0	69.4	55.0	Finland/Finlande	27.3	38.9	62.8	88.0	114.8
Norway,Svalbard and JM	52.0	17.0	30.5	100.8	49.3	Paraguay	48.3	57.5	76.0	66.4	63.8
Netherlands Antilles	14.4	44.4	41.2	90.1	56.0	Switzerland,Liechtenst.	24.9	23.4	92.6	72.1	66.2
Uruguay	51.8	44.0	40.0	45.0	58.1	Uruguay	44.3	52.8	56.3	57.7	63.0
New Zealand	27.6	37.0	54.4	61.7	55.9	Saudi Arabia	52.2	43.9	56.1	57.4	48.5
Singapore/Singapour	35.2	38.5	57.0	44.1	48.4	Australia/Australie	27.9	35.9	59.9	75.7	54.1
Austria/Autriche	37.3	33.7	41.7	38.4	54.5	Greece/Grèce	43.1	40.4	53.0	40.0	57.7
Israel/Israël	26.8	32.3	41.9	46.7	57.3	United Arab Emirates	36.4	32.1	52.7	53.8	48.2

(VALUE AS PERCENTAGE OF WORLD TOTAL)(VALEURS EN POURCENTAGE DU TOTAL MONDIAL)

	1988	1989	1990	1991	1992	1993	1994	1995	1996	1997
Africa	4.5	5.0	8.1	6.1	6.2	5.7	2.8	2.1	2.6	2.0
Americas	52.6	49.6	47.7	51.2	48.6	48.9	52.8	55.4	55.5	55.7
– Northern America	23.5	22.4	22.7	23.3	22.7	25.4	26.0	27.6	26.9	26.3
– LAIA	28.7	27.0	24.6	27.3	25.3	23.0	25.9	27.1	27.7	28.6
– CACM	0.0	0.0	0.0	0.1	0.1	0.1	0.2	0.3	0.2	0.4
– Caribbean	0.3	0.2	0.2	0.5	0.4	0.2	0.6	0.4	0.7	0.3
– Rest of America	0.0	0.1	0.1	0.1	0.1	0.1	0.0	0.1	0.0	0.1
Asia excl fmr USSR	14.6	18.8	13.8	17.7	18.9	18.4	18.8	17.7	16.8	17.1
– Middle East	0.2	0.6	0.2	0.3	0.7	1.2	0.1	0.2	0.2	0.2
Asia former USSR								0.0	0.0	0.0
Europe excl fmr USSR	27.1	25.3	29.0	23.0	23.5	23.8	22.7	22.5	22.7	23.0
– European Union	24.1	22.9	26.8	21.0	21.4	21.9	21.1	21.2	21.0	21.9
– Eastern Europe	0.4	0.4	0.5	0.3	0.4	0.3	0.4	0.2	0.3	0.2
– Rest of Europe	2.5	2.1	1.7	1.7	1.7	1.5	1.3	1.1	1.3	1.0
Europe former USSR	0.3	0.3	0.3	0.5	0.7	0.6	0.3	0.3	0.3	0.2
Oceania	0.5	0.5	0.6	0.9	0.7	1.1	1.2	1.2	1.3	1.1
Other	0.4	0.5	0.5	0.6	1.5	1.6	1.3	0.8	0.9	0.9
USA/Etats–Unis d'Amer	21.2	20.7	19.5	21.2	21.0	23.5	23.7	25.5	24.4	23.9
Argentina/Argentine	5.9	6.1	7.2	7.4	6.7	5.5	8.6	9.3	9.7	10.1
Brazil/Brésil	11.7	10.8	8.0	9.4	10.5	10.1	9.0	8.0	6.3	6.9
Japan/Japon	8.3	11.3	8.1	8.7	10.2	8.4	9.0	6.8	5.6	5.8
Germany/Allemagne				6.7	6.7	5.9	4.5	5.3	4.3	4.7
Mexico/Mexique	1.5	1.8	1.4	1.9	1.9	2.0	2.4	4.0	5.5	5.9
Italy/Italie	2.5	2.4	2.8	2.4	2.9	3.2	3.1	3.4	3.3	3.9
Korea, Republic of	2.3	2.5	1.7	2.3	2.6	3.3	3.0	3.5	3.3	3.3
France, Monaco	3.2	3.4	4.2	3.2	3.0	3.3	3.3	3.0	3.5	2.8
Spain/Espagne	2.5	2.4	2.3	2.0	2.4	2.6	3.1	3.0	3.2	3.4

	1988	1989	1990	1991	1992	1993	1994	1995	1996	1997
Afrique	0.7	1.4	1.3	1.3	0.9	0.4	0.9	0.8	0.8	0.6
Amériques	33.5	30.7	30.1	31.0	33.7	37.1	38.5	33.5	36.2	36.5
– Amérique du Nord	20.1	18.5	17.4	16.1	16.6	17.1	17.0	14.0	16.3	15.4
– ALAI	12.7	11.8	12.0	14.2	16.3	19.3	20.6	18.8	19.0	20.2
– MCAC	0.2	0.1	0.4	0.3	0.5	0.3	0.3	0.3	0.3	0.4
– Caraïbes	0.2	0.2	0.1	0.2	0.3	0.2	0.3	0.2	0.3	0.3
– Autre Amérique	0.3	0.2	0.2	0.2	0.2	0.2	0.3	0.1	0.2	0.2
Asie anc. URSS exclus	22.6	27.0	27.4	30.8	30.2	31.7	33.4	35.1	34.8	35.4
– Moyen–Orient	2.1	1.5	1.2	1.2	1.2	1.4	0.8	0.8	1.0	1.0
Asie ancienne URSS								0.0	0.0	0.0
Europe anc. URSS exclus	41.9	39.2	39.3	34.8	31.4	27.7	24.3	28.1	25.4	25.3
– Union Européenne	39.6	37.6	38.3	34.0	30.4	27.2	23.8	26.7	24.2	24.5
– Europe de l'Est	1.1	0.9	0.6	0.4	0.6	0.1	0.0	0.5	0.4	0.2
– Autre de l'Europe	1.2	0.8	0.4	0.4	0.4	0.4	0.5	0.9	0.8	0.6
Europe ancienne URSS			0.0	0.0	0.4	0.2	0.5	0.9	0.9	0.3
Océanie	0.5	0.7	0.7	0.6	0.4	0.4	0.4	0.5	0.7	0.5
Autre	0.7	0.9	1.2	1.5	3.0	2.3	2.0	1.1	1.2	1.3
Japan/Japon	12.7	13.7	16.2	18.7	17.3	16.6	17.3	17.9	16.4	16.1
USA/Etats–Unis d'Amer	19.4	17.7	16.8	15.5	16.0	16.4	16.4	13.4	15.4	14.6
United Kingdom	5.8	6.0	6.5	6.2	6.2	5.9	4.4	6.6	5.9	6.2
Brazil/Brésil	5.1	6.4	5.8	5.3	4.6	4.5	5.4	6.7	6.1	5.8
Korea, Republic of	2.0	3.2	3.0	3.0	2.5	4.5	5.2	5.6	5.8	5.9
Germany/Allemagne				8.0	6.1	5.3	4.8	5.1	4.9	4.5
Argentina/Argentine	2.4	1.3	1.3	2.9	4.6	6.3	5.6	3.7	4.5	4.7
Other Asia n.e.s.	3.5	5.0	3.3	4.4	4.8	4.4	4.7	4.3	4.2	4.6
Italy/Italie	6.4	5.1	4.8	3.8	3.8	3.6	3.1	3.8	3.2	3.0
France, Monaco	5.0	4.8	4.7	4.3	3.8	4.0	3.5	3.2	2.6	2.7

4. Special Imports C.I.F. by Commodities according to the S.I.T.C. (Rev. 2) in million U.S. Dollars
Importations Spéciales C.A.F. par Produits d'après la C.T.C.I. (Rév. 2) en millions de Dollars E.U.

SITC CTCI	COMMODITY	1994 QUANTITY QUANTITE	1994 VALUE VALEUR	1995 QUANTITY QUANTITE	1995 VALUE VALEUR	1996 QUANTITY QUANTITE	1996 VALUE VALEUR	1997 QUANTITY QUANTITE	1997 VALUE VALEUR	PRODUIT
	ALL COMMODITIES		11149.1		14903.1		16810.1		18110.9	TOUS PRODUITS
0	FOOD AND LIVE ANIMALS		634.8		824.6		1026.3		1024.1	ALIMENTS,ANIMAUX VIVANTS
01	MEAT AND PREPARATIONS		93.5		127.4		148.5		193.9	VIANDES ET PREPARATIONS
011	MEAT FRESH,CHILLD,FROZEN	W 43460	91.4	W 52297	123.7		143.9	W 82599	188.2	VIANDES FRAICHES,REF,CONGE
0111	BOVINE MEAT FRESH,FROZEN	W 40936	88.8	W 49972	120.9	W 61593	140.6	W 79592	184.6	VIANDES BOVIN FRAI,REF
01112	BOVINE MEAT BONELESS	W 40936	88.8	W 49951	120.8	W 61009	139.8	W 78179	182.2	VIANDES BOVIN DESOSSEES
02	DAIRY PRODCTS,BIRDS'EGGS		43.9		56.0		76.7		43.2	PRODUITS LAITIERS,OEUFS
022	MILK AND CREAM	W 19534	29.2	W 21429	39.2	W 26746	55.4	W 12625	22.2	LAIT ET CREME
0224	MILK,CREAM PRESERVED ETC	W 18775	28.5	W 20530	38.1	W 24950	52.9	W 11933	20.9	LAIT,CREME CONS,CONC
03	FISH AND PREPARATIONS		27.3		45.3		35.5		33.6	POISSONS ET PREPARATIONS
04	CEREALS AND PREPARATIONS		205.2		245.7		337.2		244.9	CEREALES ET PRODUITS
041	WHEAT ETC UNMILLED	W 672254	109.1	W 633398	123.6	W 714258	177.6	W 308111	55.8	FROMENT,EPEAUTRE
0412	OTHER WHEAT ETC UNMILLED	W 530504	78.4	W 561064	105.4	W 623804	153.2	W 257932	44.5	AUTRE FROMENT NON MOULU
044	MAIZE UNMILLED	W 459015	66.9	W 508673	80.8	W 404887	84.9	W 795236	119.9	MAIS NON MOULU
05	VEGETABLES AND FRUIT		60.0		79.1		90.3		95.5	LEGUMES ET FRUITS
057	FRUIT,NUTS,FRESH,DRIED	W 152668	36.4	W 151078	38.5		42.1	W 152961	43.3	FRUITS FRAIS OU SECS
0573	BANANA,PLANTAIN,FRSH,DRY	W 147946	33.8	W 144923	35.1	W 150653	37.8	W 145349	38.0	BANANES FRAICHES,SECHEES
06	SUGAR AND PREPS,HONEY		36.7		70.5		85.9		118.1	SUCRES ET PRODUITS
061	SUGAR AND HONEY	W 75924	27.0	W 136027	56.5	W 178579	70.9	W 291693	103.3	SUCRES ET MIEL
0612	REFINED SUGAR ETC	W 71214	24.9	W 129840	53.1	W 164102	65.1	W 274616	97.3	SUCRES RAFFINES
07	COFFEE,TEA,COCOA,SPICES		76.1		90.7		88.7		93.4	CAFE,THE,CACAO,EPICES
081	*FEEDING STUFF FOR ANIML	W 178281	56.6	W 237068	72.0	W 293700	118.0	W 415859	139.1	NOURRITURE POUR ANIMAUX
0813	OILCAKE AND OTH RESIDUES	W 153020	43.3	W 216092	54.8	W 255316	87.8	W 343048	96.2	TOURTEAUX
08131	— OF SOYA BEANS	W 131268	39.1	W 188647	50.5	W 217156	78.8	W 284558	85.6	TOURTEAUX DE SOJA
09	MISC EDIBLE PRODUCTS		32.3		34.6		41.9		58.1	PREP ALIMENTAIRES DIVERSES
2	CRUDE MATERLS,EXCL FUELS		278.2		445.6		317.3		334.0	MAT BRUTES NON COMESTIBLES
23	RUBBER, CRUDE		34.5		50.7		44.2		41.0	CAOUTCHOUC BRUT
26	TEXTILE FIBRES AND WASTE		111.1		138.6		122.2		115.5	FIBRES TEXTILES
263	COTTON	W 24843	37.6	W 24464	51.0	W 26678	47.9	W 27094	46.5	COTON
2631	RAW COTTON,EXCL LINTERS	W 24195	37.1	W 23871	50.4	W 26187	47.4	W 26519	45.9	COTON EN MASSE
266	SYNTHETIC FIBRES TO SPIN	W 18467	35.1	W 20656	46.5	W 19122	37.7	W 20434	35.8	FIBRES SYNTHETIQUES
28	METALLIFEROUS ORES,SCRAP		59.4		160.6		56.2		61.7	MINERAIS METAL,DECHETS
287	BASE METAL ORES,CONC NES	W 32484	56.8	W 111343	160.4	W 78180	56.0	W 29035	61.6	MINERAIS METAUX COMMUNS
2879	OTH NONFER ORE,CONCNTRTE	W 27441	55.3	W 38603	156.8	W 23483	54.1	W 24674	59.2	MINERAIS D'AUTRES METAUX
28793	MOLYBD, NIOBIUM ETC ORES	W 16330	53.9	W 18526	153.5	W 12891	51.8	W 14785	57.1	MINERAIS DE MOLYBDENE,TITANE
3	MINERAL FUELS ETC		1101.8		1341.0		1847.5		1818.3	COMBUSTIBLES MINERAUX LUB
32	COAL,COKE AND BRIQUETTES		84.2		124.7		206.9		182.7	HOUILLES,COKES,BRIQUETTES
322	COAL,LIGNITE AND PEAT	W 2344903	82.9	W 2873841	123.2	W 4674958	205.1	W 4690795	181.5	HOUILLES,LIGNITES,TOURBE
3222	OTH COAL,NOT AGGLOMERATD	W 2343237	82.2	W 2871639	122.4	W 4673570	204.4	W 4689047	180.7	AUTRES HOUILLES
33	PETROLEUM AND PRODUCTS		952.9		1129.3		1536.2		1504.5	PETROLE ET DERIVES
333	CRUDE PETROLEUM	W 5127757	748.0	W 5649080	905.7	W 6085003	1158.9	W 7964140	1131.2	HUILES BRUTES DE PETROLE
334	PETROLEUM PRODUCTS,REFIN	W 810247	187.9	W 793896	200.4	W 1255400	349.6	W 1633030	343.4	PRODUITS RAFFINES
3341	GASOLINE,OTH LIGHT OILS	W 155538	39.7	W 78672	23.2	W 231517	74.4	W 291872	72.0	ESSENCES POUR MOTEURS
33411	MOTOR,AVIATION SPIRIT	W 152345	38.3	W 73473	21.1	W 227753	72.6	W 284674	69.3	ESSENCES MOTEURS D'AVIONS
3343	GAS OILS	W 263030	56.6	W 296378	65.1	W 510195	134.6	W 794502	154.2	GAS OILS
3344	FUEL OILS,NES	W 296117	34.4	W 307640	40.4	W 358594	52.4			FUEL OILS
3345	LUBS,PETROLEUM OILS NES	W 95346	57.1	W 97185	68.6	W 105580	75.1	W 501438	108.1	HUILES LUBRIFIANTES
33451	LUBS(HIGH PETR CONT) ETC	W 93442	52.3	W 94446	61.5	W 102144	67.2	W 497446	100.1	HUILES LUBRIF,H LOURDES
341	*GAS,NATURAL AND MANUFCT	W 338486	64.8	W 414532	87.2	W 443200	104.6	W 623957	131.2	GAZ NATUREL,GAZ MANUFACT
3413	PETROLM GASES,LIQUEFIED	W 338436	64.8	W 414531	87.1	W 429944	101.2	W 472804	112.0	GAZ DE PETROLE LIQUEFIE
34131	LIQUEFIED PROPANE,BUTANE	W 268643	52.4	W 371437	78.7	W 381624	90.5	W 401525	95.0	PROPANE,BUTANE LIQUEFIES
4	ANIMAL,VEGETABLE OIL,FAT		108.3		130.7		131.4		124.7	HUILES,GRAISSES ANIM,VEG
42	FIXED VEGETABLE OIL,FAT		91.8		111.8		104.6		101.4	HUILES VEGETALES FIXES
423	FIXED VEG OILS,SOFT	W 140891	88.9	W 151607	108.5	W 157496	99.6	W 151077	95.1	HUILES VEGET DOUCES FIXES
4232	SOYA BEAN OIL	W 93679	57.0	W 91930	63.6	W 92560	56.4	W 69856	42.9	HUILE DE SOJA
5	CHEMCLS,RELATED PROD NES		1310.0		1763.6		1959.5		2024.6	PRODUITS CHIMIQUES
51	ORGANIC CHEMICALS		187.7		262.4		235.7		243.4	PROD CHIMIQ ORGANIQUES
513	CARBOXYLIC ACIDS ETC	W 29541	34.1	W 34831	54.6	W 34836	47.3	W 38488	46.0	ACIDES CARBOXYLIQUES
514	NITROGEN–FNCTN COMPOUNDS	W 14755	47.3	W 18316	65.9	W 17978	64.2	W 19943	62.8	COMPOSES FONCT AZOTES
5148	OTH NITROGN–FNCTN CMPNDS	W 11510	31.4	W 14329	45.3	W 12809	41.6	W 14181	37.6	AUTRES COMPOSES AZOTES
515	ORG–INORG COMPOUNDS ETC	W 7016	44.8	W 7840	49.8	W 6558	40.8	W 8670	51.0	COMPOSES ORGANO–MINERAUX
52	INORGANIC CHEMICALS		118.4		164.0		188.3		190.2	PROD CHIM INORGANIQUES
522	INORG ELEMNTS,OXIDES,ETC	W 147732	46.1	W 265301	68.4	W 458402	75.2	W 582166	75.4	ELEMENTS INORGANIQUES
523	OTHR INORG CHEMICALS ETC	W 163983	71.4	W 214659	94.7	W 245773	112.1	W 305814	113.4	AUT PRODUITS CHIMIQUES INORG
5232	OTH MTL CMPD OF INRG ACD	W 112332	44.8	W 161131	61.1	W 189921	76.0	W 244238	82.1	SELS METALLIQUES
53	DYES,TANNING,COLOUR PROD		116.8		146.6		184.2		203.6	PROD TEINTURE,COLORANTS
531	SYNT DYE,NAT INDGO,LAKES	W 2300	59.1	W 2688	69.6	W 2845	101.8	W 3494	98.9	MAT COLOR ORGAN,LAQUES
5311	SYNTHIC ORGNIC DYESTUFFS	W 1985	55.5	W 2143	65.5	W 2355	98.4	W 2891	95.3	MAT COLOR ORGAN SYNTHET
533	PIGMENTS,PAINTS,ETC	W 18346	53.5	W 21408	72.8	W 21702	76.9	W 32971	100.1	PIGMENTS,PEINTURES,VERNIS
541	*MEDICINAL,PHARM PRODUCT	K 4254444	137.5		182.9		214.1	MK 10695	232.6	PROD MEDICINAUX PHARMACEUT
5417	MEDICAMENTS	K 1811072	78.3	K 2444345	106.4	K 3947311	129.0	K 7253939	143.9	MEDICAMENTS
54179	— CONTNG OTH SUBSTANCES	K 1335737	50.3	K 1888954	67.9	K 3199999	82.0	K 6469500	100.1	MED CONT AUT SUBSTANCES
55	PERFUME,CLEANING ETC PRD		94.6		128.0		152.3		167.0	PROD POUR PARFUM,TOILETTE
553	PERFUMERY,COSMETICS,ETC	W 4319	38.2	W 7745	56.4	W 10423	79.4	W 16988	85.0	PRODUITS DE PARFUMERIE
562	*FERTILIZERS,MANUFACTURE	W 729404	122.3	W 822156	167.9	W 1065693	230.6	W 885120	170.0	ENGRAIS MANUFACTURES
5621	CHEM NITROGENOUS FERTLZR	W 383166	64.5	W 436059	94.3	W 582285	130.2	W 485581	89.5	ENGRAIS AZOTES
56216	UREA	W 272585	43.0	W 303016	65.2	W 401176	89.8	W 288125	44.7	UREE
58	PLASTIC MATERIALS ETC		320.2		449.4		443.5		498.9	MAT PLAST ARTIFICIELLES
582	PROD OF CONDENSATION ETC	W 33737	60.9	W 41907	88.5	W 38339	83.8	W 51320	92.6	PROD CONDENS,POLYCOND
5823	ALKYDS,OTHER POLYESTERS	W 16210	28.3	W 21434	45.9	W 17670	37.0	W 29841	46.1	ALKYDES ET AUT POLYESTERS
583	POLYMERIZATION ETC PRODS	W 224989	247.6	W 234194	346.0	W 288262	345.0	W 329634	390.5	PROD POLYMERISATION
5831	POLYETHYLENE	W 96448	82.5	W 97254	117.0	W 122869	125.3	W 143259	148.5	POLYETHYLENE
58311	— IN PRIMARY FORMS	W 90784	70.9	W 90745	101.2	W 114079	106.3	W 132146	126.3	POLYETHYLENE PRIMAIRES
5832	POLYPROPYLENE	W 31903	33.7	W 36363	63.4	W 36509	44.9	W 44155	49.6	POLYPROPYLENE
5834	POLYVINYL CHLORIDE	W 56409	56.8	W 57440	68.2	W 78614	73.4	W 83181	82.4	CHLORURE DE POLYVINYLE
58341	— IN PRIMARY FORMS	W 52028	44.8	W 50945	49.4	W 71889	54.1	W 75333	61.2	SOUS FORMES PRIMAIRES
5839	OTH POLYMRZTION ETC PROD	W 11624	34.5	W 13834	44.7	W 15276	48.5	W 18324	53.6	AUT PROD POLYMER COPOLYM
59	CHEMICAL MATERIALS NES		210.5		260.2		308.7		315.8	MAT PROD CHIMIQUES NDA
591	PESTICIDES,DISINFECTANTS	W 10199	66.0	W 12143	81.0	W 14042	93.6	W 18257	108.0	DESINF,INSECT,FONG,HERB
598	MISCEL CHEM PRODUCTS NES	W 56510	122.9	W 69779	150.6	W 74537	183.1	W 84186	176.5	PROD DIV INDUST CHIM NDA
5989	CHEM PRODUCTS,PREPS NES	W 37960	93.1	W 48717	115.7	W 53006	144.5	W 60317	138.9	PROD PREP CHIMIQUES NDA
59899	OTH CHEM PRODS,PREPS,NES	W 27824	76.0	W 34839	92.9	W 36422	114.3	W 41889	110.4	AUT PRODUITS CHIMIQUES NDA
6	BASIC MANUFACTURES		1689.2		2473.9		2471.9		2740.2	ART MANUFACTURES
62	RUBBER MANUFACTURES NES		141.8		194.0		207.0		238.1	CAOUTCHOUC MANUFACTURE
625	RUBBER TYRES, TUBES ETC	W 21046	96.0	W 28988	134.9	W 30060	146.4	W 45615	169.3	PNEUS CAOUTCHOUC VULCANISE
6252	TYRES,NEW,BUS OR LORRY	W 6757	27.2	W 10655	43.8	W 12193	53.7	W 18323	63.1	PNEUS POUR AUTOBUS,CAMIONS
6259	OTH TYRES,TYRE CASES,ETC	W 11664	57.9	W 13525	70.3	W 14102	76.1	W 20630	83.8	AUTRES PNEUS RECHAPES FLAPS
62599	TYRES NES,TYRE CASES,ETC	W 10809	54.8	W 12588	66.7	W 12811	70.9	W 19002	78.7	PNEUS,FLAPS
63	WOOD,CORK MANUFACTRS NES		36.1		51.2		58.4		78.2	OUVRAGES LIEGE ET BOIS
64	PAPER,PAPERBOARD AND MFR		233.7		401.4		337.5		387.4	PAPIERS,CARTONS & OUVRAGES
641	PAPER AND PAPERBOARD	W 235512	186.8	W 310875	336.7	W 321868	269.0	W 381260	302.5	PAPIERS ET CARTONS

4. Special Imports C.I.F. by Commodities according to the S.I.T.C. (Rev. 2) in million U.S. Dollars
Importations Spéciales C.A.F. par Produits d'après la C.T.C.I. (Rév. 2) en millions de Dollars E.U.

SITC CTCI	COMMODITY	1994			1995			1996			1997			PRODUIT
		QUANTITY QUANTITE		VALUE VALEUR	QUANTITY QUANTITE		VALUE VALEUR	QUANTITY QUANTITE		VALUE VALEUR	QUANTITY QUANTITE		VALUE VALEUR	
6412	PRINTG,WRITING PAPER NES	W	50725	47.9	W	79928	104.1	W	64088	73.2	W	111963	112.9	PAPIERS POUR L'IMPRESSION
64122	— COATED,IMPREGNATD ETC	W	44121	40.7	W	67021	85.1	W	52814	59.5	W	95731	97.7	PAPIERS IMPRESSION COUCHES
6413	KRAFT PAPER,PAPERBOARD	W	73705	35.7	W	85173	59.1	W	124735	62.1	W	105702	46.9	PAPIER ET CARTON KRAFT
6415	PAPER,PAPERBRD,BULK,NES	W	68793	51.4	W	107247	108.6	W	71817	54.6	W	91896	60.3	PAPIERS,CARTONS ROULEAUX
64159	OTHER PAPER ETC,BULK,NES	W	56248	44.6	W	79061	87.7	W	44047	41.6	W	55894	44.8	AUT PAPIER ROULEAUX FEUILLES
6418	COATED ETC PAPER NES BLK	W	17475	34.9	W	23103	48.2	W	25645	47.5	W	40551	57.8	PAP,CARTONS COUCHES,ENDUITS
642	PAPER,ETC,PRECUT,ARTS OF	W	21535	46.9	W	30141	64.8	W	32495	68.5	W	40216	85.0	PAP,CARTONS DECOUPES
65	TEXTILE YARN,FABRICS,ETC			373.1			488.0			500.2			500.8	FILS,TISSUS,ARTICLES TEXTILE
651	TEXTILE YARN	W	16389	69.9	W	21909	100.1	W	22859	96.9	W	24465	96.1	FILS TEXTILES
652	COTTON FABRICS,WOVEN	W	8136	44.6	W	9293	60.0	W	10113	67.7	W	9330	59.1	TISSUS DE COTON
6522	WOVEN COTTON BLEACHD,ETC	W	7820	43.2	W	8836	57.7	W	9596	64.9	W	8794	56.1	TISSUS COTON BLANCHIS ETC
65224	BLCHED COTTON FABRIC NES	W	7263	37.2	W	8110	49.8	W	8341	52.1	W	7360	43.9	AUT TIS PLUS 85% COT BLANCHI
653	WOVN MAN–MADE FIB FABRIC	W	13433	92.7	W	14949	110.3	W	15550	109.8	W	16706	105.4	TISSUS FIBRES SYNTH,ARTIF
6531	CONT SYNT WEAVES NONPILE	W	4914	34.5	W	5282	39.4	W	5856	42.9	W	6396	43.2	TISSUS FIBRES SYNTH CONTINUE
657	SPECIAL TXTL FABRC,PRODS	W	13370	84.3	W	16976	109.6	W	15173	105.4	W	20005	114.8	TISSUS SPECIAUX
66	NONMETAL MINERAL MFS NES			161.3			221.0			260.2			281.0	ART MIN NON METALLIQUES
661	LIME,CEMENT,BLDG PRODS	W	128830	15.6	W	147007	19.1	W	606696	42.4	W	775252	55.2	CHAUX,CIMENTS MAT CONSTR
662	CLAY,REFRACTORY BLDG PRD	W	41187	28.7	W	69403	46.2	W	88602	57.0	W	124225	60.0	MAT CONST REFRACTAIRES
664	GLASS	W	39686	50.5	W	38217	69.9	W	37402	61.5	W	49222	57.8	VERRE
67	IRON AND STEEL			328.2			538.2			481.0			577.4	FER ET ACIER
672	IRON,STEEL PRIMARY FORMS	W	91760	30.6	W	127688	52.5	W	152437	55.6	W	262665	82.6	LINGOTS FER,ACIER
6727	IRN,STL COIL FR REROLLNG	W	91181	30.4	W	118507	50.1	W	145639	53.8	W	149527	50.3	EBAUCHES POUR TOLES FER
67271	IRON,SIMPLE STEEL COILS	W	91027	30.1	W	117971	48.8	W	144423	53.0	W	142904	47.3	EBAUCHES NON EN ACIER
673	IRON,STEEL SHAPES ETC	W	153642	59.9	W	213966	91.1	W	222623	92.9	W	297452	116.7	BARRES,PROFIL FER,ACIER
6732	IRON,STEEL BARS ETC	W	79406	34.0	W	107447	51.8	W	84469	42.8	W	170464	71.3	BARRES FER,ACIER
674	IRN,STL UNIV,PLATE,SHEET	W	230041	136.6	W	376394	247.3	W	296495	188.7	W	315324	185.4	LARGES PLATS,TOLES
6744	IRN,STL HVY PLATE,ROLLED	W	62651	26.6	W	130674	63.0	W	118203	55.4	W	140141	58.7	TOLES LAMINEES PLUS 4.75 MM
67441	— OF IRON OR SIMPLE STL	W	59740	22.3	W	127900	56.2	W	112238	46.0	W	134966	48.5	TOLES NON ACIER FIN CARB
6746	IRN,STL THIN PLATE,ROLLD	W	88601	53.7	W	150346	104.0	W	82501	57.9	W	78413	54.4	TOLES LAM MOINS 3MM
67461	— OF IRON OR SIMPLE STL	W	75670	37.2	W	133435	76.9	W	63625	32.6	W	56559	26.8	TOL NON AC FIN MOINS 3 MM
6749	OTH IRN,STL PLATES,SHEET	W	43919	28.8	W	66361	52.7	W	58344	43.0	W	66450	46.8	AUTRES TOLES FER,ACIER
67491	— OF IRON OR SIMPLE STL	W	43774	28.3	W	66268	52.5	W	58233	42.7	W	66406	46.6	AUT TOLES AUTRES ACIER FIN
678	IRON,STL TUBES,PIPES,ETC	W	53920	70.8	W	66727	97.8	W	91239	107.9	W	142238	154.9	TUBES,TUYAUX EN FONTE,FER
6783	IRON,STL TUBES,PIPES NES	W	37562	37.7	W	41630	46.8	W	71457	66.3	W	97762	88.7	AUT TUBES,TUYAUX FER,ACIER
68	NON–FERROUS METALS			81.2			130.5			116.3			131.7	METAUX NON FERREUX
684	ALUMINIUM	W	22594	57.6	W	29524	93.4	W	28670	81.3	W	34727	91.3	ALUMINIUM
6842	ALUMINIUM,ALLOYS WORKED	W	8341	33.4	W	13873	59.8	W	14841	55.6	W	17543	59.5	ALUMINIUM,ALLIAGES OUVRE
69	METAL MANUFACTURES NES			310.2			414.8			479.0			507.6	ART MANUFACT EN METAL NDA
691	STRUCTURES AND PARTS NES	W	14030	25.7	W	16836	36.5	W	27958	53.5	W	34975	68.6	CONSTRUCT FER,ACIER,ALU
6911	STRUCTURES,PARTS IRN,STL	W	13577	22.6	W	16391	33.2	W	27044	48.5	W	33610	62.1	CONSTRUCT FER,ACIER,FONTE
692	METAL TANKS,BOXES,ETC	W	15318	53.0	W	19991	76.5	W	16995	63.8	W	24867	78.4	RECIPIENTS METALLIQUES
6924	MTL TRANSPORT BOXES ETC	W	13393	45.6	W	18221	71.2	W	16429	60.4	W	22798	72.6	FUTS,TAMBOURS,BIDONS
69242	ALUMNM TRNSPRT BOXES ETC	W	8332	33.3	W	12170	54.6	W	10289	44.3	W	16861	57.0	FUTS,TAMBOURS,BIDONS ALU
695	TOOLS	W	5119	60.9	W	5530	73.0	W	6186	78.2	W	8467	78.6	OUTILS A MAIN
697	BASE MTL HOUSEHOLD EQUIP	W	5826	28.4	W	8368	41.5	W	9471	49.8	W	13324	56.8	ART MENAGE MET COMMUNS
699	BASE METAL MFRS NES			82.5	W	17105	97.8	W	22070	121.7	W	26685	120.4	ART MANUFACTURES MET NDA
7	MACHINES,TRANSPORT EQUIP			4738.4			6274.0			7147.6			7875.1	MACHINES MATERIEL TRANSPORT
71	POWER GENERATING EQUIPMT			457.6			315.0			406.8			460.1	MACHINES GENERATRICES
711	STEAM BOILERS & AUX PLNT	W	14058	207.9	W	8621	75.3	W	12472	115.3	W	18314	106.6	GENERATEURS VAPEUR EAU ETC
7111	STEAM BOILERS ETC	W	13827	204.5	W	8347	71.5	W	11998	109.5	W	17436	99.3	GENERATEURS VAPEUR EAU
712	STEAM ENGINES,TURBINES	W	2651	65.5	W	854	21.3	W	1424	32.9	W	3393	73.4	MACHINES A VAPEUR D'EAU PIEC
7126	STEAM POWR UNITS,ENGINES	W	2624	64.5	W	831	20.6	W	1405	31.6	W	3390	73.1	MACHINES A VAPEUR D EAU
713	INTRNL COMBUS PSTN ENGIN	W	3618	62.9	W	3915	77.6	W	4463	86.4	W	5445	79.0	MOTEURS EXPL COMB INT, PIECE
7139	PISTON ENGINE PARTS NES	W	1660	39.9	W	2014	53.0	W	2068	53.6	W	2884	54.8	PIECES POUR 713.2,3,8
716	ROTATING ELECTRIC PLANT	W	7414	103.7	W	9740	114.6	W	8751	113.8	W	12098	129.7	APP ELECTR ROTATIFS,PIECES
7162	AC MTRS,GENRTRS,GEN SETS	W	6688	90.2	W	8523	97.5	W	7306	80.7	W	9751	95.9	MOTEURS ELECTRIQUES
71622	AC GENERATORS	W	1983	50.0	W	2107	35.3	W	1340	24.6	W	1932	26.8	GENER COURANT ALTERNATIF
72	MACHS FOR SPCL INDUSTRYS			665.5			1005.1			1174.3			1228.8	MAC SPECIALES POUR INDUST
721	AGRIC MACHY,EXC TRACTORS	W	4831	40.8	W	7017	60.1	W	8001	85.5	W	8094	60.4	MACHINES AGRICOLES
723	CIVIL ENGNEERG EQUIP ETC	W	22123	202.9	W	33156	297.4	W	40883	378.4	W	46906	354.5	APPAREILS DE GENIE CIVIL
7234	CONST,MINING MACHNRY NES	W	20391	183.6	W	30290	266.9	W	37146	343.0	W	42400	315.2	MACH POUR LA CONST, MINES
72341	SELF–PROPELLD DOZERS,ETC	W	4282	36.9	W	6323	53.6	W	6332	59.1	W	9261	69.3	BULLDOZERS
72342	SLFPRP SHOVELS,EXCAVATRS	W	13912	114.5	W	20949	172.2	W	27429	229.2	W	29355	195.3	PELLES MECANIQUES
724	TEXTILE,LEATHER MACHNRY	W	2879	55.7	W	3794	64.9	W	2993	52.8	W	3340	48.9	MACH POUR INDUSTRIE TEXTILE
725	PAPER ETC MILL MACHINERY	W	1849	34.6	W	2859	53.2	W	2133	49.1	W	8435	139.9	MACHINES FABR PATE PAPIER
7251	PAPER,PULP MAKING MACHRY	W	717	11.2	W	1786	26.5	W	975	24.4	W	7139	108.3	MACHINES FABR PATE CARTON
72512	PAPER ETC MAKING ETC MCH	W	537	8.5	W	1428	17.0	W	363	7.2	W	5564	69.7	MACH FABR FINITION DU PAP
726	PRINTG,BKBINDG MACHY,PTS	W	1893	44.8	W	2387	75.4	W	1394	41.7	W	2133	47.0	MACHINES POUR IMPRIMERIE
7264	PRINTING PRESSES	W	1310	27.4	W	1831	53.2	W	843	19.2	W	1348	24.4	MACHINES A IMPRIMER
72641	ROTARY PRINTING PRESSES	W	1310	27.4	W	1831	53.2	W	843	19.2	W	1348	24.4	MACH IMPRIMER ROTATIVES
727	FOOD MACHRY NON–DOMESTIC	W	1274	28.3	W	2667	50.6	W	1823	45.6	W	2131	34.8	MACH INDUSTRIES ALIMENT
7272	OTH FOOD PROC MCHY,PARTS	W	1093	26.2	W	2416	48.0	W	1626	43.4	W	1952	33.1	AUT MACH IND ALIMENTAIRE
72722	INDUS FOOD PROC MACH NES	W	1082	25.3	W	2383	47.8	W	1571	42.6	W	1944	32.9	MACHINES BOULANGERIE
728	OTH MACHY FOR SPCL INDUS	W	20837	228.9	W	42296	369.0	W	38524	481.5	W	63432	510.0	AUT MACH IND PARTICULIERES
7281	MACH–TOOLS FR SPCL INDUS	W	2024	25.3	W	2979	45.9	W	2848	45.6	W	2975	33.3	MACH–OUTILS SPEC IND PART
7283	OTHR MINERAL WORKG MACHY	W	12409	97.1	W	26323	166.8	W	15044	109.0	W	42410	256.5	MACH TRIER,CRIBLER,BROYER
72831	MINRAL SORTING ETC MACHY	W	4035	36.8	W	12252	69.6	W	3561	24.4	W	15599	82.3	MACH TRIER MAT MINERALES
72832	MINRL CRUSHING ETC MACHY	W	3763	30.5	W	8256	57.3	W	5280	39.2	W	16655	109.2	MACH CONCASSER MAT MINER
7284	MACHY FOR SPCL INDUS NES	W	6405	106.6	W	12994	156.4	W	20633	327.0	W	18047	220.3	MACH SPEC IND PARTICUL.
72842	RUBBER,PLASTICS WRKG MCH	W	1949	35.4	W	2706	36.9	W	2344	49.9	W	3784	61.3	MACH IND CAOUT MAT PLAST
72848	OTH MCHY WITH INDIV FNCT	W	3477	46.4	W	6271	70.8	W	15059	224.8	W	11385	106.4	AUTRES MACHINES NDA
73	METALWORKING MACHINERY			118.2			73.2			80.5			82.0	MACH TRAVAIL DES METAUX
736	METALWORKING MACH–TOOLS	W	5738	43.2	W	4791	43.5	W	5438	47.7	W	6372	44.9	MACH–OUTILS TRAVAIL METAUX
737	METALWORKING MACHNRY NES	W	3948	75.0	W	2675	29.7	W	2566	32.9	W	4577	37.2	MACH TRAV METAUX PIECES
7372	ROLLING MILLS AND ROLLS	W	2439	52.9	W	856	6.2	W	1003	8.3	W	1664	6.7	LAMINOIRS CYLINDRES PIEC
73721	ROLLING MILLS	W	1620	46.0	W	84	1.5	W	92	1.2	W	152	0.3	LAMINOIRS ET TRAINS
74	GENRL INDUSTRL MACHY NES			841.6			1152.9			1236.4			1450.1	MACH APP INDUSTRIE
741	HEATING,COOLING EQUIPMNT	W	11580	147.3	W	16289	186.6	W	23026	255.8	W	37115	316.5	MACH CHAUFFAGE,PIECES
7414	NONDOM REFRIG EQUIPT,PTS	W	2458	30.5	W	4095	45.9	W	4734	52.8	W	6367	56.3	MAT PRODUCTION DU FROID
7416	HEATING,COOLING EQU NES	W	5561	59.4	W	8518	86.7	W	13490	131.3	W	22341	166.2	APP CHANGEMENT TEMP
742	PUMPS FOR LIQUIDS ETC	W	3763	69.4	W	4851	89.8	W	4997	92.7	W	8885	114.4	POMPES MOTO–POMPES
743	PUMPS NES,CENTRFUGES ETC	W	11068	136.4	W	13875	169.2	W	15520	190.4	W	23311	216.5	POMPES COMPRES,VENT ETC
7431	PUMPS FOR GASES ETC	W	4362	42.2	W	5859	58.3	W	4961	52.9	W	8350	67.0	POMPES AIR A VIDE,COMPRES
7436	GAS,LIQUID FILTERS ETC	W	3751	52.7	W	4942	62.9	W	7039	79.3	W	9795	88.7	APP POUR FILT DES LIQUIDES
744	MECHANICAL HANDLING EQU	W	22995	187.4	W	44086	322.0	W	37758	291.4	W	54901	364.1	EQUIP MANUTENTION PIECES
7441	FORK LIFT TRCKS,ETC,PTS	W	5302	31.3	W	8172	53.9	W	9957	60.1	W	12378	66.7	CHARIOTS POUR USINES ETC
74411	FORK LIFT TRUCKS ETC	W	5300	31.3	W	8171	53.9	W	9952	60.0	W	12377	66.7	CHARIOTS POUR LES GARES
7442	LIFTING,LOADING MACH NES	W	12840	120.4	W	29591	224.3	W	20938	170.9	W	32425	224.3	APP LEVAGE,MANUTENTION
74428	OTH HANDLING ETC MCH NES	W	8156	80.0	W	23495	175.2	W	13388	111.9	W	21563	161.5	AUT APP LEVAGE ETC
7449	PTS NES OF MACHY OF 7442	W	4853	35.8	W	6323	43.9	W	6863	60.5	W	10097	73.1	PIECES DU 744.2
745	NONELEC MACHY,TOOLS NES	W	4073	102.6	W	5265	136.4	W	5101	133.3	W	7653	142.6	AUT MACH NON ELEC,PIECES

4. Special Imports C.I.F. by Commodities according to the S.I.T.C. (Rev. 2) in million U.S. Dollars
Importations Spéciales C.A.F. par Produits d'après la C.T.C.I. (Rév. 2) en millions de Dollars E.U.

SITC CTCI	COMMODITY	1994 QUANTITY QUANTITE	1994 VALUE VALEUR	1995 QUANTITY QUANTITE	1995 VALUE VALEUR	1996 QUANTITY QUANTITE	1996 VALUE VALEUR	1997 QUANTITY QUANTITE	1997 VALUE VALEUR	PRODUIT
7452	OTH NONELEC MCHS,PTS NES	W 3712	92.1	W 4835	122.5	W 4626	120.1	W 7042	129.4	AUT MACH NON ELEC,PIECES
74522	PACKAGNG,BOTTLNG,ETC MCH	W 1254	49.2	W 1997	70.4	W 1481	62.3	W 2001	64.9	MACH NETT BOUTEILLES,ETC
749	NONELEC MACH PTS,ACC NES	W 9663	198.8	W 13071	249.1	W 13679	273.0	W 21198	296.4	PIECES MACH NON ELEC NDA
7492	COCKS,VALVES ETC NES	W 3918	75.9	W 5040	94.6	W 5553	99.6	W 8480	121.1	ART ROB,SIM POUR TUYAUX
7493	SHAFT,CRANK,PULLEY ETC	W 2827	59.7	W 3792	73.4	W 3881	82.1	W 5488	81.6	ARBRES TRANS,VILEBREQUINS
75	OFFICE MACHNES,ADP EQUIP		351.0		466.0		530.0		619.2	MACH BUREAU TRAIT AUTOM
751	OFFICE MACHINES	W 1260	38.9	W 1697	53.7	W 1929	60.6	W 2478	60.6	MACH,APPAREILS DE BUREAU
752	AUTOMTIC DATA PROC EQUIP	W 3748	237.1	W 5187	319.7	W 6303	369.4	W 10927	451.3	MACH TRAIT INFORMATION
7522	DIGITAL COMPUTERS	W 831	71.4	W 936	89.1	W 1274	99.8	W 1487	92.7	MACH DIGITALES COMPLETES
7523	DIGITL CENTRL PROCESSORS	W 426	34.8	W 1029	77.0	W 887	68.8	W 1816	115.2	UNITES CENTRALES
7525	ADP PERIPHERAL UNITS	W 2173	76.4	W 2824	95.3	W 3252	109.4	W 5864	133.5	UNITES PERIPHERIQUES
759	OFFICE,ADP MCH PTS,ACCES	W 839	75.0	W 1161	92.7	W 1448	100.1	W 2490	107.4	PIECES DU 751 ET 752
7599	ACCTG,ETC,ADP MCH PTS,AC	W 668	66.1	W 881	79.5	W 1139	86.2	W 2100	92.9	PIECES DU 751 ET 752
76	TELECOMM,SOUND EQUIPMENT		426.8		585.7		699.3		865.1	EQUIPMENT DE TELECOM
761	TELEVISION RECEIVERS	W 7450	105.3	W 12269	157.0	W 12101	153.9	W 18200	169.2	RECEPTEURS DE TELEVISION
7611	COLOUR TV RECEIVERS	W 7173	102.2	W 11968	153.9	W 11998	152.6	W 18002	167.7	RECEPTEURS COULEUR
762	RADIO BROADCAST RECEIVRS	W 4113	74.2	W 5362	108.0	W 5458	107.1	W 7889	116.4	RECEPTEURS RADIODIFFUSION
7628	OTHER RADIO RECEIVERS	W 3486	52.7	W 4506	77.6	W 4572	77.2	W 6522	84.2	AUTRES RECEPT RADIO
764	TELECOM EQPT,PTS,ACC NES	W 3322	216.7	W 4314	284.4	W 6357	407.9	W 9895	526.4	EQUIP TELECOM,PIECES
7641	LINE TELEPHONE,ETC EQUIP	W 1148	72.5	W 1376	85.1	W 2055	117.0	W 3354	168.7	APP TELEPHON PAR FIL
7643	TV,RADIO TRANSMITTRS ETC	W 335	50.6	W 499	82.2	W 885	131.2	W 1391	183.0	APP EMET TELE RADIO
7649	PTS NES OF EQUIPMT OF 76	W 947	69.3	W 1039	81.2	W 1634	118.7	W 1873	138.4	PIECES DE LA DIV 76
76491	PTS NES OF APPAR OF 7641	W 277	39.7	W 451	57.3	W 1045	93.7	W 849	104.0	PIECES POUR 764.1
77	ELECTRIC MACHNRY NES ETC		534.5		695.8		710.5		836.7	MACH APP ELECT NDA
771	ELECTRIC POWER MACHY NES	W 3829	46.7	W 5290	59.3	W 4323	60.6	W 10549	93.1	MACH PROD,TRANS ELECTR
7711	TRANSFORMERS,ELECTRICAL	W 2792	24.7	W 3775	31.2	W 2322	24.5	W 7779	57.6	TRANSFO ELECTRIQUES
772	SWITCHGEAR ETC,PARTS NES	W 4680	124.9	W 6241	156.1	W 6610	166.7	W 9911	176.8	APP COUPURE,SECT ETC
7721	SWITCHGEAR ETC	W 4607	121.6	W 6152	151.9	W 6533	162.6	W 9783	170.9	APP COUPURE,SECTIONMNT
773	ELECTR DISTRIBUTNG EQUIP	W 10073	51.0	W 12782	77.1	W 16626	85.4	W 14798	64.8	EQUIPMT DISTRIBUTION ELECT
7731	INSULATED WIRE,CABLE ETC	W 8953	44.4	W 11242	67.2	W 15155	76.6	W 12227	55.1	FILS,CABLES ISOLES ELECT
775	HOUSEHOLD TYPE EQUIP NES	W 15430	118.2	W 20501	159.3	W 23063	176.1	W 36812	204.5	MACH,APP USAGE DOMESTQUE
7751	HOUSEHOLD LDRY EQUIP NES	W 5102	32.1	W 6151	41.5	W 8588	57.0	W 13033	61.8	MACH A LAVER ET SECHOIRS
77511	DOMESTIC WASHING MACHNES	W 4809	30.2	W 5924	40.2	W 8397	55.7	W 12649	59.8	MACH LAVER LINGE MOINS 6 KG
778	ELECTRICAL MACHINERY NES	W 13128	143.4	W 14837	186.4	W 16652	180.0	W 27618	240.3	AUTRES MACH ELECT NDA
7781	BATTERIES,ACCUMULATORS	W 7594	34.8	W 8536	39.9	W 9898	46.1	W 13666	50.6	PILES ET ACCUMULATEURS
7788	OTH ELEC MACHY,EQUIP NES	W 1854	49.1	W 2010	73.6	W 2025	55.1	W 6334	98.0	AUT MACH APP ELEC NDA
77886	OTH ELEC MACHINERY NES	W 405	24.4	W 548	48.0	W 461	23.4	W 3616	46.6	AUT MACH APP ELECTRIQUES
78	ROAD VEHICLES		1236.3		1824.5		2043.4		2217.7	VEHICULES ROUTIERS
781	PASS MOTOR VEH EXC BUSES	W 45558	442.7	W 73979	742.0	W 84807	862.1	W 119918	915.2	AUTO TRANSPORT PERSONNES
782	LORRIES,SPCL MTR VEH NES	W 49805	445.2	W 68941	633.7	W 75436	715.2	W 111534	775.6	VEHICULES SPECIAUX,MARCH
7821	LORRIES,TRUCKS	W 48157	423.5	W 64880	586.8	W 70398	663.6	W 103954	717.0	VEHICULES TRANSP MARCHAND
7822	SPECIAL MOTOR VEHCLS NES	W 1648	21.7	W 4061	46.9	W 5038	51.7	W 7580	58.7	VEHICULES USAGES SPECIAUX
783	ROAD MOTOR VEHICLES NES	W 15392	141.9	W 20423	211.5	W 19341	200.8	W 30882	248.6	VEHICULES ROUTIERS NDA
7831	BUSES	W 12201	109.0	W 10927	107.9	W 11152	109.8	W 18705	144.1	VOITURES TRANSPORT COMMUN
7832	TRACTORS FOR TR–TRAILERS	W 3191	33.0	W 9496	103.6	W 8190	91.0	W 12178	104.5	TRACTEURS ROUTIERS
784	MOTOR VEH PRTS,ACCES NES	W 18352	154.1	W 16331	156.6	W 18242	174.7	W 26385	188.5	PIECES 722,781,782,783
7841	MOTOR VEHICLE CHASSIS	W 4093	38.9	W 2298	25.0	W 2817	32.6	W 3632	31.1	CHASSIS 722,781,782,783
7849	OTHER MOTOR VEHCL PARTS	W 13710	113.1	W 13524	129.9	W 14772	139.9	W 21756	154.7	PIECES 722,781,782,783
79	OTHR TRANSPORT EQUIPMENT		107.4		156.3		266.8		115.7	AUTRE MATERIEL TRANSPORT
791	RAILWAY VEHICLES	W 561	2.6	W 2890	17.8	W 3316	107.8	W 3919	30.9	VEHIC MAT CHEMINS DE FER
7913	MECHAN–PROPELLED RY CARS			W 119	9.3	W 1168	98.7	W 769	13.0	AUTOMOTRICES,DRAISINES
793	SHIPS AND BOATS ETC	W 58338	94.3	W 77527	117.3	W 77290	143.8	W 61265	69.1	NAVIRES BATEAUX,ETC
7932	SHIPS AND BOATS NES	W 57619	92.3	W 70667	109.9	W 70253	137.2	W 58940	59.0	NAVIRES ET BATEAUX
79323	OTHER CARGO VESSELS	W 50725	68.1	W 29661	47.3	W 11620	17.2	W 55126	33.3	AUT BATEAUX TRANS MARCH
79324	FISHING VESSELS ETC	W 6244	15.1	W 2044	11.3	W 5155	65.4	W 2831	14.5	BATEAUX DE PECHE
8	MISC MANUFACTURED GOODS		1100.0		1419.2		1663.2		1891.5	ART MANUFACTURES DIVERS
821	*FURNITURE,PARTS THEREOF	W 5697	38.5	W 7927	55.6	W 12808	74.8	W 25562	95.5	MEUBLES ET PIECES
8219	FURNITURE AND PARTS NES	W 3312	17.5	W 4710	24.7	W 8235	39.0	W 17395	55.8	AUTRES MEUBLES ET PIECES
84	CLOTHING AND ACCESSORIES		219.3		290.5		416.4		441.8	VETEMENTS
842	MENS OUTERWEAR NOT KNIT	W 2949	36.7	W 4012	46.3	W 5106	68.0	W 6490	69.9	VET DESSUS POUR HOMMES
843	WOMENS OUTERWEAR NONKNIT	W 2233	41.8	W 3061	53.0	W 4407	82.9	W 5665	87.4	VET DESSUS FEMMES MAT TEX
845	OUTERWEAR KNIT NONELASTC	W 1890	32.7	W 2903	44.9	W 3645	68.0	W 4795	77.2	VET DESSOUS,ACCES BONNET
846	UNDER GARMENTS KNITTED	W 3445	45.3	W 4336	62.9	W 5729	83.8	W 7796	97.8	SOUS VETS DE BONNETERIE
8462	— OF COTTON NON ELASTIC	W 2559	26.2	W 3278	38.1	W 4309	50.4	W 5947	58.2	SOUS–VET BONNET COTON
84629	—— OTHER	W 2559	26.2	W 3278	38.1	W 4309	50.4	W 5947	58.2	AUT SOUS–VET BONNET COTON
848	HEADGEAR,NONTXTL CLOTHNG	W 1843	20.9	W 2637	32.0	W 3390	50.6	W 5147	54.3	VET ACCES MAT AUT QUE TEX
851	*FOOTWEAR	W 5844	86.0	W 8594	126.2	W 10281	149.3	W 16412	176.3	CHAUSSURES
85102	FOOTWEAR LEATHER	W 3973	69.4	W 5278	96.3	W 5738	108.9	W 10036	137.0	CHAUS SEMELLES EN CUIR
87	PRECISION INSTRUMNTS NES		193.9		198.7		200.3		230.2	INSTRUM,APPAR SCIENT NDA
872	MEDICAL INSTRUMENTS NES	W 1239	44.7	W 1739	54.5	W 1728	58.6	W 2409	57.9	INSTR,APP MEDIC–CHIR NDA
87202	OTH MEDICAL INSTRUMENTS	W 1090	38.5	W 1503	46.4	W 1506	50.8	W 2103	49.5	INSTRUM,APP MEDECINE
874	MEASURNG,CONTROLNG INSTR	W 2924	134.5	W 2413	128.1	W 2610	124.7	W 3907	148.4	INSTRUMENTS DE MESURE
8743	GAS,LIQUID CONTROL INSTR	W 1335	48.9	W 724	35.8	W 711	31.3	W 1351	43.7	APP,INSTR MESURE FLUIDES
8748	ELEC MEAS,CONTRL EQU NES	W 548	45.2	W 337	41.5	W 319	34.6	W 523	43.0	APP ELEC ELECTRO MESURE
88	PHOTO EQU,OPTICL GDS ETC		126.2		144.4		152.9		161.1	APP,FOURN PHOTO,OP,MONTR
882	PHOTO,CINEMA SUPPLIES	W 4011	59.7	W 4898	65.5	W 5343	70.2	W 6508	74.2	PRODUITS PHOTO,CINEMA
8822	PHOTO FILM EXC DEV CINMA	W 2697	46.5	W 2963	49.1	W 3118	50.1	W 3970	51.6	PLAQUES,PELLICULES,FILMS
89	MISC MANUFCTRD GOODS NES		395.6		545.4		599.8		702.4	ART MANUFACTURES DIVERS
892	PRINTED MATTER	W 6331	57.1	W 8830	80.1	W 9023	82.7	W 11219	85.6	IMPRIMES
8921	PRINTED BOOKS,GLOBES,ETC	W 2937	32.3	W 4720	48.8	W 4924	51.0	W 6302	53.0	LIVRES,BROCHURES,CARTES
89211	PRINTED BOOKS,PAMPHLETS	W 2815	31.6	W 4387	46.9	W 4706	49.1	W 5846	50.6	LIVRES,BROCHURES
893	ARTICLES OF PLASTIC NES		107.4		151.8		175.7		211.0	OUVRAGES EN MAT DIVIS 58
8939	MISC PLASTIC ARTICLES	W 15522	76.0	W 20291	107.9	W 24492	126.7	W 37962	155.1	ART DIVERS EN MAT DIV 58
89399	OTHR PLASTC ARTICLES NES	W 10165	68.5	W 14378	96.8	W 18022	115.5	W 28656	140.0	AUT OUV MAT DIV 58
894	TOYS,SPORTING GOODS,ETC	W 13199	95.9	W 18154	139.7	W 21056	154.3	W 33555	178.8	VOITURES ENFANTS,JOUETS
8942	TOYS,INDOOR GAMES ETC	W 10549	75.8	W 14108	108.5	W 14528	107.1	W 25110	133.8	JOUETS,JEUX ETC
89423	TOYS NES	W 6094	40.2	W 7613	53.9	W 8022	57.0	W 14635	71.8	JOUETS,MODELES REDUITS
898	MUSICAL INSTRUMENTS,PTS	W 2364	60.9	W 3130	70.5	W 3439	76.6	W 4919	108.1	INSTRUMENTS DE MUSIQUE
8983	SOUND RECRDNG TAPE,DISCS	W 1975	54.0	W 2701	62.5	W 2995	68.6	W 4229	98.4	SUPPORTS SON POUR 763
89832	RECORDED DISCS,TAPES ETC	W 435	35.8	W 708	41.1	W 849	46.4	W 1246	73.5	DISQUES,PHONO,BANDES
899	OTHER MANUFACTURED GOODS		36.3		49.5		53.4		59.8	AUT ART MANUF DIVERS NDA
9	GOODS NOT CLASSD BY KIND		162.9		188.9		206.1		230.4	ART TRANSACT NON CLASSES
931	*SPECIAL TRANSACTIONS		160.7		186.4		204.2	W 41304	227.5	TRANS.SPECIALES

5. Special Exports F.O.B. by Commodities according to the S.I.T.C. (Rev. 2) in million U.S. Dollars
Exportations Spéciales F.O.B. par Produits d'après la C.T.C.I. (Rév. 2) en millions de Dollars E.U.

SITC CTCI	COMMODITY	1994 QUANTITY QUANTITE	1994 VALUE VALEUR	1995 QUANTITY QUANTITE	1995 VALUE VALEUR	1996 QUANTITY QUANTITE	1996 VALUE VALEUR	1997 QUANTITY QUANTITE	1997 VALUE VALEUR	PRODUIT
	ALL COMMODITIES		11368.7		15901.2		15406.9		16678.3	TOUS PRODUITS
0	FOOD AND LIVE ANIMALS		2729.5		3472.0		3733.7		3634.7	ALIMENTS,ANIMAUX VIVANTS
01	MEAT AND PREPARATIONS		36.2		27.7		33.8		61.2	VIANDES ET PREPARATIONS
011	MEAT FRESH,CHILLD,FROZEN	W 19243	33.2	W 14178	24.5	W 15350	25.1	W 31432	52.1	VIANDES FRAICHES,REF,CONGE
03	FISH AND PREPARATIONS		806.1		1021.8		1042.9		1216.3	POISSONS ET PREPARATIONS
034	FISH,FRESH,CHILLED,FROZN	W 161988	571.5	W 180429	716.1	W 206872	736.2	W 264799	854.3	POISSON FRAIS, REFRIG,CONG
0341	FISH FRSH,CHLLD,EX FILLT	W 26319	98.2	W 31362	119.4	W 38926	130.1	W 40261	111.1	POISSON FRAIS,REFRIGERE
0342	FISH FROZEN,EXCL FILLETS	W 90650	284.7	W 97777	349.4	W 106134	334.0	W 126838	397.7	POISSONS CONGELES
0343	FISH FILLETS,FRESH,CHLLD	W 8789	55.3	W 11773	72.4	W 19698	103.8	W 33789	152.5	FILETS FRAIS,REFRIGERES
0344	FISH FILLETS,FROZEN	W 36230	133.5	W 39517	175.0	W 42114	168.5	W 63910	193.2	FILETS CONGELES
035	FISH SALTED,DRIED,SMOKED	W 4204	18.5	W 6789	33.5	W 10072	43.7	W 13009	55.6	POISSON SECHE,SALE,FUME
036	SHELL FISH FRESH,FROZEN	W 11723	69.1	W 12356	89.3	W 9599	80.7	W 11376	81.1	CRUSTACES,MOLLUSQUES
037	FISH ETC PREPD,PRSVD NES	W 55815	147.1	W 72192	183.0	W 68129	182.5	W 182157	225.5	POIS,CRUST,MOL PREPARES
0371	FISH PREPARD,PRESRVD NES	W 43916	50.3	W 59522	71.8	W 55740	73.0	W 165291	100.3	CONSERVES DE POISSONS
0372	SHELL FISH PREPRD,PRESVD	W 11899	96.8	W 12671	111.3	W 12389	109.5	W 16866	125.2	CRUSTACES,COQUIL PREPARES
04	CEREALS AND PREPARATIONS		75.8		94.6		123.5		139.5	CEREALES ET PRODUITS
044	MAIZE UNMILLED	W 25452	30.3	W 21406	24.9	W 29165	37.4	W 36580	50.3	MAIS NON MOULU
048	CEREAL ETC PREPARATIONS	W 77503	44.0	W 114987	67.6	W 118926	83.0	W 137951	84.8	PREPTNS A BASE CEREALES
05	VEGETABLES AND FRUIT		1170.8		1374.9		1568.6		1388.2	LEGUMES ET FRUITS
054	VEG ETC FRSH,SMPLY PRSVD	W 217884	152.4	W 279169	194.8	W 220142	172.2	W 187646	142.7	LEGUMES FRAIS,CONG,SECS
0546	VEGETABLES SIMPLY PRESVD	W 115257	101.6	W 145132	126.4	W 129824	120.5	W 121045	100.7	LEGUMES CONG,CONSER
05461	VEGETABLES FROZEN	W 110730	96.9	W 140956	121.1	W 124199	113.8	W 114512	95.1	LEGUMES CONGELES
056	VEGTBLES ETC PRSVD,PREPD	W 18610	43.3	W 15206	36.0	W 12885	32.1	W 13375	25.2	CONSERVES DE LEGUMES
057	FRUIT,NUTS,FRESH,DRIED	W 1268805	819.7	W 1361641	907.5	W 1492113	1083.6	W 1506096	1006.5	FRUITS FRAIS OU SECS
0574	APPLES FRESH	W 347103	139.6	W 432522	197.2	W 442095	223.3	W 411493	189.6	POMMES FRAICHES
0575	GRAPES FRESH OR DRIED	W 490006	386.4	W 471695	376.2	W 542776	463.8	W 566010	455.6	RAISINS FRAIS OU SECS
05751	GRAPES FRESH	W 458160	350.1	W 442818	345.4	W 513093	429.4	W 536423	414.0	RAISINS FRAIS
05752	GRAPES DRIED(RAISINS)	W 31845	36.4	W 28877	30.8	W 29682	34.5	W 29586	41.6	RAISINS SECS
0579	FRUIT FRESH OR DRIED NES	W 419443	266.1	W 441977	299.2	W 491402	353.2	W 507918	318.8	FRUITS FRAIS,SECS NDA
05792	PEARS, QUINCES FRESH	W 156871	60.0	W 146841	58.5	W 162419	73.2	W 175901	73.8	POIRES ET COINGS FRAIS
05793	STONE FRUIT FRESH NES	W 136846	103.1	W 147248	116.8	W 166689	144.6	W 156212	118.9	FRUITS A NOYAU NDA FRAIS
05798	OTHER FRESH FRUIT	W 86970	49.5	W 113054	67.5	W 121677	69.5	W 131270	66.6	AUTRES FRUITS FRAIS
05799	OTHER DRIED FRUIT	W 17446	34.7	W 19523	38.8	W 19241	41.4	W 21712	34.0	AUTRES FRUITS SECHES
058	FRUIT PRESERVED,PREPARED	W 148639	155.6	W 179976	236.7	W 193646	280.9	W 185118	214.0	CONSERVES DE FRUITS
0585	FRUIT OR VEGETABLE JUICE	W 59047	47.1	W 73714	96.9	W 81375	126.2	W 64372	86.3	JUS DE FRUITS
05857	JUICE OF OTHER FRUIT,VEG	W 57935	46.3	W 71137	95.2	W 79017	124.6	W 62449	85.1	JUS AUTRES FRUITS,LEGUMES
0586	FRUIT TEMPORARILY PRESVD	W 32683	49.5	W 37695	67.5	W 42101	70.9	W 36629	46.7	FRUITS CONSERV TEMPORAIRE
05861	FRUIT,FRZN WITHOUT SUGAR	W 30313	46.7	W 36105	65.4	W 40568	68.1	W 33985	44.0	FRUITS CONG SANS SUCRE
0589	FRUIT PREPRD,PRESRVD,NES	W 41736	44.6	W 49516	52.8	W 50885	61.6	W 62899	59.0	FRUITS PREPARES CONSERV
05899	FRUIT,NUTS NES,PRESERVED	W 41614	44.1	W 49459	52.5	W 50817	61.2	W 62834	58.6	FRUITS PREP CONSERV NDA
07	COFFEE,TEA,COCOA,SPICES		31.5		47.0		62.7		61.0	CAFE,THE,CACAO,EPICES
081	*FEEDING STUFF FOR ANIML	W 1010045	472.9	W 1134282	657.2	W 913102	639.4	W 1065984	583.5	NOURRITURE POUR ANIMAUX
0814	MEAT OR FISH MEAL FODDER	W 897551	454.2	W 1022293	633.5	W 812735	612.7	W 933293	555.4	FARINES DE VIANDES,POISSONS
08142	FISH MEAL FODDER	W 897551	454.2	W 1022192	633.4	W 812666	612.7	W 928700	552.4	FARINES DE POISSONS
09	MISC EDIBLE PRODUCTS		72.1		176.6		194.5		113.7	PREP ALIMENTAIRES DIVERSES
098	EDIBLE PRODCTS,PREPS NES	W 29617	71.8	W 67499	176.2	W 61444	193.6	W 33986	112.7	PREP ALIMENTAIRES NDA
09809	MISC FOOD PREPRTIONS NES	W 21897	53.1	W 59026	155.3	W 51051	166.9	W 22613	90.5	PREP ALIMENTAIRES NDA
1	BEVERAGES AND TOBACCO		173.8		203.6		319.9		452.1	BOISSONS ET TABACS
11	BEVERAGES		152.2		189.7		300.4		439.2	BOISSONS
112	ALCOHOLIC BEVERAGES	W 121709	147.4	W 146543	186.4	W 206624	297.4	W 336178	434.4	BOISSONS ALCOOLIQUES
1121	WINE OF FRESH GRAPES ETC	W 118500	143.7	W 142858	182.5	W 203920	294.4	W 325177	428.0	VINS DE RAISINS FRAIS
11212	WINE OF FRESH GRAPES	W 118450	143.7	W 142251	181.8	W 203368	293.8	W 321766	424.0	VINS DE MOUTS DE RAISINS
2	CRUDE MATERLS,EXCL FUELS		2906.5		4724.4		3947.5		4150.9	MAT BRUTES NON COMESTIBLES
24	CORK AND WOOD		519.0		704.1		619.6		700.3	LIEGE ET BOIS
246	PULPWOOD,CHIPS,WOODWASTE	W 3018189	163.6	W 4076520	232.9	W 2906174	171.0	W 2777954	147.1	BOIS DE TRITURATION
24602	PULPWOOD CHIPS,PARTICLES	W 3018189	163.6	W 4076496	232.9	W 2906147	170.9	W 2777952	147.1	EN FORME DE PLAQUETTES
247	OTH WOOD ROUGH,SQUARED	W 1302549	125.3	W 1626312	160.1	W 1158469	116.2	W 1698945	123.6	BOIS BRUTS EQUARRIS
2471	SAW-,VENEER-LOGS CONIFER	W 1216932	117.4	W 1447707	142.9	W 1099183	109.5	W 1498041	111.1	CONIFERES POUR SCIAGE,PLACAG
24711	— IN THE ROUGH	W 1216932	117.4	W 1447707	142.9	W 1099183	109.5	W 1498041	111.1	ECORCES OU DEGROSSIS
248	WOOD SHAPED,SLEEPERS	W 537294	230.3	W 742549	311.2	W 657465	332.6	W 1020455	429.7	BOIS SIMPLEMENT TRAVAILLES
2482	LUMBER SHAPED CONIFER	W 513436	210.3	W 719701	293.1	W 641008	318.2	W 997769	414.5	CONIFERES SCIES,RABOTES
24821	LUMBER SAWN ETC CONIFER	W 483940	170.4	W 679182	237.2	W 582123	231.5	W 909967	289.6	CONIFERES SCIES LONGITUD
24822	LUMBER PLANED ETC CONIFR	W 29496	40.0	W 40519	55.9	W 58884	86.7	W 87802	124.9	CONIFER RABOTES,RAINES
251	*PULP AND WASTE PAPER	W 1603347	720.1	W 1641259	1274.2	W 1657847	764.9	W 1650739	690.5	PATES A PAPIER,DECHETS
2517	SODA,SULPHATE WOOD PULP	W 1584218	717.7	W 1625171	1270.4	W 1653166	764.4	W 1639692	689.3	PATES CHIMIQUES AU SULFATE
25171	— UNBLEACHED	W 341098	132.2	W 272184	193.1	W 272938	106.7	W 256257	93.2	PATES ECRUES
25172	— BLEACHED,NONDISSOLVNG	W 1243120	585.6	W 1352987	1077.4	W 1380227	657.7	W 1383435	596.2	PATES BLANCHIES
27	CRUDE FERTLZR,MINRLS NES		63.6		63.0		84.5		79.4	ENGRAIS MINERAUX BRUTS
28	METALLIFEROUS ORES,SCRAP		1455.1		2501.3		2278.3		2473.9	MINERAIS METAL,DECHETS
281	IRON ORE,CONCENTRATES	W 6938960	125.9	W 6096077	123.3	W 6982429	147.6	W 6727828	150.7	MINERAIS DE FER
2815	IRON ORE,CONC,NOT AGGLOM	W 3528814	43.5	W 3099451	39.4	W 3568952	47.0	W 3163632	41.5	MINERAIS NON AGGLOMERES
2816	IRON ORE AGGLOMERATES	W 3410146	82.5	W 2996626	84.0	W 3413477	100.6	W 3564196	109.3	MINERAIS AGGLOMERES
287	BASE METAL ORES,CONC NES	W 761009	1262.6	W 911679	2312.5	W 1116138	2046.0	W 3414804	2237.5	MINERAIS METAUX COMMUNS
2871	CPR ORE ETC,CEMENT COPPR	W 678765	1130.0	W 787046	1928.7	W 1020569	1881.6	W 3289173	2017.7	MINERAIS DE CUIVRE,MATTES
28711	COPPER ORES,EXCL MATTE	W 678765	1130.0	W 783877	1920.4	W 1019778	1879.6	W 3289173	2017.7	MINERAIS DE CUIVRE
2879	OTH NONFER ORE,CONCNTRTE	W 29933	125.3	W 33911	368.5	W 29311	153.6	W 38694	200.2	MINERAIS D'AUTRES METAUX
28793	MOLYBD, NIOBIUM ETC ORES	W 29933	125.3	W 33911	368.5	W 29311	153.6	W 38610	200.2	MINERAIS DE MOLYBDENE,TITANE
289	PREC MTAL ORES,WASTE NES	MK 62674	59.4	MK 63088	58.5	MK 85935	77.2	MK 64558	57.9	MINERAIS,DECHETS MET PREC
28901	PRECIOUS METAL ORES,CONC	MK 62674	59.4	MK 63088	58.5	MK 85935	77.2	MK 64558	57.9	MINERAIS METAUX PRECIEUX
29	CRUDE ANIMAL,VEG MAT NES		129.5		157.5		179.1		187.4	MATIERES BRUTES ANIM,VEGET
292	CRUDE VEG MATERIALS NES	W 51014	124.8	W 58124	151.6	W 61849	173.5	W 67996	179.1	MAT BRUTES VEGETALES NDA
2925	SEEDS,ETC FOR PLANTING	W 2750	37.3	W 2424	37.7	W 1715	41.2	W 2587	48.5	SEMENCES NDA
2929	OTH CRUDE VEG MATERIALS	W 35977	60.9	W 41236	77.4	W 44457	88.8	W 51642	91.6	MATIERES VEGETALES NDA
29291	VEGETABLE SAPS,EXTRACTS	W 2913	40.1	W 3546	50.6	W 4009	58.7	W 4753	59.8	SUCS,EXTRAITS VEGETAUX
3	MINERAL FUELS ETC		23.9		40.0		29.2		50.8	COMBUSTIBLES MINERAUX LUB
4	ANIMAL,VEGETABLE OIL,FAT		48.6		76.1		62.5		29.0	HUILES,GRAISSES ANIM,VEG
411	*ANIMAL OILS AND FATS	W 167929	44.9	W 151649	49.7	W 129090	42.9	W 35783	15.4	HUILES,GRAISSES ANIMALES
4111	OILS OF FISH,WHALES ETC	W 165720	43.9	W 150587	49.2	W 127189	41.8	W 32354	13.3	GRAISSES,HUILES DE POISSONS
41112	OTHER FISH OILS AND FATS	W 165714	43.8	W 150587	49.2	W 127189	41.8	W 32354	13.3	AUTRES HUILES ET GRAISSES
5	CHEMCLS,RELATED PROD NES		521.4		541.4		545.3		762.2	PRODUITS CHIMIQUES
51	ORGANIC CHEMICALS		196.6		169.9		130.0		251.8	PROD CHIMIQ ORGANIQUES
512	ALCOHOLS,PHENOLS ETC	W 875489	188.7	W 723324	151.4	W 852563	106.3	W 1547257	226.4	PHENOLS,PHENOLS-ALCOOLS
5121	ACYCLIC ALCOHOLS,DERIVS	W 875453	188.6	W 723315	151.3	W 852523	106.2	W 1547119	226.1	ALCOOLS ACYCLIQUES
51211	METHYL ALCOHOL(METHANOL)	W 867172	179.1	W 715334	134.9	W 844034	92.2	W 1539392	213.9	ALCOOLS METHYLIQUES
52	INORGANIC CHEMICALS		193.8		226.1		253.5		319.8	PROD CHIM INORGANIQUES
522	INORG ELEMNTS,OXIDES,ETC	W 186827	67.3	W 110752	108.8	W 85271	131.7	W 151082	183.3	ELEMENTS INORGANIQUES
5221	CHEMICAL ELEMENTS	W 12562	40.1	W 14408	62.9	W 16730	90.9	W 43596	140.3	ELEMENTS CHIMIQUES
52214	FLUORINE,BROMINE,IODINE	W 4883	38.0	W 6401	60.8	W 6332	88.8	W 9230	135.2	FLUOR,BROME ET IODE
523	OTHR INORG CHEMICALS ETC	W 213897	126.5	W 238206	117.4	W 221640	121.9	W 276928	136.6	AUT PRODUITS CHIMIQUES INORG
5232	OTH MTL CMPD OF INRG ACD	W 193247	77.4	W 217536	91.7	W 204098	94.7	W 248423	106.2	SELS METALLIQUES
52321	NITRITES AND NITRATES	W 179867	44.8	W 203215	52.8	W 189245	55.0	W 224580	65.3	NITRITES ET NITRATES

5. Special Exports F.O.B. by Commodities according to the S.I.T.C. (Rev. 2) in million U.S. Dollars
Exportations Spéciales F.O.B. par Produits d'après la C.T.C.I. (Rév. 2) en millions de Dollars E.U.

SITC CTCI	COMMODITY	1994 QUANTITY QUANTITE	1994 VALUE VALEUR	1995 QUANTITY QUANTITE	1995 VALUE VALEUR	1996 QUANTITY QUANTITE	1996 VALUE VALEUR	1997 QUANTITY QUANTITE	1997 VALUE VALEUR	PRODUIT
5233	METALLIC ACID SALTS ETC	W 258	34.4	W 218	7.6	W 668	8.4	W 1099	8.0	SELS ACIDES D'OXYDES METAL E
55	PERFUME,CLEANING ETC PRD		34.2		33.0		34.7		36.6	PROD POUR PARFUM,TOILETTE
562	*FERTILIZERS,MANUFACTURE	W 179671	35.2	W 162459	30.3	W 175784	35.5	W 245737	45.4	ENGRAIS MANUFACTURES
5629	FERTILIZERS NES	W 177341	34.4	W 159475	29.3	W 161707	33.2	W 168307	37.2	ENGRAIS NDA
6	BASIC MANUFACTURES		3810.5		5614.9		5339.4		6111.9	ART MANUFACTURES
62	RUBBER MANUFACTURES NES		53.8		70.6		64.9		81.1	CAOUTCHOUC MANUFACTURE
625	RUBBER TYRES, TUBES ETC	W 14021	50.8	W 16945	65.7	W 14971	60.1	W 24306	75.7	PNEUS CAOUTCHOUC VULCANISE
63	WOOD,CORK MANUFACTRS NES		79.7		82.7		109.7		116.3	OUVRAGES LIEGE ET BOIS
635	WOOD MANUFACTURES NES	W 36692	55.0	W 38739	55.9	W 53352	76.9	W 57957	76.6	ART MANUF EN BOIS NDA
6353	BUILDERS WOODWRK,PREFABS	W 31633	47.4	W 30776	46.0	W 35016	62.5	W 35230	60.6	OUVRAGES DE MENUISERIE
64	PAPER,PAPERBOARD AND MFR		184.5		240.0		238.3		240.7	PAPIERS,CARTONS & OUVRAGES
641	PAPER AND PAPERBOARD	W 276354	150.4	W 252980	186.7	W 291935	186.9	W 387934	186.3	PAPIERS ET CARTONS
6411	NEWSPRINT	W 151019	77.0	W 135713	110.9	W 138134	98.0	W 151719	76.7	PAPIER JOURNAL
6416	FIBRE BUILDING BOARD	W 108750	59.5	W 97119	55.0	W 127640	65.7	W 194986	78.5	PLAQUES CONSTRUCT EN PATE
64162	INSULATING BOARD, ETC	W 82991	49.0	W 65769	41.7	W 95587	52.0	W 142462	61.3	PLAQUES CONST NON COMPR
642	PAPER,ETC,PRECUT,ARTS OF	W 16070	34.2	W 24779	53.4	W 26913	51.4	W 35614	54.4	PAP,CARTONS DECOUPES
65	TEXTILE YARN,FABRICS,ETC		81.2		94.6		122.8		147.8	FILS,TISSUS,ARTICLES TEXTILE
67	IRON AND STEEL		58.8		97.3		92.9		96.7	FER ET ACIER
671	PIG IRON ETC	W 6046	28.5	W 6806	60.8	W 6933	42.5	W 5216	35.5	FONTE,SPIEGEL,POUDRES
6716	FERRO–ALLOYS	W 6045	28.5	W 6797	60.8	W 6931	42.5	W 5155	35.5	FERRO–ALLIAGES
67169	OTHER FERRO–ALLOYS	W 4947	27.8	W 6586	60.6	W 6904	42.5	W 5040	35.4	AUTRES FERRO–ALLIAGES
68	NON–FERROUS METALS		3281.2		4928.7		4563.2		5277.3	METAUX NON FERREUX
681	SILVER,PLATINUM,ETC		114.5		134.1		153.1		127.5	ARGENT ET PLATINE
6811	SILVER UNWKD,PARTLY WRKD		114.5		134.1		153.1		127.5	ARGENT BRUT MI–OUVRE
68113	SILVER UNWROUGHT		105.0		130.3		150.9		125.3	ARGENT ET ALLIAGES BRUTS
682	COPPER EXC CEMENT COPPER	W 1437940	3160.5	W 1619048	4782.9	W 1883569	4401.1	W 2241908	5142.5	CUIVRE
6821	COPPER NES,ALLOYS,UNWRT	W 1392497	3041.4	W 1569532	4611.6	W 1836663	4263.9	W 2196240	5019.3	CUIVRE BRUT
68211	COPPER UNREF,EXC CEMENT	W 196936	418.7	W 175824	509.8	W 230606	532.8	W 178102	370.7	CUIVRE POUR AFFINAGE
68212	COPPER REFINED,UNWROUGHT	W 1195552	2622.8	W 1393704	4101.8	W 1606051	3731.1	W 2018135	4648.5	CUIVRE AFFINE BRUT
6822	COPPER,ALLOYS WORKED	W 45443	119.1	W 49516	171.3	W 46906	137.2	W 45668	123.3	CUIVRE,ALLIAGES OUVRES
68221	COPPER BARS,WIRE,ETC	W 33986	85.5	W 36379	121.4	W 33092	92.1	W 31467	82.0	BARRES,PROFILES ET FILS
69	METAL MANUFACTURES NES		51.7		69.8		111.0		97.3	ART MANUFACT EN METAL NDA
699	BASE METAL MFRS NES	W 8007	24.0		32.1		48.2		34.7	ART MANUFACTURES MET NDA
7	MACHINES,TRANSPORT EQUIP		312.2		285.9		372.3		428.6	MACHINES MATERIEL TRANSPORT
72	MACHS FOR SPCL INDUSTRYS		20.6		28.1		64.4		69.9	MAC SPECIALES POUR INDUST
74	GENRL INDUSTRL MACHY NES		37.2		52.9		55.9		66.5	MACH APP INDUSTRIE
77	ELECTRIC MACHNRY NES ETC		37.2		38.3		52.8		57.7	MACH APP ELECT NDA
78	ROAD VEHICLES		147.9		115.6		105.6		181.8	VEHICULES ROUTIERS
782	LORRIES,SPCL MTR VEH NES	W 4766	47.2	W 6449	57.9	W 4979	54.9	W 13325	107.2	VEHICULES SPECIAUX,MARCH
7821	LORRIES,TRUCKS	W 4668	46.9	W 6249	56.6	W 4870	54.0	W 13218	106.7	VEHICULES TRANSP MARCHAND
784	MOTOR VEH PRTS,ACCES NES	W 4123	55.0	W 2497	31.9	W 3047	36.1	W 4736	45.3	PIECES 722,781,782,783
7849	OTHER MOTOR VEHCL PARTS	W 4018	54.8	W 2367	31.5	W 2832	35.7	W 4255	44.6	PIECES 722,781,782,783
79	OTHR TRANSPORT EQUIPMENT		51.7		33.1		71.8		23.5	AUTRE MATERIEL TRANSPORT
793	SHIPS AND BOATS ETC	W 47246	48.5	W 51498	30.7	W 103462	60.2	W 18770	11.6	NAVIRES BATEAUX,ETC
7932	SHIPS AND BOATS NES	W 45761	46.3	W 50525	28.1	W 101373	45.3	W 18168	10.2	NAVIRES ET BATEAUX
8	MISC MANUFACTURED GOODS		345.7		357.0		344.9		378.3	ART MANUFACTURES DIVERS
821	*FURNITURE,PARTS THEREOF	W 15927	40.4	W 13268	39.5	W 21481	43.3	W 22108	59.7	MEUBLES ET PIECES
84	CLOTHING AND ACCESSORIES		75.1		66.3		60.8		58.8	VETEMENTS
89	MISC MANUFCTRD GOODS NES		175.3		203.0		196.8		217.8	ART MANUFACTURES DIVERS
892	PRINTED MATTER	W 19838	79.7	W 25951	124.0	W 27763	110.7	W 36066	125.2	IMPRIMES
8921	PRINTED BOOKS,GLOBES,ETC	W 9133	36.7	W 11537	55.9	W 13660	46.7	W 19569	55.5	LIVRES,BROCHURES,CARTES
89211	PRINTED BOOKS,PAMPHLETS	W 8684	35.3	W 11443	55.5	W 13647	46.6	W 19308	54.7	LIVRES,BROCHURES
8922	NEWSPAPERS,PERIODICALS	W 9179	34.3	W 13065	56.6	W 12949	53.7	W 14875	55.9	JOURNAUX ET PERIODIQUES
9	GOODS NOT CLASSD BY KIND		497.0		586.5		712.7		680.0	ART TRANSACT NON CLASSES
931	*SPECIAL TRANSACTIONS		183.5		211.2		272.2	W 777082	294.0	TRANS.SPECIALES
971	*GOLD,NON MONETARY NES	K 26680	309.0	K 30634	371.1	K 34261	427.7	K 54989	382.1	OR NON MONETAIRE
97101	NONMON GLD UNWRT,SEMIMFD	K 24784	303.8	K 30076	369.7	K 34261	427.7	K 54989	382.1	OR,ALLIAGES D'OR BRUTS

1. HISTORICAL SERIES, 1962–1997 SPECIAL TRADE, IMPORTS C.I.F., EXPORTS F.O.B.
SERIES HISTORIQUES, 1962–1997 COMMERCE SPECIAL, IMPORTATIONS C.A.F., EXPORTATIONS F.O.B

YEAR ANNEE	VALUE IN MILLION YUAN RENMINBI / VALEUR EN MILLION YUAN RENMINBI — MERCHANDISE –MARCHANDISE IMPORTS	EXPORTS	GOLD –OR IMPORTS	EXPORTS	CONVERSION FACTORS U.S. CENTS PER YUAN RENMINBI / FACTEURS DE CONVERSION CENTS E.U. PAR YUAN RENMINBI IMPORTS	EXPORTS	INDEX NUMBERS –INDICES QUANTUM IMPORTS	EXPORTS	UNIT VALUE / VALEUR UNITAIRE IMPORTS	EXPORTS
1962	3380.00	4710.00			40.6207	40.6207				
1963	3570.00	5000.00			40.6207	40.6207				
1964	4210.00	5540.00			40.6207	40.6207				
1965	6310.00	5530.00			40.6504	40.6504				
1966	6110.00	6600.00			40.6504	40.6504				
1967	5340.00	5880.00			40.6504	40.6504				
1968	5090.00	5760.00			40.6504	40.6504				
1969	4720.00	5980.00			40.6504	40.6504				
1970	5610.00	5680.00			41.5330	39.7887				
1971	5240.00	6850.00			42.1756	38.5401				
1972	6400.00	8290.00			44.6875	41.4958				
1973	10360.00	11690.00			49.8069	49.7861				
1974	15280.00	13940.00			49.8691	49.8565				
1975	14740.00	14300.00			50.8141	50.7692				
1976	12930.00	13480.00			50.8894	50.8902				
1977	13280.00	13970.00			54.2922	54.3307				
1978	18739.00	16765.00			58.1110	58.1395				
1979	24290.00	21168.00			64.5121	64.5253				
1980	29140.00	27240.00			67.0899	67.0705				
1981	36773.00	36761.00			59.8646	59.8651				
1982	35769.20	41433.10			52.9487	52.8883				
1983	42182.50	43832.70			50.5510	50.5342				
1984	62047.30	58055.70			42.1989	42.8399				
1985	125783.50	80931.50			33.7809	33.7854				
1986	149826.00	108210.50			28.6391	28.5926				
1987	161421.00	146995.00			26.8665	26.8665				
1988	205507.00	176672.00			26.8665	26.8665				
1989	219986.00	195606.00			26.5597	26.5597				
1990	254934.30	296731.20			20.9250	20.9250				
1991	339530.60	382744.30			18.7880	18.7880				
1992	444263.80	468272.80			18.1390	18.1390				
1993	593961.60	524141.40			17.3560	17.3560				
1994	996906.30	1043149.00			11.6040	11.6040				
1995	1077052.00	1241769.00			11.9876	11.9827				
1996	1155209.00	1257084.00			12.0276	12.0276				
1997	1180176.00	1514358.00			12.0641	12.0639				

2. IMPORTS BY BROAD ECONOMIC CATEGORY AND EXPORTS BY INDUSTRIAL ORIGIN. (PERCENTAGE OF TOTAL VALUE)
IMPORTATIONS PAR CATEGORIES ECONOMIQUES ET EXPORTATIONS PAR BRANCHE D'ACTIVITE.(EN POURCENTAGE DE LA VALEUR TOTALE)

IMPORTS – IMPORTATIONS

	1991	1992	1993	1994	1995	1996	1997
TOTAL IMPORTS–IMPORTATIONS TOTALES	100.	100.	100.	100.	100.	100.	100.
1 FOOD BEV–ALIMENTATION BOISSONS	4.8	4.0	2.3	4.0	5.6	4.5	3.5
11 PRIMARY–PRODUITS DE BASE	3.0	2.7	1.5	1.7	2.6	2.6	1.9
111 FOR INDUSTRY–POUR L'INDUSTRIE	2.6	2.2	1.0	1.1	2.0	1.9	1.2
112 FOR HOUSEHOLDS–POUR LES MENAGES	0.4	0.6	0.5	0.6	0.6	0.7	0.7
12 PROCESSED–PRODUITS ELABORES	1.9	1.2	0.8	2.3	3.0	1.8	1.6
121 FOR INDUSTRY–POUR L'INDUSTRIE	1.5	0.9	0.6	1.9	2.4	1.4	1.3
122 FOR HOUSEHOLDS–POUR LES MENAGES	0.4	0.3	0.3	0.4	0.6	0.4	0.3
2 IND SUPPLIES–APPROV INDUSTRIELS	46.4	48.1	44.9	44.0	45.5	46.6	48.2
21 PRIMARY–PRODUITS DE BASE	5.1	5.3	4.1	4.5	5.9	5.3	5.5
22 PROCESSED–PRODUITS ELABORES	41.4	42.9	40.8	39.5	39.6	41.3	42.6
3 FUELS–COMBUSTIBLES	3.3	4.4	5.6	3.5	3.9	4.9	7.1
31 PRIMARY–PRODUITS DE BASE	1.6	2.3	2.4	1.6	2.2	3.1	4.5
32 PROCESSED–PRODUITS ELABORES	1.7	2.1	3.1	1.8	1.7	1.8	2.6
321 MOTOR SPIRIT–ESSENCE	0.0	0.1		0.2		0.1	0.1
322 OTHER–AUTRES	1.6	2.0	3.1	1.6	1.7	1.7	2.5
4 MACHINERY–EQUIPEMENT	26.8	29.1	33.0	34.5	34.8	34.4	32.0
41 CAPITAL EQUIPMENT–MACHINES	23.2	24.4	28.6	29.4	29.0	27.7	23.9
42 PARTS–PIECES ACCESSOIRES	3.6	4.7	4.4	5.2	5.7	6.7	8.0
5 TRANSPORT–TRANSPORT	12.6	8.4	8.8	8.8	4.3	4.7	4.6
51 PASSENGER CARS–AUTOMOBILES	0.9	1.7	2.0	1.4	0.7	0.3	0.2
52 OTHER–AUTRES	2.6	3.4	4.2	5.6	1.8	2.1	2.2
521 INDUSTRIAL–INDUSTRIELS	2.6	3.4	3.9	5.3	1.8	2.1	2.2
522 NON INDUSTRIAL–NON INDUSTRIEL	0.0	0.0	0.4	0.4	0.0	0.0	0.0
53 PARTS–PIECES ACCESSOIRES	9.1	3.3	2.5	1.8	1.8	2.2	2.1
6 CONSUM GOODS–BIENS CONSOMMATION	5.7	5.1	4.7	4.5	4.7	4.4	3.9
61 DURABLE–DURABLES	2.3	1.9	1.9	1.9	1.7	1.4	1.1
62 SEMI DURABLE–SEMI DURABLES	2.5	2.2	2.0	2.0	2.2	2.2	2.0
63 NON DURABLE–NON DURABLES	0.9	0.9	0.7	0.5	0.8	0.9	0.8
7 GOODS NES–BIENS NDA	0.3	0.8	0.7	0.7	1.3	0.6	0.8

EXPORTS – EXPORTATIONS

	1991	1992	1993	1994	1995	1996	1997
TOTAL EXPORTS–EXPORTATIONS TOTALES	100.	100.	100.	100.	100.	100.	100.
1 AGRICULTURE	8.4	7.5	6.7	6.4	4.5	4.0	3.7
2 MINING QUARRY–INDUS EXTRACTIVES	6.2	5.2	4.4	3.3	3.5	3.8	3.5
3 MANUFACTURING–IND MANUFACTUR	85.4	87.3	88.8	90.3	92.0	92.2	92.7
31 FOOD BEV TOBACCO–ALIM BOISS TAB	5.9	5.4	5.5	5.2	5.1	5.3	4.3
32 TEXTILES–INDUSTRIES TEXTILES	32.3	35.9	36.2	35.7	31.1	30.1	30.3
33 WOOD & PRODUCTS–BOIS & PRODUITS	0.6	0.8	0.8	0.8	0.9	0.9	0.9
34 PAPER & PRODUCTS–PAPIER & PRODT	0.5	0.6	0.7	0.6	0.8	0.7	0.7
35 CHEMICALS–INDUSTRIES CHIMIQUES	9.4	9.5	9.6	9.5	10.6	10.7	10.8
36 NON METAL MIN–MIN NON METAL	2.2	1.9	1.6	1.8	2.0	2.1	2.1
37 BASIC METAL–IND METAL BASE	3.1	2.6	2.2	2.8	5.0	3.8	4.2
38 METAL MANUF–MANUF METAL	24.3	22.8	24.6	26.0	29.1	31.5	32.1
39 OTH MANUF IND–AUTRES MANUF	7.1	7.8	7.6	7.8	7.5	7.1	7.4

3. TRADE BY PRINCIPAL COUNTRIES OF ORIGIN AND SALE (VALUE IN MILLION U.S. DOLLARS)
ECHANGES SELON LES PRINCIPAUX PAYS D'ORIGINE ET DE VENTE (VALEUR EN MILLIONS DE DOLLARS EU)

COUNTRIES–PAYS	SPECIAL IMPORTS C.I.F. IMPORTATIONS SPECIALES C.A.F				
	1993	1994	1995	1996	1997
World	103959.0	115613.6	132083.5	138832.8	142370.4
Africa	1001.4	891.9	1424.7	1464.5	2463.6
Americas	14001.4	17989.8	21766.8	22335.4	22077.6
– Northern America	12070.7	15742.6	18799.8	18728.0	18309.1
– LAIA	1841.7	2118.0	2657.5	3463.2	3663.8
– CACM	2.4	2.8	69.3	3.3	2.6
– Caribbean	75.6	121.8	229.7	138.9	100.2
– Rest of America	10.9	4.7	10.5	2.0	1.9
Asia excl fmr USSR	61419.2	66992.3	75799.3	81023.6	85473.6
– Middle East	1957.6	1604.3	2129.4	2981.3	3779.3
Asia former USSR	370.3	361.5	528.5	560.2	640.5
Europe excl fmr USSR	18053.8	20360.6	22898.6	21398.1	20663.3
– European Union	15719.0	18581.4	21256.8	19867.4	19200.2
– Eastern Europe	1095.5	623.5	452.4	315.2	181.4
– Rest of Europe	1239.2	1155.8	1189.4	1215.5	1281.7
Europe former USSR	5549.8	4297.2	4384.4	5695.6	4453.0
Oceania	2360.4	2915.6	3021.6	3936.3	3673.6
Other	1202.7	1804.7	2259.7	2419.1	2925.2
Japan/Japon	23288.6	26326.9	29004.5	29180.8	28994.8
Other Asia n.e.s.	12932.1	14085.6	14784.3	16180.1	16441.2
USA/Etats–Unis d'Amer	10687.4	13893.7	16118.5	16155.2	16301.5
Korea, Republic of	5360.1	7319.1	10293.2	12481.6	14929.7
China, Hong Kong SAR	10446.5	9441.7	8590.7	7826.7	6990.3
Germany/Allemagne	6040.7	7137.4	8037.9	7324.1	6181.3
Russian Federation	4980.9	3495.2	3798.6	5151.8	4085.7
Singapore/Singapour	2645.8	2491.7	3397.8	3600.9	4464.7
Italy/Italie	2737.4	3068.5	3115.0	3245.9	2452.1
Australia/Australie	1949.5	2451.8	2584.5	3433.8	3247.6
France, Monaco	1640.9	1938.8	2648.4	2240.0	3246.7
Canada	1375.2	1848.7	2681.3	2572.6	2007.0
Indonesia/Indonésie	1468.6	1589.0	2052.2	2280.4	2673.6
Malaysia/Malaisie	1083.6	1622.0	2070.6	2243.6	2495.1
United Kingdom	1663.7	1769.9	1972.1	1880.9	1978.5
Thailand/Thaïlande	601.5	864.4	1610.8	1890.4	2013.9
Free zones/Zone franches		1775.5	2255.1		2923.2
Brazil/Brésil	863.1	1058.8	1231.5	1484.1	1489.0
Sweden/Suède	670.7	827.2	999.8	1379.7	1297.5
Belgium–Luxembourg	816.8	1066.5	1146.9	1058.6	948.4
Switzerland,Liechtenst.	1004.8	986.6	938.7	932.1	872.6
Netherlands/Pays–Bas	713.9	707.4	818.0	918.6	1072.6
Areas n.e.s.	1202.7	29.2	4.7	2419.1	2.0
Oman	561.1	413.3	481.5	811.2	1345.5
Spain/Espagne	475.2	902.5	908.6	517.4	555.5
So. African Customs Un	414.7	537.8	689.6	672.1	794.5
India/Inde	416.6	321.8	397.5	719.2	897.3
Finland/Finlande	322.4	447.6	621.7	549.6	687.0
Ukraine	485.8	742.8	539.6	507.3	334.2
Saudi Arabia	118.6	248.9	551.1	829.0	825.9
Peru/Pérou	249.1	384.3	459.5	517.6	620.9
Argentina/Argentine	219.9	268.6	370.4	517.6	722.2
Yemen/Yémen	255.1	149.2	344.2	570.3	650.9
Austria/Autriche	315.9	364.8	562.6	301.1	255.1
New Zealand	264.1	316.5	346.4	403.1	349.4
Iran (Islamic Rep of)	310.0	181.5	226.6	386.1	535.8
Kazakhstan	263.1	197.0	315.5	364.6	432.8
Chile/Chili	281.7	183.1	230.5	455.3	415.1
Denmark/Danemark	225.5	277.4	318.5	318.5	346.6
Philippines	212.9	272.4	275.8	372.9	326.8

COUNTRIES–PAYS	SPECIAL EXPORTS F.O.B. EXPORTATIONS SPECIALES F.O.B.				
	1993	1994	1995	1996	1997
Monde	91744.0	121006.3	148779.6	151047.5	182791.6
Afrique	1509.9	1723.1	2465.0	2534.6	3184.2
Amériques	19940.1	25314.6	29394.0	31416.1	39229.7
– Amérique du Nord	18171.9	22873.5	26262.1	28322.1	34648.5
– ALAI	1057.6	1466.2	2107.0	2196.7	3007.5
– MCAC	79.2	119.0	141.5	129.8	185.9
– Caraïbes	266.1	274.0	275.5	269.3	364.2
– Autre Amérique	365.3	581.9	607.9	498.2	1023.6
Asie anc. URSS exclus	52617.7	73447.9	92002.2	91242.1	108965.8
– Moyen–Orient	2417.2	2658.2	3252.5	3285.8	3954.3
Asie ancienne URSS	272.6	201.4	258.6	222.3	252.1
Europe anc. URSS exclus	13352.3	16901.7	20998.3	21885.0	26578.0
– Union Européenne	12255.3	15414.4	19126.7	19859.6	23855.3
– Europe de l'Est	663.2	935.1	1178.6	1164.3	1462.2
– Autre de l'Europe	433.8	552.3	692.9	861.0	1260.6
Europe ancienne URSS	2820.1	1693.7	1759.4	1785.8	2183.8
Océanie	1231.4	1723.8	1902.0	1961.5	2398.0
Autre					
China, Hong Kong SAR	22049.7	32361.0	35983.4	32906.3	43782.8
Japan/Japon	15776.7	21578.6	28466.7	30886.2	31838.6
USA/Etats–Unis d'Amer	16972.7	21474.8	24728.6	26705.6	32740.6
Korea, Republic of	2860.5	4402.4	6687.8	7499.9	9126.9
Germany/Allemagne	3967.5	4761.2	5671.5	5842.7	6496.9
Singapore/Singapour	2245.3	2558.1	3500.6	3748.8	4323.3
Netherlands/Pays–Bas	1608.8	2267.1	3232.1	3536.9	4406.0
United Kingdom	1928.7	2413.9	2797.7	3200.9	3815.2
Other Asia n.e.s.	1468.7	2247.5	3098.2	2801.9	3398.7
Russian Federation	2691.8	1580.8	1664.7	1692.7	2038.1
Italy/Italie	1305.4	1590.9	2067.6	1836.6	2239.0
France, Monaco	1292.4	1426.6	1843.7	1912.8	2336.8
Australia/Australie	1060.8	1487.9	1626.2	1673.0	2056.2
Canada	1197.8	1397.0	1532.5	1616.0	1906.5
Indonesia/Indonésie	691.7	1051.7	1438.1	1427.6	1841.0
Thailand/Thaïlande	750.5	1159.3	1751.8	1254.7	1501.1
Malaysia/Malaisie	704.4	1117.7	1281.0	1370.3	1921.8
United Arab Emirates	711.4	864.7	1101.1	1076.9	1301.2
Belgium–Luxembourg	611.3	822.0	1045.6	1056.7	1382.2
Spain/Espagne	551.2	774.6	1013.3	996.2	1265.9
Philippines	280.5	475.7	1030.1	1014.8	1339.6
Saudi Arabia	578.8	624.9	733.9	747.8	854.3
Pakistan	751.9	605.7	788.6	623.0	689.2
Viet Nam	274.7	341.5	720.3	842.2	1079.7
India/Inde	259.2	573.0	765.3	686.0	933.7
Macau/Macao	524.7	666.1	793.4	572.7	641.9
Brazil/Brésil	192.2	362.4	759.1	762.9	1044.4
Panama	350.1	569.0	594.9	488.2	1010.0
So. African Customs Un	250.0	366.3	637.4	688.2	800.0
Bangladesh	202.9	370.4	633.0	653.0	696.1
Korea Dem People's Rp	602.3	424.5	486.0	497.0	534.7
Myanmar	324.7	369.1	617.8	521.1	570.1
Poland/Pologne	248.5	294.2	472.0	568.5	673.7
Sweden/Suède	322.5	500.5	396.0	392.0	528.5
Switzerland,Liechtenst.	278.9	357.6	413.5	461.0	613.6
Chile/Chili	204.1	285.3	410.4	463.7	562.2
Iran (Islamic Rep of)	402.7	265.7	277.9	394.6	496.5
Egypt/Egypte	199.6	279.6	439.7	404.5	465.0
Turkey/Turquie	165.7	184.5	430.7	406.6	556.8
Argentina/Argentine	247.7	291.1	273.6	336.6	465.7

(VALUE AS PERCENTAGE OF WORLD TOTAL)(VALEURS EN POURCENTAGE DU TOTAL MONDIAL)

	1988	1989	1990	1991	1992	1993	1994	1995	1996	1997
Africa	0.5	0.7	0.7	0.7	0.6	1.0	0.8	1.1	1.1	1.7
Americas	19.3	19.1	17.9	17.6	15.8	13.5	15.6	16.5	16.1	15.5
– Northern America	15.4	15.0	15.0	15.1	13.4	11.6	13.6	14.2	13.5	12.9
– LAIA	3.4	3.7	2.2	2.1	2.1	1.8	1.8	2.0	2.5	2.6
– CACM	0.0	0.0	0.0	0.0	0.0	0.0	0.0	0.1	0.0	0.0
– Caribbean	0.5	0.4	0.6	0.3	0.2	0.1	0.1	0.2	0.1	0.1
– Rest of America	0.0	0.0	0.0	0.0	0.0	0.0	0.0	0.0	0.0	0.0
Asia excl fmr USSR	52.3	51.5	53.9	58.6	60.6	59.1	57.9	57.4	58.4	60.0
– Middle East	1.3	1.3	1.0	1.3	1.3	1.9	1.4	1.6	2.1	2.7
Asia former USSR					0.2	0.4	0.3	0.4	0.4	0.4
Europe excl fmr USSR	21.0	21.3	19.9	16.6	15.1	17.4	17.6	17.3	15.4	14.5
– European Union	15.8	16.5	16.4	14.5	13.5	15.1	16.1	16.1	14.3	13.5
– Eastern Europe	3.8	3.3	2.3	0.9	0.7	1.1	0.5	0.3	0.2	0.1
– Rest of Europe	1.4	1.4	1.2	1.2	0.9	1.2	1.0	0.9	0.9	0.9
Europe former USSR	3.2	3.6	4.0	3.2	4.6	5.3	3.7	3.3	4.1	3.1
Oceania	2.8	3.0	2.8	2.7	2.6	2.3	2.5	2.3	2.8	2.6
Other	0.9	0.7	0.8	0.7	0.5	1.2	1.6	1.7	1.7	2.1
Japan/Japon	20.0	17.8	14.2	15.7	17.0	22.4	22.8	22.0	21.0	20.4
Other Asia n.e.s.	2.3	3.1	4.2	5.7	7.3	12.4	12.2	11.2	11.7	11.5
USA/Etats–Unis d'Amer	12.0	13.3	12.3	12.5	11.0	10.3	12.0	12.2	11.6	11.5
Korea, Republic of	0.4	0.7	1.3	1.7	3.3	5.2	6.3	7.8	9.0	10.5
China, Hong Kong SAR	21.5	21.1	26.5	27.3	25.5	10.0	8.2	6.5	5.6	4.9
Germany/Allemagne				4.8	5.0	5.8	6.2	6.1	5.3	4.3
Russian Federation					4.4	4.8	3.0	2.9	3.7	2.9
Singapore/Singapour	1.8	2.5	1.6	1.6	1.5	2.5	2.2	2.6	2.6	3.1
Italy/Italie	2.8	3.1	2.0	2.3	2.2	2.6	2.7	2.4	2.3	1.7
Australia/Australie	2.0	2.5	2.5	2.4	2.1	1.9	2.1	2.0	2.5	2.3

	1988	1989	1990	1991	1992	1993	1994	1995	1996	1997
Afrique	1.4	1.2	1.1	1.2	1.5	1.6	1.4	1.7	1.7	1.7
Amériques	8.7	10.2	10.3	10.4	12.2	21.7	20.9	19.8	20.8	21.5
– Amérique du Nord	7.9	9.2	9.0	9.3	10.9	19.8	18.9	17.7	18.8	19.0
– ALAI	0.4	0.5	0.6	0.6	0.7	1.2	1.2	1.4	1.5	1.6
– MCAC	0.0	0.0	0.0	0.0	0.1	0.1	0.1	0.1	0.1	0.1
– Caraïbes	0.4	0.4	0.5	0.4	0.3	0.3	0.2	0.2	0.2	0.2
– Autre Amérique	0.1	0.1	0.2	0.1	0.2	0.4	0.5	0.4	0.3	0.6
Asie anc. URSS exclus	66.8	70.0	70.8	73.4	71.9	57.4	60.7	61.8	60.4	59.6
– Moyen–Orient	2.4	2.1	1.9	1.9	2.1	2.6	2.2	2.2	2.2	2.2
Asie ancienne URSS					0.3	0.3	0.2	0.2	0.1	0.1
Europe anc. URSS exclus	14.5	13.2	11.4	10.6	10.2	14.6	14.0	14.1	14.5	14.5
– Union Européenne	10.5	9.7	9.6	9.8	9.4	13.4	12.7	12.9	13.1	13.1
– Europe de l'Est	3.4	3.0	1.5	0.3	0.4	0.7	0.8	0.8	0.8	0.8
– Autre de l'Europe	0.6	0.5	0.4	0.4	0.4	0.5	0.5	0.5	0.6	0.7
Europe ancienne URSS	3.1	3.5	3.6	2.5	2.9	3.1	1.4	1.2	1.2	1.2
Océanie	0.9	0.9	0.9	0.9	0.9	1.3	1.4	1.3	1.3	1.3
Autre	4.6	0.9	1.9	1.0	0.1					
China, Hong Kong SAR	38.4	41.7	42.9	44.7	44.2	24.0	26.7	24.2	21.8	24.0
Japan/Japon	16.6	16.0	14.5	14.2	13.7	17.2	17.8	19.1	20.4	17.4
USA/Etats–Unis d'Amer	7.1	8.4	8.3	8.6	10.1	18.5	17.7	16.6	17.7	17.9
Korea, Republic of	0.2	0.9	2.0	3.0	2.8	3.1	3.6	4.5	5.0	5.0
Germany/Allemagne				3.3	2.9	4.3	3.9	3.8	3.9	3.6
Singapore/Singapour	3.1	3.2	3.2	2.8	2.4	2.4	2.1	2.4	2.5	2.4
Netherlands/Pays–Bas	1.6	1.4	1.5	1.5	1.4	1.8	1.9	2.2	2.3	2.4
United Kingdom	1.4	1.2	1.0	1.0	1.1	2.1	2.0	1.9	2.1	2.1
Other Asia n.e.s.	0.1	0.2	0.5	0.8	0.8	1.6	1.9	2.1	1.9	1.9
Russian Federation					2.8	2.9	1.3	1.1	1.1	1.1

4. Special Imports C.I.F. by Commodities according to the S.I.T.C. (Rev. 2) in million U.S. Dollars
Importations Spéciales C.A.F. par Produits d'après la C.T.C.I. (Rév. 2) en millions de Dollars E.U.

SITC CTCI	COMMODITY	1994 QUANTITY QUANTITE	1994 VALUE VALEUR	1995 QUANTITY QUANTITE	1995 VALUE VALEUR	1996 QUANTITY QUANTITE	1996 VALUE VALEUR	1997 QUANTITY QUANTITE	1997 VALUE VALEUR	PRODUIT
	ALL COMMODITIES		115613.7		132083.6		138832.8		142370.4	TOUS PRODUITS
0	FOOD AND LIVE ANIMALS		3132.1		6122.5		5648.9		4288.2	ALIMENTS,ANIMAUX VIVANTS
03	FISH AND PREPARATIONS		578.4		607.9		600.4		544.6	POISSONS ET PREPARATIONS
034	FISH,FRESH,CHILLED,FROZN	W 497764	368.6	W 528606	388.9	W 370544	380.9	W 406097	367.2	POISSON FRAIS, REFRIG,CONG
04	CEREALS AND PREPARATIONS		1332.6		3637.1		2601.3		941.0	CEREALES ET PRODUITS
041	WHEAT ETC UNMILLED	W 7299283	960.6	MW 11586	2026.4	W 8245961	1890.4	W 1860612	368.3	FROMENT,EPEAUTRE
0411	DURUM WHEAT UNMILLED	W 1821773	238.8	W 5603643	1014.0	W 4512381	1023.1	W 1508909	296.7	FROMENT DUR NON MOULU
0412	OTHER WHEAT ETC UNMILLED	W 5477509	721.9	W 5981937	1012.5	W 3733580	867.4	W 351703	71.7	AUTRE FROMENT NON MOULU
042	RICE	W 513816	141.5	W 1642201	433.6	W 761398	286.5	W 326173	139.8	RIZ
0422	RICE SEMI-MILLED,MILLED	W 492544	138.9	W 1623169	429.4	W 751308	283.6	W 326166	139.8	RIZ POLI,GLACE INCL BRISURES
04221	RICE MILLED UNBROKEN	W 492522	138.9	W 1610034	426.4	W 701507	270.7	W 303476	134.3	RIZ POLI,GLACE EXCL BRISURES
044	MAIZE UNMILLED	W 618	0.2	W 5181023	816.1	W 441130	73.1	W 435	0.3	MAIS NON MOULU
06	SUGAR AND PREPS,HONEY		446.2		935.5		427.7		250.7	SUCRES ET PRODUITS
061	SUGAR AND HONEY	W 1556059	411.3	W 3052177	907.5	W 1265803	399.7	W 807292	235.0	SUCRES ET MIEL
0611	RAW BEET AND CANE SUGAR	W 1484427	385.3	W 2572053	778.0	W 1204662	374.3	W 702980	199.2	SUCRES BRUTS
081	*FEEDING STUFF FOR ANIML	W 768941	349.3	W 884248	422.6	W 3478237	1299.6	W 5063501	1791.9	NOURRITURE POUR ANIMAUX
0813	OILCAKE AND OTH RESIDUES	W 3182	0.4	W 12147	1.2	W 1883561	520.7	W 3604609	1006.1	TOURTEAUX
08131	— OF SOYA BEANS	W 1380	0.2	W 1003	0.2	W 1876478	519.6	W 3469508	980.4	TOURTEAUX DE SOJA
0814	MEAT OR FISH MEAL FODDER	W 675600	276.8	W 699846	330.3	W 916284	582.0	W 1029361	644.8	FARINES DE VIANDES,POISSONS
08142	FISH MEAL FODDER	W 668792	275.3	W 693301	328.1	W 884478	569.4	W 988455	629.7	FARINES DE POISSONS
1	BEVERAGES AND TOBACCO		68.0		393.5		497.4		320.3	BOISSONS ET TABACS
12	TOBACCO AND MANUFACTURES		32.4		359.0		457.0		254.5	TABACS BRUTS FABRIQUES
2	CRUDE MATERLS,EXCL FUELS		7200.4		9868.9		10447.2		11727.6	MAT BRUTES NON COMESTIBLES
21	HIDES,SKINS,FURS UNDRSSD		268.3		410.9		369.4		405.1	CUIRS,PEAUX BRUTS
22	OIL SEEDS,OLEAGINOUS FRT		62.4		109.6		325.7		873.9	GRAINES,FRUITS OLEAGINEUX
222	SEEDS FOR'SOFT'FIXED OIL	W 215493	60.9	W 391033	103.9	W 1114516	323.4	W 2953530	870.2	GRAINES HUILES FIXES
2222	SOYA BEANS	W 51589	13.7	W 293938	75.5	W 1107539	320.4	W 2875907	843.0	FEVES DE SOJA
23	RUBBER, CRUDE		586.8		757.2		1123.6		931.8	CAOUTCHOUC BRUT
232	NATURAL RUBBER,GUMS	W 341964	332.8	W 321295	424.8	W 554021	723.1	W 432343	460.6	LATEX CAOUTCHOUC NATUREL
23202	OTHER NATURAL RUBBER	W 185495	183.1	W 177132	244.3	W 337627	464.2	W 247556	277.4	CAOUTCHOUC NATUREL
233	RUBBER,SYNTHTIC,RECLAIMD	W 258811	254.0	W 351443	332.5	W 378221	400.5	W 459174	471.2	LATEX CAOUTCH SYNTH REGEN
2331	SYNTHETIC RUBBER ETC	W 250301	250.2	W 310883	326.5	W 366835	395.7	W 452636	467.7	LATEX CAOUTCH SYNTHETIQUE
24	CORK AND WOOD		595.8		544.1		652.6		959.8	LIEGE ET BOIS
247	OTH WOOD ROUGH,SQUARED	W 2435817	430.4	W 1906091	368.4	V 3185492	457.8	W 3298965	677.1	BOIS BRUTS EQUARRIS
2472	SAW-,VENEER-LOGS NON-CON	W 1524197	317.2	W 1473932	315.1	V 2532448	409.3	W 2630211	607.7	NON CONIFERES SCIAGE,PLAC
24721	— IN THE ROUGH	W 1524197	317.2	W 1473932	315.1	V 2532448	409.3	W 2630211	607.7	BRUTS ECORCES DEGROSSIS
251	*PULP AND WASTE PAPER	W 1520763	494.5	W 1730327	844.6	W 2839852	967.9	W 3161427	923.9	PATES A PAPIER,DECHETS
2517	SODA,SULPHATE WOOD PULP	W 558166	270.8	W 647086	526.7	W 1035054	539.3	W 1105779	518.8	PATES CHIMIQUES AU SULFATE
25172	— BLEACHED,NONDISSOLVNG	W 431380	217.5	W 553295	452.9	W 941825	495.7	W 995205	474.0	PATES BLANCHIES
26	TEXTILE FIBRES AND WASTE		2782.8		3828.0		3528.1		3691.7	FIBRES TEXTILES
263	COTTON	W 615757	936.2	W 1003367	1486.8	W 751460	1276.5	W 848835	1410.4	COTON
2631	RAW COTTON,EXCL LINTERS	W 502142	880.2	W 741055	1377.9	W 650512	1196.7	W 749404	1330.9	COTON EN MASSE
266	SYNTHETIC FIBRES TO SPIN	W 684449	972.3	W 756424	1316.1	W 974250	1399.3	W 1038524	1411.5	FIBRES SYNTHETIQUES
2665	DISCN SYNTH FIBRE UNCMBD	W 527842	744.6	W 600853	1049.5	W 748932	1076.8	W 838314	1095.7	DISCONTINUES EN MASSE
26652	— POLYESTER	W 262008	330.9	W 316303	502.4	W 403743	502.9	W 547289	596.4	FIBRES EN POLYESTERS
26653	— ACRYLIC	W 239468	378.3	W 256658	498.4	W 318252	534.9	W 270508	470.8	FIBRES ACRYLIQUES
268	WOOL(EXC TOPS),ANML HAIR	W 277014	634.3	W 243421	743.8	W 190392	642.9	W 167990	549.3	LAINES ET POILS
2681	WOOL GREASY,FLEECE-WSHED	W 204006	427.5	W 173933	477.3	W 128633	416.6	W 120031	360.5	LAINE EN SUINT
28	METALLIFEROUS ORES,SCRAP		2150.8		3059.6		3069.8		3430.3	MINERAIS METAL,DECHETS
281	IRON ORE,CONCENTRATES	MW 37343	1025.5	MW 41154	1227.0	MW 43874	1320.6	MW 55106	1614.9	MINERAIS DE FER
2815	IRON ORE,CONC,NOT AGGLOM	MW 35401	956.1	MW 37624	1076.1	MW 39451	1130.3	MW 49692	1393.2	MINERAIS NON AGGLOMERES
287	BASE METAL ORES,CONC NES	W 4070307	573.0	W 4774364	1001.9	W 5136448	1115.0	W 4828872	1074.3	MINERAIS METAUX COMMUNS
288	NONFERR METAL SCRAP NES	W 955384	279.0	W 1611823	660.8	W 1037996	461.7	W 1161624	525.1	DECHETS NON FERREUX
2882	OTHER BASE MTL SCRAP NES	W 912461	270.8	W 1575557	652.5	W 1032745	460.0	W 1156510	522.9	AUTRES DECHETS
28821	COPPER WASTE AND SCRAP	W 773881	232.4	W 1188926	492.7	W 710983	318.3	W 796819	342.2	DECHETS DE CUIVRE
3	MINERAL FUELS ETC		4080.3		5172.2		6930.4		10364.3	COMBUSTIBLES MINERAUX LUB
33	PETROLEUM AND PRODUCTS		3641.5		4613.0		5974.0		9389.1	PETROLE ET DERIVES
333	CRUDE PETROLEUM	MW 12346	1573.4	MW 17090	2356.5	MW 22617	3406.6	MW 35470	5456.3	HUILES BRUTES DE PETROLE
334	PETROLEUM PRODUCTS,REFIN	MW 12917	2001.9	MW 14419	2110.8	MW 15860	2437.5	MW 23828	3740.7	PRODUITS RAFFINES
3343	GAS OILS	W 6238433	1044.9			W 4624981	901.5	W 7427898	1510.4	GAS OILS
3344	FUEL OILS,NES	W 3980870	347.5			W 8541815	830.0	MW 12672	1268.9	FUEL OILS
3345	LUBS,PETROLEUM OILS NES	W 883674	278.3			W 1281774	395.4	W 1260648	430.3	HUILES LUBRIFIANTES
341	*GAS,NATURAL AND MANUFCT	W 1407675	296.4	W 2358320	452.9	W 3695456	806.8	W 3695260	876.5	GAZ NATUREL,GAZ MANUFACT
3413	PETROLM GASES,LIQUEFIED	W 1403736	295.5	W 2339791	448.7	W 3691625	806.2	W 3694786	876.3	GAZ DE PETROLE LIQUEFIE
34139	OTH HYDROCARBON GAS LQFD	W 1026044	222.8	W 951188	186.7	W 1962139	449.2	W 2733930	659.0	HYDROCARBURES GAZEUX NDA
4	ANIMAL,VEGETABLE OIL,FAT		1804.2		2592.5		1692.1		1680.1	HUILES,GRAISSES ANIM,VEG
42	FIXED VEGETABLE OIL,FAT		1744.3		2436.2		1571.3		1572.4	HUILES VEGETALES FIXES
423	FIXED VEG OILS,SOFT	W 1622958	984.4	W 2128812	1449.5	W 1626360	964.7	W 1589778	893.8	HUILES VEGET DOUCES FIXES
4232	SOYA BEAN OIL	W 1063518	651.3	W 1481815	1024.0	W 1295396	764.5	W 1225160	684.7	HUILE DE SOJA
4239	OTH FIXED VEG OILS,SOFT	W 545180	319.7	W 631218	414.1	W 316602	188.6	W 351317	197.8	AUTRES HUILES FIXES
42391	RAPE,COLZA,MUSTARD OILS	W 544930	319.3	W 630672	413.2	W 316047	187.4	W 350635	196.9	H NAVETTE COLZA MOUTARDE
424	FIXED VEG OIL NONSOFT	W 1586171	759.9	W 1606760	986.7	W 1134320	606.6	W 1268165	678.7	AUTRES HUILES VEG FIXES
4242	PALM OIL	W 1456671	690.2	W 1396840	865.4	W 1009184	527.1	W 1156455	609.3	HUILE DE PALME
5	CHEMCLS,RELATED PROD NES		11968.0		16849.6		17898.8		19046.8	PRODUITS CHIMIQUES
51	ORGANIC CHEMICALS		1982.1		3156.3		3057.9		3013.6	PROD CHIMIQ ORGANIQUES
511	HYDROCARBONS NES,DERIVS	W 1077955	471.2	W 1639562	779.2	W 1490238	644.8	W 1581336	691.7	HYDROCARBURES NDA
5112	CYCLIC HYDROCARBONS	W 889701	380.2	W 1338207	610.4	W 1246081	501.1	W 1337959	546.4	HYDROCARBURES CYCLIQUES
512	ALCOHOLS,PHENOLS ETC		306.7		501.6		559.0		547.2	PHENOLS,PHENOLS-ALCOOLS
5121	ACYCLIC ALCOHOLS,DERIVS		233.8		382.1		430.2		424.8	ALCOOLS ACYCLIQUES
513	CARBOXYLIC ACIDS ETC	W 619627	442.8	W 875009	876.2	W 1132198	814.2	W 1165710	779.5	ACIDES CARBOXYLIQUES
5138	POLYACIDS AND DERIVATIVS	W 448082	310.8	W 629619	646.5	W 797007	561.9	W 796451	502.2	ACIDES POLYCARBOXYLIQUES
51389	OTH POLYACIDS ETC,DERIVS	W 279213	205.8	W 435173	489.3	W 512760	362.9	W 539191	333.8	ACIDES POLYCARBOXYLIQUES
514	NITROGEN-FNCTN COMPOUNDS	W 320580	366.5	W 354834	446.5	W 340968	435.9	W 353149	442.4	COMPOSES FONCT AZOTEES
52	INORGANIC CHEMICALS		304.0		371.7		507.5		535.8	PROD CHIM INORGANIQUES
53	DYES,TANNING,COLOUR PROD		702.2		791.1		856.2		1041.2	PROD TEINTURE,COLORANTS
533	PIGMENTS,PAINTS,ETC	W 248112	477.0	W 305357	561.8	W 355152	603.3	W 413457	749.3	PIGMENTS,PEINTURES,VERNIS
541	*MEDICINAL,PHARM PRODUCT	MK 17238	403.0	MK 20747	407.3	MK 19479	351.1	MK 18626	330.8	PROD MEDICINAUX PHARMACEUT
562	*FERTILIZERS,MANUFACTURE	MW 12602	1925.6	MW 19843	3732.0	MW 18365	3538.9	MW 16466	2989.3	ENGRAIS MANUFACTURES
5621	CHEM NITROGENOUS FERTLZR	W 3844718	494.7	W 8024152	1548.5	W 7253204	1398.6	W 3697058	648.5	ENGRAIS AZOTES
56216	UREA	W 3133315	423.1	W 6962529	1427.0	W 6009741	1242.1	W 3419647	618.6	UREE
5623	CHEM POTASSIC FERTILIZER	W 3502276	438.0	W 4396298	542.0	W 3855466	471.2	W 5274076	661.6	ENGRAIS POTASSIQUES
56231	POTASSIUM CHLORIDE	W 2846045	306.2	W 3858241	437.8	W 3438962	386.7	W 4625909	532.2	CHLORURE DE POTASSIUM
5629	FERTILIZERS NES	W 5194366	982.4	W 7385865	1636.0	W 7242871	1667.1	W 7491386	1678.7	ENGRAIS NDA
56291	NIT-PHOS-POT FERTLZR NES	W 1013350	189.0	W 1331350	278.1	W 2128430	462.8	W 2592345	549.9	ENGRAIS CONT N P K
56292	NITROG-PHOS FERTILZR NES	W 4114703	778.0	W 5964180	1338.8	W 5084582	1198.0	W 4898075	1128.0	ENGRAIS NDA CONT N P
58	PLASTIC MATERIALS ETC		5402.4		7111.4		7918.2		9210.4	MAT PLAST ARTIFICIELLES
582	PROD OF CONDENSATION ETC	W 720797	808.0	W 778917	1065.7	W 867761	1130.4	W 1142575	1452.5	PROD CONDENS,POLYCOND
5823	ALKYDS,OTHER POLYESTERS	W 471323	473.5	W 488359	621.7	W 520079	580.0	W 663508	692.8	ALKYDES ET AUT POLYESTERS
58231	— IN PRIMARY FORMS	W 452597	439.9	W 471355	583.0	W 499300	537.0	W 627495	635.5	SOUS FORMES PRIMAIRES
583	POLYMERIZATION ETC PRODS	W 5699022	4528.0	W 6940115	6007.0	W 7918562	6681.5	MW 9005	7648.2	PROD POLYMERISATION
5831	POLYETHYLENE	W 1456296	942.1	W 1976387	1533.7	W 2262718	1656.0	W 2348158	1846.0	POLYETHYLENE

4. Special Imports C.I.F. by Commodities according to the S.I.T.C. (Rev. 2) in million U.S. Dollars
Importations Spéciales C.A.F. par Produits d'après la C.T.C.I. (Rév. 2) en millions de Dollars E.U.

SITC CTCI	COMMODITY	1994 QUANTITY QUANTITE	1994 VALUE VALEUR	1995 QUANTITY QUANTITE	1995 VALUE VALEUR	1996 QUANTITY QUANTITE	1996 VALUE VALEUR	1997 QUANTITY QUANTITE	1997 VALUE VALEUR	PRODUIT
58311	— IN PRIMARY FORMS	W 1337170	877.2	W 1825347	1444.7	W 2194554	1582.0	W 2282972	1769.4	POLYETHYLENE PRIMAIRES
5832	POLYPROPYLENE	W 882527	594.4	W 1165687	892.2	W 1264136	920.4	W 1417991	1100.1	POLYPROPYLENE
58321	— IN PRIMARY FORMS	W 811964	527.9	W 1070428	813.1	W 1127276	814.1	W 1253237	948.3	POLYPROPYLENE PRIMAIRES
5833	POLYSTYRENE,ITS COPOLYMR	W 1884901	1580.0	W 2112571	1930.4	W 2490436	2232.1	W 2713626	2386.6	POLYPROPYLENE COPOLYMERES
58331	— IN PRIMARY FORMS	W 1776747	1541.6	W 2000936	1895.3	W 2436148	2212.0	W 2619497	2350.5	SOUS FORMES PRIMAIRES
5834	POLYVINYL CHLORIDE	W 757396	629.2	W 866829	758.3	W 1149692	923.1	W 1509389	1202.6	CHLORURE DE POLYVINYLE
58341	— IN PRIMARY FORMS	W 488742	368.3	W 576237	473.9	W 860909	625.1	W 1172809	862.4	SOUS FORMES PRIMAIRES
5839	OTH POLYMRZTION ETC PROD	W 656836	716.3	W 752305	813.2	W 662967	841.1	W 893986	944.3	AUT PROD POLYMER COPOLYM
59	CHEMICAL MATERIALS NES		1038.2		1078.1		1444.3		1667.9	MAT PROD CHIMIQUES NDA
598	MISCEL CHEM PRODUCTS NES	W 468116	696.6	W 425424	661.9	W 654012	1003.7	W 777878	1164.1	PROD DIV INDUST CHIM NDA
5989	CHEM PRODUCTS,PREPS NES	W 418387	602.4	W 358105	545.7	W 581229	882.1	W 682144	1002.5	PROD PREP CHIMIQUES NDA
59899	OTH CHEM PRODS,PREPS,NES	W 258349	377.6	W 168404	253.6	W 349466	528.0	W 409020	628.3	AUT PRODUITS CHIMIQUES NDA
6	BASIC MANUFACTURES		28732.5		29142.3		32065.1		32909.0	ART MANUFACTURES
61	LEATHER,DRESSED FUR,ETC		2203.0		2313.9		2483.1		2580.8	CUIRS,PELLETERIES
611	LEATHER	W 340507	1762.9	W 404896	1882.0	W 483455	2029.3	W 496771	2134.7	CUIRS,PEAUX PREPARES
6114	LEATHR BOVINE NES,EQUINE	W 271574	1060.2	W 338610	1241.7	W 418624	1345.4	W 446113	1530.4	CUIRS DE BOVINS
63	WOOD,CORK MANUFACTRS NES		1016.9		990.7		875.3		932.6	OUVRAGES LIEGE ET BOIS
634	VENEERS,PLYWOOD,ETC		914.2		875.2		777.9	W 1441244	854.4	PLACAGES,CONTRE–PLAQUES
6342	PLYWOOD OF WOOD SHEETS	V 2108870	816.3	V 2082926	773.7	V 1775113	643.9	W 935824	605.5	BOIS CONTRE–PLAQUES
64	PAPER,PAPERBOARD AND MFR		1976.4		2215.1		2846.1		3334.4	PAPIERS,CARTONS & OUVRAGES
641	PAPER AND PAPERBOARD	W 3389041	1634.1	W 3264491	1826.4	W 4776657	2423.8	W 5890781	2955.9	PAPIERS ET CARTONS
6412	PRINTG,WRITING PAPER NES	W 595968	380.0	W 719144	496.2	W 931531	582.8	W 1134998	736.9	PAPIERS POUR L'IMPRESSION
64122	— COATED,IMPREGNATD ETC	W 537981	346.6	W 646372	455.2	W 873670	551.3	W 1081998	707.0	PAPIERS IMPRESSION COUCHES
6413	KRAFT PAPER,PAPERBOARD	W 935746	375.6	W 790965	377.7	W 1258798	549.0	W 1487364	623.6	PAPIER ET CARTON KRAFT
64139	KRAFT PAPER PAPERBD,NES	W 744427	297.4	W 661346	316.2	W 1057434	461.0	W 1249627	519.6	PAPIER,CARTON KRAFT NDA
6415	PAPER,PAPERBRD,BULK,NES	W 1021838	426.6	W 976401	467.6	W 1360194	629.7	W 1782447	848.6	PAPIERS,CARTONS ROULEAUX
64159	OTHER PAPER ETC,BULK,NES	W 672193	330.9	W 652198	366.9	W 823308	457.5	W 1021187	609.3	AUT PAPIER ROULEAUX FEUILLES
642	PAPER,ETC,PRECUT,ARTS OF	W 396594	342.3	W 395223	388.8	W 428113	422.4	W 348868	378.6	PAP,CARTONS DECOUPES
65	TEXTILE YARN,FABRICS,ETC		9524.1		11176.6		12207.0		12527.5	FILS,TISSUS,ARTICLES TEXTILE
651	TEXTILE YARN	W 971225	2140.7	W 1088045	2461.2	W 1234394	2881.3	W 1362164	3095.4	FILS TEXTILES
6512	WOOL,HAIR YARN,INCL TOPS	W 106559	483.7	W 98121	542.9	W 99593	490.4	W 115044	532.9	FILS DE LAINE,DE POILS
6513	COTTON YARN	W 180256	366.6	W 230092	467.3	W 318335	627.6	W 369337	716.6	FILS DE COTON
6514	SYN FIB YRN,BULK,MONOFIL	W 448135	651.5	W 503980	739.3	W 568493	1052.2	W 635484	1191.2	FILS CONT 85% FIB TEXT SYNTH
65142	— NONTXT ETC CONT PAMID	W 107166	159.8	W 127418	249.6	W 283313	543.5	W 300263	549.1	FILS NON TEX FI CON POLYAMID
652	COTTON FABRICS,WOVEN		1288.5	L 1435115	1528.6	L 1678012	1697.5	L 1594529	1674.6	TISSUS DE COTON
6522	WOVEN COTTON BLEACHD,ETC		1165.2	L 1217195	1348.2	L 1405571	1503.5	L 1269499	1426.0	TISSUS COTON BLANCHIS ETC
65224	BLCHED COTTON FABRIC NES		994.9	L 1080955	1152.6	L 1272967	1295.4	L 1128966	1204.2	AUT TIS PLUS 85% COT BLANCHI
653	WOVN MAN–MADE FIB FABRIC		3146.5	L 3613368	3744.7	L 3567035	3960.6	L 3597733	3873.2	TISSUS FIBRES SYNTH,ARTIF
6531	CONT SYNT WEAVES NONPILE	L 2140124	1963.4	L 2338496	2338.1	L 2384358	2528.9	L 2502544	2489.6	TISSUS FIBRES SYNTH CONTINUE
65315	CONT SYN TXTL FABRIC NES	L 2070140	1866.1	L 2266626	2227.9	L 2305697	2412.3	L 2429031	2371.0	TIS PLUS 85% TEXT SYNT CONT
6532	DISC SYN TXTL FABRIC NES	L 680659	431.8	L 550044	477.5	L 454370	483.9	L 342421	413.0	TIS DISC MOINS 85% FIBR TEXT
6534	DISC SYN BLEND FABRC NES	L 380526	445.3	L 456498	565.3	L 469660	582.1	L 497948	609.5	TISSUS FIBRES SYNTH DISCONT
65341	DISC SYN FIB–COTTN FABRC	L 326730	330.5	L 390097	414.1	L 403964	427.9	L 426392	444.6	TISSUS FIB SYNT DIS MEL COTO
654	OTH WOVEN TEXTILE FABRIC		625.1		699.5		690.8		847.1	TISSUS AUT COTON SYNT,ARTIF
655	KNITTED,ETC FABRICS	W 288817	820.8	W 322736	975.2	W 365939	1118.1	W 425035	1199.5	ETOF BONNETERIE PIECES ETC
6552	OTHER KNIT ETC FAB NONEL	W 288817	820.8	W 322736	975.2	W 365939	1118.1	W 425035	1199.5	ETOF BON NON ELAS NON SYNT
657	SPECIAL TXTL FABRC,PRODS	W 471413	1146.7	W 528873	1321.4	W 550088	1415.2	W 553267	1388.1	TISSUS SPECIAUX
6573	COATED ETC TEXTILES NES	W 324579	818.8	W 358097	915.3	W 380312	998.7	W 381169	970.8	TISSUS,ART MATIERE TEXT NDA
65732	PLASTIC COATED TEXTILES	W 315058	771.8	W 346597	856.3	W 367206	934.2	W 363275	897.4	TISSUS IMPREGNES
66	NONMETAL MINERAL MFS NES		1066.1		1212.9		1254.7		1359.7	ART MIN NON METALLIQUES
664	GLASS		393.5		488.6		480.2		451.3	VERRE
67	IRON AND STEEL		9535.0		6583.1		7309.9		6737.8	FER ET ACIER
672	IRON,STEEL PRIMARY FORMS	W 5962337	1648.8	W 2657625	1016.3	W 3590627	1272.6	W 2438815	894.3	LINGOTS FER,ACIER
6725	IRN,STL BLOOMS,SLABS,ETC	W 1908983	437.5	W 418469	105.9	W 301720	81.7	W 316183	85.4	BLOOMS,BILLETTES FER ACIER
67251	IRN,SMPLE STL BLOOMS,ETC	W 1865197	414.5	W 396170	86.5	W 292364	61.5	W 306461	61.1	BLOOMS ETC NON ACIER FIN
6727	IRN,STL COIL FR REROLLNG	W 3132042	1004.9	W 1974574	843.6	W 3168520	1159.4	W 2034575	782.6	EBAUCHES POUR TOLES FER
67271	IRON,SIMPLE STEEL COILS	W 3003955	926.0	W 1869374	737.0	W 2993034	970.8	W 1906429	600.4	EBAUCHES NON EN ACIER
673	IRON,STEEL SHAPES ETC	MW 11706	3433.0	W 3891138	1206.0	W 4850378	1495.8	W 3451055	1057.1	BARRES,PROFIL FER,ACIER
6731	IRON,STEEL WIRE ROD	W 4389363	1238.0	W 642869	169.6	W 2596525	739.9	W 1592102	427.3	FIL MACHINE FER,ACIER
67311	IRON,SIMPLE STL WIRE ROD	W 3808239	1059.7	W 515261	127.0	W 2479114	690.1	W 1494626	382.1	FIL MACH AUT ACIER FIN
6732	IRON,STEEL BARS ETC	W 5660790	1644.9	W 2718280	778.8	W 1908550	577.8	W 1528982	456.9	BARRES FER,ACIER
67326	IRN,OTH STL BARS HOTROLD	W 5053145	1417.4	W 2454225	653.1	W 1666360	448.7	W 1323446	324.4	BARRES PLEINES FER,ACIER
6733	IRON,STEEL PROFILES ETC	W 1656008	550.2	W 529989	257.7	W 345303	178.2	W 329971	173.0	PROFILES,PALPLAN FER,ACIER
674	IRN,STL UNIV,PLATE,SHEET	W 5944955	2685.0	W 5458173	2948.1	W 7268528	3700.6	W 6811402	3708.7	LARGES PLATS,TOLES
6744	IRN,STL HVY PLATE,ROLLED	W 1444842	496.0	W 541727	273.0	W 624970	317.6	W 601353	296.1	TOLES LAMINEES PLUS 4.75 MM
67441	— OF IRON OR SIMPLE STL	W 1408001	451.3	W 502485	231.6	W 569300	271.6	W 573605	252.4	TOLES NON ACIER FIN CARB
6745	IRN,STL MED PLATE,ROLLED	W 681203	314.5	W 425720	263.9	W 823564	421.8	W 1003233	478.7	TOLES 3 A 4.75 MM
6746	IRN,STL THIN PLATE,ROLLD	W 2446869	1128.1	W 186706	261.3	W 3516525	1638.6	W 2900666	1497.0	TOLES LAM MOINS 3MM
67461	— OF IRON OR SIMPLE STL	W 2200800	847.4	W 23583	17.2	W 3306313	1373.8	W 2699585	1140.4	TOL NON AC FIN MOINS 3 MM
6749	OTH IRN,STL PLATES,SHEET	W 905129	474.4	W 3707777	1783.7	W 1752439	967.1	W 1866666	1172.2	AUTRES TOLES FER,ACIER
67491	— OF IRON OR SIMPLE STL	W 829747	383.6	W 3639129	1692.4	W 1615192	836.7	W 1727402	940.2	AUT TOLES AUTRES ACIER FIN
678	IRON,STL TUBES,PIPES,ETC	W 1406486	1271.6	W 930602	998.2	W 532796	603.0	W 730457	796.8	TUBES,TUYAUX EN FONTE,FER
6782	IRON,STL SEAMLESS TUBES	W 997351	897.2	W 666865	679.1	W 279475	317.5	W 405155	468.9	TUBES,TUYAUX SANS SOUDURE
68	NON–FERROUS METALS		1658.8		2680.3		3001.6		3183.2	METAUX NON FERREUX
682	COPPER EXC CEMENT COPPER	W 404286	889.7	W 537879	1356.5	W 714243	1673.2	W 695424	1707.5	CUIVRE
6821	COPPER NES,ALLOYS,UNWRT	W 121408	224.3	W 187504	406.5	W 290940	571.5	W 210877	433.8	CUIVRE BRUT
6822	COPPER,ALLOYS WORKED	W 282878	665.5	W 350375	950.0	W 423303	1101.8	W 484547	1273.8	CUIVRE,ALLIAGES OUVRES
68221	COPPER BARS,WIRE,ETC	W 167586	321.8	W 201829	449.0	W 262092	555.4	W 290968	620.2	BARRES,PROFILES ET FILS
684	ALUMINIUM	W 346022	588.4	W 615749	1089.2	W 634518	1052.8	W 600990	1154.8	ALUMINIUM
6841	ALUMINIUM,ALLOYS,UNWRGHT	W 168853	189.2	W 387925	513.9	W 366733	457.8	W 288891	365.4	ALUMINIUM,ALLIAGES BRUTS
6842	ALUMINIUM,ALLOYS WORKED	W 177169	399.3	W 227823	575.3	W 267785	595.0	W 312099	789.5	ALUMINIUM,ALLIAGES OUVRE
68422	ALUMNM PLATE,SHEET,STRIP	W 97481	202.7	W 127185	305.3	W 152338	327.9	W 209071	457.7	TOLES, PLANCHES EN ALU
69	METAL MANUFACTURES NES		1542.1		1726.0		1766.5		1916.7	ART MANUFACT EN METAL NDA
691	STRUCTURES AND PARTS NES	W 154501	262.0	W 153824	324.2	W 164487	361.8	W 192712	457.5	CONSTRUCT FER,ACIER,ALU
699	BASE METAL MFRS NES	W 331086	686.2	W 320888	799.5	W 315976	792.4	W 315130	825.2	ART MANUFACTURES MET NDA
7	MACHINES,TRANSPORT EQUIP		51384.8		52435.9		54705.2		52722.9	MACHINES MATERIEL TRANSPORT
71	POWER GENERATING EQUIPMT		3185.2		3111.7		3211.6		3717.9	MACHINES GENERATRICES
711	STEAM BOILERS & AUX PLNT		332.0		404.1		379.5		528.2	GENERATEURS VAPEUR EAU ETC
713	INTRNL COMBUS PSTN ENGIN		688.6		608.4		699.0		613.4	MOTEURS EXPL COMB INT, PIECE
7139	PISTON ENGINE PARTS NES	W 42543	370.1	W 39027	360.0	W 44789	426.6	W 46179	310.2	PIECES POUR 713.2,3,8
716	ROTATING ELECTRIC PLANT		1728.5		1687.4		1556.5		1747.8	APP ELECTR ROTATIFS,PIECES
7162	AC MTRS,GENRTRS,GEN SETS	MN 438415	1059.0	MN 531079	947.3	MN 565921	936.4	MN 695866	755.9	MOTEURS ELECTRIQUES
71623	GEN SETS WITH PISTN ENGN	N 28672	719.5	N 22990	508.8	N 23073	476.9	N 10756	286.2	GROUPES MOTEUR EXPLOSION
7169	PTS NES OF ROT ELEC PLNT	W 60772	526.0	W 46459	508.9	W 43578	392.9	W 55371	587.8	PIECES MAC APP ROTATIFS
72	MACHS FOR SPCL INDUSTRYS		12739.9		13247.4		14218.9		9704.9	MAC SPECIALES POUR INDUST
723	CIVIL ENGNEERG EQUIP ETC		501.6		690.9		467.1		449.9	APPAREILS DE GENIE CIVIL
7234	CONST,MINING MACHNRY NES	N 8257	393.0	N 6723	472.8	N 6897	321.2	N 9496	287.3	MACH POUR LA CONST, MINES
724	TEXTILE,LEATHER MACHNRY		3352.4		3181.5		3294.8		2227.8	MACH POUR INDUSTRIE TEXTILE
7243	SEWING MACHS,NEEDLES ETC		454.9		408.3		405.7		239.0	MACHINES A COUDRE,PIECES
72431	SEWING MACHINES	N 423506	396.3	N 349789	324.5	N 382606	337.3	N 327734	165.7	MACHINES A COUDRE
7244	SPINNING,EXTRDNG,ETC MCH		955.4		767.6		827.6		574.5	MACH POUR LE FILAGE

4. Special Imports C.I.F. by Commodities according to the S.I.T.C. (Rev. 2) in million U.S. Dollars
Importations Spéciales C.A.F. par Produits d'après la C.T.C.I. (Rév. 2) en millions de Dollars E.U.

SITC CTCI	COMMODITY	1994 QUANTITY QUANTITE	1994 VALUE VALEUR	1995 QUANTITY QUANTITE	1995 VALUE VALEUR	1996 QUANTITY QUANTITE	1996 VALUE VALEUR	1997 QUANTITY QUANTITE	1997 VALUE VALEUR	PRODUIT
7245	WEAVING,FELT MFG,ETC MCH		1044.8		1136.0		1154.6		737.9	METIERS A TISSER,PIECES
72451	WEAVING MACHINES (LOOMS)	N 20897	413.1	N 18603	499.0	N 21567	481.6	N 14516	347.4	METIERS A TISSER
7247	TEXTILE MACHINERY NES		540.4		558.2		577.3		404.6	MACH LAVAGE,TEINTURE TEX
72474	OTH TEXTILE MACHNERY NES	N 38325	470.7	N 34365	482.6	N 31287	502.7	N 19929	336.7	MACH LAVAGE ETC MAT TEXT
725	PAPER ETC MILL MACHINERY		366.1		489.3		499.2		500.6	MACHINES FABR PATE PAPIER
726	PRINTG,BKBINDG MACHY,PTS		662.7		646.2		797.0		502.0	MACHINES POUR IMPRIMERIE
7267	OTH PRINTG & ANCILL MACH	N 18379	374.5	N 15338	367.6	N 15174	418.9	N 10443	235.4	AUT MACH IMPRIMERIE,PIEC
727	FOOD MACHRY NON–DOMESTIC		567.6		640.2		797.5		409.4	MACH INDUSTRIES ALIMENT
7272	OTH FOOD PROC MCHY,PARTS		474.7		575.8	N 30577	736.5		362.5	AUT MACH IND ALIMENTAIRE
72722	INDUS FOOD PROC MACH NES	N 19703	387.0	N 21342	473.9	N 29598	680.3	N 14475	270.7	MACHINES BOULANGERIE
728	OTH MACHY FOR SPCL INDUS		7103.7		7450.5		8186.0		5479.0	AUT MACH IND PARTICULIERES
7281	MACH–TOOLS FR SPCL INDUS		591.9		509.7		706.0		329.3	MACH–OUTILS SPEC IND PART
72812	MACH–TOOLS TO WORK WOOD	N 35807	345.6	N 32301	311.2	N 40803	468.6	N 50021	221.2	MACH–OUT POUR TRAVAIL BOIS
7283	OTHR MINERAL WORKG MACHY		487.2		508.6		511.8		280.6	MACH TRIER,CRIBLER,BROYER
7284	MACHY FOR SPCL INDUS NES		6024.7		6432.2		6968.3		4869.2	MACH SPEC IND PARTICUL.
72842	RUBBER,PLASTICS WRKG MCH	N 54904	1400.1	N 47287	1272.9	N 45358	1818.2	N 115391	1195.5	MACH IND CAOUT MAT PLAST
72843	TOBACCO WORKING MACH NES	N 1651	418.2	N 484	505.3	N 284	340.9	N 147	176.1	MACH POUR IND DU TABAC
72848	OTH MCHY WITH INDIV FNCT	N 420288	3419.7	N 329161	3579.2	N 253089	3730.3	N 372844	2511.3	AUTRES MACHINES NDA
72849	PTS OF MACHS OF 7284 ETC	W 31545	422.1	W 24703	410.3	W 29291	542.4	W 28607	470.0	PIECES DU 728.4 ETC
73	METALWORKING MACHINERY		3002.9		3341.9		3637.7		2474.6	MACH TRAVAIL DES METAUX
736	METALWORKING MACH–TOOLS		2218.2		2344.3		2742.5		1795.8	MACH–OUTILS TRAVAIL METAUX
7361	METAL CUTTING MACH–TOOLS	N 86233	827.6	N 76872	915.9	N 68875	1143.8	N 56979	695.4	MACH–OUT ENLEVEMENT METAL
7362	METAL FORMING MACH–TOOLS	N 53279	730.4	N 43835	718.2	N 42335	812.5	N 34430	533.1	MACH–OUTILS DEFORM METAL
7367	OTH METALWRKG MACH–TOOLS	N 16586	487.4	N 13530	553.4	N 13756	545.4	N 9940	338.6	AUT MACH–OUT POUR METAUX
737	METALWORKING MACHNRY NES		784.8		997.6		895.3		678.8	MACH TRAV METAUX PIECES
7372	ROLLING MILLS AND ROLLS		359.5		520.9		353.0		348.1	LAMINOIRS CYLINDRES PIEC
74	GENRL INDUSTRL MACHY NES		6254.4		7196.7		7781.1		6798.2	MACH APP INDUSTRIE
741	HEATING,COOLING EQUIPMNT		1855.0		1837.9		1723.3		1481.8	MACH CHAUFFAGE,PIECES
7415	AIR–CONDITIONING MACHNRY		450.0	N 295569	398.7		298.6		203.8	GROUPES CONDITION AIR
7416	HEATING,COOLING EQU NES		802.8	N 404382	785.7	N 244303	652.4	N 125884	567.5	APP CHANGEMENT TEMP
743	PUMPS NES,CENTRFUGES ETC		864.4		1074.6		1036.2		1027.7	POMPES COMPRES,VENT ETC
7431	PUMPS FOR GASES ETC	N 2462814	415.4	N 2606282	497.9	N 2461418	443.9	N 2687654	398.5	POMPES AIR A VIDE,COMPRES
744	MECHANICAL HANDLING EQU		1233.8		1667.1		1898.1		1610.5	EQUIP MANUTENTION PIECES
7442	LIFTING,LOADING MACH NES	N 73929	860.3	N 68429	1194.5	N 71684	1360.2	N 64202	1027.8	APP LEVAGE,MANUTENTION
74424	LIFTS AND SKIP HOISTS	N 4202	307.4	N 5486	497.4	N 6936	598.8	N 4444	448.8	ASCENSEURS,MONTE–CHARGE
74428	OTH HANDLING ETC MCH NES	N 57084	336.8	N 53110	416.4	N 54730	458.9	N 50414	342.3	AUT APP LEVAGE ETC
7449	PTS NES OF MACHY OF 7442	W 29143	279.6	W 36166	353.9	W 57494	419.7	W 70681	484.8	PIECES DU 744.2
745	NONELEC MACHY,TOOLS NES		660.2		723.9		1059.4		782.2	AUT MACH NON ELEC,PIECES
7452	OTH NONELEC MCHS,PTS NES		650.7		712.6		1047.7		772.4	AUT MACH NON ELEC,PIECES
74522	PACKAGNG,BOTTLNG,ETC MCH	N 27964	428.4	N 27640	488.3	N 48373	701.8	N 21950	514.8	MACH NETT BOUTEILLES,ETC
749	NONELEC MACH PTS,ACC NES		1339.4		1519.2		1718.4		1548.4	PIECES MACH NON ELEC NDA
7499	OTH NONELEC MCHY PTS NES	W 58486	813.7	W 53510	844.1	W 65542	1026.7		752.9	PIECES NON ELECT NDA
74991	FOUNDRY MOULDS ETC NES	W 52437	726.7	W 46776	739.4	W 59169	893.2		604.6	MOULES POUR METAUX
75	OFFICE MACHNES,ADP EQUIP		2072.9		2857.9		3421.0		4475.3	MACH BUREAU TRAIT AUTOM
752	AUTOMTIC DATA PROC EQUIP	N 3322149	831.6	MN 9036	1050.6	N 8882547	964.8	MN 16433	1135.2	MACH TRAIT INFORMATION
7522	DIGITAL COMPUTERS	N 75494	421.4	N 82897	211.9	N 32103	242.6	N 30149	184.0	MACH DIGITALES COMPLETES
7528	OFF–LINE DATA PROC EQUIP	N 472323	48.5	N 3637840	397.9	N 499690	64.7	N 1432487	66.8	MACH AUXIL TRAIT INFORM
759	OFFICE,ADP MCH PTS,ACCES	W 68604	1133.4	W 72197	1725.6		2374.8	W 109067	3270.0	PIECES DU 751 ET 752
7591	OFFICE MACHINE PARTS NES	W 12471	134.4	W 19694	274.0		351.2	W 29674	454.9	PIECES DU 7511,7518
7599	ACCTG,ETC,ADP MCH PTS,AC	W 56132	999.0	W 52503	1451.7	MN 62079	2023.6	W 79393	2815.2	PIECES DU 751 ET 752
76	TELECOMM,SOUND EQUIPMENT		6805.5		7616.4		5833.4		5966.9	EQUIPMENT DE TELECOM
763	SOUND RECORDRS,PHONOGRPH	N 3082829	379.3	N 2294999	227.2	N 1119845	93.7	N 696129	42.8	PHONO,APP ENREGISTREMENT
7638	OTHR SOUND APPARATUS ETC	N 2839866	375.9	N 2167569	225.1	N 1018005	91.7	N 554306	41.2	AUT APP D'ENREGIS,REPROD
764	TELECOM EQPT,PTS,ACC NES		5960.9		6897.7		5415.8		5716.5	EQUIP TELECOM,PIECES
7641	LINE TELEPHONE,ETC EQUIP	MN 36482	2112.4	MN 38790	2177.0	MN 35687	409.8	MN 45389	214.8	APP TELEPHON PAR FIL
7643	TV,RADIO TRANSMITTRS ETC	N 524445	794.0	N 531622	941.4	N 475519	1169.1	N 1386747	1017.8	APP EMET TELE RADIO
7649	PTS NES OF EQUIPMT OF 76	W 198312	2798.9		3446.2		3587.7	W 175529	4266.2	PIECES DE LA DIV 76
76491	PTS NES OF APPAR OF 7641	W 40474	763.4	W 35818	933.6	W 30859	1025.4	W 32778	1006.3	PIECES POUR 764.1
76493	TELECOMM EQUIPMT PTS NES	W 124985	1069.9	W 72450	1312.0	MN 109627	1378.6	W 60787	1777.2	PIECES 761,762,764.3,8
76499	PARTS ETC OF SOUND EQUIP	W 657	885.1		1095.5	MN 286160	1082.4	W 52580	1365.5	PIECES NDA POUR 763
77	ELECTRIC MACHNRY NES ETC		7702.3		9741.3		11274.2		14057.0	MACH APP ELECT NDA
771	ELECTRIC POWER MACHY NES		700.8		796.7		932.9		1043.8	MACH PROD,TRANS ELECTR
7712	OTH ELEC POWER MACHY NES		465.3		555.6		609.0		670.4	AUT APP PROD TRANSF ELEC
772	SWITCHGEAR ETC,PARTS NES	W 147003	1520.0	W 122348	1888.2		2093.2		2689.4	APP COUPURE,SECT ETC
7721	SWITCHGEAR ETC	W 79669	1025.9	W 76660	1277.1		1430.8		1801.8	APP COUPURE,SECTIONMNT
7722	PRINTED CIRCUITS,PTS NES	W 47656	316.3	W 31630	398.5	MN 1917680	439.5	MN 2536884	570.6	CIRCUITS ET PIECES
773	ELECTR DISTRIBUTNG EQUIP	W 194290	640.2	W 204106	740.4	W 207192	795.9	W 239668	952.4	EQUIPMT DISTRIBUTION ELECT
7731	INSULATED WIRE,CABLE ETC	W 188704	588.1	W 199107	685.4	W 202146	734.2	W 229672	873.4	FILS,CABLES ISOLES ELECT
776	TRANSISTORS,VALVES,ETC		2917.6		3878.1		4685.5		6253.9	LAMPES,TUBES,VALVES
7761	TV PICTURE TUBES	MN 10759	605.0	MN 10851	576.2	N 7525848	474.2	N 5813427	373.4	TUBES CATHODIQUES
7762	OTH ELECTRONIC TUBES ETC	MN 77275	41.9	MN 53686	117.5	MN 22333	359.3	MN 48225	596.5	AUT LAMPES ELECTRONIQUES
7763	DIODES,TRANSISTORS,ETC	MN 13454129	335.3	MN 18580600	467.3	MN 23031630	687.2	MN 35670828	1095.8	DIODES,TRANSISTORS
7764	ELECTRONIC MICROCIRCUITS	MN 5236467	1544.5	MN 6133268	2191.0	MN 6911463	2605.1	MN 9599848	3482.2	MICROSTRUCTURES ELECTRON
7768	ELCTRNC COMP PTS,CRYSTLS		391.2		526.3		559.8		706.2	CRIST PIEZO–ELEC,PCS 776
77689	ELECTRNIC COMPON PTS NES	W 25024	350.0	W 18794	455.2	W 22263	459.8	W 27508	517.1	PIECES DU GROUPE 776
778	ELECTRICAL MACHINERY NES		1429.9		1815.0		2150.1		2620.0	AUTRES MACH ELECT NDA
7781	BATTERIES,ACCUMULATORS		168.0		201.2		386.8		523.9	PILES ET ACCUMULATEURS
7788	OTH ELEC MACHY,EQUIP NES		1109.4		1422.8		1510.4		1840.6	AUT MACH APP ELEC NDA
77884	ELECTRICAL CONDENSERS	W 24770	339.4	W 24453	429.6	W 27122	517.8	W 37739	733.3	CONDENSATEURS ELECTRIQUES
77886	OTH ELEC MACHINERY NES		310.8	N 3461404	410.5	N 5582834	446.2		395.9	AUT MACH APP ELECTRIQUES
78	ROAD VEHICLES		4774.4		2685.4		2190.3		1876.0	VEHICULES ROUTIERS
781	PASS MOTOR VEH EXC BUSES	N 188050	1637.6	N 139745	933.0	N 63637	403.6	N 35039	319.6	AUTO TRANSPORT PERSONNES
782	LORRIES,SPCL MTR VEH NES	N 71896	1226.8	N 16563	538.3	N 9913	371.8	N 9389	289.0	VEHICULES SPECIAUX,MARCH
7821	LORRIES,TRUCKS	N 69159	974.6	N 12566	152.8	N 6606	122.0	N 7296	128.4	VEHICULES TRANSP MARCHAND
783	ROAD MOTOR VEHICLES NES	N 21501	550.5	N 1815	38.4	N 1757	55.3	N 3904	109.9	VEHICULES ROUTIERS NDA
7831	BUSES	N 20086	498.4	N 1277	22.4	N 1254	33.3	N 3325	81.9	VOITURES TRANSPORT COMMUN
784	MOTOR VEH PRTS,ACCES NES		740.2		896.9		1102.6		953.7	PIECES 722,781,782,783
7849	OTHER MOTOR VEHCL PARTS	MW 30107	506.6	W 111585	748.2	W 116858	1044.0	W 144195	903.3	PIECES 722,781,782,783
785	CYCLES,ETC MOTRZD OR NOT		587.0		251.6		236.7		183.5	MOTOCYCLES SCOOTERS
7851	MOTORCYCLES ETC	N 336399	407.1	N 46248	23.9	N 2911	1.6	N 1495	2.4	MOTO VELO MOTEUR AUXIL
79	OTHR TRANSPORT EQUIPMENT		4847.7		2637.4		3137.5		3652.5	AUTRE MATERIEL TRANSPORT
792	AIRCRAFT ETC		3397.1		1359.5		2648.6		3234.3	APP NAVIGATION AERIENNE
7922	AIRCRFT NES 2000KG OR LS	N 36	6.1	N 8	1.4	N 27	551.7	N 1	27.3	AERODYNES MOINS 2000 KG
7924	AIRCRFT NES OVER 15000KG	N 56	2847.2	N 14	892.0	N 27	1419.5	N 39	2509.3	AERODYNES PLUS 15000 KG
7929	AIRCRAFT PARTS NES	W 704	172.0	W 947	237.8	W 2631	498.1	W 2495	563.9	PIECES DU 792
793	SHIPS AND BOATS ETC	N 4266	1346.5		1091.0	N 2188	425.8	N 1700	304.0	NAVIRES BATEAUX,ETC
7932	SHIPS AND BOATS NES	N 2640	1043.7	N 1151	557.6	N 1066	347.1	N 817	104.3	NAVIRES ET BATEAUX
79323	OTHER CARGO VESSELS	N 480	989.4	N 339	361.2	N 345	258.5	N 319	83.3	AUT BATEAUX TRANS MARCH
7938	TUGS,SPECIAL VESSELS ETC	N 1179	140.8		483.2	N 859	35.9	N 599	171.8	REMORQUEURS,BATEAUX SPEC
79382	SPECL PURPOSE VESSLS ETC	N 37	133.1	N 34	469.2	N 37	29.2	N 27	158.9	BAT–PHARES,–POMPES,DRAGUES
8	MISC MANUFACTURED GOODS		6496.9		7904.8		8164.9		8352.3	ART MANUFACTURES DIVERS

4. Special Imports C.I.F. by Commodities according to the S.I.T.C. (Rev. 2) in million U.S. Dollars
Importations Spéciales C.A.F. par Produits d'après la C.T.C.I. (Rév. 2) en millions de Dollars E.U.

SITC CTCI	COMMODITY	1994 QUANTITY QUANTITE	1994 VALUE VALEUR	1995 QUANTITY QUANTITE	1995 VALUE VALEUR	1996 QUANTITY QUANTITE	1996 VALUE VALEUR	1997 QUANTITY QUANTITE	1997 VALUE VALEUR	PRODUIT
84	CLOTHING AND ACCESSORIES		622.1		969.4		1044.8		1117.6	VETEMENTS
844	UNDER GARMENTS NOT KNIT		303.6		592.8		661.7		621.6	VETEMENT DESSOUS MAT TEX
8441	— MENS SHIRTS		301.9		591.2		660.9		619.3	CHEMISES HOMMES MAT TEXT
84412	—— OF SYNTHETIC FIBRES		272.1	W 43891	563.4	W 44928	621.0	W 42616	564.7	CHEMISES HOMMES FIB SYNT
87	PRECISION INSTRUMNTS NES		1736.3		2231.4		2278.3		2265.3	INSTRUM,APPAR SCIENT NDA
874	MEASURNG,CONTROLNG INSTR		1470.4		1894.0		1853.9		1747.2	INSTRUMENTS DE MESURE
8742	MEASUR,DRAW ETC INST,PTS		459.0		582.8		653.1		561.3	INST DESSIN,TRACAGE,PCS
87421	MEASURNG,DRAWNG ETC INST	N 5855053	426.2	MN 16654	546.3	N 8291979	616.8	MN 9030	520.9	INSTRUM DESSIN,TRACAGE
8748	ELEC MEAS,CONTRL EQU NES	N 675310	414.3	N 714286	505.6	N 610266	503.1	N 1194038	413.2	APP ELEC ELECTRO MESURE
87483	OTH ELCTRNC MEAS ETC EQU	N 617768	369.1	N 658721	448.7	N 548822	460.2	N 803979	373.7	AUT APP ELECTRO DE MESURE
88	PHOTO EQU,OPTICL GDS ETC		1543.3		1729.1		1721.2		1750.6	APP,FOURN PHOTO,OP,MONTR
881	PHOTO APPARAT,EQUIPT NES		346.8		425.6		522.5		580.6	APP,EQUIP PHOTO NDA
8811	CAMERAS STILL,FLASH APP		303.1		382.1		444.7		542.4	APPAREILS PHOTO,PIECES
88119	PTS NES OF APPAR OF 8811	W 9629	249.8	W 7155	347.2	W 6730	420.5	W 7253	524.0	PIECES POUR 881.1
885	WATCHES AND CLOCKS		1033.5		1094.9		979.1		910.9	HORLOGERIE
8851	WATCHES,MOVEMENTS,CASES		662.0		749.0		667.5		643.7	MONTRES,MOUVEMENTS,BOITES
88513	WATCH MOVEMENTS ASSEMBLD		504.7		568.9		509.2		506.1	MOUVEMENTS TERMINES
8852	CLOCKS,CLOCK,WATCH PARTS		371.5		346.0		311.6		267.2	HORLOGES,MOUV,PARTIES
89	MISC MANUFCTRD GOODS NES		2235.2		2647.7		2873.6		2999.8	ART MANUFACTURES DIVERS
892	PRINTED MATTER	W 156678	247.9	W 178114	341.8	W 252296	492.8	W 351847	828.7	IMPRIMES
8928	PRINTED MATTER NES	W 136163	196.1	W 149578	266.4	W 221218	417.9	W 314591	738.3	IMPRIMES NDA
893	ARTICLES OF PLASTIC NES		759.9		895.3		894.9		977.3	OUVRAGES EN MAT DIVIS 58
8939	MISC PLASTIC ARTICLES	W 300910	606.3	W 299002	683.6	W 282923	678.0	W 286630	757.3	ART DIVERS EN MAT DIV 58
89399	OTHR PLASTC ARTICLES NES	W 269802	582.6	W 257414	658.6	W 244873	655.2	W 250540	725.5	AUT OUV MAT DIV 58
894	TOYS,SPORTING GOODS,ETC		342.3		472.0		575.3		319.3	VOITURES ENFANTS,JOUETS
8942	TOYS,INDOOR GAMES ETC		253.7		373.2		461.9		208.4	JOUETS,JEUX ETC
899	OTHER MANUFACTURED GOODS		411.4		454.8		435.6		413.0	AUT ART MANUF DIVERS NDA
9	GOODS NOT CLASSD BY KIND		747.1		1602.1		783.2		959.4	ART TRANSACT NON CLASSES
931	*SPECIAL TRANSACTIONS		735.4		1583.7		755.7		935.6	TRANS.SPECIALES

5. Special Exports F.O.B. by Commodities according to the S.I.T.C. (Rev. 2) in million U.S. Dollars
Exportations Spéciales F.O.B. par Produits d'après la C.T.C.I. (Rév. 2) en millions de Dollars E.U.

SITC CTCI	COMMODITY	1994 QUANTITY QUANTITE	1994 VALUE VALEUR	1995 QUANTITY QUANTITE	1995 VALUE VALEUR	1996 QUANTITY QUANTITE	1996 VALUE VALEUR	1997 QUANTITY QUANTITE	1997 VALUE VALEUR	PRODUIT
	ALL COMMODITIES		121006.4		148779.6		151047.6		182791.7	TOUS PRODUITS
0	FOOD AND LIVE ANIMALS		9993.2		9924.0		10206.8		11050.8	ALIMENTS,ANIMAUX VIVANTS
001	*LIVE ANIMALS FOR FOOD	MN 55404	445.2	MN 55501	473.3	MN 56319	462.3	MN 55036	451.3	ANIMAUX VIVANTS
01	MEAT AND PREPARATIONS		910.1		1371.8		1437.8		1314.3	VIANDES ET PREPARATIONS
011	MEAT FRESH,CHILLD,FROZEN	W 356925	630.6	W 498535	1022.8	W 526519	1083.6	W 502051	963.1	VIANDES FRAICHES,REF,CONGE
0114	POULTRY FRESH CHLLD,FRZN	W 184486	377.5	W 282133	620.9	W 326795	690.9	W 324232	614.8	VOLAILLES MORTES
03	FISH AND PREPARATIONS		2319.5		2852.7		2855.4		2935.6	POISSONS ET PREPARATIONS
034	FISH,FRESH,CHILLED,FROZN	W 272937	661.0	W 317403	906.4	W 350796	866.7	W 432557	1023.9	POISSON FRAIS, REFRIG,CONG
0341	FISH FRSH,CHLLD,EX FILLT	W 109951	306.9	W 118357	447.9	W 115783	324.9	W 129218	344.3	POISSON FRAIS,REFRIGERE
036	SHELL FISH FRESH,FROZEN	W 280820	1002.3	W 270294	1024.8	W 269530	781.9	W 267472	764.4	CRUSTACES,MOLLUSQUES
037	FISH ETC PREPD,PRSVD NES	W 62119	523.2	W 71899	788.2	W 104158	1131.2	W 131569	1054.1	POIS,CRUST,MOL PREPARES
0371	FISH PREPARD,PRESRVD NES	W 33724	428.2	W 41407	648.7	W 64798	954.1	W 82457	847.0	CONSERVES DE POISSONS
04	CEREALS AND PREPARATIONS		1739.5		351.3		604.3		1589.4	CEREALES ET PRODUITS
042	RICE	W 1519255	514.7	W 46800	16.3	W 265162	111.7	W 939310	264.6	RIZ
044	MAIZE UNMILLED	W 8740013	944.3	W 112536	13.3	W 158656	30.3	W 6617333	859.0	MAIS NON MOULU
05	VEGETABLES AND FRUIT		2935.9		3399.4		3178.7		3138.0	LEGUMES ET FRUITS
054	VEG ETC FRSH,SMPLY PRSVD	W 3432519	1361.7	W 2411748	1373.6	W 2043929	1357.9	W 2128543	1338.4	LEGUMES FRAIS,CONG,SECS
0542	LEGUMINOUS VEGETBLES DRY	W 1461394	437.4	W 1041229	358.6	W 547117	248.2	W 593596	266.7	LEGUMES A COSSE SECS
0545	OTHER FRESH VEGETABLES	W 725484	350.5	W 678276	411.5	W 807139	457.6	W 791130	425.8	AUTRES LEGUMES FRAIS,REF
0546	VEGETABLES SIMPLY PRESVD	W 410786	336.5	W 450222	407.7	W 477621	453.7	W 531346	465.0	LEGUMES CONG,CONSER
056	VEGTBLES ETC PRSVD,PREPD	W 636585	848.7	W 738252	1148.5	W 710252	944.9	W 643649	850.9	CONSERVES DE LEGUMES
0561	VEG DRIED EXC LEGUMINOUS	W 108818	374.0	W 130033	508.5	W 112964	349.5	W 115251	355.8	LEGUM DESSECH,DESHYDRAT
0565	VEGTBLES PRSVD,PREPD NES	W 521415	467.5	W 602636	632.4	W 588609	581.6	W 519856	482.3	LEGUMES PREPARES CONSERVE
05659	OTH VEG PRESVD,PREPD NES	W 516399	464.2	W 592283	623.6	W 575492	571.4	W 508104	472.0	LEGUM PREPAP,CONSERV NDA
057	FRUIT,NUTS,FRESH,DRIED	W 494550	396.6	W 493785	444.8	W 562728	417.6	W 684235	417.2	FRUITS FRAIS OU SECS
058	FRUIT PRESERVED,PREPARED	W 319628	329.0	W 387633	432.7	W 403164	458.4	W 478892	531.6	CONSERVES DE FRUITS
06	SUGAR AND PREPS,HONEY		438.0		321.1		415.3		259.0	SUCRES ET PRODUITS
061	SUGAR AND HONEY	W 1060300	402.7	W 581473	285.2	W 764970	374.4	W 442860	210.1	SUCRES ET MIEL
07	COFFEE,TEA,COCOA,SPICES		491.0		512.0		547.3		616.2	CAFE,THE,CACAO,EPICES
081	*FEEDING STUFF FOR ANIML	W 2948266	466.5	W 2046172	351.1	W 2266987	365.5	W 1776539	310.2	NOURRITURE POUR ANIMAUX
1	BEVERAGES AND TOBACCO		1001.7		1369.2		1342.0		1048.8	BOISSONS ET TABACS
12	TOBACCO AND MANUFACTURES		686.4		999.1		975.7		657.6	TABACS BRUTS FABRIQUES
122	TOBACCO,MANUFACTURED		592.6		899.3		864.8	W 40606	461.8	TABACS FABRIQUES
1222	CIGARETTES		562.2	W 66211	864.2	MN 58816441	832.6	W 34625	436.1	CIGARETTES
2	CRUDE MATERLS,EXCL FUELS		4093.5		4347.9		4019.7		4151.6	MAT BRUTES NON COMESTIBLES
22	OIL SEEDS,OLEAGINOUS FRT		666.1		522.3		478.4		279.5	GRAINES,FRUITS OLEAGINEUX
222	SEEDS FOR'SOFT'FIXED OIL	W 1486288	635.4	W 908817	494.3	W 690196	452.4	W 414539	261.7	GRAINES HUILES FIXES
24	CORK AND WOOD		318.9		481.2		466.1		459.5	LIEGE ET BOIS
26	TEXTILE FIBRES AND WASTE		1076.5		737.8		694.7		767.4	FIBRES TEXTILES
261	SILK	W 24774	404.6	W 18404	352.9	W 18069	312.6	W 15255	312.5	SOIE
268	WOOL(EXC TOPS),ANML HAIR	W 24946	447.9	W 19525	267.2	W 22309	314.2	W 27137	321.0	LAINES ET POILS
27	CRUDE FERTLZR,MINRLS NES		696.7		979.8		953.5		1069.6	ENGRAIS MINERAUX BRUTS
278	OTHER CRUDE MINERALS	MW 9989	530.0	MW 11306	798.1	MW 10223	749.3	MW 12723	857.3	AUTRES MINERAUX BRUTS
2782	REFRACTORY MINERALS NES	W 4885564	296.6	W 5521107	483.6	W 4389486	410.3	W 5128021	460.0	ARGILE MINERAUX REFRACTAIRES
29	CRUDE ANIMAL,VEG MAT NES		1117.4		1339.7		1236.6		1279.3	MATIERES BRUTES ANIM,VEGET
291	CRUDE ANIMAL MTRIALS NES	W 175540	520.9	W 170994	690.6	W 174921	662.7	W 172671	686.9	MATIERES BRUTES ANIMALES
2919	OTH ANIMAL MATERIALS NES	W 90851	502.8	W 90771	669.4	W 86589	637.3	W 98778	666.6	MAT ORIGINE ANIMALE NDA
292	CRUDE VEG MATERIALS NES	W 392385	596.6	W 379539	649.2	W 380979	573.9		592.4	MAT BRUTES VEGETALES NDA
2924	VEG USED IN PHARMACY ETC	W 155434	410.1	W 142532	415.5	W 165023	327.9	W 165195	314.1	PLANTES MEDICINALES
3	MINERAL FUELS ETC		4072.3		5335.3		5937.6		6992.5	COMBUSTIBLES MINERAUX LUB
32	COAL,COKE AND BRIQUETTES		1054.0		1694.6		1720.9		1925.1	HOUILLES,COKES,BRIQUETTES
322	COAL,LIGNITE AND PEAT	MW 24302	771.0	MW 28618	1010.9	MW 29001	1109.3	MW 30730	1133.3	HOUILLES,LIGNITES,TOURBE
3222	OTH COAL,NOT AGGLOMERATD	MW 22437	691.5	MW 26087	904.4	MW 27268	1034.4	MW 28607	1039.1	AUTRES HOUILLES
323	BRIQUETS,COKE,SEMI–COKE	W 4049898	283.1	W 8872356	683.8	W 7688114	611.7	MW 10586	791.9	BRIQUETTES
3232	COKE,SEMI–COKE,RTRT CRBN	W 4048838	282.8	W 8871959	683.7	W 7687363	611.5	MW 10585	791.6	COKES ET SEMI–COKES
33	PETROLEUM AND PRODUCTS		2799.9		3243.7		3920.5		4252.9	PETROLE ET DERIVES
333	CRUDE PETROLEUM	MW 18552	2000.4	MW 18827	2236.4	MW 20403	2789.3	MW 19829	2734.2	HUILES BRUTES DE PETROLE
334	PETROLEUM PRODUCTS,REFIN	W 3794744	624.5	W 4151740	795.5	W 4179271	874.9	W 5593238	1207.3	PRODUITS RAFFINES
4	ANIMAL,VEGETABLE OIL,FAT		495.4		453.4		376.0		646.9	HUILES,GRAISSES ANIM,VEG
42	FIXED VEGETABLE OIL,FAT		485.2		438.9		351.2		615.0	HUILES VEGETALES FIXES
5	CHEMCLS,RELATED PROD NES		6176.4		8945.6		8771.3		10102.4	PRODUITS CHIMIQUES
51	ORGANIC CHEMICALS		1601.0		2284.8		2262.2		2579.1	PROD CHIMIQ ORGANIQUES
513	CARBOXYLIC ACIDS ETC	W 309396	332.3	W 322580	478.2	W 239241	367.7	W 344870	462.2	ACIDES CARBOXYLIQUES
514	NITROGEN–FNCTN COMPOUNDS	W 136040	389.7	W 162690	539.4	W 157236	544.0	W 216932	721.4	COMPOSES FONCT AZOTEES
515	ORG–INORG COMPOUNDS ETC	W 98671	363.8	W 109974	496.7	W 151289	645.4	W 175284	603.9	COMPOSES ORGANO–MINERAUX
52	INORGANIC CHEMICALS		1349.5		2225.1		2106.2		2383.3	PROD CHIM INORGANIQUES
522	INORG ELEMNTS,OXIDES,ETC	W 1164495	689.7	W 1545080	1067.3		1021.5		1163.3	ELEMENTS INORGANIQUES
5221	CHEMICAL ELEMENTS	W 306322	266.3	W 408878	409.2		470.3		485.5	ELEMENTS CHIMIQUES
523	OTHR INORG CHEMICALS ETC	W 2252465	567.0	W 2853949	917.6		842.7		970.0	AUT PRODUITS CHIMIQUES INORG
53	DYES,TANNING,COLOUR PROD		537.2		726.6		726.5		918.6	PROD TEINTURE,COLORANTS
531	SYNT DYE,NAT INDGO,LAKES	W 96451	351.2	W 123106	468.9	W 125522	480.2	W 165079	638.2	MAT COLOR ORGAN,LAQUES
5311	SYNTHIC ORGNIC DYESTUFFS	W 94464	342.5	W 121274	457.7	W 124564	473.6	W 162828	624.0	MAT COLOR ORGAN SYNTHET
541	*MEDICINAL,PHARM PRODUCT	MK 127362	1185.3	MK 146642	1582.0	MK 136158	1516.2	MK 137257	1536.3	PROD MEDICINAUX PHARMACEUT
5413	ANTIBIOTICS IN BULK	MK 17216	353.0	MK 19987	513.6	MK 17301	479.6	MK 17892	441.9	ANTIBIOTIQUES NDA
58	PLASTIC MATERIALS ETC		449.2		732.4		555.0		904.0	MAT PLAST ARTIFICIELLES
583	POLYMERIZATION ETC PRODS	W 318780	323.0	W 337040	466.1	W 335018	397.2	W 542556	619.1	PROD POLYMERISATION
59	CHEMICAL MATERIALS NES		542.1		698.5		826.9		994.5	MAT PROD CHIMIQUES NDA
598	MISCEL CHEM PRODUCTS NES	W 652646	324.0		381.4	W 797760	485.0	W 868129	589.8	PROD DIV INDUST CHIM NDA
6	BASIC MANUFACTURES		23780.3		32831.6		29209.7		35158.4	ART MANUFACTURES
61	LEATHER,DRESSED FUR,ETC		823.7		926.7		831.0		899.6	CUIRS,PELLETERIES
612	LEATHER ETC MANUFACTURES	W 62396	445.2	W 74126	483.2	W 69172	462.5	W 81569	479.1	OUVRAGES EN CUIRS NDA
62	RUBBER MANUFACTURES NES		422.4		693.9		753.0		850.1	CAOUTCHOUC MANUFACTURE
625	RUBBER TYRES, TUBES ETC		258.8	MN 110726	484.7	MN 118378	524.5	MN 155828	568.8	PNEUS CAOUTCHOUC VULCANISE
63	WOOD,CORK MANUFACTRS NES		705.5		927.3		940.2		1156.1	OUVRAGES LIEGE ET BOIS
635	WOOD MANUFACTURES NES	W 519119	650.3	W 611875	849.1		834.4		937.9	ART MANUF EN BOIS NDA
64	PAPER,PAPERBOARD AND MFR		611.5		916.5		796.4		977.7	PAPIERS,CARTONS & OUVRAGES
642	PAPER,ETC,PRECUT,ARTS OF	W 499720	444.9	W 540506	543.0	W 595343	613.7	W 716445	762.0	PAP,CARTONS DECOUPES
65	TEXTILE YARN,FABRICS,ETC		11942.6		14059.3		12317.6		14028.9	FILS,TISSUS,ARTICLES TEXTILE
651	TEXTILE YARN	W 525162	1778.1	W 553191	2111.5	W 504106	1935.2	W 658194	2368.6	FILS TEXTILES
6513	COTTON YARN	W 194927	514.5	W 179895	576.4	W 142044	458.6	W 153232	485.3	FILS DE COTON
652	COTTON FABRICS,WOVEN		2711.3	L 3772663	3457.5	L 3063018	2957.4	L 3039411	3091.9	TISSUS DE COTON
6521	GREY WOVEN COTTON FABRIC	L 1285053	745.6	L 1288748	860.5	L 1161670	789.9	L 1078701	760.6	TISSUS COT ECRUS NON MERCER
65214	GREY WOVEN COTTON NES	L 1012279	605.7	L 975296	676.2	L 889585	632.1	L 881689	639.1	AUT TISSUS 85% COTON ECRUS
6522	WOVEN COTTON BLEACHD,ETC		1965.8	L 2483915	2597.0	L 1901348	2167.6	L 1960710	2331.4	TISSUS COTON BLANCHIS ETC
65224	BLCHED COTTON FABRIC NES		1636.1	L 2012835	2164.4	L 1494366	1732.2	L 1468088	1706.4	AUT TIS PLUS 85% COT BLANCHI
653	WOVN MAN–MADE FIB FABRIC		2148.5	L 3516165	2474.1	L 3232562	2114.3	L 3978929	2608.3	TISSUS FIBRES SYNTH,ARTIF
6531	CONT SYNT WEAVES NONPILE	L 284952	399.7	L 278752	287.2	L 391065	300.0	L 735057	530.0	TISSUS FIBRES SYNTH CONTINUE
65315	CONT SYN TXTL FABRIC NES	L 247240	376.4	L 240097	250.2	L 368633	281.3	L 708696	507.2	TIS PLUS 85% TEXT SYNT CONT
6534	DISC SYN BLEND FABRC NES	L 1596696	897.4	L 1779785	1107.4	L 1814948	1114.0	L 2178262	1316.9	TISSUS FIBRES SYNTH DISCONT
65341	DISC SYN FIB–COTTN FABRC	L 1206575	659.9	L 1283234	778.6	L 1320867	797.8	L 1552895	936.4	TISSUS FIB SYNT DIS MEL COTO
6536	DISC REGN TXTL FABRC NES	L 1104495	628.6	L 1086077	716.4	L 675308	378.0	L 629380	333.5	TISSUS 85% TEXT ART DISC

5. Special Exports F.O.B. by Commodities according to the S.I.T.C. (Rev. 2) in million U.S. Dollars
Exportations Spéciales F.O.B. par Produits d'après la C.T.C.I. (Rév. 2) en millions de Dollars E.U.

SITC CTCI	COMMODITY	1994 QUANTITY QUANTITE	1994 VALUE VALEUR	1995 QUANTITY QUANTITE	1995 VALUE VALEUR	1996 QUANTITY QUANTITE	1996 VALUE VALEUR	1997 QUANTITY QUANTITE	1997 VALUE VALEUR	PRODUIT
654	OTH WOVEN TEXTILE FABRIC		1141.0		1141.7		826.1		960.9	TISSUS AUT COTON SYNT,ARTIF
6541	SILK FABRICS WOVEN	L 194719	676.1	L 187405	656.5	L 145529	431.9	L 149461	463.8	TISSUS DE SOIE
655	KNITTED,ETC FABRICS	W 211888	745.2	W 231776	907.4	W 214192	785.7	W 248541	831.3	ETOF BONNETERIE PIECES ETC
6552	OTHER KNIT ETC FAB NONEL	W 211888	745.2	W 231776	907.4	W 214192	785.7	W 248541	831.3	ETOF BON NON ELAS NON SYNT
657	SPECIAL TXTL FABRC,PRODS	W 121483	288.5	W 132924	463.1	W 131296	361.8	W 188428	544.6	TISSUS SPECIAUX
658	TEXTILE ARTICLES NES		2186.5		2560.7		2466.9		2684.7	ART FACONNES MAT TEXTILES
6584	LINENS ETC	MN 2094066	1398.3	MN 2426798	1597.0	MN 2176058	1482.8	MN 2373814	1652.0	LINGE DE MAISON
65841	BED LINEN OF COTTON	MN 161576	416.1	MN 156211	466.7	MN 120187	383.2	MN 126490	430.8	LINGE DE LIT DE COTON
65845	OTHER LINEN OF COTTON	MN 1384488	452.5	MN 1702584	553.1	MN 1606258	555.5	MN 1721647	586.4	LINGE DE TOILETTE COTON
659	FLOOR COVERINGS,ETC		762.3		722.5		647.7		654.3	COUVRE–PARQUETS,TAPIS ETC
6592	CARPETS ETC KNOTTED	A 14439	504.2	A 11207	427.6	A 6137	306.7	A 6106	304.3	TAPIS POINTS NOUES,ENROULES
65921	— OF WOOL OR FINE HAIR	A 11269	363.5	A 7997	294.0	A 4552	212.7	A 4342	191.4	TAP NOUES,ENROULES LAINE
66	NONMETAL MINERAL MFS NES		2523.2		3425.1		3297.1		4011.0	ART MIN NON METALLIQUES
661	LIME,CEMENT,BLDG PRODS	W 5702371	533.4	MW 9802	883.3	MW 13591	1105.5	MW 13777	1163.9	CHAUX,CIMENTS MAT CONSTR
6613	BUILDING STONE ETC WORKD	W 1044658	362.8	W 1446643	568.2	W 1632429	634.6	W 1952197	700.8	PIERRES A BATIR
66132	BUILDING STONE WORKED	W 869182	341.2	W 1222113	533.1	W 1400147	596.9	W 1558691	651.1	OUVR EN PIERRES DE TAILLE
666	POTTERY	W 780917	981.7	W 850988	1029.1	W 918593	1013.5	W 1051721	1356.4	POTERIE
6664	PORCELN,CHINA HOUSE WARE	W 497784	488.9	W 519979	506.0	W 565757	496.2	W 649877	679.5	VAISSELLE,ARTS MEN PORC
6666	CERAMIC ORNAMENTS ETC	W 249615	468.2	W 277356	482.4	W 292887	466.4	W 343145	622.1	OBJETS PORCELAINE,CERAM
667	PEARL,PREC–,SEMI–P STONE		385.8		515.1		241.9		349.4	PERLES, PIERRES GEMMES
67	IRON AND STEEL		1867.2		5467.5		4068.0		5003.8	FER ET ACIER
671	PIG IRON ETC	W 2479859	758.2	W 6850331	1770.9	W 4621266	1223.9	W 6618879	1558.8	FONTE,SPIEGEL,POUDRES
6712	PIG IRN,SPIEGELEISEN ETC	W 1541334	216.0	W 5330778	797.0	W 3553051	512.2	W 5540985	814.4	FONTES BRUTES
6716	FERRO–ALLOYS	W 922717	536.2	W 1475438	961.8	W 1031280	699.5	W 1062937	735.4	FERRO–ALLIAGES
67169	OTHER FERRO–ALLOYS	W 520641	340.9	W 906394	661.8	W 604754	446.5	W 708973	533.8	AUTRES FERRO–ALLIAGES
672	IRON,STEEL PRIMARY FORMS	W 836019	197.2	W 6353041	1699.7	W 3630883	920.1	W 5314113	1323.2	LINGOTS FER,ACIER
6725	IRN,STL BLOOMS,SLABS,ETC	W 657122	145.7	W 4432879	1071.5	W 2698954	636.6	W 3636230	846.6	BLOOMS,BILLETTES FER ACIER
67251	IRN,SMPLE STL BLOOMS,ETC	W 656178	143.6	W 4411460	1037.8	W 2692936	622.8	W 3633693	831.6	BLOOMS ETC NON ACIER FIN
6727	IRN,STL COIL FR REROLLNG	W 137796	41.7	W 1742933	586.7	W 860249	267.1	W 1162825	353.5	EBAUCHES POUR TOLES FER
67271	IRON,SIMPLE STEEL COILS	W 136752	39.1	W 1710162	568.6	W 853252	261.8	W 1157363	347.3	EBAUCHES NON EN ACIER
674	IRN,STL UNIV,PLATE,SHEET	W 289338	115.6	W 2051506	768.8	W 1312762	474.5	W 1413124	525.7	LARGES PLATS,TOLES
678	IRON,STL TUBES,PIPES,ETC	W 350152	253.7	W 589891	422.9	W 744445	544.8	W 837210	616.6	TUBES,TUYAUX EN FONTE,FER
68	NON–FERROUS METALS		1430.7		1929.5		1663.9		2558.3	METAUX NON FERREUX
684	ALUMINIUM	W 170708	242.2	W 256744	453.7	W 169170	288.3	W 349745	590.6	ALUMINIUM
686	ZINC	W 294872	251.2	W 208998	195.9	W 239898	234.3	W 568494	666.6	ZINC
6861	ZINC,ALLOYS UNWROUGHT	W 278003	236.4	W 191526	179.4	W 226777	218.3	W 556931	651.7	ZINC ET ALLIAGES BRUTS
69	METAL MANUFACTURES NES		3454.0		4486.1		4542.9		5673.3	ART MANUFACT EN METAL NDA
695	TOOLS	W 339831	635.5	W 389995	801.8	W 321064	752.2	W 377477	884.3	OUTILS A MAIN
6953	OTHER HAND TOOLS	W 254210	434.7	W 288223	546.3	W 249784	528.9	W 298403	651.4	AUTRES OUTILS A MAIN
696	CUTLERY		321.1		413.3		432.8		594.9	COUTELLERIE
697	BASE MTL HOUSEHOLD EQUIP		587.2		743.2		826.6		1091.9	ART MENAGE MET COMMUNS
6974	BASE MTL DMSTC ARTIC NES	W 171256	428.3	W 212727	555.5	W 228638	592.6	W 301223	785.9	ARTICLES NDA FONTE,FER,ETC
69741	— OF IRON OR STEEL	W 156109	367.2	W 194008	477.6	W 212140	515.7	W 281972	704.4	ART NDA EN FONTE,FER
699	BASE METAL MFRS NES	W 777834	1162.3	W 938452	1446.3	W 934690	1454.9	W 1142336	1844.8	ART MANUFACTURES MET NDA
6991	LOCKSMITHS WARES,ETC	W 223654	468.4	W 264266	563.1	W 268688	569.5	W 341675	696.4	ARTICLES DE SERRURERIE
7	MACHINES,TRANSPORT EQUIP		21830.5		31296.9		35239.2		43614.4	MACHINES MATERIEL TRANSPORT
71	POWER GENERATING EQUIPMT		981.0		1438.9		1543.3		1863.6	MACHINES GENERATRICES
716	ROTATING ELECTRIC PLANT		778.4		1080.5		1156.5		1449.2	APP ELECTR ROTATIFS,PIECES
7162	AC MTRS,GENRTRS,GEN SETS	MN 1297431	673.3	MN 1549398	888.3	MN 1472263	953.1	MN 1846608	1230.3	MOTEURS ELECTRIQUES
71621	AC MTRS,INC UNIVRSL MTRS	MN 1297362	627.2	MN 1549311	845.6	MN 1472183	926.8	MN 1846516	1185.1	MOT ELEC NON COUR CONTINU
72	MACHS FOR SPCL INDUSTRYS		820.6		1140.5		1169.1		1214.1	MAC SPECIALES POUR INDUST
74	GENRL INDUSTRL MACHY NES		1305.5		1749.0		2093.7		2568.3	MACH APP INDUSTRIE
744	MECHANICAL HANDLING EQU		300.6		356.2		453.1		574.3	EQUIP MANUTENTION PIECES
749	NONELEC MACH PTS,ACC NES		537.5		770.5		907.9		1068.2	PIECES MACH NON ELEC NDA
75	OFFICE MACHNES,ADP EQUIP		2664.5		4802.8		6716.8		9243.9	MACH BUREAU TRAIT AUTOM
751	OFFICE MACHINES	MN 259244	553.7		850.8	MN 320883	1117.2	MN 395309	1357.8	MACH,APPAREILS DE BUREAU
7518	OFFICE MACHINES NES	MN 41333	236.8	MN 44930	473.0	MN 48485	633.1	MN 60659	815.1	MACH,APP DE BUREAU NDA
75182	PHOTO,THERMOCOPY APPARAT	N 358970	163.6	N 831234	392.3	N 945621	500.9	N 1424104	663.8	APPAREILS DE PHOTOCOPIE
752	AUTOMTIC DATA PROC EQUIP	MN 26225	987.4	MN 66073	2301.6	MN 114857	3690.4	MN 197096	5361.8	MACH TRAIT INFORMATION
7524	DIGITL CENTRL STOR UNITS	N 5436367	217.4	MN 20554	822.0	MN 23619	1113.8	MN 44810	2098.5	UNITES MEMOIRE CENTRALES
7525	ADP PERIPHERAL UNITS	MN 16512	620.2	MN 36304	1061.0	MN 87071	1985.0	MN 144513	2495.8	UNITES PERIPHERIQUES
759	OFFICE,ADP MCH PTS,ACCES	W 68030	1123.4	W 112547	1650.5		1909.3	W 312343	2524.3	PIECES DU 751 ET 752
7599	ACCTG,ETC,ADP MCH PTS,AC	W 60696	1063.5	W 95835	1518.6	MN 164623	1679.2	W 268523	2198.7	PIECES DU 751 ET 752
76	TELECOMM,SOUND EQUIPMENT		6743.8		8408.6		9004.1		10303.8	EQUIPMENT DE TELECOM
761	TELEVISION RECEIVERS	MN 10788	711.5	MN 11513	807.9	MN 10323	794.4	MN 9064	654.9	RECEPTEURS DE TELEVISION
7611	COLOUR TV RECEIVERS	N 4422106	514.1	N 5660404	601.9	N 5371004	622.1	N 4299198	506.1	RECEPTEURS COULEUR
762	RADIO BROADCAST RECEIVRS	MN 254134	2305.4	MN 275499	2555.3	MN 270306	2396.7	MN 292168	2737.3	RECEPTEURS RADIODIFFUSION
7622	PORTABLE RADIO RECEIVERS	MN 84370	352.0	MN 102187	410.5	MN 112915	479.7	MN 144021	761.0	RECEPT PORTATIFS RADIO
7628	OTHER RADIO RECEIVERS	MN 154134	1724.9	MN 157393	1829.9	MN 138928	1557.2	MN 125361	1565.6	AUTRES RECEPT RADIO
763	SOUND RECORDRS,PHONOGRPH	MN 56733	790.3	MN 63259	1001.5	MN 61040	1125.5	MN 68499	1282.1	PHONO,APP ENREGISTREMENT
7638	OTHR SOUND APPARATUS ETC	MN 56549	787.8	MN 62841	997.5	MN 60477	1119.5	MN 68020	1278.2	AUT APP D'ENREGIS,REPROD
76388	DICTATING MACHINES ETC	MN 54237	633.9	MN 59133	783.3	MN 55302	734.9	MN 60284	731.7	MACHINES A DICTER
764	TELECOM EQPT,PTS,ACC NES		2936.8		4044.1		4687.7		5629.7	EQUIP TELECOM,PIECES
7641	LINE TELEPHONE,ETC EQUIP	MN 321074	962.4	MN 396293	1230.5	MN 368489	1259.1	MN 395708	1336.3	APP TELEPHON PAR FIL
7642	MICROPH,LOUDSPKR,AMPLIFR	MN 855228	386.3	MN 898271	509.2	MN 851009	574.1	MN 1025451	717.1	MICRO,HAUT–PARLEUR,AMPLI
7643	TV,RADIO TRANSMITTRS ETC	N 5375193	159.8	N 6398771	260.7	N 6502083	489.5	N 6310486	574.9	APP EMET TELE RADIO
7649	PTS NES OF EQUIPMT OF 76	W 76846	1307.2		1828.6		2199.2	W 191671	2796.0	PIECES DE LA DIV 76
76493	TELECOMM EQUIPMT PTS NES	W 57106	593.8	W 57692	812.1	MN 78442	986.6	W 76552	1156.3	PIECES 761,762,764.3,8
76499	PARTS ETC OF SOUND EQUIP	W 55	622.2		858.6	MN 311818	951.2	W 67598	1294.5	PIECES NDA POUR 763
77	ELECTRIC MACHNRY NES ETC		6436.7		9555.7		10335.9		13016.5	MACH APP ELECT NDA
771	ELECTRIC POWER MACHY NES		1087.1		1545.3		1648.5		2159.1	MACH PROD,TRANS ELECTR
7711	TRANSFORMERS,ELECTRICAL	MN 1537952	402.4	MN 2582754	633.5	MN 2754724	590.3	MN 3003494	681.3	TRANSFO ELECTRIQUES
77118	OTHER ELEC TRANSFORMERS	MN 1536012	370.3	MN 2581028	586.3	MN 2753834	542.0	MN 3003323	653.9	AUTRES TRANSFO ELECTRIQ
7712	OTH ELEC POWER MACHY NES		684.8		911.9		1058.3		1477.9	AUT APP PROD TRANSF ELEC
77121	STATIC CONVERTERS ETC	MN 117650	379.3	MN 152937	518.2	MN 177631	629.7	MN 263548	939.1	CONVERTISSEURS STATIQUES
772	SWITCHGEAR ETC,PARTS NES	W 179814	1053.1	W 195231	1630.2		1500.1		1954.4	APP COUPURE,SECT ETC
7721	SWITCHGEAR ETC	W 136378	584.5	W 156372	920.8	MN 6014286	879.2		1075.0	APP COUPURE,SECTIONMNT
7722	PRINTED CIRCUITS,PTS NES	W 33760	316.1	W 27615	415.3	MN 941564	504.8	MN 1395736	732.9	CIRCUITS ET PIECES
773	ELECTR DISTRIBUTNG EQUIP	W 188543	391.0	W 229300	545.8	W 256573	745.4	W 342916	966.6	EQUIPMT DISTRIBUTION ELECT
7731	INSULATED WIRE,CABLE ETC	W 162664	361.4	W 198425	509.6	W 229585	700.1	W 302739	861.2	FILS,CABLES ISOLES ELECT
775	HOUSEHOLD TYPE EQUIP NES		1566.1		2108.5		2464.1		2813.6	MACH,APP USAGE DOMESTQUE
7757	DOMESTIC ELECTRC EQU NES		780.0		1045.5		1175.1		1188.6	APP ELECTR DOMEST NDA
77572	DOM ELEC ROOM FANS ETC	MN 56522	510.7	MN 90446	717.1	MN 121884	794.2	MN 131277	700.5	HOTTES ASPIRANTES,VENTIL
7758	ELECTRO–THERMIC APPL NES		683.3		883.8		1060.4		1353.4	APP ELECTROTHERMIQ NDA
77586	ELECTROTHERM DOM APP NES	MN 57691	336.4	MN 73447	464.7	MN 88425	617.7	MN 115673	821.8	APP ELECTRO THERMIQUES
776	TRANSISTORS,VALVES,ETC		614.4		1294.7		1476.9		1945.8	LAMPES,TUBES,VALVES
7764	ELECTRONIC MICROCIRCUITS	MN 441543	141.3	MN 903602	407.3	MN 1282054	539.6	MN 2484014	846.6	MICROSTRUCTURES ELECTRON
778	ELECTRICAL MACHINERY NES		1701.0		2391.1		2450.4		3114.2	AUTRES MACH ELECT NDA
7781	BATTERIES,ACCUMULATORS		349.0		452.6		580.0		750.6	PILES ET ACCUMULATEURS
7788	OTH ELEC MACHY,EQUIP NES		902.6		1153.0		1117.6		1392.0	AUT MACH APP ELEC NDA
78	ROAD VEHICLES		1790.7		2699.4		2568.5		2854.6	VEHICULES ROUTIERS

5. Special Exports F.O.B. by Commodities according to the S.I.T.C. (Rev. 2) in million U.S. Dollars
Exportations Spéciales F.O.B. par Produits d'après la C.T.C.I. (Rév. 2) en millions de Dollars E.U.

SITC CTCI	COMMODITY	1994		1995		1996		1997		PRODUIT
		QUANTITY QUANTITE	VALUE VALEUR	QUANTITY QUANTITE	VALUE VALEUR	QUANTITY QUANTITE	VALUE VALEUR	QUANTITY QUANTITE	VALUE VALEUR	
785	CYCLES,ETC MOTRZD OR NOT		740.6		880.1		882.1		1070.0	MOTOCYCLES SCOOTERS
7852	CYCLES, ETC NON–MOTOR	MN 13578	507.1	MN 12823	538.8	MN 12239	465.3	MN 14618	517.9	VELOCIPEDES SANS MOTEUR
786	TRAILERS,NONMOTR VEH,NES		692.2		1286.8		1156.1		1145.4	REMORQUES,CADRES,CONTAIN
7861	TRAILERS,TRANSP CONTAINR	N 222062	631.9	N 409311	1211.5	N 368208	1079.7	N 335187	1053.9	REMORQUES TOUS VEHICULES
78613	CONTAINERS INC ROAD–RAIL	N 217797	615.7	N 406170	1195.9	N 353120	1062.4	N 330101	1030.2	CADRES ET CONTAINERS
79	OTHR TRANSPORT EQUIPMENT		766.2		1085.0		1398.1		2084.6	AUTRE MATERIEL TRANSPORT
793	SHIPS AND BOATS ETC		552.2		878.9	N 84930	1154.0		1630.1	NAVIRES BATEAUX,ETC
7932	SHIPS AND BOATS NES	N 60699	401.6	N 8146	616.9	N 16811	978.9	N 17960	1520.2	NAVIRES ET BATEAUX
79323	OTHER CARGO VESSELS	N 483	330.0	N 583	585.2	N 534	890.3	N 599	1279.4	AUT BATEAUX TRANS MARCH
8	MISC MANUFACTURED GOODS		49199.5		53726.2		55723.6		69636.4	ART MANUFACTURES DIVERS
812	*PLUMBG,HEATNG,LGHTNG EQ		820.2		1001.0		1012.9		1219.1	APPAR SANITAIRES CHAUFFAGE
8124	LIGHTING EQUIPMENT NES		808.9		984.0		999.2		1186.5	APPAREILS ECLAIRAGE ETC
81242	LAMPS,FITTINGS BASE METL	W 234488	601.6	W 316864	733.2	W 357665	752.7	W 396789	882.8	APPAREILS D'ECLAIRAGE
821	*FURNITURE,PARTS THEREOF		1495.6		1764.7		1892.2		2488.3	MEUBLES ET PIECES
8211	CHAIRS,SEATS AND PARTS		300.2		405.3		444.9		621.7	SIEGES ET PIECES
82111	CHAIRS AND OTHER SEATS	MN 41683	293.2	MN 50722	397.0	MN 53783	431.4	MN 75702	598.0	SIEGES
8212	MED FURN,STUFFD FURNSHGS		651.8		659.0		597.0		669.6	MOB MEDICO–CHIRUR,PIECES
82122	MATTRESSES ETC		649.3	W 90691	654.5		591.9		662.9	SOMMIERS,ARTICLES DE LITERIE
8219	FURNITURE AND PARTS NES		543.7		700.4		850.5		1197.1	AUTRES MEUBLES ET PIECES
82192	WOOD FURNITURE NES	MN 16659	372.1	MN 20457	439.5	MN 25553	515.4	MN 36321	722.9	MEUBLES NDA EN BOIS
831	*TRAVEL GOODS,HANDBAGS		2364.9		2869.6		2725.4		3322.1	ARTICLES DE VOYAGE ETC
83101	HANDBAGS NES	MN 293948	419.4	MN 290249	513.0	MN 270642	402.6	MN 295607	471.4	SACS A MAIN
83102	TRAVEL GDS,TOILET–CASES	MN 1077288	1563.7	MN 1309413	1886.2	MN 1390247	1871.2	MN 1654602	2306.0	ARTICLES DE VOYAGE
83109	OTHER TRAVEL BAGS,CASES		381.9		470.5		451.6		544.9	AUT CONTENANTS SIMILAIRES
84	CLOTHING AND ACCESSORIES		23793.5		24123.4		25101.0		31875.5	VETEMENTS
842	MENS OUTERWEAR NOT KNIT	MN 1095498	5464.8	MN 1087932	5168.1	MN 1118004	5476.5	MN 1124071	6321.3	VET DESSUS POUR HOMMES
8423	— TROUSERS,BREECHES ETC	MN 609473	1866.6	MN 634053	1899.5	MN 625607	1851.3	MN 565146	2101.2	PANTALONS HOMMES MAT TEX
8424	— JACKETS,BLAZERS ETC	MN 204405	1376.5	MN 166079	1147.7	MN 142833	1067.5	MN 145592	1150.1	VESTES HOMMES MAT TEXTIL
8429	— OTHER OUTER GARMENTS	MN 242811	1751.3	MN 242197	1631.9	MN 294964	2025.1	MN 349976	2429.7	AUT VET DES HOM MAT TEX
843	WOMENS OUTERWEAR NONKNIT		6613.3	MN 1622059	6306.2	MN 1639646	6269.5	MN 1573706	6880.9	VET DESSUS FEMMES MAT TEX
8431	— COATS AND JACKETS	MN 187153	1196.1	MN 185377	1287.0	MN 199700	1395.6	MN 211910	1487.1	MANT,VEST FEM MAT TEXTIL
8433	— DRESSES	MN 61622	373.7	MN 71171	375.2	MN 73473	393.2	MN 81665	471.8	ROBES EN MAT–TEXTILES
8435	— BLOUSES	MN 242670	1058.3	MN 222686	980.2	MN 214934	936.1	MN 216450	974.7	BLOUSES FEM MAT TEXTILES
8439	— OTHER OUTER GARMENTS		3479.3	MN 1020798	3122.0	MN 1033544	3037.8	MN 916550	3403.4	AUT VET DES FEM MAT TEXT
844	UNDER GARMENTS NOT KNIT		2357.3	MN 773917	2133.9	MN 725698	2074.8	MN 772355	2272.9	VETEMENT DESSOUS MAT TEX
8441	— MENS SHIRTS		1638.6	MN 491736	1459.0	MN 456486	1386.4	MN 482387	1492.7	CHEMISES HOMMES MAT TEXT
84411	—— OF COTTON	MN 225716	665.5	MN 218537	677.1	MN 198132	639.8	MN 202295	679.0	CHEMISES HOMMES DE COTON
84412	—— OF SYNTHETIC FIBRES		973.1	MN 273199	781.9	MN 258354	746.6	MN 280092	813.8	CHEMISES HOMMES FIB SYNT
8443	— WOMENS	MN 108289	410.0	MN 100213	348.2	MN 99444	355.0	MN 112453	418.7	VET DESSOUS FEM MAT TEXT
845	OUTERWEAR KNIT NONELASTC		3908.3	MN 1316941	3948.8	MN 1382633	4252.1	MN 1956251	6398.7	VET DESSOUS,ACCES BONNET
8451	— JERSEYS,PULLOVERS ETC	MN 542703	2099.7	MN 637678	2366.4	MN 729816	2535.6	MN 915582	3095.8	CHANDAILS,PULL–OVERS ETC
8459	— OTHER,CLTHG ACCESRYS		1449.9	MN 585948	1332.4	MN 560170	1466.3	MN 913604	2818.6	AUT VET DESSUS DE BONNE
846	UNDER GARMENTS KNITTED	MN 2938698	2332.4	MN 3270058	2913.5	MN 3220308	3290.2	MN 4135030	5295.1	SOUS VETS DE BONNETERIE
8462	— OF COTTON NON ELASTIC	MN 2523266	2014.7	MN 2804635	2513.9	MN 2733839	2813.1	MN 3556751	4656.0	SOUS–VET BONNET COTON
84629	—— OTHER	MN 2508633	1980.5	MN 2789255	2476.3	MN 2733839	2813.1	MN 3542179	4623.8	AUT SOUS–VET BONNET COTON
8465	CORSETS,GARTERS,ETC	MN 332877	259.6	MN 373560	343.0	MN 361682	378.9	MN 468808	557.1	CORSETS,GAINES ART SIM
847	TEXTILE CLTHNG ACCES NES		664.9		812.3		834.2		1473.1	ACCES VET MAT TEXT NDA
8471	— NOT KNITTED		380.5		446.5		439.9		988.0	ACCES VET MAT TEX NON BON
848	HEADGEAR,NONTXTL CLOTHNG		2452.9		2840.9		2904.0		3233.8	VET ACCES MAT AUT QUE TEX
8481	LEATHER CLOTHES,ACCESSOR		1674.7		1950.2	MN 570197	1947.6		2196.3	VET ACCES MAT CUIR ARTIF
851	*FOOTWEAR	MP 2368580	5706.9	MP 2540059	6273.6	MN 2634211	6704.9	MP 2996003	8149.4	CHAUSSURES
85101	FOOTWEAR RUBBER,PLASTIC	MP 977685	1851.7	MP 1148324	2214.6	MN 1281532	2476.4	MP 1559838	3151.8	CHAUS SEMELLES CAOUTCH
85102	FOOTWEAR LEATHER	MP 1247913	3637.4	MP 1238209	3812.1	MN 1179380	3969.9	MP 1254406	4720.2	CHAUS SEMELLES EN CUIR
87	PRECISION INSTRUMNTS NES		635.1		914.9		1063.4		1450.1	INSTRUM,APPAR SCIENT NDA
871	OPTICAL INSTRUMENTS		205.5	MN 1028573	314.7		395.4	MN 1561840	608.0	APPAR,INSTRUM D'OPTIQUE
874	MEASURNG,CONTROLNG INSTR		279.0		399.1		413.4		552.7	INSTRUMENTS DE MESURE
88	PHOTO EQU,OPTICL GDS ETC		2455.4		2929.9		3055.9		3489.8	APP,FOURN PHOTO,OP,MONTR
881	PHOTO APPARAT,EQUIPT NES		486.5		670.3		810.8		1083.2	APP,EQUIP PHOTO NDA
8811	CAMERAS STILL,FLASH APP		474.8		654.9		789.7		1059.3	APPAREILS PHOTO,PIECES
88111	STILL CAMERAS	MN 43209	398.9	MN 61504	571.8	MN 61804	695.8	MN 65589	925.4	APPAREILS PHOTOGRAPHIQ
885	WATCHES AND CLOCKS		1741.9		1904.5		1822.6		1877.8	HORLOGERIE
8851	WATCHES,MOVEMENTS,CASES		1328.8		1408.9		1292.6		1265.2	MONTRES,MOUVEMENTS,BOITES
88511	WATCHES		957.2		1038.7		974.1		1002.7	MONTRES POCHE,BRACELET
8852	CLOCKS,CLOCK,WATCH PARTS		413.1		495.6		530.0		612.6	HORLOGES,MOUV,PARTIES
89	MISC MANUFCTRD GOODS NES		11928.1		13849.4		14168.2		17642.4	ART MANUFACTURES DIVERS
893	ARTICLES OF PLASTIC NES		2022.4		2565.7		2791.1		3616.5	OUVRAGES EN MAT DIVIS 58
8931	PLSTC PACKG CONTNRS,LIDS	W 358551	416.6	W 421722	527.6	W 512435	609.6	W 662190	769.8	ART TRANSP EMBALLAGE ETC
8939	MISC PLASTIC ARTICLES	W 998333	1593.5	W 1198375	2024.3	W 1409690	2164.3	W 1737590	2825.3	ART DIVERS EN MAT DIV 58
89399	OTHR PLASTC ARTICLES NES	W 929083	1500.1	W 1117480	1912.8	W 1321094	2042.8	W 1627803	2669.8	AUT OUV MAT DIV 58
894	TOYS,SPORTING GOODS,ETC		5093.1		5862.0		6444.8		8045.2	VOITURES ENFANTS,JOUETS
8942	TOYS,INDOOR GAMES ETC		4519.1		5116.7		5578.7		6984.0	JOUETS,JEUX ETC
89422	DOLLS		400.2	MN 729791	516.2	MN 853756	577.1	MN 849090	662.3	POUPEES
89423	TOYS NES	W 1055970	2635.2	W 1170489	2895.3	W 1312921	3332.8	MN 15420369	4355.1	JOUETS,MODELES REDUITS
89424	INDOOR GAME EQUIPMENT		718.8		820.5		737.3		905.9	ART,JEUX DE SOCIETE
89425	XMAS DECORATIONS ETC	W 302604	736.5	W 356695	865.6	W 384791	917.0		1036.0	ART DIVERTIS,FETES
8947	OTH SPORT GDS,FAIR AMUSM		473.4		620.3		715.7		860.5	AUT ART DE SPORT
89472	OTH OUTDOOR SPORT GOODS		388.0		493.9	MN 456587	556.2		669.7	ART POUR JEUX PLEIN AIR
897	GOLD,SILVER WARE,JEWELRY		1254.8		1399.3		1151.0		1564.8	BIJOUTERIE,ORFEVRERIE
8973	PREC JEWLRY,GLD–SILVWARE		1130.9		1267.1		1012.3		1408.5	BIJOUX OR,ARGENT ORFEVRE
89731	PRECIOUS METAL JEWELLERY		829.8		950.4		878.6		1228.4	ART BIJOUTERIE,JOAILLER
898	MUSICAL INSTRUMENTS,PTS		711.5		765.7		689.5		738.9	INSTRUMENTS DE MUSIQUE
8983	SOUND RECRDNG TAPE,DISCS		606.1		586.0	MN 1899277	456.1	MN 1575569	459.2	SUPPORTS SON POUR 763
89831	PREPD SND RECORDNG MEDIA		574.6		552.1	MN 1891278	411.7	MN 1566880	409.1	SUPPORTS PREPARES
899	OTHER MANUFACTURED GOODS		2421.9		2719.4		2474.1		2852.0	AUT ART MANUF DIVERS NDA
8994	UMBRELLAS,CANES ETC		457.2		490.6		438.4		502.4	PARAPLUIES,CANNES ETC
89941	UMBRELLAS,SUNSHADES	MN 404539	418.1	MN 404918	454.5	MN 373672	414.5	MN 439334	478.4	PARAPLUIES,PARASOLS ETC
8997	BASKETWORK,BROOMS ETC		625.0		768.5		634.1		664.1	OUVRAGES VANNERIE NDA
89971	BASKETWORK,WICKERWRK,ETC	W 187599	462.4	W 200515	566.0	W 174830	414.7	W 170564	383.7	OUVRAGES DE VANNERIE
8998	SMALLWARES,TOILETRYS ETC		380.4		352.2		258.1		354.9	ART MERCERIE,TOILETTE
8999	OTHER MANUF GOODS NES		657.3		747.0		704.8		839.5	OUVRAGES DIVERS NDA
89993	ARTIFICIAL FLOWERS ETC	W 125342	468.9	W 127956	483.7	W 124177	413.3	W 142855	490.0	FLEURS ARTIFICIELLES
9	GOODS NOT CLASSD BY KIND		364.1		550.1		222.3		389.9	ART TRANSACT NON CLASSES
931	*SPECIAL TRANSACTIONS		324.1		507.4		184.9		357.9	TRANS.SPECIALES

1. HISTORICAL SERIES, 1962–1997 GENERAL TRADE, IMPORTS C.I.F., EXPORTS F.O.B.
SERIES HISTORIQUES, 1962–1997 COMMERCE GENERAL, IMPORTATIONS C.A.F., EXPORTATIONS F.O.B

YEAR ANNEE	VALUE IN MILLION HONGKONG DOLLARS / VALEUR EN MILLION HONGKONG DOLLARS: MERCHANDISE – MARCHANDISE IMPORTS	MERCHANDISE – MARCHANDISE EXPORTS	GOLD – OR IMPORTS	GOLD – OR EXPORTS	CONVERSION FACTORS U.S. CENTS PER HONG KONG DOLLAR / FACTEURS DE CONVERSION CENTS E.U. PAR HONG KONG DOLLAR IMPORTS	EXPORTS	INDEX NUMBERS – INDICES: QUANTUM IMPORTS	QUANTUM EXPORTS	UNIT VALUE – VALEUR UNITAIRE IMPORTS	UNIT VALUE – VALEUR UNITAIRE EXPORTS
1962	6657.00	4387.00	227.80	205.50	17.5000	17.5000				
1963	7412.00	4991.00	245.10	244.60	17.5000	17.5000				
1964	8551.00	5784.00	156.10	156.80	17.5000	17.5000				
1965	8965.00	6530.00	308.90	298.80	17.5000	17.5000				
1966	10097.00	7563.00	285.10	293.00	17.5000	17.5000				
1967	10449.00	8781.00	385.70	358.10	17.3600	17.3600				
1968	12472.00	10570.00	254.70	164.40	16.5000	16.5000				
1969	14893.00	13197.00	448.40	183.70	16.5000	16.5000				
1970	17607.00	15238.00	306.70	192.40	16.5000	16.5000				
1971	20256.00	17164.00	373.20	249.00	16.7406	16.7497				
1972	21764.00	19400.00	207.20	175.00	17.7797	17.7739				
1973	29005.00	25999.00	428.10	205.00	19.4929	19.5030				
1974	34120.00	30036.00	389.10	240.00	19.8345	19.8399				
1975	33472.00	29832.00			20.1870	20.1755				
1976	43292.00	41557.00			20.5157	20.5169				
1977	48701.00	44833.00			21.4726	21.4712				
1978	63056.00	53908.00			21.3328	21.3305				
1979	85837.00	75934.00			19.9650	19.9585				
1980	111651.00	98242.00			20.0746	20.0733	30	26	58	59
1981	138374.80	122162.70			17.8357	17.7939	33	30	65	64
1982	142892.60	127384.70			16.4839	16.4734	33	29	68	68
1983	175442.40	160699.40			13.6848	13.6594	36	34	76	75
1984	223370.20	221440.80			12.7909	12.7908	41	41	85	85
1985	231419.70	235152.30			12.8351	12.8355	44	43	83	85
1986	275966.80	276527.80			12.8157	12.8158	49	50	87	87
1987	377933.00	378020.40			12.8237	12.8237	65	66	90	90
1988	498774.40	493054.20			12.8106	12.8106	82	84	94	93
1989	562793.10	570512.40			12.8209	12.8201	90	92	98	98
1990	642354.10	639873.90			12.8393	12.8400	100	100	100	100
1991	778862.50	765882.60			12.8700	12.8710	119	117	102	103
1992	955119.90	924761.50			12.9206	12.9208	145	140	102	104
1993	1072541.00	1046208.00			12.9272	12.9271	164	160	102	103
1994	1250793.00	1170084.00			12.9391	12.9392	187	176	104	105
1995	1491094.00	1344122.00			12.9268	12.9267	213	197	109	108
1996	1535646.00	1397975.00			12.9294	12.9294	222	207	108	108
1997	1615096.00	1455954.00			12.9166	12.9168	238	223	106	106

2. IMPORTS BY BROAD ECONOMIC CATEGORY AND EXPORTS BY INDUSTRIAL ORIGIN. (PERCENTAGE OF TOTAL VALUE)
IMPORTATIONS PAR CATEGORIES ECONOMIQUES ET EXPORTATIONS PAR BRANCHE D'ACTIVITE.(EN POURCENTAGE DE LA VALEUR TOTALE)

IMPORTS – IMPORTATIONS

	1991	1992	1993	1994	1995	1996	1997
TOTAL IMPORTS–IMPORTATIONS TOTALES	100.	100.	100.	100.	100.	100.	100.
1 FOOD BEV–ALIMENTATION BOISSONS	5.8	5.2	4.6	4.8	4.6	4.7	5.0
11 PRIMARY–PRODUITS DE BASE	3.2	2.9	2.6	2.6	2.5	2.5	2.6
111 FOR INDUSTRY–POUR L'INDUSTRIE	0.5	0.5	0.4	0.3	0.3	0.2	0.2
112 FOR HOUSEHOLDS–POUR LES MENAGES	2.7	2.4	2.2	2.2	2.2	2.3	2.4
12 PROCESSED–PRODUITS ELABORES	2.6	2.3	2.1	2.2	2.2	2.2	2.4
121 FOR INDUSTRY–POUR L'INDUSTRIE	0.2	0.2	0.2	0.3	0.3	0.4	0.5
122 FOR HOUSEHOLDS–POUR LES MENAGES	2.4	2.1	1.9	1.9	1.8	1.9	1.9
2 IND SUPPLIES–APPROV INDUSTRIELS	35.3	32.5	30.2	31.1	31.5	30.2	28.9
21 PRIMARY–PRODUITS DE BASE	3.9	3.6	3.3	3.4	3.4	3.1	2.9
22 PROCESSED–PRODUITS ELABORES	31.4	28.9	26.9	27.6	28.1	27.1	26.1
3 FUELS–COMBUSTIBLES	2.1	2.0	1.8	1.9	1.9	2.2	2.0
31 PRIMARY–PRODUITS DE BASE	0.4	0.4	0.3	0.2	0.2	0.2	0.3
32 PROCESSED–PRODUITS ELABORES	1.6	1.6	1.5	1.7	1.7	2.0	1.7
321 MOTOR SPIRIT–ESSENCE	0.1	0.1	0.1	0.1	0.1	0.1	0.1
322 OTHER–AUTRES	1.6	1.5	1.3	1.6	1.6	1.9	1.6
4 MACHINERY–EQUIPEMENT	19.0	20.7	22.4	22.8	25.4	26.5	29.2
41 CAPITAL EQUIPMENT–MACHINES	12.2	13.8	14.9	14.7	15.8	17.0	18.6
42 PARTS–PIECES ACCESSOIRES	6.7	6.9	7.5	8.1	9.6	9.5	10.6
5 TRANSPORT–TRANSPORT	3.5	4.9	6.2	5.3	5.1	4.6	4.5
51 PASSENGER CARS–AUTOMOBILES	0.8	1.7	2.7	1.9	1.4	1.1	1.5
52 OTHER–AUTRES	1.5	1.7	2.0	1.9	2.1	1.7	1.0
521 INDUSTRIAL–INDUSTRIELS	1.0	1.1	1.2	1.1	1.4	1.2	0.6
522 NON INDUSTRIAL–NON INDUSTRIEL	0.4	0.6	0.8	0.8	0.7	0.5	0.4
53 PARTS–PIECES ACCESSOIRES	1.3	1.5	1.5	1.6	1.6	1.8	1.9
6 CONSUM GOODS–BIENS CONSOMMATION	33.9	34.3	34.4	33.7	31.0	31.2	30.0
61 DURABLE–DURABLES	9.7	9.9	9.6	10.0	9.3	8.9	8.1
62 SEMI DURABLE–SEMI DURABLES	20.9	21.1	21.8	20.7	18.9	19.5	19.5
63 NON DURABLE–NON DURABLES	3.3	3.3	3.0	2.9	2.8	2.9	2.5
7 GOODS NES–BIENS NDA	0.4	0.5	0.4	0.4	0.4	0.5	0.5

EXPORTS – EXPORTATIONS

	1991	1992	1993	1994	1995	1996	1997
TOTAL EXPORTS–EXPORTATIONS TOTALES	100.	100.	100.	100.	100.	100.	100.
1 AGRICULTURE	1.7	1.5	1.2	1.3	1.1	1.1	1.0
2 MINING QUARRY–INDUS EXTRACTIVES	1.2	0.9	0.9	0.9	0.9	0.8	0.8
3 MANUFACTURING–IND MANUFACTUR	97.1	97.6	97.9	97.9	98.0	98.1	98.2
31 FOOD BEV TOBACCO–ALIM BOISS TAB	3.2	2.9	2.6	2.7	2.5	2.6	2.4
32 TEXTILES–INDUSTRIES TEXTILES	34.0	31.8	30.2	28.9	26.6	26.6	26.5
33 WOOD & PRODUCTS–BOIS & PRODUITS	0.4	0.4	0.4	0.5	0.5	0.5	0.5
34 PAPER & PRODUCTS–PAPIER & PRODT	1.7	1.7	1.6	1.6	1.7	1.8	1.8
35 CHEMICALS–INDUSTRIES CHIMIQUES	9.9	10.2	10.0	10.7	11.7	11.6	11.3
36 NON METAL MIN–MIN NON METAL	0.7	0.9	1.0	1.0	1.0	0.9	0.9
37 BASIC METAL–IND METAL BASE	1.6	2.0	2.1	2.0	2.5	2.7	2.5
38 METAL MANUF–MANUF METAL	34.8	36.2	39.4	39.9	41.3	41.2	41.8
39 OTH MANUF IND–AUTRES MANUF	10.8	11.5	10.7	10.5	10.2	10.2	10.5

3. TRADE BY PRINCIPAL COUNTRIES OF ORIGIN AND DESTINATION (VALUE IN MILLION U.S. DOLLARS)
ECHANGES SELON LES PRINCIPAUX PAYS D'ORIGINE ET DE DESTINATION (VALEUR EN MILLIONS DE DOLLARS EU)

COUNTRIES–PAYS	GENERAL IMPORTS C.I.F. IMPORTATIONS GENERALES C.A.F					COUNTRIES–PAYS	EXPORTS EXPORTATIONS ES F.O.B.				
	1993	1994	1995	1996	1997		1993	1994	1995	1996	1997
World	141307.6	165877.6	196071.8	201284.0	213300.0	Monde	135384.6	151465.2	173870.8	180914.4	188201.3
Africa	1327.0	1462.4	1552.9	1173.4	1146.7	Afrique	2040.5	1982.5	2454.8	2322.5	2154.8
Americas	12201.0	14597.6	18102.4	18356.8	19740.1	Amériques	36940.4	41836.3	45431.1	45522.7	48947.4
– Northern America	11335.8	13669.9	16880.7	16990.8	18025.5	– Amérique du Nord	33431.5	37574.9	40504.7	40879.1	43720.8
– LAIA	843.4	897.4	1182.8	1314.9	1657.1	– ALAI	2048.1	2651.8	3357.8	3211.8	3466.4
– CACM	4.6	7.6	11.4	14.4	18.3	– MCAC	141.0	153.3	145.0	142.4	171.7
– Caribbean	4.3	11.2	6.8	5.4	11.6	– Caraïbes	192.0	182.7	196.1	189.7	202.7
– Rest of America	12.9	11.4	20.7	31.2	27.7	– Autre Amérique	1127.8	1273.5	1227.4	1099.8	1385.8
Asia excl fmr USSR	108667.5	127267.9	149541.2	153387.8	161662.7	Asie anc. URSS exclus	70185.3	79764.9	94434.5	100278.6	103390.0
– Middle East	880.7	1423.0	1256.3	1017.5	1176.0	– Moyen–Orient	2097.7	2028.3	2511.1	2646.0	2591.2
Asia former USSR	9.2	22.0	18.7	0.0	0.9	Asie ancienne URSS	4.6	5.7	3.9	7.4	9.0
Europe excl fmr USSR	16910.7	20092.6	23915.6	24937.1	26667.1	Europe anc. URSS exclus	23557.8	24812.9	28092.2	29124.9	29983.2
– European Union	14500.1	17146.4	20936.0	22472.4	23938.0	– Union Européenne	21853.3	23035.5	26083.3	26967.1	27770.1
– Eastern Europe	184.1	186.0	132.4	189.8	123.1	– Europe de l'Est	342.0	376.0	502.3	593.0	589.7
– Rest of Europe	2226.5	2760.1	2847.3	2274.9	2605.9	– Autre de l'Europe	1362.5	1401.4	1506.6	1564.8	1623.4
Europe former USSR	100.7	305.9	489.0	680.4	863.0	Europe ancienne URSS	328.8	323.5	348.1	529.0	484.1
Oceania	2074.0	2111.2	2434.4	2731.2	3199.7	Océanie	2223.3	2646.2	2983.2	3053.0	3151.6
Other	17.5	17.9	17.6	17.2	19.8	Autre	104.0	93.1	123.0	76.3	81.2
China/Chine	52003.6	60937.3	69742.6	73775.4	78598.6	China/Chine	43694.2	49674.0	57870.3	61999.0	65608.4
Japan/Japon	23031.8	25289.0	28718.5	26982.3	28690.8	USA/Etats–Unis d'Amer	31160.4	35177.1	37851.8	38368.0	40940.7
Other Asia n.e.s.	12154.2	13886.6	16710.7	15929.9	16088.9	Japan/Japon	6959.5	8437.3	10594.9	11838.5	11417.5
USA/Etats–Unis d'Amer	10636.2	12519.4	15428.6	15785.5	16444.7	Germany/Allemagne	7083.1	7054.0	7500.3	7587.5	7332.8
Korea, Republic of	6341.4	7655.2	10147.4	10844.3	10934.4	United Kingdom	4593.0	4870.7	5588.8	6029.6	6435.7
Singapore/Singapour	6189.7	8026.8	10101.7	10574.1	10378.0	Singapore/Singapour	3683.1	4215.8	4945.3	4965.9	4884.9
United Kingdom	3026.5	3736.7	4133.9	4699.6	5621.4	Other Asia n.e.s.	3669.5	3703.4	4636.6	4340.4	4749.0
Germany/Allemagne	3248.5	3719.9	4147.1	4391.6	5005.5	Netherlands/Pays–Bas	2132.7	2370.0	2825.1	2965.4	3227.3
Malaysia/Malaisie	2049.6	2606.7	3724.4	4398.9	4917.8	Korea, Republic of	2298.2	2418.6	2821.1	2980.3	2810.4
Italy/Italie	2311.3	2947.2	3572.6	4117.9	4007.4	France, Monaco	2012.9	2133.2	2666.5	2814.8	3035.9
France, Monaco	1913.7	1991.6	3739.8	3320.1	2865.8	Canada	2248.1	2377.1	2633.6	2491.7	2762.3
Thailand/Thaïlande	1682.5	2225.0	2728.9	3070.6	3378.9	Australia/Australie	1779.9	2127.4	2375.7	2438.3	2482.7
Switzerland,Liechtenst.	2137.7	2676.4	2702.7	2124.3	2436.0	Philippines	1339.1	1870.7	2009.3	2150.2	2209.0
Australia/Australie	1754.3	1711.3	1931.7	2185.9	2665.6	Italy/Italie	1479.0	1601.6	1805.1	1772.0	1881.0
India/Inde	1221.7	1463.8	1876.9	1968.2	2127.6	Macau/Macao	1411.7	1560.4	1684.4	1842.5	1553.7
Netherlands/Pays–Bas	1344.9	1536.0	1811.6	1863.5	1910.0	Thailand/Thaïlande	1021.3	1292.7	1624.2	1810.8	1869.7
Indonesia/Indonésie	943.3	1288.9	1633.4	1631.1	1709.9	Malaysia/Malaisie	901.3	1155.6	1572.2	1703.3	1727.2
Belgium–Luxembourg	1273.6	1480.2	1354.2	1248.8	1341.2	Spain/Espagne	995.7	1121.4	1330.6	1305.7	1389.1
Canada	699.3	1150.1	1450.9	1204.2	1579.7	Panama	1118.5	1266.7	1220.1	1091.6	1376.0
So. African Customs Un	1242.8	1333.4	1398.9	1001.5	923.1	United Arab Emirates	884.4	971.4	1196.3	1278.9	1284.2
Philippines	583.7	609.1	863.2	951.7	1267.8	Belgium–Luxembourg	1047.9	1051.2	1127.0	1157.1	1186.4
Israel/Israël	642.1	718.3	777.5	772.4	786.6	Switzerland,Liechtenst.	975.9	979.4	1037.4	1057.5	1111.0
Pakistan	360.1	574.4	626.5	828.8	742.3	Indonesia/Indonésie	844.8	920.6	1061.9	1006.2	917.2
Sweden/Suède	339.2	388.1	484.4	793.3	1023.7	Brazil/Brésil	306.0	548.6	1204.1	1146.7	1090.3
Spain/Espagne	343.7	424.7	478.9	602.2	613.3	Sweden/Suède	716.9	824.3	731.9	816.9	887.1
Brazil/Brésil	398.8	443.8	420.4	509.5	683.6	So. African Customs Un	633.9	697.0	855.5	797.0	724.1
Russian Federation	91.4	281.7	460.8	652.3	775.1	Austria/Autriche	656.1	745.1	828.8	779.3	691.1
Finland/Finlande	167.9	298.0	470.7	608.9	582.0	India/Inde	385.1	522.3	802.5	769.1	691.8
New Zealand	276.6	348.8	431.7	481.6	471.7	Viet Nam	510.1	523.7	636.9	601.4	634.6
United Arab Emirates	396.5	562.3	404.9	270.3	292.0	Denmark/Danemark	412.5	477.2	572.8	643.6	654.2
Denmark/Danemark	223.5	274.8	299.6	386.9	455.7	Chile/Chili	316.4	453.3	616.6	603.8	627.1
Saudi Arabia	117.6	227.7	364.0	250.2	346.4	Saudi Arabia	541.8	511.4	520.4	528.6	483.0
Argentina/Argentine	139.2	186.9	295.8	251.1	299.3	Mexico/Mexique	512.8	559.7	391.9	351.4	485.6
Austria/Autriche	183.8	212.1	263.0	239.3	237.7	Bangladesh	358.9	433.5	500.3	448.3	504.2
Turkey/Turquie	114.1	223.5	237.7	202.8	259.1	Argentina/Argentine	420.5	502.2	360.9	433.1	493.8
Macau/Macao	231.8	216.7	204.7	183.0	195.7	Israel/Israël	333.5	374.8	426.9	423.7	467.7
Viet Nam	138.8	148.0	173.6	196.4	265.2	Norway,Svalbard and JM	332.0	373.4	413.8	422.3	429.5
Mexico/Mexique	90.2	96.0	216.6	224.2	166.2	Turkey/Turquie	318.9	199.2	408.6	485.9	472.6
Chile/Chili	99.3	68.0	106.9	158.0	315.3	Russian Federation	315.6	303.4	315.5	493.7	443.3
Oman	114.5	213.5	77.4	92.6	140.3	Sri Lanka	337.2	317.7	363.5	352.6	364.2

(VALUE AS PERCENTAGE OF WORLD TOTAL)(VALEURS EN POURCENTAGE DU TOTAL MONDIAL)

	1988	1989	1990	1991	1992	1993	1994	1995	1996	1997		1988	1989	1990	1991	1992	1993	1994	1995	1996	1997
Africa	0.8	0.8	0.6	0.8	0.9	0.9	0.9	0.8	0.6	0.5	Afrique	1.7	1.5	1.7	1.7	1.9	1.5	1.3	1.4	1.3	1.1
Americas	10.1	9.8	9.8	9.8	9.0	8.6	8.8	9.2	9.1	9.3	Amériques	27.9	29.0	27.8	26.8	27.3	27.3	27.6	26.1	25.2	26.0
– Northern America	9.0	8.8	9.1	9.0	8.4	8.0	8.2	8.6	8.4	8.5	– Amérique du Nord	26.7	27.4	25.9	24.5	24.8	24.7	24.8	23.3	22.6	23.2
– LAIA	1.0	1.0	0.7	0.7	0.7	0.6	0.5	0.6	0.7	0.8	– ALAI	0.4	0.6	0.9	1.2	1.4	1.5	1.8	1.9	1.8	1.8
– CACM	0.0	0.0	0.0	0.0	0.0	0.0	0.0	0.0	0.0	0.0	– MCAC	0.1	0.1	0.1	0.1	0.1	0.1	0.1	0.1	0.1	0.1
– Caribbean	0.0	0.0	0.0	0.0	0.0	0.0	0.0	0.0	0.0	0.0	– Caraïbes	0.2	0.2	0.2	0.2	0.2	0.1	0.1	0.1	0.1	0.1
– Rest of America	0.0	0.0	0.0	0.0	0.0	0.0	0.0	0.0	0.0	0.0	– Autre Amérique	0.5	0.7	0.7	0.9	0.9	0.8	0.8	0.7	0.6	0.7
Asia excl fmr USSR	74.5	75.4	74.6	75.8	76.2	76.9	76.7	76.3	76.2	75.8	Asie anc. URSS exclus	49.2	48.7	48.1	48.9	50.4	51.8	52.7	54.3	55.4	54.9
– Middle East	0.3	0.4	0.3	0.2	0.4	0.6	0.9	0.6	0.5	0.6	– Moyen–Orient	1.5	1.5	1.4	1.5	1.5	1.5	1.3	1.4	1.5	1.4
Asia former USSR						0.0	0.0	0.0	0.0	0.0	Asie ancienne URSS						0.0	0.0	0.0	0.0	0.0
Europe excl fmr USSR	12.9	12.6	13.4	12.1	12.3	12.0	12.1	12.2	12.4	12.5	Europe anc. URSS exclus	18.6	18.3	20.3	20.5	18.4	17.4	16.4	16.2	16.1	15.9
– European Union	11.0	10.6	10.5	9.7	10.2	10.3	10.3	10.7	11.2	11.2	– Union Européenne	17.1	16.8	18.7	19.0	17.1	16.1	15.2	15.0	14.9	14.8
– Eastern Europe	0.2	0.1	0.1	0.1	0.1	0.1	0.1	0.1	0.1	0.1	– Europe de l'Est	0.2	0.3	0.2	0.3	0.2	0.3	0.2	0.3	0.3	0.3
– Rest of Europe	1.7	1.8	2.9	2.3	2.0	1.6	1.7	1.5	1.1	1.2	– Autre de l'Europe	1.3	1.3	1.4	1.3	1.1	1.0	0.9	0.9	0.9	0.9
Europe former USSR	0.2	0.1	0.1	0.1	0.1	0.1	0.2	0.2	0.3	0.4	Europe ancienne URSS	0.1	0.1	0.1	0.2	0.2	0.2	0.2	0.2	0.3	0.3
Oceania	1.4	1.2	1.3	1.6	1.5	1.5	1.3	1.2	1.4	1.5	Océanie	2.3	2.2	1.9	1.8	1.8	1.6	1.7	1.7	1.7	1.7
Other	0.1	0.1	0.0	0.0	0.0	0.0	0.0	0.0	0.0	0.0	Autre	0.2	0.1	0.1	0.1	0.1	0.1	0.1	0.1	0.0	0.0
China/Chine	31.1	35.0	35.8	36.4	36.0	36.8	36.7	35.6	36.7	36.8	China/Chine	26.9	25.7	24.7	27.1	29.6	32.3	32.8	33.3	34.3	34.9
Japan/Japon	18.8	16.4	15.7	15.8	16.9	16.3	15.2	14.6	13.4	13.5	USA/Etats–Unis d'Amer	24.8	25.3	24.1	22.7	23.1	23.0	23.2	21.8	21.2	21.8
Other Asia n.e.s.	8.9	9.2	8.8	9.2	8.8	8.6	8.4	8.5	7.9	7.5	Japan/Japon	5.9	6.2	5.7	5.4	5.2	5.1	5.6	6.1	6.5	6.1
USA/Etats–Unis d'Amer	8.5	8.3	8.4	8.3	7.7	7.5	7.5	7.9	7.8	7.7	Germany/Allemagne				6.7	5.3	5.2	4.7	4.3	4.2	3.9
Korea, Republic of	5.3	4.5	4.3	4.5	4.5	4.5	4.6	5.2	5.4	5.1	United Kingdom	4.5	4.1	4.0	3.7	3.6	3.4	3.2	3.2	3.3	3.4
Singapore/Singapour	3.7	4.0	4.0	3.9	4.0	4.4	4.8	5.2	5.3	4.9	Singapore/Singapour	2.8	3.0	3.2	2.7	2.6	2.7	2.8	2.8	2.7	2.6
United Kingdom	2.6	2.3	2.5	2.3	2.4	2.1	2.3	2.1	2.3	2.6	Other Asia n.e.s.	3.7	3.7	4.2	4.1	3.5	2.7	2.4	2.7	2.4	2.5
Germany/Allemagne				2.1	2.2	2.3	2.2	2.1	2.2	2.3	Netherlands/Pays–Bas	1.7	1.5	1.7	1.6	1.6	1.6	1.6	1.6	1.6	1.7
Malaysia/Malaisie	1.2	1.2	1.2	1.2	1.3	1.5	1.6	1.9	2.2	2.3	Korea, Republic of	2.6	2.6	2.3	2.2	1.6	1.7	1.6	1.6	1.6	1.5
Italy/Italie	1.6	1.8	1.6	1.5	1.5	1.6	1.8	1.8	2.0	1.9	France, Monaco	1.5	1.4	1.6	1.7	1.5	1.5	1.4	1.5	1.6	1.6

4. General Imports C.I.F. by Commodities according to the S.I.T.C. (Rev. 2) in million U.S. Dollars
Importations Générales C.A.F. par Produits d'après la C.T.C.I. (Rév. 2) en millions de Dollars E.U.

SITC CTCI	COMMODITY	1994 QUANTITY QUANTITE	1994 VALUE VALEUR	1995 QUANTITY QUANTITE	1995 VALUE VALEUR	1996 QUANTITY QUANTITE	1996 VALUE VALEUR	1997 QUANTITY QUANTITE	1997 VALUE VALEUR	PRODUIT
	ALL COMMODITIES		165877.6		196071.8		201284.0		213300.1	TOUS PRODUITS
0	FOOD AND LIVE ANIMALS		6552.1		7497.2		7986.7		8477.1	ALIMENTS,ANIMAUX VIVANTS
01	MEAT AND PREPARATIONS		1003.7		1380.8		1507.4		1667.7	VIANDES ET PREPARATIONS
011	MEAT FRESH,CHILLD,FROZEN	W 669084	840.7	W 931530	1194.3	W 1039580	1285.9	W 1194689	1448.6	VIANDES FRAICHES,REF,CONGE
0114	POULTRY FRESH CHLLD,FRZN	W 490146	500.8	W 688381	746.5	W 789225	832.4	W 864048	884.4	VOLAILLES MORTES
03	FISH AND PREPARATIONS		1638.0		1821.2		1914.5		2089.0	POISSONS ET PREPARATIONS
034	FISH,FRESH,CHILLED,FROZN		414.7	W 164084	455.5	W 154612	541.6		724.7	POISSON FRAIS, REFRIG,CONG
036	SHELL FISH FRESH,FROZEN	W 110148	799.4	W 111330	884.7	W 104051	869.4	W 91165	837.3	CRUSTACES,MOLLUSQUES
05	VEGETABLES AND FRUIT		1531.3		1621.8		1650.0		1733.2	LEGUMES ET FRUITS
057	FRUIT,NUTS,FRESH,DRIED	W 787349	812.3	W 831496	916.5	W 879541	999.5	W 1002816	1115.2	FRUITS FRAIS OU SECS
09	MISC EDIBLE PRODUCTS		484.3		588.5		688.2		782.4	PREP ALIMENTAIRES DIVERSES
098	EDIBLE PRODCTS,PREPS NES	W 184213	456.7	W 202839	530.2	W 218853	633.7	W 245771	723.8	PREP ALIMENTAIRES NDA
1	BEVERAGES AND TOBACCO		2481.4		2455.5		2436.4		2027.6	BOISSONS ET TABACS
11	BEVERAGES		952.4		1053.4		996.4		1129.7	BOISSONS
112	ALCOHOLIC BEVERAGES	W 212923	648.9	W 269850	710.9	W 248399	632.8	W 266588	748.5	BOISSONS ALCOOLIQUES
12	TOBACCO AND MANUFACTURES		1529.0		1402.1		1440.0		898.0	TABACS BRUTS FABRIQUES
122	TOBACCO,MANUFACTURED	W 65501	1432.7	W 60116	1295.4		1344.5		762.9	TABACS FABRIQUES
1222	CIGARETTES	W 64702	1425.0	W 59015	1285.4		1332.6		743.3	CIGARETTES
2	CRUDE MATERLS,EXCL FUELS		3034.4		4101.4		3986.8		3867.7	MAT BRUTES NON COMESTIBLES
21	HIDES,SKINS,FURS UNDRSSD		437.1		529.3		615.8		503.8	CUIRS,PEAUX BRUTS
24	CORK AND WOOD		290.0		365.3		461.7		669.0	LIEGE ET BOIS
26	TEXTILE FIBRES AND WASTE		1007.2		1256.8		1112.2		994.5	FIBRES TEXTILES
28	METALLIFEROUS ORES,SCRAP		241.8		705.6		646.1		600.7	MINERAIS METAL,DECHETS
288	NONFERR METAL SCRAP NES	W 304279	166.6	W 634801	607.7	W 542877	545.3	W 454069	492.1	DECHETS NON FERREUX
2882	OTHER BASE MTL SCRAP NES	W 258463	163.0	W 576919	600.2	W 511850	539.7	W 447684	491.1	AUTRES DECHETS
29	CRUDE ANIMAL,VEG MAT NES		566.7		588.5		559.8		500.5	MATIERES BRUTES ANIM,VEGET
3	MINERAL FUELS ETC		3166.5		3720.3		4497.8		4131.9	COMBUSTIBLES MINERAUX LUB
33	PETROLEUM AND PRODUCTS		2371.2		2877.9		3570.0		3128.3	PETROLE ET DERIVES
334	PETROLEUM PRODUCTS,REFIN	MW 14012	2343.1	MW 16516	2841.6	MW 17497	3531.9	MW 15983	3098.4	PRODUITS RAFFINES
3342	KEROSENE,OTH MEDIUM OILS	W 2827154	526.7	W 2815298	525.9	W 3018046	687.9	W 2614210	564.0	PETR LAMPANTS,AUT HUIL
33421	KEROSENE INCL JET FUEL	W 2804088	520.9	W 2808657	523.9	W 3016360	687.3	W 2614027	563.9	PETROLES LAMPANTS
3343	GAS OILS	W 6425876	1082.3	W 8631872	1474.3	MW 9092	1906.2	W 8932850	1742.8	GAS OILS
4	ANIMAL,VEGETABLE OIL,FAT		384.5		543.5		566.3		968.8	HUILES,GRAISSES ANIM,VEG
42	FIXED VEGETABLE OIL,FAT		361.7		517.4		542.9		939.6	HUILES VEGETALES FIXES
423	FIXED VEG OILS,SOFT	W 291716	222.1	W 337674	265.3	W 475607	335.0	W 1299442	839.7	HUILES VEGET DOUCES FIXES
5	CHEMCLS,RELATED PROD NES		10767.5		14308.7		13477.6		13333.5	PRODUITS CHIMIQUES
51	ORGANIC CHEMICALS		1266.0		1908.2		1741.5		1595.8	PROD CHIMIQ ORGANIQUES
52	INORGANIC CHEMICALS		567.2		625.3		580.2		577.3	PROD CHIM INORGANIQUES
53	DYES,TANNING,COLOUR PROD		1062.4		1127.6		1237.1		1262.9	PROD TEINTURE,COLORANTS
531	SYNT DYE,NAT INDGO,LAKES	W 56287	498.4	W 61714	478.6	W 64193	504.0	W 60430	484.1	MAT COLOR ORGAN,LAQUES
533	PIGMENTS,PAINTS,ETC		512.7		590.6		663.9		711.3	PIGMENTS,PEINTURES,VERNIS
541	*MEDICINAL,PHARM PRODUCT		1021.8		1178.1		1216.4		1147.2	PROD MEDICINAUX PHARMACEUT
5417	MEDICAMENTS		521.8		621.6		680.8		691.6	MEDICAMENTS
55	PERFUME,CLEANING ETC PRD		904.8		1104.0		1195.1		1199.6	PROD POUR PARFUM,TOILETTE
553	PERFUMERY,COSMETICS,ETC		538.9		652.3		711.6		721.8	PRODUITS DE PARFUMERIE
58	PLASTIC MATERIALS ETC		4889.5		7069.0		6287.6		6329.5	MAT PLAST ARTIFICIELLES
582	PROD OF CONDENSATION ETC	W 430337	832.8	W 584378	1342.6	W 611705	1266.8	W 742332	1359.8	PROD CONDENS,POLYCOND
5823	ALKYDS,OTHER POLYESTERS	W 272150	451.7	W 395391	827.9	W 387980	687.0	W 476610	714.7	ALKYDES ET AUT POLYESTERS
58231	— IN PRIMARY FORMS	W 249775	369.0	W 368641	720.0	W 359941	565.4	W 449700	613.4	SOUS FORMES PRIMAIRES
583	POLYMERIZATION ETC PRODS	W 4293074	4007.8	W 5256560	5664.9	W 5211697	4960.6	W 5734655	4901.0	PROD POLYMERISATION
5831	POLYETHYLENE	W 904952	547.2	W 1144790	877.8	W 1146092	809.5	W 1030713	751.8	POLYETHYLENE
58311	— IN PRIMARY FORMS	W 591407	398.0	W 797390	705.1	W 824307	652.6	W 738408	622.6	POLYETHYLENE PRIMAIRES
5832	POLYPROPYLENE	W 424742	383.3	W 609100	672.4	W 595326	601.8	W 611729	580.3	POLYPROPYLENE
5833	POLYSTYRENE,ITS COPOLYMR	W 1521017	1412.1	W 1728335	2054.5	W 1752935	1591.5	W 1823084	1476.4	POLYPROPYLENE COPOLYMERES
58331	— IN PRIMARY FORMS	W 1284467	1299.3	W 1487043	1908.6	W 1530370	1488.7	W 1577430	1383.7	SOUS FORMES PRIMAIRES
5834	POLYVINYL CHLORIDE	W 734987	900.0	W 829517	1073.8	W 886762	1023.7	W 990096	1109.8	CHLORURE DE POLYVINYLE
58343	— PLATES,STRIP,ETC NES	W 299794	573.8	W 305014	630.9	W 313086	604.8	W 329311	608.5	SOUS FORME DE PLAQUES
5839	OTH POLYMRZTION ETC PROD	W 633710	646.1	W 874156	848.3	W 756482	796.1	W 1202765	840.0	AUT PROD POLYMER COPOLYM
59	CHEMICAL MATERIALS NES		958.1		1220.6		1165.9		1183.8	MAT PROD CHIMIQUES NDA
598	MISCEL CHEM PRODUCTS NES		699.2		845.1		805.3		827.7	PROD DIV INDUST CHIM NDA
5989	CHEM PRODUCTS,PREPS NES		576.6		707.4		694.3		724.0	PROD PREP CHIMIQUES NDA
6	BASIC MANUFACTURES		34068.5		40059.4		40536.7		40915.4	ART MANUFACTURES
61	LEATHER,DRESSED FUR,ETC		2309.6		2773.8		3049.8		2901.7	CUIRS,PELLETERIES
611	LEATHER		1786.3		2245.8		2373.5		2248.7	CUIRS,PEAUX PREPARES
6114	LEATHR BOVINE NES,EQUINE		914.4	A 72408	1371.9		1525.5		1502.1	CUIRS DE BOVINS
62	RUBBER MANUFACTURES NES		410.2		515.0		572.7		699.0	CAOUTCHOUC MANUFACTURE
63	WOOD,CORK MANUFACTRS NES		806.6		896.3		905.0		988.8	OUVRAGES LIEGE ET BOIS
634	VENEERS,PLYWOOD,ETC		539.0		581.0		563.3		596.2	PLACAGES,CONTRE–PLAQUES
64	PAPER,PAPERBOARD AND MFR		2613.2		3313.8		3325.5		3465.2	PAPIERS,CARTONS & OUVRAGES
641	PAPER AND PAPERBOARD		1997.5		2533.9		2485.7		2600.8	PAPIERS ET CARTONS
6418	COATED ETC PAPER NES BLK	W 737644	584.8	W 799406	739.3	W 901952	705.4	W 995358	766.2	PAP,CARTONS COUCHES,ENDUITS
64189	COATED PAPER ETC NES	W 676559	503.5	W 759639	668.9	W 853142	630.0	W 947720	678.8	PAPIERS,CARTONS COUCHES
642	PAPER,ETC,PRECUT,ARTS OF		615.8		780.0		839.8		864.4	PAP,CARTONS DECOUPES
65	TEXTILE YARN,FABRICS,ETC		15349.8		16953.6		16597.0		16281.9	FILS,TISSUS,ARTICLES TEXTILE
651	TEXTILE YARN	W 913149	3124.8	W 1025891	3835.7	W 1103864	3870.0	W 1127731	3998.6	FILS TEXTILES
6512	WOOL,HAIR YARN,INCL TOPS	W 55239	559.0	W 53640	583.4	W 57933	579.0	W 60511	621.4	FILS DE LAINE,DE POILS
6513	COTTON YARN	W 292868	891.5	W 310770	1088.3	W 392477	1340.4	W 429893	1453.2	FILS DE COTON
6514	SYN FIB YRN,BULK,MONOFIL	W 384175	870.2	W 495394	1337.9	W 489170	1164.6	W 472518	1126.0	FILS CONT 85% FIB TEXT SYNTH
65144	— TEXTRD,CONT POLYESTER	W 232222	426.2	W 311581	730.8	W 345774	663.1	W 285533	496.0	FILS TEX FI CONT POLYESTERS
652	COTTON FABRICS,WOVEN	A 2431199	2272.8	A 2395198	2613.0	A 2233525	2681.1	A 2262000	2738.0	TISSUS DE COTON
6522	WOVEN COTTON BLEACHD,ETC	A 1717447	1831.7	A 1824235	2199.4	A 1645479	2210.4	A 1640497	2258.1	TISSUS COTON BLANCHIS ETC
65224	BLCHED COTTON FABRIC NES	A 1543566	1590.1	A 1625922	1899.2	A 1415454	1845.8	A 1364711	1810.3	AUT TIS PLUS 85% COT BLANCHI
653	WOVN MAN–MADE FIB FABRIC	A 4971345	4429.9	A 4965019	4908.5	A 4895258	4657.9	A 4658207	4162.9	TISSUS FIBRES SYNTH,ARTIF
6531	CONT SYNT WEAVES NONPILE	A 3024290	2817.8	A 3172170	3157.1	A 3279304	3014.7	A 3178258	2665.2	TISSUS FIBRES SYNTH CONTINUE
65315	CONT SYN TXTL FABRIC NES	A 2814443	2592.6	A 2955909	2920.0	A 3112573	2814.4	A 2990276	2446.9	TIS PLUS 85% TEXT SYNT CONT
6534	DISC SYN BLEND FABRC NES	A 985155	632.1	A 946653	680.3	A 897843	639.7	A 843323	575.9	TISSUS FIBRES SYNTH DISCONT
654	OTH WOVEN TEXTILE FABRIC		1095.9		971.4		837.8		866.8	TISSUS AUT COTON SYNT,ARTIF
655	KNITTED,ETC FABRICS	W 366574	2106.9	W 359292	2088.0	W 362741	2020.3	W 346303	2002.5	ETOF BONNETERIE PIECES ETC
6552	OTHER KNIT ETC FAB NONEL	W 366574	2106.9	W 359292	2088.0	W 362741	2020.3	W 346303	2002.5	ETOF BON NON ELAS NON SYNT
657	SPECIAL TXTL FABRC,PRODS		1156.2		1291.6		1312.9		1298.4	TISSUS SPECIAUX
6573	COATED ETC TEXTILES NES	W 220841	850.7	W 229709	960.7	W 250060	988.8	W 233494	966.2	TISSUS,ART MATIERE TEXT NDA
65732	PLASTIC COATED TEXTILES	W 213574	807.4	W 221147	910.7	W 242192	941.4	W 224935	913.6	TISSUS IMPREGNES
658	TEXTILE ARTICLES NES	MN 1241257	608.9	MN 1177809	637.7	MN 1028789	608.8	MN 1026632	599.2	ART FACONNES MAT TEXTILES
66	NONMETAL MINERAL MFS NES		5160.4		5701.2		5632.8		5815.3	ART MIN NON METALLIQUES
667	PEARL,PREC–,SEMI–P STONE		3338.3		3624.2		3362.3		3283.4	PERLES, PIERRES GEMMES
6672	DIAMONDS NONINDUST,UNSET		2915.1		3078.2		2958.4		2913.5	DIAMANTS BRUTS
66729	— CUT ETC NOT SET		2834.6		2968.9		2818.5		2739.1	DIAMANTS TAILLES
67	IRON AND STEEL		2873.9		3739.9		4081.8		3975.9	FER ET ACIER
673	IRON,STEEL SHAPES ETC	W 2683613	913.4	W 2123103	784.2	W 2233623	820.3	W 2455582	860.8	BARRES,PROFIL FER,ACIER
6732	IRON,STEEL BARS ETC	W 1771316	587.8	W 1450023	502.6	W 1553162	537.7	W 1774183	596.5	BARRES FER,ACIER
67326	IRN,OTH STL BARS HOTROLD	W 1702363	508.1	W 1343756	402.4	W 1483660	446.5	W 1699921	499.4	BARRES PLEINES FER,ACIER

4. General Imports C.I.F. by Commodities according to the S.I.T.C. (Rev. 2) in million U.S. Dollars
Importations Générales C.A.F. par Produits d'après la C.T.C.I. (Rév. 2) en millions de Dollars E.U.

SITC CTCI	COMMODITY	1994 QUANTITY QUANTITE	1994 VALUE VALEUR	1995 QUANTITY QUANTITE	1995 VALUE VALEUR	1996 QUANTITY QUANTITE	1996 VALUE VALEUR	1997 QUANTITY QUANTITE	1997 VALUE VALEUR	PRODUIT
674	IRN,STL UNIV,PLATE,SHEET	W 2014779	1474.7	W 2504396	2373.0	W 2962219	2587.8	W 3230457	2550.8	LARGES PLATS,TOLES
6746	IRN,STL THIN PLATE,ROLLD	W 1027136	941.2	W 1200973	1471.4	W 1575736	1625.3	W 1621207	1542.5	TOLES LAM MOINS 3MM
67463	— OF STAINLESS ETC STL	W 378558	652.5	W 432779	1067.6	W 601352	1141.0	W 642735	1082.8	TOL ACIER INOX MOINS 3 MM
68	NON-FERROUS METALS		1934.3		3133.1		3297.8		3530.4	METAUX NON FERREUX
682	COPPER EXC CEMENT COPPER	W 298247	926.6	W 371681	1392.1	W 435267	1424.5	W 522775	1614.4	CUIVRE
6822	COPPER,ALLOYS WORKED	W 274980	875.3	W 320418	1243.4	W 343721	1212.5	W 375956	1265.6	CUIVRE,ALLIAGES OUVRES
684	ALUMINIUM	W 250134	519.5	W 478398	1099.1	W 586552	1189.8	W 605911	1236.2	ALUMINIUM
6841	ALUMINIUM,ALLOYS,UNWRGHT	W 147913	224.0	W 362053	683.4	W 465610	742.4	W 479461	780.5	ALUMINIUM,ALLIAGES BRUTS
69	METAL MANUFACTURES NES		2610.8		3033.1		3074.7		3257.6	ART MANUFACT EN METAL NDA
697	BASE MTL HOUSEHOLD EQUIP		457.7		614.4		621.5		652.0	ART MENAGE MET COMMUNS
699	BASE METAL MFRS NES		962.4		1094.2		1074.1		1142.4	ART MANUFACTURES MET NDA
7	MACHINES,TRANSPORT EQUIP		57344.8		71542.0		73491.8		80475.3	MACHINES MATERIEL TRANSPORT
71	POWER GENERATING EQUIPMT		2318.6		2884.4		2796.5		2969.0	MACHINES GENERATRICES
713	INTRNL COMBUS PSTN ENGIN		659.5		910.4		953.3		946.5	MOTEURS EXPL COMB INT, PIECE
7139	PISTON ENGINE PARTS NES		345.7		507.7		565.2		670.9	PIECES POUR 713.2,3,8
716	ROTATING ELECTRIC PLANT		1269.8		1557.8		1427.8		1634.6	APP ELECTR ROTATIFS,PIECES
7162	AC MTRS,GENRTRS,GEN SETS	MN 1114290	932.8	MN 1215903	1059.3	MN 1144511	1040.7	MN 1351964	1172.0	MOTEURS ELECTRIQUES
71621	AC MTRS,INC UNIVRSL MTRS	MN 1114236	659.7	MN 1215861	799.3	MN 1144465	751.1	MN 1351920	865.1	MOT ELEC NON COUR CONTINU
72	MACHS FOR SPCL INDUSTRYS		2480.9		2725.3		3064.3		3395.5	MAC SPECIALES POUR INDUST
724	TEXTILE,LEATHER MACHNRY		893.4		841.4		992.5		1044.4	MACH POUR INDUSTRIE TEXTILE
728	OTH MACHY FOR SPCL INDUS		844.4		1006.9		1192.1		1313.4	AUT MACH IND PARTICULIERES
7284	MACHY FOR SPCL INDUS NES		706.2		819.5		984.1		1083.2	MACH SPEC IND PARTICUL.
73	METALWORKING MACHINERY		550.0		609.1		686.4		758.4	MACH TRAVAIL DES METAUX
74	GENRL INDUSTRL MACHY NES		4403.3		4931.5		5154.8		4934.3	MACH APP INDUSTRIE
741	HEATING,COOLING EQUIPMNT		1721.6		1794.5		1677.7		1610.8	MACH CHAUFFAGE,PIECES
7415	AIR-CONDITIONING MACHNRY		1458.9		1498.2		1352.5		1280.7	GROUPES CONDITION AIR
743	PUMPS NES,CENTRFUGES ETC		706.1		863.0		981.2		896.3	POMPES COMPRES,VENT ETC
744	MECHANICAL HANDLING EQU		812.4		905.0		965.3		902.4	EQUIP MANUTENTION PIECES
749	NONELEC MACH PTS,ACC NES		749.6		900.7		992.1		985.5	PIECES MACH NON ELEC NDA
75	OFFICE MACHNES,ADP EQUIP		6271.2		8885.5		10522.2		12920.4	MACH BUREAU TRAIT AUTOM
751	OFFICE MACHINES	MN 214862	781.8	MN 271209	1064.2	MN 270045	1070.6	MN 304813	1114.6	MACH,APPAREILS DE BUREAU
752	AUTOMTIC DATA PROC EQUIP	MN 24730	2089.1	MN 34110	2699.6	MN 70876	4461.4	MN 105360	5527.3	MACH TRAIT INFORMATION
7523	DIGITL CENTRL PROCESSORS	N 549046	762.0	N 658011	904.7	N 950319	1260.1	N 2135047	1380.5	UNITES CENTRALES
7524	DIGITL CENTRL STOR UNITS	N 8753766	559.9	MN 19184	885.7	MN 18051	933.1	MN 25172	1191.4	UNITES MEMOIRE CENTRALES
7525	ADP PERIPHERAL UNITS	MN 14914	624.6	MN 13718	724.0	MN 50198	1789.6	MN 68772	1986.2	UNITES PERIPHERIQUES
759	OFFICE,ADP MCH PTS,ACCES		3400.5		5121.8		4990.4		6278.6	PIECES DU 751 ET 752
7599	ACCTG,ETC,ADP MCH PTS,AC		3003.9		4613.0		4424.3		5652.1	PIECES DU 751 ET 752
76	TELECOMM,SOUND EQUIPMENT		15607.0		18870.0		18234.8		19682.0	EQUIPMENT DE TELECOM
761	TELEVISION RECEIVERS	MN 12313	2467.7	MN 12743	2678.1	N 8769685	2188.4	N 6065286	1696.0	RECEPTEURS DE TELEVISION
7611	COLOUR TV RECEIVERS	MN 9155	2343.3	MN 9714	2553.1	N 7334202	2137.0	N 5050212	1662.7	RECEPTEURS COULEUR
762	RADIO BROADCAST RECEIVRS	MN 214135	3329.9	MN 225463	3480.2	MN 220346	3053.9	MN 211702	2896.0	RECEPTEURS RADIODIFFUSION
7622	PORTABLE RADIO RECEIVERS	MN 171895	1875.4	MN 184364	1935.0	MN 179309	1643.8	MN 171907	1666.6	RECEPT PORTATIFS RADIO
7628	OTHER RADIO RECEIVERS	MN 26551	1237.7	MN 27002	1281.1	MN 26023	1081.9	MN 23734	866.8	AUTRES RECEPT RADIO
763	SOUND RECORDRS,PHONOGRPH	MN 51777	2193.7	MN 57317	2388.3	MN 51778	2572.5	MN 53750	2039.7	PHONO,APP ENREGISTREMENT
7638	OTHR SOUND APPARATUS ETC	MN 51674	2180.3	MN 57019	2374.7	MN 51400	2546.6	MN 53416	2036.1	AUT APP D'ENREGIS,REPROD
76381	TV IMAGE,SND RECRDRS ETC	N 7881348	1484.2	N 8390477	1622.3	N 8334782	1836.9	N 7554969	1274.0	APP ENREG,REPRO IMAG,SON
76388	DICTATING MACHINES ETC	MN 43793	696.2	MN 48629	752.4	MN 43066	709.8	MN 45861	762.1	MACHINES A DICTER
764	TELECOM EQPT,PTS,ACC NES		7615.8		10323.6		10420.2		13050.3	EQUIP TELECOM,PIECES
7641	LINE TELEPHONE,ETC EQUIP		1040.7		1510.3		2006.1		2331.5	APP TELEPHON PAR FIL
7642	MICROPH,LOUDSPKR,AMPLIFR	MN 628228	657.9	MN 735088	857.4	MN 606914	798.5	MN 576989	854.6	MICRO,HAUT-PARLEUR,AMPLI
7643	TV,RADIO TRANSMITTRS ETC	MN 25152	1227.9	MN 30913	2227.0	MN 20582	2299.5	MN 26692	3517.9	APP EMET TELE RADIO
7648	TELECOMM EQUIPMENT NES	MN 30304	1084.3	MN 34241	1526.5	MN 43091	947.6	MN 62807	1054.1	APP TELECOM NDA
76481	RADIOTELEPHONE ETC RCVRS	N 7003845	730.7	MN 9781	1016.6	N 7663481	752.2	MN 9842	797.8	RECEP RADIOTELEPHONIE
7649	PTS NES OF EQUIPMT OF 76		3605.2		4202.7		4368.7		5292.5	PIECES DE LA DIV 76
76491	PTS NES OF APPAR OF 7641		358.5		464.8		706.4		996.6	PIECES POUR 764.1
76493	TELECOMM EQUIPMT PTS NES		1453.5		1922.4		1995.2		2236.8	PIECES 761,762,764.3,8
76499	PARTS ETC OF SOUND EQUIP		1635.0		1582.1		1492.0		1872.3	PIECES NDA POUR 763
77	ELECTRIC MACHNRY NES ETC		18403.5		24575.7		25897.7		28825.9	MACH APP ELECT NDA
771	ELECTRIC POWER MACHY NES		1545.9		2200.0		2403.2		2708.1	MACH PROD,TRANS ELECTR
7712	OTH ELEC POWER MACHY NES		1176.0		1706.6		1869.2		2140.7	AUT APP PROD TRANSF ELEC
77121	STATIC CONVERTERS ETC	MN 1539010	468.7	MN 2089637	614.4	MN 1786445	767.6	MN 1544928	930.3	CONVERTISSEURS STATIQUES
77129	PTS NES OF MACHY OF 771		512.1		817.1		771.4		860.4	PIECES MACH DU 771
772	SWITCHGEAR ETC,PARTS NES		2010.5		2592.1		2693.7		2988.1	APP COUPURE,SECT ETC
7721	SWITCHGEAR ETC		1430.5		1856.5		1895.1		2053.2	APP COUPURE,SECTIONMNT
773	ELECTR DISTRIBUTNG EQUIP		901.5		1117.3		1207.9		1366.4	EQUIPMT DISTRIBUTION ELECT
7731	INSULATED WIRE,CABLE ETC		884.2		1089.7		1181.2		1340.5	FILS,CABLES ISOLES ELECT
775	HOUSEHOLD TYPE EQUIP NES		2224.3		2707.2		3008.0		2862.3	MACH,APP USAGE DOMESTQUE
7757	DOMESTIC ELECTRC EQU NES		858.7		1029.8		1137.8		1042.6	APP ELECTR DOMEST NDA
7758	ELECTRO-THERMIC APPL NES		1121.8		1397.4		1567.2		1529.7	APP ELECTROTHERMIQ NDA
77586	ELECTROTHERM DOM APP NES	MN 44764	523.2	MN 56443	712.0	MN 70033	822.0	MN 75964	828.3	APP ELECTRO THERMIQUES
776	TRANSISTORS,VALVES,ETC		8862.2		12458.8		12831.3		14830.0	LAMPES,TUBES,VALVES
7761	TV PICTURE TUBES	N 5982260	407.4	N 7806492	560.4	MN 10911	943.9	MN 9482	1090.8	TUBES CATHODIQUES
7763	DIODES,TRANSISTORS,ETC	MN 25706416	906.3	MN 30345215	1196.6	MN 31675362	1394.7	MN 111178438	1598.9	DIODES,TRANSISTORS
7764	ELECTRONIC MICROCIRCUITS	MN 10274441	6992.9	MN 10330070	9957.3	MN 10573904	9004.4	MN 58887603	10206.9	MICROSTRUCTURES ELECTRON
7768	ELCTRNC COMP PTS,CRYSTLS		551.6		740.4		1479.0		1577.8	CRIST PIEZO-ELEC,PCS 776
77689	ELECTRNIC COMPON PTS NES		393.3		517.8		1291.2		1390.8	PIECES DU GROUPE 776
778	ELECTRICAL MACHINERY NES		2667.0		3292.8		3489.3		3751.4	AUTRES MACH ELECT NDA
7781	BATTERIES,ACCUMULATORS		678.7		927.6		978.4		1060.7	PILES ET ACCUMULATEURS
7788	OTH ELEC MACHY,EQUIP NES		1344.4		1605.1		1694.5		1943.5	AUT MACH APP ELEC NDA
77884	ELECTRICAL CONDENSERS	MN 42169660	699.4	MN 241093384	866.6	MN 361906091	857.8	MN 499826394	960.6	CONDENSATEURS ELECTRIQUES
78	ROAD VEHICLES		6653.0		5967.5		5169.6		6244.4	VEHICULES ROUTIERS
781	PASS MOTOR VEH EXC BUSES	N 156653	3044.0	N 132048	2702.2	N 134838	2247.9	N 191883	3199.2	AUTO TRANSPORT PERSONNES
782	LORRIES,SPCL MTR VEH NES	N 32499	549.1	N 7185	178.4	N 7959	200.1	N 9781	224.6	VEHICULES SPECIAUX,MARCH
7821	LORRIES,TRUCKS	N 32311	535.8	N 6873	153.3	N 7685	172.7	N 9532	202.6	VEHICULES TRANSP MARCHAND
783	ROAD MOTOR VEHICLES NES	N 22366	549.4	N 10186	337.8	N 13505	377.4	N 9239	387.7	VEHICULES ROUTIERS NDA
784	MOTOR VEH PRTS,ACCES NES		719.4		785.1		843.3		1047.6	PIECES 722,781,782,783
7849	OTHER MOTOR VEHCL PARTS		639.9		707.7		715.9		864.1	PIECES 722,781,782,783
785	CYCLES,ETC MOTRZD OR NOT		1634.0		1798.1		1362.4		1226.5	MOTOCYCLES SCOOTERS
7851	MOTORCYCLES ETC	N 868607	1044.6	N 966677	1158.8	N 709055	768.7	N 768283	605.4	MOTO VELO MOTEUR AUXIL
79	OTHR TRANSPORT EQUIPMENT		657.7		2093.2		1965.7		745.8	AUTRE MATERIEL TRANSPORT
792	AIRCRAFT ETC		472.9		1933.3		1843.8		585.7	APP NAVIGATION AERIENNE
7924	AIRCRFT NES OVER 15000KG	N 4	325.2	N 16	1811.0	N 16	1675.9	N 3	357.8	AERODYNES PLUS 15000 KG
8	MISC MANUFACTURED GOODS		43393.3		47853.5		50665.3		53514.0	ART MANUFACTURES DIVERS
812	*PLUMBG,HEATNG,LGHTNG EQ		893.3		990.7		1115.9		1116.2	APPAR SANITAIRES CHAUFFAGE
8124	LIGHTING EQUIPMENT NES		823.9		921.0		1035.9		1038.9	APPAREILS ECLAIRAGE ETC
81242	LAMPS,FITTINGS BASE METL		518.6		592.7		678.0		673.7	APPAREILS D'ECLAIRAGE
821	*FURNITURE,PARTS THEREOF		966.8		996.7		1054.8		1191.5	MEUBLES ET PIECES
8219	FURNITURE AND PARTS NES		591.6		614.3		625.9		749.3	AUTRES MEUBLES ET PIECES
831	*TRAVEL GOODS,HANDBAGS	MN 1723680	3209.7	MN 1922519	3608.0	MN 1933532	3877.0	MN 1866183	3763.8	ARTICLES DE VOYAGE ETC
83101	HANDBAGS NES	MN 300039	1208.7	MN 310159	1292.7	MN 309844	1405.5	MN 283587	1261.1	SACS A MAIN
83109	OTHER TRAVEL BAGS,CASES	MN 1305778	1685.7	MN 1486786	1967.4	MN 1505923	2085.9	MN 1479679	2145.3	AUT CONTENANTS SIMILAIRES

4. General Imports C.I.F. by Commodities according to the S.I.T.C. (Rev. 2) in million U.S. Dollars
Importations Générales C.A.F. par Produits d'après la C.T.C.I. (Rév. 2) en millions de Dollars E.U.

SITC CTCI	COMMODITY	1994 QUANTITY QUANTITE	1994 VALUE VALEUR	1995 QUANTITY QUANTITE	1995 VALUE VALEUR	1996 QUANTITY QUANTITE	1996 VALUE VALEUR	1997 QUANTITY QUANTITE	1997 VALUE VALEUR	PRODUIT
84	CLOTHING AND ACCESSORIES		12475.7		12676.0		13657.6		15046.5	VETEMENTS
842	MENS OUTERWEAR NOT KNIT	MN 393968	1883.3	MN 357776	1868.7	MN 358125	2020.6	MN 376615	2116.8	VET DESSUS POUR HOMMES
8423	— TROUSERS,BREECHES ETC	MN 225126	768.5	MN 221405	852.8	MN 226972	965.6	MN 245204	1021.8	PANTALONS HOMMES MAT TEX
8429	— OTHER OUTER GARMENTS	MN 137628	710.5	MN 107175	631.9	MN 100455	634.4	MN 99820	669.6	AUT VET DES HOM MAT TEX
843	WOMENS OUTERWEAR NONKNIT	MN 573237	3358.5	MN 571426	3229.5	MN 586632	3421.2	MN 626270	3590.4	VET DESSUS FEMMES MAT TEX
8435	— BLOUSES	MN 140631	848.9	MN 116744	698.3	MN 118353	678.4	MN 125862	719.2	BLOUSES FEM MAT TEXTILES
8439	— OTHER OUTER GARMENTS	MN 330915	1374.5	MN 341055	1344.7	MN 347639	1477.7	MN 376620	1582.2	AUT VET DES FEM MAT TEXT
844	UNDER GARMENTS NOT KNIT	MN 299676	896.5		830.6		914.0		1184.9	VETEMENT DESSOUS MAT TEX
8441	— MENS SHIRTS	MN 221020	669.6		628.0		715.2		999.4	CHEMISES HOMMES MAT TEXT
845	OUTERWEAR KNIT NONELASTC	MN 662984	3067.3	MN 708668	3150.0	MN 778228	3540.5	MN 940490	4274.9	VET DESSOUS,ACCES BONNET
8451	— JERSEYS,PULLOVERS ETC	MN 324568	1962.6	MN 314198	1922.3	MN 341793	2095.7	MN 413690	2485.6	CHANDAILS,PULL–OVERS ETC
8459	— OTHER,CLTHG ACCESRYS	MN 322677	966.9	MN 374236	1087.8	MN 413352	1289.4	MN 498773	1629.6	AUT VET DESSUS DE BONNE
846	UNDER GARMENTS KNITTED		1757.9		2054.1		2210.3		2279.2	SOUS VETS DE BONNETERIE
8462	— OF COTTON NON ELASTIC	MN 1822576	1330.9	MN 1806639	1596.8	MN 1721725	1714.5	MN 1770347	1790.1	SOUS–VET BONNET COTON
84629	—— OTHER	MN 1782376	1151.8	MN 1761434	1371.0	MN 1674287	1458.4	MN 1713062	1465.4	AUT SOUS–VET BONNET COTON
848	HEADGEAR,NONTXTL CLOTHNG		1080.5		1104.8		1062.4		1052.8	VET ACCES MAT AUT QUE TEX
8481	LEATHER CLOTHES,ACCESSOR		635.6		633.4		568.2		547.1	VET ACCES MAT CUIR ARTIF
851	*FOOTWEAR	MP 1439760	5734.7	MP 1473855	6439.1	MP 1407827	6866.0	MP 1307558	6934.0	CHAUSSURES
85101	FOOTWEAR RUBBER,PLASTIC	MP 821402	2360.5	MP 862123	2627.0	MP 853256	2771.8	MP 778837	2686.8	CHAUS SEMELLES CAOUTCH
85102	FOOTWEAR LEATHER	MP 581215	3341.8	MP 576768	3780.4	MP 521011	4064.8	MP 496121	4217.2	CHAUS SEMELLES EN CUIR
87	PRECISION INSTRUMNTS NES		1311.9		1606.0		2042.1		2577.0	INSTRUM,APPAR SCIENT NDA
871	OPTICAL INSTRUMENTS		385.5		504.8		578.7		841.4	APPAR,INSTRUM D'OPTIQUE
87109	OPTICAL INSTRUMENTS NES		312.6		416.9		480.3		733.6	APP,INSTRUM OPTIQUE NDA
874	MEASURNG,CONTROLNG INSTR		690.6		818.2		1096.6		1313.7	INSTRUMENTS DE MESURE
88	PHOTO EQU,OPTICL GDS ETC		6821.8		7837.0		7808.4		7701.5	APP,FOURN PHOTO,OP,MONTR
881	PHOTO APPARAT,EQUIPT NES		1063.0		1332.2		1442.1		1640.2	APP,EQUIP PHOTO NDA
8811	CAMERAS STILL,FLASH APP		981.7		1230.8		1314.9		1511.1	APPAREILS PHOTO,PIECES
88111	STILL CAMERAS	MN 58194	617.9	MN 79344	711.1	MN 86570	777.7	MN 93541	865.1	APPAREILS PHOTOGRAPHIQ
882	PHOTO,CINEMA SUPPLIES		658.9		850.1		880.4		930.4	PRODUITS PHOTO,CINEMA
8822	PHOTO FILM EXC DEV CINMA		610.0		754.9		776.2		769.8	PLAQUES,PELLICULES,FILMS
885	WATCHES AND CLOCKS		4714.7		5205.1		4976.5		4575.0	HORLOGERIE
8851	WATCHES,MOVEMENTS,CASES		3751.1		4034.4		3785.8		3519.7	MONTRES,MOUVEMENTS,BOITES
88511	WATCHES		2349.0		2597.5		2526.5		2432.6	MONTRES POCHE,BRACELET
88513	WATCH MOVEMENTS ASSEMBLD		1221.7		1243.4		1085.6		907.9	MOUVEMENTS TERMINES
8852	CLOCKS,CLOCK,WATCH PARTS		963.6		1170.7		1190.8		1055.3	HORLOGES,MOUV,PARTIES
88529	CLOCK,WATCH PARTS NES		699.3		838.8		835.0		718.8	FOURNIT D HORLOG NDA
89	MISC MANUFCTRD GOODS NES		11979.9		13700.2		14243.8		15183.8	ART MANUFACTURES DIVERS
893	ARTICLES OF PLASTIC NES		2100.0		2422.9		2598.0		2828.2	OUVRAGES EN MAT DIVIS 58
8931	PLSTC PACKG CONTNRS,LIDS		458.6		765.0		810.6		888.8	ART TRANSP EMBALLAGE ETC
8939	MISC PLASTIC ARTICLES		1626.9		1639.7		1764.5		1909.3	ART DIVERS EN MAT DIV 58
89399	OTHR PLASTC ARTICLES NES		1493.3		1501.1		1625.2		1753.9	AUT OUV MAT DIV 58
894	TOYS,SPORTING GOODS,ETC		5366.7		6149.5		6560.0		6960.2	VOITURES ENFANTS,JOUETS
8942	TOYS,INDOOR GAMES ETC		4790.7		5400.4		5744.2		6134.6	JOUETS,JEUX ETC
89422	DOLLS		520.6	MN 554403	579.4	MN 546744	522.7	MN 564227	507.8	POUPEES
89423	TOYS NES		2737.8		2965.7		3212.5		3396.2	JOUETS,MODELES REDUITS
89424	INDOOR GAME EQUIPMENT		853.8		958.5		1045.8		1332.6	ART,JEUX DE SOCIETE
89425	XMAS DECORATIONS ETC		656.4		869.3		938.4		877.1	ART DIVERTIS,FETES
8947	OTH SPORT GDS,FAIR AMUSM		483.5		651.8		707.5		721.6	AUT ART DE SPORT
89472	OTH OUTDOOR SPORT GOODS		432.6		578.1		640.2		646.2	ART POUR JEUX PLEIN AIR
897	GOLD,SILVER WARE,JEWELRY		885.9		1042.9		1015.7		1216.2	BIJOUTERIE,ORFEVRERIE
8973	PREC JEWLRY,GLD–SILVWARE		733.2		877.2		845.2		1058.7	BIJOUX OR,ARGENT ORFEVRE
89731	PRECIOUS METAL JEWELLERY		653.2		793.3		770.3		990.7	ART BIJOUTERIE,JOAILLER
898	MUSICAL INSTRUMENTS,PTS		886.7		1016.9		958.6		914.1	INSTRUMENTS DE MUSIQUE
8983	SOUND RECRDNG TAPE,DISCS		777.4		871.2		803.2		762.8	SUPPORTS SON POUR 763
89831	PREPD SND RECORDNG MEDIA		531.2		569.6	MN 1201430	542.5	MN 1125174	471.1	SUPPORTS PREPARES
899	OTHER MANUFACTURED GOODS		1930.2		2116.4		2100.1		2086.4	AUT ART MANUF DIVERS NDA
8994	UMBRELLAS,CANES ETC		539.3		523.0		487.8		492.7	PARAPLUIES,CANNES ETC
8999	OTHER MANUF GOODS NES		553.5		651.0		621.4		654.3	OUVRAGES DIVERS NDA
9	GOODS NOT CLASSD BY KIND		4684.9		3990.9		3639.4		5589.1	ART TRANSACT NON CLASSES
931	*SPECIAL TRANSACTIONS		607.4		636.1		856.2		841.1	TRANS.SPECIALES
971	*GOLD,NON MONETARY NES		4050.9		3317.6	K 220236	2742.5		4685.3	OR NON MONETAIRE
97101	NONMON GLD UNWRT,SEMIMFD	K 326104	4041.2	K 265657	3288.7	K 217535	2715.7	K 432931	4644.4	OR,ALLIAGES D'OR BRUTS

5. General Exports F.O.B. by Commodities according to the S.I.T.C. (Rev. 2) in million U.S. Dollars
Exportations Générales F.O.B. par Produits d'après la C.T.C.I. (Rév. 2) en millions de Dollars E.U.

SITC CTCI	COMMODITY	1994 QUANTITY QUANTITE	1994 VALUE VALEUR	1995 QUANTITY QUANTITE	1995 VALUE VALEUR	1996 QUANTITY QUANTITE	1996 VALUE VALEUR	1997 QUANTITY QUANTITE	1997 VALUE VALEUR	PRODUIT
	ALL COMMODITIES		151465.2		173870.9		180914.4		188201.4	TOUS PRODUITS
0	FOOD AND LIVE ANIMALS		2434.9		2741.1		3152.1		3147.0	ALIMENTS,ANIMAUX VIVANTS
01	MEAT AND PREPARATIONS		240.1		410.0		710.8		779.4	VIANDES ET PREPARATIONS
011	MEAT FRESH,CHILLD,FROZEN	W 217820	211.4	W 360819	373.9	W 654585	676.5	W 706992	741.6	VIANDES FRAICHES,REF,CONGE
0114	POULTRY FRESH CHLLD,FRZN	W 204235	184.7	W 333554	332.6	W 567843	560.4	W 582473	574.3	VOLAILLES MORTES
03	FISH AND PREPARATIONS		615.3		577.9		583.3		572.7	POISSONS ET PREPARATIONS
05	VEGETABLES AND FRUIT		592.6		618.4		672.5		609.0	LEGUMES ET FRUITS
1	BEVERAGES AND TOBACCO		2225.8		2075.1		2174.8		1670.9	BOISSONS ET TABACS
11	BEVERAGES		633.2		615.7		520.7		591.0	BOISSONS
112	ALCOHOLIC BEVERAGES	W 124580	511.7	W 167688	511.7	W 133971	430.9	W 157850	529.8	BOISSONS ALCOOLIQUES
12	TOBACCO AND MANUFACTURES		1592.7		1459.5		1654.2		1080.0	TABACS BRUTS FABRIQUES
122	TOBACCO,MANUFACTURED	W 85133	1584.9	W 75393	1453.9		1623.1		1034.8	TABACS FABRIQUES
1222	CIGARETTES	W 84470	1579.9	W 74335	1446.9		1616.9		1021.0	CIGARETTES
2	CRUDE MATERLS,EXCL FUELS		2236.5		3066.9		2839.0		2908.1	MAT BRUTES NON COMESTIBLES
26	TEXTILE FIBRES AND WASTE		667.6		854.2		779.0		692.2	FIBRES TEXTILES
28	METALLIFEROUS ORES,SCRAP		339.5		641.9		590.1		616.3	MINERAIS METAL,DECHETS
3	MINERAL FUELS ETC		1211.6		1684.4		2013.3		2178.3	COMBUSTIBLES MINERAUX LUB
33	PETROLEUM AND PRODUCTS		1086.5		1578.4		1964.7		2130.6	PETROLE ET DERIVES
334	PETROLEUM PRODUCTS,REFIN	W 5384305	1070.4	W 8133412	1561.1	W 8816418	1946.4	MW 10280	2117.1	PRODUITS RAFFINES
3343	GAS OILS	W 2962677	557.5	W 5342492	955.8	W 6055791	1324.8	W 7252351	1453.9	GAS OILS
5	CHEMCLS,RELATED PROD NES		8369.7		10743.3		10622.8		10507.1	PRODUITS CHIMIQUES
51	ORGANIC CHEMICALS		901.0		1372.2		1378.2		1186.6	PROD CHIMIQ ORGANIQUES
53	DYES,TANNING,COLOUR PROD		845.1		895.5		977.5		984.4	PROD TEINTURE,COLORANTS
541	*MEDICINAL,PHARM PRODUCT		833.0		975.3		1020.1		967.5	PROD MEDICINAUX PHARMACEUT
5417	MEDICAMENTS		404.7		477.7		542.9		577.4	MEDICAMENTS
55	PERFUME,CLEANING ETC PRD		511.5		571.9		622.3		636.2	PROD POUR PARFUM,TOILETTE
58	PLASTIC MATERIALS ETC		4069.2		5522.6		5256.0		5369.5	MAT PLAST ARTIFICIELLES
582	PROD OF CONDENSATION ETC	W 310644	507.7	W 402796	831.5	W 424621	763.4	W 552524	888.7	PROD CONDENS,POLYCOND
5823	ALKYDS,OTHER POLYESTERS	W 204239	286.8	W 276682	538.4	W 270186	416.4	W 366403	481.2	ALKYDES ET AUT POLYESTERS
583	POLYMERIZATION ETC PRODS	W 3969293	3534.9	W 4658915	4656.3	W 4650347	4455.5	W 4776744	4436.3	PROD POLYMERISATION
5831	POLYETHYLENE	W 682114	429.9	W 828557	633.9	W 871698	658.7	W 741382	581.7	POLYETHYLENE
58311	— IN PRIMARY FORMS	W 440419	326.6	W 572559	509.2	W 677781	556.2	W 612105	515.9	POLYETHYLENE PRIMAIRES
5833	POLYSTYRENE,ITS COPOLYMR	W 1653006	1411.7	W 1777254	1810.3	W 1816747	1622.1	W 1927320	1604.3	POLYPROPYLENE COPOLYMERES
58331	— IN PRIMARY FORMS	W 1416034	1317.6	W 1513875	1681.0	W 1574141	1516.6	W 1690041	1510.4	SOUS FORMES PRIMAIRES
5834	POLYVINYL CHLORIDE	W 748333	854.9	W 869290	1029.1	W 907012	1047.1	W 960699	1082.6	CHLORURE DE POLYVINYLE
58343	— PLATES,STRIP,ETC NES	W 250837	476.4	W 268612	515.4	W 252511	520.3	W 272497	520.2	SOUS FORME DE PLAQUES
5839	OTH POLYMRZTION ETC PROD	W 514820	483.7	W 676792	614.4	W 527317	558.8	W 618633	623.9	AUT PROD POLYMER COPOLYM
59	CHEMICAL MATERIALS NES		806.7		974.6		973.0		1010.9	MAT PROD CHIMIQUES NDA
598	MISCEL CHEM PRODUCTS NES		590.1		688.4		702.3		757.6	PROD DIV INDUST CHIM NDA
5989	CHEM PRODUCTS,PREPS NES		493.3		575.7		613.3		683.5	PROD PREP CHIMIQUES NDA
6	BASIC MANUFACTURES		25318.1		29298.7		30733.2		31359.8	ART MANUFACTURES
61	LEATHER,DRESSED FUR,ETC		1738.0		1977.6		2229.6		2294.3	CUIRS,PELLETERIES
611	LEATHER		1231.4		1450.4		1557.6		1652.0	CUIRS,PEAUX PREPARES
6114	LEATHR BOVINE NES,EQUINE		740.5	A 58072	973.5		1080.4		1152.0	CUIRS DE BOVINS
63	WOOD,CORK MANUFACTRS NES		657.9		712.3		662.2		687.4	OUVRAGES LIEGE ET BOIS
64	PAPER,PAPERBOARD AND MFR		1616.9		1970.1		2241.3		2441.1	PAPIERS,CARTONS & OUVRAGES
641	PAPER AND PAPERBOARD		1004.0	W 451629	203.5	W 500593	216.8		1617.9	PAPIERS ET CARTONS
6418	COATED ETC PAPER NES BLK	W 471950	291.2	W 689098	429.0	W 836829	507.2	W 1012511	599.6	PAP,CARTONS COUCHES,ENDUITS
64189	COATED PAPER ETC NES	W 459074	266.3	W 675237	400.9	W 819881	475.3	W 994553	564.7	PAPIERS,CARTONS COUCHES
642	PAPER,ETC,PRECUT,ARTS OF		612.9		700.9		768.6		823.3	PAP,CARTONS DECOUPES
65	TEXTILE YARN,FABRICS,ETC		12616.0		13892.1		14213.6		14662.9	FILS,TISSUS,ARTICLES TEXTILE
651	TEXTILE YARN	W 732883	2370.0	W 809941	2893.1	W 927977	3135.6	W 948110	3232.4	FILS TEXTILES
6513	COTTON YARN	W 172245	537.3	W 198235	668.7	W 271751	927.2	W 310990	1068.8	FILS DE COTON
6514	SYN FIB YRN,BULK,MONOFIL	W 365314	784.8	W 419116	1119.6	W 461923	1089.9	W 443909	1027.6	FILS CONT 85% FIB TEXT SYNTH
65144	— TEXTRD,CONT POLYESTER	W 248525	417.9	W 250664	560.6	W 355079	668.3	W 305434	512.2	FILS TEX FI CONT POLYESTERS
652	COTTON FABRICS,WOVEN	A 2309326	2617.4	A 2336521	2898.1	A 2226082	3010.3	A 2397308	3323.9	TISSUS DE COTON
6522	WOVEN COTTON BLEACHD,ETC	A 1826539	2323.5	A 1910830	2600.0	A 1775075	2665.6	A 1853715	2900.0	TISSUS COTON BLANCHIS ETC
65224	BLCHED COTTON FABRIC NES	A 1690950	2117.9	A 1769312	2348.2	A 1599785	2343.1	A 1633174	2481.3	AUT TIS PLUS 85% COT BLANCHI
653	WOVN MAN-MADE FIB FABRIC	A 3577803	2815.4	A 3507599	3077.2	A 3399281	3048.9	A 3481960	3071.3	TISSUS FIBRES SYNTH,ARTIF
6531	CONT SYNT WEAVES NONPILE	A 2048395	1621.2	A 2114545	1827.9	A 2213415	1892.8	A 2314406	1934.5	TISSUS FIBRES SYNTH CONTINUE
65315	CONT SYN TXTL FABRIC NES	A 1909454	1469.6	A 1956394	1661.6	A 2065974	1727.9	A 2153211	1758.0	TIS PLUS 85% TEXT SYNT CONT
6534	DISC SYN BLEND FABRC NES	A 812753	551.5	A 787479	582.4	A 721246	534.8	A 685673	490.1	TISSUS FIBRES SYNTH DISCONT
654	OTH WOVEN TEXTILE FABRIC		929.4		813.0		708.7		758.9	TISSUS AUT COTON SYNT,ARTIF
6541	SILK FABRICS WOVEN	A 136705	463.1	A 115839	381.2	A 86209	309.0	A 75608	281.5	TISSUS DE SOIE
655	KNITTED,ETC FABRICS	W 343782	1781.7	W 344594	1920.1	W 354694	2036.2	W 335116	2024.5	ETOF BONNETERIE PIECES ETC
6552	OTHER KNIT ETC FAB NONEL	W 343782	1781.7	W 344594	1920.1	W 354694	2036.2	W 335116	2024.5	ETOF BON NON ELAS NON SYNT
657	SPECIAL TXTL FABRC,PRODS		972.8		1074.7		1084.5		1071.1	TISSUS SPECIAUX
6573	COATED ETC TEXTILES NES	W 175196	695.3	W 180406	787.0	W 193361	811.6	W 178391	791.5	TISSUS,ART MATIERE TEXT NDA
65732	PLASTIC COATED TEXTILES	W 170197	668.8	W 175168	756.8	W 187765	779.2	W 171907	753.5	TISSUS IMPREGNES
658	TEXTILE ARTICLES NES	MN 1033661	647.4	MN 1043152	670.2	MN 900119	612.7	MN 893213	605.5	ART FACONNES MAT TEXTILES
66	NONMETAL MINERAL MFS NES		2612.2		2909.0		2950.5		3026.8	ART MIN NON METALLIQUES
666	POTTERY		557.3		599.3		558.3		508.7	POTERIE
667	PEARL,PREC-,SEMI-P STONE		1350.3		1415.5		1440.9		1516.5	PERLES, PIERRES GEMMES
6672	DIAMONDS NONINDUST,UNSET		906.2		975.4		1009.7		1085.0	DIAMANTS BRUTS
66729	— CUT ETC NOT SET		807.7		835.5		806.1		939.0	DIAMANTS TAILLES
67	IRON AND STEEL		1771.4		2262.4		2642.6		2510.3	FER ET ACIER
674	IRN,STL UNIV,PLATE,SHEET	W 1604645	1167.7	W 2014461	1790.4	W 2453382	2165.3	W 2613530	2043.2	LARGES PLATS,TOLES
6746	IRN,STL THIN PLATE,ROLLD	W 906158	775.4	W 1058665	1112.2	W 1414985	1400.1	W 1469396	1294.1	TOLES LAM MOINS 3MM
67463	— OF STAINLESS ETC STL	W 279006	495.5	W 298553	720.1	W 492698	929.0	W 536048	847.0	TOL ACIER INOX MOINS 3 MM
68	NON-FERROUS METALS		1286.1		2075.4		2236.2		2161.9	METAUX NON FERREUX
682	COPPER EXC CEMENT COPPER	W 213861	585.6	W 271495	890.3	W 327373	996.3	W 358353	1065.6	CUIVRE
6822	COPPER,ALLOYS WORKED	W 193825	539.1	W 238708	794.1	W 272775	864.8	W 298518	919.5	CUIVRE,ALLIAGES OUVRES
684	ALUMINIUM	W 169994	349.0	W 334879	754.9	W 408747	853.5	W 351503	747.4	ALUMINIUM
69	METAL MANUFACTURES NES		2819.5		3238.9		3247.2		3202.9	ART MANUFACT EN METAL NDA
697	BASE MTL HOUSEHOLD EQUIP		730.1		873.1		854.4		872.9	ART MENAGE MET COMMUNS
6974	BASE MTL DMSTC ARTIC NES	W 108404	483.2	W 140153	560.9	W 135004	547.7	W 128243	557.6	ARTICLES NDA FONTE,FER,ETC
699	BASE METAL MFRS NES		1066.2		1192.5		1219.6		1238.0	ART MANUFACTURES MET NDA
7	MACHINES,TRANSPORT EQUIP		47438.0		56217.3		58194.2		61787.7	MACHINES MATERIEL TRANSPORT
71	POWER GENERATING EQUIPMT		1638.3		2000.6		1941.0		2152.6	MACHINES GENERATRICES
713	INTRNL COMBUS PSTN ENGIN		445.0		519.8		505.2		618.7	MOTEURS EXPL COMB INT, PIECE
716	ROTATING ELECTRIC PLANT		1117.1		1409.3		1316.5		1428.6	APP ELECTR ROTATIFS,PIECES
7162	AC MTRS,GENRTRS,GEN SETS	MN 717354	827.4	MN 848377	997.8	MN 796021	965.8	MN 798166	862.9	MOTEURS ELECTRIQUES
71621	AC MTRS,INC UNIVRSL MTRS	MN 717309	590.4	MN 848337	759.8	MN 795979	693.9	MN 885897	692.8	MOT ELEC NON COUR CONTINU
72	MACHS FOR SPCL INDUSTRYS		2353.0		2330.6		2723.3		2522.2	MAC SPECIALES POUR INDUST
724	TEXTILE,LEATHER MACHNRY		967.5		887.9		933.0		845.1	MACH POUR INDUSTRIE TEXTILE
728	OTH MACHY FOR SPCL INDUS		860.8		901.3		1077.9		981.3	AUT MACH IND PARTICULIERES
7284	MACHY FOR SPCL INDUS NES		731.4		762.2		907.6		821.4	MACH SPEC IND PARTICUL.
73	METALWORKING MACHINERY		577.7		570.3		637.2		619.4	MACH TRAVAIL DES METAUX
74	GENRL INDUSTRL MACHY NES		2920.9		3111.1		3350.0		2926.6	MACH APP INDUSTRIE
741	HEATING,COOLING EQUIPMNT		1085.4		1075.3		1030.1		875.2	MACH CHAUFFAGE,PIECES
7415	AIR-CONDITIONING MACHNRY		881.7		872.5		805.3		682.6	GROUPES CONDITION AIR

5. General Exports F.O.B. by Commodities according to the S.I.T.C. (Rev. 2) in million U.S. Dollars
Exportations Générales F.O.B. par Produits d'après la C.T.C.I. (Rév. 2) en millions de Dollars E.U.

SITC CTCI	COMMODITY	1994 QUANTITY QUANTITE	1994 VALUE VALEUR	1995 QUANTITY QUANTITE	1995 VALUE VALEUR	1996 QUANTITY QUANTITE	1996 VALUE VALEUR	1997 QUANTITY QUANTITE	1997 VALUE VALEUR	PRODUIT
743	PUMPS NES,CENTRFUGES ETC		496.4		548.4		630.5		567.8	POMPES COMPRES,VENT ETC
749	NONELEC MACH PTS,ACC NES		611.7		655.8		702.9		644.5	PIECES MACH NON ELEC NDA
75	OFFICE MACHNES,ADP EQUIP		7074.0		9722.7		10841.0		12487.7	MACH BUREAU TRAIT AUTOM
751	OFFICE MACHINES	MN 232767	1200.9	MN 282721	1446.9	MN 286249	1369.7	MN 331704	1502.7	MACH,APPAREILS DE BUREAU
7512	CALCULATNG,ACCTG,ETC MCH	MN 194413	507.2	MN 242108	609.7	MN 245287	711.4	MN 286045	818.9	MACHINE A CALCULER ETC
75121	CALCULATING MACHINES	MN 194288	478.3	MN 241908	567.1	MN 245084	675.8	MN 285823	777.2	MACHINES A CALCULER
7518	OFFICE MACHINES NES	MN 37995	665.9	MN 40122	804.8	MN 40309	596.8	MN 45142	644.4	MACH,APP DE BUREAU NDA
75182	PHOTO,THERMOCOPY APPARAT	N 590361	503.5	N 762216	607.3	N 564228	457.3	N 549800	491.7	APPAREILS DE PHOTOCOPIE
752	AUTOMTIC DATA PROC EQUIP	MN 24331	1323.4	MN 35061	1745.7	MN 65928	2926.5	MN 103613	3255.9	MACH TRAIT INFORMATION
7523	DIGITL CENTRL PROCESSORS	N 356588	506.0	N 602923	682.5	N 513603	821.8	N 1055187	708.1	UNITES CENTRALES
7525	ADP PERIPHERAL UNITS	MN 16778	447.3	MN 18159	525.6	MN 50403	1481.4	MN 76747	1609.3	UNITES PERIPHERIQUES
759	OFFICE,ADP MCH PTS,ACCES		4549.8		6530.2		6544.9		7729.2	PIECES DU 751 ET 752
7591	OFFICE MACHINE PARTS NES		286.9		416.0		542.6		635.9	PIECES DU 7511,7518
7599	ACCTG,ETC,ADP MCH PTS,AC		4262.9		6114.2		6002.4		7093.4	PIECES DU 751 ET 752
76	TELECOMM,SOUND EQUIPMENT		14384.8		16752.7		16102.9		16281.9	EQUIPMENT DE TELECOM
761	TELEVISION RECEIVERS	MN 10402	1553.6	MN 10428	1512.5	N 6719602	1025.9	N 5029739	847.6	RECEPTEURS DE TELEVISION
7611	COLOUR TV RECEIVERS	N 7071059	1406.1	N 7186168	1369.8	N 5196603	970.1	N 4005656	812.3	RECEPTEURS COULEUR
762	RADIO BROADCAST RECEIVRS	MN 230396	4041.4	MN 258211	4540.2	MN 242661	3827.7	MN 233776	3798.2	RECEPTEURS RADIODIFFUSION
7622	PORTABLE RADIO RECEIVERS	MN 185207	2524.5	MN 208918	2833.8	MN 195023	2293.2	MN 185775	2337.7	RECEPT PORTATIFS RADIO
7628	OTHER RADIO RECEIVERS	MN 30534	1246.6	MN 34888	1353.4	MN 32801	1082.0	MN 30944	960.3	AUTRES RECEPT RADIO
763	SOUND RECORDRS,PHONOGRPH	N 541498	6.0	MN 58777	1637.4	MN 56672	1853.6	MN 58173	1671.1	PHONO,APP ENREGISTREMENT
7638	OTHR SOUND APPARATUS ETC	MN 54586	1357.1	MN 58538	1631.4	MN 56440	1847.8	MN 57807	1662.2	AUT APP D'ENREGIS,REPROD
76381	TV IMAGE,SND RECRDRS ETC	N 2640498	380.8	N 2880120	547.4	N 4766446	757.5	N 5524367	723.3	APP ENREG,REPRO IMAG,SON
76388	DICTATING MACHINES ETC	MN 51945	976.3	MN 55658	1084.1	MN 51674	1090.4	MN 52282	938.9	MACHINES A DICTER
764	TELECOM EQPT,PTS,ACC NES		7432.2		9062.7		9394.0		9965.2	EQUIP TELECOM,PIECES
7641	LINE TELEPHONE,ETC EQUIP		1019.5		1443.4	MN 306291	2319.3	N 1435278	86.0	APP TELEPHON PAR FIL
7642	MICROPH,LOUDSPKR,AMPLIFR	MN 324353	574.2	MN 407531	867.7	MN 376516	926.1	MN 368068	914.3	MICRO,HAUT–PARLEUR,AMPLI
7643	TV,RADIO TRANSMITTRS ETC	MN 25912	1135.2	MN 29395	1464.1	MN 18594	700.3	MN 17905	650.4	APP EMET TELE RADIO
7649	PTS NES OF EQUIPMT OF 76		4397.7		4950.3		5201.5		5695.8	PIECES DE LA DIV 76
76491	PTS NES OF APPAR OF 7641		393.4		490.0		841.5		1114.3	PIECES POUR 764.1
76493	TELECOMM EQUIPMT PTS NES		2457.3		2746.7		2568.1		2507.3	PIECES 761,762,764.3,8
76499	PARTS ETC OF SOUND EQUIP		1423.0		1527.2		1621.2		1848.2	PIECES NDA POUR 763
77	ELECTRIC MACHNRY NES ETC		14551.8		19594.4		20624.9		22478.7	MACH APP ELECT NDA
771	ELECTRIC POWER MACHY NES		1765.6		2466.8		2610.4		2940.8	MACH PROD,TRANS ELECTR
7712	OTH ELEC POWER MACHY NES		1449.9		2045.1		2168.7		2417.9	AUT APP PROD TRANSF ELEC
77121	STATIC CONVERTERS ETC	MN 1102874	647.6	MN 1297640	876.7	MN 1068295	987.1	MN 940727	1092.9	CONVERTISSEURS STATIQUES
77129	PTS NES OF MACHY OF 771		465.4		702.2		704.5		838.2	PIECES MACH DU 771
772	SWITCHGEAR ETC,PARTS NES		1760.0		2302.0		2462.0		2670.7	APP COUPURE,SECT ETC
7721	SWITCHGEAR ETC		1055.5		1350.5		1439.2		1563.4	APP COUPURE,SECTIONMNT
7722	PRINTED CIRCUITS,PTS NES		592.9		800.6		877.4		939.6	CIRCUITS ET PIECES
773	ELECTR DISTRIBUTNG EQUIP		753.1		993.8		1071.7		1270.0	EQUIPMT DISTRIBUTION ELECT
7731	INSULATED WIRE,CABLE ETC		742.7		980.2		1058.3		1254.6	FILS,CABLES ISOLES ELECT
775	HOUSEHOLD TYPE EQUIP NES		2696.7		3281.6		3619.1		3447.8	MACH,APP USAGE DOMESTQUE
7757	DOMESTIC ELECTRC EQU NES		1094.9		1282.2		1416.0		1278.0	APP ELECTR DOMEST NDA
77572	DOM ELEC ROOM FANS ETC	MN 37654	509.3	MN 50541	658.0	MN 52462	709.3	MN 40825	561.0	HOTTES ASPIRANTES,VENTIL
7758	ELECTRO–THERMIC APPL NES		1480.2		1796.8		1982.9		1983.1	APP ELECTROTHERMIQ NDA
77586	ELECTROTHERM DOM APP NES	MN 46013	610.3	MN 58711	818.3	MN 69144	961.8	MN 75941	1008.7	APP ELECTRO THERMIQUES
776	TRANSISTORS,VALVES,ETC		5175.7		7576.1		7649.7		8885.0	LAMPES,TUBES,VALVES
7761	TV PICTURE TUBES	N 6510277	450.2	N 7757718	592.8	MN 10789	934.8	N 7973686	929.9	TUBES CATHODIQUES
7763	DIODES,TRANSISTORS,ETC	MN 23372812	733.1	MN 34616229	1037.3	MN 113340793	1080.6	MN 80151338	1188.8	DIODES,TRANSISTORS
7764	ELECTRONIC MICROCIRCUITS	MN 52112744	3690.4	MN 9087141	5494.0	MN 12131688	5139.6	MN 43688396	5897.3	MICROSTRUCTURES ELECTRON
778	ELECTRICAL MACHINERY NES		2271.8		2838.1		3062.9		3083.8	AUTRES MACH ELECT NDA
7781	BATTERIES,ACCUMULATORS		626.6		873.2		959.5		998.2	PILES ET ACCUMULATEURS
7788	OTH ELEC MACHY,EQUIP NES		1053.7		1306.9		1325.4		1384.7	AUT MACH APP ELEC NDA
78	ROAD VEHICLES		3830.9		2001.0		1828.0		2182.0	VEHICULES ROUTIERS
781	PASS MOTOR VEH EXC BUSES	N 45378	1092.3	N 15774	304.0	N 24212	314.2	N 34086	518.1	AUTO TRANSPORT PERSONNES
782	LORRIES,SPCL MTR VEH NES	N 29689	560.0	N 2837	70.6	N 2793	55.8	N 2347	47.9	VEHICULES SPECIAUX,MARCH
7821	LORRIES,TRUCKS	N 29388	540.1	N 2523	45.3	N 2573	38.2	N 2181	34.1	VEHICULES TRANSP MARCHAND
784	MOTOR VEH PRTS,ACCES NES		553.4		498.0		516.7		710.9	PIECES 722,781,782,783
7849	OTHER MOTOR VEHCL PARTS		334.6		361.7		420.1		577.5	PIECES 722,781,782,783
785	CYCLES,ETC MOTRZD OR NOT		1223.2		1071.9		869.4		831.8	MOTOCYCLES SCOOTERS
7851	MOTORCYCLES ETC	N 404114	583.9	N 162208	215.3	N 101418	135.2	N 84822	107.2	MOTO VELO MOTEUR AUXIL
7853	INVAL CARR, PTS OF 785		341.3		588.5		509.7		530.4	FAUTEUILS INVALIDES,PIECES
78539	PARTS,ACCES NES OF 785		341.1		587.8		507.6		528.9	PIECES DU 785
8	MISC MANUFACTURED GOODS		61001.5		66636.1		69611.3		73069.7	ART MANUFACTURES DIVERS
812	*PLUMBG,HEATNG,LGHTNG EQ		1098.2		1289.1		1424.5		1340.1	APPAR SANITAIRES CHAUFFAGE
8124	LIGHTING EQUIPMENT NES		1056.8		1235.6		1376.8		1307.9	APPAREILS ECLAIRAGE ETC
81242	LAMPS,FITTINGS BASE METL		621.5		725.5		823.6		771.6	APPAREILS D'ECLAIRAGE
821	*FURNITURE,PARTS THEREOF		709.4		770.3		789.1		864.9	MEUBLES ET PIECES
831	*TRAVEL GOODS,HANDBAGS	MN 1770872	4071.7	MN 2027468	4630.3	MN 2088968	4835.8	MN 2014528	4811.3	ARTICLES DE VOYAGE ETC
83101	HANDBAGS NES	MN 263354	1391.1	MN 265008	1449.0	MN 270079	1531.3	MN 239221	1385.8	SACS A MAIN
83109	OTHER TRAVEL BAGS,CASES	MN 1338622	2261.1	MN 1594642	2731.1	MN 1650408	2813.4	MN 1595587	2938.9	AUT CONTENANTS SIMILAIRES
84	CLOTHING AND ACCESSORIES		21428.9		21327.2		22009.1		23140.8	VETEMENTS
842	MENS OUTERWEAR NOT KNIT	MN 431468	3066.2	MN 391379	3004.4	MN 386497	3141.0	MN 403720	3300.2	VET DESSUS POUR HOMMES
8423	— TROUSERS,BREECHES ETC	MN 255994	1355.3	MN 247655	1434.5	MN 257176	1594.0	MN 269939	1640.7	PANTALONS HOMMES MAT TEX
8424	— JACKETS,BLAZERS ETC	MN 39538	554.2	MN 38533	517.8	MN 37602	518.0	MN 35757	535.8	VESTES HOMMES MAT TEXTIL
8429	— OTHER OUTER GARMENTS	MN 131747	1052.1	MN 101029	953.4	MN 88122	937.0	MN 94735	1030.2	AUT VET DES HOM MAT TEX
843	WOMENS OUTERWEAR NONKNIT	MN 670136	5764.5	MN 679921	5668.1	MN 697085	5936.2	MN 703622	5987.1	VET DESSUS FEMMES MAT TEX
8431	— COATS AND JACKETS	MN 36384	765.3	MN 34637	761.5	MN 37782	810.6	MN 39098	845.6	MANT,VEST FEM MAT TEXTIL
8435	— BLOUSES	MN 178490	1609.5	MN 156300	1423.0	MN 148688	1328.1	MN 153124	1331.2	BLOUSES FEM MAT TEXTILES
8439	— OTHER OUTER GARMENTS	MN 383216	2429.1	MN 405814	2463.0	MN 421914	2737.7	MN 429021	2801.6	AUT VET DES FEM MAT TEXT
844	UNDER GARMENTS NOT KNIT	MN 211783	760.9	MN 321221	1699.9	MN 159518	679.0	MN 131060	884.4	VETEMENT DESSOUS MAT TEX
8441	— MENS SHIRTS	MN 145183	535.6	MN 245976	1389.4	MN 101867	453.7	MN 118439	821.4	CHEMISES HOMMES MAT TEXT
84411	—— OF COTTON	MN 146941	955.5	MN 143436	985.8	MN 139675	986.7	MN 143094	955.9	CHEMISES HOMMES DE COTON
845	OUTERWEAR KNIT NONELASTC	MN 832560	6152.7	MN 847619	5914.4	MN 867672	6123.3	MN 967357	6977.9	VET DESSOUS,ACCES BONNET
8451	— JERSEYS,PULLOVERS ETC	MN 366864	3860.4	MN 340342	3552.0	MN 356324	3680.3	MN 419009	4168.0	CHANDAILS,PULL–OVERS ETC
8459	— OTHER,CLTHG ACCESRYS	MN 443977	2063.2	MN 483086	2101.8	MN 486849	2174.9	MN 522189	2532.5	AUT VET DESSUS DE BONNE
846	UNDER GARMENTS KNITTED		2659.0		2989.7		3039.4		3177.5	SOUS VETS DE BONNETERIE
8462	— OF COTTON NON ELASTIC	MN 1793581	2056.1	MN 1737039	2310.8	MN 1606817	2384.5	MN 1649396	2493.2	SOUS–VET BONNET COTON
84621	—— MENS SHIRTS	MN 65226	488.8	MN 62963	518.0	MN 59677	496.6	MN 67897	549.5	CHEMISES DE COTON
84629	—— OTHER	MN 1728355	1567.4	MN 1674076	1792.8	MN 1547140	1887.9	MN 1581499	1943.8	AUT SOUS–VET BONNET COTON
8465	CORSETS,GARTERS,ETC	MN 317621	483.5	MN 322557	539.3	MN 304656	515.9	MN 331140	521.0	CORSETS,GAINES ART SIM
847	TEXTILE CLTHNG ACCES NES		466.8		534.6		579.1		711.7	ACCES VET MAT TEXT NDA
848	HEADGEAR,NONTXTL CLOTHNG		1523.5		1516.4		1586.4		1451.5	VET ACCES MAT AUT QUE TEX
8481	LEATHER CLOTHES,ACCESSOR	N 5393401	65.6		793.6		741.9		705.3	VET ACCES MAT CUIR ARTIF
851	*FOOTWEAR	MP 1405618	6554.3	MP 1446541	7401.1	MP 1389228	7954.6	MP 1268465	8004.2	CHAUSSURES
85101	FOOTWEAR RUBBER,PLASTIC	MP 769695	2694.5	MP 836413	3111.6	MP 831405	3284.2	MP 747762	3115.0	CHAUS SEMELLES CAOUTCH
85102	FOOTWEAR LEATHER	MP 597439	3804.5	MP 579570	4246.7	MP 529032	4628.5	MP 488446	4839.7	CHAUS SEMELLES EN CUIR
87	PRECISION INSTRUMNTS NES		1226.6		1554.1		1877.9		2292.9	INSTRUM,APPAR SCIENT NDA
871	OPTICAL INSTRUMENTS		370.0		579.5		711.9		981.0	APPAR,INSTRUM D'OPTIQUE
87109	OPTICAL INSTRUMENTS NES		282.8		467.3		590.2		856.4	APP,INSTRUM OPTIQUE NDA

5. General Exports F.O.B. by Commodities according to the S.I.T.C. (Rev. 2) in million U.S. Dollars
Exportations Générales F.O.B. par Produits d'après la C.T.C.I. (Rév. 2) en millions de Dollars E.U.

SITC CTCI	COMMODITY	1994 QUANTITY QUANTITE	1994 VALUE VALEUR	1995 QUANTITY QUANTITE	1995 VALUE VALEUR	1996 QUANTITY QUANTITE	1996 VALUE VALEUR	1997 QUANTITY QUANTITE	1997 VALUE VALEUR	PRODUIT
874	MEASURNG,CONTROLNG INSTR		583.3		661.4		784.6		888.9	INSTRUMENTS DE MESURE
88	PHOTO EQU,OPTICL GDS ETC		7188.0		8379.8		8696.7		8976.1	APP,FOURN PHOTO,OP,MONTR
881	PHOTO APPARAT,EQUIPT NES		1122.0		1482.1		1627.4		1826.5	APP,EQUIP PHOTO NDA
8811	CAMERAS STILL,FLASH APP		1070.3		1423.2		1549.9		1752.2	APPAREILS PHOTO,PIECES
88111	STILL CAMERAS	MN 58962	621.9	MN 77350	814.8	MN 83973	893.8	MN 89893	1001.9	APPAREILS PHOTOGRAPHIQ
88119	PTS NES OF APPAR OF 8811		423.7		567.3		617.0		714.8	PIECES POUR 881.1
882	PHOTO,CINEMA SUPPLIES		412.2		524.5		512.4		655.4	PRODUITS PHOTO,CINEMA
884	OPTICAL GOODS NES		446.5		570.6		669.6		776.4	ELEMENTS OPTIQ,ART LUNET
8842	SPECTACLES AND FRAMES		390.6		507.9		585.5		672.2	LUNETTES ET MONTURES
885	WATCHES AND CLOCKS		5193.5		5789.7		5879.2		5712.8	HORLOGERIE
8851	WATCHES,MOVEMENTS,CASES		3971.0		4398.9		4476.6		4427.7	MONTRES,MOUVEMENTS,BOITES
88511	WATCHES		3294.1		3664.0		3822.1		3807.9	MONTRES POCHE,BRACELET
8852	CLOCKS,CLOCK,WATCH PARTS		1222.5		1390.9		1402.7		1285.2	HORLOGES,MOUV,PARTIES
88529	CLOCK,WATCH PARTS NES		758.7		810.2		769.0		676.3	FOURNIT D HORLOG NDA
89	MISC MANUFCTRD GOODS NES		18724.7		21284.6		22023.9		23639.7	ART MANUFACTURES DIVERS
892	PRINTED MATTER		772.7		888.8		901.6		961.2	IMPRIMES
893	ARTICLES OF PLASTIC NES		2742.2		3219.9		3354.9		3570.4	OUVRAGES EN MAT DIVIS 58
8931	PLSTC PACKG CONTNRS,LIDS		629.1		1107.1		1032.2		1051.2	ART TRANSP EMBALLAGE ETC
8939	MISC PLASTIC ARTICLES		2103.0		2096.7		2296.1		2492.8	ART DIVERS EN MAT DIV 58
89399	OTHR PLASTC ARTICLES NES		1952.6		1937.4		2128.7		2311.6	AUT OUV MAT DIV 58
894	TOYS,SPORTING GOODS,ETC		9702.1		11055.5		11624.1		13005.9	VOITURES ENFANTS,JOUETS
8942	TOYS,INDOOR GAMES ETC		9003.0		10127.1		10608.5		11962.2	JOUETS,JEUX ETC
89422	DOLLS		705.1	MN 503719	758.5	MN 602287	825.9	MN 687918	856.1	POUPEES
89423	TOYS NES		5855.1		6278.0		6528.6		7262.9	JOUETS,MODELES REDUITS
89424	INDOOR GAME EQUIPMENT		1077.0		1262.4		1393.0		2051.6	ART,JEUX DE SOCIETE
89425	XMAS DECORATIONS ETC		1339.2		1755.1		1792.2		1728.3	ART DIVERTIS,FETES
8947	OTH SPORT GDS,FAIR AMUSM		603.0		825.7		897.5		928.9	AUT ART DE SPORT
89472	OTH OUTDOOR SPORT GOODS		523.8		714.0		785.3		793.9	ART POUR JEUX PLEIN AIR
897	GOLD,SILVER WARE,JEWELRY		1484.6		1660.6		1690.3		1699.2	BIJOUTERIE,ORFEVRERIE
8973	PREC JEWLRY,GLD–SILVWARE		1113.0		1289.4		1335.8		1353.9	BIJOUX OR,ARGENT ORFEVRE
89731	PRECIOUS METAL JEWELLERY		963.7		1129.7		1194.2		1209.2	ART BIJOUTERIE,JOAILLER
898	MUSICAL INSTRUMENTS,PTS		783.1		915.6		901.8		765.5	INSTRUMENTS DE MUSIQUE
8983	SOUND RECRDNG TAPE,DISCS		692.2		796.4	MN 164876	121.6	MN 108161	109.9	SUPPORTS SON POUR 763
89831	PREPD SND RECORDNG MEDIA		576.6	MN 893474	555.9	MN 1245577	599.4	MN 1116986	482.8	SUPPORTS PREPARES
899	OTHER MANUFACTURED GOODS		2818.9		3079.1		3071.1		3131.3	AUT ART MANUF DIVERS NDA
8994	UMBRELLAS,CANES ETC		630.1		617.7		579.0		600.5	PARAPLUIES,CANNES ETC
89941	UMBRELLAS,SUNSHADES	MN 300263	524.1	MN 281717	523.8	MN 266155	509.7	MN 291297	542.5	PARAPLUIES,PARASOLS ETC
8998	SMALLWARES,TOILETRYS ETC		457.0		525.4		619.0		652.3	ART MERCERIE,TOILETTE
8999	OTHER MANUF GOODS NES		1104.6		1201.9		1129.6		1197.2	OUVRAGES DIVERS NDA
89993	ARTIFICIAL FLOWERS ETC		997.1		1075.3		1010.8		1075.3	FLEURS ARTIFICIELLES
9	GOODS NOT CLASSD BY KIND		974.1		1088.4		1275.4		1171.7	ART TRANSACT NON CLASSES
931	*SPECIAL TRANSACTIONS		884.9		957.1		1096.6		1022.6	TRANS.SPECIALES

1. HISTORICAL SERIES, 1962–1997 SPECIAL TRADE, IMPORTS C.I.F., EXPORTS F.O.B.
SERIES HISTORIQUES, 1962–1997 COMMERCE SPECIAL, IMPORTATIONS C.A.F., EXPORTATIONS F.O.B

YEAR ANNEE	VALUE IN MILLION U.S. DOLLARS VALEUR EN MILLION U.S. DOLLARS MERCHANDISE –MARCHANDISE		GOLD –OR		CONVERSION FACTORS FACTEURS DE CONVERSION CENTS E.U. PAR		INDEX NUMBERS –INDICES QUANTUM		UNIT VALUE VALEUR UNITAIRE	
	IMPORTS	EXPORTS	IMPORTS	EXPORTS	IMPORTS	EXPORTS	IMPORTS	EXPORTS	IMPORTS	EXPORTS
1962	540.40	463.40								
1963	506.00	446.70								
1964	586.30	548.10								
1965	453.50	539.10								
1966	674.10	507.60								
1967	496.90	509.90								
1968	643.30	558.30								
1969	685.30	607.50		4.60						
1970	843.00	727.20		7.90						
1971	929.40	688.90		0.90						
1972	858.90	969.00								
1973	1061.50	1177.30								
1974	1597.20	1416.90								
1975	1494.80	1465.20								
1976	1708.10	1745.20								
1977	2028.30	2443.20								
1978	2836.30	3002.70								
1979	3233.20	3300.40								
1980	4662.60	3945.00							10	14
1981	5199.20	2956.40							10	11
1982	5477.70	3095.00							14	16
1983	4968.10	3080.90							17	20
1984	4492.40	3483.10							22	28
1985	4130.70	3551.90							30	37
1986	3861.50	5101.60							38	57
1987	4321.90	4642.20							47	54
1988	5001.80	5037.00							60	70
1989	5004.10	5716.50							80	73
1990	5589.50	6765.80							100	100
1991	4906.10	7232.10							121	117
1992	6516.40	6916.50							130	118
1993	9831.50	7115.90							145	134
1994	11882.90	8418.50							158	174
1995	13853.10	10125.50							182	204
1996	13683.60	10587.00							209	217
1997	15377.70	11522.40							224	257

2. IMPORTS BY BROAD ECONOMIC CATEGORY AND EXPORTS BY INDUSTRIAL ORIGIN. (PERCENTAGE OF TOTAL VALUE)
IMPORTATIONS PAR CATEGORIES ECONOMIQUES ET EXPORTATIONS PAR BRANCHE D'ACTIVITE.(EN POURCENTAGE DE LA VALEUR TOTALE)

IMPORTS – IMPORTATIONS

	1991	1992	1993	1994	1995	1996	1997
TOTAL IMPORTS–IMPORTATIONS TOTALES	100.	100.	100.	100.	100.	100.	100.
1 FOOD BEV–ALIMENTATION BOISSONS	5.2	6.7	5.7	6.4	7.1	8.6	7.8
11 PRIMARY–PRODUITS DE BASE	3.4	4.5	3.2	3.3	3.7	4.7	3.9
111 FOR INDUSTRY–POUR L'INDUSTRIE	2.3	3.2	2.3	2.1	2.1	3.1	2.2
112 FOR HOUSEHOLDS–POUR LES MENAGES	1.0	1.3	0.9	1.2	1.6	1.6	1.7
12 PROCESSED–PRODUITS ELABORES	1.8	2.3	2.5	3.1	3.4	3.9	3.9
121 FOR INDUSTRY–POUR L'INDUSTRIE	0.7	0.7	0.9	0.9	0.9	1.1	0.9
122 FOR HOUSEHOLDS–POUR LES MENAGES	1.1	1.6	1.6	2.2	2.5	2.8	2.9
2 IND SUPPLIES–APPROV INDUSTRIELS	46.6	44.6	36.1	35.7	38.7	39.9	36.9
21 PRIMARY–PRODUITS DE BASE	2.6	3.9	3.0	3.2	3.3	4.3	3.6
22 PROCESSED–PRODUITS ELABORES	43.9	40.8	33.1	32.5	35.4	35.6	33.3
3 FUELS–COMBUSTIBLES	5.8	5.2	3.7	2.6	2.7	2.6	2.9
31 PRIMARY–PRODUITS DE BASE	0.0	0.4	0.3	0.0	0.0	0.0	0.0
32 PROCESSED–PRODUITS ELABORES	5.8	4.9	3.5	2.5	2.7	2.6	2.8
321 MOTOR SPIRIT–ESSENCE	4.8	4.1	2.7	1.9	1.7	1.6	2.0
322 OTHER–AUTRES	1.0	0.7	0.8	0.7	1.0	0.9	0.8
4 MACHINERY–EQUIPEMENT	25.3	24.9	24.3	25.9	27.1	28.9	27.1
41 CAPITAL EQUIPMENT–MACHINES	22.0	22.1	21.5	23.2	24.4	25.6	24.0
42 PARTS–PIECES ACCESSOIRES	3.3	2.8	2.8	2.8	2.7	3.3	3.1
5 TRANSPORT–TRANSPORT	9.4	9.7	22.7	22.1	11.7	10.7	13.2
51 PASSENGER CARS–AUTOMOBILES	2.3	2.3	8.2	7.6	3.8	3.5	4.5
52 OTHER–AUTRES	3.1	4.3	10.0	10.7	4.3	3.4	4.6
521 INDUSTRIAL–INDUSTRIELS	2.6	4.1	9.2	9.7	4.2	3.3	4.5
522 NON INDUSTRIAL–NON INDUSTRIEL	0.5	0.1	0.8	1.0	0.1	0.1	0.1
53 PARTS–PIECES ACCESSOIRES	4.1	3.1	4.4	3.8	3.6	3.8	4.2
6 CONSUM GOODS–BIENS CONSOMMATION	4.5	5.2	6.0	7.0	7.6	9.0	9.7
61 DURABLE–DURABLES	1.1	1.4	1.7	1.8	1.8	2.3	2.4
62 SEMI DURABLE–SEMI DURABLES	1.9	2.3	2.5	2.8	3.2	3.4	3.8
63 NON DURABLE–NON DURABLES	1.6	1.4	1.8	2.4	2.6	3.3	3.5
7 GOODS NES–BIENS NDA	3.2	3.7	1.4	0.4	5.1	0.3	2.4

EXPORTS – EXPORTATIONS

	1991	1992	1993	1994	1995	1996	1997
TOTAL EXPORTS–EXPORTATIONS TOTALES	100.	100.	100.	100.	100.	100.	100.
1 AGRICULTURE	33.0	33.9	29.5	36.3	30.2	25.6	31.1
2 MINING QUARRY–INDUS EXTRACTIVES	26.4	27.4	27.3	21.6	26.6	31.8	29.5
3 MANUFACTURING–IND MANUFACTUR	40.6	38.8	43.3	42.1	43.3	42.6	39.4
31 FOOD BEV TOBACCO–ALIM BOISS TAB	4.4	5.2	4.6	5.2	5.2	5.2	6.0
32 TEXTILES–INDUSTRIES TEXTILES	14.0	12.3	13.2	10.8	10.3	8.2	7.5
33 WOOD & PRODUCTS–BOIS & PRODUITS	0.2	0.2	0.2	0.1	0.1	0.2	0.1
34 PAPER & PRODUCTS–PAPIER & PRODT	2.4	2.7	2.7	2.4	2.5	2.0	2.2
35 CHEMICALS–INDUSTRIES CHIMIQUES	9.7	10.2	10.3	10.4	12.1	13.5	13.9
36 NON METAL MIN–MIN NON METAL	1.7	1.5	1.5	1.4	1.4	1.6	1.4
37 BASIC METAL–IND METAL BASE	2.5	2.2	1.8	2.2	2.4	2.1	2.1
38 METAL MANUF–MANUF METAL	4.1	4.1	7.7	8.0	8.0	8.3	5.6
39 OTH MANUF IND–AUTRES MANUF	1.6	0.4	1.3	1.6	1.2	1.4	0.5

3. TRADE BY PRINCIPAL COUNTRIES OF ORIGIN AND DESTINATION (VALUE IN MILLION U.S. DOLLARS)
ECHANGES SELON LES PRINCIPAUX PAYS D'ORIGINE ET DE DESTINATION (VALEUR EN MILLIONS DE DOLLARS EU)

COUNTRIES–PAYS	SPECIAL IMPORTS C.I.F. IMPORTATIONS SPECIALES C.A.F				
	1993	1994	1995	1996	1997
World	9840.8	11937.1	13863.1	13354.9	15378.8
Africa	50.1	88.0	46.8	72.8	44.7
Americas	5940.8	7094.5	8679.0	8676.8	9846.4
– Northern America	3520.4	4275.3	5233.8	5329.2	5885.7
– LAIA	2315.1	2680.1	3274.9	3213.7	3814.1
– CACM	15.6	15.9	21.4	24.5	28.7
– Caribbean	67.6	94.8	121.0	88.1	89.2
– Rest of America	22.2	28.5	27.9	21.2	28.6
Asia excl fmr USSR	1603.4	1827.6	1987.4	1459.7	1919.2
– Middle East	29.2	21.7	9.7	10.5	19.1
Asia former USSR	0.1	0.8	0.3	1.3	0.2
Europe excl fmr USSR	2090.9	2673.2	2892.6	2912.7	3137.9
– European Union	1859.1	2416.9	2571.6	2638.5	2839.0
– Eastern Europe	56.5	66.0	90.8	57.5	50.7
– Rest of Europe	175.3	190.3	230.2	216.7	248.2
Europe former USSR	49.9	65.2	85.9	49.9	105.3
Oceania	93.5	57.7	23.7	36.7	85.7
Other	12.1	130.0	147.4	145.0	239.6
USA/Etats–Unis d'Amer	3278.2	3837.3	4692.3	4828.4	5429.9
Venezuela	944.3	1149.6	1382.6	1309.5	1599.5
Japan/Japon	1096.1	1141.9	1230.5	728.9	951.4
Germany/Allemagne	578.1	638.6	756.8	775.4	758.8
Brazil/Brésil	456.5	427.6	452.5	428.5	514.4
Mexico/Mexique	264.3	341.8	505.4	514.4	593.9
Canada	242.0	437.9	541.5	500.8	455.7
Italy/Italie	272.2	363.9	391.1	471.5	391.3
France, Monaco	230.9	271.2	329.5	247.7	490.1
Spain/Espagne	221.1	262.0	282.3	343.7	350.8
Ecuador/Equateur	186.4	259.5	272.2	326.2	385.4
United Kingdom	175.1	389.5	248.5	284.0	270.8
Argentina/Argentine	232.1	204.7	241.1	209.0	207.6
Korea, Republic of	131.6	223.9	229.1	182.9	291.7
Switzerland,Liechtenst.	161.6	173.5	194.6	189.8	225.3
Chile/Chili	74.3	128.9	199.7	211.1	252.8
Sweden/Suède	86.5	159.3	180.2	154.5	204.5
Areas n.e.s.	12.1	130.0	147.4	145.0	239.6
Other Asia n.e.s.	105.0	114.6	132.2	141.9	150.3
Peru/Pérou	90.7	101.8	125.6	124.2	158.9
Netherlands/Pays–Bas	140.8	122.0	94.2	116.9	112.4
China/Chine	54.6	91.2	118.9	128.5	183.4
Belgium–Luxembourg	55.2	65.7	105.3	88.6	106.1
Bolivia/Bolivie	48.5	49.8	64.3	73.9	82.8
Israel/Israël	58.5	44.7	62.7	64.3	77.9
Russian Federation	35.1	49.6	72.0	44.2	91.3
Finland/Finlande	29.4	43.3	66.2	55.1	52.5
Trinidad and Tobago	37.6	47.4	51.7	50.3	40.5
So. African Customs Un	35.7	65.6	31.3	51.8	21.1
China, Hong Kong SAR	31.7	37.5	43.4	38.5	42.3
Australia/Australie	18.2	56.0	16.1	29.5	65.0
Denmark/Danemark	25.3	39.1	50.9	33.0	27.4
India/Inde	13.8	21.2	35.3	35.6	59.3
Indonesia/Indonésie	21.2	30.3	37.3	35.7	32.5
Austria/Autriche	25.2	27.6	28.1	25.0	29.3
Malaysia/Malaisie	13.0	14.9	20.6	36.8	37.1
Panama	21.9	27.0	26.7	20.6	24.3
Ireland/Irlande	14.3	23.3	28.7	24.9	26.5
Romania/Roumanie	26.5	18.9	21.6	15.9	12.7
Singapore/Singapour	10.7	12.0	28.1	18.2	24.8

COUNTRIES–PAYS	SPECIAL EXPORTS F.O.B. EXPORTATIONS SPECIALES F.O.B.				
	1993	1994	1995	1996	1997
Monde	7454.9	8916.8	10327.8	11182.4	11530.2
Afrique	21.1	10.9	36.0	29.8	33.0
Amériques	5065.9	5347.4	6770.8	7690.5	7897.3
– Amérique du Nord	3075.2	3286.4	3705.3	4567.8	4499.9
– ALAI	1474.4	1577.5	2454.6	2378.9	2647.6
– MCAC	144.5	164.7	178.2	188.7	244.3
– Caraïbes	209.9	171.5	294.7	374.2	363.7
– Autre Amérique	161.9	147.4	137.9	180.8	141.8
Asie anc. URSS exclus	410.5	571.5	647.9	544.1	584.3
– Moyen–Orient	40.4	44.7	21.4	19.7	12.1
Asie ancienne URSS	0.0	0.1	0.0	0.0	0.2
Europe anc. URSS exclus	1868.1	2875.2	2753.2	2715.1	2786.0
– Union Européenne	1758.6	2739.6	2634.0	2582.4	2618.9
– Europe de l'Est	14.7	24.1	21.3	36.8	67.7
– Autre de l'Europe	94.8	111.6	97.9	95.8	99.4
Europe ancienne URSS	27.5	11.8	27.8	44.7	68.3
Océanie	11.3	10.8	14.3	16.1	17.3
Autre	50.3	89.1	77.8	142.2	143.8
USA/Etats–Unis d'Amer	3014.8	3191.3	3539.5	4447.1	4358.5
Venezuela	716.9	562.0	962.4	827.7	988.9
Germany/Allemagne	562.6	909.7	745.1	611.9	727.1
Peru/Pérou	210.1	235.7	566.9	616.3	540.5
Ecuador/Equateur	223.1	325.8	423.3	428.4	542.2
Japan/Japon	238.0	353.6	363.9	372.4	358.8
Netherlands/Pays–Bas	212.8	357.9	344.9	366.7	337.6
Belgium–Luxembourg	220.8	359.1	296.1	294.9	339.8
France, Monaco	121.7	220.8	277.8	363.4	218.6
United Kingdom	146.4	196.7	197.9	200.1	219.2
Italy/Italie	115.6	178.0	187.9	207.0	198.4
Spain/Espagne	124.4	169.3	260.5	169.5	148.7
Chile/Chili	95.3	119.9	165.5	184.4	192.3
Panama	160.7	144.6	133.3	172.3	135.0
Canada	60.1	94.9	165.7	120.1	138.7
Mexico/Mexique	83.6	150.3	99.9	94.1	113.5
Brazil/Brésil	60.9	63.5	136.5	132.6	131.7
Areas n.e.s.	50.3	89.1	77.8	142.2	143.8
Costa Rica	84.3	92.7	93.0	104.6	128.1
Denmark/Danemark	76.5	69.6	70.7	108.3	128.1
Sweden/Suède	51.3	92.0	89.3	77.5	96.6
Argentina/Argentine	62.3	92.2	63.1	54.1	83.6
Trinidad and Tobago	50.1	16.7	55.8	131.7	90.3
Switzerland,Liechtenst.	68.1	66.0	53.3	64.2	64.1
Netherland Antilles	42.7	33.5	39.2	93.0	86.8
Finland/Finlande	39.8	70.2	56.8	69.1	58.9
Portugal	29.6	68.2	60.4	47.9	65.8
China, Hong Kong SAR	61.1	54.8	97.7	19.5	19.8
Dominican Republic	40.6	40.2	47.7	56.7	64.0
Ireland/Irlande	47.8	33.4	35.2	48.8	67.5
Aruba	32.5	11.0	105.2	23.5	50.1
Israel/Israël	30.3	30.4	38.3	49.6	73.2
Korea, Republic of	18.1	33.4	45.7	30.6	51.0
Guatemala	27.0	29.4	34.9	38.1	41.1
Russian Federation	21.1	11.4	26.0	34.0	62.6
Norway,Svalbard and JM	22.7	41.8	30.7	25.8	29.7
Bolivia/Bolivie	18.4	23.1	24.7	30.9	45.7
Cuba	20.3	35.2	18.1	23.1	19.4
El Salvador	14.7	24.5	17.3	17.8	41.5
Poland/Pologne	5.7	16.2	15.9	25.1	43.3

(VALUE AS PERCENTAGE OF WORLD TOTAL)(VALEURS EN POURCENTAGE DU TOTAL MONDIAL)

	1988	1989	1990	1991	1992	1993	1994	1995	1996	1997
Africa	0.0	0.2	0.1	0.7	0.5	0.5	0.7	0.3	0.5	0.3
Americas	61.1	62.2	60.5	60.9	63.7	60.4	59.4	62.6	65.0	64.0
– Northern America	40.0	39.7	39.0	37.7	39.1	35.8	35.8	37.8	39.9	38.3
– LAIA	18.7	20.2	18.4	19.9	21.4	23.5	22.5	23.6	24.1	24.8
– CACM	0.2	0.1	0.1	0.2	0.1	0.2	0.1	0.2	0.2	0.2
– Caribbean	0.2	0.5	1.7	2.6	2.6	0.7	0.8	0.9	0.7	0.6
– Rest of America	2.0	1.6	1.4	0.5	0.5	0.2	0.2	0.2	0.2	0.2
Asia excl fmr USSR	12.1	11.8	11.8	12.9	12.5	16.3	15.3	14.3	10.9	12.5
– Middle East	0.0	0.0	0.0	0.1	0.1	0.3	0.2	0.1	0.1	0.1
Asia former USSR						0.0	0.0	0.0	0.0	0.0
Europe excl fmr USSR	26.0	24.9	26.5	24.6	22.2	21.2	22.4	20.9	21.8	20.4
– European Union	22.0	20.9	22.4	20.4	19.5	18.9	20.2	18.5	19.8	18.5
– Eastern Europe	1.0	1.2	1.0	0.7	0.5	0.6	0.6	0.7	0.4	0.3
– Rest of Europe	3.0	2.8	3.0	3.5	2.2	1.8	1.6	1.7	1.6	1.6
Europe former USSR	0.2	0.2	0.2	0.3	0.2	0.5	0.5	0.6	0.4	0.7
Oceania	0.3	0.3	0.2	0.2	0.2	0.9	0.5	0.2	0.3	0.6
Other	0.3	0.3	0.7	0.4	0.6	0.1	1.1	1.1	1.1	1.6
USA/Etats–Unis d'Amer	36.2	36.0	35.4	35.0	35.8	33.3	32.1	33.8	36.2	35.3
Venezuela	3.5	4.1	5.8	6.9	6.5	9.6	9.6	10.0	9.8	10.4
Japan/Japon	10.8	9.4	8.9	10.2	8.7	11.1	9.6	8.9	5.5	6.2
Germany/Allemagne				5.5	6.2	5.9	5.3	5.5	5.8	4.9
Brazil/Brésil	4.6	4.2	3.3	3.2	4.2	4.6	3.6	3.3	3.2	3.3
Mexico/Mexique	4.1	2.5	2.1	3.3	2.9	2.7	2.9	3.6	3.9	3.9
Canada	3.6	3.6	3.5	2.7	3.3	2.5	3.7	3.9	3.7	3.0
Italy/Italie	1.7	1.8	1.9	2.3	2.4	2.8	3.0	2.8	3.5	2.5
France, Monaco	3.7	3.1	2.8	4.6	3.1	2.3	2.3	2.4	1.9	3.2
Spain/Espagne	2.4	2.2	2.2	1.4	1.7	2.2	2.2	2.0	2.6	2.3

	1988	1989	1990	1991	1992	1993	1994	1995	1996	1997
Afrique	1.3	0.1	0.1	0.1	0.2	0.3	0.1	0.3	0.3	0.3
Amériques	57.0	61.2	62.9	64.6	65.8	68.0	60.0	65.6	68.8	68.5
– Amérique du Nord	40.5	44.7	45.5	40.0	40.2	41.3	36.9	35.9	40.8	39.0
– ALAI	11.1	9.2	9.6	15.3	19.1	19.8	17.7	23.8	21.3	23.0
– MCAC	1.0	0.9	0.9	1.5	1.9	1.9	1.8	1.7	1.7	2.1
– Caraïbes	1.9	2.4	2.3	3.8	2.9	2.8	1.9	2.9	3.3	3.2
– Autre Amérique	2.5	4.0	4.5	4.1	1.7	2.2	1.7	1.3	1.6	1.2
Asie anc. URSS exclus	7.0	5.8	5.1	4.9	4.8	5.5	6.4	6.3	4.9	5.1
– Moyen–Orient	0.1	0.1	0.2	0.5	0.8	0.5	0.5	0.2	0.2	0.1
Asie ancienne URSS						0.0	0.0	0.0	0.0	0.0
Europe anc. URSS exclus	34.3	31.5	30.0	29.7	28.4	25.1	32.2	26.7	24.3	24.2
– Union Européenne	30.3	28.1	27.3	27.4	27.2	23.6	30.7	25.5	23.1	22.7
– Europe de l'Est	3.1	2.6	1.7	0.9	0.5	0.2	0.3	0.2	0.3	0.6
– Autre de l'Europe	0.9	0.8	1.0	1.4	0.8	1.3	1.3	0.9	0.9	0.9
Europe ancienne URSS	0.3	1.3	0.2	0.0	0.1	0.4	0.1	0.3	0.4	0.6
Océanie	0.1	0.1	0.1	0.1	0.1	0.2	0.1	0.1	0.1	0.1
Autre	0.0	0.1	1.7	0.5	0.6	0.7	1.0	0.8	1.3	1.2
USA/Etats–Unis d'Amer	39.3	43.2	44.5	38.8	39.4	40.4	35.8	34.3	39.8	37.8
Venezuela	4.4	3.2	3.0	5.9	8.5	9.6	6.3	9.3	7.4	8.6
Germany/Allemagne				7.5	8.6	7.5	10.2	7.2	5.5	6.3
Peru/Pérou	1.7	1.1	1.3	2.9	3.6	2.8	2.6	5.5	5.5	4.7
Ecuador/Equateur	0.9	1.0	1.1	1.7	2.2	3.0	3.7	4.1	3.8	4.7
Japan/Japon	5.2	4.4	3.8	3.2	2.9	3.2	4.0	3.5	3.3	3.1
Netherlands/Pays–Bas	5.0	5.7	4.3	4.3	4.0	2.9	4.0	3.3	3.3	2.9
Belgium–Luxembourg	1.5	1.4	1.7	2.4	2.6	3.0	4.0	2.9	2.6	2.9
France, Monaco	2.6	2.5	2.8	2.4	1.9	1.6	2.5	2.7	3.3	1.9
United Kingdom	1.8	1.8	2.8	2.6	2.7	2.0	2.2	1.9	1.8	1.9

4. Special Imports C.I.F. by Commodities according to the S.I.T.C. (Rev. 2) in million U.S. Dollars
Importations Spéciales C.A.F. par Produits d'après la C.T.C.I. (Rév. 2) en millions de Dollars E.U.

SITC CTCI	COMMODITY	1994		1995		1996		1997		PRODUIT
		QUANTITY QUANTITE	VALUE VALEUR	QUANTITY QUANTITE	VALUE VALEUR	QUANTITY QUANTITE	VALUE VALEUR	QUANTITY QUANTITE	VALUE VALEUR	
	ALL COMMODITIES		11937.1		13863.1		13354.9		15378.9	TOUS PRODUITS
0	FOOD AND LIVE ANIMALS		869.0		1064.7		1392.1		1385.5	ALIMENTS,ANIMAUX VIVANTS
01	MEAT AND PREPARATIONS		20.3		32.2		41.7		48.0	VIANDES ET PREPARATIONS
02	DAIRY PRODCTS,BIRDS'EGGS		15.1		30.1		33.3		64.4	PRODUITS LAITIERS,OEUFS
022	MILK AND CREAM	W 6609	9.9	W 10595	18.7	W 13036	25.5	W 25745	53.7	LAIT ET CREME
0224	MILK,CREAM PRESERVED ETC	W 5627	9.3	W 9601	18.0	W 11802	24.4	W 25743	53.7	LAIT,CREME CONS,CONC
03	FISH AND PREPARATIONS		64.5		92.6		87.7		80.5	POISSONS ET PREPARATIONS
037	FISH ETC PREPD,PRSVD NES	W 37144	44.5	W 43139	55.3	W 43509	59.2	W 42089	54.3	POIS,CRUST,MOL PREPARES
0371	FISH PREPARD,PRESRVD NES	W 36762	44.0	W 43035	54.8	W 43324	58.2	W 41944	53.5	CONSERVES DE POISSONS
04	CEREALS AND PREPARATIONS		423.4		506.3		762.9		660.9	CEREALES ET PRODUITS
041	WHEAT ETC UNMILLED	W 851207	135.3	W 990847	192.9	W 983254	230.1	W 1022866	188.5	FROMENT,EPEAUTRE
0411	DURUM WHEAT UNMILLED	W 762528	121.2	W 857324	168.3	W 835027	198.2	W 910892	169.4	FROMENT DUR NON MOULU
042	RICE	W 237852	75.0	W 123077	38.9	W 150555	55.2	W 182556	71.7	RIZ
0422	RICE SEMI–MILLED,MILLED	W 236560	74.5	W 120835	38.2	W 107825	44.1	W 116643	49.8	RIZ POLI,GLACE INCL BRISURES
04221	RICE MILLED UNBROKEN	W 221951	71.2	W 97220	33.4	W 102940	43.0	W 114905	49.3	RIZ POLI,GLACE EXCL BRISURES
043	BARLEY UNMILLED	W 201484	26.9	W 174932	28.7	W 263492	56.1	W 205799	41.7	ORGE NON MONDEE
044	MAIZE UNMILLED	W 1052942	145.4	W 1153541	176.2	W 1700141	332.6	W 1734088	272.6	MAIS NON MOULU
048	CEREAL ETC PREPARATIONS	W 22070	27.7	W 53811	51.8	W 60040	61.3	W 65158	65.3	PREPTNS A BASE CEREALES
05	VEGETABLES AND FRUIT		130.7		172.4		179.4		232.3	LEGUMES ET FRUITS
054	VEG ETC FRSH,SMPLY PRSVD	W 156208	59.1	W 134700	64.2	W 132955	69.0	W 199981	101.6	LEGUMES FRAIS,CONG,SECS
0542	LEGUMINOUS VEGETBLES DRY	W 120416	42.7	W 107489	44.2	W 101835	47.5	W 148270	73.9	LEGUMES A COSSE SECS
057	FRUIT,NUTS,FRESH,DRIED	W 109188	56.9	W 181761	88.0	W 159765	87.1	W 190443	100.9	FRUITS FRAIS OU SECS
0574	APPLES FRESH	W 47590	33.0	W 54624	40.7	W 52097	42.0	W 59671	46.5	POMMES FRAICHES
06	SUGAR AND PREPS,HONEY		29.0		50.6		22.5		23.4	SUCRES ET PRODUITS
081	*FEEDING STUFF FOR ANIML		109.9	W 332274	104.9		178.7	W 468409	179.0	NOURRITURE POUR ANIMAUX
0813	OILCAKE AND OTH RESIDUES	W 260899	63.3	W 262157	62.5	W 436435	125.3	W 366411	121.1	TOURTEAUX
08131	— OF SOYA BEANS	W 260736	63.3	W 261940	62.4	W 435892	125.2	W 359856	120.0	TOURTEAUX DE SOJA
09	MISC EDIBLE PRODUCTS		34.1		47.7		48.0		64.4	PREP ALIMENTAIRES DIVERSES
098	EDIBLE PRODCTS,PREPS NES	W 9158	27.6	W 14139	36.3	W 15116	42.5	W 18614	53.1	PREP ALIMENTAIRES NDA
1	BEVERAGES AND TOBACCO		33.8		64.5		86.7		100.8	BOISSONS ET TABACS
11	BEVERAGES		28.6		55.0		68.5		75.8	BOISSONS
112	ALCOHOLIC BEVERAGES	W 13763	25.2	W 47671	42.1	W 80745	42.4	W 72834	45.6	BOISSONS ALCOOLIQUES
2	CRUDE MATERLS,EXCL FUELS		430.8		490.0		474.4		520.4	MAT BRUTES NON COMESTIBLES
22	OIL SEEDS,OLEAGINOUS FRT		67.1		56.6		105.1		106.4	GRAINES,FRUITS OLEAGINEUX
222	SEEDS FOR'SOFT'FIXED OIL	W 159734	43.0	W 129262	35.9	W 248234	79.2	W 218525	70.8	GRAINES HUILES FIXES
2222	SOYA BEANS	W 158283	42.5	W 128847	35.4	W 245598	76.7	W 214779	67.5	FEVES DE SOJA
23	RUBBER, CRUDE		70.6		97.1		84.3		81.2	CAOUTCHOUC BRUT
232	NATURAL RUBBER,GUMS	W 24245	25.8	W 28072	44.4	W 21777	33.4	W 23356	28.7	LATEX CAOUTCHOUC NATUREL
233	RUBBER,SYNTHTIC,RECLAIMD	W 40997	44.9	W 37272	52.8	W 36318	50.9	W 42232	52.6	LATEX CAOUTCH SYNTH REGEN
2331	SYNTHETIC RUBBER ETC	W 40706	44.7	W 37118	52.7	W 36031	50.7	W 41864	52.4	LATEX CAOUTCH SYNTHETIQUE
251	*PULP AND WASTE PAPER	W 117880	57.5	W 114850	73.2	W 130188	57.4	W 120774	54.8	PATES A PAPIER,DECHETS
2517	SODA,SULPHATE WOOD PULP	W 75961	45.3	W 62171	57.5	W 66798	42.6	W 80431	45.2	PATES CHIMIQUES AU SULFATE
25172	— BLEACHED,NONDISSOLVNG	W 73770	44.0	W 60507	56.2	W 65830	42.0	W 79295	44.6	PATES BLANCHIES
26	TEXTILE FIBRES AND WASTE		101.4		133.2		90.9		131.0	FIBRES TEXTILES
263	COTTON	W 37047	56.3	W 38108	81.2	W 25948	47.8	W 48078	84.8	COTON
2631	RAW COTTON,EXCL LINTERS	W 35371	55.7	W 37747	81.0	W 25676	47.6	W 47285	84.2	COTON EN MASSE
27	CRUDE FERTLZR,MINRLS NES		58.6		58.4		69.8		68.9	ENGRAIS MINERAUX BRUTS
278	OTHER CRUDE MINERALS	W 300543	38.2	W 278065	35.4	W 426088	45.5	W 340673	42.4	AUTRES MINERAUX BRUTS
29	CRUDE ANIMAL,VEG MAT NES		32.4		38.8		41.5		46.7	MATIERES BRUTES ANIM,VEGET
3	MINERAL FUELS ETC		321.7		396.0		368.7		459.2	COMBUSTIBLES MINERAUX LUB
33	PETROLEUM AND PRODUCTS		315.7		389.0		363.1		455.5	PETROLE ET DERIVES
334	PETROLEUM PRODUCTS,REFIN	W 1731854	302.0	W 1953175	370.1	W 1497808	340.9	W 1872000	435.6	PRODUITS RAFFINES
3341	GASOLINE,OTH LIGHT OILS	W 1462188	224.3	W 1424299	239.2	W 1034341	219.3	W 1400752	314.9	ESSENCES POUR MOTEURS
33411	MOTOR,AVIATION SPIRIT	W 1461298	224.0	W 1423650	238.9	W 1033828	219.0	W 1400227	314.7	ESSENCES MOTEURS D'AVIONS
3343	GAS OILS	W 165324	26.7	W 393044	61.8	W 345934	62.8	W 334945	61.3	GAS OILS
3345	LUBS,PETROLEUM OILS NES	W 101088	50.0	W 130828	67.6	W 110280	56.5	W 128656	57.0	HUILES LUBRIFIANTES
33451	LUBS(HIGH PETR CONT) ETC	W 98853	43.7	W 127877	58.5	W 107911	49.3	W 125925	49.5	HUILES LUBRIF,H LOURDES
4	ANIMAL,VEGETABLE OIL,FAT		85.9		114.2		136.2		118.9	HUILES,GRAISSES ANIM,VEG
42	FIXED VEGETABLE OIL,FAT		56.7		84.3		98.9		87.0	HUILES VEGETALES FIXES
423	FIXED VEG OILS,SOFT	W 78895	50.3	W 118309	81.2	W 139913	90.5	W 126450	84.0	HUILES VEGET DOUCES FIXES
4232	SOYA BEAN OIL	W 63641	40.0	W 93958	62.9	W 112108	69.6	W 94292	60.6	HUILE DE SOJA
5	CHEMCLS,RELATED PROD NES		1936.5		2484.1		2454.8		2698.3	PRODUITS CHIMIQUES
51	ORGANIC CHEMICALS		715.0		952.6		874.5		901.9	PROD CHIMIQ ORGANIQUES
511	HYDROCARBONS NES,DERIVS	W 337160	189.5	W 407376	279.2	W 444745	245.1	W 477943	264.6	HYDROCARBURES NDA
5111	ACYCLIC HYDROCARBONS	W 99055	39.8	W 121980	69.9	W 135390	63.2	W 139941	72.9	HYDROCARBURES ACYCLIQUES
51112	PROPYLENE	W 96758	38.6	W 118120	67.3	W 131906	61.0	W 136151	69.9	PROPYLENE
5112	CYCLIC HYDROCARBONS	W 79401	51.2	W 78472	76.3	W 79478	61.0	W 100085	60.9	HYDROCARBURES CYCLIQUES
51125	STYRENE	W 72314	46.9	W 75513	74.0	W 75053	58.6	W 91529	56.7	STYRENE
5113	HALOG DERIV OF HYDROCARB	W 158171	97.8	W 203837	130.1	W 219646	112.0	W 235866	128.7	DERIVES HALOGENES HYDROCAR
51131	VINYL CHLORIDE	W 151371	90.0	W 198060	121.9	W 213566	103.3	W 228744	118.1	CHLORURE DE VINYLE
512	ALCOHOLS,PHENOLS ETC	W 87174	53.9	W 81103	77.7	W 84643	67.2	W 89778	70.0	PHENOLS,PHENOLS–ALCOOLS
5121	ACYCLIC ALCOHOLS,DERIVS	W 80848	46.8	W 74785	69.3	W 79108	59.6	W 83752	60.8	ALCOOLS ACYCLIQUES
513	CARBOXYLIC ACIDS ETC	W 138187	126.7	W 145100	184.7	W 126705	143.3	W 132142	133.4	ACIDES CARBOXYLIQUES
5137	MONOACIDS AND DERIVATIVS	W 41460	40.8	W 36275	53.0	W 39916	48.7	W 43605	53.6	ACIDES MONOCARBOXYLIQUES
5138	POLYACIDS AND DERIVATIVS	W 94642	69.5	W 105827	108.9	W 83768	72.8	W 85363	56.6	ACIDES POLYCARBOXYLIQUES
51384	TEREPHTHALIC ACID ESTERS	W 75343	51.8	W 84351	82.7	W 70651	57.6	W 70756	41.8	ESTERS DE L'ACIDE TEREPHTALI
514	NITROGEN–FNCTN COMPOUNDS	W 28530	143.6	W 26447	174.8	W 35590	169.8	W 38675	182.6	COMPOSES FONCT AZOTEES
5148	OTH NITROGN–FNCTN CMPNDS	W 11947	73.8	W 12551	92.6	W 16025	93.4	W 19457	97.5	AUTRES COMPOSES AZOTES
51482	IMIDE–,IMIDE–FNCT CMPNDS	W 2790	42.0	W 3480	51.0	W 3641	44.2	W 3615	42.3	COMPOSES A FONCTION IMIDE
515	ORG–INORG COMPOUNDS ETC	W 14355	148.3	W 11591	172.2	W 16772	182.9	W 17288	189.0	COMPOSES ORGANO–MINERAUX
5156	HETEROCYCLIC CMPDS ETC	W 5924	101.4	W 4756	118.6	W 5361	109.4	W 5646	117.8	COMPOSES HETEROCYCLIQUES
51569	OTH HETEROCYC CMPDS,ETC	W 4914	98.5	W 4662	116.5	W 5268	108.1	W 5573	116.6	AUT COMP HETEROCYCLIQUES
516	OTHER ORGANIC CHEMICALS	W 31678	53.3	W 31022	64.3	W 29305	66.5	W 32305	62.6	AUTRES PROD ORGANIQUES
52	INORGANIC CHEMICALS		127.1		158.0		166.6		159.1	PROD CHIM INORGANIQUES
522	INORG ELEMNTS,OXIDES,ETC	W 170762	53.4	W 195602	72.3	W 243706	70.9	W 263140	66.5	ELEMENTS INORGANIQUES
5225	INORGANIC BASES ETC NES	W 136324	25.7	W 157864	41.3	W 214072	40.6	W 235940	36.6	AUTRES BASES OXYDES METAL
523	OTHR INORG CHEMICALS ETC	W 193430	72.4	W 233323	84.3	W 245141	93.9	W 223790	89.8	AUT PRODUITS CHIMIQUES INORG
5232	OTH MTL CMPD OF INRG ACD	W 154763	45.7	W 191178	53.0	W 201746	61.6	W 182620	57.9	SELS METALLIQUES
53	DYES,TANNING,COLOUR PROD		139.5		146.0		140.8		154.4	PROD TEINTURE,COLORANTS
531	SYNT DYE,NAT INDGO,LAKES	W 5062	65.7	W 4807	64.4	W 5273	64.4	W 7840	70.7	MAT COLOR ORGAN,LAQUES
5311	SYNTHIC ORGNIC DYESTUFFS	W 4550	58.6	W 4171	56.3	W 4589	56.7	W 6515	61.2	MAT COLOR ORGAN SYNTHET
533	PIGMENTS,PAINTS,ETC	W 28228	68.4	W 27974	76.0	W 25542	70.0	W 31548	76.9	PIGMENTS,PEINTURES,VERNIS
541	*MEDICINAL,PHARM PRODUCT	K 4082238	204.0	K 4847406	268.6	K 6675034	329.7		401.0	PROD MEDICINAUX PHARMACEUT
5413	ANTIBIOTICS IN BULK	K 409285	33.5	K 616298	38.5	K 621888	44.6	K 811815	46.4	ANTIBIOTIQUES NDA
5417	MEDICAMENTS	K 2420875	102.1	K 2543849	138.2	K 4017704	180.5	K 6346622	245.0	MEDICAMENTS
54171	— CONTAINNG ANTIBIOTICS	K 1061333	30.5	K 651575	38.9	K 847809	53.0	K 1085955	58.2	MED CONTN ANTIBIOTIQUES
54179	— CONTNG OTH SUBSTANCES	K 1045053	55.4	K 1656541	80.3	K 2906809	101.5	K 4851731	151.1	MED CONT AUT SUBSTANCES
55	PERFUME,CLEANING ETC PRD		81.2		108.9		115.5		151.7	PROD POUR PARFUM,TOILETTE
551	ESSENTL OILS,PERFUME,ETC	W 2281	37.8	W 2443	45.5	W 2450	45.2	W 3169	56.2	HUILES ESSENTIELLES
5514	MIXED PERFUME SUBSTANCES	W 1754	31.7	W 2043	38.7	W 2099	37.6	W 2747	47.6	MELANGES SUBSTAN ODORIFER
553	PERFUMERY,COSMETICS,ETC	W 2595	17.2	W 3045	27.8	W 6378	37.2	W 7697	49.9	PRODUITS DE PARFUMERIE

4. Special Imports C.I.F. by Commodities according to the S.I.T.C. (Rev. 2) in million U.S. Dollars
Importations Spéciales C.A.F. par Produits d'après la C.T.C.I. (Rév. 2) en millions de Dollars E.U.

SITC CTCI	COMMODITY	1994 QUANTITY QUANTITE	1994 VALUE VALEUR	1995 QUANTITY QUANTITE	1995 VALUE VALEUR	1996 QUANTITY QUANTITE	1996 VALUE VALEUR	1997 QUANTITY QUANTITE	1997 VALUE VALEUR	PRODUIT
562	*FERTILIZERS,MANUFACTURE	W 987262	159.8	W 934549	184.8	W 875100	170.2	W 912463	163.8	ENGRAIS MANUFACTURES
5621	CHEM NITROGENOUS FERTLZR	W 450141	74.0	W 448632	99.2	W 423241	91.8	W 428077	79.4	ENGRAIS AZOTES
56216	UREA	W 407164	63.9	W 381047	82.1	W 352159	74.4	W 334939	55.9	UREE
5623	CHEM POTASSIC FERTILIZER	W 305289	39.9	W 265016	35.4	W 264431	35.1	W 285092	39.0	ENGRAIS POTASSIQUES
56231	POTASSIUM CHLORIDE	W 298059	38.7	W 252310	33.0	W 247888	32.2	W 256845	34.3	CHLORURE DE POTASSIUM
5629	FERTILIZERS NES	W 221650	44.4	W 211972	48.8	W 179844	42.0	W 193188	44.2	ENGRAIS NDA
56292	NITROG–PHOS FERTILZR NES	W 209817	41.2	W 210284	47.1	W 176415	40.4	W 188635	41.2	ENGRAIS NDA CONT N P
58	PLASTIC MATERIALS ETC		297.7		400.6		382.7		441.9	MAT PLAST ARTIFICIELLES
582	PROD OF CONDENSATION ETC	W 33242	65.7	W 32256	77.5	W 31161	77.0	W 38425	84.6	PROD CONDENS,POLYCOND
583	POLYMERIZATION ETC PRODS	W 191875	203.4	W 210213	292.4	W 232350	277.2	W 256092	331.2	PROD POLYMERISATION
5831	POLYETHYLENE	W 117799	95.3	W 145775	167.9	W 139200	136.6	W 145263	153.9	POLYETHYLENE
58311	— IN PRIMARY FORMS	W 116224	92.1	W 142703	162.3	W 136525	128.0	W 140679	141.3	POLYETHYLENE PRIMAIRES
5839	OTH POLYMRZTION ETC PROD	W 10640	30.1	W 9111	33.0	W 25038	52.3	W 34079	68.3	AUT PROD POLYMER COPOLYM
59	CHEMICAL MATERIALS NES		207.7		260.2		267.2		314.1	MAT PROD CHIMIQUES NDA
591	PESTICIDES,DISINFECTANTS	W 6657	47.3	W 7780	56.0	W 9592	63.4	W 14070	80.9	DESINF,INSECT,FONG,HERB
598	MISCEL CHEM PRODUCTS NES	W 112273	143.6	W 137234	178.8	W 130440	178.6	W 164602	203.7	PROD DIV INDUST CHIM NDA
5989	CHEM PRODUCTS,PREPS NES	W 84752	100.7	W 106254	127.8	W 102682	132.7	W 131854	147.3	PROD PREP CHIMIQUES NDA
59899	OTH CHEM PRODS,PREPS,NES	W 67306	72.5	W 84940	91.9	W 82456	95.7	W 94681	105.3	AUT PRODUITS CHIMIQUES NDA
6	BASIC MANUFACTURES		1896.2		2426.9		2316.9		2537.7	ART MANUFACTURES
62	RUBBER MANUFACTURES NES		114.3		157.8		183.8		208.5	CAOUTCHOUC MANUFACTURE
625	RUBBER TYRES, TUBES ETC	W 31688	81.5	W 36482	121.3	W 42380	140.5	W 45635	157.6	PNEUS CAOUTCHOUC VULCANISE
6252	TYRES,NEW,BUS OR LORRY	W 8694	26.1	W 13829	43.9	W 15610	51.3	W 17860	57.4	PNEUS POUR AUTOBUS,CAMIONS
6259	OTH TYRES,TYRE CASES,ETC	W 14483	27.8	W 11133	38.7	W 11680	44.5	W 13001	48.8	AUTRES PNEUS RECHAPES FLAPS
64	PAPER,PAPERBOARD AND MFR		277.1		352.8		332.6		369.6	PAPIERS,CARTONS & OUVRAGES
641	PAPER AND PAPERBOARD	W 345524	240.8	W 299847	293.6	W 327722	270.6	W 403178	305.5	PAPIERS ET CARTONS
6411	NEWSPRINT	W 96547	56.3	W 107548	79.4	W 81400	61.5	W 90833	58.7	PAPIER JOURNAL
6412	PRINTG,WRITING PAPER NES	W 44767	38.8	W 39263	48.0	W 42694	43.1	W 61807	62.8	PAPIERS POUR L'IMPRESSION
64122	— COATED,IMPREGNATD ETC	W 40453	34.9	W 36022	42.7	W 34935	36.8	W 54854	54.9	PAPIERS IMPRESSION COUCHES
6413	KRAFT PAPER,PAPERBOARD	W 102692	51.7	W 71646	51.0	W 102344	53.7	W 123720	56.4	PAPIER ET CARTON KRAFT
64139	KRAFT PAPER PAPERBD,NES	W 74026	37.8	W 51850	38.9	W 77078	41.3	W 90109	42.3	PAPIER,CARTON KRAFT NDA
6415	PAPER,PAPERBRD,BULK,NES	W 80799	59.2	W 63136	75.9	W 77184	68.1	W 99390	76.1	PAPIERS,CARTONS ROULEAUX
64159	OTHER PAPER ETC,BULK,NES	W 42749	38.7	W 35239	51.4	W 40834	46.5	W 50521	51.8	AUT PAPIER ROULEAUX FEUILLES
642	PAPER,ETC,PRECUT,ARTS OF	W 21927	36.4	W 30106	59.2	W 31733	62.0	W 35929	64.2	PAP,CARTONS DECOUPES
65	TEXTILE YARN,FABRICS,ETC		319.3		387.4		387.0		450.6	FILS,TISSUS,ARTICLES TEXTILE
651	TEXTILE YARN	W 20227	84.1	W 21982	109.4	W 21558	113.5		161.6	FILS TEXTILES
6514	SYN FIB YRN,BULK,MONOFIL	W 12130	54.1	W 11579	63.2	W 11557	70.8	W 19832	99.8	FILS CONT 85% FIB TEXT SYNTH
65142	— NONTXT ETC CONT PAMID	W 5609	28.0	W 5089	33.1	W 6253	38.2	W 11369	54.9	FILS NON TEX FI CON POLYAMID
652	COTTON FABRICS,WOVEN		60.4	W 15495	81.6	W 19152	91.2	W 17113	78.4	TISSUS DE COTON
6522	WOVEN COTTON BLEACHD,ETC		59.3	W 14998	79.2	W 18483	87.6	W 15993	72.6	TISSUS COTON BLANCHIS ETC
65224	BLCHED COTTON FABRIC NES	W 10544	52.0	W 14229	71.4	W 18091	84.1	W 15393	67.5	AUT TIS PLUS 85% COT BLANCHI
653	WOVN MAN–MADE FIB FABRIC	W 8842	68.5	W 7572	69.2	W 6954	57.3	W 8520	69.9	TISSUS FIBRES SYNTH,ARTIF
657	SPECIAL TXTL FABRC,PRODS	W 7179	35.2	W 9499	41.8	W 10807	47.0	W 13138	58.9	TISSUS SPECIAUX
66	NONMETAL MINERAL MFS NES		161.2		183.9		179.2		219.3	ART MIN NON METALLIQUES
662	CLAY,REFRACTORY BLDG PRD	W 83471	45.5	W 103291	48.7	W 67939	41.5	W 81198	47.4	MAT CONST REFRACTAIRES
664	GLASS	W 40181	33.9	W 43889	36.7	W 45256	61.3	W 58730	60.4	VERRE
665	GLASSWARE	W 61224	37.3	W 61994	44.9	W 23669	28.1	W 72042	54.6	OUVRAGES EN VERRE
67	IRON AND STEEL		547.8		751.6		645.8		618.2	FER ET ACIER
672	IRON,STEEL PRIMARY FORMS	W 265325	68.9	W 181347	51.9	W 165236	47.7	W 314488	90.8	LINGOTS FER,ACIER
6725	IRN,STL BLOOMS,SLABS,ETC	W 211454	50.0	W 147110	37.3	W 115816	30.0	W 173384	44.6	BLOOMS,BILLETTES FER ACIER
67251	IRN,SMPLE STL BLOOMS,ETC	W 211443	50.0	W 147055	37.1	W 115613	29.7	W 173240	44.2	BLOOMS ETC NON ACIER FIN
673	IRON,STEEL SHAPES ETC	W 254016	97.2	W 214477	88.3	W 163875	64.7	W 169365	69.4	BARRES,PROFIL FER,ACIER
6731	IRON,STEEL WIRE ROD	W 131295	46.3	W 97600	37.3	W 96243	33.8	W 98567	35.4	FIL MACHINE FER,ACIER
6732	IRON,STEEL BARS ETC	W 95957	39.0	W 80401	34.7	W 39179	19.2	W 44240	21.3	BARRES FER,ACIER
674	IRN,STL UNIV,PLATE,SHEET	W 499661	252.4	W 492265	293.3	W 488984	275.3	W 468597	243.9	LARGES PLATS,TOLES
6745	IRN,STL MED PLATE,ROLLED	W 79303	42.0	W 69391	43.3	W 87858	50.4	W 94143	48.8	TOLES 3 A 4.75 MM
6746	IRN,STL THIN PLATE,ROLLD	W 295325	148.7	W 334763	198.0	W 309529	173.1	W 300035	157.2	TOLES LAM MOINS 3MM
67461	— OF IRON OR SIMPLE STL	W 284094	130.3	W 324574	172.4	W 298764	149.2	W 288930	135.4	TOL NON AC FIN MOINS 3 MM
678	IRON,STL TUBES,PIPES,ETC	W 77291	99.2	W 237099	280.3	W 212354	223.7	W 132056	176.4	TUBES,TUYAUX EN FONTE,FER
6782	IRON,STL SEAMLESS TUBES	W 31095	45.9	W 44681	56.8	W 68547	89.4	W 56041	74.2	TUBES,TUYAUX SANS SOUDURE
6783	IRON,STL TUBES,PIPES NES	W 34923	26.5	W 186465	204.5	W 134712	98.8	W 60731	55.9	AUT TUBES,TUYAUX FER,ACIER
68	NON–FERROUS METALS		214.6		264.0		239.3		281.2	METAUX NON FERREUX
682	COPPER EXC CEMENT COPPER	W 32537	88.8	W 26625	99.4	W 31931	99.6	W 33658	98.2	CUIVRE
6822	COPPER,ALLOYS WORKED	W 31838	86.9	W 25449	95.4	W 31327	98.0	W 33124	96.7	CUIVRE,ALLIAGES OUVRES
68221	COPPER BARS,WIRE,ETC	W 26424	67.3	W 21253	72.2	W 25350	73.3	W 27790	74.9	BARRES,PROFILES ET FILS
684	ALUMINIUM	W 53662	92.2	W 53951	125.3	W 51540	106.3	W 65146	136.6	ALUMINIUM
6841	ALUMINIUM,ALLOYS,UNWRGHT	W 35606	49.9	W 34335	65.5	W 35293	56.4	W 42780	71.9	ALUMINIUM,ALLIAGES BRUTS
6842	ALUMINIUM,ALLOYS WORKED	W 18056	42.4	W 19616	59.9	W 16247	49.9	W 22366	64.7	ALUMINIUM,ALLIAGES OUVRE
69	METAL MANUFACTURES NES		213.9		270.2		295.6		333.3	ART MANUFACT EN METAL NDA
695	TOOLS	W 9222	68.4	W 9142	78.4	W 11006	84.5	W 6142	84.6	OUTILS A MAIN
6954	BLADES,TIPS,ETC FR TOOLS	W 2411	41.4	W 1306	49.6	W 1477	55.2	W 1510	60.1	OUTILS POUR MACHINE–OUTIL
69541	PARTS TO INSERT IN TOOLS	W 1732	35.7	W 813	44.8	W 1053	50.3	W 807	54.8	OUTILS DE FORAGE
699	BASE METAL MFRS NES	W 12121	57.2	W 16436	71.7	W 15290	73.6	W 18685	90.2	ART MANUFACTURES MET NDA
7	MACHINES,TRANSPORT EQUIP		5552.3		5171.0		5084.8		5985.8	MACHINES MATERIEL TRANSPORT
71	POWER GENERATING EQUIPMT		260.8		255.7		401.4		571.4	MACHINES GENERATRICES
712	STEAM ENGINES,TURBINES	W 296	27.4	W 1063	29.6	W 1099	37.9	W 4700	73.5	MACHINES A VAPEUR D'EAU PIEC
7126	STEAM POWR UNITS,ENGINES	W 146	16.2	W 1029	25.4	W 915	31.3	W 4685	70.6	MACHINES A VAPEUR D EAU
713	INTRNL COMBUS PSTN ENGIN	W 21094	92.7	W 20406	88.4	W 12351	91.1	W 14003	108.9	MOTEURS EXPL COMB INT, PIECE
7139	PISTON ENGINE PARTS NES	W 4754	44.4	W 4682	51.0	W 4189	53.9	W 4161	58.5	PIECES POUR 713.2,3,8
714	ENGINES AND MOTORS NES	W 261	16.8	W 1437	36.9	W 2456	87.4	W 8570	192.9	MOTEURS NON ELECTRIQUES
7148	GAS TURBINES NES	W 44	1.9	W 1327	25.6	W 1564	73.3	W 8007	170.6	TURBINES A GAZ
71488	OTHER GAS TURBINES NES	W 33	0.8	W 1313	24.9	W 1547	71.9	W 7950	164.5	AUTRES TURBINES A GAZ
716	ROTATING ELECTRIC PLANT	W 11276	116.2	W 9039	86.6	W 11319	145.8	W 12840	154.2	APP ELECTR ROTATIFS,PIECES
7161	DC MOTORS AND GENERATORS	W 3941	59.3	W 824	8.5	W 2255	46.9	W 565	6.5	MOTEURS COURANT CONTINU
7162	AC MTRS,GENRTRS,GEN SETS	W 5434	41.4	W 6535	66.5	W 7784	88.0	W 10240	132.7	MOTEURS ELECTRIQUES
71622	AC GENERATORS	W 408	2.9	W 862	16.7	W 1622	32.3	W 4976	90.3	GENER COURANT ALTERNATIF
72	MACHS FOR SPCL INDUSTRYS		655.3		826.7		648.8		569.3	MAC SPECIALES POUR INDUST
723	CIVIL ENGNEERG EQUIP ETC	W 35362	176.1	W 41314	235.1	W 38496	178.7	W 19376	143.6	APPAREILS DE GENIE CIVIL
7234	CONST,MINING MACHNRY NES	W 32202	152.2	W 37412	209.8	W 34674	154.4	W 16063	107.3	MACH POUR LA CONST, MINES
72342	SLFPRP SHOVELS,EXCAVATRS	W 20380	95.9	W 19190	100.3	W 13986	88.5	W 11665	77.8	PELLES MECANIQUES
72344	BORING,SINKING MACHINERY	W 1376	8.4	W 9553	57.7	W 13590	23.5	W 195	4.6	MACHINES DE FORAGE
724	TEXTILE,LEATHER MACHNRY	W 9061	104.3	W 7655	97.2	W 6353	76.4	W 6220	77.7	MACH POUR INDUSTRIE TEXTILE
726	PRINTG,BKBINDG MACHY,PTS	W 3799	70.0	W 2652	54.0	W 2232	39.0	W 2162	33.4	MACHINES POUR IMPRIMERIE
7264	PRINTING PRESSES	W 2716	42.1	W 1870	30.1	W 1547	20.4	W 1003	11.0	MACHINES A IMPRIMER
72641	ROTARY PRINTING PRESSES	W 2716	42.1	W 1870	30.1	W 1547	20.4	W 1003	11.0	MACH IMPRIMER ROTATIVES
727	FOOD MACHRY NON–DOMESTIC	W 2451	40.0	W 4684	66.5	W 4862	68.9	W 2056	30.8	MACH INDUSTRIES ALIMENT
7272	OTH FOOD PROC MCHY,PARTS	W 2227	36.9	W 4343	62.8	W 4267	62.4	W 1765	27.4	AUT MACH IND ALIMENTAIRE
72722	INDUS FOOD PROC MACH NES	W 2079	34.6	W 4172	61.1	W 4173	60.7	W 1738	26.6	MACHINES BOULANGERIE
728	OTH MACHY FOR SPCL INDUS	W 20766	196.6	W 26240	280.0	W 19275	219.8	W 17545	205.2	AUT MACH IND PARTICULIERES
7283	OTHR MINERAL WORKG MACHY	W 8221	50.5	W 12556	79.9	W 6324	35.0	W 5184	36.6	MACH TRIER,CRIBLER,BROYER
7284	MACHY FOR SPCL INDUS NES	W 10933	133.8	W 12587	190.3	W 11665	175.9	W 11651	160.1	MACH SPEC IND PARTICUL.
72842	RUBBER,PLASTICS WRKG MCH	W 4884	47.2	W 4098	53.5	W 3430	48.0	W 3182	45.0	MACH IND CAOUT MAT PLAST

4. Special Imports C.I.F. by Commodities according to the S.I.T.C. (Rev. 2) in million U.S. Dollars
Importations Spéciales C.A.F. par Produits d'après la C.T.C.I. (Rév. 2) en millions de Dollars E.U.

SITC CTCI	COMMODITY	1994 QUANTITY QUANTITE	1994 VALUE VALEUR	1995 QUANTITY QUANTITE	1995 VALUE VALEUR	1996 QUANTITY QUANTITE	1996 VALUE VALEUR	1997 QUANTITY QUANTITE	1997 VALUE VALEUR	PRODUIT
72848	OTH MCHY WITH INDIV FNCT	W 4324	59.1	W 4908	72.4	W 6174	84.4	W 6475	70.6	AUTRES MACHINES NDA
73	METALWORKING MACHINERY		80.4		62.7		65.7		47.7	MACH TRAVAIL DES METAUX
736	METALWORKING MACH–TOOLS	W 9767	58.4	W 7515	42.7	W 4795	32.0	W 4164	32.0	MACH–OUTILS TRAVAIL METAUX
74	GENRL INDUSTRL MACHY NES		709.4		793.9		945.8		854.5	MACH APP INDUSTRIE
741	HEATING,COOLING EQUIPMNT	W 14044	102.4	W 16775	140.1	W 17245	159.4	W 17385	138.7	MACH CHAUFFAGE,PIECES
7414	NONDOM REFRIG EQUIPT,PTS	W 2613	20.7	W 6228	40.8	W 6199	43.1	W 10114	55.9	MAT PRODUCTION DU FROID
74141	REFRIG EQUIP NONDOMESTIC	W 2001	17.2	W 5115	33.7	W 5171	35.2	W 8715	46.2	REFIG INDUSTRIELS
7416	HEATING,COOLING EQU NES	W 5320	43.9	W 5019	63.2	W 7396	81.0	W 4675	56.5	APP CHANGEMENT TEMP
742	PUMPS FOR LIQUIDS ETC	W 5437	78.0	W 4429	70.0	W 6523	110.6	W 5086	83.7	POMPES MOTO–POMPES
7422	CENTRIFUGAL PUMPS NES	W 1691	34.1	W 1297	19.7	W 2931	59.4	W 1100	19.1	POMPES CENTRIF NON 742.81
743	PUMPS NES,CENTRFUGES ETC	W 13632	146.2	W 16090	143.1	W 15280	204.0	W 16236	165.6	POMPES COMPRES,VENT ETC
7431	PUMPS FOR GASES ETC	W 7448	74.7	W 9536	69.0	W 8070	101.2	W 9718	83.2	POMPES AIR A VIDE,COMPRES
7436	GAS,LIQUID FILTERS ETC	W 2882	30.5	W 3546	37.5	W 3838	42.9	W 3601	43.7	APP POUR FILT DES LIQUIDES
7439	PTS NES OF APP OF 7435,6	W 2579	29.9	W 2044	24.1	W 2459	47.2	W 1999	27.4	PIECES 743.5 ET 743.6
744	MECHANICAL HANDLING EQU	W 20367	103.8	W 19615	111.7	W 17983	116.1	W 14542	96.6	EQUIP MANUTENTION PIECES
7442	LIFTING,LOADING MACH NES	W 9567	54.2	W 8263	52.8	W 8616	60.2	W 6075	46.2	APP LEVAGE,MANUTENTION
745	NONELEC MACHY,TOOLS NES	W 4779	104.0	W 5904	141.7	W 5586	118.9	W 5172	116.2	AUT MACH NON ELEC,PIECES
7452	OTH NONELEC MCHS,PTS NES	W 4022	84.3	W 4972	116.7	W 4577	97.7	W 4371	96.4	AUT MACH NON ELEC,PIECES
74522	PACKAGNG,BOTTLNG,ETC MCH	W 2049	55.6	W 2830	83.2	W 1921	56.1	W 1889	55.3	MACH NETT BOUTEILLES,ETC
749	NONELEC MACH PTS,ACC NES	W 14164	175.2	W 15973	187.7	W 19698	237.1	W 19048	254.1	PIECES MACH NON ELEC NDA
7491	BALL,ROLLER,ETC BEARINGS	W 3521	40.1	W 4619	44.6	W 4118	47.4	W 3643	47.9	ROULEMENTS BILLES ETC
7492	COCKS,VALVES ETC NES	W 5531	71.9	W 5392	67.6	W 9038	102.4	W 8830	123.8	ART ROB,SIM POUR TUYAUX
7493	SHAFT,CRANK,PULLEY ETC	W 3423	40.0	W 3795	42.7	W 3460	48.5	W 3450	46.2	ARBRES TRANS,VILEBREQUINS
75	OFFICE MACHNES,ADP EQUIP		415.9		469.7		457.7		549.7	MACH BUREAU TRAIT AUTOM
751	OFFICE MACHINES	W 3961	62.7	W 3237	62.1	W 2933	51.4	W 4130	66.4	MACH,APPAREILS DE BUREAU
7518	OFFICE MACHINES NES	W 1791	46.5	W 1663	45.2	W 1528	38.3	W 2964	56.0	MACH,APP DE BUREAU NDA
752	AUTOMTIC DATA PROC EQUIP	W 5904	298.6	W 6339	339.9	W 5851	342.3	W 9765	414.3	MACH TRAIT INFORMATION
7522	DIGITAL COMPUTERS	W 2042	151.4	W 1612	143.8	W 1624	131.0	W 2331	159.9	MACH DIGITALES COMPLETES
7523	DIGITL CENTRL PROCESSORS	W 523	48.0	W 770	72.3	W 706	76.1	W 1407	77.2	UNITES CENTRALES
7525	ADP PERIPHERAL UNITS	W 2998	65.4	W 3580	80.4	W 3163	86.6	W 5197	111.3	UNITES PERIPHERIQUES
759	OFFICE,ADP MCH PTS,ACCES	W 2144	54.7	W 2275	67.8	W 2228	64.1	W 3753	69.1	PIECES DU 751 ET 752
7599	ACCTG,ETC,ADP MCH PTS,AC	W 1857	44.5	W 1916	56.9	W 1928	52.1	W 2155	53.8	PIECES DU 751 ET 752
76	TELECOMM,SOUND EQUIPMENT		595.2		853.9		801.2		1020.1	EQUIPMENT DE TELECOM
761	TELEVISION RECEIVERS	W 3552	28.2	W 3934	28.1	W 4332	41.2	W 5953	55.2	RECEPTEURS DE TELEVISION
7611	COLOUR TV RECEIVERS	W 3419	27.6	W 3890	27.7	W 4290	39.4	W 5896	54.9	RECEPTEURS COULEUR
764	TELECOM EQPT,PTS,ACC NES	W 7774	536.1	W 10061	785.7	W 9831	702.1	W 14085	894.4	EQUIP TELECOM,PIECES
7641	LINE TELEPHONE,ETC EQUIP	W 2512	206.6	W 3851	309.8	W 4584	320.5	W 6622	348.1	APP TELEPHON PAR FIL
7643	TV,RADIO TRANSMITTRS ETC	W 2466	241.0	W 2365	346.3	W 2033	269.2	W 3266	423.3	APP EMET TELE RADIO
7648	TELECOMM EQUIPMENT NES	W 131	22.9	W 417	44.2	W 192	25.7	W 339	24.9	APP TELECOM NDA
7649	PTS NES OF EQUIPMT OF 76	W 2160	61.1	W 2655	79.1	W 2231	79.4	W 2440	87.4	PIECES DE LA DIV 76
76491	PTS NES OF APPAR OF 7641	W 680	26.6	W 572	37.7	W 519	41.8	W 847	53.7	PIECES POUR 764.1
77	ELECTRIC MACHNRY NES ETC		404.3		531.4		580.8		667.8	MACH APP ELECT NDA
771	ELECTRIC POWER MACHY NES	W 2900	27.8	W 4448	45.1	W 5185	54.6	W 5907	65.9	MACH PROD,TRANS ELECTR
772	SWITCHGEAR ETC,PARTS NES	W 4363	85.1	W 5467	121.4	W 5204	112.2	W 6381	129.7	APP COUPURE,SECT ETC
7721	SWITCHGEAR ETC	W 3865	74.2	W 5086	109.5	W 4912	102.2	W 6195	123.1	APP COUPURE,SECTIONMNT
773	ELECTR DISTRIBUTNG EQUIP	W 8882	38.7	W 17791	78.0	W 19569	88.4	W 18574	92.4	EQUIPMT DISTRIBUTION ELECT
7731	INSULATED WIRE,CABLE ETC	W 7802	31.4	W 16883	67.9	W 18221	75.4	W 16980	76.0	FILS,CABLES ISOLES ELECT
774	ELECTRO–MEDCL,XRAY EQUIP	W 548	39.4	W 640	44.3	W 472	43.4	W 655	61.5	APPAREILS MEDICAUX
775	HOUSEHOLD TYPE EQUIP NES	W 14888	56.0	W 17118	64.7	W 21095	93.2	W 23539	104.2	MACH,APP USAGE DOMESTQUE
7751	HOUSEHOLD LDRY EQUIP NES	W 6130	19.8	W 8358	23.8	W 12228	42.1	W 13439	49.7	MACH A LAVER ET SECHOIRS
77511	DOMESTIC WASHING MACHNES	W 6076	19.6	W 8287	23.5	W 12213	42.0	W 13384	49.5	MACH LAVER LINGE MOINS 6 KG
778	ELECTRICAL MACHINERY NES	W 16908	131.0	W 19854	150.8	W 22125	152.9	W 23174	177.7	AUTRES MACH ELECT NDA
7788	OTH ELEC MACHY,EQUIP NES	W 4169	42.0	W 4935	51.9	W 4566	45.2	W 4717	56.4	AUT MACH APP ELEC NDA
78	ROAD VEHICLES		1824.9		1115.8		925.7		1224.5	VEHICULES ROUTIERS
781	PASS MOTOR VEH EXC BUSES	W 107788	903.8	W 56394	525.7	W 51426	467.2	W 78835	684.5	AUTO TRANSPORT PERSONNES
782	LORRIES,SPCL MTR VEH NES	W 70522	459.8	W 43774	291.7	W 28136	211.6	W 28571	224.8	VEHICULES SPECIAUX,MARCH
7821	LORRIES,TRUCKS	W 66253	434.9	W 40850	273.0	W 26096	190.6	W 26737	208.2	VEHICULES TRANSP MARCHAND
783	ROAD MOTOR VEHICLES NES	W 17967	127.6	W 11221	78.0	W 5451	41.9	W 8057	61.2	VEHICULES ROUTIERS NDA
7831	BUSES	W 10547	70.0	W 6784	40.6	W 2773	18.6	W 4232	27.0	VOITURES TRANSPORT COMMUN
7832	TRACTORS FOR TR–TRAILERS	W 7420	57.7	W 4436	37.5	W 2679	23.3	W 3825	34.3	TRACTEURS ROUTIERS
784	MOTOR VEH PRTS,ACCES NES	W 36828	189.2	W 34360	173.1	W 27784	164.6	W 34072	200.6	PIECES 722,781,782,783
7841	MOTOR VEHICLE CHASSIS	W 6569	49.2	W 1711	11.0	W 4469	9.5	W 3440	22.6	CHASSIS 722,781,782,783
7849	OTHER MOTOR VEHCL PARTS	W 28382	136.4	W 29077	147.4	W 22463	152.4	W 29758	174.1	PIECES 722,781,782,783
785	CYCLES,ETC MOTRZD OR NOT	W 15562	138.0	W 8142	35.5	W 7608	32.2	W 8122	40.0	MOTOCYCLES SCOOTERS
7851	MOTORCYCLES ETC	W 9824	119.4	W 1157	10.7	W 696	7.5	W 1013	12.0	MOTO VELO MOTEUR AUXIL
79	OTHR TRANSPORT EQUIPMENT		606.4		261.5		257.9		481.2	AUTRE MATERIEL TRANSPORT
791	RAILWAY VEHICLES	W 1196	37.6	W 2152	14.5	W 1279	10.3	W 2152	16.8	VEHIC MAT CHEMINS DE FER
7914	RY COACHES NES NOT POWRD	W 1038	36.0							VOITURES A VOYAGEURS
792	AIRCRAFT ETC	W 2026	520.7	W 1681	223.7	W 873	192.4	W 2367	437.8	APP NAVIGATION AERIENNE
7921	HELICOPTERS	W 55	30.1	W 117	63.4	W 68	32.1	W 301	109.8	HELICOPTERES
7923	AIRCRFT NES2000–15000KG	W 341	113.2	W 153	44.8	W 115	57.6	W 182	62.7	AERODYNES 2000 A 15000 KG
7924	AIRCRFT NES OVER 15000KG	W 1484	353.0	W 904	67.5	W 458	73.0	W 1348	188.8	AERODYNES PLUS 15000 KG
7929	AIRCRAFT PARTS NES	W 120	22.1	W 447	41.4	W 210	28.7	W 518	66.5	PIECES DU 792
793	SHIPS AND BOATS ETC	W 30575	48.2	W 24809	23.4	W 11130	55.3	W 10052	26.7	NAVIRES BATEAUX,ETC
7938	TUGS,SPECIAL VESSELS ETC	W 4261	14.2	W 5689	18.5	W 6083	50.5	W 9070	21.2	REMORQUEURS,BATEAUX SPEC
8	MISC MANUFACTURED GOODS		772.4		950.6		1002.5		1212.5	ART MANUFACTURES DIVERS
821	*FURNITURE,PARTS THEREOF	W 5554	27.7	W 8516	44.5	W 10248	48.7	W 11056	49.6	MEUBLES ET PIECES
84	CLOTHING AND ACCESSORIES		70.0		83.1		74.4		103.4	VETEMENTS
87	PRECISION INSTRUMNTS NES		225.6		257.3		284.3		315.2	INSTRUM,APPAR SCIENT NDA
872	MEDICAL INSTRUMENTS NES	W 1710	60.2	W 2119	73.7	W 2197	67.3	W 2008	77.6	INSTR,APP MEDIC–CHIR NDA
87202	OTH MEDICAL INSTRUMENTS	W 1468	54.2	W 1712	66.0	W 1892	59.1	W 1739	67.4	INSTRUM,APP MEDECINE
874	MEASURNG,CONTROLNG INSTR	W 3541	138.9	W 3673	156.5	W 4790	179.3	W 4395	198.4	INSTRUMENTS DE MESURE
8742	MEASUR,DRAW ETC INST,PTS	W 739	27.2	W 769	31.2	W 1535	40.3	W 937	36.8	INST DESSIN,TRACAGE,PCS
8743	GAS,LIQUID CONTROL INSTR	W 1282	36.6	W 960	28.7	W 1546	42.6	W 1376	39.6	APP,INSTR MESURE FLUIDES
8748	ELEC MEAS,CONTRL EQU NES	W 492	39.1	W 587	48.7	W 622	54.0	W 570	58.0	APP ELEC ELECTRO MESURE
87483	OTH ELCTRNC MEAS ETC EQU	W 405	34.6	W 503	43.8	W 521	47.1	W 501	52.8	AUT APP ELECTRO DE MESURE
88	PHOTO EQU,OPTICL GDS ETC		112.0		122.8		115.7		137.5	APP,FOURN PHOTO,OP,MONTR
882	PHOTO,CINEMA SUPPLIES	W 6478	74.2	W 6615	79.4	W 6900	79.7	W 8920	88.2	PRODUITS PHOTO,CINEMA
8822	PHOTO FILM EXC DEV CINMA	W 4595	61.4	W 4930	65.5	W 5106	63.7	W 5774	66.5	PLAQUES,PELLICULES,FILMS
89	MISC MANUFCTRD GOODS NES		304.9		392.5		428.0		529.5	ART MANUFACTURES DIVERS
892	PRINTED MATTER	W 10653	69.8	W 11389	88.1	W 12116	89.2	W 14857	95.1	IMPRIMES
8921	PRINTED BOOKS,GLOBES,ETC	W 7682	51.4	W 7913	57.9	W 8742	60.7	W 10733	67.2	LIVRES,BROCHURES,CARTES
89211	PRINTED BOOKS,PAMPHLETS	W 7592	51.0	W 7816	57.2	W 8569	60.1	W 10631	66.8	LIVRES,BROCHURES
893	ARTICLES OF PLASTIC NES		69.2		97.8	W 30625	114.8		134.4	OUVRAGES EN MAT DIVIS 58
8931	PLSTC PACKG CONTNRS,LIDS	W 6070	21.1	W 8800	34.5	W 10911	36.7	W 13592	49.9	ART TRANSP EMBALLAGE ETC
8939	MISC PLASTIC ARTICLES	W 11351	47.2	W 12494	62.5	W 19383	77.0	W 18428	82.8	ART DIVERS EN MAT DIV 58
89399	OTHR PLASTC ARTICLES NES	W 10510	44.8	W 11376	59.2	W 17618	72.7	W 16935	78.5	AUT OUV MAT DIV 58
894	TOYS,SPORTING GOODS,ETC	W 8590	42.3	W 14456	60.9	W 17489	80.2	W 54205	89.7	VOITURES ENFANTS,JOUETS
8942	TOYS,INDOOR GAMES ETC	W 7071	33.7	W 12516	48.9	W 13784	58.6	W 15961	68.8	JOUETS,JEUX ETC
898	MUSICAL INSTRUMENTS,PTS	W 3553	71.7	W 3651	84.6	W 4684	91.6	W 5332	111.2	INSTRUMENTS DE MUSIQUE
8983	SOUND RECRDNG TAPE,DISCS	W 3172	67.0	W 3256	80.6	W 3772	85.2	W 4710	104.9	SUPPORTS SON POUR 763

4. Special Imports C.I.F. by Commodities according to the S.I.T.C. (Rev. 2) in million U.S. Dollars
Importations Spéciales C.A.F. par Produits d'après la C.T.C.I. (Rév. 2) en millions de Dollars E.U.

SITC CTCI	COMMODITY	1994			1995			1996			1997			PRODUIT
		QUANTITY QUANTITE		VALUE VALEUR	QUANTITY QUANTITE		VALUE VALEUR	QUANTITY QUANTITE		VALUE VALEUR	QUANTITY QUANTITE		VALUE VALEUR	
89832	RECORDED DISCS,TAPES ETC	W	1193	57.1	W	1102	69.8	W	1392	72.4	W	1881	90.5	DISQUES,PHONO,BANDES
899	OTHER MANUFACTURED GOODS			23.9			30.5			34.9			55.0	AUT ART MANUF DIVERS NDA
9	GOODS NOT CLASSD BY KIND			39.1			701.7			38.4			360.3	ART TRANSACT NON CLASSES
931	*SPECIAL TRANSACTIONS	W	4	0.1	W	72857	651.4			2.5			301.6	TRANS.SPECIALES
951	*WAR FIREARMS,AMMUNITION	W	2268	38.9	W	1816	50.2	W	1035	35.8	W	2406	58.5	VEHIC BLINDES ARMES

5. Special Exports F.O.B. by Commodities according to the S.I.T.C. (Rev. 2) in million U.S. Dollars
Exportations Spéciales F.O.B. par Produits d'après la C.T.C.I. (Rév. 2) en millions de Dollars E.U.

SITC CTCI	COMMODITY	1994 QUANTITY QUANTITE	1994 VALUE VALEUR	1995 QUANTITY QUANTITE	1995 VALUE VALEUR	1996 QUANTITY QUANTITE	1996 VALUE VALEUR	1997 QUANTITY QUANTITE	1997 VALUE VALEUR	PRODUIT
	ALL COMMODITIES		8916.9		10327.8		11182.4		11530.2	TOUS PRODUITS
0	FOOD AND LIVE ANIMALS		3158.4		3027.1		2779.4		3597.7	ALIMENTS,ANIMAUX VIVANTS
03	FISH AND PREPARATIONS		257.4		247.7		203.8		215.5	POISSONS ET PREPARATIONS
034	FISH,FRESH,CHILLED,FROZN	W 55083	62.6	W 55593	65.7	W 55649	63.6	W 50569	65.1	POISSON FRAIS, REFRIG,CONG
0342	FISH FROZEN,EXCL FILLETS	W 54037	53.2	W 54095	54.8	W 54741	56.2	W 50225	59.6	POISSONS CONGELES
036	SHELL FISH FRESH,FROZEN	W 12863	124.5	W 11869	118.8	W 10559	102.7	W 10823	101.7	CRUSTACES,MOLLUSQUES
037	FISH ETC PREPD,PRSVD NES	W 17525	49.4	W 20124	61.9	W 11178	35.8	W 13759	47.5	POIS,CRUST,MOL PREPARES
0371	FISH PREPARD,PRESRVD NES	W 17525	49.4	W 20121	61.8	W 11154	35.7	W 13757	47.5	CONSERVES DE POISSONS
04	CEREALS AND PREPARATIONS		22.4		32.1		37.6		43.5	CEREALES ET PRODUITS
048	CEREAL ETC PREPARATIONS	W 21165	20.5	W 28313	31.0	W 26058	36.9	W 39758	42.6	PREPTNS A BASE CEREALES
05	VEGETABLES AND FRUIT		543.4		497.1		505.8		536.6	LEGUMES ET FRUITS
054	VEG ETC FRSH,SMPLY PRSVD	W 91461	29.1	W 77052	30.3	W 62756	18.1	W 46961	12.2	LEGUMES FRAIS,CONG,SECS
057	FRUIT,NUTS,FRESH,DRIED	W 1708127	501.1	W 1370174	447.3	W 1480088	470.8	W 1588151	511.9	FRUITS FRAIS OU SECS
0573	BANANA,PLANTAIN,FRSH,DRY	W 1704078	490.3	W 1360278	431.3	W 1476523	459.2	W 1585969	503.2	BANANES FRAICHES,SECHEES
06	SUGAR AND PREPS,HONEY		186.3		217.0		267.4		314.7	SUCRES ET PRODUITS
061	SUGAR AND HONEY	W 696459	162.9	W 618803	181.1	W 794346	221.9	W 906630	243.9	SUCRES ET MIEL
0611	RAW BEET AND CANE SUGAR	W 198996	52.6	W 263947	85.5	W 460067	132.9	W 446143	123.1	SUCRES BRUTS
0612	REFINED SUGAR ETC	W 339447	99.7	W 245511	88.7	W 259542	83.9	W 376302	114.5	SUCRES RAFFINES
062	SUGAR CANDY NON–CHOCLATE	W 15547	23.5	W 21610	35.9	W 25770	45.5	W 38970	70.9	SUCRERIES
07	COFFEE,TEA,COCOA,SPICES		2125.4		1979.3		1735.0		2447.2	CAFE,THE,CACAO,EPICES
071	COFFEE AND SUBSTITUTES	W 687046	2103.0	W 569967	1953.7	W 614316	1706.1	W 632229	2422.2	CAFE ET SUCCEDANES
0711	COFFEE GREEN,ROASTED,SUB	W 674967	1998.7	W 559560	1840.8	W 600714	1579.5	W 617648	2262.4	CAFE TORREFIE OU DECAFEINE
07111	COFFEE GREEN,HUSKS,SKINS	W 673399	1993.2	W 558745	1837.3	W 600026	1577.2	W 617103	2259.6	CAFE NON TORREFIE
0712	COFFEE EXTRACTS,ESSENCES	W 12079	104.3	W 10408	113.0	W 13602	126.7	W 14581	159.9	EXTRAITS DE CAFE
1	BEVERAGES AND TOBACCO		33.2		30.9		35.2		38.7	BOISSONS ET TABACS
2	CRUDE MATERLS,EXCL FUELS		520.4		584.1		609.4		615.8	MAT BRUTES NON COMESTIBLES
26	TEXTILE FIBRES AND WASTE		23.3		43.9		40.0		16.1	FIBRES TEXTILES
29	CRUDE ANIMAL,VEG MAT NES		461.0		488.5		520.5		557.4	MATIERES BRUTES ANIM,VEGET
292	CRUDE VEG MATERIALS NES	W 139473	434.7	W 139407	480.2	W 141400	515.6	W 147524	551.8	MAT BRUTES VEGETALES NDA
2927	CUT FLOWERS AND FOLIAGE	W 138185	430.3	W 138819	477.4	W 140987	511.1	W 147045	546.8	FLEURS,FEUILLAGES COUPES
29271	CUT FLOWERS	W 138098	429.9	W 138725	476.8	W 140766	510.0	W 146569	544.6	FLEURS ET BOUTONS
3	MINERAL FUELS ETC		1788.9		2523.2		3774.5		3623.6	COMBUSTIBLES MINERAUX LUB
32	COAL,COKE AND BRIQUETTES		553.0		595.7		849.3		887.9	HOUILLES,COKES,BRIQUETTES
322	COAL,LIGNITE AND PEAT	MW 18437	545.6	MW 18274	587.5	MW 24784	839.2	MW 25785	880.0	HOUILLES,LIGNITES,TOURBE
3222	OTH COAL,NOT AGGLOMERATD	MW 18437	545.6	MW 18274	587.5	MW 24780	838.9	MW 25785	879.9	AUTRES HOUILLES
33	PETROLEUM AND PRODUCTS		1236.0		1927.0		2918.6		2729.9	PETROLE ET DERIVES
333	CRUDE PETROLEUM	MW 9141	937.0	MW 14219	1638.0	MW 16633	2438.4	MW 18638	2337.7	HUILES BRUTES DE PETROLE
334	PETROLEUM PRODUCTS,REFIN	W 3200091	295.8	W 2743223	287.9	W 3571127	447.4	W 3366485	364.3	PRODUITS RAFFINES
3343	GAS OILS	W 2742687	222.0	W 2367369	225.0	W 3279949	388.8	W 3242918	337.9	GAS OILS
3345	LUBS,PETROLEUM OILS NES	W 444943	71.4	W 361979	59.9	W 209043	41.0	W 75309	16.6	HUILES LUBRIFIANTES
33451	LUBS(HIGH PETR CONT) ETC	W 444671	70.6	W 361750	59.1	W 208640	40.2	W 74691	15.7	HUILES LUBRIF,H LOURDES
4	ANIMAL,VEGETABLE OIL,FAT		10.5		15.6		20.2		39.5	HUILES,GRAISSES ANIM,VEG
42	FIXED VEGETABLE OIL,FAT		9.6		13.5		17.1		35.8	HUILES VEGETALES FIXES
424	FIXED VEG OIL NONSOFT	W 21140	9.6	W 20416	12.5	W 31064	16.5	W 67825	35.8	AUTRES HUILES VEG FIXES
5	CHEMCLS,RELATED PROD NES		529.7		805.3		875.3		1061.7	PRODUITS CHIMIQUES
51	ORGANIC CHEMICALS		41.1		61.7		71.2		77.6	PROD CHIMIQ ORGANIQUES
52	INORGANIC CHEMICALS		26.6		39.8		82.8		131.0	PROD CHIM INORGANIQUES
523	OTHR INORG CHEMICALS ETC	W 21791	12.7	W 37148	17.5	W 34879	55.1	W 31877	100.9	AUT PRODUITS CHIMIQUES INORG
5233	METALLIC ACID SALTS ETC	W 162	2.3	W 101	0.7	W 96	41.3	W 110	87.3	SELS ACIDES D'OXYDES METAL E
52332	PRECIOUS METAL CMPDS ETC					W 11	41.1	W 15	87.1	METAUX PRECIEUX ETAT COLLOID
53	DYES,TANNING,COLOUR PROD		16.3		26.0		19.9		54.2	PROD TEINTURE,COLORANTS
533	PIGMENTS,PAINTS,ETC	W 4387	13.6	W 7805	23.3	W 5539	17.1	W 9773	51.3	PIGMENTS,PEINTURES,VERNIS
5334	VARNISHES,DISTEMPERS ETC	W 884	1.9	W 3373	7.6	W 1311	3.8	W 4111	35.6	PEINTURES A L'EAU
541	*MEDICINAL,PHARM PRODUCT	K 6339281	56.9	K 8229459	95.7	MK 13179	127.1	MK 15128	175.0	PROD MEDICINAUX PHARMACEUT
5417	MEDICAMENTS	K 5674015	49.3	K 7455829	82.7	MK 12338	113.5	MK 14665	164.5	MEDICAMENTS
54179	— CONTNG OTH SUBSTANCES	K 5236681	38.0	K 6942159	62.5	MK 11765	80.9	MK 13882	118.9	MED CONT AUT SUBSTANCES
55	PERFUME,CLEANING ETC PRD		38.1		67.6		65.8		91.3	PROD POUR PARFUM,TOILETTE
553	PERFUMERY,COSMETICS,ETC	W 6164	20.4	W 9988	29.4	W 8314	28.0	W 13161	41.4	PRODUITS DE PARFUMERIE
554	SOAP,CLEANSING ETC PREPS	W 7916	10.3	W 20261	26.4	W 18951	25.5	W 25756	35.1	SAVONS,PRODUITS DETERSIFS
58	PLASTIC MATERIALS ETC		213.9		326.4		290.5		300.6	MAT PLAST ARTIFICIELLES
582	PROD OF CONDENSATION ETC	W 39642	48.1	W 41569	67.1	W 29345	39.3	W 34881	43.0	PROD CONDENS,POLYCOND
5823	ALKYDS,OTHER POLYESTERS	W 30409	36.4	W 32582	55.7	W 21985	28.4	W 25518	29.0	ALKYDES ET AUT POLYESTERS
58231	— IN PRIMARY FORMS	W 30408	36.4	W 32582	55.7	W 21984	28.4	W 25507	28.9	SOUS FORMES PRIMAIRES
583	POLYMERIZATION ETC PRODS	W 166251	159.0	W 202124	251.8	W 246462	241.8	W 240686	249.3	PROD POLYMERISATION
5832	POLYPROPYLENE	W 36048	32.1	W 39377	55.3	W 45351	53.2	W 37841	45.7	POLYPROPYLENE
58321	— IN PRIMARY FORMS	W 31109	22.6	W 33859	39.4	W 35252	29.6	W 27763	22.9	POLYPROPYLENE PRIMAIRES
5833	POLYSTYRENE,ITS COPOLYMR	W 36092	34.2	W 41994	54.2	W 43920	40.9	W 47321	38.7	POLYPROPYLENE COPOLYMERES
58331	— IN PRIMARY FORMS	W 36083	34.2	W 41725	53.6	W 43696	40.5	W 47190	38.5	SOUS FORMES PRIMAIRES
5834	POLYVINYL CHLORIDE	W 67520	63.6	W 92380	96.1	W 124633	98.6	W 122125	113.0	CHLORURE DE POLYVINYLE
58341	— IN PRIMARY FORMS	W 64928	56.1	W 87689	82.8	W 120801	86.6	W 113982	90.0	SOUS FORMES PRIMAIRES
5839	OTH POLYMRZTION ETC PROD	W 21169	21.0	W 19912	31.5	W 22938	34.1	W 25565	38.3	AUT PROD POLYMER COPOLYM
59	CHEMICAL MATERIALS NES		130.4		179.1		204.2		219.8	MAT PROD CHIMIQUES NDA
591	PESTICIDES,DISINFECTANTS	W 22279	101.6	W 28600	141.2	W 31720	163.9	W 32766	177.2	DESINF,INSECT,FONG,HERB
5911	INSECTICIDES,FOR RETAIL	W 2344	15.6	W 3969	32.6	W 4258	37.3	W 3868	36.5	INSECTICIDES VENTE DET
5912	FUNGICIDES,FOR RETAIL	W 14486	56.1	W 16322	65.5	W 18745	78.8	W 19920	90.3	FONGICIDES VENTE AU DET
5913	HERBICIDES,FOR RETAIL	W 5111	28.4	W 7784	42.2	W 8368	46.7	W 8659	49.7	HERBICIDES VENTE AU DET
6	BASIC MANUFACTURES		1240.6		1527.0		1228.1		1214.0	ART MANUFACTURES
61	LEATHER,DRESSED FUR,ETC		94.2		115.7		74.7		71.2	CUIRS,PELLETERIES
611	LEATHER	W 4988	54.0	W 6407	62.7	W 4955	32.6	W 6035	39.2	CUIRS,PEAUX PREPARES
6118	LEATHER SPECIALLY FINSHD	W 1603	27.3	W 1662	29.1	W 664	10.2	W 850	14.0	CUIRS,PEAUX TANNES
61183	LEATHER PATENT,METALIZED	W 1586	27.0	W 1634	28.2	W 628	9.5	W 757	12.5	CUIRS,PEAUX VERNIS
612	LEATHER ETC MANUFACTURES	W 7680	40.1	W 11189	52.9	W 8939	41.9	W 6824	32.0	OUVRAGES EN CUIRS NDA
62	RUBBER MANUFACTURES NES		20.5		37.3		38.1		48.3	CAOUTCHOUC MANUFACTURE
625	RUBBER TYRES, TUBES ETC	W 6399	17.2	W 11258	33.0	W 11041	33.4	W 13941	42.2	PNEUS CAOUTCHOUC VULCANISE
64	PAPER,PAPERBOARD AND MFR		84.3		137.3		119.1		144.8	PAPIERS,CARTONS & OUVRAGES
641	PAPER AND PAPERBOARD	W 53781	41.2	W 66267	68.9	W 63949	51.0	W 82066	64.6	PAPIERS ET CARTONS
6415	PAPER,PAPERBRD,BULK,NES	W 32337	21.0	W 42297	44.3	W 46288	33.5	W 59313	43.7	PAPIERS,CARTONS ROULEAUX
64159	OTHER PAPER ETC,BULK,NES	W 30798	20.3	W 38983	42.3	W 46282	33.5	W 59277	43.6	AUT PAPIER ROULEAUX FEUILLES
642	PAPER,ETC,PRECUT,ARTS OF	W 29448	43.1	W 38442	68.4	W 38216	68.1	W 46709	80.3	PAP,CARTONS DECOUPES
6428	PAPER ETC ARTICLES NES	W 14181	17.2	W 20038	30.5	W 15736	26.0	W 23343	42.2	OUVRAGES EN PATE A PAPIER
65	TEXTILE YARN,FABRICS,ETC		211.5		280.0		283.4		291.8	FILS,TISSUS,ARTICLES TEXTILE
651	TEXTILE YARN	W 7684	34.0	W 14574	58.1	W 15467	57.8	W 10660	47.4	FILS TEXTILES
6514	SYN FIB YRN,BULK,MONOFIL	W 3735	14.6	W 9422	33.0	W 12089	38.7	W 7874	32.5	FILS CONT 85% FIB TEXT SYNTH
652	COTTON FABRICS,WOVEN	W 9523	54.5	W 11548	77.0	W 11018	71.0	W 10167	65.3	TISSUS DE COTON
6522	WOVEN COTTON BLEACHD,ETC	W 8794	50.5	W 11081	74.3	W 10786	69.4	W 10000	64.1	TISSUS COTON BLANCHIS ETC
65224	BLCHED COTTON FABRIC NES	W 7442	39.4	W 9563	59.5	W 9605	59.6	W 8455	51.2	AUT TIS PLUS 85% COT BLANCHI
657	SPECIAL TXTL FABRC,PRODS	W 13355	40.2	W 13449	43.7		51.2	W 16271	58.5	TISSUS SPECIAUX
6573	COATED ETC TEXTILES NES	W 11049	31.0	W 11056	34.0	W 13494	42.8	W 14166	49.9	TISSUS,ART MATIERE TEXT NDA
65732	PLASTIC COATED TEXTILES	W 11034	30.7	W 11001	33.6	W 12997	40.3	W 11578	37.1	TISSUS IMPREGNES
658	TEXTILE ARTICLES NES	W 5393	48.0	W 5633	55.0	W 5090	44.9	W 5871	50.4	ART FACONNES MAT TEXTILES
6584	LINENS ETC	W 4685	43.6	W 5321	50.9	W 4482	40.7	W 4914	44.5	LINGE DE MAISON

5. Special Exports F.O.B. by Commodities according to the S.I.T.C. (Rev. 2) in million U.S. Dollars
Exportations Spéciales F.O.B. par Produits d'après la C.T.C.I. (Rév. 2) en millions de Dollars E.U.

SITC CTCI	COMMODITY	1994 QUANTITY QUANTITE	1994 VALUE VALEUR	1995 QUANTITY QUANTITE	1995 VALUE VALEUR	1996 QUANTITY QUANTITE	1996 VALUE VALEUR	1997 QUANTITY QUANTITE	1997 VALUE VALEUR	PRODUIT
65845	OTHER LINEN OF COTTON	W 3406	30.4	W 3804	35.1	W 3564	30.4	W 3912	32.9	LINGE DE TOILETTE COTON
66	NONMETAL MINERAL MFS NES		532.5		580.4		343.6		295.4	ART MIN NON METALLIQUES
661	LIME,CEMENT,BLDG PRODS	W 1252388	53.2	W 1301840	58.8	W 1617738	70.3	W 1596613	75.5	CHAUX,CIMENTS MAT CONSTR
6612	CEMENT	W 1225687	45.3	W 1269566	49.8	W 1585096	61.7	W 1558622	65.1	CIMENTS HYDRAULIQUES
665	GLASSWARE	W 17093	13.3	W 25803	20.2	W 56003	43.5	W 23507	18.8	OUVRAGES EN VERRE
667	PEARL,PREC–,SEMI–P STONE		426.8		456.0		179.4		141.6	PERLES, PIERRES GEMMES
6673	PREC–,SEMI–PR STONES NES		424.3		455.4		179.3		141.5	AUTRES PIERRES NON SERTIES
67	IRON AND STEEL		142.3		217.2		203.4		214.9	FER ET ACIER
671	PIG IRON ETC	W 51668	118.9	W 56817	185.0	W 54808	168.9	W 53148	160.8	FONTE,SPIEGEL,POUDRES
6716	FERRO–ALLOYS	W 51456	118.8	W 56520	184.9	W 54155	168.7	W 52482	160.6	FERRO–ALLIAGES
67169	OTHER FERRO–ALLOYS	W 51456	118.8	W 56520	184.9	W 54129	168.7	W 52482	160.6	AUTRES FERRO–ALLIAGES
68	NON–FERROUS METALS		54.4		31.3		30.4		30.7	METAUX NON FERREUX
681	SILVER,PLATINUM,ETC		45.8		15.3		9.9		3.2	ARGENT ET PLATINE
6812	METALS OF PLATINUM GROUP		45.8		15.1		9.1		2.8	PLATINE
68123	PLATINUM,ALLOYS UNWRGHT		45.8		15.1		9.1		2.7	PLATINE,ALLIAGES BRUTS
69	METAL MANUFACTURES NES		92.1		114.8		111.5		103.6	ART MANUFACT EN METAL NDA
7	MACHINES,TRANSPORT EQUIP		514.1		581.3		680.9		442.3	MACHINES MATERIEL TRANSPORT
71	POWER GENERATING EQUIPMT		58.9		54.0		101.8		7.7	MACHINES GENERATRICES
714	ENGINES AND MOTORS NES	W 111	18.0	W 126	19.4	W 378	60.8		0.1	MOTEURS NON ELECTRIQUES
72	MACHS FOR SPCL INDUSTRYS		68.1		54.0		106.4		22.0	MAC SPECIALES POUR INDUST
723	CIVIL ENGNEERG EQUIP ETC	W 5816	29.6	W 1604	14.2	W 5554	51.2	W 197	0.8	APPAREILS DE GENIE CIVIL
7234	CONST,MINING MACHNRY NES	W 5381	24.9	W 1249	8.4	W 5001	43.6	W 179	0.7	MACH POUR LA CONST, MINES
74	GENRL INDUSTRL MACHY NES		49.5		56.6		61.7		52.5	MACH APP INDUSTRIE
77	ELECTRIC MACHNRY NES ETC		76.7		104.9		105.6		143.0	MACH APP ELECT NDA
775	HOUSEHOLD TYPE EQUIP NES	W 5555	23.1	W 8833	36.2	W 7394	32.8	W 12346	52.0	MACH,APP USAGE DOMESTQUE
7752	DOM REFRIGERATRS,FREEZRS	W 3662	12.0	W 6878	23.6	W 5450	20.0	W 10138	38.8	REFRIG,CONGEL MENAGER
77521	DOMESTIC REFRIGERATORS	W 3648	11.9	W 6870	23.5	W 5444	19.9	W 10130	38.7	REFRIGERATEURS
778	ELECTRICAL MACHINERY NES	W 8737	26.4	W 9951	34.9	W 8546	33.0	W 13115	38.2	AUTRES MACH ELECT NDA
78	ROAD VEHICLES		53.9		91.9		122.4		195.2	VEHICULES ROUTIERS
781	PASS MOTOR VEH EXC BUSES	W 1174	15.4	W 2774	35.2	W 2023	21.0	W 2703	30.6	AUTO TRANSPORT PERSONNES
782	LORRIES,SPCL MTR VEH NES	W 2479	20.2	W 3950	35.7	W 9047	77.1	W 10342	91.7	VEHICULES SPECIAUX,MARCH
7821	LORRIES,TRUCKS	W 2155	17.7	W 3620	32.6	W 8641	73.9	W 10304	91.4	VEHICULES TRANSP MARCHAND
784	MOTOR VEH PRTS,ACCES NES	W 3308	12.5	W 3327	16.4	W 3458	17.8	W 7604	40.7	PIECES 722,781,782,783
7849	OTHER MOTOR VEHCL PARTS	W 3080	10.9	W 3084	15.2	W 3421	17.5	W 7214	38.1	PIECES 722,781,782,783
79	OTHR TRANSPORT EQUIPMENT		191.6		182.1		139.5		16.8	AUTRE MATERIEL TRANSPORT
792	AIRCRAFT ETC	W 1014	137.8	W 1077	166.2	W 689	112.9	W 65	4.8	APP NAVIGATION AERIENNE
7924	AIRCRFT NES OVER 15000KG	W 883	104.6	W 903	143.7	W 481	66.6			AERODYNES PLUS 15000 KG
793	SHIPS AND BOATS ETC	W 12526	53.8	W 11136	15.8	W 8847	26.6	W 3930	12.1	NAVIRES BATEAUX,ETC
7938	TUGS,SPECIAL VESSELS ETC	W 11718	50.5	W 11120	15.7	W 8734	24.9	W 1931	6.3	REMORQUEURS,BATEAUX SPEC
79382	SPECL PURPOSE VESSLS ETC	W 11288	44.6	W 11119	15.6	W 1367	1.1	W 1931	6.3	BAT–PHARES,–POMPES,DRAGUES
8	MISC MANUFACTURED GOODS		1060.7		1046.6		970.9		820.5	ART MANUFACTURES DIVERS
831	*TRAVEL GOODS,HANDBAGS	W 1702	69.1	W 1366	56.1	W 1333	42.2	W 1396	41.8	ARTICLES DE VOYAGE ETC
83102	TRAVEL GDS,TOILET–CASES	W 826	28.1	W 694	25.8	W 648	19.8	W 505	14.4	ARTICLES DE VOYAGE
84	CLOTHING AND ACCESSORIES		522.6		553.2		476.2		439.8	VETEMENTS
842	MENS OUTERWEAR NOT KNIT	W 5157	103.5	W 5754	107.6	W 7513	128.6	W 6383	124.9	VET DESSUS POUR HOMMES
8423	— TROUSERS,BREECHES ETC	W 3917	59.3	W 4419	68.6	W 6383	90.6	W 5215	78.6	PANTALONS HOMMES MAT TEX
8424	— JACKETS,BLAZERS ETC	W 804	29.3	W 761	23.3	W 869	27.5	W 781	29.6	VESTES HOMMES MAT TEXTIL
843	WOMENS OUTERWEAR NONKNIT	W 8841	181.4	W 5908	152.1	W 5126	131.7	W 3611	94.4	VET DESSUS FEMMES MAT TEX
8439	— OTHER OUTER GARMENTS	W 6337	110.6	W 3711	80.1	W 3266	72.5	W 2298	53.5	AUT VET DES FEM MAT TEXT
844	UNDER GARMENTS NOT KNIT	W 1475	29.2	W 1967	40.2	W 622	14.5	W 438	12.1	VETEMENT DESSOUS MAT TEX
845	OUTERWEAR KNIT NONELASTC	W 1994	52.6	W 1550	49.2	W 1447	42.2	W 1606	42.9	VET DESSOUS,ACCES BONNET
8459	— OTHER,CLTHG ACCESRYS	W 1605	44.0	W 1213	40.7	W 1185	35.0	W 1214	35.4	AUT VET DESSUS DE BONNE
846	UNDER GARMENTS KNITTED	W 4718	119.7	W 5813	165.4	W 4273	139.2	W 4863	145.5	SOUS VETS DE BONNETERIE
8462	— OF COTTON NON ELASTIC	W 3729	77.0	W 4324	101.8	W 3204	89.5	W 3502	86.6	SOUS–VET BONNET COTON
84629	—— OTHER	W 3729	77.0	W 4324	101.8	W 3204	89.5	W 3502	86.6	AUT SOUS–VET BONNET COTON
8465	CORSETS,GARTERS,ETC	W 394	25.2	W 602	39.1	W 436	32.9	W 626	40.6	CORSETS,GAINES ART SIM
84651	BRASSIERES	W 376	24.3	W 576	36.5	W 369	27.0	W 523	37.8	SOUTIENS–GORGE,BUSTIERS
851	*FOOTWEAR	W 3774	63.4	W 2745	44.1	W 2100	32.1	W 1721	27.0	CHAUSSURES
85102	FOOTWEAR LEATHER	W 3252	54.3	W 2134	37.9	W 1733	27.8	W 1432	24.3	CHAUS SEMELLES EN CUIR
87	PRECISION INSTRUMNTS NES		24.4		30.5		44.7		17.4	INSTRUM,APPAR SCIENT NDA
89	MISC MANUFCTRD GOODS NES		342.3		322.8		342.0		257.8	ART MANUFACTURES DIVERS
892	PRINTED MATTER	W 22881	132.0	W 19955	119.3	W 18893	105.8	W 21234	105.6	IMPRIMES
8921	PRINTED BOOKS,GLOBES,ETC	W 18501	86.8	W 16509	89.3	W 15962	85.4	W 17775	85.3	LIVRES,BROCHURES,CARTES
89211	PRINTED BOOKS,PAMPHLETS	W 18227	85.3	W 16267	87.5	W 15922	85.1	W 17711	84.9	LIVRES,BROCHURES
8922	NEWSPAPERS,PERIODICALS	W 3519	30.3	W 2550	17.0	W 2001	9.9	W 2519	10.7	JOURNAUX ET PERIODIQUES
893	ARTICLES OF PLASTIC NES		50.3		67.8		64.7		68.1	OUVRAGES EN MAT DIVIS 58
8931	PLSTC PACKG CONTNRS,LIDS	W 5290	25.4	W 7645	37.8	W 9550	39.8	W 9855	41.5	ART TRANSP EMBALLAGE ETC
896	WORKS OF ART ETC		100.7		56.7		95.9		0.3	OBJETS D'ART
89601	HAND PAINTINGS ETC NES		1.7		31.2		9.9		0.2	TABLEAUX,PEINTURES
89606	ANTIQUES NES		98.1		25.2		77.8			OBJETS D'ANTIQUITE
9	GOODS NOT CLASSD BY KIND		60.9		187.2		208.8		76.9	ART TRANSACT NON CLASSES
971	*GOLD,NON MONETARY NES	K 3369	36.7	K 15106	175.1	K 16716	206.7	K 6968	75.7	OR NON MONETAIRE
97101	NONMON GLD UNWRT,SEMIMFD	K 3369	36.7	K 14875	174.6	K 16716	206.7	K 6956	75.6	OR,ALLIAGES D'OR BRUTS

1. HISTORICAL SERIES, 1960–1995 SPECIAL TRADE, IMPORTS C.I.F., EXPORTS F.O.B.
SERIES HISTORIQUES, 1960–1995 COMMERCE SPECIAL, IMPORTATIONS C.A.F., EXPORTATIONS F.O.B

YEAR ANNEE	VALUE IN MILLION COMORIAN FRANCS VALEUR EN MILLION COMORIAN FRANCS MERCHANDISE –MARCHANDISE		GOLD –OR		CONVERSION FACTORS U.S. CENTS PER COMORIAN FRANC FACTEURS DE CONVERSION CENTS E.U. PAR COMORIAN FRANC		INDEX NUMBERS –INDICES QUANTUM		UNIT VALUE VALEUR UNITAIRE	
	IMPORTS	EXPORTS	IMPORTS	EXPORTS	IMPORTS	EXPORTS	IMPORTS	EXPORTS	IMPORTS	EXPORTS
1960	940.30	799.60			0.4051	0.4051				
1961	908.80	686.40			0.4051	0.4051				
1962	1008.00	626.00			0.4051	0.4051				
1963	1335.00	1161.00			0.4051	0.4051				
1964	1507.00	986.00			0.4051	0.4051				
1965	1623.00	915.00			0.4051	0.4051				
1966	1783.00	953.00			0.4051	0.4051				
1967	1850.00	938.00			0.4051	0.4051				
1968	1763.00	1008.00			0.4051	0.4051				
1969	2091.70	1289.00			0.3824	0.3824				
1970	2373.30	1278.10			0.3601	0.3601				
1971	2834.70	1572.10			0.3609	0.3609				
1972	2932.00	1511.00			0.3965	0.3965				
1973	2369.00	1106.00			0.4450	0.4450				
1974	6202.90	2143.80			0.4157	0.4157				
1975	4974.00	2036.00			0.4673	0.4673				
1976	3118.60	2223.70			0.4187	0.4201				
1977	4052.50	2022.90			0.4322	0.4322				
1978	4329.00	2099.00			0.4440	0.4440				
1979	6135.00	3701.00			0.4704	0.4704				
1980	6147.00	2364.00			0.4908	0.4908				
1981	8791.00	4461.00			0.3680	0.3680				
1982	10725.00	6435.00			0.3043	0.3043				
1983	13099.00	7419.00			0.2624	0.2624				
1984	18778.00	3079.00			0.2289	0.2289				
1985	16481.00	7048.00			0.2226	0.2226				
1986	12849.00	7053.00			0.2888	0.2888				
1987	15560.00	3485.00			0.3327	0.3327				
1988	15647.00	6398.00			0.3357	0.3357				
1989	13575.00	5758.00			0.3135	0.3135				
1990	14040.00	4883.00			0.3673	0.3673				
1991	16399.00	7028.00			0.3545	0.3545				
1992	18139.01	5847.00			0.3778	0.3778				
1993	16816.90	6188.60			0.3524	0.3520				
1994	21929.30	4688.40			0.2408	0.2429				
1995	23411.20	4235.90			0.2675	0.2682				

2. IMPORTS BY BROAD ECONOMIC CATEGORY AND EXPORTS BY INDUSTRIAL ORIGIN. (PERCENTAGE OF TOTAL VALUE)
IMPORTATIONS PAR CATEGORIES ECONOMIQUES ET EXPORTATIONS PAR BRANCHE D'ACTIVITE.(EN POURCENTAGE DE LA VALEUR TOTALE)

IMPORTS – IMPORTATIONS

	1989	1990	1991	1992	1993	1994	1995
TOTAL IMPORTS–IMPORTATIONS TOTALES							
1 FOOD BEV–ALIMENTATION BOISSONS							
11 PRIMARY–PRODUITS DE BASE							
111 FOR INDUSTRY–POUR L'INDUSTRIE							
112 FOR HOUSEHOLDS–POUR LES MENAGES							
12 PROCESSED–PRODUITS ELABORES							
121 FOR INDUSTRY–POUR L'INDUSTRIE							
122 FOR HOUSEHOLDS–POUR LES MENAGES							
2 IND SUPPLIES–APPROV INDUSTRIELS							
21 PRIMARY–PRODUITS DE BASE							
22 PROCESSED–PRODUITS ELABORES							
3 FUELS–COMBUSTIBLES							
31 PRIMARY–PRODUITS DE BASE							
32 PROCESSED–PRODUITS ELABORES							
321 MOTOR SPIRIT–ESSENCE							
322 OTHER–AUTRES							
4 MACHINERY–EQUIPEMENT							
41 CAPITAL EQUIPMENT–MACHINES							
42 PARTS–PIECES ACCESSOIRES							
5 TRANSPORT–TRANSPORT							
51 PASSENGER CARS–AUTOMOBILES							
52 OTHER–AUTRES							
521 INDUSTRIAL–INDUSTRIELS							
522 NON INDUSTRIAL–NON INDUSTRIEL							
53 PARTS–PIECES ACCESSOIRES							
6 CONSUM GOODS–BIENS CONSOMMATION							
61 DURABLE–DURABLES							
62 SEMI DURABLE–SEMI DURABLES							
63 NON DURABLE–NON DURABLES							
7 GOODS NES–BIENS NDA							

EXPORTS – EXPORTATIONS

	1989	1990	1991	1992	1993	1994	1995
TOTAL EXPORTS–EXPORTATIONS TOTALES							
1 AGRICULTURE							
2 MINING QUARRY–INDUS EXTRACTIVES							
3 MANUFACTURING–IND MANUFACTUR							
31 FOOD BEV TOBACCO–ALIM BOISS TAB							
32 TEXTILES–INDUSTRIES TEXTILES							
33 WOOD & PRODUCTS–BOIS & PRODUITS							
34 PAPER & PRODUCTS–PAPIER & PRODT							
35 CHEMICALS–INDUSTRIES CHIMIQUES							
36 NON METAL MIN–MIN NON METAL							
37 BASIC METAL–IND METAL BASE							
38 METAL MANUF–MANUF METAL							
39 OTH MANUF IND–AUTRES MANUF							

3. TRADE BY PRINCIPAL COUNTRIES OF CONSIGNMENT AND DESTINATION (VALUE IN MILLION U.S. DOLLARS)
ECHANGES SELON LES PRINCIPAUX PAYS DE CONSIGNATION ET DE DESTINATION (VALEUR EN MILLIONS DE DOLLARS EU)

COUNTRIES–PAYS	SPECIAL IMPORTS C.I.F. IMPORTATIONS SPECIALES C.A.F				
	1991	1992	1993	1994	1995
World			67.8	52.8	62.6
Africa					
Americas					
– Northern America					
– LAIA					
– CACM					
– Caribbean					
– Rest of America					
Asia excl fmr USSR					
– Middle East					
Asia former USSR					
Europe excl fmr USSR					
– European Union					
– Eastern Europe					
– Rest of Europe					
Europe former USSR					
Oceania					
Other					
France, Monaco			27.6	21.1	20.0
Areas n.e.s.					
India/Inde					10.8
Saudi Arabia					5.9
Kenya				5.5	
So. African Customs Un				3.3	

COUNTRIES–PAYS	SPECIAL EXPORTS F.O.B. EXPORTATIONS SPECIALES F.O.B.				
	1991	1992	1993	1994	1995
Monde	24.9	22.1	25.1	11.4	11.4
Afrique					
Amériques		10.5	11.6	3.3	
– Amérique du Nord		10.5	11.6	3.3	
– ALAI					
– MCAC					
– Caraïbes					
– Autre Amérique					
Asie anc. URSS exclus					
– Moyen–Orient					
Asie ancienne URSS					
Europe anc. URSS exclus		10.3	12.6	6.0	
– Union Européenne		10.3	12.6	6.0	
– Europe de l'Est					
– Autre de l'Europe					
Europe ancienne URSS					
Océanie					
Autre					
USA/Etats–Unis d'Amer	10.6	10.5	11.6	3.3	3.2
France, Monaco	7.6	9.1	10.5	5.3	4.2
Germany/Allemagne		1.2	2.1	0.6	0.9

(VALUE AS PERCENTAGE OF WORLD TOTAL)(VALEURS EN POURCENTAGE DU TOTAL MONDIAL)

	1986	1987	1988	1989	1990	1991	1992	1993	1994	1995
Africa										
Americas										
– Northern America										
– LAIA										
– CACM										
– Caribbean										
– Rest of America										
Asia excl fmr USSR										
– Middle East										
Asia former USSR										
Europe excl fmr USSR										
– European Union										
– Eastern Europe										
– Rest of Europe										
Europe former USSR										
Oceania										
Other										
France, Monaco					40.0			40.8	40.0	32.0
Areas n.e.s.										
India/Inde										17.3
Saudi Arabia										9.4
Kenya									10.3	
So. African Customs Un					12.8				6.3	

	1986	1987	1988	1989	1990	1991	1992	1993	1994	1995
Afrique	2.0	12.0	1.8	0.5						
Amériques	37.0	18.0	54.2	36.3			47.4	46.1	28.7	
– Amérique du Nord	37.0	18.0	54.2	36.3			47.4	46.1	28.7	
– ALAI										
– MCAC										
– Caraïbes										
– Autre Amérique										
Asie anc. URSS exclus	2.0	4.0		2.5						
– Moyen–Orient				0.5						
Asie ancienne URSS										
Europe anc. URSS exclus	51.6	64.0	41.5	58.0			46.5	50.1	52.5	
– Union Européenne	51.6	64.0	41.5	58.0			46.5	50.1	52.5	
– Europe de l'Est										
– Autre de l'Europe										
Europe ancienne URSS										
Océanie										
Autre										
USA/Etats–Unis d'Amer	37.0	18.0	53.3	36.3	30.0	42.6	47.4	46.1	28.7	28.4
France, Monaco	41.1	35.0	31.2	46.6	41.2	30.6	41.2	41.7	46.9	36.5
Germany/Allemagne							5.3	8.4	5.6	8.0

4. Special Imports C.I.F. by Commodities according to the S.I.T.C. (Rev. 2) in million U.S. Dollars
Importations Spéciales C.A.F. par Produits d'après la C.T.C.I. (Rév. 2) en millions de Dollars E.U.

SITC CTCI	COMMODITY	1992 QUANTITY QUANTITE	1992 VALUE VALEUR	1993 QUANTITY QUANTITE	1993 VALUE VALEUR	1994 QUANTITY QUANTITE	1994 VALUE VALEUR	1995 QUANTITY QUANTITE	1995 VALUE VALEUR	PRODUIT
	ALL COMMODITIES		68.7		67.8		52.8		62.7	TOUS PRODUITS
01	MEAT AND PREPARATIONS		4.5		5.1		3.2		4.5	VIANDES ET PREPARATIONS
02	DAIRY PRODCTS,BIRDS'EGGS		2.9		2.1		2.1		1.4	PRODUITS LAITIERS,OEUFS
042	RICE	W 32493	8.2	W 30271	6.7	W 28518	6.3	W 41650	14.1	RIZ
04601	FLOUR OF WHEAT OR MESLIN	W 3617	1.1	W 3767	1.5	W 3911	1.3	W 3918	1.6	FARINE DE FROMENT
061	SUGAR AND HONEY	W 3939	2.5	W 3854	2.4	W 3629	2.0	W 3665	2.3	SUCRES ET MIEL
334	PETROLEUM PRODUCTS,REFIN	W 30536	7.2	W 21148	7.3	W 23816	6.2	W 33962	7.8	PRODUITS RAFFINES
541	*MEDICINAL,PHARM PRODUCT	K 91100	1.2	K 99800	1.4	K 89300	0.8	K 62000	0.7	PROD MEDICINAUX PHARMACEUT
6612	CEMENT	W 34568	3.4	W 41980	4.2	W 39212	4.1	W 43315	4.5	CIMENTS HYDRAULIQUES
67	IRON AND STEEL		2.5		2.6		2.1		2.4	FER ET ACIER
78	ROAD VEHICLES		7.4		6.1		3.9		4.5	VEHICULES ROUTIERS
84	CLOTHING AND ACCESSORIES		1.4		1.6		0.9		0.7	VETEMENTS
931	*SPECIAL TRANSACTIONS		26.9		27.4		20.5		18.8	TRANS.SPECIALES

5. Special Exports F.O.B. by Commodities according to the S.I.T.C. (Rev. 2) in million U.S. Dollars
Exportations Spéciales F.O.B. par Produits d'après la C.T.C.I. (Rév. 2) en millions de Dollars E.U.

SITC CTCI	COMMODITY	1992			1993			1994			1995			PRODUIT
		QUANTITY QUANTITE		VALUE VALEUR	QUANTITY QUANTITE		VALUE VALEUR	QUANTITY QUANTITE		VALUE VALEUR	QUANTITY QUANTITE		VALUE VALEUR	
	ALL COMMODITIES			22.2			25.1			11.4			11.4	TOUS PRODUITS
075	SPICES	W	710	16.0	W	1854	20.6	W	2885	8.0	W	642	6.6	EPICES
0752	SPICES,EX PEPPER,PIMENTO	W	710	16.0	W	1854	20.6	W	2885	8.0	W	642	6.6	AUTRES EPICES
07521	VANILLA	W	236	15.6	W	288	19.5	W	131	6.8	W	159	6.3	VANILLE
07523	CLOVES	W	474	0.5	W	1566	1.1	W	2754	1.3	W	483	0.4	GIROFLES
551	ESSENTL OILS,PERFUME,ETC				W	39	3.4	W	45	2.3	W	44	2.4	HUILES ESSENTIELLES
5513	ESSENTL OIL,RESINOID,ETC	W	46	4.4	W	39	3.4	W	45	2.3	W	44	2.4	HUILES ESSENTIELLES,RESIN
931	*SPECIAL TRANSACTIONS			1.8			1.3			1.2			2.5	TRANS.SPECIALES

1. HISTORICAL SERIES, 1960–1995 SPECIAL TRADE, IMPORTS C.I.F., EXPORTS F.O.B.
SERIES HISTORIQUES, 1960–1995 COMMERCE SPECIAL, IMPORTATIONS C.A.F., EXPORTATIONS F.O.B

YEAR ANNEE	VALUE IN MILLION C.F.A. FRANCS / VALEUR EN MILLION C.F.A. FRANCS — MERCHANDISE – MARCHANDISE		GOLD – OR		CONVERSION FACTORS U.S. CENTS PER C.F.A. FRANC / FACTEURS DE CONVERSION CENTS E.U. PAR C.F.A. FRANC		INDEX NUMBERS – INDICES — QUANTUM		UNIT VALUE / VALEUR UNITAIRE	
	IMPORTS	EXPORTS	IMPORTS	EXPORTS	IMPORTS	EXPORTS	IMPORTS	EXPORTS	IMPORTS	EXPORTS
1960	17316.00	4399.00	0.10	29.20	0.4051	0.4051				
1961	19492.00	4830.00	0.20	39.40	0.4051	0.4051				
1962	16010.00	8404.00	0.10	29.10	0.4051	0.4051				
1963	15245.00	10277.00		18.80	0.4051	0.4051				
1964	16006.00	11690.00		12.60	0.4051	0.4051				
1965	15974.00	11512.00		5.70	0.4051	0.4051				
1966	17170.00	10659.00			0.4051	0.4051				
1967	20231.00	11730.00			0.4051	0.4051				
1968	20605.00	12189.00			0.4051	0.4051				
1969	20291.00	11384.00			0.3854	0.3874				
1970	15910.00	8564.00			0.3601	0.3601				
1971	21910.00	10300.00			0.3601	0.3601				
1972	22608.00	13212.00			0.3970	0.3966				
1973	27730.00	19600.00			0.4501	0.4501				
1974	29900.00	45090.00			0.4160	0.4160				
1975	36380.00	38400.00			0.4673	0.4673				
1976	40240.00	43380.00			0.4185	0.4184				
1977	50450.00	42560.00			0.4071	0.4071				
1978	60364.00	69545.00			0.4432	0.4432				
1979	77209.00	105440.00			0.4701	0.4701				
1980	115191.00	192393.00			0.4733	0.4733				
1981	218362.00	291488.00			0.3680	0.3680				
1982	244560.00	364260.00			0.3043	0.3043				
1983	262090.00	406280.00			0.2624	0.2624				
1984	259820.00	516700.00			0.2289	0.2289				
1985	260871.00	488515.00			0.2226	0.2226				
1986	206648.00	268989.90			0.2888	0.2888				
1987	159083.00	155440.00			0.3327	0.3327				
1988	167985.00	279200.00			0.3357	0.3357				
1989	165130.00	397700.10			0.3131	0.3131				
1990	169023.00	267100.00			0.3652	0.3652				
1991	167684.00	290500.10			0.3570	0.3552				
1992	119480.00	312000.00			0.3777	0.3790				
1993	164789.00	302629.80			0.3535	0.3534				
1994	350405.80	532400.10			0.1809	0.1810				
1995	334182.90	585299.90			0.2006	0.2010				

2. IMPORTS BY BROAD ECONOMIC CATEGORY AND EXPORTS BY INDUSTRIAL ORIGIN. (PERCENTAGE OF TOTAL VALUE)
IMPORTATIONS PAR CATEGORIES ECONOMIQUES ET EXPORTATIONS PAR BRANCHE D'ACTIVITE.(EN POURCENTAGE DE LA VALEUR TOTALE)

IMPORTS – IMPORTATIONS

	1989	1990	1991	1992	1993	1994	1995
TOTAL IMPORTS–IMPORTATIONS TOTALES					100.	100.	100.
1 FOOD BEV–ALIMENTATION BOISSONS					18.3	25.5	20.0
11 PRIMARY–PRODUITS DE BASE					5.8	11.7	8.3
111 FOR INDUSTRY–POUR L'INDUSTRIE					0.9	0.4	0.4
112 FOR HOUSEHOLDS–POUR LES MENAGES					4.9	11.3	8.0
12 PROCESSED–PRODUITS ELABORES					12.5	13.8	11.7
121 FOR INDUSTRY–POUR L'INDUSTRIE					5.7	5.7	4.5
122 FOR HOUSEHOLDS–POUR LES MENAGES					6.9	8.1	7.2
2 IND SUPPLIES–APPROV INDUSTRIELS					22.7	28.4	19.8
21 PRIMARY–PRODUITS DE BASE					1.7	2.0	2.0
22 PROCESSED–PRODUITS ELABORES					21.0	26.4	17.9
3 FUELS–COMBUSTIBLES					0.8	0.8	19.5
31 PRIMARY–PRODUITS DE BASE					0.0	0.0	0.6
32 PROCESSED–PRODUITS ELABORES					0.8	0.8	19.0
321 MOTOR SPIRIT–ESSENCE							6.9
322 OTHER–AUTRES					0.8	0.8	12.1
4 MACHINERY–EQUIPEMENT					32.0	24.4	19.8
41 CAPITAL EQUIPMENT–MACHINES					27.8	19.6	15.1
42 PARTS–PIECES ACCESSOIRES					4.1	4.8	4.6
5 TRANSPORT–TRANSPORT					7.3	7.1	6.0
51 PASSENGER CARS–AUTOMOBILES					2.3	2.1	1.1
52 OTHER–AUTRES					2.6	2.4	1.9
521 INDUSTRIAL–INDUSTRIELS					2.5	2.3	1.8
522 NON INDUSTRIAL–NON INDUSTRIEL					0.1	0.1	0.1
53 PARTS–PIECES ACCESSOIRES					2.4	2.6	3.0
6 CONSUM GOODS–BIENS CONSOMMATION					18.7	13.7	14.8
61 DURABLE–DURABLES					1.5	0.9	1.1
62 SEMI DURABLE–SEMI DURABLES					4.7	3.4	3.4
63 NON DURABLE–NON DURABLES					12.6	9.4	10.3
7 GOODS NES–BIENS NDA					0.1	0.1	0.0

EXPORTS – EXPORTATIONS

	1989	1990	1991	1992	1993	1994	1995
TOTAL EXPORTS–EXPORTATIONS TOTALES					100.	100.	100.
1 AGRICULTURE					1.3	11.7	7.6
2 MINING QUARRY–INDUS EXTRACTIVES					92.3	82.4	86.2
3 MANUFACTURING–IND MANUFACTUR					6.4	5.9	6.2
31 FOOD BEV TOBACCO–ALIM BOISS TAB					0.9	0.8	0.8
32 TEXTILES–INDUSTRIES TEXTILES					0.0	0.0	0.0
33 WOOD & PRODUCTS–BOIS & PRODUITS					2.4	1.9	2.5
34 PAPER & PRODUCTS–PAPIER & PRODT					0.0	0.0	0.0
35 CHEMICALS–INDUSTRIES CHIMIQUES					2.2	2.2	2.0
36 NON METAL MIN–MIN NON METAL					0.0	0.0	0.0
37 BASIC METAL–IND METAL BASE					0.2	0.0	0.0
38 METAL MANUF–MANUF METAL					0.8	1.0	0.8
39 OTH MANUF IND–AUTRES MANUF					0.0	0.0	0.0

3. TRADE BY PRINCIPAL COUNTRIES OF CONSIGNMENT AND DESTINATION (VALUE IN MILLION U.S. DOLLARS)
ECHANGES SELON LES PRINCIPAUX PAYS DE CONSIGNATION ET DE DESTINATION (VALEUR EN MILLIONS DE DOLLARS EU)

COUNTRIES–PAYS	SPECIAL IMPORTS C.I.F. IMPORTATIONS SPECIALES C.A.F				
	1991	1992	1993	1994	1995
World			347.1	395.2	555.9
Africa			15.7	32.8	30.8
Americas			19.3	41.6	46.5
– Northern America			16.6	40.0	44.9
– LAIA			2.7	1.6	1.5
– CACM			0.0	0.0	0.0
– Caribbean			0.0	0.0	
– Rest of America					
Asia excl fmr USSR			27.2	24.6	32.6
– Middle East			0.3	0.5	1.2
Asia former USSR					
Europe excl fmr USSR			243.2	218.4	255.1
– European Union			240.4	213.4	252.4
– Eastern Europe			0.3	0.2	0.3
– Rest of Europe			2.6	4.7	2.4
Europe former USSR			0.1	0.5	0.0
Oceania			0.0	0.4	0.4
Other			41.6	76.8	190.6
France, Monaco			114.0	127.5	145.2
Areas n.e.s.			41.6	76.8	83.4
Italy/Italie			66.2	17.1	20.8
USA/Etats–Unis d'Amer			16.1	39.5	44.6
Netherlands/Pays–Bas			27.5	24.6	30.7
Free zones/Zone franches					56.4
Bunkers, ship stores					50.8
Belgium–Luxembourg			9.7	14.9	19.4
United Kingdom			9.0	12.7	16.6
Japan/Japon			11.1	10.2	12.3
Germany/Allemagne			8.4	9.2	15.8
Senegal/Sénégal			1.8	6.0	7.2
China, Hong Kong SAR			4.5	4.0	3.7
So. African Customs Un			2.8	8.2	0.0
Cote d'Ivoire			2.9	3.6	4.4
Viet Nam			2.9	1.7	5.4
Norway,Svalbard and JM			1.7	4.0	2.4
Singapore/Singapour			3.0	3.0	1.8
Cameroon/Cameroun			2.7	2.3	2.2
Mauritania/Mauritanie			0.0	0.7	5.9
Spain/Espagne			3.2	3.4	
Angola			0.2	3.0	3.0
Nigeria/Nigéria			2.0	1.3	2.4
Morocco/Maroc			0.8	2.6	1.5
Ireland/Irlande			0.6	1.5	2.2
China/Chine			1.3	1.0	1.4
Indonesia/Indonésie			1.0	1.3	0.9
Korea, Republic of			0.9	1.2	0.8
Guinea–Bissau				2.2	0.5
Argentina/Argentine			1.6	0.9	0.2
Brazil/Brésil			1.0	0.4	1.2
Dem Rep of the Congo			0.8	0.6	1.0
Portugal			1.3	1.0	
Benin/Bénin			0.5	0.7	1.1
India/Inde			0.1	0.3	1.7
Thailand/Thaïlande			0.7	0.6	0.7
Pakistan			0.0	0.3	1.6
Switzerland,Liechtenst.			0.9	0.7	
Sweden/Suède			0.2	0.9	0.3
Gabon			0.3	0.6	0.5

COUNTRIES–PAYS	SPECIAL EXPORTS F.O.B. EXPORTATIONS SPECIALES F.O.B.				
	1991	1992	1993	1994	1995
Monde			965.3	917.8	1089.8
Afrique			18.2	21.3	28.3
Amériques			507.9	426.4	311.1
– Amérique du Nord			507.6	386.3	311.1
– ALAI			0.1	29.7	
– MCAC					
– Caraïbes			0.2	10.5	
– Autre Amérique					
Asie anc. URSS exclus			79.7	136.5	263.2
– Moyen–Orient			0.1	1.3	1.9
Asie ancienne URSS					
Europe anc. URSS exclus			359.5	333.6	487.1
– Union Européenne			346.1	329.2	449.8
– Europe de l'Est				0.0	0.0
– Autre de l'Europe			13.4	4.3	37.3
Europe ancienne URSS			0.0	0.0	
Océanie			0.0	0.0	0.0
Autre			0.0	0.0	0.0
USA/Etats–Unis d'Amer			503.4	386.3	311.1
Italy/Italie			226.3	191.8	189.6
Other Asia n.e.s.			52.2	118.8	256.9
France, Monaco			79.5	56.3	107.3
Netherlands/Pays–Bas			16.6	11.0	130.7
Spain/Espagne			17.3	28.1	0.1
Malta/Malte					31.3
Israel/Israël			12.8	11.8	0.0
Portugal			1.6	21.9	0.4
Germany/Allemagne			2.6	8.1	11.5
Angola			10.2	5.1	6.5
Japan/Japon			14.4	3.2	3.4
Chile/Chili				15.6	
Morocco/Maroc			0.8	5.4	9.0
Belgium–Luxembourg			0.5	7.9	6.4
Brazil/Brésil			0.1	14.0	
Reunion/Réunion			4.7	4.1	3.6
Switzerland,Liechtenst.			12.3	0.0	
Dem Rep of the Congo			1.1	4.2	6.9
Norway,Svalbard and JM			1.1	4.3	6.0
Bahamas				5.5	
United Kingdom			1.1	1.7	2.4
Haiti/Haïti				5.0	
Bermuda/Bermudes			4.2		
Turkey/Turquie				1.2	1.8
Denmark/Danemark			0.7	0.6	1.4
Greece/Grèce			0.0	1.8	0.0
China/Chine			0.0	1.2	0.4
Algeria/Algérie				0.6	0.5
So. African Customs Un			0.4	0.7	
Egypt/Egypte					0.9
Guinea/Guinée			0.3	0.4	0.0
Singapore/Singapour			0.0	0.2	0.3
Tunisia/Tunisie			0.1	0.2	0.1
Gabon			0.1	0.1	0.2
Mauritius/Maurice			0.2		0.1
Nigeria/Nigéria			0.1	0.1	0.1
Zimbabwe			0.1	0.1	0.1
Trinidad and Tobago			0.2		
Korea, Republic of			0.2	0.0	0.0

(VALUE AS PERCENTAGE OF WORLD TOTAL)(VALEURS EN POURCENTAGE DU TOTAL MONDIAL)

	1986	1987	1988	1989	1990	1991	1992	1993	1994	1995
Africa	4.4	4.9		0.3	0.4			4.5	8.3	5.5
Americas	8.2	2.9		5.7	11.4			5.6	10.5	8.4
– Northern America	7.3	2.0		5.4	11.1			4.8	10.1	8.1
– LAIA	0.9	0.4		0.3	0.3			0.8	0.4	0.3
– CACM	0.0							0.0	0.0	0.0
– Caribbean	0.0							0.0	0.0	
– Rest of America	0.0	0.5								
Asia excl fmr USSR	7.1	6.2		4.4	4.4			7.8	6.2	5.9
– Middle East	0.1							0.1	0.1	0.2
Asia former USSR										
Europe excl fmr USSR	78.2	84.7		66.9	58.3			70.1	55.3	45.9
– European Union	75.9	65.9		66.9	58.3			69.3	54.0	45.4
– Eastern Europe	0.4							0.1	0.1	0.1
– Rest of Europe	1.9	18.9						0.7	1.2	0.4
Europe former USSR	1.0	1.2		1.3	0.6			0.0	0.1	0.0
Oceania	0.0							0.0	0.1	0.1
Other	1.1	0.1		6.2	7.7			12.0	19.4	34.3
France, Monaco	52.5	51.2	42.9	49.0	36.8			32.8	32.3	26.1
Areas n.e.s.	1.1	0.1	5.2	6.2	7.7			12.0	19.4	15.0
Italy/Italie	4.6	5.0	7.3	5.8	10.5			19.1	4.3	3.7
USA/Etats–Unis d'Amer	5.2	1.5	6.6	5.4	11.1			4.6	10.0	8.0
Netherlands/Pays–Bas	2.5	3.1	3.7	3.8	4.6			7.9	6.2	5.5
Free zones/Zone franches										10.1
Bunkers, ship stores										9.1
Belgium–Luxembourg	2.8							2.8	3.8	3.5
United Kingdom	3.3							2.6	3.2	3.0
Japan/Japon	4.2	3.3	4.3	4.0	4.0			3.2	2.6	2.2

	1986	1987	1988	1989	1990	1991	1992	1993	1994	1995
Afrique	2.8	4.1	1.0	0.9	1.1			1.9	2.3	2.6
Amériques	54.2	21.7	40.9	46.1	36.3			52.6	46.5	28.5
– Amérique du Nord	54.2	21.6	40.9	46.1	36.3			52.6	42.1	28.5
– ALAI	0.0	0.1	0.0	0.0	0.0			0.0	3.2	
– MCAC										
– Caraïbes	0.0							0.0	1.1	
– Autre Amérique	0.0									
Asie anc. URSS exclus	0.2	1.0	0.3	0.1	0.0			8.3	14.9	24.2
– Moyen–Orient	0.0							0.0	0.1	0.2
Asie ancienne URSS										
Europe anc. URSS exclus	42.0	71.2	40.7	41.9	45.4			37.2	36.3	44.7
– Union Européenne	41.7	59.9	40.7	41.9	45.4			35.9	35.9	41.3
– Europe de l'Est	0.2								0.0	0.0
– Autre de l'Europe	0.2	11.3						1.4	0.5	3.4
Europe ancienne URSS	0.4	1.9	0.9	0.7	0.1			0.0	0.0	
Océanie	0.2							0.0	0.0	0.0
Autre	0.1	0.1	0.3	0.2	0.1			0.0	0.0	0.0
USA/Etats–Unis d'Amer	54.2	21.6	40.9	46.1	36.3			52.1	42.1	28.5
Italy/Italie	9.0	16.5	4.4	7.7	11.5			23.4	20.9	17.4
Other Asia n.e.s.	0.0	0.4						5.4	12.9	23.6
France, Monaco	12.9	25.2	22.0	19.3	24.6			8.2	6.1	9.8
Netherlands/Pays–Bas	4.3	8.5	10.5	7.3	5.5			1.7	1.2	12.0
Spain/Espagne	11.5	7.2	1.8	6.1	2.4			1.8	3.1	0.0
Malta/Malte										2.9
Israel/Israël								1.3	1.3	0.0
Portugal	0.9							0.2	2.4	0.0
Germany/Allemagne								0.3	0.9	1.1

4. Special Imports C.I.F. by Commodities according to the S.I.T.C. (Rev. 2) in million U.S. Dollars
Importations Spéciales C.A.F. par Produits d'après la C.T.C.I. (Rév. 2) en millions de Dollars E.U.

SITC CTCI	COMMODITY	1992 QUANTITY QUANTITE	1992 VALUE VALEUR	1993 QUANTITY QUANTITE	1993 VALUE VALEUR	1994 QUANTITY QUANTITE	1994 VALUE VALEUR	1995 QUANTITY QUANTITE	1995 VALUE VALEUR	PRODUIT
	ALL COMMODITIES				347.1		395.2		556.0	TOUS PRODUITS
0	FOOD AND LIVE ANIMALS				59.6		87.9		108.6	ALIMENTS,ANIMAUX VIVANTS
01	MEAT AND PREPARATIONS				15.9		23.8		28.2	VIANDES ET PREPARATIONS
011	MEAT FRESH,CHILLD,FROZEN			W 15156	15.1	W 23964	21.7	W 23082	26.8	VIANDES FRAICHES,REF,CONGE
0111	BOVINE MEAT FRESH,FROZEN			W 173	0.4	W 14125	11.8	W 12207	14.8	VIANDES BOVIN FRAI,REF
01112	BOVINE MEAT BONELESS					W 14055	11.7	W 12199	14.8	VIANDES BOVIN DESOSSEES
0113	PIG MEAT FRESH,CHLD,FRZN			W 1909	1.4	W 2444	2.0	W 2218	2.1	VIANDE DE PORC
0114	POULTRY FRESH CHLLD,FRZN			W 12431	12.4	W 6492	7.0	W 7669	8.8	VOLAILLES MORTES
014	MEAT PREPD,PRSVD,NES ETC			W 612	0.8	W 1228	2.1	W 832	1.4	CONSERVES DE VIANDES
0149	OTH PREPARD,PRESRVD MEAT			W 612	0.8	W 963	1.6	W 832	1.4	AUTRES PREP DE VIANDES
02	DAIRY PRODCTS,BIRDS'EGGS				10.1		8.7		13.4	PRODUITS LAITIERS,OEUFS
022	MILK AND CREAM			W 6325	7.7	W 4568	7.2	W 6564	12.0	LAIT ET CREME
0224	MILK,CREAM PRESERVED ETC			W 5642	7.3	W 4021	6.8	W 5833	11.4	LAIT,CREME CONS,CONC
02243	MILK DRY,OVER 1.5% FAT					W 1597	3.7	W 1764	5.2	LAIT POUDRE SUP 1.5%
02249	MILK(EX DRY) PRSVD,SWEET			W 5558	7.1	W 2423	3.2	W 4067	6.2	LAIT CONS,CONC SUCRE
03	FISH AND PREPARATIONS				0.2		21.8		16.5	POISSONS ET PREPARATIONS
034	FISH,FRESH,CHILLED,FROZN			W 1	0.1	W 17497	10.0	W 14128	9.3	POISSON FRAIS, REFRIG,CONG
0342	FISH FROZEN,EXCL FILLETS			W 1	0.1	W 17497	10.0	W 14128	9.3	POISSONS CONGELES
035	FISH SALTED,DRIED,SMOKED			W 24	0.1	W 5489	11.1	W 3490	6.4	POISSON SECHE,SALE,FUME
03503	FISH(EX COD)DRIED,SALTED			W 24	0.1	W 5488	11.1	W 3489	6.4	POISSONS SECHES,SALES
04	CEREALS AND PREPARATIONS				27.6		23.8		36.8	CEREALES ET PRODUITS
041	WHEAT ETC UNMILLED			W 19375	3.0	W 7072	1.4	W 33903	1.8	FROMENT,EPEAUTRE
0411	DURUM WHEAT UNMILLED			W 19375	3.0	W 7072	1.4	W 33903	1.8	FROMENT DUR NON MOULU
042	RICE			W 21069	5.1	W 30907	7.0	W 36744	12.4	RIZ
0422	RICE SEMI–MILLED,MILLED			W 21068	5.1	W 30906	7.0	W 36744	12.4	RIZ POLI,GLACE INCL BRISURES
04221	RICE MILLED UNBROKEN			W 21068	5.1	W 29965	6.7	W 36744	12.4	RIZ POLI,GLACE EXCL BRISURES
046	WHEAT ETC MEAL OR FLOUR			W 65119	18.2	W 34221	8.2	W 43183	13.8	SEMOULE FARINE,FROMENT
04601	FLOUR OF WHEAT OR MESLIN			W 65114	18.1	W 34219	8.2	W 43179	13.8	FARINE DE FROMENT
047	OTHER CEREAL MEALS,FLOUR			W 1	0.1	W 3026	1.6	W 3429	2.5	AUTRES SEMOULES,FARINES
04702	MEAL OR GROATS NON–WHEAT					W 3023	1.6	W 3425	2.5	GRUAUX,SEMOULES DE CEREALES
048	CEREAL ETC PREPARATIONS			W 1349	1.4	W 6188	5.9	W 7163	6.4	PREPTNS A BASE CEREALES
0482	MALT INCLUDING FLOUR					W 4819	3.1	W 6296	5.4	MALT MEME TORREFIE
0488	OTH CEREAL PREPS,MALT EX			W 34	0.1	W 423	2.0	W 34	0.2	EXTRAITS DE MALT
05	VEGETABLES AND FRUIT				2.8		4.3		3.6	LEGUMES ET FRUITS
054	VEG ETC FRSH,SMPLY PRSVD			W 1897	1.7	W 3571	3.4	W 2679	2.7	LEGUMES FRAIS,CONG,SECS
0546	VEGETABLES SIMPLY PRESVD			W 1714	1.6	W 1830	2.4	W 1271	1.7	LEGUMES CONG,CONSER
05461	VEGETABLES FROZEN			W 1714	1.6	W 1830	2.4	W 1271	1.7	LEGUMES CONGELES
06	SUGAR AND PREPS,HONEY				1.1		1.3		1.6	SUCRES ET PRODUITS
09	MISC EDIBLE PRODUCTS				1.8		3.7		7.5	PREP ALIMENTAIRES DIVERSES
091	MARGARINE AND SHORTENING					W 1228	1.2	W 2282	3.1	MARGARINE ET GRAISSES
0914	MARGARINE,EDIBLE FAT NES					W 1228	1.2	W 2282	3.1	MARGARINES,SIMILI SAINDOUX
09141	MARGARINE					W 1211	1.2	W 2282	3.1	MARGARINE
098	EDIBLE PRODCTS,PREPS NES			W 1562	1.8	W 1111	2.5	W 1487	4.5	PREP ALIMENTAIRES NDA
09806	YEASTS,BAKING POWDERS			W 56	0.2	W 305	1.0	W 524	2.0	LEVURES
09809	MISC FOOD PREPRTIONS NES			W 910	1.0	W 293	1.0	W 545	1.8	PREP ALIMENTAIRES NDA
1	BEVERAGES AND TOBACCO				3.0		6.2		6.0	BOISSONS ET TABACS
11	BEVERAGES				2.9		2.9		2.2	BOISSONS
112	ALCOHOLIC BEVERAGES			W 3835	2.4	W 4100	2.6	W 752	1.5	BOISSONS ALCOOLIQUES
1121	WINE OF FRESH GRAPES ETC			W 3725	2.0	W 3155	1.7	W 214	0.6	VINS DE RAISINS FRAIS
11212	WINE OF FRESH GRAPES			W 3724	2.0	W 3149	1.7	W 206	0.5	VINS DE MOUTS DE RAISINS
12	TOBACCO AND MANUFACTURES				0.1		3.3		3.8	TABACS BRUTS FABRIQUES
121	TOBACCO UNMNFCTRD,REFUSE			W 19	0.1	W 621	3.3	W 589	3.8	TABACS BRUTS,DECHETS
1212	TOBACCO STRIPPED OR PART					W 591	3.3	W 583	3.8	TABACS PART ECOTES
2	CRUDE MATERLS,EXCL FUELS				6.0		5.0		7.4	MAT BRUTES NON COMESTIBLES
26	TEXTILE FIBRES AND WASTE				0.2		1.8		4.0	FIBRES TEXTILES
269	WASTE OF TEXTILE FABRICS			W 140	0.2	W 1001	1.7	W 2012	3.9	FRIPERIE DRILLES,CHIFFONS
26901	BULK TEXT WSTE,OLD CLTHG					W 954	1.7	W 1911	3.8	ART ET ACCESS D'HABILLEMENT
27	CRUDE FERTLZR,MINRLS NES				4.2		2.7		2.5	ENGRAIS MINERAUX BRUTS
278	OTHER CRUDE MINERALS			W 11586	3.0	W 11520	2.5	W 9095	2.3	AUTRES MINERAUX BRUTS
2783	COMMON SALT,ETC			W 8248	2.0	W 7910	1.8	W 6012	1.7	SEL
29	CRUDE ANIMAL,VEG MAT NES				1.6		0.4		0.5	MATIERES BRUTES ANIM,VEGET
3	MINERAL FUELS ETC				2.9		5.0		108.7	COMBUSTIBLES MINERAUX LUB
33	PETROLEUM AND PRODUCTS				2.8		4.9		106.1	PETROLE ET DERIVES
334	PETROLEUM PRODUCTS,REFIN			W 4024	2.8	W 5214	3.1	W 472482	105.5	PRODUITS RAFFINES
3341	GASOLINE,OTH LIGHT OILS							W 157533	38.5	ESSENCES POUR MOTEURS
33411	MOTOR,AVIATION SPIRIT							W 123822	30.8	ESSENCES MOTEURS D'AVIONS
33419	OTH LIGHT PETROLEUM OILS							W 33711	7.7	AUTRES HUILES LEGERES
3342	KEROSENE,OTH MEDIUM OILS							W 72399	19.3	PETR LAMPANTS,AUT HUIL
33421	KEROSENE INCL JET FUEL							W 72382	19.3	PETROLES LAMPANTS
3343	GAS OILS							W 209370	44.5	GAS OILS
3344	FUEL OILS,NES							W 32146	2.3	FUEL OILS
335	RESIDUAL PETRLM PROD NES				0.1	W 6720	1.8	W 60	0.1	PRODUITS RESIDUELS NDA
3354	PETROLM BITUMEN,COKE ETC			W 17	0.1	W 6719	1.8	W 34	0.1	BITUME,COKE DE PETROLE
33543	BITUMINOUS MIXTURES ETC			W 3	0.1	W 6432	1.7	W 3	0.1	MELANGES BITUMINEUX
341	*GAS,NATURAL AND MANUFCT			W 41	0.2	W 13	0.1	W 17824	2.7	GAZ NATUREL,GAZ MANUFACT
3413	PETROLM GASES,LIQUEFIED			W 41	0.2	W 12	0.1	W 17824	2.7	GAZ DE PETROLE LIQUEFIE
34131	LIQUEFIED PROPANE,BUTANE			W 41	0.2	W 12	0.1	W 17824	2.7	PROPANE,BUTANE LIQUEFIES
4	ANIMAL,VEGETABLE OIL,FAT				8.3		10.7		1.2	HUILES,GRAISSES ANIM,VEG
42	FIXED VEGETABLE OIL,FAT				8.3		10.5		1.2	HUILES VEGETALES FIXES
423	FIXED VEG OILS,SOFT			W 605	0.6	W 8932	8.5	W 432	0.5	HUILES VEGET DOUCES FIXES
4232	SOYA BEAN OIL					W 7550	7.1			HUILE DE SOJA
4236	SUNFLOWER SEED OIL					W 1372	1.4	W 3	0.1	HUILE DE TOURNESOL
424	FIXED VEG OIL NONSOFT			W 10966	7.8	W 2415	2.1	W 899	0.8	AUTRES HUILES VEG FIXES
4242	PALM OIL			W 1620	0.6	W 1666	1.4	W 621	0.5	HUILE DE PALME
4249	FIXED VEGETABLE OILS NES			W 9342	7.3	W 746	0.7	W 278	0.3	HUILES VEGET FIXES NDA
5	CHEMCLS,RELATED PROD NES				54.7		54.8		77.0	PRODUITS CHIMIQUES
51	ORGANIC CHEMICALS				2.0		1.4		1.7	PROD CHIMIQ ORGANIQUES
514	NITROGEN–FNCTN COMPOUNDS			W 221	1.2	W 155	0.4	W 23	0.2	COMPOSES FONCT AZOTEES
52	INORGANIC CHEMICALS				1.0		3.4		4.5	PROD CHIM INORGANIQUES
522	INORG ELEMNTS,OXIDES,ETC			W 260	0.4	W 4824	2.1	W 5319	2.5	ELEMENTS INORGANIQUES
523	OTHR INORG CHEMICALS ETC			W 678	0.6	W 3034	1.4	W 4250	2.0	AUT PRODUITS CHIMIQUES INORG
53	DYES,TANNING,COLOUR PROD				0.9		1.4		1.2	PROD TEINTURE,COLORANTS
533	PIGMENTS,PAINTS,ETC			W 478	0.8	W 422	1.4	W 471	1.2	PIGMENTS,PEINTURES,VERNIS
541	*MEDICINAL,PHARM PRODUCT			K 2104827	39.3	K 1322614	24.6	K 2032592	38.9	PROD MEDICINAUX PHARMACEUT
5417	MEDICAMENTS			K 2019362	38.5	K 1275690	24.0	K 1966604	38.0	MEDICAMENTS
54179	— CONTNG OTH SUBSTANCES			K 2001822	38.0	K 1260979	23.8	K 1947303	37.7	MED CONT AUT SUBSTANCES
55	PERFUME,CLEANING ETC PRD				4.5		5.2		8.5	PROD POUR PARFUM,TOILETTE
554	SOAP,CLEANSING ETC PREPS			W 2226	2.9	W 4551	3.5	W 3497	5.7	SAVONS,PRODUITS DETERSIFS
5541	SOAPS			W 1150	1.0	W 3872	2.1	W 2214	2.1	SAVONS,PROD TENSIO–ACTIFS
5542	WASHING PREPARATIONS ETC			W 851	1.6	W 583	1.3	W 1138	3.4	PROD ORG TENSIO–ACT NDA
572	*EXPLOSIVES,PYROTECH PRO			W 147	1.8	W 60	0.9	W 119	2.0	EXPLOSIFS

Congo

4. Special Imports C.I.F. by Commodities according to the S.I.T.C. (Rev. 2) in million U.S. Dollars
Importations Spéciales C.A.F. par Produits d'après la C.T.C.I. (Rév. 2) en millions de Dollars E.U.

SITC CTCI	COMMODITY	1992		1993		1994		1995		PRODUIT
		QUANTITY QUANTITE	VALUE VALEUR	QUANTITY QUANTITE	VALUE VALEUR	QUANTITY QUANTITE	VALUE VALEUR	QUANTITY QUANTITE	VALUE VALEUR	
5721	PREPARED EXPLOSIVES			W 147	1.8	W 53	0.9	W 98	1.6	POUDRES,EXPLOSIFS
57211	PROPELLENT POWDERS			W 89	1.5	W 49	0.7	W 57	1.2	POUDRES A TIRER
58	PLASTIC MATERIALS ETC				1.9		1.9		3.3	MAT PLAST ARTIFICIELLES
59	CHEMICAL MATERIALS NES				3.6		15.5		16.7	MAT PROD CHIMIQUES NDA
591	PESTICIDES,DISINFECTANTS			W 261	0.5	W 442	0.8	W 608	2.5	DESINF,INSECT,FONG,HERB
598	MISCEL CHEM PRODUCTS NES			W 585	3.1	W 12647	14.3	W 7474	13.2	PROD DIV INDUST CHIM NDA
5989	CHEM PRODUCTS,PREPS NES			W 133	2.0	W 12555	14.1	W 7094	12.0	PROD PREP CHIMIQUES NDA
59899	OTH CHEM PRODS,PREPS,NES			W 82	1.8	W 12279	13.4	W 6793	11.4	AUT PRODUITS CHIMIQUES NDA
6	BASIC MANUFACTURES				61.6		76.7		69.5	ART MANUFACTURES
62	RUBBER MANUFACTURES NES				4.2		7.6		5.9	CAOUTCHOUC MANUFACTURE
621	MATERIALS OF RUBBER			W 93	1.4	W 424	4.7	W 54	0.4	PRODUITS EN CAOUTCHOUC
62105	UNHARD VULC RUBBER TUBES			W 88	1.4	W 396	4.6	W 21	0.4	TUBES,TUYAUX CAOUT VULC
625	RUBBER TYRES, TUBES ETC			W 994	2.7	W 764	2.4	W 1430	4.3	PNEUS CAOUTCHOUC VULCANISE
6252	TYRES,NEW,BUS OR LORRY			W 621	1.5	W 258	1.0	W 475	2.2	PNEUS POUR AUTOBUS,CAMIONS
63	WOOD,CORK MANUFACTRS NES				6.1		0.4		3.5	OUVRAGES LIEGE ET BOIS
635	WOOD MANUFACTURES NES			W 493	6.0	W 156	0.3	W 361	3.5	ART MANUF EN BOIS NDA
6353	BUILDERS WOODWRK,PREFABS			W 445	5.9	W 115	0.2	W 347	3.4	OUVRAGES DE MENUISERIE
64	PAPER,PAPERBOARD AND MFR				8.0		4.8		7.7	PAPIERS,CARTONS & OUVRAGES
641	PAPER AND PAPERBOARD			W 465	2.3	W 1155	1.8	W 1202	2.9	PAPIERS ET CARTONS
6412	PRINTG,WRITING PAPER NES			W 76	1.4	W 522	0.9	W 535	1.2	PAPIERS POUR L'IMPRESSION
64121	— UNCOATED			W 36	1.3	W 513	0.9	W 520	1.2	PAPIERS IMPRES NON COUCHES
642	PAPER,ETC,PRECUT,ARTS OF			W 2242	5.8	W 1028	3.0	W 1508	4.8	PAP,CARTONS DECOUPES
6421	PAPER ETC CONTAINERS			W 1451	4.0	W 368	1.3	W 1005	3.0	BOITES,SACS EMBALLAGES
65	TEXTILE YARN,FABRICS,ETC				2.7		2.8		6.3	FILS,TISSUS,ARTICLES TEXTILE
652	COTTON FABRICS,WOVEN			W 264	0.8	W 314	1.0	W 499	1.9	TISSUS DE COTON
6522	WOVEN COTTON BLEACHD,ETC			W 244	0.7	W 256	0.8	W 496	1.9	TISSUS COTON BLANCHIS ETC
658	TEXTILE ARTICLES NES			W 483	1.1	W 479	1.0	W 562	2.1	ART FACONNES MAT TEXTILES
66	NONMETAL MINERAL MFS NES				5.1		4.0		5.7	ART MIN NON METALLIQUES
661	LIME,CEMENT,BLDG PRODS			W 5067	1.0	W 8859	1.5	W 6474	1.4	CHAUX,CIMENTS MAT CONSTR
662	CLAY,REFRACTORY BLDG PRD			W 2575	1.3	W 1754	0.8	W 1497	1.0	MAT CONST REFRACTAIRES
6624	BRICKS ETC NONREFRACTORY			W 2507	1.2	W 1732	0.8	W 1418	0.9	BRIQUES ETC CERAM NON REFR
665	GLASSWARE			W 1860	1.8	W 312	0.6	W 1630	1.6	OUVRAGES EN VERRE
6651	BOTTLES ETC OF GLASS			W 1406	1.2	W 14	0.1	W 1151	0.7	RECIPIENTS EN VERRE
66511	GLASS BOTTLES ETC NONVAC			W 1406	1.2	W 14	0.1	W 1151	0.7	BONBONNES,BOUTEILLES,ETC
67	IRON AND STEEL				17.8		20.6		15.6	FER ET ACIER
673	IRON,STEEL SHAPES ETC			W 4095	1.8	W 3860	1.8	W 1939	1.0	BARRES,PROFIL FER,ACIER
6732	IRON,STEEL BARS ETC			W 3147	1.3	W 2735	1.2	W 1589	0.8	BARRES FER,ACIER
674	IRN,STL UNIV,PLATE,SHEET			W 1247	1.1	W 1068	1.0	W 3994	4.4	LARGES PLATS,TOLES
6749	OTH IRN,STL PLATES,SHEET			W 30	0.1	W 168	0.2	W 2729	3.1	AUTRES TOLES FER,ACIER
67491	— OF IRON OR SIMPLE STL			W 30	0.1	W 168	0.2	W 2729	3.0	AUT TOLES AUTRES ACIER FIN
678	IRON,STL TUBES,PIPES,ETC			W 16255	14.7	W 15025	17.7	W 4797	9.8	TUBES,TUYAUX EN FONTE,FER
6782	IRON,STL SEAMLESS TUBES			W 15672	13.3	W 14039	15.9	W 3934	6.5	TUBES,TUYAUX SANS SOUDURE
6785	IRON,STEEL TUBE FITTINGS			W 199	1.2	W 168	1.3	W 391	2.8	ACCESSOIRES DE TUYAUTERIE
68	NON–FERROUS METALS				2.8		1.2		1.8	METAUX NON FERREUX
684	ALUMINIUM			W 728	2.8	W 416	1.1	W 535	1.6	ALUMINIUM
6842	ALUMINIUM,ALLOYS WORKED			W 728	2.8	W 416	1.1	W 535	1.6	ALUMINIUM,ALLIAGES OUVRE
68422	ALUMNM PLATE,SHEET,STRIP			W 656	1.8	W 383	0.8	W 467	1.1	TOLES, PLANCHES EN ALU
69	METAL MANUFACTURES NES				15.2		35.6		23.2	ART MANUFACT EN METAL NDA
691	STRUCTURES AND PARTS NES			W 108	0.3	W 4680	21.7	W 439	1.1	CONSTRUCT FER,ACIER,ALU
6911	STRUCTURES,PARTS IRN,STL			W 58	0.2	W 4663	21.6	W 413	1.0	CONSTRUCT FER,ACIER,FONTE
693	WIRE PRODUCTS NON ELECTR			W 553	0.9	W 291	0.8	W 565	2.3	OUVRAGES FILS METALLIQUES
6931	WIRE CABLES, ROPES ETC			W 253	0.8	W 137	0.6	W 349	2.0	CORDAGES EN FILS DE FER
69311	IRN,STEEL CABLE,ROPE ETC			W 251	0.7	W 136	0.6	W 349	2.0	CORDAGES FILS FER,ACIER
694	STL,COPPR NAILS,NUTS,ETC			W 186	0.8	W 159	1.0	W 285	2.1	CLOUS,VIS,ECROUS
69402	IRN,STL NUTS,BOLTS,ETC			W 183	0.8	W 128	1.0	W 238	1.9	BOULONS,VIS,ECROUS FER,AC
695	TOOLS			W 108	1.5	W 396	5.5	W 375	9.1	OUTILS A MAIN
6953	OTHER HAND TOOLS			W 47	0.6	W 82	0.7	W 77	3.4	AUTRES OUTILS A MAIN
69539	HAND TOOLS ETC NES			W 27	0.4	W 58	0.5	W 62	3.2	OUTILLAGE A MAIN NDA
6954	BLADES,TIPS,ETC FR TOOLS			W 34	0.9	W 285	4.8	W 196	5.3	OUTILS POUR MACHINE–OUTIL
69541	PARTS TO INSERT IN TOOLS			W 29	0.9	W 252	4.7	W 190	5.1	OUTILS DE FORAGE
696	CUTLERY			W 58	3.2	W 56	0.4	W 196	0.5	COUTELLERIE
69603	RAZORS,RAZOR BLADES			W 45	3.2	W 15	0.2			RASOIRS ET LAMES
697	BASE MTL HOUSEHOLD EQUIP			W 678	1.4	W 338	0.8	W 78	0.3	ART MENAGE MET COMMUNS
699	BASE METAL MFRS NES			W 1716	6.5	W 1741	4.9	W 1342	7.9	ART MANUFACTURES MET NDA
6996	BASE MTL MISC ARTICLES			W 823	3.6	W 447	1.8	W 647	3.8	ART DIVERS METAUX COMMUNS
69961	BASE MTL FLEXIBLE TUBING			W 276	1.9	W 22	0.5	W 232	2.3	TUYAUX FLEXIBLES
69963	BASE METAL STOPPERS,ETC			W 379	1.3	W 307	1.1	W 276	1.0	BOUCHONS METALLIQUES
6997	IRON,STEEL ARTICLES NES			W 406	1.3	W 661	0.7	W 265	1.1	OUV FONTE,FER,ACIER NDA
69979	IRN,STL MANUFACTURES NES			W 406	1.3	V' 659	0.7	W 227	1.1	AUT OUVRAGES EN FER NDA
6998	MFRS NES OF CPR,NIKL,ETC			W 347	1.1	W 429	1.3	W 225	0.8	OUVRAGES EN CU,NI,AL,PB,ZN
69983	ALUMINIUM MANUFACTS NES			W 304	1.0	W 422	1.3	W 210	0.7	OUVRAGES EN ALUMINIUM
7	MACHINES,TRANSPORT EQUIP				127.1		112.6		112.6	MACHINES MATERIEL TRANSPORT
71	POWER GENERATING EQUIPMT				3.1		5.2		9.2	MACHINES GENERATRICES
713	INTRNL COMBUS PSTN ENGIN			W 65	1.3	W 115	1.8	W 132	2.6	MOTEURS EXPL COMB INT, PIECE
716	ROTATING ELECTRIC PLANT			W 100	1.2	W 172	2.1	W 301	4.5	APP ELECTR ROTATIFS,PIECES
7162	AC MTRS,GENRTRS,GEN SETS			W 58	0.9	W 125	1.4	W 232	2.7	MOTEURS ELECTRIQUES
71623	GEN SETS WITH PISTN ENGN			W 20	0.2	W 75	0.8	W 191	2.1	GROUPES MOTEUR EXPLOSION
72	MACHS FOR SPCL INDUSTRYS				10.8		17.4		17.3	MAC SPECIALES POUR INDUST
722	TRACTORS NON–ROAD			W 18	0.1	W 153	1.5	W 340	2.5	TRACTEURS
7224	WHEELED TRACTORS NES			W 18	0.1	W 101	0.9	W 306	2.5	TRACTEURS A ROUES
723	CIVIL ENGNEERG EQUIP ETC			W 1507	7.3	W 1285	12.0	W 1560	10.0	APPAREILS DE GENIE CIVIL
7234	CONST,MINING MACHNRY NES			W 130	1.0	W 390	2.5	W 261	1.7	MACH POUR LA CONST, MINES
72342	SLFPRP SHOVELS,EXCAVATRS			W 29	0.1	W 253	1.3	W 99	1.0	PELLES MECANIQUES
7239	CONSTR ETC MACHY PTS NES			W 1376	6.4	W 878	9.5	W 1264	8.2	PIECES 723.41–723.46
728	OTH MACHY FOR SPCL INDUS			W 223	2.2	W 319	3.1	W 221	3.4	AUT MACH IND PARTICULIERES
7284	MACHY FOR SPCL INDUS NES			W 76	1.0	W 196	1.9	W 87	1.8	MACH SPEC IND PARTICUL.
72848	OTH MCHY WITH INDIV FNCT			W 53	0.5	W 177	1.6	W 33	1.0	AUTRES MACHINES NDA
74	GENRL INDUSTRL MACHY NES				24.9		30.4		32.1	MACH APP INDUSTRIE
741	HEATING,COOLING EQUIPMNT			W 362	3.1	W 259	2.9	W 184	2.3	MACH CHAUFFAGE,PIECES
7413	INDUS FURNACES ETC,PARTS			W 121	1.2	W 60	0.7	W 3	0.1	FOURS IND,LABOR,PIECES
7415	AIR–CONDITIONING MACHNRY			W 167	1.2	W 117	1.0	W 101	1.2	GROUPES CONDITION AIR
742	PUMPS FOR LIQUIDS ETC			W 117	2.7	W 174	4.4	W 245	4.5	POMPES MOTO–POMPES
7428	OTHER PUMPS FOR LIQUIDS			W 55	1.2	W 73	1.5	W 193	2.5	AUTRES POMPES POUR LIQ
74288	PUMPS FR LIQUIDS NES ETC			W 55	1.2	W 59	1.3	W 192	2.5	POMPES POUR LIQUIDES NDA
7429	PTS NES OF PUMPS OF 742			W 55	1.4	W 44	1.4	W 43	1.7	PIECES POUR GROUPE 742
743	PUMPS NES,CENTRFUGES ETC			W 192	5.1	W 573	9.2	W 149	4.4	POMPES COMPRES,VENT ETC
7431	PUMPS FOR GASES ETC			W 28	0.4	W 454	6.4	W 26	0.4	POMPES AIR A VIDE,COMPRES
7436	GAS,LIQUID FILTERS ETC			W 89	2.4	W 76	1.1	W 87	1.3	APP POUR FILT DES LIQUIDES
7439	PTS NES OF APP OF 7435,6			W 35	2.2	W 24	1.2	W 33	2.8	PIECES 743.5 ET 743.6
744	MECHANICAL HANDLING EQU			W 395	3.3	W 387	2.8	W 355	3.5	EQUIP MANUTENTION PIECES
7442	LIFTING,LOADING MACH NES			W 186	1.6	W 138	1.1	W 285	2.6	APP LEVAGE,MANUTENTION

4. Special Imports C.I.F. by Commodities according to the S.I.T.C. (Rev. 2) in million U.S. Dollars
Importations Spéciales C.A.F. par Produits d'après la C.T.C.I. (Rév. 2) en millions de Dollars E.U.

SITC CTCI	COMMODITY	1992		1993		1994		1995		PRODUIT
		QUANTITY QUANTITE	VALUE VALEUR	QUANTITY QUANTITE	VALUE VALEUR	QUANTITY QUANTITE	VALUE VALEUR	QUANTITY QUANTITE	VALUE VALEUR	
7449	PTS NES OF MACHY OF 7442			W 155	1.6	W 108	1.1	W 46	0.8	PIECES DU 744.2
745	NONELEC MACHY,TOOLS NES			W 83	1.2		0.9	W 85	2.3	AUT MACH NON ELEC,PIECES
7452	OTH NONELEC MCHS,PTS NES			W 67	1.1	W 39	0.7	W 66	1.8	AUT MACH NON ELEC,PIECES
749	NONELEC MACH PTS,ACC NES			W 651	9.8	W 665	10.5	W 548	15.5	PIECES MACH NON ELEC NDA
7492	COCKS,VALVES ETC NES			W 386	5.5	W 185	4.3	W 344	8.4	ART ROB,SIM POUR TUYAUX
7493	SHAFT,CRANK,PULLEY ETC			W 106	1.0	W 103	1.2	W 63	1.9	ARBRES TRANS,VILEBREQUINS
7499	OTH NONELEC MCHY PTS NES			W 118	2.8	W 287	4.3	W 85	3.7	PIECES NON ELECT NDA
74992	METAL–PLASTIC GASKETS			W 111	2.6	W 279	3.8	W 76	3.2	JOINTS METALLOPLASTIQUES
75	OFFICE MACHNES,ADP EQUIP				4.6		4.7		5.0	MACH BUREAU TRAIT AUTOM
752	AUTOMTIC DATA PROC EQUIP			W 34	2.8	W 40	2.9	W 39	3.0	MACH TRAIT INFORMATION
759	OFFICE,ADP MCH PTS,ACCES			W 15	1.5	W 13	1.2	W 28	1.2	PIECES DU 751 ET 752
7599	ACCTG,ETC,ADP MCH PTS,AC			W 15	1.5	W 7	1.1	W 11	0.9	PIECES DU 751 ET 752
76	TELECOMM,SOUND EQUIPMENT				4.0		3.9		4.6	EQUIPMENT DE TELECOM
764	TELECOM EQPT,PTS,ACC NES			W 86	2.8	W 86	3.1	W 73	3.7	EQUIP TELECOM,PIECES
77	ELECTRIC MACHNRY NES ETC				11.8		23.8		19.1	MACH APP ELECT NDA
771	ELECTRIC POWER MACHY NES			W 72	1.1	W 84	0.8	W 59	1.3	MACH PROD,TRANS ELECTR
772	SWITCHGEAR ETC,PARTS NES			W 219	5.9	W 536	11.4	W 213	5.8	APP COUPURE,SECT ETC
7721	SWITCHGEAR ETC			W 218	5.9	W 535	11.3	W 210	5.6	APP COUPURE,SECTIONMNT
773	ELECTR DISTRIBUTNG EQUIP			W 52	0.5	W 726	6.5	W 519	6.0	EQUIPMT DISTRIBUTION ELECT
7731	INSULATED WIRE,CABLE ETC			W 35	0.2	W 716	6.2	W 514	5.6	FILS,CABLES ISOLES ELECT
775	HOUSEHOLD TYPE EQUIP NES			W 507	2.1	W 267	1.0	W 294	1.5	MACH,APP USAGE DOMESTQUE
7752	DOM REFRIGERATRS,FREEZRS			W 447	1.8	W 173	0.6	W 160	0.7	REFRIG,CONGEL MENAGER
77522	DOMESTIC DEEP–FREEZERS			W 293	1.3	W 96	0.4	W 63	0.4	MEUBLES CONGELATEURS
778	ELECTRICAL MACHINERY NES			W 192	1.7	W 969	3.5	W 386	3.5	AUTRES MACH ELECT NDA
7781	BATTERIES,ACCUMULATORS			W 69	0.4	W 801	1.5	W 232	1.1	PILES ET ACCUMULATEURS
78	ROAD VEHICLES				20.4		20.7		21.2	VEHICULES ROUTIERS
781	PASS MOTOR VEH EXC BUSES			W 1536	8.1	W 1697	8.4	W 1230	6.0	AUTO TRANSPORT PERSONNES
782	LORRIES,SPCL MTR VEH NES			W 1077	3.6	W 1068	5.2	W 1269	5.5	VEHICULES SPECIAUX,MARCH
7821	LORRIES,TRUCKS			W 1048	3.4	W 1019	4.6	W 1231	5.4	VEHICULES TRANSP MARCHAND
783	ROAD MOTOR VEHICLES NES			W 727	4.4	W 541	2.9	W 498	2.9	VEHICULES ROUTIERS NDA
7831	BUSES			W 601	3.8	W 282	1.2	W 334	1.8	VOITURES TRANSPORT COMMUN
7832	TRACTORS FOR TR–TRAILERS			W 126	0.6	W 260	1.7	W 164	1.1	TRACTEURS ROUTIERS
784	MOTOR VEH PRTS,ACCES NES			W 347	3.3	W 281	3.0	W 340	5.7	PIECES 722,781,782,783
7849	OTHER MOTOR VEHCL PARTS			W 347	3.3	W 270	3.0	W 339	5.7	PIECES 722,781,782,783
79	OTHR TRANSPORT EQUIPMENT				47.1		6.5		3.8	AUTRE MATERIEL TRANSPORT
791	RAILWAY VEHICLES				0.1	W 175	2.1	W 30	0.2	VEHIC MAT CHEMINS DE FER
7919	RY TRACK FIXT,ETC,PARTS				0.1	W 175	2.1	W 30	0.2	MATER FIXE VOIES FERREES
79191	RY TRACK FIXTURES ETC					W 100	1.7		0.1	APP DE SIGNALISATION
792	AIRCRAFT ETC			W 3	0.3	W 10	1.6	W 27	3.4	APP NAVIGATION AERIENNE
7929	AIRCRAFT PARTS NES			W 3	0.2	W 8	1.5	W 20	2.4	PIECES DU 792
793	SHIPS AND BOATS ETC			W 3185	46.9	W 921	3.0	W 32	0.4	NAVIRES BATEAUX,ETC
7938	TUGS,SPECIAL VESSELS ETC			W 3152	46.7	W 890	2.9	W 32	0.4	REMORQUEURS,BATEAUX SPEC
79382	SPECL PURPOSE VESSLS ETC			W 2929	45.7			W 2	0.1	BAT–PHARES,–POMPES,DRAGUES
79383	FLOATING STRUCTURES NES			W 223	1.1	W 890	2.9	W 30	0.3	ENGINS FLOTTANTS DIVERS
8	MISC MANUFACTURED GOODS				24.2		36.4		65.2	ART MANUFACTURES DIVERS
812	*PLUMBG,HEATNG,LGHTNG EQ			W 277	0.4	W 307	1.4	W 236	1.5	APPAR SANITAIRES CHAUFFAGE
821	*FURNITURE,PARTS THEREOF			W 287	1.1	W 305	1.4	W 236	3.8	MEUBLES ET PIECES
8219	FURNITURE AND PARTS NES			W 181	0.7	W 208	0.8	W 140	2.8	AUTRES MEUBLES ET PIECES
82199	OTHR FURN,FURN PARTS NES			W 100	0.3	W 50	0.2	W 85	2.4	MEUBLES NDA AUTRES MATIERES
84	CLOTHING AND ACCESSORIES				6.1		2.4		4.5	VETEMENTS
842	MENS OUTERWEAR NOT KNIT			W 5	0.2	W 133	0.8	W 291	2.1	VET DESSUS POUR HOMMES
843	WOMENS OUTERWEAR NONKNIT			W 23	3.4	W 149	0.4	W 79	0.4	VET DESSUS FEMMES MAT TEX
8439	— OTHER OUTER GARMENTS			W 19	3.3	W 128	0.3	W 57	0.2	AUT VET DES FEM MAT TEXT
846	UNDER GARMENTS KNITTED			W 371	1.2	W 220	0.6	W 213	0.8	SOUS VETS DE BONNETERIE
851	*FOOTWEAR			W 558	1.2	W 851	1.6	W 1016	2.1	CHAUSSURES
87	PRECISION INSTRUMNTS NES				8.2		13.3		29.2	INSTRUM,APPAR SCIENT NDA
872	MEDICAL INSTRUMENTS NES			W 6	0.3	W 67	1.1	W 138	2.2	INSTR,APP MEDIC–CHIR NDA
87202	OTH MEDICAL INSTRUMENTS			W 2	0.1	W 63	0.8	W 101	1.9	INSTRUM,APP MEDECINE
874	MEASURNG,CONTROLNG INSTR			W 245	7.6	W 564	11.7	W 1044	26.4	INSTRUMENTS DE MESURE
8741	SURVEYING INSTRUMENTS			W 21	0.8	W 31	1.1	W 69	4.7	INST GEODESIE,TOPO ETC
87412	SURVEY INSTR ETC NONELEC			W 20	0.4	W 27	0.3	W 66	4.1	INSTR GEODESIE,TOPO ETC
8742	MEASUR,DRAW ETC INST,PTS			W 83	1.3	W 71	1.3	W 180	5.5	INST DESSIN,TRACAGE,PCS
87421	MEASURNG,DRAWNG ETC INST			W 83	1.2	W 67	1.2	W 179	5.4	INSTRUM DESSIN,TRACAGE
8743	GAS,LIQUID CONTROL INSTR			W 88	2.9	W 217	3.7	W 269	6.1	APP,INSTR MESURE FLUIDES
8748	ELEC MEAS,CONTRL EQU NES			W 32	1.4	W 196	3.8	W 379	7.4	APP ELEC ELECTRO MESURE
87483	OTH ELCTRNC MEAS ETC EQU			W 3	0.3	W 88	2.1	W 223	4.2	AUT APP ELECTRO DE MESURE
87489	ELEC MEASUR ETC INST NES			W 28	1.1	W 108	1.7	W 155	3.0	AUT INSTRUM ELEC NDA
8749	INSTR PTS NES,ACCESSORYS			W 14	1.2	W 16	1.5	W 82	2.3	PIECES 873,874.3,54,874.8
89	MISC MANUFCTRD GOODS NES				6.4		15.4		23.2	ART MANUFACTURES DIVERS
892	PRINTED MATTER			W 83	1.0	W 229	2.1	W 511	5.2	IMPRIMES
8921	PRINTED BOOKS,GLOBES,ETC			W 8	0.3	W 72	0.7	W 272	2.5	LIVRES,BROCHURES,CARTES
89211	PRINTED BOOKS,PAMPHLETS			W 6	0.2	W 70	0.7	W 271	2.5	LIVRES,BROCHURES
8928	PRINTED MATTER NES			W 75	0.8	W 138	1.3	W 144	1.3	IMPRIMES NDA
893	ARTICLES OF PLASTIC NES				1.6	W 2511	4.5	W 5951	4.8	OUVRAGES EN MAT DIVIS 58
8939	MISC PLASTIC ARTICLES			W 173	0.8	W 1971	3.8	W 5052	3.2	ART DIVERS EN MAT DIV 58
89399	OTHR PLASTC ARTICLES NES			W 130	0.5	W 1946	3.7	W 2395	2.6	AUT OUV MAT DIV 58
894	TOYS,SPORTING GOODS,ETC			W 60	0.3	W 702	2.8	W 1257	5.5	VOITURES ENFANTS,JOUETS
8946	NON–MILITARY ARMS,AMMO			W 3	0.1	W 607	2.4	W 1191	5.1	ARMES NON MILITAIRES
89463	HUNTNG,SPORTNG AMMUNTION			W 3	0.1	W 607	2.4	W 1190	5.1	MUNITIONS
895	OFFICE SUPPLIES NES			W 109	1.2	W 130	1.3	W 232	2.2	ART PAPET NDA
899	OTHER MANUFACTURED GOODS				1.7		4.2		4.5	AUT ART MANUF DIVERS NDA
8997	BASKETWORK,BROOMS ETC			W 186	0.6	W 597	3.1	W 582	3.6	OUVRAGES VANNERIE NDA
89972	BRUSHES,BROOMS,MOPS ETC			W 186	0.6	W 579	3.1	W 581	3.6	BALAIS ET BALAYETTES

5. Special Exports F.O.B. by Commodities according to the S.I.T.C. (Rev. 2) in million U.S. Dollars
Exportations Spéciales F.O.B. par Produits d'après la C.T.C.I. (Rév. 2) en millions de Dollars E.U.

SITC CTCI	COMMODITY	1992		1993		1994		1995		PRODUIT
		QUANTITY QUANTITE	VALUE VALEUR	QUANTITY QUANTITE	VALUE VALEUR	QUANTITY QUANTITE	VALUE VALEUR	QUANTITY QUANTITE	VALUE VALEUR	
	ALL COMMODITIES				965.4		917.9		1089.8	TOUS PRODUITS
0	FOOD AND LIVE ANIMALS				12.1		8.1		10.8	ALIMENTS,ANIMAUX VIVANTS
03	FISH AND PREPARATIONS				3.7		1.3		0.2	POISSONS ET PREPARATIONS
036	SHELL FISH FRESH,FROZEN			W 1062	3.7	W 660	1.2	W 44	0.1	CRUSTACES,MOLLUSQUES
06	SUGAR AND PREPS,HONEY				8.2		6.3		8.4	SUCRES ET PRODUITS
061	SUGAR AND HONEY			W 18210	8.2	W 11000	6.3	W 13715	8.4	SUCRES ET MIEL
0611	RAW BEET AND CANE SUGAR			W 18210	8.2	W 11000	6.3	W 13700	8.4	SUCRES BRUTS
2	CRUDE MATERLS,EXCL FUELS				18.4		124.6		94.2	MAT BRUTES NON COMESTIBLES
24	CORK AND WOOD				17.9		114.6		90.7	LIEGE ET BOIS
247	OTH WOOD ROUGH,SQUARED			W 119351	8.8	W 510522	106.1	W 562409	80.3	BOIS BRUTS EQUARRIS
2472	SAW-,VENEER-LOGS NON-CON			W 119351	8.8	W 509783	105.9	W 562409	80.3	NON CONIFERES SCIAGE,PLAC
24721	— IN THE ROUGH			W 119351	8.8	W 509783	105.9	W 562409	80.3	BRUTS ECORCES DEGROSSIS
248	WOOD SHAPED,SLEEPERS			W 22105	9.1	W 15102	8.6	W 18003	10.4	BOIS SIMPLEMENT TRAVAILLES
2483	LUMBER SHAPED NON-CONIFR			W 22105	9.1	W 15102	8.6	W 18003	10.4	NON CONIFERES SCIES,RABOTES
24831	LUMBER SAWN ETC NON-CON			W 22105	9.1	W 14206	7.6	W 16790	9.1	SCIES LONGITUDINALEMENT
27	CRUDE FERTLZR,MINRLS NES				0.4		9.7		3.2	ENGRAIS MINERAUX BRUTS
277	NATURAL ABRASIVES NES						9.6		3.1	ABRASIFS NATURELS NDA
2771	INDUSTRIAL DIAMONDS						9.6		3.1	DIAMANTS INDUSTRIELS
3	MINERAL FUELS ETC				911.2		765.3		955.2	COMBUSTIBLES MINERAUX LUB
33	PETROLEUM AND PRODUCTS				911.2		765.3		955.2	PETROLE ET DERIVES
333	CRUDE PETROLEUM			MW 9002	890.9	W 8621539	746.8	W 7806172	936.3	HUILES BRUTES DE PETROLE
334	PETROLEUM PRODUCTS,REFIN			W 267623	20.4	W 226859	18.6	W 191163	18.9	PRODUITS RAFFINES
3344	FUEL OILS,NES							W 182997	17.5	FUEL OILS
6	BASIC MANUFACTURES				16.5		11.4		19.4	ART MANUFACTURES
63	WOOD,CORK MANUFACTRS NES				13.7		8.9		17.2	OUVRAGES LIEGE ET BOIS
634	VENEERS,PLYWOOD,ETC			W 13501	13.7	W 8564	8.9	W 13915	17.1	PLACAGES,CONTRE-PLAQUES
6341	VENEER SHEETS ETC			W 13490	13.7	W 8515	8.9	W 13440	16.6	BOIS SIMPLEMENT SCIES
7	MACHINES,TRANSPORT EQUIP				5.4		3.9		4.1	MACHINES MATERIEL TRANSPORT
8	MISC MANUFACTURED GOODS				1.2		3.2		3.2	ART MANUFACTURES DIVERS

1. HISTORICAL SERIES, 1960–1995 GENERAL TRADE, IMPORTS C.I.F., EXPORTS F.O.B.
SERIES HISTORIQUES, 1960–1995 COMMERCE GENERAL, IMPORTATIONS C.A.F., EXPORTATIONS F.O.B

YEAR ANNEE	VALUE IN MILLION N.Z. DOLLARS / VALEUR EN MILLION N.Z. DOLLARS — MERCHANDISE – MARCHANDISE		GOLD – OR		CONVERSION FACTORS U.S. CENTS PER N.Z. DOLLAR / FACTEURS DE CONVERSION CENTS E.U. PAR N.Z. DOLLAR		INDEX NUMBERS – INDICES — QUANTUM		UNIT VALUE – VALEUR UNITAIRE	
	IMPORTS	EXPORTS	IMPORTS	EXPORTS	IMPORTS	EXPORTS	IMPORTS	EXPORTS	IMPORTS	EXPORTS
1960	1.79	0.93			140.0000	140.0000				
1961	2.04	1.20			140.0000	140.0000				
1962	1.88	1.42			139.0000	139.0000				
1963	2.45	1.67			139.0000	139.0000				
1964	3.00	1.87			139.0000	139.0000				
1965	3.07	1.99			139.0000	139.0000				
1966	3.15	1.74			139.0000	139.0000				
1967	2.99	1.78			137.0000	137.0000				
1968	3.38	1.92			112.0000	112.0000				
1969	3.40	2.40			112.0000	112.0000				
1970	5.77	2.69			112.0000	112.0000				
1971	5.79	2.01			113.6080	113.6080				
1972	6.20	1.89			119.5000	119.5000				
1973	4.95	2.51			136.1970	136.3000				
1974	6.22	2.58			140.1000	140.1000				
1975	10.52	2.39			121.4560	121.4560				
1976	13.37	2.20			99.6380	99.4150				
1977	17.50	2.39			97.0830	96.9160				
1978	18.23	2.41			103.7760	104.0350				
1979	22.46	3.78			101.8410	102.0700				
1980	23.61	4.19			97.0800	97.2800				
1981	28.73	5.01			86.9619	86.8414				
1982	26.85	4.98			75.7608	75.5292				
1983	35.09	4.89			66.8717	66.6792				
1984	36.17	6.51			56.9005	57.6534				
1985	47.16	6.07			49.7975	50.8231				
1986	50.31	9.23			52.3131	52.3408				
1987	56.98	12.04			59.3850	58.9991				
1988	64.53	6.63			65.4367	65.9262				
1989	73.08	4.67			59.6126	59.5968				
1990	86.33	8.17			59.5778	59.8340				
1991	94.51	9.43			57.9200	57.9200				
1992	109.16	5.11			53.8119	53.8205				
1993	124.25	7.16			54.1631	53.9514				
1994	135.98	11.57			59.5157	59.3695				
1995	112.39	10.57			65.6409	65.7145				

2. IMPORTS BY BROAD ECONOMIC CATEGORY AND EXPORTS BY INDUSTRIAL ORIGIN. (PERCENTAGE OF TOTAL VALUE)
IMPORTATIONS PAR CATEGORIES ECONOMIQUES ET EXPORTATIONS PAR BRANCHE D'ACTIVITE. (EN POURCENTAGE DE LA VALEUR TOTALE)

IMPORTS – IMPORTATIONS

	1989	1990	1991	1992	1993	1994	1995
TOTAL IMPORTS–IMPORTATIONS TOTALES						100.	100.
1 FOOD BEV–ALIMENTATION BOISSONS						25.7	29.2
11 PRIMARY–PRODUITS DE BASE						6.1	6.3
111 FOR INDUSTRY–POUR L'INDUSTRIE						0.1	0.1
112 FOR HOUSEHOLDS–POUR LES MENAGES						6.0	6.2
12 PROCESSED–PRODUITS ELABORES						19.7	22.8
121 FOR INDUSTRY–POUR L'INDUSTRIE						2.3	2.4
122 FOR HOUSEHOLDS–POUR LES MENAGES						17.4	20.5
2 IND SUPPLIES–APPROV INDUSTRIELS						23.5	22.6
21 PRIMARY–PRODUITS DE BASE						1.1	0.3
22 PROCESSED–PRODUITS ELABORES						22.5	22.3
3 FUELS–COMBUSTIBLES						6.1	12.1
31 PRIMARY–PRODUITS DE BASE						0.5	0.7
32 PROCESSED–PRODUITS ELABORES						5.7	11.4
321 MOTOR SPIRIT–ESSENCE							2.3
322 OTHER–AUTRES						5.7	9.0
4 MACHINERY–EQUIPEMENT						12.0	9.8
41 CAPITAL EQUIPMENT–MACHINES						11.4	9.3
42 PARTS–PIECES ACCESSOIRES						0.5	0.5
5 TRANSPORT–TRANSPORT						12.4	6.5
51 PASSENGER CARS–AUTOMOBILES						1.5	0.7
52 OTHER–AUTRES						6.2	2.6
521 INDUSTRIAL–INDUSTRIELS						5.3	1.8
522 NON INDUSTRIAL–NON INDUSTRIEL						0.9	0.8
53 PARTS–PIECES ACCESSOIRES						4.7	3.2
6 CONSUM GOODS–BIENS CONSOMMATION						19.9	18.1
61 DURABLE–DURABLES						5.0	4.0
62 SEMI DURABLE–SEMI DURABLES						8.9	8.6
63 NON DURABLE–NON DURABLES						6.0	5.4
7 GOODS NES–BIENS NDA						0.3	1.7

EXPORTS – EXPORTATIONS

	1989	1990	1991	1992	1993	1994	1995
TOTAL EXPORTS–EXPORTATIONS TOTALES						100.	100.
1 AGRICULTURE						86.6	87.5
2 MINING QUARRY–INDUS EXTRACTIVES						0.3	1.9
3 MANUFACTURING–IND MANUFACTUR						13.1	10.6
31 FOOD BEV TOBACCO–ALIM BOISS TAB						0.3	0.0
32 TEXTILES–INDUSTRIES TEXTILES						3.5	5.0
33 WOOD & PRODUCTS–BOIS & PRODUITS							0.0
34 PAPER & PRODUCTS–PAPIER & PRODT						0.0	0.0
35 CHEMICALS–INDUSTRIES CHIMIQUES						0.2	0.0
36 NON METAL MIN–MIN NON METAL							
37 BASIC METAL–IND METAL BASE							
38 METAL MANUF–MANUF METAL						2.7	2.1
39 OTH MANUF IND–AUTRES MANUF						6.4	3.4

3. TRADE BY PRINCIPAL COUNTRIES OF ORIGIN AND DESTINATION (VALUE IN MILLION U.S. DOLLARS)
ECHANGES SELON LES PRINCIPAUX PAYS D'ORIGINE ET DE DESTINATION (VALEUR EN MILLIONS DE DOLLARS EU)

COUNTRIES–PAYS	GENERAL IMPORTS C.I.F. IMPORTATIONS GENERALES C.A.F				
	1991	1992	1993	1994	1995
World	54.7				
Africa					
Americas					
– Northern America					
– LAIA					
– CACM					
– Caribbean					
– Rest of America					
Asia excl fmr USSR					
– Middle East					
Asia former USSR					
Europe excl fmr USSR					
– European Union					
– Eastern Europe					
– Rest of Europe					
Europe former USSR					
Oceania					
Other					
New Zealand	23.0				
Australia/Australie	3.0				
USA/Etats–Unis d'Amer	2.9				
Japan/Japon	2.8				
Fiji/Fidji	2.7				
Singapore/Singapour	0.8				
Italy/Italie	0.8				
French Polynesia	0.7				
France, Monaco	0.7				
China, Hong Kong SAR	0.5				
China/Chine	0.5				
Samoa	0.4				
Other Asia n.e.s.	0.3				
United Kingdom	0.2				
Korea, Republic of	0.2				
Thailand/Thaïlande	0.2				
Canada	0.1				

COUNTRIES–PAYS	GENERAL EXPORTS F.O.B. EXPORTATIONS GENERALES F.O.B.				
	1991	1992	1993	1994	1995
Monde	5.5	3.2			
Afrique					
Amériques	0.2	0.2			
– Amérique du Nord	0.2	0.2			
– ALAI					
– MCAC					
– Caraïbes					
– Autre Amérique					
Asie anc. URSS exclus	3.6	1.4			
– Moyen–Orient					
Asie ancienne URSS					
Europe anc. URSS exclus	0.2	0.0			
– Union Européenne	0.0	0.0			
– Europe de l'Est					
– Autre de l'Europe	0.2	0.0			
Europe ancienne URSS					
Océanie	1.5	1.2			
Autre					
Japan/Japon	2.8	0.6			
New Zealand	1.1	1.1			
China, Hong Kong SAR	0.8	0.7			
USA/Etats–Unis d'Amer	0.2	0.2			
Australia/Australie	0.3	0.0			
Other Europe n.e.s.	0.2				
French Polynesia	0.1	0.0			
Fiji/Fidji	0.0	0.0			
Switzerland,Liechtenst.		0.0			
United Kingdom	0.0	0.0			
Samoa		0.0			

(VALUE AS PERCENTAGE OF WORLD TOTAL)(VALEURS EN POURCENTAGE DU TOTAL MONDIAL)

	1986	1987	1988	1989	1990	1991	1992	1993	1994	1995
Africa					0.0					
Americas					7.0					
– Northern America					6.8					
– LAIA					0.1					
– CACM					0.0					
– Caribbean					0.1					
– Rest of America										
Asia excl fmr USSR					8.9					
– Middle East					0.0					
Asia former USSR										
Europe excl fmr USSR					36.2					
– European Union					35.8					
– Eastern Europe					0.0					
– Rest of Europe					0.4					
Europe former USSR										
Oceania					47.8					
Other										
New Zealand					37.7	42.1				
Australia/Australie					5.4	5.4				
USA/Etats–Unis d'Amer					6.4	5.4				
Japan/Japon					3.3	5.1				
Fiji/Fidji					3.8	5.0				
Singapore/Singapour					1.5	1.5				
Italy/Italie					32.5	1.4				
French Polynesia					0.3	1.3				
France, Monaco					1.5	1.2				

	1986	1987	1988	1989	1990	1991	1992	1993	1994	1995
Afrique										
Amériques						3.5	5.8			
– Amérique du Nord						3.5	5.8			
– ALAI										
– MCAC										
– Caraïbes										
– Autre Amérique										
Asie anc. URSS exclus						65.4	41.6			
– Moyen–Orient										
Asie ancienne URSS										
Europe anc. URSS exclus						3.3	1.1			
– Union Européenne						0.0	0.3			
– Europe de l'Est										
– Autre de l'Europe						3.2	0.8			
Europe ancienne URSS										
Océanie						27.8	36.4			
Autre										
Japan/Japon						51.0	18.9			
New Zealand						20.0	33.9			
China, Hong Kong SAR						14.2	21.3			
USA/Etats–Unis d'Amer						3.5	5.8			
Australia/Australie						5.1	1.4			
Other Europe n.e.s.						3.2				
French Polynesia						1.9	0.7			
Fiji/Fidji						0.7	0.1			
Switzerland,Liechtenst.							0.8			

4. General Imports C.I.F. by Commodities according to the S.I.T.C. (Rev. 2) in million U.S. Dollars
Importations Générales C.A.F. par Produits d'après la C.T.C.I. (Rév. 2) en millions de Dollars E.U.

SITC CTCI	COMMODITY	1992 QUANTITY QUANTITE	1992 VALUE VALEUR	1993 QUANTITY QUANTITE	1993 VALUE VALEUR	1994 QUANTITY QUANTITE	1994 VALUE VALEUR	1995 QUANTITY QUANTITE	1995 VALUE VALEUR	PRODUIT
	ALL COMMODITIES		58.8		67.3		81.0		73.8	TOUS PRODUITS
0	FOOD AND LIVE ANIMALS		12.2		14.0		17.9		19.3	ALIMENTS,ANIMAUX VIVANTS
01	MEAT AND PREPARATIONS						5.6		5.8	VIANDES ET PREPARATIONS
011	MEAT FRESH,CHILLD,FROZEN					W 859	3.0	W 1103	2.9	VIANDES FRAICHES,REF,CONGE
0111	BOVINE MEAT FRESH,FROZEN					W 97	0.8	W 111	0.6	VIANDES BOVIN FRAI,REF
01112	BOVINE MEAT BONELESS					W 92	0.7	W 110	0.6	VIANDES BOVIN DESOSSEES
0112	MUTTON ETC FRSH,CHLD,FRN					W 220	0.8	W 299	0.6	VIANDE DE MOUTON
0114	POULTRY FRESH CHLLD,FRZN					W 234	0.6	W 109	0.5	VOLAILLES MORTES
0118	MEAT NES FRESH,CHLD,FRZN					W 305	0.9	W 574	1.2	AUTRES VIANDES,ABATS
01181	POULTRY LIVER FRESH,ETC					W 305	0.9	W 574	1.2	FOIES DE VOLAILLES
014	MEAT PREPD,PRSVD,NES ETC					W 413	2.6	W 1204	2.9	CONSERVES DE VIANDES
0142	SAUSAGES INCLDING TINNED					W 63	0.4	W 67	0.4	SAUCISSES,SAUCISSONS
0149	OTH PREPARD,PRESRVD MEAT					W 350	2.3	W 1137	2.6	AUTRES PREP DE VIANDES
02	DAIRY PRODCTS,BIRDS'EGGS						1.8		1.8	PRODUITS LAITIERS,OEUFS
022	MILK AND CREAM					W 621	1.2	W 1593	1.3	LAIT ET CREME
0223	MILK AND CREAM FRESH					W 153	0.4	W 164	0.4	LAIT,CREME FRAIS
0224	MILK,CREAM PRESERVED ETC					W 469	0.8	W 1429	0.9	LAIT,CREME CONS,CONC
02243	MILK DRY,OVER 1.5% FAT					W 98	0.5	W 316	0.4	LAIT POUDRE SUP 1.5%
02249	MILK(EX DRY) PRSVD,SWEET					W 364	0.3	W 1086	0.4	LAIT CONS,CONC SUCRE
023	BUTTER					W 52	0.3	W 91	0.3	BEURRE
024	CHEESE AND CURD					W 51	0.4	W 403	0.3	FROMAGE ET CAILLEBOTTE
03	FISH AND PREPARATIONS						1.3		1.2	POISSONS ET PREPARATIONS
036	SHELL FISH FRESH,FROZEN					W 48	0.4	W 55	0.3	CRUSTACES,MOLLUSQUES
037	FISH ETC PREPD,PRSVD NES					W 281	0.9	W 315	0.9	POIS,CRUST,MOL PREPARES
0371	FISH PREPARD,PRESRVD NES					W 281	0.9	W 314	0.9	CONSERVES DE POISSONS
04	CEREALS AND PREPARATIONS						2.9		3.2	CEREALES ET PRODUITS
042	RICE					W 396	0.2	W 264	0.3	RIZ
0422	RICE SEMI-MILLED,MILLED					W 395	0.2	W 264	0.3	RIZ POLI,GLACE INCL BRISURES
04221	RICE MILLED UNBROKEN					W 394	0.2	W 263	0.3	RIZ POLI,GLACE EXCL BRISURES
046	WHEAT ETC MEAL OR FLOUR					W 107400	0.8	W 160465	0.9	SEMOULE FARINE,FROMENT
04601	FLOUR OF WHEAT OR MESLIN					W 107400	0.8	W 160465	0.9	FARINE DE FROMENT
048	CEREAL ETC PREPARATIONS						1.9		2.1	PREPTNS A BASE CEREALES
0481	PREPD BREAKFAST FOOD ETC						0.6		0.6	CEREALES TRAVAILLEES
04812	CEREAL ROASTED, PUFFED						0.6		0.6	PRODTS BASE CEREALES
0483	MACARONI,SPAGHETTI ETC					W 276	0.5	W 311	0.5	PATES ALMENTAIRES
0484	BAKERY PRODUCTS						0.6		0.7	PRODUITS DE BOULANGERIE
04841	BREAD,BISCUIT,COM WAFERS						0.4		0.5	PAINS,BISCUITS DE MER
04842	PASTRY, CAKES ETC						0.3		0.3	PATISSERIE ETC.
0488	OTH CEREAL PREPS,MALT EX					W 290	0.4	W 480	0.4	EXTRAITS DE MALT
05	VEGETABLES AND FRUIT						2.2		2.3	LEGUMES ET FRUITS
054	VEG ETC FRSH,SMPLY PRSVD					W 592	1.0	W 1153	1.1	LEGUMES FRAIS,CONG,SECS
0545	OTHER FRESH VEGETABLES					W 236	0.5	W 169	0.5	AUTRES LEGUMES FRAIS,REF
05459	FRESH VEGETABLES NES					W 95	0.4	W 88	0.4	LEGUMES FRAIS,REFRI NDA
0546	VEGETABLES SIMPLY PRESVD					W 180	0.4	W 175	0.4	LEGUMES CONG,CONSER
05461	VEGETABLES FROZEN					W 180	0.4	W 174	0.4	LEGUMES CONGELES
056	VEGTBLES ETC PRSVD,PREPD					W 88	0.3	W 119	0.3	CONSERVES DE LEGUMES
0565	VEGTBLES PRSVD,PREPD NES					W 77	0.3	W 116	0.3	LEGUMES PREPARES CONSERVE
057	FRUIT,NUTS,FRESH,DRIED					W 153	0.3		0.3	FRUITS FRAIS OU SECS
058	FRUIT PRESERVED,PREPARED					W 270	0.7	W 583	0.8	CONSERVES DE FRUITS
0585	FRUIT OR VEGETABLE JUICE					W 163	0.3	W 380	0.5	JUS DE FRUITS
05858	MIXTURES OF DIFF JUICES					W 129	0.3	W 321	0.4	MELANGES JUS FRUITS,LEGUMES
06	SUGAR AND PREPS,HONEY						0.9		0.9	SUCRES ET PRODUITS
061	SUGAR AND HONEY					W 401	0.6	W 673	0.6	SUCRES ET MIEL
0611	RAW BEET AND CANE SUGAR					W 385	0.5	W 535	0.6	SUCRES BRUTS
062	SUGAR CANDY NON-CHOCLATE					W 35	0.4	W 117	0.4	SUCRERIES
07	COFFEE,TEA,COCOA,SPICES						0.7		0.7	CAFE,THE,CACAO,EPICES
071	COFFEE AND SUBSTITUTES						0.3		0.3	CAFE ET SUCCEDANES
0712	COFFEE EXTRACTS,ESSENCES						0.3		0.3	EXTRAITS DE CAFE
073	CHOCOLATE AND PRODUCTS					W 16	0.2	W 80	0.4	CHOCOLAT
081	*FEEDING STUFF FOR ANIML					W 1706	1.1	W 1412	1.5	NOURRITURE POUR ANIMAUX
0819	FOOD WASTE AND FEED NES					W 1706	1.1	W 1412	1.5	DECHETS,ALIMENTS NDA
08199	FODDER NES,INCL SWEETNED					W 1706	1.1	W 1412	1.5	PREPARATIONS FOURRAGERES
09	MISC EDIBLE PRODUCTS						1.8		2.1	PREP ALIMENTAIRES DIVERSES
091	MARGARINE AND SHORTENING					W 106	0.3	W 98	0.3	MARGARINE ET GRAISSES
0914	MARGARINE,EDIBLE FAT NES					W 106	0.3	W 98	0.3	MARGARINES,SIMILI SAINDOUX
09141	MARGARINE					W 84	0.3	W 66	0.3	MARGARINE
098	EDIBLE PRODCTS,PREPS NES						1.6		1.8	PREP ALIMENTAIRES NDA
09804	SAUCES,MIXED SEASONINGS					W 127	0.4	W 1172	0.5	SAUCES,ASSAISONNEMENTS
09809	MISC FOOD PREPRTIONS NES						1.0		1.2	PREP ALIMENTAIRES NDA
1	BEVERAGES AND TOBACCO		3.5		4.0		4.6		4.4	BOISSONS ET TABACS
11	BEVERAGES						3.9		3.6	BOISSONS
111	NON-ALCOHL BEVERAGES NES					W 1357	1.0	W 3916	0.9	BOISSONS NON ALCOOLIQUES
11102	FLAVORED WATERS NON-ALCO					W 1321	0.9	W 3675	0.8	LIMONADES,EAUX GAZEUSES
112	ALCOHOLIC BEVERAGES					W 3043	3.0	W 170	2.7	BOISSONS ALCOOLIQUES
1121	WINE OF FRESH GRAPES ETC					W 52	0.4	W 87	0.4	VINS DE RAISINS FRAIS
11212	WINE OF FRESH GRAPES					W 21	0.2	W 64	0.4	VINS DE MOUTS DE RAISINS
1123	BEER,ALE,STOUT,PORTER					W 2935	1.9	W 54	1.8	BIERES
1124	DISTILLED ALCOHOLIC BEVS					W 57	0.8	W 29	0.6	ALCOOLS,EAUX-DE-VIE
11241	WHISKY					W 20	0.4	W 6	0.2	WHISKY
11249	OTH ALCOHOLC BEVS,CMPNDS					W 33	0.4	W 20	0.4	BOISSONS ALCOOLIQUES NDA
12	TOBACCO AND MANUFACTURES						0.7		0.9	TABACS BRUTS FABRIQUES
122	TOBACCO,MANUFACTURED					W 23	0.7	W 27	0.9	TABACS FABRIQUES
1222	CIGARETTES					W 23	0.7	W 20	0.6	CIGARETTES
2	CRUDE MATERLS,EXCL FUELS		1.3		1.5		3.0		1.9	MAT BRUTES NON COMESTIBLES
23	RUBBER, CRUDE						0.3		0.1	CAOUTCHOUC BRUT
233	RUBBER,SYNTHTIC,RECLAIMD						0.3			LATEX CAOUTCH SYNTH REGEN
2332	RCLMD,SCRAP UNHARDND RUB						0.3			CAOUTCHOUC REGENERE ETC
23322	SCRAP UNHARDENED RUBBER						0.3			DECHETS ET ROGNURES
24	CORK AND WOOD						2.2		1.7	LIEGE ET BOIS
248	WOOD SHAPED,SLEEPERS						2.1		1.7	BOIS SIMPLEMENT TRAVAILLES
2482	LUMBER SHAPED CONIFER						2.0		1.6	CONIFERES SCIES,RABOTES
24821	LUMBER SAWN ETC CONIFER					W 760889	1.9	W 499690	1.5	CONIFERES SCIES LONGITUD
27	CRUDE FERTLZR,MINRLS NES						0.4		0.1	ENGRAIS MINERAUX BRUTS
278	OTHER CRUDE MINERALS					W 293	0.3	W 458	0.1	AUTRES MINERAUX BRUTS
2789	MINERALS CRUDE NES					W 261	0.3			MINERAUX BRUTS NDA
27896	NATURAL ASPHALT,BITUMEN					W 260	0.3			BITUMES,ASPHALTES NATURELS
3	MINERAL FUELS ETC		7.0		8.0		5.1		9.0	COMBUSTIBLES MINERAUX LUB
33	PETROLEUM AND PRODUCTS						4.7		8.4	PETROLE ET DERIVES
334	PETROLEUM PRODUCTS,REFIN						4.6	W 17902	8.4	PRODUITS RAFFINES
3341	GASOLINE,OTH LIGHT OILS					W 10611	4.3	W 9667	4.6	ESSENCES POUR MOTEURS
33411	MOTOR,AVIATION SPIRIT							W 3301	1.8	ESSENCES MOTEURS D'AVIONS

4. General Imports C.I.F. by Commodities according to the S.I.T.C. (Rev. 2) in million U.S. Dollars
Importations Générales C.A.F. par Produits d'après la C.T.C.I. (Rév. 2) en millions de Dollars E.U.

SITC CTCI	COMMODITY	1992 QUANTITY QUANTITE	1992 VALUE VALEUR	1993 QUANTITY QUANTITE	1993 VALUE VALEUR	1994 QUANTITY QUANTITE	1994 VALUE VALEUR	1995 QUANTITY QUANTITE	1995 VALUE VALEUR	PRODUIT
33412	SPIRIT TYPE JET FUEL					W 10611	4.3	W 6366	2.9	CARBUREACTEURS
3344	FUEL OILS,NES						0.1	W 7910	3.3	FUEL OILS
3345	LUBS,PETROLEUM OILS NES					W 134	0.4	W 231	0.5	HUILES LUBRIFIANTES
33451	LUBS(HIGH PETR CONT) ETC					W 134	0.4	W 228	0.5	HUILES LUBRIF,H LOURDES
341	*GAS,NATURAL AND MANUFCT						0.4		0.6	GAZ NATUREL,GAZ MANUFACT
3413	PETROLM GASES,LIQUEFIED					W 160	0.4	W 124	0.6	GAZ DE PETROLE LIQUEFIE
34131	LIQUEFIED PROPANE,BUTANE					W 160	0.4	W 124	0.6	PROPANE,BUTANE LIQUEFIES
4	ANIMAL,VEGETABLE OIL,FAT		0.4		0.4		0.3		0.3	HUILES,GRAISSES ANIM,VEG
42	FIXED VEGETABLE OIL,FAT						0.2		0.3	HUILES VEGETALES FIXES
5	CHEMCLS,RELATED PROD NES		4.2		4.8		6.1		4.5	PRODUITS CHIMIQUES
53	DYES,TANNING,COLOUR PROD						0.9		0.9	PROD TEINTURE,COLORANTS
533	PIGMENTS,PAINTS,ETC						0.9		0.8	PIGMENTS,PEINTURES,VERNIS
5334	VARNISHES,DISTEMPERS ETC						0.8		0.7	PEINTURES A L'EAU
53341	WATER–THINNED PAINTS						0.3		0.3	PEINTURES DILUEES
53342	OTH PAINTS,VARNISHES ETC						0.5		0.4	AUTRES PEINTURES,VERNIS
541	*MEDICINAL,PHARM PRODUCT						1.1		1.1	PROD MEDICINAUX PHARMACEUT
5417	MEDICAMENTS						0.9		0.9	MEDICAMENTS
54173	— CONTAINING ALKALOIDS						0.9		0.9	MED CONTEN ALCALOIDES
55	PERFUME,CLEANING ETC PRD						2.1		1.4	PROD POUR PARFUM,TOILETTE
553	PERFUMERY,COSMETICS,ETC						1.4		0.7	PRODUITS DE PARFUMERIE
554	SOAP,CLEANSING ETC PREPS						0.8		0.7	SAVONS,PRODUITS DETERSIFS
5542	WASHING PREPARATIONS ETC					W 125	0.5	W 124	0.5	PROD ORG TENSIO–ACT NDA
58	PLASTIC MATERIALS ETC						1.1		0.3	MAT PLAST ARTIFICIELLES
583	POLYMERIZATION ETC PRODS					W 25	1.1		0.2	PROD POLYMERISATION
5832	POLYPROPYLENE						1.0			POLYPROPYLENE
58321	— IN PRIMARY FORMS						1.0			POLYPROPYLENE PRIMAIRES
59	CHEMICAL MATERIALS NES						0.7		0.7	MAT PROD CHIMIQUES NDA
591	PESTICIDES,DISINFECTANTS						0.5		0.5	DESINF,INSECT,FONG,HERB
5911	INSECTICIDES,FOR RETAIL						0.3		0.3	INSECTICIDES VENTE DET
6	BASIC MANUFACTURES		11.7		13.4		13.2		11.9	ART MANUFACTURES
62	RUBBER MANUFACTURES NES						0.5		0.4	CAOUTCHOUC MANUFACTURE
625	RUBBER TYRES, TUBES ETC					W 29	0.4	W 34	0.3	PNEUS CAOUTCHOUC VULCANISE
63	WOOD,CORK MANUFACTRS NES						1.8		1.8	OUVRAGES LIEGE ET BOIS
634	VENEERS,PLYWOOD,ETC						0.9		0.5	PLACAGES,CONTRE–PLAQUES
6342	PLYWOOD OF WOOD SHEETS					A 471	0.7	A 89	0.4	BOIS CONTRE–PLAQUES
635	WOOD MANUFACTURES NES						0.9		1.4	ART MANUF EN BOIS NDA
6353	BUILDERS WOODWRK,PREFABS						0.7	N 801	1.2	OUVRAGES DE MENUISERIE
64	PAPER,PAPERBOARD AND MFR						2.5		2.3	PAPIERS,CARTONS & OUVRAGES
641	PAPER AND PAPERBOARD						0.5		0.5	PAPIERS ET CARTONS
642	PAPER,ETC,PRECUT,ARTS OF						2.0		1.8	PAP,CARTONS DECOUPES
6421	PAPER ETC CONTAINERS						0.7		0.6	BOITES,SACS EMBALLAGES
6423	EXERCISE BOOKS ETC						0.4		0.3	REGISTRES,CAHIERS,CARNETS
6424	PAPER ETC CT TO SIZE NES						0.4		0.4	PAP,CARTONS DECOUPES
64243	TOILET PAPER CUT TO SIZE						0.3		0.3	PAPIER HYGIENIQUE
6428	PAPER ETC ARTICLES NES						0.7		0.6	OUVRAGES EN PATE A PAPIER
64285	PAPER ETC DIAPERS ETC						0.5		0.4	SERVIETTES HYGIENIQUES
65	TEXTILE YARN,FABRICS,ETC						1.6		1.7	FILS,TISSUS,ARTICLES TEXTILE
652	COTTON FABRICS,WOVEN						0.8		0.8	TISSUS DE COTON
6521	GREY WOVEN COTTON FABRIC					A 593	0.8	A 418	0.8	TISSUS COT ECRUS NON MERCER
65214	GREY WOVEN COTTON NES					A 466	0.5	A 334	0.6	AUT TISSUS 85% COTON ECRUS
657	SPECIAL TXTL FABRC,PRODS						0.2		0.3	TISSUS SPECIAUX
658	TEXTILE ARTICLES NES						0.5		0.4	ART FACONNES MAT TEXTILES
6584	LINENS ETC						0.3		0.3	LINGE DE MAISON
66	NONMETAL MINERAL MFS NES						2.6		2.5	ART MIN NON METALLIQUES
661	LIME,CEMENT,BLDG PRODS						1.3		1.1	CHAUX,CIMENTS MAT CONSTR
6612	CEMENT					W 1865	0.9	W 1678	0.8	CIMENTS HYDRAULIQUES
6618	MNRL BLDG PRD UNFIRD NES						0.3		0.2	MAT CONST AMIANTE–CIMENT
662	CLAY,REFRACTORY BLDG PRD						0.4		0.4	MAT CONST REFRACTAIRES
664	GLASS						0.7		0.8	VERRE
6642	OPTICAL GLASS UNWRKD ETC					A 157	0.4	L 335	0.6	VERRE OPTIQUE,LUNETTERIE
67	IRON AND STEEL						1.1		0.9	FER ET ACIER
673	IRON,STEEL SHAPES ETC					W 166	0.4	W 146	0.3	BARRES,PROFIL FER,ACIER
674	IRN,STL UNIV,PLATE,SHEET					W 194	0.5	W 110	0.6	LARGES PLATS,TOLES
6749	OTH IRN,STL PLATES,SHEET					W 169	0.4	W 98	0.5	AUTRES TOLES FER,ACIER
67491	— OF IRON OR SIMPLE STL					W 155	0.4	W 96	0.5	AUT TOLES AUTRES ACIER FIN
69	METAL MANUFACTURES NES						3.1		2.4	ART MANUFACT EN METAL NDA
691	STRUCTURES AND PARTS NES						0.8		0.5	CONSTRUCT FER,ACIER,ALU
6912	STRUCTURES,PARTS ALUMNM						0.6		0.5	CONSTRUCT ALUMINIUM
693	WIRE PRODUCTS NON ELECTR						0.2		0.6	OUVRAGES FILS METALLIQUES
6935	METAL FENCING,GAUZE,ETC					W 57	0.2	W 51	0.5	TOILES EN FER,ACIER,CUIVRE
69351	IRN,STL FENCNG,GAUZE ETC					W 57	0.2	W 51	0.5	TOILES EN FER,ACIER
694	STL,COPPR NAILS,NUTS,ETC						0.4		0.2	CLOUS,VIS,ECROUS
695	TOOLS						0.3		0.3	OUTILS A MAIN
697	BASE MTL HOUSEHOLD EQUIP						0.8		0.5	ART MENAGE MET COMMUNS
6973	DMSTC HEATG,COOKG APPARA						0.4		0.3	APPS CHAUF NON ELECTRIQ
69731	IRN,STL DOM COOKG APPARA					N 830	0.4	N 626	0.3	APPS CUISSON FER,ACIER
699	BASE METAL MFRS NES						0.5		0.4	ART MANUFACTURES MET NDA
7	MACHINES,TRANSPORT EQUIP		10.6		12.2		20.5		13.0	MACHINES MATERIEL TRANSPORT
71	POWER GENERATING EQUIPMT						3.6		1.7	MACHINES GENERATRICES
713	INTRNL COMBUS PSTN ENGIN						2.4		1.3	MOTEURS EXPL COMB INT, PIECE
7131	AIRCRAFT PSTN ENGINS,PTS						1.5		1.0	MOTEURS EXPL P.AVIATION, PIE
71311	AIRCRAFT PISTON ENGINES					N 173	1.5	N 8	1.0	MOTEURS EXPL P.AVIATION
7133	MARINE PISTON ENGINES					N 109	0.4	N 73	0.2	MOTEURS EXPL POUR BATEAUX
71331	—— OUTBOARD					N 105	0.3	N 70	0.2	MOTEURS BATEAUX HORSBORD
7139	PISTON ENGINE PARTS NES						0.6		0.1	PIECES POUR 713.2,3,8
716	ROTATING ELECTRIC PLANT						1.2		0.4	APP ELECTR ROTATIFS,PIECES
7162	AC MTRS,GENRTRS,GEN SETS					N 122	0.6	N 77	0.2	MOTEURS ELECTRIQUES
71621	AC MTRS,INC UNIVRSL MTRS					N 122	0.6	N 77	0.2	MOT ELEC NON COUR CONTINU
7169	PTS NES OF ROT ELEC PLNT						0.6		0.2	PIECES MAC APP ROTATIFS
72	MACHS FOR SPCL INDUSTRYS						1.0		0.7	MAC SPECIALES POUR INDUST
728	OTH MACHY FOR SPCL INDUS						0.1		0.4	AUT MACH IND PARTICULIERES
7284	MACHY FOR SPCL INDUS NES						0.1		0.4	MACH SPEC IND PARTICUL.
74	GENRL INDUSTRL MACHY NES						2.0		1.5	MACH APP INDUSTRIE
741	HEATING,COOLING EQUIPMNT						0.6		0.6	MACH CHAUFFAGE,PIECES
744	MECHANICAL HANDLING EQU						0.6		0.2	EQUIP MANUTENTION PIECES
7441	FORK LIFT TRCKS,ETC,PTS						0.5		0.1	CHARIOTS POUR USINES ETC
74411	FORK LIFT TRUCKS ETC					N 2009	0.4	N 908	0.1	CHARIOTS POUR LES GARES
745	NONELEC MACHY,TOOLS NES						0.4		0.3	AUT MACH NON ELEC,PIECES
75	OFFICE MACHNES,ADP EQUIP						1.5		1.3	MACH BUREAU TRAIT AUTOM
751	OFFICE MACHINES						0.3		0.2	MACH,APPAREILS DE BUREAU
752	AUTOMTIC DATA PROC EQUIP						1.0		1.0	MACH TRAIT INFORMATION

4. General Imports C.I.F. by Commodities according to the S.I.T.C. (Rev. 2) in million U.S. Dollars
Importations Générales C.A.F. par Produits d'après la C.T.C.I. (Rév. 2) en millions de Dollars E.U.

SITC CTCI	COMMODITY	1992 QUANTITY QUANTITE	1992 VALUE VALEUR	1993 QUANTITY QUANTITE	1993 VALUE VALEUR	1994 QUANTITY QUANTITE	1994 VALUE VALEUR	1995 QUANTITY QUANTITE	1995 VALUE VALEUR	PRODUIT
7521	ANALOG,HYBRID COMPUTERS						1.0		1.0	MACH POUR TRAIT INFORMAT
76	TELECOMM,SOUND EQUIPMENT						2.3		2.9	EQUIPMENT DE TELECOM
761	TELEVISION RECEIVERS					N 375	0.3	N 624	0.4	RECEPTEURS DE TELEVISION
7611	COLOUR TV RECEIVERS					N 369	0.3	N 615	0.4	RECEPTEURS COULEUR
763	SOUND RECORDRS,PHONOGRPH					N 1868	0.5	N 943	0.5	PHONO,APP ENREGISTREMENT
7638	OTHR SOUND APPARATUS ETC					N 1867	0.5	N 940	0.5	AUT APP D'ENREGIS,REPROD
76388	DICTATING MACHINES ETC					N 943	0.2	N 727	0.3	MACHINES A DICTER
764	TELECOM EQPT,PTS,ACC NES						1.6		2.1	EQUIP TELECOM,PIECES
7642	MICROPH,LOUDSPKR,AMPLIFR					N 291	0.1		0.4	MICRO,HAUT–PARLEUR,AMPLI
7643	TV,RADIO TRANSMITTRS ETC						1.3		1.4	APP EMET TELE RADIO
77	ELECTRIC MACHNRY NES ETC						3.2		2.0	MACH APP ELECT NDA
772	SWITCHGEAR ETC,PARTS NES						1.6		0.6	APP COUPURE,SECT ETC
7721	SWITCHGEAR ETC						1.6		0.6	APP COUPURE,SECTIONMNT
775	HOUSEHOLD TYPE EQUIP NES						1.0		0.9	MACH,APP USAGE DOMESTQUE
7752	DOM REFRIGERATRS,FREEZRS					N 653	0.5	N 631	0.4	REFRIG,CONGEL MENAGER
77521	DOMESTIC REFRIGERATORS					N 405	0.3	N 272	0.3	REFRIGERATEURS
778	ELECTRICAL MACHINERY NES						0.6		0.5	AUTRES MACH ELECT NDA
7781	BATTERIES,ACCUMULATORS					N 69645	0.2	N 125357	0.3	PILES ET ACCUMULATEURS
78	ROAD VEHICLES						5.9		2.7	VEHICULES ROUTIERS
781	PASS MOTOR VEH EXC BUSES					N 104	1.2	N 46	0.6	AUTO TRANSPORT PERSONNES
782	LORRIES,SPCL MTR VEH NES					N 1607	3.3	N 57	1.1	VEHICULES SPECIAUX,MARCH
7821	LORRIES,TRUCKS					N 1603	2.0	N 57	1.1	VEHICULES TRANSP MARCHAND
7822	SPECIAL MOTOR VEHCLS NES					N 4	1.3			VEHICULES USAGES SPECIAUX
784	MOTOR VEH PRTS,ACCES NES					N 8179	0.4	N 2933	0.3	PIECES 722,781,782,783
7849	OTHER MOTOR VEHCL PARTS					N 8144	0.4	N 2802	0.3	PIECES 722,781,782,783
785	CYCLES,ETC MOTRZD OR NOT						0.9		0.7	MOTOCYCLES SCOOTERS
7851	MOTORCYCLES ETC					N 373	0.7	N 289	0.5	MOTO VELO MOTEUR AUXIL
79	OTHR TRANSPORT EQUIPMENT						1.2		0.5	AUTRE MATERIEL TRANSPORT
792	AIRCRAFT ETC						0.4		0.3	APP NAVIGATION AERIENNE
7929	AIRCRAFT PARTS NES						0.3		0.3	PIECES DU 792
793	SHIPS AND BOATS ETC						0.9	N 19002	0.3	NAVIRES BATEAUX,ETC
7932	SHIPS AND BOATS NES					N 295	0.8	N 1289	0.2	NAVIRES ET BATEAUX
79321	YACHTS,SPORTS VESSLS ETC					N 95	0.8	N 89	0.2	BATEAUX DE PLAISANCE
8	MISC MANUFACTURED GOODS		8.1		9.3		10.7		9.9	ART MANUFACTURES DIVERS
812	*PLUMBG,HEATNG,LGHTNG EQ						0.4		0.3	APPAR SANITAIRES CHAUFFAGE
8124	LIGHTING EQUIPMENT NES						0.3		0.3	APPAREILS ECLAIRAGE ETC
821	*FURNITURE,PARTS THEREOF						1.2		0.7	MEUBLES ET PIECES
8211	CHAIRS,SEATS AND PARTS						0.3		0.2	SIEGES ET PIECES
82111	CHAIRS AND OTHER SEATS					N 2578	0.3	N 2247	0.2	SIEGES
8212	MED FURN,STUFFD FURNSHGS						0.3		0.3	MOB MEDICO–CHIRUR,PIECES
8219	FURNITURE AND PARTS NES						0.7		0.3	AUTRES MEUBLES ET PIECES
82192	WOOD FURNITURE NES						0.5		0.2	MEUBLES NDA EN BOIS
84	CLOTHING AND ACCESSORIES						2.1		2.0	VETEMENTS
842	MENS OUTERWEAR NOT KNIT						0.3		0.3	VET DESSUS POUR HOMMES
8422	— SUITS							N 25563	0.3	COMPLETS HOMMES MAT TEXT
84223	—— OF MAN–MADE FIBRES							N 25563	0.3	COMPLETS HOMMES FIB SYNT
843	WOMENS OUTERWEAR NONKNIT						0.4		0.4	VET DESSUS FEMMES MAT TEX
845	OUTERWEAR KNIT NONELASTC					N 36608	0.4	N 30920	0.3	VET DESSOUS,ACCES BONNET
846	UNDER GARMENTS KNITTED						0.8		0.7	SOUS VETS DE BONNETERIE
8462	— OF COTTON NON ELASTIC					N 168415	0.6	N 132423	0.5	SOUS–VET BONNET COTON
84629	—— OTHER					N 168415	0.6	N 132423	0.5	AUT SOUS–VET BONNET COTON
851	*FOOTWEAR						0.8	P 54980	0.6	CHAUSSURES
85101	FOOTWEAR RUBBER,PLASTIC						0.4	P 35622	0.3	CHAUS SEMELLES CAOUTCH
85102	FOOTWEAR LEATHER						0.3	P 13133	0.3	CHAUS SEMELLES EN CUIR
87	PRECISION INSTRUMNTS NES						0.4		0.5	INSTRUM,APPAR SCIENT NDA
88	PHOTO EQU,OPTICL GDS ETC						0.6		0.5	APP,FOURN PHOTO,OP,MONTR
89	MISC MANUFCTRD GOODS NES						5.4		5.5	ART MANUFACTURES DIVERS
892	PRINTED MATTER						1.3		2.1	IMPRIMES
8921	PRINTED BOOKS,GLOBES,ETC						0.6		0.4	LIVRES,BROCHURES,CARTES
89211	PRINTED BOOKS,PAMPHLETS						0.6		0.4	LIVRES,BROCHURES
8928	PRINTED MATTER NES						0.4		1.5	IMPRIMES NDA
89283	UNISSUED BANKNOTES ETC						0.2		1.3	TIMBRES–POSTE FISCAUX
893	ARTICLES OF PLASTIC NES						1.8		1.5	OUVRAGES EN MAT DIVIS 58
8931	PLSTC PACKG CONTNRS,LIDS						0.3		0.4	ART TRANSP EMBALLAGE ETC
8939	MISC PLASTIC ARTICLES						1.3		1.0	ART DIVERS EN MAT DIV 58
89399	OTHR PLASTC ARTICLES NES						1.1		0.9	AUT OUV MAT DIV 58
894	TOYS,SPORTING GOODS,ETC						0.4		0.6	VOITURES ENFANTS,JOUETS
8942	TOYS,INDOOR GAMES ETC						0.2		0.3	JOUETS,JEUX ETC
8947	OTH SPORT GDS,FAIR AMUSM						0.3		0.3	AUT ART DE SPORT
897	GOLD,SILVER WARE,JEWELRY						0.7		0.5	BIJOUTERIE,ORFEVRERIE
8973	PREC JEWLRY,GLD–SILVWARE						0.6		0.4	BIJOUX OR,ARGENT ORFEVRE
89731	PRECIOUS METAL JEWELLERY						0.4		0.3	ART BIJOUTERIE,JOAILLER
898	MUSICAL INSTRUMENTS,PTS						0.7		0.5	INSTRUMENTS DE MUSIQUE
8983	SOUND RECRDNG TAPE,DISCS						0.5		0.5	SUPPORTS SON POUR 763
89832	RECORDED DISCS,TAPES ETC						0.5		0.5	DISQUES,PHONO,BANDES
899	OTHER MANUFACTURED GOODS						0.5		0.4	AUT ART MANUF DIVERS NDA

5. General Exports F.O.B. by Commodities according to the S.I.T.C. (Rev. 2) in million U.S. Dollars
Exportations Générales F.O.B. par Produits d'après la C.T.C.I. (Rév. 2) en millions de Dollars E.U.

SITC CTCI	COMMODITY	1992		1993		1994		1995		PRODUIT
		QUANTITY QUANTITE	VALUE VALEUR	QUANTITY QUANTITE	VALUE VALEUR	QUANTITY QUANTITE	VALUE VALEUR	QUANTITY QUANTITE	VALUE VALEUR	
	ALL COMMODITIES		3.3		3.9		6.9		7.0	TOUS PRODUITS
0	FOOD AND LIVE ANIMALS		1.0		1.1		1.6		2.3	ALIMENTS,ANIMAUX VIVANTS
03	FISH AND PREPARATIONS						0.7		1.3	POISSONS ET PREPARATIONS
034	FISH,FRESH,CHILLED,FROZN					W 103	0.7	W 171	1.3	POISSON FRAIS, REFRIG,CONG
0341	FISH FRSH,CHLLD,EX FILLT					W 103	0.7	W 171	1.3	POISSON FRAIS,REFRIGERE
05	VEGETABLES AND FRUIT		0.9		1.0		1.0		1.0	LEGUMES ET FRUITS
054	VEG ETC FRSH,SMPLY PRSVD					W 41	0.1	W 79	0.1	LEGUMES FRAIS,CONG,SECS
0542	LEGUMINOUS VEGETBLES DRY		0.1		0.1					LEGUMES A COSSE SECS
05459	FRESH VEGETABLES NES		0.1		0.1	W 2	0.1			LEGUMES FRAIS,REFRI NDA
0548	EDIBLE VEG NES FRESH,DRY					W 39	0.1	W 79	0.1	RACINES,TUBERCULES
05481	ROOTS,TUBERS FRESH,DRY		0.1			W 39	0.1	W 79	0.1	RACINES DE MANIOC ETC
057	FRUIT,NUTS,FRESH,DRIED					W 517	0.9	W 417	0.9	FRUITS FRAIS OU SECS
0579	FRUIT FRESH OR DRIED NES					W 493	0.9	W 417	0.9	FRUITS FRAIS,SECS NDA
05797	OTH TROP FRUIT,FRESH,DRY		0.1		0.1					AVOCATS,MANGUES,GOYAVES
05798	OTHER FRESH FRUIT		0.8		0.9	W 493	0.9	W 417	0.9	AUTRES FRUITS FRAIS
0751	PEPPER AND PIMENTO		0.1		0.1					POIVRE,PIMENTS
2	CRUDE MATERLS,EXCL FUELS		0.2		0.2		0.3		0.1	MAT BRUTES NON COMESTIBLES
29	CRUDE ANIMAL,VEG MAT NES						0.3		0.1	MATIERES BRUTES ANIM,VEGET
29199	ANIMAL PRODUCTS,NES		0.1		0.2					PROD ORIGINE ANIMALE NDA
292	CRUDE VEG MATERIALS NES					W 13	0.3	W 35	0.1	MAT BRUTES VEGETALES NDA
2927	CUT FLOWERS AND FOLIAGE					W 13	0.3	W 35	0.1	FLEURS,FEUILLAGES COUPES
29272	CUT FOLIAGE					W 13	0.3	W 35	0.1	FEUILLAGES,RAMEAUX ETC
5	CHEMCLS,RELATED PROD NES		0.1		0.1		0.1		0.1	PRODUITS CHIMIQUES
6	BASIC MANUFACTURES		1.8		2.1		4.2		4.0	ART MANUFACTURES
65	TEXTILE YARN,FABRICS,ETC						0.1		0.1	FILS,TISSUS,ARTICLES TEXTILE
658	TEXTILE ARTICLES NES								0.1	ART FACONNES MAT TEXTILES
6584	LINENS ETC								0.1	LINGE DE MAISON
65842	BED LINEN OF OTHR FIBRES								0.1	LINGE DE LIT AUT FIBRES
66	NONMETAL MINERAL MFS NES						4.2		3.9	ART MIN NON METALLIQUES
667	PEARL,PREC–,SEMI–P STONE						4.2		3.9	PERLES, PIERRES GEMMES
6671	PEARLS UNSET,UNSTRUNG						4.2		3.8	PERLES FINES NON SERTIES
6673	PREC–,SEMI–PR STONES NES								0.2	AUTRES PIERRES NON SERTIES
7	MACHINES,TRANSPORT EQUIP		0.1		0.1		0.2		0.1	MACHINES MATERIEL TRANSPORT
72	MACHS FOR SPCL INDUSTRYS						0.1		0.1	MAC SPECIALES POUR INDUST
721	AGRIC MACHY,EXC TRACTORS					W 20	0.1			MACHINES AGRICOLES
7219	AGRICULTURE MACHINES NES					W 20	0.1			ENGINS AGRICOLES NDA
72191	WINE–MAKING ETC MACHNERY					W 20	0.1			APPAREILS DE VINIFICATION
76	TELECOMM,SOUND EQUIPMENT						0.1		0.1	EQUIPMENT DE TELECOM
764	TELECOM EQPT,PTS,ACC NES						0.1		0.1	EQUIP TELECOM,PIECES
7643	TV,RADIO TRANSMITTRS ETC						0.1		0.1	APP EMET TELE RADIO
8	MISC MANUFACTURED GOODS		0.4		0.5		0.8		0.7	ART MANUFACTURES DIVERS
84	CLOTHING AND ACCESSORIES						0.3		0.4	VETEMENTS
842	MENS OUTERWEAR NOT KNIT					W 6	0.2	W 7	0.2	VET DESSUS POUR HOMMES
8422	— SUITS					W 6	0.2	W 7	0.2	COMPLETS HOMMES MAT TEXT
84223	—— OF MAN–MADE FIBRES					W 6	0.2	W 7	0.2	COMPLETS HOMMES FIB SYNT
843	WOMENS OUTERWEAR NONKNIT						0.1	W 1	0.2	VET DESSUS FEMMES MAT TEX
8432	— SUITS AND COSTUMES						0.1		0.1	COSTUMES–TAIL MAT TEXIL
8439	— OTHER OUTER GARMENTS						0.1		0.1	AUT VET DES FEM MAT TEXT
844	UNDER GARMENTS NOT KNIT					W 1	0.1	W 2	0.1	VETEMENT DESSOUS MAT TEX
8441	— MENS SHIRTS					W 1	0.1	W 2	0.1	CHEMISES HOMMES MAT TEXT
84412	—— OF SYNTHETIC FIBRES					W 1	0.1	W 2	0.1	CHEMISES HOMMES FIB SYNT
845	OUTERWEAR KNIT NONELASTC					W 1	0.1		0.1	VET DESSOUS,ACCES BONNET
8459	— OTHER,CLTHG ACCESRYS					W 1	0.1		0.1	AUT VET DESSUS DE BONNE
87	PRECISION INSTRUMNTS NES						0.1		0.1	INSTRUM,APPAR SCIENT NDA
874	MEASURNG,CONTROLNG INSTR					W 1	0.1		0.1	INSTRUMENTS DE MESURE
8741	SURVEYING INSTRUMENTS					W 1	0.1		0.1	INST GEODESIE,TOPO ETC
87412	SURVEY INSTR ETC NONELEC					W 1	0.1		0.1	INSTR GEODESIE,TOPO ETC
89	MISC MANUFCTRD GOODS NES						0.5		0.4	ART MANUFACTURES DIVERS
897	GOLD,SILVER WARE,JEWELRY						0.1		0.2	BIJOUTERIE,ORFEVRERIE
8973	PREC JEWLRY,GLD–SILVWARE						0.1		0.2	BIJOUX OR,ARGENT ORFEVRE
89731	PRECIOUS METAL JEWELLERY						0.1		0.1	ART BIJOUTERIE,JOAILLER
89733	JEWELLERY NES								0.2	OUV PERLES,PIERRES
898	MUSICAL INSTRUMENTS,PTS						0.1		0.1	INSTRUMENTS DE MUSIQUE
8983	SOUND RECRDNG TAPE,DISCS						0.1		0.1	SUPPORTS SON POUR 763
89832	RECORDED DISCS,TAPES ETC						0.1		0.1	DISQUES,PHONO,BANDES
899	OTHER MANUFACTURED GOODS					W 43	0.5	W 11	0.1	AUT ART MANUF DIVERS NDA
8991	CARVED,MOULDED GOODS					W 43	0.5	W 9	0.1	MAT A TAILLER,A MOULER
89911	GOODS OF ANML CARVNG MTL					W 43	0.5		0.1	ECAILLE,NACRE,IVOIRE ETC
89919	MOULDED,CARVED GOODS NES						0.1	W 9	0.1	MAT VEGET,MINE A TAILLER

1. HISTORICAL SERIES, 1962–1997 SPECIAL TRADE, IMPORTS C.I.F., EXPORTS F.O.B.
SERIES HISTORIQUES, 1962–1997 COMMERCE SPECIAL, IMPORTATIONS C.A.F., EXPORTATIONS F.O.B

YEAR ANNEE	VALUE IN MILLION U.S. DOLLARS / VALEUR EN MILLION U.S. DOLLARS — MERCHANDISE – MARCHANDISE: IMPORTS	MERCHANDISE – MARCHANDISE: EXPORTS	GOLD – OR: IMPORTS	GOLD – OR: EXPORTS	CONVERSION FACTORS FACTEURS DE CONVERSION CENTS E.U. PAR: IMPORTS	CONVERSION FACTORS: EXPORTS	INDEX NUMBERS – INDICES — QUANTUM: IMPORTS	QUANTUM: EXPORTS	UNIT VALUE / VALEUR UNITAIRE: IMPORTS	UNIT VALUE / VALEUR UNITAIRE: EXPORTS
1962	113.40	93.00								
1963	123.90	95.00								
1964	138.60	113.90								
1965	178.20	111.80								
1966	178.50	135.50								
1967	190.70	143.80								
1968	213.90	170.80								
1969	245.10	189.70								
1970	316.70	231.20								
1971	349.70	225.40								
1972	342.80	278.50								
1973	455.30	344.50								
1974	719.70	440.30								
1975	694.00	493.30								
1976	770.40	592.90								
1977	1026.20	828.20								
1978	1165.70	864.90								
1979	1396.80	934.30								
1980	1523.80	1001.70								
1981	1208.50	1008.10								
1982	893.10	871.00								
1983	987.80	866.10								
1984	1084.50	978.50								
1985	1098.20	988.90								
1986	1147.50	1120.50								
1987	1382.50	1158.30								
1988	1409.80	1245.70								
1989	1717.40	1414.60								
1990	1989.70	1448.20								
1991	1876.60	1597.70								
1992	2440.70	1840.80								
1993	2885.80	1995.30								
1994	3025.10	2242.50								
1995	3252.80	2701.60								
1996	3479.40	3013.80								
1997	4088.20	3280.50								

2. IMPORTS BY BROAD ECONOMIC CATEGORY AND EXPORTS BY INDUSTRIAL ORIGIN. (PERCENTAGE OF TOTAL VALUE)
IMPORTATIONS PAR CATEGORIES ECONOMIQUES ET EXPORTATIONS PAR BRANCHE D'ACTIVITE.(EN POURCENTAGE DE LA VALEUR TOTALE)

IMPORTS – IMPORTATIONS

	1990	1991	1992	1993	1994	1995	1996
TOTAL IMPORTS–IMPORTATIONS TOTALES	100.	100.	100.	100.	100.	100.	100.
1 FOOD BEV–ALIMENTATION BOISSONS	6.0	5.9	6.2	7.8	8.5	8.3	10.0
11 PRIMARY–PRODUITS DE BASE	3.3	3.1	3.1	4.3	4.2	4.6	6.5
111 FOR INDUSTRY–POUR L'INDUSTRIE	2.0	2.1	2.0	2.6	2.9	3.3	4.5
112 FOR HOUSEHOLDS–POUR LES MENAGES	1.4	1.0	1.1	1.7	1.3	1.3	2.0
12 PROCESSED–PRODUITS ELABORES	2.7	2.8	3.1	3.5	4.3	3.6	3.5
121 FOR INDUSTRY–POUR L'INDUSTRIE	0.3	0.3	0.3	0.3	0.4	0.4	0.4
122 FOR HOUSEHOLDS–POUR LES MENAGES	2.4	2.5	2.8	3.2	3.9	3.2	3.1
2 IND SUPPLIES–APPROV INDUSTRIELS	36.3	37.6	35.4	36.3	37.7	41.2	37.2
21 PRIMARY–PRODUITS DE BASE	2.6	2.9	2.4	2.6	2.6	2.7	3.7
22 PROCESSED–PRODUITS ELABORES	33.7	34.7	33.0	33.6	35.1	38.4	33.5
3 FUELS–COMBUSTIBLES	9.5	9.3	8.6	8.4	8.9	8.5	9.4
31 PRIMARY–PRODUITS DE BASE	3.2	2.7	3.1	2.6	2.4	3.0	3.2
32 PROCESSED–PRODUITS ELABORES	6.3	6.6	5.5	5.7	6.5	5.5	6.1
321 MOTOR SPIRIT–ESSENCE	2.2	2.1	1.5	1.8	2.3	2.2	2.7
322 OTHER–AUTRES	4.2	4.5	4.0	3.9	4.2	3.2	3.4
4 MACHINERY–EQUIPEMENT	16.3	14.1	16.2	20.5	17.6	17.9	16.0
41 CAPITAL EQUIPMENT–MACHINES	13.9	12.0	13.8	17.8	15.0	15.5	13.6
42 PARTS–PIECES ACCESSOIRES	2.4	2.1	2.4	2.7	2.6	2.5	2.4
5 TRANSPORT–TRANSPORT	7.5	6.0	9.8	11.1	10.9	8.6	9.9
51 PASSENGER CARS–AUTOMOBILES	4.3	2.8	6.6	7.6	4.4	2.6	5.2
52 OTHER–AUTRES	0.6	0.7	0.6	0.8	3.7	3.5	2.3
521 INDUSTRIAL–INDUSTRIELS	0.5	0.5	0.4	0.5	3.3	3.2	2.1
522 NON INDUSTRIAL–NON INDUSTRIEL	0.1	0.1	0.2	0.3	0.4	0.3	0.3
53 PARTS–PIECES ACCESSOIRES	2.7	2.5	2.5	2.8	2.8	2.5	2.4
6 CONSUM GOODS–BIENS CONSOMMATION	9.4	9.7	10.6	13.3	16.1	15.1	14.6
61 DURABLE–DURABLES	1.6	1.7	2.2	3.1	4.1	3.3	2.9
62 SEMI DURABLE–SEMI DURABLES	3.8	3.8	4.3	5.4	6.5	6.3	6.3
63 NON DURABLE–NON DURABLES	4.0	4.2	4.2	4.9	5.4	5.5	5.5
7 GOODS NES–BIENS NDA	15.0	17.5	13.2	2.7	0.3	0.4	3.0

EXPORTS – EXPORTATIONS

	1990	1991	1992	1993	1994	1995	1996
TOTAL EXPORTS–EXPORTATIONS TOTALES	100.	100.	100.	100.	100.	100.	100.
1 AGRICULTURE	52.9	54.3	53.9	57.3	54.5	56.3	57.3
2 MINING QUARRY–INDUS EXTRACTIVES	0.1	0.0	0.1	0.2	0.2	0.1	0.2
3 MANUFACTURING–IND MANUFACTUR	47.0	45.7	46.0	42.6	45.3	43.6	42.5
31 FOOD BEV TOBACCO–ALIM BOISS TAB	10.7	11.5	11.7	13.7	11.7	12.0	14.9
32 TEXTILES–INDUSTRIES TEXTILES	6.3	5.4	5.8	5.9	5.8	4.0	3.5
33 WOOD & PRODUCTS–BOIS & PRODUITS	0.9	0.7	0.9	1.1	1.4	1.3	1.4
34 PAPER & PRODUCTS–PAPIER & PRODT	1.3	1.6	1.9	1.8	1.6	2.2	1.9
35 CHEMICALS–INDUSTRIES CHIMIQUES	9.3	8.9	9.6	10.1	9.8	9.8	10.5
36 NON METAL MIN–MIN NON METAL	1.2	1.1	1.1	1.1	1.1	1.2	1.3
37 BASIC METAL–IND METAL BASE	1.6	1.5	1.6	1.5	1.4	1.5	1.4
38 METAL MANUF–MANUF METAL	5.3	5.1	5.3	5.5	5.2	5.0	6.0
39 OTH MANUF IND–AUTRES MANUF	10.3	9.8	8.1	1.8	7.3	6.5	1.6

3. TRADE BY PRINCIPAL COUNTRIES OF ORIGIN AND DESTINATION (VALUE IN MILLION U.S. DOLLARS)
ECHANGES SELON LES PRINCIPAUX PAYS D'ORIGINE ET DE DESTINATION (VALEUR EN MILLIONS DE DOLLARS EU)

COUNTRIES–PAYS	SPECIAL IMPORTS C.I.F. IMPORTATIONS SPECIALES C.A.F				
	1992	1993	1994	1995	1996
World	2789.1	2938.7	3024.3	3205.5	3561.0
Africa	0.6	2.9	2.3	4.0	8.0
Americas	2104.9	2124.5	2273.2	2496.4	2835.1
– Northern America	1411.6	1340.5	1384.2	1492.4	1699.9
– LAIA	445.0	492.0	571.4	641.1	759.5
– CACM	216.3	206.0	231.2	235.6	249.7
– Caribbean	10.0	11.0	21.2	26.6	25.5
– Rest of America	22.0	75.0	65.2	100.6	100.4
Asia excl fmr USSR	325.8	400.3	333.7	272.4	296.8
– Middle East	0.3	2.4	3.1	1.4	2.2
Asia former USSR			0.0	0.2	0.0
Europe excl fmr USSR	340.7	388.8	381.0	407.5	412.7
– European Union	306.2	357.7	342.6	374.5	375.9
– Eastern Europe	4.0	3.4	9.5	10.2	11.5
– Rest of Europe	30.5	27.8	29.0	22.8	25.2
Europe former USSR	3.1	4.8	11.1	11.2	2.8
Oceania	0.9	0.9	1.4	6.2	1.4
Other	13.1	16.4	21.5	7.5	4.2
USA/Etats–Unis d'Amer	1385.7	1306.6	1341.9	1453.0	1651.2
Venezuela	113.0	139.1	164.9	211.3	252.3
Japan/Japon	168.9	217.8	166.5	122.9	145.6
Mexico/Mexique	123.8	116.5	136.8	176.8	251.1
Guatemala	96.8	104.2	109.3	112.1	116.2
Brazil/Brésil	98.7	110.3	124.4	101.6	78.9
Germany/Allemagne	86.5	101.3	100.3	99.9	88.9
Colombia/Colombie	56.5	77.5	86.8	98.6	110.9
El Salvador	60.8	69.2	76.4	84.1	93.2
Panama	22.0	74.9	65.1	99.4	97.8
Other Asia n.e.s.	54.2	72.0	54.7	44.7	45.1
Italy/Italie	36.5	47.3	50.8	61.9	64.1
Spain/Espagne	32.4	46.1	42.6	57.2	50.1
France, Monaco	38.3	55.4	40.7	33.3	47.2
Canada	25.9	33.8	42.0	39.3	47.8
Netherlands/Pays–Bas	24.1	25.7	28.2	43.4	30.7
United Kingdom	29.3	29.9	30.5	26.0	32.6
Korea, Republic of	56.6	0.2	50.2	2.7	32.1
Nicaragua	50.5	21.6	22.7	17.1	15.3
China, Hong Kong SAR	27.4	32.6	16.7	23.0	20.5
Switzerland,Liechtenst.	28.6	26.1	25.0	18.1	18.8
Belgium–Luxembourg	17.5	22.9	15.4	28.3	29.3
Chile/Chili	19.0	15.4	17.6	12.7	32.3
Korea Dem People's Rp	0.1	52.0	0.2	39.8	2.8
Honduras	8.2	11.0	22.8	22.3	25.0
Argentina/Argentine	9.4	9.7	19.4	27.1	21.4
China/Chine	0.3	0.4	20.8	17.2	23.3
Sweden/Suède	11.1	7.9	9.7	8.4	10.9
Ecuador/Equateur	15.6	12.7	10.0	3.4	3.5
Peru/Pérou	7.8	8.9	11.1	9.0	8.1
Israel/Israël	6.3	7.7	7.2	7.1	9.7
Ireland/Irlande	5.9	7.3	7.5	6.1	9.0
Trinidad and Tobago	7.8	5.6	10.3	9.5	1.5
Areas n.e.s.			21.5	7.5	4.2
Denmark/Danemark	5.7	4.7	9.1	3.1	6.4
Austria/Autriche	12.7	5.0	4.3	2.6	4.2
Singapore/Singapour	5.8	8.1	4.9	5.2	3.2
Russian Federation	3.1	4.8	7.2	8.5	2.8
Jamaica/Jamaïque	0.1	0.1	0.0	8.3	12.1
Poland/Pologne	1.2	1.3	5.3	5.8	6.1

COUNTRIES–PAYS	SPECIAL EXPORTS F.O.B. EXPORTATIONS SPECIALES F.O.B.				
	1992	1993	1994	1995	1996
Monde	1833.7	1941.7	2220.4	2701.8	2779.8
Afrique	1.9	3.4	12.6	5.9	7.2
Amériques	1322.1	1345.7	1451.8	1692.2	1738.1
– Amérique du Nord	917.4	908.4	991.7	1118.3	1079.9
– ALAI	50.9	76.9	80.9	91.1	137.5
– MCAC	308.7	269.4	285.9	349.7	384.2
– Caraïbes	29.3	26.5	26.4	33.0	47.1
– Autre Amérique	15.9	64.4	67.0	100.1	89.4
Asie anc. URSS exclus	40.7	36.6	41.4	106.4	105.4
– Moyen–Orient	5.3	3.5	1.3	4.6	8.5
Asie ancienne URSS				0.1	
Europe anc. URSS exclus	467.5	552.7	697.9	858.3	879.8
– Union Européenne	454.2	541.9	683.4	830.5	858.0
– Europe de l'Est	3.3	4.0	2.2	5.9	7.0
– Autre de l'Europe	10.0	6.8	12.2	21.8	14.8
Europe ancienne URSS	0.4	0.5	4.1	33.2	22.8
Océanie	0.9	1.6	3.1	3.8	3.9
Autre	0.3	1.3	9.6	1.9	22.5
USA/Etats–Unis d'Amer	887.5	871.7	963.0	1084.7	1026.7
Germany/Allemagne	173.3	188.0	197.8	172.9	206.5
Belgium–Luxembourg	78.3	124.4	148.1	177.6	127.0
Italy/Italie	83.3	87.8	105.4	132.1	150.4
Guatemala	75.3	84.8	102.6	117.0	123.5
Nicaragua	134.4	69.4	67.5	87.3	102.0
El Salvador	55.7	62.9	72.3	90.9	93.3
Netherlands/Pays–Bas	35.2	42.4	60.0	87.6	111.9
United Kingdom	24.0	38.1	66.6	101.2	92.9
Panama	0.3	63.4	65.6	84.6	85.4
Honduras	43.3	52.3	43.4	54.6	65.4
France, Monaco	19.2	24.2	35.5	51.1	59.7
Canada	29.7	36.5	28.5	33.4	53.0
Mexico/Mexique	17.6	28.7	22.1	16.5	52.8
Japan/Japon	13.4	11.6	19.5	28.1	35.1
Spain/Espagne	14.5	11.5	21.2	25.9	27.8
Sweden/Suède	6.7	7.1	13.2	24.5	45.2
Finland/Finlande	8.7	7.7	16.7	35.8	16.5
China, Hong Kong SAR	2.6	5.8	12.8	22.0	39.6
Colombia/Colombie	6.8	8.8	10.9	16.5	21.0
Chile/Chili	4.4	9.4	12.0	16.3	18.1
Russian Federation	0.4	0.5	4.1	33.1	20.8
Dominican Republic	11.2	7.7	8.3	12.3	15.7
Venezuela	7.8	10.8	8.0	14.5	11.5
Switzerland,Liechtenst.	8.3	5.3	7.9	16.9	12.4
Portugal	8.3	6.1	11.0	11.9	11.2
Jamaica/Jamaïque	5.1	5.7	9.5	9.0	11.7
Areas n.e.s.		1.1	9.6	1.9	22.5
Argentina/Argentine	4.8	6.8	9.9	5.1	8.4
China/Chine		0.2	0.3	33.0	0.5
Belize/Bélize	15.4	0.6	0.9	14.5	2.3
Peru/Pérou	1.8	4.4	6.0	7.1	13.7
Ecuador/Equateur	4.1	4.1	7.3	7.2	7.2
Israel/Israël	4.4	4.6	2.5	9.5	7.2
Denmark/Danemark	1.1	2.0	4.3	5.6	6.5
Poland/Pologne	1.8	3.7	1.6	4.3	5.8
Norway,Svalbard and JM	1.6	1.4	4.2	4.8	2.4
Brazil/Brésil	2.8	1.2	0.3	6.7	3.4
Other Asia n.e.s.	8.1	1.7	0.9	1.6	1.2
Morocco/Maroc	0.6	0.7	10.1	1.3	0.5

(VALUE AS PERCENTAGE OF WORLD TOTAL)(VALEURS EN POURCENTAGE DU TOTAL MONDIAL)

	1987	1988	1989	1990	1991	1992	1993	1994	1995	1996
Africa	0.0	0.0	0.0	0.0	0.0	0.0	0.1	0.1	0.1	0.2
Americas	67.5	72.0	74.9	73.0	77.1	75.5	72.3	75.2	77.9	79.6
– Northern America	39.2	40.4	48.3	48.6	52.6	50.6	45.6	45.8	46.6	47.7
– LAIA	17.8	20.9	17.5	16.4	16.0	16.0	16.7	18.9	20.0	21.3
– CACM	8.5	8.4	6.9	6.5	6.9	7.8	7.0	7.6	7.4	7.0
– Caribbean	0.2	0.4	0.5	0.1	0.2	0.4	0.4	0.7	0.8	0.7
– Rest of America	1.8	1.8	1.7	1.2	1.4	0.8	2.6	2.2	3.1	2.8
Asia excl fmr USSR	14.2	12.3	11.2	12.2	10.4	11.7	13.6	11.0	8.5	8.3
– Middle East	0.1	0.0	0.0	0.0	0.0	0.0	0.1	0.1	0.0	0.1
Asia former USSR								0.0	0.0	0.0
Europe excl fmr USSR	17.1	14.9	12.9	13.6	11.3	12.2	13.2	12.6	12.7	11.6
– European Union	15.8	13.5	11.5	12.3	10.0	11.0	12.2	11.3	11.7	10.6
– Eastern Europe	0.2	0.2	0.3	0.3	0.2	0.1	0.1	0.3	0.3	0.3
– Rest of Europe	1.2	1.2	1.1	1.0	1.2	1.1	0.9	1.0	0.7	0.7
Europe former USSR	0.2	0.1	0.1	0.1	0.1	0.1	0.2	0.4	0.4	0.1
Oceania	0.0	0.0	0.0	0.0	0.0	0.0	0.0	0.0	0.2	0.0
Other	0.9	0.6	0.8	1.1	1.0	0.5	0.6	0.7	0.2	0.1
USA/Etats–Unis d'Amer	37.2	38.8	47.1	47.3	51.3	49.7	44.5	44.4	45.3	46.4
Venezuela	7.0	7.4	6.8	7.4	5.2	4.1	4.7	5.5	6.6	7.1
Japan/Japon	8.5	6.7	6.1	7.2	5.3	6.1	7.4	5.5	3.8	4.1
Mexico/Mexique	5.0	6.0	4.8	2.8	3.9	4.4	4.0	4.5	5.5	7.1
Guatemala	4.7	4.7	3.6	3.5	3.7	3.5	3.5	3.6	3.5	3.3
Brazil/Brésil	2.7	4.0	3.1	2.5	3.1	3.5	3.8	4.1	3.2	2.2
Germany/Allemagne					2.8	3.1	3.4	3.3	3.1	2.5
Colombia/Colombie	1.2	1.6	1.0	0.8	1.6	2.0	2.6	2.9	3.1	3.1
El Salvador	2.7	2.6	2.2	2.2	2.3	2.2	2.4	2.5	2.6	2.6
Panama	1.8	1.8	1.7	1.2	1.4	0.8	2.5	2.2	3.1	2.7

	1987	1988	1989	1990	1991	1992	1993	1994	1995	1996
Afrique	0.2	0.3	0.2	0.1	0.1	0.1	0.2	0.6	0.2	0.3
Amériques	63.4	61.5	66.5	66.0	68.0	72.1	69.3	65.4	62.6	62.5
– Amérique du Nord	47.0	44.1	49.3	49.0	50.2	50.0	46.8	44.7	41.4	38.8
– ALAI	1.1	2.0	2.1	1.9	1.8	2.8	4.0	3.6	3.4	4.9
– MCAC	9.8	11.0	10.3	9.5	11.0	16.8	13.9	12.9	12.9	13.8
– Caraïbes	1.2	1.5	1.7	2.0	1.5	1.6	1.4	1.2	1.2	1.7
– Autre Amérique	4.3	3.0	3.0	3.6	3.4	0.9	3.3	3.0	3.7	3.2
Asie anc. URSS exclus	2.4	3.4	1.9	2.6	2.9	2.2	1.9	1.9	3.9	3.8
– Moyen–Orient	0.3	0.5	0.2	0.1	0.1	0.3	0.2	0.1	0.2	0.3
Asie ancienne URSS									0.0	
Europe anc. URSS exclus	32.1	32.9	29.0	30.3	28.4	25.5	28.5	31.4	31.8	31.7
– Union Européenne	29.4	29.7	26.8	29.5	27.7	24.8	27.9	30.8	30.7	30.9
– Europe de l'Est	1.7	2.8	1.9	0.3	0.2	0.2	0.2	0.1	0.2	0.3
– Autre de l'Europe	1.0	0.5	0.3	0.5	0.6	0.5	0.3	0.6	0.8	0.5
Europe ancienne URSS	0.6	0.5	0.8	0.0	0.0	0.0	0.0	0.2	1.2	0.8
Océanie	0.1	0.1	0.1	0.1	0.1	0.0	0.1	0.1	0.1	0.1
Autre	1.3	1.2	1.6	0.8	0.6	0.0	0.1	0.4	0.1	0.8
USA/Etats–Unis d'Amer	45.3	41.7	45.4	45.1	47.6	48.4	44.9	43.4	40.1	36.9
Germany/Allemagne					10.7	9.4	9.7	8.9	6.4	7.4
Belgium–Luxembourg	1.0	0.9	1.9	4.5	4.7	4.3	6.4	6.7	6.6	4.6
Italy/Italie	3.0	4.4	4.3	4.3	4.5	4.5	4.5	4.7	4.9	5.4
Guatemala	3.9	4.7	4.2	3.6	3.6	4.1	4.4	4.6	4.3	4.4
Nicaragua	1.1	1.4	1.7	2.1	3.6	7.3	3.6	3.0	3.2	3.7
El Salvador	3.2	3.7	3.2	2.5	2.7	3.0	3.2	3.3	3.4	3.4
Netherlands/Pays–Bas	2.7	3.0	2.3	3.0	2.6	1.9	2.2	2.7	3.2	4.0
United Kingdom	2.2	2.3	2.2	2.0	1.9	1.3	2.0	3.0	3.7	3.3
Panama	4.2	2.9	2.9	3.5	3.3	0.0	3.3	3.0	3.1	3.1

4. Special Imports C.I.F. by Commodities according to the S.I.T.C. (Rev. 2) in million U.S. Dollars
Importations Spéciales C.A.F. par Produits d'après la C.T.C.I. (Rév. 2) en millions de Dollars E.U.

SITC CTCI	COMMODITY	1993 QUANTITY QUANTITE	1993 VALUE VALEUR	1994 QUANTITY QUANTITE	1994 VALUE VALEUR	1995 QUANTITY QUANTITE	1995 VALUE VALEUR	1996 QUANTITY QUANTITE	1996 VALUE VALEUR	PRODUIT
	ALL COMMODITIES		2938.7		3024.4		3205.5		3561.1	TOUS PRODUITS
0	FOOD AND LIVE ANIMALS		224.9		252.8		256.2		367.2	ALIMENTS,ANIMAUX VIVANTS
001	*LIVE ANIMALS FOR FOOD	W 13728	13.5	W 10002	10.3	W 1361	2.1	W 149	1.8	ANIMAUX VIVANTS
0011	BOVINE SPECIES,LIVE	W 13488	11.6	W 9847	8.6	W 1234	1.1	W 44	0.1	ESPECE BOVINE
00119	— OTHR THAN FR BREEDING	W 13464	11.5	W 9815	8.4	W 1218	1.1			BOVINS NON REPRODUCTEURS
02	DAIRY PRODCTS,BIRDS'EGGS		9.0		9.4		9.9		10.3	PRODUITS LAITIERS,OEUFS
03	FISH AND PREPARATIONS		33.8		23.2		21.3		38.1	POISSONS ET PREPARATIONS
034	FISH,FRESH,CHILLED,FROZN	W 22080	31.2	W 59406	20.9	W 20337	18.6	W 160482	33.5	POISSON FRAIS, REFRIG,CONG
0341	FISH FRSH,CHLLD,EX FILLT	W 22080	31.2	W 415	0.6	W 514	0.7	W 1314	0.4	POISSON FRAIS,REFRIGERE
0342	FISH FROZEN,EXCL FILLETS			W 58949	20.3	W 19635	17.9	W 159167	33.2	POISSONS CONGELES
04	CEREALS AND PREPARATIONS		96.8		127.0		130.8		206.1	CEREALES ET PRODUITS
041	WHEAT ETC UNMILLED	W 113471	25.4	W 152451	30.1	W 162137	34.5	W 1052561	56.6	FROMENT,EPEAUTRE
0411	DURUM WHEAT UNMILLED					W 56732	13.1	W 156411	34.0	FROMENT DUR NON MOULU
0412	OTHER WHEAT ETC UNMILLED			W 152451	30.1	W 105405	21.5	W 896150	22.6	AUTRE FROMENT NON MOULU
042	RICE	W 36469	6.4	W 52691	19.9	W 156209	16.3	W 90561	28.7	RIZ
0421	RICE IN HUSK OR HUSKED	W 46	0.1	W 10199	2.0	W 155248	15.9	W 87512	28.5	RIZ SANS AUTRE PREPARATION
04211	RICE IN THE HUSK			W 10195	2.0	W 155233	15.9	W 87507	28.5	RIZ PADDY
0422	RICE SEMI–MILLED,MILLED	W 36423	6.4	W 42493	18.0	W 960	0.5	W 3048	0.2	RIZ POLI,GLACE INCL BRISURES
04221	RICE MILLED UNBROKEN			W 42485	17.9	W 960	0.5	W 3048	0.2	RIZ POLI,GLACE EXCL BRISURES
044	MAIZE UNMILLED	W 336720	45.9	W 383111	50.1	W 345017	52.2	W 451425	90.7	MAIS NON MOULU
048	CEREAL ETC PREPARATIONS	W 20690	17.7	W 24275	24.6	W 25714	25.5	W 219322	28.0	PREPTNS A BASE CEREALES
0481	PREPD BREAKFAST FOOD ETC	W 5428	9.5	W 5817	11.1	W 6098	9.8	W 53726	11.0	CEREALES TRAVAILLEES
04812	CEREAL ROASTED, PUFFED	W 2558	7.7	W 3205	9.4	W 3735	8.1	W 31288	8.9	PRODTS BASE CEREALES
05	VEGETABLES AND FRUIT		26.5		30.8		37.3		49.2	LEGUMES ET FRUITS
054	VEG ETC FRSH,SMPLY PRSVD	W 6936	3.2	W 10654	7.8	W 21940	12.3	W 303159	20.1	LEGUMES FRAIS,CONG,SECS
0542	LEGUMINOUS VEGETBLES DRY	W 2149	1.2	W 5461	3.7	W 8052	5.0	W 167386	12.1	LEGUMES A COSSE SECS
057	FRUIT,NUTS,FRESH,DRIED	W 16259	8.0	W 17207	8.5	W 20897	10.5	W 187812	13.6	FRUITS FRAIS OU SECS
058	FRUIT PRESERVED,PREPARED	W 8538	10.3	W 8805	10.3	W 9250	10.5	W 74662	10.6	CONSERVES DE FRUITS
06	SUGAR AND PREPS,HONEY		8.6		10.0		9.9		10.8	SUCRES ET PRODUITS
07	COFFEE,TEA,COCOA,SPICES		6.9		10.3		12.3		12.9	CAFE,THE,CACAO,EPICES
09	MISC EDIBLE PRODUCTS		24.8		23.6		25.5		29.0	PREP ALIMENTAIRES DIVERSES
098	EDIBLE PRODCTS,PREPS NES	W 11391	24.7	W 13814	23.3	W 12930	25.0	W 84056	28.3	PREP ALIMENTAIRES NDA
09804	SAUCES,MIXED SEASONINGS	W 5142	6.6	W 6076	7.9	W 6127	8.6	W 54101	11.0	SAUCES,ASSAISONNEMENTS
09809	MISC FOOD PREPRTIONS NES	W 5729	17.6	W 4605	7.5	W 3899	9.4	W 13034	12.2	PREP ALIMENTAIRES NDA
1	BEVERAGES AND TOBACCO		16.3		15.5		17.2		18.1	BOISSONS ET TABACS
11	BEVERAGES		15.1		15.1		15.4		14.7	BOISSONS
112	ALCOHOLIC BEVERAGES	W 6052	11.5	W 7157	11.3	W 6496	11.1	W 38134	10.9	BOISSONS ALCOOLIQUES
2	CRUDE MATERLS,EXCL FUELS		80.3		86.6		96.8		120.2	MAT BRUTES NON COMESTIBLES
22	OIL SEEDS,OLEAGINOUS FRT		36.6		41.8		47.3		67.1	GRAINES,FRUITS OLEAGINEUX
222	SEEDS FOR'SOFT'FIXED OIL	W 130201	36.0	W 143037	40.6	W 161448	46.2	W 219845	66.4	GRAINES HUILES FIXES
2222	SOYA BEANS	W 129071	35.5	W 141041	39.4	W 159823	45.0	W 201403	64.8	FEVES DE SOJA
23	RUBBER, CRUDE		10.6		13.6		15.0		14.6	CAOUTCHOUC BRUT
233	RUBBER,SYNTHTIC,RECLAIMD	W 8274	7.5	W 9453	9.2	W 7909	9.8	W 69722	9.4	LATEX CAOUTCH SYNTH REGEN
2331	SYNTHETIC RUBBER ETC	W 8199	7.4	W 9318	9.0	W 7903	9.8	W 69680	9.4	LATEX CAOUTCH SYNTHETIQUE
27	CRUDE FERTLZR,MINRLS NES		9.3		9.7		9.7		8.6	ENGRAIS MINERAUX BRUTS
29	CRUDE ANIMAL,VEG MAT NES		7.8		7.6		9.4		11.3	MATIERES BRUTES ANIM,VEGET
3	MINERAL FUELS ETC		248.8		271.7		273.6		335.8	COMBUSTIBLES MINERAUX LUB
33	PETROLEUM AND PRODUCTS		242.4		263.5		265.5		322.1	PETROLE ET DERIVES
333	CRUDE PETROLEUM	W 569026	71.3	W 553852	64.3	W 706133	88.7	W 675909	101.4	HUILES BRUTES DE PETROLE
334	PETROLEUM PRODUCTS,REFIN	W 856040	167.9	W 1044246	196.1	W 885215	173.7	MW 9014	217.0	PRODUITS RAFFINES
3341	GASOLINE,OTH LIGHT OILS	W 347788	68.0	W 387557	70.2	W 380459	70.8	W 4186639	96.7	ESSENCES POUR MOTEURS
33411	MOTOR,AVIATION SPIRIT	W 269613	52.7							ESSENCES MOTEURS D'AVIONS
33412	SPIRIT TYPE JET FUEL	W 78080	15.2							CARBUREACTEURS
33419	OTH LIGHT PETROLEUM OILS	W 95	0.1	W 387557	70.2	W 380459	70.8	W 4186639	96.7	AUTRES HUILES LEGERES
3343	GAS OILS	W 401613	67.0							GAS OILS
3344	FUEL OILS,NES	W 83522	10.2	W 614740	93.6	W 459205	70.6	W 4374584	86.0	FUEL OILS
3345	LUBS,PETROLEUM OILS NES	W 22820	22.6	W 41292	32.0	W 45145	32.2	W 448885	34.1	HUILES LUBRIFIANTES
33451	LUBS(HIGH PETR CONT) ETC	W 22371	21.7	W 40700	31.0	W 44552	31.3	W 447347	33.1	HUILES LUBRIF,H LOURDES
341	*GAS,NATURAL AND MANUFCT	W 29786	6.3	W 31261	6.5	W 42082	8.1	W 442326	13.1	GAZ NATUREL,GAZ MANUFACT
3413	PETROLM GASES,LIQUEFIED	W 29786	6.3	W 31260	6.5	W 42058	8.1	W 442306	13.1	GAZ DE PETROLE LIQUEFIE
34131	LIQUEFIED PROPANE,BUTANE			W 31253	6.5	W 40953	7.8	W 399201	11.9	PROPANE,BUTANE LIQUEFIES
5	CHEMCLS,RELATED PROD NES		521.5		537.5		622.2		642.5	PRODUITS CHIMIQUES
51	ORGANIC CHEMICALS		58.9		57.6		67.5		72.0	PROD CHIMIQ ORGANIQUES
512	ALCOHOLS,PHENOLS ETC	W 37864	11.9	W 35795	11.2	W 55039	18.8	W 310698	14.4	PHENOLS,PHENOLS–ALCOOLS
5121	ACYCLIC ALCOHOLS,DERIVS	W 37732	11.2	W 34197	9.9	W 54773	17.8	W 309382	13.3	ALCOOLS ACYCLIQUES
51216	ETHYL ALC,DENATRD SPIRIT	W 34047	7.9	W 29108	5.6	W 50563	12.8	W 272221	8.5	ALCOOL ETHYLIQUE NON DENAT
513	CARBOXYLIC ACIDS ETC	W 8572	13.0	W 9098	15.1	W 6943	14.1	W 60227	16.3	ACIDES CARBOXYLIQUES
514	NITROGEN–FNCTN COMPOUNDS	W 2173	7.5	W 2807	12.3	W 3187	13.5	W 16745	15.6	COMPOSES FONCT AZOTEES
515	ORG–INORG COMPOUNDS ETC	W 1458	12.7	W 1810	8.3	W 1912	9.1	W 10787	9.6	COMPOSES ORGANO–MINERAUX
5156	HETEROCYCLIC CMPDS ETC	W 962	9.2	W 1103	5.7	W 1127	6.1	W 7388	6.2	COMPOSES HETEROCYCLIQUES
516	OTHER ORGANIC CHEMICALS	W 3570	8.4		5.6		5.6		10.8	AUTRES PROD ORGANIQUES
52	INORGANIC CHEMICALS		36.7		38.2		42.9		46.1	PROD CHIM INORGANIQUES
522	INORG ELEMNTS,OXIDES,ETC	W 72678	22.0	W 56858	21.7	W 63379	26.4	W 388669	28.1	ELEMENTS INORGANIQUES
5225	INORGANIC BASES ETC NES	W 59699	10.8	W 43077	10.0	W 49351	15.3	W 224549	15.9	AUTRES BASES OXYDES METAL
52251	AMMONIA,ANHYDROUS ETC	W 48662	8.7	W 35014	8.0	W 43572	12.0	W 162906	13.1	AMMONIAC LIQUEFIE
523	OTHR INORG CHEMICALS ETC	W 37859	14.4	W 37453	16.1	W 45096	16.2	W 419411	17.7	AUT PRODUITS CHIMIQUES INORG
5232	OTH MTL CMPD OF INRG ACD	W 22288	8.5	W 20440	8.7	W 30108	9.9	W 245994	9.9	SELS METALLIQUES
53	DYES,TANNING,COLOUR PROD		27.1		25.1		25.0		28.3	PROD TEINTURE,COLORANTS
533	PIGMENTS,PAINTS,ETC	W 5292	16.8	W 5270	16.0	W 6784	17.3	W 37088	20.0	PIGMENTS,PEINTURES,VERNIS
541	*MEDICINAL,PHARM PRODUCT	K 3769173	95.5	K 3139377	98.4	K 3686335	103.2	K 8665987	114.1	PROD MEDICINAUX PHARMACEUT
5417	MEDICAMENTS	K 2508286	74.2	K 2342088	81.3	K 2707163	85.4	K 7710410	92.7	MEDICAMENTS
54171	— CONTAINNG ANTIBIOTICS			K 640631	20.2	K 551628	16.5	K 1356495	13.2	MED CONTN ANTIBIOTIQUES
54179	— CONTNG OTH SUBSTANCES			K 1528530	53.5	K 1890324	62.4	K 2971016	70.7	MED CONT AUT SUBSTANCES
55	PERFUME,CLEANING ETC PRD		47.0		55.5		64.6		71.5	PROD POUR PARFUM,TOILETTE
551	ESSENTL OILS,PERFUME,ETC	W 477	8.9	W 598	10.8	W 699	10.3	W 1447	10.4	HUILES ESSENTIELLES
5514	MIXED PERFUME SUBSTANCES	W 399	8.1	W 497	9.5	W 617	9.3	W 1372	9.5	MELANGES SUBSTAN ODORIFER
553	PERFUMERY,COSMETICS,ETC	W 3733	17.3	W 4147	19.0	W 5974	28.5	W 44556	31.6	PRODUITS DE PARFUMERIE
554	SOAP,CLEANSING ETC PREPS	W 15435	21.0	W 19468	25.8	W 22990	25.8	W 70518	29.6	SAVONS,PRODUITS DETERSIFS
5542	WASHING PREPARATIONS ETC	W 12364	15.6	W 15854	18.7	W 17222	19.2	W 29577	21.0	PROD ORG TENSIO–ACT NDA
562	*FERTILIZERS,MANUFACTURE	W 215754	36.5	W 243540	41.0	W 272784	59.8	W 2465252	57.1	ENGRAIS MANUFACTURES
5621	CHEM NITROGENOUS FERTLZR	W 96882	16.0	W 102026	17.5	W 128095	30.8	W 1104696	27.5	ENGRAIS AZOTES
56216	UREA			W 72890	11.7	W 79468	19.4	W 845242	21.6	UREE
56219	CHEM NITROG FERTILZR NES	W 90462	15.1	W 13093	3.3	W 11729	6.0	W 8099	0.7	ENGRAIS AZOTES NDA
5623	CHEM POTASSIC FERTILIZER	W 86360	13.3	W 98110	13.9	W 94322	15.6	W 902412	15.2	ENGRAIS POTASSIQUES
56239	CHEM POTASS FERTILZR NES	W 86360	13.3	W 38955	5.8	W 13602	3.2	W 119191	2.9	ENGRAIS POTASSIQUES NDA
5629	FERTILIZERS NES	W 5137	3.0	W 27463	6.8	W 36154	10.1	W 356066	11.8	ENGRAIS NDA
58	PLASTIC MATERIALS ETC		114.2		119.3		142.0		136.1	MAT PLAST ARTIFICIELLES
582	PROD OF CONDENSATION ETC	W 15180	22.8	W 13896	19.1	W 13748	22.8	W 164939	23.7	PROD CONDENS,POLYCOND
5823	ALKYDS,OTHER POLYESTERS	W 13669	18.3	W 7313	10.2	W 7277	12.8	W 65189	12.4	ALKYDES ET AUT POLYESTERS
58231	— IN PRIMARY FORMS			W 7015	8.8	W 6868	10.7	W 64812	10.6	SOUS FORMES PRIMAIRES
583	POLYMERIZATION ETC PRODS	W 85545	82.9	W 96142	96.3	W 90123	115.9	W 359648	108.5	PROD POLYMERISATION

4. Special Imports C.I.F. by Commodities according to the S.I.T.C. (Rev. 2) in million U.S. Dollars
Importations Spéciales C.A.F. par Produits d'après la C.T.C.I. (Rév. 2) en millions de Dollars E.U.

SITC CTCI	COMMODITY	1993 QUANTITY QUANTITE	1993 VALUE VALEUR	1994 QUANTITY QUANTITE	1994 VALUE VALEUR	1995 QUANTITY QUANTITE	1995 VALUE VALEUR	1996 QUANTITY QUANTITE	1996 VALUE VALEUR	PRODUIT
5831	POLYETHYLENE	W 728	1.9	W 42378	36.2	W 37224	43.8	W 132390	36.9	POLYETHYLENE
58311	— IN PRIMARY FORMS			W 40456	32.9	W 35460	40.2	W 115562	32.2	POLYETHYLENE PRIMAIRES
5832	POLYPROPYLENE			W 13217	12.7	W 15276	19.6	W 32827	19.5	POLYPROPYLENE
58321	— IN PRIMARY FORMS			W 11614	8.4	W 13646	14.6	W 14342	13.2	POLYPROPYLENE PRIMAIRES
5834	POLYVINYL CHLORIDE	W 20644	16.1	W 23749	21.0	W 18584	20.5	W 37587	19.0	CHLORURE DE POLYVINYLE
58341	— IN PRIMARY FORMS			W 22544	18.6	W 17521	18.1	W 34765	16.3	SOUS FORMES PRIMAIRES
5839	OTH POLYMRZTION ETC PROD	W 63286	64.1	W 7495	13.8	W 9754	17.1	W 65002	16.1	AUT PROD POLYMER COPOLYM
59	CHEMICAL MATERIALS NES		105.3		102.2		117.3		116.2	MAT PROD CHIMIQUES NDA
591	PESTICIDES,DISINFECTANTS	W 13184	69.5	W 13742	72.0	W 15861	85.3	W 29738	79.4	DESINF,INSECT,FONG,HERB
5911	INSECTICIDES,FOR RETAIL	W 3093	14.4	W 2392	12.5	W 4158	17.0	W 2780	16.7	INSECTICIDES VENTE DET
5912	FUNGICIDES,FOR RETAIL	W 5592	34.6	W 5385	34.1	W 5777	41.2	W 5807	38.7	FONGICIDES VENTE AU DET
5913	HERBICIDES,FOR RETAIL	W 2414	13.0	W 3193	16.5	W 3211	16.7	W 2456	17.4	HERBICIDES VENTE AU DET
5914	DISINFECTANTS,ETC,FR RET	W 2085	7.5	W 2772	9.1	W 2715	10.4	W 18696	6.7	DESINFECTANTS VENTE DET
59149	RAT POISONS ETC FR RTAIL	W 1843	6.9	W 2385	8.3	W 2337	9.8	W 12426	5.7	ANTIPARASITES VENTE DET
598	MISCEL CHEM PRODUCTS NES	W 10017	28.8	W 10600	21.9	W 11782	23.0	W 79429	26.7	PROD DIV INDUST CHIM NDA
5989	CHEM PRODUCTS,PREPS NES	W 8407	23.4	W 8618	15.6	W 8604	18.1	W 70534	21.9	PROD PREP CHIMIQUES NDA
59899	OTH CHEM PRODS,PREPS,NES	W 6353	19.1	W 6260	12.2	W 5797	14.2	W 55171	17.7	AUT PRODUITS CHIMIQUES NDA
6	BASIC MANUFACTURES		581.0		640.4		744.3		707.2	ART MANUFACTURES
62	RUBBER MANUFACTURES NES		31.1		33.5		35.0		39.9	CAOUTCHOUC MANUFACTURE
625	RUBBER TYRES, TUBES ETC	W 5657	18.9	W 6402	21.0	W 6048	20.1	W 43669	22.9	PNEUS CAOUTCHOUC VULCANISE
6251	TYRES NEW FOR MOTOR CARS	W 3884	13.5	W 2299	7.5	W 2153	6.8	W 18524	7.1	PNEUS POUR VOITURES
63	WOOD,CORK MANUFACTRS NES		6.4		9.7		9.6		9.0	OUVRAGES LIEGE ET BOIS
64	PAPER,PAPERBOARD AND MFR		155.1		202.2		259.2		242.0	PAPIERS,CARTONS & OUVRAGES
641	PAPER AND PAPERBOARD	W 179969	126.0	W 311140	157.6	W 264573	208.3	W 797944	182.1	PAPIERS ET CARTONS
6411	NEWSPRINT			W 27511	17.0	W 19579	16.0	W 216239	18.7	PAPIER JOURNAL
6412	PRINTG,WRITING PAPER NES	W 20242	13.2	W 9209	8.9	W 10861	13.2	W 80082	10.0	PAPIERS POUR L'IMPRESSION
64121	— UNCOATED	W 20242	13.2	W 1328	1.5	W 1522	2.6	W 10358	1.7	PAPIERS IMPRES NON COUCHES
64122	— COATED,IMPREGNATD ETC			W 7882	7.5	W 9339	10.6	W 69724	8.3	PAPIERS IMPRESSION COUCHES
6413	KRAFT PAPER,PAPERBOARD	W 119459	54.8	W 199213	88.9	W 188199	128.4	W 342598	105.4	PAPIER ET CARTON KRAFT
64131	KRAFT LINER IN BULK			W 139321	60.3	W 125848	87.8	W 220622	74.6	PAP KRAFT POUR COUVERTURES
64139	KRAFT PAPER PAPERBD,NES			W 55848	25.7	W 56980	36.0	W 85795	27.5	PAPIER,CARTON KRAFT NDA
6415	PAPER,PAPERBRD,BULK,NES	W 19820	16.0	W 59382	17.0	W 22515	23.4	W 54515	21.2	PAPIERS,CARTONS ROULEAUX
64159	OTHER PAPER ETC,BULK,NES	W 19666	15.6	W 58871	16.1	W 21424	21.9	W 44931	19.7	AUT PAPIER ROULEAUX FEUILLES
6418	COATED ETC PAPER NES BLK	W 18735	40.4	W 11112	22.9	W 20653	24.8	W 73372	23.8	PAP,CARTONS COUCHES,ENDUITS
64181	PLASTIC COATED PAPER ETC			W 4620	14.1	W 4608	14.6	W 40877	16.3	PAP,CARTONS ENDUITS,RESINES
64189	COATED PAPER ETC NES			W 6405	8.8	W 16031	10.3	W 32478	7.5	PAPIERS,CARTONS COUCHES
642	PAPER,ETC,PRECUT,ARTS OF	W 21610	29.2	W 43534	44.6	W 44492	51.0	W 286219	60.0	PAP,CARTONS DECOUPES
6421	PAPER ETC CONTAINERS	W 9807	10.6	W 31065	23.9	W 31489	28.9	W 189505	33.6	BOITES,SACS EMBALLAGES
6428	PAPER ETC ARTICLES NES	W 4711	7.6	W 7821	11.8	W 7929	12.4	W 59877	14.6	OUVRAGES EN PATE A PAPIER
65	TEXTILE YARN,FABRICS,ETC		102.3		79.9		87.7		84.3	FILS,TISSUS,ARTICLES TEXTILE
651	TEXTILE YARN	W 4014	14.1	W 6949	9.4	W 2299	9.1	W 13430	10.4	FILS TEXTILES
652	COTTON FABRICS,WOVEN	W 6433	27.5	W 3840	16.9	W 4017	21.1	W 19875	15.3	TISSUS DE COTON
6521	GREY WOVEN COTTON FABRIC	W 5032	22.7	W 515	3.0	W 333	1.9	W 131	0.6	TISSUS COT ECRUS NON MERCER
65215	GREY WOVN COTN BLEND NES	W 4991	22.5	W 36	0.2	W 110	0.7	W 23	0.2	AUT TIS MOINS 85% COT ECRUS
6522	WOVEN COTTON BLEACHD,ETC	W 1401	4.9	W 3325	13.9	W 3684	19.2	W 19744	14.8	TISSUS COTON BLANCHIS ETC
65224	BLCHED COTTON FABRIC NES	W 1381	4.8	W 2117	9.5	W 2360	11.6	W 17279	12.0	AUT TIS PLUS 85% COT BLANCHI
653	WOVN MAN–MADE FIB FABRIC	W 4270	23.8	W 2647	15.5	W 3367	17.8	W 7755	16.3	TISSUS FIBRES SYNTH,ARTIF
6531	CONT SYNT WEAVES NONPILE	W 2539	13.4	W 797	4.3	W 1155	5.5	W 4893	5.1	TISSUS FIBRES SYNTH CONTINUE
6534	DISC SYN BLEND FABRC NES	W 1680	10.1	W 1023	7.2	W 1266	7.6	W 2075	7.6	TISSUS FIBRES SYNTH DISCONT
657	SPECIAL TXTL FABRC,PRODS	W 3340	12.5	W 4326	16.8	W 4532	17.1	W 25092	19.1	TISSUS SPECIAUX
6573	COATED ETC TEXTILES NES	W 1230	3.6	W 1985	9.5	W 2388	9.0	W 10831	9.2	TISSUS,ART MATIERE TEXT NDA
658	TEXTILE ARTICLES NES	W 1811	9.0	W 1757	9.5	W 2557	11.1	W 14481	13.1	ART FACONNES MAT TEXTILES
66	NONMETAL MINERAL MFS NES		46.3		53.1		53.6		52.4	ART MIN NON METALLIQUES
662	CLAY,REFRACTORY BLDG PRD	W 24787	12.3	W 38398	14.4	W 48097	18.6	W 94746	17.2	MAT CONST REFRACTAIRES
6624	BRICKS ETC NONREFRACTORY	W 23307	11.1	W 37171	13.4	W 47225	17.9	W 82238	16.0	BRIQUES ETC CERAM NON REFR
66245	GLAZED CERAMIC SETTS ETC	W 21965	10.6	W 32984	12.4	W 42529	16.9	W 56190	15.2	AUT CARREAUX CERAMIQUE
664	GLASS	W 15414	8.9	W 19842	11.3	W 14164	10.3	W 135544	12.2	VERRE
665	GLASSWARE	W 13175	12.7	W 14785	12.1	W 9337	10.0	W 46294	9.0	OUVRAGES EN VERRE
67	IRON AND STEEL		114.8		116.4		145.0		122.4	FER ET ACIER
672	IRON,STEEL PRIMARY FORMS	W 95033	28.6	W 144352	41.9	W 104897	39.4	W 358204	26.1	LINGOTS FER,ACIER
6724	IRN,STL INGOTS,LUMPS,ETC	W 58257	17.1	W 75678	19.6	W 50816	13.9	W 53004	13.9	FER,ACIER LINGOTS,MASSES
67241	IRON,SIMPLE STEEL INGOTS			W 75669	19.6	W 50688	13.7	W 52931	13.7	LINGOTS EN FER ET ACIER
67245	IRN,STL BLOCKS,LUMPS,ETC	W 58257	17.1	W 7	0.1	W 120	0.2	W 8	0.1	FER,ACIER EN MASSES
6727	IRN,STL COIL FR REROLLNG	W 36775	11.5	W 68667	22.3	W 53953	25.5	W 305171	12.2	EBAUCHES POUR TOLES FER
67271	IRON,SIMPLE STEEL COILS	W 36775	11.5	W 68429	22.1	W 53793	25.3	W 305102	12.0	EBAUCHES NON EN ACIER
673	IRON,STEEL SHAPES ETC	W 36994	15.9	W 34960	15.2	W 44387	21.0	W 336126	18.3	BARRES,PROFIL FER,ACIER
6731	IRON,STEEL WIRE ROD	W 13299	5.6	W 16405	5.9	W 25914	11.5	W 131453	4.5	FIL MACHINE FER,ACIER
67311	IRON,SIMPLE STL WIRE ROD	W 7225	2.4	W 16404	5.8	W 25913	11.4	W 129338	4.3	FIL MACH AUT ACIER FIN
674	IRN,STL UNIV,PLATE,SHEET	W 108338	51.2	W 83028	41.8	W 106732	65.5	W 740152	55.6	LARGES PLATS,TOLES
6746	IRN,STL THIN PLATE,ROLLD			W 44684	19.4	W 67155	37.9	W 514778	26.6	TOLES LAM MOINS 3MM
67461	— OF IRON OR SIMPLE STL			W 43449	18.1	W 65691	35.9	W 512225	25.1	TOL NON AC FIN MOINS 3 MM
6747	TINNED PLATES,SHEETS			W 7976	6.4	W 11726	10.1	W 22121	11.8	TOLES ETAMEES EN ACIER
6749	OTH IRN,STL PLATES,SHEET	W 106222	49.9	W 12196	8.5	W 11288	8.7	W 84023	9.2	AUTRES TOLES FER,ACIER
67491	— OF IRON OR SIMPLE STL	W 106222	49.9	W 11539	7.8	W 10476	7.9	W 66732	7.2	AUT TOLES AUTRES ACIER FIN
678	IRON,STL TUBES,PIPES,ETC	W 13457	9.4	W 9233	13.0	W 8133	13.2	W 122681	16.8	TUBES,TUYAUX EN FONTE,FER
68	NON–FERROUS METALS		40.6		43.8		53.1		50.6	METAUX NON FERREUX
682	COPPER EXC CEMENT COPPER	W 4997	12.9	W 6391	16.5	W 4661	16.5	W 7469	20.3	CUIVRE
6822	COPPER,ALLOYS WORKED	W 4996	12.9	W 6354	16.3	W 4649	16.4	W 7467	20.2	CUIVRE,ALLIAGES OUVRES
68221	COPPER BARS,WIRE,ETC	W 4558	10.8	W 5905	14.2	W 4198	14.2	W 6073	17.6	BARRES,PROFILES ET FILS
684	ALUMINIUM	W 10652	20.3	W 10036	21.4	W 13357	29.5	W 33400	25.1	ALUMINIUM
6841	ALUMINIUM,ALLOYS,UNWRGHT	W 7206	9.1	W 6620	9.7	W 7891	14.8	W 15379	12.1	ALUMINIUM,ALLIAGES BRUTS
6842	ALUMINIUM,ALLOYS WORKED	W 3446	11.2	W 3416	11.8	W 5466	14.7	W 18020	13.1	ALUMINIUM,ALLIAGES OUVRE
69	METAL MANUFACTURES NES		82.2		94.6		92.9		98.3	ART MANUFACT EN METAL NDA
692	METAL TANKS,BOXES,ETC	W 5161	10.0	W 4913	13.3	W 5029	13.1	W 56605	15.6	RECIPIENTS METALLIQUES
6924	MTL TRANSPORT BOXES ETC	W 4983	9.4	W 4403	11.8	W 4536	11.9	W 52402	14.0	FUTS,TAMBOURS,BIDONS
695	TOOLS	W 1960	15.7	W 2091	15.9	W 2348	16.0	W 6149	17.7	OUTILS A MAIN
6953	OTHER HAND TOOLS	W 1201	8.9	W 1292	9.4	W 1311	9.9	W 3399	10.0	AUTRES OUTILS A MAIN
699	BASE METAL MFRS NES	W 6371	26.0	W 7579	29.2	W 8095	30.9	W 30167	28.0	ART MANUFACTURES MET NDA
6991	LOCKSMITHS WARES,ETC	W 1735	9.7	W 2319	10.9	W 1806	10.7	W 2288	8.7	ARTICLES DE SERRURERIE
7	MACHINES,TRANSPORT EQUIP		923.0		889.5		850.5		902.8	MACHINES MATERIEL TRANSPORT
71	POWER GENERATING EQUIPMT		67.4		37.4		72.4		41.0	MACHINES GENERATRICES
711	STEAM BOILERS & AUX PLNT	W 908	12.2	W 416	1.5	W 674	2.2	W 1237	1.4	GENERATEURS VAPEUR EAU ETC
7111	STEAM BOILERS ETC	W 868	11.9	W 245	1.0	W 427	1.3	W 121	0.9	GENERATEURS VAPEUR EAU
713	INTRNL COMBUS PSTN ENGIN	W 1842	14.1	W 1641	14.4	W 1596	13.9	W 6941	14.9	MOTEURS EXPL COMB INT, PIECE
7139	PISTON ENGINE PARTS NES			W 539	10.4	W 593	9.9	W 2438	11.2	PIECES POUR 713.2,3,8
714	ENGINES AND MOTORS NES	W 7	0.4	W 37	1.5	W 968	21.1	W 1054	2.7	MOTEURS NON ELECTRIQUES
7148	GAS TURBINES NES			W 9	0.1	W 549	12.8	W 1	0.1	TURBINES A GAZ
71488	OTHER GAS TURBINES NES			W 8	0.1	W 549	12.8		0.1	AUTRES TURBINES A GAZ
716	ROTATING ELECTRIC PLANT	W 3124	26.8	W 1610	18.1	W 1979	18.7	W 3006	12.7	APP ELECTR ROTATIFS,PIECES
7162	AC MTRS,GENRTRS,GEN SETS			W 1411	15.4	W 1583	14.4	W 2753	8.6	MOTEURS ELECTRIQUES
71622	AC GENERATORS			W 889	11.3	W 954	9.7	W 2144	3.8	GENER COURANT ALTERNATIF

4. Special Imports C.I.F. by Commodities according to the S.I.T.C. (Rev. 2) in million U.S. Dollars
Importations Spéciales C.A.F. par Produits d'après la C.T.C.I. (Rév. 2) en millions de Dollars E.U.

SITC CTCI	COMMODITY	1993 QUANTITY QUANTITE	1993 VALUE VALEUR	1994 QUANTITY QUANTITE	1994 VALUE VALEUR	1995 QUANTITY QUANTITE	1995 VALUE VALEUR	1996 QUANTITY QUANTITE	1996 VALUE VALEUR	PRODUIT
718	OTH POWER GENERATG MACHY	W 432	13.6	W 77	2.1	W 653	15.2	W 1102	2.4	AUTRES MOTEURS PARTIES
7188	WIND,WATER,ETC ENGINES	W 432	13.6	W 77	2.1	W 649	15.1	W 1102	2.4	MOT MACHINES MOTRICES NDA
71882	OTH HYDRAULIC ENGNS,MTRS	W 432	13.6	W 9	0.3	W 391	6.8	W 5	0.1	MACH MOTRICES HYDRAULQUES
72	MACHS FOR SPCL INDUSTRYS		147.3		105.1		99.9		101.4	MAC SPECIALES POUR INDUST
721	AGRIC MACHY,EXC TRACTORS	W 1599	9.8	W 1568	10.3	W 1554	9.5	W 10105	12.6	MACHINES AGRICOLES
722	TRACTORS NON–ROAD	W 7240	26.8	W 2005	10.2	W 1777	9.4	W 10652	10.5	TRACTEURS
723	CIVIL ENGNEERG EQUIP ETC	W 5402	26.5	W 3575	17.4	W 3149	17.8	W 12544	18.7	APPAREILS DE GENIE CIVIL
7234	CONST,MINING MACHNRY NES	W 5376	26.1	W 3405	16.5	W 2927	16.1	W 11258	14.4	MACH POUR LA CONST, MINES
72342	SLFPRP SHOVELS,EXCAVATRS			W 1965	9.9	W 1788	9.7	W 8588	8.7	PELLES MECANIQUES
724	TEXTILE,LEATHER MACHNRY	W 5428	29.4	W 962	8.6	W 859	9.3	W 770	7.3	MACH POUR INDUSTRIE TEXTILE
7247	TEXTILE MACHINERY NES	W 4388	18.5	W 395	3.1	W 310	2.5	W 225	2.3	MACH LAVAGE,TEINTURE TEX
726	PRINTG,BKBINDG MACHY,PTS	W 874	13.9	W 660	12.8	W 595	9.8	W 544	7.7	MACHINES POUR IMPRIMERIE
7264	PRINTING PRESSES	W 673	10.7	W 378	6.7	W 247	3.7	W 217	2.3	MACHINES A IMPRIMER
727	FOOD MACHRY NON–DOMESTIC	W 1138	10.3	W 1100	10.0	W 1347	12.7	W 10057	12.2	MACH INDUSTRIES ALIMENT
7272	OTH FOOD PROC MCHY,PARTS	W 915	8.3	W 1067	9.5	W 1225	11.4	W 9952	11.3	AUT MACH IND ALIMENTAIRE
728	OTH MACHY FOR SPCL INDUS	W 2827	25.3	W 3150	32.0	W 3150	28.0	W 7169	27.3	AUT MACH IND PARTICULIERES
7284	MACHY FOR SPCL INDUS NES	W 1099	14.9	W 1002	18.5	W 1191	22.0	W 2993	18.9	MACH SPEC IND PARTICUL.
72842	RUBBER,PLASTICS WRKG MCH			W 453	9.6	W 394	6.1	W 1490	8.3	MACH IND CAOUT MAT PLAST
72848	OTH MCHY WITH INDIV FNCT	W 1032	13.0	W 352	4.4	W 345	5.1	W 1246	4.8	AUTRES MACHINES NDA
73	METALWORKING MACHINERY		11.6		9.5		10.8		9.5	MACH TRAVAIL DES METAUX
736	METALWORKING MACH–TOOLS	W 1223	10.0	W 914	6.9	W 945	8.2	W 981	7.6	MACH–OUTILS TRAVAIL METAUX
74	GENRL INDUSTRL MACHY NES		147.6		122.4		132.1		130.9	MACH APP INDUSTRIE
741	HEATING,COOLING EQUIPMNT	W 5234	34.9	W 2949	25.0	W 3281	29.2	W 15082	25.8	MACH CHAUFFAGE,PIECES
7414	NONDOM REFRIG EQUIPT,PTS	W 3701	19.6	W 1464	10.1	W 1257	9.0	W 10923	11.7	MAT PRODUCTION DU FROID
7416	HEATING,COOLING EQU NES	W 686	7.0	W 606	7.9	W 1001	9.9	W 1467	7.3	APP CHANGEMENT TEMP
742	PUMPS FOR LIQUIDS ETC	W 772	12.0	W 780	10.7	W 1004	13.4	W 2699	13.1	POMPES MOTO–POMPES
7428	OTHER PUMPS FOR LIQUIDS			W 663	8.7	W 851	10.8	W 2561	9.9	AUTRES POMPES POUR LIQ
74288	PUMPS FR LIQUIDS NES ETC			W 596	7.5	W 812	10.1	W 2527	9.3	POMPES POUR LIQUIDES NDA
743	PUMPS NES,CENTRFUGES ETC	W 2768	22.6	W 2548	18.2	W 3072	19.3	W 21277	20.2	POMPES COMPRES,VENT ETC
7431	PUMPS FOR GASES ETC	W 1757	14.3	W 1195	6.3	W 1681	8.8	W 15351	8.6	POMPES AIR A VIDE,COMPRES
744	MECHANICAL HANDLING EQU	W 2462	13.1	W 3125	16.5	W 4023	16.5	W 11890	17.0	EQUIP MANUTENTION PIECES
745	NONELEC MACHY,TOOLS NES	W 1586	24.8	W 1309	20.3	W 1269	20.0	W 1190	17.9	AUT MACH NON ELEC,PIECES
7452	OTH NONELEC MCHS,PTS NES	W 1431	21.2	W 1172	17.3	W 1126	17.3	W 1071	15.5	AUT MACH NON ELEC,PIECES
74522	PACKAGNG,BOTTLNG,ETC MCH	W 578	12.3	W 372	7.6	W 237	6.6	W 219	5.1	MACH NETT BOUTEILLES,ETC
749	NONELEC MACH PTS,ACC NES	W 2611	40.5	W 2269	31.9	W 2449	33.9	W 8726	37.2	PIECES MACH NON ELEC NDA
7492	COCKS,VALVES ETC NES	W 1088	18.3	W 999	11.9	W 1048	13.2	W 7206	13.9	ART ROB,SIM POUR TUYAUX
7499	OTH NONELEC MCHY PTS NES	W 629	9.0	W 497	7.7	W 533	8.2	W 545	8.8	PIECES NON ELECT NDA
75	OFFICE MACHNES,ADP EQUIP		58.7		70.9		78.1		90.0	MACH BUREAU TRAIT AUTOM
751	OFFICE MACHINES	W 335	5.3	W 506	10.3	W 520	9.7	W 1417	9.5	MACH,APPAREILS DE BUREAU
752	AUTOMTIC DATA PROC EQUIP	W 832	38.4	W 945	41.8	W 1127	47.6	W 5736	61.6	MACH TRAIT INFORMATION
7522	DIGITAL COMPUTERS			W 258	16.6	W 475	19.9	W 330	24.1	MACH DIGITALES COMPLETES
7525	ADP PERIPHERAL UNITS			W 445	11.4	W 294	7.4	W 3083	7.3	UNITES PERIPHERIQUES
759	OFFICE,ADP MCH PTS,ACCES	W 373	15.1	W 500	19.0	W 479	20.8	W 373	19.0	PIECES DU 751 ET 752
7591	OFFICE MACHINE PARTS NES	W 373	15.1	W 50	1.7	W 59	1.8	W 52	1.8	PIECES DU 7511,7518
75911	TYPEWRTR PARTS,ACCES NES	W 373	15.1	W 1	0.1	W 3	0.1	W 1	0.1	PIECES DU 7511
7599	ACCTG,ETC,ADP MCH PTS,AC			W 450	17.3	W 420	19.1	W 321	17.3	PIECES DU 751 ET 752
76	TELECOMM,SOUND EQUIPMENT		93.7		94.4		82.1		88.2	EQUIPMENT DE TELECOM
761	TELEVISION RECEIVERS	W 1544	14.7	W 1931	19.3	W 1544	15.2	W 902	11.9	RECEPTEURS DE TELEVISION
7611	COLOUR TV RECEIVERS			W 1859	18.7	W 1472	14.8	W 857	11.5	RECEPTEURS COULEUR
762	RADIO BROADCAST RECEIVRS	W 1199	13.3	W 1250	12.9	W 1087	10.6	W 4544	10.0	RECEPTEURS RADIODIFFUSION
7628	OTHER RADIO RECEIVERS			W 988	9.8	W 905	8.5	W 4359	7.1	AUTRES RECEPT RADIO
764	TELECOM EQPT,PTS,ACC NES	W 1635	58.5	W 1517	54.4	W 1504	50.3	W 3403	62.2	EQUIP TELECOM,PIECES
7641	LINE TELEPHONE,ETC EQUIP	W 872	43.5	W 549	19.0	W 665	26.9	W 1529	31.7	APP TELEPHON PAR FIL
7643	TV,RADIO TRANSMITTRS ETC	W 18	0.2	W 117	11.7	W 46	3.8	W 1098	6.4	APP EMET TELE RADIO
7648	TELECOMM EQUIPMENT NES	W 271	9.4	W 21	1.8	W 22	2.7	W 36	3.0	APP TELECOM NDA
7649	PTS NES OF EQUIPMT OF 76	W 183	2.7	W 480	18.7	W 414	13.5	W 397	17.5	PIECES DE LA DIV 76
76491	PTS NES OF APPAR OF 7641			W 169	12.7	W 210	10.2	W 169	13.9	PIECES POUR 764.1
77	ELECTRIC MACHNRY NES ETC		99.5		170.6		147.1		142.2	MACH APP ELECT NDA
771	ELECTRIC POWER MACHY NES			W 3320	18.8	W 2367	13.4	W 13813	11.0	MACH PROD,TRANS ELECTR
7711	TRANSFORMERS,ELECTRICAL			W 2490	15.1	W 1683	8.8	W 9539	6.7	TRANSFO ELECTRIQUES
77111	LIQUID DIELEC TRANSFRMRS			W 1540	9.5	W 985	5.2	W 6136	3.5	TRANSFO DIELEC LIQUIDE
772	SWITCHGEAR ETC,PARTS NES	W 1803	22.8	W 1887	25.8	W 2228	31.9	W 3277	23.8	APP COUPURE,SECT ETC
7721	SWITCHGEAR ETC	W 1594	20.2	W 1882	25.4	W 2219	31.3	W 3268	23.3	APP COUPURE,SECTIONMNT
773	ELECTR DISTRIBUTNG EQUIP	W 2637	9.1	W 6924	21.2	W 3213	12.6	W 14634	12.1	EQUIPMT DISTRIBUTION ELECT
7731	INSULATED WIRE,CABLE ETC	W 2022	7.5	W 6474	20.1	W 2803	11.6	W 14167	10.7	FILS,CABLES ISOLES ELECT
775	HOUSEHOLD TYPE EQUIP NES	W 4768	28.2	W 10969	53.2	W 9964	44.4	W 53695	40.9	MACH,APP USAGE DOMESTQUE
7751	HOUSEHOLD LDRY EQUIP NES			W 3344	14.0	W 3824	12.7	W 16744	10.1	MACH A LAVER ET SECHOIRS
77511	DOMESTIC WASHING MACHNES			W 3235	13.5	W 3736	12.3	W 15738	9.7	MACH LAVER LINGE MOINS 6 KG
7752	DOM REFRIGERATRS,FREEZRS			W 3155	12.6	W 2176	10.0	W 9920	8.6	REFRIG,CONGEL MENAGER
77521	DOMESTIC REFRIGERATORS			W 2503	11.0	W 1914	8.6	W 9740	7.8	REFRIGERATEURS
7758	ELECTRO–THERMIC APPL NES	W 3170	19.3	W 2866	17.6	W 2540	15.1	W 15177	15.6	APP ELECTROTHERMIQ NDA
77586	ELECTROTHERM DOM APP NES	W 1747	11.8	W 2110	12.7	W 1808	10.1	W 12688	10.4	APP ELECTRO THERMIQUES
776	TRANSISTORS,VALVES,ETC	W 418	9.7	W 452	13.0	W 357	9.6	W 2180	12.7	LAMPES,TUBES,VALVES
778	ELECTRICAL MACHINERY NES	W 4288	29.1	W 4926	32.4	W 5131	31.1	W 32183	37.4	AUTRES MACH ELECT NDA
78	ROAD VEHICLES		273.8		274.2		209.9		294.2	VEHICULES ROUTIERS
781	PASS MOTOR VEH EXC BUSES	W 51043	221.7	W 30936	131.6	W 15686	82.5	W 20809	183.2	AUTO TRANSPORT PERSONNES
782	LORRIES,SPCL MTR VEH NES	W 491	2.5	W 13257	57.1	W 12049	53.2	W 19123	42.3	VEHICULES SPECIAUX,MARCH
7821	LORRIES,TRUCKS			W 12586	54.5	W 11504	50.7	W 18895	41.5	VEHICULES TRANSP MARCHAND
783	ROAD MOTOR VEHICLES NES			W 8470	32.5	W 6572	25.3	W 51042	22.9	VEHICULES ROUTIERS NDA
7831	BUSES			W 4116	20.6	W 3212	16.6	W 6774	14.8	VOITURES TRANSPORT COMMUN
7832	TRACTORS FOR TR–TRAILERS			W 4354	11.9	W 3361	8.8	W 44268	8.1	TRACTEURS ROUTIERS
784	MOTOR VEH PRTS,ACCES NES	W 5028	31.7	W 4647	30.3	W 4389	28.1	W 22557	26.8	PIECES 722,781,782,783
7849	OTHER MOTOR VEHCL PARTS	W 4086	28.4	W 3971	26.5	W 3830	25.4	W 21203	24.7	PIECES 722,781,782,783
785	CYCLES,ETC MOTRZD OR NOT	W 2979	13.1	W 3451	17.6	W 3127	16.3	W 12809	15.9	MOTOCYCLES SCOOTERS
79	OTHR TRANSPORT EQUIPMENT		23.8		5.2		18.5		5.6	AUTRE MATERIEL TRANSPORT
793	SHIPS AND BOATS ETC	W 7752	18.2	W 1529	3.5	W 2030	16.0	W 6345	2.8	NAVIRES BATEAUX,ETC
7932	SHIPS AND BOATS NES	W 1177	2.4	W 1518	3.5	W 2021	15.9	W 6322	2.7	NAVIRES ET BATEAUX
7938	TUGS,SPECIAL VESSELS ETC	W 6575	15.9	W 9	0.1	W 9	0.1	W 23	0.2	REMORQUEURS,BATEAUX SPEC
79382	SPECL PURPOSE VESSLS ETC	W 6571	15.8	W 4	0.1		0.1	W 16	0.1	BAT–PHARES,–POMPES,DRAGUES
8	MISC MANUFACTURED GOODS		319.7		300.3		315.8		341.0	ART MANUFACTURES DIVERS
812	*PLUMBG,HEATNG,LGHTNG EQ	W 3355	7.0	W 3507	9.7	W 3556	8.7	W 13769	8.5	APPAR SANITAIRES CHAUFFAGE
821	*FURNITURE,PARTS THEREOF	W 3806	8.8	W 6540	16.2	W 6489	15.7	W 38382	21.7	MEUBLES ET PIECES
8219	FURNITURE AND PARTS NES	W 2705	5.2	W 5087	10.3	W 5124	10.2	W 34093	12.4	AUTRES MEUBLES ET PIECES
84	CLOTHING AND ACCESSORIES		28.6		38.2		37.5		41.3	VETEMENTS
846	UNDER GARMENTS KNITTED	W 557	5.9	W 992	10.4	W 1243	11.3	W 909	11.8	SOUS VETS DE BONNETERIE
851	*FOOTWEAR	W 2274	14.8	W 3181	21.0	W 4399	24.3	W 14340	30.2	CHAUSSURES
85102	FOOTWEAR LEATHER	W 1582	11.1	W 2242	16.3	W 3084	17.6	W 10948	22.8	CHAUS SEMELLES EN CUIR
87	PRECISION INSTRUMNTS NES		40.3		41.4		46.9		52.4	INSTRUM,APPAR SCIENT NDA
872	MEDICAL INSTRUMENTS NES	W 548	14.7	W 673	14.3	W 857	17.7	W 2621	18.5	INSTR,APP MEDIC–CHIR NDA
87202	OTH MEDICAL INSTRUMENTS	W 501	13.9	W 587	13.2	W 780	16.4	W 2566	17.3	INSTRUM,APP MEDECINE
874	MEASURNG,CONTROLNG INSTR	W 783	19.9	W 759	21.5	W 1016	24.0	W 1744	25.6	INSTRUMENTS DE MESURE

Costa Rica

4. Special Imports C.I.F. by Commodities according to the S.I.T.C. (Rev. 2) in million U.S. Dollars
Importations Spéciales C.A.F. par Produits d'après la C.T.C.I. (Rév. 2) en millions de Dollars E.U.

SITC CTCI	COMMODITY	1993			1994			1995			1996			PRODUIT
		QUANTITY QUANTITE		VALUE VALEUR	QUANTITY QUANTITE		VALUE VALEUR	QUANTITY QUANTITE		VALUE VALEUR	QUANTITY QUANTITE		VALUE VALEUR	
88	PHOTO EQU,OPTICL GDS ETC			27.4			19.8			20.1			23.4	APP,FOURN PHOTO,OP,MONTR
882	PHOTO,CINEMA SUPPLIES	W	795	10.8	W	875	11.6	W	879	12.1	W	4565	12.7	PRODUITS PHOTO,CINEMA
89	MISC MANUFCTRD GOODS NES			191.1			151.1			160.0			160.9	ART MANUFACTURES DIVERS
892	PRINTED MATTER	W	2669	94.0	W	3790	33.5	W	4155	38.3	W	29067	29.2	IMPRIMES
8921	PRINTED BOOKS,GLOBES,ETC	W	1522	16.2	W	1979	22.0	W	1927	17.1	W	12895	17.4	LIVRES,BROCHURES,CARTES
89211	PRINTED BOOKS,PAMPHLETS	W	1484	16.1	W	1862	20.9	W	1797	16.4	W	12795	17.0	LIVRES,BROCHURES
8928	PRINTED MATTER NES	W	655	75.8	W	1058	7.8	W	1159	16.4	W	3721	7.1	IMPRIMES NDA
89283	UNISSUED BANKNOTES ETC	W	96	71.0	W	95	2.0	W	105	9.8	W	60	1.3	TIMBRES–POSTE FISCAUX
893	ARTICLES OF PLASTIC NES	W	8524	33.6			48.1			52.0			56.4	OUVRAGES EN MAT DIVIS 58
8931	PLSTC PACKG CONTNRS,LIDS	W	4432	14.9	W	5679	17.8	W	5603	18.8	W	42258	19.6	ART TRANSP EMBALLAGE ETC
8939	MISC PLASTIC ARTICLES	W	2957	14.4	W	7303	29.1	W	8662	31.9	W	39351	35.2	ART DIVERS EN MAT DIV 58
89399	OTHR PLASTC ARTICLES NES	W	2042	10.9	W	6304	27.7	W	7677	30.2	W	34829	33.7	AUT OUV MAT DIV 58
894	TOYS,SPORTING GOODS,ETC	W	5106	26.7	W	5883	29.7	W	5934	28.6	W	24790	25.9	VOITURES ENFANTS,JOUETS
8942	TOYS,INDOOR GAMES ETC	W	4095	22.4	W	4610	24.4	W	4726	23.6	W	18726	20.4	JOUETS,JEUX ETC
89423	TOYS NES	W	2804	14.9	W	2788	15.0	W	2957	15.3	W	12371	12.2	JOUETS,MODELES REDUITS
895	OFFICE SUPPLIES NES	W	921	8.2	W	874	8.7	W	1260	8.9	W	1119	10.8	ART PAPET NDA
898	MUSICAL INSTRUMENTS,PTS	W	748	15.0	W	760	14.8	W	878	16.9	W	1842	22.6	INSTRUMENTS DE MUSIQUE
8983	SOUND RECRDNG TAPE,DISCS	W	543	12.5	W	585	12.5	W	675	14.7	W	1663	20.4	SUPPORTS SON POUR 763
89832	RECORDED DISCS,TAPES ETC	W	268	11.1	W	241	8.3	W	316	11.5	W	1277	16.9	DISQUES,PHONO,BANDES
899	OTHER MANUFACTURED GOODS			8.3			13.0			11.8			12.4	AUT ART MANUF DIVERS NDA
9	GOODS NOT CLASSD BY KIND			19.1			25.2			23.5			120.2	ART TRANSACT NON CLASSES
931	*SPECIAL TRANSACTIONS	W	2098	5.3	W	6111	5.6	W	67	2.2	W	7387	104.3	TRANS.SPECIALES
971	*GOLD,NON MONETARY NES	K	33736	11.9	K	121622	19.1	K	16246	20.5	K	1277	14.9	OR NON MONETAIRE
97101	NONMON GLD UNWRT,SEMIMFD	K	33736	11.9	K	121130	19.1	K	16212	20.3	K	1266	14.9	OR,ALLIAGES D'OR BRUTS

5. Special Exports F.O.B. by Commodities according to the S.I.T.C. (Rev. 2) in million U.S. Dollars*
Exportations Spéciales F.O.B. par Produits d'après la C.T.C.I. (Rév. 2) en millions de Dollars E.U.

SITC CTCI	COMMODITY	1993 QUANTITY QUANTITE	1993 VALUE VALEUR	1994 QUANTITY QUANTITE	1994 VALUE VALEUR	1995 QUANTITY QUANTITE	1995 VALUE VALEUR	1996 QUANTITY QUANTITE	1996 VALUE VALEUR	PRODUIT
	ALL COMMODITIES		1941.8		2220.5		2701.8		2779.8	TOUS PRODUITS
0	FOOD AND LIVE ANIMALS		1255.7		1326.7		1673.4		1776.7	ALIMENTS,ANIMAUX VIVANTS
01	MEAT AND PREPARATIONS		68.3		55.8		49.2		46.3	VIANDES ET PREPARATIONS
011	MEAT FRESH,CHILLD,FROZEN	W 26975	65.4	W 23980	53.1	W 23582	46.7	W 28148	44.3	VIANDES FRAICHES,REF,CONGE
0111	BOVINE MEAT FRESH,FROZEN	W 25745	63.8	W 22604	51.2	W 21242	43.8	W 20307	42.5	VIANDES BOVIN FRAI,REF
01112	BOVINE MEAT BONELESS			W 22470	51.0	W 21158	43.7	W 20168	42.2	VIANDES BOVIN DESOSSEES
02	DAIRY PRODCTS,BIRDS'EGGS		13.1		7.4		9.0		17.2	PRODUITS LAITIERS,OEUFS
022	MILK AND CREAM	W 9165	12.1	W 8286	6.5	W 11400	7.8	W 134148	15.6	LAIT ET CREME
0224	MILK,CREAM PRESERVED ETC	W 3493	9.1	W 1442	2.9	W 1133	2.7	W 43586	10.3	LAIT,CREME CONS,CONC
03	FISH AND PREPARATIONS		135.0		104.8		125.9		215.8	POISSONS ET PREPARATIONS
034	FISH,FRESH,CHILLED,FROZN	W 6748	41.2	W 7288	35.5	W 18979	35.2	W 95534	60.0	POISSON FRAIS, REFRIG,CONG
0341	FISH FRSH,CHLLD,EX FILLT	W 6748	41.2	W 4441	20.8	W 15424	20.9	W 56630	29.4	POISSON FRAIS,REFRIGERE
0342	FISH FROZEN,EXCL FILLETS			W 136	0.8	W 794	1.2	W 10370	14.5	POISSONS CONGELES
0343	FISH FILLETS,FRESH,CHLLD			W 2534	12.8	W 2538	11.9	W 28163	14.1	FILETS FRAIS,REFRIGERES
035	FISH SALTED,DRIED,SMOKED	W 232	16.4	W 117	12.5	W 151	24.0	W 1143	46.6	POISSON SECHE,SALE,FUME
03503	FISH(EX COD)DRIED,SALTED	W 232	16.4	W 114	12.4	W 150	23.9	W 1142	46.5	POISSONS SECHES,SALES
036	SHELL FISH FRESH,FROZEN	W 3219	48.6	W 3765	31.0	W 3824	33.0	W 62865	63.7	CRUSTACES,MOLLUSQUES
037	FISH ETC PREPD,PRSVD NES	W 10563	28.8	W 9871	26.0	W 13073	33.9	W 155531	45.7	POIS,CRUST,MOL PREPARES
0371	FISH PREPARD,PRESRVD NES	W 10563	28.8	W 9871	26.0	W 13073	33.9	W 155530	45.7	CONSERVES DE POISSONS
04	CEREALS AND PREPARATIONS		12.8		13.9		21.6		27.2	CEREALES ET PRODUITS
048	CEREAL ETC PREPARATIONS	W 8791	11.5	W 9383	12.5	W 13891	18.0	W 42376	19.8	PREPTNS A BASE CEREALES
0484	BAKERY PRODUCTS	W 7090	9.7	W 7455	10.2	W 11457	15.2	W 14266	15.6	PRODUITS DE BOULANGERIE
04842	PASTRY, CAKES ETC	W 7081	9.7	W 7141	9.6	W 10975	14.3	W 10961	15.0	PATISSERIE ETC.
05	VEGETABLES AND FRUIT		750.4		757.9		942.9		946.8	LEGUMES ET FRUITS
054	VEG ETC FRSH,SMPLY PRSVD	W 95133	46.4	W 88871	52.4	W 133938	67.2	W 154581	72.7	LEGUMES FRAIS,CONG,SECS
0545	OTHER FRESH VEGETABLES	W 30016	11.9	W 26656	13.7	W 28679	17.6	W 53911	18.4	AUTRES LEGUMES FRAIS,REF
05459	FRESH VEGETABLES NES	W 30016	11.9	W 23249	12.5	W 26718	14.6	W 43491	14.6	LEGUMES FRAIS,REFRI NDA
0548	EDIBLE VEG NES FRESH,DRY	W 57821	29.9	W 60286	38.2	W 72901	46.3	W 81781	52.2	RACINES,TUBERCULES
05481	ROOTS,TUBERS FRESH,DRY	W 57783	29.9	W 60264	38.1	W 72832	46.2	W 81743	52.2	RACINES DE MANIOC ETC
056	VEGTBLES ETC PRSVD,PREPD	W 6365	13.4	W 2703	5.6	W 746	1.2	W 8429	2.9	CONSERVES DE LEGUMES
0565	VEGTBLES PRSVD,PREPD NES	W 6166	13.2	W 2398	5.3	W 408	0.9	W 5336	2.6	LEGUMES PREPARES CONSERVE
05651	VEGTBLS,FRUIT IN VINEGAR	W 5996	13.0	W 2325	5.2	W 357	0.8	W 5281	2.5	LEGUM CONSERV AU VINAIGRE
057	FRUIT,NUTS,FRESH,DRIED	W 2073558	656.5	W 2172690	650.4	W 2322018	800.9	W 2820383	778.1	FRUITS FRAIS OU SECS
0573	BANANA,PLANTAIN,FRSH,DRY			W 1891050	543.4	W 2038411	686.7	W 2123777	644.4	BANANES FRAICHES,SECHEES
0579	FRUIT FRESH OR DRIED NES	W 2072558	654.0	W 278493	103.2	W 280732	110.0	W 345342	126.5	FRUITS FRAIS,SECS NDA
05795	PINEAPPLES,FRESH,DRIED			W 160526	56.6	W 177604	58.7	W 178775	69.0	ANANAS FRAIS OU SECS
05797	OTH TROP FRUIT,FRESH,DRY	W 1991940	621.1	W 2072	2.4	W 2500	3.5	W 34313	5.2	AVOCATS,MANGUES,GOYAVES
05798	OTHER FRESH FRUIT	W 80282	31.9	W 115563	43.2	W 100331	47.0	W 130038	51.3	AUTRES FRUITS FRAIS
058	FRUIT PRESERVED,PREPARED	W 42553	34.4	W 57053	49.8	W 76468	73.7	W 263041	93.3	CONSERVES DE FRUITS
0583	FRUIT JAMS,JELLIES ETC	W 26644	18.1	W 34929	22.3	W 45259	28.2	W 55863	35.5	PATES DE FRUITS CONFITURES
0585	FRUIT OR VEGETABLE JUICE	W 11343	10.8	W 13169	14.6	W 18232	22.6	W 157327	26.6	JUS DE FRUITS
05851	ORANGE JUICE			W 4643	6.5	W 10005	12.9	W 83342	13.4	JUS D'ORANGE
05854	PINEAPPLE JUICE			W 6234	6.3	W 6158	7.7	W 58386	11.4	JUS D'ANANAS
05857	JUICE OF OTHER FRUIT,VEG	W 11343	10.8	W 627	0.8	W 625	0.8	W 4296	0.9	JUS AUTRES FRUITS,LEGUMES
0589	FRUIT PREPRD,PRESRVD,NES	W 1117	1.8	W 5189	8.9	W 9202	18.2	W 16067	25.5	FRUITS PREPARES CONSERV
05899	FRUIT,NUTS NES,PRESERVED	W 1117	1.8	W 4047	6.8	W 8066	16.0	W 9726	23.2	FRUITS PREP CONSERV NDA
06	SUGAR AND PREPS,HONEY		34.1		36.3		53.7		57.9	SUCRES ET PRODUITS
061	SUGAR AND HONEY	W 96279	28.0	W 96290	28.9	W 146046	46.2	W 1483441	48.1	SUCRES ET MIEL
0611	RAW BEET AND CANE SUGAR	W 96263	27.9	W 90010	28.4	W 145823	46.1	W 1127354	44.5	SUCRES BRUTS
062	SUGAR CANDY NON–CHOCLATE	W 3461	6.2	W 4302	7.5	W 3651	7.5	W 34002	9.9	SUCRERIES
07	COFFEE,TEA,COCOA,SPICES		220.5		327.1		443.3		426.6	CAFE,THE,CACAO,EPICES
071	COFFEE AND SUBSTITUTES	W 145350	204.0	W 132540	308.6	W 128728	418.7	W 156903	385.7	CAFE ET SUCCEDANES
0711	COFFEE GREEN,ROASTED,SUB	W 145350	204.0	W 132539	308.6	W 128728	418.7	W 156903	385.7	CAFE TORREFIE OU DECAFEINE
07111	COFFEE GREEN,HUSKS,SKINS			W 132417	307.7	W 128495	417.5	W 155642	384.1	CAFE NON TORREFIE
072	COCOA	W 2548	4.2	W 2403	5.4	W 4286	8.7	W 30530	7.8	CACAO
075	SPICES	W 4621	5.9	W 4297	10.1	W 6197	13.0	W 126687	29.2	EPICES
0752	SPICES,EX PEPPER,PIMENTO	W 2973	4.4	W 2617	8.6	W 4456	11.0	W 108571	27.0	AUTRES EPICES
07526	GINGER (EXCPT SWEETENED)			W 2366	3.3	W 4217	5.5	W 104394	18.5	GINGEMBRE
09	MISC EDIBLE PRODUCTS		18.3		19.6		24.9		34.7	PREP ALIMENTAIRES DIVERSES
098	EDIBLE PRODCTS,PREPS NES	W 6684	16.9	W 6000	19.5	W 7473	24.8	W 68332	34.3	PREP ALIMENTAIRES NDA
09809	MISC FOOD PREPRTIONS NES	W 2274	11.7	W 1423	14.3	W 2018	18.2	W 13300	25.3	PREP ALIMENTAIRES NDA
1	BEVERAGES AND TOBACCO		7.9		4.3		1.6		3.1	BOISSONS ET TABACS
2	CRUDE MATERLS,EXCL FUELS		101.0		125.9		146.4		201.3	MAT BRUTES NON COMESTIBLES
21	HIDES,SKINS,FURS UNDRSSD		8.2		0.1		0.4		0.4	CUIRS,PEAUX BRUTS
211	HIDES,SKINS,EXC FURS,RAW	W 3891	8.2	W 14	0.1	W 196	0.4	W 2332	0.4	CUIRS ET PEAUX
2111	BOVINE,EQUINE HIDES,RAW	W 1127	7.9	W 11	0.1	W 125	0.2	W 1199	0.2	PEAUX DE BOVINS
28	METALLIFEROUS ORES,SCRAP		3.1		7.3		7.1		8.2	MINERAIS METAL,DECHETS
29	CRUDE ANIMAL,VEG MAT NES		87.7		112.6		130.0		183.9	MATIERES BRUTES ANIM,VEGET
291	CRUDE ANIMAL MTRIALS NES	W 1183	3.1	W 1500	7.5	W 1631	7.4	W 16476	34.0	MATIERES BRUTES ANIMALES
2919	OTH ANIMAL MATERIALS NES	W 1162	2.8	W 1446	7.0	W 1525	6.9	W 16437	33.5	MAT ORIGINE ANIMALE NDA
29198	AMBERGRIS,CIVET,MUSK,ETC	W 813	0.6	W 812	1.3	W 1066	1.0	W 13129	17.9	AMBRE GRIS,CIVETTE,MUSC
29199	ANIMAL PRODUCTS,NES	W 148	1.7	W 373	4.3	W 134	3.9	W 177	8.5	PROD ORIGINE ANIMALE NDA
292	CRUDE VEG MATERIALS NES	W 48815	84.7		105.2	W 68964	122.6	W 312044	150.0	MAT BRUTES VEGETALES NDA
2924	VEG USED IN PHARMACY ETC	W 124	5.0	W 253	2.4	W 1739	4.1	W 1208	10.3	PLANTES MEDICINALES
2925	SEEDS,ETC FOR PLANTING	W 483	7.3	W 533	6.0	W 248	6.3	W 2302	5.9	SEMENCES NDA
2926	LIVE PLANTS,BULBS,ETC	W 28110	30.5	W 35035	36.1	W 36702	41.0	W 118436	48.0	BULBES,TUBERCULES
29269	LIVE PLANTS NES	W 28076	30.5	W 34961	36.0	W 36610	40.8	W 118354	47.8	AUTRES PLANTES VIVANTES
2927	CUT FLOWERS AND FOLIAGE	W 20076	42.0	W 25764	60.8	W 30202	71.3	W 190021	85.8	FLEURS,FEUILLAGES COUPES
29271	CUT FLOWERS	W 5051	11.8	W 7432	21.0	W 7617	22.4	W 8206	24.6	FLEURS ET BOUTONS
29272	CUT FOLIAGE	W 15024	30.2	W 18332	39.8	W 22585	49.0	W 181815	61.3	FEUILLAGES,RAMEAUX ETC
3	MINERAL FUELS ETC		7.7		12.9		21.0		24.2	COMBUSTIBLES MINERAUX LUB
33	PETROLEUM AND PRODUCTS		7.7		12.9		21.0		24.2	PETROLE ET DERIVES
334	PETROLEUM PRODUCTS,REFIN	W 33492	7.7	W 100130	12.9	W 163086	21.0	W 302027	24.1	PRODUITS RAFFINES
3344	FUEL OILS,NES	W 3744	0.4	W 81311	7.6	W 145482	15.7	W 142599	18.2	FUEL OILS
4	ANIMAL,VEGETABLE OIL,FAT		17.7		24.3		34.0		38.0	HUILES,GRAISSES ANIM,VEG
42	FIXED VEGETABLE OIL,FAT		17.6		21.8		29.1		35.0	HUILES VEGETALES FIXES
424	FIXED VEG OIL NONSOFT	W 37259	15.1	W 34704	16.7	W 40579	23.0	W 59351	31.1	AUTRES HUILES VEG FIXES
4242	PALM OIL	W 20	0.1	W 34703	16.7	W 40579	23.0	W 59350	31.1	HUILE DE PALME
4249	FIXED VEGETABLE OILS NES	W 37220	15.1						0.1	HUILES VEGET FIXES NDA
5	CHEMCLS,RELATED PROD NES		118.8		130.2		164.5		179.4	PRODUITS CHIMIQUES
51	ORGANIC CHEMICALS		14.1		12.0		19.4		20.2	PROD CHIMIQ ORGANIQUES
512	ALCOHOLS,PHENOLS ETC	W 37420	13.9	W 77521	11.6	W 77308	18.7	W 98788	19.1	PHENOLS,PHENOLS–ALCOOLS
5121	ACYCLIC ALCOHOLS,DERIVS	W 37420	13.9	W 77520	11.6	W 77308	18.7	W 98769	19.0	ALCOOLS ACYCLIQUES
51216	ETHYL ALC,DENATRD SPIRIT	W 37407	13.9	W 77489	11.6	W 77194	18.5	W 98508	18.7	ALCOOL ETHYLIQUE NON DENAT
53	DYES,TANNING,COLOUR PROD		6.7		8.0		11.9		14.6	PROD TEINTURE,COLORANTS
541	*MEDICINAL,PHARM PRODUCT	K 2690683	46.1	K 2904204	48.8	K 2990975	54.5	K 2844756	51.8	PROD MEDICINAUX PHARMACEUT
5417	MEDICAMENTS	K 2586956	44.9	K 2724717	47.9	K 2945305	52.5	K 2806350	50.5	MEDICAMENTS
54171	— CONTAINNG ANTIBIOTICS			K 1493255	16.2	K 1382289	19.6	K 247655	7.0	MED CONTN ANTIBIOTIQUES
54179	— CONTNG OTH SUBSTANCES			K 1167171	30.4	K 1500791	32.0	K 2403217	42.3	MED CONT AUT SUBSTANCES
55	PERFUME,CLEANING ETC PRD		10.9		13.9		18.1		21.8	PROD POUR PARFUM,TOILETTE
554	SOAP,CLEANSING ETC PREPS	W 4142	4.9	W 9216	7.4	W 8144	9.4	W 59678	15.5	SAVONS,PRODUITS DETERSIFS

5. Special Exports F.O.B. by Commodities according to the S.I.T.C. (Rev. 2) in million U.S. Dollars
Exportations Spéciales F.O.B. par Produits d'après la C.T.C.I. (Rév. 2) en millions de Dollars E.U.

SITC CTCI	COMMODITY	1993		1994		1995		1996		PRODUIT
		QUANTITY QUANTITE	VALUE VALEUR	QUANTITY QUANTITE	VALUE VALEUR	QUANTITY QUANTITE	VALUE VALEUR	QUANTITY QUANTITE	VALUE VALEUR	
562	*FERTILIZERS,MANUFACTURE	W 83001	15.2	W 139784	15.7	W 94542	22.1	W 1085878	30.7	ENGRAIS MANUFACTURES
5621	CHEM NITROGENOUS FERTLZR	W 82646	15.0	W 138338	15.1	W 91122	20.9	W 960123	27.3	ENGRAIS AZOTES
56211	AMMONIUM NITRATE	W 1253	0.3	W 927	0.2	W 939	0.3	W 509579	11.8	NITRATE D'AMMONIUM
56212	AMMONIUM SULPHONITRATE			W 135313	14.5	W 87093	19.9	W 418187	14.6	SULFONITRATE D'AMMONIUM
56219	CHEM NITROG FERTILZR NES	W 81393	14.7	W 1156	0.3	W 1586	0.4	W 173	0.1	ENGRAIS AZOTES NDA
58	PLASTIC MATERIALS ETC		15.1		18.1		18.6		18.3	MAT PLAST ARTIFICIELLES
583	POLYMERIZATION ETC PRODS	W 6572	10.7	W 8372	13.8	W 7054	14.3	W 49972	14.0	PROD POLYMERISATION
59	CHEMICAL MATERIALS NES		9.6		12.6		18.1		19.8	MAT PROD CHIMIQUES NDA
591	PESTICIDES,DISINFECTANTS	W 3359	7.1	W 4056	9.4	W 4507	14.4	W 20565	14.0	DESINF,INSECT,FONG,HERB
6	BASIC MANUFACTURES		191.6		226.7		267.8		283.6	ART MANUFACTURES
61	LEATHER,DRESSED FUR,ETC		8.3		22.5		22.4		26.6	CUIRS,PELLETERIES
611	LEATHER	W 497	5.3	W 14502	18.7	W 3269	18.3	W 27796	21.1	CUIRS,PEAUX PREPARES
6114	LEATHR BOVINE NES,EQUINE			W 12030	9.9	W 1713	9.3	W 10858	7.8	CUIRS DE BOVINS
6118	LEATHER SPECIALLY FINSHD	W 492	5.3	W 1525	8.1	W 1125	8.6	W 5668	11.4	CUIRS,PEAUX TANNES
61183	LEATHER PATENT,METALIZED	W 486	5.2	W 1510	8.1	W 1087	8.5	W 5613	11.1	CUIRS,PEAUX VERNIS
62	RUBBER MANUFACTURES NES		43.9		46.0		45.6		53.0	CAOUTCHOUC MANUFACTURE
625	RUBBER TYRES, TUBES ETC	W 5032	14.5	W 6133	17.2	W 5691	18.1	W 32843	22.5	PNEUS CAOUTCHOUC VULCANISE
6251	TYRES NEW FOR MOTOR CARS	W 4392	13.2	W 2513	7.7	W 2279	7.5	W 26362	9.6	PNEUS POUR VOITURES
6252	TYRES,NEW,BUS OR LORRY			W 2663	7.7	W 2601	8.6	W 3028	10.9	PNEUS POUR AUTOBUS,CAMIONS
628	RUBBER ARTICLES NES	W 6725	28.5	W 7376	27.9	W 7698	26.6	W 7952	29.5	OUVRAGES CAOUTCHOUC NDA
6289	OTH RUBBER ARTICLES NES	W 6724	28.5	W 7375	27.9	W 7694	26.6	W 7950	29.5	AUT OUVR CAOUTCHOUC NDA
62898	UNHARD RUBBER PRODS NES	W 6723	28.5	W 7374	27.9	W 7682	26.6	W 7942	29.5	OUV CAOUT VULC NON DURCI
63	WOOD,CORK MANUFACTRS NES		21.9		30.9		34.9		38.2	OUVRAGES LIEGE ET BOIS
634	VENEERS,PLYWOOD,ETC	W 17615	8.6	W 17554	8.7	W 20218	9.9	W 180904	9.1	PLACAGES,CONTRE–PLAQUES
635	WOOD MANUFACTURES NES	W 3541	13.3	W 6387	22.2	W 9373	25.0	W 89562	29.1	ART MANUF EN BOIS NDA
6353	BUILDERS WOODWRK,PREFABS	W 1531	6.7	W 2060	9.5	W 2885	8.4	W 11271	7.8	OUVRAGES DE MENUISERIE
6354	WOOD MFRS DOMESTIC ETC	W 154	3.1	W 117	5.8	W 109	6.5	W 360	8.9	ART MANUF USAGE DOMESTIQUE
63549	WOOD MFRS,DOMESTIC NES	W 139	3.1	W 113	5.8	W 105	6.5	W 356	8.9	OUVRAGES DE TABLETTERIE
6359	OTHER WOOD MANUFACTURES	W 1799	3.6	W 1037	5.8	W 1178	8.6	W 5496	9.4	OUVRAGES EN BOIS NDA
63599	OTHER WOOD ARTICLES NES	W 1728	3.4	W 968	5.6	W 1131	8.4	W 5479	9.3	AUTRES OUVRAGES EN BOIS NDA
64	PAPER,PAPERBOARD AND MFR		26.7		27.9		44.3		43.0	PAPIERS,CARTONS & OUVRAGES
642	PAPER,ETC,PRECUT,ARTS OF	W 13213	23.9	W 16977	25.6	W 24801	38.9	W 173914	37.8	PAP,CARTONS DECOUPES
6421	PAPER ETC CONTAINERS	W 3972	4.2	W 7080	5.7	W 13791	16.1	W 115222	13.7	BOITES,SACS EMBALLAGES
6424	PAPER ETC CT TO SIZE NES	W 4314	6.6	W 4553	7.3	W 4725	7.5	W 40550	8.0	PAP,CARTONS DECOUPES
6428	PAPER ETC ARTICLES NES	W 4384	12.1	W 4738	11.5	W 5641	13.5	W 13458	13.5	OUVRAGES EN PATE A PAPIER
64285	PAPER ETC DIAPERS ETC		0.1	W 2918	8.3	W 3420	9.5	W 3633	10.3	SERVIETTES HYGIENIQUES
64289	OTHER ARTICLES OF PAPER	W 4363	12.1	W 61	0.4	W 171	0.3	W 125	0.3	ARTICLES,OUVRAGES EN PAPIER
65	TEXTILE YARN,FABRICS,ETC		25.5		27.2		28.3		29.5	FILS,TISSUS,ARTICLES TEXTILE
651	TEXTILE YARN	W 5267	13.0	W 4942	12.8	W 5165	14.5	W 44716	13.1	FILS TEXTILES
6514	SYN FIB YRN,BULK,MONOFIL	W 4797	12.2	W 4609	11.6	W 4797	12.8	W 44586	12.6	FILS CONT 85% FIB TEXT SYNTH
65142	— NONTXT ETC CONT PAMID	W 1	0.1	W 4255	10.5	W 4531	12.1	W 44395	12.3	FILS NON TEX FI CON POLYAMID
65145	— NONTXT ETC CONT PESTR	W 4715	12.0							FILS NON TEX CONT POLYESTER
653	WOVN MAN–MADE FIB FABRIC	W 926	6.8	W 1036	7.9	W 801	6.6	W 2544	6.9	TISSUS FIBRES SYNTH,ARTIF
6534	DISC SYN BLEND FABRC NES	W 672	5.0	W 822	6.8	W 672	6.2	W 2528	6.9	TISSUS FIBRES SYNTH DISCONT
65341	DISC SYN FIB–COTTN FABRC			W 822	6.8	W 672	6.2	W 2517	6.8	TISSUS FIB SYNT DIS MEL COTO
66	NONMETAL MINERAL MFS NES		17.1		17.8		24.3		25.2	ART MIN NON METALLIQUES
665	GLASSWARE	W 27204	14.1	W 26397	14.0	W 36137	18.9	W 36222	19.6	OUVRAGES EN VERRE
6651	BOTTLES ETC OF GLASS	W 26164	13.4	W 25720	13.2	W 36093	18.8	W 36047	19.5	RECIPIENTS EN VERRE
66511	GLASS BOTTLES ETC NONVAC	W 26164	13.4	W 25720	13.2	W 36093	18.8	W 36047	19.5	BONBONNES,BOUTEILLES,ETC
67	IRON AND STEEL		13.6		17.2		18.8		15.9	FER ET ACIER
674	IRN,STL UNIV,PLATE,SHEET	W 7181	6.3	W 9474	7.6	W 9976	9.1	W 104650	9.9	LARGES PLATS,TOLES
6749	OTH IRN,STL PLATES,SHEET	W 1358	1.7	W 9470	7.6	W 9962	9.1	W 104577	9.8	AUTRES TOLES FER,ACIER
67491	— OF IRON OR SIMPLE STL	W 1358	1.7	W 9470	7.6	W 9962	9.1	W 104567	9.7	AUT TOLES AUTRES ACIER FIN
678	IRON,STL TUBES,PIPES,ETC	W 8739	6.1	W 11833	7.5	W 9375	6.5	W 50838	4.3	TUBES,TUYAUX EN FONTE,FER
6783	IRON,STL TUBES,PIPES NES	W 8551	5.9	W 11651	7.3	W 9216	6.2	W 50693	4.0	AUT TUBES,TUYAUX FER,ACIER
68	NON–FERROUS METALS		16.2		13.5		20.8		24.2	METAUX NON FERREUX
684	ALUMINIUM	W 7248	14.9	W 5855	13.5	W 7286	20.6	W 18090	23.8	ALUMINIUM
6842	ALUMINIUM,ALLOYS WORKED	W 6116	14.1	W 5855	13.5	W 7245	20.6	W 18090	23.8	ALUMINIUM,ALLIAGES OUVRE
68423	ALUMINIUM FOIL	W 5523	12.5	W 4847	10.6	W 5192	15.0	W 6208	18.7	FEUILLES,BANDES MINCES AL
69	METAL MANUFACTURES NES		19.0		24.1		28.8		28.3	ART MANUFACT EN METAL NDA
692	METAL TANKS,BOXES,ETC	W 2971	10.0	W 3068	11.1	W 4338	15.8	W 24895	13.6	RECIPIENTS METALLIQUES
6924	MTL TRANSPORT BOXES ETC	W 2907	9.8	W 3005	10.8	W 4329	15.7	W 24871	13.5	FUTS,TAMBOURS,BIDONS
69242	ALUMNM TRNSPRT BOXES ETC	W 390	4.1	W 687	5.7	W 1084	8.4	W 3539	7.1	FUTS,TAMBOURS,BIDONS ALU
7	MACHINES,TRANSPORT EQUIP		56.0		72.4		85.9		115.7	MACHINES MATERIEL TRANSPORT
72	MACHS FOR SPCL INDUSTRYS		2.1		4.4		5.8		13.9	MAC SPECIALES POUR INDUST
74	GENRL INDUSTRL MACHY NES		10.8		4.3		5.8		9.7	MACH APP INDUSTRIE
741	HEATING,COOLING EQUIPMNT	W 1749	6.7	W 214	0.8	W 156	0.8	W 263	0.9	MACH CHAUFFAGE,PIECES
77	ELECTRIC MACHNRY NES ETC		38.9		59.2		66.6		73.5	MACH APP ELECT NDA
772	SWITCHGEAR ETC,PARTS NES	W 1603	18.9	W 1701	21.9	W 1834	25.6	W 3637	22.4	APP COUPURE,SECT ETC
7721	SWITCHGEAR ETC	W 1453	18.4	W 1699	21.9	W 1793	24.1	W 3637	22.4	APP COUPURE,SECTIONMNT
773	ELECTR DISTRIBUTNG EQUIP	W 2016	6.3	W 3118	9.6	W 3567	12.6	W 5349	19.0	EQUIPMT DISTRIBUTION ELECT
7731	INSULATED WIRE,CABLE ETC	W 2015	6.2	W 3116	9.6	W 3567	12.6	W 5345	18.9	FILS,CABLES ISOLES ELECT
775	HOUSEHOLD TYPE EQUIP NES	W 137	0.6	W 2005	7.5	W 2394	9.1	W 17926	10.8	MACH,APP USAGE DOMESTQUE
7752	DOM REFRIGERATRS,FREEZRS			W 1927	7.2	W 2270	8.6	W 16665	9.7	REFRIG,CONGEL MENAGER
77521	DOMESTIC REFRIGERATORS			W 1926	7.2	W 2268	8.6	W 16663	9.7	REFRIGERATEURS
778	ELECTRICAL MACHINERY NES	W 3799	12.1	W 4698	20.1	W 5519	16.1	W 16163	17.1	AUTRES MACH ELECT NDA
7781	BATTERIES,ACCUMULATORS	W 3487	6.6	W 4303	7.4	W 5197	7.7	W 13071	8.5	PILES ET ACCUMULATEURS
77811	PRIMARY BATTERIES,CELLS	W 3403	6.6	W 3779	7.3	W 3948	7.6	W 3832	8.4	PILES ELECTRIQUES,PIECES
7783	AUTOMOTIVE ELECTR EQUIP	W 39	4.0	W 141	9.4	W 110	7.0	W 2010	7.7	EQUIP ELECT MOTEURS EXPL
77831	IGNITION,STARTING EQUIP	W 39	4.0	W 137	9.4	W 109	7.0	W 2003	7.7	APP ELEC ALLUM,DEMARRAGE
8	MISC MANUFACTURED GOODS		171.9		179.9		179.7		150.4	ART MANUFACTURES DIVERS
812	*PLUMBG,HEATNG,LGHTNG EQ	W 3341	5.5	W 3987	7.8	W 4136	9.7	W 36978	11.6	APPAR SANITAIRES CHAUFFAGE
821	*FURNITURE,PARTS THEREOF	W 2925	11.4	W 2693	9.9	W 3039	11.6	W 16275	12.3	MEUBLES ET PIECES
8219	FURNITURE AND PARTS NES	W 2485	10.4	W 2417	9.2	W 2603	10.4	W 15012	11.2	AUTRES MEUBLES ET PIECES
82199	OTHR FURN,FURN PARTS NES			W 1835	7.6	W 2005	8.0	W 14336	8.2	MEUBLES NDA AUTRES MATIERES
84	CLOTHING AND ACCESSORIES		75.3		70.7		50.4		31.9	VETEMENTS
842	MENS OUTERWEAR NOT KNIT	W 1667	19.8	W 1045	12.0	W 971	11.5	W 4426	11.2	VET DESSUS POUR HOMMES
8423	— TROUSERS,BREECHES ETC			W 646	7.3	W 816	9.5	W 4317	9.8	PANTALONS HOMMES MAT TEX
843	WOMENS OUTERWEAR NONKNIT	W 3322	42.8	W 2350	27.1	W 1026	12.5	W 11295	7.3	VET DESSUS FEMMES MAT TEX
8439	— OTHER OUTER GARMENTS			W 2330	26.9	W 962	11.8	W 11206	6.0	AUT VET DES FEM MAT TEXT
844	UNDER GARMENTS NOT KNIT	W 579	7.6	W 304	4.4	W 646	10.0	W 220	4.0	VETEMENT DESSOUS MAT TEX
8441	— MENS SHIRTS			W 286	4.0	W 635	9.8	W 211	3.9	CHEMISES HOMMES MAT TEXT
8442	— MENS,OTHR THAN SHIRTS	W 516	6.4	W 16	0.4	W 11	0.2	W 9	0.2	SOUS–VET HOMMES MAT TEXT
845	OUTERWEAR KNIT NONELASTC	W 150	2.0	W 840	14.1	W 404	5.0	W 94	1.9	VET DESSOUS,ACCES BONNET
8459	— OTHER,CLTHG ACCESRYS			W 616	11.8	W 248	4.1	W 63	1.4	AUT VET DESSUS DE BONNE
846	UNDER GARMENTS KNITTED	W 66	1.8	W 747	10.7	W 508	8.3	W 2116	4.8	SOUS VETS DE BONNETERIE
8462	— OF COTTON NON ELASTIC			W 741	10.7	W 488	8.0	W 2104	4.6	SOUS–VET BONNET COTON
84629	—— OTHER			W 545	8.1	W 486	7.9	W 2100	4.5	AUT SOUS–VET BONNET COTON
851	*FOOTWEAR	W 682	5.7	W 690	8.0	W 673	8.2	W 4259	8.9	CHAUSSURES
85102	FOOTWEAR LEATHER	W 314	4.4	W 456	7.0	W 522	7.4	W 4177	8.7	CHAUS SEMELLES EN CUIR
88	PHOTO EQU,OPTICL GDS ETC		10.1		1.9		3.2		2.8	APP,FOURN PHOTO,OP,MONTR

Costa Rica

5. Special Exports F.O.B. by Commodities according to the S.I.T.C. (Rev. 2) in million U.S. Dollars
Exportations Spéciales F.O.B. par Produits d'après la C.T.C.I. (Rév. 2) en millions de Dollars E.U.

SITC CTCI	COMMODITY	1993		1994		1995		1996		PRODUIT
		QUANTITY QUANTITE	VALUE VALEUR	QUANTITY QUANTITE	VALUE VALEUR	QUANTITY QUANTITE	VALUE VALEUR	QUANTITY QUANTITE	VALUE VALEUR	
885	WATCHES AND CLOCKS		10.0		1.7		3.0		2.4	HORLOGERIE
8851	WATCHES,MOVEMENTS,CASES		10.0		1.7		3.0		2.4	MONTRES,MOUVEMENTS,BOITES
88511	WATCHES		10.0		0.4					MONTRES POCHE,BRACELET
89	MISC MANUFCTRD GOODS NES		59.1		80.3		95.8		81.6	ART MANUFACTURES DIVERS
892	PRINTED MATTER	W 2969	7.3	W 4132	6.6	W 2920	13.0	W 21017	9.3	IMPRIMES
8921	PRINTED BOOKS,GLOBES,ETC	W 2758	5.9	W 2775	5.3	W 2463	7.5	W 20566	6.9	LIVRES,BROCHURES,CARTES
893	ARTICLES OF PLASTIC NES	W 11212	24.5		27.9		33.1		34.1	OUVRAGES EN MAT DIVIS 58
8931	PLSTC PACKG CONTNRS,LIDS	W 5925	13.2	W 5771	13.0	W 6553	17.1	W 47461	16.7	ART TRANSP EMBALLAGE ETC
8939	MISC PLASTIC ARTICLES	W 4792	10.2	W 6245	14.8	W 6299	15.9	W 50478	17.3	ART DIVERS EN MAT DIV 58
89391	PVC FLOORING TILES ETC	W 2737	6.0	W 1	0.1	W 1	0.1			CHLORURE POLYVINYL PLAQ
89399	OTHR PLASTC ARTICLES NES	W 2054	4.3	W 6242	14.7	W 6296	15.8	W 50478	17.3	AUT OUV MAT DIV 58
897	GOLD,SILVER WARE,JEWELRY		18.8		39.8		42.2		25.4	BIJOUTERIE,ORFEVRERIE
8973	PREC JEWLRY,GLD–SILVWARE		17.8		39.1		42.1		24.8	BIJOUX OR,ARGENT ORFEVRE
89731	PRECIOUS METAL JEWELLERY		17.8		39.1		42.1		24.8	ART BIJOUTERIE,JOAILLER
898	MUSICAL INSTRUMENTS,PTS	W 41	5.9	W 53	2.1	W 57	1.7	W 46	1.7	INSTRUMENTS DE MUSIQUE
8983	SOUND RECRDNG TAPE,DISCS	W 40	5.9	W 38	2.0	W 37	1.5	W 37	1.6	SUPPORTS SON POUR 763
89832	RECORDED DISCS,TAPES ETC	W 40	5.9	W 35	1.7	W 36	1.4	W 36	1.5	DISQUES,PHONO,BANDES
9	GOODS NOT CLASSD BY KIND		13.9		117.5		127.9		7.9	ART TRANSACT NON CLASSES
931	*SPECIAL TRANSACTIONS	W 4288	13.8	W 36558	117.2	W 43669	127.5	W 29173	7.5	TRANS.SPECIALES

Côte d'Ivoire

1. HISTORICAL SERIES, 1962–1997 SPECIAL TRADE, IMPORTS C.I.F., EXPORTS F.O.B.
SERIES HISTORIQUES, 1962–1997 COMMERCE SPECIAL, IMPORTATIONS C.A.F., EXPORTATIONS F.O.B

YEAR ANNEE	VALUE IN MILLION C.F.A. FRANCS / VALEUR EN MILLION C.F.A. FRANCS — MERCHANDISE –MARCHANDISE		GOLD –OR		CONVERSION FACTORS U.S. CENTS PER C.F.A. FRANC FACTEURS DE CONVERSION CENTS E.U. PAR C.F.A. FRANC		INDEX NUMBERS –INDICES — QUANTUM		UNIT VALUE VALEUR UNITAIRE	
	IMPORTS	EXPORTS	IMPORTS	EXPORTS	IMPORTS	EXPORTS	IMPORTS	EXPORTS	IMPORTS	EXPORTS
1962	38515.00	47693.00			0.4051	0.4051				
1963	41900.00	56858.00			0.4051	0.4051				
1964	58834.00	74501.00			0.4051	0.4051				
1965	58301.00	68418.00			0.4051	0.4051				
1966	63533.00	76657.00			0.4051	0.4051				
1967	64872.00	80262.00			0.4051	0.4051				
1968	75676.00	104890.00			0.4051	0.4051				
1969	86235.00	118223.00			0.3872	0.3833				
1970	107704.00	130190.00			0.3601	0.3601				
1971	110838.00	126558.00			0.3601	0.3601				
1972	114317.00	139541.00			0.3970	0.3963				
1973	157524.00	190860.00			0.4510	0.4494				
1974	232286.00	291770.00			0.4162	0.4162				
1975	241393.00	254572.00			0.4668	0.4641				
1976	311608.00	392501.00			0.4164	0.4157				
1977	429566.00	529212.00			0.4083	0.4076				
1978	522502.00	524382.00			0.4449	0.4429				
1979	528850.00	534847.00			0.4714	0.4703				
1980	636960.00	663920.00			0.4733	0.4733				
1981	653320.00	689301.00			0.3648	0.3678				
1982	718593.00	747452.00			0.2909	0.2990				
1983	704248.00	796774.00			0.2568	0.2594				
1984	658570.00	1184339.00			0.2294	0.2278				
1985	772979.00	1318060.00			0.2254	0.2230				
1986	709040.10	1160440.00			0.2900	0.2891				
1987	673900.00	929139.90			0.3327	0.3347				
1988	619920.10	826469.80			0.3388	0.3378				
1989	673449.90	895600.10			0.3245	0.3273				
1990	571099.90	836430.00			0.3673	0.3673				
1991	593370.10	757760.00			0.3570	0.3570				
1992	613169.90	751699.90			0.3777	0.3777				
1993	570469.80	750000.10			0.3541	0.3541				
1994	1064600.00	1522500.00			0.1810	0.1810				
1995	1463000.00	1819300.00			0.2002	0.2007				
1996	1524400.00	2236199.00			0.1955	0.1955				
1997	1703099.00	2375800.00			0.1713	0.1713				

2. IMPORTS BY BROAD ECONOMIC CATEGORY AND EXPORTS BY INDUSTRIAL ORIGIN. (PERCENTAGE OF TOTAL VALUE)
IMPORTATIONS PAR CATEGORIES ECONOMIQUES ET EXPORTATIONS PAR BRANCHE D'ACTIVITE.(EN POURCENTAGE DE LA VALEUR TOTALE)

IMPORTS – IMPORTATIONS

	1990	1991	1992	1993	1994	1995	1996
TOTAL IMPORTS–IMPORTATIONS TOTALES							100.
1 FOOD BEV–ALIMENTATION BOISSONS							16.6
11 PRIMARY–PRODUITS DE BASE							8.4
111 FOR INDUSTRY–POUR L'INDUSTRIE							2.4
112 FOR HOUSEHOLDS–POUR LES MENAGES							5.9
12 PROCESSED–PRODUITS ELABORES							8.2
121 FOR INDUSTRY–POUR L'INDUSTRIE							1.2
122 FOR HOUSEHOLDS–POUR LES MENAGES							7.0
2 IND SUPPLIES–APPROV INDUSTRIELS							28.6
21 PRIMARY–PRODUITS DE BASE							2.9
22 PROCESSED–PRODUITS ELABORES							25.7
3 FUELS–COMBUSTIBLES							23.0
31 PRIMARY–PRODUITS DE BASE							16.9
32 PROCESSED–PRODUITS ELABORES							6.1
321 MOTOR SPIRIT–ESSENCE							6.1
322 OTHER–AUTRES							0.0
4 MACHINERY–EQUIPEMENT							12.1
41 CAPITAL EQUIPMENT–MACHINES							10.5
42 PARTS–PIECES ACCESSOIRES							1.6
5 TRANSPORT–TRANSPORT							10.2
51 PASSENGER CARS–AUTOMOBILES							3.9
52 OTHER–AUTRES							3.2
521 INDUSTRIAL–INDUSTRIELS							3.0
522 NON INDUSTRIAL–NON INDUSTRIEL							0.2
53 PARTS–PIECES ACCESSOIRES							3.0
6 CONSUM GOODS–BIENS CONSOMMATION							8.8
61 DURABLE–DURABLES							1.1
62 SEMI DURABLE–SEMI DURABLES							2.0
63 NON DURABLE–NON DURABLES							5.7
7 GOODS NES–BIENS NDA							0.7

EXPORTS – EXPORTATIONS

	1990	1991	1992	1993	1994	1995	1996
TOTAL EXPORTS–EXPORTATIONS TOTALES							
1 AGRICULTURE							
2 MINING QUARRY–INDUS EXTRACTIVES							
3 MANUFACTURING–IND MANUFACTUR							
31 FOOD BEV TOBACCO–ALIM BOISS TAB							
32 TEXTILES–INDUSTRIES TEXTILES							
33 WOOD & PRODUCTS–BOIS & PRODUITS							
34 PAPER & PRODUCTS–PAPIER & PRODT							
35 CHEMICALS–INDUSTRIES CHIMIQUES							
36 NON METAL MIN–MIN NON METAL							
37 BASIC METAL–IND METAL BASE							
38 METAL MANUF–MANUF METAL							
39 OTH MANUF IND–AUTRES MANUF							

Côte d'Ivoire

3. TRADE BY PRINCIPAL COUNTRIES OF ORIGIN AND DESTINATION (VALUE IN MILLION U.S. DOLLARS)
ECHANGES SELON LES PRINCIPAUX PAYS D'ORIGINE ET DE DESTINATION (VALEUR EN MILLIONS DE DOLLARS EU)

COUNTRIES–PAYS	SPECIAL IMPORTS C.I.F. IMPORTATIONS SPECIALES C.A.F					COUNTRIES–PAYS	SPECIAL EXPORTS F.O.B. EXPORTATIONS SPECIALES F.O.B.				
	1992	1993	1994	1995	1996		1992	1993	1994	1995	1996
World					2812.0	Monde					
Africa					655.1	Afrique					
Americas					268.9	Amériques					
– Northern America					182.8	– Amérique du Nord					
– LAIA					80.4	– ALAI					
– CACM					3.9	– MCAC					
– Caribbean					1.9	– Caraïbes					
– Rest of America						– Autre Amérique					
Asia excl fmr USSR					382.3	Asie anc. URSS exclus					
– Middle East					19.8	– Moyen–Orient					
Asia former USSR						Asie ancienne URSS					
Europe excl fmr USSR					1457.3	Europe anc. URSS exclus					
– European Union					1403.4	– Union Européenne					
– Eastern Europe					23.1	– Europe de l'Est					
– Rest of Europe					30.8	– Autre de l'Europe					
Europe former USSR					40.7	Europe ancienne URSS					
Oceania					6.3	Océanie					
Other					1.4	Autre					
France, Monaco					704.9						
Nigeria/Nigéria					532.8						
USA/Etats–Unis d'Amer					166.4						
Germany/Allemagne					161.6						
Italy/Italie					131.2						
Japan/Japon					115.7						
Netherlands/Pays–Bas					96.5						
Belgium–Luxembourg					83.0						
United Kingdom					81.9						
Spain/Espagne					79.7						
China/Chine					50.7						
India/Inde					42.8						
Russian Federation					40.7						
Korea, Republic of					39.1						
Viet Nam					39.0						
Venezuela					35.0						
Brazil/Brésil					29.7						
Switzerland,Liechtenst.					26.5						
Senegal/Sénégal					22.5						
Thailand/Thaïlande					20.7						
Mauritania/Mauritanie					20.1						
Ireland/Irlande					18.4						
So. African Customs Un					16.8						
Canada					16.4						
Sweden/Suède					14.8						
Other Asia n.e.s.					14.7						
Cameroon/Cameroun					14.4						
Argentina/Argentine					13.2						
Finland/Finlande					11.4						
Morocco/Maroc					10.8						
Poland/Pologne					9.5						
Malaysia/Malaisie					9.3						
Bangladesh					8.4						
Pakistan					7.7						
Tunisia/Tunisie					7.6						
Greece/Grèce					7.4						
Guinea/Guinée					6.9						
Turkey/Turquie					6.5						
Romania/Roumanie					6.3						
United Arab Emirates					5.7						

(VALUE AS PERCENTAGE OF WORLD TOTAL)(VALEURS EN POURCENTAGE DU TOTAL MONDIAL)

	1987	1988	1989	1990	1991	1992	1993	1994	1995	1996		1987	1988	1989	1990	1991	1992	1993	1994	1995	1996
Africa	15.0	13.2	19.2							23.3	Afrique	16.0	16.1	13.4							
Americas	6.2	6.0	6.4							9.6	Amériques	10.6	7.5	6.7							
– Northern America	4.9	4.5	5.3							6.5	– Amérique du Nord	10.6	7.5	6.7							
– LAIA	1.3	1.5	1.1							2.9	– ALAI										
– CACM										0.1	– MCAC										
– Caribbean										0.1	– Caraïbes										
– Rest of America											– Autre Amérique	0.0									
Asia excl fmr USSR	11.3	7.3	3.9							13.6	Asie anc. URSS exclus	1.6	1.0	2.0							
– Middle East	0.0									0.7	– Moyen–Orient										
Asia former USSR											Asie ancienne URSS										
Europe excl fmr USSR	59.7	61.6	55.6							51.8	Europe anc. URSS exclus	63.6	57.1	62.4							
– European Union	57.3	59.5	53.9							49.9	– Union Européenne	63.1	57.0	62.2							
– Eastern Europe	0.7	0.6	0.6							0.8	– Europe de l'Est	0.2	0.1	0.0							
– Rest of Europe	1.7	1.5	1.1							1.1	– Autre de l'Europe	0.3	0.0	0.1							
Europe former USSR	0.3	0.5	0.4							1.4	Europe ancienne URSS	5.1	4.8	5.0							
Oceania	0.0	0.1	0.1							0.2	Océanie	0.0	0.1	0.2							
Other	1.2	2.4	2.6							0.0	Autre		3.7	1.2							
France, Monaco	31.7	31.2	28.7							25.1											
Nigeria/Nigéria	10.9	9.5	16.0							18.9											
USA/Etats–Unis d'Amer	4.4	3.9	4.3							5.9											
Germany/Allemagne										5.7											
Italy/Italie	5.4	5.0	5.3							4.7											
Japan/Japon	5.5	4.5	2.7							4.1											
Netherlands/Pays–Bas	5.1	5.6	4.7							3.4											
Belgium–Luxembourg	2.6	2.7	2.5							3.0											
United Kingdom	2.3	3.5	2.4							2.9											
Spain/Espagne	3.5	4.7	3.8							2.8											

4. Special Imports C.I.F. by Commodities according to the S.I.T.C. (Rev. 2) in million U.S. Dollars
Importations Spéciales C.A.F. par Produits d'après la C.T.C.I. (Rév. 2) en millions de Dollars E.U.

SITC CTCI	COMMODITY	1993 QUANTITY QUANTITE	1993 VALUE VALEUR	1994 QUANTITY QUANTITE	1994 VALUE VALEUR	1995 QUANTITY QUANTITE	1995 VALUE VALEUR	1996 QUANTITY QUANTITE	1996 VALUE VALEUR	PRODUIT
	ALL COMMODITIES								2812.0	TOUS PRODUITS
0	FOOD AND LIVE ANIMALS								447.7	ALIMENTS,ANIMAUX VIVANTS
02	DAIRY PRODCTS,BIRDS'EGGS								54.2	PRODUITS LAITIERS,OEUFS
022	MILK AND CREAM							W 30031	50.1	LAIT ET CREME
0224	MILK,CREAM PRESERVED ETC							W 26683	47.3	LAIT,CREME CONS,CONC
02243	MILK DRY,OVER 1.5% FAT							W 10479	25.5	LAIT POUDRE SUP 1.5%
02249	MILK(EX DRY) PRSVD,SWEET							W 15447	20.1	LAIT CONS,CONC SUCRE
03	FISH AND PREPARATIONS								145.9	POISSONS ET PREPARATIONS
034	FISH,FRESH,CHILLED,FROZN							W 209230	141.3	POISSON FRAIS, REFRIG,CONG
0342	FISH FROZEN,EXCL FILLETS							W 209192	141.1	POISSONS CONGELES
04	CEREALS AND PREPARATIONS								184.7	CEREALES ET PRODUITS
041	WHEAT ETC UNMILLED							W 201275	52.9	FROMENT,EPEAUTRE
0412	OTHER WHEAT ETC UNMILLED							W 192280	50.5	AUTRE FROMENT NON MOULU
042	RICE							W 300395	101.2	RIZ
0421	RICE IN HUSK OR HUSKED							W 34270	13.9	RIZ SANS AUTRE PREPARATION
04212	RICE HUSKED							W 34270	13.9	RIZ CARGO
0422	RICE SEMI-MILLED,MILLED							W 266125	87.4	RIZ POLI,GLACE INCL BRISURES
04221	RICE MILLED UNBROKEN							W 259108	85.1	RIZ POLI,GLACE EXCL BRISURES
048	CEREAL ETC PREPARATIONS							W 25763	21.1	PREPTNS A BASE CEREALES
0482	MALT INCLUDING FLOUR							W 17013	12.9	MALT MEME TORREFIE
05	VEGETABLES AND FRUIT								22.3	LEGUMES ET FRUITS
054	VEG ETC FRSH,SMPLY PRSVD							W 31995	15.2	LEGUMES FRAIS,CONG,SECS
06	SUGAR AND PREPS,HONEY								10.8	SUCRES ET PRODUITS
061	SUGAR AND HONEY							W 21164	10.2	SUCRES ET MIEL
09	MISC EDIBLE PRODUCTS								13.9	PREP ALIMENTAIRES DIVERSES
098	EDIBLE PRODCTS,PREPS NES							W 5668	13.8	PREP ALIMENTAIRES NDA
1	BEVERAGES AND TOBACCO								33.6	BOISSONS ET TABACS
11	BEVERAGES								15.4	BOISSONS
112	ALCOHOLIC BEVERAGES							W 21805	14.0	BOISSONS ALCOOLIQUES
1121	WINE OF FRESH GRAPES ETC							W 21329	12.4	VINS DE RAISINS FRAIS
11212	WINE OF FRESH GRAPES							W 21309	12.4	VINS DE MOUTS DE RAISINS
12	TOBACCO AND MANUFACTURES								18.3	TABACS BRUTS FABRIQUES
121	TOBACCO UNMNFCTRD,REFUSE							W 2462	18.0	TABACS BRUTS,DECHETS
1212	TOBACCO STRIPPED OR PART							W 1874	17.1	TABACS PART ECOTES
2	CRUDE MATERLS,EXCL FUELS								66.4	MAT BRUTES NON COMESTIBLES
26	TEXTILE FIBRES AND WASTE								19.3	FIBRES TEXTILES
264	JUTE,OTH TEX BAST FIBRES							W 15522	8.7	JUTE
27	CRUDE FERTLZR,MINRLS NES								15.8	ENGRAIS MINERAUX BRUTS
278	OTHER CRUDE MINERALS							W 282254	12.5	AUTRES MINERAUX BRUTS
29	CRUDE ANIMAL,VEG MAT NES								27.8	MATIERES BRUTES ANIM,VEGET
291	CRUDE ANIMAL MTRIALS NES							W 24712	24.8	MATIERES BRUTES ANIMALES
2919	OTH ANIMAL MATERIALS NES							W 24698	24.8	MAT ORIGINE ANIMALE NDA
29194	FISH WASTE							W 24695	24.7	DECHETS DE POISSONS
3	MINERAL FUELS ETC								650.4	COMBUSTIBLES MINERAUX LUB
33	PETROLEUM AND PRODUCTS								649.3	PETROLE ET DERIVES
333	CRUDE PETROLEUM							W 3025749	474.1	HUILES BRUTES DE PETROLE
334	PETROLEUM PRODUCTS,REFIN							W 1069899	172.1	PRODUITS RAFFINES
3341	GASOLINE,OTH LIGHT OILS							W 1069736	171.6	ESSENCES POUR MOTEURS
33411	MOTOR,AVIATION SPIRIT							W 1069736	171.6	ESSENCES MOTEURS D'AVIONS
4	ANIMAL,VEGETABLE OIL,FAT								9.5	HUILES,GRAISSES ANIM,VEG
5	CHEMCLS,RELATED PROD NES								444.2	PRODUITS CHIMIQUES
51	ORGANIC CHEMICALS								55.7	PROD CHIMIQ ORGANIQUES
513	CARBOXYLIC ACIDS ETC							W 10917	12.2	ACIDES CARBOXYLIQUES
5138	POLYACIDS AND DERIVATIVS							W 10078	10.0	ACIDES POLYCARBOXYLIQUES
514	NITROGEN-FNCTN COMPOUNDS							W 5687	20.1	COMPOSES FONCT AZOTEES
5148	OTH NITROGN-FNCTN CMPNDS							W 1618	12.3	AUTRES COMPOSES AZOTES
515	ORG-INORG COMPOUNDS ETC							W 889	10.0	COMPOSES ORGANO-MINERAUX
52	INORGANIC CHEMICALS								24.5	PROD CHIM INORGANIQUES
522	INORG ELEMNTS,OXIDES,ETC							W 31592	11.9	ELEMENTS INORGANIQUES
5225	INORGANIC BASES ETC NES							W 24504	8.6	AUTRES BASES OXYDES METAL
523	OTHR INORG CHEMICALS ETC							W 23533	12.6	AUT PRODUITS CHIMIQUES INORG
53	DYES,TANNING,COLOUR PROD								19.8	PROD TEINTURE,COLORANTS
531	SYNT DYE,NAT INDGO,LAKES							W 570	8.9	MAT COLOR ORGAN,LAQUES
533	PIGMENTS,PAINTS,ETC							W 3663	10.8	PIGMENTS,PEINTURES,VERNIS
541	*MEDICINAL,PHARM PRODUCT							K 5537782	119.9	PROD MEDICINAUX PHARMACEUT
5417	MEDICAMENTS							K 5230829	109.9	MEDICAMENTS
54171	— CONTAINNG ANTIBIOTICS							K 593780	13.1	MED CONTN ANTIBIOTIQUES
54179	— CONTNG OTH SUBSTANCES							K 4527560	94.5	MED CONT AUT SUBSTANCES
55	PERFUME,CLEANING ETC PRD								27.3	PROD POUR PARFUM,TOILETTE
551	ESSENTL OILS,PERFUME,ETC							W 1934	19.5	HUILES ESSENTIELLES
5514	MIXED PERFUME SUBSTANCES							W 1923	19.4	MELANGES SUBSTAN ODORIFER
562	*FERTILIZERS,MANUFACTURE							W 202373	43.2	ENGRAIS MANUFACTURES
5621	CHEM NITROGENOUS FERTLZR							W 93501	18.7	ENGRAIS AZOTES
56216	UREA							W 61040	14.3	UREE
5629	FERTILIZERS NES							W 59920	16.0	ENGRAIS NDA
56292	NITROG-PHOS FERTILZR NES							W 49852	13.0	ENGRAIS NDA CONT N P
58	PLASTIC MATERIALS ETC								102.8	MAT PLAST ARTIFICIELLES
583	POLYMERIZATION ETC PRODS							W 93577	93.6	PROD POLYMERISATION
5831	POLYETHYLENE							W 35001	33.8	POLYETHYLENE
58311	— IN PRIMARY FORMS							W 34440	32.6	POLYETHYLENE PRIMAIRES
5832	POLYPROPYLENE							W 21838	22.6	POLYPROPYLENE
58321	— IN PRIMARY FORMS							W 21165	19.7	POLYPROPYLENE PRIMAIRES
5834	POLYVINYL CHLORIDE							W 24951	21.0	CHLORURE DE POLYVINYLE
58341	— IN PRIMARY FORMS							W 23979	18.7	SOUS FORMES PRIMAIRES
5839	OTH POLYMRZTION ETC PROD							W 8655	11.7	AUT PROD POLYMER COPOLYM
59	CHEMICAL MATERIALS NES								51.1	MAT PROD CHIMIQUES NDA
591	PESTICIDES,DISINFECTANTS							W 5325	20.1	DESINF,INSECT,FONG,HERB
5911	INSECTICIDES,FOR RETAIL							W 2061	9.0	INSECTICIDES VENTE DET
5913	HERBICIDES,FOR RETAIL							W 2964	8.8	HERBICIDES VENTE AU DET
598	MISCEL CHEM PRODUCTS NES							W 11148	27.3	PROD DIV INDUST CHIM NDA
5982	ANTI-KNOCK PREPARTNS ETC							W 2890	11.3	PREPARAT ANTIDETONANTES
5989	CHEM PRODUCTS,PREPS NES							W 7336	13.9	PROD PREP CHIMIQUES NDA
59899	OTH CHEM PRODS,PREPS,NES							W 4683	9.5	AUT PRODUITS CHIMIQUES NDA
6	BASIC MANUFACTURES								426.8	ART MANUFACTURES
62	RUBBER MANUFACTURES NES								41.1	CAOUTCHOUC MANUFACTURE
625	RUBBER TYRES, TUBES ETC							W 8271	31.2	PNEUS CAOUTCHOUC VULCANISE
6251	TYRES NEW FOR MOTOR CARS							W 2129	9.3	PNEUS POUR VOITURES
6252	TYRES,NEW,BUS OR LORRY							W 3735	14.9	PNEUS POUR AUTOBUS,CAMIONS
64	PAPER,PAPERBOARD AND MFR								79.9	PAPIERS,CARTONS & OUVRAGES
641	PAPER AND PAPERBOARD							W 77065	65.5	PAPIERS ET CARTONS
6412	PRINTG,WRITING PAPER NES							W 7715	9.4	PAPIERS POUR L'IMPRESSION

4. Special Imports C.I.F. by Commodities according to the S.I.T.C. (Rev. 2) in million U.S. Dollars
Importations Spéciales C.A.F. par Produits d'après la C.T.C.I. (Rév. 2) en millions de Dollars E.U.

SITC CTCI	COMMODITY	1993 QUANTITY QUANTITE	1993 VALUE VALEUR	1994 QUANTITY QUANTITE	1994 VALUE VALEUR	1995 QUANTITY QUANTITE	1995 VALUE VALEUR	1996 QUANTITY QUANTITE	1996 VALUE VALEUR	PRODUIT
6413	KRAFT PAPER,PAPERBOARD							W 27580	19.5	PAPIER ET CARTON KRAFT
64131	KRAFT LINER IN BULK							W 19299	11.0	PAP KRAFT POUR COUVERTURES
6415	PAPER,PAPERBRD,BULK,NES							W 32062	23.6	PAPIERS,CARTONS ROULEAUX
64151	SEMI-CHEM FLUTING PAPER							W 18184	10.0	PAPIER FLUTING
64159	OTHER PAPER ETC,BULK,NES							W 13839	13.5	AUT PAPIER ROULEAUX FEUILLES
642	PAPER,ETC,PRECUT,ARTS OF							W 4319	14.5	PAP,CARTONS DECOUPES
65	TEXTILE YARN,FABRICS,ETC								46.4	FILS,TISSUS,ARTICLES TEXTILE
651	TEXTILE YARN							W 2420	10.2	FILS TEXTILES
652	COTTON FABRICS,WOVEN							W 2416	12.2	TISSUS DE COTON
6522	WOVEN COTTON BLEACHD,ETC							W 1679	9.2	TISSUS COTON BLANCHIS ETC
65224	BLCHED COTTON FABRIC NES							W 1547	9.0	AUT TIS PLUS 85% COT BLANCHI
653	WOVN MAN-MADE FIB FABRIC							W 5130	10.0	TISSUS FIBRES SYNTH,ARTIF
66	NONMETAL MINERAL MFS NES								88.3	ART MIN NON METALLIQUES
661	LIME,CEMENT,BLDG PRODS							W 1082556	55.3	CHAUX,CIMENTS MAT CONSTR
6612	CEMENT							W 1070307	51.1	CIMENTS HYDRAULIQUES
665	GLASSWARE							W 14573	15.7	OUVRAGES EN VERRE
6651	BOTTLES ETC OF GLASS							W 12900	13.4	RECIPIENTS EN VERRE
66511	GLASS BOTTLES ETC NONVAC							W 12899	13.4	BONBONNES,BOUTEILLES,ETC
67	IRON AND STEEL								82.7	FER ET ACIER
673	IRON,STEEL SHAPES ETC							W 62744	21.2	BARRES,PROFIL FER,ACIER
6731	IRON,STEEL WIRE ROD							W 51145	15.6	FIL MACHINE FER,ACIER
67311	IRON,SIMPLE STL WIRE ROD							W 51084	15.6	FIL MACH AUT ACIER FIN
674	IRN,STL UNIV,PLATE,SHEET							W 59822	48.5	LARGES PLATS,TOLES
6746	IRN,STL THIN PLATE,ROLLD							W 20547	10.8	TOLES LAM MOINS 3MM
67461	— OF IRON OR SIMPLE STL							W 20291	10.2	TOL NON AC FIN MOINS 3 MM
6747	TINNED PLATES,SHEETS							W 9009	9.5	TOLES ETAMEES EN ACIER
6749	OTH IRN,STL PLATES,SHEET							W 23060	23.2	AUTRES TOLES FER,ACIER
67491	— OF IRON OR SIMPLE STL							W 22969	23.2	AUT TOLES AUTRES ACIER FIN
68	NON-FERROUS METALS								21.6	METAUX NON FERREUX
684	ALUMINIUM							W 3979	16.9	ALUMINIUM
6842	ALUMINIUM,ALLOYS WORKED							W 3979	16.9	ALUMINIUM,ALLIAGES OUVRE
68423	ALUMINIUM FOIL							W 1165	8.8	FEUILLES,BANDES MINCES AL
69	METAL MANUFACTURES NES								64.6	ART MANUFACT EN METAL NDA
692	METAL TANKS,BOXES,ETC							W 3326	9.6	RECIPIENTS METALLIQUES
6924	MTL TRANSPORT BOXES ETC							W 3266	8.9	FUTS,TAMBOURS,BIDONS
695	TOOLS							W 2287	13.0	OUTILS A MAIN
699	BASE METAL MFRS NES							W 6841	19.5	ART MANUFACTURES MET NDA
7	MACHINES,TRANSPORT EQUIP								588.2	MACHINES MATERIEL TRANSPORT
71	POWER GENERATING EQUIPMT								18.3	MACHINES GENERATRICES
713	INTRNL COMBUS PSTN ENGIN							W 609	10.3	MOTEURS EXPL COMB INT, PIECE
72	MACHS FOR SPCL INDUSTRYS								83.6	MAC SPECIALES POUR INDUST
723	CIVIL ENGNEERG EQUIP ETC							W 2918	14.5	APPAREILS DE GENIE CIVIL
7234	CONST,MINING MACHNRY NES							W 2432	12.3	MACH POUR LA CONST, MINES
724	TEXTILE,LEATHER MACHNRY							W 1185	13.4	MACH POUR INDUSTRIE TEXTILE
728	OTH MACHY FOR SPCL INDUS							W 3722	27.1	AUT MACH IND PARTICULIERES
7284	MACHY FOR SPCL INDUS NES							W 2283	19.9	MACH SPEC IND PARTICUL.
72842	RUBBER,PLASTICS WRKG MCH							W 1803	14.4	MACH IND CAOUT MAT PLAST
74	GENRL INDUSTRL MACHY NES								102.2	MACH APP INDUSTRIE
741	HEATING,COOLING EQUIPMNT							W 2017	18.8	MACH CHAUFFAGE,PIECES
742	PUMPS FOR LIQUIDS ETC							W 435	11.1	POMPES MOTO-POMPES
743	PUMPS NES,CENTRFUGES ETC							W 1227	12.1	POMPES COMPRES,VENT ETC
744	MECHANICAL HANDLING EQU							W 3063	19.6	EQUIP MANUTENTION PIECES
7441	FORK LIFT TRCKS,ETC,PTS							W 1582	8.9	CHARIOTS POUR USINES ETC
74411	FORK LIFT TRUCKS ETC							W 1581	8.9	CHARIOTS POUR LES GARES
745	NONELEC MACHY,TOOLS NES							W 880	12.7	AUT MACH NON ELEC,PIECES
7452	OTH NONELEC MCHS,PTS NES							W 849	11.8	AUT MACH NON ELEC,PIECES
749	NONELEC MACH PTS,ACC NES							W 1623	28.2	PIECES MACH NON ELEC NDA
75	OFFICE MACHNES,ADP EQUIP								32.9	MACH BUREAU TRAIT AUTOM
752	AUTOMTIC DATA PROC EQUIP							W 315	21.7	MACH TRAIT INFORMATION
7522	DIGITAL COMPUTERS							W 154	11.7	MACH DIGITALES COMPLETES
76	TELECOMM,SOUND EQUIPMENT								35.2	EQUIPMENT DE TELECOM
764	TELECOM EQPT,PTS,ACC NES							W 454	24.4	EQUIP TELECOM,PIECES
7641	LINE TELEPHONE,ETC EQUIP							W 140	9.3	APP TELEPHON PAR FIL
77	ELECTRIC MACHNRY NES ETC								73.9	MACH APP ELECT NDA
772	SWITCHGEAR ETC,PARTS NES							W 885	19.4	APP COUPURE,SECT ETC
7721	SWITCHGEAR ETC							W 879	18.5	APP COUPURE,SECTIONMNT
773	ELECTR DISTRIBUTNG EQUIP							W 2847	13.2	EQUIPMT DISTRIBUTION ELECT
7731	INSULATED WIRE,CABLE ETC							W 2772	12.6	FILS,CABLES ISOLES ELECT
775	HOUSEHOLD TYPE EQUIP NES							W 3127	10.1	MACH,APP USAGE DOMESTQUE
778	ELECTRICAL MACHINERY NES							W 7053	22.2	AUTRES MACH ELECT NDA
7781	BATTERIES,ACCUMULATORS							W 6130	10.6	PILES ET ACCUMULATEURS
78	ROAD VEHICLES								232.3	VEHICULES ROUTIERS
781	PASS MOTOR VEH EXC BUSES							W 32590	110.9	AUTO TRANSPORT PERSONNES
782	LORRIES,SPCL MTR VEH NES							W 12859	56.9	VEHICULES SPECIAUX,MARCH
7821	LORRIES,TRUCKS							W 12533	55.0	VEHICULES TRANSP MARCHAND
783	ROAD MOTOR VEHICLES NES							W 6495	19.8	VEHICULES ROUTIERS NDA
7832	TRACTORS FOR TR-TRAILERS							W 4302	11.4	TRACTEURS ROUTIERS
784	MOTOR VEH PRTS,ACCES NES							W 2218	28.7	PIECES 722,781,782,783
7849	OTHER MOTOR VEHCL PARTS							W 1773	24.8	PIECES 722,781,782,783
785	CYCLES,ETC MOTRZD OR NOT							W 3402	10.6	MOTOCYCLES SCOOTERS
8	MISC MANUFACTURED GOODS								126.1	ART MANUFACTURES DIVERS
87	PRECISION INSTRUMNTS NES								29.5	INSTRUM,APPAR SCIENT NDA
872	MEDICAL INSTRUMENTS NES							W 888	8.8	INSTR,APP MEDIC-CHIR NDA
874	MEASURNG,CONTROLNG INSTR							W 333	14.1	INSTRUMENTS DE MESURE
88	PHOTO EQU,OPTICL GDS ETC								8.7	APP,FOURN PHOTO,OP,MONTR
89	MISC MANUFCTRD GOODS NES								62.3	ART MANUFACTURES DIVERS
892	PRINTED MATTER							W 2546	28.4	IMPRIMES
8921	PRINTED BOOKS,GLOBES,ETC							W 1128	13.5	LIVRES,BROCHURES,CARTES
89211	PRINTED BOOKS,PAMPHLETS							W 1115	13.3	LIVRES,BROCHURES
893	ARTICLES OF PLASTIC NES								15.9	OUVRAGES EN MAT DIVIS 58
8939	MISC PLASTIC ARTICLES							W 2422	9.3	ART DIVERS EN MAT DIV 58
9	GOODS NOT CLASSD BY KIND								19.6	ART TRANSACT NON CLASSES
931	*SPECIAL TRANSACTIONS							W 2438	19.6	TRANS.SPECIALES

Côte d'Ivoire

5. Special Exports F.O.B. by Commodities according to the S.I.T.C. (Rev. 2) in million U.S. Dollars
Exportations Spéciales F.O.B. par Produits d'après la C.T.C.I. (Rév. 2) en millions de Dollars E.U.

SITC CTCI	COMMODITY	1993		1994		1995		1996		PRODUIT
		QUANTITY QUANTITE	VALUE VALEUR	QUANTITY QUANTITE	VALUE VALEUR	QUANTITY QUANTITE	VALUE VALEUR	QUANTITY QUANTITE	VALUE VALEUR	
	ALL COMMODITIES									TOUS PRODUITS

1. HISTORICAL SERIES, 1992–1997 GENERAL TRADE, IMPORTS C.I.F., EXPORTS F.O.B.
SERIES HISTORIQUES, 1992–1997 COMMERCE GENERAL, IMPORTATIONS C.A.F., EXPORTATIONS F.O.B

YEAR ANNEE	VALUE IN MILLION U.S. DOLLARS VALEUR EN MILLION U.S. DOLLARS MERCHANDISE –MARCHANDISE		GOLD –OR		CONVERSION FACTORS FACTEURS DE CONVERSION CENTS E.U. PAR		INDEX NUMBERS –INDICES QUANTUM		UNIT VALUE VALEUR UNITAIRE	
	IMPORTS	EXPORTS	IMPORTS	EXPORTS	IMPORTS	EXPORTS	IMPORTS	EXPORTS	IMPORTS	EXPORTS
1992	4460.70	4597.50								
1993	4666.40	3903.80								
1994	5229.30	4260.40								
1995	7509.90	4632.70								
1996	7787.90	4511.80								
1997	9122.50	4340.90								

2. IMPORTS BY BROAD ECONOMIC CATEGORY AND EXPORTS BY INDUSTRIAL ORIGIN. (PERCENTAGE OF TOTAL VALUE)
IMPORTATIONS PAR CATEGORIES ECONOMIQUES ET EXPORTATIONS PAR BRANCHE D'ACTIVITE.(EN POURCENTAGE DE LA VALEUR TOTALE)

IMPORTS – IMPORTATIONS

	1991	1992	1993	1994	1995	1996	1997
TOTAL IMPORTS–IMPORTATIONS TOTALES		100.	100.	100.	100.	100.	100.
1 FOOD BEV–ALIMENTATION BOISSONS		11.2	7.7	10.0	10.9	10.3	9.5
11 PRIMARY–PRODUITS DE BASE		5.6	3.5	4.6	5.3	4.8	5.1
111 FOR INDUSTRY–POUR L'INDUSTRIE		2.5	0.9	1.4	1.7	1.6	2.4
112 FOR HOUSEHOLDS–POUR LES MENAGES		3.1	2.6	3.2	3.6	3.2	2.8
12 PROCESSED–PRODUITS ELABORES		5.6	4.3	5.5	5.6	5.5	4.4
121 FOR INDUSTRY–POUR L'INDUSTRIE		0.9	0.7	0.8	0.9	0.9	0.5
122 FOR HOUSEHOLDS–POUR LES MENAGES		4.7	3.6	4.7	4.7	4.6	3.8
2 IND SUPPLIES–APPROV INDUSTRIELS		39.4	33.8	35.8	28.2	29.1	27.7
21 PRIMARY–PRODUITS DE BASE		3.9	3.0	2.2	1.8	1.7	1.7
22 PROCESSED–PRODUITS ELABORES		35.5	30.8	33.6	26.4	27.4	26.0
3 FUELS–COMBUSTIBLES		9.6	9.8	11.2	11.5	11.0	9.2
31 PRIMARY–PRODUITS DE BASE		8.7	9.1	9.6	9.6	9.7	7.9
32 PROCESSED–PRODUITS ELABORES		0.9	0.8	1.6	1.9	1.3	1.4
321 MOTOR SPIRIT–ESSENCE		0.1	0.0	0.1	0.1	0.1	0.3
322 OTHER–AUTRES		0.8	0.7	1.5	1.9	1.2	1.1
4 MACHINERY–EQUIPEMENT		12.6	16.3	16.8	18.0	18.4	19.4
41 CAPITAL EQUIPMENT–MACHINES		10.5	13.5	14.7	15.8	16.4	17.3
42 PARTS–PIECES ACCESSOIRES		2.1	2.8	2.1	2.2	2.0	2.1
5 TRANSPORT–TRANSPORT		4.7	9.0	9.6	8.9	9.3	14.4
51 PASSENGER CARS–AUTOMOBILES		1.5	3.1	2.7	2.0	2.4	6.5
52 OTHER–AUTRES		1.2	3.8	4.7	4.3	4.5	5.7
521 INDUSTRIAL–INDUSTRIELS		1.1	3.7	4.6	4.1	4.3	5.5
522 NON INDUSTRIAL–NON INDUSTRIEL		0.1	0.1	0.2	0.2	0.1	0.2
53 PARTS–PIECES ACCESSOIRES		1.9	2.1	2.1	2.5	2.4	2.2
6 CONSUM GOODS–BIENS CONSOMMATION		16.0	16.3	16.6	16.7	17.2	16.2
61 DURABLE–DURABLES		2.1	2.2	3.1	3.8	3.8	4.1
62 SEMI DURABLE–SEMI DURABLES		11.0	11.7	10.7	9.6	9.9	8.9
63 NON DURABLE–NON DURABLES		2.9	2.4	2.9	3.4	3.5	3.1
7 GOODS NES–BIENS NDA		6.5	7.0	0.0	5.8	4.8	3.6

EXPORTS – EXPORTATIONS

	1991	1992	1993	1994	1995	1996	1997
TOTAL EXPORTS–EXPORTATIONS TOTALES		100.	100.	100.	100.	100.	100.
1 AGRICULTURE		4.5	3.4	3.0	3.2	3.0	3.2
2 MINING QUARRY–INDUS EXTRACTIVES		2.4	2.0	1.4	1.1	1.3	2.4
3 MANUFACTURING–IND MANUFACTUR		93.2	94.6	95.6	95.7	95.7	94.4
31 FOOD BEV TOBACCO–ALIM BOISS TAB		9.3	9.5	9.1	8.7	9.7	10.6
32 TEXTILES–INDUSTRIES TEXTILES		18.6	25.1	24.9	22.6	22.0	22.7
33 WOOD & PRODUCTS–BOIS & PRODUITS		4.3	5.3	4.5	4.4	4.4	5.5
34 PAPER & PRODUCTS–PAPIER & PRODT		2.5	2.8	3.3	2.9	1.9	2.1
35 CHEMICALS–INDUSTRIES CHIMIQUES		22.6	23.7	22.4	26.1	23.1	22.1
36 NON METAL MIN–MIN NON METAL		2.9	2.8	3.1	2.9	3.1	3.2
37 BASIC METAL–IND METAL BASE		7.0	2.9	2.9	2.9	2.7	3.0
38 METAL MANUF–MANUF METAL		24.0	20.9	24.0	23.7	27.6	23.9
39 OTH MANUF IND–AUTRES MANUF		1.9	1.7	1.5	1.4	1.4	1.3

3. TRADE BY PRINCIPAL COUNTRIES OF ORIGIN AND DESTINATION (VALUE IN MILLION U.S. DOLLARS)
ECHANGES SELON LES PRINCIPAUX PAYS D'ORIGINE ET DE DESTINATION (VALEUR EN MILLIONS DE DOLLARS EU)

COUNTRIES–PAYS	GENERAL IMPORTS C.I.F. IMPORTATIONS GENERALES C.A.F				
	1993	1994	1995	1996	1997
World	4666.4	5229.1	7509.2	7787.8	9122.3
Africa	109.3	110.6	265.9	291.9	200.5
Americas	204.0	273.9	359.2	372.8	501.3
– Northern America	146.2	192.8	214.3	229.9	321.6
– LAIA	52.3	67.2	121.9	129.1	164.9
– CACM	2.5	6.2	7.7	6.3	8.2
– Caribbean	0.6	7.1	12.6	6.6	6.1
– Rest of America	2.3	0.5	2.7	0.9	0.6
Asia excl fmr USSR	361.7	493.4	439.6	606.1	652.3
– Middle East	248.0	324.8	162.9	299.2	229.0
Asia former USSR	1.0	4.4	2.6	6.5	8.9
Europe excl fmr USSR	3723.6	4090.5	6205.8	6242.1	7255.3
– European Union	2630.3	3096.1	4663.3	4625.4	5430.8
– Eastern Europe	235.2	306.8	464.9	567.5	633.2
– Rest of Europe	858.1	687.6	1077.6	1049.1	1191.2
Europe former USSR	260.1	249.7	221.4	246.5	489.5
Oceania	6.2	6.7	14.7	21.9	14.4
Other	0.5		0.0	0.1	0.0
Germany/Allemagne	990.7	1109.8	1509.0	1601.8	1840.8
Italy/Italie	881.7	994.6	1366.0	1421.6	1724.7
Slovenia/Slovénie	712.5	540.9	804.8	769.2	755.5
Austria/Autriche	310.6	352.7	574.1	597.4	708.9
Russian Federation	226.9	183.0	157.0	214.1	456.6
United Kingdom	89.7	179.1	455.3	225.4	188.9
USA/Etats–Unis d'Amer	123.8	173.2	202.3	212.8	272.9
France, Monaco	97.6	117.6	188.6	199.0	292.9
Iran (Islamic Rep of)	236.5	292.4	89.6	165.2	11.6
Hungary/Hongrie	78.2	100.1	158.0	192.6	238.5
Czech Republic	93.5	91.9	147.1	207.1	207.7
Switzerland,Liechtenst.	81.1	103.7	174.6	151.7	222.0
Netherlands/Pays–Bas	91.7	114.6	174.2	176.5	170.2
Libyan Arab Jamahiriya	32.6	67.7	189.7	242.5	133.4
Sweden/Suède	60.2	81.4	147.5	117.1	147.4
Japan/Japon	42.1	54.1	79.8	104.5	139.4
Belgium–Luxembourg	47.8	55.6	88.1	105.2	100.0
Slovakia/Slovaquie	24.4	53.1	77.9	83.7	81.0
Syrian Arab Republic	0.2	11.8	32.7	102.4	113.9
Spain/Espagne	20.1	30.7	50.9	62.1	94.0
Brazil/Brésil	23.9	29.1	56.7	64.7	78.9
Bosnia and Herzegovina	13.9	4.1	8.7	63.5	136.8
Poland/Pologne	25.2	37.6	45.3	49.7	59.1
China/Chine	16.7	30.0	44.3	54.7	67.4
Denmark/Danemark	16.1	31.0	51.2	48.0	62.1
TFYR Macedonia	45.6	27.3	36.4	33.6	42.0
Korea, Republic of	8.4	13.9	35.5	32.4	69.2
Other Asia n.e.s.	11.4	21.5	36.3	32.6	47.2
Ukraine	11.8	50.5	40.6	11.3	16.3
Turkey/Turquie	8.6	15.8	27.9	27.1	31.1
Ireland/Irlande	7.9	13.2	16.6	28.1	42.2
Canada	10.4	19.4	11.7	16.8	48.5
Norway,Svalbard and JM	4.6	8.0	44.1	26.6	20.8
Finland/Finlande	8.4	6.9	24.5	26.3	31.7
India/Inde	8.2	14.6	23.5	21.9	24.4
Ecuador/Equateur	7.3	14.2	22.5	21.8	23.8
Belarus/Bélarus	19.6	13.2	21.7	19.5	13.9
Romania/Roumanie	3.7	10.6	12.6	19.1	29.3
Morocco/Maroc	15.7	11.5	15.5	13.8	18.8
Iraq	0.0	0.0	6.1	0.0	64.0

COUNTRIES–PAYS	GENERAL EXPORTS F.O.B. EXPORTATIONS GENERALES F.O.B.				
	1993	1994	1995	1996	1997
Monde	3903.8	4260.4	4632.7	4511.7	4340.9
Afrique	77.1	94.3	151.0	311.2	163.4
Amériques	122.5	161.2	144.6	127.7	132.9
– Amérique du Nord	88.9	100.0	96.1	100.7	105.9
– ALAI	10.4	20.7	13.6	18.8	14.2
– MCAC	1.2	0.7	0.9	0.6	0.1
– Caraïbes	2.2	4.1	31.9	5.4	10.1
– Autre Amérique	19.8	35.7	2.1	2.1	2.5
Asie anc. URSS exclus	110.9	67.4	119.1	142.9	71.2
– Moyen–Orient	48.6	33.2	64.5	84.0	31.9
Asie ancienne URSS	5.5	7.2	10.1	5.7	5.1
Europe anc. URSS exclus	3413.4	3756.6	4026.2	3753.5	3769.3
– Union Européenne	2245.1	2530.7	2671.9	2302.6	2221.0
– Europe de l'Est	133.7	177.8	190.2	190.1	194.3
– Autre de l'Europe	1034.7	1048.1	1164.1	1260.8	1354.0
Europe ancienne URSS	167.8	168.6	175.4	166.1	193.4
Océanie	5.8	5.2	6.2	4.7	5.6
Autre	0.8				0.0
Italy/Italie	828.4	910.2	1098.2	949.7	904.9
Germany/Allemagne	895.1	941.5	996.9	839.5	774.6
Slovenia/Slovénie	711.6	555.9	607.8	611.4	529.6
Bosnia and Herzegovina	188.9	338.5	383.2	548.5	648.7
Austria/Autriche	130.1	149.4	200.3	198.1	222.9
Russian Federation	144.5	151.0	152.1	130.5	163.8
Liberia/Libéria	39.5	54.8	104.9	265.7	123.9
France, Monaco	133.9	112.0	112.1	84.5	79.8
USA/Etats–Unis d'Amer	83.9	94.6	88.7	92.4	97.3
Netherlands/Pays–Bas	92.2	94.1	80.2	68.8	61.7
TFYR Macedonia	62.8	73.4	69.7	59.0	77.5
United Kingdom	73.1	67.7	57.3	70.2	67.2
Hungary/Hongrie	54.0	68.4	71.1	55.3	48.8
Switzerland,Liechtenst.	41.9	61.3	54.2	37.5	44.7
Poland/Pologne	37.2	45.1	48.6	56.0	46.8
Sweden/Suède	25.3	163.8	14.2	12.8	16.3
Belgium–Luxembourg	29.1	37.9	43.3	41.1	38.8
Czech Republic	24.2	34.2	35.6	40.3	46.4
Malta/Malte	24.8	14.6	38.9	1.1	28.4
China/Chine	28.8	12.9	27.1	30.4	8.6
Slovakia/Slovaquie	8.1	16.2	21.5	22.3	22.1
Cyprus/Chypre	3.0	1.6	19.8	53.9	2.1
Egypt/Egypte	10.2	12.5	13.7	13.9	22.4
Greece/Grèce	15.9	12.5	18.9	7.0	15.3
Ireland/Irlande	5.7	5.0	16.3	13.7	22.2
Panama	19.7	35.6	2.1	2.0	2.4
Spain/Espagne	6.1	17.2	20.5	9.6	8.2
Turkey/Turquie	20.5	13.9	4.6	12.7	9.3
Belarus/Bélarus	12.4	4.6	9.0	21.7	12.7
Ukraine	9.9	11.7	12.8	8.6	12.2
Ecuador/Equateur	7.1	9.7	9.5	5.5	3.4
Iran (Islamic Rep of)	3.7	2.6	18.7	4.3	5.7
Canada	5.0	5.2	7.5	8.3	8.5
Denmark/Danemark	7.0	9.9	6.8	4.3	5.9
Romania/Roumanie	3.4	5.1	4.6	5.7	15.1
Saudi Arabia	4.8	6.3	8.3	6.5	6.2
Nigeria/Nigéria	9.5	11.7	5.6	1.2	2.6
Bulgaria/Bulgarie	3.6	5.0	6.3	4.8	9.7
India/Inde	10.2	1.4	6.6	8.2	2.5
Bahamas	0.0	0.1	26.9	0.1	0.2

(VALUE AS PERCENTAGE OF WORLD TOTAL)(VALEURS EN POURCENTAGE DU TOTAL MONDIAL)

	1988	1989	1990	1991	1992	1993	1994	1995	1996	1997
Africa					2.4	2.3	2.1	3.5	3.7	2.2
Americas					3.8	4.4	5.2	4.8	4.8	5.5
– Northern America					2.5	3.1	3.7	2.9	3.0	3.5
– LAIA					1.3	1.1	1.3	1.6	1.7	1.8
– CACM					0.0	0.1	0.1	0.1	0.1	0.1
– Caribbean					0.0	0.0	0.1	0.2	0.1	0.1
– Rest of America					0.0	0.0	0.0	0.0	0.0	0.0
Asia excl fmr USSR					7.6	7.8	9.4	5.9	7.8	7.2
– Middle East					5.8	5.3	6.2	2.2	3.8	2.5
Asia former USSR					0.0	0.0	0.1	0.0	0.1	0.1
Europe excl fmr USSR					80.5	79.8	78.2	82.6	80.2	79.5
– European Union					47.5	56.4	59.2	62.1	59.4	59.5
– Eastern Europe					8.5	5.0	5.9	6.2	7.3	6.9
– Rest of Europe					24.6	18.4	13.2	14.4	13.5	13.1
Europe former USSR					5.2	5.6	4.8	2.9	3.2	5.4
Oceania					0.2	0.1	0.1	0.2	0.3	0.2
Other					0.3	0.0		0.0	0.0	0.0
Germany/Allemagne					17.2	21.2	21.2	20.1	20.6	20.2
Italy/Italie					17.1	18.9	19.0	18.2	18.3	18.9
Slovenia/Slovénie					19.6	15.3	10.3	10.7	9.9	8.3
Austria/Autriche					4.3	6.7	6.7	7.6	7.7	7.8
Russian Federation					4.5	4.9	3.5	2.1	2.7	5.0
United Kingdom					1.4	1.9	3.4	6.1	2.9	2.1
USA/Etats–Unis d'Amer					2.4	2.7	3.3	2.7	2.7	3.0
France, Monaco					1.6	2.1	2.2	2.5	2.6	3.2
Iran (Islamic Rep of)					5.2	5.1	5.6	1.2	2.1	0.1
Hungary/Hongrie					2.3	1.7	1.9	2.1	2.5	2.6

	1988	1989	1990	1991	1992	1993	1994	1995	1996	1997
Afrique					2.0	2.0	2.2	3.3	6.9	3.8
Amériques					2.4	3.1	3.8	3.1	2.8	3.1
– Amérique du Nord					1.7	2.3	2.3	2.1	2.2	2.4
– ALAI					0.3	0.3	0.5	0.3	0.4	0.3
– MCAC					0.0	0.0	0.0	0.0	0.0	0.0
– Caraïbes					0.0	0.1	0.1	0.7	0.1	0.2
– Autre Amérique					0.5	0.5	0.8	0.0	0.0	0.1
Asie anc. URSS exclus					3.9	2.8	1.6	2.6	3.2	1.6
– Moyen–Orient					0.8	1.2	0.8	1.4	1.9	0.7
Asie ancienne URSS					0.0	0.1	0.2	0.2	0.1	0.1
Europe anc. URSS exclus					87.6	87.4	88.2	86.9	83.2	86.8
– Union Européenne					52.5	57.5	59.4	57.7	51.0	51.2
– Europe de l'Est					2.4	3.4	4.2	4.1	4.2	4.5
– Autre de l'Europe					32.7	26.5	24.6	25.1	27.9	31.2
Europe ancienne URSS					3.3	4.3	4.0	3.8	3.7	4.5
Océanie					0.1	0.1	0.1	0.1	0.1	0.1
Autre					0.7	0.0				0.0
Italy/Italie					19.8	21.2	21.4	23.7	21.0	20.8
Germany/Allemagne					16.8	22.9	22.1	21.5	18.6	17.8
Slovenia/Slovénie					23.9	18.2	13.0	13.1	13.6	12.2
Bosnia and Herzegovina					4.2	4.8	7.9	8.3	12.2	14.9
Austria/Autriche					2.3	3.3	3.5	4.3	4.4	5.1
Russian Federation					3.1	3.7	3.5	3.3	2.9	3.8
Liberia/Libéria					1.1	1.0	1.3	2.3	5.9	2.9
France, Monaco					1.3	3.4	2.6	2.4	1.9	1.8
USA/Etats–Unis d'Amer					1.6	2.1	2.2	1.9	2.0	2.2
Netherlands/Pays–Bas					2.1	2.4	2.2	1.7	1.5	1.4

4. General Imports C.I.F. by Commodities according to the S.I.T.C. (Rev. 2) in million U.S. Dollars
Importations Générales C.A.F. par Produits d'après la C.T.C.I. (Rév. 2) en millions de Dollars E.U.

SITC CTCI	COMMODITY	1994 QUANTITY QUANTITE	1994 VALUE VALEUR	1995 QUANTITY QUANTITE	1995 VALUE VALEUR	1996 QUANTITY QUANTITE	1996 VALUE VALEUR	1997 QUANTITY QUANTITE	1997 VALUE VALEUR	PRODUIT
	ALL COMMODITIES		5229.2		7509.3		7787.8		9122.4	TOUS PRODUITS
0	FOOD AND LIVE ANIMALS		499.0		780.2		767.5		832.5	ALIMENTS,ANIMAUX VIVANTS
001	*LIVE ANIMALS FOR FOOD		17.9	W 14172	27.0	W 24733	45.1	W 36839	65.9	ANIMAUX VIVANTS
0011	BOVINE SPECIES,LIVE	W 10761	15.9	W 13102	23.1	W 18779	33.9	W 31720	53.0	ESPECE BOVINE
00119	— OTHR THAN FR BREEDING	W 10196	15.0	W 11405	19.5	W 13652	22.5	W 20081	31.2	BOVINS NON REPRODUCTEURS
01	MEAT AND PREPARATIONS		75.9		114.5		98.0		117.8	VIANDES ET PREPARATIONS
011	MEAT FRESH,CHILLD,FROZEN		49.7	W 34709	77.9		63.2	W 33940	77.6	VIANDES FRAICHES,REF,CONGE
0111	BOVINE MEAT FRESH,FROZEN		24.6	W 10176	23.7	W 6974	16.2	W 9520	21.9	VIANDES BOVIN FRAI,REF
0113	PIG MEAT FRESH,CHLD,FRZN		18.3	W 17909	40.9	W 16417	39.3	W 20800	48.5	VIANDE DE PORC
014	MEAT PREPD,PRSVD,NES ETC		24.2	W 9647	33.7	W 10032	30.7	W 11757	32.4	CONSERVES DE VIANDES
0142	SAUSAGES INCLDING TINNED		17.3	W 6887	25.3	W 6628	22.1	W 8717	25.8	SAUCISSES,SAUCISSONS
02	DAIRY PRODCTS,BIRDS'EGGS		34.5		65.7		76.7		79.7	PRODUITS LAITIERS,OEUFS
022	MILK AND CREAM		22.5	W 108683	45.0	W 118124	50.3	W 123050	55.3	LAIT ET CREME
0223	MILK AND CREAM FRESH		16.7	W 70408	30.8	W 91167	38.5	W 85956	37.2	LAIT,CREME FRAIS
024	CHEESE AND CURD		10.8	W 6408	19.3	W 9382	23.4	W 8190	22.1	FROMAGE ET CAILLEBOTTE
03	FISH AND PREPARATIONS		19.0		23.3		28.1		30.3	POISSONS ET PREPARATIONS
04	CEREALS AND PREPARATIONS		42.8		52.8		66.8		95.1	CEREALES ET PRODUITS
048	CEREAL ETC PREPARATIONS		30.2	W 46608	42.4	W 61244	51.3	W 69627	55.6	PREPTNS A BASE CEREALES
05	VEGETABLES AND FRUIT		131.5		221.9		194.3		179.2	LEGUMES ET FRUITS
054	VEG ETC FRSH,SMPLY PRSVD		30.2		62.4	W 95654	44.5		42.6	LEGUMES FRAIS,CONG,SECS
056	VEGTBLES ETC PRSVD,PREPD		19.1	W 15834	26.1	W 15941	26.7	W 15428	22.6	CONSERVES DE LEGUMES
057	FRUIT,NUTS,FRESH,DRIED		61.0		93.6		84.4	W 165058	80.2	FRUITS FRAIS OU SECS
0573	BANANA,PLANTAIN,FRSH,DRY		18.3	W 67373	28.0	W 58037	27.8	W 59456	27.3	BANANES FRAICHES,SECHEES
0579	FRUIT FRESH OR DRIED NES		13.7	W 36120	23.4	W 37698	18.4	W 35013	17.9	FRUITS FRAIS,SECS NDA
058	FRUIT PRESERVED,PREPARED		21.4	W 42032	40.0		38.8		34.0	CONSERVES DE FRUITS
0585	FRUIT OR VEGETABLE JUICE		13.0	W 32230	25.2	W 27410	23.8	W 19682	18.7	JUS DE FRUITS
06	SUGAR AND PREPS,HONEY		47.6		62.6		39.4		23.4	SUCRES ET PRODUITS
061	SUGAR AND HONEY		34.4	W 129941	46.0	W 75427	27.9	W 48844	11.9	SUCRES ET MIEL
07	COFFEE,TEA,COCOA,SPICES		51.7		97.9		89.0		109.8	CAFE,THE,CACAO,EPICES
071	COFFEE AND SUBSTITUTES		30.0	W 19033	64.0	W 18907	56.2	W 22399	72.2	CAFE ET SUCCEDANES
0711	COFFEE GREEN,ROASTED,SUB		29.7	W 18960	62.9	W 18698	52.8	W 22016	66.7	CAFE TORREFIE OU DECAFEINE
07111	COFFEE GREEN,HUSKS,SKINS		27.0	W 18221	59.0	W 18196	49.6	W 21388	63.1	CAFE NON TORREFIE
081	*FEEDING STUFF FOR ANIML		34.1		38.2	W 108023	53.1		56.0	NOURRITURE POUR ANIMAUX
09	MISC EDIBLE PRODUCTS		44.4		76.7		77.5		75.8	PREP ALIMENTAIRES DIVERSES
098	EDIBLE PRODCTS,PREPS NES		41.7		72.1		73.4		71.9	PREP ALIMENTAIRES NDA
09809	MISC FOOD PREPRTIONS NES		34.5	W 13736	61.5	W 15294	61.5	W 21186	59.4	PREP ALIMENTAIRES NDA
1	BEVERAGES AND TOBACCO		62.9		66.3		57.7		57.0	BOISSONS ET TABACS
11	BEVERAGES		48.0		44.4		41.1		34.8	BOISSONS
112	ALCOHOLIC BEVERAGES		33.5		25.0	W 33210	26.3	W 29316	24.6	BOISSONS ALCOOLIQUES
1123	BEER,ALE,STOUT,PORTER		26.5	W 23392	14.5	W 22028	13.8	W 20780	11.5	BIERES
2	CRUDE MATERLS,EXCL FUELS		147.8		191.6		214.6		267.1	MAT BRUTES NON COMESTIBLES
22	OIL SEEDS,OLEAGINOUS FRT		11.7		13.4		14.0		37.2	GRAINES,FRUITS OLEAGINEUX
222	SEEDS FOR'SOFT'FIXED OIL		10.8	W 37943	12.3	W 35285	13.0	W 104021	36.0	GRAINES HUILES FIXES
2222	SOYA BEANS		9.4	W 36552	10.5	W 31993	10.6	W 88094	30.7	FEVES DE SOJA
24	CORK AND WOOD		19.5		26.9		52.0		65.0	LIEGE ET BOIS
248	WOOD SHAPED,SLEEPERS		16.1	W 65355	22.8	W 145951	48.6	W 209203	60.8	BOIS SIMPLEMENT TRAVAILLES
2482	LUMBER SHAPED CONIFER		12.0	W 57769	17.4	W 131711	39.4	W 191145	52.0	CONIFERES SCIES,RABOTES
24821	LUMBER SAWN ETC CONIFER		11.4	W 55606	16.0	W 128371	36.9	W 184592	47.3	CONIFERES SCIES LONGITUD
251	*PULP AND WASTE PAPER		13.1	W 74716	22.6	W 51913	9.1		9.3	PATES A PAPIER,DECHETS
26	TEXTILE FIBRES AND WASTE		25.2		25.7		24.0		28.8	FIBRES TEXTILES
27	CRUDE FERTLZR,MINRLS NES		38.1		50.6		55.7		56.2	ENGRAIS MINERAUX BRUTS
29	CRUDE ANIMAL,VEG MAT NES		25.3		38.8		42.8		47.1	MATIERES BRUTES ANIM,VEGET
292	CRUDE VEG MATERIALS NES		16.5	W 9340	26.7		28.1	W 18849	32.5	MAT BRUTES VEGETALES NDA
3	MINERAL FUELS ETC		591.4		874.2		860.7		853.9	COMBUSTIBLES MINERAUX LUB
32	COAL,COKE AND BRIQUETTES		29.8		17.4		16.2		18.8	HOUILLES,COKES,BRIQUETTES
322	COAL,LIGNITE AND PEAT	W 481553	27.1	W 245467	13.6	W 204577	12.2	W 218439	11.5	HOUILLES,LIGNITES,TOURBE
3222	OTH COAL,NOT AGGLOMERATD	W 350570	21.2	W 89387	4.8	W 61406	4.3	W 128355	6.7	AUTRES HOUILLES
33	PETROLEUM AND PRODUCTS		437.8		739.2		710.1		675.8	PETROLE ET DERIVES
333	CRUDE PETROLEUM		381.9	W 4929170	674.9	W 4098141	635.3	W 4008272	580.7	HUILES BRUTES DE PETROLE
334	PETROLEUM PRODUCTS,REFIN		50.6	W 324659	57.0		67.3	W 345711	84.7	PRODUITS RAFFINES
3341	GASOLINE,OTH LIGHT OILS		3.4	W 18412	5.0	W 37314	8.2	W 141936	29.5	ESSENCES POUR MOTEURS
3343	GAS OILS	W 107151	17.7	W 151496	11.1	W 77139	14.5	W 96971	20.0	GAS OILS
3345	LUBS,PETROLEUM OILS NES		14.7	W 28419	23.0	W 51219	28.4	W 48151	26.4	HUILES LUBRIFIANTES
33451	LUBS(HIGH PETR CONT) ETC		12.6	W 27473	19.9	W 50328	25.1	W 46565	22.4	HUILES LUBRIF,H LOURDES
341	*GAS,NATURAL AND MANUFCT		95.0		33.8		107.1	W 601162	124.3	GAZ NATUREL,GAZ MANUFACT
3414	PETROLEUM GASES, GASEOUS		92.0	W 143032	32.3	W 509725	105.8	W 558033	118.3	GAZ DE PETROLE GAZEUX
351	*ELECTRIC CURRENT		29.1		83.8		27.6		35.1	ENERGIE ELECTRIQUE
4	ANIMAL,VEGETABLE OIL,FAT		11.7		25.2		36.9		26.0	HUILES,GRAISSES ANIM,VEG
42	FIXED VEGETABLE OIL,FAT		6.0		16.5		27.3		16.8	HUILES VEGETALES FIXES
5	CHEMCLS,RELATED PROD NES		521.8		777.0		818.7		933.3	PRODUITS CHIMIQUES
51	ORGANIC CHEMICALS		80.8		114.0		118.7		123.1	PROD CHIMIQ ORGANIQUES
513	CARBOXYLIC ACIDS ETC		17.4	W 11630	20.4	W 12804	19.7	W 14190	19.2	ACIDES CARBOXYLIQUES
514	NITROGEN–FNCTN COMPOUNDS		27.5	W 10723	37.9		48.3	W 11150	44.3	COMPOSES FONCT AZOTEES
52	INORGANIC CHEMICALS		35.2		50.9		46.5		49.3	PROD CHIM INORGANIQUES
523	OTHR INORG CHEMICALS ETC		24.2		34.3		28.6		25.9	AUT PRODUITS CHIMIQUES INORG
5232	OTH MTL CMPD OF INRG ACD		17.3	W 104786	25.7	W 66941	19.8	W 62164	17.6	SELS METALLIQUES
53	DYES,TANNING,COLOUR PROD		43.9		64.3		68.3		71.4	PROD TEINTURE,COLORANTS
533	PIGMENTS,PAINTS,ETC		34.2	W 26964	50.7	W 36089	55.5	W 51332	58.7	PIGMENTS,PEINTURES,VERNIS
5334	VARNISHES,DISTEMPERS ETC		19.6	W 12924	29.5	W 13402	30.7	W 13694	30.3	PEINTURES A L'EAU
541	*MEDICINAL,PHARM PRODUCT		98.7		176.6		188.3		185.2	PROD MEDICINAUX PHARMACEUT
5413	ANTIBIOTICS IN BULK		9.8	K 432000	22.7	K 289622	26.4	K 235241	26.3	ANTIBIOTIQUES NDA
5417	MEDICAMENTS		69.3	K 1739000	122.7	K 1870611	125.6	K 2085873	122.5	MEDICAMENTS
54171	— CONTAINNG ANTIBIOTICS		12.3	K 310000	23.9	K 275477	21.7	K 290214	18.7	MED CONTN ANTIBIOTIQUES
54179	— CONTNG OTH SUBSTANCES		49.6	K 1298000	79.8	K 1406207	86.3	K 1574781	82.7	MED CONT AUT SUBSTANCES
55	PERFUME,CLEANING ETC PRD		69.4		105.6		122.8		141.4	PROD POUR PARFUM,TOILETTE
553	PERFUMERY,COSMETICS,ETC		30.2	W 8043	51.9	W 8347	56.8	W 10984	66.5	PRODUITS DE PARFUMERIE
554	SOAP,CLEANSING ETC PREPS		33.1	W 34668	46.6	W 40432	53.0	W 48490	56.5	SAVONS,PRODUITS DETERSIFS
5542	WASHING PREPARATIONS ETC		28.0	W 31920	39.6	W 37424	45.3	W 44503	48.1	PROD ORG TENSIO–ACT NDA
562	*FERTILIZERS,MANUFACTURE		15.2		22.5	W 172595	20.3		28.3	ENGRAIS MANUFACTURES
58	PLASTIC MATERIALS ETC		97.1		118.1		118.5		183.7	MAT PLAST ARTIFICIELLES
582	PROD OF CONDENSATION ETC		17.8	W 18081	26.9	W 19644	29.4	W 27217	36.8	PROD CONDENS,POLYCOND
583	POLYMERIZATION ETC PRODS		75.9	W 49611	86.1	W 50119	84.5	W 128558	140.4	PROD POLYMERISATION
5831	POLYETHYLENE		21.7	W 19106	22.7	W 20018	23.1	W 62192	48.6	POLYETHYLENE
58311	— IN PRIMARY FORMS	W 17695	19.7	W 17535	19.0	W 17411	17.7	W 58339	41.5	POLYETHYLENE PRIMAIRES
5834	POLYVINYL CHLORIDE		21.5	W 12120	19.9	W 10084	16.1	W 24544	26.6	CHLORURE DE POLYVINYLE
5839	OTH POLYMRZTION ETC PROD		15.8	W 6582	19.5	W 6954	20.5	W 8473	26.3	AUT PROD POLYMER COPOLYM
59	CHEMICAL MATERIALS NES		78.9		121.1		130.9		145.4	MAT PROD CHIMIQUES NDA
598	MISCEL CHEM PRODUCTS NES		56.7		86.6	W 58089	93.0	W 97653	105.1	PROD DIV INDUST CHIM NDA
5989	CHEM PRODUCTS,PREPS NES		42.0	W 31959	64.6	W 51423	70.9	W 90403	83.7	PROD PREP CHIMIQUES NDA
59899	OTH CHEM PRODS,PREPS,NES		26.2	W 24078	36.0	W 43644	39.7	W 79194	51.1	AUT PRODUITS CHIMIQUES NDA
6	BASIC MANUFACTURES		1321.9		1395.3		1481.5		1605.8	ART MANUFACTURES

4. General Imports C.I.F. by Commodities according to the S.I.T.C. (Rev. 2) in million U.S. Dollars
Importations Générales C.A.F. par Produits d'après la C.T.C.I. (Rév. 2) en millions de Dollars E.U.

SITC CTCI	COMMODITY	1994		1995		1996		1997		PRODUIT
		QUANTITY QUANTITE	VALUE VALEUR	QUANTITY QUANTITE	VALUE VALEUR	QUANTITY QUANTITE	VALUE VALEUR	QUANTITY QUANTITE	VALUE VALEUR	
61	LEATHER,DRESSED FUR,ETC		83.1		87.1		88.8		86.6	CUIRS,PELLETERIES
612	LEATHER ETC MANUFACTURES		69.1	W 3669	68.2	W 3414	70.1	W 3541	68.9	OUVRAGES EN CUIRS NDA
6123	PREPRD PARTS OF FOOTWEAR		68.4	W 3633	67.3	W 3375	69.2	W 3511	68.2	PARTIES DE CHAUSSURES
62	RUBBER MANUFACTURES NES		53.4		86.0		88.7		92.0	CAOUTCHOUC MANUFACTURE
625	RUBBER TYRES, TUBES ETC		32.9	W 13247	52.8	W 13475	58.1	W 15541	57.7	PNEUS CAOUTCHOUC VULCANISE
6252	TYRES,NEW,BUS OR LORRY		16.0	W 5489	23.7	W 5744	25.7	W 6378	24.4	PNEUS POUR AUTOBUS,CAMIONS
63	WOOD,CORK MANUFACTRS NES		34.7		51.0		62.3		65.0	OUVRAGES LIEGE ET BOIS
635	WOOD MANUFACTURES NES		22.4	W 17006	33.1	W 18221	38.5	W 23037	36.3	ART MANUF EN BOIS NDA
6353	BUILDERS WOODWRK,PREFABS		19.0	W 13881	27.3	W 13794	32.3	W 17096	29.4	OUVRAGES DE MENUISERIE
64	PAPER,PAPERBOARD AND MFR		136.3		238.8		252.8		256.3	PAPIERS,CARTONS & OUVRAGES
641	PAPER AND PAPERBOARD		90.5	W 132977	155.4	W 150638	159.4	W 173037	154.5	PAPIERS ET CARTONS
6411	NEWSPRINT		11.1	W 34119	26.0	W 33645	26.7	W 33602	18.7	PAPIER JOURNAL
6412	PRINTG,WRITING PAPER NES		17.1	W 19786	32.5	W 22307	26.7	W 37222	35.9	PAPIERS POUR L'IMPRESSION
64122	— COATED,IMPREGNATD ETC		15.2	W 16238	26.7	W 18526	21.3	W 32354	30.3	PAPIERS IMPRESSION COUCHES
6415	PAPER,PAPERBRD,BULK,NES		23.8	W 34543	39.8	W 37754	34.9	W 31100	23.5	PAPIERS,CARTONS ROULEAUX
64159	OTHER PAPER ETC,BULK,NES		22.2	W 32569	37.1	W 34725	32.1	W 28017	21.4	AUT PAPIER ROULEAUX FEUILLES
6418	COATED ETC PAPER NES BLK		22.3	W 17714	36.3	W 23062	45.9	W 31669	49.9	PAP,CARTONS COUCHES,ENDUITS
642	PAPER,ETC,PRECUT,ARTS OF		45.9		83.5		93.4	W 48965	101.9	PAP,CARTONS DECOUPES
6421	PAPER ETC CONTAINERS		17.4	W 14770	26.3	W 15561	30.0	W 16911	29.6	BOITES,SACS EMBALLAGES
6428	PAPER ETC ARTICLES NES		14.5		30.9		37.8	W 17773	46.5	OUVRAGES EN PATE A PAPIER
64285	PAPER ETC DIAPERS ETC		7.5	W 4668	17.3	W 6239	23.7	W 9360	32.3	SERVIETTES HYGIENIQUES
65	TEXTILE YARN,FABRICS,ETC		582.0		216.5		209.2		218.6	FILS,TISSUS,ARTICLES TEXTILE
651	TEXTILE YARN		48.6		55.2		53.4		58.7	FILS TEXTILES
6513	COTTON YARN		22.1	W 4070	18.9	W 4330	19.8	W 4892	19.8	FILS DE COTON
652	COTTON FABRICS,WOVEN		449.6		34.8		32.7		36.0	TISSUS DE COTON
6521	GREY WOVEN COTTON FABRIC		432.6	W 1218	6.4	W 625	3.0		4.7	TISSUS COT ECRUS NON MERCER
65215	GREY WOVN COTN BLEND NES		430.7	W 262	1.3	W 41	0.4	W 132	0.9	AUT TIS MOINS 85% COT ECRUS
6522	WOVEN COTTON BLEACHD,ETC		17.1		28.4		29.8	W 4208	31.3	TISSUS COTON BLANCHIS ETC
653	WOVN MAN–MADE FIB FABRIC		18.5	W 2072	27.3	W 1931	26.7	W 2430	26.4	TISSUS FIBRES SYNTH,ARTIF
657	SPECIAL TXTL FABRC,PRODS		21.5		30.9		33.6		30.7	TISSUS SPECIAUX
659	FLOOR COVERINGS,ETC		11.6		26.1		18.9		20.4	COUVRE–PARQUETS,TAPIS ETC
66	NONMETAL MINERAL MFS NES		84.1		131.2		153.4		195.7	ART MIN NON METALLIQUES
661	LIME,CEMENT,BLDG PRODS		12.3	W 220797	25.0	W 187832	26.5	W 343351	40.2	CHAUX,CIMENTS MAT CONSTR
662	CLAY,REFRACTORY BLDG PRD		18.5	W 63750	28.1	W 145655	38.4	W 297263	59.5	MAT CONST REFRACTAIRES
6624	BRICKS ETC NONREFRACTORY		13.5	W 51880	23.4	W 130267	32.9	W 278496	51.6	BRIQUES ETC CERAM NON REFR
66245	GLAZED CERAMIC SETTS ETC		11.5	W 35254	20.0	W 46105	24.7	W 71962	36.3	AUT CARREAUX CERAMIQUE
663	MINERAL MANUFCTURES NES		15.6	W 54204	25.0		28.6	W 139430	35.3	ART MIN MANUF NDA
664	GLASS		19.9	W 27709	27.3	W 28730	34.2	W 35771	32.8	VERRE
67	IRON AND STEEL		145.3		248.2		260.9		291.1	FER ET ACIER
672	IRON,STEEL PRIMARY FORMS		21.2		19.4		16.9		20.9	LINGOTS FER,ACIER
673	IRON,STEEL SHAPES ETC		23.5	W 83230	41.5		52.2	W 157170	60.3	BARRES,PROFIL FER,ACIER
6732	IRON,STEEL BARS ETC		10.5	W 33498	19.5	W 57195	25.3	W 78670	29.8	BARRES FER,ACIER
674	IRN,STL UNIV,PLATE,SHEET		48.2	W 156291	95.9	W 169190	108.6	W 231061	129.8	LARGES PLATS,TOLES
6744	IRN,STL HVY PLATE,ROLLED		14.4	W 90176	41.7	W 85350	42.1	W 132043	56.2	TOLES LAMINEES PLUS 4.75 MM
67441	— OF IRON OR SIMPLE STL		13.2	W 89136	39.6	W 84778	40.5	W 131503	54.6	TOLES NON ACIER FIN CARB
678	IRON,STL TUBES,PIPES,ETC		29.7	W 53859	61.3	W 43635	48.5	W 55436	54.7	TUBES,TUYAUX EN FONTE,FER
6781	CAST IRON TUBES,PIPES		7.3	W 27583	27.1	W 13874	12.1	W 18309	14.3	TUBES,TUYAUX EN FONTE
68	NON–FERROUS METALS		81.3		137.0		133.5		140.3	METAUX NON FERREUX
682	COPPER EXC CEMENT COPPER		20.3	W 10076	40.3	W 11876	40.7	W 13594	46.1	CUIVRE
6822	COPPER,ALLOYS WORKED		20.1	W 9877	39.5	W 11687	40.0	W 13434	45.4	CUIVRE,ALLIAGES OUVRES
68221	COPPER BARS,WIRE,ETC		12.3	W 6986	23.8	W 7540	21.0	W 7171	19.8	BARRES,PROFILES ET FILS
684	ALUMINIUM		55.8	W 35512	88.2	W 35928	82.8	W 36591	82.8	ALUMINIUM
6841	ALUMINIUM,ALLOYS,UNWRGHT	W 26895	34.4	W 25129	48.8	W 23558	39.4	W 24516	40.8	ALUMINIUM,ALLIAGES BRUTS
6842	ALUMINIUM,ALLOYS WORKED		21.5	W 10383	39.4	W 12370	43.4	W 12075	42.0	ALUMINIUM,ALLIAGES OUVRE
69	METAL MANUFACTURES NES		122.2		199.8		232.3		260.8	ART MANUFACT EN METAL NDA
691	STRUCTURES AND PARTS NES		14.0	W 12560	26.9	W 18956	30.7	W 25848	43.2	CONSTRUCT FER,ACIER,ALU
6911	STRUCTURES,PARTS IRN,STL		9.4	W 11033	18.0	W 17600	22.6	W 23361	29.1	CONSTRUCT FER,ACIER,FONTE
695	TOOLS		17.1	W 2081	27.8		29.5		30.3	OUTILS A MAIN
697	BASE MTL HOUSEHOLD EQUIP		22.5	W 4859	35.4		42.1	W 7645	39.6	ART MENAGE MET COMMUNS
6974	BASE MTL DMSTC ARTIC NES		13.2	W 2054	21.9		25.3	W 2646	19.3	ARTICLES NDA FONTE,FER,ETC
69741	— OF IRON OR STEEL		12.6	W 1956	21.2	W 2367	24.6	W 2361	18.2	ART NDA EN FONTE,FER
699	BASE METAL MFRS NES		38.2		62.6		72.5		82.1	ART MANUFACTURES MET NDA
6991	LOCKSMITHS WARES,ETC		13.0	W 2553	23.5	W 3069	26.8	W 4890	34.9	ARTICLES DE SERRURERIE
7	MACHINES,TRANSPORT EQUIP		1358.6		2000.0		2115.7		3053.7	MACHINES MATERIEL TRANSPORT
71	POWER GENERATING EQUIPMT		50.5		48.5		44.4		56.8	MACHINES GENERATRICES
713	INTRNL COMBUS PSTN ENGIN		17.5	W 1297	28.4		22.5		29.9	MOTEURS EXPL COMB INT, PIECE
716	ROTATING ELECTRIC PLANT		19.6	W 712	8.4		8.6		13.3	APP ELECTR ROTATIFS,PIECES
7162	AC MTRS,GENRTRS,GEN SETS		17.3	W 319	4.5		5.0		9.1	MOTEURS ELECTRIQUES
72	MACHS FOR SPCL INDUSTRYS		175.1		279.4		315.2		376.1	MAC SPECIALES POUR INDUST
721	AGRIC MACHY,EXC TRACTORS		14.0		36.9		24.4		30.2	MACHINES AGRICOLES
722	TRACTORS NON–ROAD		14.7	W 3930	20.2	W 3427	14.5	W 7388	28.4	TRACTEURS
7224	WHEELED TRACTORS NES		14.7	W 3927	20.2	W 3424	14.5	W 7367	28.2	TRACTEURS A ROUES
723	CIVIL ENGNEERG EQUIP ETC		26.7	W 9052	45.7		65.4	W 19225	82.7	APPAREILS DE GENIE CIVIL
7234	CONST,MINING MACHNRY NES		23.2	W 8319	40.1	W 13437	58.9	W 18011	75.7	MACH POUR LA CONST, MINES
72342	SLFPRP SHOVELS,EXCAVATRS		16.8	W 6476	27.9	W 11023	42.7	W 14818	54.6	PELLES MECANIQUES
724	TEXTILE,LEATHER MACHNRY		21.6	W 2107	28.8		31.4		26.8	MACH POUR INDUSTRIE TEXTILE
726	PRINTG,BKBINDG MACHY,PTS		11.9	W 3387	30.9		27.5		42.6	MACHINES POUR IMPRIMERIE
7264	PRINTING PRESSES		4.1	W 2672	21.6	W 905	17.9	W 1595	29.0	MACHINES A IMPRIMER
72641	ROTARY PRINTING PRESSES		4.1	W 2672	21.6	W 905	17.9	W 1595	29.0	MACH IMPRIMER ROTATIVES
727	FOOD MACHRY NON–DOMESTIC		15.8	W 907	17.5		29.7	W 2169	35.9	MACH INDUSTRIES ALIMENT
7272	OTH FOOD PROC MCHY,PARTS		13.3	W 797	16.4		27.4	W 1915	34.5	AUT MACH IND ALIMENTAIRE
72722	INDUS FOOD PROC MACH NES		13.2	W 742	15.9	W 1319	27.4	W 1814	33.5	MACHINES BOULANGERIE
728	OTH MACHY FOR SPCL INDUS		63.1	W 11251	90.6	W 18969	112.2	W 15282	114.6	AUT MACH IND PARTICULIERES
7281	MACH–TOOLS FR SPCL INDUS		14.1	W 1815	17.2	W 2654	22.6	W 3708	27.9	MACH–OUTILS SPEC IND PART
7284	MACHY FOR SPCL INDUS NES		42.1	W 7524	61.6	W 13134	72.1	W 6230	61.4	MACH SPEC IND PARTICUL.
72848	OTH MCHY WITH INDIV FNCT		16.6	W 5876	29.7	W 11464	51.5	W 3273	34.4	AUTRES MACHINES NDA
73	METALWORKING MACHINERY		23.3		26.7		29.7		42.0	MACH TRAVAIL DES METAUX
736	METALWORKING MACH–TOOLS		18.6	W 2976	18.6		22.1	W 4332	27.4	MACH–OUTILS TRAVAIL METAUX
74	GENRL INDUSTRL MACHY NES		217.5		330.5		371.9		460.6	MACH APP INDUSTRIE
741	HEATING,COOLING EQUIPMNT		52.6	W 7221	86.1	W 9906	104.7	W 17050	144.5	MACH CHAUFFAGE,PIECES
7414	NONDOM REFRIG EQUIPT,PTS		15.2	W 2966	24.4	W 3867	26.5	W 4616	31.2	MAT PRODUCTION DU FROID
74141	REFRIG EQUIP NONDOMESTIC		13.7	W 2525	21.4	W 3366	23.5	W 3775	25.9	REFIG INDUSTRIELS
7415	AIR–CONDITIONING MACHNRY		12.0	W 1274	20.3	W 1336	21.7	W 2175	31.2	GROUPES CONDITION AIR
7416	HEATING,COOLING EQU NES		18.9	W 2103	31.8	W 3433	46.0	W 5479	57.7	APP CHANGEMENT TEMP
742	PUMPS FOR LIQUIDS ETC		17.0	W 1351	26.8	W 1562	25.1	W 1784	33.0	POMPES MOTO–POMPES
743	PUMPS NES,CENTRFUGES ETC		29.3	W 3286	40.1	W 3553	48.0	W 4365	50.6	POMPES COMPRES,VENT ETC
744	MECHANICAL HANDLING EQU		27.0	W 6545	33.2	W 8785	41.5	W 11715	51.5	EQUIP MANUTENTION PIECES
745	NONELEC MACHY,TOOLS NES		41.3	W 2495	63.6		76.5	W 4159	87.4	AUT MACH NON ELEC,PIECES
7452	OTH NONELEC MCHS,PTS NES		37.2	W 2308	56.9		67.6	W 3739	76.6	AUT MACH NON ELEC,PIECES
74522	PACKAGNG,BOTTLNG,ETC MCH		27.5	W 992	36.6	W 1607	46.9	W 1768	48.9	MACH NETT BOUTEILLES,ETC
749	NONELEC MACH PTS,ACC NES		50.7	W 5160	81.0	W 5003	76.4		93.8	PIECES MACH NON ELEC NDA

4. General Imports C.I.F. by Commodities according to the S.I.T.C. (Rev. 2) in million U.S. Dollars
Importations Générales C.A.F. par Produits d'après la C.T.C.I. (Rév. 2) en millions de Dollars E.U.

SITC CTCI	COMMODITY	1994 QUANTITY QUANTITE	1994 VALUE VALEUR	1995 QUANTITY QUANTITE	1995 VALUE VALEUR	1996 QUANTITY QUANTITE	1996 VALUE VALEUR	1997 QUANTITY QUANTITE	1997 VALUE VALEUR	PRODUIT
7492	COCKS,VALVES ETC NES		28.4	W 2368	41.7	W 2963	44.0	W 3956	53.9	ART ROB,SIM POUR TUYAUX
75	OFFICE MACHNES,ADP EQUIP		120.3		183.7		185.1		247.0	MACH BUREAU TRAIT AUTOM
752	AUTOMTIC DATA PROC EQUIP		82.2		129.7		130.8		179.0	MACH TRAIT INFORMATION
7523	DIGITL CENTRL PROCESSORS		19.4	W 250	36.4	W 241	32.4	W 338	42.1	UNITES CENTRALES
7524	DIGITL CENTRL STOR UNITS		14.7	W 148	24.7	W 156	22.2	W 222	29.6	UNITES MEMOIRE CENTRALES
7525	ADP PERIPHERAL UNITS		31.5	W 1062	40.7	W 1456	49.4	W 2079	63.0	UNITES PERIPHERIQUES
759	OFFICE,ADP MCH PTS,ACCES		22.9		33.8		34.8		43.1	PIECES DU 751 ET 752
7599	ACCTG,ETC,ADP MCH PTS,AC		20.3	W 536	29.3	W 657	29.4	W 983	37.3	PIECES DU 751 ET 752
76	TELECOMM,SOUND EQUIPMENT		108.3		200.2		161.6		251.1	EQUIPMENT DE TELECOM
761	TELEVISION RECEIVERS		14.4	W 1615	24.4		24.3		39.2	RECEPTEURS DE TELEVISION
7611	COLOUR TV RECEIVERS		14.4	W 1610	24.3	W 1736	24.2	W 3102	39.1	RECEPTEURS COULEUR
764	TELECOM EQPT,PTS,ACC NES		83.6	W 1897	157.6		114.9		176.9	EQUIP TELECOM,PIECES
7641	LINE TELEPHONE,ETC EQUIP		37.4	W 494	42.1	W 380	25.5	W 525	33.6	APP TELEPHON PAR FIL
7643	TV,RADIO TRANSMITTRS ETC		17.6	W 108	25.0	W 75	28.5	W 139	44.9	APP EMET TELE RADIO
7649	PTS NES OF EQUIPMT OF 76		22.6	W 1021	77.6		50.7		88.8	PIECES DE LA DIV 76
76491	PTS NES OF APPAR OF 7641		16.3	W 476	64.3	W 295	41.3	W 394	75.7	PIECES POUR 764.1
77	ELECTRIC MACHNRY NES ETC		234.5		370.2		387.8		420.7	MACH APP ELECT NDA
771	ELECTRIC POWER MACHY NES		14.8	W 3020	38.1	W 1911	19.9	W 2077	25.7	MACH PROD,TRANS ELECTR
7711	TRANSFORMERS,ELECTRICAL		6.3	W 474	27.7	W 866	9.7	W 1049	14.8	TRANSFO ELECTRIQUES
77118	OTHER ELEC TRANSFORMERS		6.2	W 400	27.6	W 537	7.9	W 476	8.3	AUTRES TRANSFO ELECTRIQ
772	SWITCHGEAR ETC,PARTS NES		49.6	W 3319	77.2		86.2		81.5	APP COUPURE,SECT ETC
7721	SWITCHGEAR ETC		45.6	W 3275	71.9	W 3910	80.3	W 3011	73.6	APP COUPURE,SECTIONMNT
773	ELECTR DISTRIBUTNG EQUIP		52.5	W 11576	68.9	W 13463	62.4	W 14412	56.6	EQUIPMT DISTRIBUTION ELECT
7731	INSULATED WIRE,CABLE ETC		43.0	W 10351	54.7	W 12030	51.6	W 13194	46.7	FILS,CABLES ISOLES ELECT
774	ELECTRO–MEDCL,XRAY EQUIP		8.9	W 133	17.8	W 339	38.4	W 398	30.2	APPAREILS MEDICAUX
7742	X–RAY APPARATUS ETC		5.8	W 91	11.2	W 213	25.0	W 217	13.2	APPAREILS A RAYONS X
775	HOUSEHOLD TYPE EQUIP NES		49.1		88.2		95.7		123.9	MACH,APP USAGE DOMESTQUE
7752	DOM REFRIGERATRS,FREEZRS		13.8	W 4959	25.1	W 5314	25.0	W 7533	31.0	REFRIG,CONGEL MENAGER
7758	ELECTRO–THERMIC APPL NES		15.5		26.5		31.6		39.0	APP ELECTROTHERMIQ NDA
778	ELECTRICAL MACHINERY NES		47.1		64.5		71.3		84.5	AUTRES MACH ELECT NDA
7788	OTH ELEC MACHY,EQUIP NES		13.2		17.5		22.0		32.3	AUT MACH APP ELEC NDA
78	ROAD VEHICLES		390.4		438.5		477.0		946.6	VEHICULES ROUTIERS
781	PASS MOTOR VEH EXC BUSES	W 17271	143.0	W 21929	153.2	W 33390	188.0	W 75556	588.8	AUTO TRANSPORT PERSONNES
782	LORRIES,SPCL MTR VEH NES		115.9	W 32421	139.1	W 42212	136.2	W 43914	175.0	VEHICULES SPECIAUX,MARCH
7821	LORRIES,TRUCKS		104.0	W 29090	113.1	W 37635	112.8	W 38774	144.3	VEHICULES TRANSP MARCHAND
7822	SPECIAL MOTOR VEHCLS NES	W 2217	11.9	W 3331	26.0	W 4578	23.5	W 5140	30.8	VEHICULES USAGES SPECIAUX
783	ROAD MOTOR VEHICLES NES	W 14425	72.4	W 7643	49.5	W 10071	54.7	W 10799	71.3	VEHICULES ROUTIERS NDA
7831	BUSES	W 10644	51.8	W 5584	37.3	W 5945	35.5	W 4735	36.5	VOITURES TRANSPORT COMMUN
7832	TRACTORS FOR TR–TRAILERS	W 3781	20.6	W 2059	12.3	W 4126	19.3	W 6064	34.9	TRACTEURS ROUTIERS
784	MOTOR VEH PRTS,ACCES NES		32.3	W 6903	63.9	W 8574	65.5	W 8879	65.5	PIECES 722,781,782,783
7849	OTHER MOTOR VEHCL PARTS		30.2	W 6379	58.0	W 8206	63.1	W 8405	60.4	PIECES 722,781,782,783
786	TRAILERS,NONMOTR VEH,NES		17.1	W 5853	14.6	W 8808	18.1	W 9801	28.1	REMORQUES,CADRES,CONTAIN
79	OTHR TRANSPORT EQUIPMENT		39.0		122.7		143.2		253.1	AUTRE MATERIEL TRANSPORT
792	AIRCRAFT ETC		13.6		22.9		31.2		126.4	APP NAVIGATION AERIENNE
7922	AIRCRFT NES 2000KG OR LS		0.8	W 5	0.5	W 7	8.2	W 29	50.3	AERODYNES MOINS 2000 KG
7924	AIRCRFT NES OVER 15000KG		4.4	W 3	0.8	W 21	14.8	W 66	34.8	AERODYNES PLUS 15000 KG
793	SHIPS AND BOATS ETC		20.9	W 86364	82.4	W 42068	98.3	W 52276	115.9	NAVIRES BATEAUX,ETC
7932	SHIPS AND BOATS NES		18.7	W 85548	79.4	W 41770	96.2	W 48762	110.3	NAVIRES ET BATEAUX
79322	TANKERS OF ALL KINDS		8.9	W 81608	60.1	W 22701	70.8	W 18828	42.6	BATEAUX–CITERNES
79323	OTHER CARGO VESSELS		2.7	W 2496	3.6	W 18115	15.4	W 27694	43.9	AUT BATEAUX TRANS MARCH
8	MISC MANUFACTURED GOODS		714.0		967.2		1066.0		1163.8	ART MANUFACTURES DIVERS
812	*PLUMBG,HEATNG,LGHTNG EQ		19.2	W 7854	38.5	W 7803	44.6	W 14231	66.9	APPAR SANITAIRES CHAUFFAGE
8124	LIGHTING EQUIPMENT NES		9.6	W 2087	19.6	W 1581	21.4	W 6072	39.5	APPAREILS ECLAIRAGE ETC
81242	LAMPS,FITTINGS BASE METL		7.2	W 1277	15.6	W 1123	16.4	W 5527	34.4	APPAREILS D'ECLAIRAGE
821	*FURNITURE,PARTS THEREOF		56.4	W 28024	97.5	W 28903	96.9	W 38842	127.5	MEUBLES ET PIECES
8211	CHAIRS,SEATS AND PARTS		15.0	W 6159	26.1	W 7140	26.1	W 8627	34.7	SIEGES ET PIECES
82111	CHAIRS AND OTHER SEATS		12.0	W 4413	22.7	W 6254	22.9	W 7245	30.0	SIEGES
8219	FURNITURE AND PARTS NES		33.7	W 20069	62.2	W 19783	59.2	W 27881	79.2	AUTRES MEUBLES ET PIECES
82192	WOOD FURNITURE NES		21.3	W 13318	39.5	W 13638	38.8	W 19369	52.7	MEUBLES NDA EN BOIS
84	CLOTHING AND ACCESSORIES		231.6		271.3		285.7		270.6	VETEMENTS
842	MENS OUTERWEAR NOT KNIT		68.6	W 2961	64.5	W 2712	59.6	W 2692	54.9	VET DESSUS POUR HOMMES
8423	— TROUSERS,BREECHES ETC		23.3	W 1421	22.8	W 1406	24.3	W 1300	24.5	PANTALONS HOMMES MAT TEX
8424	— JACKETS,BLAZERS ETC		28.1	W 830	22.1	W 635	17.5	W 592	13.6	VESTES HOMMES MAT TEXTIL
843	WOMENS OUTERWEAR NONKNIT		72.0	W 2582	78.5	W 2944	81.8	W 3230	72.8	VET DESSUS FEMMES MAT TEX
8431	— COATS AND JACKETS		25.3	W 697	25.7	W 733	23.4	W 752	21.8	MANT,VEST FEM MAT TEXTIL
8439	— OTHER OUTER GARMENTS		26.9	W 1083	27.5	W 1433	34.3	W 1717	31.7	AUT VET DES FEM MAT TEXT
844	UNDER GARMENTS NOT KNIT		15.4	W 1285	18.0	W 1348	26.1	W 1382	16.6	VETEMENT DESSOUS MAT TEX
845	OUTERWEAR KNIT NONELASTC		30.0	W 1714	37.7		32.9	W 2254	42.7	VET DESSOUS,ACCES BONNET
8451	— JERSEYS,PULLOVERS ETC		19.9	W 834	20.3	W 808	15.8	W 1376	25.5	CHANDAILS,PULL–OVERS ETC
846	UNDER GARMENTS KNITTED		24.6	W 2633	38.1	W 2603	51.8	W 2376	54.6	SOUS VETS DE BONNETERIE
8462	— OF COTTON NON ELASTIC		14.8	W 2121	23.4	W 2073	34.8	W 1765	38.3	SOUS–VET BONNET COTON
84629	—— OTHER		14.8	W 2121	23.4	W 2073	34.8	W 1765	38.3	AUT SOUS–VET BONNET COTON
848	HEADGEAR,NONTXTL CLOTHNG		16.9	W 1564	27.9		27.5	W 1150	23.4	VET ACCES MAT AUT QUE TEX
851	*FOOTWEAR		133.2	W 10976	147.3	W 12070	171.3	W 13593	178.2	CHAUSSURES
85102	FOOTWEAR LEATHER		117.9	W 9006	131.1	W 9993	151.5	W 11235	157.1	CHAUS SEMELLES EN CUIR
87	PRECISION INSTRUMNTS NES		77.6		110.6		129.6		155.8	INSTRUM,APPAR SCIENT NDA
872	MEDICAL INSTRUMENTS NES		26.3	W 800	33.3	W 1020	47.5	W 1260	62.5	INSTR,APP MEDIC–CHIR NDA
87202	OTH MEDICAL INSTRUMENTS		24.2	W 677	28.1	W 873	38.3	W 928	51.6	INSTRUM,APP MEDECINE
874	MEASURNG,CONTROLNG INSTR		43.3		66.5		68.6		72.3	INSTRUMENTS DE MESURE
8743	GAS,LIQUID CONTROL INSTR		18.5	W 1056	25.9	W 827	23.7	W 789	21.4	APP,INSTR MESURE FLUIDES
88	PHOTO EQU,OPTICL GDS ETC		31.0		43.6		58.2		50.3	APP,FOURN PHOTO,OP,MONTR
89	MISC MANUFCTRD GOODS NES		156.5		246.4		265.0		299.5	ART MANUFACTURES DIVERS
892	PRINTED MATTER		11.2		23.5		23.2		25.1	IMPRIMES
893	ARTICLES OF PLASTIC NES		54.5		100.1		112.4		118.4	OUVRAGES EN MAT DIVIS 58
8931	PLSTC PACKG CONTNRS,LIDS		11.3	W 6257	19.0	W 8281	24.5	W 10753	27.7	ART TRANSP EMBALLAGE ETC
8939	MISC PLASTIC ARTICLES		39.6	W 16264	74.9	W 16841	80.0	W 19432	80.8	ART DIVERS EN MAT DIV 58
89399	OTHR PLASTC ARTICLES NES		36.9	W 15079	70.2	W 15354	74.7	W 17411	74.3	AUT OUV MAT DIV 58
894	TOYS,SPORTING GOODS,ETC		46.5	W 7538	54.7		52.7		51.7	VOITURES ENFANTS,JOUETS
8942	TOYS,INDOOR GAMES ETC		40.5	W 6504	44.5	W 6800	40.4	W 5051	34.6	JOUETS,JEUX ETC
89423	TOYS NES		30.2	W 5183	33.2	W 3520	24.3	W 2712	19.3	JOUETS,MODELES REDUITS
898	MUSICAL INSTRUMENTS,PTS		14.3		23.1		26.5		53.8	INSTRUMENTS DE MUSIQUE
8983	SOUND RECRDNG TAPE,DISCS		13.4	W 567	20.8	W 717	23.3	W 1002	50.6	SUPPORTS SON POUR 763
89832	RECORDED DISCS,TAPES ETC		8.6	W 130	13.5	W 163	15.4	W 323	43.0	DISQUES,PHONO,BANDES
899	OTHER MANUFACTURED GOODS		17.5		26.1		28.2		27.7	AUT ART MANUF DIVERS NDA
9	GOODS NOT CLASSD BY KIND		0.6		432.8		369.1		329.7	ART TRANSACT NON CLASSES
931	*SPECIAL TRANSACTIONS		0.1	W 724372	431.4	W 228957	367.7	W 245572	326.9	TRANS.SPECIALES

5. General Exports F.O.B. by Commodities according to the S.I.T.C. (Rev. 2) in million U.S. Dollars
Exportations Générales F.O.B. par Produits d'après la C.T.C.I. (Rév. 2) en millions de Dollars E.U.

SITC CTCI	COMMODITY	1994		1995		1996		1997		PRODUIT
		QUANTITY QUANTITE	VALUE VALEUR	QUANTITY QUANTITE	VALUE VALEUR	QUANTITY QUANTITE	VALUE VALEUR	QUANTITY QUANTITE	VALUE VALEUR	
	ALL COMMODITIES		4260.4		4632.7		4511.8		4340.9	TOUS PRODUITS
0	FOOD AND LIVE ANIMALS		400.8		396.1		411.6		385.3	ALIMENTS,ANIMAUX VIVANTS
01	MEAT AND PREPARATIONS		60.7		50.6		47.5		55.0	VIANDES ET PREPARATIONS
011	MEAT FRESH,CHILLD,FROZEN		31.7	W 5757	20.0	W 3698	12.3	W 4293	14.7	VIANDES FRAICHES,REF,CONGE
0111	BOVINE MEAT FRESH,FROZEN		18.1	W 2187	11.9	W 1374	7.1	W 1609	8.3	VIANDES BOVIN FRAI,REF
01111	BOVINE MEAT WITH BONE IN	W 3643	17.3	W 2126	11.7	W 1178	6.7	W 1599	8.3	VIANDES BOVIN NON DESOSS
014	MEAT PREPD,PRSVD,NES ETC		28.2	W 8178	30.0	W 9892	33.9	W 11398	38.6	CONSERVES DE VIANDES
0149	OTH PREPARD,PRESRVD MEAT		22.5	W 6694	24.0	W 7817	26.1	W 7733	27.1	AUTRES PREP DE VIANDES
02	DAIRY PRODCTS,BIRDS'EGGS		16.2		18.3		23.6		35.5	PRODUITS LAITIERS,OEUFS
022	MILK AND CREAM		6.6	W 6457	6.6	W 12090	11.3	W 22978	18.4	LAIT ET CREME
0223	MILK AND CREAM FRESH		5.7	W 5747	5.3	W 11576	10.1	W 22335	16.8	LAIT,CREME FRAIS
024	CHEESE AND CURD		6.6	W 2016	8.1	W 2551	9.1	W 3669	13.9	FROMAGE ET CAILLEBOTTE
03	FISH AND PREPARATIONS		50.3		44.8		49.0		60.3	POISSONS ET PREPARATIONS
034	FISH,FRESH,CHILLED,FROZN		25.5	W 6163	20.5	W 5886	19.8		26.6	POISSON FRAIS, REFRIG,CONG
0341	FISH FRSH,CHLLD,EX FILLT		25.4	W 6104	20.4	W 5782	19.6	W 9322	22.9	POISSON FRAIS,REFRIGERE
037	FISH ETC PREPD,PRSVD NES		19.0	W 8213	19.8		22.6	W 12957	26.8	POIS,CRUST,MOL PREPARES
0371	FISH PREPARD,PRESRVD NES		19.0	W 8212	19.8	W 9804	22.6	W 12955	26.8	CONSERVES DE POISSONS
04	CEREALS AND PREPARATIONS		68.6		79.3		69.3		40.4	CEREALES ET PRODUITS
041	WHEAT ETC UNMILLED	W 28312	5.5	W 226856	32.3	W 138943	22.1	W 695	0.3	FROMENT,EPEAUTRE
0412	OTHER WHEAT ETC UNMILLED	W 17561	2.4	W 221411	31.2	W 125377	19.6	W 648	0.3	AUTRE FROMENT NON MOULU
044	MAIZE UNMILLED	W 19522	12.0	W 35526	11.3	W 68829	14.5	W 14275	4.3	MAIS NON MOULU
046	WHEAT ETC MEAL OR FLOUR		22.2	W 19875	5.9	W 8049	2.8	W 5934	2.1	SEMOULE FARINE,FROMENT
04601	FLOUR OF WHEAT OR MESLIN		22.2	W 19808	5.9	W 7392	2.4	W 5310	1.8	FARINE DE FROMENT
048	CEREAL ETC PREPARATIONS		27.0	W 11195	28.5	W 11180	28.5		32.7	PREPTNS A BASE CEREALES
0484	BAKERY PRODUCTS		21.4	W 8543	22.6	W 8278	22.2	W 10487	26.7	PRODUITS DE BOULANGERIE
04842	PASTRY, CAKES ETC		16.5	W 7125	18.3	W 6841	18.2	W 9127	22.8	PATISSERIE ETC.
05	VEGETABLES AND FRUIT		40.1		41.6		39.6		28.2	LEGUMES ET FRUITS
058	FRUIT PRESERVED,PREPARED		16.2		13.7		12.1		11.9	CONSERVES DE FRUITS
07	COFFEE,TEA,COCOA,SPICES		29.8		34.4		30.7		31.1	CAFE,THE,CACAO,EPICES
073	CHOCOLATE AND PRODUCTS		18.6	W 4529	20.5	W 4512	21.0	W 5210	21.5	CHOCOLAT
081	*FEEDING STUFF FOR ANIML		21.0	W 83235	14.6		15.4	W 100391	21.0	NOURRITURE POUR ANIMAUX
0819	FOOD WASTE AND FEED NES		17.5	W 61259	11.6	W 47450	12.0	W 67556	13.0	DECHETS,ALIMENTS NDA
08199	FODDER NES,INCL SWEETNED		15.6	W 16389	6.6	W 16177	8.5	W 20973	9.5	PREPARATIONS FOURRAGERES
09	MISC EDIBLE PRODUCTS		101.0		99.2		117.8		102.9	PREP ALIMENTAIRES DIVERSES
098	EDIBLE PRODCTS,PREPS NES		94.5	W 37533	94.8	W 43465	113.0		96.2	PREP ALIMENTAIRES NDA
09804	SAUCES,MIXED SEASONINGS		60.1	W 23194	59.8	W 27666	72.3	W 22387	56.2	SAUCES,ASSAISONNEMENTS
09809	MISC FOOD PREPRTIONS NES		20.7	W 5606	18.1	W 6579	20.8	W 7524	21.3	PREP ALIMENTAIRES NDA
1	BEVERAGES AND TOBACCO		68.5		90.1		91.6		121.3	BOISSONS ET TABACS
11	BEVERAGES		40.0		67.7		74.4		73.3	BOISSONS
111	NON-ALCOHL BEVERAGES NES		5.5	W 23472	10.2	W 39202	14.9	W 59388	20.2	BOISSONS NON ALCOOLIQUES
11102	FLAVORED WATERS NON-ALCO		5.2	W 18765	8.6	W 31170	12.3	W 49608	17.5	LIMONADES,EAUX GAZEUSES
112	ALCOHOLIC BEVERAGES		34.6	W 61600	57.5		59.5		53.2	BOISSONS ALCOOLIQUES
1121	WINE OF FRESH GRAPES ETC		12.1	W 24907	26.0	W 27066	17.7	W 19320	14.7	VINS DE RAISINS FRAIS
11212	WINE OF FRESH GRAPES		9.4	W 19294	23.9	W 21664	15.4	W 10657	11.0	VINS DE MOUTS DE RAISINS
1123	BEER,ALE,STOUT,PORTER		8.9	W 24747	12.3	W 39552	19.2	W 43936	18.2	BIERES
1124	DISTILLED ALCOHOLIC BEVS		13.6	W 11930	19.2		22.6		19.2	ALCOOLS,EAUX-DE-VIE
11242	DISTILLD WINE,GRAPE MARC		10.0	W 8429	14.2	W 9358	17.1	W 8679	14.3	EAUX-DE-VIE NATURELLES
12	TOBACCO AND MANUFACTURES		28.5		22.4		17.3		48.0	TABACS BRUTS FABRIQUES
121	TOBACCO UNMNFCTRD,REFUSE	W 8223	14.4	W 3471	4.3	W 4179	4.9	W 8906	20.8	TABACS BRUTS,DECHETS
1212	TOBACCO STRIPPED OR PART	W 3170	6.6	W 1008	2.4	W 1346	2.7	W 6593	18.3	TABACS PART ECOTES
122	TOBACCO,MANUFACTURED	W 1639	14.2	W 2011	18.1	W 1476	12.4	W 3022	27.3	TABACS FABRIQUES
1222	CIGARETTES	W 1609	14.1	W 1627	17.9	W 1035	12.0	W 2462	26.2	CIGARETTES
2	CRUDE MATERLS,EXCL FUELS		214.1		250.4		247.5		323.1	MAT BRUTES NON COMESTIBLES
21	HIDES,SKINS,FURS UNDRSSD		6.3		9.8		14.5		13.8	CUIRS,PEAUX BRUTS
211	HIDES,SKINS,EXC FURS,RAW		6.2	W 4557	9.8	W 7013	14.5		13.7	CUIRS ET PEAUX
24	CORK AND WOOD		143.8		160.9		166.4		230.4	LIEGE ET BOIS
247	OTH WOOD ROUGH,SQUARED		17.9	W 189363	24.2	W 194670	22.4	W 225829	46.7	BOIS BRUTS EQUARRIS
2472	SAW-,VENEER-LOGS NON-CON	W 134330	17.0	W 171879	22.9	W 192842	22.1	W 223510	46.3	NON CONIFERES SCIAGE,PLAC
24721	— IN THE ROUGH	W 134330	17.0	W 171879	22.9	W 192842	22.1	W 223510	46.3	BRUTS ECORCES DEGROSSIS
248	WOOD SHAPED,SLEEPERS		122.0	W 294184	133.8	W 292260	140.7	W 337600	180.9	BOIS SIMPLEMENT TRAVAILLES
2483	LUMBER SHAPED NON-CONIFR	W 304909	120.3	W 291486	132.8	W 290277	140.1	W 335976	180.5	NON CONIFERES SCIES,RABOTES
24831	LUMBER SAWN ETC NON-CON	W 289634	101.5	W 281404	117.6	W 279507	124.6	W 323824	150.5	SCIES LONGITUDINALEMENT
24832	LUMBER PLANED ETC NONCON	W 15275	18.8	W 10082	15.2	W 10770	15.6	W 12153	30.1	RABOTES,RAINES,LANGUETES
251	*PULP AND WASTE PAPER	W 44571	11.0	W 50810	17.2	W 48113	13.0	W 47630	9.5	PATES A PAPIER,DECHETS
2512	MECHANICAL WOOD PULP	W 32717	9.6	W 36750	14.0	W 36406	11.3	W 36484	8.4	PATES MECANIQUES DE BOIS
27	CRUDE FERTLZR,MINRLS NES		12.8		13.5		13.4		19.0	ENGRAIS MINERAUX BRUTS
273	STONE,SAND AND GRAVEL		9.4	W 944033	10.5	W 816425	10.4	W 2002476	14.8	PIERRES,SABLES,GRAVIERS
28	METALLIFEROUS ORES,SCRAP		20.4		21.7		19.6		31.2	MINERAIS METAL,DECHETS
282	IRON AND STEEL SCRAP	W 59584	13.4	W 100206	9.6	W 106093	9.1	W 124452	10.9	FERRAILLES
29	CRUDE ANIMAL,VEG MAT NES		12.2		17.2		15.9		13.9	MATIERES BRUTES ANIM,VEGET
3	MINERAL FUELS ETC		386.7		396.6		416.5		426.9	COMBUSTIBLES MINERAUX LUB
32	COAL,COKE AND BRIQUETTES		23.3		0.8		0.2		0.2	HOUILLES,COKES,BRIQUETTES
323	BRIQUETS,COKE,SEMI-COKE		23.2	W 7232	0.8		0.1		0.1	BRIQUETTES
3232	COKE,SEMI-COKE,RTRT CRBN		23.2	W 7227	0.8	W 710	0.1	W 683	0.1	COKES ET SEMI-COKES
33	PETROLEUM AND PRODUCTS		343.8		372.0		371.2		385.2	PETROLE ET DERIVES
333	CRUDE PETROLEUM	W 46761	5.9	W 123039	15.8	W 117526	17.7	W 296337	44.5	HUILES BRUTES DE PETROLE
334	PETROLEUM PRODUCTS,REFIN		320.3	W 1978659	336.0		331.3	W 1529946	321.6	PRODUITS RAFFINES
3341	GASOLINE,OTH LIGHT OILS		146.5	W 964533	160.9	W 692470	140.4	W 925286	193.8	ESSENCES POUR MOTEURS
33411	MOTOR,AVIATION SPIRIT		109.8	W 607424	103.1	W 457794	103.9	W 480255	109.0	ESSENCES MOTEURS D'AVIONS
33419	OTH LIGHT PETROLEUM OILS		36.8	W 357109	57.9	W 234676	36.5	W 445031	84.9	AUTRES HUILES LEGERES
3342	KEROSENE,OTH MEDIUM OILS		23.8	W 133139	20.5		43.0	W 58483	13.3	PETR LAMPANTS,AUT HUIL
33429	OTH MEDIUM PETROLEUM OIL	W 157717	23.8	W 133125	20.5	W 233467	43.0	W 28541	6.2	AUTRES HUILES MOYENNES
3343	GAS OILS	W 435577	80.1	W 533479	85.2	W 468508	97.9	W 327414	65.8	GAS OILS
3344	FUEL OILS,NES	W 433443	44.0	W 289062	33.1	W 142694	20.0	W 156147	20.7	FUEL OILS
3345	LUBS,PETROLEUM OILS NES		26.0	W 58446	36.5	W 50986	30.2	W 62616	28.1	HUILES LUBRIFIANTES
33451	LUBS(HIGH PETR CONT) ETC		25.8	W 54287	30.7	W 50851	29.7	W 62475	27.7	HUILES LUBRIF,H LOURDES
335	RESIDUAL PETRLM PROD NES		17.8		20.3	W 157910	22.2		19.2	PRODUITS RESIDUELS NDA
3354	PETROLM BITUMEN,COKE ETC		12.9	W 177453	15.3	W 146977	17.2	W 129124	16.2	BITUME,COKE DE PETROLE
33541	PETROLEUM BITUMEN, ETC	W 132234	10.8	W 104265	11.3	W 116195	14.6	W 101661	13.1	BITUME DE PETROLE
341	*GAS,NATURAL AND MANUFCT		16.5		22.3		28.4	W 214265	40.3	GAZ NATUREL,GAZ MANUFACT
3413	PETROLM GASES,LIQUEFIED		16.5	W 161768	22.2	W 149377	28.4	W 214257	40.3	GAZ DE PETROLE LIQUEFIE
34131	LIQUEFIED PROPANE,BUTANE	W 50006	6.5	W 60374	8.5	W 66152	13.6	W 54602	12.2	PROPANE,BUTANE LIQUEFIES
34139	OTH HYDROCARBON GAS LQFD		10.0	W 101394	13.8	W 83225	14.8	W 159655	28.2	HYDROCARBURES GAZEUX NDA
351	*ELECTRIC CURRENT		3.2		1.6		16.9		1.3	ENERGIE ELECTRIQUE
4	ANIMAL,VEGETABLE OIL,FAT		3.7		8.5		9.0		13.4	HUILES,GRAISSES ANIM,VEG
5	CHEMCLS,RELATED PROD NES		526.4		784.8		626.1		550.6	PRODUITS CHIMIQUES
51	ORGANIC CHEMICALS		42.9		53.3		43.7		35.8	PROD CHIMIQ ORGANIQUES
511	HYDROCARBONS NES,DERIVS		19.1	W 58977	27.5		20.1		19.9	HYDROCARBURES NDA
5112	CYCLIC HYDROCARBONS		0.1	W 38603	14.0		13.6		5.1	HYDROCARBURES CYCLIQUES
5113	HALOG DERIV OF HYDROCARB		18.8	W 19913	13.2	W 16163	6.2	W 49230	14.5	DERIVES HALOGENES HYDROCAR
51131	VINYL CHLORIDE	W 47780	18.8	W 19877	13.1	W 16145	6.2	W 49149	14.3	CHLORURE DE VINYLE

5. General Exports F.O.B. by Commodities according to the S.I.T.C. (Rev. 2) in million U.S. Dollars
Exportations Générales F.O.B. par Produits d'après la C.T.C.I. (Rév. 2) en millions de Dollars E.U.

SITC CTCI	COMMODITY	1994 QUANTITY QUANTITE	1994 VALUE VALEUR	1995 QUANTITY QUANTITE	1995 VALUE VALEUR	1996 QUANTITY QUANTITE	1996 VALUE VALEUR	1997 QUANTITY QUANTITE	1997 VALUE VALEUR	PRODUIT
52	INORGANIC CHEMICALS		12.7		22.0		17.2		14.4	PROD CHIM INORGANIQUES
522	INORG ELEMNTS,OXIDES,ETC		11.7		21.3		16.5		13.7	ELEMENTS INORGANIQUES
5221	CHEMICAL ELEMENTS		10.6		20.5		15.6		12.8	ELEMENTS CHIMIQUES
52218	CARBON NES, CARBON BLACK	W 21081	9.8	W 26738	15.0	W 25723	14.9	W 23106	11.9	CARBONE NDA
53	DYES,TANNING,COLOUR PROD		13.8		18.2		22.5		23.3	PROD TEINTURE,COLORANTS
533	PIGMENTS,PAINTS,ETC		13.0	W 11427	17.4	W 16443	21.8	W 18711	22.2	PIGMENTS,PEINTURES,VERNIS
541	*MEDICINAL,PHARM PRODUCT		133.4		137.2		139.4		156.6	PROD MEDICINAUX PHARMACEUT
5411	PROVITAMINS AND VITAMINS		17.0	K 1423000	15.8	K 616286	5.9	K 156963	1.2	PROVITAMINES,VITAMINES
5413	ANTIBIOTICS IN BULK		16.9		33.2		56.6		61.5	ANTIBIOTIQUES NDA
54139	OTHER ANTIBIOTICS		10.9	K 49000	27.7	K 90110	51.9	K 90030	55.7	AUTRES ANTIBIOTIQUES
5417	MEDICAMENTS		87.0	K 2253000	73.4	K 2212363	65.4	K 1887758	84.3	MEDICAMENTS
54171	— CONTAINNG ANTIBIOTICS		31.8	K 533000	30.4	K 479903	26.3	K 469464	39.8	MED CONTN ANTIBIOTIQUES
54179	— CONTNG OTH SUBSTANCES		47.9	K 1663000	37.4	K 1648718	34.7	K 1356485	40.1	MED CONT AUT SUBSTANCES
55	PERFUME,CLEANING ETC PRD		20.1		18.4		21.0		20.7	PROD POUR PARFUM,TOILETTE
562	*FERTILIZERS,MANUFACTURE		86.2		112.2		118.2		87.0	ENGRAIS MANUFACTURES
5621	CHEM NITROGENOUS FERTLZR		38.3		60.6	W 415610	67.1		50.6	ENGRAIS AZOTES
56216	UREA	W 232338	22.6	W 234984	38.1	W 269295	47.5	W 262804	36.1	UREE
56219	CHEM NITROG FERTILZR NES		14.0	W 161986	21.0	W 142415	18.7	W 106578	12.5	ENGRAIS AZOTES NDA
5629	FERTILIZERS NES		48.0	W 324853	51.6	W 282296	51.2	W 224983	36.4	ENGRAIS NDA
56291	NIT-PHOS-POT FERTLZR NES	W 36585	47.9	W 323840	51.3	W 282133	51.1	W 224796	36.3	ENGRAIS CONT N P K
58	PLASTIC MATERIALS ETC		190.5		387.6		226.2		191.8	MAT PLAST ARTIFICIELLES
583	POLYMERIZATION ETC PRODS		184.9		373.4		217.7		184.1	PROD POLYMERISATION
5831	POLYETHYLENE		78.7	W 125891	142.9		98.6		103.4	POLYETHYLENE
58311	— IN PRIMARY FORMS	W 104664	75.4	W 124285	138.6	W 126135	94.7	W 120107	98.3	POLYETHYLENE PRIMAIRES
5833	POLYSTYRENE,ITS COPOLYMR	W 61811	49.8		138.9	W 56166	82.4	W 58321	46.0	POLYPROPYLENE COPOLYMERES
58331	— IN PRIMARY FORMS	W 61776	49.8	W 48854	138.9	W 56127	82.3	W 58207	45.8	SOUS FORMES PRIMAIRES
5834	POLYVINYL CHLORIDE		51.4	W 83328	85.1	W 41980	29.7	W 30420	25.3	CHLORURE DE POLYVINYLE
58341	— IN PRIMARY FORMS		45.9	W 79818	69.0	W 38598	23.0	W 27059	18.2	SOUS FORMES PRIMAIRES
58343	— PLATES,STRIP,ETC NES		4.8	W 3135	14.9	W 2982	5.9	W 2764	5.5	SOUS FORME DE PLAQUES
59	CHEMICAL MATERIALS NES		26.8		35.8		37.6		21.0	MAT PROD CHIMIQUES NDA
591	PESTICIDES,DISINFECTANTS		10.4	W 2417	12.9	W 3054	14.1	W 2373	10.1	DESINF,INSECT,FONG,HERB
598	MISCEL CHEM PRODUCTS NES		15.2		21.4		21.8		9.4	PROD DIV INDUST CHIM NDA
5989	CHEM PRODUCTS,PREPS NES		13.8		20.7		19.5		7.0	PROD PREP CHIMIQUES NDA
6	BASIC MANUFACTURES		762.3		760.7		684.8		674.9	ART MANUFACTURES
61	LEATHER,DRESSED FUR,ETC		128.3		100.9		96.4		92.6	CUIRS,PELLETERIES
611	LEATHER		21.1		12.9		9.5		8.1	CUIRS,PEAUX PREPARES
6114	LEATHR BOVINE NES,EQUINE		17.0	W 1689	11.2	W 966	7.7	W 990	6.5	CUIRS DE BOVINS
612	LEATHER ETC MANUFACTURES		106.9		87.9		86.7	W 3196	83.5	OUVRAGES EN CUIRS NDA
6123	PREPRD PARTS OF FOOTWEAR		106.9	W 2610	87.8	W 2808	86.6	W 3190	83.4	PARTIES DE CHAUSSURES
62	RUBBER MANUFACTURES NES		13.0		9.2		9.4		7.8	CAOUTCHOUC MANUFACTURE
63	WOOD,CORK MANUFACTRS NES		67.9		67.7		57.6		59.3	OUVRAGES LIEGE ET BOIS
634	VENEERS,PLYWOOD,ETC		37.1	W 18175	31.7	W 16559	28.0	W 24098	32.5	PLACAGES,CONTRE-PLAQUES
6341	VENEER SHEETS ETC		29.0	W 9347	21.5	W 7933	18.2	W 9205	19.1	BOIS SIMPLEMENT SCIES
635	WOOD MANUFACTURES NES		30.9	W 21779	36.1	W 16222	29.6	W 17647	26.8	ART MANUF EN BOIS NDA
6353	BUILDERS WOODWRK,PREFABS		27.0	W 14917	31.3	W 12100	25.8	W 13710	23.3	OUVRAGES DE MENUISERIE
64	PAPER,PAPERBOARD AND MFR		97.7		107.6		62.4		72.0	PAPIERS,CARTONS & OUVRAGES
641	PAPER AND PAPERBOARD		63.0	W 111748	65.5	W 82107	31.0		37.6	PAPIERS ET CARTONS
6415	PAPER,PAPERBRD,BULK,NES		53.6	W 105107	56.9	W 78453	25.6	W 107466	30.4	PAPIERS,CARTONS ROULEAUX
64151	SEMI-CHEM FLUTING PAPER	W 106860	35.4	W 92683	50.6	W 64646	19.9	W 82684	21.6	PAPIER FLUTING
64159	OTHER PAPER ETC,BULK,NES		18.2	W 12363	6.2	W 13746	5.6	W 24728	8.7	AUT PAPIER ROULEAUX FEUILLES
642	PAPER,ETC,PRECUT,ARTS OF		34.7		42.2		31.4	W 22328	34.5	PAP,CARTONS DECOUPES
6421	PAPER ETC CONTAINERS		15.1	W 9897	16.7	W 9797	15.2	W 11435	17.0	BOITES,SACS EMBALLAGES
6424	PAPER ETC CT TO SIZE NES		13.5	W 6841	14.6	W 1923	4.4	W 2424	6.2	PAP,CARTONS DECOUPES
65	TEXTILE YARN,FABRICS,ETC		129.3		123.9		110.4		90.6	FILS,TISSUS,ARTICLES TEXTILE
651	TEXTILE YARN		45.5		35.9		25.3		29.2	FILS TEXTILES
6513	COTTON YARN		15.6	W 2315	18.2	W 1542	15.3	W 2096	14.3	FILS DE COTON
6514	SYN FIB YRN,BULK,MONOFIL		16.0	W 2254	8.0		5.9		8.8	FILS CONT 85% FIB TEXT SYNTH
652	COTTON FABRICS,WOVEN		13.8		13.5		9.2		10.9	TISSUS DE COTON
653	WOVN MAN-MADE FIB FABRIC		14.9	W 1337	13.4		13.5		9.9	TISSUS FIBRES SYNTH,ARTIF
654	OTH WOVEN TEXTILE FABRIC		12.9		17.1		20.7		6.1	TISSUS AUT COTON SYNT,ARTIF
657	SPECIAL TXTL FABRC,PRODS		13.3		16.3		16.4		9.3	TISSUS SPECIAUX
658	TEXTILE ARTICLES NES		25.7	W 2641	23.6		20.5		22.0	ART FACONNES MAT TEXTILES
6584	LINENS ETC		19.6	W 1453	14.3	W 1118	12.7		12.8	LINGE DE MAISON
66	NONMETAL MINERAL MFS NES		125.8		126.3		135.8		133.6	ART MIN NON METALLIQUES
661	LIME,CEMENT,BLDG PRODS		44.4	W 638249	37.9	W 411089	35.2	W 598268	55.1	CHAUX,CIMENTS MAT CONSTR
6612	CEMENT		38.0	W 613559	31.3	W 372043	26.0	W 539811	43.7	CIMENTS HYDRAULIQUES
662	CLAY,REFRACTORY BLDG PRD		25.2	W 120035	17.3	W 125966	19.5	W 142530	17.4	MAT CONST REFRACTAIRES
6624	BRICKS ETC NONREFRACTORY		24.6	W 110116	16.7	W 123854	19.0	W 141420	17.0	BRIQUES ETC CERAM NON REFR
66245	GLAZED CERAMIC SETTS ETC		13.1	W 22433	10.5	W 21335	8.4	W 26042	8.7	AUT CARREAUX CERAMIQUE
663	MINERAL MANUFCTURES NES		13.4		16.0		20.3	W 63561	15.9	ART MIN MANUF NDA
665	GLASSWARE		34.2	W 105461	44.1		36.6		33.5	OUVRAGES EN VERRE
6651	BOTTLES ETC OF GLASS		25.7	W 104086	35.1	W 75575	29.7	W 69029	22.9	RECIPIENTS EN VERRE
66511	GLASS BOTTLES ETC NONVAC	W 92713	25.7	W 104086	35.1	W 75575	29.7	W 69029	22.9	BONBONNES,BOUTEILLES,ETC
666	POTTERY		5.0	W 2499	6.6	W 2568	15.3	W 2439	5.2	POTERIE
6664	PORCELN,CHINA HOUSE WARE		4.4	W 1694	5.3	W 1638	14.1	W 1466	4.0	VAISSELLE,ARTS MEN PORC
67	IRON AND STEEL		73.3		62.7		54.2		67.4	FER ET ACIER
671	PIG IRON ETC		24.8		21.3		8.1	W 24486	14.8	FONTE,SPIEGEL,POUDRES
6716	FERRO-ALLOYS		24.8		21.2		8.1	W 24010	14.7	FERRO-ALLIAGES
67169	OTHER FERRO-ALLOYS	W 27556	24.0	W 27655	21.2	W 12608	8.1	W 24009	14.7	AUTRES FERRO-ALLIAGES
678	IRON,STL TUBES,PIPES,ETC		39.9	W 39582	31.8	W 34874	31.3	W 45742	37.2	TUBES,TUYAUX EN FONTE,FER
6782	IRON,STL SEAMLESS TUBES		9.2	W 8035	6.2	W 13763	10.0	W 22181	13.8	TUBES,TUYAUX SANS SOUDURE
6783	IRON,STL TUBES,PIPES NES		20.9	W 27502	14.4	W 16310	11.0	W 17565	10.4	AUT TUBES,TUYAUX FER,ACIER
68	NON-FERROUS METALS		50.4		73.3		65.5		62.1	METAUX NON FERREUX
684	ALUMINIUM		47.9	W 21480	70.5	W 24245	62.1	W 20612	57.8	ALUMINIUM
6842	ALUMINIUM,ALLOYS WORKED		45.4	W 20749	69.2	W 21367	58.1	W 18134	53.8	ALUMINIUM,ALLIAGES OUVRE
68422	ALUMNM PLATE,SHEET,STRIP		21.9	W 11950	35.7	W 12067	29.6	W 9214	21.7	TOLES, PLANCHES EN ALU
68423	ALUMINIUM FOIL		12.3	W 4417	17.7	W 5300	17.1	W 4073	18.0	FEUILLES,BANDES MINCES AL
69	METAL MANUFACTURES NES		77.0		89.5		93.5		89.9	ART MANUFACT EN METAL NDA
691	STRUCTURES AND PARTS NES		25.5	W 11356	22.4	W 11467	20.7	W 10587	17.0	CONSTRUCT FER,ACIER,ALU
6911	STRUCTURES,PARTS IRN,STL		20.1	W 10843	16.5	W 10837	15.5	W 10067	13.7	CONSTRUCT FER,ACIER,FONTE
699	BASE METAL MFRS NES		24.0		35.0		37.9		39.3	ART MANUFACTURES MET NDA
6997	IRON,STEEL ARTICLES NES		11.3	W 6583	16.4	W 7345	17.1	W 8143	14.6	OUV FONTE,FER,ACIER NDA
69979	IRN,STL MANUFACTURES NES		10.6	W 6190	15.7	W 7111	16.6	W 7850	14.1	AUT OUVRAGES EN FER NDA
6998	MFRS NES OF CPR,NIKL,ETC		7.1		9.6		10.6		13.2	OUVRAGES EN CU,NI,AL,PB,ZN
7	MACHINES,TRANSPORT EQUIP		731.4		777.1		963.5		751.7	MACHINES MATERIEL TRANSPORT
71	POWER GENERATING EQUIPMT		66.7		60.9		58.3		57.6	MACHINES GENERATRICES
713	INTRNL COMBUS PSTN ENGIN		15.8		13.1		10.1		10.5	MOTEURS EXPL COMB INT, PIECE
714	ENGINES AND MOTORS NES		15.8	W 2029	15.1		19.5	W 1954	19.3	MOTEURS NON ELECTRIQUES
7149	ENGINE & MOTOR PARTS NES		15.8	W 2029	15.1		19.5	W 1954	19.3	PIECES 714 ET 718.88
71499	PARTS NES,OF 71488,71888		15.8	W 2029	15.1	W 2223	19.1	W 1923	16.7	PIECES 714.88 ET 718.88
716	ROTATING ELECTRIC PLANT		20.0		18.4		19.5		17.8	APP ELECTR ROTATIFS,PIECES

5. General Exports F.O.B. by Commodities according to the S.I.T.C. (Rev. 2) in million U.S. Dollars
Exportations Générales F.O.B. par Produits d'après la C.T.C.I. (Rév. 2) en millions de Dollars E.U.

SITC CTCI	COMMODITY	1994 QUANTITY QUANTITE	1994 VALUE VALEUR	1995 QUANTITY QUANTITE	1995 VALUE VALEUR	1996 QUANTITY QUANTITE	1996 VALUE VALEUR	1997 QUANTITY QUANTITE	1997 VALUE VALEUR	PRODUIT
7162	AC MTRS,GENRTRS,GEN SETS		16.0	W 2869	14.8	W 2846	15.5	W 2391	13.6	MOTEURS ELECTRIQUES
72	MACHS FOR SPCL INDUSTRYS		40.4		37.5		45.6		37.4	MAC SPECIALES POUR INDUST
728	OTH MACHY FOR SPCL INDUS		27.8	W 10111	20.9		26.2		17.9	AUT MACH IND PARTICULIERES
7284	MACHY FOR SPCL INDUS NES		26.1	W 8181	17.3		20.8	W 5599	14.6	MACH SPEC IND PARTICUL.
72848	OTH MCHY WITH INDIV FNCT		22.9	W 6935	12.9	W 8604	14.4	W 3496	6.1	AUTRES MACHINES NDA
73	METALWORKING MACHINERY		14.1		27.7		23.1		30.4	MACH TRAVAIL DES METAUX
736	METALWORKING MACH–TOOLS		11.2		18.7		19.9		26.9	MACH–OUTILS TRAVAIL METAUX
74	GENRL INDUSTRL MACHY NES		48.2		60.2		59.8		64.6	MACH APP INDUSTRIE
744	MECHANICAL HANDLING EQU		14.4		20.8		17.3		15.7	EQUIP MANUTENTION PIECES
749	NONELEC MACH PTS,ACC NES		15.4	W 4583	16.8		19.4		20.7	PIECES MACH NON ELEC NDA
76	TELECOMM,SOUND EQUIPMENT		47.6		57.3		80.2		92.8	EQUIPMENT DE TELECOM
764	TELECOM EQPT,PTS,ACC NES		47.5		57.0		79.9		92.5	EQUIP TELECOM,PIECES
7641	LINE TELEPHONE,ETC EQUIP		19.6	W 459	23.9	W 902	21.1	W 262	14.3	APP TELEPHON PAR FIL
7649	PTS NES OF EQUIPMT OF 76		26.2		32.4		55.0		75.6	PIECES DE LA DIV 76
76491	PTS NES OF APPAR OF 7641		25.6	W 451	31.3	W 655	54.1	W 790	75.1	PIECES POUR 764.1
77	ELECTRIC MACHNRY NES ETC		171.9		211.2		219.1		226.9	MACH APP ELECT NDA
771	ELECTRIC POWER MACHY NES		36.0	W 6561	49.0	W 7954	52.5	W 9218	59.0	MACH PROD,TRANS ELECTR
7711	TRANSFORMERS,ELECTRICAL		25.9	W 5366	41.9	W 7235	46.7	W 8101	49.9	TRANSFO ELECTRIQUES
77111	LIQUID DIELEC TRANSFRMRS		17.1	W 4853	29.2	W 6739	34.7	W 7342	37.9	TRANSFO DIELEC LIQUIDE
772	SWITCHGEAR ETC,PARTS NES		55.1	W 4600	75.7		78.8		81.0	APP COUPURE,SECT ETC
7721	SWITCHGEAR ETC		49.1	W 4570	68.1	W 4902	70.6	W 6045	66.6	APP COUPURE,SECTIONMNT
7723	FIXED,VARIABLE RESISTORS		6.0	W 29	7.5	W 32	8.1	W 54	14.2	POTENTIOMETRES PIECES
773	ELECTR DISTRIBUTNG EQUIP		52.4	W 8788	52.6	W 9285	53.1	W 10237	51.4	EQUIPMT DISTRIBUTION ELECT
7731	INSULATED WIRE,CABLE ETC		51.8	W 8688	51.8	W 9154	52.0	W 10074	50.3	FILS,CABLES ISOLES ELECT
775	HOUSEHOLD TYPE EQUIP NES		15.7		16.9		17.4		16.7	MACH,APP USAGE DOMESTQUE
7758	ELECTRO–THERMIC APPL NES		15.2		16.6		16.9		16.3	APP ELECTROTHERMIQ NDA
778	ELECTRICAL MACHINERY NES		11.8		15.3		15.3		16.1	AUTRES MACH ELECT NDA
78	ROAD VEHICLES		36.3		57.6		61.7		70.1	VEHICULES ROUTIERS
784	MOTOR VEH PRTS,ACCES NES		29.6	W 7653	49.2	W 7890	53.6		56.9	PIECES 722,781,782,783
7849	OTHER MOTOR VEHCL PARTS		29.1	W 7614	49.0	W 7716	53.0	W 8521	56.5	PIECES 722,781,782,783
79	OTHR TRANSPORT EQUIPMENT		304.3		261.5		410.5		165.3	AUTRE MATERIEL TRANSPORT
793	SHIPS AND BOATS ETC		302.8	W 184248	260.4	W 226668	409.7	W 91593	162.6	NAVIRES BATEAUX,ETC
7932	SHIPS AND BOATS NES		301.6	W 183335	258.2	W 226554	408.1	W 88079	160.5	NAVIRES ET BATEAUX
79322	TANKERS OF ALL KINDS		62.2	W 119897	226.0	W 90014	296.7	W 44294	94.7	BATEAUX–CITERNES
79323	OTHER CARGO VESSELS		238.0	W 63251	30.7	W 136352	110.1	W 43477	64.4	AUT BATEAUX TRANS MARCH
8	MISC MANUFACTURED GOODS		1165.1		1166.1		1059.8		1091.5	ART MANUFACTURES DIVERS
812	*PLUMBG,HEATNG,LGHTNG EQ		16.3	W 5974	17.5	W 5162	15.3	W 5304	14.4	APPAR SANITAIRES CHAUFFAGE
821	*FURNITURE,PARTS THEREOF		138.4	W 45133	151.6	W 38149	120.2	W 44769	124.9	MEUBLES ET PIECES
8211	CHAIRS,SEATS AND PARTS		66.1	W 17960	71.5	W 15906	55.8	W 17535	55.6	SIEGES ET PIECES
82111	CHAIRS AND OTHER SEATS		57.6	W 14272	64.0	W 12925	49.9	W 13743	49.5	SIEGES
8219	FURNITURE AND PARTS NES		69.0	W 26113	76.5	W 21191	60.4	W 26182	65.9	AUTRES MEUBLES ET PIECES
82192	WOOD FURNITURE NES		50.4	W 16302	46.1	W 12530	37.2	W 15455	41.4	MEUBLES NDA EN BOIS
82199	OTHR FURN,FURN PARTS NES		17.8	W 9158	28.3	W 8117	21.1	W 10443	23.3	MEUBLES NDA AUTRES MATIERES
84	CLOTHING AND ACCESSORIES		629.1		672.9		632.7		633.2	VETEMENTS
842	MENS OUTERWEAR NOT KNIT		227.2	W 5152	241.9	W 5202	236.3	W 4894	192.1	VET DESSUS POUR HOMMES
8421	— OVERCOATS,OTHER COATS		16.7	W 255	12.9	W 207	10.7	W 203	8.0	MANTEAUX HOMMES MAT TEXT
8422	— SUITS		33.8	W 554	35.3	W 708	37.7	W 723	33.4	COMPLETS HOMMES MAT TEXT
84221	—— OF WOOL,FINE HAIR		18.2	W 273	19.5	W 364	21.1	W 427	20.6	COMPLETS HOMMES LAINE
84223	—— OF MAN–MADE FIBRES		15.6	W 281	15.9	W 344	16.7	W 296	12.8	COMPLETS HOMMES FIB SYNT
8423	— TROUSERS,BREECHES ETC		58.0	W 1974	56.8	W 1996	52.9	W 1579	46.8	PANTALONS HOMMES MAT TEX
8424	— JACKETS,BLAZERS ETC		108.3	W 2035	119.6	W 1945	115.6	W 2045	88.3	VESTES HOMMES MAT TEXTIL
8429	— OTHER OUTER GARMENTS		10.6	W 334	17.4	W 347	19.6	W 343	15.8	AUT VET DES HOM MAT TEX
843	WOMENS OUTERWEAR NONKNIT		192.2	W 4011	215.2	W 3779	190.1	W 4013	174.9	VET DESSUS FEMMES MAT TEX
8431	— COATS AND JACKETS		72.4	W 1455	81.0	W 1289	70.4	W 1342	62.2	MANT,VEST FEM MAT TEXTIL
8433	— DRESSES		9.8	W 259	16.3	W 291	16.5	W 238	13.1	ROBES EN MAT–TEXTILES
8434	— SKIRTS		26.7	W 552	29.3	W 450	23.7	W 377	18.0	JUPES EN MAT TEXTILES
8435	— BLOUSES		23.9	W 404	22.3	W 307	16.8	W 356	17.0	BLOUSES FEM MAT TEXTILES
8439	— OTHER OUTER GARMENTS		54.1	W 1195	57.5	W 1296	54.4	W 1386	53.2	AUT VET DES FEM MAT TEXT
844	UNDER GARMENTS NOT KNIT		28.5	W 1121	34.4	W 780	23.9	W 636	18.3	VETEMENT DESSOUS MAT TEX
8441	— MENS SHIRTS		24.8	W 814	30.3	W 614	20.6	W 481	14.8	CHEMISES HOMMES MAT TEXT
84411	—— OF COTTON		17.7	W 495	20.9	W 406	16.7	W 353	12.1	CHEMISES HOMMES DE COTON
845	OUTERWEAR KNIT NONELASTC		67.2	W 2446	61.2	W 2491	66.1	W 3376	80.6	VET DESSOUS,ACCES BONNET
8451	— JERSEYS,PULLOVERS ETC		33.9	W 1469	29.9	W 1524	34.6	W 2318	43.0	CHANDAILS,PULL–OVERS ETC
8459	— OTHER,CLTHG ACCESRYS		31.0	W 854	27.0	W 835	26.9	W 938	33.8	AUT VET DESSUS DE BONNE
846	UNDER GARMENTS KNITTED		77.8	W 2820	95.5		95.0	W 6938	144.6	SOUS VETS DE BONNETERIE
8462	— OF COTTON NON ELASTIC		61.0	W 2430	59.0	W 2993	64.8	W 6473	130.2	SOUS–VET BONNET COTON
84629	—— OTHER		61.0	W 2430	59.0	W 2993	64.8	W 6473	130.2	AUT SOUS–VET BONNET COTON
8463	— OF SYNTH FBR NONELAST		6.0	W 317	6.4		20.7	W 362	5.6	SOUS–VET BONNET FIB SYNT
84631	—— PANTY HOSE (TIGHTS)		5.2	W 309	6.1		20.2	W 344	5.0	COLLANTS BON FIBR SYNT
8465	CORSETS,GARTERS,ETC		10.9	W 73	30.2	W 101	9.5	W 104	9.0	CORSETS,GAINES ART SIM
84651	BRASSIERES		5.7	W 47	28.5	W 78	7.8	W 83	7.7	SOUTIENS–GORGE,BUSTIERS
848	HEADGEAR,NONTXTL CLOTHNG		31.1		18.6		17.1		17.8	VET ACCES MAT AUT QUE TEX
8481	LEATHER CLOTHES,ACCESSOR		26.2	W 104	14.0	W 135	10.7	W 187	12.3	VET ACCES MAT CUIR ARTIF
851	*FOOTWEAR		171.7	W 6627	146.0	W 6193	148.7	W 6553	165.0	CHAUSSURES
85102	FOOTWEAR LEATHER		161.5	W 5532	135.4	W 5423	142.0	W 5646	158.4	CHAUS SEMELLES EN CUIR
87	PRECISION INSTRUMNTS NES		17.1		28.1		21.8		22.7	INSTRUM,APPAR SCIENT NDA
874	MEASURNG,CONTROLNG INSTR		13.5		23.8		17.9		19.7	INSTRUMENTS DE MESURE
8743	GAS,LIQUID CONTROL INSTR		11.6	W 813	20.6	W 562	15.8	W 653	16.8	APP,INSTR MESURE FLUIDES
88	PHOTO EQU,OPTICL GDS ETC		23.1		14.0		12.2		11.4	APP,FOURN PHOTO,OP,MONTR
885	WATCHES AND CLOCKS		19.9		8.5		5.3		5.2	HORLOGERIE
8852	CLOCKS,CLOCK,WATCH PARTS		19.9		8.4		5.2		5.1	HORLOGES,MOUV,PARTIES
88524	TIME SWITCHES		19.7		8.2		5.2		5.0	APP DECLENC MECANISME
89	MISC MANUFCTRD GOODS NES		166.3		130.0		103.6		115.1	ART MANUFACTURES DIVERS
892	PRINTED MATTER		31.9		10.3		8.9		9.4	IMPRIMES
8928	PRINTED MATTER NES		26.2		3.6		4.0		3.2	IMPRIMES NDA
89283	UNISSUED BANKNOTES ETC		24.0		0.1	W 23	0.5		0.1	TIMBRES–POSTE FISCAUX
893	ARTICLES OF PLASTIC NES		68.7	W 19138	48.9	W 18272	43.2	W 24907	52.4	OUVRAGES EN MAT DIVIS 58
8931	PLSTC PACKG CONTNRS,LIDS		39.8	W 8245	12.6	W 8242	11.9	W 10838	15.7	ART TRANSP EMBALLAGE ETC
8939	MISC PLASTIC ARTICLES		28.1	W 10363	33.9	W 9066	27.3	W 12697	31.9	ART DIVERS EN MAT DIV 58
89399	OTHR PLASTC ARTICLES NES		27.6	W 10263	33.3	W 8862	26.1	W 12513	31.0	AUT OUV MAT DIV 58
894	TOYS,SPORTING GOODS,ETC		33.3		28.1		16.2		10.8	VOITURES ENFANTS,JOUETS
8942	TOYS,INDOOR GAMES ETC		33.1	W 5760	27.5	W 3141	15.8	W 1348	7.9	JOUETS,JEUX ETC
89423	TOYS NES		27.7	W 5282	25.4	W 2735	14.2	W 823	5.0	JOUETS,MODELES REDUITS
899	OTHER MANUFACTURED GOODS		23.4		28.0		20.8		28.6	AUT ART MANUF DIVERS NDA
8997	BASKETWORK,BROOMS ETC		12.2	W 2295	14.3	W 1868	8.8	W 2578	8.3	OUVRAGES VANNERIE NDA

1. HISTORICAL SERIES, 1961–1996 SPECIAL TRADE, IMPORTS C.I.F., EXPORTS F.O.B.
SERIES HISTORIQUES, 1961–1996 COMMERCE SPECIAL, IMPORTATIONS C.A.F., EXPORTATIONS F.O.B

YEAR ANNEE	VALUE IN MILLION CUBAN PESOS VALEUR EN MILLION CUBAN PESOS MERCHANDISE –MARCHANDISE IMPORTS	EXPORTS	GOLD –OR IMPORTS	EXPORTS	CONVERSION FACTORS U.S. CENTS PER CUBAN PESO FACTEURS DE CONVERSION CENTS E.U. PAR CUBAN PESO IMPORTS	EXPORTS	INDEX NUMBERS –INDICES QUANTUM IMPORTS	EXPORTS	UNIT VALUE VALEUR UNITAIRE IMPORTS	EXPORTS
1961	638.70	624.70			100.0000	100.0000				
1962	759.30	520.70			100.0000	100.0000				
1963	867.30	543.80			100.0000	100.0000				
1964	1018.80	713.80			100.0000	100.0000				
1965	866.20	690.60			100.0000	100.0000				
1966	925.50	597.80			100.0000	100.0000				
1967	999.10	705.00			100.0000	100.0000				
1968	1102.30	651.40			100.0000	100.0000				
1969	1221.60	666.70			100.0000	100.0000				
1970	1311.00	1049.50			100.0000	100.0000				
1971	1386.60	861.20			100.0000	100.0000				
1972	1189.80	770.90			108.6960	108.6960				
1973	1467.00	1153.00			122.2080	122.2730				
1974	2225.90	2236.50			118.9770	118.9360				
1975	3113.10	2952.20			124.7420	124.7790				
1976	3179.70	2692.30			132.6390	132.6400				
1977	3461.60	2918.40			121.9980	121.4550				
1978	3573.80	3440.10			131.7390	130.4170				
1979	3687.00	3500.40			137.9100	137.9100				
1980	4627.00	3967.00			140.5880	140.5880				
1981	5114.00	4223.80			127.9750	127.9750				
1982	5530.60	4933.20			120.0050	120.0050				
1983	6222.10	5534.90			115.8940	116.2040				
1984	7227.50	5476.50			113.0010	113.4480				
1985	8035.00	5991.50			108.8880	108.5040				
1986	7569.00	5325.00			121.1911	118.2647				
1987	7611.50	5401.00			100.0000	100.0000				
1988	7579.00	5518.00			100.0000	100.0000				
1989	8124.00	5392.00			100.0000	100.0000				
1990	6745.00	4910.00			100.0000	100.0000				
1991	3690.00	3550.00			100.0000	100.0000				
1992	2185.00	2050.00			100.0000	100.0000				
1993	1990.00	1275.00			100.0000	100.0000				
1994	2055.00	1385.00			100.0000	100.0000				
1995	2825.00	1600.00			100.0000	100.0000				
1996	3205.00	2015.00			100.0000	100.0000				

2. IMPORTS BY BROAD ECONOMIC CATEGORY AND EXPORTS BY INDUSTRIAL ORIGIN. (PERCENTAGE OF TOTAL VALUE)
IMPORTATIONS PAR CATEGORIES ECONOMIQUES ET EXPORTATIONS PAR BRANCHE D'ACTIVITE.(EN POURCENTAGE DE LA VALEUR TOTALE)

IMPORTS – IMPORTATIONS

	1990	1991	1992	1993	1994	1995	1996
TOTAL IMPORTS–IMPORTATIONS TOTALES							
1 FOOD BEV–ALIMENTATION BOISSONS							
11 PRIMARY–PRODUITS DE BASE							
111 FOR INDUSTRY–POUR L'INDUSTRIE							
112 FOR HOUSEHOLDS–POUR LES MENAGES							
12 PROCESSED–PRODUITS ELABORES							
121 FOR INDUSTRY–POUR L'INDUSTRIE							
122 FOR HOUSEHOLDS–POUR LES MENAGES							
2 IND SUPPLIES–APPROV INDUSTRIELS							
21 PRIMARY–PRODUITS DE BASE							
22 PROCESSED–PRODUITS ELABORES							
3 FUELS–COMBUSTIBLES							
31 PRIMARY–PRODUITS DE BASE							
32 PROCESSED–PRODUITS ELABORES							
321 MOTOR SPIRIT–ESSENCE							
322 OTHER–AUTRES							
4 MACHINERY–EQUIPEMENT							
41 CAPITAL EQUIPMENT–MACHINES							
42 PARTS–PIECES ACCESSOIRES							
5 TRANSPORT–TRANSPORT							
51 PASSENGER CARS–AUTOMOBILES							
52 OTHER–AUTRES							
521 INDUSTRIAL–INDUSTRIELS							
522 NON INDUSTRIAL–NON INDUSTRIEL							
53 PARTS–PIECES ACCESSOIRES							
6 CONSUM GOODS–BIENS CONSOMMATION							
61 DURABLE–DURABLES							
62 SEMI DURABLE–SEMI DURABLES							
63 NON DURABLE–NON DURABLES							
7 GOODS NES–BIENS NDA							

EXPORTS – EXPORTATIONS

	1990	1991	1992	1993	1994	1995	1996
TOTAL EXPORTS–EXPORTATIONS TOTALES							
1 AGRICULTURE							
2 MINING QUARRY–INDUS EXTRACTIVES							
3 MANUFACTURING–IND MANUFACTUR							
31 FOOD BEV TOBACCO–ALIM BOISS TAB							
32 TEXTILES–INDUSTRIES TEXTILES							
33 WOOD & PRODUCTS–BOIS & PRODUITS							
34 PAPER & PRODUCTS–PAPIER & PRODT							
35 CHEMICALS–INDUSTRIES CHIMIQUES							
36 NON METAL MIN–MIN NON METAL							
37 BASIC METAL–IND METAL BASE							
38 METAL MANUF–MANUF METAL							
39 OTH MANUF IND–AUTRES MANUF							

3. TRADE BY PRINCIPAL COUNTRIES OF PURCHASE AND SALE (VALUE IN MILLION U.S. DOLLARS)
ECHANGES SELON LES PRINCIPAUX PAYS D'ACHAT ET DE VENTE (VALEUR EN MILLIONS DE DOLLARS EU)

COUNTRIES–PAYS	SPECIAL IMPORTS C.I.F. IMPORTATIONS SPECIALES C.A.F				
	1992	1993	1994	1995	1996
World		1990.0	2055.0	2805.0	3205.0
Africa			6.0		
Americas			588.0		
– Northern America			88.0		
– LAIA			490.0		
– CACM			1.0		
– Caribbean			7.0		
– Rest of America			2.0		
Asia excl fmr USSR			192.0		
– Middle East			2.0		
Asia former USSR					
Europe excl fmr USSR			699.0		
– European Union			670.0		
– Eastern Europe			15.0		
– Rest of Europe			14.0		
Europe former USSR			249.0		
Oceania			8.0		
Other					
Spain/Espagne		191.0	289.0	396.0	465.0
Mexico/Mexique		189.0	271.0	355.0	318.0
Russian Federation			249.0	237.0	465.0
France, Monaco		127.0	133.0	148.0	197.0
Canada		107.0	84.0	200.0	197.0
China/Chine		177.0	147.0	146.0	101.0
Italy/Italie		64.0	63.0	81.0	114.0
Venezuela		120.0	90.0	112.0	
Argentina/Argentine		72.0	48.0	65.0	125.0
Netherlands/Pays–Bas		55.0	50.0	71.0	54.0
Germany/Allemagne		40.0	41.0	70.0	70.0
Belgium–Luxembourg		52.0	33.0	69.0	41.0
United Kingdom		21.0	40.0	30.0	38.0
Brazil/Brésil		19.0	25.0	42.0	
Japan/Japon		18.0	24.0	19.0	24.0
Colombia/Colombie		20.0	35.0	18.0	
Sweden/Suède		8.0	8.0	11.0	11.0
Chile/Chili		5.0	15.0	18.0	
Switzerland,Liechtenst.		12.0	8.0	8.0	6.0
New Zealand		5.0	8.0	16.0	
Indonesia/Indonésie		14.0	14.0	1.0	
Thailand/Thaïlande				27.0	
Other Asia n.e.s.		1.0	1.0	7.0	17.0
Portugal		2.0	1.0	12.0	7.0
Denmark/Danemark		5.0	5.0	6.0	5.0
USA/Etats–Unis d'Amer		3.0	4.0	6.0	6.0
Kyrgyzstan/Kirghizistan				19.0	
Ireland/Irlande		6.0	4.0	8.0	
Trinidad and Tobago		9.0	7.0		
Tunisia/Tunisie		9.0	6.0		
Romania/Roumanie		5.0	9.0		
China, Hong Kong SAR		1.0	3.0	6.0	
Turkey/Turquie		1.0	2.0	6.0	
Ecuador/Equateur		4.0	5.0		
Poland/Pologne		3.0	2.0	3.0	
Belarus/Bélarus		5.0		3.0	
Croatia/Croatie		2.0	6.0		
Panama		2.0	2.0	3.0	
Finland/Finlande		2.0	1.0	2.0	1.0
Austria/Autriche		1.0	2.0		2.0

COUNTRIES–PAYS	SPECIAL EXPORTS F.O.B. EXPORTATIONS SPECIALES F.O.B.				
	1992	1993	1994	1995	1996
Monde		1325.0	1465.0	1625.0	2015.0
Afrique		61.0	126.0	41.0	
Amériques		162.0	295.0	329.0	
– Amérique du Nord		132.0	142.0	234.0	
– ALAI		22.0	142.0	91.0	
– MCAC		8.0	9.0	2.0	
– Caraïbes			2.0	2.0	
– Autre Amérique					
Asie anc. URSS exclus		131.0	198.0	312.0	
– Moyen–Orient		1.0			
Asie ancienne URSS		4.0	12.0	23.0	
Europe anc. URSS exclus		341.0	429.0	475.0	
– Union Européenne		321.0	396.0	463.0	
– Europe de l'Est		8.0	17.0	1.0	
– Autre de l'Europe		12.0	16.0	11.0	
Europe ancienne URSS		443.0	316.0	225.0	
Océanie			3.0		
Autre					
Russian Federation		436.0	301.0	225.0	523.0
Canada		132.0	142.0	234.0	294.0
Netherlands/Pays–Bas		89.0	101.0	172.0	230.0
China/Chine		74.0	121.0	214.0	138.0
Spain/Espagne		65.0	78.0	96.0	131.0
Japan/Japon		51.0	63.0	89.0	67.0
France, Monaco		39.0	44.0	57.0	48.0
Italy/Italie		33.0	50.0	54.0	38.0
Egypt/Egypte		1.0	83.0	41.0	16.0
Portugal		35.0	48.0	24.0	12.0
Brazil/Brésil		10.0	57.0	40.0	
Germany/Allemagne		14.0	25.0	31.0	22.0
Algeria/Algérie		49.0	31.0		
United Kingdom		13.0	16.0	13.0	30.0
Argentina/Argentine		2.0	48.0	7.0	8.0
Mexico/Mexique		4.0	12.0	6.0	23.0
Finland/Finlande		18.0	21.0	5.0	
Colombia/Colombie		3.0	13.0	20.0	
Switzerland,Liechtenst.		7.0	8.0	11.0	10.0
Kyrgyzstan/Kirghizistan			12.0	23.0	
Romania/Roumanie		8.0	17.0		
Belgium–Luxembourg		5.0	7.0	7.0	6.0
Tunisia/Tunisie		10.0	8.0		
Latvia/Lettonie			14.0		
India/Inde		4.0	3.0	5.0	
Sweden/Suède		5.0	1.0	2.0	4.0
Uruguay			5.0	5.0	
Venezuela		3.0	5.0	2.0	
Costa Rica		4.0	6.0		
Ecuador/Equateur			1.0	9.0	
Slovenia/Slovénie		5.0	4.0		
Belarus/Bélarus		7.0	1.0		
Malaysia/Malaisie			7.0		
Ireland/Irlande		2.0	1.0	1.0	2.0
Austria/Autriche		2.0	3.0		1.0
Nicaragua		3.0	1.0	1.0	
So. African Customs Un			4.0		
Kazakhstan		4.0			
China, Hong Kong SAR		1.0	1.0	2.0	
Other Asia n.e.s.			3.0	1.0	

(VALUE AS PERCENTAGE OF WORLD TOTAL)(VALEURS EN POURCENTAGE DU TOTAL MONDIAL)

	1987	1988	1989	1990	1991	1992	1993	1994	1995	1996
Africa								0.3		
Americas								28.6		
– Northern America								4.3		
– LAIA								23.8		
– CACM								0.0		
– Caribbean								0.3		
– Rest of America								0.1		
Asia excl fmr USSR								9.3		
– Middle East								0.1		
Asia former USSR										
Europe excl fmr USSR								34.0		
– European Union								32.6		
– Eastern Europe								0.7		
– Rest of Europe								0.7		
Europe former USSR								12.1		
Oceania								0.4		
Other										
Spain/Espagne							9.6	14.1	14.1	14.5
Mexico/Mexique							9.5	13.2	12.7	9.9
Russian Federation								12.1	8.4	14.5
France, Monaco							6.4	6.5	5.3	6.1
Canada							5.4	4.1	7.1	6.1
China/Chine							8.9	7.2	5.2	3.2
Italy/Italie							3.2	3.1	2.9	3.6
Venezuela							6.0	4.4	4.0	
Argentina/Argentine							3.6	2.3	2.3	3.9
Netherlands/Pays–Bas							2.8	2.4	2.5	1.7

	1987	1988	1989	1990	1991	1992	1993	1994	1995	1996
Afrique							4.6	8.6	2.5	
Amériques							12.2	20.1	20.2	
– Amérique du Nord							10.0	9.7	14.4	
– ALAI							1.7	9.7	5.6	
– MCAC							0.6	0.6	0.1	
– Caraïbes								0.1	0.1	
– Autre Amérique										
Asie anc. URSS exclus							9.9	13.5	19.2	
– Moyen–Orient							0.1			
Asie ancienne URSS							0.3	0.8	1.4	
Europe anc. URSS exclus							25.7	29.3	29.2	
– Union Européenne							24.2	27.0	28.5	
– Europe de l'Est							0.6	1.2	0.1	
– Autre de l'Europe							0.9	1.1	0.7	
Europe ancienne URSS							33.4	21.6	13.8	
Océanie								0.2		
Autre										
Russian Federation							32.9	20.5	13.8	26.0
Canada							10.0	9.7	14.4	14.6
Netherlands/Pays–Bas							6.7	6.9	10.6	11.4
China/Chine							5.6	8.3	13.2	6.8
Spain/Espagne							4.9	5.3	5.9	6.5
Japan/Japon							3.8	4.3	5.5	3.3
France, Monaco							2.9	3.0	3.5	2.4
Italy/Italie							2.5	3.4	3.3	1.9
Egypt/Egypte							0.1	5.7	2.5	0.8
Portugal							2.6	3.3	1.5	0.6

4. Special Imports C.I.F. by Commodities according to the S.I.T.C. (Rev. 2) in million U.S. Dollars
Importations Spéciales C.A.F. par Produits d'après la C.T.C.I. (Rév. 2) en millions de Dollars E.U.

SITC CTCI	COMMODITY	1993		1994		1995		1996		PRODUIT
		QUANTITY QUANTITE	VALUE VALEUR	QUANTITY QUANTITE	VALUE VALEUR	QUANTITY QUANTITE	VALUE VALEUR	QUANTITY QUANTITE	VALUE VALEUR	
	ALL COMMODITIES									TOUS PRODUITS

 Cuba

5. Special Exports F.O.B. by Commodities according to the S.I.T.C. (Rev. 2) in million U.S. Dollars
Exportations Spéciales F.O.B. par Produits d'après la C.T.C.I. (Rév. 2) en millions de Dollars E.U.

SITC CTCI	COMMODITY	1993 QUANTITY QUANTITE	1993 VALUE VALEUR	1994 QUANTITY QUANTITE	1994 VALUE VALEUR	1995 QUANTITY QUANTITE	1995 VALUE VALEUR	1996 QUANTITY QUANTITE	1996 VALUE VALEUR	PRODUIT
	ALL COMMODITIES		1325.0		1465.0		1625.0		2015.0	TOUS PRODUITS
03	FISH AND PREPARATIONS		90.1		110.1		115.0		125.0	POISSONS ET PREPARATIONS
05	VEGETABLES AND FRUIT		50.1		80.1		45.1		50.1	LEGUMES ET FRUITS
061	SUGAR AND HONEY		820.0		785.0		855.0		1095.0	SUCRES ET MIEL
12	TOBACCO AND MANUFACTURES		75.1		80.1		90.1		90.1	TABACS BRUTS FABRIQUES
541	*MEDICINAL,PHARM PRODUCT		20.1		110.1		40.1		85.1	PROD MEDICINAUX PHARMACEUT
683	NICKEL		170.0		190.0		345.0		450.0	NICKEL
931	*SPECIAL TRANSACTIONS		100.1		110.1		135.0		120.0	TRANS.SPECIALES

1. HISTORICAL SERIES, 1962–1997 GENERAL TRADE, IMPORTS C.I.F., EXPORTS F.O.B.
SERIES HISTORIQUES, 1962–1997 COMMERCE GENERAL, IMPORTATIONS C.A.F., EXPORTATIONS F.O.B

YEAR ANNEE	VALUE IN MILLION CYPRUS POUNDS VALEUR EN MILLION CYPRUS POUNDS MERCHANDISE–MARCHANDISE IMPORTS	EXPORTS	GOLD–OR IMPORTS	EXPORTS	CONVERSION FACTORS U.S. CENTS PER CYPRUS POUND FACTEURS DE CONVERSION CENTS E.U. PAR CYPRUS POUND IMPORTS	EXPORTS	INDEX NUMBERS–INDICES QUANTUM IMPORTS	EXPORTS	UNIT VALUE VALEUR UNITAIRE IMPORTS	EXPORTS
1962	44.90	20.80			280.0000	280.0000				
1963	47.00	21.90			280.0000	280.0000				
1964	37.50	20.60			280.0000	280.0000				
1965	51.20	25.30			280.0000	280.0000				
1966	55.20	29.20			280.0000	280.0000				
1967	59.50	29.70			275.8700	276.2700				
1968	70.70	37.00			240.0000	240.0000				
1969	86.20	40.90			240.0000	240.0000				
1970	98.00	45.20			240.0000	240.0000				
1971	106.50	47.30			243.2200	242.8800				
1972	121.00	51.30			260.7410	260.7940				
1973	157.40	60.50			286.2230	286.1890				
1974	148.00	55.30			274.7380	275.2740				
1975	113.70	56.00			270.8630	271.1040				
1976	177.80	106.30			243.1160	242.4900				
1977	254.00	129.80			245.2150	244.7970				
1978	282.70	128.40			268.1270	267.7890				
1979	357.60	161.90			282.1910	281.7830				
1980	424.30	188.00			283.3130	283.3600				77
1981	489.50	234.80			238.0484	236.6654				94
1982	577.60	263.80			210.4190	210.2771				92
1983	642.00	260.50			189.8973	189.6373				91
1984	796.50	336.80			171.2021	170.6190				101
1985	762.30	290.60			163.5775	163.9238				97
1986	659.07	260.16			193.3665	193.6711				92
1987	711.42	297.99			208.5753	208.4327				95
1988	866.76	330.86			214.2754	214.9259				
1989	1130.30	393.05			202.1515	202.3059				
1990	1174.54	435.60			218.7020	217.7073				
1991	1215.83	441.79			215.6854	215.8765				
1992	1490.75	443.72			221.4602	221.7269				
1993	1260.05	431.40			201.1368	200.9395				
1994	1481.66	475.47			203.6779	203.5009				
1995	1668.40	554.71			221.1538	221.5009				
1996	1855.94	647.20			214.4023	214.3448				
1997	1897.59	565.20			194.7033	195.3581				

2. IMPORTS BY BROAD ECONOMIC CATEGORY AND EXPORTS BY INDUSTRIAL ORIGIN. (PERCENTAGE OF TOTAL VALUE)
IMPORTATIONS PAR CATEGORIES ECONOMIQUES ET EXPORTATIONS PAR BRANCHE D'ACTIVITE.(EN POURCENTAGE DE LA VALEUR TOTALE)

IMPORTS – IMPORTATIONS

	1991	1992	1993	1994	1995	1996	1997
TOTAL IMPORTS–IMPORTATIONS TOTALES	100.	100.	100.	100.	100.	100.	100.
1 FOOD BEV–ALIMENTATION BOISSONS	9.0	8.5	9.6	9.1	8.9	8.6	9.0
11 PRIMARY–PRODUITS DE BASE	3.9	3.3	3.4	3.5	3.3	3.6	3.6
111 FOR INDUSTRY–POUR L'INDUSTRIE	2.1	1.4	1.6	1.7	1.6	2.4	2.3
112 FOR HOUSEHOLDS–POUR LES MENAGES	1.9	1.9	1.8	1.8	1.7	1.2	1.3
12 PROCESSED–PRODUITS ELABORES	5.1	5.2	6.2	5.6	5.6	5.0	5.3
121 FOR INDUSTRY–POUR L'INDUSTRIE	0.8	0.7	1.2	0.9	0.8	0.6	0.6
122 FOR HOUSEHOLDS–POUR LES MENAGES	4.3	4.5	5.0	4.6	4.8	4.4	4.7
2 IND SUPPLIES–APPROV INDUSTRIELS	32.1	29.6	30.1	27.8	27.3	23.7	22.6
21 PRIMARY–PRODUITS DE BASE	2.0	1.7	2.1	1.9	1.6	1.7	1.8
22 PROCESSED–PRODUITS ELABORES	30.1	27.9	28.0	25.8	25.8	22.0	20.8
3 FUELS–COMBUSTIBLES	10.3	8.5	10.1	8.4	7.7	8.4	8.3
31 PRIMARY–PRODUITS DE BASE	4.9	3.6	3.8	3.8	3.1	3.2	4.3
32 PROCESSED–PRODUITS ELABORES	5.4	4.9	6.4	4.6	4.6	5.2	3.9
321 MOTOR SPIRIT–ESSENCE	5.3	4.8	6.3	0.4	0.4	0.6	0.3
322 OTHER–AUTRES	0.0	0.0	0.1	4.2	4.1	4.6	3.6
4 MACHINERY–EQUIPEMENT	15.0	16.2	15.7	16.7	15.0	13.9	12.7
41 CAPITAL EQUIPMENT–MACHINES	13.6	14.9	14.3	15.5	13.8	12.7	11.6
42 PARTS–PIECES ACCESSOIRES	1.4	1.3	1.3	1.3	1.2	1.2	1.1
5 TRANSPORT–TRANSPORT	12.2	15.3	10.8	10.0	11.6	10.0	8.9
51 PASSENGER CARS–AUTOMOBILES	5.7	5.9	3.5	4.5	5.1	4.8	4.0
52 OTHER–AUTRES	4.3	7.2	4.8	3.3	4.3	3.3	3.1
521 INDUSTRIAL–INDUSTRIELS	4.0	6.9	4.6	3.1	4.1	3.1	2.8
522 NON INDUSTRIAL–NON INDUSTRIEL	0.3	0.3	0.2	0.2	0.2	0.2	0.2
53 PARTS–PIECES ACCESSOIRES	2.1	2.2	2.5	2.2	2.2	1.9	1.9
6 CONSUM GOODS–BIENS CONSOMMATION	21.4	21.8	23.7	23.6	26.2	29.8	33.4
61 DURABLE–DURABLES	5.1	5.0	5.5	4.4	4.5	3.6	3.6
62 SEMI DURABLE–SEMI DURABLES	7.1	6.9	7.8	7.3	7.5	7.8	8.8
63 NON DURABLE–NON DURABLES	9.2	9.9	10.5	11.9	14.2	18.5	21.0
7 GOODS NES–BIENS NDA	0.1	0.1	0.1	4.5	3.3	5.6	5.1

EXPORTS – EXPORTATIONS

	1991	1992	1993	1994	1995	1996	1997
TOTAL EXPORTS–EXPORTATIONS TOTALES	100.	100.	100.	100.	100.	100.	100.
1 AGRICULTURE	14.2	11.1	10.5	10.1	12.7	8.7	6.1
2 MINING QUARRY–INDUS EXTRACTIVES	0.5	0.9	1.1	1.5	0.4	0.7	0.9
3 MANUFACTURING–IND MANUFACTUR	85.3	88.0	88.4	88.4	86.8	90.7	93.0
31 FOOD BEV TOBACCO–ALIM BOISS TAB	22.3	26.7	28.5	33.5	38.1	48.6	53.5
32 TEXTILES–INDUSTRIES TEXTILES	29.0	26.6	22.7	19.3	15.6	11.4	10.0
33 WOOD & PRODUCTS–BOIS & PRODUITS	0.1	0.1	0.0	0.0	0.1	0.1	0.0
34 PAPER & PRODUCTS–PAPIER & PRODT	1.9	1.4	1.4	1.6	1.7	1.4	1.6
35 CHEMICALS–INDUSTRIES CHIMIQUES	11.9	12.7	13.3	13.0	12.0	11.6	11.3
36 NON METAL MIN–MIN NON METAL	1.5	1.7	1.5	2.6	1.6	1.6	2.2
37 BASIC METAL–IND METAL BASE	0.2	0.3	0.3	0.3	0.8	0.7	1.1
38 METAL MANUF–MANUF METAL	17.1	17.3	19.7	17.4	16.4	14.8	12.6
39 OTH MANUF IND–AUTRES MANUF	1.2	1.1	1.0	0.8	0.6	0.5	0.7

3. TRADE BY PRINCIPAL COUNTRIES OF ORIGIN AND DESTINATION (VALUE IN MILLION U.S. DOLLARS)
ECHANGES SELON LES PRINCIPAUX PAYS D'ORIGINE ET DE DESTINATION (VALEUR EN MILLIONS DE DOLLARS EU)

COUNTRIES–PAYS	GENERAL IMPORTS C.I.F. IMPORTATIONS GENERALES C.A.F				
	1993	1994	1995	1996	1997
World	2535.9	3014.1	3693.8	3981.9	3698.1
Africa	26.8	37.4	35.6	89.0	34.9
Americas	278.3	379.7	553.3	743.4	761.5
– Northern America	250.4	335.4	506.1	684.4	712.7
– LAIA	27.0	43.6	46.1	57.7	44.9
– CACM	0.1	0.2	0.2	0.2	0.3
– Caribbean	0.8	0.5	0.8	0.9	2.3
– Rest of America	0.0	0.0	0.1	0.3	1.2
Asia excl fmr USSR	550.2	636.8	770.8	707.0	646.4
– Middle East	71.5	85.0	86.1	92.0	61.3
Asia former USSR	0.1	3.1	0.1	0.2	0.1
Europe excl fmr USSR	1543.5	1677.5	2024.4	2056.5	1860.0
– European Union	1436.1	1587.6	1907.8	1934.2	1758.5
– Eastern Europe	56.0	41.3	57.9	65.7	49.8
– Rest of Europe	51.5	48.6	58.6	56.6	51.7
Europe former USSR	128.1	137.6	177.3	153.3	197.7
Oceania	7.5	10.1	12.7	10.2	9.9
Other	1.4	131.9	119.7	222.4	187.6
USA/Etats–Unis d'Amer	235.4	311.6	480.9	670.7	701.3
United Kingdom	319.0	343.6	434.7	447.6	422.6
Italy/Italie	264.4	297.9	361.8	364.4	304.3
Germany/Allemagne	204.8	247.8	301.4	280.9	220.7
Greece/Grèce	211.0	205.1	265.5	287.1	264.7
Japan/Japon	205.6	205.3	246.9	237.5	195.0
France, Monaco	146.5	128.0	151.9	156.7	155.6
Russian Federation	125.7	121.1	146.9	111.9	167.3
Areas n.e.s.	1.4	131.9	119.7	222.4	187.6
Spain/Espagne	53.1	71.5	78.9	93.3	96.5
Netherlands/Pays–Bas	63.8	90.5	75.7	68.0	65.3
Belgium–Luxembourg	48.4	60.4	68.8	59.7	67.2
Korea, Republic of	37.1	67.1	101.2	53.2	41.0
Israel/Israël	34.8	38.4	53.8	66.7	102.5
China/Chine	45.9	57.1	69.8	59.2	60.0
Other Asia n.e.s.	44.4	50.1	52.1	52.1	47.5
Sweden/Suède	29.9	37.7	55.4	63.9	56.7
Syrian Arab Republic	43.0	45.8	54.5	69.0	22.0
Switzerland,Liechtenst.	41.9	39.0	46.3	39.8	39.9
Denmark/Danemark	28.8	30.9	31.9	29.9	28.2
Ireland/Irlande	23.2	25.8	30.4	24.9	23.4
Thailand/Thaïlande	16.0	19.4	24.8	27.3	30.1
Malaysia/Malaisie	19.9	23.0	36.1	23.6	15.0
Egypt/Egypte	7.9	9.6	15.7	66.3	15.8
India/Inde	12.8	17.8	29.2	28.0	27.0
Argentina/Argentine	15.4	25.7	21.9	23.5	26.6
China, Hong Kong SAR	20.0	16.8	21.8	21.5	25.1
Austria/Autriche	21.6	17.0	22.1	21.2	19.1
Indonesia/Indonésie	14.1	17.7	21.0	21.3	17.8
Canada	15.0	23.8	25.2	13.6	11.4
Ukraine	2.1	15.1	17.0	28.0	26.5
Finland/Finlande	10.8	18.4	14.8	20.1	20.0
Romania/Roumanie	16.7	10.5	14.6	23.1	17.6
Portugal	10.8	12.9	14.7	16.5	14.2
Singapore/Singapour	15.1	12.6	13.7	12.6	11.7
Brazil/Brésil	8.0	13.7	14.6	14.7	9.5
Czech Republic	14.3	10.3	12.8	8.1	7.8
Saudi Arabia	10.3	11.5	12.2	9.0	10.1
Hungary/Hongrie	9.4	5.5	8.6	11.9	9.6
Bulgaria/Bulgarie	7.6	7.9	9.5	9.3	9.0

COUNTRIES–PAYS	EXPORTS EXPORTATIONS ES F.O.B.				
	1993	1994	1995	1996	1997
Monde	867.3	961.2	1230.5	1390.6	1250.1
Afrique	59.4	63.2	71.2	68.5	72.9
Amériques	22.7	18.7	18.3	15.4	20.5
– Amérique du Nord	18.0	15.9	15.9	10.7	14.8
– ALAI	1.3	2.4	1.5	1.0	1.1
– MCAC	0.8	0.0	0.1	0.9	0.4
– Caraïbes	2.6	0.3	0.5	0.4	0.4
– Autre Amérique	0.0	0.1	0.2	2.4	3.7
Asie anc. URSS exclus	263.4	225.1	222.5	251.0	285.9
– Moyen–Orient	223.1	174.2	172.0	187.5	208.5
Asie ancienne URSS	0.8	0.5	3.9	1.3	3.3
Europe anc. URSS exclus	402.5	460.3	635.1	684.1	538.0
– Union Européenne	335.8	354.2	426.9	394.8	338.6
– Europe de l'Est	54.1	87.6	184.6	247.6	133.9
– Autre de l'Europe	12.6	18.5	23.6	41.8	65.5
Europe ancienne URSS	28.1	105.1	177.6	257.0	260.4
Océanie	0.7	1.1	0.9	1.3	1.5
Autre	89.6	87.3	101.2	111.9	67.5
Russian Federation	26.4	98.0	168.1	243.7	244.8
United Kingdom	136.1	142.5	164.1	144.5	117.8
Bulgaria/Bulgarie	34.5	56.0	112.4	209.4	98.5
Areas n.e.s.	89.6	87.3	101.2	111.9	67.5
Greece/Grèce	66.6	72.8	73.9	80.5	89.8
Lebanon/Liban	111.4	82.9	53.1	54.6	68.6
Germany/Allemagne	44.8	56.6	65.4	61.0	40.0
United Arab Emirates	20.1	21.4	47.7	38.5	70.5
Egypt/Egypte	26.4	26.0	28.0	34.0	32.7
Israel/Israël	21.3	26.3	23.0	33.6	39.4
Romania/Roumanie	11.1	19.6	58.8	22.7	22.8
Saudi Arabia	27.3	19.5	13.5	40.1	18.9
Syrian Arab Republic	19.4	20.5	22.4	21.1	16.4
Belgium–Luxembourg	13.7	15.2	23.1	17.6	14.7
Netherlands/Pays–Bas	14.6	13.6	20.6	18.4	15.0
France, Monaco	14.3	14.8	17.4	18.6	13.2
Italy/Italie	10.8	10.5	15.7	22.1	16.2
USA/Etats–Unis d'Amer	17.0	15.0	15.3	10.1	14.2
Libyan Arab Jamahiriya	16.8	17.0	13.6	9.1	13.4
Yugoslavia/Yougoslavie	1.9	0.2	1.4	16.5	49.7
Jordan/Jordanie	9.8	10.3	13.7	10.3	11.9
Spain/Espagne	14.1	10.7	11.9	8.3	6.2
China, Hong Kong SAR	4.9	5.7	8.7	9.2	14.8
Switzerland,Liechtenst.	7.7	9.8	10.3	8.4	6.6
Kuwait/ Koweït	9.0	8.1	7.8	7.8	6.2
Ukraine	0.9	5.0	8.8	11.7	11.9
Austria/Autriche	6.1	4.9	14.5	6.7	5.0
Morocco/Maroc	4.7	5.7	13.6	6.8	1.6
Ireland/Irlande	4.9	5.3	6.6	6.4	7.4
Denmark/Danemark	3.8	3.0	6.4	3.7	6.0
Poland/Pologne	2.9	6.6	6.3	4.2	2.5
Turkey/Turquie	9.5	2.7	2.6	3.7	3.3
Singapore/Singapour	2.1	5.3	2.0	6.7	2.8
Sweden/Suède	3.5	2.3	4.1	4.1	4.0
Oman	4.2	2.8	3.0	3.3	4.6
Yemen/Yémen	5.3	2.5	3.0	3.7	3.4
Norway,Svalbard and JM	0.4	2.9	8.1	4.0	1.8
Nigeria/Nigéria	5.0	3.5	3.1	2.8	2.3
Tunisia/Tunisie	2.1	3.4	4.7	3.5	2.8
Czech Republic	3.4	2.0	3.3	3.7	2.3

(VALUE AS PERCENTAGE OF WORLD TOTAL)(VALEURS EN POURCENTAGE DU TOTAL MONDIAL)

	1988	1989	1990	1991	1992	1993	1994	1995	1996	1997
Africa	2.2	1.6	1.9	2.0	1.4	1.1	1.2	1.0	2.2	0.9
Americas	6.0	7.0	8.3	9.2	9.7	11.0	12.6	15.0	18.7	20.6
– Northern America	4.8	5.9	7.5	8.4	8.9	9.9	11.1	13.7	17.2	19.3
– LAIA	1.1	1.0	0.8	0.7	0.7	1.1	1.4	1.2	1.4	1.2
– CACM	0.1	0.0	0.0	0.0	0.0	0.0	0.0	0.0	0.0	0.0
– Caribbean	0.0	0.0	0.0	0.1	0.0	0.0	0.0	0.0	0.0	0.1
– Rest of America	0.0	0.0	0.0	0.0	0.0	0.0	0.0	0.0	0.0	0.0
Asia excl fmr USSR	22.6	23.2	24.2	23.6	22.9	21.7	21.1	20.9	17.8	17.5
– Middle East	3.3	4.3	3.6	2.5	2.5	2.8	2.8	2.3	2.3	1.7
Asia former USSR						0.0	0.1	0.0	0.0	0.0
Europe excl fmr USSR	66.1	65.5	62.4	60.1	61.0	60.9	55.7	54.8	51.6	50.3
– European Union	58.7	58.7	56.5	54.4	56.0	56.6	52.7	51.6	48.6	47.6
– Eastern Europe	4.4	4.6	3.5	3.1	2.5	2.2	1.4	1.6	1.7	1.3
– Rest of Europe	3.0	2.2	2.5	2.6	2.5	2.0	1.6	1.6	1.4	1.4
Europe former USSR	2.8	2.5	2.9	4.8	4.7	5.1	4.6	4.8	3.8	5.3
Oceania	0.2	0.2	0.2	0.2	0.3	0.3	0.3	0.3	0.3	0.3
Other	0.0	0.1	0.1	0.0	0.1	0.1	4.4	3.2	5.6	5.1
USA/Etats–Unis d'Amer	4.6	5.6	7.1	7.9	8.4	9.3	10.3	13.0	16.8	19.0
United Kingdom	13.9	11.4	12.7	13.0	11.3	12.6	11.4	11.8	11.2	11.4
Italy/Italie	10.3	9.5	10.0	10.1	9.7	10.4	9.9	9.8	9.2	8.2
Germany/Allemagne				9.6	9.0	8.1	8.2	8.2	7.1	6.0
Greece/Grèce	7.3	6.1	7.0	6.9	6.8	8.3	6.8	7.2	7.2	7.2
Japan/Japon	11.6	10.8	11.5	11.4	10.5	8.1	6.8	6.7	6.0	5.3
France, Monaco	5.0	11.8	6.5	3.7	7.9	5.8	4.2	4.1	3.9	4.2
Russian Federation					4.7	5.0	4.0	4.0	2.8	4.5
Areas n.e.s.	0.0	0.1	0.1	0.0	0.1	0.1	4.4	3.2	5.6	5.1
Spain/Espagne	2.0	1.9	2.2	1.6	1.9	2.1	2.4	2.1	2.3	2.6

	1988	1989	1990	1991	1992	1993	1994	1995	1996	1997
Afrique	13.8	6.6	5.1	8.2	9.1	6.9	6.6	5.8	4.9	5.8
Amériques	3.0	2.1	2.7	1.8	1.8	2.6	1.9	1.5	1.1	1.6
– Amérique du Nord	2.5	1.8	1.7	1.5	1.6	2.1	1.7	1.3	0.8	1.2
– ALAI	0.3	0.0	0.9	0.2	0.1	0.2	0.2	0.1	0.1	0.1
– MCAC		0.0	0.0		0.0	0.1	0.0	0.0	0.1	0.0
– Caraïbes	0.1	0.0	0.0	0.0	0.0	0.3	0.0	0.0	0.0	0.0
– Autre Amérique	0.2	0.2	0.0	0.0	0.0	0.0	0.0	0.0	0.2	0.3
Asie anc. URSS exclus	24.2	25.8	23.5	28.7	28.0	30.4	23.4	18.1	18.0	22.9
– Moyen–Orient	21.0	22.4	19.9	24.9	24.0	25.7	18.1	14.0	13.5	16.7
Asie ancienne URSS						0.1	0.0	0.3	0.1	0.3
Europe anc. URSS exclus	47.6	51.5	54.4	50.8	48.2	46.4	47.9	51.6	49.2	43.0
– Union Européenne	44.4	48.0	49.0	45.1	42.2	38.7	36.8	34.7	28.4	27.1
– Europe de l'Est	1.9	1.8	2.3	3.2	4.1	6.2	9.1	15.0	17.8	10.7
– Autre de l'Europe	1.3	1.7	3.1	2.5	1.8	1.5	1.9	1.9	3.0	5.2
Europe ancienne URSS	2.2	3.9	3.2	1.7	2.6	3.2	10.9	14.4	18.5	20.8
Océanie	0.1	0.1	0.1	0.2	0.1	0.1	0.1	0.1	0.1	0.1
Autre	9.1	10.0	11.0	8.6	10.3	10.3	9.1	8.2	8.0	5.4
Russian Federation					2.6	3.0	10.2	13.7	17.5	19.6
United Kingdom	21.6	23.4	23.1	21.0	19.2	15.7	14.8	13.3	10.4	9.4
Bulgaria/Bulgarie	0.6	0.5	0.6	0.8	1.7	4.0	5.8	9.1	15.1	7.9
Areas n.e.s.	9.1	10.0	11.0	8.6	10.3	10.3	9.1	8.2	8.0	5.4
Greece/Grèce	8.3	10.2	9.9	8.4	8.3	7.7	7.6	6.0	5.8	7.2
Lebanon/Liban	6.3	8.6	9.7	12.7	12.1	12.8	8.6	4.3	3.9	5.5
Germany/Allemagne				5.2	4.6	5.2	5.9	5.3	4.4	3.2
United Arab Emirates	2.5	2.2	1.5	2.0	2.2	2.3	2.2	3.9	2.8	5.6
Egypt/Egypte	3.3	3.0	2.4	4.8	6.5	3.0	2.7	2.3	2.4	2.6
Israel/Israël	0.9	1.3	1.2	1.5	2.0	2.5	2.7	1.9	2.4	3.2

4. General Imports C.I.F. by Commodities according to the S.I.T.C. (Rev. 2) in million U.S. Dollars
Importations Générales C.A.F. par Produits d'après la C.T.C.I. (Rév. 2) en millions de Dollars E.U.

SITC CTCI	COMMODITY	1994 QUANTITY QUANTITE	1994 VALUE VALEUR	1995 QUANTITY QUANTITE	1995 VALUE VALEUR	1996 QUANTITY QUANTITE	1996 VALUE VALEUR	1997 QUANTITY QUANTITE	1997 VALUE VALEUR	PRODUIT
	ALL COMMODITIES		3014.1		3693.8		3981.9		3698.1	TOUS PRODUITS
0	FOOD AND LIVE ANIMALS		258.6		311.5		339.9		325.6	ALIMENTS,ANIMAUX VIVANTS
01	MEAT AND PREPARATIONS		19.3		22.7		11.9		14.8	VIANDES ET PREPARATIONS
011	MEAT FRESH,CHILLD,FROZEN	W 4212	15.5	W 3561	18.1	W 1910	7.6	W 2603	10.4	VIANDES FRAICHES,REF,CONGE
0111	BOVINE MEAT FRESH,FROZEN	W 2613	11.7	W 1911	14.0	W 1340	5.9	W 1565	6.9	VIANDES BOVIN FRAI,REF
01112	BOVINE MEAT BONELESS	W 2613	11.7	W 1911	14.0	W 1321	5.8	W 1550	6.9	VIANDES BOVIN DESOSSEES
02	DAIRY PRODCTS,BIRDS'EGGS		18.2		21.9		22.0		22.6	PRODUITS LAITIERS,OEUFS
024	CHEESE AND CURD	W 3287	11.1	W 3356	13.3	W 2900	13.1	W 2985	13.5	FROMAGE ET CAILLEBOTTE
03	FISH AND PREPARATIONS		26.0		33.2		29.3		26.8	POISSONS ET PREPARATIONS
034	FISH,FRESH,CHILLED,FROZN	W 2591	9.6	W 3062	12.5	W 2519	9.9	W 2394	8.7	POISSON FRAIS, REFRIG,CONG
04	CEREALS AND PREPARATIONS		82.8		100.2		139.6		127.6	CEREALES ET PRODUITS
041	WHEAT ETC UNMILLED	W 89025	13.3	W 77605	13.8	W 104891	24.1	W 94054	18.1	FROMENT,EPEAUTRE
0412	OTHER WHEAT ETC UNMILLED	W 48048	6.8	W 22354	3.5	W 70247	15.3	W 60546	10.5	AUTRE FROMENT NON MOULU
043	BARLEY UNMILLED	W 323781	26.4	W 270806	32.2	W 323985	53.2	W 364429	54.1	ORGE NON MONDEE
044	MAIZE UNMILLED	W 130987	16.8	W 168873	23.3	W 144256	30.1	W 168650	23.5	MAIS NON MOULU
048	CEREAL ETC PREPARATIONS	W 9267	22.7	W 10575	27.1	W 10783	28.3	W 10757	28.0	PREPTNS A BASE CEREALES
05	VEGETABLES AND FRUIT		25.5		30.5		31.4		30.4	LEGUMES ET FRUITS
054	VEG ETC FRSH,SMPLY PRSVD		14.1	W 14411	13.0	W 17284	11.1	W 18658	11.2	LEGUMES FRAIS,CONG,SECS
0541	POTATOES FRSH EXCL SWEET	W 16546	9.3	W 8996	6.5	W 11876	5.8	W 4813	2.0	POMMES DE TERRE
06	SUGAR AND PREPS,HONEY		15.2		18.6		17.3		15.2	SUCRES ET PRODUITS
061	SUGAR AND HONEY	W 31616	12.0	W 32996	14.5	W 32278	13.7	W 28999	11.8	SUCRES ET MIEL
0612	REFINED SUGAR ETC	W 30430	11.2	W 31662	13.6	W 31152	12.8	W 27673	10.8	SUCRES RAFFINES
07	COFFEE,TEA,COCOA,SPICES		21.0		24.5		23.6		22.2	CAFE,THE,CACAO,EPICES
071	COFFEE AND SUBSTITUTES	W 2706	11.1	W 2489	13.1	W 2664	13.4	W 2125	11.4	CAFE ET SUCCEDANES
081	*FEEDING STUFF FOR ANIML	W 79094	28.7	W 86911	32.1	W 75905	33.2	W 113072	37.7	NOURRITURE POUR ANIMAUX
0813	OILCAKE AND OTH RESIDUES	W 54820	14.5	W 60836	14.0	W 50721	14.9	W 54733	16.4	TOURTEAUX
08131	— OF SOYA BEANS	W 53020	14.2	W 58317	13.4	W 47770	14.4	W 48072	15.3	TOURTEAUX DE SOJA
0819	FOOD WASTE AND FEED NES	W 11575	8.8	W 13082	11.8	W 12855	11.8	W 31783	11.8	DECHETS,ALIMENTS NDA
08199	FODDER NES,INCL SWEETNED	W 11575	8.8	W 13063	11.8	W 12854	11.8	W 31749	11.8	PREPARATIONS FOURRAGERES
09	MISC EDIBLE PRODUCTS		21.0		26.8		30.7		27.4	PREP ALIMENTAIRES DIVERSES
098	EDIBLE PRODCTS,PREPS NES		18.3		23.5		27.5		24.3	PREP ALIMENTAIRES NDA
09809	MISC FOOD PREPRTIONS NES		11.5	W 1553	16.1	W 3897	20.0	W 3944	16.6	PREP ALIMENTAIRES NDA
1	BEVERAGES AND TOBACCO		256.8		397.6		598.4		638.7	BOISSONS ET TABACS
11	BEVERAGES		28.0		31.4		30.5		35.1	BOISSONS
112	ALCOHOLIC BEVERAGES	W 6247	23.4	W 5602	26.1	W 6496	25.2	W 6749	28.6	BOISSONS ALCOOLIQUES
1124	DISTILLED ALCOHOLIC BEVS	W 3038	18.3	W 2380	20.0	W 2529	18.1	W 2944	21.8	ALCOOLS,EAUX–DE–VIE
11241	WHISKY	W 1768	12.6	W 1630	15.7	W 1594	13.4	W 1638	15.6	WHISKY
12	TOBACCO AND MANUFACTURES		228.8		366.2		568.0		603.6	TABACS BRUTS FABRIQUES
122	TOBACCO,MANUFACTURED	W 17504	224.4	W 26021	363.2	W 41745	563.3	W 39056	600.3	TABACS FABRIQUES
1222	CIGARETTES	W 16497	216.1	W 24577	350.5	W 40463	552.2	W 36931	584.3	CIGARETTES
1223	OTH MANUFACTURED TOBACCO	W 970	6.8	W 1406	10.5	W 1185	8.4	W 2092	13.5	TABACS FUMER,CHIQUER,PRISER
2	CRUDE MATERLS,EXCL FUELS		60.7		69.3		64.2		59.5	MAT BRUTES NON COMESTIBLES
22	OIL SEEDS,OLEAGINOUS FRT		9.4		11.9		15.9		13.4	GRAINES,FRUITS OLEAGINEUX
24	CORK AND WOOD		26.9		33.3		27.2		25.6	LIEGE ET BOIS
248	WOOD SHAPED,SLEEPERS		23.1		29.4	W 73105	23.6	W 199461	22.1	BOIS SIMPLEMENT TRAVAILLES
2482	LUMBER SHAPED CONIFER		13.8		19.3	W 57114	12.2	W 160621	11.0	CONIFERES SCIES,RABOTES
24821	LUMBER SAWN ETC CONIFER		11.9		16.5	W 54395	9.5	W 157656	8.4	CONIFERES SCIES LONGITUD
2483	LUMBER SHAPED NON–CONIFR		9.4		10.1	W 15991	11.5	W 38840	11.2	NON CONIFERES SCIES,RABOTES
27	CRUDE FERTLZR,MINRLS NES		11.8		8.2		7.1		7.2	ENGRAIS MINERAUX BRUTS
3	MINERAL FUELS ETC		254.1		286.6		338.8		308.7	COMBUSTIBLES MINERAUX LUB
33	PETROLEUM AND PRODUCTS		243.5		270.9		322.1		294.0	PETROLE ET DERIVES
333	CRUDE PETROLEUM	W 875423	103.2	W 808725	100.2	W 748947	113.4	W 1039834	146.2	HUILES BRUTES DE PETROLE
334	PETROLEUM PRODUCTS,REFIN		136.7		166.9	W 1224083	204.8	W 7494775	143.4	PRODUITS RAFFINES
3341	GASOLINE,OTH LIGHT OILS	W 59427	12.3	W 72978	16.0	W 101122	23.4	W 46061	12.4	ESSENCES POUR MOTEURS
33411	MOTOR,AVIATION SPIRIT	W 57876	11.7	W 72449	15.7	W 98598	22.5	W 28564	7.0	ESSENCES MOTEURS D'AVIONS
3342	KEROSENE,OTH MEDIUM OILS	W 401393	55.1	W 436219	58.2	W 285911	60.2	W 251366	50.2	PETR LAMPANTS,AUT HUIL
33421	KEROSENE INCL JET FUEL	W 401367	55.1	W 436217	58.2	W 285892	60.2	W 251305	50.2	PETROLES LAMPANTS
3343	GAS OILS	W 84734	13.4	W 151624	24.8	W 224509	43.7	W 6799630	28.0	GAS OILS
3344	FUEL OILS,NES	W 545737	46.1	W 538783	56.8	W 599181	65.4	W 384599	42.3	FUEL OILS
3345	LUBS,PETROLEUM OILS NES		10.0		11.4	W 13360	12.3	W 13119	10.7	HUILES LUBRIFIANTES
33451	LUBS(HIGH PETR CONT) ETC		9.4	W 10634	10.6	W 13131	11.5	W 12894	10.0	HUILES LUBRIF,H LOURDES
4	ANIMAL,VEGETABLE OIL,FAT		23.4		31.7		20.9		20.6	HUILES,GRAISSES ANIM,VEG
42	FIXED VEGETABLE OIL,FAT		20.8		28.3		19.0		19.1	HUILES VEGETALES FIXES
423	FIXED VEG OILS,SOFT	W 20988	17.4	W 23007	22.5	W 16636	15.1	W 21567	14.9	HUILES VEGET DOUCES FIXES
4232	SOYA BEAN OIL	W 13487	10.6	W 8459	7.8	W 6773	5.8	W 7440	4.7	HUILE DE SOJA
4236	SUNFLOWER SEED OIL	W 4969	4.3	W 11438	11.3	W 7944	7.2	W 11514	8.0	HUILE DE TOURNESOL
5	CHEMCLS,RELATED PROD NES		245.7		313.2		298.7		296.0	PRODUITS CHIMIQUES
51	ORGANIC CHEMICALS		19.6		24.0		22.5		22.9	PROD CHIMIQ ORGANIQUES
514	NITROGEN–FNCTN COMPOUNDS		9.7	W 1177	11.7		11.0	W 1935	12.9	COMPOSES FONCT AZOTEES
52	INORGANIC CHEMICALS		11.2		14.0		13.2		11.8	PROD CHIM INORGANIQUES
53	DYES,TANNING,COLOUR PROD		14.5		17.4		16.8		16.4	PROD TEINTURE,COLORANTS
533	PIGMENTS,PAINTS,ETC	W 4608	11.5	W 5815	14.4	W 6562	14.2	W 7273	14.0	PIGMENTS,PEINTURES,VERNIS
541	*MEDICINAL,PHARM PRODUCT		61.9		77.7		84.1		80.6	PROD MEDICINAUX PHARMACEUT
5413	ANTIBIOTICS IN BULK	K 158893	9.8	K 174222	12.4	K 179523	13.8	K 145880	10.5	ANTIBIOTIQUES NDA
5417	MEDICAMENTS		46.6		58.9	K 2127823	63.4	K 2441000	64.2	MEDICAMENTS
54179	— CONTNG OTH SUBSTANCES		34.7		45.1	K 1704712	48.0	K 2038452	49.3	MED CONT AUT SUBSTANCES
55	PERFUME,CLEANING ETC PRD		42.1		50.8		51.5		60.6	PROD POUR PARFUM,TOILETTE
553	PERFUMERY,COSMETICS,ETC		27.9		33.1	W 3332	33.7	W 3421	40.8	PRODUITS DE PARFUMERIE
554	SOAP,CLEANSING ETC PREPS		9.5		12.3	W 7038	13.6	W 8633	14.8	SAVONS,PRODUITS DETERSIFS
562	*FERTILIZERS,MANUFACTURE	W 71917	11.6	W 91018	19.2	W 58958	14.6	W 51413	13.1	ENGRAIS MANUFACTURES
5629	FERTILIZERS NES	W 45180	8.3	W 60398	13.7	W 45839	11.7	W 38723	10.5	ENGRAIS NDA
58	PLASTIC MATERIALS ETC		52.4		71.6		60.6		57.7	MAT PLAST ARTIFICIELLES
582	PROD OF CONDENSATION ETC	W 6514	10.9	W 7422	14.2	W 6320	12.0	W 7254	11.9	PROD CONDENS,POLYCOND
583	POLYMERIZATION ETC PRODS		39.7	W 35073	55.2	W 35139	46.7	W 33733	44.0	PROD POLYMERISATION
5831	POLYETHYLENE	W 14598	12.1	W 16808	20.1	W 17668	17.0	W 15919	16.4	POLYETHYLENE
58311	— IN PRIMARY FORMS	W 13948	10.7	W 15947	17.6	W 16787	14.8	W 15041	14.3	POLYETHYLENE PRIMAIRES
5834	POLYVINYL CHLORIDE	W 8823	10.8	W 8764	13.6	W 8347	10.1	W 9303	10.3	CHLORURE DE POLYVINYLE
59	CHEMICAL MATERIALS NES		30.9		36.9		33.7		31.6	MAT PROD CHIMIQUES NDA
591	PESTICIDES,DISINFECTANTS	W 2932	12.9	W 2790	16.1	W 2485	13.0	W 1916	10.6	DESINF,INSECT,FONG,HERB
598	MISCEL CHEM PRODUCTS NES		14.6		16.5		16.4	W 6149	16.9	PROD DIV INDUST CHIM NDA
5989	CHEM PRODUCTS,PREPS NES		11.8		13.5		13.1	W 4510	12.7	PROD PREP CHIMIQUES NDA
59899	OTH CHEM PRODS,PREPS,NES		10.0		11.7	W 4403	11.5	W 3998	11.4	AUT PRODUITS CHIMIQUES NDA
6	BASIC MANUFACTURES		621.7		727.5		687.8		592.6	ART MANUFACTURES
61	LEATHER,DRESSED FUR,ETC		21.4		19.8		17.7		15.2	CUIRS,PELLETERIES
611	LEATHER	A 930	15.5	A 707	13.6	W 675	11.9	W 587	9.2	CUIRS,PEAUX PREPARES
6114	LEATHR BOVINE NES,EQUINE	A 613	10.9	A 428	9.2	W 555	8.9	W 473	7.0	CUIRS DE BOVINS
62	RUBBER MANUFACTURES NES		31.2		37.6		34.0		30.8	CAOUTCHOUC MANUFACTURE
625	RUBBER TYRES, TUBES ETC	N 608715	20.3	N 657700	25.8	N 641073	22.4	N 655724	20.2	PNEUS CAOUTCHOUC VULCANISE
6251	TYRES NEW FOR MOTOR CARS	N 288163	12.8	N 352498	15.7	N 308829	14.3	N 341657	13.4	PNEUS POUR VOITURES
63	WOOD,CORK MANUFACTRS NES		16.5		21.7		23.5		21.3	OUVRAGES LIEGE ET BOIS
634	VENEERS,PLYWOOD,ETC		10.8		13.4		13.1		12.3	PLACAGES,CONTRE–PLAQUES

4. General Imports C.I.F. by Commodities according to the S.I.T.C. (Rev. 2) in million U.S. Dollars
Importations Générales C.A.F. par Produits d'après la C.T.C.I. (Rév. 2) en millions de Dollars E.U.

SITC CTCI	COMMODITY	1994 QUANTITY QUANTITE	1994 VALUE VALEUR	1995 QUANTITY QUANTITE	1995 VALUE VALEUR	1996 QUANTITY QUANTITE	1996 VALUE VALEUR	1997 QUANTITY QUANTITE	1997 VALUE VALEUR	PRODUIT
64	PAPER,PAPERBOARD AND MFR		85.8		113.1		103.5		91.5	PAPIERS,CARTONS & OUVRAGES
641	PAPER AND PAPERBOARD		62.3		83.9	W 72609	72.5	W 66645	62.3	PAPIERS ET CARTONS
6412	PRINTG,WRITING PAPER NES		8.2		14.7	W 10268	11.2	W 13065	12.2	PAPIERS POUR L'IMPRESSION
64122	— COATED,IMPREGNATD ETC	W 7838	6.7	W 9852	11.2	W 7856	8.3	W 9870	8.6	PAPIERS IMPRESSION COUCHES
6415	PAPER,PAPERBRD,BULK,NES		9.3	W 12677	14.6	W 11346	11.2	W 10022	8.5	PAPIERS,CARTONS ROULEAUX
64159	OTHER PAPER ETC,BULK,NES		7.9	W 8958	11.6	W 6176	8.1	W 5681	6.3	AUT PAPIER ROULEAUX FEUILLES
6416	FIBRE BUILDING BOARD		10.8	V 29650	10.2	W 17377	8.5	W 15600	7.0	PLAQUES CONSTRUCT EN PATE
64162	INSULATING BOARD, ETC		10.1	V 24029	9.2	W 16475	7.6	W 14393	6.0	PLAQUES CONST NON COMPR
6418	COATED ETC PAPER NES BLK	W 7628	17.7	W 8205	21.2	W 6882	18.5	W 6820	17.6	PAP,CARTONS COUCHES,ENDUITS
64181	PLASTIC COATED PAPER ETC	W 3232	10.6	W 3616	14.1	W 3267	12.5	W 2901	11.4	PAP,CARTONS ENDUITS,RESINES
642	PAPER,ETC,PRECUT,ARTS OF		23.6		29.2	W 10077	31.1	W 10073	29.2	PAP,CARTONS DECOUPES
6428	PAPER ETC ARTICLES NES		10.1		13.5	W 4211	15.0	W 3664	13.7	OUVRAGES EN PATE A PAPIER
65	TEXTILE YARN,FABRICS,ETC		194.4		204.1		166.1		142.8	FILS,TISSUS,ARTICLES TEXTILE
651	TEXTILE YARN		26.3		27.9	W 3333	18.3	W 3369	17.7	FILS TEXTILES
6513	COTTON YARN		9.2	W 2650	10.1	W 1371	6.0	W 1242	5.6	FILS DE COTON
6516	DISCON SYN FIB BLEND YRN	W 2116	9.3	W 1702	8.2	W 1205	6.8	W 1202	6.6	FILS FIBR TEX SYNT DIS MOINS
652	COTTON FABRICS,WOVEN		24.3	A 10460	23.9	W 2808	20.6	W 2538	17.9	TISSUS DE COTON
6522	WOVEN COTTON BLEACHD,ETC		23.9	A 10095	23.3	W 2697	19.9	W 2406	16.8	TISSUS COTON BLANCHIS ETC
65224	BLCHED COTTON FABRIC NES		17.0	A 8517	17.9	W 2290	15.3	W 1979	12.3	AUT TIS PLUS 85% COT BLANCHI
653	WOVN MAN-MADE FIB FABRIC		86.2	A 62260	94.0	W 9194	71.2	W 7108	56.5	TISSUS FIBRES SYNTH,ARTIF
6531	CONT SYNT WEAVES NONPILE	A 8365	12.3	A 7161	11.1	W 1077	11.7	W 862	9.3	TISSUS FIBRES SYNTH CONTINUE
65315	CONT SYN TXTL FABRIC NES	A 7054	9.6	A 5268	8.5	W 841	9.6	W 741	7.9	TIS PLUS 85% TEXT SYNT CONT
6532	DISC SYN TXTL FABRIC NES	A 17694	23.6	A 19533	29.6	W 3505	22.3	W 1902	14.9	TIS DISC MOINS 85% FIBR TEXT
6534	DISC SYN BLEND FABRC NES	A 31651	39.2	A 29544	39.5	W 3686	25.7	W 3599	22.5	TISSUS FIBRES SYNTH DISCONT
65341	DISC SYN FIB-COTTN FABRC	A 10224	9.6	A 8617	10.1	W 908	6.6	W 783	5.8	TISSUS FIB SYNT DIS MEL COTO
65349	OTH DISC SYN BLEND FABRC	A 15720	18.4	A 16215	19.7	W 2033	11.9	W 2486	13.7	TISSUS FIB SYNT MEL MAT AUT
655	KNITTED,ETC FABRICS		15.2	A 6071	14.4	W 1450	13.3	W 1453	12.1	ETOF BONNETERIE PIECES ETC
6552	OTHER KNIT ETC FAB NONEL		15.2	A 6071	14.4	W 1450	13.3	W 1453	12.1	ETOF BON NON ELAS NON SYNT
657	SPECIAL TXTL FABRC,PRODS		11.5		13.0	W 2426	12.2	W 2435	10.8	TISSUS SPECIAUX
658	TEXTILE ARTICLES NES		8.7		10.1	W 1498	11.3	W 1492	11.6	ART FACONNES MAT TEXTILES
66	NONMETAL MINERAL MFS NES		81.2		93.4		100.0		91.3	ART MIN NON METALLIQUES
661	LIME,CEMENT,BLDG PRODS		12.6		18.0		18.4	W 28829	16.5	CHAUX,CIMENTS MAT CONSTR
6613	BUILDING STONE ETC WORKD		8.2		11.2	W 20819	13.1	W 19034	11.5	PIERRES A BATIR
66132	BUILDING STONE WORKED		8.0		10.9	W 20329	12.9	W 18561	11.3	OUVR EN PIERRES DE TAILLE
662	CLAY,REFRACTORY BLDG PRD		19.0		23.9		28.2		23.2	MAT CONST REFRACTAIRES
6624	BRICKS ETC NONREFRACTORY		17.6		22.5		26.6		22.2	BRIQUES ETC CERAM NON REFR
66245	GLAZED CERAMIC SETTS ETC		15.4		20.1	A 5030	23.9	A 2954	20.2	AUT CARREAUX CERAMIQUE
664	GLASS		9.9		11.7		10.8		8.7	VERRE
665	GLASSWARE		11.8		15.2		15.7		13.7	OUVRAGES EN VERRE
667	PEARL,PREC-,SEMI-P STONE		12.4		8.0		9.9		14.5	PERLES, PIERRES GEMMES
6672	DIAMONDS NONINDUST,UNSET		11.4		6.3		8.4		13.2	DIAMANTS BRUTS
66729	— CUT ETC NOT SET		9.4		4.8		6.8		11.3	DIAMANTS TAILLES
67	IRON AND STEEL		76.0		99.9		98.1		79.9	FER ET ACIER
673	IRON,STEEL SHAPES ETC		42.7	W 167050	51.3	W 158703	50.2	W 131675	40.2	BARRES,PROFIL FER,ACIER
6732	IRON,STEEL BARS ETC		32.4	W 130165	38.4	W 124360	38.7	W 104277	30.8	BARRES FER,ACIER
67326	IRN,OTH STL BARS HOTROLD		25.7	W 114681	31.8	W 122996	37.3	W 103409	29.8	BARRES PLEINES FER,ACIER
674	IRN,STL UNIV,PLATE,SHEET		19.2	W 38818	28.5	W 28727	22.1	W 28988	19.2	LARGES PLATS,TOLES
6749	OTH IRN,STL PLATES,SHEET	W 16070	11.2	W 20173	16.0	W 16247	13.8	W 15851	11.7	AUTRES TOLES FER,ACIER
67491	— OF IRON OR SIMPLE STL	W 15594	10.0	W 19733	14.8	W 15906	12.9	W 15571	11.0	AUT TOLES AUTRES ACIER FIN
678	IRON,STL TUBES,PIPES,ETC	W 7681	8.0	W 9222	9.2	W 18219	17.3	W 16537	14.0	TUBES,TUYAUX EN FONTE,FER
68	NON-FERROUS METALS		26.0		37.8		37.7		32.1	METAUX NON FERREUX
682	COPPER EXC CEMENT COPPER		7.4	W 2656	10.6		12.0	W 2553	8.7	CUIVRE
684	ALUMINIUM	W 7376	15.0	W 7980	22.1	W 8083	19.5	W 7770	18.1	ALUMINIUM
6841	ALUMINIUM,ALLOYS,UNWRGHT	W 5013	7.8	W 5389	11.9	W 5280	9.7	W 5299	9.7	ALUMINIUM,ALLIAGES BRUTS
69	METAL MANUFACTURES NES		89.5		100.5		107.4		88.2	ART MANUFACT EN METAL NDA
691	STRUCTURES AND PARTS NES		9.8	W 7257	13.9	W 8420	15.1	W 7225	12.0	CONSTRUCT FER,ACIER,ALU
6911	STRUCTURES,PARTS IRN,STL	W 4627	7.1	W 7010	11.6	W 8056	12.8	W 6860	10.2	CONSTRUCT FER,ACIER,FONTE
692	METAL TANKS,BOXES,ETC		17.6		17.1	W 4387	18.4	W 3937	16.7	RECIPIENTS METALLIQUES
6924	MTL TRANSPORT BOXES ETC		15.3		16.6	W 3774	17.2	W 3809	15.8	FUTS,TAMBOURS,BIDONS
69242	ALUMNM TRNSPRT BOXES ETC		12.4		13.5	W 2425	13.2	W 2470	12.7	FUTS,TAMBOURS,BIDONS ALU
695	TOOLS		9.6		10.0	W 778	8.3	W 714	6.8	OUTILS A MAIN
697	BASE MTL HOUSEHOLD EQUIP		17.1		17.9		19.4		16.6	ART MENAGE MET COMMUNS
699	BASE METAL MFRS NES		23.8		27.9	W 5482	30.6		25.2	ART MANUFACTURES MET NDA
6991	LOCKSMITHS WARES,ETC		10.9		12.6	W 1764	13.2	W 1777	11.7	ARTICLES DE SERRURERIE
7	MACHINES,TRANSPORT EQUIP		820.6		1018.8		963.5		804.0	MACHINES MATERIEL TRANSPORT
71	POWER GENERATING EQUIPMT		38.1		28.1		23.1		23.9	MACHINES GENERATRICES
712	STEAM ENGINES,TURBINES		11.8		2.0		0.7		0.1	MACHINES A VAPEUR D'EAU PIEC
7126	STEAM POWR UNITS,ENGINES	N 2	9.4			N 54	0.1	N 257	0.1	MACHINES A VAPEUR D EAU
713	INTRNL COMBUS PSTN ENGIN		11.3		12.7		10.4		11.1	MOTEURS EXPL COMB INT, PIECE
716	ROTATING ELECTRIC PLANT		14.0		12.3		10.9		10.7	APP ELECTR ROTATIFS,PIECES
7162	AC MTRS,GENRTRS,GEN SETS	N 244490	12.7	N 164399	10.9	N 155434	10.0	N 176823	9.9	MOTEURS ELECTRIQUES
72	MACHS FOR SPCL INDUSTRYS		64.9		75.2		71.4		57.2	MAC SPECIALES POUR INDUST
723	CIVIL ENGNEERG EQUIP ETC		9.2		9.8		10.9		10.7	APPAREILS DE GENIE CIVIL
728	OTH MACHY FOR SPCL INDUS		24.7		28.3		25.6		18.9	AUT MACH IND PARTICULIERES
7284	MACHY FOR SPCL INDUS NES		11.0		13.9		14.1		11.0	MACH SPEC IND PARTICUL.
74	GENRL INDUSTRL MACHY NES		132.9		162.0		176.5		136.0	MACH APP INDUSTRIE
741	HEATING,COOLING EQUIPMNT		43.7		59.3		74.9		45.0	MACH CHAUFFAGE,PIECES
7414	NONDOM REFRIG EQUIPT,PTS		9.2		13.2		20.5		12.3	MAT PRODUCTION DU FROID
74141	REFRIG EQUIP NONDOMESTIC	N 24196	8.1	N 33834	11.3		18.6		10.2	REFIG INDUSTRIELS
7415	AIR-CONDITIONING MACHNRY		20.7	N 83699	29.4	N 106352	36.2	N 61444	20.9	GROUPES CONDITION AIR
7416	HEATING,COOLING EQU NES		7.2		12.1	N 28981	12.8	N 22180	8.3	APP CHANGEMENT TEMP
742	PUMPS FOR LIQUIDS ETC		9.7		10.9		15.2		10.6	POMPES MOTO-POMPES
743	PUMPS NES,CENTRFUGES ETC		24.3		20.5		25.9		26.7	POMPES COMPRES,VENT ETC
7436	GAS,LIQUID FILTERS ETC	N 628833	8.5	N 734059	7.8	N 791279	13.4	N 1066309	13.6	APP POUR FILT DES LIQUIDES
744	MECHANICAL HANDLING EQU		17.8		27.8		18.0		20.5	EQUIP MANUTENTION PIECES
7442	LIFTING,LOADING MACH NES		7.5	N 32881	19.7	N 16628	7.7	N 15694	8.7	APP LEVAGE,MANUTENTION
74422	SHIP DERRICKS,CRANES ETC	N 41	0.7	N 1994	12.7	N 123	0.6	N 42	0.6	GRUES,PONTS ROULANTS
745	NONELEC MACHY,TOOLS NES		17.6		20.1		20.1		14.3	AUT MACH NON ELEC,PIECES
7452	OTH NONELEC MCHS,PTS NES		16.4		18.7		18.7		13.2	AUT MACH NON ELEC,PIECES
749	NONELEC MACH PTS,ACC NES		20.2		23.6		22.6		19.3	PIECES MACH NON ELEC NDA
7492	COCKS,VALVES ETC NES		12.1		14.2	W 1201	12.8	W 1089	11.4	ART ROB,SIM POUR TUYAUX
75	OFFICE MACHNES,ADP EQUIP		55.5		70.0		74.9		77.0	MACH BUREAU TRAIT AUTOM
752	AUTOMTIC DATA PROC EQUIP		39.2		50.1	N 133324	50.7	N 169390	52.0	MACH TRAIT INFORMATION
7522	DIGITAL COMPUTERS		8.4		11.1	N 3149	4.6	N 4089	5.3	MACH DIGITALES COMPLETES
7523	DIGITL CENTRL PROCESSORS		6.3		11.3	N 11244	16.4	N 13851	16.0	UNITES CENTRALES
7528	OFF-LINE DATA PROC EQUIP	N 36942	13.4	N 47457	14.2	N 53206	12.4	N 63496	11.8	MACH AUXIL TRAIT INFORM
759	OFFICE,ADP MCH PTS,ACCES		8.4		11.0	W 249	16.1	W 293	15.1	PIECES DU 751 ET 752
7599	ACCTG,ETC,ADP MCH PTS,AC		6.6		8.6	W 202	13.6	W 220	12.5	PIECES DU 751 ET 752
76	TELECOMM,SOUND EQUIPMENT		110.2		121.5		114.7		93.5	EQUIPMENT DE TELECOM
761	TELEVISION RECEIVERS	N 92911	28.6	N 100610	30.3	N 112871	18.4	N 36066	11.2	RECEPTEURS DE TELEVISION
7611	COLOUR TV RECEIVERS	N 92818	28.5	N 100425	30.3	N 111846	18.4	N 35698	11.1	RECEPTEURS COULEUR

4. General Imports C.I.F. by Commodities according to the S.I.T.C. (Rev. 2) in million U.S. Dollars
Importations Générales C.A.F. par Produits d'après la C.T.C.I. (Rév. 2) en millions de Dollars E.U.

SITC CTCI	COMMODITY	1994		1995		1996		1997		PRODUIT
		QUANTITY QUANTITE	VALUE VALEUR	QUANTITY QUANTITE	VALUE VALEUR	QUANTITY QUANTITE	VALUE VALEUR	QUANTITY QUANTITE	VALUE VALEUR	
762	RADIO BROADCAST RECEIVRS	N 216074	12.0	N 324178	19.4	N 239688	12.9	N 224521	9.2	RECEPTEURS RADIODIFFUSION
7628	OTHER RADIO RECEIVERS	N 112758	7.2	N 189516	12.5	N 114897	8.8	N 88097	5.6	AUTRES RECEPT RADIO
764	TELECOM EQPT,PTS,ACC NES		63.5		62.6		76.2		67.4	EQUIP TELECOM,PIECES
7641	LINE TELEPHONE,ETC EQUIP		13.2	N 146206	12.9	N 332335	12.4	N 149769	10.1	APP TELEPHON PAR FIL
7643	TV,RADIO TRANSMITTRS ETC	N 18591	10.0	N 40385	17.5	N 39759	16.2	N 46647	14.5	APP EMET TELE RADIO
7649	PTS NES OF EQUIPMT OF 76		31.6		23.5	W 716	41.7	W 544	36.2	PIECES DE LA DIV 76
76491	PTS NES OF APPAR OF 7641	N 956892	16.8	N 251865	12.7	W 190	20.0	W 187	16.4	PIECES POUR 764.1
76493	TELECOMM EQUIPMT PTS NES		14.4		10.4	W 515	21.4	W 332	19.4	PIECES 761,762,764.3,8
77	ELECTRIC MACHNRY NES ETC		153.0		177.8		144.7		123.3	MACH APP ELECT NDA
771	ELECTRIC POWER MACHY NES		9.2		9.0		10.3		7.8	MACH PROD,TRANS ELECTR
772	SWITCHGEAR ETC,PARTS NES		19.9		25.7	W 1679	31.7	W 1686	22.3	APP COUPURE,SECT ETC
7721	SWITCHGEAR ETC		19.6		25.4	W 1674	31.4	W 1675	22.0	APP COUPURE,SECTIONMNT
773	ELECTR DISTRIBUTNG EQUIP		11.8		22.3	W 6985	20.1	W 6671	17.6	EQUIPMT DISTRIBUTION ELECT
7731	INSULATED WIRE,CABLE ETC		11.3		21.3	W 6837	19.8	W 6521	17.1	FILS,CABLES ISOLES ELECT
775	HOUSEHOLD TYPE EQUIP NES		39.2		51.6		45.8		39.7	MACH,APP USAGE DOMESTQUE
7752	DOM REFRIGERATRS,FREEZRS	N 27727	9.3	N 34553	13.6	N 31696	12.8	N 26121	9.3	REFRIG,CONGEL MENAGER
77521	DOMESTIC REFRIGERATORS	N 23618	8.1	N 29288	12.0	N 26742	11.2	N 22046	8.4	REFRIGERATEURS
7758	ELECTRO–THERMIC APPL NES		16.7		21.4		18.5		16.4	APP ELECTROTHERMIQ NDA
77586	ELECTROTHERM DOM APP NES	N 208613	10.9	N 290918	13.9	N 213747	11.6	N 189382	10.0	APP ELECTRO THERMIQUES
778	ELECTRICAL MACHINERY NES		67.5		63.4		31.0		25.1	AUTRES MACH ELECT NDA
7788	OTH ELEC MACHY,EQUIP NES		50.9		43.5		10.1		6.5	AUT MACH APP ELEC NDA
77886	OTH ELEC MACHINERY NES		47.5		40.6	N 108256	6.6	N 375284	4.1	AUT MACH APP ELECTRIQUES
78	ROAD VEHICLES		247.8		360.5		340.1		275.1	VEHICULES ROUTIERS
781	PASS MOTOR VEH EXC BUSES	N 12840	134.3	N 18740	187.3	N 23562	188.9	N 21596	146.3	AUTO TRANSPORT PERSONNES
782	LORRIES,SPCL MTR VEH NES	N 6990	77.3	N 10020	123.2	N 8149	100.4	N 7152	86.8	VEHICULES SPECIAUX,MARCH
7821	LORRIES,TRUCKS	N 6939	74.2	N 9960	119.1	N 8075	94.2	N 7065	80.3	VEHICULES TRANSP MARCHAND
784	MOTOR VEH PRTS,ACCES NES		24.3		30.1		29.3		24.6	PIECES 722,781,782,783
7849	OTHER MOTOR VEHCL PARTS		22.2		27.1	W 2317	27.3	W 2678	23.8	PIECES 722,781,782,783
79	OTHR TRANSPORT EQUIPMENT		12.0		18.0		11.9		11.4	AUTRE MATERIEL TRANSPORT
793	SHIPS AND BOATS ETC	N 7823	9.5	N 6161	15.3	N 7259	8.2	N 7812	3.5	NAVIRES BATEAUX,ETC
8	MISC MANUFACTURED GOODS		310.6		389.0		423.4		445.5	ART MANUFACTURES DIVERS
812	*PLUMBG,HEATNG,LGHTNG EQ		23.8		30.0		31.1		26.8	APPAR SANITAIRES CHAUFFAGE
8124	LIGHTING EQUIPMENT NES		10.5		14.6		16.3		14.0	APPAREILS ECLAIRAGE ETC
81242	LAMPS,FITTINGS BASE METL		9.7		13.4	W 1679	14.6	W 1223	12.4	APPAREILS D'ECLAIRAGE
821	*FURNITURE,PARTS THEREOF		16.3		23.3		31.0		32.5	MEUBLES ET PIECES
8219	FURNITURE AND PARTS NES		9.2		14.1		19.3		20.8	AUTRES MEUBLES ET PIECES
82192	WOOD FURNITURE NES		4.7		7.2	N 162731	11.4	N 218138	13.6	MEUBLES NDA EN BOIS
84	CLOTHING AND ACCESSORIES		49.9		70.5		95.7		113.3	VETEMENTS
842	MENS OUTERWEAR NOT KNIT	N 428187	5.8	N 554398	8.1		12.3		13.8	VET DESSUS POUR HOMMES
843	WOMENS OUTERWEAR NONKNIT	N 1379340	13.5	N 1512917	18.1	N 2029234	28.3	N 2210328	37.8	VET DESSUS FEMMES MAT TEX
8439	— OTHER OUTER GARMENTS	N 464266	4.5	N 469025	5.6	N 845571	9.7	N 748428	12.5	AUT VET DES FEM MAT TEXT
845	OUTERWEAR KNIT NONELASTC		10.5	N 1236981	15.3	N 1460425	19.4	N 1584659	22.8	VET DESSOUS,ACCES BONNET
8459	— OTHER,CLTHG ACCESRYS		5.6	N 830392	8.9	N 912932	10.7	N 947331	11.8	AUT VET DESSUS DE BONNE
846	UNDER GARMENTS KNITTED		11.3		15.3		17.9		19.3	SOUS VETS DE BONNETERIE
8462	— OF COTTON NON ELASTIC	N 4703903	7.2	N 4487786	9.7	N 3438348	11.0	N 2330725	12.1	SOUS–VET BONNET COTON
84629	—— OTHER	N 4703903	7.2	N 4487786	9.7	N 3438348	11.0	N 2330725	12.1	AUT SOUS–VET BONNET COTON
851	*FOOTWEAR	P 1141952	17.0	P 1557463	23.2	P 1570766	26.4	P 2094509	34.2	CHAUSSURES
85102	FOOTWEAR LEATHER	P 787817	13.1	P 1269221	20.0	P 1274344	22.9	P 1626192	29.7	CHAUS SEMELLES EN CUIR
87	PRECISION INSTRUMNTS NES		23.2		27.7		27.8		26.0	INSTRUM,APPAR SCIENT NDA
874	MEASURNG,CONTROLNG INSTR		13.7		14.8		16.4		13.1	INSTRUMENTS DE MESURE
88	PHOTO EQU,OPTICL GDS ETC		35.8		41.3		34.9		33.4	APP,FOURN PHOTO,OP,MONTR
882	PHOTO,CINEMA SUPPLIES		12.7		13.7		11.4		11.0	PRODUITS PHOTO,CINEMA
8822	PHOTO FILM EXC DEV CINMA		10.6		11.3		9.0		8.5	PLAQUES,PELLICULES,FILMS
885	WATCHES AND CLOCKS		11.4		12.7		8.9		10.1	HORLOGERIE
8851	WATCHES,MOVEMENTS,CASES		9.9		11.0		7.3		8.7	MONTRES,MOUVEMENTS,BOITES
88511	WATCHES		9.7		10.9		7.2		8.4	MONTRES POCHE,BRACELET
89	MISC MANUFCTRD GOODS NES		140.0		167.5		169.0		170.5	ART MANUFACTURES DIVERS
892	PRINTED MATTER		30.4		37.5	W 5130	41.6	W 5343	42.4	IMPRIMES
8921	PRINTED BOOKS,GLOBES,ETC		12.5		15.9	W 2444	22.0	W 2053	19.8	LIVRES,BROCHURES,CARTES
89211	PRINTED BOOKS,PAMPHLETS		12.3		15.5	W 2382	21.6	W 2007	19.5	LIVRES,BROCHURES
8922	NEWSPAPERS,PERIODICALS		10.2		11.7	W 1756	10.8	W 2307	12.7	JOURNAUX ET PERIODIQUES
893	ARTICLES OF PLASTIC NES		34.2		44.0		43.8		41.4	OUVRAGES EN MAT DIVIS 58
8939	MISC PLASTIC ARTICLES		26.4		34.7	W 6962	34.8	W 7508	32.8	ART DIVERS EN MAT DIV 58
89399	OTHR PLASTC ARTICLES NES		24.3		32.1	W 6323	32.2	W 6895	30.4	AUT OUV MAT DIV 58
894	TOYS,SPORTING GOODS,ETC		32.6		37.5		34.6		33.4	VOITURES ENFANTS,JOUETS
8942	TOYS,INDOOR GAMES ETC		20.1		25.0		21.6		21.9	JOUETS,JEUX ETC
89423	TOYS NES		10.8		13.9	N 7764918	10.8	N 7951999	11.0	JOUETS,MODELES REDUITS
898	MUSICAL INSTRUMENTS,PTS		18.9		20.8		20.9		21.0	INSTRUMENTS DE MUSIQUE
8983	SOUND RECRDNG TAPE,DISCS	N 5620779	16.4	N 6879190	18.3	N 5295831	18.3	N 6639082	18.9	SUPPORTS SON POUR 763
89832	RECORDED DISCS,TAPES ETC	N 2380792	13.2	N 3781017	14.9	N 3093078	15.7	N 3860163	16.2	DISQUES,PHONO,BANDES
899	OTHER MANUFACTURED GOODS		13.5		16.1		15.1		13.2	AUT ART MANUF DIVERS NDA
9	GOODS NOT CLASSD BY KIND		162.5		149.1		246.9		207.3	ART TRANSACT NON CLASSES
951	*WAR FIREARMS,AMMUNITION		131.5		119.2		221.5		186.6	VEHIC BLINDES ARMES
95102	MILITARY FIREARMS NES		131.0	N 11821	118.6	N 34471	220.9	N 59135	186.2	ARMES DE GUERRE
971	*GOLD,NON MONETARY NES	K 2696	30.2	K 2451	29.6	K 3406	24.6	K 4280	20.6	OR NON MONETAIRE
97101	NONMON GLD UNWRT,SEMIMFD	K 2696	30.2	K 2400	29.5	K 3382	24.6	K 4175	20.6	OR,ALLIAGES D'OR BRUTS

5. General Exports F.O.B. by Commodities according to the S.I.T.C. (Rev. 2) in million U.S. Dollars
Exportations Générales F.O.B. par Produits d'après la C.T.C.I. (Rév. 2) en millions de Dollars E.U.

SITC CTCI	COMMODITY	1994		1995		1996		1997		PRODUIT
		QUANTITY QUANTITE	VALUE VALEUR	QUANTITY QUANTITE	VALUE VALEUR	QUANTITY QUANTITE	VALUE VALEUR	QUANTITY QUANTITE	VALUE VALEUR	
	ALL COMMODITIES		961.3		1230.6		1390.7		1250.2	TOUS PRODUITS
0	FOOD AND LIVE ANIMALS		139.5		205.1		168.9		116.6	ALIMENTS,ANIMAUX VIVANTS
001	*LIVE ANIMALS FOR FOOD	N 138637	0.5	N 504954	1.4	N 91461	0.9	N 142363	7.9	ANIMAUX VIVANTS
0011	BOVINE SPECIES,LIVE			N 729	0.6	N 893	0.6	N 12751	3.9	ESPECE BOVINE
01	MEAT AND PREPARATIONS		3.4		3.2		5.1		7.7	VIANDES ET PREPARATIONS
011	MEAT FRESH,CHILLD,FROZEN	W 1823	2.4	W 1583	2.8	W 2918	4.8	W 3904	7.1	VIANDES FRAICHES,REF,CONGE
02	DAIRY PRODCTS,BIRDS'EGGS		10.3		12.4		12.5		13.7	PRODUITS LAITIERS,OEUFS
024	CHEESE AND CURD	W 2154	9.3	W 2291	11.1	W 2419	11.2	W 2902	12.9	FROMAGE ET CAILLEBOTTE
05	VEGETABLES AND FRUIT		110.9		171.2		135.4		75.7	LEGUMES ET FRUITS
054	VEG ETC FRSH,SMPLY PRSVD	W 244	0.2	W 198328	105.0	W 189721	68.7	W 45654	25.0	LEGUMES FRAIS,CONG,SECS
0541	POTATOES FRSH EXCL SWEET	W 96224	48.0	W 186969	95.5	W 178287	59.4	W 34776	16.6	POMMES DE TERRE
0545	OTHER FRESH VEGETABLES	W 6883	6.3	W 6598	6.1	W 6291	6.3	W 6007	5.7	AUTRES LEGUMES FRAIS,REF
05459	FRESH VEGETABLES NES	W 6554	6.2	W 6589	6.1	W 6282	6.3	W 5966	5.6	LEGUMES FRAIS,REFRI NDA
057	FRUIT,NUTS,FRESH,DRIED	W 200	0.5	W 98136	43.5	W 91965	45.1	W 83995	37.6	FRUITS FRAIS OU SECS
0571	ORANGES, MANDARINS ETC		6.5	W 25629	10.2	W 27169	12.3	W 27890	11.9	ORANGES,MAND,CLEMENTINES
05711	ORANGES,FRESH OR DRIED		6.2	W 24149	9.3	W 24591	10.2	W 21945	8.8	ORANGES FRAICHES,SECHEES
0572	LEMONS,GRAPEFRUIT ETC		21.4	W 65702	27.1	W 57877	26.6	W 51683	22.0	AUTRES AGRUMES FRAIS,SECS
05721	LEMONS,LIMES,FRESH,DRIED	W 19781	7.6	W 16099	7.6	W 17124	9.1	W 12867	6.8	CITRONS ET LIMES
05722	GRAPEFRUITS,FRESH,DRIED	W 33204	10.4	W 41409	14.8	W 33233	13.0	W 33003	11.7	PAMPLEMOUSSES,POMELOS
05729	CITRUS NES, FRESH,DRIED		3.5	W 8194	4.8	W 7519	4.5	W 5813	3.6	AGRUMES N.D.A
0575	GRAPES FRESH OR DRIED	W 5423	4.8	W 5554	5.4	W 5251	5.4	W 2937	2.8	RAISINS FRAIS OU SECS
05751	GRAPES FRESH	W 5039	4.3	W 4958	4.7	W 4635	4.7	W 2712	2.5	RAISINS FRAIS
058	FRUIT PRESERVED,PREPARED	W 27597	19.5	W 28361	22.3	W 27069	21.4	W 16111	12.9	CONSERVES DE FRUITS
0585	FRUIT OR VEGETABLE JUICE	W 21924	13.6	W 23641	17.3	W 21728	15.8	W 12761	9.3	JUS DE FRUITS
05851	ORANGE JUICE	W 5946	3.5	W 6844	4.0	W 6040	3.7	W 3164	1.9	JUS D'ORANGE
05852	GRAPEFRUIT JUICE	W 3761	3.3	W 3216	2.9	W 2246	2.0	W 1347	1.0	JUS DE PAMPLEMOUSSE
05857	JUICE OF OTHER FRUIT,VEG	W 5941	4.2	W 6456	6.7	W 6989	6.4	W 4495	4.2	JUS AUTRES FRUITS,LEGUMES
0589	FRUIT PREPRD,PRESRVD,NES	W 5078	5.2	W 4149	4.4	W 4452	4.8	W 3055	3.3	FRUITS PREPARES CONSERV
05899	FRUIT,NUTS NES,PRESERVED	W 5069	5.2	W 4147	4.4	W 4437	4.7	W 3051	3.2	FRUITS PREP CONSERV NDA
07	COFFEE,TEA,COCOA,SPICES		4.8		4.2		5.3		2.5	CAFE,THE,CACAO,EPICES
073	CHOCOLATE AND PRODUCTS	W 575	3.8	W 359	3.4	W 374	3.2	W 175	0.6	CHOCOLAT
1	BEVERAGES AND TOBACCO		262.9		402.9		612.7		615.1	BOISSONS ET TABACS
11	BEVERAGES		37.7		43.3		41.0		26.6	BOISSONS
112	ALCOHOLIC BEVERAGES	W 56258	35.5	W 55125	42.1	W 50039	40.2	W 37220	26.1	BOISSONS ALCOOLIQUES
1121	WINE OF FRESH GRAPES ETC	W 52831	17.6	W 51691	21.6	W 46512	22.2	W 34296	16.3	VINS DE RAISINS FRAIS
11212	WINE OF FRESH GRAPES	W 52805	17.5	W 50389	20.9	W 16187	11.0	W 11847	8.1	VINS DE MOUTS DE RAISINS
11213	VERMOUTHS ETC	W 23	0.2	W 1256	0.7	W 29469	10.3	W 22446	8.2	VERMOUTHS
1124	DISTILLED ALCOHOLIC BEVS	W 1967	16.2	W 1927	18.7	W 1663	15.8	W 1242	8.0	ALCOOLS,EAUX-DE-VIE
11241	WHISKY	W 1004	9.6	W 978	12.0	W 888	9.9	W 533	5.3	WHISKY
11249	OTH ALCOHOLC BEVS,CMPNDS	W 816	5.1	W 782	5.0	W 636	4.5	W 665	2.4	BOISSONS ALCOOLIQUES NDA
12	TOBACCO AND MANUFACTURES		225.3		359.7		571.7		588.5	TABACS BRUTS FABRIQUES
122	TOBACCO,MANUFACTURED	W 17386	225.0	W 25607	359.0	W 41523	571.2	W 38869	588.2	TABACS FABRIQUES
1222	CIGARETTES	W 17340	222.3	W 25541	356.1	W 41424	567.9	W 38830	587.3	CIGARETTES
2	CRUDE MATERLS,EXCL FUELS		17.0		19.0		18.8		21.6	MAT BRUTES NON COMESTIBLES
27	CRUDE FERTLZR,MINRLS NES		3.4		3.2		4.5		5.9	ENGRAIS MINERAUX BRUTS
28	METALLIFEROUS ORES,SCRAP		7.9		9.2		8.1		9.6	MINERAIS METAL,DECHETS
282	IRON AND STEEL SCRAP	W 22166	2.8	W 25902	3.6	W 34373	3.5	W 21344	4.2	FERRAILLES
28202	— OF ALLOY STEEL	W 6725	1.0	W 16616	2.4	W 32146	3.2	W 21118	4.1	FERRAILLES D'ACIERS ALLIES
288	NONFERR METAL SCRAP NES	W 111937	5.1	W 22538	5.6	W 23436	4.5	W 4026	4.5	DECHETS NON FERREUX
2882	OTHER BASE MTL SCRAP NES	W 59826	4.6	W 22538	5.6	W 23436	4.5	W 4026	4.5	AUTRES DECHETS
3	MINERAL FUELS ETC		38.0		45.9		60.6		55.6	COMBUSTIBLES MINERAUX LUB
33	PETROLEUM AND PRODUCTS		38.0		45.9		60.5		55.6	PETROLE ET DERIVES
334	PETROLEUM PRODUCTS,REFIN	W 154216	11.4	W 241289	45.8	W 284810	60.5	W 260534	55.5	PRODUITS RAFFINES
3342	KEROSENE,OTH MEDIUM OILS	W 140390	28.6	W 164726	34.8	W 160821	42.0	W 158360	38.7	PETR LAMPANTS,AUT HUIL
33421	KEROSENE INCL JET FUEL	W 140390	28.6	W 164726	34.8	W 160821	42.0	W 158360	38.7	PETROLES LAMPANTS
3343	GAS OILS	W 15866	3.0	W 18203	3.3	W 34352	7.1	W 26419	6.5	GAS OILS
3344	FUEL OILS,NES	W 123599	5.1	W 54736	5.9	W 85283	9.8	W 70467	7.8	FUEL OILS
4	ANIMAL,VEGETABLE OIL,FAT		12.1		12.4		10.6		8.7	HUILES,GRAISSES ANIM,VEG
42	FIXED VEGETABLE OIL,FAT		11.2		11.6		9.7		7.8	HUILES VEGETALES FIXES
423	FIXED VEG OILS,SOFT	W 14101	10.6	W 10520	9.9	W 10209	8.6	W 7638	6.3	HUILES VEGET DOUCES FIXES
4232	SOYA BEAN OIL	W 10834	7.9	W 3542	3.2	W 2964	2.3	W 1259	1.0	HUILE DE SOJA
4236	SUNFLOWER SEED OIL	W 3265	2.8	W 6821	6.3	W 7210	6.3	W 6349	5.2	HUILE DE TOURNESOL
5	CHEMCLS,RELATED PROD NES		63.5		76.4		80.9		67.6	PRODUITS CHIMIQUES
51	ORGANIC CHEMICALS		0.3		0.4		3.1		5.1	PROD CHIMIQ ORGANIQUES
541	*MEDICINAL,PHARM PRODUCT		33.2		39.9		43.5	K 1223626	38.6	PROD MEDICINAUX PHARMACEUT
5417	MEDICAMENTS		33.2		39.9	K 1178406	41.8	K 1228659	38.7	MEDICAMENTS
54171	— CONTAINNG ANTIBIOTICS		5.2		6.5	K 319108	8.2	K 130984	2.8	MED CONTN ANTIBIOTIQUES
54179	— CONTNG OTH SUBSTANCES		28.0		33.3	K 858850	33.6	K 1095862	35.9	MED CONT AUT SUBSTANCES
55	PERFUME,CLEANING ETC PRD		22.2		25.7		22.9		9.5	PROD POUR PARFUM,TOILETTE
553	PERFUMERY,COSMETICS,ETC		20.0		22.7	W 1705	20.5	W 2304	7.8	PRODUITS DE PARFUMERIE
59	CHEMICAL MATERIALS NES		4.6		6.6		7.1		7.2	MAT PROD CHIMIQUES NDA
598	MISCEL CHEM PRODUCTS NES		2.2		3.5	W 38311	4.1	W 50480	4.3	PROD DIV INDUST CHIM NDA
5989	CHEM PRODUCTS,PREPS NES		2.2		3.5	W 38296	4.1	W 50471	4.3	PROD PREP CHIMIQUES NDA
59892	ACTIVTED NAT MINRL PROD	W 28299	1.8	W 36830	2.7	W 38059	3.5	W 50316	3.9	CHARBONS ACTIVES
6	BASIC MANUFACTURES		130.2		128.9		117.9		111.7	ART MANUFACTURES
61	LEATHER,DRESSED FUR,ETC		3.5		3.2		3.3		5.1	CUIRS,PELLETERIES
64	PAPER,PAPERBOARD AND MFR		11.1		14.7		13.7		12.5	PAPIERS,CARTONS & OUVRAGES
642	PAPER,ETC,PRECUT,ARTS OF		10.7		13.8	W 5103	13.3	W 5084	12.1	PAP,CARTONS DECOUPES
6421	PAPER ETC CONTAINERS		5.0		4.4	W 1388	3.1	W 1839	4.2	BOITES,SACS EMBALLAGES
6428	PAPER ETC ARTICLES NES		5.3		9.1	W 3537	9.9	W 3194	7.8	OUVRAGES EN PATE A PAPIER
64285	PAPER ETC DIAPERS ETC		5.0		8.8	W 3399	9.6	W 3144	7.6	SERVIETTES HYGIENIQUES
65	TEXTILE YARN,FABRICS,ETC		65.4		67.5		55.0		39.6	FILS,TISSUS,ARTICLES TEXTILE
651	TEXTILE YARN	W 1	0.1		5.9	W 1485	3.4	W 1064	3.5	FILS TEXTILES
6514	SYN FIB YRN,BULK,MONOFIL	W 1	0.1		3.2	W 858	1.7	W 300	1.3	FILS CONT 85% FIB TEXT SYNTH
652	COTTON FABRICS,WOVEN	A 6770	5.1	A 3603	3.6	W 1560	4.4	W 539	2.0	TISSUS DE COTON
6522	WOVEN COTTON BLEACHD,ETC	A 6202	4.8	A 3487	3.5	W 1468	4.0	W 508	1.9	TISSUS COTON BLANCHIS ETC
65224	BLCHED COTTON FABRIC NES	A 4761	3.9	A 3015	3.1	W 1432	3.7	W 456	1.6	AUT TIS PLUS 85% COT BLANCHI
653	WOVN MAN-MADE FIB FABRIC	A 39958	43.0	A 37285	44.6	W 7553	36.6	W 5259	27.0	TISSUS FIBRES SYNTH,ARTIF
6531	CONT SYNT WEAVES NONPILE	A 4265	5.3	A 1371	2.6	W 485	3.1	W 409	3.0	TISSUS FIBRES SYNTH CONTINUE
65315	CONT SYN TXTL FABRIC NES	A 4241	5.2	A 1257	2.4	W 476	3.0	W 379	2.9	TIS PLUS 85% TEXT SYNT CONT
6532	DISC SYN TXTL FABRIC NES	A 8441	10.1	A 11524	15.0	W 2052	14.4	W 1733	9.8	TIS DISC MOINS 85% FIBR TEXT
6534	DISC SYN BLEND FABRC NES	A 26554	27.1	A 23578	26.1	W 4833	18.6	W 2911	13.5	TISSUS FIBRES SYNTH DISCONT
65341	DISC SYN FIB-COTTN FABRC	A 6625	5.7	A 6697	5.4	W 642	2.3	W 408	1.9	TISSUS FIB SYNT DIS MEL COTO
65343	DISC SYN-CONT MAN-MD FAB	A 2607	3.7	A 3242	4.6	W 419	3.8	W 131	0.9	TISSUS FIB SYNT MEL TEXT SY
65349	OTH DISC SYN BLEND FABRC	A 16829	17.2	A 13460	16.0	W 3711	12.4	W 2285	10.5	TISSUS FIB SYNT MEL MAT AUT
655	KNITTED,ETC FABRICS	A 6	0.1	A 1786	4.1	W 481	2.9	W 522	2.8	ETOF BONNETERIE PIECES ETC
6552	OTHER KNIT ETC FAB NONEL	A 6	0.1	A 1786	4.1	W 481	2.9	W 522	2.8	ETOF BON NON ELAS NON SYNT
658	TEXTILE ARTICLES NES		7.7		6.3	W 915	5.8	W 275	1.9	ART FACONNES MAT TEXTILES
6589	OTH TEXTILE ARTICLES NES		5.9		5.3	W 424	3.5	W 173	1.4	AUT ART EN TEXTILES NDA
65898	KNITTED ETC ARTICLES NES		5.9		5.3	W 415	3.4	W 170	1.3	ART BONNET NON ELASTIQUE
66	NONMETAL MINERAL MFS NES		35.5		21.5		25.9		31.6	ART MIN NON METALLIQUES

5. General Exports F.O.B. by Commodities according to the S.I.T.C. (Rev. 2) in million U.S. Dollars
Exportations Générales F.O.B. par Produits d'après la C.T.C.I. (Rév. 2) en millions de Dollars E.U.

SITC CTCI	COMMODITY	1994 QUANTITY QUANTITE	1994 VALUE VALEUR	1995 QUANTITY QUANTITE	1995 VALUE VALEUR	1996 QUANTITY QUANTITE	1996 VALUE VALEUR	1997 QUANTITY QUANTITE	1997 VALUE VALEUR	PRODUIT
661	LIME,CEMENT,BLDG PRODS		23.4		18.2	W 529756	19.5	W 646135	25.3	CHAUX,CIMENTS MAT CONSTR
6612	CEMENT	W 699963	22.6	W 528716	17.3	W 529407	18.9	W 644873	24.4	CIMENTS HYDRAULIQUES
667	PEARL,PREC–,SEMI–P STONE		11.1		2.4		4.8		5.1	PERLES, PIERRES GEMMES
6672	DIAMONDS NONINDUST,UNSET		10.9		2.3		4.4		4.9	DIAMANTS BRUTS
66721	— ROUGH,UNSORTED		10.2		2.3		4.2		4.7	DIAMANTS BRUTS NON TRIES
68	NON–FERROUS METALS		1.9		2.6		5.8		13.2	METAUX NON FERREUX
682	COPPER EXC CEMENT COPPER	W 15	0.1	W 27	0.1	W 1542	3.1	W 4084	9.2	CUIVRE
6821	COPPER NES,ALLOYS,UNWRT					W 1491	2.9	W 4048	9.2	CUIVRE BRUT
68212	COPPER REFINED,UNWROUGHT					W 1491	2.9	W 4048	9.2	CUIVRE AFFINE BRUT
69	METAL MANUFACTURES NES		9.3		13.4		10.3		7.6	ART MANUFACT EN METAL NDA
699	BASE METAL MFRS NES		3.4		8.9	W 188	3.2	W 1505	3.3	ART MANUFACTURES MET NDA
6999	OTHR BASE METAL MFRS ETC		0.1	W 26	5.4	W 9	1.9			OUVRAGES EN TUNGST,MOLYB
69999	BASE MTLS NES WRGHT,MFRS		0.1	W 26	5.4	W 9	1.9			MET COMMUNS OUVRES NDA
7	MACHINES,TRANSPORT EQUIP		117.5		148.9		153.2		109.9	MACHINES MATERIEL TRANSPORT
71	POWER GENERATING EQUIPMT		3.2		3.4		3.1		3.6	MACHINES GENERATRICES
72	MACHS FOR SPCL INDUSTRYS		6.2		10.6		8.0		7.8	MAC SPECIALES POUR INDUST
74	GENRL INDUSTRL MACHY NES		19.9		21.2		28.3		28.4	MACH APP INDUSTRIE
741	HEATING,COOLING EQUIPMNT		5.6		6.5		15.7		13.5	MACH CHAUFFAGE,PIECES
7414	NONDOM REFRIG EQUIPT,PTS		1.4		1.9		9.5		5.6	MAT PRODUCTION DU FROID
74141	REFRIG EQUIP NONDOMESTIC	N 3467	1.3	N 6610	1.8	N 21623	9.4	N 15264	5.5	REFIG INDUSTRIELS
7415	AIR–CONDITIONING MACHNRY	N 1249	0.7	N 11070	4.5	N 23997	6.1	N 16990	7.5	GROUPES CONDITION AIR
742	PUMPS FOR LIQUIDS ETC		6.1		7.9		5.1		5.4	POMPES MOTO–POMPES
7422	CENTRIFUGAL PUMPS NES	N 4321	4.5	N 6890	6.3	N 4644	3.7	N 5616	4.0	POMPES CENTRIF NON 742.81
743	PUMPS NES,CENTRFUGES ETC		3.2		3.1		4.3		4.1	POMPES COMPRES,VENT ETC
75	OFFICE MACHNES,ADP EQUIP		2.5		3.5		5.8		4.3	MACH BUREAU TRAIT AUTOM
76	TELECOMM,SOUND EQUIPMENT		41.5		48.5		33.4		9.9	EQUIPMENT DE TELECOM
761	TELEVISION RECEIVERS	N 47525	18.9	N 60178	21.7	N 35104	12.6	N 4022	2.0	RECEPTEURS DE TELEVISION
7611	COLOUR TV RECEIVERS	N 47512	18.9	N 60172	21.7	N 35102	12.6	N 4007	2.0	RECEPTEURS COULEUR
762	RADIO BROADCAST RECEIVRS	N 64742	8.8	N 120435	10.8	N 87537	8.3	N 12982	1.4	RECEPTEURS RADIODIFFUSION
7621	MTR VEHC RADIO RECEIVERS	N 31515	2.9	N 81790	4.8	N 6601	1.1	N 1717	0.3	RECEPTEURS RADIO AUTO
7628	OTHER RADIO RECEIVERS	N 29375	5.7	N 34065	5.8	N 75046	7.0	N 10383	1.1	AUTRES RECEPT RADIO
763	SOUND RECORDRS,PHONOGRPH		3.8	N 35155	5.3	N 26818	5.5	N 5548	1.4	PHONO,APP ENREGISTREMENT
7638	OTHR SOUND APPARATUS ETC		3.7	N 35112	5.3	N 26730	5.5	N 5519	1.4	AUT APP D'ENREGIS,REPROD
76381	TV IMAGE,SND RECRDRS ETC	N 8866	2.7	N 19070	4.6	N 20103	5.0	N 3989	1.3	APP ENREG,REPRO IMAG,SON
764	TELECOM EQPT,PTS,ACC NES		10.1		10.8	N 120	0.1		5.3	EQUIP TELECOM,PIECES
7648	TELECOMM EQUIPMENT NES	N 6768	3.1	N 17725	2.7	N 60015	1.7	N 2453	0.4	APP TELECOM NDA
7649	PTS NES OF EQUIPMT OF 76		3.7		2.7	W 74	1.8	W 32	1.4	PIECES DE LA DIV 76
76493	TELECOMM EQUIPMT PTS NES		3.4		2.4	W 72	1.6	W 28	1.3	PIECES 761,762,764.3,8
77	ELECTRIC MACHNRY NES ETC		20.7		46.3		48.1		16.1	MACH APP ELECT NDA
772	SWITCHGEAR ETC,PARTS NES		6.5		3.5	W 219	3.2	W 244	4.0	APP COUPURE,SECT ETC
7721	SWITCHGEAR ETC		6.5		3.5	W 216	3.1	W 243	3.9	APP COUPURE,SECTIONMNT
775	HOUSEHOLD TYPE EQUIP NES		4.3		4.7		1.5		0.7	MACH,APP USAGE DOMESTQUE
7752	DOM REFRIGERATRS,FREEZRS	N 8491	3.6	N 8479	4.0	N 2241	1.0	N 387	0.1	REFRIG,CONGEL MENAGER
77522	DOMESTIC DEEP–FREEZERS	N 7737	3.4	N 8209	3.8	N 2050	0.9	N 81	0.1	MEUBLES CONGELATEURS
778	ELECTRICAL MACHINERY NES		9.1		37.6		42.4		10.0	AUTRES MACH ELECT NDA
7788	OTH ELEC MACHY,EQUIP NES		7.2		35.2		0.1		6.2	AUT MACH APP ELEC NDA
77886	OTH ELEC MACHINERY NES		6.7		35.0	N 47171	38.8	N 13052	5.8	AUT MACH APP ELECTRIQUES
78	ROAD VEHICLES		21.8		14.5		16.2		37.0	VEHICULES ROUTIERS
781	PASS MOTOR VEH EXC BUSES	N 543	10.2	N 177	4.8	N 354	6.6	N 2120	23.3	AUTO TRANSPORT PERSONNES
782	LORRIES,SPCL MTR VEH NES	N 453	7.8	N 340	6.1	N 407	6.4	N 613	9.7	VEHICULES SPECIAUX,MARCH
7821	LORRIES,TRUCKS	N 438	7.1	N 330	5.5	N 397	5.7	N 603	8.6	VEHICULES TRANSP MARCHAND
79	OTHR TRANSPORT EQUIPMENT		1.8		0.5		9.8		1.1	AUTRE MATERIEL TRANSPORT
793	SHIPS AND BOATS ETC	N 42	1.7	N 85	0.5	N 220	9.6	N 223	0.8	NAVIRES BATEAUX,ETC
7938	TUGS,SPECIAL VESSELS ETC	N 7	1.6	N 10	0.1	N 36	8.7	N 7	0.5	REMORQUEURS,BATEAUX SPEC
79381	TUGS	N 2	0.9			N 16	8.6	N 2	0.4	BATEAUX REMORQUEURS
8	MISC MANUFACTURED GOODS		180.4		191.2		166.6		143.5	ART MANUFACTURES DIVERS
812	*PLUMBG,HEATNG,LGHTNG EQ		3.6		4.4	W 1245	4.1		4.5	APPAR SANITAIRES CHAUFFAGE
8124	LIGHTING EQUIPMENT NES		3.5		4.3	W 1243	4.1	W 1552	4.1	APPAREILS ECLAIRAGE ETC
81242	LAMPS,FITTINGS BASE METL		3.2		4.0	W 1228	3.2	W 1541	3.9	APPAREILS D'ECLAIRAGE
821	*FURNITURE,PARTS THEREOF		10.3		12.0		11.9		13.8	MEUBLES ET PIECES
8211	CHAIRS,SEATS AND PARTS		4.3		4.4		4.9		6.2	SIEGES ET PIECES
82111	CHAIRS AND OTHER SEATS		4.2	N 86108	4.2	N 122045	4.9	N 170484	6.1	SIEGES
8219	FURNITURE AND PARTS NES		5.7		7.2		6.6		7.1	AUTRES MEUBLES ET PIECES
82191	METAL FURNITURE NES		3.2		3.0	W 723	3.5	W 680	3.4	MEUBLES NDA EN METAL
82192	WOOD FURNITURE NES		2.5		4.1	N 124609	3.0	N 379466	3.7	MEUBLES NDA EN BOIS
831	*TRAVEL GOODS,HANDBAGS		3.6		1.2		1.1		0.8	ARTICLES DE VOYAGE ETC
83102	TRAVEL GDS,TOILET–CASES		3.2		0.7	N 30385	0.5	N 9595	0.1	ARTICLES DE VOYAGE
84	CLOTHING AND ACCESSORIES		99.7		109.1		88.5		67.5	VETEMENTS
842	MENS OUTERWEAR NOT KNIT	N 1241367	12.6	N 942837	8.8	N 546457	5.4	N 163296	1.6	VET DESSUS POUR HOMMES
8423	— TROUSERS,BREECHES ETC	N 1092158	9.6	N 801727	6.7	N 567032	4.7	N 443320	3.7	PANTALONS HOMMES MAT TEX
843	WOMENS OUTERWEAR NONKNIT	N 5130572	51.2	N 5643861	65.9	N 4619902	53.1	N 2779396	35.5	VET DESSUS FEMMES MAT TEX
8432	— SUITS AND COSTUMES	N 326904	5.1	N 204092	4.3	N 214219	4.0	N 111881	2.1	COSTUMES–TAIL MAT TEXIL
8433	— DRESSES	N 478216	6.3	N 658068	9.8	N 535172	8.4	N 374415	6.6	ROBES EN MAT–TEXTILES
8434	— SKIRTS	N 514887	5.1	N 544874	6.0	N 344293	3.7	N 210316	2.5	JUPES EN MAT TEXTILES
8435	— BLOUSES	N 3373009	29.5	N 3585189	37.7	N 3044985	30.4	N 1737998	18.9	BLOUSES FEM MAT TEXTILES
8439	— OTHER OUTER GARMENTS	N 481939	5.6	N 583601	6.8	N 438034	6.2	N 269925	4.4	AUT VET DES FEM MAT TEXT
844	UNDER GARMENTS NOT KNIT		4.9	N 493158	4.6	N 406003	4.2	N 535815	4.6	VETEMENT DESSOUS MAT TEX
8441	— MENS SHIRTS	\	4.5	N 410901	4.1	N 501369	4.3	N 531038	4.5	CHEMISES HOMMES MAT TEXT
845	OUTERWEAR KNIT NONELASTC		22.0	N 2521344	19.5	N 118222	1.1	N 74530	0.8	VET DESSOUS,ACCES BONNET
8451	— JERSEYS,PULLOVERS ETC		14.1	N 1735039	12.4	N 1644882	11.2	N 34203	0.4	CHANDAILS,PULL–OVERS ETC
8452	— WOMENS DRESSES ETC	N 371356	4.7	N 211264	2.7	N 165395	2.1	N 150765	2.0	ROBES,JUPES BONNETERIE
8459	— OTHER,CLTHG ACCESRYS		3.3	N 720041	5.5	N 108153	1.0	N 37468	0.4	AUT VET DESSUS DE BONNE
846	UNDER GARMENTS KNITTED		5.9		7.3		3.4		1.4	SOUS VETS DE BONNETERIE
8462	— OF COTTON NON ELASTIC	N 284761	1.5	N 5078398	5.9	N 2226786	3.0	N 559609	1.1	SOUS–VET BONNET COTON
84629	—— OTHER	N 284761	1.5	N 5078398	5.9	N 2226786	3.0	N 559609	1.1	AUT SOUS–VET BONNET COTON
848	HEADGEAR,NONTXTL CLOTHNG		0.6		1.0	W 14	1.8	W 76	3.9	VET ACCES MAT AUT QUE TEX
851	*FOOTWEAR	P 2397745	19.0	P 1857762	15.5	P 1822544	15.6	P 2041121	16.5	CHAUSSURES
85101	FOOTWEAR RUBBER,PLASTIC	P 1043599	5.8	P 1032153	4.7	P 911098	4.3	P 933477	3.9	CHAUS SEMELLES CAOUTCH
85102	FOOTWEAR LEATHER	P 1324139	13.0	P 818568	10.7	P 907048	11.3	P 1090350	12.6	CHAUS SEMELLES EN CUIR
87	PRECISION INSTRUMNTS NES		1.8		1.7		4.6		2.8	INSTRUM,APPAR SCIENT NDA
88	PHOTO EQU,OPTICL GDS ETC		17.2		17.1		11.6		7.5	APP,FOURN PHOTO,OP,MONTR
882	PHOTO,CINEMA SUPPLIES	N 16	0.1		5.1		0.1		0.1	PRODUITS PHOTO,CINEMA
8822	PHOTO FILM EXC DEV CINMA	N 16	0.1		5.0				0.1	PLAQUES,PELLICULES,FILMS
88222	PHOTO FILM ROLL UNEXPOSD		4.4		4.9	L 1109	2.4	L 1289	2.2	PEL SENSIB PERF OU NON
884	OPTICAL GOODS NES		3.5		3.1	N 625	0.1		1.2	ELEMENTS OPTIQ,ART LUNET
8842	SPECTACLES AND FRAMES		3.1		2.9	N 72654	2.3	N 47921	1.1	LUNETTES ET MONTURES
885	WATCHES AND CLOCKS		8.1		7.3		5.8		3.6	HORLOGERIE
8851	WATCHES,MOVEMENTS,CASES		7.9		7.2		5.7		3.5	MONTRES,MOUVEMENTS,BOITES
88511	WATCHES		7.8		7.1		5.7		3.5	MONTRES POCHE,BRACELET
89	MISC MANUFCTRD GOODS NES		25.7		30.6		29.3		30.4	ART MANUFACTURES DIVERS
892	PRINTED MATTER		3.5		4.9	W 762	4.1	W 761	6.0	IMPRIMES

5. General Exports F.O.B. by Commodities according to the S.I.T.C. (Rev. 2) in million U.S. Dollars
Exportations Générales F.O.B. par Produits d'après la C.T.C.I. (Rév. 2) en millions de Dollars E.U.

SITC CTCI	COMMODITY	1994		1995		1996		1997		PRODUIT
		QUANTITY QUANTITE	VALUE VALEUR	QUANTITY QUANTITE	VALUE VALEUR	QUANTITY QUANTITE	VALUE VALEUR	QUANTITY QUANTITE	VALUE VALEUR	
893	ARTICLES OF PLASTIC NES		6.6		10.0		9.6	W 2907	7.6	OUVRAGES EN MAT DIVIS 58
8939	MISC PLASTIC ARTICLES		4.0		6.3	W 2307	6.5	W 2215	6.7	ART DIVERS EN MAT DIV 58
89399	OTHR PLASTC ARTICLES NES		3.9		6.1	W 2286	6.4	W 2212	6.7	AUT OUV MAT DIV 58
894	TOYS,SPORTING GOODS,ETC		6.8		7.2		7.0		7.5	VOITURES ENFANTS,JOUETS
8946	NON–MILITARY ARMS,AMMO		5.6	MN 20534	2.2	W 838	2.3	W 755	2.2	ARMES NON MILITAIRES
899	OTHER MANUFACTURED GOODS		3.3		3.1		2.5		2.9	AUT ART MANUF DIVERS NDA

1. HISTORICAL SERIES, 1993–1997 GENERAL TRADE, IMPORTS F.O.B., EXPORTS F.O.B.
SERIES HISTORIQUES, 1993–1997 COMMERCE GENERAL, IMPORTATIONS F.O.B., EXPORTATIONS F.O.B

YEAR ANNEE	VALUE IN MILLION CZECH. KORUNY / VALEUR EN MILLION CZECH. KORUNY: MERCHANDISE –MARCHANDISE		GOLD –OR		CONVERSION FACTORS U.S. CENTS PER CZECH. KORUNA / FACTEURS DE CONVERSION CENTS E.U. PAR CZECH. KORUNA		INDEX NUMBERS –INDICES: QUANTUM		UNIT VALUE / VALEUR UNITAIRE	
	IMPORTS	EXPORTS	IMPORTS	EXPORTS	IMPORTS	EXPORTS	IMPORTS	EXPORTS	IMPORTS	EXPORTS
1993	374877.90	384965.80			3.4271	3.4312				
1994	428638.90	410249.90			3.4892	3.4808				
1995	670407.90	574722.00			3.7744	3.7733				
1996	763926.00	698932.90			3.6852	3.6865				
1997	855508.90	714680.00			3.1545	3.1487				

2. IMPORTS BY BROAD ECONOMIC CATEGORY AND EXPORTS BY INDUSTRIAL ORIGIN. (PERCENTAGE OF TOTAL VALUE)
IMPORTATIONS PAR CATEGORIES ECONOMIQUES ET EXPORTATIONS PAR BRANCHE D'ACTIVITE.(EN POURCENTAGE DE LA VALEUR TOTALE)

IMPORTS – IMPORTATIONS

	1991	1992	1993	1994	1995	1996	1997
TOTAL IMPORTS–IMPORTATIONS TOTALES			100.	100.	100.	100.	100.
1 FOOD BEV–ALIMENTATION BOISSONS			6.1	6.9	5.4	5.6	5.1
11 PRIMARY–PRODUITS DE BASE			3.3	3.5	2.6	2.6	2.4
111 FOR INDUSTRY–POUR L'INDUSTRIE			1.2	1.0	0.8	0.8	0.8
112 FOR HOUSEHOLDS–POUR LES MENAGES			2.1	2.4	1.8	1.8	1.6
12 PROCESSED–PRODUITS ELABORES			2.9	3.4	2.9	3.0	2.7
121 FOR INDUSTRY–POUR L'INDUSTRIE			0.4	0.4	0.4	0.4	0.3
122 FOR HOUSEHOLDS–POUR LES MENAGES			2.4	3.0	2.5	2.6	2.4
2 IND SUPPLIES–APPROV INDUSTRIELS			30.0	31.1	34.3	32.6	33.2
21 PRIMARY–PRODUITS DE BASE			4.1	4.0	3.5	3.0	3.2
22 PROCESSED–PRODUITS ELABORES			25.9	27.1	30.8	29.6	30.0
3 FUELS–COMBUSTIBLES			10.8	9.9	7.7	8.6	8.6
31 PRIMARY–PRODUITS DE BASE			8.4	7.6	6.1	7.0	6.6
32 PROCESSED–PRODUITS ELABORES			2.4	2.2	1.7	1.7	2.0
321 MOTOR SPIRIT–ESSENCE			2.2	1.8	1.2	1.3	1.5
322 OTHER–AUTRES			0.2	0.4	0.4	0.4	0.4
4 MACHINERY–EQUIPEMENT			30.3	29.0	28.8	28.5	26.7
41 CAPITAL EQUIPMENT–MACHINES			26.1	25.1	24.3	24.2	22.4
42 PARTS–PIECES ACCESSOIRES			4.3	3.9	4.6	4.4	4.2
5 TRANSPORT–TRANSPORT			6.7	6.8	7.9	9.4	10.8
51 PASSENGER CARS–AUTOMOBILES			2.2	2.7	2.5	3.0	2.9
52 OTHER–AUTRES			1.6	1.7	2.2	2.2	2.6
521 INDUSTRIAL–INDUSTRIELS			1.4	1.6	2.1	2.1	2.5
522 NON INDUSTRIAL–NON INDUSTRIEL			0.2	0.2	0.1	0.1	0.1
53 PARTS–PIECES ACCESSOIRES			3.0	2.3	3.3	4.1	5.4
6 CONSUM GOODS–BIENS CONSOMMATION			15.3	15.8	14.6	15.3	15.6
61 DURABLE–DURABLES			4.7	4.7	4.1	4.2	4.6
62 SEMI DURABLE–SEMI DURABLES			6.2	6.2	6.4	6.9	6.6
63 NON DURABLE–NON DURABLES			4.4	5.0	4.1	4.2	4.4
7 GOODS NES–BIENS NDA			0.7	0.5	1.2	0.0	0.1

EXPORTS – EXPORTATIONS

	1991	1992	1993	1994	1995	1996	1997
TOTAL EXPORTS–EXPORTATIONS TOTALES			100.	100.	100.	100.	100.
1 AGRICULTURE			3.1	3.5	3.0	2.1	1.8
2 MINING QUARRY–INDUS EXTRACTIVES			5.7	4.7	3.6	3.7	2.7
3 MANUFACTURING–IND MANUFACTUR			91.2	91.8	93.5	94.1	95.4
31 FOOD BEV TOBACCO–ALIM BOISS TAB			6.2	5.5	4.3	4.3	4.4
32 TEXTILES–INDUSTRIES TEXTILES			9.0	9.2	10.6	9.1	8.3
33 WOOD & PRODUCTS–BOIS & PRODUITS			3.0	3.7	3.0	3.0	2.7
34 PAPER & PRODUCTS–PAPIER & PRODT			2.4	2.3	3.2	2.9	2.8
35 CHEMICALS–INDUSTRIES CHIMIQUES			13.0	14.2	13.5	13.7	13.2
36 NON METAL MIN–MIN NON METAL			6.2	6.4	5.1	5.6	4.8
37 BASIC METAL–IND METAL BASE			11.8	11.2	11.2	9.3	8.7
38 METAL MANUF–MANUF METAL			34.7	33.6	38.6	43.7	47.8
39 OTH MANUF IND–AUTRES MANUF			5.0	5.6	4.0	2.5	2.8

3. TRADE BY PRINCIPAL COUNTRIES OF ORIGIN AND DESTINATION (VALUE IN MILLION U.S. DOLLARS)
ECHANGES SELON LES PRINCIPAUX PAYS D'ORIGINE ET DE DESTINATION (VALEUR EN MILLIONS DE DOLLARS EU)

COUNTRIES–PAYS	GENERAL IMPORTS F.O.B. IMPORTATIONS GENERALES F.O.B.				
	1993	1994	1995	1996	1997
World	12703.9	14951.0	25303.4	27717.3	27183.6
Africa	52.2	72.0	93.4	144.1	198.8
Americas	590.6	755.7	1172.2	1297.9	1359.1
– Northern America	435.9	568.1	930.2	1028.2	1114.7
– LAIA	125.7	141.7	188.6	216.4	214.3
– CACM	24.0	35.0	40.5	39.2	22.1
– Caribbean	2.0	2.3	4.2	7.2	3.5
– Rest of America	3.0	8.6	8.6	7.0	4.4
Asia excl fmr USSR	783.6	1005.6	1513.1	1850.5	1897.8
– Middle East	58.6	72.4	109.5	168.8	129.6
Asia former USSR	38.2	70.4	88.7	87.5	109.6
Europe excl fmr USSR	9771.0	11568.1	20136.9	21846.5	21069.1
– European Union	6720.6	8307.8	15454.8	17300.2	16711.7
– Eastern Europe	2646.9	2753.9	3922.4	3772.1	3546.2
– Rest of Europe	403.5	506.4	759.7	774.2	811.2
Europe former USSR	1405.4	1404.4	2141.3	2273.7	2078.7
Oceania	55.4	31.6	35.9	49.6	57.6
Other	7.6	43.2	122.0	167.5	412.8
Germany/Allemagne	3259.9	3795.5	8015.7	8262.1	8672.0
Slovakia/Slovaquie	2127.2	2131.2	2988.4	2650.7	2273.8
Russian Federation	1268.9	1256.5	1879.2	2059.9	1843.3
Austria/Autriche	1001.2	1207.1	1747.5	1594.0	1646.9
Italy/Italie	605.1	768.5	1344.5	1633.4	1495.2
France, Monaco	394.2	548.0	1018.5	1162.1	1120.8
United Kingdom	348.8	452.3	953.4	1043.0	1054.9
USA/Etats–Unis d'Amer	386.2	506.8	853.2	940.0	1030.4
Poland/Pologne	322.5	426.2	683.1	806.5	870.9
Netherlands/Pays–Bas	360.2	437.2	665.5	630.1	655.7
Belgium–Luxembourg	210.8	314.8	507.7	503.0	595.7
Switzerland,Liechtenst.	295.5	343.4	494.1	493.1	459.3
Japan/Japon	225.1	303.1	442.1	473.6	524.1
Sweden/Suède	144.2	203.4	312.9	336.1	344.7
Spain/Espagne	98.3	159.2	275.6	358.0	399.4
Hungary/Hongrie	174.3	170.9	218.5	275.6	355.0
European Union n.e.s.				1082.8	
China/Chine	76.6	101.9	209.6	298.2	377.6
Finland/Finlande	94.2	168.3	213.5	266.9	301.9
Denmark/Danemark	118.9	142.0	203.3	224.7	219.2
Other Asia n.e.s.	131.2	145.7	190.7	222.7	198.3
Ukraine	115.7	113.9	216.6	175.4	196.0
Areas n.e.s.	7.6	43.2	122.0	167.5	412.8
Korea, Republic of	58.1	95.5	120.0	179.8	192.4
Slovenia/Slovénie	51.3	72.3	131.1	153.5	151.9
Ireland/Irlande	46.3	66.1	116.4	129.9	128.9
China, Hong Kong SAR	64.8	73.0	104.0	108.8	84.5
Brazil/Brésil	33.0	55.8	90.2	111.7	100.8
Canada	49.6	61.2	76.8	88.0	84.3
Norway,Svalbard and JM	33.4	46.9	73.4	66.3	128.9
Turkey/Turquie	42.3	44.2	61.4	78.6	70.2
India/Inde	34.1	48.5	61.1	82.7	63.6
Singapore/Singapour	24.6	39.4	70.3	54.4	53.7
Malaysia/Malaisie	21.2	29.4	48.1	67.5	74.5
Greece/Grèce	32.9	37.3	63.7	49.5	50.8
Israel/Israël	21.0	27.2	40.5	50.1	46.7
Thailand/Thaïlande	20.8	24.5	42.4	44.9	41.7
Uzbekistan/Ouzbékistan	17.3	32.0	42.3	40.5	42.0
Croatia/Croatie	19.4	29.8	40.6	36.9	43.0
Indonesia/Indonésie	12.8	20.5	37.3	47.3	45.1

COUNTRIES–PAYS	GENERAL EXPORTS F.O.B. EXPORTATIONS GENERALES F.O.B.				
	1993	1994	1995	1996	1997
Monde	12892.2	14081.5	21685.6	21907.3	22746.4
Afrique	255.3	222.5	230.7	341.6	172.0
Amériques	401.8	483.2	634.7	693.8	801.4
– Amérique du Nord	279.1	345.7	471.1	522.3	639.6
– ALAI	102.2	112.9	135.2	140.2	126.3
– MCAC	6.4	12.7	9.7	8.7	9.0
– Caraïbes	7.3	8.8	15.5	19.8	22.3
– Autre Amérique	6.7	3.1	3.1	2.9	4.2
Asie anc. URSS exclus	1149.1	922.0	1100.4	1056.8	984.8
– Moyen–Orient	356.9	265.7	312.6	366.4	407.7
Asie ancienne URSS	96.5	78.4	76.4	94.8	90.9
Europe anc. URSS exclus	10231.4	11526.4	18534.5	18495.2	19372.0
– Union Européenne	6410.7	7633.4	13217.5	12762.1	13634.7
– Europe de l'Est	3440.0	3342.1	4493.9	4862.3	4824.9
– Autre de l'Europe	380.6	550.9	823.1	870.8	912.3
Europe ancienne URSS	717.1	795.0	1014.7	1107.9	1228.1
Océanie	37.1	37.8	45.8	41.8	34.9
Autre	4.0	16.2	48.3	75.6	62.3
Germany/Allemagne	3352.4	4153.1	8144.9	7892.0	8131.6
Slovakia/Slovaquie	2704.9	2319.4	3009.4	3120.9	2937.9
Austria/Autriche	779.4	1013.1	1426.4	1411.2	1461.4
Poland/Pologne	351.9	548.6	966.9	1205.4	1305.1
Italy/Italie	666.1	628.6	809.2	722.4	833.4
Russian Federation	575.4	548.2	632.0	692.8	771.4
United Kingdom	388.8	392.6	687.9	551.8	688.8
France, Monaco	250.5	359.3	570.2	628.2	724.9
Netherlands/Pays–Bas	307.6	358.1	518.0	454.6	550.4
USA/Etats–Unis d'Amer	236.2	302.6	415.5	463.2	583.3
Hungary/Hongrie	292.8	363.3	378.3	390.7	427.1
Belgium–Luxembourg	173.1	218.8	345.6	373.6	434.6
Switzerland,Liechtenst.	152.4	198.3	290.5	264.9	278.6
Slovenia/Slovénie	111.8	162.3	244.4	227.8	208.4
Ukraine	98.8	133.6	223.1	224.6	227.2
Spain/Espagne	159.0	130.1	166.3	161.6	186.2
Sweden/Suède	85.0	105.7	162.8	176.0	224.9
Croatia/Croatie	68.4	97.3	139.7	154.1	182.1
Denmark/Danemark	80.9	97.7	132.5	135.0	130.7
China/Chine	251.6	85.5	94.7	71.4	48.4
Egypt/Egypte	149.0	123.8	81.0	93.1	89.4
Japan/Japon	64.7	88.6	139.7	95.4	95.8
China, Hong Kong SAR	109.3	118.0	70.8	103.9	66.0
Turkey/Turquie	135.0	53.1	70.6	90.6	79.7
Greece/Grèce	75.5	66.4	91.1	92.8	85.7
Finland/Finlande	52.0	68.2	96.8	90.7	89.7
India/Inde	49.7	56.5	81.1	83.6	65.1
Singapore/Singapour	36.6	32.4	122.3	70.4	73.1
Norway,Svalbard and JM	30.4	42.3	69.8	85.4	98.2
Bulgaria/Bulgarie	53.4	61.6	75.8	66.8	61.0
Lithuania/Lituanie	13.9	43.7	59.7	85.8	106.4
Romania/Roumanie	32.7	46.4	57.1	72.6	91.7
Thailand/Thaïlande	73.8	82.5	42.3	48.7	38.5
Iran (Islamic Rep of)	57.9	45.1	59.0	68.3	32.8
Syrian Arab Republic	38.2	67.2	58.7	48.9	44.2
Canada	42.9	42.9	55.6	59.1	56.3
Lebanon/Liban	50.0	35.4	53.4	61.4	44.2
United Arab Emirates	19.7	20.5	18.2	37.3	146.0
Other Asia n.e.s.	49.3	39.6	54.3	50.5	47.8
Belarus/Bélarus	17.5	39.9	54.2	59.0	66.4

(VALUE AS PERCENTAGE OF WORLD TOTAL)(VALEURS EN POURCENTAGE DU TOTAL MONDIAL)

	1988	1989	1990	1991	1992	1993	1994	1995	1996	1997
Africa						0.4	0.5	0.4	0.5	0.7
Americas						4.6	5.1	4.6	4.7	5.0
– Northern America						3.4	3.8	3.7	3.7	4.1
– LAIA						1.0	0.9	0.7	0.8	0.8
– CACM						0.2	0.2	0.2	0.1	0.1
– Caribbean						0.0	0.0	0.0	0.0	0.0
– Rest of America						0.0	0.1	0.0	0.0	0.0
Asia excl fmr USSR						6.2	6.7	6.0	6.7	7.0
– Middle East						0.5	0.5	0.4	0.6	0.5
Asia former USSR						0.3	0.5	0.4	0.3	0.4
Europe excl fmr USSR						76.9	77.4	79.6	78.8	77.5
– European Union						52.9	55.6	61.1	62.4	61.5
– Eastern Europe						20.8	18.4	15.5	13.6	13.0
– Rest of Europe						3.2	3.4	3.0	2.8	3.0
Europe former USSR						11.1	9.4	8.5	8.2	7.6
Oceania						0.4	0.2	0.1	0.2	0.2
Other						0.1	0.3	0.5	0.6	1.5
Germany/Allemagne						25.7	25.4	31.7	29.8	31.9
Slovakia/Slovaquie						16.7	14.3	11.8	9.6	8.4
Russian Federation						10.0	8.4	7.4	7.4	6.8
Austria/Autriche						7.9	8.1	6.9	5.8	6.1
Italy/Italie						4.8	5.1	5.3	5.9	5.5
France, Monaco						3.1	3.7	4.0	4.2	4.1
United Kingdom						2.7	3.0	3.8	3.8	3.9
USA/Etats–Unis d'Amer						3.0	3.4	3.4	3.4	3.8
Poland/Pologne						2.5	2.9	2.7	2.9	3.2
Netherlands/Pays–Bas						2.8	2.9	2.6	2.3	2.4

	1988	1989	1990	1991	1992	1993	1994	1995	1996	1997
Afrique						2.0	1.6	1.1	1.6	0.8
Amériques						3.1	3.4	2.9	3.2	3.5
– Amérique du Nord						2.2	2.5	2.2	2.4	2.8
– ALAI						0.8	0.8	0.6	0.6	0.6
– MCAC						0.0	0.1	0.0	0.0	0.0
– Caraïbes						0.1	0.1	0.1	0.1	0.1
– Autre Amérique						0.1	0.0	0.0	0.0	0.0
Asie anc. URSS exclus						8.9	6.5	5.1	4.8	4.3
– Moyen–Orient						2.8	1.9	1.4	1.7	1.8
Asie ancienne URSS						0.7	0.6	0.4	0.4	0.4
Europe anc. URSS exclus						79.4	81.9	85.5	84.4	85.2
– Union Européenne						49.7	54.2	61.0	58.3	59.9
– Europe de l'Est						26.7	23.7	20.7	22.2	21.2
– Autre de l'Europe						3.0	3.9	3.8	4.0	4.0
Europe ancienne URSS						5.6	5.6	4.7	5.1	5.4
Océanie						0.3	0.3	0.2	0.2	0.2
Autre						0.0	0.1	0.2	0.3	0.3
Germany/Allemagne						26.0	29.5	37.6	36.0	35.7
Slovakia/Slovaquie						21.0	16.5	13.9	14.2	12.9
Austria/Autriche						6.0	7.2	6.6	6.4	6.4
Poland/Pologne						2.7	3.9	4.5	5.5	5.7
Italy/Italie						5.2	4.5	3.7	3.3	3.7
Russian Federation						4.5	3.9	2.9	3.2	3.4
United Kingdom						3.0	2.8	3.2	2.5	3.0
France, Monaco						1.9	2.6	2.6	2.9	3.2
Netherlands/Pays–Bas						2.4	2.5	2.4	2.1	2.4
USA/Etats–Unis d'Amer						1.8	2.1	1.9	2.1	2.6

4. General Imports F.O.B. by Commodities according to the S.I.T.C. (Rev. 2) in million U.S. Dollars
Importations Générales F.O.B. par Produits d'après la C.T.C.I. (Rév. 2) en millions de Dollars E.U.

SITC CTCI	COMMODITY	1994		1995		1996		1997		PRODUIT
		QUANTITY QUANTITE	VALUE VALEUR	QUANTITY QUANTITE	VALUE VALEUR	QUANTITY QUANTITE	VALUE VALEUR	QUANTITY QUANTITE	VALUE VALEUR	
	ALL COMMODITIES		14951.0		25303.5		27717.4		27183.6	TOUS PRODUITS
0	FOOD AND LIVE ANIMALS		1037.8		1400.9		1585.1		1404.8	ALIMENTS,ANIMAUX VIVANTS
01	MEAT AND PREPARATIONS		53.7		56.7		60.8		51.4	VIANDES ET PREPARATIONS
03	FISH AND PREPARATIONS		62.6		72.4		84.7		79.8	POISSONS ET PREPARATIONS
04	CEREALS AND PREPARATIONS		91.9		121.5		184.6		181.2	CEREALES ET PRODUITS
048	CEREAL ETC PREPARATIONS	W 35191	51.1	W 50015	71.3	W 65768	80.8	W 52817	79.2	PREPTNS A BASE CEREALES
05	VEGETABLES AND FRUIT		370.1		487.9		535.4		459.8	LEGUMES ET FRUITS
054	VEG ETC FRSH,SMPLY PRSVD	W 255393	104.7	W 341283	156.5	W 358124	155.1	W 302731	132.1	LEGUMES FRAIS,CONG,SECS
0545	OTHER FRESH VEGETABLES	W 155676	54.6	W 153086	63.3	W 169840	75.6	W 171556	71.1	AUTRES LEGUMES FRAIS,REF
057	FRUIT,NUTS,FRESH,DRIED	W 387383	180.6	W 454254	219.9	W 460857	255.6	W 437397	223.7	FRUITS FRAIS OU SECS
0573	BANANA,PLANTAIN,FRSH,DRY	W 121057	55.1	W 161194	67.6	W 148543	73.7	W 133350	60.4	BANANES FRAICHES,SECHEES
058	FRUIT PRESERVED,PREPARED	W 92572	68.3	W 99891	87.8	W 104573	99.6	W 101187	82.0	CONSERVES DE FRUITS
07	COFFEE,TEA,COCOA,SPICES		166.8		218.9		214.7		211.1	CAFE,THE,CACAO,EPICES
071	COFFEE AND SUBSTITUTES	W 30667	83.7	W 30284	115.7	W 33564	96.2	W 36978	103.2	CAFE ET SUCCEDANES
0711	COFFEE GREEN,ROASTED,SUB	W 29221	74.6	W 28588	99.6	W 31091	76.6	W 33169	78.8	CAFE TORREFIE OU DECAFEINE
07111	COFFEE GREEN,HUSKS,SKINS	W 26743	65.7	W 25973	86.5	W 28538	66.8	W 30593	69.0	CAFE NON TORREFIE
081	*FEEDING STUFF FOR ANIML	W 417639	121.6	W 514736	157.1		206.3	W 501616	185.6	NOURRITURE POUR ANIMAUX
0813	OILCAKE AND OTH RESIDUES	W 321174	67.6	W 389167	78.7	W 423230	117.8	W 377390	107.9	TOURTEAUX
08131	— OF SOYA BEANS	W 308613	65.7	W 374711	76.8	W 413809	116.4	W 365836	106.0	TOURTEAUX DE SOJA
09	MISC EDIBLE PRODUCTS		96.1		145.3		157.4		138.0	PREP ALIMENTAIRES DIVERSES
098	EDIBLE PRODCTS,PREPS NES	W 34578	91.7	W 44255	140.0		151.6	W 61134	133.7	PREP ALIMENTAIRES NDA
09809	MISC FOOD PREPRTIONS NES	W 19170	68.3	W 24758	101.1	W 31307	113.0	W 37201	96.5	PREP ALIMENTAIRES NDA
1	BEVERAGES AND TOBACCO		191.8		198.4		241.7		287.3	BOISSONS ET TABACS
11	BEVERAGES		67.6		75.3		101.3		100.3	BOISSONS
112	ALCOHOLIC BEVERAGES	W 69400	53.5	W 64337	60.2	W 95081	85.4	W 113831	88.6	BOISSONS ALCOOLIQUES
12	TOBACCO AND MANUFACTURES		124.2		123.1		140.4		187.0	TABACS BRUTS FABRIQUES
121	TOBACCO UNMNFCTRD,REFUSE	W 17502	46.6	W 17030	59.1	W 20648	87.3	W 27486	131.7	TABACS BRUTS,DECHETS
1212	TOBACCO STRIPPED OR PART	W 12099	39.2	W 10346	43.1	W 12438	65.1	W 19175	116.3	TABACS PART ECOTES
122	TOBACCO,MANUFACTURED	W 8000	77.6	W 7863	64.1	W 7593	53.2	W 8772	55.3	TABACS FABRIQUES
1222	CIGARETTES	W 5954	55.3	W 6688	55.2	W 4312	34.0	W 4338	31.6	CIGARETTES
2	CRUDE MATERLS,EXCL FUELS		724.1		1109.1		1004.4		992.5	MAT BRUTES NON COMESTIBLES
23	RUBBER, CRUDE		56.1		101.0		89.6		83.3	CAOUTCHOUC BRUT
251	*PULP AND WASTE PAPER	W 133545	72.2	W 134877	110.9	W 150732	81.6	W 150673	73.3	PATES A PAPIER,DECHETS
2517	SODA,SULPHATE WOOD PULP	W 91784	46.2	W 83771	72.9	W 85628	43.0	W 95271	44.8	PATES CHIMIQUES AU SULFATE
26	TEXTILE FIBRES AND WASTE		161.8		254.4		237.6		234.2	FIBRES TEXTILES
263	COTTON	W 54533	85.2	W 61389	132.5	W 59523	110.6	W 65957	112.9	COTON
2631	RAW COTTON,EXCL LINTERS	W 52149	83.2	W 58757	129.4	W 56949	107.4	W 62755	109.7	COTON EN MASSE
27	CRUDE FERTLZR,MINRLS NES		79.6		104.2		102.1		89.9	ENGRAIS MINERAUX BRUTS
278	OTHER CRUDE MINERALS	W 1094484	51.9	W 1309621	68.9	W 1492307	72.3	W 1525196	62.9	AUTRES MINERAUX BRUTS
28	METALLIFEROUS ORES,SCRAP		209.6		316.0		257.9		283.1	MINERAIS METAL,DECHETS
281	IRON ORE,CONCENTRATES	W 7368775	157.5	MW 9146	214.7	W 8079384	187.0	W 7383349	204.1	MINERAIS DE FER
2815	IRON ORE,CONC,NOT AGGLOM	W 2443117	58.9	W 2709980	71.3	W 2569950	62.9	W 3046306	74.6	MINERAIS NON AGGLOMERES
2816	IRON ORE AGGLOMERATES	W 4925658	98.7	W 6436127	143.4	W 5509434	124.1	W 4337043	129.6	MINERAIS AGGLOMERES
29	CRUDE ANIMAL,VEG MAT NES		62.6		89.3		102.2		96.0	MATIERES BRUTES ANIM,VEGET
292	CRUDE VEG MATERIALS NES	W 10330	49.6	W 14047	67.6	W 18570	78.1	W 20974	72.4	MAT BRUTES VEGETALES NDA
3	MINERAL FUELS ETC		1508.6		1999.2		2433.5		2369.6	COMBUSTIBLES MINERAUX LUB
32	COAL,COKE AND BRIQUETTES		71.4		113.2		118.2		97.5	HOUILLES,COKES,BRIQUETTES
322	COAL,LIGNITE AND PEAT	W 1746431	56.2	W 2683306	86.3	W 3233878	107.7	W 2297215	70.9	HOUILLES,LIGNITES,TOURBE
3222	OTH COAL,NOT AGGLOMERATD	W 1730771	55.7	W 2661238	85.5	W 3174020	104.6	W 2263443	69.5	AUTRES HOUILLES
33	PETROLEUM AND PRODUCTS		992.1		1175.0		1453.5		1364.6	PETROLE ET DERIVES
333	CRUDE PETROLEUM	W 6493361	673.0	W 7072167	805.0	W 7644963	1045.6	W 7023306	893.1	HUILES BRUTES DE PETROLE
334	PETROLEUM PRODUCTS,REFIN	W 1578295	286.8	W 1505324	325.1	W 1547760	368.8	W 1912949	436.0	PRODUITS RAFFINES
3341	GASOLINE,OTH LIGHT OILS	W 1571474	274.8	W 1497688	306.9	W 1541363	351.2	W 1905736	416.3	ESSENCES POUR MOTEURS
341	*GAS,NATURAL AND MANUFCT		412.1	W 8114629	645.8	MW 9537	782.3	MW 9677	838.5	GAZ NATUREL,GAZ MANUFACT
3414	PETROLEUM GASES, GASEOUS		402.1	W 8049135	628.8	MW 9439	758.8	MW 9524	806.2	GAZ DE PETROLE GAZEUX
4	ANIMAL,VEGETABLE OIL,FAT		53.2		75.9		76.3		63.7	HUILES,GRAISSES ANIM,VEG
5	CHEMCLS,RELATED PROD NES		1869.1		2826.4		3063.3		3100.7	PRODUITS CHIMIQUES
51	ORGANIC CHEMICALS		252.9		373.6		328.2		348.1	PROD CHIMIQ ORGANIQUES
512	ALCOHOLS,PHENOLS ETC	W 95994	46.8	W 99932	69.6	W 94286	54.3	W 103241	53.7	PHENOLS,PHENOLS–ALCOOLS
514	NITROGEN–FNCTN COMPOUNDS	W 19404	63.6	W 22770	88.7	W 25156	85.2	W 26125	88.2	COMPOSES FONCT AZOTEES
516	OTHER ORGANIC CHEMICALS	W 66424	44.9	W 80931	72.4		64.1	W 66748	63.6	AUTRES PROD ORGANIQUES
52	INORGANIC CHEMICALS		175.2		254.0		259.6		264.1	PROD CHIM INORGANIQUES
522	INORG ELEMNTS,OXIDES,ETC	W 454100	88.7	W 513828	122.4	W 436118	124.7	W 433518	111.4	ELEMENTS INORGANIQUES
523	OTHR INORG CHEMICALS ETC	W 320041	82.3	W 390040	125.2		132.9	W 443755	120.6	AUT PRODUITS CHIMIQUES INORG
5232	OTH MTL CMPD OF INRG ACD	W 238375	48.0	W 280844	73.0	W 287807	78.2	W 322284	75.7	SELS METALLIQUES
53	DYES,TANNING,COLOUR PROD		181.9		277.5		307.6		302.9	PROD TEINTURE,COLORANTS
533	PIGMENTS,PAINTS,ETC	W 60936	153.2	W 105808	243.0	W 119628	267.9	W 120384	265.2	PIGMENTS,PEINTURES,VERNIS
5334	VARNISHES,DISTEMPERS ETC	W 32232	91.1	W 42470	143.8	W 46320	159.3	W 51016	162.1	PEINTURES A L'EAU
53342	OTH PAINTS,VARNISHES ETC	W 19239	56.5	W 25186	94.6	W 25692	104.0	W 28563	101.9	AUTRES PEINTURES,VERNIS
541	*MEDICINAL,PHARM PRODUCT	MK 16556	450.8	MK 18429	629.3		711.1	MK 20164	694.2	PROD MEDICINAUX PHARMACEUT
5416	GLYCOSIDES,GLANDS,SERA	K 477595	44.1	K 1066272	80.1	K 584797	82.7	K 531315	75.4	HETEROSIDES
5417	MEDICAMENTS	MK 13455	343.4	MK 14450	471.3	MK 16309	542.6	MK 16726	547.0	MEDICAMENTS
54171	— CONTAINNG ANTIBIOTICS	K 1255763	48.8	K 1572104	58.7	K 1665803	64.9	K 1520908	68.8	MED CONTN ANTIBIOTIQUES
54172	— CONTAINING HORMONES	K 833529	48.4	K 650825	69.6	K 629332	73.4	K 607936	78.3	MED CONTENANT HORMONES
54179	— CONTNG OTH SUBSTANCES	MK 11022	233.4	MK 11724	320.4	MK 13525	378.4	MK 14112	377.2	MED CONT AUT SUBSTANCES
55	PERFUME,CLEANING ETC PRD		190.7		253.9		290.9		306.7	PROD POUR PARFUM,TOILETTE
553	PERFUMERY,COSMETICS,ETC	W 22037	88.1	W 25933	117.2	W 27518	130.8	W 34463	136.4	PRODUITS DE PARFUMERIE
554	SOAP,CLEANSING ETC PREPS	W 84398	78.4	W 89925	100.4	W 100104	109.6	W 120065	111.0	SAVONS,PRODUITS DETERSIFS
5542	WASHING PREPARATIONS ETC	W 75406	65.6	W 80163	83.9	W 89015	91.0	W 107676	93.0	PROD ORG TENSIO–ACT NDA
562	*FERTILIZERS,MANUFACTURE	W 627748	59.4	W 705434	81.3	W 749081	89.8	W 720167	75.5	ENGRAIS MANUFACTURES
58	PLASTIC MATERIALS ETC		343.6		636.3		705.1		730.8	MAT PLAST ARTIFICIELLES
582	PROD OF CONDENSATION ETC	W 62815	85.0	W 89600	170.0	W 104311	180.6	W 121640	182.7	PROD CONDENS,POLYCOND
5823	ALKYDS,OTHER POLYESTERS	W 14116	31.6	W 27963	77.7	W 31866	71.4	W 40857	71.1	ALKYDES ET AUT POLYESTERS
583	POLYMERIZATION ETC PRODS	W 157783	241.4	W 238371	447.6	W 297086	507.7	W 336628	531.9	PROD POLYMERISATION
5831	POLYETHYLENE	W 63684	57.7	W 82197	103.6	W 98957	111.1	W 108419	122.1	POLYETHYLENE
5834	POLYVINYL CHLORIDE	W 33509	47.4	W 66330	109.2	W 76977	113.7	W 76927	114.1	CHLORURE DE POLYVINYLE
5839	OTH POLYMRZTION ETC PROD	W 18406	62.0	W 31748	116.4	W 43361	136.0	W 59518	146.6	AUT PROD POLYMER COPOLYM
59	CHEMICAL MATERIALS NES		213.3		318.2		364.0		373.2	MAT PROD CHIMIQUES NDA
591	PESTICIDES,DISINFECTANTS	W 9250	68.8	W 9142	86.5	W 10509	104.5	W 10844	95.2	DESINF,INSECT,FONG,HERB
5913	HERBICIDES,FOR RETAIL	W 5705	46.0	W 5263	56.3	W 5705	66.6	W 5925	62.5	HERBICIDES VENTE AU DET
598	MISCEL CHEM PRODUCTS NES	W 82595	120.2	W 128507	190.0	W 160122	211.4	W 218832	229.4	PROD DIV INDUST CHIM NDA
5989	CHEM PRODUCTS,PREPS NES	W 70231	100.6	W 112569	161.7	W 140826	176.7	W 199288	200.6	PROD PREP CHIMIQUES NDA
59899	OTH CHEM PRODS,PREPS,NES	W 41871	58.9	W 75060	103.0	W 103265	117.8	W 156828	134.2	AUT PRODUITS CHIMIQUES NDA
6	BASIC MANUFACTURES		2520.7		5282.1		5481.9		5405.5	ART MANUFACTURES
61	LEATHER,DRESSED FUR,ETC		64.8		221.5		203.5		166.8	CUIRS,PELLETERIES
611	LEATHER	W 3185	31.9	W 8707	113.3	W 8490	111.8	W 6573	102.3	CUIRS,PEAUX PREPARES
6114	LEATHR BOVINE NES,EQUINE	W 1608	20.0	W 4928	87.6	W 4889	77.6	W 4441	78.9	CUIRS DE BOVINS
612	LEATHER ETC MANUFACTURES	W 3275	24.9	W 8052	88.5	W 6547	75.4	W 6245	54.1	OUVRAGES EN CUIRS NDA
6123	PREPRD PARTS OF FOOTWEAR	W 3179	23.8	W 7813	83.8	W 6281	66.8	W 6060	49.6	PARTIES DE CHAUSSURES
62	RUBBER MANUFACTURES NES		143.1		261.7		296.9		315.0	CAOUTCHOUC MANUFACTURE
621	MATERIALS OF RUBBER	W 13211	34.7	W 22906	68.5	W 26168	85.6	W 33101	100.1	PRODUITS EN CAOUTCHOUC

4. General Imports F.O.B. by Commodities according to the S.I.T.C. (Rev. 2) in million U.S. Dollars
Importations Générales F.O.B. par Produits d'après la C.T.C.I. (Rév. 2) en millions de Dollars E.U.

SITC CTCI	COMMODITY	1994 QUANTITY QUANTITE	1994 VALUE VALEUR	1995 QUANTITY QUANTITE	1995 VALUE VALEUR	1996 QUANTITY QUANTITE	1996 VALUE VALEUR	1997 QUANTITY QUANTITE	1997 VALUE VALEUR	PRODUIT
625	RUBBER TYRES, TUBES ETC	W 26954	63.1	W 35736	94.8	W 35775	110.1	W 38263	106.5	PNEUS CAOUTCHOUC VULCANISE
628	RUBBER ARTICLES NES	W 12451	45.4	W 15114	98.5	W 14533	101.3	W 16741	108.5	OUVRAGES CAOUTCHOUC NDA
63	WOOD,CORK MANUFACTRS NES		72.3		122.4		137.4		153.0	OUVRAGES LIEGE ET BOIS
64	PAPER,PAPERBOARD AND MFR		313.3		526.5		594.9		584.0	PAPIERS,CARTONS & OUVRAGES
641	PAPER AND PAPERBOARD	W 292496	216.9	W 290153	329.5	W 353019	359.4	W 459364	380.5	PAPIERS ET CARTONS
6412	PRINTG,WRITING PAPER NES	W 55549	64.3	W 63105	90.9	W 85516	96.6	W 103148	95.7	PAPIERS POUR L'IMPRESSION
64122	— COATED,IMPREGNATD ETC	W 52755	60.0	W 56978	81.4	W 75113	83.6	W 89390	82.1	PAPIERS IMPRESSION COUCHES
6415	PAPER,PAPERBRD,BULK,NES	W 103371	56.5	W 125311	104.9	W 132827	102.1	W 138259	80.1	PAPIERS,CARTONS ROULEAUX
64159	OTHER PAPER ETC,BULK,NES	W 80824	48.1	W 102187	89.4	W 103911	87.1	W 108581	66.3	AUT PAPIER ROULEAUX FEUILLES
6418	COATED ETC PAPER NES BLK	W 81125	66.1	W 49523	88.6	W 63841	106.9	W 77725	119.2	PAP,CARTONS COUCHES,ENDUITS
642	PAPER,ETC,PRECUT,ARTS OF	W 76246	96.5	W 100799	197.1	W 113477	235.6	W 115154	203.5	PAP,CARTONS DECOUPES
6421	PAPER ETC CONTAINERS	W 30924	34.3	W 51968	94.5	W 54371	117.9	W 49525	85.5	BOITES,SACS EMBALLAGES
65	TEXTILE YARN,FABRICS,ETC		319.5		955.7		1022.7		990.6	FILS,TISSUS,ARTICLES TEXTILE
651	TEXTILE YARN	W 40227	140.0	W 55713	253.8		253.0	W 64446	248.2	FILS TEXTILES
6514	SYN FIB YRN,BULK,MONOFIL	W 26505	90.6	W 33306	140.6	W 31766	135.2	W 38110	127.7	FILS CONT 85% FIB TEXT SYNTH
65142	— NONTXT ETC CONT PAMID	W 16150	52.1	W 20800	75.7	W 18547	65.6	W 24502	68.2	FILS NON TEX FI CON POLYAMID
652	COTTON FABRICS,WOVEN	W 4671	18.7	W 13289	123.4		115.8	W 11723	103.5	TISSUS DE COTON
6522	WOVEN COTTON BLEACHD,ETC	W 2418	12.9	W 10010	106.0		98.7	W 8730	85.9	TISSUS COTON BLANCHIS ETC
653	WOVN MAN-MADE FIB FABRIC	W 4132	42.0	W 10851	162.4	W 12413	176.2	W 11961	157.5	TISSUS FIBRES SYNTH,ARTIF
654	OTH WOVEN TEXTILE FABRIC	W 1082	8.6	W 4270	89.1	W 4104	80.9	W 4514	75.5	TISSUS AUT COTON SYNT,ARTIF
657	SPECIAL TXTL FABRC,PRODS	W 4790	33.6	W 16076	137.2		168.7	W 24497	178.9	TISSUS SPECIAUX
6573	COATED ETC TEXTILES NES	W 1282	11.7	W 6532	67.4	W 7766	92.9	W 8970	99.4	TISSUS,ART MATIERE TEXT NDA
65732	PLASTIC COATED TEXTILES	W 710	6.3	W 5624	58.1	W 6588	81.6	W 7699	89.4	TISSUS IMPREGNES
66	NONMETAL MINERAL MFS NES		284.9		478.7		535.9		538.6	ART MIN NON METALLIQUES
662	CLAY,REFRACTORY BLDG PRD	W 187705	92.4	W 223682	120.0	W 217003	112.4	W 255534	97.2	MAT CONST REFRACTAIRES
6623	REFRACTORY BUILDING PROD	W 132488	69.8	W 156186	91.3	W 135621	76.8	W 137941	61.0	BRIQUES REFRACTAIRES
66232	REFRACTRY BRICKS ETC NES	W 103267	54.9	W 110461	67.9	W 85199	53.3	W 77369	39.4	BRIQUES ETC REFRACTAIRES
663	MINERAL MANUFCTURES NES	W 244609	70.5	W 273403	105.1	W 321608	119.5	W 415058	117.9	ART MIN MANUF NDA
664	GLASS	W 98260	51.2	W 132434	117.2	W 157979	135.8	W 186612	155.4	VERRE
67	IRON AND STEEL		571.4		1271.2		1150.2		1143.6	FER ET ACIER
671	PIG IRON ETC	W 164805	72.8	W 189994	111.0	W 139446	85.8	W 142637	73.1	FONTE,SPIEGEL,POUDRES
6716	FERRO-ALLOYS	W 99228	64.0	W 117200	98.7	W 105213	79.6	W 108957	67.7	FERRO-ALLIAGES
672	IRON,STEEL PRIMARY FORMS	W 396666	95.6	W 551824	178.3		97.3	W 403792	111.2	LINGOTS FER,ACIER
6725	IRN,STL BLOOMS,SLABS,ETC	W 208185	45.2	W 364661	107.9	W 95524	39.4	W 153384	44.0	BLOOMS,BILLETTES FER ACIER
67251	IRN,SMPLE STL BLOOMS,ETC	W 207294	43.4	W 357877	97.7	W 91211	30.9	W 150284	39.9	BLOOMS ETC NON ACIER FIN
673	IRON,STEEL SHAPES ETC	W 58403	34.0	W 154685	113.5	W 192410	126.8	W 308067	158.4	BARRES,PROFIL FER,ACIER
674	IRN,STL UNIV,PLATE,SHEET	W 562582	248.5	W 996711	601.5	W 899938	559.2	W 1016438	535.2	LARGES PLATS,TOLES
6744	IRN,STL HVY PLATE,ROLLED	W 115259	41.3	W 183075	93.9	W 161062	86.5	W 180742	84.3	TOLES LAMINEES PLUS 4.75 MM
67441	— OF IRON OR SIMPLE STL	W 112902	36.2	W 178659	82.4	W 147556	67.0	W 167872	68.2	TOLES NON ACIER FIN CARB
6745	IRN,STL MED PLATE,ROLLED	W 113982	37.7	W 202247	92.8	W 256495	122.6	W 308634	125.7	TOLES 3 A 4.75 MM
67451	— OF IRON OR SIMPLE STL	W 111900	34.0	W 190799	80.3	W 237192	103.2	W 268314	100.4	TOLES AUT NON ACIER FIN
6746	IRN,STL THIN PLATE,ROLLD	W 195012	90.3	W 361250	227.7	W 230132	163.5	W 236562	138.6	TOLES LAM MOINS 3MM
67461	— OF IRON OR SIMPLE STL	W 181937	71.8	W 325634	172.7	W 200515	114.5	W 200809	93.5	TOL NON AC FIN MOINS 3 MM
6749	OTH IRN,STL PLATES,SHEET	W 93856	50.5	W 208700	154.0	W 207885	151.3	W 247963	156.6	AUTRES TOLES FER,ACIER
67491	— OF IRON OR SIMPLE STL	W 91059	42.7	W 203696	141.1	W 204142	144.4	W 239798	146.4	AUT TOLES AUTRES ACIER FIN
678	IRON,STL TUBES,PIPES,ETC	W 88603	99.3	W 143742	204.2	W 150054	208.9	W 184947	197.9	TUBES,TUYAUX EN FONTE,FER
6783	IRON,STL TUBES,PIPES NES	W 54945	46.3	W 84465	88.2	W 84200	82.3	W 101791	78.4	AUT TUBES,TUYAUX FER,ACIER
68	NON-FERROUS METALS		330.2		636.0		609.0		638.9	METAUX NON FERREUX
682	COPPER EXC CEMENT COPPER	W 43210	111.0	W 59414	192.3	W 66632	189.6	W 62225	175.8	CUIVRE
6822	COPPER,ALLOYS WORKED	W 32652	86.8	W 41270	140.4	W 47393	148.4	W 50022	148.0	CUIVRE,ALLIAGES OUVRES
68221	COPPER BARS,WIRE,ETC	W 25175	60.1	W 31498	94.2	W 35228	91.0	W 36645	89.2	BARRES,PROFILES ET FILS
684	ALUMINIUM	W 94723	165.9	W 116352	300.9	W 116329	281.2	W 134728	308.7	ALUMINIUM
6841	ALUMINIUM,ALLOYS,UNWRGHT	W 71346	85.3	W 82718	156.1	W 76394	125.0	W 81079	133.9	ALUMINIUM,ALLIAGES BRUTS
6842	ALUMINIUM,ALLOYS WORKED	W 23377	80.7	W 33635	144.9	W 39934	156.3	W 53649	174.8	ALUMINIUM,ALLIAGES OUVRE
69	METAL MANUFACTURES NES		421.8		808.7		931.8		875.5	ART MANUFACT EN METAL NDA
691	STRUCTURES AND PARTS NES	W 36215	68.4	W 63344	123.8	W 71927	145.5	W 66799	124.6	CONSTRUCT FER,ACIER,ALU
6911	STRUCTURES,PARTS IRN,STL	W 33384	49.6	W 60100	94.8	W 68225	117.8	W 62128	95.1	CONSTRUCT FER,ACIER,FONTE
692	METAL TANKS,BOXES,ETC	W 23804	58.0	W 28221	72.4	W 28266	78.4	W 23192	61.3	RECIPIENTS METALLIQUES
6924	MTL TRANSPORT BOXES ETC	W 16880	47.3	W 19731	58.9	W 20637	62.8	W 17875	44.2	FUTS,TAMBOURS,BIDONS
694	STL,COPPR NAILS,NUTS,ETC	W 10954	21.4	W 22504	69.8	W 24913	79.9	W 26963	83.8	CLOUS,VIS,ECROUS
695	TOOLS	W 6197	65.3	W 91107	100.9	W 8499	110.7	W 8313	101.7	OUTILS A MAIN
697	BASE MTL HOUSEHOLD EQUIP	W 8656	50.5	W 11207	65.2		74.4	W 13263	56.0	ART MENAGE MET COMMUNS
699	BASE METAL MFRS NES	W 31520	123.0	W 72401	311.8		367.4	W 113050	379.9	ART MANUFACTURES MET NDA
6991	LOCKSMITHS WARES,ETC	W 7197	55.0	W 18747	138.5	W 21660	147.8	W 26614	148.9	ARTICLES DE SERRURERIE
69913	BASE MTL DOOR,ETC FITTNG	W 4752	35.2	W 11470	79.6	W 14435	91.8	W 17419	92.4	GARNITURES POUR MEUBLES
6997	IRON,STEEL ARTICLES NES	W 11870	20.6	W 31817	62.5	W 49687	93.9	W 57882	99.4	OUV FONTE,FER,ACIER NDA
69979	IRN,STL MANUFACTURES NES	W 11682	20.1	W 31674	62.3	W 49125	93.4	W 57544	98.9	AUT OUVRAGES EN FER NDA
7	MACHINES,TRANSPORT EQUIP		5162.3		9107.9		10534.6		10269.8	MACHINES MATERIEL TRANSPORT
71	POWER GENERATING EQUIPMT		82.6		331.0		490.9		549.5	MACHINES GENERATRICES
713	INTRNL COMBUS PSTN ENGIN	W 2535	28.5	W 6245	71.6	W 15709	146.5	W 27450	231.0	MOTEURS EXPL COMB INT, PIECE
7132	MOTOR VEHCL PISTN ENGINS	W 614	3.8	W 1612	13.5	W 6949	52.9	W 17129	129.2	MOTEURS EXPL POUR VEHICULES
716	ROTATING ELECTRIC PLANT	W 2034	21.0	W 13628	135.0	W 18227	154.5	W 23815	164.0	APP ELECTR ROTATIFS,PIECES
718	OTH POWER GENERATG MACHY	W 260	8.0	W 1216	61.4	W 2731	94.0	W 3678	57.3	AUTRES MOTEURS PARTIES
72	MACHS FOR SPCL INDUSTRYS		887.7		1364.5		1329.3		1128.1	MAC SPECIALES POUR INDUST
721	AGRIC MACHY,EXC TRACTORS	W 19789	108.4	W 25213	184.1		231.1	W 27080	165.3	MACHINES AGRICOLES
7212	HARVESTING ETC MACHINES	W 12573	57.5	W 15735	107.5	W 20982	151.8	W 17938	112.7	ENGINS POUR LA RECOLTE
723	CIVIL ENGNEERG EQUIP ETC	W 16939	106.2	W 27656	180.1	W 26753	161.5	W 25102	129.7	APPAREILS DE GENIE CIVIL
7234	CONST,MINING MACHNRY NES	W 15256	95.0	W 22650	158.1	W 22007	143.7	W 20332	113.9	MACH POUR LA CONST, MINES
72342	SLFPRP SHOVELS,EXCAVATRS	W 9418	42.9	W 15308	86.2	W 15713	84.7	W 13817	61.9	PELLES MECANIQUES
724	TEXTILE,LEATHER MACHNRY	W 10056	136.2	W 17812	211.8	W 19001	198.6	W 17503	191.0	MACH POUR INDUSTRIE TEXTILE
7247	TEXTILE MACHINERY NES	W 3910	45.9	W 4099	36.9	W 4556	40.8	W 5114	39.7	MACH LAVAGE,TEINTURE TEX
725	PAPER ETC MILL MACHINERY	W 2082	33.6	W 5244	79.6	W 3997	61.5	W 4221	57.2	MACHINES FABR PATE PAPIER
726	PRINTG,BKBINDG MACHY,PTS	W 4337	99.4	W 4695	123.6		84.6	W 4002	86.5	MACHINES POUR IMPRIMERIE
727	FOOD MACHRY NON-DOMESTIC	W 3892	73.4	W 3806	66.7	W 5543	80.3	W 4249	60.2	MACH INDUSTRIES ALIMENT
7272	OTH FOOD PROC MCHY,PARTS	W 3654	70.7	W 3632	66.0	W 5340	77.6	W 4116	57.9	AUT MACH IND ALIMENTAIRE
72722	INDUS FOOD PROC MACH NES	W 3186	60.5	W 3008	51.8	W 4428	60.8	W 3095	45.7	MACHINES BOULANGERIE
728	OTH MACHY FOR SPCL INDUS	W 28691	301.0	W 42938	477.8	W 36438	460.1	W 37009	393.2	AUT MACH IND PARTICULIERES
7281	MACH-TOOLS FR SPCL INDUS	W 7599	60.0	W 7643	75.1	W 6497	74.1	W 6071	53.8	MACH-OUTILS SPEC IND PART
7284	MACHY FOR SPCL INDUS NES	W 16248	204.8	W 26156	339.1	W 22607	330.6	W 21708	283.5	MACH SPEC IND PARTICUL.
72842	RUBBER,PLASTICS WRKG MCH	W 5945	69.3	W 6574	82.3	W 7022	80.6	W 7671	81.3	MACH IND CAOUT MAT PLAST
72848	OTH MCHY WITH INDIV FNCT	W 6369	60.3	W 13753	118.7	W 8427	105.7	W 6742	93.4	AUTRES MACHINES NDA
73	METALWORKING MACHINERY		217.2		300.9		313.7		313.0	MACH TRAVAIL DES METAUX
736	METALWORKING MACH-TOOLS	W 17096	154.1	W 27883	225.8	W 26337	241.1	W 28661	228.4	MACH-OUTILS TRAVAIL METAUX
7361	METAL CUTTING MACH-TOOLS	W 5505	51.2	W 8823	76.1	W 8257	70.4	W 8228	70.9	MACH-OUT ENLEVEMENT METAL
737	METALWORKING MACHNRY NES	W 3946	63.2	W 8287	75.2	W 7805	72.6	W 11569	84.7	MACH TRAV METAUX PIECES
7373	WELDING,BRAZING,ETC MCHS	W 1933	46.3	W 2885	57.4	W 3283	58.2	W 2682	54.8	MACH SOUDAGE ETC PIECES
74	GENRL INDUSTRL MACHY NES		1025.1		1641.3		1794.4		1640.5	MACH APP INDUSTRIE
741	HEATING,COOLING EQUIPMNT	W 15251	202.6	W 29457	325.5		350.0	W 29166	301.2	MACH CHAUFFAGE,PIECES
7414	NONDOM REFRIG EQUIPT,PTS	W 3123	61.8	W 12283	108.9	W 11789	111.0	W 9627	86.6	MAT PRODUCTION DU FROID
74141	REFRIG EQUIP NONDOMESTIC	W 1954	52.9	W 8275	70.5	W 8271	75.8	W 6816	58.0	REFIG INDUSTRIELS
7416	HEATING,COOLING EQU NES	W 3196	42.9	W 6292	84.5	W 10684	92.4	W 9134	80.7	APP CHANGEMENT TEMP

4. General Imports F.O.B. by Commodities according to the S.I.T.C. (Rev. 2) in million U.S. Dollars
Importations Générales F.O.B. par Produits d'après la C.T.C.I. (Rév. 2) en millions de Dollars E.U.

SITC CTCI	COMMODITY	1994 QUANTITY QUANTITE	1994 VALUE VALEUR	1995 QUANTITY QUANTITE	1995 VALUE VALEUR	1996 QUANTITY QUANTITE	1996 VALUE VALEUR	1997 QUANTITY QUANTITE	1997 VALUE VALEUR	PRODUIT
742	PUMPS FOR LIQUIDS ETC	W 4030	61.4	W 6623	125.7	W 7929	164.4	W 9114	173.7	POMPES MOTO-POMPES
743	PUMPS NES,CENTRFUGES ETC	W 12478	216.6	W 25992	275.0	W 29664	322.5	W 27267	289.0	POMPES COMPRES,VENT ETC
7436	GAS,LIQUID FILTERS ETC	W 6153	132.2	W 15132	150.6	W 17600	196.0	W 14131	160.0	APP POUR FILT DES LIQUIDES
744	MECHANICAL HANDLING EQU	W 19196	126.2	W 40935	217.6	W 44443	232.4	W 51033	211.3	EQUIP MANUTENTION PIECES
7442	LIFTING,LOADING MACH NES	W 7748	51.7	W 13204	72.3	W 13096	89.3	W 14254	92.5	APP LEVAGE,MANUTENTION
7449	PTS NES OF MACHY OF 7442	W 7412	53.0	W 22017	112.5	W 23672	101.8	W 29078	82.3	PIECES DU 744.2
745	NONELEC MACHY,TOOLS NES	W 8023	177.7	W 9910	222.1	W 12240	239.2	W 12994	212.5	AUT MACH NON ELEC,PIECES
7452	OTH NONELEC MCHS,PTS NES	W 7374	159.2	W 9214	197.4	W 11448	212.5	W 12121	187.1	AUT MACH NON ELEC,PIECES
74522	PACKAGNG,BOTTLNG,ETC MCH	W 2702	83.8	W 2497	99.0	W 3129	96.4	W 2318	67.1	MACH NETT BOUTEILLES,ETC
749	NONELEC MACH PTS,ACC NES	W 20959	240.8	W 34288	475.6	W 39283	486.1	W 39567	453.0	PIECES MACH NON ELEC NDA
7491	BALL,ROLLER,ETC BEARINGS	W 5689	52.0	W 7576	100.0	W 7622	103.9	W 6800	94.2	ROULEMENTS BILLES ETC
7492	COCKS,VALVES ETC NES	W 9296	121.7	W 11249	190.3	W 13396	220.6	W 14608	208.2	ART ROB,SIM POUR TUYAUX
7493	SHAFT,CRANK,PULLEY ETC	W 3603	32.3	W 10152	91.5	W 12041	95.3	W 12166	76.9	ARBRES TRANS,VILEBREQUINS
7499	OTH NONELEC MCHY PTS NES	W 2372	34.9	W 5310	93.9	W 6225	66.5	W 5993	73.9	PIECES NON ELECT NDA
75	OFFICE MACHNES,ADP EQUIP		729.1		1024.9		1035.2		879.9	MACH BUREAU TRAIT AUTOM
751	OFFICE MACHINES	W 2327	73.8	W 4235	86.9	W 4167	84.1	W 3824	64.9	MACH,APPAREILS DE BUREAU
7518	OFFICE MACHINES NES	W 1617	52.4	W 3473	63.8	W 3540	65.2	W 3268	49.3	MACH,APP DE BUREAU NDA
752	AUTOMTIC DATA PROC EQUIP	W 7926	541.9	W 10182	743.1	W 11495	732.8	W 10944	610.3	MACH TRAIT INFORMATION
7522	DIGITAL COMPUTERS	W 1573	169.2	W 1593	202.3	W 1741	173.3	W 1080	101.9	MACH DIGITALES COMPLETES
7523	DIGITL CENTRL PROCESSORS	W 864	90.8	W 902	137.5	W 550	85.5	W 769	94.0	UNITES CENTRALES
7524	DIGITL CENTRL STOR UNITS	W 403	75.6	W 513	92.7	W 612	112.1	W 636	106.4	UNITES MEMOIRE CENTRALES
7525	ADP PERIPHERAL UNITS	W 3629	138.2	W 5342	224.8	W 5327	202.7	W 5785	181.2	UNITES PERIPHERIQUES
7528	OFF-LINE DATA PROC EQUIP	W 1358	55.5	W 1766	79.2	W 3011	126.2	W 2443	95.4	MACH AUXIL TRAIT INFORM
759	OFFICE,ADP MCH PTS,ACCES	W 2845	113.4	W 6517	194.9	W 7125	218.4	W 7436	204.7	PIECES DU 751 ET 752
7599	ACCTG,ETC,ADP MCH PTS,AC	W 2162	86.0	W 5220	153.1	W 4940	154.9	W 5842	163.3	PIECES DU 751 ET 752
76	TELECOMM,SOUND EQUIPMENT		478.6		719.4		985.6		892.5	EQUIPMENT DE TELECOM
761	TELEVISION RECEIVERS	W 6639	51.2	W 5732	56.8	W 7451	78.9	W 7479	80.1	RECEPTEURS DE TELEVISION
7611	COLOUR TV RECEIVERS	W 6600	50.6	W 5701	56.1	W 7412	78.2	W 7443	79.6	RECEPTEURS COULEUR
762	RADIO BROADCAST RECEIVRS	W 3180	49.1	W 3431	67.6	W 4459	80.8	W 4152	72.9	RECEPTEURS RADIODIFFUSION
763	SOUND RECORDRS,PHONOGRPH	W 2004	48.4	W 1225	56.0		74.9	W 1552	71.1	PHONO,APP ENREGISTREMENT
7638	OTHR SOUND APPARATUS ETC	W 1985	48.1	W 1205	55.5	W 1512	74.4	W 1526	70.7	AUT APP D'ENREGIS,REPROD
764	TELECOM EQPT,PTS,ACC NES	W 7329	330.0	W 9711	539.2		751.3	W 11611	668.6	EQUIP TELECOM,PIECES
7641	LINE TELEPHONE,ETC EQUIP	W 1356	80.1	W 1786	129.0	W 2114	161.2	W 2076	170.5	APP TELEPHON PAR FIL
7643	TV,RADIO TRANSMITTRS ETC	W 203	36.4	W 253	55.6	W 567	142.8	W 846	178.9	APP EMET TELE RADIO
7649	PTS NES OF EQUIPMT OF 76	W 4821	190.8	W 6117	314.6	W 7299	367.8	W 6174	278.3	PIECES DE LA DIV 76
76491	PTS NES OF APPAR OF 7641	W 2179	134.4	W 2060	194.1	W 2096	220.1	W 1438	131.0	PIECES POUR 764.1
76493	TELECOMM EQUIPMT PTS NES	W 2563	55.3	W 3530	103.9	W 3841	128.7	W 3470	127.3	PIECES 761,762,764.3,8
77	ELECTRIC MACHNRY NES ETC		853.8		2024.9		2441.5		2509.8	MACH APP ELECT NDA
771	ELECTRIC POWER MACHY NES	W 9737	60.3	W 15394	140.6	W 18791	176.8	W 19746	178.3	MACH PROD,TRANS ELECTR
7712	OTH ELEC POWER MACHY NES	W 3210	26.5	W 7563	95.5	W 10127	133.1	W 11245	135.1	AUT APP PROD TRANSF ELEC
772	SWITCHGEAR ETC,PARTS NES	W 7947	152.2	W 110292	512.6	W 26774	636.1	W 31408	703.0	APP COUPURE,SECT ETC
7721	SWITCHGEAR ETC	W 7853	148.6	W 108666	459.5	W 24923	566.8	W 28061	623.3	APP COUPURE,SECTIONMNT
773	ELECTR DISTRIBUTNG EQUIP	W 14864	57.3	W 35730	250.8	W 50066	343.0	W 51004	320.3	EQUIPMT DISTRIBUTION ELECT
7731	INSULATED WIRE,CABLE ETC	W 13150	46.7	W 32507	214.1	W 45951	284.1	W 46783	259.8	FILS,CABLES ISOLES ELECT
774	ELECTRO-MEDCL,XRAY EQUIP	W 623	99.4	W 626	82.9	W 560	80.7	W 554	61.7	APPAREILS MEDICAUX
7741	ELECTRO-MEDICAL EQUIPMNT	W 332	61.9	W 325	48.4	W 247	41.1	W 198	23.8	APP ELECTRICITE MEDICALE
775	HOUSEHOLD TYPE EQUIP NES	W 42427	218.3	W 54044	317.1	W 64242	388.4	W 64043	337.9	MACH,APP USAGE DOMESTQUE
7752	DOM REFRIGERATRS,FREEZRS	W 15265	61.9	W 18809	84.1	W 19923	90.9	W 17844	70.6	REFRIG,CONGEL MENAGER
7758	ELECTRO-THERMIC APPL NES	W 13143	81.6	W 16017	120.4	W 17919	140.0	W 17865	118.3	APP ELECTROTHERMIQ NDA
776	TRANSISTORS,VALVES,ETC	W 1360	94.8	W 2824	217.9		221.4	W 4017	220.0	LAMPES,TUBES,VALVES
7764	ELECTRONIC MICROCIRCUITS	W 417	79.4	W 409	155.6	W 350	151.6	W 388	134.5	MICROSTRUCTURES ELECTRON
778	ELECTRICAL MACHINERY NES	W 18925	171.7	W 34388	503.3		595.4	W 37176	689.0	AUTRES MACH ELECT NDA
7781	BATTERIES,ACCUMULATORS	W 6525	25.7	W 11467	95.8	W 15194	131.2	W 16341	201.4	PILES ET ACCUMULATEURS
77812	ELECTRIC ACCUMULATORS	W 2787	11.9	W 5507	37.8	W 8363	69.8	W 9263	105.4	ACCUMULATEURS ELECTRIQ
7788	OTH ELEC MACHY,EQUIP NES	W 7537	80.8	W 14826	284.3		315.3	W 10123	327.2	AUT MACH APP ELEC NDA
77884	ELECTRICAL CONDENSERS	W 189	4.9	W 5383	158.5	W 1260	177.8	W 1343	201.8	CONDENSATEURS ELECTRIQUES
78	ROAD VEHICLES		875.0		1567.8		1972.6		2131.5	VEHICULES ROUTIERS
781	PASS MOTOR VEH EXC BUSES	W 83012	407.0	W 110239	621.4	W 160790	823.8	W 157008	778.4	AUTO TRANSPORT PERSONNES
782	LORRIES,SPCL MTR VEH NES	W 24196	113.5	W 37786	232.4	W 38567	274.4	W 47698	287.1	VEHICULES SPECIAUX,MARCH
7821	LORRIES,TRUCKS	W 18126	91.7	W 28614	191.4	W 32433	235.0	W 38108	246.0	VEHICULES TRANSP MARCHAND
783	ROAD MOTOR VEHICLES NES	W 6913	69.6	W 11772	118.9	W 12620	114.7	W 16013	128.5	VEHICULES ROUTIERS NDA
7832	TRACTORS FOR TR-TRAILERS	W 5606	53.2	W 9011	99.2	W 10034	97.5	W 13584	113.5	TRACTEURS ROUTIERS
784	MOTOR VEH PRTS,ACCES NES	W 39957	186.0	W 80588	437.8	W 108381	583.0	W 180528	769.1	PIECES 722,781,782,783
7849	OTHER MOTOR VEHCL PARTS	W 36732	175.7	W 73020	410.1	W 103913	562.5	W 174059	740.2	PIECES 722,781,782,783
785	CYCLES,ETC MOTRZD OR NOT	W 7952	51.9	W 14210	81.0	W 15230	87.3	W 12415	74.6	MOTOCYCLES SCOOTERS
786	TRAILERS,NONMOTR VEH,NES	W 12690	47.4	W 19883	76.6	W 21672	89.6	W 26518	94.1	REMORQUES,CADRES,CONTAIN
79	OTHR TRANSPORT EQUIPMENT		13.4		133.7		171.8		225.6	AUTRE MATERIEL TRANSPORT
791	RAILWAY VEHICLES	W 9445	11.2	W 42944	130.3	W 30406	68.6	W 31155	83.0	VEHIC MAT CHEMINS DE FER
792	AIRCRAFT ETC	W 2	0.2	W 11	0.6		98.9	W 1164	136.4	APP NAVIGATION AERIENNE
7924	AIRCRFT NES OVER 15000KG					W 419	42.5	W 774	108.2	AERODYNES PLUS 15000 KG
8	MISC MANUFACTURED GOODS		1805.7		3001.5		3282.8		3270.8	ART MANUFACTURES DIVERS
812	*PLUMBG,HEATNG,LGHTNG EQ	W 19313	105.9	W 24849	153.2	W 30200	182.4	W 36750	176.3	APPAR SANITAIRES CHAUFFAGE
8121	CENTRAL HEATING EQUIPMNT	W 7700	31.4	W 13161	57.6	W 18373	80.3	W 25049	90.1	CHAUDIERES,RADIATEURS
8124	LIGHTING EQUIPMENT NES	W 11108	72.5	W 10960	92.3	W 10714	97.8	W 9353	79.9	APPAREILS ECLAIRAGE ETC
81242	LAMPS,FITTINGS BASE METL	W 8423	48.7	W 7131	55.2	W 7027	62.7	W 5943	49.6	APPAREILS D'ECLAIRAGE
821	*FURNITURE,PARTS THEREOF	W 68788	175.5	W 177736	258.7	W 98193	308.9	W 107312	309.0	MEUBLES ET PIECES
8211	CHAIRS,SEATS AND PARTS	W 12988	47.2	W 115891	97.9	W 27178	132.7	W 36123	150.7	SIEGES ET PIECES
82119	PTS NES OF CHAIRS ETC	W 1394	5.1	W 101626	40.1	W 10878	67.3	W 19082	95.3	PIECES DU 821.11
8219	FURNITURE AND PARTS NES	W 53795	107.2	W 59536	136.4	W 68430	150.2	W 68593	138.7	AUTRES MEUBLES ET PIECES
82192	WOOD FURNITURE NES	W 32039	57.7	W 35704	73.2	W 41491	83.1	W 42357	73.9	MEUBLES NDA EN BOIS
84	CLOTHING AND ACCESSORIES		227.6		462.2		502.3		434.0	VETEMENTS
843	WOMENS OUTERWEAR NONKNIT	W 6504	56.1	W 6925	94.1	W 7502	107.2	W 7815	94.5	VET DESSUS FEMMES MAT TEX
845	OUTERWEAR KNIT NONELASTC	W 6880	47.8	W 8765	76.1	W 9656	78.1	W 7303	65.1	VET DESSOUS,ACCES BONNET
846	UNDER GARMENTS KNITTED	W 8183	43.7	W 10161	94.6	W 10307	101.6	W 8349	88.0	SOUS VETS DE BONNETERIE
851	*FOOTWEAR	W 12029	93.9	W 14994	133.0	W 17286	167.1	W 19071	168.1	CHAUSSURES
85102	FOOTWEAR LEATHER	W 7203	63.6	W 8839	88.5	W 10531	117.2	W 12616	123.5	CHAUS SEMELLES EN CUIR
87	PRECISION INSTRUMNTS NES		385.1		623.9		594.8		502.4	INSTRUM,APPAR SCIENT NDA
872	MEDICAL INSTRUMENTS NES	W 2998	110.8	W 4603	127.6	W 5548	136.1	W 4016	104.6	INSTR,APP MEDIC-CHIR NDA
87202	OTH MEDICAL INSTRUMENTS	W 2080	93.9	W 3085	108.3	W 3645	113.0	W 3219	88.3	INSTRUM,APP MEDECINE
874	MEASURNG,CONTROLNG INSTR	W 3815	225.6	W 6992	437.6		398.2	W 6853	340.2	INSTRUMENTS DE MESURE
8742	MEASUR,DRAW ETC INST,PTS	W 1182	58.1	W 1880	119.0	W 1887	97.0	W 1743	73.6	INST DESSIN,TRACAGE,PCS
87421	MEASURNG,DRAWNG ETC INST	W 981	49.0	W 1592	103.6	W 1388	77.8	W 1404	60.4	INSTRUM DESSIN,TRACAGE
8743	GAS,LIQUID CONTROL INSTR	W 1105	55.4	W 1818	97.5	W 2035	92.2	W 2054	88.6	APP,INSTR MESURE FLUIDES
8748	ELEC MEAS,CONTRL EQU NES	W 451	61.6	W 720	107.2	W 670	107.3	W 580	83.7	APP ELEC ELECTRO MESURE
87483	OTH ELCTRNC MEAS ETC EQU	W 348	52.9	W 571	94.0	W 530	88.8	W 472	72.3	AUT APP ELECTRO DE MESURE
88	PHOTO EQU,OPTICL GDS ETC		112.3		157.2		183.6		175.3	APP,FOURN PHOTO,OP,MONTR
882	PHOTO,CINEMA SUPPLIES	W 3147	46.2	W 4200	63.0		64.3	W 5348	67.8	PRODUITS PHOTO,CINEMA
89	MISC MANUFCTRD GOODS NES		680.7		1175.7		1302.2		1466.2	ART MANUFACTURES DIVERS
892	PRINTED MATTER	W 30156	119.4	W 43873	188.7		222.1	W 67808	217.9	IMPRIMES
8921	PRINTED BOOKS,GLOBES,ETC	W 12789	47.2	W 16477	67.7	W 17694	69.4	W 19410	64.0	LIVRES,BROCHURES,CARTES
8928	PRINTED MATTER NES	W 7844	48.3	W 15195	80.5		103.7	W 34053	113.3	IMPRIMES NDA

4. General Imports F.O.B. by Commodities according to the S.I.T.C. (Rev. 2) in million U.S. Dollars
Importations Générales F.O.B. par Produits d'après la C.T.C.I. (Rév. 2) en millions de Dollars E.U.

SITC CTCI	COMMODITY	1994 QUANTITY QUANTITE	1994 VALUE VALEUR	1995 QUANTITY QUANTITE	1995 VALUE VALEUR	1996 QUANTITY QUANTITE	1996 VALUE VALEUR	1997 QUANTITY QUANTITE	1997 VALUE VALEUR	PRODUIT
893	ARTICLES OF PLASTIC NES		227.3		417.2		518.2		566.1	OUVRAGES EN MAT DIVIS 58
8931	PLSTC PACKG CONTNRS,LIDS	W 22348	62.1	W 29563	110.9	W 37218	115.0	W 42730	122.3	ART TRANSP EMBALLAGE ETC
8939	MISC PLASTIC ARTICLES	W 54484	151.7	W 83445	285.6	W 87490	382.4	W 102525	423.4	ART DIVERS EN MAT DIV 58
89399	OTHR PLASTC ARTICLES NES	W 49904	140.5	W 78592	269.6	W 82293	364.5	W 96648	406.4	AUT OUV MAT DIV 58
894	TOYS,SPORTING GOODS,ETC	W 12384	100.2	W 17929	175.3	W 22432	193.5	W 27083	167.7	VOITURES ENFANTS,JOUETS
8942	TOYS,INDOOR GAMES ETC	W 9197	74.0	W 12313	106.9	W 14194	108.2	W 14148	92.3	JOUETS,JEUX ETC
896	WORKS OF ART ETC		4.4		73.2		2.8		158.8	OBJETS D'ART
89601	HAND PAINTINGS ETC NES		3.5		27.9		0.8		121.6	TABLEAUX,PEINTURES
898	MUSICAL INSTRUMENTS,PTS	W 4082	98.2	W 5375	126.7		145.9	W 5893	146.8	INSTRUMENTS DE MUSIQUE
8983	SOUND RECRDNG TAPE,DISCS	W 3696	86.0	W 4720	110.4	W 5252	127.3	W 5195	132.0	SUPPORTS SON POUR 763
89832	RECORDED DISCS,TAPES ETC	W 1051	57.2	W 1322	77.1	W 1724	91.8	W 1629	100.9	DISQUES,PHONO,BANDES
899	OTHER MANUFACTURED GOODS		80.2		120.7		131.0		119.5	AUT ART MANUF DIVERS NDA
9	GOODS NOT CLASSD BY KIND		78.2		302.5		14.1		19.3	ART TRANSACT NON CLASSES
931	*SPECIAL TRANSACTIONS	W 4721	67.8	W 12525	279.2					TRANS.SPECIALES

5. General Exports F.O.B. by Commodities according to the S.I.T.C. (Rev. 2) in million U.S. Dollars
Exportations Générales F.O.B. par Produits d'après la C.T.C.I. (Rév. 2) en millions de Dollars E.U.

SITC CTCI	COMMODITY	1994 QUANTITY QUANTITE	1994 VALUE VALEUR	1995 QUANTITY QUANTITE	1995 VALUE VALEUR	1996 QUANTITY QUANTITE	1996 VALUE VALEUR	1997 QUANTITY QUANTITE	1997 VALUE VALEUR	PRODUIT
	ALL COMMODITIES		14081.5		21685.7		21907.4		22746.4	TOUS PRODUITS
0	FOOD AND LIVE ANIMALS		743.3		1038.5		875.7		824.9	ALIMENTS,ANIMAUX VIVANTS
001	*LIVE ANIMALS FOR FOOD	W 37896	57.4	W 25900	52.3	W 17163	35.8	W 34456	51.7	ANIMAUX VIVANTS
0011	BOVINE SPECIES,LIVE	W 29897	45.2	W 21580	39.6	W 11666	20.7	W 22270	28.1	ESPECE BOVINE
01	MEAT AND PREPARATIONS		47.6		54.0		52.3		63.2	VIANDES ET PREPARATIONS
02	DAIRY PRODCTS,BIRDS'EGGS		180.1		229.3		213.0		171.5	PRODUITS LAITIERS,OEUFS
022	MILK AND CREAM	W 117594	117.8	W 111528	143.7	W 104479	125.7	W 99224	89.9	LAIT ET CREME
0224	MILK,CREAM PRESERVED ETC	W 98996	110.6	W 88751	135.4	W 81286	117.8	W 64806	79.0	LAIT,CREME CONS,CONC
02242	MILK DRY,1.5% FAT OR LES	W 58376	72.0	W 53930	94.8	W 43504	75.2	W 28648	43.2	LAIT POUDRE INF 1.5%
04	CEREALS AND PREPARATIONS		89.5		263.7		157.4		124.7	CEREALES ET PRODUITS
041	WHEAT ETC UNMILLED	W 28722	3.7	W 1018274	117.5	W 145320	21.5	W 3532	0.7	FROMENT,EPEAUTRE
0412	OTHER WHEAT ETC UNMILLED	W 27259	3.4	W 1000441	115.2	W 144588	21.4	W 3532	0.7	AUTRE FROMENT NON MOULU
048	CEREAL ETC PREPARATIONS	W 214522	73.9	W 254238	105.5	W 234306	117.3	W 221090	111.5	PREPTNS A BASE CEREALES
05	VEGETABLES AND FRUIT		137.1		143.7		147.7		135.9	LEGUMES ET FRUITS
054	VEG ETC FRSH,SMPLY PRSVD	W 277726	91.0	W 137294	76.7		75.9	W 93694	55.0	LEGUMES FRAIS,CONG,SECS
0548	EDIBLE VEG NES FRESH,DRY	W 68228	55.8	W 7413	48.7		51.3	W 6107	33.1	RACINES,TUBERCULES
05484	HOP CONES AND LUPULIN	W 7483	54.5	W 6723	48.2	W 7286	49.3	W 6039	33.0	HOUBLON
06	SUGAR AND PREPS,HONEY		58.7		66.3		42.4		69.2	SUCRES ET PRODUITS
07	COFFEE,TEA,COCOA,SPICES		60.6		84.2		76.3		66.5	CAFE,THE,CACAO,EPICES
073	CHOCOLATE AND PRODUCTS	W 15428	45.2	W 17162	53.8	W 18949	55.0	W 18601	44.0	CHOCOLAT
081	*FEEDING STUFF FOR ANIML	W 287170	43.7	W 342728	48.4	W 342490	51.9	W 289378	43.7	NOURRITURE POUR ANIMAUX
09	MISC EDIBLE PRODUCTS		43.9		66.6		67.4		70.3	PREP ALIMENTAIRES DIVERSES
1	BEVERAGES AND TOBACCO		173.8		174.2		223.5		289.4	BOISSONS ET TABACS
11	BEVERAGES		112.5		116.3		136.8		128.2	BOISSONS
112	ALCOHOLIC BEVERAGES	W 313320	99.6	W 211313	101.9		114.7	W 224967	104.9	BOISSONS ALCOOLIQUES
1123	BEER,ALE,STOUT,PORTER	W 273720	67.9	W 178385	79.9	W 212148	98.3	W 214995	94.5	BIERES
12	TOBACCO AND MANUFACTURES		61.3		57.9		86.7		161.2	TABACS BRUTS FABRIQUES
122	TOBACCO,MANUFACTURED	W 6576	61.0	W 8031	57.5		85.4	W 22214	161.2	TABACS FABRIQUES
1222	CIGARETTES	W 6337	56.9	W 8025	57.4	W 11671	79.0	W 18509	144.5	CIGARETTES
2	CRUDE MATERLS,EXCL FUELS		966.7		1110.5		1048.4		901.2	MAT BRUTES NON COMESTIBLES
23	RUBBER, CRUDE		62.1		68.6		63.5		50.2	CAOUTCHOUC BRUT
233	RUBBER,SYNTHETIC,RECLAIMD	W 68681	45.9	W 60072	68.1		63.0	W 66655	49.1	LATEX CAOUTCH SYNTH REGEN
2331	SYNTHETIC RUBBER ETC	W 61140	43.8	W 53972	65.9		60.8	W 58337	47.1	LATEX CAOUTCH SYNTHETIQUE
24	CORK AND WOOD		368.2		424.2		408.6		379.4	LIEGE ET BOIS
247	OTH WOOD ROUGH,SQUARED	W 1826532	136.0	W 1674819	163.2	W 1692751	138.6	W 1929607	141.0	BOIS BRUTS EQUARRIS
2471	SAW–,VENEER–LOGS CONIFER	W 1570911	125.6	W 1332723	146.2	W 1335376	122.3	W 1480038	125.0	CONIFERES POUR SCIAGE,PLACAG
24711	— IN THE ROUGH	W 1570911	125.6	W 1332723	146.2	W 1335376	122.3	W 1480038	125.0	ECORCES OU DEGROSSIS
248	WOOD SHAPED,SLEEPERS	W 820998	218.8	W 866596	242.7	W 805878	250.5	W 877160	220.7	BOIS SIMPLEMENT TRAVAILLES
2482	LUMBER SHAPED CONIFER	W 782203	206.8	W 820359	223.1	W 770113	234.1	W 844205	207.3	CONIFERES SCIES,RABOTES
24821	LUMBER SAWN ETC CONIFER	W 763453	196.8	W 798832	207.3	W 748424	217.1	W 822607	191.2	CONIFERES SCIES LONGITUD
251	*PULP AND WASTE PAPER	W 253564	91.6	W 240049	155.0	W 270552	101.1	W 273829	89.4	PATES A PAPIER,DECHETS
2518	SULPHITE WOOD PULP	W 182406	75.4	W 161096	120.2	W 190654	77.1	W 185780	66.4	PATES AU BISULFITE
25182	— BLEACHED,NONDISSOLVNG	W 162924	72.0	W 152895	116.6	W 185260	75.7	W 179127	65.0	PATES BLANCHES
26	TEXTILE FIBRES AND WASTE		103.8		91.7		60.5		59.0	FIBRES TEXTILES
263	COTTON	W 36936	45.8	W 5544	7.6	W 4722	4.7	W 5944	5.3	COTON
2631	RAW COTTON,EXCL LINTERS	W 33312	44.1	W 2583	5.7	W 1482	2.5	W 1995	3.0	COTON EN MASSE
27	CRUDE FERTLZR,MINRLS NES		73.5		84.9		150.4		71.5	ENGRAIS MINERAUX BRUTS
278	OTHER CRUDE MINERALS	W 780660	48.8	W 779003	57.6		91.1	W 806713	52.0	AUTRES MINERAUX BRUTS
28	METALLIFEROUS ORES,SCRAP		182.7		181.6		160.1		155.6	MINERAIS METAL,DECHETS
282	IRON AND STEEL SCRAP	W 994036	127.4	W 826669	96.1	W 906236	96.7	W 977455	96.6	FERRAILLES
28209	— OF OTHR IRON OR STEEL	W 919221	84.6	W 767948	84.6	W 807921	82.1	W 870713	80.4	FERRAILLES DE FER
288	NONFERR METAL SCRAP NES	W 50709	51.8	W 54470	72.6	W 49847	56.2	W 57466	54.2	DECHETS NON FERREUX
2882	OTHER BASE MTL SCRAP NES	W 46490	50.7	W 50133	70.7	W 46788	55.2	W 53462	52.5	AUTRES DECHETS
3	MINERAL FUELS ETC		786.8		927.2		993.8		855.8	COMBUSTIBLES MINERAUX LUB
32	COAL,COKE AND BRIQUETTES		563.9		652.9		649.8		530.7	HOUILLES,COKES,BRIQUETTES
322	COAL,LIGNITE AND PEAT	MW 12660	423.0	MW 13489	489.1	MW 12373	480.1	MW 11342	423.9	HOUILLES,LIGNITES,TOURBE
3222	OTH COAL,NOT AGGLOMERATD	W 6449540	301.0	W 6975637	357.1	W 6730650	361.8	W 6633642	334.7	AUTRES HOUILLES
3223	LIGNITE,NOT AGGLOMERATED	W 6131627	118.5	W 6455319	128.8	W 5606695	115.8	W 4664842	86.4	LIGNITES
323	BRIQUETS,COKE,SEMI–COKE	W 1774278	141.0	W 1848627	163.9	W 1895907	169.8	W 1404059	106.9	BRIQUETTES
3232	COKE,SEMI–COKE,RTRT CRBN	W 1442295	125.7	W 1406223	140.0	W 1329646	139.3	W 1037618	89.4	COKES ET SEMI–COKES
33	PETROLEUM AND PRODUCTS		147.1		192.4		237.7		208.0	PETROLE ET DERIVES
334	PETROLEUM PRODUCTS,REFIN	W 791222	106.6	W 826940	122.3	W 1507659	175.4	W 948079	142.7	PRODUITS RAFFINES
3341	GASOLINE,OTH LIGHT OILS	W 790011	104.8	W 825997	120.3	W 1506554	173.8	W 946514	141.4	ESSENCES POUR MOTEURS
351	*ELECTRIC CURRENT		68.7	H 2020	71.8		98.4		110.4	ENERGIE ELECTRIQUE
5	CHEMCLS,RELATED PROD NES		1376.5		1937.4		1911.5		1863.9	PRODUITS CHIMIQUES
51	ORGANIC CHEMICALS		413.8		590.1		555.5		535.8	PROD CHIMIQ ORGANIQUES
511	HYDROCARBONS NES,DERIVS	W 367411	142.3	W 421922	181.3	W 476725	190.3	W 407429	175.4	HYDROCARBURES NDA
5111	ACYCLIC HYDROCARBONS	W 166434	76.6	W 212743	106.7	W 254916	127.3	W 235601	119.9	HYDROCARBURES ACYCLIQUES
5112	CYCLIC HYDROCARBONS	W 191515	59.1	W 200577	67.1	W 212737	56.7	W 157418	45.2	HYDROCARBURES CYCLIQUES
512	ALCOHOLS,PHENOLS ETC	W 93146	56.7	W 94088	57.6		52.5	W 72226	39.2	PHENOLS,PHENOLS–ALCOOLS
513	CARBOXYLIC ACIDS ETC	W 74769	74.5	W 95392	141.7	W 105674	123.7	W 106564	117.7	ACIDES CARBOXYLIQUES
5137	MONOACIDS AND DERIVATIVS	W 36653	42.2	W 57765	93.3	W 59759	76.7	W 62603	71.9	ACIDES MONOCARBOXYLIQUES
51379	OTH MONOACIDS ETC,DERIVS	W 29223	37.1	W 51224	86.5	W 50655	68.8	W 53197	63.4	AUTRES MONOCARBOXYLIQUES
514	NITROGEN–FNCTN COMPOUNDS	W 70841	75.0	W 81616	112.5		101.2	W 90908	116.6	COMPOSES FONCT AZOTEES
5145	AMINE–FUNCTION COMPOUNDS	W 67167	58.2	W 76704	80.1	W 77150	70.2	W 80497	66.5	COMPOSES FONCTION AMINE
515	ORG–INORG COMPOUNDS ETC	W 36687	50.4	W 74663	74.7	W 43676	69.7	W 44055	68.7	COMPOSES ORGANO–MINERAUX
5156	HETEROCYCLIC CMPDS ETC	W 36553	49.5	W 73961	72.4	W 42658	66.9	W 42949	65.8	COMPOSES HETEROCYCLIQUES
52	INORGANIC CHEMICALS		112.5		150.4		140.8		182.2	PROD CHIM INORGANIQUES
522	INORG ELEMNTS,OXIDES,ETC	W 320514	68.6	W 350791	75.0		80.3	W 429872	75.5	ELEMENTS INORGANIQUES
523	OTHR INORG CHEMICALS ETC	W 131310	43.1	W 168346	74.0		56.6	W 134634	43.0	AUT PRODUITS CHIMIQUES INORG
53	DYES,TANNING,COLOUR PROD		126.8		182.5		155.5		148.4	PROD TEINTURE,COLORANTS
531	SYNT DYE,NAT INDGO,LAKES	W 6122	59.4	W 6205	64.9	W 6932	64.1	W 7838	64.9	MAT COLOR ORGAN,LAQUES
5311	SYNTHIC ORGNIC DYESTUFFS	W 5853	57.8	W 5853	62.6	W 6595	62.1	W 6817	62.5	MAT COLOR ORGAN SYNTHET
533	PIGMENTS,PAINTS,ETC	W 79658	66.8	W 86213	116.8	W 72998	90.7	W 67920	83.1	PIGMENTS,PEINTURES,VERNIS
541	*MEDICINAL,PHARM PRODUCT	MK 9331	150.4	MK 11743	185.7		218.1	MK 10797	213.8	PROD MEDICINAUX PHARMACEUT
5417	MEDICAMENTS	K 5869966	96.2	K 7072207	109.8	K 5898324	127.6	K 6184640	131.4	MEDICAMENTS
54179	— CONTNG OTH SUBSTANCES	K 5097315	82.0	K 6580630	90.0	K 4738556	75.6	K 4928306	77.1	MED CONT AUT SUBSTANCES
55	PERFUME,CLEANING ETC PRD		147.4		168.0		214.5		228.0	PROD POUR PARFUM,TOILETTE
554	SOAP,CLEANSING ETC PREPS	W 123309	107.6	W 151438	119.0	W 206099	164.1	W 238964	176.6	SAVONS,PRODUITS DETERSIFS
5542	WASHING PREPARATIONS ETC	W 106344	94.9	W 130456	99.5	W 184469	142.5	W 222689	159.5	PROD ORG TENSIO–ACT NDA
562	*FERTILIZERS,MANUFACTURE	W 590081	57.5	W 761599	92.6		102.4	W 697537	70.6	ENGRAIS MANUFACTURES
5621	CHEM NITROGENOUS FERTLZR	W 504085	44.7	W 634517	70.3		84.1	W 596984	55.3	ENGRAIS AZOTES
58	PLASTIC MATERIALS ETC		296.0		468.0		413.8		380.8	MAT PLAST ARTIFICIELLES
582	PROD OF CONDENSATION ETC	W 15482	23.0	W 30660	71.8	W 27686	51.0	W 34960	47.6	PROD CONDENS,POLYCOND
583	POLYMERIZATION ETC PRODS	W 520310	262.0	W 333484	382.1	W 364923	350.1	W 366963	321.5	PROD POLYMERISATION
5831	POLYETHYLENE	W 105347	60.9	W 97223	87.5	W 100553	84.3	W 98455	80.1	POLYETHYLENE
58311	— IN PRIMARY FORMS	W 97314	53.6	W 81765	68.5	W 89497	68.0	W 85110	63.5	POLYETHYLENE PRIMAIRES
5832	POLYPROPYLENE	W 75913	44.6	W 59370	53.1	W 58050	65.3	W 55666	44.0	POLYPROPYLENE
5833	POLYSTYRENE,ITS COPOLYMR	W 53756	51.9	W 55529	74.1	W 60534	59.9	W 65266	55.5	POLYPROPYLENE COPOLYMERES
58331	— IN PRIMARY FORMS	W 52855	51.3	W 54381	72.0	W 59188	57.4	W 62073	50.2	SOUS FORMES PRIMAIRES
5834	POLYVINYL CHLORIDE	W 268016	73.5	W 90664	96.5	W 117391	83.1	W 116253	86.4	CHLORURE DE POLYVINYLE

5. General Exports F.O.B. by Commodities according to the S.I.T.C. (Rev. 2) in million U.S. Dollars
Exportations Générales F.O.B. par Produits d'après la C.T.C.I. (Rév. 2) en millions de Dollars E.U.

SITC CTCI	COMMODITY	1994 QUANTITY QUANTITE	1994 VALUE VALEUR	1995 QUANTITY QUANTITE	1995 VALUE VALEUR	1996 QUANTITY QUANTITE	1996 VALUE VALEUR	1997 QUANTITY QUANTITE	1997 VALUE VALEUR	PRODUIT
58341	— IN PRIMARY FORMS	W 260614	64.5	W 73051	65.7	W 105655	64.0	W 105962	68.5	SOUS FORMES PRIMAIRES
59	CHEMICAL MATERIALS NES		72.0		99.6		92.4		82.9	MAT PROD CHIMIQUES NDA
598	MISCEL CHEM PRODUCTS NES	W 137815	35.3	W 201003	67.7	W 172397	52.2	W 189688	51.5	PROD DIV INDUST CHIM NDA
6	BASIC MANUFACTURES		4444.3		7252.7		6570.7		6303.6	ART MANUFACTURES
61	LEATHER,DRESSED FUR,ETC		74.2		232.6		150.3		116.5	CUIRS,PELLETERIES
611	LEATHER	W 10838	41.4	W 13596	120.2		52.6	W 7160	32.4	CUIRS,PEAUX PREPARES
6114	LEATHR BOVINE NES,EQUINE	W 3690	21.4	W 5977	83.7	W 3586	29.6	W 2564	18.7	CUIRS DE BOVINS
612	LEATHER ETC MANUFACTURES	W 5159	29.6	W 11884	102.2	W 8268	91.9	W 7129	74.6	OUVRAGES EN CUIRS NDA
6123	PREPRD PARTS OF FOOTWEAR	W 4913	27.3	W 11398	96.5	W 7978	86.4	W 6817	68.1	PARTIES DE CHAUSSURES
62	RUBBER MANUFACTURES NES		172.0		328.4		332.6		344.1	CAOUTCHOUC MANUFACTURE
625	RUBBER TYRES, TUBES ETC	W 51093	118.6	W 178379	202.3	W 70964	205.3	W 78836	197.5	PNEUS CAOUTCHOUC VULCANISE
6251	TYRES NEW FOR MOTOR CARS	W 16560	45.5	W 25280	80.0	W 21078	75.4	W 23665	76.2	PNEUS POUR VOITURES
6252	TYRES,NEW,BUS OR LORRY	W 13659	33.1	W 127586	69.2	W 24186	71.7	W 26142	66.4	PNEUS POUR AUTOBUS,CAMIONS
628	RUBBER ARTICLES NES	W 11804	37.3	W 16631	76.7	W 16524	78.1	W 21257	84.9	OUVRAGES CAOUTCHOUC NDA
6289	OTH RUBBER ARTICLES NES	W 10630	30.2	W 14963	65.2	W 14781	65.2	W 19642	73.5	AUT OUVR CAOUTCHOUC NDA
62898	UNHARD RUBBER PRODS NES	W 8091	28.8	W 11166	62.5	W 10725	61.8	W 15004	69.7	OUV CAOUT VULC NON DURCI
63	WOOD,CORK MANUFACTRS NES		299.4		404.8		408.2		381.0	OUVRAGES LIEGE ET BOIS
634	VENEERS,PLYWOOD,ETC	W 199448	54.9	W 262727	98.1	W 285648	100.1	W 340269	106.5	PLACAGES,CONTRE–PLAQUES
635	WOOD MANUFACTURES NES	W 404253	243.9	W 424064	306.0	W 433001	307.4	W 459590	273.9	ART MANUF EN BOIS NDA
6351	BOXES,CASES,CRATES,ETC	W 201803	45.5	W 240421	64.9	W 248392	64.5	W 279641	63.1	CAISSES EMBALLAGES BOIS
6353	BUILDERS WOODWRK,PREFABS	W 185234	177.7	W 161391	205.6	W 163551	209.1	W 157779	179.3	OUVRAGES DE MENUISERIE
64	PAPER,PAPERBOARD AND MFR		181.6		439.0		406.2		386.0	PAPIERS,CARTONS & OUVRAGES
641	PAPER AND PAPERBOARD	W 271473	142.1	W 371107	289.6	W 354451	252.0	W 445987	246.2	PAPIERS ET CARTONS
6415	PAPER,PAPERBRD,BULK,NES	W 87240	53.4	W 133787	114.8	W 128997	91.1	W 142294	86.8	PAPIERS,CARTONS ROULEAUX
64159	OTHER PAPER ETC,BULK,NES	W 64535	37.0	W 98969	78.1	W 99292	63.1	W 108831	59.4	AUT PAPIER ROULEAUX FEUILLES
642	PAPER,ETC,PRECUT,ARTS OF	W 39321	39.6	W 108166	149.5	W 101681	154.3	W 110193	139.9	PAP,CARTONS DECOUPES
6421	PAPER ETC CONTAINERS	W 19011	14.4	W 68743	89.6	W 53396	81.3	W 55513	57.3	BOITES,SACS EMBALLAGES
65	TEXTILE YARN,FABRICS,ETC		671.9		1352.2		991.4		997.7	FILS,TISSUS,ARTICLES TEXTILE
651	TEXTILE YARN	W 24827	71.1	W 43677	172.7		123.8	W 43759	140.7	FILS TEXTILES
652	COTTON FABRICS,WOVEN	W 24580	157.3	W 37705	308.4		216.7	W 30203	221.5	TISSUS DE COTON
6522	WOVEN COTTON BLEACHD,ETC	W 18358	127.7	W 28755	257.8		174.5	W 22194	177.4	TISSUS COTON BLANCHIS ETC
65224	BLCHED COTTON FABRIC NES	W 12901	94.8	W 19661	182.5	W 13927	129.9	W 15682	130.0	AUT TIS PLUS 85% COT BLANCHI
653	WOVN MAN–MADE FIB FABRIC	W 13909	91.0	W 21524	210.6	W 14515	124.2	W 16517	116.4	TISSUS FIBRES SYNTH,ARTIF
6534	DISC SYN BLEND FABRC NES	W 3570	31.3	W 7333	70.8	W 4641	53.6	W 4739	50.0	TISSUS FIBRES SYNTH DISCONT
654	OTH WOVEN TEXTILE FABRIC	W 16296	108.5	W 18966	182.5		101.0	W 18375	98.9	TISSUS AUT COTON SYNT,ARTIF
6542	WOVEN WOOL,HAIR NONPILE	W 2563	32.5	W 3889	85.5	W 2174	35.0	W 2179	33.0	TIS PLUS 85% LAINE,POILS
655	KNITTED,ETC FABRICS	W 4733	29.5	W 7817	65.4	W 5091	45.1	W 5366	38.7	ETOF BONNETERIE PIECES ETC
6552	OTHER KNIT ETC FAB NONEL	W 4733	29.5	W 7817	65.4	W 5091	45.1	W 5366	38.7	ETOF BON NON ELAS NON SYNT
657	SPECIAL TXTL FABRC,PRODS	W 28490	96.8	W 47185	228.1		167.1	W 41179	152.6	TISSUS SPECIAUX
6573	COATED ETC TEXTILES NES	W 13711	54.2	W 23192	132.8	W 18258	95.2	W 17191	73.8	TISSUS,ART MATIERE TEXT NDA
65732	PLASTIC COATED TEXTILES	W 4123	13.3	W 11143	73.4	W 7772	35.6	W 8080	28.3	TISSUS IMPREGNES
658	TEXTILE ARTICLES NES	W 20216	86.0	W 27652	120.6		158.4	W 26761	178.7	ART FACONNES MAT TEXTILES
6584	LINENS ETC	W 6432	37.3	W 11234	48.2	W 9073	77.1	W 10224	91.3	LINGE DE MAISON
66	NONMETAL MINERAL MFS NES		882.8		1034.9		1159.0		1023.1	ART MIN NON METALLIQUES
661	LIME,CEMENT,BLDG PRODS	W 2500024	140.7	W 1847245	123.1	W 1819996	193.1	W 1778860	106.3	CHAUX,CIMENTS MAT CONSTR
6612	CEMENT	W 2130974	107.7	W 1469507	83.5	W 1417898	152.6	W 1319781	59.3	CIMENTS HYDRAULIQUES
662	CLAY,REFRACTORY BLDG PRD	W 1168351	138.6	W 631064	116.3	W 444342	121.0	W 497916	118.1	MAT CONST REFRACTAIRES
6624	BRICKS ETC NONREFRACTORY	W 1064206	119.6	W 579978	102.1	W 383568	104.2	W 425153	97.3	BRIQUES ETC CERAM NON REFR
66245	GLAZED CERAMIC SETTS ETC	W 84908	71.9	W 97897	49.8	W 98616	49.9	W 116567	48.2	AUT CARREAUX CERAMIQUE
663	MINERAL MANUFCTURES NES	W 536397	89.9	W 572775	121.9	W 557481	126.4	W 548215	121.1	ART MIN MANUF NDA
6633	MINRL MFS NES NONCERAMIC	W 456004	47.8	W 497022	65.9	W 468434	70.3	W 451288	61.4	OUVR MAT MINERALE NDA
66332	CEMENT,ARTFCL STONE PROD	W 446592	43.3	W 470471	56.1	W 427935	58.3	W 398249	49.0	OUVRAGES EN CIMENT
664	GLASS	W 234322	116.7	W 302742	201.1	W 323019	199.9	W 381001	198.5	VERRE
665	GLASSWARE	W 209175	317.5	W 226343	386.9	W 169799	410.1	W 198839	368.1	OUVRAGES EN VERRE
6651	BOTTLES ETC OF GLASS	W 156714	45.3	W 168703	56.1	W 110513	41.2	W 136042	40.8	RECIPIENTS EN VERRE
66511	GLASS BOTTLES ETC NONVAC	W 156628	45.0	W 168456	55.0	W 110462	40.9	W 135905	40.3	BONBONNES,BOUTEILLES,ETC
6652	HOUSEHLD,HOTEL ETC GLASS	W 42616	175.1	W 46141	193.1	W 47750	204.8	W 48051	193.2	OBJETS VERRE TABLE,CUISINE
6658	GLASS ARTICLES NES	W 9845	97.3	W 11499	137.7	W 11535	164.2	W 14747	134.2	ARTICLES FAB EN VERRE NDA
66582	GLASS ORNAMENTS NES	W 4172	83.3	W 3978	116.3	W 3888	143.5	W 3974	111.7	PERLES DE VERRE
666	POTTERY	W 18369	46.8	W 24554	82.8	W 22784	106.4	W 26600	109.2	POTERIE
6664	PORCELN,CHINA HOUSE WARE	W 17335	42.9	W 23027	77.6	W 20665	99.1	W 24587	101.3	VAISSELLE,ARTS MEN PORC
67	IRON AND STEEL		1412.0		2066.0		1733.6		1592.1	FER ET ACIER
671	PIG IRON ETC	W 217098	51.6	W 226982	79.8	W 195131	79.3	W 259765	76.0	FONTE,SPIEGEL,POUDRES
672	IRON,STEEL PRIMARY FORMS	W 1172640	149.2	W 390846	130.6		108.1	W 521436	125.8	LINGOTS FER,ACIER
6725	IRN,STL BLOOMS,SLABS,ETC	W 1100078	130.3	W 317874	103.0	W 296995	77.9	W 368491	85.2	BLOOMS,BILLETTES FER ACIER
67251	IRN,SMPLE STL BLOOMS,ETC	W 1094674	127.4	W 306320	89.1	W 289530	68.6	W 359063	75.9	BLOOMS ETC NON ACIER FIN
673	IRON,STEEL SHAPES ETC	W 2980650	585.5	W 2320951	727.0	W 1905557	592.2	W 1691373	467.8	BARRES,PROFIL FER,ACIER
6731	IRON,STEEL WIRE ROD	W 1592913	208.0	W 775856	229.5	W 806739	221.5	W 609062	154.8	FIL MACHINE FER,ACIER
67311	IRON,SIMPLE STL WIRE ROD	W 1581592	203.4	W 727385	208.1	W 805574	220.0	W 608221	154.3	FIL MACH AUT ACIER FIN
6732	IRON,STEEL BARS ETC	W 1038967	265.8	W 925076	342.2	W 760384	264.7	W 669493	194.0	BARRES FER,ACIER
67325	OTH ALLOY STEEL BARS ETC	W 84075	42.4	W 170491	122.4	W 98332	76.5	W 70925	36.5	BARRES NON ACIERS ALLIES
67326	IRN,OTH STL BARS HOTROLD	W 930226	210.3	W 719452	192.4	W 642881	171.8	W 576168	145.3	BARRES PLEINES FER,ACIER
6733	IRON,STEEL PROFILES ETC	W 348769	111.8	W 620020	155.4	W 338434	106.0	W 412818	119.1	PROFILES,PALPLAN FER,ACIER
67332	LARGE U,I,H SECTIONS ETC	W 221001	60.7	W 283754	93.5	W 240069	69.1	W 288393	77.3	PROFILES PLUS 80MM
674	IRN,STL UNIV,PLATE,SHEET	W 771367	233.2	W 879206	450.4	W 639739	275.8	W 880531	316.7	LARGES PLATS,TOLES
6744	IRN,STL HVY PLATE,ROLLED	W 654035	165.5	W 504892	222.8	W 470903	179.5	W 636125	216.5	TOLES LAMINEES PLUS 4.75 MM
67441	— OF IRON OR SIMPLE STL	W 653224	164.2	W 501193	215.9	W 469079	175.2	W 634304	212.7	TOLES NON ACIER FIN CARB
6746	IRN,STL THIN PLATE,ROLLD	W 75384	29.3	W 198011	117.4	W 65671	38.9	W 101066	44.4	TOLES LAM MOINS 3MM
67461	— OF IRON OR SIMPLE STL	W 73903	27.4	W 182519	100.1	W 62413	33.6	W 98496	40.5	TOL NON AC FIN MOINS 3 MM
677	IRN,STL WIRE(EXCL W ROD)	W 155182	61.6	W 201405	102.0	W 211235	99.8	W 263980	102.9	FILS EN FER,ACIER
67701	IRON, SIMPLE STEEL WIRE	W 135309	50.0	W 169257	74.9	W 195103	83.4	W 244824	86.8	FILS NON ACIER FIN CARBONE
678	IRON,STL TUBES,PIPES,ETC	W 384102	187.5	W 590506	346.9	W 508301	333.4	W 471705	280.7	TUBES,TUYAUX EN FONTE,FER
6782	IRON,STL SEAMLESS TUBES	W 196096	97.3	W 352883	188.8	W 305912	200.7	W 247877	156.6	TUBES,TUYAUX SANS SOUDURE
6783	IRON,STL TUBES,PIPES NES	W 169709	69.3	W 208469	116.1	W 181276	92.1	W 204660	87.1	AUT TUBES,TUYAUX FER,ACIER
679	IRN,STL CASTINGS UNWORKD	W 105957	118.6	W 147937	187.9	W 140220	202.8	W 153284	184.8	OUVRAGES EN FONTE,FER,ACIER
6794	IRON,STL CASTINGS ROUGH	W 84410	93.1	W 119939	144.8	W 114788	162.7	W 127615	148.0	OUVRAGES COULES,MOULES
67941	IRON CASTINGS ROUGH	W 84410	93.1	W 119939	144.8	W 114788	162.7	W 127615	148.0	OUVRAGES A L'ETAT BRUT
68	NON–FERROUS METALS		152.8		337.0		231.3		281.8	METAUX NON FERREUX
684	ALUMINIUM	W 61951	106.7	W 66413	179.3	W 64963	161.8	W 86932	195.1	ALUMINIUM
6842	ALUMINIUM,ALLOYS WORKED	W 34237	70.9	W 42552	135.3	W 40348	128.9	W 49806	140.9	ALUMINIUM,ALLIAGES OUVRE
69	METAL MANUFACTURES NES		598.1		1058.2		1158.5		1181.6	ART MANUFACT EN METAL NDA
691	STRUCTURES AND PARTS NES	W 177939	120.6	W 230093	200.5	W 214374	225.5	W 232871	225.6	CONSTRUCT FER,ACIER,ALU
6911	STRUCTURES,PARTS IRN,STL	W 176365	115.8	W 227887	188.9	W 212246	210.7	W 230035	206.6	CONSTRUCT FER,ACIER,FONTE
692	METAL TANKS,BOXES,ETC	W 53860	63.8	W 66418	94.4	W 68056	123.4	W 62204	109.2	RECIPIENTS METALLIQUES
6924	MTL TRANSPORT BOXES ETC	W 28433	36.6	W 35420	56.2	W 40445	82.5	W 41613	77.9	FUTS,TAMBOURS,BIDONS
694	STL,COPPR NAILS,NUTS,ETC	W 50375	42.2	W 66816	89.8	W 59622	75.3	W 65267	72.5	CLOUS,VIS,ECROUS
69402	IRN,STL NUTS,BOLTS,ETC	W 31982	32.4	W 47597	73.8	W 40439	60.5	W 44444	57.9	BOULONS,VIS,ECROUS FER,AC
695	TOOLS	W 11174	50.2	W 11509	75.8	W 10604	84.2	W 12068	82.5	OUTILS A MAIN
697	BASE MTL HOUSEHOLD EQUIP	W 22883	66.8	W 30086	71.3		77.2	W 27251	67.9	ART MENAGE MET COMMUNS
699	BASE METAL MFRS NES	W 137998	214.3	W 208802	470.5		506.6	W 228616	550.8	ART MANUFACTURES MET NDA
6991	LOCKSMITHS WARES,ETC	W 15203	46.7	W 28880	133.4	W 26134	122.8	W 32170	129.9	ARTICLES DE SERRURERIE

5. General Exports F.O.B. by Commodities according to the S.I.T.C. (Rev. 2) in million U.S. Dollars
Exportations Générales F.O.B. par Produits d'après la C.T.C.I. (Rév. 2) en millions de Dollars E.U.

SITC CTCI	COMMODITY	1994 QUANTITY QUANTITE	1994 VALUE VALEUR	1995 QUANTITY QUANTITE	1995 VALUE VALEUR	1996 QUANTITY QUANTITE	1996 VALUE VALEUR	1997 QUANTITY QUANTITE	1997 VALUE VALEUR	PRODUIT
69911	LOCKS,KEYS AND PARTS	W 4203	23.1	W 10073	74.3	W 6472	58.0	W 6481	49.7	SERRURES,VERROUS,CADENAS
6997	IRON,STEEL ARTICLES NES	W 88121	85.1	W 132846	166.2	W 133330	181.3	W 151128	180.4	OUV FONTE,FER,ACIER NDA
69979	IRN,STL MANUFACTURES NES	W 87928	84.9	W 132681	165.9	W 133225	181.1	W 151026	180.2	AUT OUVRAGES EN FER NDA
6998	MFRS NES OF CPR,NIKL,ETC	W 8912	32.8	W 12448	65.0		58.3	W 15176	72.1	OUVRAGES EN CU,NI,AL,PB,ZN
6999	OTHR BASE METAL MFRS ETC	W 318	6.3	W 502	14.5	W 590	64.0	W 709	88.9	OUVRAGES EN TUNGST,MOLYB
69993	TANTALUM WRGHT,MFRS NES	W 99	3.4	W 383	11.7	W 390	61.5	W 600	86.9	TANTALE OUVRE NDA
7	MACHINES,TRANSPORT EQUIP		3428.4		6336.4		7147.1		8556.7	MACHINES MATERIEL TRANSPORT
71	POWER GENERATING EQUIPMT		257.6		454.0		578.5		554.0	MACHINES GENERATRICES
713	INTRNL COMBUS PSTN ENGIN	W 9821	63.6	W 13117	100.0		131.8	W 25421	136.2	MOTEURS EXPL COMB INT, PIECE
7139	PISTON ENGINE PARTS NES	W 4957	43.2	W 7370	62.5	W 14595	87.3	W 17457	84.4	PIECES POUR 713.2,3,8
716	ROTATING ELECTRIC PLANT	W 46217	126.6	W 64805	256.1		278.4	W 66798	276.1	APP ELECTR ROTATIFS,PIECES
7162	AC MTRS,GENRTRS,GEN SETS	W 31302	87.0	W 36839	133.7	W 39850	143.6	W 40708	137.9	MOTEURS ELECTRIQUES
71621	AC MTRS,INC UNIVRSL MTRS	W 25663	63.5	W 32806	115.6	W 34526	117.0	W 35070	111.9	MOT ELEC NON COUR CONTINU
7169	PTS NES OF ROT ELEC PLNT	W 13510	34.0	W 23591	72.6	W 20135	83.4	W 20175	89.9	PIECES MAC APP ROTATIFS
72	MACHS FOR SPCL INDUSTRYS		467.1		783.9		862.9		890.6	MAC SPECIALES POUR INDUST
721	AGRIC MACHY,EXC TRACTORS	W 25790	63.7	W 34507	86.8	W 37654	95.4	W 38811	103.3	MACHINES AGRICOLES
722	TRACTORS NON–ROAD	W 11208	37.2	W 31573	118.6	W 28809	108.1	W 32077	110.8	TRACTEURS
7224	WHEELED TRACTORS NES	W 11103	37.0	W 31427	118.6	W 28742	108.1	W 31890	110.8	TRACTEURS A ROUES
723	CIVIL ENGNEERG EQUIP ETC	W 12565	31.6	W 18583	47.8	W 28820	66.3	W 27375	59.1	APPAREILS DE GENIE CIVIL
724	TEXTILE,LEATHER MACHNRY	W 19993	139.9	W 26745	216.1	W 23478	224.9	W 26948	230.6	MACH POUR INDUSTRIE TEXTILE
7244	SPINNING,EXTRDNG,ETC MCH	W 7316	46.6	W 9853	80.2	W 8970	77.4	W 10643	74.8	MACH POUR LE FILAGE
726	PRINTG,BKBINDG MACHY,PTS	W 7584	46.6	W 5078	58.7		71.9	W 6152	79.7	MACHINES POUR IMPRIMERIE
728	OTH MACHY FOR SPCL INDUS	W 26157	108.8	W 39840	196.6	W 40005	219.1	W 40775	202.8	AUT MACH IND PARTICULIERES
7284	MACHY FOR SPCL INDUS NES	W 7806	43.8	W 15937	112.0	W 15801	125.8	W 16303	111.9	MACH SPEC IND PARTICUL.
73	METALWORKING MACHINERY		223.5		351.4		384.7		405.6	MACH TRAVAIL DES METAUX
736	METALWORKING MACH–TOOLS	W 49056	175.8	W 61588	271.9	W 56284	326.5	W 61060	350.4	MACH–OUTILS TRAVAIL METAUX
7361	METAL CUTTING MACH–TOOLS	W 16516	75.7	W 17256	105.6	W 20271	150.8	W 23290	161.1	MACH–OUT ENLEVEMENT METAL
73614	REAMING ETC MCHS,MTLWRKG	W 7008	34.8	W 6894	48.6	W 10787	79.9	W 10998	79.6	MACH POUR ALESER FRAISER
7369	PTS NES OF TOOLS OF 736	W 22458	54.9	W 33844	115.2	W 26815	98.4	W 27804	114.4	PIECES GROUPE 736
737	METALWORKING MACHNRY NES	W 10257	47.7	W 20491	79.6	W 13897	58.3	W 13677	55.3	MACH TRAV METAUX PIECES
74	GENRL INDUSTRL MACHY NES		502.4		957.4		1065.4		1198.8	MACH APP INDUSTRIE
741	HEATING,COOLING EQUIPMNT	W 18220	79.8	W 29082	168.6	W 28120	218.9	W 35099	262.5	MACH CHAUFFAGE,PIECES
7414	NONDOM REFRIG EQUIPT,PTS	W 3956	31.4	W 9533	85.0	W 8333	85.7	W 9299	84.4	MAT PRODUCTION DU FROID
7415	AIR–CONDITIONING MACHNRY	W 2671	12.4	W 4690	21.3	W 4558	53.9	W 7337	95.2	GROUPES CONDITION AIR
742	PUMPS FOR LIQUIDS ETC	W 8525	55.5	W 11574	105.9	W 10597	140.0	W 11719	173.6	POMPES MOTO–POMPES
7428	OTHER PUMPS FOR LIQUIDS	W 1979	14.5	W 2631	25.1	W 3515	73.6	W 4444	100.8	AUTRES POMPES POUR LIQ
74288	PUMPS FR LIQUIDS NES ETC	W 1472	9.0	W 2005	16.7	W 2865	64.4	W 3710	90.4	POMPES POUR LIQUIDES NDA
743	PUMPS NES,CENTRFUGES ETC	W 11005	56.8	W 17116	88.7	W 21745	107.0	W 24407	110.5	POMPES COMPRES,VENT ETC
744	MECHANICAL HANDLING EQU	W 59569	112.7	W 131776	195.7	W 83673	197.2	W 102290	213.9	EQUIP MANUTENTION PIECES
7442	LIFTING,LOADING MACH NES	W 14304	32.9	W 56979	48.6	W 13967	47.5	W 23517	72.9	APP LEVAGE,MANUTENTION
7449	PTS NES OF MACHY OF 7442	W 40499	64.9	W 70523	132.4	W 66799	138.9	W 76291	132.9	PIECES DU 744.2
745	NONELEC MACHY,TOOLS NES	W 8142	39.0	W 11748	64.8	W 11569	68.1	W 11693	79.7	AUT MACH NON ELEC,PIECES
7452	OTH NONELEC MCHS,PTS NES	W 7996	36.7	W 11406	60.8	W 11390	64.0	W 11425	75.3	AUT MACH NON ELEC,PIECES
749	NONELEC MACH PTS,ACC NES	W 36550	158.8	W 55369	333.9	W 54227	334.4	W 58290	358.9	PIECES MACH NON ELEC NDA
7492	COCKS,VALVES ETC NES	W 16332	60.9	W 19915	99.9	W 20450	121.1	W 19978	133.7	ART ROB,SIM POUR TUYAUX
7493	SHAFT,CRANK,PULLEY ETC	W 11752	44.6	W 23412	109.0	W 21365	93.9	W 27100	111.2	ARBRES TRANS,VILEBREQUINS
7499	OTH NONELEC MCHY PTS NES	W 3917	28.5	W 5996	65.5	W 6106	63.3	W 6025	69.3	PIECES NON ELECT NDA
75	OFFICE MACHNES,ADP EQUIP		116.6		200.9		227.2		208.5	MACH BUREAU TRAIT AUTOM
752	AUTOMTIC DATA PROC EQUIP	W 4932	68.4	W 3597	79.4		85.5	W 2131	94.3	MACH TRAIT INFORMATION
759	OFFICE,ADP MCH PTS,ACCES	W 4136	24.4	W 8760	100.0	W 7579	117.2	W 7245	103.0	PIECES DU 751 ET 752
7599	ACCTG,ETC,ADP MCH PTS,AC	W 2682	17.4	W 6653	81.7	W 5544	96.3	W 5641	90.2	PIECES DU 751 ET 752
76	TELECOMM,SOUND EQUIPMENT		80.6		139.8		165.4		166.9	EQUIPMENT DE TELECOM
764	TELECOM EQPT,PTS,ACC NES	W 4088	67.4	W 6501	126.1		160.1	W 9892	140.1	EQUIP TELECOM,PIECES
7649	PTS NES OF EQUIPMT OF 76	W 3011	41.7	W 4178	96.8	W 5220	125.6	W 5386	104.2	PIECES DE LA DIV 76
76493	TELECOMM EQUIPMT PTS NES	W 1444	8.8	W 2284	55.2	W 1800	72.4	W 1978	60.4	PIECES 761,762,764.3,8
77	ELECTRIC MACHNRY NES ETC		504.5		1554.5		1521.8		1839.3	MACH APP ELECT NDA
771	ELECTRIC POWER MACHY NES	W 7597	32.0	W 11526	87.0	W 9292	97.3	W 11348	96.6	MACH PROD,TRANS ELECTR
7712	OTH ELEC POWER MACHY NES	W 3758	18.7	W 7945	74.0	W 5425	72.7	W 6379	72.1	AUT APP PROD TRANSF ELEC
772	SWITCHGEAR ETC,PARTS NES	W 19427	114.3	W 36230	458.7	W 28025	459.5	W 34186	534.8	APP COUPURE,SECT ETC
7721	SWITCHGEAR ETC	W 17437	100.4	W 33025	394.1	W 26034	402.0	W 30906	464.8	APP COUPURE,SECTIONMNT
773	ELECTR DISTRIBUTNG EQUIP	W 28642	79.6	W 92710	247.2		308.6	W 53757	342.5	EQUIPMT DISTRIBUTION ELECT
7731	INSULATED WIRE,CABLE ETC	W 26172	73.4	W 87617	222.3	W 39238	284.7	W 47422	318.8	FILS,CABLES ISOLES ELECT
775	HOUSEHOLD TYPE EQUIP NES	W 16842	73.0	W 18286	86.9		95.7	W 22342	94.0	MACH,APP USAGE DOMESTQUE
776	TRANSISTORS,VALVES,ETC	W 6111	54.4	W 10121	144.5		117.0	W 8489	131.3	LAMPES,TUBES,VALVES
778	ELECTRICAL MACHINERY NES	W 21795	145.3	W 43015	519.8		436.7	W 43809	634.8	AUTRES MACH ELECT NDA
7781	BATTERIES,ACCUMULATORS	W 9957	21.2	W 24216	84.3	W 22612	87.2	W 28823	210.6	PILES ET ACCUMULATEURS
77812	ELECTRIC ACCUMULATORS	W 7319	13.6	W 12021	39.7	W 18955	71.9	W 22717	157.6	ACCUMULATEURS ELECTRIQ
7783	AUTOMOTIVE ELECTR EQUIP	W 4123	29.8	W 7075	62.6	W 5045	64.1	W 5674	70.6	EQUIP ELECT MOTEURS EXPL
7788	OTH ELEC MACHY,EQUIP NES	W 3857	62.5	W 6799	327.9		239.2	W 5644	308.2	AUT MACH APP ELEC NDA
77884	ELECTRICAL CONDENSERS	W 726	38.5	W 2315	271.9	W 945	190.9	W 1927	239.9	CONDENSATEURS ELECTRIQUES
78	ROAD VEHICLES		1119.0		1593.3		2034.5		2815.3	VEHICULES ROUTIERS
781	PASS MOTOR VEH EXC BUSES	W 96556	536.2	W 121339	720.9	W 143435	948.2	W 207455	1357.1	AUTO TRANSPORT PERSONNES
782	LORRIES,SPCL MTR VEH NES	W 63528	207.7	W 44164	171.7	W 44044	191.8	W 69714	322.3	VEHICULES SPECIAUX,MARCH
7821	LORRIES,TRUCKS	W 50505	182.9	W 34800	141.3	W 38519	178.5	W 62043	306.8	VEHICULES TRANSP MARCHAND
783	ROAD MOTOR VEHICLES NES	W 11065	38.1	W 13848	60.6	W 12402	75.4	W 11491	68.7	VEHICULES ROUTIERS NDA
7831	BUSES	W 8789	32.7	W 11822	51.9	W 10905	68.3	W 9836	60.9	VOITURES TRANSPORT COMMUN
784	MOTOR VEH PRTS,ACCES NES	W 106716	218.0	W 126660	487.5	W 143698	665.5	W 214476	899.1	PIECES 722,781,782,783
7842	MOTOR VEHICLE BODIES	W 3360	12.8	W 6767	37.4	W 12814	75.7	W 17699	108.3	CARROS 722,781,782,783
7849	OTHER MOTOR VEHCL PARTS	W 102322	189.9	W 115945	430.5	W 123541	563.4	W 182190	739.4	PIECES 722,781,782,783
785	CYCLES,ETC MOTRZD OR NOT	W 15093	61.7	W 21698	85.3	W 17392	83.8	W 18051	81.2	MOTOCYCLES SCOOTERS
786	TRAILERS,NONMOTR VEH,NES	W 41890	57.6	W 52037	67.5	W 47405	70.1	W 61848	87.1	REMORQUES,CADRES,CONTAIN
79	OTHR TRANSPORT EQUIPMENT		157.6		301.6		307.1		478.1	AUTRE MATERIEL TRANSPORT
791	RAILWAY VEHICLES	W 69840	139.4	W 114203	293.4	W 84993	178.7	W 96773	207.9	VEHIC MAT CHEMINS DE FER
7919	RY TRACK FIXT,ETC,PARTS	W 41406	74.0	W 69530	139.7	W 60373	124.3	W 63277	125.6	MATER FIXE VOIES FERREES
79199	PARTS NES OF 7911–7915	W 40751	73.3	W 67935	138.1	W 59231	123.2	W 62056	123.9	PIECES 791.1 ET 5
792	AIRCRAFT ETC	W 51	2.5	W 49	2.0		115.6	W 2070	242.3	APP NAVIGATION AERIENNE
7924	AIRCRFT NES OVER 15000KG					W 276	14.2	W 1265	178.0	AERODYNES PLUS 15000 KG
8	MISC MANUFACTURED GOODS		1856.7		2513.6		3045.0		3067.9	ART MANUFACTURES DIVERS
812	*PLUMBG,HEATNG,LGHTNG EQ	W 50410	111.7	W 57815	140.6	W 68300	175.6	W 78995	188.4	APPAR SANITAIRES CHAUFFAGE
8124	LIGHTING EQUIPMENT NES	W 10170	54.0	W 12015	70.1	W 11691	81.2	W 12113	85.1	APPAREILS ECLAIRAGE ETC
821	*FURNITURE,PARTS THEREOF	W 140127	291.7	W 208773	402.2	W 149959	519.1	W 164276	535.5	MEUBLES ET PIECES
8211	CHAIRS,SEATS AND PARTS	W 46391	123.3	W 108921	196.3	W 51972	291.8	W 58218	308.1	SIEGES ET PIECES
82111	CHAIRS AND OTHER SEATS	W 33004	104.9	W 30446	87.9	W 22601	82.0	W 23008	78.2	SIEGES
82119	PTS NES OF CHAIRS ETC	W 13387	18.5	W 78475	108.5	W 29371	209.9	W 35211	229.9	PIECES DU 821.11
8219	FURNITURE AND PARTS NES	W 87733	150.7	W 94970	185.0	W 93198	200.1	W 100320	197.6	AUTRES MEUBLES ET PIECES
82191	METAL FURNITURE NES	W 30912	51.8	W 24861	36.8	W 20977	32.5	W 21870	31.7	MEUBLES NDA EN METAL
82192	WOOD FURNITURE NES	W 44111	83.8	W 51151	115.8	W 51790	126.8	W 55374	119.4	MEUBLES NDA EN BOIS
84	CLOTHING AND ACCESSORIES		367.8		524.0		622.5		620.0	VETEMENTS
842	MENS OUTERWEAR NOT KNIT	W 6395	103.5	W 7466	95.9	W 6242	127.2	W 7476	162.9	VET DESSUS POUR HOMMES
8429	— OTHER OUTER GARMENTS	W 1499	44.7	W 1900	18.9	W 1605	30.9	W 1761	30.6	AUT VET DES HOM MAT TEX
843	WOMENS OUTERWEAR NONKNIT	W 6761	77.4	W 7673	101.7	W 6287	154.8	W 5593	138.1	VET DESSUS FEMMES MAT TEX

5. General Exports F.O.B. by Commodities according to the S.I.T.C. (Rev. 2) in million U.S. Dollars
Exportations Générales F.O.B. par Produits d'après la C.T.C.I. (Rév. 2) en millions de Dollars E.U.

SITC CTCI	COMMODITY	1994 QUANTITY QUANTITE	1994 VALUE VALEUR	1995 QUANTITY QUANTITE	1995 VALUE VALEUR	1996 QUANTITY QUANTITE	1996 VALUE VALEUR	1997 QUANTITY QUANTITE	1997 VALUE VALEUR	PRODUIT
845	OUTERWEAR KNIT NONELASTC	W 3810	44.4	W 5313	63.8	W 4319	87.0	W 3854	79.4	VET DESSOUS,ACCES BONNET
846	UNDER GARMENTS KNITTED	W 7266	47.3	W 7343	86.2	W 4446	93.8	W 4416	81.5	SOUS VETS DE BONNETERIE
847	TEXTILE CLTHNG ACCES NES	W 3234	27.3	W 4432	74.3	W 2920	49.7	W 2794	49.4	ACCES VET MAT TEXT NDA
851	*FOOTWEAR	W 20585	208.8	W 16596	215.2	W 14507	254.2	W 12781	165.4	CHAUSSURES
85102	FOOTWEAR LEATHER	W 15848	182.2	W 12725	180.7	W 10572	215.0	W 9010	140.2	CHAUS SEMELLES EN CUIR
87	PRECISION INSTRUMNTS NES		82.7		210.1		186.2		182.0	INSTRUM,APPAR SCIENT NDA
874	MEASURNG,CONTROLNG INSTR	W 5317	59.0	W 9646	166.1		129.6	W 7422	124.2	INSTRUMENTS DE MESURE
88	PHOTO EQU,OPTICL GDS ETC		37.4		57.3		73.9		81.4	APP,FOURN PHOTO,OP,MONTR
89	MISC MANUFCTRD GOODS NES		724.5		925.1		1170.5		1258.3	ART MANUFACTURES DIVERS
892	PRINTED MATTER	W 23844	56.4	W 41261	111.6		133.1	W 46511	162.9	IMPRIMES
8928	PRINTED MATTER NES	W 8363	21.4	W 20024	51.2		68.8	W 21909	90.9	IMPRIMES NDA
893	ARTICLES OF PLASTIC NES		147.9		309.9		356.9		455.8	OUVRAGES EN MAT DIVIS 58
8931	PLSTC PACKG CONTNRS,LIDS	W 21255	30.6	W 31297	76.2	W 43008	90.6	W 50273	101.8	ART TRANSP EMBALLAGE ETC
8939	MISC PLASTIC ARTICLES	W 70511	112.9	W 78823	224.7	W 70001	256.7	W 85594	340.2	ART DIVERS EN MAT DIV 58
89399	OTHR PLASTC ARTICLES NES	W 62402	102.9	W 69381	206.4	W 61620	238.8	W 77315	324.2	AUT OUV MAT DIV 58
894	TOYS,SPORTING GOODS,ETC	W 17749	111.3	W 21231	150.9	W 24518	220.9	W 32459	203.1	VOITURES ENFANTS,JOUETS
8942	TOYS,INDOOR GAMES ETC	W 12004	61.5	W 11135	73.7	W 10300	80.1	W 11819	80.0	JOUETS,JEUX ETC
8947	OTH SPORT GDS,FAIR AMUSM	W 5364	36.6	W 9779	67.7	W 7668	91.2	W 9537	80.7	AUT ART DE SPORT
89472	OTH OUTDOOR SPORT GOODS	W 4767	33.5	W 8071	63.4	W 7173	84.7	W 7475	73.5	ART POUR JEUX PLEIN AIR
896	WORKS OF ART ETC		208.4		80.6		17.3		131.8	OBJETS D'ART
89601	HAND PAINTINGS ETC NES		173.7		22.7		7.0		63.0	TABLEAUX,PEINTURES
897	GOLD,SILVER WARE,JEWELRY		49.6		55.8		55.6		50.9	BIJOUTERIE,ORFEVRERIE
898	MUSICAL INSTRUMENTS,PTS	W 6939	78.1	W 8641	103.1		239.6	W 7759	102.7	INSTRUMENTS DE MUSIQUE
8983	SOUND RECRDNG TAPE,DISCS	W 2752	28.7	W 3532	44.4		176.5	W 3444	47.9	SUPPORTS SON POUR 763
89832	RECORDED DISCS,TAPES ETC	W 2532	26.5	W 3318	42.4	W 2902	174.8	W 3337	46.4	DISQUES,PHONO,BANDES
899	OTHER MANUFACTURED GOODS		46.9		75.3		89.4		84.6	AUT ART MANUF DIVERS NDA
9	GOODS NOT CLASSD BY KIND		263.5		361.8		57.3		52.1	ART TRANSACT NON CLASSES
931	*SPECIAL TRANSACTIONS	W 19556	251.0	W 17152	335.3					TRANS.SPECIALES

1. HISTORICAL SERIES, 1962–1997 GENERAL TRADE, IMPORTS C.I.F., EXPORTS F.O.B.
SERIES HISTORIQUES, 1962–1997 COMMERCE GENERAL, IMPORTATIONS C.A.F., EXPORTATIONS F.O.B

YEAR ANNEE	VALUE IN MILLION DANISH KRONER / VALEUR EN MILLION DANISH KRONER — MERCHANDISE –MARCHANDISE		GOLD –OR		CONVERSION FACTORS U.S. CENTS PER DANISH KRONE FACTEURS DE CONVERSION CENTS E.U. PAR DANISH KRONE		INDEX NUMBERS –INDICES — QUANTUM		UNIT VALUE VALEUR UNITAIRE	
	IMPORTS	EXPORTS	IMPORTS	EXPORTS	IMPORTS	EXPORTS	IMPORTS	EXPORTS	IMPORTS	EXPORTS
1962	14715.00	11525.00	26.50	1.00	14.4778	14.4778				
1963	14703.00	13176.00	27.90	1.00	14.4778	14.4778				
1964	18077.00	14651.00	35.20	1.00	14.4778	14.4778				
1965	19495.00	16025.00	41.30	1.00	14.4778	14.4778				
1966	20739.00	16944.00	40.60	1.00	14.4778	14.4778				
1967	21940.00	17660.00	41.80	1.00	14.3395	14.3360				
1968	24274.00	19799.00	43.90	3.00	13.3333	13.3333				
1969	28594.00	22654.00	52.70	2.00	13.3333	13.3333				
1970	32909.00	24673.00	45.40	3.00	13.3333	13.3333				
1971	34013.00	26739.00	39.50	3.00	13.4939	13.4982				
1972	35155.00	30136.00	54.50	4.00	14.3444	14.3436				
1973	46734.00	36817.00	58.60	6.00	16.6115	16.6413				
1974	60480.00	46922.00	51.40	8.00	16.4133	16.4515				
1975	59708.00	50031.00			17.3671	17.4150				
1976	75011.00	55034.00			16.5668	16.5625				
1977	79637.00	60436.00			16.6572	16.6551				
1978	81405.00	65308.00			18.1952	18.1981				
1979	98292.00	78160.00			19.0034	19.0078				
1980	111143.00	96986.00			17.7333	17.7333	76	65	77	69
1981	126274.20	115605.90			14.0445	14.0445	72	67	90	79
1982	141356.50	129996.00			11.9963	11.9963	75	68	99	88
1983	148896.00	146798.00			10.9313	10.9313	79	74	102	91
1984	171826.00	165346.00			9.6520	9.6520	84	77	111	99
1985	187701.20	174415.20			9.4340	9.4340	90	80	111	102
1986	184733.00	171720.00			12.3541	12.3541	96	82	103	98
1987	174033.00	175187.00			14.6118	14.6118	95	83	96	97
1988	174429.00	185819.00			14.8739	14.8836	94	87	97	96
1989	195328.00	205300.00			13.6822	13.6937	94	92	105	103
1990	198782.00	216444.00			16.2139	16.2329	100	100	100	100
1991	206799.00	229764.00			15.6727	15.6730	108	111	99	100
1992	212088.00	247254.00			16.5900	16.6091	113	116	96	98
1993	197957.00	241034.00			15.4304	15.4219	104	113	93	96
1994	220769.00	262365.00			15.8002	15.7878	118	122	95	97
1995	252343.00	278514.90			17.8687	17.8673	126	128	97	97
1996	257655.00	290543.10			17.2460	17.2439	128	132	98	99
1997	291816.90	317110.00			15.1491	15.1500	139	140	101	101

2. IMPORTS BY BROAD ECONOMIC CATEGORY AND EXPORTS BY INDUSTRIAL ORIGIN. (PERCENTAGE OF TOTAL VALUE)
IMPORTATIONS PAR CATEGORIES ECONOMIQUES ET EXPORTATIONS PAR BRANCHE D'ACTIVITE.(EN POURCENTAGE DE LA VALEUR TOTALE)

IMPORTS – IMPORTATIONS

	1991	1992	1993	1994	1995	1996	1997
TOTAL IMPORTS–IMPORTATIONS TOTALES	100.	100.	100.	100.	100.	100.	100.
1 FOOD BEV–ALIMENTATION BOISSONS	10.1	10.5	10.6	10.1	10.0	10.1	10.4
11 PRIMARY–PRODUITS DE BASE	5.4	5.4	5.2	5.1	4.9	4.9	4.9
111 FOR INDUSTRY–POUR L'INDUSTRIE	0.6	0.8	0.9	0.9	0.9	0.8	0.7
112 FOR HOUSEHOLDS–POUR LES MENAGES	4.8	4.6	4.3	4.2	4.0	4.1	4.2
12 PROCESSED–PRODUITS ELABORES	4.7	5.2	5.4	5.0	5.2	5.2	5.5
121 FOR INDUSTRY–POUR L'INDUSTRIE	0.8	0.9	0.9	0.9	0.9	0.9	0.9
122 FOR HOUSEHOLDS–POUR LES MENAGES	3.9	4.3	4.5	4.2	4.3	4.4	4.6
2 IND SUPPLIES–APPROV INDUSTRIELS	32.3	33.3	30.5	30.4	31.0	28.4	30.1
21 PRIMARY–PRODUITS DE BASE	2.2	2.4	2.3	2.2	2.2	2.3	2.4
22 PROCESSED–PRODUITS ELABORES	30.1	30.9	28.1	28.2	28.8	26.2	27.6
3 FUELS–COMBUSTIBLES	5.1	4.6	4.9	4.1	3.3	3.7	3.7
31 PRIMARY–PRODUITS DE BASE	2.4	2.2	2.2	1.8	1.6	1.9	1.7
32 PROCESSED–PRODUITS ELABORES	2.7	2.5	2.7	2.3	1.6	1.8	2.0
321 MOTOR SPIRIT–ESSENCE	0.6	2.1	2.5	2.2	1.4	1.5	1.8
322 OTHER–AUTRES	2.2	0.4	0.3	0.1	0.2	0.3	0.2
4 MACHINERY–EQUIPEMENT	19.9	20.0	20.0	20.0	21.5	21.4	22.8
41 CAPITAL EQUIPMENT–MACHINES	16.0	15.9	15.9	15.9	16.8	16.9	18.4
42 PARTS–PIECES ACCESSOIRES	3.9	4.1	4.1	4.2	4.6	4.5	4.3
5 TRANSPORT–TRANSPORT	11.6	9.7	9.1	11.1	10.6	10.8	10.8
51 PASSENGER CARS–AUTOMOBILES	2.5	2.8	2.8	4.1	3.9	4.0	3.9
52 OTHER–AUTRES	6.1	3.8	3.2	3.9	3.8	3.9	3.7
521 INDUSTRIAL–INDUSTRIELS	5.9	3.7	3.0	3.8	3.6	3.6	3.5
522 NON INDUSTRIAL–NON INDUSTRIEL	0.2	0.2	0.2	0.2	0.2	0.2	0.2
53 PARTS–PIECES ACCESSOIRES	3.0	3.0	3.1	3.0	3.0	3.0	3.2
6 CONSUM GOODS–BIENS CONSOMMATION	16.4	17.2	17.4	17.0	16.7	17.1	18.7
61 DURABLE–DURABLES	3.6	3.6	3.8	3.8	3.7	3.9	4.1
62 SEMI DURABLE–SEMI DURABLES	9.4	9.8	10.0	9.6	9.4	9.5	10.8
63 NON DURABLE–NON DURABLES	3.4	3.8	3.6	3.6	3.5	3.7	3.8
7 GOODS NES–BIENS NDA	4.7	4.6	7.5	7.4	6.9	8.4	3.6

EXPORTS – EXPORTATIONS

	1991	1992	1993	1994	1995	1996	1997
TOTAL EXPORTS–EXPORTATIONS TOTALES	100.	100.	100.	100.	100.	100.	100.
1 AGRICULTURE	9.7	8.4	7.9	7.5	7.1	7.2	7.1
2 MINING QUARRY–INDUS EXTRACTIVES	1.9	1.8	1.3	1.0	1.5	1.7	2.1
3 MANUFACTURING–IND MANUFACTUR	88.4	89.8	90.8	91.5	91.4	91.1	90.7
31 FOOD BEV TOBACCO–ALIM BOISS TAB	20.8	20.7	20.4	20.2	19.5	18.6	19.0
32 TEXTILES–INDUSTRIES TEXTILES	5.3	5.4	5.1	4.8	4.9	5.0	5.8
33 WOOD & PRODUCTS–BOIS & PRODUITS	1.6	1.6	1.6	1.7	1.9	1.7	1.8
34 PAPER & PRODUCTS–PAPIER & PRODT	2.2	2.0	2.1	2.1	2.2	2.0	2.0
35 CHEMICALS–INDUSTRIES CHIMIQUES	11.9	12.6	12.7	12.5	12.8	13.3	13.6
36 NON METAL MIN–MIN NON METAL	1.7	1.8	1.6	1.5	1.5	1.3	1.4
37 BASIC METAL–IND METAL BASE	2.0	1.9	1.6	1.8	2.1	1.9	2.0
38 METAL MANUF–MANUF METAL	36.5	37.6	35.0	35.4	36.2	36.2	38.2
39 OTH MANUF IND–AUTRES MANUF	6.3	6.1	10.6	11.5	10.4	11.1	6.9

3. TRADE BY PRINCIPAL COUNTRIES OF ORIGIN AND DESTINATION (VALUE IN MILLION U.S. DOLLARS)
ECHANGES SELON LES PRINCIPAUX PAYS D'ORIGINE ET DE DESTINATION (VALEUR EN MILLIONS DE DOLLARS EU)

COUNTRIES–PAYS	GENERAL IMPORTS C.I.F. IMPORTATIONS GENERALES C.A.F					COUNTRIES–PAYS	GENERAL EXPORTS F.O.B. EXPORTATIONS GENERALES F.O.B.				
	1993	1994	1995	1996	1997		1993	1994	1995	1996	1997
World	30535.7	35436.5	43141.6	43126.4	44492.4	Monde	37171.0	41602.4	48789.2	48884.6	48800.5
Africa	143.2	249.2	201.4	188.5	131.6	Afrique	456.0	747.6	850.8	511.3	531.3
Americas	2316.6	2728.7	3035.9	3195.1	3357.8	Amériques	2748.6	3156.5	2986.4	2974.6	3231.3
– Northern America	1743.6	2120.7	2396.2	2523.5	2637.7	– Amérique du Nord	2082.1	2377.2	2160.7	2253.7	2453.1
– LAIA	463.4	573.0	614.0	635.4	647.1	– ALAI	337.2	478.1	507.5	426.9	463.7
– CACM	13.2	15.2	20.6	30.3	21.5	– MCAC	16.8	26.2	28.8	21.3	24.8
– Caribbean	94.3	18.8	3.8	5.4	51.2	– Caraïbes	297.8	258.9	205.6	131.6	244.5
– Rest of America	2.0	1.0	1.3	0.5	0.3	– Autre Amérique	14.7	16.0	83.8	141.2	45.2
Asia excl fmr USSR	3183.5	3756.3	3895.9	3823.7	3902.2	Asie anc. URSS exclus	3614.4	4124.9	5009.3	4923.6	4553.0
– Middle East	122.0	141.4	175.3	182.9	199.3	– Moyen–Orient	870.0	811.8	907.3	827.8	824.4
Asia former USSR	4.8	11.2	8.1	7.3	4.3	Asie ancienne URSS	37.5	22.8	87.7	40.5	47.7
Europe excl fmr USSR	23623.7	27262.5	34170.5	34152.5	35242.6	Europe anc. URSS exclus	27021.7	29619.6	34971.2	35484.0	35063.4
– European Union	20625.6	23805.8	30113.6	30029.3	31178.5	– Union Européenne	22898.1	25169.6	29863.5	29983.6	29725.4
– Eastern Europe	533.2	686.7	857.5	874.5	886.1	– Europe de l'Est	712.4	856.5	1051.3	1193.6	1187.9
– Rest of Europe	2464.9	2770.0	3199.4	3248.8	3178.0	– Autre de l'Europe	3411.3	3593.5	4056.3	4306.7	4150.2
Europe former USSR	507.0	531.2	667.5	652.0	646.7	Europe ancienne URSS	400.5	613.4	957.0	1158.6	1441.4
Oceania	41.7	53.3	94.0	105.8	76.1	Océanie	210.2	266.0	286.2	296.0	313.0
Other	715.2	844.0	1068.2	1001.5	1131.1	Autre	2682.1	3051.7	3640.5	3496.1	3619.3
Germany/Allemagne	6592.3	7249.5	9186.0	8697.6	9466.1	Germany/Allemagne	7987.5	8302.8	10219.4	9699.3	9673.7
Sweden/Suède	3180.6	3891.7	5024.7	4969.5	5597.3	Sweden/Suède	3386.7	3918.2	4404.2	4734.1	5355.3
Netherlands/Pays–Bas	1880.3	2248.4	3023.7	2829.5	3441.8	United Kingdom	2941.3	3036.8	3537.1	4006.9	4404.2
United Kingdom	2184.1	2191.4	2810.6	2897.5	3308.0	Areas n.e.s.	2682.1	3051.7	3640.5	3496.1	3619.3
France, Monaco	1530.5	1811.5	2220.7	2240.5	2451.9	Norway,Svalbard and JM	2425.9	2483.3	2771.4	2994.6	2926.3
Norway,Svalbard and JM	1506.0	1709.9	2120.7	2205.3	2291.5	France, Monaco	1721.0	1955.4	2360.7	2174.3	2293.4
USA/Etats–Unis d'Amer	1383.9	1715.8	1942.6	2033.5	2216.2	USA/Etats–Unis d'Amer	1701.4	1953.4	1727.6	1759.9	1961.8
Italy/Italie	1106.8	1310.9	1756.1	1740.4	1941.6	Netherlands/Pays–Bas	1404.3	1431.1	1936.2	1845.1	2015.1
Belgium–Luxembourg	1055.8	1187.3	1509.0	1428.2	1629.3	Italy/Italie	1341.8	1466.5	1633.6	1614.4	1629.9
European Union n.e.s.	1022.9	1469.8	1515.2	2188.2		Japan/Japon	1315.0	1466.9	1675.8	1523.3	1435.5
Finland/Finlande	840.9	1040.8	1222.0	1149.4	1279.0	European Union n.e.s.	1256.6	1771.6	1567.4	1766.6	
Japan/Japon	1008.5	1160.3	1122.3	960.8	869.8	Finland/Finlande	644.6	907.3	1175.5	1173.5	1245.9
Areas n.e.s.	715.2	844.0	1068.2	1001.5	1131.1	Belgium–Luxembourg	638.4	664.1	856.8	822.9	902.5
China/Chine	569.2	656.4	758.5	807.6	902.3	Spain/Espagne	617.7	660.0	840.5	862.9	869.4
Switzerland,Liechtenst.	658.8	640.1	730.1	692.6	594.5	Switzerland,Liechtenst.	600.6	697.5	813.5	707.1	634.5
Poland/Pologne	388.1	477.2	591.5	591.5	597.8	Poland/Pologne	452.2	533.3	634.3	798.3	824.7
Spain/Espagne	332.1	376.2	488.1	506.6	597.1	Russian Federation	268.4	409.2	624.6	702.6	874.3
Portugal	324.7	373.1	470.3	430.8	471.2	Austria/Autriche	349.5	385.8	456.2	449.2	435.5
Austria/Autriche	345.6	347.5	407.6	381.7	424.6	China, Hong Kong SAR	240.3	303.3	347.2	443.1	448.2
Ireland/Irlande	178.1	251.8	424.7	511.9	497.4	Korea, Republic of	194.3	315.1	368.0	460.6	380.9
Russian Federation	307.7	313.1	431.1	363.2	279.7	Greece/Grèce	278.2	287.7	326.8	331.7	370.0
Greenland/Groenland	242.0	276.0	307.1	327.9	262.8	Saudi Arabia	242.4	242.0	284.3	234.1	241.6
Other Asia n.e.s.	235.3	234.2	274.6	312.5	334.7	Greenland/Groenland	217.6	219.2	239.0	247.7	291.5
Korea, Republic of	235.0	348.9	232.6	229.2	190.9	Ireland/Irlande	161.9	182.9	247.5	242.8	341.3
Brazil/Brésil	210.8	243.2	268.3	219.6	262.3	China/Chine	126.9	162.5	245.2	286.0	314.8
China, Hong Kong SAR	154.0	170.7	204.3	229.3	218.4	Portugal	168.6	199.6	301.5	260.0	189.1
Argentina/Argentine	150.9	204.0	174.1	215.1	177.5	Australia/Australie	162.6	202.3	217.6	229.3	247.3
Thailand/Thaïlande	122.7	157.9	189.8	202.5	239.1	Iceland/Islande	141.5	160.1	193.9	200.9	214.2
India/Inde	111.7	160.4	205.3	194.0	196.1	Canada	160.8	186.1	173.6	182.4	197.6
Indonesia/Indonésie	135.9	142.9	170.6	176.9	199.1	Singapore/Singapour	119.6	182.3	201.9	216.5	178.4
Malaysia/Malaisie	97.3	140.9	172.1	161.9	161.5	Thailand/Thaïlande	164.6	162.3	205.8	185.7	164.9
Canada	117.7	128.9	146.5	161.0	158.6	India/Inde	70.5	139.0	338.4	181.5	98.8
Faeroe Islds/Is Féroé	178.4	151.5	136.3	136.0	110.1	Other Asia n.e.s.	129.0	134.1	166.9	170.1	150.2
Turkey/Turquie	78.3	115.8	144.6	152.7	182.2	Czech Republic	107.4	131.4	172.7	179.3	154.7
Singapore/Singapour	182.5	199.9	84.3	93.1	80.1	Turkey/Turquie	124.0	119.9	157.0	145.6	150.3
Iceland/Islande	86.1	109.6	149.4	146.0	118.9	Faeroe Islds/Is Féroé	92.0	98.7	136.8	155.3	183.9
Czech Republic	67.9	105.5	131.9	133.4	138.1	Egypt/Egypte	113.7	120.2	152.9	126.4	130.6
Lithuania/Lituanie	44.9	74.5	94.0	107.5	114.7	Bahamas	234.4	147.9	85.9	46.3	113.4
Latvia/Lettonie	85.6	62.2	51.5	68.5	89.9	Lithuania/Lituanie	29.5	67.6	122.4	159.7	238.3
Hungary/Hongrie	41.0	47.6	57.6	68.8	81.6	United Arab Emirates	103.4	116.3	129.3	131.8	135.8

(VALUE AS PERCENTAGE OF WORLD TOTAL)(VALEURS EN POURCENTAGE DU TOTAL MONDIAL)

	1988	1989	1990	1991	1992	1993	1994	1995	1996	1997		1988	1989	1990	1991	1992	1993	1994	1995	1996	1997
Africa	0.6	0.9	0.7	0.5	0.4	0.5	0.7	0.5	0.4	0.3	Afrique	2.3	1.8	2.7	1.1	1.8	1.2	1.8	1.7	1.0	1.1
Americas	8.9	9.7	8.9	8.4	8.2	7.6	7.7	7.0	7.4	7.5	Amériques	8.5	7.7	6.7	6.8	6.7	7.4	7.6	6.1	6.1	6.6
– Northern America	7.0	7.8	7.1	6.9	6.3	5.7	6.0	5.6	5.9	5.9	– Amérique du Nord	7.5	6.5	5.8	5.2	5.3	5.6	5.7	4.4	4.6	5.0
– LAIA	1.4	1.6	1.3	1.4	1.5	1.5	1.6	1.4	1.5	1.5	– ALAI	0.6	0.7	0.5	0.8	0.9	0.9	1.1	1.0	0.9	1.0
– CACM	0.1	0.1	0.1	0.1	0.1	0.0	0.0	0.0	0.1	0.0	– MCAC	0.1	0.1	0.1	0.1	0.0	0.0	0.1	0.1	0.0	0.1
– Caribbean	0.3	0.2	0.2	0.0	0.3	0.3	0.1	0.0	0.0	0.1	– Caraïbes	0.2	0.3	0.2	0.6	0.2	0.8	0.6	0.4	0.3	0.5
– Rest of America	0.1	0.0	0.2	0.0	0.0	0.0	0.0	0.0	0.0	0.0	– Autre Amérique	0.2	0.1	0.1	0.0	0.3	0.0	0.0	0.2	0.3	0.1
Asia excl fmr USSR	10.9	11.2	10.5	10.5	10.1	10.4	10.6	9.0	8.9	8.8	Asie anc. URSS exclus	9.1	9.5	8.5	8.8	9.4	9.7	9.9	10.3	10.1	9.3
– Middle East	1.6	1.9	1.2	0.4	0.3	0.4	0.4	0.4	0.4	0.4	– Moyen–Orient	1.9	2.3	2.1	2.1	2.1	2.3	2.0	1.9	1.7	1.7
Asia former USSR					0.0	0.0	0.0	0.0	0.0	0.0	Asie ancienne URSS					0.0	0.1	0.1	0.2	0.1	0.1
Europe excl fmr USSR	76.6	74.5	76.7	77.1	77.5	77.4	76.9	79.2	79.2	79.2	Europe anc. URSS exclus	73.1	73.0	74.6	75.7	74.3	72.7	71.2	71.7	72.6	71.9
– European Union	67.3	65.6	67.2	67.0	67.6	67.5	67.2	69.8	69.6	70.1	– Union Européenne	60.9	62.6	64.7	64.9	64.1	61.6	60.5	61.2	61.3	60.9
– Eastern Europe	1.8	1.8	1.8	1.6	1.7	1.7	1.9	2.0	2.0	2.0	– Europe de l'Est	1.2	1.4	1.3	2.3	1.8	1.9	2.1	2.2	2.4	2.4
– Rest of Europe	7.5	7.2	7.6	8.5	8.2	8.1	7.8	7.4	7.5	7.1	– Autre de l'Europe	11.0	9.0	8.6	8.4	8.4	9.2	8.6	8.3	8.8	8.5
Europe former USSR	0.5	0.8	0.7	0.8	1.1	1.7	1.5	1.5	1.5	1.5	Europe ancienne URSS	0.5	0.8	1.0	0.6	0.9	1.1	1.5	2.0	2.4	3.0
Oceania	0.2	0.2	0.1	0.1	0.1	0.1	0.2	0.2	0.2	0.2	Océanie	0.9	0.7	0.5	0.5	0.5	0.6	0.6	0.6	0.6	0.6
Other	2.3	2.7	2.3	2.6	2.4	2.3	2.4	2.5	2.3	2.5	Autre	5.5	6.4	6.0	6.5	6.3	7.2	7.3	7.5	7.2	7.4
Germany/Allemagne				21.9	22.9	21.6	20.5	21.3	20.2	21.3	Germany/Allemagne				21.0	22.3	21.5	20.0	20.9	19.8	19.8
Sweden/Suède	12.2	12.0	11.5	10.8	10.8	10.4	11.0	11.6	11.5	12.6	Sweden/Suède	11.1	11.7	12.3	10.9	10.0	9.1	9.4	9.0	9.7	11.0
Netherlands/Pays–Bas	6.0	5.6	5.8	5.7	5.5	6.2	6.3	7.0	6.6	7.7	United Kingdom	11.1	11.5	10.2	9.8	9.6	7.9	7.3	7.2	8.2	9.0
United Kingdom	6.9	6.8	7.5	8.0	8.1	7.2	6.2	6.5	6.7	7.4	Areas n.e.s.	5.4	6.3	5.9	6.5	6.3	7.2	7.3	7.5	7.2	7.4
France, Monaco	4.9	4.9	5.3	6.2	5.5	5.0	5.1	5.1	5.2	5.5	Norway,Svalbard and JM	6.9	5.6	5.6	5.4	5.6	6.5	6.0	5.7	6.1	6.0
Norway,Svalbard and JM	4.4	4.3	4.6	5.6	5.3	4.9	4.8	4.9	5.1	5.2	France, Monaco	5.3	5.6	5.6	5.4	5.2	4.6	4.7	4.8	4.4	4.7
USA/Etats–Unis d'Amer	5.5	6.3	5.7	5.6	5.1	4.5	4.8	4.5	4.7	5.0	USA/Etats–Unis d'Amer	5.4	5.0	4.6	4.2	4.2	4.6	4.7	3.5	3.6	4.0
Italy/Italie	3.9	3.9	4.1	4.2	4.1	3.6	3.7	4.1	4.0	4.4	Netherlands/Pays–Bas	3.8	3.9	4.5	4.5	4.1	3.8	3.4	4.0	3.8	4.1
Belgium–Luxembourg	3.3	3.2	3.3	3.1	3.2	3.5	3.4	3.5	3.3	3.7	Italy/Italie	4.4	4.5	4.7	4.6	4.3	3.6	3.5	3.3	3.3	3.3
European Union n.e.s.						3.3	4.1	3.5	5.1		Japan/Japon	3.9	4.1	3.2	3.4	3.4	3.5	3.5	3.4	3.1	2.9

4. General Imports C.I.F. by Commodities according to the S.I.T.C. (Rev. 2) in million U.S. Dollars
Importations Générales C.A.F. par Produits d'après la C.T.C.I. (Rév. 2) en millions de Dollars E.U.

SITC CTCI	COMMODITY	1994 QUANTITY QUANTITE	1994 VALUE VALEUR	1995 QUANTITY QUANTITE	1995 VALUE VALEUR	1996 QUANTITY QUANTITE	1996 VALUE VALEUR	1997 QUANTITY QUANTITE	1997 VALUE VALEUR	PRODUIT
	ALL COMMODITIES		35436.5		43141.6		43126.4		44492.4	TOUS PRODUITS
0	FOOD AND LIVE ANIMALS		3744.5		4329.9		4394.6		4603.7	ALIMENTS,ANIMAUX VIVANTS
01	MEAT AND PREPARATIONS		327.6		431.4		436.3		530.0	VIANDES ET PREPARATIONS
011	MEAT FRESH,CHILLD,FROZEN	W 78549	285.1	W 99080	375.3	W 106131	369.9	W 150842	444.3	VIANDES FRAICHES,REF,CONGE
0111	BOVINE MEAT FRESH,FROZEN	W 41274	173.5	W 47984	227.3	W 52341	213.2	W 66363	238.9	VIANDES BOVIN FRAI,REF
01111	BOVINE MEAT WITH BONE IN	W 27825	109.5	W 29499	123.2	W 31536	109.7	W 45368	143.1	VIANDES BOVIN NON DESOSS
02	DAIRY PRODCTS,BIRDS'EGGS		159.1		233.6		228.8		243.4	PRODUITS LAITIERS,OEUFS
03	FISH AND PREPARATIONS		1076.6		1225.9		1243.2		1132.4	POISSONS ET PREPARATIONS
034	FISH,FRESH,CHILLED,FROZN	W 337416	550.3	W 327366	620.3	W 311099	608.2	W 330431	589.0	POISSON FRAIS, REFRIG,CONG
0341	FISH FRSH,CHLLD,EX FILLT	W 241007	314.9	W 241600	370.6	W 229874	364.2	W 247849	351.0	POISSON FRAIS,REFRIGERE
036	SHELL FISH FRESH,FROZEN	W 66651	236.3	W 59987	262.4	W 71292	291.1	W 77484	269.3	CRUSTACES,MOLLUSQUES
037	FISH ETC PREPD,PRSVD NES	W 40434	229.5	W 41014	278.4	W 45270	278.0	W 49326	231.0	POIS,CRUST,MOL PREPARES
0372	SHELL FISH PREPRD,PRESVD	W 25537	170.4	W 24227	209.5	W 24433	197.6	W 24342	157.0	CRUSTACES,COQUIL PREPARES
04	CEREALS AND PREPARATIONS		302.7		374.7		342.6		349.6	CEREALES ET PRODUITS
048	CEREAL ETC PREPARATIONS	W 149268	169.4	W 167558	217.4	W 134915	203.4	W 166742	215.7	PREPTNS A BASE CEREALES
05	VEGETABLES AND FRUIT		540.8		596.8		628.3		729.0	LEGUMES ET FRUITS
054	VEG ETC FRSH,SMPLY PRSVD	W 233312	172.9	W 213870	187.8	W 227619	194.2	W 329774	255.1	LEGUMES FRAIS,CONG,SECS
057	FRUIT,NUTS,FRESH,DRIED	W 232295	225.8	W 211086	232.5	W 245945	264.7	W 277736	288.2	FRUITS FRAIS OU SECS
06	SUGAR AND PREPS,HONEY		136.9		173.1		195.7		227.0	SUCRES ET PRODUITS
061	SUGAR AND HONEY	W 420040	86.3	W 453649	105.0	W 457555	122.9	W 527729	141.9	SUCRES ET MIEL
07	COFFEE,TEA,COCOA,SPICES		344.4		407.7		359.9		384.9	CAFE,THE,CACAO,EPICES
071	COFFEE AND SUBSTITUTES	W 58922	169.1	W 50613	192.1	W 57925	170.1	W 54601	201.5	CAFE ET SUCCEDANES
0711	COFFEE GREEN,ROASTED,SUB	W 57142	152.7	W 49528	179.0	W 56439	154.5	W 53242	184.9	CAFE TORREFIE OU DECAFEINE
07111	COFFEE GREEN,HUSKS,SKINS	W 54974	145.8	W 47477	169.0	W 54692	145.0	W 51245	174.1	CAFE NON TORREFIE
073	CHOCOLATE AND PRODUCTS	W 33454	139.7	W 35075	172.4	W 32189	147.5	W 34804	133.0	CHOCOLAT
081	*FEEDING STUFF FOR ANIML	W 3070948	670.1	W 2924388	669.0	W 2831323	744.0	W 2909279	775.7	NOURRITURE POUR ANIMAUX
0813	OILCAKE AND OTH RESIDUES	W 2388427	465.2	W 2228836	421.5	W 2098537	465.7	W 2015716	469.6	TOURTEAUX
08131	— OF SOYA BEANS	W 1518308	331.2	W 1581610	324.6	W 1355132	337.0	W 1308471	351.2	TOURTEAUX DE SOJA
0819	FOOD WASTE AND FEED NES	W 517483	148.5	W 437893	163.3	W 453760	166.9	W 564320	192.8	DECHETS,ALIMENTS NDA
09	MISC EDIBLE PRODUCTS		174.5		195.7		196.3		220.2	PREP ALIMENTAIRES DIVERSES
098	EDIBLE PRODCTS,PREPS NES	W 49777	152.1	W 69622	166.1	W 54361	171.2	W 73323	189.2	PREP ALIMENTAIRES NDA
09809	MISC FOOD PREPRTIONS NES	W 35701	115.4	W 48338	115.8	W 31558	120.3	W 39486	133.7	PREP ALIMENTAIRES NDA
1	BEVERAGES AND TOBACCO		451.8		546.4		574.4		697.0	BOISSONS ET TABACS
11	BEVERAGES		341.0		432.5		462.8		571.6	BOISSONS
112	ALCOHOLIC BEVERAGES	W 152147	327.3	W 168832	413.6	W 181464	445.0	W 224269	549.7	BOISSONS ALCOOLIQUES
1121	WINE OF FRESH GRAPES ETC	W 128452	258.4	W 144529	341.3	W 154511	368.7	W 188731	459.8	VINS DE RAISINS FRAIS
11212	WINE OF FRESH GRAPES	W 123422	249.2	W 139332	331.0	W 149489	359.2	W 182286	447.7	VINS DE MOUTS DE RAISINS
12	TOBACCO AND MANUFACTURES		110.9		114.0		111.7		125.5	TABACS BRUTS FABRIQUES
2	CRUDE MATERLS,EXCL FUELS		1345.0		1609.2		1478.6		1693.3	MAT BRUTES NON COMESTIBLES
21	HIDES,SKINS,FURS UNDRSSD		82.3		104.7		122.5		152.5	CUIRS,PEAUX BRUTS
212	FURSKINS,RAW	W 541	78.8	W 478	101.7	W 495	116.5	W 672	149.0	PELLETERIES BRUTES
24	CORK AND WOOD		635.0		685.7		553.6		703.9	LIEGE ET BOIS
248	WOOD SHAPED,SLEEPERS	W 1316943	588.1	W 1097042	596.8	W 929912	470.1	W 1244948	578.6	BOIS SIMPLEMENT TRAVAILLES
2482	LUMBER SHAPED CONIFER	W 1252465	531.0	W 1025983	529.3	W 870694	410.8	W 1180019	516.6	CONIFERES SCIES,RABOTES
24821	LUMBER SAWN ETC CONIFER	W 1246801	525.5	W 1016601	519.3	W 856993	395.9	W 1158376	493.9	CONIFERES SCIES LONGITUD
27	CRUDE FERTLZR,MINRLS NES		111.2		148.1		170.8		177.8	ENGRAIS MINERAUX BRUTS
29	CRUDE ANIMAL,VEG MAT NES		263.9		338.7		327.7		371.5	MATIERES BRUTES ANIM,VEGET
292	CRUDE VEG MATERIALS NES	W 65173	186.0	W 65213	240.2	W 64113	221.0	W 80024	259.4	MAT BRUTES VEGETALES NDA
3	MINERAL FUELS ETC		1485.0		1454.2		1667.5		1728.3	COMBUSTIBLES MINERAUX LUB
33	PETROLEUM AND PRODUCTS		1420.9		1350.6		1553.1		1616.7	PETROLE ET DERIVES
333	CRUDE PETROLEUM	W 4986799	602.0	W 5236573	689.2	W 5174129	803.2	W 4768350	740.1	HUILES BRUTES DE PETROLE
334	PETROLEUM PRODUCTS,REFIN	W 5110345	769.4	W 3645454	610.6	W 3530037	685.2	W 4086870	796.7	PRODUITS RAFFINES
3341	GASOLINE,OTH LIGHT OILS					W 3524104	666.6			ESSENCES POUR MOTEURS
33419	OTH LIGHT PETROLEUM OILS					W 3524104	666.6			AUTRES HUILES LEGERES
4	ANIMAL,VEGETABLE OIL,FAT		171.1		208.8		232.5		245.8	HUILES,GRAISSES ANIM,VEG
42	FIXED VEGETABLE OIL,FAT		98.8		128.1		148.6		149.0	HUILES VEGETALES FIXES
5	CHEMCLS,RELATED PROD NES		3687.0		4636.5		4293.1		4483.0	PRODUITS CHIMIQUES
51	ORGANIC CHEMICALS		379.9		481.0		461.9		479.3	PROD CHIMIQ ORGANIQUES
514	NITROGEN–FNCTN COMPOUNDS	W 30000	99.2	W 31697	129.7	W 33604	123.9	W 39591	125.2	COMPOSES FONCT AZOTEES
516	OTHER ORGANIC CHEMICALS	W 67747	80.3	W 55465	90.5	W 55305	112.4	W 52322	136.4	AUTRES PROD ORGANIQUES
52	INORGANIC CHEMICALS		242.5		321.5		265.5		276.7	PROD CHIM INORGANIQUES
522	INORG ELEMNTS,OXIDES,ETC	W 545968	128.6	W 711410	187.1	W 537846	140.1	W 713704	155.2	ELEMENTS INORGANIQUES
523	OTHR INORG CHEMICALS ETC	W 335367	106.8	W 354569	128.2	W 352843	119.8	W 359706	113.9	AUT PRODUITS CHIMIQUES INORG
53	DYES,TANNING,COLOUR PROD		335.9		425.4		398.4		437.9	PROD TEINTURE,COLORANTS
531	SYNT DYE,NAT INDGO,LAKES	W 6851	132.2	W 7360	171.5	W 8030	156.9	W 9687	185.0	MAT COLOR ORGAN,LAQUES
5311	SYNTHIC ORGNIC DYESTUFFS	W 6411	129.3	W 6642	166.5	W 7371	152.3	W 8322	178.3	MAT COLOR ORGAN SYNTHET
533	PIGMENTS,PAINTS,ETC	W 74393	195.3	W 71096	238.8	W 76649	225.5	W 88118	237.2	PIGMENTS,PEINTURES,VERNIS
541	*MEDICINAL,PHARM PRODUCT	MK 17154	726.9	MK 15981	897.7	MK 19498	847.2	MK 22152	835.1	PROD MEDICINAUX PHARMACEUT
5411	PROVITAMINS AND VITAMINS	K 5851705	108.4	K 6289336	134.4	K 7137294	91.6	MK 9279	127.6	PROVITAMINES,VITAMINES
5417	MEDICAMENTS	K 8397754	475.3	K 7026452	606.6	MK 9455	584.1	K 8563862	544.5	MEDICAMENTS
54179	— CONTNG OTH SUBSTANCES	K 6570188	321.3	K 4943992	347.6	K 7150645	380.6	K 6490027	374.7	MED CONT AUT SUBSTANCES
55	PERFUME,CLEANING ETC PRD		380.6		409.2		438.7		473.4	PROD POUR PARFUM,TOILETTE
553	PERFUMERY,COSMETICS,ETC	W 24680	220.2	W 24404	228.8	W 27291	268.5	W 34258	278.7	PRODUITS DE PARFUMERIE
554	SOAP,CLEANSING ETC PREPS	W 80975	124.6	W 81580	136.7	W 84018	130.2	W 101969	149.8	SAVONS,PRODUITS DETERSIFS
562	*FERTILIZERS,MANUFACTURE	W 1278782	180.4	W 1134785	202.2	W 962460	177.7	W 981601	154.1	ENGRAIS MANUFACTURES
58	PLASTIC MATERIALS ETC		1001.8		1358.0		1209.9		1293.7	MAT PLAST ARTIFICIELLES
582	PROD OF CONDENSATION ETC	W 96236	229.2	W 105035	307.5	W 110725	293.7	W 143542	297.5	PROD CONDENS,POLYCOND
5823	ALKYDS,OTHER POLYESTERS	W 39373	102.0	W 41724	141.6	W 42738	130.9	W 62785	128.0	ALKYDES ET AUT POLYESTERS
583	POLYMERIZATION ETC PRODS	W 580244	743.6	W 594414	1014.7	W 619995	883.4	W 694437	956.0	PROD POLYMERISATION
5831	POLYETHYLENE	W 207462	188.6	W 208805	267.4	W 214584	224.7	W 232410	240.2	POLYETHYLENE
58311	— IN PRIMARY FORMS	W 173113	143.0	W 178224	213.9	W 176565	171.9	W 185228	183.5	POLYETHYLENE PRIMAIRES
5832	POLYPROPYLENE	W 118057	109.9	W 133040	178.6	W 136464	151.0	W 146389	153.6	POLYPROPYLENE
5834	POLYVINYL CHLORIDE	W 80161	119.9	W 66839	140.2	W 80668	119.9	W 90007	143.6	CHLORURE DE POLYVINYLE
5839	OTH POLYMRZTION ETC PROD	W 72278	159.4	W 80310	212.2	W 77861	192.7	W 99656	217.8	AUT PROD POLYMER COPOLYM
59	CHEMICAL MATERIALS NES		431.7		532.3		483.2		523.1	MAT PROD CHIMIQUES NDA
591	PESTICIDES,DISINFECTANTS	W 8571	111.4	W 12691	148.7	W 12336	122.0	W 12236	114.3	DESINF,INSECT,FONG,HERB
598	MISCEL CHEM PRODUCTS NES	W 137574	232.8	W 130555	273.9	W 134266	252.9	W 147126	286.2	PROD DIV INDUST CHIM NDA
5989	CHEM PRODUCTS,PREPS NES	W 83038	159.2	W 82602	195.6	W 99404	190.4	W 105927	215.6	PROD PREP CHIMIQUES NDA
59899	OTH CHEM PRODS,PREPS,NES	W 59780	121.1	W 62791	153.2	W 76790	148.4	W 75226	169.0	AUT PRODUITS CHIMIQUES NDA
6	BASIC MANUFACTURES		6159.4		7966.7		7170.0		7779.4	ART MANUFACTURES
62	RUBBER MANUFACTURES NES		293.4		379.8		358.8		398.5	CAOUTCHOUC MANUFACTURE
625	RUBBER TYRES, TUBES ETC	W 46248	174.4	W 52716	237.1	W 51355	225.6	W 55745	228.3	PNEUS CAOUTCHOUC VULCANISE
63	WOOD,CORK MANUFACTRS NES		332.4		403.6		364.1		446.2	OUVRAGES LIEGE ET BOIS
634	VENEERS,PLYWOOD,ETC	W 332833	206.9	W 335408	244.9	W 309394	203.6	W 400406	232.9	PLACAGES,CONTRE–PLAQUES
635	WOOD MANUFACTURES NES	W 96898	120.1	W 108585	153.6	W 109112	155.5	W 124677	208.0	ART MANUF EN BOIS NDA
64	PAPER,PAPERBOARD AND MFR		1251.9		1605.7		1506.9		1440.1	PAPIERS,CARTONS & OUVRAGES
641	PAPER AND PAPERBOARD	W 1175663	894.9	W 1133034	1156.9	W 1129742	1059.7	W 1243901	982.0	PAPIERS ET CARTONS
6411	NEWSPRINT	W 267545	132.3	W 262814	181.5	W 256117	204.5	W 291467	176.1	PAPIER JOURNAL
6412	PRINTG,WRITING PAPER NES	W 168579	166.0	W 223709	287.6	W 190841	218.9	W 209680	200.3	PAPIERS POUR L'IMPRESSION
64122	— COATED,IMPREGNATD ETC	W 146676	140.7	W 195948	241.3	W 164259	183.3	W 189064	173.0	PAPIERS IMPRESSION COUCHES
6413	KRAFT PAPER,PAPERBOARD	W 187342	119.2	W 158388	136.3	W 175953	129.6	W 174938	107.9	PAPIER ET CARTON KRAFT

4. General Imports C.I.F. by Commodities according to the S.I.T.C. (Rev. 2) in million U.S. Dollars
Importations Générales C.A.F. par Produits d'après la C.T.C.I. (Rév. 2) en millions de Dollars E.U.

SITC CTCI	COMMODITY	1994 QUANTITY QUANTITE	1994 VALUE VALEUR	1995 QUANTITY QUANTITE	1995 VALUE VALEUR	1996 QUANTITY QUANTITE	1996 VALUE VALEUR	1997 QUANTITY QUANTITE	1997 VALUE VALEUR	PRODUIT
6415	PAPER,PAPERBRD,BULK,NES	W 327257	216.4	W 286503	266.7	W 297199	238.8	W 337064	230.4	PAPIERS,CARTONS ROULEAUX
64159	OTHER PAPER ETC,BULK,NES	W 256804	180.5	W 219070	216.9	W 244598	205.6	W 284891	203.0	AUT PAPIER ROULEAUX FEUILLES
6418	COATED ETC PAPER NES BLK	W 129118	200.1	W 115026	218.3	W 128891	210.6	W 131118	200.9	PAP,CARTONS COUCHES,ENDUITS
64189	COATED PAPER ETC NES	W 78728	117.3	W 79050	148.9	W 86861	138.6	W 85884	132.4	PAPIERS,CARTONS COUCHES
642	PAPER,ETC,PRECUT,ARTS OF	W 176603	357.1	W 188232	448.8	W 207135	447.3	W 226611	458.2	PAP,CARTONS DECOUPES
6421	PAPER ETC CONTAINERS	W 52637	92.5	W 67135	137.4	W 73829	130.0	W 83479	152.1	BOITES,SACS EMBALLAGES
6428	PAPER ETC ARTICLES NES	W 64659	152.4	W 64433	182.2	W 70504	184.7	W 72947	167.8	OUVRAGES EN PATE A PAPIER
65	TEXTILE YARN,FABRICS,ETC		861.7		1061.1		1005.2		1133.6	FILS,TISSUS,ARTICLES TEXTILE
651	TEXTILE YARN	W 49078	235.2	W 51494	282.5	W 54692	271.6	W 64426	277.2	FILS TEXTILES
6514	SYN FIB YRN,BULK,MONOFIL	W 24283	102.4	W 26614	129.8	W 30607	128.7	W 37583	138.7	FILS CONT 85% FIB TEXT SYNTH
653	WOVN MAN–MADE FIB FABRIC	W 10854	131.5	W 12058	165.0	W 11445	146.0	W 16309	171.8	TISSUS FIBRES SYNTH,ARTIF
657	SPECIAL TXTL FABRC,PRODS	W 21623	118.2	W 22650	155.4	W 26202	146.1	W 33682	167.3	TISSUS SPECIAUX
658	TEXTILE ARTICLES NES	W 15260	113.2	W 17530	145.7	W 16862	137.6	W 21972	173.3	ART FACONNES MAT TEXTILES
66	NONMETAL MINERAL MFS NES		446.1		568.8		552.8		640.3	ART MIN NON METALLIQUES
664	GLASS	W 158807	129.3	W 191587	174.7	W 176840	163.2	W 170545	174.7	VERRE
67	IRON AND STEEL		1371.4		1869.5		1426.1		1587.0	FER ET ACIER
672	IRON,STEEL PRIMARY FORMS	W 292990	112.1	W 394185	186.8	W 284383	135.5	W 358795	137.2	LINGOTS FER,ACIER
6727	IRN,STL COIL FR REROLLNG	W 272414	103.6	W 281143	147.7	W 262002	127.5	W 315187	123.8	EBAUCHES POUR TOLES FER
673	IRON,STEEL SHAPES ETC	W 400033	226.8	W 398634	296.4	W 351895	225.5	W 423378	228.2	BARRES,PROFIL FER,ACIER
6732	IRON,STEEL BARS ETC	W 175602	112.8	W 165366	151.6	W 144997	116.2	W 175693	114.7	BARRES FER,ACIER
674	IRN,STL UNIV,PLATE,SHEET	W 956695	632.6	W 1001805	847.7	W 792619	618.8	W 991621	658.3	LARGES PLATS,TOLES
6744	IRN,STL HVY PLATE,ROLLED	W 290805	151.3	W 271335	194.1	W 197490	121.1	W 291829	154.0	TOLES LAMINEES PLUS 4.75 MM
67441	— OF IRON OR SIMPLE STL	W 279843	129.7	W 259586	158.8	W 186613	94.9	W 274133	125.1	TOLES NON ACIER FIN CARB
6746	IRN,STL THIN PLATE,ROLLD	W 268714	192.4	W 270889	245.0	W 206313	172.4	W 244514	182.1	TOLES LAM MOINS 3MM
67461	— OF IRON OR SIMPLE STL	W 217950	102.3	W 225629	134.3	W 159969	85.8	W 185113	84.6	TOL NON AC FIN MOINS 3 MM
6749	OTH IRN,STL PLATES,SHEET	W 221869	151.3	W 261942	223.2	W 212391	171.9	W 263838	186.4	AUTRES TOLES FER,ACIER
67491	— OF IRON OR SIMPLE STL	W 218433	142.5	W 256629	206.7	W 209390	164.1	W 259672	178.0	AUT TOLES AUTRES ACIER FIN
678	IRON,STL TUBES,PIPES,ETC	W 267515	289.7	W 305848	401.6	W 255692	339.2	W 594551	444.5	TUBES,TUYAUX EN FONTE,FER
6782	IRON,STL SEAMLESS TUBES	W 33853	49.9	W 34725	64.2	W 30616	52.7	W 321871	140.1	TUBES,TUYAUX SANS SOUDURE
6783	IRON,STL TUBES,PIPES NES	W 218241	166.9	W 255681	249.6	W 206645	192.1	W 249887	199.2	AUT TUBES,TUYAUX FER,ACIER
68	NON–FERROUS METALS		511.2		654.6		574.8		620.3	METAUX NON FERREUX
682	COPPER EXC CEMENT COPPER	W 51005	159.2	W 54419	209.5	W 51188	182.0	W 58336	195.1	CUIVRE
6822	COPPER,ALLOYS WORKED	W 49120	155.1	W 52527	204.4	W 49130	175.4	W 55903	188.6	CUIVRE,ALLIAGES OUVRES
684	ALUMINIUM	W 100000	288.2	W 101722	368.7	W 98635	321.0	W 114176	349.5	ALUMINIUM
6842	ALUMINIUM,ALLOYS WORKED	W 70453	241.0	W 66326	292.2	W 65041	259.0	W 73159	282.2	ALUMINIUM,ALLIAGES OUVRE
68421	ALUMINIUM BARS,WIRE,ETC	W 28770	95.7	W 28444	123.4	W 28548	108.4	W 36595	137.4	BARRES,PROFILES FILS ALU
69	METAL MANUFACTURES NES		990.1		1324.7		1283.4		1399.3	ART MANUFACT EN METAL NDA
691	STRUCTURES AND PARTS NES	W 69683	142.9	W 92267	248.4	W 107346	266.6	W 129046	263.8	CONSTRUCT FER,ACIER,ALU
6911	STRUCTURES,PARTS IRN,STL	W 66791	126.3	W 89871	230.3	W 104029	245.3	W 122908	236.6	CONSTRUCT FER,ACIER,FONTE
692	METAL TANKS,BOXES,ETC	W 36804	115.2	W 40478	162.5	W 41771	147.5	W 36279	138.6	RECIPIENTS METALLIQUES
6924	MTL TRANSPORT BOXES ETC	W 34323	107.9	W 38090	150.1	W 36058	134.0	W 34172	131.1	FUTS,TAMBOURS,BIDONS
694	STL,COPPR NAILS,NUTS,ETC	W 29427	91.4	W 37290	131.8	W 46779	112.2	W 40298	126.5	CLOUS,VIS,ECROUS
695	TOOLS	W 8668	144.9	W 9780	191.0	W 10636	196.2	W 13166	206.9	OUTILS A MAIN
699	BASE METAL MFRS NES	W 70517	333.1	W 72361	387.9	W 73346	366.0	W 91959	436.8	ART MANUFACTURES MET NDA
6991	LOCKSMITHS WARES,ETC	W 22778	135.0	W 22654	150.9	W 22037	140.8	W 31196	176.7	ARTICLES DE SERRURERIE
69913	BASE MTL DOOR,ETC FITTNG	W 19677	111.6	W 19509	123.3	W 18619	113.0	W 27492	143.3	GARNITURES POUR MEUBLES
7	MACHINES,TRANSPORT EQUIP		11020.6		13806.3		13984.5		14973.7	MACHINES MATERIEL TRANSPORT
71	POWER GENERATING EQUIPMT		512.0		711.6		669.9		705.9	MACHINES GENERATRICES
713	INTRNL COMBUS PSTN ENGIN	W 16998	234.5	W 22505	285.9	W 22465	265.5	W 26100	299.4	MOTEURS EXPL COMB INT, PIECE
7139	PISTON ENGINE PARTS NES	W 5677	102.6	W 8005	133.2	W 9808	144.1	W 10720	157.2	PIECES POUR 713.2,3,8
716	ROTATING ELECTRIC PLANT	W 19108	182.1	W 26318	260.7	W 26029	249.1	W 41310	282.2	APP ELECTR ROTATIFS,PIECES
7162	AC MTRS,GENRTRS,GEN SETS	W 14716	126.3	W 18021	174.6	W 17156	157.3	W 22931	163.0	MOTEURS ELECTRIQUES
72	MACHS FOR SPCL INDUSTRYS		888.1		1226.3		1272.7		1386.2	MAC SPECIALES POUR INDUST
721	AGRIC MACHY,EXC TRACTORS	W 21818	148.7	W 31768	234.8	W 33847	248.1	W 38734	261.2	MACHINES AGRICOLES
7212	HARVESTING ETC MACHINES	W 10324	77.2	W 15330	125.5	W 16949	131.3	W 17605	123.5	ENGINS POUR LA RECOLTE
722	TRACTORS NON–ROAD	W 14196	93.9	W 18672	147.4	W 22735	178.2	W 24017	177.2	TRACTEURS
7224	WHEELED TRACTORS NES	W 14196	93.9	W 18559	146.7	W 22735	178.2	W 24017	177.2	TRACTEURS A ROUES
723	CIVIL ENGNEERG EQUIP ETC	W 16648	128.2	W 19298	186.2	W 25098	216.4	W 29464	241.1	APPAREILS DE GENIE CIVIL
7234	CONST,MINING MACHNRY NES	W 13164	76.2	W 15890	120.6	W 21453	142.7	W 24378	147.7	MACH POUR LA CONST, MINES
726	PRINTG,BKBINDG MACHY,PTS	W 3477	118.1	W 4497	145.5	W 4303	150.3	W 5357	160.5	MACHINES POUR IMPRIMERIE
728	OTH MACHY FOR SPCL INDUS	W 16332	248.4	W 18491	324.2	W 17092	307.0	W 20913	334.2	AUT MACH IND PARTICULIERES
7284	MACHY FOR SPCL INDUS NES	W 7912	161.8	W 9283	209.2	W 8997	201.1	W 12385	234.5	MACH SPEC IND PARTICUL.
73	METALWORKING MACHINERY		163.5		246.2		209.4		181.8	MACH TRAVAIL DES METAUX
736	METALWORKING MACH–TOOLS	W 7843	128.7	W 10314	197.2	W 9520	173.0	W 9124	147.5	MACH–OUTILS TRAVAIL METAUX
74	GENRL INDUSTRL MACHY NES		1400.0		1859.5		1783.6		1965.9	MACH APP INDUSTRIE
741	HEATING,COOLING EQUIPMNT	W 14900	191.6	W 16836	249.4	W 18667	252.9	W 26670	308.1	MACH CHAUFFAGE,PIECES
742	PUMPS FOR LIQUIDS ETC	W 7337	147.5	W 17574	208.1	W 35642	204.3	W 48414	221.0	POMPES MOTO–POMPES
743	PUMPS NES,CENTRFUGES ETC	W 32158	276.9	W 31889	315.2	W 60508	302.2	W 49000	341.2	POMPES COMPRES,VENT ETC
744	MECHANICAL HANDLING EQU	W 26257	206.6	W 28752	250.4	W 35957	271.8	W 43573	347.3	EQUIP MANUTENTION PIECES
745	NONELEC MACHY,TOOLS NES	W 7459	161.7	W 9333	237.4	W 9738	222.2	W 11174	233.8	AUT MACH NON ELEC,PIECES
7452	OTH NONELEC MCHS,PTS NES	W 6558	133.0	W 8365	202.6	W 8665	194.3	W 9665	201.2	AUT MACH NON ELEC,PIECES
749	NONELEC MACH PTS,ACC NES	W 34275	415.8	W 47601	599.3	W 41377	530.4	W 44984	514.7	PIECES MACH NON ELEC NDA
7492	COCKS,VALVES ETC NES	W 16868	180.4	W 20592	248.8	W 17031	234.6	W 23052	269.4	ART ROB,SIM POUR TUYAUX
7493	SHAFT,CRANK,PULLEY ETC	W 11941	109.8	W 20721	204.5	W 17007	159.9	W 15086	127.1	ARBRES TRANS,VILEBREQUINS
75	OFFICE MACHNES,ADP EQUIP		1863.6		2319.7		2320.9		2458.5	MACH BUREAU TRAIT AUTOM
751	OFFICE MACHINES	W 3236	113.0	W 3036	121.4	W 3202	119.1	W 3872	124.8	MACH,APPAREILS DE BUREAU
752	AUTOMTIC DATA PROC EQUIP	W 15103	1097.9	W 17040	1291.2	W 20906	1322.4	W 22039	1529.4	MACH TRAIT INFORMATION
7522	DIGITAL COMPUTERS	W 626	85.1	W 886	137.6	W 693	132.4	W 955	152.1	MACH DIGITALES COMPLETES
7523	DIGITL CENTRL PROCESSORS	W 4393	465.5	W 4645	512.4	W 4143	446.3	W 5837	522.6	UNITES CENTRALES
7524	DIGITL CENTRL STOR UNITS	W 1038	123.3	W 991	144.5	W 4218	226.7	W 2000	308.7	UNITES MEMOIRE CENTRALES
7525	ADP PERIPHERAL UNITS	W 7855	333.6	W 8503	332.9	W 9859	342.8	W 11888	415.3	UNITES PERIPHERIQUES
7528	OFF–LINE DATA PROC EQUIP	W 1132	86.0	W 1885	139.6	W 1635	132.2	W 1063	102.5	MACH AUXIL TRAIT INFORM
759	OFFICE,ADP MCH PTS,ACCES	W 7545	652.8	W 10211	907.2	W 11196	879.5	W 10275	804.5	PIECES DU 751 ET 752
7591	OFFICE MACHINE PARTS NES	W 1564	83.1	W 2592	148.1	W 2002	95.3	W 2091	98.5	PIECES DU 7511,7518
75919	COPY MACH PRTS,ACCES NES	W 1454	74.6	W 2420	135.0	W 1637	63.7	W 1601	65.7	PIECES DU 751.82
7599	ACCTG,ETC,ADP MCH PTS,AC	W 5981	569.7	W 7620	759.1	W 9194	784.2	W 8184	706.0	PIECES DU 751 ET 752
76	TELECOMM,SOUND EQUIPMENT		1191.0		1467.6		1691.0		1857.3	EQUIPMENT DE TELECOM
761	TELEVISION RECEIVERS	W 11376	158.8	W 11390	176.3	W 14944	219.0	W 16665	213.6	RECEPTEURS DE TELEVISION
7611	COLOUR TV RECEIVERS	W 11345	157.9	W 11346	174.7	W 14906	217.6	W 16637	212.5	RECEPTEURS COULEUR
762	RADIO BROADCAST RECEIVRS	W 6039	128.3	W 6191	144.5	W 6304	135.5	W 7071	130.0	RECEPTEURS RADIODIFFUSION
763	SOUND RECORDRS,PHONOGRPH	W 4246	177.2	W 4510	193.5	W 4470	210.9	W 4961	188.5	PHONO,APP ENREGISTREMENT
7638	OTHR SOUND APPARATUS ETC	W 4146	175.3	W 4439	192.1	W 4375	209.2	W 4872	186.5	AUT APP D'ENREGIS,REPROD
76381	TV IMAGE,SND RECRDRS ETC	W 2089	106.9	W 2089	111.3	W 2321	136.8	W 2466	104.5	APP ENREG,REPRO IMAG,SON
764	TELECOM EQPT,PTS,ACC NES	W 15001	726.9	W 18242	953.5	W 23325	1125.7	W 25532	1325.3	EQUIP TELECOM,PIECES
7641	LINE TELEPHONE,ETC EQUIP	W 1553	171.8	W 1416	111.4	W 1881	177.3	W 2247	199.4	APP TELEPHON PAR FIL
7642	MICROPH,LOUDSPKR,AMPLIFR	W 7620	97.0	W 9731	113.0	W 12972	142.8	W 13539	163.1	MICRO,HAUT–PARLEUR,AMPLI
7643	TV,RADIO TRANSMITTRS ETC	W 379	108.4	W 859	307.6	W 1026	331.7	W 1474	433.6	APP EMET TELE RADIO
7649	PTS NES OF EQUIPMT OF 76	W 5180	293.3	W 5921	341.5	W 7297	440.9	W 8116	501.2	PIECES DE LA DIV 76
76491	PTS NES OF APPAR OF 7641	W 855	126.3	W 899	152.4	W 1283	205.2	W 1667	223.5	PIECES POUR 764.1
76493	TELECOMM EQUIPMT PTS NES	W 2791	127.6	W 3249	136.7	W 3993	182.0	W 4110	215.4	PIECES 761,762,764.3,8
77	ELECTRIC MACHNRY NES ETC		1605.1		2039.9		1992.9		2313.8	MACH APP ELECT NDA

4. General Imports C.I.F. by Commodities according to the S.I.T.C. (Rev. 2) in million U.S. Dollars
Importations Générales C.A.F. par Produits d'après la C.T.C.I. (Rév. 2) en millions de Dollars E.U.

SITC CTCI	COMMODITY	1994 QUANTITY QUANTITE	1994 VALUE VALEUR	1995 QUANTITY QUANTITE	1995 VALUE VALEUR	1996 QUANTITY QUANTITE	1996 VALUE VALEUR	1997 QUANTITY QUANTITE	1997 VALUE VALEUR	PRODUIT
771	ELECTRIC POWER MACHY NES	W 8279	124.1	W 11822	186.8	W 9380	133.1	W 9781	170.3	MACH PROD,TRANS ELECTR
772	SWITCHGEAR ETC,PARTS NES	W 8195	293.6	W 10118	385.7	W 12733	363.4	W 12552	421.6	APP COUPURE,SECT ETC
7721	SWITCHGEAR ETC	W 7758	258.5	W 9682	336.3	W 12274	314.0	W 11909	363.7	APP COUPURE,SECTIONMNT
773	ELECTR DISTRIBUTNG EQUIP	W 21066	120.6	W 27584	167.2	W 38426	177.9	W 40337	215.3	EQUIPMT DISTRIBUTION ELECT
7731	INSULATED WIRE,CABLE ETC	W 19993	107.1	W 26274	150.4	W 37052	160.1	W 38552	194.1	FILS,CABLES ISOLES ELECT
775	HOUSEHOLD TYPE EQUIP NES	W 46395	372.7	W 49093	434.6	W 49353	422.6	W 57216	448.0	MACH,APP USAGE DOMESTQUE
7758	ELECTRO-THERMIC APPL NES	W 13260	133.1	W 13804	149.9	W 14947	157.7	W 19168	178.6	APP ELECTROTHERMIQ NDA
776	TRANSISTORS,VALVES,ETC	W 2842	252.1	W 2371	318.6	W 3079	323.3	W 2526	410.5	LAMPES,TUBES,VALVES
7764	ELECTRONIC MICROCIRCUITS	W 269	175.1	W 320	228.1	W 297	213.0	W 1228	308.1	MICROSTRUCTURES ELECTRON
778	ELECTRICAL MACHINERY NES	W 28938	377.4	W 31617	471.2	W 36389	500.6	W 46510	571.8	AUTRES MACH ELECT NDA
7788	OTH ELEC MACHY,EQUIP NES	W 5341	144.7	W 5172	179.9	W 5823	168.4	W 5751	199.1	AUT MACH APP ELEC NDA
78	ROAD VEHICLES		2626.6		3284.1		3309.3		3506.0	VEHICULES ROUTIERS
781	PASS MOTOR VEH EXC BUSES	W 180740	1469.8	W 171656	1666.2	W 177022	1718.9	W 197314	1715.8	AUTO TRANSPORT PERSONNES
782	LORRIES,SPCL MTR VEH NES	W 56498	483.4	W 74026	751.4	W 67000	681.6	W 88503	747.1	VEHICULES SPECIAUX,MARCH
7821	LORRIES,TRUCKS	W 55887	478.2	W 73348	745.1	W 66387	675.9	W 87468	737.6	VEHICULES TRANSP MARCHAND
784	MOTOR VEH PRTS,ACCES NES	W 46681	375.7	W 54396	449.6	W 57907	456.8	W 62325	501.6	PIECES 722,781,782,783
7849	OTHER MOTOR VEHCL PARTS	W 45055	358.0	W 52821	426.6	W 56206	435.0	W 58833	465.9	PIECES 722,781,782,783
785	CYCLES,ETC MOTRZD OR NOT	W 10401	119.7	W 13222	155.3	W 13688	163.7	W 15280	180.6	MOTOCYCLES SCOOTERS
786	TRAILERS,NONMOTR VEH,NES	W 29012	125.1	W 45328	205.0	W 56001	246.1	W 69852	289.6	REMORQUES,CADRES,CONTAIN
7861	TRAILERS,TRANSP CONTAINR	W 17898	68.6	W 31224	127.5	W 38708	165.9	W 51196	201.1	REMORQUES TOUS VEHICULES
78612	OTHER TRAILERS	W 8873	33.0	W 17777	79.5	W 23932	114.6	W 33319	135.9	REMORQUES TRANSP MARCH
79	OTHR TRANSPORT EQUIPMENT		771.1		651.8		735.2		598.8	AUTRE MATERIEL TRANSPORT
792	AIRCRAFT ETC	W 605	180.0	W 1342	382.3	W 819	405.9	W 816	341.8	APP NAVIGATION AERIENNE
7924	AIRCRFT NES OVER 15000KG	W 212	96.2	W 894	282.2	W 449	289.2	W 211	184.9	AERODYNES PLUS 15000 KG
793	SHIPS AND BOATS ETC	W 239141	559.0	W 65126	227.0	W 128843	303.9	W 38800	189.8	NAVIRES BATEAUX,ETC
7932	SHIPS AND BOATS NES	W 237592	548.4	W 60530	201.8	W 122099	254.9	W 33968	147.0	NAVIRES ET BATEAUX
79322	TANKERS OF ALL KINDS	W 65601	221.5			W 63118	82.2			BATEAUX-CITERNES
79323	OTHER CARGO VESSELS	W 170523	312.5	W 59504	189.6	W 57651	152.4	W 30646	106.9	AUT BATEAUX TRANS MARCH
8	MISC MANUFACTURED GOODS		4741.7		5607.3		5738.9		6721.1	ART MANUFACTURES DIVERS
812	*PLUMBG,HEATNG,LGHTNG EQ	W 17498	141.0	W 18140	164.4	W 22341	179.3	W 28171	223.6	APPAR SANITAIRES CHAUFFAGE
8124	LIGHTING EQUIPMENT NES	W 8345	82.0	W 9853	102.1	W 10653	104.9	W 14097	143.2	APPAREILS ECLAIRAGE ETC
821	*FURNITURE,PARTS THEREOF	W 93743	359.3	W 105556	442.8	W 112008	472.8	W 157611	612.2	MEUBLES ET PIECES
8211	CHAIRS,SEATS AND PARTS	W 23131	121.2	W 27046	156.0	W 27543	160.1	W 36378	196.5	SIEGES ET PIECES
82111	CHAIRS AND OTHER SEATS	W 20605	105.0	W 24420	137.0	W 24243	137.0	W 31827	166.0	SIEGES
8219	FURNITURE AND PARTS NES	W 60300	164.4	W 69133	205.5	W 73874	224.9	W 107421	311.6	AUTRES MEUBLES ET PIECES
82192	WOOD FURNITURE NES	W 25143	74.9	W 28417	92.1	W 35670	119.1	W 52085	161.3	MEUBLES NDA EN BOIS
84	CLOTHING AND ACCESSORIES		1483.5		1808.8		1834.6		2173.4	VETEMENTS
842	MENS OUTERWEAR NOT KNIT	W 11757	248.7	W 12622	310.2	W 12372	310.4	W 14977	346.9	VET DESSUS POUR HOMMES
8423	— TROUSERS,BREECHES ETC	W 6109	110.5	W 6321	137.0	W 6558	149.8	W 7742	161.2	PANTALONS HOMMES MAT TEX
843	WOMENS OUTERWEAR NONKNIT	W 17926	406.2	W 17859	486.8	W 18090	481.7	W 21787	564.9	VET DESSUS FEMMES MAT TEX
8439	— OTHER OUTER GARMENTS	W 12106	225.6	W 11055	246.3	W 11030	242.1	W 13145	283.0	AUT VET DES FEM MAT TEXT
845	OUTERWEAR KNIT NONELASTC	W 19574	367.3	W 21236	432.7	W 22547	461.3	W 25685	586.4	VET DESSOUS,ACCES BONNET
8451	— JERSEYS,PULLOVERS ETC	W 8859	177.2	W 10075	214.5	W 10915	231.4	W 11516	281.6	CHANDAILS,PULL-OVERS ETC
8459	— OTHER,CLTHG ACCESRYS	W 9622	163.6	W 9666	181.2	W 10186	195.3	W 12642	260.7	AUT VET DESSUS DE BONNE
846	UNDER GARMENTS KNITTED	W 13077	230.6	W 14532	288.8	W 15433	307.9	W 14819	338.9	SOUS VETS DE BONNETERIE
8462	— OF COTTON NON ELASTIC	W 11091	164.7	W 12414	212.5	W 13095	220.7	W 12828	249.5	SOUS-VET BONNET COTON
84629	—— OTHER	W 11091	164.7	W 12414	212.5	W 13095	220.7	W 12828	249.5	AUT SOUS-VET BONNET COTON
848	HEADGEAR,NONTXTL CLOTHNG	W 7370	101.6	W 7871	117.0	W 7317	113.4	W 9739	140.5	VET ACCES MAT AUT QUE TEX
851	*FOOTWEAR	W 18086	325.4	W 18081	366.8	W 17671	365.9	W 20549	429.4	CHAUSSURES
85102	FOOTWEAR LEATHER	W 13754	290.0	W 13647	322.1	W 13406	319.3	W 15751	377.6	CHAUS SEMELLES EN CUIR
87	PRECISION INSTRUMNTS NES		538.3		596.0		569.9		658.7	INSTRUM,APPAR SCIENT NDA
872	MEDICAL INSTRUMENTS NES	W 3811	147.0	W 3390	153.4	W 3347	157.2	W 3118	163.0	INSTR,APP MEDIC-CHIR NDA
87202	OTH MEDICAL INSTRUMENTS	W 3183	130.9	W 2778	134.2	W 2628	138.6	W 2321	140.8	INSTRUM,APP MEDECINE
874	MEASURNG,CONTROLNG INSTR	W 3485	324.4	W 3885	364.6	W 3677	326.7	W 5165	407.8	INSTRUMENTS DE MESURE
88	PHOTO EQU,OPTICL GDS ETC		271.2		321.9		326.5		392.3	APP,FOURN PHOTO,OP,MONTR
882	PHOTO,CINEMA SUPPLIES	W 8044	135.4	W 8405	148.9	W 8853	136.4	W 10383	174.4	PRODUITS PHOTO,CINEMA
89	MISC MANUFCTRD GOODS NES		1557.6		1826.8		1871.0		2135.7	ART MANUFACTURES DIVERS
892	PRINTED MATTER	W 48239	233.4	W 65063	271.9	W 80229	299.0	W 84910	357.6	IMPRIMES
8928	PRINTED MATTER NES	W 28969	112.5	W 41937	134.8	W 58454	153.9	W 57466	174.8	IMPRIMES NDA
893	ARTICLES OF PLASTIC NES		501.6		630.1		607.3		706.7	OUVRAGES EN MAT DIVIS 58
8931	PLSTC PACKG CONTNRS,LIDS	W 46579	132.1	W 52048	183.2	W 71629	172.1	W 69020	205.8	ART TRANSP EMBALLAGE ETC
8939	MISC PLASTIC ARTICLES	W 69176	359.9	W 76055	429.8	W 102924	420.8	W 90731	480.8	ART DIVERS EN MAT DIV 58
89399	OTHR PLASTC ARTICLES NES	W 59149	325.9	W 65454	389.2	W 90622	382.1	W 80026	434.4	AUT OUV MAT DIV 58
894	TOYS,SPORTING GOODS,ETC	W 26752	249.3	W 27941	285.8	W 31579	316.1	W 35769	338.1	VOITURES ENFANTS,JOUETS
8942	TOYS,INDOOR GAMES ETC	W 20726	179.6	W 21490	206.5	W 23735	226.5	W 26186	233.3	JOUETS,JEUX ETC
89423	TOYS NES	W 11898	112.4	W 12084	125.9	W 13318	138.8	W 15232	129.8	JOUETS,MODELES REDUITS
898	MUSICAL INSTRUMENTS,PTS	W 12404	295.6	W 12735	324.3	W 15272	312.5	W 16981	348.8	INSTRUMENTS DE MUSIQUE
8983	SOUND RECRDNG TAPE,DISCS	W 11744	278.3	W 11851	298.1	W 14194	283.9	W 15818	323.4	SUPPORTS SON POUR 763
89832	RECORDED DISCS,TAPES ETC	W 4579	194.3	W 4553	207.4	W 5381	208.0	W 4789	253.2	DISQUES,PHONO,BANDES
899	OTHER MANUFACTURED GOODS		164.3		198.9		218.4		240.0	AUT ART MANUF DIVERS NDA
9	GOODS NOT CLASSD BY KIND		2630.9		2976.6		3592.7		1567.6	ART TRANSACT NON CLASSES
931	*SPECIAL TRANSACTIONS		2596.3		2951.5		3567.9		1537.9	TRANS.SPECIALES

5. General Exports F.O.B. by Commodities according to the S.I.T.C. (Rev. 2) in million U.S. Dollars
Exportations Générales F.O.B. par Produits d'après la C.T.C.I. (Rév. 2) en millions de Dollars E.U.

SITC CTCI	COMMODITY	1994 QUANTITY QUANTITE	1994 VALUE VALEUR	1995 QUANTITY QUANTITE	1995 VALUE VALEUR	1996 QUANTITY QUANTITE	1996 VALUE VALEUR	1997 QUANTITY QUANTITE	1997 VALUE VALEUR	PRODUIT
	ALL COMMODITIES		41602.5		48789.2		48884.6		48800.5	TOUS PRODUITS
0	FOOD AND LIVE ANIMALS		9812.3		10879.4		10465.6		10639.1	ALIMENTS,ANIMAUX VIVANTS
001	*LIVE ANIMALS FOR FOOD	W 33021	70.1	W 50924	116.3	W 61342	136.5	W 85012	180.4	ANIMAUX VIVANTS
01	MEAT AND PREPARATIONS		3875.9		4118.9		3995.4		4133.9	VIANDES ET PREPARATIONS
011	MEAT FRESH,CHILLD,FROZEN	W 1089111	2878.0	W 1053837	3055.7	W 1007639	2888.7	W 1174131	3055.8	VIANDES FRAICHES,REF,CONGE
0111	BOVINE MEAT FRESH,FROZEN	W 127660	442.4	W 111580	417.5	W 98693	309.5	W 125142	356.6	VIANDES BOVIN FRAI,REF
01111	BOVINE MEAT WITH BONE IN	W 72841	256.3	W 69296	242.6	W 48922	152.8	W 61211	170.6	VIANDES BOVIN NON DESOSS
01112	BOVINE MEAT BONELESS	W 54819	186.2	W 42284	174.9	W 49771	156.7	W 63930	186.1	VIANDES BOVIN DESOSSEES
0113	PIG MEAT FRESH,CHLD,FRZN	W 774202	2195.8	W 739781	2374.6	W 711103	2302.6	W 821955	2406.2	VIANDE DE PORC
0114	POULTRY FRESH CHLLD,FRZN	W 103600	158.5	W 105268	164.5	W 102291	179.2	W 103113	176.7	VOLAILLES MORTES
012	MEAT DRIED,SALTED,SMOKED	W 127584	359.4	W 120990	425.5	W 121582	465.3	W 130183	452.6	VIANDE,ABATS SALES,SECHES
0121	PIG MEAT DRIED,SLTD,SMKD	W 127582	359.4	W 120990	425.5	W 121582	465.3	W 130112	452.3	LARD,JAMBONS
014	MEAT PREPD,PRSVD,NES ETC	W 216976	638.6	W 191284	637.8	W 191170	641.6	W 193925	625.6	CONSERVES DE VIANDES
0142	SAUSAGES INCLDING TINNED	W 52430	143.1	W 50795	155.0	W 55522	174.3	W 55390	169.6	SAUCISSES,SAUCISSONS
0149	OTH PREPARD,PRESRVD MEAT	W 164516	495.2	W 140429	482.3	W 135619	467.0	W 138502	455.7	AUTRES PREP DE VIANDES
02	DAIRY PRODCTS,BIRDS'EGGS		1362.2		1623.3		1596.3		1505.1	PRODUITS LAITIERS,OEUFS
022	MILK AND CREAM	W 177660	376.1	W 168191	398.6	W 158665	376.4	W 168783	379.7	LAIT ET CREME
0224	MILK,CREAM PRESERVED ETC	W 137009	324.3	W 129479	345.2	W 123836	325.6	W 129098	321.7	LAIT,CREME CONS,CONC
02243	MILK DRY,OVER 1.5% FAT	W 105905	272.8	W 92650	271.7	W 85886	253.0	W 92336	257.6	LAIT POUDRE SUP 1.5%
023	BUTTER	W 49412	170.0	W 50978	190.5	W 54593	199.5	W 43756	137.3	BEURRE
024	CHEESE AND CURD	W 236773	808.4	W 254974	1014.2	W 241724	999.0	W 250467	965.3	FROMAGE ET CAILLEBOTTE
03	FISH AND PREPARATIONS		2259.5		2193.3		2123.0		2093.5	POISSONS ET PREPARATIONS
034	FISH,FRESH,CHILLED,FROZN	W 369985	1104.3	W 339225	1053.0	W 355167	965.0	W 356521	990.5	POISSON FRAIS, REFRIG,CONG
0341	FISH FRSH,CHLLD,EX FILLT	W 166551	540.9	W 158134	510.3	W 188290	429.8	W 184962	466.0	POISSON FRAIS,REFRIGERE
0342	FISH FROZEN,EXCL FILLETS	W 74581	145.3	W 66065	131.8	W 49812	123.0	W 56535	123.1	POISSONS CONGELES
0343	FISH FILLETS,FRESH,CHLLD	W 65441	165.1	W 61982	172.6	W 57871	176.0	W 62758	182.9	FILETS FRAIS,REFRIGERES
0344	FISH FILLETS,FROZEN	W 63413	253.1	W 53044	238.5	W 59193	236.5	W 52265	218.7	FILETS CONGELES
035	FISH SALTED,DRIED,SMOKED	W 56177	359.2	W 40030	298.3	W 42154	289.0	W 40414	275.0	POISSON SECHE,SALE,FUME
03504	FISH SMOKED	W 11676	158.2	W 13192	187.2	W 15032	186.6	W 19210	203.7	POISSONS FUMES
036	SHELL FISH FRESH,FROZEN	W 72421	313.5	W 70061	330.9	W 85389	385.8	W 103669	376.3	CRUSTACES,MOLLUSQUES
037	FISH ETC PREPD,PRSVD NES	W 113479	482.7	W 102528	511.2	W 96573	483.3	W 101006	451.9	POIS,CRUST,MOL PREPARES
0371	FISH PREPARD,PRESRVD NES	W 74554	265.9	W 70580	285.4	W 69963	273.6	W 73440	259.4	CONSERVES DE POISSONS
0372	SHELL FISH PREPRD,PRESVD	W 38925	216.8	W 31948	225.8	W 26609	209.8	W 27565	192.6	CRUSTACES,COQUIL PREPARES
04	CEREALS AND PREPARATIONS		754.6		1035.1		953.6		917.3	CEREALES ET PRODUITS
041	WHEAT ETC UNMILLED	W 794429	103.2	W 1585305	229.1	W 823946	154.7	W 1061819	163.9	FROMENT,EPEAUTRE
0412	OTHER WHEAT ETC UNMILLED	W 770661	99.2	W 1579196	228.0	W 823436	154.6	W 1061800	163.9	AUTRE FROMENT NON MOULU
043	BARLEY UNMILLED	W 691825	112.7	W 791420	190.6	W 699612	163.5	W 801292	140.2	ORGE NON MONDEE
048	CEREAL ETC PREPARATIONS	W 282995	512.4	W 294136	574.8	W 310574	551.0	W 374375	572.0	PREPTNS A BASE CEREALES
0484	BAKERY PRODUCTS	W 113574	301.7	W 121549	340.7	W 115323	325.1	W 149023	341.4	PRODUITS DE BOULANGERIE
04841	BREAD,BISCUIT,COM WAFERS	W 55874	120.4	W 69444	160.0	W 63854	151.3	W 89531	167.1	PAINS,BISCUITS DE MER
04842	PASTRY, CAKES ETC	W 57700	181.3	W 52105	180.7	W 51468	173.8	W 59492	174.4	PATISSERIE ETC.
05	VEGETABLES AND FRUIT		231.5		229.6		213.9		259.6	LEGUMES ET FRUITS
06	SUGAR AND PREPS,HONEY		278.4		312.5		268.0		250.3	SUCRES ET PRODUITS
062	SUGAR CANDY NON–CHOCLATE	W 45568	170.2	W 45723	206.4	W 38851	167.2	W 38199	139.4	SUCRERIES
081	*FEEDING STUFF FOR ANIML	W 851879	446.7	W 994642	584.5	W 920861	581.6	W 1034963	588.2	NOURRITURE POUR ANIMAUX
0814	MEAT OR FISH MEAL FODDER	W 366270	190.7	W 439261	254.1	W 402307	252.1	W 379622	232.1	FARINES DE VIANDES,POISSONS
08142	FISH MEAL FODDER	W 285361	163.8	W 355664	224.5	W 331591	225.2	W 286234	198.4	FARINES DE POISSONS
0819	FOOD WASTE AND FEED NES	W 266860	228.4	W 280627	290.6	W 283617	290.9	W 408583	312.4	DECHETS,ALIMENTS NDA
08199	FODDER NES,INCL SWEETNED	W 246720	223.7	W 259716	286.5	W 267419	286.2	W 356109	304.8	PREPARATIONS FOURRAGERES
09	MISC EDIBLE PRODUCTS		418.9		543.6		484.9		601.5	PREP ALIMENTAIRES DIVERSES
098	EDIBLE PRODCTS,PREPS NES	W 104852	377.4	W 109781	484.7	W 113746	436.5	W 146053	549.2	PREP ALIMENTAIRES NDA
09809	MISC FOOD PREPRTIONS NES	W 76722	331.2	W 85315	434.7	W 83733	378.1	W 109087	481.2	PREP ALIMENTAIRES NDA
1	BEVERAGES AND TOBACCO		430.6		539.5		483.7		492.2	BOISSONS ET TABACS
11	BEVERAGES		285.8		356.1		311.4		321.8	BOISSONS
112	ALCOHOLIC BEVERAGES	W 288730	259.8	W 331353	323.0	W 301170	284.2	W 306066	290.2	BOISSONS ALCOOLIQUES
1123	BEER,ALE,STOUT,PORTER	W 265737	204.1	W 311227	254.1	W 283832	221.4	W 280906	208.5	BIERES
12	TOBACCO AND MANUFACTURES		144.9		183.4		172.4		170.4	TABACS BRUTS FABRIQUES
122	TOBACCO,MANUFACTURED	W 5628	132.5	W 6331	166.8	W 5821	156.3	W 6076	153.0	TABACS FABRIQUES
2	CRUDE MATERLS,EXCL FUELS		1460.8		1760.4		1779.4		1776.7	MAT BRUTES NON COMESTIBLES
21	HIDES,SKINS,FURS UNDRSSD		396.5		393.1		534.9		479.7	CUIRS,PEAUX BRUTS
212	FURSKINS,RAW	W 1587	344.1	W 1625	330.5	W 1523	482.5	W 1823	425.2	PELLETERIES BRUTES
21201	MINK SKINS,RAW	W 1245	293.2	W 1289	276.5	W 1120	406.4	W 1360	374.5	PEAUX DE VISON BRUTES
24	CORK AND WOOD		112.9		145.2		121.0		161.2	LIEGE ET BOIS
28	METALLIFEROUS ORES,SCRAP		158.9		245.3		161.9		181.9	MINERAIS METAL,DECHETS
288	NONFERR METAL SCRAP NES	W 103832	98.4	W 118671	154.7	W 77930	84.9	W 82662	86.3	DECHETS NON FERREUX
2882	OTHER BASE MTL SCRAP NES	W 98559	97.3	W 115010	152.9	W 72513	82.5	W 76986	84.3	AUTRES DECHETS
29	CRUDE ANIMAL,VEG MAT NES		619.5		767.1		784.4		795.4	MATIERES BRUTES ANIM,VEGET
292	CRUDE VEG MATERIALS NES	W 184031	511.6	W 214920	665.9	W 228352	672.4	W 264847	681.2	MAT BRUTES VEGETALES NDA
2925	SEEDS,ETC FOR PLANTING	W 57207	117.4	W 68162	155.2	W 77447	167.4	W 89080	185.4	SEMENCES NDA
2926	LIVE PLANTS,BULBS,ETC	W 80605	314.6	W 101975	416.6	W 108393	427.6	W 118625	400.1	BULBES,TUBERCULES
29269	LIVE PLANTS NES	W 80177	312.6	W 101582	414.3	W 108072	426.6	W 118084	397.9	AUTRES PLANTES VIVANTES
3	MINERAL FUELS ETC		1041.6		1270.7		2108.2		1839.7	COMBUSTIBLES MINERAUX LUB
33	PETROLEUM AND PRODUCTS		890.2		1151.3		1538.9		1560.6	PETROLE ET DERIVES
333	CRUDE PETROLEUM	W 2897144	338.2	W 5130018	641.4	W 4616379	717.8	W 6545596	919.5	HUILES BRUTES DE PETROLE
334	PETROLEUM PRODUCTS,REFIN	W 3769416	548.4	W 3212929	505.3	W 4340760	810.5	W 3455021	630.6	PRODUITS RAFFINES
3341	GASOLINE,OTH LIGHT OILS					W 4335474	799.6			ESSENCES POUR MOTEURS
33419	OTH LIGHT PETROLEUM OILS					W 4335474	799.6			AUTRES HUILES LEGERES
351	*ELECTRIC CURRENT		143.1		108.1		547.8		251.2	ENERGIE ELECTRIQUE
4	ANIMAL,VEGETABLE OIL,FAT		175.0		261.3		248.8		264.2	HUILES,GRAISSES ANIM,VEG
5	CHEMCLS,RELATED PROD NES		3701.9		4587.9		4556.6		4854.3	PRODUITS CHIMIQUES
51	ORGANIC CHEMICALS		648.7		680.3		662.2		686.1	PROD CHIMIQ ORGANIQUES
516	OTHER ORGANIC CHEMICALS	W 61468	475.8	W 57042	475.9	W 64587	473.6	W 68515	459.4	AUTRES PROD ORGANIQUES
5169	ORGANIC CHEMICALS,NES	W 59730	465.1	W 56399	470.8	W 64119	470.4	W 68149	453.7	PROD CHIM ORGANIQUES NDA
51691	ENZYMES	W 58682	461.8	W 55312	467.4	W 62393	465.5	W 66602	449.9	ENZYMES
53	DYES,TANNING,COLOUR PROD		363.5		467.6		449.1		498.3	PROD TEINTURE,COLORANTS
531	SYNT DYE,NAT INDGO,LAKES	W 15823	163.5	W 19655	219.3	W 26323	196.2	W 24752	200.1	MAT COLOR ORGAN,LAQUES
5311	SYNTHIC ORGNIC DYESTUFFS	W 15733	163.0	W 19581	218.8	W 26243	195.8	W 24668	199.6	MAT COLOR ORGAN SYNTHET
533	PIGMENTS,PAINTS,ETC	W 79602	190.2	W 81919	231.4	W 88656	233.0	W 120936	278.4	PIGMENTS,PEINTURES,VERNIS
5334	VARNISHES,DISTEMPERS ETC	W 56219	149.0	W 59159	182.0	W 59456	182.2	W 69797	203.4	PEINTURES A L'EAU
53342	OTH PAINTS,VARNISHES ETC	W 46608	119.1	W 48996	147.3	W 48464	145.8	W 55165	157.1	AUTRES PEINTURES,VERNIS
541	*MEDICINAL,PHARM PRODUCT	MK 15593	1615.2	MK 16531	2160.9		2214.7	MK 18715	2272.5	PROD MEDICINAUX PHARMACEUT
5417	MEDICAMENTS	MK 10324	1258.9	MK 10945	1767.4	MK 11620	1768.5	MK 11676	1751.9	MEDICAMENTS
54172	— CONTAINING HORMONES	K 2911955	858.4	K 3815242	1196.2	K 3737229	1069.3	K 3872463	1087.6	MED CONTENANT HORMONES
54179	— CONTNG OTH SUBSTANCES	K 6296014	349.0	K 5905131	499.4	K 6747460	632.8	K 6287652	596.5	MED CONT AUT SUBSTANCES
55	PERFUME,CLEANING ETC PRD		264.5		292.0		279.0		323.8	PROD POUR PARFUM,TOILETTE
554	SOAP,CLEANSING ETC PREPS	W 111879	149.8	W 114974	174.2	W 117248	153.0	W 137070	176.8	SAVONS,PRODUITS DETERSIFS
5542	WASHING PREPARATIONS ETC	W 108546	137.8	W 110130	158.0	W 112562	138.1	W 130015	156.5	PROD ORG TENSIO–ACT NDA
58	PLASTIC MATERIALS ETC		316.9		397.6		415.7		417.8	MAT PLAST ARTIFICIELLES
583	POLYMERIZATION ETC PRODS	W 106685	266.7	W 104546	333.3	W 115900	355.5	W 143659	359.2	PROD POLYMERISATION
5839	OTH POLYMRZTION ETC PROD	W 35844	139.5	W 37832	179.6	W 43562	199.0	W 45725	181.8	AUT PROD POLYMER COPOLYM
59	CHEMICAL MATERIALS NES		390.9		457.6		439.3		523.7	MAT PROD CHIMIQUES NDA

5. General Exports F.O.B. by Commodities according to the S.I.T.C. (Rev. 2) in million U.S. Dollars
Exportations Générales F.O.B. par Produits d'après la C.T.C.I. (Rév. 2) en millions de Dollars E.U.

SITC CTCI	COMMODITY	1994 QUANTITY QUANTITE	1994 VALUE VALEUR	1995 QUANTITY QUANTITE	1995 VALUE VALEUR	1996 QUANTITY QUANTITE	1996 VALUE VALEUR	1997 QUANTITY QUANTITE	1997 VALUE VALEUR	PRODUIT
592	STARCH,INULIN,GLUTEN,ETC	W 208518	159.9	W 156615	172.3	W 169225	188.2	W 203837	201.0	AMIDONS,INUL,GLUT FROM
5922	ALBUMINOID SUBSTAN,GLUES	W 88604	119.6	W 91280	138.0	W 83769	140.0	W 92142	154.1	MAT ALBUMIN,COLLES
598	MISCEL CHEM PRODUCTS NES	W 80505	214.7	W 82881	261.4	W 82219	223.4	W 95253	280.2	PROD DIV INDUST CHIM NDA
5989	CHEM PRODUCTS,PREPS NES	W 34765	116.6	W 34715	139.8	W 43126	127.3	W 54438	201.6	PROD PREP CHIMIQUES NDA
6	BASIC MANUFACTURES		4247.6		5385.2		5126.4		5403.0	ART MANUFACTURES
62	RUBBER MANUFACTURES NES		113.0		128.5		145.1		156.0	CAOUTCHOUC MANUFACTURE
63	WOOD,CORK MANUFACTRS NES		634.1		797.9		750.0		764.8	OUVRAGES LIEGE ET BOIS
635	WOOD MANUFACTURES NES	W 187540	557.1	W 204108	710.3	W 196103	668.1	W 211634	680.0	ART MANUF EN BOIS NDA
6353	BUILDERS WOODWRK,PREFABS	W 148055	462.1	W 157959	587.4	W 148600	546.5	W 172256	569.1	OUVRAGES DE MENUISERIE
64	PAPER,PAPERBOARD AND MFR		484.9		610.4		593.4		578.6	PAPIERS,CARTONS & OUVRAGES
641	PAPER AND PAPERBOARD	W 293105	217.8	W 279015	282.0	W 274792	233.7	W 296425	226.8	PAPIERS ET CARTONS
6415	PAPER,PAPERBRD,BULK,NES	W 209293	120.8	W 203787	179.9	W 190690	124.9	W 185126	108.1	PAPIERS,CARTONS ROULEAUX
64159	OTHER PAPER ETC,BULK,NES	W 207873	117.8	W 201792	177.0	W 189977	122.8	W 184708	105.6	AUT PAPIER ROULEAUX FEUILLES
642	PAPER,ETC,PRECUT,ARTS OF	W 149807	267.2	W 157607	328.4	W 175230	359.8	W 187787	351.8	PAP,CARTONS DECOUPES
6421	PAPER ETC CONTAINERS	W 75082	123.1	W 83815	159.6	W 92199	169.0	W 93645	156.4	BOITES,SACS EMBALLAGES
6428	PAPER ETC ARTICLES NES	W 69064	126.0	W 69933	152.4	W 78634	162.2	W 88575	173.8	OUVRAGES EN PATE A PAPIER
65	TEXTILE YARN,FABRICS,ETC		669.1		819.8		855.1		908.8	FILS,TISSUS,ARTICLES TEXTILE
651	TEXTILE YARN	W 18171	128.7	W 20783	171.2	W 22149	183.4	W 26268	187.4	FILS TEXTILES
6514	SYN FIB YRN,BULK,MONOFIL	W 14047	97.1	W 16181	133.0	W 17908	148.0	W 21173	147.1	FILS CONT 85% FIB TEXT SYNTH
659	FLOOR COVERINGS,ETC	W 24317	124.5	W 25960	146.5	W 26855	148.8	W 17392	143.5	COUVRE–PARQUETS,TAPIS ETC
66	NONMETAL MINERAL MFS NES		583.0		675.3		616.3		649.9	ART MIN NON METALLIQUES
663	MINERAL MANUFCTURES NES	W 874178	226.8	W 826367	253.9	W 834885	248.3	W 956289	237.0	ART MIN MANUF NDA
6633	MINRL MFS NES NONCERAMIC	W 742273	169.6	W 728670	182.1	W 742639	181.1	W 760362	166.0	OUVR MAT MINERALE NDA
67	IRON AND STEEL		560.3		769.8		701.5		745.2	FER ET ACIER
674	IRN,STL UNIV,PLATE,SHEET	W 373766	188.5	W 439442	268.5	W 455374	269.0	W 550470	281.5	LARGES PLATS,TOLES
6744	IRN,STL HVY PLATE,ROLLED	W 293332	130.0	W 343939	191.6	W 366384	195.6	W 460197	213.0	TOLES LAMINEES PLUS 4.75 MM
67441	— OF IRON OR SIMPLE STL	W 290628	124.8	W 339831	178.6	W 358362	177.6	W 450244	195.2	TOLES NON ACIER FIN CARB
678	IRON,STL TUBES,PIPES,ETC	W 137978	204.3	W 158281	281.8	W 134190	254.9	W 155048	247.7	TUBES,TUYAUX EN FONTE,FER
6783	IRON,STL TUBES,PIPES NES	W 121542	134.6	W 136779	182.8	W 114543	157.6	W 130634	144.1	AUT TUBES,TUYAUX FER,ACIER
68	NON–FERROUS METALS		169.2		265.1		208.2		217.0	METAUX NON FERREUX
684	ALUMINIUM	W 42357	132.6	W 53089	209.6	W 44846	176.1	W 56848	182.2	ALUMINIUM
6842	ALUMINIUM,ALLOYS WORKED	W 25002	105.5	W 29293	164.1	W 24163	145.5	W 27224	134.7	ALUMINIUM,ALLIAGES OUVRE
69	METAL MANUFACTURES NES		974.0		1250.5		1179.3		1307.0	ART MANUFACT EN METAL NDA
691	STRUCTURES AND PARTS NES	W 102906	342.7	W 110971	441.4	W 106762	385.5	W 116324	374.5	CONSTRUCT FER,ACIER,ALU
6911	STRUCTURES,PARTS IRN,STL	W 85151	209.0	W 91163	274.2	W 88162	235.5	W 96550	229.2	CONSTRUCT FER,ACIER,FONTE
6912	STRUCTURES,PARTS ALUMNM	W 17756	133.7	W 19808	167.3	W 18600	150.1	W 19773	145.4	CONSTRUCT ALUMINIUM
699	BASE METAL MFRS NES	W 53254	332.1	W 62414	430.4	W 69377	415.8	W 79639	452.0	ART MANUFACTURES MET NDA
6991	LOCKSMITHS WARES,ETC	W 16871	118.6	W 19401	143.9	W 27313	140.2	W 30794	153.6	ARTICLES DE SERRURERIE
7	MACHINES,TRANSPORT EQUIP		10259.6		12248.2		12486.4		13140.2	MACHINES MATERIEL TRANSPORT
71	POWER GENERATING EQUIPMT		656.5		934.0		926.8		940.0	MACHINES GENERATRICES
713	INTRNL COMBUS PSTN ENGIN	W 7123	120.4	W 6293	143.4	W 7560	174.7	W 8469	200.0	MOTEURS EXPL COMB INT, PIECE
7139	PISTON ENGINE PARTS NES	W 3140	82.4	W 3872	106.8	W 5485	145.3	W 6422	172.3	PIECES POUR 713.2,3,8
716	ROTATING ELECTRIC PLANT	W 36295	417.4	W 55576	691.8	W 55284	617.9	W 73468	615.5	APP ELECTR ROTATIFS,PIECES
7161	DC MOTORS AND GENERATORS	W 21076	229.6	W 36705	439.9	W 39524	413.0	W 55992	431.2	MOTEURS COURANT CONTINU
72	MACHS FOR SPCL INDUSTRYS		1550.5		1911.3		1947.4		1819.4	MAC SPECIALES POUR INDUST
721	AGRIC MACHY,EXC TRACTORS	W 41931	442.0	W 43016	561.2	W 50207	603.1	W 55269	530.0	MACHINES AGRICOLES
7212	HARVESTING ETC MACHINES	W 25480	207.8	W 24364	222.3	W 30335	273.6	W 31269	219.4	ENGINS POUR LA RECOLTE
7213	DAIRY MACHINERY NES	W 4833	165.8	W 8337	267.3	W 7117	248.8	W 6259	201.7	MACHINES DE LAITERIE NDA
72139	PTS NES OF MACHY OF 7213	W 3583	129.4	W 4994	186.1	W 3881	153.6	W 3085	120.3	PIECES POUR MACH 721.3
726	PRINTG,BKBINDG MACHY,PTS	W 3649	125.6	W 4057	182.5	W 4439	209.0	W 5233	224.2	MACHINES POUR IMPRIMERIE
727	FOOD MACHRY NON–DOMESTIC	W 12783	291.6	W 13152	354.3	W 14146	359.3	W 12780	315.3	MACH INDUSTRIES ALIMENT
7272	OTH FOOD PROC MCHY,PARTS	W 10885	274.1	W 11239	328.9	W 12333	336.8	W 11256	292.8	AUT MACH IND ALIMENTAIRE
72722	INDUS FOOD PROC MACH NES	W 10420	263.2	W 10763	314.9	W 11504	315.7	W 10456	273.6	MACHINES BOULANGERIE
728	OTH MACHY FOR SPCL INDUS	W 32112	478.9	W 31370	568.9	W 32362	537.1	W 31766	499.8	AUT MACH IND PARTICULIERES
7283	OTHR MINERAL WORKG MACHY	W 18607	247.4	W 18408	308.3	W 19307	288.7	W 17140	239.6	MACH TRIER,CRIBLER,BROYER
72839	PTS NES OF MACHY OF 7283	W 10814	155.1	W 10308	189.3	W 14060	199.8	W 13129	186.8	PIECES MACH DU 728.3
7284	MACHY FOR SPCL INDUS NES	W 11200	205.7	W 10628	229.5	W 11108	216.3	W 11680	226.6	MACH SPEC IND PARTICUL.
74	GENRL INDUSTRL MACHY NES		2789.6		3534.1		3431.0		3472.6	MACH APP INDUSTRIE
741	HEATING,COOLING EQUIPMNT	W 61518	794.0	W 67354	1022.2	W 69854	995.6	W 79620	960.5	MACH CHAUFFAGE,PIECES
7414	NONDOM REFRIG EQUIPT,PTS	W 34781	349.0	W 37831	469.5	W 38004	427.3	W 45687	422.6	MAT PRODUCTION DU FROID
74141	REFRIG EQUIP NONDOMESTIC	W 28713	265.1	W 30335	339.9	W 30788	317.2	W 37564	321.3	REFIG INDUSTRIELS
7416	HEATING,COOLING EQU NES	W 18983	320.3	W 19702	378.8	W 19506	375.3	W 20306	331.2	APP CHANGEMENT TEMP
742	PUMPS FOR LIQUIDS ETC	W 27765	375.6	W 30001	456.3	W 30482	478.9	W 31740	468.6	POMPES MOTO–POMPES
7422	CENTRIFUGAL PUMPS NES	W 12953	178.5	W 13569	213.5	W 14204	228.3	W 15358	221.8	POMPES CENTRIF NON 742.81
7429	PTS NES OF PUMPS OF 742	W 14064	179.4	W 15705	218.8	W 14948	222.7	W 15215	219.1	PIECES POUR GROUPE 742
743	PUMPS NES,CENTRFUGES ETC	W 22520	353.9	W 28634	467.9	W 27604	443.3	W 43603	466.2	POMPES COMPRES,VENT ETC
7439	PTS NES OF APP OF 7435,6	W 10306	142.8	W 14407	201.0	W 13072	188.1	W 19747	202.8	PIECES 743.5 ET 743.6
744	MECHANICAL HANDLING EQU	W 42641	416.2	W 40190	450.5	W 40881	431.0	W 44779	467.1	EQUIP MANUTENTION PIECES
7442	LIFTING,LOADING MACH NES	W 30543	315.1	W 27934	320.4	W 27768	297.5	W 28062	302.6	APP LEVAGE,MANUTENTION
74428	OTH HANDLING ETC MCH NES	W 25662	283.6	W 23944	282.3	W 24769	270.5	W 24844	272.2	AUT APP LEVAGE ETC
745	NONELEC MACHY,TOOLS NES	W 17219	310.3	W 21739	449.7	W 22311	445.7	W 24833	451.3	AUT MACH NON ELEC,PIECES
7452	OTH NONELEC MCHS,PTS NES	W 16990	304.0	W 21559	442.0	W 22120	438.5	W 24605	442.6	AUT MACH NON ELEC,PIECES
74527	SPRAYING MACHINERY	W 12550	142.3	W 14593	192.9	W 16094	209.8	W 18095	200.6	APP PROJETER ETC LIQUID
749	NONELEC MACH PTS,ACC NES	W 29286	539.9	W 37254	687.6	W 34060	636.8	W 40016	659.1	PIECES MACH NON ELEC NDA
7492	COCKS,VALVES ETC NES	W 20350	452.9	W 26049	580.6	W 22487	536.0	W 28392	545.9	ART ROB,SIM POUR TUYAUX
75	OFFICE MACHNES,ADP EQUIP		876.0		857.2		901.8		1040.5	MACH BUREAU TRAIT AUTOM
752	AUTOMTIC DATA PROC EQUIP	W 5793	498.0	W 4013	388.7	W 9186	461.8	W 102503	520.8	MACH TRAIT INFORMATION
7523	DIGITL CENTRL PROCESSORS	W 1903	166.3	W 799	102.8	W 6022	138.3	W 906	138.6	UNITES CENTRALES
7525	ADP PERIPHERAL UNITS	W 2192	152.6	W 1434	82.5	W 1418	89.2	W 99856	121.9	UNITES PERIPHERIQUES
759	OFFICE,ADP MCH PTS,ACCES	W 4160	350.0	W 4514	432.2	W 4999	409.5	W 446239	491.6	PIECES DU 751 ET 752
7599	ACCTG,ETC,ADP MCH PTS,AC	W 3642	334.3	W 4074	416.7	W 3711	378.6	W 441863	437.9	PIECES DU 751 ET 752
76	TELECOMM,SOUND EQUIPMENT		944.1		1323.7		1395.0		1781.5	EQUIPMENT DE TELECOM
761	TELEVISION RECEIVERS	W 5031	96.1	W 7602	170.1	W 6197	125.7	W 7642	154.1	RECEPTEURS DE TELEVISION
7611	COLOUR TV RECEIVERS	W 5024	96.0	W 7582	168.7	W 6194	125.5	W 7639	153.8	RECEPTEURS COULEUR
762	RADIO BROADCAST RECEIVRS	W 2330	87.9	W 4255	147.4	W 3092	107.0	W 4198	120.1	RECEPTEURS RADIODIFFUSION
764	TELECOM EQPT,PTS,ACC NES	W 23040	711.7	W 29252	921.3	W 34355	1110.1	W 31284	1448.8	EQUIP TELECOM,PIECES
7641	LINE TELEPHONE,ETC EQUIP	W 658	132.6	W 740	108.5	W 802	114.6	W 2164	188.1	APP TELEPHON PAR FIL
7642	MICROPH,LOUDSPKR,AMPLIFR	W 14960	177.0	W 19119	239.3	W 22108	303.0	W 18774	364.5	MICRO,HAUT–PARLEUR,AMPLI
7643	TV,RADIO TRANSMITTRS ETC	W 628	156.7	W 745	246.2	W 1229	335.8	W 1842	514.1	APP EMET TELE RADIO
7649	PTS NES OF EQUIPMT OF 76	W 6633	214.8	W 8471	284.5	W 10091	320.6	W 8397	351.0	PIECES DE LA DIV 76
76493	TELECOMM EQUIPMT PTS NES	W 5538	160.9	W 7250	217.4	W 7989	241.3	W 6061	205.9	PIECES 761,762,764.3,8
77	ELECTRIC MACHNRY NES ETC		1347.8		1580.8		1607.2		1806.3	MACH APP ELECT NDA
771	ELECTRIC POWER MACHY NES	W 5202	169.5	W 7096	210.2	W 7482	229.9	W 21626	262.3	MACH PROD,TRANS ELECTR
7712	OTH ELEC POWER MACHY NES	W 3844	145.2	W 5259	173.2	W 5713	192.2	W 20090	215.4	AUT APP PROD TRANSF ELEC
77121	STATIC CONVERTERS ETC	W 2075	117.3	W 2630	142.9	W 2842	157.0	W 17772	178.1	CONVERTISSEURS STATIQUES
772	SWITCHGEAR ETC,PARTS NES	W 6321	230.1	W 7257	299.6	W 8009	316.6	W 11682	327.8	APP COUPURE,SECT ETC
7721	SWITCHGEAR ETC	W 5817	159.7	W 6645	204.8	W 7396	220.6	W 10855	220.6	APP COUPURE,SECTIONMNT
774	ELECTRO–MEDCL,XRAY EQUIP	W 1145	154.7	W 1246	190.0	W 1106	168.3	W 1393	186.6	APPAREILS MEDICAUX
7741	ELECTRO–MEDICAL EQUIPMNT	W 863	125.3	W 865	142.1	W 822	137.0	W 1104	159.5	APP ELECTRICITE MEDICALE
775	HOUSEHOLD TYPE EQUIP NES	W 71279	413.3	W 74372	464.0	W 61362	408.9	W 72543	419.5	MACH,APP USAGE DOMESTQUE
7752	DOM REFRIGERATRS,FREEZRS	W 62460	294.6	W 64408	334.5	W 49611	252.2	W 59427	262.4	REFRIG,CONGEL MENAGER

5. General Exports F.O.B. by Commodities according to the S.I.T.C. (Rev. 2) in million U.S. Dollars
Exportations Générales F.O.B. par Produits d'après la C.T.C.I. (Rév. 2) en millions de Dollars E.U.

SITC CTCI	COMMODITY	1994 QUANTITY QUANTITE	1994 VALUE VALEUR	1995 QUANTITY QUANTITE	1995 VALUE VALEUR	1996 QUANTITY QUANTITE	1996 VALUE VALEUR	1997 QUANTITY QUANTITE	1997 VALUE VALEUR	PRODUIT
77522	DOMESTIC DEEP–FREEZERS	W 50108	234.7	W 52095	266.4	W 39164	194.8	W 44191	184.5	MEUBLES CONGELATEURS
776	TRANSISTORS,VALVES,ETC	W 475	108.2	W 395	99.7	W 422	120.7	W 488	152.6	LAMPES,TUBES,VALVES
778	ELECTRICAL MACHINERY NES	W 11565	203.2	W 12282	241.3	W 14092	276.7	W 31489	364.8	AUTRES MACH ELECT NDA
78	ROAD VEHICLES		725.9		903.0		959.2		1069.5	VEHICULES ROUTIERS
781	PASS MOTOR VEH EXC BUSES	W 9519	96.2	W 9394	114.9	W 12334	143.6	W 15173	149.1	AUTO TRANSPORT PERSONNES
784	MOTOR VEH PRTS,ACCES NES	W 90062	372.1	W 102873	457.9	W 188329	470.4	W 118496	528.7	PIECES 722,781,782,783
7849	OTHER MOTOR VEHCL PARTS	W 86737	356.3	W 99126	434.5	W 185133	450.2	W 114897	507.7	PIECES 722,781,782,783
786	TRAILERS,NONMOTR VEH,NES	W 28399	110.8	W 37077	141.4	W 39367	144.7	W 51462	155.7	REMORQUES,CADRES,CONTAIN
79	OTHR TRANSPORT EQUIPMENT		1254.6		1071.5		1189.7		1081.2	AUTRE MATERIEL TRANSPORT
792	AIRCRAFT ETC	W 960	213.7	W 631	101.3	W 628	238.6	W 613	225.7	APP NAVIGATION AERIENNE
7924	AIRCRFT NES OVER 15000KG	W 508	127.0	W 206	10.8	W 273	141.4	W 340	135.5	AERODYNES PLUS 15000 KG
793	SHIPS AND BOATS ETC	W 573615	1035.8	W 390656	945.8	W 317389	897.0	W 278940	830.1	NAVIRES BATEAUX,ETC
7932	SHIPS AND BOATS NES	W 550603	939.3	W 378278	850.7	W 310282	837.5	W 264657	693.5	NAVIRES ET BATEAUX
79322	TANKERS OF ALL KINDS	W 289993	388.6	W 77251	272.0	W 172672	529.6	W 120888	368.9	BATEAUX–CITERNES
79323	OTHER CARGO VESSELS	W 259210	524.4	W 298503	545.9	W 136301	273.1	W 141015	269.7	AUT BATEAUX TRANS MARCH
8	MISC MANUFACTURED GOODS		6079.0		7196.4		7047.1		7629.2	ART MANUFACTURES DIVERS
812	*PLUMBG,HEATNG,LGHTNG EQ	W 27697	181.6	W 26596	218.2	W 26772	223.0	W 30551	247.7	APPAR SANITAIRES CHAUFFAGE
8124	LIGHTING EQUIPMENT NES	W 7760	115.3	W 8104	149.8	W 9009	158.2	W 10599	178.3	APPAREILS ECLAIRAGE ETC
821	*FURNITURE,PARTS THEREOF	W 432151	1786.2	W 451407	2160.3	W 449792	2024.4	W 690962	2021.8	MEUBLES ET PIECES
8211	CHAIRS,SEATS AND PARTS	W 22350	237.6	W 26754	313.6	W 23350	279.8	W 28603	285.3	SIEGES ET PIECES
82111	CHAIRS AND OTHER SEATS	W 20597	223.3	W 25217	298.3	W 21447	260.7	W 25841	262.2	SIEGES
8212	MED FURN,STUFFD FURNSHGS	W 19669	140.7	W 19153	171.2	W 22241	168.6	W 18358	162.5	MOB MEDICO–CHIRUR,PIECES
8219	FURNITURE AND PARTS NES	W 390132	1408.1	W 405500	1675.6	W 404201	1576.1	W 644001	1574.1	AUTRES MEUBLES ET PIECES
82192	WOOD FURNITURE NES	W 340323	1218.3	W 353172	1439.6	W 353238	1370.5	W 594947	1372.9	MEUBLES NDA EN BOIS
82199	OTHR FURN,FURN PARTS NES	W 40757	141.0	W 43494	181.2	W 36835	142.5	W 34186	136.5	MEUBLES NDA AUTRES MATIERES
84	CLOTHING AND ACCESSORIES		1064.9		1274.3		1287.8		1587.0	VETEMENTS
842	MENS OUTERWEAR NOT KNIT	W 4242	138.9	W 5001	177.2	W 5552	201.0	W 6687	223.7	VET DESSUS POUR HOMMES
843	WOMENS OUTERWEAR NONKNIT	W 7347	296.6	W 7765	369.1	W 7608	350.5	W 11538	453.4	VET DESSUS FEMMES MAT TEX
8439	— OTHER OUTER GARMENTS	W 4859	146.9	W 4797	175.2	W 4321	151.4	W 6533	218.3	AUT VET DES FEM MAT TEXT
845	OUTERWEAR KNIT NONELASTC	W 12179	412.2	W 14093	498.1	W 14877	471.5	W 13708	549.7	VET DESSOUS,ACCES BONNET
8451	— JERSEYS,PULLOVERS ETC	W 6272	218.7	W 7206	259.8	W 7314	240.8	W 6486	286.5	CHANDAILS,PULL–OVERS ETC
8459	— OTHER,CLTHG ACCESRYS	W 4918	149.3	W 5487	182.7	W 6340	182.3	W 6157	213.1	AUT VET DESSUS DE BONNE
846	UNDER GARMENTS KNITTED	W 3640	122.5	W 3779	125.3	W 4884	166.4	W 5216	208.0	SOUS VETS DE BONNETERIE
8462	— OF COTTON NON ELASTIC	W 3200	95.8	W 3385	102.7	W 4206	126.7	W 4668	169.4	SOUS–VET BONNET COTON
84629	—— OTHER	W 3200	95.8	W 3385	102.7	W 4206	126.7	W 4668	169.4	AUT SOUS–VET BONNET COTON
851	*FOOTWEAR	W 6486	211.5	W 6302	224.5	W 6285	213.2	W 7691	252.0	CHAUSSURES
85102	FOOTWEAR LEATHER	W 5812	202.2	W 5638	214.2	W 5601	203.0	W 6927	241.3	CHAUS SEMELLES EN CUIR
87	PRECISION INSTRUMNTS NES		837.6		926.3		964.6		1010.5	INSTRUM,APPAR SCIENT NDA
872	MEDICAL INSTRUMENTS NES	W 7953	235.8	W 7394	256.1	W 7084	295.7	W 9461	290.8	INSTR,APP MEDIC–CHIR NDA
87202	OTH MEDICAL INSTRUMENTS	W 7619	212.6	W 6908	233.2	W 6436	270.1	W 8698	262.8	INSTRUM,APP MEDECINE
874	MEASURNG,CONTROLNG INSTR	W 3842	569.0	W 3977	622.9	W 4562	587.9	W 5143	623.1	INSTRUMENTS DE MESURE
8742	MEASUR,DRAW ETC INST,PTS	W 703	142.0	W 808	157.6	W 1136	142.7	W 1055	155.3	INST DESSIN,TRACAGE,PCS
87421	MEASURNG,DRAWNG ETC INST	W 547	134.3	W 729	150.8	W 1018	132.5	W 917	143.5	INSTRUM DESSIN,TRACAGE
8743	GAS,LIQUID CONTROL INSTR	W 1170	95.2	W 1430	123.7	W 1748	137.2	W 2325	149.3	APP,INSTR MESURE FLUIDES
8748	ELEC MEAS,CONTRL EQU NES	W 839	182.3	W 534	172.2	W 495	147.9	W 491	141.7	APP ELEC ELECTRO MESURE
87483	OTH ELCTRNC MEAS ETC EQU	W 742	174.8	W 408	160.1	W 370	137.1	W 372	133.7	AUT APP ELECTRO DE MESURE
88	PHOTO EQU,OPTICL GDS ETC		191.8		224.7		237.7		249.7	APP,FOURN PHOTO,OP,MONTR
89	MISC MANUFCTRD GOODS NES		1789.2		2144.8		2073.6		2232.9	ART MANUFACTURES DIVERS
892	PRINTED MATTER	W 48937	319.4	W 51313	365.1	W 63778	326.9	W 619447	340.8	IMPRIMES
8921	PRINTED BOOKS,GLOBES,ETC	W 20160	129.5	W 19989	139.6	W 16541	127.2	W 498701	121.4	LIVRES,BROCHURES,CARTES
8928	PRINTED MATTER NES	W 21792	132.5	W 20116	156.8	W 35345	149.5	W 109939	180.2	IMPRIMES NDA
893	ARTICLES OF PLASTIC NES		837.9		1047.6		1010.0		1039.3	OUVRAGES EN MAT DIVIS 58
8931	PLSTC PACKG CONTNRS,LIDS	W 53008	230.8	W 53999	273.8	W 158647	264.9	W 140108	281.1	ART TRANSP EMBALLAGE ETC
8939	MISC PLASTIC ARTICLES	W 92996	596.9	W 103229	764.1	W 97830	735.8	W 123648	747.8	ART DIVERS EN MAT DIV 58
89399	OTHR PLASTC ARTICLES NES	W 78688	540.6	W 84478	677.7	W 79653	663.3	W 105835	675.5	AUT OUV MAT DIV 58
898	MUSICAL INSTRUMENTS,PTS	W 10316	197.3	W 10425	248.5	W 10243	184.6	W 10044	224.5	INSTRUMENTS DE MUSIQUE
8983	SOUND RECRDNG TAPE,DISCS	W 10180	192.6	W 10171	236.6	W 9876	171.7	W 9610	208.1	SUPPORTS SON POUR 763
89832	RECORDED DISCS,TAPES ETC	W 6277	146.3	W 6194	182.6	W 6394	139.8	W 6170	171.1	DISQUES,PHONO,BANDES
899	OTHER MANUFACTURED GOODS		217.6		259.4		325.2		375.1	AUT ART MANUF DIVERS NDA
8996	HEARING,ORTHOPAEDIC AIDS		151.6		168.9		242.9		264.9	APPAREILS D'ORTHOPEDIE
89961	HEARING AIDS		108.8		120.0		183.7		201.4	APPAREILS POUR LES SOURDS
9	GOODS NOT CLASSD BY KIND		4394.5		4660.6		4582.9		2762.4	ART TRANSACT NON CLASSES
931	*SPECIAL TRANSACTIONS		4376.1		4643.4		4568.6		2744.1	TRANS.SPECIALES

1. HISTORICAL SERIES, 1959–1995 SPECIAL TRADE, IMPORTS C.I.F., EXPORTS F.O.B.
SERIES HISTORIQUES, 1959–1995 COMMERCE SPECIAL, IMPORTATIONS C.A.F., EXPORTATIONS F.O.B

YEAR ANNEE	VALUE IN MILLION DJIB. FRANCS VALEUR EN MILLION DJIB. FRANCS MERCHANDISE –MARCHANDISE		GOLD –OR		CONVERSION FACTORS U.S. CENTS PER DJIB. FRANC FACTEURS DE CONVERSION CENTS E.U. PAR DJIB. FRANC		INDEX NUMBERS –INDICES QUANTUM		UNIT VALUE VALEUR UNITAIRE	
	IMPORTS	EXPORTS	IMPORTS	EXPORTS	IMPORTS	EXPORTS	IMPORTS	EXPORTS	IMPORTS	EXPORTS
1959	6659.00	4108.00			0.4665	0.4665				
1960	7157.00	4483.00			0.4665	0.4665				
1961	8075.00	4784.00			0.4665	0.4665				
1962	9318.80	5786.90			0.4665	0.4665				
1963	11437.00	4891.80			0.4665	0.4665				
1964	12201.60	4833.90			0.4665	0.4665				
1965	13116.80	5985.80			0.4665	0.4665				
1966	12628.60	5776.40			0.4665	0.4665				
1967	12289.80	4954.20			0.4665	0.4665				
1968	10752.80	2580.10			0.4665	0.4665				
1969	10475.10	2521.90			0.4665	0.4665				
1970	10592.90	4523.20			0.4665	0.4665				
1971	11335.00	3219.30			0.4664	0.4664				
1972	12934.90	3829.10			0.5138	0.5138				
1973	14495.60	5498.60			0.5836	0.5836				
1974	24932.70	6732.90			0.5382	0.5382				
1975	24166.30	2639.20			0.6082	0.6070				
1976	21284.40	2835.20			0.6063	0.6052				
1977	18948.60	3364.10			0.5269	0.5268				
1978	29117.40	3154.20			0.5592	0.5621				
1979	33454.30	2023.20			0.5630	0.5630				
1980	37890.00	2220.50			0.5630	0.5630				
1981	39865.00	1553.70			0.5630	0.5630				
1982	40197.50	2234.20			0.5630	0.5630				
1983	39306.90	1918.80			0.5630	0.5630				
1984	40462.00	2362.00			0.5630	0.5630				
1985	35670.00	2488.00			0.5630	0.5630				
1986	32731.01	3628.00			0.5627	0.5627				
1987	36487.01	4976.00			0.5627	0.5627				
1988	35771.01	4116.00			0.5627	0.5627				
1989	34920.00	4423.00			0.5627	0.5627				
1990	38174.00	4420.00			0.5627	0.5627				
1991	38103.01	3083.00			0.5627	0.5627				
1992	38860.00	2800.00			0.5627	0.5627				
1994	73218.41	15816.60			0.5627	0.5627				
1995	76417.27	19193.18			0.5627	0.5627				

2. IMPORTS BY BROAD ECONOMIC CATEGORY AND EXPORTS BY INDUSTRIAL ORIGIN. (PERCENTAGE OF TOTAL VALUE)
IMPORTATIONS PAR CATEGORIES ECONOMIQUES ET EXPORTATIONS PAR BRANCHE D'ACTIVITE.(EN POURCENTAGE DE LA VALEUR TOTALE)

IMPORTS – IMPORTATIONS

	1989	1990	1991	1992	1993	1994	1995
TOTAL IMPORTS–IMPORTATIONS TOTALES	100.	100.	100.	100.			
1 FOOD BEV–ALIMENTATION BOISSONS	24.6	26.6	24.8	24.2			
11 PRIMARY–PRODUITS DE BASE	6.9	8.1	6.9	3.4			
111 FOR INDUSTRY–POUR L'INDUSTRIE	3.3	4.1	3.6	0.3			
112 FOR HOUSEHOLDS–POUR LES MENAGES	3.5	4.0	3.2	3.0			
12 PROCESSED–PRODUITS ELABORES	17.7	18.5	17.9	20.9			
121 FOR INDUSTRY–POUR L'INDUSTRIE	3.0	4.9	4.1	3.5			
122 FOR HOUSEHOLDS–POUR LES MENAGES	14.7	13.6	13.8	17.4			
2 IND SUPPLIES–APPROV INDUSTRIELS	27.3	24.8	26.2	27.9			
21 PRIMARY–PRODUITS DE BASE	12.6	11.6	10.4	10.4			
22 PROCESSED–PRODUITS ELABORES	14.7	13.2	15.8	17.5			
3 FUELS–COMBUSTIBLES	6.6	7.0	9.0	8.0			
31 PRIMARY–PRODUITS DE BASE	0.1	0.1	0.1	0.1			
32 PROCESSED–PRODUITS ELABORES	6.4	6.8	8.8	7.9			
321 MOTOR SPIRIT–ESSENCE	0.8	0.9	1.2	2.2			
322 OTHER–AUTRES	5.6	5.9	7.7	5.7			
4 MACHINERY–EQUIPEMENT	8.5	8.6	8.6	7.9			
41 CAPITAL EQUIPMENT–MACHINES	8.0	7.8	7.9	7.1			
42 PARTS–PIECES ACCESSOIRES	0.5	0.8	0.7	0.8			
5 TRANSPORT–TRANSPORT	7.9	8.7	7.5	8.6			
51 PASSENGER CARS–AUTOMOBILES	2.9	4.5	4.5	0.6			
52 OTHER–AUTRES	2.5	1.8	1.0	5.9			
521 INDUSTRIAL–INDUSTRIELS	2.3	1.6	0.8	5.7			
522 NON INDUSTRIAL–NON INDUSTRIEL	0.2	0.2	0.2	0.2			
53 PARTS–PIECES ACCESSOIRES	2.5	2.4	2.1	2.1			
6 CONSUM GOODS–BIENS CONSOMMATION	22.0	21.1	20.8	19.2			
61 DURABLE–DURABLES	2.2	2.6	2.1	2.1			
62 SEMI DURABLE–SEMI DURABLES	8.9	6.9	7.8	7.5			
63 NON DURABLE–NON DURABLES	11.0	11.5	10.9	9.6			
7 GOODS NES–BIENS NDA	3.1	3.3	3.1	4.1			

EXPORTS – EXPORTATIONS

	1989	1990	1991	1992	1993	1994	1995
TOTAL EXPORTS–EXPORTATIONS TOTALES	100.	100.	100.	100.			
1 AGRICULTURE	43.2	39.3	25.1	21.4			
2 MINING QUARRY–INDUS EXTRACTIVES	0.0		0.0	0.1			
3 MANUFACTURING–IND MANUFACTUR	56.7	60.7	74.8	78.5			
31 FOOD BEV TOBACCO–ALIM BOISS TAB	7.6	5.0	7.1	3.3			
32 TEXTILES–INDUSTRIES TEXTILES	0.1	0.0	0.6	2.3			
33 WOOD & PRODUCTS–BOIS & PRODUITS	0.0	0.0	0.0	0.0			
34 PAPER & PRODUCTS–PAPIER & PRODT	0.1	0.2	0.2	0.2			
35 CHEMICALS–INDUSTRIES CHIMIQUES	0.5	0.4	0.5	0.8			
36 NON METAL MIN–MIN NON METAL	0.1	0.1	0.2	0.1			
37 BASIC METAL–IND METAL BASE	0.1	0.1	0.6	0.1			
38 METAL MANUF–MANUF METAL	10.4	7.1	10.6	10.5			
39 OTH MANUF IND–AUTRES MANUF	37.8	47.7	55.1	61.3			

3. TRADE BY PRINCIPAL COUNTRIES OF ORIGIN AND DESTINATION (VALUE IN MILLION U.S. DOLLARS)
ECHANGES SELON LES PRINCIPAUX PAYS D'ORIGINE ET DE DESTINATION (VALEUR EN MILLIONS DE DOLLARS EU)

COUNTRIES–PAYS	SPECIAL IMPORTS C.I.F. IMPORTATIONS SPECIALES C.A.F				
	1991	1992	1993	1994	1995
World	214.4	219.9		412.0	430.0
Africa	20.8	20.5			
Americas	9.3	8.8			
– Northern America	8.6	7.1			
– LAIA	0.7	1.1			
– CACM	0.0				
– Caribbean	0.0				
– Rest of America		0.6			
Asia excl fmr USSR	74.5	56.4			
– Middle East	24.1	17.7			
Asia former USSR					
Europe excl fmr USSR	104.5	101.1			
– European Union	99.9	98.5			
– Eastern Europe	1.0	0.3			
– Rest of Europe	3.6	2.3			
Europe former USSR	0.6	0.1			
Oceania	0.3	0.5			
Other	4.4	32.5			
France, Monaco	56.0	58.0			
Saudi Arabia	10.8	8.8		51.0	25.0
Areas n.e.s.	4.2	32.4			
Ethiopia, incl Eritrea	17.8	17.2			
Japan/Japon	15.4	14.8			
Bahrain/Bahreïn	5.7	3.9		9.0	11.0
Italy/Italie	13.9	12.1			
United Arab Emirates	4.9	1.5		6.0	7.0
Netherlands/Pays–Bas	7.5	7.8			
Pakistan	3.2	0.5		6.0	5.0
USA/Etats–Unis d'Amer	7.9	6.8			
China/Chine	6.6	6.7			
United Kingdom	5.8	7.0			
Thailand/Thaïlande	6.5	6.2			
Singapore/Singapour	5.4	4.4			
Germany/Allemagne	4.6	4.4			
Belgium–Luxembourg	5.2	3.5			
Egypt/Egypte	0.6	1.7		4.0	2.0
Yemen/Yémen	2.0	3.0			1.0
Denmark/Danemark	3.3	2.5			
India/Inde	3.0	2.2			
Korea, Republic of	3.3	1.7			
Switzerland,Liechtenst.	2.9	2.0			
Other Asia n.e.s.	3.1	1.0			
Lebanon/Liban	0.4	0.6		1.0	1.0
China, Hong Kong SAR	2.5	0.3			
Kenya	1.5	1.3			
Austria/Autriche	1.2	1.1			
Malaysia/Malaisie	0.0				2.0
Ireland/Irlande	0.7	0.9			
Turkey/Turquie	0.2			1.0	
Korea Dem People's Rp	0.4	0.8			
Spain/Espagne	0.6	0.5			
Canada	0.7	0.3			
Jordan/Jordanie	0.0			1.0	
Brazil/Brésil	0.0	0.9			
Sweden/Suède	0.7	0.2			
Chile/Chili	0.6	0.2			
Australia/Australie	0.3	0.5			
Greece/Grèce	0.3	0.4			

COUNTRIES–PAYS	SPECIAL EXPORTS F.O.B. EXPORTATIONS SPECIALES F.O.B.				
	1991	1992	1993	1994	1995
Monde	17.3	15.9		89.0	108.0
Afrique	1.6	1.4			
Amériques	0.2				
– Amérique du Nord	0.2				
– ALAI					
– MCAC					
– Caraïbes	0.0				
– Autre Amérique					
Asie anc. URSS exclus	4.1	2.6			
– Moyen–Orient	3.9	2.3			
Asie ancienne URSS					
Europe anc. URSS exclus	11.1	9.4			
– Union Européenne	10.9	9.4			
– Europe de l'Est	0.0				
– Autre de l'Europe	0.2				
Europe ancienne URSS					
Océanie	0.0				
Autre	0.4	2.5			
Somalia/Somalie	0.7	0.7		35.0	45.0
Yemen/Yémen	2.9	0.7		18.0	8.0
France, Monaco	9.9	9.1			
Saudi Arabia	1.0	1.6		1.0	3.0
Pakistan				1.0	3.0
Areas n.e.s.		2.4			
Egypt/Egypte	0.0			1.0	1.0
Ethiopia, incl Eritrea	0.3	0.5			
Italy/Italie	0.6				
Belgium–Luxembourg	0.2	0.2			
Bunkers, ship stores	0.4				
Reunion/Réunion	0.2	0.1			
Thailand/Thaïlande	0.0	0.3			
Japan/Japon	0.2	0.1			
Switzerland,Liechtenst.	0.2				
Madagascar	0.2				
Germany/Allemagne	0.1				
USA/Etats–Unis d'Amer	0.1				
Kenya	0.0	0.1			
United Kingdom	0.0	0.1			
Free zones/Zone franches		0.1			
Greece/Grèce	0.1				
India/Inde	0.1				
United Arab Emirates	0.0				
Tunisia/Tunisie	0.0				
Canada	0.0				
Qatar	0.0				
Netherlands/Pays–Bas	0.0				
Special Categories	0.0				
Lebanon/Liban	0.0				
Cote d'Ivoire	0.0				
Australia/Australie	0.0				
Sweden/Suède	0.0				
Norway,Svalbard and JM	0.0				
Denmark/Danemark	0.0				
Philippines	0.0				
Former Czechoslovakia	0.0				
Jordan/Jordanie	0.0				
Poland/Pologne	0.0				
China/Chine	0.0				

(VALUE AS PERCENTAGE OF WORLD TOTAL)(VALEURS EN POURCENTAGE DU TOTAL MONDIAL)

	1986	1987	1988	1989	1990	1991	1992	1993	1994	1995
Africa	12.1	11.5	11.2	13.8	12.6	9.7	9.3			
Americas	2.5	2.5	3.0	2.2	3.7	4.4	4.0			
– Northern America	2.5	2.3	2.7	1.8	3.5	4.0	3.2			
– LAIA	0.1	0.2	0.3	0.4	0.2	0.3	0.5			
– CACM	0.0	0.0	0.0	0.0		0.0				
– Caribbean	0.0	0.0		0.0		0.0				
– Rest of America			0.0	0.0			0.3			
Asia excl fmr USSR	26.2	29.9	32.0	33.0	30.8	34.7	25.7			
– Middle East	8.2	8.5	10.5	10.8	10.9	11.3	8.0			
Asia former USSR										
Europe excl fmr USSR	55.9	53.3	51.1	48.6	49.9	48.7	46.0			
– European Union	53.8	51.1	49.2	46.7	47.9	46.6	44.8			
– Eastern Europe	0.4	0.5	0.4	0.4	0.4	0.5	0.1			
– Rest of Europe	1.7	1.7	1.5	1.5	1.7	1.7	1.1			
Europe former USSR	0.0	0.0	0.0	0.4	0.3	0.3	0.1			
Oceania	0.6	0.1	0.2	0.0	0.1	0.1	0.2			
Other	2.6	2.7	2.5	1.9	2.5	2.0	14.8			
France, Monaco	30.7	28.7	28.7	27.8	29.3	26.1	26.4			
Saudi Arabia	4.6	4.7	5.5	5.0	5.0	5.0	4.0		12.4	5.8
Areas n.e.s.	2.5	2.7	1.7	1.4	1.1	2.0	14.7			
Ethiopia, incl Eritrea	11.4	9.5	10.1	12.6	11.1	8.3	7.8			
Japan/Japon	4.7	6.3	6.3	5.0	5.4	7.2	6.7			
Bahrain/Bahreïn	3.0	2.9	3.0	3.1	2.5	2.7	1.8		2.2	2.6
Italy/Italie	7.9	6.0	5.0	6.3	5.3	6.5	5.5			
United Arab Emirates	0.3	0.5	1.1	1.7	2.6	2.3	0.7		1.5	1.6
Netherlands/Pays–Bas	3.4	4.5	4.4	3.8	2.9	3.5	3.5			
Pakistan	0.5	0.4	0.4	0.7	0.5	1.5	0.2		1.5	1.2

	1986	1987	1988	1989	1990	1991	1992	1993	1994	1995
Afrique	12.7	15.7	7.6	7.2	6.6	9.2	8.8			
Amériques	0.9	0.6	0.2	0.4	0.3	0.9				
– Amérique du Nord	0.7	0.4	0.1	0.4	0.2	0.9				
– ALAI	0.0	0.0		0.0						
– MCAC			0.0	0.0						
– Caraïbes	0.1	0.1		0.0	0.0	0.1				
– Autre Amérique	0.0		0.0		0.0					
Asie anc. URSS exclus	33.4	23.3	27.7	39.2	36.3	23.8	16.5			
– Moyen–Orient	28.7	22.9	26.5	38.8	35.9	22.3	14.3			
Asie ancienne URSS										
Europe anc. URSS exclus	52.4	60.2	60.2	50.7	55.6	63.9	59.0			
– Union Européenne	51.6	59.1	58.3	47.6	54.5	62.6	59.0			
– Europe de l'Est	0.1	0.0	0.0	0.0		0.0				
– Autre de l'Europe	0.7	1.1	1.9	3.1	1.1	1.3				
Europe ancienne URSS			0.0							
Océanie	0.0	0.0	0.0	0.0	0.1	0.0				
Autre	0.6	0.2	4.4	2.4	1.2	2.2	15.6			
Somalia/Somalie	6.5	9.4	2.8	3.6	1.7	4.1	4.2		39.3	41.7
Yemen/Yémen						16.4	4.3		20.2	7.4
France, Monaco	45.3	53.1	50.4	40.9	49.0	57.1	57.4			
Saudi Arabia	0.6	0.5	1.1	1.3	1.1	5.6	10.0		1.1	2.8
Pakistan	0.1	0.0	0.0	0.0	0.0				1.1	2.8
Areas n.e.s.	0.5	0.2			0.0		15.2			
Egypt/Egypte	0.0	0.1	0.2	0.1	0.3	0.0			1.1	0.9
Ethiopia, incl Eritrea	2.5	5.4	2.7	1.5	1.6	1.8	3.3			
Italy/Italie	3.8	3.5	3.5	3.4	3.6	3.2				
Belgium–Luxembourg	1.1	0.6	1.2	1.1	0.7	1.0	1.2			

4. Special Imports C.I.F. by Commodities according to the S.I.T.C. (Rev. 2) in million U.S. Dollars
Importations Spéciales C.A.F. par Produits d'après la C.T.C.I. (Rév. 2) en millions de Dollars E.U.

SITC CTCI	COMMODITY	1992 QUANTITY QUANTITE	1992 VALUE VALEUR	1993 QUANTITY QUANTITE	1993 VALUE VALEUR	1994 QUANTITY QUANTITE	1994 VALUE VALEUR	1995 QUANTITY QUANTITE	1995 VALUE VALEUR	PRODUIT
	ALL COMMODITIES		220.0							TOUS PRODUITS
0	FOOD AND LIVE ANIMALS		43.8							ALIMENTS,ANIMAUX VIVANTS
01	MEAT AND PREPARATIONS		2.9							VIANDES ET PREPARATIONS
011	MEAT FRESH,CHILLD,FROZEN	W 455	1.7							VIANDES FRAICHES,REF,CONGE
014	MEAT PREPD,PRSVD,NES ETC	W 216	1.2							CONSERVES DE VIANDES
0142	SAUSAGES INCLDING TINNED	W 143	1.0							SAUCISSES,SAUCISSONS
02	DAIRY PRODCTS,BIRDS'EGGS		7.4							PRODUITS LAITIERS,OEUFS
022	MILK AND CREAM	W 3124	5.2							LAIT ET CREME
0224	MILK,CREAM PRESERVED ETC	W 2497	4.6							LAIT,CREME CONS,CONC
02242	MILK DRY,1.5% FAT OR LES	W 1661	3.6							LAIT POUDRE INF 1.5%
024	CHEESE AND CURD	W 187	1.2							FROMAGE ET CAILLEBOTTE
03	FISH AND PREPARATIONS		1.1							POISSONS ET PREPARATIONS
037	FISH ETC PREPD,PRSVD NES	W 443	0.9							POIS,CRUST,MOL PREPARES
0371	FISH PREPARD,PRESRVD NES	W 425	0.8							CONSERVES DE POISSONS
04	CEREALS AND PREPARATIONS		16.4							CEREALES ET PRODUITS
042	RICE	W 16470	5.8							RIZ
046	WHEAT ETC MEAL OR FLOUR	W 17108	4.5							SEMOULE FARINE,FROMENT
04601	FLOUR OF WHEAT OR MESLIN	W 17108	4.5							FARINE DE FROMENT
048	CEREAL ETC PREPARATIONS	W 6759	4.9							PREPTNS A BASE CEREALES
0483	MACARONI,SPAGHETTI ETC	W 5956	3.1							PATES ALMENTAIRES
0484	BAKERY PRODUCTS	W 512	1.2							PRODUITS DE BOULANGERIE
05	VEGETABLES AND FRUIT		6.3							LEGUMES ET FRUITS
054	VEG ETC FRSH,SMPLY PRSVD	W 2291	0.9							LEGUMES FRAIS,CONG,SECS
056	VEGTBLES ETC PRSVD,PREPD	W 2771	2.7							CONSERVES DE LEGUMES
0565	VEGTBLES PRSVD,PREPD NES	W 2771	2.7							LEGUMES PREPARES CONSERVE
05659	OTH VEG PRESVD,PREPD NES	W 2291	2.4							LEGUM PREPAP,CONSERV NDA
057	FRUIT,NUTS,FRESH,DRIED	W 912	1.7							FRUITS FRAIS OU SECS
0579	FRUIT FRESH OR DRIED NES	W 535	0.9							FRUITS FRAIS,SECS NDA
058	FRUIT PRESERVED,PREPARED	W 897	1.2							CONSERVES DE FRUITS
0589	FRUIT PREPRD,PRESRVD,NES	W 632	0.8							FRUITS PREPARES CONSERV
05899	FRUIT,NUTS NES,PRESERVED	W 632	0.8							FRUITS PREP CONSERV NDA
06	SUGAR AND PREPS,HONEY		5.2							SUCRES ET PRODUITS
061	SUGAR AND HONEY	W 14479	4.8							SUCRES ET MIEL
0612	REFINED SUGAR ETC	W 13629	4.5							SUCRES RAFFINES
07	COFFEE,TEA,COCOA,SPICES		1.7							CAFE,THE,CACAO,EPICES
09	MISC EDIBLE PRODUCTS		3.1							PREP ALIMENTAIRES DIVERSES
098	EDIBLE PRODCTS,PREPS NES	W 1049	3.0							PREP ALIMENTAIRES NDA
09809	MISC FOOD PREPRTIONS NES	W 750	2.4							PREP ALIMENTAIRES NDA
1	BEVERAGES AND TOBACCO		12.5							BOISSONS ET TABACS
11	BEVERAGES		7.3							BOISSONS
111	NON–ALCOHL BEVERAGES NES	W 5925	3.5							BOISSONS NON ALCOOLIQUES
11101	WATERS,ICE AND SNOW	W 3537	1.0							EAU,EAUX MINERALES
11102	FLAVORED WATERS NON–ALCO	W 2388	2.5							LIMONADES,EAUX GAZEUSES
112	ALCOHOLIC BEVERAGES	W 2944	3.9							BOISSONS ALCOOLIQUES
1121	WINE OF FRESH GRAPES ETC	W 455	0.8							VINS DE RAISINS FRAIS
11212	WINE OF FRESH GRAPES	W 455	0.8							VINS DE MOUTS DE RAISINS
1123	BEER,ALE,STOUT,PORTER	W 2209	2.5							BIERES
12	TOBACCO AND MANUFACTURES		5.2							TABACS BRUTS FABRIQUES
122	TOBACCO,MANUFACTURED	W 405	5.1							TABACS FABRIQUES
1222	CIGARETTES	W 405	5.1							CIGARETTES
2	CRUDE MATERLS,EXCL FUELS		23.5							MAT BRUTES NON COMESTIBLES
24	CORK AND WOOD		1.1							LIEGE ET BOIS
248	WOOD SHAPED,SLEEPERS	W 1831	0.9							BOIS SIMPLEMENT TRAVAILLES
2483	LUMBER SHAPED NON–CONIFR	W 1831	0.9							NON CONIFERES SCIES,RABOTES
24831	LUMBER SAWN ETC NON–CON	W 1831	0.9							SCIES LONGITUDINALEMENT
26	TEXTILE FIBRES AND WASTE		5.2							FIBRES TEXTILES
269	WASTE OF TEXTILE FABRICS	W 5978	5.2							FRIPERIE DRILLES,CHIFFONS
26901	BULK TEXT WSTE,OLD CLTHG	W 5634	4.9							ART ET ACCESS D'HABILLEMENT
29	CRUDE ANIMAL,VEG MAT NES		17.2							MATIERES BRUTES ANIM,VEGET
292	CRUDE VEG MATERIALS NES		17.2							MAT BRUTES VEGETALES NDA
2924	VEG USED IN PHARMACY ETC	W 2657	16.5							PLANTES MEDICINALES
3	MINERAL FUELS ETC		17.8							COMBUSTIBLES MINERAUX LUB
33	PETROLEUM AND PRODUCTS		17.5							PETROLE ET DERIVES
334	PETROLEUM PRODUCTS,REFIN	W 97065	17.4							PRODUITS RAFFINES
3341	GASOLINE,OTH LIGHT OILS	W 20356	4.9							ESSENCES POUR MOTEURS
33419	OTH LIGHT PETROLEUM OILS	W 20356	4.9							AUTRES HUILES LEGERES
3343	GAS OILS	W 32787	6.0							GAS OILS
3344	FUEL OILS,NES	W 41555	4.3							FUEL OILS
3345	LUBS,PETROLEUM OILS NES	W 2367	2.3							HUILES LUBRIFIANTES
33451	LUBS(HIGH PETR CONT) ETC	W 2367	2.3							HUILES LUBRIF,H LOURDES
4	ANIMAL,VEGETABLE OIL,FAT		3.3							HUILES,GRAISSES ANIM,VEG
42	FIXED VEGETABLE OIL,FAT		3.2							HUILES VEGETALES FIXES
424	FIXED VEG OIL NONSOFT	W 4543	3.0							AUTRES HUILES VEG FIXES
4242	PALM OIL	W 3504	2.3							HUILE DE PALME
5	CHEMCLS,RELATED PROD NES		14.9							PRODUITS CHIMIQUES
53	DYES,TANNING,COLOUR PROD		0.9							PROD TEINTURE,COLORANTS
533	PIGMENTS,PAINTS,ETC	W 708	0.9							PIGMENTS,PEINTURES,VERNIS
5334	VARNISHES,DISTEMPERS ETC	W 648	0.8							PEINTURES A L'EAU
541	*MEDICINAL,PHARM PRODUCT		8.6							PROD MEDICINAUX PHARMACEUT
5417	MEDICAMENTS	K 445000	6.9							MEDICAMENTS
54173	— CONTAINING ALKALOIDS	K 278000	2.8							MED CONTEN ALCALOIDES
54179	— CONTNG OTH SUBSTANCES	K 167000	4.1							MED CONT AUT SUBSTANCES
5419	PHARMACEUTICAL GOODS NES	K 62000	1.5							PREP,ART PHARMACEUTIQUES
54199	OTH PHARMACEUTICAL GOODS	K 47000	1.4							AUT PREP PHARMACEUTIQUES
55	PERFUME,CLEANING ETC PRD		4.1							PROD POUR PARFUM,TOILETTE
553	PERFUMERY,COSMETICS,ETC	W 305	1.6							PRODUITS DE PARFUMERIE
554	SOAP,CLEANSING ETC PREPS	W 2693	2.6							SAVONS,PRODUITS DETERSIFS
5541	SOAPS	W 2266	1.8							SAVONS,PROD TENSIO–ACTIFS
59	CHEMICAL MATERIALS NES		1.1							MAT PROD CHIMIQUES NDA
6	BASIC MANUFACTURES		35.2							ART MANUFACTURES
62	RUBBER MANUFACTURES NES		1.6							CAOUTCHOUC MANUFACTURE
625	RUBBER TYRES, TUBES ETC	W 342	1.2							PNEUS CAOUTCHOUC VULCANISE
6252	TYRES,NEW,BUS OR LORRY	W 255	0.9							PNEUS POUR AUTOBUS,CAMIONS
63	WOOD,CORK MANUFACTRS NES		2.2							OUVRAGES LIEGE ET BOIS
635	WOOD MANUFACTURES NES	W 931	1.6							ART MANUF EN BOIS NDA
64	PAPER,PAPERBOARD AND MFR		3.0							PAPIERS,CARTONS & OUVRAGES
642	PAPER,ETC,PRECUT,ARTS OF	W 802	2.5							PAP,CARTONS DECOUPES
6423	EXERCISE BOOKS ETC	W 288	1.3							REGISTRES,CAHIERS,CARNETS
65	TEXTILE YARN,FABRICS,ETC		10.0							FILS,TISSUS,ARTICLES TEXTILE
651	TEXTILE YARN	W 567	3.1							FILS TEXTILES
6515	YARN OF 6514 FOR RETAIL	W 484	2.8							FILS CONT 85% FI SYNTHETIQ

4. Special Imports C.I.F. by Commodities according to the S.I.T.C. (Rev. 2) in million U.S. Dollars
Importations Spéciales C.A.F. par Produits d'après la C.T.C.I. (Rév. 2) en millions de Dollars E.U.

SITC CTCI	COMMODITY	1992 QUANTITY QUANTITE	1992 VALUE VALEUR	1993 QUANTITY QUANTITE	1993 VALUE VALEUR	1994 QUANTITY QUANTITE	1994 VALUE VALEUR	1995 QUANTITY QUANTITE	1995 VALUE VALEUR	PRODUIT
65152	— OF DISCONTIN FIBRES	W 484	2.8							FILS CONT 85% FI TEXT SYNT
652	COTTON FABRICS,WOVEN	W 232	1.3							TISSUS DE COTON
6522	WOVEN COTTON BLEACHD,ETC	W 224	1.1							TISSUS COTON BLANCHIS ETC
65225	BLCHD COTN BLEND FAB NES	W 224	1.1							AUT TIS MOINS 85% COT BLANCH
653	WOVN MAN-MADE FIB FABRIC	W 361	1.8							TISSUS FIBRES SYNTH,ARTIF
6531	CONT SYNT WEAVES NONPILE	W 340	1.7							TISSUS FIBRES SYNTH CONTINUE
658	TEXTILE ARTICLES NES	W 940	3.2							ART FACONNES MAT TEXTILES
6582	MADE-UP CANVAS GOODS	W 294	0.9							BACHES,TENTES ETC
65821	MADE-UP COTTN CANVAS GDS	W 294	0.9							BACHES,TENTES DE COTON
6583	BLANKETS ETC NON ELECTRC	W 281	1.1							COUVERTURES
65839	BLANKETS ETC NES	W 211	0.8							COUVERTURES AUTRES FIBRES
6589	OTH TEXTILE ARTICLES NES	W 219	0.8							AUT ART EN TEXTILES NDA
65899	TXTL ARTCLES NONKNIT NES	W 219	0.8							ART TIS AUT QUE BONNETERIE
66	NONMETAL MINERAL MFS NES		5.7							ART MIN NON METALLIQUES
661	LIME,CEMENT,BLDG PRODS	W 29278	2.1							CHAUX,CIMENTS MAT CONSTR
6612	CEMENT	W 29233	2.1							CIMENTS HYDRAULIQUES
662	CLAY,REFRACTORY BLDG PRD	W 1789	1.1							MAT CONST REFRACTAIRES
6624	BRICKS ETC NONREFRACTORY	W 1623	0.9							BRIQUES ETC CERAM NON REFR
66245	GLAZED CERAMIC SETTS ETC	W 1224	0.7							AUT CARREAUX CERAMIQUE
664	GLASS	W 1761	1.4							VERRE
6649	GLASS NES	W 1680	1.3							VERRE NDA
66494	GLASS FIBRE AND PROD NES	W 1680	1.3							LAINE DE VERRE,FIBRES
67	IRON AND STEEL		4.8							FER ET ACIER
673	IRON,STEEL SHAPES ETC	W 3439	1.9							BARRES,PROFIL FER,ACIER
6732	IRON,STEEL BARS ETC	W 2734	1.5							BARRES FER,ACIER
67326	IRN,OTH STL BARS HOTROLD	W 2348	1.2							BARRES PLEINES FER,ACIER
674	IRN,STL UNIV,PLATE,SHEET	W 824	1.1							LARGES PLATS,TOLES
6744	IRN,STL HVY PLATE,ROLLED	W 524	0.9							TOLES LAMINEES PLUS 4.75 MM
67441	— OF IRON OR SIMPLE STL	W 524	0.9							TOLES NON ACIER FIN CARB
678	IRON,STL TUBES,PIPES,ETC	W 1148	1.6							TUBES,TUYAUX EN FONTE,FER
6783	IRON,STL TUBES,PIPES NES	W 992	1.0							AUT TUBES,TUYAUX FER,ACIER
68	NON-FERROUS METALS		0.9							METAUX NON FERREUX
684	ALUMINIUM	W 284	0.9							ALUMINIUM
6842	ALUMINIUM,ALLOYS WORKED	W 284	0.9							ALUMINIUM,ALLIAGES OUVRE
68421	ALUMINIUM BARS,WIRE,ETC	W 206	0.8							BARRES,PROFILES FILS ALU
69	METAL MANUFACTURES NES		7.3							ART MANUFACT EN METAL NDA
691	STRUCTURES AND PARTS NES	W 1109	1.7							CONSTRUCT FER,ACIER,ALU
6911	STRUCTURES,PARTS IRN,STL	W 1018	1.4							CONSTRUCT FER,ACIER,FONTE
695	TOOLS	W 477	2.0							OUTILS A MAIN
6953	OTHER HAND TOOLS	W 225	1.1							AUTRES OUTILS A MAIN
69539	HAND TOOLS ETC NES	W 138	0.8							OUTILLAGE A MAIN NDA
697	BASE MTL HOUSEHOLD EQUIP	W 616	1.4							ART MENAGE MET COMMUNS
6974	BASE MTL DMSTC ARTIC NES	W 569	1.3							ARTICLES NDA FONTE,FER,ETC
69741	— OF IRON OR STEEL	W 532	1.1							ART NDA EN FONTE,FER
699	BASE METAL MFRS NES		1.6							ART MANUFACTURES MET NDA
7	MACHINES,TRANSPORT EQUIP		42.2							MACHINES MATERIEL TRANSPORT
71	POWER GENERATING EQUIPMT		3.2							MACHINES GENERATRICES
716	ROTATING ELECTRIC PLANT	W 65	2.8							APP ELECTR ROTATIFS,PIECES
7162	AC MTRS,GENRTRS,GEN SETS	W 37	1.0							MOTEURS ELECTRIQUES
71623	GEN SETS WITH PISTN ENGN	W 34	0.8							GROUPES MOTEUR EXPLOSION
7169	PTS NES OF ROT ELEC PLNT	W 28	1.9							PIECES MAC APP ROTATIFS
72	MACHS FOR SPCL INDUSTRYS		0.9							MAC SPECIALES POUR INDUST
74	GENRL INDUSTRL MACHY NES		3.8							MACH APP INDUSTRIE
741	HEATING,COOLING EQUIPMNT	W 145	1.4							MACH CHAUFFAGE,PIECES
7415	AIR-CONDITIONING MACHNRY	W 137	1.2							GROUPES CONDITION AIR
742	PUMPS FOR LIQUIDS ETC	W 73	1.2							POMPES MOTO-POMPES
7429	PTS NES OF PUMPS OF 742	W 49	0.8							PIECES POUR GROUPE 742
75	OFFICE MACHNES,ADP EQUIP		2.9							MACH BUREAU TRAIT AUTOM
752	AUTOMTIC DATA PROC EQUIP	W 11	0.8							MACH TRAIT INFORMATION
759	OFFICE,ADP MCH PTS,ACCES	W 28	1.7							PIECES DU 751 ET 752
7591	OFFICE MACHINE PARTS NES	W 28	1.7							PIECES DU 7511,7518
75911	TYPEWRTR PARTS,ACCES NES	W 15	1.5							PIECES DU 7511
76	TELECOMM,SOUND EQUIPMENT		6.4							EQUIPMENT DE TELECOM
764	TELECOM EQPT,PTS,ACC NES	W 78	6.3							EQUIP TELECOM,PIECES
7641	LINE TELEPHONE,ETC EQUIP	W 29	1.1							APP TELEPHON PAR FIL
7649	PTS NES OF EQUIPMT OF 76	W 29	5.1							PIECES DE LA DIV 76
76499	PARTS ETC OF SOUND EQUIP	W 21	4.8							PIECES NDA POUR 763
77	ELECTRIC MACHNRY NES ETC		7.9							MACH APP ELECT NDA
772	SWITCHGEAR ETC,PARTS NES	W 377	4.0							APP COUPURE,SECT ETC
7721	SWITCHGEAR ETC	W 377	4.0							APP COUPURE,SECTIONMNT
773	ELECTR DISTRIBUTNG EQUIP	W 234	1.2							EQUIPMT DISTRIBUTION ELECT
7731	INSULATED WIRE,CABLE ETC	W 234	1.2							FILS,CABLES ISOLES ELECT
775	HOUSEHOLD TYPE EQUIP NES	W 268	1.2							MACH,APP USAGE DOMESTQUE
7752	DOM REFRIGERATRS,FREEZRS	W 218	1.0							REFRIG,CONGEL MENAGER
77521	DOMESTIC REFRIGERATORS	W 202	0.9							REFRIGERATEURS
778	ELECTRICAL MACHINERY NES	W 406	1.3							AUTRES MACH ELECT NDA
7781	BATTERIES,ACCUMULATORS	W 334	0.9							PILES ET ACCUMULATEURS
78	ROAD VEHICLES		17.1							VEHICULES ROUTIERS
781	PASS MOTOR VEH EXC BUSES	W 440	1.5							AUTO TRANSPORT PERSONNES
782	LORRIES,SPCL MTR VEH NES	W 1349	11.7							VEHICULES SPECIAUX,MARCH
7821	LORRIES,TRUCKS	W 1349	11.7							VEHICULES TRANSP MARCHAND
784	MOTOR VEH PRTS,ACCES NES	W 223	2.7							PIECES 722,781,782,783
7849	OTHER MOTOR VEHCL PARTS	W 223	2.7							PIECES 722,781,782,783
8	MISC MANUFACTURED GOODS		18.2							ART MANUFACTURES DIVERS
821	*FURNITURE,PARTS THEREOF	W 1195	2.7							MEUBLES ET PIECES
8219	FURNITURE AND PARTS NES	W 1032	2.5							AUTRES MEUBLES ET PIECES
82192	WOOD FURNITURE NES	W 895	1.7							MEUBLES NDA EN BOIS
84	CLOTHING AND ACCESSORIES		3.7							VETEMENTS
842	MENS OUTERWEAR NOT KNIT	W 214	1.2							VET DESSUS POUR HOMMES
8429	— OTHER OUTER GARMENTS	W 156	0.9							AUT VET DES HOM MAT TEX
843	WOMENS OUTERWEAR NONKNIT	W 151	0.9							VET DESSUS FEMMES MAT TEX
8439	— OTHER OUTER GARMENTS	W 126	0.7							AUT VET DES FEM MAT TEXT
851	*FOOTWEAR	W 935	3.3							CHAUSSURES
85101	FOOTWEAR RUBBER,PLASTIC	W 500	1.4							CHAUS SEMELLES CAOUTCH
85102	FOOTWEAR LEATHER	W 404	1.7							CHAUS SEMELLES EN CUIR
87	PRECISION INSTRUMNTS NES		0.8							INSTRUM,APPAR SCIENT NDA
88	PHOTO EQU,OPTICL GDS ETC		0.8							APP,FOURN PHOTO,OP,MONTR
89	MISC MANUFCTRD GOODS NES		6.1							ART MANUFACTURES DIVERS
892	PRINTED MATTER	W 279	2.1							IMPRIMES
8921	PRINTED BOOKS,GLOBES,ETC	W 141	1.4							LIVRES,BROCHURES,CARTES
89211	PRINTED BOOKS,PAMPHLETS	W 141	1.4							LIVRES,BROCHURES

4. Special Imports C.I.F. by Commodities according to the S.I.T.C. (Rev. 2) in million U.S. Dollars
Importations Spéciales C.A.F. par Produits d'après la C.T.C.I. (Rév. 2) en millions de Dollars E.U.

SITC CTCI	COMMODITY	1992 QUANTITY QUANTITE	1992 VALUE VALEUR	1993 QUANTITY QUANTITE	1993 VALUE VALEUR	1994 QUANTITY QUANTITE	1994 VALUE VALEUR	1995 QUANTITY QUANTITE	1995 VALUE VALEUR	PRODUIT
893	ARTICLES OF PLASTIC NES	W 610	1.8							OUVRAGES EN MAT DIVIS 58
8939	MISC PLASTIC ARTICLES	W 283	0.8							ART DIVERS EN MAT DIV 58
9	GOODS NOT CLASSD BY KIND		9.0							ART TRANSACT NON CLASSES
931	*SPECIAL TRANSACTIONS	W 1073	7.9							TRANS.SPECIALES
961	*COIN NONGOLD,NONCURRENT		0.7							MONNAIES NON EMISES

5. Special Exports F.O.B. by Commodities according to the S.I.T.C. (Rev. 2) in million U.S. Dollars
Exportations Spéciales F.O.B. par Produits d'après la C.T.C.I. (Rév. 2) en millions de Dollars E.U.

SITC CTCI	COMMODITY	1992 QUANTITY QUANTITE	1992 VALUE VALEUR	1993 QUANTITY QUANTITE	1993 VALUE VALEUR	1994 QUANTITY QUANTITE	1994 VALUE VALEUR	1995 QUANTITY QUANTITE	1995 VALUE VALEUR	PRODUIT
	ALL COMMODITIES		16.0							TOUS PRODUITS
0	FOOD AND LIVE ANIMALS		3.3							ALIMENTS,ANIMAUX VIVANTS
001	*LIVE ANIMALS FOR FOOD	W 308	0.4							ANIMAUX VIVANTS
0011	BOVINE SPECIES,LIVE	W 307	0.4							ESPECE BOVINE
00111	— PURE BRED FR BREEDING	W 307	0.4							BOVINS REPRODUCTEURS
02	DAIRY PRODCTS,BIRDS'EGGS		0.1							PRODUITS LAITIERS,OEUFS
022	MILK AND CREAM	W 28	0.1							LAIT ET CREME
0224	MILK,CREAM PRESERVED ETC	W 28	0.1							LAIT,CREME CONS,CONC
02242	MILK DRY,1.5% FAT OR LES	W 28	0.1							LAIT POUDRE INF 1.5%
03	FISH AND PREPARATIONS		0.1							POISSONS ET PREPARATIONS
034	FISH,FRESH,CHILLED,FROZN	W 18	0.1							POISSON FRAIS, REFRIG,CONG
04	CEREALS AND PREPARATIONS		0.8							CEREALES ET PRODUITS
042	RICE	W 2258	0.8							RIZ
05	VEGETABLES AND FRUIT		0.2							LEGUMES ET FRUITS
054	VEG ETC FRSH,SMPLY PRSVD	W 228	0.1							LEGUMES FRAIS,CONG,SECS
0542	LEGUMINOUS VEGETBLES DRY	W 228	0.1							LEGUMES A COSSE SECS
07	COFFEE,TEA,COCOA,SPICES		1.9							CAFE,THE,CACAO,EPICES
071	COFFEE AND SUBSTITUTES	W 2000	1.8							CAFE ET SUCCEDANES
0711	COFFEE GREEN,ROASTED,SUB	W 2000	1.8							CAFE TORREFIE OU DECAFEINE
075	SPICES		0.1							EPICES
0752	SPICES,EX PEPPER,PIMENTO		0.1							AUTRES EPICES
09	MISC EDIBLE PRODUCTS		0.1							PREP ALIMENTAIRES DIVERSES
098	EDIBLE PRODCTS,PREPS NES	W 15	0.1							PREP ALIMENTAIRES NDA
09801	HOMOGENZD COMPOSITE FOOD	W 15	0.1							PREP ALIM COMPOSITES
2	CRUDE MATERLS,EXCL FUELS		0.9							MAT BRUTES NON COMESTIBLES
21	HIDES,SKINS,FURS UNDRSSD		0.2							CUIRS,PEAUX BRUTS
211	HIDES,SKINS,EXC FURS,RAW	W 286	0.2							CUIRS ET PEAUX
2111	BOVINE,EQUINE HIDES,RAW	W 144	0.2							PEAUX DE BOVINS
2119	SKIN NES,WASTE,USED LTHR	W 142	0.1							CUIRS ET PEAUX NDA
21199	HIDES AND SKINS NES,RAW	W 142	0.1							CUIRS,PEAUX NDA
26	TEXTILE FIBRES AND WASTE		0.4							FIBRES TEXTILES
269	WASTE OF TEXTILE FABRICS	W 259	0.3							FRIPERIE DRILLES,CHIFFONS
26901	BULK TEXT WSTE,OLD CLTHG	W 250	0.3							ART ET ACCESS D'HABILLEMENT
29	CRUDE ANIMAL,VEG MAT NES		0.4							MATIERES BRUTES ANIM,VEGET
291	CRUDE ANIMAL MTRIALS NES		0.2							MATIERES BRUTES ANIMALES
2919	OTH ANIMAL MATERIALS NES		0.2							MAT ORIGINE ANIMALE NDA
29198	AMBERGRIS,CIVET,MUSK,ETC		0.2							AMBRE GRIS,CIVETTE,MUSC
292	CRUDE VEG MATERIALS NES	W 271	0.3							MAT BRUTES VEGETALES NDA
2922	NAT GUMS,RESINS,LACS,ETC	W 199	0.3							GOMME LAQUE
6	BASIC MANUFACTURES		0.8							ART MANUFACTURES
65	TEXTILE YARN,FABRICS,ETC		0.3							FILS,TISSUS,ARTICLES TEXTILE
658	TEXTILE ARTICLES NES	W 74	0.3							ART FACONNES MAT TEXTILES
6582	MADE-UP CANVAS GOODS	W 30	0.1							BACHES,TENTES ETC
65821	MADE-UP COTTN CANVAS GDS	W 30	0.1							BACHES,TENTES DE COTON
6589	OTH TEXTILE ARTICLES NES	W 44	0.2							AUT ART EN TEXTILES NDA
65899	TXTL ARTCLES NONKNIT NES	W 44	0.2							ART TIS AUT QUE BONNETERIE
69	METAL MANUFACTURES NES		0.5							ART MANUFACT EN METAL NDA
692	METAL TANKS,BOXES,ETC	W 61	0.2							RECIPIENTS METALLIQUES
6924	MTL TRANSPORT BOXES ETC	W 61	0.2							FUTS,TAMBOURS,BIDONS
69241	STL TRANSPORT BOXES ETC	W 61	0.2							FUTS,TAMBOURS,BIDONS FER
695	TOOLS	W 78	0.2							OUTILS A MAIN
6953	OTHER HAND TOOLS	W 78	0.2							AUTRES OUTILS A MAIN
69539	HAND TOOLS ETC NES	W 78	0.2							OUTILLAGE A MAIN NDA
699	BASE METAL MFRS NES	W 158	0.2							ART MANUFACTURES MET NDA
6997	IRON,STEEL ARTICLES NES	W 137	0.2							OUV FONTE,FER,ACIER NDA
69979	IRN,STL MANUFACTURES NES	W 137	0.2							AUT OUVRAGES EN FER NDA
7	MACHINES,TRANSPORT EQUIP		1.3							MACHINES MATERIEL TRANSPORT
76	TELECOMM,SOUND EQUIPMENT		0.2							EQUIPMENT DE TELECOM
764	TELECOM EQPT,PTS,ACC NES	W 11	0.2							EQUIP TELECOM,PIECES
7649	PTS NES OF EQUIPMT OF 76	W 11	0.2							PIECES DE LA DIV 76
76493	TELECOMM EQUIPMT PTS NES	W 11	0.2							PIECES 761,762,764.3,8
78	ROAD VEHICLES		0.6							VEHICULES ROUTIERS
781	PASS MOTOR VEH EXC BUSES	W 75	0.5							AUTO TRANSPORT PERSONNES
784	MOTOR VEH PRTS,ACCES NES	W 7	0.2							PIECES 722,781,782,783
7849	OTHER MOTOR VEHCL PARTS	W 7	0.2							PIECES 722,781,782,783
79	OTHR TRANSPORT EQUIPMENT		0.6							AUTRE MATERIEL TRANSPORT
792	AIRCRAFT ETC		0.5							APP NAVIGATION AERIENNE
7929	AIRCRAFT PARTS NES	W 2	0.5							PIECES DU 792
793	SHIPS AND BOATS ETC		0.1							NAVIRES BATEAUX,ETC
7932	SHIPS AND BOATS NES		0.1							NAVIRES ET BATEAUX
79321	YACHTS,SPORTS VESSLS ETC	W 8	0.1							BATEAUX DE PLAISANCE
8	MISC MANUFACTURED GOODS		0.1							ART MANUFACTURES DIVERS
89	MISC MANUFCTRD GOODS NES		0.1							ART MANUFACTURES DIVERS
9	GOODS NOT CLASSD BY KIND		9.5							ART TRANSACT NON CLASSES
931	*SPECIAL TRANSACTIONS	W 787	9.5							TRANS.SPECIALES

1. HISTORICAL SERIES, 1962–1997 SPECIAL TRADE, IMPORTS C.I.F., EXPORTS F.O.B.
SERIES HISTORIQUES, 1962–1997 COMMERCE SPECIAL, IMPORTATIONS C.A.F., EXPORTATIONS F.O.B.

YEAR ANNEE	VALUE IN MILLION E.C. DOLLARS / VALEUR EN MILLION E.C. DOLLARS — MERCHANDISE –MARCHANDISE: IMPORTS	EXPORTS	GOLD –OR: IMPORTS	EXPORTS	CONVERSION FACTORS U.S. CENTS PER E.C. DOLLAR / FACTEURS DE CONVERSION CENTS E.U. PAR E.C. DOLLAR: IMPORTS	EXPORTS	INDEX NUMBERS –INDICES — QUANTUM: IMPORTS	EXPORTS	UNIT VALUE / VALEUR UNITAIRE: IMPORTS	EXPORTS
1962	12.80	7.70			58.3340	58.3340				
1963	12.00	7.80			58.3340	58.3340				
1964	15.00	8.60			58.3340	58.3340				
1965	17.20	9.50			58.3340	58.3340				
1966	16.90	10.10			58.3340	58.3340				
1967	17.20	10.80			57.6500	57.6500				
1968	20.10	12.40			50.0000	50.0000				
1969	24.70	14.20			50.0000	50.0000				
1970	31.50	11.80			50.0000	50.0000				
1971	33.00	12.30			50.7166	50.7166				
1972	32.90	13.50			52.1216	52.1216				
1973	32.30	16.70			51.0808	51.0808				
1974	38.90	20.90			48.7301	48.7301				
1975	45.00	24.60			46.2878	46.2878				
1976	49.80	29.10			38.0480	38.0480				
1977	59.10	32.30			37.0370	37.0370				
1978	76.80	42.90			37.0370	37.0370				
1979	60.00	25.40			37.0370	37.0370				
1980	128.70	26.30			37.0370	37.0370	54	27	89	73
1981	134.10	51.80			37.0370	37.0370	56	53	90	71
1982	128.20	66.00			37.0370	37.0370	47	57	89	76
1983	121.70	74.20			37.0370	37.0370	45	58	88	84
1984	156.10	69.20			37.0370	37.0370	62	59	91	74
1985	149.40	76.80			37.0370	37.0370	57	62	79	81
1986	150.69	117.24			37.0370	37.0370	63	83	77	91
1987	179.22	129.59			37.0370	37.0370	75	96	86	92
1988	236.34	146.41			37.0370	37.0370	80	107	93	99
1989	289.08	121.77			37.0370	37.0370	93	88	94	93
1990	318.39	148.59			37.0370	37.0370	100	100	100	100
1991	295.98	146.62			37.0370	37.0370	90	94	104	105
1992	300.02	150.81			37.0370	37.0370		97		100
1993	253.00	129.00			37.0370	37.0370		95		89
1994	260.00	122.00			37.0370	37.0370		107		97
1995	317.10	122.16			37.0370	37.0370		68		100
1996	350.85	138.46			37.0370	37.0370				
1997	362.33	143.01			37.0370	37.0370				

2. IMPORTS BY BROAD ECONOMIC CATEGORY AND EXPORTS BY INDUSTRIAL ORIGIN. (PERCENTAGE OF TOTAL VALUE)
IMPORTATIONS PAR CATEGORIES ECONOMIQUES ET EXPORTATIONS PAR BRANCHE D'ACTIVITE.(EN POURCENTAGE DE LA VALEUR TOTALE)

IMPORTS – IMPORTATIONS

	1990	1991	1992	1993	1994	1995	1996
TOTAL IMPORTS–IMPORTATIONS TOTALES	100.	100.		100.	100.	100.	100.
1 FOOD BEV–ALIMENTATION BOISSONS	20.7	22.9		22.9	24.4	23.1	21.9
11 PRIMARY–PRODUITS DE BASE	4.8	5.0		6.1	7.0	6.5	6.4
111 FOR INDUSTRY–POUR L'INDUSTRIE	0.2	0.3		0.5	0.6	0.6	0.6
112 FOR HOUSEHOLDS–POUR LES MENAGES	4.6	4.7		5.5	6.5	5.9	5.8
12 PROCESSED–PRODUITS ELABORES	15.9	18.0		16.8	17.3	16.5	15.5
121 FOR INDUSTRY–POUR L'INDUSTRIE	3.8	4.1		4.1	3.7	3.5	3.8
122 FOR HOUSEHOLDS–POUR LES MENAGES	12.1	13.9		12.7	13.6	13.0	11.7
2 IND SUPPLIES–APPROV INDUSTRIELS	37.1	35.6		39.0	36.5	36.5	37.9
21 PRIMARY–PRODUITS DE BASE	0.8	0.7		0.6	0.6	0.8	0.4
22 PROCESSED–PRODUITS ELABORES	36.3	34.9		38.5	35.9	35.7	37.5
3 FUELS–COMBUSTIBLES	6.1	7.9		6.1	6.4	5.3	6.3
31 PRIMARY–PRODUITS DE BASE	0.7	1.2		0.8	0.8	0.6	0.8
32 PROCESSED–PRODUITS ELABORES	5.3	6.7		5.3	5.6	4.7	5.5
321 MOTOR SPIRIT–ESSENCE				2.5	2.6	2.1	2.5
322 OTHER–AUTRES	5.3	6.7		2.8	3.0	2.6	3.0
4 MACHINERY–EQUIPEMENT	16.7	13.5		10.3	11.8	16.1	13.3
41 CAPITAL EQUIPMENT–MACHINES	16.7	13.5		9.2	10.8	14.8	12.0
42 PARTS–PIECES ACCESSOIRES				1.1	1.1	1.3	1.3
5 TRANSPORT–TRANSPORT	10.5	9.1		7.9	7.7	6.8	7.9
51 PASSENGER CARS–AUTOMOBILES				2.5	2.0	1.9	2.6
52 OTHER–AUTRES	0.5	0.6		3.0	3.4	2.9	3.1
521 INDUSTRIAL–INDUSTRIELS	0.5	0.6		2.9	3.3	2.8	3.0
522 NON INDUSTRIAL–NON INDUSTRIEL				0.1	0.1	0.0	0.1
53 PARTS–PIECES ACCESSOIRES	10.0	8.5		2.4	2.3	2.1	2.2
6 CONSUM GOODS–BIENS CONSOMMATION	8.9	11.1		13.6	13.1	12.1	12.5
61 DURABLE–DURABLES	1.3	1.9		3.4	3.1	2.6	2.6
62 SEMI DURABLE–SEMI DURABLES	4.9	5.7		5.7	5.6	5.3	5.5
63 NON DURABLE–NON DURABLES	2.7	3.5		4.5	4.4	4.2	4.4
7 GOODS NES–BIENS NDA	0.0	0.0		0.1	0.1	0.1	0.1

EXPORTS – EXPORTATIONS

	1990	1991	1992	1993	1994	1995	1996
TOTAL EXPORTS–EXPORTATIONS TOTALES	100.	100.		100.	100.	100.	100.
1 AGRICULTURE	62.4	64.4		64.5	55.5	47.8	46.3
2 MINING QUARRY–INDUS EXTRACTIVES	0.1	0.4		0.1	0.5	1.3	1.6
3 MANUFACTURING–IND MANUFACTUR	37.6	35.2		35.4	44.0	51.0	52.1
31 FOOD BEV TOBACCO–ALIM BOISS TAB	3.0	2.7		1.6	2.6	2.8	2.2
32 TEXTILES–INDUSTRIES TEXTILES	4.2	1.1		0.6	0.7	0.8	0.3
33 WOOD & PRODUCTS–BOIS & PRODUITS	1.6	2.1		0.0	0.1	0.0	0.4
34 PAPER & PRODUCTS–PAPIER & PRODT	0.1	0.1		2.4	1.6	0.1	0.1
35 CHEMICALS–INDUSTRIES CHIMIQUES	24.2	23.8		28.2	37.0	44.0	47.6
36 NON METAL MIN–MIN NON METAL	0.0	0.0		0.0	0.0	0.0	0.0
37 BASIC METAL–IND METAL BASE				0.0	0.0	0.0	
38 METAL MANUF–MANUF METAL	4.2	4.9		2.4	1.7	3.0	1.4
39 OTH MANUF IND–AUTRES MANUF	0.2	0.4		0.3	0.2	0.1	0.1

3. TRADE BY PRINCIPAL COUNTRIES OF ORIGIN AND DESTINATION (VALUE IN MILLION U.S. DOLLARS)
ECHANGES SELON LES PRINCIPAUX PAYS D'ORIGINE ET DE DESTINATION (VALEUR EN MILLIONS DE DOLLARS EU)

COUNTRIES–PAYS	SPECIAL IMPORTS C.I.F. IMPORTATIONS SPECIALES C.A.F				
	1992	1993	1994	1995	1996
World		93.8	96.3	117.3	129.9
Africa		0.0	0.2	0.1	0.1
Americas		67.2	69.7	78.6	94.0
– Northern America		37.3	36.5	41.4	55.8
– LAIA		2.0	1.6	2.1	3.0
– CACM		0.7	0.8	1.0	1.3
– Caribbean		26.2	29.8	32.2	33.0
– Rest of America		0.9	1.1	1.9	0.9
Asia excl fmr USSR		6.2	7.0	7.3	9.4
– Middle East		0.0	0.0	0.1	0.0
Asia former USSR					
Europe excl fmr USSR		20.4	19.3	31.1	26.3
– European Union		18.4	17.5	29.4	24.4
– Eastern Europe		0.1	0.1	0.1	0.1
– Rest of Europe		1.9	1.7	1.6	1.8
Europe former USSR		0.0	0.0	0.1	0.0
Oceania		0.0	0.0	0.1	0.2
Other		0.0	0.0	0.0	0.0
USA/Etats–Unis d'Amer		35.2	34.5	38.9	53.2
United Kingdom		11.8	12.2	15.8	16.9
Trinidad and Tobago		10.4	12.1	12.9	16.3
Japan/Japon		4.0	4.5	5.4	7.2
Saint Lucia/Ste–Lucie		3.0	5.0	5.9	3.6
Barbados/Barbade		3.2	3.7	4.3	4.8
St Vincent & Grenadines		3.0	3.0	3.0	2.6
France, Monaco		0.5	0.9	7.7	2.4
Canada		2.1	2.0	2.4	2.6
Germany/Allemagne		1.2	1.4	3.1	2.1
Jamaica/Jamaïque		1.8	1.9	1.8	2.1
Netherlands/Pays–Bas		1.7	1.4	1.5	1.7
Netherlands Antilles		1.0	0.7	1.0	0.9
Grenada/Grenade		0.8	0.6	0.9	1.1
Brazil/Brésil		1.0	0.8	0.8	0.7
Switzerland,Liechtenst.		1.0	0.8	0.9	0.6
Venezuela		0.6	0.4	1.1	1.1
Guyana		0.6	0.7	1.3	0.4
Antigua and Barbuda		0.8	0.7	0.5	0.5
China/Chine		0.6	0.7	0.6	0.5
Costa Rica		0.4	0.4	0.5	0.8
Guadeloupe		0.8	0.7	0.6	
Italy/Italie		0.4	0.7	0.5	0.4
Spain/Espagne		1.7	0.1	0.2	0.1
Saint Kitts and Nevis		0.4	0.5	0.5	0.5
Martinique		0.8	0.7	0.4	
TFYR Macedonia		0.6	0.5	0.4	0.2
Other Asia n.e.s.		0.4	0.4	0.3	0.5
Colombia/Colombie		0.1	0.3	0.2	1.1
China, Hong Kong SAR		0.5	0.4	0.3	0.3
Guatemala		0.2	0.3	0.6	0.5
Norway,Svalbard and JM		0.3	0.4	0.4	0.3
Denmark/Danemark		0.4	0.4	0.2	0.4
Panama		0.3	0.3	0.4	0.3
Dominican Republic		0.1	0.1	0.2	0.5
Belgium–Luxembourg		0.4	0.1	0.1	0.2
Korea, Republic of		0.2	0.2	0.2	0.2
Malta/Malte					0.6
Israel/Israël		0.0	0.3	0.1	0.2
Singapore/Singapour		0.2	0.1	0.1	0.1

COUNTRIES–PAYS	EXPORTS EXPORTATIONS ES F.O.B.				
	1992	1993	1994	1995	1996
Monde		48.0	45.2	45.2	51.2
Afrique		0.0	0.0		
Amériques		22.0	23.5	27.5	28.7
– Amérique du Nord		2.8	3.5	3.7	3.7
– ALAI		0.0	0.0	0.0	
– MCAC		0.0	0.0	0.1	0.0
– Caraïbes		17.7	18.4	21.0	22.5
– Autre Amérique		1.5	1.7	2.8	2.4
Asie anc. URSS exclus		0.0	0.1	0.0	0.0
– Moyen–Orient					
Asie ancienne URSS					
Europe anc. URSS exclus		26.0	21.5	17.6	22.2
– Union Européenne		26.0	21.5	17.6	22.2
– Europe de l'Est					
– Autre de l'Europe		0.0	0.0		0.0
Europe ancienne URSS					
Océanie					0.0
Autre		0.0	0.1	0.1	0.2
United Kingdom		24.4	21.5	17.3	18.2
Jamaica/Jamaïque		4.4	4.5	5.4	10.7
USA/Etats–Unis d'Amer		2.7	3.4	3.7	3.7
Saint Lucia/Ste–Lucie		1.6	2.4	2.7	2.2
Guyana		1.5	1.6	2.7	2.4
Trinidad and Tobago		1.5	1.8	2.3	2.1
Antigua and Barbuda		1.5	1.5	1.9	2.6
Guadeloupe		2.3	2.1	2.8	
Barbados/Barbade		1.2	1.6	1.6	1.4
Netherlands Antilles		1.9	1.3	0.9	0.7
France, Monaco		0.0	0.0	0.2	4.0
Grenada/Grenade		1.2	0.9	0.7	0.7
Saint Kitts and Nevis		0.6	0.7	0.8	1.0
St Vincent & Grenadines		0.7	0.9	0.9	0.6
Italy/Italie		1.6			
Martinique		0.5	0.4	0.5	
Montserrat		0.1	0.1	0.1	0.1
Areas n.e.s.		0.0	0.1	0.1	0.2
British Virgin Islds		0.0	0.1	0.1	0.1
Bahamas		0.0	0.1	0.1	0.1
Cuba		0.2	0.1		
Belize/Bélize		0.0	0.1	0.1	0.0
Haiti/Haïti				0.0	0.1
Japan/Japon		0.0	0.1	0.0	0.0
Dominican Republic			0.1	0.0	0.0
Venezuela		0.0	0.0	0.0	
Canada		0.0	0.0	0.0	0.0
El Salvador				0.1	
Germany/Allemagne				0.0	0.0
Netherlands/Pays–Bas		0.0	0.0		0.0
Israel/Israël			0.0		
Mexico/Mexique			0.0	0.0	
Portugal				0.0	
Costa Rica		0.0	0.0		0.0
Belgium–Luxembourg		0.0			
Brazil/Brésil			0.0		
TFYR Macedonia		0.0	0.0		
Switzerland,Liechtenst.			0.0		0.0
Ireland/Irlande					0.0
Malta/Malte			0.0		

(VALUE AS PERCENTAGE OF WORLD TOTAL)(VALEURS EN POURCENTAGE DU TOTAL MONDIAL)

	1987	1988	1989	1990	1991	1992	1993	1994	1995	1996
Africa		0.0	0.0	0.1	0.0		0.0	0.3	0.1	0.1
Americas		62.0	65.2	65.6	68.8		71.6	72.4	67.0	72.3
– Northern America		28.5	37.8	35.8	35.8		39.8	37.9	35.3	43.0
– LAIA		1.5	2.6	2.2	2.6		2.2	1.6	1.8	2.3
– CACM		0.4	0.5	0.7	0.5		0.7	0.8	0.9	1.0
– Caribbean		30.7	23.6	26.4	29.6		27.9	31.0	27.5	25.4
– Rest of America		1.0	0.8	0.4	0.3		1.0	1.1	1.6	0.7
Asia excl fmr USSR		11.6	11.1	10.1	8.3		6.6	7.2	6.3	7.2
– Middle East			0.0	0.0	0.0		0.0	0.0	0.1	0.0
Asia former USSR										
Europe excl fmr USSR		25.9	23.5	24.2	22.8		21.7	20.0	26.6	20.2
– European Union		25.3	22.7	22.9	21.3		19.6	18.2	25.0	18.8
– Eastern Europe		0.1	0.1	0.2	0.3		0.1	0.1	0.1	0.1
– Rest of Europe		0.6	0.7	1.1	1.2		2.0	1.8	1.4	1.4
Europe former USSR		0.3	0.1	0.0	0.0		0.0	0.0	0.0	0.0
Oceania		0.1	0.1	0.1	0.0		0.0	0.0	0.1	0.1
Other			0.0	0.0	0.0		0.0	0.0	0.0	0.0
USA/Etats–Unis d'Amer		25.3	31.2	33.3	31.4		37.6	35.8	33.2	40.9
United Kingdom		18.4	14.4	14.4	13.8		12.6	12.6	13.5	13.0
Trinidad and Tobago		8.4	7.2	9.2	10.0		11.1	12.5	11.0	12.5
Japan/Japon		5.3	5.8	6.2	5.6		4.3	4.7	4.6	5.6
Saint Lucia/Ste–Lucie		8.1	3.9	4.2	4.2		3.2	5.2	5.1	2.7
Barbados/Barbade		3.6	3.2	2.5	3.3		3.4	3.9	3.6	3.7
St Vincent & Grenadines		1.8	2.0	2.1	2.5		3.2	3.1	2.6	2.0
France, Monaco		1.3	3.4	1.5	1.3		0.6	0.9	6.5	1.8
Canada		3.2	6.6	2.5	4.4		2.2	2.1	2.1	2.0
Germany/Allemagne					2.8		1.3	1.5	2.7	1.6

	1987	1988	1989	1990	1991	1992	1993	1994	1995	1996
Afrique							0.0	0.0		
Amériques		29.8	42.0	42.9	38.7		45.8	52.1	60.8	56.1
– Amérique du Nord		5.7	8.6	11.4	5.4		5.7	7.6	8.1	7.3
– ALAI		0.0	0.0		0.0		0.1	0.1	0.0	
– MCAC							0.0	0.0	0.1	0.0
– Caraïbes		22.7	32.8	30.5	33.1		36.9	40.6	46.3	44.0
– Autre Amérique		1.4	0.6	1.0	0.2		3.1	3.7	6.2	4.8
Asie anc. URSS exclus		0.0	0.0	0.0	0.0		0.0	0.3	0.0	0.1
– Moyen–Orient										
Asie ancienne URSS										
Europe anc. URSS exclus		70.2	57.9	56.9	61.2		54.2	47.5	38.9	43.5
– Union Européenne		70.2	57.9	56.9	61.2		54.1	47.5	38.9	43.5
– Europe de l'Est				0.0	0.0					
– Autre de l'Europe				0.0	0.0		0.0	0.0		0.0
Europe ancienne URSS				0.2						
Océanie			0.0	0.0						0.0
Autre				0.0	0.0		0.0	0.2	0.3	0.3
United Kingdom		60.9	52.1	49.6	53.5		50.8	47.5	38.2	35.6
Jamaica/Jamaïque		10.4	13.9	12.3	10.3		9.1	9.9	11.9	20.8
USA/Etats–Unis d'Amer		5.3	8.1	11.2	5.2		5.7	7.6	8.1	7.3
Saint Lucia/Ste–Lucie		1.8	3.0	2.0	3.0		3.4	5.3	6.0	4.3
Guyana		1.4	0.6	1.0	0.2		3.0	3.4	6.1	4.7
Trinidad and Tobago		1.4	2.5	2.6	3.1		3.1	4.0	5.2	4.2
Antigua and Barbuda		1.4	1.9	2.1	3.1		3.0	3.3	4.1	5.0
Guadeloupe		1.8	2.7	4.3	5.5		4.7	4.6	6.1	
Barbados/Barbade		2.1	2.9	2.1	2.2		2.4	3.6	3.5	2.8
Netherlands Antilles		0.9	1.1	1.4	1.0		3.9	2.8	2.0	1.3

4. Special Imports C.I.F. by Commodities according to the S.I.T.C. (Rev. 2) in million U.S. Dollars
Importations Spéciales C.A.F. par Produits d'après la C.T.C.I. (Rév. 2) en millions de Dollars E.U.

SITC CTCI	COMMODITY	1993 QUANTITY QUANTITE	1993 VALUE VALEUR	1994 QUANTITY QUANTITE	1994 VALUE VALEUR	1995 QUANTITY QUANTITE	1995 VALUE VALEUR	1996 QUANTITY QUANTITE	1996 VALUE VALEUR	PRODUIT
	ALL COMMODITIES				96.4		117.3		130.0	TOUS PRODUITS
0	FOOD AND LIVE ANIMALS				19.5		22.7		24.7	ALIMENTS,ANIMAUX VIVANTS
01	MEAT AND PREPARATIONS				4.4		4.9		5.8	VIANDES ET PREPARATIONS
011	MEAT FRESH,CHILLD,FROZEN			W 2418	3.4	W 2798	3.8	W 3154	4.5	VIANDES FRAICHES,REF,CONGE
0114	POULTRY FRESH CHLLD,FRZN			W 2117	2.9	W 2505	3.3	W 2818	4.0	VOLAILLES MORTES
014	MEAT PREPD,PRSVD,NES ETC			W 492	1.0	W 519	1.2	W 563	1.3	CONSERVES DE VIANDES
0142	SAUSAGES INCLDING TINNED			W 175	0.5	W 198	0.5	W 210	0.6	SAUCISSES,SAUCISSONS
0149	OTH PREPARD,PRESRVD MEAT			W 317	0.6	W 320	0.7	W 353	0.8	AUTRES PREP DE VIANDES
02	DAIRY PRODCTS,BIRDS'EGGS				3.1		3.8		4.0	PRODUITS LAITIERS,OEUFS
022	MILK AND CREAM			W 1499	2.4	W 1520	2.9	W 1668	3.2	LAIT ET CREME
0223	MILK AND CREAM FRESH			W 834	1.1	W 685	1.0	W 757	1.1	LAIT,CREME FRAIS
0224	MILK,CREAM PRESERVED ETC			W 665	1.3	W 836	2.0	W 911	2.1	LAIT,CREME CONS,CONC
02242	MILK DRY,1.5% FAT OR LES			W 330	0.8	W 326	1.1	W 387	1.3	LAIT POUDRE INF 1.5%
02243	MILK DRY,OVER 1.5% FAT			W 78	0.2	W 149	0.4	W 29	0.1	LAIT POUDRE SUP 1.5%
02249	MILK(EX DRY) PRSVD,SWEET			W 256	0.4	W 361	0.6	W 495	0.8	LAIT CONS,CONC SUCRE
024	CHEESE AND CURD			W 204	0.7	W 217	0.9	W 240	0.9	FROMAGE ET CAILLEBOTTE
03	FISH AND PREPARATIONS				1.4		1.4		1.7	POISSONS ET PREPARATIONS
035	FISH SALTED,DRIED,SMOKED			W 278	0.9	W 241	0.9	W 301	1.1	POISSON SECHE,SALE,FUME
03502	COD(NOT IN FILLETS)DRIED			W 168	0.7	W 108	0.5	W 138	0.7	MORUE SECHEE,SALEE
037	FISH ETC PREPD,PRSVD NES			W 148	0.5	W 340	0.5	W 210	0.5	POIS,CRUST,MOL PREPARES
0371	FISH PREPARD,PRESRVD NES			W 148	0.4	W 339	0.5	W 210	0.5	CONSERVES DE POISSONS
04	CEREALS AND PREPARATIONS				4.6		5.4		5.7	CEREALES ET PRODUITS
042	RICE			W 963	0.7	W 1776	0.7	W 1018	0.8	RIZ
0421	RICE IN HUSK OR HUSKED			W 845	0.6	W 1638	0.6	W 866	0.6	RIZ SANS AUTRE PREPARATION
04212	RICE HUSKED			W 844	0.6	W 1618	0.6	W 866	0.6	RIZ CARGO
046	WHEAT ETC MEAL OR FLOUR			W 4237	2.3	W 4592	2.6	W 4392	2.6	SEMOULE FARINE,FROMENT
04601	FLOUR OF WHEAT OR MESLIN			W 4183	2.3	W 4580	2.6	W 4380	2.6	FARINE DE FROMENT
048	CEREAL ETC PREPARATIONS			W 799	1.6	W 1647	1.9	W 1105	2.2	PREPTNS A BASE CEREALES
0481	PREPD BREAKFAST FOOD ETC			W 109	0.4	W 200	0.5	W 143	0.5	CEREALES TRAVAILLEES
0484	BAKERY PRODUCTS			W 311	0.6	W 1168	0.9	W 439	0.9	PRODUITS DE BOULANGERIE
04841	BREAD,BISCUIT,COM WAFERS			W 311	0.6	W 1168	0.9	W 439	0.9	PAINS,BISCUITS DE MER
0488	OTH CEREAL PREPS,MALT EX			W 243	0.4	W 132	0.4	W 168	0.5	EXTRAITS DE MALT
05	VEGETABLES AND FRUIT				1.7		2.4		1.9	LEGUMES ET FRUITS
054	VEG ETC FRSH,SMPLY PRSVD			W 1107	0.9	W 1358	1.4	W 1075	0.9	LEGUMES FRAIS,CONG,SECS
0542	LEGUMINOUS VEGETBLES DRY			W 291	0.3	W 395	0.7	W 269	0.3	LEGUMES A COSSE SECS
058	FRUIT PRESERVED,PREPARED			W 384	0.6	W 321	0.6	W 327	0.7	CONSERVES DE FRUITS
06	SUGAR AND PREPS,HONEY				1.4		1.9		2.0	SUCRES ET PRODUITS
061	SUGAR AND HONEY			W 1800	1.2	W 3517	1.6	W 3461	1.7	SUCRES ET MIEL
0611	RAW BEET AND CANE SUGAR			W 150	0.4	W 1446	0.7	W 650	0.3	SUCRES BRUTS
0612	REFINED SUGAR ETC			W 1633	0.8	W 2036	1.0	W 2799	1.4	SUCRES RAFFINES
07	COFFEE,TEA,COCOA,SPICES				0.6		0.5		0.6	CAFE,THE,CACAO,EPICES
081	*FEEDING STUFF FOR ANIML			W 1959	0.8	W 2037	0.8	W 2113	0.9	NOURRITURE POUR ANIMAUX
0819	FOOD WASTE AND FEED NES			W 1959	0.8	W 2037	0.8	W 2103	0.9	DECHETS,ALIMENTS NDA
08199	FODDER NES,INCL SWEETNED			W 1959	0.8	W 2028	0.8	W 2103	0.9	PREPARATIONS FOURRAGERES
09	MISC EDIBLE PRODUCTS				1.8		2.2		2.4	PREP ALIMENTAIRES DIVERSES
091	MARGARINE AND SHORTENING			W 302	0.6	W 310	0.6	W 334	0.6	MARGARINE ET GRAISSES
0914	MARGARINE,EDIBLE FAT NES			W 302	0.6	W 310	0.6	W 334	0.6	MARGARINES,SIMILI SAINDOUX
09141	MARGARINE			W 237	0.5	W 222	0.5	W 277	0.5	MARGARINE
098	EDIBLE PRODCTS,PREPS NES			W 481	1.3	W 649	1.6	W 659	1.8	PREP ALIMENTAIRES NDA
09804	SAUCES,MIXED SEASONINGS			W 212	0.5	W 234	0.5	W 254	0.6	SAUCES,ASSAISONNEMENTS
09809	MISC FOOD PREPRTIONS NES			W 138	0.6	W 273	0.8	W 264	0.9	PREP ALIMENTAIRES NDA
1	BEVERAGES AND TOBACCO				4.4		4.9		3.2	BOISSONS ET TABACS
11	BEVERAGES				4.2		4.6		3.0	BOISSONS
111	NON-ALCOHL BEVERAGES NES			W 1138	1.1	W 1451	1.2	W 1039	1.1	BOISSONS NON ALCOOLIQUES
11102	FLAVORED WATERS NON-ALCO			W 1138	1.1	W 1320	1.1	W 949	1.1	LIMONADES,EAUX GAZEUSES
112	ALCOHOLIC BEVERAGES			W 2479	3.1	W 3614	3.5	W 1132	2.0	BOISSONS ALCOOLIQUES
1121	WINE OF FRESH GRAPES ETC			W 320	0.5	W 375	0.6	W 266	0.6	VINS DE RAISINS FRAIS
11212	WINE OF FRESH GRAPES			W 315	0.5	W 373	0.6	W 245	0.5	VINS DE MOUTS DE RAISINS
1123	BEER,ALE,STOUT,PORTER			W 1853	2.0	W 2582	2.0	W 454	0.6	BIERES
1124	DISTILLED ALCOHOLIC BEVS			W 275	0.7	W 630	0.9	W 364	0.8	ALCOOLS,EAUX-DE-VIE
11249	OTH ALCOHOLC BEVS,CMPNDS			W 171	0.4	W 483	0.5	W 195	0.5	BOISSONS ALCOOLIQUES NDA
2	CRUDE MATERLS,EXCL FUELS				2.1		2.7		2.8	MAT BRUTES NON COMESTIBLES
24	CORK AND WOOD				1.8		2.2		2.3	LIEGE ET BOIS
248	WOOD SHAPED,SLEEPERS			W 2814	1.7	W 2954	1.9	W 5972	2.3	BOIS SIMPLEMENT TRAVAILLES
2482	LUMBER SHAPED CONIFER			W 1387	0.9	W 1698	1.2	W 4053	1.3	CONIFERES SCIES,RABOTES
24822	LUMBER PLANED ETC CONIFR			W 1387	0.9	W 1698	1.2	W 4053	1.3	CONIFER RABOTES,RAINES
2483	LUMBER SHAPED NON-CONIFR			W 1427	0.9	W 1256	0.8	W 1919	1.0	NON CONIFERES SCIES,RABOTES
24831	LUMBER SAWN ETC NON-CON			W 1311	0.8	W 1066	0.7	W 1778	0.9	SCIES LONGITUDINALEMENT
3	MINERAL FUELS ETC				6.4		6.7		8.6	COMBUSTIBLES MINERAUX LUB
33	PETROLEUM AND PRODUCTS				5.6		6.0		7.5	PETROLE ET DERIVES
334	PETROLEUM PRODUCTS,REFIN			W 22830	5.4	W 22124	5.6	W 17404	7.2	PRODUITS RAFFINES
3341	GASOLINE,OTH LIGHT OILS			W 11057	2.6	W 8989	2.5	W 7322	3.3	ESSENCES POUR MOTEURS
33411	MOTOR,AVIATION SPIRIT			W 11057	2.6	W 8961	2.5	W 7322	3.3	ESSENCES MOTEURS D'AVIONS
3343	GAS OILS			W 9291	1.8	W 9904	1.8	W 7725	2.6	GAS OILS
3344	FUEL OILS,NES			W 1766	0.6	W 2558	0.8	W 1553	0.8	FUEL OILS
3345	LUBS,PETROLEUM OILS NES			W 332	0.5	W 429	0.6	W 444	0.6	HUILES LUBRIFIANTES
33451	LUBS(HIGH PETR CONT) ETC			W 328	0.5	W 421	0.5	W 437	0.6	HUILES LUBRIF,H LOURDES
335	RESIDUAL PETRLM PROD NES			W 10741	0.2	W 720	0.4	W 3620	0.4	PRODUITS RESIDUELS NDA
341	*GAS,NATURAL AND MANUFCT			W 202339	0.9	W 1532	0.7	W 2108	1.1	GAZ NATUREL,GAZ MANUFACT
3413	PETROLM GASES,LIQUEFIED			W 202339	0.9	W 1532	0.7	W 2108	1.1	GAZ DE PETROLE LIQUEFIE
34131	LIQUEFIED PROPANE,BUTANE			W 202334	0.9	W 1518	0.7	W 2094	1.1	PROPANE,BUTANE LIQUEFIES
4	ANIMAL,VEGETABLE OIL,FAT				3.2		3.2		8.3	HUILES,GRAISSES ANIM,VEG
411	*ANIMAL OILS AND FATS			W 4506	2.5	W 2733	2.7	W 9628	6.6	HUILES,GRAISSES ANIMALES
4113	ANIML OIL,FAT,GREASE NES			W 4495	2.5	W 2733	2.7	W 9628	6.6	HUILES,GRAISSES ANIMALES NDA
41132	FATS OF BOVINE,SHEEP,ETC			W 3395	2.0	W 2732	2.7	W 9625	6.6	SUIFS BRUTS FONDUS
41133	LARD STEARIN AND OIL,ETC			W 1100	0.5					STEARINE SOLAIRE
42	FIXED VEGETABLE OIL,FAT				0.6		0.5		1.7	HUILES VEGETALES FIXES
423	FIXED VEG OILS,SOFT			W 175	0.3	W 260	0.5	W 351	0.7	HUILES VEGET DOUCES FIXES
4232	SOYA BEAN OIL			W 156	0.3	W 256	0.5	W 334	0.6	HUILE DE SOJA
424	FIXED VEG OIL NONSOFT			W 538	0.3	W 33	0.1	W 1649	1.1	AUTRES HUILES VEG FIXES
4242	PALM OIL			W 537	0.3			W 1200	0.6	HUILE DE PALME
4243	COCONUT (COPRA) OIL					W 17	0.1	W 436	0.5	HJUILE DE COPRAH
5	CHEMCLS,RELATED PROD NES				13.0		15.8		16.5	PRODUITS CHIMIQUES
51	ORGANIC CHEMICALS				0.5		0.6		0.6	PROD CHIMIQ ORGANIQUES
512	ALCOHOLS,PHENOLS ETC			W 285	0.4	W 309	0.4	W 284	0.4	PHENOLS,PHENOLS-ALCOOLS
5121	ACYCLIC ALCOHOLS,DERIVS			W 285	0.4	W 307	0.4	W 274	0.4	ALCOOLS ACYCLIQUES
52	INORGANIC CHEMICALS				0.9		1.6		1.5	PROD CHIM INORGANIQUES
522	INORG ELEMNTS,OXIDES,ETC			W 1298	0.7	W 3064	1.4	W 7318	1.3	ELEMENTS INORGANIQUES
5225	INORGANIC BASES ETC NES			W 1050	0.4	W 2816	0.9	W 7043	0.8	AUTRES BASES OXYDES METAL
52253	SODIUM HYDROXIDE, OTHER			W 532	0.3	W 2514	0.7	W 6967	0.7	HYDROXYDE SODIUM AQUEUX
53	DYES,TANNING,COLOUR PROD				1.0		1.0		1.3	PROD TEINTURE,COLORANTS

4. Special Imports C.I.F. by Commodities according to the S.I.T.C. (Rev. 2) in million U.S. Dollars
Importations Spéciales C.A.F. par Produits d'après la C.T.C.I. (Rév. 2) en millions de Dollars E.U.

SITC CTCI	COMMODITY	1993 QUANTITY QUANTITE	1993 VALUE VALEUR	1994 QUANTITY QUANTITE	1994 VALUE VALEUR	1995 QUANTITY QUANTITE	1995 VALUE VALEUR	1996 QUANTITY QUANTITE	1996 VALUE VALEUR	PRODUIT
533	PIGMENTS,PAINTS,ETC			W 542	1.0	W 397	1.0	W 418	1.2	PIGMENTS,PEINTURES,VERNIS
5334	VARNISHES,DISTEMPERS ETC			W 210	0.7	W 215	0.8	W 257	0.9	PEINTURES A L'EAU
53342	OTH PAINTS,VARNISHES ETC			W 70	0.3	W 131	0.5	W 151	0.6	AUTRES PEINTURES,VERNIS
541	*MEDICINAL,PHARM PRODUCT			K 97799	1.2	K 190981	1.3	K 116392	1.5	PROD MEDICINAUX PHARMACEUT
5417	MEDICAMENTS			K 93403	1.0	K 182630	1.2	K 105619	1.2	MEDICAMENTS
54179	— CONTNG OTH SUBSTANCES			K 92703	1.0	K 179283	1.2	K 102999	1.1	MED CONT AUT SUBSTANCES
55	PERFUME,CLEANING ETC PRD				3.0		3.5		3.6	PROD POUR PARFUM,TOILETTE
551	ESSENTL OILS,PERFUME,ETC			W 64	1.1	W 106	1.4	W 95	1.3	HUILES ESSENTIELLES
5514	MIXED PERFUME SUBSTANCES			W 63	1.0	W 104	1.4	W 94	1.3	MELANGES SUBSTAN ODORIFER
553	PERFUMERY,COSMETICS,ETC			W 206	1.0	W 199	1.0	W 215	1.2	PRODUITS DE PARFUMERIE
554	SOAP,CLEANSING ETC PREPS			W 783	1.0	W 853	1.2	W 1062	1.2	SAVONS,PRODUITS DETERSIFS
5542	WASHING PREPARATIONS ETC			W 717	0.8	W 806	1.0	W 982	1.0	PROD ORG TENSIO-ACT NDA
562	*FERTILIZERS,MANUFACTURE			W 6263	2.1	W 7233	2.7	W 6059	2.0	ENGRAIS MANUFACTURES
5629	FERTILIZERS NES			W 6259	2.1	W 7189	2.7	W 6035	2.0	ENGRAIS NDA
56291	NIT-PHOS-POT FERTLZR NES			W 6258	2.1	W 7189	2.7	W 6034	2.0	ENGRAIS CONT N P K
58	PLASTIC MATERIALS ETC				1.3		1.7		2.0	MAT PLAST ARTIFICIELLES
582	PROD OF CONDENSATION ETC			W 386	0.5	W 407	0.6	W 455	0.6	PROD CONDENS,POLYCOND
5825	POLYURETHANES			W 344	0.4	W 309	0.4	W 381	0.4	POLYURETHANES
58251	— IN PRIMARY FORMS			W 344	0.4	W 309	0.4	W 381	0.4	POLYURETHANES PRIMAIRES
583	POLYMERIZATION ETC PRODS			W 421	0.8	W 561	1.1	W 585	1.5	PROD POLYMERISATION
5839	OTH POLYMRZTION ETC PROD			W 421	0.8	W 544	1.1	W 585	1.5	AUT PROD POLYMER COPOLYM
59	CHEMICAL MATERIALS NES				3.4		3.7		4.3	MAT PROD CHIMIQUES NDA
591	PESTICIDES,DISINFECTANTS			W 352	2.2	W 516	2.6	W 585	2.7	DESINF,INSECT,FONG,HERB
5911	INSECTICIDES,FOR RETAIL			W 134	0.7	W 284	1.5	W 317	1.2	INSECTICIDES VENTE DET
5912	FUNGICIDES,FOR RETAIL			W 47	0.9	W 14	0.3	W 50	0.7	FONGICIDES VENTE AU DET
5913	HERBICIDES,FOR RETAIL			W 154	0.6	W 192	0.8	W 185	0.9	HERBICIDES VENTE AU DET
598	MISCEL CHEM PRODUCTS NES			W 276	0.9	W 301	0.9	W 390	1.3	PROD DIV INDUST CHIM NDA
5989	CHEM PRODUCTS,PREPS NES			W 271	0.9	W 286	0.8	W 317	1.1	PROD PREP CHIMIQUES NDA
59899	OTH CHEM PRODS,PREPS,NES			W 171	0.7	W 176	0.6	W 208	0.9	AUT PRODUITS CHIMIQUES NDA
6	BASIC MANUFACTURES				20.0		23.8		26.3	ART MANUFACTURES
62	RUBBER MANUFACTURES NES				1.2		1.5		1.8	CAOUTCHOUC MANUFACTURE
625	RUBBER TYRES, TUBES ETC			W 337	0.9	W 502	1.1	W 399	1.3	PNEUS CAOUTCHOUC VULCANISE
6252	TYRES,NEW,BUS OR LORRY			W 128	0.5	W 294	0.6	W 158	0.7	PNEUS POUR AUTOBUS,CAMIONS
6259	OTH TYRES,TYRE CASES,ETC			W 169	0.3	W 163	0.4	W 184	0.5	AUTRES PNEUS RECHAPES FLAPS
62599	TYRES NES,TYRE CASES,ETC			W 163	0.2	W 154	0.3	W 177	0.5	PNEUS,FLAPS
628	RUBBER ARTICLES NES			W 24	0.2	W 23	0.4	W 43	0.4	OUVRAGES CAOUTCHOUC NDA
63	WOOD,CORK MANUFACTRS NES				1.8		1.9		2.6	OUVRAGES LIEGE ET BOIS
634	VENEERS,PLYWOOD,ETC			W 1581	1.3	W 1662	1.1	W 1506	1.3	PLACAGES,CONTRE-PLAQUES
6342	PLYWOOD OF WOOD SHEETS			W 1550	1.3	W 1532	1.0	W 1480	1.3	BOIS CONTRE-PLAQUES
635	WOOD MANUFACTURES NES			W 452	0.6	W 336	0.9	W 382	1.3	ART MANUF EN BOIS NDA
6353	BUILDERS WOODWRK,PREFABS			W 399	0.5	W 280	0.8	W 257	1.0	OUVRAGES DE MENUISERIE
64	PAPER,PAPERBOARD AND MFR				6.1		7.1		7.8	PAPIERS,CARTONS & OUVRAGES
641	PAPER AND PAPERBOARD			W 2050	2.0	W 658	1.5	W 3728	3.8	PAPIERS ET CARTONS
6413	KRAFT PAPER,PAPERBOARD			W 1116	0.7	W 61	0.1	W 146	0.2	PAPIER ET CARTON KRAFT
64132	SACK KRAFT PAPER IN BULK			W 1116	0.7	W 61	0.1	W 146	0.2	PAPIER KRAFT POUR SACS
6415	PAPER,PAPERBRD,BULK,NES			W 348	0.4	W 65	0.2	W 3026	2.1	PAPIERS,CARTONS ROULEAUX
64159	OTHER PAPER ETC,BULK,NES			W 347	0.4	W 63	0.2	W 3025	2.0	AUT PAPIER ROULEAUX FEUILLES
6418	COATED ETC PAPER NES BLK			W 118	0.5	W 152	0.7	W 174	1.1	PAP,CARTONS COUCHES,ENDUITS
64181	PLASTIC COATED PAPER ETC			W 33	0.2	W 66	0.6	W 91	0.9	PAP,CARTONS ENDUITS,RESINES
64189	COATED PAPER ETC NES			W 84	0.4	W 85	0.2	W 83	0.3	PAPIERS,CARTONS COUCHES
642	PAPER,ETC,PRECUT,ARTS OF			W 3423	4.1	W 4009	5.7	W 2447	4.1	PAP,CARTONS DECOUPES
6421	PAPER ETC CONTAINERS			W 3052	2.7	W 3500	4.1	W 1994	2.4	BOITES,SACS EMBALLAGES
6423	EXERCISE BOOKS ETC			W 64	0.5	W 76	0.5	W 61	0.4	REGISTRES,CAHIERS,CARNETS
6424	PAPER ETC CT TO SIZE NES			W 110	0.3	W 123	0.4	W 185	0.5	PAP,CARTONS DECOUPES
6428	PAPER ETC ARTICLES NES			W 183	0.6	W 287	0.8	W 192	0.8	OUVRAGES EN PATE A PAPIER
64285	PAPER ETC DIAPERS ETC			W 87	0.4	W 175	0.4	W 140	0.6	SERVIETTES HYGIENIQUES
65	TEXTILE YARN,FABRICS,ETC				1.8		1.4		1.4	FILS,TISSUS,ARTICLES TEXTILE
652	COTTON FABRICS,WOVEN			W 51	0.4	W 45	0.4	W 35	0.3	TISSUS DE COTON
653	WOVN MAN-MADE FIB FABRIC			W 62	0.5	W 57	0.4	W 42	0.4	TISSUS FIBRES SYNTH,ARTIF
658	TEXTILE ARTICLES NES			W 62	0.4	W 31	0.3	W 36	0.4	ART FACONNES MAT TEXTILES
66	NONMETAL MINERAL MFS NES				2.9		3.3		3.5	ART MIN NON METALLIQUES
661	LIME,CEMENT,BLDG PRODS			W 13589	1.0	W 22684	1.6	W 20217	1.3	CHAUX,CIMENTS MAT CONSTR
6612	CEMENT			W 13370	0.8	W 22543	1.5	W 20116	1.2	CIMENTS HYDRAULIQUES
662	CLAY,REFRACTORY BLDG PRD			W 819	0.6	W 753	0.6	W 765	0.7	MAT CONST REFRACTAIRES
6624	BRICKS ETC NONREFRACTORY			W 817	0.6	W 753	0.6	W 765	0.7	BRIQUES ETC CERAM NON REFR
66245	GLAZED CERAMIC SETTS ETC			W 580	0.5	W 681	0.6	W 628	0.6	AUT CARREAUX CERAMIQUE
664	GLASS			W 185	0.7	W 147	0.4	W 96	0.4	VERRE
6642	OPTICAL GLASS UNWRKD ETC			W 95	0.4	W 13	0.2	W 22	0.2	VERRE OPTIQUE,LUNETTERIE
665	GLASSWARE			W 537	0.6	W 550	0.6	W 839	1.0	OUVRAGES EN VERRE
6651	BOTTLES ETC OF GLASS			W 476	0.4	W 481	0.4	W 784	0.8	RECIPIENTS EN VERRE
66511	GLASS BOTTLES ETC NONVAC			W 476	0.4	W 481	0.4	W 784	0.8	BONBONNES,BOUTEILLES,ETC
67	IRON AND STEEL				2.4		4.1		3.2	FER ET ACIER
673	IRON,STEEL SHAPES ETC			W 2154	1.3	W 2380	1.2	W 3125	1.6	BARRES,PROFIL FER,ACIER
6732	IRON,STEEL BARS ETC			W 1328	0.7	W 2277	1.1	W 2404	1.2	BARRES FER,ACIER
67325	OTH ALLOY STEEL BARS ETC			W 807	0.4	W 1777	0.9	W 1783	0.9	BARRES NON ACIERS ALLIES
67327	IRN, OTH STL BARS FORGED			W 522	0.4	W 493	0.3	W 618	0.3	BARRES FORGEES CREUSES
6733	IRON,STEEL PROFILES ETC			W 638	0.5	W 28	0.1	W 440	0.4	PROFILES,PALPLAN FER,ACIER
67336	IRN,SMPL STL SHEET PILNG			W 614	0.5	W 8	0.1	W 228	0.2	PALPLANCHES EN FER,ACIER
674	IRN,STL UNIV,PLATE,SHEET			W 712	0.9	W 751	0.9	W 785	1.1	LARGES PLATS,TOLES
6749	OTH IRN,STL PLATES,SHEET			W 683	0.8	W 746	0.9	W 713	1.0	AUTRES TOLES FER,ACIER
67491	— OF IRON OR SIMPLE STL			W 683	0.8	W 719	0.9	W 713	1.0	AUT TOLES AUTRES ACIER FIN
678	IRON,STL TUBES,PIPES,ETC			W 131	0.4	W 1362	2.1	W 230	0.5	TUBES,TUYAUX EN FONTE,FER
6781	CAST IRON TUBES,PIPES			W 5	0.1	W 836	1.1	W 5	0.1	TUBES,TUYAUX EN FONTE
6783	IRON,STL TUBES,PIPES NES			W 86	0.2	W 329	0.5	W 159	0.3	AUT TUBES,TUYAUX FER,ACIER
6785	IRON,STEEL TUBE FITTINGS			W 17	0.2	W 173	0.5	W 30	0.2	ACCESSOIRES DE TUYAUTERIE
69	METAL MANUFACTURES NES				4.0		4.3		6.0	ART MANUFACT EN METAL NDA
691	STRUCTURES AND PARTS NES			W 499	1.4	W 515	1.5	W 488	2.5	CONSTRUCT FER,ACIER,ALU
6911	STRUCTURES,PARTS IRN,STL			W 321	0.6	W 327	0.8	W 277	1.4	CONSTRUCT FER,ACIER,FONTE
6912	STRUCTURES,PARTS ALUMNM			W 178	0.9	W 188	0.8	W 211	1.2	CONSTRUCT ALUMINIUM
693	WIRE PRODUCTS NON ELECTR			W 260	0.4	W 259	0.4	W 297	0.5	OUVRAGES FILS METALLIQUES
694	STL,COPPR NAILS,NUTS,ETC			W 184	0.4	W 203	0.4	W 181	0.5	CLOUS,VIS,ECROUS
695	TOOLS			W 47	0.5	W 49	0.4	W 72	0.6	OUTILS A MAIN
697	BASE MTL HOUSEHOLD EQUIP			W 116	0.6	W 83	0.5	W 90	0.6	ART MENAGE MET COMMUNS
6973	DMSTC HEATG,COOKG APPARA			W 66	0.4	W 37	0.3	W 48	0.4	APPS CHAUF NON ELECTRIQ
69731	IRN,STL DOM COOKG APPARA			W 65	0.4	W 36	0.3	W 48	0.4	APPS CUISSON FER,ACIER
699	BASE METAL MFRS NES			W 162	0.7	W 192	0.9	W 223	1.1	ART MANUFACTURES MET NDA
6991	LOCKSMITHS WARES,ETC			W 34	0.3	W 62	0.4	W 51	0.4	ARTICLES DE SERRURERIE
7	MACHINES,TRANSPORT EQUIP				19.6		28.0		28.1	MACHINES MATERIEL TRANSPORT
71	POWER GENERATING EQUIPMT				1.4		0.9		2.7	MACHINES GENERATRICES
713	INTRNL COMBUS PSTN ENGIN			W 16	0.4	W 15	0.3	W 17	0.4	MOTEURS EXPL COMB INT, PIECE
716	ROTATING ELECTRIC PLANT			W 43	1.0	W 50	0.6	W 127	2.4	APP ELECTR ROTATIFS,PIECES

4. Special Imports C.I.F. by Commodities according to the S.I.T.C. (Rev. 2) in million U.S. Dollars
Importations Spéciales C.A.F. par Produits d'après la C.T.C.I. (Rév. 2) en millions de Dollars E.U.

SITC CTCI	COMMODITY	1993 QUANTITY QUANTITE	1993 VALUE VALEUR	1994 QUANTITY QUANTITE	1994 VALUE VALEUR	1995 QUANTITY QUANTITE	1995 VALUE VALEUR	1996 QUANTITY QUANTITE	1996 VALUE VALEUR	PRODUIT
7161	DC MOTORS AND GENERATORS			W 20	0.2	W 38	0.3	W 91	2.0	MOTEURS COURANT CONTINU
7162	AC MTRS,GENRTRS,GEN SETS			W 14	0.6	W 8	0.1	W 15	0.2	MOTEURS ELECTRIQUES
71622	AC GENERATORS			W 4	0.5	W 3	0.1	W 5	0.1	GENER COURANT ALTERNATIF
72	MACHS FOR SPCL INDUSTRYS				3.3		6.7		2.8	MAC SPECIALES POUR INDUST
723	CIVIL ENGNEERG EQUIP ETC			W 509	1.2	W 460	5.5	W 313	1.3	APPAREILS DE GENIE CIVIL
7234	CONST,MINING MACHNRY NES			W 470	1.1	W 449	5.4	W 303	1.3	MACH POUR LA CONST, MINES
72342	SLFPRP SHOVELS,EXCAVATRS			W 348	0.7	W 114	0.5	W 215	0.9	PELLES MECANIQUES
72345	PILE DRIVERS,ETC					W 314	4.9		0.1	CHASSE-NEIGE
726	PRINTG,BKBINDG MACHY,PTS			W 14	0.5	W 10	0.1	W 5	0.1	MACHINES POUR IMPRIMERIE
728	OTH MACHY FOR SPCL INDUS			W 115	1.1	W 27	0.7	W 113	0.9	AUT MACH IND PARTICULIERES
7283	OTHR MINERAL WORKG MACHY			W 60	0.4	W 15	0.2	W 99	0.6	MACH TRIER,CRIBLER,BROYER
7284	MACHY FOR SPCL INDUS NES			W 53	0.7	W 11	0.5	W 13	0.3	MACH SPEC IND PARTICUL.
72848	OTH MCHY WITH INDIV FNCT			W 47	0.7	W 6	0.3	W 3	0.1	AUTRES MACHINES NDA
74	GENRL INDUSTRL MACHY NES				2.2		4.9		3.3	MACH APP INDUSTRIE
741	HEATING,COOLING EQUIPMNT			W 89	0.8	W 722	1.7	W 114	0.8	MACH CHAUFFAGE,PIECES
7414	NONDOM REFRIG EQUIPT,PTS			W 46	0.3	W 667	1.0	W 29	0.2	MAT PRODUCTION DU FROID
74149	PTS NES OF REFRIG EQUIPT			W 23	0.1	W 647	0.9	W 6	0.1	PIECES POUR MACH FROID
744	MECHANICAL HANDLING EQU			W 515	0.4	W 79	0.5	W 99	0.6	EQUIP MANUTENTION PIECES
745	NONELEC MACHY,TOOLS NES			W 23	0.3	W 53	1.4	W 104	0.7	AUT MACH NON ELEC,PIECES
7452	OTH NONELEC MCHS,PTS NES			W 19	0.3	W 48	1.3	W 96	0.6	AUT MACH NON ELEC,PIECES
74522	PACKAGNG,BOTTLNG,ETC MCH			W 4	0.1	W 23	0.9	W 43	0.1	MACH NETT BOUTEILLES,ETC
749	NONELEC MACH PTS,ACC NES			W 63	0.5	W 76	0.9	W 60	0.8	PIECES MACH NON ELEC NDA
7492	COCKS,VALVES ETC NES			W 49	0.3	W 64	0.7	W 47	0.5	ART ROB,SIM POUR TUYAUX
75	OFFICE MACHNES,ADP EQUIP				1.5		1.8		3.0	MACH BUREAU TRAIT AUTOM
751	OFFICE MACHINES			W 11	0.4	W 9	0.3	W 18	0.4	MACH,APPAREILS DE BUREAU
752	AUTOMTIC DATA PROC EQUIP			W 16	0.9	W 22	1.0	W 38	1.8	MACH TRAIT INFORMATION
7522	DIGITAL COMPUTERS			W 8	0.4	W 11	0.6	W 22	1.0	MACH DIGITALES COMPLETES
759	OFFICE,ADP MCH PTS,ACCES			W 9	0.4	W 15	0.6	W 26	0.9	PIECES DU 751 ET 752
7599	ACCTG,ETC,ADP MCH PTS,AC			W 7	0.3	W 10	0.5	W 21	0.8	PIECES DU 751 ET 752
76	TELECOMM,SOUND EQUIPMENT				2.3		2.9		3.8	EQUIPMENT DE TELECOM
761	TELEVISION RECEIVERS			W 36	0.4	W 38	0.4	W 45	0.5	RECEPTEURS DE TELEVISION
7611	COLOUR TV RECEIVERS			W 34	0.4	W 38	0.4	W 44	0.5	RECEPTEURS COULEUR
764	TELECOM EQPT,PTS,ACC NES			W 56	1.7	W 56	2.2	W 64	3.0	EQUIP TELECOM,PIECES
7641	LINE TELEPHONE,ETC EQUIP			W 19	1.0	W 14	0.8	W 19	1.1	APP TELEPHON PAR FIL
7649	PTS NES OF EQUIPMT OF 76			W 11	0.4	W 19	1.0	W 29	1.7	PIECES DE LA DIV 76
76491	PTS NES OF APPAR OF 7641			W 8	0.3	W 15	1.0	W 20	1.5	PIECES POUR 764.1
77	ELECTRIC MACHNRY NES ETC				2.9		4.5		4.2	MACH APP ELECT NDA
772	SWITCHGEAR ETC,PARTS NES			W 35	0.5	W 47	1.0	W 42	0.9	APP COUPURE,SECT ETC
7721	SWITCHGEAR ETC			W 34	0.5	W 44	0.9	W 41	0.7	APP COUPURE,SECTIONMNT
773	ELECTR DISTRIBUTNG EQUIP			W 117	0.5	W 251	1.1	W 157	0.9	EQUIPMT DISTRIBUTION ELECT
7731	INSULATED WIRE,CABLE ETC			W 112	0.5	W 239	1.1	W 149	0.9	FILS,CABLES ISOLES ELECT
775	HOUSEHOLD TYPE EQUIP NES			W 154	1.0	W 184	1.1	W 168	1.1	MACH,APP USAGE DOMESTQUE
7752	DOM REFRIGERATRS,FREEZRS			W 82	0.5	W 104	0.6	W 94	0.6	REFRIG,CONGEL MENAGER
77521	DOMESTIC REFRIGERATORS			W 68	0.4	W 86	0.5	W 77	0.5	REFRIGERATEURS
778	ELECTRICAL MACHINERY NES			W 132	0.8	W 159	1.0	W 141	1.0	AUTRES MACH ELECT NDA
7781	BATTERIES,ACCUMULATORS			W 91	0.3	W 123	0.5	W 93	0.4	PILES ET ACCUMULATEURS
78	ROAD VEHICLES				5.8		6.1		8.2	VEHICULES ROUTIERS
781	PASS MOTOR VEH EXC BUSES			W 386	2.0	W 456	2.3	W 733	3.5	AUTO TRANSPORT PERSONNES
782	LORRIES,SPCL MTR VEH NES			W 301	1.7	W 437	1.8	W 454	2.3	VEHICULES SPECIAUX,MARCH
7821	LORRIES,TRUCKS			W 211	1.4	W 347	1.5	W 434	2.2	VEHICULES TRANSP MARCHAND
783	ROAD MOTOR VEHICLES NES			W 146	1.2	W 122	1.1	W 203	1.3	VEHICULES ROUTIERS NDA
7831	BUSES			W 135	1.2	W 116	1.1	W 148	1.2	VOITURES TRANSPORT COMMUN
784	MOTOR VEH PRTS,ACCES NES			W 65	0.8	W 98	0.9	W 70	0.9	PIECES 722,781,782,783
7849	OTHER MOTOR VEHCL PARTS			W 64	0.8	W 90	0.9	W 64	0.9	PIECES 722,781,782,783
79	OTHR TRANSPORT EQUIPMENT				0.4		0.6		0.2	AUTRE MATERIEL TRANSPORT
793	SHIPS AND BOATS ETC			W 75	0.4	W 43	0.6	W 35	0.2	NAVIRES BATEAUX,ETC
7932	SHIPS AND BOATS NES			W 43	0.2	W 37	0.4	W 34	0.2	NAVIRES ET BATEAUX
8	MISC MANUFACTURED GOODS				8.6		10.0		12.0	ART MANUFACTURES DIVERS
812	*PLUMBG,HEATNG,LGHTNG EQ			W 134	0.6	W 103	0.5	W 110	0.5	APPAR SANITAIRES CHAUFFAGE
821	*FURNITURE,PARTS THEREOF			W 184	0.9	W 142	0.9	W 258	1.3	MEUBLES ET PIECES
8219	FURNITURE AND PARTS NES			W 113	0.5	W 96	0.6	W 104	0.9	AUTRES MEUBLES ET PIECES
82191	METAL FURNITURE NES			W 58	0.3	W 60	0.4	W 54	0.6	MEUBLES NDA EN METAL
84	CLOTHING AND ACCESSORIES				1.2		1.4		1.4	VETEMENTS
851	*FOOTWEAR			W 52	0.6	W 50	0.7	W 88	0.8	CHAUSSURES
85101	FOOTWEAR RUBBER,PLASTIC			W 36	0.4	W 19	0.3	W 44	0.4	CHAUS SEMELLES CAOUTCH
85102	FOOTWEAR LEATHER			W 14	0.2	W 24	0.4	W 38	0.5	CHAUS SEMELLES EN CUIR
87	PRECISION INSTRUMNTS NES				0.6		0.7		0.8	INSTRUM,APPAR SCIENT NDA
874	MEASURNG,CONTROLNG INSTR			W 21	0.3	W 16	0.4	W 12	0.4	INSTRUMENTS DE MESURE
88	PHOTO EQU,OPTICL GDS ETC				0.3		0.4		0.4	APP,FOURN PHOTO,OP,MONTR
89	MISC MANUFCTRD GOODS NES				4.7		5.5		6.8	ART MANUFACTURES DIVERS
892	PRINTED MATTER			W 159	1.7	W 126	1.8	W 186	2.4	IMPRIMES
8921	PRINTED BOOKS,GLOBES,ETC			W 76	1.0	W 80	1.1	W 122	1.4	LIVRES,BROCHURES,CARTES
89211	PRINTED BOOKS,PAMPHLETS			W 72	1.0	W 78	1.1	W 121	1.4	LIVRES,BROCHURES
8928	PRINTED MATTER NES			W 69	0.5	W 33	0.5	W 43	0.8	IMPRIMES NDA
89281	LABELS PAPER,PAPERBOARD			W 28	0.3	W 21	0.3	W 22	0.5	ETIQUETTES TOUS GENRES
893	ARTICLES OF PLASTIC NES			W 894	2.1		2.6		3.0	OUVRAGES EN MAT DIVIS 58
8931	PLSTC PACKG CONTNRS,LIDS			W 189	0.6	W 221	0.9	W 344	1.2	ART TRANSP EMBALLAGE ETC
8939	MISC PLASTIC ARTICLES			W 689	1.5	W 557	1.8	W 547	1.9	ART DIVERS EN MAT DIV 58
89399	OTHR PLASTC ARTICLES NES			W 556	1.3	W 479	1.7	W 414	1.7	AUT OUV MAT DIV 58
894	TOYS,SPORTING GOODS,ETC			W 40	0.3	W 40	0.3	W 60	0.6	VOITURES ENFANTS,JOUETS
899	OTHER MANUFACTURED GOODS				0.4		0.4		0.4	AUT ART MANUF DIVERS NDA

5. Special Exports F.O.B. by Commodities according to the S.I.T.C. (Rev. 2) in million U.S. Dollars
Exportations Spéciales F.O.B. par Produits d'après la C.T.C.I. (Rév. 2) en millions de Dollars E.U.

SITC CTCI	COMMODITY	1993 QUANTITY QUANTITE	1993 VALUE VALEUR	1994 QUANTITY QUANTITE	1994 VALUE VALEUR	1995 QUANTITY QUANTITE	1995 VALUE VALEUR	1996 QUANTITY QUANTITE	1996 VALUE VALEUR	PRODUIT
	ALL COMMODITIES				45.3		45.3		51.2	TOUS PRODUITS
0	FOOD AND LIVE ANIMALS				25.9		22.5		24.4	ALIMENTS,ANIMAUX VIVANTS
04	CEREALS AND PREPARATIONS				0.3		0.2		0.2	CEREALES ET PRODUITS
048	CEREAL ETC PREPARATIONS			W 107	0.3	W 79	0.2	W 67	0.2	PREPTNS A BASE CEREALES
0483	MACARONI,SPAGHETTI ETC			W 96	0.2	W 79	0.2	W 67	0.2	PATES ALMENTAIRES
05	VEGETABLES AND FRUIT				24.8		21.4		23.4	LEGUMES ET FRUITS
054	VEG ETC FRSH,SMPLY PRSVD			W 1834	1.3	W 1803	1.8	W 1833	2.3	LEGUMES FRAIS,CONG,SECS
0545	OTHER FRESH VEGETABLES			W 392	0.2	W 418	0.4	W 557	0.6	AUTRES LEGUMES FRAIS,REF
05459	FRESH VEGETABLES NES			W 388	0.2	W 418	0.4	W 557	0.6	LEGUMES FRAIS,REFRI NDA
0548	EDIBLE VEG NES FRESH,DRY			W 1439	1.1	W 1384	1.4	W 1274	1.7	RACINES,TUBERCULES
05481	ROOTS,TUBERS FRESH,DRY			W 1438	1.1	W 1384	1.4	W 1273	1.7	RACINES DE MANIOC ETC
057	FRUIT,NUTS,FRESH,DRIED			W 50046	23.3	W 37377	19.4	W 46988	20.9	FRUITS FRAIS OU SECS
0571	ORANGES, MANDARINS ETC			W 572	0.2	W 583	0.3	W 503	0.5	ORANGES,MAND,CLEMENTINES
05711	ORANGES,FRESH OR DRIED			W 549	0.2	W 567	0.3	W 475	0.4	ORANGES FRAICHES,SECHEES
0572	LEMONS,GRAPEFRUIT ETC			W 1384	0.5	W 1110	0.5	W 1008	0.6	AUTRES AGRUMES FRAIS,SECS
05721	LEMONS,LIMES,FRESH,DRIED			W 160	0.1	W 152	0.2	W 153	0.3	CITRONS ET LIMES
05722	GRAPEFRUITS,FRESH,DRIED			W 1223	0.4	W 958	0.4	W 855	0.4	PAMPLEMOUSSES,POMELOS
0573	BANANA,PLANTAIN,FRSH,DRY			W 46744	22.2	W 34844	17.9	W 44708	19.4	BANANES FRAICHES,SECHEES
0577	NUTS EDIBLE,FRESH,DRIED			W 495	0.2	W 255	0.1	W 300	0.2	FRUITS A COQUES
05771	COCONUTS FRESH OR DRIED			W 491	0.2	W 253	0.1	W 297	0.2	NOIX DE COCO
0579	FRUIT FRESH OR DRIED NES			W 851	0.4	W 585	0.7	W 470	0.5	FRUITS FRAIS,SECS NDA
05797	OTH TROP FRUIT,FRESH,DRY			W 706	0.4	W 447	0.6	W 357	0.4	AVOCATS,MANGUES,GOYAVES
058	FRUIT PRESERVED,PREPARED			W 89	0.3	W 116	0.3	W 116	0.3	CONSERVES DE FRUITS
0585	FRUIT OR VEGETABLE JUICE			W 78	0.2	W 106	0.3	W 109	0.3	JUS DE FRUITS
07	COFFEE,TEA,COCOA,SPICES				0.5		0.4		0.4	CAFE,THE,CACAO,EPICES
075	SPICES			W 109	0.4	W 94	0.4	W 57	0.4	EPICES
0752	SPICES,EX PEPPER,PIMENTO			W 103	0.4	W 81	0.4	W 48	0.4	AUTRES EPICES
07521	VANILLA			W 1	0.2	W 1	0.2	W 1	0.3	VANILLE
09	MISC EDIBLE PRODUCTS				0.5		0.6		0.5	PREP ALIMENTAIRES DIVERSES
098	EDIBLE PRODCTS,PREPS NES			W 283	0.5	W 372	0.6	W 212	0.5	PREP ALIMENTAIRES NDA
09804	SAUCES,MIXED SEASONINGS			W 279	0.5	W 368	0.6	W 209	0.4	SAUCES,ASSAISONNEMENTS
1	BEVERAGES AND TOBACCO				0.3		0.3		0.4	BOISSONS ET TABACS
11	BEVERAGES				0.3		0.1		0.1	BOISSONS
111	NON–ALCOHL BEVERAGES NES			W 444	0.3	W 76	0.1	W 74	0.1	BOISSONS NON ALCOOLIQUES
11101	WATERS,ICE AND SNOW			W 440	0.2	W 73	0.1	W 53	0.1	EAU,EAUX MINERALES
12	TOBACCO AND MANUFACTURES				0.1		0.3		0.3	TABACS BRUTS FABRIQUES
122	TOBACCO,MANUFACTURED			W 2	0.1	W 8	0.3	W 7	0.2	TABACS FABRIQUES
1222	CIGARETTES			W 2	0.1	W 8	0.3	W 7	0.2	CIGARETTES
2	CRUDE MATERLS,EXCL FUELS				0.4		0.8		1.2	MAT BRUTES NON COMESTIBLES
24	CORK AND WOOD				0.1		0.1		0.2	LIEGE ET BOIS
248	WOOD SHAPED,SLEEPERS			W 2	0.1	W 2	0.1	W 349	0.2	BOIS SIMPLEMENT TRAVAILLES
2483	LUMBER SHAPED NON–CONIFR			W 2	0.1	W 2	0.1	W 349	0.2	NON CONIFERES SCIES,RABOTES
24831	LUMBER SAWN ETC NON–CON			W 2	0.1			W 345	0.2	SCIES LONGITUDINALEMENT
27	CRUDE FERTLZR,MINRLS NES				0.3		0.6		0.9	ENGRAIS MINERAUX BRUTS
273	STONE,SAND AND GRAVEL			W 41113	0.3	W 101479	0.6	W 136700	0.9	PIERRES,SABLES,GRAVIERS
2733	SAND,EXCL METAL–BEARING			W 21000	0.2	W 15459	0.1	W 61600	0.4	SABLES NATURELS
2734	GRAVEL,CRUSHED STONE,ETC			W 20113	0.1	W 86020	0.5	W 75100	0.5	PIERRES CONCASSEES
5	CHEMCLS,RELATED PROD NES				16.2		19.4		23.7	PRODUITS CHIMIQUES
51	ORGANIC CHEMICALS				0.2		0.2		0.2	PROD CHIMIQ ORGANIQUES
512	ALCOHOLS,PHENOLS ETC			W 290	0.2	W 202	0.2	W 201	0.2	PHENOLS,PHENOLS–ALCOOLS
5121	ACYCLIC ALCOHOLS,DERIVS			W 290	0.2	W 202	0.2	W 201	0.2	ALCOOLS ACYCLIQUES
51218	GLYCEROL,GLYCEROL LYES			W 290	0.2	W 202	0.2	W 201	0.2	GLYCERINE
53	DYES,TANNING,COLOUR PROD				1.0		1.6		1.7	PROD TEINTURE,COLORANTS
533	PIGMENTS,PAINTS,ETC			W 303	1.0	W 483	1.6	W 689	1.7	PIGMENTS,PEINTURES,VERNIS
5334	VARNISHES,DISTEMPERS ETC			W 301	1.0	W 481	1.6	W 689	1.7	PEINTURES A L'EAU
53342	OTH PAINTS,VARNISHES ETC			W 299	1.0	W 463	1.5	W 683	1.7	AUTRES PEINTURES,VERNIS
55	PERFUME,CLEANING ETC PRD				14.7		17.1		21.3	PROD POUR PARFUM,TOILETTE
551	ESSENTL OILS,PERFUME,ETC			W 11	0.5	W 13	0.6	W 19	1.0	HUILES ESSENTIELLES
5513	ESSENTL OIL,RESINOID,ETC			W 11	0.5	W 13	0.6	W 19	1.0	HUILES ESSENTIELLES,RESIN
553	PERFUMERY,COSMETICS,ETC			W 157	0.7	W 133	0.6	W 92	0.6	PRODUITS DE PARFUMERIE
554	SOAP,CLEANSING ETC PREPS			W 11484	13.5	W 12023	15.9	W 14911	19.8	SAVONS,PRODUITS DETERSIFS
5541	SOAPS			W 10450	12.4	W 11088	14.9	W 13826	18.5	SAVONS,PROD TENSIO–ACTIFS
5542	WASHING PREPARATIONS ETC			W 1034	1.2	W 935	1.1	W 1047	1.3	PROD ORG TENSIO–ACT NDA
58	PLASTIC MATERIALS ETC				0.3		0.3		0.1	MAT PLAST ARTIFICIELLES
583	POLYMERIZATION ETC PRODS			W 117	0.3	W 98	0.3	W 26	0.1	PROD POLYMERISATION
5839	OTH POLYMRZTION ETC PROD			W 117	0.3	W 98	0.3	W 26	0.1	AUT PROD POLYMER COPOLYM
59	CHEMICAL MATERIALS NES				0.2		0.4		0.7	MAT PROD CHIMIQUES NDA
591	PESTICIDES,DISINFECTANTS			W 117	0.2	W 317	0.4	W 486	0.7	DESINF,INSECT,FONG,HERB
5914	DISINFECTANTS,ETC,FR RET			W 117	0.2	W 317	0.4	W 486	0.7	DESINFECTANTS VENTE DET
59141	DISINFECTANTS FOR RETAIL			W 117	0.2	W 317	0.4	W 486	0.7	DESINFECTANTS VENTE DET
6	BASIC MANUFACTURES				0.8		0.3		0.2	ART MANUFACTURES
64	PAPER,PAPERBOARD AND MFR				0.5		0.1		0.1	PAPIERS,CARTONS & OUVRAGES
642	PAPER,ETC,PRECUT,ARTS OF			W 1180	0.5	W 1	0.1	W 18	0.1	PAP,CARTONS DECOUPES
6421	PAPER ETC CONTAINERS			W 791	0.5				0.1	BOITES,SACS EMBALLAGES
7	MACHINES,TRANSPORT EQUIP				0.6		1.3		0.6	MACHINES MATERIEL TRANSPORT
72	MACHS FOR SPCL INDUSTRYS				0.1		0.3		0.1	MAC SPECIALES POUR INDUST
723	CIVIL ENGNEERG EQUIP ETC			W 6	0.1	W 36	0.2	W 10	0.1	APPAREILS DE GENIE CIVIL
7234	CONST,MINING MACHNRY NES			W 5	0.1	W 18	0.2	W 10	0.1	MACH POUR LA CONST, MINES
72343	SLFPRP CONST ETC MCH NES					W 17	0.2			AUT MACH EXTR,TERRASSEM
74	GENRL INDUSTRL MACHY NES				0.2		0.4		0.3	MACH APP INDUSTRIE
741	HEATING,COOLING EQUIPMNT			W 10	0.2	W 9	0.2	W 29	0.1	MACH CHAUFFAGE,PIECES
7416	HEATING,COOLING EQU NES			W 9	0.2	W 9	0.2	W 25	0.1	APP CHANGEMENT TEMP
78	ROAD VEHICLES				0.2		0.3		0.2	VEHICULES ROUTIERS
8	MISC MANUFACTURED GOODS				1.3		1.1		1.0	ART MANUFACTURES DIVERS
84	CLOTHING AND ACCESSORIES				0.3		0.3		0.2	VETEMENTS
847	TEXTILE CLTHNG ACCES NES			W 90	0.2	W 91	0.2			ACCES VET MAT TEXT NDA
8472	CLTHNG ACCESRYS ETC KNIT			W 90	0.2	W 91	0.2			ACCES VET BONNE NDA
84721	KNIT GLOVES,ETC NONELAST			W 90	0.2	W 91	0.2			GANTERIE BONNET NON ELAS
851	*FOOTWEAR			W 36	0.3	W 50	0.3	W 32	0.3	CHAUSSURES
85101	FOOTWEAR RUBBER,PLASTIC			W 35	0.3	W 50	0.3	W 32	0.3	CHAUS SEMELLES CAOUTCH
89	MISC MANUFCTRD GOODS NES				0.7		0.5		0.6	ART MANUFACTURES DIVERS
892	PRINTED MATTER			W 1	0.3	W 2	0.1	W 10	0.1	IMPRIMES
8928	PRINTED MATTER NES				0.3	W 1	0.1		0.1	IMPRIMES NDA
89283	UNISSUED BANKNOTES ETC				0.3					TIMBRES–POSTE FISCAUX
893	ARTICLES OF PLASTIC NES			W 74	0.2	W 48	0.2	W 85	0.3	OUVRAGES EN MAT DIVIS 58
8931	PLSTC PACKG CONTNRS,LIDS			W 74	0.2	W 46	0.2	W 79	0.3	ART TRANSP EMBALLAGE ETC
899	OTHER MANUFACTURED GOODS			W 103	0.3	W 163	0.3	W 109	0.3	AUT ART MANUF DIVERS NDA
8993	COMBUSTIBLE PRODUCTS ETC			W 98	0.2	W 160	0.3	W 106	0.2	BOUGIES,ALLUMETTES ETC
89931	CANDLES,TAPERS,ETC			W 98	0.2	W 160	0.3	W 106	0.2	BOUGIES,CHANDELLES,CIERG

1. HISTORICAL SERIES, 1962–1997 GENERAL TRADE, IMPORTS F.O.B., EXPORTS F.O.B.
SERIES HISTORIQUES, 1962–1997 COMMERCE GENERAL, IMPORTATIONS F.O.B., EXPORTATIONS F.O.B

YEAR ANNEE	VALUE IN MILLION U.S. DOLLARS VALEUR EN MILLION U.S. DOLLARS MERCHANDISE –MARCHANDISE		GOLD –OR		CONVERSION FACTORS FACTEURS DE CONVERSION CENTS E.U. PAR		INDEX NUMBERS –INDICES QUANTUM		UNIT VALUE VALEUR UNITAIRE	
	IMPORTS	EXPORTS	IMPORTS	EXPORTS	IMPORTS	EXPORTS	IMPORTS	EXPORTS	IMPORTS	EXPORTS
1962	129.10	172.40								
1963	160.30	174.10								
1964	192.40	179.40								
1965	86.70	125.50								
1966	160.80	136.70								
1967	174.70	156.20								
1968	196.90	163.50								
1969	217.20	184.10								
1970	278.00	213.60								
1971	309.70	240.70								
1972	337.70	347.60								
1973	421.90	442.20								
1974	673.00	636.80								
1975	772.70	893.80								
1976	763.60	716.40								
1977	847.80	780.50								
1978	860.90	675.50								
1979	1080.40	868.60								
1980	1498.40	961.90						99		92
1981	1450.20	1188.00						109		118
1982	1255.80	767.70						104		76
1983	1279.00	785.20						121		72
1984	1257.10	868.10						122		83
1985	1285.90	738.50						110		71
1986	1432.70	717.61						91		76
1987	1830.20	711.25						111		63
1988	1849.20	889.70						114		90
1989	2258.40	924.39						117		104
1990	2061.70	734.54						100		100
1991	1988.10	658.32						95		95
1992	2500.80	562.40						90		82
1993	2436.20	511.04						94		75
1994	2626.40	644.03						94		89
1995	2976.20	766.67						97		101
1996	3685.90	816.74						101		103
1997	4120.00	881.72						100		105

2. IMPORTS BY BROAD ECONOMIC CATEGORY AND EXPORTS BY INDUSTRIAL ORIGIN. (PERCENTAGE OF TOTAL VALUE)
IMPORTATIONS PAR CATEGORIES ECONOMIQUES ET EXPORTATIONS PAR BRANCHE D'ACTIVITE.(EN POURCENTAGE DE LA VALEUR TOTALE)

IMPORTS – IMPORTATIONS

	1988	1989	1990	1991	1992	1993	1994
TOTAL IMPORTS–IMPORTATIONS TOTALES							
1 FOOD BEV–ALIMENTATION BOISSONS							
11 PRIMARY–PRODUITS DE BASE							
111 FOR INDUSTRY–POUR L'INDUSTRIE							
112 FOR HOUSEHOLDS–POUR LES MENAGES							
12 PROCESSED–PRODUITS ELABORES							
121 FOR INDUSTRY–POUR L'INDUSTRIE							
122 FOR HOUSEHOLDS–POUR LES MENAGES							
2 IND SUPPLIES–APPROV INDUSTRIELS							
21 PRIMARY–PRODUITS DE BASE							
22 PROCESSED–PRODUITS ELABORES							
3 FUELS–COMBUSTIBLES							
31 PRIMARY–PRODUITS DE BASE							
32 PROCESSED–PRODUITS ELABORES							
321 MOTOR SPIRIT–ESSENCE							
322 OTHER–AUTRES							
4 MACHINERY–EQUIPEMENT							
41 CAPITAL EQUIPMENT–MACHINES							
42 PARTS–PIECES ACCESSOIRES							
5 TRANSPORT–TRANSPORT							
51 PASSENGER CARS–AUTOMOBILES							
52 OTHER–AUTRES							
521 INDUSTRIAL–INDUSTRIELS							
522 NON INDUSTRIAL–NON INDUSTRIEL							
53 PARTS–PIECES ACCESSOIRES							
6 CONSUM GOODS–BIENS CONSOMMATION							
61 DURABLE–DURABLES							
62 SEMI DURABLE–SEMI DURABLES							
63 NON DURABLE–NON DURABLES							
7 GOODS NES–BIENS NDA							

EXPORTS – EXPORTATIONS

	1988	1989	1990	1991	1992	1993	1994
TOTAL EXPORTS–EXPORTATIONS TOTALES	100.				100.	100.	100.
1 AGRICULTURE	16.3				9.0	8.4	9.7
2 MINING QUARRY–INDUS EXTRACTIVES	0.6				0.5	0.3	0.2
3 MANUFACTURING–IND MANUFACTUR	83.1				90.5	91.3	90.0
31 FOOD BEV TOBACCO–ALIM BOISS TAB	19.2				12.8	12.3	10.9
32 TEXTILES–INDUSTRIES TEXTILES	22.1				38.9	40.5	37.1
33 WOOD & PRODUCTS–BOIS & PRODUITS	0.0				0.0	0.0	0.0
34 PAPER & PRODUCTS–PAPIER & PRODT	0.8				0.7	0.7	0.7
35 CHEMICALS–INDUSTRIES CHIMIQUES	4.5				3.9	3.6	3.4
36 NON METAL MIN–MIN NON METAL	0.3				0.3	0.3	0.3
37 BASIC METAL–IND METAL BASE	23.2				8.6	7.7	9.6
38 METAL MANUF–MANUF METAL	10.7				17.9	20.5	21.1
39 OTH MANUF IND–AUTRES MANUF	2.3				7.4	5.7	6.9

3. TRADE BY PRINCIPAL COUNTRIES OF CONSIGNMENT AND DESTINATION (VALUE IN MILLION U.S. DOLLARS)
ECHANGES SELON LES PRINCIPAUX PAYS DE CONSIGNATION ET DE DESTINATION (VALEUR EN MILLIONS DE DOLLARS EU)

COUNTRIES–PAYS	SPECIAL IMPORTS C.I.F. IMPORTATIONS SPECIALES C.A.F					COUNTRIES–PAYS	GENERAL EXPORTS F.O.B. # 1 EXPORTATIONS GENERALES F.O.B.				
	1990	1991	1992	1993	1994		1990	1991	1992	1993	1994
World						Monde			1715.4	1758.9	2007.8
Africa						Afrique			11.3	0.9	2.2
Americas						Amériques			1566.5	1565.7	1767.0
– Northern America						– Amérique du Nord			1530.3	1511.2	1717.6
– LAIA						– ALAI			7.6	11.1	7.4
– CACM						– MCAC			9.5	7.6	10.0
– Caribbean						– Caraïbes			14.9	31.2	24.7
– Rest of America						– Autre Amérique			4.2	4.7	7.3
Asia excl fmr USSR						Asie anc. URSS exclus			34.4	45.7	62.1
– Middle East						– Moyen–Orient			0.2	0.6	0.3
Asia former USSR						Asie ancienne URSS					
Europe excl fmr USSR						Europe anc. URSS exclus			101.8	142.5	174.9
– European Union						– Union Européenne			100.4	141.6	174.2
– Eastern Europe						– Europe de l'Est				0.1	0.1
– Rest of Europe						– Autre de l'Europe			1.5	0.8	0.6
Europe former USSR						Europe ancienne URSS			1.0	3.4	0.5
Oceania						Océanie			0.2	0.7	0.6
Other						Autre			0.1	0.1	0.5
						USA/Etats–Unis d'Amer			1437.4	1488.8	1698.2
						Netherlands/Pays–Bas			9.3	42.4	103.7
						Canada			92.9	22.1	19.0
						Belgium–Luxembourg			39.9	44.9	21.6
						Korea, Republic of			23.3	22.9	37.6
						United Kingdom			16.5	17.8	12.9
						Japan/Japon			5.3	19.5	15.5
						Spain/Espagne			12.1	12.4	9.4
						Italy/Italie			9.5	10.3	11.3
						Honduras			5.8	6.2	6.7
						Netherlands Antilles			0.6	13.6	4.3
						Germany/Allemagne			6.7	5.4	4.7
						Jamaica/Jamaïque			5.2	4.6	5.9
						Panama			3.4	3.8	6.8
						Portugal			2.8	5.8	4.6
						Haiti/Haïti			0.3	5.9	7.0
						France, Monaco			3.3	2.5	5.2
						Thailand/Thaïlande			4.8	1.4	4.3
						Guadeloupe			3.1	3.2	3.2
						Mexico/Mexique			1.8	2.0	3.6
						Morocco/Maroc			5.6		1.1
						Costa Rica			2.8	0.8	2.5
						Brazil/Brésil			2.4	1.4	1.2
						Russian Federation			1.0	3.4	0.5
						Uruguay				4.8	0.0
						China, Hong Kong SAR			0.2	0.4	3.3
						Venezuela			1.7	1.1	1.1
						Colombia/Colombie			1.4	1.2	0.7
						Mauritius/Maurice			3.0	0.3	
						Algeria/Algérie			2.6	0.1	
						Martinique			0.7	1.1	0.9
						Switzerland,Liechtenst.			1.4	0.7	0.5
						Trinidad and Tobago			1.1	0.7	0.9
						British Virgin Islds			1.0	0.0	0.3
						Cameroon/Cameroun			0.1	0.5	0.7
						Cuba			1.1	0.1	0.1
						El Salvador			0.5	0.3	0.4
						Australia/Australie			0.1	0.4	0.6
						Barbados/Barbade			0.3	0.4	0.4
						Guyana			0.3	0.4	0.3

(VALUE AS PERCENTAGE OF WORLD TOTAL)(VALEURS EN POURCENTAGE DU TOTAL MONDIAL)

	1985	1986	1987	1988	1989	1990	1991	1992	1993	1994		1985	1986	1987	1988	1989	1990	1991	1992	1993	1994
Africa											Afrique								0.7	0.1	0.1
Americas											Amériques								91.3	89.0	88.0
– Northern America											– Amérique du Nord								89.2	85.9	85.5
– LAIA											– ALAI								0.4	0.6	0.4
– CACM											– MCAC								0.6	0.4	0.5
– Caribbean											– Caraïbes								0.9	1.8	1.2
– Rest of America											– Autre Amérique								0.2	0.3	0.4
Asia excl fmr USSR											Asie anc. URSS exclus								2.0	2.6	3.1
– Middle East											– Moyen–Orient								0.0	0.0	0.0
Asia former USSR											Asie ancienne URSS										
Europe excl fmr USSR											Europe anc. URSS exclus								5.9	8.1	8.7
– European Union											– Union Européenne								5.9	8.0	8.7
– Eastern Europe											– Europe de l'Est									0.0	0.0
– Rest of Europe											– Autre de l'Europe								0.1	0.0	0.0
Europe former USSR											Europe ancienne URSS								0.1	0.2	0.0
Oceania											Océanie								0.0	0.0	0.0
Other											Autre								0.0	0.0	0.0
											USA/Etats–Unis d'Amer								83.8	84.6	84.6
											Netherlands/Pays–Bas								0.5	2.4	5.2
											Canada								5.4	1.3	0.9
											Belgium–Luxembourg								2.3	2.6	1.1
											Korea, Republic of								1.4	1.3	1.9
											United Kingdom								1.0	1.0	0.6
											Japan/Japon								0.3	1.1	0.8
											Spain/Espagne								0.7	0.7	0.5
											Italy/Italie								0.6	0.6	0.6
											Honduras								0.3	0.4	0.3

4. General Imports F.O.B. by Commodities according to the S.I.T.C. (Rev. 2) in million U.S. Dollars
Importations Générales F.O.B. par Produits d'après la C.T.C.I. (Rév. 2) en millions de Dollars E.U.

SITC CTCI	COMMODITY	1991		1992		1993		1994		PRODUIT
		QUANTITY QUANTITE	VALUE VALEUR	QUANTITY QUANTITE	VALUE VALEUR	QUANTITY QUANTITE	VALUE VALEUR	QUANTITY QUANTITE	VALUE VALEUR	
	ALL COMMODITIES		1728.8		2174.6		2118.4		2275.8	TOUS PRODUITS
041	WHEAT ETC UNMILLED		36.4		41.9		40.7		39.2	FROMENT,EPEAUTRE
061	SUGAR AND HONEY								8.7	SUCRES ET MIEL
3	MINERAL FUELS ETC		448.5		500.8		463.3		525.8	COMBUSTIBLES MINERAUX LUB
33	PETROLEUM AND PRODUCTS		436.8		487.8		453.0		521.7	PETROLE ET DERIVES

5. General Exports F.O.B. by Commodities according to the S.I.T.C. (Rev. 2) in million U.S. Dollars
Exportations Générales F.O.B. par Produits d'après la C.T.C.I. (Rév. 2) en millions de Dollars E.U.

SITC CTCI	COMMODITY	1991		1992		1993		1994		PRODUIT
		QUANTITY QUANTITE	VALUE VALEUR	QUANTITY QUANTITE	VALUE VALEUR	QUANTITY QUANTITE	VALUE VALEUR	QUANTITY QUANTITE	VALUE VALEUR	
	ALL COMMODITIES #1				1715.4		1758.9		2007.8	TOUS PRODUITS
0	FOOD AND LIVE ANIMALS				284.8		285.8		335.0	ALIMENTS,ANIMAUX VIVANTS
01	MEAT AND PREPARATIONS				13.8		14.3		13.0	VIANDES ET PREPARATIONS
011	MEAT FRESH,CHILLD,FROZEN			W 5985	12.4	W 6533	13.5	W 5153	9.7	VIANDES FRAICHES,REF,CONGE
0111	BOVINE MEAT FRESH,FROZEN			W 5985	12.4	W 6533	13.5	W 5091	9.6	VIANDES BOVIN FRAI,REF
01111	BOVINE MEAT WITH BONE IN			W 5985	12.4	W 6533	13.5	W 5091	9.6	VIANDES BOVIN NON DESOSS
04	CEREALS AND PREPARATIONS				2.2		12.8		4.9	CEREALES ET PRODUITS
042	RICE					W 29508	11.1	W 5827	2.2	RIZ
0422	RICE SEMI–MILLED,MILLED					W 29508	11.1	W 5827	2.2	RIZ POLI,GLACE INCL BRISURES
04222	RICE BROKEN					W 29508	11.1	W 5827	2.2	BRISURES DE RIZ
05	VEGETABLES AND FRUIT				53.9		54.1		55.4	LEGUMES ET FRUITS
054	VEG ETC FRSH,SMPLY PRSVD			W 37206	11.0	W 35738	10.5	W 34906	9.7	LEGUMES FRAIS,CONG,SECS
0548	EDIBLE VEG NES FRESH,DRY			W 25813	6.3	W 22571	5.3	W 23477	5.4	RACINES,TUBERCULES
05481	ROOTS,TUBERS FRESH,DRY			W 25317	6.0	W 22051	5.0	W 23061	5.2	RACINES DE MANIOC ETC
056	VEGTBLES ETC PRSVD,PREPD			W 13098	5.7	W 6847	3.6	W 11164	6.5	CONSERVES DE LEGUMES
0565	VEGTBLES PRSVD,PREPD NES			W 12467	5.6	W 5608	3.3	W 10013	6.3	LEGUMES PREPARES CONSERVE
05659	OTH VEG PRESVD,PREPD NES			W 12467	5.6	W 5608	3.3	W 10013	6.3	LEGUM PREPAP,CONSERV NDA
057	FRUIT,NUTS,FRESH,DRIED			W 154869	30.5	W 175626	32.0	W 177523	32.6	FRUITS FRAIS OU SECS
0579	FRUIT FRESH OR DRIED NES			W 142849	27.3	W 164008	29.1	W 165672	29.8	FRUITS FRAIS,SECS NDA
05796	DATES,FRESH OR DRIED			W 132331	25.0	W 154072	27.3	W 152243	27.5	DATTES FRAICHES OU SECHES
058	FRUIT PRESERVED,PREPARED			W 11845	6.9	W 16918	8.3	W 12751	6.7	CONSERVES DE FRUITS
06	SUGAR AND PREPS,HONEY				138.7		127.2		129.1	SUCRES ET PRODUITS
061	SUGAR AND HONEY			W 511381	138.3	W 530607	126.9	W 491399	128.7	SUCRES ET MIEL
0612	REFINED SUGAR ETC			W 351711	123.8	W 316600	109.7	W 319735	113.4	SUCRES RAFFINES
0615	MOLASSES			W 144044	11.5	W 169854	12.9	W 148018	11.0	MELASSES
07	COFFEE,TEA,COCOA,SPICES				63.5		63.2		118.7	CAFE,THE,CACAO,EPICES
071	COFFEE AND SUBSTITUTES			W 23265	27.1	W 20009	25.7	W 20364	63.0	CAFE ET SUCCEDANES
0711	COFFEE GREEN,ROASTED,SUB			W 23265	27.1	W 20009	25.7	W 20364	63.0	CAFE TORREFIE OU DECAFEINE
07111	COFFEE GREEN,HUSKS,SKINS			W 23265	27.1	W 20009	25.7	W 20364	63.0	CAFE NON TORREFIE
072	COCOA			W 47275	35.3	W 46641	37.0	W 52115	55.1	CACAO
0721	COCOA BEANS,RAW,ROASTED			W 46327	33.3	W 45210	33.9	W 50780	51.4	CACAO EN FEVES
09	MISC EDIBLE PRODUCTS				10.3		11.2		11.4	PREP ALIMENTAIRES DIVERSES
098	EDIBLE PRODCTS,PREPS NES			W 12378	10.3	W 12407	11.2	W 12305	11.4	PREP ALIMENTAIRES NDA
09809	MISC FOOD PREPRTIONS NES			W 11400	9.6	W 11702	10.2	W 11444	10.7	PREP ALIMENTAIRES NDA
1	BEVERAGES AND TOBACCO				76.9		69.5		64.2	BOISSONS ET TABACS
12	TOBACCO AND MANUFACTURES				72.8		66.3		60.3	TABACS BRUTS FABRIQUES
121	TOBACCO UNMNFCTRD,REFUSE			W 10950	42.3	W 12702	39.1	W 6153	29.7	TABACS BRUTS,DECHETS
1211	TOBACCO,NOT STRIPPED			W 10950	42.3	W 12702	39.1	W 6153	29.7	TABACS NON ECOTES
12111	— VIRGI TYPE,FLUE–CURED			W 9819	41.4	W 11612	37.5	W 5145	28.4	VIRGINIE SECHES AIR CHAUD
122	TOBACCO,MANUFACTURED			W 4004	30.6	W 2818	27.3	W 2412	30.6	TABACS FABRIQUES
1221	CIGARS,CHEROOTS,ETC			W 3614	30.2	W 2487	24.4	W 2147	26.1	CIGARES
2	CRUDE MATERLS,EXCL FUELS				8.6		9.3		11.5	MAT BRUTES NON COMESTIBLES
29	CRUDE ANIMAL,VEG MAT NES				5.3		4.3		5.0	MATIERES BRUTES ANIM,VEGET
5	CHEMCLS,RELATED PROD NES				46.6		50.1		51.8	PRODUITS CHIMIQUES
51	ORGANIC CHEMICALS				15.7		22.2		19.1	PROD CHIMIQ ORGANIQUES
515	ORG–INORG COMPOUNDS ETC			W 29724	14.6	W 36150	16.5	W 30977	12.5	COMPOSES ORGANO–MINERAUX
5156	HETEROCYCLIC CMPDS ETC			W 29724	14.6	W 36150	16.5	W 30977	12.5	COMPOSES HETEROCYCLIQUES
51569	OTH HETEROCYC CMPDS,ETC			W 29724	14.6	W 36150	16.5	W 30977	12.5	AUT COMP HETEROCYCLIQUES
541	*MEDICINAL,PHARM PRODUCT			K 1280100	20.8	K 1241023	17.2	K 1675687	18.6	PROD MEDICINAUX PHARMACEUT
5417	MEDICAMENTS			K 1229673	20.1	K 1123268	15.7	K 1112086	12.6	MEDICAMENTS
54179	— CONTNG OTH SUBSTANCES			K 1055472	17.1	K 991065	15.2	K 862472	11.2	MED CONT AUT SUBSTANCES
58	PLASTIC MATERIALS ETC				4.7		5.8		6.8	MAT PLAST ARTIFICIELLES
585	PLASTIC MATERIAL NES			W 1585	4.1	W 2021	5.5	W 2457	6.6	RESINES ARTIFICIELLES
5851	MODIFIED NATL RESINS ETC			W 1562	4.1	W 2020	5.5	W 2457	6.6	RESINES
6	BASIC MANUFACTURES				314.1		316.9		400.2	ART MANUFACTURES
61	LEATHER,DRESSED FUR,ETC				94.9		95.9		110.3	CUIRS,PELLETERIES
612	LEATHER ETC MANUFACTURES			W 5399	94.7	W 4243	94.8	W 4421	108.5	OUVRAGES EN CUIRS NDA
6123	PREPRD PARTS OF FOOTWEAR			W 5399	94.7	W 4242	94.7	W 4414	108.5	PARTIES DE CHAUSSURES
64	PAPER,PAPERBOARD AND MFR				10.2		10.1		11.2	PAPIERS,CARTONS & OUVRAGES
642	PAPER,ETC,PRECUT,ARTS OF			W 1761	9.9	W 1479	10.0	W 2851	10.9	PAP,CARTONS DECOUPES
6428	PAPER ETC ARTICLES NES			W 1174	9.0	W 1213	9.7	W 1435	10.3	OUVRAGES EN PATE A PAPIER
64289	OTHER ARTICLES OF PAPER			W 1165	9.0	W 1213	9.7	W 1435	10.3	ARTICLES,OUVRAGES EN PAPIER
65	TEXTILE YARN,FABRICS,ETC				41.9		52.4		64.8	FILS,TISSUS,ARTICLES TEXTILE
651	TEXTILE YARN			W 1287	10.3	W 1315	10.7	W 1380	10.8	FILS TEXTILES
6514	SYN FIB YRN,BULK,MONOFIL			W 1281	10.2	W 1315	10.7	W 1380	10.8	FILS CONT 85% FIB TEXT SYNTH
65141	— TEXTRD,CONT POLYAMIDE			W 1254	9.9	W 1302	10.6	W 1331	10.7	FILS TEXT FIB CONT POLYAMID
656	LACE,RIBBONS,TULLE,ETC			W 491	4.8	W 488	5.9	W 360	3.9	TULLES,BRODERIE
657	SPECIAL TXTL FABRC,PRODS			W 708	7.6	W 1264	16.3	W 1825	26.8	TISSUS SPECIAUX
6576	HAT BODIES			W 474	7.6	W 1060	16.2	W 1592	26.8	CLOCHES POUR CHAPEAUX
65761	WOOL,FUR FELT HAT BODIES			W 464	7.6	W 1060	16.2	W 1592	26.8	CLOCHES NON DRESSEES
658	TEXTILE ARTICLES NES			W 2487	12.8	W 2832	13.3	W 3852	17.5	ART FACONNES MAT TEXTILES
6582	MADE–UP CANVAS GOODS			W 2411	11.4	W 2795	13.0	W 3825	17.5	BACHES,TENTES ETC
65829	OTH MADE–UP CANVAS GOODS			W 2411	11.4	W 2795	13.0	W 3825	17.5	BACHES,TENTES EXC COTON
66	NONMETAL MINERAL MFS NES				9.3		6.5		6.5	ART MIN NON METALLIQUES
667	PEARL,PREC–,SEMI–P STONE				6.8		3.6		2.7	PERLES, PIERRES GEMMES
6672	DIAMONDS NONINDUST,UNSET				6.8		3.6		2.7	DIAMANTS BRUTS
66721	— ROUGH,UNSORTED				6.8		3.6		2.7	DIAMANTS BRUTS NON TRIES
67	IRON AND STEEL				144.5		133.7		190.2	FER ET ACIER
671	PIG IRON ETC			W 56020	144.0	W 64691	127.0	W 83031	182.5	FONTE,SPIEGEL,POUDRES
6716	FERRO–ALLOYS			W 56020	144.0	W 64691	127.0	W 83031	182.5	FERRO–ALLIAGES
67169	OTHER FERRO–ALLOYS			W 56020	144.0	W 64691	127.0	W 83031	182.5	AUTRES FERRO–ALLIAGES
674	IRN,STL UNIV,PLATE,SHEET			W 12	0.3	W 4243	6.2	W 472	6.7	LARGES PLATS,TOLES
6744	IRN,STL HVY PLATE,ROLLED			W 12	0.3	W 4240	6.2	W 464	6.7	TOLES LAMINEES PLUS 4.75 MM
67441	— OF IRON OR SIMPLE STL			W 12	0.3	W 4240	6.2	W 464	6.7	TOLES NON ACIER FIN CARB
69	METAL MANUFACTURES NES				12.5		16.7		16.6	ART MANUFACT EN METAL NDA
694	STL,COPPR NAILS,NUTS,ETC			W 2545	8.6	W 4587	14.4	W 4582	14.0	CLOUS,VIS,ECROUS
69401	IRON,STEEL NAILS ETC			W 2534	8.6	W 4587	14.4	W 4581	14.0	CLOUS,POINTES FER,ACIER
7	MACHINES,TRANSPORT EQUIP				171.5		190.4		232.5	MACHINES MATERIEL TRANSPORT
75	OFFICE MACHNES,ADP EQUIP				6.2		3.3		3.4	MACH BUREAU TRAIT AUTOM
759	OFFICE,ADP MCH PTS,ACCES			W 160	6.2	W 17	3.3	W 77	3.4	PIECES DU 751 ET 752
7591	OFFICE MACHINE PARTS NES			W 160	6.2	W 17	3.3	W 77	3.4	PIECES DU 7511,7518
75911	TYPEWRTR PARTS,ACCES NES			W 160	6.2	W 17	3.3	W 77	3.4	PIECES DU 7511
76	TELECOMM,SOUND EQUIPMENT				11.0		20.6		30.5	EQUIPMENT DE TELECOM
764	TELECOM EQPT,PTS,ACC NES			W 401	10.8	W 687	20.6	W 1014	30.2	EQUIP TELECOM,PIECES
7643	TV,RADIO TRANSMITTRS ETC			W 179	5.7	W 390	12.4	W 701	20.0	APP EMET TELE RADIO
7649	PTS NES OF EQUIPMT OF 76			W 221	5.2	W 296	8.3	W 313	10.2	PIECES DE LA DIV 76
76493	TELECOMM EQUIPMT PTS NES			W 217	5.2	W 292	8.0	W 313	10.2	PIECES 761,762,764.3,8
77	ELECTRIC MACHNRY NES ETC				152.8		163.5		192.3	MACH APP ELECT NDA
772	SWITCHGEAR ETC,PARTS NES			W 6818	117.1	W 6941	103.8	W 7244	116.0	APP COUPURE,SECT ETC
7721	SWITCHGEAR ETC			W 305	9.4	W 852	24.9	W 995	34.0	APP COUPURE,SECTIONMNT
7722	PRINTED CIRCUITS,PTS NES			W 6513	107.7	W 6089	78.9	W 6249	82.1	CIRCUITS ET PIECES

5. General Exports F.O.B. by Commodities according to the S.I.T.C. (Rev. 2) in million U.S. Dollars
Exportations Générales F.O.B. par Produits d'après la C.T.C.I. (Rév. 2) en millions de Dollars E.U.

SITC CTCI	COMMODITY	1991 QUANTITY QUANTITE	1991 VALUE VALEUR	1992 QUANTITY QUANTITE	1992 VALUE VALEUR	1993 QUANTITY QUANTITE	1993 VALUE VALEUR	1994 QUANTITY QUANTITE	1994 VALUE VALEUR	PRODUIT
773	ELECTR DISTRIBUTNG EQUIP			W 80	6.8	W 194	8.5	W 174	8.8	EQUIPMT DISTRIBUTION ELECT
7731	INSULATED WIRE,CABLE ETC			W 80	6.8	W 194	8.5	W 174	8.8	FILS,CABLES ISOLES ELECT
778	ELECTRICAL MACHINERY NES			W 2154	29.1	W 2272	51.3	W 2428	67.0	AUTRES MACH ELECT NDA
7788	OTH ELEC MACHY,EQUIP NES			W 1040	27.1	W 1703	50.1	W 1905	66.1	AUT MACH APP ELEC NDA
77883	ELEC SIGNALLING EQU NES			W 1040	27.1	W 1703	50.1	W 1870	66.0	APP ELECT SIGNAL ACOUS
8	MISC MANUFACTURED GOODS				783.5		822.4		847.6	ART MANUFACTURES DIVERS
821	*FURNITURE,PARTS THEREOF			W 3729	6.2	W 3118	5.3	W 3070	5.8	MEUBLES ET PIECES
831	*TRAVEL GOODS,HANDBAGS			W 4859	30.4	W 4883	27.9	W 4700	28.5	ARTICLES DE VOYAGE ETC
83101	HANDBAGS NES			W 698	5.7	W 1137	7.0	W 592	4.0	SACS A MAIN
83109	OTHER TRAVEL BAGS,CASES			W 4013	23.5	W 3597	20.0	W 4030	24.1	AUT CONTENANTS SIMILAIRES
84	CLOTHING AND ACCESSORIES				486.6		527.0		509.3	VETEMENTS
842	MENS OUTERWEAR NOT KNIT			W 31845	148.6	W 35626	160.8	W 40128	173.7	VET DESSUS POUR HOMMES
8421	— OVERCOATS,OTHER COATS			W 2174	25.7	W 1809	22.8	W 2011	21.8	MANTEAUX HOMMES MAT TEXT
84211	—— OF WOOL,FINE HAIR			W 1598	21.3	W 1247	17.4	W 1496	18.2	MANTEAUX HOMMES DE LAINE
84219	—— OF OTHER FIBRES			W 576	4.4	W 562	5.5	W 515	3.6	MANTEAUX HOMMES AUT FIBR
8422	— SUITS			W 27844	112.3	W 30846	120.1	W 34826	137.7	COMPLETS HOMMES MAT TEXT
84223	—— OF MAN–MADE FIBRES			W 27788	112.1	W 30843	120.1	W 34815	137.7	COMPLETS HOMMES FIB SYNT
8429	— OTHER OUTER GARMENTS			W 1822	10.6	W 2936	17.9	W 3263	14.3	AUT VET DES HOM MAT TEX
84299	—— OF OTHER FIBRES			W 1632	8.7	W 2637	14.7	W 2975	11.1	VET DES HOM NDA AUT FIB
843	WOMENS OUTERWEAR NONKNIT			W 13275	76.9	W 17960	104.5	W 16397	91.5	VET DESSUS FEMMES MAT TEX
8431	— COATS AND JACKETS			W 5398	40.4	W 7880	55.7	W 7175	47.2	MANT,VEST FEM MAT TEXTIL
84311	—— OF WOOL,FINE HAIR			W 3228	25.4	W 5069	39.3	W 4008	28.8	MANT,VEST FEMMES LAINE
84312	—— OF COTTON			W 1119	10.2	W 1591	11.4	W 1579	11.4	MANT,VEST FEMMES COTON
84313	—— OF MAN–MADE FIBRES			W 1051	4.8	W 1220	5.2	W 1589	7.1	MANT,VEST FEM FIBR SYNT
8432	— SUITS AND COSTUMES			W 6961	33.2	W 9096	43.7	W 8013	38.4	COSTUMES–TAIL MAT TEXIL
84321	—— OF WOOL,FINE HAIR			W 1722	9.1	W 1558	9.1	W 1280	7.5	COSTUMES–TAIL LAINE
84322	—— OF COTTON			W 5239	24.2	W 7538	34.6	W 6733	31.0	COSTUMES–TAIL COTON
844	UNDER GARMENTS NOT KNIT			W 23370	153.9	W 27574	158.3	W 26294	151.6	VETEMENT DESSOUS MAT TEX
8441	— MENS SHIRTS			W 15586	112.8	W 18085	112.4	W 15791	101.6	CHEMISES HOMMES MAT TEXT
84411	—— OF COTTON			W 11167	99.7	W 10895	89.0	W 9138	80.5	CHEMISES HOMMES DE COTON
84412	—— OF SYNTHETIC FIBRES			W 449	1.4	W 2526	10.3	W 1432	5.0	CHEMISES HOMMES FIB SYNT
84419	—— OF OTHER FIBRES			W 3969	11.7	W 4664	13.2	W 5221	16.3	CHEMISES HOMMES AUT FIBR
8442	— MENS,OTHR THAN SHIRTS			W 3933	13.1	W 5562	18.4	W 5496	19.4	SOUS–VET HOMMES MAT TEXT
84421	—— OF COTTON			W 3488	9.1	W 4726	14.1	W 4667	16.4	SOUS–VET HOMMES DE COTON
8443	— WOMENS			W 3851	28.2	W 3927	27.6	W 5007	30.7	VET DESSOUS FEM MAT TEXT
84431	— OF COTTON			W 1065	7.3	W 842	13.1	W 1270	9.9	VET DESSOUS FEM DE COTON
84439	— OF OTHER FIBRES			W 2786	21.0	W 3085	14.6	W 3737	20.9	VET DESSOUS FEM AUT FIBR
845	OUTERWEAR KNIT NONELASTC			W 2282	11.1	W 5268	21.9	W 7715	31.3	VET DESSOUS,ACCES BONNET
8451	— JERSEYS,PULLOVERS ETC			W 2282	11.1	W 5268	21.9	W 7715	31.3	CHANDAILS,PULL–OVERS ETC
84519	—— OF OTHER FIBRES			W 2282	11.1	W 5268	21.9	W 7715	31.3	CHANDAILS,PULL AUT FIBR
846	UNDER GARMENTS KNITTED			W 1740	30.8	W 1997	21.2	W 2461	28.6	SOUS VETS DE BONNETERIE
8465	CORSETS,GARTERS,ETC			W 1740	30.8	W 1997	21.2	W 2461	28.6	CORSETS,GAINES ART SIM
84652	CORSETS,BRACES ETC			W 1719	30.7	W 1972	21.0	W 2385	27.9	CORSETS,GAINES,JARRETEL
848	HEADGEAR,NONTXTL CLOTHNG			W 2910	65.3	W 2671	59.5	W 1578	29.7	VET ACCES MAT AUT QUE TEX
8481	LEATHER CLOTHES,ACCESSOR			W 984	23.4	W 653	17.4	W 314	5.9	VET ACCES MAT CUIR ARTIF
8484	HEADGEAR			W 1896	41.2	W 2017	42.1	W 1264	23.8	COIFFURES ET PARTIES NDA
84843	HEADGEAR TEXTILE NONFELT			W 1890	41.2	W 2005	42.1	W 1259	23.8	CHAPEAUX EN BONNETERIE
851	*FOOTWEAR			W 2993	18.8	W 2563	14.8	W 4919	35.3	CHAUSSURES
85101	FOOTWEAR RUBBER,PLASTIC			W 2353	14.8	W 1969	7.8	W 3182	11.3	CHAUS SEMELLES CAOUTCH
85102	FOOTWEAR LEATHER			W 543	3.4	W 585	7.0	W 1727	24.0	CHAUS SEMELLES EN CUIR
87	PRECISION INSTRUMNTS NES				111.8		145.1		159.2	INSTRUM,APPAR SCIENT NDA
872	MEDICAL INSTRUMENTS NES			W 7955	111.7	W 8615	145.0	W 8961	159.0	INSTR,APP MEDIC–CHIR NDA
87202	OTH MEDICAL INSTRUMENTS			W 7955	111.7	W 8615	145.0	W 8961	159.0	INSTRUM,APP MEDECINE
89	MISC MANUFCTRD GOODS NES				127.1		99.8		107.2	ART MANUFACTURES DIVERS
893	ARTICLES OF PLASTIC NES			W 1325	4.3	W 1111	4.3	W 1778	9.7	OUVRAGES EN MAT DIVIS 58
8939	MISC PLASTIC ARTICLES			W 1325	4.3	W 1111	4.3	W 1778	9.7	ART DIVERS EN MAT DIV 58
89399	OTHR PLASTC ARTICLES NES			W 1325	4.3	W 1111	4.3	W 1778	9.7	AUT OUV MAT DIV 58
897	GOLD,SILVER WARE,JEWELRY				113.3		85.8		87.5	BIJOUTERIE,ORFEVRERIE
8972	IMITATION JEWELLERY				0.8		6.1		3.9	BIJOUTERIE DE FANTAISIE
8973	PREC JEWLRY,GLD–SILVWARE				84.1		60.5		71.6	BIJOUX OR,ARGENT ORFEVRE
89731	PRECIOUS METAL JEWELLERY				80.9		41.7		38.2	ART BIJOUTERIE,JOAILLER
89732	GOLD,SILVER,ETC WARE				3.2		18.9		33.4	ORFEVRERIE MET PRECIEUX
8974	PREC MTL INDUS,LAB EQUIP				28.6		19.4		12.2	AUT OUV METAUX PRECIEUX
9	GOODS NOT CLASSD BY KIND				28.9		12.8		61.1	ART TRANSACT NON CLASSES
931	*SPECIAL TRANSACTIONS			W 787	3.8	W 5630	6.9	W 9687	41.6	TRANS.SPECIALES
971	*GOLD,NON MONETARY NES			K 72192	25.0	K 3184	5.9	K 13124	19.5	OR NON MONETAIRE
97101	NONMON GLD UNWRT,SEMIMFD			K 72192	25.0	K 3184	5.9	K 13085	19.4	OR,ALLIAGES D'OR BRUTS

FOOT NOTES – NOTES

TABLE 3 –
1 Export data for 1992, 1993 and 1994 include exports from the Industrial Free Zones.
TABLE 5 –
1 Data for 1992, 1993 and 1994 include exports from the Industrial Free Zones.
TABLEAU 3 –
1 En 1992, 1993 et 1994 les exportations incluent les données des zones franches et industrielles.
TABLEAU 5 –
1 Y compris en 1992, 1993 et 1994 les données des zones franches et industrielles.

1. HISTORICAL SERIES, 1962–1997 SPECIAL TRADE, IMPORTS C.I.F., EXPORTS F.O.B.
SERIES HISTORIQUES, 1962–1997 COMMERCE SPECIAL, IMPORTATIONS C.A.F., EXPORTATIONS F.O.B

YEAR ANNEE	VALUE IN MILLION U.S. DOLLARS VALEUR EN MILLION U.S. DOLLARS MERCHANDISE – MARCHANDISE IMPORTS	EXPORTS	GOLD – OR IMPORTS	EXPORTS	CONVERSION FACTORS FACTEURS DE CONVERSION CENTS E.U. PAR IMPORTS	EXPORTS	INDEX NUMBERS – INDICES QUANTUM IMPORTS	EXPORTS	UNIT VALUE VALEUR UNITAIRE IMPORTS	EXPORTS
1962	97.10	142.80								
1963	128.00	148.20								
1964	151.90	159.00								
1965	168.90	169.50								
1966	171.90	184.10								
1967	214.20	189.70								
1968	255.50	226.30								
1969	241.80	152.50								
1970	273.80	189.90								
1971	340.20	199.10								
1972	318.60	326.30								
1973	537.10	486.90								
1974	962.50	962.40								
1975	943.00	897.00								
1976	958.80	1257.60								
1977	1189.00	1436.30								
1978	1627.30	1493.80								
1979	1985.60	2067.00								
1980	2253.30	2480.80						58		165
1981	2246.10	2541.60						67		152
1982	2189.00	2340.80						57		164
1983	1465.00	2202.60						76		138
1984	1716.00	2581.30						81		132
1985	1674.40	2779.80						98		128
1986	1810.20	2171.50						105		76
1987	2251.50	1927.80						68		86
1988	1713.50	2192.40						100		72
1989	1854.80	2353.80						98		85
1990	1861.90	2714.30						100		100
1991	2397.40	2851.50						107		88
1992	2500.50	3007.40						116		97
1993	2561.90	2903.70						124		75
1994	3690.30	3819.90					103	138		83
1995	4193.30	4307.20					138	154		84
1996	3934.50	4899.70					133	158		96
1997	4945.30	5213.70					185	158		90

2. IMPORTS BY BROAD ECONOMIC CATEGORY AND EXPORTS BY INDUSTRIAL ORIGIN. (PERCENTAGE OF TOTAL VALUE)
IMPORTATIONS PAR CATEGORIES ECONOMIQUES ET EXPORTATIONS PAR BRANCHE D'ACTIVITE.(EN POURCENTAGE DE LA VALEUR TOTALE)

IMPORTS – IMPORTATIONS

	1991	1992	1993	1994	1995	1996	1997
TOTAL IMPORTS–IMPORTATIONS TOTALES	100.	100.	100.	100.	100.	100.	100.
1 FOOD BEV–ALIMENTATION BOISSONS	6.8	4.2	4.5	5.9	6.6	7.9	7.6
11 PRIMARY–PRODUITS DE BASE	3.5	1.6	2.7	2.6	3.0	3.8	3.2
111 FOR INDUSTRY–POUR L'INDUSTRIE	3.3	1.4	2.3	1.6	2.1	2.6	2.3
112 FOR HOUSEHOLDS–POUR LES MENAGES	0.2	0.2	0.4	0.9	0.9	1.2	0.9
12 PROCESSED–PRODUITS ELABORES	3.3	2.6	1.8	3.4	3.6	4.1	4.4
121 FOR INDUSTRY–POUR L'INDUSTRIE	1.6	1.1	0.4	0.8	0.8	1.1	1.1
122 FOR HOUSEHOLDS–POUR LES MENAGES	1.7	1.5	1.4	2.6	2.8	3.0	3.3
2 IND SUPPLIES–APPROV INDUSTRIELS	41.1	34.9	31.7	32.0	36.1	38.5	34.9
21 PRIMARY–PRODUITS DE BASE	1.6	1.3	1.7	1.4	2.4	2.8	2.4
22 PROCESSED–PRODUITS ELABORES	39.5	33.6	30.1	30.6	33.6	35.7	32.5
3 FUELS–COMBUSTIBLES	0.9	3.9	1.5	2.9	5.8	4.3	7.6
31 PRIMARY–PRODUITS DE BASE	0.0	0.0	0.8	1.5	2.0	3.0	1.9
32 PROCESSED–PRODUITS ELABORES	0.9	3.8	0.7	1.4	3.8	1.3	5.7
321 MOTOR SPIRIT–ESSENCE	0.0	0.0	0.0		0.6	0.1	0.5
322 OTHER–AUTRES	0.9	3.8	0.7	1.4	3.2	1.2	5.2
4 MACHINERY–EQUIPEMENT	26.3	25.7	27.2	20.1	20.2	20.6	22.7
41 CAPITAL EQUIPMENT–MACHINES	22.5	21.6	23.3	17.4	18.2	18.5	20.6
42 PARTS–PIECES ACCESSOIRES	3.8	4.0	3.9	2.6	1.9	2.1	2.1
5 TRANSPORT–TRANSPORT	15.7	19.7	22.4	28.4	19.9	14.6	12.9
51 PASSENGER CARS–AUTOMOBILES	3.2	8.4	10.4	11.6	7.0	5.8	4.9
52 OTHER–AUTRES	6.2	5.7	6.2	11.8	8.5	5.1	3.9
521 INDUSTRIAL–INDUSTRIELS	6.1	5.6	6.1	11.5	8.2	4.9	3.8
522 NON INDUSTRIAL–NON INDUSTRIEL	0.1	0.1	0.2	0.3	0.2	0.1	0.1
53 PARTS–PIECES ACCESSOIRES	6.3	5.6	5.8	5.1	4.4	3.7	4.1
6 CONSUM GOODS–BIENS CONSOMMATION	9.1	11.6	11.9	10.7	11.4	13.8	14.1
61 DURABLE–DURABLES	1.1	1.5	2.0	2.4	2.1	2.6	3.0
62 SEMI DURABLE–SEMI DURABLES	2.4	3.1	3.6	3.5	4.1	4.9	4.9
63 NON DURABLE–NON DURABLES	5.6	7.0	6.4	4.7	5.2	6.3	6.2
7 GOODS NES–BIENS NDA	0.1	0.1	0.7	0.0	0.1	0.2	0.2

EXPORTS – EXPORTATIONS

	1991	1992	1993	1994	1995	1996	1997
TOTAL EXPORTS–EXPORTATIONS TOTALES	100.	100.	100.	100.	100.	100.	100.
1 AGRICULTURE	51.1	46.0	42.8	49.8	47.4	44.1	52.1
2 MINING QUARRY–INDUS EXTRACTIVES	37.2	41.8	38.8	31.4	32.8	32.0	27.3
3 MANUFACTURING–IND MANUFACTUR	11.6	12.2	18.3	18.8	19.8	23.9	20.6
31 FOOD BEV TOBACCO–ALIM BOISS TAB	5.3	5.1	6.9	7.3	8.1	9.9	8.9
32 TEXTILES–INDUSTRIES TEXTILES	0.5	0.9	1.3	1.4	1.3	1.3	1.4
33 WOOD & PRODUCTS–BOIS & PRODUITS	1.0	0.7	1.4	1.2	1.3	1.5	1.3
34 PAPER & PRODUCTS–PAPIER & PRODT	0.0	0.4	0.4	0.3	0.4	0.4	0.3
35 CHEMICALS–INDUSTRIES CHIMIQUES	3.8	3.5	4.5	4.4	4.8	7.3	4.8
36 NON METAL MIN–MIN NON METAL	0.1	0.1	0.3	0.5	0.5	0.5	0.6
37 BASIC METAL–IND METAL BASE	0.1	0.2	0.2	0.3	0.3	0.2	0.2
38 METAL MANUF–MANUF METAL	0.7	1.2	2.9	3.1	2.8	2.5	2.8
39 OTH MANUF IND–AUTRES MANUF	0.2	0.2	0.4	0.3	0.3	0.3	0.4

3. TRADE BY PRINCIPAL COUNTRIES OF ORIGIN AND DESTINATION (VALUE IN MILLION U.S. DOLLARS)
ECHANGES SELON LES PRINCIPAUX PAYS D'ORIGINE ET DE DESTINATION (VALEUR EN MILLIONS DE DOLLARS EU)

COUNTRIES–PAYS	SPECIAL IMPORTS C.I.F. IMPORTATIONS SPECIALES C.A.F				
	1993	1994	1995	1996	1997
World	2552.7	3622.0	4195.2	3733.0	4510.6
Africa	11.2	27.0	31.9	9.1	57.8
Americas	1386.3	2111.2	2741.2	2526.2	3048.6
– Northern America	839.7	1004.1	1374.8	1223.8	1430.4
– LAIA	435.7	1010.0	1248.2	1164.0	1388.6
– CACM	5.4	4.6	8.7	12.0	13.2
– Caribbean	24.5	17.7	40.8	29.0	104.0
– Rest of America	81.0	74.7	68.8	97.4	112.4
Asia excl fmr USSR	459.1	756.9	619.0	411.3	513.6
– Middle East	5.4	26.0	21.6	13.0	23.3
Asia former USSR				0.3	0.3
Europe excl fmr USSR	676.1	677.3	706.3	724.5	816.3
– European Union	621.5	608.7	643.8	654.7	755.5
– Eastern Europe	17.8	26.5	18.7	28.5	21.2
– Rest of Europe	36.9	42.0	43.9	41.3	39.6
Europe former USSR	13.9	20.3		19.7	41.5
Oceania	5.6	25.1	4.6	18.6	21.6
Other	0.5	4.3	92.1	23.3	10.9
USA/Etats–Unis d'Amer	810.2	950.3	1289.8	1174.1	1376.3
Japan/Japon	344.7	515.5	361.2	209.8	263.0
Colombia/Colombie	99.6	297.9	399.6	378.5	478.9
Venezuela	46.9	160.0	262.6	172.6	301.9
Germany/Allemagne	131.2	217.0	190.5	155.5	188.2
Brazil/Brésil	99.3	227.0	187.8	142.6	134.0
Mexico/Mexique	59.2	150.8	158.5	197.7	149.9
Italy/Italie	227.4	138.2	103.2	98.1	124.5
Spain/Espagne	119.2	82.9	93.1	170.1	161.1
Chile/Chili	48.4	66.6	111.5	135.2	152.1
Panama	80.7	74.0	68.7	97.1	112.3
Korea, Republic of	43.4	102.8	102.1	60.2	61.5
Argentina/Argentine	41.1	50.0	75.7	81.2	90.4
Canada	29.4	53.6	84.7	49.5	53.3
France, Monaco	49.3	37.5	59.3	34.6	81.1
Other Asia n.e.s.	34.4	59.9	61.3	35.3	49.7
Peru/Pérou	34.7	52.4	39.8	40.4	59.7
Belgium–Luxembourg	20.3	34.5	59.2	64.5	46.4
United Kingdom	37.6	35.0	51.3	45.7	54.3
Switzerland,Liechtenst.	35.5	40.2	42.1	40.0	37.5
Netherlands/Pays–Bas	13.8	24.0	39.7	49.8	49.2
Areas n.e.s.	0.5	4.3	92.1	23.3	10.9
China, Hong Kong SAR	9.9	10.0	20.0	30.1	29.0
Russian Federation	13.9	20.3		19.6	35.6
Sweden/Suède	10.0	16.9	19.2	13.5	29.6
Aruba				4.4	80.9
China/Chine	8.9	2.5	26.6	0.8	45.3
Netherlands Antilles	18.0	10.7	19.6	9.5	18.8
Australia/Australie	3.2	24.5	2.0	17.5	19.5
Israel/Israël	5.5	7.1	8.7	13.0	16.7
So. African Customs Un	9.1	11.3	14.7	7.4	4.9
Turkey/Turquie	5.1	20.5	4.9	2.1	14.0
Poland/Pologne	2.8	7.3	13.4	13.1	8.6
Uruguay	6.2	4.6	7.2	8.2	16.9
Angola		12.9		0.0	28.5
Korea Dem People's Rp		12.6		24.9	0.2
Trinidad and Tobago	5.8	5.7	10.3	6.7	2.8
Romania/Roumanie	3.8	6.5	4.1	12.5	4.0
Indonesia/Indonésie	3.5	4.3	2.3	10.1	10.4
Denmark/Danemark	3.8	6.4	5.9	6.6	6.4

COUNTRIES–PAYS	SPECIAL EXPORTS F.O.B. EXPORTATIONS SPECIALES F.O.B.				
	1993	1994	1995	1996	1997
Monde	3020.0	3843.4	4361.5	4889.8	5214.1
Afrique	5.1	4.6	9.1	9.6	1.9
Amériques	2047.4	2499.8	2841.6	3158.2	3365.5
– Amérique du Nord	1405.8	1640.8	1871.0	1870.3	2011.9
– ALAI	517.4	717.3	761.3	854.8	1021.7
– MCAC	25.9	30.1	33.2	112.3	95.7
– Caraïbes	9.6	10.0	14.4	108.8	61.2
– Autre Amérique	88.7	101.5	161.7	211.9	175.0
Asie anc. URSS exclus	398.2	442.8	482.0	602.1	579.5
– Moyen–Orient	23.1	24.8	28.8	27.0	41.1
Asie ancienne URSS				0.1	0.4
Europe anc. URSS exclus	531.2	824.7	886.1	1009.2	1037.3
– Union Européenne	493.6	760.0	843.4	942.6	1005.5
– Europe de l'Est	30.1	56.2	32.2	36.6	21.2
– Autre de l'Europe	7.5	8.5	10.5	30.1	10.7
Europe ancienne URSS	24.2	38.4	86.4	87.2	178.0
Océanie	10.1	9.7	19.3	20.9	24.9
Autre	3.7	23.4	36.9	2.5	26.7
USA/Etats–Unis d'Amer	1397.5	1625.1	1853.4	1851.5	1992.0
Korea, Republic of	281.6	289.6	290.4	314.4	171.4
Colombia/Colombie	141.4	226.0	251.9	300.5	352.1
Chile/Chili	116.3	166.5	194.4	220.5	237.9
Italy/Italie	121.0	155.3	173.4	195.4	271.4
Germany/Allemagne	70.6	188.8	167.2	176.0	204.0
Panama	88.1	101.4	161.6	211.7	175.0
Peru/Pérou	130.3	156.8	69.2	53.3	222.8
Spain/Espagne	82.2	114.6	150.1	133.2	127.5
Japan/Japon	51.3	76.0	118.3	138.7	155.7
Belgium–Luxembourg	59.4	105.8	93.9	108.2	98.9
United Kingdom	45.7	50.4	95.7	125.1	94.3
Argentina/Argentine	53.4	71.5	89.9	84.1	76.0
France, Monaco	45.7	64.0	79.1	82.9	87.6
Russian Federation	24.2	38.4	65.1	82.5	141.2
Netherlands/Pays–Bas	43.3	49.3	57.3	77.4	86.7
Mexico/Mexique	42.7	76.4	54.0	57.7	41.8
China/Chine	4.1	13.6	15.8	67.1	157.3
Venezuela	9.7	8.0	34.1	72.4	49.8
Brazil/Brésil	21.0	7.5	54.1	43.9	25.9
Other Asia n.e.s.	34.3	26.5	15.8	22.2	45.3
Poland/Pologne	14.3	41.7	28.3	32.0	19.6
El Salvador	0.7	2.8	2.1	53.5	76.1
Areas n.e.s.	3.7	23.4	36.9	2.5	26.7
Guatemala	15.2	17.9	17.3	21.8	12.5
Canada	8.3	15.4	17.6	18.7	19.9
Netherlands Antilles	4.0	0.7	0.2	35.4	37.1
Portugal	11.2	18.1	16.5	19.6	7.3
New Zealand	8.7	8.2	17.9	15.6	21.7
Cuba	3.8	5.0	6.8	38.5	4.6
Lithuania/Lituanie			17.0	2.8	35.7
Saudi Arabia	0.5	1.6	3.4	11.7	36.4
Greece/Grèce	0.8	0.2	1.6	16.7	23.0
Iran (Islamic Rep of)	18.2	12.7	10.3	0.1	
Nicaragua	0.4	0.3	8.5	28.9	2.6
Uruguay	0.2	0.5	8.4	16.2	8.7
Switzerland,Liechtenst.	6.1	4.6	7.1	6.5	6.5
Costa Rica	8.5	7.9	2.7	3.6	2.7
Aruba				23.9	0.1
Turkey/Turquie	3.9	1.3	4.2	13.5	0.1

(VALUE AS PERCENTAGE OF WORLD TOTAL)(VALEURS EN POURCENTAGE DU TOTAL MONDIAL)

	1988	1989	1990	1991	1992	1993	1994	1995	1996	1997
Africa	1.0	1.9	0.6	1.2	0.5	0.4	0.7	0.8	0.2	1.3
Americas	54.0	59.1	58.2	56.3	56.8	54.3	58.3	65.3	67.7	67.6
– Northern America	35.0	36.2	34.8	34.0	34.4	32.9	27.7	32.8	32.8	31.7
– LAIA	17.3	20.7	20.7	19.8	19.5	17.1	27.9	29.8	31.2	30.8
– CACM	1.0	1.3	1.5	1.0	1.0	0.2	0.1	0.2	0.3	0.3
– Caribbean	0.2	0.4	0.7	0.9	0.7	1.0	0.5	1.0	0.8	2.3
– Rest of America	0.6	0.4	0.5	0.5	1.1	3.2	2.1	1.6	2.6	2.5
Asia excl fmr USSR	18.7	11.7	13.0	14.9	17.4	18.0	20.9	14.8	11.0	11.4
– Middle East	1.6	0.1	0.1	0.5	0.7	0.2	0.7	0.5	0.3	0.5
Asia former USSR									0.0	0.0
Europe excl fmr USSR	24.9	26.3	27.7	27.1	24.5	26.5	18.7	16.8	19.4	18.1
– European Union	21.9	22.2	23.8	23.2	22.1	24.3	16.8	15.3	17.5	16.7
– Eastern Europe	0.9	1.4	0.8	1.1	0.4	0.7	0.7	0.4	0.8	0.5
– Rest of Europe	2.2	2.7	3.1	2.8	2.0	1.4	1.2	1.0	1.1	0.9
Europe former USSR	0.1	0.3	0.2	0.3	0.6	0.5	0.6		0.5	0.9
Oceania	0.6	0.7	0.2	0.1	0.2	0.2	0.7	0.1	0.5	0.5
Other	0.6	0.1	0.0	0.1	0.0	0.0	0.1	2.2	0.6	0.2
USA/Etats–Unis d'Amer	33.1	33.9	32.6	31.9	32.5	31.7	26.2	30.7	31.5	30.5
Japan/Japon	13.9	8.2	9.5	10.0	13.1	13.5	14.2	8.6	5.6	5.8
Colombia/Colombie	2.0	2.4	3.2	4.1	4.1	3.9	8.2	9.5	10.1	10.6
Venezuela	1.3	0.9	1.8	1.8	1.7	1.8	4.4	6.3	4.6	6.7
Germany/Allemagne				6.1	5.3	5.1	6.0	4.5	4.2	4.2
Brazil/Brésil	6.4	9.3	7.5	5.9	4.8	3.9	6.3	4.5	3.8	3.0
Mexico/Mexique	3.3	2.9	2.9	1.4	2.3	2.3	4.2	3.8	5.3	3.3
Italy/Italie	3.7	4.5	5.8	6.2	5.1	8.9	3.8	2.5	2.6	2.8
Spain/Espagne	4.0	2.9	2.5	2.3	5.3	4.7	2.3	2.2	4.6	3.6
Chile/Chili	2.0	1.6	1.9	2.7	2.4	1.9	1.8	2.7	3.6	3.4

	1988	1989	1990	1991	1992	1993	1994	1995	1996	1997
Afrique	0.4	0.5	0.5	0.1	0.1	0.2	0.1	0.2	0.2	0.0
Amériques	67.3	79.1	81.9	66.7	65.1	67.8	65.0	65.2	64.6	64.5
– Amérique du Nord	46.0	60.7	53.3	49.3	46.9	46.5	42.7	42.9	38.2	38.6
– ALAI	12.5	13.3	10.8	12.3	13.3	17.1	18.7	17.5	17.5	19.6
– MCAC	0.6	1.9	1.8	0.9	1.3	0.9	0.8	0.8	2.3	1.8
– Caraïbes	6.6	0.5	10.9	0.4	0.4	0.3	0.3	0.3	2.2	1.2
– Autre Amérique	1.6	2.6	5.0	3.8	3.3	2.9	2.6	3.7	4.3	3.4
Asie anc. URSS exclus	5.6	5.4	5.5	15.0	16.2	13.2	11.5	11.1	12.3	11.1
– Moyen–Orient	0.4	0.6	0.2	0.3	0.4	0.8	0.6	0.7	0.6	0.8
Asie ancienne URSS									0.0	0.0
Europe anc. URSS exclus	10.4	9.8	11.5	17.6	18.0	17.6	21.5	20.3	20.6	19.9
– Union Européenne	9.4	9.0	10.2	17.1	16.4	16.3	19.8	19.3	19.3	19.3
– Europe de l'Est	0.9	0.5	0.9	0.4	1.4	1.0	1.5	0.7	0.7	0.4
– Autre de l'Europe	0.1	0.2	0.5	0.2	0.1	0.2	0.2	0.2	0.6	0.2
Europe ancienne URSS	0.2	0.2	0.1		0.2	0.8	1.0	2.0	1.8	3.4
Océanie	0.5	0.4	0.5	0.6	0.5	0.3	0.3	0.4	0.4	0.5
Autre	15.6	4.6	0.0	0.0	0.0	0.1	0.6	0.8	0.1	0.5
USA/Etats–Unis d'Amer	45.9	60.6	53.0	49.2	46.7	46.3	42.3	42.5	37.9	38.2
Korea, Republic of	0.0	0.0	0.9	10.4	11.4	9.3	7.5	6.7	6.4	3.3
Colombia/Colombie	2.0	1.8	1.2	1.1	2.0	4.7	5.9	5.8	6.1	6.8
Chile/Chili	2.7	3.5	2.9	3.7	5.0	3.9	4.3	4.5	4.5	4.6
Italy/Italie	1.3	1.1	1.3	2.1	3.1	4.0	4.0	4.0	4.0	5.2
Germany/Allemagne				4.8	3.5	2.3	4.9	3.8	3.6	3.9
Panama	1.6	2.6	5.0	3.7	3.2	2.9	2.6	3.7	4.3	3.4
Peru/Pérou	5.9	5.7	5.1	5.8	3.3	4.3	4.1	1.6	1.1	4.3
Spain/Espagne	1.1	1.7	2.5	4.0	3.7	2.7	3.0	3.4	2.7	2.4
Japan/Japon	2.5	2.5	1.9	2.2	2.1	1.7	2.0	2.7	2.8	3.0

4. Special Imports C.I.F. by Commodities according to the S.I.T.C. (Rev. 2) in million U.S. Dollars
Importations Spéciales C.A.F. par Produits d'après la C.T.C.I. (Rév. 2) en millions de Dollars E.U.

SITC CTCI	COMMODITY	1994 QUANTITY QUANTITE	1994 VALUE VALEUR	1995 QUANTITY QUANTITE	1995 VALUE VALEUR	1996 QUANTITY QUANTITE	1996 VALUE VALEUR	1997 QUANTITY QUANTITE	1997 VALUE VALEUR	PRODUIT
	ALL COMMODITIES		3622.1		4195.2		3733.1		4510.7	TOUS PRODUITS
0	FOOD AND LIVE ANIMALS		179.0		263.2		308.8		359.2	ALIMENTS,ANIMAUX VIVANTS
02	DAIRY PRODCTS,BIRDS'EGGS		7.5		7.2		11.6		13.6	PRODUITS LAITIERS,OEUFS
03	FISH AND PREPARATIONS		9.8		11.0		15.9		1.9	POISSONS ET PREPARATIONS
034	FISH,FRESH,CHILLED,FROZN	W 11374	9.1	W 12704	9.9	W 17610	14.8	W 541	0.6	POISSON FRAIS, REFRIG,CONG
0342	FISH FROZEN,EXCL FILLETS	W 11346	8.9	W 12674	9.8	W 17592	14.6	W 517	0.5	POISSONS CONGELES
04	CEREALS AND PREPARATIONS		70.7		113.5		134.4		139.7	CEREALES ET PRODUITS
041	WHEAT ETC UNMILLED	W 253428	47.2	W 303986	71.4	W 351020	86.0	W 492637	88.3	FROMENT,EPEAUTRE
0411	DURUM WHEAT UNMILLED	W 253428	47.2	W 298986	70.3	W 334120	82.0	W 489337	87.8	FROMENT DUR NON MOULU
044	MAIZE UNMILLED	W 11855	2.7	W 18348	17.3	W 26333	20.5	W 116885	20.1	MAIS NON MOULU
048	CEREAL ETC PREPARATIONS	W 4626	10.8	W 6994	12.2	W 8618	16.5	W 40076	27.5	PREPTNS A BASE CEREALES
05	VEGETABLES AND FRUIT		19.1		29.1		32.5		41.4	LEGUMES ET FRUITS
057	FRUIT,NUTS,FRESH,DRIED	W 17027	10.9	W 19435	15.9	W 22385	17.8	W 34280	22.9	FRUITS FRAIS OU SECS
06	SUGAR AND PREPS,HONEY		26.3		40.6		22.9		45.4	SUCRES ET PRODUITS
061	SUGAR AND HONEY	W 175939	20.4	W 75728	33.9	W 21824	12.9	W 54329	34.2	SUCRES ET MIEL
0612	REFINED SUGAR ETC	W 163410	15.8	W 63410	27.8	W 12151	8.3	W 34756	28.8	SUCRES RAFFINES
07	COFFEE,TEA,COCOA,SPICES		12.7		14.1		12.5		18.0	CAFE,THE,CACAO,EPICES
081	*FEEDING STUFF FOR ANIML	W 8107	6.3	W 29127	13.9	W 59415	43.4	W 50820	55.0	NOURRITURE POUR ANIMAUX
0813	OILCAKE AND OTH RESIDUES	W 16	0.1	W 19377	6.2	W 55383	36.8	W 40135	43.6	TOURTEAUX
08131	— OF SOYA BEANS	W 2	0.1	W 19377	6.2	W 55383	36.8	W 38987	43.3	TOURTEAUX DE SOJA
09	MISC EDIBLE PRODUCTS		16.5		23.7		28.0		34.6	PREP ALIMENTAIRES DIVERSES
098	EDIBLE PRODCTS,PREPS NES	W 4081	16.4	W 7438	23.5	W 5522	27.7	W 5791	34.1	PREP ALIMENTAIRES NDA
09809	MISC FOOD PREPRTIONS NES	W 2943	14.3	W 4005	19.7	W 4000	24.7	W 4087	30.7	PREP ALIMENTAIRES NDA
1	BEVERAGES AND TOBACCO		28.7		23.7		20.6		14.8	BOISSONS ET TABACS
11	BEVERAGES		28.3		23.5		20.2		13.8	BOISSONS
112	ALCOHOLIC BEVERAGES	W 37222	27.2	W 21207	22.5	W 20528	19.8	W 14080	12.1	BOISSONS ALCOOLIQUES
2	CRUDE MATERLS,EXCL FUELS		84.4		137.9		128.1		143.4	MAT BRUTES NON COMESTIBLES
23	RUBBER, CRUDE		11.0		18.5		16.2		16.4	CAOUTCHOUC BRUT
251	*PULP AND WASTE PAPER	W 14298	5.4	W 26246	14.5	W 28024	7.8	W 30368	6.6	PATES A PAPIER,DECHETS
26	TEXTILE FIBRES AND WASTE		37.8		56.3		53.3		60.7	FIBRES TEXTILES
263	COTTON	W 4350	7.5	W 9349	17.3	W 7912	16.4	W 12478	22.0	COTON
2631	RAW COTTON,EXCL LINTERS	W 4147	7.4	W 9137	17.2	W 7811	16.4	W 12359	21.9	COTON EN MASSE
266	SYNTHETIC FIBRES TO SPIN	W 17020	27.6	W 19094	35.9	W 18541	33.7	W 24677	36.1	FIBRES SYNTHETIQUES
2665	DISCN SYNTH FIBRE UNCMBD	W 8274	12.3	W 9698	18.2	W 8358	15.1	W 12654	17.4	DISCONTINUES EN MASSE
26652	— POLYESTER	W 7135	10.3	W 8543	16.0	W 7192	12.8	W 11023	14.4	FIBRES EN POLYESTERS
2666	CONTIN FILAMNT TOW SYNTH	W 6780	11.4	W 7343	14.1	W 8654	15.7	W 9739	15.5	CABLES POUR DISCONTINUS
26663	— OF ACRYLIC FIBRES	W 6459	10.8	W 6901	13.0	W 8085	14.3	W 9307	14.6	DE FIBRES ACRYLIQUES
27	CRUDE FERTLZR,MINRLS NES		11.5		14.1		9.3		8.9	ENGRAIS MINERAUX BRUTS
29	CRUDE ANIMAL,VEG MAT NES		15.5		27.7		37.9		38.6	MATIERES BRUTES ANIM,VEGET
292	CRUDE VEG MATERIALS NES	W 1572	12.4	W 2331	23.6	W 2214	33.6	W 2432	35.1	MAT BRUTES VEGETALES NDA
2926	LIVE PLANTS,BULBS,ETC	W 815	8.8	W 1356	17.9	W 1322	28.9	W 1183	27.4	BULBES,TUBERCULES
29269	LIVE PLANTS NES	W 735	8.2	W 1287	17.4	W 1137	27.4	W 1002	26.4	AUTRES PLANTES VIVANTES
3	MINERAL FUELS ETC		108.5		249.5		165.6		385.2	COMBUSTIBLES MINERAUX LUB
33	PETROLEUM AND PRODUCTS		54.7		170.9		53.2		299.0	PETROLE ET DERIVES
334	PETROLEUM PRODUCTS,REFIN	W 155307	50.3	W 724958	158.8	W 114099	47.9	W 1347860	257.8	PRODUITS RAFFINES
3341	GASOLINE,OTH LIGHT OILS			W 97292	25.9	W 6317	2.4	W 110690	24.5	ESSENCES POUR MOTEURS
33411	MOTOR,AVIATION SPIRIT			W 96629	25.7	W 6284	2.3	W 110660	24.5	ESSENCES MOTEURS D'AVIONS
3342	KEROSENE,OTH MEDIUM OILS			W 413160	73.7	W 55342	15.1	W 1175383	206.4	PETR LAMPANTS,AUT HUIL
33429	OTH MEDIUM PETROLEUM OIL			W 413160	73.7	W 55342	15.1	W 1170853	205.6	AUTRES HUILES MOYENNES
3343	GAS OILS			W 162592	24.5					GAS OILS
3344	FUEL OILS,NES	W 154935	49.7	W 2	0.1					FUEL OILS
3345	LUBS,PETROLEUM OILS NES	W 372	0.7	W 51912	34.9	W 52441	30.5	W 61787	27.0	HUILES LUBRIFIANTES
33451	LUBS(HIGH PETR CONT) ETC			W 50945	32.8	W 51812	29.1	W 60969	25.3	HUILES LUBRIF,H LOURDES
335	RESIDUAL PETRLM PROD NES	W 8374	4.5	W 7299	5.5	W 5892	5.3	W 170271	41.2	PRODUITS RESIDUELS NDA
3352	MINERAL TARS AND PRODCTS	W 226	0.3	W 219	0.3	W 248	0.3	W 160893	35.2	GOUDRONS MINERAUX
33525	MINERAL TAR OILS ETC NES	W 195	0.3	W 207	0.3	W 227	0.3	W 160860	35.2	AUTRES PRODUITS NDA
341	*GAS,NATURAL AND MANUFCT	W 142899	53.7	W 290884	78.4	W 391175	112.3	W 396044	86.1	GAZ NATUREL,GAZ MANUFACT
3413	PETROLM GASES,LIQUEFIED	W 142898	53.7	W 290883	78.3	W 391121	111.6	W 396043	86.1	GAZ DE PETROLE LIQUEFIE
34131	LIQUEFIED PROPANE,BUTANE	W 142874	53.2	W 290882	78.3	W 261271	71.0	W 1	0.1	PROPANE,BUTANE LIQUEFIES
34139	OTH HYDROCARBON GAS LQFD	W 24	0.6	W 1	0.1	W 129850	40.6	W 396041	86.1	HYDROCARBURES GAZEUX NDA
4	ANIMAL,VEGETABLE OIL,FAT		21.5		27.0		40.6		39.1	HUILES,GRAISSES ANIM,VEG
42	FIXED VEGETABLE OIL,FAT		17.9		24.3		37.3		36.4	HUILES VEGETALES FIXES
423	FIXED VEG OILS,SOFT	W 29388	17.3	W 31151	22.8	W 56116	35.3	W 60618	34.0	HUILES VEGET DOUCES FIXES
4232	SOYA BEAN OIL	W 29052	16.4	W 30621	21.7	W 54562	33.3	W 59280	32.0	HUILE DE SOJA
5	CHEMCLS,RELATED PROD NES		602.7		729.8		700.1		820.1	PRODUITS CHIMIQUES
51	ORGANIC CHEMICALS		90.3		99.9		94.0		106.0	PROD CHIMIQ ORGANIQUES
512	ALCOHOLS,PHENOLS ETC	W 14630	9.8	W 25314	13.0	W 43806	10.2	W 19354	12.0	PHENOLS,PHENOLS–ALCOOLS
513	CARBOXYLIC ACIDS ETC	W 14617	21.3	W 15540	24.5	W 14808	23.4	W 16996	26.1	ACIDES CARBOXYLIQUES
5137	MONOACIDS AND DERIVATIVS	W 6572	12.5	W 10244	15.2	W 7057	9.3	W 9229	9.8	ACIDES MONOCARBOXYLIQUES
514	NITROGEN–FNCTN COMPOUNDS	W 6489	19.5	W 6896	23.4	W 5532	23.0	W 7118	26.4	COMPOSES FONCT AZOTEES
5148	OTH NITROGN–FNCTN CMPNDS	W 4840	12.0	W 4846	14.9	W 3571	12.8	W 5294	14.7	AUTRES COMPOSES AZOTES
515	ORG–INORG COMPOUNDS ETC	W 3626	25.1	W 2744	19.4	W 3044	21.7	W 3164	23.2	COMPOSES ORGANO–MINERAUX
5155	OTH ORG–INORG COMPOUNDS	W 2426	12.5	W 1187	6.4	W 1376	7.7	W 1421	7.3	AUTR COMP ORG–MINERAUX
52	INORGANIC CHEMICALS		39.8		49.0		44.9		45.5	PROD CHIM INORGANIQUES
522	INORG ELEMNTS,OXIDES,ETC	W 38964	15.6	W 37133	18.6	W 43085	18.1	W 52458	16.6	ELEMENTS INORGANIQUES
523	OTHR INORG CHEMICALS ETC	W 54320	24.1	W 56102	30.4	W 65956	26.8	W 64018	28.8	AUT PRODUITS CHIMIQUES INORG
5232	OTH MTL CMPD OF INRG ACD	W 36648	15.0	W 36017	19.1	W 26770	16.5	W 40129	18.1	SELS METALLIQUES
53	DYES,TANNING,COLOUR PROD		34.2		34.0		31.7		39.4	PROD TEINTURE,COLORANTS
531	SYNT DYE,NAT INDGO,LAKES	W 1459	13.1	W 2997	13.1	W 2861	10.0	W 3526	12.0	MAT COLOR ORGAN,LAQUES
533	PIGMENTS,PAINTS,ETC	W 6229	18.7	W 7794	19.5	W 15157	20.4	W 9793	25.6	PIGMENTS,PEINTURES,VERNIS
541	*MEDICINAL,PHARM PRODUCT		115.2		164.3	MK 10770	173.3	MK 11376	206.9	PROD MEDICINAUX PHARMACEUT
5413	ANTIBIOTICS IN BULK	K 199455	11.9	K 316044	19.0	K 251848	13.7	K 263018	14.5	ANTIBIOTIQUES NDA
5417	MEDICAMENTS	K 6940291	84.3	K 6301873	124.9	K 6623306	138.1	MK 9159	166.8	MEDICAMENTS
54171	— CONTAINNG ANTIBIOTICS	K 961124	13.0	K 446405	22.2	K 533001	22.2	K 621924	26.0	MED CONTN ANTIBIOTIQUES
54172	— CONTAINING HORMONES	K 744304	9.5	K 368772	13.8	K 464761	18.9	K 469950	20.4	MED CONTENANT HORMONES
54179	— CONTNG OTH SUBSTANCES	K 5194590	60.9	K 5441159	87.7	K 5541310	94.6	K 7969425	117.7	MED CONT AUT SUBSTANCES
55	PERFUME,CLEANING ETC PRD		32.6		37.0		40.2		54.3	PROD POUR PARFUM,TOILETTE
551	ESSENTL OILS,PERFUME,ETC	W 1997	12.0	W 2834	13.5	W 1004	11.8	W 1236	14.6	HUILES ESSENTIELLES
553	PERFUMERY,COSMETICS,ETC	W 3019	8.4	W 3994	11.4	W 3707	17.2	W 7557	22.7	PRODUITS DE PARFUMERIE
554	SOAP,CLEANSING ETC PREPS	W 5481	12.2	W 6420	12.1	W 5855	11.3	W 11866	17.1	SAVONS,PRODUITS DETERSIFS
562	*FERTILIZERS,MANUFACTURE		53.0	W 261263	73.6	W 262853	63.7	W 408401	63.1	ENGRAIS MANUFACTURES
5621	CHEM NITROGENOUS FERTLZR	W 140035	28.4	W 133809	39.6	W 151290	37.7	W 280121	31.2	ENGRAIS AZOTES
56216	UREA	W 133340	26.3	W 114541	34.6	W 122281	31.0	W 248478	24.8	UREE
5629	FERTILIZERS NES		15.0	W 53689	21.7	W 37658	14.7	W 50247	18.9	ENGRAIS NDA
56292	NITROG–PHOS FERTILZR NES		8.2	W 33381	14.4	W 29101	9.9	W 34847	11.4	ENGRAIS NDA CONT N P
58	PLASTIC MATERIALS ETC		140.7		139.5		120.6		144.7	MAT PLAST ARTIFICIELLES
582	PROD OF CONDENSATION ETC	W 22146	56.7	W 17018	29.0	W 12151	21.8	W 18431	26.4	PROD CONDENS,POLYCOND
5823	ALKYDS,OTHER POLYESTERS	W 12465	43.6	W 6362	12.6	W 4520	7.6	W 6441	8.0	ALKYDES ET AUT POLYESTERS
58231	— IN PRIMARY FORMS	W 12341	43.1	W 6290	12.2	W 4438	7.3	W 6356	7.6	SOUS FORMES PRIMAIRES
583	POLYMERIZATION ETC PRODS	W 87929	79.1	W 80919	104.6	W 91193	93.8	W 117419	113.2	PROD POLYMERISATION
5831	POLYETHYLENE	W 27036	20.5	W 28104	33.6	W 32874	32.9	W 46266	44.1	POLYETHYLENE

4. Special Imports C.I.F. by Commodities according to the S.I.T.C. (Rev. 2) in million U.S. Dollars
Importations Spéciales C.A.F. par Produits d'après la C.T.C.I. (Rév. 2) en millions de Dollars E.U.

SITC CTCI	COMMODITY	1994 QUANTITY QUANTITE	1994 VALUE VALEUR	1995 QUANTITY QUANTITE	1995 VALUE VALEUR	1996 QUANTITY QUANTITE	1996 VALUE VALEUR	1997 QUANTITY QUANTITE	1997 VALUE VALEUR	PRODUIT
58311	— IN PRIMARY FORMS	W 26175	19.0	W 25993	30.1	W 30424	27.4	W 41807	36.4	POLYETHYLENE PRIMAIRES
5832	POLYPROPYLENE	W 19299	15.2	W 16295	19.7	W 16000	16.6	W 21621	17.0	POLYPROPYLENE
58321	— IN PRIMARY FORMS	W 18976	14.3	W 15882	18.7	W 15689	15.9	W 21249	15.7	POLYPROPYLENE PRIMAIRES
5834	POLYVINYL CHLORIDE	W 30536	25.4	W 25768	27.9	W 31010	25.1	W 36091	29.5	CHLORURE DE POLYVINYLE
58341	— IN PRIMARY FORMS	W 29679	23.4	W 24454	24.4	W 30001	22.6	W 34701	25.7	SOUS FORMES PRIMAIRES
59	CHEMICAL MATERIALS NES		96.2		131.2		130.1		158.1	MAT PROD CHIMIQUES NDA
591	PESTICIDES,DISINFECTANTS	W 11013	58.4	W 15702	86.3	W 14059	81.6	W 31516	104.6	DESINF,INSECT,FONG,HERB
5911	INSECTICIDES,FOR RETAIL	W 2993	13.3	W 5311	25.6	W 4520	21.9	W 5344	26.1	INSECTICIDES VENTE DET
5912	FUNGICIDES,FOR RETAIL	W 2970	22.9	W 3611	29.8	W 2627	28.4	W 12425	40.9	FONGICIDES VENTE AU DET
5913	HERBICIDES,FOR RETAIL	W 4363	20.0	W 6233	29.1	W 6381	29.9	W 12175	35.3	HERBICIDES VENTE AU DET
598	MISCEL CHEM PRODUCTS NES	W 22823	33.5	W 25816	39.9	W 25912	42.5	W 31863	47.4	PROD DIV INDUST CHIM NDA
5989	CHEM PRODUCTS,PREPS NES	W 14589	21.6	W 16516	25.0	W 17659	29.0	W 22368	32.6	PROD PREP CHIMIQUES NDA
59899	OTH CHEM PRODS,PREPS,NES	W 7349	14.9	W 10008	17.1	W 11072	21.9	W 13782	22.8	AUT PRODUITS CHIMIQUES NDA
6	BASIC MANUFACTURES		576.7		788.2		738.6		778.5	ART MANUFACTURES
62	RUBBER MANUFACTURES NES		43.5		55.7		54.5		77.8	CAOUTCHOUC MANUFACTURE
625	RUBBER TYRES, TUBES ETC	W 12651	30.2	W 14636	40.1	W 14534	39.2	W 19627	57.6	PNEUS CAOUTCHOUC VULCANISE
6251	TYRES NEW FOR MOTOR CARS	W 3588	9.8	W 3806	11.6	W 5797	11.7	W 5756	17.1	PNEUS POUR VOITURES
6252	TYRES,NEW,BUS OR LORRY	W 4889	13.0	W 6285	19.8	W 5840	20.4	W 9282	29.7	PNEUS POUR AUTOBUS,CAMIONS
628	RUBBER ARTICLES NES	W 1514	8.0	W 2381	10.2	W 1808	10.7	W 3141	15.3	OUVRAGES CAOUTCHOUC NDA
64	PAPER,PAPERBOARD AND MFR		103.6		144.6		124.1		108.7	PAPIERS,CARTONS & OUVRAGES
641	PAPER AND PAPERBOARD	W 97460	91.1	W 117818	125.8	W 130055	100.6	W 103074	82.0	PAPIERS ET CARTONS
6411	NEWSPRINT	W 45220	46.4	W 47351	43.9	W 28988	24.2	W 33516	18.8	PAPIER JOURNAL
6412	PRINTG,WRITING PAPER NES	W 9889	8.4	W 10760	12.7	W 9269	9.8	W 15382	13.3	PAPIERS POUR L'IMPRESSION
6413	KRAFT PAPER,PAPERBOARD	W 4096	2.9	W 24859	19.8	W 36276	21.5	W 8841	6.9	PAPIER ET CARTON KRAFT
64131	KRAFT LINER IN BULK	W 7	0.1	W 16332	12.7	W 30643	16.0	W 32	0.1	PAP KRAFT POUR COUVERTURES
6415	PAPER,PAPERBRD,BULK,NES	W 31811	24.3	W 25146	33.3	W 36838	30.6	W 31263	24.4	PAPIERS,CARTONS ROULEAUX
64159	OTHER PAPER ETC,BULK,NES	W 31399	23.7	W 24377	32.4	W 24708	24.1	W 30662	23.6	AUT PAPIER ROULEAUX FEUILLES
642	PAPER,ETC,PRECUT,ARTS OF	W 5396	12.5	W 8399	18.8	W 16083	23.6	W 13256	26.7	PAP,CARTONS DECOUPES
6428	PAPER ETC ARTICLES NES	W 1853	5.1	W 2794	8.2	W 9960	11.8	W 5775	13.8	OUVRAGES EN PATE A PAPIER
65	TEXTILE YARN,FABRICS,ETC		52.8		60.4		65.4		86.4	FILS,TISSUS,ARTICLES TEXTILE
651	TEXTILE YARN	W 5683	14.8	W 6045	18.4	W 12980	17.3		19.0	FILS TEXTILES
6514	SYN FIB YRN,BULK,MONOFIL	W 3739	10.4	W 4823	13.0	W 3899	12.8	W 5284	15.1	FILS CONT 85% FIB TEXT SYNTH
652	COTTON FABRICS,WOVEN	W 1202	6.4	W 1427	5.0	W 2626	11.3	W 2818	12.8	TISSUS DE COTON
657	SPECIAL TXTL FABRC,PRODS	W 3735	15.3	W 3814	19.4	W 14079	21.4	W 6613	27.9	TISSUS SPECIAUX
6573	COATED ETC TEXTILES NES	W 2374	8.5	W 2138	9.5	W 3171	13.0	W 3948	15.1	TISSUS,ART MATIERE TEXT NDA
66	NONMETAL MINERAL MFS NES		66.7		87.0		82.5		83.0	ART MIN NON METALLIQUES
661	LIME,CEMENT,BLDG PRODS	W 77033	11.9	W 180143	19.0	W 113038	17.8	W 75096	16.9	CHAUX,CIMENTS MAT CONSTR
662	CLAY,REFRACTORY BLDG PRD	W 11885	7.3	W 20576	13.1	W 18362	13.6	W 26064	13.1	MAT CONST REFRACTAIRES
663	MINERAL MANUFCTURES NES	W 5729	14.3	W 4545	8.4	W 4298	8.3	W 5996	9.7	ART MIN MANUF NDA
664	GLASS	W 31648	18.9	W 36894	25.6	W 35467	23.3	W 42397	24.1	VERRE
665	GLASSWARE	W 12334	11.2	W 16015	15.7	W 15851	14.3	W 13451	13.5	OUVRAGES EN VERRE
67	IRON AND STEEL		187.0		279.2		262.3		237.2	FER ET ACIER
672	IRON,STEEL PRIMARY FORMS	W 169945	58.7	W 283807	120.9		84.9	W 262868	65.4	LINGOTS FER,ACIER
6725	IRN,STL BLOOMS,SLABS,ETC	W 95884	35.5	W 205403	86.2	W 191702	59.0	W 158068	42.0	BLOOMS,BILLETTES FER ACIER
67251	IRN,SMPLE STL BLOOMS,ETC	W 95872	35.4	W 205084	85.9	W 191648	58.9	W 158066	42.0	BLOOMS ETC NON ACIER FIN
6727	IRN,STL COIL FR REROLLNG	W 74050	23.2	W 77371	34.4	W 62794	24.9	W 102154	22.7	EBAUCHES POUR TOLES FER
67271	IRON,SIMPLE STEEL COILS	W 73689	23.0	W 77144	34.3	W 60785	23.6	W 102096	22.6	EBAUCHES NON EN ACIER
673	IRON,STEEL SHAPES ETC	W 94049	35.9	W 102273	42.1	W 95589	37.8	W 140074	48.4	BARRES,PROFIL FER,ACIER
6731	IRON,STEEL WIRE ROD	W 45324	19.2	W 61072	25.1	W 63274	21.3	W 66231	19.8	FIL MACHINE FER,ACIER
67311	IRON,SIMPLE STL WIRE ROD	W 41935	17.9	W 58543	24.0	W 63210	21.3	W 65996	19.7	FIL MACH AUT ACIER FIN
6732	IRON,STEEL BARS ETC	W 30385	10.3	W 30965	12.3	W 22909	11.7	W 60795	23.9	BARRES FER,ACIER
67326	IRN,OTH STL BARS HOTROLD	W 25600	7.4	W 26787	8.6	W 20208	8.1	W 56473	20.0	BARRES PLEINES FER,ACIER
674	IRN,STL UNIV,PLATE,SHEET	W 106201	54.1	W 111960	73.8	W 106056	67.0	W 132441	65.9	LARGES PLATS,TOLES
6745	IRN,STL MED PLATE,ROLLED	W 14914	6.0	W 13577	8.0	W 23620	12.4	W 11323	5.0	TOLES 3 A 4.75 MM
6746	IRN,STL THIN PLATE,ROLLD	W 48605	23.6	W 51640	32.5	W 36849	23.2	W 64476	26.9	TOLES LAM MOINS 3MM
67461	— OF IRON OR SIMPLE STL	W 47058	21.9	W 49970	28.6	W 35792	20.6	W 63059	24.2	TOL NON AC FIN MOINS 3 MM
6749	OTH IRN,STL PLATES,SHEET	W 27014	16.7	W 25120	20.2	W 26330	19.7	W 37177	24.6	AUTRES TOLES FER,ACIER
67491	— OF IRON OR SIMPLE STL	W 26872	16.4	W 24805	19.3	W 25638	19.0	W 36616	23.8	AUT TOLES AUTRES ACIER FIN
678	IRON,STL TUBES,PIPES,ETC	W 29098	33.2	W 32398	38.5	W 52226	67.6	W 43593	52.4	TUBES,TUYAUX EN FONTE,FER
6782	IRON,STL SEAMLESS TUBES	W 20939	18.4	W 28656	29.6	W 30986	38.6	W 29933	34.4	TUBES,TUYAUX SANS SOUDURE
6783	IRON,STL TUBES,PIPES NES	W 3322	5.9	W 1877	2.6	W 9796	11.8	W 10384	9.4	AUT TUBES,TUYAUX FER,ACIER
6785	IRON,STEEL TUBE FITTINGS	W 4077	7.4	W 1864	6.4	W 5840	12.7	W 2788	8.4	ACCESSOIRES DE TUYAUTERIE
68	NON–FERROUS METALS		43.4		61.2		47.4		57.4	METAUX NON FERREUX
682	COPPER EXC CEMENT COPPER	W 5516	15.3	W 5573	19.9	W 6237	17.1	W 6724	19.2	CUIVRE
6822	COPPER,ALLOYS WORKED	W 5381	15.1	W 5566	19.8	W 6223	17.1	W 6720	19.2	CUIVRE,ALLIAGES OUVRES
68221	COPPER BARS,WIRE,ETC	W 4575	12.2	W 4665	15.4	W 5525	14.0	W 5532	14.4	BARRES,PROFILES ET FILS
684	ALUMINIUM	W 12502	23.1	W 12557	34.0	W 10599	23.9	W 12927	28.7	ALUMINIUM
6841	ALUMINIUM,ALLOYS,UNWRGHT	W 8106	13.1	W 9513	22.7	W 6675	13.3	W 8388	15.2	ALUMINIUM,ALLIAGES BRUTS
69	METAL MANUFACTURES NES		75.4		92.2		91.4		117.4	ART MANUFACT EN METAL NDA
695	TOOLS	W 5680	20.7	W 4784	20.6	W 3707	19.0	W 4273	21.0	OUTILS A MAIN
697	BASE MTL HOUSEHOLD EQUIP	W 3189	8.0	W 2997	9.1	W 4068	12.1	W 4920	13.9	ART MENAGE MET COMMUNS
699	BASE METAL MFRS NES		17.4	W 8255	24.5	W 9012	25.2	W 17321	40.7	ART MANUFACTURES MET NDA
7	MACHINES,TRANSPORT EQUIP		1737.4		1679.0		1323.3		1624.9	MACHINES MATERIEL TRANSPORT
71	POWER GENERATING EQUIPMT		99.3		141.8		133.5		167.1	MACHINES GENERATRICES
711	STEAM BOILERS & AUX PLNT	W 566	3.4	W 1301	6.6	W 2703	25.1	W 747	3.9	GENERATEURS VAPEUR EAU ETC
7111	STEAM BOILERS ETC	W 527	2.9	W 1268	6.0	W 2396	20.4	W 652	3.1	GENERATEURS VAPEUR EAU
712	STEAM ENGINES,TURBINES		2.3	W 169	1.5	W 288	19.9	W 264	11.3	MACHINES A VAPEUR D'EAU PIEC
7126	STEAM POWR UNITS,ENGINES		0.1	W 115	0.5	W 287	19.8	W 192	7.0	MACHINES A VAPEUR D EAU
713	INTRNL COMBUS PSTN ENGIN	W 16683	56.5	W 13648	57.4	W 4510	34.4	W 4524	43.4	MOTEURS EXPL COMB INT, PIECE
7139	PISTON ENGINE PARTS NES	W 6726	35.1	W 7220	38.6	W 2478	25.4	W 3123	30.7	PIECES POUR 713.2,3,8
714	ENGINES AND MOTORS NES	W 118	3.4	W 432	18.6	W 546	13.2	W 116	9.2	MOTEURS NON ELECTRIQUES
7148	GAS TURBINES NES	W 9	0.5	W 386	16.3	W 512	10.7	W 30	3.0	TURBINES A GAZ
71488	OTHER GAS TURBINES NES	W 6	0.2	W 380	15.6	W 510	10.6	W 28	3.0	AUTRES TURBINES A GAZ
716	ROTATING ELECTRIC PLANT	W 3298	32.4	W 6233	55.3	W 3507	38.6	W 7283	96.5	APP ELECTR ROTATIFS,PIECES
7161	DC MOTORS AND GENERATORS	W 656	14.6	W 771	6.4	W 696	6.0	W 1472	18.1	MOTEURS COURANT CONTINU
7162	AC MTRS,GENRTRS,GEN SETS	W 2453	15.9	W 5207	47.3	W 2747	30.6	W 5493	73.1	MOTEURS ELECTRIQUES
71623	GEN SETS WITH PSTN ENGN	W 677	6.7	W 2800	30.5	W 1346	18.8	W 4317	64.1	GROUPES MOTEUR EXPLOSION
72	MACHS FOR SPCL INDUSTRYS		184.1		201.1		167.7		179.2	MAC SPECIALES POUR INDUST
721	AGRIC MACHY,EXC TRACTORS	W 2646	11.9	W 3522	17.2	W 1901	12.7	W 3388	17.6	MACHINES AGRICOLES
722	TRACTORS NON–ROAD	W 2361	12.1	W 2301	13.5	W 1524	10.3	W 2243	12.8	TRACTEURS
7224	WHEELED TRACTORS NES	W 2063	11.0	W 1874	10.9	W 916	6.2	W 1741	9.6	TRACTEURS A ROUES
723	CIVIL ENGNEERG EQUIP ETC	W 16032	48.8	W 9627	47.6		26.2	W 5405	32.0	APPAREILS DE GENIE CIVIL
7234	CONST,MINING MACHNRY NES	W 15633	46.5	W 8767	39.5		19.4	W 4660	23.5	MACH POUR LA CONST, MINES
72341	SELF–PROPELLD DOZERS,ETC	W 2011	12.4	W 1975	11.3	W 600	4.9	W 565	3.4	BULLDOZERS
72342	SLFPRP SHOVELS,EXCAVATRS	W 12947	30.1	W 6277	24.1	W 1639	11.1	W 3174	14.9	PELLES MECANIQUES
724	TEXTILE,LEATHER MACHNRY	W 4242	30.4	W 3250	22.6	W 2521	24.1	W 3222	29.5	MACH POUR INDUSTRIE TEXTILE
726	PRINTG,BKBINDG MACHY,PTS	W 1074	18.3	W 1735	32.0	W 559	9.8	W 517	8.9	MACHINES POUR IMPRIMERIE
7264	PRINTING PRESSES	W 537	13.0	W 1232	25.0	W 296	4.9	W 255	3.6	MACHINES A IMPRIMER
72641	ROTARY PRINTING PRESSES	W 537	13.0	W 1232	25.0	W 296	4.9	W 255	3.6	MACH IMPRIMER ROTATIVES
727	FOOD MACHRY NON–DOMESTIC	W 2992	18.5	W 2187	16.2	W 2026	15.0	W 2020	14.4	MACH INDUSTRIES ALIMENT
7272	OTH FOOD PROC MCHY,PARTS	W 1142	13.7	W 1466	12.6	W 1390	11.6	W 1188	10.1	AUT MACH IND ALIMENTAIRE

4. Special Imports C.I.F. by Commodities according to the S.I.T.C. (Rev. 2) in million U.S. Dollars
Importations Spéciales C.A.F. par Produits d'après la C.T.C.I. (Rév. 2) en millions de Dollars E.U.

SITC CTCI	COMMODITY	1994 QUANTITY QUANTITE	1994 VALUE VALEUR	1995 QUANTITY QUANTITE	1995 VALUE VALEUR	1996 QUANTITY QUANTITE	1996 VALUE VALEUR	1997 QUANTITY QUANTITE	1997 VALUE VALEUR	PRODUIT
72722	INDUS FOOD PROC MACH NES	W 961	11.6	W 1449	12.2	W 1185	11.3	W 731	8.2	MACHINES BOULANGERIE
728	OTH MACHY FOR SPCL INDUS	W 4373	39.6	W 5312	46.9	W 6242	67.3	W 6003	57.1	AUT MACH IND PARTICULIERES
7283	OTHR MINERAL WORKG MACHY	W 804	4.5	W 1271	8.3	W 1801	14.3	W 2117	10.4	MACH TRIER,CRIBLER,BROYER
7284	MACHY FOR SPCL INDUS NES	W 2506	27.6	W 3535	34.6	W 3896	48.7	W 3344	42.2	MACH SPEC IND PARTICUL.
72842	RUBBER,PLASTICS WRKG MCH	W 843	10.7	W 928	13.7	W 1352	16.2	W 1169	17.4	MACH IND CAOUT MAT PLAST
72848	OTH MCHY WITH INDIV FNCT	W 901	7.7	W 1523	12.1	W 1278	13.1	W 1928	20.3	AUTRES MACHINES NDA
73	METALWORKING MACHINERY		19.7		17.0		13.2		23.0	MACH TRAVAIL DES METAUX
736	METALWORKING MACH-TOOLS	W 3173	16.3	W 2571	12.2	W 1650	8.2	W 1188	5.9	MACH-OUTILS TRAVAIL METAUX
737	METALWORKING MACHNRY NES	W 770	3.4	W 753	4.9	W 713	5.0	W 1704	17.1	MACH TRAV METAUX PIECES
7372	ROLLING MILLS AND ROLLS	W 35	0.4	W 138	0.7	W 63	0.3	W 1168	13.7	LAMINOIRS CYLINDRES PIEC
74	GENRL INDUSTRL MACHY NES		235.0		249.2		231.0		282.3	MACH APP INDUSTRIE
741	HEATING,COOLING EQUIPMNT	W 4934	40.6	W 5361	36.1	W 4759	41.0	W 8774	58.0	MACH CHAUFFAGE,PIECES
7414	NONDOM REFRIG EQUIPT,PTS	W 1656	15.4	W 1907	12.8	W 1405	10.4	W 2729	18.1	MAT PRODUCTION DU FROID
74141	REFRIG EQUIP NONDOMESTIC	W 623	11.1	W 599	6.7	W 697	6.6	W 1671	12.6	REFIG INDUSTRIELS
7415	AIR-CONDITIONING MACHNRY	W 1570	11.5	W 1530	7.9	W 1181	6.8	W 3044	14.7	GROUPES CONDITION AIR
7416	HEATING,COOLING EQU NES	W 1074	9.4	W 1159	8.6	W 1217	17.9	W 1840	16.2	APP CHANGEMENT TEMP
742	PUMPS FOR LIQUIDS ETC	W 6223	50.4	W 5107	47.3	W 4008	43.9	W 5464	51.6	POMPES MOTO-POMPES
7428	OTHER PUMPS FOR LIQUIDS	W 4228	31.1	W 2710	26.3	W 1936	20.8	W 3424	23.0	AUTRES POMPES POUR LIQ
74288	PUMPS FR LIQUIDS NES ETC	W 4109	30.0	W 2271	17.8	W 1749	17.3	W 3312	21.1	POMPES POUR LIQUIDES NDA
7429	PTS NES OF PUMPS OF 742	W 1160	11.1	W 1193	13.0	W 1121	15.6	W 991	19.7	PIECES POUR GROUPE 742
743	PUMPS NES,CENTRFUGES ETC	W 5399	29.8	W 5765	33.1	W 5328	40.3	W 6025	46.5	POMPES COMPRES,VENT ETC
7431	PUMPS FOR GASES ETC	W 2954	14.4	W 3051	15.0	W 2446	17.3	W 3145	25.3	POMPES AIR A VIDE,COMPRES
7436	GAS,LIQUID FILTERS ETC	W 1699	10.1	W 1866	10.0	W 2160	14.5	W 2170	13.1	APP POUR FILT DES LIQUIDES
744	MECHANICAL HANDLING EQU	W 6805	25.9	W 6284	33.2	W 3178	20.6	W 3961	21.1	EQUIP MANUTENTION PIECES
7442	LIFTING,LOADING MACH NES	W 4304	9.0	W 2833	18.6	W 1624	11.1	W 2310	13.1	APP LEVAGE,MANUTENTION
7449	PTS NES OF MACHY OF 7442	W 1251	11.8	W 1741	7.9	W 754	5.8	W 588	3.7	PIECES DU 744.2
745	NONELEC MACHY,TOOLS NES	W 4068	37.7	W 4587	46.0	W 5745	30.2	W 3491	34.9	AUT MACH NON ELEC,PIECES
7452	OTH NONELEC MCHS,PTS NES	W 3819	.33.1	W 4315	40.3	W 5501	26.4	W 3257	30.6	AUT MACH NON ELEC,PIECES
74522	PACKAGNG,BOTTLNG,ETC MCH	W 1156	19.2	W 511	13.1	W 514	10.6	W 490	9.6	MACH NETT BOUTEILLES,ETC
74527	SPRAYING MACHINERY	W 2265	9.5	W 3232	21.2	W 4576	10.6	W 2245	13.2	APP PROJETER ETC LIQUID
749	NONELEC MACH PTS,ACC NES	W 7671	50.8	W 6907	53.7	W 5153	55.3	W 7711	70.6	PIECES MACH NON ELEC NDA
7492	COCKS,VALVES ETC NES	W 2061	19.7	W 1991	20.7	W 2551	23.8	W 3455	31.3	ART ROB,SIM POUR TUYAUX
7493	SHAFT,CRANK,PULLEY ETC	W 2245	9.8	W 2067	11.6	W 936	11.8	W 1874	13.4	ARBRES TRANS,VILEBREQUINS
7499	OTH NONELEC MCHY PTS NES	W 1773	11.9	W 1659	11.3	W 917	10.7	W 1384	14.2	PIECES NON ELECT NDA
75	OFFICE MACHNES,ADP EQUIP		59.5		65.1		72.9		90.3	MACH BUREAU TRAIT AUTOM
752	AUTOMTIC DATA PROC EQUIP	W 1284	40.4	W 1253	46.0	W 1238	55.5	W 2305	71.7	MACH TRAIT INFORMATION
7522	DIGITAL COMPUTERS	W 524	21.2	W 436	21.8	W 222	13.6	W 214	10.1	MACH DIGITALES COMPLETES
7523	DIGITL CENTRL PROCESSORS	W 216	6.4	W 118	8.3	W 348	20.8	W 578	34.7	UNITES CENTRALES
7525	ADP PERIPHERAL UNITS	W 167	4.2	W 519	7.1	W 421	12.3	W 1200	17.9	UNITES PERIPHERIQUES
76	TELECOMM,SOUND EQUIPMENT		93.2		86.5		89.7		235.9	EQUIPEMENT DE TELECOM
761	TELEVISION RECEIVERS	W 2749	14.2	W 2289	9.3	W 2902	15.9	W 15180	23.6	RECEPTEURS DE TELEVISION
7611	COLOUR TV RECEIVERS	W 2257	12.7	W 1340	7.3	W 2393	14.7	W 3180	21.6	RECEPTEURS COULEUR
762	RADIO BROADCAST RECEIVRS	W 2622	9.8	W 2657	9.8	W 2258	10.9	W 2283	18.5	RECEPTEURS RADIODIFFUSION
7628	OTHER RADIO RECEIVERS	W 1370	6.0	W 1622	7.1	W 1485	8.6	W 1815	15.7	AUTRES RECEPT RADIO
764	TELECOM EQPT,PTS,ACC NES	W 4480	64.7	W 2945	64.4	W 2441	59.3	W 3861	188.2	EQUIP TELECOM,PIECES
7641	LINE TELEPHONE,ETC EQUIP	W 1446	17.6	W 617	11.1	W 948	15.1	W 1308	73.9	APP TELEPHON PAR FIL
7643	TV,RADIO TRANSMITTRS ETC	W 663	24.5	W 347	33.1	W 329	28.2	W 906	96.8	APP EMET TELE RADIO
7649	PTS NES OF EQUIPMT OF 76	W 1664	17.8	W 1425	16.6	W 700	12.2	W 872	10.4	PIECES DE LA DIV 76
76493	TELECOMM EQUIPMT PTS NES	W 966	13.5	W 763	12.6	W 396	9.5	W 652	7.2	PIECES 761,762,764.3,8
77	ELECTRIC MACHNRY NES ETC		117.1		197.1		160.1		183.0	MACH APP ELECT NDA
771	ELECTRIC POWER MACHY NES	W 2224	16.1	W 3657	41.5	W 2168	15.9	W 2652	17.2	MACH PROD,TRANS ELECTR
7711	TRANSFORMERS,ELECTRICAL	W 1553	10.8	W 2478	32.5	W 1490	9.3	W 1703	8.7	TRANSFO ELECTRIQUES
77118	OTHER ELEC TRANSFORMERS	W 648	4.2	W 1455	23.5	W 615	3.2	W 690	4.2	AUTRES TRANSFO ELECTRIQ
772	SWITCHGEAR ETC,PARTS NES	W 4176	22.5	W 3433	39.8	W 2852	31.4	W 3960	35.5	APP COUPURE,SECT ETC
7721	SWITCHGEAR ETC	W 4118	21.8	W 3396	39.2	W 2786	30.7	W 3913	34.7	APP COUPURE,SECTIONMNT
773	ELECTR DISTRIBUTNG EQUIP	W 2264	9.1	W 6449	29.3	W 5339	25.0	W 3806	18.2	EQUIPMT DISTRIBUTION ELECT
7731	INSULATED WIRE,CABLE ETC	W 1483	7.4	W 5323	27.2	W 4376	22.6	W 3182	16.1	FILS,CABLES ISOLES ELECT
775	HOUSEHOLD TYPE EQUIP NES	W 7710	28.8	W 11521	36.2	W 11654	36.9		52.3	MACH,APP USAGE DOMESTQUE
7752	DOM REFRIGERATRS,FREEZRS	W 2998	10.9	W 5059	19.9	W 5127	17.6	W 6805	24.9	REFRIG,CONGEL MENAGER
77521	DOMESTIC REFRIGERATORS	W 2783	10.0	W 4683	18.3	W 4933	16.7	W 6554	24.1	REFRIGERATEURS
778	ELECTRICAL MACHINERY NES	W 15382	29.0	W 16486	37.6	W 8560	37.2	W 11544	47.3	AUTRES MACH ELECT NDA
7781	BATTERIES,ACCUMULATORS	W 4705	9.1	W 5582	12.7	W 5221	12.8	W 7383	17.4	PILES ET ACCUMULATEURS
78	ROAD VEHICLES		915.9		695.0		440.6		454.1	VEHICULES ROUTIERS
781	PASS MOTOR VEH EXC BUSES	W 55717	418.5	W 32976	294.3	W 30165	218.2	W 27763	222.4	AUTO TRANSPORT PERSONNES
782	LORRIES,SPCL MTR VEH NES	W 45621	297.6	W 28849	216.9	W 14859	121.0	W 19184	147.1	VEHICULES SPECIAUX,MARCH
7821	LORRIES,TRUCKS	W 41689	287.5	W 27028	206.2	W 13637	114.4	W 18646	139.3	VEHICULES TRANSP MARCHAND
783	ROAD MOTOR VEHICLES NES	W 17309	98.5	W 14709	99.8	W 4567	46.2	W 1735	12.8	VEHICULES ROUTIERS NDA
7831	BUSES	W 9476	71.8	W 9535	74.4	W 3505	40.4	W 713	5.7	VOITURES TRANSPORT COMMUN
7832	TRACTORS FOR TR-TRAILERS	W 7833	26.7	W 5175	25.4	W 1062	5.9	W 1022	7.2	TRACTEURS ROUTIERS
784	MOTOR VEH PRTS,ACCES NES	W 35512	77.3	W 15292	65.9	W 9296	45.0	W 10741	59.7	PIECES 722,781,782,783
7841	MOTOR VEHICLE CHASSIS	W 14404	35.1	W 3653	18.7	W 1358	9.9	W 2503	15.9	CHASSIS 722,781,782,783
7849	OTHER MOTOR VEHCL PARTS	W 21106	42.3	W 11583	47.2	W 7905	34.6	W 8195	43.6	PIECES 722,781,782,783
785	CYCLES,ETC MOTRZD OR NOT	W 8753	16.5	W 6658	15.6	W 2947	8.5	W 3858	9.5	MOTOCYCLES SCOOTERS
79	OTHR TRANSPORT EQUIPMENT		14.0		26.5		15.0		10.3	AUTRE MATERIEL TRANSPORT
792	AIRCRAFT ETC	W 180	10.7	W 316	21.4	W 13	2.2	W 10	1.3	APP NAVIGATION AERIENNE
793	SHIPS AND BOATS ETC	W 537	3.3	W 2006	5.0	W 8858	12.7	W 4190	8.9	NAVIRES BATEAUX,ETC
7932	SHIPS AND BOATS NES	W 519	2.8	W 1992	4.1	W 8854	12.7	W 3465	6.8	NAVIRES ET BATEAUX
8	MISC MANUFACTURED GOODS		281.9		295.4		301.1		338.9	ART MANUFACTURES DIVERS
812	*PLUMBG,HEATNG,LGHTNG EQ	W 3552	8.4	W 4274	12.8	W 3253	11.1	W 3264	12.0	APPAR SANITAIRES CHAUFFAGE
821	*FURNITURE,PARTS THEREOF	W 4738	16.4	W 3412	14.1	W 3683	14.3	W 4182	15.3	MEUBLES ET PIECES
8219	FURNITURE AND PARTS NES	W 4124	13.2	W 2326	8.6	W 2667	8.6	W 2992	9.6	AUTRES MEUBLES ET PIECES
84	CLOTHING AND ACCESSORIES		15.1		25.4		24.3		31.8	VETEMENTS
851	*FOOTWEAR	W 4230	16.5	W 3431	15.1	W 3177	15.9	W 4978	25.8	CHAUSSURES
85102	FOOTWEAR LEATHER	W 3008	12.2	W 2508	11.3	W 2005	11.9	W 3425	20.7	CHAUS SEMELLES EN CUIR
87	PRECISION INSTRUMNTS NES		52.2		52.3		44.5		44.4	INSTRUM,APPAR SCIENT NDA
872	MEDICAL INSTRUMENTS NES	W 963	11.7	W 825	11.4	W 1989	12.3	W 818	10.9	INSTR,APP MEDIC-CHIR NDA
874	MEASURNG,CONTROLNG INSTR	W 2153	35.9	W 1745	34.7	W 1686	26.0	W 1771	28.6	INSTRUMENTS DE MESURE
88	PHOTO EQU,OPTICL GDS ETC		15.9		20.6		22.2		25.9	APP,FOURN PHOTO,OP,MONTR
882	PHOTO,CINEMA SUPPLIES	W 1634	9.7	W 2170	12.8	W 1490	15.3	W 1642	16.4	PRODUITS PHOTO,CINEMA
8822	PHOTO FILM EXC DEV CINMA	W 1273	8.5	W 1792	10.8	W 1030	12.9	W 1147	13.7	PLAQUES,PELLICULES,FILMS
89	MISC MANUFCTRD GOODS NES		155.7		153.3		166.0		179.0	ART MANUFACTURES DIVERS
892	PRINTED MATTER	W 18605	73.0	W 7314	44.9	W 6658	39.4	W 8245	40.7	IMPRIMES
8921	PRINTED BOOKS,GLOBES,ETC	W 6515	40.9	W 5485	35.4	W 4858	31.1	W 6073	30.9	LIVRES,BROCHURES,CARTES
89211	PRINTED BOOKS,PAMPHLETS	W 6469	40.8	W 5334	35.1	W 4757	30.9	W 5961	30.6	LIVRES,BROCHURES
8928	PRINTED MATTER NES	W 11368	27.0	W 669	4.7	W 823	3.7	W 936	4.8	IMPRIMES NDA
89281	LABELS PAPER,PAPERBOARD	W 11093	25.4	W 245	1.4	W 193	1.2	W 360	2.1	ETIQUETTES TOUS GENRES
893	ARTICLES OF PLASTIC NES		31.8		43.2		49.9		56.4	OUVRAGES EN MAT DIVIS 58
8931	PLSTC PACKG CONTNRS,LIDS	W 2774	9.4	W 5122	19.2	W 4607	20.7	W 6398	24.3	ART TRANSP EMBALLAGE ETC
8939	MISC PLASTIC ARTICLES	W 7182	21.6	W 7349	22.8	W 8643	27.9	W 11051	30.7	ART DIVERS EN MAT DIV 58
89399	OTHR PLASTC ARTICLES NES	W 5115	19.3	W 5753	20.6	W 7299	25.7	W 8398	27.5	AUT OUV MAT DIV 58
894	TOYS,SPORTING GOODS,ETC	W 7675	27.6	W 10114	39.8	W 21202	41.2	W 14056	41.0	VOITURES ENFANTS,JOUETS

4. Special Imports C.I.F. by Commodities according to the S.I.T.C. (Rev. 2) in million U.S. Dollars
Importations Spéciales C.A.F. par Produits d'après la C.T.C.I. (Rév. 2) en millions de Dollars E.U.

SITC CTCI	COMMODITY	1994			1995			1996			1997			PRODUIT
		QUANTITY QUANTITE		VALUE VALEUR	QUANTITY QUANTITE		VALUE VALEUR	QUANTITY QUANTITE		VALUE VALEUR	QUANTITY QUANTITE		VALUE VALEUR	
8942	TOYS,INDOOR GAMES ETC	W	6832	23.5	W	8851	34.6	W	19535	35.6	W	12385	34.3	JOUETS,JEUX ETC
89423	TOYS NES	W	3883	14.5	W	5139	21.0	W	3577	19.5	W	3645	17.3	JOUETS,MODELES REDUITS
898	MUSICAL INSTRUMENTS,PTS	W	1281	8.2	W	1498	8.5	W	1862	16.5	W	2524	18.0	INSTRUMENTS DE MUSIQUE
8983	SOUND RECRDNG TAPE,DISCS	W	1066	6.1	W	1225	6.8	W	1628	14.9	W	2139	16.2	SUPPORTS SON POUR 763
89832	RECORDED DISCS,TAPES ETC	W	265	3.1	W	367	4.5	W	536	12.4	W	716	12.3	DISQUES,PHONO,BANDES

5. Special Exports F.O.B. by Commodities according to the S.I.T.C. (Rev. 2) in million U.S. Dollars
Exportations Spéciales F.O.B. par Produits d'après la C.T.C.I. (Rév. 2) en millions de Dollars E.U.

SITC CTCI	COMMODITY	1994 QUANTITY QUANTITE	1994 VALUE VALEUR	1995 QUANTITY QUANTITE	1995 VALUE VALEUR	1996 QUANTITY QUANTITE	1996 VALUE VALEUR	1997 QUANTITY QUANTITE	1997 VALUE VALEUR	PRODUIT
	ALL COMMODITIES		3843.4		4361.5		4889.9		5214.2	TOUS PRODUITS
0	FOOD AND LIVE ANIMALS		2056.5		2235.9		2415.1		2953.0	ALIMENTS,ANIMAUX VIVANTS
03	FISH AND PREPARATIONS		734.9		890.3		871.0		1155.1	POISSONS ET PREPARATIONS
034	FISH,FRESH,CHILLED,FROZN	W 29253	73.1	W 41086	90.5	W 41344	87.4	W 46562	102.5	POISSON FRAIS, REFRIG,CONG
0341	FISH FRSH,CHLLD,EX FILLT	W 10289	44.2	W 10474	48.2	W 10671	50.0	W 12685	52.6	POISSON FRAIS,REFRIGERE
0342	FISH FROZEN,EXCL FILLETS	W 15690	16.5	W 26562	27.1	W 27901	26.3	W 26884	26.5	POISSONS CONGELES
0344	FISH FILLETS,FROZEN	W 2570	9.1	W 3404	12.2	W 1564	5.7	W 5507	17.8	FILETS CONGELES
036	SHELL FISH FRESH,FROZEN	W 78123	557.4	W 89629	678.7	W 86786	631.4	W 110002	874.5	CRUSTACES,MOLLUSQUES
037	FISH ETC PREPD,PRSVD NES	W 50529	102.8	W 61516	118.3	W 75644	151.0	W 78359	176.5	POIS,CRUST,MOL PREPARES
0371	FISH PREPARD,PRESRVD NES	W 50469	102.3	W 61435	117.3	W 75592	150.4	W 78237	175.0	CONSERVES DE POISSONS
04	CEREALS AND PREPARATIONS		27.3		19.1		53.3		80.2	CEREALES ET PRODUITS
042	RICE	W 31700	16.7	W 26853	8.9	W 92728	33.9	W 112671	46.5	RIZ
0422	RICE SEMI–MILLED,MILLED	W 27456	15.4	W 24853	8.3	W 83453	31.8	W 106721	43.9	RIZ POLI,GLACE INCL BRISURES
04221	RICE MILLED UNBROKEN	W 27276	15.3	W 24853	8.3	W 83393	31.8	W 105581	43.7	RIZ POLI,GLACE EXCL BRISURES
044	MAIZE UNMILLED	W 45048	8.0	W 36530	6.0	W 75467	15.5	W 131210	31.2	MAIS NON MOULU
05	VEGETABLES AND FRUIT		742.6		898.5		1054.5		1420.0	LEGUMES ET FRUITS
054	VEG ETC FRSH,SMPLY PRSVD	W 6192	4.6	W 14240	9.5	W 27683	17.2	W 37359	19.8	LEGUMES FRAIS,CONG,SECS
057	FRUIT,NUTS,FRESH,DRIED	W 3136503	712.4	W 3747173	850.3	W 3969399	985.1	W 4587780	1331.8	FRUITS FRAIS OU SECS
0573	BANANA,PLANTAIN,FRSH,DRY	W 3123084	708.4	W 3732008	845.2	W 3931217	973.1	W 4563233	1327.0	BANANES FRAICHES,SECHEES
058	FRUIT PRESERVED,PREPARED	W 20941	19.8	W 27819	33.0	W 49464	48.5	W 47539	65.4	CONSERVES DE FRUITS
0585	FRUIT OR VEGETABLE JUICE	W 6454	9.4	W 6419	15.0	W 9341	24.5	W 17265	36.0	JUS DE FRUITS
05857	JUICE OF OTHER FRUIT,VEG	W 1613	1.9	W 5806	14.0	W 8403	23.1	W 16414	34.8	JUS AUTRES FRUITS,LEGUMES
0589	FRUIT PREPRD,PRESRVD,NES	W 1567	1.9	W 9434	9.0	W 28061	15.1	W 16394	19.9	FRUITS PREPARES CONSERV
05899	FRUIT,NUTS NES,PRESERVED	W 1559	1.9	W 9432	9.0	W 28061	15.1	W 16393	19.9	FRUITS PREP CONSERV NDA
06	SUGAR AND PREPS,HONEY		15.8		27.2		42.5		18.5	SUCRES ET PRODUITS
061	SUGAR AND HONEY	W 15721	4.5	W 10311	4.6	W 57293	22.1	W 5472	2.5	SUCRES ET MIEL
0611	RAW BEET AND CANE SUGAR	W 6977	2.9	W 5880	2.6	W 35806	18.6	W 5442	2.4	SUCRES BRUTS
062	SUGAR CANDY NON–CHOCLATE	W 5551	11.3	W 10330	22.7	W 8726	20.5	W 7485	16.0	SUCRERIES
07	COFFEE,TEA,COCOA,SPICES		517.4		378.3		324.3		246.8	CAFE,THE,CACAO,EPICES
071	COFFEE AND SUBSTITUTES	W 125067	413.9	W 88285	243.9	W 77669	159.1	W 46299	114.1	CAFE ET SUCCEDANES
0711	COFFEE GREEN,ROASTED,SUB	W 114677	368.8	W 77702	185.8	W 70137	129.1	W 39506	86.3	CAFE TORREFIE OU DECAFEINE
07111	COFFEE GREEN,HUSKS,SKINS	W 113848	365.8	W 77585	185.4	W 70093	129.0	W 39505	86.3	CAFE NON TORREFIE
0712	COFFEE EXTRACTS,ESSENCES	W 10390	45.1	W 10583	58.2	W 7532	30.0	W 6793	27.8	EXTRAITS DE CAFE
072	COCOA	W 75910	101.1	W 87088	130.6	W 100676	157.6	W 72723	126.3	CACAO
0721	COCOA BEANS,RAW,ROASTED	W 56184	66.5	W 63623	82.0	W 71100	91.1	W 42300	59.2	CACAO EN FEVES
0723	COCOA BUTTER AND PASTE	W 16717	32.4	W 20777	46.7	W 25454	63.8	W 26722	64.7	BEURRE ET PATE DE CACAO
07231	COCOA PASTE	W 11397	17.9	W 13249	20.2	W 12827	19.2	W 16996	27.7	CACAO EN MASSE
07232	COCOA BUTTER	W 5320	14.6	W 7528	26.5	W 12627	44.7	W 9726	37.0	BEURRE DE CACAO
081	*FEEDING STUFF FOR ANIML	W 27747	10.8	W 30766	13.3		55.9	W 46556	23.3	NOURRITURE POUR ANIMAUX
0814	MEAT OR FISH MEAL FODDER	W 25765	10.0	W 25989	11.9	W 109953	53.5	W 44333	22.2	FARINES DE VIANDES,POISSONS
08142	FISH MEAL FODDER	W 25765	10.0	W 25989	11.9	W 109953	53.5	W 44328	22.2	FARINES DE POISSONS
2	CRUDE MATERLS,EXCL FUELS		101.4		139.4		160.9		194.4	MAT BRUTES NON COMESTIBLES
24	CORK AND WOOD		23.0		33.9		30.9		41.6	LIEGE ET BOIS
247	OTH WOOD ROUGH,SQUARED	W 67103	6.4	W 84552	14.1	W 77914	11.6	W 153330	20.0	BOIS BRUTS EQUARRIS
248	WOOD SHAPED,SLEEPERS	W 13739	16.7	W 18626	19.8	W 21482	19.4	W 19967	21.6	BOIS SIMPLEMENT TRAVAILLES
2483	LUMBER SHAPED NON–CONIFR	W 10205	14.4	W 13392	17.6	W 14306	16.5	W 14937	18.7	NON CONIFERES SCIES,RABOTES
24831	LUMBER SAWN ETC NON–CON	W 9877	14.1	W 10435	16.3	W 11084	14.9	W 11037	16.9	SCIES LONGITUDINALEMENT
26	TEXTILE FIBRES AND WASTE		11.7		14.5		22.3		19.5	FIBRES TEXTILES
265	VEG FIBRE,EXCL COTN,JUTE	W 13576	10.8	W 12432	12.5	W 14215	14.9	W 13626	14.8	FIBRES VEGETALES
2655	MANILA FIBRE,TOW,WASTE	W 13521	10.7	W 12368	12.5	W 14178	14.9	W 13605	14.7	ABACA BRUT
29	CRUDE ANIMAL,VEG MAT NES		60.8		81.4		101.3		128.1	MATIERES BRUTES ANIM,VEGET
292	CRUDE VEG MATERIALS NES	W 26971	60.5	W 31546	80.4	W 67224	100.5	W 128137	127.4	MAT BRUTES VEGETALES NDA
2927	CUT FLOWERS AND FOLIAGE	W 22763	59.6	W 30400	79.5	W 64549	99.2	W 43927	119.1	FLEURS,FEUILLAGES COUPES
29271	CUT FLOWERS	W 22754	59.6	W 30395	79.5	W 64544	99.1	W 43923	119.1	FLEURS ET BOUTONS
3	MINERAL FUELS ETC		1305.0		1529.9		1776.1		1550.0	COMBUSTIBLES MINERAUX LUB
33	PETROLEUM AND PRODUCTS		1305.0		1529.9		1776.1		1550.0	PETROLE ET DERIVES
333	CRUDE PETROLEUM		1185.1	MW 11698	1395.5	MW 11801	1520.9	MW 12729	1404.3	HUILES BRUTES DE PETROLE
334	PETROLEUM PRODUCTS,REFIN		119.9	W 1563477	134.4	W 2117708	216.6	W 1248748	118.0	PRODUITS RAFFINES
3343	GAS OILS					W 1810279	185.7	W 1247917	117.4	GAS OILS
3344	FUEL OILS,NES		116.8	W 1563428	134.4					FUEL OILS
3345	LUBS,PETROLEUM OILS NES	W 63	0.1	W 49	0.1	W 278462	27.7	W 832	0.7	HUILES LUBRIFIANTES
33451	LUBS(HIGH PETR CONT) ETC	W 56	0.1	W 46	0.1	W 278449	27.7	W 831	0.7	HUILES LUBRIF,H LOURDES
335	RESIDUAL PETRLM PROD NES	W 33	0.1	W 36	0.1	W 281552	38.8	W 206640	27.7	PRODUITS RESIDUELS NDA
3352	MINERAL TARS AND PRODCTS	W 8	0.1			W 281490	38.7	W 206543	27.7	GOUDRONS MINERAUX
33525	MINERAL TAR OILS ETC NES	W 8	0.1			W 281490	38.7	W 206543	27.7	AUTRES PRODUITS NDA
4	ANIMAL,VEGETABLE OIL,FAT		12.6		15.9		15.2		13.0	HUILES,GRAISSES ANIM,VEG
42	FIXED VEGETABLE OIL,FAT		9.6		15.3		14.5		10.9	HUILES VEGETALES FIXES
424	FIXED VEG OIL NONSOFT	W 11850	6.7	W 22092	14.8	W 25632	13.9	W 18419	10.4	AUTRES HUILES VEG FIXES
5	CHEMCLS,RELATED PROD NES		39.5		54.1		62.4		70.7	PRODUITS CHIMIQUES
541	*MEDICINAL,PHARM PRODUCT	K 940056	12.3		22.3	K 1154529	23.1	K 1542411	25.1	PROD MEDICINAUX PHARMACEUT
5417	MEDICAMENTS	K 528683	10.0	K 1074273	21.5	K 1131089	22.3	K 1504646	24.6	MEDICAMENTS
58	PLASTIC MATERIALS ETC		5.3		10.6		10.3		17.3	MAT PLAST ARTIFICIELLES
583	POLYMERIZATION ETC PRODS	W 2816	5.0	W 4563	10.1	W 5130	9.8	W 9151	16.7	PROD POLYMERISATION
6	BASIC MANUFACTURES		118.8		150.9		187.9		190.5	ART MANUFACTURES
62	RUBBER MANUFACTURES NES		2.5		12.8		22.7		21.9	CAOUTCHOUC MANUFACTURE
625	RUBBER TYRES, TUBES ETC	W 833	2.5	W 4264	12.8	W 9718	22.6	W 48983	21.6	PNEUS CAOUTCHOUC VULCANISE
6252	TYRES,NEW,BUS OR LORRY	W 449	1.3	W 2652	8.0	W 6638	15.6	W 16168	13.3	PNEUS POUR AUTOBUS,CAMIONS
63	WOOD,CORK MANUFACTRS NES		28.6		36.4		54.5		45.2	OUVRAGES LIEGE ET BOIS
634	VENEERS,PLYWOOD,ETC	W 44395	24.2	W 59520	31.7	W 146719	49.8	W 91563	39.9	PLACAGES,CONTRE–PLAQUES
6341	VENEER SHEETS ETC	W 2761	4.1	W 21013	6.2	W 99217	19.6	W 893	2.1	BOIS SIMPLEMENT SCIES
6342	PLYWOOD OF WOOD SHEETS	W 21126	14.5	W 30391	22.5	W 37516	26.6	W 43063	30.4	BOIS CONTRE–PLAQUES
64	PAPER,PAPERBOARD AND MFR		12.2		13.7		19.3		15.0	PAPIERS,CARTONS & OUVRAGES
65	TEXTILE YARN,FABRICS,ETC		30.0		34.9		38.4		42.7	FILS,TISSUS,ARTICLES TEXTILE
651	TEXTILE YARN	W 1877	6.8	W 3590	11.9	W 2814	11.9	W 3787	15.7	FILS TEXTILES
66	NONMETAL MINERAL MFS NES		12.5		14.0		17.7		24.1	ART MIN NON METALLIQUES
69	METAL MANUFACTURES NES		19.9		24.7		22.6		29.0	ART MANUFACT EN METAL NDA
7	MACHINES,TRANSPORT EQUIP		91.5		86.0		87.5		106.0	MACHINES MATERIEL TRANSPORT
78	ROAD VEHICLES		72.6		63.6		54.3		82.8	VEHICULES ROUTIERS
781	PASS MOTOR VEH EXC BUSES	W 7072	64.8	W 5093	48.8	W 4185	43.5	W 7378	80.6	AUTO TRANSPORT PERSONNES
782	LORRIES,SPCL MTR VEH NES	W 1537	7.5	W 2945	14.3	W 1948	9.6	W 126	0.7	VEHICULES SPECIAUX,MARCH
7821	LORRIES,TRUCKS	W 1524	7.5	W 2871	14.2	W 1941	9.6	W 94	0.7	VEHICULES TRANSP MARCHAND
8	MISC MANUFACTURED GOODS		44.2		48.3		50.8		63.5	ART MANUFACTURES DIVERS
84	CLOTHING AND ACCESSORIES		19.2		17.5		18.6		23.6	VETEMENTS
89	MISC MANUFCTRD GOODS NES		14.7		17.7		19.5		26.5	ART MANUFACTURES DIVERS
9	GOODS NOT CLASSD BY KIND		70.3		96.2		127.5		65.2	ART TRANSACT NON CLASSES
971	*GOLD,NON MONETARY NES	K 278495	70.2	K 647277	95.9	K 383577	127.5	K 802885	65.2	OR NON MONETAIRE
97101	NONMON GLD UNWRT,SEMIMFD	K 278394	70.2	K 647277	95.9	K 383577	127.5	K 588080	65.1	OR,ALLIAGES D'OR BRUTS

1. HISTORICAL SERIES, 1962–1997 SPECIAL TRADE, IMPORTS C.I.F., EXPORTS F.O.B.
SERIES HISTORIQUES, 1962–1997 COMMERCE SPECIAL, IMPORTATIONS C.A.F., EXPORTATIONS F.O.B

YEAR ANNEE	VALUE IN MILLION EGYPTIAN POUNDS VALEUR EN MILLION EGYPTIAN POUNDS MERCHANDISE –MARCHANDISE IMPORTS	EXPORTS	GOLD –OR IMPORTS	EXPORTS	CONVERSION FACTORS U.S. CENTS PER EGYPTIAN POUND FACTEURS DE CONVERSION CENTS E.U. PAR EGYPTIAN POUND IMPORTS	EXPORTS	INDEX NUMBERS –INDICES QUANTUM IMPORTS	EXPORTS	UNIT VALUE VALEUR UNITAIRE IMPORTS	EXPORTS
1962	300.90	157.80			245.9099	252.1699				
1963	398.30	225.90			229.9999	229.9999				
1964	414.30	233.60			229.9999	229.9999				
1965	405.80	262.50			229.9999	229.9999				
1966	465.30	262.50			229.9999	229.9999				
1967	344.30	245.90			229.9999	229.9999				
1968	289.50	270.30			229.9999	229.9999				
1969	277.20	323.90			229.9999	229.9999				
1970	342.00	331.20			230.0011	230.0012				
1971	399.90	343.20			230.0012	230.0012				
1972	390.70	358.80			230.0012	230.0012				
1973	361.10	444.20			254.0006	253.3092				
1974	920.20	593.30			255.5578	255.5579				
1975	1539.30	548.60			255.5580	255.5578				
1976	1489.90	595.50			255.5580	255.5582				
1977	1884.30	668.50			255.5554	255.5556				
1978	2632.20	679.80			255.5568	255.5558				
1979	2686.20	1287.80			142.8567	142.8568				
1980	3402.00	2132.20			142.8567	142.8567				39
1981	6187.50	2263.00			142.8568	142.8568				41
1982	6354.60	2184.10			142.8582	142.8581				39
1983	7192.00	2250.60			142.8598	142.8598				37
1984	7536.10	2198.00			142.8598	142.8597				37
1985	7772.80	2599.90			70.6999	70.6999				
1986	8051.40	2053.90			107.8061	107.8054				
1987	11357.80	3046.00			66.8809	66.8806				
1988	16308.60	3994.40			53.0843	53.0840				
1989	16623.70	5734.70			44.7205	44.7207				
1990	24823.20	6953.80			67.6087	71.2798				
1991	25216.21	11764.60			32.9540	32.2140				
1992	27656.10	10173.40			30.1004	30.1080				
1993	27553.81	7558.80			29.8115	29.7929				
1994	34598.90	11767.90			29.5339	29.5330				
1995	39892.00	11703.80			29.4791	29.4755				
1996	44218.00	12004.10			29.4865	29.4856				
1997	44766.69	13285.90			29.5094	29.5093				

2. IMPORTS BY BROAD ECONOMIC CATEGORY AND EXPORTS BY INDUSTRIAL ORIGIN. (PERCENTAGE OF TOTAL VALUE)
IMPORTATIONS PAR CATEGORIES ECONOMIQUES ET EXPORTATIONS PAR BRANCHE D'ACTIVITE.(EN POURCENTAGE DE LA VALEUR TOTALE)

IMPORTS – IMPORTATIONS

	1991	1992	1993	1994	1995	1996	1997
TOTAL IMPORTS–IMPORTATIONS TOTALES	100.	100.	100.	100.	100.	100.	100.
1 FOOD BEV–ALIMENTATION BOISSONS	20.1	23.1	17.0	21.0	22.4	22.5	19.9
11 PRIMARY–PRODUITS DE BASE	12.3	15.3	10.2	14.8	14.1	15.0	11.7
111 FOR INDUSTRY–POUR L'INDUSTRIE	6.9	9.0	5.4	10.0	9.5	11.1	7.7
112 FOR HOUSEHOLDS–POUR LES MENAGES	5.4	6.3	4.8	4.7	4.6	3.9	4.0
12 PROCESSED–PRODUITS ELABORES	7.8	7.8	6.8	6.2	8.3	7.5	8.2
121 FOR INDUSTRY–POUR L'INDUSTRIE	2.3	2.7	3.0	3.3	4.6	4.0	4.0
122 FOR HOUSEHOLDS–POUR LES MENAGES	5.5	5.1	3.8	2.9	3.7	3.5	4.2
2 IND SUPPLIES–APPROV INDUSTRIELS	48.3	43.7	45.7	43.7	46.1	45.7	44.7
21 PRIMARY–PRODUITS DE BASE	7.1	6.9	11.4	6.7	6.8	7.9	6.7
22 PROCESSED–PRODUITS ELABORES	41.1	36.8	34.3	37.0	39.4	37.8	38.0
3 FUELS–COMBUSTIBLES	2.2	1.4	1.7	1.4	1.1	1.3	1.7
31 PRIMARY–PRODUITS DE BASE	1.2	1.0	1.1	1.1	0.9	0.9	1.2
32 PROCESSED–PRODUITS ELABORES	1.0	0.4	0.5	0.3	0.2	0.4	0.6
321 MOTOR SPIRIT–ESSENCE	0.0	0.0		0.0	0.0	0.0	0.0
322 OTHER–AUTRES	1.0	0.4	0.5	0.3	0.2	0.4	0.5
4 MACHINERY–EQUIPEMENT	18.9	20.7	23.5	20.0	18.0	19.2	21.6
41 CAPITAL EQUIPMENT–MACHINES	15.1	16.7	19.4	16.5	15.1	16.2	18.4
42 PARTS–PIECES ACCESSOIRES	3.7	4.0	4.1	3.5	3.0	3.1	3.2
5 TRANSPORT–TRANSPORT	6.2	6.6	7.5	9.2	7.3	6.6	6.5
51 PASSENGER CARS–AUTOMOBILES	1.3	1.4	2.0	2.2	1.8	1.5	1.4
52 OTHER–AUTRES	0.8	1.2	1.2	2.5	1.5	1.4	1.9
521 INDUSTRIAL–INDUSTRIELS	0.8	1.2	1.2	2.5	1.5	1.4	1.9
522 NON INDUSTRIAL–NON INDUSTRIEL	0.0	0.0	0.0	0.0	0.0	0.0	0.0
53 PARTS–PIECES ACCESSOIRES	4.0	4.0	4.3	4.5	3.9	3.6	3.2
6 CONSUM GOODS–BIENS CONSOMMATION	4.4	4.5	4.6	4.7	5.0	4.7	5.5
61 DURABLE–DURABLES	1.3	1.2	1.7	1.5	1.7	1.5	1.5
62 SEMI DURABLE–SEMI DURABLES	0.9	1.0	1.1	1.4	1.4	1.3	1.6
63 NON DURABLE–NON DURABLES	2.1	2.4	1.9	1.8	1.9	1.9	2.4
7 GOODS NES–BIENS NDA	0.0	0.0	0.0	0.0	0.0	0.0	0.0

EXPORTS – EXPORTATIONS

	1991	1992	1993	1994	1995	1996	1997
TOTAL EXPORTS–EXPORTATIONS TOTALES	100.	100.	100.	100.	100.	100.	100.
1 AGRICULTURE	8.1	10.9	9.1	11.3	11.3	8.8	7.0
2 MINING QUARRY–INDUS EXTRACTIVES	50.1	38.8	43.5	24.4	22.9	25.1	19.1
3 MANUFACTURING–IND MANUFACTUR	41.9	50.3	47.4	64.3	65.8	66.1	73.9
31 FOOD BEV TOBACCO–ALIM BOISS TAB	2.8	3.1	3.2	4.8	4.4	6.0	4.4
32 TEXTILES–INDUSTRIES TEXTILES	19.1	19.4	19.4	25.4	24.7	19.5	21.0
33 WOOD & PRODUCTS–BOIS & PRODUITS	0.1	0.1	0.1	0.1	0.2	0.1	0.1
34 PAPER & PRODUCTS–PAPIER & PRODT	0.4	0.4	0.5	0.5	0.6	0.5	0.4
35 CHEMICALS–INDUSTRIES CHIMIQUES	9.0	11.3	10.7	20.3	21.3	29.0	33.6
36 NON METAL MIN–MIN NON METAL	0.8	1.0	1.1	1.1	1.2	1.2	3.8
37 BASIC METAL–IND METAL BASE	6.0	11.0	8.8	8.7	10.5	7.2	6.6
38 METAL MANUF–MANUF METAL	3.6	3.9	3.4	3.2	2.7	2.4	3.3
39 OTH MANUF IND–AUTRES MANUF	0.1	0.1	0.1	0.1	0.2	0.2	0.7

3. TRADE BY PRINCIPAL COUNTRIES OF CONSIGNMENT AND DESTINATION (VALUE IN MILLION U.S. DOLLARS)
ECHANGES SELON LES PRINCIPAUX PAYS DE CONSIGNATION ET DE DESTINATION (VALEUR EN MILLIONS DE DOLLARS EU)

COUNTRIES–PAYS	SPECIAL IMPORTS C.I.F. IMPORTATIONS SPECIALES C.A.F				
	1993	1994	1995	1996	1997
World	8175.3	9586.7	11739.0	13019.6	13168.5
Africa	119.8	170.9	287.5	281.4	266.4
Americas	1472.7	2020.2	2658.5	3261.1	2543.6
– Northern America	1275.7	1659.3	2280.9	2706.5	1820.8
– LAIA	195.3	277.6	336.1	536.8	645.2
– CACM	0.3	0.6	0.7	1.1	0.9
– Caribbean	1.4	82.6	40.6	16.5	76.2
– Rest of America	0.0	0.1	0.2	0.2	0.5
Asia excl fmr USSR	1572.9	1755.3	2209.0	2404.7	2671.2
– Middle East	326.8	423.0	523.4	654.5	753.1
Asia former USSR	5.7	0.7	8.4	4.7	4.7
Europe excl fmr USSR	4214.7	4383.1	5325.5	5615.2	5987.2
– European Union	3714.0	3834.7	4562.8	4711.3	5030.9
– Eastern Europe	206.5	258.5	315.8	402.5	412.4
– Rest of Europe	294.2	289.9	446.9	501.3	543.9
Europe former USSR	201.9	345.7	515.8	492.0	624.4
Oceania	232.9	430.7	152.3	432.3	511.4
Other	354.7	480.1	581.8	528.2	559.5
USA/Etats–Unis d'Amer	1227.7	1616.0	2211.1	2608.8	1719.8
Germany/Allemagne	887.8	913.4	1044.6	1089.2	1141.8
Italy/Italie	678.7	613.8	731.1	870.9	929.9
France, Monaco	542.9	592.3	685.2	577.1	805.4
Free zones/Zone franches	345.1	468.5	570.2	512.4	546.8
United Kingdom	336.0	349.6	379.8	441.4	427.0
Japan/Japon	366.9	400.9	314.0	344.9	446.5
Netherlands/Pays–Bas	283.6	285.5	381.4	363.5	379.2
Australia/Australie	198.9	403.1	123.8	386.2	480.3
Russian Federation	144.5	273.8	405.3	370.8	379.2
Switzerland,Liechtenst.	220.0	211.5	311.9	334.1	340.8
Saudi Arabia	132.6	194.1	248.9	290.5	440.3
Sweden/Suède	220.6	157.5	259.6	306.6	299.8
China/Chine	160.2	194.4	295.9	283.6	295.6
Belgium–Luxembourg	180.5	214.5	236.8	211.9	206.4
Brazil/Brésil	118.8	158.1	189.9	265.6	257.3
Spain/Espagne	135.7	143.1	184.5	210.8	221.4
Turkey/Turquie	137.1	143.4	179.6	252.9	174.1
Korea, Republic of	125.8	107.0	227.1	192.9	233.1
Malaysia/Malaisie	93.0	93.7	220.4	241.0	232.5
Argentina/Argentine	71.8	93.4	115.1	237.7	339.4
India/Inde	117.8	123.8	160.7	184.4	223.1
Ireland/Irlande	112.9	200.1	217.9	131.7	140.2
Finland/Finlande	114.5	135.7	183.0	166.4	177.4
Romania/Roumanie	75.3	121.4	160.4	197.0	218.5
Other Asia n.e.s.	140.6	140.6	137.8	151.5	126.4
Ukraine	53.8	67.3	102.9	112.0	230.9
Denmark/Danemark	88.1	96.3	95.0	94.2	105.4
Austria/Autriche	62.9	74.5	82.4	125.9	81.4
Indonesia/Indonésie	66.9	55.8	78.8	100.9	95.9
Greece/Grèce	64.5	51.8	71.1	106.2	104.0
Canada	48.0	43.3	69.8	97.8	100.6
Libyan Arab Jamahiriya	27.5	47.9	99.6	76.8	75.2
Kenya	48.2	52.7	78.7	67.1	73.8
China, Hong Kong SAR	56.3	66.8	66.9	51.6	50.7
Poland/Pologne	42.0	47.4	48.4	67.9	72.4
Singapore/Singapour	43.9	44.6	48.9	52.7	51.3
Other Europe n.e.s.	6.1	7.9	62.3	66.8	80.4
Cuba	1.1	82.5	40.6	16.4	76.0
Czech Republic	39.0	37.8	34.5	48.4	43.0

COUNTRIES–PAYS	SPECIAL EXPORTS F.O.B. EXPORTATIONS SPECIALES F.O.B.				
	1993	1994	1995	1996	1997
Monde	3105.2	3472.5	3444.1	3534.5	3908.0
Afrique	164.1	170.0	179.4	170.1	192.2
Amériques	458.2	388.6	542.9	474.9	472.4
– Amérique du Nord	436.9	374.2	530.2	464.4	453.2
– ALAI	3.5	8.6	11.9	9.6	18.2
– MCAC	0.0	5.2	0.0	0.5	0.3
– Caraïbes	0.4	0.6	0.7	0.4	0.7
– Autre Amérique	17.4	0.0	0.0	0.0	0.0
Asie anc. URSS exclus	986.0	1125.4	939.4	1084.4	1265.6
– Moyen–Orient	425.6	452.2	420.6	494.9	461.8
Asie ancienne URSS	1.1	0.7	1.0	3.4	6.8
Europe anc. URSS exclus	1382.5	1667.8	1682.6	1735.8	1724.7
– Union Européenne	1245.4	1526.4	1577.4	1613.3	1621.3
– Europe de l'Est	68.9	69.7	57.5	59.1	75.4
– Autre de l'Europe	68.2	71.7	47.6	63.4	28.0
Europe ancienne URSS	43.4	46.0	36.4	49.0	33.5
Océanie	1.4	1.3	1.6	1.8	3.2
Autre	68.4	72.7	60.8	15.2	209.8
USA/Etats–Unis d'Amer	430.4	364.4	522.1	459.9	447.2
Italy/Italie	399.7	426.4	458.8	438.4	438.0
Israel/Israël	229.9	188.9	176.3	351.8	327.9
Netherlands/Pays–Bas	172.1	207.0	166.7	364.8	264.4
Germany/Allemagne	131.5	209.7	207.1	162.9	265.6
France, Monaco	155.4	138.2	144.3	144.7	150.2
Saudi Arabia	196.3	155.0	113.1	122.7	138.5
Greece/Grèce	125.2	117.1	137.3	142.4	175.0
United Kingdom	84.9	143.9	142.4	165.7	90.2
Spain/Espagne	100.7	149.0	157.3	98.2	111.9
Singapore/Singapour	128.1	146.6	92.8	90.1	152.7
Turkey/Turquie	25.8	71.5	82.7	115.3	96.6
Bunkers, ship stores	66.4	65.1	52.3	1.0	194.9
Belgium–Luxembourg	43.4	71.2	110.5	50.5	62.8
Korea, Republic of	44.5	106.2	51.6	35.6	60.4
Libyan Arab Jamahiriya	62.4	44.1	52.9	51.7	69.6
Japan/Japon	54.5	49.8	43.7	41.4	90.8
Syrian Arab Republic	49.1	57.5	56.1	55.0	34.6
Romania/Roumanie	49.9	43.4	41.3	36.9	64.3
India/Inde	35.7	66.1	53.0	14.1	44.0
United Arab Emirates	24.8	40.8	41.0	44.4	34.2
Russian Federation	40.5	40.9	31.9	37.7	24.4
Lebanon/Liban	26.7	35.1	43.5	33.0	32.3
Jordan/Jordanie	14.5	21.0	30.9	44.6	26.1
Sudan/Soudan	30.0	28.9	24.5	21.0	25.5
Yemen/Yémen	20.7	19.1	12.5	36.5	32.5
Kuwait/ Koweït	35.5	26.1	16.9	19.3	19.0
Tunisia/Tunisie	20.5	23.4	27.5	24.1	18.8
Portugal	5.6	20.6	21.5	24.0	40.4
Algeria/Algérie	24.4	32.8	31.3	15.8	6.9
Sri Lanka	15.3	29.6	18.5	11.7	25.1
Other Asia n.e.s.	10.4	26.6	29.0	14.2	5.4
So. African Customs Un	3.2	1.9	4.6	35.0	40.3
Switzerland,Liechtenst.	25.4	27.7	16.7	6.7	4.3
China/Chine	30.7	10.6	6.3	7.6	16.7
Cyprus/Chypre	15.2	13.1	13.4	12.6	12.7
Thailand/Thaïlande	4.6	9.5	4.7	1.0	44.2
Denmark/Danemark	11.0	20.0	14.9	5.0	10.9
Morocco/Maroc	10.1	12.7	15.2	8.1	11.4
Gibraltar	24.5	23.0	0.1	2.8	0.2

(VALUE AS PERCENTAGE OF WORLD TOTAL)(VALEURS EN POURCENTAGE DU TOTAL MONDIAL)

	1988	1989	1990	1991	1992	1993	1994	1995	1996	1997
Africa	1.3	1.4	1.4	1.8	1.9	1.5	1.8	2.4	2.2	2.0
Americas	15.4	20.2	17.8	19.3	21.6	18.0	21.1	22.6	25.0	19.3
– Northern America	12.7	18.0	14.8	17.1	18.5	15.6	17.3	19.4	20.8	13.8
– LAIA	2.5	1.9	2.3	2.1	3.0	2.4	2.9	2.9	4.1	4.9
– CACM	0.0	0.1	0.0	0.0	0.1	0.0	0.0	0.0	0.0	0.0
– Caribbean	0.2	0.2	0.6	0.1	0.1	0.0	0.9	0.3	0.1	0.6
– Rest of America	0.0	0.0	0.0	0.0	0.0	0.0	0.0	0.0	0.0	0.0
Asia excl fmr USSR	16.4	14.7	16.0	17.9	19.2	19.2	18.3	18.8	18.5	20.3
– Middle East	3.7	3.4	3.2	4.7	3.7	4.0	4.4	4.5	5.0	5.7
Asia former USSR					0.0	0.1	0.0	0.1	0.0	0.0
Europe excl fmr USSR	58.1	53.7	52.3	51.1	49.3	51.6	45.7	45.4	43.1	45.5
– European Union	45.5	42.7	43.1	42.7	41.1	45.4	40.0	38.9	36.2	38.2
– Eastern Europe	6.8	6.4	4.5	4.0	3.2	2.5	2.7	2.7	3.1	3.1
– Rest of Europe	5.8	4.6	4.7	4.4	5.0	3.6	3.0	3.8	3.9	4.1
Europe former USSR	3.1	3.5	3.0	1.8	0.5	2.5	3.6	4.4	3.8	4.7
Oceania	2.9	2.8	4.9	3.5	3.5	2.8	4.5	1.3	3.3	3.9
Other	2.8	3.7	4.5	4.5	3.9	4.3	5.0	5.0	4.1	4.2
USA/Etats–Unis d'Amer	11.9	17.6	14.1	16.1	17.5	15.0	16.9	18.8	20.0	13.1
Germany/Allemagne				10.4	10.4	10.9	9.5	8.9	8.4	8.7
Italy/Italie	7.0	5.8	6.5	6.8	6.6	8.3	6.4	6.2	6.7	7.1
France, Monaco	8.4	9.0	9.4	6.9	5.0	6.6	6.2	5.8	4.4	6.1
Free zones/Zone franches	2.7	3.4	4.4	4.4	3.7	4.2	4.9	4.9	3.9	4.2
United Kingdom	4.2	4.2	4.0	4.5	4.4	4.1	3.6	3.2	3.4	3.2
Japan/Japon	5.0	3.9	3.7	4.1	4.3	4.5	4.2	2.7	2.6	3.4
Netherlands/Pays–Bas	3.7	3.2	3.1	3.4	3.6	3.5	3.0	3.2	2.8	2.9
Australia/Australie	2.5	2.6	4.2	3.4	3.3	2.4	4.2	1.1	3.0	3.6
Russian Federation					0.4	1.8	2.9	3.5	2.8	2.9

	1988	1989	1990	1991	1992	1993	1994	1995	1996	1997
Afrique	3.5	2.3	3.7	5.7	6.3	5.3	4.9	5.2	4.8	4.9
Amériques	6.7	5.6	9.6	8.6	9.8	14.8	11.2	15.8	13.4	12.1
– Amérique du Nord	6.5	5.3	8.8	7.8	9.6	14.1	10.8	15.4	13.1	11.6
– ALAI	0.0	0.2	0.0	0.4	0.1	0.1	0.2	0.3	0.3	0.5
– MCAC		0.0	0.7	0.2	0.0	0.0	0.1	0.0	0.0	0.0
– Caraïbes	0.0	0.0		0.0	0.0	0.0	0.0	0.0	0.0	0.0
– Autre Amérique	0.3	0.1	0.0	0.2	0.1	0.6	0.0	0.0	0.0	0.0
Asie anc. URSS exclus	29.3	26.8	24.7	28.9	33.4	31.8	32.4	27.3	30.7	32.4
– Moyen–Orient	9.3	9.9	8.8	8.0	13.7	13.7	13.0	12.2	14.0	11.8
Asie ancienne URSS					0.0	0.0	0.0	0.0	0.1	0.2
Europe anc. URSS exclus	45.0	49.8	45.2	49.0	45.9	44.5	48.0	48.9	49.1	44.1
– Union Européenne	38.1	43.8	38.9	43.1	39.7	40.1	44.0	45.8	45.6	41.5
– Europe de l'Est	5.6	3.8	4.5	4.6	4.0	2.2	2.0	1.7	1.7	1.9
– Autre de l'Europe	1.3	2.1	1.9	1.3	2.2	2.2	2.1	1.4	1.8	0.7
Europe ancienne URSS	12.2	13.3	15.8	6.3	2.5	1.4	1.3	1.1	1.4	0.9
Océanie	0.1	0.0	0.0	0.0	0.0	0.0	0.0	0.0	0.1	0.1
Autre	3.1	2.1	0.9	1.4	2.1	2.2	2.1	1.8	0.4	5.4
USA/Etats–Unis d'Amer	6.3	5.2	8.6	7.6	9.4	13.9	10.5	15.2	13.0	11.4
Italy/Italie	11.1	13.8	12.2	14.8	14.2	12.9	12.3	13.3	12.4	11.2
Israel/Israël	6.9	6.4	6.5	10.1	9.5	7.4	5.4	5.1	10.0	8.4
Netherlands/Pays–Bas	6.9	5.7	6.3	3.8	5.7	5.5	6.0	4.8	10.3	6.8
Germany/Allemagne				3.7	4.2	4.2	6.0	6.0	4.6	6.8
France, Monaco	5.8	7.1	4.0	5.9	4.2	5.0	4.0	4.2	4.1	3.8
Saudi Arabia	3.2	3.0	3.0	3.1	6.6	6.3	4.5	3.3	3.5	3.5
Greece/Grèce	2.3	2.3	1.5	3.8	2.3	4.0	3.4	4.0	4.0	4.5
United Kingdom	2.7	2.6	3.0	2.2	3.4	2.7	4.1	4.1	4.7	2.3
Spain/Espagne	0.8	1.4	1.4	4.8	2.4	3.2	4.3	4.6	2.8	2.9

4. Special Imports C.I.F. by Commodities according to the S.I.T.C. (Rev. 2) in million U.S. Dollars
Importations Spéciales C.A.F. par Produits d'après la C.T.C.I. (Rév. 2) en millions de Dollars E.U.

SITC CTCI	COMMODITY	1994 QUANTITY QUANTITE	1994 VALUE VALEUR	1995 QUANTITY QUANTITE	1995 VALUE VALEUR	1996 QUANTITY QUANTITE	1996 VALUE VALEUR	1997 QUANTITY QUANTITE	1997 VALUE VALEUR	PRODUIT
	ALL COMMODITIES		9586.7		11739.0		13019.6		13168.5	TOUS PRODUITS
0	FOOD AND LIVE ANIMALS		2262.0		2611.8		3058.1		2698.6	ALIMENTS,ANIMAUX VIVANTS
001	*LIVE ANIMALS FOR FOOD	W 111206	146.8	W 101294	150.2	W 48318	79.5	W 33720	61.9	ANIMAUX VIVANTS
0011	BOVINE SPECIES,LIVE	W 110618	138.2	W 101044	140.2	W 47351	68.1	W 32197	48.8	ESPECE BOVINE
00119	— OTHR THAN FR BREEDING	W 102680	126.0	W 99220	137.6	W 45686	63.2	W 32197	48.8	BOVINS NON REPRODUCTEURS
01	MEAT AND PREPARATIONS		181.3		214.2		175.7		194.9	VIANDES ET PREPARATIONS
011	MEAT FRESH,CHILLD,FROZEN	W 156856	177.3	W 140009	207.4	W 110859	168.5	W 128743	192.4	VIANDES FRAICHES,REF,CONGE
0111	BOVINE MEAT FRESH,FROZEN	W 128827	155.5	W 113438	175.8	W 90728	145.7	W 102384	161.6	VIANDES BOVIN FRAI,REF
01112	BOVINE MEAT BONELESS	W 106761	131.4	W 113413	175.8	W 88888	142.9	W 102314	161.4	VIANDES BOVIN DESOSSEES
02	DAIRY PRODCTS,BIRDS'EGGS		151.0		169.0		181.3		149.5	PRODUITS LAITIERS,OEUFS
022	MILK AND CREAM	W 21820	36.8	W 27342	54.8	W 25330	53.7	W 27972	53.5	LAIT ET CREME
0224	MILK,CREAM PRESERVED ETC	W 21548	36.5	W 27270	54.8	W 25220	53.4	W 27792	53.2	LAIT,CREME CONS,CONC
023	BUTTER	W 52649	75.5	W 48816	77.3	W 50225	92.2	W 37758	58.6	BEURRE
024	CHEESE AND CURD	W 21877	38.3	W 16623	36.9	W 14626	35.2	W 15698	36.6	FROMAGE ET CAILLEBOTTE
03	FISH AND PREPARATIONS		72.8		74.6		109.1		96.4	POISSONS ET PREPARATIONS
034	FISH,FRESH,CHILLED,FROZN	W 135395	56.5	W 113437	56.9	W 173356	89.4	W 144400	75.1	POISSON FRAIS, REFRIG,CONG
0342	FISH FROZEN,EXCL FILLETS	W 131120	54.3	W 108918	54.5	W 163384	84.1	W 143936	73.2	POISSONS CONGELES
04	CEREALS AND PREPARATIONS		1126.0		1309.8		1720.2		1257.6	CEREALES ET PRODUITS
041	WHEAT ETC UNMILLED	W 6597382	766.3	W 5069599	875.7	W 5546184	1232.1	W 4841796	821.1	FROMENT,EPEAUTRE
0411	DURUM WHEAT UNMILLED	W 6363851	738.7	W 5069599	875.7	W 4958247	1100.6	W 4579297	777.7	FROMENT DUR NON MOULU
0412	OTHER WHEAT ETC UNMILLED	W 233530	27.6			W 587936	131.5	W 262499	43.5	AUTRE FROMENT NON MOULU
044	MAIZE UNMILLED	W 2021007	263.7	W 2425162	349.3	W 2296699	435.5	W 2637976	385.4	MAIS NON MOULU
046	WHEAT ETC MEAL OR FLOUR	W 379858	70.8	W 289959	61.8	W 56567	14.8	W 63912	18.0	SEMOULE FARINE,FROMENT
04601	FLOUR OF WHEAT OR MESLIN	W 374051	69.6	W 281699	59.6	W 43689	12.6	W 61743	17.3	FARINE DE FROMENT
05	VEGETABLES AND FRUIT		127.9		160.5		169.5		167.5	LEGUMES ET FRUITS
054	VEG ETC FRSH,SMPLY PRSVD	W 240816	93.4	W 260996	124.5	W 271272	130.5	W 253702	121.5	LEGUMES FRAIS,CONG,SECS
0541	POTATOES FRSH EXCL SWEET	W 34903	18.6	W 74108	50.0	W 48643	30.2	W 78311	36.5	POMMES DE TERRE
0542	LEGUMINOUS VEGETBLES DRY	W 200746	71.9	W 174271	67.3	W 187490	90.1	W 123182	69.5	LEGUMES A COSSE SECS
057	FRUIT,NUTS,FRESH,DRIED	W 39055	29.2	W 38688	29.8	W 48791	31.6	W 51477	37.1	FRUITS FRAIS OU SECS
06	SUGAR AND PREPS,HONEY		130.4		219.2		260.6		358.3	SUCRES ET PRODUITS
061	SUGAR AND HONEY	W 439354	129.7	W 566539	218.5	W 774235	260.0	W 1535413	357.6	SUCRES ET MIEL
0611	RAW BEET AND CANE SUGAR	W 381408	109.7	W 392494	144.0	W 646186	208.7	W 1275722	263.2	SUCRES BRUTS
0612	REFINED SUGAR ETC	W 53690	16.7	W 170051	71.1	W 120878	47.9	W 256182	91.9	SUCRES RAFFINES
07	COFFEE,TEA,COCOA,SPICES		118.1		153.5		121.6		143.8	CAFE,THE,CACAO,EPICES
074	TEA AND MATE	W 57230	90.0	W 79964	118.6	W 65041	86.8	W 77892	104.1	THE ET MATE
0741	TEA	W 57230	90.0	W 79964	118.6	W 65041	86.8	W 77892	104.1	THE
081	*FEEDING STUFF FOR ANIML	W 672006	184.2	W 474635	137.0	W 696047	211.5	W 681108	237.1	NOURRITURE POUR ANIMAUX
0813	OILCAKE AND OTH RESIDUES	W 498470	112.7	W 309347	65.1	W 521878	134.5	W 478098	154.4	TOURTEAUX
08131	— OF SOYA BEANS	W 474962	106.6	W 305670	64.7	W 436905	120.3	W 476098	154.1	TOURTEAUX DE SOJA
0819	FOOD WASTE AND FEED NES	W 100177	44.3	W 94389	44.7	W 101193	46.9	W 90157	43.8	DECHETS,ALIMENTS NDA
08199	FODDER NES,INCL SWEETNED	W 100102	41.8	W 92989	44.3	W 90263	43.6	W 89655	43.8	PREPARATIONS FOURRAGERES
1	BEVERAGES AND TOBACCO		146.6		143.3		174.5		166.5	BOISSONS ET TABACS
12	TOBACCO AND MANUFACTURES		144.2		142.0		173.8		163.6	TABACS BRUTS FABRIQUES
121	TOBACCO UNMNFCTRD,REFUSE	W 47693	142.3	W 48286	134.2	W 53084	146.4	W 53756	128.5	TABACS BRUTS,DECHETS
1211	TOBACCO,NOT STRIPPED	W 28472	69.0	W 26070	61.0	W 30382	72.9	W 37994	89.1	TABACS NON ECOTES
1212	TOBACCO STRIPPED OR PART	W 18551	72.9	W 21376	72.8	W 22367	73.3	W 13958	38.0	TABACS PART ECOTES
2	CRUDE MATERLS,EXCL FUELS		715.9		1059.1		1142.1		1119.8	MAT BRUTES NON COMESTIBLES
22	OIL SEEDS,OLEAGINOUS FRT		34.4		66.8		91.7		110.5	GRAINES,FRUITS OLEAGINEUX
222	SEEDS FOR'SOFT'FIXED OIL	W 95889	31.3	W 103963	64.5	W 185074	89.2	W 190095	89.1	GRAINES HUILES FIXES
2222	SOYA BEANS	W 79591	21.6	W 54856	14.1	W 124178	37.9	W 139476	42.6	FEVES DE SOJA
2225	SESAME SEEDS	W 10679	7.1	W 34979	40.3	W 39360	44.9	W 45800	44.7	GRAINES DE SESAME
23	RUBBER, CRUDE		23.6		37.0		42.8		39.6	CAOUTCHOUC BRUT
24	CORK AND WOOD		377.2		551.0		502.2		538.1	LIEGE ET BOIS
247	OTH WOOD ROUGH,SQUARED	W 118222	30.5	W 108118	28.6	W 189793	49.6	W 148089	35.7	BOIS BRUTS EQUARRIS
248	WOOD SHAPED,SLEEPERS	W 1001438	344.7	W 1420120	522.3	W 1299151	452.5	W 1412024	502.3	BOIS SIMPLEMENT TRAVAILLES
2482	LUMBER SHAPED CONIFER	W 791699	256.1	W 1246669	445.7	W 1061790	346.7	W 1195678	410.3	CONIFERES SCIES,RABOTES
24821	LUMBER SAWN ETC CONIFER	W 791387	256.0	W 1246641	445.6	W 1061702	346.7	W 1195572	410.2	CONIFERES SCIES LONGITUD
2483	LUMBER SHAPED NON–CONIFR	W 209447	88.5	W 173036	76.6	W 236926	105.6	W 208102	88.9	NON CONIFERES SCIES,RABOTES
24831	LUMBER SAWN ETC NON–CON	W 204148	86.2	W 171236	75.4	W 235357	104.4	W 206592	87.8	SCIES LONGITUDINALEMENT
251	*PULP AND WASTE PAPER	W 58123	30.5	W 57194	48.7	W 82249	49.3	W 73494	37.1	PATES A PAPIER,DECHETS
2512	MECHANICAL WOOD PULP	W 49191	26.1	W 48543	44.0	W 69390	44.1	W 64416	35.3	PATES MECANIQUES DE BOIS
26	TEXTILE FIBRES AND WASTE		88.7		159.1		163.8		133.4	FIBRES TEXTILES
263	COTTON	W 398	0.7	W 30710	37.7	W 127624	47.0	W 15862	9.0	COTON
2631	RAW COTTON,EXCL LINTERS			W 30555	37.7	W 126966	46.2	W 14184	7.3	COTON EN MASSE
266	SYNTHETIC FIBRES TO SPIN	W 37158	64.9	W 40881	91.0	W 43099	78.9	W 58442	99.5	FIBRES SYNTHETIQUES
2665	DISCN SYNTH FIBRE UNCMBD	W 30403	50.7	W 36417	77.6	W 38703	68.1	W 52695	85.7	DISCONTINUES EN MASSE
26653	— ACRYLIC	W 17565	32.1	W 19505	43.0	W 26307	49.8	W 33021	62.8	FIBRES ACRYLIQUES
27	CRUDE FERTLZR,MINRLS NES		34.7		41.5		73.0		73.2	ENGRAIS MINERAUX BRUTS
278	OTHER CRUDE MINERALS	W 127712	24.8	W 105230	25.6	W 149795	40.6	W 157798	36.8	AUTRES MINERAUX BRUTS
28	METALLIFEROUS ORES,SCRAP		100.5		123.2		184.0		155.6	MINERAIS METAL,DECHETS
281	IRON ORE,CONCENTRATES	W 1113675	44.7	W 639228	31.2	W 881265	50.7	W 877995	50.8	MINERAIS DE FER
287	BASE METAL ORES,CONC NES	W 138924	39.5	W 244930	76.2	W 416628	116.6	W 331315	93.0	MINERAIS METAUX COMMUNS
2873	ALUMINIUM ORES,ALUMINA	W 135658	37.4	W 242410	74.4	W 402268	113.1	W 324603	89.8	MINERAIS D'ALUMINIUM
28731	ALUMINIUM ORE,CONCNTRATE	W 134854	36.8	W 240687	72.9	W 400670	112.0	W 322724	88.7	MINERAIS D'ALUMINIUM
3	MINERAL FUELS ETC		139.0		145.5		190.5		243.5	COMBUSTIBLES MINERAUX LUB
32	COAL,COKE AND BRIQUETTES		106.7		99.9		124.3		96.2	HOUILLES,COKES,BRIQUETTES
322	COAL,LIGNITE AND PEAT	W 1863918	106.5	W 1558748	99.8	W 1884863	123.8	W 1635782	94.6	HOUILLES,LIGNITES,TOURBE
3222	OTH COAL,NOT AGGLOMERATD	W 1852275	104.4	W 1539147	96.0	W 1874735	121.6	W 1532439	87.3	AUTRES HOUILLES
33	PETROLEUM AND PRODUCTS		31.6		39.0		64.8		88.8	PETROLE ET DERIVES
334	PETROLEUM PRODUCTS,REFIN	W 53527	25.3	W 49129	28.6	W 182423	52.0	W 261763	71.8	PRODUITS RAFFINES
341	*GAS,NATURAL AND MANUFCT	W 2493	0.7	W 25797	6.7	W 6992	1.5	W 198405	58.5	GAZ NATUREL,GAZ MANUFACT
3413	PETROLM GASES,LIQUEFIED	W 2301	0.7	W 25796	6.7	W 6992	1.5	W 198385	58.5	GAZ DE PETROLE LIQUEFIE
34131	LIQUEFIED PROPANE,BUTANE	W 11	0.1	W 25796	6.7	W 6992	1.5	W 198385	58.5	PROPANE,BUTANE LIQUEFIES
4	ANIMAL,VEGETABLE OIL,FAT		193.3		510.1		512.9		484.3	HUILES,GRAISSES ANIM,VEG
42	FIXED VEGETABLE OIL,FAT		172.4		466.7		482.0		444.7	HUILES VEGETALES FIXES
423	FIXED VEG OILS,SOFT	W 140171	75.2	W 349418	235.1	W 360265	225.2	W 390764	231.2	HUILES VEGET DOUCES FIXES
4232	SOYA BEAN OIL	W 64647	37.6	W 81168	52.3	W 106202	65.6	W 33695	18.6	HUILE DE SOJA
4233	COTTON SEED OIL	W 1238	0.8	W 96091	62.1	W 21336	13.2	W 190	0.3	HUILE DE COTON
4236	SUNFLOWER SEED OIL	W 73805	36.2	W 171792	120.1	W 232444	145.4	W 356150	211.1	HUILE DE TOURNESOL
424	FIXED VEG OIL NONSOFT	W 222702	97.3	W 379012	231.7	W 424243	256.9	W 362822	213.5	AUTRES HUILES VEG FIXES
4242	PALM OIL	W 149204	68.5	W 248624	163.8	W 272250	164.4	W 308663	178.9	HUILE DE PALME
4249	FIXED VEGETABLE OILS NES	W 35753	15.3	W 79980	38.5	W 122449	67.2	W 25976	13.8	HUILES VEGET FIXES NDA
5	CHEMCLS,RELATED PROD NES		1153.9		1526.4		1596.2		1727.3	PRODUITS CHIMIQUES
51	ORGANIC CHEMICALS		190.6		289.2		277.4		285.9	PROD CHIMIQ ORGANIQUES
513	CARBOXYLIC ACIDS ETC	W 34345	35.1	W 53548	73.3	W 54878	69.0	W 57161	59.9	ACIDES CARBOXYLIQUES
5138	POLYACIDS AND DERIVATIVS	W 17056	13.1	W 39494	47.1	W 36665	38.8	W 37507	26.7	ACIDES POLYCARBOXYLIQUES
514	NITROGEN–FNCTN COMPOUNDS	W 10285	42.7	W 12981	72.4	W 9964	66.8	W 13793	63.9	COMPOSES FONCT AZOTEES
5148	OTH NITROGN–FNCTN CMPNDS	W 4444	22.9	W 7543	40.2	W 5272	40.2	W 8874	38.8	AUTRES COMPOSES AZOTES
515	ORG–INORG COMPOUNDS ETC	W 5705	54.3	W 13043	70.0	W 5933	79.2	W 7363	71.3	COMPOSES ORGANO–MINERAUX
5156	HETEROCYCLIC CMPDS ETC	W 2552	25.1	W 9081	32.2	W 2280	36.9	W 2829	40.4	COMPOSES HETEROCYCLIQUES
516	OTHER ORGANIC CHEMICALS	W 9513	31.3	W 12104	31.4	W 10766	24.8	W 112084	50.4	AUTRES PROD ORGANIQUES

4. Special Imports C.I.F. by Commodities according to the S.I.T.C. (Rev. 2) in million U.S. Dollars
Importations Spéciales C.A.F. par Produits d'après la C.T.C.I. (Rév. 2) en millions de Dollars E.U.

SITC CTCI	COMMODITY	1994		1995		1996		1997		PRODUIT
		QUANTITY QUANTITE	VALUE VALEUR	QUANTITY QUANTITE	VALUE VALEUR	QUANTITY QUANTITE	VALUE VALEUR	QUANTITY QUANTITE	VALUE VALEUR	
52	INORGANIC CHEMICALS		79.0		91.8		97.9		113.1	PROD CHIM INORGANIQUES
523	OTHR INORG CHEMICALS ETC	W 105238	54.0	W 133958	66.4	W 148512	72.0	W 159599	75.3	AUT PRODUITS CHIMIQUES INORG
5232	OTH MTL CMPD OF INRG ACD	W 73782	39.3	W 90398	46.4	W 106446	51.3	W 112966	49.4	SELS METALLIQUES
53	DYES,TANNING,COLOUR PROD		124.0		153.1		160.5		161.3	PROD TEINTURE,COLORANTS
531	SYNT DYE,NAT INDGO,LAKES	W 7444	37.5	W 8357	38.1	W 6374	37.5	W 5387	35.8	MAT COLOR ORGAN,LAQUES
5311	SYNTHIC ORGNIC DYESTUFFS	W 6425	30.3	W 7590	33.1	W 5974	33.7	W 4733	32.4	MAT COLOR ORGAN SYNTHET
533	PIGMENTS,PAINTS,ETC	W 73627	82.6	W 99176	110.2	W 107140	119.2	W 119780	121.0	PIGMENTS,PEINTURES,VERNIS
5331	COLOURING MATERIAL NES	W 38124	31.5	W 57820	48.0	W 50624	46.8	W 47070	41.4	AUT MATIERES COLORANTES
5335	GLAZES,DRIERS,PUTTY ETC	W 27305	27.1	W 31748	31.4	W 46416	42.5	W 60256	47.3	PREPTNS COLOR UTILISES CERAM
541	*MEDICINAL,PHARM PRODUCT	K 4307094	181.4	MK 9423	227.6	K 4728952	238.5	K 5570286	315.2	PROD MEDICINAUX PHARMACEUT
5413	ANTIBIOTICS IN BULK	K 572270	36.4	K 664107	46.4	K 504661	44.7	K 794845	63.1	ANTIBIOTIQUES NDA
54139	OTHER ANTIBIOTICS	K 301322	24.2	K 388297	32.9	K 338047	36.4	K 454278	45.8	AUTRES ANTIBIOTIQUES
5417	MEDICAMENTS	K 2413130	100.8	K 7574920	132.1	K 2591894	137.4	K 2900404	175.4	MEDICAMENTS
54179	— CONTNG OTH SUBSTANCES	K 2178243	91.7	K 7394749	115.0	K 2377373	115.3	K 2386696	131.2	MED CONT AUT SUBSTANCES
55	PERFUME,CLEANING ETC PRD		45.5		55.3		47.6		52.5	PROD POUR PARFUM,TOILETTE
58	PLASTIC MATERIALS ETC		358.2		498.5		549.4		584.2	MAT PLAST ARTIFICIELLES
582	PROD OF CONDENSATION ETC	W 38879	62.2	W 56384	106.9	W 64537	111.1	W 69206	105.1	PROD CONDENS,POLYCOND
5823	ALKYDS,OTHER POLYESTERS	W 19151	27.6	W 37730	65.8	W 41945	62.1	W 41970	52.3	ALKYDES ET AUT POLYESTERS
58231	— IN PRIMARY FORMS	W 18593	25.9	W 37202	63.6	W 41306	60.1	W 41346	50.4	SOUS FORMES PRIMAIRES
583	POLYMERIZATION ETC PRODS	W 336575	288.2	W 311089	381.9	W 435325	427.8	W 471135	469.5	PROD POLYMERISATION
5831	POLYETHYLENE	W 127584	90.3	W 138353	143.5	W 184525	162.2	W 204562	190.0	POLYETHYLENE
58311	— IN PRIMARY FORMS	W 126775	87.7	W 137331	140.1	W 183257	159.5	W 203009	187.0	POLYETHYLENE PRIMAIRES
5832	POLYPROPYLENE	W 101830	72.9	W 72913	88.4	W 110615	98.7	W 110742	96.6	POLYPROPYLENE
58321	— IN PRIMARY FORMS	W 100709	69.9	W 71318	83.2	W 109231	95.2	W 107796	90.1	POLYPROPYLENE PRIMAIRES
5833	POLYSTYRENE,ITS COPOLYMR	W 32938	31.7	W 28383	38.9	W 36692	36.8	W 37985	36.8	POLYPROPYLENE COPOLYMERES
58331	— IN PRIMARY FORMS	W 32931	31.7	W 28210	38.5	W 36518	36.5	W 37879	36.6	SOUS FORMES PRIMAIRES
5834	POLYVINYL CHLORIDE	W 14680	16.5	W 26308	29.5	W 48605	41.6	W 53016	41.2	CHLORURE DE POLYVINYLE
5839	OTH POLYMRZTION ETC PROD	W 41357	56.3	W 26330	52.4	W 29254	55.7	W 40992	71.1	AUT PROD POLYMER COPOLYM
59	CHEMICAL MATERIALS NES		162.0		191.0		207.4		204.3	MAT PROD CHIMIQUES NDA
591	PESTICIDES,DISINFECTANTS	W 6952	48.3	W 7535	60.2	W 10811	77.9	W 11102	91.4	DESINF,INSECT,FONG,HERB
5911	INSECTICIDES,FOR RETAIL	W 3887	33.7	W 4522	42.1	W 6155	52.6	W 7132	70.9	INSECTICIDES VENTE DET
598	MISCEL CHEM PRODUCTS NES	W 54851	102.5	W 62909	116.0	W 71030	115.8	W 54768	99.2	PROD DIV INDUST CHIM NDA
5989	CHEM PRODUCTS,PREPS NES	W 36401	78.1	W 38280	82.8	W 42549	80.7	W 38576	80.9	PROD PREP CHIMIQUES NDA
59899	OTH CHEM PRODS,PREPS,NES	W 25052	61.9	W 24204	63.2	W 30387	63.7	W 25905	63.4	AUT PRODUITS CHIMIQUES NDA
6	BASIC MANUFACTURES		1820.4		2375.5		2602.8		2574.7	ART MANUFACTURES
62	RUBBER MANUFACTURES NES		125.7		143.0		161.1		176.6	CAOUTCHOUC MANUFACTURE
625	RUBBER TYRES, TUBES ETC	W 30707	81.5	W 40538	98.9	W 38752	115.6	W 42519	120.6	PNEUS CAOUTCHOUC VULCANISE
6252	TYRES,NEW,BUS OR LORRY	W 9272	27.3	W 7836	21.3	W 10141	29.7	W 17735	52.6	PNEUS POUR AUTOBUS,CAMIONS
6259	OTH TYRES,TYRE CASES,ETC	W 14883	35.7	W 22425	52.8	W 19848	60.4	W 14408	37.2	AUTRES PNEUS RECHAPES FLAPS
62599	TYRES NES,TYRE CASES,ETC	W 11070	27.0	W 15634	41.7	W 12721	46.4	W 9421	25.5	PNEUS,FLAPS
63	WOOD,CORK MANUFACTRS NES		114.8		81.3		91.5		100.4	OUVRAGES LIEGE ET BOIS
634	VENEERS,PLYWOOD,ETC	W 226336	111.6	W 131086	76.2	W 140142	82.8	W 157366	89.4	PLACAGES,CONTRE–PLAQUES
6342	PLYWOOD OF WOOD SHEETS	W 129174	70.2	W 120418	57.1	W 124170	64.8	W 140993	72.5	BOIS CONTRE–PLAQUES
64	PAPER,PAPERBOARD AND MFR		282.5		534.8		413.7		388.7	PAPIERS,CARTONS & OUVRAGES
641	PAPER AND PAPERBOARD	W 469897	261.7	W 556351	499.6	W 485659	365.5	W 512523	355.5	PAPIERS ET CARTONS
6411	NEWSPRINT	W 69776	30.8	W 59654	48.9	W 34178	21.0	W 18938	9.9	PAPIER JOURNAL
6412	PRINTG,WRITING PAPER NES	W 55840	39.2	W 26213	30.8	W 22988	25.0	W 39132	34.0	PAPIERS POUR L'IMPRESSION
6413	KRAFT PAPER,PAPERBOARD	W 47176	21.9	W 107885	105.9	W 111591	77.0	W 104251	57.4	PAPIER ET CARTON KRAFT
64132	SACK KRAFT PAPER IN BULK	W 8415	5.0	W 64852	71.9	W 43099	42.7	W 32947	24.8	PAPIER KRAFT POUR SACS
6415	PAPER,PAPERBRD,BULK,NES	W 187797	101.7	W 257065	226.1	W 204403	158.0	W 233031	168.7	PAPIERS,CARTONS ROULEAUX
64159	OTHER PAPER ETC,BULK,NES	W 184116	98.1	W 254153	221.5	W 202511	156.1	W 230214	166.2	AUT PAPIER ROULEAUX FEUILLES
6418	COATED ETC PAPER NES BLK	W 96708	62.6	W 90134	80.9	W 91048	76.5	W 95718	77.6	PAP,CARTONS COUCHES,ENDUITS
64189	COATED PAPER ETC NES	W 93468	55.0	W 86287	70.0	W 87513	62.3	W 90446	60.7	PAPIERS,CARTONS COUCHES
642	PAPER,ETC,PRECUT,ARTS OF	W 15719	20.9	W 18868	35.2	W 26976	48.3	W 16556	33.3	PAP,CARTONS DECOUPES
65	TEXTILE YARN,FABRICS,ETC		242.2		279.7		289.7		300.3	FILS,TISSUS,ARTICLES TEXTILE
651	TEXTILE YARN	W 67607	133.4	W 63452	173.6	W 81545	198.7	W 83106	196.8	FILS TEXTILES
6513	COTTON YARN	W 3526	11.7	W 8946	35.3	W 14983	57.3	W 19450	70.1	FILS DE COTON
6514	SYN FIB YRN,BULK,MONOFIL	W 50203	89.1	W 44263	110.3	W 50272	99.8	W 49235	92.2	FILS CONT 85% FIB TEXT SYNTH
65142	— NONTXT ETC CONT PAMID	W 35503	58.8	W 32565	76.4	W 41673	72.9	W 39529	61.4	FILS NON TEX FI CON POLYAMID
652	COTTON FABRICS,WOVEN	W 6677	34.7	W 6394	37.3	W 4560	29.0	W 5035	33.1	TISSUS DE COTON
6522	WOVEN COTTON BLEACHD,ETC	W 6270	32.4	W 6227	36.4	W 4442	28.4	W 4820	32.3	TISSUS COTON BLANCHIS ETC
657	SPECIAL TXTL FABRC,PRODS	W 10132	39.4	W 7348	27.1	W 6290	26.3	W 7789	26.7	TISSUS SPECIAUX
66	NONMETAL MINERAL MFS NES		106.6		160.8		234.5		247.7	ART MIN NON METALLIQUES
661	LIME,CEMENT,BLDG PRODS	W 379124	18.3	W 1262224	54.3	W 2284452	98.0	W 2258108	96.3	CHAUX,CIMENTS MAT CONSTR
6612	CEMENT	W 374135	15.3	W 1255673	48.7	W 2275746	91.1	W 2246552	89.7	CIMENTS HYDRAULIQUES
662	CLAY,REFRACTORY BLDG PRD	W 34223	24.9	W 44561	25.2	W 43274	31.4	W 69491	41.7	MAT CONST REFRACTAIRES
664	GLASS	W 76880	30.1	W 95733	38.3	W 145111	56.4	W 101833	51.3	VERRE
67	IRON AND STEEL		545.8		782.8		1012.3		919.8	FER ET ACIER
671	PIG IRON ETC	W 336935	62.5	W 303240	68.9	W 297883	84.7	W 131759	45.0	FONTE,SPIEGEL,POUDRES
6712	PIG IRN,SPIEGELEISEN ETC	W 204495	33.7	W 100264	19.7	W 153370	32.3	W 94208	21.6	FONTES BRUTES
672	IRON,STEEL PRIMARY FORMS	W 439461	98.5	W 409936	129.5	W 834514	234.6	W 1282437	322.1	LINGOTS FER,ACIER
6725	IRN,STL BLOOMS,SLABS,ETC	W 339121	72.0	W 282592	68.1	W 629646	144.7	W 1205623	288.5	BLOOMS,BILLETTES FER ACIER
67251	IRN,SMPLE STL BLOOMS,ETC	W 338445	71.3	W 282518	67.9	W 626594	143.6	W 1205622	288.5	BLOOMS ETC NON ACIER FIN
6727	IRN,STL COIL FR REROLLNG	W 27437	13.2	W 118988	57.8	W 191953	84.0	W 73006	31.4	EBAUCHES POUR TOLES FER
67271	IRON,SIMPLE STEEL COILS	W 23551	8.7	W 115329	50.0	W 189837	70.6	W 71028	27.8	EBAUCHES NON EN ACIER
673	IRON,STEEL SHAPES ETC	W 429186	132.2	W 676739	210.7	W 971470	274.3	W 517775	161.3	BARRES,PROFIL FER,ACIER
6731	IRON,STEEL WIRE ROD	W 232628	67.4	W 509822	149.8	W 448700	126.2	W 73807	21.7	FIL MACHINE FER,ACIER
67311	IRON,SIMPLE STL WIRE ROD	W 227255	64.9	W 479808	139.3	W 442197	124.2	W 66040	19.4	FIL MACH AUT ACIER FIN
6732	IRON,STEEL BARS ETC	W 134509	45.6	W 124154	42.4	W 479302	130.6	W 386076	113.8	BARRES FER,ACIER
67326	IRN,OTH STL BARS HOTROLD	W 98252	26.6	W 105010	31.6	W 440494	112.4	W 369603	105.6	BARRES PLEINES FER,ACIER
674	IRN,STL UNIV,PLATE,SHEET	W 181055	103.5	W 369325	244.9	W 429502	281.7	W 353911	219.1	LARGES PLATS,TOLES
6744	IRN,STL HVY PLATE,ROLLED	W 28252	16.6	W 90961	46.9	W 96518	51.1	W 129494	54.8	TOLES LAMINEES PLUS 4.75 MM
67441	— OF IRON OR SIMPLE STL	W 27250	14.7	W 89829	43.8	W 94617	44.9	W 127756	51.5	TOLES NON ACIER FIN CARB
6746	IRN,STL THIN PLATE,ROLLD	W 16932	14.4	W 80581	64.9	W 97129	75.7	W 34390	35.8	TOLES LAM MOINS 3MM
67461	— OF IRON OR SIMPLE STL	W 12745	5.3	W 70946	41.8	W 82505	42.1	W 26454	12.5	TOL NON AC FIN MOINS 3 MM
6747	TINNED PLATES,SHEETS	W 49999	30.4	W 58615	40.4	W 68955	54.4	W 64325	45.1	TOLES ETAMEES EN ACIER
6749	OTH IRN,STL PLATES,SHEET	W 59420	29.4	W 111501	74.9	W 117425	72.4	W 80989	56.9	AUTRES TOLES FER,ACIER
67491	— OF IRON OR SIMPLE STL	W 44165	20.7	W 103398	63.2	W 112401	64.0	W 70554	46.4	AUT TOLES AUTRES ACIER FIN
678	IRON,STL TUBES,PIPES,ETC	W 117439	135.5	W 102040	112.1	W 106365	122.7	W 172112	155.2	TUBES,TUYAUX EN FONTE,FER
6781	CAST IRON TUBES,PIPES	W 2686	4.2	W 21149	20.5	W 34071	30.6	W 64446	40.9	TUBES,TUYAUX EN FONTE
6782	IRON,STL SEAMLESS TUBES	W 29990	30.8	W 25768	22.2	W 36417	33.8	W 37829	32.4	TUBES,TUYAUX SANS SOUDURE
6783	IRON,STL TUBES,PIPES NES	W 75970	75.8	W 41871	45.0	W 24964	28.9	W 56452	56.2	AUT TUBES,TUYAUX FER,ACIER
68	NON–FERROUS METALS		169.4		153.7		146.4		161.7	METAUX NON FERREUX
682	COPPER EXC CEMENT COPPER	W 16644	51.2	W 24961	90.8	W 23956	84.9	W 31336	90.8	CUIVRE
6822	COPPER,ALLOYS WORKED	W 16224	50.0	W 24955	90.7	W 23862	84.7	W 30296	89.1	CUIVRE,ALLIAGES OUVRES
68221	COPPER BARS,WIRE,ETC	W 10949	32.6	W 18260	62.6	W 14881	48.2	W 20544	57.2	BARRES,PROFILES ET FILS
684	ALUMINIUM	W 73561	102.3	W 7241	29.2	W 9829	33.8	W 7318	27.6	ALUMINIUM
6841	ALUMINIUM,ALLOYS,UNWRGHT	W 67693	81.6	W 52	0.1	W 2645	4.4	W 41	0.1	ALUMINIUM,ALLIAGES BRUTS
69	METAL MANUFACTURES NES		230.2		236.8		249.6		276.6	ART MANUFACT EN METAL NDA
691	STRUCTURES AND PARTS NES	W 23044	34.5	W 11553	26.7	W 12403	32.6	W 25535	38.0	CONSTRUCT FER,ACIER,ALU
6911	STRUCTURES,PARTS IRN,STL	W 22936	33.9	W 11188	25.6	W 11837	30.8	W 25073	33.0	CONSTRUCT FER,ACIER,FONTE

4. Special Imports C.I.F. by Commodities according to the S.I.T.C. (Rev. 2) in million U.S. Dollars
Importations Spéciales C.A.F. par Produits d'après la C.T.C.I. (Rév. 2) en millions de Dollars E.U.

SITC CTCI	COMMODITY	1994 QUANTITY QUANTITE	1994 VALUE VALEUR	1995 QUANTITY QUANTITE	1995 VALUE VALEUR	1996 QUANTITY QUANTITE	1996 VALUE VALEUR	1997 QUANTITY QUANTITE	1997 VALUE VALEUR	PRODUIT
693	WIRE PRODUCTS NON ELECTR	W 26896	31.8	W 11214	20.6	W 16907	27.1	W 21588	33.6	OUVRAGES FILS METALLIQUES
695	TOOLS	W 10649	26.7	W 9450	30.0	W 11214	32.2	W 13906	41.8	OUTILS A MAIN
699	BASE METAL MFRS NES	W 26244	91.6	W 29339	101.8	W 22981	98.7	W 30859	99.7	ART MANUFACTURES MET NDA
6997	IRON,STEEL ARTICLES NES	W 10945	47.9	W 11968	45.8	W 5966	45.7	W 10869	42.7	OUV FONTE,FER,ACIER NDA
69979	IRN,STL MANUFACTURES NES	W 10940	47.9	W 11936	45.8	W 5919	45.6	W 10797	42.5	AUT OUVRAGES EN FER NDA
7	MACHINES,TRANSPORT EQUIP		2782.8		2957.7		3302.8		3547.0	MACHINES MATERIEL TRANSPORT
71	POWER GENERATING EQUIPMT		150.3		183.6		235.0		231.8	MACHINES GENERATRICES
713	INTRNL COMBUS PSTN ENGIN	W 18784	66.1	W 18995	86.0	W 23548	92.4	W 24608	88.8	MOTEURS EXPL COMB INT, PIECE
7139	PISTON ENGINE PARTS NES	W 7859	34.0	W 6864	43.1	W 8297	43.8	W 8739	42.3	PIECES POUR 713.2,3,8
716	ROTATING ELECTRIC PLANT	W 12427	67.3	W 16402	84.2	W 16534	96.7	W 20092	119.6	APP ELECTR ROTATIFS,PIECES
7162	AC MTRS,GENRTRS,GEN SETS	W 10370	54.2	W 14568	66.0	W 14274	79.3	W 17763	93.8	MOTEURS ELECTRIQUES
71621	AC MTRS,INC UNIVRSL MTRS	W 9478	45.2	W 13250	51.5	W 11578	51.7	W 13134	56.7	MOT ELEC NON COUR CONTINU
72	MACHS FOR SPCL INDUSTRYS		438.9		475.9		608.7		768.0	MAC SPECIALES POUR INDUST
723	CIVIL ENGNEERG EQUIP ETC	W 23873	92.0	W 25443	96.1	W 34020	118.4	W 55544	205.7	APPAREILS DE GENIE CIVIL
7234	CONST,MINING MACHNRY NES	W 20576	74.8	W 23070	82.3	W 31831	102.7	W 50258	174.1	MACH POUR LA CONST, MINES
72341	SELF-PROPELLD DOZERS,ETC	W 10849	34.9	W 10220	31.0	W 11349	33.7	W 16200	55.4	BULLDOZERS
72342	SLFPRP SHOVELS,EXCAVATRS	W 2226	7.1	W 5961	20.0	W 8447	25.6	W 15113	61.0	PELLES MECANIQUES
724	TEXTILE,LEATHER MACHNRY	W 13551	124.6	W 12295	105.9	W 18112	135.9	W 15444	122.1	MACH POUR INDUSTRIE TEXTILE
7245	WEAVING,FELT MFG,ETC MCH	W 4745	40.3	W 4072	34.4	W 6078	46.1	W 5214	39.9	METIERS A TISSER,PIECES
7247	TEXTILE MACHINERY NES	W 3861	38.4	W 3899	25.4	W 4980	38.0	W 3723	25.1	MACH LAVAGE,TEINTURE TEX
726	PRINTG,BKBINDG MACHY,PTS	W 2521	26.3	W 1886	21.6	W 3590	43.3	W 4314	47.9	MACHINES POUR IMPRIMERIE
728	OTH MACHY FOR SPCL INDUS	W 17172	137.8	W 21656	181.0	W 28322	212.3	W 35899	293.9	AUT MACH IND PARTICULIERES
7283	OTHR MINERAL WORKG MACHY	W 2692	13.0	W 4553	20.3	W 5714	23.3	W 9665	56.0	MACH TRIER,CRIBLER,BROYER
7284	MACHY FOR SPCL INDUS NES	W 11867	114.0	W 14757	150.7	W 18510	174.1	W 22742	220.6	MACH SPEC IND PARTICUL.
72848	OTH MCHY WITH INDIV FNCT	W 7553	79.2	W 9274	112.0	W 10226	109.6	W 13048	129.5	AUTRES MACHINES NDA
73	METALWORKING MACHINERY		55.7		54.5		82.2		71.6	MACH TRAVAIL DES METAUX
736	METALWORKING MACH-TOOLS	W 101173	42.7	W 11944	41.1	W 12384	58.0	W 11369	44.5	MACH-OUTILS TRAVAIL METAUX
74	GENRL INDUSTRL MACHY NES		657.2		786.0		845.4		791.2	MACH APP INDUSTRIE
741	HEATING,COOLING EQUIPMNT	W 12585	144.6	W 55299	238.3	W 17716	154.1	W 19583	138.0	MACH CHAUFFAGE,PIECES
7414	NONDOM REFRIG EQUIPT,PTS	W 2883	23.2	W 41540	31.3	W 5610	36.7	W 5920	41.4	MAT PRODUCTION DU FROID
7416	HEATING,COOLING EQU NES	W 5720	86.8	W 9241	176.4	W 8006	84.3	W 6857	64.3	APP CHANGEMENT TEMP
742	PUMPS FOR LIQUIDS ETC	W 8538	62.0	W 8407	76.6	W 10260	93.8	W 11136	106.6	POMPES MOTO-POMPES
7422	CENTRIFUGAL PUMPS NES	W 706	8.9	W 839	7.6	W 2357	17.4	W 2939	42.0	POMPES CENTRIF NON 742.81
7428	OTHER PUMPS FOR LIQUIDS	W 6756	41.2	W 4800	45.1	W 5669	51.7	W 5937	37.1	AUTRES POMPES POUR LIQ
74288	PUMPS FR LIQUIDS NES ETC	W 6280	34.6	W 4455	41.0	W 5385	47.9	W 5516	31.8	POMPES POUR LIQUIDES NDA
743	PUMPS NES,CENTRFUGES ETC	W 24667	122.0	W 19466	110.9	W 26359	176.4	W 23020	124.5	POMPES COMPRES,VENT ETC
7431	PUMPS FOR GASES ETC	W 11730	85.2	W 12232	63.5	W 12928	69.8	W 11581	62.7	POMPES AIR A VIDE,COMPRES
7436	GAS,LIQUID FILTERS ETC	W 1945	17.5	W 2446	20.6	W 3726	64.5	W 2055	22.4	APP POUR FILT DES LIQUIDES
744	MECHANICAL HANDLING EQU	W 13778	56.6	W 16163	80.6	W 20047	77.8	W 28060	97.0	EQUIP MANUTENTION PIECES
7442	LIFTING,LOADING MACH NES	W 7277	35.1	W 9289	50.6	W 9051	41.3	W 17795	58.4	APP LEVAGE,MANUTENTION
745	NONELEC MACHY,TOOLS NES	W 2933	33.7	W 3483	48.4	W 7248	88.4	W 4223	71.6	AUT MACH NON ELEC,PIECES
7452	OTH NONELEC MCHS,PTS NES	W 2855	32.5	W 3407	47.2	W 7116	86.8	W 4090	69.5	AUT MACH NON ELEC,PIECES
74522	PACKAGNG,BOTTLNG,ETC MCH	W 757	18.6	W 933	26.6	W 2286	54.8	W 1148	25.0	MACH NETT BOUTEILLES,ETC
749	NONELEC MACH PTS,ACC NES	W 29744	238.6	W 22930	231.5	W 27600	255.2	W 28634	253.8	PIECES MACH NON ELEC NDA
7492	COCKS,VALVES ETC NES	W 7516	47.3	W 8615	60.4	W 8875	59.1	W 11008	68.7	ART ROB,SIM POUR TUYAUX
7493	SHAFT,CRANK,PULLEY ETC	W 6511	45.3	W 6080	50.2	W 7331	58.5	W 5665	55.7	ARBRES TRANS,VILEBREQUINS
7499	OTH NONELEC MCHY PTS NES	W 13984	130.3	W 5904	102.4	W 8036	113.6	W 7601	102.2	PIECES NON ELECT NDA
74999	MACH PARTS NONELEC NES	W 12101	110.7	W 4229	80.3	W 6135	91.8	W 5469	76.2	PIECES MACHINES NDA
75	OFFICE MACHNES,ADP EQUIP		116.6		133.2		136.3		188.6	MACH BUREAU TRAIT AUTOM
752	AUTOMTIC DATA PROC EQUIP	W 904	50.9	W 1255	57.0	W 1562	63.3	W 2740	89.3	MACH TRAIT INFORMATION
759	OFFICE,ADP MCH PTS,ACCES	W 1066	41.3	W 1732	50.6	W 1712	49.6	W 2296	66.7	PIECES DU 751 ET 752
7599	ACCTG,ETC,ADP MCH PTS,AC	W 559	28.3	W 837	35.8	W 873	32.9	W 1232	47.5	PIECES DU 751 ET 752
76	TELECOMM,SOUND EQUIPMENT		201.3		212.1		238.0		278.9	EQUIPMENT DE TELECOM
761	TELEVISION RECEIVERS	W 4098	41.6	W 7948	78.8	W 7358	70.7	W 7519	67.1	RECEPTEURS DE TELEVISION
7611	COLOUR TV RECEIVERS	W 3136	36.8	W 6237	72.0	W 5523	62.2	W 5574	60.3	RECEPTEURS COULEUR
764	TELECOM EQPT,PTS,ACC NES	W 14158	150.2	W 5729	118.5	W 6302	154.5	W 9055	198.6	EQUIP TELECOM,PIECES
7641	LINE TELEPHONE,ETC EQUIP	W 1258	29.3	W 1290	16.4	W 1484	26.6	W 2556	30.6	APP TELEPHON PAR FIL
7649	PTS NES OF EQUIPMT OF 76	W 12383	101.6	W 3939	93.6	W 4220	94.0	W 5544	130.8	PIECES DE LA DIV 76
76491	PTS NES OF APPAR OF 7641	W 10860	78.4	W 1551	76.4	W 1603	76.5	W 1617	91.4	PIECES POUR 764.1
77	ELECTRIC MACHNRY NES ETC		444.5		463.4		532.5		517.4	MACH APP ELECT NDA
771	ELECTRIC POWER MACHY NES	W 3588	22.6	W 4298	27.7	W 5595	40.9	W 8575	46.8	MACH PROD,TRANS ELECTR
772	SWITCHGEAR ETC,PARTS NES	W 8456	139.5	W 10014	133.4	W 10090	146.6	W 9923	147.8	APP COUPURE,SECT ETC
7721	SWITCHGEAR ETC	W 7036	121.9	W 7970	107.3	W 9237	134.3	W 9432	142.5	APP COUPURE,SECTIONMNT
773	ELECTR DISTRIBUTNG EQUIP	W 33267	132.2	W 29755	118.5	W 44144	129.5	W 39237	104.6	EQUIPMT DISTRIBUTION ELECT
7731	INSULATED WIRE,CABLE ETC	W 28681	110.1	W 23523	91.2	W 29719	92.3	W 29802	76.5	FILS,CABLES ISOLES ELECT
775	HOUSEHOLD TYPE EQUIP NES	W 7001	32.2	W 7533	34.5	W 8375	38.7	W 7729	40.8	MACH,APP USAGE DOMESTQUE
776	TRANSISTORS,VALVES,ETC	W 593	12.4	W 2575	23.2	W 6380	46.2	W 4296	38.6	LAMPES,TUBES,VALVES
778	ELECTRICAL MACHINERY NES	W 22381	86.3	W 21162	96.3	W 20948	97.5	W 22238	108.6	AUTRES MACH ELECT NDA
7788	OTH ELEC MACHY,EQUIP NES	W 9822	42.7	W 10977	46.4	W 10124	44.5	W 9498	52.0	AUT MACH APP ELEC NDA
78	ROAD VEHICLES		667.0		624.7		601.2		596.1	VEHICULES ROUTIERS
781	PASS MOTOR VEH EXC BUSES	W 27813	213.5	W 32067	216.7	W 40887	201.3	W 23430	181.9	AUTO TRANSPORT PERSONNES
782	LORRIES,SPCL MTR VEH NES	W 15063	101.7	W 5248	44.8	W 13374	82.9	W 17097	125.2	VEHICULES SPECIAUX,MARCH
7821	LORRIES,TRUCKS	W 12770	83.8	W 3840	29.9	W 10912	64.0	W 11785	87.5	VEHICULES TRANSP MARCHAND
783	ROAD MOTOR VEHICLES NES	W 9011	97.9	W 8888	102.7	W 8197	79.4	W 10689	94.5	VEHICULES ROUTIERS NDA
7831	BUSES	W 8814	96.5	W 8487	99.4	W 7987	78.2	W 8386	89.5	VOITURES TRANSPORT COMMUN
784	MOTOR VEH PRTS,ACCES NES	W 48743	228.0	W 55558	228.4	W 59076	201.7	W 49205	160.2	PIECES 722,781,782,783
7849	OTHER MOTOR VEHCL PARTS	W 48072	225.1	W 54555	223.8	W 58364	198.6	W 48408	158.9	PIECES 722,781,782,783
79	OTHR TRANSPORT EQUIPMENT		51.6		24.8		24.0		103.8	AUTRE MATERIEL TRANSPORT
793	SHIPS AND BOATS ETC		30.8	W 5978	8.8	W 704	3.9	W 11262	83.3	NAVIRES BATEAUX,ETC
7938	TUGS,SPECIAL VESSELS ETC	W 2637	25.0	W 161	3.5	W 218	2.4	W 10250	80.8	REMORQUEURS,BATEAUX SPEC
79382	SPECL PURPOSE VESSLS ETC	W 1058	3.0	W 151	3.4	W 185	2.1	W 10022	80.3	BAT-PHARES,-POMPES,DRAGUES
8	MISC MANUFACTURED GOODS		370.5		409.1		439.2		533.8	ART MANUFACTURES DIVERS
87	PRECISION INSTRUMNTS NES		134.2		137.3		165.6		191.7	INSTRUM,APPAR SCIENT NDA
872	MEDICAL INSTRUMENTS NES	W 1742	57.5	W 2297	68.3	W 2869	89.8	W 2817	101.1	INSTR,APP MEDIC-CHIR NDA
87202	OTH MEDICAL INSTRUMENTS	W 1462	48.5	W 2088	62.3	W 2500	80.6	W 2462	93.1	INSTRUM,APP MEDECINE
874	MEASURNG,CONTROLNG INSTR	W 2412	64.0	W 2359	59.2	W 3340	65.9	W 3484	80.8	INSTRUMENTS DE MESURE
88	PHOTO EQU,OPTICL GDS ETC		64.6		72.9		68.6		82.8	APP,FOURN PHOTO,OP,MONTR
882	PHOTO,CINEMA SUPPLIES	W 3350	35.2	W 3988	37.6	W 4189	35.4	W 4650	39.2	PRODUITS PHOTO,CINEMA
89	MISC MANUFCTRD GOODS NES		136.4		164.4		164.9		190.6	ART MANUFACTURES DIVERS
893	ARTICLES OF PLASTIC NES	W 14855	41.9	W 25610	56.9	W 17241	55.4		64.5	OUVRAGES EN MAT DIVIS 58
8939	MISC PLASTIC ARTICLES	W 13891	37.6	W 23814	48.9	W 14264	45.8	W 21145	51.9	ART DIVERS EN MAT DIV 58
89399	OTHR PLASTC ARTICLES NES	W 12778	36.0	W 22676	46.9	W 13158	43.8	W 20182	50.4	AUT OUV MAT DIV 58
894	TOYS,SPORTING GOODS,ETC	W 9112	29.5	W 12473	39.0	W 11934	35.2	W 12342	44.6	VOITURES ENFANTS,JOUETS
9	GOODS NOT CLASSD BY KIND		2.8		1.0		1.0		73.5	ART TRANSACT NON CLASSES
971	*GOLD,NON MONETARY NES	K 350	0.2	K 60	0.1			K 6663	73.2	OR NON MONETAIRE
97101	NONMON GLD UNWRT,SEMIMFD	K 350	0.2	K 60	0.1			K 6663	73.2	OR,ALLIAGES D'OR BRUTS

5. Special Exports F.O.B. by Commodities according to the S.I.T.C. (Rev. 2) in million U.S. Dollars
Exportations Spéciales F.O.B. par Produits d'après la C.T.C.I. (Rév. 2) en millions de Dollars E.U.

SITC CTCI	COMMODITY	1994 QUANTITY QUANTITE	1994 VALUE VALEUR	1995 QUANTITY QUANTITE	1995 VALUE VALEUR	1996 QUANTITY QUANTITE	1996 VALUE VALEUR	1997 QUANTITY QUANTITE	1997 VALUE VALEUR	PRODUIT
	ALL COMMODITIES		3472.6		3444.2		3534.5		3908.0	TOUS PRODUITS
0	FOOD AND LIVE ANIMALS		266.2		321.0		355.0		269.6	ALIMENTS,ANIMAUX VIVANTS
04	CEREALS AND PREPARATIONS		86.0		63.2		124.1		77.2	CEREALES ET PRODUITS
042	RICE	W 248193	79.2	W 156787	56.8	W 328834	117.8	W 202604	71.4	RIZ
0422	RICE SEMI-MILLED,MILLED	W 234169	75.2	W 156756	56.8	W 325621	116.2	W 202484	71.4	RIZ POLI,GLACE INCL BRISURES
04221	RICE MILLED UNBROKEN	W 229626	74.1	W 156756	56.8	W 325621	116.2	W 201308	71.3	RIZ POLI,GLACE EXCL BRISURES
05	VEGETABLES AND FRUIT		121.0		206.9		170.1		140.5	LEGUMES ET FRUITS
054	VEG ETC FRSH,SMPLY PRSVD	W 335041	75.6	W 609864	152.9	W 581057	121.0	W 407642	89.6	LEGUMES FRAIS,CONG,SECS
0541	POTATOES FRSH EXCL SWEET	W 131865	26.6	W 418744	102.2	W 411172	80.0	W 232963	41.3	POMMES DE TERRE
0545	OTHER FRESH VEGETABLES	W 153151	29.9	W 139622	25.6	W 124855	17.9	W 120908	18.3	AUTRES LEGUMES FRAIS,REF
05451	ALLIACEOUS VEGTBLS,FRESH	W 137829	23.3	W 118483	18.5	W 111169	13.7	W 108844	14.8	OIGNONS,ECHALOTES,AULX
0546	VEGETABLES SIMPLY PRESVD	W 12395	9.2	W 12942	10.9	W 14532	11.3	W 17113	17.9	LEGUMES CONG,CONSER
05461	VEGETABLES FROZEN	W 11582	8.8	W 12768	10.8	W 14480	11.2	W 17098	17.9	LEGUMES CONGELES
056	VEGTBLES ETC PRSVD,PREPD	W 25503	19.1	W 15922	25.1	W 13810	19.5	W 12249	17.6	CONSERVES DE LEGUMES
0561	VEG DRIED EXC LEGUMINOUS	W 22975	17.4	W 11411	22.5	W 10166	17.6	W 7931	13.5	LEGUM DESSECH,DESHYDRAT
057	FRUIT,NUTS,FRESH,DRIED	W 65478	23.2	W 82124	25.4	W 86408	25.9	W 78195	24.8	FRUITS FRAIS OU SECS
0571	ORANGES, MANDARINS ETC	W 28347	8.4	W 42641	13.3	W 53669	17.4	W 44405	14.2	ORANGES,MAND,CLEMENTINES
05711	ORANGES,FRESH OR DRIED	W 27957	8.3	W 41969	13.0	W 53598	17.4	W 44301	14.1	ORANGES FRAICHES,SECHEES
06	SUGAR AND PREPS,HONEY		14.9		12.8		13.4		7.2	SUCRES ET PRODUITS
07	COFFEE,TEA,COCOA,SPICES		11.6		10.4		15.0		10.3	CAFE,THE,CACAO,EPICES
2	CRUDE MATERLS,EXCL FUELS		305.1		241.0		180.1		203.0	MAT BRUTES NON COMESTIBLES
22	OIL SEEDS,OLEAGINOUS FRT		10.7		9.2		7.0		10.2	GRAINES,FRUITS OLEAGINEUX
26	TEXTILE FIBRES AND WASTE		250.4		169.1		102.5		117.5	FIBRES TEXTILES
263	COTTON	W 116318	237.5	W 71498	157.9	W 23600	92.6	W 41999	111.2	COTON
2631	RAW COTTON,EXCL LINTERS	W 113371	233.7	W 67417	152.3	W 23289	91.9	W 41790	110.3	COTON EN MASSE
27	CRUDE FERTLZR,MINRLS NES		14.6		19.3		21.9		36.4	ENGRAIS MINERAUX BRUTS
273	STONE,SAND AND GRAVEL	W 129314	7.0	W 312074	13.1	W 339162	14.6	W 435855	24.7	PIERRES,SABLES,GRAVIERS
29	CRUDE ANIMAL,VEG MAT NES		23.5		32.3		44.7		28.4	MATIERES BRUTES ANIM,VEGET
292	CRUDE VEG MATERIALS NES	W 27131	20.5	W 28728	29.0	W 34079	41.1	W 27435	25.8	MAT BRUTES VEGETALES NDA
2924	VEG USED IN PHARMACY ETC	W 10547	11.4	W 12086	13.6	W 13319	16.1	W 13841	18.2	PLANTES MEDICINALES
2929	OTH CRUDE VEG MATERIALS	W 1271	1.2	W 2556	6.7	W 1620	14.7	W 981	0.8	MATIERES VEGETALES NDA
29291	VEGETABLE SAPS,EXTRACTS	W 122	0.4	W 1707	5.9	W 457	13.5			SUCS,EXTRAITS VEGETAUX
3	MINERAL FUELS ETC		1360.2		1283.0		1682.2		1772.4	COMBUSTIBLES MINERAUX LUB
32	COAL,COKE AND BRIQUETTES		34.5		48.9		47.4		40.5	HOUILLES,COKES,BRIQUETTES
323	BRIQUETS,COKE,SEMI-COKE	W 364236	34.4	W 466690	48.8	W 394405	47.3	W 364789	40.4	BRIQUETTES
3232	COKE,SEMI-COKE,RTRT CRBN	W 347412	32.9	W 466690	48.8	W 394403	47.3	W 364789	40.4	COKES ET SEMI-COKES
33	PETROLEUM AND PRODUCTS		1320.5		1231.8		1634.8		1731.9	PETROLE ET DERIVES
333	CRUDE PETROLEUM	W 7867128	793.0	W 7242853	719.2	W 6684826	816.6	W 6147800	668.2	HUILES BRUTES DE PETROLE
334	PETROLEUM PRODUCTS,REFIN	W 6072480	503.5	W 6077973	496.4	W 5964300	810.2	W 6701564	968.4	PRODUITS RAFFINES
3341	GASOLINE,OTH LIGHT OILS	W 2972	0.4	W 212555	21.8			W 82462	16.9	ESSENCES POUR MOTEURS
33412	SPIRIT TYPE JET FUEL	W 2936	0.3	W 179506	17.9			W 81300	16.1	CARBUREACTEURS
3343	GAS OILS	W 97369	15.6	W 74121	12.4			W 120300	23.5	GAS OILS
3344	FUEL OILS,NES	W 5970689	486.4	W 5788043	461.6	W 5962517	809.3	W 6324610	886.3	FUEL OILS
3345	LUBS,PETROLEUM OILS NES	W 1450	1.3	W 3241	0.7	W 1783	0.9	W 174193	41.9	HUILES LUBRIFIANTES
33451	LUBS(HIGH PETR CONT) ETC	W 1450	1.3	W 3241	0.7	W 1783	0.9	W 174192	41.9	HUILES LUBRIF,H LOURDES
335	RESIDUAL PETRLM PROD NES	W 193100	24.0	W 39341	16.3	W 44892	8.2	W 104275	95.3	PRODUITS RESIDUELS NDA
3351	PETRLM JELLY,MINERAL WAX	W 23744	3.5	W 26980	13.5	W 40390	7.4	W 89942	13.3	VASELINE,CIRES MINERALES
33512	MINERAL WAXES	W 23744	3.5	W 26980	13.5	W 40390	7.4	W 89942	13.3	PARAFFINES,CIRES DE PETROLE
3352	MINERAL TARS AND PRODCTS	W 28586	4.7	W 12334	2.9	W 4502	0.8	W 14068	82.0	GOUDRONS MINERAUX
33522	BENZOLE	W 27051	4.3	W 11357	2.6	W 4042	0.6	W 13695	81.9	BENZOLS
3353	MIN TAR PITCH,PITCH COKE	W 107950	11.4							BRAI,COKE DE BRAI
33531	PITCH FROM MINERAL TARS	W 107941	11.4							BRAI DE GOUDRON
4	ANIMAL,VEGETABLE OIL,FAT		4.6		4.1		6.5		12.8	HUILES,GRAISSES ANIM,VEG
5	CHEMCLS,RELATED PROD NES		159.2		200.9		176.6		197.8	PRODUITS CHIMIQUES
51	ORGANIC CHEMICALS		7.0		8.5		13.9		5.6	PROD CHIMIQ ORGANIQUES
52	INORGANIC CHEMICALS		14.7		22.2		33.2		39.4	PROD CHIM INORGANIQUES
522	INORG ELEMNTS,OXIDES,ETC	W 51196	7.7	W 49396	14.5	W 60908	19.0	W 87216	26.9	ELEMENTS INORGANIQUES
5221	CHEMICAL ELEMENTS	W 1869	0.9	W 17143	9.3	W 22782	13.9	W 34017	20.1	ELEMENTS CHIMIQUES
52218	CARBON NES, CARBON BLACK	W 1717	0.9	W 16874	9.2	W 21722	13.1	W 33586	20.0	CARBONE NDA
523	OTHR INORG CHEMICALS ETC	W 43835	7.0	W 57089	7.7	W 78751	14.3	W 70069	12.5	AUT PRODUITS CHIMIQUES INORG
541	*MEDICINAL,PHARM PRODUCT	K 5065492	28.1	K 5442286	35.2	K 6525653	41.1	K 7634576	55.7	PROD MEDICINAUX PHARMACEUT
5417	MEDICAMENTS	K 3559319	23.0	K 3289350	28.7	K 5339944	36.6	K 6596457	49.1	MEDICAMENTS
54179	— CONTNG OTH SUBSTANCES	K 3522295	22.8	K 3249382	28.5	K 5336444	36.6	K 6586957	49.0	MED CONT AUT SUBSTANCES
55	PERFUME,CLEANING ETC PRD		33.9		34.7		39.2		41.8	PROD POUR PARFUM,TOILETTE
553	PERFUMERY,COSMETICS,ETC	W 2361	11.9	W 1771	9.5	W 3430	17.3	W 2609	11.9	PRODUITS DE PARFUMERIE
554	SOAP,CLEANSING ETC PREPS	W 14374	12.0	W 17678	15.4	W 12461	12.6	W 21452	19.9	SAVONS,PRODUITS DETERSIFS
5542	WASHING PREPARATIONS ETC	W 11019	8.5	W 11115	10.8	W 9225	9.5	W 8649	8.3	PROD ORG TENSIO-ACT NDA
562	*FERTILIZERS,MANUFACTURE	W 518681	53.0	W 481615	65.2	W 87286	14.8	W 146414	20.7	ENGRAIS MANUFACTURES
5621	CHEM NITROGENOUS FERTLZR	W 413644	45.5	W 316235	45.9	W 36515	6.5	W 106868	14.3	ENGRAIS AZOTES
56211	AMMONIUM NITRATE	W 197363	19.6	W 175818	19.5	W 24132	3.8	W 76901	11.5	NITRATE D'AMMONIUM
56216	UREA	W 113596	13.4	W 115528	22.5	W 11136	2.6	W 29254	2.8	UREE
56219	CHEM NITROG FERTILZR NES	W 97435	12.1	W 24889	4.0	W 1247	0.2	W 116	0.1	ENGRAIS AZOTES NDA
5622	CHEM PHOSPHATIC FERTILZR	W 104822	7.3	W 164787	19.2	W 45791	7.9	W 38826	6.3	ENGRAIS PHOSPHATES
56222	SUPERPHOSPHATES	W 104822	7.3	W 155861	18.6	W 45791	7.9	W 38483	6.2	SUPERPHOSPHATES
59	CHEMICAL MATERIALS NES		15.1		22.5		21.7		26.6	MAT PROD CHIMIQUES NDA
598	MISCEL CHEM PRODUCTS NES	W 16690	11.3	W 24267	16.7	W 24169	16.9	W 33773	23.7	PROD DIV INDUST CHIM NDA
5989	CHEM PRODUCTS,PREPS NES	W 16381	11.1	W 24241	16.7	W 24143	16.9	W 33633	23.7	PROD PREP CHIMIQUES NDA
59899	OTH CHEM PRODS,PREPS,NES	W 16351	11.0	W 24193	16.6	W 24023	16.8	W 33505	23.6	AUT PRODUITS CHIMIQUES NDA
6	BASIC MANUFACTURES		1046.9		1035.7		788.7		1004.0	ART MANUFACTURES
61	LEATHER,DRESSED FUR,ETC		12.3		7.3		9.5		18.5	CUIRS,PELLETERIES
611	LEATHER	W 1976	10.0	W 2208	6.0	W 1356	7.8	W 2287	15.3	CUIRS,PEAUX PREPARES
6114	LEATHR BOVINE NES,EQUINE	W 1342	7.8	W 1732	4.4	W 825	3.9	W 1748	13.3	CUIRS DE BOVINS
64	PAPER,PAPERBOARD AND MFR		5.4		11.1		10.9		9.8	PAPIERS,CARTONS & OUVRAGES
65	TEXTILE YARN,FABRICS,ETC		618.9		571.3		426.5		533.5	FILS,TISSUS,ARTICLES TEXTILE
651	TEXTILE YARN	W 115558	386.9	W 74023	322.6	W 47621	204.2	W 66344	285.0	FILS TEXTILES
6513	COTTON YARN	W 112084	377.9	W 69390	305.8	W 44612	193.5	W 64945	280.7	FILS DE COTON
652	COTTON FABRICS,WOVEN	W 31422	121.3	W 23823	109.3	W 20461	88.8	W 22188	104.9	TISSUS DE COTON
6521	GREY WOVEN COTTON FABRIC	W 29205	111.6	W 23131	105.9	W 19492	83.9	W 21145	97.7	TISSUS COT ECRUS NON MERCER
65214	GREY WOVEN COTTON NES	W 27965	106.2	W 19232	88.1	W 16603	70.5	W 18248	83.7	AUT TISSUS 85% COTON ECRUS
65215	GREY WOVN COTN BLEND NES	W 1240	5.5	W 3899	17.9	W 2889	13.4	W 2897	14.0	AUT TIS MOINS 85% COT ECRUS
658	TEXTILE ARTICLES NES	W 13288	64.8	W 17038	91.9	W 17918	89.8	W 21078	95.3	ART FACONNES MAT TEXTILES
6584	LINENS ETC	W 11835	59.3	W 14995	83.8	W 13949	78.8	W 16562	77.8	LINGE DE MAISON
65841	BED LINEN OF COTTON	W 6688	30.9	W 7762	42.0	W 7178	35.3	W 4998	32.4	LINGE DE LIT DE COTON
65845	OTHER LINEN OF COTTON	W 4428	24.6	W 6187	35.7	W 5556	34.3	W 10498	38.7	LINGE DE TOILETTE COTON
659	FLOOR COVERINGS,ETC	W 8948	34.1	W 7364	34.0	W 6457	30.8	W 5278	31.4	COUVRE-PARQUETS,TAPIS ETC
6595	MAN-MADE TXTL CARPTS NES	W 5869	21.2	W 4905	23.8	W 3739	16.0	W 4103	20.3	TAPIS MAT TEXT SYNT ARTIF
65951	— TUFTED	W 3708	10.9	W 134	0.5	W 91	0.4	W 32	0.2	TAPIS MAT TEXT SYNT TOUFFT
65952	— WOVEN	W 2161	10.3	W 4771	23.4	W 3648	15.6	W 4071	20.2	TAPIS MAT TEXT SYNT TISSES
66	NONMETAL MINERAL MFS NES		28.6		27.5		28.0		121.2	ART MIN NON METALLIQUES
662	CLAY,REFRACTORY BLDG PRD	W 11610	4.5	W 15942	4.7	W 18805	6.1	W 16560	79.1	MAT CONST REFRACTAIRES
6624	BRICKS ETC NONREFRACTORY	W 7831	3.4	W 10273	3.5	W 11972	4.4	W 10796	75.4	BRIQUES ETC CERAM NON REFR

5. Special Exports F.O.B. by Commodities according to the S.I.T.C. (Rev. 2) in million U.S. Dollars
Exportations Spéciales F.O.B. par Produits d'après la C.T.C.I. (Rév. 2) en millions de Dollars E.U.

SITC CTCI	COMMODITY	1994 QUANTITY QUANTITE	1994 VALUE VALEUR	1995 QUANTITY QUANTITE	1995 VALUE VALEUR	1996 QUANTITY QUANTITE	1996 VALUE VALEUR	1997 QUANTITY QUANTITE	1997 VALUE VALEUR	PRODUIT
66245	GLAZED CERAMIC SETTS ETC	W 7174	3.2	W 10203	3.4	W 11604	4.2	W 10686	75.3	AUT CARREAUX CERAMIQUE
665	GLASSWARE	W 8088	17.2	W 16465	15.6	W 15337	14.0	W 7493	20.8	OUVRAGES EN VERRE
67	IRON AND STEEL		134.8		160.0		69.1		108.6	FER ET ACIER
671	PIG IRON ETC	W 31799	16.4	W 42120	27.0	W 34070	24.3	W 32521	20.9	FONTE,SPIEGEL,POUDRES
6716	FERRO–ALLOYS	W 31332	16.2	W 41937	26.9	W 32898	24.2	W 32511	20.8	FERRO–ALLIAGES
67162	FERRO–SILICON	W 9698	5.3	W 41341	26.5	W 31745	23.5	W 32450	20.8	FERRO–SILICIUM
67169	OTHER FERRO–ALLOYS	W 20834	10.9	W 576	0.4			W 20	0.1	AUTRES FERRO–ALLIAGES
672	IRON,STEEL PRIMARY FORMS	W 5903	1.8	W 39498	10.8	W 578	0.2	W 90193	22.9	LINGOTS FER,ACIER
6727	IRN,STL COIL FR REROLLNG	W 4992	1.5	W 31494	8.9	W 576	0.2	W 90110	22.8	EBAUCHES POUR TOLES FER
67274	STNLESS STEEL ETC COILS	W 70	0.1	W 31212	8.8	W 576	0.2	W 80881	20.4	EBAUCHES ACIER INOXYDBLE
673	IRON,STEEL SHAPES ETC	W 229709	68.7	W 191085	58.5	W 73382	23.8	W 122061	36.5	BARRES,PROFIL FER,ACIER
6731	IRON,STEEL WIRE ROD	W 148577	44.3	W 35818	10.5	W 22957	6.7	W 620	0.2	FIL MACHINE FER,ACIER
67311	IRON,SIMPLE STL WIRE ROD	W 87774	27.1	W 35688	10.4	W 22957	6.7	W 620	0.2	FIL MACH AUT ACIER FIN
67315	OTHER ALLOY STL WIRE ROD	W 57963	16.5							FIL MACH NON ACIERS ALL
6732	IRON,STEEL BARS ETC	W 45379	13.3	W 87882	25.8	W 27823	8.2	W 92182	26.3	BARRES FER,ACIER
67326	IRN,OTH STL BARS HOTROLD	W 19382	6.2	W 84586	24.8	W 27619	8.2	W 92100	26.2	BARRES PLEINES FER,ACIER
6733	IRON,STEEL PROFILES ETC	W 35753	11.3	W 67385	22.3	W 22602	9.0	W 29260	10.1	PROFILES,PALPLAN FER,ACIER
67332	LARGE U,I,H SECTIONS ETC	W 12622	4.2	W 66412	21.7	W 21660	8.6	W 27927	9.5	PROFILES PLUS 80MM
674	IRN,STL UNIV,PLATE,SHEET	W 23236	6.3	W 37427	10.8	W 682	0.2	W 34021	9.0	LARGES PLATS,TOLES
6744	IRN,STL HVY PLATE,ROLLED	W 17978	5.2	W 36517	10.6	W 27	0.1	W 32151	8.4	TOLES LAMINEES PLUS 4.75 MM
67441	— OF IRON OR SIMPLE STL	W 17978	5.2	W 36517	10.6	W 27	0.1	W 31905	8.3	TOLES NON ACIER FIN CARB
677	IRN,STL WIRE(EXCL W ROD)	W 102530	29.9	W 152342	47.9	W 44530	12.7	W 34593	9.9	FILS EN FER,ACIER
67702	HIGH CARBON STEEL WIRE	W 72420	20.8	W 122575	38.4	W 42799	12.0	W 30863	8.5	FILS ACIER FIN CARBONE
678	IRON,STL TUBES,PIPES,ETC	W 24622	11.6	W 7472	5.1	W 12294	7.9	W 14052	9.2	TUBES,TUYAUX EN FONTE,FER
68	NON–FERROUS METALS		168.3		199.8		186.9		151.1	METAUX NON FERREUX
684	ALUMINIUM	W 111239	167.2	W 93258	197.6	W 107368	185.1	W 81640	148.8	ALUMINIUM
6841	ALUMINIUM,ALLOYS,UNWRGHT	W 15934	27.9	W 70282	149.8	W 96880	164.8	W 71237	125.5	ALUMINIUM,ALLIAGES BRUTS
6842	ALUMINIUM,ALLOYS WORKED	W 95305	139.4	W 22976	47.9	W 10488	20.4	W 10404	23.3	ALUMINIUM,ALLIAGES OUVRE
68421	ALUMINIUM BARS,WIRE,ETC	W 86788	125.6	W 10826	20.3	W 7675	14.6	W 5897	13.7	BARRES,PROFILES FILS ALU
68422	ALUMNM PLATE,SHEET,STRIP	W 4703	8.9	W 10303	23.7	W 2266	4.7	W 3684	8.2	TOLES, PLANCHES EN ALU
69	METAL MANUFACTURES NES		70.7		47.6		44.0		50.0	ART MANUFACT EN METAL NDA
696	CUTLERY	W 966	11.2	W 954	11.2	W 1053	13.4	W 1334	16.8	COUTELLERIE
69603	RAZORS,RAZOR BLADES	W 945	11.1	W 924	11.1	W 1043	13.3	W 1323	16.8	RASOIRS ET LAMES
697	BASE MTL HOUSEHOLD EQUIP	W 5967	13.6	W 4445	12.5	W 4207	13.0	W 6177	15.7	ART MENAGE MET COMMUNS
699	BASE METAL MFRS NES	W 78703	31.5	W 9717	11.5	W 5960	6.1	W 4289	6.4	ART MANUFACTURES MET NDA
6997	IRON,STEEL ARTICLES NES	W 73153	22.0	W 5503	2.8	W 4301	2.2	W 2038	1.7	OUV FONTE,FER,ACIER NDA
69979	IRN,STL MANUFACTURES NES	W 73153	22.0	W 5503	2.8	W 4301	2.2	W 2038	1.7	AUT OUVRAGES EN FER NDA
7	MACHINES,TRANSPORT EQUIP		18.7		22.2		15.6		47.4	MACHINES MATERIEL TRANSPORT
78	ROAD VEHICLES		2.6		1.4		2.2		27.6	VEHICULES ROUTIERS
784	MOTOR VEH PRTS,ACCES NES	W 663	2.3	W 772	1.3	W 544	1.6	W 884	25.8	PIECES 722,781,782,783
7849	OTHER MOTOR VEHCL PARTS	W 663	2.3	W 772	1.3	W 544	1.6	W 884	25.8	PIECES 722,781,782,783
8	MISC MANUFACTURED GOODS		305.3		330.0		323.5		395.3	ART MANUFACTURES DIVERS
812	*PLUMBG,HEATNG,LGHTNG EQ	W 7717	10.5	W 9668	15.4	W 10559	16.4	W 10179	29.6	APPAR SANITAIRES CHAUFFAGE
8122	CERAMIC PLUMBNG FIXTURES	W 7572	9.4	W 9188	12.3	W 10107	13.6	W 9691	26.0	EVIERS,LAVABOS,CUVETTES
821	*FURNITURE,PARTS THEREOF	W 9004	15.0	W 8081	13.2	W 9161	13.7	W 10248	16.4	MEUBLES ET PIECES
8219	FURNITURE AND PARTS NES	W 8966	14.8	W 7966	13.0	W 9039	13.5	W 10122	16.0	AUTRES MEUBLES ET PIECES
82192	WOOD FURNITURE NES	W 8741	14.1	W 7504	12.1	W 8808	13.2	W 9751	15.4	MEUBLES NDA EN BOIS
84	CLOTHING AND ACCESSORIES		230.6		252.6		239.4		259.0	VETEMENTS
842	MENS OUTERWEAR NOT KNIT	W 2654	25.9	W 3630	35.6	W 5168	46.7	W 4211	41.6	VET DESSUS POUR HOMMES
8423	— TROUSERS,BREECHES ETC	W 1669	14.3	W 2467	21.4	W 3387	29.4	W 2890	28.6	PANTALONS HOMMES MAT TEX
8429	— OTHER OUTER GARMENTS	W 552	7.4	W 887	11.6	W 1335	14.2	W 1114	11.4	AUT VET DES HOM MAT TEX
843	WOMENS OUTERWEAR NONKNIT	W 7530	66.7	W 7530	75.1	W 6493	64.6	W 5163	53.9	VET DESSUS FEMMES MAT TEX
8435	— BLOUSES	W 1603	15.1	W 1903	21.1	W 2415	26.0	W 1589	16.7	BLOUSES FEM MAT TEXTILES
8439	— OTHER OUTER GARMENTS	W 4873	41.2	W 4913	46.6	W 3545	32.8	W 3093	31.7	AUT VET DES FEM MAT TEXT
844	UNDER GARMENTS NOT KNIT	W 7015	52.3	W 6972	64.8	W 5869	51.2	W 7096	67.1	VETEMENT DESSOUS MAT TEX
8441	— MENS SHIRTS	W 4327	34.1	W 4476	44.0	W 3432	31.5	W 3566	36.3	CHEMISES HOMMES MAT TEXT
84411	—— OF COTTON	W 4193	33.1	W 4422	43.6	W 3339	30.7	W 3210	33.8	CHEMISES HOMMES DE COTON
8442	— MENS,OTHR THAN SHIRTS	W 2104	13.2	W 1863	15.2	W 1889	15.0	W 2878	25.7	SOUS–VET HOMMES MAT TEXT
845	OUTERWEAR KNIT NONELASTC	W 1383	11.0	W 123	1.3	W 251	2.5	W 114	1.2	VET DESSOUS,ACCES BONNET
846	UNDER GARMENTS KNITTED	W 8010	73.0	W 7837	75.1	W 7344	73.8	W 8861	94.9	SOUS VETS DE BONNETERIE
8462	— OF COTTON NON ELASTIC	W 8006	72.9	W 7832	75.0	W 7343	73.8	W 8861	94.9	SOUS–VET BONNET COTON
84629	—— OTHER	W 7619	69.1	W 7734	74.1	W 7195	72.4	W 8859	94.9	AUT SOUS–VET BONNET COTON
851	*FOOTWEAR	W 1800	10.9	W 1940	9.6	W 2061	10.2	W 1062	7.1	CHAUSSURES
89	MISC MANUFCTRD GOODS NES		33.7		34.9		37.6		79.8	ART MANUFACTURES DIVERS
892	PRINTED MATTER	W 9703	10.7	W 6615	8.4	W 6162	8.6	W 4761	7.2	IMPRIMES
893	ARTICLES OF PLASTIC NES		17.5		19.8		20.1		45.6	OUVRAGES EN MAT DIVIS 58
8932	PLSTC SANITRY,TOILET ART	W 4360	9.1	W 4755	13.2	W 4813	14.5	W 6969	39.0	OBJETS HYGIEN MAT DU 58
895	OFFICE SUPPLIES NES	W 240	0.9	W 479	2.2	W 305	1.1	W 3544	19.5	ART PAPET NDA
8952	PENS,PENCILS,FOUNTN PENS	W 174	0.8	W 421	2.2	W 205	1.0	W 3542	19.5	PLUMES,CRAYONS,STYLOS
89521	FOUNTAIN PENS,ETC	W 158	0.7	W 396	2.0	W 198	1.0	W 3536	19.4	PORTE PLUME,STYLO ETC

1. HISTORICAL SERIES, 1962–1997 SPECIAL TRADE, IMPORTS C.I.F., EXPORTS F.O.B.
SERIES HISTORIQUES, 1962–1997 COMMERCE SPECIAL, IMPORTATIONS C.A.F., EXPORTATIONS F.O.B

YEAR ANNEE	VALUE IN MILLION EL SALV. COLONES / VALEUR EN MILLION EL SALV. COLONES — MERCHANDISE –MARCHANDISE		GOLD –OR		CONVERSION FACTORS U.S. CENTS PER EL SALV. COLON FACTEURS DE CONVERSION CENTS E.U. PAR EL SALV. COLON		INDEX NUMBERS –INDICES — QUANTUM		UNIT VALUE VALEUR UNITAIRE	
	IMPORTS	EXPORTS	IMPORTS	EXPORTS	IMPORTS	EXPORTS	IMPORTS	EXPORTS	IMPORTS	EXPORTS
1962	312.00	340.80			40.0000	40.0000				
1963	379.40	384.60			40.0000	40.0000				
1964	477.80	445.20			40.0000	40.0000				
1965	501.40	471.80			40.0000	40.0000				
1966	550.00	472.30			40.0000	40.0000				
1967	559.80	518.10			40.0000	40.0000				
1968	533.80	529.30			40.0000	40.0000				
1969	523.10	505.30			40.0000	40.0000				
1970	534.00	570.80			40.0000	40.0000				
1971	618.60	607.90			40.0000	40.0000				
1972	695.20	754.30			40.0000	40.0000				
1973	927.60	895.80			40.0000	40.0000				
1974	1408.50	1156.20			40.0000	40.0000				
1975	1495.10	1283.40			40.0000	40.0000				
1976	1794.70	1801.80			40.0000	40.0000				
1977	2356.10	2431.90			40.0000	40.0000				
1978	2559.90	1577.40			40.0000	40.0000				
1979	2529.90	2579.30			40.0000	40.0000				
1980	2404.30	2684.00			40.0000	40.0000				64
1981	2461.40	1991.80			40.0000	40.0000				59
1982	2141.90	1748.60			40.0000	40.0000				56
1983	2228.70	1838.20			40.0000	40.0000				45
1984	3285.50	1517.80			40.0000	40.0000				
1985	2403.40	1697.40			40.0000	40.0000				
1986	4674.40	3774.60			20.0000	20.0000				
1987	4970.30	2954.70			20.0000	20.0000				
1988	5034.90	3043.80			20.0000	20.0000				
1989	5806.50	2482.50			20.0000	20.0000				
1990	8816.20	3891.68			14.3202	14.9422				
1991	11359.71	4751.05			12.3762	12.3762				
1992	14210.10	4983.71			11.9528	11.9891				
1993	16630.62	6364.73			11.4981	11.4962				
1994	22491.54	7373.35								
1995	24977.29	8736.10								
1996	23383.85	8968.67			11.4220	11.4220				
1997	26032.25	11898.98			11.4220	11.4220				

2. IMPORTS BY BROAD ECONOMIC CATEGORY AND EXPORTS BY INDUSTRIAL ORIGIN. (PERCENTAGE OF TOTAL VALUE)
IMPORTATIONS PAR CATEGORIES ECONOMIQUES ET EXPORTATIONS PAR BRANCHE D'ACTIVITE.(EN POURCENTAGE DE LA VALEUR TOTALE)

IMPORTS – IMPORTATIONS

	1991	1992	1993	1994	1995	1996	1997
TOTAL IMPORTS–IMPORTATIONS TOTALES	100.	100.	100.	100.	100.	100.	100.
1 FOOD BEV–ALIMENTATION BOISSONS	12.4	11.7	10.0	11.7	11.5	13.0	12.5
11 PRIMARY–PRODUITS DE BASE	5.7	4.3	2.6	3.9	3.1	3.9	3.5
111 FOR INDUSTRY–POUR L'INDUSTRIE	4.4	2.5	1.6	2.6	1.8	2.3	1.7
112 FOR HOUSEHOLDS–POUR LES MENAGES	1.3	1.8	1.0	1.4	1.3	1.6	1.8
12 PROCESSED–PRODUITS ELABORES	6.8	7.5	7.4	7.7	8.5	9.1	9.0
121 FOR INDUSTRY–POUR L'INDUSTRIE	1.7	2.1	2.0	2.2	2.4	2.4	2.1
122 FOR HOUSEHOLDS–POUR LES MENAGES	5.1	5.4	5.4	5.5	6.1	6.7	6.9
2 IND SUPPLIES–APPROV INDUSTRIELS	37.7	34.3	33.0	33.6	33.3	33.8	34.7
21 PRIMARY–PRODUITS DE BASE	4.3	2.8	2.3	3.3	2.7	3.9	4.4
22 PROCESSED–PRODUITS ELABORES	33.4	31.4	30.7	30.3	30.6	29.8	30.3
3 FUELS–COMBUSTIBLES	12.5	13.9	11.2	9.4	9.1	12.1	11.3
31 PRIMARY–PRODUITS DE BASE	10.1	10.2	8.0	5.6	4.2	5.5	4.9
32 PROCESSED–PRODUITS ELABORES	2.4	3.7	3.2	3.8	4.9	6.6	6.4
321 MOTOR SPIRIT–ESSENCE	0.5	1.2	0.4	0.6	0.7	1.5	1.3
322 OTHER–AUTRES	2.0	2.5	2.8	3.2	4.2	5.1	5.1
4 MACHINERY–EQUIPEMENT	14.0	14.1	16.8	16.1	15.1	15.4	15.7
41 CAPITAL EQUIPMENT–MACHINES	12.4	12.6	14.9	14.3	13.0	13.5	13.1
42 PARTS–PIECES ACCESSOIRES	1.6	1.5	1.9	1.8	2.2	1.9	2.6
5 TRANSPORT–TRANSPORT	10.7	12.8	14.6	14.4	14.5	11.0	10.3
51 PASSENGER CARS–AUTOMOBILES	7.0	8.9	5.2	4.3	4.6	3.0	2.6
52 OTHER–AUTRES	0.5	0.6	5.8	6.7	6.7	5.1	4.6
521 INDUSTRIAL–INDUSTRIELS	0.2	0.2	5.5	6.5	6.4	4.8	4.5
522 NON INDUSTRIAL–NON INDUSTRIEL	0.3	0.3	0.3	0.2	0.2	0.2	0.2
53 PARTS–PIECES ACCESSOIRES	3.2	3.4	3.6	3.4	3.2	3.0	3.0
6 CONSUM GOODS–BIENS CONSOMMATION	12.5	13.1	14.4	14.7	16.2	14.5	15.3
61 DURABLE–DURABLES	1.9	2.4	3.2	3.5	3.9	2.9	3.7
62 SEMI DURABLE–SEMI DURABLES	3.5	3.6	4.0	4.3	5.2	4.5	4.8
63 NON DURABLE–NON DURABLES	7.1	7.2	7.2	6.9	7.1	7.1	6.8
7 GOODS NES–BIENS NDA	0.1	0.0	0.0	0.1	0.1	0.2	0.2

EXPORTS – EXPORTATIONS

	1991	1992	1993	1994	1995	1996	1997
TOTAL EXPORTS–EXPORTATIONS TOTALES	100.	100.	100.	100.	100.	100.	100.
1 AGRICULTURE	45.3	33.7	38.6	39.2	46.3	40.3	43.2
2 MINING QUARRY–INDUS EXTRACTIVES	0.1	0.3	0.1	0.1	0.1	0.0	0.0
3 MANUFACTURING–IND MANUFACTUR	54.6	66.0	61.3	60.7	53.6	59.6	56.8
31 FOOD BEV TOBACCO–ALIM BOISS TAB	10.9	15.6	12.4	12.6	11.5	12.7	12.6
32 TEXTILES–INDUSTRIES TEXTILES	17.0	18.0	15.3	15.4	12.0	11.1	10.6
33 WOOD & PRODUCTS–BOIS & PRODUITS	0.1	0.2	0.1	0.1	0.1	0.0	0.1
34 PAPER & PRODUCTS–PAPIER & PRODT	6.0	7.6	8.0	7.6	6.3	6.0	5.1
35 CHEMICALS–INDUSTRIES CHIMIQUES	11.9	14.8	14.4	14.5	13.2	18.9	17.1
36 NON METAL MIN–MIN NON METAL	0.2	0.3	0.5	0.2	0.2	0.2	0.6
37 BASIC METAL–IND METAL BASE	3.1	3.3	3.9	3.6	4.3	4.1	3.7
38 METAL MANUF–MANUF METAL	5.1	5.3	5.9	5.9	5.2	5.8	6.2
39 OTH MANUF IND–AUTRES MANUF	0.4	0.9	0.8	0.9	0.8	0.8	1.0

3. TRADE BY PRINCIPAL COUNTRIES OF CONSIGNMENT AND DESTINATION (VALUE IN MILLION U.S. DOLLARS)
ECHANGES SELON LES PRINCIPAUX PAYS DE CONSIGNATION ET DE DESTINATION (VALEUR EN MILLIONS DE DOLLARS EU)

COUNTRIES–PAYS	SPECIAL IMPORTS C.I.F. IMPORTATIONS SPECIALES C.A.F					COUNTRIES–PAYS	SPECIAL EXPORTS F.O.B. EXPORTATIONS SPECIALES F.O.B.				
	1993	1994	1995	1996	1997		1993	1994	1995	1996	1997
World	1860.8	2261.8	2627.7	2670.1	2961.5	Monde	717.3	812.7	985.2	1024.3	1353.9
Africa	1.5	1.4	6.1	1.2	0.9	Afrique	8.2	0.1	0.0	0.0	6.6
Americas	1493.8	1767.6	2052.2	2159.9	2401.2	Amériques	575.1	601.9	656.9	724.5	925.3
– Northern America	805.1	950.5	1177.9	1093.9	1245.6	– Amérique du Nord	218.9	195.9	187.7	202.9	271.4
– LAIA	294.1	316.1	311.5	347.8	478.1	– ALAI	25.4	38.4	26.1	26.0	32.0
– CACM	323.5	399.1	470.1	505.9	576.2	– MCAC	306.4	343.4	415.9	455.1	576.1
– Caribbean	4.8	21.0	29.7	36.2	35.4	– Caraïbes	9.7	9.5	8.3	13.2	18.2
– Rest of America	66.4	80.9	63.1	176.1	66.0	– Autre Amérique	14.6	14.7	19.0	27.3	27.5
Asia excl fmr USSR	162.0	216.6	230.2	202.1	185.6	Asie anc. URSS exclus	15.0	6.8	20.9	14.0	20.0
– Middle East	0.1	2.9	1.0	0.8	0.6	– Moyen–Orient	0.0	0.0	0.1		0.0
Asia former USSR					2.3	Asie ancienne URSS					
Europe excl fmr USSR	184.9	260.5	263.1	271.8	290.2	Europe anc. URSS exclus	119.0	203.7	307.1	285.7	401.1
– European Union	167.0	239.9	244.3	257.3	262.7	– Union Européenne	118.6	203.1	304.3	285.5	400.2
– Eastern Europe	2.2	5.8	4.5	3.4	5.8	– Europe de l'Est	0.0	0.2	0.4	0.1	0.2
– Rest of Europe	15.7	14.8	14.4	11.0	21.6	– Autre de l'Europe	0.4	0.4	2.5	0.1	0.8
Europe former USSR	4.2	5.6	2.9	20.6	22.1	Europe ancienne URSS					0.0
Oceania	6.4	7.8	9.0	13.5	13.3	Océanie	0.1	0.2	0.1	0.1	0.2
Other	8.1	2.4	64.1	1.0	45.9	Autre	0.0	0.0	0.1	0.0	0.6
USA/Etats–Unis d'Amer	790.1	938.2	1161.5	1067.6	1224.6	USA/Etats–Unis d'Amer	212.7	183.4	172.6	197.4	260.1
Guatemala	205.8	242.5	284.5	279.8	323.7	Guatemala	157.8	178.1	204.2	210.7	264.1
Mexico/Mexique	103.7	105.6	150.4	172.3	235.3	Germany/Allemagne	75.3	120.8	143.2	159.0	237.5
Japan/Japon	97.7	143.3	133.6	114.1	91.2	Costa Rica	66.0	72.3	77.5	93.3	111.4
Venezuela	133.7	138.4	76.6	59.6	63.6	Honduras	47.1	56.3	70.3	97.5	136.0
Costa Rica	66.3	78.9	91.1	101.7	116.3	Nicaragua	35.5	36.7	63.9	53.7	64.6
Panama	66.4	80.9	62.7	175.9	65.5	Belgium–Luxembourg	17.9	34.1	48.3	60.6	60.9
Germany/Allemagne	65.0	73.1	91.9	97.2	93.6	Netherlands/Pays–Bas	15.6	22.3	73.4	31.3	29.1
Honduras	34.8	46.1	59.7	70.3	85.1	Panama	12.9	12.1	17.0	24.5	24.5
Nicaragua	16.6	31.7	34.8	54.1	51.1	Mexico/Mexique	17.2	21.3	8.3	12.6	17.8
Brazil/Brésil	24.6	40.3	30.8	29.4	23.6	Japan/Japon	14.6	6.3	14.6	10.3	14.1
Spain/Espagne	16.1	29.0	31.1	24.2	39.5	Canada	6.1	12.5	15.0	5.3	11.3
Italy/Italie	17.4	22.8	28.9	31.2	31.2	United Kingdom	1.6	2.6	4.5	9.9	29.9
Other Asia n.e.s.	27.4	23.8	29.2	23.2	25.9	France, Monaco	2.3	7.3	11.5	4.7	16.8
Ecuador/Equateur	4.8	5.2	5.0	29.2	79.3	Dominican Republic	6.6	7.4	7.0	8.1	11.4
Korea, Republic of	19.6	20.3	28.2	22.9	26.9	Venezuela	5.7	11.4	10.4	5.6	2.8
United Kingdom	17.9	25.1	25.8	24.1	25.0	Italy/Italie	3.8	4.6	5.8	7.5	10.1
Colombia/Colombie	12.1	15.2	22.5	19.0	42.2	Spain/Espagne	1.6	5.6	9.0	6.1	8.6
Netherlands/Pays–Bas	18.7	14.6	18.3	30.4	18.2	Belize/Bélize	1.7	2.6	2.0	2.7	3.0
Netherlands Antilles	0.6	15.8	23.2	30.3	20.7	Peru/Pérou	0.2	1.7	0.4	3.6	3.3
Canada	15.0	11.9	16.3	26.0	20.4	Denmark/Danemark	0.0	2.0	2.3	1.3	2.7
France, Monaco	8.1	14.1	17.1	16.9	20.1	Colombia/Colombie	1.4	0.8	3.9	0.8	1.3
Switzerland,Liechtenst.	15.1	14.5	13.7	10.7	20.8	Finland/Finlande		0.6	3.8	1.3	2.4
Areas n.e.s.	8.1	2.4	5.5	1.0	45.9	Morocco/Maroc	4.9				2.7
Belgium–Luxembourg	9.6	16.5	12.0	11.3	12.7	Ecuador/Equateur	0.2	0.6	1.5	2.5	2.6
China, Hong Kong SAR	8.3	8.6	13.7	12.3	16.7	Sweden/Suède	0.3	0.2	2.4	3.7	0.5
Free zones/Zone franches			58.6			Chile/Chili	0.5	0.4	0.9	0.4	3.7
Russian Federation	4.2	5.6	2.9	20.6	22.0	Netherlands Antilles	0.7	0.6	0.7	2.7	0.7
Argentina/Argentine	5.7	3.8	8.7	19.2	12.6	Portugal	0.0	3.1	0.0	0.0	1.6
New Zealand	6.4	7.8	8.8	13.3	13.2	China/Chine		0.1	3.9	0.3	0.1
China/Chine	0.2	12.4	9.2	7.9	14.0	Bahamas	0.6	0.4		0.5	2.8
Chile/Chili	5.5	5.1	14.6	8.0	8.4	Sri Lanka			0.0		4.0
Finland/Finlande	1.5	30.8	3.1	1.7	2.9	Haiti/Haïti	1.3	0.6	0.2	0.5	1.2
Peru/Pérou	4.1	2.5	2.7	10.6	12.5	Egypt/Egypte	3.1				
Sweden/Suède	6.1	5.6	5.0	5.7	8.8	China, Hong Kong SAR	0.2	0.2	0.6	0.8	1.4
Denmark/Danemark	1.9	2.2	3.2	4.8	5.4	Norway,Svalbard and JM		0.1	2.1	0.0	0.7
Malaysia/Malaisie	1.5		6.6	6.1	0.0	Kenya					2.6
Singapore/Singapour	2.1	1.3	3.9	4.3	1.4	Jamaica/Jamaïque	0.4	0.3	0.2	0.4	0.8
Trinidad and Tobago	3.7	2.8	2.3	2.3	1.4	Korea, Republic of	0.1	0.0	0.2	1.2	0.3
Austria/Autriche	1.7	3.1	2.0	3.4	1.6	Bolivia/Bolivie		1.6	0.1	0.1	0.0

(VALUE AS PERCENTAGE OF WORLD TOTAL)(VALEURS EN POURCENTAGE DU TOTAL MONDIAL)

	1988	1989	1990	1991	1992	1993	1994	1995	1996	1997		1988	1989	1990	1991	1992	1993	1994	1995	1996	1997
Africa	0.0	0.0	0.0	0.1	0.1	0.1	0.1	0.2	0.0	0.0	Afrique	0.0		0.0	0.0	0.6	1.1	0.0	0.0	0.0	0.5
Americas	79.7	77.0	66.5	78.0	66.5	80.3	78.1	78.1	80.9	81.1	Amériques	70.0	75.7	70.9	74.8	64.6	80.2	74.1	66.7	70.7	68.3
– Northern America	37.9	40.1	38.8	42.1	40.8	43.3	42.0	44.8	41.0	42.1	– Amérique du Nord	42.9	38.5	35.1	35.7	34.3	30.5	24.1	19.0	19.8	20.0
– LAIA	18.8	15.7	10.0	17.7	15.5	15.8	14.0	11.9	13.0	16.1	– ALAI	0.3	1.1	1.3	1.9	3.9	3.5	4.7	2.6	2.5	2.4
– CACM	19.8	18.2	17.0	17.0	6.4	17.4	17.6	17.9	18.9	19.5	– MCAC	24.8	32.8	31.0	33.6	22.6	42.7	42.3	42.2	44.4	42.6
– Caribbean	0.1	0.0	0.0	0.2	0.1	0.3	0.9	1.1	1.4	1.2	– Caraïbes	0.6	1.8	1.3	1.2	1.1	1.4	1.2	0.8	1.3	1.3
– Rest of America	3.2	2.9	0.7	1.0	3.6	3.6	3.6	2.4	6.6	2.2	– Autre Amérique	1.4	1.5	2.3	2.4	2.7	2.0	1.8	1.9	2.7	2.0
Asia excl fmr USSR	7.5	6.7	4.8	7.3	8.2	8.7	9.6	8.8	7.6	6.3	Asie anc. URSS exclus	4.7	3.1	1.2	3.1	0.8	2.1	0.8	2.1	1.4	1.5
– Middle East		0.0	0.0	0.0	0.1	0.0	0.1	0.0	0.0	0.0	– Moyen–Orient		0.0	0.0			0.0	0.0	0.0		0.0
Asia former USSR										0.1	Asie ancienne URSS										
Europe excl fmr USSR	12.3	15.6	11.5	11.9	11.7	9.9	11.5	10.0	10.2	9.8	Europe anc. URSS exclus	24.2	21.1	27.7	21.8	10.5	16.6	25.1	31.2	27.9	29.6
– European Union	11.4	14.2	10.5	11.0	10.5	9.0	10.6	9.3	9.6	8.9	– Union Européenne	24.2	21.1	27.6	21.5	10.4	16.5	25.0	30.9	27.9	29.6
– Eastern Europe	0.1	0.0	0.0	0.1	0.4	0.1	0.3	0.2	0.1	0.2	– Europe de l'Est				0.2	0.0	0.0	0.0	0.0	0.0	0.0
– Rest of Europe	0.8	1.4	1.0	0.8	0.8	0.8	0.7	0.5	0.4	0.7	– Autre de l'Europe	0.0	0.0	0.1	0.1	0.1	0.1	0.0	0.2	0.0	0.1
Europe former USSR	0.0	0.0			0.2	0.2	0.2	0.1	0.8	0.7	Europe ancienne URSS	1.0									0.0
Oceania	0.3	0.4	0.4	0.3	0.3	0.3	0.3	0.3	0.5	0.4	Océanie	0.0	0.0	0.1	0.3	0.0	0.0	0.0	0.0	0.0	0.0
Other	0.2	0.3	16.8	2.4	13.0	0.4	0.1	2.4	0.0	1.5	Autre		0.1	0.0	0.0	23.6	0.0	0.0	0.0	0.0	0.0
USA/Etats–Unis d'Amer	36.9	39.4	37.9	41.1	40.0	42.5	41.5	44.2	40.0	41.4	USA/Etats–Unis d'Amer	39.7	35.9	34.1	34.8	33.6	29.6	22.6	17.5	19.3	19.2
Guatemala	13.4	11.6	11.8	11.6		11.1	10.7	10.8	10.5	10.9	Guatemala	16.3	21.1	17.8	18.4		22.0	21.9	20.7	20.6	19.5
Mexico/Mexique	9.1	7.9	4.9	9.7	7.3	5.6	4.7	5.7	6.5	7.9	Germany/Allemagne				18.0	7.7	10.5	14.9	14.5	15.5	17.5
Japan/Japon	4.7	4.3	3.1	4.8	5.2	5.2	6.3	5.1	4.3	3.1	Costa Rica	5.7	8.2	8.5	7.6	9.9	9.2	8.9	7.9	9.1	8.2
Venezuela	6.6	5.2	3.2	4.1	5.3	7.2	6.1	2.9	2.2	2.1	Honduras	2.2	3.0	3.1	3.7	5.7	6.6	6.9	7.1	9.5	10.0
Costa Rica	4.8	4.5	3.1	2.9	3.7	3.6	3.5	3.5	3.8	3.9	Nicaragua	0.6	0.6	1.6	4.0	7.0	5.0	4.5	6.5	5.2	4.8
Panama	3.2	2.9	0.6	1.0	3.6	3.6	3.6	2.4	6.6	2.2	Belgium–Luxembourg	0.2	0.2	0.7	0.7	0.7	2.5	4.2	4.9	5.9	4.5
Germany/Allemagne				4.3	4.5	3.5	3.2	3.5	3.6	3.2	Netherlands/Pays–Bas	0.2	0.9	0.7	0.9	0.7	2.2	2.7	7.4	3.1	2.1
Honduras	1.4	1.1	1.3	1.3	1.9	1.9	2.0	2.3	2.6	2.9	Panama	1.2	1.1	1.6	1.7	2.0	1.8	1.5	1.7	2.4	1.8
Nicaragua	0.2	1.0	0.8	1.2	0.9	0.9	1.4	1.3	2.0	1.7	Mexico/Mexique	0.2	0.7	0.8	1.4	2.2	2.4	2.6	0.8	1.2	1.3

4. Special Imports C.I.F. by Commodities according to the S.I.T.C. (Rev. 2) in million U.S. Dollars
Importations Spéciales C.A.F. par Produits d'après la C.T.C.I. (Rév. 2) en millions de Dollars E.U.

SITC CTCI	COMMODITY	1994 QUANTITY QUANTITE	1994 VALUE VALEUR	1995 QUANTITY QUANTITE	1995 VALUE VALEUR	1996 QUANTITY QUANTITE	1996 VALUE VALEUR	1997 * QUANTITY QUANTITE	1997 * VALUE VALEUR	PRODUIT
	ALL COMMODITIES		2261.9		2627.7		2670.1		2961.5	TOUS PRODUITS
0	FOOD AND LIVE ANIMALS		257.5		290.9		358.6		403.0	ALIMENTS,ANIMAUX VIVANTS
01	MEAT AND PREPARATIONS		12.8		19.1		27.4		25.8	VIANDES ET PREPARATIONS
011	MEAT FRESH,CHILLD,FROZEN	W 4157	10.8	W 7211	16.4	W 12090	23.7	W 8951	21.0	VIANDES FRAICHES,REF,CONGE
0111	BOVINE MEAT FRESH,FROZEN	W 4086	10.7	W 6832	15.8	W 11289	22.4	W 8437	20.2	VIANDES BOVIN FRAI,REF
02	DAIRY PRODCTS,BIRDS'EGGS		33.4		46.2		52.0		61.4	PRODUITS LAITIERS,OEUFS
022	MILK AND CREAM	W 14015	27.2	W 16389	37.1	W 16979	37.7	W 20978	42.7	LAIT ET CREME
0224	MILK,CREAM PRESERVED ETC	W 13271	26.7	W 14960	36.1	W 14863	36.2	W 17971	40.3	LAIT,CREME CONS,CONC
024	CHEESE AND CURD	W 1293	4.7	W 2363	7.6	W 4801	13.0	W 6955	17.5	FROMAGE ET CAILLEBOTTE
04	CEREALS AND PREPARATIONS		100.2		99.6		128.7		140.1	CEREALES ET PRODUITS
041	WHEAT ETC UNMILLED	W 260294	43.2		31.4	W 164151	42.4	W 173164	33.5	FROMENT,EPEAUTRE
0411	DURUM WHEAT UNMILLED	W 232584	40.2	W 165809	31.4	W 164151	42.4	W 173162	33.5	FROMENT DUR NON MOULU
042	RICE	W 27172	8.3	W 26519	7.3	W 32422	10.8	W 34277	11.3	RIZ
0421	RICE IN HUSK OR HUSKED	W 22341	6.6	W 23481	6.0	W 23229	7.1	W 30893	9.2	RIZ SANS AUTRE PREPARATION
044	MAIZE UNMILLED	W 146408	22.6	W 194655	28.8	W 156244	35.3	W 325936	55.5	MAIS NON MOULU
048	CEREAL ETC PREPARATIONS	W 16050	20.9	W 22141	26.9	W 21416	31.4	W 23015	33.8	PREPTNS A BASE CEREALES
0484	BAKERY PRODUCTS	W 5273	7.4	W 7513	9.9	W 8552	11.8	W 8447	11.6	PRODUITS DE BOULANGERIE
04842	PASTRY, CAKES ETC	W 4186	5.8	W 6198	8.3	W 6890	9.8	W 6965	9.9	PATISSERIE ETC.
0488	OTH CEREAL PREPS,MALT EX	W 1867	6.3	W 1678	6.9	W 2746	8.2	W 3239	9.1	EXTRAITS DE MALT
05	VEGETABLES AND FRUIT		29.8		29.9		30.3		43.0	LEGUMES ET FRUITS
054	VEG ETC FRSH,SMPLY PRSVD	W 24339	12.9	W 25645	6.4	W 16239	5.3	W 30187	10.5	LEGUMES FRAIS,CONG,SECS
0542	LEGUMINOUS VEGETBLES DRY	W 15608	9.3	W 5137	3.4	W 3214	2.2	W 6250	5.4	LEGUMES A COSSE SECS
057	FRUIT,NUTS,FRESH,DRIED	W 42888	6.2		8.8	W 36737	11.4	W 73359	16.4	FRUITS FRAIS OU SECS
058	FRUIT PRESERVED,PREPARED	W 7480	8.2	W 8461	11.8	W 11115	10.5	W 13956	12.5	CONSERVES DE FRUITS
06	SUGAR AND PREPS,HONEY		7.9		10.1		10.7		11.0	SUCRES ET PRODUITS
062	SUGAR CANDY NON-CHOCLATE	W 2634	5.5	W 4431	8.2	W 4538	8.4	W 4034	7.2	SUCRERIES
07	COFFEE,TEA,COCOA,SPICES		5.6		8.8		9.9		9.5	CAFE,THE,CACAO,EPICES
081	*FEEDING STUFF FOR ANIML	W 84010	23.2		21.3	W 113894	39.8	W 135413	45.0	NOURRITURE POUR ANIMAUX
0813	OILCAKE AND OTH RESIDUES	W 67546	17.2	W 71796	15.5	W 95066	31.8	W 111163	34.6	TOURTEAUX
08131	— OF SOYA BEANS	W 61560	16.0	W 71079	15.4	W 86978	30.4	W 104348	33.5	TOURTEAUX DE SOJA
09	MISC EDIBLE PRODUCTS		36.9		46.5		49.4		56.2	PREP ALIMENTAIRES DIVERSES
098	EDIBLE PRODCTS,PREPS NES	W 12758	34.4	W 15435	43.6	W 17498	45.9	W 20186	53.7	PREP ALIMENTAIRES NDA
09804	SAUCES,MIXED SEASONINGS	W 3501	4.9	W 5604	8.0	W 6586	8.9	W 7700	9.2	SAUCES,ASSAISONNEMENTS
09809	MISC FOOD PREPRTIONS NES	W 5378	20.7	W 5251	26.4	W 5379	26.2	W 6493	32.7	PREP ALIMENTAIRES NDA
1	BEVERAGES AND TOBACCO		14.3		15.1		16.5		16.1	BOISSONS ET TABACS
11	BEVERAGES		6.6		9.0		8.6		10.2	BOISSONS
12	TOBACCO AND MANUFACTURES		7.8		6.2		7.9		5.9	TABACS BRUTS FABRIQUES
2	CRUDE MATERLS,EXCL FUELS		81.8		67.4		95.2		100.3	MAT BRUTES NON COMESTIBLES
22	OIL SEEDS,OLEAGINOUS FRT		10.3		7.5		2.5		2.3	GRAINES,FRUITS OLEAGINEUX
223	SEEDS FOR OTH FIXED OILS	W 34155	9.2	W 24607	6.5	W 1652	0.7	W 2427	1.0	GRAINES AUTRES HUILES FIXES
2239	OIL SEED FLOUR AND MEAL	W 33886	9.0	W 24328	6.4	W 1448	0.5	W 2184	0.8	FARINES GRAINES OLEAG
24	CORK AND WOOD		11.6		6.2		13.4		12.9	LIEGE ET BOIS
248	WOOD SHAPED,SLEEPERS	W 41238	10.7	W 21509	5.8	W 42065	12.9	W 33565	12.1	BOIS SIMPLEMENT TRAVAILLES
2482	LUMBER SHAPED CONIFER	W 37941	9.3	W 17132	3.8	W 38444	10.9	W 30909	9.8	CONIFERES SCIES,RABOTES
24821	LUMBER SAWN ETC CONIFER	W 35833	8.2	W 16105	3.3	W 36135	9.9	W 28587	8.7	CONIFERES SCIES LONGITUD
251	*PULP AND WASTE PAPER	W 14144	5.8	W 16173	10.4	W 18400	8.2	W 19025	6.9	PATES A PAPIER,DECHETS
26	TEXTILE FIBRES AND WASTE		38.2		29.0		55.2		61.6	FIBRES TEXTILES
263	COTTON	W 16448	24.6	W 8466	15.3	W 21506	41.2	W 25756	45.9	COTON
2631	RAW COTTON,EXCL LINTERS	W 16111	24.5	W 7907	14.9	W 21110	41.0	W 25476	45.6	COTON EN MASSE
266	SYNTHETIC FIBRES TO SPIN	W 4979	7.3	W 5286	7.2	W 5524	9.3	W 6839	9.7	FIBRES SYNTHETIQUES
2665	DISCN SYNTH FIBRE UNCMBD	W 4896	7.1	W 4872	6.6	W 5076	8.3	W 6606	9.5	DISCONTINUES EN MASSE
27	CRUDE FERTLZR,MINRLS NES		7.3		6.6		7.8		8.2	ENGRAIS MINERAUX BRUTS
3	MINERAL FUELS ETC		215.4		243.3		325.4		336.7	COMBUSTIBLES MINERAUX LUB
33	PETROLEUM AND PRODUCTS		201.5		226.6		299.7		311.5	PETROLE ET DERIVES
333	CRUDE PETROLEUM	W 802905	112.1	W 402482	94.9	W 720862	121.6	W 789345	119.6	HUILES BRUTES DE PETROLE
334	PETROLEUM PRODUCTS,REFIN	W 419438	86.8		128.6	W 789808	175.2	W 861103	188.5	PRODUITS RAFFINES
3341	GASOLINE,OTH LIGHT OILS	W 60976	14.0	W 38457	19.2	W 161900	40.6	W 142730	39.4	ESSENCES POUR MOTEURS
3343	GAS OILS	W 334925	56.6							GAS OILS
3344	FUEL OILS,NES	W 272	0.4	W 470058	92.8	W 599570	114.0	W 683223	125.2	FUEL OILS
3345	LUBS,PETROLEUM OILS NES	W 15181	14.3	W 13479	15.8	W 28319	20.7	W 35150	24.0	HUILES LUBRIFIANTES
341	*GAS,NATURAL AND MANUFCT	W 57418	13.7		16.5	W 83198	25.0	W 82173	24.1	GAZ NATUREL,GAZ MANUFACT
3413	PETROLM GASES,LIQUEFIED	W 57410	13.7	W 52475	16.5	W 82891	24.9	W 82113	24.1	GAZ DE PETROLE LIQUEFIE
4	ANIMAL,VEGETABLE OIL,FAT		59.6		74.4		76.2		76.9	HUILES,GRAISSES ANIM,VEG
411	*ANIMAL OILS AND FATS	W 55799	23.2	W 45287	27.1	W 44991	22.9	W 35495	18.6	HUILES,GRAISSES ANIMALES
4113	ANIML OIL,FAT,GREASE NES	W 55778	23.1	W 45260	27.1	W 42871	21.9	W 35479	18.6	HUILES,GRAISSES ANIMALES NDA
41132	FATS OF BOVINE,SHEEP,ETC	W 55767	23.1	W 45219	27.0	W 42825	21.8	W 35450	18.5	SUIFS BRUTS FONDUS
42	FIXED VEGETABLE OIL,FAT		32.6		44.2		47.6		50.8	HUILES VEGETALES FIXES
423	FIXED VEG OILS,SOFT	W 33347	22.6	W 41773	32.7	W 44509	32.4	W 45591	31.7	HUILES VEGET DOUCES FIXES
4233	COTTON SEED OIL	W 29701	19.5	W 36941	28.2	W 39307	28.0	W 30927	21.0	HUILE DE COTON
424	FIXED VEG OIL NONSOFT	W 19643	10.1	W 13868	11.6	W 22425	15.2	W 30080	19.2	AUTRES HUILES VEG FIXES
4242	PALM OIL	W 18907	9.5	W 12986	10.6	W 20871	13.7	W 27775	17.1	HUILE DE PALME
5	CHEMCLS,RELATED PROD NES		373.1		441.5		455.4		503.4	PRODUITS CHIMIQUES
51	ORGANIC CHEMICALS		32.3		41.7		42.6		48.3	PROD CHIMIQ ORGANIQUES
511	HYDROCARBONS NES,DERIVS	W 5318	3.5	W 7379	5.3	W 8761	8.3	W 10550	9.2	HYDROCARBURES NDA
512	ALCOHOLS,PHENOLS ETC	W 13533	6.3		6.1	W 22995	9.2	W 16566	8.4	PHENOLS,PHENOLS-ALCOOLS
5121	ACYCLIC ALCOHOLS,DERIVS	W 13285	5.7		5.7	W 22630	8.6	W 15866	7.3	ALCOOLS ACYCLIQUES
514	NITROGEN-FNCTN COMPOUNDS	W 1466	4.0		7.2	W 1967	8.4	W 2755	10.4	COMPOSES FONCT AZOTEES
515	ORG-INORG COMPOUNDS ETC	W 952	6.6	W 1249	9.3	W 754	5.7	W 1078	6.8	COMPOSES ORGANO-MINERAUX
52	INORGANIC CHEMICALS		20.9		25.6		27.7		29.6	PROD CHIM INORGANIQUES
522	INORG ELEMNTS,OXIDES,ETC	W 22761	7.9		9.2	W 15954	7.0	W 18018	7.9	ELEMENTS INORGANIQUES
523	OTHR INORG CHEMICALS ETC	W 30816	13.1	W 33956	16.2	W 47074	20.6	W 55286	21.7	AUT PRODUITS CHIMIQUES INORG
5232	OTH MTL CMPD OF INRG ACD	W 18495	8.1	W 20177	10.3	W 26888	13.2	W 24731	12.2	SELS METALLIQUES
52322	PHOSPHITES,PHOSPHATES	W 8506	5.4	W 10609	7.6	W 12347	8.6	W 10166	7.3	PHOSPHITES,PHOSPHATES
53	DYES,TANNING,COLOUR PROD		23.2		24.6		27.1		29.8	PROD TEINTURE,COLORANTS
531	SYNT DYE,NAT INDGO,LAKES	W 1006	9.1	W 1454	8.0	W 1025	8.9	W 1661	10.4	MAT COLOR ORGAN,LAQUES
5311	SYNTHIC ORGNIC DYESTUFFS	W 617	7.4	W 895	6.2	W 711	7.1	W 1127	7.9	MAT COLOR ORGAN SYNTHET
533	PIGMENTS,PAINTS,ETC	W 5580	13.1		15.5	W 8589	16.6	W 10281	18.0	PIGMENTS,PEINTURES,VERNIS
5334	VARNISHES,DISTEMPERS ETC	W 3551	5.8	W 5433	8.0	W 6725	9.3	W 7877	10.9	PEINTURES A L'EAU
541	*MEDICINAL,PHARM PRODUCT	K 4169557	97.1	MK 11865	110.8	K 4882220	109.7	K 5874032	115.2	PROD MEDICINAUX PHARMACEUT
5413	ANTIBIOTICS IN BULK	K 77303	5.5	K 126039	8.1	K 103636	6.0	K 135628	7.9	ANTIBIOTIQUES NDA
5417	MEDICAMENTS	K 3344969	79.6	MK 10429	88.8	K 3614222	89.9	K 4093287	90.8	MEDICAMENTS
55	PERFUME,CLEANING ETC PRD		53.5		70.0		70.6		80.3	PROD POUR PARFUM,TOILETTE
551	ESSENTL OILS,PERFUME,ETC	W 673	7.2	W 687	9.0	W 564	8.1	W 749	9.6	HUILES ESSENTIELLES
5514	MIXED PERFUME SUBSTANCES	W 581	6.1	W 616	8.0	W 495	7.3	W 539	8.3	MELANGES SUBSTAN ODORIFER
553	PERFUMERY,COSMETICS,ETC	W 4565	23.5	W 9452	30.6	W 6007	29.5	W 7634	32.8	PRODUITS DE PARFUMERIE
554	SOAP,CLEANSING ETC PREPS	W 25279	22.9	W 28904	30.5	W 32451	33.1	W 36336	38.1	SAVONS,PRODUITS DETERSIFS
5541	SOAPS	W 18672	13.9	W 19829	18.6	W 25058	22.2	W 25585	23.3	SAVONS,PROD TENSIO-ACTIFS
5542	WASHING PREPARATIONS ETC	W 6026	7.6	W 8231	10.0	W 6663	9.0	W 9790	12.5	PROD ORG TENSIO-ACT NDA
562	*FERTILIZERS,MANUFACTURE	W 290072	36.6	W 264981	32.6	W 276891	51.4	W 374806	57.9	ENGRAIS MANUFACTURES
5621	CHEM NITROGENOUS FERTLZR	W 235815	27.5	W 188965	26.1	W 207994	36.1	W 284520	38.4	ENGRAIS AZOTES
56213	AMMONIUM SULPHATE	W 191930	21.4	W 120835	13.0	W 162484	25.3	W 223158	26.5	SULFATE D'AMMONIUM

4. Special Imports C.I.F. by Commodities according to the S.I.T.C. (Rev. 2) in million U.S. Dollars
Importations Spéciales C.A.F. par Produits d'après la C.T.C.I. (Rév. 2) en millions de Dollars E.U.

SITC CTCI	COMMODITY	1994 QUANTITY QUANTITE	1994 VALUE VALEUR	1995 QUANTITY QUANTITE	1995 VALUE VALEUR	1996 QUANTITY QUANTITE	1996 VALUE VALEUR	1997 QUANTITY QUANTITE	1997 VALUE VALEUR	PRODUIT
56216	UREA	W 41091	5.7	W 58318	11.2	W 36748	8.9	W 52001	10.1	UREE
5629	FERTILIZERS NES	W 34883	6.8	W 54395	3.0	W 16321	6.2	W 49653	11.8	ENGRAIS NDA
58	PLASTIC MATERIALS ETC		73.8		93.3		85.2		95.3	MAT PLAST ARTIFICIELLES
582	PROD OF CONDENSATION ETC	W 4891	8.3	W 4152	8.7	W 5687	9.0	W 6016	10.8	PROD CONDENS,POLYCOND
583	POLYMERIZATION ETC PRODS	W 58604	61.7	W 58201	80.2	W 59949	71.8	W 67176	80.2	PROD POLYMERISATION
5831	POLYETHYLENE	W 25095	19.8	W 20842	22.6	W 22170	22.0	W 28067	30.4	POLYETHYLENE
5832	POLYPROPYLENE	W 5354	5.6	W 4423	6.8	W 5252	6.6	W 7782	9.4	POLYPROPYLENE
5834	POLYVINYL CHLORIDE	W 11607	11.6	W 13269	17.4	W 13710	13.3	W 15139	14.5	CHLORURE DE POLYVINYLE
5839	OTH POLYMRZTION ETC PROD	W 10758	16.5	W 14306	24.5	W 13715	21.7	W 8862	16.3	AUT PROD POLYMER COPOLYM
59	CHEMICAL MATERIALS NES		35.6		42.5		40.9		46.4	MAT PROD CHIMIQUES NDA
591	PESTICIDES,DISINFECTANTS	W 4491	14.3	W 8188	17.9	W 5907	17.0	W 6868	18.6	DESINF,INSECT,FONG,HERB
5911	INSECTICIDES,FOR RETAIL	W 3016	7.9	W 5362	7.9	W 3013	6.2	W 3521	8.6	INSECTICIDES VENTE DET
5913	HERBICIDES,FOR RETAIL	W 1031	4.6	W 1820	7.6	W 2237	8.7	W 2027	7.2	HERBICIDES VENTE AU DET
598	MISCEL CHEM PRODUCTS NES	W 9151	16.5	W 9180	17.6	W 10101	18.4	W 11915	21.8	PROD DIV INDUST CHIM NDA
5989	CHEM PRODUCTS,PREPS NES	W 7781	11.9	W 7905	13.2	W 8395	14.4	W 9946	17.4	PROD PREP CHIMIQUES NDA
59899	OTH CHEM PRODS,PREPS,NES	W 6042	9.0	W 6403	10.6	W 6758	11.4	W 7819	12.9	AUT PRODUITS CHIMIQUES NDA
6	BASIC MANUFACTURES		399.8		487.2		435.4		499.5	ART MANUFACTURES
61	LEATHER,DRESSED FUR,ETC		8.9		6.3		13.8		12.4	CUIRS,PELLETERIES
611	LEATHER	W 1016	6.9		4.6	W 2704	11.1	W 2809	10.0	CUIRS,PEAUX PREPARES
62	RUBBER MANUFACTURES NES		31.3		39.2		37.7		41.4	CAOUTCHOUC MANUFACTURE
625	RUBBER TYRES, TUBES ETC	W 9690	24.9	W 25435	30.5	W 12291	30.9	W 13911	32.3	PNEUS CAOUTCHOUC VULCANISE
6251	TYRES NEW FOR MOTOR CARS	W 2568	8.4	W 2079	9.1	W 2371	7.6	W 2179	7.4	PNEUS POUR VOITURES
6252	TYRES,NEW,BUS OR LORRY	W 2940	9.5	W 18803	13.2	W 4092	14.2	W 4549	15.1	PNEUS POUR AUTOBUS,CAMIONS
6259	OTH TYRES,TYRE CASES,ETC	W 3951	6.4	W 4417	7.6	W 5605	8.4	W 6872	9.1	AUTRES PNEUS RECHAPES FLAPS
63	WOOD,CORK MANUFACTRS NES		8.7		9.1		10.0		12.9	OUVRAGES LIEGE ET BOIS
64	PAPER,PAPERBOARD AND MFR		81.6		127.5		90.3		94.1	PAPIERS,CARTONS & OUVRAGES
641	PAPER AND PAPERBOARD	W 82661	67.5	W 106133	103.6	W 72576	68.4	W 84464	68.2	PAPIERS ET CARTONS
6411	NEWSPRINT	W 16215	10.7	W 19076	20.0	W 19854	15.7	W 17065	10.5	PAPIER JOURNAL
6412	PRINTG,WRITING PAPER NES	W 15227	15.1	W 18371	21.5	W 13021	14.0	W 16215	16.0	PAPIERS POUR L'IMPRESSION
64122	— COATED,IMPREGNATD ETC	W 13904	12.5	W 16718	18.5	W 10959	10.5	W 11615	11.0	PAPIERS IMPRESSION COUCHES
6413	KRAFT PAPER,PAPERBOARD	W 28700	16.7	W 47388	32.0	W 24092	16.5	W 31108	16.7	PAPIER ET CARTON KRAFT
6415	PAPER,PAPERBRD,BULK,NES	W 13068	12.5	W 10094	14.5	W 7681	9.5	W 11239	10.5	PAPIERS,CARTONS ROULEAUX
64159	OTHER PAPER ETC,BULK,NES	W 12700	11.7	W 9643	13.3	W 7288	8.6	W 10775	9.4	AUT PAPIER ROULEAUX FEUILLES
6418	COATED ETC PAPER NES BLK	W 5703	8.9	W 8553	12.5	W 5644	10.0	W 6599	11.9	PAP,CARTONS COUCHES,ENDUITS
642	PAPER,ETC,PRECUT,ARTS OF	W 7586	14.2	W 11559	24.0	W 11664	22.0	W 14395	25.9	PAP,CARTONS DECOUPES
6424	PAPER ETC CT TO SIZE NES	W 2769	5.2	W 4339	8.3	W 3605	6.0	W 4268	7.1	PAP,CARTONS DECOUPES
6428	PAPER ETC ARTICLES NES	W 1885	4.7	W 3027	6.8	W 3104	7.0	W 4724	10.1	OUVRAGES EN PATE A PAPIER
65	TEXTILE YARN,FABRICS,ETC		54.4		59.2		45.9		64.3	FILS,TISSUS,ARTICLES TEXTILE
651	TEXTILE YARN	W 5612	15.1		12.0	W 3558	10.9	W 6809	21.8	FILS TEXTILES
6514	SYN FIB YRN,BULK,MONOFIL	W 5134	13.5	W 3459	9.3	W 2890	8.4	W 4685	13.8	FILS CONT 85% FIB TEXT SYNTH
65142	— NONTXT ETC CONT PAMID	W 3622	8.4	W 3087	7.6	W 2058	5.9	W 2963	9.2	FILS NON TEX FI CON POLYAMID
652	COTTON FABRICS,WOVEN	W 2092	9.6		12.4	W 1870	9.5	W 1893	9.5	TISSUS DE COTON
6522	WOVEN COTTON BLEACHD,ETC	W 1806	8.3		11.3	W 1653	8.5	W 1778	8.9	TISSUS COTON BLANCHIS ETC
65224	BLCHED COTTON FABRIC NES	W 1394	5.9	W 1691	8.8	W 1236	6.4	W 1334	6.2	AUT TIS PLUS 85% COT BLANCHI
653	WOVN MAN–MADE FIB FABRIC	W 2194	12.0		13.9	W 2072	10.9	W 2623	15.3	TISSUS FIBRES SYNTH,ARTIF
657	SPECIAL TXTL FABRC,PRODS	W 2510	10.3		10.1	W 2047	7.5	W 2471	8.9	TISSUS SPECIAUX
66	NONMETAL MINERAL MFS NES		44.6		51.7		43.9		51.7	ART MIN NON METALLIQUES
661	LIME,CEMENT,BLDG PRODS	W 49139	6.3		10.9	W 64991	8.3	W 58250	7.3	CHAUX,CIMENTS MAT CONSTR
662	CLAY,REFRACTORY BLDG PRD	W 20259	9.1		9.5	W 16774	7.0	W 22051	9.7	MAT CONST REFRACTAIRES
6624	BRICKS ETC NONREFRACTORY	W 15599	7.2		7.5	W 14130	5.5	W 15871	7.3	BRIQUES ETC CERAM NON REFR
664	GLASS	W 9626	7.1	W 10646	8.8	W 9788	7.8	W 10408	8.2	VERRE
665	GLASSWARE	W 20798	16.0	W 18694	15.3	W 15672	12.8	W 23878	17.4	OUVRAGES EN VERRE
6651	BOTTLES ETC OF GLASS	W 18129	11.1	W 15957	9.9	W 13266	9.0	W 20816	12.2	RECIPIENTS EN VERRE
66511	GLASS BOTTLES ETC NONVAC	W 18128	11.1	W 15946	9.9	W 13265	9.0	W 20815	12.2	BONBONNES,BOUTEILLES,ETC
67	IRON AND STEEL		82.0		80.8		99.0		111.6	FER ET ACIER
672	IRON,STEEL PRIMARY FORMS	W 31975	10.4	W 23122	7.7	W 57681	17.9	W 70401	21.9	LINGOTS FER,ACIER
6724	IRN,STL INGOTS,LUMPS,ETC	W 18722	5.1	W 15943	4.3	W 43635	12.0	W 33952	9.1	FER,ACIER LINGOTS,MASSES
67244	OTHER ALLOY STEEL INGOTS	W 18069	4.7	W 9085	2.4	W 29489	8.3	W 2019	0.6	LINGOTS AUT ACIERS ALLIES
6727	IRN,STL COIL FR REROLLNG	W 10464	4.4	W 3981	2.2	W 11091	4.7	W 29788	10.4	EBAUCHES POUR TOLES FER
673	IRON,STEEL SHAPES ETC	W 69631	28.2	W 64592	30.2	W 54534	22.3	W 58618	24.5	BARRES,PROFIL FER,ACIER
6731	IRON,STEEL WIRE ROD	W 31056	10.9	W 23862	10.7	W 22446	7.6	W 29737	10.1	FIL MACHINE FER,ACIER
67311	IRON,SIMPLE STL WIRE ROD	W 30407	10.5	W 23688	10.1	W 21520	7.3	W 26332	9.0	FIL MACH AUT ACIER FIN
6732	IRON,STEEL BARS ETC	W 25852	11.2	W 26029	11.9	W 17877	7.5	W 12814	6.0	BARRES FER,ACIER
67326	IRN,OTH STL BARS HOTROLD	W 24226	9.8	W 23610	10.1	W 16891	6.6	W 10878	4.6	BARRES PLEINES FER,ACIER
674	IRN,STL UNIV,PLATE,SHEET	W 41719	25.3	W 29266	23.9	W 65817	39.0	W 57936	34.8	LARGES PLATS,TOLES
6746	IRN,STL THIN PLATE,ROLLD	W 16673	8.3	W 5606	4.4	W 34075	16.7	W 25490	11.5	TOLES LAM MOINS 3MM
67461	— OF IRON OR SIMPLE STL	W 15541	7.6	W 4573	3.5	W 33186	16.1	W 24066	10.6	TOL NON AC FIN MOINS 3 MM
6749	OTH IRN,STL PLATES,SHEET	W 17332	13.0	W 19154	16.0	W 18672	16.6	W 24297	19.4	AUTRES TOLES FER,ACIER
67491	— OF IRON OR SIMPLE STL	W 17149	12.8	W 18837	15.5	W 18617	16.5	W 23672	18.8	AUT TOLES AUTRES ACIER FIN
678	IRON,STL TUBES,PIPES,ETC	W 15777	12.4	W 15540	13.5	W 14090	15.0	W 25515	25.1	TUBES,TUYAUX EN FONTE,FER
6783	IRON,STL TUBES,PIPES NES	W 11940	8.2	W 13311	9.5	W 10490	8.0	W 14286	11.2	AUT TUBES,TUYAUX FER,ACIER
68	NON–FERROUS METALS		26.4		32.8		24.0		29.1	METAUX NON FERREUX
682	COPPER EXC CEMENT COPPER	W 3103	8.9	W 2344	8.8	W 2229	6.8	W 3490	10.2	CUIVRE
6822	COPPER,ALLOYS WORKED	W 3075	8.8	W 2292	8.6	W 2197	6.7	W 3432	10.0	CUIVRE,ALLIAGES OUVRES
68221	COPPER BARS,WIRE,ETC	W 2750	7.5	W 2110	7.3	W 2061	5.9	W 3148	8.6	BARRES,PROFILES ET FILS
684	ALUMINIUM	W 7257	16.0	W 7784	23.1	W 7832	16.3	W 7866	17.5	ALUMINIUM
6842	ALUMINIUM,ALLOYS WORKED	W 4343	11.0	W 5103	16.3	W 3663	12.1	W 3083	10.9	ALUMINIUM,ALLIAGES OUVRE
69	METAL MANUFACTURES NES		62.3		81.1		71.1		82.6	ART MANUFACT EN METAL NDA
691	STRUCTURES AND PARTS NES	W 2889	4.0	W 5299	6.4	W 5732	10.0	W 5936	10.6	CONSTRUCT FER,ACIER,ALU
6911	STRUCTURES,PARTS IRN,STL	W 2805	3.6	W 5112	5.5	W 5519	9.2	W 5762	9.9	CONSTRUCT FER,ACIER,FONTE
692	METAL TANKS,BOXES,ETC	W 3495	10.2	W 4766	14.4	W 4888	14.3	W 7212	18.3	RECIPIENTS METALLIQUES
6924	MTL TRANSPORT BOXES ETC	W 3382	10.0	W 4601	13.5	W 4480	13.4	W 6761	17.7	FUTS,TAMBOURS,BIDONS
69242	ALUMNM TRNSPRT BOXES ETC	W 993	4.6	W 1794	8.1	W 1238	6.6	W 1847	8.4	FUTS,TAMBOURS,BIDONS ALU
695	TOOLS	W 1283	7.0	W 1084	7.7	W 1089	6.5	W 1233	7.2	OUTILS A MAIN
697	BASE MTL HOUSEHOLD EQUIP	W 2915	10.8	W 5264	14.3	W 3194	10.5	W 4255	12.9	ART MENAGE MET COMMUNS
6973	DMSTC HEATG,COOKG APPARA	W 1993	7.1	W 2745	8.8	W 1829	5.8	W 2931	8.2	APPS CHAUF NON ELECTRIQ
699	BASE METAL MFRS NES	W 5730	17.1		22.7	W 4780	15.7	W 6561	20.5	ART MANUFACTURES MET NDA
7	MACHINES,TRANSPORT EQUIP		695.7		790.1		700.1		783.8	MACHINES MATERIEL TRANSPORT
71	POWER GENERATING EQUIPMT		55.7		34.3		58.1		44.0	MACHINES GENERATRICES
713	INTRNL COMBUS PSTN ENGIN	W 1944	10.5	W 2918	12.8	W 1789	14.1	W 2160	21.5	MOTEURS EXPL COMB INT, PIECE
714	ENGINES AND MOTORS NES	W 141	5.3	W 119	6.4	W 426	19.2	W 66	4.0	MOTEURS NON ELECTRIQUES
716	ROTATING ELECTRIC PLANT	W 903	37.0	W 739	8.6	W 601	5.9	W 1316	11.6	APP ELECTR ROTATIFS,PIECES
72	MACHS FOR SPCL INDUSTRYS		84.5		106.1		87.2		136.0	MAC SPECIALES POUR INDUST
723	CIVIL ENGNEERG EQUIP ETC	W 2022	9.9	W 2227	11.9	W 1288	8.7	W 7822	29.6	APPAREILS DE GENIE CIVIL
7234	CONST,MINING MACHNRY NES	W 1771	8.3	W 1926	9.5	W 1100	6.9	W 7010	23.3	MACH POUR LA CONST, MINES
724	TEXTILE,LEATHER MACHNRY	W 3514	34.2	W 3539	45.5	W 2206	24.7	W 3764	49.9	MACH POUR INDUSTRIE TEXTILE
7243	SEWING MACHS,NEEDLES ETC	W 1626	16.4	W 1726	20.5	W 1107	10.8	W 1426	19.9	MACHINES A COUDRE,PIECES
7244	SPINNING,EXTRDNG,ETC MCH	W 893	8.2	W 801	10.0	W 400	5.3	W 1258	11.5	MACH POUR LE FILAGE
7247	TEXTILE MACHINERY NES	W 317	3.1	W 404	4.6	W 219	2.3	W 611	9.3	MACH LAVAGE,TEINTURE TEX
726	PRINTG,BKBINDG MACHY,PTS	W 955	11.4		13.8	W 565	6.6	W 759	12.4	MACHINES POUR IMPRIMERIE
727	FOOD MACHRY NON–DOMESTIC	W 1202	5.1	W 813	8.2	W 1031	21.2	W 1011	11.0	MACH INDUSTRIES ALIMENT

4. Special Imports C.I.F. by Commodities according to the S.I.T.C. (Rev. 2) in million U.S. Dollars
Importations Spéciales C.A.F. par Produits d'après la C.T.C.I. (Rév. 2) en millions de Dollars E.U.

SITC CTCI	COMMODITY	1994 QUANTITY QUANTITE	1994 VALUE VALEUR	1995 QUANTITY QUANTITE	1995 VALUE VALEUR	1996 QUANTITY QUANTITE	1996 VALUE VALEUR	1997 QUANTITY QUANTITE	1997 VALUE VALEUR	PRODUIT
7272	OTH FOOD PROC MCHY,PARTS	W 1141	4.6	W 772	7.5	W 952	20.6	W 789	6.4	AUT MACH IND ALIMENTAIRE
72722	INDUS FOOD PROC MACH NES	W 1080	3.4	W 545	6.1	W 767	18.0	W 734	5.7	MACHINES BOULANGERIE
728	OTH MACHY FOR SPCL INDUS	W 1761	13.4		16.5	W 1897	18.5	W 2224	18.3	AUT MACH IND PARTICULIERES
7284	MACHY FOR SPCL INDUS NES	W 726	7.5		12.3	W 1204	13.5	W 1034	12.3	MACH SPEC IND PARTICUL.
73	METALWORKING MACHINERY		7.0		6.8		10.0		8.0	MACH TRAVAIL DES METAUX
736	METALWORKING MACH–TOOLS	W 1004	4.5	W 568	4.7	W 1114	8.2	W 991	6.4	MACH–OUTILS TRAVAIL METAUX
74	GENRL INDUSTRL MACHY NES		71.2		92.4		85.2		114.7	MACH APP INDUSTRIE
741	HEATING,COOLING EQUIPMNT	W 2577	20.2	W 2970	25.7	W 3049	20.9	W 4507	24.5	MACH CHAUFFAGE,PIECES
7414	NONDOM REFRIG EQUIPT,PTS	W 1266	8.6	W 1535	11.0	W 1551	9.8	W 3127	12.2	MAT PRODUCTION DU FROID
7415	AIR–CONDITIONING MACHNRY	W 930	6.9	W 883	6.6	W 986	6.5	W 915	6.8	GROUPES CONDITION AIR
742	PUMPS FOR LIQUIDS ETC	W 1006	7.4	W 720	9.1	W 894	10.8	W 817	10.1	POMPES MOTO–POMPES
743	PUMPS NES,CENTRFUGES ETC	W 2311	13.7	W 2812	16.2	W 2654	16.2	W 2959	17.9	POMPES COMPRES,VENT ETC
7431	PUMPS FOR GASES ETC	W 1371	6.9	W 1414	7.7	W 1423	7.0	W 1272	7.1	POMPES AIR A VIDE,COMPRES
744	MECHANICAL HANDLING EQU	W 1259	7.9	W 2035	11.2	W 1855	11.6	W 2959	14.9	EQUIP MANUTENTION PIECES
745	NONELEC MACHY,TOOLS NES	W 475	6.4	W 616	9.9	W 733	8.9	W 1614	22.5	AUT MACH NON ELEC,PIECES
7452	OTH NONELEC MCHS,PTS NES	W 452	6.0	W 594	9.3	W 711	8.5	W 1585	22.0	AUT MACH NON ELEC,PIECES
74522	PACKAGNG,BOTTLNG,ETC MCH	W 167	2.3	W 142	4.1	W 144	3.7	W 890	15.7	MACH NETT BOUTEILLES,ETC
749	NONELEC MACH PTS,ACC NES	W 1496	15.9	W 1311	20.6	W 1396	17.0	W 1860	24.9	PIECES MACH NON ELEC NDA
7492	COCKS,VALVES ETC NES	W 636	5.4	W 578	6.7	W 702	6.4	W 949	9.3	ART ROB,SIM POUR TUYAUX
7499	OTH NONELEC MCHY PTS NES	W 397	5.6	W 422	8.4	W 342	5.2	W 402	8.9	PIECES NON ELECT NDA
75	OFFICE MACHNES,ADP EQUIP		45.4		55.2		57.7		76.5	MACH BUREAU TRAIT AUTOM
751	OFFICE MACHINES	W 456	7.3	W 467	9.1	W 627	10.3	W 591	10.4	MACH,APPAREILS DE BUREAU
752	AUTOMTIC DATA PROC EQUIP	W 395	19.9	W 453	20.6	W 341	20.4	W 498	23.3	MACH TRAIT INFORMATION
759	OFFICE,ADP MCH PTS,ACCES	W 465	18.3	W 476	25.7	W 677	27.0	W 941	42.9	PIECES DU 751 ET 752
7599	ACCTG,ETC,ADP MCH PTS,AC	W 397	16.5	W 427	23.7	W 613	24.9	W 868	40.7	PIECES DU 751 ET 752
76	TELECOMM,SOUND EQUIPMENT		68.2		73.9		68.5		67.2	EQUIPMENT DE TELECOM
761	TELEVISION RECEIVERS	W 1241	10.6	W 1339	15.3	W 1463	13.1	W 2065	17.3	RECEPTEURS DE TELEVISION
762	RADIO BROADCAST RECEIVRS	W 757	7.2	W 932	11.8	W 929	8.4	W 1062	10.8	RECEPTEURS RADIODIFFUSION
764	TELECOM EQPT,PTS,ACC NES	W 1127	47.7	W 1272	43.2	W 2142	43.6	W 1124	35.3	EQUIP TELECOM,PIECES
7641	LINE TELEPHONE,ETC EQUIP	W 317	18.4	W 493	25.6	W 1353	17.8	W 285	14.5	APP TELEPHON PAR FIL
7649	PTS NES OF EQUIPMT OF 76	W 450	22.0	W 412	9.4	W 361	16.0	W 236	5.0	PIECES DE LA DIV 76
76491	PTS NES OF APPAR OF 7641	W 246	19.3	W 64	4.7	W 182	13.7	W 44	2.5	PIECES POUR 764.1
77	ELECTRIC MACHNRY NES ETC		82.0		94.3		94.1		97.4	MACH APP ELECT NDA
771	ELECTRIC POWER MACHY NES	W 1964	8.9	W 2656	9.1	W 2746	13.0	W 1951	9.8	MACH PROD,TRANS ELECTR
7711	TRANSFORMERS,ELECTRICAL	W 1447	6.3	W 2305	6.8	W 2305	10.1	W 1505	6.7	TRANSFO ELECTRIQUES
772	SWITCHGEAR ETC,PARTS NES	W 1008	12.1	W 1818	20.1	W 1261	15.0	W 1214	15.2	APP COUPURE,SECT ETC
7721	SWITCHGEAR ETC	W 1003	11.8	W 1813	18.5	W 1255	14.6	W 1209	14.7	APP COUPURE,SECTIONMNT
773	ELECTR DISTRIBUTNG EQUIP	W 1549	6.8	W 1430	7.6	W 3010	11.5	W 3568	13.7	EQUIPMT DISTRIBUTION ELECT
7731	INSULATED WIRE,CABLE ETC	W 1358	6.3	W 1099	6.9	W 2568	10.7	W 3091	12.3	FILS,CABLES ISOLES ELECT
774	ELECTRO–MEDCL,XRAY EQUIP	W 257	11.2	W 120	4.6	W 143	8.1	W 92	4.1	APPAREILS MEDICAUX
7741	ELECTRO–MEDICAL EQUIPMNT	W 196	7.8	W 63	2.8	W 80	3.4	W 52	3.2	APP ELECTRICITE MEDICALE
775	HOUSEHOLD TYPE EQUIP NES	W 3574	16.6		21.1	W 3401	16.1	W 4753	22.0	MACH,APP USAGE DOMESTQUE
7752	DOM REFRIGERATRS,FREEZRS	W 1921	8.5	W 1834	9.1	W 1213	6.1	W 1995	9.6	REFRIG,CONGEL MENAGER
778	ELECTRICAL MACHINERY NES	W 6868	25.5		30.3	W 6909	28.6	W 7928	30.7	AUTRES MACH ELECT NDA
7781	BATTERIES,ACCUMULATORS	W 4864	10.7	W 6500	11.6	W 5026	11.2	W 5932	13.4	PILES ET ACCUMULATEURS
77811	PRIMARY BATTERIES,CELLS	W 3182	7.5	W 4007	8.1	W 2920	7.3	W 2927	8.0	PILES ELECTRIQUES,PIECES
78	ROAD VEHICLES		279.5		322.9		237.2		234.6	VEHICULES ROUTIERS
781	PASS MOTOR VEH EXC BUSES	W 15580	96.4	W 21215	120.9	W 18510	79.0	W 17428	78.5	AUTO TRANSPORT PERSONNES
782	LORRIES,SPCL MTR VEH NES	W 31623	108.4	W 36861	122.2	W 35648	96.4	W 35705	90.0	VEHICULES SPECIAUX,MARCH
7821	LORRIES,TRUCKS	W 31064	106.3	W 36144	120.0	W 34426	89.0	W 34912	86.0	VEHICULES TRANSP MARCHAND
783	ROAD MOTOR VEHICLES NES	W 11354	33.7	W 16902	39.9	W 11621	26.5	W 14053	34.0	VEHICULES ROUTIERS NDA
7831	BUSES	W 7667	28.1	W 9436	34.7	W 8039	21.9	W 8953	26.8	VOITURES TRANSPORT COMMUN
784	MOTOR VEH PRTS,ACCES NES	W 3416	29.7	W 2396	29.2	W 3189	23.7	W 3304	21.9	PIECES 722,781,782,783
7849	OTHER MOTOR VEHCL PARTS	W 3194	29.1	W 2286	28.5	W 2969	22.2	W 3169	21.4	PIECES 722,781,782,783
785	CYCLES,ETC MOTRZD OR NOT	W 2256	9.0	W 3884	8.4	W 1836	8.2	W 1789	7.3	MOTOCYCLES SCOOTERS
8	MISC MANUFACTURED GOODS		163.5		214.8		204.8		237.0	ART MANUFACTURES DIVERS
812	*PLUMBG,HEATNG,LGHTNG EQ	W 2706	8.5	W 4822	9.1	W 2822	9.4	W 3228	9.3	APPAR SANITAIRES CHAUFFAGE
821	*FURNITURE,PARTS THEREOF	W 9349	14.9	W 7050	17.1	W 5037	15.2	W 8030	23.8	MEUBLES ET PIECES
8219	FURNITURE AND PARTS NES	W 3872	11.5	W 5738	12.9	W 3618	11.3	W 6336	18.2	AUTRES MEUBLES ET PIECES
84	CLOTHING AND ACCESSORIES		19.4		30.3		24.8		30.1	VETEMENTS
851	*FOOTWEAR	W 2713	13.7	W 3738	19.5	W 3840	19.7	W 4559	24.0	CHAUSSURES
85101	FOOTWEAR RUBBER,PLASTIC	W 1262	4.9	W 1926	7.6	W 2087	8.3	W 2679	10.7	CHAUS SEMELLES CAOUTCH
85102	FOOTWEAR LEATHER	W 1283	7.5	W 1505	10.4	W 1419	9.2	W 1546	10.9	CHAUS SEMELLES EN CUIR
87	PRECISION INSTRUMNTS NES		22.6		24.8		25.1		25.4	INSTRUM,APPAR SCIENT NDA
872	MEDICAL INSTRUMENTS NES	W 532	6.9	W 1752	8.8	W 597	9.1	W 469	8.6	INSTR,APP MEDIC–CHIR NDA
87202	OTH MEDICAL INSTRUMENTS	W 517	6.3	W 986	7.3	W 575	8.1	W 434	7.5	INSTRUM,APP MEDECINE
874	MEASURNG,CONTROLNG INSTR	W 528	11.3	W 380	12.4	W 424	11.7	W 531	12.8	INSTRUMENTS DE MESURE
88	PHOTO EQU,OPTICL GDS ETC		11.9		17.2		14.5		14.5	APP,FOURN PHOTO,OP,MONTR
882	PHOTO,CINEMA SUPPLIES	W 549	6.7	W 672	9.9	W 763	8.9	W 598	8.1	PRODUITS PHOTO,CINEMA
8822	PHOTO FILM EXC DEV CINMA	W 316	5.7	W 365	8.1	W 336	7.6	W 364	6.9	PLAQUES,PELLICULES,FILMS
89	MISC MANUFCTRD GOODS NES		71.3		94.2		94.0		107.8	ART MANUFACTURES DIVERS
892	PRINTED MATTER	W 3179	12.6	W 2653	16.7	W 3587	22.6	W 3092	20.5	IMPRIMES
8921	PRINTED BOOKS,GLOBES,ETC	W 2500	8.2	W 1548	10.2	W 2193	15.0	W 2051	13.7	LIVRES,BROCHURES,CARTES
89211	PRINTED BOOKS,PAMPHLETS	W 2120	7.9	W 1502	10.0	W 2017	14.6	W 1920	13.3	LIVRES,BROCHURES
893	ARTICLES OF PLASTIC NES		24.5		30.7		30.3		36.8	OUVRAGES EN MAT DIVIS 58
8931	PLSTC PACKG CONTNRS,LIDS	W 3696	7.5	W 4435	10.3	W 3463	11.0	W 4178	13.8	ART TRANSP EMBALLAGE ETC
8939	MISC PLASTIC ARTICLES	W 5050	16.5	W 20359	19.7	W 6652	18.6	W 7193	22.4	ART DIVERS EN MAT DIV 58
89399	OTHR PLASTC ARTICLES NES	W 4708	15.9	W 20210	19.2	W 6482	18.0	W 6922	21.5	AUT OUV MAT DIV 58
894	TOYS,SPORTING GOODS,ETC	W 2513	11.0	W 10447	17.6	W 2741	12.6	W 3871	17.1	VOITURES ENFANTS,JOUETS
8942	TOYS,INDOOR GAMES ETC	W 2124	8.4	W 10067	13.2	W 2202	9.3	W 3123	12.0	JOUETS,JEUX ETC
89423	TOYS NES	W 1235	4.8	W 8898	8.2	W 1299	5.9	W 1906	7.1	JOUETS,MODELES REDUITS
895	OFFICE SUPPLIES NES	W 2008	6.9	W 1240	9.6	W 1126	10.0	W 1449	12.0	ART PAPET NDA
898	MUSICAL INSTRUMENTS,PTS	W 402	6.8		8.1	W 677	7.7	W 522	8.0	INSTRUMENTS DE MUSIQUE
899	OTHER MANUFACTURED GOODS		7.8		9.9		9.1		11.8	AUT ART MANUF DIVERS NDA

5. Special Exports F.O.B. by Commodities according to the S.I.T.C. (Rev. 2) in million U.S. Dollars
Exportations Spéciales F.O.B. par Produits d'après la C.T.C.I. (Rév. 2) en millions de Dollars E.U.

SITC CTCI	COMMODITY	1994		1995		1996		1997		PRODUIT
		QUANTITY QUANTITE	VALUE VALEUR	QUANTITY QUANTITE	VALUE VALEUR	QUANTITY QUANTITE	VALUE VALEUR	QUANTITY QUANTITE	VALUE VALEUR	
	ALL COMMODITIES		812.8		985.3		1024.3		1354.0	TOUS PRODUITS
0	FOOD AND LIVE ANIMALS		399.1		540.5		509.1		715.5	ALIMENTS,ANIMAUX VIVANTS
001	*LIVE ANIMALS FOR FOOD	W 972	4.3	W 864	3.7	W 806	3.8	W 903	4.4	ANIMAUX VIVANTS
0014	LIVE POULTRY	W 928	4.2	W 841	3.7	W 792	3.8	W 893	4.4	VOLAILLES VIVANTES
00141	LIVE PLTRY 185 GR OR LES	W 529	3.5	W 541	3.3	W 614	3.6	W 606	4.0	VOL VIVANTES MOINS 185 GR.
02	DAIRY PRODCTS,BIRDS'EGGS		1.9		3.6		5.1		7.6	PRODUITS LAITIERS,OEUFS
025	EGGS,BIRDS,FRESH,PRSRVD	W 2202	1.8	W 4416	3.4	W 5465	4.8	W 7254	6.5	OEUFS
0251	— IN SHELL	W 2184	1.8	W 4416	3.4	W 5465	4.8	W 7156	6.4	OEUFS EN COQUILLE
03	FISH AND PREPARATIONS		31.3		30.3		43.7		34.2	POISSONS ET PREPARATIONS
034	FISH,FRESH,CHILLED,FROZN	W 1430	4.5		1.4	W 309	0.9	W 171	0.6	POISSON FRAIS, REFRIG,CONG
0341	FISH FRSH,CHLLD,EX FILLT	W 1318	3.9	W 466	1.4	W 279	0.8	W 121	0.4	POISSON FRAIS,REFRIGERE
036	SHELL FISH FRESH,FROZEN	W 3725	25.1	W 4367	27.5	W 5615	40.9	W 3559	31.6	CRUSTACES,MOLLUSQUES
04	CEREALS AND PREPARATIONS		17.2		34.8		19.6		23.8	CEREALES ET PRODUITS
044	MAIZE UNMILLED	W 471	0.2	W 15678	3.0	W 3068	0.7	W 1559	0.4	MAIS NON MOULU
048	CEREAL ETC PREPARATIONS	W 13993	15.8	W 29755	31.1	W 14389	17.6	W 18402	21.9	PREPTNS A BASE CEREALES
0481	PREPD BREAKFAST FOOD ETC	W 6471	9.1	W 23084	25.1	W 7414	10.5	W 8604	12.2	CEREALES TRAVAILLEES
04811	CEREAL FLAKED,ROLLED,ETC	W 23	0.1	W 16784	16.4	W 10	0.1	W 6	0.1	GRAINS GERMES DE CEREALES
04812	CEREAL ROASTED, PUFFED	W 6448	9.0	W 6300	8.8	W 7404	10.4	W 8598	12.2	PRODTS BASE CEREALES
0484	BAKERY PRODUCTS	W 5068	5.3	W 4132	4.5	W 4822	5.7	W 6501	7.7	PRODUITS DE BOULANGERIE
04842	PASTRY, CAKES ETC	W 3764	4.5	W 2351	3.3	W 2656	3.9	W 3041	4.5	PATISSERIE ETC.
05	VEGETABLES AND FRUIT		7.7		9.2		9.7		9.2	LEGUMES ET FRUITS
054	VEG ETC FRSH,SMPLY PRSVD	W 4480	3.4	W 5287	3.5	W 7004	4.4	W 4827	4.5	LEGUMES FRAIS,CONG,SECS
057	FRUIT,NUTS,FRESH,DRIED	W 7866	3.1		3.8	W 7695	3.3	W 5845	2.3	FRUITS FRAIS OU SECS
06	SUGAR AND PREPS,HONEY		44.1		49.9		53.1		74.8	SUCRES ET PRODUITS
061	SUGAR AND HONEY	W 162303	35.9		43.4	W 176532	45.7	W 276033	68.0	SUCRES ET MIEL
0611	RAW BEET AND CANE SUGAR	W 101911	27.7	W 49831	36.3	W 81382	31.6	W 163792	52.9	SUCRES BRUTS
0612	REFINED SUGAR ETC	W 10073	2.9	W 1825	0.7	W 16241	5.2	W 10224	3.1	SUCRES RAFFINES
0615	MOLASSES	W 48229	3.5	W 42442	3.4	W 77140	5.8	W 99861	8.2	MELASSES
0616	NATURAL HONEY	W 2078	2.0	W 2573	3.1	W 1756	3.3	W 2154	4.0	MIEL NATUREL
062	SUGAR CANDY NON-CHOCLATE	W 7506	8.2	W 5701	6.5	W 6107	7.5	W 5409	6.8	SUCRERIES
07	COFFEE,TEA,COCOA,SPICES		268.8		396.3		341.9		519.8	CAFE,THE,CACAO,EPICES
071	COFFEE AND SUBSTITUTES	W 121095	267.8	W 113628	373.1	W 138370	340.0	W 165795	517.5	CAFE ET SUCCEDANES
0711	COFFEE GREEN,ROASTED,SUB	W 119068	264.0	W 113393	371.8	W 138186	339.1	W 165620	515.9	CAFE TORREFIE OU DECAFEINE
0712	COFFEE EXTRACTS,ESSENCES	W 2027	3.9	W 235	1.3	W 184	0.9	W 175	1.7	EXTRAITS DE CAFE
072	COCOA	W 138	0.2		22.4	W 503	0.7	W 360	0.5	CACAO
0721	COCOA BEANS,RAW,ROASTED	W 23	0.1		22.0	W 3	0.1	W 1	0.1	CACAO EN FEVES
081	*FEEDING STUFF FOR ANIML	W 13200	3.6		2.4	W 11916	2.2	W 9508	1.8	NOURRITURE POUR ANIMAUX
0819	FOOD WASTE AND FEED NES	W 12534	2.9	W 13657	2.4	W 9782	1.6	W 8814	1.6	DECHETS,ALIMENTS NDA
08199	FODDER NES,INCL SWEETNED	W 12279	2.8	W 13294	2.3	W 9469	1.6	W 8532	1.6	PREPARATIONS FOURRAGERES
09	MISC EDIBLE PRODUCTS		20.4		9.2		28.4		36.8	PREP ALIMENTAIRES DIVERSES
098	EDIBLE PRODCTS,PREPS NES	W 17493	20.0		7.9	W 24728	27.7	W 28490	33.2	PREP ALIMENTAIRES NDA
09809	MISC FOOD PREPRTIONS NES	W 15227	16.5	W 2640	3.5	W 22490	23.4	W 26313	27.9	PREP ALIMENTAIRES NDA
1	BEVERAGES AND TOBACCO		8.4		10.5		14.0		16.2	BOISSONS ET TABACS
11	BEVERAGES		7.1		6.8		9.2		11.7	BOISSONS
111	NON-ALCOHL BEVERAGES NES	W 11403	6.0		5.4	W 16318	7.8	W 21867	10.4	BOISSONS NON ALCOOLIQUES
11102	FLAVORED WATERS NON-ALCO	W 11332	6.0	W 11871	5.4	W 16316	7.8	W 21867	10.4	LIMONADES,EAUX GAZEUSES
12	TOBACCO AND MANUFACTURES		1.4		3.8		4.8		4.5	TABACS BRUTS FABRIQUES
122	TOBACCO,MANUFACTURED	W 119	0.8	W 599	3.2	W 820	4.6	W 511	3.0	TABACS FABRIQUES
1222	CIGARETTES	W 115	0.7	W 597	3.2	W 820	4.6	W 511	3.0	CIGARETTES
2	CRUDE MATERLS,EXCL FUELS		13.5		18.1		17.6		19.9	MAT BRUTES NON COMESTIBLES
22	OIL SEEDS,OLEAGINOUS FRT		5.6		5.3		6.6		5.9	GRAINES,FRUITS OLEAGINEUX
222	SEEDS FOR'SOFT'FIXED OIL	W 5236	5.1	W 4476	5.0	W 5935	6.4	W 7605	5.6	GRAINES HUILES FIXES
2225	SESAME SEEDS	W 4372	4.8	W 4474	5.0	W 5703	6.3	W 7206	5.2	GRAINES DE SESAME
26	TEXTILE FIBRES AND WASTE		4.0		7.4		3.0		3.3	FIBRES TEXTILES
263	COTTON	W 1628	3.6	W 3196	7.2	W 1151	2.5	W 1610	2.8	COTON
2631	RAW COTTON,EXCL LINTERS	W 450	0.7	W 1365	3.2	W 11	0.1	W 64	0.2	COTON EN MASSE
2634	COTTON,CARDED OR COMBED	W 986	2.8	W 1347	3.6	W 741	2.1	W 648	1.9	COTON CARDE OU PEIGNE
29	CRUDE ANIMAL,VEG MAT NES		2.8		3.6		4.4		5.2	MATIERES BRUTES ANIM,VEGET
292	CRUDE VEG MATERIALS NES	W 1735	2.5		3.3	W 2412	4.2	W 2729	4.9	MAT BRUTES VEGETALES NDA
3	MINERAL FUELS ETC		4.5		0.7		33.2		44.5	COMBUSTIBLES MINERAUX LUB
33	PETROLEUM AND PRODUCTS		4.5		0.7		33.2		44.4	PETROLE ET DERIVES
334	PETROLEUM PRODUCTS,REFIN	W 17092	4.4	W 2357	0.6	W 157619	33.1	W 241072	44.3	PRODUITS RAFFINES
3342	KEROSENE,OTH MEDIUM OILS	W 16468	3.9			W 29303	7.9	W 23066	7.5	PETR LAMPANTS,AUT HUIL
3344	FUEL OILS,NES			W 1677	0.2	W 106115	12.0	W 191663	22.5	FUEL OILS
3345	LUBS,PETROLEUM OILS NES	W 454	0.4	W 613	0.5	W 15429	11.3	W 25873	14.2	HUILES LUBRIFIANTES
4	ANIMAL,VEGETABLE OIL,FAT		3.4		5.4		6.5		8.0	HUILES,GRAISSES ANIM,VEG
42	FIXED VEGETABLE OIL,FAT		1.7		4.7		5.1		4.5	HUILES VEGETALES FIXES
423	FIXED VEG OILS,SOFT	W 1316	1.4	W 3985	4.0	W 4620	4.5	W 3569	3.7	HUILES VEGET DOUCES FIXES
4233	COTTON SEED OIL	W 1056	1.0	W 3336	3.1	W 4082	3.6	W 2823	2.5	HUILE DE COTON
5	CHEMCLS,RELATED PROD NES		97.5		110.7		141.2		166.5	PRODUITS CHIMIQUES
51	ORGANIC CHEMICALS		6.4		3.2		7.7		6.6	PROD CHIMIQ ORGANIQUES
512	ALCOHOLS,PHENOLS ETC	W 17928	6.2	W 8882	3.1	W 20304	7.4	W 15378	5.9	PHENOLS,PHENOLS-ALCOOLS
5121	ACYCLIC ALCOHOLS,DERIVS	W 17908	6.2	W 8882	3.1	W 20276	7.4	W 15378	5.9	ALCOOLS ACYCLIQUES
51216	ETHYL ALC,DENATRD SPIRIT	W 17842	6.1	W 8860	3.1	W 20236	7.3	W 15205	5.8	ALCOOL ETHYLIQUE NON DENAT
53	DYES,TANNING,COLOUR PROD		5.8		7.2		9.1		8.6	PROD TEINTURE,COLORANTS
533	PIGMENTS,PAINTS,ETC	W 4562	5.5	W 4681	6.9	W 5958	8.9	W 5715	8.0	PIGMENTS,PEINTURES,VERNIS
5334	VARNISHES,DISTEMPERS ETC	W 1169	2.1	W 891	2.3	W 5574	7.8	W 5262	6.9	PEINTURES A L'EAU
53341	WATER-THINNED PAINTS	W 579	0.6	W 292	0.4	W 4566	5.2	W 3100	2.8	PEINTURES DILUEES
53342	OTH PAINTS,VARNISHES ETC	W 563	1.5	W 571	1.9	W 1007	2.6	W 2159	4.1	AUTRES PEINTURES,VERNIS
5335	GLAZES,DRIERS,PUTTY ETC	W 3367	3.4	W 3673	4.1	W 240	0.5	W 347	0.7	PREPTNS COLOR UTILISES CERAM
53351	PREPRD PIGMENT,GLAZE ETC	W 3360	3.4	W 3655	4.1	W 23	0.2	W 29	0.2	PIGMENTS OPACIFIANTS
541	*MEDICINAL,PHARM PRODUCT	K 3984058	34.5		40.5	K 6738629	49.7	K 8056010	53.2	PROD MEDICINAUX PHARMACEUT
5416	GLYCOSIDES,GLANDS,SERA	K 1051291	1.5	K 2911903	2.5	K 4011456	3.6	K 5449043	4.8	HETEROSIDES
54164	ANTISERA,MICROB VACCINES	K 1048990	1.3	K 2909741	2.4	K 3913214	3.5	K 5445902	4.7	SERUMS,VACCINS
5417	MEDICAMENTS	K 2872061	32.6	K 3882900	37.5	K 2658460	45.7	K 2547670	48.0	MEDICAMENTS
55	PERFUME,CLEANING ETC PRD		28.0		36.6		48.4		63.7	PROD POUR PARFUM,TOILETTE
553	PERFUMERY,COSMETICS,ETC	W 2435	5.8	W 3232	11.6	W 3555	14.5	W 4652	20.8	PRODUITS DE PARFUMERIE
554	SOAP,CLEANSING ETC PREPS	W 21257	22.1		24.9	W 33284	33.8	W 42361	42.9	SAVONS,PRODUITS DETERSIFS
5541	SOAPS	W 9493	9.2	W 13870	12.6	W 17596	17.4	W 19549	19.6	SAVONS,PROD TENSIO-ACTIFS
5542	WASHING PREPARATIONS ETC	W 11763	13.0	W 11765	12.4	W 15683	16.5	W 22796	23.3	PROD ORG TENSIO-ACT NDA
58	PLASTIC MATERIALS ETC		12.9		12.8		14.7		17.1	MAT PLAST ARTIFICIELLES
583	POLYMERIZATION ETC PRODS	W 6170	11.4	W 5432	11.8	W 7008	13.4	W 8536	16.3	PROD POLYMERISATION
5834	POLYVINYL CHLORIDE	W 4050	5.1	W 3441	5.1	W 4491	5.6	W 5155	6.1	CHLORURE DE POLYVINYLE
5839	OTH POLYMRZTION ETC PROD	W 1671	4.6	W 1557	5.1	W 2053	5.6	W 2459	6.0	AUT PROD POLYMER COPOLYM
59	CHEMICAL MATERIALS NES		7.5		7.8		9.4		13.8	MAT PROD CHIMIQUES NDA
591	PESTICIDES,DISINFECTANTS	W 2596	6.6	W 3384	7.0	W 3512	8.6	W 3914	11.4	DESINF,INSECT,FONG,HERB
5911	INSECTICIDES,FOR RETAIL	W 1122	4.5	W 1283	4.8	W 1427	5.3	W 1872	7.1	INSECTICIDES VENTE DET
6	BASIC MANUFACTURES		171.1		189.3		188.6		232.6	ART MANUFACTURES
61	LEATHER,DRESSED FUR,ETC		2.6		2.7		2.3		1.8	CUIRS,PELLETERIES
64	PAPER,PAPERBOARD AND MFR		56.6		58.2		57.0		64.4	PAPIERS,CARTONS & OUVRAGES
641	PAPER AND PAPERBOARD	W 8298	12.7	W 8869	15.2	W 8239	16.4	W 10587	18.6	PAPIERS ET CARTONS

5. Special Exports F.O.B. by Commodities according to the S.I.T.C. (Rev. 2) in million U.S. Dollars
Exportations Spéciales F.O.B. par Produits d'après la C.T.C.I. (Rév. 2) en millions de Dollars E.U.

SITC CTCI	COMMODITY	1994 QUANTITY QUANTITE	1994 VALUE VALEUR	1995 QUANTITY QUANTITE	1995 VALUE VALEUR	1996 QUANTITY QUANTITE	1996 VALUE VALEUR	1997 QUANTITY QUANTITE	1997 VALUE VALEUR	PRODUIT
6417	CORRUGATED PAPER ETC,BLK	W 2828	2.0	W 3596	2.6	W 3412	3.2	W 5346	4.0	PAPIERS,CARTONS ONDULES
6418	COATED ETC PAPER NES BLK	W 1607	6.6	W 1793	7.7	W 1553	7.9	W 1806	9.9	PAP,CARTONS COUCHES,ENDUITS
642	PAPER,ETC,PRECUT,ARTS OF	W 30551	44.0	W 23511	43.0	W 23369	40.6	W 27944	45.8	PAP,CARTONS DECOUPES
6421	PAPER ETC CONTAINERS	W 21314	29.4	W 14246	25.8	W 12923	19.8	W 15921	22.3	BOITES,SACS EMBALLAGES
6424	PAPER ETC CT TO SIZE NES	W 5464	6.5	W 4682	7.1	W 4757	8.1	W 4958	8.3	PAP,CARTONS DECOUPES
64243	TOILET PAPER CUT TO SIZE	W 5395	6.3	W 4633	7.0	W 4680	7.9	W 4884	8.1	PAPIER HYGIENIQUE
6428	PAPER ETC ARTICLES NES	W 1974	5.7	W 2943	7.2	W 4334	10.5	W 4394	11.5	OUVRAGES EN PATE A PAPIER
64284	PAPER TISSUES,TOWELS ETC	W 977	2.1	W 1251	3.1	W 1847	4.2	W 1741	4.2	MOUCHOIRS SERVIETTES EN PAP
64285	PAPER ETC DIAPERS ETC	W 741	3.2	W 809	3.2	W 969	4.8	W 1028	6.1	SERVIETTES HYGIENIQUES
65	TEXTILE YARN,FABRICS,ETC		61.7		64.3		67.3		84.2	FILS,TISSUS,ARTICLES TEXTILE
651	TEXTILE YARN	W 7244	21.9		18.7	W 6361	22.1	W 7851	27.5	FILS TEXTILES
6513	COTTON YARN	W 4916	14.0	W 3920	13.0	W 4870	16.2	W 5604	19.0	FILS DE COTON
6516	DISCON SYN FIB BLEND YRN	W 1842	5.7	W 1182	3.5	W 1051	3.7	W 1764	6.0	FILS FIBR TEX SYNT DIS MOINS
65166	DISCON SYN FIB–COTTN YRN	W 1842	5.7	W 1178	3.5	W 767	2.8	W 1627	5.6	FILS TEXT SYNT MELANGE COTON
652	COTTON FABRICS,WOVEN	W 850	3.8	W 1507	7.8	W 805	4.9	W 1786	9.3	TISSUS DE COTON
6522	WOVEN COTTON BLEACHD,ETC	W 392	1.8	W 955	5.5	W 634	4.1	W 1110	7.1	TISSUS COTON BLANCHIS ETC
65224	BLCHED COTTON FABRIC NES	W 314	1.3	W 728	4.2	W 523	3.2	W 1024	6.5	AUT TIS PLUS 85% COT BLANCHI
653	WOVN MAN–MADE FIB FABRIC	W 2185	15.1		15.0	W 2013	14.4	W 2422	17.1	TISSUS FIBRES SYNTH,ARTIF
6534	DISC SYN BLEND FABRC NES	W 1931	13.5	W 1968	13.4	W 1861	13.3	W 2007	14.9	TISSUS FIBRES SYNTH DISCONT
655	KNITTED,ETC FABRICS	W 156	1.4	W 1137	2.8	W 396	3.3	W 664	5.3	ETOF BONNETERIE PIECES ETC
6552	OTHER KNIT ETC FAB NONEL	W 156	1.4	W 1137	2.8	W 396	3.3	W 664	5.3	ETOF BON NON ELAS NON SYNT
658	TEXTILE ARTICLES NES	W 2682	17.3	W 2967	17.4	W 2833	20.3	W 3246	21.9	ART FACONNES MAT TEXTILES
6584	LINENS ETC	W 2022	14.8	W 2486	15.1	W 2059	17.9	W 2247	19.1	LINGE DE MAISON
66	NONMETAL MINERAL MFS NES		1.9		2.0		2.4		7.8	ART MIN NON METALLIQUES
661	LIME,CEMENT,BLDG PRODS	W 3453	0.8	W 1700	0.5	W 5199	0.9	W 42068	4.3	CHAUX,CIMENTS MAT CONSTR
67	IRON AND STEEL		9.7		16.1		21.6		26.9	FER ET ACIER
673	IRON,STEEL SHAPES ETC	W 5358	2.1	W 6445	2.6	W 14502	5.5	W 15513	6.3	BARRES,PROFIL FER,ACIER
6732	IRON,STEEL BARS ETC	W 3944	1.5	W 6114	2.5	W 14216	5.3	W 14226	5.5	BARRES FER,ACIER
67326	IRN,OTH STL BARS HOTROLD	W 3878	1.5	W 6018	2.4	W 14027	5.2	W 13714	5.2	BARRES PLEINES FER,ACIER
674	IRN,STL UNIV,PLATE,SHEET	W 12667	6.1	W 22799	11.9	W 26832	12.9	W 34440	15.4	LARGES PLATS,TOLES
6745	IRN,STL MED PLATE,ROLLED	W 6652	2.7	W 9360	4.7	W 12004	5.7	W 14570	6.3	TOLES 3 A 4.75 MM
67451	— OF IRON OR SIMPLE STL	W 6652	2.7	W 9360	4.7	W 12004	5.7	W 14570	6.3	TOLES AUT NON ACIER FIN
6746	IRN,STL THIN PLATE,ROLLD	W 3166	2.0	W 7454	4.1	W 7814	4.0	W 9434	4.5	TOLES LAM MOINS 3MM
67461	— OF IRON OR SIMPLE STL	W 3166	2.0	W 7435	4.1	W 7814	4.0	W 9434	4.5	TOL NON AC FIN MOINS 3 MM
68	NON–FERROUS METALS		19.4		26.8		21.0		23.0	METAUX NON FERREUX
684	ALUMINIUM	W 3926	18.5	W 4335	26.4	W 3861	20.7	W 4263	22.1	ALUMINIUM
6842	ALUMINIUM,ALLOYS WORKED	W 3921	18.5	W 4331	26.4	W 3861	20.7	W 4263	22.1	ALUMINIUM,ALLIAGES OUVRE
68421	ALUMINIUM BARS,WIRE,ETC	W 1688	5.5	W 1767	6.7	W 1685	6.3	W 1919	6.8	BARRES,PROFILES FILS ALU
68423	ALUMINIUM FOIL	W 2186	12.8	W 2564	19.8	W 2170	14.5	W 2298	15.2	FEUILLES,BANDES MINCES AL
69	METAL MANUFACTURES NES		18.2		17.6		15.9		23.5	ART MANUFACT EN METAL NDA
691	STRUCTURES AND PARTS NES	W 6444	4.8	W 3655	3.7	W 1315	2.1	W 2509	3.6	CONSTRUCT FER,ACIER,ALU
6911	STRUCTURES,PARTS IRN,STL	W 6025	2.8	W 3254	1.9	W 1024	0.7	W 2009	1.3	CONSTRUCT FER,ACIER,FONTE
693	WIRE PRODUCTS NON ELECTR	W 1356	3.1		1.9	W 601	0.9	W 924	0.6	OUVRAGES FILS METALLIQUES
6931	WIRE CABLES, ROPES ETC	W 1051	2.8		1.7	W 291	0.7	W 8	0.1	CORDAGES EN FILS DE FER
695	TOOLS	W 1648	5.5	W 1634	5.7	W 1850	5.7	W 2757	8.0	OUTILS A MAIN
6951	HAND TOOLS,AGRIC,FOREST	W 1506	4.6	W 1530	4.5	W 1813	5.3	W 2652	7.4	BECHES,PELLES,PIOCHES
699	BASE METAL MFRS NES	W 1348	2.4		2.8	W 1542	2.9	W 2449	4.3	ART MANUFACTURES MET NDA
7	MACHINES,TRANSPORT EQUIP		24.8		27.6		35.3		50.2	MACHINES MATERIEL TRANSPORT
72	MACHS FOR SPCL INDUSTRYS		1.2		1.6		2.3		5.0	MAC SPECIALES POUR INDUST
74	GENRL INDUSTRL MACHY NES		2.5		3.0		2.6		4.6	MACH APP INDUSTRIE
77	ELECTRIC MACHNRY NES ETC		20.3		21.7		29.2		38.5	MACH APP ELECT NDA
773	ELECTR DISTRIBUTNG EQUIP	W 2373	8.5	W 1908	6.8	W 2836	10.9	W 4880	17.8	EQUIPMT DISTRIBUTION ELECT
7731	INSULATED WIRE,CABLE ETC	W 2373	8.5	W 1908	6.8	W 2836	10.9	W 4880	17.8	FILS,CABLES ISOLES ELECT
775	HOUSEHOLD TYPE EQUIP NES	W 2053	8.3		9.7	W 2901	11.4	W 3092	11.9	MACH,APP USAGE DOMESTQUE
7752	DOM REFRIGERATRS,FREEZRS	W 2051	8.3	W 2612	9.7	W 2897	11.3	W 3054	11.8	REFRIG,CONGEL MENAGER
77521	DOMESTIC REFRIGERATORS	W 2051	8.3	W 2607	9.7	W 2890	11.3	W 3051	11.7	REFRIGERATEURS
778	ELECTRICAL MACHINERY NES	W 1084	3.4		5.2	W 2598	6.8	W 3544	8.6	AUTRES MACH ELECT NDA
7781	BATTERIES,ACCUMULATORS	W 590	1.1	W 1123	2.1	W 1966	3.3	W 2793	4.5	PILES ET ACCUMULATEURS
7782	ELECTRIC LAMPS,BULBS	W 493	2.4	W 533	3.0	W 629	3.5	W 744	4.2	LAMPES, TUBES ELECTRIQUES
77821	ELEC FILAMENT LAMPS NES	W 480	2.4	W 528	3.0	W 628	3.4	W 726	4.1	LAMPES NON INFRAROUGES
8	MISC MANUFACTURED GOODS		89.6		81.6		77.3		98.5	ART MANUFACTURES DIVERS
821	*FURNITURE,PARTS THEREOF	W 1025	2.0	W 1597	3.4	W 1500	3.2	W 2390	4.7	MEUBLES ET PIECES
831	*TRAVEL GOODS,HANDBAGS	W 516	4.7	W 494	3.6	W 104	0.9	W 194	1.5	ARTICLES DE VOYAGE ETC
84	CLOTHING AND ACCESSORIES		37.6		33.1		27.5		39.4	VETEMENTS
843	WOMENS OUTERWEAR NONKNIT	W 155	2.8	W 75	1.7	W 66	1.7	W 110	2.6	VET DESSUS FEMMES MAT TEX
844	UNDER GARMENTS NOT KNIT	W 508	6.2	W 1108	7.3	W 347	4.6	W 325	4.9	VETEMENT DESSOUS MAT TEX
8442	— MENS,OTHR THAN SHIRTS	W 384	3.7	W 718	5.1	W 268	2.6	W 253	2.9	SOUS–VET HOMMES MAT TEXT
845	OUTERWEAR KNIT NONELASTC	W 553	9.6	W 328	7.7	W 292	5.5	W 607	11.0	VET DESSOUS,ACCES BONNET
846	UNDER GARMENTS KNITTED	W 1455	16.1	W 956	12.8	W 736	11.3	W 1229	16.1	SOUS VETS DE BONNETERIE
8462	— OF COTTON NON ELASTIC	W 1400	15.1	W 882	11.7	W 670	10.4	W 1186	15.1	SOUS–VET BONNET COTON
84621	—— MENS SHIRTS	W 76	1.2	W 183	3.1	W 88	1.4	W 290	2.5	CHEMISES DE COTON
84629	—— OTHER	W 1324	13.9	W 699	8.6	W 582	9.0	W 896	12.7	AUT SOUS–VET BONNET COTON
851	*FOOTWEAR	W 3018	17.8	W 2476	13.1	W 1975	14.0	W 2269	15.3	CHAUSSURES
85101	FOOTWEAR RUBBER,PLASTIC	W 857	2.6	W 862	2.6	W 764	1.8	W 1096	2.5	CHAUS SEMELLES CAOUTCH
85102	FOOTWEAR LEATHER	W 1161	7.8	W 894	7.1	W 901	8.5	W 989	9.4	CHAUS SEMELLES EN CUIR
85103	SHOES WOOD–,CORK–SOLED	W 228	3.5	W 74	0.5	W 206	3.3	W 183	3.5	CHAUS SEMELLES BOIS,LIEGE
85104	FOOTWEAR NES	W 773	4.1	W 646	3.1	W 103	0.6	W 1	0.1	CHAUS SEMELLES AUT MAT
89	MISC MANUFCTRD GOODS NES		25.6		27.3		28.7		35.6	ART MANUFACTURES DIVERS
892	PRINTED MATTER	W 697	4.9	W 676	3.9	W 600	3.9	W 702	4.4	IMPRIMES
8928	PRINTED MATTER NES	W 348	3.1	W 320	2.0	W 248	1.7	W 464	2.6	IMPRIMES NDA
893	ARTICLES OF PLASTIC NES	W 4839	10.4		12.8		14.3	W 7217	15.4	OUVRAGES EN MAT DIVIS 58
8931	PLSTC PACKG CONTNRS,LIDS	W 2378	5.7	W 3209	7.5	W 2981	7.4	W 3065	6.8	ART TRANSP EMBALLAGE ETC
8939	MISC PLASTIC ARTICLES	W 2453	4.7	W 2496	5.3	W 3003	7.0	W 4147	8.7	ART DIVERS EN MAT DIV 58
89399	OTHR PLASTC ARTICLES NES	W 2427	4.6	W 2469	5.3	W 2941	6.8	W 4114	8.5	AUT OUV MAT DIV 58
895	OFFICE SUPPLIES NES	W 609	2.8		3.5	W 464	2.8	W 536	3.3	ART PAPET NDA
899	OTHER MANUFACTURED GOODS		5.5		5.7		5.9	W 2502	10.6	AUT ART MANUF DIVERS NDA
8997	BASKETWORK,BROOMS ETC	W 685	2.4	W 1019	2.9	W 1218	2.9	W 1698	4.5	OUVRAGES VANNERIE NDA
8998	SMALLWARES,TOILETRYS ETC	W 278	2.6		2.5	W 230	2.5	W 392	5.6	ART MERCERIE,TOILETTE
89984	SLIDE FASTENERS,PARTS	W 168	1.7	W 119	1.3	W 166	2.3	W 291	4.9	FERMETURES A GLISSIERE

1. HISTORICAL SERIES, 1992–1997 GENERAL TRADE, IMPORTS C.I.F., EXPORTS F.O.B.
SERIES HISTORIQUES, 1992–1997 COMMERCE GENERAL, IMPORTATIONS C.A.F., EXPORTATIONS F.O.B.

YEAR ANNEE	VALUE IN MILLION KROONS VALEUR EN MILLION KROONS MERCHANDISE –MARCHANDISE IMPORTS	EXPORTS	GOLD –OR IMPORTS	EXPORTS	CONVERSION FACTORS U.S. CENTS PER KROON FACTEURS DE CONVERSION CENTS E.U. PAR KROON IMPORTS	EXPORTS	INDEX NUMBERS –INDICES QUANTUM IMPORTS	EXPORTS	UNIT VALUE VALEUR UNITAIRE IMPORTS	EXPORTS
1992	5128.00	5549.00			8.0319	8.0167				
1993	11848.00	10642.00			7.5670	7.5670				
1994	21561.01	16872.00			7.7140	7.7140				
1995	29101.01	21040.00			8.7449	8.7338				
1996	38367.01	24586.00			8.3424	8.3431				
1997	59435.01	39320.00			7.1901	7.1908				

2. IMPORTS BY BROAD ECONOMIC CATEGORY AND EXPORTS BY INDUSTRIAL ORIGIN. (PERCENTAGE OF TOTAL VALUE)
IMPORTATIONS PAR CATEGORIES ECONOMIQUES ET EXPORTATIONS PAR BRANCHE D'ACTIVITE.(EN POURCENTAGE DE LA VALEUR TOTALE)

IMPORTS – IMPORTATIONS

	1991	1992	1993	1994	1995	1996	1997
TOTAL IMPORTS–IMPORTATIONS TOTALES					100.	100.	100.
1 FOOD BEV–ALIMENTATION BOISSONS					12.5	13.6	14.8
11 PRIMARY–PRODUITS DE BASE					3.6	4.7	6.7
111 FOR INDUSTRY–POUR L'INDUSTRIE					1.3	2.0	3.4
112 FOR HOUSEHOLDS–POUR LES MENAGES					2.3	2.8	3.4
12 PROCESSED–PRODUITS ELABORES					8.9	8.9	8.1
121 FOR INDUSTRY–POUR L'INDUSTRIE					1.3	1.2	1.0
122 FOR HOUSEHOLDS–POUR LES MENAGES					7.6	7.7	7.1
2 IND SUPPLIES–APPROV INDUSTRIELS					30.8	31.5	29.2
21 PRIMARY–PRODUITS DE BASE					3.1	2.9	2.9
22 PROCESSED–PRODUITS ELABORES					27.8	28.6	26.3
3 FUELS–COMBUSTIBLES					10.9	9.3	8.0
31 PRIMARY–PRODUITS DE BASE					2.2	2.1	1.4
32 PROCESSED–PRODUITS ELABORES					8.7	7.2	6.6
321 MOTOR SPIRIT–ESSENCE							
322 OTHER–AUTRES					8.7	7.2	6.6
4 MACHINERY–EQUIPEMENT					20.2	19.0	19.8
41 CAPITAL EQUIPMENT–MACHINES					15.0	14.9	15.5
42 PARTS–PIECES ACCESSOIRES					5.1	4.2	4.3
5 TRANSPORT–TRANSPORT					8.8	8.4	12.8
51 PASSENGER CARS–AUTOMOBILES					3.8	3.1	7.0
52 OTHER–AUTRES					2.4	2.7	3.3
521 INDUSTRIAL–INDUSTRIELS					2.3	2.6	3.2
522 NON INDUSTRIAL–NON INDUSTRIEL					0.1	0.1	0.1
53 PARTS–PIECES ACCESSOIRES					2.6	2.6	2.4
6 CONSUM GOODS–BIENS CONSOMMATION					16.6	18.1	15.3
61 DURABLE–DURABLES					4.4	5.5	4.6
62 SEMI DURABLE–SEMI DURABLES					7.8	7.8	6.4
63 NON DURABLE–NON DURABLES					4.5	4.7	4.4
7 GOODS NES–BIENS NDA					0.1	0.0	0.1

EXPORTS – EXPORTATIONS

	1991	1992	1993	1994	1995	1996	1997
TOTAL EXPORTS–EXPORTATIONS TOTALES					100.	100.	100.
1 AGRICULTURE					9.6	7.3	10.6
2 MINING QUARRY–INDUS EXTRACTIVES					1.4	1.3	1.3
3 MANUFACTURING–IND MANUFACTUR					89.0	91.4	88.1
31 FOOD BEV TOBACCO–ALIM BOISS TAB					13.1	12.5	10.3
32 TEXTILES–INDUSTRIES TEXTILES					15.0	16.2	12.8
33 WOOD & PRODUCTS–BOIS & PRODUITS					6.9	7.8	7.6
34 PAPER & PRODUCTS–PAPIER & PRODT					1.5	2.4	2.6
35 CHEMICALS–INDUSTRIES CHIMIQUES					15.4	15.4	14.8
36 NON METAL MIN–MIN NON METAL					2.4	2.3	1.9
37 BASIC METAL–IND METAL BASE					2.4	1.6	1.8
38 METAL MANUF–MANUF METAL					29.6	30.6	34.2
39 OTH MANUF IND–AUTRES MANUF					2.7	2.7	2.1

3. TRADE BY PRINCIPAL COUNTRIES OF ORIGIN AND DESTINATION (VALUE IN MILLION U.S. DOLLARS)
ECHANGES SELON LES PRINCIPAUX PAYS D'ORIGINE ET DE DESTINATION (VALEUR EN MILLIONS DE DOLLARS EU)

COUNTRIES–PAYS	GENERAL IMPORTS C.I.F. IMPORTATIONS GENERALES C.A.F				
	1993	1994	1995	1996	1997
World	894.0	1660.4	2545.5	3197.0	4438.7
Africa	0.2	4.7	3.6	22.6	114.3
Americas	31.2	55.8	86.5	102.3	229.6
– Northern America	26.6	48.0	68.5	84.4	183.4
– LAIA	4.1	6.7	13.4	13.6	43.6
– CACM	0.3	0.7	2.0	1.9	1.0
– Caribbean	0.1	0.2	1.8	1.9	1.2
– Rest of America	0.1	0.2	0.9	0.4	0.4
Asia excl fmr USSR	54.2	92.5	109.9	191.6	333.5
– Middle East	1.7	1.8	4.5	8.5	12.6
Asia former USSR	8.2	17.0	24.3	40.3	71.0
Europe excl fmr USSR	562.0	1100.5	1774.0	2226.0	2829.7
– European Union	540.2	1050.0	1680.8	2070.9	2624.2
– Eastern Europe	12.6	28.2	48.8	83.3	105.7
– Rest of Europe	9.2	22.3	44.4	71.8	99.8
Europe former USSR	234.4	389.3	546.1	610.4	848.9
Oceania	0.2	0.6	1.1	3.8	11.8
Other	3.1				0.0
Finland/Finlande	249.6	496.0	829.4	934.6	1038.3
Russian Federation	153.6	279.1	410.0	431.5	640.5
Germany/Allemagne	96.2	165.2	243.4	318.6	444.0
Sweden/Suède	79.7	147.3	215.5	261.3	402.6
USA/Etats–Unis d'Amer	24.4	41.5	62.7	73.3	169.6
Netherlands/Pays–Bas	32.4	51.0	79.1	91.2	113.7
Italy/Italie	18.5	40.1	66.3	103.2	132.0
Japan/Japon	37.6	48.4	47.5	64.8	148.4
United Kingdom	13.1	35.4	56.2	105.5	135.8
Denmark/Danemark	23.2	43.9	71.0	90.2	114.4
France, Monaco	10.5	24.8	37.1	64.7	99.2
Latvia/Lettonie	20.2	24.1	50.5	62.0	77.3
Lithuania/Lituanie	29.6	42.7	41.1	50.0	67.3
Belgium–Luxembourg	9.5	23.4	39.6	45.4	60.1
Ukraine	14.5	27.9	26.8	51.3	45.3
Korea, Republic of	2.1	5.2	12.7	52.6	76.0
Switzerland,Liechtenst.	4.7	9.8	20.8	38.8	47.4
Poland/Pologne	3.6	10.0	15.1	34.8	50.0
Norway,Svalbard and JM	4.2	10.5	21.3	29.1	47.3
Cote d'Ivoire		2.3	2.1	14.7	82.4
Uzbekistan/Ouzbékistan	1.1	7.8	10.7	25.0	31.7
Belarus/Bélarus	12.9	14.0	15.7	13.8	17.0
Austria/Autriche	2.2	10.4	17.2	18.3	24.6
Czech Republic	3.8	8.9	15.1	19.3	20.3
China/Chine	3.5	8.5	11.1	16.2	23.8
Hungary/Hongrie	3.8	6.4	13.0	20.6	18.8
Spain/Espagne	2.1	4.2	11.0	17.3	24.1
Ireland/Irlande	1.5	5.2	10.7	12.8	26.9
Other Asia n.e.s.	2.4	5.5	7.9	9.6	16.2
Kazakhstan	2.0	3.1	5.0	8.7	22.1
Canada	2.2	6.3	5.5	10.9	13.5
Brazil/Brésil	3.8	3.2	2.5	3.3	24.4
China, Hong Kong SAR	1.4	5.5	9.2	9.1	12.0
India/Inde	1.5	4.6	3.7	8.4	10.4
Slovakia/Slovaquie	0.2	1.3	3.3	5.0	11.8
Malaysia/Malaisie	0.2	1.2	1.7	6.3	10.6
Turkey/Turquie	0.4	0.9	2.7	6.6	8.7
Indonesia/Indonésie	0.4	4.0	2.0	5.5	7.4
Tajikistan/Tadjikistan	0.3	1.7	4.7	1.6	10.8
Portugal	0.9	2.4	3.2	5.7	6.1

COUNTRIES–PAYS	GENERAL EXPORTS F.O.B. EXPORTATIONS GENERALES F.O.B.				
	1993	1994	1995	1996	1997
Monde	803.9	1305.9	1838.8	2074.1	2926.5
Afrique	14.4	10.2	8.1	8.0	14.7
Amériques	18.6	29.8	49.7	55.9	67.8
– Amérique du Nord	16.2	25.7	46.1	47.9	58.8
– ALAI	0.6	0.3	0.5	0.4	2.4
– MCAC			0.0	0.1	0.1
– Caraïbes	1.7	2.8	2.6	1.2	1.3
– Autre Amérique	0.1	1.0	0.5	6.4	5.2
Asie anc. URSS exclus	10.8	17.2	27.6	47.4	74.3
– Moyen–Orient	4.1	2.9	13.8	10.1	17.1
Asie ancienne URSS	22.1	24.8	18.4	23.8	30.3
Europe anc. URSS exclus	416.7	674.1	1070.2	1153.5	1568.1
– Union Européenne	388.3	624.5	995.7	1060.0	1422.3
– Europe de l'Est	19.9	20.8	30.6	30.8	32.0
– Autre de l'Europe	8.5	28.8	44.0	62.7	113.8
Europe ancienne URSS	320.9	549.5	664.7	785.1	1170.5
Océanie	0.1	0.3	0.1	0.3	0.8
Autre					
Russian Federation	182.0	301.8	322.7	340.8	549.1
Finland/Finlande	166.4	233.0	395.6	380.8	460.2
Sweden/Suède	76.1	141.5	200.0	240.0	394.5
Latvia/Lettonie	69.1	107.4	137.4	171.4	252.4
Germany/Allemagne	64.3	89.1	132.9	146.6	163.2
Lithuania/Lituanie	29.8	70.8	86.2	118.8	178.1
Ukraine	28.6	40.0	69.0	104.2	145.6
Netherlands/Pays–Bas	32.6	41.1	86.0	61.2	98.8
Denmark/Danemark	19.1	44.3	60.5	73.5	93.6
United Kingdom	11.2	36.4	60.4	71.9	107.3
USA/Etats–Unis d'Amer	14.9	23.8	44.0	45.8	53.8
Belarus/Bélarus	9.1	26.7	45.7	40.2	40.2
Norway,Svalbard and JM	4.8	19.5	34.2	31.3	47.4
Switzerland,Liechtenst.	2.9	6.3	5.4	24.7	60.9
Belgium–Luxembourg	5.0	14.2	16.4	25.8	34.1
Poland/Pologne	8.5	8.9	21.1	24.2	26.6
Italy/Italie	5.2	11.5	15.5	19.5	22.1
France, Monaco	2.4	5.9	14.0	23.5	20.6
Japan/Japon	3.5	5.9	8.9	14.7	15.8
Kazakhstan	7.4	7.1	8.9	7.7	11.4
Korea, Republic of		0.2	0.5	10.2	22.8
Uzbekistan/Ouzbékistan	2.6	5.3	5.2	8.1	12.5
Turkey/Turquie	2.1	0.2	9.4	8.0	11.0
Republic of Moldova	2.3	2.8	3.6	9.6	5.2
Austria/Autriche	2.2	1.9	5.3	5.0	8.2
Ireland/Irlande	0.4	0.4	4.2	5.5	8.3
So. African Customs Un	3.9	4.8	6.2	0.6	0.9
Portugal	1.9	3.6	2.9	3.5	4.0
Czech Republic	4.9	3.0	2.7	2.4	2.5
Canada	1.3	1.9	2.1	2.1	5.0
Spain/Espagne	0.4	1.2	1.8	2.1	6.6
Hungary/Hongrie	3.6	2.6	2.6	1.4	1.4
Tajikistan/Tadjikistan	3.0	3.9	1.3	1.3	1.7
Azerbaijan/Azerbaïdjan	3.7	3.0	1.7	1.5	1.1
Iceland/Islande	0.4	1.6	3.8	1.8	3.0
Mauritania/Mauritanie	6.7	2.9	0.2	0.6	0.0
Egypt/Egypte	2.0	1.1	0.0	2.0	5.1
China/Chine	2.0	4.1	1.4	0.5	1.9
Turkmenistan/Turkménistn	3.8	1.8	0.5	2.1	0.8
Bulgaria/Bulgarie	2.1	1.3	1.2	2.2	0.5

(VALUE AS PERCENTAGE OF WORLD TOTAL)(VALEURS EN POURCENTAGE DU TOTAL MONDIAL)

	1988	1989	1990	1991	1992	1993	1994	1995	1996	1997
Africa						0.0	0.3	0.1	0.7	2.6
Americas					4.9	3.5	3.4	3.4	3.2	5.2
– Northern America					4.9	3.0	2.9	2.7	2.6	4.1
– LAIA						0.5	0.4	0.5	0.4	1.0
– CACM						0.0	0.0	0.1	0.1	0.0
– Caribbean						0.0	0.0	0.1	0.1	0.0
– Rest of America						0.0	0.0	0.0	0.0	0.0
Asia excl fmr USSR					2.7	6.1	5.6	4.3	6.0	7.5
– Middle East						0.2	0.1	0.2	0.3	0.3
Asia former USSR						0.9	1.0	1.0	1.3	1.6
Europe excl fmr USSR					44.0	62.9	66.3	69.7	69.6	63.7
– European Union					44.0	60.4	63.2	66.0	64.8	59.1
– Eastern Europe						1.4	1.7	1.9	2.6	2.4
– Rest of Europe						1.0	1.3	1.7	2.2	2.2
Europe former USSR					43.2	26.2	23.4	21.5	19.1	19.1
Oceania						0.0	0.0	0.0	0.1	0.3
Other						0.3				0.0
Finland/Finlande					22.6	27.9	29.9	32.6	29.2	23.4
Russian Federation					28.4	17.2	16.8	16.1	13.5	14.4
Germany/Allemagne					8.3	10.8	9.9	9.6	10.0	10.0
Sweden/Suède					5.9	8.9	8.9	8.5	8.2	9.1
USA/Etats–Unis d'Amer					4.9	2.7	2.5	2.5	2.3	3.8
Netherlands/Pays–Bas					1.8	3.6	3.1	3.1	2.9	2.6
Italy/Italie					0.5	2.1	2.4	2.6	3.2	3.0
Japan/Japon					2.7	4.2	2.9	1.9	2.0	3.3
United Kingdom					1.6	1.5	2.1	2.2	3.3	3.1
Denmark/Danemark					1.7	2.6	2.6	2.8	2.8	2.6

	1988	1989	1990	1991	1992	1993	1994	1995	1996	1997
Afrique						1.8	0.8	0.4	0.4	0.5
Amériques					1.9	2.3	2.3	2.7	2.7	2.3
– Amérique du Nord					1.9	2.0	2.0	2.5	2.3	2.0
– ALAI						0.1	0.0	0.0	0.0	0.1
– MCAC								0.0	0.0	0.0
– Caraïbes						0.2	0.2	0.1	0.1	0.0
– Autre Amérique						0.0	0.1	0.0	0.3	0.2
Asie anc. URSS exclus						1.3	1.3	1.5	2.3	2.5
– Moyen–Orient						0.5	0.2	0.8	0.5	0.6
Asie ancienne URSS					1.0	2.7	1.9	1.0	1.1	1.0
Europe anc. URSS exclus					44.0	51.8	51.6	58.2	55.6	53.6
– Union Européenne					41.8	48.3	47.8	54.1	51.1	48.6
– Europe de l'Est					1.9	2.5	1.6	1.7	1.5	1.1
– Autre de l'Europe					0.3	1.1	2.2	2.4	3.0	3.9
Europe ancienne URSS					41.3	39.9	42.1	36.1	37.9	40.0
Océanie						0.0	0.0	0.0	0.0	0.0
Autre										
Russian Federation					20.8	22.6	23.1	17.5	16.4	18.8
Finland/Finlande					21.1	20.7	17.8	21.5	18.4	15.7
Sweden/Suède					7.7	9.5	10.8	10.9	11.6	13.5
Latvia/Lettonie					10.6	8.6	8.2	7.5	8.3	8.6
Germany/Allemagne					3.9	8.0	6.8	7.2	7.1	5.6
Lithuania/Lituanie					1.5	3.7	5.4	4.7	5.7	6.1
Ukraine					6.9	3.6	3.1	3.8	5.0	5.0
Netherlands/Pays–Bas					5.1	4.1	3.1	4.7	2.9	3.4
Denmark/Danemark					2.4	2.4	3.4	3.3	3.5	3.2
United Kingdom					0.8	1.4	2.8	3.3	3.5	3.7

4. General Imports C.I.F. by Commodities according to the S.I.T.C. (Rev. 2) in million U.S. Dollars
Importations Générales C.A.F. par Produits d'après la C.T.C.I. (Rév. 2) en millions de Dollars E.U.

SITC CTCI	COMMODITY	1994 QUANTITY QUANTITE	1994 VALUE VALEUR	1995 QUANTITY QUANTITE	1995 VALUE VALEUR	1996 QUANTITY QUANTITE	1996 VALUE VALEUR	1997 QUANTITY QUANTITE	1997 VALUE VALEUR	PRODUIT
	ALL COMMODITIES		1660.4		2545.5		3197.1		4438.8	TOUS PRODUITS
0	FOOD AND LIVE ANIMALS				280.6		400.1		600.8	ALIMENTS,ANIMAUX VIVANTS
01	MEAT AND PREPARATIONS				19.3		39.0		90.4	VIANDES ET PREPARATIONS
011	MEAT FRESH,CHILLD,FROZEN	W 10511	11.5	W 12394	14.3		32.5		74.7	VIANDES FRAICHES,REF,CONGE
0113	PIG MEAT FRESH,CHLD,FRZN			W 2013	2.9		9.7		10.6	VIANDE DE PORC
0114	POULTRY FRESH CHLLD,FRZN			W 8493	9.3		15.2		57.0	VOLAILLES MORTES
014	MEAT PREPD,PRSVD,NES ETC			W 2469	5.0		6.4		15.5	CONSERVES DE VIANDES
0141	MEAT,FISH EXTRCTS,JUICES		7.1		0.1		0.1		0.1	EXTRAITS DE VIANDE
02	DAIRY PRODCTS,BIRDS'EGGS				30.2		39.7		69.5	PRODUITS LAITIERS,OEUFS
022	MILK AND CREAM			W 23037	16.3		18.0		18.0	LAIT ET CREME
0224	MILK,CREAM PRESERVED ETC			W 7965	11.0		12.3		13.8	LAIT,CREME CONS,CONC
02242	MILK DRY,1.5% FAT OR LES			W 6181	8.5		11.0		10.1	LAIT POUDRE INF 1.5%
023	BUTTER			W 4392	8.4		14.0		43.3	BEURRE
03	FISH AND PREPARATIONS		11.3		14.5		21.4		39.4	POISSONS ET PREPARATIONS
034	FISH,FRESH,CHILLED,FROZN			W 19735	11.2		17.4		34.8	POISSON FRAIS, REFRIG,CONG
0342	FISH FROZEN,EXCL FILLETS			W 13614	7.6		12.7		28.1	POISSONS CONGELES
04	CEREALS AND PREPARATIONS				38.2		72.3		60.1	CEREALES ET PRODUITS
043	BARLEY UNMILLED			W 55199	4.0		12.4		3.8	ORGE NON MONDEE
046	WHEAT ETC MEAL OR FLOUR			W 39281	7.8		10.0		8.0	SEMOULE FARINE,FROMENT
048	CEREAL ETC PREPARATIONS		13.4	W 20317	20.8		36.4		35.9	PREPTNS A BASE CEREALES
0484	BAKERY PRODUCTS			W 6208	11.4		23.7		17.8	PRODUITS DE BOULANGERIE
04842	PASTRY, CAKES ETC			W 4490	8.2		18.2		13.0	PATISSERIE ETC.
0488	OTH CEREAL PREPS,MALT EX		13.4	W 1550	2.2		2.2		2.4	EXTRAITS DE MALT
05	VEGETABLES AND FRUIT				39.4		50.5		53.3	LEGUMES ET FRUITS
057	FRUIT,NUTS,FRESH,DRIED		12.1	W 31919	17.4		20.8		20.4	FRUITS FRAIS OU SECS
058	FRUIT PRESERVED,PREPARED		10.8	W 13600	10.9		14.8		16.6	CONSERVES DE FRUITS
06	SUGAR AND PREPS,HONEY		33.6		28.4		36.0		43.6	SUCRES ET PRODUITS
061	SUGAR AND HONEY			W 41479	15.4		21.1		28.6	SUCRES ET MIEL
0612	REFINED SUGAR ETC			W 23153	9.3		19.7		26.5	SUCRES RAFFINES
062	SUGAR CANDY NON-CHOCLATE			W 3235	13.0		14.9		15.0	SUCRERIES
07	COFFEE,TEA,COCOA,SPICES		44.9		50.7		71.5		173.4	CAFE,THE,CACAO,EPICES
071	COFFEE AND SUBSTITUTES			W 4849	26.0		24.0		29.6	CAFE ET SUCCEDANES
0711	COFFEE GREEN,ROASTED,SUB			W 4093	21.8		20.0		27.1	CAFE TORREFIE OU DECAFEINE
07112	COFFEE ROASTED			W 2649	16.1		15.7		17.3	CAFE TORREFIE
072	COCOA			W 2846	4.3		25.9		116.7	CACAO
0721	COCOA BEANS,RAW,ROASTED			W 2426	3.3		20.6		103.6	CACAO EN FEVES
073	CHOCOLATE AND PRODUCTS			W 4220	16.3		16.7		20.8	CHOCOLAT
081	*FEEDING STUFF FOR ANIML			W 78220	19.1		26.1		20.5	NOURRITURE POUR ANIMAUX
0819	FOOD WASTE AND FEED NES		7.9	W 19086	9.0		11.6		11.6	DECHETS,ALIMENTS NDA
08199	FODDER NES,INCL SWEETNED			W 18926	9.0		11.5		11.5	PREPARATIONS FOURRAGERES
09	MISC EDIBLE PRODUCTS		20.5		40.3		43.5		50.2	PREP ALIMENTAIRES DIVERSES
091	MARGARINE AND SHORTENING			W 12458	14.7		15.1		10.7	MARGARINE ET GRAISSES
0914	MARGARINE,EDIBLE FAT NES			W 12403	14.6		15.0		10.6	MARGARINES,SIMILI SAINDOUX
09141	MARGARINE			W 11768	13.8		14.5		10.2	MARGARINE
098	EDIBLE PRODCTS,PREPS NES				25.7		28.4		39.5	PREP ALIMENTAIRES NDA
09809	MISC FOOD PREPRTIONS NES			W 6864	16.7		18.6		28.0	PREP ALIMENTAIRES NDA
1	BEVERAGES AND TOBACCO				53.9		70.0		93.9	BOISSONS ET TABACS
11	BEVERAGES		32.1		41.2		46.8		55.8	BOISSONS
112	ALCOHOLIC BEVERAGES			W 11169	33.8		37.9		44.2	BOISSONS ALCOOLIQUES
1121	WINE OF FRESH GRAPES ETC			W 5189	10.3		12.5		13.9	VINS DE RAISINS FRAIS
11212	WINE OF FRESH GRAPES			W 4604	8.8		10.8		12.0	VINS DE MOUTS DE RAISINS
1124	DISTILLED ALCOHOLIC BEVS			W 2183	19.8		19.5		22.2	ALCOOLS,EAUX-DE-VIE
11249	OTH ALCOHOLC BEVS,CMPNDS			W 966	12.9		9.5		10.3	BOISSONS ALCOOLIQUES NDA
12	TOBACCO AND MANUFACTURES		11.7		12.7		23.2		38.2	TABACS BRUTS FABRIQUES
122	TOBACCO,MANUFACTURED				10.9		22.7		38.2	TABACS FABRIQUES
1222	CIGARETTES			W 676	10.7		22.2		37.3	CIGARETTES
2	CRUDE MATERLS,EXCL FUELS				93.3		111.4		168.4	MAT BRUTES NON COMESTIBLES
24	CORK AND WOOD				9.5		13.3		17.7	LIEGE ET BOIS
248	WOOD SHAPED,SLEEPERS	W 345	2.4		7.5		9.6		12.1	BOIS SIMPLEMENT TRAVAILLES
26	TEXTILE FIBRES AND WASTE				49.8		48.1		53.8	FIBRES TEXTILES
263	COTTON			W 18520	37.8		39.2		44.5	COTON
2631	RAW COTTON,EXCL LINTERS			W 18245	37.3		39.1		44.3	COTON EN MASSE
27	CRUDE FERTLZR,MINRLS NES				11.2		13.3		22.8	ENGRAIS MINERAUX BRUTS
278	OTHER CRUDE MINERALS			W 234085	4.4		9.8		18.4	AUTRES MINERAUX BRUTS
28	METALLIFEROUS ORES,SCRAP				7.4		10.3		31.5	MINERAIS METAL,DECHETS
282	IRON AND STEEL SCRAP			W 3900	1.5		3.8		18.3	FERRAILLES
28209	— OF OTHR IRON OR STEEL			W 1014	0.2		2.5		16.6	FERRAILLES DE FER
29	CRUDE ANIMAL,VEG MAT NES				9.1		10.2		11.7	MATIERES BRUTES ANIM,VEGET
292	CRUDE VEG MATERIALS NES				8.0		9.1		10.2	MAT BRUTES VEGETALES NDA
3	MINERAL FUELS ETC				279.8		299.6		362.5	COMBUSTIBLES MINERAUX LUB
33	PETROLEUM AND PRODUCTS				223.9		233.2		298.5	PETROLE ET DERIVES
334	PETROLEUM PRODUCTS,REFIN			W 561300	214.4		222.0		281.9	PRODUITS RAFFINES
335	RESIDUAL PETRLM PROD NES			W 77750	9.5		11.1		16.1	PRODUITS RESIDUELS NDA
341	*GAS,NATURAL AND MANUFCT				50.9		58.8		58.8	GAZ NATUREL,GAZ MANUFACT
3414	PETROLEUM GASES, GASEOUS			MV 71786572	49.5		57.3		57.2	GAZ DE PETROLE GAZEUX
4	ANIMAL,VEGETABLE OIL,FAT				16.9		15.9		17.5	HUILES,GRAISSES ANIM,VEG
42	FIXED VEGETABLE OIL,FAT				15.3		14.0		14.1	HUILES VEGETALES FIXES
423	FIXED VEG OILS,SOFT			W 17104	13.9		12.7		13.2	HUILES VEGET DOUCES FIXES
4239	OTH FIXED VEG OILS,SOFT			W 10681	10.2		9.1		8.5	AUTRES HUILES FIXES
42391	RAPE,COLZA,MUSTARD OILS			W 10663	10.2		9.1		8.5	H NAVETTE COLZA MOUTARDE
5	CHEMCLS,RELATED PROD NES				232.2		328.9		411.0	PRODUITS CHIMIQUES
51	ORGANIC CHEMICALS				17.0		25.2		34.8	PROD CHIMIQ ORGANIQUES
515	ORG-INORG COMPOUNDS ETC			W 325	0.7		8.6		13.6	COMPOSES ORGANO-MINERAUX
5156	HETEROCYCLIC CMPDS ETC			W 129	0.3		8.4		13.4	COMPOSES HETEROCYCLIQUES
52	INORGANIC CHEMICALS				16.6		22.0		26.4	PROD CHIM INORGANIQUES
53	DYES,TANNING,COLOUR PROD				32.1		41.9		48.8	PROD TEINTURE,COLORANTS
533	PIGMENTS,PAINTS,ETC			W 14135	29.7		38.9		45.2	PIGMENTS,PEINTURES,VERNIS
5334	VARNISHES,DISTEMPERS ETC			W 6770	20.9		27.9		29.5	PEINTURES A L'EAU
53342	OTH PAINTS,VARNISHES ETC			W 5474	17.6		24.2		26.4	AUTRES PEINTURES,VERNIS
541	*MEDICINAL,PHARM PRODUCT			K 4090153	51.4		58.4		70.3	PROD MEDICINAUX PHARMACEUT
5417	MEDICAMENTS			K 2993830	45.2		51.1		60.4	MEDICAMENTS
54179	— CONTNG OTH SUBSTANCES			K 2269480	35.3		38.8		48.3	MED CONT AUT SUBSTANCES
55	PERFUME,CLEANING ETC PRD				38.5		48.8		62.7	PROD POUR PARFUM,TOILETTE
553	PERFUMERY,COSMETICS,ETC			W 3348	21.7		31.7		43.3	PRODUITS DE PARFUMERIE
554	SOAP,CLEANSING ETC PREPS			W 9667	15.6		16.1		17.9	SAVONS,PRODUITS DETERSIFS
5542	WASHING PREPARATIONS ETC			W 8245	12.3		10.9		12.7	PROD ORG TENSIO-ACT NDA
562	*FERTILIZERS,MANUFACTURE				8.3		34.2		60.7	ENGRAIS MANUFACTURES
5629	FERTILIZERS NES			W 14544	2.7		25.3		52.8	ENGRAIS NDA
56292	NITROG-PHOS FERTILZR NES			W 2368	0.5		21.3		47.3	ENGRAIS NDA CONT N P
572	*EXPLOSIVES,PYROTECH PRO			W 19372	14.2		19.9		21.0	EXPLOSIFS
5721	PREPARED EXPLOSIVES			W 18739	11.8		16.9		18.0	POUDRES,EXPLOSIFS

4. General Imports C.I.F. by Commodities according to the S.I.T.C. (Rev. 2) in million U.S. Dollars
Importations Générales C.A.F. par Produits d'après la C.T.C.I. (Rév. 2) en millions de Dollars E.U.

SITC CTCI	COMMODITY	1994		1995		1996		1997		PRODUIT
		QUANTITY QUANTITE	VALUE VALEUR	QUANTITY QUANTITE	VALUE VALEUR	QUANTITY QUANTITE	VALUE VALEUR	QUANTITY QUANTITE	VALUE VALEUR	
57212	PREPARED EXPLOSIVES NES			W 18739	11.8		16.9		18.0	EXPLOSIFS PREPARES
58	PLASTIC MATERIALS ETC				38.0		47.0		57.2	MAT PLAST ARTIFICIELLES
582	PROD OF CONDENSATION ETC			W 5396	7.1		10.7		13.0	PROD CONDENS,POLYCOND
583	POLYMERIZATION ETC PRODS			W 14914	29.1		34.3		41.5	PROD POLYMERISATION
5831	POLYETHYLENE			W 6020	9.2		9.3		15.2	POLYETHYLENE
5839	OTH POLYMRZTION ETC PROD			W 2881	9.9		12.4		10.8	AUT PROD POLYMER COPOLYM
59	CHEMICAL MATERIALS NES				16.7		31.8		29.6	MAT PROD CHIMIQUES NDA
598	MISCEL CHEM PRODUCTS NES			W 9114	10.0		19.7		18.9	PROD DIV INDUST CHIM NDA
5989	CHEM PRODUCTS,PREPS NES			W 6905	8.7		12.3		13.0	PROD PREP CHIMIQUES NDA
6	BASIC MANUFACTURES				523.0		649.5		831.8	ART MANUFACTURES
61	LEATHER,DRESSED FUR,ETC				17.2		20.7		22.4	CUIRS,PELLETERIES
611	LEATHER				7.5		11.4		11.3	CUIRS,PEAUX PREPARES
612	LEATHER ETC MANUFACTURES			W 998	8.9		8.5		10.6	OUVRAGES EN CUIRS NDA
6123	PREPRD PARTS OF FOOTWEAR			W 954	8.5		8.0		9.9	PARTIES DE CHAUSSURES
62	RUBBER MANUFACTURES NES				25.7		30.9		43.1	CAOUTCHOUC MANUFACTURE
625	RUBBER TYRES, TUBES ETC				16.8		21.1		31.1	PNEUS CAOUTCHOUC VULCANISE
6251	TYRES NEW FOR MOTOR CARS			N 190588	9.8		9.9		16.5	PNEUS POUR VOITURES
63	WOOD,CORK MANUFACTRS NES				30.7		33.8		40.7	OUVRAGES LIEGE ET BOIS
634	VENEERS,PLYWOOD,ETC				20.7		23.1		25.9	PLACAGES,CONTRE–PLAQUES
6342	PLYWOOD OF WOOD SHEETS		8.7	V 62145	13.8		16.0		16.0	BOIS CONTRE–PLAQUES
635	WOOD MANUFACTURES NES			W 5395	9.8		10.6		14.6	ART MANUF EN BOIS NDA
6353	BUILDERS WOODWRK,PREFABS		3.7	W 3045	8.1		8.6		12.0	OUVRAGES DE MENUISERIE
64	PAPER,PAPERBOARD AND MFR				69.9		87.3		146.2	PAPIERS,CARTONS & OUVRAGES
641	PAPER AND PAPERBOARD				40.1		53.1		102.0	PAPIERS ET CARTONS
6411	NEWSPRINT			W 10404	6.0		6.6		38.7	PAPIER JOURNAL
6412	PRINTG,WRITING PAPER NES			W 9377	11.7		10.7		15.1	PAPIERS POUR L'IMPRESSION
64122	— COATED,IMPREGNATD ETC			W 7945	9.6		8.4		10.1	PAPIERS IMPRESSION COUCHES
6415	PAPER,PAPERBRD,BULK,NES			W 5695	6.5		11.3		14.0	PAPIERS,CARTONS ROULEAUX
64159	OTHER PAPER ETC,BULK,NES			W 5487	6.0		10.5		12.6	AUT PAPIER ROULEAUX FEUILLES
6418	COATED ETC PAPER NES BLK			W 3308	5.3		9.1		17.3	PAP,CARTONS COUCHES,ENDUITS
642	PAPER,ETC,PRECUT,ARTS OF			W 13820	29.8		34.2		44.2	PAP,CARTONS DECOUPES
6421	PAPER ETC CONTAINERS			W 7666	12.6		13.4		15.7	BOITES,SACS EMBALLAGES
6428	PAPER ETC ARTICLES NES			W 2562	9.5		10.6		14.8	OUVRAGES EN PATE A PAPIER
65	TEXTILE YARN,FABRICS,ETC				154.2		170.6		188.9	FILS,TISSUS,ARTICLES TEXTILE
651	TEXTILE YARN			W 2213	12.0		15.8		20.7	FILS TEXTILES
652	COTTON FABRICS,WOVEN				33.0		31.3		35.3	TISSUS DE COTON
6522	WOVEN COTTON BLEACHD,ETC				25.4		24.0		23.9	TISSUS COTON BLANCHIS ETC
65224	BLCHED COTTON FABRIC NES				18.6		15.9		16.5	AUT TIS PLUS 85% COT BLANCHI
653	WOVN MAN–MADE FIB FABRIC				50.9		54.7		60.4	TISSUS FIBRES SYNTH,ARTIF
6531	CONT SYNT WEAVES NONPILE				16.6		18.4		22.4	TISSUS FIBRES SYNTH CONTINUE
65315	CONT SYN TXTL FABRIC NES				15.4		17.1		20.0	TIS PLUS 85% TEXT SYNT CONT
6534	DISC SYN BLEND FABRC NES				17.0		16.8		21.3	TISSUS FIBRES SYNTH DISCONT
65342	DISC SYN FIB–WOOL FABRIC				9.1		8.7		10.2	TISSUS FIB SYNT MEL LAINE
6535	CONT REGN WEAVES NONPILE				9.6		9.6		7.4	TISSUS FIB TEXT ART CONTINU
65355	CONT REGN TXTL FABRC NES				8.1		7.9		6.1	TISSUS 85% TEXT ART CONT
654	OTH WOVEN TEXTILE FABRIC				9.3		10.4		10.5	TISSUS AUT COTON SYNT,ARTIF
655	KNITTED,ETC FABRICS			W 852	9.9		11.4		14.8	ETOF BONNETERIE PIECES ETC
6552	OTHER KNIT ETC FAB NONEL			W 852	9.9		11.4		14.8	ETOF BON NON ELAS NON SYNT
657	SPECIAL TXTL FABRC,PRODS				20.3		26.5		25.9	TISSUS SPECIAUX
6573	COATED ETC TEXTILES NES				9.4		9.1		12.0	TISSUS,ART MATIERE TEXT NDA
658	TEXTILE ARTICLES NES				10.0		9.0		8.6	ART FACONNES MAT TEXTILES
66	NONMETAL MINERAL MFS NES				52.5		66.2		69.6	ART MIN NON METALLIQUES
661	LIME,CEMENT,BLDG PRODS				7.7		10.3		10.8	CHAUX,CIMENTS MAT CONSTR
662	CLAY,REFRACTORY BLDG PRD				8.7		11.6		10.8	MAT CONST REFRACTAIRES
663	MINERAL MANUFCTURES NES				12.9		14.4		17.4	ART MIN MANUF NDA
6633	MINRL MFS NES NONCERAMIC				7.7		7.7		9.1	OUVR MAT MINERALE NDA
664	GLASS				15.1		20.6		20.8	VERRE
67	IRON AND STEEL				78.0		110.4		151.7	FER ET ACIER
673	IRON,STEEL SHAPES ETC	W 31480	6.1	W 22807	9.1		15.4		19.7	BARRES,PROFIL FER,ACIER
674	IRN,STL UNIV,PLATE,SHEET			W 84668	42.9		58.0		87.4	LARGES PLATS,TOLES
6744	IRN,STL HVY PLATE,ROLLED			W 35697	13.0		11.5		15.4	TOLES LAMINEES PLUS 4.75 MM
67441	— OF IRON OR SIMPLE STL			W 28949	9.1		9.8		14.0	TOLES NON ACIER FIN CARB
6747	TINNED PLATES,SHEETS			W 21445	12.5		12.0		21.3	TOLES ETAMEES EN ACIER
6749	OTH IRN,STL PLATES,SHEET			W 12936	10.8		20.0		29.5	AUTRES TOLES FER,ACIER
67491	— OF IRON OR SIMPLE STL			W 11999	9.5		19.6		29.0	AUT TOLES AUTRES ACIER FIN
678	IRON,STL TUBES,PIPES,ETC			W 16553	14.1		24.0		25.6	TUBES,TUYAUX EN FONTE,FER
6782	IRON,STL SEAMLESS TUBES	W 5726	6.7	W 4293	3.4		5.1		5.2	TUBES,TUYAUX SANS SOUDURE
6783	IRON,STL TUBES,PIPES NES	W 7778	4.4	W 11730	8.5		12.2		13.9	AUT TUBES,TUYAUX FER,ACIER
68	NON–FERROUS METALS				16.1		15.9		35.3	METAUX NON FERREUX
684	ALUMINIUM			W 3124	11.6		10.6		23.5	ALUMINIUM
6842	ALUMINIUM,ALLOYS WORKED			W 2695	11.0		9.8		13.5	ALUMINIUM,ALLIAGES OUVRE
69	METAL MANUFACTURES NES				79.0		114.1		134.4	ART MANUFACT EN METAL NDA
691	STRUCTURES AND PARTS NES	W 8462	7.4	W 7222	17.2		25.9		30.7	CONSTRUCT FER,ACIER,ALU
6911	STRUCTURES,PARTS IRN,STL			W 6981	15.7		23.6		27.3	CONSTRUCT FER,ACIER,FONTE
692	METAL TANKS,BOXES,ETC			W 3799	6.9		10.7		14.7	RECIPIENTS METALLIQUES
695	TOOLS			W 1103	8.7		11.0		12.5	OUTILS A MAIN
697	BASE MTL HOUSEHOLD EQUIP				8.4		14.9		14.8	ART MENAGE MET COMMUNS
699	BASE METAL MFRS NES				26.6		35.1		41.3	ART MANUFACTURES MET NDA
6991	LOCKSMITHS WARES,ETC				13.7		19.1		23.1	ARTICLES DE SERRURERIE
69913	BASE MTL DOOR,ETC FITTNG			W 1641	9.5		14.7		18.2	GARNITURES POUR MEUBLES
69979	IRN,STL MANUFACTURES NES	W 4060	5.2	W 3117	4.1		4.3		4.1	AUT OUVRAGES EN FER NDA
7	MACHINES,TRANSPORT EQUIP				757.3		942.6		1509.2	MACHINES MATERIEL TRANSPORT
71	POWER GENERATING EQUIPMT				21.6		18.3		21.7	MACHINES GENERATRICES
711	STEAM BOILERS & AUX PLNT			W 12670	10.9		5.7		6.3	GENERATEURS VAPEUR EAU ETC
72	MACHS FOR SPCL INDUSTRYS				63.1		78.5		126.8	MAC SPECIALES POUR INDUST
721	AGRIC MACHY,EXC TRACTORS				9.5		13.4		18.7	MACHINES AGRICOLES
722	TRACTORS NON–ROAD			N 433	5.1		4.2		15.8	TRACTEURS
7224	WHEELED TRACTORS NES			N 432	5.1		4.2		15.6	TRACTEURS A ROUES
723	CIVIL ENGNEERG EQUIP ETC				6.5		7.1		19.8	APPAREILS DE GENIE CIVIL
7234	CONST,MINING MACHNRY NES				5.5		6.3		17.9	MACH POUR LA CONST, MINES
724	TEXTILE,LEATHER MACHNRY				11.1		12.7		16.1	MACH POUR INDUSTRIE TEXTILE
727	FOOD MACHRY NON–DOMESTIC			W 512	6.4		10.4		9.4	MACH INDUSTRIES ALIMENT
7272	OTH FOOD PROC MCHY,PARTS			W 467	6.2		10.2		9.2	AUT MACH IND ALIMENTAIRE
728	OTH MACHY FOR SPCL INDUS				19.7		24.7		34.3	AUT MACH IND PARTICULIERES
7281	MACH–TOOLS FR SPCL INDUS				11.2		7.8		12.6	MACH–OUTILS SPEC IND PART
72812	MACH–TOOLS TO WORK WOOD			N 18554	9.2		5.6		10.0	MACH–OUT POUR TRAVAIL BOIS
7284	MACHY FOR SPCL INDUS NES			W 633	7.2		14.2		18.9	MACH SPEC IND PARTICUL.
73	METALWORKING MACHINERY				6.9		9.0		13.8	MACH TRAVAIL DES METAUX
74	GENRL INDUSTRL MACHY NES				83.5		111.3		136.4	MACH APP INDUSTRIE
741	HEATING,COOLING EQUIPMNT				21.0		27.1		36.0	MACH CHAUFFAGE,PIECES
742	PUMPS FOR LIQUIDS ETC				8.3		12.0		11.5	POMPES MOTO–POMPES

4. General Imports C.I.F. by Commodities according to the S.I.T.C. (Rev. 2) in million U.S. Dollars
Importations Générales C.A.F. par Produits d'après la C.T.C.I. (Rév. 2) en millions de Dollars E.U.

SITC CTCI	COMMODITY	1994 QUANTITY QUANTITE	1994 VALUE VALEUR	1995 QUANTITY QUANTITE	1995 VALUE VALEUR	1996 QUANTITY QUANTITE	1996 VALUE VALEUR	1997 QUANTITY QUANTITE	1997 VALUE VALEUR	PRODUIT
743	PUMPS NES,CENTRFUGES ETC				12.6		20.6		17.3	POMPES COMPRES,VENT ETC
7436	GAS,LIQUID FILTERS ETC			W 771	5.7		11.8		7.6	APP POUR FILT DES LIQUIDES
744	MECHANICAL HANDLING EQU				15.3		18.4		25.3	EQUIP MANUTENTION PIECES
745	NONELEC MACHY,TOOLS NES				11.7		13.6		22.5	AUT MACH NON ELEC,PIECES
7452	OTH NONELEC MCHS,PTS NES				8.6		11.2		17.8	AUT MACH NON ELEC,PIECES
749	NONELEC MACH PTS,ACC NES			W 3017	14.8		19.9		23.9	PIECES MACH NON ELEC NDA
7492	COCKS,VALVES ETC NES			W 2346	9.9		14.5		18.0	ART ROB,SIM POUR TUYAUX
75	OFFICE MACHNES,ADP EQUIP				145.4		137.3		173.2	MACH BUREAU TRAIT AUTOM
751	OFFICE MACHINES				8.0		8.6		11.6	MACH,APPAREILS DE BUREAU
752	AUTOMTIC DATA PROC EQUIP			N 493852	31.6		34.4		50.7	MACH TRAIT INFORMATION
7525	ADP PERIPHERAL UNITS			N 144194	14.1		12.3		18.3	UNITES PERIPHERIQUES
7528	OFF-LINE DATA PROC EQUIP			N 291891	6.5		8.4		13.7	MACH AUXIL TRAIT INFORM
759	OFFICE,ADP MCH PTS,ACCES			W 1811	105.9		94.4		110.9	PIECES DU 751 ET 752
7591	OFFICE MACHINE PARTS NES			W 480	26.0		13.9		5.9	PIECES DU 7511,7518
75915	OTH OFF MCH PTS,ACC NES			W 383	23.7		10.7		2.4	PIECES DU 751.18,81,88
7599	ACCTG,ETC,ADP MCH PTS,AC			W 1331	80.0		80.5		105.1	PIECES DU 751 ET 752
76	TELECOMM,SOUND EQUIPMENT				118.3		186.5		228.7	EQUIPMENT DE TELECOM
761	TELEVISION RECEIVERS				12.3		38.2		41.6	RECEPTEURS DE TELEVISION
7611	COLOUR TV RECEIVERS				11.8		38.2		41.6	RECEPTEURS COULEUR
763	SOUND RECORDRS,PHONOGRPH				4.6		9.6		14.5	PHONO,APP ENREGISTREMENT
7638	OTHR SOUND APPARATUS ETC				4.5		9.4		14.4	AUT APP D'ENREGIS,REPROD
764	TELECOM EQPT,PTS,ACC NES				97.6		130.9		160.7	EQUIP TELECOM,PIECES
7641	LINE TELEPHONE,ETC EQUIP			W 229	33.5		31.1		40.1	APP TELEPHON PAR FIL
7643	TV,RADIO TRANSMITTRS ETC				6.5		12.4		29.2	APP EMET TELE RADIO
7649	PTS NES OF EQUIPMT OF 76				54.2		79.8		80.8	PIECES DE LA DIV 76
76491	PTS NES OF APPAR OF 7641			W 55	7.8		14.5		21.1	PIECES POUR 764.1
76493	TELECOMM EQUIPMT PTS NES				44.3		55.9		57.9	PIECES 761,762,764.3,8
77	ELECTRIC MACHNRY NES ETC				123.0		168.5		292.7	MACH APP ELECT NDA
771	ELECTRIC POWER MACHY NES				4.2		9.1		26.7	MACH PROD,TRANS ELECTR
7712	OTH ELEC POWER MACHY NES				3.3		7.5		24.2	AUT APP PROD TRANSF ELEC
77121	STATIC CONVERTERS ETC				2.4		6.3		19.1	CONVERTISSEURS STATIQUES
772	SWITCHGEAR ETC,PARTS NES			W 1508	18.2		25.3		49.9	APP COUPURE,SECT ETC
7721	SWITCHGEAR ETC			W 1480	17.8		24.4		32.0	APP COUPURE,SECTIONMNT
773	ELECTR DISTRIBUTNG EQUIP			W 4715	21.5		29.1		40.3	EQUIPMT DISTRIBUTION ELECT
7731	INSULATED WIRE,CABLE ETC			W 4483	21.1		28.3		39.6	FILS,CABLES ISOLES ELECT
774	ELECTRO-MEDCL,XRAY EQUIP				13.5		12.6		11.3	APPAREILS MEDICAUX
7742	X-RAY APPARATUS ETC				8.0		5.7		4.4	APPAREILS A RAYONS X
775	HOUSEHOLD TYPE EQUIP NES				36.0		55.9		62.6	MACH,APP USAGE DOMESTQUE
7751	HOUSEHOLD LDRY EQUIP NES				5.0		10.5		13.6	MACH A LAVER ET SECHOIRS
77511	DOMESTIC WASHING MACHNES				4.9		10.4		13.6	MACH LAVER LINGE MOINS 6 KG
7757	DOMESTIC ELECTRC EQU NES				11.2		16.2		14.6	APP ELECTR DOMEST NDA
7758	ELECTRO-THERMIC APPL NES				14.1		21.7		23.5	APP ELECTROTHERMIQ NDA
77586	ELECTROTHERM DOM APP NES			N 124936	5.6		10.9		12.6	APP ELECTRO THERMIQUES
776	TRANSISTORS,VALVES,ETC				2.1		6.5		42.0	LAMPES,TUBES,VALVES
7764	ELECTRONIC MICROCIRCUITS				1.5		5.3		27.7	MICROSTRUCTURES ELECTRON
778	ELECTRICAL MACHINERY NES				27.8		30.2		60.0	AUTRES MACH ELECT NDA
7781	BATTERIES,ACCUMULATORS				7.7		9.9		13.7	PILES ET ACCUMULATEURS
7788	OTH ELEC MACHY,EQUIP NES				10.0		10.5		33.5	AUT MACH APP ELEC NDA
77884	ELECTRICAL CONDENSERS			W 19	0.4		0.3		17.3	CONDENSATEURS ELECTRIQUES
78	ROAD VEHICLES				188.6		223.2		492.6	VEHICULES ROUTIERS
781	PASS MOTOR VEH EXC BUSES		70.8	N 45142	96.3		98.6		311.8	AUTO TRANSPORT PERSONNES
782	LORRIES,SPCL MTR VEH NES			N 14443	41.7		59.6		84.5	VEHICULES SPECIAUX,MARCH
7821	LORRIES,TRUCKS		20.6	N 13141	32.3		48.6		77.8	VEHICULES TRANSP MARCHAND
7822	SPECIAL MOTOR VEHCLS NES		1.9	N 1302	9.4		11.0		6.8	VEHICULES USAGES SPECIAUX
783	ROAD MOTOR VEHICLES NES			N 519	5.6		7.4		18.8	VEHICULES ROUTIERS NDA
784	MOTOR VEH PRTS,ACCES NES				34.0		41.4		48.6	PIECES 722,781,782,783
7849	OTHER MOTOR VEHCL PARTS			W 3637	33.3		39.0		45.8	PIECES 722,781,782,783
786	TRAILERS,NONMOTR VEH,NES				9.3		12.7		23.0	REMORQUES,CADRES,CONTAIN
7861	TRAILERS,TRANSP CONTAINR				5.5		8.3		15.0	REMORQUES TOUS VEHICULES
79	OTHR TRANSPORT EQUIPMENT				7.3		10.5		23.8	AUTRE MATERIEL TRANSPORT
8	MISC MANUFACTURED GOODS				305.8		377.8		443.0	ART MANUFACTURES DIVERS
812	*PLUMBG,HEATNG,LGHTNG EQ			W 4271	22.0		26.1		32.3	APPAR SANITAIRES CHAUFFAGE
8124	LIGHTING EQUIPMENT NES			W 1454	14.1		17.4		19.1	APPAREILS ECLAIRAGE ETC
81242	LAMPS,FITTINGS BASE METL			W 1000	10.8		14.3		16.2	APPAREILS D'ECLAIRAGE
821	*FURNITURE,PARTS THEREOF			W 8758	38.2		42.8		52.1	MEUBLES ET PIECES
8219	FURNITURE AND PARTS NES			W 7093	27.8		28.7		33.8	AUTRES MEUBLES ET PIECES
82192	WOOD FURNITURE NES		13.7	W 4059	15.8		16.8		20.1	MEUBLES NDA EN BOIS
84	CLOTHING AND ACCESSORIES				66.2		89.6		99.8	VETEMENTS
842	MENS OUTERWEAR NOT KNIT				11.9		14.8		18.2	VET DESSUS POUR HOMMES
843	WOMENS OUTERWEAR NONKNIT				15.5		20.0		18.6	VET DESSUS FEMMES MAT TEX
8439	— OTHER OUTER GARMENTS				6.6		10.0		9.7	AUT VET DES FEM MAT TEXT
844	UNDER GARMENTS NOT KNIT				11.7		14.0		16.8	VETEMENT DESSOUS MAT TEX
8441	— MENS SHIRTS				11.4		13.4		16.5	CHEMISES HOMMES MAT TEXT
84412	—— OF SYNTHETIC FIBRES			W 450	9.5		10.3		13.4	CHEMISES HOMMES FIB SYNT
845	OUTERWEAR KNIT NONELASTC				9.5		17.3		18.6	VET DESSOUS,ACCES BONNET
8459	— OTHER,CLTHG ACCESRYS				5.5		12.3		13.2	AUT VET DESSUS DE BONNE
846	UNDER GARMENTS KNITTED				7.7		9.0		11.9	SOUS VETS DE BONNETERIE
851	*FOOTWEAR			P 2062437	22.2		27.7		33.6	CHAUSSURES
85102	FOOTWEAR LEATHER			P 1283994	15.1		19.4		20.8	CHAUS SEMELLES EN CUIR
87	PRECISION INSTRUMNTS NES				30.1		42.3		47.5	INSTRUM,APPAR SCIENT NDA
872	MEDICAL INSTRUMENTS NES			W 307	10.9		14.2		9.7	INSTR,APP MEDIC-CHIR NDA
87202	OTH MEDICAL INSTRUMENTS			W 280	9.6		12.5		8.5	INSTRUM,APP MEDECINE
874	MEASURNG,CONTROLNG INSTR				15.4		21.9		25.7	INSTRUMENTS DE MESURE
88	PHOTO EQU,OPTICL GDS ETC				15.6		18.1		21.4	APP,FOURN PHOTO,OP,MONTR
882	PHOTO,CINEMA SUPPLIES				7.9		8.7		8.3	PRODUITS PHOTO,CINEMA
89	MISC MANUFCTRD GOODS NES				108.2		126.6		151.6	ART MANUFACTURES DIVERS
892	PRINTED MATTER			W 3015	16.2		18.3		23.5	IMPRIMES
8928	PRINTED MATTER NES			W 1393	10.6		9.8		13.8	IMPRIMES NDA
893	ARTICLES OF PLASTIC NES				50.6		59.3		71.3	OUVRAGES EN MAT DIVIS 58
8931	PLSTC PACKG CONTNRS,LIDS			W 3435	12.4		17.3		19.9	ART TRANSP EMBALLAGE ETC
8939	MISC PLASTIC ARTICLES			W 7323	35.6		39.5		48.0	ART DIVERS EN MAT DIV 58
89399	OTHR PLASTC ARTICLES NES			W 5993	29.6		32.2		39.5	AUT OUV MAT DIV 58
894	TOYS,SPORTING GOODS,ETC				12.8		14.6		18.7	VOITURES ENFANTS,JOUETS
8942	TOYS,INDOOR GAMES ETC				9.0		10.0		11.6	JOUETS,JEUX ETC
899	OTHER MANUFACTURED GOODS				13.7		18.3		17.8	AUT ART MANUF DIVERS NDA

5. General Exports F.O.B. by Commodities according to the S.I.T.C. (Rev. 2) in million U.S. Dollars
Exportations Générales F.O.B. par Produits d'après la C.T.C.I. (Rév. 2) en millions de Dollars E.U.

SITC CTCI	COMMODITY	1994 QUANTITY QUANTITE	1994 VALUE VALEUR	1995 QUANTITY QUANTITE	1995 VALUE VALEUR	1996 QUANTITY QUANTITE	1996 VALUE VALEUR	1997 QUANTITY QUANTITE	1997 VALUE VALEUR	PRODUIT
	ALL COMMODITIES		1305.9		1838.9		2074.1		2926.5	TOUS PRODUITS
0	FOOD AND LIVE ANIMALS				272.6		290.3		448.5	ALIMENTS,ANIMAUX VIVANTS
01	MEAT AND PREPARATIONS				16.1		8.5		48.3	VIANDES ET PREPARATIONS
011	MEAT FRESH,CHILLD,FROZEN	W 2416	3.5	W 5643	7.7		3.9		36.1	VIANDES FRAICHES,REF,CONGE
0114	POULTRY FRESH CHLLD,FRZN			W 3945	4.8		3.0		30.3	VOLAILLES MORTES
014	MEAT PREPD,PRSVD,NES ETC			W 3404	8.2		4.6		12.2	CONSERVES DE VIANDES
0141	MEAT,FISH EXTRCTS,JUICES		69.9		0.1		0.1		0.1	EXTRAITS DE VIANDE
0142	SAUSAGES INCLDING TINNED			W 2229	5.6		3.1		10.7	SAUCISSES,SAUCISSONS
02	DAIRY PRODCTS,BIRDS'EGGS				88.2		94.8		105.4	PRODUITS LAITIERS,OEUFS
022	MILK AND CREAM			W 33705	50.2		52.6		60.1	LAIT ET CREME
0223	MILK AND CREAM FRESH			W 7422	5.1		13.3		17.2	LAIT,CREME FRAIS
0224	MILK,CREAM PRESERVED ETC			W 26284	45.2		39.3		42.9	LAIT,CREME CONS,CONC
02242	MILK DRY,1.5% FAT OR LES			W 23893	41.7		37.7		38.9	LAIT POUDRE INF 1.5%
023	BUTTER			W 13204	27.0		28.2		37.0	BEURRE
024	CHEESE AND CURD			W 4649	10.4		13.3		7.8	FROMAGE ET CAILLEBOTTE
03	FISH AND PREPARATIONS		36.5		104.6		99.0		80.8	POISSONS ET PREPARATIONS
034	FISH,FRESH,CHILLED,FROZN			W 51103	39.0		25.6		37.3	POISSON FRAIS, REFRIG,CONG
0342	FISH FROZEN,EXCL FILLETS			W 47021	24.2		9.9		19.6	POISSONS CONGELES
0343	FISH FILLETS,FRESH,CHLLD			W 1031	7.0		8.8		9.9	FILETS FRAIS,REFRIGERES
037	FISH ETC PREPD,PRSVD NES			W 42327	62.6		69.9		37.9	POIS,CRUST,MOL PREPARES
0371	FISH PREPARD,PRESRVD NES			W 42215	61.7		69.3		37.2	CONSERVES DE POISSONS
04	CEREALS AND PREPARATIONS				5.9		13.2		16.1	CEREALES ET PRODUITS
048	CEREAL ETC PREPARATIONS			W 6774	4.6		9.4		10.5	PREPTNS A BASE CEREALES
0484	BAKERY PRODUCTS			W 1465	2.7		7.9		4.9	PRODUITS DE BOULANGERIE
04842	PASTRY, CAKES ETC			W 1173	2.3		7.3		4.4	PATISSERIE ETC.
05	VEGETABLES AND FRUIT				8.3		13.1		13.1	LEGUMES ET FRUITS
057	FRUIT,NUTS,FRESH,DRIED		7.5	W 2315	1.9		2.8		4.0	FRUITS FRAIS OU SECS
058	FRUIT PRESERVED,PREPARED		6.3	W 5101	3.9		7.8		7.0	CONSERVES DE FRUITS
06	SUGAR AND PREPS,HONEY		19.0		9.4		12.8		21.8	SUCRES ET PRODUITS
061	SUGAR AND HONEY			W 4724	2.2		4.2		11.0	SUCRES ET MIEL
0612	REFINED SUGAR ETC			W 3848	1.8		4.0		10.7	SUCRES RAFFINES
062	SUGAR CANDY NON–CHOCLATE			W 1467	7.2		8.6		10.9	SUCRERIES
07	COFFEE,TEA,COCOA,SPICES		33.6		22.0		31.2		145.4	CAFE,THE,CACAO,EPICES
071	COFFEE AND SUBSTITUTES			W 1013	7.1		7.3		9.1	CAFE ET SUCCEDANES
0711	COFFEE GREEN,ROASTED,SUB			W 796	5.6		5.4		6.7	CAFE TORREFIE OU DECAFEINE
072	COCOA			W 2131	3.4		15.2		121.8	CACAO
0721	COCOA BEANS,RAW,ROASTED			W 1939	2.9		14.1		110.1	CACAO EN FEVES
0723	COCOA BUTTER AND PASTE			W 185	0.5		1.1		10.9	BEURRE ET PATE DE CACAO
073	CHOCOLATE AND PRODUCTS			W 3904	10.9		6.7		11.7	CHOCOLAT
081	*FEEDING STUFF FOR ANIML			W 13191	6.0		2.7		2.8	NOURRITURE POUR ANIMAUX
09	MISC EDIBLE PRODUCTS				10.5		14.9		14.5	PREP ALIMENTAIRES DIVERSES
091	MARGARINE AND SHORTENING			W 4419	5.7		5.2		1.9	MARGARINE ET GRAISSES
0914	MARGARINE,EDIBLE FAT NES			W 4380	5.6		5.2		1.9	MARGARINES,SIMILI SAINDOUX
098	EDIBLE PRODCTS,PREPS NES				4.9		9.8		12.7	PREP ALIMENTAIRES NDA
09809	MISC FOOD PREPRTIONS NES			W 2419	3.5		8.1		9.7	PREP ALIMENTAIRES NDA
1	BEVERAGES AND TOBACCO		26.2		15.3		21.9		20.0	BOISSONS ET TABACS
11	BEVERAGES		17.5		13.7		17.2		15.5	BOISSONS
111	NON–ALCOHL BEVERAGES NES			W 22935	7.6		12.6		11.9	BOISSONS NON ALCOOLIQUES
11102	FLAVORED WATERS NON–ALCO			W 22411	7.4		12.4		11.2	LIMONADES,EAUX GAZEUSES
112	ALCOHOLIC BEVERAGES			W 2701	6.2		4.6		3.7	BOISSONS ALCOOLIQUES
12	TOBACCO AND MANUFACTURES		8.8		1.6		4.7		4.5	TABACS BRUTS FABRIQUES
2	CRUDE MATERLS,EXCL FUELS				219.3		210.3		343.4	MAT BRUTES NON COMESTIBLES
21	HIDES,SKINS,FURS UNDRSSD				11.3		10.0		9.9	CUIRS,PEAUX BRUTS
211	HIDES,SKINS,EXC FURS,RAW				7.5		5.5		5.9	CUIRS ET PEAUX
23	RUBBER, CRUDE				0.2		3.5		9.2	CAOUTCHOUC BRUT
233	RUBBER,SYNTHTIC,RECLAIMD			W 103	0.2		3.5		9.1	LATEX CAOUTCH SYNTH REGEN
2331	SYNTHETIC RUBBER ETC			W 103	0.2		3.5		9.1	LATEX CAOUTCH SYNTHETIQUE
24	CORK AND WOOD				155.4		149.9		242.4	LIEGE ET BOIS
246	PULPWOOD,CHIPS,WOODWASTE			W 71159	3.2		6.6		11.6	BOIS DE TRITURATION
247	OTH WOOD ROUGH,SQUARED			W 1907408	102.6		76.3		118.7	BOIS BRUTS EQUARRIS
2471	SAW–,VENEER–LOGS CONIFER			W 989520	60.0		49.3		78.1	CONIFERES POUR SCIAGE,PLACAG
24711	— IN THE ROUGH			W 989520	60.0		49.3		78.1	ECORCES OU DEGROSSIS
2472	SAW–,VENEER–LOGS NON–CON			W 917888	42.6		27.0		40.6	NON CONIFERES SCIAGE,PLAC
24721	— IN THE ROUGH			W 917888	42.6		27.0		40.6	BRUTS ECORCES DEGROSSIS
248	WOOD SHAPED,SLEEPERS	W 6838	40.1		49.2		66.5		110.8	BOIS SIMPLEMENT TRAVAILLES
2482	LUMBER SHAPED CONIFER				46.3		61.4		103.5	CONIFERES SCIES,RABOTES
24821	LUMBER SAWN ETC CONIFER				45.1		56.8		90.8	CONIFERES SCIES LONGITUD
24822	LUMBER PLANED ETC CONIFR				1.2		4.7		12.8	CONIFER RABOTES,RAINES
27861	SLAG ETC FRM IRN,STL MFR	W 191413	16.8				0.1			SCORIES,LAITIER,BATTIT
28	METALLIFEROUS ORES,SCRAP				38.0		36.5		60.4	MINERAIS METAL,DECHETS
282	IRON AND STEEL SCRAP			W 255649	22.0		22.3		38.0	FERRAILLES
28209	— OF OTHR IRON OR STEEL			W 227232	16.7		15.8		31.1	FERRAILLES DE FER
288	NONFERR METAL SCRAP NES			W 19708	13.3		10.6		11.9	DECHETS NON FERREUX
2882	OTHER BASE MTL SCRAP NES			W 19708	13.3		10.6		11.9	AUTRES DECHETS
28821	COPPER WASTE AND SCRAP			W 5320	6.4		4.6		5.4	DECHETS DE CUIVRE
29	CRUDE ANIMAL,VEG MAT NES				6.8		5.1		4.5	MATIERES BRUTES ANIM,VEGET
292	CRUDE VEG MATERIALS NES				6.2		4.9		4.2	MAT BRUTES VEGETALES NDA
3	MINERAL FUELS ETC				130.4		132.1		185.3	COMBUSTIBLES MINERAUX LUB
32	COAL,COKE AND BRIQUETTES				21.3		24.1		22.0	HOUILLES,COKES,BRIQUETTES
322	COAL,LIGNITE AND PEAT			W 410700	14.3		16.2		16.1	HOUILLES,LIGNITES,TOURBE
3224	PEAT,NOT AGGLOMERATED			W 368399	12.9		14.2		14.0	TOURBE
323	BRIQUETS,COKE,SEMI–COKE			W 39216	7.0		8.0		5.9	BRIQUETTES
3232	COKE,SEMI–COKE,RTRT CRBN			W 39215	7.0		8.0		5.9	COKES ET SEMI–COKES
33	PETROLEUM AND PRODUCTS				87.6		80.7		135.3	PETROLE ET DERIVES
334	PETROLEUM PRODUCTS,REFIN			W 405149	59.7		63.0		117.8	PRODUITS RAFFINES
335	RESIDUAL PETRLM PROD NES			W 219016	28.0		17.3		16.7	PRODUITS RESIDUELS NDA
3352	MINERAL TARS AND PRODCTS			W 194977	24.1		11.5		9.5	GOUDRONS MINERAUX
33521	MINERAL TAR			W 133826	9.8		8.5			GOUDRONS DE HOUILLE
33522	BENZOLE			W 44455	11.2		1.8		8.5	BENZOLS
351	*ELECTRIC CURRENT			H 1004593	21.5		27.3		27.9	ENERGIE ELECTRIQUE
5	CHEMCLS,RELATED PROD NES				150.6		198.0		246.4	PRODUITS CHIMIQUES
51	ORGANIC CHEMICALS				20.6		35.6		37.6	PROD CHIMIQ ORGANIQUES
511	HYDROCARBONS NES,DERIVS			W 12096	2.8		7.8		2.6	HYDROCARBURES NDA
512	ALCOHOLS,PHENOLS ETC				4.2		6.3		2.9	PHENOLS,PHENOLS–ALCOOLS
513	CARBOXYLIC ACIDS ETC			W 22710	12.6		12.6		17.1	ACIDES CARBOXYLIQUES
5137	MONOACIDS AND DERIVATIVS			W 22601	12.4		12.4		17.1	ACIDES MONOCARBOXYLIQUES
51379	OTH MONOACIDS ETC,DERIVS			W 22311	12.1		12.2		17.1	AUTRES MONOCARBOXYLIQUES
515	ORG–INORG COMPOUNDS ETC			W 188	0.5		7.6		13.1	COMPOSES ORGANO–MINERAUX
5156	HETEROCYCLIC CMPDS ETC						7.6		13.1	COMPOSES HETEROCYCLIQUES
51561	LACTAMS						7.6		13.1	LACTAMES .
52	INORGANIC CHEMICALS				35.3		37.5		36.4	PROD CHIM INORGANIQUES

5. General Exports F.O.B. by Commodities according to the S.I.T.C. (Rev. 2) in million U.S. Dollars
Exportations Générales F.O.B. par Produits d'après la C.T.C.I. (Rév. 2) en millions de Dollars E.U.

SITC CTCI	COMMODITY	1994 QUANTITY QUANTITE	1994 VALUE VALEUR	1995 QUANTITY QUANTITE	1995 VALUE VALEUR	1996 QUANTITY QUANTITE	1996 VALUE VALEUR	1997 QUANTITY QUANTITE	1997 VALUE VALEUR	PRODUIT
522	INORG ELEMNTS,OXIDES,ETC				21.1		23.3		24.7	ELEMENTS INORGANIQUES
5225	INORGANIC BASES ETC NES			W 120083	19.8		21.0		20.4	AUTRES BASES OXYDES METAL
52251	AMMONIA,ANHYDROUS ETC			W 120075	19.8		19.8		18.6	AMMONIAC LIQUEFIE
524	RADIOACTIVE ETC MATERIAL				12.8		12.1		4.2	MATIERES RADIOACTIVES
5249	OTH RADIOACTIVE ETC MTLS				12.8		12.1		4.2	AUT MATIERES RADIOACTIVES
52492	OTH CHEMS ASSOC RADIOACT				12.8		12.1		4.2	COMPOSES THORIUM,URANIUM
53	DYES,TANNING,COLOUR PROD				25.9		36.8		39.4	PROD TEINTURE,COLORANTS
533	PIGMENTS,PAINTS,ETC			W 9047	25.3		36.3		38.9	PIGMENTS,PEINTURES,VERNIS
5334	VARNISHES,DISTEMPERS ETC			W 5644	18.1		24.3		24.6	PEINTURES A L'EAU
53342	OTH PAINTS,VARNISHES ETC			W 4558	15.6		22.4		22.5	AUTRES PEINTURES,VERNIS
5335	GLAZES,DRIERS,PUTTY ETC			W 3355	7.0		11.6		14.1	PREPTNS COLOR UTILISES CERAM
53354	PUTTY,OTHER FILLINGS ETC			W 3255	6.8		11.6		13.8	MASTICS ENDUITS
541	*MEDICINAL,PHARM PRODUCT			K 2046350	19.9		26.0		31.8	PROD MEDICINAUX PHARMACEUT
5417	MEDICAMENTS			K 1903344	18.8		24.3		30.4	MEDICAMENTS
54179	— CONTNG OTH SUBSTANCES			K 1802565	16.7		20.7		25.6	MED CONT AUT SUBSTANCES
55	PERFUME,CLEANING ETC PRD				10.5		8.9		9.8	PROD POUR PARFUM,TOILETTE
554	SOAP,CLEANSING ETC PREPS			W 4386	6.7		4.3		3.3	SAVONS,PRODUITS DETERSIFS
562	*FERTILIZERS,MANUFACTURE				18.7		32.6		59.3	ENGRAIS MANUFACTURES
5621	CHEM NITROGENOUS FERTLZR				16.8		15.7		9.8	ENGRAIS AZOTES
56216	UREA				15.0		13.2		7.2	UREE
5629	FERTILIZERS NES			W 3733	0.6		16.9		49.5	ENGRAIS NDA
56292	NITROG–PHOS FERTILZR NES			W 2410	0.5		16.1		46.8	ENGRAIS NDA CONT N P
58	PLASTIC MATERIALS ETC				13.1		14.8		18.1	MAT PLAST ARTIFICIELLES
582	PROD OF CONDENSATION ETC			W 8570	6.4		8.1		10.6	PROD CONDENS,POLYCOND
583	POLYMERIZATION ETC PRODS			W 7193	6.4		6.7		7.5	PROD POLYMERISATION
59	CHEMICAL MATERIALS NES				6.9		6.1		14.4	MAT PROD CHIMIQUES NDA
598	MISCEL CHEM PRODUCTS NES			W 4240	4.1		1.9		10.4	PROD DIV INDUST CHIM NDA
6	BASIC MANUFACTURES				363.8		451.4		557.0	ART MANUFACTURES
61	LEATHER,DRESSED FUR,ETC				14.1		19.7		21.1	CUIRS,PELLETERIES
612	LEATHER ETC MANUFACTURES			W 504	8.2		8.4		9.0	OUVRAGES EN CUIRS NDA
6123	PREPRD PARTS OF FOOTWEAR			W 489	7.6		7.9		8.4	PARTIES DE CHAUSSURES
613	FUR SKINS TANNED,DRESSED			N 32994	1.8		7.5		8.3	PELLETERIES
62	RUBBER MANUFACTURES NES				10.8		7.1		8.7	CAOUTCHOUC MANUFACTURE
625	RUBBER TYRES, TUBES ETC				8.5		4.1		4.5	PNEUS CAOUTCHOUC VULCANISE
63	WOOD,CORK MANUFACTRS NES				77.0		92.2		103.8	OUVRAGES LIEGE ET BOIS
634	VENEERS,PLYWOOD,ETC				41.0		46.0		47.6	PLACAGES,CONTRE–PLAQUES
6342	PLYWOOD OF WOOD SHEETS		19.4	V 64460	25.5		28.5		28.1	BOIS CONTRE–PLAQUES
6343	IMPROVED,RECONSTIT WOOD			V 93692	13.3		14.4		15.5	BOIS AMELIORES,RECONST
63432	RECONSTITUTED WOOD		2.9	V 92970	13.1		14.4		15.5	BOIS RECONSTITUES
635	WOOD MANUFACTURES NES			W 54316	36.0		46.2		56.3	ART MANUF EN BOIS NDA
6351	BOXES,CASES,CRATES,ETC		4.2	W 31067	8.5		10.0		12.9	CAISSES EMBALLAGES BOIS
6353	BUILDERS WOODWRK,PREFABS		9.7	W 19963	19.6		26.0		32.4	OUVRAGES DE MENUISERIE
6354	WOOD MFRS DOMESTIC ETC			W 1621	5.4		7.1		7.9	ART MANUF USAGE DOMESTIQUE
64	PAPER,PAPERBOARD AND MFR				23.3		45.3		68.3	PAPIERS,CARTONS & OUVRAGES
641	PAPER AND PAPERBOARD				13.0		31.0		49.8	PAPIERS ET CARTONS
6413	KRAFT PAPER,PAPERBOARD			W 651	0.5		9.4		16.0	PAPIER ET CARTON KRAFT
64132	SACK KRAFT PAPER IN BULK			W 183	0.2		2.5		10.4	PAPIER KRAFT POUR SACS
6416	FIBRE BUILDING BOARD			A 8478	7.0		9.9		10.6	PLAQUES CONSTRUCT EN PATE
64161	HARDBOARD			A 8028	6.5		7.5		7.7	PLAQUES CONSTR COMPRIMES
64162	INSULATING BOARD, ETC		4.4	A 449	0.5		2.5		3.0	PLAQUES CONST NON COMPR
642	PAPER,ETC,PRECUT,ARTS OF			W 4319	10.3		14.3		18.6	PAP,CARTONS DECOUPES
65	TEXTILE YARN,FABRICS,ETC				105.9		141.7		159.8	FILS,TISSUS,ARTICLES TEXTILE
651	TEXTILE YARN			W 2102	9.2		10.9		18.3	FILS TEXTILES
6513	COTTON YARN			W 1635	5.5		6.6		7.2	FILS DE COTON
652	COTTON FABRICS,WOVEN				45.4		61.1		68.1	TISSUS DE COTON
6521	GREY WOVEN COTTON FABRIC				15.6		29.1		32.8	TISSUS COT ECRUS NON MERCER
65214	GREY WOVEN COTTON NES				15.5		28.9		32.6	AUT TISSUS 85% COTON ECRUS
6522	WOVEN COTTON BLEACHD,ETC				29.8		32.0		35.3	TISSUS COTON BLANCHIS ETC
65224	BLCHED COTTON FABRIC NES				28.2		28.9		34.5	AUT TIS PLUS 85% COT BLANCHI
657	SPECIAL TXTL FABRC,PRODS				17.2		26.1		24.4	TISSUS SPECIAUX
6577	TEXTILES FOR MACHINERY			W 948	5.3		13.1		12.4	OUATES,MECHES ART TEXT
65771	TEXTILE WADDING NES ETC			W 899	5.2		12.9		11.0	OUATES,ARTICLES EN OUATE
658	TEXTILE ARTICLES NES				27.3		33.7		38.4	ART FACONNES MAT TEXTILES
6584	LINENS ETC				21.2		24.4		27.1	LINGE DE MAISON
65841	BED LINEN OF COTTON			W 1656	10.6		10.7		11.4	LINGE DE LIT DE COTON
65845	OTHER LINEN OF COTTON			W 802	5.5		7.1		7.5	LINGE DE TOILETTE COTON
66	NONMETAL MINERAL MFS NES				42.6		46.4		52.9	ART MIN NON METALLIQUES
661	LIME,CEMENT,BLDG PRODS				15.6		16.2		16.1	CHAUX,CIMENTS MAT CONSTR
6612	CEMENT			W 515946	15.0		15.2		15.1	CIMENTS HYDRAULIQUES
663	MINERAL MANUFCTURES NES				6.9		6.5		8.7	ART MIN MANUF NDA
6633	MINRL MFS NES NONCERAMIC				6.3		5.8		7.7	OUVR MAT MINERALE NDA
66332	CEMENT,ARTFCL STONE PROD				5.7		5.0		7.1	OUVRAGES EN CIMENT
664	GLASS				10.5		10.7		9.2	VERRE
665	GLASSWARE				8.0		11.1		17.1	OUVRAGES EN VERRE
6651	BOTTLES ETC OF GLASS				6.6		9.4		15.6	RECIPIENTS EN VERRE
66511	GLASS BOTTLES ETC NONVAC				6.6		9.4		15.6	BONBONNES,BOUTEILLES,ETC
67	IRON AND STEEL				23.3		21.3		30.3	FER ET ACIER
674	IRN,STL UNIV,PLATE,SHEET			W 17272	6.2		10.9		15.8	LARGES PLATS,TOLES
68	NON–FERROUS METALS				15.6		10.7		21.8	METAUX NON FERREUX
683	NICKEL			W 2028	7.9		2.1		0.3	NICKEL
6832	NICKEL,ALLOYS WORKED			W 2002	7.9		2.1		0.2	NICKEL,ALLIAGES OUVRES
68322	NICKEL SHEET,POWDER,FOIL			W 1722	7.1		2.0		0.2	TOLES,PLANCHES, FEUILLES NI
684	ALUMINIUM			W 2412	2.3		3.0		12.9	ALUMINIUM
6841	ALUMINIUM,ALLOYS,UNWRGHT			W 334	0.5		0.6		10.4	ALUMINIUM,ALLIAGES BRUTS
69	METAL MANUFACTURES NES				51.6		67.5		90.7	ART MANUFACT EN METAL NDA
691	STRUCTURES AND PARTS NES	W 8005	6.8	W 11202	15.5		35.4		56.7	CONSTRUCT FER,ACIER,ALU
6911	STRUCTURES,PARTS IRN,STL			W 11025	14.9		34.3		56.1	CONSTRUCT FER,ACIER,FONTE
699	BASE METAL MFRS NES				24.6		17.8		15.8	ART MANUFACTURES MET NDA
6991	LOCKSMITHS WARES,ETC				6.2		6.9		6.2	ARTICLES DE SERRURERIE
6997	IRON,STEEL ARTICLES NES			W 5893	9.2		7.3		5.2	OUV FONTE,FER,ACIER NDA
69979	IRN,STL MANUFACTURES NES	W 5710	3.9	W 5893	9.2		7.3		5.1	AUT OUVRAGES EN FER NDA
6999	OTHR BASE METAL MFRS ETC			W 345	6.1		0.9		1.8	OUVRAGES EN TUNGST,MOLYB
7	MACHINES,TRANSPORT EQUIP				366.7		410.6		718.6	MACHINES MATERIEL TRANSPORT
71	POWER GENERATING EQUIPMT				12.9		14.7		14.8	MACHINES GENERATRICES
711	STEAM BOILERS & AUX PLNT			W 1456	5.9		5.3		6.9	GENERATEURS VAPEUR EAU ETC
72	MACHS FOR SPCL INDUSTRYS				21.8		24.3		38.6	MAC SPECIALES POUR INDUST
728	OTH MACHY FOR SPCL INDUS				3.7		6.5		16.0	AUT MACH IND PARTICULIERES
7284	MACHY FOR SPCL INDUS NES				1.5		3.7		12.6	MACH SPEC IND PARTICUL.
74	GENRL INDUSTRL MACHY NES				27.5		29.7		41.5	MACH APP INDUSTRIE
741	HEATING,COOLING EQUIPMNT				12.5		11.4		14.4	MACH CHAUFFAGE,PIECES
7416	HEATING,COOLING EQU NES			W 3310	10.4		8.4		8.4	APP CHANGEMENT TEMP

5. General Exports F.O.B. by Commodities according to the S.I.T.C. (Rev. 2) in million U.S. Dollars
Exportations Générales F.O.B. par Produits d'après la C.T.C.I. (Rév. 2) en millions de Dollars E.U.

SITC CTCI	COMMODITY	1994 QUANTITY QUANTITE	1994 VALUE VALEUR	1995 QUANTITY QUANTITE	1995 VALUE VALEUR	1996 QUANTITY QUANTITE	1996 VALUE VALEUR	1997 QUANTITY QUANTITE	1997 VALUE VALEUR	PRODUIT
749	NONELEC MACH PTS,ACC NES			W 1330	5.4		6.5		8.7	PIECES MACH NON ELEC NDA
75	OFFICE MACHNES,ADP EQUIP				89.4		71.5		42.0	MACH BUREAU TRAIT AUTOM
752	AUTOMTIC DATA PROC EQUIP			N 13718	2.8		4.7		10.7	MACH TRAIT INFORMATION
759	OFFICE,ADP MCH PTS,ACCES			W 1425	85.5		66.1		28.9	PIECES DU 751 ET 752
7591	OFFICE MACHINE PARTS NES			W 892	59.3		9.0		1.8	PIECES DU 7511,7518
75915	OTH OFF MCH PTS,ACC NES			W 876	58.5		8.1		0.9	PIECES DU 751.18,81,88
7599	ACCTG,ETC,ADP MCH PTS,AC			W 533	26.2		57.2		27.1	PIECES DU 751 ET 752
76	TELECOMM,SOUND EQUIPMENT				47.9		82.6		271.0	EQUIPMENT DE TELECOM
761	TELEVISION RECEIVERS				4.0		9.7		31.2	RECEPTEURS DE TELEVISION
7611	COLOUR TV RECEIVERS				4.0		9.7		31.2	RECEPTEURS COULEUR
764	TELECOM EQPT,PTS,ACC NES				42.8		70.7		227.5	EQUIP TELECOM,PIECES
7641	LINE TELEPHONE,ETC EQUIP				2.7		9.3		3.5	APP TELEPHON PAR FIL
7643	TV,RADIO TRANSMITTRS ETC				2.3		4.7		72.4	APP EMET TELE RADIO
7649	PTS NES OF EQUIPMT OF 76				36.6		55.9		150.3	PIECES DE LA DIV 76
76493	TELECOMM EQUIPMT PTS NES				34.3		48.6		145.5	PIECES 761,762,764.3,8
76499	PARTS ETC OF SOUND EQUIP			W 10	1.9		6.8		3.2	PIECES NDA POUR 763
77	ELECTRIC MACHNRY NES ETC				39.0		54.1		83.2	MACH APP ELECT NDA
771	ELECTRIC POWER MACHY NES				0.9		3.2		10.4	MACH PROD,TRANS ELECTR
7712	OTH ELEC POWER MACHY NES				0.8		3.2		10.2	AUT APP PROD TRANSF ELEC
77121	STATIC CONVERTERS ETC				0.6		1.9		9.0	CONVERTISSEURS STATIQUES
772	SWITCHGEAR ETC,PARTS NES			W 432	4.4		7.0		10.3	APP COUPURE,SECT ETC
773	ELECTR DISTRIBUTNG EQUIP			W 1705	13.9		21.7		31.5	EQUIPMT DISTRIBUTION ELECT
7731	INSULATED WIRE,CABLE ETC			W 1679	13.8		21.4		31.4	FILS,CABLES ISOLES ELECT
775	HOUSEHOLD TYPE EQUIP NES				5.2		8.6		14.2	MACH,APP USAGE DOMESTQUE
778	ELECTRICAL MACHINERY NES				10.8		10.1		11.4	AUTRES MACH ELECT NDA
7788	OTH ELEC MACHY,EQUIP NES				8.2		3.6		3.5	AUT MACH APP ELEC NDA
78	ROAD VEHICLES				113.8		115.9		213.0	VEHICULES ROUTIERS
781	PASS MOTOR VEH EXC BUSES		43.2	N 9655	59.9		59.9		147.3	AUTO TRANSPORT PERSONNES
782	LORRIES,SPCL MTR VEH NES			N 366	10.3		6.6		7.7	VEHICULES SPECIAUX,MARCH
7822	SPECIAL MOTOR VEHCLS NES		4.8	N 186	7.6		4.3		1.3	VEHICULES USAGES SPECIAUX
784	MOTOR VEH PRTS,ACCES NES				37.3		40.7		47.0	PIECES 722,781,782,783
7849	OTHER MOTOR VEHCL PARTS				37.2		40.6		47.0	PIECES 722,781,782,783
79	OTHR TRANSPORT EQUIPMENT				12.2		14.6		10.1	AUTRE MATERIEL TRANSPORT
793	SHIPS AND BOATS ETC				10.0		11.1		6.8	NAVIRES BATEAUX,ETC
7932	SHIPS AND BOATS NES				9.4		10.6		6.5	NAVIRES ET BATEAUX
8	MISC MANUFACTURED GOODS				314.6		354.7		403.9	ART MANUFACTURES DIVERS
812	*PLUMBG,HEATNG,LGHTNG EQ			W 1092	7.4		7.9		9.8	APPAR SANITAIRES CHAUFFAGE
8124	LIGHTING EQUIPMENT NES			W 663	6.2		6.3		7.2	APPAREILS ECLAIRAGE ETC
821	*FURNITURE,PARTS THEREOF			W 31645	69.0		86.8		93.1	MEUBLES ET PIECES
8211	CHAIRS,SEATS AND PARTS			W 5006	12.9		18.2		20.2	SIEGES ET PIECES
82111	CHAIRS AND OTHER SEATS			W 4709	12.1		16.8		18.1	SIEGES
8212	MED FURN,STUFFD FURNSHGS			W 1513	6.4		7.3		10.6	MOB MEDICO–CHIRUR,PIECES
82122	MATTRESSES ETC			W 1420	5.9		6.9		10.3	SOMMIERS,ARTICLES DE LITERIE
8219	FURNITURE AND PARTS NES			W 25126	49.9		61.4		62.4	AUTRES MEUBLES ET PIECES
82192	WOOD FURNITURE NES		35.6	W 19487	39.1		43.9		49.1	MEUBLES NDA EN BOIS
82199	OTHR FURN,FURN PARTS NES			W 4864	9.1		15.4		11.4	MEUBLES NDA AUTRES MATIERES
84	CLOTHING AND ACCESSORIES				145.2		158.7		179.9	VETEMENTS
842	MENS OUTERWEAR NOT KNIT				35.3		47.1		56.5	VET DESSUS POUR HOMMES
8423	— TROUSERS,BREECHES ETC			N 864248	10.7		15.3		19.3	PANTALONS HOMMES MAT TEX
8424	— JACKETS,BLAZERS ETC				6.5		7.1		7.1	VESTES HOMMES MAT TEXTIL
8429	— OTHER OUTER GARMENTS				10.9		15.6		21.0	AUT VET DES HOM MAT TEX
843	WOMENS OUTERWEAR NONKNIT				58.4		55.8		56.5	VET DESSUS FEMMES MAT TEX
8431	— COATS AND JACKETS				7.9		7.6		12.0	MANT,VEST FEM MAT TEXTIL
8435	— BLOUSES			N 987614	13.9		13.2		7.5	BLOUSES FEM MAT TEXTILES
8439	— OTHER OUTER GARMENTS				31.1		29.2		30.0	AUT VET DES FEM MAT TEXT
845	OUTERWEAR KNIT NONELASTC				26.1		26.8		32.6	VET DESSOUS,ACCES BONNET
8451	— JERSEYS,PULLOVERS ETC				7.9		9.0		11.1	CHANDAILS,PULL–OVERS ETC
8459	— OTHER,CLTHG ACCESRYS				16.2		15.9		18.8	AUT VET DESSUS DE BONNE
846	UNDER GARMENTS KNITTED				14.0		15.4		18.8	SOUS VETS DE BONNETERIE
8462	— OF COTTON NON ELASTIC				10.8		11.2		11.9	SOUS–VET BONNET COTON
84629	—— OTHER			N 3597157	10.4		10.8		11.6	AUT SOUS–VET BONNET COTON
851	*FOOTWEAR			P 1189939	16.2		21.8		21.2	CHAUSSURES
85101	FOOTWEAR RUBBER,PLASTIC			P 523639	6.6		9.0		9.3	CHAUS SEMELLES CAOUTCH
85102	FOOTWEAR LEATHER			P 418334	7.4		11.7		10.9	CHAUS SEMELLES EN CUIR
87	PRECISION INSTRUMNTS NES				12.2		21.5		30.0	INSTRUM,APPAR SCIENT NDA
874	MEASURNG,CONTROLNG INSTR				6.6		12.8		18.2	INSTRUMENTS DE MESURE
8748	ELEC MEAS,CONTRL EQU NES			W 45	2.1		5.7		10.1	APP ELEC ELECTRO MESURE
89	MISC MANUFCTRD GOODS NES				61.4		53.8		66.1	ART MANUFACTURES DIVERS
893	ARTICLES OF PLASTIC NES				24.9		19.5		22.3	OUVRAGES EN MAT DIVIS 58
8931	PLSTC PACKG CONTNRS,LIDS			W 4292	14.7		7.7		8.9	ART TRANSP EMBALLAGE ETC
8939	MISC PLASTIC ARTICLES			W 2012	8.3		9.8		11.1	ART DIVERS EN MAT DIV 58
89399	OTHR PLASTC ARTICLES NES			W 1216	5.5		6.8		7.7	AUT OUV MAT DIV 58
894	TOYS,SPORTING GOODS,ETC				16.9		14.7		17.8	VOITURES ENFANTS,JOUETS
8947	OTH SPORT GDS,FAIR AMUSM				14.2		11.5		14.2	AUT ART DE SPORT
89472	OTH OUTDOOR SPORT GOODS				13.3		11.1		12.5	ART POUR JEUX PLEIN AIR
899	OTHER MANUFACTURED GOODS				7.6		8.5		10.1	AUT ART MANUF DIVERS NDA

1. HISTORICAL SERIES, 1993–1996 GENERAL TRADE, IMPORTS C.I.F., EXPORTS F.O.B.
SERIES HISTORIQUES, 1993–1996 COMMERCE GENERAL, IMPORTATIONS C.A.F., EXPORTATIONS F.O.B

YEAR ANNEE	VALUE IN MILLION BIRR VALEUR EN MILLION BIRR MERCHANDISE –MARCHANDISE		GOLD –OR		CONVERSION FACTORS U.S. CENTS PER BIRR FACTEURS DE CONVERSION CENTS E.U. PAR BIRR		INDEX NUMBERS –INDICES QUANTUM		UNIT VALUE VALEUR UNITAIRE	
	IMPORTS	EXPORTS	IMPORTS	EXPORTS	IMPORTS	EXPORTS	IMPORTS	EXPORTS	IMPORTS	EXPORTS
1993	3936.70	994.16			20.0000	20.0000		125		157
1994	5658.00	2062.38			18.2554	18.0565				
1995	7052.50	2602.91			16.1905	16.2139				
1996		2650.55				15.7506				

2. IMPORTS BY BROAD ECONOMIC CATEGORY AND EXPORTS BY INDUSTRIAL ORIGIN. (PERCENTAGE OF TOTAL VALUE)
IMPORTATIONS PAR CATEGORIES ECONOMIQUES ET EXPORTATIONS PAR BRANCHE D'ACTIVITE.(EN POURCENTAGE DE LA VALEUR TOTALE)

IMPORTS – IMPORTATIONS

	1989	1990	1991	1992	1993	1994	1995
TOTAL IMPORTS–IMPORTATIONS TOTALES					100.		100.
1 FOOD BEV–ALIMENTATION BOISSONS					12.5		12.6
11 PRIMARY–PRODUITS DE BASE					9.0		10.5
111 FOR INDUSTRY–POUR L'INDUSTRIE					8.3		10.3
112 FOR HOUSEHOLDS–POUR LES MENAGES					0.7		0.1
12 PROCESSED–PRODUITS ELABORES					3.5		2.2
121 FOR INDUSTRY–POUR L'INDUSTRIE					1.2		1.2
122 FOR HOUSEHOLDS–POUR LES MENAGES					2.3		1.0
2 IND SUPPLIES–APPROV INDUSTRIELS					26.7		28.8
21 PRIMARY–PRODUITS DE BASE					1.4		1.5
22 PROCESSED–PRODUITS ELABORES					25.3		27.4
3 FUELS–COMBUSTIBLES					21.4		11.1
31 PRIMARY–PRODUITS DE BASE					9.4		6.0
32 PROCESSED–PRODUITS ELABORES					12.0		5.1
321 MOTOR SPIRIT–ESSENCE					0.6		
322 OTHER–AUTRES					11.4		5.1
4 MACHINERY–EQUIPEMENT					11.6		17.0
41 CAPITAL EQUIPMENT–MACHINES					10.0		15.1
42 PARTS–PIECES ACCESSOIRES					1.6		1.9
5 TRANSPORT–TRANSPORT					17.1		20.2
51 PASSENGER CARS–AUTOMOBILES					3.8		2.5
52 OTHER–AUTRES					7.1		12.6
521 INDUSTRIAL–INDUSTRIELS					7.1		12.1
522 NON INDUSTRIAL–NON INDUSTRIEL					0.1		0.4
53 PARTS–PIECES ACCESSOIRES					6.1		5.1
6 CONSUM GOODS–BIENS CONSOMMATION					10.7		10.1
61 DURABLE–DURABLES					1.4		2.2
62 SEMI DURABLE–SEMI DURABLES					2.9		3.3
63 NON DURABLE–NON DURABLES					6.3		4.7
7 GOODS NES–BIENS NDA					0.0		0.2

EXPORTS – EXPORTATIONS

	1989	1990	1991	1992	1993	1994	1995
TOTAL EXPORTS–EXPORTATIONS TOTALES					100.		100.
1 AGRICULTURE					76.5		79.2
2 MINING QUARRY–INDUS EXTRACTIVES							
3 MANUFACTURING–IND MANUFACTUR					23.5		20.8
31 FOOD BEV TOBACCO–ALIM BOISS TAB					18.8		3.7
32 TEXTILES–INDUSTRIES TEXTILES					0.6		13.8
33 WOOD & PRODUCTS–BOIS & PRODUITS					0.0		
34 PAPER & PRODUCTS–PAPIER & PRODT					0.0		
35 CHEMICALS–INDUSTRIES CHIMIQUES					4.1		3.2
36 NON METAL MIN–MIN NON METAL							0.0
37 BASIC METAL–IND METAL BASE					0.0		
38 METAL MANUF–MANUF METAL					0.0		0.1
39 OTH MANUF IND–AUTRES MANUF					0.0		0.0

3. TRADE BY PRINCIPAL COUNTRIES OF ORIGIN AND DESTINATION (VALUE IN MILLION U.S. DOLLARS)
ECHANGES SELON LES PRINCIPAUX PAYS D'ORIGINE ET DE DESTINATION (VALEUR EN MILLIONS DE DOLLARS EU)

COUNTRIES–PAYS	GENERAL IMPORTS C.I.F. IMPORTATIONS GENERALES C.A.F 1991	1992	1993	1994	1995
World			771.6		1141.0
Africa			64.3		75.0
Americas			87.9		153.0
– Northern America			87.9		150.9
– LAIA			0.1		1.7
– CACM					
– Caribbean			0.0		0.2
– Rest of America			0.0		0.3
Asia excl fmr USSR			273.1		397.8
– Middle East			188.4		189.8
Asia former USSR					
Europe excl fmr USSR			321.6		483.9
– European Union			302.9		452.4
– Eastern Europe			4.5		5.2
– Rest of Europe			14.1		26.3
Europe former USSR			0.9		1.7
Oceania			5.9		0.6
Other			17.9		28.9
Saudi Arabia			145.2		134.3
USA/Etats–Unis d'Amer			73.3		147.5
Italy/Italie			79.6		140.0
Germany/Allemagne			81.6		87.4
Japan/Japon			31.3		96.2
United Kingdom			29.8		67.7
Djibouti			34.5		28.2
Netherlands/Pays–Bas			28.3		31.5
Kenya			21.2		34.8
Belgium–Luxembourg			20.7		35.2
Sweden/Suède			19.1		32.2
Areas n.e.s.			17.9		28.9
France, Monaco			12.0		31.4
India/Inde			10.9		28.7
China/Chine			11.7		26.2
Middle East n.e.s.					35.2
Korea, Republic of			5.5		25.2
Yemen/Yémen			23.3		2.2
Denmark/Danemark			14.1		10.7
Switzerland,Liechtenst.			12.4		12.2
Canada			14.6		3.3
United Arab Emirates			16.2		
Greece/Grèce			8.0		6.3
Thailand/Thaïlande			8.7		2.2
Korea Dem People's Rp			3.1		7.0
Indonesia/Indonésie			3.5		6.5
Norway,Svalbard and JM			1.3		8.6
Spain/Espagne			4.0		5.6
Jordan/Jordanie			0.1		8.5
Turkey/Turquie			2.2		5.9
Egypt/Egypte			2.4		5.6
Singapore/Singapour			3.9		3.7
Australia/Australie			5.4		0.6
Other Europe n.e.s.			0.0		5.1
Other Asia n.e.s.			0.7		3.5
Ireland/Irlande			1.6		2.4
Malaysia/Malaisie			0.5		3.3
Austria/Autriche			2.1		0.9
Kuwait/ Koweït			0.0		3.0
Poland/Pologne			1.3		1.6

COUNTRIES–PAYS	GENERAL EXPORTS F.O.B. EXPORTATIONS GENERALES F.O.B. 1991	1992	1993	1994	1995
Monde			201.7		421.9
Afrique			27.1		48.5
Amériques			20.3		29.6
– Amérique du Nord			20.2		29.6
– ALAI			0.0		
– MCAC					
– Caraïbes			0.1		
– Autre Amérique			0.0		
Asie anc. URSS exclus			69.4		120.3
– Moyen–Orient			24.7		46.2
Asie ancienne URSS					
Europe anc. URSS exclus			84.7		222.5
– Union Européenne			84.0		218.1
– Europe de l'Est			0.6		1.9
– Autre de l'Europe			0.2		2.5
Europe ancienne URSS			0.0		
Océanie			0.1		0.7
Autre			0.0		0.4
Germany/Allemagne			39.7		122.7
Japan/Japon			38.3		54.8
Djibouti			24.3		38.5
Saudi Arabia			19.9		38.0
Italy/Italie			15.3		36.5
USA/Etats–Unis d'Amer			18.6		27.0
France, Monaco			7.4		21.2
United Kingdom			9.3		15.3
Belgium–Luxembourg			6.0		7.4
Netherlands/Pays–Bas			4.2		6.6
Yemen/Yémen			3.9		3.5
Thailand/Thaïlande			0.2		6.9
Malaysia/Malaisie			1.8		3.3
India/Inde			2.2		2.7
Tunisia/Tunisie					4.2
Canada			1.6		2.6
Sudan/Soudan			2.6		1.2
Spain/Espagne			0.3		3.4
Finland/Finlande			1.2		2.2
Egypt/Egypte			0.0		3.0
Middle East n.e.s.					2.7
Korea, Republic of			0.9		1.8
Portugal			0.1		2.2
Switzerland,Liechtenst.			0.2		2.1
Indonesia/Indonésie			0.4		1.7
Romania/Roumanie			0.4		1.4
Israel/Israël			0.1		1.4
Kuwait/ Koweït					1.3
So. African Customs Un			0.0		0.9
Australia/Australie			0.1		0.7
China, Hong Kong SAR			0.2		0.5
Turkey/Turquie			0.3		0.3
China/Chine			0.1		0.6
United Arab Emirates			0.6		
Sweden/Suède			0.2		0.3
Lebanon/Liban			0.0		0.5
Greece/Grèce			0.2		0.3
Areas n.e.s.			0.0		0.4
Czech Republic					0.4
Yugoslavia/Yougoslavie					0.4

(VALUE AS PERCENTAGE OF WORLD TOTAL)(VALEURS EN POURCENTAGE DU TOTAL MONDIAL)

	1986	1987	1988	1989	1990	1991	1992	1993	1994	1995
Africa								8.3		6.6
Americas								11.4		13.4
– Northern America								11.4		13.2
– LAIA								0.0		0.1
– CACM										
– Caribbean								0.0		0.0
– Rest of America								0.0		0.0
Asia excl fmr USSR								35.4		34.9
– Middle East								24.4		16.6
Asia former USSR										
Europe excl fmr USSR								41.7		42.4
– European Union								39.3		39.6
– Eastern Europe								0.6		0.5
– Rest of Europe								1.8		2.3
Europe former USSR								0.1		0.1
Oceania								0.8		0.1
Other								2.3		2.5
Saudi Arabia								18.8		11.8
USA/Etats–Unis d'Amer								9.5		12.9
Italy/Italie								10.3		12.3
Germany/Allemagne								10.6		7.7
Japan/Japon								4.1		8.4
United Kingdom								3.9		5.9
Djibouti								4.5		2.5
Netherlands/Pays–Bas								3.7		2.8
Kenya								2.7		3.1
Belgium–Luxembourg								2.7		3.1

	1986	1987	1988	1989	1990	1991	1992	1993	1994	1995
Afrique								13.4		11.5
Amériques								10.1		7.0
– Amérique du Nord								10.0		7.0
– ALAI								0.0		
– MCAC										
– Caraïbes								0.1		
– Autre Amérique								0.0		
Asie anc. URSS exclus								34.4		28.5
– Moyen–Orient								12.2		11.0
Asie ancienne URSS										
Europe anc. URSS exclus								42.0		52.7
– Union Européenne								41.6		51.7
– Europe de l'Est								0.3		0.4
– Autre de l'Europe								0.1		0.6
Europe ancienne URSS								0.0		
Océanie								0.0		0.2
Autre								0.0		0.1
Germany/Allemagne								19.7		29.1
Japan/Japon								19.0		13.0
Djibouti								12.1		9.1
Saudi Arabia								9.9		9.0
Italy/Italie								7.6		8.6
USA/Etats–Unis d'Amer								9.2		6.4
France, Monaco								3.7		5.0
United Kingdom								4.6		3.6
Belgium–Luxembourg								3.0		1.7
Netherlands/Pays–Bas								2.1		1.6

4. General Imports C.I.F. by Commodities according to the S.I.T.C. (Rev. 2) in million U.S. Dollars
Importations Générales C.A.F. par Produits d'après la C.T.C.I. (Rév. 2) en millions de Dollars E.U.

SITC CTCI	COMMODITY	1992 QUANTITY QUANTITE	1992 VALUE VALEUR	1993 QUANTITY QUANTITE	1993 VALUE VALEUR	1994 QUANTITY QUANTITE	1994 VALUE VALEUR	1995 QUANTITY QUANTITE	1995 VALUE VALEUR	PRODUIT
	ALL COMMODITIES				771.6				1141.1	TOUS PRODUITS
0	FOOD AND LIVE ANIMALS				94.0				132.6	ALIMENTS,ANIMAUX VIVANTS
02	DAIRY PRODCTS,BIRDS'EGGS				2.6				2.0	PRODUITS LAITIERS,OEUFS
022	MILK AND CREAM			W 1811	2.5			W 517	1.4	LAIT ET CREME
0224	MILK,CREAM PRESERVED ETC			W 1801	2.4			W 515	1.4	LAIT,CREME CONS,CONC
04	CEREALS AND PREPARATIONS				79.0				122.3	CEREALES ET PRODUITS
041	WHEAT ETC UNMILLED			W 233880	62.6			W 376975	94.1	FROMENT,EPEAUTRE
0411	DURUM WHEAT UNMILLED			W 722	3.0			W 18852	4.7	FROMENT DUR NON MOULU
0412	OTHER WHEAT ETC UNMILLED			W 233158	59.7			W 358123	89.5	AUTRE FROMENT NON MOULU
042	RICE			W 13170	6.2			W 1256	0.7	RIZ
0422	RICE SEMI–MILLED,MILLED			W 13121	6.2			W 709	0.5	RIZ POLI,GLACE INCL BRISURES
045	CEREALS NES UNMILLED			W 891	0.6			W 100921	23.2	AUTRES CEREALES NON MOULUES
0459	OTHER CEREALS UNMILLED			W 891	0.6			W 100921	23.2	SARRASIN,MILLET,SORGHO
04592	SORGHUM UNMILLED			W 3	0.1			W 100354	22.8	SORGHO NON MOULU
046	WHEAT ETC MEAL OR FLOUR			W 26114	5.2			W 2870	0.9	SEMOULE FARINE,FROMENT
04601	FLOUR OF WHEAT OR MESLIN			W 25814	5.1			W 621	0.2	FARINE DE FROMENT
048	CEREAL ETC PREPARATIONS			W 7517	3.8			W 3790	3.0	PREPTNS A BASE CEREALES
05	VEGETABLES AND FRUIT				6.7				4.2	LEGUMES ET FRUITS
054	VEG ETC FRSH,SMPLY PRSVD			W 7698	5.5			W 1950	1.5	LEGUMES FRAIS,CONG,SECS
0542	LEGUMINOUS VEGETBLES DRY			W 7609	4.9			W 1816	1.1	LEGUMES A COSSE SECS
09	MISC EDIBLE PRODUCTS				5.7				1.8	PREP ALIMENTAIRES DIVERSES
098	EDIBLE PRODCTS,PREPS NES			W 2044	4.3			W 620	1.7	PREP ALIMENTAIRES NDA
09809	MISC FOOD PREPRTIONS NES			W 1165	3.1			W 239	0.3	PREP ALIMENTAIRES NDA
1	BEVERAGES AND TOBACCO				3.9				5.4	BOISSONS ET TABACS
11	BEVERAGES				2.0				3.8	BOISSONS
112	ALCOHOLIC BEVERAGES			W 239	2.0			W 738	3.6	BOISSONS ALCOOLIQUES
2	CRUDE MATERLS,EXCL FUELS				11.6				23.9	MAT BRUTES NON COMESTIBLES
23	RUBBER, CRUDE				2.2				6.3	CAOUTCHOUC BRUT
232	NATURAL RUBBER,GUMS			W 1611	1.7			W 2877	4.4	LATEX CAOUTCHOUC NATUREL
26	TEXTILE FIBRES AND WASTE				7.1				11.2	FIBRES TEXTILES
266	SYNTHETIC FIBRES TO SPIN			W 46	0.2			W 1216	3.7	FIBRES SYNTHETIQUES
268	WOOL(EXC TOPS),ANML HAIR			W 78	0.1			W 4011	4.4	LAINES ET POILS
2686	WASTE OF WOOL,HAIR NES			W 78	0.1			W 3961	4.4	DECHETS LAINE ET POILS
26861	— NOT PULLD OR GARNETTD			W 78	0.1			W 3961	4.4	DECHETS LAINE ET POILS
269	WASTE OF TEXTILE FABRICS			W 4823	5.9			W 17	0.1	FRIPERIE DRILLES,CHIFFONS
26901	BULK TEXT WSTE,OLD CLTHG			W 4817	5.9			W 17	0.1	ART ET ACCESS D'HABILLEMENT
3	MINERAL FUELS ETC				166.7				126.5	COMBUSTIBLES MINERAUX LUB
33	PETROLEUM AND PRODUCTS				165.7				126.4	PETROLE ET DERIVES
333	CRUDE PETROLEUM			W 584714	71.4			W 516899	68.4	HUILES BRUTES DE PETROLE
334	PETROLEUM PRODUCTS,REFIN			W 340309	92.8			W 279543	56.4	PRODUITS RAFFINES
3341	GASOLINE,OTH LIGHT OILS			W 21600	4.5					ESSENCES POUR MOTEURS
33411	MOTOR,AVIATION SPIRIT			W 21600	4.5					ESSENCES MOTEURS D'AVIONS
3342	KEROSENE,OTH MEDIUM OILS			W 95991	33.2					PETR LAMPANTS,AUT HUIL
33421	KEROSENE INCL JET FUEL			W 95991	33.2					PETROLES LAMPANTS
3343	GAS OILS			W 185206	37.9					GAS OILS
3345	LUBS,PETROLEUM OILS NES			W 37506	17.4					HUILES LUBRIFIANTES
33451	LUBS(HIGH PETR CONT) ETC			W 37496	17.4					HUILES LUBRIF,H LOURDES
4	ANIMAL,VEGETABLE OIL,FAT				26.0				20.0	HUILES,GRAISSES ANIM,VEG
42	FIXED VEGETABLE OIL,FAT				20.8				8.2	HUILES VEGETALES FIXES
424	FIXED VEG OIL NONSOFT			W 19609	20.3			W 9743	7.6	AUTRES HUILES VEG FIXES
4241	LINSEED OIL			W 4	0.1			W 6964	5.9	HUILE DE LIN
4249	FIXED VEGETABLE OILS NES			W 19605	20.3			W 1977	1.4	HUILES VEGET FIXES NDA
431	*PROCESD ANML VEG OIL,ET			W 6536	5.2			W 13680	11.8	HUILES,GRAISSES PREPAREES
4312	HYDROGENATED OIL,FAT			W 37	0.1			W 7238	7.1	HUILES HYDROGENEES
4313	FATTY ACIDS ETC,RESIDUES			W 6499	5.2			W 6442	4.8	ACIDES GRAS INDUST,RESIDUS
43131	FATTY ACIDS,ACID OILS			W 6499	5.2			W 6334	4.7	ACIDES GRAS INDUSTRIELS
5	CHEMCLS,RELATED PROD NES				106.2				160.0	PRODUITS CHIMIQUES
52	INORGANIC CHEMICALS				20.9				20.0	PROD CHIM INORGANIQUES
522	INORG ELEMNTS,OXIDES,ETC			W 12314	15.0			W 8567	8.0	ELEMENTS INORGANIQUES
5221	CHEMICAL ELEMENTS			W 1146	0.7			W 3970	3.9	ELEMENTS CHIMIQUES
5222	INORGANIC ACIDS ETC			W 4905	5.9			W 1152	1.0	ACIDES INORGANIQUES
52229	OTH INORGANIC ACIDS ETC			W 3657	5.2			W 216	0.4	AUTRES ACIDES INORGANIQUES
5223	HALGN,SULPHR CMPD NONMET			W 3208	3.9			W 207	0.2	DERIVES HALOGENES
52231	HALOGEN CMPNDS NON–METAL			W 3208	3.9			W 207	0.2	CHLORURES,OXYCHLORURES
5224	ZINC,IRON,LEAD ETC OXIDE			W 848	2.6			W 1088	1.8	OXYDES METALLIQUES
52247	LEAD OXIDES			W 842	2.6			W 64	0.1	OXYDES DE PLOMB
523	OTHR INORG CHEMICALS ETC			W 4255	5.9			W 9881	12.0	AUT PRODUITS CHIMIQUES INORG
5239	INORG CHEM PRODUCTS NES			W 2166	3.2			W 4004	7.3	PROD CHIM INORGANIQ NDA
52399	OTH INORG CMPNDS NES ETC			W 1896	3.0			W 2879	6.7	AUT COMP INORGANIQUES NDA
53	DYES,TANNING,COLOUR PROD				8.8				7.7	PROD TEINTURE,COLORANTS
532	DYES NES,TANNING PROD			W 2663	4.0			W 1505	2.6	EXTRAITS TEINTURE,TANNAGE
5322	DYE,TANN EXTRCTS,TANNINS			W 1941	3.1			W 415	0.7	EXT TAN ORIG VEG,TANNINS
53222	DYEING EXTRCTS VEG,ANMAL			W 1910	3.0			W 190	0.3	MATI COLOR VEGET ANIMALE
533	PIGMENTS,PAINTS,ETC			W 2146	3.8			W 2108	3.6	PIGMENTS,PEINTURES,VERNIS
541	*MEDICINAL,PHARM PRODUCT			K 2282082	31.6			K 3556994	30.0	PROD MEDICINAUX PHARMACEUT
5417	MEDICAMENTS			K 2185471	31.0			K 3412456	28.0	MEDICAMENTS
54172	— CONTAINING HORMONES			K 661905	6.3			K 1826194	21.5	MED CONTENANT HORMONES
54173	— CONTAINING ALKALOIDS			K 1457730	22.6			K 577435	2.0	MED CONTEN ALCALOIDES
54179	— CONTNG OTH SUBSTANCES			K 14254	0.6			K 574985	3.6	MED CONT AUT SUBSTANCES
55	PERFUME,CLEANING ETC PRD				8.6				11.5	PROD POUR PARFUM,TOILETTE
554	SOAP,CLEANSING ETC PREPS			W 11928	6.7			W 11227	5.9	SAVONS,PRODUITS DETERSIFS
5541	SOAPS			W 11592	6.2			W 10248	4.8	SAVONS,PROD TENSIO–ACTIFS
562	*FERTILIZERS,MANUFACTURE			W 88526	18.8			W 239363	62.1	ENGRAIS MANUFACTURES
5621	CHEM NITROGENOUS FERTLZR			W 76657	15.1			W 171491	42.6	ENGRAIS AZOTES
56211	AMMONIUM NITRATE							W 25237	6.9	NITRATE D'AMMONIUM
56212	AMMONIUM SULPHONITRATE							W 57096	14.2	SULFONITRATE D'AMMONIUM
56213	AMMONIUM SULPHATE							W 38549	11.1	SULFATE D'AMMONIUM
56216	UREA			W 52000	10.1			W 50504	10.5	UREE
56219	CHEM NITROG FERTILZR NES			W 24657	5.1			W 105	0.1	ENGRAIS AZOTES NDA
5629	FERTILIZERS NES			W 11869	3.7			W 67872	19.5	ENGRAIS NDA
56292	NITROG–PHOS FERTILZR NES			W 10238	2.7			W 67872	19.5	ENGRAIS NDA CONT N P
58	PLASTIC MATERIALS ETC				5.8				11.5	MAT PLAST ARTIFICIELLES
583	POLYMERIZATION ETC PRODS			W 5311	5.6			W 6430	9.5	PROD POLYMERISATION
5831	POLYETHYLENE			W 5311	5.6			W 540	0.7	POLYETHYLENE
5839	OTH POLYMRZTION ETC PROD							W 4274	6.4	AUT PROD POLYMER COPOLYM
59	CHEMICAL MATERIALS NES				10.5				15.2	MAT PROD CHIMIQUES NDA
591	PESTICIDES,DISINFECTANTS			W 4543	5.9			W 2278	6.4	DESINF,INSECT,FONG,HERB
5913	HERBICIDES,FOR RETAIL			W 2828	2.8			W 475	2.6	HERBICIDES VENTE AU DET
598	MISCEL CHEM PRODUCTS NES			W 1867	2.5			W 4131	6.9	PROD DIV INDUST CHIM NDA
5989	CHEM PRODUCTS,PREPS NES			W 1194	2.1			W 3661	3.9	PROD PREP CHIMIQUES NDA
6	BASIC MANUFACTURES				124.3				207.6	ART MANUFACTURES

4. General Imports C.I.F. by Commodities according to the S.I.T.C. (Rev. 2) in million U.S. Dollars
Importations Générales C.A.F. par Produits d'après la C.T.C.I. (Rév. 2) en millions de Dollars E.U.

SITC CTCI	COMMODITY	1992 QUANTITY QUANTITE	1992 VALUE VALEUR	1993 QUANTITY QUANTITE	1993 VALUE VALEUR	1994 QUANTITY QUANTITE	1994 VALUE VALEUR	1995 QUANTITY QUANTITE	1995 VALUE VALEUR	PRODUIT
62	RUBBER MANUFACTURES NES				17.6				30.7	CAOUTCHOUC MANUFACTURE
625	RUBBER TYRES, TUBES ETC			W 4516	14.1			W 7877	25.2	PNEUS CAOUTCHOUC VULCANISE
6251	TYRES NEW FOR MOTOR CARS			W 2223	7.6			W 1797	5.1	PNEUS POUR VOITURES
6252	TYRES,NEW,BUS OR LORRY			W 1912	5.0			W 4651	15.2	PNEUS POUR AUTOBUS,CAMIONS
6259	OTH TYRES,TYRE CASES,ETC			W 279	1.2			W 1407	4.9	AUTRES PNEUS RECHAPES FLAPS
62599	TYRES NES,TYRE CASES,ETC			W 64	0.5			W 1358	4.4	PNEUS,FLAPS
628	RUBBER ARTICLES NES			W 548	2.6			W 656	4.2	OUVRAGES CAOUTCHOUC NDA
64	PAPER,PAPERBOARD AND MFR				7.9				10.4	PAPIERS,CARTONS & OUVRAGES
641	PAPER AND PAPERBOARD			W 4552	5.3			W 3067	4.5	PAPIERS ET CARTONS
642	PAPER,ETC,PRECUT,ARTS OF			W 1755	2.7			W 4175	6.0	PAP,CARTONS DECOUPES
65	TEXTILE YARN,FABRICS,ETC				22.6				38.0	FILS,TISSUS,ARTICLES TEXTILE
651	TEXTILE YARN			W 2543	9.2			W 4738	20.7	FILS TEXTILES
6511	SILK YARN, SILKWORM GUT			W 1508	6.3			W 35	0.2	FILS DE SOIE
6516	DISCON SYN FIB BLEND YRN							W 3188	13.4	FILS FIBR TEX SYNT DIS MOINS
65166	DISCON SYN FIB–COTTN YRN							W 1388	5.9	FILS TEXT SYNT MELANGE COTON
65168	OTH DISC SYN BLEND YARN							W 1799	7.6	FILS TEXT SYNT MELANGE AUT F
653	WOVN MAN–MADE FIB FABRIC			W 2001	6.9			W 2891	11.2	TISSUS FIBRES SYNTH,ARTIF
6532	DISC SYN TXTL FABRIC NES			W 1617	5.4			W 31	0.2	TIS DISC MOINS 85% FIBR TEXT
6534	DISC SYN BLEND FABRC NES							W 1157	3.7	TISSUS FIBRES SYNTH DISCONT
65341	DISC SYN FIB–COTTN FABRC							W 1146	3.6	TISSUS FIB SYNT DIS MEL COTO
6538	DISC REG BLEND FABRC NES							W 1668	7.2	TIS MOINS 85% TEXT ART DISC
65389	OTH DISC REG BLEND FABRC							W 1637	7.1	TISSUS TEX ART CONT MEL AUT
657	SPECIAL TXTL FABRC,PRODS			W 999	3.2				2.7	TISSUS SPECIAUX
658	TEXTILE ARTICLES NES			W 1642	2.4			W 3352	2.2	ART FACONNES MAT TEXTILES
66	NONMETAL MINERAL MFS NES				6.9				13.1	ART MIN NON METALLIQUES
663	MINERAL MANUFCTURES NES			W 1744	2.9			W 3394	5.6	ART MIN MANUF NDA
6631	GRINDING STONES ETC			W 1609	2.6			W 2073	4.5	PIERRES A AIGUISER,MEULES
67	IRON AND STEEL				38.6				70.0	FER ET ACIER
673	IRON,STEEL SHAPES ETC			W 14556	9.3			W 14462	8.8	BARRES,PROFIL FER,ACIER
6731	IRON,STEEL WIRE ROD			W 9207	6.1			W 1021	0.5	FIL MACHINE FER,ACIER
67311	IRON,SIMPLE STL WIRE ROD			W 9207	6.1			W 959	0.4	FIL MACH AUT ACIER FIN
6732	IRON,STEEL BARS ETC			W 3145	1.9			W 7723	4.9	BARRES FER,ACIER
6733	IRON,STEEL PROFILES ETC			W 2205	1.4			W 5719	3.5	PROFILES,PALPLAN FER,ACIER
674	IRN,STL UNIV,PLATE,SHEET			W 29863	22.5			W 52465	45.6	LARGES PLATS,TOLES
6744	IRN,STL HVY PLATE,ROLLED							W 8430	5.2	TOLES LAMINEES PLUS 4.75 MM
67441	— OF IRON OR SIMPLE STL							W 8425	5.2	TOLES NON ACIER FIN CARB
6747	TINNED PLATES,SHEETS			W 11849	10.4			W 1345	1.0	TOLES ETAMEES EN ACIER
6749	OTH IRN,STL PLATES,SHEET			W 14637	10.5			W 39498	37.5	AUTRES TOLES FER,ACIER
67491	— OF IRON OR SIMPLE STL							W 39005	37.2	AUT TOLES AUTRES ACIER FIN
675	IRON,STEEL HOOP,STRIP			W 6913	3.7					FEUILLARDS LAMINES
67501	IRN,SMPLE STL HOOP,STRIP			W 6913	3.7					FEUILLARDS NON ACIER FIN
678	IRON,STL TUBES,PIPES,ETC			W 2262	2.3			W 7141	9.6	TUBES,TUYAUX EN FONTE,FER
6783	IRON,STL TUBES,PIPES NES							W 3283	3.8	AUT TUBES,TUYAUX FER,ACIER
68	NON–FERROUS METALS				2.3				6.9	METAUX NON FERREUX
69	METAL MANUFACTURES NES				26.3				35.7	ART MANUFACT EN METAL NDA
691	STRUCTURES AND PARTS NES			W 6435	9.0			W 1163	4.8	CONSTRUCT FER,ACIER,ALU
6911	STRUCTURES,PARTS IRN,STL			W 6375	8.7			W 1038	3.4	CONSTRUCT FER,ACIER,FONTE
694	STL,COPPR NAILS,NUTS,ETC			W 13435	2.9			W 6134	4.6	CLOUS,VIS,ECROUS
695	TOOLS			W 764	3.2			W 2176	7.2	OUTILS A MAIN
697	BASE MTL HOUSEHOLD EQUIP			W 1055	3.4			W 2345	5.4	ART MENAGE MET COMMUNS
6974	BASE MTL DMSTC ARTIC NES			W 697	2.3			W 1869	4.2	ARTICLES NDA FONTE,FER,ETC
699	BASE METAL MFRS NES			W 3375	5.4			W 4782	9.6	ART MANUFACTURES MET NDA
6991	LOCKSMITHS WARES,ETC			W 1006	2.4			W 2016	5.1	ARTICLES DE SERRURERIE
7	MACHINES,TRANSPORT EQUIP				208.9				405.1	MACHINES MATERIEL TRANSPORT
71	POWER GENERATING EQUIPMT				3.2				13.9	MACHINES GENERATRICES
713	INTRNL COMBUS PSTN ENGIN			W 48	0.4			W 808	4.4	MOTEURS EXPL COMB INT, PIECE
716	ROTATING ELECTRIC PLANT			W 847	2.2			W 1104	7.5	APP ELECTR ROTATIFS,PIECES
7162	AC MTRS,GENRTRS,GEN SETS			W 293	1.1			W 820	5.2	MOTEURS ELECTRIQUES
72	MACHS FOR SPCL INDUSTRYS				34.4				86.1	MAC SPECIALES POUR INDUST
721	AGRIC MACHY,EXC TRACTORS			W 492	1.9			W 1487	7.6	MACHINES AGRICOLES
7219	AGRICULTURE MACHINES NES			W 311	0.7			W 449	4.5	ENGINS AGRICOLES NDA
72198	PTS NES OF MCHY OF 72191			W 93	0.3			W 322	3.9	PIECES DES APP 721.91
722	TRACTORS NON–ROAD			W 60	0.3			W 801	7.0	TRACTEURS
7223	TRACK–LAYING TRACTORS			W 10	0.1			W 723	6.4	TRACTEURS A CHENILLES
723	CIVIL ENGNEERG EQUIP ETC			W 1452	9.7			W 3104	33.2	APPAREILS DE GENIE CIVIL
7234	CONST,MINING MACHNRY NES			W 657	2.9			W 2763	30.3	MACH POUR LA CONST, MINES
72341	SELF–PROPELLD DOZERS,ETC			W 265	1.4			W 1967	20.4	BULLDOZERS
72342	SLFPRP SHOVELS,EXCAVATRS			W 48	0.3			W 504	4.0	PELLES MECANIQUES
72344	BORING,SINKING MACHINERY			W 1	0.1			W 113	4.5	MACHINES DE FORAGE
7239	CONSTR ETC MACHY PTS NES			W 796	6.8			W 33	0.6	PIECES 723.41–723.46
724	TEXTILE,LEATHER MACHNRY			W 2313	9.7			W 1275	9.2	MACH POUR INDUSTRIE TEXTILE
7246	AUXIL TXTL MCH,PARTS NES			W 1437	4.6			W 47	1.6	MACH PR 724.51,52,53,61
72469	LOOM,KNT MCH ETC PTS NES			W 1437	4.6			W 36	1.2	PIECES 724.51,52,53,61
7248	SKIN,LEATHER WORKNG MACH			W 247	3.1			W 346	3.2	MACHINES TRAVAIL DES CUIRS
727	FOOD MACHRY NON–DOMESTIC			W 816	4.9			W 1718	9.2	MACH INDUSTRIES ALIMENT
7271	GRAIN WORKING MCHY,PARTS			W 498	2.9			W 893	4.1	MACH POUR MINOTERIE,PIEC
7272	OTH FOOD PROC MCHY,PARTS			W 318	2.1			W 825	5.1	AUT MACH IND ALIMENTAIRE
728	OTH MACHY FOR SPCL INDUS			W 1385	6.5			W 2976	17.7	AUT MACH IND PARTICULIERES
7283	OTHR MINERAL WORKG MACHY			W 908	3.3			W 1569	5.9	MACH TRIER,CRIBLER,BROYER
7284	MACHY FOR SPCL INDUS NES			W 332	2.5			W 963	10.0	MACH SPEC IND PARTICUL.
72849	PTS OF MACHS OF 7284 ETC			W 287	2.3			W 223	3.5	PIECES DU 728.4 ETC
73	METALWORKING MACHINERY				1.4				6.5	MACH TRAVAIL DES METAUX
736	METALWORKING MACH–TOOLS			W 215	0.9			W 871	6.0	MACH–OUTILS TRAVAIL METAUX
74	GENRL INDUSTRL MACHY NES				14.4				34.7	MACH APP INDUSTRIE
742	PUMPS FOR LIQUIDS ETC			W 344	3.8			W 798	6.8	POMPES MOTO–POMPES
7428	OTHER PUMPS FOR LIQUIDS			W 148	1.9			W 476	3.6	AUTRES POMPES POUR LIQ
743	PUMPS NES,CENTRFUGES ETC			W 94	0.8			W 2139	4.0	POMPES COMPRES,VENT ETC
744	MECHANICAL HANDLING EQU			W 590	4.2			W 1588	11.2	EQUIP MANUTENTION PIECES
7441	FORK LIFT TRCKS,ETC,PTS			W 418	2.9			W 108	1.2	CHARIOTS POUR USINES ETC
74411	FORK LIFT TRUCKS ETC			W 336	2.5			W 96	0.9	CHARIOTS POUR LES GARES
7449	PTS NES OF MACHY OF 7442			W 101	0.7			W 800	6.9	PIECES DU 744.2
745	NONELEC MACHY,TOOLS NES			W 235	1.3			W 670	3.7	AUT MACH NON ELEC,PIECES
7452	OTH NONELEC MCHS,PTS NES			W 178	1.1			W 653	3.7	AUT MACH NON ELEC,PIECES
749	NONELEC MACH PTS,ACC NES			W 573	4.2			W 950	6.6	PIECES MACH NON ELEC NDA
7499	OTH NONELEC MCHY PTS NES			W 239	2.4			W 359	2.0	PIECES NON ELECT NDA
75	OFFICE MACHNES,ADP EQUIP				6.1				12.5	MACH BUREAU TRAIT AUTOM
751	OFFICE MACHINES			W 54	1.8			W 189	4.3	MACH,APPAREILS DE BUREAU
752	AUTOMTIC DATA PROC EQUIP			W 49	2.2			W 86	5.4	MACH TRAIT INFORMATION
7522	DIGITAL COMPUTERS							W 63	3.9	MACH DIGITALES COMPLETES
76	TELECOMM,SOUND EQUIPMENT				8.2				19.2	EQUIPMENT DE TELECOM
763	SOUND RECORDRS,PHONOGRPH			W 29	0.9			W 212	3.8	PHONO,APP ENREGISTREMENT

4. General Imports C.I.F. by Commodities according to the S.I.T.C. (Rev. 2) in million U.S. Dollars
Importations Générales C.A.F. par Produits d'après la C.T.C.I. (Rév. 2) en millions de Dollars E.U.

SITC CTCI	COMMODITY	1992		1993		1994		1995		PRODUIT
		QUANTITY QUANTITE	VALUE VALEUR	QUANTITY QUANTITE	VALUE VALEUR	QUANTITY QUANTITE	VALUE VALEUR	QUANTITY QUANTITE	VALUE VALEUR	
7638	OTHR SOUND APPARATUS ETC			W 5	0.2			W 211	3.8	AUT APP D'ENREGIS,REPROD
764	TELECOM EQPT,PTS,ACC NES			W 583	4.1			W 449	11.3	EQUIP TELECOM,PIECES
7649	PTS NES OF EQUIPMT OF 76			W 374	2.9			W 282	4.9	PIECES DE LA DIV 76
77	ELECTRIC MACHNRY NES ETC				25.8				34.2	MACH APP ELECT NDA
772	SWITCHGEAR ETC,PARTS NES			W 935	5.5			W 937	7.2	APP COUPURE,SECT ETC
7721	SWITCHGEAR ETC							W 928	7.1	APP COUPURE,SECTIONMNT
774	ELECTRO-MEDCL,XRAY EQUIP			W 146	7.6			W 238	4.0	APPAREILS MEDICAUX
7741	ELECTRO-MEDICAL EQUIPMNT			W 143	7.6			W 138	2.5	APP ELECTRICITE MEDICALE
775	HOUSEHOLD TYPE EQUIP NES			W 636	2.9			W 841	6.8	MACH,APP USAGE DOMESTQUE
778	ELECTRICAL MACHINERY NES			W 3772	8.7			W 6429	12.4	AUTRES MACH ELECT NDA
7781	BATTERIES,ACCUMULATORS			W 2566	4.2			W 5666	8.5	PILES ET ACCUMULATEURS
77811	PRIMARY BATTERIES,CELLS			W 1894	2.4			W 4997	6.9	PILES ELECTRIQUES,PIECES
7782	ELECTRIC LAMPS,BULBS			W 958	2.7			W 445	1.6	LAMPES, TUBES ELECTRIQUES
77821	ELEC FILAMENT LAMPS NES			W 935	2.6			W 137	0.5	LAMPES NON INFRAROUGES
78	ROAD VEHICLES				113.5				196.3	VEHICULES ROUTIERS
781	PASS MOTOR VEH EXC BUSES			W 4981	29.6			W 4887	28.9	AUTO TRANSPORT PERSONNES
782	LORRIES,SPCL MTR VEH NES			W 13879	50.6			W 21858	108.2	VEHICULES SPECIAUX,MARCH
7821	LORRIES,TRUCKS			W 13557	49.0			W 21347	104.0	VEHICULES TRANSP MARCHAND
7822	SPECIAL MOTOR VEHCLS NES			W 323	1.6			W 512	4.2	VEHICULES USAGES SPECIAUX
783	ROAD MOTOR VEHICLES NES			W 449	1.8			W 3548	15.3	VEHICULES ROUTIERS NDA
7831	BUSES			W 379	1.6			W 3509	15.1	VOITURES TRANSPORT COMMUN
784	MOTOR VEH PRTS,ACCES NES			W 5006	28.9			W 2122	24.1	PIECES 722,781,782,783
7849	OTHER MOTOR VEHCL PARTS			W 4999	28.8			W 2008	23.8	PIECES 722,781,782,783
785	CYCLES,ETC MOTRZD OR NOT			W 233	1.1			W 1375	5.4	MOTOCYCLES SCOOTERS
786	TRAILERS,NONMOTR VEH,NES			W 798	1.7			W 4324	14.6	REMORQUES,CADRES,CONTAIN
7861	TRAILERS,TRANSP CONTAINR			W 740	1.4			W 2001	5.2	REMORQUES TOUS VEHICULES
78612	OTHER TRAILERS			W 2	0.1			W 1823	5.0	REMORQUES TRANSP MARCH
7868	OTH NONMOTR VEHICLES ETC			W 59	0.3			W 2323	9.5	AUT VEHIC NON AUTO,PIECES
78681	OTH NONMOTORIZED VEHCLS							W 2295	9.4	AUTRES VEHIC NON AUTO
79	OTHR TRANSPORT EQUIPMENT				2.4				2.0	AUTRE MATERIEL TRANSPORT
8	MISC MANUFACTURED GOODS				30.5				60.4	ART MANUFACTURES DIVERS
821	*FURNITURE,PARTS THEREOF			W 362	1.2			W 2236	5.3	MEUBLES ET PIECES
8219	FURNITURE AND PARTS NES			W 64	0.3			W 1736	3.9	AUTRES MEUBLES ET PIECES
84	CLOTHING AND ACCESSORIES				4.3				9.2	VETEMENTS
87	PRECISION INSTRUMNTS NES				6.4				11.7	INSTRUM,APPAR SCIENT NDA
872	MEDICAL INSTRUMENTS NES			W 469	4.2			W 282	6.0	INSTR,APP MEDIC-CHIR NDA
87202	OTH MEDICAL INSTRUMENTS			W 344	2.6			W 279	5.9	INSTRUM,APP MEDECINE
874	MEASURNG,CONTROLNG INSTR			W 133	2.0			W 173	5.1	INSTRUMENTS DE MESURE
88	PHOTO EQU,OPTICL GDS ETC				2.9				6.1	APP,FOURN PHOTO,OP,MONTR
882	PHOTO,CINEMA SUPPLIES			W 179	1.7			W 330	3.6	PRODUITS PHOTO,CINEMA
89	MISC MANUFCTRD GOODS NES				12.9				22.4	ART MANUFACTURES DIVERS
892	PRINTED MATTER			W 1075	2.7			W 1069	7.7	IMPRIMES
8921	PRINTED BOOKS,GLOBES,ETC			W 929	2.1			W 704	4.7	LIVRES,BROCHURES,CARTES
89211	PRINTED BOOKS,PAMPHLETS			W 929	2.1			W 697	4.6	LIVRES,BROCHURES
893	ARTICLES OF PLASTIC NES			W 3415	6.4			W 5312	8.3	OUVRAGES EN MAT DIVIS 58
8939	MISC PLASTIC ARTICLES			W 3215	5.9			W 3796	6.3	ART DIVERS EN MAT DIV 58
89399	OTHR PLASTC ARTICLES NES			W 3167	5.8			W 3145	5.5	AUT OUV MAT DIV 58

5. General Exports F.O.B. by Commodities according to the S.I.T.C. (Rev. 2) in million U.S. Dollars
Exportations Générales F.O.B. par Produits d'après la C.T.C.I. (Rév. 2) en millions de Dollars E.U.

SITC CTCI	COMMODITY	1992 QUANTITY QUANTITE	1992 VALUE VALEUR	1993 QUANTITY QUANTITE	1993 VALUE VALEUR	1994 QUANTITY QUANTITE	1994 VALUE VALEUR	1995 QUANTITY QUANTITE	1995 VALUE VALEUR	PRODUIT
	ALL COMMODITIES				201.8				422.0	TOUS PRODUITS
0	FOOD AND LIVE ANIMALS				138.6				294.9	ALIMENTS,ANIMAUX VIVANTS
001	*LIVE ANIMALS FOR FOOD			W 1048	1.0			W 430	0.9	ANIMAUX VIVANTS
0011	BOVINE SPECIES,LIVE			W 784	0.7			W 8	0.1	ESPECE BOVINE
00111	— PURE BRED FR BREEDING			W 784	0.7			W 8	0.1	BOVINS REPRODUCTEURS
05	VEGETABLES AND FRUIT				3.1				16.5	LEGUMES ET FRUITS
054	VEG ETC FRSH,SMPLY PRSVD			W 13621	2.9			W 35171	16.2	LEGUMES FRAIS,CONG,SECS
0542	LEGUMINOUS VEGETBLES DRY			W 3808	2.0			W 22691	15.2	LEGUMES A COSSE SECS
06	SUGAR AND PREPS,HONEY				4.9				0.1	SUCRES ET PRODUITS
061	SUGAR AND HONEY			W 23632	4.9				0.1	SUCRES ET MIEL
0612	REFINED SUGAR ETC			W 13631	4.7					SUCRES RAFFINES
07	COFFEE,TEA,COCOA,SPICES				129.4				275.9	CAFE,THE,CACAO,EPICES
071	COFFEE AND SUBSTITUTES			W 70007	129.2			W 76567	275.7	CAFE ET SUCCEDANES
0711	COFFEE GREEN,ROASTED,SUB			W 70007	129.2			W 76567	275.7	CAFE TORREFIE OU DECAFEINE
07111	COFFEE GREEN,HUSKS,SKINS							W 76567	275.7	CAFE NON TORREFIE
2	CRUDE MATERLS,EXCL FUELS				52.8				66.6	MAT BRUTES NON COMESTIBLES
21	HIDES,SKINS,FURS UNDRSSD				32.7				13.6	CUIRS,PEAUX BRUTS
211	HIDES,SKINS,EXC FURS,RAW			W 7577	32.7			W 2627	13.6	CUIRS ET PEAUX
2111	BOVINE,EQUINE HIDES,RAW			W 2306	4.6					PEAUX DE BOVINS
2114	GOAT AND KID SKINS,RAW			W 2275	5.5			W 2627	13.6	PEAUX DE CAPRINS
2116	SHEEP SKIN WITH WOOL			W 2839	22.6					PEAUX LAINEES D'OVINS
22	OIL SEEDS,OLEAGINOUS FRT				0.3				9.9	GRAINES,FRUITS OLEAGINEUX
222	SEEDS FOR'SOFT'FIXED OIL			W 372	0.3			W 7059	6.4	GRAINES HUILES FIXES
2225	SESAME SEEDS			W 372	0.3			W 6989	6.4	GRAINES DE SESAME
223	SEEDS FOR OTH FIXED OILS			W 77	0.1			W 4539	3.6	GRAINES AUTRES HUILES FIXES
2238	OIL SEEDS AND FRUITS NES			W 77	0.1			W 4391	3.5	GRAINES D'OLEAGINEUX NDA
26	TEXTILE FIBRES AND WASTE								12.9	FIBRES TEXTILES
263	COTTON							W 7619	12.9	COTON
2634	COTTON,CARDED OR COMBED							W 7619	12.9	COTON CARDE OU PEIGNE
29	CRUDE ANIMAL,VEG MAT NES				19.8				30.0	MATIERES BRUTES ANIM,VEGET
292	CRUDE VEG MATERIALS NES			W 3001	19.6			W 5301	29.7	MAT BRUTES VEGETALES NDA
2922	NAT GUMS,RESINS,LACS,ETC			W 182	0.5			W 933	1.4	GOMME LAQUE
2924	VEG USED IN PHARMACY ETC			W 2711	18.8					PLANTES MEDICINALES
2929	OTH CRUDE VEG MATERIALS			W 5	0.1			W 4080	27.9	MATIERES VEGETALES NDA
29298	OTH CRD VEG MATERIAL NES			W 5	0.1			W 4080	27.9	PRODUITS ORIGINE VEGET NDA
3	MINERAL FUELS ETC				8.1				12.1	COMBUSTIBLES MINERAUX LUB
33	PETROLEUM AND PRODUCTS				8.1				12.1	PETROLE ET DERIVES
334	PETROLEUM PRODUCTS,REFIN			W 148049	8.1			W 123862	12.1	PRODUITS RAFFINES
3344	FUEL OILS,NES			W 148049	8.1					FUEL OILS
4	ANIMAL,VEGETABLE OIL,FAT				0.9				1.3	HUILES,GRAISSES ANIM,VEG
431	*PROCESD ANML VEG OIL,ET			W 246	0.9			W 328	1.3	HUILES,GRAISSES PREPAREES
4314	ANIMAL,VEGETABLE WAXES			W 246	0.9			W 328	1.3	CIRES ANIMALES,VEGETALES
43144	INSECT WAXES,SPERMACETI			W 246	0.9			W 328	1.3	BLANC DE BALEINE
5	CHEMCLS,RELATED PROD NES				0.2				1.4	PRODUITS CHIMIQUES
6	BASIC MANUFACTURES				0.2				45.2	ART MANUFACTURES
61	LEATHER,DRESSED FUR,ETC				0.1				44.1	CUIRS,PELLETERIES
611	LEATHER							W 5610	44.0	CUIRS,PEAUX PREPARES
6114	LEATHR BOVINE NES,EQUINE							W 2877	9.0	CUIRS DE BOVINS
6115	LEATHER FROM SHEEP,LAMBS							W 2732	35.0	PEAUX D'OVINS PREPAREES
8	MISC MANUFACTURED GOODS				1.3				0.6	ART MANUFACTURES DIVERS
84	CLOTHING AND ACCESSORIES				1.2				0.4	VETEMENTS
845	OUTERWEAR KNIT NONELASTC			W 63	0.7					VET DESSOUS,ACCES BONNET
8452	— WOMENS DRESSES ETC			W 63	0.7					ROBES,JUPES BONNETERIE
84529	—— OF OTHER FIBRES			W 63	0.7					ROBES JUPES AUTRES FIBR

1. HISTORICAL SERIES, 1961–1996 GENERAL TRADE, IMPORTS C.I.F., EXPORTS F.O.B.
SERIES HISTORIQUES, 1961–1996 COMMERCE GENERAL, IMPORTATIONS C.A.F., EXPORTATIONS F.O.B

YEAR ANNEE	VALUE IN MILLION KRONER VALEUR EN MILLION KRONER MERCHANDISE –MARCHANDISE		GOLD –OR		CONVERSION FACTORS U.S. CENTS PER KRONE FACTEURS DE CONVERSION CENTS E.U. PAR KRONE		INDEX NUMBERS –INDICES QUANTUM		UNIT VALUE VALEUR UNITAIRE	
	IMPORTS	EXPORTS	IMPORTS	EXPORTS	IMPORTS	EXPORTS	IMPORTS	EXPORTS	IMPORTS	EXPORTS
1961	129.60	97.30			14.4778	14.4778				
1962	135.70	126.30			14.4778	14.4778				
1963	138.40	137.00			14.4778	14.4778				
1964	161.90	135.90			14.4778	14.4778				
1965	182.30	177.80			14.4778	14.4778				
1966	195.30	152.70			14.4778	14.4778				
1967	186.30	177.80			14.3395	14.3360				
1968	211.30	154.10			13.3333	13.3333				
1969	243.80	182.20			13.3333	13.3333				
1970	228.40	251.00			13.3333	13.3333				
1971	301.10	278.70			13.4867	13.4867				
1972	325.70	322.10			14.3368	14.3368				
1973	412.30	471.40			16.5893	16.5893				
1974	606.90	487.20			16.4323	16.4323				
1975	651.20	464.30			17.4028	17.4028				
1976	791.70	632.00			16.5426	16.5500				
1977	910.90	863.70			16.6343	16.6341				
1978	1008.20	776.30			18.2438	18.2402				
1979	1075.50	759.10			19.0032	19.0161				
1980	1235.40	1057.70			17.7333	17.7333	92	62	73	68
1981	1482.70	1140.30			14.0445	14.0445	93	62	84	79
1982	1659.00	1254.90			11.9963	11.9963	99	65	93	86
1983	2222.50	1572.90			10.9313	10.9313	101	79	97	91
1984	2719.50	1640.40			9.6520	9.6520	106	81	105	92
1985	2630.50	1899.00			9.4340	9.4340	112	86	108	97
1986	2664.43	1960.28			12.6216	12.6900	136	86	101	97
1987	3513.10	2359.00			14.6118	14.6118	146	83	116	103
1988	3220.69	2344.66			14.8544	14.8544	146	89	99	100
1989	2530.29	2530.22			13.6807	13.6807	125	102	103	99
1990	2084.21	2578.46			16.2278	16.2278	100	100	100	100
1991	1936.21	2781.37			15.6351	15.6351	100	104	100	110
1992	2008.86	2640.88			16.6050	16.6050				
1993	1421.53	2125.71			15.3971	15.3971				
1994	1539.83	2076.34			15.7208	15.7208				
1995	1767.26	2026.27			17.8508	17.8508				
1996	2117.98	2530.59			17.2428	17.2514				

2. IMPORTS BY BROAD ECONOMIC CATEGORY AND EXPORTS BY INDUSTRIAL ORIGIN. (PERCENTAGE OF TOTAL VALUE)
IMPORTATIONS PAR CATEGORIES ECONOMIQUES ET EXPORTATIONS PAR BRANCHE D'ACTIVITE.(EN POURCENTAGE DE LA VALEUR TOTALE)

IMPORTS – IMPORTATIONS

	1989	1990	1991	1992	1993	1994	1995
TOTAL IMPORTS–IMPORTATIONS TOTALES	100.	100.	100.	100.	100.	100.	
1 FOOD BEV–ALIMENTATION BOISSONS	11.4	13.9	17.6	20.7	20.5	20.2	
11 PRIMARY–PRODUITS DE BASE	5.1	6.9	10.0	12.2	9.7	10.3	
111 FOR INDUSTRY–POUR L'INDUSTRIE	0.3	0.3	0.4	0.4	0.5	0.6	
112 FOR HOUSEHOLDS–POUR LES MENAGES	4.8	6.5	9.6	11.8	9.3	9.8	
12 PROCESSED–PRODUITS ELABORES	6.3	7.1	7.6	8.5	10.8	9.9	
121 FOR INDUSTRY–POUR L'INDUSTRIE	0.7	0.7	0.7	0.7	0.9	0.8	
122 FOR HOUSEHOLDS–POUR LES MENAGES	5.6	6.4	7.0	7.8	9.9	9.0	
2 IND SUPPLIES–APPROV INDUSTRIELS	28.4	26.9	28.5	31.1	30.6	29.2	
21 PRIMARY–PRODUITS DE BASE	2.2	1.5	1.6	2.1	2.5	2.7	
22 PROCESSED–PRODUITS ELABORES	26.1	25.4	26.9	29.1	28.1	26.5	
3 FUELS–COMBUSTIBLES	10.0	12.0	12.8	12.5	15.4	11.8	
31 PRIMARY–PRODUITS DE BASE	0.0	0.0	0.0	0.0	0.0	0.0	
32 PROCESSED–PRODUITS ELABORES	10.0	12.0	12.8	12.5	15.4	11.8	
321 MOTOR SPIRIT–ESSENCE	9.9	12.0	1.1	0.9	1.2	0.8	
322 OTHER–AUTRES	0.0	0.0	11.7	11.6	14.2	11.0	
4 MACHINERY–EQUIPEMENT	17.0	10.6	11.1	12.8	11.4	16.6	
41 CAPITAL EQUIPMENT–MACHINES	15.1	9.2	9.6	11.7	10.2	15.2	
42 PARTS–PIECES ACCESSOIRES	1.9	1.5	1.5	1.1	1.2	1.4	
5 TRANSPORT–TRANSPORT	12.5	13.8	6.7	7.9	5.0	4.7	
51 PASSENGER CARS–AUTOMOBILES	2.4	0.8	1.1	1.3	0.4	0.7	
52 OTHER–AUTRES	7.8	10.8	3.5	4.0	0.7	0.6	
521 INDUSTRIAL–INDUSTRIELS	7.7	10.7	3.4	3.9	0.6	0.5	
522 NON INDUSTRIAL–NON INDUSTRIEL	0.1	0.1	0.1	0.1	0.1	0.1	
53 PARTS–PIECES ACCESSOIRES	2.2	2.2	2.1	2.6	3.9	3.4	
6 CONSUM GOODS–BIENS CONSOMMATION	16.1	13.2	13.4	14.4	16.7	17.1	
61 DURABLE–DURABLES	4.5	3.2	3.0	3.1	3.0	2.6	
62 SEMI DURABLE–SEMI DURABLES	7.1	5.3	5.3	6.5	7.5	8.4	
63 NON DURABLE–NON DURABLES	4.5	4.7	5.1	4.8	6.2	6.1	
7 GOODS NES–BIENS NDA	4.7	9.5	9.9	0.6	0.3	0.4	

EXPORTS – EXPORTATIONS

	1989	1990	1991	1992	1993	1994	1995
TOTAL EXPORTS–EXPORTATIONS TOTALES	100.	100.	100.	100.	100.	100.	
1 AGRICULTURE	81.2	84.0	87.9	81.2	84.8	85.7	
2 MINING QUARRY–INDUS EXTRACTIVES	0.1	0.0					
3 MANUFACTURING–IND MANUFACTUR	18.7	16.0	12.1	18.8	15.2	14.3	
31 FOOD BEV TOBACCO–ALIM BOISS TAB	12.0	9.2	6.6	9.5	11.0	11.1	
32 TEXTILES–INDUSTRIES TEXTILES	0.0	0.0	0.0	0.1	0.1	0.2	
33 WOOD & PRODUCTS–BOIS & PRODUITS					0.0	0.1	
34 PAPER & PRODUCTS–PAPIER & PRODT			0.0	0.0	0.0		
35 CHEMICALS–INDUSTRIES CHIMIQUES		0.1	0.1	0.1	0.1	0.1	
36 NON METAL MIN–MIN NON METAL							
37 BASIC METAL–IND METAL BASE							
38 METAL MANUF–MANUF METAL	6.6	6.7	5.4	9.1	3.9	2.6	
39 OTH MANUF IND–AUTRES MANUF	0.1	0.0	0.0	0.0	0.1	0.2	

3. TRADE BY PRINCIPAL COUNTRIES OF ORIGIN AND DESTINATION (VALUE IN MILLION U.S. DOLLARS)
ECHANGES SELON LES PRINCIPAUX PAYS D'ORIGINE ET DE DESTINATION (VALEUR EN MILLIONS DE DOLLARS EU)

COUNTRIES–PAYS	GENERAL IMPORTS C.I.F. IMPORTATIONS GENERALES C.A.F				
	1991	1992	1993	1994	1995
World	302.7	333.6	218.9	242.1	306.8
Africa	0.1	0.2	0.2	0.2	0.2
Americas	13.2	19.7	8.2	7.0	7.8
– Northern America	12.4	18.4	7.0	4.5	6.0
– LAIA	0.3	0.5	0.4	0.6	0.6
– CACM	0.4	0.3	0.2	0.1	0.1
– Caribbean	0.0	0.0	0.1	0.1	0.1
– Rest of America	0.0	0.5	0.4	1.8	1.1
Asia excl fmr USSR	11.1	17.0	9.9	13.1	20.6
– Middle East	0.1	0.2	0.2	0.2	0.4
Asia former USSR			0.0	0.3	0.0
Europe excl fmr USSR	274.1	286.2	194.7	213.2	267.6
– European Union	200.4	212.4	145.9	163.4	207.5
– Eastern Europe	1.0	1.7	1.9	1.1	1.5
– Rest of Europe	72.7	72.2	47.0	48.7	58.6
Europe former USSR	3.0	9.3	5.2	7.6	9.9
Oceania	1.0	0.9	0.7	0.7	0.6
Other	0.2	0.2	0.0		
Denmark/Danemark	137.1	118.7	80.6	85.7	105.8
Norway,Svalbard and JM	57.4	64.4	41.8	42.2	48.4
United Kingdom	14.3	19.8	15.8	26.1	24.9
Germany/Allemagne	14.0	25.4	15.5	15.9	24.2
Sweden/Suède	14.0	18.5	11.3	11.3	17.7
USA/Etats–Unis d'Amer	11.6	13.1	6.5	3.4	4.7
Iceland/Islande	14.1	5.9	3.4	4.9	8.2
Japan/Japon	6.7	8.3	3.6	4.8	9.6
Russian Federation		9.3	5.1	4.4	9.8
France, Monaco	4.3	6.6	4.8	4.7	8.2
Netherlands/Pays–Bas	4.7	6.8	5.1	5.3	6.3
Italy/Italie	2.7	3.8	2.6	3.2	4.9
Belgium–Luxembourg	2.3	3.1	2.3	3.1	4.8
Portugal	1.8	2.8	2.1	2.4	3.0
Finland/Finlande	2.0	2.8	2.0	2.0	2.2
China/Chine	0.7	1.5	1.6	2.7	3.9
Spain/Espagne	1.8	1.8	1.4	2.3	2.8
Canada	0.8	5.2	0.6	1.1	1.3
Switzerland,Liechtenst.	1.3	1.9	1.7	1.6	2.0
China, Hong Kong SAR	1.0	1.6	1.1	1.2	1.3
Ireland/Irlande	0.5	1.1	1.5	0.6	1.6
Other Asia n.e.s.	0.5	1.5	0.8	0.8	1.2
Poland/Pologne	0.3	1.0	0.6	0.7	1.0
Lithuania/Lituanie		0.0	0.0	3.1	0.0
New Zealand	0.7	0.7	0.6	0.6	0.5
Former USSR/Anc. URSS	3.0				
Korea, Republic of	0.5	0.8	0.5	0.5	0.7
Austria/Autriche	0.6	0.7	0.4	0.4	0.6
Falkland Isl (Malvinas)		0.4	0.4	0.9	1.0
Indonesia/Indonésie	0.3	0.5	0.4	0.4	0.6
India/Inde	0.2	0.3	0.3	0.6	0.7
Malaysia/Malaisie	0.2	0.5	0.3	0.4	0.6
Greece/Grèce	0.2	0.4	0.3	0.3	0.5
Thailand/Thaïlande	0.2	0.5	0.3	0.3	0.4
Czech Republic			1.0	0.2	0.3
Costa Rica	0.4	0.2	0.2	0.1	0.1
Hungary/Hongrie	0.4	0.3	0.1	0.1	0.1
Pakistan	0.1	0.2	0.2	0.2	0.3
Belize/Bélize	0.0			0.9	0.0
Singapore/Singapour	0.2	0.3	0.1	0.2	0.2

COUNTRIES–PAYS	GENERAL EXPORTS F.O.B. EXPORTATIONS GENERALES F.O.B.				
	1991	1992	1993	1994	1995
Monde	434.9	438.2	328.3	326.4	351.5
Afrique	0.5	1.0	0.8		0.9
Amériques	42.7	23.7	15.8	12.1	12.0
– Amérique du Nord	42.7	23.7	14.0	10.5	11.9
– ALAI			1.0		
– MCAC					
– Caraïbes			0.0	0.1	
– Autre Amérique			0.7	1.5	0.1
Asie anc. URSS exclus	17.5	12.8	13.6	9.5	14.0
– Moyen–Orient		0.0	1.1	0.1	0.0
Asie ancienne URSS					
Europe anc. URSS exclus	372.4	392.9	297.3	300.7	323.2
– Union Européenne	358.7	353.9	284.9	287.3	294.9
– Europe de l'Est			0.0	0.0	0.0
– Autre de l'Europe	13.7	39.0	12.4	13.4	28.2
Europe ancienne URSS	1.7	5.1	0.9	0.4	0.7
Océanie		2.6		3.7	0.8
Autre				0.0	
Denmark/Danemark	81.7	77.3	83.9	86.6	80.4
United Kingdom	53.6	73.9	64.1	66.7	90.2
Germany/Allemagne	78.3	65.1	45.5	37.2	35.0
France, Monaco	39.6	39.0	36.8	36.7	29.8
Italy/Italie	33.2	26.6	16.3	18.6	18.1
Spain/Espagne	29.9	28.6	17.5	15.0	17.4
USA/Etats–Unis d'Amer	30.9	22.5	8.2	9.4	7.2
Norway,Svalbard and JM	5.6	18.3	5.4	9.7	17.3
Japan/Japon	15.1	10.1	8.5	8.7	13.1
Sweden/Suède	12.4	8.2	3.9	9.7	9.4
Netherlands/Pays–Bas	6.7	11.0	8.5	6.7	6.1
Iceland/Islande	5.3	17.4	0.7	0.7	8.7
Belgium–Luxembourg	7.1	7.5	4.2	3.2	1.2
Greece/Grèce	8.7	7.2	1.6	1.9	1.0
Finland/Finlande	7.3	4.2	1.4	3.9	2.6
Switzerland,Liechtenst.	2.4	3.3	4.8	3.0	2.3
Greenland/Groenland	10.3	0.6	0.4	0.8	0.8
Canada	1.5	0.6	5.4	0.3	3.9
Portugal	0.3	4.7	0.9	1.2	3.3
Other Asia n.e.s.	2.2	2.4	1.9	0.3	0.3
Russian Federation		5.1	0.9	0.4	0.6
New Zealand		2.6		2.9	
So. African Customs Un		1.0	0.8		0.5
Panama			0.7	1.3	
Malta/Malte	0.5	0.0	1.3		
Israel/Israël	0.2	0.3	1.2		
Former USSR/Anc. URSS	1.7				
Australia/Australie				0.7	0.8
Cyprus/Chypre			1.1		
Ireland/Irlande	0.0	0.4	0.2		0.4
Chile/Chili			1.0		
China, Hong Kong SAR			0.8	0.1	0.0
Malaysia/Malaisie				0.2	0.5
Guinea/Guinée	0.5				
Egypt/Egypte					0.4
Belize/Bélize				0.3	0.1
Dominican Republic			0.0	0.1	
Singapore/Singapour			0.0	0.1	
Czech Republic				0.0	0.0
Estonia/Estonie					0.0

(VALUE AS PERCENTAGE OF WORLD TOTAL)(VALEURS EN POURCENTAGE DU TOTAL MONDIAL)

	1986	1987	1988	1989	1990	1991	1992	1993	1994	1995
Africa	0.0	0.0	0.0	0.0	0.0	0.0	0.1	0.1	0.1	0.1
Americas	2.6	1.8	2.0	3.2	2.0	4.3	5.9	3.7	2.9	2.5
– Northern America	2.4	1.6	1.7	3.0	1.7	4.1	5.5	3.2	1.8	1.9
– LAIA	0.1	0.1	0.1	0.2	0.1	0.1	0.1	0.2	0.3	0.2
– CACM	0.1	0.1	0.1	0.1	0.2	0.1	0.1	0.1	0.1	0.0
– Caribbean	0.0	0.0	0.0	0.0	0.0	0.0	0.0	0.0	0.0	0.0
– Rest of America	0.0	0.0	0.1	0.0	0.0	0.0	0.2	0.2	0.7	0.4
Asia excl fmr USSR	6.1	5.2	5.0	4.6	3.3	3.7	5.1	4.5	5.4	6.7
– Middle East	0.1	0.0	0.0	0.0	0.1	0.0	0.1	0.1	0.1	0.1
Asia former USSR								0.0	0.1	0.0
Europe excl fmr USSR	90.9	92.9	91.1	91.3	93.3	90.5	85.8	89.0	88.1	87.2
– European Union	74.4	57.7	66.5	68.6	64.0	66.2	63.7	66.6	67.5	67.6
– Eastern Europe	0.6	0.7	0.5	0.6	3.3	0.3	0.5	0.8	0.4	0.5
– Rest of Europe	16.0	34.5	24.1	22.1	26.0	24.0	21.6	21.5	20.1	19.1
Europe former USSR	0.2	0.0	1.7	0.6	1.2	1.0	2.8	2.4	3.1	3.2
Oceania	0.0	0.0	0.1	0.1	0.1	0.3	0.3	0.3	0.3	0.2
Other	0.1	0.1	0.1	0.1	0.0	0.1	0.1	0.0		
Denmark/Danemark	45.5	32.7	39.6	44.4	43.8	45.3	35.6	36.8	35.4	34.5
Norway,Svalbard and JM	13.1	32.6	21.1	16.3	19.8	18.9	19.3	19.1	17.4	15.8
United Kingdom	4.3	3.3	8.2	3.7	4.8	4.7	5.9	7.2	10.8	8.1
Germany/Allemagne						4.6	7.6	7.1	6.6	7.9
Sweden/Suède	7.9	7.3	6.3	5.8	4.9	4.6	5.6	5.2	4.7	5.8
USA/Etats–Unis d'Amer	2.3	1.5	1.6	2.8	1.4	3.8	3.9	3.0	1.4	1.5
Iceland/Islande	2.1	1.4	2.4	4.3	5.5	4.6	1.8	1.6	2.0	2.7
Japan/Japon	4.8	3.9	3.5	3.1	2.0	2.2	2.5	1.6	2.0	3.1
Russian Federation							2.8	2.3	1.8	3.2
France, Monaco	1.1	1.3	0.9	2.5	1.2	1.4	2.0	2.2	2.0	2.7

	1986	1987	1988	1989	1990	1991	1992	1993	1994	1995
Afrique						0.1	0.2	0.2		0.3
Amériques	18.8	12.0	13.3	11.9	8.4	9.8	5.4	4.8	3.7	3.4
– Amérique du Nord	18.8	11.0	12.8	11.5	8.4	9.8	5.4	4.3	3.2	3.4
– ALAI		1.0	0.6	0.3				0.3		
– MCAC										
– Caraïbes								0.0	0.0	
– Autre Amérique	0.1							0.2	0.5	0.0
Asie anc. URSS exclus	2.3	2.3	8.3	5.8	3.4	4.0	2.9	4.1	2.9	4.0
– Moyen–Orient							0.0	0.3	0.0	0.0
Asie ancienne URSS										
Europe anc. URSS exclus	78.4	83.6	77.3	79.2	88.1	85.6	89.7	90.5	92.1	91.9
– Union Européenne	75.3	80.3	68.4	75.2	85.5	82.5	80.8	86.8	88.0	83.9
– Europe de l'Est		0.2			0.3			0.0	0.0	0.0
– Autre de l'Europe	3.1	3.0	8.9	4.0	2.3	3.2	8.9	3.8	4.1	8.0
Europe ancienne URSS	0.5	0.4	1.0	3.1		0.4	1.2	0.3	0.1	0.2
Océanie		1.7	0.0	0.0	0.1		0.6		1.1	0.2
Autre									0.0	
Denmark/Danemark	17.9	16.2	18.6	16.2	20.8	18.8	17.6	25.6	26.5	22.9
United Kingdom	13.3	7.6	11.5	13.6	14.3	12.3	16.9	19.5	20.4	25.6
Germany/Allemagne						18.0	14.9	13.9	11.4	10.0
France, Monaco	10.1	8.5	7.6	9.2	11.2	9.1	8.9	11.2	11.2	8.5
Italy/Italie	6.5	7.1	7.2	7.0	4.8	7.6	6.1	5.0	5.7	5.1
Spain/Espagne	2.0	4.5	6.7	7.3	7.9	6.9	6.5	5.3	4.6	5.0
USA/Etats–Unis d'Amer	14.0	10.2	9.1	9.8	4.5	7.1	5.1	2.5	2.9	2.0
Norway,Svalbard and JM	1.8	2.3	8.0	3.5	1.0	1.3	4.2	1.7	3.0	4.9
Japan/Japon	2.0	2.0	4.9	5.2	3.0	3.5	2.3	2.6	2.7	3.7
Sweden/Suède	2.3	2.0	1.9	3.2	4.0	2.8	1.9	1.2	3.0	2.7

4. General Imports C.I.F. by Commodities according to the S.I.T.C. (Rev. 2) in million U.S. Dollars
Importations Générales C.A.F. par Produits d'après la C.T.C.I. (Rév. 2) en millions de Dollars E.U.

SITC CTCI	COMMODITY	1992 QUANTITY QUANTITE	1992 VALUE VALEUR	1993 QUANTITY QUANTITE	1993 VALUE VALEUR	1994 QUANTITY QUANTITE	1994 VALUE VALEUR	1995 QUANTITY QUANTITE	1995 VALUE VALEUR	PRODUIT
	ALL COMMODITIES		333.6		218.9		242.1			TOUS PRODUITS
0	FOOD AND LIVE ANIMALS		86.6		55.9		62.7			ALIMENTS,ANIMAUX VIVANTS
01	MEAT AND PREPARATIONS		9.1		7.4		8.0			VIANDES ET PREPARATIONS
011	MEAT FRESH,CHILLD,FROZEN	W 2394	6.3	W 1967	4.9	W 1916	5.4			VIANDES FRAICHES,REF,CONGE
0111	BOVINE MEAT FRESH,FROZEN	W 730	2.0	W 660	1.7	W 645	1.7			VIANDES BOVIN FRAI,REF
01112	BOVINE MEAT BONELESS	W 490	1.5	W 517	1.3	W 551	1.4			VIANDES BOVIN DESOSSEES
0112	MUTTON ETC FRSH,CHLD,FRN	W 601	1.9	W 397	1.3	W 510	1.7			VIANDE DE MOUTON
0113	PIG MEAT FRESH,CHLD,FRZN	W 329	1.1	W 330	1.0	W 376	1.2			VIANDE DE PORC
0114	POULTRY FRESH CHLLD,FRZN	W 555	1.0	W 428	0.7	W 239	0.6			VOLAILLES MORTES
014	MEAT PREPD,PRSVD,NES ETC	W 701	2.7	W 682	2.4	W 736	2.6			CONSERVES DE VIANDES
0142	SAUSAGES INCLDING TINNED	W 315	1.2	W 294	1.0	W 311	1.1			SAUCISSES,SAUCISSONS
0149	OTH PREPARD,PRESRVD MEAT	W 384	1.6	W 387	1.4	W 425	1.6			AUTRES PREP DE VIANDES
02	DAIRY PRODCTS,BIRDS'EGGS		4.4		3.5		3.3			PRODUITS LAITIERS,OEUFS
022	MILK AND CREAM	W 1246	1.3	W 876	0.9	W 670	0.8			LAIT ET CREME
0223	MILK AND CREAM FRESH	W 1188	1.1	W 823	0.7	W 606	0.6			LAIT,CREME FRAIS
024	CHEESE AND CURD	W 483	1.9	W 463	1.7	W 434	1.6			FROMAGE ET CAILLEBOTTE
025	EGGS,BIRDS,FRESH,PRSRVD	W 616	0.9	W 538	0.7	W 487	0.7			OEUFS
0251	— IN SHELL	W 613	0.8	W 536	0.7	W 485	0.7			OEUFS EN COQUILLE
03	FISH AND PREPARATIONS		26.8		10.7		13.4			POISSONS ET PREPARATIONS
034	FISH,FRESH,CHILLED,FROZN	W 14046	23.4	W 7243	7.5	W 9221	9.5			POISSON FRAIS, REFRIG,CONG
0341	FISH FRSH,CHLLD,EX FILLT	W 4690	7.0	W 2430	1.8	W 2083	1.0			POISSON FRAIS,REFRIGERE
0342	FISH FROZEN,EXCL FILLETS	W 9272	16.1	W 4233	4.6	W 6707	7.6			POISSONS CONGELES
0343	FISH FILLETS,FRESH,CHLLD		0.1	W 505	1.1	W 37	0.1			FILETS FRAIS,REFRIGERES
0344	FISH FILLETS,FROZEN	W 84	0.4	W 75	0.2	W 394	0.9			FILETS CONGELES
035	FISH SALTED,DRIED,SMOKED	W 15	0.1	W 7	0.1	W 591	1.0			POISSON SECHE,SALE,FUME
03503	FISH(EX COD)DRIED,SALTED	W 14	0.1	W 5	0.1	W 436	0.9			POISSONS SECHES,SALES
036	SHELL FISH FRESH,FROZEN	W 2569	2.9	W 2007	2.8	W 1811	2.6			CRUSTACES,MOLLUSQUES
04	CEREALS AND PREPARATIONS		5.0		4.8		4.9			CEREALES ET PRODUITS
046	WHEAT ETC MEAL OR FLOUR	W 1995	0.8	W 1886	0.7	W 2092	0.8			SEMOULE FARINE,FROMENT
04601	FLOUR OF WHEAT OR MESLIN	W 1975	0.8	W 1879	0.7	W 2086	0.8			FARINE DE FROMENT
048	CEREAL ETC PREPARATIONS	W 2059	3.7	W 2260	3.8	W 2461	3.9			PREPTNS A BASE CEREALES
0484	BAKERY PRODUCTS	W 760	2.3	W 954	2.5	W 1101	2.6			PRODUITS DE BOULANGERIE
04841	BREAD,BISCUIT,COM WAFERS	W 435	1.0	W 553	1.1	W 693	1.2			PAINS,BISCUITS DE MER
04842	PASTRY, CAKES ETC	W 325	1.4	W 401	1.4	W 408	1.5			PATISSERIE ETC.
05	VEGETABLES AND FRUIT		8.0		6.5		6.8			LEGUMES ET FRUITS
054	VEG ETC FRSH,SMPLY PRSVD	W 4825	2.9	W 4630	2.4	W 4236	2.7			LEGUMES FRAIS,CONG,SECS
0541	POTATOES FRSH EXCL SWEET	W 3130	0.9	W 3058	0.7	W 2820	1.1			POMMES DE TERRE
0545	OTHER FRESH VEGETABLES	W 934	1.0	W 924	0.9	W 828	0.9			AUTRES LEGUMES FRAIS,REF
05459	FRESH VEGETABLES NES	W 718	0.8	W 705	0.8	W 612	0.7			LEGUMES FRAIS,REFRI NDA
056	VEGTBLES ETC PRSVD,PREPD	W 427	1.2	W 395	1.0	W 393	1.0			CONSERVES DE LEGUMES
0565	VEGTBLES PRSVD,PREPD NES	W 416	1.2	W 382	1.0	W 382	1.0			LEGUMES PREPARES CONSERVE
05659	OTH VEG PRESVD,PREPD NES	W 244	0.9	W 206	0.7	W 223	0.8			LEGUM PREPAP,CONSERV NDA
057	FRUIT,NUTS,FRESH,DRIED	W 1763	2.3	W 1621	1.8	W 1520	1.9			FRUITS FRAIS OU SECS
058	FRUIT PRESERVED,PREPARED	W 1298	1.7	W 1291	1.4	W 1198	1.4			CONSERVES DE FRUITS
06	SUGAR AND PREPS,HONEY		2.6		2.0		2.2			SUCRES ET PRODUITS
062	SUGAR CANDY NON-CHOCLATE	W 325	1.9	W 259	1.4	W 286	1.5			SUCRERIES
07	COFFEE,TEA,COCOA,SPICES		3.7		2.8		3.4			CAFE,THE,CACAO,EPICES
071	COFFEE AND SUBSTITUTES	W 272	1.3	W 226	0.9	W 256	1.3			CAFE ET SUCCEDANES
0711	COFFEE GREEN,ROASTED,SUB	W 267	1.2	W 223	0.9	W 254	1.3			CAFE TORREFIE OU DECAFEINE
07112	COFFEE ROASTED	W 264	1.2	W 214	0.9	W 250	1.2			CAFE TORREFIE
073	CHOCOLATE AND PRODUCTS	W 252	1.6	W 221	1.3	W 268	1.5			CHOCOLAT
081	*FEEDING STUFF FOR ANIML	W 27712	23.0	W 19414	14.4	W 19948	17.0			NOURRITURE POUR ANIMAUX
0819	FOOD WASTE AND FEED NES	W 26545	22.4	W 18649	14.0	W 19125	16.6			DECHETS,ALIMENTS NDA
08199	FODDER NES,INCL SWEETNED	W 26545	22.4	W 18643	14.0	W 19124	16.6			PREPARATIONS FOURRAGERES
09	MISC EDIBLE PRODUCTS		4.3		4.1		4.2			PREP ALIMENTAIRES DIVERSES
091	MARGARINE AND SHORTENING	W 823	1.0	W 781	0.9	W 733	0.8			MARGARINE ET GRAISSES
0914	MARGARINE,EDIBLE FAT NES	W 821	0.9	W 780	0.8	W 732	0.8			MARGARINES,SIMILI SAINDOUX
09141	MARGARINE	W 742	0.8	W 715	0.8	W 672	0.7			MARGARINE
098	EDIBLE PRODCTS,PREPS NES	W 953	3.4	W 930	3.3	W 844	3.4			PREP ALIMENTAIRES NDA
09809	MISC FOOD PREPRTIONS NES	W 557	2.0	W 528	2.1	W 440	2.1			PREP ALIMENTAIRES NDA
1	BEVERAGES AND TOBACCO		7.2		4.9		4.4			BOISSONS ET TABACS
11	BEVERAGES		5.3		3.2		2.8			BOISSONS
111	NON-ALCOHL BEVERAGES NES	W 1079	1.1	W 1172	1.1	W 862	0.9			BOISSONS NON ALCOOLIQUES
11102	FLAVORED WATERS NON-ALCO	W 994	1.0	W 1101	1.0	W 768	0.8			LIMONADES,EAUX GAZEUSES
112	ALCOHOLIC BEVERAGES	W 1316	4.2	W 1369	2.2	W 1482	2.0			BOISSONS ALCOOLIQUES
1121	WINE OF FRESH GRAPES ETC	W 464	1.3	W 216	0.5	W 241	0.5			VINS DE RAISINS FRAIS
11212	WINE OF FRESH GRAPES	W 448	1.2	W 201	0.5	W 230	0.5			VINS DE MOUTS DE RAISINS
1124	DISTILLED ALCOHOLIC BEVS	W 389	2.5	W 447	1.4	W 395	1.1			ALCOOLS,EAUX-DE-VIE
11249	OTH ALCOHOLC BEVS,CMPNDS	W 381	2.4	W 409	1.2	W 357	1.0			BOISSONS ALCOOLIQUES NDA
12	TOBACCO AND MANUFACTURES		2.0		1.7		1.7			TABACS BRUTS FABRIQUES
122	TOBACCO,MANUFACTURED	W 90	2.0	W 86	1.7	W 79	1.7			TABACS FABRIQUES
1222	CIGARETTES	W 57	1.5	W 49	1.2	W 45	1.1			CIGARETTES
2	CRUDE MATERLS,EXCL FUELS		11.9		7.0		8.6			MAT BRUTES NON COMESTIBLES
24	CORK AND WOOD		5.6		1.7		1.5			LIEGE ET BOIS
248	WOOD SHAPED,SLEEPERS	W 6674	4.7	W 2647	1.4	W 1757	1.2			BOIS SIMPLEMENT TRAVAILLES
2482	LUMBER SHAPED CONIFER	W 6519	4.4	W 2544	1.2	W 1679	1.0			CONIFERES SCIES,RABOTES
24821	LUMBER SAWN ETC CONIFER	W 5073	3.3	W 2116	1.0	W 1196	0.7			CONIFERES SCIES LONGITUD
24822	LUMBER PLANED ETC CONIFR	W 1446	1.1	W 428	0.3	W 483	0.4			CONIFER RABOTES,RAINES
26	TEXTILE FIBRES AND WASTE		0.5		0.2		1.0			FIBRES TEXTILES
266	SYNTHETIC FIBRES TO SPIN	W 76	0.3	W 11	0.1	W 109	0.9			FIBRES SYNTHETIQUES
2666	CONTIN FILAMNT TOW SYNTH	W 76	0.3	W 11	0.1	W 109	0.9			CABLES POUR DISCONTINUS
26669	— OF OTH SYNTHTC FIBRES		0.1	W 8	0.1	W 87	0.8			D'AUTRES FIBRES TEXT SYNT
27	CRUDE FERTLZR,MINRLS NES		2.2		1.4		1.6			ENGRAIS MINERAUX BRUTS
278	OTHER CRUDE MINERALS	W 22080	1.8	W 16767	1.2	W 19049	1.5			AUTRES MINERAUX BRUTS
2783	COMMON SALT,ETC	W 16680	1.2	W 10644	0.7	W 17756	1.3			SEL
29	CRUDE ANIMAL,VEG MAT NES		3.6		3.8		4.6			MATIERES BRUTES ANIM,VEGET
291	CRUDE ANIMAL MTRIALS NES	W 25148	2.6	W 29203	2.9	W 39574	3.7			MATIERES BRUTES ANIMALES
2919	OTH ANIMAL MATERIALS NES	W 25148	2.6	W 29203	2.9	W 39574	3.7			MAT ORIGINE ANIMALE NDA
29194	FISH WASTE	W 25127	2.5	W 29100	2.8	W 39466	3.6			DECHETS DE POISSONS
292	CRUDE VEG MATERIALS NES	W 256	1.1	W 230	0.9	W 195	0.9			MAT BRUTES VEGETALES NDA
3	MINERAL FUELS ETC		41.9		33.9		28.8			COMBUSTIBLES MINERAUX LUB
33	PETROLEUM AND PRODUCTS		41.7		33.8		28.7			PETROLE ET DERIVES
334	PETROLEUM PRODUCTS,REFIN	W 196090	41.6	W 189938	33.8	W 169248	28.6			PRODUITS RAFFINES
3341	GASOLINE,OTH LIGHT OILS	W 12976	3.1	W 12690	2.7	W 10406	2.1			ESSENCES POUR MOTEURS
33419	OTH LIGHT PETROLEUM OILS	W 12968	3.1	W 12682	2.6	W 10392	2.0			AUTRES HUILES LEGERES
3343	GAS OILS	W 175445	33.5	W 138387	25.1	W 133354	21.7			GAS OILS
3344	FUEL OILS,NES	W 1	0.1	W 35756	3.7	W 22494	2.2			FUEL OILS
3345	LUBS,PETROLEUM OILS NES	W 6076	4.8	W 1517	2.2	W 1646	2.5			HUILES LUBRIFIANTES
33451	LUBS(HIGH PETR CONT) ETC	W 6069	4.7	W 1489	2.1	W 1625	2.4			HUILES LUBRIF,H LOURDES
5	CHEMCLS,RELATED PROD NES		27.4		20.2		20.2			PRODUITS CHIMIQUES
51	ORGANIC CHEMICALS		1.3		0.6		0.6			PROD CHIMIQ ORGANIQUES

4. General Imports C.I.F. by Commodities according to the S.I.T.C. (Rev. 2) in million U.S. Dollars
Importations Générales C.A.F. par Produits d'après la C.T.C.I. (Rév. 2) en millions de Dollars E.U.

SITC CTCI	COMMODITY	1992 QUANTITY QUANTITE	1992 VALUE VALEUR	1993 QUANTITY QUANTITE	1993 VALUE VALEUR	1994 QUANTITY QUANTITE	1994 VALUE VALEUR	1995 QUANTITY QUANTITE	1995 VALUE VALEUR	PRODUIT
52	INORGANIC CHEMICALS		2.1		1.4		1.1			PROD CHIM INORGANIQUES
522	INORG ELEMNTS,OXIDES,ETC	W 441	0.7	W 451	0.8	W 468	0.9			ELEMENTS INORGANIQUES
523	OTHR INORG CHEMICALS ETC	W 1078	1.4	W 247	0.6	W 155	0.3			AUT PRODUITS CHIMIQUES INORG
5239	INORG CHEM PRODUCTS NES	W 930	1.3	W 72	0.5	W 15	0.1			PROD CHIM INORGANIQ NDA
52391	HYDROGEN PEROXIDE	W 929	1.3	W 71	0.5	W 14	0.1			PEROXYDE D'HYDROGENE
53	DYES,TANNING,COLOUR PROD		4.5		4.0		3.4			PROD TEINTURE,COLORANTS
531	SYNT DYE,NAT INDGO,LAKES	W 15	1.6	W 18	1.8	W 10	1.3			MAT COLOR ORGAN,LAQUES
5311	SYNTHIC ORGNIC DYESTUFFS	W 8	1.6	W 10	1.8	W 7	1.3			MAT COLOR ORGAN SYNTHET
533	PIGMENTS,PAINTS,ETC	W 704	2.9	W 602	2.2	W 539	2.1			PIGMENTS,PEINTURES,VERNIS
5334	VARNISHES,DISTEMPERS ETC	W 566	2.3	W 518	1.8	W 463	1.8			PEINTURES A L'EAU
53342	OTH PAINTS,VARNISHES ETC	W 330	1.4	W 306	1.2	W 299	1.2			AUTRES PEINTURES,VERNIS
541	*MEDICINAL,PHARM PRODUCT	K 180931	9.6	K 91647	6.7	K 139964	7.4			PROD MEDICINAUX PHARMACEUT
5416	GLYCOSIDES,GLANDS,SERA	K 31691	2.7	K 6187	0.8	K 59554	1.6			HETEROSIDES
54164	ANTISERA,MICROB VACCINES	K 9046	1.8	K 1623	0.3	K 55215	1.1			SERUMS,VACCINS
5417	MEDICAMENTS	K 123529	6.0	K 53193	5.1	K 60167	5.1			MEDICAMENTS
54179	— CONTNG OTH SUBSTANCES	K 115507	5.1	K 50006	4.5	K 56251	4.5			MED CONT AUT SUBSTANCES
55	PERFUME,CLEANING ETC PRD		4.1		3.5		3.6			PROD POUR PARFUM,TOILETTE
553	PERFUMERY,COSMETICS,ETC	W 162	1.9	W 158	1.6	W 158	1.7			PRODUITS DE PARFUMERIE
554	SOAP,CLEANSING ETC PREPS	W 947	2.2	W 915	1.9	W 884	1.8			SAVONS,PRODUITS DETERSIFS
5542	WASHING PREPARATIONS ETC	W 858	1.8	W 840	1.6	W 772	1.4			PROD ORG TENSIO–ACT NDA
58	PLASTIC MATERIALS ETC		3.6		2.6		2.4			MAT PLAST ARTIFICIELLES
583	POLYMERIZATION ETC PRODS	W 1594	3.2	W 1390	2.4	W 1316	2.2			PROD POLYMERISATION
5833	POLYSTYRENE,ITS COPOLYMR	W 771	1.5	W 774	1.2	W 667	1.0			POLYPROPYLENE COPOLYMERES
58331	— IN PRIMARY FORMS	W 770	1.5	W 774	1.2	W 666	1.0			SOUS FORMES PRIMAIRES
59	CHEMICAL MATERIALS NES		1.2		1.1		1.2			MAT PROD CHIMIQUES NDA
6	BASIC MANUFACTURES		53.1		35.2		35.5			ART MANUFACTURES
62	RUBBER MANUFACTURES NES		2.5		1.7		2.0			CAOUTCHOUC MANUFACTURE
625	RUBBER TYRES, TUBES ETC	W 272	1.7	W 216	1.2	W 280	1.4			PNEUS CAOUTCHOUC VULCANISE
6251	TYRES NEW FOR MOTOR CARS	W 155	1.0	W 113	0.7	W 141	0.8			PNEUS POUR VOITURES
63	WOOD,CORK MANUFACTRS NES		6.3		3.3		2.1			OUVRAGES LIEGE ET BOIS
634	VENEERS,PLYWOOD,ETC	W 3136	3.4	W 1517	1.5	W 995	1.0			PLACAGES,CONTRE–PLAQUES
6342	PLYWOOD OF WOOD SHEETS	W 2125	2.0	W 930	0.9	W 515	0.6			BOIS CONTRE–PLAQUES
635	WOOD MANUFACTURES NES	W 1725	2.9	W 1012	1.8	W 509	1.1			ART MANUF EN BOIS NDA
6353	BUILDERS WOODWRK,PREFABS	W 442	2.1	W 275	1.4	W 153	0.8			OUVRAGES DE MENUISERIE
64	PAPER,PAPERBOARD AND MFR		12.6		9.5		10.0			PAPIERS,CARTONS & OUVRAGES
641	PAPER AND PAPERBOARD	W 3892	5.2	W 2056	2.9	W 1539	2.7			PAPIERS ET CARTONS
6418	COATED ETC PAPER NES BLK	W 664	1.4	W 349	0.9	W 267	0.9			PAP,CARTONS COUCHES,ENDUITS
64189	COATED PAPER ETC NES	W 269	0.9	W 216	0.7	W 183	0.8			PAPIERS,CARTONS COUCHES
642	PAPER,ETC,PRECUT,ARTS OF	W 2681	7.5	W 2759	6.6	W 3229	7.4			PAP,CARTONS DECOUPES
6421	PAPER ETC CONTAINERS	W 1966	4.2	W 1976	3.6	W 2349	4.2			BOITES,SACS EMBALLAGES
6428	PAPER ETC ARTICLES NES	W 438	2.0	W 435	1.7	W 441	1.9			OUVRAGES EN PATE A PAPIER
64285	PAPER ETC DIAPERS ETC	W 259	1.1	W 262	1.1	W 249	1.2			SERVIETTES HYGIENIQUES
65	TEXTILE YARN,FABRICS,ETC		8.6		6.9		7.2			FILS,TISSUS,ARTICLES TEXTILE
654	OTH WOVEN TEXTILE FABRIC	W 137	4.1	W 276	3.6	W 124	3.5			TISSUS AUT COTON SYNT,ARTIF
6549	WOVEN FABRICS NES	W 127	4.0	W 259	3.5	W 116	3.5			TISSUS NDA
65499	PILE,CHENILLE FABRIC NES	W 127	4.0	W 258	3.5	W 116	3.5			VELOURS NDA
657	SPECIAL TXTL FABRC,PRODS	W 430	2.7	W 328	1.9	W 293	1.9			TISSUS SPECIAUX
6575	CORDAGE AND MANUFACTURES	W 396	2.4	W 309	1.7	W 271	1.6			FICELLES,CORDES,CORDAGES
65751	CORDAGE,CABLE,ROPE,TWINE	W 227	1.1	W 114	0.5	W 76	0.3			CORDAGES TRESSES OU NON
65752	NETTING OF ROPE,TWINE	W 168	1.3	W 192	1.2	W 190	1.3			FILETS MAT DU 657.51
66	NONMETAL MINERAL MFS NES		5.6		3.3		2.7			ART MIN NON METALLIQUES
661	LIME,CEMENT,BLDG PRODS	W 12081	1.9	W 7112	1.1	W 4807	0.8			CHAUX,CIMENTS MAT CONSTR
6612	CEMENT	W 11346	1.2	W 6790	0.7	W 4517	0.5			CIMENTS HYDRAULIQUES
663	MINERAL MANUFCTURES NES	W 3053	1.7	W 1775	0.8	W 804	0.6			ART MIN MANUF NDA
664	GLASS	W 573	1.0	W 298	0.8	W 217	0.5			VERRE
67	IRON AND STEEL		3.7		2.0		2.2			FER ET ACIER
674	IRN,STL UNIV,PLATE,SHEET	W 720	1.1	W 364	0.4	W 396	0.5			LARGES PLATS,TOLES
68	NON–FERROUS METALS		1.9		1.1		1.0			METAUX NON FERREUX
684	ALUMINIUM	W 216	1.3	W 121	0.7	W 134	0.7			ALUMINIUM
6842	ALUMINIUM,ALLOYS WORKED	W 216	1.3	W 121	0.7	W 132	0.7			ALUMINIUM,ALLIAGES OUVRE
69	METAL MANUFACTURES NES		12.2		7.6		8.4			ART MANUFACT EN METAL NDA
691	STRUCTURES AND PARTS NES	W 562	2.0	W 286	1.2	W 233	1.0			CONSTRUCT FER,ACIER,ALU
6911	STRUCTURES,PARTS IRN,STL	W 483	1.3	W 267	1.0	W 215	0.9			CONSTRUCT FER,ACIER,FONTE
693	WIRE PRODUCTS NON ELECTR	W 1538	2.8	W 974	1.6	W 1045	1.8			OUVRAGES FILS METALLIQUES
6931	WIRE CABLES, ROPES ETC	W 1198	2.4	W 683	1.3	W 882	1.6			CORDAGES EN FILS DE FER
69311	IRN,STEEL CABLE,ROPE ETC	W 1169	2.3	W 659	1.2	W 846	1.5			CORDAGES FILS FER,ACIER
699	BASE METAL MFRS NES	W 685	4.0	W 418	2.6	W 532	3.2			ART MANUFACTURES MET NDA
6991	LOCKSMITHS WARES,ETC	W 106	1.1	W 53	0.7	W 47	0.6			ARTICLES DE SERRURERIE
6997	IRON,STEEL ARTICLES NES	W 263	1.7	W 132	1.0	W 261	1.6			OUV FONTE,FER,ACIER NDA
69979	IRN,STL MANUFACTURES NES	W 222	1.5	W 124	1.0	W 246	1.6			AUT OUVRAGES EN FER NDA
7	MACHINES,TRANSPORT EQUIP		68.0		33.2		47.9			MACHINES MATERIEL TRANSPORT
71	POWER GENERATING EQUIPMT		3.3		4.6		3.8			MACHINES GENERATRICES
713	INTRNL COMBUS PSTN ENGIN	W 64	2.2	W 64	4.1	W 121	3.3			MOTEURS EXPL COMB INT, PIECE
7131	AIRCRAFT PSTN ENGINS,PTS			W 2	2.1		0.1			MOTEURS EXPL P.AVIATION, PIE
71311	AIRCRAFT PISTON ENGINES			W 1	1.0		0.1			MOTEURS EXPL P.AVIATION
71319	PTS NES OF ENGN OF 71311			W 1	1.1		0.1			PIECES POUR 713.11
7139	PISTON ENGINE PARTS NES	W 27	1.7	W 36	1.8	W 39	2.2			PIECES POUR 713.2,3,8
72	MACHS FOR SPCL INDUSTRYS		7.4		3.7		5.3			MAC SPECIALES POUR INDUST
727	FOOD MACHRY NON–DOMESTIC	W 84	2.7	W 28	0.7	W 68	1.8			MACH INDUSTRIES ALIMENT
7272	OTH FOOD PROC MCHY,PARTS	W 80	2.6	W 27	0.6	W 66	1.8			AUT MACH IND ALIMENTAIRE
72722	INDUS FOOD PROC MACH NES	W 80	2.6	W 27	0.6	W 66	1.8			MACHINES BOULANGERIE
728	OTH MACHY FOR SPCL INDUS	W 96	2.9	W 191	2.6	W 85	2.7			AUT MACH IND PARTICULIERES
7284	MACHY FOR SPCL INDUS NES	W 61	2.4	W 175	2.3	W 78	2.6			MACH SPEC IND PARTICUL.
72848	OTH MCHY WITH INDIV FNCT	W 54	2.1	W 167	2.2	W 65	2.4			AUTRES MACHINES NDA
74	GENRL INDUSTRL MACHY NES		10.5		5.5		7.4			MACH APP INDUSTRIE
741	HEATING,COOLING EQUIPMNT	W 156	2.6	W 43	0.9	W 63	1.2			MACH CHAUFFAGE,PIECES
7414	NONDOM REFRIG EQUIPT,PTS	W 100	1.6	W 20	0.3	W 38	0.6			MAT PRODUCTION DU FROID
74141	REFRIG EQUIP NONDOMESTIC	W 94	1.4	W 18	0.2	W 27	0.4			REFIG INDUSTRIELS
742	PUMPS FOR LIQUIDS ETC	W 32	1.3	W 28	0.9	W 25	0.8			POMPES MOTO–POMPES
743	PUMPS NES,CENTRFUGES ETC	W 73	1.5	W 36	0.8	W 46	1.2			POMPES COMPRES,VENT ETC
744	MECHANICAL HANDLING EQU	W 249	2.5	W 75	1.5	W 303	2.4			EQUIP MANUTENTION PIECES
7442	LIFTING,LOADING MACH NES	W 112	1.1	W 28	0.4	W 94	1.0			APP LEVAGE,MANUTENTION
7449	PTS NES OF MACHY OF 7442	W 38	0.9	W 42	1.1	W 30	0.8			PIECES DU 744.2
745	NONELEC MACHY,TOOLS NES	W 40	1.1	W 19	0.6	W 27	1.0			AUT MACH NON ELEC,PIECES
7452	OTH NONELEC MCHS,PTS NES	W 38	1.1	W 19	0.6	W 26	1.0			AUT MACH NON ELEC,PIECES
749	NONELEC MACH PTS,ACC NES	W 59	1.7	W 28	1.0	W 27	1.0			PIECES MACH NON ELEC NDA
75	OFFICE MACHNES,ADP EQUIP		8.1		4.8		6.0			MACH BUREAU TRAIT AUTOM
751	OFFICE MACHINES	W 21	0.8	W 15	0.6	W 19	0.9			MACH,APPAREILS DE BUREAU
752	AUTOMTIC DATA PROC EQUIP	W 57	5.9	W 37	2.9	W 37	3.2			MACH TRAIT INFORMATION
7522	DIGITAL COMPUTERS	W 14	1.6	W 10	0.8	W 7	0.8			MACH DIGITALES COMPLETES
7523	DIGITL CENTRL PROCESSORS	W 9	1.1	W 4	0.4	W 3	0.3			UNITES CENTRALES

4. General Imports C.I.F. by Commodities according to the S.I.T.C. (Rev. 2) in million U.S. Dollars
Importations Générales C.A.F. par Produits d'après la C.T.C.I. (Rév. 2) en millions de Dollars E.U.

SITC CTCI	COMMODITY	1992 QUANTITY QUANTITE	1992 VALUE VALEUR	1993 QUANTITY QUANTITE	1993 VALUE VALEUR	1994 QUANTITY QUANTITE	1994 VALUE VALEUR	1995 QUANTITY QUANTITE	1995 VALUE VALEUR	PRODUIT
7525	ADP PERIPHERAL UNITS	W 16	1.4	W 11	0.9	W 15	1.2			UNITES PERIPHERIQUES
759	OFFICE,ADP MCH PTS,ACCES	W 19	1.5	W 14	1.3	W 21	2.1			PIECES DU 751 ET 752
7599	ACCTG,ETC,ADP MCH PTS,AC	W 8	1.1	W 10	1.0	W 16	1.7			PIECES DU 751 ET 752
76	TELECOMM,SOUND EQUIPMENT		7.7		3.7		13.2			EQUIPMENT DE TELECOM
764	TELECOM EQPT,PTS,ACC NES	W 70	6.0	W 42	3.0	W 59	12.3			EQUIP TELECOM,PIECES
7641	LINE TELEPHONE,ETC EQUIP	W 7	1.1	W 7	0.7	W 7	1.8			APP TELEPHON PAR FIL
7643	TV,RADIO TRANSMITTRS ETC	W 6	1.3	W 2	0.5	W 3	0.6			APP EMET TELE RADIO
7648	TELECOMM EQUIPMENT NES	W 3	0.5	W 2	0.3	W 16	2.6			APP TELECOM NDA
76483	RADAR APPARATUS ETC	W 2	0.4	W 2	0.2	W 15	2.5			APP DE RADIOGUIDAGE ETC
7649	PTS NES OF EQUIPMT OF 76	W 40	2.9	W 24	1.5	W 25	7.3			PIECES DE LA DIV 76
76491	PTS NES OF APPAR OF 7641	W 7	1.2	W 3	0.4	W 9	5.9			PIECES POUR 764.1
76493	TELECOMM EQUIPMT PTS NES	W 32	1.7	W 21	1.1	W 15	1.4			PIECES 761,762,764.3,8
77	ELECTRIC MACHNRY NES ETC		8.9		5.7		5.9			MACH APP ELECT NDA
772	SWITCHGEAR ETC,PARTS NES	W 85	2.0	W 49	1.2	W 51	1.4			APP COUPURE,SECT ETC
7721	SWITCHGEAR ETC	W 85	1.9	W 48	1.2	W 51	1.4			APP COUPURE,SECTIONMNT
773	ELECTR DISTRIBUTNG EQUIP	W 179	1.2	W 106	0.7	W 93	0.6			EQUIPMT DISTRIBUTION ELECT
775	HOUSEHOLD TYPE EQUIP NES	W 246	2.4	W 186	1.6	W 188	1.6			MACH,APP USAGE DOMESTQUE
778	ELECTRICAL MACHINERY NES	W 156	2.1	W 146	1.8	W 180	2.0			AUTRES MACH ELECT NDA
7781	BATTERIES,ACCUMULATORS	W 115	0.8	W 112	0.6	W 136	0.8			PILES ET ACCUMULATEURS
78	ROAD VEHICLES		9.8		4.6		5.6			VEHICULES ROUTIERS
781	PASS MOTOR VEH EXC BUSES	W 513	4.3	W 119	1.0	W 177	1.7			AUTO TRANSPORT PERSONNES
782	LORRIES,SPCL MTR VEH NES	W 180	2.0	W 64	0.9	W 83	0.9			VEHICULES SPECIAUX,MARCH
7821	LORRIES,TRUCKS	W 106	1.1	W 19	0.3	W 52	0.2			VEHICULES TRANSP MARCHAND
7822	SPECIAL MOTOR VEHCLS NES	W 75	1.0	W 45	0.7	W 31	0.7			VEHICULES USAGES SPECIAUX
784	MOTOR VEH PRTS,ACCES NES	W 211	2.9	W 155	2.2	W 160	2.4			PIECES 722,781,782,783
7849	OTHER MOTOR VEHCL PARTS	W 208	2.9	W 154	2.2	W 156	2.4			PIECES 722,781,782,783
79	OTHR TRANSPORT EQUIPMENT		12.3		0.8		0.8			AUTRE MATERIEL TRANSPORT
792	AIRCRAFT ETC	W 5	1.3	W 3	0.7	W 6	0.5			APP NAVIGATION AERIENNE
7929	AIRCRAFT PARTS NES	W 4	1.2	W 2	0.7	W 6	0.5			PIECES DU 792
793	SHIPS AND BOATS ETC	W 2027	11.1	W 10	0.1	W 21	0.3			NAVIRES BATEAUX,ETC
7932	SHIPS AND BOATS NES	W 1990	10.7		0.1		0.1			NAVIRES ET BATEAUX
79324	FISHING VESSELS ETC	W 1984	10.5							BATEAUX DE PECHE
8	MISC MANUFACTURED GOODS		36.2		28.1		33.4			ART MANUFACTURES DIVERS
812	*PLUMBG,HEATNG,LGHTNG EQ	W 293	2.3	W 169	1.3	W 119	1.1			APPAR SANITAIRES CHAUFFAGE
8124	LIGHTING EQUIPMENT NES	W 60	1.2	W 48	0.8	W 51	0.8			APPAREILS ECLAIRAGE ETC
81242	LAMPS,FITTINGS BASE METL	W 50	1.1	W 44	0.7	W 47	0.8			APPAREILS D'ECLAIRAGE
821	*FURNITURE,PARTS THEREOF	W 958	5.6	W 677	3.6	W 610	3.4			MEUBLES ET PIECES
8211	CHAIRS,SEATS AND PARTS	W 147	1.4	W 96	0.8	W 106	0.9			SIEGES ET PIECES
82111	CHAIRS AND OTHER SEATS	W 145	1.4	W 96	0.8	W 105	0.9			SIEGES
8219	FURNITURE AND PARTS NES	W 752	3.6	W 524	2.3	W 430	1.8			AUTRES MEUBLES ET PIECES
82192	WOOD FURNITURE NES	W 618	2.7	W 410	1.6	W 337	1.4			MEUBLES NDA EN BOIS
84	CLOTHING AND ACCESSORIES		7.4		6.4		8.6			VETEMENTS
842	MENS OUTERWEAR NOT KNIT	W 28	1.1	W 28	1.0	W 47	1.4			VET DESSUS POUR HOMMES
8423	— TROUSERS,BREECHES ETC	W 17	0.7	W 19	0.6	W 31	0.8			PANTALONS HOMMES MAT TEX
843	WOMENS OUTERWEAR NONKNIT	W 40	1.9	W 33	1.4	W 46	1.9			VET DESSUS FEMMES MAT TEX
8439	— OTHER OUTER GARMENTS	W 25	1.0	W 18	0.7	W 27	1.0			AUT VET DES FEM MAT TEXT
845	OUTERWEAR KNIT NONELASTC	W 49	2.2	W 47	1.9	W 60	2.4			VET DESSOUS,ACCES BONNET
8451	— JERSEYS,PULLOVERS ETC	W 15	0.8	W 21	0.9	W 27	1.1			CHANDAILS,PULL–OVERS ETC
8459	— OTHER,CLTHG ACCESRYS	W 30	1.3	W 21	0.8	W 28	1.1			AUT VET DESSUS DE BONNE
846	UNDER GARMENTS KNITTED	W 23	1.0	W 24	0.8	W 35	1.0			SOUS VETS DE BONNETERIE
848	HEADGEAR,NONTXTL CLOTHNG	W 27	0.6	W 54	1.1	W 78	1.4			VET ACCES MAT AUT QUE TEX
8484	HEADGEAR	W 3	0.1	W 35	0.8	W 47	0.9			COIFFURES ET PARTIES NDA
84843	HEADGEAR TEXTILE NONFELT	W 2	0.1	W 35	0.8	W 44	0.9			CHAPEAUX EN BONNETERIE
851	*FOOTWEAR	W 91	2.3	W 56	1.3	W 64	1.4			CHAUSSURES
85102	FOOTWEAR LEATHER	W 68	1.8	W 29	0.9	W 39	1.0			CHAUS SEMELLES EN CUIR
87	PRECISION INSTRUMNTS NES		2.9		3.5		4.5			INSTRUM,APPAR SCIENT NDA
872	MEDICAL INSTRUMENTS NES	W 5	0.5	W 8	0.9	W 11	0.9			INSTR,APP MEDIC–CHIR NDA
87202	OTH MEDICAL INSTRUMENTS	W 4	0.4	W 7	0.6	W 10	0.8			INSTRUM,APP MEDECINE
874	MEASURNG,CONTROLNG INSTR	W 23	2.3	W 24	2.4	W 43	3.5			INSTRUMENTS DE MESURE
8741	SURVEYING INSTRUMENTS	W 4	0.6	W 2	0.4	W 5	1.0			INST GEODESIE,TOPO ETC
8745	MEAS,CONTRL,SCI INST NES	W 9	0.8	W 13	1.0	W 29	1.1			APP SCIENT MESURE NDA
87453	MECHANCL TESTING APPARAT	W 8	0.7	W 11	0.9	W 27	0.9			MACH NON ELEC ESSAIS MEC
8748	ELEC MEAS,CONTRL EQU NES	W 1	0.2	W 3	0.7	W 2	1.0			APP ELEC ELECTRO MESURE
87483	OTH ELCTRNC MEAS ETC EQU	W 1	0.2	W 2	0.6	W 2	1.0			AUT APP ELECTRO DE MESURE
88	PHOTO EQU,OPTICL GDS ETC		1.5		1.0		1.1			APP,FOURN PHOTO,OP,MONTR
89	MISC MANUFCTRD GOODS NES		14.1		11.3		13.4			ART MANUFACTURES DIVERS
892	PRINTED MATTER	W 281	3.4	W 281	2.8	W 404	3.9			IMPRIMES
8921	PRINTED BOOKS,GLOBES,ETC	W 79	1.4	W 70	1.0	W 63	1.1			LIVRES,BROCHURES,CARTES
89211	PRINTED BOOKS,PAMPHLETS	W 77	1.3	W 68	1.0	W 58	1.0			LIVRES,BROCHURES
8922	NEWSPAPERS,PERIODICALS	W 57	0.4	W 78	0.6	W 201	1.6			JOURNAUX ET PERIODIQUES
8928	PRINTED MATTER NES	W 137	1.6	W 130	1.3	W 136	1.3			IMPRIMES NDA
893	ARTICLES OF PLASTIC NES		5.1	W 692	3.6		3.8			OUVRAGES EN MAT DIVIS 58
8931	PLSTC PACKG CONTNRS,LIDS	W 388	1.7	W 283	1.3	W 382	1.6			ART TRANSP EMBALLAGE ETC
8939	MISC PLASTIC ARTICLES	W 523	3.3	W 404	2.3	W 361	2.2			ART DIVERS EN MAT DIV 58
89399	OTHR PLASTC ARTICLES NES	W 410	2.7	W 284	1.9	W 266	1.8			AUT OUV MAT DIV 58
894	TOYS,SPORTING GOODS,ETC	W 154	2.1	W 108	1.4	W 178	1.9			VOITURES ENFANTS,JOUETS
8942	TOYS,INDOOR GAMES ETC	W 79	1.1	W 68	0.9	W 99	1.1			JOUETS,JEUX ETC
898	MUSICAL INSTRUMENTS,PTS	W 37	1.1	W 30	1.5	W 34	1.5			INSTRUMENTS DE MUSIQUE
8983	SOUND RECRDNG TAPE,DISCS	W 30	0.9	W 24	1.1	W 29	1.3			SUPPORTS SON POUR 763
89832	RECORDED DISCS,TAPES ETC	W 13	0.6	W 7	0.5	W 10	1.0			DISQUES,PHONO,BANDES
899	OTHER MANUFACTURED GOODS		1.4		1.1		1.4			AUT ART MANUF DIVERS NDA
9	GOODS NOT CLASSD BY KIND		1.5		0.6		0.8			ART TRANSACT NON CLASSES
931	*SPECIAL TRANSACTIONS	W 238	1.5	W 39	0.6	W 30	0.8			TRANS.SPECIALES

5. General Exports F.O.B. by Commodities according to the S.I.T.C. (Rev. 2) in million U.S. Dollars
Exportations Générales F.O.B. par Produits d'après la C.T.C.I. (Rév. 2) en millions de Dollars E.U.

SITC CTCI	COMMODITY	1992 QUANTITY QUANTITE	1992 VALUE VALEUR	1993 QUANTITY QUANTITE	1993 VALUE VALEUR	1994 QUANTITY QUANTITE	1994 VALUE VALEUR	1995 QUANTITY QUANTITE	1995 VALUE VALEUR	PRODUIT
	ALL COMMODITIES		438.2		328.4		326.5			TOUS PRODUITS
0	FOOD AND LIVE ANIMALS		389.8		306.9		310.2			ALIMENTS,ANIMAUX VIVANTS
03	FISH AND PREPARATIONS		379.7		296.6		297.5			POISSONS ET PREPARATIONS
034	FISH,FRESH,CHILLED,FROZN	W 88013	275.5	W 85319	217.6	W 74079	202.6			POISSON FRAIS, REFRIG,CONG
0341	FISH FRSH,CHLLD,EX FILLT	W 39850	100.5	W 41851	92.9	W 33165	77.1			POISSON FRAIS,REFRIGERE
0342	FISH FROZEN,EXCL FILLETS	W 9099	34.9	W 10704	23.6	W 5583	13.8			POISSONS CONGELES
0343	FISH FILLETS,FRESH,CHLLD	W 6319	26.5	W 5210	19.1	W 5863	23.4			FILETS FRAIS,REFRIGERES
0344	FISH FILLETS,FROZEN	W 32744	113.8	W 27554	82.1	W 29468	88.5			FILETS CONGELES
035	FISH SALTED,DRIED,SMOKED	W 12284	61.3	W 7516	30.4	W 10371	42.7			POISSON SECHE,SALE,FUME
03503	FISH(EX COD)DRIED,SALTED	W 11922	57.7	W 7118	26.8	W 9664	35.8			POISSONS SECHES,SALES
03504	FISH SMOKED	W 343	3.4	W 398	3.6	W 660	6.8			POISSONS FUMES
036	SHELL FISH FRESH,FROZEN	W 2929	19.3	W 5643	30.5	W 8971	34.7			CRUSTACES,MOLLUSQUES
037	FISH ETC PREPD,PRSVD NES	W 4287	23.7	W 3870	18.3	W 3908	17.6			POIS,CRUST,MOL PREPARES
0371	FISH PREPARD,PRESRVD NES	W 1839	6.1	W 2062	6.9	W 2287	6.6			CONSERVES DE POISSONS
0372	SHELL FISH PREPRD,PRESVD	W 2448	17.7	W 1808	11.4	W 1621	11.1			CRUSTACES,COQUIL PREPARES
081	*FEEDING STUFF FOR ANIML	W 19016	10.2	W 22328	10.3	W 23829	11.9			NOURRITURE POUR ANIMAUX
0814	MEAT OR FISH MEAL FODDER	W 19015	10.2	W 22325	10.3	W 22416	10.8			FARINES DE VIANDES,POISSONS
08142	FISH MEAL FODDER	W 19015	10.2	W 22325	10.3	W 22416	10.8			FARINES DE POISSONS
0819	FOOD WASTE AND FEED NES		0.1	W 3	0.1	W 1413	1.2			DECHETS,ALIMENTS NDA
08199	FODDER NES,INCL SWEETNED		0.1	W 3	0.1	W 1413	1.2			PREPARATIONS FOURRAGERES
2	CRUDE MATERLS,EXCL FUELS		4.4		2.2		3.1			MAT BRUTES NON COMESTIBLES
29	CRUDE ANIMAL,VEG MAT NES		4.2		2.0		2.6			MATIERES BRUTES ANIM,VEGET
291	CRUDE ANIMAL MTRIALS NES	W 45697	4.2	W 27126	2.0	W 29311	2.6			MATIERES BRUTES ANIMALES
2919	OTH ANIMAL MATERIALS NES	W 45697	4.2	W 27126	2.0	W 29311	2.6			MAT ORIGINE ANIMALE NDA
29194	FISH WASTE	W 45697	4.2	W 27126	2.0	W 29311	2.6			DECHETS DE POISSONS
4	ANIMAL,VEGETABLE OIL,FAT		3.4		5.5		3.0			HUILES,GRAISSES ANIM,VEG
411	*ANIMAL OILS AND FATS	W 9463	3.4	W 16487	5.5	W 10278	3.0			HUILES,GRAISSES ANIMALES
4111	OILS OF FISH,WHALES ETC	W 9463	3.4	W 16487	5.5	W 10278	3.0			GRAISSES,HUILES DE POISSONS
41112	OTHER FISH OILS AND FATS	W 9463	3.4	W 16487	5.5	W 10278	3.0			AUTRES HUILES ET GRAISSES
6	BASIC MANUFACTURES		0.3		0.4		1.1			ART MANUFACTURES
7	MACHINES,TRANSPORT EQUIP		40.0		12.9		8.1			MACHINES MATERIEL TRANSPORT
79	OTHR TRANSPORT EQUIPMENT		40.0		12.4		8.0			AUTRE MATERIEL TRANSPORT
793	SHIPS AND BOATS ETC	W 6996	40.0	W 7962	12.4	W 4286	8.0			NAVIRES BATEAUX,ETC
7932	SHIPS AND BOATS NES	W 6706	39.7	W 7962	12.4	W 4286	8.0			NAVIRES ET BATEAUX
79323	OTHER CARGO VESSELS	W 964	4.4	W 3158	3.3	W 2128	2.8			AUT BATEAUX TRANS MARCH
79324	FISHING VESSELS ETC	W 5742	35.4	W 4722	9.1	W 2156	5.2			BATEAUX DE PECHE

1. HISTORICAL SERIES, 1961–1996 GENERAL TRADE, IMPORTS C.I.F., EXPORTS F.O.B.
SERIES HISTORIQUES, 1961–1996 COMMERCE GENERAL, IMPORTATIONS C.A.F., EXPORTATIONS F.O.B

YEAR ANNEE	VALUE IN MILLION FIJI DOLLARS VALEUR EN MILLION FIJI DOLLARS MERCHANDISE – MARCHANDISE		GOLD – OR		CONVERSION FACTORS U.S. CENTS PER FIJI DOLLAR FACTEURS DE CONVERSION CENTS E.U. PAR FIJI DOLLAR		INDEX NUMBERS – INDICES QUANTUM		UNIT VALUE VALEUR UNITAIRE	
	IMPORTS	EXPORTS	IMPORTS	EXPORTS	IMPORTS	EXPORTS	IMPORTS	EXPORTS	IMPORTS	EXPORTS
1961	34.40	23.90	0.01	2.40	126.1250	126.1250				
1962	34.80	29.10	0.01	2.30	126.1250	126.1250				
1963	40.40	41.20		3.10	126.1250	126.1250				
1964	55.20	49.50	0.01	2.70	126.1250	126.1250				
1965	58.20	39.40		3.00	126.1250	126.1250				
1966	50.50	35.90	0.01	3.00	126.1250	126.1250				
1967	56.30	39.50	0.01	3.10	125.0600	125.0150				
1968	68.40	45.70	0.01	3.40	114.8320	114.8320				
1969	77.90	49.90	0.01	3.30	114.8320	114.8320				
1970	90.50	59.00	0.01	3.30	114.8320	114.8320				
1971	111.50	59.00	0.02	2.60	116.7380	117.2200				
1972	131.50	61.60	0.02	3.90	121.2040	119.5080				
1973	174.70	74.40	0.02	6.10	126.0050	127.0040				
1974	219.30	123.70	0.04	8.60	124.5230	124.8030				
1975	221.80	142.30	0.12	8.50	121.0680	119.1930				
1976	238.00	122.50	0.16	7.20	110.4230	110.0350				
1977	281.00	164.30	0.14	6.50	109.1210	109.8100				
1978	300.00	166.50	0.21	4.90	118.3640	119.2430				
1979	392.90	215.00	0.35	6.40	119.6580	119.5820				
1980	458.80	305.60	0.23	12.00	122.5530	123.3810				
1981	539.90	269.00	0.48	11.60	117.0591	115.7757				
1982	475.60	267.60			108.2365	106.8719				
1983	493.20	244.90			98.1908	97.8534				
1984	487.10	279.40			92.3739	91.4452				
1985	508.00	271.40			86.9212	87.1189				
1986	493.60	383.02			88.1690	87.5722				
1987	465.11	483.12			81.4973	78.9356				
1988	658.82	531.19			70.0407	70.0158				
1989	860.44	658.62			67.5036	67.3683				
1990	1112.90	731.86			67.7531	68.0514				
1991	961.77	664.60			67.7923	67.8170				
1992	947.11	666.98			66.5841	66.4621				
1993	1109.81	692.40			64.8944	64.9260				
1994	1209.85	800.49			68.5257	68.7404				
1995	1218.93	869.94			71.1090	71.1100				
1996	1380.07	1048.49			71.3118	71.3225				

2. IMPORTS BY BROAD ECONOMIC CATEGORY AND EXPORTS BY INDUSTRIAL ORIGIN. (PERCENTAGE OF TOTAL VALUE)
IMPORTATIONS PAR CATEGORIES ECONOMIQUES ET EXPORTATIONS PAR BRANCHE D'ACTIVITE.(EN POURCENTAGE DE LA VALEUR TOTALE)

IMPORTS – IMPORTATIONS

	1990	1991	1992	1993	1994	1995	1996
TOTAL IMPORTS–IMPORTATIONS TOTALES	100.	100.	100.	100.	100.		
1 FOOD BEV–ALIMENTATION BOISSONS	13.8	16.1	15.5	17.0	14.8		
11 PRIMARY–PRODUITS DE BASE	8.6	9.9	7.9	9.4	8.6		
111 FOR INDUSTRY–POUR L'INDUSTRIE	2.5	2.9	2.9	2.7	2.7		
112 FOR HOUSEHOLDS–POUR LES MENAGES	6.1	7.0	5.1	6.6	5.9		
12 PROCESSED–PRODUITS ELABORES	5.2	6.2	7.5	7.7	6.2		
121 FOR INDUSTRY–POUR L'INDUSTRIE	1.4	1.6	2.4	1.7	1.4		
122 FOR HOUSEHOLDS–POUR LES MENAGES	3.9	4.7	5.1	6.0	4.8		
2 IND SUPPLIES–APPROV INDUSTRIELS	27.1	30.4	31.0	27.5	28.1		
21 PRIMARY–PRODUITS DE BASE	0.8	1.0	1.1	0.8	0.6		
22 PROCESSED–PRODUITS ELABORES	26.3	29.5	29.8	26.7	27.4		
3 FUELS–COMBUSTIBLES	14.1	15.0	14.0	13.6	11.2		
31 PRIMARY–PRODUITS DE BASE	0.4	0.7	0.6	0.7	0.6		
32 PROCESSED–PRODUITS ELABORES	13.7	14.3	13.4	12.9	10.6		
321 MOTOR SPIRIT–ESSENCE							
322 OTHER–AUTRES	13.7	14.3	13.4	12.9	10.6		
4 MACHINERY–EQUIPEMENT	13.0	12.9	11.2	14.6	12.3		
41 CAPITAL EQUIPMENT–MACHINES	11.2	10.5	9.3	12.5	10.5		
42 PARTS–PIECES ACCESSOIRES	1.8	2.5	1.9	2.1	1.7		
5 TRANSPORT–TRANSPORT	16.9	8.9	12.9	9.9	18.6		
51 PASSENGER CARS–AUTOMOBILES	2.1	1.9	2.4	2.5	1.9		
52 OTHER–AUTRES	11.0	3.5	7.5	4.0	12.7		
521 INDUSTRIAL–INDUSTRIELS	10.9	3.4	7.5	3.9	12.6		
522 NON INDUSTRIAL–NON INDUSTRIEL	0.1	0.1	0.1	0.1	0.1		
53 PARTS–PIECES ACCESSOIRES	3.8	3.5	2.9	3.4	4.0		
6 CONSUM GOODS–BIENS CONSOMMATION	14.0	15.6	14.5	16.2	13.9		
61 DURABLE–DURABLES	5.1	5.2	4.6	5.0	4.1		
62 SEMI DURABLE–SEMI DURABLES	5.7	6.9	6.2	7.4	6.1		
63 NON DURABLE–NON DURABLES	3.2	3.5	3.7	3.7	3.6		
7 GOODS NES–BIENS NDA	1.1	1.0	1.0	1.2	1.1		

EXPORTS – EXPORTATIONS

	1990	1991	1992	1993	1994	1995	1996
TOTAL EXPORTS–EXPORTATIONS TOTALES	100.	100.	100.	100.	100.		
1 AGRICULTURE	4.8	3.4	3.7	3.0	4.3		
2 MINING QUARRY–INDUS EXTRACTIVES	0.0	0.0	0.0	0.0	0.0		
3 MANUFACTURING–IND MANUFACTUR	95.1	96.6	96.3	97.0	95.7		
31 FOOD BEV TOBACCO–ALIM BOISS TAB	45.0	51.7	47.7	46.0	45.1		
32 TEXTILES–INDUSTRIES TEXTILES	20.1	22.1	22.1	27.6	22.9		
33 WOOD & PRODUCTS–BOIS & PRODUITS	5.5	4.5	5.8	3.6	4.8		
34 PAPER & PRODUCTS–PAPIER & PRODT	0.7	1.0	1.0	1.3	0.8		
35 CHEMICALS–INDUSTRIES CHIMIQUES	13.5	11.5	10.9	12.9	10.1		
36 NON METAL MIN–MIN NON METAL	0.7	0.4	0.2	0.2	0.1		
37 BASIC METAL–IND METAL BASE	1.0	0.4	0.8	0.6	0.7		
38 METAL MANUF–MANUF METAL	7.5	4.1	6.7	3.7	9.8		
39 OTH MANUF IND–AUTRES MANUF	1.1	1.0	1.0	1.2	1.3		

3. TRADE BY PRINCIPAL COUNTRIES OF PURCHASE AND SALE (VALUE IN MILLION U.S. DOLLARS)
ECHANGES SELON LES PRINCIPAUX PAYS D'ACHAT ET DE VENTE (VALEUR EN MILLIONS DE DOLLARS EU)

COUNTRIES–PAYS	GENERAL IMPORTS C.I.F. IMPORTATIONS GENERALES C.A.F				
	1992	1993	1994	1995	1996
World	630.7	526.6	837.8	866.8	986.5
Africa	0.7	0.8	1.0		
Americas	58.7	26.6	129.1	65.7	98.6
– Northern America	57.2	24.9	126.7	65.7	98.6
– LAIA	1.0	0.9	1.8		
– CACM	0.0	0.0	0.0		
– Caribbean	0.4	0.7	0.5		
– Rest of America	0.1	0.0	0.0		
Asia excl fmr USSR	210.2	181.1	247.4	235.2	211.2
– Middle East	0.3	0.2	0.2		
Asia former USSR					
Europe excl fmr USSR	48.6	33.7	34.6	32.3	32.2
– European Union	45.3	31.1	32.7	32.3	32.2
– Eastern Europe	1.4	1.3	0.5		
– Rest of Europe	1.9	1.3	1.4		
Europe former USSR	0.4	0.0	0.1		
Oceania	309.9	282.6	421.7	474.5	582.6
Other	2.3	1.8	4.0		
Australia/Australie	202.2	172.9	275.9	336.6	437.1
New Zealand	106.1	108.3	141.0	137.9	145.5
USA/Etats–Unis d'Amer	55.1	22.5	123.7	61.5	91.8
Japan/Japon	65.0	63.4	66.9	62.3	51.6
Singapore/Singapour	40.4	28.4	62.2	61.9	49.7
China/Chine	21.3	19.0	26.5	25.0	24.7
Other Asia n.e.s.	16.9	11.7	20.3	27.3	25.3
China, Hong Kong SAR	20.2	16.8	17.7	24.0	17.0
United Kingdom	19.9	15.8	14.5	18.0	17.6
Thailand/Thaïlande	11.5	11.6	12.9	12.4	17.9
Korea, Republic of	11.4	7.7	9.4	12.6	12.7
Malaysia/Malaisie	5.7	5.3	8.3	9.8	12.4
Germany/Allemagne	9.6	5.3	6.5	9.8	8.9
France, Monaco	8.5	3.3	3.1	4.5	5.7
India/Inde	7.0	7.4	10.0		
Indonesia/Indonésie	7.1	7.0	9.6		
Canada	2.1	2.5	2.9	4.1	6.8
Belgium–Luxembourg	2.9	2.2	3.1		
Areas n.e.s.	2.3	1.8	4.0		
Italy/Italie	1.7	1.3	1.9		
Netherlands/Pays–Bas	1.4	1.4	2.0		
Papua New Guinea	0.9	1.1	2.7		
Switzerland,Liechtenst.	1.7	1.3	1.2		
Sri Lanka	1.4	1.2	1.3		
Brazil/Brésil	0.8	0.7	1.3		
Pakistan	1.1	0.8	0.8		
Philippines	0.5	0.6	0.9		
Sweden/Suède	0.6	0.7	0.6		
Czech Republic		1.2	0.4		
Solomon Islands	0.4	0.2	0.9		
Dominica/Dominique	0.3	0.3	0.5		
Spain/Espagne	0.2	0.4	0.3		
Kiribati	0.0	0.0	0.8		
So. African Customs Un	0.2	0.2	0.5		
Poland/Pologne	0.7	0.0	0.0		
Mali	0.3	0.2	0.1		
Finland/Finlande	0.1	0.3	0.2		
Former Czechoslovakia	0.5				
Mexico/Mexique	0.1	0.1	0.2		
Korea Dem People's Rp	0.2	0.2	0.1		

COUNTRIES–PAYS	GENERAL EXPORTS F.O.B. EXPORTATIONS GENERALES F.O.B.				
	1992	1993	1994	1995	1996
Monde	428.0	297.7	550.3	618.6	747.4
Afrique	0.2	0.1	0.7		
Amériques	71.7	47.8	124.4	90.5	77.4
– Amérique du Nord	71.5	47.8	124.3	90.5	77.4
– ALAI	0.0	0.0	0.1		
– MCAC	0.0	0.0	0.0		
– Caraïbes	0.2	0.0	0.0		
– Autre Amérique	0.0				
Asie anc. URSS exclus	58.9	23.7	81.4	95.4	112.5
– Moyen–Orient	0.0	0.0	0.1		
Asie ancienne URSS					
Europe anc. URSS exclus	136.4	85.8	111.7	137.7	131.1
– Union Européenne	136.3	85.8	111.5	137.7	131.1
– Europe de l'Est	0.0				
– Autre de l'Europe	0.0	0.0	0.3		
Europe ancienne URSS	0.0	0.0	0.1		
Océanie	145.8	122.0	207.7	181.1	292.2
Autre	15.0	18.1	24.3		
Australia/Australie	61.7	63.0	118.6	148.2	202.0
United Kingdom	132.5	81.8	106.9	124.9	104.3
USA/Etats–Unis d'Amer	59.7	34.0	98.6	71.2	61.3
New Zealand	24.8	17.3	29.3	32.9	90.2
Japan/Japon	22.5	14.8	37.6	36.1	48.4
Malaysia/Malaisie	27.1	3.4	26.2	29.4	21.6
Canada	11.8	13.8	25.6	19.4	16.1
Tonga	13.7	9.3	15.2		
Portugal		0.0		9.6	24.8
Other Asia n.e.s.	0.4	0.2	4.3	13.2	14.2
Areas n.e.s.	4.5	9.8	17.9		
Bunkers, ship stores	10.5	8.4	6.4		
US Misc Pacific Islands	9.0	5.4	7.8		
Samoa	8.2	5.3	7.2		
China/Chine	3.5	0.0	1.2	6.0	9.5
China, Hong Kong SAR	4.0	1.8	2.4	5.4	5.4
Korea, Republic of	0.2	0.6	7.2	4.3	6.6
Kiribati	5.5	4.3	5.0		
Vanuatu	4.0	3.4	4.5		
Cook Islands/Iles Cook	4.6	2.9	3.4		
Singapore/Singapour	1.0	1.9	0.6	0.8	6.5
Germany/Allemagne	3.3	1.6	1.3	2.7	1.6
Tuvalu	3.5	2.5	3.0		
French Polynesia	2.3	1.8	2.5		
Papua New Guinea	1.1	0.9	4.3		
New Caledonia	2.0	1.4	2.1		
Norfolk Island	1.4	1.4	1.7		
Solomon Islands	1.4	1.4	1.3		
Netherlands/Pays–Bas	0.2	2.0	1.4		
Nauru	0.9	0.7	0.8		
Wallis and Futuna Is	1.3	0.4	0.5		
France, Monaco	0.2	0.2	0.7	0.5	0.5
Indonesia/Indonésie	0.1	0.6	0.8		
Niue/Nioué	0.3	0.5	0.3		
Italy/Italie	0.1	0.1	0.9		
Thailand/Thaïlande	0.1	0.2	0.2	0.3	0.2
Cote d'Ivoire	0.1	0.0	0.5		
Sri Lanka	0.0	0.0	0.4		
Spain/Espagne	0.1	0.0	0.2		
Oceania n.e.s.	0.1	0.1	0.1		

(VALUE AS PERCENTAGE OF WORLD TOTAL)(VALEURS EN POURCENTAGE DU TOTAL MONDIAL)

	1987	1988	1989	1990	1991	1992	1993	1994	1995	1996
Africa	0.1	0.1	0.1	0.1	0.1	0.1	0.1	0.1		
Americas	6.1	5.4	5.8	13.6	5.2	9.3	5.0	15.4	7.6	10.0
– Northern America	5.9	5.3	5.6	13.5	4.9	9.1	4.7	15.1	7.6	10.0
– LAIA	0.2	0.1	0.2	0.1	0.2	0.2	0.2	0.2		
– CACM	0.0		0.0	0.0	0.0	0.0	0.0	0.0		
– Caribbean	0.0	0.0	0.0	0.0	0.0	0.1	0.1	0.1		
– Rest of America	0.0	0.0	0.0	0.0	0.0	0.0	0.0	0.0		
Asia excl fmr USSR	37.9	33.0	39.0	33.2	36.8	33.3	34.4	29.5	27.1	21.4
– Middle East	0.1	0.1	0.1	0.0	0.0	0.1	0.0	0.0		
Asia former USSR										
Europe excl fmr USSR	9.4	12.0	7.4	7.8	6.6	7.7	6.4	4.1	3.7	3.3
– European Union	8.7	11.4	6.7	7.2	6.0	7.2	5.9	3.9	3.7	3.3
– Eastern Europe	0.2	0.2	0.3	0.2	0.3	0.2	0.2	0.1		
– Rest of Europe	0.4	0.3	0.3	0.3	0.3	0.3	0.3	0.2		
Europe former USSR	0.0	0.0	0.0	0.0	0.0	0.1	0.0	0.0		
Oceania	46.4	49.6	47.6	45.1	51.0	49.1	53.7	50.3	54.7	59.1
Other	0.0	0.0	0.1	0.1	0.2	0.4	0.3	0.5		
Australia/Australie	28.7	29.4	30.2	27.8	31.6	32.1	32.8	32.9	38.8	44.3
New Zealand	16.9	18.9	16.5	16.3	18.2	16.8	20.6	16.8	15.9	14.7
USA/Etats–Unis d'Amer	5.3	4.9	5.3	13.0	4.4	8.7	4.3	14.8	7.1	9.3
Japan/Japon	12.1	10.2	13.6	11.1	11.3	10.3	12.0	8.0	7.2	5.2
Singapore/Singapour	11.4	4.2	5.4	5.8	6.1	6.4	5.4	7.4	7.1	5.0
China/Chine	2.5	2.7	3.3	2.8	2.9	3.4	3.6	3.2	2.9	2.5
Other Asia n.e.s.	4.0	5.3	5.0	4.3	5.5	2.7	2.2	2.4	3.1	2.6
China, Hong Kong SAR	2.0	3.3	3.3	2.9	3.6	3.2	3.2	2.1	2.8	1.7
United Kingdom	4.4	3.7	3.0	3.1	3.0	3.2	3.0	1.7	2.1	1.8
Thailand/Thaïlande	1.1	1.2	1.6	1.7	2.3	1.8	2.2	1.5	1.4	1.8

	1987	1988	1989	1990	1991	1992	1993	1994	1995	1996
Afrique	0.0	0.0	0.0	0.0	0.0	0.0	0.0	0.1		
Amériques	7.1	6.7	8.1	10.9	13.4	16.8	16.1	22.6	14.6	10.4
– Amérique du Nord	6.8	6.7	8.1	10.9	13.3	16.7	16.1	22.6	14.6	10.4
– ALAI	0.2	0.0	0.0		0.0	0.0	0.0	0.0		
– MCAC			0.0	0.0		0.0	0.0	0.0		
– Caraïbes	0.0	0.0	0.0		0.0	0.0	0.0	0.0		
– Autre Amérique		0.0				0.0				
Asie anc. URSS exclus	17.4	15.6	15.5	16.2	13.5	13.8	8.0	14.8	15.4	15.0
– Moyen–Orient	0.0	0.0	0.4	0.0	0.0	0.0	0.0	0.0		
Asie ancienne URSS										
Europe anc. URSS exclus	35.1	29.3	25.3	23.9	33.4	31.9	28.8	20.3	22.3	17.5
– Union Européenne	35.0	29.3	25.3	23.9	33.4	31.9	28.8	20.3	22.3	17.5
– Europe de l'Est	0.1	0.0	0.0	0.0		0.0				
– Autre de l'Europe	0.0	0.0	0.0	0.0	0.0	0.0	0.0	0.1		
Europe ancienne URSS			0.0			0.0	0.0	0.0		
Océanie	34.5	40.9	45.6	43.0	34.7	34.1	41.0	37.7	29.3	39.1
Autre	5.9	7.5	5.5	6.0	5.0	3.5	6.1	4.4		
Australia/Australie	17.8	22.2	20.4	17.7	14.2	14.4	21.2	21.6	24.0	27.0
United Kingdom	34.0	28.6	24.5	23.1	32.6	30.9	27.5	19.4	20.2	14.0
USA/Etats–Unis d'Amer	5.5	3.0	5.6	8.5	10.3	14.0	11.4	17.9	11.5	8.2
New Zealand	5.7	7.4	14.1	11.8	8.4	5.8	5.8	5.3	5.3	12.1
Japan/Japon	3.0	4.9	6.1	5.9	5.2	5.3	5.0	6.8	5.8	6.5
Malaysia/Malaisie	7.4	4.1	5.9	4.9	4.0	6.3	1.1	4.8	4.8	2.9
Canada	1.4	3.7	2.5	2.3	3.0	2.7	4.6	4.7	3.1	2.2
Tonga	2.9	2.7	2.7	2.9	2.9	3.2	3.1	2.8		
Portugal	0.0			0.0			0.0		1.6	3.3
Other Asia n.e.s.	2.5	2.1	0.7	0.7	1.6	0.1	0.1	0.8	2.1	1.9

4. General Imports C.I.F. by Commodities according to the S.I.T.C. (Rev. 2) in million U.S. Dollars
Importations Générales C.A.F. par Produits d'après la C.T.C.I. (Rév. 2) en millions de Dollars E.U.

SITC CTCI	COMMODITY	1993 QUANTITY QUANTITE	1993 VALUE VALEUR	1994 QUANTITY QUANTITE	1994 VALUE VALEUR	1995 QUANTITY QUANTITE	1995 VALUE VALEUR	1996 QUANTITY QUANTITE	1996 VALUE VALEUR	PRODUIT
	ALL COMMODITIES		526.7		837.8		866.8		986.6	TOUS PRODUITS
0	FOOD AND LIVE ANIMALS		84.0		115.2		129.7		139.1	ALIMENTS,ANIMAUX VIVANTS
01	MEAT AND PREPARATIONS		14.2		15.7					VIANDES ET PREPARATIONS
011	MEAT FRESH,CHILLD,FROZEN	W 11918	13.7	W 12427	14.9					VIANDES FRAICHES,REF,CONGE
0112	MUTTON ETC FRSH,CHLD,FRN	W 8956	9.2	W 10916	12.2					VIANDE DE MOUTON
0114	POULTRY FRESH CHLLD,FRZN	W 1740	3.0	W 446	0.9					VOLAILLES MORTES
02	DAIRY PRODCTS,BIRDS'EGGS		9.8		12.2					PRODUITS LAITIERS,OEUFS
022	MILK AND CREAM	W 3174	5.8	W 3452	6.2					LAIT ET CREME
0224	MILK,CREAM PRESERVED ETC	W 2603	5.7	W 3121	5.9					LAIT,CREME CONS,CONC
02243	MILK DRY,OVER 1.5% FAT	W 2183	5.1	W 2416	5.0					LAIT POUDRE SUP 1.5%
023	BUTTER	W 1750	3.1	W 2248	4.1					BEURRE
03	FISH AND PREPARATIONS		8.5		18.1					POISSONS ET PREPARATIONS
034	FISH,FRESH,CHILLED,FROZN		5.3	W 12400	14.3					POISSON FRAIS, REFRIG,CONG
0341	FISH FRSH,CHLLD,EX FILLT		2.5	W 5125	5.1					POISSON FRAIS,REFRIGERE
0342	FISH FROZEN,EXCL FILLETS		2.5	W 6898	8.7					POISSONS CONGELES
037	FISH ETC PREPD,PRSVD NES	W 2003	2.5	W 1654	2.7					POIS,CRUST,MOL PREPARES
0371	FISH PREPARD,PRESRVD NES	W 2001	2.5	W 1653	2.7					CONSERVES DE POISSONS
04	CEREALS AND PREPARATIONS		22.5		31.1					CEREALES ET PRODUITS
041	WHEAT ETC UNMILLED		7.6	W 78504	14.9					FROMENT,EPEAUTRE
0412	OTHER WHEAT ETC UNMILLED		7.6	W 78504	14.9					AUTRE FROMENT NON MOULU
042	RICE		7.3		8.0					RIZ
0421	RICE IN HUSK OR HUSKED	W 12086	4.1	W 56973	5.1					RIZ SANS AUTRE PREPARATION
04212	RICE HUSKED	W 12086	4.1	W 56542	4.9					RIZ CARGO
0422	RICE SEMI-MILLED,MILLED		3.3		3.0					RIZ POLI,GLACE INCL BRISURES
04221	RICE MILLED UNBROKEN	W 9511	2.7		2.4					RIZ POLI,GLACE EXCL BRISURES
046	WHEAT ETC MEAL OR FLOUR	W 8915	2.2	W 9500	1.9					SEMOULE FARINE,FROMENT
048	CEREAL ETC PREPARATIONS	W 3246	3.6	W 3925	4.8					PREPTNS A BASE CEREALES
05	VEGETABLES AND FRUIT		15.7		19.8					LEGUMES ET FRUITS
054	VEG ETC FRSH,SMPLY PRSVD	W 27962	10.6		13.1					LEGUMES FRAIS,CONG,SECS
0541	POTATOES FRSH EXCL SWEET	W 14424	3.4	W 15950	4.4					POMMES DE TERRE
0542	LEGUMINOUS VEGETBLES DRY	W 5425	1.9	W 6802	2.5					LEGUMES A COSSE SECS
0545	OTHER FRESH VEGETABLES	W 7284	4.5	W 8372	5.2					AUTRES LEGUMES FRAIS,REF
05451	ALLIACEOUS VEGTBLS,FRESH	W 5771	3.5	W 6415	3.9					OIGNONS,ECHALOTES,AULX
057	FRUIT,NUTS,FRESH,DRIED	W 2548	2.7	W 3117	3.4					FRUITS FRAIS OU SECS
058	FRUIT PRESERVED,PREPARED	W 1205	2.0	W 1998	2.7					CONSERVES DE FRUITS
07	COFFEE,TEA,COCOA,SPICES		4.0		5.1					CAFE,THE,CACAO,EPICES
081	*FEEDING STUFF FOR ANIML		2.5		4.0					NOURRITURE POUR ANIMAUX
09	MISC EDIBLE PRODUCTS		4.4		6.3					PREP ALIMENTAIRES DIVERSES
098	EDIBLE PRODCTS,PREPS NES		3.1		4.7					PREP ALIMENTAIRES NDA
1	BEVERAGES AND TOBACCO		4.8		7.2		9.4		9.5	BOISSONS ET TABACS
11	BEVERAGES		4.0		5.5					BOISSONS
112	ALCOHOLIC BEVERAGES		3.3		4.2					BOISSONS ALCOOLIQUES
1124	DISTILLED ALCOHOLIC BEVS		1.7		1.9					ALCOOLS,EAUX-DE-VIE
2	CRUDE MATERLS,EXCL FUELS		3.4		4.9		6.5		6.3	MAT BRUTES NON COMESTIBLES
3	MINERAL FUELS ETC		71.8		94.3		97.8		132.1	COMBUSTIBLES MINERAUX LUB
33	PETROLEUM AND PRODUCTS		68.1		89.4					PETROLE ET DERIVES
334	PETROLEUM PRODUCTS,REFIN	W 332360	67.8	W 479797	88.9					PRODUITS RAFFINES
341	*GAS,NATURAL AND MANUFCT	W 7390	2.7	W 9716	3.5					GAZ NATUREL,GAZ MANUFACT
3413	PETROLM GASES,LIQUEFIED	W 7390	2.7	W 9716	3.5					GAZ DE PETROLE LIQUEFIE
34139	OTH HYDROCARBON GAS LQFD	W 7390	2.7	W 9716	3.5					HYDROCARBURES GAZEUX NDA
4	ANIMAL,VEGETABLE OIL,FAT		6.1		8.8		11.8		10.6	HUILES,GRAISSES ANIM,VEG
42	FIXED VEGETABLE OIL,FAT		4.8		6.9					HUILES VEGETALES FIXES
423	FIXED VEG OILS,SOFT		3.8		5.8					HUILES VEGET DOUCES FIXES
4232	SOYA BEAN OIL		3.4	W 7065	5.3					HUILE DE SOJA
5	CHEMCLS,RELATED PROD NES		38.1		58.7		66.1		73.4	PRODUITS CHIMIQUES
52	INORGANIC CHEMICALS		4.3		4.7					PROD CHIM INORGANIQUES
522	INORG ELEMNTS,OXIDES,ETC		2.3		2.4					ELEMENTS INORGANIQUES
523	OTHR INORG CHEMICALS ETC	W 3160	2.1	W 3353	2.4					AUT PRODUITS CHIMIQUES INORG
53	DYES,TANNING,COLOUR PROD		2.3		3.3					PROD TEINTURE,COLORANTS
533	PIGMENTS,PAINTS,ETC		2.0		3.0					PIGMENTS,PEINTURES,VERNIS
541	*MEDICINAL,PHARM PRODUCT		7.1		11.3					PROD MEDICINAUX PHARMACEUT
5417	MEDICAMENTS		5.5		8.9					MEDICAMENTS
54171	— CONTAINNG ANTIBIOTICS		5.5		8.9					MED CONTN ANTIBIOTIQUES
55	PERFUME,CLEANING ETC PRD		7.4		11.4					PROD POUR PARFUM,TOILETTE
553	PERFUMERY,COSMETICS,ETC		4.3		7.0					PRODUITS DE PARFUMERIE
554	SOAP,CLEANSING ETC PREPS		2.0		3.3					SAVONS,PRODUITS DETERSIFS
562	*FERTILIZERS,MANUFACTURE	W 22517	3.5	W 55319	8.2					ENGRAIS MANUFACTURES
5621	CHEM NITROGENOUS FERTLZR	W 7463	1.0	W 30592	3.8					ENGRAIS AZOTES
56213	AMMONIUM SULPHATE	W 7011	0.8	W 28438	3.5					SULFATE D'AMMONIUM
58	PLASTIC MATERIALS ETC		6.4		10.3					MAT PLAST ARTIFICIELLES
583	POLYMERIZATION ETC PRODS		4.9		8.3					PROD POLYMERISATION
5831	POLYETHYLENE		1.7		2.2					POLYETHYLENE
5839	OTH POLYMRZTION ETC PROD		1.6		3.0					AUT PROD POLYMER COPOLYM
59	CHEMICAL MATERIALS NES		4.8		5.9					MAT PROD CHIMIQUES NDA
591	PESTICIDES,DISINFECTANTS		1.7		2.1					DESINF,INSECT,FONG,HERB
6	BASIC MANUFACTURES		120.9		198.7		239.7		255.2	ART MANUFACTURES
61	LEATHER,DRESSED FUR,ETC		1.2		3.9					CUIRS,PELLETERIES
62	RUBBER MANUFACTURES NES		8.4		13.5					CAOUTCHOUC MANUFACTURE
625	RUBBER TYRES, TUBES ETC	N 205963	4.8	N 370819	8.3					PNEUS CAOUTCHOUC VULCANISE
6252	TYRES,NEW,BUS OR LORRY	N 19096	2.2	N 38845	3.9					PNEUS POUR AUTOBUS,CAMIONS
628	RUBBER ARTICLES NES		2.1		3.0					OUVRAGES CAOUTCHOUC NDA
64	PAPER,PAPERBOARD AND MFR		17.5		25.6					PAPIERS,CARTONS & OUVRAGES
641	PAPER AND PAPERBOARD		13.1		19.7					PAPIERS ET CARTONS
6412	PRINTG,WRITING PAPER NES		3.9	W 5109	5.7					PAPIERS POUR L'IMPRESSION
64121	— UNCOATED		3.9	W 5109	5.7					PAPIERS IMPRES NON COUCHES
6417	CORRUGATED PAPER ETC,BLK	W 4912	4.3	W 5427	6.3					PAPIERS,CARTONS ONDULES
64171	KRAFT PAPER CREPED ETC	W 4912	4.3	W 5427	6.3					PAPIER KRAFT CREPE ROULEAU
642	PAPER,ETC,PRECUT,ARTS OF		4.4		6.0					PAP,CARTONS DECOUPES
6421	PAPER ETC CONTAINERS		2.1		2.4					BOITES,SACS EMBALLAGES
65	TEXTILE YARN,FABRICS,ETC		44.6		86.1					FILS,TISSUS,ARTICLES TEXTILE
651	TEXTILE YARN		2.8		3.6					FILS TEXTILES
652	COTTON FABRICS,WOVEN		12.3		20.8					TISSUS DE COTON
6521	GREY WOVEN COTTON FABRIC	A 6609	5.9	A 8627	8.8					TISSUS COT ECRUS NON MERCER
65214	GREY WOVEN COTTON NES	A 6269	5.7	A 7487	7.7					AUT TISSUS 85% COTON ECRUS
6522	WOVEN COTTON BLEACHD,ETC		6.5		12.0					TISSUS COTON BLANCHIS ETC
65225	BLCHD COTN BLEND FAB NES	A 19903	6.5	A 22292	11.9					AUT TIS MOINS 85% COT BLANCH
653	WOVN MAN-MADE FIB FABRIC		15.9		26.3					TISSUS FIBRES SYNTH,ARTIF
6531	CONT SYNT WEAVES NONPILE	A 4274	7.1	A 4847	6.7					TISSUS FIBRES SYNTH CONTINUE
65315	CONT SYN TXTL FABRIC NES	A 4274	7.1	A 4847	6.7					TIS PLUS 85% TEXT SYNT CONT
6532	DISC SYN TXTL FABRIC NES	A 2296	3.4	A 2763	5.9					TIS DISC MOINS 85% FIBR TEXT
6534	DISC SYN BLEND FABRC NES		5.3		11.1					TISSUS FIBRES SYNTH DISCONT

4. General Imports C.I.F. by Commodities according to the S.I.T.C. (Rev. 2) in million U.S. Dollars
Importations Générales C.A.F. par Produits d'après la C.T.C.I. (Rév. 2) en millions de Dollars E.U.

SITC CTCI	COMMODITY	1993 QUANTITY QUANTITE	1993 VALUE VALEUR	1994 QUANTITY QUANTITE	1994 VALUE VALEUR	1995 QUANTITY QUANTITE	1995 VALUE VALEUR	1996 QUANTITY QUANTITE	1996 VALUE VALEUR	PRODUIT
65341	DISC SYN FIB–COTTN FABRC	A 669	1.0	A 1696	3.2					TISSUS FIB SYNT DIS MEL COTO
65342	DISC SYN FIB–WOOL FABRIC		4.3		8.0					TISSUS FIB SYNT MEL LAINE
655	KNITTED,ETC FABRICS		8.0		26.1					ETOF BONNETERIE PIECES ETC
6552	OTHER KNIT ETC FAB NONEL		8.0		26.1					ETOF BON NON ELAS NON SYNT
656	LACE,RIBBONS,TULLE,ETC		1.1		2.8					TULLES,BRODERIE
657	SPECIAL TXTL FABRC,PRODS		1.6		2.9					TISSUS SPECIAUX
658	TEXTILE ARTICLES NES		1.7		2.0					ART FACONNES MAT TEXTILES
66	NONMETAL MINERAL MFS NES		8.4		10.6					ART MIN NON METALLIQUES
662	CLAY,REFRACTORY BLDG PRD		1.9		2.5					MAT CONST REFRACTAIRES
664	GLASS		1.8		2.1					VERRE
665	GLASSWARE		2.6		2.9					OUVRAGES EN VERRE
6651	BOTTLES ETC OF GLASS		1.8		2.0					RECIPIENTS EN VERRE
66511	GLASS BOTTLES ETC NONVAC		1.8		2.0					BONBONNES,BOUTEILLES,ETC
67	IRON AND STEEL		15.9		21.9					FER ET ACIER
672	IRON,STEEL PRIMARY FORMS	W 4349	1.7	W 8598	3.0					LINGOTS FER,ACIER
6724	IRN,STL INGOTS,LUMPS,ETC	W 3995	1.4	W 8149	2.7					FER,ACIER LINGOTS,MASSES
67241	IRON,SIMPLE STEEL INGOTS	W 3967	1.3	W 8149	2.7					LINGOTS EN FER ET ACIER
673	IRON,STEEL SHAPES ETC	W 5663	2.9	W 8467	4.1					BARRES,PROFIL FER,ACIER
674	IRN,STL UNIV,PLATE,SHEET		6.4	W 10544	9.0					LARGES PLATS,TOLES
6747	TINNED PLATES,SHEETS	W 2011	1.7	W 2150	2.1					TOLES ETAMEES EN ACIER
6749	OTH IRN,STL PLATES,SHEET		4.6	W 7840	6.6					AUTRES TOLES FER,ACIER
67491	— OF IRON OR SIMPLE STL		4.5	W 7835	6.6					AUT TOLES AUTRES ACIER FIN
678	IRON,STL TUBES,PIPES,ETC		3.0		4.2					TUBES,TUYAUX EN FONTE,FER
6782	IRON,STL SEAMLESS TUBES	W 1354	2.0	W 3093	2.7					TUBES,TUYAUX SANS SOUDURE
68	NON–FERROUS METALS		6.0		8.3					METAUX NON FERREUX
687	TIN	W 2243	3.5	W 2794	3.7					ETAIN
6872	TIN,ALLOYS WORKED	W 2243	3.5	W 2793	3.7					ETAIN ET ALLIAGES OUVRES
68722	TIN SHEET,PLATE,STRIP	W 2243	3.5	W 2790	3.7					TABLES,PLANCHES ETAIN
69	METAL MANUFACTURES NES		18.5		26.7					ART MANUFACT EN METAL NDA
691	STRUCTURES AND PARTS NES		1.9		3.1					CONSTRUCT FER,ACIER,ALU
6911	STRUCTURES,PARTS IRN,STL		1.5		2.8					CONSTRUCT FER,ACIER,FONTE
692	METAL TANKS,BOXES,ETC		2.8		3.9					RECIPIENTS METALLIQUES
6924	MTL TRANSPORT BOXES ETC		2.6		3.7					FUTS,TAMBOURS,BIDONS
69241	STL TRANSPORT BOXES ETC	MN 13422	1.7	MN 18953	2.3					FUTS,TAMBOURS,BIDONS FER
694	STL,COPPR NAILS,NUTS,ETC		2.1		2.7					CLOUS,VIS,ECROUS
69402	IRN,STL NUTS,BOLTS,ETC		1.8		2.4					BOULONS,VIS,ECROUS FER,AC
695	TOOLS		2.5		3.9					OUTILS A MAIN
697	BASE MTL HOUSEHOLD EQUIP		2.8		3.8					ART MENAGE MET COMMUNS
699	BASE METAL MFRS NES		4.7		7.2					ART MANUFACTURES MET NDA
7	MACHINES,TRANSPORT EQUIP		129.2		259.0		197.6		250.0	MACHINES MATERIEL TRANSPORT
71	POWER GENERATING EQUIPMT		7.7		11.2					MACHINES GENERATRICES
713	INTRNL COMBUS PSTN ENGIN		4.2		5.3					MOTEURS EXPL COMB INT, PIECE
7139	PISTON ENGINE PARTS NES		1.8		2.2					PIECES POUR 713.2,3,8
716	ROTATING ELECTRIC PLANT		2.0		4.4					APP ELECTR ROTATIFS,PIECES
7162	AC MTRS,GENRTRS,GEN SETS	N 772	1.0	N 547	3.1					MOTEURS ELECTRIQUES
71623	GEN SETS WITH PSTN ENGN	N 719	1.0	N 522	3.1					GROUPES MOTEUR EXPLOSION
72	MACHS FOR SPCL INDUSTRYS		14.3		18.9					MAC SPECIALES POUR INDUST
723	CIVIL ENGNEERG EQUIP ETC		5.8		4.8					APPAREILS DE GENIE CIVIL
7234	CONST,MINING MACHNRY NES		4.9		3.7					MACH POUR LA CONST, MINES
72341	SELF–PROPELLD DOZERS,ETC	N 39	1.7	N 21	1.0					BULLDOZERS
72342	SLFPRP SHOVELS,EXCAVATRS	N 101	2.6	N 65	1.8					PELLES MECANIQUES
724	TEXTILE,LEATHER MACHNRY		2.0		4.5					MACH POUR INDUSTRIE TEXTILE
7243	SEWING MACHS,NEEDLES ETC		1.0		2.9					MACHINES A COUDRE,PIECES
727	FOOD MACHRY NON–DOMESTIC		1.3		3.6					MACH INDUSTRIES ALIMENT
7272	OTH FOOD PROC MCHY,PARTS		1.3		3.4					AUT MACH IND ALIMENTAIRE
72722	INDUS FOOD PROC MACH NES		1.3		3.4					MACHINES BOULANGERIE
728	OTH MACHY FOR SPCL INDUS		2.9		3.2					AUT MACH IND PARTICULIERES
73	METALWORKING MACHINERY		2.4		4.8					MACH TRAVAIL DES METAUX
736	METALWORKING MACH–TOOLS		2.0		4.2					MACH–OUTILS TRAVAIL METAUX
7361	METAL CUTTING MACH–TOOLS		1.4		2.8					MACH–OUT ENLEVEMENT METAL
74	GENRL INDUSTRL MACHY NES		18.5		31.5					MACH APP INDUSTRIE
741	HEATING,COOLING EQUIPMNT		3.0		7.1					MACH CHAUFFAGE,PIECES
742	PUMPS FOR LIQUIDS ETC		2.2		3.2					POMPES MOTO–POMPES
743	PUMPS NES,CENTRFUGES ETC		2.5		3.7					POMPES COMPRES,VENT ETC
744	MECHANICAL HANDLING EQU		2.1		5.2					EQUIP MANUTENTION PIECES
7442	LIFTING,LOADING MACH NES		1.3		3.1					APP LEVAGE,MANUTENTION
745	NONELEC MACHY,TOOLS NES		2.9		4.5					AUT MACH NON ELEC,PIECES
7452	OTH NONELEC MCHS,PTS NES		1.7		2.5					AUT MACH NON ELEC,PIECES
749	NONELEC MACH PTS,ACC NES		6.1		8.0					PIECES MACH NON ELEC NDA
7492	COCKS,VALVES ETC NES		2.1		2.7					ART ROB,SIM POUR TUYAUX
75	OFFICE MACHNES,ADP EQUIP		8.1		12.0					MACH BUREAU TRAIT AUTOM
751	OFFICE MACHINES		1.8		2.5					MACH,APPAREILS DE BUREAU
752	AUTOMTIC DATA PROC EQUIP		4.0		6.2					MACH TRAIT INFORMATION
7522	DIGITAL COMPUTERS		2.9		3.5					MACH DIGITALES COMPLETES
7528	OFF–LINE DATA PROC EQUIP		1.0		2.6					MACH AUXIL TRAIT INFORM
759	OFFICE,ADP MCH PTS,ACCES		2.5		3.4					PIECES DU 751 ET 752
7599	ACCTG,ETC,ADP MCH PTS,AC		2.5		3.3					PIECES DU 751 ET 752
76	TELECOMM,SOUND EQUIPMENT		19.6		17.7					EQUIPMENT DE TELECOM
761	TELEVISION RECEIVERS	N 12973	2.9	N 7030	2.3					RECEPTEURS DE TELEVISION
7611	COLOUR TV RECEIVERS	N 12973	2.9	N 7030	2.3					RECEPTEURS COULEUR
762	RADIO BROADCAST RECEIVRS	N 69648	2.9	N 41444	2.0					RECEPTEURS RADIODIFFUSION
7622	PORTABLE RADIO RECEIVERS	N 66162	2.8	N 33931	1.6					RECEPT PORTATIFS RADIO
763	SOUND RECORDRS,PHONOGRPH		3.0		3.6					PHONO,APP ENREGISTREMENT
7638	OTHR SOUND APPARATUS ETC		2.6		3.3					AUT APP D'ENREGIS,REPROD
76381	TV IMAGE,SND RECRDRS ETC		1.8		1.5					APP ENREG,REPRO IMAG,SON
764	TELECOM EQPT,PTS,ACC NES		10.9		9.9					EQUIP TELECOM,PIECES
7641	LINE TELEPHONE,ETC EQUIP		6.0		5.6					APP TELEPHON PAR FIL
7649	PTS NES OF EQUIPMT OF 76		3.2		1.8					PIECES DE LA DIV 76
76491	PTS NES OF APPAR OF 7641		2.1		0.9					PIECES POUR 764.1
77	ELECTRIC MACHNRY NES ETC		16.8		22.7					MACH APP ELECT NDA
772	SWITCHGEAR ETC,PARTS NES		3.4		6.3					APP COUPURE,SECT ETC
7721	SWITCHGEAR ETC		3.3		6.2					APP COUPURE,SECTIONMNT
773	ELECTR DISTRIBUTNG EQUIP		2.3		2.1					EQUIPMT DISTRIBUTION ELECT
7731	INSULATED WIRE,CABLE ETC		2.2		1.9					FILS,CABLES ISOLES ELECT
775	HOUSEHOLD TYPE EQUIP NES		5.3		6.3					MACH,APP USAGE DOMESTQUE
7752	DOM REFRIGERATRS,FREEZRS	N 9487	2.7	N 10096	3.1					REFRIG,CONGEL MENAGER
77521	DOMESTIC REFRIGERATORS	N 7806	2.1	N 9374	2.8					REFRIGERATEURS
778	ELECTRICAL MACHINERY NES		4.9		6.6					AUTRES MACH ELECT NDA
7781	BATTERIES,ACCUMULATORS		2.1		2.6					PILES ET ACCUMULATEURS
78	ROAD VEHICLES		35.3		43.9					VEHICULES ROUTIERS
781	PASS MOTOR VEH EXC BUSES	N 1541	13.4	N 1891	15.9					AUTO TRANSPORT PERSONNES

4. General Imports C.I.F. by Commodities according to the S.I.T.C. (Rev. 2) in million U.S. Dollars
Importations Générales C.A.F. par Produits d'après la C.T.C.I. (Rév. 2) en millions de Dollars E.U.

SITC CTCI	COMMODITY	1993		1994		1995		1996		PRODUIT
		QUANTITY QUANTITE	VALUE VALEUR	QUANTITY QUANTITE	VALUE VALEUR	QUANTITY QUANTITE	VALUE VALEUR	QUANTITY QUANTITE	VALUE VALEUR	
782	LORRIES,SPCL MTR VEH NES	N 1368	14.6	N 1487	18.6					VEHICULES SPECIAUX,MARCH
7821	LORRIES,TRUCKS	N 1355	14.2	N 1427	18.0					VEHICULES TRANSP MARCHAND
784	MOTOR VEH PRTS,ACCES NES	N 304322	5.0	N 472898	6.9					PIECES 722,781,782,783
7849	OTHER MOTOR VEHCL PARTS	N 303929	4.3	N 472581	6.1					PIECES 722,781,782,783
79	OTHR TRANSPORT EQUIPMENT		6.7		96.7					AUTRE MATERIEL TRANSPORT
792	AIRCRAFT ETC		1.9		93.3					APP NAVIGATION AERIENNE
7924	AIRCRFT NES OVER 15000KG			N 1	81.0					AERODYNES PLUS 15000 KG
7929	AIRCRAFT PARTS NES		1.9		10.6					PIECES DU 792
793	SHIPS AND BOATS ETC	N 5516	4.7	N 5897	2.7					NAVIRES BATEAUX,ETC
7932	SHIPS AND BOATS NES	N 353	4.3	N 1046	2.2					NAVIRES ET BATEAUX
79323	OTHER CARGO VESSELS	N 4	3.6	N 63	1.1					AUT BATEAUX TRANS MARCH
8	MISC MANUFACTURED GOODS		61.9		81.2		99.1		115.1	ART MANUFACTURES DIVERS
812	*PLUMBG,HEATNG,LGHTNG EQ		2.1		2.8					APPAR SANITAIRES CHAUFFAGE
821	*FURNITURE,PARTS THEREOF		2.7		2.5					MEUBLES ET PIECES
831	*TRAVEL GOODS,HANDBAGS		1.8		2.4					ARTICLES DE VOYAGE ETC
84	CLOTHING AND ACCESSORIES		10.5		15.2					VETEMENTS
843	WOMENS OUTERWEAR NONKNIT		2.9		3.8					VET DESSUS FEMMES MAT TEX
844	UNDER GARMENTS NOT KNIT		1.3		2.7					VETEMENT DESSOUS MAT TEX
845	OUTERWEAR KNIT NONELASTC		2.1	N 1140350	2.6					VET DESSOUS,ACCES BONNET
846	UNDER GARMENTS KNITTED		1.8		3.1					SOUS VETS DE BONNETERIE
8462	— OF COTTON NON ELASTIC	N 1642764	1.4	N 2547156	2.6					SOUS–VET BONNET COTON
84629	—— OTHER	N 1642764	1.4	N 2547156	2.6					AUT SOUS–VET BONNET COTON
851	*FOOTWEAR	P 1431481	5.7	P 1687996	6.4					CHAUSSURES
85101	FOOTWEAR RUBBER,PLASTIC	P 853545	2.5	P 742202	2.4					CHAUS SEMELLES CAOUTCH
85102	FOOTWEAR LEATHER	P 563420	3.2	P 928655	4.0					CHAUS SEMELLES EN CUIR
87	PRECISION INSTRUMNTS NES		7.9		5.8					INSTRUM,APPAR SCIENT NDA
872	MEDICAL INSTRUMENTS NES		5.3		1.5					INSTR,APP MEDIC–CHIR NDA
87202	OTH MEDICAL INSTRUMENTS		5.1		1.1					INSTRUM,APP MEDECINE
874	MEASURNG,CONTROLNG INSTR		2.1		3.6					INSTRUMENTS DE MESURE
88	PHOTO EQU,OPTICL GDS ETC		5.0		8.6					APP,FOURN PHOTO,OP,MONTR
882	PHOTO,CINEMA SUPPLIES		1.7		2.8					PRODUITS PHOTO,CINEMA
885	WATCHES AND CLOCKS		2.0		3.5					HORLOGERIE
8851	WATCHES,MOVEMENTS,CASES		1.8		3.3					MONTRES,MOUVEMENTS,BOITES
88511	WATCHES		1.7		3.2					MONTRES POCHE,BRACELET
89	MISC MANUFCTRD GOODS NES		26.5		37.9					ART MANUFACTURES DIVERS
892	PRINTED MATTER		3.3		5.7					IMPRIMES
8921	PRINTED BOOKS,GLOBES,ETC		2.3		3.4					LIVRES,BROCHURES,CARTES
89211	PRINTED BOOKS,PAMPHLETS		2.2		3.4					LIVRES,BROCHURES
893	ARTICLES OF PLASTIC NES		9.0		11.9					OUVRAGES EN MAT DIVIS 58
8931	PLSTC PACKG CONTNRS,LIDS		2.7		3.7					ART TRANSP EMBALLAGE ETC
8939	MISC PLASTIC ARTICLES		6.2		7.9					ART DIVERS EN MAT DIV 58
89399	OTHR PLASTC ARTICLES NES		5.4		6.6					AUT OUV MAT DIV 58
894	TOYS,SPORTING GOODS,ETC		2.6		3.1					VOITURES ENFANTS,JOUETS
897	GOLD,SILVER WARE,JEWELRY		6.6		9.5					BIJOUTERIE,ORFEVRERIE
8973	PREC JEWLRY,GLD–SILVWARE		5.7		8.2					BIJOUX OR,ARGENT ORFEVRE
89731	PRECIOUS METAL JEWELLERY		5.6		8.1					ART BIJOUTERIE,JOAILLER
898	MUSICAL INSTRUMENTS,PTS		1.8		2.7					INSTRUMENTS DE MUSIQUE
899	OTHER MANUFACTURED GOODS		2.2		3.1					AUT ART MANUF DIVERS NDA
9	GOODS NOT CLASSD BY KIND		6.9		10.2		9.6		9.9	ART TRANSACT NON CLASSES
931	*SPECIAL TRANSACTIONS		6.5		8.6					TRANS.SPECIALES

5. General Exports F.O.B. by Commodities according to the S.I.T.C. (Rev. 2) in million U.S. Dollars
Exportations Générales F.O.B. par Produits d'après la C.T.C.I. (Rév. 2) en millions de Dollars E.U.

SITC CTCI	COMMODITY	1993		1994		1995		1996		PRODUIT
		QUANTITY QUANTITE	VALUE VALEUR	QUANTITY QUANTITE	VALUE VALEUR	QUANTITY QUANTITE	VALUE VALEUR	QUANTITY QUANTITE	VALUE VALEUR	
	ALL COMMODITIES		297.7		550.4		618.7		747.5	TOUS PRODUITS
0	FOOD AND LIVE ANIMALS		130.3		243.0		282.9		303.4	ALIMENTS,ANIMAUX VIVANTS
01	MEAT AND PREPARATIONS		1.1		1.5					VIANDES ET PREPARATIONS
014	MEAT PREPD,PRSVD,NES ETC	W 876	1.0	W 489	1.2					CONSERVES DE VIANDES
0149	OTH PREPARD,PRESRVD MEAT	W 867	1.0	W 485	1.2					AUTRES PREP DE VIANDES
03	FISH AND PREPARATIONS		22.6		38.9					POISSONS ET PREPARATIONS
034	FISH,FRESH,CHILLED,FROZN	W 1	0.1	W 3356	9.0		15.8			POISSON FRAIS, REFRIG,CONG
0341	FISH FRSH,CHLLD,EX FILLT		0.5	W 2870	7.2					POISSON FRAIS,REFRIGERE
0343	FISH FILLETS,FRESH,CHLLD	W 693	2.3	W 222	0.9					FILETS FRAIS,REFRIGERES
036	SHELL FISH FRESH,FROZEN	W 272	1.4	W 465	2.4					CRUSTACES,MOLLUSQUES
037	FISH ETC PREPD,PRSVD NES	W 14501	17.6	W 9918	27.4					POIS,CRUST,MOL PREPARES
0371	FISH PREPARD,PRESRVD NES	W 14495	17.6	W 9901	27.4					CONSERVES DE POISSONS
04	CEREALS AND PREPARATIONS		6.0		7.8					CEREALES ET PRODUITS
048	CEREAL ETC PREPARATIONS	W 4936	5.5	W 5877	7.1					PREPTNS A BASE CEREALES
0481	PREPD BREAKFAST FOOD ETC	W 400	1.3	W 644	2.6					CEREALES TRAVAILLEES
04812	CEREAL ROASTED, PUFFED	W 400	1.3	W 644	2.6					PRODTS BASE CEREALES
0483	MACARONI,SPAGHETTI ETC	W 3278	2.9	W 4133	3.3					PATES ALMENTAIRES
0484	BAKERY PRODUCTS	W 1216	1.3	W 1099	1.3					PRODUITS DE BOULANGERIE
04842	PASTRY, CAKES ETC	W 1121	1.1	W 965	1.1					PATISSERIE ETC.
05	VEGETABLES AND FRUIT		2.6		7.3					LEGUMES ET FRUITS
054	VEG ETC FRSH,SMPLY PRSVD	W 777	0.7	W 4302	4.6					LEGUMES FRAIS,CONG,SECS
0548	EDIBLE VEG NES FRESH,DRY	W 392	0.4	W 3747	4.1					RACINES,TUBERCULES
05488	VEG PRODTS NES FRESH,DRY	W 319	0.3	W 3578	4.0					PROD VEGET ALIM HUMAINE
058	FRUIT PRESERVED,PREPARED	W 854	1.7	W 1346	2.3					CONSERVES DE FRUITS
0582	FRUIT PRESERVED BY SUGAR	W 518	1.4	W 391	1.2					FRUITS CONFITS AU SUCRE
06	SUGAR AND PREPS,HONEY		95.7		185.5					SUCRES ET PRODUITS
061	SUGAR AND HONEY	W 254482	95.0				196.4			SUCRES ET MIEL
0611	RAW BEET AND CANE SUGAR	W 201585	91.8	W 460353	173.4					SUCRES BRUTS
0615	MOLASSES	W 44546	2.5	W 140316	9.4		15.2			MELASSES
062	SUGAR CANDY NON–CHOCLATE	W 1140	0.7	W 1310	2.7					SUCRERIES
07	COFFEE,TEA,COCOA,SPICES		1.4		1.7					CAFE,THE,CACAO,EPICES
075	SPICES	W 923	1.0	W 1122	1.3					EPICES
0752	SPICES,EX PEPPER,PIMENTO	W 915	1.0	W 1110	1.3					AUTRES EPICES
2	CRUDE MATERLS,EXCL FUELS		10.0		25.6		36.7		30.6	MAT BRUTES NON COMESTIBLES
24	CORK AND WOOD		7.5		21.6		32.1			LIEGE ET BOIS
246	PULPWOOD,CHIPS,WOODWASTE		3.3		11.8					BOIS DE TRITURATION
24602	PULPWOOD CHIPS,PARTICLES		3.3		10.9					EN FORME DE PLAQUETTES
248	WOOD SHAPED,SLEEPERS	W 331	0.1		8.9					BOIS SIMPLEMENT TRAVAILLES
2481	RAILWAY SLEEPERS,TIES	W 93451	3.4	W 28975	7.6					TRAVERSES VOIES FERREES
28	METALLIFEROUS ORES,SCRAP		1.0		0.8					MINERAIS METAL,DECHETS
29	CRUDE ANIMAL,VEG MAT NES		1.3		2.7					MATIERES BRUTES ANIM,VEGET
292	CRUDE VEG MATERIALS NES									MAT BRUTES VEGETALES NDA
2924	VEG USED IN PHARMACY ETC	W 186	0.9	W 340	1.8					PLANTES MEDICINALES
3	MINERAL FUELS ETC		30.2		40.7		46.4		60.5	COMBUSTIBLES MINERAUX LUB
33	PETROLEUM AND PRODUCTS		30.2		40.7					PETROLE ET DERIVES
334	PETROLEUM PRODUCTS,REFIN	W 125441	30.2	W 189572	40.7					PRODUITS RAFFINES
4	ANIMAL,VEGETABLE OIL,FAT		2.5		2.9		3.2		4.4	HUILES,GRAISSES ANIM,VEG
42	FIXED VEGETABLE OIL,FAT		2.5		2.8					HUILES VEGETALES FIXES
424	FIXED VEG OIL NONSOFT	W 300	0.2		2.7					AUTRES HUILES VEG FIXES
4243	COCONUT (COPRA) OIL	W 300	0.2	W 4169	2.7		2.8			HJUILE DE COPRAH
5	CHEMCLS,RELATED PROD NES		3.6		5.2		5.3		6.2	PRODUITS CHIMIQUES
53	DYES,TANNING,COLOUR PROD		1.0		1.0					PROD TEINTURE,COLORANTS
533	PIGMENTS,PAINTS,ETC		1.0		1.0					PIGMENTS,PEINTURES,VERNIS
55	PERFUME,CLEANING ETC PRD		1.8		3.2					PROD POUR PARFUM,TOILETTE
553	PERFUMERY,COSMETICS,ETC		1.0		1.7					PRODUITS DE PARFUMERIE
6	BASIC MANUFACTURES		18.1		27.3		31.1		39.9	ART MANUFACTURES
61	LEATHER,DRESSED FUR,ETC		1.4		2.2					CUIRS,PELLETERIES
612	LEATHER ETC MANUFACTURES		1.3		2.1					OUVRAGES EN CUIRS NDA
6123	PREPRD PARTS OF FOOTWEAR		1.2		1.6					PARTIES DE CHAUSSURES
63	WOOD,CORK MANUFACTRS NES		2.8		4.8					OUVRAGES LIEGE ET BOIS
634	VENEERS,PLYWOOD,ETC		2.7	V 437	0.1					PLACAGES,CONTRE–PLAQUES
6341	VENEER SHEETS ETC		0.1	V 687	0.1		2.9			BOIS SIMPLEMENT SCIES
6342	PLYWOOD OF WOOD SHEETS		2.7	V 24	0.1		1.8			BOIS CONTRE–PLAQUES
64	PAPER,PAPERBOARD AND MFR		3.3		3.8					PAPIERS,CARTONS & OUVRAGES
642	PAPER,ETC,PRECUT,ARTS OF		3.1		3.4					PAP,CARTONS DECOUPES
6421	PAPER ETC CONTAINERS		2.8		3.1					BOITES,SACS EMBALLAGES
65	TEXTILE YARN,FABRICS,ETC		7.2		9.8					FILS,TISSUS,ARTICLES TEXTILE
652	COTTON FABRICS,WOVEN	A 2938	2.6	A 3045	2.6					TISSUS DE COTON
6521	GREY WOVEN COTTON FABRIC	A 1000	1.0	A 769	0.8					TISSUS COT ECRUS NON MERCER
65214	GREY WOVEN COTTON NES	A 990	1.0	A 762	0.7					AUT TISSUS 85% COTON ECRUS
6522	WOVEN COTTON BLEACHD,ETC	A 1959	1.7	A 2303	1.9					TISSUS COTON BLANCHIS ETC
65225	BLCHD COTN BLEND FAB NES	A 1962	1.7	A 2735	2.0					AUT TIS MOINS 85% COT BLANCH
658	TEXTILE ARTICLES NES		3.0		5.0					ART FACONNES MAT TEXTILES
6584	LINENS ETC		1.1		4.2					LINGE DE MAISON
65842	BED LINEN OF OTHR FIBRES		0.7		3.6					LINGE DE LIT AUT FIBRES
6589	OTH TEXTILE ARTICLES NES		1.0		0.7					AUT ART EN TEXTILES NDA
65898	KNITTED ETC ARTICLES NES		1.0		0.4					ART BONNET NON ELASTIQUE
67	IRON AND STEEL		1.5		2.8					FER ET ACIER
674	IRN,STL UNIV,PLATE,SHEET		1.0		1.8					LARGES PLATS,TOLES
6749	OTH IRN,STL PLATES,SHEET		0.9		1.7					AUTRES TOLES FER,ACIER
67491	— OF IRON OR SIMPLE STL		0.9		1.7					AUT TOLES AUTRES ACIER FIN
69	METAL MANUFACTURES NES		1.5		2.3					ART MANUFACT EN METAL NDA
7	MACHINES,TRANSPORT EQUIP		6.2		43.9		13.1		81.9	MACHINES MATERIEL TRANSPORT
77	ELECTRIC MACHNRY NES ETC		1.7		2.2					MACH APP ELECT NDA
79	OTHR TRANSPORT EQUIPMENT		0.7		36.9					AUTRE MATERIEL TRANSPORT
792	AIRCRAFT ETC		0.4		36.6					APP NAVIGATION AERIENNE
7923	AIRCRFT NES2000–15000KG	N 2	0.1	N 1	34.4					AERODYNES 2000 A 15000 KG
7929	AIRCRAFT PARTS NES		0.4		2.3					PIECES DU 792
8	MISC MANUFACTURED GOODS		71.7		114.9		153.5		156.5	ART MANUFACTURES DIVERS
821	*FURNITURE,PARTS THEREOF		1.1		1.7					MEUBLES ET PIECES
8219	FURNITURE AND PARTS NES		1.1		1.6					AUTRES MEUBLES ET PIECES
84	CLOTHING AND ACCESSORIES		63.0		98.8					VETEMENTS
842	MENS OUTERWEAR NOT KNIT		19.0		40.9					VET DESSUS POUR HOMMES
8421	— OVERCOATS,OTHER COATS	N 69540	1.5	N 545458	1.2					MANTEAUX HOMMES MAT TEXT
84211	—— OF WOOL,FINE HAIR	N 69540	1.5	N 545458	1.2					MANTEAUX HOMMES DE LAINE
8422	— SUITS	N 139944	1.7	N 115730	3.4					COMPLETS HOMMES MAT TEXT
84221	—— OF WOOL,FINE HAIR	N 139944	1.7	N 115730	3.4					COMPLETS HOMMES LAINE
8423	— TROUSERS,BREECHES ETC	N 1668468	13.0	MN 11452	27.7					PANTALONS HOMMES MAT TEX
8429	— OTHER OUTER GARMENTS		3.0		8.7					AUT VET DES HOM MAT TEX
843	WOMENS OUTERWEAR NONKN!T		13.4		22.5					VET DESSUS FEMMES MAT TEX
8432	— SUITS AND COSTUMES	N 279360	1.2	N 235800	1.1					COSTUMES–TAIL MAT TEXIL

5. General Exports F.O.B. by Commodities according to the S.I.T.C. (Rev. 2) in million U.S. Dollars
Exportations Générales F.O.B. par Produits d'après la C.T.C.I. (Rév. 2) en millions de Dollars E.U.

SITC CTCI	COMMODITY	1993		1994		1995		1996		PRODUIT
		QUANTITY QUANTITE	VALUE VALEUR	QUANTITY QUANTITE	VALUE VALEUR	QUANTITY QUANTITE	VALUE VALEUR	QUANTITY QUANTITE	VALUE VALEUR	
8434	— SKIRTS	N 287796	1.7	N 948120	2.4					JUPES EN MAT TEXTILES
8435	— BLOUSES	N 753504	2.5	N 3138324	4.4					BLOUSES FEM MAT TEXTILES
8439	— OTHER OUTER GARMENTS		7.9		13.4					AUT VET DES FEM MAT TEXT
844	UNDER GARMENTS NOT KNIT		11.1		9.2					VETEMENT DESSOUS MAT TEX
8441	— MENS SHIRTS		8.1		6.5					CHEMISES HOMMES MAT TEXT
84411	—— OF COTTON	MN 13965	8.1	N 2787936	6.3					CHEMISES HOMMES DE COTON
8442	— MENS,OTHR THAN SHIRTS	N 752412	2.5	N 619620	1.6					SOUS–VET HOMMES MAT TEXT
845	OUTERWEAR KNIT NONELASTC	N 2499660	8.0	N 4324213	13.3					VET DESSOUS,ACCES BONNET
8451	— JERSEYS,PULLOVERS ETC	N 451392	1.3	N 339336	1.0					CHANDAILS,PULL–OVERS ETC
8459	— OTHER,CLTHG ACCESRYS	N 1981332	6.3	N 3874438	11.7					AUT VET DESSUS DE BONNE
846	UNDER GARMENTS KNITTED	N 305604	0.4	N 762972	1.1					SOUS VETS DE BONNETERIE
8462	— OF COTTON NON ELASTIC	N 3055344	9.5	N 4145688	6.5					SOUS–VET BONNET COTON
84629	—— OTHER	N 3055344	9.5	N 4145688	6.5					AUT SOUS–VET BONNET COTON
8463	— OF SYNTH FBR NONELAST	N 346932	2.0	N 996	0.1					SOUS–VET BONNET FIB SYNT
84632	—— MENS SHIRTS	N 346932	2.0	N 1359156	6.4					CHEMISES DE BON FIB SYNMT
851	*FOOTWEAR	P 592908	4.5	P 958578	8.9					CHAUSSURES
85101	FOOTWEAR RUBBER,PLASTIC	P 208421	0.6	P 503580	3.9					CHAUS SEMELLES CAOUTCH
85102	FOOTWEAR LEATHER	P 253585	2.8	P 300366	4.1					CHAUS SEMELLES EN CUIR
85103	SHOES WOOD–,CORK–SOLED	P 129872	1.2	P 154243	1.0					CHAUS SEMELLES BOIS,LIEGE
89	MISC MANUFCTRD GOODS NES		2.1		3.3					ART MANUFACTURES DIVERS
9	GOODS NOT CLASSD BY KIND		25.2		46.7		46.4		63.8	ART TRANSACT NON CLASSES
931	*SPECIAL TRANSACTIONS		2.3		5.0					TRANS.SPECIALES
971	*GOLD,NON MONETARY NES	K 1927	22.9	K 3924	41.8					OR NON MONETAIRE
97101	NONMON GLD UNWRT,SEMIMFD	K 1927	22.9	K 3924	41.8					OR,ALLIAGES D'OR BRUTS

1. HISTORICAL SERIES, 1962–1997 GENERAL TRADE, IMPORTS C.I.F., EXPORTS F.O.B.
SERIES HISTORIQUES, 1962–1997 COMMERCE GENERAL, IMPORTATIONS C.A.F., EXPORTATIONS F.O.B

YEAR ANNEE	VALUE IN MILLION NEW MARKKAA / VALEUR EN MILLION NEW MARKKAA: MERCHANDISE –MARCHANDISE IMPORTS	MERCHANDISE –MARCHANDISE EXPORTS	GOLD # 1 –OR IMPORTS	GOLD # 1 –OR EXPORTS	CONVERSION FACTORS U.S. CENTS PER NEW MARKKA / FACTEURS DE CONVERSION CENTS E.U. PAR NEW MARKKA: IMPORTS	EXPORTS	INDEX NUMBERS –INDICES: QUANTUM IMPORTS	QUANTUM EXPORTS	UNIT VALUE / VALEUR UNITAIRE IMPORTS	UNIT VALUE / VALEUR UNITAIRE EXPORTS
1962	3928.70	3533.10	0.01		31.2500	31.2500				
1963	3866.90	3678.00	0.01		31.2500	31.2500				
1964	4816.50	4131.90	0.37		31.2500	31.2500				
1965	5265.10	4566.00	0.68		31.2500	31.2500				
1966	5524.40	4816.90	0.50	0.01	31.2500	31.2500				
1967	5794.40	5231.20	10.18	0.11	29.3000	29.3400				
1968	6710.90	6874.20	5.45		23.8100	23.8100				
1969	8504.80	8344.70	8.43	0.02	23.8100	23.8100				
1970	11071.40	9686.70	7.41		23.8100	23.8100				
1971	11734.40	9897.20	8.60	0.45	23.8100	23.8100				
1972	13106.70	12082.00	12.20		24.1136	24.1129				
1973	16599.00	14605.20	16.64		26.2331	26.2650				
1974	25666.30	20686.40	13.57		26.5351	26.5368				
1975	28002.00	20247.40			27.2324	27.1769				
1976	28555.10	24504.60			25.8863	25.8788				
1977	30707.80	30931.40			24.7733	24.7804				
1978	32337.70	35206.20			24.3313	24.3484				
1979	44222.10	43430.00			25.7787	25.7322				
1980	58250.40	52794.60			26.8519	26.8076	72	80	78	65
1981	61269.40	60308.00			23.1795	23.2386	68	82	88	72
1982	64751.40	63026.00			20.6752	20.8364	68	80	92	77
1983	71527.90	69692.30			17.9731	17.9636	71	83	98	82
1984	74681.60	80904.10			16.6608	16.6927	71	92	102	87
1985	81520.20	84027.90			16.2333	16.2049	75	92	106	89
1986	77600.99	82578.99			19.7586	19.7824	80	93	95	88
1987	82806.99	85516.00			22.8509	22.8730	86	94	93	90
1988	92118.00	92902.00			23.7120	23.8430	94	97	95	94
1989	105518.70	99781.84			23.3260	23.3211	104	96	99	101
1990	103066.00	101380.00			26.1994	26.2107	100	100	100	100
1991	87821.01	93088.00			24.8318	24.7924	83	91	102	100
1992	94984.00	107471.00			22.3029	22.2893	81	99	113	106
1993	103162.00	133962.00			17.4801	17.5028	79	117	127	113
1994	119897.00	153690.00			19.3617	19.2972	95	133	123	113
1995	122428.00	172380.00			22.9636	22.9571	102	143	123	121
1996	134422.00	176592.00			21.7707	21.7649	110	151	125	121
1997	154681.00	204202.00			19.2561	19.2546			125	121

2. IMPORTS BY BROAD ECONOMIC CATEGORY AND EXPORTS BY INDUSTRIAL ORIGIN. (PERCENTAGE OF TOTAL VALUE)
IMPORTATIONS PAR CATEGORIES ECONOMIQUES ET EXPORTATIONS PAR BRANCHE D'ACTIVITE.(EN POURCENTAGE DE LA VALEUR TOTALE)

IMPORTS – IMPORTATIONS

	1991	1992	1993	1994	1995	1996	1997
TOTAL IMPORTS–IMPORTATIONS TOTALES	100.	100.	100.	100.	100.	100.	100.
1 FOOD BEV–ALIMENTATION BOISSONS	5.3	5.5	5.9	6.2	5.4	6.0	6.1
11 PRIMARY–PRODUITS DE BASE	2.6	2.6	2.9	3.3	2.5	2.8	2.8
111 FOR INDUSTRY–POUR L'INDUSTRIE	0.8	0.8	1.1	1.3	1.0	1.1	1.3
112 FOR HOUSEHOLDS–POUR LES MENAGES	1.7	1.8	1.8	1.9	1.5	1.7	1.5
12 PROCESSED–PRODUITS ELABORES	2.7	2.9	3.0	2.9	2.9	3.2	3.3
121 FOR INDUSTRY–POUR L'INDUSTRIE	0.4	0.4	0.6	0.6	0.5	0.5	0.5
122 FOR HOUSEHOLDS–POUR LES MENAGES	2.3	2.4	2.4	2.3	2.5	2.7	2.8
2 IND SUPPLIES–APPROV INDUSTRIELS	28.7	30.7	31.5	31.5	32.0	28.3	28.8
21 PRIMARY–PRODUITS DE BASE	4.9	6.1	6.1	5.6	6.1	5.9	5.9
22 PROCESSED–PRODUITS ELABORES	23.8	24.5	25.5	25.8	25.9	22.4	22.9
3 FUELS–COMBUSTIBLES	13.3	12.8	12.7	11.5	8.7	10.5	9.6
31 PRIMARY–PRODUITS DE BASE	9.6	8.5	8.6	8.1	6.3	7.3	6.9
32 PROCESSED–PRODUITS ELABORES	3.7	4.3	4.0	3.4	2.4	3.2	2.7
321 MOTOR SPIRIT–ESSENCE	0.4	0.6	0.6	0.2	0.2	0.2	0.2
322 OTHER–AUTRES	3.3	3.8	3.4	3.2	2.3	3.0	2.5
4 MACHINERY–EQUIPEMENT	23.4	23.5	24.8	27.0	29.0	27.9	28.2
41 CAPITAL EQUIPMENT–MACHINES	19.0	18.2	17.7	18.9	20.0	20.4	20.3
42 PARTS–PIECES ACCESSOIRES	4.4	5.3	7.0	8.1	9.1	7.5	7.8
5 TRANSPORT–TRANSPORT	11.7	10.4	9.9	9.6	10.3	11.6	11.4
51 PASSENGER CARS–AUTOMOBILES	3.4	2.6	2.2	2.8	3.0	3.5	3.4
52 OTHER–AUTRES	3.3	2.4	3.6	2.1	2.7	2.8	2.2
521 INDUSTRIAL–INDUSTRIELS	3.1	2.3	3.4	1.9	2.6	2.6	2.0
522 NON INDUSTRIAL–NON INDUSTRIEL	0.2	0.2	0.1	0.1	0.1	0.2	0.2
53 PARTS–PIECES ACCESSOIRES	5.0	5.4	4.1	4.7	4.6	5.3	5.8
6 CONSUM GOODS–BIENS CONSOMMATION	16.7	15.4	14.1	13.6	12.6	13.7	13.7
61 DURABLE–DURABLES	3.9	3.3	2.8	2.8	2.7	3.1	3.2
62 SEMI DURABLE–SEMI DURABLES	8.9	8.0	7.4	7.0	6.5	6.8	6.9
63 NON DURABLE–NON DURABLES	3.9	4.1	4.0	3.7	3.4	3.8	3.6
7 GOODS NES–BIENS NDA	0.9	1.8	1.0	0.8	1.9	2.1	2.2

EXPORTS – EXPORTATIONS

	1991	1992	1993	1994	1995	1996	1997
TOTAL EXPORTS–EXPORTATIONS TOTALES	100.	100.	100.	100.	100.	100.	100.
1 AGRICULTURE	1.2	1.1	1.5	2.2	1.4	1.7	1.4
2 MINING QUARRY–INDUS EXTRACTIVES	0.5	0.4	0.4	0.4	0.3	0.3	0.4
3 MANUFACTURING–IND MANUFACTUR	98.3	98.4	98.1	97.4	98.3	98.0	98.2
31 FOOD BEV TOBACCO–ALIM BOISS TAB	2.0	2.1	2.5	2.4	2.1	2.4	2.5
32 TEXTILES–INDUSTRIES TEXTILES	2.9	2.7	2.3	2.3	2.0	2.1	2.0
33 WOOD & PRODUCTS–BOIS & PRODUITS	7.0	6.8	7.5	8.3	7.0	6.2	6.6
34 PAPER & PRODUCTS–PAPIER & PRODT	32.0	30.3	27.9	26.8	27.7	23.9	23.5
35 CHEMICALS–INDUSTRIES CHIMIQUES	11.4	11.3	10.6	10.2	9.0	9.9	9.8
36 NON METAL MIN–MIN NON METAL	1.2	1.3	1.4	1.3	1.2	1.2	1.3
37 BASIC METAL–IND METAL BASE	9.4	9.7	8.9	8.4	8.0	7.7	7.6
38 METAL MANUF–MANUF METAL	31.8	33.6	36.3	37.0	40.0	43.0	43.9
39 OTH MANUF IND–AUTRES MANUF	0.7	0.6	0.6	0.7	1.4	1.6	1.1

3. TRADE BY PRINCIPAL COUNTRIES OF ORIGIN AND DESTINATION (VALUE IN MILLION U.S. DOLLARS)
ECHANGES SELON LES PRINCIPAUX PAYS D'ORIGINE ET DE DESTINATION (VALEUR EN MILLIONS DE DOLLARS EU)

COUNTRIES–PAYS	GENERAL IMPORTS C.I.F. IMPORTATIONS GENERALES C.A.F				
	1993	1994	1995	1996	1997
World	18032.8	23358.2	29519.9	30859.6	31001.0
Africa	149.3	149.9	143.6	204.0	265.6
Americas	1825.7	2533.6	2872.1	3039.2	3146.3
– Northern America	1439.6	1943.4	2320.7	2441.3	2470.1
– LAIA	284.8	414.8	401.7	441.6	512.5
– CACM	37.5	78.6	80.7	94.1	116.1
– Caribbean	31.8	53.4	47.5	32.7	27.1
– Rest of America	32.0	43.4	21.6	29.6	20.5
Asia excl fmr USSR	2220.4	3139.9	3680.6	3445.8	3538.5
– Middle East	53.9	79.5	61.4	74.5	87.9
Asia former USSR	69.0	32.3	54.5	126.1	172.9
Europe excl fmr USSR	11917.9	14857.1	19353.2	20441.5	20127.3
– European Union	10282.4	12782.3	17015.4	18089.8	17830.2
– Eastern Europe	379.3	510.5	571.6	541.4	619.2
– Rest of Europe	1256.3	1564.3	1766.2	1810.3	1677.9
Europe former USSR	1540.6	2265.4	2597.0	2605.2	2766.7
Oceania	108.6	168.2	239.8	317.3	239.2
Other	201.4	211.8	578.9	680.4	744.6
Germany/Allemagne	2938.9	3425.4	4584.7	4634.3	4497.7
Sweden/Suède	1838.9	2435.3	3415.2	3680.8	3746.3
United Kingdom	1590.3	1924.6	2420.7	2728.8	2420.8
Russian Federation	1482.5	1968.3	2121.4	2137.2	2264.3
USA/Etats–Unis d'Amer	1312.8	1780.5	2127.8	2257.7	2266.2
Japan/Japon	1042.9	1517.9	1876.2	1591.9	1655.3
France, Monaco	708.3	924.1	1192.6	1381.7	1486.5
Norway,Svalbard and JM	862.6	1108.8	1216.1	1226.8	1097.5
Italy/Italie	666.6	907.3	1174.0	1254.3	1245.2
Netherlands/Pays–Bas	649.2	801.1	1091.1	1103.8	1246.0
Denmark/Danemark	565.2	710.3	947.6	1080.9	1053.1
Belgium–Luxembourg	528.0	637.2	862.1	902.7	781.0
Switzerland,Liechtenst.	356.7	405.8	500.9	530.5	516.7
China/Chine	256.5	354.2	393.3	454.5	549.6
Areas n.e.s.		211.8	483.8	505.6	744.6
Spain/Espagne	231.2	307.3	390.7	434.6	434.3
Austria/Autriche	206.3	261.2	368.4	330.5	326.4
Poland/Pologne	241.7	300.0	315.5	284.1	345.5
Estonia/Estonie		218.3	358.6	364.1	421.5
Other Asia n.e.s.	178.8	221.9	258.6	269.7	251.2
Portugal	190.6	211.4	241.7	225.4	235.9
Ireland/Irlande	120.4	173.6	248.2	252.0	280.2
Australia/Australie	71.9	134.4	213.7	269.7	196.5
Canada	126.5	162.5	191.2	183.0	202.7
Korea, Republic of	127.2	177.4	227.6	172.4	135.9
Malaysia/Malaisie	115.0	176.0	197.6	127.1	115.0
China, Hong Kong SAR	112.3	162.6	164.0	150.9	122.2
Brazil/Brésil	103.2	175.7	121.2	126.6	157.8
Singapore/Singapour	102.0	122.1	132.6	118.3	110.9
Colombia/Colombie	84.2	119.1	114.2	118.1	126.7
Thailand/Thaïlande	72.3	99.9	114.5	125.3	122.4
Special Categories	201.4		95.2	174.8	
Czech Republic	58.4	84.9	106.3	109.1	110.8
Hungary/Hongrie	55.4	79.4	77.7	88.7	99.9
Chile/Chili	39.5	38.0	73.8	107.8	124.1
Kazakhstan	22.5	18.9	42.2	125.8	172.7
Greece/Grèce	48.5	63.5	78.6	80.0	76.9
Indonesia/Indonésie	23.9	42.5	50.4	114.0	115.8
India/Inde	45.9	48.2	56.4	68.5	73.7
Philippines	29.8	58.8	53.4	53.5	58.5

COUNTRIES–PAYS	GENERAL EXPORTS F.O.B. EXPORTATIONS GENERALES F.O.B.				
	1993	1994	1995	1996	1997
Monde	23473.4	29764.9	40408.5	40561.5	40980.0
Afrique	425.7	501.9	624.8	544.1	629.4
Amériques	2406.7	2733.2	3920.0	4048.0	3864.1
– Amérique du Nord	2014.7	2294.0	2933.0	3416.3	3211.2
– ALAI	290.6	371.5	541.4	553.4	602.7
– MCAC	11.9	39.1	39.7	10.0	13.3
– Caraïbes	80.6	25.1	252.1	55.0	32.1
– Autre Amérique	8.9	3.6	153.8	13.3	4.7
Asie anc. URSS exclus	2970.0	3525.9	5516.8	6019.8	5866.9
– Moyen–Orient	497.5	460.8	747.2	1054.7	863.5
Asie ancienne URSS	17.4	37.6	42.7	84.3	99.5
Europe anc. URSS exclus	15473.0	19310.2	25179.9	24219.1	24066.7
– Union Européenne	13672.7	16894.8	22417.3	21383.4	21092.3
– Europe de l'Est	639.7	972.9	978.9	1129.6	1293.9
– Autre de l'Europe	1160.6	1442.5	1783.7	1706.1	1680.6
Europe ancienne URSS	1528.3	2483.0	3310.2	4048.0	4824.3
Océanie	325.2	414.6	594.0	536.8	591.4
Autre	327.1	758.6	1220.2	1061.4	1037.9
Germany/Allemagne	2993.2	3883.2	5306.8	4796.0	4416.5
Sweden/Suède	2699.6	3177.5	4036.4	4264.1	3963.4
United Kingdom	2391.5	2996.9	4110.3	4052.6	4019.8
USA/Etats–Unis d'Amer	1831.7	2101.2	2658.2	3189.8	2822.0
Russian Federation	1372.8	1530.7	1917.4	2439.7	2951.3
France, Monaco	1206.7	1450.0	1770.9	1666.7	1687.3
Netherlands/Pays–Bas	1147.7	1475.8	1661.5	1559.0	1645.0
Denmark/Danemark	771.2	1005.7	1271.0	1215.7	1242.6
Norway,Svalbard and JM	734.7	917.2	1181.5	1130.3	1175.4
Italy/Italie	731.7	858.1	1169.4	1007.9	1182.4
Belgium–Luxembourg	486.7	625.5	1138.7	981.6	913.1
Estonia/Estonie		647.2	939.1	1099.5	1291.0
Spain/Espagne	605.7	662.5	996.5	855.1	845.0
Japan/Japon	378.3	609.1	1022.7	1044.1	758.1
Poland/Pologne	353.3	483.4	506.9	577.3	706.3
China/Chine	256.5	435.3	596.1	587.8	730.1
China, Hong Kong SAR	206.8	351.2	557.9	659.3	760.2
Areas n.e.s.	0.0	758.6	357.2	240.7	1037.9
Korea, Republic of	246.0	403.5	514.7	587.6	467.8
Switzerland,Liechtenst.	359.2	435.6	513.1	447.0	393.1
Australia/Australie	289.1	374.9	530.4	440.7	510.5
Special Categories	327.1		863.0	820.7	
Austria/Autriche	246.7	306.3	346.5	347.1	383.5
Thailand/Thaïlande	280.2	208.3	373.7	375.9	381.9
Singapore/Singapour	184.1	276.7	328.5	368.2	386.9
Indonesia/Indonésie	220.6	101.9	360.1	302.4	482.8
Canada	181.1	192.2	273.4	226.1	388.5
United Arab Emirates	37.3	43.4	238.4	477.5	257.2
Ireland/Irlande	119.6	136.4	204.5	238.1	335.5
Greece/Grèce	126.2	169.4	213.8	206.4	236.9
Malaysia/Malaisie	109.1	156.3	225.2	178.8	281.7
Czech Republic	77.6	163.6	177.7	246.2	285.0
Other Asia n.e.s.	148.3	144.7	203.9	233.1	199.4
Latvia/Lettonie	43.7	151.8	220.9	230.6	274.3
Portugal	146.4	147.4	191.0	193.2	221.4
Hungary/Hongrie	132.0	218.3	177.2	178.1	190.4
Turkey/Turquie	133.2	105.2	153.5	209.3	289.1
India/Inde	71.4	135.7	192.8	207.9	237.7
So. African Customs Un	61.7	158.2	188.7	158.3	201.9
Brazil/Brésil	71.4	106.2	182.7	176.0	219.0

(VALUE AS PERCENTAGE OF WORLD TOTAL)(VALEURS EN POURCENTAGE DU TOTAL MONDIAL)

	1988	1989	1990	1991	1992	1993	1994	1995	1996	1997
Africa	0.5	0.5	0.4	0.7	1.0	0.8	0.6	0.5	0.7	0.9
Americas	9.4	9.2	9.3	9.4	9.3	10.1	10.8	9.7	9.8	10.1
– Northern America	7.1	7.2	7.6	7.4	6.7	8.0	8.3	7.9	7.9	8.0
– LAIA	1.8	1.5	1.3	1.5	1.8	1.6	1.8	1.4	1.4	1.7
– CACM	0.3	0.3	0.2	0.2	0.2	0.2	0.3	0.3	0.3	0.4
– Caribbean	0.2	0.3	0.2	0.2	0.5	0.2	0.2	0.2	0.1	0.1
– Rest of America	0.1	0.0	0.1	0.1	0.1	0.2	0.2	0.1	0.1	0.1
Asia excl fmr USSR	12.0	11.9	11.8	12.6	12.3	12.3	13.4	12.5	11.2	11.4
– Middle East	0.6	0.6	1.2	1.4	1.1	0.3	0.3	0.2	0.2	0.3
Asia former USSR					0.2	0.4	0.1	0.2	0.4	0.6
Europe excl fmr USSR	65.1	66.0	67.7	67.4	67.2	66.1	63.6	65.6	66.2	64.9
– European Union	57.8	59.0	60.1	58.8	58.9	57.0	54.7	57.6	58.6	57.5
– Eastern Europe	2.6	2.5	2.4	2.2	2.2	2.1	2.2	1.9	1.8	2.0
– Rest of Europe	4.7	4.4	5.3	6.4	6.1	7.0	6.7	6.0	5.9	5.4
Europe former USSR	11.5	11.1	9.5	8.5	7.5	8.5	9.7	8.8	8.4	8.9
Oceania	0.6	0.4	0.5	0.6	0.7	0.6	0.7	0.8	1.0	0.8
Other	1.0	0.9	0.8	0.8	1.8	1.1	0.9	2.0	2.2	2.4
Germany/Allemagne				16.9	16.6	16.3	14.7	15.5	15.0	14.5
Sweden/Suède	13.3	13.6	12.9	12.0	11.4	10.2	10.4	11.6	11.9	12.1
United Kingdom	6.7	6.5	7.6	7.6	8.6	8.8	8.2	8.2	8.8	7.8
Russian Federation					7.3	8.2	8.4	7.2	6.9	7.3
USA/Etats–Unis d'Amer	6.3	6.3	6.8	6.8	6.1	7.3	7.6	7.2	7.3	7.3
Japan/Japon	7.4	7.3	6.4	6.0	5.5	5.8	6.5	6.4	5.2	5.3
France, Monaco	4.0	4.1	4.2	4.0	4.1	3.9	4.0	4.0	4.5	4.8
Norway,Svalbard and JM	2.2	2.2	3.3	4.5	3.9	4.8	4.7	4.1	4.0	3.5
Italy/Italie	4.4	4.6	4.6	4.2	3.6	3.7	3.9	4.0	4.1	4.0
Netherlands/Pays–Bas	3.2	3.2	3.2	3.4	3.5	3.6	3.4	3.7	3.6	4.0

	1988	1989	1990	1991	1992	1993	1994	1995	1996	1997
Afrique	1.5	1.6	1.8	1.5	1.7	1.8	1.7	1.5	1.3	1.5
Amériques	8.9	8.8	8.4	8.6	8.0	10.3	9.2	9.7	10.0	9.4
– Amérique du Nord	8.1	7.7	6.9	6.8	6.5	8.6	7.7	7.3	8.4	7.8
– ALAI	0.7	0.9	1.3	1.3	1.1	1.2	1.2	1.3	1.4	1.5
– MCAC	0.1	0.1	0.1	0.1	0.1	0.1	0.1	0.1	0.0	0.0
– Caraïbes	0.1	0.1	0.1	0.4	0.2	0.3	0.1	0.6	0.1	0.1
– Autre Amérique	0.0	0.0	0.0	0.0	0.0	0.0	0.0	0.4	0.0	0.0
Asie anc. URSS exclus	6.7	7.3	7.2	9.4	9.1	12.7	11.8	13.7	14.8	14.3
– Moyen–Orient	1.4	1.3	1.6	1.9	1.8	2.1	1.5	1.8	2.6	2.1
Asie ancienne URSS					0.1	0.1	0.1	0.1	0.2	0.2
Europe anc. URSS exclus	65.0	64.5	66.7	72.1	73.4	65.9	64.9	62.3	59.7	58.7
– Union Européenne	58.1	58.1	60.2	64.7	65.5	58.2	56.8	55.5	52.7	51.5
– Europe de l'Est	1.4	1.6	1.4	1.8	2.3	2.7	3.3	2.4	2.8	3.2
– Autre de l'Europe	5.4	4.8	5.1	5.6	5.6	4.9	4.8	4.4	4.2	4.1
Europe ancienne URSS	14.7	14.3	12.5	4.8	4.1	6.5	8.3	8.2	10.0	11.8
Océanie	1.2	1.3	1.0	1.1	1.2	1.4	1.4	1.5	1.3	1.4
Autre	2.0	2.1	2.4	2.5	2.4	1.4	2.5	3.0	2.6	2.5
Germany/Allemagne				15.0	15.2	12.8	13.0	13.1	11.8	10.8
Sweden/Suède	14.0	14.1	14.0	13.6	12.6	11.5	10.7	10.0	10.5	9.7
United Kingdom	12.9	11.8	10.4	10.1	10.4	10.2	10.1	10.2	10.0	9.8
USA/Etats–Unis d'Amer	5.7	6.4	5.8	6.1	5.9	7.8	7.1	6.6	7.9	6.9
Russian Federation					3.6	5.8	5.1	4.7	6.0	7.2
France, Monaco	5.2	5.3	6.0	5.7	6.5	5.1	4.9	4.4	4.1	4.1
Netherlands/Pays–Bas	3.6	3.9	4.2	4.8	5.1	4.9	5.0	4.1	3.8	4.0
Denmark/Danemark	3.5	3.2	3.5	3.7	3.5	3.3	3.4	3.1	3.0	3.0
Norway,Svalbard and JM	3.4	2.9	3.0	3.3	3.5	3.1	3.1	2.9	2.8	2.9
Italy/Italie	2.6	2.9	3.1	3.4	3.9	3.1	2.9	2.9	2.5	2.9

4. General Imports C.I.F. by Commodities according to the S.I.T.C. (Rev. 2) in million U.S. Dollars
Importations Générales C.A.F. par Produits d'après la C.T.C.I. (Rév. 2) en millions de Dollars E.U.

SITC CTCI	COMMODITY	1994 QUANTITY QUANTITE	1994 VALUE VALEUR	1995 QUANTITY QUANTITE	1995 VALUE VALEUR	1996 QUANTITY QUANTITE	1996 VALUE VALEUR	1997 QUANTITY QUANTITE	1997 VALUE VALEUR	PRODUIT
	ALL COMMODITIES		23358.3		29519.9		30859.7		31001.1	TOUS PRODUITS
0	FOOD AND LIVE ANIMALS		1400.1		1441.4		1719.3		1735.8	ALIMENTS,ANIMAUX VIVANTS
01	MEAT AND PREPARATIONS		15.2		93.7		109.5		92.4	VIANDES ET PREPARATIONS
02	DAIRY PRODCTS,BIRDS'EGGS		21.8		61.4		86.7		101.0	PRODUITS LAITIERS,OEUFS
03	FISH AND PREPARATIONS		116.4		92.1		111.8		102.1	POISSONS ET PREPARATIONS
04	CEREALS AND PREPARATIONS		87.5		147.3		209.1		203.0	CEREALES ET PRODUITS
048	CEREAL ETC PREPARATIONS	W 22310	50.1	W 39141	95.4	W 61657	126.8	W 86524	142.0	PREPTNS A BASE CEREALES
05	VEGETABLES AND FRUIT		555.3		438.8		543.5		485.9	LEGUMES ET FRUITS
054	VEG ETC FRSH,SMPLY PRSVD	W 128013	119.5	W 95916	109.6	W 116289	136.7	W 120497	128.1	LEGUMES FRAIS,CONG,SECS
057	FRUIT,NUTS,FRESH,DRIED	W 411689	295.1	W 227974	213.5		263.8	W 249855	234.5	FRUITS FRAIS OU SECS
0573	BANANA,PLANTAIN,FRSH,DRY	W 168552	95.5	W 66194	44.1	W 58489	53.4	W 59951	55.6	BANANES FRAICHES,SECHEES
058	FRUIT PRESERVED,PREPARED	W 96291	125.9	W 58323	96.2	W 77366	121.6	W 77244	103.3	CONSERVES DE FRUITS
06	SUGAR AND PREPS,HONEY		61.4		83.0		98.6		81.8	SUCRES ET PRODUITS
07	COFFEE,TEA,COCOA,SPICES		319.1		281.5		291.1		385.2	CAFE,THE,CACAO,EPICES
071	COFFEE AND SUBSTITUTES	W 80870	238.8	W 49709	185.2	W 66980	194.6	W 67266	286.4	CAFE ET SUCCEDANES
0711	COFFEE GREEN,ROASTED,SUB	W 80480	234.0	W 49389	180.4	W 66586	189.8	W 65026	264.0	CAFE TORREFIE OU DECAFEINE
07111	COFFEE GREEN,HUSKS,SKINS	W 78921	227.2	W 47613	169.7	W 64081	176.3	W 62249	248.4	CAFE NON TORREFIE
081	*FEEDING STUFF FOR ANIML	W 186340	101.7	W 156290	103.3	W 184872	123.8	W 183102	115.4	NOURRITURE POUR ANIMAUX
09	MISC EDIBLE PRODUCTS		120.1		139.9		144.6		168.0	PREP ALIMENTAIRES DIVERSES
098	EDIBLE PRODCTS,PREPS NES	W 42633	118.4	W 36400	130.3	W 35105	135.0	W 43719	141.6	PREP ALIMENTAIRES NDA
09809	MISC FOOD PREPRTIONS NES	W 30072	80.7	W 22359	84.9	W 18958	84.6	W 24428	89.8	PREP ALIMENTAIRES NDA
1	BEVERAGES AND TOBACCO		144.9		193.2		206.5		210.8	BOISSONS ET TABACS
11	BEVERAGES		76.3		144.6		141.3		147.1	BOISSONS
112	ALCOHOLIC BEVERAGES	W 37804	70.7	W 48423	139.2	W 50122	135.1	W 61329	143.0	BOISSONS ALCOOLIQUES
2	CRUDE MATERLS,EXCL FUELS		1544.3		2173.2		2081.5		2115.7	MAT BRUTES NON COMESTIBLES
21	HIDES,SKINS,FURS UNDRSSD		32.3		96.1		110.0		111.8	CUIRS,PEAUX BRUTS
212	FURSKINS,RAW	W 141	16.2	W 533	82.2	W 471	100.4	W 570	103.7	PELLETERIES BRUTES
24	CORK AND WOOD		329.9		581.2		392.5		393.4	LIEGE ET BOIS
246	PULPWOOD,CHIPS,WOODWASTE	W 4687052	194.9	W 506676	21.3	W 574115	22.4	W 734771	24.8	BOIS DE TRITURATION
24601	PULPWOOD ROUGH OR SPLIT	W 4209022	175.8							EN RONDINS REFENDUS
247	OTH WOOD ROUGH,SQUARED	W 1547894	76.1	W 8796076	492.2	W 6032356	312.0	W 6321019	292.5	BOIS BRUTS EQUARRIS
2471	SAW–,VENEER–LOGS CONIFER	W 1547894	76.1	W 2133041	124.0	W 2452392	128.9	W 2475976	120.4	CONIFERES POUR SCIAGE,PLACAG
24711	— IN THE ROUGH	W 1547894	76.1	W 2133041	124.0	W 2452392	128.9	W 2475976	120.4	ECORCES OU DEGROSSIS
2472	SAW–,VENEER–LOGS NON–CON		0.1	W 6663036	368.3	W 3579965	183.1	W 3845043	172.1	NON CONIFERES SCIAGE,PLAC
24721	— IN THE ROUGH		0.1	W 6663036	368.3	W 3579965	183.1	W 3845043	172.1	BRUTS ECORCES DEGROSSIS
251	*PULP AND WASTE PAPER		94.7		157.7		68.0		66.8	PATES A PAPIER,DECHETS
27	CRUDE FERTLZR,MINRLS NES		269.4		295.3		258.8		286.1	ENGRAIS MINERAUX BRUTS
278	OTHER CRUDE MINERALS	W 2219630	237.7	W 2229213	256.9	W 1939041	222.4	W 2261188	249.8	AUTRES MINERAUX BRUTS
2782	REFRACTORY MINERALS NES	W 1426197	188.8	W 1458938	205.7	W 1284504	177.5	W 1529178	207.3	ARGILE MINERAUX REFRACTAIRES
27821	CLAY ETC	W 1385071	183.8	W 1418272	200.2	W 1237922	170.9	W 1473237	201.4	ARGILES
28	METALLIFEROUS ORES,SCRAP		572.8		747.2		961.6		962.9	MINERAIS METAL,DECHETS
281	IRON ORE,CONCENTRATES	W 3617586	90.4	W 2964994	81.3	W 3305776	103.5	W 3732484	116.0	MINERAIS DE FER
2815	IRON ORE,CONC,NOT AGGLOM	W 2753445	71.0	W 2359725	65.8	W 2647692	86.6	W 2962462	94.7	MINERAIS NON AGGLOMERES
282	IRON AND STEEL SCRAP	W 335731	53.4	W 294589	62.0	W 226197	92.8	W 347906	112.2	FERRAILLES
28202	— OF ALLOY STEEL	W 143710	30.1	W 159721	46.0	W 144229	83.4	W 189503	94.1	FERRAILLES D'ACIERS ALLIES
287	BASE METAL ORES,CONC NES		304.7		424.0		574.6		563.0	MINERAIS METAUX COMMUNS
2871	CPR ORE ETC,CEMENT COPPR	W 292801	128.4	W 293680	178.1	W 494218	267.4	W 487486	267.1	MINERAIS DE CUIVRE,MATTES
28711	COPPER ORES,EXCL MATTE	W 292791	128.4	W 293676	178.1	W 494217	267.4	W 487477	267.0	MINERAIS DE CUIVRE
2872	NICKEL ORES,CONCENTRATES	W 114022	54.2	W 138918	121.3	W 210452	193.4	W 171276	145.2	MINERAIS DE NICKEL
28721	NICKEL ORES,EXCL MATTE	W 111084	43.3	W 134831	100.4	W 200610	151.4	W 163962	112.9	MINERAIS DE NICKEL
2875	ZINC ORES,CONCENTRATES	W 337393	88.9	W 211074	61.4	W 288603	77.1	W 295485	107.9	MINERAIS DE ZINC
288	NONFERR METAL SCRAP NES	W 197637	124.4	W 88341	180.0	W 118886	190.6	W 112514	171.8	DECHETS NON FERREUX
2881	METALIFEROUS NONFER WSTE	W 116950	69.3	W 15647	102.9	W 36208	119.6	W 20618	78.9	CENDRES ET RESIDUS
29	CRUDE ANIMAL,VEG MAT NES		112.1		114.8		121.0		121.4	MATIERES BRUTES ANIM,VEGET
292	CRUDE VEG MATERIALS NES	W 18627	90.9	W 15437	93.7	W 17504	95.7	W 19014	91.9	MAT BRUTES VEGETALES NDA
3	MINERAL FUELS ETC		2709.6		2609.1		3272.7		3005.1	COMBUSTIBLES MINERAUX LUB
32	COAL,COKE AND BRIQUETTES		347.6		325.2		329.6		393.1	HOUILLES,COKES,BRIQUETTES
322	COAL,LIGNITE AND PEAT	W 8114981	305.2	W 5891598	289.8	W 6253644	290.1	W 7487675	342.7	HOUILLES,LIGNITES,TOURBE
3222	OTH COAL,NOT AGGLOMERATD	W 8087168	304.1	W 5887173	289.1	W 6250334	289.7	W 7470953	342.0	AUTRES HOUILLES
33	PETROLEUM AND PRODUCTS		1881.2		1734.8		2309.3		2015.0	PETROLE ET DERIVES
333	CRUDE PETROLEUM	MW 9837	1267.3	W 8394853	1209.1	MW 9498	1569.4	MW 9980	1406.5	HUILES BRUTES DE PETROLE
334	PETROLEUM PRODUCTS,REFIN	W 4446042	577.8	W 3366834	490.1	W 4248363	706.6	W 3667115	580.8	PRODUITS RAFFINES
3343	GAS OILS	W 1329366	203.6	W 723268	75.9	W 1043368	153.9	W 722897	107.9	GAS OILS
3344	FUEL OILS,NES	W 2090613	198.6	W 2300222	289.8	W 2727918	393.3	W 2438470	316.8	FUEL OILS
3345	LUBS,PETROLEUM OILS NES	W 649246	113.8	W 118370	74.5	W 142990	82.5	W 173570	82.5	HUILES LUBRIFIANTES
33451	LUBS(HIGH PETR CONT) ETC	W 644519	99.7	W 113142	57.5	W 135993	62.3	W 165564	62.1	HUILES LUBRIF,H LOURDES
341	*GAS,NATURAL AND MANUFCT		312.1		357.3		393.2		385.2	GAZ NATUREL,GAZ MANUFACT
3414	PETROLEUM GASES, GASEOUS		250.3		313.9		335.2		310.2	GAZ DE PETROLE GAZEUX
351	*ELECTRIC CURRENT	H 7170561	168.8		192.0		240.8		211.9	ENERGIE ELECTRIQUE
5	CHEMCLS,RELATED PROD NES		2895.0		3511.4		3399.1		3494.1	PRODUITS CHIMIQUES
51	ORGANIC CHEMICALS		550.4		629.9		528.7		619.1	PROD CHIMIQ ORGANIQUES
511	HYDROCARBONS NES,DERIVS		160.0		191.6		143.3		219.2	HYDROCARBURES NDA
5111	ACYCLIC HYDROCARBONS	W 69955	17.4	W 94066	35.0	W 145003	35.0	W 276049	94.4	HYDROCARBURES ACYCLIQUES
5112	CYCLIC HYDROCARBONS	W 137935	82.9	W 105908	100.1	W 112451	66.9	W 147729	81.2	HYDROCARBURES CYCLIQUES
51125	STYRENE	W 106244	74.2	W 94408	95.4	W 97447	61.1	W 127401	73.9	STYRENE
512	ALCOHOLS,PHENOLS ETC		84.2		107.6		85.9		92.5	PHENOLS,PHENOLS–ALCOOLS
5121	ACYCLIC ALCOHOLS,DERIVS		73.5		89.0		66.5		69.1	ALCOOLS ACYCLIQUES
513	CARBOXYLIC ACIDS ETC		85.8		122.8		99.2		94.9	ACIDES CARBOXYLIQUES
514	NITROGEN–FNCTN COMPOUNDS		71.7		84.1		81.7		84.6	COMPOSES FONCT AZOTEES
516	OTHER ORGANIC CHEMICALS		113.5		89.9		79.3		94.1	AUTRES PROD ORGANIQUES
52	INORGANIC CHEMICALS		293.4		402.8		341.2		330.1	PROD CHIM INORGANIQUES
522	INORG ELEMNTS,OXIDES,ETC		173.4		265.8		211.6		178.3	ELEMENTS INORGANIQUES
5225	INORGANIC BASES ETC NES		116.0		203.9		154.3		120.6	AUTRES BASES OXYDES METAL
52253	SODIUM HYDROXIDE, OTHER	W 634118	43.3	W 656430	115.7	W 622159	79.5	W 736476	56.6	HYDROXYDE SODIUM AQUEUX
523	OTHR INORG CHEMICALS ETC		115.4		131.3		124.4		147.5	AUT PRODUITS CHIMIQUES INORG
53	DYES,TANNING,COLOUR PROD		215.0		259.2		263.4		269.3	PROD TEINTURE,COLORANTS
531	SYNT DYE,NAT INDGO,LAKES	W 17722	74.9	W 17873	92.9	W 19181	83.8	W 27365	90.5	MAT COLOR ORGAN,LAQUES
533	PIGMENTS,PAINTS,ETC	W 49012	136.0	W 47653	162.3	W 55393	175.5	W 63998	175.1	PIGMENTS,PEINTURES,VERNIS
5334	VARNISHES,DISTEMPERS ETC	W 19019	69.5	W 20575	84.3	W 24053	93.3	W 23729	89.5	PEINTURES A L'EAU
541	*MEDICINAL,PHARM PRODUCT	MK 11393	482.5		591.3		630.6	MK 12174	618.6	PROD MEDICINAUX PHARMACEUT
5417	MEDICAMENTS	MK 9542	396.4	MK 9536	496.8	MK 10780	532.5	MK 10052	522.5	MEDICAMENTS
54179	— CONTNG OTH SUBSTANCES	K 8855203	306.8	K 8578677	378.4	MK 9827	412.7	MK 9108	423.1	MED CONT AUT SUBSTANCES
55	PERFUME,CLEANING ETC PRD		212.0		248.3		327.1		286.6	PROD POUR PARFUM,TOILETTE
553	PERFUMERY,COSMETICS,ETC	W 13468	101.9	W 14305	126.6	W 29005	197.5	W 24608	158.2	PRODUITS DE PARFUMERIE
554	SOAP,CLEANSING ETC PREPS	W 52170	90.3	W 54093	101.6	W 55903	102.8	W 60729	102.1	SAVONS,PRODUITS DETERSIFS
5542	WASHING PREPARATIONS ETC	W 47339	77.2	W 48739	85.7	W 51130	87.5	W 55899	87.3	PROD ORG TENSIO–ACT NDA
58	PLASTIC MATERIALS ETC		680.3		845.1		770.1		809.7	MAT PLAST ARTIFICIELLES
582	PROD OF CONDENSATION ETC	W 71665	180.8	W 67940	215.8	W 70024	212.0	W 83092	210.8	PROD CONDENS,POLYCOND
583	POLYMERIZATION ETC PRODS	W 369371	484.8	W 366106	614.2	W 366723	540.4		580.1	PROD POLYMERISATION
5831	POLYETHYLENE	W 158970	145.9	W 138582	181.1	W 135656	152.2	W 139560	152.5	POLYETHYLENE
58311	— IN PRIMARY FORMS	W 146784	120.8	W 127866	153.2	W 122002	124.5	W 123817	123.7	POLYETHYLENE PRIMAIRES

4. General Imports C.I.F. by Commodities according to the S.I.T.C. (Rev. 2) in million U.S. Dollars
Importations Générales C.A.F. par Produits d'après la C.T.C.I. (Rév. 2) en millions de Dollars E.U.

SITC CTCI	COMMODITY	1994		1995		1996		1997		PRODUIT
		QUANTITY QUANTITE	VALUE VALEUR	QUANTITY QUANTITE	VALUE VALEUR	QUANTITY QUANTITE	VALUE VALEUR	QUANTITY QUANTITE	VALUE VALEUR	
5836	ACRYLIC POLYMERS,ETC	W 49045	71.2	W 49840	85.9	W 52738	83.9	W 57221	82.6	POLYM ACRYLIQ METHACRYLI
5839	OTH POLYMRZTION ETC PROD	W 39547	115.6	W 46069	145.4	W 47450	129.3	W 62717	148.8	AUT PROD POLYMER COPOLYM
59	CHEMICAL MATERIALS NES		397.0		480.3		476.3		501.9	MAT PROD CHIMIQUES NDA
592	STARCH,INULIN,GLUTEN,ETC	W 158473	111.3	W 130747	133.2	W 140129	142.3	W 170541	139.0	AMIDONS,INUL,GLUT FROM
5922	ALBUMINOID SUBSTAN,GLUES	W 126914	100.2	W 108777	118.8	W 119191	128.5	W 128808	119.0	MAT ALBUMIN,COLLES
598	MISCEL CHEM PRODUCTS NES		243.4		297.2		284.3		319.0	PROD DIV INDUST CHIM NDA
5989	CHEM PRODUCTS,PREPS NES	W 122944	179.0		229.8	W 158722	219.6	W 259173	250.8	PROD PREP CHIMIQUES NDA
59899	OTH CHEM PRODS,PREPS,NES	W 86696	120.0		162.0	W 131524	153.6	W 229556	179.9	AUT PRODUITS CHIMIQUES NDA
6	BASIC MANUFACTURES		3472.5		4556.8		4144.9		4189.7	ART MANUFACTURES
62	RUBBER MANUFACTURES NES		208.8		261.7		258.4		273.3	CAOUTCHOUC MANUFACTURE
625	RUBBER TYRES, TUBES ETC	W 29956	107.1	W 34056	143.8	W 35193	144.7	W 40514	157.1	PNEUS CAOUTCHOUC VULCANISE
64	PAPER,PAPERBOARD AND MFR		373.1		517.1		498.6		490.2	PAPIERS,CARTONS & OUVRAGES
641	PAPER AND PAPERBOARD	W 243714	238.0	W 253080	322.1	W 298155	327.6	W 367774	335.9	PAPIERS ET CARTONS
6418	COATED ETC PAPER NES BLK	W 40070	95.2	W 46474	125.3	W 40243	111.1	W 55188	115.2	PAP,CARTONS COUCHES,ENDUITS
642	PAPER,ETC,PRECUT,ARTS OF	W 44543	135.2	W 45882	195.1	W 52289	171.1	W 54498	154.4	PAP,CARTONS DECOUPES
6428	PAPER ETC ARTICLES NES	W 26181	80.4	W 27814	130.1	W 31763	103.7	W 33237	92.2	OUVRAGES EN PATE A PAPIER
64285	PAPER ETC DIAPERS ETC	W 13887	52.7	W 15465	93.0	W 17199	63.4	W 16384	50.9	SERVIETTES HYGIENIQUES
65	TEXTILE YARN,FABRICS,ETC		576.0		605.6		610.2		586.9	FILS,TISSUS,ARTICLES TEXTILE
651	TEXTILE YARN	W 23805	124.4		125.0		113.4		103.5	FILS TEXTILES
653	WOVN MAN-MADE FIB FABRIC	W 6058	89.8	W 5414	91.2	W 5602	90.4	W 6482	86.7	TISSUS FIBRES SYNTH,ARTIF
657	SPECIAL TXTL FABRC,PRODS	W 16456	152.5	W 15887	164.0	W 17774	175.1	W 18549	164.5	TISSUS SPECIAUX
66	NONMETAL MINERAL MFS NES		296.9		348.7		355.1		392.5	ART MIN NON METALLIQUES
663	MINERAL MANUFCTURES NES	W 78316	81.6	W 75397	92.0	W 79592	85.8	W 106272	92.0	ART MIN MANUF NDA
664	GLASS	W 61947	61.3	W 71798	72.3	W 69023	76.9	W 145884	103.1	VERRE
67	IRON AND STEEL		895.4		1362.2		1153.7		1096.9	FER ET ACIER
671	PIG IRON ETC	W 164336	183.6	W 208361	257.7	W 191152	218.2	W 170740	208.5	FONTE,SPIEGEL,POUDRES
6716	FERRO-ALLOYS	W 130247	176.1	W 128660	243.3	W 117137	204.3	W 120080	198.7	FERRO-ALLIAGES
67169	OTHER FERRO-ALLOYS	W 98032	156.4	W 104430	221.9	W 90725	181.7	W 91219	176.6	AUTRES FERRO-ALLIAGES
672	IRON,STEEL PRIMARY FORMS	W 349829	94.4	W 653756	201.4	W 576604	152.7	W 351147	104.0	LINGOTS FER,ACIER
6725	IRN,STL BLOOMS,SLABS,ETC	W 227805	52.5	W 561386	161.1	W 461729	110.1	W 224141	61.0	BLOOMS,BILLETTES FER ACIER
67251	IRN,SMPLE STL BLOOMS,ETC	W 222807	48.4	W 556053	152.4	W 459717	107.0	W 216288	51.4	BLOOMS ETC NON ACIER FIN
673	IRON,STEEL SHAPES ETC	W 217823	127.0	W 261973	189.1	W 255370	164.6	W 371166	182.7	BARRES,PROFIL FER,ACIER
6732	IRON,STEEL BARS ETC	W 104841	73.2	W 119254	114.1	W 126283	101.4	W 195108	107.9	BARRES FER,ACIER
674	IRN,STL UNIV,PLATE,SHEET	W 306517	258.5	W 335055	373.6	W 304058	314.4	W 347303	295.6	LARGES PLATS,TOLES
6744	IRN,STL HVY PLATE,ROLLED	W 82508	72.4	W 81662	123.7	W 68761	95.2	W 82452	82.0	TOLES LAMINEES PLUS 4.75 MM
67443	— OF STAINLESS ETC STL	W 19179	44.8	W 25095	90.4	W 20921	69.0	W 21447	52.3	TOLES ACIER INOXYDABLE
6749	OTH IRN,STL PLATES,SHEET	W 86214	72.6	W 97554	102.3	W 87538	80.6	W 103214	82.4	AUTRES TOLES FER,ACIER
67491	— OF IRON OR SIMPLE STL	W 84174	65.7	W 95244	92.1	W 85530	73.8	W 98710	74.9	AUT TOLES AUTRES ACIER FIN
678	IRON,STL TUBES,PIPES,ETC	W 121011	173.3	W 139376	260.2	W 127782	219.9	W 160826	221.2	TUBES,TUYAUX EN FONTE,FER
6782	IRON,STL SEAMLESS TUBES	W 40747	64.2	W 50331	96.9	W 41472	75.9	W 56162	82.4	TUBES,TUYAUX SANS SOUDURE
6783	IRON,STL TUBES,PIPES NES	W 70130	59.9	W 78264	98.3	W 75194	79.2	W 91697	74.1	AUT TUBES,TUYAUX FER,ACIER
68	NON-FERROUS METALS		465.4		633.3		461.9		514.2	METAUX NON FERREUX
682	COPPER EXC CEMENT COPPER	W 72253	198.9	W 80855	291.3	W 67352	198.1	W 68746	209.2	CUIVRE
6821	COPPER NES,ALLOYS,UNWRT	W 38383	86.2	W 43801	132.9	W 24882	57.2	W 26773	64.8	CUIVRE BRUT
68212	COPPER REFINED,UNWROUGHT	W 37460	84.6	W 43141	130.4	W 24547	55.9	W 26397	63.4	CUIVRE AFFINE BRUT
6822	COPPER,ALLOYS WORKED	W 33870	112.7	W 37054	158.4	W 42470	141.0	W 41972	144.5	CUIVRE,ALLIAGES OUVRES
683	NICKEL	W 7797	51.3	W 12170	103.7	W 7808	59.9	W 9681	68.0	NICKEL
684	ALUMINIUM	W 79063	190.6	W 63773	214.0	W 66187	170.9	W 79912	197.4	ALUMINIUM
6842	ALUMINIUM,ALLOYS WORKED	W 40305	131.0	W 40750	165.5	W 33149	115.4	W 46364	139.0	ALUMINIUM,ALLIAGES OUVRE
69	METAL MANUFACTURES NES		528.1		692.4		670.2		688.9	ART MANUFACT EN METAL NDA
694	STL,COPPR NAILS,NUTS,ETC	W 20142	67.1	W 25006	93.3	W 25651	90.2	W 29246	89.1	CLOUS,VIS,ECROUS
695	TOOLS	W 7420	108.3	W 9614	144.8	W 8789	143.6	W 8835	135.2	OUTILS A MAIN
699	BASE METAL MFRS NES	W 39975	201.8		257.9		241.0	W 51068	244.1	ART MANUFACTURES MET NDA
7	MACHINES,TRANSPORT EQUIP		8380.0		11414.8		12065.7		12186.4	MACHINES MATERIEL TRANSPORT
71	POWER GENERATING EQUIPMT		502.5		548.9		782.4		601.3	MACHINES GENERATRICES
712	STEAM ENGINES,TURBINES	W 1045	12.6	W 1065	22.3	W 4004	171.2	W 956	34.0	MACHINES A VAPEUR D'EAU PIEC
7129	STM ENGINE ETC PARTS NES	W 197	5.5	W 159	6.8	W 3100	143.5	W 815	27.0	PARTIES,PIECES DU 712.6
713	INTRNL COMBUS PSTN ENGIN	W 17450	183.6	W 25233	242.6	W 19246	225.0	W 24184	268.4	MOTEURS EXPL COMB INT, PIECE
7139	PISTON ENGINE PARTS NES	W 10736	99.5	W 17232	134.2	W 11707	123.7	W 12891	124.9	PIECES POUR 713.2,3,8
714	ENGINES AND MOTORS NES	W 926	97.5	W 575	53.5	W 853	123.0	W 574	96.2	MOTEURS NON ELECTRIQUES
716	ROTATING ELECTRIC PLANT	W 11026	125.6	W 10443	120.4	W 12219	131.5	W 12630	119.6	APP ELECTR ROTATIFS,PIECES
7162	AC MTRS,GENRTRS,GEN SETS	W 7411	73.6	W 8164	87.4	W 8922	91.7	W 9123	85.3	MOTEURS ELECTRIQUES
718	OTH POWER GENERATG MACHY	W 2287	72.0	W 1865	87.7	W 2049	114.1	W 1831	75.0	AUTRES MOTEURS PARTIES
72	MACHS FOR SPCL INDUSTRYS		650.7		936.4		987.9		1020.9	MAC SPECIALES POUR INDUST
721	AGRIC MACHY,EXC TRACTORS	W 9198	48.7	W 12583	94.6	W 15296	100.8	W 17634	114.8	MACHINES AGRICOLES
722	TRACTORS NON-ROAD	W 9188	69.5	W 13708	99.1	W 15331	118.2	W 17036	128.6	TRACTEURS
7224	WHEELED TRACTORS NES	W 9151	69.4	W 13603	98.6	W 15302	117.9	W 16931	128.4	TRACTEURS A ROUES
723	CIVIL ENGNEERG EQUIP ETC	W 11818	60.0	W 17052	106.8	W 16439	95.6	W 21800	107.0	APPAREILS DE GENIE CIVIL
7234	CONST,MINING MACHNRY NES	W 11105	55.1	W 15902	98.1	W 15330	86.5	W 20470	97.9	MACH POUR LA CONST, MINES
725	PAPER ETC MILL MACHINERY	W 5693	77.0	W 8193	118.7	W 11491	182.2	W 10543	115.8	MACHINES FABR PATE PAPIER
7259	PTS NES OF MACHS OF 725	W 3938	44.3	W 6469	78.5	W 8834	113.3	W 8659	77.7	PIECES GROUPE 725
72591	PTS NES OF MACHS OF 7251	W 3824	39.9	W 6169	69.8	W 8482	102.3	W 8356	68.7	PIECES DU 725.1
726	PRINTG,BKBINDG MACHY,PTS	W 1508	44.8	W 2380	75.9	W 2129	78.1	W 3187	107.5	MACHINES POUR IMPRIMERIE
728	OTH MACHY FOR SPCL INDUS	W 16055	291.8	W 15908	348.4	W 17943	326.9	W 20129	356.0	AUT MACH IND PARTICULIERES
7284	MACHY FOR SPCL INDUS NES	W 10357	245.3	W 8881	274.1	W 10240	250.3	W 11183	259.9	MACH SPEC IND PARTICUL.
72848	OTH MCHY WITH INDIV FNCT	W 6358	149.1	W 5160	168.3	W 4852	121.2	W 6405	147.6	AUTRES MACHINES NDA
73	METALWORKING MACHINERY		142.4		233.1		207.6		228.0	MACH TRAVAIL DES METAUX
736	METALWORKING MACH-TOOLS	W 7563	99.0	W 10094	159.9	W 12154	156.6	W 11136	152.9	MACH-OUTILS TRAVAIL METAUX
74	GENRL INDUSTRL MACHY NES		1157.2		1458.2		1538.4		1514.9	MACH APP INDUSTRIE
741	HEATING,COOLING EQUIPMNT	W 11850	176.6	W 15457	222.8	W 17690	232.1	W 19848	236.7	MACH CHAUFFAGE,PIECES
7416	HEATING,COOLING EQU NES	W 4538	77.8	W 4947	88.4	W 4414	88.2	W 5576	88.0	APP CHANGEMENT TEMP
742	PUMPS FOR LIQUIDS ETC	W 5083	109.3	W 6042	133.3	W 6438	138.2	W 6464	132.4	POMPES MOTO-POMPES
743	PUMPS NES,CENTRFUGES ETC	W 14790	191.6	W 14135	200.5	W 15249	227.0	W 16603	239.2	POMPES COMPRES,VENT ETC
744	MECHANICAL HANDLING EQU	W 22930	155.7	W 28354	217.2	W 31043	230.8	W 36168	242.6	EQUIP MANUTENTION PIECES
7442	LIFTING,LOADING MACH NES	W 6682	55.9	W 9847	78.6	W 11613	94.3	W 12287	93.4	APP LEVAGE,MANUTENTION
7449	PTS NES OF MACHY OF 7442	W 12508	79.0	W 13894	107.7	W 14733	103.7	W 17757	112.5	PIECES DU 744.2
745	NONELEC MACHY,TOOLS NES	W 6637	147.3	W 8984	169.4	W 10671	198.0	W 12476	188.1	AUT MACH NON ELEC,PIECES
7452	OTH NONELEC MCHS,PTS NES	W 5745	121.0	W 7990	134.2	W 9393	161.6	W 11033	150.9	AUT MACH NON ELEC,PIECES
749	NONELEC MACH PTS,ACC NES	W 25282	377.0	W 32025	515.2	W 33210	512.5	W 37106	476.2	PIECES MACH NON ELEC NDA
7492	COCKS,VALVES ETC NES	W 7001	151.1	W 8439	205.1	W 9139	202.6	W 8939	185.1	ART ROB,SIM POUR TUYAUX
7493	SHAFT,CRANK,PULLEY ETC	W 12172	123.3	W 16272	170.2	W 16710	166.7	W 19673	161.0	ARBRES TRANS,VILEBREQUINS
75	OFFICE MACHNES,ADP EQUIP		1196.0		1597.9		1486.6		1591.5	MACH BUREAU TRAIT AUTOM
751	OFFICE MACHINES	W 2403	81.2	W 2513	84.5	W 2552	81.7	W 3232	101.0	MACH,APPAREILS DE BUREAU
752	AUTOMTIC DATA PROC EQUIP	W 9123	671.7	W 10865	885.4	W 12288	948.6	W 12995	1026.8	MACH TRAIT INFORMATION
7522	DIGITAL COMPUTERS	W 519	72.2	W 420	93.5	W 976	137.2	W 666	134.2	MACH DIGITALES COMPLETES
7523	DIGITL CENTRL PROCESSORS	W 2205	206.7	W 2299	275.4	W 2195	259.8	W 2254	269.7	UNITES CENTRALES
7524	DIGITL CENTRL STOR UNITS	W 840	151.4	W 1093	170.9	W 1000	176.7	W 1374	227.2	UNITES MEMOIRE CENTRALES
7525	ADP PERIPHERAL UNITS	W 5086	186.3	W 6361	279.7	W 7240	293.7	W 8086	315.7	UNITES PERIPHERIQUES
759	OFFICE,ADP MCH PTS,ACCES	W 4020	443.2	W 5814	628.1	W 6785	456.4	W 7112	463.7	PIECES DU 751 ET 752
7599	ACCTG,ETC,ADP MCH PTS,AC	W 3419	409.9	W 5069	589.4	W 6110	422.2	W 6214	428.2	PIECES DU 751 ET 752
76	TELECOMM,SOUND EQUIPMENT		684.5		912.8		1042.7		1047.4	EQUIPMENT DE TELECOM

4. General Imports C.I.F. by Commodities according to the S.I.T.C. (Rev. 2) in million U.S. Dollars
Importations Générales C.A.F. par Produits d'après la C.T.C.I. (Rév. 2) en millions de Dollars E.U.

SITC CTCI	COMMODITY	1994 QUANTITY QUANTITE	1994 VALUE VALEUR	1995 QUANTITY QUANTITE	1995 VALUE VALEUR	1996 QUANTITY QUANTITE	1996 VALUE VALEUR	1997 QUANTITY QUANTITE	1997 VALUE VALEUR	PRODUIT
764	TELECOM EQPT,PTS,ACC NES	W 6349	515.8	W 7799	699.3	W 8667	790.6	W 10106	811.1	EQUIP TELECOM,PIECES
7641	LINE TELEPHONE,ETC EQUIP	W 948	94.1	W 1068	120.0	W 1188	137.5	W 1527	184.9	APP TELEPHON PAR FIL
7643	TV,RADIO TRANSMITTRS ETC	W 335	103.3	W 323	122.9	W 430	190.4	W 655	165.0	APP EMET TELE RADIO
7649	PTS NES OF EQUIPMT OF 76	W 3048	261.3	W 3542	379.0	W 3705	393.1	W 4572	392.3	PIECES DE LA DIV 76
76491	PTS NES OF APPAR OF 7641	W 1240	86.3	W 1453	117.8	W 1176	119.8	W 713	113.9	PIECES POUR 764.1
76493	TELECOMM EQUIPMT PTS NES	W 1517	170.3	W 1969	255.5	W 2397	259.6	W 3703	270.7	PIECES 761,762,764.3,8
77	ELECTRIC MACHNRY NES ETC		2317.6		3325.3		3122.0		3338.7	MACH APP ELECT NDA
771	ELECTRIC POWER MACHY NES	W 7343	148.3	W 8605	229.1	W 8149	206.5	W 9505	214.7	MACH PROD,TRANS ELECTR
7712	OTH ELEC POWER MACHY NES	W 4608	113.0	W 5918	187.6	W 5807	170.1	W 6946	166.7	AUT APP PROD TRANSF ELEC
77121	STATIC CONVERTERS ETC	W 1675	66.5	W 2134	99.6	W 1937	96.2	W 2466	86.1	CONVERTISSEURS STATIQUES
772	SWITCHGEAR ETC,PARTS NES	W 8923	389.9	W 11410	580.4	W 11368	544.7	W 13896	552.6	APP COUPURE,SECT ETC
7721	SWITCHGEAR ETC	W 8068	291.1	W 9717	400.8	W 10159	398.1	W 12333	401.1	APP COUPURE,SECTIONMNT
7722	PRINTED CIRCUITS,PTS NES	W 574	69.4	W 1015	133.0	W 785	110.6	W 1083	112.2	CIRCUITS ET PIECES
773	ELECTR DISTRIBUTNG EQUIP	W 21933	150.2	W 25637	204.6	W 24282	209.3	W 30683	235.7	EQUIPMT DISTRIBUTION ELECT
7731	INSULATED WIRE,CABLE ETC	W 20603	137.2	W 24437	192.6	W 23054	194.7	W 29200	218.6	FILS,CABLES ISOLES ELECT
775	HOUSEHOLD TYPE EQUIP NES	W 29369	207.8	W 31671	246.6	W 42315	333.7	W 57438	353.0	MACH,APP USAGE DOMESTQUE
7758	ELECTRO-THERMIC APPL NES	W 9219	83.4	W 8952	89.6	W 12544	124.1	W 14295	118.7	APP ELECTROTHERMIQ NDA
776	TRANSISTORS,VALVES,ETC	W 15225	889.8	W 16794	1316.9	W 13708	1105.3	W 22550	1265.4	LAMPES,TUBES,VALVES
7762	OTH ELECTRONIC TUBES ETC	W 6402	137.9	W 8271	205.2	W 7649	184.4	W 11353	244.6	AUT LAMPES ELECTRONIQUES
7763	DIODES,TRANSISTORS,ETC	W 455	123.0	W 633	189.6	W 521	147.2	W 629	155.4	DIODES,TRANSISTORS
7764	ELECTRONIC MICROCIRCUITS	W 471	562.1	W 740	826.9	W 586	706.6	W 690	786.9	MICROSTRUCTURES ELECTRON
778	ELECTRICAL MACHINERY NES	W 30508	482.9	W 31094	692.1	W 33782	652.8	W 36303	653.1	AUTRES MACH ELECT NDA
7781	BATTERIES,ACCUMULATORS	W 17682	161.6	W 17307	223.8	W 20050	210.9	W 21350	169.1	PILES ET ACCUMULATEURS
77812	ELECTRIC ACCUMULATORS	W 14902	142.8	W 14372	198.0	W 16942	190.1	W 18688	149.7	ACCUMULATEURS ELECTRIQ
7788	OTH ELEC MACHY,EQUIP NES	W 5845	193.6	W 5762	316.5	W 5128	291.7	W 4999	329.7	AUT MACH APP ELEC NDA
77883	ELEC SIGNALLING EQU NES	W 439	56.4	W 524	93.2	W 484	97.3	W 640	112.0	APP ELECT SIGNAL ACOUS
77884	ELECTRICAL CONDENSERS	W 908	72.8	W 1290	114.8	W 995	91.4	W 1406	105.5	CONDENSATEURS ELECTRIQUES
78	ROAD VEHICLES		1424.9		1928.4		2142.4		2216.7	VEHICULES ROUTIERS
781	PASS MOTOR VEH EXC BUSES	W 84746	649.7	W 96034	878.3	W 120033	1077.6	W 132401	1061.2	AUTO TRANSPORT PERSONNES
782	LORRIES,SPCL MTR VEH NES	W 22556	200.0	W 37312	396.0	W 39529	406.1	W 48009	422.6	VEHICULES SPECIAUX,MARCH
7821	LORRIES,TRUCKS	W 21949	194.0	W 36307	388.5	W 38739	396.3	W 46908	410.8	VEHICULES TRANSP MARCHAND
784	MOTOR VEH PRTS,ACCES NES	W 53848	474.2	W 59003	529.0	W 58115	512.1	W 69804	587.3	PIECES 722,781,782,783
7841	MOTOR VEHICLE CHASSIS	W 6212	76.6	W 3219	46.4	W 2959	44.3	W 4669	62.8	CHASSIS 722,781,782,783
7849	OTHER MOTOR VEHCL PARTS	W 47425	396.9	W 55706	481.9	W 54993	467.0	W 64793	519.5	PIECES 722,781,782,783
79	OTHR TRANSPORT EQUIPMENT		304.4		474.1		756.2		627.5	AUTRE MATERIEL TRANSPORT
792	AIRCRAFT ETC	W 447	217.2	W 619	300.0	W 956	572.9	W 771	487.0	APP NAVIGATION AERIENNE
7923	AIRCRFT NES2000-15000KG	W 36	53.5	W 63	130.7	W 52	102.6	W 30	10.4	AERODYNES 2000 A 15000 KG
7924	AIRCRFT NES OVER 15000KG	W 153	83.0	W 89	42.7	W 162	83.9	W 72	31.5	AERODYNES PLUS 15000 KG
7929	AIRCRAFT PARTS NES	W 207	69.0	W 394	109.9	W 721	377.5	W 658	443.4	PIECES DU 792
793	SHIPS AND BOATS ETC		40.8		120.8	W 24106	137.5	W 9115	94.7	NAVIRES BATEAUX,ETC
7932	SHIPS AND BOATS NES	W 34043	35.0	W 31801	100.3	W 22000	120.5	W 6995	78.9	NAVIRES ET BATEAUX
79323	OTHER CARGO VESSELS	W 28073	25.8	W 31077	93.0	W 21286	110.5	W 5911	67.6	AUT BATEAUX TRANS MARCH
8	MISC MANUFACTURED GOODS		2591.0		3017.4		3267.1		3313.7	ART MANUFACTURES DIVERS
812	*PLUMBG,HEATNG,LGHTNG EQ	W 10810	77.7	W 11463	101.4	W 13474	113.3	W 15569	115.3	APPAR SANITAIRES CHAUFFAGE
821	*FURNITURE,PARTS THEREOF	W 36330	162.2	W 37118	199.4	W 43882	238.3	W 51100	254.5	MEUBLES ET PIECES
8211	CHAIRS,SEATS AND PARTS	W 13057	66.4	W 12708	76.3	W 13756	86.2	W 15251	97.7	SIEGES ET PIECES
8219	FURNITURE AND PARTS NES	W 20011	62.1	W 21436	81.2	W 26220	105.0	W 30889	109.7	AUTRES MEUBLES ET PIECES
84	CLOTHING AND ACCESSORIES		704.0		796.7		878.8		904.6	VETEMENTS
842	MENS OUTERWEAR NOT KNIT	W 5218	115.7	W 5120	138.7	W 5353	153.3	W 5743	158.6	VET DESSUS POUR HOMMES
843	WOMENS OUTERWEAR NONKNIT	W 5932	179.2	W 6569	208.3	W 6436	223.6	W 7378	237.5	VET DESSUS FEMMES MAT TEX
8439	— OTHER OUTER GARMENTS	W 3846	96.8	W 3870	101.7	W 3719	104.0	W 4528	120.6	AUT VET DES FEM MAT TEXT
845	OUTERWEAR KNIT NONELASTC	W 7322	163.3	W 7064	180.2	W 7867	194.0	W 8540	204.1	VET DESSOUS,ACCES BONNET
8451	— JERSEYS,PULLOVERS ETC	W 3857	89.3	W 3564	93.7	W 3736	97.5	W 3935	100.0	CHANDAILS,PULL-OVERS ETC
846	UNDER GARMENTS KNITTED	W 5264	102.2	W 4963	117.5	W 5558	135.2	W 5891	131.1	SOUS VETS DE BONNETERIE
8462	— OF COTTON NON ELASTIC	W 4368	75.8	W 4125	86.1	W 4486	93.3	W 4977	96.9	SOUS-VET BONNET COTON
84629	—— OTHER	W 4208	72.9	W 4125	86.1	W 4486	93.3	W 4726	91.6	AUT SOUS-VET BONNET COTON
851	*FOOTWEAR	W 11697	157.8	W 8458	147.6	W 9425	177.2	W 10105	177.7	CHAUSSURES
85102	FOOTWEAR LEATHER	W 7586	122.1	W 5602	115.4	W 6359	139.0	W 6628	138.3	CHAUS SEMELLES EN CUIR
87	PRECISION INSTRUMNTS NES		412.6		532.8		544.9		538.9	INSTRUM,APPAR SCIENT NDA
872	MEDICAL INSTRUMENTS NES	W 1637	81.8	W 3306	96.3	W 1882	104.9	W 1744	106.9	INSTR,APP MEDIC-CHIR NDA
87202	OTH MEDICAL INSTRUMENTS	W 1462	74.0	W 3052	84.4	W 1622	90.2	W 1463	94.0	INSTRUM,APP MEDECINE
874	MEASURNG,CONTROLNG INSTR	W 3418	286.0	W 3674	365.7	W 4185	379.2	W 4589	367.8	INSTRUMENTS DE MESURE
8743	GAS,LIQUID CONTROL INSTR	W 1221	94.3	W 1237	113.5	W 1650	131.5	W 1868	116.3	APP,INSTR MESURE FLUIDES
8748	ELEC MEAS,CONTRL EQU NES	W 497	76.1	W 610	112.1	W 649	100.9	W 660	100.7	APP ELEC ELECTRO MESURE
87483	OTH ELCTRNC MEAS ETC EQU	W 413	68.7	W 521	102.5	W 567	90.1	W 578	93.4	AUT APP ELECTRO DE MESURE
88	PHOTO EQU,OPTICL GDS ETC		202.2		227.3		229.4		221.2	APP,FOURN PHOTO,OP,MONTR
882	PHOTO,CINEMA SUPPLIES	W 8506	101.9	W 8018	112.3	W 8190	113.8	W 8805	103.9	PRODUITS PHOTO,CINEMA
8822	PHOTO FILM EXC DEV CINMA	W 5048	78.5	W 5046	87.4	W 5094	89.5	W 5631	79.8	PLAQUES,PELLICULES,FILMS
89	MISC MANUFCTRD GOODS NES		851.3		980.1		1044.9		1059.2	ART MANUFACTURES DIVERS
892	PRINTED MATTER	W 16267	132.5	W 13045	124.3	W 14863	140.0	W 16819	140.8	IMPRIMES
893	ARTICLES OF PLASTIC NES		273.9		317.3		344.5		356.9	OUVRAGES EN MAT DIVIS 58
8939	MISC PLASTIC ARTICLES	W 37623	208.0	W 38975	242.3	W 42152	254.2	W 50331	270.8	ART DIVERS EN MAT DIV 58
89399	OTHR PLASTC ARTICLES NES	W 27742	175.8	W 28138	201.8	W 32597	220.0	W 38964	232.3	AUT OUV MAT DIV 58
894	TOYS,SPORTING GOODS,ETC	W 14646	135.4	W 14820	160.7	W 16686	175.2	W 17023	184.3	VOITURES ENFANTS,JOUETS
8942	TOYS,INDOOR GAMES ETC	W 9433	80.7	W 9807	98.1	W 10576	99.7	W 11141	103.7	JOUETS,JEUX ETC
898	MUSICAL INSTRUMENTS,PTS	W 5156	138.5	W 5366	201.2	W 5509	190.9	W 5865	188.0	INSTRUMENTS DE MUSIQUE
8983	SOUND RECRDNG TAPE,DISCS	W 4450	122.7	W 4686	185.6	W 4847	175.5	W 5135	171.5	SUPPORTS SON POUR 763
89832	RECORDED DISCS,TAPES ETC	W 2015	91.3	W 2184	157.7	W 2236	143.9	W 2442	139.1	DISQUES,PHONO,BANDES
899	OTHER MANUFACTURED GOODS		94.8		96.6		107.5		104.9	AUT ART MANUF DIVERS NDA
9	GOODS NOT CLASSD BY KIND		180.0		547.3		644.5		696.8	ART TRANSACT NON CLASSES
931	*SPECIAL TRANSACTIONS				484.4		506.1		517.6	TRANS.SPECIALES
951	*WAR FIREARMS,AMMUNITION		168.4		51.2		130.5		168.2	VEHIC BLINDES ARMES
95106	AMMUNITION NES		110.6		10.1		103.6		157.5	PROJECTILES,MUNITIONS

5. General Exports F.O.B. by Commodities according to the S.I.T.C. (Rev. 2) in million U.S. Dollars *
Exportations Générales F.O.B. par Produits d'après la C.T.C.I. (Rév. 2) en millions de Dollars E.U.

SITC CTCI	COMMODITY	1994 QUANTITY QUANTITE	1994 VALUE VALEUR	1995 QUANTITY QUANTITE	1995 VALUE VALEUR	1996 QUANTITY QUANTITE	1996 VALUE VALEUR	1997 QUANTITY QUANTITE	1997 VALUE VALEUR	PRODUIT
	ALL COMMODITIES		29764.9		40408.6		40561.6		40980.1	TOUS PRODUITS
0	FOOD AND LIVE ANIMALS		870.4		800.3		947.8		981.3	ALIMENTS,ANIMAUX VIVANTS
02	DAIRY PRODCTS,BIRDS'EGGS		150.6		205.4		228.8		262.6	PRODUITS LAITIERS,OEUFS
04	CEREALS AND PREPARATIONS		144.7		144.0		207.0		210.4	CEREALES ET PRODUITS
05	VEGETABLES AND FRUIT		188.6		66.7		70.6		63.9	LEGUMES ET FRUIT
057	FRUIT,NUTS,FRESH,DRIED	W 150119	124.7	W 21676	19.1	W 12307	12.9	W 4713	5.4	FRUITS FRAIS OU SECS
07	COFFEE,TEA,COCOA,SPICES		149.8		144.2		155.8		157.9	CAFE,THE,CACAO,EPICES
073	CHOCOLATE AND PRODUCTS	W 30394	102.2	W 24587	104.6	W 25407	106.1	W 25482	93.0	CHOCOLAT
09	MISC EDIBLE PRODUCTS		105.1		109.0		124.2		104.7	PREP ALIMENTAIRES DIVERSES
1	BEVERAGES AND TOBACCO		111.4		115.6		151.8		133.5	BOISSONS ET TABACS
11	BEVERAGES		92.5		91.7		113.9		94.0	BOISSONS
2	CRUDE MATERLS,EXCL FUELS		2945.3		3608.5		3100.0		3294.8	MAT BRUTES NON COMESTIBLES
21	HIDES,SKINS,FURS UNDRSSD		235.0		325.7		450.1		331.1	CUIRS,PEAUX BRUTS
212	FURSKINS,RAW	W 1232	209.9	W 1762	301.1	W 1827	428.5	W 2075	309.3	PELLETERIES BRUTES
21201	MINK SKINS,RAW	W 180	41.5	W 391	69.5	W 457	146.9	W 431	108.2	PEAUX DE VISON BRUTES
21209	OTHER FURSKINS,RAW	W 1051	168.5	W 1371	231.7	W 1370	281.7	W 1644	201.1	AUTRES PELLETERIES BRUTES
24	CORK AND WOOD		1705.3		1896.9		1567.3		1758.0	LIEGE ET BOIS
247	OTH WOOD ROUGH,SQUARED	W 1130272	130.0	W 797090	108.6	W 491345	79.8	W 549556	79.1	BOIS BRUTS EQUARRIS
2471	SAW–,VENEER–LOGS CONIFER	W 1130272	130.0	W 749327	100.2	W 479710	76.1	W 529331	74.1	CONIFERES POUR SCIAGE,PLACAG
24711	— IN THE ROUGH	W 1130272	130.0	W 749327	100.2	W 479710	76.1	W 529331	74.1	ECORCES OU DEGROSSIS
248	WOOD SHAPED,SLEEPERS	W 3974439	1565.7	W 3842438	1777.5	W 3614750	1474.9	W 3905336	1669.0	BOIS SIMPLEMENT TRAVAILLES
2482	LUMBER SHAPED CONIFER	W 3939331	1546.2	W 3818023	1761.2	W 3593658	1460.9	W 3886601	1655.5	CONIFERES SCIES,RABOTES
24821	LUMBER SAWN ETC CONIFER	W 3851729	1484.9	W 3761967	1710.9	W 3535199	1415.2	W 3836185	1613.4	CONIFERES SCIES LONGITUD
251	*PULP AND WASTE PAPER		723.9	W 1346886	1043.2	W 1585882	761.6	W 1802835	809.6	PATES A PAPIER,DECHETS
2517	SODA,SULPHATE WOOD PULP	W 1418851	689.0	W 1231911	985.2	W 1472017	723.2	W 1661633	764.9	PATES CHIMIQUES AU SULFATE
25172	— BLEACHED,NONDISSOLVNG	W 1382683	667.8	W 1200671	959.1	W 1442475	704.5	W 1630814	748.2	PATES BLANCHIES
26	TEXTILE FIBRES AND WASTE		97.9		103.3		80.2		96.7	FIBRES TEXTILES
267	OTHER MAN–MADE FIBRES		95.2		99.0		76.7		90.8	AUTR FIBR TEXT ARTIF SYNTH
27	CRUDE FERTLZR,MINRLS NES		93.3		99.0		97.7		97.8	ENGRAIS MINERAUX BRUTS
28	METALLIFEROUS ORES,SCRAP		81.2		130.2		131.4		189.9	MINERAIS METAL,DECHETS
3	MINERAL FUELS ETC		673.3		768.5		1250.1		965.1	COMBUSTIBLES MINERAUX LUB
33	PETROLEUM AND PRODUCTS		645.0		750.7		1050.8		904.1	PETROLE ET DERIVES
334	PETROLEUM PRODUCTS,REFIN	W 3571649	636.0	W 3889325	738.4	W 4688942	1035.6	W 4003138	887.8	PRODUITS RAFFINES
3341	GASOLINE,OTH LIGHT OILS	W 2356323	419.2	W 2356163	440.8	W 2897592	620.4	W 2432774	509.8	ESSENCES POUR MOTEURS
33411	MOTOR,AVIATION SPIRIT	W 2134974	381.5	W 887651	170.0	W 1451904	309.9	W 685478	143.4	ESSENCES MOTEURS D'AVIONS
33419	OTH LIGHT PETROLEUM OILS	W 221349	37.7	W 1468259	270.6	W 1445555	310.3	W 1747262	366.4	AUTRES HUILES LEGERES
3343	GAS OILS	W 1165089	184.9	W 36796	6.0	W 134	0.2	W 8	0.1	GAS OILS
3344	FUEL OILS,NES	W 207	0.1	W 1055624	177.8	W 1458727	292.3	W 1288454	250.7	FUEL OILS
351	*ELECTRIC CURRENT	H 630177	13.9		6.6		184.1		44.0	ENERGIE ELECTRIQUE
5	CHEMCLS,RELATED PROD NES		1894.4		2332.9		2431.1		2550.2	PRODUITS CHIMIQUES
51	ORGANIC CHEMICALS		337.4		382.4		366.8		387.1	PROD CHIMIQ ORGANIQUES
512	ALCOHOLS,PHENOLS ETC		102.8		106.9		84.9		94.8	PHENOLS,PHENOLS–ALCOOLS
516	OTHER ORGANIC CHEMICALS		105.9		124.5		143.7		155.4	AUTRES PROD ORGANIQUES
52	INORGANIC CHEMICALS		224.8		321.8		359.1		363.8	PROD CHIM INORGANIQUES
522	INORG ELEMNTS,OXIDES,ETC		102.3		134.2		154.6		171.7	ELEMENTS INORGANIQUES
523	OTHR INORG CHEMICALS ETC		119.3		184.3		201.3		189.1	AUT PRODUITS CHIMIQUES INORG
53	DYES,TANNING,COLOUR PROD		262.1		317.5		332.4		378.8	PROD TEINTURE,COLORANTS
533	PIGMENTS,PAINTS,ETC		249.8		298.3		309.9		352.8	PIGMENTS,PEINTURES,VERNIS
5331	COLOURING MATERIAL NES		157.5		184.5		160.7		155.2	AUT MATIERES COLORANTES
5334	VARNISHES,DISTEMPERS ETC		69.8		86.2	W 27993	107.2	W 37485	130.5	PEINTURES A L'EAU
541	*MEDICINAL,PHARM PRODUCT		192.2		214.4		205.0		214.5	PROD MEDICINAUX PHARMACEUT
5417	MEDICAMENTS	K 1218642	128.2	K 1618014	159.2	K 908164	143.8	K 1387056	151.5	MEDICAMENTS
54179	— CONTNG OTH SUBSTANCES	K 1048651	118.3	K 1566832	152.4	K 859751	134.3	K 1279109	139.6	MED CONT AUT SUBSTANCES
58	PLASTIC MATERIALS ETC		566.3		699.3		698.3		707.0	MAT PLAST ARTIFICIELLES
583	POLYMERIZATION ETC PRODS		471.2		579.4		571.0		582.6	PROD POLYMERISATION
5831	POLYETHYLENE		84.6		100.5		117.0		146.7	POLYETHYLENE
5839	OTH POLYMRZTION ETC PROD		195.0		224.9	W 131362	248.7	W 120974	239.5	AUT PROD POLYMER COPOLYM
59	CHEMICAL MATERIALS NES		162.4		224.4		237.5		258.3	MAT PROD CHIMIQUES NDA
598	MISCEL CHEM PRODUCTS NES		132.3		172.7		183.2		205.9	PROD DIV INDUST CHIM NDA
5989	CHEM PRODUCTS,PREPS NES	W 36052	83.0	W 56413	113.1	W 171057	124.5	W 125755	134.1	PROD PREP CHIMIQUES NDA
6	BASIC MANUFACTURES		11726.4		15730.0		14473.2		14426.8	ART MANUFACTURES
62	RUBBER MANUFACTURES NES		125.9		176.5		181.6		191.1	CAOUTCHOUC MANUFACTURE
625	RUBBER TYRES, TUBES ETC	W 25230	92.1	W 28832	128.8	W 28950	138.5	W 32183	149.3	PNEUS CAOUTCHOUC VULCANISE
63	WOOD,CORK MANUFACTRS NES		888.3		1021.4		1009.6		1036.6	OUVRAGES LIEGE ET BOIS
634	VENEERS,PLYWOOD,ETC	W 613425	529.0	W 570479	642.4	W 621888	615.9	W 652771	624.4	PLACAGES,CONTRE–PLAQUES
6342	PLYWOOD OF WOOD SHEETS	W 431536	459.0	W 387782	545.1	W 436605	529.7	W 482690	544.3	BOIS CONTRE–PLAQUES
635	WOOD MANUFACTURES NES		359.1	W 147548	378.8	W 172803	393.3	W 202185	412.1	ART MANUF EN BOIS NDA
6353	BUILDERS WOODWRK,PREFABS	W 161254	347.6	W 140210	366.6	W 163981	381.7	W 192162	400.0	OUVRAGES DE MENUISERIE
64	PAPER,PAPERBOARD AND MFR		6997.0		9772.9		8554.5		8434.5	PAPIERS,CARTONS & OUVRAGES
641	PAPER AND PAPERBOARD	MW 9930	6689.2	MW 9771	9313.1	MW 9231	8070.6	MW 10983	7967.6	PAPIERS ET CARTONS
6411	NEWSPRINT	W 1252541	559.9	W 1098951	727.9	W 1050550	734.0	W 1210942	629.9	PAPIER JOURNAL
6412	PRINTG,WRITING PAPER NES	W 3256025	2371.8	W 3425718	3585.7	W 3209289	2943.4	W 4136590	3115.2	PAPIERS POUR L'IMPRESSION
64121	— UNCOATED	W 377638	277.6	W 411937	466.3	W 464244	402.8	W 521924	410.9	PAPIERS IMPRES NON COUCHES
64122	— COATED,IMPREGNATD ETC	W 2878387	2094.2	W 3013781	3119.5	W 2745045	2540.6	W 3614665	2704.3	PAPIERS IMPRESSION COUCHES
6413	KRAFT PAPER,PAPERBOARD	W 797034	554.3	W 744027	693.5	W 655594	543.0	W 716750	519.7	PAPIER ET CARTON KRAFT
64131	KRAFT LINER IN BULK	W 196979	109.6	W 187997	149.9	W 193218	124.3	W 163388	93.3	PAP KRAFT POUR COUVERTURES
64139	KRAFT PAPER PAPERBD,NES	W 479026	370.2	W 446531	448.9	W 370930	338.7	W 438983	341.7	PAPIER,CARTON KRAFT NDA
6415	PAPER,PAPERBRD,BULK,NES	W 3289967	1903.3	W 3216617	2703.1	W 2936749	2263.8	W 3391451	2131.2	PAPIERS,CARTONS ROULEAUX
64151	SEMI–CHEM FLUTING PAPER	W 416730	133.7	W 403394	209.2	W 383778	145.1	W 406616	126.1	PAPIER FLUTING
64153	GREASEPROOF ETC PAPER	W 46634	71.4	W 38707	74.3	W 47588	81.4	W 88484	125.9	PAP,CARTONS PARCHEMINES
64159	OTHER PAPER ETC,BULK,NES	W 2826595	1698.3	W 2774375	2419.3	W 2504992	2036.3	W 2895524	1878.2	AUT PAPIER ROULEAUX FEUILLES
6418	COATED ETC PAPER NES BLK	W 1159051	1166.2	W 1129630	1437.3	W 1226770	1437.1	W 1374758	1441.9	PAP,CARTONS COUCHES,ENDUITS
64181	PLASTIC COATED PAPER ETC	W 334290	351.4	W 248981	348.5	W 260839	338.9	W 344544	390.7	PAP,CARTONS ENDUITS,RESINES
64189	COATED PAPER ETC NES	W 809182	797.7	W 870066	1073.6	W 957140	1087.4	W 1019985	1040.0	PAPIERS,CARTONS COUCHES
642	PAPER,ETC,PRECUT,ARTS OF	W 250941	307.9	W 263469	459.9	W 299026	484.0	W 316851	466.9	PAP,CARTONS DECOUPES
6421	PAPER ETC CONTAINERS	W 37878	68.6	W 48584	112.1	W 58138	129.7	W 69156	134.5	BOITES,SACS EMBALLAGES
6428	PAPER ETC ARTICLES NES	W 169019	166.4	W 162345	242.7	W 190096	252.3	W 202765	251.9	OUVRAGES EN PATE A PAPIER
65	TEXTILE YARN,FABRICS,ETC		290.0		365.2		375.7		379.0	FILS,TISSUS,ARTICLES TEXTILE
657	SPECIAL TXTL FABRC,PRODS	W 30259	143.4	W 31180	187.6	W 36837	201.5	W 42202	208.3	TISSUS SPECIAUX
66	NONMETAL MINERAL MFS NES		363.0		457.1		463.6		482.9	ART MIN NON METALLIQUES
663	MINERAL MANUFCTURES NES		92.5		117.1		115.9		118.1	ART MIN MANUF NDA
664	GLASS		191.2		243.3		252.9		253.1	VERRE
6647	SAFETY GLASS CUT OR NOT	W 27555	110.9	W 27225	126.4	W 26785	120.9	W 32836	130.0	GLACES DE SECURITE
67	IRON AND STEEL		1707.9		2224.1		2085.9		1922.8	FER ET ACIER
672	IRON,STEEL PRIMARY FORMS		231.6		265.6		259.9		265.0	LINGOTS FER,ACIER
6727	IRN,STL COIL FR REROLLNG		186.7		209.4		185.5		177.8	EBAUCHES POUR TOLES FER
67274	STNLESS STEEL ETC COILS	W 66450	100.7	W 52951	143.6	W 54477	99.7	W 79978	119.4	EBAUCHES ACIER INOXYDBLE
673	IRON,STEEL SHAPES ETC	W 386441	166.8	W 409836	227.4	W 416080	221.4	W 465397	212.6	BARRES,PROFIL FER,ACIER
6732	IRON,STEEL BARS ETC	W 165808	82.3	W 197856	131.2	W 162505	105.8	W 179312	97.7	BARRES FER,ACIER
674	IRN,STL UNIV,PLATE,SHEET		989.5		1287.6		1220.0		1057.8	LARGES PLATS,TOLES
6744	IRN,STL HVY PLATE,ROLLED		175.7		213.3		250.9		198.3	TOLES LAMINEES PLUS 4.75 MM

5. General Exports F.O.B. by Commodities according to the S.I.T.C. (Rev. 2) in million U.S. Dollars
Exportations Générales F.O.B. par Produits d'après la C.T.C.I. (Rév. 2) en millions de Dollars E.U.

SITC CTCI	COMMODITY	1994 QUANTITY QUANTITE	1994 VALUE VALEUR	1995 QUANTITY QUANTITE	1995 VALUE VALEUR	1996 QUANTITY QUANTITE	1996 VALUE VALEUR	1997 QUANTITY QUANTITE	1997 VALUE VALEUR	PRODUIT
67441	— OF IRON OR SIMPLE STL		135.9		127.4		175.9		128.6	TOLES NON ACIER FIN CARB
6745	IRN,STL MED PLATE,ROLLED		102.2		159.6		133.3		101.4	TOLES 3 A 4.75 MM
67453	— OF STAINLESS ETC STL	W 43533	78.4	W 43320	123.9	W 42101	90.2	W 38900	70.6	TOLES ACIER INOXYDABLE
6746	IRN,STL THIN PLATE,ROLLD		479.7		616.5		543.2		517.6	TOLES LAM MOINS 3MM
67463	— OF STAINLESS ETC STL	W 216890	373.4	W 195766	509.1	W 198801	411.9	W 231068	419.0	TOL ACIER INOX MOINS 3 MM
6749	OTH IRN,STL PLATES,SHEET		231.9		297.9	W 366901	292.6		240.2	AUTRES TOLES FER,ACIER
67491	— OF IRON OR SIMPLE STL		198.2		242.5	W 334162	249.8		195.0	AUT TOLES AUTRES ACIER FIN
678	IRON,STL TUBES,PIPES,ETC		233.0		322.7		292.6		293.5	TUBES,TUYAUX EN FONTE,FER
6783	IRON,STL TUBES,PIPES NES		192.8		269.0		242.2		244.9	AUT TUBES,TUYAUX FER,ACIER
68	NON-FERROUS METALS		791.9		1008.5		1029.6		1173.1	METAUX NON FERREUX
682	COPPER EXC CEMENT COPPER	W 128454	392.6	W 123928	509.9	W 153622	480.0	W 199441	568.8	CUIVRE
6821	COPPER NES,ALLOYS,UNWRT	W 48235	115.3	W 39010	120.4	W 76765	181.2	W 106946	217.6	CUIVRE BRUT
6822	COPPER,ALLOYS WORKED	W 80219	277.4	W 84918	389.5	W 76857	298.9	W 92495	351.2	CUIVRE,ALLIAGES OUVRES
68222	COPPER PLATE,SHEET,STRIP	W 30763	104.4	W 33382	147.0	W 42368	155.7	W 38718	137.8	TOLES DE PLUS 0.15 MM
68225	COPPER TUBES,PIPES,ETC	W 29573	105.6	W 31598	149.3	W 19832	81.9	W 30703	121.2	TUBES,TUYAUX EN CUIVRE
683	NICKEL	W 12617	77.2	W 13103	108.9	W 22092	169.7	W 24748	172.5	NICKEL
6831	NICKEL,ALLOYS UNWROUGHT	W 12532	76.5	W 12847	106.7	W 21475	164.9	W 23692	165.6	NICKEL ET ALLIAGES BRUTS
684	ALUMINIUM	W 47259	104.6	W 46491	138.6	W 47789	112.6	W 56258	132.0	ALUMINIUM
686	ZINC	W 142234	137.9		137.3		146.5		173.6	ZINC
6861	ZINC,ALLOYS UNWROUGHT	W 141693	136.6	W 130308	135.7	W 140236	143.9	W 133588	171.4	ZINC ET ALLIAGES BRUTS
69	METAL MANUFACTURES NES		494.2		632.6		668.6		705.4	ART MANUFACT EN METAL NDA
691	STRUCTURES AND PARTS NES	W 99176	195.8	W 124153	289.3	W 137015	296.2	W 185488	327.3	CONSTRUCT FER,ACIER,ALU
6911	STRUCTURES,PARTS IRN,STL	W 95868	173.0	W 120780	257.2	W 133749	268.6	W 182224	301.2	CONSTRUCT FER,ACIER,FONTE
699	BASE METAL MFRS NES	W 41062	150.9		170.7		176.2	W 34892	191.0	ART MANUFACTURES MET NDA
7	MACHINES,TRANSPORT EQUIP		9474.8		14264.0		15532.6		15884.2	MACHINES MATERIEL TRANSPORT
71	POWER GENERATING EQUIPMT		832.7		1079.4		1215.0		1105.4	MACHINES GENERATRICES
711	STEAM BOILERS & AUX PLNT	W 10737	100.5	W 14806	123.5	W 16544	123.0	W 15482	125.3	GENERATEURS VAPEUR EAU ETC
713	INTRNL COMBUS PSTN ENGIN	W 11980	194.6	W 15602	215.0	W 16451	235.2	W 18945	265.5	MOTEURS EXPL COMB INT, PIECE
7139	PISTON ENGINE PARTS NES	W 5964	130.4	W 8677	119.0	W 6106	97.4	W 8147	136.9	PIECES POUR 713.2,3,8
716	ROTATING ELECTRIC PLANT	W 47073	507.5	W 59217	692.8	W 68801	797.6	W 63654	663.7	APP ELECTR ROTATIFS,PIECES
7162	AC MTRS,GENRTRS,GEN SETS	W 43419	457.3	W 53329	619.8	W 60362	692.1	W 56362	594.9	MOTEURS ELECTRIQUES
71621	AC MTRS,INC UNIVRSL MTRS	W 21825	158.4	W 25094	187.2	W 28472	225.3	W 27825	196.7	MOT ELEC NON COUR CONTINU
71623	GEN SETS WITH PISTN ENGN	W 20305	280.0	W 24874	408.7	W 28188	430.8	W 23772	360.5	GROUPES MOTEUR EXPLOSION
72	MACHS FOR SPCL INDUSTRYS		1557.4		2252.5		2292.2		2449.7	MAC SPECIALES POUR INDUST
722	TRACTORS NON-ROAD	W 19730	142.3	W 24738	238.8	W 26626	263.7	W 31570	275.1	TRACTEURS
7224	WHEELED TRACTORS NES	W 19583	140.8	W 24738	238.8	W 26589	263.6	W 31414	274.9	TRACTEURS A ROUES
723	CIVIL ENGNEERG EQUIP ETC	W 21043	215.7	W 19741	295.8	W 21342	306.1	W 24508	335.9	APPAREILS DE GENIE CIVIL
7234	CONST,MINING MACHNRY NES	W 19851	181.3	W 18088	248.6	W 19553	255.4	W 22222	276.9	MACH POUR LA CONST, MINES
72343	SLFPRP CONST ETC MCH NES	W 5762	83.2	W 5787	108.0	W 6296	114.3	W 7909	133.8	AUT MACH EXTR,TERRASSEM
725	PAPER ETC MILL MACHINERY	W 40611	526.8	W 76637	921.3	W 55005	884.6	W 62689	885.0	MACHINES FABR PATE PAPIER
7251	PAPER,PULP MAKING MACHRY	W 24483	305.1	W 50421	491.1	W 35540	501.5	W 40724	519.8	MACHINES FABR PATE CARTON
72511	CELLULOSE PULP MFG MACHY	W 10846	147.5	W 31011	258.9	W 14970	221.0	W 21297	190.6	MACH FABR PATE CELLULOSE
72512	PAPER ETC MAKING ETC MCH	W 13637	157.6	W 19409	232.3	W 20570	280.6	W 19427	329.3	MACH FABR FINITION DU PAP
7259	PTS NES OF MACHS OF 725	W 13423	187.6	W 22538	376.0	W 16064	320.2	W 18281	294.5	PIECES GROUPE 725
72591	PTS NES OF MACHS OF 7251	W 12585	173.6	W 21655	355.8	W 15517	306.1	W 17634	277.6	PIECES DU 725.1
728	OTH MACHY FOR SPCL INDUS	W 44725	560.6	W 45589	684.7	W 43989	710.8	W 57484	805.7	AUT MACH IND PARTICULIERES
7281	MACH-TOOLS FR SPCL INDUS	W 8740	97.8	W 5163	78.3	W 4977	65.1	W 7055	86.0	MACH-OUTILS SPEC IND PART
7283	OTHR MINERAL WORKG MACHY	W 15245	92.9	W 18095	137.3	W 15917	123.4	W 18334	139.4	MACH TRIER,CRIBLER,BROYER
7284	MACHY FOR SPCL INDUS NES	W 20739	370.0	W 22331	469.3	W 23094	522.4	W 32095	580.4	MACH SPEC IND PARTICUL.
72848	OTH MCHY WITH INDIV FNCT	W 11299	240.2	W 10510	268.1	W 12369	325.9	W 14984	351.9	AUTRES MACHINES NDA
73	METALWORKING MACHINERY		153.1		209.1		232.2		221.9	MACH TRAVAIL DES METAUX
736	METALWORKING MACH-TOOLS	W 6229	86.2	W 7686	134.6	W 8753	161.2	W 9887	143.9	MACH-OUTILS TRAVAIL METAUX
74	GENRL INDUSTRL MACHY NES		1322.5		1765.4		1778.6		1763.8	MACH APP INDUSTRIE
741	HEATING,COOLING EQUIPMNT	W 21165	199.8	W 22872	255.9	W 23110	264.7	W 25974	265.6	MACH CHAUFFAGE,PIECES
742	PUMPS FOR LIQUIDS ETC	W 4829	74.2	W 6038	101.3	W 6428	123.2	W 6461	113.3	POMPES MOTO-POMPES
743	PUMPS NES,CENTRFUGES ETC	W 8193	128.5	W 8416	153.6	W 8720	176.6	W 10916	194.0	POMPES COMPRES,VENT ETC
7436	GAS,LIQUID FILTERS ETC	W 4713	81.5	W 4857	90.9	W 5013	106.8	W 6945	126.2	APP POUR FILT DES LIQUIDES
744	MECHANICAL HANDLING EQU	W 73804	588.4	W 85421	782.3	W 77794	729.6	W 87389	745.8	EQUIP MANUTENTION PIECES
7441	FORK LIFT TRCKS,ETC,PTS	W 12435	85.9	W 19424	157.6	W 20818	181.6	W 18886	144.6	CHARIOTS POUR USINES ETC
74411	FORK LIFT TRUCKS ETC	W 12416	85.7	W 19393	157.3	W 20737	180.8	W 18819	144.1	CHARIOTS POUR LES GARES
7442	LIFTING,LOADING MACH NES	W 40531	282.7	W 41648	345.5	W 36575	316.1	W 44621	346.1	APP LEVAGE,MANUTENTION
74428	OTH HANDLING ETC MCH NES	W 22048	172.2	W 23206	218.4	W 20886	204.5	W 23800	202.3	AUT APP LEVAGE ETC
7449	PTS NES OF MACHY OF 7442	W 20838	220.0	W 24348	279.2	W 20402	231.9	W 23882	255.3	PIECES DU 744.2
745	NONELEC MACHY,TOOLS NES	W 4518	71.8	W 7009	126.7	W 6385	110.8	W 4743	100.6	AUT MACH NON ELEC,PIECES
749	NONELEC MACH PTS,ACC NES	W 14541	260.0	W 17555	345.9	W 18701	373.9	W 18814	344.8	PIECES MACH NON ELEC NDA
7492	COCKS,VALVES ETC NES	W 8477	173.4	W 8978	222.2	W 9444	232.4	W 10194	220.5	ART ROB,SIM POUR TUYAUX
75	OFFICE MACHNES,ADP EQUIP		868.7		1070.2		998.0		1146.9	MACH BUREAU TRAIT AUTOM
752	AUTOMTIC DATA PROC EQUIP	W 16581	721.7	W 23396	918.5	W 22590	884.5	W 27993	1019.6	MACH TRAIT INFORMATION
7522	DIGITAL COMPUTERS	W 81	10.6	W 5986	404.3	W 315	49.6	W 329	75.2	MACH DIGITALES COMPLETES
7523	DIGITL CENTRL PROCESSORS	W 3531	335.4	W 287	23.9	W 3404	307.4	W 3273	299.1	UNITES CENTRALES
7525	ADP PERIPHERAL UNITS	W 12683	329.9	W 16874	463.5	W 18515	487.3	W 24054	601.0	UNITES PERIPHERIQUES
759	OFFICE,ADP MCH PTS,ACCES	W 1261	128.1	W 1530	137.2	W 1919	100.0	W 1962	103.3	PIECES DU 751 ET 752
7599	ACCTG,ETC,ADP MCH PTS,AC	W 1102	123.0	W 1409	133.7	W 1670	94.9	W 1806	98.9	PIECES DU 751 ET 752
76	TELECOMM,SOUND EQUIPMENT		1980.6		3482.5		4103.7		4798.5	EQUIPMENT DE TELECOM
761	TELEVISION RECEIVERS	W 10804	159.4	W 10444	190.9	W 6674	129.6	W 11692	178.5	RECEPTEURS DE TELEVISION
7611	COLOUR TV RECEIVERS	W 10794	159.0	W 10441	190.6	W 6666	128.5	W 11674	175.4	RECEPTEURS COULEUR
764	TELECOM EQPT,PTS,ACC NES	W 9246	1797.0	W 12281	3277.9	W 14448	3946.2	W 19180	4575.9	EQUIP TELECOM,PIECES
7641	LINE TELEPHONE,ETC EQUIP	W 1631	422.1	W 2171	853.7	W 2429	1092.8	W 2988	1454.0	APP TELEPHON PAR FIL
7643	TV,RADIO TRANSMITTRS ETC	W 3395	874.0	W 4571	1689.8	W 4895	2017.4	W 6301	2230.9	APP EMET TELE RADIO
7649	PTS NES OF EQUIPMT OF 76	W 3340	486.8	W 4088	701.8	W 5396	797.9	W 8247	863.3	PIECES DE LA DIV 76
76491	PTS NES OF APPAR OF 7641	W 713	209.9	W 737	192.3	W 933	260.5	W 907	356.4	PIECES POUR 764.1
76493	TELECOMM EQUIPMT PTS NES	W 2561	272.9	W 3324	505.7	W 3996	524.7	W 7310	503.5	PIECES 761,762,764.3,8
77	ELECTRIC MACHNRY NES ETC		1282.3		1810.3		1981.0		2100.2	MACH APP ELECT NDA
771	ELECTRIC POWER MACHY NES	W 30787	357.7	W 37455	577.5	W 34580	625.4	W 37796	626.7	MACH PROD,TRANS ELECTR
7712	OTH ELEC POWER MACHY NES	W 22617	306.8	W 29294	494.5	W 26827	542.4	W 30438	563.3	AUT APP PROD TRANSF ELEC
77121	STATIC CONVERTERS ETC	W 4631	216.5	W 11354	371.5	W 7417	420.3	W 9298	445.0	CONVERTISSEURS STATIQUES
772	SWITCHGEAR ETC,PARTS NES	W 8483	226.1	W 8805	271.3	W 9380	291.3	W 10747	313.5	APP COUPURE,SECT ETC
7721	SWITCHGEAR ETC	W 8052	198.7	W 8511	245.4	W 9075	266.3	W 10128	272.5	APP COUPURE,SECTIONMNT
773	ELECTR DISTRIBUTNG EQUIP	W 29450	140.5	W 28233	175.9	W 35780	205.0	W 44640	244.8	EQUIPMT DISTRIBUTION ELECT
7731	INSULATED WIRE,CABLE ETC	W 29156	137.8	W 27997	172.8	W 35493	200.8	W 44236	239.5	FILS,CABLES ISOLES ELECT
774	ELECTRO-MEDCL,XRAY EQUIP	W 1377	182.2	W 1433	215.4	W 1885	250.6	W 2362	282.1	APPAREILS MEDICAUX
7741	ELECTRO-MEDICAL EQUIPMNT	W 422	99.7	W 551	123.1	W 928	157.2	W 1274	180.4	APP ELECTRICITE MEDICALE
775	HOUSEHOLD TYPE EQUIP NES	W 12173	85.1	W 13001	111.7	W 19037	194.6	W 33078	236.2	MACH,APP USAGE DOMESTQUE
776	TRANSISTORS,VALVES,ETC	W 238	87.5	W 673	119.7	W 922	121.9	W 2453	141.3	LAMPES,TUBES,VALVES
778	ELECTRICAL MACHINERY NES	W 7974	203.4	W 7670	339.1	W 6998	292.6	W 14423	255.9	AUTRES MACH ELECT NDA
7781	BATTERIES,ACCUMULATORS	W 4375	75.1	W 3758	187.2	W 2943	141.0	W 9087	79.4	PILES ET ACCUMULATEURS
77812	ELECTRIC ACCUMULATORS	W 4118	73.7	W 3464	182.5	W 2359	136.7	W 8413	74.5	ACCUMULATEURS ELECTRIQ
7788	OTH ELEC MACHY,EQUIP NES	W 2020	95.5	W 2225	113.3	W 2135	111.7	W 2823	130.9	AUT MACH APP ELEC NDA
78	ROAD VEHICLES		901.3		1166.7		1197.1		1260.8	VEHICULES ROUTIERS
781	PASS MOTOR VEH EXC BUSES	W 43246	372.2	W 46206	559.5	W 49366	609.3	W 59120	645.1	AUTO TRANSPORT PERSONNES
782	LORRIES,SPCL MTR VEH NES	W 32532	191.3	W 23595	198.5	W 19018	177.5	W 22371	204.7	VEHICULES SPECIAUX,MARCH

5. General Exports F.O.B. by Commodities according to the S.I.T.C. (Rev. 2) in million U.S. Dollars
Exportations Générales F.O.B. par Produits d'après la C.T.C.I. (Rév. 2) en millions de Dollars E.U.

SITC CTCI	COMMODITY	1994		1995		1996		1997		PRODUIT
		QUANTITY QUANTITE	VALUE VALEUR	QUANTITY QUANTITE	VALUE VALEUR	QUANTITY QUANTITE	VALUE VALEUR	QUANTITY QUANTITE	VALUE VALEUR	
7821	LORRIES,TRUCKS	W 27015	128.0	W 18444	119.3	W 15056	117.9	W 17624	129.7	VEHICULES TRANSP MARCHAND
784	MOTOR VEH PRTS,ACCES NES	W 31470	159.8	W 37964	222.8	W 32927	224.0	W 37186	223.3	PIECES 722,781,782,783
7849	OTHER MOTOR VEHCL PARTS	W 30172	146.5	W 37076	210.2	W 31197	203.9	W 35562	204.6	PIECES 722,781,782,783
79	OTHR TRANSPORT EQUIPMENT		576.6		1428.3		1735.4		1037.3	AUTRE MATERIEL TRANSPORT
793	SHIPS AND BOATS ETC		519.6		1292.9		1645.6	W 96684	911.9	NAVIRES BATEAUX,ETC
7932	SHIPS AND BOATS NES	W 248945	431.3	W 169415	1199.2	W 171313	1515.0	W 76287	713.0	NAVIRES ET BATEAUX
79322	TANKERS OF ALL KINDS	W 52811	36.1	W 48610	221.9	W 70000	402.1	W 35000	200.0	BATEAUX–CITERNES
79323	OTHER CARGO VESSELS	W 72068	316.0	W 118342	913.7	W 98204	1040.9	W 37483	429.1	AUT BATEAUX TRANS MARCH
7938	TUGS,SPECIAL VESSELS ETC		4.1	W 329	2.7	W 36418	124.9	W 10955	113.8	REMORQUEURS,BATEAUX SPEC
79382	SPECL PURPOSE VESSLS ETC	N 9	2.3	W 125	1.7	W 36110	123.6	W 10114	112.0	BAT–PHARES,–POMPES,DRAGUES
8	MISC MANUFACTURED GOODS		2028.5		2339.2		2345.5		2437.0	ART MANUFACTURES DIVERS
812	*PLUMBG,HEATNG,LGHTNG EQ		220.3		210.2		223.2		210.5	APPAR SANITAIRES CHAUFFAGE
8121	CENTRAL HEATING EQUIPMNT	W 36847	110.1	W 30906	87.1	W 34302	94.9	W 31414	79.4	CHAUDIERES,RADIATEURS
821	*FURNITURE,PARTS THEREOF	W 72982	328.1	W 63340	366.9	W 60310	326.8	W 65639	320.2	MEUBLES ET PIECES
8219	FURNITURE AND PARTS NES	W 62734	214.6	W 54738	231.0	W 51956	213.0	W 55872	205.9	AUTRES MEUBLES ET PIECES
82192	WOOD FURNITURE NES	W 41366	153.8	W 33974	156.4	W 31934	141.2	W 35431	130.4	MEUBLES NDA EN BOIS
84	CLOTHING AND ACCESSORIES		251.8		273.2		261.6		251.4	VETEMENTS
87	PRECISION INSTRUMNTS NES		369.3		493.6		496.6		582.3	INSTRUM,APPAR SCIENT NDA
874	MEASURNG,CONTROLNG INSTR	W 2178	298.3	W 3345	412.2	W 2587	384.5	W 3542	460.4	INSTRUMENTS DE MESURE
8743	GAS,LIQUID CONTROL INSTR	W 838	104.3	W 1326	144.0	W 1119	127.3	W 1767	156.2	APP,INSTR MESURE FLUIDES
89	MISC MANUFCTRD GOODS NES		747.8		869.2		897.0		944.2	ART MANUFACTURES DIVERS
892	PRINTED MATTER	W 101867	243.3	W 127612	360.7	W 132831	377.3	W 157774	371.2	IMPRIMES
8922	NEWSPAPERS,PERIODICALS	W 40564	83.8	W 68073	152.9	W 79136	173.0	W 70500	156.5	JOURNAUX ET PERIODIQUES
8928	PRINTED MATTER NES	W 47238	112.6	W 45559	138.6	W 41206	140.1	W 74022	153.6	IMPRIMES NDA
893	ARTICLES OF PLASTIC NES		261.7		253.6		263.9		277.5	OUVRAGES EN MAT DIVIS 58
8939	MISC PLASTIC ARTICLES	W 37538	187.8	W 30069	176.2	W 32494	182.7	W 35724	193.6	ART DIVERS EN MAT DIV 58
89399	OTHR PLASTC ARTICLES NES	W 32452	172.2	W 26121	159.6	W 28513	167.0	W 31451	178.5	AUT OUV MAT DIV 58
894	TOYS,SPORTING GOODS,ETC	W 12998	124.8	W 10861	135.4	W 11703	133.4	W 12326	123.5	VOITURES ENFANTS,JOUETS
9	GOODS NOT CLASSD BY KIND		22.2		418.8		297.0		263.9	ART TRANSACT NON CLASSES
931	*SPECIAL TRANSACTIONS				357.3		240.8		210.2	TRANS.SPECIALES

FOOT NOTES – NOTES

TABLE 1 –

1 The gold trade excludes partly–worked gold, which is included in merchandise trade.

TABLEAU 1 –

1 Le commerce de l'or exclut l'or partiellement travail lé qui est compris dans le commerce de marchandises.

1. HISTORICAL SERIES, 1962–1997 SPECIAL TRADE, IMPORTS C.I.F., EXPORTS F.O.B.
SERIES HISTORIQUES, 1962–1997 COMMERCE SPECIAL, IMPORTATIONS C.A.F., EXPORTATIONS F.O.B

YEAR ANNEE	VALUE IN MILLION FRENCH FRANCS / VALEUR EN MILLION FRENCH FRANCS: MERCHANDISE –MARCHANDISE IMPORTS	MERCHANDISE –MARCHANDISE EXPORTS	GOLD # 1 –OR IMPORTS	GOLD # 1 –OR EXPORTS	CONVERSION FACTORS U.S. CENTS PER FRENCH FRANC FACTEURS DE CONVERSION CENTS E.U. PAR FRENCH FRANC IMPORTS	EXPORTS	INDEX NUMBERS –INDICES: QUANTUM IMPORTS	QUANTUM EXPORTS	UNIT VALUE VALEUR UNITAIRE IMPORTS	UNIT VALUE VALEUR UNITAIRE EXPORTS
1962	37101.00	36333.00	449.00	115.00	20.2550	20.2550				
1963	43073.00	39890.00	1688.00	135.00	20.2550	20.2550				
1964	49700.00	44386.00			20.2550	20.2550				
1965	51029.00	49609.00			20.2550	20.2550				
1966	58453.00	53782.00			20.2550	20.2550				
1967	61251.00	56198.00			20.2550	20.2550				
1968	69029.00	62723.00			20.2550	20.2550				
1969	90023.00	77759.00			19.3200	19.3200				
1970	106190.00	99641.00			18.0000	18.0000				
1971	117997.00	113970.00			18.0700	18.0700				
1972	135606.00	131497.00			19.8269	19.8315				
1973	166123.00	159714.00			22.5579	22.5660				
1974	254651.00	220213.00			20.8098	20.8216				
1975	231269.00	223362.00			23.3459	23.3824				
1976	308012.00	266228.00			20.9027	20.9217				
1977	346207.00	311550.00			20.3537	20.3616				
1978	368401.00	344594.00			22.1937	22.2006				
1979	457128.00	414677.00			23.5355	23.5297				
1980	570778.00	469694.00			23.6663	23.6566	71	70	68	63
1981	654239.00	549500.00			18.4753	18.4478	68	72	82	70
1982	757595.00	606094.00			15.2647	15.2829	69	70	92	80
1983	799754.00	694659.00			13.1784	13.1332	67	72	100	87
1984	905421.00	813003.00			11.4744	11.4655	69	76	110	95
1985	962746.00	870812.00			11.1984	11.2117	72	79	111	98
1986	895891.90	863539.90			14.4476	14.4594	77	78	93	94
1987	949817.00	888912.90			16.6873	16.6948	82	81	92	93
1988	1053798.00	997648.90			16.8237	16.8208	90	88	95	96
1989	1216839.00	1102501.00			15.6933	15.6982	95	95	101	102
1990	1266788.00	1142182.00			18.4093	18.4007	100	100	100	100
1991	1297131.00	1200488.00			17.7956	17.7795	102	105	99	100
1992	1263933.00	1227504.00			18.8993	18.8930	104	109	95	97
1993	1135291.00	1166648.00			17.6827	17.6773	107	111	91	94
1994	1276609.00	1306033.00			18.0665	18.0755	117	120	94	100
1995	1381278.00	1432334.00			20.0525	20.0605	123	129	96	102
1996	1434754.00	1476998.00			19.5459	19.5436	126	134	96	102
1997	1560308.00	1684318.00			17.1567	17.1504			98	103

2. IMPORTS BY BROAD ECONOMIC CATEGORY AND EXPORTS BY INDUSTRIAL ORIGIN. (PERCENTAGE OF TOTAL VALUE)
IMPORTATIONS PAR CATEGORIES ECONOMIQUES ET EXPORTATIONS PAR BRANCHE D'ACTIVITE.(EN POURCENTAGE DE LA VALEUR TOTALE)

IMPORTS – IMPORTATIONS

	1991	1992	1993	1994	1995	1996	1997
TOTAL IMPORTS–IMPORTATIONS TOTALES	100.	100.	100.	100.	100.	100.	100.
1 FOOD BEV–ALIMENTATION BOISSONS	9.1	9.3	9.7	9.7	9.4	9.0	8.6
11 PRIMARY–PRODUITS DE BASE	5.0	5.0	5.1	5.2	4.8	4.4	4.2
111 FOR INDUSTRY–POUR L'INDUSTRIE	0.8	0.7	0.8	1.0	0.9	0.8	0.8
112 FOR HOUSEHOLDS–POUR LES MENAGES	4.3	4.2	4.3	4.2	3.9	3.6	3.4
12 PROCESSED–PRODUITS ELABORES	4.0	4.3	4.6	4.6	4.6	4.6	4.4
121 FOR INDUSTRY–POUR L'INDUSTRIE	0.6	0.6	0.6	0.6	0.6	0.6	0.6
122 FOR HOUSEHOLDS–POUR LES MENAGES	3.5	3.7	4.0	3.9	4.0	4.0	3.8
2 IND SUPPLIES–APPROV INDUSTRIELS	29.5	29.4	28.7	30.0	31.3	29.0	29.3
21 PRIMARY–PRODUITS DE BASE	2.5	2.4	2.3	2.4	2.4	2.1	2.1
22 PROCESSED–PRODUITS ELABORES	26.9	27.0	26.4	27.6	28.9	27.0	27.2
3 FUELS–COMBUSTIBLES	9.6	8.5	8.8	7.6	6.7	8.2	8.1
31 PRIMARY–PRODUITS DE BASE	7.1	6.2	6.5	5.6	5.2	6.4	6.5
32 PROCESSED–PRODUITS ELABORES	2.5	2.3	2.3	1.9	1.5	1.8	1.6
321 MOTOR SPIRIT–ESSENCE					0.4	0.4	0.4
322 OTHER–AUTRES	2.5	2.3	2.3	1.9	1.1	1.3	1.2
4 MACHINERY–EQUIPEMENT	20.4	20.2	19.8	20.1	21.0	21.5	22.3
41 CAPITAL EQUIPMENT–MACHINES	16.2	16.0	15.3	15.3	15.7	16.2	16.7
42 PARTS–PIECES ACCESSOIRES	4.2	4.2	4.4	4.8	5.3	5.3	5.6
5 TRANSPORT–TRANSPORT	14.6	15.2	15.0	15.5	14.7	15.1	14.4
51 PASSENGER CARS–AUTOMOBILES	5.0	5.7	5.8	5.6	5.4	5.9	4.5
52 OTHER–AUTRES	3.2	2.8	2.5	3.0	3.2	2.9	2.8
521 INDUSTRIAL–INDUSTRIELS	2.9	2.5	2.2	2.7	3.0	2.6	2.5
522 NON INDUSTRIAL–NON INDUSTRIEL	0.3	0.3	0.4	0.3	0.3	0.3	0.3
53 PARTS–PIECES ACCESSOIRES	6.3	6.7	6.6	6.9	6.1	6.3	7.0
6 CONSUM GOODS–BIENS CONSOMMATION	16.9	17.3	18.1	17.0	16.9	17.1	17.3
61 DURABLE–DURABLES	4.6	4.4	4.5	4.2	4.0	4.0	3.9
62 SEMI DURABLE–SEMI DURABLES	9.2	9.6	10.0	9.2	9.0	9.2	9.4
63 NON DURABLE–NON DURABLES	3.1	3.3	3.6	3.6	3.8	3.9	4.0
7 GOODS NES–BIENS NDA	0.2	0.1	0.1	0.1	0.1	0.1	0.1

EXPORTS – EXPORTATIONS

	1991	1992	1993	1994	1995	1996	1997
TOTAL EXPORTS–EXPORTATIONS TOTALES	100.	100.	100.	100.	100.	100.	100.
1 AGRICULTURE	5.8	5.7	5.7	4.7	4.4	4.5	4.2
2 MINING QUARRY–INDUS EXTRACTIVES	0.6	0.6	0.6	0.5	0.5	0.5	0.4
3 MANUFACTURING–IND MANUFACTUR	93.6	93.7	93.8	94.8	95.1	95.1	95.4
31 FOOD BEV TOBACCO–ALIM BOISS TAB	10.3	10.5	11.0	10.9	10.4	10.3	9.9
32 TEXTILES–INDUSTRIES TEXTILES	6.1	6.1	6.0	5.9	5.7	5.6	5.4
33 WOOD & PRODUCTS–BOIS & PRODUITS	0.6	0.6	0.6	0.6	0.6	0.6	0.6
34 PAPER & PRODUCTS–PAPIER & PRODT	2.9	2.9	2.8	2.9	3.1	2.8	2.7
35 CHEMICALS–INDUSTRIES CHIMIQUES	18.0	17.8	18.8	18.8	16.8	18.8	17.3
36 NON METAL MIN–MIN NON METAL	1.9	1.9	2.0	2.0	1.9	1.9	1.8
37 BASIC METAL–IND METAL BASE	5.9	5.5	5.3	5.5	5.4	5.3	5.0
38 METAL MANUF–MANUF METAL	45.2	45.7	44.5	45.5	45.8	46.8	47.7
39 OTH MANUF IND–AUTRES MANUF	2.6	2.6	2.8	2.7	5.4	3.0	4.8

3. TRADE BY PRINCIPAL COUNTRIES OF ORIGIN AND DESTINATION (VALUE IN MILLION U.S. DOLLARS)
ECHANGES SELON LES PRINCIPAUX PAYS D'ORIGINE ET DE DESTINATION (VALEUR EN MILLIONS DE DOLLARS EU)

COUNTRIES–PAYS	SPECIAL IMPORTS C.I.F. IMPORTATIONS SPECIALES C.A.F				
	1993	1994	1995	1996	1997
World	200796.7	228281.6	273387.3	274913.5	266575.4
Africa	9402.0	10397.2	11397.4	12021.4	11546.1
Americas	22830.5	25978.7	29051.0	29513.5	30447.1
– Northern America	18769.7	21106.2	23432.3	24208.0	25076.6
– LAIA	3418.4	4053.2	4567.2	4354.8	4493.1
– CACM	109.0	178.5	216.9	208.3	230.7
– Caribbean	445.5	573.2	615.3	542.7	557.0
– Rest of America	88.0	67.7	219.4	199.6	89.7
Asia excl fmr USSR	27997.4	29431.3	34398.4	35768.1	36525.4
– Middle East	5698.9	5455.8	5855.8	6322.7	6332.2
Asia former USSR	166.9	230.4	229.9	203.9	267.4
Europe excl fmr USSR	133792.8	154808.7	189622.9	190928.0	178738.9
– European Union	123304.5	142619.5	174572.7	174586.9	162663.1
– Eastern Europe	1814.8	2179.1	2865.3	3465.1	3722.5
– Rest of Europe	8673.5	10010.1	12184.9	12876.1	12353.3
Europe former USSR	2946.3	3106.4	3795.7	4418.1	3893.1
Oceania	856.9	1045.9	1242.1	1169.7	1243.4
Other	2803.8	3282.9	3649.9	891.1	3914.0
Germany/Allemagne	35379.5	40657.4	50549.4	48265.9	44115.2
Italy/Italie	19828.6	22999.7	27283.6	28125.1	26070.5
Belgium–Luxembourg	17845.7	20791.1	24506.2	23345.4	21414.3
USA/Etats–Unis d'Amer	17565.2	19476.2	21320.2	22420.9	23358.3
United Kingdom	16153.2	18219.3	21897.7	23128.9	22229.3
Spain/Espagne	10923.9	13929.2	17811.9	19176.8	17727.1
Netherlands/Pays–Bas	10264.3	11331.8	14493.6	14419.3	13366.3
Japan/Japon	8274.1	8507.4	9589.3	8967.0	8928.4
Switzerland,Liechtenst.	4982.9	5752.2	7096.2	6872.3	6362.7
China/Chine	3751.7	4105.5	5142.2	6028.3	6636.8
Norway,Svalbard and JM	2679.3	3109.5	3794.8	4621.8	4864.3
Sweden/Suède	2884.9	3101.3	4060.8	3928.8	3842.9
Ireland/Irlande	2446.8	2731.2	3487.8	3810.9	4077.7
Russian Federation	2620.3	2811.6	3486.0	3975.8	3484.5
Areas n.e.s.	2803.8	3282.9	3649.9	891.1	3914.0
Portugal	2168.8	2615.4	3090.9	3196.5	3035.0
Saudi Arabia	2679.5	2781.9	2554.6	2907.9	2642.0
Morocco/Maroc	1920.9	2143.1	2595.9	2568.7	2457.0
Denmark/Danemark	1782.4	2032.0	2439.8	2437.2	2227.1
Austria/Autriche	1812.3	2055.9	2264.1	2249.7	2112.9
Other Asia n.e.s.	1710.6	1794.3	1978.4	2109.7	2227.3
Brazil/Brésil	1483.0	1891.9	1997.5	1839.9	1975.5
Singapore/Singapour	1223.2	1548.8	1899.1	2249.6	2259.9
Finland/Finlande	1342.5	1650.2	2076.3	1918.7	1994.0
Canada	1192.2	1602.1	2094.4	1778.9	1709.3
Algeria/Algérie	1376.5	1496.6	1509.2	1720.5	2168.7
Korea, Republic of	1248.7	1335.6	1899.0	1659.8	1792.9
Tunisia/Tunisie	1078.3	1206.3	1452.4	1513.4	1479.2
Thailand/Thaïlande	1017.2	1163.4	1357.5	1505.7	1431.7
Malaysia/Malaisie	916.7	1081.0	1479.9	1510.4	1424.3
Iran (Islamic Rep of)	1434.6	1034.1	1374.1	1289.4	928.8
Turkey/Turquie	818.1	936.1	1147.7	1187.3	1301.9
Poland/Pologne	663.7	814.3	1026.1	1298.4	1256.6
India/Inde	762.4	904.4	1107.3	1143.5	1096.5
Nigeria/Nigéria	765.5	1087.9	781.9	1389.2	711.2
Indonesia/Indonésie	807.9	807.7	909.4	1023.4	1033.8
Australia/Australie	595.2	755.7	887.7	767.0	846.5
Israel/Israël	663.6	692.6	869.8	832.2	755.6
Cote d'Ivoire	581.9	653.0	915.2	814.0	775.4
So. African Customs Un	504.4	595.8	703.4	830.7	743.3

COUNTRIES–PAYS	SPECIAL EXPORTS F.O.B. EXPORTATIONS SPECIALES F.O.B.				
	1993	1994	1995	1996	1997
Monde	206275.0	233307.3	284045.6	283901.2	283345.7
Afrique	13599.9	14256.2	17770.3	16192.1	15069.7
Amériques	24180.8	26762.8	29087.3	25273.9	27609.7
– Amérique du Nord	16343.1	18188.2	18724.5	19263.9	20868.7
– ALAI	3706.2	4789.4	4830.2	5058.9	5666.3
– MCAC	172.1	109.5	191.9	145.7	249.9
– Caraïbes	2581.5	2565.6	3092.1	573.7	631.5
– Autre Amérique	1377.9	1110.1	2248.5	231.7	193.3
Asie anc. URSS exclus	24057.2	26886.9	34257.1	33705.3	35618.5
– Moyen–Orient	7382.6	6922.1	7916.6	8218.4	8996.1
Asie ancienne URSS	157.7	193.0	144.7	309.1	281.1
Europe anc. URSS exclus	140536.7	161586.1	198115.2	200533.2	197268.2
– Union Européenne	128030.4	147630.9	180281.3	181001.5	177877.7
– Europe de l'Est	2503.6	2788.1	3979.6	5136.2	5622.0
– Autre de l'Europe	10002.7	11167.1	13854.2	14395.5	13768.4
Europe ancienne URSS	1819.7	1518.5	2133.7	2544.4	3250.2
Océanie	1688.3	1890.2	2335.4	2439.9	2452.7
Autre	234.7	213.6	202.0	2903.2	1795.4
Germany/Allemagne	35741.9	39975.0	50152.2	49120.4	44979.0
United Kingdom	19369.6	23112.4	26292.9	26853.1	28640.8
Italy/Italie	19370.3	21926.8	27405.3	26420.9	26309.8
Belgium–Luxembourg	17673.2	20431.0	24258.1	24147.4	22759.6
Spain/Espagne	13776.0	16691.7	20880.1	22712.2	22763.1
USA/Etats–Unis d'Amer	14787.3	16423.0	16763.6	17311.9	18446.3
Netherlands/Pays–Bas	9885.3	10813.3	13118.5	13028.8	13262.6
Switzerland,Liechtenst.	7859.0	8799.3	11044.6	11084.4	9970.7
Japan/Japon	4074.8	4583.2	5590.1	5353.9	4875.6
Portugal	3158.4	3473.7	3973.2	3897.7	3992.3
Sweden/Suède	2125.7	2682.8	3656.2	4050.4	4143.7
China, Hong Kong SAR	1989.1	2340.0	3783.3	3516.2	2944.4
Austria/Autriche	2098.1	2548.0	3270.7	3143.2	2969.6
China/Chine	1602.0	2168.0	2640.2	2422.6	3421.4
Algeria/Algérie	2104.2	2414.0	2855.6	2460.5	2290.5
Morocco/Maroc	2014.3	2175.4	2590.3	2394.4	2433.3
Denmark/Danemark	1664.0	2041.4	2538.6	2577.4	2489.6
Turkey/Turquie	1894.0	1383.3	1834.6	2553.8	2861.3
Greece/Grèce	1610.2	1678.4	2162.5	2272.6	2432.1
Singapore/Singapour	1574.9	1445.3	1800.8	2513.0	2623.7
Canada	1507.1	1636.5	1878.8	1918.3	2371.4
Tunisia/Tunisie	1610.7	1779.7	1968.6	1869.0	2000.7
Russian Federation	1474.6	1213.8	1674.7	2002.4	2535.3
Korea, Republic of	1281.8	1700.3	1968.2	1974.2	1912.6
Other Asia n.e.s.	1104.7	1419.0	1683.5	1620.9	2433.2
Poland/Pologne	823.3	961.4	1408.5	2055.8	2328.9
Ireland/Irlande	921.5	1439.4	1449.8	1451.3	1825.8
Saudi Arabia	1397.2	1320.3	1329.7	1411.8	1484.9
Malaysia/Malaisie	553.8	1067.0	2385.5	1337.7	1251.7
Brazil/Brésil	755.4	966.1	1410.7	1511.3	1588.0
Egypt/Egypte	1034.1	861.3	1188.6	1423.4	1431.5
Australia/Australie	862.9	1049.1	1259.2	1400.3	1312.5
Norway,Svalbard and JM	894.5	973.1	1161.6	1209.7	1591.6
Argentina/Argentine	817.8	1082.3	1024.5	1258.3	1272.4
Indonesia/Indonésie	803.7	756.0	1037.5	1273.1	1489.4
Areas n.e.s.	234.7	213.6	202.0	2903.2	1795.4
Thailand/Thaïlande	783.0	902.1	1712.2	978.6	950.8
Finland/Finlande	636.2	817.0	1123.2	1326.1	1309.8
Israel/Israël	769.7	1011.8	1130.3	1150.8	1056.2
United Arab Emirates	855.7	859.3	1285.8	1064.8	1039.6

(VALUE AS PERCENTAGE OF WORLD TOTAL)(VALEURS EN POURCENTAGE DU TOTAL MONDIAL)

	1988	1989	1990	1991	1992	1993	1994	1995	1996	1997
Africa	5.1	4.9	5.2	5.1	4.7	4.7	4.6	4.2	4.4	4.3
Americas	10.9	10.8	11.0	12.5	11.1	11.4	11.4	10.6	10.7	11.4
– Northern America	8.5	8.5	8.8	10.4	9.1	9.3	9.2	8.6	8.8	9.4
– LAIA	2.0	2.0	1.9	1.8	1.7	1.7	1.8	1.7	1.6	1.7
– CACM	0.0	0.0	0.0	0.0	0.0	0.1	0.1	0.1	0.1	0.1
– Caribbean	0.3	0.2	0.2	0.2	0.2	0.2	0.3	0.2	0.2	0.2
– Rest of America	0.0	0.0	0.0	0.0	0.1	0.0	0.0	0.1	0.1	0.0
Asia excl fmr USSR	11.3	11.9	11.8	12.8	12.6	13.9	12.9	12.6	13.0	13.7
– Middle East	2.0	2.8	2.9	2.9	2.5	2.8	2.4	2.1	2.3	2.4
Asia former USSR					0.0	0.1	0.1	0.1	0.1	0.1
Europe excl fmr USSR	68.8	68.6	68.2	66.1	67.6	66.6	67.8	69.4	69.5	67.1
– European Union	63.7	63.2	62.9	61.1	62.8	61.4	62.5	63.9	63.5	61.0
– Eastern Europe	1.1	1.1	1.0	0.8	0.8	0.9	1.0	1.0	1.3	1.4
– Rest of Europe	4.1	4.3	4.3	4.2	4.1	4.3	4.4	4.5	4.7	4.6
Europe former USSR	1.6	1.4	1.4	1.3	1.5	1.5	1.4	1.4	1.6	1.5
Oceania	0.8	0.8	0.5	0.5	0.5	0.4	0.5	0.5	0.4	0.5
Other	1.6	1.7	1.9	1.7	1.9	1.4	1.4	1.3	0.3	1.5
Germany/Allemagne				17.8	18.7	17.6	17.8	18.5	17.6	16.5
Italy/Italie	11.6	11.5	11.6	10.9	10.6	9.9	10.1	10.0	10.2	9.8
Belgium–Luxembourg	9.1	9.2	8.8	8.4	8.6	8.9	9.1	9.0	8.5	8.0
USA/Etats–Unis d'Amer	7.7	7.7	8.1	9.6	8.4	8.7	8.5	7.8	8.2	8.8
United Kingdom	7.3	7.1	7.3	7.5	7.7	8.0	8.0	8.0	8.4	8.3
Spain/Espagne	4.2	4.4	4.7	5.1	5.4	5.4	6.1	6.5	7.0	6.6
Netherlands/Pays–Bas	5.3	5.2	5.1	5.2	5.1	5.1	5.0	5.3	5.2	5.0
Japan/Japon	4.2	4.1	4.0	4.1	4.1	4.1	3.7	3.5	3.3	3.3
Switzerland,Liechtenst.	2.5	2.5	2.5	2.3	2.3	2.5	2.5	2.6	2.5	2.4
China/Chine	0.8	0.9	0.9	1.3	1.5	1.9	1.8	1.9	2.2	2.5

	1988	1989	1990	1991	1992	1993	1994	1995	1996	1997
Afrique	7.3	7.4	7.3	6.9	6.6	6.6	6.1	6.3	5.7	5.3
Amériques	11.7	10.5	10.0	10.8	11.0	11.7	11.5	10.2	8.9	9.7
– Amérique du Nord	8.6	7.6	7.1	7.5	7.5	7.9	7.8	6.6	6.8	7.4
– ALAI	1.5	1.4	1.3	1.5	1.7	1.8	2.1	1.7	1.8	2.0
– MCAC	0.1	0.1	0.0	0.1	0.1	0.1	0.0	0.1	0.1	0.1
– Caraïbes	1.2	1.2	1.2	1.1	1.2	1.3	1.1	1.1	0.2	0.2
– Autre Amérique	0.2	0.3	0.4	0.6	0.6	0.7	0.5	0.8	0.1	0.1
Asie anc. URSS exclus	8.5	9.7	9.4	9.6	9.9	11.7	11.5	12.1	11.9	12.6
– Moyen–Orient	2.5	2.7	2.8	2.7	3.0	3.6	3.0	2.8	2.9	3.2
Asie ancienne URSS					0.0	0.1	0.1	0.1	0.1	0.1
Europe anc. URSS exclus	70.4	70.3	71.6	71.1	70.7	68.1	69.3	69.7	70.6	69.6
– Union Européenne	64.3	64.0	65.3	65.3	65.0	62.1	63.3	63.5	63.8	62.8
– Europe de l'Est	0.9	1.0	0.8	1.0	1.2	1.2	1.2	1.4	1.8	2.0
– Autre de l'Europe	5.2	5.3	5.5	4.8	4.5	4.8	4.8	4.9	5.1	4.9
Europe ancienne URSS	1.2	1.0	0.7	0.7	0.9	0.9	0.7	0.8	0.9	1.1
Océanie	0.9	1.0	0.9	0.9	0.9	0.8	0.8	0.8	0.9	0.9
Autre	0.0	0.0	0.0	0.0	0.0	0.1	0.1	0.1	1.0	0.6
Germany/Allemagne				18.6	17.6	17.3	17.1	17.7	17.3	15.9
United Kingdom	9.8	9.6	9.4	8.9	9.2	9.4	9.9	9.3	9.5	10.1
Italy/Italie	12.2	12.1	11.4	11.0	10.9	9.4	9.4	9.6	9.3	9.3
Belgium–Luxembourg	9.0	8.9	9.4	9.0	9.2	8.6	8.8	8.5	8.5	8.0
Spain/Espagne	5.5	5.8	6.4	6.9	7.2	6.7	7.2	7.4	8.0	8.0
USA/Etats–Unis d'Amer	7.3	6.6	6.1	6.4	6.5	7.2	7.0	5.9	6.1	6.5
Netherlands/Pays–Bas	5.6	5.7	5.6	4.9	4.9	4.8	4.6	4.6	4.6	4.7
Switzerland,Liechtenst.	4.2	4.2	4.2	3.7	3.5	3.8	3.8	3.9	3.9	3.5
Japan/Japon	1.7	1.9	1.9	2.0	1.8	2.0	2.0	2.0	1.9	1.7
Portugal	1.2	1.4	1.3	1.5	1.7	1.5	1.5	1.4	1.4	1.4

4. Special Imports C.I.F. by Commodities according to the S.I.T.C. (Rev. 2) in million U.S. Dollars
Importations Spéciales C.A.F. par Produits d'après la C.T.C.I. (Rév. 2) en millions de Dollars E.U.

SITC CTCI	COMMODITY	1994 QUANTITY QUANTITE	1994 VALUE VALEUR	1995 QUANTITY QUANTITE	1995 VALUE VALEUR	1996 QUANTITY QUANTITE	1996 VALUE VALEUR	1997 QUANTITY QUANTITE	1997 VALUE VALEUR	PRODUIT
	ALL COMMODITIES		228281.7		273387.4		274913.8		266575.4	TOUS PRODUITS
0	FOOD AND LIVE ANIMALS		21435.5		24605.8		23611.2		22026.5	ALIMENTS,ANIMAUX VIVANTS
01	MEAT AND PREPARATIONS		3922.4		4214.1		3652.6		3253.8	VIANDES ET PREPARATIONS
011	MEAT FRESH,CHILLD,FROZEN	W 1084577	3503.2	W 1085730	3716.8	W 973532	3134.1	W 951598	2782.6	VIANDES FRAICHES,REF,CONGE
0111	BOVINE MEAT FRESH,FROZEN	W 426454	1661.2	W 394097	1653.0	W 265474	982.3	W 241380	835.9	VIANDES BOVIN FRAI,REF
01111	BOVINE MEAT WITH BONE IN	W 352617	1255.3	W 306741	1167.7	W 194906	644.7	W 170962	525.1	VIANDES BOVIN NON DESOSS
02	DAIRY PRODCTS,BIRDS'EGGS		1759.5		2179.3		2013.1		1906.1	PRODUITS LAITIERS,OEUFS
03	FISH AND PREPARATIONS		2705.8		3159.1		3206.2		3009.3	POISSONS ET PREPARATIONS
034	FISH,FRESH,CHILLED,FROZN	W 395450	1208.5	W 403990	1347.7	W 455778	1415.5	W 427672	1333.8	POISSON FRAIS, REFRIG,CONG
036	SHELL FISH FRESH,FROZEN	W 148684	790.8	W 156826	917.6	W 168604	890.8	W 173312	864.9	CRUSTACES,MOLLUSQUES
04	CEREALS AND PREPARATIONS		1785.5		2001.1		2196.1		2028.5	CEREALES ET PRODUITS
048	CEREAL ETC PREPARATIONS	W 646852	1273.[illegible]	W 711755	1496.9	W 798385	1609.6	W 850374	1493.6	PREPTNS A BASE CEREALES
0484	BAKERY PRODUCTS	W 266880	731.6	W 287734	860.3	W 322005	915.5	W 335726	824.4	PRODUITS DE BOULANGERIE
05	VEGETABLES AND FRUIT		5431.3		6318.6		6063.0		5549.8	LEGUMES ET FRUITS
054	VEG ETC FRSH,SMPLY PRSVD	W 2645440	1597.0		1943.9		1849.8	W 2317727	1598.4	LEGUMES FRAIS,CONG,SECS
057	FRUIT,NUTS,FRESH,DRIED	W 2641139	2374.9	W 2660950	2648.2	W 2455972	2512.2	W 2490583	2357.0	FRUITS FRAIS OU SECS
0579	FRUIT FRESH OR DRIED NES	W 655330	745.3	W 675251	874.2	W 698706	847.8	W 740649	804.2	FRUITS FRAIS,SECS NDA
058	FRUIT PRESERVED,PREPARED	W 990975	1038.1	W 1040630	1217.8	W 971702	1189.9	W 1054270	1124.6	CONSERVES DE FRUITS
07	COFFEE,TEA,COCOA,SPICES		2331.1		2981.3		2728.9		2794.2	CAFE,THE,CACAO,EPICES
071	COFFEE AND SUBSTITUTES	W 376837	1051.9	W 357580	1377.1	W 380165	1110.2	W 380976	1250.0	CAFE ET SUCCEDANES
0711	COFFEE GREEN,ROASTED,SUB	W 364551	937.8	W 345128	1238.4	W 367550	971.0	W 365418	1110.0	CAFE TORREFIE OU DECAFEINE
07111	COFFEE GREEN,HUSKS,SKINS	W 317530	748.9	W 293944	965.4	W 315509	748.5	W 313483	885.7	CAFE NON TORREFIE
073	CHOCOLATE AND PRODUCTS	W 219917	770.9	W 243435	980.3	W 254276	961.6	W 272898	903.5	CHOCOLAT
081	*FEEDING STUFF FOR ANIML	W 6142762	1531.5	W 5850902	1491.7		1701.7	W 5819665	1716.3	NOURRITURE POUR ANIMAUX
0813	OILCAKE AND OTH RESIDUES	W 4776944	998.6	W 4548361	910.4	W 4467280	1134.1	W 4495183	1143.2	TOURTEAUX
08131	— OF SOYA BEANS	W 3943069	863.1	W 3635689	767.0	W 3386625	934.8	W 3201347	923.9	TOURTEAUX DE SOJA
09	MISC EDIBLE PRODUCTS		792.0		906.3		918.8		878.9	PREP ALIMENTAIRES DIVERSES
1	BEVERAGES AND TOBACCO		2711.7		3234.4		3388.1		3207.8	BOISSONS ET TABACS
11	BEVERAGES		1282.7		1568.2		1651.5		1552.9	BOISSONS
112	ALCOHOLIC BEVERAGES	W 1206808	1096.4	W 1167729	1304.3	W 1156950	1372.9	W 1180393	1280.2	BOISSONS ALCOOLIQUES
12	TOBACCO AND MANUFACTURES		1429.0		1666.3		1736.6		1655.0	TABACS BRUTS FABRIQUES
122	TOBACCO,MANUFACTURED	W 68258	1296.9	W 63961	1544.8	W 65746	1620.9	W 69244	1564.7	TABACS FABRIQUES
1222	CIGARETTES	W 62585	1124.7	W 58296	1342.0	W 58055	1382.5	W 60900	1343.0	CIGARETTES
2	CRUDE MATERLS,EXCL FUELS		8067.7		10009.8		8697.3		8525.7	MAT BRUTES NON COMESTIBLES
23	RUBBER, CRUDE		602.3		826.2		809.5		692.8	CAOUTCHOUC BRUT
24	CORK AND WOOD		1151.6		1310.8		1112.5		1124.3	LIEGE ET BOIS
248	WOOD SHAPED,SLEEPERS	W 1237900	748.0	W 1231042	824.4	W 1356488	764.2	W 1434078	784.2	BOIS SIMPLEMENT TRAVAILLES
251	*PULP AND WASTE PAPER	W 3331097	1170.2	W 3220411	1831.3	W 3129831	1176.2	W 3172878	1150.9	PATES A PAPIER,DECHETS
2517	SODA,SULPHATE WOOD PULP	W 1884609	935.4	W 1768928	1425.1	W 1880661	992.7	W 1976701	976.7	PATES CHIMIQUES AU SULFATE
25172	— BLEACHED,NONDISSOLVNG	W 1868784	928.3	W 1757944	1416.9	W 1868591	986.5	W 1952168	965.3	PATES BLANCHIES
26	TEXTILE FIBRES AND WASTE		1024.6		1163.9		945.9		957.5	FIBRES TEXTILES
27	CRUDE FERTLZR,MINRLS NES		686.9		763.1		761.6		693.5	ENGRAIS MINERAUX BRUTS
28	METALLIFEROUS ORES,SCRAP		1549.2		1969.1		1688.4		1862.3	MINERAIS METAL,DECHETS
29	CRUDE ANIMAL,VEG MAT NES		1300.9		1594.7		1621.6		1500.8	MATIERES BRUTES ANIM,VEGET
292	CRUDE VEG MATERIALS NES	W 278001	1011.6	W 303520	1251.7	W 334733	1285.6	W 356225	1202.1	MAT BRUTES VEGETALES NDA
3	MINERAL FUELS ETC		17592.5		18633.6		22857.6		21891.9	COMBUSTIBLES MINERAUX LUB
32	COAL,COKE AND BRIQUETTES		931.5		965.7		1068.6		985.4	HOUILLES,COKES,BRIQUETTES
322	COAL,LIGNITE AND PEAT	MW 13044	772.6	MW 13656	836.8	MW 16224	943.7	MW 14118	822.9	HOUILLES,LIGNITES,TOURBE
33	PETROLEUM AND PRODUCTS		13166.5		13814.1		17691.3		16651.2	PETROLE ET DERIVES
333	CRUDE PETROLEUM	MW 75360	8784.1	MW 75743	9614.6	MW 83131	12746.4	MW 86965	12379.1	HUILES BRUTES DE PETROLE
334	PETROLEUM PRODUCTS;REFIN	MW 25136	4064.4	MW 21956	3812.0	MW 22054	4545.5	MW 19507	3907.6	PRODUITS RAFFINES
3341	GASOLINE,OTH LIGHT OILS			W 6156672	1154.7	W 6792303	1454.0	W 5247450	1125.5	ESSENCES POUR MOTEURS
3343	GAS OILS			MW 11352	1856.1	W 67703	17.4	MW 10512	1986.5	GAS OILS
3344	FUEL OILS,NES			W 3685300	441.7	MW 14291	2642.1	W 2632704	316.3	FUEL OILS
341	*GAS,NATURAL AND MANUFCT	MW 26629	3301.8	MW 25930	3626.9	MW 27492	3884.6	MW 28429	4045.3	GAZ NATUREL,GAZ MANUFACT
3413	PETROLM GASES,LIQUEFIED	W 8665397	1173.8	W 7168311	1126.7	W 6611738	1151.8	W 8139287	1361.0	GAZ DE PETROLE LIQUEFIE
34139	OTH HYDROCARBON GAS LQFD	W 6474479	819.0	W 5433249	766.8	W 4980505	739.1	W 6652294	951.6	HYDROCARBURES GAZEUX NDA
3414	PETROLEUM GASES, GASEOUS	MW 17964	2126.4	MW 18761	2498.5	MW 20880	2731.5	MW 20284	2683.6	GAZ DE PETROLE GAZEUX
4	ANIMAL,VEGETABLE OIL,FAT		849.5		1125.8		1076.8		1039.3	HUILES,GRAISSES ANIM,VEG
5	CHEMCLS,RELATED PROD NES		26758.3		33559.2		32862.7		32322.4	PRODUITS CHIMIQUES
51	ORGANIC CHEMICALS		6235.4		7571.1		7431.9		7495.3	PROD CHIMIQ ORGANIQUES
511	HYDROCARBONS NES,DERIVS	W 1506536	830.7	W 1585121	1100.6	W 1503904	898.9	W 1465598	826.2	HYDROCARBURES NDA
512	ALCOHOLS,PHENOLS ETC	W 1308740	768.9	W 1284922	885.5	W 1395056	811.4	W 1450485	801.6	PHENOLS,PHENOLS–ALCOOLS
513	CARBOXYLIC ACIDS ETC	W 603024	897.6	W 599884	1158.2	W 574380	1011.4	W 656324	979.0	ACIDES CARBOXYLIQUES
514	NITROGEN–FNCTN COMPOUNDS	W 324721	1760.9	W 353605	2134.4	W 370945	2083.4	W 379132	2037.3	COMPOSES FONCT AZOTEES
5148	OTH NITROGN–FNCTN CMPNDS	W 124808	912.8	W 127170	1153.6	W 130368	1102.4	W 125941	1011.9	AUTRES COMPOSES AZOTES
51482	IMIDE–,IMIDE–FNCT CMPNDS	W 34930	640.3	W 40200	837.0	W 38212	774.2	W 35675	733.4	COMPOSES A FONCTION IMIDE
515	ORG–INORG COMPOUNDS ETC	W 102829	1404.8	W 116026	1599.9	W 121107	1989.8	W 126069	2157.8	COMPOSES ORGANO–MINERAUX
5156	HETEROCYCLIC CMPDS ETC	W 45260	890.9	W 52853	1140.8	W 48154	1421.7	W 45722	1660.4	COMPOSES HETEROCYCLIQUES
51569	OTH HETEROCYC CMPDS,ETC	W 39811	869.1	W 46263	1108.5	W 42140	1391.5	W 39705	1634.6	AUT COMP HETEROCYCLIQUES
52	INORGANIC CHEMICALS		2194.1		2657.2		2600.1		2502.8	PROD CHIM INORGANIQUES
522	INORG ELEMNTS,OXIDES,ETC	W 2711748	812.4	W 3006139	1030.2	W 2792533	1011.0	W 2724184	938.1	ELEMENTS INORGANIQUES
523	OTHR INORG CHEMICALS ETC	W 1760352	774.6	W 1733553	890.5	W 1759473	848.4	W 1979850	798.2	AUT PRODUITS CHIMIQUES INORG
53	DYES,TANNING,COLOUR PROD		1639.6		2036.0		2014.4		1970.4	PROD TEINTURE,COLORANTS
533	PIGMENTS,PAINTS,ETC	W 353497	1008.7	W 366481	1211.3	W 406314	1247.1	W 463520	1160.8	PIGMENTS,PEINTURES,VERNIS
541	*MEDICINAL,PHARM PRODUCT		4203.5	MK 103452	5626.3		5723.0		5875.4	PROD MEDICINAUX PHARMACEUT
5417	MEDICAMENTS	MK 43963	2203.6	MK 55623	3210.7	MK 58509	3418.7	MK 56342	3645.2	MEDICAMENTS
54179	— CONTNG OTH SUBSTANCES	MK 37233	1615.5	MK 47216	2349.1	MK 46572	2507.7	MK 47292	2679.1	MED CONT AUT SUBSTANCES
55	PERFUME,CLEANING ETC PRD		2097.5		2418.6		2399.2		2533.5	PROD POUR PARFUM,TOILETTE
553	PERFUMERY,COSMETICS,ETC	W 149844	966.6	W 154830	1007.8	W 163537	989.2	W 177808	1048.6	PRODUITS DE PARFUMERIE
554	SOAP,CLEANSING ETC PREPS	W 627597	733.9	W 673288	854.4	W 686904	825.3	W 762914	815.5	SAVONS,PRODUITS DETERSIFS
562	*FERTILIZERS,MANUFACTURE	W 7011316	911.8	W 7817956	1252.9	W 8168639	1305.6	W 7702606	1033.1	ENGRAIS MANUFACTURES
58	PLASTIC MATERIALS ETC		5882.3		7499.3		6938.6		6692.2	MAT PLAST ARTIFICIELLES
582	PROD OF CONDENSATION ETC	W 810136	1616.3	W 879271	2151.9	W 901092	1983.0	W 1059719	1881.6	PROD CONDENS,POLYCOND
5823	ALKYDS,OTHER POLYESTERS	W 275385	659.5	W 318610	957.9	W 340188	854.0	W 434320	812.6	ALKYDES ET AUT POLYESTERS
583	POLYMERIZATION ETC PRODS	W 2851570	4070.8	W 2822789	5133.2	W 2992092	4750.8	W 3210179	4621.3	PROD POLYMERISATION
5831	POLYETHYLENE	W 930288	913.5	W 876152	1146.3	W 922569	1018.4	W 941034	1018.7	POLYETHYLENE
5839	OTH POLYMRZTION ETC PROD	W 548885	1202.5	W 569698	1555.7	W 652793	1577.9	W 725110	1524.3	AUT PROD POLYMER COPOLYM
59	CHEMICAL MATERIALS NES		3560.9		4455.8		4408.3		4183.0	MAT PROD CHIMIQUES NDA
591	PESTICIDES,DISINFECTANTS	W 155949	1132.8	W 174450	1480.5	W 183323	1484.5	W 176410	1244.6	DESINF,INSECT,FONG,HERB
598	MISCEL CHEM PRODUCTS NES	W 2666889	1980.8	W 2686313	2465.0	W 1829023	2430.9	W 2118333	2479.0	PROD DIV INDUST CHIM NDA
5989	CHEM PRODUCTS,PREPS NES	W 2329484	1545.0	W 2346104	1940.5	W 1525923	1926.6	W 1789251	1960.5	PROD PREP CHIMIQUES NDA
59899	OTH CHEM PRODS,PREPS,NES	W 2093390	1169.7	W 1938831	1479.6	W 1260533	1493.2	W 1500277	1531.4	AUT PRODUITS CHIMIQUES NDA
6	BASIC MANUFACTURES		37072.2		46502.6		42980.7		42267.0	ART MANUFACTURES
61	LEATHER,DRESSED FUR,ETC		797.5		868.2		827.3		822.9	CUIRS,PELLETERIES
62	RUBBER MANUFACTURES NES		1847.2		2181.2		2245.5		2205.1	CAOUTCHOUC MANUFACTURE
625	RUBBER TYRES, TUBES ETC	W 274154	1076.9	W 303546	1263.1	W 342178	1343.1	W 365685	1270.7	PNEUS CAOUTCHOUC VULCANISE
63	WOOD,CORK MANUFACTRS NES		1080.1		1318.3		1308.7		1283.2	OUVRAGES LIEGE ET BOIS
64	PAPER,PAPERBOARD AND MFR		5573.9		7317.1		6790.0		6454.7	PAPIERS,CARTONS & OUVRAGES
641	PAPER AND PAPERBOARD	W 4917626	4124.2	W 4786928	5452.1	W 4931701	4894.4	W 5705717	4636.1	PAPIERS ET CARTONS
6412	PRINTG,WRITING PAPER NES	W 1276252	1171.6	W 1382741	1700.3	W 1444595	1505.2	W 1710952	1441.9	PAPIERS POUR L'IMPRESSION

4. Special Imports C.I.F. by Commodities according to the S.I.T.C. (Rev. 2) in million U.S. Dollars
Importations Spéciales C.A.F. par Produits d'après la C.T.C.I. (Rév. 2) en millions de Dollars E.U.

SITC CTCI	COMMODITY	1994		1995		1996		1997		PRODUIT
		QUANTITY QUANTITE	VALUE VALEUR	QUANTITY QUANTITE	VALUE VALEUR	QUANTITY QUANTITE	VALUE VALEUR	QUANTITY QUANTITE	VALUE VALEUR	
64122	— COATED,IMPREGNATD ETC	W 1125314	1038.5	W 1195893	1451.8	W 1249380	1301.7	W 1503519	1250.2	PAPIERS IMPRESSION COUCHES
6415	PAPER,PAPERBRD,BULK,NES	W 1712631	1095.6	W 1567704	1467.0	W 1609654	1250.2	W 1872615	1195.4	PAPIERS,CARTONS ROULEAUX
64159	OTHER PAPER ETC,BULK,NES	W 1601229	1011.6	W 1477282	1363.1	W 1506857	1152.7	W 1755168	1098.8	AUT PAPIER ROULEAUX FEUILLES
6418	COATED ETC PAPER NES BLK	W 666856	885.3	W 636516	1050.0	W 651575	959.4	W 735182	934.2	PAP,CARTONS COUCHES,ENDUITS
642	PAPER,ETC,PRECUT,ARTS OF	W 698321	1449.7	W 733872	1865.0	W 841031	1895.7	W 931508	1818.6	PAP,CARTONS DECOUPES
65	TEXTILE YARN,FABRICS,ETC		6621.2		7542.9		7083.5		6989.6	FILS,TISSUS,ARTICLES TEXTILE
651	TEXTILE YARN	W 427242	1874.4	W 411562	2146.7	W 405526	2035.1	W 444907	1943.0	FILS TEXTILES
6514	SYN FIB YRN,BULK,MONOFIL	W 165854	747.6	W 162221	885.6	W 169309	861.8	W 192699	861.1	FILS CONT 85% FIB TEXT SYNTH
652	COTTON FABRICS,WOVEN	W 109833	762.0	W 101643	825.4	W 96831	788.6		815.8	TISSUS DE COTON
653	WOVN MAN-MADE FIB FABRIC	W 90879	954.4	W 97961	1139.6	W 88327	1005.8	W 94383	1006.0	TISSUS FIBRES SYNTH,ARTIF
657	SPECIAL TXTL FABRC,PRODS	W 171555	863.8	W 173018	1057.5	W 174215	1001.3	W 192870	945.5	TISSUS SPECIAUX
658	TEXTILE ARTICLES NES	W 91701	693.2	W 98472	820.2	W 92864	820.0	W 100933	802.7	ART FACONNES MAT TEXTILES
66	NONMETAL MINERAL MFS NES		4027.5		4695.4		4553.2		4419.5	ART MIN NON METALLIQUES
662	CLAY,REFRACTORY BLDG PRD	W 1225414	752.6	W 1248739	852.5	W 1347017	866.1	W 1455810	783.7	MAT CONST REFRACTAIRES
664	GLASS	W 756295	835.9	W 786829	1004.4	W 833573	983.6	W 955858	994.1	VERRE
665	GLASSWARE	W 984933	709.0	W 1005390	871.8	W 931336	818.3	W 1043110	788.5	OUVRAGES EN VERRE
67	IRON AND STEEL		7001.9		9370.5		8010.4		7872.9	FER ET ACIER
672	IRON,STEEL PRIMARY FORMS	W 3249843	1304.0	W 3634878	1760.5	W 3345005	1460.0	W 3845442	1469.0	LINGOTS FER,ACIER
6727	IRN,STL COIL FR REROLLNG	W 2316077	993.3	W 2579349	1336.8	W 2541874	1154.4	W 2949908	1140.0	EBAUCHES POUR TOLES FER
67271	IRON,SIMPLE STEEL COILS	W 2111249	769.6	W 2384467	1074.9	W 2327110	878.8	W 2710006	852.6	EBAUCHES NON EN ACIER
673	IRON,STEEL SHAPES ETC	W 2614601	1296.4	W 2955378	1822.4	W 2808422	1526.6	W 3029062	1452.5	BARRES,PROFIL FER,ACIER
6732	IRON,STEEL BARS ETC	W 1003927	572.1	W 1174366	857.2	W 1000498	682.4	W 1169322	660.5	BARRES FER,ACIER
674	IRN,STL UNIV,PLATE,SHEET	W 3977608	2624.5	W 4042165	3378.0	W 3794205	2742.5	W 4341192	2730.7	LARGES PLATS,TOLES
6746	IRN,STL THIN PLATE,ROLLD	W 1174227	816.8	W 1234225	1143.9	W 1071939	795.0	W 1241349	855.5	TOLES LAM MOINS 3MM
6749	OTH IRN,STL PLATES,SHEET	W 1241836	809.1	W 1275157	1007.9	W 1306540	941.3	W 1546106	933.8	AUTRES TOLES FER,ACIER
67491	— OF IRON OR SIMPLE STL	W 1227419	781.8	W 1256083	970.1	W 1292272	909.0	W 1535380	906.8	AUT TOLES AUTRES ACIER FIN
678	IRON,STL TUBES,PIPES,ETC	W 812220	853.3	W 855107	1130.6	W 941369	1119.3	W 1084053	1110.9	TUBES,TUYAUX EN FONTE,FER
68	NON-FERROUS METALS		4934.5		6787.1		5766.7		6084.6	METAUX NON FERREUX
682	COPPER EXC CEMENT COPPER	W 744209	1879.7	W 779684	2599.0	W 707474	1963.1	W 811920	2182.8	CUIVRE
6821	COPPER NES,ALLOYS,UNWRT	W 480209	1032.8	W 516014	1520.0	W 477146	1094.5	W 552790	1278.7	CUIVRE BRUT
68212	COPPER REFINED,UNWROUGHT	W 467631	1005.3	W 499550	1479.1	W 456320	1052.6	W 537017	1248.6	CUIVRE AFFINE BRUT
6822	COPPER,ALLOYS WORKED	W 264000	847.0	W 263671	1079.1	W 230328	868.6	W 259130	904.1	CUIVRE,ALLIAGES OUVRES
684	ALUMINIUM	W 849735	1920.6	W 881416	2610.7	W 904513	2351.5	W 955764	2262.6	ALUMINIUM
6841	ALUMINIUM,ALLOYS,UNWRGHT	W 444828	674.5	W 469305	964.3	W 491124	861.9	W 497674	849.6	ALUMINIUM,ALLIAGES BRUTS
6842	ALUMINIUM,ALLOYS WORKED	W 404907	1246.2	W 412111	1646.5	W 413389	1489.7	W 458090	1413.0	ALUMINIUM,ALLIAGES OUVRE
69	METAL MANUFACTURES NES		5188.7		6422.4		6395.7		6135.0	ART MANUFACT EN METAL NDA
695	TOOLS	W 65058	754.2	W 68143	920.3	W 72288	898.5	W 65130	845.6	OUTILS A MAIN
699	BASE METAL MFRS NES	W 482040	2021.9	W 513433	2532.2	W 509947	2570.8	W 532360	2497.2	ART MANUFACTURES MET NDA
7	MACHINES,TRANSPORT EQUIP		80445.2		96726.1		99648.4		96774.9	MACHINES MATERIEL TRANSPORT
71	POWER GENERATING EQUIPMT		7053.7		6821.6		6713.4		7666.2	MACHINES GENERATRICES
713	INTRNL COMBUS PSTN ENGIN	W 222768	2151.7		2664.6	W 235573	2623.8	W 226652	2416.2	MOTEURS EXPL COMB INT, PIECE
7132	MOTOR VEHCL PISTN ENGINS	W 80843	887.1	W 85607	1093.0	W 89515	1118.6	W 86218	1013.4	MOTEURS EXPL POUR VEHICULES
7139	PISTON ENGINE PARTS NES	W 111310	859.6	W 114423	1122.7	W 114301	1068.7	W 105087	960.8	PIECES POUR 713.2,3,8
714	ENGINES AND MOTORS NES	W 6980	3412.8	W 24526	2560.3	W 8018	2618.3	W 10557	3730.1	MOTEURS NON ELECTRIQUES
7144	REACTION ENGINES	W 1294	1622.3	W 531	767.4	W 499	646.7	W 927	1272.3	PROPULSEURS A REACTION
7149	ENGINE & MOTOR PARTS NES	W 5471	1656.7	W 23625	1630.5	W 6990	1800.1	W 7170	2293.9	PIECES 714 ET 718.88
71491	PARTS NES OF 7144,71481	W 1638	1337.4	W 1662	1287.8	W 2229	1383.9	W 2756	2029.9	PIECES DES PROPULSEURS
716	ROTATING ELECTRIC PLANT	W 62786	760.7	W 78070	944.1	W 81604	1034.2	W 90754	1013.7	APP ELECTR ROTATIFS,PIECES
72	MACHS FOR SPCL INDUSTRYS		5440.1		7132.8		7501.3		6834.8	MAC SPECIALES POUR INDUST
721	AGRIC MACHY,EXC TRACTORS	W 163464	1010.1	W 170129	1217.1	W 180111	1310.1	W 186864	1214.2	MACHINES AGRICOLES
7212	HARVESTING ETC MACHINES	W 99237	723.8	W 107123	840.9	W 115415	923.4	W 116613	844.2	ENGINS POUR LA RECOLTE
722	TRACTORS NON-ROAD	W 88184	596.2	W 120793	922.2	W 139469	1122.8	W 131403	984.9	TRACTEURS
7224	WHEELED TRACTORS NES	W 87989	594.8	W 120468	919.3	W 139177	1118.7	W 130677	980.3	TRACTEURS A ROUES
723	CIVIL ENGNEERG EQUIP ETC	W 97528	628.5	W 126174	902.8	W 107117	784.1	W 102768	672.9	APPAREILS DE GENIE CIVIL
728	OTH MACHY FOR SPCL INDUS	W 105867	1633.9	W 125087	2134.2	W 123709	2221.5	W 124948	2062.7	AUT MACH IND PARTICULIERES
7284	MACHY FOR SPCL INDUS NES	W 67639	1281.1	W 77548	1663.7	W 74535	1749.5	W 75261	1639.9	MACH SPEC IND PARTICUL.
73	METALWORKING MACHINERY		1282.6		1742.4		1925.8		1798.8	MACH TRAVAIL DES METAUX
736	METALWORKING MACH-TOOLS	W 62826	1011.9	W 71296	1390.1	W 78059	1564.4	W 79561	1381.3	MACH-OUTILS TRAVAIL METAUX
74	GENRL INDUSTRL MACHY NES		9018.2		11412.4		11801.2		11259.2	MACH APP INDUSTRIE
741	HEATING,COOLING EQUIPMNT	W 96521	1222.5	W 117547	1568.8	W 132710	1751.8	W 138045	1592.0	MACH CHAUFFAGE,PIECES
742	PUMPS FOR LIQUIDS ETC	W 58089	1139.4		1448.8	W 65579	1471.5	W 73463	1482.4	POMPES MOTO-POMPES
743	PUMPS NES,CENTRFUGES ETC	W 129689	1417.6	W 167107	1678.4	W 153429	1797.3	W 156741	1714.6	POMPES COMPRES,VENT ETC
744	MECHANICAL HANDLING EQU	W 213623	1432.7	W 276427	2000.1	W 278153	2059.6	W 300015	1857.8	EQUIP MANUTENTION PIECES
7449	PTS NES OF MACHY OF 7442	W 108412	663.2	W 147859	972.5	W 129275	987.9	W 153993	879.7	PIECES DU 744.2
745	NONELEC MACHY,TOOLS NES	W 69040	1237.9	W 81707	1517.1	W 82337	1518.5	W 85874	1474.8	AUT MACH NON ELEC,PIECES
7452	OTH NONELEC MCHS,PTS NES	W 61563	1030.0	W 73697	1266.9	W 73868	1285.9	W 77798	1250.5	AUT MACH NON ELEC,PIECES
749	NONELEC MACH PTS,ACC NES	W 241016	2568.3	W 267947	3199.5	W 275049	3202.7	W 282669	3137.9	PIECES MACH NON ELEC NDA
7492	COCKS,VALVES ETC NES	W 63757	991.6	W 69515	1189.7	W 72847	1194.1	W 81090	1218.3	ART ROB,SIM POUR TUYAUX
75	OFFICE MACHNES,ADP EQUIP		10796.3		13215.1		13342.5		13681.2	MACH BUREAU TRAIT AUTOM
751	OFFICE MACHINES	W 26294	843.8	W 27193	955.4	W 26364	818.1	W 29236	805.4	MACH,APPAREILS DE BUREAU
7518	OFFICE MACHINES NES	W 21722	688.8	W 23023	778.5	W 22537	674.6	W 24745	650.2	MACH,APP DE BUREAU NDA
752	AUTOMTIC DATA PROC EQUIP	W 92868	6416.1	W 106022	7566.2	W 135604	7936.1	W 166413	8212.4	MACH TRAIT INFORMATION
7522	DIGITAL COMPUTERS	W 5224	789.3	W 5443	844.4	W 6183	992.4	W 7538	1076.0	MACH DIGITALES COMPLETES
7523	DIGITL CENTRL PROCESSORS	W 10747	1824.3	W 11420	1762.4	W 13763	1548.5	W 20667	1659.3	UNITES CENTRALES
7524	DIGITL CENTRL STOR UNITS	W 12767	1145.1	W 10003	1433.4	W 11064	1449.8	W 14240	1787.0	UNITES MEMOIRE CENTRALES
7525	ADP PERIPHERAL UNITS	W 58074	2150.4	W 70961	2762.0	W 90110	3022.8	W 112210	2873.4	UNITES PERIPHERIQUES
759	OFFICE,ADP MCH PTS,ACCES	W 42521	3536.5	W 49153	4693.5	W 56699	4588.4	W 67327	4663.5	PIECES DU 751 ET 752
7591	OFFICE MACHINE PARTS NES	W 20209	662.1	W 22752	811.8	W 24426	774.1	W 23312	823.9	PIECES DU 7511,7518
7599	ACCTG,ETC,ADP MCH PTS,AC	W 22312	2874.5	W 26400	3881.7	W 32273	3814.4	W 44015	3839.6	PIECES DU 751 ET 752
76	TELECOMM,SOUND EQUIPMENT		5282.3		6422.3		6686.6		7418.8	EQUIPMENT DE TELECOM
761	TELEVISION RECEIVERS	W 55411	831.7	W 69324	1062.4	W 64756	1057.4	W 69740	1030.6	RECEPTEURS DE TELEVISION
7611	COLOUR TV RECEIVERS	W 54879	817.4	W 68630	1040.5	W 64107	1038.4	W 69015	1009.6	RECEPTEURS COULEUR
762	RADIO BROADCAST RECEIVRS	W 34481	809.4	W 39334	904.8	W 32628	750.0	W 33558	633.7	RECEPTEURS RADIODIFFUSION
763	SOUND RECORDRS,PHONOGRPH	W 19699	836.2	W 21289	872.1	W 20597	970.3	W 19779	876.7	PHONO,APP ENREGISTREMENT
7638	OTHR SOUND APPARATUS ETC	W 19201	828.5	W 20815	863.1	W 20072	961.3	W 19228	867.8	AUT APP D'ENREGIS,REPROD
764	TELECOM EQPT,PTS,ACC NES	W 66597	2805.2	W 82834	3583.2	W 83337	3909.1	W 104113	4877.9	EQUIP TELECOM,PIECES
7641	LINE TELEPHONE,ETC EQUIP	W 7377	454.2	W 8095	674.9	W 10356	950.4	W 11797	1088.7	APP TELEPHON PAR FIL
7643	TV,RADIO TRANSMITTRS ETC	W 2428	458.3	W 3544	635.3	W 2595	586.7	W 9761	1071.9	APP EMET TELE RADIO
7649	PTS NES OF EQUIPMT OF 76	W 33370	1186.1	W 42953	1437.7	W 41176	1743.1	W 52236	2078.0	PIECES DE LA DIV 76
76493	TELECOMM EQUIPMT PTS NES	W 22197	660.4	W 30210	772.6	W 27574	960.1	W 37873	1319.2	PIECES 761,762,764.3,8
77	ELECTRIC MACHNRY NES ETC		13544.4		17221.3		17339.2		18001.9	MACH APP ELECT NDA
771	ELECTRIC POWER MACHY NES	W 52841	731.1	W 71762	1002.5	W 75860	1053.3	W 85614	1161.6	MACH PROD,TRANS ELECTR
7712	OTH ELEC POWER MACHY NES	W 34865	542.8	W 42886	766.4	W 54526	844.7	W 59329	930.6	AUT APP PROD TRANSF ELEC
772	SWITCHGEAR ETC,PARTS NES	W 71411	2164.9	W 84535	2527.5	W 88700	2586.3	W 89127	2856.2	APP COUPURE,SECT ETC
7721	SWITCHGEAR ETC	W 62907	1634.8	W 75023	2026.7	W 77407	2084.5	W 79969	2297.0	APP COUPURE,SECTIONMNT
773	ELECTR DISTRIBUTNG EQUIP	W 137430	1072.0	W 158403	1375.3	W 161914	1388.3	W 175676	1371.9	EQUIPMT DISTRIBUTION ELECT
7731	INSULATED WIRE,CABLE ETC	W 128494	955.7	W 147762	1232.5	W 150296	1247.7	W 164529	1241.1	FILS,CABLES ISOLES ELECT
775	HOUSEHOLD TYPE EQUIP NES	W 348816	2072.6	W 401641	2438.9	W 374989	2413.7	W 394862	2287.8	MACH,APP USAGE DOMESTQUE
776	TRANSISTORS,VALVES,ETC	W 62233	3762.2	W 74330	5195.5	W 72441	5292.2	W 68006	5682.1	LAMPES,TUBES,VALVES
7763	DIODES,TRANSISTORS,ETC	W 3747	637.9	W 5828	851.0	W 5735	835.9	W 6117	898.9	DIODES,TRANSISTORS
7764	ELECTRONIC MICROCIRCUITS	W 8430	2540.6	W 8934	3616.4	W 8907	3754.8	W 8489	4128.7	MICROSTRUCTURES ELECTRON

4. Special Imports C.I.F. by Commodities according to the S.I.T.C. (Rev. 2) in million U.S. Dollars
Importations Spéciales C.A.F. par Produits d'après la C.T.C.I. (Rév. 2) en millions de Dollars E.U.

SITC CTCI	COMMODITY	1994		1995		1996		1997		PRODUIT
		QUANTITY QUANTITE	VALUE VALEUR	QUANTITY QUANTITE	VALUE VALEUR	QUANTITY QUANTITE	VALUE VALEUR	QUANTITY QUANTITE	VALUE VALEUR	
778	ELECTRICAL MACHINERY NES	W 272320	3114.6	W 276134	3961.0	W 347215	3881.2	W 396601	3960.2	AUTRES MACH ELECT NDA
7788	OTH ELEC MACHY,EQUIP NES	W 54965	1236.8	W 64047	1662.2	W 64339	1613.9	W 55027	1670.2	AUT MACH APP ELEC NDA
78	ROAD VEHICLES		22031.0		27490.4		28485.8		23474.7	VEHICULES ROUTIERS
781	PASS MOTOR VEH EXC BUSES	W 1204083	12638.1	W 1234561	14589.8	W 1454558	16043.8	W 1232301	12103.7	AUTO TRANSPORT PERSONNES
782	LORRIES,SPCL MTR VEH NES	W 272767	2409.3	W 284441	3033.3	W 311260	3094.4	W 338500	2843.8	VEHICULES SPECIAUX,MARCH
7821	LORRIES,TRUCKS	W 263905	2324.1	W 273473	2920.2	W 299305	2975.9	W 324449	2723.8	VEHICULES TRANSP MARCHAND
783	ROAD MOTOR VEHICLES NES	W 84276	1001.9	W 170789	2443.2	W 142184	1997.2	W 118472	1222.8	VEHICULES ROUTIERS NDA
7832	TRACTORS FOR TR–TRAILERS	W 67671	767.6	W 152495	2177.6	W 125324	1758.5	W 97499	970.3	TRACTEURS ROUTIERS
784	MOTOR VEH PRTS,ACCES NES	W 716999	4587.1	W 785303	5731.2	W 787689	5618.0	W 826489	5576.8	PIECES 722,781,782,783
7849	OTHER MOTOR VEHCL PARTS	W 694255	4405.9	W 761470	5461.8	W 768012	5348.1	W 805130	5300.6	PIECES 722,781,782,783
785	CYCLES,ETC MOTRZD OR NOT	W 82452	1006.1	W 96991	1202.0	W 137977	1283.7	W 92739	1284.6	MOTOCYCLES SCOOTERS
79	OTHR TRANSPORT EQUIPMENT		5997.0		5268.3		5853.0		6639.6	AUTRE MATERIEL TRANSPORT
791	RAILWAY VEHICLES	W 71215	1278.3	W 41475	357.1		130.0	W 37584	210.3	VEHIC MAT CHEMINS DE FER
7915	FRT,MAINT CARS NOT POWRD	W 39124	876.3	W 9604	226.5	W 6040	19.9	W 6511	34.3	WAGONS DE SERVICE
79152	RAILWAY FREIGHT CARS NES	W 38440	863.8	W 9032	218.0	W 5250	3.1	W 4347	6.5	WAGONS MARCHANDISES
792	AIRCRAFT ETC	W 11090	4398.4	W 10525	4289.7	W 11201	5021.8	W 12830	5732.7	APP NAVIGATION AERIENNE
7924	AIRCRFT NES OVER 15000KG	W 1470	782.4	W 1960	991.3	W 1942	740.8	W 1680	881.4	AERODYNES PLUS 15000 KG
7929	AIRCRAFT PARTS NES	W 9043	3461.1	W 7984	3051.6	W 8714	4017.4	W 10414	4331.4	PIECES DU 792
8	MISC MANUFACTURED GOODS		32575.0		38090.0		38828.3		37995.6	ART MANUFACTURES DIVERS
812	*PLUMBG,HEATNG,LGHTNG EQ	W 159335	773.1	W 163005	906.0	W 180677	1029.5	W 204132	961.1	APPAR SANITAIRES CHAUFFAGE
821	*FURNITURE,PARTS THEREOF	W 687987	2737.6	W 754699	3205.8	W 783992	3377.9	W 880425	3140.9	MEUBLES ET PIECES
8211	CHAIRS,SEATS AND PARTS	W 162792	974.5	W 176595	1115.8	W 176987	1193.7	W 182961	1046.8	SIEGES ET PIECES
82111	CHAIRS AND OTHER SEATS	W 135085	814.0	W 144110	911.4	W 148469	973.1	W 147340	821.7	SIEGES
8219	FURNITURE AND PARTS NES	W 496082	1487.4	W 547795	1775.5	W 566617	1821.2	W 659574	1797.7	AUTRES MEUBLES ET PIECES
82192	WOOD FURNITURE NES	W 320484	917.4	W 345546	1094.2	W 360184	1130.7	W 427203	1128.7	MEUBLES NDA EN BOIS
831	*TRAVEL GOODS,HANDBAGS	W 61290	677.9	W 72630	827.6	W 78129	858.2	W 80102	831.5	ARTICLES DE VOYAGE ETC
84	CLOTHING AND ACCESSORIES		9128.5		10292.2		10897.9		10759.9	VETEMENTS
842	MENS OUTERWEAR NOT KNIT	W 81730	1691.6	W 80248	1889.4	W 81804	1983.8	W 88101	1949.0	VET DESSUS POUR HOMMES
8423	— TROUSERS,BREECHES ETC	W 49056	833.9	W 46626	926.8	W 49682	1015.0	W 54795	1011.8	PANTALONS HOMMES MAT TEX
843	WOMENS OUTERWEAR NONKNIT	W 67912	1923.7	W 72597	2288.3	W 81440	2498.8	W 89942	2526.1	VET DESSUS FEMMES MAT TEX
8439	— OTHER OUTER GARMENTS	W 41218	919.2	W 43254	1062.2	W 47993	1185.7	W 52000	1249.1	AUT VET DES FEM MAT TEXT
845	OUTERWEAR KNIT NONELASTC	W 108999	2337.8	W 99034	2541.1	W 104979	2653.9	W 112866	2703.7	VET DESSOUS,ACCES BONNET
8451	— JERSEYS,PULLOVERS ETC	W 57956	1260.2	W 49295	1311.7	W 52505	1388.2	W 60821	1488.4	CHANDAILS,PULL–OVERS ETC
8459	— OTHER,CLTHG ACCESRYS	W 44834	927.3	W 45147	1073.9	W 46483	1123.3	W 47929	1085.7	AUT VET DESSUS DE BONNE
846	UNDER GARMENTS KNITTED	W 70114	1558.2	W 74140	1792.9	W 82290	1956.1	W 88397	1888.3	SOUS VETS DE BONNETERIE
8462	— OF COTTON NON ELASTIC	W 52368	986.6	W 56159	1168.6	W 63644	1282.6	W 68282	1225.8	SOUS–VET BONNET COTON
84629	—— OTHER	W 52368	986.6	W 56159	1168.6	W 63644	1282.6	W 68282	1225.8	AUT SOUS–VET BONNET COTON
851	*FOOTWEAR	W 142978	2153.7	W 147500	2427.5	W 145144	2452.3	W 165115	2559.0	CHAUSSURES
85102	FOOTWEAR LEATHER	W 112544	1865.2	W 110861	2043.5	W 105506	2010.6	W 112916	2029.5	CHAUS SEMELLES EN CUIR
87	PRECISION INSTRUMNTS NES		3956.8		4732.6		4853.6		4802.7	INSTRUM,APPAR SCIENT NDA
872	MEDICAL INSTRUMENTS NES	W 20264	986.7	W 23334	1214.3	W 23579	1295.0	W 23835	1310.0	INSTR,APP MEDIC–CHIR NDA
87202	OTH MEDICAL INSTRUMENTS	W 18186	909.1	W 20880	1121.5	W 20576	1194.4	W 20677	1199.1	INSTRUM,APP MEDECINE
874	MEASURNG,CONTROLNG INSTR	W 35538	2656.5	W 37946	3076.1	W 41483	3090.4	W 37924	2989.7	INSTRUMENTS DE MESURE
8748	ELEC MEAS,CONTRL EQU NES	W 4589	696.8	W 5725	835.4	W 5131	828.9	W 3767	725.9	APP ELEC ELECTRO MESURE
88	PHOTO EQU,OPTICL GDS ETC		2651.6		3025.2		2869.1		2801.6	APP,FOURN PHOTO,OP,MONTR
882	PHOTO,CINEMA SUPPLIES	W 94296	1137.3	W 99000	1307.3	W 97039	1240.8	W 102843	1212.3	PRODUITS PHOTO,CINEMA
8822	PHOTO FILM EXC DEV CINMA	W 62720	921.4	W 67703	1060.6	W 64026	999.3	W 70218	985.6	PLAQUES,PELLICULES,FILMS
89	MISC MANUFCTRD GOODS NES		10496.1		12673.5		12490.3		12139.3	ART MANUFACTURES DIVERS
892	PRINTED MATTER	W 420685	1683.6	W 481119	2131.3	W 485194	1965.4	W 507044	1782.2	IMPRIMES
8928	PRINTED MATTER NES	W 220852	708.6	W 232998	866.6	W 231776	846.9	W 249145	727.6	IMPRIMES NDA
893	ARTICLES OF PLASTIC NES		3026.3		3831.4		3847.7		3752.7	OUVRAGES EN MAT DIVIS 58
8931	PLSTC PACKG CONTNRS,LIDS	W 328075	929.4	W 338273	1212.8	W 360951	1198.0	W 396418	1164.4	ART TRANSP EMBALLAGE ETC
8939	MISC PLASTIC ARTICLES	W 472698	2014.3	W 474466	2509.0	W 531227	2524.1	W 582647	2462.1	ART DIVERS EN MAT DIV 58
89399	OTHR PLASTC ARTICLES NES	W 370615	1795.1	W 377247	2263.0	W 426634	2267.6	W 465337	2211.8	AUT OUV MAT DIV 58
894	TOYS,SPORTING GOODS,ETC	W 206344	1856.7	W 220159	2105.5	W 215413	2143.6	W 234549	2268.0	VOITURES ENFANTS,JOUETS
8942	TOYS,INDOOR GAMES ETC	W 157023	1378.3	W 164742	1530.4	W 154480	1527.1	W 164940	1641.7	JOUETS,JEUX ETC
898	MUSICAL INSTRUMENTS,PTS	W 88252	1580.0	W 111100	1957.8	W 105888	1935.1	W 143538	1826.8	INSTRUMENTS DE MUSIQUE
8983	SOUND RECRDNG TAPE,DISCS	W 77763	1391.4	W 100021	1763.9	W 95855	1740.7	W 134908	1671.9	SUPPORTS SON POUR 763
89832	RECORDED DISCS,TAPES ETC	W 27309	871.0	W 34552	1180.3	W 35596	1210.7	W 35023	1196.7	DISQUES,PHONO,BANDES
899	OTHER MANUFACTURED GOODS		997.9		1182.2		1199.7		1146.3	AUT ART MANUF DIVERS NDA
9	GOODS NOT CLASSD BY KIND		774.6		900.6		963.3		524.7	ART TRANSACT NON CLASSES
971	*GOLD,NON MONETARY NES	K 645600	670.1	K 870297	791.9	K 267067	825.3	K 86964	410.9	OR NON MONETAIRE

5. Special Exports F.O.B. by Commodities according to the S.I.T.C. (Rev. 2) in million U.S. Dollars
Exportations Spéciales F.O.B. par Produits d'après la C.T.C.I. (Rév. 2) en millions de Dollars E.U.

SITC CTCI	COMMODITY	1994 QUANTITY QUANTITE	1994 VALUE VALEUR	1995 QUANTITY QUANTITE	1995 VALUE VALEUR	1996 QUANTITY QUANTITE	1996 VALUE VALEUR	1997 QUANTITY QUANTITE	1997 VALUE VALEUR	PRODUIT
	ALL COMMODITIES		233307.3		284045.8		283901.4		283345.8	TOUS PRODUITS
0	FOOD AND LIVE ANIMALS		26054.4		30460.6		29974.8		27870.4	ALIMENTS,ANIMAUX VIVANTS
001	*LIVE ANIMALS FOR FOOD	W 562907	1812.6	W 597829	1912.4	W 630760	1706.7	W 654859	1650.0	ANIMAUX VIVANTS
0011	BOVINE SPECIES,LIVE	W 466658	1558.8	W 494778	1620.4	W 533414	1408.5	W 554580	1358.6	ESPECE BOVINE
00119	— OTHR THAN FR BREEDING	W 446875	1502.9	W 470040	1546.5	W 505909	1336.4	W 539281	1320.1	BOVINS NON REPRODUCTEURS
01	MEAT AND PREPARATIONS		4090.1		4613.2		4321.6		4219.7	VIANDES ET PREPARATIONS
011	MEAT FRESH,CHILLD,FROZEN	W 1563020	3551.5	W 1543992	3926.1	W 1471271	3664.6	W 1585556	3574.3	VIANDES FRAICHES,REF,CONGE
0111	BOVINE MEAT FRESH,FROZEN	W 518663	1531.3	W 431532	1574.4	W 351863	1117.1	W 363987	1081.8	VIANDES BOVIN FRAI,REF
01111	BOVINE MEAT WITH BONE IN	W 339864	1024.8	W 271502	1073.0	W 206595	742.0	W 206866	692.9	VIANDES BOVIN NON DESOSS
0114	POULTRY FRESH CHLLD,FRZN	W 684287	1264.1	W 737476	1408.8	W 752235	1564.9	W 776672	1464.4	VOLAILLES MORTES
02	DAIRY PRODCTS,BIRDS'EGGS		4010.4		4717.3		4346.0		4113.9	PRODUITS LAITIERS,OEUFS
022	MILK AND CREAM	W 1824319	1678.5	W 1738573	2035.6	W 1618105	1726.1	W 1795576	1770.1	LAIT ET CREME
0224	MILK,CREAM PRESERVED ETC	W 667583	1049.6	W 685941	1328.3	W 668207	1087.3	W 746796	1134.2	LAIT,CREME CONS,CONC
024	CHEESE AND CURD	W 438383	1972.5	W 457975	2243.5	W 464881	2238.2	W 472130	2003.1	FROMAGE ET CAILLEBOTTE
03	FISH AND PREPARATIONS		884.5		973.4		980.7		1088.5	POISSONS ET PREPARATIONS
04	CEREALS AND PREPARATIONS		6129.0		7483.8		7600.3		6630.1	CEREALES ET PRODUITS
041	WHEAT ETC UNMILLED	MW 12600	1999.0	MW 16333	2964.4	MW 14733	2883.0	MW 14585	2364.7	FROMENT,EPEAUTRE
0412	OTHER WHEAT ETC UNMILLED	MW 12226	1918.7	MW 15572	2770.4	MW 14064	2725.5	MW 13930	2235.8	AUTRE FROMENT NON MOULU
044	MAIZE UNMILLED	W 8009015	1655.1	W 6474232	1641.8	W 6601528	1616.9	W 7347502	1392.9	MAIS NON MOULU
048	CEREAL ETC PREPARATIONS	W 1625982	1382.4	W 1655810	1664.0	W 1654796	1733.3	W 1861386	1713.2	PREPTNS A BASE CEREALES
05	VEGETABLES AND FRUIT		3145.4		3632.9		3701.5		3513.0	LEGUMES ET FRUITS
054	VEG ETC FRSH,SMPLY PRSVD	W 2432797	1149.3	W 2526627	1328.6	W 2562467	1304.9	W 2761507	1178.7	LEGUMES FRAIS,CONG,SECS
057	FRUIT,NUTS,FRESH,DRIED	W 1292611	1190.0	W 1373583	1348.3		1487.1	W 1750192	1460.6	FRUITS FRAIS OU SECS
06	SUGAR AND PREPS,HONEY		1823.1		2026.6		2077.0		1664.6	SUCRES ET PRODUITS
061	SUGAR AND HONEY	W 3135688	1653.4	W 2929236	1849.9	W 3422340	1913.1	W 2921589	1511.1	SUCRES ET MIEL
0612	REFINED SUGAR ETC	W 2469110	1346.5	W 2770802	1783.0	W 2615531	1491.7	W 2760362	1441.6	SUCRES RAFFINES
07	COFFEE,TEA,COCOA,SPICES		1305.7		1682.5		1731.8		1356.5	CAFE,THE,CACAO,EPICES
073	CHOCOLATE AND PRODUCTS	W 199421	734.1	W 235107	1123.4	W 242912	1028.2	W 238470	824.9	CHOCOLAT
081	*FEEDING STUFF FOR ANIML	W 2886109	1175.8	W 2898381	1377.9	W 2949321	1365.1	W 3062258	1312.2	NOURRITURE POUR ANIMAUX
0819	FOOD WASTE AND FEED NES	W 1744489	1014.9	W 1722520	1196.4	W 1833620	1180.5	W 1978319	1153.1	DECHETS,ALIMENTS NDA
08199	FODDER NES,INCL SWEETNED	W 1039174	913.5	W 1131697	1099.0	W 1174950	1077.5	W 1369871	1071.4	PREPARATIONS FOURRAGERES
09	MISC EDIBLE PRODUCTS		1678.2		2041.1		2144.7		2322.3	PREP ALIMENTAIRES DIVERSES
098	EDIBLE PRODCTS,PREPS NES	W 388722	1617.4	W 412612	1978.0	W 413926	2092.5	W 467822	2272.4	PREP ALIMENTAIRES NDA
09809	MISC FOOD PREPRTIONS NES	W 286526	1435.0	W 306441	1761.2	W 303020	1864.9	W 349656	2057.0	PREP ALIMENTAIRES NDA
1	BEVERAGES AND TOBACCO		7365.7		8333.0		8378.7		8608.6	BOISSONS ET TABACS
11	BEVERAGES		7145.3		8064.7		8087.0		8277.3	BOISSONS
111	NON–ALCOHL BEVERAGES NES	W 5035485	747.2	W 4724930	871.0	W 3897877	758.6	W 3560764	784.5	BOISSONS NON ALCOOLIQUES
112	ALCOHOLIC BEVERAGES	W 1795687	6398.2	W 1825259	7193.7	W 1969299	7328.5	W 2267097	7492.9	BOISSONS ALCOOLIQUES
1121	WINE OF FRESH GRAPES ETC	W 1275567	3974.0	W 1258469	4606.7	W 1383242	4814.8	W 1670952	5211.3	VINS DE RAISINS FRAIS
11212	WINE OF FRESH GRAPES	W 1248626	3937.0	W 1226920	4565.2	W 1365205	4785.4	W 1635763	5180.0	VINS DE MOUTS DE RAISINS
1124	DISTILLED ALCOHOLIC BEVS	W 374049	2294.4	W 389690	2417.7	W 383298	2316.7	W 364720	2095.4	ALCOOLS,EAUX–DE–VIE
11242	DISTILLD WINE,GRAPE MARC	W 226169	1902.6	W 224477	1941.7	W 222337	1829.9	W 200532	1626.2	EAUX–DE–VIE NATURELLES
2	CRUDE MATERLS,EXCL FUELS		5564.7		6305.5		6081.9		5702.0	MAT BRUTES NON COMESTIBLES
22	OIL SEEDS,OLEAGINOUS FRT		430.3		578.2		743.6		921.9	GRAINES,FRUITS OLEAGINEUX
222	SEEDS FOR'SOFT'FIXED OIL	W 1285119	412.6	W 1770838	561.0	W 2430410	726.0	W 3337181	906.6	GRAINES HUILES FIXES
24	CORK AND WOOD		749.6		871.1		788.0		730.8	LIEGE ET BOIS
28	METALLIFEROUS ORES,SCRAP		1162.4		1378.5		1137.2		1088.6	MINERAIS METAL,DECHETS
3	MINERAL FUELS ETC		5784.1		6854.3		7429.4		7234.1	COMBUSTIBLES MINERAUX LUB
33	PETROLEUM AND PRODUCTS		2546.3		2589.4		3314.4		3522.9	PETROLE ET DERIVES
334	PETROLEUM PRODUCTS,REFIN	MW 13145	2328.4	MW 11442	2352.0	MW 14087	3073.5		3266.4	PRODUITS RAFFINES
3341	GASOLINE,OTH LIGHT OILS			W 4375031	799.0	W 5111258	1059.9		1243.5	ESSENCES POUR MOTEURS
33411	MOTOR,AVIATION SPIRIT			W 3565643	634.8	W 4260064	871.6	W 5027181	1025.3	ESSENCES MOTEURS D'AVIONS
3344	FUEL OILS,NES			W 2814772	270.4	W 6276249	948.0	W 4485301	451.1	FUEL OILS
351	*ELECTRIC CURRENT		2881.3		3839.1		3671.2		3169.3	ENERGIE ELECTRIQUE
5	CHEMCLS,RELATED PROD NES		33269.4		35794.0		40217.5		36319.7	PRODUITS CHIMIQUES
51	ORGANIC CHEMICALS		7004.9		5770.1		8732.2		5835.7	PROD CHIMIQ ORGANIQUES
511	HYDROCARBONS NES,DERIVS	W 3103550	3074.6	W 1219641	868.2	W 3360099	3659.9	W 1258940	705.2	HYDROCARBURES NDA
5112	CYCLIC HYDROCARBONS	W 2383297	2666.2	W 479579	337.3	W 2558652	3202.6	W 383397	179.9	HYDROCARBURES CYCLIQUES
51129	OTH CYCLIC HYDROCARBONS	W 9327	14.5	W 16947	24.1	W 2184267	3042.6	W 17400	28.9	AUT HYDROCARBURES CYCLIQUES
514	NITROGEN–FNCTN COMPOUNDS	W 257720	1177.3	W 252450	1398.2	W 203658	1433.9	W 192331	1346.1	COMPOSES FONCT AZOTEES
515	ORG–INORG COMPOUNDS ETC	W 123525	1157.1	W 132249	1555.6	W 136391	1683.7	W 143056	1824.2	COMPOSES ORGANO–MINERAUX
5156	HETEROCYCLIC CMPDS ETC	W 22661	793.8	W 33608	1046.5	W 25701	1153.1	W 27541	1347.7	COMPOSES HETEROCYCLIQUES
51569	OTH HETEROCYC CMPDS,ETC	W 17052	766.3	W 29430	1020.1	W 21059	1124.7	W 23423	1325.0	AUT COMP HETEROCYCLIQUES
52	INORGANIC CHEMICALS		2508.3		2209.1		2053.7		1837.6	PROD CHIM INORGANIQUES
522	INORG ELEMNTS,OXIDES,ETC	W 3450638	1100.0		561.8		510.4	W 1495997	493.8	ELEMENTS INORGANIQUES
524	RADIOACTIVE ETC MATERIAL		1058.9		1217.4		1125.9		978.5	MATIERES RADIOACTIVES
5241	RADIOACTIVE ELEMENTS ETC		989.4		1142.6		1093.7		954.7	RADIOELEMENTS,ISOTOPES
53	DYES,TANNING,COLOUR PROD		1626.8		1894.3		2021.9		1801.0	PROD TEINTURE,COLORANTS
533	PIGMENTS,PAINTS,ETC	W 406397	972.4	W 427035	1229.7	W 424750	1149.6	W 495565	1153.7	PIGMENTS,PEINTURES,VERNIS
541	*MEDICINAL,PHARM PRODUCT	MK 153106	5415.4	MK 178057	6864.4		7244.8		7900.9	PROD MEDICINAUX PHARMACEUT
5417	MEDICAMENTS	MK 121855	3912.0	MK 143051	5065.1	MK 137654	5324.9	MK 156203	5936.4	MEDICAMENTS
54179	— CONTNG OTH SUBSTANCES	MK 106697	3118.9	MK 129209	4086.8	MK 124725	4261.1	MK 141360	4799.7	MED CONT AUT SUBSTANCES
55	PERFUME,CLEANING ETC PRD		6287.1		7557.4		7636.8		7630.6	PROD POUR PARFUM,TOILETTE
551	ESSENTL OILS,PERFUME,ETC	W 27919	574.5	W 35098	717.2	W 35483	743.5	W 46503	888.4	HUILES ESSENTIELLES
553	PERFUMERY,COSMETICS,ETC	W 294817	4836.7	W 334703	5782.2	W 377853	5877.3	W 398644	5762.9	PRODUITS DE PARFUMERIE
554	SOAP,CLEANSING ETC PREPS	W 628933	875.9	W 679426	1058.0	W 693309	1016.1	W 783599	979.4	SAVONS,PRODUITS DETERSIFS
5542	WASHING PREPARATIONS ETC	W 544298	691.4	W 597808	857.0	W 613445	824.2	W 699234	797.6	PROD ORG TENSIO–ACT NDA
58	PLASTIC MATERIALS ETC		5642.4		6113.6		6883.1		5765.0	MAT PLAST ARTIFICIELLES
583	POLYMERIZATION ETC PRODS	W 4212098	5106.1	W 3783974	5389.6	W 4461610	6208.6	W 4456783	5056.2	PROD POLYMERISATION
5831	POLYETHYLENE	W 1050107	814.9	W 970644	1083.4	W 955763	957.5	W 933966	904.3	POLYETHYLENE
58311	— IN PRIMARY FORMS	W 959868	667.3	W 882981	924.3	W 861259	801.9	W 821868	730.2	POLYETHYLENE PRIMAIRES
5834	POLYVINYL CHLORIDE	W 722400	739.0	W 692795	966.8	W 832668	858.8	W 923835	904.2	CHLORURE DE POLYVINYLE
5839	OTH POLYMRZTION ETC PROD	W 924224	1968.3	W 662491	1247.2	W 1143366	2528.9	W 914953	1392.5	AUT PROD POLYMER COPOLYM
59	CHEMICAL MATERIALS NES		4442.4		5035.2		5283.3		5232.6	MAT PROD CHIMIQUES NDA
591	PESTICIDES,DISINFECTANTS	W 188681	1336.5	W 179100	1518.0	W 199918	1665.1	W 203081	1676.3	DESINF,INSECT,FONG,HERB
592	STARCH,INULIN,GLUTEN,ETC	W 696373	744.0	W 536316	818.6	W 745699	952.5	W 575336	777.4	AMIDONS,INUL,GLUT FROM
598	MISCEL CHEM PRODUCTS NES	W 1597991	2362.0	W 1517888	2698.6	W 1491100	2665.8	W 1578556	2779.0	PROD DIV INDUST CHIM NDA
5982	ANTI–KNOCK PREPARTNS ETC	W 474969	809.9	W 515686	928.4	W 519764	871.3	W 511667	882.5	PREPARAT ANTIDETONANTES
5989	CHEM PRODUCTS,PREPS NES	W 879390	1292.6	W 927422	1626.4	W 894759	1657.0	W 990424	1758.8	PROD PREP CHIMIQUES NDA
59899	OTH CHEM PRODS,PREPS,NES	W 693987	866.5	W 744577	1158.3	W 714854	1234.0	W 773758	1354.3	AUT PRODUITS CHIMIQUES NDA
6	BASIC MANUFACTURES		38359.9		46603.9		45742.1		43998.6	ART MANUFACTURES
62	RUBBER MANUFACTURES NES		3389.2		3879.4		4076.5		3986.6	CAOUTCHOUC MANUFACTURE
625	RUBBER TYRES, TUBES ETC	W 556082	2365.9	W 569684	2639.3	W 614298	2760.0	W 685856	2704.1	PNEUS CAOUTCHOUC VULCANISE
6251	TYRES NEW FOR MOTOR CARS	W 266929	1339.9	W 283749	1541.8	W 303242	1623.1	W 336169	1577.2	PNEUS POUR VOITURES
63	WOOD,CORK MANUFACTRS NES		1027.1		1305.9		1316.4		1322.4	OUVRAGES LIEGE ET BOIS
64	PAPER,PAPERBOARD AND MFR		4897.1		6368.7		5924.7		5637.3	PAPIERS,CARTONS & OUVRAGES
641	PAPER AND PAPERBOARD	W 3970478	3556.0	W 3885962	4711.2	W 4199997	4324.9	W 4636689	4138.1	PAPIERS ET CARTONS
6412	PRINTG,WRITING PAPER NES	W 1122423	1070.3	W 1109985	1449.2	W 1195015	1236.4	W 1241158	1175.2	PAPIERS POUR L'IMPRESSION
64122	— COATED,IMPREGNATD ETC	W 965803	908.7	W 962974	1233.9	W 1034194	1042.7	W 1077500	993.6	PAPIERS IMPRESSION COUCHES
6415	PAPER,PAPERBRD,BULK,NES	W 1074324	850.4	W 1016618	1117.5	W 1205309	1021.0	W 1321461	985.0	PAPIERS,CARTONS ROULEAUX
64159	OTHER PAPER ETC,BULK,NES	W 924189	721.2	W 868383	942.9	W 1055253	863.2	W 1125557	795.6	AUT PAPIER ROULEAUX FEUILLES

5. Special Exports F.O.B. by Commodities according to the S.I.T.C. (Rev. 2) in million U.S. Dollars
Exportations Spéciales F.O.B. par Produits d'après la C.T.C.I. (Rév. 2) en millions de Dollars E.U.

SITC CTCI	COMMODITY	1994 QUANTITY QUANTITE	1994 VALUE VALEUR	1995 QUANTITY QUANTITE	1995 VALUE VALEUR	1996 QUANTITY QUANTITE	1996 VALUE VALEUR	1997 QUANTITY QUANTITE	1997 VALUE VALEUR	PRODUIT
6418	COATED ETC PAPER NES BLK	W 436223	761.0	W 421530	931.6	W 459485	940.9	W 529191	947.8	PAP,CARTONS COUCHES,ENDUITS
642	PAPER,ETC,PRECUT,ARTS OF	W 703193	1341.1		1657.6	W 654306	1599.9	W 713527	1499.2	PAP,CARTONS DECOUPES
65	TEXTILE YARN,FABRICS,ETC		6541.7		7911.9		7644.7		7545.3	FILS,TISSUS,ARTICLES TEXTILE
651	TEXTILE YARN	W 293067	1551.5	W 316048	1845.0	W 323924	1679.4	W 365723	1632.6	FILS TEXTILES
652	COTTON FABRICS,WOVEN	W 90538	1054.7		1192.1	W 92243	1185.7	W 104514	1170.9	TISSUS DE COTON
6522	WOVEN COTTON BLEACHD,ETC	W 72301	937.5	W 75779	1064.7	W 72173	1050.2	W 81775	1032.4	TISSUS COTON BLANCHIS ETC
653	WOVN MAN–MADE FIB FABRIC	W 98096	1250.5	W 94980	1581.2	W 97467	1579.6	W 101825	1538.1	TISSUS FIBRES SYNTH,ARTIF
657	SPECIAL TXTL FABRC,PRODS	W 97127	726.1	W 110977	910.5	W 115653	907.2	W 125063	882.0	TISSUS SPECIAUX
66	NONMETAL MINERAL MFS NES		4468.7		5208.1		5251.5		5014.6	ART MIN NON METALLIQUES
664	GLASS	W 728149	817.7	W 831659	1039.8	W 829800	1047.9	W 958434	1014.3	VERRE
665	GLASSWARE	W 815480	1542.8	W 807662	1728.0	W 840742	1734.1	W 948034	1703.7	OUVRAGES EN VERRE
6652	HOUSEHLD,HOTEL ETC GLASS	W 345884	999.1	W 364728	1104.5	W 377673	1106.2	W 406187	1073.3	OBJETS VERRE TABLE,CUISINE
67	IRON AND STEEL		8800.9		10575.6		10343.4		9775.3	FER ET ACIER
672	IRON,STEEL PRIMARY FORMS	W 4144926	1508.0	W 3783397	1790.9		1600.0	W 4956822	1624.7	LINGOTS FER,ACIER
6727	IRN,STL COIL FR REROLLNG	W 2580193	904.8	W 2496446	1076.7	W 2848115	986.8	W 3262197	1053.5	EBAUCHES POUR TOLES FER
67271	IRON,SIMPLE STEEL COILS	W 2485018	834.2	W 2409745	990.1	W 2755758	927.1	W 3151272	999.7	EBAUCHES NON EN ACIER
673	IRON,STEEL SHAPES ETC	W 2966371	1531.4	W 2859689	1976.4	W 2823957	1695.2	W 2951127	1659.0	BARRES,PROFIL FER,ACIER
6732	IRON,STEEL BARS ETC	W 1192906	692.8	W 1168843	961.7	W 1156964	867.5	W 1278272	878.4	BARRES FER,ACIER
674	IRN,STL UNIV,PLATE,SHEET	W 4322690	3192.9	W 4827314	4235.5	W 4648888	3768.0	W 5264754	3690.0	LARGES PLATS,TOLES
6746	IRN,STL THIN PLATE,ROLLD	W 1432482	1098.1	W 1335427	1407.6	W 1284993	1193.4	W 1496246	1169.3	TOLES LAM MOINS 3MM
6749	OTH IRN,STL PLATES,SHEET	W 1623373	1112.3	W 1812880	1450.6	W 1799561	1285.6	W 2357333	1474.6	AUTRES TOLES FER,ACIER
67491	— OF IRON OR SIMPLE STL	W 1546100	976.7	W 1740629	1277.9	W 1656827	1087.1	W 1906015	1103.6	AUT TOLES AUTRES ACIER FIN
678	IRON,STL TUBES,PIPES,ETC	W 1375592	1550.3	W 1018728	1542.7	W 1452241	1894.4	W 1331752	1686.3	TUBES,TUYAUX EN FONTE,FER
68	NON–FERROUS METALS		3861.5		4698.2		4626.3		4309.8	METAUX NON FERREUX
682	COPPER EXC CEMENT COPPER	W 473904	1311.7	W 474012	1729.1	W 462112	1455.1	W 522310	1562.6	CUIVRE
6822	COPPER,ALLOYS WORKED	W 443446	1254.5	W 447496	1669.5	W 435946	1401.9	W 492104	1497.2	CUIVRE,ALLIAGES OUVRES
68221	COPPER BARS,WIRE,ETC	W 344255	861.5	W 355328	1151.1	W 349512	977.4	W 393218	1042.8	BARRES,PROFILES ET FILS
684	ALUMINIUM	W 671438	1683.1	W 661007	2185.6	W 701751	1990.7	W 680826	1856.9	ALUMINIUM
6842	ALUMINIUM,ALLOYS WORKED	W 459459	1343.1	W 456442	1727.8	W 419261	1483.1	W 453969	1455.6	ALUMINIUM,ALLIAGES OUVRE
68422	ALUMNM PLATE,SHEET,STRIP	W 340729	905.4	W 336614	1163.4	W 309687	997.6	W 328164	954.8	TOLES, PLANCHES EN ALU
69	METAL MANUFACTURES NES		4882.2		6108.9		5990.2		5821.3	ART MANUFACT EN METAL NDA
699	BASE METAL MFRS NES	W 320305	1835.7		2380.2		2392.8		2393.3	ART MANUFACTURES MET NDA
7	MACHINES,TRANSPORT EQUIP		91760.7		112492.0		115326.9		117947.7	MACHINES MATERIEL TRANSPORT
71	POWER GENERATING EQUIPMT		8724.7		9207.7		9098.1		9084.3	MACHINES GENERATRICES
713	INTRNL COMBUS PSTN ENGIN	W 306468	3283.5		3639.1	W 346263	3944.4	W 374519	3760.8	MOTEURS EXPL COMB INT, PIECE
7132	MOTOR VEHCL PISTN ENGINS	W 156360	1724.2	W 155394	2103.1	W 218509	2474.4	W 222539	2284.0	MOTEURS EXPL POUR VEHICULES
7139	PISTON ENGINE PARTS NES	W 126442	1202.8	W 113196	1283.4	W 109023	1250.5	W 132651	1232.3	PIECES POUR 713.2,3,8
714	ENGINES AND MOTORS NES	W 19703	3324.9	W 22300	3141.8	W 19623	2958.3	W 12666	3314.0	MOTEURS NON ELECTRIQUES
7144	REACTION ENGINES	W 968	1311.6	W 477	730.4	W 451	687.6	W 672	1086.0	PROPULSEURS A REACTION
7149	ENGINE & MOTOR PARTS NES	W 13480	1613.5	W 16418	1836.6	W 15421	1941.8	W 9937	2035.2	PIECES 714 ET 718.88
71491	PARTS NES OF 7144,71481	W 1099	1188.1	W 1203	1206.1	W 1224	1317.2	W 1887	1670.9	PIECES DES PROPULSEURS
716	ROTATING ELECTRIC PLANT	W 132457	1396.1	W 144573	1605.7	W 157261	1546.6	W 159039	1412.7	APP ELECTR ROTATIFS,PIECES
7162	AC MTRS,GENRTRS,GEN SETS	W 78426	823.2	W 88229	1018.1	W 95803	1014.0	W 91909	914.7	MOTEURS ELECTRIQUES
72	MACHS FOR SPCL INDUSTRYS		6007.6		7279.8		7497.5		7367.4	MAC SPECIALES POUR INDUST
723	CIVIL ENGNEERG EQUIP ETC	W 190168	1270.7	W 208300	1435.5	W 206637	1320.5	W 275681	1537.9	APPAREILS DE GENIE CIVIL
7234	CONST,MINING MACHNRY NES	W 163005	1066.8	W 172674	1183.1	W 170798	1069.8	W 227200	1259.9	MACH POUR LA CONST, MINES
72342	SLFPRP SHOVELS,EXCAVATRS	W 122858	741.0	W 131808	825.1	W 129922	739.8	W 163068	800.7	PELLES MECANIQUES
724	TEXTILE,LEATHER MACHNRY	W 49457	863.3	W 49065	979.7	W 53145	1006.7	W 63933	987.6	MACH POUR INDUSTRIE TEXTILE
728	OTH MACHY FOR SPCL INDUS	W 110523	1903.5	W 118141	2366.3	W 140889	2503.4	W 131254	2271.2	AUT MACH IND PARTICULIERES
7284	MACHY FOR SPCL INDUS NES	W 58726	1449.5	W 69154	1947.5	W 75928	1902.9	W 76522	1871.2	MACH SPEC IND PARTICUL.
73	METALWORKING MACHINERY		951.3		1367.6		1322.8		1425.9	MACH TRAVAIL DES METAUX
736	METALWORKING MACH–TOOLS	W 42601	591.0		880.3	W 58032	777.2	W 73223	821.5	MACH–OUTILS TRAVAIL METAUX
74	GENRL INDUSTRL MACHY NES		10010.0		12597.1		13292.8		13150.4	MACH APP INDUSTRIE
741	HEATING,COOLING EQUIPMNT	W 174770	2014.2	W 223867	2551.1	W 220369	2644.3	W 243930	2685.5	MACH CHAUFFAGE,PIECES
7416	HEATING,COOLING EQU NES	W 77257	823.6	W 67597	886.9	W 77661	914.6	W 91686	999.8	APP CHANGEMENT TEMP
742	PUMPS FOR LIQUIDS ETC	W 44219	1064.3	W 57989	1268.7	W 60035	1437.8	W 69681	1430.5	POMPES MOTO–POMPES
743	PUMPS NES,CENTRFUGES ETC	W 108907	1609.3	W 123773	2030.2	W 141942	2179.1	W 146406	2219.0	POMPES COMPRES,VENT ETC
744	MECHANICAL HANDLING EQU	W 281766	1711.1	W 333858	2259.8	W 342100	2303.7	W 357480	2186.8	EQUIP MANUTENTION PIECES
7442	LIFTING,LOADING MACH NES	W 107529	685.0	W 110961	839.0	W 120182	869.5	W 121285	818.3	APP LEVAGE,MANUTENTION
7449	PTS NES OF MACHY OF 7442	W 121448	731.0	W 155649	986.6	W 145730	975.6	W 148716	916.8	PIECES DU 744.2
749	NONELEC MACH PTS,ACC NES	W 217353	2963.8	W 237727	3721.4	W 247618	3879.3	W 275913	3843.0	PIECES MACH NON ELEC NDA
7491	BALL,ROLLER,ETC BEARINGS	W 59280	761.7	W 64050	972.5	W 67913	1043.6	W 73462	993.0	ROULEMENTS BILLES ETC
7492	COCKS,VALVES ETC NES	W 56905	1116.4	W 63778	1331.7	W 68021	1416.8	W 73702	1414.7	ART ROB,SIM POUR TUYAUX
75	OFFICE MACHNES,ADP EQUIP		6766.1		8964.1		9815.4		10279.8	MACH BUREAU TRAIT AUTOM
752	AUTOMTIC DATA PROC EQUIP	W 42612	3882.9	W 59759	5714.3	W 91567	6496.9	W 92314	6925.1	MACH TRAIT INFORMATION
7523	DIGITL CENTRL PROCESSORS	W 13749	2011.5	W 22319	2804.2	W 22018	2911.6	W 28219	3072.5	UNITES CENTRALES
7524	DIGITL CENTRL STOR UNITS	W 2380	357.4	W 3288	471.8	W 4062	601.5	W 4346	870.9	UNITES MEMOIRE CENTRALES
7525	ADP PERIPHERAL UNITS	W 22716	980.9	W 28296	1584.2	W 58009	1997.8	W 53752	1897.0	UNITES PERIPHERIQUES
759	OFFICE,ADP MCH PTS,ACCES	W 29429	2255.8	W 24588	2474.9	W 32575	2617.9	W 35698	2721.3	PIECES DU 751 ET 752
7599	ACCTG,ETC,ADP MCH PTS,AC	W 19103	1968.3	W 13218	2116.0	W 20623	2242.2	W 24835	2313.6	PIECES DU 751 ET 752
76	TELECOMM,SOUND EQUIPMENT		4682.6		6327.9		6797.3		8075.5	EQUIPMENT DE TELECOM
761	TELEVISION RECEIVERS	W 50257	690.3	W 61043	898.6	W 65850	899.6	W 85516	1097.7	RECEPTEURS DE TELEVISION
7611	COLOUR TV RECEIVERS	W 50148	685.9	W 60860	892.3	W 65781	896.9	W 85366	1094.8	RECEPTEURS COULEUR
764	TELECOM EQPT,PTS,ACC NES	W 37913	3329.1	W 44356	4588.7	W 52093	5081.5	W 60267	6319.9	EQUIP TELECOM,PIECES
7641	LINE TELEPHONE,ETC EQUIP	W 12357	1217.5	W 11702	1503.6	W 11772	1530.0	W 13243	1348.0	APP TELEPHON PAR FIL
7643	TV,RADIO TRANSMITTRS ETC	W 1701	458.4	W 3199	901.7	W 5224	1307.3	W 10139	2153.5	APP EMET TELE RADIO
7649	PTS NES OF EQUIPMT OF 76	W 16988	1225.5	W 20872	1718.5	W 27362	1797.0	W 27606	1936.1	PIECES DE LA DIV 76
76493	TELECOMM EQUIPMT PTS NES	W 9574	622.2	W 13375	925.9	W 20157	1022.9	W 16573	1122.0	PIECES 761,762,764.3,8
77	ELECTRIC MACHNRY NES ETC		14935.3		19401.0		20307.4		20870.5	MACH APP ELECT NDA
771	ELECTRIC POWER MACHY NES	W 67214	846.0	W 70108	985.6	W 82068	1061.8	W 92873	1118.0	MACH PROD,TRANS ELECTR
772	SWITCHGEAR ETC,PARTS NES	W 133079	3907.3	W 143995	4715.6	W 147305	4700.4	W 164371	4753.8	APP COUPURE,SECT ETC
7721	SWITCHGEAR ETC	W 131427	3748.3	W 141960	4485.7	W 144531	4436.3	W 161449	4505.0	APP COUPURE,SECTIONMNT
773	ELECTR DISTRIBUTNG EQUIP	W 202156	990.1	W 212487	1315.1	W 207487	1385.1	W 226160	1421.9	EQUIPMT DISTRIBUTION ELECT
7731	INSULATED WIRE,CABLE ETC	W 178805	853.8	W 184740	1121.1	W 186744	1233.2	W 203256	1265.0	FILS,CABLES ISOLES ELECT
774	ELECTRO–MEDCL,XRAY EQUIP	W 6046	725.7	W 5883	768.9	W 6136	790.2	W 6912	718.8	APPAREILS MEDICAUX
775	HOUSEHOLD TYPE EQUIP NES	W 214358	1850.2	W 224615	2204.3	W 233067	2349.5	W 249265	2286.7	MACH,APP USAGE DOMESTQUE
7758	ELECTRO–THERMIC APPL NES	W 99267	974.8	W 110065	1176.5	W 118333	1305.4	W 125972	1259.3	APP ELECTROTHERMIQ NDA
77586	ELECTROTHERM DOM APP NES	W 71393	647.8	W 78444	770.8	W 84704	874.1	W 88566	841.4	APP ELECTRO THERMIQUES
776	TRANSISTORS,VALVES,ETC	W 45955	3739.0	W 53158	5641.7	W 59321	6113.9	W 57439	6729.7	LAMPES,TUBES,VALVES
7763	DIODES,TRANSISTORS,ETC	W 3467	704.3	W 3556	923.4	W 5283	909.7	W 4273	1002.9	DIODES,TRANSISTORS
7764	ELECTRONIC MICROCIRCUITS	W 5255	2465.6	W 6357	4035.1	W 8197	4492.8	W 8267	5107.3	MICROSTRUCTURES ELECTRON
778	ELECTRICAL MACHINERY NES	W 388742	2877.4	W 392807	3770.1	W 409286	3906.8	W 424589	3842.0	AUTRES MACH ELECT NDA
7783	AUTOMOTIVE ELECTR EQUIP	W 60720	914.0	W 72498	1112.9	W 75218	1160.8	W 80001	1146.0	EQUIP ELECT MOTEURS EXPL
7788	OTH ELEC MACHY,EQUIP NES	W 87679	1005.5	W 105188	1403.0	W 99287	1414.4	W 99515	1370.6	AUT MACH APP ELEC NDA
78	ROAD VEHICLES		26647.9		31377.1		31618.6		32235.3	VEHICULES ROUTIERS
781	PASS MOTOR VEH EXC BUSES	W 1447587	13789.5	W 1357653	15212.3	W 1449977	15803.8	W 1805761	17345.3	AUTO TRANSPORT PERSONNES
782	LORRIES,SPCL MTR VEH NES	W 232062	1790.5	W 289709	2434.4	W 286414	2457.0	W 359390	2503.4	VEHICULES SPECIAUX,MARCH
7821	LORRIES,TRUCKS	W 217180	1641.4	W 272017	2226.2	W 266822	2237.9	W 333063	2263.2	VEHICULES TRANSP MARCHAND
783	ROAD MOTOR VEHICLES NES	W 115951	839.6	W 208421	2240.1	W 192728	1908.0	W 172446	1263.8	VEHICULES ROUTIERS NDA
7832	TRACTORS FOR TR–TRAILERS	W 103637	714.3	W 192214	2073.1	W 174515	1763.3	W 150398	1112.8	TRACTEURS ROUTIERS
784	MOTOR VEH PRTS,ACCES NES	W 1214006	9294.3	W 1265663	10323.7	W 1339267	10346.6	W 1480713	9942.2	PIECES 722,781,782,783

5. Special Exports F.O.B. by Commodities according to the S.I.T.C. (Rev. 2) in million U.S. Dollars
Exportations Spéciales F.O.B. par Produits d'après la C.T.C.I. (Rév. 2) en millions de Dollars E.U.

SITC CTCI	COMMODITY	1994		1995		1996		1997		PRODUIT
		QUANTITY QUANTITE	VALUE VALEUR	QUANTITY QUANTITE	VALUE VALEUR	QUANTITY QUANTITE	VALUE VALEUR	QUANTITY QUANTITE	VALUE VALEUR	
7849	OTHER MOTOR VEHCL PARTS	W 1190619	9098.1	W 1234343	10021.2	W 1309146	10069.9	W 1447975	9685.6	PIECES 722,781,782,783
79	OTHR TRANSPORT EQUIPMENT		13035.5		15970.3		15577.3		15458.9	AUTRE MATERIEL TRANSPORT
791	RAILWAY VEHICLES	W 85189	1233.4	W 70359	644.3	W 79851	489.9	W 68636	573.2	VEHIC MAT CHEMINS DE FER
792	AIRCRAFT ETC	W 16094	11080.2	W 16656	13548.4	W 24775	13223.9	W 21848	13613.9	APP NAVIGATION AERIENNE
7923	AIRCRFT NES2000–15000KG	W 1156	1216.2	W 1178	1181.0	W 1048	1161.4	W 1169	1363.3	AERODYNES 2000 A 15000 KG
7924	AIRCRFT NES OVER 15000KG	W 10836	7865.4	W 11132	10059.0	W 11462	7679.6	W 15671	10306.9	AERODYNES PLUS 15000 KG
7928	AIRCRAFT NES,ASSOC EQUIP	W 76	7.0	W 235	20.1	W 256	1215.0	W 164	37.5	APP NAVIG AERIENNE NDA
79283	AIRCRAFT LAUNCHERS ETC	W 55	5.5	W 211	19.2	W 205	1212.5	W 136	35.9	CATAPULTES
7929	AIRCRAFT PARTS NES	W 3658	1800.4	W 3724	2057.7	W 11693	2899.7	W 4442	1608.5	PIECES DU 792
793	SHIPS AND BOATS ETC	W 292991	722.1	W 795429	1777.7	W 226241	1863.6	W 321137	1271.9	NAVIRES BATEAUX,ETC
7932	SHIPS AND BOATS NES	W 248219	648.3	W 761211	1414.2	W 196924	1054.5	W 300028	1184.7	NAVIRES ET BATEAUX
8	MISC MANUFACTURED GOODS		23918.8		28166.7		28201.2		27507.8	ART MANUFACTURES DIVERS
812	*PLUMBG,HEATNG,LGHTNG EQ	W 162480	988.1	W 166151	1143.3	W 181461	1162.2	W 198339	1092.2	APPAR SANITAIRES CHAUFFAGE
821	*FURNITURE,PARTS THEREOF	W 363036	1807.9	W 340201	2080.3	W 372888	2197.6	W 429115	2198.9	MEUBLES ET PIECES
8219	FURNITURE AND PARTS NES	W 234419	948.9	W 212340	1076.9	W 239453	1136.9	W 282255	1144.2	AUTRES MEUBLES ET PIECES
831	*TRAVEL GOODS,HANDBAGS	W 20749	972.5	W 22977	1206.8	W 22035	1232.6	W 26025	1145.0	ARTICLES DE VOYAGE ETC
84	CLOTHING AND ACCESSORIES		4975.5		5622.5		5529.9		5345.8	VETEMENTS
843	WOMENS OUTERWEAR NONKNIT	W 29395	1910.4	W 28492	2116.3	W 27178	2038.4	W 28573	1961.2	VET DESSUS FEMMES MAT TEX
8439	— OTHER OUTER GARMENTS	W 19264	1209.0	W 17615	1321.6	W 17453	1276.8	W 18799	1253.1	AUT VET DES FEM MAT TEXT
845	OUTERWEAR KNIT NONELASTC	W 23416	1039.7	W 21199	1141.5	W 22176	1166.5	W 25493	1181.9	VET DESSOUS,ACCES BONNET
846	UNDER GARMENTS KNITTED	W 14703	799.0	W 15551	970.2	W 18890	978.4	W 25167	956.6	SOUS VETS DE BONNETERIE
851	*FOOTWEAR	W 44298	958.7	W 41724	1038.6	W 39137	952.4	W 41580	895.3	CHAUSSURES
85102	FOOTWEAR LEATHER	W 31477	756.8	W 29348	824.0	W 27285	762.5	W 28915	717.2	CHAUS SEMELLES EN CUIR
87	PRECISION INSTRUMNTS NES		3463.0		4307.8		4365.6		4614.8	INSTRUM,APPAR SCIENT NDA
874	MEASURNG,CONTROLNG INSTR	W 38011	2515.6	W 36405	3038.5	W 36410	3039.0	W 40826	3162.5	INSTRUMENTS DE MESURE
88	PHOTO EQU,OPTICL GDS ETC		2068.0		2244.8		2278.4		2144.1	APP,FOURN PHOTO,OP,MONTR
882	PHOTO,CINEMA SUPPLIES	W 73394	904.4	W 76186	981.6	W 75023	1050.8	W 81721	1018.8	PRODUITS PHOTO,CINEMA
8822	PHOTO FILM EXC DEV CINMA	W 44832	825.4	W 46856	891.7	W 46075	950.6	W 51455	913.2	PLAQUES,PELLICULES,FILMS
89	MISC MANUFCTRD GOODS NES		8685.4		10522.9		10483.1		10072.1	ART MANUFACTURES DIVERS
892	PRINTED MATTER	W 268853	1601.7	W 314690	2004.3	W 331892	1904.9	W 371600	1756.7	IMPRIMES
893	ARTICLES OF PLASTIC NES		2698.6		3458.3		3452.1		3423.8	OUVRAGES EN MAT DIVIS 58
8931	PLSTC PACKG CONTNRS,LIDS	W 230321	812.6	W 203947	965.8	W 201526	939.0	W 251633	961.0	ART TRANSP EMBALLAGE ETC
8939	MISC PLASTIC ARTICLES	W 365395	1788.7	W 446930	2377.5	W 406543	2398.5	W 464080	2367.9	ART DIVERS EN MAT DIV 58
89399	OTHR PLASTC ARTICLES NES	W 304919	1609.5	W 382090	2155.5	W 342958	2181.0	W 382724	2129.6	AUT OUV MAT DIV 58
894	TOYS,SPORTING GOODS,ETC	W 90842	1061.6	W 94410	1175.2	W 90206	1107.3	W 97735	1050.4	VOITURES ENFANTS,JOUETS
897	GOLD,SILVER WARE,JEWELRY		785.3		802.3		844.1		662.1	BIJOUTERIE,ORFEVRERIE
898	MUSICAL INSTRUMENTS,PTS	W 53576	848.5		1163.9		1157.5	W 69599	1143.4	INSTRUMENTS DE MUSIQUE
8983	SOUND RECRDNG TAPE,DISCS	W 52572	756.4	W 65483	1058.7	W 63275	1050.9	W 68522	1042.8	SUPPORTS SON POUR 763
899	OTHER MANUFACTURED GOODS		814.3		970.3		988.9		973.0	AUT ART MANUF DIVERS NDA
9	GOODS NOT CLASSD BY KIND		653.9		8257.6		1888.0		7507.5	ART TRANSACT NON CLASSES
931	*SPECIAL TRANSACTIONS	W 14207	38.5	W 8664404	7684.3		1174.8	W 8565792	6965.6	TRANS.SPECIALES

FOOT NOTES – NOTES

TABLE 1 –
1 The gold trade includes crude gold, gold specie and partly–worked gold.
TABLEAU 1 –
1 Le commerce d'or comprend l'or brut, les monnaies en or e t l'or partiellement travaillé.

1. HISTORICAL SERIES, 1960–1995 GENERAL TRADE, IMPORTS C.I.F., EXPORTS F.O.B. # 1
SERIES HISTORIQUES, 1960–1995 COMMERCE GENERAL, IMPORTATIONS C.A.F., EXPORTATIONS F.O.B

YEAR ANNEE	VALUE IN MILLION C.F.P. FRANCS VALEUR EN MILLION C.F.P. FRANCS MERCHANDISE –MARCHANDISE IMPORTS	EXPORTS	GOLD –OR IMPORTS	EXPORTS	CONVERSION FACTORS U.S. CENTS PER C.F.P. FRANC FACTEURS DE CONVERSION CENTS E.U. PAR C.F.P. FRANC IMPORTS	EXPORTS	INDEX NUMBERS –INDICES QUANTUM IMPORTS	EXPORTS	UNIT VALUE VALEUR UNITAIRE IMPORTS	EXPORTS
1960	1644.00	1125.00			1.1140	1.1140				
1961	2097.00	1035.00			1.1140	1.1140				
1962	2226.00	972.00			1.1140	1.1140				
1963	2894.00	919.00			1.1140	1.1140				
1964	6391.00	997.00			1.1140	1.1140				
1965	9637.00	920.00			1.1140	1.1140				
1966	14946.00	1560.00			1.1140	1.1140				
1967	10227.00	1167.00			1.1140	1.1140				
1968	15617.00	1039.00			1.1140	1.1140				
1969	10368.00	1303.00			1.0523	1.0821				
1970	13642.00	1840.00			0.9902	0.9902				
1971	14073.00	1749.00			0.9902	0.9902				
1972	14271.00	1341.00			1.0915	1.0934				
1973	16898.00	1497.00			1.2512	1.2638				
1974	25151.00	2775.00			1.1442	1.1530				
1975	22322.00	1969.00			1.2855	1.2859				
1976	25700.00	1911.00			1.1480	1.1481				
1977	29187.00	1464.00			1.1207	1.1188				
1978	33070.00	2978.00			1.2193	1.2288				
1979	36705.00	2215.00			1.2975	1.3011				
1980	42030.00	2340.00			1.3025	1.2899				
1981	53877.00	2861.00			1.0143	1.0098				
1982	62307.00	3349.00			0.8342	0.8339				
1983	74242.10	4820.00			0.7183	0.7147				
1984	85622.80	5083.10			0.6293	0.6211				
1985	88940.00	6564.40			0.6169	0.6193				
1986	92666.99	5112.00			0.7941	0.7941				
1987	90586.98	9095.00			0.9132	0.9143				
1988	87486.72	8111.99			0.9240	0.9212				
1989	91664.00	10308.00			0.8632	0.8616				
1990	91926.00	11011.18			1.0105	1.0048				
1991	93865.33	13148.00			0.9744	0.9686				
1992	86046.00	10184.00			1.0392	1.0494				
1993	86904.99	15183.00			0.9806	0.9766				
1994	87866.00	22286.99			1.0023	1.0147				
1995	91382.98	17548.00			1.1152	1.1186				

2. IMPORTS BY BROAD ECONOMIC CATEGORY AND EXPORTS BY INDUSTRIAL ORIGIN. (PERCENTAGE OF TOTAL VALUE)
IMPORTATIONS PAR CATEGORIES ECONOMIQUES ET EXPORTATIONS PAR BRANCHE D'ACTIVITE.(EN POURCENTAGE DE LA VALEUR TOTALE)

IMPORTS – IMPORTATIONS

	1989	1990	1991	1992	1993	1994	1995
TOTAL IMPORTS–IMPORTATIONS TOTALES							
1 FOOD BEV–ALIMENTATION BOISSONS							
11 PRIMARY–PRODUITS DE BASE							
111 FOR INDUSTRY–POUR L'INDUSTRIE							
112 FOR HOUSEHOLDS–POUR LES MENAGES							
12 PROCESSED–PRODUITS ELABORES							
121 FOR INDUSTRY–POUR L'INDUSTRIE							
122 FOR HOUSEHOLDS–POUR LES MENAGES							
2 IND SUPPLIES–APPROV INDUSTRIELS							
21 PRIMARY–PRODUITS DE BASE							
22 PROCESSED–PRODUITS ELABORES							
3 FUELS–COMBUSTIBLES							
31 PRIMARY–PRODUITS DE BASE							
32 PROCESSED–PRODUITS ELABORES							
321 MOTOR SPIRIT–ESSENCE							
322 OTHER–AUTRES							
4 MACHINERY–EQUIPEMENT							
41 CAPITAL EQUIPMENT–MACHINES							
42 PARTS–PIECES ACCESSOIRES							
5 TRANSPORT–TRANSPORT							
51 PASSENGER CARS–AUTOMOBILES							
52 OTHER–AUTRES							
521 INDUSTRIAL–INDUSTRIELS							
522 NON INDUSTRIAL–NON INDUSTRIEL							
53 PARTS–PIECES ACCESSOIRES							
6 CONSUM GOODS–BIENS CONSOMMATION							
61 DURABLE–DURABLES							
62 SEMI DURABLE–SEMI DURABLES							
63 NON DURABLE–NON DURABLES							
7 GOODS NES–BIENS NDA							

EXPORTS – EXPORTATIONS

	1989	1990	1991	1992	1993	1994	1995
TOTAL EXPORTS–EXPORTATIONS TOTALES							
1 AGRICULTURE							
2 MINING QUARRY–INDUS EXTRACTIVES							
3 MANUFACTURING–IND MANUFACTUR							
31 FOOD BEV TOBACCO–ALIM BOISS TAB							
32 TEXTILES–INDUSTRIES TEXTILES							
33 WOOD & PRODUCTS–BOIS & PRODUITS							
34 PAPER & PRODUCTS–PAPIER & PRODT							
35 CHEMICALS–INDUSTRIES CHIMIQUES							
36 NON METAL MIN–MIN NON METAL							
37 BASIC METAL–IND METAL BASE							
38 METAL MANUF–MANUF METAL							
39 OTH MANUF IND–AUTRES MANUF							

3. TRADE BY PRINCIPAL COUNTRIES OF ORIGIN AND DESTINATION (VALUE IN MILLION U.S. DOLLARS)
ECHANGES SELON LES PRINCIPAUX PAYS D'ORIGINE ET DE DESTINATION (VALEUR EN MILLIONS DE DOLLARS EU)

COUNTRIES–PAYS	GENERAL IMPORTS C.I.F. IMPORTATIONS GENERALES C.A.F				
	1991	1992	1993	1994	1995
World	913.9	893.8	852.2	880.7	
Africa					
Americas	112.0	121.1	117.0	122.8	
– Northern America	112.0	121.1	117.0	122.8	
– LAIA					
– CACM					
– Caribbean					
– Rest of America					
Asia excl fmr USSR	61.0	53.6	41.1	35.5	
– Middle East					
Asia former USSR					
Europe excl fmr USSR	536.3	520.6	497.1	508.8	
– European Union	433.9	406.4	393.1	394.2	
– Eastern Europe					
– Rest of Europe	102.4	114.2	103.9	114.5	
Europe former USSR					
Oceania	113.6	113.8	108.4	125.5	
Other	91.0	84.6	88.5	88.1	
France, Monaco	433.9	406.4	393.1	394.2	
Areas n.e.s.	91.0	84.6	88.5	88.1	
USA/Etats–Unis d'Amer	112.0	121.1	117.0	122.8	
Other Europe n.e.s.	102.4	114.2	103.9	114.5	
Australia/Australie	63.8	61.9	46.0	60.1	
New Zealand	49.8	51.9	62.5	65.4	
Israel/Israël	46.7	44.4			
Japan/Japon			41.1	35.5	
Singapore/Singapour	14.3	9.2			

COUNTRIES–PAYS	GENERAL EXPORTS F.O.B. EXPORTATIONS GENERALES F.O.B.				
	1991	1992	1993	1994	1995
Monde	127.2	106.8	149.0	226.2	
Afrique					
Amériques	13.4	11.5	11.8	19.0	
– Amérique du Nord	13.4	11.5	11.8	19.0	
– ALAI					
– MCAC					
– Caraïbes					
– Autre Amérique					
Asie anc. URSS exclus			63.0	103.5	
– Moyen–Orient					
Asie ancienne URSS					
Europe anc. URSS exclus	62.7	40.1	53.0	84.1	
– Union Européenne	61.4	36.3	51.0	74.0	
– Europe de l'Est					
– Autre de l'Europe	1.4	3.8	1.9	10.1	
Europe ancienne URSS					
Océanie	4.0	4.2	2.8	2.8	
Autre	47.2	51.0	18.4	16.8	
Areas n.e.s.	47.2	51.0	18.4	16.8	
France, Monaco	61.4	36.3	51.0	74.0	
Japan/Japon			63.0	103.5	
USA/Etats–Unis d'Amer	13.4	11.5	11.8	19.0	
Other Europe n.e.s.	1.4	3.8	1.9	10.1	
New Caledonia	4.0	4.2	2.8	2.8	

(VALUE AS PERCENTAGE OF WORLD TOTAL)(VALEURS EN POURCENTAGE DU TOTAL MONDIAL)

	1986	1987	1988	1989	1990	1991	1992	1993	1994	1995
Africa	0.4	0.5								
Americas	14.6	1.1		12.5	10.9	12.3	13.6	13.7	13.9	
– Northern America	13.8	0.5		12.5	10.9	12.3	13.6	13.7	13.9	
– LAIA	0.4	0.5								
– CACM										
– Caribbean	0.5	0.1								
– Rest of America	0.0	0.0								
Asia excl fmr USSR	11.1	10.9		4.0	5.7	6.7	6.0	4.8	4.0	
– Middle East										
Asia former USSR										
Europe excl fmr USSR	64.8	66.3		63.3	63.9	58.7	58.2	58.3	57.8	
– European Union	64.3	65.8		63.3	51.6	47.5	45.5	46.1	44.8	
– Eastern Europe										
– Rest of Europe	0.5	0.5			12.4	11.2	12.8	12.2	13.0	
Europe former USSR										
Oceania	9.0	10.7		10.7	11.0	12.4	12.7	12.7	14.2	
Other	0.0	0.0		9.5	8.4	10.0	9.5	10.4	10.0	
France, Monaco	50.1	52.2		52.3	51.6	47.5	45.5	46.1	44.8	
Areas n.e.s.	0.0	0.0		9.5	8.4	10.0	9.5	10.4	10.0	
USA/Etats–Unis d'Amer	13.6			12.5	10.9	12.3	13.6	13.7	13.9	
Other Europe n.e.s.	0.2	0.2			12.4	11.2	12.8	12.2	13.0	
Australia/Australie	4.3	5.5		5.9	6.4	7.0	6.9	5.4	6.8	
New Zealand	4.4	4.9		4.8	4.7	5.4	5.8	7.3	7.4	
Israel/Israël					4.5	5.1	5.0			
Japan/Japon	5.1	4.2		4.0				4.8	4.0	
Singapore/Singapour	2.4	2.5			1.2	1.6	1.0			

	1986	1987	1988	1989	1990	1991	1992	1993	1994	1995
Afrique	0.1	0.1								
Amériques	11.7	19.5		13.9	10.1	10.5	10.8	7.9	8.4	
– Amérique du Nord	11.6	18.8		13.9	10.1	10.5	10.8	7.9	8.4	
– ALAI	0.0	0.7								
– MCAC										
– Caraïbes										
– Autre Amérique										
Asie anc. URSS exclus	18.6	18.0						42.3	45.8	
– Moyen–Orient										
Asie ancienne URSS										
Europe anc. URSS exclus	53.6	54.9		48.9	50.9	49.3	37.5	35.6	37.2	
– Union Européenne	53.5	53.2		35.5	29.6	48.2	34.0	34.3	32.7	
– Europe de l'Est										
– Autre de l'Europe	0.1	1.7		13.4	21.3	1.1	3.6	1.3	4.5	
Europe ancienne URSS										
Océanie	15.2	6.7		3.5	3.1	3.1	3.9	1.9	1.2	
Autre	0.0	0.0		33.7	36.0	37.1	47.8	12.3	7.4	
Areas n.e.s.	0.0	0.0		33.7	36.0	37.1	47.8	12.3	7.4	
France, Monaco	52.1	52.9		35.5	29.6	48.2	34.0	34.3	32.7	
Japan/Japon	18.2	17.0						42.3	45.8	
USA/Etats–Unis d'Amer	11.6	18.8		13.9	10.1	10.5	10.8	7.9	8.4	
Other Europe n.e.s.	0.0	0.0		13.4	21.3	1.1	3.6	1.3	4.5	
New Caledonia	14.3	5.9		3.5	3.1	3.1	3.9	1.9	1.2	

4. General Imports C.I.F. by Commodities according to the S.I.T.C. (Rev. 2) in million U.S. Dollars
Importations Générales C.A.F. par Produits d'après la C.T.C.I. (Rév. 2) en millions de Dollars E.U.

SITC CTCI	COMMODITY	1992		1993		1994		1995		PRODUIT
		QUANTITY QUANTITE	VALUE VALEUR	QUANTITY QUANTITE	VALUE VALEUR	QUANTITY QUANTITE	VALUE VALEUR	QUANTITY QUANTITE	VALUE VALEUR	
	ALL COMMODITIES		893.8		852.2		880.7		1019.2	TOUS PRODUITS
011	MEAT FRESH,CHILLD,FROZEN		39.9		39.4		42.2		49.1	VIANDES FRAICHES,REF,CONGE
1	BEVERAGES AND TOBACCO				19.8		20.0			BOISSONS ET TABACS
11	BEVERAGES		16.4		16.3		16.4		20.5	BOISSONS
12	TOBACCO AND MANUFACTURES		3.6		3.5		3.7		4.2	TABACS BRUTS FABRIQUES
541	*MEDICINAL,PHARM PRODUCT		21.2		21.4		22.5		29.4	PROD MEDICINAUX PHARMACEUT
67	IRON AND STEEL		31.5		28.4		25.9		30.7	FER ET ACIER
7	MACHINES,TRANSPORT EQUIP		174.2		159.8		170.9		185.0	MACHINES MATERIEL TRANSPORT

5. General Exports F.O.B. by Commodities according to the S.I.T.C. (Rev. 2) in million U.S. Dollars
Exportations Générales F.O.B. par Produits d'après la C.T.C.I. (Rév. 2) en millions de Dollars E.U.

SITC CTCI	COMMODITY	1992		1993		1994		1995		PRODUIT
		QUANTITY QUANTITE	VALUE VALEUR	QUANTITY QUANTITE	VALUE VALEUR	QUANTITY QUANTITE	VALUE VALEUR	QUANTITY QUANTITE	VALUE VALEUR	
	ALL COMMODITIES		106.8		149.0		226.2		196.3	TOUS PRODUITS
0	FOOD AND LIVE ANIMALS				1.2		0.9			ALIMENTS,ANIMAUX VIVANTS
07521	VANILLA		0.5	W 15	1.2	W 10	0.9		1.5	VANILLE
29	CRUDE ANIMAL,VEG MAT NES				2.0		2.6			MATIERES BRUTES ANIM,VEGET
4243	COCONUT (COPRA) OIL		2.2	W 5050	1.8	W 7744	3.9		3.0	HJUILE DE COPRAH
553	PERFUMERY,COSMETICS,ETC		1.0		1.2	W 264	1.7		2.0	PRODUITS DE PARFUMERIE
6671	PEARLS UNSET,UNSTRUNG		44.7		76.0		120.9		110.8	PERLES FINES NON SERTIES
89911	GOODS OF ANML CARVNG MTL		1.5	W 181	2.0	W 541	2.6		2.1	ECAILLE,NACRE,IVOIRE ETC
931	*SPECIAL TRANSACTIONS			W 1191	2.4	W 892	2.2			TRANS.SPECIALES

FOOT NOTES – NOTES

TABLE 1 –
1 Prior to 1983, special trade.
TABLEAU 1 –
1 Avant 1983, commerce spécial.

1. HISTORICAL SERIES, 1961–1996 SPECIAL TRADE, IMPORTS C.I.F., EXPORTS F.O.B.
SERIES HISTORIQUES, 1961–1996 COMMERCE SPECIAL, IMPORTATIONS C.A.F., EXPORTATIONS F.O.B

YEAR ANNEE	VALUE IN MILLION C.F.A. FRANCS VALEUR EN MILLION C.F.A. FRANCS MERCHANDISE –MARCHANDISE		GOLD –OR		CONVERSION FACTORS U.S. CENTS PER C.F.A. FRANC FACTEURS DE CONVERSION CENTS E.U. PAR C.F.A. FRANC		INDEX NUMBERS –INDICES QUANTUM		UNIT VALUE VALEUR UNITAIRE	
	IMPORTS	EXPORTS	IMPORTS	EXPORTS	IMPORTS	EXPORTS	IMPORTS	EXPORTS	IMPORTS	EXPORTS
1961	8831.00	13767.00	0.10	97.80	0.4051	0.4051				
1962	10061.00	14535.00	0.30	92.60	0.4051	0.4051				
1963	11874.00	17859.00		266.00	0.4051	0.4051				
1964	13742.00	22253.00		287.60	0.4051	0.4051				
1965	15425.00	23686.00		253.00	0.4051	0.4051				
1966	16209.00	24669.00		212.70	0.4051	0.4051				
1967	16585.00	29516.00		163.00	0.4051	0.4051				
1968	15875.00	30714.00		89.40	0.4051	0.4051				
1969	20127.00	36663.00		56.10	0.3853	0.3853				
1970	22232.00	33662.00		53.90	0.3601	0.3601				
1971	25309.00	49428.00			0.3616	0.3610				
1972	35001.00	50279.00			0.3970	0.3970				
1973	36978.00	63926.00		26.60	0.4641	0.4529				
1974	110626.00	204227.00			0.4175	0.4167				
1975	100559.00	201921.00			0.4681	0.4665				
1976	120238.00	271447.00			0.4163	0.4186				
1977	176000.00	329840.00			0.4071	0.4071				
1978	139174.00	249850.00			0.4277	0.4277				
1979	113108.00	393186.00			0.4704	0.4704				
1980	142310.00	459060.00			0.4733	0.4733				
1981	228600.00	597900.00			0.3680	0.3680				
1982	237500.00	709900.00			0.3043	0.3043				
1983	324900.00	752700.00			0.2624	0.2624				
1984	387950.00	881700.00			0.2289	0.2289				
1985	438400.00	876700.00			0.2226	0.2226				
1986	300000.00	440000.00			0.2888	0.2888				
1987	219900.00	386599.90			0.3327	0.3327				
1988	235700.00	356100.10			0.3357	0.3357				
1989	244600.00	509600.00			0.3137	0.3137				
1990	250000.00	600000.00			0.3688	0.3688				
1991	235400.00	632699.90			0.3545	0.3545				
1992	185200.00	551099.90			0.3778	0.3778				
1993	239300.00	649799.90			0.3832	0.3540				
1994	420000.00	1304900.00			0.1806	0.1800				
1995	440199.90	1354400.00			0.2002	0.2002				
1996	459482.80	1609523.00			0.1955	0.1954				

2. IMPORTS BY BROAD ECONOMIC CATEGORY AND EXPORTS BY INDUSTRIAL ORIGIN. (PERCENTAGE OF TOTAL VALUE)
IMPORTATIONS PAR CATEGORIES ECONOMIQUES ET EXPORTATIONS PAR BRANCHE D'ACTIVITE.(EN POURCENTAGE DE LA VALEUR TOTALE)

IMPORTS – IMPORTATIONS

	1990	1991	1992	1993	1994	1995	1996
TOTAL IMPORTS–IMPORTATIONS TOTALES				100.	100.		100.
1 FOOD BEV–ALIMENTATION BOISSONS				18.3	16.5		18.2
11 PRIMARY–PRODUITS DE BASE				7.0	6.6		6.6
111 FOR INDUSTRY–POUR L'INDUSTRIE				1.2	1.3		1.4
112 FOR HOUSEHOLDS–POUR LES MENAGES				5.7	5.3		5.2
12 PROCESSED–PRODUITS ELABORES				11.3	9.9		11.7
121 FOR INDUSTRY–POUR L'INDUSTRIE				1.7	1.6		2.0
122 FOR HOUSEHOLDS–POUR LES MENAGES				9.6	8.3		9.6
2 IND SUPPLIES–APPROV INDUSTRIELS				22.5	22.0		21.8
21 PRIMARY–PRODUITS DE BASE				1.1	1.1		1.0
22 PROCESSED–PRODUITS ELABORES				21.4	20.9		20.7
3 FUELS–COMBUSTIBLES				1.9	2.4		3.4
31 PRIMARY–PRODUITS DE BASE				0.0	0.0		0.4
32 PROCESSED–PRODUITS ELABORES				1.8	2.4		3.1
321 MOTOR SPIRIT–ESSENCE							0.1
322 OTHER–AUTRES				1.8	2.4		3.0
4 MACHINERY–EQUIPEMENT				28.8	32.6		28.6
41 CAPITAL EQUIPMENT–MACHINES				23.9	26.5		23.1
42 PARTS–PIECES ACCESSOIRES				4.9	6.1		5.5
5 TRANSPORT–TRANSPORT				13.7	14.1		14.1
51 PASSENGER CARS–AUTOMOBILES				4.0	2.6		3.3
52 OTHER–AUTRES				6.0	6.7		5.3
521 INDUSTRIAL–INDUSTRIELS				5.9	6.6		5.2
522 NON INDUSTRIAL–NON INDUSTRIEL				0.0	0.1		0.1
53 PARTS–PIECES ACCESSOIRES				3.8	4.8		5.5
6 CONSUM GOODS–BIENS CONSOMMATION				14.7	12.3		13.5
61 DURABLE–DURABLES				3.1	2.6		2.6
62 SEMI DURABLE–SEMI DURABLES				4.4	4.1		4.3
63 NON DURABLE–NON DURABLES				7.2	5.5		6.6
7 GOODS NES–BIENS NDA				0.1	0.2		0.3

EXPORTS – EXPORTATIONS

	1990	1991	1992	1993	1994	1995	1996
TOTAL EXPORTS–EXPORTATIONS TOTALES				100.	100.		100.
1 AGRICULTURE				3.1	8.9		13.0
2 MINING QUARRY–INDUS EXTRACTIVES				94.3	89.1		83.3
3 MANUFACTURING–IND MANUFACTUR				2.6	2.0		3.6
31 FOOD BEV TOBACCO–ALIM BOISS TAB				0.1	0.0		0.1
32 TEXTILES–INDUSTRIES TEXTILES				0.1	0.1		0.1
33 WOOD & PRODUCTS–BOIS & PRODUITS				0.1	0.1		0.8
34 PAPER & PRODUCTS–PAPIER & PRODT				0.0	0.0		0.0
35 CHEMICALS–INDUSTRIES CHIMIQUES				1.7	1.3		1.9
36 NON METAL MIN–MIN NON METAL				0.0	0.0		0.0
37 BASIC METAL–IND METAL BASE				0.0	0.0		0.0
38 METAL MANUF–MANUF METAL				0.6	0.4		0.6
39 OTH MANUF IND–AUTRES MANUF				0.0	0.0		0.0

3. TRADE BY PRINCIPAL COUNTRIES OF ORIGIN AND DESTINATION (VALUE IN MILLION U.S. DOLLARS)
ECHANGES SELON LES PRINCIPAUX PAYS D'ORIGINE ET DE DESTINATION (VALEUR EN MILLIONS DE DOLLARS EU)

COUNTRIES–PAYS	SPECIAL IMPORTS C.I.F. IMPORTATIONS SPECIALES C.A.F					COUNTRIES–PAYS	SPECIAL EXPORTS F.O.B. EXPORTATIONS SPECIALES F.O.B.				
	1992	1993	1994	1995	1996		1992	1993	1994	1995	1996
World		774.9	707.5		898.1	Monde		2637.0	2391.0		3145.6
Africa		43.2	41.6		60.6	Afrique		59.5	99.9		72.4
Americas		91.4	107.7		113.0	Amériques		1549.5	1220.8		2173.4
– Northern America		77.2	89.5		101.2	– Amérique du Nord		1440.5	1193.0		2015.3
– LAIA		14.1	6.8		7.3	– ALAI		108.9	26.8		19.0
– CACM		0.0	0.0		0.2	– MCAC					
– Caribbean		0.0	0.1		4.2	– Caraïbes		0.0	0.0		139.0
– Rest of America		0.0	11.3		0.0	– Autre Amérique		0.1	1.0		
Asia excl fmr USSR		29.5	24.7		100.5	Asie anc. URSS exclus		102.0	179.8		335.6
– Middle East		1.6	2.3		4.0	– Moyen–Orient		7.6	7.6		23.7
Asia former USSR						Asie ancienne URSS					
Europe excl fmr USSR		539.0	482.2		617.9	Europe anc. URSS exclus		682.5	783.5		401.0
– European Union		533.3	478.4		611.2	– Union Européenne		651.3	721.9		361.8
– Eastern Europe		0.5	0.6		2.2	– Europe de l'Est		0.2	0.0		2.3
– Rest of Europe		5.3	3.2		4.5	– Autre de l'Europe		31.0	61.6		37.0
Europe former USSR		3.3	1.2		0.6	Europe ancienne URSS					0.1
Oceania		1.0	2.5		1.4	Océanie		21.5			11.6
Other		67.6	47.7		4.2	Autre		222.0	107.0		151.6
France, Monaco		370.4	281.4		384.8	USA/Etats–Unis d'Amer		1388.2	1192.9		2015.3
USA/Etats–Unis d'Amer		71.0	83.5		93.4	France, Monaco		505.6	361.6		239.8
Areas n.e.s.		67.6	47.7		4.2	Areas n.e.s.		222.0	107.0		151.6
United Kingdom		29.4	45.1		42.8	China/Chine		29.4	54.5		136.2
Netherlands/Pays–Bas		36.0	35.1		40.8	United Kingdom		93.1	61.8		7.3
Germany/Allemagne		27.8	39.7		41.1	Spain/Espagne		32.9	92.5		36.8
Italy/Italie		24.3	29.6		31.3	Netherlands/Pays–Bas		2.9	89.0		30.7
Belgium–Luxembourg		22.5	24.5		37.1	Chile/Chili		81.6	22.6		17.5
Japan/Japon					53.8	Netherlands Antilles					121.4
Spain/Espagne		11.2	11.4		21.0	Morocco/Maroc		14.5	76.2		16.8
Cameroon/Cameroun		6.3	12.0		12.1	Portugal		1.9	91.2		6.3
Cote d'Ivoire		6.3	7.6		13.7	Korea, Republic of		16.1	35.4		24.2
Thailand/Thaïlande		4.3	3.3		15.3	Japan/Japon					66.1
Morocco/Maroc		10.1	4.5		6.6	Israel/Israël		9.9	19.8		34.5
Canada		6.2	6.0		7.8	Singapore/Singapour		17.1	40.6		2.0
So. African Customs Un		3.5	4.5		9.3	Gibraltar		17.2	42.0		
Senegal/Sénégal		4.4	4.6		7.6	Switzerland,Liechtenst.		10.8	9.8		34.7
Nigeria/Nigéria		5.8	3.0		6.4	Canada		52.3	0.1		0.0
Ireland/Irlande		4.3	5.0		5.7	Philippines		1.9	12.1		30.5
China, Hong Kong SAR		5.5	3.8		4.8	Turkey/Turquie		7.6	5.7		23.0
Brazil/Brésil		7.3	3.7		2.9	Australia/Australie		21.5			11.6
Viet Nam		4.1	5.9		2.0	Greece/Grèce		4.2	9.7		18.8
Panama		0.0	11.3		0.0	Guinea/Guinée		5.5	4.1		22.7
Korea, Republic of		3.8	2.7		4.7	Argentina/Argentine		25.4	0.1		0.0
Argentina/Argentine		5.3	2.3		3.3	Italy/Italie		3.6	10.5		11.2
China/Chine		4.3	2.4		4.0	Dem Rep of the Congo		9.6	5.6		6.4
Sweden/Suède		4.0	2.9		2.6	Senegal/Sénégal		15.0	0.4		3.1
Switzerland,Liechtenst.		2.2	2.2		2.9	Korea Dem People's Rp		16.2	0.0		0.9
Norway,Svalbard and JM		3.0	0.9		1.5	Norway,Svalbard and JM		3.0	9.8		2.3
Other Asia n.e.s.		1.9	1.1		2.0	Belgium–Luxembourg		5.8	1.7		6.2
Russian Federation		3.3	1.2		0.3	Trinidad and Tobago					12.2
Singapore/Singapour		1.1	0.9		2.7	Other Asia n.e.s.		2.6	3.1		5.2
Aruba					4.2	Germany/Allemagne		1.3	3.9		4.5
Portugal		0.8	2.1		1.1	India/Inde		0.3	5.1		2.6
Congo		1.0	1.3		1.2	Thailand/Thaïlande		0.6	0.4		6.4
Denmark/Danemark		1.2	0.7		1.4	Togo		1.9	2.9		1.7
Turkey/Turquie		0.7	0.8		1.6	Algeria/Algérie		0.3	2.3		3.6
Lebanon/Liban		0.7	0.8		1.5	Congo		0.0	0.2		5.5
Indonesia/Indonésie		0.8	0.8		1.3	Aruba					5.4
Pakistan		0.0	0.0		2.8	So. African Customs Un		0.0	0.7		4.1

(VALUE AS PERCENTAGE OF WORLD TOTAL)(VALEURS EN POURCENTAGE DU TOTAL MONDIAL)

	1987	1988	1989	1990	1991	1992	1993	1994	1995	1996		1987	1988	1989	1990	1991	1992	1993	1994	1995	1996
Africa							5.6	5.9		6.8	Afrique							2.3	4.2		2.3
Americas							11.8	15.2		12.6	Amériques							58.8	51.1		69.1
– Northern America							10.0	12.7		11.3	– Amérique du Nord							54.6	49.9		64.1
– LAIA							1.8	1.0		0.8	– ALAI							4.1	1.1		0.6
– CACM							0.0	0.0		0.0	– MCAC										
– Caribbean							0.0	0.0		0.5	– Caraïbes							0.0	0.0		4.4
– Rest of America							0.0	1.6		0.0	– Autre Amérique							0.0	0.0		
Asia excl fmr USSR							3.8	3.5		11.2	Asie anc. URSS exclus							3.9	7.5		10.7
– Middle East							0.2	0.3		0.4	– Moyen–Orient							0.3	0.3		0.8
Asia former USSR											Asie ancienne URSS										
Europe excl fmr USSR							69.6	68.2		68.8	Europe anc. URSS exclus							25.9	32.8		12.7
– European Union							68.8	67.6		68.1	– Union Européenne							24.7	30.2		11.5
– Eastern Europe							0.1	0.1		0.2	– Europe de l'Est							0.0	0.0		0.1
– Rest of Europe							0.7	0.4		0.5	– Autre de l'Europe							1.2	2.6		1.2
Europe former USSR							0.4	0.2		0.1	Europe ancienne URSS										0.0
Oceania							0.1	0.4		0.2	Océanie							0.8			0.4
Other							8.7	6.7		0.5	Autre							8.4	4.5		4.8
France, Monaco							47.8	39.8		42.8	USA/Etats–Unis d'Amer							52.6	49.9		64.1
USA/Etats–Unis d'Amer							9.2	11.8		10.4	France, Monaco							19.2	15.1		7.6
Areas n.e.s.							8.7	6.7		0.5	Areas n.e.s.							8.4	4.5		4.8
United Kingdom							3.8	6.4		4.8	China/Chine							1.1	2.3		4.3
Netherlands/Pays–Bas							4.6	5.0		4.5	United Kingdom							3.5	2.6		0.2
Germany/Allemagne							3.6	5.6		4.6	Spain/Espagne							1.2	3.9		1.2
Italy/Italie							3.1	4.2		3.5	Netherlands/Pays–Bas							0.1	3.7		1.0
Belgium–Luxembourg							2.9	3.5		4.1	Chile/Chili							3.1	0.9		0.6
Japan/Japon										6.0	Netherlands Antilles										3.9
Spain/Espagne							1.4	1.6		2.3	Morocco/Maroc							0.5	3.2		0.5

4. Special Imports C.I.F. by Commodities according to the S.I.T.C. (Rev. 2) in million U.S. Dollars
Importations Spéciales C.A.F. par Produits d'après la C.T.C.I. (Rév. 2) en millions de Dollars E.U.

SITC CTCI	COMMODITY	1993		1994		1995		1996		PRODUIT
		QUANTITY QUANTITE	VALUE VALEUR	QUANTITY QUANTITE	VALUE VALEUR	QUANTITY QUANTITE	VALUE VALEUR	QUANTITY QUANTITE	VALUE VALEUR	
	ALL COMMODITIES		775.0		707.6				898.2	TOUS PRODUITS
0	FOOD AND LIVE ANIMALS		131.6		105.9				145.7	ALIMENTS,ANIMAUX VIVANTS
01	MEAT AND PREPARATIONS		34.9		32.1				37.9	VIANDES ET PREPARATIONS
011	MEAT FRESH,CHILLD,FROZEN	W 26742	31.5	W 26952	29.0			W 22270	32.9	VIANDES FRAICHES,REF,CONGE
0111	BOVINE MEAT FRESH,FROZEN	W 14595	16.8	W 12804	13.2			W 6738	10.2	VIANDES BOVIN FRAI,REF
01111	BOVINE MEAT WITH BONE IN	W 1852	2.9	W 1126	1.6			W 850	1.8	VIANDES BOVIN NON DESOSS
01112	BOVINE MEAT BONELESS	W 12743	13.9	W 11678	11.6			W 5887	8.5	VIANDES BOVIN DESOSSEES
0113	PIG MEAT FRESH,CHLD,FRZN	W 2470	2.6	W 2960	2.8			W 2848	3.1	VIANDE DE PORC
0114	POULTRY FRESH CHLLD,FRZN	W 4015	4.1	W 7582	8.3			W 10020	15.7	VOLAILLES MORTES
0116	EDIBLE OFFAL FRESH,CH,FR	W 4816	6.4	W 2767	3.2			W 2255	2.8	ABATS COMESTIBLES
014	MEAT PREPD,PRSVD,NES ETC	W 1281	3.2	W 1063	2.9			W 1483	4.8	CONSERVES DE VIANDES
0149	OTH PREPARD,PRESRVD MEAT	W 1075	2.5	W 733	2.0			W 1081	3.5	AUTRES PREP DE VIANDES
02	DAIRY PRODCTS,BIRDS'EGGS		16.1		10.8				15.5	PRODUITS LAITIERS,OEUFS
022	MILK AND CREAM	W 8099	12.1	W 5190	7.7			W 7297	11.7	LAIT ET CREME
0224	MILK,CREAM PRESERVED ETC	W 7342	11.3	W 4487	7.1			W 5694	10.0	LAIT,CREME CONS,CONC
02243	MILK DRY,OVER 1.5% FAT	W 1225	3.2	W 838	1.8			W 1079	3.3	LAIT POUDRE SUP 1.5%
02249	MILK(EX DRY) PRSVD,SWEET	W 5841	7.5	W 3295	4.3			W 4342	6.1	LAIT CONS,CONC SUCRE
024	CHEESE AND CURD	W 524	2.4	W 457	1.8			W 561	2.5	FROMAGE ET CAILLEBOTTE
03	FISH AND PREPARATIONS		15.5		8.7				13.6	POISSONS ET PREPARATIONS
034	FISH,FRESH,CHILLED,FROZN	W 4106	4.3	W 5207	4.1			W 8577	7.2	POISSON FRAIS, REFRIG,CONG
0342	FISH FROZEN,EXCL FILLETS	W 4102	4.3	W 5202	4.1			W 8173	6.9	POISSONS CONGELES
037	FISH ETC PREPD,PRSVD NES	W 5196	8.8	W 2607	4.0			W 3208	5.5	POIS,CRUST,MOL PREPARES
0371	FISH PREPARD,PRESRVD NES	W 5177	8.7	W 2595	4.0			W 3203	5.5	CONSERVES DE POISSONS
04	CEREALS AND PREPARATIONS		35.5		32.3				48.5	CEREALES ET PRODUITS
041	WHEAT ETC UNMILLED	W 40296	8.0	W 42602	8.0			W 39283	10.9	FROMENT,EPEAUTRE
0412	OTHER WHEAT ETC UNMILLED	W 40202	8.0	W 42602	8.0			W 39283	10.9	AUTRE FROMENT NON MOULU
042	RICE	W 27934	7.7	W 31068	8.6			W 43444	16.3	RIZ
0422	RICE SEMI–MILLED,MILLED	W 27932	7.7	W 31066	8.6			W 43443	16.3	RIZ POLI,GLACE INCL BRISURES
04221	RICE MILLED UNBROKEN	W 27932	7.7	W 30777	8.5			W 43188	16.2	RIZ POLI,GLACE EXCL BRISURES
047	OTHER CEREAL MEALS,FLOUR	W 4475	2.2	W 4084	2.2			W 5402	3.6	AUTRES SEMOULES,FARINES
04702	MEAL OR GROATS NON–WHEAT	W 4450	2.2	W 4081	2.2			W 5391	3.6	GRUAUX,SEMOULES DE CEREALES
048	CEREAL ETC PREPARATIONS	W 14715	15.5	W 28837	12.7			W 13660	15.2	PREPTNS A BASE CEREALES
0482	MALT INCLUDING FLOUR	W 10584	6.3	W 25550	6.2			W 9600	7.8	MALT MEME TORREFIE
0488	OTH CEREAL PREPS,MALT EX	W 1408	6.2	W 819	3.5			W 674	3.4	EXTRAITS DE MALT
05	VEGETABLES AND FRUIT		12.8		10.0				13.4	LEGUMES ET FRUITS
054	VEG ETC FRSH,SMPLY PRSVD	W 9584	7.4	W 7038	5.7			W 8573	7.9	LEGUMES FRAIS,CONG,SECS
0546	VEGETABLES SIMPLY PRESVD	W 4056	3.3	W 3746	3.3			W 4760	4.7	LEGUMES CONG,CONSER
05461	VEGETABLES FROZEN	W 4053	3.3	W 3745	3.3			W 4759	4.7	LEGUMES CONGELES
07	COFFEE,TEA,COCOA,SPICES		3.0		1.8				2.6	CAFE,THE,CACAO,EPICES
081	*FEEDING STUFF FOR ANIML	W 5871	3.8	W 2669	1.6			W 3335	1.9	NOURRITURE POUR ANIMAUX
0819	FOOD WASTE AND FEED NES	W 4575	2.9	W 2175	1.4			W 1759	1.4	DECHETS,ALIMENTS NDA
08199	FODDER NES,INCL SWEETNED	W 4575	2.9	W 2175	1.4			W 1759	1.4	PREPARATIONS FOURRAGERES
09	MISC EDIBLE PRODUCTS		9.5		8.0				11.7	PREP ALIMENTAIRES DIVERSES
098	EDIBLE PRODCTS,PREPS NES	W 2855	7.9	W 2379	6.2			W 3173	9.3	PREP ALIMENTAIRES NDA
09809	MISC FOOD PREPRTIONS NES	W 1239	4.4	W 847	2.8			W 1204	4.8	PREP ALIMENTAIRES NDA
1	BEVERAGES AND TOBACCO		17.7		15.6				23.2	BOISSONS ET TABACS
11	BEVERAGES		13.1		11.6				17.1	BOISSONS
112	ALCOHOLIC BEVERAGES	W 12192	11.8	W 10087	10.2			W 13811	15.6	BOISSONS ALCOOLIQUES
1121	WINE OF FRESH GRAPES ETC	W 9961	5.5	W 8039	5.5			W 10426	9.4	VINS DE RAISINS FRAIS
11212	WINE OF FRESH GRAPES	W 9873	5.2	W 7988	5.3			W 10382	9.2	VINS DE MOUTS DE RAISINS
1124	DISTILLED ALCOHOLIC BEVS	W 758	4.7	W 812	3.4			W 1682	4.1	ALCOOLS,EAUX–DE–VIE
11249	OTH ALCOHOLC BEVS,CMPNDS	W 420	2.4	W 444	1.7			W 1200	2.4	BOISSONS ALCOOLIQUES NDA
12	TOBACCO AND MANUFACTURES		4.6		4.1				6.1	TABACS BRUTS FABRIQUES
122	TOBACCO,MANUFACTURED	W 331	4.3	W 301	4.1			W 350	5.9	TABACS FABRIQUES
1223	OTH MANUFACTURED TOBACCO	W 294	3.7	W 253	3.3			W 301	4.6	TABACS FUMER,CHIQUER,PRISER
2	CRUDE MATERLS,EXCL FUELS		8.2		8.2				9.6	MAT BRUTES NON COMESTIBLES
26	TEXTILE FIBRES AND WASTE		3.1		2.8				4.5	FIBRES TEXTILES
269	WASTE OF TEXTILE FABRICS	W 1310	3.0	W 2200	2.8			W 3431	4.4	FRIPERIE DRILLES,CHIFFONS
26901	BULK TEXT WSTE,OLD CLTHG	W 1209	2.9	W 2090	2.6			W 3312	4.3	ART ET ACCESS D'HABILLEMENT
27	CRUDE FERTLZR,MINRLS NES		3.8		3.8				3.4	ENGRAIS MINERAUX BRUTS
278	OTHER CRUDE MINERALS	W 9418	2.5	W 10982	3.3			W 8044	2.5	AUTRES MINERAUX BRUTS
3	MINERAL FUELS ETC		14.6		17.2				31.6	COMBUSTIBLES MINERAUX LUB
33	PETROLEUM AND PRODUCTS		14.4		17.0				28.3	PETROLE ET DERIVES
334	PETROLEUM PRODUCTS,REFIN	W 56669	14.2	W 54782	16.8			W 108944	27.5	PRODUITS RAFFINES
3342	KEROSENE,OTH MEDIUM OILS							W 23021	5.3	PETR LAMPANTS,AUT HUIL
33421	KEROSENE INCL JET FUEL							W 22266	4.7	PETROLES LAMPANTS
3343	GAS OILS							W 76823	15.4	GAS OILS
3345	LUBS,PETROLEUM OILS NES	W 195	0.8	W 165	0.5			W 8227	6.4	HUILES LUBRIFIANTES
33451	LUBS(HIGH PETR CONT) ETC							W 7976	5.7	HUILES LUBRIF,H LOURDES
341	*GAS,NATURAL AND MANUFCT	W 77	0.2	W 80	0.2			W 9910	3.3	GAZ NATUREL,GAZ MANUFACT
3413	PETROLM GASES,LIQUEFIED	W 76	0.2	W 80	0.2			W 9900	3.3	GAZ DE PETROLE LIQUEFIE
34131	LIQUEFIED PROPANE,BUTANE	W 76	0.2	W 80	0.2			W 9899	3.3	PROPANE,BUTANE LIQUEFIES
4	ANIMAL,VEGETABLE OIL,FAT		1.1		1.2				2.9	HUILES,GRAISSES ANIM,VEG
42	FIXED VEGETABLE OIL,FAT		1.1		1.1				2.9	HUILES VEGETALES FIXES
5	CHEMCLS,RELATED PROD NES		83.6		70.1				93.1	PRODUITS CHIMIQUES
51	ORGANIC CHEMICALS		3.9		3.3				4.5	PROD CHIMIQ ORGANIQUES
52	INORGANIC CHEMICALS		5.5		5.1				4.9	PROD CHIM INORGANIQUES
522	INORG ELEMNTS,OXIDES,ETC	W 2075	2.4	W 2347	2.6			W 1945	2.2	ELEMENTS INORGANIQUES
523	OTHR INORG CHEMICALS ETC	W 4773	2.6	W 2952	2.2			W 3694	2.6	AUT PRODUITS CHIMIQUES INORG
53	DYES,TANNING,COLOUR PROD		3.0		2.1				4.0	PROD TEINTURE,COLORANTS
533	PIGMENTS,PAINTS,ETC	W 1266	2.7	W 982	2.0			W 1950	3.6	PIGMENTS,PEINTURES,VERNIS
541	*MEDICINAL,PHARM PRODUCT	K 1328736	30.8	K 883575	18.5			K 1482824	33.4	PROD MEDICINAUX PHARMACEUT
5417	MEDICAMENTS	K 1237687	28.3	K 820185	16.7			K 1368240	30.7	MEDICAMENTS
54171	— CONTAINNG ANTIBIOTICS	K 81222	3.1	K 34599	1.0			K 74046	1.7	MED CONTN ANTIBIOTIQUES
54179	— CONTNG OTH SUBSTANCES	K 1093543	23.6	K 769115	15.1			K 1266601	27.9	MED CONT AUT SUBSTANCES
55	PERFUME,CLEANING ETC PRD		12.6		12.4				13.6	PROD POUR PARFUM,TOILETTE
551	ESSENTL OILS,PERFUME,ETC	W 147	2.3	W 155	3.6			W 208	4.4	HUILES ESSENTIELLES
5514	MIXED PERFUME SUBSTANCES	W 138	2.3	W 143	3.5			W 202	4.3	MELANGES SUBSTAN ODORIFER
553	PERFUMERY,COSMETICS,ETC	W 1061	2.8	W 1022	2.9			W 1281	2.9	PRODUITS DE PARFUMERIE
554	SOAP,CLEANSING ETC PREPS	W 4034	7.5	W 3414	6.0			W 3505	6.4	SAVONS,PRODUITS DETERSIFS
5542	WASHING PREPARATIONS ETC	W 3273	6.1	W 2662	4.9			W 2676	5.0	PROD ORG TENSIO–ACT NDA
58	PLASTIC MATERIALS ETC		7.3		9.9				10.0	MAT PLAST ARTIFICIELLES
582	PROD OF CONDENSATION ETC	W 1415	2.3	W 2074	3.0			W 2364	3.8	PROD CONDENS,POLYCOND
583	POLYMERIZATION ETC PRODS	W 2218	3.7	W 2548	4.3			W 2328	4.6	PROD POLYMERISATION
59	CHEMICAL MATERIALS NES		18.3		16.3				19.9	MAT PROD CHIMIQUES NDA
591	PESTICIDES,DISINFECTANTS	W 776	3.1	W 944	2.7			W 1107	4.0	DESINF,INSECT,FONG,HERB
598	MISCEL CHEM PRODUCTS NES	W 4659	13.3	W 4568	12.4			W 3979	13.9	PROD DIV INDUST CHIM NDA
5982	ANTI–KNOCK PREPARTNS ETC	W 934	2.8	W 1440	4.4			W 1337	5.0	PREPARAT ANTIDETONANTES
5989	CHEM PRODUCTS,PREPS NES	W 3672	10.4	W 3051	7.9			W 2620	8.9	PROD PREP CHIMIQUES NDA
59899	OTH CHEM PRODS,PREPS,NES	W 3290	9.3	W 2625	6.8			W 2218	7.8	AUT PRODUITS CHIMIQUES NDA
6	BASIC MANUFACTURES		123.8		112.2				150.3	ART MANUFACTURES

4. Special Imports C.I.F. by Commodities according to the S.I.T.C. (Rev. 2) in million U.S. Dollars
Importations Spéciales C.A.F. par Produits d'après la C.T.C.I. (Rév. 2) en millions de Dollars E.U.

SITC CTCI	COMMODITY	1993		1994		1995		1996		PRODUIT
		QUANTITY QUANTITE	VALUE VALEUR	QUANTITY QUANTITE	VALUE VALEUR	QUANTITY QUANTITE	VALUE VALEUR	QUANTITY QUANTITE	VALUE VALEUR	
62	RUBBER MANUFACTURES NES		10.0		12.3				17.1	CAOUTCHOUC MANUFACTURE
621	MATERIALS OF RUBBER	W 237	2.4	W 229	3.0			W 155	2.2	PRODUITS EN CAOUTCHOUC
62105	UNHARD VULC RUBBER TUBES	W 160	2.0	W 188	2.6			W 108	1.9	TUBES,TUYAUX CAOUT VULC
625	RUBBER TYRES, TUBES ETC	W 1592	5.6	W 1936	7.1			W 2580	11.5	PNEUS CAOUTCHOUC VULCANISE
6252	TYRES,NEW,BUS OR LORRY	W 654	3.0	W 790	3.5			W 1144	6.4	PNEUS POUR AUTOBUS,CAMIONS
6259	OTH TYRES,TYRE CASES,ETC	W 672	1.4	W 906	2.5			W 1246	4.1	AUTRES PNEUS RECHAPES FLAPS
62599	TYRES NES,TYRE CASES,ETC	W 558	1.0	W 793	2.1			W 1032	3.0	PNEUS,FLAPS
628	RUBBER ARTICLES NES	W 176	2.1	W 155	2.3			W 239	3.4	OUVRAGES CAOUTCHOUC NDA
64	PAPER,PAPERBOARD AND MFR		19.5		14.1				16.8	PAPIERS,CARTONS & OUVRAGES
641	PAPER AND PAPERBOARD		8.1	W 2424	5.2			W 2928	6.9	PAPIERS ET CARTONS
6415	PAPER,PAPERBRD,BULK,NES	W 1172	2.9	W 482	1.2			W 908	2.2	PAPIERS,CARTONS ROULEAUX
64159	OTHER PAPER ETC,BULK,NES	W 1155	2.8	W 467	1.2			W 893	2.1	AUT PAPIER ROULEAUX FEUILLES
642	PAPER,ETC,PRECUT,ARTS OF	W 4384	11.4	W 3378	8.9			W 3619	10.0	PAP,CARTONS DECOUPES
6421	PAPER ETC CONTAINERS	W 2656	5.2	W 1606	3.2			W 1957	4.4	BOITES,SACS EMBALLAGES
6423	EXERCISE BOOKS ETC	W 850	2.6	W 899	2.8			W 724	2.4	REGISTRES,CAHIERS,CARNETS
6428	PAPER ETC ARTICLES NES	W 636	2.7	W 635	2.1			W 589	2.0	OUVRAGES EN PATE A PAPIER
65	TEXTILE YARN,FABRICS,ETC		10.1		6.9				10.4	FILS,TISSUS,ARTICLES TEXTILE
652	COTTON FABRICS,WOVEN		3.1	W 528	1.6			W 302	1.7	TISSUS DE COTON
6522	WOVEN COTTON BLEACHD,ETC	W 674	3.0	W 526	1.6			W 299	1.7	TISSUS COTON BLANCHIS ETC
658	TEXTILE ARTICLES NES	W 832	2.8	W 592	2.1			W 797	4.1	ART FACONNES MAT TEXTILES
66	NONMETAL MINERAL MFS NES		12.0		13.2				18.2	ART MIN NON METALLIQUES
661	LIME,CEMENT,BLDG PRODS	W 7573	2.7	W 8783	2.0			W 11939	3.6	CHAUX,CIMENTS MAT CONSTR
662	CLAY,REFRACTORY BLDG PRD	W 5879	3.4	W 5372	2.8			W 8769	4.5	MAT CONST REFRACTAIRES
6624	BRICKS ETC NONREFRACTORY	W 5635	3.2	W 5071	2.6			W 8237	4.0	BRIQUES ETC CERAM NON REFR
66245	GLAZED CERAMIC SETTS ETC	W 4911	2.7	W 4539	2.3			W 7783	3.8	AUT CARREAUX CERAMIQUE
665	GLASSWARE	W 1052	2.1	W 3792	3.4			W 5621	4.4	OUVRAGES EN VERRE
6651	BOTTLES ETC OF GLASS	W 72	0.2	W 3175	2.0			W 4932	2.9	RECIPIENTS EN VERRE
66511	GLASS BOTTLES ETC NONVAC	W 71	0.2	W 3175	2.0			W 4932	2.9	BONBONNES,BOUTEILLES,ETC
67	IRON AND STEEL		30.9		27.3				37.4	FER ET ACIER
673	IRON,STEEL SHAPES ETC	W 7878	3.5	W 8388	4.0			W 14764	8.1	BARRES,PROFIL FER,ACIER
6732	IRON,STEEL BARS ETC	W 5443	2.2	W 6510	2.9			W 10627	4.5	BARRES FER,ACIER
67326	IRN,OTH STL BARS HOTROLD	W 3193	1.2	W 4840	2.0			W 9471	3.9	BARRES PLEINES FER,ACIER
6733	IRON,STEEL PROFILES ETC	W 1817	1.1	W 1545	1.0			W 4065	3.6	PROFILES,PALPLAN FER,ACIER
67332	LARGE U,I,H SECTIONS ETC	W 1148	0.7	W 1048	0.7			W 3083	2.8	PROFILES PLUS 80MM
674	IRN,STL UNIV,PLATE,SHEET	W 3696	2.8	W 3204	2.4			W 3875	3.0	LARGES PLATS,TOLES
678	IRON,STL TUBES,PIPES,ETC	W 12345	23.8	W 7058	19.8			W 13618	24.3	TUBES,TUYAUX EN FONTE,FER
6782	IRON,STL SEAMLESS TUBES	W 9740	13.7	W 5729	10.3			W 11335	17.6	TUBES,TUYAUX SANS SOUDURE
6783	IRON,STL TUBES,PIPES NES	W 1284	2.6	W 666	0.9			W 1319	1.5	AUT TUBES,TUYAUX FER,ACIER
6785	IRON,STEEL TUBE FITTINGS	W 535	6.9	W 511	8.6			W 431	4.6	ACCESSOIRES DE TUYAUTERIE
68	NON–FERROUS METALS		7.3		6.5				6.8	METAUX NON FERREUX
684	ALUMINIUM	W 2273	6.8	W 2817	6.0			W 1976	5.9	ALUMINIUM
6842	ALUMINIUM,ALLOYS WORKED	W 2273	6.8	W 2817	6.0			W 1975	5.9	ALUMINIUM,ALLIAGES OUVRE
68422	ALUMNM PLATE,SHEET,STRIP	W 2103	5.7	W 2639	5.0			W 1739	4.3	TOLES, PLANCHES EN ALU
69	METAL MANUFACTURES NES		32.6		31.0				42.3	ART MANUFACT EN METAL NDA
691	STRUCTURES AND PARTS NES	W 1462	3.7	W 756	2.4			W 574	1.5	CONSTRUCT FER,ACIER,ALU
6911	STRUCTURES,PARTS IRN,STL	W 1361	3.2	W 719	1.9			W 541	1.3	CONSTRUCT FER,ACIER,FONTE
692	METAL TANKS,BOXES,ETC	W 781	2.5	W 885	2.3			W 1233	5.3	RECIPIENTS METALLIQUES
6924	MTL TRANSPORT BOXES ETC	W 658	1.9	W 715	2.0			W 845	3.4	FUTS,TAMBOURS,BIDONS
693	WIRE PRODUCTS NON ELECTR	W 1199	3.1	W 1475	3.7			W 1940	4.8	OUVRAGES FILS METALLIQUES
6931	WIRE CABLES, ROPES ETC	W 839	2.5	W 1067	2.8			W 1444	4.1	CORDAGES EN FILS DE FER
69311	IRN,STEEL CABLE,ROPE ETC	W 824	2.4	W 1055	2.7			W 1276	3.5	CORDAGES FILS FER,ACIER
694	STL,COPPR NAILS,NUTS,ETC	W 860	2.9	W 755	3.5			W 1012	3.6	CLOUS,VIS,ECROUS
69402	IRN,STL NUTS,BOLTS,ETC	W 415	2.5	W 359	3.1			W 464	3.0	BOULONS,VIS,ECROUS FER,AC
695	TOOLS	W 390	5.0	W 385	6.6			W 669	9.2	OUTILS A MAIN
6953	OTHER HAND TOOLS	W 213	2.3	W 160	2.3			W 311	3.4	AUTRES OUTILS A MAIN
6954	BLADES,TIPS,ETC FR TOOLS	W 118	2.5	W 162	4.2			W 237	5.4	OUTILS POUR MACHINE–OUTIL
69541	PARTS TO INSERT IN TOOLS	W 112	2.4	W 154	4.0			W 231	5.2	OUTILS DE FORAGE
697	BASE MTL HOUSEHOLD EQUIP	W 1025	4.5	W 602	2.9			W 738	3.0	ART MENAGE MET COMMUNS
699	BASE METAL MFRS NES	W 2252	10.1	W 1966	9.1			W 3090	14.0	ART MANUFACTURES MET NDA
6996	BASE MTL MISC ARTICLES	W 682	3.0	W 775	2.6			W 821	3.3	ART DIVERS METAUX COMMUNS
6997	IRON,STEEL ARTICLES NES	W 555	2.0	W 395	2.0			W 1396	5.3	OUV FONTE,FER,ACIER NDA
69979	IRN,STL MANUFACTURES NES	W 471	1.9	W 395	2.0			W 1393	5.3	AUT OUVRAGES EN FER NDA
7	MACHINES,TRANSPORT EQUIP		316.4		314.3				352.0	MACHINES MATERIEL TRANSPORT
71	POWER GENERATING EQUIPMT		26.9		25.9				26.3	MACHINES GENERATRICES
713	INTRNL COMBUS PSTN ENGIN	W 370	8.9	W 357	8.5			W 563	14.8	MOTEURS EXPL COMB INT, PIECE
7131	AIRCRAFT PSTN ENGINS,PTS	W 10	1.6	W 4	0.9			W 16	3.2	MOTEURS EXPL P.AVIATION, PIE
7133	MARINE PISTON ENGINES	W 131	2.5	W 80	1.6			W 129	2.5	MOTEURS EXPL POUR BATEAUX
7139	PISTON ENGINE PARTS NES	W 163	4.3	W 198	5.6			W 253	8.1	PIECES POUR 713.2,3,8
714	ENGINES AND MOTORS NES	W 160	9.6	W 18	2.0			W 54	5.7	MOTEURS NON ELECTRIQUES
7148	GAS TURBINES NES	W 134	8.6	W 7	1.0			W 38	3.9	TURBINES A GAZ
71488	OTHER GAS TURBINES NES	W 134	8.6	W 7	1.0			W 37	3.7	AUTRES TURBINES A GAZ
716	ROTATING ELECTRIC PLANT	W 416	5.9	W 491	14.4			W 321	4.8	APP ELECTR ROTATIFS,PIECES
7161	DC MOTORS AND GENERATORS	W 134	2.7	W 44	0.7			W 53	0.7	MOTEURS COURANT CONTINU
7162	AC MTRS,GENRTRS,GEN SETS	W 270	3.0	W 433	13.2			W 257	3.7	MOTEURS ELECTRIQUES
71622	AC GENERATORS	W 18	0.2	W 243	11.0			W 18	0.5	GENER COURANT ALTERNATIF
72	MACHS FOR SPCL INDUSTRYS		21.1		46.4				36.9	MAC SPECIALES POUR INDUST
722	TRACTORS NON–ROAD	W 215	1.2	W 833	6.3			W 610	4.1	TRACTEURS
7224	WHEELED TRACTORS NES	W 132	1.2	W 664	6.1			W 527	4.0	TRACTEURS A ROUES
723	CIVIL ENGNEERG EQUIP ETC	W 1979	12.1	W 5680	30.9			W 3397	23.3	APPAREILS DE GENIE CIVIL
7234	CONST,MINING MACHNRY NES	W 1440	8.4	W 3669	22.4			W 2425	15.4	MACH POUR LA CONST, MINES
72341	SELF–PROPELLD DOZERS,ETC	W 800	5.2	W 2182	14.9			W 1079	7.1	BULLDOZERS
72342	SLFPRP SHOVELS,EXCAVATRS	W 423	2.3	W 1294	6.9			W 1122	7.1	PELLES MECANIQUES
7239	CONSTR ETC MACHY PTS NES	W 403	3.3	W 1862	8.1			W 771	7.2	PIECES 723.41–723.46
728	OTH MACHY FOR SPCL INDUS	W 730	3.3	W 996	6.5			W 833	6.6	AUT MACH IND PARTICULIERES
7281	MACH–TOOLS FR SPCL INDUS	W 41	0.5	W 490	3.2			W 186	1.7	MACH–OUTILS SPEC IND PART
72812	MACH–TOOLS TO WORK WOOD	W 34	0.4	W 386	2.5			W 158	1.3	MACH–OUT POUR TRAVAIL BOIS
74	GENRL INDUSTRL MACHY NES		67.1		82.2				105.9	MACH APP INDUSTRIE
741	HEATING,COOLING EQUIPMNT	W 484	5.8	W 657	5.1			W 780	8.0	MACH CHAUFFAGE,PIECES
7415	AIR–CONDITIONING MACHNRY	W 106	1.2	W 159	1.7			W 340	3.7	GROUPES CONDITION AIR
7416	HEATING,COOLING EQU NES	W 260	3.4	W 235	1.3			W 140	1.5	APP CHANGEMENT TEMP
742	PUMPS FOR LIQUIDS ETC	W 436	10.8	W 627	14.1			W 752	10.1	POMPES MOTO–POMPES
7428	OTHER PUMPS FOR LIQUIDS	W 189	4.0	W 342	6.7			W 633	5.3	AUTRES POMPES POUR LIQ
74288	PUMPS FR LIQUIDS NES ETC	W 176	3.7	W 331	6.4			W 622	5.0	POMPES POUR LIQUIDES NDA
7429	PTS NES OF PUMPS OF 742	W 105	3.6	W 251	6.5			W 71	3.5	PIECES POUR GROUPE 742
743	PUMPS NES,CENTRFUGES ETC	W 985	14.6		18.6			W 1533	35.9	POMPES COMPRES,VENT ETC
7431	PUMPS FOR GASES ETC	W 327	3.4	W 383	4.1			W 1076	27.3	POMPES AIR A VIDE,COMPRES
7436	GAS,LIQUID FILTERS ETC	W 565	7.5	W 265	3.0			W 376	5.1	APP POUR FILT DES LIQUIDES
7439	PTS NES OF APP OF 7435,6	W 71	3.5	W 463	11.3			W 47	3.3	PIECES 743.5 ET 743.6
744	MECHANICAL HANDLING EQU	W 1184	4.9	W 1715	9.2			W 1916	10.6	EQUIP MANUTENTION PIECES
7442	LIFTING,LOADING MACH NES	W 505	2.2	W 903	4.8			W 775	4.4	APP LEVAGE,MANUTENTION
74428	OTH HANDLING ETC MCH NES	W 137	0.9	W 274	2.4			W 429	2.8	AUT APP LEVAGE ETC

4. Special Imports C.I.F. by Commodities according to the S.I.T.C. (Rev. 2) in million U.S. Dollars
Importations Spéciales C.A.F. par Produits d'après la C.T.C.I. (Rév. 2) en millions de Dollars E.U.

SITC CTCI	COMMODITY	1993 QUANTITY QUANTITE		1993 VALUE VALEUR	1994 QUANTITY QUANTITE		1994 VALUE VALEUR	1995 QUANTITY QUANTITE	1995 VALUE VALEUR	1996 QUANTITY QUANTITE		1996 VALUE VALEUR	PRODUIT
7449	PTS NES OF MACHY OF 7442	W	186	1.7	W	382	3.8			W	463	4.6	PIECES DU 744.2
745	NONELEC MACHY,TOOLS NES	W	154	2.8	W	141	3.1			W	398	8.0	AUT MACH NON ELEC,PIECES
7452	OTH NONELEC MCHS,PTS NES	W	98	1.6	W	91	1.8			W	340	6.1	AUT MACH NON ELEC,PIECES
74522	PACKAGNG,BOTTLNG,ETC MCH	W	23	0.4	W	24	0.5			W	194	3.0	MACH NETT BOUTEILLES,ETC
749	NONELEC MACH PTS,ACC NES	W	1287	28.4	W	2161	32.4			W	1344	33.6	PIECES MACH NON ELEC NDA
7491	BALL,ROLLER,ETC BEARINGS	W	131	2.4	W	295	3.3			W	251	4.1	ROULEMENTS BILLES ETC
7492	COCKS,VALVES ETC NES	W	758	17.6	W	1200	17.6			W	659	15.9	ART ROB,SIM POUR TUYAUX
7493	SHAFT,CRANK,PULLEY ETC	W	197	4.3	W	526	6.4			W	204	7.3	ARBRES TRANS,VILEBREQUINS
7499	OTH NONELEC MCHY PTS NES	W	201	4.3	W	139	5.2			W	230	6.5	PIECES NON ELECT NDA
74992	METAL-PLASTIC GASKETS	W	154	3.8	W	117	4.4			W	186	6.2	JOINTS METALLOPLASTIQUES
75	OFFICE MACHNES,ADP EQUIP			15.2			12.3					19.7	MACH BUREAU TRAIT AUTOM
751	OFFICE MACHINES	W	103	2.4	W	71	1.8			W	89	2.4	MACH,APPAREILS DE BUREAU
752	AUTOMTIC DATA PROC EQUIP	W	113	9.0	W	93	8.0			W	180	13.9	MACH TRAIT INFORMATION
7522	DIGITAL COMPUTERS	W	37	2.9	W	43	4.6			W	93	7.0	MACH DIGITALES COMPLETES
7523	DIGITL CENTRL PROCESSORS	W	30	3.6	W	5	0.4			W	9	0.8	UNITES CENTRALES
7525	ADP PERIPHERAL UNITS	W	18	1.4	W	20	1.7			W	51	3.8	UNITES PERIPHERIQUES
759	OFFICE,ADP MCH PTS,ACCES	W	30	3.9	W	22	2.5			W	36	3.5	PIECES DU 751 ET 752
7599	ACCTG,ETC,ADP MCH PTS,AC	W	20	3.4	W	14	2.1			W	26	2.9	PIECES DU 751 ET 752
76	TELECOMM,SOUND EQUIPMENT			19.0			16.6					22.9	EQUIPMENT DE TELECOM
761	TELEVISION RECEIVERS	W	353	2.7	W	234	2.0			W	476	3.2	RECEPTEURS DE TELEVISION
7611	COLOUR TV RECEIVERS	W	275	2.4	W	229	2.0			W	442	2.9	RECEPTEURS COULEUR
764	TELECOM EQPT,PTS,ACC NES	W	210	13.4	W	202	12.4			W	188	17.1	EQUIP TELECOM,PIECES
7641	LINE TELEPHONE,ETC EQUIP	W	33	3.8	W	26	2.1			W	26	2.6	APP TELEPHON PAR FIL
7643	TV,RADIO TRANSMITTRS ETC	W	25	3.5	W	16	2.1			W	35	6.3	APP EMET TELE RADIO
7648	TELECOMM EQUIPMENT NES	W	6	0.5	W	63	4.4			W	16	2.1	APP TELECOM NDA
76483	RADAR APPARATUS ETC	W	2	0.4	W	56	4.2			W	10	1.7	APP DE RADIOGUIDAGE ETC
7649	PTS NES OF EQUIPMT OF 76	W	118	5.2	W	69	3.7			W	93	5.5	PIECES DE LA DIV 76
76491	PTS NES OF APPAR OF 7641	W	16	2.6	W	5	1.2			W	13	4.0	PIECES POUR 764.1
76493	TELECOMM EQUIPMT PTS NES	W	87	2.1	W	64	2.4			W	75	1.4	PIECES 761,762,764.3,8
77	ELECTRIC MACHNRY NES ETC			40.1			29.8					42.8	MACH APP ELECT NDA
771	ELECTRIC POWER MACHY NES	W	153	2.2	W	202	2.7			W	392	4.3	MACH PROD,TRANS ELECTR
772	SWITCHGEAR ETC,PARTS NES	W	550	15.3	W	350	9.2			W	426	12.0	APP COUPURE,SECT ETC
7721	SWITCHGEAR ETC	W	548	15.2	W	348	9.0			W	422	11.6	APP COUPURE,SECTIONMNT
773	ELECTR DISTRIBUTNG EQUIP	W	1424	6.7	W	1511	5.9			W	1409	8.1	EQUIPMT DISTRIBUTION ELECT
7731	INSULATED WIRE,CABLE ETC	W	1405	6.5	W	1506	5.8			W	1315	7.6	FILS,CABLES ISOLES ELECT
775	HOUSEHOLD TYPE EQUIP NES	W	1298	6.8			4.6			W	1319	7.1	MACH,APP USAGE DOMESTQUE
7752	DOM REFRIGERATRS,FREEZRS	W	914	4.8	W	484	2.7			W	791	4.4	REFRIG,CONGEL MENAGER
77522	DOMESTIC DEEP-FREEZERS	W	515	2.7	W	287	1.6			W	422	2.5	MEUBLES CONGELATEURS
778	ELECTRICAL MACHINERY NES	W	921	6.6	W	936	6.7			W	1104	9.4	AUTRES MACH ELECT NDA
7781	BATTERIES,ACCUMULATORS	W	657	2.3	W	691	2.6			W	755	4.0	PILES ET ACCUMULATEURS
77812	ELECTRIC ACCUMULATORS	W	518	1.8	W	524	1.9			W	527	3.2	ACCUMULATEURS ELECTRIQ
78	ROAD VEHICLES			68.8			57.7					84.2	VEHICULES ROUTIERS
781	PASS MOTOR VEH EXC BUSES	W	3883	30.8	W	2333	18.7			W	4604	29.4	AUTO TRANSPORT PERSONNES
782	LORRIES,SPCL MTR VEH NES	W	3190	18.9	W	2637	14.2			W	3924	23.4	VEHICULES SPECIAUX,MARCH
7821	LORRIES,TRUCKS	W	2933	17.8	W	2437	13.3			W	3328	19.8	VEHICULES TRANSP MARCHAND
7822	SPECIAL MOTOR VEHCLS NES	W	257	1.1	W	200	0.9			W	596	3.6	VEHICULES USAGES SPECIAUX
783	ROAD MOTOR VEHICLES NES	W	1194	8.1	W	1645	12.0			W	2502	16.6	VEHICULES ROUTIERS NDA
7831	BUSES	W	753	5.5	W	563	4.4			W	1468	9.8	VOITURES TRANSPORT COMMUN
7832	TRACTORS FOR TR-TRAILERS	W	441	2.7	W	1082	7.7			W	1034	6.9	TRACTEURS ROUTIERS
784	MOTOR VEH PRTS,ACCES NES	W	683	9.5	W	821	11.1			W	748	11.7	PIECES 722,781,782,783
7849	OTHER MOTOR VEHCL PARTS	W	654	9.3	W	815	11.0			W	740	11.5	PIECES 722,781,782,783
79	OTHR TRANSPORT EQUIPMENT			57.8			42.8					12.4	AUTRE MATERIEL TRANSPORT
791	RAILWAY VEHICLES	W	1645	4.9	W	58	1.6			W	140	1.0	VEHIC MAT CHEMINS DE FER
7915	FRT,MAINT CARS NOT POWRD	W	1524	4.0									WAGONS DE SERVICE
79152	RAILWAY FREIGHT CARS NES	W	1506	3.5									WAGONS MARCHANDISES
792	AIRCRAFT ETC	W	22	2.1	W	32	3.4			W	41	7.3	APP NAVIGATION AERIENNE
7929	AIRCRAFT PARTS NES	W	17	1.7	W	21	2.3			W	27	5.3	PIECES DU 792
793	SHIPS AND BOATS ETC	W	5453	50.9	W	21863	37.9			W	6048	4.1	NAVIRES BATEAUX,ETC
7932	SHIPS AND BOATS NES	W	3197	13.3	W	8648	18.4			W	1298	1.3	NAVIRES ET BATEAUX
79323	OTHER CARGO VESSELS	W	2328	12.2	W	8581	18.0			W	1277	1.0	AUT BATEAUX TRANS MARCH
7938	TUGS,SPECIAL VESSELS ETC	W	2246	37.6	W	13212	19.6			W	1881	1.4	REMORQUEURS,BATEAUX SPEC
79382	SPECL PURPOSE VESSLS ETC	W	2099	37.3	W	13002	19.3			W	985	0.1	BAT-PHARES,-POMPES,DRAGUES
8	MISC MANUFACTURED GOODS			77.9			62.3					89.2	ART MANUFACTURES DIVERS
812	*PLUMBG,HEATNG,LGHTNG EQ	W	552	3.1	W	476	2.6			W	707	3.7	APPAR SANITAIRES CHAUFFAGE
8124	LIGHTING EQUIPMENT NES	W	268	2.3	W	211	2.0			W	333	2.8	APPAREILS ECLAIRAGE ETC
821	*FURNITURE,PARTS THEREOF	W	1483	9.4	W	1382	7.9			W	1430	9.2	MEUBLES ET PIECES
8219	FURNITURE AND PARTS NES	W	1044	6.0	W	1070	5.8			W	914	4.5	AUTRES MEUBLES ET PIECES
82192	WOOD FURNITURE NES	W	318	1.9	W	394	2.6			W	382	2.4	MEUBLES NDA EN BOIS
82199	OTHR FURN,FURN PARTS NES	W	639	3.5	W	550	2.4			W	362	1.2	MEUBLES NDA AUTRES MATIERES
84	CLOTHING AND ACCESSORIES			6.3			5.3					7.3	VETEMENTS
851	*FOOTWEAR			3.7	W	1386	2.8			W	1445	3.8	CHAUSSURES
87	PRECISION INSTRUMNTS NES			21.4			17.0					29.8	INSTRUM,APPAR SCIENT NDA
872	MEDICAL INSTRUMENTS NES	W	110	3.6	W	92	1.9			W	153	3.9	INSTR,APP MEDIC-CHIR NDA
87202	OTH MEDICAL INSTRUMENTS	W	105	3.4	W	78	1.7			W	96	3.3	INSTRUM,APP MEDECINE
874	MEASURNG,CONTROLNG INSTR	W	440	15.4	W	759	14.4			W	594	24.3	INSTRUMENTS DE MESURE
8741	SURVEYING INSTRUMENTS	W	27	1.1	W	10	1.1			W	14	3.5	INST GEODESIE,TOPO ETC
8742	MEASUR,DRAW ETC INST,PTS	W	215	4.9	W	540	5.6			W	262	7.9	INST DESSIN,TRACAGE,PCS
87421	MEASURNG,DRAWNG ETC INST	W	209	4.7	W	530	5.3			W	255	7.6	INSTRUM DESSIN,TRACAGE
8743	GAS,LIQUID CONTROL INSTR	W	98	4.2	W	30	1.8			W	49	2.9	APP,INSTR MESURE FLUIDES
8748	ELEC MEAS,CONTRL EQU NES	W	70	4.0	W	145	4.5			W	218	6.3	APP ELEC ELECTRO MESURE
87483	OTH ELCTRNC MEAS ETC EQU	W	60	3.0	W	108	3.5			W	165	4.6	AUT APP ELECTRO DE MESURE
8749	INSTR PTS NES,ACCESSORYS	W	14	0.8	W	20	1.0			W	43	3.4	PIECES 873,874.3,54,874.8
88	PHOTO EQU,OPTICL GDS ETC			3.2			2.1					3.1	APP,FOURN PHOTO,OP,MONTR
89	MISC MANUFCTRD GOODS NES			29.9			23.9					31.0	ART MANUFACTURES DIVERS
892	PRINTED MATTER			13.6	W	805	9.2			W	829	11.6	IMPRIMES
8921	PRINTED BOOKS,GLOBES,ETC	W	398	7.8	W	422	5.5			W	372	6.1	LIVRES,BROCHURES,CARTES
89211	PRINTED BOOKS,PAMPHLETS	W	386	7.6	W	416	5.4			W	366	6.0	LIVRES,BROCHURES
8922	NEWSPAPERS,PERIODICALS			4.1	W	267	2.5			W	303	3.5	JOURNAUX ET PERIODIQUES
893	ARTICLES OF PLASTIC NES			7.3			6.9					8.9	OUVRAGES EN MAT DIVIS 58
8931	PLSTC PACKG CONTNRS,LIDS	W	534	2.1	W	851	2.1			W	1110	2.9	ART TRANSP EMBALLAGE ETC
8939	MISC PLASTIC ARTICLES	W	1415	4.9	W	2041	4.7			W	1770	5.8	ART DIVERS EN MAT DIV 58
89399	OTHR PLASTC ARTICLES NES	W	1139	4.4	W	1761	4.2			W	1391	5.2	AUT OUV MAT DIV 58
894	TOYS,SPORTING GOODS,ETC	W	362	2.2	W	310	2.3			W	484	3.2	VOITURES ENFANTS,JOUETS
895	OFFICE SUPPLIES NES	W	188	2.4	W	174	2.1			W	224	3.0	ART PAPET NDA

 Gabon

5. Special Exports F.O.B. by Commodities according to the S.I.T.C. (Rev. 2) in million U.S. Dollars
Exportations Spéciales F.O.B. par Produits d'après la C.T.C.I. (Rév. 2) en millions de Dollars E.U.

SITC CTCI	COMMODITY	1993		1994		1995		1996		PRODUIT
		QUANTITY QUANTITE	VALUE VALEUR	QUANTITY QUANTITE	VALUE VALEUR	QUANTITY QUANTITE	VALUE VALEUR	QUANTITY QUANTITE	VALUE VALEUR	
	ALL COMMODITIES		2637.1		2391.1				3145.7	TOUS PRODUITS
2	CRUDE MATERLS,EXCL FUELS		240.1		292.8				476.0	MAT BRUTES NON COMESTIBLES
23	RUBBER, CRUDE		1.1		2.9				9.7	CAOUTCHOUC BRUT
232	NATURAL RUBBER,GUMS	W 1391	1.1	W 2964	2.9			W 8254	9.7	LATEX CAOUTCHOUC NATUREL
23202	OTHER NATURAL RUBBER	W 1391	1.1	W 2601	2.6			W 8254	9.7	CAOUTCHOUC NATUREL
24	CORK AND WOOD		77.3		208.1				402.3	LIEGE ET BOIS
247	OTH WOOD ROUGH,SQUARED	W 429167	77.3	W 533963	207.9			W 1713213	398.7	BOIS BRUTS EQUARRIS
2472	SAW–,VENEER–LOGS NON–CON	W 429167	77.3	W 533963	207.9			W 1713213	398.7	NON CONIFERES SCIAGE,PLAC
24721	— IN THE ROUGH	W 429167	77.3	W 533963	207.9			W 1713213	398.7	BRUTS ECORCES DEGROSSIS
28	METALLIFEROUS ORES,SCRAP		161.1		81.4				63.6	MINERAIS METAL,DECHETS
287	BASE METAL ORES,CONC NES	W 2688583	161.1	W 3095671	81.3			W 2119146	63.4	MINERAIS METAUX COMMUNS
2877	MANGANESE ORE,CONCENTRTE	W 2688583	161.1	W 3095671	81.3			W 2119146	63.4	MINERAIS DE MANGANESE
3	MINERAL FUELS ETC		2355.4		2070.7				2602.7	COMBUSTIBLES MINERAUX LUB
33	PETROLEUM AND PRODUCTS		2355.4		2070.7				2602.6	PETROLE ET DERIVES
333	CRUDE PETROLEUM	MW 14258	2326.1	MW 15834	2048.2			MW 18571	2557.5	HUILES BRUTES DE PETROLE
334	PETROLEUM PRODUCTS,REFIN	W 258772	29.4	W 258953	22.5			W 315783	45.2	PRODUITS RAFFINES
3344	FUEL OILS,NES							W 210180	23.8	FUEL OILS
5	CHEMCLS,RELATED PROD NES		15.7		8.9				13.4	PRODUITS CHIMIQUES
52	INORGANIC CHEMICALS		15.2		8.4				11.7	PROD CHIM INORGANIQUES
524	RADIOACTIVE ETC MATERIAL		12.6		7.6				10.9	MATIERES RADIOACTIVES
5241	RADIOACTIVE ELEMENTS ETC		12.6		7.6				10.9	RADIOELEMENTS,ISOTOPES
6	BASIC MANUFACTURES		5.7		6.4				26.0	ART MANUFACTURES
63	WOOD,CORK MANUFACTRS NES		3.3		3.1				21.5	OUVRAGES LIEGE ET BOIS
634	VENEERS,PLYWOOD,ETC	W 14675	3.1	W 13637	3.1			W 19591	21.3	PLACAGES,CONTRE–PLAQUES
6342	PLYWOOD OF WOOD SHEETS	W 13290	2.9	W 12640	2.9			W 17000	19.7	BOIS CONTRE–PLAQUES
7	MACHINES,TRANSPORT EQUIP		6.6		5.1				12.3	MACHINES MATERIEL TRANSPORT
8	MISC MANUFACTURED GOODS		9.2		4.9				9.8	ART MANUFACTURES DIVERS

1. HISTORICAL SERIES, 1962–1997 GENERAL TRADE, IMPORTS C.I.F., EXPORTS F.O.B.
SERIES HISTORIQUES, 1962–1997 COMMERCE GENERAL, IMPORTATIONS C.A.F., EXPORTATIONS F.O.B

YEAR ANNEE	VALUE IN MILLION DALASIS VALEUR EN MILLION DALASIS MERCHANDISE –MARCHANDISE		GOLD –OR		CONVERSION FACTORS U.S. CENTS PER DALASI FACTEURS DE CONVERSION CENTS E.U. PAR DALASI		INDEX NUMBERS –INDICES QUANTUM		UNIT VALUE VALEUR UNITAIRE	
	IMPORTS	EXPORTS	IMPORTS	EXPORTS	IMPORTS	EXPORTS	IMPORTS	EXPORTS	IMPORTS	EXPORTS
1962	22.41	18.29			56.0000	56.0000				
1963	21.15	16.04			56.0000	56.0000				
1964	21.68	17.10			56.0000	56.0000				
1965	28.97	25.06			56.0000	56.0000				
1966	32.29	29.85			56.0000	56.0000				
1967	34.97	32.17			51.1120	51.1120				
1968	43.90	27.85			48.0000	48.0000				
1969	40.65	35.16			48.0000	48.0000				
1970	37.42	35.34			48.0000	48.0000				
1971	44.75	28.03			48.1962	48.1617				
1972	49.53	38.53			50.0036	51.4010				
1973	53.69	36.92			58.1678	61.4582				
1974	76.06	80.49			58.4883	59.4121				
1975	108.72	85.66			55.1795	57.7407				
1976	165.51	82.12			45.1182	46.4692				
1977	177.72	116.66			44.0684	43.5635				
1978	209.78	86.89			47.8669	47.2971				
1979	265.51	120.91			53.0001	52.9652				
1980	280.46	69.07			57.9783	57.4819				
1981	238.89	65.13			51.2267	52.9547				
1982	227.90	145.97			43.8131	44.7099				
1983	304.25	190.20			37.8920	38.2103				
1984	354.16	230.81			27.8110	28.8198				
1985	362.25	267.26			25.7522	24.9827				
1986	733.39	235.73			14.2578	14.7828				
1987	897.24	281.39			14.1748	14.1098				
1988	919.36	388.72			14.9054	14.9054				
1989	1221.01	198.05			13.2014	13.5615				
1990	1482.11	244.80			12.6777	12.5770				
1991	1759.38	333.45			11.4934	11.4258				
1992	1944.94	510.52			11.1802	11.1753				
1993	2372.27	604.73			10.9751	11.0312				
1994	2002.89	337.80			10.3691	10.3691				
1995	1339.84	155.23			10.4696	10.5203				
1996	2340.75	180.22			10.2171	10.2539				
1997	2833.28	145.98			9.8211	9.9016				

2. IMPORTS BY BROAD ECONOMIC CATEGORY AND EXPORTS BY INDUSTRIAL ORIGIN. (PERCENTAGE OF TOTAL VALUE)
IMPORTATIONS PAR CATEGORIES ECONOMIQUES ET EXPORTATIONS PAR BRANCHE D'ACTIVITE.(EN POURCENTAGE DE LA VALEUR TOTALE)

IMPORTS – IMPORTATIONS

	1989	1990	1991	1992	1993	1994	1995
TOTAL IMPORTS–IMPORTATIONS TOTALES							
1 FOOD BEV–ALIMENTATION BOISSONS							
11 PRIMARY–PRODUITS DE BASE							
111 FOR INDUSTRY–POUR L'INDUSTRIE							
112 FOR HOUSEHOLDS–POUR LES MENAGES							
12 PROCESSED–PRODUITS ELABORES							
121 FOR INDUSTRY–POUR L'INDUSTRIE							
122 FOR HOUSEHOLDS–POUR LES MENAGES							
2 IND SUPPLIES–APPROV INDUSTRIELS							
21 PRIMARY–PRODUITS DE BASE							
22 PROCESSED–PRODUITS ELABORES							
3 FUELS–COMBUSTIBLES							
31 PRIMARY–PRODUITS DE BASE							
32 PROCESSED–PRODUITS ELABORES							
321 MOTOR SPIRIT–ESSENCE							
322 OTHER–AUTRES							
4 MACHINERY–EQUIPEMENT							
41 CAPITAL EQUIPMENT–MACHINES							
42 PARTS–PIECES ACCESSOIRES							
5 TRANSPORT–TRANSPORT							
51 PASSENGER CARS–AUTOMOBILES							
52 OTHER–AUTRES							
521 INDUSTRIAL–INDUSTRIELS							
522 NON INDUSTRIAL–NON INDUSTRIEL							
53 PARTS–PIECES ACCESSOIRES							
6 CONSUM GOODS–BIENS CONSOMMATION							
61 DURABLE–DURABLES							
62 SEMI DURABLE–SEMI DURABLES							
63 NON DURABLE–NON DURABLES							
7 GOODS NES–BIENS NDA							

EXPORTS – EXPORTATIONS

	1989	1990	1991	1992	1993	1994	1995
TOTAL EXPORTS–EXPORTATIONS TOTALES							
1 AGRICULTURE							
2 MINING QUARRY–INDUS EXTRACTIVES							
3 MANUFACTURING–IND MANUFACTUR							
31 FOOD BEV TOBACCO–ALIM BOISS TAB							
32 TEXTILES–INDUSTRIES TEXTILES							
33 WOOD & PRODUCTS–BOIS & PRODUITS							
34 PAPER & PRODUCTS–PAPIER & PRODT							
35 CHEMICALS–INDUSTRIES CHIMIQUES							
36 NON METAL MIN–MIN NON METAL							
37 BASIC METAL–IND METAL BASE							
38 METAL MANUF–MANUF METAL							
39 OTH MANUF IND–AUTRES MANUF							

Gambia — Gambie

3. TRADE BY PRINCIPAL COUNTRIES OF ORIGIN AND DESTINATION (VALUE IN MILLION U.S. DOLLARS)
ECHANGES SELON LES PRINCIPAUX PAYS D'ORIGINE ET DE DESTINATION (VALEUR EN MILLIONS DE DOLLARS EU)

GENERAL IMPORTS C.I.F. IMPORTATIONS GENERALES C.A.F

COUNTRIES–PAYS	1991	1992	1993	1994	1995
World	202.2		260.0	226.6	140.3
Africa	11.2			46.1	27.3
Americas	6.8			10.5	10.8
– Northern America	6.8			7.1	7.5
– LAIA				3.4	3.2
– CACM					
– Caribbean				0.0	0.0
– Rest of America					0.1
Asia excl fmr USSR	59.2			53.0	34.0
– Middle East				1.5	1.3
Asia former USSR					
Europe excl fmr USSR	98.7			115.0	67.5
– European Union	96.4			113.2	66.3
– Eastern Europe	0.9			0.6	0.3
– Rest of Europe	1.3			1.2	0.9
Europe former USSR				1.9	0.6
Oceania				0.1	0.1
Other	26.3				
United Kingdom	26.6			24.4	19.9
France, Monaco	16.8			32.8	11.1
Cote d'Ivoire	3.3			35.6	19.0
China/Chine	29.5			11.8	8.8
Netherlands/Pays–Bas	21.3			13.5	7.1
Germany/Allemagne	13.6			13.2	8.9
Belgium–Luxembourg	8.6			14.1	10.2
China, Hong Kong SAR	13.1			10.1	5.1
Senegal/Sénégal	5.2		16.0	2.7	4.1
Areas n.e.s.	26.3				
Japan/Japon	8.1			8.7	4.9
USA/Etats–Unis d'Amer	6.8			6.9	7.3
Thailand/Thaïlande	6.1			6.5	4.9
Pakistan			1.0	10.2	0.8
Spain/Espagne	1.7			5.5	4.5
Italy/Italie	5.4			3.0	2.5
Denmark/Danemark	1.0			4.4	1.5
Malawi	2.7			2.1	2.0
Brazil/Brésil				3.4	2.1
India/Inde				1.3	3.8
Sweden/Suède	1.4			2.2	0.5
Viet Nam				1.2	2.5
Cameroon/Cameroun				2.7	0.1
Russian Federation				1.9	0.6
Norway,Svalbard and JM	0.9			0.9	0.4
Nigeria/Nigéria			1.0	0.5	0.4
Indonesia/Indonésie			1.0	0.3	0.3
Gabon				1.0	0.5
Brunei Darussalam				0.6	0.8
Guinea/Guinée			1.0	0.2	0.0
Myanmar	1.1				
Syrian Arab Republic				0.6	0.5
Switzerland,Liechtenst.	0.4			0.3	0.4
Argentina/Argentine					1.0
Poland/Pologne	0.3			0.4	0.2
Morocco/Maroc			1.0		
Singapore/Singapour	0.3			0.4	0.2
Middle East n.e.s.				0.5	0.4
Other Asia n.e.s.	0.9				
Former Czechoslovakia	0.6				

GENERAL EXPORTS F.O.B. EXPORTATIONS GENERALES F.O.B.

COUNTRIES–PAYS	1991	1992	1993	1994	1995
Monde	39.8		67.0	38.4	
Afrique	10.1				
Amériques	0.1				
– Amérique du Nord	0.1				
– ALAI					
– MCAC					
– Caraïbes					
– Autre Amérique					
Asie anc. URSS exclus	1.1				
– Moyen–Orient					
Asie ancienne URSS					
Europe anc. URSS exclus	15.2				
– Union Européenne	14.3				
– Europe de l'Est					
– Autre de l'Europe	0.9				
Europe ancienne URSS					
Océanie					
Autre	13.3				
Areas n.e.s.	13.3				
Guinea/Guinée	0.8		10.0	1.0	
Senegal/Sénégal	0.9		2.0	6.0	
Guinea–Bissau	6.9				
United Kingdom	5.8				
Netherlands/Pays–Bas	3.1				
Indonesia/Indonésie				3.0	
France, Monaco	3.0				
Malaysia/Malaisie			2.0		
Belgium–Luxembourg	1.8				
Mali	1.2				
Switzerland,Liechtenst.	0.9				
China/Chine	0.9				
Germany/Allemagne	0.4				
Ghana	0.3				
Italy/Italie	0.2				
China, Hong Kong SAR	0.2				
USA/Etats–Unis d'Amer	0.1				

(VALUE AS PERCENTAGE OF WORLD TOTAL)(VALEURS EN POURCENTAGE DU TOTAL MONDIAL)

	1986	1987	1988	1989	1990	1991	1992	1993	1994	1995
Africa	4.6	5.3	5.4	6.0	5.0	5.6			20.4	19.5
Americas	5.2	3.1	9.0	4.5	5.8	3.4			4.6	7.7
– Northern America	5.2	3.1	9.0	4.5	5.8	3.4			3.1	5.3
– LAIA									1.5	2.3
– CACM										
– Caribbean									0.0	0.0
– Rest of America										0.1
Asia excl fmr USSR	20.0	24.3	19.5	15.5	21.7	29.3			23.4	24.3
– Middle East									0.6	0.9
Asia former USSR										
Europe excl fmr USSR	53.7	58.1	56.2	59.2	50.0	48.8			50.7	48.1
– European Union	50.6	52.8	54.0	56.0	48.2	47.7			49.9	47.3
– Eastern Europe	2.1	1.4	1.7	2.9	0.8	0.4			0.2	0.2
– Rest of Europe	1.0	3.8	0.5	0.3	1.0	0.7			0.5	0.6
Europe former USSR									0.8	0.4
Oceania									0.0	0.0
Other	16.6	9.2	9.9	14.7	17.5	13.0				
United Kingdom	15.6	19.1	19.7	18.9	17.4	13.1			10.8	14.2
France, Monaco	12.2	9.5	8.9	9.8	12.0	8.3			14.5	7.9
Cote d'Ivoire	0.8	2.5	1.1	0.6	0.4	1.6			15.7	13.6
China/Chine	6.7	5.6	5.2	1.1	12.6	14.6			5.2	6.3
Netherlands/Pays–Bas	5.7	4.2	7.6	9.2	0.9	10.5			5.9	5.0
Germany/Allemagne						6.7			5.8	6.3
Belgium–Luxembourg	4.0	3.6	3.0	3.7	3.7	4.2			6.2	7.2
China, Hong Kong SAR	1.7	1.6	3.6	4.1	2.2	6.5			4.4	3.7
Senegal/Sénégal	3.0	2.2	3.2	3.4	3.3	2.6		6.2	1.2	2.9
Areas n.e.s.	16.6	9.2	9.9	14.7	17.5	13.0				

	1986	1987	1988	1989	1990	1991	1992	1993	1994	1995
Afrique	7.9	30.3	16.1	2.1	16.4	25.5				
Amériques	0.2	2.7	0.1	0.2		0.2				
– Amérique du Nord	0.2	2.7	0.1	0.2		0.2				
– ALAI										
– MCAC										
– Caraïbes										
– Autre Amérique										
Asie anc. URSS exclus			0.5	0.9	0.9	2.7				
– Moyen–Orient										
Asie ancienne URSS										
Europe anc. URSS exclus	51.0	47.8	64.8	22.2	57.0	38.2				
– Union Européenne	30.1	30.4	41.4	22.2	43.6	35.9				
– Europe de l'Est										
– Autre de l'Europe	20.9	17.4	23.4		13.5	2.3				
Europe ancienne URSS										
Océanie										
Autre	40.8	19.2	18.6	74.6	25.6	33.4				
Areas n.e.s.	40.8	19.2	18.6	74.6	25.6	33.4				
Guinea/Guinée	2.2	5.1	4.0	0.3	2.1	1.9		14.9	2.6	
Senegal/Sénégal	1.0	12.1	3.2	1.2	3.5	2.4		3.0	15.6	
Guinea–Bissau		9.8	5.2		7.9	17.3				
United Kingdom	6.4	15.7	21.6	5.3	8.1	14.7				
Netherlands/Pays–Bas	13.6	10.9	10.2	6.5	16.7	7.7				
Indonesia/Indonésie									7.8	
France, Monaco	3.8	1.9	5.0	5.2	8.4	7.5				
Malaysia/Malaisie								3.0		
Belgium–Luxembourg	1.5	0.5	0.9	3.1	8.9	4.5				

4. General Imports C.I.F. by Commodities according to the S.I.T.C. (Rev. 2) in million U.S. Dollars
Importations Générales C.A.F. par Produits d'après la C.T.C.I. (Rév. 2) en millions de Dollars E.U.

SITC CTCI	COMMODITY	1992 QUANTITY QUANTITE	1992 VALUE VALEUR	1993 QUANTITY QUANTITE	1993 VALUE VALEUR	1994 QUANTITY QUANTITE	1994 VALUE VALEUR	1995 QUANTITY QUANTITE	1995 VALUE VALEUR	PRODUIT
	ALL COMMODITIES						226.7		140.4	TOUS PRODUITS
0	FOOD AND LIVE ANIMALS						61.2		37.4	ALIMENTS,ANIMAUX VIVANTS
001	*LIVE ANIMALS FOR FOOD						1.1		0.1	ANIMAUX VIVANTS
0011	BOVINE SPECIES,LIVE						1.0		0.1	ESPECE BOVINE
01	MEAT AND PREPARATIONS						1.7		0.5	VIANDES ET PREPARATIONS
011	MEAT FRESH,CHILLD,FROZEN						0.8		0.4	VIANDES FRAICHES,REF,CONGE
014	MEAT PREPD,PRSVD,NES ETC						0.9		0.1	CONSERVES DE VIANDES
0149	OTH PREPARD,PRESRVD MEAT						0.9		0.1	AUTRES PREP DE VIANDES
02	DAIRY PRODCTS,BIRDS'EGGS						5.8		4.0	PRODUITS LAITIERS,OEUFS
022	MILK AND CREAM						3.5		3.5	LAIT ET CREME
0223	MILK AND CREAM FRESH						1.8		1.1	LAIT,CREME FRAIS
0224	MILK,CREAM PRESERVED ETC						1.7		2.4	LAIT,CREME CONS,CONC
025	EGGS,BIRDS,FRESH,PRSRVD						2.0		0.3	OEUFS
0251	— IN SHELL						1.9		0.3	OEUFS EN COQUILLE
03	FISH AND PREPARATIONS						1.0		0.4	POISSONS ET PREPARATIONS
04	CEREALS AND PREPARATIONS						23.0		16.1	CEREALES ET PRODUITS
041	WHEAT ETC UNMILLED						3.4		0.1	FROMENT,EPEAUTRE
0411	DURUM WHEAT UNMILLED						3.4		0.1	FROMENT DUR NON MOULU
042	RICE						14.6		11.3	RIZ
046	WHEAT ETC MEAL OR FLOUR						0.1		0.6	SEMOULE FARINE,FROMENT
04602	MEAL,GROATS OF WHEAT ETC						0.1		0.6	GRUAUX,SEMOULES FROMENT
047	OTHER CEREAL MEALS,FLOUR						4.4		3.3	AUTRES SEMOULES,FARINES
04701	CEREAL FLOUR(NON-WHEAT)						4.4		3.3	FARINES DE CEREALES
048	CEREAL ETC PREPARATIONS						0.8		1.1	PREPTNS A BASE CEREALES
0488	OTH CEREAL PREPS,MALT EX						0.1		0.6	EXTRAITS DE MALT
05	VEGETABLES AND FRUIT						8.7		4.7	LEGUMES ET FRUITS
054	VEG ETC FRSH,SMPLY PRSVD						3.8		1.3	LEGUMES FRAIS,CONG,SECS
0545	OTHER FRESH VEGETABLES						3.3		0.8	AUTRES LEGUMES FRAIS,REF
05451	ALLIACEOUS VEGTBLS,FRESH						3.3		0.7	OIGNONS,ECHALOTES,AULX
056	VEGTBLES ETC PRSVD,PREPD						2.7		1.9	CONSERVES DE LEGUMES
0564	FLOUR ETC OF FRUIT,VEGET						0.8		0.1	FARINES,SEMOULES,FLOCONS
05643	POTATO FLOUR,MEAL,FLAKES						0.8		0.1	FLOCONS DE POMMES DE TERRE
0565	VEGTBLES PRSVD,PREPD NES						1.9		1.8	LEGUMES PREPARES CONSERVE
05659	OTH VEG PRESVD,PREPD NES						1.9		1.8	LEGUM PREPAP,CONSERV NDA
057	FRUIT,NUTS,FRESH,DRIED						1.8		1.2	FRUITS FRAIS OU SECS
0577	NUTS EDIBLE,FRESH,DRIED						1.3		1.1	FRUITS A COQUES
06	SUGAR AND PREPS,HONEY						14.4		8.7	SUCRES ET PRODUITS
061	SUGAR AND HONEY						14.3		8.5	SUCRES ET MIEL
0611	RAW BEET AND CANE SUGAR						14.1		8.5	SUCRES BRUTS
07	COFFEE,TEA,COCOA,SPICES						2.1		1.4	CAFE,THE,CACAO,EPICES
074	TEA AND MATE						1.6		1.2	THE ET MATE
0741	TEA						1.6		1.2	THE
09	MISC EDIBLE PRODUCTS						3.4		1.7	PREP ALIMENTAIRES DIVERSES
091	MARGARINE AND SHORTENING						1.7		0.6	MARGARINE ET GRAISSES
0914	MARGARINE,EDIBLE FAT NES						1.7		0.6	MARGARINES,SIMILI SAINDOUX
09141	MARGARINE						1.7		0.6	MARGARINE
098	EDIBLE PRODCTS,PREPS NES						1.7		1.2	PREP ALIMENTAIRES NDA
09809	MISC FOOD PREPRTIONS NES						1.0		0.6	PREP ALIMENTAIRES NDA
1	BEVERAGES AND TOBACCO						20.6		6.5	BOISSONS ET TABACS
11	BEVERAGES						1.8		0.8	BOISSONS
111	NON-ALCOHL BEVERAGES NES						1.0		0.5	BOISSONS NON ALCOOLIQUES
112	ALCOHOLIC BEVERAGES						0.9		0.4	BOISSONS ALCOOLIQUES
12	TOBACCO AND MANUFACTURES						18.8		5.7	TABACS BRUTS FABRIQUES
121	TOBACCO UNMNFCTRD,REFUSE						2.4		2.1	TABACS BRUTS,DECHETS
1211	TOBACCO,NOT STRIPPED						2.4		2.1	TABACS NON ECOTES
122	TOBACCO,MANUFACTURED						16.5		3.7	TABACS FABRIQUES
1222	CIGARETTES						16.5		3.6	CIGARETTES
2	CRUDE MATERLS,EXCL FUELS						2.1		1.9	MAT BRUTES NON COMESTIBLES
26	TEXTILE FIBRES AND WASTE						0.9		1.0	FIBRES TEXTILES
269	WASTE OF TEXTILE FABRICS						0.9		1.0	FRIPERIE DRILLES,CHIFFONS
26901	BULK TEXT WSTE,OLD CLTHG						0.9		1.0	ART ET ACCESS D'HABILLEMENT
3	MINERAL FUELS ETC						36.9		20.3	COMBUSTIBLES MINERAUX LUB
32	COAL,COKE AND BRIQUETTES						0.9			HOUILLES,COKES,BRIQUETTES
322	COAL,LIGNITE AND PEAT						0.9			HOUILLES,LIGNITES,TOURBE
3221	ANTHRACITE,NOT AGGLOMRTD						0.9			ANTHRACITE
33	PETROLEUM AND PRODUCTS						29.5		19.8	PETROLE ET DERIVES
334	PETROLEUM PRODUCTS,REFIN						28.8		19.4	PRODUITS RAFFINES
341	*GAS,NATURAL AND MANUFCT						6.6		0.5	GAZ NATUREL,GAZ MANUFACT
4	ANIMAL,VEGETABLE OIL,FAT						3.7		3.9	HUILES,GRAISSES ANIM,VEG
42	FIXED VEGETABLE OIL,FAT						2.7		3.3	HUILES VEGETALES FIXES
423	FIXED VEG OILS,SOFT						0.8		2.0	HUILES VEGET DOUCES FIXES
4234	GROUNDNUT(PEANUT) OIL						0.4		0.8	HUILE D'ARACHIDE
4239	OTH FIXED VEG OILS,SOFT						0.2		0.9	AUTRES HUILES FIXES
42391	RAPE,COLZA,MUSTARD OILS						0.2		0.9	H NAVETTE COLZA,MOUTARDE
424	FIXED VEG OIL NONSOFT						1.9		1.4	AUTRES HUILES VEG FIXES
431	*PROCESD ANML VEG OIL,ET						1.1		0.6	HUILES,GRAISSES PREPAREES
4312	HYDROGENATED OIL,FAT						1.1		0.6	HUILES HYDROGENEES
5	CHEMCLS,RELATED PROD NES						12.3		7.9	PRODUITS CHIMIQUES
52	INORGANIC CHEMICALS						1.1		1.9	PROD CHIM INORGANIQUES
522	INORG ELEMNTS,OXIDES,ETC						0.7		1.8	ELEMENTS INORGANIQUES
5222	INORGANIC ACIDS ETC						0.4		1.4	ACIDES INORGANIQUES
52223	NITRIC,SULPHONITRIC ACID						0.4		1.3	ACIDE NITRIQUE
53	DYES,TANNING,COLOUR PROD						0.8		0.8	PROD TEINTURE,COLORANTS
533	PIGMENTS,PAINTS,ETC						0.8		0.7	PIGMENTS,PEINTURES,VERNIS
5334	VARNISHES,DISTEMPERS ETC						0.7		0.6	PEINTURES A L'EAU
541	*MEDICINAL,PHARM PRODUCT						3.6		3.0	PROD MEDICINAUX PHARMACEUT
5417	MEDICAMENTS						3.3		2.6	MEDICAMENTS
55	PERFUME,CLEANING ETC PRD						1.6		0.8	PROD POUR PARFUM,TOILETTE
553	PERFUMERY,COSMETICS,ETC						0.9		0.2	PRODUITS DE PARFUMERIE
562	*FERTILIZERS,MANUFACTURE						1.8		0.1	ENGRAIS MANUFACTURES
5621	CHEM NITROGENOUS FERTLZR						1.7			ENGRAIS AZOTES
56216	UREA						1.7			UREE
59	CHEMICAL MATERIALS NES						2.8		1.0	MAT PROD CHIMIQUES NDA
591	PESTICIDES,DISINFECTANTS						1.6		0.8	DESINF,INSECT,FONG,HERB
5911	INSECTICIDES,FOR RETAIL						1.6		0.8	INSECTICIDES VENTE DET
598	MISCEL CHEM PRODUCTS NES						1.2		0.1	PROD DIV INDUST CHIM NDA
5989	CHEM PRODUCTS,PREPS NES						1.1		0.1	PROD PREP CHIMIQUES NDA
59893	CULTURE MEDIA,PREPARED						1.0			MILIEUX DE CULTURE
6	BASIC MANUFACTURES						32.7		21.0	ART MANUFACTURES
62	RUBBER MANUFACTURES NES						1.1		1.5	CAOUTCHOUC MANUFACTURE
621	MATERIALS OF RUBBER						0.1		0.7	PRODUITS EN CAOUTCHOUC

4. General Imports C.I.F. by Commodities according to the S.I.T.C. (Rev. 2) in million U.S. Dollars
Importations Générales C.A.F. par Produits d'après la C.T.C.I. (Rév. 2) en millions de Dollars E.U.

SITC CTCI	COMMODITY	1992 QUANTITY QUANTITE	1992 VALUE VALEUR	1993 QUANTITY QUANTITE	1993 VALUE VALEUR	1994 QUANTITY QUANTITE	1994 VALUE VALEUR	1995 QUANTITY QUANTITE	1995 VALUE VALEUR	PRODUIT
62105	UNHARD VULC RUBBER TUBES						0.1		0.7	TUBES,TUYAUX CAOUT VULC
625	RUBBER TYRES, TUBES ETC						1.0		0.9	PNEUS CAOUTCHOUC VULCANISE
6251	TYRES NEW FOR MOTOR CARS						0.8		0.7	PNEUS POUR VOITURES
63	WOOD,CORK MANUFACTRS NES						0.8		0.4	OUVRAGES LIEGE ET BOIS
64	PAPER,PAPERBOARD AND MFR						2.1		1.7	PAPIERS,CARTONS & OUVRAGES
641	PAPER AND PAPERBOARD						0.8		0.5	PAPIERS ET CARTONS
642	PAPER,ETC,PRECUT,ARTS OF						1.4		1.2	PAP,CARTONS DECOUPES
6421	PAPER ETC CONTAINERS						0.6		0.5	BOITES,SACS EMBALLAGES
65	TEXTILE YARN,FABRICS,ETC						14.8		8.7	FILS,TISSUS,ARTICLES TEXTILE
651	TEXTILE YARN						1.1		0.3	FILS TEXTILES
6513	COTTON YARN						1.0		0.2	FILS DE COTON
65135	— PUT UP FOR RETAIL						0.8		0.1	FILS CONDS VENTE DETAIL
652	COTTON FABRICS,WOVEN						8.9		6.2	TISSUS DE COTON
6522	WOVEN COTTON BLEACHD,ETC						8.2		6.1	TISSUS COTON BLANCHIS ETC
65224	BLCHED COTTON FABRIC NES						7.9		5.8	AUT TIS PLUS 85% COT BLANCHI
653	WOVN MAN-MADE FIB FABRIC						3.1		1.8	TISSUS FIBRES SYNTH,ARTIF
6535	CONT REGN WEAVES NONPILE						0.7		0.8	TISSUS FIB TEXT ART CONTINU
654	OTH WOVEN TEXTILE FABRIC						0.7		0.1	TISSUS AUT COTON SYNT,ARTIF
658	TEXTILE ARTICLES NES						0.8		0.2	ART FACONNES MAT TEXTILES
66	NONMETAL MINERAL MFS NES						4.8		3.4	ART MIN NON METALLIQUES
661	LIME,CEMENT,BLDG PRODS						3.1		2.4	CHAUX,CIMENTS MAT CONSTR
6612	CEMENT						3.0		2.2	CIMENTS HYDRAULIQUES
662	CLAY,REFRACTORY BLDG PRD						1.0		0.6	MAT CONST REFRACTAIRES
6624	BRICKS ETC NONREFRACTORY						0.4		0.5	BRIQUES ETC CERAM NON REFR
67	IRON AND STEEL						2.9		2.8	FER ET ACIER
673	IRON,STEEL SHAPES ETC						1.1		1.7	BARRES,PROFIL FER,ACIER
6732	IRON,STEEL BARS ETC						0.5		0.7	BARRES FER,ACIER
67326	IRN,OTH STL BARS HOTROLD						0.4		0.7	BARRES PLEINES FER,ACIER
6733	IRON,STEEL PROFILES ETC						0.6		0.8	PROFILES,PALPLAN FER,ACIER
67336	IRN,SMPL STL SHEET PILNG						0.6		0.7	PALPLANCHES EN FER,ACIER
674	IRN,STL UNIV,PLATE,SHEET						0.9		0.9	LARGES PLATS,TOLES
678	IRON,STL TUBES,PIPES,ETC						0.8		0.2	TUBES,TUYAUX EN FONTE,FER
68	NON-FERROUS METALS						1.7		0.7	METAUX NON FERREUX
684	ALUMINIUM						0.9		0.6	ALUMINIUM
6842	ALUMINIUM,ALLOYS WORKED						0.4		0.6	ALUMINIUM,ALLIAGES OUVRE
687	TIN						0.8			ETAIN
6872	TIN,ALLOYS WORKED						0.8			ETAIN ET ALLIAGES OUVRES
68724	TIN TUBES,FITTINGS,ETC						0.8			TUBES,TUYAUX EN ETAIN
69	METAL MANUFACTURES NES						4.8		2.2	ART MANUFACT EN METAL NDA
691	STRUCTURES AND PARTS NES						0.8		0.1	CONSTRUCT FER,ACIER,ALU
692	METAL TANKS,BOXES,ETC						0.8		0.2	RECIPIENTS METALLIQUES
697	BASE MTL HOUSEHOLD EQUIP						0.5		0.6	ART MENAGE MET COMMUNS
699	BASE METAL MFRS NES						2.1		0.5	ART MANUFACTURES MET NDA
6991	LOCKSMITHS WARES,ETC						1.0		0.2	ARTICLES DE SERRURERIE
6998	MFRS NES OF CPR,NIKL,ETC						0.8		0.2	OUVRAGES EN CU,NI,AL,PB,ZN
69985	ZINC MANUFACTURES NES						0.8		0.2	OUVRAGES EN ZINC
7	MACHINES,TRANSPORT EQUIP						40.0		28.5	MACHINES MATERIEL TRANSPORT
71	POWER GENERATING EQUIPMT						2.2		1.2	MACHINES GENERATRICES
716	ROTATING ELECTRIC PLANT						1.3		0.8	APP ELECTR ROTATIFS,PIECES
7169	PTS NES OF ROT ELEC PLNT						0.8		0.3	PIECES MAC APP ROTATIFS
72	MACHS FOR SPCL INDUSTRYS						2.3		2.2	MAC SPECIALES POUR INDUST
721	AGRIC MACHY,EXC TRACTORS						0.6		0.6	MACHINES AGRICOLES
723	CIVIL ENGNEERG EQUIP ETC						0.6		0.8	APPAREILS DE GENIE CIVIL
74	GENRL INDUSTRL MACHY NES						3.6		3.1	MACH APP INDUSTRIE
741	HEATING,COOLING EQUIPMNT						0.8		0.4	MACH CHAUFFAGE,PIECES
742	PUMPS FOR LIQUIDS ETC						0.8		1.4	POMPES MOTO-POMPES
7428	OTHER PUMPS FOR LIQUIDS						0.8		1.4	AUTRES POMPES POUR LIQ
74281	GARAGE-TYPE FUEL PUMPS						0.8		1.4	POMPES DISTRIB CARBURNTS
743	PUMPS NES,CENTRFUGES ETC						0.8		0.2	POMPES COMPRES,VENT ETC
744	MECHANICAL HANDLING EQU						0.7		0.6	EQUIP MANUTENTION PIECES
75	OFFICE MACHNES,ADP EQUIP						2.0		1.5	MACH BUREAU TRAIT AUTOM
752	AUTOMTIC DATA PROC EQUIP						1.4		1.0	MACH TRAIT INFORMATION
7521	ANALOG,HYBRID COMPUTERS						1.4		1.0	MACH POUR TRAIT INFORMAT
76	TELECOMM,SOUND EQUIPMENT						5.0		4.3	EQUIPMENT DE TELECOM
763	SOUND RECORDRS,PHONOGRPH						0.8		0.5	PHONO,APP ENREGISTREMENT
7638	OTHR SOUND APPARATUS ETC						0.8		0.5	AUT APP D'ENREGIS,REPROD
764	TELECOM EQPT,PTS,ACC NES						3.3		3.5	EQUIP TELECOM,PIECES
7641	LINE TELEPHONE,ETC EQUIP						2.8		1.8	APP TELEPHON PAR FIL
7643	TV,RADIO TRANSMITTRS ETC						0.1		0.5	APP EMET TELE RADIO
7649	PTS NES OF EQUIPMT OF 76						0.2		1.3	PIECES DE LA DIV 76
76493	TELECOMM EQUIPMT PTS NES						0.2		1.2	PIECES 761,762,764.3,8
77	ELECTRIC MACHNRY NES ETC						6.2		4.3	MACH APP ELECT NDA
772	SWITCHGEAR ETC,PARTS NES						0.7		0.5	APP COUPURE,SECT ETC
7721	SWITCHGEAR ETC						0.7		0.5	APP COUPURE,SECTIONMNT
774	ELECTRO-MEDCL,XRAY EQUIP						0.5		1.1	APPAREILS MEDICAUX
7741	ELECTRO-MEDICAL EQUIPMNT						0.5		1.0	APP ELECTRICITE MEDICALE
775	HOUSEHOLD TYPE EQUIP NES						0.9		0.8	MACH,APP USAGE DOMESTQUE
7752	DOM REFRIGERATRS,FREEZRS						0.7		0.7	REFRIG,CONGEL MENAGER
77521	DOMESTIC REFRIGERATORS						0.7		0.7	REFRIGERATEURS
776	TRANSISTORS,VALVES,ETC						0.8		0.1	LAMPES,TUBES,VALVES
7763	DIODES,TRANSISTORS,ETC						0.7		0.1	DIODES,TRANSISTORS
778	ELECTRICAL MACHINERY NES						2.9		1.7	AUTRES MACH ELECT NDA
7781	BATTERIES,ACCUMULATORS						1.6		1.5	PILES ET ACCUMULATEURS
77811	PRIMARY BATTERIES,CELLS						1.4		1.4	PILES ELECTRIQUES,PIECES
7788	OTH ELEC MACHY,EQUIP NES						0.9		0.1	AUT MACH APP ELEC NDA
77881	ELECTRO-MAGNETS ETC						0.8		0.1	ELECTRO-AIMANTS
78	ROAD VEHICLES						18.4		11.5	VEHICULES ROUTIERS
781	PASS MOTOR VEH EXC BUSES						9.2		8.1	AUTO TRANSPORT PERSONNES
782	LORRIES,SPCL MTR VEH NES						1.6		0.7	VEHICULES SPECIAUX,MARCH
7821	LORRIES,TRUCKS						1.0		0.4	VEHICULES TRANSP MARCHAND
783	ROAD MOTOR VEHICLES NES						1.7		0.3	VEHICULES ROUTIERS NDA
7831	BUSES						1.7		0.3	VOITURES TRANSPORT COMMUN
784	MOTOR VEH PRTS,ACCES NES						2.1		1.6	PIECES 722,781,782,783
7849	OTHER MOTOR VEHCL PARTS						2.1		1.6	PIECES 722,781,782,783
785	CYCLES,ETC MOTRZD OR NOT						3.8		0.9	MOTOCYCLES SCOOTERS
7851	MOTORCYCLES ETC						3.4		0.6	MOTO VELO MOTEUR AUXIL
79	OTHR TRANSPORT EQUIPMENT						0.6		0.6	AUTRE MATERIEL TRANSPORT
793	SHIPS AND BOATS ETC						0.4		0.5	NAVIRES BATEAUX,ETC
8	MISC MANUFACTURED GOODS						15.6		11.2	ART MANUFACTURES DIVERS
821	*FURNITURE,PARTS THEREOF						1.4		0.7	MEUBLES ET PIECES
8219	FURNITURE AND PARTS NES						0.9		0.5	AUTRES MEUBLES ET PIECES

4. General Imports C.I.F. by Commodities according to the S.I.T.C. (Rev. 2) in million U.S. Dollars
Importations Générales C.A.F. par Produits d'après la C.T.C.I. (Rév. 2) en millions de Dollars E.U.

SITC CTCI	COMMODITY	1992 QUANTITY QUANTITE	1992 VALUE VALEUR	1993 QUANTITY QUANTITE	1993 VALUE VALEUR	1994 QUANTITY QUANTITE	1994 VALUE VALEUR	1995 QUANTITY QUANTITE	1995 VALUE VALEUR	PRODUIT
82191	METAL FURNITURE NES						0.9		0.5	MEUBLES NDA EN METAL
84	CLOTHING AND ACCESSORIES						1.7		1.0	VETEMENTS
851	*FOOTWEAR						2.4		1.7	CHAUSSURES
85101	FOOTWEAR RUBBER,PLASTIC						1.3		0.9	CHAUS SEMELLES CAOUTCH
85102	FOOTWEAR LEATHER						1.1		0.8	CHAUS SEMELLES EN CUIR
88	PHOTO EQU,OPTICL GDS ETC						0.7		0.6	APP,FOURN PHOTO,OP,MONTR
89	MISC MANUFCTRD GOODS NES						8.3		6.4	ART MANUFACTURES DIVERS
892	PRINTED MATTER						3.1		2.3	IMPRIMES
8921	PRINTED BOOKS,GLOBES,ETC						0.4		1.0	LIVRES,BROCHURES,CARTES
89211	PRINTED BOOKS,PAMPHLETS						0.3		1.0	LIVRES,BROCHURES
8922	NEWSPAPERS,PERIODICALS						1.7		0.7	JOURNAUX ET PERIODIQUES
8928	PRINTED MATTER NES						1.2		0.7	IMPRIMES NDA
89286	TRADE ADV MATRL,CATALOGS						0.4		0.6	IMPRIMES PUBLICITAIRES
893	ARTICLES OF PLASTIC NES						1.6		1.3	OUVRAGES EN MAT DIVIS 58
8939	MISC PLASTIC ARTICLES						1.0		1.1	ART DIVERS EN MAT DIV 58
89399	OTHR PLASTC ARTICLES NES						0.8		0.9	AUT OUV MAT DIV 58
894	TOYS,SPORTING GOODS,ETC						0.8		0.2	VOITURES ENFANTS,JOUETS
899	OTHER MANUFACTURED GOODS						2.5		2.1	AUT ART MANUF DIVERS NDA
8993	COMBUSTIBLE PRODUCTS ETC						2.3		1.9	BOUGIES,ALLUMETTES ETC
89931	CANDLES,TAPERS,ETC						1.5		1.3	BOUGIES,CHANDELLES,CIERG
89932	MATCHES						0.8		0.6	ALLUMETTES
9	GOODS NOT CLASSD BY KIND								2.3	ART TRANSACT NON CLASSES
931	*SPECIAL TRANSACTIONS						1.7		2.3	TRANS.SPECIALES

5. General Exports F.O.B. by Commodities according to the S.I.T.C. (Rev. 2) in million U.S. Dollars
Exportations Générales F.O.B. par Produits d'après la C.T.C.I. (Rév. 2) en millions de Dollars E.U.

SITC CTCI	COMMODITY	1992 QUANTITY QUANTITE	1992 VALUE VALEUR	1993 QUANTITY QUANTITE	1993 VALUE VALEUR	1994 QUANTITY QUANTITE	1994 VALUE VALEUR	1995 QUANTITY QUANTITE	1995 VALUE VALEUR	PRODUIT
	ALL COMMODITIES						38.5		27.8	TOUS PRODUITS
0	FOOD AND LIVE ANIMALS						6.1		4.8	ALIMENTS,ANIMAUX VIVANTS
02	DAIRY PRODCTS,BIRDS'EGGS						0.3		0.1	PRODUITS LAITIERS,OEUFS
022	MILK AND CREAM						0.3		0.1	LAIT ET CREME
0223	MILK AND CREAM FRESH						0.3		0.1	LAIT,CREME FRAIS
03	FISH AND PREPARATIONS						2.8		2.6	POISSONS ET PREPARATIONS
034	FISH,FRESH,CHILLED,FROZN						0.3		0.1	POISSON FRAIS, REFRIG,CONG
0342	FISH FROZEN,EXCL FILLETS						0.3		0.1	POISSONS CONGELES
035	FISH SALTED,DRIED,SMOKED						0.4		0.4	POISSON SECHE,SALE,FUME
03503	FISH(EX COD)DRIED,SALTED						0.4		0.4	POISSONS SECHES,SALES
036	SHELL FISH FRESH,FROZEN						2.1		2.1	CRUSTACES,MOLLUSQUES
04	CEREALS AND PREPARATIONS						0.4		0.1	CEREALES ET PRODUITS
048	CEREAL ETC PREPARATIONS						0.4		0.1	PREPTNS A BASE CEREALES
0484	BAKERY PRODUCTS						0.4		0.1	PRODUITS DE BOULANGERIE
04842	PASTRY, CAKES ETC						0.4		0.1	PATISSERIE ETC.
05	VEGETABLES AND FRUIT						1.6		1.9	LEGUMES ET FRUITS
054	VEG ETC FRSH,SMPLY PRSVD						0.8		1.4	LEGUMES FRAIS,CONG,SECS
0542	LEGUMINOUS VEGETBLES DRY						0.3		1.0	LEGUMES A COSSE SECS
0545	OTHER FRESH VEGETABLES						0.5		0.5	AUTRES LEGUMES FRAIS,REF
05459	FRESH VEGETABLES NES						0.5		0.5	LEGUMES FRAIS,REFRI NDA
056	VEGTBLES ETC PRSVD,PREPD						0.2		0.1	CONSERVES DE LEGUMES
0565	VEGTBLES PRSVD,PREPD NES						0.2		0.1	LEGUMES PREPARES CONSERVE
05659	OTH VEG PRESVD,PREPD NES						0.2		0.1	LEGUM PREPAP,CONSERV NDA
057	FRUIT,NUTS,FRESH,DRIED						0.8		0.5	FRUITS FRAIS OU SECS
0577	NUTS EDIBLE,FRESH,DRIED						0.3		0.2	FRUITS A COQUES
05773	CASHEW NUTS,FRESH,DRIED						0.3		0.2	NOIX DE CAJOU
0579	FRUIT FRESH OR DRIED NES						0.5		0.3	FRUITS FRAIS,SECS NDA
05797	OTH TROP FRUIT,FRESH,DRY						0.4		0.3	AVOCATS,MANGUES,GOYAVES
06	SUGAR AND PREPS,HONEY						1.1		0.3	SUCRES ET PRODUITS
061	SUGAR AND HONEY						0.5		0.1	SUCRES ET MIEL
0619	SUGARS AND SYRUPS NES						0.4			AUTRES SUCRES SIROPS
062	SUGAR CANDY NON-CHOCLATE						0.7		0.3	SUCRERIES
1	BEVERAGES AND TOBACCO						0.3		0.2	BOISSONS ET TABACS
12	TOBACCO AND MANUFACTURES						0.3		0.2	TABACS BRUTS FABRIQUES
121	TOBACCO UNMNFCTRD,REFUSE						0.2		0.1	TABACS BRUTS,DECHETS
1211	TOBACCO,NOT STRIPPED						0.2		0.1	TABACS NON ECOTES
2	CRUDE MATERLS,EXCL FUELS						14.4		11.9	MAT BRUTES NON COMESTIBLES
21	HIDES,SKINS,FURS UNDRSSD						0.1		0.1	CUIRS,PEAUX BRUTS
211	HIDES,SKINS,EXC FURS,RAW						0.1		0.1	CUIRS ET PEAUX
2112	CALF AND KIP SKINS,RAW						0.1		0.1	PEAUX DE VEAUX
22	OIL SEEDS,OLEAGINOUS FRT						8.5		10.1	GRAINES,FRUITS OLEAGINEUX
222	SEEDS FOR'SOFT'FIXED OIL						8.5		10.1	GRAINES HUILES FIXES
2221	GROUNDNUTS,GREEN						8.2		10.0	ARACHIDES NON GRILLEES
2223	COTTON SEEDS						0.3		0.1	GRAINES DE COTON
26	TEXTILE FIBRES AND WASTE						5.6		1.8	FIBRES TEXTILES
263	COTTON						5.6		1.8	COTON
2631	RAW COTTON,EXCL LINTERS						3.6			COTON EN MASSE
2632	COTTON LINTERS						2.0		1.8	LINTERS DE COTON
29	CRUDE ANIMAL,VEG MAT NES						0.4			MATIERES BRUTES ANIM,VEGET
292	CRUDE VEG MATERIALS NES						0.4			MAT BRUTES VEGETALES NDA
2927	CUT FLOWERS AND FOLIAGE						0.3			FLEURS,FEUILLAGES COUPES
29271	CUT FLOWERS						0.3			FLEURS ET BOUTONS
5	CHEMCLS,RELATED PROD NES						0.8		0.4	PRODUITS CHIMIQUES
562	*FERTILIZERS,MANUFACTURE								0.3	ENGRAIS MANUFACTURES
5621	CHEM NITROGENOUS FERTLZR								0.2	ENGRAIS AZOTES
56216	UREA								0.2	UREE
5629	FERTILIZERS NES								0.2	ENGRAIS NDA
56291	NIT-PHOS-POT FERTLZR NES								0.2	ENGRAIS CONT N P K
572	*EXPLOSIVES,PYROTECH PRO						0.3			EXPLOSIFS
5723	PYROTECHNIC ARTICLES						0.3			ARTICLES DE PYROTECHNIE
59	CHEMICAL MATERIALS NES						0.6		0.1	MAT PROD CHIMIQUES NDA
591	PESTICIDES,DISINFECTANTS						0.6		0.1	DESINF,INSECT,FONG,HERB
5914	DISINFECTANTS,ETC,FR RET						0.6		0.1	DESINFECTANTS VENTE DET
59149	RAT POISONS ETC FR RTAIL						0.6		0.1	ANTIPARASITES VENTE DET
6	BASIC MANUFACTURES						2.7		1.4	ART MANUFACTURES
65	TEXTILE YARN,FABRICS,ETC						2.6		1.3	FILS,TISSUS,ARTICLES TEXTILE
652	COTTON FABRICS,WOVEN						0.4		0.3	TISSUS DE COTON
6521	GREY WOVEN COTTON FABRIC						0.1		0.2	TISSUS COT ECRUS NON MERCER
65215	GREY WOVN COTN BLEND NES						0.1		0.2	AUT TIS MOINS 85% COT ECRUS
6522	WOVEN COTTON BLEACHD,ETC						0.4		0.1	TISSUS COTON BLANCHIS ETC
65225	BLCHD COTN BLEND FAB NES						0.4		0.1	AUT TIS MOINS 85% COT BLANCH
653	WOVN MAN-MADE FIB FABRIC						1.7		0.6	TISSUS FIBRES SYNTH,ARTIF
6535	CONT REGN WEAVES NONPILE						1.6		0.4	TISSUS FIB TEXT ART CONTINU
65356	CONT REG BLEND FABRC NES						1.5		0.4	TIS MOINS 85% TEXT ART CONT
6538	DISC REG BLEND FABRC NES						0.1		0.3	TIS MOINS 85% TEXT ART DISC
65389	OTH DISC REG BLEND FABRC						0.1		0.3	TISSUS TEX ART CONT MEL AUT
654	OTH WOVEN TEXTILE FABRIC						0.5		0.3	TISSUS AUT COTON SYNT,ARTIF
6542	WOVEN WOOL,HAIR NONPILE						0.5		0.3	TIS PLUS 85% LAINE,POILS
65422	WOVN COMB WOOL,FINE HAIR						0.5		0.3	TISSUS 85% LAINE,PLS PEIG
69	METAL MANUFACTURES NES						0.1		0.2	ART MANUFACT EN METAL NDA
7	MACHINES,TRANSPORT EQUIP						0.9		0.6	MACHINES MATERIEL TRANSPORT
71	POWER GENERATING EQUIPMT						0.3		0.1	MACHINES GENERATRICES
716	ROTATING ELECTRIC PLANT						0.3			APP ELECTR ROTATIFS,PIECES
7169	PTS NES OF ROT ELEC PLNT						0.3			PIECES MAC APP ROTATIFS
72	MACHS FOR SPCL INDUSTRYS						0.3			MAC SPECIALES POUR INDUST
723	CIVIL ENGNEERG EQUIP ETC						0.3			APPAREILS DE GENIE CIVIL
7234	CONST,MINING MACHNRY NES						0.3			MACH POUR LA CONST, MINES
72341	SELF-PROPELLD DOZERS,ETC						0.3			BULLDOZERS
77	ELECTRIC MACHNRY NES ETC						0.2		0.3	MACH APP ELECT NDA
778	ELECTRICAL MACHINERY NES						0.2		0.3	AUTRES MACH ELECT NDA
7781	BATTERIES,ACCUMULATORS						0.2		0.3	PILES ET ACCUMULATEURS
77811	PRIMARY BATTERIES,CELLS						0.2		0.3	PILES ELECTRIQUES,PIECES
78	ROAD VEHICLES						0.1		0.2	VEHICULES ROUTIERS
781	PASS MOTOR VEH EXC BUSES						0.1		0.2	AUTO TRANSPORT PERSONNES
8	MISC MANUFACTURED GOODS						5.3		2.1	ART MANUFACTURES DIVERS
87	PRECISION INSTRUMNTS NES						0.2		0.2	INSTRUM,APPAR SCIENT NDA
874	MEASURNG,CONTROLNG INSTR						0.2		0.2	INSTRUMENTS DE MESURE
8741	SURVEYING INSTRUMENTS								0.2	INST GEODESIE,TOPO ETC
87412	SURVEY INSTR ETC NONELEC								0.2	INSTR GEODESIE,TOPO ETC
89	MISC MANUFCTRD GOODS NES						5.1		1.9	ART MANUFACTURES DIVERS
892	PRINTED MATTER						3.5			IMPRIMES

5. General Exports F.O.B. by Commodities according to the S.I.T.C. (Rev. 2) in million U.S. Dollars
Exportations Générales F.O.B. par Produits d'après la C.T.C.I. (Rév. 2) en millions de Dollars E.U.

SITC CTCI	COMMODITY	1992 QUANTITY QUANTITE	1992 VALUE VALEUR	1993 QUANTITY QUANTITE	1993 VALUE VALEUR	1994 QUANTITY QUANTITE	1994 VALUE VALEUR	1995 QUANTITY QUANTITE	1995 VALUE VALEUR	PRODUIT
8928	PRINTED MATTER NES						3.4			IMPRIMES NDA
89283	UNISSUED BANKNOTES ETC						3.4			TIMBRES–POSTE FISCAUX
899	OTHER MANUFACTURED GOODS						1.7		1.9	AUT ART MANUF DIVERS NDA
8993	COMBUSTIBLE PRODUCTS ETC						1.7		1.8	BOUGIES,ALLUMETTES ETC
89931	CANDLES,TAPERS,ETC						1.7		1.8	BOUGIES,CHANDELLES,CIERG
9	GOODS NOT CLASSD BY KIND						8.2		6.7	ART TRANSACT NON CLASSES
931	*SPECIAL TRANSACTIONS						8.2		6.7	TRANS.SPECIALES

1. HISTORICAL SERIES, 1992–1996 GENERAL TRADE, IMPORTS C.I.F., EXPORTS F.O.B.
SERIES HISTORIQUES, 1992–1996 COMMERCE GENERAL, IMPORTATIONS C.A.F., EXPORTATIONS F.O.B

YEAR ANNEE	VALUE IN MILLION U.S. DOLLARS VALEUR EN MILLION U.S. DOLLARS MERCHANDISE –MARCHANDISE		GOLD –OR		CONVERSION FACTORS FACTEURS DE CONVERSION CENTS E.U. PAR		INDEX NUMBERS –INDICES QUANTUM		UNIT VALUE VALEUR UNITAIRE	
	IMPORTS	EXPORTS	IMPORTS	EXPORTS	IMPORTS	EXPORTS	IMPORTS	EXPORTS	IMPORTS	EXPORTS
1992	227.00	68.00								
1993	167.00	69.00								
1994	471.00	70.00								
1995	250.00	140.00								
1996	718.40	199.40								

2. IMPORTS BY BROAD ECONOMIC CATEGORY AND EXPORTS BY INDUSTRIAL ORIGIN. (PERCENTAGE OF TOTAL VALUE)
IMPORTATIONS PAR CATEGORIES ECONOMIQUES ET EXPORTATIONS PAR BRANCHE D'ACTIVITE.(EN POURCENTAGE DE LA VALEUR TOTALE)

IMPORTS – IMPORTATIONS

	1990	1991	1992	1993	1994	1995	1996
TOTAL IMPORTS–IMPORTATIONS TOTALES							
1 FOOD BEV–ALIMENTATION BOISSONS							
11 PRIMARY–PRODUITS DE BASE							
111 FOR INDUSTRY–POUR L'INDUSTRIE							
112 FOR HOUSEHOLDS–POUR LES MENAGES							
12 PROCESSED–PRODUITS ELABORES							
121 FOR INDUSTRY–POUR L'INDUSTRIE							
122 FOR HOUSEHOLDS–POUR LES MENAGES							
2 IND SUPPLIES–APPROV INDUSTRIELS							
21 PRIMARY–PRODUITS DE BASE							
22 PROCESSED–PRODUITS ELABORES							
3 FUELS–COMBUSTIBLES							
31 PRIMARY–PRODUITS DE BASE							
32 PROCESSED–PRODUITS ELABORES							
321 MOTOR SPIRIT–ESSENCE							
322 OTHER–AUTRES							
4 MACHINERY–EQUIPEMENT							
41 CAPITAL EQUIPMENT–MACHINES							
42 PARTS–PIECES ACCESSOIRES							
5 TRANSPORT–TRANSPORT							
51 PASSENGER CARS–AUTOMOBILES							
52 OTHER–AUTRES							
521 INDUSTRIAL–INDUSTRIELS							
522 NON INDUSTRIAL–NON INDUSTRIEL							
53 PARTS–PIECES ACCESSOIRES							
6 CONSUM GOODS–BIENS CONSOMMATION							
61 DURABLE–DURABLES							
62 SEMI DURABLE–SEMI DURABLES							
63 NON DURABLE–NON DURABLES							
7 GOODS NES–BIENS NDA							

EXPORTS – EXPORTATIONS

	1990	1991	1992	1993	1994	1995	1996
TOTAL EXPORTS–EXPORTATIONS TOTALES							
1 AGRICULTURE							
2 MINING QUARRY–INDUS EXTRACTIVES							
3 MANUFACTURING–IND MANUFACTUR							
31 FOOD BEV TOBACCO–ALIM BOISS TAB							
32 TEXTILES–INDUSTRIES TEXTILES							
33 WOOD & PRODUCTS–BOIS & PRODUITS							
34 PAPER & PRODUCTS–PAPIER & PRODT							
35 CHEMICALS–INDUSTRIES CHIMIQUES							
36 NON METAL MIN–MIN NON METAL							
37 BASIC METAL–IND METAL BASE							
38 METAL MANUF–MANUF METAL							
39 OTH MANUF IND–AUTRES MANUF							

3. TRADE BY PRINCIPAL COUNTRIES OF ORIGIN AND DESTINATION (VALUE IN MILLION U.S. DOLLARS)
ECHANGES SELON LES PRINCIPAUX PAYS D'ORIGINE ET DE DESTINATION (VALEUR EN MILLIONS DE DOLLARS EU)

GENERAL IMPORTS C.I.F. IMPORTATIONS GENERALES C.A.F

COUNTRIES–PAYS	1992	1993	1994	1995	1996
World	175.9	238.5	337.8	385.4	718.4
Africa			0.2		0.7
Americas	2.1	3.1	5.1	14.5	52.7
– Northern America	2.1	3.1	5.1	14.5	48.3
– LAIA					
– CACM					
– Caribbean					4.4
– Rest of America					
Asia excl fmr USSR	7.4	37.7	40.5	92.9	111.8
– Middle East	7.2	34.6	40.3	87.4	92.5
Asia former USSR	98.1	141.6	241.2	96.1	101.7
Europe excl fmr USSR	1.3	27.3	18.5	121.0	278.1
– European Union	1.0	22.5	12.5	58.7	172.4
– Eastern Europe	0.2	4.3	5.8	59.7	90.1
– Rest of Europe	0.1	0.5	0.2	2.6	15.6
Europe former USSR	66.8	24.7	31.1	58.1	169.8
Oceania		1.6	0.6	0.1	0.9
Other					
Turkmenistan/Turkménistn	80.7	132.6	215.8	41.2	4.7
Russian Federation	45.8	9.7	26.5	48.8	127.3
Turkey/Turquie	7.1	34.5	38.6	84.6	80.3
Azerbaijan/Azerbaïdjan	12.5	2.5	23.5	42.8	77.9
Ukraine	12.4	13.2	4.2	7.7	38.8
Romania/Roumanie			3.3	31.4	40.8
USA/Etats–Unis d'Amer	2.1	2.7	5.1	14.5	48.3
Bulgaria/Bulgarie	0.1	0.2	2.1	26.6	43.3
United Kingdom		4.1	0.3	11.8	34.3
Germany/Allemagne	0.4	1.6	4.8	10.6	27.1
Italy/Italie	0.3	1.7	2.7	1.1	33.1
Armenia/Arménie	0.6	4.7	1.1	11.4	17.3
France, Monaco		6.9	0.3	1.6	25.4
Greece/Grèce			1.8	10.7	17.8
Netherlands/Pays–Bas		6.2	0.9	3.9	12.9
Austria/Autriche		1.6	0.3	10.1	8.4
Switzerland,Liechtenst.		0.5	0.2	2.6	9.2
India/Inde	0.1			0.1	8.3
Belgium–Luxembourg		0.2	1.2	1.8	5.1
Lebanon/Liban				0.5	6.9
Belarus/Bélarus	2.6	0.4	0.4	1.1	2.7
Czech Republic		3.9	0.1	0.5	2.4
Kazakhstan	2.8	1.7	0.5	0.2	0.8
Israel/Israël			0.1	4.1	1.6
Denmark/Danemark			0.2	2.1	3.4
Iran (Islamic Rep of)			0.7	1.3	2.8
China/Chine		2.9	0.1	0.1	1.4
Spain/Espagne		0.1		3.7	0.3
Malta/Malte					3.8
Estonia/Estonie	3.7	0.1			
Ireland/Irlande	0.3			0.2	3.1
Indonesia/Indonésie					3.6
Hungary/Hongrie		0.1	0.1	0.8	2.6
Singapore/Singapour				1.2	2.1
Australia/Australie		1.6	0.6	0.1	0.9
Uzbekistan/Ouzbékistan	1.2		0.3	0.5	1.0
British Virgin Islds					3.0
Yugoslavia/Yougoslavie	0.1				2.6
Lithuania/Lituanie	0.8	0.1		0.5	1.0
Portugal				1.1	1.2

GENERAL EXPORTS F.O.B. EXPORTATIONS GENERALES F.O.B.

COUNTRIES–PAYS	1992	1993	1994	1995	1996
Monde	87.0	226.7	155.8	154.3	199.4
Afrique					
Amériques		1.3	3.7	0.6	1.3
– Amérique du Nord		0.7	3.7	0.6	1.3
– ALAI					
– MCAC					
– Caraïbes		0.6			
– Autre Amérique					
Asie anc. URSS exclus	0.2	24.1	29.4	37.0	29.2
– Moyen–Orient	0.2	22.6	28.4	35.7	28.1
Asie ancienne URSS	20.2	56.5	55.2	41.7	64.9
Europe anc. URSS exclus	9.1	18.0	5.3	19.1	39.2
– Union Européenne	7.7	4.1	1.4	7.2	16.9
– Europe de l'Est	0.4	13.5	1.8	5.8	14.8
– Autre de l'Europe	1.0	0.4	2.1	6.1	7.5
Europe ancienne URSS	57.4	120.2	62.1	55.1	64.6
Océanie					
Autre					
Russian Federation	43.6	103.3	52.3	47.0	56.8
Turkey/Turquie	0.2	21.9	23.6	34.9	25.9
Azerbaijan/Azerbaïdjan	4.4	14.8	14.7	12.7	24.9
Armenia/Arménie	0.8	10.2	12.9	18.9	20.5
Turkmenistan/Turkménistn	8.2	12.4	15.5	6.9	13.4
Ukraine	10.3	12.7	6.1	5.6	5.4
Kazakhstan	3.6	12.9	9.0	1.8	2.4
Bulgaria/Bulgarie		3.4	0.1	5.7	12.2
Switzerland,Liechtenst.	1.0	0.4	2.1	6.1	7.5
Uzbekistan/Ouzbékistan	1.7	4.7	2.7	0.6	2.9
Belarus/Bélarus	2.3	2.2	3.3	2.1	1.4
Czech Republic		9.9	0.2		
United Kingdom		0.7		0.4	8.4
Iran (Islamic Rep of)			4.8	0.8	2.2
Germany/Allemagne	0.7	1.0	0.1	1.2	4.6
USA/Etats–Unis d'Amer		0.7	3.7	0.6	1.3
Sweden/Suède	5.6				
Italy/Italie		0.3	0.1	2.8	1.7
Netherlands/Pays–Bas		1.2	0.7	1.1	0.6
China/Chine		1.5	1.0	0.7	0.3
Tajikistan/Tadjikistan	0.7	0.7	0.3	0.3	0.5
Kyrgyzstan/Kirghizistan	0.8	0.8	0.1	0.5	0.3
Romania/Roumanie					2.1
Hungary/Hongrie	0.4		1.3		0.3
Lithuania/Lituanie	0.4	0.7	0.1	0.1	0.4
Austria/Autriche	1.4	0.1			
France, Monaco		0.3	0.2	0.9	0.1
Republic of Moldova	0.4	0.4	0.2	0.2	0.1
Latvia/Lettonie	0.3	0.6	0.1		0.3
Denmark/Danemark		0.3	0.1	0.3	0.6
Greece/Grèce			0.1	0.4	0.4
Syrian Arab Republic		0.7			
Estonia/Estonie	0.1	0.3		0.1	0.2
Poland/Pologne		0.2	0.1	0.1	0.2
Cuba		0.6			
India/Inde				0.3	0.2
Mongolia/Mongolie				0.2	0.2
Portugal				0.1	0.2
Belgium–Luxembourg		0.1			0.2
Ireland/Irlande			0.1		0.1

(VALUE AS PERCENTAGE OF WORLD TOTAL)(VALEURS EN POURCENTAGE DU TOTAL MONDIAL)

Imports

	1987	1988	1989	1990	1991	1992	1993	1994	1995	1996
Africa								0.1		0.1
Americas						1.2	1.3	1.5	3.8	7.3
– Northern America						1.2	1.3	1.5	3.8	6.7
– LAIA										
– CACM										
– Caribbean										0.6
– Rest of America										
Asia excl fmr USSR						4.2	15.8	12.0	24.1	15.6
– Middle East						4.1	14.5	11.9	22.7	12.9
Asia former USSR						55.8	59.4	71.4	24.9	14.2
Europe excl fmr USSR						0.7	11.4	5.5	31.4	38.7
– European Union						0.6	9.4	3.7	15.2	24.0
– Eastern Europe						0.1	1.8	1.7	15.5	12.5
– Rest of Europe						0.1	0.2	0.1	0.7	2.2
Europe former USSR						38.0	10.4	9.2	15.1	23.6
Oceania							0.7	0.2	0.0	0.1
Other										
Turkmenistan/Turkménistn						45.9	55.6	63.9	10.7	0.7
Russian Federation						26.0	4.1	7.8	12.7	17.7
Turkey/Turquie						4.0	14.5	11.4	22.0	11.2
Azerbaijan/Azerbaïdjan						7.1	1.0	7.0	11.1	10.8
Ukraine						7.0	5.5	1.2	2.0	5.4
Romania/Roumanie								1.0	8.1	5.7
USA/Etats–Unis d'Amer						1.2	1.1	1.5	3.8	6.7
Bulgaria/Bulgarie						0.1	0.1	0.6	6.9	6.0
United Kingdom							1.7	0.1	3.1	4.8
Germany/Allemagne						0.2	0.7	1.4	2.8	3.8

Exports

	1987	1988	1989	1990	1991	1992	1993	1994	1995	1996
Afrique										
Amériques							0.6	2.4	0.4	0.7
– Amérique du Nord							0.3	2.4	0.4	0.7
– ALAI										
– MCAC										
– Caraïbes							0.3			
– Autre Amérique										
Asie anc. URSS exclus						0.2	10.6	18.9	24.0	14.6
– Moyen–Orient						0.2	10.0	18.2	23.1	14.1
Asie ancienne URSS						23.2	24.9	35.4	27.0	32.5
Europe anc. URSS exclus						10.5	7.9	3.4	12.4	19.7
– Union Européenne						8.9	1.8	0.9	4.7	8.5
– Europe de l'Est						0.5	6.0	1.2	3.8	7.4
– Autre de l'Europe						1.1	0.2	1.3	4.0	3.8
Europe ancienne URSS						66.0	53.0	39.9	35.7	32.4
Océanie										
Autre										
Russian Federation						50.1	45.6	33.6	30.5	28.5
Turkey/Turquie						0.2	9.7	15.1	22.6	13.0
Azerbaijan/Azerbaïdjan						5.1	6.5	9.4	8.2	12.5
Armenia/Arménie						0.9	4.5	8.3	12.2	10.3
Turkmenistan/Turkménistn						9.4	5.5	9.9	4.5	6.7
Ukraine						11.8	5.6	3.9	3.6	2.7
Kazakhstan						4.1	5.7	5.8	1.2	1.2
Bulgaria/Bulgarie							1.5	0.1	3.7	6.1
Switzerland,Liechtenst.						1.1	0.2	1.3	4.0	3.8
Uzbekistan/Ouzbékistan						2.0	2.1	1.7	0.4	1.5

4. General Imports C.I.F. by Commodities according to the S.I.T.C. (Rev. 2) in million U.S. Dollars
Importations Générales C.A.F. par Produits d'après la C.T.C.I. (Rév. 2) en millions de Dollars E.U.

SITC CTCI	COMMODITY	1993		1994		1995		1996		PRODUIT
		QUANTITY QUANTITE	VALUE VALEUR	QUANTITY QUANTITE	VALUE VALEUR	QUANTITY QUANTITE	VALUE VALEUR	QUANTITY QUANTITE	VALUE VALEUR	
	ALL COMMODITIES						385.4		718.4	TOUS PRODUITS
01	MEAT AND PREPARATIONS						4.1		5.1	VIANDES ET PREPARATIONS
02	DAIRY PRODCTS,BIRDS'EGGS						5.1		9.1	PRODUITS LAITIERS,OEUFS
04	CEREALS AND PREPARATIONS						22.1		120.0	CEREALES ET PRODUITS
054	VEG ETC FRSH,SMPLY PRSVD						2.1		4.1	LEGUMES FRAIS,CONG,SECS
06	SUGAR AND PREPS,HONEY						28.1		36.1	SUCRES ET PRODUITS
07	COFFEE,TEA,COCOA,SPICES						1.1		12.1	CAFE,THE,CACAO,EPICES
11	BEVERAGES						17.1		17.1	BOISSONS
12	TOBACCO AND MANUFACTURES						22.1		31.1	TABACS BRUTS FABRIQUES
3	MINERAL FUELS ETC						204.0		266.0	COMBUSTIBLES MINERAUX LUB
4	ANIMAL,VEGETABLE OIL,FAT						10.1		7.1	HUILES,GRAISSES ANIM,VEG
52	INORGANIC CHEMICALS						1.1		5.1	PROD CHIM INORGANIQUES
541	*MEDICINAL,PHARM PRODUCT						3.1		16.1	PROD MEDICINAUX PHARMACEUT
572	*EXPLOSIVES,PYROTECH PRO						4.1		5.1	EXPLOSIFS
62	RUBBER MANUFACTURES NES						1.1		3.1	CAOUTCHOUC MANUFACTURE
64	PAPER,PAPERBOARD AND MFR						2.1		7.1	PAPIERS,CARTONS & OUVRAGES
65	TEXTILE YARN,FABRICS,ETC						1.1		4.1	FILS,TISSUS,ARTICLES TEXTILE
66	NONMETAL MINERAL MFS NES						4.1		10.1	ART MIN NON METALLIQUES
67	IRON AND STEEL						1.1		4.1	FER ET ACIER
69	METAL MANUFACTURES NES								5.1	ART MANUFACT EN METAL NDA
7	MACHINES,TRANSPORT EQUIP						22.1		66.1	MACHINES MATERIEL TRANSPORT
78	ROAD VEHICLES						2.1		9.1	VEHICULES ROUTIERS
821	*FURNITURE,PARTS THEREOF						1.1		5.1	MEUBLES ET PIECES
84	CLOTHING AND ACCESSORIES						2.1		4.1	VETEMENTS
851	*FOOTWEAR						2.1		3.1	CHAUSSURES
892	PRINTED MATTER								4.1	IMPRIMES

5. General Exports F.O.B. by Commodities according to the S.I.T.C. (Rev. 2) in million U.S. Dollars
Exportations Générales F.O.B. par Produits d'après la C.T.C.I. (Rév. 2) en millions de Dollars E.U.

SITC CTCI	COMMODITY	1993		1994		1995		1996		PRODUIT
		QUANTITY QUANTITE	VALUE VALEUR	QUANTITY QUANTITE	VALUE VALEUR	QUANTITY QUANTITE	VALUE VALEUR	QUANTITY QUANTITE	VALUE VALEUR	
	ALL COMMODITIES						154.3		199.4	TOUS PRODUITS
04	CEREALS AND PREPARATIONS								6.1	CEREALES ET PRODUITS
057	FRUIT,NUTS,FRESH,DRIED						9.1		11.1	FRUITS FRAIS OU SECS
06	SUGAR AND PREPS,HONEY								1.1	SUCRES ET PRODUITS
07	COFFEE,TEA,COCOA,SPICES						10.1		19.1	CAFE,THE,CACAO,EPICES
11	BEVERAGES						14.1		16.1	BOISSONS
12	TOBACCO AND MANUFACTURES						3.1		2.1	TABACS BRUTS FABRIQUES
24	CORK AND WOOD								3.1	LIEGE ET BOIS
3	MINERAL FUELS ETC						15.1		38.1	COMBUSTIBLES MINERAUX LUB
51	ORGANIC CHEMICALS						1.1			PROD CHIMIQ ORGANIQUES
52	INORGANIC CHEMICALS						3.1		5.1	PROD CHIM INORGANIQUES
53	DYES,TANNING,COLOUR PROD						1.1		1.1	PROD TEINTURE,COLORANTS
541	*MEDICINAL,PHARM PRODUCT						1.1		1.1	PROD MEDICINAUX PHARMACEUT
572	*EXPLOSIVES,PYROTECH PRO						1.1		2.1	EXPLOSIFS
611	LEATHER						1.1		2.1	CUIRS,PEAUX PREPARES
64	PAPER,PAPERBOARD AND MFR						1.1			PAPIERS,CARTONS & OUVRAGES
65	TEXTILE YARN,FABRICS,ETC						1.1		2.1	FILS,TISSUS,ARTICLES TEXTILE
658	TEXTILE ARTICLES NES						1.1			ART FACONNES MAT TEXTILES
66	NONMETAL MINERAL MFS NES						2.1		1.1	ART MIN NON METALLIQUES
67	IRON AND STEEL						36.1		12.1	FER ET ACIER
684	ALUMINIUM						5.1		1.1	ALUMINIUM
69	METAL MANUFACTURES NES						16.1		17.1	ART MANUFACT EN METAL NDA
7	MACHINES,TRANSPORT EQUIP						11.1		9.1	MACHINES MATERIEL TRANSPORT
78	ROAD VEHICLES						2.1		2.1	VEHICULES ROUTIERS
792	AIRCRAFT ETC						1.1			APP NAVIGATION AERIENNE
821	*FURNITURE,PARTS THEREOF								1.1	MEUBLES ET PIECES
84	CLOTHING AND ACCESSORIES						3.1		3.1	VETEMENTS
851	*FOOTWEAR								1.1	CHAUSSURES
892	PRINTED MATTER						2.1		10.1	IMPRIMES

1. HISTORICAL SERIES, 1991–1997 SPECIAL TRADE, IMPORTS C.I.F., EXPORTS F.O.B.
SERIES HISTORIQUES, 1991–1997 COMMERCE SPECIAL, IMPORTATIONS C.A.F., EXPORTATIONS F.O.B

YEAR ANNEE	VALUE IN MILLION DEUTSCHE MARK / VALEUR EN MILLION DEUTSCHE MARK — MERCHANDISE –MARCHANDISE		GOLD –OR		CONVERSION FACTORS U.S. CENTS PER DEUTSCHE MARK FACTEURS DE CONVERSION CENTS E.U. PAR DEUTSCHE MARK		INDEX NUMBERS –INDICES — QUANTUM		UNIT VALUE VALEUR UNITAIRE	
	IMPORTS	EXPORTS	IMPORTS	EXPORTS	IMPORTS	EXPORTS	IMPORTS	EXPORTS	IMPORTS	EXPORTS
1991	645410.00	666170.10			60.4923	60.4923	113	100	102	99
1992	628189.90	658469.80			64.1952	64.1952	115	102	99	99
1993	571909.80	632219.90			60.5218	60.5218	104	98	93	94
1994	622919.90	694690.00			61.7649	61.7649	114	112	95	93
1995	635889.90	727300.10			69.9105	69.9020	115	116	98	95
1996	690400.00	788940.00			66.4557	66.4471	125	128	98	94
1997	765540.10	887280.10			57.7118	57.6724				

2. IMPORTS BY BROAD ECONOMIC CATEGORY AND EXPORTS BY INDUSTRIAL ORIGIN. (PERCENTAGE OF TOTAL VALUE)
IMPORTATIONS PAR CATEGORIES ECONOMIQUES ET EXPORTATIONS PAR BRANCHE D'ACTIVITE.(EN POURCENTAGE DE LA VALEUR TOTALE)

IMPORTS – IMPORTATIONS

	1991	1992	1993	1994	1995	1996	1997
TOTAL IMPORTS–IMPORTATIONS TOTALES	100.	100.	100.	100.	100.	100.	100.
1 FOOD BEV–ALIMENTATION BOISSONS	9.0	9.3	8.7	9.3	9.0	9.0	8.2
11 PRIMARY–PRODUITS DE BASE	4.9	5.0	4.6	5.0	4.9	4.9	4.4
111 FOR INDUSTRY–POUR L'INDUSTRIE	1.1	1.1	0.9	1.3	1.3	1.2	1.2
112 FOR HOUSEHOLDS–POUR LES MENAGES	3.8	3.9	3.7	3.7	3.6	3.6	3.2
12 PROCESSED–PRODUITS ELABORES	4.1	4.3	4.2	4.3	4.1	4.1	3.8
121 FOR INDUSTRY–POUR L'INDUSTRIE	0.5	0.5	0.5	0.5	0.5	0.5	0.5
122 FOR HOUSEHOLDS–POUR LES MENAGES	3.6	3.8	3.7	3.8	3.6	3.6	3.3
2 IND SUPPLIES–APPROV INDUSTRIELS	27.3	27.6	25.4	27.5	28.8	25.8	25.2
21 PRIMARY–PRODUITS DE BASE	2.9	3.0	2.7	2.9	2.9	2.6	2.6
22 PROCESSED–PRODUITS ELABORES	24.4	24.7	22.7	24.6	25.9	23.3	22.6
3 FUELS–COMBUSTIBLES	8.2	7.4	7.9	6.9	6.3	7.5	7.5
31 PRIMARY–PRODUITS DE BASE	5.4	5.1	5.6	5.1	4.7	5.6	5.5
32 PROCESSED–PRODUITS ELABORES	2.8	2.3	2.3	1.8	1.6	2.0	2.0
321 MOTOR SPIRIT–ESSENCE	0.9	0.8	0.7	0.6	0.5	0.5	0.6
322 OTHER–AUTRES	1.9	1.5	1.6	1.3	1.1	1.5	1.4
4 MACHINERY–EQUIPEMENT	18.9	19.2	18.8	19.7	20.4	20.0	19.3
41 CAPITAL EQUIPMENT–MACHINES	14.5	14.7	14.2	14.4	14.5	14.5	14.0
42 PARTS–PIECES ACCESSOIRES	4.4	4.4	4.6	5.3	5.9	5.5	5.3
5 TRANSPORT–TRANSPORT	16.2	15.6	14.3	14.2	14.2	14.6	13.5
51 PASSENGER CARS–AUTOMOBILES	6.2	5.8	5.1	4.8	5.2	5.3	5.3
52 OTHER–AUTRES	4.6	4.0	3.3	3.0	2.7	2.7	2.7
521 INDUSTRIAL–INDUSTRIELS	4.3	3.7	2.9	2.6	2.3	2.3	2.4
522 NON INDUSTRIAL–NON INDUSTRIEL	0.3	0.3	0.4	0.4	0.4	0.4	0.3
53 PARTS–PIECES ACCESSOIRES	5.4	5.8	5.9	6.4	6.3	6.5	5.5
6 CONSUM GOODS–BIENS CONSOMMATION	19.0	19.0	19.7	19.1	17.8	17.9	16.8
61 DURABLE–DURABLES	5.0	5.0	5.1	4.9	4.6	4.7	4.2
62 SEMI DURABLE–SEMI DURABLES	11.5	11.5	12.0	11.4	10.5	10.5	9.9
63 NON DURABLE–NON DURABLES	2.5	2.6	2.6	2.8	2.7	2.7	2.7
7 GOODS NES–BIENS NDA	1.5	1.9	4.8	3.2	3.6	5.2	9.4

EXPORTS – EXPORTATIONS

	1991	1992	1993	1994	1995	1996	1997
TOTAL EXPORTS–EXPORTATIONS TOTALES	100.	100.	100.	100.	100.	100.	100.
1 AGRICULTURE	1.2	1.3	1.1	1.2	1.1	1.2	1.0
2 MINING QUARRY–INDUS EXTRACTIVES	0.7	0.6	0.5	0.5	0.5	0.7	0.6
3 MANUFACTURING–IND MANUFACTUR	97.9	97.9	97.9	98.1	98.1	97.9	98.3
31 FOOD BEV TOBACCO–ALIM BOISS TAB	4.6	4.6	4.8	4.6	4.3	4.4	4.0
32 TEXTILES–INDUSTRIES TEXTILES	5.8	5.8	5.4	5.2	4.8	4.6	4.5
33 WOOD & PRODUCTS–BOIS & PRODUITS	0.5	0.5	0.4	0.5	0.5	0.5	0.5
34 PAPER & PRODUCTS–PAPIER & PRODT	3.0	3.0	2.9	3.1	3.3	3.1	2.8
35 CHEMICALS–INDUSTRIES CHIMIQUES	16.3	16.2	16.3	17.0	16.8	16.4	16.5
36 NON METAL MIN–MIN NON METAL	1.6	1.6	1.5	1.5	1.5	1.5	1.4
37 BASIC METAL–IND METAL BASE	5.4	5.0	5.0	5.0	5.4	4.7	4.8
38 METAL MANUF–MANUF METAL	57.8	58.5	56.9	57.6	58.0	57.6	55.4
39 OTH MANUF IND–AUTRES MANUF	2.9	2.7	4.7	3.7	3.5	5.1	8.4

3. TRADE BY PRINCIPAL COUNTRIES OF ORIGIN AND CONSUMPTION (VALUE IN MILLION U.S. DOLLARS)
ECHANGES SELON LES PRINCIPAUX PAYS D'ORIGINE ET DE COMSOMMATION (VALEUR EN MILLIONS DE DOLLARS EU)

COUNTRIES–PAYS	SPECIAL IMPORTS C.I.F. IMPORTATIONS SPECIALES C.A.F				
	1993	1994	1995	1996	1997
World	342558.5	381538.8	464145.2	458641.7	436458.0
Africa	8638.7	8800.6	9550.6	9765.1	9302.4
Americas	34342.7	39181.7	45852.4	45578.6	46384.9
– Northern America	26782.5	30292.7	35357.6	36191.6	36771.5
– LAIA	6605.9	7653.9	8881.1	7910.6	8153.7
– CACM	541.8	819.0	956.9	816.4	823.3
– Caribbean	249.8	222.3	295.0	327.2	400.7
– Rest of America	162.7	193.8	361.8	332.8	235.7
Asia excl fmr USSR	60359.5	64691.4	75180.2	73384.3	71169.1
– Middle East	7183.1	7415.1	8354.5	8389.0	8310.2
Asia former USSR	464.2	482.0	418.2	319.2	538.2
Europe excl fmr USSR	229687.1	257012.6	319208.4	315145.5	294743.6
– European Union	192239.9	212496.9	262159.7	258149.8	236835.4
– Eastern Europe	13927.3	17884.4	25204.2	25290.0	27102.7
– Rest of Europe	23519.9	26631.3	31844.7	31705.8	30805.6
Europe former USSR	7421.0	9459.2	11424.8	12051.0	11986.0
Oceania	1515.8	1784.9	2068.9	1829.5	1855.3
Other	129.7	126.5	441.7	568.6	478.6
France, Monaco	39636.7	42243.2	51076.7	48969.6	45785.3
Netherlands/Pays–Bas	30217.7	31929.2	40669.2	40578.1	37041.3
Italy/Italie	29132.4	32085.8	39734.8	38777.8	34031.9
USA/Etats–Unis d'Amer	24395.5	27591.7	31616.5	32876.3	33807.3
United Kingdom	21448.7	23918.7	30453.0	31531.0	30370.8
Belgium–Luxembourg	20598.3	23532.8	30734.7	29169.4	26867.3
Japan/Japon	20636.7	21116.1	24758.9	22902.5	21277.3
Switzerland,Liechtenst.	14566.5	16472.8	19898.7	18459.1	17519.4
Austria/Autriche	15961.7	18194.1	18195.1	18104.2	16007.1
Spain/Espagne	8994.5	10794.8	14661.8	15190.8	14703.6
China/Chine	8344.4	9501.7	11155.8	11974.0	12379.0
Russian Federation	6483.9	8164.3	9499.9	10245.9	9896.0
Sweden/Suède	7591.6	8690.8	9745.1	9696.5	8267.2
Denmark/Danemark	6381.1	7124.5	8929.3	8659.0	8024.1
Norway,Svalbard and JM	5564.0	6396.5	7552.0	9031.3	9026.5
Poland/Pologne	5219.1	6279.4	8681.8	8104.7	8286.5
Czech Republic	3889.9	5270.9	7406.4	7559.2	7973.0
Turkey/Turquie	4025.6	4478.7	5558.4	5618.2	5727.3
Other Asia n.e.s.	4484.9	4468.3	5486.7	5472.0	5192.8
Ireland/Irlande	3601.8	4252.3	5904.2	5532.3	4765.9
Hungary/Hongrie	2734.4	3359.8	4831.5	5274.6	6265.1
Portugal	3236.0	3446.4	4895.1	5382.2	5033.0
Finland/Finlande	3416.6	4339.2	4997.7	4531.0	4141.3
Korea, Republic of	3440.3	4216.1	5284.2	4314.8	3801.3
Brazil/Brésil	2670.4	3193.1	3495.1	3264.1	3687.8
Canada	2382.9	2696.4	3736.8	3309.0	2941.6
Singapore/Singapour	2448.1	2964.0	2974.7	2893.1	3202.5
Malaysia/Malaisie	2063.7	2460.3	3161.8	3100.5	3000.1
China, Hong Kong SAR	2631.1	2412.0	2554.0	2348.2	2118.8
India/Inde	1956.8	2150.6	2516.2	2645.9	2397.8
Slovenia/Slovénie	1813.0	2069.2	2540.9	2422.2	2377.5
Thailand/Thaïlande	1897.5	2087.1	2267.9	2181.0	2061.4
Indonesia/Indonésie	1618.2	1857.7	1995.7	2191.1	2354.8
Greece/Grèce	2022.9	1944.9	2163.0	2028.0	1796.7
So. African Customs Un	1621.2	1660.1	2027.1	2079.1	2070.1
Slovakia/Slovaquie	899.4	1363.2	2196.4	2275.7	2415.5
Libyan Arab Jamahiriya	1587.9	1521.3	1518.2	1989.2	1795.4
Romania/Roumanie	827.2	1134.9	1505.3	1522.3	1607.9
Australia/Australie	949.0	1094.1	1185.2	1029.4	1100.9
Philippines	780.7	934.2	1057.4	1253.1	1310.9

COUNTRIES–PAYS	SPECIAL EXPORTS F.O.B. EXPORTATIONS SPECIALES F.O.B.				
	1993	1994	1995	1996	1997
Monde	380074.8	427099.9	523696.6	524080.6	511941.9
Afrique	8651.5	9077.5	11084.5	10169.6	10079.4
Amériques	39828.2	46710.4	54149.0	55079.0	61937.0
– Amérique du Nord	30673.8	36247.8	41050.2	42732.6	48115.3
– ALAI	8262.2	9505.5	11646.5	11527.4	12986.4
– MCAC	286.6	313.4	350.2	333.4	336.0
– Caraïbes	340.0	319.6	446.9	387.7	400.9
– Autre Amérique	265.5	324.2	655.2	97.9	98.4
Asie anc. URSS exclus	52237.3	58895.9	72369.3	73832.1	69049.3
– Moyen–Orient	13696.0	12721.9	15063.8	15833.7	16344.7
Asie ancienne URSS	694.9	1016.3	889.4	1116.2	1121.2
Europe anc. URSS exclus	265920.6	298023.4	368750.3	367241.7	350474.5
– Union Européenne	222923.9	247842.5	304762.6	301538.3	283880.2
– Europe de l'Est	16129.5	19557.8	26977.2	30729.1	33329.4
– Autre de l'Europe	26867.2	30623.1	37010.6	34974.2	33265.0
Europe ancienne URSS	8937.1	9219.6	10500.8	11065.7	13824.8
Océanie	2854.3	3435.1	4596.8	4086.1	4016.1
Autre	950.9	721.8	1356.5	1490.2	1439.7
France, Monaco	46819.1	51329.4	61364.3	58431.3	54520.4
United Kingdom	30423.2	34258.2	43299.1	42298.4	43302.9
USA/Etats–Unis d'Amer	28243.6	33512.3	38170.3	39921.4	44232.7
Italy/Italie	28756.1	32416.1	39747.8	39421.2	37746.6
Netherlands/Pays–Bas	29246.6	32618.0	39894.3	40059.4	35807.5
Belgium–Luxembourg	25908.9	28927.1	34324.3	33100.9	29792.5
Austria/Autriche	22537.5	24570.7	29110.6	30231.2	26514.7
Switzerland,Liechtenst.	20422.5	22941.7	27952.0	25371.3	23252.4
Spain/Espagne	12642.7	13741.0	18262.3	19260.5	19088.0
Japan/Japon	9521.4	11118.5	13163.5	14088.5	11822.2
Sweden/Suède	7667.3	9500.2	12841.5	12656.0	11911.5
Poland/Pologne	5864.3	6418.9	8877.9	10861.7	11933.3
Denmark/Danemark	6839.3	7988.6	10026.4	9626.6	9009.6
Russian Federation	6875.8	6643.5	7197.1	7601.7	9488.1
Czech Republic	4623.2	5975.7	8264.7	9199.1	9526.1
China/Chine	5795.7	6350.8	7538.5	7223.1	6135.5
Turkey/Turquie	5086.2	3875.9	6359.2	7573.9	7949.8
Korea, Republic of	3452.4	4581.3	6116.7	6557.8	5331.4
Hungary/Hongrie	3116.9	3951.3	4911.6	5541.0	6734.9
Portugal	3740.1	3651.9	4737.3	5424.4	5448.9
Other Asia n.e.s.	3515.2	4106.8	5079.8	4454.1	4714.1
Brazil/Brésil	2556.7	3148.7	5057.6	4801.0	5285.3
Finland/Finlande	2816.1	3336.3	4824.6	5022.6	4704.6
Norway,Svalbard and JM	3108.0	3695.9	4281.4	4419.1	4466.9
China, Hong Kong SAR	3009.2	3586.0	4038.3	4239.8	4561.2
Greece/Grèce	3848.7	3554.5	3882.6	3714.0	3553.1
So. African Customs Un	2636.9	3150.7	4101.9	3706.5	3443.2
Singapore/Singapour	2253.0	2809.5	3669.7	3859.7	3571.1
Australia/Australie	2466.3	2924.0	3674.1	3488.1	3464.8
Thailand/Thaïlande	2036.5	2791.7	3758.8	3513.8	2617.6
Canada	2388.3	2716.2	2869.7	2798.5	3871.5
Mexico/Mexique	2602.4	2783.6	2388.5	2560.9	3119.8
India/Inde	1816.6	2074.6	3194.4	3116.3	2572.6
Indonesia/Indonésie	1897.0	2189.3	2747.7	2656.9	3007.2
Malaysia/Malaisie	1440.2	2096.9	2862.4	2809.5	2773.3
Saudi Arabia	2177.9	2558.5	2472.6	2552.8	2121.9
Israel/Israël	1890.2	2232.8	2482.6	2549.4	2522.5
Ireland/Irlande	1678.2	1950.4	2447.6	2291.9	2480.2
Slovenia/Slovénie	1489.2	1735.7	2194.2	2057.8	2063.8
Slovakia/Slovaquie	846.9	1265.5	2158.1	2443.2	2635.8

(VALUE AS PERCENTAGE OF WORLD TOTAL)(VALEURS EN POURCENTAGE DU TOTAL MONDIAL)

	1988	1989	1990	1991	1992	1993	1994	1995	1996	1997
Africa				2.7	2.6	2.5	2.3	2.1	2.1	2.1
Americas				9.7	9.6	10.0	10.3	9.9	9.9	10.6
– Northern America				7.3	7.3	7.8	7.9	7.6	7.9	8.4
– LAIA				2.2	2.1	1.9	2.0	1.9	1.7	1.9
– CACM				0.2	0.1	0.2	0.2	0.2	0.2	0.2
– Caribbean				0.1	0.1	0.1	0.1	0.1	0.1	0.1
– Rest of America				0.1	0.1	0.0	0.1	0.1	0.1	0.1
Asia excl fmr USSR				15.9	15.7	17.6	17.0	16.2	16.0	16.3
– Middle East				1.9	1.9	2.1	1.9	1.8	1.8	1.9
Asia former USSR					0.0	0.1	0.1	0.1	0.1	0.1
Europe excl fmr USSR				69.0	69.6	67.1	67.4	68.8	68.7	67.5
– European Union				59.5	59.7	56.1	55.7	56.5	56.3	54.3
– Eastern Europe				2.9	3.5	4.1	4.7	5.4	5.5	6.2
– Rest of Europe				6.6	6.5	6.9	7.0	6.9	6.9	7.1
Europe former USSR				2.2	2.0	2.2	2.5	2.5	2.6	2.7
Oceania				0.5	0.5	0.4	0.5	0.4	0.4	0.4
Other				0.0	0.0	0.0	0.0	0.1	0.1	0.1
France, Monaco				12.3	12.0	11.6	11.1	11.0	10.7	10.5
Netherlands/Pays–Bas				9.8	9.6	8.8	8.4	8.8	8.8	8.5
Italy/Italie				9.3	9.2	8.5	8.4	8.6	8.5	7.8
USA/Etats–Unis d'Amer				6.5	6.6	7.1	7.2	6.8	7.2	7.7
United Kingdom				6.6	6.8	6.3	6.3	6.6	6.9	7.0
Belgium–Luxembourg				7.1	7.0	6.0	6.2	6.6	6.4	6.2
Japan/Japon				6.1	6.0	6.0	5.5	5.3	5.0	4.9
Switzerland,Liechtenst.				3.9	4.0	4.3	4.3	4.3	4.0	4.0
Austria/Autriche				4.2	4.4	4.7	4.8	3.9	3.9	3.7
Spain/Espagne				2.7	2.7	2.6	2.8	3.2	3.3	3.4

	1988	1989	1990	1991	1992	1993	1994	1995	1996	1997
Afrique				2.4	2.3	2.3	2.1	2.1	1.9	2.0
Amériques				9.0	9.1	10.5	10.9	10.3	10.5	12.1
– Amérique du Nord				7.0	7.0	8.1	8.5	7.8	8.2	9.4
– ALAI				1.8	1.9	2.2	2.2	2.2	2.2	2.5
– MCAC				0.1	0.1	0.1	0.1	0.1	0.1	0.1
– Caraïbes				0.1	0.1	0.1	0.1	0.1	0.1	0.1
– Autre Amérique				0.1	0.1	0.1	0.1	0.1	0.0	0.0
Asie anc. URSS exclus				11.4	11.8	13.7	13.8	13.8	14.1	13.5
– Moyen–Orient				3.4	3.7	3.6	3.0	2.9	3.0	3.2
Asie ancienne URSS					0.1	0.2	0.2	0.2	0.2	0.2
Europe anc. URSS exclus				73.8	73.9	70.0	69.8	70.4	70.1	68.5
– Union Européenne				63.2	63.4	58.7	58.0	58.2	57.5	55.5
– Europe de l'Est				3.0	3.5	4.2	4.6	5.2	5.9	6.5
– Autre de l'Europe				7.6	7.0	7.1	7.2	7.1	6.7	6.5
Europe ancienne URSS				2.7	2.0	2.4	2.2	2.0	2.1	2.7
Océanie				0.6	0.7	0.8	0.8	0.9	0.8	0.8
Autre				0.2	0.1	0.3	0.2	0.3	0.3	0.3
France, Monaco				13.2	13.0	12.3	12.0	11.7	11.1	10.6
United Kingdom				7.6	7.7	8.0	8.0	8.3	8.1	8.5
USA/Etats–Unis d'Amer				6.3	6.4	7.4	7.8	7.3	7.6	8.6
Italy/Italie				9.2	9.3	7.6	7.6	7.6	7.5	7.4
Netherlands/Pays–Bas				8.4	8.3	7.7	7.6	7.6	7.6	7.0
Belgium–Luxembourg				7.3	7.4	6.8	6.8	6.6	6.3	5.8
Austria/Autriche				5.9	6.0	5.9	5.8	5.6	5.8	5.2
Switzerland,Liechtenst.				5.6	5.3	5.4	5.4	5.3	4.8	4.5
Spain/Espagne				4.1	4.2	3.3	3.2	3.5	3.7	3.7
Japan/Japon				2.5	2.2	2.5	2.6	2.5	2.7	2.3

4. Special Imports C.I.F. by Commodities according to the S.I.T.C. (Rev. 2) in million U.S. Dollars
Importations Spéciales C.A.F. par Produits d'après la C.T.C.I. (Rév. 2) en millions de Dollars E.U.

SITC CTCI	COMMODITY	1994		1995		1996		1997		PRODUIT
		QUANTITY QUANTITE	VALUE VALEUR	QUANTITY QUANTITE	VALUE VALEUR	QUANTITY QUANTITE	VALUE VALEUR	QUANTITY QUANTITE	VALUE VALEUR	
	ALL COMMODITIES		381539.0		464145.4		458642.0		436458.2	TOUS PRODUITS
0	FOOD AND LIVE ANIMALS		32400.2		38093.1		37679.7		32238.6	ALIMENTS,ANIMAUX VIVANTS
01	MEAT AND PREPARATIONS		5260.1		5836.3		5852.7		4581.7	VIANDES ET PREPARATIONS
011	MEAT FRESH,CHILLD,FROZEN		4460.8		4984.2	W 1668325	5014.8		3913.4	VIANDES FRAICHES,REF,CONGE
0111	BOVINE MEAT FRESH,FROZEN	W 266891	1239.7	W 241499	1213.7	W 219489	930.3	W 169543	669.7	VIANDES BOVIN FRAI,REF
0113	PIG MEAT FRESH,CHLD,FRZN	W 838653	1770.5	W 836259	2141.8	W 861526	2317.0	W 748383	1847.5	VIANDE DE PORC
02	DAIRY PRODCTS,BIRDS'EGGS		3319.6		4183.6		3988.7		3512.9	PRODUITS LAITIERS,OEUFS
024	CHEESE AND CURD	W 432767	2085.6	W 478849	2588.9	W 488855	2463.9	W 476358	2112.2	FROMAGE ET CAILLEBOTTE
03	FISH AND PREPARATIONS		2186.9		2362.2		2455.0		2178.9	POISSONS ET PREPARATIONS
034	FISH,FRESH,CHILLED,FROZN	W 498038	1277.9	W 491102	1375.0	W 517800	1406.7	W 506636	1269.8	POISSON FRAIS, REFRIG,CONG
04	CEREALS AND PREPARATIONS		2339.3		2744.7		2832.9		2126.8	CEREALES ET PRODUITS
048	CEREAL ETC PREPARATIONS	W 1085209	1430.4	W 1174669	1676.7	W 1181361	1666.9	W 1123835	1404.7	PREPTNS A BASE CEREALES
05	VEGETABLES AND FRUIT		11014.5		12924.9		12973.1		10921.6	LEGUMES ET FRUITS
054	VEG ETC FRSH,SMPLY PRSVD	W 5282463	3668.9	W 5248102	4393.7	W 5069315	4285.1	W 4471795	3419.0	LEGUMES FRAIS,CONG,SECS
0545	OTHER FRESH VEGETABLES	W 2049128	1835.0	W 2155141	2199.0	W 2233997	2265.2	W 1990303	1830.6	AUTRES LEGUMES FRAIS,REF
05459	FRESH VEGETABLES NES	W 1698108	1662.1	W 1765630	1987.1	W 1831887	2087.6	W 1693933	1676.9	LEGUMES FRAIS,REFRI NDA
057	FRUIT,NUTS,FRESH,DRIED	W 5029235	4703.4	W 5475042	5521.9	W 5410514	5603.1	W 5022284	4855.2	FRUITS FRAIS OU SECS
0579	FRUIT FRESH OR DRIED NES	W 1282745	1354.2	W 1308796	1533.2	W 1368971	1495.2	W 1298128	1373.4	FRUITS FRAIS,SECS NDA
058	FRUIT PRESERVED,PREPARED	W 1624570	1690.2	W 1573102	1968.4	W 1663286	2076.0	W 1756230	1869.5	CONSERVES DE FRUITS
07	COFFEE,TEA,COCOA,SPICES		3854.2		4791.8		4117.9		4645.5	CAFE,THE,CACAO,EPICES
071	COFFEE AND SUBSTITUTES	W 800043	2039.3	W 756921	2858.9	W 792039	2145.1	W 809470	2693.2	CAFE ET SUCCEDANES
0711	COFFEE GREEN,ROASTED,SUB	W 782715	1912.5	W 742602	2725.1	W 773625	1993.2	W 792828	2561.7	CAFE TORREFIE OU DECAFEINE
07111	COFFEE GREEN,HUSKS,SKINS	W 775506	1875.4	W 736556	2681.0	W 764231	1938.5	W 782327	2503.5	CAFE NON TORREFIE
081	*FEEDING STUFF FOR ANIML	W 6887115	1599.8	W 6856945	1794.0	W 6671690	1969.2	W 6192466	1731.6	NOURRITURE POUR ANIMAUX
09	MISC EDIBLE PRODUCTS		1570.2		1924.2		1782.4		1424.6	PREP ALIMENTAIRES DIVERSES
098	EDIBLE PRODCTS,PREPS NES		1522.3		1855.1	W 442612	1710.8		1360.3	PREP ALIMENTAIRES NDA
09809	MISC FOOD PREPRTIONS NES	W 240498	1250.5	W 253744	1494.9	W 249566	1378.8	W 236314	1075.1	PREP ALIMENTAIRES NDA
1	BEVERAGES AND TOBACCO		3995.0		4415.7		4390.7		4203.1	BOISSONS ET TABACS
11	BEVERAGES		2752.9		3021.2		3123.1		2888.8	BOISSONS
112	ALCOHOLIC BEVERAGES	W 1603904	2322.4	W 1571937	2654.8	W 1660315	2849.2	W 1694368	2659.8	BOISSONS ALCOOLIQUES
1121	WINE OF FRESH GRAPES ETC	W 1129601	1447.1	W 1064934	1726.8	W 1168587	1938.9	W 1179315	1789.5	VINS DE RAISINS FRAIS
11212	WINE OF FRESH GRAPES	W 1012474	1392.3	W 987553	1680.2	W 1103259	1890.4	W 1122294	1754.1	VINS DE MOUTS DE RAISINS
12	TOBACCO AND MANUFACTURES		1242.2		1394.5		1267.7		1314.4	TABACS BRUTS FABRIQUES
2	CRUDE MATERLS,EXCL FUELS		16962.8		20290.2		17807.4		17262.5	MAT BRUTES NON COMESTIBLES
22	OIL SEEDS,OLEAGINOUS FRT		1467.4		1476.7		1672.6		1644.0	GRAINES,FRUITS OLEAGINEUX
222	SEEDS FOR'SOFT'FIXED OIL	W 4507237	1333.3		1315.9	W 4917100	1526.3	W 4841985	1504.0	GRAINES HUILES FIXES
24	CORK AND WOOD		2295.9		2276.4		1872.2		1905.3	LIEGE ET BOIS
248	WOOD SHAPED,SLEEPERS	W 3939435	1979.9	W 3517694	1904.9	W 3361402	1589.0	W 3584034	1615.9	BOIS SIMPLEMENT TRAVAILLES
2482	LUMBER SHAPED CONIFER	W 3357932	1500.2	W 2930313	1397.2	W 2873014	1179.7	W 3040000	1194.4	CONIFERES SCIES,RABOTES
24821	LUMBER SAWN ETC CONIFER	W 3146128	1339.7	W 2803850	1284.0	W 2742430	1081.7	W 2903376	1097.9	CONIFERES SCIES LONGITUD
251	*PULP AND WASTE PAPER	W 5190434	2343.3	W 5152310	3594.7	W 4924079	2401.2	W 4963854	2196.6	PATES A PAPIER,DECHETS
2517	SODA,SULPHATE WOOD PULP	W 3635334	1804.6	W 3365602	2738.1	W 3293062	1846.5	W 3388658	1699.5	PATES CHIMIQUES AU SULFATE
25172	— BLEACHED,NONDISSOLVNG	W 3545026	1763.5	W 3314294	2700.1	W 3241188	1818.2	W 3323339	1670.9	PATES BLANCHIES
26	TEXTILE FIBRES AND WASTE		1381.6		1546.2		1273.5		1263.9	FIBRES TEXTILES
27	CRUDE FERTLZR,MINRLS NES		1370.9		1527.7		1382.3		1229.6	ENGRAIS MINERAUX BRUTS
28	METALLIFEROUS ORES,SCRAP		4179.7		5156.5		4626.1		4992.5	MINERAIS METAL,DECHETS
281	IRON ORE,CONCENTRATES	MW 42773	1250.2	MW 43316	1410.1	MW 39376	1208.4	MW 41782	1238.4	MINERAIS DE FER
288	NONFERR METAL SCRAP NES		1203.7		1578.7	W 1064689	1254.3		1553.0	DECHETS NON FERREUX
2882	OTHER BASE MTL SCRAP NES	W 683749	967.7	W 731259	1307.2	W 738579	1102.9	W 1043394	1428.6	AUTRES DECHETS
29	CRUDE ANIMAL,VEG MAT NES		2928.9		3457.2		3454.6		2993.9	MATIERES BRUTES ANIM,VEGET
292	CRUDE VEG MATERIALS NES		2352.8		2791.1	W 874025	2807.3		2395.2	MAT BRUTES VEGETALES NDA
2927	CUT FLOWERS AND FOLIAGE	W 248696	1197.8	W 249838	1359.6	W 261917	1310.3	W 254280	1092.2	FLEURS,FEUILLAGES COUPES
3	MINERAL FUELS ETC		26754.4		28875.1		35105.3		33314.8	COMBUSTIBLES MINERAUX LUB
33	PETROLEUM AND PRODUCTS		19331.9		19929.3		24505.5		22967.8	PETROLE ET DERIVES
333	CRUDE PETROLEUM	MW 107579	12878.2	MW 100549	13054.3	MW 103729	16042.9	MW 100738	14555.2	HUILES BRUTES DE PETROLE
334	PETROLEUM PRODUCTS,REFIN	MW 37097	5914.8	MW 37095	6288.5	MW 39260	7814.9	MW 40384	7815.1	PRODUITS RAFFINES
3341	GASOLINE,OTH LIGHT OILS	MW 12793	2124.4	MW 12790	2271.3	MW 11773	2392.2	MW 13731	2818.5	ESSENCES POUR MOTEURS
33411	MOTOR,AVIATION SPIRIT	W 6978491	1172.4	W 6880952	1228.2	W 6570132	1368.1	W 7254413	1499.5	ESSENCES MOTEURS D'AVIONS
33419	OTH LIGHT PETROLEUM OILS	W 5814909	952.1	W 5901735	1041.9	W 5196642	1023.0	W 6465079	1316.6	AUTRES HUILES LEGERES
3343	GAS OILS	MW 16309	2508.6	MW 17271	2741.0	MW 20634	4010.1	MW 19404	3554.6	GAS OILS
341	*GAS,NATURAL AND MANUFCT	MW 47886	5542.3	MW 52744	6834.6	MW 68485	8421.9	MW 60654	8359.4	GAZ NATUREL,GAZ MANUFACT
3414	PETROLEUM GASES, GASEOUS	MW 46774	5360.7	MW 51820	6639.4	MW 67257	8124.5	MW 59415	8024.8	GAZ DE PETROLE GAZEUX
4	ANIMAL,VEGETABLE OIL,FAT		1159.3		1336.8		1332.2		1292.7	HUILES,GRAISSES ANIM,VEG
5	CHEMCLS,RELATED PROD NES		33052.0		41256.6		39325.6		37217.9	PRODUITS CHIMIQUES
51	ORGANIC CHEMICALS		8030.8		9885.6		9101.6		9347.5	PROD CHIMIQ ORGANIQUES
511	HYDROCARBONS NES,DERIVS	W 2453065	1150.2	W 2498323	1595.1	W 2499712	1231.1	W 2963334	1433.9	HYDROCARBURES NDA
513	CARBOXYLIC ACIDS ETC	W 855354	1128.8		1565.5	W 942033	1391.8		1317.9	ACIDES CARBOXYLIQUES
514	NITROGEN–FNCTN COMPOUNDS		2895.9		3369.1	W 779215	3208.1		3348.8	COMPOSES FONCT AZOTEES
5148	OTH NITROGN–FNCTN CMPNDS	W 286635	1248.2	W 249142	1547.2	W 267447	1445.2	W 306895	1607.2	AUTRES COMPOSES AZOTES
515	ORG–INORG COMPOUNDS ETC		1128.8		1343.1		1484.8		1481.5	COMPOSES ORGANO–MINERAUX
52	INORGANIC CHEMICALS		2454.8		2617.1		2589.0		2431.1	PROD CHIM INORGANIQUES
53	DYES,TANNING,COLOUR PROD		1746.6		2115.6		2046.5		1871.0	PROD TEINTURE,COLORANTS
533	PIGMENTS,PAINTS,ETC		1165.0		1395.4	W 440747	1264.1		1154.4	PIGMENTS,PEINTURES,VERNIS
541	*MEDICINAL,PHARM PRODUCT	MK 118737	5349.2		6663.2		7157.9		6978.0	PROD MEDICINAUX PHARMACEUT
5417	MEDICAMENTS	MK 73045	3321.6	MK 81053	4046.3	MK 79348	4212.7	MK 91247	4113.3	MEDICAMENTS
54179	— CONTNG OTH SUBSTANCES	MK 65195	2499.8	MK 73213	2971.3	MK 71138	3033.7	MK 83090	3011.4	MED CONT AUT SUBSTANCES
55	PERFUME,CLEANING ETC PRD		2553.7		3160.7		3158.7		2501.1	PROD POUR PARFUM,TOILETTE
553	PERFUMERY,COSMETICS,ETC	W 142761	1398.6	W 168758	1743.6	W 196265	1713.4	W 169928	1425.4	PRODUITS DE PARFUMERIE
58	PLASTIC MATERIALS ETC		8517.9		10991.0		9624.1		9079.1	MAT PLAST ARTIFICIELLES
582	PROD OF CONDENSATION ETC	W 1294103	2525.0	W 1352096	3282.4	W 1346444	3045.3	W 1471225	2818.6	PROD CONDENS,POLYCOND
583	POLYMERIZATION ETC PRODS	W 4658632	5708.0	W 4478189	7351.7	W 4419888	6239.3	W 4657956	5971.2	PROD POLYMERISATION
5831	POLYETHYLENE	W 1599147	1396.2	W 1479018	1810.8	W 1398633	1470.7	W 1410768	1449.3	POLYETHYLENE
58311	— IN PRIMARY FORMS	W 1428392	1111.4	W 1311196	1446.4	W 1242996	1168.2	W 1259608	1196.3	POLYETHYLENE PRIMAIRES
5839	OTH POLYMRZTION ETC PROD	W 763715	1614.5	W 782961	2075.9	W 756021	1889.0	W 907467	1920.0	AUT PROD POLYMER COPOLYM
59	CHEMICAL MATERIALS NES		3537.6		4536.0		4576.7		4149.0	MAT PROD CHIMIQUES NDA
598	MISCEL CHEM PRODUCTS NES		2418.5		2992.5	W 2322062	3036.5		2816.6	PROD DIV INDUST CHIM NDA
5989	CHEM PRODUCTS,PREPS NES	W 1391086	1934.4	W 1557084	2420.9	W 1837539	2490.6	W 1608714	2269.0	PROD PREP CHIMIQUES NDA
59899	OTH CHEM PRODS,PREPS,NES	W 1016830	1390.8	W 1228875	1801.7	W 1531572	1861.2	W 1262067	1704.4	AUT PRODUITS CHIMIQUES NDA
6	BASIC MANUFACTURES		63351.1		79868.7		71297.8		64510.5	ART MANUFACTURES
61	LEATHER,DRESSED FUR,ETC		1350.7		1481.8		1429.4		1302.3	CUIRS,PELLETERIES
62	RUBBER MANUFACTURES NES		3613.4		4385.7		4387.8		4132.7	CAOUTCHOUC MANUFACTURE
625	RUBBER TYRES, TUBES ETC	W 551516	2182.1	W 617492	2660.6	W 621536	2653.9	W 650913	2407.5	PNEUS CAOUTCHOUC VULCANISE
6251	TYRES NEW FOR MOTOR CARS	W 258270	1286.1	W 287298	1556.4	W 289466	1544.1	W 311007	1423.0	PNEUS POUR VOITURES
63	WOOD,CORK MANUFACTRS NES		3898.2		4425.4		4062.9		3666.3	OUVRAGES LIEGE ET BOIS
634	VENEERS,PLYWOOD,ETC	W 1899514	1290.3	W 1958612	1592.8	W 1767978	1322.4	W 1835533	1265.0	PLACAGES,CONTRE–PLAQUES
635	WOOD MANUFACTURES NES	W 1937897	2493.6	W 1909708	2697.5	W 1899336	2619.4	W 2054567	2286.1	ART MANUF EN BOIS NDA
6353	BUILDERS WOODWRK,PREFABS	W 858211	1763.7	W 755826	1815.3	W 786706	1745.0	W 804616	1434.9	OUVRAGES DE MENUISERIE
64	PAPER,PAPERBOARD AND MFR		7539.8		10042.6		9062.9		7595.2	PAPIERS,CARTONS & OUVRAGES
641	PAPER AND PAPERBOARD		6100.4	W 7949300	8252.1	W 7899101	7203.0	W 7913383	5983.4	PAPIERS ET CARTONS
6412	PRINTG,WRITING PAPER NES	W 1709409	1554.2	W 1719519	2136.5	W 1760623	1819.4	W 1840596	1574.7	PAPIERS POUR L'IMPRESSION
64122	— COATED,IMPREGNATD ETC	W 1454781	1317.4	W 1436568	1752.8	W 1458276	1488.7	W 1512651	1273.3	PAPIERS IMPRESSION COUCHES

4. Special Imports C.I.F. by Commodities according to the S.I.T.C. (Rev. 2) in million U.S. Dollars
Importations Spéciales C.A.F. par Produits d'après la C.T.C.I. (Rév. 2) en millions de Dollars E.U.

SITC CTCI	COMMODITY	1994			1995			1996			1997			PRODUIT
		QUANTITY QUANTITE		VALUE VALEUR	QUANTITY QUANTITE		VALUE VALEUR	QUANTITY QUANTITE		VALUE VALEUR	QUANTITY QUANTITE		VALUE VALEUR	
6415	PAPER,PAPERBRD,BULK,NES	W	2529527	1664.4	W	2467850	2334.8	W	2411290	1903.0	W	2288205	1528.6	PAPIERS,CARTONS ROULEAUX
64159	OTHER PAPER ETC,BULK,NES	W	2314386	1532.7	W	2265491	2150.6	W	2210005	1771.9	W	2092694	1412.9	AUT PAPIER ROULEAUX FEUILLES
642	PAPER,ETC,PRECUT,ARTS OF	W	738029	1439.5	W	743043	1790.6	W	817767	1859.9	W	839679	1611.8	PAP,CARTONS DECOUPES
65	TEXTILE YARN,FABRICS,ETC			11113.3			12654.5			12069.5			10549.1	FILS,TISSUS,ARTICLES TEXTILE
651	TEXTILE YARN			2168.4			2569.5	W	458271	2400.0			2261.8	FILS TEXTILES
653	WOVN MAN–MADE FIB FABRIC	W	118874	1553.9	W	118695	1857.3	W	116842	1651.3	W	117541	1429.4	TISSUS FIBRES SYNTH,ARTIF
654	OTH WOVEN TEXTILE FABRIC	W	71805	1172.9	W	70155	1220.4	W	63797	1061.1	W	66729	915.5	TISSUS AUT COTON SYNT,ARTIF
657	SPECIAL TXTL FABRC,PRODS	W	183272	1179.5	W	186339	1417.0	W	195613	1366.6	W	190138	1210.2	TISSUS SPECIAUX
658	TEXTILE ARTICLES NES	W	172199	1462.2	W	179709	1675.3	W	199828	1719.1	W	202563	1543.8	ART FACONNES MAT TEXTILES
659	FLOOR COVERINGS,ETC			1833.1			2023.2			1985.6			1539.6	COUVRE–PARQUETS,TAPIS ETC
66	NONMETAL MINERAL MFS NES			6834.2			8088.2			7513.0			6355.2	ART MIN NON METALLIQUES
661	LIME,CEMENT,BLDG PRODS	MW	11502	1223.3			1400.3	MW	10072	1252.4			1021.2	CHAUX,CIMENTS MAT CONSTR
662	CLAY,REFRACTORY BLDG PRD	W	3896348	1475.7	W	3755192	1712.8	W	3354586	1504.0			1224.3	MAT CONST REFRACTAIRES
6624	BRICKS ETC NONREFRACTORY	W	3636988	1285.4	W	3495454	1497.2	W	3068550	1280.3	W	2983836	1044.9	BRIQUES ETC CERAM NON REFR
663	MINERAL MANUFCTURES NES			1306.4			1613.3			1532.4			1311.1	ART MIN MANUF NDA
664	GLASS	W	1023176	1143.7	W	1071655	1442.9	W	1022379	1402.4	W	1022649	1183.3	VERRE
67	IRON AND STEEL			11342.2			16103.6			12826.4			11397.0	FER ET ACIER
671	PIG IRON ETC			955.1			1411.8	W	1296032	1078.5			1063.1	FONTE,SPIEGEL,POUDRES
672	IRON,STEEL PRIMARY FORMS	W	3053207	1377.5	W	3681187	2137.5	W	2624879	1482.1	W	3112941	1402.2	LINGOTS FER,ACIER
673	IRON,STEEL SHAPES ETC	W	5993709	2651.3	W	6646442	3753.7	W	5124502	2620.6	W	5068950	2237.2	BARRES,PROFIL FER,ACIER
6732	IRON,STEEL BARS ETC	W	2681985	1264.6	W	2978964	1907.2	W	2293525	1365.0	W	2313871	1131.8	BARRES FER,ACIER
674	IRN,STL UNIV,PLATE,SHEET	W	6256114	3913.0	W	6890273	5601.9	W	6264548	4672.1	W	6772883	4117.5	LARGES PLATS,TOLES
6746	IRN,STL THIN PLATE,ROLLD	W	1668224	1221.2	W	1798628	1837.6	W	1786566	1616.5	W	1837018	1355.4	TOLES LAM MOINS 3MM
6749	OTH IRN,STL PLATES,SHEET	W	1850800	1196.2	W	2098960	1606.1	W	1964672	1384.3	W	2408763	1425.5	AUTRES TOLES FER,ACIER
67491	— OF IRON OR SIMPLE STL	W	1840640	1153.6	W	2087336	1544.9	W	1950269	1310.2	W	2333397	1329.6	AUT TOLES AUTRES ACIER FIN
678	IRON,STL TUBES,PIPES,ETC			1649.7			2169.9	W	1715891	2001.2			1713.5	TUBES,TUYAUX EN FONTE,FER
68	NON–FERROUS METALS			8661.8			11767.9			9298.1			9843.9	METAUX NON FERREUX
682	COPPER EXC CEMENT COPPER			2888.8			3695.2	W	969280	2786.3			2753.2	CUIVRE
6821	COPPER NES,ALLOYS,UNWRT	W	652222	1421.1	W	656442	1898.3	W	584343	1396.4	W	628984	1437.9	CUIVRE BRUT
68212	COPPER REFINED,UNWROUGHT	W	563161	1217.8	W	602323	1730.3	W	496961	1167.7	W	560051	1272.8	CUIVRE AFFINE BRUT
6822	COPPER,ALLOYS WORKED	W	473264	1467.8	W	443420	1796.9	W	384937	1390.0	W	406906	1315.3	CUIVRE,ALLIAGES OUVRES
684	ALUMINIUM	W	1890170	3814.8	W	2057119	5466.6	W	1791951	4264.3	W	2127218	4606.0	ALUMINIUM
6841	ALUMINIUM,ALLOYS,UNWRGHT	W	1203073	1820.1	W	1340855	2758.1	W	1127627	1953.5	W	1400210	2391.0	ALUMINIUM,ALLIAGES BRUTS
6842	ALUMINIUM,ALLOYS WORKED	W	687097	1994.7	W	716264	2708.5	W	664324	2310.8	W	727008	2215.0	ALUMINIUM,ALLIAGES OUVRE
69	METAL MANUFACTURES NES			8997.9			10919.4			10648.3			9669.3	ART MANUFACT EN METAL NDA
691	STRUCTURES AND PARTS NES	W	805049	1545.3	W	868662	1794.8	W	852797	1784.7	W	765052	1367.0	CONSTRUCT FER,ACIER,ALU
6911	STRUCTURES,PARTS IRN,STL	W	759964	1172.3	W	819158	1390.1	W	799276	1357.7	W	714325	1028.1	CONSTRUCT FER,ACIER,FONTE
695	TOOLS	W	113207	1503.3	W	118773	1851.3	W	113453	1785.3	W	111597	1618.4	OUTILS A MAIN
699	BASE METAL MFRS NES			2920.5			3606.5			3598.0			3469.9	ART MANUFACTURES MET NDA
7	MACHINES,TRANSPORT EQUIP			129136.1			155439.1			157536.4			149115.1	MACHINES MATERIEL TRANSPORT
71	POWER GENERATING EQUIPMT			8092.7			9850.5			10984.6			11568.3	MACHINES GENERATRICES
713	INTRNL COMBUS PSTN ENGIN	W	310816	3622.7	W	350185	4357.6	W	421089	4759.8	W	502034	5212.9	MOTEURS EXPL COMB INT, PIECE
7132	MOTOR VEHCL PISTN ENGINS	W	197112	2309.1	W	222342	2718.4	W	260723	3002.8	W	283570	3333.9	MOTEURS EXPL POUR VEHICULES
7139	PISTON ENGINE PARTS NES	W	81985	960.9	W	95425	1242.4	W	133734	1420.5	W	186393	1572.2	PIECES POUR 713.2,3,8
714	ENGINES AND MOTORS NES	W	12677	2372.1	W	15851	2969.6	W	20205	3527.9	W	18778	3870.7	MOTEURS NON ELECTRIQUES
7144	REACTION ENGINES	W	1253	933.5	W	1091	1182.5	W	1575	1530.7	W	1845	1820.7	PROPULSEURS A REACTION
7149	ENGINE & MOTOR PARTS NES	W	10687	1125.6	W	13765	1366.5	W	17134	1632.9	W	15943	1698.1	PIECES 714 ET 718.88
716	ROTATING ELECTRIC PLANT	W	198198	1664.3	W	236078	2027.4	W	237090	2031.8	W	250979	1840.1	APP ELECTR ROTATIFS,PIECES
72	MACHS FOR SPCL INDUSTRYS			6841.1			8031.6			7744.4			6658.3	MAC SPECIALES POUR INDUST
728	OTH MACHY FOR SPCL INDUS	W	199135	2452.1	W	212042	2934.5	W	204010	2938.4	W	193344	2582.8	AUT MACH IND PARTICULIERES
7284	MACHY FOR SPCL INDUS NES	W	92278	1707.9	W	102769	2133.6	W	108780	2161.1	W	107419	2014.2	MACH SPEC IND PARTICUL.
73	METALWORKING MACHINERY			1812.5			2489.2			2731.1			2420.1	MACH TRAVAIL DES METAUX
736	METALWORKING MACH–TOOLS	W	106606	1408.2	W	128679	1982.8	W	134038	2199.9	W	142731	1937.4	MACH–OUTILS TRAVAIL METAUX
74	GENRL INDUSTRL MACHY NES			12583.7			15535.3			15773.5			14287.4	MACH APP INDUSTRIE
741	HEATING,COOLING EQUIPMNT	W	165760	1830.3	W	181431	2291.5	W	204414	2596.3			2179.6	MACH CHAUFFAGE,PIECES
742	PUMPS FOR LIQUIDS ETC	W	85976	1148.2	W	97233	1471.6	W	109135	1627.4	W	108617	1533.3	POMPES MOTO–POMPES
743	PUMPS NES,CENTRFUGES ETC	W	175305	1976.8	W	191632	2423.0	W	203299	2550.6	W	218916	2492.4	POMPES COMPRES,VENT ETC
744	MECHANICAL HANDLING EQU	W	441326	2088.4	W	478280	2489.1	W	461625	2273.5	W	475042	2020.1	EQUIP MANUTENTION PIECES
745	NONELEC MACHY,TOOLS NES			1276.6			1444.8	W	85763	1442.5			1232.7	AUT MACH NON ELEC,PIECES
749	NONELEC MACH PTS,ACC NES	W	349386	4263.6	W	439563	5415.5	W	455613	5283.4	W	454127	4829.6	PIECES MACH NON ELEC NDA
7491	BALL,ROLLER,ETC BEARINGS	W	83510	980.9	W	111937	1436.8	W	115349	1406.9	W	109300	1168.1	ROULEMENTS BILLES ETC
7492	COCKS,VALVES ETC NES	W	99445	1633.2	W	105309	1925.6	W	108354	1892.2	W	112696	1751.4	ART ROB,SIM POUR TUYAUX
75	OFFICE MACHNES,ADP EQUIP			18105.8			22120.7			21611.6			20387.5	MACH BUREAU TRAIT AUTOM
751	OFFICE MACHINES	W	39518	1273.8	W	45005	1541.8	W	42399	1339.9	W	42675	1162.8	MACH,APPAREILS DE BUREAU
752	AUTOMTIC DATA PROC EQUIP	W	143902	11113.9	W	177881	13362.6	W	183244	13193.3	W	191351	12482.8	MACH TRAIT INFORMATION
7523	DIGITL CENTRL PROCESSORS	W	16588	2830.1	W	20987	3237.9	W	23238	3344.8	W	19828	2820.6	UNITES CENTRALES
7524	DIGITL CENTRL STOR UNITS	W	14007	2546.8	W	18142	3354.4	W	14810	3081.2	W	23487	3815.9	UNITES MEMOIRE CENTRALES
7525	ADP PERIPHERAL UNITS	W	104713	4255.4	W	129687	5264.6	W	135963	4921.3	W	140535	4083.3	UNITES PERIPHERIQUES
759	OFFICE,ADP MCH PTS,ACCES	W	78798	5718.2	W	91510	7216.4	W	97735	7078.5	W	106697	6742.0	PIECES DU 751 ET 752
7599	ACCTG,ETC,ADP MCH PTS,AC	W	55709	4871.5	W	66086	6216.0	W	76750	6321.0	W	81601	6070.4	PIECES DU 751 ET 752
76	TELECOMM,SOUND EQUIPMENT			11122.3			12238.8			12167.4			10491.9	EQUIPMENT DE TELECOM
761	TELEVISION RECEIVERS	W	114945	1684.2	W	118692	1905.0	W	118175	1807.8	W	99308	1303.7	RECEPTEURS DE TELEVISION
7611	COLOUR TV RECEIVERS	W	114106	1661.9	W	117859	1878.5	W	117425	1786.3	W	98310	1278.7	RECEPTEURS COULEUR
762	RADIO BROADCAST RECEIVRS	W	62820	1494.9	W	61802	1710.6	W	66731	1584.8	W	59174	1322.0	RECEPTEURS RADIODIFFUSION
763	SOUND RECORDRS,PHONOGRPH	W	37627	1495.1	W	33732	1411.3	W	38073	1757.7	W	30800	1074.7	PHONO,APP ENREGISTREMENT
7638	OTHR SOUND APPARATUS ETC	W	36556	1478.4	W	32923	1397.9	W	37328	1745.5	W	29927	1062.7	AUT APP D'ENREGIS,REPROD
764	TELECOM EQPT,PTS,ACC NES	W	130137	6448.3	W	124766	7212.0	W	131708	7017.3	W	134469	6791.6	EQUIP TELECOM,PIECES
7641	LINE TELEPHONE,ETC EQUIP	W	18754	1261.3	W	21912	1969.9	W	23682	2138.3	W	22367	1869.8	APP TELEPHON PAR FIL
7649	PTS NES OF EQUIPMT OF 76	W	57947	3114.1	W	46705	2744.1	W	47476	2620.0	W	46101	2400.2	PIECES DE LA DIV 76
76491	PTS NES OF APPAR OF 7641	W	7088	1294.7	W	4769	923.2	W	4920	872.3	W	4384	673.1	PIECES POUR 764.1
77	ELECTRIC MACHNRY NES ETC			25414.5			32699.3			31590.7			29970.1	MACH APP ELECT NDA
771	ELECTRIC POWER MACHY NES	W	79456	1252.0	W	82335	1624.6	W	90794	1776.8	W	93810	1892.9	MACH PROD,TRANS ELECTR
7712	OTH ELEC POWER MACHY NES	W	51924	926.7	W	52626	1220.9	W	60773	1395.1	W	59032	1527.3	AUT APP PROD TRANSF ELEC
772	SWITCHGEAR ETC,PARTS NES	W	95483	3870.0	W	112342	4868.1	W	120799	4902.9	W	131541	4750.4	APP COUPURE,SECT ETC
7721	SWITCHGEAR ETC	W	85456	3039.3	W	101624	3870.0	W	110152	3970.3	W	119387	3796.5	APP COUPURE,SECTIONMNT
773	ELECTR DISTRIBUTNG EQUIP	W	354262	2435.3	W	373694	2996.7	W	377114	3156.0	W	377375	3164.2	EQUIPMT DISTRIBUTION ELECT
7731	INSULATED WIRE,CABLE ETC	W	343272	2305.5	W	361778	2851.9	W	363922	2987.8	W	362500	2998.9	FILS,CABLES ISOLES ELECT
775	HOUSEHOLD TYPE EQUIP NES			3180.1			3651.8	W	514279	3671.7			3190.7	MACH,APP USAGE DOMESTQUE
7758	ELECTRO–THERMIC APPL NES	W	172879	1419.6	W	177549	1565.2	W	191151	1614.1	W	197799	1462.2	APP ELECTROTHERMIQ NDA
776	TRANSISTORS,VALVES,ETC	W	71841	7245.5	W	72840	9793.0	W	73900	9309.5	W	53293	8992.9	LAMPES,TUBES,VALVES
7764	ELECTRONIC MICROCIRCUITS	W	5978	5593.4	W	8903	7694.8	W	17532	7386.5	W	9435	7167.9	MICROSTRUCTURES ELECTRON
778	ELECTRICAL MACHINERY NES			6646.2			8785.6	W	401237	7736.8			7074.4	AUTRES MACH ELECT NDA
7788	OTH ELEC MACHY,EQUIP NES	W	90756	3818.4	W	100426	5270.6	W	89334	4347.6	W	71553	3560.8	AUT MACH APP ELEC NDA
77889	ELEC PARTS OF MACHY NES	W	934	1503.9	W	1102	2231.8	W	1229	1318.1	W	1411	622.1	PIECES ELEC DE MACH NDA
78	ROAD VEHICLES			34760.2			44171.9			46112.2			43018.9	VEHICULES ROUTIERS
781	PASS MOTOR VEH EXC BUSES	W	1720333	18274.3	W	1862018	23255.2	W	2092257	24380.8	W	2174328	23064.3	AUTO TRANSPORT PERSONNES
782	LORRIES,SPCL MTR VEH NES	W	298714	2677.5	W	319815	3416.8	W	369935	3861.7	W	424006	3970.1	VEHICULES SPECIAUX,MARCH
7821	LORRIES,TRUCKS	W	279903	2515.2	W	307373	3285.9	W	356550	3735.8	W	410332	3847.7	VEHICULES TRANSP MARCHAND
783	ROAD MOTOR VEHICLES NES	W	47784	681.3	W	85400	1592.4	W	83106	1416.1	W	53098	562.4	VEHICULES ROUTIERS NDA
7832	TRACTORS FOR TR–TRAILERS	W	36382	503.0	W	76813	1452.9	W	71437	1258.6	W	40689	409.7	TRACTEURS ROUTIERS
784	MOTOR VEH PRTS,ACCES NES	W	1309233	10738.4	W	1578333	12926.4	W	1611152	13453.9	W	1771730	12825.0	PIECES 722,781,782,783

4. Special Imports C.I.F. by Commodities according to the S.I.T.C. (Rev. 2) in million U.S. Dollars
Importations Spéciales C.A.F. par Produits d'après la C.T.C.I. (Rév. 2) en millions de Dollars E.U.

SITC CTCI	COMMODITY	1994 QUANTITY QUANTITE	1994 VALUE VALEUR	1995 QUANTITY QUANTITE	1995 VALUE VALEUR	1996 QUANTITY QUANTITE	1996 VALUE VALEUR	1997 QUANTITY QUANTITE	1997 VALUE VALEUR	PRODUIT
7849	OTHER MOTOR VEHCL PARTS	W 1272953	10417.0	W 1549336	12616.7	W 1580882	13168.2	W 1738159	12562.8	PIECES 722,781,782,783
785	CYCLES,ETC MOTRZD OR NOT	W 132290	1834.9	W 141108	2250.7	W 146571	2218.4	W 138503	1890.7	MOTOCYCLES SCOOTERS
79	OTHR TRANSPORT EQUIPMENT		10403.8		8302.1		8821.3		10313.0	AUTRE MATERIEL TRANSPORT
792	AIRCRAFT ETC	W 20257	9431.9	W 17749	7514.8	W 15842	8124.5	W 18960	9689.9	APP NAVIGATION AERIENNE
7924	AIRCRFT NES OVER 15000KG	W 6926	5404.9	W 4809	3693.9	W 4844	3835.8	W 5119	4550.7	AERODYNES PLUS 15000 KG
7929	AIRCRAFT PARTS NES	W 12557	3837.6	W 12144	3458.9	W 10210	3918.5	W 13160	4850.6	PIECES DU 792
8	MISC MANUFACTURED GOODS		61155.7		67971.2		68945.2		62334.6	ART MANUFACTURES DIVERS
812	*PLUMBG,HEATNG,LGHTNG EQ	W 482688	2056.9	W 474014	2300.2	W 466854	2221.7	W 451654	1883.6	APPAR SANITAIRES CHAUFFAGE
821	*FURNITURE,PARTS THEREOF	W 1578200	5714.9	W 1715075	6910.8	W 1826552	7277.7	W 1801935	6294.6	MEUBLES ET PIECES
8211	CHAIRS,SEATS AND PARTS	W 455880	2057.8	W 524895	2648.2	W 559391	2852.3	W 562537	2564.3	SIEGES ET PIECES
82111	CHAIRS AND OTHER SEATS	W 374546	1422.2	W 422827	1671.7	W 444535	1726.0	W 438064	1479.3	SIEGES
8219	FURNITURE AND PARTS NES	W 1059016	3139.3	W 1126326	3697.9	W 1200613	3842.5	W 1173141	3215.4	AUTRES MEUBLES ET PIECES
82192	WOOD FURNITURE NES	W 706360	2085.9	W 728087	2387.7	W 785252	2475.5	W 759225	2034.6	MEUBLES NDA EN BOIS
84	CLOTHING AND ACCESSORIES		22717.2		24553.7		24655.0		22501.3	VETEMENTS
842	MENS OUTERWEAR NOT KNIT	W 155061	3861.7	W 146684	4032.6	W 155273	4168.3	W 157374	3895.1	VET DESSUS POUR HOMMES
8423	— TROUSERS,BREECHES ETC	W 87321	1852.5	W 84813	1976.0	W 93205	2101.4	W 90740	1862.7	PANTALONS HOMMES MAT TEX
843	WOMENS OUTERWEAR NONKNIT	W 198999	6641.6	W 196280	7223.0	W 208208	7058.2	W 218810	6536.5	VET DESSUS FEMMES MAT TEX
8431	— COATS AND JACKETS	W 32076	1299.6	W 30064	1335.2	W 30250	1258.6	W 35798	1261.1	MANT,VEST FEM MAT TEXTIL
8435	— BLOUSES	W 33753	1432.1	W 32916	1504.0	W 33428	1318.2	W 35004	1214.6	BLOUSES FEM MAT TEXTILES
8439	— OTHER OUTER GARMENTS	W 105872	2822.2	W 99959	2933.2	W 111157	3147.3	W 119710	3083.7	AUT VET DES FEM MAT TEXT
844	UNDER GARMENTS NOT KNIT	W 62764	1380.0	W 64490	1526.4	W 59188	1351.2	W 55296	1143.6	VETEMENT DESSOUS MAT TEX
8441	— MENS SHIRTS	W 56765	1242.4	W 58950	1372.6	W 53419	1203.6	W 49112	1008.6	CHEMISES HOMMES MAT TEXT
845	OUTERWEAR KNIT NONELASTC	W 191597	5154.1	W 186632	5524.4	W 216427	5739.2	W 216946	5200.9	VET DESSOUS,ACCES BONNET
8451	— JERSEYS,PULLOVERS ETC	W 110114	3139.5	W 104395	3155.6	W 123866	3401.2	W 129570	3195.8	CHANDAILS,PULL–OVERS ETC
8459	— OTHER,CLTHG ACCESRYS	W 69622	1670.0	W 68150	1868.4	W 75296	1926.0	W 77984	1727.9	AUT VET DESSUS DE BONNE
846	UNDER GARMENTS KNITTED	W 142952	3076.4	W 148560	3570.0	W 159582	3643.6	W 152871	3184.9	SOUS VETS DE BONNETERIE
8462	— OF COTTON NON ELASTIC	W 112327	2165.7	W 117444	2523.1	W 128339	2605.1	W 122358	2274.7	SOUS–VET BONNET COTON
84629	—— OTHER	W 112327	2165.7	W 117444	2523.1	W 128339	2605.1	W 122358	2274.7	AUT SOUS–VET BONNET COTON
848	HEADGEAR,NONTXTL CLOTHNG	W 80254	1710.3	W 80171	1690.2	W 81592	1655.5	W 88881	1624.1	VET ACCES MAT AUT QUE TEX
8481	LEATHER CLOTHES,ACCESSOR	W 40024	1167.6	W 37114	1123.3	W 34126	1030.8	W 36332	1031.6	VET ACCES MAT CUIR ARTIF
851	*FOOTWEAR	W 253470	4473.2	W 231101	4460.8	W 243441	4685.7	W 242912	4246.9	CHAUSSURES
85102	FOOTWEAR LEATHER	W 198820	3869.9	W 180379	3890.6	W 187364	4039.7	W 185340	3655.0	CHAUS SEMELLES EN CUIR
87	PRECISION INSTRUMNTS NES		5937.9		6946.4		7432.1		7114.1	INSTRUM,APPAR SCIENT NDA
872	MEDICAL INSTRUMENTS NES	W 32219	1450.5	W 35548	1767.8	W 38057	1839.8	W 40917	1730.2	INSTR,APP MEDIC–CHIR NDA
87202	OTH MEDICAL INSTRUMENTS	W 26861	1311.3	W 29452	1600.7	W 31060	1668.6	W 33156	1536.2	INSTRUM,APP MEDECINE
874	MEASURNG,CONTROLNG INSTR	W 51516	3761.5	W 54881	4309.9	W 57900	4604.3	W 62727	4423.1	INSTRUMENTS DE MESURE
88	PHOTO EQU,OPTICL GDS ETC		4259.7		4812.5		4713.0		4280.3	APP,FOURN PHOTO,OP,MONTR
882	PHOTO,CINEMA SUPPLIES	W 114932	1587.2	W 116552	1804.2	W 108973	1685.1	W 107243	1473.4	PRODUITS PHOTO,CINEMA
8822	PHOTO FILM EXC DEV CINMA	W 73552	1237.5	W 79192	1413.7	W 67376	1263.2	W 66038	1086.8	PLAQUES,PELLICULES,FILMS
89	MISC MANUFCTRD GOODS NES		14918.7		16745.9		16750.5		14933.5	ART MANUFACTURES DIVERS
892	PRINTED MATTER	W 381178	1467.8	W 279484	1525.8	W 290275	1535.0	W 294351	1352.0	IMPRIMES
893	ARTICLES OF PLASTIC NES		4357.5		5264.6		5234.7		4637.8	OUVRAGES EN MAT DIVIS 58
8939	MISC PLASTIC ARTICLES	W 622489	3231.4	W 691288	3943.0	W 688623	3929.7	W 681142	3506.3	ART DIVERS EN MAT DIV 58
89399	OTHR PLASTC ARTICLES NES	W 544560	2978.0	W 600857	3625.6	W 588501	3598.2	W 594092	3254.5	AUT OUV MAT DIV 58
894	TOYS,SPORTING GOODS,ETC	W 301106	2863.5	W 316326	3219.9	W 339547	3321.9	W 323696	3220.9	VOITURES ENFANTS,JOUETS
8942	TOYS,INDOOR GAMES ETC	W 237263	2203.1	W 242835	2450.9	W 249401	2359.8	W 248061	2447.2	JOUETS,JEUX ETC
898	MUSICAL INSTRUMENTS,PTS	W 129267	2919.0	W 133614	3093.5	W 137270	2989.1	W 116819	2279.1	INSTRUMENTS DE MUSIQUE
8983	SOUND RECRDNG TAPE,DISCS	W 115103	2617.7	W 118916	2755.5	W 122325	2667.0	W 102212	1994.9	SUPPORTS SON POUR 763
89832	RECORDED DISCS,TAPES ETC	W 40804	1652.0	W 38599	1746.0	W 38543	1700.7	W 36925	1314.0	DISQUES,PHONO,BANDES
899	OTHER MANUFACTURED GOODS		1632.6		1882.5		1954.0		1784.2	AUT ART MANUF DIVERS NDA
9	GOODS NOT CLASSD BY KIND		13572.8		26599.4		25222.2		34968.9	ART TRANSACT NON CLASSES
931	*SPECIAL TRANSACTIONS	W 644086	12139.8	W 448091	25066.4	W 510186	23729.5	W 468468	33733.5	TRANS.SPECIALES
971	*GOLD,NON MONETARY NES	K 303369	1264.0	K 223940	1377.1	K 276585	1355.5		1138.9	OR NON MONETAIRE
97101	NONMON GLD UNWRT,SEMIMFD	K 95612	1182.7	K 100377	1260.5	K 94900	1193.4	K 92593	967.7	OR,ALLIAGES D'OR BRUTS

5. Special Exports F.O.B. by Commodities according to the S.I.T.C. (Rev. 2) in million U.S. Dollars
Exportations Spéciales F.O.B. par Produits d'après la C.T.C.I. (Rév. 2) en millions de Dollars E.U.

SITC CTCI	COMMODITY	1994		1995		1996		1997		PRODUIT
		QUANTITY QUANTITE	VALUE VALEUR	QUANTITY QUANTITE	VALUE VALEUR	QUANTITY QUANTITE	VALUE VALEUR	QUANTITY QUANTITE	VALUE VALEUR	
	ALL COMMODITIES		427100.1		523696.8		524080.8		511942.1	TOUS PRODUITS
0	FOOD AND LIVE ANIMALS		18147.2	-	21178.1		22293.8		19448.9	ALIMENTS,ANIMAUX VIVANTS
01	MEAT AND PREPARATIONS		2027.6		2196.4		2183.1		2001.4	VIANDES ET PREPARATIONS
011	MEAT FRESH,CHILLD,FROZEN	W 667075	1642.8	W 637062	1738.5	W 657940	1683.4	W 689280	1587.3	VIANDES FRAICHES,REF,CONGE
02	DAIRY PRODCTS,BIRDS'EGGS		4105.5		5063.5		5197.3		4620.2	PRODUITS LAITIERS,OEUFS
022	MILK AND CREAM	W 3328515	2461.3	W 3577986	3137.6	W 3823675	3092.2	W 3777397	2709.4	LAIT ET CREME
0224	MILK,CREAM PRESERVED ETC	W 1176360	1301.4	W 1154378	1677.9	W 1364388	1636.5	W 1226826	1277.1	LAIT,CREME CONS,CONC
024	CHEESE AND CURD	W 386940	1413.4	W 406632	1611.5	W 483881	1801.2	W 510775	1673.0	FROMAGE ET CAILLEBOTTE
04	CEREALS AND PREPARATIONS		3069.9		3667.9		4081.6		3055.0	CEREALES ET PRODUITS
048	CEREAL ETC PREPARATIONS	W 1058192	1618.6	W 1170945	1807.9	W 1180797	1863.0	W 1329025	1768.6	PREPTNS A BASE CEREALES
05	VEGETABLES AND FRUIT		1801.6		2104.0		2249.0		1871.2	LEGUMES ET FRUITS
07	COFFEE,TEA,COCOA,SPICES		2294.1		2612.7		2877.5		2648.5	CAFE,THE,CACAO,EPICES
073	CHOCOLATE AND PRODUCTS	W 326139	1142.1	W 330280	1251.8	W 440117	1583.4	W 382393	1270.9	CHOCOLAT
081	*FEEDING STUFF FOR ANIML	W 4319251	1343.4	W 4501174	1446.6	W 4677169	1525.3	W 4722818	1490.5	NOURRITURE POUR ANIMAUX
1	BEVERAGES AND TOBACCO		3280.2		3478.3		3653.0		3098.2	BOISSONS ET TABACS
11	BEVERAGES		1860.1		2027.5		1971.2		1659.6	BOISSONS
112	ALCOHOLIC BEVERAGES	W 1410227	1609.4	W 1354068	1760.6	W 1346036	1694.1	W 1279774	1420.0	BOISSONS ALCOOLIQUES
12	TOBACCO AND MANUFACTURES		1420.1		1450.8		1681.8		1438.6	TABACS BRUTS FABRIQUES
122	TOBACCO,MANUFACTURED	W 100703	1325.5	W 93539	1341.2	W 109516	1527.1	W 103700	1305.5	TABACS FABRIQUES
2	CRUDE MATERLS,EXCL FUELS		7814.1		9736.9		8584.9		8131.3	MAT BRUTES NON COMESTIBLES
26	TEXTILE FIBRES AND WASTE		1417.9		1651.4		1569.0		1372.2	FIBRES TEXTILES
28	METALLIFEROUS ORES,SCRAP		2137.8		2734.2		2246.7		2458.0	MINERAIS METAL,DECHETS
3	MINERAL FUELS ETC		5219.6		5502.6		7170.4		6460.0	COMBUSTIBLES MINERAUX LUB
33	PETROLEUM AND PRODUCTS		3685.5		3752.7		4216.3		3772.4	PETROLE ET DERIVES
334	PETROLEUM PRODUCTS,REFIN	MW 15695	3133.6		3149.0	MW 14074	3543.4	MW 12710	3143.9	PRODUITS RAFFINES
341	*GAS,NATURAL AND MANUFCT	W 2293277	403.7	W 5289548	741.3	MW 14865	1710.9	MW 14510	1742.2	GAZ NATUREL,GAZ MANUFACT
3414	PETROLEUM GASES, GASEOUS	W 1533355	279.0	W 4593295	601.0	MW 14227	1574.0	MW 13857	1601.5	GAZ DE PETROLE GAZEUX
5	CHEMCLS,RELATED PROD NES		55584.6		67211.7		66015.5		65181.5	PRODUITS CHIMIQUES
51	ORGANIC CHEMICALS		11753.2		14534.0		13641.4		13030.6	PROD CHIMIQ ORGANIQUES
512	ALCOHOLS,PHENOLS ETC		1757.7		2300.0		2008.7		2015.5	PHENOLS,PHENOLS–ALCOOLS
5121	ACYCLIC ALCOHOLS,DERIVS	W 1604298	1395.3	W 1518281	1841.7	W 1760910	1593.3	W 1770867	1561.3	ALCOOLS ACYCLIQUES
513	CARBOXYLIC ACIDS ETC		1746.4		2290.0		2029.5		1805.1	ACIDES CARBOXYLIQUES
514	NITROGEN–FNCTN COMPOUNDS		3739.7		4497.2	W 1072021	4423.2		4319.1	COMPOSES FONCT AZOTEES
5148	OTH NITROGN–FNCTN CMPNDS	W 502926	2014.1	W 562066	2528.1	W 569772	2635.3	W 554578	2512.0	AUTRES COMPOSES AZOTES
51482	IMIDE–,IMIDE–FNCT CMPNDS	W 156639	1244.3	W 187584	1515.2	W 164521	1612.4	W 160567	1610.4	COMPOSES A FONCTION IMIDE
515	ORG–INORG COMPOUNDS ETC		1950.5		2140.3		2198.3		1985.8	COMPOSES ORGANO–MINERAUX
516	OTHER ORGANIC CHEMICALS	W 1097149	1444.7		1802.6		1794.6	W 1318222	1677.3	AUTRES PROD ORGANIQUES
52	INORGANIC CHEMICALS		3306.7		3871.5		3823.6		3539.9	PROD CHIM INORGANIQUES
522	INORG ELEMNTS,OXIDES,ETC		1661.1		2082.0		1994.6		1888.8	ELEMENTS INORGANIQUES
523	OTHR INORG CHEMICALS ETC		1471.4		1655.4		1634.8		1537.1	AUT PRODUITS CHIMIQUES INORG
53	DYES,TANNING,COLOUR PROD		5687.9		6412.3		6370.5		6391.5	PROD TEINTURE,COLORANTS
531	SYNT DYE,NAT INDGO,LAKES	W 194155	2337.9	W 197041	2483.8	W 215588	2428.2	W 234248	2387.6	MAT COLOR ORGAN,LAQUES
5311	SYNTHIC ORGNIC DYESTUFFS	W 135090	2109.3	W 133091	2228.9	W 139750	2139.5	W 151727	2131.8	MAT COLOR ORGAN SYNTHET
533	PIGMENTS,PAINTS,ETC	W 1185664	3197.0	W 1192213	3762.0	W 1265848	3761.0		3843.0	PIGMENTS,PEINTURES,VERNIS
5334	VARNISHES,DISTEMPERS ETC	W 318452	1417.3	W 339554	1708.0	W 365884	1727.5	W 422784	1734.9	PEINTURES A L'EAU
541	*MEDICINAL,PHARM PRODUCT		8739.2		10268.3		10711.9		11553.5	PROD MEDICINAUX PHARMACEUT
5417	MEDICAMENTS	MK 122871	5218.6	MK 122573	6305.2	MK 126414	6681.4	MK 144169	7642.1	MEDICAMENTS
54179	— CONTNG OTH SUBSTANCES	MK 113978	4348.0	MK 113483	5187.1	MK 116857	5459.1	MK 136074	6528.1	MED CONT AUT SUBSTANCES
55	PERFUME,CLEANING ETC PRD		3791.2		4542.6		4523.2		4372.5	PROD POUR PARFUM,TOILETTE
553	PERFUMERY,COSMETICS,ETC	W 221467	1674.3	W 256320	2047.8	W 261851	2042.7	W 303258	2091.6	PRODUITS DE PARFUMERIE
554	SOAP,CLEANSING ETC PREPS	W 988556	1598.2	W 1016974	1887.8	W 1097126	1866.4	W 1128747	1724.4	SAVONS,PRODUITS DETERSIFS
5542	WASHING PREPARATIONS ETC	W 885304	1343.9	W 904236	1577.6	W 964492	1531.0	W 1009787	1459.5	PROD ORG TENSIO–ACT NDA
58	PLASTIC MATERIALS ETC		13609.8		17018.5		16337.0		16185.0	MAT PLAST ARTIFICIELLES
582	PROD OF CONDENSATION ETC	W 1859489	4243.5	W 1939487	5448.4	W 2026334	5343.1	W 2346578	5337.4	PROD CONDENS,POLYCOND
5823	ALKYDS,OTHER POLYESTERS	W 539945	1290.6	W 607520	1841.4	W 613543	1728.1	W 776575	1719.9	ALKYDES ET AUT POLYESTERS
583	POLYMERIZATION ETC PRODS	W 5722340	8942.9	W 5747217	11086.1	W 6026660	10523.3	W 6502427	10416.0	PROD POLYMERISATION
5831	POLYETHYLENE	W 1392354	1386.1	W 1485371	1867.8	W 1538238	1797.2	W 1574042	1749.0	POLYETHYLENE
5834	POLYVINYL CHLORIDE	W 990245	1630.4	W 1002276	2096.7	W 1062901	1941.4	W 1142385	1938.2	CHLORURE DE POLYVINYLE
5839	OTH POLYMRZTION ETC PROD	W 1144819	2775.8	W 1102048	3282.2	W 1167205	3220.7	W 1332464	3273.0	AUT PROD POLYMER COPOLYM
59	CHEMICAL MATERIALS NES		7576.3		9286.3		9358.9		8988.2	MAT PROD CHIMIQUES NDA
591	PESTICIDES,DISINFECTANTS	W 191159	1571.5	W 198979	1861.1	W 206466	1826.7	W 207091	1655.6	DESINF,INSECT,FONG,HERB
598	MISCEL CHEM PRODUCTS NES		5088.4		6297.5	W 3252406	6403.0		6274.9	PROD DIV INDUST CHIM NDA
5989	CHEM PRODUCTS,PREPS NES	W 2760916	4468.7	W 2923744	5600.6	W 2873749	5701.5	W 3162284	5565.6	PROD PREP CHIMIQUES NDA
59899	OTH CHEM PRODS,PREPS,NES	W 2241691	3244.9	W 2367419	4160.8	W 2353758	4293.2	W 2604444	4215.6	AUT PRODUITS CHIMIQUES NDA
6	BASIC MANUFACTURES		69572.8		86887.9		81638.3		78420.0	ART MANUFACTURES
62	RUBBER MANUFACTURES NES		3772.0		4566.5		4649.4		4572.5	CAOUTCHOUC MANUFACTURE
625	RUBBER TYRES, TUBES ETC	W 424755	1767.2	W 437724	2022.2	W 468698	2112.7	W 508473	2057.3	PNEUS CAOUTCHOUC VULCANISE
63	WOOD,CORK MANUFACTRS NES		1435.8		1801.2		1790.5		1752.0	OUVRAGES LIEGE ET BOIS
64	PAPER,PAPERBOARD AND MFR		9507.0		12817.9		11728.7		10791.7	PAPIERS,CARTONS & OUVRAGES
641	PAPER AND PAPERBOARD	W 6684919	6173.8	W 7115270	8790.3	W 7495276	7958.4	W 8696766	7870.4	PAPIERS ET CARTONS
6412	PRINTG,WRITING PAPER NES	W 1996194	1856.0	W 2298662	2877.9	W 2309480	2460.7	W 2768812	2561.3	PAPIERS POUR L'IMPRESSION
64122	— COATED,IMPREGNATD ETC	W 1866735	1718.2	W 2145137	2649.4	W 2158049	2271.3	W 2619055	2386.3	PAPIERS IMPRESSION COUCHES
6415	PAPER,PAPERBRD,BULK,NES	W 2796757	1906.4	W 2709416	2626.7	W 2766760	2178.1	W 3144636	2026.0	PAPIERS,CARTONS ROULEAUX
64159	OTHER PAPER ETC,BULK,NES	W 2722267	1799.6	W 2642986	2505.8	W 2696306	2063.9	W 3066338	1916.6	AUT PAPIER ROULEAUX FEUILLES
6418	COATED ETC PAPER NES BLK	W 857088	1514.0	W 879234	1928.5	W 964108	1872.0	W 1079844	1884.4	PAP,CARTONS COUCHES,ENDUITS
642	PAPER,ETC,PRECUT,ARTS OF	W 1390517	3333.3	W 1388377	4027.7	W 1428432	3770.3	W 1309100	2921.3	PAP,CARTONS DECOUPES
6428	PAPER ETC ARTICLES NES	W 516228	1543.9	W 546687	1895.7	W 561925	1739.5	W 458374	1125.6	OUVRAGES EN PATE A PAPIER
65	TEXTILE YARN,FABRICS,ETC		12863.8		14647.9		14041.6		13286.0	FILS,TISSUS,ARTICLES TEXTILE
651	TEXTILE YARN	W 623069	3250.0	W 585988	3676.7		3580.3	W 692969	3436.8	FILS TEXTILES
6514	SYN FIB YRN,BULK,MONOFIL	W 358019	1673.9	W 338857	1918.6	W 370201	1922.9	W 425211	1901.6	FILS CONT 85% FIB TEXT SYNTH
652	COTTON FABRICS,WOVEN	W 127211	1528.5	W 116226	1637.7	W 121780	1609.1	W 129102	1537.5	TISSUS DE COTON
6522	WOVEN COTTON BLEACHD,ETC	W 88211	1334.1	W 82637	1430.5	W 87107	1414.6	W 91243	1349.1	TISSUS COTON BLANCHIS ETC
653	WOVN MAN–MADE FIB FABRIC	W 161950	2782.4	W 158540	3152.6	W 154820	2776.3	W 158736	2449.2	TISSUS FIBRES SYNTH,ARTIF
657	SPECIAL TXTL FABRC,PRODS	W 260590	2050.9	W 273319	2473.7	W 287618	2427.3	W 305068	2381.4	TISSUS SPECIAUX
66	NONMETAL MINERAL MFS NES		6457.9		7740.8		7528.0		7132.1	ART MIN NON METALLIQUES
663	MINERAL MANUFCTURES NES		1711.1		2084.8	W 1921192	2086.3	W 2178558	2005.1	ART MIN MANUF NDA
664	GLASS	W 1078726	1546.3	W 1098870	1916.0	W 1197761	2019.9		2015.5	VERRE
67	IRON AND STEEL		13955.2		18124.0		15777.8		15557.6	FER ET ACIER
672	IRON,STEEL PRIMARY FORMS	W 4564887	2325.8	W 4650303	2970.1	W 5094865	2281.4	W 5675229	2379.3	LINGOTS FER,ACIER
6727	IRN,STL COIL FR REROLLNG	W 2885267	1738.7	W 2788317	2155.5	W 2828265	1497.6	W 3419636	1563.7	EBAUCHES POUR TOLES FER
673	IRON,STEEL SHAPES ETC	W 4144746	2195.5	W 4602963	2935.9	W 4363465	2504.8	W 5136695	2550.6	BARRES,PROFIL FER,ACIER
674	IRN,STL UNIV,PLATE,SHEET	W 8398589	5638.0	W 8771547	7461.4	W 8438048	6401.4	MW 9563	6156.2	LARGES PLATS,TOLES
6746	IRN,STL THIN PLATE,ROLLD	W 2928875	2047.1	W 2832049	2715.3	W 2760842	2330.2	W 3367285	2369.7	TOLES LAM MOINS 3MM
6749	OTH IRN,STL PLATES,SHEET	W 2507855	1677.5	W 2741567	2170.4	W 2711553	1887.9	W 2812440	1712.8	AUTRES TOLES FER,ACIER
67491	— OF IRON OR SIMPLE STL	W 2469666	1606.0	W 2721396	2083.9	W 2695793	1815.1	W 2780064	1649.9	AUT TOLES AUTRES ACIER FIN
678	IRON,STL TUBES,PIPES,ETC		2882.7		3601.5		3504.4		3494.1	TUBES,TUYAUX EN FONTE,FER
68	NON–FERROUS METALS		7197.9		9704.7		8757.3		9005.1	METAUX NON FERREUX
682	COPPER EXC CEMENT COPPER		2742.9		3654.1	W 921256	3333.6		3300.9	CUIVRE
6822	COPPER,ALLOYS WORKED	W 626770	2330.5	W 688449	3192.1	W 651036	2661.5	W 783614	2886.8	CUIVRE,ALLIAGES OUVRES
684	ALUMINIUM		3175.2	W 1223155	4462.9	W 1220189	4056.7	W 1365713	4140.9	ALUMINIUM
6842	ALUMINIUM,ALLOYS WORKED	W 794284	2726.6	W 923767	3787.6	W 920031	3507.3	W 1136096	3720.4	ALUMINIUM,ALLIAGES OUVRE

5. Special Exports F.O.B. by Commodities according to the S.I.T.C. (Rev. 2) in million U.S. Dollars
Exportations Spéciales F.O.B. par Produits d'après la C.T.C.I. (Rév. 2) en millions de Dollars E.U.

SITC CTCI	COMMODITY	1994		1995		1996		1997		PRODUIT
		QUANTITY QUANTITE	VALUE VALEUR	QUANTITY QUANTITE	VALUE VALEUR	QUANTITY QUANTITE	VALUE VALEUR	QUANTITY QUANTITE	VALUE VALEUR	
68422	ALUMNM PLATE,SHEET,STRIP	W 458405	1273.1	W 588443	1978.1	W 581015	1797.9	W 721572	1996.2	TOLES, PLANCHES EN ALU
69	METAL MANUFACTURES NES		12846.5		15632.0		15751.6		14725.4	ART MANUFACT EN METAL NDA
691	STRUCTURES AND PARTS NES	W 554079	1537.2	W 598546	1895.0	W 649255	2012.5	W 693100	1960.9	CONSTRUCT FER,ACIER,ALU
695	TOOLS	W 107105	2546.1	W 109061	3071.8	W 115280	3124.7	W 125285	2921.0	OUTILS A MAIN
6954	BLADES,TIPS,ETC FR TOOLS	W 47212	1640.2	W 46144	1961.9	W 48246	1995.6	W 49661	1875.4	OUTILS POUR MACHINE–OUTIL
699	BASE METAL MFRS NES	W 730317	5029.4		6207.4		6331.7	W 926137	6057.5	ART MANUFACTURES MET NDA
6991	LOCKSMITHS WARES,ETC	W 229460	2292.9	W 244940	2757.8	W 267820	2818.3	W 297059	2711.9	ARTICLES DE SERRURERIE
69913	BASE MTL DOOR,ETC FITTNG	W 194228	1695.7	W 206896	2010.3	W 226056	2047.3	W 251717	1982.4	GARNITURES POUR MEUBLES
7	MACHINES,TRANSPORT EQUIP		209185.7		255995.8		257834.8		253630.2	MACHINES MATERIEL TRANSPORT
71	POWER GENERATING EQUIPMT		12344.3		14398.4		15993.3		15808.1	MACHINES GENERATRICES
713	INTRNL COMBUS PSTN ENGIN	W 545101	5974.8	W 608489	7360.7	W 647348	8107.7	W 738812	8174.5	MOTEURS EXPL COMB INT, PIECE
7132	MOTOR VEHCL PISTN ENGINS	W 195380	2044.5	W 206782	2544.7	W 227830	2807.2	W 266873	2960.5	MOTEURS EXPL POUR VEHICULES
7139	PISTON ENGINE PARTS NES	W 275863	2895.9	W 320595	3577.6	W 337059	3927.2	W 397728	3945.3	PIECES POUR 713.2,3,8
714	ENGINES AND MOTORS NES	W 20648	2257.9	W 16493	2218.2	W 25706	2997.7	W 21145	3184.8	MOTEURS NON ELECTRIQUES
7149	ENGINE & MOTOR PARTS NES	W 17531	1127.5	W 14983	1225.2	W 21597	1627.1	W 17988	1676.7	PIECES 714 ET 718.88
716	ROTATING ELECTRIC PLANT	W 199020	2675.6	W 223417	3180.9	W 230380	3215.9	W 243108	2942.4	APP ELECTR ROTATIFS,PIECES
7162	AC MTRS,GENRTRS,GEN SETS	W 132213	1749.9	W 145232	2020.1	W 151640	2075.5	W 158680	1895.9	MOTEURS ELECTRIQUES
71621	AC MTRS,INC UNIVRSL MTRS	W 105096	1316.0	W 127411	1720.7	W 129226	1768.4	W 139082	1651.0	MOT ELEC NON COUR CONTINU
72	MACHS FOR SPCL INDUSTRYS		24307.0		30020.1		30829.1		28720.1	MAC SPECIALES POUR INDUST
721	AGRIC MACHY,EXC TRACTORS	W 203258	1548.0	W 210333	1870.0	W 236536	1984.3	W 297984	2140.7	MACHINES AGRICOLES
722	TRACTORS NON–ROAD	W 172405	1278.7	W 199070	1663.0	W 213763	1692.3	W 201236	1487.6	TRACTEURS
7224	WHEELED TRACTORS NES	W 172360	1278.4	W 199035	1662.8	W 213686	1691.5	W 197972	1423.2	TRACTEURS A ROUES
723	CIVIL ENGNEERG EQUIP ETC	W 222000	1677.8	W 253694	2161.1	W 271153	2106.0	W 329459	2149.7	APPAREILS DE GENIE CIVIL
7234	CONST,MINING MACHNRY NES	W 178552	1343.0	W 205342	1737.8	W 222708	1706.8	W 272196	1737.5	MACH POUR LA CONST, MINES
724	TEXTILE,LEATHER MACHNRY	W 259615	5677.6	W 266914	6459.8	W 255344	6000.5	W 254817	5494.8	MACH POUR INDUSTRIE TEXTILE
7244	SPINNING,EXTRDNG,ETC MCH	W 110863	2258.9	W 120165	2655.3	W 105653	2254.0	W 102313	1963.9	MACH POUR LE FILAGE
725	PAPER ETC MILL MACHINERY	W 62488	1302.5	W 72403	1712.7	W 80935	1993.5	W 79496	1682.3	MACHINES FABR PATE PAPIER
726	PRINTG,BKBINDG MACHY,PTS	W 129852	3440.4	W 148879	4447.1	W 170421	4778.1	W 178025	4632.1	MACHINES POUR IMPRIMERIE
7264	PRINTING PRESSES	W 85723	2196.4	W 100515	2969.2	W 120473	3338.8	W 126400	3326.6	MACHINES A IMPRIMER
72641	ROTARY PRINTING PRESSES	W 85723	2196.4	W 100515	2969.2	W 120473	3338.8	W 126400	3326.6	MACH IMPRIMER ROTATIVES
728	OTH MACHY FOR SPCL INDUS		8304.9		10461.3		10861.9		9962.5	AUT MACH IND PARTICULIERES
7284	MACHY FOR SPCL INDUS NES	W 272275	6128.9	W 320387	7919.4	W 330879	8323.0	W 334473	7611.6	MACH SPEC IND PARTICUL.
72842	RUBBER,PLASTICS WRKG MCH	W 90413	1911.7	W 105295	2421.3	W 112447	2507.8	W 119490	2303.5	MACH IND CAOUT MAT PLAST
72848	OTH MCHY WITH INDIV FNCT	W 101040	2181.4	W 104259	2671.4	W 114473	2946.6	W 120162	2840.5	AUTRES MACHINES NDA
72849	PTS OF MACHS OF 7284 ETC	W 39259	1173.5	W 48609	1550.9	W 50005	1578.5	W 53104	1558.9	PIECES DU 728.4 ETC
73	METALWORKING MACHINERY		5522.2		7004.3		7534.1		6564.2	MACH TRAVAIL DES METAUX
736	METALWORKING MACH–TOOLS	W 242341	4291.5	W 259658	5383.3	W 273878	5883.5	W 261452	5026.8	MACH–OUTILS TRAVAIL METAUX
7361	METAL CUTTING MACH–TOOLS	W 100902	1601.6	W 101543	2040.2	W 101733	2108.6	W 92029	1764.0	MACH–OUT ENLEVEMENT METAL
737	METALWORKING MACHNRY NES	W 118042	1230.8	W 117253	1621.0	W 121950	1650.6	W 111895	1537.5	MACH TRAV METAUX PIECES
74	GENRL INDUSTRL MACHY NES		29931.8		37251.8		38139.6		35888.2	MACH APP INDUSTRIE
741	HEATING,COOLING EQUIPMNT	W 220396	3673.3	W 238759	4452.6	W 298820	4958.1	W 290492	4433.5	MACH CHAUFFAGE,PIECES
7416	HEATING,COOLING EQU NES	W 101083	1867.8	W 109008	2192.3	W 137437	2514.2	W 141958	2294.6	APP CHANGEMENT TEMP
742	PUMPS FOR LIQUIDS ETC	W 126457	3727.9	W 138601	4573.3	W 144464	4608.6	W 159989	4459.2	POMPES MOTO–POMPES
7428	OTHER PUMPS FOR LIQUIDS	W 30003	1371.3	W 31117	1670.5	W 31348	1607.2	W 34619	1609.8	AUTRES POMPES POUR LIQ
74288	PUMPS FR LIQUIDS NES ETC	W 27677	1314.5	W 28980	1609.9	W 29431	1559.9	W 32225	1558.1	POMPES POUR LIQUIDES NDA
743	PUMPS NES,CENTRFUGES ETC	W 238363	4318.8	W 279881	5446.9	W 295944	5563.6	W 341123	5420.9	POMPES COMPRES,VENT ETC
7431	PUMPS FOR GASES ETC	W 76121	1233.0	W 94888	1578.9	W 94701	1525.2	W 110712	1518.9	POMPES AIR A VIDE,COMPRES
7436	GAS,LIQUID FILTERS ETC	W 74650	1295.6	W 82266	1620.9	W 90889	1691.1	W 105025	1627.0	APP POUR FILT DES LIQUIDES
744	MECHANICAL HANDLING EQU	W 517159	4232.7	W 601845	5476.4	W 639351	5610.1	W 702660	5356.7	EQUIP MANUTENTION PIECES
7442	LIFTING,LOADING MACH NES	W 171451	1724.8	W 205889	2265.2	W 218713	2273.9	W 246033	2204.1	APP LEVAGE,MANUTENTION
7449	PTS NES OF MACHY OF 7442	W 215473	1659.6	W 242982	2103.7	W 251710	2148.9	W 276639	2070.5	PIECES DU 744.2
745	NONELEC MACHY,TOOLS NES	W 171340	4835.1	W 181934	5619.3	W 181672	5777.6	W 196066	5353.2	AUT MACH NON ELEC,PIECES
7452	OTH NONELEC MCHS,PTS NES	W 161625	4426.2	W 172302	5172.5	W 171881	5339.9	W 184327	4909.1	AUT MACH NON ELEC,PIECES
74522	PACKAGNG,BOTTLNG,ETC MCH	W 56416	2190.3	W 56631	2519.5	W 57847	2685.5	W 58512	2361.1	MACH NETT BOUTEILLES,ETC
749	NONELEC MACH PTS,ACC NES	W 610857	9144.3	W 675347	11683.5	W 698388	11622.0	W 743092	10864.9	PIECES MACH NON ELEC NDA
7491	BALL,ROLLER,ETC BEARINGS	W 107679	1586.0	W 134062	2208.1	W 128879	2090.1	W 139479	1940.3	ROULEMENTS BILLES ETC
7492	COCKS,VALVES ETC NES	W 122047	3038.5	W 128932	3767.8	W 133878	3696.5	W 141857	3432.3	ART ROB,SIM POUR TUYAUX
7493	SHAFT,CRANK,PULLEY ETC	W 283924	2626.0	W 327156	3420.1	W 329503	3466.1	W 334849	3219.5	ARBRES TRANS,VILEBREQUINS
7499	OTH NONELEC MCHY PTS NES	W 97207	1894.0	W 85198	2287.7	W 106127	2369.4	W 126907	2272.9	PIECES NON ELECT NDA
75	OFFICE MACHNES,ADP EQUIP		9920.9		12951.7		12297.1		12177.6	MACH BUREAU TRAIT AUTOM
752	AUTOMTIC DATA PROC EQUIP	W 57331	5722.2		7390.1	W 73421	7034.2	W 86836	7429.9	MACH TRAIT INFORMATION
7523	DIGITL CENTRL PROCESSORS	W 11582	1771.1	W 17531	2345.0	W 17526	2138.2	W 21099	2322.7	UNITES CENTRALES
7524	DIGITL CENTRL STOR UNITS	W 6458	1151.4	W 9753	1635.3	W 7986	1439.7	W 9746	1522.0	UNITES MEMOIRE CENTRALES
7525	ADP PERIPHERAL UNITS	W 33322	1731.1	W 40024	2155.2	W 41991	2066.9	W 50100	2019.0	UNITES PERIPHERIQUES
759	OFFICE,ADP MCH PTS,ACCES	W 34078	3157.3	W 40954	4206.4	W 43110	4053.4	W 44715	3563.7	PIECES DU 751 ET 752
7599	ACCTG,ETC,ADP MCH PTS,AC	W 16889	2670.7	W 24541	3656.3	W 27772	3600.2	W 30638	3148.3	PIECES DU 751 ET 752
76	TELECOMM,SOUND EQUIPMENT		9182.4		11169.0		12078.4		12094.8	EQUIPMENT DE TELECOM
764	TELECOM EQPT,PTS,ACC NES	W 79562	6924.4	W 76913	8636.9	W 91590	9494.4	W 93345	10202.3	EQUIP TELECOM,PIECES
7641	LINE TELEPHONE,ETC EQUIP	W 18096	1853.5	W 19668	2386.2	W 23420	2755.1	W 22587	2377.8	APP TELEPHON PAR FIL
7643	TV,RADIO TRANSMITTRS ETC	W 4507	1441.3	W 5793	2550.3	W 7654	3071.3	W 12648	3947.9	APP EMET TELE RADIO
7649	PTS NES OF EQUIPMT OF 76	W 42597	3075.8	W 35558	3052.4	W 40427	2968.7	W 37386	3193.2	PIECES DE LA DIV 76
76491	PTS NES OF APPAR OF 7641	W 14675	1796.7	W 10565	1616.0	W 9811	1475.0	W 8585	1825.1	PIECES POUR 764.1
77	ELECTRIC MACHNRY NES ETC		33046.0		42573.4		41242.7		40495.5	MACH APP ELECT NDA
771	ELECTRIC POWER MACHY NES	W 109763	1743.7	W 114345	2333.5	W 130658	2525.6	W 143564	2426.0	MACH PROD,TRANS ELECTR
7712	OTH ELEC POWER MACHY NES	W 71294	1298.5	W 77654	1831.2	W 85221	1982.5	W 98176	1956.4	AUT APP PROD TRANSF ELEC
772	SWITCHGEAR ETC,PARTS NES	W 223108	8625.6	W 254018	10838.3	W 272986	11006.0	W 303206	10667.3	APP COUPURE,SECT ETC
7721	SWITCHGEAR ETC	W 215421	7795.1	W 245264	10005.3	W 264607	10215.9	W 293307	9879.7	APP COUPURE,SECTIONMNT
773	ELECTR DISTRIBUTNG EQUIP	W 255829	2067.8	W 297808	2785.0	W 323494	2994.5	W 349823	2795.1	EQUIPMT DISTRIBUTION ELECT
7731	INSULATED WIRE,CABLE ETC	W 230244	1709.1	W 268041	2274.0	W 293456	2473.0	W 317885	2299.9	FILS,CABLES ISOLES ELECT
774	ELECTRO–MEDCL,XRAY EQUIP	W 16100	2228.5	W 17273	2666.1	W 18917	2704.6	W 18015	2475.4	APPAREILS MEDICAUX
7742	X–RAY APPARATUS ETC	W 11995	1589.2	W 12547	1876.8	W 13363	1898.0	W 13681	1735.9	APPAREILS A RAYONS X
775	HOUSEHOLD TYPE EQUIP NES	W 433563	4122.6	W 439029	4755.4	W 458111	4603.2	W 524662	4635.4	MACH,APP USAGE DOMESTQUE
776	TRANSISTORS,VALVES,ETC	W 93042	5943.1	W 93788	8003.4	W 116483	7399.3	W 141223	7955.5	LAMPES,TUBES,VALVES
7764	ELECTRONIC MICROCIRCUITS	W 3972	4312.5	W 4724	5798.2	W 4216	5214.9	W 5360	5685.6	MICROSTRUCTURES ELECTRON
778	ELECTRICAL MACHINERY NES	W 496896	8315.2	W 547544	11192.0	W 571085	10009.8	W 588504	9541.2	AUTRES MACH ELECT NDA
7783	AUTOMOTIVE ELECTR EQUIP	W 106946	1817.6	W 127346	2349.1	W 131393	2456.1	W 145766	2420.9	EQUIP ELECT MOTEURS EXPL
7788	OTH ELEC MACHY,EQUIP NES	W 164641	3738.5	W 179417	5550.8	W 166542	4252.6	W 156210	3879.1	AUT MACH APP ELEC NDA
77889	ELEC PARTS OF MACHY NES	W 2226	1309.7	W 2567	2316.4	W 3050	1078.9	W 3259	653.6	PIECES ELEC DE MACH NDA
78	ROAD VEHICLES		68802.7		83140.5		85033.1		85233.4	VEHICULES ROUTIERS
781	PASS MOTOR VEH EXC BUSES	W 2955382	42225.6	W 3163109	48602.1	W 3571536	51864.1	W 3981586	52651.8	AUTO TRANSPORT PERSONNES
782	LORRIES,SPCL MTR VEH NES	W 621650	4661.4	W 670602	6111.0	W 805729	6547.5	W 950677	6896.3	VEHICULES SPECIAUX,MARCH
7821	LORRIES,TRUCKS	W 536936	3922.8	W 567905	5152.4	W 674855	5442.4	W 786347	5584.4	VEHICULES TRANSP MARCHAND
783	ROAD MOTOR VEHICLES NES	W 236702	2286.3	W 326722	4172.0	W 309513	3411.2	W 348742	2872.8	VEHICULES ROUTIERS NDA
7832	TRACTORS FOR TR–TRAILERS	W 169887	1586.4	W 268978	3536.4	W 241073	2674.2	W 276164	2180.9	TRACTEURS ROUTIERS
784	MOTOR VEH PRTS,ACCES NES	W 2129405	17778.4	W 2323321	21931.6	W 2162676	20802.2	W 2504959	20468.2	PIECES 722,781,782,783
7849	OTHER MOTOR VEHCL PARTS	W 2090944	17334.7	W 2270403	21317.0	W 2110379	20213.9	W 2428329	19835.8	PIECES 722,781,782,783
786	TRAILERS,NONMOTR VEH,NES	W 302816	1415.6	W 321770	1775.8	W 344761	1728.1	W 408477	1760.3	REMORQUES,CADRES,CONTAIN
79	OTHR TRANSPORT EQUIPMENT		12298.3		12868.4		10412.5		12617.9	AUTRE MATERIEL TRANSPORT
791	RAILWAY VEHICLES	W 172300	2091.5	W 98679	1261.6	W 99126	951.2	W. 110544	799.6	VEHIC MAT CHEMINS DE FER
792	AIRCRAFT ETC	W 16302	8441.3	W 16580	9015.2	W 14579	7966.8	W 18582	10401.8	APP NAVIGATION AERIENNE
7924	AIRCRFT NES OVER 15000KG	W 6394	4747.7	W 6657	4994.8	W 5210	4174.2	W 7052	6134.6	AERODYNES PLUS 15000 KG

5. Special Exports F.O.B. by Commodities according to the S.I.T.C. (Rev. 2) in million U.S. Dollars
Exportations Spéciales F.O.B. par Produits d'après la C.T.C.I. (Rév. 2) en millions de Dollars E.U.

SITC CTCI	COMMODITY	1994		1995		1996		1997		PRODUIT
		QUANTITY QUANTITE	VALUE VALEUR	QUANTITY QUANTITE	VALUE VALEUR	QUANTITY QUANTITE	VALUE VALEUR	QUANTITY QUANTITE	VALUE VALEUR	
7929	AIRCRAFT PARTS NES	W 9146	3462.0	W 8888	3556.3	W 8391	3375.7	W 10532	3823.1	PIECES DU 792
793	SHIPS AND BOATS ETC	W 827053	1765.7	W 344297	2591.6	W 203973	1494.6	W 255199	1416.5	NAVIRES BATEAUX,ETC
7932	SHIPS AND BOATS NES	W 331726	1498.6	W 310125	2531.3	W 189053	1443.5	W 208003	1355.3	NAVIRES ET BATEAUX
79323	OTHER CARGO VESSELS	W 292840	1164.7	W 270736	2189.0	W 184577	1356.5	W 179381	1058.7	AUT BATEAUX TRANS MARCH
8	MISC MANUFACTURED GOODS		45746.5		52986.0		53841.2		50567.0	ART MANUFACTURES DIVERS
812	*PLUMBG,HEATNG,LGHTNG EQ	W 189888	1782.5	W 192183	2014.8	W 220268	2149.0	W 229148	1950.9	APPAR SANITAIRES CHAUFFAGE
821	*FURNITURE,PARTS THEREOF	W 778625	4356.5	W 808935	4983.3	W 826971	4951.6	W 898755	4489.9	MEUBLES ET PIECES
8211	CHAIRS,SEATS AND PARTS	W 156632	1300.4	W 165947	1548.0	W 169990	1566.7	W 179742	1396.3	SIEGES ET PIECES
8219	FURNITURE AND PARTS NES	W 591722	2383.7	W 611025	2774.2	W 624477	2764.2	W 686955	2523.4	AUTRES MEUBLES ET PIECES
82192	WOOD FURNITURE NES	W 424509	1626.2	W 426219	1850.4	W 429083	1858.6	W 472863	1680.1	MEUBLES NDA EN BOIS
84	CLOTHING AND ACCESSORIES		6671.8		7502.8		7582.4		7293.0	VETEMENTS
843	WOMENS OUTERWEAR NONKNIT	W 32127	2655.0	W 32289	2963.7	W 35081	2941.4	W 42212	2833.6	VET DESSUS FEMMES MAT TEX
87	PRECISION INSTRUMNTS NES		10318.9		12386.0		12992.4		12576.7	INSTRUM,APPAR SCIENT NDA
872	MEDICAL INSTRUMENTS NES	W 25403	1839.8	W 27982	2258.2	W 31109	2350.9	W 33168	2249.7	INSTR,APP MEDIC–CHIR NDA
87202	OTH MEDICAL INSTRUMENTS	W 21460	1606.2	W 23174	1920.0	W 25878	1988.6	W 27586	1910.3	INSTRUM,APP MEDECINE
874	MEASURNG,CONTROLNG INSTR		7192.4		8583.2	W 80651	9070.4		8740.1	INSTRUMENTS DE MESURE
8742	MEASUR,DRAW ETC INST,PTS	W 22068	1742.3	W 23542	2089.7	W 24933	2219.5	W 28580	2122.8	INST DESSIN,TRACAGE,PCS
87421	MEASURNG,DRAWNG ETC INST	W 19055	1500.9	W 20481	1797.8	W 21734	1869.5	W 25066	1800.5	INSTRUM DESSIN,TRACAGE
8743	GAS,LIQUID CONTROL INSTR	W 19717	1858.2	W 21502	2237.9	W 22684	2287.1	W 25288	2238.1	APP,INSTR MESURE FLUIDES
8748	ELEC MEAS,CONTRL EQU NES	W 8144	1770.5	W 9242	2174.3	W 10020	2286.9	W 10420	2194.7	APP ELEC ELECTRO MESURE
87483	OTH ELCTRNC MEAS ETC EQU	W 6867	1606.7	W 7616	1963.3	W 8114	2067.1	W 8429	1974.3	AUT APP ELECTRO DE MESURE
88	PHOTO EQU,OPTICL GDS ETC		4298.5		4862.3		4852.7		4695.8	APP,FOURN PHOTO,OP,MONTR
882	PHOTO,CINEMA SUPPLIES		2000.9		2178.1		2245.4		2152.9	PRODUITS PHOTO,CINEMA
8822	PHOTO FILM EXC DEV CINMA	W 141221	1681.8	W 144792	1815.6	W 131107	1818.5	W 134441	1698.9	PLAQUES,PELLICULES,FILMS
89	MISC MANUFCTRD GOODS NES		16694.6		19400.4		19606.5		17970.4	ART MANUFACTURES DIVERS
892	PRINTED MATTER	W 740606	3385.8	W 739767	3837.8	W 809383	3975.3	W 758750	3309.2	IMPRIMES
8928	PRINTED MATTER NES	W 410613	1352.1	W 403761	1604.3	W 463971	1712.9	W 453977	1459.0	IMPRIMES NDA
893	ARTICLES OF PLASTIC NES		5876.8		7196.4		7196.9		6929.0	OUVRAGES EN MAT DIVIS 58
8931	PLSTC PACKG CONTNRS,LIDS	W 381594	1519.5	W 387203	1798.5	W 400644	1711.6	W 432351	1610.7	ART TRANSP EMBALLAGE ETC
8939	MISC PLASTIC ARTICLES	W 634232	4166.1	W 667462	5180.5	W 727511	5244.7	W 789189	5088.1	ART DIVERS EN MAT DIV 58
89399	OTHR PLASTC ARTICLES NES	W 556996	3848.7	W 587641	4805.2	W 637625	4868.4	W 686995	4709.7	AUT OUV MAT DIV 58
894	TOYS,SPORTING GOODS,ETC	W 116735	1512.2	W 124744	1779.0	W 127747	1750.5	W 131407	1752.0	VOITURES ENFANTS,JOUETS
898	MUSICAL INSTRUMENTS,PTS	W 126249	2375.2	W 129411	2474.9	W 142018	2835.1	W 173423	2313.7	INSTRUMENTS DE MUSIQUE
8983	SOUND RECRDNG TAPE,DISCS	W 119553	2093.7	W 122372	2146.2	W 134790	2498.2	W 165965	2003.6	SUPPORTS SON POUR 763
899	OTHER MANUFACTURED GOODS		1404.7		1639.5		1628.4		1580.0	AUT ART MANUF DIVERS NDA
9	GOODS NOT CLASSD BY KIND		11399.9		19248.2		21807.3		25793.0	ART TRANSACT NON CLASSES
931	*SPECIAL TRANSACTIONS	W 680480	10190.2	W 548019	17705.7	W 532736	20279.4	W 527372	24608.1	TRANS.SPECIALES

1. HISTORICAL SERIES, 1962–1997 SPECIAL TRADE, IMPORTS C.I.F., EXPORTS F.O.B.
SERIES HISTORIQUES, 1962–1997 COMMERCE SPECIAL, IMPORTATIONS C.A.F., EXPORTATIONS F.O.B

YEAR ANNEE	VALUE IN MILLION DRACHMAS VALEUR EN MILLION DRACHMAS MERCHANDISE – MARCHANDISE IMPORTS	EXPORTS	GOLD – OR IMPORTS	EXPORTS	CONVERSION FACTORS U.S. CENTS PER DRACHMA FACTEURS DE CONVERSION CENTS E.U. PAR DRACHMA IMPORTS	EXPORTS	INDEX NUMBERS – INDICES QUANTUM IMPORTS	EXPORTS	UNIT VALUE VALEUR UNITAIRE IMPORTS	EXPORTS
1962	21038.00	7503.00			3.3330	3.3330				
1963	24129.00	8703.00			3.3330	3.3330				
1964	26553.00	9257.00			3.3330	3.3330				
1965	34012.00	9833.00			3.3330	3.3330				
1966	36686.00	12180.00			3.3330	3.3330				
1967	35589.00	14856.00			3.3330	3.3330				
1968	41831.00	14047.00			3.3330	3.3330				
1969	47825.00	16609.00			3.3330	3.3330				
1970	58750.00	19276.00			3.3330	3.3330				
1971	62943.00	19874.00			3.3330	3.3330				
1972	70374.00	26126.00			3.3333	3.3333				
1973	102979.00	42812.00			3.3836	3.4012				
1974	132181.00	60891.00			3.3333	3.3333				
1975	172041.00	74441.00			3.0936	3.0716				
1976	223160.00	93812.00			2.7108	2.7108				
1977	253231.00	101331.00			2.6880	2.6880				
1978	287729.00	123727.00			2.7285	2.7280				
1979	356820.00	144239.00			2.6727	2.6727				
1980	452881.00	221109.00			2.3254	2.3254	45	74	25	25
1981	493765.00	237928.50			1.7817	1.7848	45	62	29	30
1982	665920.00	286281.00			1.5051	1.5010	50	62	36	36
1983	848294.00	392652.00			1.1220	1.1237	55	71	42	43
1984	1083940.00	542665.70			0.8704	0.8865	55	87	52	50
1985	1412797.00	629188.10			0.7177	0.7219	62	86	60	57
1986	1587399.00	790000.10			0.7152	0.7151	58	101	68	62
1987	1773400.00	880999.90			0.7423	0.7414	73	114	66	66
1988	1758000.00	776400.10			0.7010	0.6994	58	77	82	80
1989	2629400.00	1231000.00			0.6142	0.6128	78	106	91	92
1990	3137900.00	1280999.00			0.6304	0.6328	100	100	100	100
1991	3921900.00	1584600.00			0.5503	0.5475	113	115	109	109
1992	4442300.00	1880800.00			0.5230	0.5231	130	147	110	106
1993	5051600.00	1934200.00			0.4356	0.4538	143	143	112	109
1994	5207601.00	2276600.00			0.4127	0.4125	150	149	110	121
1995	5908369.00	2540890.00			0.4317	0.4317				
1996	6839687.00	2859110.00			0.4155	0.4155				
1997	6904574.00	2955778.00			0.3651	0.3652				

2. IMPORTS BY BROAD ECONOMIC CATEGORY AND EXPORTS BY INDUSTRIAL ORIGIN. (PERCENTAGE OF TOTAL VALUE)
IMPORTATIONS PAR CATEGORIES ECONOMIQUES ET EXPORTATIONS PAR BRANCHE D'ACTIVITE.(EN POURCENTAGE DE LA VALEUR TOTALE)

IMPORTS – IMPORTATIONS

	1991	1992	1993	1994	1995	1996	1997
TOTAL IMPORTS–IMPORTATIONS TOTALES	100.	100.	100.	100.	100.	100.	100.
1 FOOD BEV–ALIMENTATION BOISSONS	12.4	12.8	12.2	13.9	13.9	13.1	13.2
11 PRIMARY–PRODUITS DE BASE	6.0	6.6	5.9	6.8	7.0	6.8	7.2
111 FOR INDUSTRY–POUR L'INDUSTRIE	1.7	1.3	1.3	1.5	1.7	1.9	1.9
112 FOR HOUSEHOLDS–POUR LES MENAGES	4.3	5.3	4.6	5.3	5.3	4.9	5.2
12 PROCESSED–PRODUITS ELABORES	6.4	6.2	6.3	7.1	6.9	6.3	6.1
121 FOR INDUSTRY–POUR L'INDUSTRIE	0.3	0.3	0.3	0.4	0.4	0.5	0.4
122 FOR HOUSEHOLDS–POUR LES MENAGES	6.1	5.8	6.0	6.7	6.5	5.8	5.7
2 IND SUPPLIES–APPROV INDUSTRIELS	31.8	28.5	26.8	29.9	31.9	29.1	30.7
21 PRIMARY–PRODUITS DE BASE	2.9	2.1	2.0	2.1	2.3	2.2	2.3
22 PROCESSED–PRODUITS ELABORES	28.9	26.4	24.8	27.9	29.6	26.9	28.3
3 FUELS–COMBUSTIBLES	9.5	9.7	10.6	9.8	7.2	8.7	6.4
31 PRIMARY–PRODUITS DE BASE	6.7	7.6	7.9	7.1	5.4	7.4	4.8
32 PROCESSED–PRODUITS ELABORES	2.8	2.1	2.7	2.7	1.8	1.3	1.6
321 MOTOR SPIRIT–ESSENCE	2.7	1.9	2.6	0.3	0.3	0.1	0.1
322 OTHER–AUTRES	0.2	0.2	0.2	2.3	1.5	1.2	1.5
4 MACHINERY–EQUIPEMENT	14.0	14.8	14.4	14.8	14.5	15.9	16.1
41 CAPITAL EQUIPMENT–MACHINES	12.1	12.8	12.5	12.8	12.6	13.9	13.9
42 PARTS–PIECES ACCESSOIRES	1.9	2.0	1.9	2.0	2.0	2.0	2.2
5 TRANSPORT–TRANSPORT	18.9	19.5	20.2	13.1	12.8	14.3	13.9
51 PASSENGER CARS–AUTOMOBILES	7.1	8.7	7.0	4.6	4.9	5.1	5.1
52 OTHER–AUTRES	7.9	6.6	9.3	4.5	3.7	5.3	5.0
521 INDUSTRIAL–INDUSTRIELS	7.5	6.2	8.9	4.1	3.2	4.9	4.4
522 NON INDUSTRIAL–NON INDUSTRIEL	0.4	0.4	0.4	0.4	0.4	0.4	0.5
53 PARTS–PIECES ACCESSOIRES	3.9	4.2	3.9	3.9	4.2	3.8	3.8
6 CONSUM GOODS–BIENS CONSOMMATION	13.1	14.2	15.3	17.7	19.1	18.8	19.4
61 DURABLE–DURABLES	3.7	3.8	4.2	4.6	4.3	4.5	4.5
62 SEMI DURABLE–SEMI DURABLES	6.4	6.7	6.8	8.0	8.0	8.6	9.1
63 NON DURABLE–NON DURABLES	3.0	3.7	4.3	5.1	6.8	5.8	5.9
7 GOODS NES–BIENS NDA	0.1	0.5	0.4	0.7	0.5	0.1	0.2

EXPORTS – EXPORTATIONS

	1991	1992	1993	1994	1995	1996	1997
TOTAL EXPORTS–EXPORTATIONS TOTALES	100.	100.	100.	100.	100.	100.	100.
1 AGRICULTURE	18.5	16.6	15.6	16.4	15.1	14.9	14.4
2 MINING QUARRY–INDUS EXTRACTIVES	2.6	2.0	2.5	1.8	2.1	2.4	2.2
3 MANUFACTURING–IND MANUFACTUR	78.8	81.4	81.9	81.7	82.8	82.7	83.4
31 FOOD BEV TOBACCO–ALIM BOISS TAB	14.2	18.5	16.8	16.3	18.2	19.1	15.4
32 TEXTILES–INDUSTRIES TEXTILES	28.0	28.8	27.5	23.7	22.9	21.4	20.0
33 WOOD & PRODUCTS–BOIS & PRODUITS	0.5	0.5	0.7	0.6	0.5	0.4	0.3
34 PAPER & PRODUCTS–PAPIER & PRODT	0.9	0.8	0.9	0.9	1.5	1.3	4.9
35 CHEMICALS–INDUSTRIES CHIMIQUES	13.3	9.8	13.3	16.0	12.7	14.3	15.2
36 NON METAL MIN–MIN NON METAL	3.9	4.3	4.3	4.8	4.0	4.2	4.6
37 BASIC METAL–IND METAL BASE	8.9	8.3	6.8	7.5	8.7	7.5	8.2
38 METAL MANUF–MANUF METAL	6.4	6.8	9.0	9.2	11.4	11.8	12.0
39 OTH MANUF IND–AUTRES MANUF	2.8	3.5	2.5	2.7	2.9	2.6	2.7

3. TRADE BY PRINCIPAL COUNTRIES OF CONSIGNMENT AND DESTINATION (VALUE IN MILLION U.S. DOLLARS)
ECHANGES SELON LES PRINCIPAUX PAYS DE CONSIGNATION ET DE DESTINATION (VALEUR EN MILLIONS DE DOLLARS EU)

COUNTRIES–PAYS	SPECIAL IMPORTS C.I.F. IMPORTATIONS SPECIALES C.A.F					COUNTRIES–PAYS	SPECIAL EXPORTS F.O.B. EXPORTATIONS SPECIALES F.O.B.				
	1993	1994	1995	1996	1997		1993	1994	1995	1996	1997
World	22004.5	21491.6	25926.8	28418.9	25208.6	Monde	8783.7	9399.0	10954.6	11879.6	10794.5
Africa	975.4	1059.3	805.7	1262.2	849.9	Afrique	292.0	348.8	282.4	337.9	335.2
Americas	1180.6	1051.7	1408.7	1492.5	1537.2	Amériques	617.8	708.5	570.0	706.8	714.5
– Northern America	884.5	747.8	935.7	1049.0	1073.1	– Amérique du Nord	434.6	509.5	392.1	512.2	548.8
– LAIA	210.6	269.2	390.3	397.1	404.2	– ALAI	86.2	76.7	93.6	98.8	51.7
– CACM	6.5	5.0	3.1	3.7	4.2	– MCAC	7.3	13.3	7.2	3.7	4.6
– Caribbean	55.2	10.8	3.1	7.9	17.9	– Caraïbes	44.3	61.3	35.8	33.5	52.9
– Rest of America	23.8	19.0	76.5	34.9	37.8	– Autre Amérique	45.4	47.7	41.3	58.7	56.5
Asia excl fmr USSR	4218.4	2870.2	3228.4	4288.2	3843.7	Asie anc. URSS exclus	1200.8	1317.6	1407.0	1810.6	1650.8
– Middle East	1401.8	986.4	1111.9	1398.7	1056.7	– Moyen–Orient	836.1	906.6	943.7	1220.8	1157.4
Asia former USSR	1.0	15.8	25.7	62.9	95.7	Asie ancienne URSS	5.9	18.5	42.9	54.5	65.5
Europe excl fmr USSR	15003.4	15740.7	19609.0	20445.5	18133.1	Europe anc. URSS exclus	6294.9	6581.1	8174.7	8348.8	7299.7
– European Union	13846.9	14584.2	18126.2	18853.7	16397.8	– Union Européenne	5175.7	5356.2	6645.1	6544.9	5122.1
– Eastern Europe	471.6	638.1	911.2	883.5	943.3	– Europe de l'Est	687.8	876.6	1083.6	1003.4	986.1
– Rest of Europe	684.8	518.3	571.5	708.2	792.0	– Autre de l'Europe	431.4	348.4	446.0	800.4	1191.5
Europe former USSR	547.8	709.4	804.4	814.5	684.2	Europe ancienne URSS	233.4	333.7	391.0	529.7	584.6
Oceania	42.7	41.0	39.0	50.7	61.6	Océanie	44.5	44.0	53.3	74.5	68.5
Other	35.1	3.6	5.9	2.5	3.2	Autre	94.3	46.8	33.4	16.9	75.8
Italy/Italie	3081.7	3576.0	4849.0	4973.3	4166.4	Germany/Allemagne	2083.0	1983.1	2421.8	2207.2	1650.8
Germany/Allemagne	3722.1	3522.0	4289.7	4147.0	3522.0	Italy/Italie	1161.7	1299.1	1544.0	1597.8	1333.2
France, Monaco	1735.9	1731.9	2106.3	2280.4	2260.5	United Kingdom	500.5	550.7	667.5	706.4	666.7
Netherlands/Pays–Bas	1458.9	1603.2	1796.8	1821.2	1536.0	France, Monaco	546.3	501.7	597.4	598.5	447.1
United Kingdom	1337.5	1335.8	1683.3	1921.6	1598.1	USA/Etats–Unis d'Amer	392.4	455.4	343.7	454.8	487.2
Japan/Japon	1497.4	821.4	682.2	909.8	946.1	Bulgaria/Bulgarie	315.6	413.4	447.0	312.1	316.4
Belgium–Luxembourg	740.4	819.8	938.3	1011.7	905.8	Cyprus/Chypre	274.1	305.7	322.4	417.0	386.2
USA/Etats–Unis d'Amer	819.3	688.0	840.4	940.8	960.7	Russian Federation	193.1	243.3	269.8	360.5	411.8
Spain/Espagne	590.3	675.6	876.4	978.3	879.7	Spain/Espagne	152.3	216.6	378.8	380.5	197.4
Russian Federation	509.3	548.4	703.0	694.2	613.8	Netherlands/Pays–Bas	219.4	233.7	297.2	304.8	250.1
Iran (Islamic Rep of)	737.3	524.7	468.0	500.0	141.6	Turkey/Turquie	154.4	138.2	221.0	354.0	431.8
Egypt/Egypte	438.5	470.7	323.3	617.7	399.9	Albania/Albanie	131.4	213.4	261.0	322.9	288.9
Switzerland,Liechtenst.	419.8	397.3	439.8	474.8	456.8	Switzerland,Liechtenst.	124.9	106.3	146.1	105.0	456.3
Korea, Republic of	445.1	188.3	343.1	635.4	456.7	Belgium–Luxembourg	133.9	152.7	212.3	183.4	139.9
China/Chine	291.0	280.7	337.0	461.7	468.9	Lebanon/Liban	106.3	172.2	183.8	189.7	106.8
Sweden/Suède	278.2	346.5	379.7	415.0	392.3	Romania/Roumanie	92.9	93.4	180.2	173.8	175.4
Bulgaria/Bulgarie	198.0	318.1	483.8	368.3	403.2	TFYR Macedonia	145.3	14.2	36.6	232.1	272.6
Denmark/Danemark	299.4	311.6	374.8	381.6	375.0	Austria/Autriche	126.7	132.5	149.3	151.3	109.8
Saudi Arabia	290.6	190.5	268.9	390.5	497.0	Israel/Israël	93.6	109.4	120.6	128.8	129.0
Austria/Autriche	232.4	223.9	268.5	329.5	256.4	Sweden/Suède	85.4	88.6	127.9	142.3	135.1
Libyan Arab Jamahiriya	350.5	281.7	157.8	206.0	107.6	Saudi Arabia	145.2	142.1	83.8	107.2	80.8
Ireland/Irlande	163.4	183.8	266.0	252.4	197.4	Malta/Malte	93.9	123.7	101.8	110.6	107.9
Turkey/Turquie	138.4	170.8	209.7	231.3	291.0	Ukraine	33.0	81.5	103.2	138.5	130.4
Finland/Finlande	138.1	178.4	207.5	224.2	219.1	Egypt/Egypte	76.9	105.8	81.0	86.9	102.8
Other Asia n.e.s.	148.0	119.8	150.4	184.1	227.6	Japan/Japon	77.9	94.0	84.4	82.0	73.9
Brazil/Brésil	78.9	117.6	193.5	166.3	177.5	Yugoslavia/Yougoslavie		0.0	21.8	168.5	201.7
Romania/Roumanie	65.6	93.3	134.2	143.8	196.3	Denmark/Danemark	65.9	77.5	86.0	86.1	66.7
Israel/Israël	82.0	86.9	129.1	111.9	114.6	Poland/Pologne	57.2	69.8	85.3	75.7	85.8
Czech Republic	76.3	74.7	92.1	104.5	97.9	Gibraltar	0.3	52.2	47.0	123.0	75.1
Portugal	68.7	75.7	90.0	117.4	89.3	Finland/Finlande	46.1	53.3	62.8	71.1	61.6
Canada	61.9	58.8	95.3	107.9	112.4	Portugal	36.3	36.7	64.9	82.3	39.0
Ukraine	34.0	151.4	88.1	104.8	57.5	Australia/Australie	40.1	39.3	48.5	68.1	60.6
Indonesia/Indonésie	47.9	64.3	83.6	115.8	113.5	Panama	45.1	47.5	40.9	58.3	53.9
India/Inde	50.0	55.8	87.4	114.2	108.7	Libyan Arab Jamahiriya	64.9	49.8	35.2	55.9	39.7
Argentina/Argentine	65.9	72.8	81.0	104.5	80.6	Tunisia/Tunisie	33.6	48.6	51.1	63.3	41.1
Cyprus/Chypre	171.2	51.4	75.1	49.9	54.8	Canada	41.8	44.4	42.8	51.7	56.2
Norway,Svalbard and JM	78.1	54.8	57.3	62.7	97.1	Brazil/Brésil	47.8	32.2	62.0	70.8	23.8
Thailand/Thaïlande	45.7	51.7	65.7	78.1	106.0	Hungary/Hongrie	37.9	40.8	47.0	54.4	56.4
Poland/Pologne	46.5	47.8	66.3	99.9	86.5	Czech Republic	34.4	36.2	53.3	47.2	49.6
Hungary/Hongrie	47.7	47.5	67.0	95.8	88.9	United Arab Emirates	39.7	50.4	40.7	44.2	43.7

(VALUE AS PERCENTAGE OF WORLD TOTAL)(VALEURS EN POURCENTAGE DU TOTAL MONDIAL)

	1988	1989	1990	1991	1992	1993	1994	1995	1996	1997		1988	1989	1990	1991	1992	1993	1994	1995	1996	1997
Africa	4.0	3.9	3.6	4.5	4.8	4.4	4.9	3.1	4.4	3.4	Afrique	4.2	3.7	3.8	3.7	3.6	3.3	3.7	2.6	2.8	3.1
Americas	6.5	5.8	5.8	6.8	5.2	5.4	4.9	5.4	5.3	6.1	Amériques	7.7	7.3	7.2	7.5	5.5	7.0	7.5	5.2	5.9	6.6
– Northern America	4.3	3.9	4.0	4.6	3.8	4.0	3.5	3.6	3.7	4.3	– Amérique du Nord	6.8	6.4	6.2	6.2	4.4	4.9	5.4	3.6	4.3	5.1
– LAIA	1.8	1.6	1.6	1.6	1.0	1.0	1.3	1.5	1.4	1.6	– ALAI	0.4	0.1	0.1	0.2	0.5	1.0	0.8	0.9	0.8	0.5
– CACM	0.0	0.0	0.0	0.0	0.1	0.0	0.0	0.0	0.0	0.0	– MCAC	0.0	0.1	0.1	0.1	0.1	0.1	0.1	0.1	0.0	0.0
– Caribbean	0.1	0.1	0.0	0.2	0.1	0.3	0.1	0.0	0.0	0.1	– Caraïbes	0.2	0.3	0.3	0.3	0.2	0.5	0.7	0.3	0.3	0.5
– Rest of America	0.3	0.2	0.0	0.3	0.1	0.1	0.1	0.3	0.1	0.1	– Autre Amérique	0.3	0.4	0.5	0.6	0.3	0.5	0.5	0.4	0.5	0.5
Asia excl fmr USSR	13.7	15.5	14.6	16.8	16.6	19.2	13.4	12.5	15.1	15.2	Asie anc. URSS exclus	11.8	10.2	10.4	11.1	11.2	13.7	14.0	12.8	15.2	15.3
– Middle East	2.5	4.7	4.9	5.6	5.4	6.4	4.6	4.3	4.9	4.2	– Moyen–Orient	8.2	6.8	7.4	8.1	8.2	9.5	9.6	8.6	10.3	10.7
Asia former USSR					0.0	0.0	0.1	0.1	0.2	0.4	Asie ancienne URSS					0.0	0.1	0.2	0.4	0.5	0.6
Europe excl fmr USSR	73.1	73.0	73.9	69.8	71.0	68.2	73.2	75.6	71.9	71.9	Europe anc. URSS exclus	73.8	75.8	75.3	75.4	77.1	71.7	70.0	74.6	70.3	67.6
– European Union	66.2	66.4	67.7	63.9	66.4	62.9	67.9	69.9	66.3	65.0	– Union Européenne	67.9	68.8	67.7	67.2	68.7	58.9	57.0	60.7	55.1	47.5
– Eastern Europe	3.2	2.8	2.4	2.7	2.2	2.1	3.0	3.5	3.1	3.7	– Europe de l'Est	2.7	3.4	3.1	3.9	4.9	7.8	9.3	9.9	8.4	9.1
– Rest of Europe	3.7	3.7	3.8	3.2	2.5	3.1	2.4	2.2	2.5	3.1	– Autre de l'Europe	3.2	3.6	4.6	4.3	3.4	4.9	3.7	4.1	6.7	11.0
Europe former USSR	2.1	1.5	1.8	1.9	1.9	2.5	3.3	3.1	2.9	2.7	Europe ancienne URSS	1.6	1.8	1.6	1.0	1.3	2.7	3.6	3.6	4.5	5.4
Oceania	0.6	0.4	0.3	0.2	0.2	0.2	0.2	0.2	0.2	0.2	Océanie	0.4	0.6	0.9	0.5	0.5	0.5	0.5	0.5	0.6	0.6
Other	0.1	0.1	0.1	0.0	0.3	0.2	0.0	0.0	0.0	0.0	Autre	0.5	0.7	0.9	0.8	0.8	1.1	0.5	0.3	0.1	0.7
Italy/Italie	14.5	14.9	15.4	14.2	14.3	14.0	16.6	18.7	17.5	16.5	Germany/Allemagne				23.9	23.7	23.7	21.1	22.1	18.6	15.3
Germany/Allemagne				19.4	20.4	16.9	16.4	16.5	14.6	14.0	Italy/Italie	14.2	20.3	17.1	16.7	18.4	13.2	13.8	14.1	13.5	12.4
France, Monaco	8.0	6.9	8.1	7.8	7.9	7.9	8.1	8.1	8.0	9.0	United Kingdom	7.7	7.4	7.3	6.8	7.0	5.7	5.9	6.1	5.9	6.2
Netherlands/Pays–Bas	6.9	6.9	6.7	6.0	6.9	6.6	7.5	6.9	6.4	6.1	France, Monaco	8.6	8.8	9.6	7.5	7.2	6.2	5.3	5.5	5.0	4.1
United Kingdom	5.0	5.8	5.3	5.4	5.5	6.1	6.2	6.5	6.8	6.3	USA/Etats–Unis d'Amer	6.3	5.7	5.6	5.7	3.9	4.5	4.8	3.1	3.8	4.5
Japan/Japon	5.7	6.6	5.9	6.6	6.4	6.8	3.8	2.6	3.2	3.8	Bulgaria/Bulgarie	0.6	0.9	0.7	1.0	1.7	3.6	4.4	4.1	2.6	2.9
Belgium–Luxembourg	3.7	3.9	3.7	3.4	3.5	3.4	3.8	3.6	3.6	3.6	Cyprus/Chypre	2.6	2.3	2.5	2.9	3.3	3.1	3.3	2.9	3.5	3.6
USA/Etats–Unis d'Amer	3.8	3.4	3.7	4.3	3.6	3.7	3.2	3.2	3.3	3.8	Russian Federation					1.1	2.2	2.6	2.5	3.0	3.8
Spain/Espagne	2.1	1.9	2.0	2.2	2.2	2.7	3.1	3.4	3.4	3.5	Spain/Espagne	1.4	1.3	1.5	1.7	2.5	1.7	2.3	3.5	3.2	1.8
Russian Federation					1.7	2.3	2.6	2.7	2.4	2.4	Netherlands/Pays–Bas	3.4	3.2	3.5	3.4	2.8	2.5	2.5	2.7	2.6	2.3

4. Special Imports C.I.F. by Commodities according to the S.I.T.C. (Rev. 2) in million U.S. Dollars
Importations Spéciales C.A.F. par Produits d'après la C.T.C.I. (Rév. 2) en millions de Dollars E.U.

SITC CTCI	COMMODITY	1994		1995		1996		1997		PRODUIT
		QUANTITY QUANTITE	VALUE VALEUR	QUANTITY QUANTITE	VALUE VALEUR	QUANTITY QUANTITE	VALUE VALEUR	QUANTITY QUANTITE	VALUE VALEUR	
	ALL COMMODITIES		21491.6		25926.8		28419.0		25208.6	TOUS PRODUITS
0	FOOD AND LIVE ANIMALS		2758.3		3399.0		3410.1		3087.9	ALIMENTS,ANIMAUX VIVANTS
01	MEAT AND PREPARATIONS		824.2		946.5		856.5		808.1	VIANDES ET PREPARATIONS
011	MEAT FRESH,CHILLD,FROZEN	W 481478	780.7	W 308265	896.5	W 286372	815.8	W 346847	770.4	VIANDES FRAICHES,REF,CONGE
0111	BOVINE MEAT FRESH,FROZEN	W 336306	474.6	W 145377	524.8	W 110202	390.4	W 122801	392.7	VIANDES BOVIN FRAI,REF
01111	BOVINE MEAT WITH BONE IN	W 93476	344.0	W 108818	390.6	W 85907	312.6	W 94349	302.7	VIANDES BOVIN NON DESOSS
01112	BOVINE MEAT BONELESS	W 242830	130.6	W 36559	134.3	W 24295	77.9	W 28452	90.0	VIANDES BOVIN DESOSSEES
0113	PIG MEAT FRESH,CHLD,FRZN	W 85939	180.0	W 107827	250.1	W 109731	289.9	W 164208	255.6	VIANDE DE PORC
02	DAIRY PRODCTS,BIRDS'EGGS		593.2		615.9		578.9		507.3	PRODUITS LAITIERS,OEUFS
022	MILK AND CREAM	W 166580	277.9	W 158050	286.4	W 161217	273.2	W 177491	231.1	LAIT ET CREME
0224	MILK,CREAM PRESERVED ETC	W 132113	226.7	W 129080	238.5	W 121880	217.7	W 122042	174.6	LAIT,CREME CONS,CONC
02249	MILK(EX DRY) PRSVD,SWEET	W 115148	186.5	W 112835	193.7	W 103572	176.0	W 104982	137.1	LAIT CONS,CONC SUCRE
024	CHEESE AND CURD	W 64676	278.3	W 62011	286.0	W 139414	265.6	W 101731	241.7	FROMAGE ET CAILLEBOTTE
03	FISH AND PREPARATIONS		153.7		202.1		271.6		272.2	POISSONS ET PREPARATIONS
034	FISH,FRESH,CHILLED,FROZN	W 23873	50.5	W 30963	76.1	W 41812	113.1	W 42802	111.9	POISSON FRAIS, REFRIG,CONG
036	SHELL FISH FRESH,FROZEN	W 13395	37.2	W 16937	60.2	W 23318	83.2	W 26664	87.5	CRUSTACES,MOLLUSQUES
04	CEREALS AND PREPARATIONS		309.7		485.8		461.6		411.1	CEREALES ET PRODUITS
041	WHEAT ETC UNMILLED	W 382630	79.1	W 744296	173.4	W 658859	148.6	W 752493	139.9	FROMENT,EPEAUTRE
0412	OTHER WHEAT ETC UNMILLED	W 381696	78.6	W 647881	145.9	W 639863	141.5	W 716585	132.0	AUTRE FROMENT NON MOULU
044	MAIZE UNMILLED	W 153244	44.4	W 304658	90.7	W 208729	63.1	W 345005	71.1	MAIS NON MOULU
048	CEREAL ETC PREPARATIONS	W 124169	151.5	W 100129	178.1	W 154816	181.0	W 132551	156.2	PREPTNS A BASE CEREALES
05	VEGETABLES AND FRUIT		314.0		389.2		430.4		371.4	LEGUMES ET FRUITS
054	VEG ETC FRSH,SMPLY PRSVD	W 248035	123.8	W 228202	154.8	W 254163	151.5	W 257892	134.3	LEGUMES FRAIS,CONG,SECS
057	FRUIT,NUTS,FRESH,DRIED	W 116085	118.7	W 130105	149.7	W 161301	184.9	W 145379	164.8	FRUITS FRAIS OU SECS
06	SUGAR AND PREPS,HONEY		38.5		115.9		77.2		71.1	SUCRES ET PRODUITS
061	SUGAR AND HONEY	W 16781	12.2	W 94403	85.3	W 112264	46.2	W 58557	44.5	SUCRES ET MIEL
07	COFFEE,TEA,COCOA,SPICES		164.0		233.9		271.5		251.4	CAFE,THE,CACAO,EPICES
071	COFFEE AND SUBSTITUTES	W 18259	93.6	W 20607	131.9	W 36059	160.7	W 43684	147.5	CAFE ET SUCCEDANES
0711	COFFEE GREEN,ROASTED,SUB	W 11091	34.7	W 14187	55.0	W 27798	82.6	W 36816	90.3	CAFE TORREFIE OU DECAFEINE
081	*FEEDING STUFF FOR ANIML	W 402324	161.8	W 378050	171.0	W 368838	183.4	W 349750	172.6	NOURRITURE POUR ANIMAUX
0819	FOOD WASTE AND FEED NES	W 96986	83.8	W 105216	96.3	W 100413	95.1	W 109113	92.5	DECHETS,ALIMENTS NDA
08199	FODDER NES,INCL SWEETNED	W 88247	82.6	W 98269	95.2	W 92111	93.8	W 106470	92.1	PREPARATIONS FOURRAGERES
09	MISC EDIBLE PRODUCTS		144.9		180.6		199.5		160.8	PREP ALIMENTAIRES DIVERSES
098	EDIBLE PRODCTS,PREPS NES	W 38421	133.1	W 42213	164.7	W 56016	184.6	W 71515	143.2	PREP ALIMENTAIRES NDA
09809	MISC FOOD PREPRTIONS NES	W 22498	112.6	W 25242	139.4	W 27496	152.9	W 27192	118.9	PREP ALIMENTAIRES NDA
1	BEVERAGES AND TOBACCO		452.2		532.6		578.9		502.7	BOISSONS ET TABACS
11	BEVERAGES		250.1		285.6		299.3		273.9	BOISSONS
112	ALCOHOLIC BEVERAGES	W 68077	228.0	W 78359	264.6	W 83132	274.0	W 95846	249.3	BOISSONS ALCOOLIQUES
1124	DISTILLED ALCOHOLIC BEVS	W 38548	192.1	W 43758	221.3	W 46344	227.1	W 42593	194.8	ALCOOLS,EAUX–DE–VIE
11241	WHISKY	W 25669	142.3	W 29674	162.3	W 31235	163.3	W 29220	140.1	WHISKY
12	TOBACCO AND MANUFACTURES		202.1		247.0		279.6		228.9	TABACS BRUTS FABRIQUES
121	TOBACCO UNMNFCTRD,REFUSE	W 18016	77.1	W 19846	98.1	W 24143	128.2	W 14891	98.8	TABACS BRUTS,DECHETS
1212	TOBACCO STRIPPED OR PART	W 9406	49.4	W 8741	66.4	W 9372	89.7	W 9171	74.5	TABACS PART ECOTES
122	TOBACCO,MANUFACTURED	W 11905	125.1	W 13495	148.9	W 30402	151.4	W 22252	130.1	TABACS FABRIQUES
1222	CIGARETTES	W 10967	114.0	W 11747	132.8	W 12343	135.3	W 19242	114.3	CIGARETTES
2	CRUDE MATERLS,EXCL FUELS		719.0		903.2		934.2		886.9	MAT BRUTES NON COMESTIBLES
22	OIL SEEDS,OLEAGINOUS FRT		121.2		116.5		171.2		154.9	GRAINES,FRUITS OLEAGINEUX
222	SEEDS FOR'SOFT'FIXED OIL	W 370039	119.7	W 289530	115.0	W 385874	168.8	W 348559	153.6	GRAINES HUILES FIXES
2222	SOYA BEANS	W 275471	76.3	W 219483	59.8	W 234404	78.7	W 249740	89.7	FEVES DE SOJA
24	CORK AND WOOD		199.8		218.6		218.6		228.0	LIEGE ET BOIS
248	WOOD SHAPED,SLEEPERS	W 308409	145.8	W 335883	171.1	W 369491	162.5	W 438108	175.7	BOIS SIMPLEMENT TRAVAILLES
2482	LUMBER SHAPED CONIFER	W 244160	109.4	W 269507	129.2	W 286639	117.6	W 340654	128.5	CONIFERES SCIES,RABOTES
24821	LUMBER SAWN ETC CONIFER	W 233272	102.5	W 261654	122.3	W 277242	110.5	W 328628	121.3	CONIFERES SCIES LONGITUD
251	*PULP AND WASTE PAPER	W 108862	58.9	W 155895	127.1	W 136002	79.6	W 137003	69.8	PATES A PAPIER,DECHETS
2517	SODA,SULPHATE WOOD PULP	W 79967	44.6	W 109430	97.3	W 102646	62.9	W 109292	57.0	PATES CHIMIQUES AU SULFATE
25172	— BLEACHED,NONDISSOLVNG	W 79069	44.1	W 108974	97.0	W 101950	62.6	W 109002	56.9	PATES BLANCHIES
26	TEXTILE FIBRES AND WASTE		76.0		89.4		79.3		70.1	FIBRES TEXTILES
27	CRUDE FERTLZR,MINRLS NES		54.1		76.3		93.4		92.6	ENGRAIS MINERAUX BRUTS
28	METALLIFEROUS ORES,SCRAP		51.2		80.7		85.5		96.4	MINERAIS METAL,DECHETS
29	CRUDE ANIMAL,VEG MAT NES		76.7		91.0		98.3		84.7	MATIERES BRUTES ANIM,VEGET
292	CRUDE VEG MATERIALS NES	W 23073	66.3	W 26533	80.4	W 28780	86.5	W 24406	74.1	MAT BRUTES VEGETALES NDA
3	MINERAL FUELS ETC		2115.9		1890.8		2500.2		1642.5	COMBUSTIBLES MINERAUX LUB
32	COAL,COKE AND BRIQUETTES		61.0		69.6		80.5		76.3	HOUILLES,COKES,BRIQUETTES
33	PETROLEUM AND PRODUCTS		2035.7		1797.0		2378.7		1498.8	PETROLE ET DERIVES
333	CRUDE PETROLEUM	MW 13375	1468.9	MW 11356	1329.9	MW 17850	2014.9	MW 10753	1124.9	HUILES BRUTES DE PETROLE
334	PETROLEUM PRODUCTS,REFIN	W 4194946	549.5	W 2831412	438.8	W 1489688	330.8	W 1936341	334.1	PRODUITS RAFFINES
3341	GASOLINE,OTH LIGHT OILS	W 399745	67.7	W 420255	71.6	W 92257	19.8	W 85019	14.2	ESSENCES POUR MOTEURS
3343	GAS OILS	W 1147616	174.0	W 684197	107.8			W 6492	1.2	GAS OILS
3344	FUEL OILS,NES	W 2440152	214.4	W 1536432	161.7	W 1208183	204.8	W 1661632	227.8	FUEL OILS
3345	LUBS,PETROLEUM OILS NES	W 158097	84.7	W 147587	92.1	W 163949	99.1	W 181142	89.8	HUILES LUBRIFIANTES
33451	LUBS(HIGH PETR CONT) ETC	W 151793	70.4	W 141770	77.4	W 154212	83.8	W 174091	75.5	HUILES LUBRIF,H LOURDES
4	ANIMAL,VEGETABLE OIL,FAT		87.8		89.6		108.3		97.3	HUILES,GRAISSES ANIM,VEG
42	FIXED VEGETABLE OIL,FAT		74.6		73.5		89.4		82.6	HUILES VEGETALES FIXES
5	CHEMCLS,RELATED PROD NES		2667.9		3344.6		3496.5		3245.4	PRODUITS CHIMIQUES
51	ORGANIC CHEMICALS		385.9		471.1		504.4		385.0	PROD CHIMIQ ORGANIQUES
511	HYDROCARBONS NES,DERIVS	W 133096	74.5	W 104125	77.3	W 123865	70.6	W 139840	76.9	HYDROCARBURES NDA
513	CARBOXYLIC ACIDS ETC	W 47916	55.8	W 51044	80.6	W 50724	65.8	W 55177	57.8	ACIDES CARBOXYLIQUES
514	NITROGEN–FNCTN COMPOUNDS	W 13163	100.0	W 13013	113.7	W 13020	128.9	W 13122	92.3	COMPOSES FONCT AZOTEES
515	ORG–INORG COMPOUNDS ETC	W 4113	93.8	W 4678	115.0	W 4585	136.8	W 8844	90.4	COMPOSES ORGANO–MINERAUX
5156	HETEROCYCLIC CMPDS ETC	W 1022	65.0	W 1339	80.8	W 961	86.2	W 880	63.5	COMPOSES HETEROCYCLIQUES
52	INORGANIC CHEMICALS		142.7		187.4		186.1		144.4	PROD CHIM INORGANIQUES
522	INORG ELEMNTS,OXIDES,ETC	W 379858	72.7	W 417707	101.6	W 499224	101.8	W 438076	80.8	ELEMENTS INORGANIQUES
5225	INORGANIC BASES ETC NES	W 305486	52.6	W 353172	78.0	W 368716	76.5	W 326345	60.3	AUTRES BASES OXYDES METAL
523	OTHR INORG CHEMICALS ETC	W 157328	63.5	W 178772	78.5	W 193519	76.5	W 158615	58.1	AUT PRODUITS CHIMIQUES INORG
53	DYES,TANNING,COLOUR PROD		202.8		239.9		237.7		246.5	PROD TEINTURE,COLORANTS
533	PIGMENTS,PAINTS,ETC	W 69913	153.8	W 76299	183.1	W 84629	174.0	W 194541	188.6	PIGMENTS,PEINTURES,VERNIS
5334	VARNISHES,DISTEMPERS ETC	W 21249	65.4	W 25778	78.6	W 23174	80.3	W 137757	98.7	PEINTURES A L'EAU
53342	OTH PAINTS,VARNISHES ETC	W 16566	53.5	W 19602	63.1	W 16812	62.8	W 130563	81.9	AUTRES PEINTURES,VERNIS
541	*MEDICINAL,PHARM PRODUCT	MK 15697	664.7	MK 10869	824.0	MK 17804	937.2	MK 22956	957.6	PROD MEDICINAUX PHARMACEUT
5417	MEDICAMENTS	MK 12328	505.6	K 7626087	646.6	MK 11982	759.5	MK 15581	796.0	MEDICAMENTS
54171	— CONTAINNG ANTIBIOTICS	K 4791042	74.7	K 1129871	78.7	K 1329786	108.8	K 932352	94.5	MED CONTN ANTIBIOTIQUES
54179	— CONTNG OTH SUBSTANCES	K 7117435	377.3	K 5930482	500.4	MK 10016	572.3	MK 14210	623.9	MED CONT AUT SUBSTANCES
55	PERFUME,CLEANING ETC PRD		308.2		359.0		381.5		387.4	PROD POUR PARFUM,TOILETTE
553	PERFUMERY,COSMETICS,ETC	W 20361	177.9	W 25672	205.7	W 363173	219.9	W 31399	222.6	PRODUITS DE PARFUMERIE
554	SOAP,CLEANSING ETC PREPS	W 73365	98.6	W 81619	114.7	W 134998	120.6	W 259647	119.1	SAVONS,PRODUITS DETERSIFS
5542	WASHING PREPARATIONS ETC	W 63952	81.6	W 68377	92.6	W 121514	96.9	W 246909	96.1	PROD ORG TENSIO–ACT NDA
562	*FERTILIZERS,MANUFACTURE	W 719509	103.0	W 722943	122.9	W 798171	141.9	W 747088	124.4	ENGRAIS MANUFACTURES
58	PLASTIC MATERIALS ETC		525.9		730.0		692.2		631.0	MAT PLAST ARTIFICIELLES
582	PROD OF CONDENSATION ETC	W 81501	98.3	W 106516	143.7	W 70023	130.9	W 71808	111.7	PROD CONDENS,POLYCOND
5823	ALKYDS,OTHER POLYESTERS	W 41442	46.0	W 68884	78.0	W 33790	64.5	W 32528	51.7	ALKYDES ET AUT POLYESTERS
583	POLYMERIZATION ETC PRODS	W 399628	414.4	W 427127	569.2	W 457848	547.1	W 489307	506.5	PROD POLYMERISATION

4. Special Imports C.I.F. by Commodities according to the S.I.T.C. (Rev. 2) in million U.S. Dollars
Importations Spéciales C.A.F. par Produits d'après la C.T.C.I. (Rév. 2) en millions de Dollars E.U.

SITC CTCI	COMMODITY	1994 QUANTITY QUANTITE	1994 VALUE VALEUR	1995 QUANTITY QUANTITE	1995 VALUE VALEUR	1996 QUANTITY QUANTITE	1996 VALUE VALEUR	1997 QUANTITY QUANTITE	1997 VALUE VALEUR	PRODUIT
5831	POLYETHYLENE	W 196181	152.4	W 189584	217.8	W 219968	211.7	W 218094	200.8	POLYETHYLENE
58311	— IN PRIMARY FORMS	W 181332	136.1	W 174041	194.6	W 201817	188.2	W 202806	181.7	POLYETHYLENE PRIMAIRES
5832	POLYPROPYLENE	W 56842	54.3	W 89977	78.0	W 60854	71.2	W 73317	70.4	POLYPROPYLENE
5834	POLYVINYL CHLORIDE	W 63933	69.8	W 64907	97.3	W 65578	79.3	W 73724	80.2	CHLORURE DE POLYVINYLE
5839	OTH POLYMRZTION ETC PROD	W 37983	77.7	W 38984	105.0	W 45103	109.4	W 50186	85.8	AUT PROD POLYMER COPOLYM
59	CHEMICAL MATERIALS NES		329.8		402.6		408.8		360.8	MAT PROD CHIMIQUES NDA
591	PESTICIDES,DISINFECTANTS	W 17562	113.4	W 26553	137.7	W 23390	153.9	W 65625	117.4	DESINF,INSECT,FONG,HERB
598	MISCEL CHEM PRODUCTS NES	W 80894	170.0	W 96301	210.9	W 132422	201.8	W 101566	195.9	PROD DIV INDUST CHIM NDA
5989	CHEM PRODUCTS,PREPS NES	W 60239	132.2	W 70160	163.9	W 96998	153.5	W 70259	154.0	PROD PREP CHIMIQUES NDA
59899	OTH CHEM PRODS,PREPS,NES	W 43433	105.0	W 50064	129.1	W 79812	122.9	W 51768	124.8	AUT PRODUITS CHIMIQUES NDA
6	BASIC MANUFACTURES		3929.1		5093.3		5213.2		4934.0	ART MANUFACTURES
61	LEATHER,DRESSED FUR,ETC		215.7		208.7		278.2		256.2	CUIRS,PELLETERIES
613	FUR SKINS TANNED,DRESSED	W 1886	153.0	W 1778	136.7	W 2058	207.4	W 2205	194.0	PELLETERIES
62	RUBBER MANUFACTURES NES		175.9		240.9		267.5		226.3	CAOUTCHOUC MANUFACTURE
625	RUBBER TYRES, TUBES ETC	W 33003	134.6	W 40089	184.9	W 45806	206.0	W 44640	175.4	PNEUS CAOUTCHOUC VULCANISE
6251	TYRES NEW FOR MOTOR CARS	W 12149	62.3	W 15029	89.0	W 15893	95.5	W 14969	80.8	PNEUS POUR VOITURES
63	WOOD,CORK MANUFACTRS NES		75.2		93.2		103.2		91.7	OUVRAGES LIEGE ET BOIS
64	PAPER,PAPERBOARD AND MFR		579.3		859.1		784.9		700.2	PAPIERS,CARTONS & OUVRAGES
641	PAPER AND PAPERBOARD	W 566261	425.6	W 666892	673.8	W 808845	593.1	W 709169	516.4	PAPIERS ET CARTONS
6411	NEWSPRINT	W 101363	54.9	W 90069	78.0	W 114262	90.9	W 96492	53.5	PAPIER JOURNAL
6412	PRINTG,WRITING PAPER NES	W 127349	115.4	W 128973	178.5	W 223541	147.7	W 151001	137.7	PAPIERS POUR L'IMPRESSION
64122	— COATED,IMPREGNATD ETC	W 111891	101.3	W 112698	156.0	W 207000	128.7	W 129564	116.9	PAPIERS IMPRESSION COUCHES
6415	PAPER,PAPERBRD,BULK,NES	W 91976	65.1	W 125900	117.7	W 185492	102.5	W 142711	100.7	PAPIERS,CARTONS ROULEAUX
6418	COATED ETC PAPER NES BLK	W 52516	89.7	W 58736	128.5	W 58705	121.5	W 71350	103.7	PAP,CARTONS COUCHES,ENDUITS
642	PAPER,ETC,PRECUT,ARTS OF	W 65763	153.8	W 68776	185.3	W 69907	191.8	W 153047	183.8	PAP,CARTONS DECOUPES
6428	PAPER ETC ARTICLES NES	W 30115	74.0	W 32144	90.7	W 33591	92.4	W 50328	92.9	OUVRAGES EN PATE A PAPIER
65	TEXTILE YARN,FABRICS,ETC		1052.0		1168.5		1181.7		1094.9	FILS,TISSUS,ARTICLES TEXTILE
651	TEXTILE YARN	W 47049	212.2	W 44325	243.5	W 62927	249.3	W 80967	269.9	FILS TEXTILES
6513	COTTON YARN	W 13761	57.0	W 10579	54.3	W 14417	63.8	W 18996	78.4	FILS DE COTON
6514	SYN FIB YRN,BULK,MONOFIL	W 9941	57.4	W 11310	70.6	W 16897	68.6	W 15271	77.9	FILS CONT 85% FIB TEXT SYNTH
652	COTTON FABRICS,WOVEN	W 12427	118.9	W 11867	131.1	W 13794	131.9	W 15367	115.5	TISSUS DE COTON
6522	WOVEN COTTON BLEACHD,ETC	W 10854	106.7	W 10675	120.7	W 12019	118.4	W 13611	104.4	TISSUS COTON BLANCHIS ETC
65224	BLCHED COTTON FABRIC NES	W 9180	82.3	W 8631	89.8	W 9968	88.8	W 11176	76.8	AUT TIS PLUS 85% COT BLANCHI
653	WOVN MAN–MADE FIB FABRIC	W 22328	308.7	W 23632	336.3	W 29402	308.7	W 26079	253.8	TISSUS FIBRES SYNTH,ARTIF
6531	CONT SYNT WEAVES NONPILE	W 8011	103.7	W 8819	121.7	W 11423	118.8	W 10525	99.1	TISSUS FIBRES SYNTH CONTINUE
65315	CONT SYN TXTL FABRIC NES	W 6754	92.4	W 7135	104.7	W 9641	102.5	W 8038	82.4	TIS PLUS 85% TEXT SYNT CONT
654	OTH WOVEN TEXTILE FABRIC	W 4166	81.6	W 3975	72.6	W 3959	69.0	W 4777	52.3	TISSUS AUT COTON SYNT,ARTIF
655	KNITTED,ETC FABRICS	W 7324	60.0	W 5467	80.0	W 8478	85.8	W 10144	104.5	ETOF BONNETERIE PIECES ETC
6552	OTHER KNIT ETC FAB NONEL	W 7324	60.0	W 5467	80.0	W 8478	85.8	W 10144	104.5	ETOF BON NON ELAS NON SYNT
657	SPECIAL TXTL FABRC,PRODS	W 14669	95.4	W 14637	96.8	W 20224	102.1	W 16982	89.3	TISSUS SPECIAUX
658	TEXTILE ARTICLES NES	W 14348	74.8	W 12015	86.3	W 16350	109.1	W 13627	89.1	ART FACONNES MAT TEXTILES
659	FLOOR COVERINGS,ETC	W 16477	71.7	W 18736	89.5	W 20451	95.1	W 19937	85.7	COUVRE–PARQUETS,TAPIS ETC
66	NONMETAL MINERAL MFS NES		396.3		477.4		546.3		465.9	ART MIN NON METALLIQUES
662	CLAY,REFRACTORY BLDG PRD	W 375056	150.8	W 424113	177.4	W 582661	186.0	W 546380	164.5	MAT CONST REFRACTAIRES
6624	BRICKS ETC NONREFRACTORY	W 351576	136.1	W 399016	160.7	W 556411	166.9	W 516986	146.6	BRIQUES ETC CERAM NON REFR
66245	GLAZED CERAMIC SETTS ETC	W 341557	132.5	W 390495	156.5	W 539394	161.6	W 483755	140.5	AUT CARREAUX CERAMIQUE
664	GLASS	W 105559	60.8	W 124282	81.1	W 128775	83.9	W 131226	80.2	VERRE
665	GLASSWARE	W 86691	89.0	W 105409	101.6	W 196892	132.9	W 153451	102.4	OUVRAGES EN VERRE
67	IRON AND STEEL		601.9		894.7		939.3		902.7	FER ET ACIER
672	IRON,STEEL PRIMARY FORMS	W 667639	165.4	W 847130	267.3	W 958432	283.1	W 1009398	296.5	LINGOTS FER,ACIER
6725	IRN,STL BLOOMS,SLABS,ETC	W 549834	127.9	W 626425	178.9	W 455448	110.0	W 464786	115.4	BLOOMS,BILLETTES FER ACIER
67251	IRN,SMPLE STL BLOOMS,ETC	W 549421	127.6	W 624496	178.1	W 454725	109.1	W 463563	114.7	BLOOMS ETC NON ACIER FIN
6727	IRN,STL COIL FR REROLLNG	W 113210	36.8	W 220120	88.3	W 502843	173.0	W 544550	181.1	EBAUCHES POUR TOLES FER
67271	IRON,SIMPLE STEEL COILS	W 112581	36.2	W 219730	87.6	W 502342	172.6	W 544286	180.8	EBAUCHES NON EN ACIER
673	IRON,STEEL SHAPES ETC	W 435554	150.5	W 572106	225.4	W 605857	208.3	W 692401	222.3	BARRES,PROFIL FER,ACIER
6732	IRON,STEEL BARS ETC	W 289585	97.4	W 384343	148.3	W 408178	136.6	W 442879	140.1	BARRES FER,ACIER
67326	IRN,OTH STL BARS HOTROLD	W 279101	86.4	W 362281	128.3	W 385420	116.5	W 425914	125.3	BARRES PLEINES FER,ACIER
674	IRN,STL UNIV,PLATE,SHEET	W 298349	188.0	W 348209	267.4		296.2		264.1	LARGES PLATS,TOLES
6746	IRN,STL THIN PLATE,ROLLD	W 67020	49.2	W 86049	83.7	W 92140	67.1	W 121181	67.6	TOLES LAM MOINS 3MM
6749	OTH IRN,STL PLATES,SHEET	W 95399	59.2	W 100766	80.6	W 108126	84.5	W 146924	88.8	AUTRES TOLES FER,ACIER
67491	— OF IRON OR SIMPLE STL	W 94340	54.7	W 99108	74.2	W 105784	75.9	W 144208	81.9	AUT TOLES AUTRES ACIER FIN
678	IRON,STL TUBES,PIPES,ETC	W 56881	56.7	W 54861	66.1	W 143342	93.1	W 138077	74.9	TUBES,TUYAUX EN FONTE,FER
68	NON–FERROUS METALS		388.0		613.5		528.3		641.2	METAUX NON FERREUX
682	COPPER EXC CEMENT COPPER	W 79093	193.6	W 103371	315.9	W 114914	277.3	W 116601	296.7	CUIVRE
6821	COPPER NES,ALLOYS,UNWRT	W 62332	141.2	W 79959	237.5	W 90187	213.1	W 97752	240.0	CUIVRE BRUT
68212	COPPER REFINED,UNWROUGHT	W 62193	140.8	W 79677	236.6	W 90055	212.7	W 97566	239.4	CUIVRE AFFINE BRUT
6822	COPPER,ALLOYS WORKED	W 16761	52.4	W 23412	78.5	W 24727	64.2	W 18849	56.8	CUIVRE,ALLIAGES OUVRES
684	ALUMINIUM	W 87391	146.5	W 109230	240.3	W 104855	194.1	W 162114	290.1	ALUMINIUM
6841	ALUMINIUM,ALLOYS,UNWRGHT	W 56689	81.0	W 79667	148.5	W 71457	111.3	W 119450	201.3	ALUMINIUM,ALLIAGES BRUTS
6842	ALUMINIUM,ALLOYS WORKED	W 30702	65.5	W 29563	91.9	W 33398	82.8	W 42664	88.9	ALUMINIUM,ALLIAGES OUVRE
69	METAL MANUFACTURES NES		445.1		537.6		584.3		555.4	ART MANUFACT EN METAL NDA
695	TOOLS	W 8299	59.0	W 11772	73.3	W 14295	86.9	W 94588	79.2	OUTILS A MAIN
697	BASE MTL HOUSEHOLD EQUIP	W 17710	73.4	W 24617	85.5	W 20913	92.8	W 20545	88.1	ART MENAGE MET COMMUNS
699	BASE METAL MFRS NES	W 35155	151.6	W 45932	190.1	W 78915	197.1	W 64190	191.6	ART MANUFACTURES MET NDA
6991	LOCKSMITHS WARES,ETC	W 12890	74.9	W 14069	91.2	W 20485	93.8	W 18277	93.6	ARTICLES DE SERRURERIE
7	MACHINES,TRANSPORT EQUIP		6120.6		7111.1		8597.6		7501.6	MACHINES MATERIEL TRANSPORT
71	POWER GENERATING EQUIPMT		321.5		412.9		438.2		348.6	MACHINES GENERATRICES
713	INTRNL COMBUS PSTN ENGIN	W 10275	88.7	W 27826	213.5	W 10598	109.1	W 14784	116.4	MOTEURS EXPL COMB INT, PIECE
7139	PISTON ENGINE PARTS NES	W 4362	45.0	W 22471	170.7	W 4206	62.4	W 7194	57.1	PIECES POUR 713.2,3,8
714	ENGINES AND MOTORS NES	W 325	113.6	W 223	79.0	W 4864	124.1	W 2695	122.2	MOTEURS NON ELECTRIQUES
7144	REACTION ENGINES	W 121	76.1	W 105	60.0	W 3802	81.3	W 127	64.3	PROPULSEURS A REACTION
716	ROTATING ELECTRIC PLANT	W 7497	54.5	W 7394	60.2	W 13246	101.9	W 11163	83.1	APP ELECTR ROTATIFS,PIECES
72	MACHS FOR SPCL INDUSTRYS		572.1		734.2		932.7		874.2	MAC SPECIALES POUR INDUST
722	TRACTORS NON–ROAD	W 9475	32.9	W 12204	55.4	W 16284	80.5	W 21607	111.9	TRACTEURS
7224	WHEELED TRACTORS NES	W 9426	32.8	W 12133	55.1	W 16215	80.1	W 21505	111.6	TRACTEURS A ROUES
723	CIVIL ENGNEERG EQUIP ETC	W 25760	69.4	W 30960	90.0	W 31273	105.0	W 47684	80.9	APPAREILS DE GENIE CIVIL
724	TEXTILE,LEATHER MACHNRY	W 7486	130.5	W 13834	200.6	W 10763	202.6	W 11347	182.3	MACH POUR INDUSTRIE TEXTILE
7244	SPINNING,EXTRDNG,ETC MCH	W 2752	34.8	W 5585	78.1	W 3922	63.8	W 2233	51.6	MACH POUR LE FILAGE
727	FOOD MACHRY NON–DOMESTIC	W 3520	64.0	W 3077	65.4	W 4026	85.9	W 3956	87.9	MACH INDUSTRIES ALIMENT
7272	OTH FOOD PROC MCHY,PARTS	W 3170	58.8	W 2827	60.7	W 3502	77.3	W 3393	80.4	AUT MACH IND ALIMENTAIRE
728	OTH MACHY FOR SPCL INDUS	W 13740	144.8	W 17207	181.3	W 22978	236.4	W 28307	224.3	AUT MACH IND PARTICULIERES
7284	MACHY FOR SPCL INDUS NES	W 6848	98.2	W 8980	125.2	W 8258	153.8	W 9821	146.0	MACH SPEC IND PARTICUL.
73	METALWORKING MACHINERY		63.7		81.2		102.1		97.9	MACH TRAVAIL DES METAUX
74	GENRL INDUSTRL MACHY NES		793.4		1006.9		1119.0		1047.0	MACH APP INDUSTRIE
741	HEATING,COOLING EQUIPMNT	W 22467	261.1	W 28846	351.6	W 29684	349.4	W 32306	345.0	MACH CHAUFFAGE,PIECES
7415	AIR–CONDITIONING MACHNRY	W 10819	145.8	W 14037	192.1	W 13285	179.0	W 15451	195.5	GROUPES CONDITION AIR
742	PUMPS FOR LIQUIDS ETC	W 5572	56.4	W 6067	73.4	W 7380	93.3	W 13047	72.0	POMPES MOTO–POMPES
743	PUMPS NES,CENTRFUGES ETC	W 12116	109.3	W 14528	140.8	W 19568	141.6	W 16374	148.7	POMPES COMPRES,VENT ETC
744	MECHANICAL HANDLING EQU	W 20244	76.9	W 20510	106.1	W 32406	138.2	W 27285	129.5	EQUIP MANUTENTION PIECES
745	NONELEC MACHY,TOOLS NES	W 9487	126.0	W 9012	140.9	W 9617	177.6	W 8757	150.8	AUT MACH NON ELEC,PIECES
7452	OTH NONELEC MCHS,PTS NES	W 8794	111.9	W 8251	123.3	W 8182	155.6	W 7562	129.3	AUT MACH NON ELEC,PIECES

4. Special Imports C.I.F. by Commodities according to the S.I.T.C. (Rev. 2) in million U.S. Dollars
Importations Spéciales C.A.F. par Produits d'après la C.T.C.I. (Rév. 2) en millions de Dollars E.U.

SITC CTCI	COMMODITY	1994 QUANTITY QUANTITE	1994 VALUE VALEUR	1995 QUANTITY QUANTITE	1995 VALUE VALEUR	1996 QUANTITY QUANTITE	1996 VALUE VALEUR	1997 QUANTITY QUANTITE	1997 VALUE VALEUR	PRODUIT
749	NONELEC MACH PTS,ACC NES	W 14939	164.0	W 18763	194.5	W 18145	219.1	W 33849	201.2	PIECES MACH NON ELEC NDA
7492	COCKS,VALVES ETC NES	W 9506	94.4	W 12918	111.2	W 11006	117.0	W 27645	126.3	ART ROB,SIM POUR TUYAUX
75	OFFICE MACHNES,ADP EQUIP		364.8		451.7		513.4		461.7	MACH BUREAU TRAIT AUTOM
752	AUTOMTIC DATA PROC EQUIP	W 3338	191.4	W 4576	233.4	W 12335	275.5	W 3985	196.9	MACH TRAIT INFORMATION
759	OFFICE,ADP MCH PTS,ACCES	W 2731	121.8	W 3049	156.9	W 6060	181.1	W 4987	207.2	PIECES DU 751 ET 752
7599	ACCTG,ETC,ADP MCH PTS,AC	W 2033	106.7	W 2479	137.0	W 4925	156.6	W 4190	186.7	PIECES DU 751 ET 752
76	TELECOMM,SOUND EQUIPMENT		716.7		695.6		847.9		667.7	EQUIPMENT DE TELECOM
761	TELEVISION RECEIVERS	W 10249	144.5	W 9969	121.8	W 10442	150.7	W 7566	93.2	RECEPTEURS DE TELEVISION
7611	COLOUR TV RECEIVERS	W 10013	141.2	W 9864	118.8	W 10206	148.5	W 7316	91.9	RECEPTEURS COULEUR
762	RADIO BROADCAST RECEIVRS	W 3117	62.7	W 3624	70.4	W 8318	96.1	W 4154	73.5	RECEPTEURS RADIODIFFUSION
764	TELECOM EQPT,PTS,ACC NES	W 38225	464.0	W 10134	456.9	W 33584	522.9	W 13993	446.6	EQUIP TELECOM,PIECES
7641	LINE TELEPHONE,ETC EQUIP	W 1601	55.5	W 2412	68.6	W 16511	114.0	W 2685	129.2	APP TELEPHON PAR FIL
7643	TV,RADIO TRANSMITTRS ETC	W 376	71.4	W 847	98.0	W 2924	138.9	W 2010	104.6	APP EMET TELE RADIO
7649	PTS NES OF EQUIPMT OF 76	W 33659	282.9	W 3937	226.8	W 5544	161.9	W 4198	121.7	PIECES DE LA DIV 76
76491	PTS NES OF APPAR OF 7641	W 1469	184.9	W 1806	150.4	W 1818	99.7	W 2775	84.5	PIECES POUR 764.1
76493	TELECOMM EQUIPMT PTS NES	W 32060	91.6	W 1967	71.1	W 2299	57.4	W 1196	34.0	PIECES 761,762,764.3,8
77	ELECTRIC MACHNRY NES ETC		845.1		950.1		1086.1		927.4	MACH APP ELECT NDA
772	SWITCHGEAR ETC,PARTS NES	W 5931	118.6	W 6179	124.6	W 8913	167.0	W 7942	137.0	APP COUPURE,SECT ETC
7721	SWITCHGEAR ETC	W 5838	113.8	W 6071	119.3	W 8807	162.4	W 7837	132.4	APP COUPURE,SECTIONMNT
775	HOUSEHOLD TYPE EQUIP NES	W 58537	352.6	W 71737	401.7		423.5	W 173678	366.5	MACH,APP USAGE DOMESTQUE
7751	HOUSEHOLD LDRY EQUIP NES	W 18590	74.6	W 19467	78.3	W 19671	76.7	W 18444	67.1	MACH A LAVER ET SECHOIRS
77511	DOMESTIC WASHING MACHNES	W 18456	73.7	W 19368	77.5	W 19481	75.5	W 18259	66.1	MACH LAVER LINGE MOINS 6 KG
7752	DOM REFRIGERATRS,FREEZRS	W 19075	94.3	W 28047	111.3	W 29930	118.9	W 124846	105.2	REFRIG,CONGEL MENAGER
77521	DOMESTIC REFRIGERATORS	W 16531	81.8	W 24245	94.3	W 20310	96.8	W 120231	84.4	REFRIGERATEURS
7758	ELECTRO–THERMIC APPL NES	W 12088	104.0	W 13513	121.5		130.8	W 19323	111.7	APP ELECTROTHERMIQ NDA
77586	ELECTROTHERM DOM APP NES	W 7022	65.4	W 8050	75.0	W 13378	83.9	W 12738	73.1	APP ELECTRO THERMIQUES
778	ELECTRICAL MACHINERY NES	W 35806	221.8	W 38628	253.0	W 43220	297.9	W 32929	236.9	AUTRES MACH ELECT NDA
7788	OTH ELEC MACHY,EQUIP NES	W 12323	72.4	W 10958	70.8	W 10757	105.2	W 6726	68.6	AUT MACH APP ELEC NDA
78	ROAD VEHICLES		1704.6		2216.3		2478.0		2237.5	VEHICULES ROUTIERS
781	PASS MOTOR VEH EXC BUSES	W 102238	992.3	W 121221	1279.0	W 144281	1459.8	W 233334	1287.3	AUTO TRANSPORT PERSONNES
782	LORRIES,SPCL MTR VEH NES	W 52555	164.6	W 65399	250.1	W 86932	314.4	W 100726	295.0	VEHICULES SPECIAUX,MARCH
7821	LORRIES,TRUCKS	W 47631	146.9	W 57372	225.2	W 74461	264.6	W 91230	267.3	VEHICULES TRANSP MARCHAND
784	MOTOR VEH PRTS,ACCES NES	W 56986	376.6	W 70347	461.6	W 148633	458.7	W 60916	421.0	PIECES 722,781,782,783
7849	OTHER MOTOR VEHCL PARTS	W 55132	363.1	W 67424	451.9	W 143486	437.0	W 58381	405.6	PIECES 722,781,782,783
785	CYCLES,ETC MOTRZD OR NOT	W 15792	116.0	W 16366	141.4	W 24293	151.2	W 17756	164.6	MOTOCYCLES SCOOTERS
7851	MOTORCYCLES ETC	W 9812	78.0	W 9894	96.4	W 10940	107.4	W 12911	126.9	MOTO VELO MOTEUR AUXIL
79	OTHR TRANSPORT EQUIPMENT		739.1		562.6		1080.6		840.1	AUTRE MATERIEL TRANSPORT
792	AIRCRAFT ETC	W 445	119.6	W 506	101.2	W 464	112.6	W 475	145.0	APP NAVIGATION AERIENNE
7923	AIRCRFT NES2000–15000KG	W 63	13.3	W 42	5.8	W 7	6.0	W 102	77.1	AERODYNES 2000 A 15000 KG
793	SHIPS AND BOATS ETC	W 9076	603.8	W 4647	429.7	W 26635	943.3	W 6957	635.5	NAVIRES BATEAUX,ETC
7932	SHIPS AND BOATS NES	W 4597	599.7	W 3607	425.3	W 26179	939.1	W 5722	630.1	NAVIRES ET BATEAUX
79322	TANKERS OF ALL KINDS	W 557	193.7	W 125	91.0	W 588	368.1	W 194	187.6	BATEAUX–CITERNES
79323	OTHER CARGO VESSELS	W 2210	376.6	W 1544	303.6	W 10978	531.4	W 3870	409.3	AUT BATEAUX TRANS MARCH
8	MISC MANUFACTURED GOODS		2452.7		3384.9		3522.1		3250.8	ART MANUFACTURES DIVERS
812	*PLUMBG,HEATNG,LGHTNG EQ	W 31478	98.2	W 44584	120.6	W 83197	133.7	W 58250	134.6	APPAR SANITAIRES CHAUFFAGE
821	*FURNITURE,PARTS THEREOF	W 30144	140.3	W 55057	196.5	W 89025	218.6	W 155061	215.2	MEUBLES ET PIECES
8219	FURNITURE AND PARTS NES	W 20218	86.2	W 44608	125.7	W 77089	145.5	W 141860	143.7	AUTRES MEUBLES ET PIECES
82192	WOOD FURNITURE NES	W 13385	59.5	W 27105	82.3	W 54429	98.4	W 129756	103.6	MEUBLES NDA EN BOIS
84	CLOTHING AND ACCESSORIES		615.8		794.1		952.3		934.7	VETEMENTS
842	MENS OUTERWEAR NOT KNIT	W 4175	107.1	W 4328	130.5	W 8923	161.4	W 8733	153.6	VET DESSUS POUR HOMMES
843	WOMENS OUTERWEAR NONKNIT	W 3866	137.2	W 4600	174.2	W 7175	203.4	W 9573	189.9	VET DESSUS FEMMES MAT TEX
8439	— OTHER OUTER GARMENTS	W 1361	48.2	W 1923	59.5	W 2840	80.2	W 4642	80.6	AUT VET DES FEM MAT TEXT
845	OUTERWEAR KNIT NONELASTC	W 3844	121.4	W 5600	164.6	W 12284	221.0	W 11898	234.0	VET DESSOUS,ACCES BONNET
8451	— JERSEYS,PULLOVERS ETC	W 1061	40.4	W 1627	53.0	W 5228	72.7	W 3972	80.9	CHANDAILS,PULL–OVERS ETC
8459	— OTHER,CLTHG ACCESRYS	W 2434	69.0	W 3509	97.6	W 5977	132.3	W 7237	136.8	AUT VET DESSUS DE BONNE
846	UNDER GARMENTS KNITTED	W 4210	95.6	W 4466	121.8	W 7349	140.5	W 13245	158.1	SOUS VETS DE BONNETERIE
8462	— OF COTTON NON ELASTIC	W 2689	48.6	W 2957	58.9	W 5231	76.8	W 10600	95.0	SOUS–VET BONNET COTON
84629	—— OTHER	W 2689	48.6	W 2957	58.9	W 5231	76.8	W 10600	95.0	AUT SOUS–VET BONNET COTON
848	HEADGEAR,NONTXTL CLOTHNG	W 4087	72.9	W 4625	98.1	W 7141	116.6	W 7511	104.5	VET ACCES MAT AUT QUE TEX
851	*FOOTWEAR	W 13592	162.0	W 13292	198.5	W 24102	254.6	W 19513	264.3	CHAUSSURES
85102	FOOTWEAR LEATHER	W 10553	129.6	W 9824	159.4	W 19562	203.2	W 14220	203.7	CHAUS SEMELLES EN CUIR
87	PRECISION INSTRUMNTS NES		282.8		336.8		382.5		372.3	INSTRUM,APPAR SCIENT NDA
872	MEDICAL INSTRUMENTS NES	W 6897	119.9	W 4756	147.0	W 7078	173.9	W 6811	182.5	INSTR,APP MEDIC–CHIR NDA
87202	OTH MEDICAL INSTRUMENTS	W 6635	111.5	W 4431	136.7	W 6692	159.8	W 6412	161.7	INSTRUM,APP MEDECINE
874	MEASURNG,CONTROLNG INSTR	W 3806	145.5		170.2	W 6468	183.8	W 5099	169.5	INSTRUMENTS DE MESURE
88	PHOTO EQU,OPTICL GDS ETC		216.0		684.4		412.5		256.2	APP,FOURN PHOTO,OP,MONTR
882	PHOTO,CINEMA SUPPLIES	W 7369	80.3		533.2	W 17631	242.2	W 9873	86.8	PRODUITS PHOTO,CINEMA
8822	PHOTO FILM EXC DEV CINMA	W 4468	69.1		519.5	W 7684	229.0	W 5718	74.3	PLAQUES,PELLICULES,FILMS
88222	PHOTO FILM ROLL UNEXPOSD	W 612	24.5		451.3	W 3137	165.1	W 823	29.3	PEL SENSIB PERF OU NON
885	WATCHES AND CLOCKS		65.0		72.6		77.1		80.3	HORLOGERIE
89	MISC MANUFCTRD GOODS NES		903.9		1013.5		1110.2		1017.7	ART MANUFACTURES DIVERS
892	PRINTED MATTER	W 14296	113.6	W 14160	122.4	W 17252	132.4	W 13864	113.3	IMPRIMES
893	ARTICLES OF PLASTIC NES		218.0		280.1		292.7		268.7	OUVRAGES EN MAT DIVIS 58
8939	MISC PLASTIC ARTICLES	W 33759	144.5	W 84801	193.3	W 91908	201.1	W 56414	179.7	ART DIVERS EN MAT DIV 58
89399	OTHR PLASTC ARTICLES NES	W 26728	126.9	W 76580	173.5	W 45063	182.0	W 47153	162.3	AUT OUV MAT DIV 58
894	TOYS,SPORTING GOODS,ETC	W 24224	232.1	W 27334	236.3	W 29774	253.8	W 34876	230.3	VOITURES ENFANTS,JOUETS
8942	TOYS,INDOOR GAMES ETC	W 20258	194.5	W 22924	192.9	W 24570	202.8	W 29060	183.1	JOUETS,JEUX ETC
89424	INDOOR GAME EQUIPMENT	W 7953	112.1	W 7762	91.5	W 5787	80.0	W 11623	76.8	ART,JEUX DE SOCIETE
898	MUSICAL INSTRUMENTS,PTS	W 6776	111.5	W 9972	123.4	W 9071	147.7	W 6433	118.9	INSTRUMENTS DE MUSIQUE
8983	SOUND RECRDNG TAPE,DISCS	W 5843	99.4	W 7421	107.0	W 7814	129.0	W 4862	100.5	SUPPORTS SON POUR 763
89832	RECORDED DISCS,TAPES ETC	W 2976	70.3	W 2411	77.5	W 3846	99.5	W 1855	76.2	DISQUES,PHONO,BANDES
899	OTHER MANUFACTURED GOODS		130.5		137.8		161.8		153.0	AUT ART MANUF DIVERS NDA
9	GOODS NOT CLASSD BY KIND		188.6		178.1		58.4		59.8	ART TRANSACT NON CLASSES
931	*SPECIAL TRANSACTIONS		143.6	W 246498	127.9		14.6		24.0	TRANS.SPECIALES

5. Special Exports F.O.B. by Commodities according to the S.I.T.C. (Rev. 2) in million U.S. Dollars
Exportations Spéciales F.O.B. par Produits d'après la C.T.C.I. (Rév. 2) en millions de Dollars E.U.

SITC CTCI	COMMODITY	1994		1995		1996		1997		PRODUIT
		QUANTITY QUANTITE	VALUE VALEUR	QUANTITY QUANTITE	VALUE VALEUR	QUANTITY QUANTITE	VALUE VALEUR	QUANTITY QUANTITE	VALUE VALEUR	
	ALL COMMODITIES		9399.0		10954.7		11879.7		10794.6	TOUS PRODUITS
0	FOOD AND LIVE ANIMALS		1888.0		1985.3		2016.9		1805.1	ALIMENTS,ANIMAUX VIVANTS
01	MEAT AND PREPARATIONS		56.2		51.2		31.9		69.4	VIANDES ET PREPARATIONS
014	MEAT PREPD,PRSVD,NES ETC	W 6561	31.6	W 7915	27.3	W 3700	9.3	W 8496	51.6	CONSERVES DE VIANDES
0149	OTH PREPARD,PRESRVD MEAT	W 3072	27.0	W 3789	20.5	W 1022	3.5	W 6724	48.9	AUTRES PREP DE VIANDES
02	DAIRY PRODCTS,BIRDS'EGGS		96.6		112.8		107.8		100.9	PRODUITS LAITIERS,OEUFS
024	CHEESE AND CURD	W 13757	79.0	W 16078	92.9	W 22708	87.7	W 109780	80.5	FROMAGE ET CAILLEBOTTE
03	FISH AND PREPARATIONS		152.9		175.0		208.0		218.0	POISSONS ET PREPARATIONS
034	FISH,FRESH,CHILLED,FROZN	W 14647	105.2	W 15693	117.4	W 20412	143.0	W 27805	159.2	POISSON FRAIS, REFRIG,CONG
0341	FISH FRSH,CHLLD,EX FILLT	W 13063	96.6	W 13744	105.6	W 17224	126.1	W 22945	144.1	POISSON FRAIS,REFRIGERE
04	CEREALS AND PREPARATIONS		326.0		215.3		225.7		233.4	CEREALES ET PRODUITS
041	WHEAT ETC UNMILLED	W 952736	172.3	W 334765	89.0	W 366651	86.5	W 377825	83.0	FROMENT,EPEAUTRE
0411	DURUM WHEAT UNMILLED	W 929765	168.1	W 334713	89.0	W 359248	84.6	W 329201	73.2	FROMENT DUR NON MOULU
042	RICE	W 83712	38.5	W 117383	59.0	W 73065	35.7	W 86186	31.6	RIZ
0421	RICE IN HUSK OR HUSKED	W 76590	35.8	W 108659	54.6	W 64275	31.1	W 67033	24.3	RIZ SANS AUTRE PREPARATION
04211	RICE IN THE HUSK	W 76162	35.7	W 108622	54.5	W 64138	30.9	W 63571	21.9	RIZ PADDY
044	MAIZE UNMILLED	W 285606	41.1	W 16002	2.9	W 35083	7.7	W 165093	26.7	MAIS NON MOULU
048	CEREAL ETC PREPARATIONS	W 80700	56.4	W 45772	55.9	W 61488	66.6	W 55920	62.8	PREPTNS A BASE CEREALES
0484	BAKERY PRODUCTS	W 11608	32.9	W 12383	32.3	W 13962	35.7	W 13376	37.1	PRODUITS DE BOULANGERIE
05	VEGETABLES AND FRUIT		1125.1		1275.2		1298.1		1052.7	LEGUMES ET FRUITS
054	VEG ETC FRSH,SMPLY PRSVD	W 256048	218.3	W 254006	260.4	W 279674	272.2	W 277446	235.4	LEGUMES FRAIS,CONG,SECS
0545	OTHER FRESH VEGETABLES	W 64770	74.3	W 56304	100.6	W 63343	104.3	W 71460	81.4	AUTRES LEGUMES FRAIS,REF
05459	FRESH VEGETABLES NES	W 60277	72.6	W 52698	99.7	W 62825	104.0	W 60469	79.2	LEGUMES FRAIS,REFRI NDA
0546	VEGETABLES SIMPLY PRESVD	W 168661	131.3	W 147403	138.0	W 165837	152.8	W 175737	143.3	LEGUMES CONG,CONSER
05461	VEGETABLES FROZEN	W 167931	130.3	W 146802	136.8	W 164406	149.8	W 172849	138.4	LEGUMES CONGELES
056	VEGTBLES ETC PRSVD,PREPD	W 95051	128.6	W 82797	132.6	W 92802	193.1	W 81376	118.3	CONSERVES DE LEGUMES
0565	VEGTBLES PRSVD,PREPD NES	W 94275	127.3	W 81009	130.4	W 92219	191.8	W 78220	116.6	LEGUMES PREPARES CONSERVE
05659	OTH VEG PRESVD,PREPD NES	W 64947	101.0	W 56471	106.3	W 64256	162.4	W 53239	91.5	LEGUM PREPAP,CONSERV NDA
057	FRUIT,NUTS,FRESH,DRIED	W 1106738	461.7	W 848027	482.6	W 829275	472.0	W 858855	420.0	FRUITS FRAIS OU SECS
0571	ORANGES, MANDARINS ETC	W 572836	135.5	W 281555	86.1	W 313071	119.5	W 373813	120.9	ORANGES,MAND,CLEMENTINES
05711	ORANGES,FRESH OR DRIED	W 555155	128.6	W 263072	74.9	W 283683	102.0	W 349404	110.7	ORANGES FRAICHES,SECHEES
0575	GRAPES FRESH OR DRIED	W 167655	151.4	W 172882	194.7	W 158319	181.1	W 162291	169.0	RAISINS FRAIS OU SECS
05751	GRAPES FRESH	W 102784	79.0	W 111916	108.1	W 103334	102.2	W 102574	105.3	RAISINS FRAIS
05752	GRAPES DRIED(RAISINS)	W 64872	72.5	W 60966	86.7	W 54984	79.0	W 59718	63.7	RAISINS SECS
0579	FRUIT FRESH OR DRIED NES	W 244533	112.9	W 293422	135.1	W 241108	103.4	W 224629	73.1	FRUITS FRAIS,SECS NDA
05793	STONE FRUIT FRESH NES	W 83322	63.2	W 92382	83.7	W 57707	44.7	W 22927	22.4	FRUITS A NOYAU NDA FRAIS
05798	OTHER FRESH FRUIT	W 160191	48.8	W 199601	50.2	W 180348	56.7	W 199932	49.3	AUTRES FRUITS FRAIS
058	FRUIT PRESERVED,PREPARED	W 459976	316.7	W 480606	399.8	W 516581	360.9	W 370063	279.2	CONSERVES DE FRUITS
0589	FRUIT PREPRD,PRESRVD,NES	W 410523	274.9	W 413111	333.5	W 441630	301.4	W 306738	228.0	FRUITS PREPARES CONSERV
05899	FRUIT,NUTS NES,PRESERVED	W 406944	267.5	W 407274	321.0	W 435102	287.7	W 300982	216.7	FRUITS PREP CONSERV NDA
07	COFFEE,TEA,COCOA,SPICES		54.8		62.5		45.8		34.0	CAFE,THE,CACAO,EPICES
09	MISC EDIBLE PRODUCTS		42.0		54.1		58.4		43.8	PREP ALIMENTAIRES DIVERSES
098	EDIBLE PRODCTS,PREPS NES	W 18221	40.5	W 20032	47.3	W 23425	44.1	W 21001	32.5	PREP ALIMENTAIRES NDA
09809	MISC FOOD PREPRTIONS NES	W 14837	37.6	W 14372	42.8	W 12975	37.7	W 10265	26.4	PREP ALIMENTAIRES NDA
1	BEVERAGES AND TOBACCO		516.7		615.4		720.2		646.2	BOISSONS ET TABACS
11	BEVERAGES		174.6		210.5		214.8		146.4	BOISSONS
111	NON–ALCOHL BEVERAGES NES	W 131831	36.2	W 95967	19.8	W 96370	26.5	W 70604	12.2	BOISSONS NON ALCOOLIQUES
11102	FLAVORED WATERS NON–ALCO	W 63252	33.9	W 29912	17.0	W 34506	22.4	W 37874	8.9	LIMONADES,EAUX GAZEUSES
112	ALCOHOLIC BEVERAGES	W 141778	138.4	W 152349	190.8	W 161669	188.3	W 87034	134.2	BOISSONS ALCOOLIQUES
1121	WINE OF FRESH GRAPES ETC	W 65920	62.2	W 66237	80.6	W 60856	78.1	W 47367	70.4	VINS DE RAISINS FRAIS
11212	WINE OF FRESH GRAPES	W 54694	58.9	W 60580	78.1	W 60825	78.0	W 46362	70.0	VINS DE MOUTS DE RAISINS
1124	DISTILLED ALCOHOLIC BEVS	W 31753	53.0	W 58594	87.3	W 81734	94.2	W 29779	55.7	ALCOOLS,EAUX–DE–VIE
11242	DISTILLD WINE,GRAPE MARC	W 11091	25.6	W 19504	34.6	W 37717	30.1	W 6969	17.5	EAUX–DE–VIE NATURELLES
11249	OTH ALCOHOLC BEVS,CMPNDS	W 19957	24.4	W 38684	49.5	W 43058	57.3	W 21404	28.1	BOISSONS ALCOOLIQUES NDA
12	TOBACCO AND MANUFACTURES		342.2		405.0		505.5		499.9	TABACS BRUTS FABRIQUES
121	TOBACCO UNMNFCTRD,REFUSE	W 106195	292.5	W 121408	308.9	W 130934	353.5	W 94794	347.2	TABACS BRUTS,DECHETS
1211	TOBACCO,NOT STRIPPED	W 68103	235.8	W 88952	264.0	W 96989	301.9	W 67939	284.6	TABACS NON ECOTES
1212	TOBACCO STRIPPED OR PART	W 31239	53.5	W 26202	42.2	W 23488	47.2	W 21317	60.0	TABACS PART ECOTES
122	TOBACCO,MANUFACTURED	W 7046	49.7	W 13420	96.1	W 22600	152.0	W 19721	152.7	TABACS FABRIQUES
1222	CIGARETTES	W 7044	49.7	W 13399	96.0	W 22411	151.1	W 19232	150.1	CIGARETTES
2	CRUDE MATERLS,EXCL FUELS		601.3		777.6		861.2		663.5	MAT BRUTES NON COMESTIBLES
21	HIDES,SKINS,FURS UNDRSSD		29.0		37.5		48.7		31.9	CUIRS,PEAUX BRUTS
211	HIDES,SKINS,EXC FURS,RAW	W 6831	28.5	W 6716	35.8	W 8562	47.4	W 7874	30.9	CUIRS ET PEAUX
2116	SHEEP SKIN WITH WOOL	W 5456	21.7	W 4648	25.2	W 6724	37.6	W 4490	21.3	PEAUX LAINEES D'OVINS
26	TEXTILE FIBRES AND WASTE		295.9		408.7		511.1		344.2	FIBRES TEXTILES
263	COTTON	W 209325	283.3	W 211894	394.8	W 313073	497.5	W 213535	331.1	COTON
2631	RAW COTTON,EXCL LINTERS	W 187534	264.2	W 191246	370.7	W 284160	464.3	W 190898	309.7	COTON EN MASSE
27	CRUDE FERTLZR,MINRLS NES		107.2		128.7		124.8		111.4	ENGRAIS MINERAUX BRUTS
278	OTHER CRUDE MINERALS	W 743080	71.0	W 971075	92.2	W 988176	91.7	W 911021	80.0	AUTRES MINERAUX BRUTS
2782	REFRACTORY MINERALS NES	W 284230	31.8	W 350892	38.2	W 271760	33.8	W 210484	30.1	ARGILE MINERAUX REFRACTAIRES
27824	MAGNESITE, ETC	W 196140	28.8	W 205972	32.4	W 179446	30.9	W 182126	28.9	CARBONATE DE MAGNESIUM
28	METALLIFEROUS ORES,SCRAP		107.4		136.5		123.1		126.8	MINERAIS METAL,DECHETS
287	BASE METAL ORES,CONC NES	W 1058984	72.4	W 1170197	106.3	W 1177583	100.4	W 869598	89.4	MINERAIS METAUX COMMUNS
2873	ALUMINIUM ORES,ALUMINA	W 1031282	65.9	W 1122330	97.2	W 1164232	97.0	W 834249	75.5	MINERAIS D'ALUMINIUM
28732	ALUMINA(ALUMINIUM OXIDE)	W 290431	42.9	W 344875	71.6	W 344821	67.6	W 297238	58.6	ALUMINE (OXYDE ALUMINIUM)
3	MINERAL FUELS ETC		972.1		713.5		1000.2		939.6	COMBUSTIBLES MINERAUX LUB
33	PETROLEUM AND PRODUCTS		962.4		700.3		973.1		913.4	PETROLE ET DERIVES
333	CRUDE PETROLEUM	W 269997	26.6	W 517877	50.2	W 894507	100.9	W 700026	72.1	HUILES BRUTES DE PETROLE
334	PETROLEUM PRODUCTS,REFIN	W 7037736	932.9	W 4386648	648.6	W 5192824	866.5	W 4890922	833.2	PRODUITS RAFFINES
3341	GASOLINE,OTH LIGHT OILS	W 1798674	284.2	W 1297558	210.1	W 1498593	296.1	W 1470093	297.4	ESSENCES POUR MOTEURS
33411	MOTOR,AVIATION SPIRIT	W 577017	103.8	W 370937	62.2	W 670348	141.0	W 539839	114.7	ESSENCES MOTEURS D'AVIONS
33419	OTH LIGHT PETROLEUM OILS	W 1221656	180.5	W 926601	147.9	W 741571	138.3	W 830292	162.8	AUTRES HUILES LEGERES
3342	KEROSENE,OTH MEDIUM OILS	W 746201	117.9	W 477715	78.3	W 667390	137.5	W 662653	159.9	PETR LAMPANTS,AUT HUIL
33421	KEROSENE INCL JET FUEL	W 745892	117.7	W 476338	76.9	W 663291	134.0	W 659742	157.9	PETROLES LAMPANTS
3343	GAS OILS	W 1139179	186.3	W 719434	113.2					GAS OILS
3344	FUEL OILS,NES	W 3124539	254.4	W 1734834	169.8	W 2872588	348.4	W 2627576	309.8	FUEL OILS
3345	LUBS,PETROLEUM OILS NES	W 229144	90.2	W 157107	77.4	W 154253	84.6	W 130600	66.3	HUILES LUBRIFIANTES
33451	LUBS(HIGH PETR CONT) ETC	W 228982	90.0	W 156960	77.0	W 154070	84.2	W 130163	65.6	HUILES LUBRIF,H LOURDES
4	ANIMAL,VEGETABLE OIL,FAT		345.1		605.5		758.7		390.8	HUILES,GRAISSES ANIM,VEG
42	FIXED VEGETABLE OIL,FAT		344.3		604.1		756.9		387.9	HUILES VEGETALES FIXES
423	FIXED VEG OILS,SOFT	W 145462	344.0	W 214200	598.5	W 185891	754.6	W 163324	386.7	HUILES VEGET DOUCES FIXES
4235	OLIVE OIL	W 123168	327.9	W 183750	574.5	W 165397	738.4	W 127598	362.6	HUILE D'OLIVE
5	CHEMCLS,RELATED PROD NES		366.1		481.9		566.7		589.0	PRODUITS CHIMIQUES
51	ORGANIC CHEMICALS		50.2		32.1		34.3		40.8	PROD CHIMIQ ORGANIQUES
511	HYDROCARBONS NES,DERIVS	W 70517	29.6	W 25036	19.8	W 22417	20.0	W 29686	22.8	HYDROCARBURES NDA
5113	HALOG DERIV OF HYDROCARB	W 70350	29.5	W 24521	19.6	W 22288	19.9	W 27214	20.9	DERIVES HALOGENES HYDROCAR
51139	OTH HALOG HYDRCARB DERIV	W 70343	29.5	W 24489	19.5	W 22123	19.8	W 27137	20.9	AUTRE DERIVES HALOGENES
53	DYES,TANNING,COLOUR PROD		45.4		56.4		60.9		59.7	PROD TEINTURE,COLORANTS
541	*MEDICINAL,PHARM PRODUCT	K 2037372	73.7	K 2191430	77.9	K 2281563	87.3	K 2323677	77.9	PROD MEDICINAUX PHARMACEUT
5417	MEDICAMENTS	K 1931476	72.0	K 1971443	68.6	K 1907101	75.5	K 1823180	67.7	MEDICAMENTS
55	PERFUME,CLEANING ETC PRD		50.6		65.2		109.0		124.3	PROD POUR PARFUM,TOILETTE

5. Special Exports F.O.B. by Commodities according to the S.I.T.C. (Rev. 2) in million U.S. Dollars
Exportations Spéciales F.O.B. par Produits d'après la C.T.C.I. (Rév. 2) en millions de Dollars E.U.

SITC CTCI	COMMODITY	1994 QUANTITY QUANTITE	1994 VALUE VALEUR	1995 QUANTITY QUANTITE	1995 VALUE VALEUR	1996 QUANTITY QUANTITE	1996 VALUE VALEUR	1997 QUANTITY QUANTITE	1997 VALUE VALEUR	PRODUIT
553	PERFUMERY,COSMETICS,ETC	W 7794	23.9	W 9090	35.5	W 14203	70.3	W 18226	81.3	PRODUITS DE PARFUMERIE
554	SOAP,CLEANSING ETC PREPS	W 22953	23.1	W 21078	25.9	W 24546	35.0	W 31079	38.4	SAVONS,PRODUITS DETERSIFS
562	*FERTILIZERS,MANUFACTURE	W 153046	17.7	W 421577	68.3	W 503305	82.0	W 417639	70.6	ENGRAIS MANUFACTURES
5629	FERTILIZERS NES	W 91799	12.5	W 198775	36.7	W 336922	60.1	W 322376	56.5	ENGRAIS NDA
56291	NIT–PHOS–POT FERTLZR NES	W 91397	12.4	W 150945	28.3	W 201930	38.1	W 268848	47.9	ENGRAIS CONT N P K
58	PLASTIC MATERIALS ETC		61.7		82.3		93.0		113.7	MAT PLAST ARTIFICIELLES
583	POLYMERIZATION ETC PRODS	W 42321	52.4	W 43174	69.3	W 70968	81.7	W 134263	101.1	PROD POLYMERISATION
5834	POLYVINYL CHLORIDE	W 18568	14.7	W 18028	18.1	W 33879	24.7	W 42403	36.9	CHLORURE DE POLYVINYLE
58341	— IN PRIMARY FORMS	W 17572	14.0	W 17431	16.6	W 32570	21.9	W 40893	33.4	SOUS FORMES PRIMAIRES
59	CHEMICAL MATERIALS NES		53.0		78.7		83.1		82.9	MAT PROD CHIMIQUES NDA
598	MISCEL CHEM PRODUCTS NES	W 514199	40.3	W 702397	58.8	W 743909	62.0	W 768777	66.0	PROD DIV INDUST CHIM NDA
5989	CHEM PRODUCTS,PREPS NES	W 510436	35.6	W 698773	53.8	W 740089	56.4	W 763918	60.1	PROD PREP CHIMIQUES NDA
59892	ACTIVTED NAT MINRL PROD	W 502268	27.2	W 690060	41.5	W 725589	41.8	W 754018	45.9	CHARBONS ACTIVES
6	BASIC MANUFACTURES		1917.6		2325.5		2356.2		2130.7	ART MANUFACTURES
61	LEATHER,DRESSED FUR,ETC		60.0		55.3		63.9		61.3	CUIRS,PELLETERIES
613	FUR SKINS TANNED,DRESSED	W 346	33.1	W 389	29.1	W 409	41.1	W 392	36.1	PELLETERIES
62	RUBBER MANUFACTURES NES		42.1		57.4		50.7		24.0	CAOUTCHOUC MANUFACTURE
63	WOOD,CORK MANUFACTRS NES		39.3		46.6		40.9		24.9	OUVRAGES LIEGE ET BOIS
634	VENEERS,PLYWOOD,ETC	W 41127	32.4	W 52428	41.6	W 42166	34.8	W 29548	17.6	PLACAGES,CONTRE–PLAQUES
64	PAPER,PAPERBOARD AND MFR		60.3		92.7		105.9		97.7	PAPIERS,CARTONS & OUVRAGES
641	PAPER AND PAPERBOARD	W 51405	34.1	W 59046	49.7	W 61971	49.1	W 65651	42.5	PAPIERS ET CARTONS
642	PAPER,ETC,PRECUT,ARTS OF	W 12295	26.3	W 16778	43.0	W 20707	56.9	W 21988	55.3	PAP,CARTONS DECOUPES
6428	PAPER ETC ARTICLES NES	W 6509	16.0	W 9513	29.8	W 12400	40.4	W 12672	37.7	OUVRAGES EN PATE A PAPIER
65	TEXTILE YARN,FABRICS,ETC		430.7		520.8		507.2		389.1	FILS,TISSUS,ARTICLES TEXTILE
651	TEXTILE YARN	W 50566	210.9	W 52188	265.2	W 68510	242.6	W 44250	187.7	FILS TEXTILES
6513	COTTON YARN	W 35334	146.0	W 38522	182.2	W 56129	171.6	W 30661	126.8	FILS DE COTON
6517	REGEN FIBRE YARN,MONOFIL	W 4132	25.9	W 4611	38.5	W 4078	30.1	W 4233	23.6	FILS TEXT ART NON VENTE DT
65171	CONT VISCOSE RAYON YARN	W 4082	25.7	W 4604	38.4	W 4042	29.8	W 4121	23.0	FILS RAY,VIS NON VENTE DET
652	COTTON FABRICS,WOVEN	W 13820	69.8	W 13801	76.7	W 12672	70.0	W 5374	26.6	TISSUS DE COTON
6522	WOVEN COTTON BLEACHD,ETC	W 10510	53.3	W 9884	55.4	W 10149	58.1	W 4391	21.2	TISSUS COTON BLANCHIS ETC
65224	BLCHED COTTON FABRIC NES	W 10430	52.5	W 9776	54.0	W 10065	57.1	W 4268	20.2	AUT TIS PLUS 85% COT BLANCHI
655	KNITTED,ETC FABRICS	W 3344	26.6	W 4136	36.4	W 6002	32.6	W 10250	32.8	ETOF BONNETERIE PIECES ETC
6552	OTHER KNIT ETC FAB NONEL	W 3344	26.6	W 4136	36.4	W 6002	32.6	W 10250	32.8	ETOF BON NON ELAS NON SYNT
658	TEXTILE ARTICLES NES	W 7923	57.6	W 8480	72.0	W 9610	73.7	W 10040	60.3	ART FACONNES MAT TEXTILES
6589	OTH TEXTILE ARTICLES NES	W 4535	36.3	W 4826	45.7	W 5550	48.4	W 5055	41.2	AUT ART EN TEXTILES NDA
65898	KNITTED ETC ARTICLES NES	W 4517	36.1	W 4811	45.5	W 5493	48.2	W 4919	40.9	ART BONNET NON ELASTIQUE
659	FLOOR COVERINGS,ETC	W 6658	28.8	W 5904	28.4	W 7743	32.4	W 6451	26.1	COUVRE–PARQUETS,TAPIS ETC
66	NONMETAL MINERAL MFS NES		442.2		423.1		490.0		477.8	ART MIN NON METALLIQUES
661	LIME,CEMENT,BLDG PRODS	W 7933680	373.2	W 6850244	336.7	W 7387316	383.9	W 6684224	374.3	CHAUX,CIMENTS MAT CONSTR
6612	CEMENT	W 7713873	269.0	W 6647568	232.9	W 7146669	269.3	W 6451120	252.9	CIMENTS HYDRAULIQUES
6613	BUILDING STONE ETC WORKD	W 208283	99.6	W 188189	97.9	W 224649	107.2	W 211767	112.1	PIERRES A BATIR
66132	BUILDING STONE WORKED	W 207616	99.4	W 187571	97.7	W 223196	107.0	W 211517	112.0	OUVR EN PIERRES DE TAILLE
662	CLAY,REFRACTORY BLDG PRD	W 65885	18.8	W 101604	28.4	W 158563	40.8	W 173530	46.5	MAT CONST REFRACTAIRES
67	IRON AND STEEL		282.7		353.7		338.9		308.6	FER ET ACIER
672	IRON,STEEL PRIMARY FORMS	W 243133	75.6	W 225883	82.3	W 226095	63.7	W 107035	32.2	LINGOTS FER,ACIER
6727	IRN,STL COIL FR REROLLNG	W 228352	72.3	W 205869	77.5	W 166059	48.6	W 100890	30.7	EBAUCHES POUR TOLES FER
67271	IRON,SIMPLE STEEL COILS	W 228339	72.2	W 205866	77.5	W 166021	48.5	W 100867	30.7	EBAUCHES NON EN ACIER
674	IRN,STL UNIV,PLATE,SHEET	W 282888	150.5	W 329068	209.3		191.0		186.6	LARGES PLATS,TOLES
6746	IRN,STL THIN PLATE,ROLLD	W 125811	59.5	W 112647	62.8	W 110966	48.8	W 109461	57.1	TOLES LAM MOINS 3MM
67461	— OF IRON OR SIMPLE STL	W 125575	59.0	W 112574	62.7	W 110621	47.7	W 108738	55.7	TOL NON AC FIN MOINS 3 MM
6747	TINNED PLATES,SHEETS	W 49502	29.6	W 90087	64.3	W 73706	48.0	W 69977	44.8	TOLES ETAMEES EN ACIER
6749	OTH IRN,STL PLATES,SHEET	W 103651	59.9	W 101299	72.4	W 109215	70.5	W 104586	68.1	AUTRES TOLES FER,ACIER
67491	— OF IRON OR SIMPLE STL	W 103537	59.6	W 100817	71.7	W 109004	70.2	W 104237	67.6	AUT TOLES AUTRES ACIER FIN
678	IRON,STL TUBES,PIPES,ETC	W 27771	17.3	W 43951	29.5	W 80892	55.5	W 93218	59.7	TUBES,TUYAUX EN FONTE,FER
6783	IRON,STL TUBES,PIPES NES	W 26383	13.8	W 38296	22.8	W 75084	48.5	W 87534	55.0	AUT TUBES,TUYAUX FER,ACIER
68	NON–FERROUS METALS		419.3		598.3		550.3		576.2	METAUX NON FERREUX
682	COPPER EXC CEMENT COPPER	W 33003	95.9	W 43981	159.1	W 50576	160.6	W 55741	162.5	CUIVRE
6822	COPPER,ALLOYS WORKED	W 32811	95.5	W 43637	158.5	W 50443	160.4	W 55443	161.9	CUIVRE,ALLIAGES OUVRES
68221	COPPER BARS,WIRE,ETC	W 8989	20.2	W 13583	39.8	W 15060	37.4	W 17659	40.8	BARRES,PROFILES ET FILS
68222	COPPER PLATE,SHEET,STRIP	W 9847	29.5	W 12667	47.1	W 14691	47.1	W 16126	47.9	TOLES DE PLUS 0.15 MM
68225	COPPER TUBES,PIPES,ETC	W 13793	44.8	W 17260	70.9	W 20604	75.3	W 21542	72.4	TUBES,TUYAUX EN CUIVRE
684	ALUMINIUM	W 159189	322.8	W 155802	436.3	W 153125	383.6	W 172317	410.4	ALUMINIUM
6841	ALUMINIUM,ALLOYS,UNWRGHT	W 52975	78.7	W 49311	103.5	W 44389	80.1	W 46868	84.2	ALUMINIUM,ALLIAGES BRUTS
6842	ALUMINIUM,ALLOYS WORKED	W 106214	244.1	W 106490	332.9	W 108736	303.5	W 125449	326.3	ALUMINIUM,ALLIAGES OUVRE
68421	ALUMINIUM BARS,WIRE,ETC	W 24850	65.8	W 25756	95.3	W 26637	87.5	W 24752	80.3	BARRES,PROFILES FILS ALU
68422	ALUMNM PLATE,SHEET,STRIP	W 52110	109.0	W 52671	146.6	W 58818	145.5	W 73588	170.5	TOLES, PLANCHES EN ALU
68423	ALUMINIUM FOIL	W 22856	54.1	W 24425	77.6	W 22706	68.4	W 26942	74.9	FEUILLES,BANDES MINCES AL
69	METAL MANUFACTURES NES		141.2		178.0		208.7		171.6	ART MANUFACT EN METAL NDA
691	STRUCTURES AND PARTS NES	W 9167	19.7	W 12834	30.2	W 18680	36.4	W 16949	33.6	CONSTRUCT FER,ACIER,ALU
692	METAL TANKS,BOXES,ETC	W 9096	27.8	W 10393	43.2	W 11698	44.7	W 11762	40.5	RECIPIENTS METALLIQUES
6924	MTL TRANSPORT BOXES ETC	W 8340	27.2	W 9508	41.5	W 10062	41.4	W 9799	37.2	FUTS,TAMBOURS,BIDONS
697	BASE MTL HOUSEHOLD EQUIP	W 4890	35.5	W 3919	31.2	W 4182	33.3	W 3434	16.8	ART MENAGE MET COMMUNS
699	BASE METAL MFRS NES	W 8707	34.6	W 9056	40.9	W 17933	53.8	W 13623	52.1	ART MANUFACTURES MET NDA
7	MACHINES,TRANSPORT EQUIP		577.3		878.0		960.7		898.8	MACHINES MATERIEL TRANSPORT
71	POWER GENERATING EQUIPMT		57.0		141.0		165.1		81.8	MACHINES GENERATRICES
713	INTRNL COMBUS PSTN ENGIN	W 4873	42.3	W 6301	55.6	W 7935	67.3	W 7446	57.0	MOTEURS EXPL COMB INT, PIECE
7139	PISTON ENGINE PARTS NES	W 4711	38.2	W 6083	52.3	W 7549	64.5	W 7231	55.5	PIECES POUR 713.2,3,8
714	ENGINES AND MOTORS NES	W 23	7.8	W 181	80.2	W 179	91.4	W 36	15.7	MOTEURS NON ELECTRIQUES
7144	REACTION ENGINES	W 11	0.6	W 163	53.1	W 103	51.2	W 15	9.2	PROPULSEURS A REACTION
72	MACHS FOR SPCL INDUSTRYS		61.8		68.2		98.4		107.9	MAC SPECIALES POUR INDUST
724	TEXTILE,LEATHER MACHNRY	W 2872	18.3	W 3853	21.4	W 5308	28.3	W 7800	37.0	MACH POUR INDUSTRIE TEXTILE
728	OTH MACHY FOR SPCL INDUS	W 3432	15.9	W 4951	22.6	W 8806	31.6	W 6195	34.3	AUT MACH IND PARTICULIERES
74	GENRL INDUSTRL MACHY NES		66.4		104.7		114.4		117.5	MACH APP INDUSTRIE
741	HEATING,COOLING EQUIPMNT	W 3248	25.5	W 5174	48.6	W 6132	49.4	W 7027	48.5	MACH CHAUFFAGE,PIECES
75	OFFICE MACHNES,ADP EQUIP		18.7		20.5		30.2		33.7	MACH BUREAU TRAIT AUTOM
76	TELECOMM,SOUND EQUIPMENT		60.9		70.3		86.8		101.8	EQUIPMENT DE TELECOM
764	TELECOM EQPT,PTS,ACC NES	W 573	56.5	W 1109	65.7	W 751	79.5	W 1426	95.0	EQUIP TELECOM,PIECES
7649	PTS NES OF EQUIPMT OF 76	W 488	50.4	W 830	30.8	W 274	19.5	W 803	28.6	PIECES DE LA DIV 76
76491	PTS NES OF APPAR OF 7641	W 400	46.1	W 730	26.4	W 142	16.8	W 602	23.8	PIECES POUR 764.1
77	ELECTRIC MACHNRY NES ETC		215.3		300.6		309.2		289.9	MACH APP ELECT NDA
772	SWITCHGEAR ETC,PARTS NES	W 2057	31.5	W 2993	46.5	W 3171	49.1	W 3013	41.5	APP COUPURE,SECT ETC
7721	SWITCHGEAR ETC	W 2027	30.0	W 2954	44.4	W 3108	46.4	W 2956	40.1	APP COUPURE,SECTIONMNT
773	ELECTR DISTRIBUTNG EQUIP	W 42137	92.0	W 45848	132.1	W 41175	110.9	W 44538	108.7	EQUIPMT DISTRIBUTION ELECT
7731	INSULATED WIRE,CABLE ETC	W 42096	90.4	W 45758	130.0	W 41105	108.4	W 44390	107.6	FILS,CABLES ISOLES ELECT
775	HOUSEHOLD TYPE EQUIP NES	W 11439	60.9	W 14575	84.5	W 17266	102.2	W 16620	90.9	MACH,APP USAGE DOMESTQUE
7752	DOM REFRIGERATRS,FREEZRS	W 6762	32.5	W 7975	41.0	W 8318	44.5	W 8350	41.3	REFRIG,CONGEL MENAGER
7758	ELECTRO–THERMIC APPL NES	W 2442	16.9	W 4322	29.0	W 5923	41.6	W 5920	35.7	APP ELECTROTHERMIQ NDA
77586	ELECTROTHERM DOM APP NES	W 1661	11.6	W 3406	24.6	W 5238	36.3	W 5236	31.8	APP ELECTRO THERMIQUES
78	ROAD VEHICLES		42.7		61.7		65.8		90.3	VEHICULES ROUTIERS
79	OTHR TRANSPORT EQUIPMENT		48.3		100.4		82.8		68.4	AUTRE MATERIEL TRANSPORT
792	AIRCRAFT ETC	W 71	17.4	W 156	69.1	W 106	43.1	W 114	19.0	APP NAVIGATION AERIENNE

5. Special Exports F.O.B. by Commodities according to the S.I.T.C. (Rev. 2) in million U.S. Dollars
Exportations Spéciales F.O.B. par Produits d'après la C.T.C.I. (Rév. 2) en millions de Dollars E.U.

SITC CTCI	COMMODITY	1994 QUANTITY QUANTITE	1994 VALUE VALEUR	1995 QUANTITY QUANTITE	1995 VALUE VALEUR	1996 QUANTITY QUANTITE	1996 VALUE VALEUR	1997 QUANTITY QUANTITE	1997 VALUE VALEUR	PRODUIT
7924	AIRCRFT NES OVER 15000KG			W 60	35.6	W 36	16.0	W 64	5.9	AERODYNES PLUS 15000 KG
793	SHIPS AND BOATS ETC	W 996	29.3	W 732	30.5	W 693	39.3	W 1823	48.8	NAVIRES BATEAUX,ETC
7932	SHIPS AND BOATS NES	W 868	25.4	W 523	26.9	W 515	36.2	W 1645	46.7	NAVIRES ET BATEAUX
8	MISC MANUFACTURED GOODS		1995.1		2284.9		2365.6		2512.3	ART MANUFACTURES DIVERS
812	*PLUMBG,HEATNG,LGHTNG EQ	W 5230	22.6	W 6800	28.4	W 6999	29.6	W 9160	33.0	APPAR SANITAIRES CHAUFFAGE
821	*FURNITURE,PARTS THEREOF	W 10641	31.2	W 8604	35.8	W 11219	41.4	W 9183	36.4	MEUBLES ET PIECES
84	CLOTHING AND ACCESSORIES		1670.3		1844.8		1878.5		1632.0	VETEMENTS
842	MENS OUTERWEAR NOT KNIT	W 3762	93.3	W 3044	81.0	W 3260	76.5	W 3078	80.8	VET DESSUS POUR HOMMES
8423	— TROUSERS,BREECHES ETC	W 2287	43.0	W 1684	36.7	W 1803	36.4	W 1611	30.1	PANTALONS HOMMES MAT TEX
843	WOMENS OUTERWEAR NONKNIT	W 8717	299.0	W 9526	281.5	W 8618	257.8	W 8933	174.2	VET DESSUS FEMMES MAT TEX
8431	— COATS AND JACKETS	W 988	40.5	W 783	36.1	W 614	27.0	W 449	16.8	MANT,VEST FEM MAT TEXTIL
8434	— SKIRTS	W 2347	65.5	W 2065	68.2	W 3202	71.7	W 3329	29.0	JUPES EN MAT TEXTILES
8435	— BLOUSES	W 2467	100.7	W 4148	90.5	W 1852	72.1	W 1828	57.3	BLOUSES FEM MAT TEXTILES
8439	— OTHER OUTER GARMENTS	W 2274	67.4	W 1905	62.4	W 2428	65.5	W 2898	54.2	AUT VET DES FEM MAT TEXT
845	OUTERWEAR KNIT NONELASTC	W 23368	581.3	W 27140	687.0	W 43193	683.1	W 66847	576.8	VET DESSOUS,ACCES BONNET
8451	— JERSEYS,PULLOVERS ETC	W 5273	124.2	W 5314	133.9	W 6165	132.2	W 8733	100.3	CHANDAILS,PULL–OVERS ETC
8452	— WOMENS DRESSES ETC	W 2076	58.4	W 2389	78.8	W 3797	66.3	W 4973	35.4	ROBES,JUPES BONNETERIE
8459	— OTHER,CLTHG ACCESRYS	W 16020	398.8	W 19437	474.5	W 33231	484.7	W 53141	441.2	AUT VET DESSUS DE BONNE
846	UNDER GARMENTS KNITTED	W 20174	481.0	W 23154	596.9	W 57600	593.5	W 49724	479.1	SOUS VETS DE BONNETERIE
8462	— OF COTTON NON ELASTIC	W 18836	443.1	W 22092	552.7	W 52786	552.7	W 48523	440.5	SOUS–VET BONNET COTON
84629	—— OTHER	W 18836	443.1	W 22092	552.7	W 52786	552.7	W 48523	440.5	AUT SOUS–VET BONNET COTON
848	HEADGEAR,NONTXTL CLOTHNG	W 934	199.5	W 970	181.2	W 1405	252.1	W 2327	303.9	VET ACCES MAT AUT QUE TEX
8483	FUR ETC,CLOTHES,PRODUCTS	W 740	194.0	W 621	173.3	W 974	240.8	W 1584	294.0	VETEMENTS DE FOURRURE
84831	ARTICLES OF FURSKIN,NES	W 737	193.8	W 615	173.1	W 962	240.1	W 1569	293.0	PELLETERIES OUVREES NDA
851	*FOOTWEAR	W 1987	34.9	W 1753	38.5	W 3175	47.9	W 2414	49.9	CHAUSSURES
85102	FOOTWEAR LEATHER	W 989	23.2	W 1076	27.5	W 1315	33.3	W 1542	35.0	CHAUS SEMELLES EN CUIR
87	PRECISION INSTRUMNTS NES		33.9		48.7		64.2		60.3	INSTRUM,APPAR SCIENT NDA
89	MISC MANUFCTRD GOODS NES		191.8		275.0		285.6		681.4	ART MANUFACTURES DIVERS
892	PRINTED MATTER	W 3438	23.0		65.3	W 4598	45.0	W 5570	430.5	IMPRIMES
8928	PRINTED MATTER NES	W 653	5.2		44.8	W 1151	21.4	W 1319	405.9	IMPRIMES NDA
89283	UNISSUED BANKNOTES ETC	W 78	0.7		39.6	W 5	9.5	W 16	396.8	TIMBRES–POSTE FISCAUX
893	ARTICLES OF PLASTIC NES		95.4		121.6		127.4		113.2	OUVRAGES EN MAT DIVIS 58
8939	MISC PLASTIC ARTICLES	W 24231	71.3	W 28912	100.2	W 32143	103.6	W 34373	89.4	ART DIVERS EN MAT DIV 58
89399	OTHR PLASTC ARTICLES NES	W 23660	68.7	W 28256	97.1	W 31313	99.2	W 32895	82.3	AUT OUV MAT DIV 58
898	MUSICAL INSTRUMENTS,PTS	W 369	13.8	W 287	29.5	W 458	36.0	W 457	41.8	INSTRUMENTS DE MUSIQUE
8983	SOUND RECRDNG TAPE,DISCS	W 339	13.6	W 281	29.4	W 443	35.7	W 431	41.5	SUPPORTS SON POUR 763
89832	RECORDED DISCS,TAPES ETC	W 247	13.1	W 216	28.6	W 311	34.3	W 356	40.7	DISQUES,PHONO,BANDES
9	GOODS NOT CLASSD BY KIND		220.1		287.4		273.8		218.9	ART TRANSACT NON CLASSES
931	*SPECIAL TRANSACTIONS		199.7		260.1		233.6		198.8	TRANS.SPECIALES
951	*WAR FIREARMS,AMMUNITION	W 63	20.0	W 49	20.3		39.6		14.0	VEHIC BLINDES ARMES
95109	PARTS OF ARMS NES	W 9	17.8	W 8	15.5		37.3		9.6	PIECES POUR ARMES

1. HISTORICAL SERIES, 1962–1997 GENERAL TRADE, IMPORTS C.I.F., EXPORTS F.O.B.
SERIES HISTORIQUES, 1962–1997 COMMERCE GENERAL, IMPORTATIONS C.A.F., EXPORTATIONS F.O.B

YEAR ANNEE	VALUE IN MILLION DANISH KRONER / VALEUR EN MILLION DANISH KRONER — MERCHANDISE –MARCHANDISE		GOLD –OR		CONVERSION FACTORS U.S. CENTS PER DANISH KRONE FACTEURS DE CONVERSION CENTS E.U. PAR DANISH KRONE		INDEX NUMBERS –INDICES — QUANTUM		UNIT VALUE VALEUR UNITAIRE	
	IMPORTS	EXPORTS	IMPORTS	EXPORTS	IMPORTS	EXPORTS	IMPORTS	EXPORTS	IMPORTS	EXPORTS
1962	153.90	61.80			14.4800	14.4800				
1963	174.10	75.60			14.4800	14.4800				
1964	197.00	72.50			14.4800	14.4800				
1965	234.80	89.80			14.4800	14.4800				
1966	269.00	103.00			14.4800	14.4800				
1967	320.90	91.30			14.3360	14.3360				
1968	360.00	90.00			13.3300	13.3300				
1969	375.00	88.00			13.3300	13.3300				
1970	397.50	105.00			13.3300	13.3300				
1971	452.80	139.00			13.4800	13.4800				
1972	502.70	152.60			14.3330	14.3330				
1973	565.70	191.10			16.5300	16.5300				
1974	633.70	551.10			16.7900	16.7900				
1975	741.90	509.40			17.3900	17.3900				
1976	777.90	516.50			16.5800	16.6500				
1977	964.60	555.20			16.6100	16.5600				
1978	980.30	559.30			18.2730	18.3530				
1979	1447.60	921.20			18.9730	18.9540				
1980	1846.20	1167.60			17.7280	17.7110				
1981	2101.80	1442.20			14.0445	14.0445				
1982	2286.50	1422.30			11.9963	11.9963				
1983	2421.00	1644.70			10.9313	10.9313				
1984	2836.30	1750.60			9.6520	9.6520				
1985	3140.20	1841.80			9.4340	9.4340				
1986	2911.83	2078.46			12.3541	12.3541				
1987	3470.68	2369.48			14.6118	14.6118				
1988	3494.66	2630.63			14.8544	14.8544				
1989	2914.96	3055.94			13.6807	13.6807				
1990	2755.68	2794.69			16.2278	16.2278				
1991	2609.04	2179.20			15.6351	15.6351				
1992	2754.17	2008.60			16.5861	16.5861				
1993	2243.61	2029.66			15.4242	15.4242				
1994	2311.78	1810.72			16.9403	16.9403				
1995	2357.37	2035.42			17.8635	17.8657				
1996	2705.22	2140.93			17.2398	17.2413				
1997	2542.22	1937.23			14.7145	14.7225				

2. IMPORTS BY BROAD ECONOMIC CATEGORY AND EXPORTS BY INDUSTRIAL ORIGIN. (PERCENTAGE OF TOTAL VALUE)
IMPORTATIONS PAR CATEGORIES ECONOMIQUES ET EXPORTATIONS PAR BRANCHE D'ACTIVITE.(EN POURCENTAGE DE LA VALEUR TOTALE)

IMPORTS – IMPORTATIONS

	1991	1992	1993	1994	1995	1996	1997
TOTAL IMPORTS–IMPORTATIONS TOTALES	100.	100.	100.	100.	100.	100.	100.
1 FOOD BEV–ALIMENTATION BOISSONS	18.4	18.1	15.2	14.2	13.2	13.9	14.3
11 PRIMARY–PRODUITS DE BASE	6.3	7.2	5.5	5.2	4.7	4.2	4.9
111 FOR INDUSTRY–POUR L'INDUSTRIE	0.5	0.4	0.1	0.2	0.2	0.2	0.5
112 FOR HOUSEHOLDS–POUR LES MENAGES	5.8	6.8	5.3	5.0	4.5	3.9	4.4
12 PROCESSED–PRODUITS ELABORES	12.1	11.0	9.7	9.0	8.5	9.7	9.4
121 FOR INDUSTRY–POUR L'INDUSTRIE	0.6	0.5	0.4	0.4	0.3	0.4	0.3
122 FOR HOUSEHOLDS–POUR LES MENAGES	11.5	10.4	9.3	8.6	8.2	9.3	9.1
2 IND SUPPLIES–APPROV INDUSTRIELS	21.2	18.1	21.2	18.5	21.5	18.0	17.5
21 PRIMARY–PRODUITS DE BASE	0.5	0.4	0.4	0.4	0.4	0.4	0.5
22 PROCESSED–PRODUITS ELABORES	20.7	17.7	20.8	18.1	21.1	17.5	17.0
3 FUELS–COMBUSTIBLES	11.9	9.8	11.1	9.8	5.8	9.9	9.7
31 PRIMARY–PRODUITS DE BASE	0.1	0.1	0.2	0.1	0.1	0.1	0.1
32 PROCESSED–PRODUITS ELABORES	11.8	9.7	10.9	9.7	5.7	9.8	9.6
321 MOTOR SPIRIT–ESSENCE	11.8	9.7	10.9				
322 OTHER–AUTRES	0.0	0.0	0.0	9.7	5.7	9.8	9.6
4 MACHINERY–EQUIPEMENT	13.7	15.5	15.1	15.7	14.1	14.0	15.4
41 CAPITAL EQUIPMENT–MACHINES	11.7	13.8	13.1	13.6	12.1	11.9	12.9
42 PARTS–PIECES ACCESSOIRES	2.0	1.7	2.0	2.2	2.0	2.1	2.5
5 TRANSPORT–TRANSPORT	6.5	12.9	7.0	7.3	10.2	15.5	11.0
51 PASSENGER CARS–AUTOMOBILES	0.7	0.5	0.4	0.4	0.6	0.7	0.8
52 OTHER–AUTRES	2.0	9.0	3.3	3.3	6.3	10.5	5.8
521 INDUSTRIAL–INDUSTRIELS	1.9	8.9	3.2	3.1	6.2	10.4	5.7
522 NON INDUSTRIAL–NON INDUSTRIEL	0.1	0.1	0.1	0.2	0.1	0.1	0.1
53 PARTS–PIECES ACCESSOIRES	3.8	3.5	3.4	3.6	3.3	4.3	4.4
6 CONSUM GOODS–BIENS CONSOMMATION	15.1	14.1	16.5	16.6	16.1	13.5	14.9
61 DURABLE–DURABLES	4.1	3.7	4.5	4.0	4.5	3.7	4.1
62 SEMI DURABLE–SEMI DURABLES	6.6	6.1	7.5	7.9	7.2	6.2	6.7
63 NON DURABLE–NON DURABLES	4.4	4.2	4.5	4.7	4.4	3.7	4.2
7 GOODS NES–BIENS NDA	13.2	11.5	13.9	17.9	19.2	15.3	17.2

EXPORTS – EXPORTATIONS

	1991	1992	1993	1994	1995	1996	1997
TOTAL EXPORTS–EXPORTATIONS TOTALES	100.	100.	100.	100.	100.	100.	100.
1 AGRICULTURE	68.6	63.2	59.7	63.5	62.4	59.9	64.5
2 MINING QUARRY–INDUS EXTRACTIVES	0.0	0.0					0.0
3 MANUFACTURING–IND MANUFACTUR	31.4	36.8	40.3	36.5	37.6	40.1	35.5
31 FOOD BEV TOBACCO–ALIM BOISS TAB	26.9	31.6	33.0	30.5	33.3	32.6	28.7
32 TEXTILES–INDUSTRIES TEXTILES	0.1	0.2	0.2	0.3	0.2	0.3	0.2
33 WOOD & PRODUCTS–BOIS & PRODUITS			0.0	0.0	0.0		
34 PAPER & PRODUCTS–PAPIER & PRODT	0.1	0.0	0.0	0.0	0.0	0.0	0.0
35 CHEMICALS–INDUSTRIES CHIMIQUES	0.9	1.0	1.2	1.1	0.8	1.2	1.1
36 NON METAL MIN–MIN NON METAL	0.0	0.0	0.0	0.0	0.0	0.0	0.0
37 BASIC METAL–IND METAL BASE	0.0	0.0	0.0	0.0	0.0	0.0	0.0
38 METAL MANUF–MANUF METAL	1.4	1.8	1.7	0.5	0.4	2.4	2.0
39 OTH MANUF IND–AUTRES MANUF	2.1	2.1	4.1	4.1	2.8	3.6	3.4

3. TRADE BY PRINCIPAL COUNTRIES OF ORIGIN AND DESTINATION (VALUE IN MILLION U.S. DOLLARS)
ECHANGES SELON LES PRINCIPAUX PAYS D'ORIGINE ET DE DESTINATION (VALEUR EN MILLIONS DE DOLLARS EU)

COUNTRIES–PAYS	GENERAL IMPORTS C.I.F. IMPORTATIONS GENERALES C.A.F				
	1993	1994	1995	1996	1997
World	346.1	391.6	421.1	466.4	374.1
Africa	0.1	0.1	0.2	0.2	0.2
Americas	17.2	22.3	15.3	31.3	17.7
– Northern America	16.6	21.4	14.3	30.2	16.9
– LAIA	0.5	0.8	0.9	0.8	0.4
– CACM	0.2	0.0	0.0	0.3	0.3
– Caribbean	0.0	0.0	0.0	0.0	0.1
– Rest of America	0.0	0.0	0.0	0.0	0.0
Asia excl fmr USSR	19.0	19.5	21.9	20.6	20.5
– Middle East	0.1	0.1	0.2	0.2	0.2
Asia former USSR	0.0	0.0	0.0	0.0	0.0
Europe excl fmr USSR	306.4	346.8	381.5	411.8	334.1
– European Union	290.5	332.4	350.3	355.6	284.2
– Eastern Europe	0.4	0.4	0.4	0.8	0.8
– Rest of Europe	15.5	14.0	30.9	55.4	49.1
Europe former USSR	2.1	1.4	0.3	0.3	0.2
Oceania	0.8	0.5	0.8	0.9	0.2
Other	0.5	0.9	1.0	1.2	1.2
Denmark/Danemark	258.7	299.5	314.9	309.8	245.0
Norway,Svalbard and JM	14.0	11.5	13.1	53.9	46.4
USA/Etats–Unis d'Amer	13.9	12.9	10.2	16.8	11.6
Japan/Japon	12.4	12.8	14.1	11.4	10.9
Germany/Allemagne	8.4	8.7	9.9	10.3	8.8
Canada	2.7	8.5	4.1	13.4	5.3
Sweden/Suède	5.0	6.0	7.5	7.7	6.3
United Kingdom	5.9	4.7	5.0	5.7	4.5
France, Monaco	2.9	2.7	2.7	7.1	8.7
Iceland/Islande	0.8	1.0	15.9	0.8	1.8
Netherlands/Pays–Bas	2.6	3.5	3.2	4.5	3.4
Italy/Italie	2.3	2.5	2.6	4.6	2.2
China/Chine	1.2	1.8	1.8	2.5	2.2
Korea, Republic of	2.2	1.8	1.7	1.6	1.7
Finland/Finlande	1.5	1.4	1.3	1.7	1.1
Other Asia n.e.s.	0.6	0.8	1.7	1.4	1.5
Portugal	1.3	1.2	1.1	1.1	1.0
Belgium–Luxembourg	0.9	1.0	1.0	1.1	0.9
Areas n.e.s.	0.5	0.9	0.9	1.2	1.2
China, Hong Kong SAR	1.4	0.8	0.8	1.0	0.7
Russian Federation	2.1	1.4	0.3	0.2	0.2
Switzerland,Liechtenst.	0.4	0.6	0.7	0.4	0.8
Spain/Espagne	0.3	0.3	0.4	0.9	0.9
Indonesia/Indonésie	0.2	0.2	0.2	0.5	1.3
New Zealand	0.5	0.4	0.5	0.8	0.2
Ireland/Irlande	0.2	0.4	0.4	0.4	0.9
India/Inde	0.2	0.3	0.3	0.6	0.4
Faeroe Islds/Is Féroé	0.1	0.6	1.0	0.1	0.0
Austria/Autriche	0.4	0.3	0.2	0.4	0.3
Ecuador/Equateur	0.2	0.4	0.4	0.3	0.2
Malaysia/Malaisie	0.2	0.2	0.3	0.3	0.5
Thailand/Thaïlande	0.2	0.2	0.3	0.2	0.3
Chile/Chili	0.1	0.3	0.3	0.2	0.1
Australia/Australie	0.3	0.1	0.4	0.1	0.0
Poland/Pologne	0.1	0.1	0.2	0.3	0.1
Slovenia/Slovénie	0.1	0.3	0.2	0.2	0.1
Singapore/Singapour	0.1	0.1	0.2	0.2	0.2
Hungary/Hongrie	0.2	0.1	0.0	0.2	0.3
Czech Republic	0.1	0.1	0.1	0.2	0.2
Greece/Grèce	0.1	0.1	0.2	0.2	0.2

COUNTRIES–PAYS	GENERAL EXPORTS F.O.B. EXPORTATIONS GENERALES F.O.B.				
	1993	1994	1995	1996	1997
Monde	313.1	306.7	363.6	369.1	285.2
Afrique					
Amériques	8.1	3.0	2.2	1.0	6.1
– Amérique du Nord	8.1	3.0	2.2	1.0	6.1
– ALAI					
– MCAC					
– Caraïbes					
– Autre Amérique					
Asie anc. URSS exclus	40.9	18.2	17.8	17.2	10.1
– Moyen–Orient					
Asie ancienne URSS					
Europe anc. URSS exclus	253.6	280.7	340.8	343.1	265.9
– Union Européenne	253.2	280.5	339.5	333.7	260.3
– Europe de l'Est					
– Autre de l'Europe	0.5	0.2	1.3	9.4	5.6
Europe ancienne URSS					
Océanie	3.9				
Autre	6.5	4.9	2.9	7.8	3.0
Denmark/Danemark	236.9	262.2	322.5	318.3	250.1
Japan/Japon	40.9	18.2	16.9	16.3	9.6
United Kingdom	14.2	17.7	16.9	15.0	10.0
Areas n.e.s.	6.5	4.9	2.9	7.8	3.0
USA/Etats–Unis d'Amer	6.0	3.0	2.2	0.5	6.0
Norway,Svalbard and JM	0.0	0.1	0.9	3.6	4.5
Iceland/Islande	0.5	0.1	0.4	5.7	1.1
New Zealand	3.9				
Canada	2.1	0.0	0.1	0.5	0.1
Germany/Allemagne	2.1	0.6	0.0		0.0
Other Asia n.e.s.			0.9	0.6	
Thailand/Thaïlande				0.3	0.3
Netherlands/Pays–Bas					0.3
Sweden/Suède		0.0		0.2	0.0
China/Chine					0.2
France, Monaco	0.0			0.1	0.0
Ireland/Irlande				0.1	
Faeroe Islds/Is Féroé					0.0
China, Hong Kong SAR	0.0	0.0			
Belgium–Luxembourg	0.0	0.0			
Finland/Finlande	0.0				
Austria/Autriche				0.0	
Korea, Republic of		0.0			
Switzerland,Liechtenst.	0.0				
Italy/Italie	0.0				

(VALUE AS PERCENTAGE OF WORLD TOTAL)(VALEURS EN POURCENTAGE DU TOTAL MONDIAL)

	1988	1989	1990	1991	1992	1993	1994	1995	1996	1997
Africa	0.1	0.1	0.1	0.1	0.1	0.0	0.0	0.1	0.1	0.0
Americas	4.7	4.6	5.4	3.9	3.3	5.0	5.7	3.6	6.7	4.7
– Northern America	4.4	4.3	5.1	3.6	3.1	4.8	5.5	3.4	6.5	4.5
– LAIA	0.1	0.2	0.2	0.2	0.1	0.1	0.2	0.2	0.2	0.1
– CACM	0.1	0.1	0.1	0.1	0.1	0.0	0.0	0.0	0.1	0.1
– Caribbean	0.0	0.0	0.0	0.0	0.0	0.0	0.0	0.0	0.0	0.0
– Rest of America	0.0	0.0	0.0	0.0	0.0	0.0	0.0	0.0	0.0	0.0
Asia excl fmr USSR	5.8	5.3	5.3	5.6	4.8	5.5	5.0	5.2	4.4	5.5
– Middle East	0.1	0.0	0.0	0.0	0.0	0.0	0.0	0.0	0.0	0.1
Asia former USSR					0.0	0.0	0.0	0.0	0.0	0.0
Europe excl fmr USSR	89.1	89.5	88.9	90.0	91.0	88.5	88.6	90.6	88.3	89.3
– European Union	82.2	84.6	79.0	78.7	83.8	83.9	84.9	83.2	76.3	76.0
– Eastern Europe	0.2	0.3	0.2	0.2	0.1	0.1	0.1	0.1	0.2	0.2
– Rest of Europe	6.7	4.7	9.7	11.1	7.1	4.5	3.6	7.3	11.9	13.1
Europe former USSR	0.1	0.1	0.0	0.1	0.6	0.6	0.4	0.1	0.1	0.1
Oceania	0.1	0.2	0.1	0.2	0.2	0.2	0.1	0.2	0.2	0.1
Other	0.1	0.1	0.1	0.1	0.1	0.1	0.2	0.2	0.3	0.3
Denmark/Danemark	66.0	69.2	65.6	66.8	73.3	74.8	76.5	74.8	66.4	65.5
Norway,Svalbard and JM	5.2	3.8	8.8	10.3	6.6	4.1	2.9	3.1	11.6	12.4
USA/Etats–Unis d'Amer	2.8	3.7	4.6	2.7	2.5	4.0	3.3	2.4	3.6	3.1
Japan/Japon	3.8	3.5	3.9	4.0	3.2	3.6	3.3	3.3	2.4	2.9
Germany/Allemagne				3.2	2.9	2.4	2.2	2.3	2.2	2.4
Canada	1.7	0.6	0.5	1.0	0.6	0.8	2.2	1.0	2.9	1.4
Sweden/Suède	3.6	3.0	2.5	2.2	1.7	1.4	1.5	1.8	1.7	1.7
United Kingdom	1.6	2.2	1.8	1.5	1.6	1.7	1.2	1.2	1.2	1.2
France, Monaco	1.2	1.2	1.4	1.5	1.0	0.8	0.7	0.6	1.5	2.3
Iceland/Islande	1.1	0.5	0.6	0.4	0.3	0.2	0.3	3.8	0.2	0.5

	1988	1989	1990	1991	1992	1993	1994	1995	1996	1997
Afrique										
Amériques	0.0	0.0	0.0	0.0	2.9	2.6	1.0	0.6	0.3	2.1
– Amérique du Nord	0.0	0.0	0.0	0.0	2.9	2.6	1.0	0.6	0.3	2.1
– ALAI										
– MCAC										
– Caraïbes										
– Autre Amérique										
Asie anc. URSS exclus	0.0	0.4	0.9	0.9	3.7	13.1	5.9	4.9	4.7	3.6
– Moyen–Orient										
Asie ancienne URSS										
Europe anc. URSS exclus	98.6	98.7	97.6	97.5	90.7	81.0	91.5	93.7	92.9	93.2
– Union Européenne	96.2	97.5	97.5	96.8	90.4	80.9	91.4	93.3	90.4	91.3
– Europe de l'Est										
– Autre de l'Europe	2.4	1.3	0.1	0.7	0.3	0.1	0.1	0.4	2.5	2.0
Europe ancienne URSS					1.0					
Océanie				0.0		1.3				
Autre	1.4	0.9	1.5	1.6	1.7	2.1	1.6	0.8	2.1	1.1
Denmark/Danemark	76.8	73.8	91.1	93.5	88.2	75.7	85.5	88.7	86.2	87.7
Japan/Japon	0.0	0.4	0.9	0.9	3.7	13.1	5.9	4.6	4.4	3.4
United Kingdom	1.4	2.1	4.1	2.7	2.2	4.5	5.8	4.7	4.1	3.5
Areas n.e.s.	1.4	0.9	1.5	1.6	1.7	2.1	1.6	0.8	2.1	1.1
USA/Etats–Unis d'Amer				0.0	2.3	1.9	1.0	0.6	0.1	2.1
Norway,Svalbard and JM	2.4	1.2	0.1	0.0	0.0	0.0	0.0	0.2	1.0	1.6
Iceland/Islande	0.0	0.0	0.0	0.7	0.3	0.1	0.0	0.1	1.6	0.4
New Zealand				0.0		1.3				
Canada	0.0	0.0	0.0		0.7	0.7	0.0	0.0	0.1	0.0
Germany/Allemagne				0.1	0.0	0.7	0.2	0.0		0.0

4. General Imports C.I.F. by Commodities according to the S.I.T.C. (Rev. 2) in million U.S. Dollars
Importations Générales C.A.F. par Produits d'après la C.T.C.I. (Rév. 2) en millions de Dollars E.U.

SITC CTCI	COMMODITY	1994		1995		1996		1997		PRODUIT
		QUANTITY QUANTITE	VALUE VALEUR	QUANTITY QUANTITE	VALUE VALEUR	QUANTITY QUANTITE	VALUE VALEUR	QUANTITY QUANTITE	VALUE VALEUR	
	ALL COMMODITIES		391.7		421.2		466.4		374.1	TOUS PRODUITS
0	FOOD AND LIVE ANIMALS		44.6		44.5		54.9		43.4	ALIMENTS,ANIMAUX VIVANTS
01	MEAT AND PREPARATIONS		14.6		14.7		16.3		13.9	VIANDES ET PREPARATIONS
011	MEAT FRESH,CHILLD,FROZEN	W 2286	9.3	W 2098	9.4	W 2278	10.2	W 2358	9.3	VIANDES FRAICHES,REF,CONGE
0111	BOVINE MEAT FRESH,FROZEN	W 490	3.0	W 522	3.3	W 630	3.9	W 598	3.1	VIANDES BOVIN FRAI,REF
01112	BOVINE MEAT BONELESS	W 451	2.7	W 430	2.9	W 570	3.4	W 550	2.9	VIANDES BOVIN DESOSSEES
0113	PIG MEAT FRESH,CHLD,FRZN	W 1125	4.4	W 1054	4.5	W 944	4.3	W 1006	4.3	VIANDE DE PORC
014	MEAT PREPD,PRSVD,NES ETC	W 993	4.6	W 918	4.7	W 1075	5.5	W 936	4.2	CONSERVES DE VIANDES
0142	SAUSAGES INCLDING TINNED	W 557	2.4	W 510	2.4	W 577	2.8	W 486	2.1	SAUCISSES,SAUCISSONS
0149	OTH PREPARD,PRESRVD MEAT	W 435	2.3	W 409	2.3	W 498	2.7	W 451	2.2	AUTRES PREP DE VIANDES
02	DAIRY PRODCTS,BIRDS'EGGS		7.8		7.7		8.8		7.4	PRODUITS LAITIERS,OEUFS
022	MILK AND CREAM	W 3109	3.9	W 2687	3.7	W 3058	4.3	W 3066	3.8	LAIT ET CREME
0223	MILK AND CREAM FRESH	W 3017	3.5	W 2590	3.2	W 2964	3.8	W 3001	3.4	LAIT,CREME FRAIS
024	CHEESE AND CURD	W 450	2.4	W 412	2.5	W 419	2.8	W 432	2.5	FROMAGE ET CAILLEBOTTE
03	FISH AND PREPARATIONS		3.9		4.1		6.3		0.7	POISSONS ET PREPARATIONS
034	FISH,FRESH,CHILLED,FROZN	W 741	1.5	W 1574	2.6	W 28	0.3	W 14	0.1	POISSON FRAIS, REFRIG,CONG
0342	FISH FROZEN,EXCL FILLETS	W 734	1.5	W 1568	2.5	W 22	0.2	W 6	0.1	POISSONS CONGELES
036	SHELL FISH FRESH,FROZEN	W 1446	1.9	W 376	0.8	W 523	0.9	W 209	0.3	CRUSTACES,MOLLUSQUES
037	FISH ETC PREPD,PRSVD NES	W 53	0.3	W 73	0.4	W 3553	5.0	W 79	0.4	POIS,CRUST,MOL PREPARES
0372	SHELL FISH PREPRD,PRESVD	W 4	0.1	W 7	0.1	W 3470	4.6	W 8	0.1	CRUSTACES,COQUIL PREPARES
04	CEREALS AND PREPARATIONS		3.9		4.2		6.3		4.6	CEREALES ET PRODUITS
048	CEREAL ETC PREPARATIONS	W 868	2.6	W 869	3.2	W 1319	4.7	W 1028	3.3	PREPTNS A BASE CEREALES
0484	BAKERY PRODUCTS	W 584	1.8	W 506	1.8	W 622	2.3	W 568	2.1	PRODUITS DE BOULANGERIE
04841	BREAD,BISCUIT,COM WAFERS	W 500	1.4	W 410	1.3	W 497	1.7	W 427	1.4	PAINS,BISCUITS DE MER
05	VEGETABLES AND FRUIT		5.7		5.2		5.3		5.8	LEGUMES ET FRUITS
054	VEG ETC FRSH,SMPLY PRSVD	W 420	0.8	W 475	1.0	W 558	1.0	W 1588	1.8	LEGUMES FRAIS,CONG,SECS
056	VEGTBLES ETC PRSVD,PREPD	W 313	1.2	W 267	1.1	W 348	1.2	W 394	1.3	CONSERVES DE LEGUMES
0565	VEGTBLES PRSVD,PREPD NES	W 312	1.2	W 264	1.1	W 347	1.2	W 393	1.3	LEGUMES PREPARES CONSERVE
057	FRUIT,NUTS,FRESH,DRIED	W 1205	2.0	W 771	1.3	W 899	1.6	W 982	1.4	FRUITS FRAIS OU SECS
058	FRUIT PRESERVED,PREPARED	W 1467	1.9	W 1302	1.9	W 955	1.6	W 903	1.4	CONSERVES DE FRUITS
0585	FRUIT OR VEGETABLE JUICE	W 1349	1.6	W 1197	1.6	W 781	1.2	W 713	1.0	JUS DE FRUITS
06	SUGAR AND PREPS,HONEY		2.9		2.7		3.3		3.2	SUCRES ET PRODUITS
061	SUGAR AND HONEY	W 1359	1.3	W 1205	1.3	W 1529	1.5	W 1666	1.4	SUCRES ET MIEL
0612	REFINED SUGAR ETC	W 1345	1.2	W 1194	1.2	W 1521	1.5	W 1650	1.4	SUCRES RAFFINES
062	SUGAR CANDY NON–CHOCLATE	W 219	1.6	W 191	1.4	W 270	1.9	W 299	1.9	SUCRERIES
07	COFFEE,TEA,COCOA,SPICES		1.7		1.8		2.3		2.8	CAFE,THE,CACAO,EPICES
071	COFFEE AND SUBSTITUTES	W 111	0.7	W 101	0.9	W 123	0.9	W 254	1.8	CAFE ET SUCCEDANES
0711	COFFEE GREEN,ROASTED,SUB	W 109	0.7	W 99	0.9	W 118	0.8	W 245	1.7	CAFE TORREFIE OU DECAFEINE
07112	COFFEE ROASTED	W 109	0.7	W 99	0.9	W 118	0.8	W 245	1.7	CAFE TORREFIE
09	MISC EDIBLE PRODUCTS		3.9		3.9		5.4		4.4	PREP ALIMENTAIRES DIVERSES
098	EDIBLE PRODCTS,PREPS NES	W 614	2.9	W 634	3.0	W 1038	4.5	W 1042	3.6	PREP ALIMENTAIRES NDA
09809	MISC FOOD PREPRTIONS NES	W 500	2.5	W 508	2.5	W 850	3.9	W 867	3.0	PREP ALIMENTAIRES NDA
1	BEVERAGES AND TOBACCO		16.1		15.3		15.9		14.9	BOISSONS ET TABACS
11	BEVERAGES		11.5		11.5		11.0		10.9	BOISSONS
111	NON–ALCOHL BEVERAGES NES	W 1900	2.5	W 1192	1.8	W 1284	1.9	W 1185	1.4	BOISSONS NON ALCOOLIQUES
11102	FLAVORED WATERS NON–ALCO	W 1883	2.5	W 1174	1.8	W 1243	1.9	W 1157	1.4	LIMONADES,EAUX GAZEUSES
112	ALCOHOLIC BEVERAGES	W 8767	9.0	W 7674	9.8	W 6802	9.1	W 8051	9.5	BOISSONS ALCOOLIQUES
1121	WINE OF FRESH GRAPES ETC	W 168	0.8	W 182	1.0	W 258	1.3	W 322	1.4	VINS DE RAISINS FRAIS
11212	WINE OF FRESH GRAPES	W 164	0.8	W 178	1.0	W 251	1.3	W 313	1.4	VINS DE MOUTS DE RAISINS
1123	BEER,ALE,STOUT,PORTER	W 8542	7.8	W 7435	8.3	W 6458	7.1	W 7624	7.2	BIERES
12	TOBACCO AND MANUFACTURES		4.7		3.8		5.0		4.1	TABACS BRUTS FABRIQUES
122	TOBACCO,MANUFACTURED	W 165	4.7	W 128	3.8	W 168	5.0	W 160	4.1	TABACS FABRIQUES
1222	CIGARETTES	W 148	4.2	W 116	3.5	W 153	4.6	W 144	3.8	CIGARETTES
2	CRUDE MATERLS,EXCL FUELS		5.8		6.4		6.5		4.9	MAT BRUTES NON COMESTIBLES
24	CORK AND WOOD		4.0		4.6		4.7		2.9	LIEGE ET BOIS
248	WOOD SHAPED,SLEEPERS	W 3865	3.9	W 3783	4.3	W 3713	4.1	W 3080	2.8	BOIS SIMPLEMENT TRAVAILLES
2482	LUMBER SHAPED CONIFER	W 3327	3.4	W 3474	4.0	W 3094	3.6	W 2858	2.6	CONIFERES SCIES,RABOTES
24821	LUMBER SAWN ETC CONIFER	W 3252	3.2	W 3367	3.8	W 3051	3.4	W 2824	2.6	CONIFERES SCIES LONGITUD
27	CRUDE FERTLZR,MINRLS NES		1.2		1.3		1.2		1.6	ENGRAIS MINERAUX BRUTS
278	OTHER CRUDE MINERALS	W 2795	1.2	W 2735	1.2	W 2486	1.1	W 4183	1.5	AUTRES MINERAUX BRUTS
2783	COMMON SALT,ETC	W 2693	1.1	W 2685	1.2	W 2425	1.0	W 4057	1.4	SEL
3	MINERAL FUELS ETC		38.3		24.4		46.7		36.3	COMBUSTIBLES MINERAUX LUB
33	PETROLEUM AND PRODUCTS		37.9		24.0		46.3		35.9	PETROLE ET DERIVES
334	PETROLEUM PRODUCTS,REFIN	W 163141	37.3	W 105682	23.4	W 185073	45.8	W 170036	35.4	PRODUITS RAFFINES
5	CHEMCLS,RELATED PROD NES		15.7		17.0		15.3		13.4	PRODUITS CHIMIQUES
53	DYES,TANNING,COLOUR PROD		3.0		3.9		3.3		2.5	PROD TEINTURE,COLORANTS
532	DYES NES,TANNING PROD	W 112	1.1	W 74	1.4	W 65	0.6	W 63	0.6	EXTRAITS TEINTURE,TANNAGE
5322	DYE,TANN EXTRCTS,TANNINS	W 109	1.1	W 74	1.4	W 65	0.6	W 63	0.6	EXT TAN ORIG VEG,TANNINS
53222	DYEING EXTRCTS VEG,ANMAL	W 109	1.1	W 74	1.4	W 65	0.6	W 63	0.6	MATI COLOR VEGET ANIMALE
533	PIGMENTS,PAINTS,ETC	W 368	1.9	W 449	2.5	W 553	2.7	W 448	2.0	PIGMENTS,PEINTURES,VERNIS
5334	VARNISHES,DISTEMPERS ETC	W 323	1.7	W 417	2.2	W 522	2.5	W 413	1.8	PEINTURES A L'EAU
53342	OTH PAINTS,VARNISHES ETC	W 136	0.8	W 209	1.1	W 356	1.6	W 282	1.2	AUTRES PEINTURES,VERNIS
541	*MEDICINAL,PHARM PRODUCT	K 89360	5.9	K 79614	6.2	K 77387	5.4	K 89473	5.0	PROD MEDICINAUX PHARMACEUT
5417	MEDICAMENTS	K 74699	5.2	K 71955	5.6	K 69549	4.9	K 80880	4.4	MEDICAMENTS
54179	— CONTNG OTH SUBSTANCES	K 74699	5.2	K 71954	5.6	K 69501	4.9	K 80840	4.4	MED CONT AUT SUBSTANCES
55	PERFUME,CLEANING ETC PRD		3.1		3.0		2.4		2.8	PROD POUR PARFUM,TOILETTE
553	PERFUMERY,COSMETICS,ETC	W 58	1.4	W 50	1.3	W 37	1.0	W 59	0.9	PRODUITS DE PARFUMERIE
554	SOAP,CLEANSING ETC PREPS	W 667	1.7	W 650	1.7	W 537	1.5	W 767	1.8	SAVONS,PRODUITS DETERSIFS
5542	WASHING PREPARATIONS ETC	W 601	1.5	W 593	1.5	W 488	1.3	W 712	1.6	PROD ORG TENSIO–ACT NDA
58	PLASTIC MATERIALS ETC		1.6		1.7		1.4		1.3	MAT PLAST ARTIFICIELLES
6	BASIC MANUFACTURES		61.3		77.1		70.4		56.1	ART MANUFACTURES
62	RUBBER MANUFACTURES NES		1.1		1.3		1.5		1.2	CAOUTCHOUC MANUFACTURE
63	WOOD,CORK MANUFACTRS NES		11.3		13.4		10.0		8.5	OUVRAGES LIEGE ET BOIS
634	VENEERS,PLYWOOD,ETC	W 3459	5.0	W 2503	4.2	W 2649	3.4	W 2647	2.8	PLACAGES,CONTRE–PLAQUES
6342	PLYWOOD OF WOOD SHEETS	W 3146	4.5	W 2168	3.6	W 2403	2.9	W 2326	2.5	BOIS CONTRE–PLAQUES
635	WOOD MANUFACTURES NES	W 1491	6.3	W 2014	9.3	W 1695	6.7	W 1542	5.7	ART MANUF EN BOIS NDA
6353	BUILDERS WOODWRK,PREFABS	W 1107	5.9	W 1583	8.7	W 1053	5.9	W 1129	5.2	OUVRAGES DE MENUISERIE
64	PAPER,PAPERBOARD AND MFR		9.5		8.7		9.3		6.8	PAPIERS,CARTONS & OUVRAGES
641	PAPER AND PAPERBOARD	W 851	1.7	W 747	1.6	W 940	1.9	W 763	1.4	PAPIERS ET CARTONS
642	PAPER,ETC,PRECUT,ARTS OF	W 3682	7.9	W 2999	7.1	W 3491	7.5	W 2886	5.4	PAP,CARTONS DECOUPES
6421	PAPER ETC CONTAINERS	W 3195	6.1	W 2495	5.3	W 2952	5.5	W 2257	3.3	BOITES,SACS EMBALLAGES
6428	PAPER ETC ARTICLES NES	W 192	0.9	W 197	0.9	W 250	1.1	W 273	1.2	OUVRAGES EN PATE A PAPIER
65	TEXTILE YARN,FABRICS,ETC		6.0		5.7		4.9		4.3	FILS,TISSUS,ARTICLES TEXTILE
657	SPECIAL TXTL FABRC,PRODS	W 358	3.1	W 291	2.3	W 277	2.1	W 402	2.2	TISSUS SPECIAUX
6575	CORDAGE AND MANUFACTURES	W 338	2.9	W 273	2.2	W 256	2.0	W 371	2.1	FICELLES,CORDES,CORDAGES
65752	NETTING OF ROPE,TWINE	W 189	1.8	W 168	1.5	W 155	1.4	W 245	1.5	FILETS MAT DU 657.51
659	FLOOR COVERINGS,ETC	W 224	1.3	W 233	1.5	W 255	1.6	W 196	1.0	COUVRE–PARQUETS,TAPIS ETC
66	NONMETAL MINERAL MFS NES		13.9		24.6		23.5		15.2	ART MIN NON METALLIQUES
661	LIME,CEMENT,BLDG PRODS	W 3785	1.4	W 5112	1.9	W 8046	2.7	W 9412	2.7	CHAUX,CIMENTS MAT CONSTR
6612	CEMENT	W 3737	1.3	W 5065	1.8	W 7958	2.6	W 9166	2.5	CIMENTS HYDRAULIQUES
663	MINERAL MANUFCTURES NES	W 4182	9.2	W 34616	18.8	W 31920	16.8	W 19822	9.5	ART MIN MANUF NDA

4. General Imports C.I.F. by Commodities according to the S.I.T.C. (Rev. 2) in million U.S. Dollars
Importations Générales C.A.F. par Produits d'après la C.T.C.I. (Rév. 2) en millions de Dollars E.U.

SITC CTCI	COMMODITY	1994 QUANTITY QUANTITE	1994 VALUE VALEUR	1995 QUANTITY QUANTITE	1995 VALUE VALEUR	1996 QUANTITY QUANTITE	1996 VALUE VALEUR	1997 QUANTITY QUANTITE	1997 VALUE VALEUR	PRODUIT
6633	MINRL MFS NES NONCERAMIC	W 4110	8.8	W 34537	18.4	W 31870	16.5	W 19718	8.9	OUVR MAT MINERALE NDA
66331	ARTICLES OF PLASTER	W 1491	0.8	W 3186	1.8	W 574	0.8	W 989	0.9	OUVRAGES EN PLATRE
66332	CEMENT,ARTFCL STONE PROD	W 2617	8.0	W 31350	16.6	W 31296	15.7	W 18729	8.1	OUVRAGES EN CIMENT
664	GLASS	W 425	2.3	W 512	2.8	W 515	2.8	W 471	2.2	VERRE
6649	GLASS NES	W 367	2.1	W 440	2.7	W 456	2.6	W 434	2.0	VERRE NDA
66494	GLASS FIBRE AND PROD NES	W 316	2.0	W 364	2.5	W 387	2.5	W 321	1.8	LAINE DE VERRE,FIBRES
67	IRON AND STEEL		3.4		4.7		4.0		2.4	FER ET ACIER
678	IRON,STL TUBES,PIPES,ETC	W 331	1.7	W 383	2.5	W 514	2.6	W 321	1.4	TUBES,TUYAUX EN FONTE,FER
69	METAL MANUFACTURES NES		15.8		18.2		16.6		17.3	ART MANUFACT EN METAL NDA
691	STRUCTURES AND PARTS NES	W 772	3.2	W 1294	3.7	W 721	2.7	W 1521	4.3	CONSTRUCT FER,ACIER,ALU
6911	STRUCTURES,PARTS IRN,STL	W 752	2.9	W 1263	3.4	W 688	2.3	W 1459	3.8	CONSTRUCT FER,ACIER,FONTE
692	METAL TANKS,BOXES,ETC	W 503	1.8	W 298	1.4	W 323	1.4	W 337	1.2	RECIPIENTS METALLIQUES
6924	MTL TRANSPORT BOXES ETC	W 427	1.4	W 282	1.2	W 308	1.2	W 274	1.0	FUTS,TAMBOURS,BIDONS
693	WIRE PRODUCTS NON ELECTR	W 636	1.7	W 564	1.7	W 546	1.4	W 501	1.2	OUVRAGES FILS METALLIQUES
6931	WIRE CABLES, ROPES ETC	W 591	1.6	W 530	1.6	W 536	1.4	W 491	1.1	CORDAGES EN FILS DE FER
69311	IRN,STEEL CABLE,ROPE ETC	W 591	1.6	W 526	1.5	W 536	1.4	W 491	1.1	CORDAGES FILS FER,ACIER
695	TOOLS	W 48	1.1	W 90	1.7	W 75	2.0	W 199	2.5	OUTILS A MAIN
6953	OTHER HAND TOOLS	W 43	1.0	W 77	1.5	W 67	1.7	W 92	1.5	AUTRES OUTILS A MAIN
69539	HAND TOOLS ETC NES	W 38	0.9	W 66	1.4	W 61	1.6	W 86	1.4	OUTILLAGE A MAIN NDA
697	BASE MTL HOUSEHOLD EQUIP	W 126	1.5	W 122	1.7	W 115	1.2	W 107	1.1	ART MENAGE MET COMMUNS
699	BASE METAL MFRS NES	W 1028	5.8	W 1104	7.0	W 1159	7.1	W 1214	6.5	ART MANUFACTURES MET NDA
6991	LOCKSMITHS WARES,ETC	W 110	1.0	W 139	1.2	W 174	1.4	W 162	1.2	ARTICLES DE SERRURERIE
6997	IRON,STEEL ARTICLES NES	W 695	3.2	W 719	3.6	W 703	3.4	W 793	3.4	OUV FONTE,FER,ACIER NDA
69979	IRN,STL MANUFACTURES NES	W 694	3.2	W 718	3.6	W 701	3.4	W 787	3.4	AUT OUVRAGES EN FER NDA
6998	MFRS NES OF CPR,NIKL,ETC	W 71	1.0	W 103	1.6	W 129	1.8	W 114	1.3	OUVRAGES EN CU,NI,AL,PB,ZN
69983	ALUMINIUM MANUFACTS NES	W 44	0.9	W 82	1.5	W 106	1.7	W 88	1.3	OUVRAGES EN ALUMINIUM
7	MACHINES,TRANSPORT EQUIP		91.1		103.7		137.5		98.1	MACHINES MATERIEL TRANSPORT
71	POWER GENERATING EQUIPMT		10.4		8.6		10.4		8.5	MACHINES GENERATRICES
713	INTRNL COMBUS PSTN ENGIN	W 180	6.7	W 167	6.4	W 197	7.0	W 188	6.8	MOTEURS EXPL COMB INT, PIECE
7133	MARINE PISTON ENGINES	W 89	2.8	W 77	2.7	W 72	2.3	W 75	2.3	MOTEURS EXPL POUR BATEAUX
71331	——OUTBOARD	W 57	2.0	W 52	2.0	W 49	1.7	W 53	1.6	MOTEURS BATEAUX HORSBORD
7139	PISTON ENGINE PARTS NES	W 61	3.3	W 67	3.1	W 100	3.6	W 98	3.5	PIECES POUR 713.2,3,8
716	ROTATING ELECTRIC PLANT	W 98	2.5	W 78	2.0	W 145	2.9	W 53	1.2	APP ELECTR ROTATIFS,PIECES
7162	AC MTRS,GENRTRS,GEN SETS	W 71	1.7	W 70	1.8	W 54	1.2	W 33	0.7	MOTEURS ELECTRIQUES
71623	GEN SETS WITH PISTN ENGN	W 59	1.5	W 61	1.5	W 46	1.1	W 22	0.6	GROUPES MOTEUR EXPLOSION
72	MACHS FOR SPCL INDUSTRYS		8.1		7.6		11.6		9.2	MAC SPECIALES POUR INDUST
723	CIVIL ENGNEERG EQUIP ETC	W 128	1.1	W 257	2.4	W 292	2.5	W 429	3.6	APPAREILS DE GENIE CIVIL
7234	CONST,MINING MACHNRY NES	W 114	0.9	W 215	2.1	W 247	2.1	W 410	3.2	MACH POUR LA CONST, MINES
72342	SLFPRP SHOVELS,EXCAVATRS	W 102	0.7	W 206	2.0	W 225	1.8	W 375	2.9	PELLES MECANIQUES
727	FOOD MACHRY NON–DOMESTIC	W 150	4.6	W 132	3.0	W 178	7.2	W 136	4.0	MACH INDUSTRIES ALIMENT
7272	OTH FOOD PROC MCHY,PARTS	W 149	4.6	W 111	2.8	W 178	7.2	W 136	4.0	AUT MACH IND ALIMENTAIRE
72722	INDUS FOOD PROC MACH NES	W 149	4.6	W 111	2.8	W 178	7.2	W 136	4.0	MACHINES BOULANGERIE
74	GENRL INDUSTRL MACHY NES		12.4		13.5		11.5		11.9	MACH APP INDUSTRIE
741	HEATING,COOLING EQUIPMNT	W 319	5.6	W 352	6.0	W 277	3.6	W 273	3.3	MACH CHAUFFAGE,PIECES
7414	NONDOM REFRIG EQUIPT,PTS	W 182	3.8	W 185	3.8	W 61	1.4	W 108	1.9	MAT PRODUCTION DU FROID
74141	REFRIG EQUIP NONDOMESTIC	W 158	3.1	W 146	2.6	W 21	0.4	W 51	0.8	REFIG INDUSTRIELS
74149	PTS NES OF REFRIG EQUIPT	W 24	0.8	W 39	1.2	W 40	1.0	W 57	1.2	PIECES POUR MACH FROID
7416	HEATING,COOLING EQU NES	W 34	1.0	W 64	1.3	W 127	1.5	W 22	0.7	APP CHANGEMENT TEMP
743	PUMPS NES,CENTRFUGES ETC	W 57	1.1	W 63	1.5	W 78	1.3	W 63	1.6	POMPES COMPRES,VENT ETC
744	MECHANICAL HANDLING EQU	W 155	2.7	W 166	2.7	W 232	3.2	W 349	3.8	EQUIP MANUTENTION PIECES
7441	FORK LIFT TRCKS,ETC,PTS	W 71	0.7	W 58	0.5	W 122	0.8	W 181	1.5	CHARIOTS POUR USINES ETC
74411	FORK LIFT TRUCKS ETC	W 68	0.6	W 56	0.4	W 122	0.8	W 181	1.5	CHARIOTS POUR LES GARES
7449	PTS NES OF MACHY OF 7442	W 53	1.5	W 51	1.7	W 84	2.0	W 88	1.7	PIECES DU 744.2
745	NONELEC MACHY,TOOLS NES	W 46	1.3	W 60	1.9	W 51	1.4	W 74	1.6	AUT MACH NON ELEC,PIECES
7452	OTH NONELEC MCHS,PTS NES	W 37	1.1	W 49	1.7	W 43	1.2	W 60	1.3	AUT MACH NON ELEC,PIECES
75	OFFICE MACHNES,ADP EQUIP		13.5		11.3		10.8		10.5	MACH BUREAU TRAIT AUTOM
751	OFFICE MACHINES	W 26	2.7	W 20	1.3	W 18	1.0	W 22	1.1	MACH,APPAREILS DE BUREAU
7512	CALCULATNG,ACCTG,ETC MCH	W 8	1.8	W 2	0.2	W 2	0.2	W 2	0.2	MACHINE A CALCULER ETC
75123	CASH REGISTERS	W 5	1.4	W 1	0.2	W 1	0.1	W 1	0.1	CAISSES ENREGISTREUSES
752	AUTOMTIC DATA PROC EQUIP	W 24	3.4	W 26	2.8	W 20	2.0	W 31	2.3	MACH TRAIT INFORMATION
7523	DIGITL CENTRL PROCESSORS	W 6	1.4	W 5	0.9	W 3	0.5	W 4	0.4	UNITES CENTRALES
7528	OFF–LINE DATA PROC EQUIP	W 2	0.2	W 2	0.2	W 3	0.4	W 18	1.3	MACH AUXIL TRAIT INFORM
759	OFFICE,ADP MCH PTS,ACCES	W 61	7.4	W 57	7.3	W 71	8.0	W 88	7.2	PIECES DU 751 ET 752
7591	OFFICE MACHINE PARTS NES	W 18	1.4	W 10	0.8	W 5	0.5	W 6	0.4	PIECES DU 7511,7518
7599	ACCTG,ETC,ADP MCH PTS,AC	W 44	6.0	W 47	6.6	W 66	7.5	W 83	6.8	PIECES DU 751 ET 752
76	TELECOMM,SOUND EQUIPMENT		13.0		11.5		14.6		12.7	EQUIPMENT DE TELECOM
761	TELEVISION RECEIVERS	W 48	1.0	W 66	1.7	W 62	1.4	W 71	1.3	RECEPTEURS DE TELEVISION
7611	COLOUR TV RECEIVERS	W 48	1.0	W 66	1.6	W 61	1.3	W 71	1.3	RECEPTEURS COULEUR
764	TELECOM EQPT,PTS,ACC NES	W 132	10.7	W 118	8.5	W 135	12.0	W 109	9.6	EQUIP TELECOM,PIECES
7641	LINE TELEPHONE,ETC EQUIP	W 16	3.7	W 10	2.0	W 11	1.7	W 27	3.7	APP TELEPHON PAR FIL
7643	TV,RADIO TRANSMITTRS ETC	W 3	0.9	W 2	0.8	W 4	0.7	W 5	1.2	APP EMET TELE RADIO
7648	TELECOMM EQUIPMENT NES	W 62	2.2	W 50	1.5	W 11	0.7	W 3	0.5	APP TELECOM NDA
76482	TELEVISION CAMERAS	W 60	1.6	W 48	1.0	W 10	0.4		0.1	APP PRISE DE VUES TELE
7649	PTS NES OF EQUIPMT OF 76	W 28	3.7	W 45	4.2	W 91	8.6	W 53	4.0	PIECES DE LA DIV 76
76491	PTS NES OF APPAR OF 7641	W 12	2.6	W 10	0.8	W 17	2.3	W 9	1.6	PIECES POUR 764.1
76493	TELECOMM EQUIPMT PTS NES	W 15	1.1	W 35	3.3	W 73	6.2	W 44	2.4	PIECES 761,762,764.3,8
77	ELECTRIC MACHNRY NES ETC		13.0		15.7		14.6		12.2	MACH APP ELECT NDA
772	SWITCHGEAR ETC,PARTS NES	W 141	3.6	W 188	5.7	W 164	5.6	W 223	4.1	APP COUPURE,SECT ETC
7721	SWITCHGEAR ETC	W 141	3.6	W 188	5.6	W 164	5.5	W 223	4.1	APP COUPURE,SECTIONMNT
773	ELECTR DISTRIBUTNG EQUIP	W 212	1.7	W 324	2.4	W 216	1.8	W 170	1.2	EQUIPMT DISTRIBUTION ELECT
7731	INSULATED WIRE,CABLE ETC	W 212	1.7	W 240	2.3	W 215	1.8	W 166	1.2	FILS,CABLES ISOLES ELECT
775	HOUSEHOLD TYPE EQUIP NES	W 305	3.3	W 275	3.3	W 276	3.0	W 284	2.7	MACH,APP USAGE DOMESTQUE
7758	ELECTRO–THERMIC APPL NES	W 88	1.1	W 90	1.3	W 79	1.0	W 87	1.1	APP ELECTROTHERMIQ NDA
778	ELECTRICAL MACHINERY NES	W 165	3.5	W 147	3.4	W 170	3.3	W 164	3.1	AUTRES MACH ELECT NDA
7788	OTH ELEC MACHY,EQUIP NES	W 19	1.6	W 11	1.1	W 10	0.9	W 18	1.1	AUT MACH APP ELEC NDA
78	ROAD VEHICLES		10.7		12.1		12.4		11.8	VEHICULES ROUTIERS
781	PASS MOTOR VEH EXC BUSES	W 114	1.7	W 157	2.4	W 230	3.5	W 242	3.2	AUTO TRANSPORT PERSONNES
782	LORRIES,SPCL MTR VEH NES	W 349	5.2	W 377	5.6	W 332	4.8	W 519	5.2	VEHICULES SPECIAUX,MARCH
7821	LORRIES,TRUCKS	W 305	4.2	W 356	5.1	W 289	4.3	W 407	4.7	VEHICULES TRANSP MARCHAND
784	MOTOR VEH PRTS,ACCES NES	W 104	2.5	W 120	2.9	W 113	2.6	W 140	2.5	PIECES 722,781,782,783
7849	OTHER MOTOR VEHCL PARTS	W 104	2.5	W 120	2.9	W 111	2.6	W 139	2.5	PIECES 722,781,782,783
79	OTHR TRANSPORT EQUIPMENT		10.1		23.3		51.4		21.4	AUTRE MATERIEL TRANSPORT
792	AIRCRAFT ETC	W 25	8.3	W 25	7.0	W 51	21.1	W 58	5.8	APP NAVIGATION AERIENNE
7921	HELICOPTERS			W 14	3.8	W 22	12.6			HELICOPTERES
7923	AIRCRFT NES2000–15000KG	W 15	5.2							AERODYNES 2000 A 15000 KG
7929	AIRCRAFT PARTS NES	W 10	3.1	W 12	3.2	W 25	8.5	W 56	5.8	PIECES DU 792
793	SHIPS AND BOATS ETC	W 242	1.9	W 22851	16.4	W 3552	30.3	W 2013	15.6	NAVIRES BATEAUX,ETC
7932	SHIPS AND BOATS NES	W 233	1.6	W 22845	16.1	W 3548	30.2	W 1982	15.4	NAVIRES ET BATEAUX
79321	YACHTS,SPORTS VESSLS ETC	W 51	1.1	W 38	1.0	W 62	1.6	W 86	1.6	BATEAUX DE PLAISANCE
79324	FISHING VESSELS ETC	W 182	0.5	W 22807	15.2	W 3486	28.6	W 1860	13.8	BATEAUX DE PECHE
8	MISC MANUFACTURED GOODS		48.9		52.3		48.3		42.9	ART MANUFACTURES DIVERS

4. General Imports C.I.F. by Commodities according to the S.I.T.C. (Rev. 2) in million U.S. Dollars
Importations Générales C.A.F. par Produits d'après la C.T.C.I. (Rév. 2) en millions de Dollars E.U.

SITC CTCI	COMMODITY	1994 QUANTITY QUANTITE	1994 VALUE VALEUR	1995 QUANTITY QUANTITE	1995 VALUE VALEUR	1996 QUANTITY QUANTITE	1996 VALUE VALEUR	1997 QUANTITY QUANTITE	1997 VALUE VALEUR	PRODUIT
812	*PLUMBG,HEATNG,LGHTNG EQ	W 184	2.2	W 255	3.0	W 131	2.3	W 140	2.0	APPAR SANITAIRES CHAUFFAGE
8124	LIGHTING EQUIPMENT NES	W 46	1.3	W 44	1.7	W 40	1.4	W 32	0.9	APPAREILS ECLAIRAGE ETC
81242	LAMPS,FITTINGS BASE METL	W 41	1.2	W 41	1.7	W 37	1.3	W 29	0.9	APPAREILS D'ECLAIRAGE
821	*FURNITURE,PARTS THEREOF	W 928	7.3	W 1282	10.2	W 1252	9.2	W 1019	7.8	MEUBLES ET PIECES
8211	CHAIRS,SEATS AND PARTS	W 219	2.3	W 165	2.4	W 222	2.5	W 178	2.0	SIEGES ET PIECES
82111	CHAIRS AND OTHER SEATS	W 219	2.3	W 164	2.3	W 221	2.5	W 177	2.0	SIEGES
8219	FURNITURE AND PARTS NES	W 669	4.4	W 1051	6.9	W 981	5.7	W 799	5.1	AUTRES MEUBLES ET PIECES
82192	WOOD FURNITURE NES	W 550	3.3	W 923	5.7	W 807	4.3	W 613	3.8	MEUBLES NDA EN BOIS
84	CLOTHING AND ACCESSORIES		11.9		10.2		10.5		8.8	VETEMENTS
842	MENS OUTERWEAR NOT KNIT	W 60	2.9	W 47	2.5	W 51	2.3	W 51	2.0	VET DESSUS POUR HOMMES
843	WOMENS OUTERWEAR NONKNIT	W 54	2.2	W 48	2.3	W 64	2.7	W 54	2.0	VET DESSUS FEMMES MAT TEX
8439	— OTHER OUTER GARMENTS	W 40	1.6	W 39	1.6	W 53	2.0	W 41	1.5	AUT VET DES FEM MAT TEXT
845	OUTERWEAR KNIT NONELASTC	W 97	3.5	W 51	2.8	W 65	3.0	W 69	2.6	VET DESSOUS,ACCES BONNET
8451	— JERSEYS,PULLOVERS ETC	W 38	1.5	W 24	1.4	W 35	1.7	W 35	1.5	CHANDAILS,PULL–OVERS ETC
8459	— OTHER,CLTHG ACCESRYS	W 57	1.9	W 25	1.3	W 29	1.3	W 33	1.1	AUT VET DESSUS DE BONNE
848	HEADGEAR,NONTXTL CLOTHNG	W 52	1.2	W 42	1.0	W 47	1.0	W 56	1.0	VET ACCES MAT AUT QUE TEX
851	*FOOTWEAR	W 105	3.2	W 84	2.8	W 105	3.1	W 104	2.7	CHAUSSURES
85102	FOOTWEAR LEATHER	W 54	2.0	W 52	1.9	W 78	2.5	W 82	2.3	CHAUS SEMELLES EN CUIR
87	PRECISION INSTRUMNTS NES		3.4		3.6		3.5		3.4	INSTRUM,APPAR SCIENT NDA
874	MEASURNG,CONTROLNG INSTR	W 22	1.9	W 23	2.4	W 16	2.0	W 30	2.3	INSTRUMENTS DE MESURE
88	PHOTO EQU,OPTICL GDS ETC		1.7		2.0		1.8		1.8	APP,FOURN PHOTO,OP,MONTR
89	MISC MANUFCTRD GOODS NES		19.1		20.5		17.9		16.4	ART MANUFACTURES DIVERS
892	PRINTED MATTER	W 187	3.1	W 222	3.6	W 288	3.5	W 1073	3.5	IMPRIMES
8921	PRINTED BOOKS,GLOBES,ETC	W 105	1.9	W 73	1.8	W 77	1.8	W 117	1.9	LIVRES,BROCHURES,CARTES
89211	PRINTED BOOKS,PAMPHLETS	W 105	1.9	W 72	1.8	W 75	1.7	W 115	1.8	LIVRES,BROCHURES
8928	PRINTED MATTER NES	W 80	1.2	W 135	1.6	W 209	1.7	W 88	1.4	IMPRIMES NDA
893	ARTICLES OF PLASTIC NES		5.0		6.1	W 1052	4.8		5.1	OUVRAGES EN MAT DIVIS 58
8931	PLSTC PACKG CONTNRS,LIDS	W 760	2.3	W 786	2.8	W 613	2.1	W 503	1.6	ART TRANSP EMBALLAGE ETC
8939	MISC PLASTIC ARTICLES	W 325	2.7	W 392	3.3	W 434	2.7	W 587	3.4	ART DIVERS EN MAT DIV 58
89399	OTHR PLASTC ARTICLES NES	W 223	2.0	W 282	2.4	W 227	1.8	W 499	2.8	AUT OUV MAT DIV 58
894	TOYS,SPORTING GOODS,ETC	W 293	4.9	W 289	4.9	W 334	4.5	W 250	4.2	VOITURES ENFANTS,JOUETS
8942	TOYS,INDOOR GAMES ETC	W 115	1.9	W 137	2.1	W 182	2.4	W 116	1.8	JOUETS,JEUX ETC
89423	TOYS NES	W 64	1.1	W 69	0.9	W 120	1.5	W 62	1.1	JOUETS,MODELES REDUITS
8946	NON–MILITARY ARMS,AMMO	W 139	2.0	W 112	2.1	W 86	1.4	W 84	1.5	ARMES NON MILITAIRES
89463	HUNTNG,SPORTNG AMMUNTION	W 132	1.4	W 107	1.7	W 81	1.0	W 78	1.0	MUNITIONS
898	MUSICAL INSTRUMENTS,PTS	W 38	3.0	W 40	3.1	W 50	2.8	W 49	1.9	INSTRUMENTS DE MUSIQUE
8983	SOUND RECRDNG TAPE,DISCS	W 35	2.8	W 37	2.9	W 47	2.6	W 44	1.7	SUPPORTS SON POUR 763
89832	RECORDED DISCS,TAPES ETC	W 28	2.7	W 25	2.7	W 27	2.4	W 28	1.5	DISQUES,PHONO,BANDES
899	OTHER MANUFACTURED GOODS		2.2		1.9		1.5		1.2	AUT ART MANUF DIVERS NDA
8996	HEARING,ORTHOPAEDIC AIDS		1.2		1.0		0.7		0.6	APPAREILS D'ORTHOPEDIE
9	GOODS NOT CLASSD BY KIND		70.1		80.7		71.2		64.3	ART TRANSACT NON CLASSES
931	*SPECIAL TRANSACTIONS	W 332532	70.1	W 2013095	80.7	W 2025819	71.1	W 7196281	64.3	TRANS.SPECIALES

5. General Exports F.O.B. by Commodities according to the S.I.T.C. (Rev. 2) in million U.S. Dollars
Exportations Générales F.O.B. par Produits d'après la C.T.C.I. (Rév. 2) en millions de Dollars E.U.

SITC CTCI	COMMODITY	1994		1995		1996		1997		PRODUIT
		QUANTITY QUANTITE	VALUE VALEUR	QUANTITY QUANTITE	VALUE VALEUR	QUANTITY QUANTITE	VALUE VALEUR	QUANTITY QUANTITE	VALUE VALEUR	
	ALL COMMODITIES		306.8		363.7		369.2		285.3	TOUS PRODUITS
0	FOOD AND LIVE ANIMALS		287.3		345.7		336.2		261.9	ALIMENTS,ANIMAUX VIVANTS
03	FISH AND PREPARATIONS		287.2		344.8		334.9		260.7	POISSONS ET PREPARATIONS
034	FISH,FRESH,CHILLED,FROZN	W 11047	49.4	W 13534	64.8	W 16946	60.6	W 26572	61.7	POISSON FRAIS, REFRIG,CONG
0342	FISH FROZEN,EXCL FILLETS	W 2393	8.6	W 4738	18.6	W 5869	19.4	W 5602	19.4	POISSONS CONGELES
0344	FISH FILLETS,FROZEN	W 8635	40.8	W 8672	45.9	W 7824	40.3	W 9479	41.3	FILETS CONGELES
035	FISH SALTED,DRIED,SMOKED	W 141	0.7	W 80	0.8	W 94	1.0	W 240	2.4	POISSON SECHE,SALE,FUME
03502	COD(NOT IN FILLETS)DRIED	W 91	0.6	W 71	0.8	W 87	1.0	W 132	1.2	MORUE SECHEE,SALEE
03504	FISH SMOKED		0.1			W 6	0.1	W 103	1.2	POISSONS FUMES
036	SHELL FISH FRESH,FROZEN	W 34826	144.1	W 33948	160.7	W 35330	158.7	W 33181	118.1	CRUSTACES,MOLLUSQUES
037	FISH ETC PREPD,PRSVD NES	W 12729	93.0	W 14229	118.7	W 13001	114.7	W 12004	78.7	POIS,CRUST,MOL PREPARES
0372	SHELL FISH PREPRD,PRESVD	W 12729	93.0	W 14229	118.7	W 13001	114.7	W 12004	78.7	CRUSTACES,COQUIL PREPARES
081	*FEEDING STUFF FOR ANIML	W 74	0.1	W 790	0.9	W 1135	1.2	W 1219	1.1	NOURRITURE POUR ANIMAUX
0814	MEAT OR FISH MEAL FODDER	W 74	0.1	W 790	0.9	W 1135	1.2	W 1219	1.1	FARINES DE VIANDES,POISSONS
08142	FISH MEAL FODDER	W 74	0.1	W 790	0.9	W 1135	1.2	W 1219	1.1	FARINES DE POISSONS
2	CRUDE MATERLS,EXCL FUELS		1.0		2.5		5.3		4.1	MAT BRUTES NON COMESTIBLES
21	HIDES,SKINS,FURS UNDRSSD		0.6		1.1		1.3		2.3	CUIRS,PEAUX BRUTS
212	FURSKINS,RAW	W 16	0.5	W 20	0.9	W 32	1.0	W 49	2.1	PELLETERIES BRUTES
21209	OTHER FURSKINS,RAW	W 16	0.5	W 20	0.9	W 32	1.0	W 49	2.1	AUTRES PELLETERIES BRUTES
29	CRUDE ANIMAL,VEG MAT NES		0.4		1.3		4.1		1.9	MATIERES BRUTES ANIM,VEGET
291	CRUDE ANIMAL MTRIALS NES	W 55	0.4	W 220	1.3	W 334	4.1	W 122	1.9	MATIERES BRUTES ANIMALES
2919	OTH ANIMAL MATERIALS NES	W 54	0.3	W 220	1.3	W 334	4.0	W 122	1.9	MAT ORIGINE ANIMALE NDA
29199	ANIMAL PRODUCTS,NES	W 52	0.3	W 81	1.3	W 333	4.0	W 122	1.9	PROD ORIGINE ANIMALE NDA
3	MINERAL FUELS ETC		3.4		2.9		4.3		3.1	COMBUSTIBLES MINERAUX LUB
33	PETROLEUM AND PRODUCTS		3.4		2.9		4.3		3.1	PETROLE ET DERIVES
334	PETROLEUM PRODUCTS,REFIN	W 6308	3.4	W 5755	2.9	W 6933	4.3	W 5482	3.1	PRODUITS RAFFINES
7	MACHINES,TRANSPORT EQUIP		1.2		1.0		8.5		5.6	MACHINES MATERIEL TRANSPORT
79	OTHR TRANSPORT EQUIPMENT		0.1		0.1		6.5		4.4	AUTRE MATERIEL TRANSPORT
792	AIRCRAFT ETC		0.1		0.1	W 4	1.2	W 13	4.4	APP NAVIGATION AERIENNE
7921	HELICOPTERS					W 3	1.1	W 13	4.3	HELICOPTERES
793	SHIPS AND BOATS ETC		0.1	W 16	0.1	W 1246	5.4	W 6	0.1	NAVIRES BATEAUX,ETC
7932	SHIPS AND BOATS NES		0.1	W 16	0.1	W 1246	5.4	W 6	0.1	NAVIRES ET BATEAUX
79324	FISHING VESSELS ETC					W 1246	5.4			BATEAUX DE PECHE
8	MISC MANUFACTURED GOODS		3.6		4.4		5.8		2.0	ART MANUFACTURES DIVERS
84	CLOTHING AND ACCESSORIES		1.0		0.8		1.0		0.7	VETEMENTS
848	HEADGEAR,NONTXTL CLOTHNG	W 4	1.0	W 4	0.8	W 4	1.0	W 2	0.7	VET ACCES MAT AUT QUE TEX
8483	FUR ETC,CLOTHES,PRODUCTS	W 4	1.0	W 3	0.8	W 4	1.0	W 2	0.7	VETEMENTS DE FOURRURE
84831	ARTICLES OF FURSKIN,NES	W 4	1.0	W 3	0.8	W 4	1.0	W 2	0.7	PELLETERIES OUVREES NDA
89	MISC MANUFCTRD GOODS NES		2.5		3.4		4.7		1.2	ART MANUFACTURES DIVERS
896	WORKS OF ART ETC		2.2		3.2		4.4		1.0	OBJETS D'ART
89604	STAMPS FOR PHILATELY		2.2		3.2		4.4		1.0	TIMBRES–POSTE
9	GOODS NOT CLASSD BY KIND		10.2		7.2		8.9		8.7	ART TRANSACT NON CLASSES
931	*SPECIAL TRANSACTIONS	W 803	10.2	W 656	7.2	W 746	8.9	W 791	8.7	TRANS.SPECIALES

1. HISTORICAL SERIES, 1971–1996 SPECIAL TRADE, IMPORTS C.I.F., EXPORTS F.O.B.
SERIES HISTORIQUES, 1971–1996 COMMERCE SPECIAL, IMPORTATIONS C.A.F., EXPORTATIONS F.O.B

YEAR ANNEE	VALUE IN MILLION E.C. DOLLARS VALEUR EN MILLION E.C. DOLLARS MERCHANDISE –MARCHANDISE IMPORTS	EXPORTS	GOLD –OR IMPORTS	EXPORTS	CONVERSION FACTORS U.S. CENTS PER E.C. DOLLAR FACTEURS DE CONVERSION CENTS E.U. PAR E.C. DOLLAR IMPORTS	EXPORTS	INDEX NUMBERS –INDICES QUANTUM IMPORTS	EXPORTS	UNIT VALUE VALEUR UNITAIRE IMPORTS	EXPORTS
1971	46.10	10.20			50.0000	50.0000				
1972	42.80	10.50			52.1387	52.1387				
1973	42.50	14.50			51.0808	51.0808				
1974	38.10	19.30			48.7301	48.7301				
1975	52.80	26.90			46.2878	46.2878				
1976	66.30	33.80			38.0480	38.0480				
1977	84.80	38.80			37.0370	37.0370				
1978	96.50	45.60			37.0370	37.0370				
1979	118.00	57.80			37.0370	37.0370				
1980	135.60	46.90			37.0370	37.0370				
1981	146.70	51.40			37.0370	37.0370				
1982	152.40	50.10			37.0370	37.0370				
1983	154.50	51.80			37.0370	37.0370				
1984	151.10	49.10			37.0370	37.0370				
1985	187.00	60.30			37.0370	37.0370				
1986	225.72	84.36			37.0370	37.0370				
1987	239.17	86.10			37.0370	37.0370				
1988	248.80	88.50			37.0370	37.0370				
1989	267.90	75.40			37.0370	37.0370				
1990	283.80	71.60			37.0370	37.0370				
1991	327.00	61.50			37.0370	37.0370				
1992	287.80	53.90			37.0370	37.0370				
1993	338.13	60.52			37.0370	37.0370				
1994	321.51	63.04			37.0370	37.0370				
1995	348.05	58.69			37.0370	37.0370				
1996	411.10	56.70			37.0370	37.0370				

2. IMPORTS BY BROAD ECONOMIC CATEGORY AND EXPORTS BY INDUSTRIAL ORIGIN. (PERCENTAGE OF TOTAL VALUE)
IMPORTATIONS PAR CATEGORIES ECONOMIQUES ET EXPORTATIONS PAR BRANCHE D'ACTIVITE.(EN POURCENTAGE DE LA VALEUR TOTALE)

IMPORTS – IMPORTATIONS

	1990	1991	1992	1993	1994	1995	1996
TOTAL IMPORTS–IMPORTATIONS TOTALES	100.	100.		100.	100.	100.	100.
1 FOOD BEV–ALIMENTATION BOISSONS	27.0	25.1		24.5	25.7	26.6	25.3
11 PRIMARY–PRODUITS DE BASE	9.1	8.2		8.0	8.8	8.1	8.6
111 FOR INDUSTRY–POUR L'INDUSTRIE	2.9	2.2		2.5	2.1	1.4	2.5
112 FOR HOUSEHOLDS–POUR LES MENAGES	6.2	6.0		5.5	6.7	6.7	6.1
12 PROCESSED–PRODUITS ELABORES	17.9	16.9		16.5	17.0	18.6	16.7
121 FOR INDUSTRY–POUR L'INDUSTRIE	2.0	2.1		2.2	2.3	2.6	2.2
122 FOR HOUSEHOLDS–POUR LES MENAGES	15.9	14.8		14.3	14.7	15.9	14.5
2 IND SUPPLIES–APPROV INDUSTRIELS	28.1	27.8		26.8	27.5	26.4	25.7
21 PRIMARY–PRODUITS DE BASE	0.9	0.6		0.9	0.8	0.6	0.9
22 PROCESSED–PRODUITS ELABORES	27.2	27.1		25.9	26.7	25.8	24.8
3 FUELS–COMBUSTIBLES	6.5	6.9		12.0	7.6	7.7	9.7
31 PRIMARY–PRODUITS DE BASE	1.2	1.2		0.9	1.2	1.1	1.2
32 PROCESSED–PRODUITS ELABORES	5.3	5.7		11.1	6.5	6.6	8.5
321 MOTOR SPIRIT–ESSENCE	2.9	2.6		2.7	2.8	2.6	3.0
322 OTHER–AUTRES	2.4	3.1		8.4	3.7	3.9	5.5
4 MACHINERY–EQUIPEMENT	11.5	14.7		12.2	12.2	12.3	13.2
41 CAPITAL EQUIPMENT–MACHINES	10.4	13.6		11.0	11.0	11.1	11.9
42 PARTS–PIECES ACCESSOIRES	1.1	1.1		1.2	1.2	1.2	1.3
5 TRANSPORT–TRANSPORT	9.7	9.3		7.2	9.0	8.4	8.9
51 PASSENGER CARS–AUTOMOBILES	3.0	2.1		2.3	3.0	3.1	3.1
52 OTHER–AUTRES	4.0	4.6		2.2	3.1	2.6	3.5
521 INDUSTRIAL–INDUSTRIELS	3.9	4.5		2.1	3.1	2.6	3.4
522 NON INDUSTRIAL–NON INDUSTRIEL	0.1	0.1		0.0	0.1	0.1	0.1
53 PARTS–PIECES ACCESSOIRES	2.8	2.6		2.8	2.8	2.7	2.3
6 CONSUM GOODS–BIENS CONSOMMATION	17.0	16.1		17.2	18.0	18.2	17.2
61 DURABLE–DURABLES	3.7	2.6		4.1	3.9	3.7	3.8
62 SEMI DURABLE–SEMI DURABLES	7.6	7.7		7.8	7.8	7.8	7.8
63 NON DURABLE–NON DURABLES	5.8	5.8		5.3	6.3	6.7	5.6
7 GOODS NES–BIENS NDA	0.1	0.1		0.2	0.1	0.4	0.1

EXPORTS – EXPORTATIONS

	1990	1991	1992	1993	1994	1995	1996
TOTAL EXPORTS–EXPORTATIONS TOTALES	100.	100.		100.	100.	100.	100.
1 AGRICULTURE	61.4	59.7		54.8	63.0	66.1	63.6
2 MINING QUARRY–INDUS EXTRACTIVES				0.0			
3 MANUFACTURING–IND MANUFACTUR	38.5	40.2		45.2	37.0	33.9	36.4
31 FOOD BEV TOBACCO–ALIM BOISS TAB	4.7	7.8		10.5	8.4	13.4	16.9
32 TEXTILES–INDUSTRIES TEXTILES	14.8	11.8		9.9	6.8	1.4	1.1
33 WOOD & PRODUCTS–BOIS & PRODUITS	0.4	0.6		0.1	0.1	0.0	
34 PAPER & PRODUCTS–PAPIER & PRODT	4.7	4.1		4.8	5.6	7.4	6.5
35 CHEMICALS–INDUSTRIES CHIMIQUES	4.4	4.9		6.6	8.0	3.6	5.0
36 NON METAL MIN–MIN NON METAL	0.2	0.0		0.0		0.0	0.0
37 BASIC METAL–IND METAL BASE	0.5	0.1		0.4	0.2	1.4	2.4
38 METAL MANUF–MANUF METAL	8.5	10.7		12.8	7.8	6.6	4.5
39 OTH MANUF IND–AUTRES MANUF	0.4	0.2		0.1	0.1	0.0	0.0

3. TRADE BY PRINCIPAL COUNTRIES OF ORIGIN AND DESTINATION (VALUE IN MILLION U.S. DOLLARS)
ECHANGES SELON LES PRINCIPAUX PAYS D'ORIGINE ET DE DESTINATION (VALEUR EN MILLIONS DE DOLLARS EU)

COUNTRIES–PAYS	SPECIAL IMPORTS C.I.F. IMPORTATIONS SPECIALES C.A.F					COUNTRIES–PAYS	EXPORTS EXPORTATIONS ES F.O.B.				
	1992	1993	1994	1995	1996		1992	1993	1994	1995	1996
World		125.2	119.1	128.9	151.4	Monde		22.4	23.3	21.7	19.8
Africa		0.1	0.1	0.0	0.1	Afrique		0.0	0.1		
Americas		94.8	85.6	99.9	116.4	Amériques		15.8	16.2	15.0	11.8
– Northern America		48.0	44.6	58.6	69.2	– Amérique du Nord		8.2	8.1	7.4	4.6
– LAIA		2.9	3.7	3.0	2.9	– ALAI		0.3	0.7	0.4	0.8
– CACM		1.7	1.7	1.3	1.9	– MCAC			0.0		
– Caribbean		40.6	33.6	35.1	41.4	– Caraïbes		7.1	7.1	7.0	6.1
– Rest of America		1.6	2.0	1.7	1.0	– Autre Amérique		0.2	0.4	0.2	0.2
Asia excl fmr USSR		8.1	9.2	7.8	9.9	Asie anc. URSS exclus		0.1	0.0	0.1	0.1
– Middle East		0.1	0.1	0.1	0.2	– Moyen–Orient		0.1	0.0	0.0	0.1
Asia former USSR						Asie ancienne URSS					
Europe excl fmr USSR		21.0	22.8	20.4	24.0	Europe anc. URSS exclus		6.4	7.0	6.7	7.8
– European Union		20.0	21.8	19.6	22.9	– Union Européenne		6.4	7.0	6.7	7.7
– Eastern Europe		0.2	0.4	0.2	0.3	– Europe de l'Est					
– Rest of Europe		0.8	0.6	0.6	0.9	– Autre de l'Europe		0.0	0.0	0.0	0.2
Europe former USSR		0.0	0.0	0.0	0.0	Europe ancienne URSS		0.1			
Oceania		1.2	1.4	0.8	1.0	Océanie		0.0	0.0		
Other						Autre					
USA/Etats–Unis d'Amer		43.6	41.6	53.6	64.5	USA/Etats–Unis d'Amer		7.8	7.7	7.1	4.2
Trinidad and Tobago		27.8	23.5	26.2	32.1	United Kingdom		3.0	3.0	2.4	1.6
United Kingdom		13.8	14.1	13.3	14.6	Netherlands/Pays–Bas		1.9	1.5	2.3	3.5
Japan/Japon		4.7	5.7	4.1	5.7	Saint Lucia/Ste–Lucie		1.5	1.5	1.8	1.8
Canada		4.3	3.0	5.0	4.7	Germany/Allemagne		1.3	1.9	1.5	1.7
Barbados/Barbade		3.4	3.4	3.5	4.1	Barbados/Barbade		1.2	1.4	1.7	0.7
Germany/Allemagne		1.7	2.8	1.7	1.4	Dominica/Dominique		1.0	0.6	0.7	1.0
Venezuela		1.2	2.2	1.7	1.2	Trinidad and Tobago		1.4	0.6	0.4	0.3
Jamaica/Jamaïque		2.1	1.7	0.9	1.1	St Vincent & Grenadines		0.5	0.5	0.4	0.8
Guyana		1.4	2.0	1.6	0.8	Antigua and Barbuda		0.5	0.4	0.5	0.5
Honduras		1.2	1.6	1.2	1.6	France, Monaco		0.1	0.5	0.4	0.8
St Vincent & Grenadines		1.8	1.3	0.8	1.0	Dominican Republic		0.2	1.0	0.1	0.5
France, Monaco		1.0	1.1	0.9	1.5	Canada		0.4	0.4	0.3	0.4
Korea, Republic of		0.6	1.1	1.4	1.5	Argentina/Argentine		0.2	0.5	0.1	0.4
Netherlands/Pays–Bas		1.3	1.0	0.9	1.2	Jamaica/Jamaïque		0.1	0.4	0.3	0.3
New Zealand		1.1	1.4	0.7	0.8	Saint Kitts and Nevis		0.6	0.3	0.2	0.0
Saint Lucia/Ste–Lucie		1.0	1.0	1.3	0.6	Guyana		0.2	0.4	0.2	0.2
Netherlands Antilles		0.7	0.9	0.9	1.4	Guadeloupe		0.0	0.1	0.5	
China/Chine		0.8	1.0	0.9	1.0	Brazil/Brésil			0.1	0.2	0.3
Brazil/Brésil		0.9	1.0	0.9	0.6	Martinique		0.0	0.1	0.2	
Denmark/Danemark		0.8	0.9	0.7	0.9	Montserrat		0.0	0.1	0.0	0.0
Dominica/Dominique		1.2	0.9	0.7	0.5	Jordan/Jordanie		0.1	0.0	0.0	0.1
Other Asia n.e.s.		0.7	0.7	0.6	0.6	Uruguay		0.1	0.1		
Italy/Italie		0.4	0.6	0.5	1.0	Switzerland,Liechtenst.		0.0	0.0	0.0	0.2
Spain/Espagne		0.1	0.1	0.9	1.1	Colombia/Colombie					0.2
Ireland/Irlande		0.5	0.4	0.5	0.6	Belgium–Luxembourg		0.0	0.1	0.0	0.0
Bahamas		1.7	0.0	0.0	0.0	Netherlands Antilles		0.1	0.0	0.0	0.0
Norway,Svalbard and JM		0.3	0.4	0.4	0.6	Spain/Espagne		0.1			
Dominican Republic		0.5	0.3	0.4	0.3	Italy/Italie			0.0		0.1
Colombia/Colombie		0.1	0.1	0.1	0.8	Japan/Japon		0.0			
Belgium–Luxembourg		0.1	0.4	0.1	0.3	Suriname/Surinam			0.0		0.0
China, Hong Kong SAR		0.3	0.2	0.2	0.2	China/Chine			0.0		0.0
Mexico/Mexique		0.4	0.1	0.1	0.2	New Zealand		0.0			
Guatemala		0.5	0.1	0.1	0.1	Venezuela		0.0			
Argentina/Argentine		0.2	0.2	0.2	0.2	Korea, Republic of		0.0	0.0		
Switzerland,Liechtenst.		0.2	0.2	0.1	0.2	Honduras			0.0		
Antigua and Barbuda		0.3	0.2	0.1	0.1	Denmark/Danemark		0.0	0.0	0.0	0.0
Saint Kitts and Nevis		0.2	0.2	0.1	0.0	Austria/Autriche		0.0	0.0	0.0	
Sweden/Suède		0.1	0.2	0.1	0.2	Ireland/Irlande				0.0	
Hungary/Hongrie		0.0	0.3	0.1	0.1	Madagascar			0.0		

(VALUE AS PERCENTAGE OF WORLD TOTAL)(VALEURS EN POURCENTAGE DU TOTAL MONDIAL)

	1987	1988	1989	1990	1991	1992	1993	1994	1995	1996		1987	1988	1989	1990	1991	1992	1993	1994	1995	1996
Africa	0.2	0.0	0.1	0.0	0.0		0.1	0.1	0.0	0.0	Afrique					0.0		0.0	0.2		
Americas	59.8	60.8	62.2	64.0	67.4		75.7	71.9	77.5	76.9	Amériques	30.4	41.3	44.2	50.4	59.0		70.7	69.5	69.0	59.7
– Northern America	33.5	30.9	33.8	35.3	37.5		38.3	37.4	45.5	45.7	– Amérique du Nord	9.4	16.1	18.5	18.3	19.4		36.6	34.5	34.1	23.4
– LAIA	2.9	4.3	3.0	3.6	3.8		2.3	3.1	2.4	1.9	– ALAI	5.7	3.8	3.7	5.4	3.6		1.4	2.9	1.8	4.1
– CACM	1.3	2.5	0.5	0.2	0.8		1.3	1.4	1.0	1.2	– MCAC					0.0			0.0		
– Caribbean	21.2	22.5	24.2	24.6	25.1		32.5	28.2	27.3	27.3	– Caraïbes	14.8	21.1	21.6	25.9	36.0		31.9	30.3	32.4	30.9
– Rest of America	0.9	0.5	0.6	0.3	0.2		1.3	1.7	1.3	0.7	– Autre Amérique	0.5	0.3	0.3	0.7	0.0		0.9	1.8	0.8	1.2
Asia excl fmr USSR	12.7	11.5	11.4	11.6	10.2		6.5	7.7	6.0	6.5	Asie anc. URSS exclus	2.5	1.1	1.6	3.0	2.3		0.4	0.1	0.2	0.6
– Middle East	0.0	0.1	0.1	0.0	0.0		0.1	0.1	0.1	0.1	– Moyen–Orient	0.3	0.4	0.4	0.4			0.3	0.1	0.2	0.6
Asia former USSR											Asie ancienne URSS										
Europe excl fmr USSR	26.0	26.1	25.6	22.2	21.1		16.8	19.2	15.9	15.9	Europe anc. URSS exclus	67.1	57.6	54.0	46.6	38.7		28.4	30.1	30.7	39.7
– European Union	25.0	25.2	24.7	21.3	20.3		16.0	18.3	15.2	15.1	– Union Européenne	66.9	55.8	54.0	45.2	38.7		28.4	30.1	30.7	38.8
– Eastern Europe	0.3	0.2	0.3	0.3	0.1		0.1	0.3	0.2	0.2	– Europe de l'Est	0.2	1.8	0.0	1.3						
– Rest of Europe	0.7	0.7	0.6	0.7	0.8		0.7	0.5	0.4	0.6	– Autre de l'Europe	0.0			0.0	0.0		0.0	0.0	0.0	0.9
Europe former USSR	0.0	0.0	0.0	0.0	0.0		0.0	0.0	0.0	0.0	Europe ancienne URSS							0.4			
Oceania	1.2	1.5	0.7	2.1	1.2		1.0	1.2	0.6	0.6	Océanie				0.0			0.1	0.0		
Other	0.0	0.0	0.0	0.0	0.0						Autre			0.2							
USA/Etats–Unis d'Amer	26.9	25.5	29.9	30.6	32.2		34.9	34.9	41.6	42.6	USA/Etats–Unis d'Amer	6.1	13.1	14.8	16.3	18.0		35.0	32.9	32.7	21.4
Trinidad and Tobago	11.9	12.4	13.2	15.7	15.9		22.2	19.7	20.3	21.2	United Kingdom	23.1	23.2	20.6	20.3	20.2		13.3	12.9	11.1	8.1
United Kingdom	16.9	16.4	17.1	14.6	13.8		11.0	11.9	10.3	9.7	Netherlands/Pays–Bas	23.5	20.3	25.2	19.6	8.2		8.3	6.6	10.8	17.5
Japan/Japon	7.2	5.9	6.4	7.1	7.1		3.8	4.8	3.2	3.7	Saint Lucia/Ste–Lucie	0.7	1.1	3.3	4.8	7.9		6.6	6.6	8.5	9.3
Canada	6.6	5.4	3.9	4.7	5.2		3.5	2.5	3.9	3.1	Germany/Allemagne					9.4		5.6	8.0	6.9	8.8
Barbados/Barbade	3.2	4.0	4.0	3.3	3.5		2.7	2.9	2.7	2.7	Barbados/Barbade	1.6	1.7	2.0	3.6	4.5		5.4	5.9	7.7	3.3
Germany/Allemagne					1.2		1.3	2.3	1.3	0.9	Dominica/Dominique	1.8	1.8	1.2	1.6	2.0		4.7	2.7	3.4	5.2
Venezuela	0.9	1.7	1.4	1.1	2.0		1.0	1.9	1.3	0.8	Trinidad and Tobago	9.6	13.0	12.4	11.0	12.6		6.4	2.5	1.8	1.7
Jamaica/Jamaïque	1.8	1.5	1.7	1.4	1.2		1.7	1.4	0.7	0.7	St Vincent & Grenadines	0.6	0.7	1.2	2.4	4.0		2.3	1.9	1.9	4.1
Guyana	0.3	0.3	0.4	0.3	0.2		1.1	1.7	1.3	0.5	Antigua and Barbuda	0.1	0.3	0.2	0.5	3.2		2.1	1.8	2.4	2.6

4. Special Imports C.I.F. by Commodities according to the S.I.T.C. (Rev. 2) in million U.S. Dollars
Importations Spéciales C.A.F. par Produits d'après la C.T.C.I. (Rév. 2) en millions de Dollars E.U.

SITC CTCI	COMMODITY	1993 QUANTITY QUANTITE	1993 VALUE VALEUR	1994 QUANTITY QUANTITE	1994 VALUE VALEUR	1995 QUANTITY QUANTITE	1995 VALUE VALEUR	1996 QUANTITY QUANTITE	1996 VALUE VALEUR	PRODUIT
	ALL COMMODITIES		125.3		119.1		129.0		151.4	TOUS PRODUITS
0	FOOD AND LIVE ANIMALS		28.3		28.6		32.0		35.9	ALIMENTS,ANIMAUX VIVANTS
01	MEAT AND PREPARATIONS		5.8		6.8		7.5		8.0	VIANDES ET PREPARATIONS
011	MEAT FRESH,CHILLD,FROZEN	W 3830	4.2	W 3978	5.0	W 4113	5.3	W 4584	6.0	VIANDES FRAICHES,REF,CONGE
0111	BOVINE MEAT FRESH,FROZEN	W 109	0.4	W 196	0.5	W 110	0.5	W 98	0.5	VIANDES BOVIN FRAI,REF
01112	BOVINE MEAT BONELESS	W 99	0.4	W 188	0.5	W 104	0.4	W 85	0.4	VIANDES BOVIN DESOSSEES
0114	POULTRY FRESH CHLLD,FRZN	W 3570	3.7	W 3575	4.2	W 3824	4.6	W 4309	5.3	VOLAILLES MORTES
012	MEAT DRIED,SALTED,SMOKED	W 296	0.7	W 458	0.7	W 501	0.8	W 859	0.8	VIANDE,ABATS SALES,SECHES
0121	PIG MEAT DRIED,SLTD,SMKD	W 240	0.5	W 358	0.5	W 427	0.6	W 770	0.6	LARD,JAMBONS
014	MEAT PREPD,PRSVD,NES ETC	W 394	1.0	W 578	1.3	W 549	1.5	W 430	1.4	CONSERVES DE VIANDES
0142	SAUSAGES INCLDING TINNED	W 202	0.5	W 177	0.5	W 185	0.5	W 240	0.6	SAUCISSES,SAUCISSONS
0149	OTH PREPARD,PRESRVD MEAT	W 191	0.5	W 401	0.9	W 364	1.1	W 190	0.8	AUTRES PREP DE VIANDES
02	DAIRY PRODCTS,BIRDS'EGGS		5.0		4.8		5.4		5.6	PRODUITS LAITIERS,OEUFS
022	MILK AND CREAM	W 2232	3.8	W 2484	3.5	W 1606	3.8	W 1910	4.1	LAIT ET CREME
0223	MILK AND CREAM FRESH	W 248	0.3	W 354	0.5	W 424	0.5	W 354	0.5	LAIT,CREME FRAIS
0224	MILK,CREAM PRESERVED ETC	W 1984	3.5	W 2131	3.1	W 1182	3.3	W 1556	3.7	LAIT,CREME CONS,CONC
02243	MILK DRY,OVER 1.5% FAT	W 572	1.6	W 974	1.5	W 612	1.8	W 577	1.9	LAIT POUDRE SUP 1.5%
02249	MILK(EX DRY) PRSVD,SWEET	W 1368	1.8	W 1122	1.5	W 566	1.5	W 947	1.7	LAIT CONS,CONC SUCRE
024	CHEESE AND CURD	W 386	1.2	W 401	1.3	W 347	1.5	W 330	1.5	FROMAGE ET CAILLEBOTTE
03	FISH AND PREPARATIONS		1.8		1.9		1.8		2.2	POISSONS ET PREPARATIONS
035	FISH SALTED,DRIED,SMOKED	W 387	1.3	W 402	1.3	W 338	1.3	W 561	1.5	POISSON SECHE,SALE,FUME
03502	COD(NOT IN FILLETS)DRIED	W 237	0.9	W 101	0.5	W 54	0.4	W 57	0.4	MORUE SECHEE,SALEE
03503	FISH(EX COD)DRIED,SALTED	W 72	0.3	W 208	0.7	W 156	0.8	W 402	1.0	POISSONS SECHES,SALES
037	FISH ETC PREPD,PRSVD NES	W 155	0.5	W 152	0.5	W 95	0.5	W 158	0.6	POIS,CRUST,MOL PREPARES
0371	FISH PREPARD,PRESRVD NES	W 150	0.5	W 150	0.5	W 94	0.5	W 157	0.6	CONSERVES DE POISSONS
04	CEREALS AND PREPARATIONS		6.9		6.0		7.0		9.2	CEREALES ET PRODUITS
041	WHEAT ETC UNMILLED	W 14413	2.0	W 11110	1.9	W 15687	1.6	W 12333	3.5	FROMENT,EPEAUTRE
0412	OTHER WHEAT ETC UNMILLED	W 14413	2.0	W 11110	1.9	W 15687	1.6	W 12333	3.5	AUTRE FROMENT NON MOULU
042	RICE	W 3694	1.4	W 1359	0.9	W 1189	1.4	W 3710	1.2	RIZ
0421	RICE IN HUSK OR HUSKED	W 2989	1.1	W 747	0.5	W 175	0.2	W 844	0.2	RIZ SANS AUTRE PREPARATION
04212	RICE HUSKED	W 2947	1.1	W 747	0.5	W 157	0.2	W 844	0.2	RIZ CARGO
0422	RICE SEMI-MILLED,MILLED	W 705	0.3	W 612	0.4	W 1013	1.3	W 2866	1.1	RIZ POLI,GLACE INCL BRISURES
04221	RICE MILLED UNBROKEN	W 657	0.3	W 612	0.4	W 1002	1.3	W 2412	1.1	RIZ POLI,GLACE EXCL BRISURES
044	MAIZE UNMILLED	W 6281	0.4	W 3214	0.4	W 1333	0.4	W 4122	0.6	MAIS NON MOULU
046	WHEAT ETC MEAL OR FLOUR	W 2275	0.7	W 2177	0.7	W 1260	0.8	W 1643	0.5	SEMOULE FARINE,FROMENT
04601	FLOUR OF WHEAT OR MESLIN	W 2125	0.7	W 1889	0.6	W 678	0.6	W 1317	0.4	FARINE DE FROMENT
048	CEREAL ETC PREPARATIONS	W 1345	2.5	W 1425	2.3	W 1697	2.9	W 2327	3.3	PREPTNS A BASE CEREALES
0481	PREPD BREAKFAST FOOD ETC	W 184	0.6	W 194	0.6	W 169	0.6	W 334	0.7	CEREALES TRAVAILLEES
0484	BAKERY PRODUCTS	W 588	1.2	W 680	1.1	W 685	1.4	W 1122	1.6	PRODUITS DE BOULANGERIE
04841	BREAD,BISCUIT,COM WAFERS	W 274	0.6	W 202	0.5	W 326	0.7	W 319	0.8	PAINS,BISCUITS DE MER
04842	PASTRY, CAKES ETC	W 314	0.6	W 478	0.7	W 359	0.8	W 803	0.9	PATISSERIE ETC.
0488	OTH CEREAL PREPS,MALT EX	W 132	0.5	W 104	0.5	W 104	0.5	W 114	0.5	EXTRAITS DE MALT
05	VEGETABLES AND FRUIT		2.4		2.6		3.2		2.9	LEGUMES ET FRUITS
054	VEG ETC FRSH,SMPLY PRSVD	W 2302	1.0	W 1742	1.2	W 2084	1.5	W 1678	1.2	LEGUMES FRAIS,CONG,SECS
0541	POTATOES FRSH EXCL SWEET	W 1588	0.5	W 987	0.6	W 969	0.6	W 697	0.5	POMMES DE TERRE
058	FRUIT PRESERVED,PREPARED	W 817	1.1	W 922	1.2	W 879	1.2	W 1103	1.3	CONSERVES DE FRUITS
0585	FRUIT OR VEGETABLE JUICE	W 717	0.8	W 781	0.8	W 771	0.9	W 844	1.0	JUS DE FRUITS
05851	ORANGE JUICE	W 434	0.5	W 457	0.5	W 451	0.5	W 467	0.5	JUS D'ORANGE
06	SUGAR AND PREPS,HONEY		2.2		2.5		2.7		2.9	SUCRES ET PRODUITS
061	SUGAR AND HONEY	W 4847	2.1	W 5043	2.3	W 11630	2.5	W 5666	2.5	SUCRES ET MIEL
0611	RAW BEET AND CANE SUGAR	W 2542	1.0	W 2651	1.2	W 8801	1.1	W 2064	1.1	SUCRES BRUTS
0612	REFINED SUGAR ETC	W 2299	1.1	W 2383	1.1	W 2608	1.4	W 2276	1.2	SUCRES RAFFINES
07	COFFEE,TEA,COCOA,SPICES		0.5		0.6		0.7		0.6	CAFE,THE,CACAO,EPICES
081	*FEEDING STUFF FOR ANIML	W 3473	0.5	W 1167	0.4	W 1699	0.4	W 3384	0.4	NOURRITURE POUR ANIMAUX
09	MISC EDIBLE PRODUCTS		3.4		3.3		3.7		4.2	PREP ALIMENTAIRES DIVERSES
091	MARGARINE AND SHORTENING	W 818	1.2	W 844	1.3	W 865	1.3	W 834	1.5	MARGARINE ET GRAISSES
0914	MARGARINE,EDIBLE FAT NES	W 818	1.2	W 844	1.3	W 860	1.3	W 834	1.5	MARGARINES,SIMILI SAINDOUX
09141	MARGARINE	W 517	0.8	W 615	0.9	W 565	1.0	W 588	1.1	MARGARINE
09149	OTH PREPARED EDIBLE FATS	W 302	0.4	W 230	0.4	W 295	0.4	W 246	0.4	SIMILI-SAINDOUX
098	EDIBLE PRODCTS,PREPS NES	W 3910	2.2	W 1480	2.0	W 1757	2.5	W 6355	2.7	PREP ALIMENTAIRES NDA
09804	SAUCES,MIXED SEASONINGS	W 925	0.6	W 310	0.6	W 473	0.8	W 608	0.7	SAUCES,ASSAISONNEMENTS
09809	MISC FOOD PREPRTIONS NES	W 2857	1.2	W 1042	1.2	W 1151	1.4	W 5512	1.6	PREP ALIMENTAIRES NDA
1	BEVERAGES AND TOBACCO		3.2		2.7		2.8		3.1	BOISSONS ET TABACS
11	BEVERAGES		2.9		2.3		2.4		2.7	BOISSONS
111	NON-ALCOHL BEVERAGES NES	W 1311	1.1	W 1067	0.8	W 869	0.8	W 982	0.9	BOISSONS NON ALCOOLIQUES
11102	FLAVORED WATERS NON-ALCO	W 1173	1.0	W 842	0.7	W 777	0.8	W 813	0.8	LIMONADES,EAUX GAZEUSES
112	ALCOHOLIC BEVERAGES	W 1570	1.9	W 1156	1.6	W 896	1.6	W 1058	1.8	BOISSONS ALCOOLIQUES
1121	WINE OF FRESH GRAPES ETC	W 162	0.3	W 207	0.5	W 239	0.4	W 265	0.5	VINS DE RAISINS FRAIS
11212	WINE OF FRESH GRAPES	W 161	0.3	W 186	0.4	W 224	0.4	W 244	0.5	VINS DE MOUTS DE RAISINS
1123	BEER,ALE,STOUT,PORTER	W 1228	1.1	W 721	0.6	W 443	0.5	W 476	0.5	BIERES
1124	DISTILLED ALCOHOLIC BEVS	W 179	0.5	W 224	0.6	W 210	0.8	W 316	0.9	ALCOOLS,EAUX-DE-VIE
11249	OTH ALCOHOLC BEVS,CMPNDS	W 152	0.4	W 186	0.5	W 175	0.6	W 275	0.7	BOISSONS ALCOOLIQUES NDA
12	TOBACCO AND MANUFACTURES		0.3		0.4		0.5		0.5	TABACS BRUTS FABRIQUES
122	TOBACCO,MANUFACTURED	W 13	0.2	W 16	0.3	W 30	0.4	W 41	0.4	TABACS FABRIQUES
2	CRUDE MATERLS,EXCL FUELS		3.8		4.6		3.6		4.9	MAT BRUTES NON COMESTIBLES
24	CORK AND WOOD		3.2		4.1		3.2		4.1	LIEGE ET BOIS
248	WOOD SHAPED,SLEEPERS	W 6116	3.1	W 6766	4.1	W 4490	3.2	W 6791	4.1	BOIS SIMPLEMENT TRAVAILLES
2482	LUMBER SHAPED CONIFER	W 5232	2.8	W 5852	3.6	W 3928	2.8	W 5862	3.7	CONIFERES SCIES,RABOTES
24821	LUMBER SAWN ETC CONIFER	W 1771	0.7	W 2735	1.5	W 1446	0.9	W 2334	1.4	CONIFERES SCIES LONGITUD
24822	LUMBER PLANED ETC CONIFR	W 3461	2.2	W 3117	2.1	W 2481	2.0	W 3528	2.3	CONIFER RABOTES,RAINES
2483	LUMBER SHAPED NON-CONIFR	W 884	0.4	W 914	0.5	W 562	0.5	W 930	0.5	NON CONIFERES SCIES,RABOTES
27	CRUDE FERTLZR,MINRLS NES		0.5		0.4		0.3		0.6	ENGRAIS MINERAUX BRUTS
278	OTHER CRUDE MINERALS	W 1131	0.4	W 1020	0.3	W 950	0.3	W 1661	0.5	AUTRES MINERAUX BRUTS
3	MINERAL FUELS ETC		15.1		9.2		10.1		14.8	COMBUSTIBLES MINERAUX LUB
33	PETROLEUM AND PRODUCTS		14.0		7.8		8.6		13.0	PETROLE ET DERIVES
334	PETROLEUM PRODUCTS,REFIN	W 46284	13.9	W 27901	7.7	W 37341	8.5	W 42362	12.9	PRODUITS RAFFINES
3341	GASOLINE,OTH LIGHT OILS	W 13852	3.4	W 14136	3.4	W 14756	3.5	W 19394	4.6	ESSENCES POUR MOTEURS
33411	MOTOR,AVIATION SPIRIT	W 13440	3.2	W 14048	3.3	W 14688	3.4	W 19333	4.5	ESSENCES MOTEURS D'AVIONS
3342	KEROSENE,OTH MEDIUM OILS	W 472	0.1	W 319	0.1	W 305	0.1	W 3679	1.8	PETR LAMPANTS,AUT HUIL
33421	KEROSENE INCL JET FUEL	W 180	0.1	W 141	0.1	W 305	0.1	W 3500	1.7	PETROLES LAMPANTS
3343	GAS OILS	W 31113	9.7	W 12853	3.6	W 21871	4.5	W 18848	6.0	GAS OILS
3345	LUBS,PETROLEUM OILS NES	W 847	0.8	W 593	0.8	W 409	0.6	W 440	0.7	HUILES LUBRIFIANTES
33451	LUBS(HIGH PETR CONT) ETC	W 846	0.8	W 592	0.8	W 379	0.6	W 437	0.7	HUILES LUBRIF,H LOURDES
341	*GAS,NATURAL AND MANUFCT	W 3555	1.2	W 3577	1.4	W 3757	1.5	W 6010	1.8	GAZ NATUREL,GAZ MANUFACT
3413	PETROLM GASES,LIQUEFIED	W 3555	1.2	W 3577	1.4	W 3757	1.5	W 6010	1.8	GAZ DE PETROLE LIQUEFIE
34131	LIQUEFIED PROPANE,BUTANE	W 3265	1.0	W 3272	1.3	W 2854	1.2	W 3696	0.5	PROPANE,BUTANE LIQUEFIES
34139	OTH HYDROCARBON GAS LQFD	W 290	0.3	W 305	0.2	W 903	0.4	W 2314	1.4	HYDROCARBURES GAZEUX NDA
4	ANIMAL,VEGETABLE OIL,FAT		0.5		0.5		0.7		0.7	HUILES,GRAISSES ANIM,VEG
42	FIXED VEGETABLE OIL,FAT		0.5		0.5		0.7		0.7	HUILES VEGETALES FIXES
423	FIXED VEG OILS,SOFT	W 185	0.3	W 206	0.4	W 216	0.6	W 259	0.6	HUILES VEGET DOUCES FIXES
4232	SOYA BEAN OIL	W 182	0.3	W 201	0.4	W 213	0.5	W 251	0.5	HUILE DE SOJA

4. Special Imports C.I.F. by Commodities according to the S.I.T.C. (Rev. 2) in million U.S. Dollars
Importations Spéciales C.A.F. par Produits d'après la C.T.C.I. (Rév. 2) en millions de Dollars E.U.

SITC CTCI	COMMODITY	1993 QUANTITY QUANTITE	1993 VALUE VALEUR	1994 QUANTITY QUANTITE	1994 VALUE VALEUR	1995 QUANTITY QUANTITE	1995 VALUE VALEUR	1996 QUANTITY QUANTITE	1996 VALUE VALEUR	PRODUIT
5	CHEMCLS,RELATED PROD NES		10.2		9.9		10.7		11.5	PRODUITS CHIMIQUES
53	DYES,TANNING,COLOUR PROD		1.9		1.7		1.5		1.9	PROD TEINTURE,COLORANTS
531	SYNT DYE,NAT INDGO,LAKES	W 105	0.3	W 200	0.4	W 164	0.4	W 253	0.6	MAT COLOR ORGAN,LAQUES
5312	SYNTH LUMIN,INDIGO,LAKES	W 105	0.3	W 200	0.4	W 164	0.4	W 253	0.6	LUMINOPHORES ORGAN SYNTH
53121	SYN ORG LUMIN ETC,INDIGO	W 105	0.3	W 200	0.4	W 164	0.4	W 253	0.6	PROD ORGANIQ SYNTH LUMIN
533	PIGMENTS,PAINTS,ETC	W 871	1.6	W 505	1.3	W 861	1.1	W 526	1.4	PIGMENTS,PEINTURES,VERNIS
5334	VARNISHES,DISTEMPERS ETC	W 811	1.4	W 404	1.1	W 620	0.9	W 407	1.2	PEINTURES A L'EAU
53342	OTH PAINTS,VARNISHES ETC	W 377	0.8	W 187	0.6	W 190	0.5	W 192	0.7	AUTRES PEINTURES,VERNIS
53344	DISTEMPERS,DYES NES ETC	W 395	0.5	W 158	0.4	W 259	0.3	W 187	0.4	PEINTURES A L'EAU
541	*MEDICINAL,PHARM PRODUCT	K 149601	2.0	K 158493	2.4	K 202123	2.6	K 178101	2.6	PROD MEDICINAUX PHARMACEUT
5417	MEDICAMENTS	K 123148	1.7	K 132723	2.1	K 121463	2.3	K 135546	2.2	MEDICAMENTS
54179	— CONTNG OTH SUBSTANCES	K 100825	1.5	K 120620	1.7	K 108834	1.9	K 122125	1.9	MED CONT AUT SUBSTANCES
55	PERFUME,CLEANING ETC PRD		3.3		3.4		3.6		3.7	PROD POUR PARFUM,TOILETTE
553	PERFUMERY,COSMETICS,ETC	W 181	1.1	W 213	1.2	W 226	1.3	W 283	1.3	PRODUITS DE PARFUMERIE
554	SOAP,CLEANSING ETC PREPS	W 1685	2.2	W 1588	2.2	W 1536	2.3	W 1867	2.4	SAVONS,PRODUITS DETERSIFS
5541	SOAPS	W 520	0.7	W 362	0.6	W 320	0.7	W 357	0.7	SAVONS,PROD TENSIO-ACTIFS
5542	WASHING PREPARATIONS ETC	W 1124	1.5	W 1199	1.5	W 1175	1.6	W 1473	1.7	PROD ORG TENSIO-ACT NDA
562	*FERTILIZERS,MANUFACTURE	W 6840	0.7	W 2118	0.4	W 2581	0.5	W 1717	0.5	ENGRAIS MANUFACTURES
5629	FERTILIZERS NES	W 5550	0.5	W 866	0.3	W 1360	0.4	W 1015	0.3	ENGRAIS NDA
56299	OTHER FERTILIZERS NES	W 5438	0.4	W 405	0.1	W 53	0.1	W 21	0.1	AUTRES ENGRAIS NDA
58	PLASTIC MATERIALS ETC		0.6		0.6		0.7		0.7	MAT PLAST ARTIFICIELLES
583	POLYMERIZATION ETC PRODS	W 310	0.5	W 360	0.5	W 280	0.7	W 140	0.6	PROD POLYMERISATION
5839	OTH POLYMRZTION ETC PROD	W 310	0.5	W 360	0.5	W 279	0.7	W 140	0.6	AUT PROD POLYMER COPOLYM
59	CHEMICAL MATERIALS NES		1.5		1.5		1.7		1.7	MAT PROD CHIMIQUES NDA
591	PESTICIDES,DISINFECTANTS	W 321	0.8	W 328	0.8	W 455	0.9	W 381	0.9	DESINF,INSECT,FONG,HERB
5911	INSECTICIDES,FOR RETAIL	W 214	0.5	W 188	0.5	W 219	0.6	W 233	0.6	INSECTICIDES VENTE DET
598	MISCEL CHEM PRODUCTS NES	W 166	0.5	W 254	0.5	W 308	0.5	W 181	0.6	PROD DIV INDUST CHIM NDA
5989	CHEM PRODUCTS,PREPS NES	W 162	0.5	W 240	0.5	W 275	0.5	W 176	0.5	PROD PREP CHIMIQUES NDA
6	BASIC MANUFACTURES		24.2		23.8		25.6		29.0	ART MANUFACTURES
62	RUBBER MANUFACTURES NES		1.8		1.7		1.9		2.0	CAOUTCHOUC MANUFACTURE
625	RUBBER TYRES, TUBES ETC	W 694	1.4	W 599	1.4	W 1162	1.7	W 746	1.6	PNEUS CAOUTCHOUC VULCANISE
6259	OTH TYRES,TYRE CASES,ETC	W 562	0.9	W 442	0.9	W 969	1.2	W 594	1.0	AUTRES PNEUS RECHAPES FLAPS
62599	TYRES NES,TYRE CASES,ETC	W 554	0.9	W 431	0.8	W 963	1.2	W 586	0.9	PNEUS,FLAPS
63	WOOD,CORK MANUFACTRS NES		2.8		2.5		2.5		3.3	OUVRAGES LIEGE ET BOIS
634	VENEERS,PLYWOOD,ETC	W 2019	1.6	W 2237	1.7	W 1908	1.8	W 5171	2.2	PLACAGES,CONTRE-PLAQUES
6342	PLYWOOD OF WOOD SHEETS	W 1756	1.6	W 1830	1.5	W 1636	1.7	W 4930	2.1	BOIS CONTRE-PLAQUES
635	WOOD MANUFACTURES NES	W 541	1.2	W 290	0.9	W 178	0.8	W 431	1.2	ART MANUF EN BOIS NDA
6353	BUILDERS WOODWRK,PREFABS	W 445	1.0	W 175	0.7	W 152	0.6	W 373	0.9	OUVRAGES DE MENUISERIE
64	PAPER,PAPERBOARD AND MFR		3.9		3.7		4.8		3.7	PAPIERS,CARTONS & OUVRAGES
641	PAPER AND PAPERBOARD		1.4	W 586	1.2	W 1379	2.0	W 1986	1.1	PAPIERS ET CARTONS
6417	CORRUGATED PAPER ETC,BLK		0.7	W 318	0.6	W 957	1.2	W 1548	0.5	PAPIERS,CARTONS ONDULES
64172	CREPED HSHOLD PAPER ETC	W 284	0.7	W 263	0.6	W 891	1.2	W 1529	0.4	PAPIER NON KRAFT CREPE
642	PAPER,ETC,PRECUT,ARTS OF	W 1718	2.6	W 1289	2.6	W 1351	2.8	W 843	2.7	PAP,CARTONS DECOUPES
6421	PAPER ETC CONTAINERS	W 1289	1.1	W 954	1.2	W 943	1.3	W 415	0.9	BOITES,SACS EMBALLAGES
6423	EXERCISE BOOKS ETC	W 81	0.5	W 106	0.6	W 154	0.5	W 107	0.6	REGISTRES,CAHIERS,CARNETS
6428	PAPER ETC ARTICLES NES	W 221	0.8	W 163	0.7	W 170	0.8	W 225	0.9	OUVRAGES EN PATE A PAPIER
64285	PAPER ETC DIAPERS ETC	W 92	0.5	W 93	0.5	W 78	0.5	W 106	0.6	SERVIETTES HYGIENIQUES
65	TEXTILE YARN,FABRICS,ETC		2.4		2.5		2.9		2.9	FILS,TISSUS,ARTICLES TEXTILE
652	COTTON FABRICS,WOVEN	W 98	0.5	W 141	0.7	W 173	0.9	W 165	0.9	TISSUS DE COTON
6522	WOVEN COTTON BLEACHD,ETC	W 92	0.5	W 135	0.7	W 168	0.9	W 163	0.8	TISSUS COTON BLANCHIS ETC
65224	BLCHED COTTON FABRIC NES	W 91	0.5	W 130	0.7	W 146	0.8	W 156	0.8	AUT TIS PLUS 85% COT BLANCHI
653	WOVN MAN-MADE FIB FABRIC	W 115	0.7	W 98	0.7	W 93	0.9	W 95	0.8	TISSUS FIBRES SYNTH,ARTIF
6534	DISC SYN BLEND FABRC NES	W 52	0.4	W 43	0.4	W 50	0.5	W 38	0.4	TISSUS FIBRES SYNTH DISCONT
65341	DISC SYN FIB-COTTN FABRC	W 51	0.4	W 42	0.4	W 50	0.5	W 37	0.4	TISSUS FIB SYNT DIS MEL COTO
658	TEXTILE ARTICLES NES	W 156	0.5	W 79	0.5	W 175	0.6	W 334	0.6	ART FACONNES MAT TEXTILES
66	NONMETAL MINERAL MFS NES		5.0		4.8		5.4		6.8	ART MIN NON METALLIQUES
661	LIME,CEMENT,BLDG PRODS	W 57744	2.7	W 39932	2.7	W 32129	2.6	W 35917	3.3	CHAUX,CIMENTS MAT CONSTR
6612	CEMENT	W 56710	2.4	W 39530	2.5	W 31733	2.5	W 35377	3.1	CIMENTS HYDRAULIQUES
662	CLAY,REFRACTORY BLDG PRD	W 1314	0.9	W 1060	0.8	W 1438	0.9	W 6109	1.0	MAT CONST REFRACTAIRES
6624	BRICKS ETC NONREFRACTORY	W 1272	0.9	W 1048	0.8	W 1433	0.9	W 6015	1.0	BRIQUES ETC CERAM NON REFR
66245	GLAZED CERAMIC SETTS ETC	W 805	0.7	W 622	0.6	W 650	0.6	W 5035	0.7	AUT CARREAUX CERAMIQUE
663	MINERAL MANUFCTURES NES	W 846	0.3	W 171	0.2	W 1023	0.3	W 1017	0.8	ART MIN MANUF NDA
6633	MINRL MFS NES NONCERAMIC	W 823	0.2	W 158	0.1	W 1007	0.3	W 1001	0.7	OUVR MAT MINERALE NDA
66332	CEMENT,ARTFCL STONE PROD	W 815	0.2	W 145	0.1	W 996	0.2	W 920	0.7	OUVRAGES EN CIMENT
664	GLASS	W 229	0.6	W 115	0.3	W 126	0.5	W 155	0.3	VERRE
665	GLASSWARE	W 622	0.5	W 918	0.9	W 1220	1.0	W 1712	1.3	OUVRAGES EN VERRE
6651	BOTTLES ETC OF GLASS	W 551	0.4	W 872	0.7	W 1181	0.8	W 1643	1.0	RECIPIENTS EN VERRE
66511	GLASS BOTTLES ETC NONVAC	W 550	0.4	W 872	0.7	W 1181	0.8	W 1643	1.0	BONBONNES,BOUTEILLES,ETC
67	IRON AND STEEL		2.4		2.8		2.8		3.9	FER ET ACIER
672	IRON,STEEL PRIMARY FORMS	W 1161	0.3	W 591	0.4	W 555	0.8	W 871	0.9	LINGOTS FER,ACIER
6727	IRN,STL COIL FR REROLLNG	W 1161	0.3	W 591	0.4	W 555	0.8	W 871	0.9	EBAUCHES POUR TOLES FER
67271	IRON,SIMPLE STEEL COILS	W 1159	0.3	W 588	0.4	W 555	0.8	W 857	0.9	EBAUCHES NON EN ACIER
673	IRON,STEEL SHAPES ETC	W 1797	1.1	W 2664	0.9	W 3614	1.2	W 6547	1.6	BARRES,PROFIL FER,ACIER
6731	IRON,STEEL WIRE ROD	W 1009	0.5	W 994	0.4	W 1730	0.7	W 4512	0.5	FIL MACHINE FER,ACIER
67311	IRON,SIMPLE STL WIRE ROD	W 992	0.5	W 994	0.4	W 1730	0.7	W 4512	0.5	FIL MACH AUT ACIER FIN
6732	IRON,STEEL BARS ETC	W 693	0.4	W 1645	0.5	W 1854	0.6	W 1992	1.1	BARRES FER,ACIER
67322	HIGH CARBON STL BARS ETC	W 524	0.2	W 1527	0.4	W 1739	0.5	W 1710	0.9	BARRES ACIER FIN CARBONE
674	IRN,STL UNIV,PLATE,SHEET	W 222	0.3	W 320	0.5	W 160	0.4	W 557	0.7	LARGES PLATS,TOLES
6749	OTH IRN,STL PLATES,SHEET	W 173	0.3	W 275	0.4	W 126	0.3	W 339	0.4	AUTRES TOLES FER,ACIER
678	IRON,STL TUBES,PIPES,ETC	W 1037	0.8	W 694	1.1	W 249	0.5	W 319	0.8	TUBES,TUYAUX EN FONTE,FER
6781	CAST IRON TUBES,PIPES	W 807	0.5	W 407	0.4	W 1	0.1	W 49	0.2	TUBES,TUYAUX EN FONTE
6785	IRON,STEEL TUBE FITTINGS	W 57	0.2	W 126	0.5	W 34	0.2	W 109	0.3	ACCESSOIRES DE TUYAUTERIE
69	METAL MANUFACTURES NES		6.1		5.8		5.5		6.6	ART MANUFACT EN METAL NDA
691	STRUCTURES AND PARTS NES	W 427	1.8	W 660	1.9	W 366	1.3	W 387	1.4	CONSTRUCT FER,ACIER,ALU
6911	STRUCTURES,PARTS IRN,STL	W 178	1.0	W 265	0.8	W 219	0.6	W 172	0.4	CONSTRUCT FER,ACIER,FONTE
6912	STRUCTURES,PARTS ALUMNM	W 249	0.9	W 396	1.1	W 147	0.8	W 214	1.0	CONSTRUCT ALUMINIUM
692	METAL TANKS,BOXES,ETC	W 153	0.3	W 144	0.4	W 144	0.4	W 338	1.1	RECIPIENTS METALLIQUES
6921	METAL STORAGE TANKS ETC	W 24	0.1	W 15	0.1	W 18	0.1	W 173	0.8	CUVES EN FONTE,FER,ALU
69211	STEEL STORAGE TANKS ETC	W 19	0.1	W 15	0.1	W 18	0.1	W 173	0.8	CUVES EN FONTE FER OU ACIER
693	WIRE PRODUCTS NON ELECTR	W 557	0.6	W 501	0.6	W 489	0.5	W 480	0.6	OUVRAGES FILS METALLIQUES
6935	METAL FENCING,GAUZE,ETC	W 469	0.4	W 471	0.5	W 450	0.4	W 449	0.5	TOILES EN FER,ACIER,CUIVRE
69351	IRN,STL FENCNG,GAUZE ETC	W 468	0.4	W 471	0.5	W 450	0.4	W 449	0.5	TOILES EN FER,ACIER
694	STL,COPPR NAILS,NUTS,ETC	W 200	0.4	W 164	0.4	W 261	0.4	W 149	0.5	CLOUS,VIS,ECROUS
695	TOOLS	W 76	0.5	W 71	0.5	W 145	0.7	W 123	0.7	OUTILS A MAIN
6953	OTHER HAND TOOLS	W 44	0.3	W 39	0.4	W 123	0.5	W 52	0.5	AUTRES OUTILS A MAIN
697	BASE MTL HOUSEHOLD EQUIP	W 458	1.3	W 227	1.0	W 264	1.1	W 182	1.0	ART MENAGE MET COMMUNS
6973	DMSTC HEATG,COOKG APPARA	W 398	0.9	W 169	0.7	W 178	0.8	W 118	0.6	APPS CHAUF NON ELECTRIQ
69731	IRN,STL DOM COOKG APPARA	W 395	0.9	W 167	0.7	W 170	0.8	W 88	0.5	APPS CUISSON FER,ACIER
699	BASE METAL MFRS NES	W 303	1.2	W 311	1.2	W 320	1.2	W 396	1.4	ART MANUFACTURES MET NDA
6991	LOCKSMITHS WARES,ETC	W 83	0.5	W 121	0.6	W 71	0.5	W 104	0.6	ARTICLES DE SERRURERIE
7	MACHINES,TRANSPORT EQUIP		25.0		25.9		27.3		33.4	MACHINES MATERIEL TRANSPORT

4. Special Imports C.I.F. by Commodities according to the S.I.T.C. (Rev. 2) in million U.S. Dollars
Importations Spéciales C.A.F. par Produits d'après la C.T.C.I. (Rév. 2) en millions de Dollars E.U.

SITC CTCI	COMMODITY	1993		1994		1995		1996		PRODUIT
		QUANTITY QUANTITE	VALUE VALEUR	QUANTITY QUANTITE	VALUE VALEUR	QUANTITY QUANTITE	VALUE VALEUR	QUANTITY QUANTITE	VALUE VALEUR	
71	POWER GENERATING EQUIPMT		2.1		3.5		1.2		1.2	MACHINES GENERATRICES
713	INTRNL COMBUS PSTN ENGIN	W 40	0.9	W 50	0.8	W 38	0.7	W 38	0.5	MOTEURS EXPL COMB INT, PIECE
7139	PISTON ENGINE PARTS NES	W 23	0.6	W 24	0.5	W 7	0.3	W 11	0.2	PIECES POUR 713.2,3,8
716	ROTATING ELECTRIC PLANT	W 138	1.2	W 387	2.7	W 40	0.6	W 59	0.6	APP ELECTR ROTATIFS,PIECES
7162	AC MTRS,GENRTRS,GEN SETS	W 92	1.0	W 378	2.6	W 31	0.3	W 42	0.3	MOTEURS ELECTRIQUES
71623	GEN SETS WITH PSTN ENGN	W 82	0.9	W 370	2.5	W 11	0.1	W 10	0.1	GROUPES MOTEUR EXPLOSION
72	MACHS FOR SPCL INDUSTRYS		2.8		1.5		1.2		3.4	MAC SPECIALES POUR INDUST
722	TRACTORS NON-ROAD			W 18	0.5	W 13	0.1	W 13	0.1	TRACTEURS
7224	WHEELED TRACTORS NES			W 15	0.5	W 11	0.1	W 3	0.1	TRACTEURS A ROUES
723	CIVIL ENGNEERG EQUIP ETC	W 55	0.3	W 35	0.2	W 70	0.6	W 336	2.0	APPAREILS DE GENIE CIVIL
7234	CONST,MINING MACHNRY NES	W 49	0.3	W 28	0.1	W 60	0.5	W 327	2.0	MACH POUR LA CONST, MINES
72342	SLFPRP SHOVELS,EXCAVATRS	W 44	0.3	W 6	0.1	W 49	0.3	W 284	1.8	PELLES MECANIQUES
728	OTH MACHY FOR SPCL INDUS	W 497	2.1	W 72	0.5	W 24	0.2	W 53	0.6	AUT MACH IND PARTICULIERES
7283	OTHR MINERAL WORKG MACHY	W 463	1.9	W 38	0.2	W 9	0.1	W 31	0.3	MACH TRIER,CRIBLER,BROYER
72833	MNRL MIXING,KNEADING MCH	W 441	1.6	W 30	0.2	W 5	0.1	W 25	0.2	MACH MELANGER MAT MINER
74	GENRL INDUSTRL MACHY NES		4.3		3.4		3.6		4.8	MACH APP INDUSTRIE
741	HEATING,COOLING EQUIPMNT	W 168	1.8	W 124	1.2	W 151	1.4	W 176	1.4	MACH CHAUFFAGE,PIECES
7414	NONDOM REFRIG EQUIPT,PTS	W 21	0.4	W 28	0.3	W 41	0.5	W 95	0.8	MAT PRODUCTION DU FROID
74149	PTS NES OF REFRIG EQUIPT	W 6	0.2	W 12	0.2	W 21	0.3	W 54	0.6	PIECES POUR MACH FROID
7415	AIR-CONDITIONING MACHNRY	W 104	0.7	W 42	0.3	W 63	0.5	W 49	0.4	GROUPES CONDITION AIR
7416	HEATING,COOLING EQU NES	W 41	0.8	W 38	0.5	W 44	0.4	W 18	0.2	APP CHANGEMENT TEMP
742	PUMPS FOR LIQUIDS ETC	W 25	0.4	W 17	0.4	W 29	0.4	W 36	0.6	POMPES MOTO-POMPES
7428	OTHER PUMPS FOR LIQUIDS	W 18	0.3	W 14	0.3	W 27	0.3	W 30	0.6	AUTRES POMPES POUR LIQ
743	PUMPS NES,CENTRFUGES ETC	W 50	0.5	W 47	0.6	W 33	0.4	W 62	0.8	POMPES COMPRES,VENT ETC
7436	GAS,LIQUID FILTERS ETC	W 29	0.3	W 17	0.4	W 14	0.3	W 22	0.3	APP POUR FILT DES LIQUIDES
744	MECHANICAL HANDLING EQU	W 47	0.4	W 63	0.5	W 268	0.6	W 114	0.6	EQUIP MANUTENTION PIECES
745	NONELEC MACHY,TOOLS NES	W 47	0.6	W 35	0.4	W 17	0.3	W 37	0.7	AUT MACH NON ELEC,PIECES
7452	OTH NONELEC MCHS,PTS NES	W 41	0.5	W 22	0.3	W 10	0.3	W 23	0.6	AUT MACH NON ELEC,PIECES
749	NONELEC MACH PTS,ACC NES	W 209	0.8	W 54	0.7	W 36	0.7	W 111	0.9	PIECES MACH NON ELEC NDA
7492	COCKS,VALVES ETC NES	W 190	0.5	W 41	0.4	W 22	0.4	W 93	0.6	ART ROB,SIM POUR TUYAUX
75	OFFICE MACHNES,ADP EQUIP		2.0		2.4		3.1		3.5	MACH BUREAU TRAIT AUTOM
751	OFFICE MACHINES	W 21	0.5	W 16	0.4	W 18	0.6	W 11	0.5	MACH,APPAREILS DE BUREAU
7518	OFFICE MACHINES NES	W 11	0.4	W 8	0.3	W 11	0.5	W 7	0.4	MACH,APP DE BUREAU NDA
752	AUTOMTIC DATA PROC EQUIP	W 27	1.0	W 34	1.5	W 35	1.8	W 62	2.1	MACH TRAIT INFORMATION
7522	DIGITAL COMPUTERS	W 20	0.6	W 21	1.1	W 18	1.1	W 30	1.5	MACH DIGITALES COMPLETES
7525	ADP PERIPHERAL UNITS	W 5	0.3	W 10	0.3	W 13	0.5	W 20	0.5	UNITES PERIPHERIQUES
759	OFFICE,ADP MCH PTS,ACCES	W 8	0.5	W 32	0.7	W 12	0.8	W 15	1.0	PIECES DU 751 ET 752
7599	ACCTG,ETC,ADP MCH PTS,AC	W 5	0.4	W 28	0.5	W 9	0.7	W 13	0.9	PIECES DU 751 ET 752
76	TELECOMM,SOUND EQUIPMENT		2.4		1.9		4.6		4.7	EQUIPMENT DE TELECOM
761	TELEVISION RECEIVERS	W 30	0.4	W 30	0.4	W 40	0.5	W 52	0.5	RECEPTEURS DE TELEVISION
7611	COLOUR TV RECEIVERS	W 28	0.4	W 29	0.4	W 39	0.5	W 52	0.5	RECEPTEURS COULEUR
764	TELECOM EQPT,PTS,ACC NES	W 38	1.8	W 32	1.3	W 75	3.8	W 98	3.8	EQUIP TELECOM,PIECES
7641	LINE TELEPHONE,ETC EQUIP	W 28	1.5	W 20	1.0	W 58	3.1	W 73	2.6	APP TELEPHON PAR FIL
7649	PTS NES OF EQUIPMT OF 76	W 3	0.1	W 3	0.1	W 12	0.5	W 17	1.0	PIECES DE LA DIV 76
76491	PTS NES OF APPAR OF 7641	W 1	0.1		0.1	W 4	0.4	W 5	0.9	PIECES POUR 764.1
77	ELECTRIC MACHNRY NES ETC		4.9		4.8		5.2		5.0	MACH APP ELECT NDA
771	ELECTRIC POWER MACHY NES	W 60	0.5	W 80	0.5	W 93	0.6	W 51	0.4	MACH PROD,TRANS ELECTR
7711	TRANSFORMERS,ELECTRICAL	W 55	0.4	W 75	0.4	W 85	0.4	W 47	0.3	TRANSFO ELECTRIQUES
772	SWITCHGEAR ETC,PARTS NES	W 47	0.8	W 99	1.0	W 58	0.7	W 131	0.9	APP COUPURE,SECT ETC
7721	SWITCHGEAR ETC	W 47	0.8	W 99	1.0	W 58	0.7	W 131	0.8	APP COUPURE,SECTIONMNT
773	ELECTR DISTRIBUTNG EQUIP		1.0	W 152	0.8	W 242	1.0	W 235	1.0	EQUIPMT DISTRIBUTION ELECT
7731	INSULATED WIRE,CABLE ETC	W 303	0.9	W 151	0.8	W 242	0.9	W 223	0.9	FILS,CABLES ISOLES ELECT
775	HOUSEHOLD TYPE EQUIP NES	W 448	1.7	W 380	1.6	W 298	1.5	W 315	1.7	MACH,APP USAGE DOMESTQUE
7752	DOM REFRIGERATRS,FREEZRS	W 376	1.2	W 275	1.1	W 230	1.0	W 210	0.9	REFRIG,CONGEL MENAGER
77521	DOMESTIC REFRIGERATORS	W 325	1.1	W 257	1.0	W 185	0.8	W 185	0.8	REFRIGERATEURS
778	ELECTRICAL MACHINERY NES	W 168	0.9	W 149	0.9	W 124	1.3	W 264	1.0	AUTRES MACH ELECT NDA
7782	ELECTRIC LAMPS,BULBS	W 48	0.3	W 24	0.3	W 18	0.5	W 21	0.2	LAMPES, TUBES ELECTRIQUES
77822	ELEC DISCHARGE LAMPS NES	W 40	0.2	W 18	0.2	W 12	0.4	W 15	0.2	LAMPES NON ULTRA-VIOLETS
78	ROAD VEHICLES		6.4		8.2		8.0		10.8	VEHICULES ROUTIERS
781	PASS MOTOR VEH EXC BUSES	W 571	2.9	W 771	3.6	W 827	4.0	W 1278	4.7	AUTO TRANSPORT PERSONNES
782	LORRIES,SPCL MTR VEH NES	W 337	1.5	W 542	2.3	W 459	1.9	W 852	3.3	VEHICULES SPECIAUX,MARCH
7821	LORRIES,TRUCKS	W 300	1.1	W 513	2.1	W 447	1.9	W 767	2.8	VEHICULES TRANSP MARCHAND
7822	SPECIAL MOTOR VEHCLS NES	W 37	0.4	W 30	0.2	W 11	0.1	W 85	0.6	VEHICULES USAGES SPECIAUX
783	ROAD MOTOR VEHICLES NES	W 132	1.1	W 149	1.2	W 123	1.1	W 200	1.7	VEHICULES ROUTIERS NDA
7831	BUSES	W 132	1.1	W 149	1.2	W 123	1.1	W 200	1.7	VOITURES TRANSPORT COMMUN
784	MOTOR VEH PRTS,ACCES NES	W 113	0.9	W 103	0.9	W 104	0.9	W 186	1.0	PIECES 722,781,782,783
7849	OTHER MOTOR VEHCL PARTS	W 108	0.9	W 96	0.9	W 94	0.9	W 184	1.0	PIECES 722,781,782,783
79	OTHR TRANSPORT EQUIPMENT		0.3		0.1		0.7		0.3	AUTRE MATERIEL TRANSPORT
793	SHIPS AND BOATS ETC	W 56	0.3	W 29	0.1	W 34	0.7	W 17	0.2	NAVIRES BATEAUX,ETC
8	MISC MANUFACTURED GOODS		15.4		14.3		16.3		18.4	ART MANUFACTURES DIVERS
812	*PLUMBG,HEATNG,LGHTNG EQ	W 149	0.8	W 176	0.8	W 128	0.8	W 184	0.8	APPAR SANITAIRES CHAUFFAGE
8124	LIGHTING EQUIPMENT NES	W 47	0.5	W 72	0.5	W 50	0.5	W 70	0.6	APPAREILS ECLAIRAGE ETC
81242	LAMPS,FITTINGS BASE METL	W 41	0.5	W 64	0.4	W 40	0.4	W 58	0.5	APPAREILS D'ECLAIRAGE
821	*FURNITURE,PARTS THEREOF	W 673	1.8	W 392	1.3	W 390	1.4	W 501	2.0	MEUBLES ET PIECES
8211	CHAIRS,SEATS AND PARTS	W 114	0.5	W 77	0.4	W 135	0.4	W 98	0.5	SIEGES ET PIECES
82111	CHAIRS AND OTHER SEATS	W 112	0.5	W 77	0.4	W 135	0.4	W 98	0.5	SIEGES
8219	FURNITURE AND PARTS NES	W 505	1.2	W 232	0.8	W 204	0.9	W 317	1.3	AUTRES MEUBLES ET PIECES
82191	METAL FURNITURE NES	W 68	0.3	W 82	0.3	W 80	0.4	W 116	0.7	MEUBLES NDA EN METAL
82192	WOOD FURNITURE NES	W 333	0.6	W 59	0.2	W 41	0.2	W 94	0.4	MEUBLES NDA EN BOIS
84	CLOTHING AND ACCESSORIES		2.3		2.3		2.1		2.0	VETEMENTS
842	MENS OUTERWEAR NOT KNIT	W 20	0.3	W 20	0.4	W 211	0.5	W 30	0.5	VET DESSUS POUR HOMMES
843	WOMENS OUTERWEAR NONKNIT	W 105	0.5	W 210	0.5	W 112	0.6	W 112	0.6	VET DESSUS FEMMES MAT TEX
846	UNDER GARMENTS KNITTED	W 36	0.4	W 20	0.4	W 25	0.5	W 19	0.3	SOUS VETS DE BONNETERIE
848	HEADGEAR,NONTXTL CLOTHNG	W 180	0.9	W 105	0.6	W 26	0.2	W 17	0.2	VET ACCES MAT AUT QUE TEX
8484	HEADGEAR	W 173	0.8	W 92	0.5	W 2	0.1	W 3	0.1	COIFFURES ET PARTIES NDA
84843	HEADGEAR TEXTILE NONFELT	W 171	0.8	W 91	0.5	W 1	0.1	W 1	0.1	CHAPEAUX EN BONNETERIE
851	*FOOTWEAR	W 131	1.3	W 108	1.1	W 154	1.3	W 202	1.4	CHAUSSURES
85102	FOOTWEAR LEATHER	W 76	0.9	W 51	0.7	W 102	0.9	W 154	1.1	CHAUS SEMELLES EN CUIR
87	PRECISION INSTRUMNTS NES		1.2		0.8		1.2		1.2	INSTRUM,APPAR SCIENT NDA
874	MEASURNG,CONTROLNG INSTR	W 13	0.6	W 10	0.5	W 9	0.6	W 24	0.6	INSTRUMENTS DE MESURE
88	PHOTO EQU,OPTICL GDS ETC		0.5		0.5		0.5		0.6	APP,FOURN PHOTO,OP,MONTR
89	MISC MANUFCTRD GOODS NES		7.6		7.8		9.1		10.5	ART MANUFACTURES DIVERS
892	PRINTED MATTER	W 191	2.1	W 217	2.5	W 312	2.9	W 367	3.2	IMPRIMES
8921	PRINTED BOOKS,GLOBES,ETC	W 121	1.4	W 137	1.6	W 153	1.8	W 168	2.0	LIVRES,BROCHURES,CARTES
89211	PRINTED BOOKS,PAMPHLETS	W 116	1.4	W 134	1.6	W 149	1.7	W 165	2.0	LIVRES,BROCHURES
8922	NEWSPAPERS,PERIODICALS	W 24	0.2	W 42	0.3	W 54	0.5	W 110	0.4	JOURNAUX ET PERIODIQUES
8928	PRINTED MATTER NES	W 41	0.5	W 32	0.6	W 88	0.6	W 68	0.7	IMPRIMES NDA
893	ARTICLES OF PLASTIC NES		4.4		4.0		4.7		5.8	OUVRAGES EN MAT DIVIS 58
8931	PLSTC PACKG CONTNRS,LIDS	W 311	1.0	W 327	0.9	W 361	1.1	W 1218	1.4	ART TRANSP EMBALLAGE ETC
8939	MISC PLASTIC ARTICLES	W 1099	3.4	W 741	3.1	W 779	3.6	W 1294	4.4	ART DIVERS EN MAT DIV 58
89399	OTHR PLASTC ARTICLES NES	W 872	3.1	W 614	2.9	W 641	3.3	W 1199	4.2	AUT OUV MAT DIV 58

4. Special Imports C.I.F. by Commodities according to the S.I.T.C. (Rev. 2) in million U.S. Dollars
Importations Spéciales C.A.F. par Produits d'après la C.T.C.I. (Rév. 2) en millions de Dollars E.U.

SITC CTCI	COMMODITY	1993			1994			1995			1996			PRODUIT
		QUANTITY QUANTITE		VALUE VALEUR	QUANTITY QUANTITE		VALUE VALEUR	QUANTITY QUANTITE		VALUE VALEUR	QUANTITY QUANTITE		VALUE VALEUR	
894	TOYS,SPORTING GOODS,ETC	W	39	0.3	W	56	0.3	W	114	0.6	W	76	0.5	VOITURES ENFANTS,JOUETS
899	OTHER MANUFACTURED GOODS			0.5			0.6			0.6			0.6	AUT ART MANUF DIVERS NDA

5. Special Exports F.O.B. by Commodities according to the S.I.T.C. (Rev. 2) in million U.S. Dollars
Exportations Spéciales F.O.B. par Produits d'après la C.T.C.I. (Rév. 2) en millions de Dollars E.U.

SITC CTCI	COMMODITY	1993 QUANTITY QUANTITE	1993 VALUE VALEUR	1994 QUANTITY QUANTITE	1994 VALUE VALEUR	1995 QUANTITY QUANTITE	1995 VALUE VALEUR	1996 QUANTITY QUANTITE	1996 VALUE VALEUR	PRODUIT
	ALL COMMODITIES		22.5		23.4		21.8		19.8	TOUS PRODUITS
0	FOOD AND LIVE ANIMALS		14.1		16.2		16.2		14.9	ALIMENTS,ANIMAUX VIVANTS
03	FISH AND PREPARATIONS		2.6		3.6		3.8		3.1	POISSONS ET PREPARATIONS
034	FISH,FRESH,CHILLED,FROZN	W 443	2.3	W 403	2.8	W 445	3.5	W 396	3.0	POISSON FRAIS, REFRIG,CONG
0341	FISH FRSH,CHLLD,EX FILLT	W 234	1.3	W 318	2.2	W 352	2.9	W 396	3.0	POISSON FRAIS,REFRIGERE
0342	FISH FROZEN,EXCL FILLETS	W 208	1.0	W 85	0.6	W 93	0.6			POISSONS CONGELES
036	SHELL FISH FRESH,FROZEN	W 33	0.3	W 83	0.9	W 44	0.4	W 20	0.2	CRUSTACES,MOLLUSQUES
04	CEREALS AND PREPARATIONS		1.4		1.0		1.4		1.8	CEREALES ET PRODUITS
046	WHEAT ETC MEAL OR FLOUR	W 2857	1.4	W 2381	1.0	W 3025	1.4	W 4208	1.8	SEMOULE FARINE,FROMENT
04601	FLOUR OF WHEAT OR MESLIN	W 2857	1.4	W 2381	1.0	W 3025	1.4	W 4208	1.8	FARINE DE FROMENT
05	VEGETABLES AND FRUIT		3.3		3.0		3.2		1.6	LEGUMES ET FRUITS
054	VEG ETC FRSH,SMPLY PRSVD	W 36	0.1	W 53	0.1	W 49	0.1	W 37	0.1	LEGUMES FRAIS,CONG,SECS
057	FRUIT,NUTS,FRESH,DRIED	W 7097	3.2	W 5622	2.9	W 6328	3.1	W 3024	1.5	FRUITS FRAIS OU SECS
0573	BANANA,PLANTAIN,FRSH,DRY	W 4871	1.9	W 4571	2.2	W 4737	1.9	W 1975	0.6	BANANES FRAICHES,SECHEES
0579	FRUIT FRESH OR DRIED NES	W 2053	1.2	W 1021	0.8	W 1581	1.3	W 1049	0.9	FRUITS FRAIS,SECS NDA
05797	OTH TROP FRUIT,FRESH,DRY	W 581	0.5	W 318	0.3	W 689	0.6	W 535	0.5	AVOCATS,MANGUES,GOYAVES
05798	OTHER FRESH FRUIT	W 1429	0.8	W 703	0.5	W 861	0.7	W 491	0.4	AUTRES FRUITS FRAIS
07	COFFEE,TEA,COCOA,SPICES		6.6		8.2		7.6		8.0	CAFE,THE,CACAO,EPICES
072	COCOA	W 1855	3.3	W 1110	2.7	W 1387	3.3	W 1633	2.7	CACAO
0721	COCOA BEANS,RAW,ROASTED	W 1855	3.3	W 1110	2.7	W 1387	3.3	W 1633	2.7	CACAO EN FEVES
075	SPICES	W 2312	3.4	W 3341	5.6	W 1868	4.2	W 2198	5.3	EPICES
0752	SPICES,EX PEPPER,PIMENTO	W 2311	3.4	W 3340	5.6	W 1868	4.2	W 2198	5.3	AUTRES EPICES
07522	CINNAMON,ETC	W 5	0.1	W 12	0.1	W 5	0.1	W 4	0.1	CANNELLE
07524	NUTMEG,MACE,CARDAMOMS	W 2298	3.3	W 3316	5.4	W 1860	4.2	W 2191	5.3	NOIX MUSCADES
081	*FEEDING STUFF FOR ANIML	W 1140	0.4	W 1446	0.4	W 1435	0.4	W 2892	0.6	NOURRITURE POUR ANIMAUX
0819	FOOD WASTE AND FEED NES	W 935	0.4	W 1135	0.4	W 1411	0.4	W 2892	0.6	DECHETS,ALIMENTS NDA
08199	FODDER NES,INCL SWEETNED	W 935	0.4	W 1134	0.4	W 1411	0.4	W 2892	0.6	PREPARATIONS FOURRAGERES
1	BEVERAGES AND TOBACCO		0.6		0.5		1.2		1.1	BOISSONS ET TABACS
11	BEVERAGES		0.6		0.5		1.2		1.1	BOISSONS
111	NON–ALCOHL BEVERAGES NES	W 559	0.6	W 686	0.5	W 1599	0.9	W 947	0.6	BOISSONS NON ALCOOLIQUES
11102	FLAVORED WATERS NON–ALCO	W 559	0.6	W 686	0.5	W 1599	0.9	W 946	0.6	LIMONADES,EAUX GAZEUSES
112	ALCOHOLIC BEVERAGES	W 29	0.1	W 9	0.1	W 192	0.3	W 793	0.5	BOISSONS ALCOOLIQUES
1123	BEER,ALE,STOUT,PORTER	W 21	0.1			W 139	0.2	W 779	0.5	BIERES
1124	DISTILLED ALCOHOLIC BEVS	W 8	0.1	W 9	0.1	W 54	0.1	W 14	0.1	ALCOOLS,EAUX–DE–VIE
11249	OTH ALCOHOLC BEVS,CMPNDS	W 8	0.1	W 8	0.1	W 54	0.1	W 14	0.1	BOISSONS ALCOOLIQUES NDA
5	CHEMCLS,RELATED PROD NES		0.8		0.9		0.6		0.5	PRODUITS CHIMIQUES
53	DYES,TANNING,COLOUR PROD		0.8		0.9		0.6		0.4	PROD TEINTURE,COLORANTS
533	PIGMENTS,PAINTS,ETC	W 328	0.8	W 357	0.9	W 208	0.6	W 164	0.4	PIGMENTS,PEINTURES,VERNIS
5334	VARNISHES,DISTEMPERS ETC	W 323	0.7	W 357	0.9	W 208	0.6	W 164	0.4	PEINTURES A L'EAU
53342	OTH PAINTS,VARNISHES ETC	W 317	0.7	W 345	0.8	W 191	0.5	W 133	0.3	AUTRES PEINTURES,VERNIS
55	PERFUME,CLEANING ETC PRD		0.1		0.1		0.1		0.1	PROD POUR PARFUM,TOILETTE
6	BASIC MANUFACTURES		2.8		2.1		2.3		2.0	ART MANUFACTURES
62	RUBBER MANUFACTURES NES		0.2		0.1				0.1	CAOUTCHOUC MANUFACTURE
628	RUBBER ARTICLES NES		0.2		0.1					OUVRAGES CAOUTCHOUC NDA
6281	HYGIENIC UNHRDND RUBBER		0.2		0.1					ART HYGIENE PHARM CAOUT
64	PAPER,PAPERBOARD AND MFR		1.1		1.3		1.6		1.3	PAPIERS,CARTONS & OUVRAGES
642	PAPER,ETC,PRECUT,ARTS OF	W 246	1.1	W 322	1.3	W 375	1.6	W 308	1.3	PAP,CARTONS DECOUPES
6424	PAPER ETC CT TO SIZE NES	W 210	0.9	W 261	1.1	W 299	1.2	W 258	1.1	PAP,CARTONS DECOUPES
64243	TOILET PAPER CUT TO SIZE	W 210	0.9	W 261	1.1	W 299	1.2	W 258	1.1	PAPIER HYGIENIQUE
6428	PAPER ETC ARTICLES NES	W 31	0.2	W 58	0.2	W 75	0.4	W 49	0.3	OUVRAGES EN PATE A PAPIER
64284	PAPER TISSUES,TOWELS ETC	W 23	0.2	W 42	0.2	W 61	0.3	W 34	0.2	MOUCHOIRS SERVIETTES EN PAP
64285	PAPER ETC DIAPERS ETC	W 9	0.1	W 6	0.1	W 14	0.1	W 16	0.1	SERVIETTES HYGIENIQUES
67	IRON AND STEEL		0.1		0.1		0.4		0.5	FER ET ACIER
674	IRN,STL UNIV,PLATE,SHEET	W 107	0.1	W 45	0.1	W 253	0.3	W 394	0.5	LARGES PLATS,TOLES
6749	OTH IRN,STL PLATES,SHEET	W 107	0.1	W 45	0.1	W 253	0.3	W 394	0.5	AUTRES TOLES FER,ACIER
67491	— OF IRON OR SIMPLE STL	W 107	0.1	W 45	0.1	W 253	0.3	W 394	0.5	AUT TOLES AUTRES ACIER FIN
69	METAL MANUFACTURES NES		1.5		0.8		0.4		0.3	ART MANUFACT EN METAL NDA
695	TOOLS		0.1	W 7	0.1	W 16	0.1	W 16	0.2	OUTILS A MAIN
6953	OTHER HAND TOOLS		0.1	W 7	0.1	W 16	0.1	W 16	0.2	AUTRES OUTILS A MAIN
69539	HAND TOOLS ETC NES			W 7	0.1	W 16	0.1	W 16	0.2	OUTILLAGE A MAIN NDA
696	CUTLERY	W 58	0.9	W 13	0.2		0.1		0.1	COUTELLERIE
69605	CLIPPERS,CLEAVERS,ETC	W 58	0.9	W 13	0.2					AUT ART DE COUTELLERIE
697	BASE MTL HOUSEHOLD EQUIP	W 51	0.7	W 50	0.5	W 33	0.4	W 2	0.1	ART MENAGE MET COMMUNS
6973	DMSTC HEATG,COOKG APPARA	W 51	0.7	W 49	0.5	W 33	0.4	W 2	0.1	APPS CHAUF NON ELECTRIQ
69731	IRN,STL DOM COOKG APPARA	W 51	0.7	W 49	0.5	W 33	0.4	W 2	0.1	APPS CUISSON FER,ACIER
7	MACHINES,TRANSPORT EQUIP		1.4		1.0		0.9		0.7	MACHINES MATERIEL TRANSPORT
71	POWER GENERATING EQUIPMT		0.4		0.1		0.1		0.1	MACHINES GENERATRICES
713	INTRNL COMBUS PSTN ENGIN	W 13	0.1	W 2	0.1		0.1		0.1	MOTEURS EXPL COMB INT, PIECE
7139	PISTON ENGINE PARTS NES	W 13	0.1				0.1		0.1	PIECES POUR 713.2,3,8
716	ROTATING ELECTRIC PLANT	W 1	0.4		0.1	W 4	0.1		0.1	APP ELECTR ROTATIFS,PIECES
7161	DC MOTORS AND GENERATORS	W 1	0.4			W 3	0.1			MOTEURS COURANT CONTINU
72	MACHS FOR SPCL INDUSTRYS		0.1		0.1		0.1		0.5	MAC SPECIALES POUR INDUST
722	TRACTORS NON–ROAD							W 22	0.2	TRACTEURS
7224	WHEELED TRACTORS NES							W 22	0.2	TRACTEURS A ROUES
723	CIVIL ENGNEERG EQUIP ETC			W 2	0.1	W 51	0.1	W 18	0.3	APPAREILS DE GENIE CIVIL
7234	CONST,MINING MACHNRY NES			W 2	0.1	W 50	0.1	W 10	0.3	MACH POUR LA CONST, MINES
72344	BORING,SINKING MACHINERY							W 10	0.3	MACHINES DE FORAGE
74	GENRL INDUSTRL MACHY NES		0.1		0.2		0.1		0.1	MACH APP INDUSTRIE
741	HEATING,COOLING EQUIPMNT			W 3	0.2		0.1		0.1	MACH CHAUFFAGE,PIECES
7411	GAS GENERATORS,PARTS NES			W 3	0.1					GAZOGENES
77	ELECTRIC MACHNRY NES ETC		0.8		0.7		0.5		0.1	MACH APP ELECT NDA
775	HOUSEHOLD TYPE EQUIP NES	W 33	0.4	W 41	0.6	W 37	0.5	W 2	0.1	MACH,APP USAGE DOMESTQUE
7752	DOM REFRIGERATRS,FREEZRS	W 32	0.4	W 41	0.6	W 37	0.5	W 2	0.1	REFRIG,CONGEL MENAGER
77521	DOMESTIC REFRIGERATORS	W 32	0.4	W 41	0.6	W 37	0.5	W 2	0.1	REFRIGERATEURS
776	TRANSISTORS,VALVES,ETC		0.4		0.1				0.1	LAMPES,TUBES,VALVES
7764	ELECTRONIC MICROCIRCUITS		0.4		0.1				0.1	MICROSTRUCTURES ELECTRON
78	ROAD VEHICLES		0.1		0.2		0.2		0.1	VEHICULES ROUTIERS
781	PASS MOTOR VEH EXC BUSES	W 4	0.1	W 9	0.2	W 8	0.1	W 10	0.1	AUTO TRANSPORT PERSONNES
8	MISC MANUFACTURED GOODS		2.9		2.8		0.8		0.9	ART MANUFACTURES DIVERS
831	*TRAVEL GOODS,HANDBAGS	W 10	0.2	W 7	0.2	W 11	0.2	W 7	0.1	ARTICLES DE VOYAGE ETC
83101	HANDBAGS NES	W 10	0.2	W 7	0.2	W 11	0.2	W 6	0.1	SACS A MAIN
84	CLOTHING AND ACCESSORIES		2.1		1.5		0.2		0.2	VETEMENTS
843	WOMENS OUTERWEAR NONKNIT	W 6	0.1	W 6	0.1	W 1	0.1	W 1	0.1	VET DESSUS FEMMES MAT TEX
8439	— OTHER OUTER GARMENTS	W 6	0.1	W 6	0.1	W 1	0.1	W 1	0.1	AUT VET DES FEM MAT TEXT
844	UNDER GARMENTS NOT KNIT	W 6	0.2	W 5	0.1	W 1	0.1	W 1	0.1	VETEMENT DESSOUS MAT TEX
8443	— WOMENS	W 6	0.2	W 5	0.1	W 1	0.1	W 1	0.1	VET DESSOUS FEM MAT TEXT
846	UNDER GARMENTS KNITTED	W 24	0.3	W 13	0.2	W 8	0.2	W 4	0.1	SOUS VETS DE BONNETERIE
8462	— OF COTTON NON ELASTIC	W 23	0.3	W 13	0.2	W 8	0.2	W 4	0.1	SOUS–VET BONNET COTON
84629	—— OTHER	W 23	0.3	W 13	0.2	W 8	0.2	W 4	0.1	AUT SOUS–VET BONNET COTON
848	HEADGEAR,NONTXTL CLOTHNG	W 134	1.6	W 127	1.2		0.1		0.1	VET ACCES MAT AUT QUE TEX
8484	HEADGEAR	W 134	1.6	W 127	1.2		0.1		0.1	COIFFURES ET PARTIES NDA

5. Special Exports F.O.B. by Commodities according to the S.I.T.C. (Rev. 2) in million U.S. Dollars
Exportations Spéciales F.O.B. par Produits d'après la C.T.C.I. (Rév. 2) en millions de Dollars E.U.

SITC CTCI	COMMODITY	1993		1994		1995		1996		PRODUIT
		QUANTITY QUANTITE	VALUE VALEUR	QUANTITY QUANTITE	VALUE VALEUR	QUANTITY QUANTITE	VALUE VALEUR	QUANTITY QUANTITE	VALUE VALEUR	
84843	HEADGEAR TEXTILE NONFELT	W 132	1.5	W 127	1.2		0.1		0.1	CHAPEAUX EN BONNETERIE
84848	HEAD–BANDS,LININGS,ETC	W 2	0.1		0.1					BANDES POUR GARNIT INTER
88	PHOTO EQU,OPTICL GDS ETC		0.1		0.1		0.3			APP,FOURN PHOTO,OP,MONTR
881	PHOTO APPARAT,EQUIPT NES				0.1	W 2	0.3			APP,EQUIP PHOTO NDA
8812	CINEMA CAMERAS,PROJ,ETC				0.1	W 2	0.3			APPAREILS CINEMA,PIECES
88121	— FOR FILM UNDER 16MM					W 2	0.3			APP CINEMA MOINS 16 MM
89	MISC MANUFCTRD GOODS NES		0.7		1.1		0.3		0.6	ART MANUFACTURES DIVERS
892	PRINTED MATTER	W 5	0.1	W 4	0.1	W 11	0.1	W 2	0.1	IMPRIMES
893	ARTICLES OF PLASTIC NES	W 45	0.6	W 72	1.1	W 18	0.3	W 40	0.6	OUVRAGES EN MAT DIVIS 58
8939	MISC PLASTIC ARTICLES	W 35	0.6	W 71	1.1	W 17	0.3	W 40	0.6	ART DIVERS EN MAT DIV 58
89399	OTHR PLASTC ARTICLES NES	W 35	0.6	W 71	1.1	W 17	0.3	W 40	0.6	AUT OUV MAT DIV 58

1. HISTORICAL SERIES, 1962–1997 SPECIAL TRADE, IMPORTS C.I.F., EXPORTS F.O.B.
SERIES HISTORIQUES, 1962–1997 COMMERCE SPECIAL, IMPORTATIONS C.A.F., EXPORTATIONS F.O.B

YEAR ANNEE	VALUE IN MILLION U.S. DOLLARS / VALEUR EN MILLION U.S. DOLLARS — MERCHANDISE –MARCHANDISE IMPORTS	EXPORTS	GOLD –OR IMPORTS	EXPORTS	CONVERSION FACTORS U.S. CENTS PER QUETZAL FACTEURS DE CONVERSION CENTS E.U. PAR QUETZAL IMPORTS	EXPORTS	INDEX NUMBERS –INDICES — QUANTUM IMPORTS	EXPORTS	UNIT VALUE VALEUR UNITAIRE IMPORTS	EXPORTS
1962	136.00	117.80								
1963	171.10	154.00								
1964	202.10	164.50								
1965	228.30	187.90								
1966	207.60	228.70								
1967	247.10	202.20								
1968	249.40	226.70								
1969	250.20	258.60								
1970	284.30	290.20								
1971	303.30	283.20								
1972	324.00	327.50								
1973	431.00	436.20								
1974	700.50	572.10								
1975	732.70	623.50								
1976	838.90	760.40								
1977	1052.50	1160.20								
1978	1309.60	1092.40								
1979	1503.90	1241.40								
1980	1598.20	1519.80					89	92	109	142
1981	1673.50	1226.10					87	88	116	120
1982	1388.00	1119.80					70	95	120	101
1983	1135.00	1158.80					62	98	111	102
1984	1278.50	1122.30					48	122	138	92
1985	1174.90	1020.60					70	81	101	109
1986	958.50	1043.80					57	113	101	81
1987	1447.20	987.30					88	90	100	94
1988	1557.00	1021.70					62	91	128	96
1989	1653.80	1108.00					92	101	117	106
1990	1648.80	1163.00					100	100	100	100
1991	1851.30	1202.20					117	125	96	79
1992	2531.50	1295.30					125	145	123	77
1993	2599.30	1340.40					133	136	119	85
1994	2604.20	1521.50					148	147	109	88
1995	3292.50	2155.50								98
1996	3146.10	2030.80								89
1997	3467.10	2149.40								

2. IMPORTS BY BROAD ECONOMIC CATEGORY AND EXPORTS BY INDUSTRIAL ORIGIN. (PERCENTAGE OF TOTAL VALUE)
IMPORTATIONS PAR CATEGORIES ECONOMIQUES ET EXPORTATIONS PAR BRANCHE D'ACTIVITE.(EN POURCENTAGE DE LA VALEUR TOTALE)

IMPORTS – IMPORTATIONS

	1991	1992	1993	1994	1995	1996	1997
TOTAL IMPORTS–IMPORTATIONS TOTALES	100.	100.	100.	100.	100.	100.	100.
1 FOOD BEV–ALIMENTATION BOISSONS	9.0	9.0	9.0	10.9	9.5	10.9	10.4
11 PRIMARY–PRODUITS DE BASE	2.5	2.7	2.9	3.2	2.6	4.0	2.8
111 FOR INDUSTRY–POUR L'INDUSTRIE	2.0	1.9	2.1	2.5	1.9	3.4	1.7
112 FOR HOUSEHOLDS–POUR LES MENAGES	0.5	0.8	0.7	0.6	0.7	0.7	1.1
12 PROCESSED–PRODUITS ELABORES	6.5	6.3	6.2	7.7	6.9	6.9	7.6
121 FOR INDUSTRY–POUR L'INDUSTRIE	1.7	1.2	1.1	1.5	1.0	1.1	0.8
122 FOR HOUSEHOLDS–POUR LES MENAGES	4.8	5.1	5.1	6.2	5.9	5.8	6.8
2 IND SUPPLIES–APPROV INDUSTRIELS	39.2	35.5	33.1	34.5	34.7	32.8	35.2
21 PRIMARY–PRODUITS DE BASE	2.6	1.7	2.1	1.9	2.1	2.8	2.9
22 PROCESSED–PRODUITS ELABORES	36.6	33.8	30.9	32.7	32.6	30.0	32.3
3 FUELS–COMBUSTIBLES	16.4	13.5	11.7	11.3	12.2	14.6	10.5
31 PRIMARY–PRODUITS DE BASE	7.3	6.1	4.7	5.1	4.5	5.4	4.5
32 PROCESSED–PRODUITS ELABORES	9.1	7.5	6.9	6.1	7.7	9.2	6.0
321 MOTOR SPIRIT–ESSENCE	3.0	2.3	3.0	2.5	2.6	3.9	0.9
322 OTHER–AUTRES	6.0	5.2	3.9	3.7	5.0	5.3	5.2
4 MACHINERY–EQUIPEMENT	16.6	19.1	18.5	14.4	14.6	15.4	17.3
41 CAPITAL EQUIPMENT–MACHINES	14.5	17.0	16.5	12.2	12.4	13.0	14.7
42 PARTS–PIECES ACCESSOIRES	2.1	2.1	2.0	2.2	2.2	2.4	2.6
5 TRANSPORT–TRANSPORT	10.5	13.6	17.4	16.4	16.6	14.1	13.0
51 PASSENGER CARS–AUTOMOBILES	6.1	9.4	7.1	6.4	6.1	5.0	4.1
52 OTHER–AUTRES	0.7	0.7	6.8	6.7	6.9	5.8	5.3
521 INDUSTRIAL–INDUSTRIELS	0.4	0.4	6.5	6.4	6.6	5.5	5.1
522 NON INDUSTRIAL–NON INDUSTRIEL	0.2	0.3	0.3	0.3	0.3	0.3	0.2
53 PARTS–PIECES ACCESSOIRES	3.7	3.5	3.4	3.2	3.6	3.4	3.6
6 CONSUM GOODS–BIENS CONSOMMATION	8.3	9.0	10.2	12.4	12.3	12.0	13.5
61 DURABLE–DURABLES	1.4	1.7	2.4	2.9	3.1	2.6	3.4
62 SEMI DURABLE–SEMI DURABLES	3.1	3.5	3.9	4.6	4.6	4.4	5.0
63 NON DURABLE–NON DURABLES	3.8	3.8	3.9	4.8	4.6	5.0	5.2
7 GOODS NES–BIENS NDA	0.1	0.3	0.2	0.1	0.1	0.1	0.1

EXPORTS – EXPORTATIONS

	1991	1992	1993	1994	1995	1996	1997
TOTAL EXPORTS–EXPORTATIONS TOTALES	100.	100.	100.	100.	100.	100.	100.
1 AGRICULTURE	46.5	44.2	43.9	43.7	47.2	45.0	44.2
2 MINING QUARRY–INDUS EXTRACTIVES	1.9	1.8	2.0	1.9	2.1	3.4	4.5
3 MANUFACTURING–IND MANUFACTUR	51.6	54.0	54.1	54.5	50.7	51.6	51.2
31 FOOD BEV TOBACCO–ALIM BOISS TAB	22.4	22.8	22.3	22.1	21.6	20.1	20.4
32 TEXTILES–INDUSTRIES TEXTILES	6.3	6.1	6.1	5.6	4.4	4.9	4.4
33 WOOD & PRODUCTS–BOIS & PRODUITS	1.2	1.4	1.2	1.1	0.8	0.9	0.8
34 PAPER & PRODUCTS–PAPIER & PRODT	1.3	1.3	1.5	1.5	1.5	2.2	2.0
35 CHEMICALS–INDUSTRIES CHIMIQUES	13.8	14.0	14.0	14.4	13.3	14.2	14.0
36 NON METAL MIN–MIN NON METAL	1.5	2.1	2.6	2.8	2.3	2.2	2.1
37 BASIC METAL–IND METAL BASE	1.5	2.4	2.4	2.6	2.7	3.0	3.1
38 METAL MANUF–MANUF METAL	3.1	3.1	3.4	3.8	3.5	3.7	4.1
39 OTH MANUF IND–AUTRES MANUF	0.4	0.5	0.5	0.6	0.5	0.6	0.5

3. TRADE BY PRINCIPAL COUNTRIES OF ORIGIN AND DESTINATION (VALUE IN MILLION U.S. DOLLARS)
ECHANGES SELON LES PRINCIPAUX PAYS D'ORIGINE ET DE DESTINATION (VALEUR EN MILLIONS DE DOLLARS EU)

COUNTRIES–PAYS	SPECIAL IMPORTS C.I.F. IMPORTATIONS SPECIALES C.A.F					COUNTRIES–PAYS	SPECIAL EXPORTS F.O.B. EXPORTATIONS SPECIALES F.O.B.				
	1993	1994	1995	1996	1997		1993	1994	1995	1996	1997
World	2668.1	2647.2	3292.5	3146.2	3851.9	Monde	1338.2	1502.4	1935.5	2030.7	2344.1
Africa	7.5	5.1	2.9	2.4	5.2	Afrique	21.4	19.2	13.2	8.5	35.4
Americas	2075.5	2058.3	2631.3	2541.8	3122.7	Amériques	1078.7	1176.7	1404.7	1616.7	1845.3
– Northern America	1345.5	1197.9	1528.8	1465.8	1685.8	– Amérique du Nord	523.2	498.3	628.9	787.8	898.8
– LAIA	430.1	444.3	615.7	637.0	773.6	– ALAI	78.2	141.6	139.8	150.0	168.2
– CACM	235.2	292.3	291.5	243.0	411.4	– MCAC	418.2	474.9	565.8	578.0	683.3
– Caribbean	14.9	55.4	107.8	115.7	138.0	– Caraïbes	23.7	23.9	29.0	47.4	44.3
– Rest of America	49.7	68.3	87.5	80.3	113.9	– Autre Amérique	35.4	37.9	41.3	53.6	50.6
Asia excl fmr USSR	239.4	203.0	252.1	212.3	269.0	Asie anc. URSS exclus	62.6	111.8	195.3	91.3	126.3
– Middle East	0.7	1.3	1.0	1.4	2.9	– Moyen–Orient	29.3	34.1	32.8	34.3	32.5
Asia former USSR						Asie ancienne URSS					
Europe excl fmr USSR	331.2	342.7	371.9	365.4	407.8	Europe anc. URSS exclus	170.8	187.1	315.1	293.3	330.7
– European Union	298.3	313.0	343.9	337.3	365.2	– Union Européenne	163.5	182.4	303.8	271.6	308.3
– Eastern Europe	3.0	8.1	7.8	4.1	10.9	– Europe de l'Est	3.4	0.9	5.0	8.4	7.2
– Rest of Europe	29.8	21.5	20.1	23.9	31.8	– Autre de l'Europe	3.9	3.8	6.3	13.3	15.2
Europe former USSR	9.8	27.2	24.7	10.5	29.0	Europe ancienne URSS	3.9	3.2	5.6	19.6	3.2
Oceania	4.6	8.0	9.6	11.9	16.4	Océanie	1.0	3.7	1.7	1.1	1.6
Other		3.0		1.9	1.8	Autre		0.8		0.2	1.5
USA/Etats–Unis d'Amer	1313.2	1169.0	1478.5	1409.4	1613.6	USA/Etats–Unis d'Amer	510.6	483.4	605.8	746.7	841.2
Mexico/Mexique	168.5	185.9	308.2	322.5	438.4	El Salvador	191.2	229.0	268.9	258.0	310.9
El Salvador	138.9	165.0	161.2	128.8	228.5	Honduras	77.0	87.0	124.8	140.2	177.3
Venezuela	130.9	137.2	151.7	165.3	180.5	Costa Rica	95.5	97.6	101.0	99.8	111.9
Japan/Japon	138.0	100.6	121.2	99.3	130.0	Germany/Allemagne	59.3	65.3	112.5	102.6	113.5
Germany/Allemagne	102.2	104.8	116.1	99.6	114.2	Nicaragua	54.6	61.3	71.0	79.9	83.2
Panama	49.5	68.1	86.4	79.8	111.9	Mexico/Mexique	47.6	67.2	45.0	80.0	77.0
Costa Rica	65.0	83.8	69.3	62.0	108.0	Japan/Japon	23.3	38.8	53.5	42.1	53.3
Aruba	8.6	2.0	102.0	107.0	127.4	Panama	28.5	32.7	37.0	46.3	42.6
Canada	32.2	28.9	50.3	56.2	72.1	Netherlands/Pays–Bas	20.8	27.9	38.4	29.4	39.7
Brazil/Brésil	56.7	48.4	50.8	42.8	38.9	Canada	12.6	14.9	22.2	37.7	51.2
Honduras	27.6	37.6	53.3	44.0	65.6	Belgium–Luxembourg	15.1	16.6	32.7	27.3	36.2
Other Asia n.e.s.	39.6	32.2	50.0	41.2	55.7	Venezuela	4.1	29.5	37.8	12.5	34.6
Italy/Italie	46.2	39.5	36.9	38.5	52.2	Peru/Pérou	16.4	17.9	28.6	29.5	13.2
United Kingdom	37.2	34.6	39.5	31.5	43.1	Italy/Italie	14.5	18.4	23.3	21.2	27.0
Spain/Espagne	23.7	26.1	32.2	40.9	44.0	Saudi Arabia	18.6	19.8	19.8	18.8	19.0
Netherlands/Pays–Bas	24.6	29.0	30.2	46.5	24.8	France, Monaco	15.4	15.0	21.5	21.6	20.6
Colombia/Colombie	25.9	24.4	32.1	31.4	35.1	Sweden/Suède	5.4	10.3	25.6	21.5	22.3
Korea, Republic of	20.2	22.5	34.8	27.8	26.3	Dominican Republic	12.0	14.8	16.8	14.2	17.9
Belgium–Luxembourg	17.4	19.0	32.4	31.4	23.8	United Kingdom	15.8	11.2	13.2	18.3	14.0
Ecuador/Equateur	16.4	21.0	29.9	28.9	21.6	Chile/Chili	0.3	11.3	19.0	13.5	26.8
Argentina/Argentine	19.3	12.5	21.5	28.5	32.9	Other Asia n.e.s.	0.7	4.8	52.4	1.3	0.5
China, Hong Kong SAR	21.2	19.5	22.9	20.1	24.8	Sri Lanka	1.2	23.6	12.4	0.1	21.8
France, Monaco	19.1	24.1	21.3	17.4	21.5	Finland/Finlande	7.5	7.3	16.1	13.8	13.9
Switzerland,Liechtenst.	24.6	14.6	15.2	18.6	24.8	Spain/Espagne	4.9	6.4	11.9	7.5	11.5
Russian Federation	9.8	27.2	24.7	10.5	19.0	Morocco/Maroc	4.8	0.1	4.9	4.9	24.3
Chile/Chili	7.5	8.8	11.0	11.3	15.3	Haiti/Haïti	4.5	5.1	5.1	12.8	8.6
Netherlands Antilles	0.0	47.3	1.0	2.6	0.1	China/Chine		0.0	34.0	0.1	0.3
Ireland/Irlande	8.1	11.4	9.4	8.2	12.1	Colombia/Colombie	4.4	4.6	6.6	9.6	8.7
New Zealand	3.9	7.4	8.9	11.4	14.1	Russian Federation	3.9	3.2	5.6	19.6	0.1
Sweden/Suède	7.2	9.1	11.2	8.7	7.9	Belize/Bélize	6.2	5.1	3.9	6.3	6.9
Denmark/Danemark	4.6	3.9	8.4	4.5	15.6	Switzerland,Liechtenst.	2.9	3.3	4.4	4.5	6.2
Nicaragua	3.7	5.9	7.7	8.2	9.3	Norway,Svalbard and JM	1.0	0.5	1.9	8.7	9.0
Peru/Pérou	4.6	5.4	9.2	5.3	10.2	Singapore/Singapour	4.2	2.6	4.1	4.2	5.3
Israel/Israël	4.3	6.5	5.2	5.8	8.2	United Arab Emirates	4.3	4.8	4.9	2.9	3.4
Norway,Svalbard and JM	4.9	6.7	4.6	5.4	6.9	Algeria/Algérie	5.0	8.8	3.0		3.4
China/Chine	2.0	4.1	3.6	4.9	5.9	Portugal	2.8	2.3	4.7	4.1	4.1
Finland/Finlande	3.6	8.4	1.9	5.2	1.1	Jamaica/Jamaïque	0.9	0.8	2.0	6.8	5.5
So. African Customs Un	6.0	3.5	2.6	2.1	2.6	So. African Customs Un	6.8	0.5	4.3	3.1	1.0
Trinidad and Tobago	4.0	4.2	1.2	2.6	4.6	Poland/Pologne	0.4	0.8	3.5	4.5	5.5

(VALUE AS PERCENTAGE OF WORLD TOTAL)(VALEURS EN POURCENTAGE DU TOTAL MONDIAL)

	1988	1989	1990	1991	1992	1993	1994	1995	1996	1997		1988	1989	1990	1991	1992	1993	1994	1995	1996	1997
Africa	0.3	0.5	0.5	0.3	0.2	0.3	0.2	0.1	0.1	0.1	Afrique	1.3	0.9	2.0	2.2	3.7	1.6	1.3	0.7	0.4	1.5
Americas	62.7	64.9	71.7	73.4	75.7	77.8	77.8	79.9	80.8	81.1	Amériques	61.1	71.1	76.0	78.0	77.9	80.6	78.3	72.6	79.6	78.7
– Northern America	39.0	40.7	41.8	43.7	46.3	50.4	45.3	46.4	46.6	43.8	– Amérique du Nord	28.2	36.4	41.2	39.1	36.5	39.1	33.2	32.5	38.8	38.3
– LAIA	13.1	12.8	18.2	17.9	17.3	16.1	16.8	18.7	20.2	20.1	– ALAI	3.7	7.1	4.7	6.8	6.3	5.8	9.4	7.2	7.4	7.2
– CACM	9.8	10.2	8.2	8.5	9.8	8.8	11.0	8.9	7.7	10.7	– MCAC	23.5	23.6	24.8	27.0	30.5	31.3	31.6	29.2	28.5	29.2
– Caribbean	0.3	0.2	2.7	2.5	1.0	0.6	2.1	3.3	3.7	3.6	– Caraïbes	3.1	1.4	2.3	2.1	1.9	1.8	1.6	1.5	2.3	1.9
– Rest of America	0.5	1.0	0.8	0.8	1.4	1.9	2.6	2.7	2.6	3.0	– Autre Amérique	2.6	2.5	3.0	3.1	2.7	2.6	2.5	2.1	2.6	2.2
Asia excl fmr USSR	12.7	12.0	9.8	10.6	9.8	9.0	7.7	7.7	6.7	7.0	Asie anc. URSS exclus	10.4	6.7	7.5	7.2	4.8	4.7	7.4	10.1	4.5	5.4
– Middle East	0.2	0.0	0.0	0.0	0.1	0.0	0.1	0.0	0.0	0.1	– Moyen–Orient	4.7	2.7	2.7	2.5	2.3	2.2	2.3	1.7	1.7	1.4
Asia former USSR											Asie ancienne URSS										
Europe excl fmr USSR	23.5	21.9	17.7	15.5	14.0	12.4	12.9	11.3	11.6	10.6	Europe anc. URSS exclus	22.9	18.5	13.9	12.5	12.2	12.8	12.5	16.3	14.4	14.1
– European Union	20.5	18.5	15.3	13.6	12.4	11.2	11.8	10.4	10.7	9.5	– Union Européenne	17.6	16.6	13.6	12.2	11.8	12.2	12.1	15.7	13.4	13.2
– Eastern Europe	1.3	1.2	0.6	0.3	0.3	0.1	0.3	0.2	0.1	0.3	– Europe de l'Est	4.9	1.4	0.0	0.0	0.1	0.3	0.1	0.3	0.4	0.3
– Rest of Europe	1.7	2.2	1.8	1.6	1.3	1.1	0.8	0.6	0.8	0.8	– Autre de l'Europe	0.3	0.5	0.4	0.3	0.3	0.3	0.3	0.3	0.7	0.6
Europe former USSR	0.0	0.2	0.2	0.0	0.1	0.4	1.0	0.8	0.3	0.8	Europe ancienne URSS	4.1	2.5	0.6		0.4	0.3	0.2	0.3	1.0	0.1
Oceania	0.2	0.2	0.1	0.2	0.1	0.2	0.3	0.3	0.4	0.4	Océanie	0.0	0.0	0.0	0.0	1.0	0.1	0.2	0.1	0.1	0.1
Other	0.6	0.5					0.1		0.1	0.0	Autre	0.2	0.3					0.1		0.0	0.1
USA/Etats–Unis d'Amer	37.3	38.7	40.3	42.6	45.4	49.2	44.2	44.9	44.8	41.9	USA/Etats–Unis d'Amer	27.3	34.8	39.8	37.8	35.4	38.2	32.2	31.3	36.8	35.9
Mexico/Mexique	6.2	5.9	6.7	6.6	5.8	6.3	7.0	9.4	10.3	11.4	El Salvador	12.8	12.0	12.4	12.9	14.1	14.3	15.2	13.9	12.7	13.3
El Salvador	5.4	5.6	4.9	5.3	5.7	5.2	6.2	4.9	4.1	5.9	Honduras	3.1	3.3	3.3	3.6	4.7	5.8	5.8	6.5	6.9	7.6
Venezuela	1.4	2.1	7.2	4.5	4.1	4.9	5.2	4.6	5.3	4.7	Costa Rica	6.5	6.9	6.3	6.3	6.9	7.1	6.5	5.2	4.9	4.8
Japan/Japon	7.3	6.0	6.0	6.6	6.0	5.2	3.8	3.7	3.2	3.4	Germany/Allemagne				3.8	3.4	4.4	4.3	5.8	5.1	4.8
Germany/Allemagne				4.7	4.6	3.8	4.0	3.5	3.2	3.0	Nicaragua	1.2	1.5	2.8	4.2	4.8	4.1	4.1	3.7	3.9	3.6
Panama	0.5	1.0	0.7	0.8	1.4	1.9	2.6	2.6	2.5	2.9	Mexico/Mexique	2.2	5.0	3.1	5.2	4.5	3.6	4.5	2.3	3.9	3.3
Costa Rica	3.3	3.2	2.3	2.3	3.0	2.4	3.2	2.1	2.0	2.8	Japan/Japon	2.1	2.5	3.0	2.8	1.7	1.7	2.6	2.8	2.1	2.3
Aruba			2.6	1.8	0.6	0.3	0.1	3.1	3.4	3.3	Panama	2.4	2.1	2.4	2.3	2.1	2.1	2.2	1.9	2.3	1.8
Canada	1.7	1.9	1.5	1.1	1.0	1.2	1.1	1.5	1.8	1.9	Netherlands/Pays–Bas	2.5	2.2	2.0	2.3	1.7	1.6	1.9	2.0	1.4	1.7

4. Special Imports C.I.F. by Commodities according to the S.I.T.C. (Rev. 2) in million U.S. Dollars
Importations Spéciales C.A.F. par Produits d'après la C.T.C.I. (Rév. 2) en millions de Dollars E.U.

SITC CTCI	COMMODITY	1994		1995		1996		1997		PRODUIT
		QUANTITY QUANTITE	VALUE VALEUR	QUANTITY QUANTITE	VALUE VALEUR	QUANTITY QUANTITE	VALUE VALEUR	QUANTITY QUANTITE	VALUE VALEUR	
	ALL COMMODITIES		2647.2		3292.5		3146.3		3852.0	TOUS PRODUITS
0	FOOD AND LIVE ANIMALS		284.5		308.5		369.6		414.0	ALIMENTS,ANIMAUX VIVANTS
01	MEAT AND PREPARATIONS		6.2		10.0		10.1		24.5	VIANDES ET PREPARATIONS
011	MEAT FRESH,CHILLD,FROZEN	W 3835	3.8	W 5349	5.9	W 5837	4.7	W 15727	17.0	VIANDES FRAICHES,REF,CONGE
02	DAIRY PRODCTS,BIRDS'EGGS		36.9		34.7		40.3		54.1	PRODUITS LAITIERS,OEUFS
022	MILK AND CREAM	W 20154	33.4	W 17755	29.9	W 17168	34.2	W 27581	46.7	LAIT ET CREME
0224	MILK,CREAM PRESERVED ETC	W 14715	29.5	W 12296	25.4	W 13924	31.0	W 21015	41.5	LAIT,CREME CONS,CONC
02243	MILK DRY,OVER 1.5% FAT	W 11962	26.0	W 9149	20.9	W 11028	27.5	W 15283	33.7	LAIT POUDRE SUP 1.5%
04	CEREALS AND PREPARATIONS		123.9		123.7		176.8		147.0	CEREALES ET PRODUITS
041	WHEAT ETC UNMILLED	W 356259	55.9	W 232804	48.5	W 354069	84.8	W 277713	54.8	FROMENT,EPEAUTRE
0411	DURUM WHEAT UNMILLED	W 340430	54.0	W 232804	48.5	W 335637	80.9	W 171524	34.7	FROMENT DUR NON MOULU
0412	OTHER WHEAT ETC UNMILLED	W 15829	1.9		0.1	W 18433	4.0	W 106189	20.2	AUTRE FROMENT NON MOULU
042	RICE	W 16535	6.5	W 33532	10.3	W 25016	7.1	W 26632	8.7	RIZ
044	MAIZE UNMILLED	W 151161	23.0	W 174254	25.0	W 216852	43.8	W 251420	38.4	MAIS NON MOULU
048	CEREAL ETC PREPARATIONS	W 26277	30.0	W 44068	36.8	W 39025	38.1	W 38716	41.9	PREPTNS A BASE CEREALES
0481	PREPD BREAKFAST FOOD ETC	W 6250	9.2	W 9429	10.3	W 10910	10.7	W 10691	13.0	CEREALES TRAVAILLEES
04812	CEREAL ROASTED, PUFFED	W 5437	8.3	W 5178	7.8	W 4328	7.0	W 6680	9.8	PRODTS BASE CEREALES
0484	BAKERY PRODUCTS	W 9100	12.6	W 8165	11.6	W 7599	11.0	W 12270	16.8	PRODUITS DE BOULANGERIE
04842	PASTRY, CAKES ETC	W 5979	8.5	W 5014	7.3	W 4189	6.4	W 6679	10.0	PATISSERIE ETC.
05	VEGETABLES AND FRUIT		18.5		25.6		29.0		42.7	LEGUMES ET FRUITS
057	FRUIT,NUTS,FRESH,DRIED	W 14693	4.1	W 19904	6.8	W 22241	8.2	W 29823	13.9	FRUITS FRAIS OU SECS
058	FRUIT PRESERVED,PREPARED	W 4952	5.0	W 6871	6.5	W 10698	9.3	W 15444	14.4	CONSERVES DE FRUITS
06	SUGAR AND PREPS,HONEY		9.9		9.7		9.4		12.5	SUCRES ET PRODUITS
081	*FEEDING STUFF FOR ANIML	W 77333	22.8	W 98614	28.9	W 107941	38.1	W 110959	40.1	NOURRITURE POUR ANIMAUX
0813	OILCAKE AND OTH RESIDUES	W 64785	16.4	W 84310	20.3	W 97231	31.0	W 91462	30.4	TOURTEAUX
08131	— OF SOYA BEANS	W 64679	16.4	W 84284	20.3	W 96764	30.9	W 90108	29.8	TOURTEAUX DE SOJA
09	MISC EDIBLE PRODUCTS		52.9		60.9		52.2		79.7	PREP ALIMENTAIRES DIVERSES
098	EDIBLE PRODCTS,PREPS NES	W 21046	52.6	W 22259	59.6	W 21309	51.3	W 30007	75.4	PREP ALIMENTAIRES NDA
09809	MISC FOOD PREPRTIONS NES	W 16272	45.9	W 16850	51.2	W 15249	43.2	W 21497	63.7	PREP ALIMENTAIRES NDA
1	BEVERAGES AND TOBACCO		14.5		19.8		20.5		29.2	BOISSONS ET TABACS
11	BEVERAGES		13.3		16.2		16.4		22.5	BOISSONS
112	ALCOHOLIC BEVERAGES	W 5928	9.3	W 6184	11.4	W 4938	11.6	W 5454	12.2	BOISSONS ALCOOLIQUES
2	CRUDE MATERLS,EXCL FUELS		41.8		64.5		63.3		91.9	MAT BRUTES NON COMESTIBLES
22	OIL SEEDS,OLEAGINOUS FRT		4.6		5.2		9.7		6.6	GRAINES,FRUITS OLEAGINEUX
26	TEXTILE FIBRES AND WASTE		16.9		30.3		28.5		55.1	FIBRES TEXTILES
263	COTTON	W 3634	4.5	W 7678	12.0	W 8827	13.2	W 22346	33.0	COTON
2631	RAW COTTON,EXCL LINTERS	W 3419	4.4	W 6704	11.4	W 7313	12.3	W 20497	31.5	COTON EN MASSE
269	WASTE OF TEXTILE FABRICS	W 6228	4.9	W 9615	8.6	W 9384	8.4	W 13778	12.3	FRIPERIE DRILLES,CHIFFONS
3	MINERAL FUELS ETC		305.2		410.5		466.7		412.6	COMBUSTIBLES MINERAUX LUB
33	PETROLEUM AND PRODUCTS		275.0		374.4		423.4		366.3	PETROLE ET DERIVES
333	CRUDE PETROLEUM	W 788478	106.2	W 781135	114.1	W 738980	128.1	W 778628	126.4	HUILES BRUTES DE PETROLE
334	PETROLEUM PRODUCTS,REFIN	W 831898	162.1	W 1205421	251.6	W 1129647	288.9	W 898910	231.8	PRODUITS RAFFINES
3341	GASOLINE,OTH LIGHT OILS	W 308187	65.2	W 367059	86.2	W 379252	123.7	W 126389	33.4	ESSENCES POUR MOTEURS
33419	OTH LIGHT PETROLEUM OILS			W 367059	86.2	W 379252	123.7	W 126389	33.4	AUTRES HUILES LEGERES
3342	KEROSENE,OTH MEDIUM OILS	W 1601	0.4	W 59839	11.9	W 68474	16.1	W 44732	9.5	PETR LAMPANTS,AUT HUIL
33429	OTH MEDIUM PETROLEUM OIL			W 59839	11.9	W 68474	16.1	W 44732	9.5	AUTRES HUILES MOYENNES
3344	FUEL OILS,NES	W 503600	83.6	W 753521	136.1	W 658703	132.4	W 328717	63.0	FUEL OILS
3345	LUBS,PETROLEUM OILS NES	W 16612	12.8	W 25002	17.6	W 23219	16.8	W 399071	125.9	HUILES LUBRIFIANTES
33451	LUBS(HIGH PETR CONT) ETC	W 16314	12.2	W 24623	17.0	W 22523	15.8	W 398398	124.6	HUILES LUBRIF,H LOURDES
341	*GAS,NATURAL AND MANUFCT	W 117569	29.9	W 134099	35.5	W 144303	42.8	W 147742	45.7	GAZ NATUREL,GAZ MANUFACT
3413	PETROLM GASES,LIQUEFIED	W 117484	29.9	W 134064	35.5	W 144240	42.8	W 147741	45.7	GAZ DE PETROLE LIQUEFIE
34131	LIQUEFIED PROPANE,BUTANE	W 117431	29.8	W 133950	35.4	W 144173	42.7	W 147588	45.6	PROPANE,BUTANE LIQUEFIES
4	ANIMAL,VEGETABLE OIL,FAT		48.6		57.0		49.7		58.2	HUILES,GRAISSES ANIM,VEG
411	*ANIMAL OILS AND FATS	W 30363	13.4	W 43004	17.7	W 29635	16.8	W 35612	19.9	HUILES,GRAISSES ANIMALES
4113	ANIML OIL,FAT,GREASE NES	W 29948	13.2	W 42412	17.3	W 29334	16.6	W 35276	19.6	HUILES,GRAISSES ANIMALES NDA
41132	FATS OF BOVINE,SHEEP,ETC	W 29769	12.9	W 41900	16.7	W 28100	15.3	W 33846	18.3	SUIFS BRUTS FONDUS
42	FIXED VEGETABLE OIL,FAT		32.9		37.5		31.6		35.6	HUILES VEGETALES FIXES
423	FIXED VEG OILS,SOFT	W 36498	24.7	W 37129	29.3	W 37580	26.0	W 42562	30.6	HUILES VEGET DOUCES FIXES
4232	SOYA BEAN OIL	W 13687	9.1	W 7386	5.3	W 5747	3.8	W 7516	5.5	HUILE DE SOJA
4233	COTTON SEED OIL	W 10982	7.9	W 4113	3.1	W 13272	10.5	W 608	0.5	HUILE DE COTON
4236	SUNFLOWER SEED OIL	W 11667	7.5	W 25249	20.2	W 18173	10.6	W 33794	23.5	HUILE DE TOURNESOL
424	FIXED VEG OIL NONSOFT	W 14992	8.3	W 10529	8.2	W 7476	5.6	W 7235	5.0	AUTRES HUILES VEG FIXES
5	CHEMCLS,RELATED PROD NES		459.4		558.9		528.3		684.7	PRODUITS CHIMIQUES
51	ORGANIC CHEMICALS		49.1		61.8		56.2		72.5	PROD CHIMIQ ORGANIQUES
513	CARBOXYLIC ACIDS ETC	W 6454	9.8	W 7610	12.4	W 8130	10.8	W 8707	12.6	ACIDES CARBOXYLIQUES
514	NITROGEN–FNCTN COMPOUNDS	W 3055	10.1	W 3900	15.1	W 3444	14.5	W 5271	18.6	COMPOSES FONCT AZOTEES
5148	OTH NITROGN–FNCTN CMPNDS	W 1108	5.2	W 1916	10.2	W 1850	10.1	W 2259	11.2	AUTRES COMPOSES AZOTES
515	ORG–INORG COMPOUNDS ETC	W 2116	10.4	W 1692	10.7	W 1751	11.1	W 7739	16.3	COMPOSES ORGANO–MINERAUX
516	OTHER ORGANIC CHEMICALS	W 4808	8.1	W 1604846	10.2	W 3752	7.7	W 3673	8.8	AUTRES PROD ORGANIQUES
52	INORGANIC CHEMICALS		33.7		38.3		36.6		45.4	PROD CHIM INORGANIQUES
522	INORG ELEMNTS,OXIDES,ETC	W 42515	12.3	W 1248735	17.9	W 45426	14.9	W 55339	17.5	ELEMENTS INORGANIQUES
523	OTHR INORG CHEMICALS ETC	W 56410	21.3	W 1256268	20.4	W 63185	21.6	W 76511	27.7	AUT PRODUITS CHIMIQUES INORG
5232	OTH MTL CMPD OF INRG ACD	W 27766	13.5	W 32094	12.5	W 39974	13.7	W 44253	16.0	SELS METALLIQUES
52322	PHOSPHITES,PHOSPHATES	W 13225	8.2	W 11745	7.0	W 14684	7.8	W 18255	9.5	PHOSPHITES,PHOSPHATES
53	DYES,TANNING,COLOUR PROD		29.8		33.4		30.9		41.1	PROD TEINTURE,COLORANTS
531	SYNT DYE,NAT INDGO,LAKES	W 1539	10.4	W 2853	10.7	W 2321	9.8	W 2612	13.1	MAT COLOR ORGAN,LAQUES
533	PIGMENTS,PAINTS,ETC	W 8504	16.6	W 9597	19.8	W 9938	18.7	W 14037	25.5	PIGMENTS,PEINTURES,VERNIS
5334	VARNISHES,DISTEMPERS ETC	W 2871	5.0	W 3941	7.3	W 5754	8.4	W 8228	12.5	PEINTURES A L'EAU
541	*MEDICINAL,PHARM PRODUCT	K 5727455	90.8	K 7123817	106.1	K 6489352	107.4	K 6977726	124.6	PROD MEDICINAUX PHARMACEUT
5417	MEDICAMENTS	K 3423864	69.0	K 4839679	81.4	K 5457295	86.3	K 4301125	100.3	MEDICAMENTS
54171	— CONTAINNG ANTIBIOTICS	K 733652	17.0	K 544149	17.7	K 543407	14.7	K 316692	13.7	MED CONTN ANTIBIOTIQUES
54179	— CONTNG OTH SUBSTANCES	K 2502335	47.0	K 4058570	57.8	K 4476935	64.5	K 3720631	77.9	MED CONT AUT SUBSTANCES
55	PERFUME,CLEANING ETC PRD		46.6		53.7		53.1		86.0	PROD POUR PARFUM,TOILETTE
551	ESSENTL OILS,PERFUME,ETC	W 1380	15.5	W 1237	17.8	W 1306	17.9	W 2039	26.1	HUILES ESSENTIELLES
5514	MIXED PERFUME SUBSTANCES	W 1200	13.2	W 1071	15.4	W 1068	15.7	W 1762	22.3	MELANGES SUBSTAN ODORIFER
553	PERFUMERY,COSMETICS,ETC	W 3994	14.3	W 4301	16.2	W 5082	15.8	W 6185	21.7	PRODUITS DE PARFUMERIE
554	SOAP,CLEANSING ETC PREPS	W 17569	17.0	W 21565	19.8	W 19943	19.5	W 39746	38.4	SAVONS,PRODUITS DETERSIFS
5541	SOAPS	W 10082	7.2	W 13750	9.5	W 11310	9.2	W 24225	20.7	SAVONS,PROD TENSIO–ACTIFS
5542	WASHING PREPARATIONS ETC	W 7127	8.9	W 7588	9.8	W 8310	9.5	W 14869	16.6	PROD ORG TENSIO–ACT NDA
562	*FERTILIZERS,MANUFACTURE	W 473611	66.6	W 438065	74.9	W 382738	67.2	W 514395	94.8	ENGRAIS MANUFACTURES
5621	CHEM NITROGENOUS FERTLZR	W 379655	49.6	W 285493	46.2	W 263065	43.6	W 330647	57.9	ENGRAIS AZOTES
56213	AMMONIUM SULPHATE	W 142683	13.4	W 114542	12.9	W 125708	13.8	W 136506	17.4	SULFATE D'AMMONIUM
56216	UREA	W 126881	20.8	W 93418	19.0	W 92922	20.0	W 140107	29.9	UREE
56219	CHEM NITROG FERTILZR NES	W 76057	9.4	W 29543	5.8	W 23334	5.0	W 27106	6.2	ENGRAIS AZOTES NDA
5623	CHEM POTASSIC FERTILIZER	W 46548	8.0	W 55071	7.7	W 54753	8.8	W 69156	9.5	ENGRAIS POTASSIQUES
5629	FERTILIZERS NES	W 20589	4.1	W 62834	13.3	W 30494	7.4	W 79491	21.2	ENGRAIS NDA
56292	NITROG–PHOS FERTILZR NES	W 8752	2.1	W 15260	3.9	W 19397	4.9	W 55668	15.3	ENGRAIS NDA CONT N P
58	PLASTIC MATERIALS ETC		78.5		112.0		99.4		135.5	MAT PLAST ARTIFICIELLES
582	PROD OF CONDENSATION ETC	W 6049	9.5	W 8773	13.7	W 8004	12.5	W 8435	14.5	PROD CONDENS,POLYCOND
583	POLYMERIZATION ETC PRODS	W 67682	64.8	W 74523	93.9	W 81239	82.7	W 108428	117.1	PROD POLYMERISATION
5831	POLYETHYLENE	W 27270	21.2	W 32352	37.0	W 31654	30.6	W 40387	43.0	POLYETHYLENE

4. Special Imports C.I.F. by Commodities according to the S.I.T.C. (Rev. 2) in million U.S. Dollars
Importations Spéciales C.A.F. par Produits d'après la C.T.C.I. (Rév. 2) en millions de Dollars E.U.

SITC CTCI	COMMODITY	1994 QUANTITY QUANTITE	1994 VALUE VALEUR	1995 QUANTITY QUANTITE	1995 VALUE VALEUR	1996 QUANTITY QUANTITE	1996 VALUE VALEUR	1997 QUANTITY QUANTITE	1997 VALUE VALEUR	PRODUIT
58311	— IN PRIMARY FORMS	W 26931	20.3	W 31825	35.3	W 31252	29.0	W 39372	40.1	POLYETHYLENE PRIMAIRES
5832	POLYPROPYLENE	W 10161	10.2	W 10206	15.0	W 10819	12.5	W 18232	18.8	POLYPROPYLENE
58321	— IN PRIMARY FORMS	W 8738	6.6	W 8116	9.0	W 9463	8.8	W 16070	13.5	POLYPROPYLENE PRIMAIRES
5834	POLYVINYL CHLORIDE	W 14208	13.7	W 12998	14.5	W 18268	15.2	W 23500	21.9	CHLORURE DE POLYVINYLE
58341	— IN PRIMARY FORMS	W 13173	11.5	W 12058	12.3	W 17096	12.7	W 22272	19.2	SOUS FORMES PRIMAIRES
5839	OTH POLYMRZTION ETC PROD	W 10853	13.5	W 13500	19.4	W 14650	17.3	W 19249	24.9	AUT PROD POLYMER COPOLYM
59	CHEMICAL MATERIALS NES		64.0		78.3		77.0		84.0	MAT PROD CHIMIQUES NDA
591	PESTICIDES,DISINFECTANTS	W 8897	40.8	W 10797	50.2	W 9063	47.6	W 10187	49.0	DESINF,INSECT,FONG,HERB
5911	INSECTICIDES,FOR RETAIL	W 1805	12.3	W 1884	13.1	W 1693	12.6	W 1682	13.1	INSECTICIDES VENTE DET
5912	FUNGICIDES,FOR RETAIL	W 2252	12.1	W 3414	17.6	W 2447	15.6	W 3437	16.8	FONGICIDES VENTE AU DET
5913	HERBICIDES,FOR RETAIL	W 3913	14.9	W 4488	17.5	W 4146	18.0	W 3897	17.1	HERBICIDES VENTE AU DET
598	MISCEL CHEM PRODUCTS NES	W 11687	18.1	W 12764	22.1	W 12975	22.2	W 12345	24.5	PROD DIV INDUST CHIM NDA
5989	CHEM PRODUCTS,PREPS NES	W 8063	11.8	W 8694	14.9	W 9593	15.7	W 9798	19.5	PROD PREP CHIMIQUES NDA
59899	OTH CHEM PRODS,PREPS,NES	W 4777	8.5	W 4761	10.8	W 5455	11.5	W 6980	14.4	AUT PRODUITS CHIMIQUES NDA
6	BASIC MANUFACTURES		479.3		605.4		500.8		672.3	ART MANUFACTURES
62	RUBBER MANUFACTURES NES		33.0		47.1		42.6		53.7	CAOUTCHOUC MANUFACTURE
625	RUBBER TYRES, TUBES ETC	W 8702	22.5	W 12401	34.3	W 16196	31.1	W 17826	38.8	PNEUS CAOUTCHOUC VULCANISE
6252	TYRES,NEW,BUS OR LORRY	W 2797	8.0	W 4534	14.6	W 4947	15.1	W 5236	15.7	PNEUS POUR AUTOBUS,CAMIONS
64	PAPER,PAPERBOARD AND MFR		115.6		166.3		117.2		161.5	PAPIERS,CARTONS & OUVRAGES
641	PAPER AND PAPERBOARD	W 120755	79.9	W 132950	126.4	W 99486	84.2	W 149101	107.2	PAPIERS ET CARTONS
6411	NEWSPRINT	W 21202	13.1	W 20495	18.2	W 18314	16.6	W 31123	19.0	PAPIER JOURNAL
6412	PRINTG,WRITING PAPER NES	W 10371	9.1	W 13256	15.4	W 12700	10.7	W 18975	15.1	PAPIERS POUR L'IMPRESSION
64122	— COATED,IMPREGNATD ETC	W 10052	8.5	W 12815	14.1	W 12196	9.7	W 17987	13.7	PAPIERS IMPRESSION COUCHES
6413	KRAFT PAPER,PAPERBOARD	W 57301	27.7	W 62317	45.4	W 30639	19.5	W 47066	26.2	PAPIER ET CARTON KRAFT
64131	KRAFT LINER IN BULK	W 23757	11.2	W 33992	23.9	W 20267	10.7	W 32447	14.9	PAP KRAFT POUR COUVERTURES
64139	KRAFT PAPER PAPERBD,NES	W 28173	13.2	W 22563	16.0	W 5329	4.1	W 5866	4.0	PAPIER,CARTON KRAFT NDA
6415	PAPER,PAPERBRD,BULK,NES	W 22443	17.7	W 28110	31.2	W 28567	24.6	W 39948	30.2	PAPIERS,CARTONS ROULEAUX
64159	OTHER PAPER ETC,BULK,NES	W 18059	14.7	W 18556	24.2	W 19832	19.4	W 27741	23.7	AUT PAPIER ROULEAUX FEUILLES
6418	COATED ETC PAPER NES BLK	W 8411	11.2	W 6841	14.5	W 6741	10.8	W 8524	14.5	PAP,CARTONS COUCHES,ENDUITS
64189	COATED PAPER ETC NES	W 6915	8.0	W 5038	9.6	W 4997	7.6	W 7041	11.0	PAPIERS,CARTONS COUCHES
642	PAPER,ETC,PRECUT,ARTS OF	W 24973	35.7	W 27264	40.0	W 22493	33.0	W 37317	54.3	PAP,CARTONS DECOUPES
6421	PAPER ETC CONTAINERS	W 13873	17.2	W 15797	18.7	W 10619	12.7	W 19754	20.4	BOITES,SACS EMBALLAGES
6428	PAPER ETC ARTICLES NES	W 3278	7.6	W 4874	10.0	W 5179	9.9	W 8312	18.6	OUVRAGES EN PATE A PAPIER
65	TEXTILE YARN,FABRICS,ETC		48.8		52.0		43.0		60.4	FILS,TISSUS,ARTICLES TEXTILE
651	TEXTILE YARN	W 4264	13.8	W 4218	14.0	W 3910	10.4	W 4912	14.9	FILS TEXTILES
653	WOVN MAN-MADE FIB FABRIC	W 2138	10.1	W 2249	11.9	W 1579	7.4	W 3152	13.8	TISSUS FIBRES SYNTH,ARTIF
657	SPECIAL TXTL FABRC,PRODS	W 2832	9.4	W 2812	9.9	W 2794	9.9	W 3945	14.2	TISSUS SPECIAUX
66	NONMETAL MINERAL MFS NES		53.8		60.0		60.3		74.9	ART MIN NON METALLIQUES
661	LIME,CEMENT,BLDG PRODS	W 196371	16.1	W 228085	15.0	W 278981	19.4	W 334754	25.3	CHAUX,CIMENTS MAT CONSTR
6612	CEMENT	W 195334	15.4	W 226682	14.3	W 276518	18.4	W 331343	23.9	CIMENTS HYDRAULIQUES
662	CLAY,REFRACTORY BLDG PRD	W 14951	7.0	W 16782	8.3	W 18062	9.1	W 24894	12.7	MAT CONST REFRACTAIRES
664	GLASS	W 16824	8.2	W 28171	13.1	W 25123	11.9	W 22917	12.3	VERRE
665	GLASSWARE	W 15951	12.3	W 11019	11.0	W 8268	8.9	W 12702	11.9	OUVRAGES EN VERRE
67	IRON AND STEEL		112.2		142.5		116.9		154.6	FER ET ACIER
672	IRON,STEEL PRIMARY FORMS	W 81876	30.7	W 48527	20.0	W 57310	21.2	W 52091	21.7	LINGOTS FER,ACIER
6724	IRN,STL INGOTS,LUMPS,ETC	W 53939	19.6	W 26442	10.9	W 32760	11.9	W 34522	15.0	FER,ACIER LINGOTS,MASSES
67241	IRON,SIMPLE STEEL INGOTS	W 53617	19.5	W 25256	10.5	W 32608	11.8	W 34453	14.9	LINGOTS EN FER ET ACIER
673	IRON,STEEL SHAPES ETC	W 41298	15.2	W 62951	26.8	W 54384	22.5	W 73311	27.3	BARRES,PROFIL FER,ACIER
6731	IRON,STEEL WIRE ROD	W 21169	8.6	W 26164	14.5	W 24429	10.5	W 38600	12.8	FIL MACHINE FER,ACIER
674	IRN,STL UNIV,PLATE,SHEET	W 161698	53.6	W 129634	81.8	W 88727	55.7	W 134754	78.4	LARGES PLATS,TOLES
6746	IRN,STL THIN PLATE,ROLLD	W 113289	32.7	W 69188	46.3	W 51539	32.8	W 60256	35.7	TOLES LAM MOINS 3MM
67461	— OF IRON OR SIMPLE STL	W 111620	31.7	W 66471	44.6	W 50225	31.6	W 57884	34.3	TOL NON AC FIN MOINS 3 MM
6749	OTH IRN,STL PLATES,SHEET	W 14052	9.6	W 27189	18.8	W 19236	14.1	W 39048	24.8	AUTRES TOLES FER,ACIER
67491	— OF IRON OR SIMPLE STL	W 9104	6.6	W 24663	16.6	W 17302	12.3	W 36425	22.6	AUT TOLES AUTRES ACIER FIN
678	IRON,STL TUBES,PIPES,ETC	W 8887	8.6	W 7903	8.8	W 10726	13.9	W 15138	19.0	TUBES,TUYAUX EN FONTE,FER
68	NON-FERROUS METALS		25.5		29.5		24.3		39.3	METAUX NON FERREUX
684	ALUMINIUM	W 4398	16.1	W 15049	17.8	W 4990	13.7	W 5165	20.3	ALUMINIUM
6842	ALUMINIUM,ALLOYS WORKED	W 3941	15.3	W 14639	17.6	W 4510	13.5	W 4723	20.0	ALUMINIUM,ALLIAGES OUVRE
68423	ALUMINIUM FOIL	W 1769	9.5	W 1663	9.7	W 1091	6.6	W 1832	11.0	FEUILLES,BANDES MINCES AL
686	ZINC	W 4690	5.6	W 5055	6.4	W 4985	6.0	W 27450	12.3	ZINC
69	METAL MANUFACTURES NES		81.5		99.1		88.8		114.4	ART MANUFACT EN METAL NDA
692	METAL TANKS,BOXES,ETC	W 3487	9.5	W 4732	16.2	W 4668	13.3	W 7351	17.0	RECIPIENTS METALLIQUES
6924	MTL TRANSPORT BOXES ETC	W 3284	9.0	W 3992	14.3	W 4192	12.0	W 7063	16.1	FUTS,TAMBOURS,BIDONS
69242	ALUMNM TRNSPRT BOXES ETC	W 1563	5.6	W 2574	10.7	W 2724	7.8	W 2966	9.4	FUTS,TAMBOURS,BIDONS ALU
695	TOOLS	W 4056	15.6	W 3755	15.9	W 3508	16.3	W 4060	20.8	OUTILS A MAIN
6953	OTHER HAND TOOLS	W 2547	10.3	W 2157	10.2	W 2109	9.8	W 2192	12.1	AUTRES OUTILS A MAIN
697	BASE MTL HOUSEHOLD EQUIP	W 5125	13.1	W 6779	14.7	W 5273	11.9	W 7019	16.7	ART MENAGE MET COMMUNS
699	BASE METAL MFRS NES	W 6938	20.4	W 9644	30.2	W 9069	26.3	W 10727	32.5	ART MANUFACTURES MET NDA
7	MACHINES,TRANSPORT EQUIP		826.5		1033.3		921.3		1187.4	MACHINES MATERIEL TRANSPORT
71	POWER GENERATING EQUIPMT		34.9		58.7		46.8		78.0	MACHINES GENERATRICES
713	INTRNL COMBUS PSTN ENGIN	W 2757	19.2	W 2980	22.9	W 3514	22.4	W 5287	29.7	MOTEURS EXPL COMB INT, PIECE
7139	PISTON ENGINE PARTS NES	W 1207	13.4	W 1228	16.5	W 2000	17.5	W 1741	22.2	PIECES POUR 713.2,3,8
714	ENGINES AND MOTORS NES	W 38	1.1	W 52	1.3	W 33	0.8	W 1237	20.1	MOTEURS NON ELECTRIQUES
7148	GAS TURBINES NES	W 1	0.1	W 3	0.1	W 2	0.1	W 1210	19.9	TURBINES A GAZ
71488	OTHER GAS TURBINES NES	W 1	0.1	W 3	0.1		0.1	W 1210	19.9	AUTRES TURBINES A GAZ
716	ROTATING ELECTRIC PLANT	W 1708	12.2	W 3229	29.2	W 4964	17.1	W 2550	20.1	APP ELECTR ROTATIFS,PIECES
7161	DC MOTORS AND GENERATORS	W 404	3.4	W 1340	14.3	W 484	2.9	W 513	5.9	MOTEURS COURANT CONTINU
7162	AC MTRS,GENRTRS,GEN SETS	W 1157	6.3	W 1652	12.3	W 4171	7.1	W 1874	12.5	MOTEURS ELECTRIQUES
72	MACHS FOR SPCL INDUSTRYS		88.5		104.1		113.0		159.0	MAC SPECIALES POUR INDUST
721	AGRIC MACHY,EXC TRACTORS	W 1787	8.3	W 2127	8.0	W 1449	7.8	W 1772	10.8	MACHINES AGRICOLES
722	TRACTORS NON-ROAD	W 2156	10.8	W 2101	10.4	W 1469	6.9	W 2075	10.3	TRACTEURS
7224	WHEELED TRACTORS NES	W 1765	9.2	W 1837	9.2	W 1165	6.0	W 1434	8.7	TRACTEURS A ROUES
723	CIVIL ENGNEERG EQUIP ETC	W 2147	10.8	W 3886	17.9	W 6353	24.9	W 7822	38.1	APPAREILS DE GENIE CIVIL
7234	CONST,MINING MACHNRY NES	W 2000	10.0	W 3562	16.8	W 5918	22.8	W 6055	32.4	MACH POUR LA CONST, MINES
72342	SLFPRP SHOVELS,EXCAVATRS	W 1167	5.8	W 1778	8.6	W 3590	10.8	W 2470	13.0	PELLES MECANIQUES
724	TEXTILE,LEATHER MACHNRY	W 2235	14.6	W 2210	14.7	W 2006	17.7	W 2457	17.4	MACH POUR INDUSTRIE TEXTILE
726	PRINTG,BKBINDG MACHY,PTS	W 655	5.5	W 1005	8.7	W 804	10.1	W 883	13.1	MACHINES POUR IMPRIMERIE
727	FOOD MACHRY NON-DOMESTIC	W 2309	16.5	W 1996	15.6	W 3229	15.2	W 3168	20.3	MACH INDUSTRIES ALIMENT
7272	OTH FOOD PROC MCHY,PARTS	W 2198	15.3	W 1683	11.4	W 2367	10.8	W 2812	16.4	AUT MACH IND ALIMENTAIRE
72722	INDUS FOOD PROC MACH NES	W 1141	9.9	W 1296	7.9	W 1909	6.0	W 2300	12.0	MACHINES BOULANGERIE
728	OTH MACHY FOR SPCL INDUS	W 2574	20.8	W 3956	27.9	W 5350	26.8	W 5411	46.2	AUT MACH IND PARTICULIERES
7283	OTHR MINERAL WORKG MACHY	W 791	4.3	W 754	4.8	W 1168	6.1	W 3349	23.8	MACH TRIER,CRIBLER,BROYER
72839	PTS NES OF MACHY OF 7283	W 194	1.6	W 246	1.7	W 214	2.0	W 2438	19.0	PIECES MACH DU 728.3
7284	MACHY FOR SPCL INDUS NES	W 883	11.7	W 2345	18.2	W 1384	16.5	W 1376	18.4	MACH SPEC IND PARTICUL.
72842	RUBBER,PLASTICS WRKG MCH	W 269	3.1	W 1676	11.3	W 677	5.7	W 649	6.5	MACH IND CAOUT MAT PLAST
74	GENRL INDUSTRL MACHY NES		108.0		128.3		123.8		165.9	MACH APP INDUSTRIE
741	HEATING,COOLING EQUIPMNT	W 2104	13.4	W 2814	16.4	W 3138	14.5	W 3335	24.7	MACH CHAUFFAGE,PIECES
742	PUMPS FOR LIQUIDS ETC	W 1363	14.5	W 1472	15.7	W 2133	18.8	W 2335	19.0	POMPES MOTO-POMPES
7428	OTHER PUMPS FOR LIQUIDS	W 1118	10.9	W 1176	11.1	W 1714	14.1	W 1920	13.9	AUTRES POMPES POUR LIQ
74288	PUMPS FR LIQUIDS NES ETC	W 1026	9.1	W 1094	9.8	W 1564	11.7	W 1777	12.6	POMPES POUR LIQUIDES NDA
743	PUMPS NES,CENTRFUGES ETC	W 2042	14.1	W 3005	17.3	W 3030	19.3	W 3342	22.0	POMPES COMPRES,VENT ETC

4. Special Imports C.I.F. by Commodities according to the S.I.T.C. (Rev. 2) in million U.S. Dollars
Importations Spéciales C.A.F. par Produits d'après la C.T.C.I. (Rév. 2) en millions de Dollars E.U.

SITC CTCI	COMMODITY	1994 QUANTITY QUANTITE	1994 VALUE VALEUR	1995 QUANTITY QUANTITE	1995 VALUE VALEUR	1996 QUANTITY QUANTITE	1996 VALUE VALEUR	1997 QUANTITY QUANTITE	1997 VALUE VALEUR	PRODUIT
744	MECHANICAL HANDLING EQU	W 4163	17.9	W 4405	19.4	W 3499	20.4	W 6340	30.7	EQUIP MANUTENTION PIECES
7442	LIFTING,LOADING MACH NES	W 2156	8.5	W 2090	8.9	W 1378	6.7	W 2909	13.0	APP LEVAGE,MANUTENTION
7449	PTS NES OF MACHY OF 7442	W 900	6.9	W 1271	6.7	W 1248	9.1	W 1743	14.0	PIECES DU 744.2
745	NONELEC MACHY,TOOLS NES	W 1795	21.5	W 1858	26.6	W 1607	20.0	W 2400	29.4	AUT MACH NON ELEC,PIECES
7452	OTH NONELEC MCHS,PTS NES	W 1489	19.4	W 1675	24.6	W 1395	17.9	W 2227	26.7	AUT MACH NON ELEC,PIECES
74522	PACKAGNG,BOTTLNG,ETC MCH	W 543	10.9	W 641	13.4	W 425	7.8	W 518	9.3	MACH NETT BOUTEILLES,ETC
749	NONELEC MACH PTS,ACC NES	W 2758	26.9	W 3845	33.1	W 3219	30.9	W 4049	40.2	PIECES MACH NON ELEC NDA
7492	COCKS,VALVES ETC NES	W 1136	9.9	W 1327	11.3	W 1698	11.9	W 1746	15.7	ART ROB,SIM POUR TUYAUX
7499	OTH NONELEC MCHY PTS NES	W 595	7.4	W 866	9.3	W 748	8.6	W 1132	11.7	PIECES NON ELECT NDA
75	OFFICE MACHNES,ADP EQUIP		52.9		61.9		71.2		90.9	MACH BUREAU TRAIT AUTOM
751	OFFICE MACHINES	W 888	12.8	W 1103	13.2	W 896	13.2	W 1093	15.3	MACH,APPAREILS DE BUREAU
752	AUTOMTIC DATA PROC EQUIP	W 711	21.7	W 551	23.6	W 557	27.8	W 868	33.9	MACH TRAIT INFORMATION
7522	DIGITAL COMPUTERS	W 394	16.1	W 383	18.6	W 405	19.3	W 330	12.0	MACH DIGITALES COMPLETES
759	OFFICE,ADP MCH PTS,ACCES	W 1105	18.5	W 1408	25.2	W 1914	30.3	W 3342	41.8	PIECES DU 751 ET 752
7599	ACCTG,ETC,ADP MCH PTS,AC	W 1029	16.7	W 1303	22.6	W 1705	27.4	W 2387	38.8	PIECES DU 751 ET 752
76	TELECOMM,SOUND EQUIPMENT		68.0		94.9		85.3		122.6	EQUIPMENT DE TELECOM
761	TELEVISION RECEIVERS	W 1806	10.9	W 2273	16.1	W 1505	11.3	W 2982	21.6	RECEPTEURS DE TELEVISION
7611	COLOUR TV RECEIVERS	W 1550	10.3	W 2067	15.4	W 1318	10.7	W 2750	20.8	RECEPTEURS COULEUR
762	RADIO BROADCAST RECEIVRS	W 1438	9.5	W 1848	16.3	W 1060	8.5	W 1624	13.6	RECEPTEURS RADIODIFFUSION
7622	PORTABLE RADIO RECEIVERS	W 963	6.9	W 1429	12.7	W 549	3.2	W 742	3.7	RECEPT PORTATIFS RADIO
764	TELECOM EQPT,PTS,ACC NES	W 2497	43.8	W 2668	56.9	W 2440	62.7	W 2798	81.8	EQUIP TELECOM,PIECES
7641	LINE TELEPHONE,ETC EQUIP	W 617	29.8	W 759	37.3	W 925	42.1	W 1075	50.2	APP TELEPHON PAR FIL
7649	PTS NES OF EQUIPMT OF 76	W 593	5.0	W 847	10.3	W 885	11.3	W 818	17.8	PIECES DE LA DIV 76
76491	PTS NES OF APPAR OF 7641	W 49	1.9	W 317	5.3	W 221	6.8	W 330	13.5	PIECES POUR 764.1
77	ELECTRIC MACHNRY NES ETC		86.5		102.0		96.0		149.2	MACH APP ELECT NDA
771	ELECTRIC POWER MACHY NES	W 1789	6.2	W 2100	8.9	W 2491	9.2	W 5925	16.5	MACH PROD,TRANS ELECTR
7711	TRANSFORMERS,ELECTRICAL	W 1506	4.8	W 1709	7.0	W 1888	7.0	W 5364	12.7	TRANSFO ELECTRIQUES
772	SWITCHGEAR ETC,PARTS NES	W 1159	11.6	W 1271	11.5	W 1978	12.9	W 1661	20.1	APP COUPURE,SECT ETC
7721	SWITCHGEAR ETC	W 1148	11.4	W 1265	11.3	W 1964	12.7	W 1647	19.8	APP COUPURE,SECTIONMNT
773	ELECTR DISTRIBUTNG EQUIP	W 4318	12.5	W 4242	13.5	W 7496	13.0	W 7745	24.9	EQUIPMT DISTRIBUTION ELECT
7731	INSULATED WIRE,CABLE ETC	W 4114	12.0	W 3969	12.7	W 7035	11.9	W 7209	22.9	FILS,CABLES ISOLES ELECT
775	HOUSEHOLD TYPE EQUIP NES	W 6934	24.0	W 7638	28.3	W 5577	22.5	W 9550	38.5	MACH,APP USAGE DOMESTQUE
7752	DOM REFRIGERATRS,FREEZRS	W 3626	12.7	W 3798	13.7	W 2480	9.8	W 5003	19.1	REFRIG,CONGEL MENAGER
77521	DOMESTIC REFRIGERATORS	W 3459	12.0	W 3548	12.7	W 2267	8.9	W 4633	17.1	REFRIGERATEURS
778	ELECTRICAL MACHINERY NES	W 5945	27.5	W 6907	33.9	W 9262	33.8	W 9603	42.3	AUTRES MACH ELECT NDA
7781	BATTERIES,ACCUMULATORS	W 2761	6.3	W 2874	6.8	W 3517	8.2	W 4593	12.0	PILES ET ACCUMULATEURS
7783	AUTOMOTIVE ELECTR EQUIP	W 697	8.0	W 1126	11.4	W 2379	9.5	W 1094	10.8	EQUIP ELECT MOTEURS EXPL
78	ROAD VEHICLES		372.5		469.0		371.5		408.7	VEHICULES ROUTIERS
781	PASS MOTOR VEH EXC BUSES	W 37061	170.6	W 40309	201.1	W 44142	157.1	W 34011	158.8	AUTO TRANSPORT PERSONNES
782	LORRIES,SPCL MTR VEH NES	W 34792	131.1	W 46632	163.4	W 49574	126.1	W 44953	143.4	VEHICULES SPECIAUX,MARCH
7821	LORRIES,TRUCKS	W 34498	130.5	W 45994	161.6	W 49440	125.7	W 44715	142.8	VEHICULES TRANSP MARCHAND
783	ROAD MOTOR VEHICLES NES	W 9541	26.4	W 14857	44.4	W 13755	38.0	W 35718	43.2	VEHICULES ROUTIERS NDA
7831	BUSES	W 4798	15.5	W 6815	22.7	W 5499	17.0	W 25857	19.2	VOITURES TRANSPORT COMMUN
7832	TRACTORS FOR TR--TRAILERS	W 4743	11.0	W 8042	21.8	W 8256	21.1	W 9861	24.1	TRACTEURS ROUTIERS
784	MOTOR VEH PRTS,ACCES NES	W 4618	24.7	W 6868	32.2	W 5168	30.0	W 6346	34.5	PIECES 722,781,782,783
7849	OTHER MOTOR VEHCL PARTS	W 4470	24.1	W 6583	30.9	W 4738	28.9	W 6067	33.8	PIECES 722,781,782,783
785	CYCLES,ETC MOTRZD OR NOT	W 4062	15.3	W 5949	22.7	W 3830	16.5	W 6477	23.6	MOTOCYCLES SCOOTERS
7853	INVAL CARR, PTS OF 785	W 2478	7.7	W 4070	12.8	W 2375	8.3	W 4785	15.7	FAUTEUILS INVALIDES,PIECES
78539	PARTS,ACCES NES OF 785	W 2466	7.6	W 4045	12.7	W 2346	8.3	W 4770	15.6	PIECES DU 785
79	OTHR TRANSPORT EQUIPMENT		8.3		6.5		6.5		6.2	AUTRE MATERIEL TRANSPORT
8	MISC MANUFACTURED GOODS		184.8		231.3		222.3		298.7	ART MANUFACTURES DIVERS
821	*FURNITURE,PARTS THEREOF	W 5429	12.8	W 8098	18.7	W 8907	17.4	W 10293	26.1	MEUBLES ET PIECES
8219	FURNITURE AND PARTS NES	W 3910	9.5	W 5958	13.9	W 5955	13.9	W 8937	21.4	AUTRES MEUBLES ET PIECES
84	CLOTHING AND ACCESSORIES		22.3		24.8		27.3		42.3	VETEMENTS
851	*FOOTWEAR	W 3794	12.2	W 2903	12.8	W 2615	9.6	W 4863	15.7	CHAUSSURES
87	PRECISION INSTRUMNTS NES		19.2		22.6		21.3		29.3	INSTRUM,APPAR SCIENT NDA
874	MEASURNG,CONTROLNG INSTR	W 929	11.2	W 833	12.1	W 1050	12.1	W 959	17.2	INSTRUMENTS DE MESURE
88	PHOTO EQU,OPTICL GDS ETC		17.0		20.5		19.9		23.9	APP,FOURN PHOTO,OP,MONTR
882	PHOTO,CINEMA SUPPLIES	W 844	10.6	W 1072	12.6	W 923	12.7	W 1206	14.3	PRODUITS PHOTO,CINEMA
8822	PHOTO FILM EXC DEV CINMA	W 478	8.3	W 645	9.8	W 602	9.8	W 804	10.6	PLAQUES,PELLICULES,FILMS
89	MISC MANUFCTRD GOODS NES		92.5		121.1		115.8		147.0	ART MANUFACTURES DIVERS
892	PRINTED MATTER	W 3058	16.5	W 3558	21.0	W 3633	21.4	W 3994	24.5	IMPRIMES
8921	PRINTED BOOKS,GLOBES,ETC	W 1791	10.1	W 2329	14.2	W 2051	13.6	W 2085	14.5	LIVRES,BROCHURES,CARTES
89211	PRINTED BOOKS,PAMPHLETS	W 1715	9.8	W 2195	13.6	W 1936	13.0	W 1965	14.2	LIVRES,BROCHURES
893	ARTICLES OF PLASTIC NES		29.7		40.2		36.3		49.1	OUVRAGES EN MAT DIVIS 58
8931	PLSTC PACKG CONTNRS,LIDS	W 3787	11.9	W 4728	17.3	W 5714	14.6	W 6507	17.5	ART TRANSP EMBALLAGE ETC
8939	MISC PLASTIC ARTICLES	W 5763	17.1	W 6410	21.8	W 7364	20.9	W 8993	30.1	ART DIVERS EN MAT DIV 58
89399	OTHR PLASTC ARTICLES NES	W 5334	16.3	W 5742	20.4	W 6572	19.8	W 8482	28.6	AUT OUV MAT DIV 58
894	TOYS,SPORTING GOODS,ETC	W 5273	16.5	W 6213	23.0	W 5533	22.7	W 6957	27.1	VOITURES ENFANTS,JOUETS
8942	TOYS,INDOOR GAMES ETC	W 4252	11.0	W 4922	15.7	W 4147	15.7	W 5507	20.3	JOUETS,JEUX ETC
89423	TOYS NES	W 2780	6.6	W 3150	9.5	W 2180	8.4	W 2893	12.0	JOUETS,MODELES REDUITS
895	OFFICE SUPPLIES NES	W 1435	8.8	W 1771	10.5	W 1945	9.9	W 2457	14.8	ART PAPET NDA
898	MUSICAL INSTRUMENTS,PTS	W 1085	9.2	W 1222	13.7	W 1425	11.9	W 1182	15.3	INSTRUMENTS DE MUSIQUE
8983	SOUND RECRDNG TAPE,DISCS	W 824	7.5	W 918	11.5	W 1071	9.9	W 923	13.2	SUPPORTS SON POUR 763
899	OTHER MANUFACTURED GOODS		8.8		9.7		9.7		12.2	AUT ART MANUF DIVERS NDA

5. Special Exports F.O.B. by Commodities according to the S.I.T.C. (Rev. 2) in million U.S. Dollars
Exportations Spéciales F.O.B. par Produits d'après la C.T.C.I. (Rév. 2) en millions de Dollars E.U.

SITC CTCI	COMMODITY	1994 QUANTITY QUANTITE	1994 VALUE VALEUR	1995 QUANTITY QUANTITE	1995 VALUE VALEUR	1996 QUANTITY QUANTITE	1996 VALUE VALEUR	1997 QUANTITY QUANTITE	1997 VALUE VALEUR	PRODUIT
	ALL COMMODITIES		1502.5		1935.6		2030.8		2344.1	TOUS PRODUITS
0	FOOD AND LIVE ANIMALS		859.9		1191.3		1139.2		1323.2	ALIMENTS,ANIMAUX VIVANTS
01	MEAT AND PREPARATIONS		10.0		7.8		4.7		5.8	VIANDES ET PREPARATIONS
011	MEAT FRESH,CHILLD,FROZEN	W 6258	8.9	W 4613	6.5	W 2202	3.1	W 2148	3.4	VIANDES FRAICHES,REF,CONGE
0111	BOVINE MEAT FRESH,FROZEN	W 5687	8.3	W 3984	5.9	W 1590	2.6	W 900	1.6	VIANDES BOVIN FRAI,REF
01112	BOVINE MEAT BONELESS	W 5532	8.1	W 3679	5.4	W 1590	2.6	W 897	1.6	VIANDES BOVIN DESOSSEES
03	FISH AND PREPARATIONS		31.4		23.3		27.6		20.0	POISSONS ET PREPARATIONS
036	SHELL FISH FRESH,FROZEN	W 6401	29.9	W 4219	22.6	W 5090	26.8	W 3257	18.6	CRUSTACES,MOLLUSQUES
04	CEREALS AND PREPARATIONS		32.3		45.7		53.2		77.4	CEREALES ET PRODUITS
044	MAIZE UNMILLED	W 1816	0.9	W 49718	8.0	W 15473	4.5	W 84223	24.4	MAIS NON MOULU
047	OTHER CEREAL MEALS,FLOUR	W 1032	1.2	W 5115	3.0	W 11652	6.5	W 10614	6.8	AUTRES SEMOULES,FARINES
048	CEREAL ETC PREPARATIONS	W 14147	27.6	W 19568	31.9	W 24873	39.7	W 26943	44.0	PREPTNS A BASE CEREALES
0481	PREPD BREAKFAST FOOD ETC	W 6617	17.9	W 8328	19.2	W 8679	22.0	W 8937	22.9	CEREALES TRAVAILLEES
04812	CEREAL ROASTED, PUFFED	W 5319	16.2	W 5533	16.7	W 6522	18.8	W 6704	19.8	PRODTS BASE CEREALES
0484	BAKERY PRODUCTS	W 4680	5.0	W 7505	7.7	W 10663	10.4	W 11768	12.4	PRODUITS DE BOULANGERIE
04842	PASTRY, CAKES ETC	W 3108	3.4	W 4321	4.8	W 5905	6.6	W 6396	7.5	PATISSERIE ETC.
05	VEGETABLES AND FRUIT		190.0		215.8		251.8		248.5	LEGUMES ET FRUITS
054	VEG ETC FRSH,SMPLY PRSVD	W 113223	43.6	W 132174	44.4	W 169888	54.0	W 160898	53.3	LEGUMES FRAIS,CONG,SECS
0545	OTHER FRESH VEGETABLES	W 49048	13.3	W 65170	15.8	W 93341	22.9	W 98255	31.2	AUTRES LEGUMES FRAIS,REF
05459	FRESH VEGETABLES NES	W 40282	11.8	W 54151	14.4	W 80071	21.1	W 89243	29.6	LEGUMES FRAIS,REFRI NDA
0546	VEGETABLES SIMPLY PRESVD	W 45732	29.0	W 41755	27.2	W 43846	29.1	W 28333	19.0	LEGUMES CONG,CONSER
05461	VEGETABLES FROZEN	W 44915	28.7	W 41282	27.1	W 43630	29.0	W 28279	19.0	LEGUMES CONGELES
057	FRUIT,NUTS,FRESH,DRIED	W 648880	135.1	W 745834	159.9	W 786197	185.5	W 786659	182.1	FRUITS FRAIS OU SECS
0573	BANANA,PLANTAIN,FRSH,DRY	W 577463	114.4	W 665426	139.3	W 669686	156.3	W 684287	152.5	BANANES FRAICHES,SECHEES
0579	FRUIT FRESH OR DRIED NES	W 66441	18.7	W 65775	18.7	W 105140	27.9	W 92048	28.3	FRUITS FRAIS,SECS NDA
05798	OTHER FRESH FRUIT	W 55512	14.4	W 49341	12.8	W 84324	19.9	W 72221	20.4	AUTRES FRUITS FRAIS
058	FRUIT PRESERVED,PREPARED	W 8981	7.5	W 9551	6.8	W 9967	6.6	W 8376	6.7	CONSERVES DE FRUITS
0585	FRUIT OR VEGETABLE JUICE	W 5301	5.1	W 4467	4.5	W 4292	4.0	W 5033	4.2	JUS DE FRUITS
06	SUGAR AND PREPS,HONEY		181.6		261.7		228.9		278.1	SUCRES ET MIEL
061	SUGAR AND HONEY	W 913872	170.0	W 1173716	250.9	W 1109470	222.0	W 1332868	272.1	SUCRES ET MIEL
0611	RAW BEET AND CANE SUGAR	W 692793	161.5	W 866937	238.2	W 796195	202.1	W 1033010	255.4	SUCRES BRUTS
0615	MOLASSES	W 218330	6.7	W 305443	11.5	W 311259	17.0	W 298386	14.8	MELASSES
062	SUGAR CANDY NON–CHOCLATE	W 6123	11.6	W 5796	10.8	W 4967	7.0	W 4079	6.1	SUCRERIES
07	COFFEE,TEA,COCOA,SPICES		362.7		583.0		514.8		629.9	CAFE,THE,CACAO,EPICES
071	COFFEE AND SUBSTITUTES	W 179455	318.6	W 206963	539.8	W 241604	473.1	W 249992	589.6	CAFE ET SUCCEDANES
0711	COFFEE GREEN,ROASTED,SUB	W 179454	318.6	W 206963	539.8	W 241573	473.0	W 249973	589.6	CAFE TORREFIE OU DECAFEINE
07111	COFFEE GREEN,HUSKS,SKINS	W 179363	318.3	W 206791	539.3	W 241295	472.5	W 249929	589.5	CAFE NON TORREFIE
075	SPICES	W 14002	42.8	W 14624	41.2	W 22509	40.1	W 22059	38.6	EPICES
0752	SPICES,EX PEPPER,PIMENTO	W 13826	42.6	W 14252	40.9	W 22088	39.7	W 21534	38.2	AUTRES EPICES
07524	NUTMEG,MACE,CARDAMOMS	W 13293	42.4	W 13923	40.8	W 21556	39.4	W 21415	38.0	NOIX MUSCADES
09	MISC EDIBLE PRODUCTS		44.2		47.2		51.3		55.1	PREP ALIMENTAIRES DIVERSES
098	EDIBLE PRODCTS,PREPS NES	W 19776	40.7	W 21328	42.2	W 23347	46.0	W 26783	51.4	PREP ALIMENTAIRES NDA
09805	SOUPS AND BROTHS	W 11696	27.4	W 12717	29.0	W 13843	31.7	W 14613	34.4	SOUPES,POTAGES,BOUILLONS
09809	MISC FOOD PREPRTIONS NES	W 3485	7.7	W 3298	6.7	W 3108	6.7	W 5059	9.1	PREP ALIMENTAIRES NDA
1	BEVERAGES AND TOBACCO		34.3		28.5		38.2		52.0	BOISSONS ET TABACS
11	BEVERAGES		4.9		6.2		6.7		8.0	BOISSONS
12	TOBACCO AND MANUFACTURES		29.5		22.4		31.6		44.1	TABACS BRUTS FABRIQUES
121	TOBACCO UNMNFCTRD,REFUSE	W 9832	24.6	W 5439	18.0	W 10038	27.2	W 8636	28.9	TABACS BRUTS,DECHETS
1211	TOBACCO,NOT STRIPPED	W 5139	12.1	W 2150	7.4	W 4358	12.2	W 4263	15.4	TABACS NON ECOTES
1212	TOBACCO STRIPPED OR PART	W 4091	12.3	W 2976	10.6	W 5072	14.8	W 3667	11.4	TABACS PART ECOTES
122	TOBACCO,MANUFACTURED	W 813	4.9	W 618	4.4	W 580	4.4	W 3820	15.3	TABACS FABRIQUES
1222	CIGARETTES	W 807	4.9	W 611	4.4	W 580	4.4	W 3112	12.7	CIGARETTES
2	CRUDE MATERLS,EXCL FUELS		99.6		122.2		146.0		136.3	MAT BRUTES NON COMESTIBLES
22	OIL SEEDS,OLEAGINOUS FRT		28.3		33.7		36.5		35.0	GRAINES,FRUITS OLEAGINEUX
222	SEEDS FOR'SOFT'FIXED OIL	W 33087	23.7	W 35042	30.7	W 32969	32.5	W 45550	31.1	GRAINES HUILES FIXES
2225	SESAME SEEDS	W 32170	23.1	W 34519	30.4	W 32169	31.5	W 44454	30.1	GRAINES DE SESAME
223	SEEDS FOR OTH FIXED OILS	W 8243	4.6	W 3106	3.1	W 1691	4.1	W 456	3.9	GRAINES AUTRES HUILES FIXES
23	RUBBER, CRUDE		27.4		36.2		48.7		38.7	CAOUTCHOUC BRUT
232	NATURAL RUBBER,GUMS	W 39145	27.3	W 29772	36.1	W 40060	48.6	W 35460	38.7	LATEX CAOUTCHOUC NATUREL
23201	NATURAL RUBBER LATEX	W 19363	16.0	W 20945	21.8	W 28001	30.8	W 23256	23.8	LATEX NATUREL
23202	OTHER NATURAL RUBBER	W 19153	9.3	W 8547	13.5	W 11900	17.4	W 12122	14.7	CAOUTCHOUC NATUREL
24	CORK AND WOOD		8.6		9.4		8.9		7.7	LIEGE ET BOIS
248	WOOD SHAPED,SLEEPERS	W 28820	8.5	W 35363	9.1	W 32091	8.4	W 27080	7.4	BOIS SIMPLEMENT TRAVAILLES
2483	LUMBER SHAPED NON–CONIFR	W 11534	5.0	W 9496	4.1	W 7953	3.5	W 6519	3.1	NON CONIFERES SCIES,RABOTES
24831	LUMBER SAWN ETC NON–CON	W 11346	4.9	W 9051	3.8	W 7519	3.1	W 6401	3.0	SCIES LONGITUDINALEMENT
27	CRUDE FERTLZR,MINRLS NES		4.9		6.2		6.2		6.4	ENGRAIS MINERAUX BRUTS
29	CRUDE ANIMAL,VEG MAT NES		25.2		30.1		38.3		40.2	MATIERES BRUTES ANIM,VEGET
292	CRUDE VEG MATERIALS NES	W 19416	24.9	W 22378	30.0	W 27594	38.2	W 29089	40.1	MAT BRUTES VEGETALES NDA
2925	SEEDS,ETC FOR PLANTING	W 248	6.0	W 354	7.1	W 144	6.6	W 96	6.9	SEMENCES NDA
2926	LIVE PLANTS,BULBS,ETC	W 9202	5.7	W 11781	7.5	W 13857	10.0	W 13338	10.6	BULBES,TUBERCULES
29269	LIVE PLANTS NES	W 9173	5.7	W 11658	7.4	W 13727	10.0	W 13206	10.6	AUTRES PLANTES VIVANTES
2927	CUT FLOWERS AND FOLIAGE	W 8445	12.2	W 8891	14.0	W 11915	19.5	W 13467	20.3	FLEURS,FEUILLAGES COUPES
29271	CUT FLOWERS	W 3465	7.9	W 3320	8.9	W 3815	10.8	W 3641	11.1	FLEURS ET BOUTONS
29272	CUT FOLIAGE	W 4981	4.4	W 5570	5.1	W 8100	8.8	W 9826	9.2	FEUILLAGES,RAMEAUX ETC
3	MINERAL FUELS ETC		27.8		39.7		65.8		98.7	COMBUSTIBLES MINERAUX LUB
33	PETROLEUM AND PRODUCTS		27.8		39.7		65.8		98.7	PETROLE ET DERIVES
333	CRUDE PETROLEUM	W 185592	22.3	W 126816	32.9	W 530434	60.5	W 893216	96.5	HUILES BRUTES DE PETROLE
334	PETROLEUM PRODUCTS,REFIN	W 6133	5.6	W 7294	6.9	W 6884	5.3	W 2145	2.0	PRODUITS RAFFINES
3345	LUBS,PETROLEUM OILS NES	W 5925	5.5	W 7294	6.9	W 4679	4.6	W 2076	2.0	HUILES LUBRIFIANTES
33451	LUBS(HIGH PETR CONT) ETC	W 5223	4.8	W 6524	6.2	W 4047	4.0	W 1869	1.7	HUILES LUBRIF,H LOURDES
4	ANIMAL,VEGETABLE OIL,FAT		9.7		8.2		16.0		23.0	HUILES,GRAISSES ANIM,VEG
42	FIXED VEGETABLE OIL,FAT		7.2		6.0		10.6		16.0	HUILES VEGETALES FIXES
423	FIXED VEG OILS,SOFT	W 6018	5.2	W 4176	4.3	W 5734	5.5	W 7490	6.9	HUILES VEGET DOUCES FIXES
424	FIXED VEG OIL NONSOFT	W 3709	2.0	W 1418	1.7	W 6838	5.1	W 13895	9.2	AUTRES HUILES VEG FIXES
4242	PALM OIL	W 2955	1.1	W 847	0.8	W 5476	3.5	W 12023	7.5	HUILE DE PALME
431	*PROCESD ANML VEG OIL,ET	W 3192	2.5	W 2234	2.1	W 7124	5.4	W 9190	7.1	HUILES,GRAISSES PREPAREES
5	CHEMCLS,RELATED PROD NES		173.5		207.3		236.7		263.4	PRODUITS CHIMIQUES
51	ORGANIC CHEMICALS		7.0		11.0		19.5		19.5	PROD CHIMIQ ORGANIQUES
512	ALCOHOLS,PHENOLS ETC	W 10794	5.0	W 13566	7.3	W 21270	11.6	W 22102	11.0	PHENOLS,PHENOLS–ALCOOLS
5121	ACYCLIC ALCOHOLS,DERIVS	W 10779	5.0	W 13565	7.3	W 21158	11.6	W 21885	11.0	ALCOOLS ACYCLIQUES
51216	ETHYL ALC,DENATRD SPIRIT	W 10485	4.7	W 13166	6.7	W 20331	10.4	W 21369	10.4	ALCOOL ETHYLIQUE NON DENAT
53	DYES,TANNING,COLOUR PROD		6.9		7.8		8.1		9.4	PROD TEINTURE,COLORANTS
533	PIGMENTS,PAINTS,ETC	W 5959	6.4	W 6488	6.9	W 7152	7.7	W 7904	8.9	PIGMENTS,PEINTURES,VERNIS
5334	VARNISHES,DISTEMPERS ETC	W 5829	6.3	W 6394	6.7	W 7009	7.4	W 7765	8.5	PEINTURES A L'EAU
53342	OTH PAINTS,VARNISHES ETC	W 5105	5.2	W 5610	5.5	W 6335	6.3	W 7136	7.5	AUTRES PEINTURES,VERNIS
541	*MEDICINAL,PHARM PRODUCT	K 6618386	64.7	K 5785152	75.0	K 6788963	74.4	MK 15251	68.6	PROD MEDICINAUX PHARMACEUT
5417	MEDICAMENTS	K 5610561	60.7	K 4799453	70.7	K 5929850	70.3	MK 14361	64.7	MEDICAMENTS
54171	— CONTAINNG ANTIBIOTICS	K 342084	4.9	K 197727	10.4	K 265217	10.7	K 2251510	9.9	MED CONTN ANTIBIOTIQUES
54172	— CONTAINING HORMONES	K 1013881	10.7	K 786425	10.1	K 226335	5.0	K 126668	1.8	MED CONTENANT HORMONES
54179	— CONTNG OTH SUBSTANCES	K 4249952	45.0	K 3802822	49.9	K 5421733	54.4	MK 11975	52.9	MED CONT AUT SUBSTANCES
55	PERFUME,CLEANING ETC PRD		52.9		58.0		69.4		84.2	PROD POUR PARFUM,TOILETTE

5. Special Exports F.O.B. by Commodities according to the S.I.T.C. (Rev. 2) in million U.S. Dollars
Exportations Spéciales F.O.B. par Produits d'après la C.T.C.I. (Rév. 2) en millions de Dollars E.U.

SITC CTCI	COMMODITY	1994		1995		1996		1997		PRODUIT
		QUANTITY QUANTITE	VALUE VALEUR	QUANTITY QUANTITE	VALUE VALEUR	QUANTITY QUANTITE	VALUE VALEUR	QUANTITY QUANTITE	VALUE VALEUR	
553	PERFUMERY,COSMETICS,ETC	W 6963	25.6	W 7402	29.0	W 18492	31.7	W 10746	39.9	PRODUITS DE PARFUMERIE
554	SOAP,CLEANSING ETC PREPS	W 24423	25.4	W 24391	26.5	W 65317	36.0	W 34276	41.9	SAVONS,PRODUITS DETERSIFS
5541	SOAPS	W 16853	18.4	W 14932	17.4	W 57289	28.1	W 24891	33.5	SAVONS,PROD TENSIO–ACTIFS
5542	WASHING PREPARATIONS ETC	W 6569	6.1	W 7437	7.3	W 7125	6.8	W 8996	7.7	PROD ORG TENSIO–ACT NDA
58	PLASTIC MATERIALS ETC		11.2		12.0		12.2		13.3	MAT PLAST ARTIFICIELLES
583	POLYMERIZATION ETC PRODS	W 8273	10.1	W 7498	10.6	W 7612	10.8	W 8009	12.4	PROD POLYMERISATION
59	CHEMICAL MATERIALS NES		25.2		37.8		46.0		57.3	MAT PROD CHIMIQUES NDA
591	PESTICIDES,DISINFECTANTS	W 6631	17.2	W 9420	28.6	W 11100	38.4	W 14833	49.6	DESINF,INSECT,FONG,HERB
5911	INSECTICIDES,FOR RETAIL	W 4022	9.5	W 4469	10.8	W 4973	12.3	W 5955	16.1	INSECTICIDES VENTE DET
5912	FUNGICIDES,FOR RETAIL	W 63	0.5	W 350	5.4	W 710	10.5	W 1238	11.4	FONGICIDES VENTE AU DET
5913	HERBICIDES,FOR RETAIL	W 2215	6.9	W 4171	12.0	W 4977	15.1	W 6206	21.0	HERBICIDES VENTE AU DET
6	BASIC MANUFACTURES		180.7		202.2		232.9		261.9	ART MANUFACTURES
62	RUBBER MANUFACTURES NES		15.5		19.5		18.5		29.5	CAOUTCHOUC MANUFACTURE
625	RUBBER TYRES, TUBES ETC	W 5118	13.5	W 5770	17.3	W 5262	16.4	W 9590	27.7	PNEUS CAOUTCHOUC VULCANISE
6251	TYRES NEW FOR MOTOR CARS	W 1784	4.8	W 1507	4.9	W 1490	5.0	W 3847	11.5	PNEUS POUR VOITURES
6252	TYRES,NEW,BUS OR LORRY	W 2156	6.3	W 2562	8.3	W 2365	7.9	W 3263	10.5	PNEUS POUR AUTOBUS,CAMIONS
63	WOOD,CORK MANUFACTRS NES		8.3		6.6		9.0		10.4	OUVRAGES LIEGE ET BOIS
635	WOOD MANUFACTURES NES	W 2270	5.0	W 2485	4.5	W 19953	5.8	W 3022	6.5	ART MANUF EN BOIS NDA
64	PAPER,PAPERBOARD AND MFR		18.1		24.7		38.4		40.3	PAPIERS,CARTONS & OUVRAGES
642	PAPER,ETC,PRECUT,ARTS OF	W 13438	14.5	W 17871	20.8	W 39337	33.4	W 39274	34.1	PAP,CARTONS DECOUPES
6421	PAPER ETC CONTAINERS	W 8667	8.9	W 12210	13.2	W 33691	25.6	W 30383	25.5	BOITES,SACS EMBALLAGES
65	TEXTILE YARN,FABRICS,ETC		44.5		40.4		50.3		45.5	FILS,TISSUS,ARTICLES TEXTILE
652	COTTON FABRICS,WOVEN	W 3843	16.3	W 2959	13.0	W 5011	21.9	W 3374	14.1	TISSUS DE COTON
6522	WOVEN COTTON BLEACHD,ETC	W 3572	15.5	W 2776	12.4	W 4585	20.8	W 3266	13.7	TISSUS COTON BLANCHIS ETC
65224	BLCHED COTTON FABRIC NES	W 1924	7.3	W 1411	5.9	W 1969	7.2	W 1942	7.5	AUT TIS PLUS 85% COT BLANCHI
65225	BLCHD COTN BLEND FAB NES	W 1547	7.7	W 1197	5.9	W 2468	13.1	W 1164	5.7	AUT TIS MOINS 85% COT BLANCH
653	WOVN MAN–MADE FIB FABRIC	W 4198	17.3	W 2982	14.3	W 4079	17.0	W 3608	16.3	TISSUS FIBRES SYNTH,ARTIF
6531	CONT SYNT WEAVES NONPILE	W 1879	5.4	W 1235	5.9	W 2634	9.7	W 1623	7.2	TISSUS FIBRES SYNTH CONTINUE
65315	CONT SYN TXTL FABRIC NES	W 1876	5.4	W 1235	5.9	W 2610	9.6	W 1620	7.2	TIS PLUS 85% TEXT SYNT CONT
6534	DISC SYN BLEND FABRC NES	W 1252	6.2	W 1062	4.3	W 801	3.0	W 1165	4.4	TISSUS FIBRES SYNTH DISCONT
65341	DISC SYN FIB–COTTN FABRC	W 1128	5.6	W 1025	4.1	W 800	3.0	W 819	3.5	TISSUS FIB SYNT DIS MEL COTO
66	NONMETAL MINERAL MFS NES		34.4		36.3		34.1		38.0	ART MIN NON METALLIQUES
665	GLASSWARE	W 53138	26.7	W 61900	29.6	W 55064	26.9	W 58351	29.6	OUVRAGES EN VERRE
6651	BOTTLES ETC OF GLASS	W 48882	23.9	W 59708	27.8	W 52237	24.6	W 53647	26.5	RECIPIENTS EN VERRE
66511	GLASS BOTTLES ETC NONVAC	W 48882	23.9	W 59708	27.8	W 52237	24.6	W 53647	26.5	BONBONNES,BOUTEILLES,ETC
67	IRON AND STEEL		39.1		52.2		58.2		69.3	FER ET ACIER
673	IRON,STEEL SHAPES ETC	W 41827	17.0	W 46277	19.2	W 52385	15.9	W 50548	20.0	BARRES,PROFIL FER,ACIER
6732	IRON,STEEL BARS ETC	W 32406	12.1	W 36342	14.5	W 31103	11.0	W 41836	15.9	BARRES FER,ACIER
67326	IRN,OTH STL BARS HOTROLD	W 32376	12.1	W 36192	14.4	W 30786	10.9	W 39923	15.0	BARRES PLEINES FER,ACIER
6733	IRON,STEEL PROFILES ETC	W 9420	4.9	W 9903	4.8	W 21205	4.8	W 8511	4.1	PROFILES,PALPLAN FER,ACIER
674	IRN,STL UNIV,PLATE,SHEET	W 17625	13.2	W 47038	19.5	W 30051	24.8	W 37925	29.8	LARGES PLATS,TOLES
6749	OTH IRN,STL PLATES,SHEET	W 16340	12.6	W 44609	18.1	W 28325	23.9	W 35697	28.6	AUTRES TOLES FER,ACIER
67491	— OF IRON OR SIMPLE STL	W 16340	12.6	W 44588	18.1	W 28302	23.9	W 35695	28.5	AUT TOLES AUTRES ACIER FIN
678	IRON,STL TUBES,PIPES,ETC	W 12174	7.4	W 17643	11.8	W 18511	11.3	W 27910	17.2	TUBES,TUYAUX EN FONTE,FER
6783	IRON,STL TUBES,PIPES NES	W 11738	7.1	W 17400	11.6	W 18342	11.1	W 27328	16.5	AUT TUBES,TUYAUX FER,ACIER
69	METAL MANUFACTURES NES		18.7		19.8		20.2		22.9	ART MANUFACT EN METAL NDA
692	METAL TANKS,BOXES,ETC	W 2645	5.2	W 4399	7.2	W 4898	8.9	W 4949	10.1	RECIPIENTS METALLIQUES
6924	MTL TRANSPORT BOXES ETC	W 2635	5.2	W 4290	7.0	W 4828	8.9	W 4936	10.1	FUTS,TAMBOURS,BIDONS
69241	STL TRANSPORT BOXES ETC	W 1380	2.9	W 2002	4.1	W 2669	5.6	W 3296	7.7	FUTS,TAMBOURS,BIDONS FER
7	MACHINES,TRANSPORT EQUIP		27.6		35.6		37.4		52.6	MACHINES MATERIEL TRANSPORT
74	GENRL INDUSTRL MACHY NES		5.6		10.4		10.1		16.6	MACH APP INDUSTRIE
741	HEATING,COOLING EQUIPMNT	W 796	4.6	W 1609	9.3	W 1433	7.8	W 2565	13.8	MACH CHAUFFAGE,PIECES
7414	NONDOM REFRIG EQUIPT,PTS	W 783	4.5	W 1595	9.1	W 1400	7.5	W 2488	12.7	MAT PRODUCTION DU FROID
74141	REFRIG EQUIP NONDOMESTIC	W 667	4.1	W 1462	8.7	W 1266	7.0	W 2286	12.1	REFIG INDUSTRIELS
77	ELECTRIC MACHNRY NES ETC		12.5		15.0		15.6		17.2	MACH APP ELECT NDA
775	HOUSEHOLD TYPE EQUIP NES	W 598	3.2	W 1028	6.0	W 1186	6.3	W 949	5.2	MACH,APP USAGE DOMESTQUE
778	ELECTRICAL MACHINERY NES	W 4105	9.2	W 3805	8.5	W 3576	9.1	W 4500	11.5	AUTRES MACH ELECT NDA
7781	BATTERIES,ACCUMULATORS	W 4098	9.1	W 3791	8.4	W 3533	8.7	W 4472	11.3	PILES ET ACCUMULATEURS
77811	PRIMARY BATTERIES,CELLS	W 3802	9.1	W 3429	8.2	W 3354	8.6	W 4302	11.3	PILES ELECTRIQUES,PIECES
78	ROAD VEHICLES		6.5		7.0		8.4		10.3	VEHICULES ROUTIERS
8	MISC MANUFACTURED GOODS		89.7		100.9		118.9		133.3	ART MANUFACTURES DIVERS
812	*PLUMBG,HEATNG,LGHTNG EQ	W 5223	8.1	W 6068	8.8	W 8580	11.2	W 8517	11.1	APPAR SANITAIRES CHAUFFAGE
8122	CERAMIC PLUMBNG FIXTURES	W 5173	8.0	W 6032	8.8	W 8574	11.1	W 8358	10.9	EVIERS,LAVABOS,CUVETTES
821	*FURNITURE,PARTS THEREOF	W 3264	7.6	W 4156	8.7	W 5410	13.2	W 6377	17.1	MEUBLES ET PIECES
8219	FURNITURE AND PARTS NES	W 1954	5.0	W 2308	5.3	W 3241	8.1	W 3585	11.7	AUTRES MEUBLES ET PIECES
82192	WOOD FURNITURE NES	W 1211	3.2	W 1456	3.4	W 2316	6.3	W 2305	9.1	MEUBLES NDA EN BOIS
84	CLOTHING AND ACCESSORIES		30.6		35.6		38.7		43.9	VETEMENTS
843	WOMENS OUTERWEAR NONKNIT	W 477	7.0	W 470	6.5	W 1180	7.2	W 793	10.7	VET DESSUS FEMMES MAT TEX
845	OUTERWEAR KNIT NONELASTC	W 276	4.0	W 351	5.5	W 450	6.2	W 507	7.4	VET DESSOUS,ACCES BONNET
846	UNDER GARMENTS KNITTED	W 675	9.2	W 948	11.1	W 938	10.6	W 771	10.0	SOUS VETS DE BONNETERIE
8463	— OF SYNTH FBR NONELAST	W 392	5.0	W 309	4.8	W 348	4.8	W 124	2.3	SOUS–VET BONNET FIB SYNT
848	HEADGEAR,NONTXTL CLOTHNG	W 890	5.7	W 677	5.5	W 1055	9.4	W 741	7.1	VET ACCES MAT AUT QUE TEX
851	*FOOTWEAR	W 1167	7.0	W 1228	7.9	W 1463	9.0	W 1797	11.9	CHAUSSURES
85102	FOOTWEAR LEATHER	W 528	4.0	W 601	5.3	W 646	5.8	W 835	7.6	CHAUS SEMELLES EN CUIR
89	MISC MANUFCTRD GOODS NES		34.8		38.3		44.8		47.2	ART MANUFACTURES DIVERS
893	ARTICLES OF PLASTIC NES	W 13131	21.2		23.6		25.5		28.3	OUVRAGES EN MAT DIVIS 58
8931	PLSTC PACKG CONTNRS,LIDS	W 7347	9.3	W 6875	13.0	W 8002	14.2	W 8816	14.8	ART TRANSP EMBALLAGE ETC
8939	MISC PLASTIC ARTICLES	W 5712	11.8	W 4152	10.2	W 4854	10.6	W 6811	12.9	ART DIVERS EN MAT DIV 58
89399	OTHR PLASTC ARTICLES NES	W 5632	11.6	W 4126	10.1	W 4808	10.5	W 6794	12.8	AUT OUV MAT DIV 58

1. HISTORICAL SERIES, 1957–1995 SPECIAL TRADE, IMPORTS C.I.F., EXPORTS F.O.B.
SERIES HISTORIQUES, 1957–1995 COMMERCE SPECIAL, IMPORTATIONS C.A.F., EXPORTATIONS F.O.B

YEAR ANNEE	VALUE IN MILLION U.S. DOLLARS / VALEUR EN MILLION U.S. DOLLARS — MERCHANDISE –MARCHANDISE		GOLD –OR		CONVERSION FACTORS FACTEURS DE CONVERSION CENTS E.U. PAR		INDEX NUMBERS –INDICES — QUANTUM		UNIT VALUE VALEUR UNITAIRE	
	IMPORTS	EXPORTS	IMPORTS	EXPORTS	IMPORTS	EXPORTS	IMPORTS	EXPORTS	IMPORTS	EXPORTS
1957	52.00	29.26								
1958	61.90	23.21								
1959	61.90	28.80								
1960	49.94	51.63								
1961	72.89	61.47								
1962	65.48	44.91								
1963	46.10	55.13								
1964	49.00	42.99								
1965	52.59	53.95								
1966	70.08	58.24								
1967	55.01	51.00								
1968	45.01	53.00								
1969	60.00	57.00								
1970	55.01	44.99								
1971	65.00	55.01								
1972	69.93	45.08								
1973	64.98	54.11								
1974	85.03	99.94								
1976	269.81	251.24								
1977	247.03	304.68								
1978	259.36	318.91								
1979	296.01	363.65								
1981	378.62	421.72								
1987	308.56	313.35								
1988	331.20	322.59								
1989	325.36	321.44								
1990	337.91	325.38								
1991	340.26	326.55								
1992	352.77	337.69								
1993	410.00	392.00								
1994	774.00	713.00								
1995	884.00	800.00								

2. IMPORTS BY BROAD ECONOMIC CATEGORY AND EXPORTS BY INDUSTRIAL ORIGIN. (PERCENTAGE OF TOTAL VALUE)
IMPORTATIONS PAR CATEGORIES ECONOMIQUES ET EXPORTATIONS PAR BRANCHE D'ACTIVITE.(EN POURCENTAGE DE LA VALEUR TOTALE)

IMPORTS – IMPORTATIONS	1989	1990	1991	1992	1993	1994	1995
TOTAL IMPORTS–IMPORTATIONS TOTALES							
1 FOOD BEV–ALIMENTATION BOISSONS							
11 PRIMARY–PRODUITS DE BASE							
111 FOR INDUSTRY–POUR L'INDUSTRIE							
112 FOR HOUSEHOLDS–POUR LES MENAGES							
12 PROCESSED–PRODUITS ELABORES							
121 FOR INDUSTRY–POUR L'INDUSTRIE							
122 FOR HOUSEHOLDS–POUR LES MENAGES							
2 IND SUPPLIES–APPROV INDUSTRIELS							
21 PRIMARY–PRODUITS DE BASE							
22 PROCESSED–PRODUITS ELABORES							
3 FUELS–COMBUSTIBLES							
31 PRIMARY–PRODUITS DE BASE							
32 PROCESSED–PRODUITS ELABORES							
321 MOTOR SPIRIT–ESSENCE							
322 OTHER–AUTRES							
4 MACHINERY–EQUIPEMENT							
41 CAPITAL EQUIPMENT–MACHINES							
42 PARTS–PIECES ACCESSOIRES							
5 TRANSPORT–TRANSPORT							
51 PASSENGER CARS–AUTOMOBILES							
52 OTHER–AUTRES							
521 INDUSTRIAL–INDUSTRIELS							
522 NON INDUSTRIAL–NON INDUSTRIEL							
53 PARTS–PIECES ACCESSOIRES							
6 CONSUM GOODS–BIENS CONSOMMATION							
61 DURABLE–DURABLES							
62 SEMI DURABLE–SEMI DURABLES							
63 NON DURABLE–NON DURABLES							
7 GOODS NES–BIENS NDA							

EXPORTS – EXPORTATIONS	1989	1990	1991	1992	1993	1994	1995
TOTAL EXPORTS–EXPORTATIONS TOTALES							
1 AGRICULTURE							
2 MINING QUARRY–INDUS EXTRACTIVES							
3 MANUFACTURING–IND MANUFACTUR							
31 FOOD BEV TOBACCO–ALIM BOISS TAB							
32 TEXTILES–INDUSTRIES TEXTILES							
33 WOOD & PRODUCTS–BOIS & PRODUITS							
34 PAPER & PRODUCTS–PAPIER & PRODT							
35 CHEMICALS–INDUSTRIES CHIMIQUES							
36 NON METAL MIN–MIN NON METAL							
37 BASIC METAL–IND METAL BASE							
38 METAL MANUF–MANUF METAL							
39 OTH MANUF IND–AUTRES MANUF							

3. TRADE BY PRINCIPAL COUNTRIES OF CONSIGNMENT AND DESTINATION (VALUE IN MILLION U.S. DOLLARS)
ECHANGES SELON LES PRINCIPAUX PAYS DE CONSIGNATION ET DE DESTINATION (VALEUR EN MILLIONS DE DOLLARS EU)

COUNTRIES–PAYS	SPECIAL IMPORTS C.I.F. IMPORTATIONS SPECIALES C.A.F					COUNTRIES–PAYS	SPECIAL EXPORTS F.O.B. EXPORTATIONS SPECIALES F.O.B.				
	1991	1992	1993	1994	1995		1991	1992	1993	1994	1995
World			410.0	774.0	884.0	Monde			392.0	713.0	800.0
Africa						Afrique					
Americas						Amériques					
– Northern America						– Amérique du Nord					
– LAIA						– ALAI					
– CACM						– MCAC					
– Caribbean						– Caraïbes					
– Rest of America						– Autre Amérique					
Asia excl fmr USSR						Asie anc. URSS exclus					
– Middle East						– Moyen–Orient					
Asia former USSR						Asie ancienne URSS					
Europe excl fmr USSR						Europe anc. URSS exclus					
– European Union						– Union Européenne					
– Eastern Europe						– Europe de l'Est					
– Rest of Europe						– Autre de l'Europe					
Europe former USSR						Europe ancienne URSS					
Oceania						Océanie					
Other						Autre					
Nigeria/Nigéria			18.0	19.0	21.0	Cameroon/Cameroun			29.0	29.0	29.0
Senegal/Sénégal			20.0	23.0	13.0	Morocco/Maroc			2.0	2.0	22.0
Morocco/Maroc			7.0	8.0	12.0	Tunisia/Tunisie				1.0	2.0
Pakistan			3.0	2.0		Nigeria/Nigéria			1.0	1.0	1.0
Tunisia/Tunisie			2.0	1.0	1.0	Senegal/Sénégal			1.0	1.0	
Malaysia/Malaisie				2.0	1.0	Saudi Arabia					1.0
Cameroon/Cameroun			1.0	1.0	1.0	Malaysia/Malaisie					1.0
Algeria/Algérie			1.0	1.0							
Somalia/Somalie				1.0	1.0						
Gambia/Gambie				1.0	1.0						
Turkey/Turquie				1.0	1.0						

(VALUE AS PERCENTAGE OF WORLD TOTAL)(VALEURS EN POURCENTAGE DU TOTAL MONDIAL)

	1986	1987	1988	1989	1990	1991	1992	1993	1994	1995		1986	1987	1988	1989	1990	1991	1992	1993	1994	1995
Africa											Afrique										
Americas											Amériques										
– Northern America											– Amérique du Nord										
– LAIA											– ALAI										
– CACM											– MCAC										
– Caribbean											– Caraïbes										
– Rest of America											– Autre Amérique										
Asia excl fmr USSR											Asie anc. URSS exclus										
– Middle East											– Moyen–Orient										
Asia former USSR											Asie ancienne URSS										
Europe excl fmr USSR											Europe anc. URSS exclus										
– European Union											– Union Européenne										
– Eastern Europe											– Europe de l'Est										
– Rest of Europe											– Autre de l'Europe										
Europe former USSR											Europe ancienne URSS										
Oceania											Océanie										
Other											Autre										
Nigeria/Nigéria								4.4	2.5	2.4	Cameroon/Cameroun								7.4	4.1	3.6
Senegal/Sénégal								4.9	3.0	1.5	Morocco/Maroc								0.5	0.3	2.7
Morocco/Maroc								1.7	1.0	1.4	Tunisia/Tunisie									0.1	0.2
Pakistan								0.7	0.3		Nigeria/Nigéria								0.3	0.1	0.1
Tunisia/Tunisie								0.5	0.1	0.1	Senegal/Sénégal								0.3	0.1	
Malaysia/Malaisie									0.3	0.1	Saudi Arabia										0.1
Cameroon/Cameroun								0.2	0.1	0.1	Malaysia/Malaisie										0.1
Algeria/Algérie								0.2	0.1												
Somalia/Somalie									0.1	0.1											
Gambia/Gambie									0.1	0.1											

4. Special Imports C.I.F. by Commodities according to the S.I.T.C. (Rev. 2) in million U.S. Dollars
Importations Spéciales C.A.F. par Produits d'après la C.T.C.I. (Rév. 2) en millions de Dollars E.U.

SITC CTCI	COMMODITY	1992		1993		1994		1995		PRODUIT
		QUANTITY QUANTITE	VALUE VALEUR	QUANTITY QUANTITE	VALUE VALEUR	QUANTITY QUANTITE	VALUE VALEUR	QUANTITY QUANTITE	VALUE VALEUR	
	ALL COMMODITIES									TOUS PRODUITS

5. Special Exports F.O.B. by Commodities according to the S.I.T.C. (Rev. 2) in million U.S. Dollars
Exportations Spéciales F.O.B. par Produits d'après la C.T.C.I. (Rév. 2) en millions de Dollars E.U.

SITC CTCI	COMMODITY	1992		1993		1994		1995		PRODUIT
		QUANTITY QUANTITE	VALUE VALEUR	QUANTITY QUANTITE	VALUE VALEUR	QUANTITY QUANTITE	VALUE VALEUR	QUANTITY QUANTITE	VALUE VALEUR	
	ALL COMMODITIES									TOUS PRODUITS

1. HISTORICAL SERIES, 1962–1997 SPECIAL TRADE, IMPORTS C.I.F., EXPORTS F.O.B.
SERIES HISTORIQUES, 1962–1997 COMMERCE SPECIAL, IMPORTATIONS C.A.F., EXPORTATIONS F.O.B

YEAR ANNEE	VALUE IN MILLION GUYANA DOLLARS / VALEUR EN MILLION GUYANA DOLLARS — MERCHANDISE – MARCHANDISE: IMPORTS	EXPORTS	GOLD – OR: IMPORTS	EXPORTS	CONVERSION FACTORS U.S. CENTS PER GUYANA DOLLAR / FACTEURS DE CONVERSION CENTS E.U. PAR GUYANA DOLLAR: IMPORTS	EXPORTS	INDEX NUMBERS – INDICES — QUANTUM: IMPORTS	EXPORTS	UNIT VALUE / VALEUR UNITAIRE: IMPORTS	EXPORTS
1962	126.30	161.10			58.3330	58.3330				
1963	118.50	172.90			58.3330	58.3330				
1964	149.80	166.60			58.3330	58.3330				
1965	180.10	165.80			58.3330	58.3330				
1966	202.00	182.60			58.3330	58.3330				
1967	225.30	192.00			57.5180	57.1730				
1968	219.30	228.50			50.0000	50.0000				
1969	235.80	233.70			50.0000	50.0000				
1970	268.20	265.60			50.0000	50.0000				
1971	267.60	287.80			50.0000	50.0000				
1972	297.90	299.90			47.9194	47.8191				
1973	372.50	287.00			47.1090	46.8918				
1974	567.10	602.40			44.9641	44.9512				
1975	810.60	858.10			42.4310	42.5940				
1976	927.40	711.30			39.2157	39.2157				
1977	804.30	661.80			39.2157	39.2157				
1978	711.10	750.20			39.2157	39.2157				
1979	810.20	746.40			39.2157	39.2157				
1980	1010.00	992.40			39.2157	39.2157				
1981	1236.50	974.30			35.2851	35.5166				
1982	841.10	724.00			33.3333	33.3333				
1983	691.50	567.60			33.3333	33.3333				
1984	945.30	807.80			26.6905	26.0105				
1985	1082.30	874.70			23.5441	23.6298				
1986	1030.00	953.20			23.2558	23.3311				
1987	2590.00	2596.30			10.1767	10.2726				
1988	2156.00	2295.60			10.0000	10.0000				
1989	7012.00	6123.20			3.6765	3.7129				
1990	12290.00	10207.70			2.5316	2.5086				
1991	34274.90	28107.10			0.9562	0.8793				
1992	55319.81	36567.20			0.7960	0.7942				
1993	61376.00	52506.90			0.7898	0.7882				
1994	70000.59	63389.81			0.7227	0.7198				
1995	74911.50	64581.30			0.7054	0.7048				
1996	83894.99	72597.90			0.7123	0.7121				
1997	91053.22	91808.70			0.7008	0.7007				

2. IMPORTS BY BROAD ECONOMIC CATEGORY AND EXPORTS BY INDUSTRIAL ORIGIN. (PERCENTAGE OF TOTAL VALUE)
IMPORTATIONS PAR CATEGORIES ECONOMIQUES ET EXPORTATIONS PAR BRANCHE D'ACTIVITE.(EN POURCENTAGE DE LA VALEUR TOTALE)

IMPORTS – IMPORTATIONS

	1991	1992	1993	1994	1995	1996	1997
TOTAL IMPORTS–IMPORTATIONS TOTALES	100.	100.					
1 FOOD BEV–ALIMENTATION BOISSONS	7.7	6.2					
11 PRIMARY–PRODUITS DE BASE	1.3	1.6					
111 FOR INDUSTRY–POUR L'INDUSTRIE	0.2	0.2					
112 FOR HOUSEHOLDS–POUR LES MENAGES	1.1	1.4					
12 PROCESSED–PRODUITS ELABORES	6.4	4.7					
121 FOR INDUSTRY–POUR L'INDUSTRIE	4.0	0.6					
122 FOR HOUSEHOLDS–POUR LES MENAGES	2.4	4.0					
2 IND SUPPLIES–APPROV INDUSTRIELS	25.5	22.9					
21 PRIMARY–PRODUITS DE BASE	1.1	0.8					
22 PROCESSED–PRODUITS ELABORES	24.5	22.1					
3 FUELS–COMBUSTIBLES	16.2	10.7					
31 PRIMARY–PRODUITS DE BASE	0.9	0.1					
32 PROCESSED–PRODUITS ELABORES	15.4	10.7					
321 MOTOR SPIRIT–ESSENCE	3.3	2.9					
322 OTHER–AUTRES	12.1	7.8					
4 MACHINERY–EQUIPEMENT	29.0	37.0					
41 CAPITAL EQUIPMENT–MACHINES	26.1	33.0					
42 PARTS–PIECES ACCESSOIRES	2.8	4.0					
5 TRANSPORT–TRANSPORT	15.2	14.9					
51 PASSENGER CARS–AUTOMOBILES	2.9	2.4					
52 OTHER–AUTRES	6.5	7.2					
521 INDUSTRIAL–INDUSTRIELS	5.3	6.0					
522 NON INDUSTRIAL–NON INDUSTRIEL	1.2	1.1					
53 PARTS–PIECES ACCESSOIRES	5.8	5.3					
6 CONSUM GOODS–BIENS CONSOMMATION	6.0	8.0					
61 DURABLE–DURABLES	1.1	1.2					
62 SEMI DURABLE–SEMI DURABLES	2.9	4.6					
63 NON DURABLE–NON DURABLES	2.0	2.2					
7 GOODS NES–BIENS NDA	0.3	0.2					

EXPORTS – EXPORTATIONS

	1991	1992	1993	1994	1995	1996	1997
TOTAL EXPORTS–EXPORTATIONS TOTALES							
1 AGRICULTURE							
2 MINING QUARRY–INDUS EXTRACTIVES							
3 MANUFACTURING–IND MANUFACTUR							
31 FOOD BEV TOBACCO–ALIM BOISS TAB							
32 TEXTILES–INDUSTRIES TEXTILES							
33 WOOD & PRODUCTS–BOIS & PRODUITS							
34 PAPER & PRODUCTS–PAPIER & PRODT							
35 CHEMICALS–INDUSTRIES CHIMIQUES							
36 NON METAL MIN–MIN NON METAL							
37 BASIC METAL–IND METAL BASE							
38 METAL MANUF–MANUF METAL							
39 OTH MANUF IND–AUTRES MANUF							

3. TRADE BY PRINCIPAL COUNTRIES OF ORIGIN AND DESTINATION (VALUE IN MILLION U.S. DOLLARS)
ECHANGES SELON LES PRINCIPAUX PAYS D'ORIGINE ET DE DESTINATION (VALEUR EN MILLIONS DE DOLLARS EU)

COUNTRIES–PAYS	SPECIAL IMPORTS C.I.F. IMPORTATIONS SPECIALES C.A.F				
	1993	1994	1995	1996	1997
World					
Africa					
Americas					
– Northern America					
– LAIA					
– CACM					
– Caribbean					
– Rest of America					
Asia excl fmr USSR					
– Middle East					
Asia former USSR					
Europe excl fmr USSR					
– European Union					
– Eastern Europe					
– Rest of Europe					
Europe former USSR					
Oceania					
Other					

COUNTRIES–PAYS	SPECIAL EXPORTS F.O.B. EXPORTATIONS SPECIALES F.O.B.				
	1993	1994	1995	1996	1997
Monde	422.7	459.4			
Afrique					
Amériques					
– Amérique du Nord					
– ALAI					
– MCAC					
– Caraïbes					
– Autre Amérique					
Asie anc. URSS exclus					
– Moyen–Orient					
Asie ancienne URSS					
Europe anc. URSS exclus					
– Union Européenne					
– Europe de l'Est					
– Autre de l'Europe					
Europe ancienne URSS					
Océanie					
Autre					
Canada	108.7	138.0			
United Kingdom	102.7	6.1			
Caribbean n.e.s.	12.4	8.8			
USA/Etats–Unis d'Amer	6.4	7.8			
Japan/Japon	0.0				

(VALUE AS PERCENTAGE OF WORLD TOTAL)(VALEURS EN POURCENTAGE DU TOTAL MONDIAL)

	1988	1989	1990	1991	1992	1993	1994	1995	1996	1997
Africa				0.0	0.0					
Americas				67.6	71.9					
– Northern America				34.3	48.3					
– LAIA				7.5	3.8					
– CACM				3.2	0.4					
– Caribbean				22.5	19.2					
– Rest of America				0.2	0.2					
Asia excl fmr USSR				8.3	8.2					
– Middle East				0.1	0.0					
Asia former USSR					1.8					
Europe excl fmr USSR				23.7	17.7					
– European Union				23.3	17.0					
– Eastern Europe				0.1	0.1					
– Rest of Europe				0.3	0.6					
Europe former USSR				0.0	0.0					
Oceania				0.4	0.4					
Other										

	1988	1989	1990	1991	1992	1993	1994	1995	1996	1997
Afrique										
Amériques				32.4						
– Amérique du Nord				26.6						
– ALAI										
– MCAC										
– Caraïbes				5.8						
– Autre Amérique										
Asie anc. URSS exclus				4.2						
– Moyen–Orient										
Asie ancienne URSS										
Europe anc. URSS exclus				38.5						
– Union Européenne				38.5						
– Europe de l'Est										
– Autre de l'Europe										
Europe ancienne URSS										
Océanie										
Autre				24.9						
Areas n.e.s.				24.9						
Canada				10.3		25.7	30.0			
United Kingdom				38.5		24.3	1.3			
Caribbean n.e.s.				5.8		2.9	1.9			
USA/Etats–Unis d'Amer				16.3		1.5	1.7			
Japan/Japon				4.2		0.0				

4. Special Imports C.I.F. by Commodities according to the S.I.T.C. (Rev. 2) in million U.S. Dollars
Importations Spéciales C.A.F. par Produits d'après la C.T.C.I. (Rév. 2) en millions de Dollars E.U.

SITC CTCI	COMMODITY	1994		1995		1996		1997		PRODUIT
		QUANTITY QUANTITE	VALUE VALEUR	QUANTITY QUANTITE	VALUE VALEUR	QUANTITY QUANTITE	VALUE VALEUR	QUANTITY QUANTITE	VALUE VALEUR	
	ALL COMMODITIES		506.7				597.6		638.2	TOUS PRODUITS
1	BEVERAGES AND TOBACCO						8.9		9.7	BOISSONS ET TABACS
3	MINERAL FUELS ETC		82.4				90.3		97.6	COMBUSTIBLES MINERAUX LUB
5	CHEMCLS,RELATED PROD NES						31.8		33.3	PRODUITS CHIMIQUES
781	PASS MOTOR VEH EXC BUSES						14.9		14.3	AUTO TRANSPORT PERSONNES

5. Special Exports F.O.B. by Commodities according to the S.I.T.C. (Rev. 2) in million U.S. Dollars
Exportations Spéciales F.O.B. par Produits d'après la C.T.C.I. (Rév. 2) en millions de Dollars E.U.

SITC CTCI	COMMODITY	1994 QUANTITY QUANTITE	1994 VALUE VALEUR	1995 QUANTITY QUANTITE	1995 VALUE VALEUR	1996 QUANTITY QUANTITE	1996 VALUE VALEUR	1997 QUANTITY QUANTITE	1997 VALUE VALEUR	PRODUIT
	ALL COMMODITIES		459.5		455.0		574.5		600.7	TOUS PRODUITS
03	FISH AND PREPARATIONS								20.6	POISSONS ET PREPARATIONS
036	SHELL FISH FRESH,FROZEN	W 3525	13.0	W 827	2.8	W 3100	12.6	W 4880	20.6	CRUSTACES,MOLLUSQUES
04	CEREALS AND PREPARATIONS								85.5	CEREALES ET PRODUITS
042	RICE	W 182587	52.8	W 200544	72.3	W 261823	93.5	W 261823	85.5	RIZ
061	SUGAR AND HONEY	W 238354	120.0	W 225421	124.2		151.2		135.4	SUCRES ET MIEL
0611	RAW BEET AND CANE SUGAR		119.5			W 255529	150.8	W 256241	134.7	SUCRES BRUTS
098	EDIBLE PRODCTS,PREPS NES		3.3							PREP ALIMENTAIRES NDA
1124	DISTILLED ALCOHOLIC BEVS						11.6			ALCOOLS,EAUX–DE–VIE
11249	OTH ALCOHOLC BEVS,CMPNDS		11.2						8.7	BOISSONS ALCOOLIQUES NDA
24	CORK AND WOOD		7.6		5.8		10.2		44.8	LIEGE ET BOIS
28	METALLIFEROUS ORES,SCRAP						86.2			MINERAIS METAL,DECHETS
287	BASE METAL ORES,CONC NES	W 1996492	79.5			W 2100568	86.2			MINERAIS METAUX COMMUNS
2873	ALUMINIUM ORES,ALUMINA	W 1996492	79.5	W 1971063	77.5	W 2100568	86.2			MINERAIS D'ALUMINIUM
28731	ALUMINIUM ORE,CONCNTRATE	W 1996492	79.5	W 1971063	77.5	W 2100568	86.2	W 2200300	90.2	MINERAIS D'ALUMINIUM
63	WOOD,CORK MANUFACTRS NES		15.0							OUVRAGES LIEGE ET BOIS
6672	DIAMONDS NONINDUST,UNSET		2.7							DIAMANTS BRUTS
84	CLOTHING AND ACCESSORIES		5.4							VETEMENTS
9	GOODS NOT CLASSD BY KIND						103.6			ART TRANSACT NON CLASSES
931	*SPECIAL TRANSACTIONS		5.4							TRANS.SPECIALES
971	*GOLD,NON MONETARY NES		126.0		94.7		103.6			OR NON MONETAIRE
97101	NONMON GLD UNWRT,SEMIMFD		126.0		94.7		103.6		140.8	OR,ALLIAGES D'OR BRUTS

1. HISTORICAL SERIES, 1962–1997 SPECIAL TRADE, IMPORTS C.I.F., EXPORTS F.O.B.
SERIES HISTORIQUES, 1962–1997 COMMERCE SPECIAL, IMPORTATIONS C.A.F., EXPORTATIONS F.O.B

YEAR ANNEE	VALUE IN MILLION U.S. DOLLARS / VALEUR EN MILLION U.S. DOLLARS — MERCHANDISE –MARCHANDISE		GOLD –OR		CONVERSION FACTORS FACTEURS DE CONVERSION CENTS E.U. PAR		INDEX NUMBERS –INDICES — QUANTUM		UNIT VALUE VALEUR UNITAIRE	
	IMPORTS	EXPORTS	IMPORTS	EXPORTS	IMPORTS	EXPORTS	IMPORTS	EXPORTS	IMPORTS	EXPORTS
1962	79.80	81.45		0.21						
1963	95.10	83.30		0.23						
1964	101.65	93.80		0.20						
1965	121.95	126.60		0.27						
1966	149.05	145.50		0.23						
1967	164.75	158.05		0.29						
1968	184.70	178.95		0.08						
1969	184.25	165.85								
1970	220.67	179.04		0.32						
1971	193.39	188.78								
1972	192.79	204.04								
1973	262.25	261.35								
1974	380.10	294.25								
1975	404.28	303.20								
1976	453.08	397.21								
1977	579.41	518.57								
1978	699.21	612.77								
1979	825.78	733.62								
1980	1008.70	829.50						118		112
1981	949.10	760.70						115		95
1982	700.50	659.50						113		93
1983	802.60	671.80						108		87
1984	893.40	725.30						105		96
1985	888.10	780.00						115		98
1986	875.00	854.20						107		127
1987	827.40	791.40						123		100
1988	940.10	841.90						109		108
1989	968.60	858.50						99		105
1990	934.80	831.00						100		100
1991	955.10	792.40						88		98
1992	1036.60	801.50						102		77
1993	1130.00	814.00						90		78
1994	1055.90	842.00						79		89
1995	1218.60	1060.70						83		123
1996	1839.90	1320.80						98		107
1997	2048.40	1442.80						81		120

2. IMPORTS BY BROAD ECONOMIC CATEGORY AND EXPORTS BY INDUSTRIAL ORIGIN. (PERCENTAGE OF TOTAL VALUE)
IMPORTATIONS PAR CATEGORIES ECONOMIQUES ET EXPORTATIONS PAR BRANCHE D'ACTIVITE.(EN POURCENTAGE DE LA VALEUR TOTALE)

IMPORTS – IMPORTATIONS

	1991	1992	1993	1994	1995	1996	1997
TOTAL IMPORTS–IMPORTATIONS TOTALES	100.	100.	100.	100.	100.	100.	100.
1 FOOD BEV–ALIMENTATION BOISSONS	9.2	8.5	10.3	12.4	10.1	12.4	12.4
11 PRIMARY–PRODUITS DE BASE	3.1	3.3	4.0	4.0	3.0	3.8	4.2
111 FOR INDUSTRY–POUR L'INDUSTRIE	2.7	2.7	3.1	3.3	2.1	2.6	2.9
112 FOR HOUSEHOLDS–POUR LES MENAGES	0.4	0.6	0.9	0.7	0.9	1.1	1.2
12 PROCESSED–PRODUITS ELABORES	6.0	5.2	6.3	8.4	7.1	8.6	8.2
121 FOR INDUSTRY–POUR L'INDUSTRIE	0.5	0.6	0.8	1.9	1.2	1.2	0.7
122 FOR HOUSEHOLDS–POUR LES MENAGES	5.5	4.6	5.6	6.5	5.9	7.4	7.6
2 IND SUPPLIES–APPROV INDUSTRIELS	39.0	37.3	34.2	32.3	34.1	34.5	34.6
21 PRIMARY–PRODUITS DE BASE	3.4	2.8	2.0	1.6	2.1	2.6	4.4
22 PROCESSED–PRODUITS ELABORES	35.6	34.5	32.3	30.7	32.1	31.9	30.2
3 FUELS–COMBUSTIBLES	15.3	12.9	13.5	12.6	11.4	13.4	10.2
31 PRIMARY–PRODUITS DE BASE	6.6	3.8	0.5	1.0	0.3	0.4	0.5
32 PROCESSED–PRODUITS ELABORES	8.7	9.1	13.1	11.6	11.0	13.0	9.7
321 MOTOR SPIRIT–ESSENCE	0.6	0.6	5.2	3.7	2.0	3.0	2.8
322 OTHER–AUTRES	8.0	8.4	7.8	7.9	9.1	10.0	7.0
4 MACHINERY–EQUIPEMENT	13.2	15.3	14.9	17.7	19.6	13.7	15.2
41 CAPITAL EQUIPMENT–MACHINES	11.8	13.7	13.3	16.0	18.1	12.2	13.8
42 PARTS–PIECES ACCESSOIRES	1.4	1.5	1.7	1.7	1.5	1.6	1.4
5 TRANSPORT–TRANSPORT	9.8	12.2	12.4	11.6	9.7	9.8	10.6
51 PASSENGER CARS–AUTOMOBILES	5.5	7.6	2.6	2.4	1.3	1.4	1.5
52 OTHER–AUTRES	0.5	0.7	6.1	5.7	5.3	5.4	6.2
521 INDUSTRIAL–INDUSTRIELS	0.2	0.3	5.8	5.4	5.0	5.1	5.8
522 NON INDUSTRIAL–NON INDUSTRIEL	0.3	0.4	0.3	0.3	0.3	0.3	0.3
53 PARTS–PIECES ACCESSOIRES	3.8	3.9	3.8	3.5	3.1	2.9	2.9
6 CONSUM GOODS–BIENS CONSOMMATION	12.8	13.8	14.4	13.3	15.0	16.0	16.7
61 DURABLE–DURABLES	1.2	1.6	1.9	1.8	2.5	2.7	3.3
62 SEMI DURABLE–SEMI DURABLES	5.3	6.0	5.9	5.7	6.8	7.9	8.5
63 NON DURABLE–NON DURABLES	6.3	6.2	6.6	5.8	5.7	5.4	4.9
7 GOODS NES–BIENS NDA	0.8	0.1	0.2	0.0	0.1	0.2	0.3

EXPORTS – EXPORTATIONS

	1991	1992	1993	1994	1995	1996	1997
TOTAL EXPORTS–EXPORTATIONS TOTALES	100.	100.	100.	100.	100.	100.	100.
1 AGRICULTURE	75.2	74.7	72.3	71.6	83.7	59.7	59.8
2 MINING QUARRY–INDUS EXTRACTIVES	0.4	2.6	1.1	1.0	0.0	1.5	2.8
3 MANUFACTURING–IND MANUFACTUR	24.3	22.7	26.6	27.4	16.3	38.7	37.4
31 FOOD BEV TOBACCO–ALIM BOISS TAB	11.0	8.7	12.2	11.5	5.7	7.2	8.2
32 TEXTILES–INDUSTRIES TEXTILES	3.2	3.4	2.0	2.4	1.2	4.3	3.5
33 WOOD & PRODUCTS–BOIS & PRODUITS	2.0	2.2	3.8	4.2	2.6	2.2	2.2
34 PAPER & PRODUCTS–PAPIER & PRODT	1.8	1.7	1.9	2.2	1.2	16.7	15.4
35 CHEMICALS–INDUSTRIES CHIMIQUES	3.1	3.1	2.3	2.6	2.1	2.1	2.1
36 NON METAL MIN–MIN NON METAL	0.5	0.5	0.3	0.3	0.3	0.3	0.2
37 BASIC METAL–IND METAL BASE	1.1	0.3	0.2	0.3	0.3	0.2	0.2
38 METAL MANUF–MANUF METAL	1.4	2.1	3.7	3.9	2.8	5.6	4.5
39 OTH MANUF IND–AUTRES MANUF	0.1	0.6	0.1	0.1	0.1	0.1	1.1

3. TRADE BY PRINCIPAL COUNTRIES OF ORIGIN AND DESTINATION (VALUE IN MILLION U.S. DOLLARS)
ECHANGES SELON LES PRINCIPAUX PAYS D'ORIGINE ET DE DESTINATION (VALEUR EN MILLIONS DE DOLLARS EU)

COUNTRIES–PAYS	SPECIAL IMPORTS C.I.F. IMPORTATIONS SPECIALES C.A.F				
	1993	1994	1995	1996	1997
World	1304.4	1334.6	1727.5	1922.2	2435.0
Africa	0.7	3.3	2.1	9.4	1.6
Americas	1054.8	1027.0	1319.4	1567.0	2162.4
– Northern America	678.9	645.2	816.0	1004.3	1498.1
– LAIA	96.3	100.6	152.3	166.0	182.8
– CACM	165.4	156.1	244.1	296.7	349.4
– Caribbean	80.7	96.0	63.6	54.9	58.2
– Rest of America	33.6	29.1	43.4	45.0	73.8
Asia excl fmr USSR	111.7	109.4	107.7	129.9	127.7
– Middle East	0.2	0.1	0.3	0.1	0.3
Asia former USSR				0.0	
Europe excl fmr USSR	125.0	170.2	266.0	151.1	116.8
– European Union	112.7	155.8	251.1	133.2	103.7
– Eastern Europe	1.9	3.8	2.6	7.5	5.6
– Rest of Europe	10.4	10.6	12.3	10.4	7.5
Europe former USSR	6.6	3.6	5.0	3.4	6.5
Oceania	1.4	2.1	4.1	6.9	7.1
Other	4.3	19.0	23.2	54.4	13.1
USA/Etats–Unis d'Amer	666.1	633.4	804.7	995.1	1491.2
Guatemala	76.7	83.1	118.2	133.0	157.1
El Salvador	44.1	46.4	68.3	88.8	116.5
Mexico/Mexique	34.8	40.4	72.2	88.4	107.6
Japan/Japon	70.3	55.7	59.2	78.4	69.9
Netherlands Antilles	62.1	79.2	48.7	31.0	7.9
Panama	33.5	28.9	43.3	45.0	73.7
Costa Rica	37.6	21.8	44.8	58.6	54.7
Germany/Allemagne	37.3	47.4	42.3	38.1	22.3
Netherlands/Pays–Bas	11.7	21.3	129.8	16.6	6.6
Brazil/Brésil	24.6	24.6	26.3	21.5	21.5
Spain/Espagne	6.9	27.5	27.0	20.3	20.5
Areas n.e.s.	1.7	11.1	20.8	50.7	13.1
Venezuela	11.6	11.5	21.7	23.1	27.1
Colombia/Colombie	15.2	15.2	18.7	17.5	11.8
Belgium–Luxembourg	9.6	19.3	14.8	14.8	11.2
Nicaragua	7.0	4.7	12.7	16.3	21.1
Other Asia n.e.s.	11.7	14.2	16.6	11.3	7.5
Italy/Italie	14.2	8.5	12.0	12.5	13.6
Canada	12.6	11.7	10.9	9.0	6.9
Switzerland,Liechtenst.	10.2	10.5	12.0	10.3	7.3
United Kingdom	10.4	9.7	7.3	6.9	13.5
China/Chine	6.7	6.8	8.0	9.7	10.6
France, Monaco	8.8	8.6	5.2	9.7	6.0
China, Hong Kong SAR	9.7	7.7	4.8	7.3	5.4
Korea Dem People's Rp	7.7	5.8	8.4	4.9	7.7
Dominican Republic	1.2	1.4	4.8	12.9	12.9
Jamaica/Jamaïque	0.6	0.1	0.3	4.3	23.6
Aruba	6.1	9.4	6.4	3.8	0.9
Korea, Republic of	1.3	4.5	4.4	9.0	7.1
Russian Federation	6.6	3.6	5.0	3.4	6.4
Trinidad and Tobago	4.1	2.7	1.5	1.3	11.7
Ireland/Irlande	2.8	5.2	3.9	5.3	4.0
Chile/Chili	2.6	3.0	4.9	5.5	5.0
New Zealand	1.3	2.1	3.3	6.7	6.9
Sweden/Suède	3.1	4.1	3.9	4.7	2.8
Argentina/Argentine	3.6	1.8	2.5	3.0	5.2
Indonesia/Indonésie	0.3	0.4	0.5	1.4	10.9
Denmark/Danemark	3.9	1.8	3.1	2.0	2.0
Bunkers, ship stores	2.3	7.8	2.3		

COUNTRIES–PAYS	SPECIAL EXPORTS F.O.B. EXPORTATIONS SPECIALES F.O.B.				
	1993	1994	1995	1996	1997
Monde	664.8	614.0	656.0	846.0	1033.3
Afrique	0.2	0.3	0.4	1.1	1.2
Amériques	454.1	396.0	342.4	565.2	758.0
– Amérique du Nord	382.3	335.5	288.0	508.1	708.5
– ALAI	5.9	4.0	4.9	6.3	4.7
– MCAC	51.3	40.1	36.8	34.6	33.3
– Caraïbes	11.1	11.6	10.0	5.0	4.6
– Autre Amérique	3.5	4.9	2.7	11.2	6.9
Asie anc. URSS exclus	28.9	38.8	67.5	38.2	51.3
– Moyen–Orient	1.2	0.0	0.1	0.1	0.0
Asie ancienne URSS				0.0	
Europe anc. URSS exclus	179.4	173.4	242.2	219.9	221.1
– Union Européenne	177.5	170.9	238.4	214.6	218.2
– Europe de l'Est	0.2	0.1	2.6	2.4	0.9
– Autre de l'Europe	1.7	2.4	1.3	2.9	2.0
Europe ancienne URSS		0.2	0.1	7.7	0.7
Océanie	0.2	0.2	0.0	0.2	0.3
Autre	1.9	5.2	3.4	13.8	0.7
USA/Etats–Unis d'Amer	381.0	331.0	279.9	499.1	702.3
Germany/Allemagne	93.1	76.0	126.7	93.9	82.2
Japan/Japon	19.2	24.9	44.2	22.4	27.7
Belgium–Luxembourg	30.0	18.6	23.2	23.9	16.8
Spain/Espagne	13.7	22.1	25.3	24.9	24.7
United Kingdom	10.6	12.7	10.8	14.4	31.8
Italy/Italie	5.7	9.6	15.4	16.7	22.2
El Salvador	18.2	14.0	9.0	15.1	10.7
Netherlands/Pays–Bas	8.8	12.9	10.9	20.1	11.6
Nicaragua	13.5	10.6	18.4	7.9	7.1
France, Monaco	5.1	9.8	11.8	9.8	16.0
Korea Dem People's Rp	8.0	11.9	18.1	2.7	6.1
Guatemala	13.6	6.8	4.3	6.8	7.3
Costa Rica	6.0	8.6	5.1	5.0	8.1
Korea, Republic of	0.2	0.3	4.0	11.8	13.7
Canada	1.1	4.5	8.1	9.0	6.2
Panama	2.7	3.4	2.3	10.8	6.6
Finland/Finlande	1.3	4.0	7.4	3.9	6.0
Portugal	7.8	3.4	4.0	2.8	3.0
Areas n.e.s.	0.8	1.5	2.3	8.2	0.7
Mexico/Mexique	4.2	1.9	2.1	2.6	2.1
Switzerland,Liechtenst.	1.7	2.2	1.2	2.9	1.9
Russian Federation		0.2	0.1	7.7	0.7
Colombia/Colombie	1.4	1.6	2.0	2.5	0.8
Dominican Republic	0.5	1.0	1.1	3.1	2.2
Trinidad and Tobago	1.4	2.4	2.4	0.2	0.7
Guadeloupe	2.2	2.1	1.5		
Free zones/Zone franches	0.0			5.5	
Bunkers, ship stores	1.1	3.7	0.6		
Ireland/Irlande	0.2	0.3	0.5	1.6	2.2
Denmark/Danemark	0.0	0.6	1.0	1.9	0.6
Saint Lucia/Ste–Lucie	0.9	1.7	1.3		
Israel/Israël	0.2	0.8	0.9	0.6	1.2
Belize/Bélize	0.7	1.5	0.4	0.4	0.2
Poland/Pologne	0.0	0.0	1.6	0.9	0.5
Martinique	1.1	0.9	1.1		
Barbados/Barbade	1.1	0.8	0.8	0.1	0.2
Jamaica/Jamaïque	1.1	0.8	0.1	0.5	0.5
Grenada/Grenade	0.6	0.9	0.9	0.5	
China, Hong Kong SAR	0.0	0.5	0.0	0.2	1.9

(VALUE AS PERCENTAGE OF WORLD TOTAL)(VALEURS EN POURCENTAGE DU TOTAL MONDIAL)

	1988	1989	1990	1991	1992	1993	1994	1995	1996	1997
Africa	0.1	0.0	0.0	0.0	0.0	0.1	0.2	0.1	0.5	0.1
Americas	69.1	72.0	72.7	75.5	82.2	80.9	77.0	76.4	81.5	88.8
– Northern America	42.5	44.6	43.7	49.6	54.1	52.1	48.3	47.2	52.2	61.5
– LAIA	17.4	16.0	16.6	14.4	12.3	7.4	7.5	8.8	8.6	7.5
– CACM	6.6	8.4	8.1	9.6	10.8	12.7	11.7	14.1	15.4	14.4
– Caribbean	0.1	0.2	0.2	0.2	2.1	6.2	7.2	3.7	2.9	2.4
– Rest of America	2.5	2.7	4.1	1.7	2.9	2.6	2.2	2.5	2.3	3.0
Asia excl fmr USSR	12.6	11.6	10.5	9.1	8.3	8.6	8.2	6.2	6.8	5.2
– Middle East	0.0	0.0	0.0	0.0	0.0	0.0	0.0	0.0	0.0	0.0
Asia former USSR									0.0	
Europe excl fmr USSR	13.9	11.8	11.5	10.7	8.6	9.6	12.8	15.4	7.9	4.8
– European Union	12.2	10.1	10.1	9.5	7.5	8.6	11.7	14.5	6.9	4.3
– Eastern Europe	0.8	0.4	0.2	0.3	0.2	0.1	0.3	0.2	0.4	0.2
– Rest of Europe	1.0	1.3	1.2	1.0	0.8	0.8	0.8	0.7	0.5	0.3
Europe former USSR	0.0	0.1	0.0	0.0	0.1	0.5	0.3	0.3	0.2	0.3
Oceania	0.1	0.1	0.1	0.2	0.1	0.1	0.2	0.2	0.4	0.3
Other	4.1	4.5	5.2	4.4	0.7	0.3	1.4	1.3	2.8	0.5
USA/Etats–Unis d'Amer	41.6	43.5	43.3	48.7	53.4	51.1	47.5	46.6	51.8	61.2
Guatemala	3.6	4.9	3.7	4.4	4.6	5.9	6.2	6.8	6.9	6.5
El Salvador	1.4	1.5	1.7	2.1	2.9	3.4	3.5	4.0	4.6	4.8
Mexico/Mexique	7.2	6.4	4.8	5.5	6.3	2.7	3.0	4.2	4.6	4.4
Japan/Japon	9.2	8.2	7.0	6.0	5.0	5.4	4.2	3.4	4.1	2.9
Netherlands Antilles				0.0	1.3	4.8	5.9	2.8	1.6	0.3
Panama	2.5	2.7	4.1	1.6	2.8	2.6	2.2	2.5	2.3	3.0
Costa Rica	1.4	1.6	1.6	2.1	2.5	2.9	1.6	2.6	3.1	2.2
Germany/Allemagne				2.9	2.2	2.9	3.6	2.5	2.0	0.9
Netherlands/Pays–Bas	2.1	1.3	1.3	1.7	0.5	0.9	1.6	7.5	0.9	0.3

	1988	1989	1990	1991	1992	1993	1994	1995	1996	1997
Afrique	0.9	0.4	0.0	0.0	0.1	0.0	0.0	0.1	0.1	0.1
Amériques	52.9	52.3	59.7	62.4	62.0	68.3	64.5	52.2	66.8	73.4
– Amérique du Nord	44.6	44.7	52.1	54.4	53.7	57.5	54.6	43.9	60.1	68.6
– ALAI	1.2	0.4	0.9	1.3	0.6	0.9	0.6	0.8	0.7	0.5
– MCAC	3.9	4.8	4.4	5.2	6.5	7.7	6.5	5.6	4.1	3.2
– Caraïbes	2.7	2.3	1.9	0.9	0.7	1.7	1.9	1.5	0.6	0.4
– Autre Amérique	0.6	0.2	0.5	0.6	0.6	0.5	0.8	0.4	1.3	0.7
Asie anc. URSS exclus	8.4	10.6	7.3	9.0	5.9	4.4	6.3	10.3	4.5	5.0
– Moyen–Orient	1.2	1.1	0.8	0.6	1.8	0.2	0.0	0.0	0.0	0.0
Asie ancienne URSS									0.0	
Europe anc. URSS exclus	36.6	35.5	29.8	27.6	31.0	27.0	28.2	36.9	26.0	21.4
– Union Européenne	27.8	26.7	28.1	26.0	30.3	26.7	27.8	36.3	25.4	21.1
– Europe de l'Est	8.8	8.2	1.0	0.7	0.3	0.0	0.0	0.4	0.3	0.1
– Autre de l'Europe	0.1	0.5	0.7	0.9	0.5	0.3	0.4	0.2	0.3	0.2
Europe ancienne URSS	1.0	0.3	2.3		0.2		0.0	0.0	0.9	0.1
Océanie	0.1	0.8	0.6	0.0	0.0	0.0	0.0	0.0	0.0	0.0
Autre	0.0	0.1	0.3	0.9	0.8	0.3	0.8	0.5	1.6	0.1
USA/Etats–Unis d'Amer	44.1	44.3	51.6	53.9	53.0	57.3	53.9	42.7	59.0	68.0
Germany/Allemagne				7.0	13.2	14.0	12.4	19.3	11.1	8.0
Japan/Japon	5.9	7.6	5.1	5.7	2.5	2.9	4.1	6.7	2.7	2.7
Belgium–Luxembourg	6.9	6.1	5.9	6.1	4.7	4.5	3.0	3.5	2.8	1.6
Spain/Espagne	2.3	1.6	1.7	1.8	1.5	2.1	3.6	3.9	2.9	2.4
United Kingdom	2.4	3.3	2.1	1.8	2.0	1.6	2.1	1.6	1.7	3.1
Italy/Italie	3.7	2.4	3.3	4.0	4.7	0.9	1.6	2.4	2.0	2.1
El Salvador	1.8	1.8	1.8	2.7	3.1	2.7	2.3	1.4	1.8	1.0
Netherlands/Pays–Bas	2.0	1.8	1.1	2.2	0.9	1.3	2.1	1.7	2.4	1.1
Nicaragua	0.2	0.4	0.3	0.7	1.2	2.0	1.7	2.8	0.9	0.7

4. Special Imports C.I.F. by Commodities according to the S.I.T.C. (Rev. 2) in million U.S. Dollars
Importations Spéciales C.A.F. par Produits d'après la C.T.C.I. (Rév. 2) en millions de Dollars E.U.

SITC CTCI	COMMODITY	1994 QUANTITY QUANTITE	1994 VALUE VALEUR	1995 QUANTITY QUANTITE	1995 VALUE VALEUR	1996 QUANTITY QUANTITE	1996 VALUE VALEUR	1997 QUANTITY QUANTITE	1997 VALUE VALEUR	PRODUIT
	ALL COMMODITIES		1334.7		1727.6		1922.2		2435.1	TOUS PRODUITS
0	FOOD AND LIVE ANIMALS		178.1		184.0		243.4		354.4	ALIMENTS,ANIMAUX VIVANTS
01	MEAT AND PREPARATIONS		2.5		5.5		5.6		10.6	VIANDES ET PREPARATIONS
011	MEAT FRESH,CHILLD,FROZEN	W 1436	2.0	W 3475	4.6	W 3076	4.2	W 5385	7.4	VIANDES FRAICHES,REF,CONGE
02	DAIRY PRODCTS,BIRDS'EGGS		20.3		22.5		30.5		36.5	PRODUITS LAITIERS,OEUFS
022	MILK AND CREAM	W 7306	15.2	W 8185	16.8	W 8399	20.7	W 9770	25.1	LAIT ET CREME
0224	MILK,CREAM PRESERVED ETC	W 7245	15.1	W 7923	16.6	W 7876	20.3	W 9274	24.6	LAIT,CREME CONS,CONC
02243	MILK DRY,OVER 1.5% FAT			W 6720	14.3	W 6182	17.2	W 6648	19.1	LAIT POUDRE SUP 1.5%
025	EGGS,BIRDS,FRESH,PRSRVD	W 2636	2.4	W 5167	3.8	W 6038	6.4	W 6999	8.2	OEUFS
0251	— IN SHELL	W 2634	2.4	W 5129	3.8	W 6033	6.4	W 6929	8.1	OEUFS EN COQUILLE
03	FISH AND PREPARATIONS		3.2		5.9		4.9		7.3	POISSONS ET PREPARATIONS
04	CEREALS AND PREPARATIONS		72.9		68.3		97.5		153.5	CEREALES ET PRODUITS
041	WHEAT ETC UNMILLED	W 225002	38.0	W 99556	24.6	W 111959	31.2	W 155133	44.6	FROMENT,EPEAUTRE
0411	DURUM WHEAT UNMILLED	W 30588	3.7	W 16301	4.7	W 8568	4.3	W 54790	13.4	FROMENT DUR NON MOULU
0412	OTHER WHEAT ETC UNMILLED	W 194415	34.3	W 83256	20.0	W 103391	26.9	W 100343	31.3	AUTRE FROMENT NON MOULU
042	RICE	W 9459	6.3	W 21060	7.9	W 48105	19.6	W 57970	28.3	RIZ
0421	RICE IN HUSK OR HUSKED	W 4563	1.5	W 17130	6.7	W 29222	10.9	W 27067	10.6	RIZ SANS AUTRE PREPARATION
04211	RICE IN THE HUSK			W 16816	6.6	W 29050	10.8	W 24513	9.5	RIZ PADDY
0422	RICE SEMI–MILLED,MILLED	W 4895	4.9	W 3930	1.3	W 18883	8.8	W 30903	17.8	RIZ POLI,GLACE INCL BRISURES
04221	RICE MILLED UNBROKEN			W 2965	1.1	W 16255	7.8	W 30680	17.7	RIZ POLI,GLACE EXCL BRISURES
044	MAIZE UNMILLED	W 33977	5.1	W 17383	9.6	W 43488	9.4	W 116065	25.4	MAIS NON MOULU
045	CEREALS NES UNMILLED	W 23143	0.4	W 1205	0.6	W 8765	1.9	W 70711	10.7	AUTRES CEREALES NON MOULUES
0459	OTHER CEREALS UNMILLED	W 23083	0.3	W 756	0.4	W 7717	1.8	W 70604	10.6	SARRASIN,MILLET,SORGHO
04592	SORGHUM UNMILLED	W 23073	0.3	W 745	0.4	W 7702	1.8	W 70597	10.6	SORGHO NON MOULU
047	OTHER CEREAL MEALS,FLOUR	W 25644	9.2	W 697	0.5	W 1986	1.4	W 4091	2.2	AUTRES SEMOULES,FARINES
04702	MEAL OR GROATS NON–WHEAT	W 13045	6.5	W 49	0.1	W 100	0.1	W 1367	0.6	GRUAUX,SEMOULES DE CEREALES
048	CEREAL ETC PREPARATIONS	W 18366	14.1	W 29924	24.8	W 32874	34.0	W 38944	42.2	PREPTNS A BASE CEREALES
0481	PREPD BREAKFAST FOOD ETC	W 4903	5.2	W 9887	8.7	W 9695	11.3	W 13865	16.5	CEREALES TRAVAILLEES
04811	CEREAL FLAKED,ROLLED,ETC	W 3396	2.1	W 7322	4.5	W 6503	5.5	W 9428	8.9	GRAINS GERMES DE CEREALES
04812	CEREAL ROASTED, PUFFED	W 1507	3.1	W 2565	4.2	W 3192	5.8	W 4437	7.7	PRODTS BASE CEREALES
0484	BAKERY PRODUCTS	W 1705	2.3	W 5151	6.1	W 8169	9.4	W 10001	11.8	PRODUITS DE BOULANGERIE
04841	BREAD,BISCUIT,COM WAFERS	W 143	0.2	W 2908	3.5	W 5560	5.9	W 5724	6.6	PAINS,BISCUITS DE MER
05	VEGETABLES AND FRUIT		8.4		12.9		21.5		28.0	LEGUMES ET FRUITS
054	VEG ETC FRSH,SMPLY PRSVD	W 5227	3.6	W 8114	6.0	W 16073	11.9	W 19015	12.6	LEGUMES FRAIS,CONG,SECS
0546	VEGETABLES SIMPLY PRESVD	W 3539	2.7	W 4407	4.7	W 6332	6.4	W 11045	9.2	LEGUMES CONG,CONSER
05461	VEGETABLES FROZEN	W 3410	2.6	W 4233	4.4	W 6094	6.2	W 10779	9.0	LEGUMES CONGELES
058	FRUIT PRESERVED,PREPARED	W 2551	2.7	W 4107	4.8	W 4719	6.6	W 7151	7.9	CONSERVES DE FRUITS
06	SUGAR AND PREPS,HONEY		10.4		6.8		5.9		6.8	SUCRES ET PRODUITS
061	SUGAR AND HONEY	W 21469	7.4	W 6981	2.9	W 3390	1.4	W 3605	1.8	SUCRES ET MIEL
0611	RAW BEET AND CANE SUGAR	W 19626	6.5	W 3547	1.4	W 52	0.1	W 604	0.3	SUCRES BRUTS
081	*FEEDING STUFF FOR ANIML	W 55381	16.5	W 70689	18.1	W 59983	17.7	W 111057	41.9	NOURRITURE POUR ANIMAUX
0813	OILCAKE AND OTH RESIDUES	W 30642	9.4	W 31379	8.2	W 21376	7.0	W 65401	23.9	TOURTEAUX
08131	— OF SOYA BEANS	W 30641	9.4	W 31160	8.2	W 21261	6.9	W 65084	23.8	TOURTEAUX DE SOJA
0819	FOOD WASTE AND FEED NES	W 17894	5.1	W 21248	6.3	W 16988	7.2	W 17719	9.1	DECHETS,ALIMENTS NDA
08199	FODDER NES,INCL SWEETNED	W 17878	5.1	W 21174	6.3	W 16380	6.9	W 17372	8.9	PREPARATIONS FOURRAGERES
09	MISC EDIBLE PRODUCTS		40.0		39.3		53.2		62.0	PREP ALIMENTAIRES DIVERSES
098	EDIBLE PRODCTS,PREPS NES	W 9226	39.3	W 10189	38.5	W 14997	52.8	W 17575	61.7	PREP ALIMENTAIRES NDA
09805	SOUPS AND BROTHS	W 2192	5.5	W 2204	5.5	W 2510	6.7	W 2671	7.7	SOUPES,POTAGES,BOUILLONS
09809	MISC FOOD PREPRTIONS NES	W 4363	30.7	W 4587	29.0	W 6367	39.8	W 8928	46.3	PREP ALIMENTAIRES NDA
1	BEVERAGES AND TOBACCO		6.8		11.8		29.1		63.6	BOISSONS ET TABACS
11	BEVERAGES		3.1		5.9		6.8		8.1	BOISSONS
12	TOBACCO AND MANUFACTURES		3.7		5.9		22.3		55.5	TABACS BRUTS FABRIQUES
121	TOBACCO UNMNFCTRD,REFUSE	W 1260	3.4	W 1249	5.7	W 4463	20.2	W 7803	53.7	TABACS BRUTS,DECHETS
1211	TOBACCO,NOT STRIPPED	W 946	2.6	W 837	3.8	W 2780	14.9	W 6604	48.0	TABACS NON ECOTES
2	CRUDE MATERLS,EXCL FUELS		19.6		28.8		36.1		65.6	MAT BRUTES NON COMESTIBLES
22	OIL SEEDS,OLEAGINOUS FRT		3.4		6.5		9.8		1.6	GRAINES,FRUITS OLEAGINEUX
223	SEEDS FOR OTH FIXED OILS		2.9	W 11186	5.7	W 25455	9.6	W 977	1.5	GRAINES AUTRES HUILES FIXES
2239	OIL SEED FLOUR AND MEAL	W 9435	2.2	W 11047	4.6	W 25069	8.2	W 933	0.5	FARINES GRAINES OLEAG
24	CORK AND WOOD		0.1		0.7		2.6		35.9	LIEGE ET BOIS
248	WOOD SHAPED,SLEEPERS	W 265	0.1	W 2855	0.6	W 12399	2.4	W 88893	35.8	BOIS SIMPLEMENT TRAVAILLES
2481	RAILWAY SLEEPERS,TIES				0.1	W 734	0.3	W 73615	32.5	TRAVERSES VOIES FERREES
26	TEXTILE FIBRES AND WASTE		4.8		8.4		10.4		14.2	FIBRES TEXTILES
269	WASTE OF TEXTILE FABRICS	W 996	1.0	W 3071	3.7	W 4799	5.3	W 6525	8.6	FRIPERIE DRILLES,CHIFFONS
29	CRUDE ANIMAL,VEG MAT NES		6.2		4.6		4.6		6.1	MATIERES BRUTES ANIM,VEGET
3	MINERAL FUELS ETC		173.2		199.2		259.6		252.2	COMBUSTIBLES MINERAUX LUB
33	PETROLEUM AND PRODUCTS		159.4		193.2		251.4		238.1	PETROLE ET DERIVES
334	PETROLEUM PRODUCTS,REFIN	W 654151	154.6	W 827491	190.4	W 1065575	248.7	W 1040683	233.2	PRODUITS RAFFINES
3341	GASOLINE,OTH LIGHT OILS	W 183066	49.8	W 146598	34.0	W 229837	57.7	W 248342	67.7	ESSENCES POUR MOTEURS
33419	OTH LIGHT PETROLEUM OILS			W 146598	34.0	W 229837	57.7	W 248342	67.7	AUTRES HUILES LEGERES
3342	KEROSENE,OTH MEDIUM OILS	W 60337	17.3	W 41407	8.4	W 56974	14.0	W 61446	14.4	PETR LAMPANTS,AUT HUIL
33429	OTH MEDIUM PETROLEUM OIL			W 41407	8.4	W 56974	14.0	W 61446	14.4	AUTRES HUILES MOYENNES
3343	GAS OILS	W 400813	79.5							GAS OILS
3344	FUEL OILS,NES	W 93	0.1	W 623436	137.7	W 763878	165.4	W 715723	138.6	FUEL OILS
3345	LUBS,PETROLEUM OILS NES	W 9841	8.1	W 16051	10.5	W 14886	11.7	W 15172	12.6	HUILES LUBRIFIANTES
33451	LUBS(HIGH PETR CONT) ETC			W 15989	10.3	W 14722	11.4	W 15001	12.3	HUILES LUBRIF,H LOURDES
335	RESIDUAL PETRLM PROD NES	W 19343	4.8	W 11178	2.9	W 11476	2.7	W 11027	3.3	PRODUITS RESIDUELS NDA
341	*GAS,NATURAL AND MANUFCT	W 72807	13.6	W 21022	5.7	W 22221	6.8	W 32394	10.1	GAZ NATUREL,GAZ MANUFACT
3413	PETROLM GASES,LIQUEFIED	W 54651	10.3	W 21018	5.7	W 21808	6.7	W 32380	10.0	GAZ DE PETROLE LIQUEFIE
34131	LIQUEFIED PROPANE,BUTANE			W 21018	5.7	W 21798	6.7	W 32378	10.0	PROPANE,BUTANE LIQUEFIES
4	ANIMAL,VEGETABLE OIL,FAT		5.3		16.2		15.5		16.0	HUILES,GRAISSES ANIM,VEG
411	*ANIMAL OILS AND FATS	W 4757	2.4	W 15153	9.0	W 15851	9.2	W 16546	9.7	HUILES,GRAISSES ANIMALES
4113	ANIML OIL,FAT,GREASE NES	W 4455	2.2	W 14809	8.8	W 15586	9.0	W 16083	9.4	HUILES,GRAISSES ANIMALES NDA
41132	FATS OF BOVINE,SHEEP,ETC	W 4440	2.2	W 14792	8.8	W 15553	9.0	W 15764	9.1	SUIFS BRUTS FONDUS
42	FIXED VEGETABLE OIL,FAT		2.0		5.5		4.2		4.1	HUILES VEGETALES FIXES
5	CHEMCLS,RELATED PROD NES		224.4		292.8		318.2		334.1	PRODUITS CHIMIQUES
51	ORGANIC CHEMICALS		11.7		20.0		19.7		21.2	PROD CHIMIQ ORGANIQUES
511	HYDROCARBONS NES,DERIVS	W 6055	4.9	W 9741	9.9	W 10536	10.3	W 10988	9.9	HYDROCARBURES NDA
5112	CYCLIC HYDROCARBONS	W 5307	3.9	W 6492	5.7	W 6644	5.2	W 6434	3.9	HYDROCARBURES CYCLIQUES
52	INORGANIC CHEMICALS		14.7		19.6		21.9		21.1	PROD CHIM INORGANIQUES
522	INORG ELEMNTS,OXIDES,ETC	W 18416	6.1	W 302129	9.6	W 28064	10.1	W 46378	9.9	ELEMENTS INORGANIQUES
523	OTHR INORG CHEMICALS ETC	W 17822	8.7	W 22539	10.0	W 22620	11.8	W 23576	11.2	AUT PRODUITS CHIMIQUES INORG
5232	OTH MTL CMPD OF INRG ACD	W 9483	5.0	W 11653	5.7	W 15370	7.6	W 12109	6.6	SELS METALLIQUES
53	DYES,TANNING,COLOUR PROD		10.5		14.2		15.8		17.8	PROD TEINTURE,COLORANTS
533	PIGMENTS,PAINTS,ETC	W 3368	6.2	W 4811	9.4	W 5896	10.7	W 7552	12.5	PIGMENTS,PEINTURES,VERNIS
5334	VARNISHES,DISTEMPERS ETC	W 2543	4.0	W 3505	6.0	W 4928	7.7	W 6399	8.9	PEINTURES A L'EAU
541	*MEDICINAL,PHARM PRODUCT	K 7917774	58.6	MK 12017	74.8	K 7684276	72.5	K 4785351	76.1	PROD MEDICINAUX PHARMACEUT
5417	MEDICAMENTS	K 6989161	51.9	MK 11047	65.8	K 6083906	62.4	K 3579345	66.4	MEDICAMENTS
54171	— CONTAINNG ANTIBIOTICS			K 1613278	9.6	K 372285	8.3	K 703933	8.3	MED CONTN ANTIBIOTIQUES
54172	— CONTAINING HORMONES			K 3408420	11.1	K 824978	11.2	K 324461	9.7	MED CONTENANT HORMONES
54179	— CONTNG OTH SUBSTANCES			K 5403850	45.0	K 4877953	43.0	K 2549020	48.4	MED CONT AUT SUBSTANCES
55	PERFUME,CLEANING ETC PRD		15.2		22.9		29.7		36.8	PROD POUR PARFUM,TOILETTE

4. Special Imports C.I.F. by Commodities according to the S.I.T.C. (Rev. 2) in million U.S. Dollars
Importations Spéciales C.A.F. par Produits d'après la C.T.C.I. (Rév. 2) en millions de Dollars E.U.

SITC CTCI	COMMODITY	1994 QUANTITY QUANTITE	1994 VALUE VALEUR	1995 QUANTITY QUANTITE	1995 VALUE VALEUR	1996 QUANTITY QUANTITE	1996 VALUE VALEUR	1997 QUANTITY QUANTITE	1997 VALUE VALEUR	PRODUIT
551	ESSENTL OILS,PERFUME,ETC	W 648	3.9	W 1038	6.6	W 949	6.9	W 1637	6.9	HUILES ESSENTIELLES
553	PERFUMERY,COSMETICS,ETC	W 2073	7.3	W 3040	9.9	W 3259	12.1	W 5088	17.1	PRODUITS DE PARFUMERIE
554	SOAP,CLEANSING ETC PREPS	W 4291	4.1	W 5737	6.5	W 9287	10.8	W 11672	12.9	SAVONS,PRODUITS DETERSIFS
562	*FERTILIZERS,MANUFACTURE	W 135763	26.5	W 124782	27.9	W 158460	42.2	W 192920	42.5	ENGRAIS MANUFACTURES
5621	CHEM NITROGENOUS FERTLZR	W 55777	9.5	W 60002	12.3	W 69506	21.0	W 68362	14.9	ENGRAIS AZOTES
56216	UREA	W 35047	6.4	W 27534	7.0	W 48562	16.3	W 17926	6.3	UREE
5623	CHEM POTASSIC FERTILIZER	W 28442	5.5	W 18156	3.4	W 8028	1.7	W 26182	4.3	ENGRAIS POTASSIQUES
5629	FERTILIZERS NES	W 48854	10.6	W 45872	11.8	W 75890	17.7	W 88857	19.8	ENGRAIS NDA
56291	NIT-PHOS-POT FERTLZR NES	W 27375	5.6	W 28477	6.4	W 43681	8.1	W 62937	13.7	ENGRAIS CONT N P K
56292	NITROG-PHOS FERTILZR NES	W 19204	4.2	W 15817	4.8	W 28650	8.2	W 15150	3.8	ENGRAIS NDA CONT N P
58	PLASTIC MATERIALS ETC		41.6		60.7		60.5		62.9	MAT PLAST ARTIFICIELLES
582	PROD OF CONDENSATION ETC	W 4605	5.2	W 4895	7.4	W 5124	7.0	W 3849	6.3	PROD CONDENS,POLYCOND
583	POLYMERIZATION ETC PRODS	W 35465	33.5	W 38965	50.1	W 50134	50.5	W 46200	53.5	PROD POLYMERISATION
5831	POLYETHYLENE	W 11631	9.9	W 13715	16.9	W 18303	19.2	W 18332	20.5	POLYETHYLENE
58311	— IN PRIMARY FORMS			W 13049	15.6	W 17482	17.5	W 16239	16.1	POLYETHYLENE PRIMAIRES
5832	POLYPROPYLENE	W 4476	4.6	W 4714	7.5	W 6136	8.5	W 6588	8.4	POLYPROPYLENE
58321	— IN PRIMARY FORMS	W 4020	3.3	W 4152	5.4	W 5524	5.9	W 5322	4.2	POLYPROPYLENE PRIMAIRES
5834	POLYVINYL CHLORIDE	W 10992	9.1	W 10248	11.2	W 9141	7.4	W 8997	8.2	CHLORURE DE POLYVINYLE
58341	— IN PRIMARY FORMS			W 9982	10.4	W 7677	6.2	W 8300	7.2	SOUS FORMES PRIMAIRES
5839	OTH POLYMRZTION ETC PROD	W 6109	7.3	W 7253	10.0	W 12317	10.5	W 7994	10.7	AUT PROD POLYMER COPOLYM
59	CHEMICAL MATERIALS NES		45.0		52.1		55.0		55.1	MAT PROD CHIMIQUES NDA
591	PESTICIDES,DISINFECTANTS	W 9894	34.0	W 13295	39.5	W 12778	41.2	W 13317	37.5	DESINF,INSECT,FONG,HERB
5911	INSECTICIDES,FOR RETAIL	W 1264	5.9	W 2073	7.4	W 2586	9.6	W 2955	7.8	INSECTICIDES VENTE DET
5912	FUNGICIDES,FOR RETAIL	W 5918	17.4	W 7479	19.6	W 6119	18.3	W 5311	16.8	FONGICIDES VENTE AU DET
5913	HERBICIDES,FOR RETAIL	W 1984	8.3	W 2529	9.0	W 2821	11.1	W 2917	10.5	HERBICIDES VENTE AU DET
598	MISCEL CHEM PRODUCTS NES	W 4664	8.4	W 5352	9.4	W 5780	10.1	W 8471	13.3	PROD DIV INDUST CHIM NDA
5989	CHEM PRODUCTS,PREPS NES	W 3538	6.4	W 4572	7.4	W 4958	8.0	W 7032	10.2	PROD PREP CHIMIQUES NDA
59899	OTH CHEM PRODS,PREPS,NES	W 1893	4.4	W 2820	4.8	W 2745	3.9	W 2879	5.9	AUT PRODUITS CHIMIQUES NDA
6	BASIC MANUFACTURES		242.8		341.5		372.4		449.6	ART MANUFACTURES
62	RUBBER MANUFACTURES NES		20.5		25.3		28.6		35.3	CAOUTCHOUC MANUFACTURE
625	RUBBER TYRES, TUBES ETC	W 8208	16.8	W 10646	20.4	W 11385	22.9	W 13812	28.2	PNEUS CAOUTCHOUC VULCANISE
6252	TYRES,NEW,BUS OR LORRY	W 2908	7.6	W 3505	8.6	W 3848	9.8	W 4093	11.8	PNEUS POUR AUTOBUS,CAMIONS
6259	OTH TYRES,TYRE CASES,ETC	W 3617	4.9	W 5057	6.3	W 5375	7.3	W 7889	11.4	AUTRES PNEUS RECHAPES FLAPS
62599	TYRES NES,TYRE CASES,ETC	W 3291	4.0	W 4483	5.3	W 4867	6.2	W 7251	10.0	PNEUS,FLAPS
63	WOOD,CORK MANUFACTRS NES		1.8		2.6		5.8		6.9	OUVRAGES LIEGE ET BOIS
64	PAPER,PAPERBOARD AND MFR		62.1		97.9		97.7		105.0	PAPIERS,CARTONS & OUVRAGES
641	PAPER AND PAPERBOARD	W 81319	45.1	W 93581	73.6	W 95937	64.5	W 95187	62.2	PAPIERS ET CARTONS
6411	NEWSPRINT	W 6687	4.5	W 7582	6.2	W 7124	5.8	W 11334	8.3	PAPIER JOURNAL
6412	PRINTG,WRITING PAPER NES	W 3129	2.8	W 3948	4.8	W 5310	6.1	W 5549	6.2	PAPIERS POUR L'IMPRESSION
6413	KRAFT PAPER,PAPERBOARD	W 53132	24.3	W 52212	36.2	W 44256	24.6	W 32986	18.9	PAPIER ET CARTON KRAFT
64131	KRAFT LINER IN BULK			W 44667	29.6	W 22468	11.9	W 5971	3.6	PAP KRAFT POUR COUVERTURES
64139	KRAFT PAPER PAPERBD,NES			W 3005	2.4	W 17814	8.3	W 22962	11.6	PAPIER,CARTON KRAFT NDA
6415	PAPER,PAPERBRD,BULK,NES	W 10362	7.7	W 18664	17.5	W 13677	11.4	W 17957	12.9	PAPIERS,CARTONS ROULEAUX
64159	OTHER PAPER ETC,BULK,NES	W 8644	6.6	W 11732	11.9	W 8640	7.8	W 12961	10.3	AUT PAPIER ROULEAUX FEUILLES
6417	CORRUGATED PAPER ETC,BLK	W 2806	2.1	W 4421	3.8	W 13306	7.8	W 18592	9.8	PAPIERS,CARTONS ONDULES
642	PAPER,ETC,PRECUT,ARTS OF	W 12533	17.0	W 15954	24.3	W 21982	33.3	W 34072	42.8	PAP,CARTONS DECOUPES
6421	PAPER ETC CONTAINERS	W 9231	11.2	W 11174	15.3	W 15664	20.5	W 26006	26.6	BOITES,SACS EMBALLAGES
6428	PAPER ETC ARTICLES NES	W 1813	3.2	W 3274	5.8	W 4238	8.3	W 4613	10.1	OUVRAGES EN PATE A PAPIER
65	TEXTILE YARN,FABRICS,ETC		31.0		45.8		56.2		76.5	FILS,TISSUS,ARTICLES TEXTILE
651	TEXTILE YARN	W 1993	5.4	W 1873	6.4	W 1875	5.6	W 2026	7.6	FILS TEXTILES
652	COTTON FABRICS,WOVEN	W 2628	8.8	W 27168	10.5	W 14352	20.1	W 4088	19.0	TISSUS DE COTON
6522	WOVEN COTTON BLEACHD,ETC	W 2413	8.0	W 27105	10.1	W 13914	17.4	W 3447	15.7	TISSUS COTON BLANCHIS ETC
65224	BLCHED COTTON FABRIC NES	W 1986	6.3	W 26485	7.7	W 12927	8.6	W 2827	11.9	AUT TIS PLUS 85% COT BLANCHI
65225	BLCHD COTN BLEND FAB NES	W 405	1.6	W 598	2.4	W 955	8.6	W 579	3.8	AUT TIS MOINS 85% COT BLANCH
653	WOVN MAN-MADE FIB FABRIC	W 2333	7.2	W 3106	11.6	W 2108	8.6	W 4266	17.7	TISSUS FIBRES SYNTH,ARTIF
6534	DISC SYN BLEND FABRC NES	W 1421	4.6	W 1681	7.3	W 975	5.0	W 2143	9.8	TISSUS FIBRES SYNTH DISCONT
65341	DISC SYN FIB-COTTN FABRC			W 1320	5.5	W 735	3.7	W 1767	8.2	TISSUS FIB SYNT DIS MEL COTO
655	KNITTED,ETC FABRICS	W 349	1.4	W 701	4.6	W 1288	5.7	W 1317	8.0	ETOF BONNETERIE PIECES ETC
6552	OTHER KNIT ETC FAB NONEL	W 349	1.4	W 701	4.6	W 1288	5.7	W 1317	8.0	ETOF BON NON ELAS NON SYNT
657	SPECIAL TXTL FABRC,PRODS	W 1169	4.3	W 1721	6.5	W 1655	6.3	W 1923	7.5	TISSUS SPECIAUX
658	TEXTILE ARTICLES NES	W 853	1.8	W 1054	2.4	W 1569	4.6	W 2559	10.2	ART FACONNES MAT TEXTILES
66	NONMETAL MINERAL MFS NES		23.3		37.2		34.3		40.2	ART MIN NON METALLIQUES
662	CLAY,REFRACTORY BLDG PRD	W 8272	4.0	W 10919	5.1	W 11690	4.8	W 18572	7.7	MAT CONST REFRACTAIRES
665	GLASSWARE	W 18236	10.9	W 37484	21.0	W 31938	17.9	W 26703	16.6	OUVRAGES EN VERRE
6651	BOTTLES ETC OF GLASS	W 16656	8.7	W 35754	18.3	W 29708	14.8	W 24670	13.2	RECIPIENTS EN VERRE
66511	GLASS BOTTLES ETC NONVAC	W 16650	8.6	W 35754	18.3	W 29707	14.8	W 24668	13.2	BONBONNES,BOUTEILLES,ETC
67	IRON AND STEEL		50.1		61.3		82.1		89.5	FER ET ACIER
672	IRON,STEEL PRIMARY FORMS	W 7566	4.0	W 10843	3.0	W 14742	5.0	W 40281	12.2	LINGOTS FER,ACIER
6725	IRN,STL BLOOMS,SLABS,ETC	W 3257	1.6	W 8019	1.4	W 6510	1.7	W 36046	10.0	BLOOMS,BILLETTES FER ACIER
67251	IRN,SMPLE STL BLOOMS,ETC	W 2967	1.0	W 7846	1.2	W 6267	1.4	W 35116	9.3	BLOOMS ETC NON ACIER FIN
673	IRON,STEEL SHAPES ETC	W 54214	19.1	W 48702	20.2	W 51648	20.4	W 78608	31.2	BARRES,PROFIL FER,ACIER
6731	IRON,STEEL WIRE ROD	W 37532	12.3	W 21028	7.9	W 26303	9.3	W 32481	10.8	FIL MACHINE FER,ACIER
67311	IRON,SIMPLE STL WIRE ROD	W 33542	10.9	W 19160	7.2	W 25065	8.7	W 25625	8.5	FIL MACH AUT ACIER FIN
6732	IRON,STEEL BARS ETC	W 8009	3.4	W 16677	7.1	W 16231	7.2	W 34507	14.9	BARRES FER,ACIER
67326	IRN,OTH STL BARS HOTROLD	W 6853	2.7	W 16030	6.5	W 15228	6.0	W 32818	12.9	BARRES PLEINES FER,ACIER
6733	IRON,STEEL PROFILES ETC	W 8673	3.6	W 10996	5.4	W 9115	4.0	W 11620	5.7	PROFILES,PALPLAN FER,ACIER
674	IRN,STL UNIV,PLATE,SHEET	W 33849	19.5	W 37516	24.1	W 35335	23.5	W 47083	30.6	LARGES PLATS,TOLES
6746	IRN,STL THIN PLATE,ROLLD	W 14576	7.0	W 8451	5.1	W 9382	4.3	W 7996	3.4	TOLES LAM MOINS 3MM
67461	— OF IRON OR SIMPLE STL	W 11037	5.3	W 7623	4.6	W 8088	3.5	W 6721	2.6	TOL NON AC FIN MOINS 3 MM
6749	OTH IRN,STL PLATES,SHEET	W 13527	9.2	W 13981	11.0	W 16716	14.2	W 25308	19.7	AUTRES TOLES FER,ACIER
67491	— OF IRON OR SIMPLE STL	W 13484	9.1	W 13750	10.8	W 16435	13.9	W 24723	19.3	AUT TOLES AUTRES ACIER FIN
678	IRON,STL TUBES,PIPES,ETC	W 4142	4.0	W 8261	10.8	W 8692	30.9	W 11935	11.0	TUBES,TUYAUX EN FONTE,FER
6783	IRON,STL TUBES,PIPES NES	W 3011	2.1	W 6612	6.3	W 6421	4.5	W 9179	6.8	AUT TUBES,TUYAUX FER,ACIER
6785	IRON,STEEL TUBE FITTINGS	W 304	1.0	W 961	3.6	W 718	24.9	W 633	1.8	ACCESSOIRES DE TUYAUTERIE
68	NON-FERROUS METALS		15.1		17.3		17.2		25.7	METAUX NON FERREUX
684	ALUMINIUM	W 2669	8.4	W 2986	11.9	W 3502	12.1	W 6505	19.2	ALUMINIUM
6842	ALUMINIUM,ALLOYS WORKED	W 2667	8.4	W 2974	11.8	W 3445	12.0	W 6490	19.0	ALUMINIUM,ALLIAGES OUVRE
68421	ALUMINIUM BARS,WIRE,ETC	W 1317	3.2	W 1291	4.4	W 1996	5.0	W 4495	10.5	BARRES,PROFILES FILS ALU
68423	ALUMINIUM FOIL	W 1116	4.6	W 1214	6.4	W 1228	6.4	W 1521	7.2	FEUILLES,BANDES MINCES AL
69	METAL MANUFACTURES NES		38.0		52.8		49.5		68.8	ART MANUFACT EN METAL NDA
691	STRUCTURES AND PARTS NES	W 815	1.3	W 1703	6.1	W 947	1.8	W 2232	3.3	CONSTRUCT FER,ACIER,ALU
6911	STRUCTURES,PARTS IRN,STL	W 677	1.0	W 1589	5.6	W 754	1.1	W 2048	2.3	CONSTRUCT FER,ACIER,FONTE
692	METAL TANKS,BOXES,ETC	W 2485	8.3	W 3787	11.2	W 4018	10.7	W 5376	15.0	RECIPIENTS METALLIQUES
6924	MTL TRANSPORT BOXES ETC	W 1947	5.5	W 3099	9.0	W 3718	9.8	W 5083	14.1	FUTS,TAMBOURS,BIDONS
69242	ALUMNM TRNSPRT BOXES ETC	W 671	3.0	W 1045	5.5	W 1319	6.0	W 2529	9.5	FUTS,TAMBOURS,BIDONS ALU
695	TOOLS	W 1451	5.5	W 1975	8.2	W 1956	7.2	W 2623	10.3	OUTILS A MAIN
697	BASE MTL HOUSEHOLD EQUIP	W 1597	4.5	W 1949	4.9	W 2224	5.2	W 2177	6.2	ART MENAGE MET COMMUNS
699	BASE METAL MFRS NES	W 5645	9.8	W 5655	13.2	W 4719	14.1	W 7354	22.2	ART MANUFACTURES MET NDA
7	MACHINES,TRANSPORT EQUIP		386.4		502.8		457.8		636.3	MACHINES MATERIEL TRANSPORT
71	POWER GENERATING EQUIPMT		55.5		130.8		23.9		27.9	MACHINES GENERATRICES
713	INTRNL COMBUS PSTN ENGIN	W 1958	6.1	W 1348	7.6	W 1053	8.2	W 3340	11.0	MOTEURS EXPL COMB INT, PIECE

4. Special Imports C.I.F. by Commodities according to the S.I.T.C. (Rev. 2) in million U.S. Dollars
Importations Spéciales C.A.F. par Produits d'après la C.T.C.I. (Rév. 2) en millions de Dollars E.U.

SITC CTCI	COMMODITY	1994 QUANTITY QUANTITE	1994 VALUE VALEUR	1995 QUANTITY QUANTITE	1995 VALUE VALEUR	1996 QUANTITY QUANTITE	1996 VALUE VALEUR	1997 QUANTITY QUANTITE	1997 VALUE VALEUR	PRODUIT
716	ROTATING ELECTRIC PLANT	W 5845	45.4	W 2346	113.4	W 1248	12.0	W 1146	10.3	APP ELECTR ROTATIFS,PIECES
7161	DC MOTORS AND GENERATORS			W 949	15.7	W 242	1.1	W 175	1.0	MOTEURS COURANT CONTINU
7169	PTS NES OF ROT ELEC PLNT			W 652	93.1	W 202	6.6	W 87	3.3	PIECES MAC APP ROTATIFS
718	OTH POWER GENERATG MACHY	W 72	0.5	W 86	6.3	W 79	0.4	W 33	0.4	AUTRES MOTEURS PARTIES
7188	WIND,WATER,ETC ENGINES	W 70	0.5	W 86	6.3	W 79	0.4	W 33	0.4	MOT MACHINES MOTRICES NDA
71882	OTH HYDRAULIC ENGNS,MTRS	W 4	0.1	W 64	5.6	W 6	0.1	W 13	0.2	MACH MOTRICES HYDRAULQUES
72	MACHS FOR SPCL INDUSTRYS		44.3		57.5		59.0		127.4	MAC SPECIALES POUR INDUST
721	AGRIC MACHY,EXC TRACTORS	W 1573	6.3	W 1930	7.9	W 1724	8.3	W 3557	15.9	MACHINES AGRICOLES
7219	AGRICULTURE MACHINES NES	W 446	2.4	W 732	3.3	W 663	2.2	W 2146	8.8	ENGINS AGRICOLES NDA
72197	OTH AGRIC ETC MACHINERY			W 401	1.8	W 367	1.4	W 1833	8.2	AUT APP POUR AGRICULTURE
722	TRACTORS NON–ROAD	W 1373	5.1	W 1261	4.6	W 1996	5.0	W 5055	25.2	TRACTEURS
7224	WHEELED TRACTORS NES			W 1157	4.4	W 1863	4.6	W 4349	23.2	TRACTEURS A ROUES
723	CIVIL ENGNEERG EQUIP ETC	W 1446	5.5	W 1791	7.3	W 2357	11.1	W 4529	21.3	APPAREILS DE GENIE CIVIL
7234	CONST,MINING MACHNRY NES	W 1318	4.8	W 1509	5.8	W 2126	9.7	W 4247	19.8	MACH POUR LA CONST, MINES
72341	SELF–PROPELLD DOZERS,ETC			W 499	1.6	W 585	2.9	W 1669	8.5	BULLDOZERS
72342	SLFPRP SHOVELS,EXCAVATRS			W 779	3.1	W 1212	5.5	W 1732	7.4	PELLES MECANIQUES
724	TEXTILE,LEATHER MACHNRY	W 1756	10.0	W 1430	11.4	W 1724	10.6	W 1854	15.5	MACH POUR INDUSTRIE TEXTILE
7243	SEWING MACHS,NEEDLES ETC	W 862	3.9	W 891	5.7	W 1231	6.4	W 1136	7.4	MACHINES A COUDRE,PIECES
727	FOOD MACHRY NON–DOMESTIC	W 671	4.6	W 1164	7.6	W 960	6.9	W 1303	12.8	MACH INDUSTRIES ALIMENT
7272	OTH FOOD PROC MCHY,PARTS	W 602	3.9	W 1119	6.9	W 872	6.2	W 1255	12.2	AUT MACH IND ALIMENTAIRE
72722	INDUS FOOD PROC MACH NES	W 292	1.7	W 1106	6.4	W 610	3.3	W 1028	7.9	MACHINES BOULANGERIE
728	OTH MACHY FOR SPCL INDUS	W 1224	8.5	W 3680	14.2	W 1807	11.5	W 3844	31.4	AUT MACH IND PARTICULIERES
7284	MACHY FOR SPCL INDUS NES	W 368	3.7	W 521	6.2	W 689	5.5	W 1383	19.9	MACH SPEC IND PARTICUL.
72848	OTH MCHY WITH INDIV FNCT	W 88	0.7	W 140	1.2	W 108	0.7	W 789	12.5	AUTRES MACHINES NDA
74	GENRL INDUSTRL MACHY NES		55.2		70.8		67.8		87.4	MACH APP INDUSTRIE
741	HEATING,COOLING EQUIPMNT	W 1674	9.0	W 3267	17.5	W 2355	14.5	W 3124	19.9	MACH CHAUFFAGE,PIECES
7414	NONDOM REFRIG EQUIPT,PTS	W 540	2.6	W 1573	10.7	W 870	7.6	W 1017	6.3	MAT PRODUCTION DU FROID
74141	REFRIG EQUIP NONDOMESTIC			W 1335	9.5	W 667	6.3	W 711	4.1	REFIG INDUSTRIELS
742	PUMPS FOR LIQUIDS ETC	W 779	6.2	W 2195	8.4	W 1900	9.7	W 1067	10.4	POMPES MOTO–POMPES
7428	OTHER PUMPS FOR LIQUIDS			W 1926	6.0	W 1650	6.6	W 853	7.6	AUTRES POMPES POUR LIQ
743	PUMPS NES,CENTRFUGES ETC	W 1335	6.2	W 1477	9.9	W 1654	9.9	W 1932	10.5	POMPES COMPRES,VENT ETC
744	MECHANICAL HANDLING EQU	W 2100	15.5	W 1354	6.9	W 1911	10.5	W 2679	15.6	EQUIP MANUTENTION PIECES
7442	LIFTING,LOADING MACH NES	W 1310	10.3	W 600	2.1	W 1057	4.4	W 1571	6.8	APP LEVAGE,MANUTENTION
745	NONELEC MACHY,TOOLS NES	W 1040	8.7	W 1854	17.2	W 1364	11.5	W 1321	15.6	AUT MACH NON ELEC,PIECES
7452	OTH NONELEC MCHS,PTS NES	W 1005	7.8	W 1776	16.0	W 1240	10.5	W 1242	14.3	AUT MACH NON ELEC,PIECES
74522	PACKAGNG,BOTTLNG,ETC MCH	W 113	1.9	W 754	9.1	W 376	3.0	W 262	4.9	MACH NETT BOUTEILLES,ETC
749	NONELEC MACH PTS,ACC NES	W 1301	9.9	W 1287	11.1	W 1449	11.9	W 2308	15.6	PIECES MACH NON ELEC NDA
75	OFFICE MACHNES,ADP EQUIP		21.9		26.7		40.3		47.5	MACH BUREAU TRAIT AUTOM
752	AUTOMTIC DATA PROC EQUIP	W 326	11.0	W 575	14.8	W 618	24.0	W 1071	29.0	MACH TRAIT INFORMATION
7521	ANALOG,HYBRID COMPUTERS			W 193	8.3	W 210	12.4	W 277	9.4	MACH POUR TRAIT INFORMAT
759	OFFICE,ADP MCH PTS,ACCES	W 281	8.3	W 331	8.1	W 373	11.5	W 654	12.1	PIECES DU 751 ET 752
7599	ACCTG,ETC,ADP MCH PTS,AC	W 246	7.5	W 241	6.8	W 272	9.8	W 575	10.5	PIECES DU 751 ET 752
76	TELECOMM,SOUND EQUIPMENT		38.2		23.7		45.5		50.8	EQUIPMENT DE TELECOM
761	TELEVISION RECEIVERS	W 280	1.2	W 915	4.3	W 1167	6.1	W 2231	13.2	RECEPTEURS DE TELEVISION
7611	COLOUR TV RECEIVERS			W 760	3.9	W 1039	5.8	W 2049	12.8	RECEPTEURS COULEUR
764	TELECOM EQPT,PTS,ACC NES	W 844	34.8	W 745	14.2	W 1116	34.1	W 1067	27.1	EQUIP TELECOM,PIECES
7641	LINE TELEPHONE,ETC EQUIP	W 206	14.1	W 263	4.2	W 257	7.5	W 400	4.7	APP TELEPHON PAR FIL
7643	TV,RADIO TRANSMITTRS ETC	W 47	1.5	W 81	2.7	W 126	8.4	W 125	13.7	APP EMET TELE RADIO
7648	TELECOMM EQUIPMENT NES	W 47	6.8	W 20	0.5	W 16	0.8	W 14	1.4	APP TELECOM NDA
7649	PTS NES OF EQUIPMT OF 76	W 505	12.3	W 268	6.3	W 604	16.8	W 344	6.5	PIECES DE LA DIV 76
76491	PTS NES OF APPAR OF 7641	W 428	10.7	W 101	2.9	W 359	12.4	W 66	2.4	PIECES POUR 764.1
77	ELECTRIC MACHNRY NES ETC		42.4		55.4		66.0		79.7	MACH APP ELECT NDA
771	ELECTRIC POWER MACHY NES	W 1006	3.3	W 1332	7.5	W 4000	12.7	W 1865	5.8	MACH PROD,TRANS ELECTR
7711	TRANSFORMERS,ELECTRICAL	W 703	2.2	W 1014	6.0	W 3649	10.9	W 1399	4.1	TRANSFO ELECTRIQUES
77111	LIQUID DIELEC TRANSFRMRS	W 308	1.0	W 155	0.7	W 2554	8.3	W 415	1.6	TRANSFO DIELEC LIQUIDE
77118	OTHER ELEC TRANSFORMERS	W 395	1.3	W 859	5.4	W 1096	2.7	W 984	2.5	AUTRES TRANSFO ELECTRIQ
772	SWITCHGEAR ETC,PARTS NES	W 815	6.7	W 987	7.7	W 843	5.7	W 1374	8.5	APP COUPURE,SECT ETC
7721	SWITCHGEAR ETC	W 807	6.6	W 964	7.5	W 828	5.6	W 1367	8.4	APP COUPURE,SECTIONMNT
773	ELECTR DISTRIBUTNG EQUIP	W 2092	9.4	W 1385	5.3	W 2752	9.3	W 2639	10.8	EQUIPMT DISTRIBUTION ELECT
7731	INSULATED WIRE,CABLE ETC	W 1626	8.5	W 1133	4.5	W 2441	8.8	W 2400	10.2	FILS,CABLES ISOLES ELECT
775	HOUSEHOLD TYPE EQUIP NES	W 3617	10.7	W 5513	18.7	W 6218	21.4	W 8605	29.3	MACH,APP USAGE DOMESTQUE
7752	DOM REFRIGERATRS,FREEZRS	W 1971	6.0	W 3355	12.3	W 3653	13.5	W 4390	15.9	REFRIG,CONGEL MENAGER
77521	DOMESTIC REFRIGERATORS	W 1499	4.2	W 2066	6.3	W 2330	7.5	W 3214	10.9	REFRIGERATEURS
77522	DOMESTIC DEEP–FREEZERS	W 472	1.8	W 1289	6.1	W 1322	6.0	W 1176	5.0	MEUBLES CONGELATEURS
778	ELECTRICAL MACHINERY NES	W 3081	10.5	W 3673	14.9	W 3849	14.6	W 4381	18.8	AUTRES MACH ELECT NDA
78	ROAD VEHICLES		120.0		132.5		150.0		208.3	VEHICULES ROUTIERS
781	PASS MOTOR VEH EXC BUSES	W 7386	31.7	W 4343	22.5	W 6606	27.7	W 8164	37.8	AUTO TRANSPORT PERSONNES
782	LORRIES,SPCL MTR VEH NES	W 15449	50.5	W 17490	64.6	W 22742	81.2	W 38480	118.3	VEHICULES SPECIAUX,MARCH
7821	LORRIES,TRUCKS	W 14745	48.9	W 16118	59.9	W 21940	75.1	W 37302	115.2	VEHICULES TRANSP MARCHAND
7822	SPECIAL MOTOR VEHCLS NES	W 704	1.7	W 1372	4.8	W 802	6.1	W 1177	3.1	VEHICULES USAGES SPECIAUX
783	ROAD MOTOR VEHICLES NES	W 4310	14.4	W 5042	17.6	W 5068	14.1	W 5542	18.0	VEHICULES ROUTIERS NDA
7831	BUSES	W 3193	13.4	W 3630	14.6	W 2878	8.2	W 4624	13.7	VOITURES TRANSPORT COMMUN
7832	TRACTORS FOR TR–TRAILERS	W 1116	1.1	W 1412	3.0	W 2191	6.0	W 918	4.4	TRACTEURS ROUTIERS
784	MOTOR VEH PRTS,ACCES NES	W 2640	15.3	W 4220	18.2	W 4414	16.7	W 3371	19.2	PIECES 722,781,782,783
7849	OTHER MOTOR VEHCL PARTS	W 2346	14.6	W 4093	17.9	W 4274	16.5	W 3139	19.0	PIECES 722,781,782,783
785	CYCLES,ETC MOTRZD OR NOT	W 2786	7.0	W 9200	7.8	W 2324	7.9	W 3361	10.7	MOTOCYCLES SCOOTERS
79	OTHR TRANSPORT EQUIPMENT		6.7		1.8		1.8		2.4	AUTRE MATERIEL TRANSPORT
793	SHIPS AND BOATS ETC	W 1462	5.6	W 117	0.6	W 95	0.6	W 181	0.8	NAVIRES BATEAUX,ETC
8	MISC MANUFACTURED GOODS		98.2		150.3		187.7		260.0	ART MANUFACTURES DIVERS
812	*PLUMBG,HEATNG,LGHTNG EQ	W 2253	3.9	W 3127	6.2	W 2721	5.1	W 3190	6.8	APPAR SANITAIRES CHAUFFAGE
821	*FURNITURE,PARTS THEREOF	W 1158	3.3	W 7692	5.8	W 8082	7.9	W 4997	15.7	MEUBLES ET PIECES
8219	FURNITURE AND PARTS NES	W 845	2.4	W 7050	4.0	W 7433	6.4	W 3683	9.9	AUTRES MEUBLES ET PIECES
84	CLOTHING AND ACCESSORIES		37.6		61.7		88.3		103.8	VETEMENTS
842	MENS OUTERWEAR NOT KNIT	W 166	1.4	W 898	5.2	W 608	5.1	W 1230	8.9	VET DESSUS POUR HOMMES
8423	— TROUSERS,BREECHES ETC			W 750	4.7	W 517	4.4	W 959	7.4	PANTALONS HOMMES MAT TEX
843	WOMENS OUTERWEAR NONKNIT	W 332	2.8	W 1125	5.2	W 1523	8.9	W 1577	9.7	VET DESSUS FEMMES MAT TEX
8439	— OTHER OUTER GARMENTS			W 747	3.4	W 1094	5.9	W 1166	7.2	AUT VET DES FEM MAT TEXT
844	UNDER GARMENTS NOT KNIT	W 1265	7.8	W 2786	21.7	W 3942	34.8	W 4079	31.9	VETEMENT DESSOUS MAT TEX
8441	— MENS SHIRTS	W 1205	7.6	W 2665	20.9	W 3819	33.9	W 3910	30.6	CHEMISES HOMMES MAT TEXT
84411	—— OF COTTON	W 145	1.2	W 1311	9.8	W 2211	20.1	W 3047	20.6	CHEMISES HOMMES DE COTON
84412	—— OF SYNTHETIC FIBRES	W 1061	6.5	W 1354	11.1	W 1609	13.9	W 863	10.0	CHEMISES HOMMES FIB SYNT
845	OUTERWEAR KNIT NONELASTC	W 1187	10.2	W 1409	11.7	W 584	4.8	W 861	6.7	VET DESSOUS,ACCES BONNET
8459	— OTHER,CLTHG ACCESRYS			W 1227	11.0	W 499	4.2	W 697	5.4	AUT VET DESSUS DE BONNE
846	UNDER GARMENTS KNITTED		5.7	W 1628	11.1	W 5912	32.8	W 7275	43.5	SOUS VETS DE BONNETERIE
8462	— OF COTTON NON ELASTIC		5.1	W 685	5.0	W 1027	8.0	W 1234	9.4	SOUS–VET BONNET COTON
84621	—— MENS SHIRTS	W 386	4.1							CHEMISES DE COTON
84629	—— OTHER		1.1	W 685	5.0	W 1027	8.0	W 1234	9.4	AUT SOUS–VET BONNET COTON
8463	— OF SYNTH FBR NONELAST	W 66	0.5	W 833	5.8	W 4820	24.4	W 5905	33.4	SOUS–VET BONNET FIB SYNT
84632	—— MENS SHIRTS	W 28	0.2	W 760	5.4	W 4741	24.0	W 5647	32.2	CHEMISES DE BON FIB SYNMT
847	TEXTILE CLTHNG ACCES NES	W 918	8.8	W 721	5.7	W 266	1.0	W 359	1.8	ACCES VET MAT TEXT NDA
8471	— NOT KNITTED	W 844	8.2	W 582	5.3	W 81	0.4	W 125	0.7	ACCES VET MAT TEX NON BON

4. Special Imports C.I.F. by Commodities according to the S.I.T.C. (Rev. 2) in million U.S. Dollars
Importations Spéciales C.A.F. par Produits d'après la C.T.C.I. (Rév. 2) en millions de Dollars E.U.

SITC CTCI	COMMODITY	1994			1995			1996			1997			PRODUIT
		QUANTITY QUANTITE		VALUE VALEUR	QUANTITY QUANTITE		VALUE VALEUR	QUANTITY QUANTITE		VALUE VALEUR	QUANTITY QUANTITE		VALUE VALEUR	
84713	TIES,CRAVATS ETC,NOT KNT	W	824	8.1	W	530	4.9	W	2	0.1	W	9	0.1	CRAVATES MAT TEX NON BON
851	*FOOTWEAR	W	605	2.2	W	1456	4.4	W	1433	5.6	W	2439	12.8	CHAUSSURES
85102	FOOTWEAR LEATHER	W	418	1.4	W	804	2.6	W	814	3.2	W	1618	8.0	CHAUS SEMELLES EN CUIR
87	PRECISION INSTRUMNTS NES			7.3			9.0			10.6			18.7	INSTRUM,APPAR SCIENT NDA
872	MEDICAL INSTRUMENTS NES	W	293	2.0	W	274	2.3	W	598	3.5	W	429	8.0	INSTR,APP MEDIC–CHIR NDA
874	MEASURNG,CONTROLNG INSTR	W	320	3.3	W	472	4.7	W	601	6.0	W	611	6.5	INSTRUMENTS DE MESURE
88	PHOTO EQU,OPTICL GDS ETC			4.8			5.7			6.6			11.3	APP,FOURN PHOTO,OP,MONTR
89	MISC MANUFCTRD GOODS NES			38.7			56.3			62.6			88.6	ART MANUFACTURES DIVERS
892	PRINTED MATTER	W	1465	6.5	W	2051	8.6	W	1767	10.1	W	2837	13.4	IMPRIMES
893	ARTICLES OF PLASTIC NES			18.0			27.3			30.6			39.0	OUVRAGES EN MAT DIVIS 58
8931	PLSTC PACKG CONTNRS,LIDS	W	3019	8.9	W	4404	13.9	W	5033	14.3	W	4598	15.8	ART TRANSP EMBALLAGE ETC
8939	MISC PLASTIC ARTICLES	W	2915	8.7	W	12553	13.0	W	4578	15.7	W	7495	22.3	ART DIVERS EN MAT DIV 58
89399	OTHR PLASTC ARTICLES NES	W	2696	8.1	W	12002	11.6	W	4354	14.8	W	7249	21.6	AUT OUV MAT DIV 58
894	TOYS,SPORTING GOODS,ETC	W	1810	5.0	W	2146	7.5	W	2401	7.8	W	3820	14.8	VOITURES ENFANTS,JOUETS
8942	TOYS,INDOOR GAMES ETC	W	1182	3.7	W	1656	6.0	W	1716	6.3	W	3035	11.4	JOUETS,JEUX ETC
895	OFFICE SUPPLIES NES	W	530	3.5	W	879	5.5	W	24045	5.0	W	1321	7.3	ART PAPET NDA
899	OTHER MANUFACTURED GOODS			3.4			4.4			5.2			7.8	AUT ART MANUF DIVERS NDA

5. Special Exports F.O.B. by Commodities according to the S.I.T.C. (Rev. 2) in million U.S. Dollars
Exportations Spéciales F.O.B. par Produits d'après la C.T.C.I. (Rév. 2) en millions de Dollars E.U.

SITC CTCI	COMMODITY	1994 QUANTITY QUANTITE	1994 VALUE VALEUR	1995 QUANTITY QUANTITE	1995 VALUE VALEUR	1996 QUANTITY QUANTITE	1996 VALUE VALEUR	1997 QUANTITY QUANTITE	1997 VALUE VALEUR	PRODUIT
	ALL COMMODITIES		614.1		656.1		846.0		1033.3	TOUS PRODUITS
0	FOOD AND LIVE ANIMALS		473.2		561.2		524.6		627.5	ALIMENTS,ANIMAUX VIVANTS
01	MEAT AND PREPARATIONS		39.5		14.3		11.3		5.5	VIANDES ET PREPARATIONS
011	MEAT FRESH,CHILLD,FROZEN	W 17004	39.5	W 6391	14.3	W 5982	11.1	W 3058	5.5	VIANDES FRAICHES,REF,CONGE
0111	BOVINE MEAT FRESH,FROZEN	W 16087	37.8	W 5925	13.2	W 5776	10.7	W 2956	5.3	VIANDES BOVIN FRAI,REF
01112	BOVINE MEAT BONELESS			W 5925	13.2	W 5571	10.4	W 1708	3.2	VIANDES BOVIN DESOSSEES
03	FISH AND PREPARATIONS		74.9		37.8		63.3		77.6	POISSONS ET PREPARATIONS
034	FISH,FRESH,CHILLED,FROZN	W 858	1.7	W 930	1.9	W 1553	5.9	W 922	2.2	POISSON FRAIS, REFRIG,CONG
0344	FISH FILLETS,FROZEN					W 652	3.6	W 7	0.1	FILETS CONGELES
036	SHELL FISH FRESH,FROZEN	W 11851	73.2	W 5741	35.9	W 9227	57.5	W 11077	75.4	CRUSTACES,MOLLUSQUES
05	VEGETABLES AND FRUIT		153.8		158.5		196.6		196.9	LEGUMES ET FRUITS
054	VEG ETC FRSH,SMPLY PRSVD		3.7	W 23604	4.3	W 23813	4.7	W 22763	5.2	LEGUMES FRAIS,CONG,SECS
0545	OTHER FRESH VEGETABLES	W 2876	0.7	W 10000	2.1	W 15317	3.2	W 6191	1.9	AUTRES LEGUMES FRAIS,REF
05459	FRESH VEGETABLES NES	W 2517	0.7	W 9965	2.1	W 15315	3.2	W 5210	1.4	LEGUMES FRAIS,REFRI NDA
0546	VEGETABLES SIMPLY PRESVD		2.6	W 4784	1.0	W 2222	0.8	W 3716	1.0	LEGUMES CONG,CONSER
05462	VEG PRSVD UNFRZN UNTINND	W 13525	2.4	W 4646	0.9	W 1563	0.3	W 3250	0.7	LEGUMES CONSER PROVISOIR
057	FRUIT,NUTS,FRESH,DRIED	W 640042	145.4	W 683231	150.3	W 806800	175.0	W 736223	176.5	FRUITS FRAIS OU SECS
0572	LEMONS,GRAPEFRUIT ETC	W 6752	1.8	W 10148	2.1	W 15497	3.3	W 3692	0.8	AUTRES AGRUMES FRAIS,SECS
05722	GRAPEFRUITS,FRESH,DRIED			W 9817	2.1	W 15404	3.1	W 3381	0.7	PAMPLEMOUSSES,POMELOS
0573	BANANA,PLANTAIN,FRSH,DRY	W 475274	112.4	W 530893	121.0	W 575315	137.9	W 578287	144.4	BANANES FRAICHES,SECHEES
0577	NUTS EDIBLE,FRESH,DRIED	W 1663	0.4	W 700	0.4	W 36640	8.5	W 4745	1.1	FRUITS A COQUES
05773	CASHEW NUTS,FRESH,DRIED	W 752	0.3	W 15	0.1	W 36026	8.3	W 15	0.1	NOIX DE CAJOU
0579	FRUIT FRESH OR DRIED NES	W 141981	30.5	W 124221	26.1	W 176292	25.5	W 143021	29.9	FRUITS FRAIS,SECS NDA
05793	STONE FRUIT FRESH NES							W 69612	12.1	FRUITS A NOYAU NDA FRAIS
05795	PINEAPPLES,FRESH,DRIED	W 42915	9.5	W 44228	11.8	W 30636	8.8	W 22949	5.7	ANANAS FRAIS OU SECS
05798	OTHER FRESH FRUIT	W 98470	20.9	W 79691	14.3	W 143871	16.1	W 48712	11.7	AUTRES FRUITS FRAIS
058	FRUIT PRESERVED,PREPARED	W 7262	4.3	W 6903	4.0	W 20499	16.6	W 18510	15.2	CONSERVES DE FRUITS
0583	FRUIT JAMS,JELLIES ETC	W 2800	1.3	W 2632	1.1	W 12704	5.7	W 15054	11.3	PATES DE FRUITS CONFITURES
0585	FRUIT OR VEGETABLE JUICE	W 2825	1.9	W 3296	2.1	W 6284	9.7	W 658	1.1	JUS DE FRUITS
05851	ORANGE JUICE	W 2121	1.4	W 3030	2.0	W 5262	6.2	W 419	0.8	JUS D'ORANGE
05854	PINEAPPLE JUICE	W 101	0.1	W 20	0.1	W 734	3.4	W 139	0.3	JUS D'ANANAS
06	SUGAR AND PREPS,HONEY		6.5		8.5		8.7		16.1	SUCRES ET PRODUITS
061	SUGAR AND HONEY	W 28431	6.1	W 34473	7.8	W 14066	8.0	W 54006	14.8	SUCRES ET MIEL
0611	RAW BEET AND CANE SUGAR	W 8978	3.7	W 11529	5.2	W 5031	3.6	W 2249	0.9	SUCRES BRUTS
0612	REFINED SUGAR ETC	W 1465	0.7					W 31760	12.3	SUCRES RAFFINES
0615	MOLASSES	W 17989	1.8	W 22944	2.6	W 9015	4.4	W 19993	1.7	MELASSES
07	COFFEE,TEA,COCOA,SPICES		194.9		337.6		239.9		328.1	CAFE,THE,CACAO,EPICES
071	COFFEE AND SUBSTITUTES	W 102657	192.2	W 106557	335.7	W 114768	237.7	W 110319	322.1	CAFE ET SUCCEDANES
0711	COFFEE GREEN,ROASTED,SUB	W 102654	192.2	W 106557	335.7	W 114768	237.7	W 110319	322.1	CAFE TORREFIE OU DECAFEINE
07111	COFFEE GREEN,HUSKS,SKINS			W 106557	335.7	W 114767	237.7	W 98953	289.6	CAFE NON TORREFIE
07113	COFFEE SUBST CONT COFFEE							W 11361	32.6	SUCCEDANES DU CAFE
072	COCOA	W 1306	1.4	W 1127	1.3	W 874	1.1	W 1952	4.0	CACAO
1	BEVERAGES AND TOBACCO		10.0		3.4		18.7		44.5	BOISSONS ET TABACS
12	TOBACCO AND MANUFACTURES		9.8		3.2		18.1		43.3	TABACS BRUTS FABRIQUES
121	TOBACCO UNMNFCTRD,REFUSE	W 1374	2.9	W 590	1.2	W 960	1.8	W 2001	5.3	TABACS BRUTS,DECHETS
1211	TOBACCO,NOT STRIPPED	W 1341	2.9	W 575	1.2	W 904	1.8	W 1790	5.1	TABACS NON ECOTES
122	TOBACCO,MANUFACTURED	W 1998	6.9	W 594	2.0	W 3113	16.3	W 5104	38.1	TABACS FABRIQUES
1221	CIGARS,CHEROOTS,ETC	W 1711	6.4	W 457	2.0	W 2652	15.8	W 2606	18.3	CIGARES
1222	CIGARETTES	W 31	0.2	W 1	0.1	W 8	0.2	W 2142	19.6	CIGARETTES
2	CRUDE MATERLS,EXCL FUELS		35.2		26.1		40.9		62.0	MAT BRUTES NON COMESTIBLES
24	CORK AND WOOD		22.5		17.8		20.5		18.0	LIEGE ET BOIS
247	OTH WOOD ROUGH,SQUARED	W 48845	12.6	W 47156	13.0	W 22255	14.7	W 26584	15.2	BOIS BRUTS EQUARRIS
2471	SAW–,VENEER–LOGS CONIFER	W 48160	12.4	W 44977	12.2	W 22023	14.7	W 4440	1.4	CONIFERES POUR SCIAGE,PLACAG
24711	— IN THE ROUGH	W 48160	12.4	W 44977	12.2	W 22023	14.7	W 4440	1.4	ECORCES OU DEGROSSIS
2472	SAW–,VENEER–LOGS NON–CON	W 685	0.2	W 2179	0.9	W 232	0.1	W 22144	13.9	NON CONIFERES SCIAGE,PLAC
24721	— IN THE ROUGH	W 685	0.2	W 2179	0.9	W 232	0.1	W 22144	13.9	BRUTS ECORCES DEGROSSIS
248	WOOD SHAPED,SLEEPERS	W 31181	9.7	W 14574	4.6	W 10438	5.5	W 4160	2.1	BOIS SIMPLEMENT TRAVAILLES
2482	LUMBER SHAPED CONIFER	W 28441	9.0	W 13681	4.4	W 9291	5.1	W 3877	2.0	CONIFERES SCIES,RABOTES
24821	LUMBER SAWN ETC CONIFER	W 26556	8.5	W 13030	4.2	W 3403	3.5	W 3437	1.5	CONIFERES SCIES LONGITUD
26	TEXTILE FIBRES AND WASTE		0.1		0.3		1.4		7.4	FIBRES TEXTILES
261	SILK	W 4	0.1					W 1	5.1	SOIE
2614	SILK WORM COCOONS,WASTE	W 4	0.1					W 1	5.1	COCONS ET DECHETS
26141	SILK WORM COCOONS							W 1	5.1	COCONS DE VER A SOIE
28	METALLIFEROUS ORES,SCRAP		6.4		2.3		13.9		30.6	MINERAIS METAL,DECHETS
287	BASE METAL ORES,CONC NES		4.6	W 183	0.1	W 21382	10.7	W 15289	16.3	MINERAIS METAUX COMMUNS
2874	LEAD ORES,CONCENTRATES					W 2037	1.7	W 1733	9.5	MINERAIS DE PLOMB
2875	ZINC ORES,CONCENTRATES		4.3	W 163	0.1	W 19301	9.0	W 13544	6.8	MINERAIS DE ZINC
288	NONFERR METAL SCRAP NES	W 793	0.2	W 1219	2.2	W 1702	0.9	W 2228	1.4	DECHETS NON FERREUX
2882	OTHER BASE MTL SCRAP NES	W 793	0.2	W 1159	2.2	W 1702	0.9	W 2228	1.4	AUTRES DECHETS
289	PREC MTAL ORES,WASTE NES	K 23194	1.5			K 2592390	2.4	MK 27137	12.9	MINERAIS,DECHETS MET PREC
.28901	PRECIOUS METAL ORES,CONC	K 23194	1.5			K 2592390	2.4	MK 27137	12.9	MINERAIS METAUX PRECIEUX
29	CRUDE ANIMAL,VEG MAT NES		3.0		2.2		2.6		3.7	MATIERES BRUTES ANIM,VEGET
292	CRUDE VEG MATERIALS NES	W 3574	2.8	W 2011	2.1	W 2653	2.5	W 5390	3.6	MAT BRUTES VEGETALES NDA
4	ANIMAL,VEGETABLE OIL,FAT		6.7		3.7		2.2		2.0	HUILES,GRAISSES ANIM,VEG
42	FIXED VEGETABLE OIL,FAT		6.2		3.3		1.9		1.9	HUILES VEGETALES FIXES
424	FIXED VEG OIL NONSOFT	W 9724	4.7	W 4271	3.2	W 2561	1.7	W 222	0.2	AUTRES HUILES VEG FIXES
4242	PALM OIL	W 8686	4.4	W 4075	3.1	W 2223	1.5	W 194	0.1	HUILE DE PALME
5	CHEMCLS,RELATED PROD NES		13.4		11.0		13.5		15.5	PRODUITS CHIMIQUES
55	PERFUME,CLEANING ETC PRD		4.0		4.7		7.8		5.9	PROD POUR PARFUM,TOILETTE
554	SOAP,CLEANSING ETC PREPS	W 5472	3.9	W 6529	4.5	W 10592	7.4	W 5360	5.6	SAVONS,PRODUITS DETERSIFS
5541	SOAPS	W 4400	2.7	W 5197	3.3	W 9340	6.3	W 3706	3.3	SAVONS,PROD TENSIO–ACTIFS
562	*FERTILIZERS,MANUFACTURE	W 14920	2.9	W 3791	1.0	W 2425	0.7	W 654	0.4	ENGRAIS MANUFACTURES
5623	CHEM POTASSIC FERTILIZER	W 9490	2.1	W 2063	0.6	W 529	0.2			ENGRAIS POTASSIQUES
56239	CHEM POTASS FERTILZR NES	W 9490	2.1	W 2063	0.6	W 529	0.2			ENGRAIS POTASSIQUES NDA
59	CHEMICAL MATERIALS NES		4.1		2.0		2.9		3.9	MAT PROD CHIMIQUES NDA
598	MISCEL CHEM PRODUCTS NES	W 4413	2.5	W 2329	1.5	W 3323	2.6	W 4489	3.7	PROD DIV INDUST CHIM NDA
5981	CHEMCLS FROM WOOD,RESIN	W 4169	2.4	W 2096	1.4	W 3159	2.5	W 4456	3.5	PROD CHIM BASE BOIS RESIN
59814	ROSIN,RESIN ACIDS,ETC	W 3731	2.1	W 1925	1.2	W 2724	2.1	W 3830	3.0	COLOPHANES RESINIQUES
6	BASIC MANUFACTURES		37.9		28.9		36.0		41.1	ART MANUFACTURES
63	WOOD,CORK MANUFACTRS NES		16.1		12.3		13.3		20.2	OUVRAGES LIEGE ET BOIS
634	VENEERS,PLYWOOD,ETC	W 26234	5.5	W 17751	4.1	W 20278	4.7	W 26686	6.8	PLACAGES,CONTRE–PLAQUES
6349	WOOD SIMPLY SHAPED NES	W 23618	4.0	W 15685	2.8	W 17347	3.2	W 20512	4.4	BOIS SIMPL TRAVAILLES NDA
63491	HOOPWOOD,SPLIT POLES ETC	W 23618	4.0	W 15685	2.8	W 17345	3.2	W 20479	4.3	BOIS ETC
635	WOOD MANUFACTURES NES	W 25972	10.6	W 18524	8.2	W 17910	8.7	W 35445	13.4	ART MANUF EN BOIS NDA
6359	OTHER WOOD MANUFACTURES	W 23227	8.7	W 15350	6.1	W 14614	7.2	W 21684	10.4	OUVRAGES EN BOIS NDA
63591	TOOLS,HANDLES ETC WOOD	W 12734	3.8	W 9138	2.9	W 5571	2.3	W 14299	6.3	OUTILS MANCHES D'OUTILS
63599	OTHER WOOD ARTICLES NES	W 10493	4.9	W 6212	3.2	W 9043	4.9	W 7385	4.1	AUTRES OUVRAGES EN BOIS NDA
64	PAPER,PAPERBOARD AND MFR		9.6		6.4		7.2		7.8	PAPIERS,CARTONS & OUVRAGES
642	PAPER,ETC,PRECUT,ARTS OF	W 14234	8.6	W 7976	5.4	W 10250	6.5	W 11128	7.3	PAP,CARTONS DECOUPES
6421	PAPER ETC CONTAINERS	W 13478	7.8	W 7122	4.7	W 8835	5.5	W 10617	6.8	BOITES,SACS EMBALLAGES
65	TEXTILE YARN,FABRICS,ETC		4.9		3.9		8.1		5.2	FILS,TISSUS,ARTICLES TEXTILE

5. Special Exports F.O.B. by Commodities according to the S.I.T.C. (Rev. 2) in million U.S. Dollars
Exportations Spéciales F.O.B. par Produits d'après la C.T.C.I. (Rév. 2) en millions de Dollars E.U.

SITC CTCI	COMMODITY	1994		1995		1996		1997		PRODUIT
		QUANTITY QUANTITE	VALUE VALEUR	QUANTITY QUANTITE	VALUE VALEUR	QUANTITY QUANTITE	VALUE VALEUR	QUANTITY QUANTITE	VALUE VALEUR	
67	IRON AND STEEL		1.9		1.0		1.7		1.8	FER ET ACIER
69	METAL MANUFACTURES NES		3.4		2.6		3.4		2.7	ART MANUFACT EN METAL NDA
7	MACHINES,TRANSPORT EQUIP		3.2		4.6		28.0		19.8	MACHINES MATERIEL TRANSPORT
71	POWER GENERATING EQUIPMT		0.1		0.5		9.6		0.5	MACHINES GENERATRICES
716	ROTATING ELECTRIC PLANT	W 6	0.1	W 64	0.5	W 895	9.3	W 113	0.4	APP ELECTR ROTATIFS,PIECES
7162	AC MTRS,GENRTRS,GEN SETS			W 55	0.4	W 754	9.0	W 99	0.3	MOTEURS ELECTRIQUES
71621	AC MTRS,INC UNIVRSL MTRS			W 12	0.1	W 437	5.0	W 30	0.1	MOT ELEC NON COUR CONTINU
71623	GEN SETS WITH PISTN ENGN					W 281	4.0	W 57	0.3	GROUPES MOTEUR EXPLOSION
72	MACHS FOR SPCL INDUSTRYS		0.6		1.1		5.8		6.9	MAC SPECIALES POUR INDUST
723	CIVIL ENGNEERG EQUIP ETC	W 22	0.1	W 136	0.4	W 922	3.0	W 231	0.8	APPAREILS DE GENIE CIVIL
724	TEXTILE,LEATHER MACHNRY	W 37	0.1	W 89	0.1	W 74	0.6	W 331	5.0	MACH POUR INDUSTRIE TEXTILE
7243	SEWING MACHS,NEEDLES ETC	W 24	0.1		0.1	W 47	0.5	W 321	5.0	MACHINES A COUDRE,PIECES
72431	SEWING MACHINES				0.1	W 41	0.5	W 320	5.0	MACHINES A COUDRE
78	ROAD VEHICLES		0.3		0.6		4.3		4.9	VEHICULES ROUTIERS
8	MISC MANUFACTURED GOODS		33.2		16.3		180.5		208.7	ART MANUFACTURES DIVERS
821	*FURNITURE,PARTS THEREOF	W 5383	16.8	W 2866	9.2	W 5225	15.0	W 5505	21.8	MEUBLES ET PIECES
8219	FURNITURE AND PARTS NES	W 4738	15.5	W 2545	8.5	W 5075	14.9	W 5265	20.7	AUTRES MEUBLES ET PIECES
82192	WOOD FURNITURE NES			W 1984	6.8	W 1878·	5.4	W 464	1.4	MEUBLES NDA EN BOIS
82199	OTHR FURN,FURN PARTS NES			W 435	1.3	W 3009	8.9	W 4763	19.2	MEUBLES NDA AUTRES MATIERES
84	CLOTHING AND ACCESSORIES		9.6		4.0		27.4		29.5	VETEMENTS
843	WOMENS OUTERWEAR NONKNIT	W 51	0.4	W 68	0.4	W 1096	3.5	W 1118	2.9	VET DESSUS FEMMES MAT TEX
844	UNDER GARMENTS NOT KNIT	W 90	0.6	W 156	0.5	W 1020	2.7	W 1501	5.7	VETEMENT DESSOUS MAT TEX
8441	— MENS SHIRTS	W 73	0.4	W 45	0.2	W 627	2.0	W 690	3.5	CHEMISES HOMMES MAT TEXT
845	OUTERWEAR KNIT NONELASTC	W 1797	3.6	W 263	1.2	W 1595	5.3	W 1122	4.4	VET DESSOUS,ACCES BONNET
8459	— OTHER,CLTHG ACCESRYS			W 257	1.1	W 1479	4.8	W 1025	4.2	AUT VET DESSUS DE BONNE
846	UNDER GARMENTS KNITTED	W 900	3.2	W 326	1.5	W 12646	13.8	W 7434	14.4	SOUS VETS DE BONNETERIE
8462	— OF COTTON NON ELASTIC	W 839	2.6	W 45	0.4	W 10208	9.1	W 2513	7.2	SOUS–VET BONNET COTON
84629	—— OTHER	W 199	0.9	W 45	0.4	W 10208	9.1	W 2513	7.2	AUT SOUS–VET BONNET COTON
8463	— OF SYNTH FBR NONELAST	W 55	0.2	W 267	0.6	W 2431	4.4	W 4913	7.0	SOUS–VET BONNET FIB SYNT
84632	—— MENS SHIRTS	W 55	0.2	W 267	0.6	W 2348	4.2	W 4908	6.9	CHEMISES DE BON FIB SYNMT
89	MISC MANUFCTRD GOODS NES		6.3		2.7		137.2		154.4	ART MANUFACTURES DIVERS
892	PRINTED MATTER	W 53	3.7	W 57	0.1	W 144	133.5	W 64	150.9	IMPRIMES
8928	PRINTED MATTER NES	W 50	3.7	W 52	0.1	W 81	133.4	W 50	150.9	IMPRIMES NDA
89283	UNISSUED BANKNOTES ETC	W 1	3.6			W 25	133.1	W 6	140.8	TIMBRES–POSTE FISCAUX
89289	OTHER PRINTED MATTER			W 1	0.1			W 1	10.1	GRAVURES,PHOTO AUT IMPR
893	ARTICLES OF PLASTIC NES		2.2	W 1613	2.4		3.4	W 1026	1.8	OUVRAGES EN MAT DIVIS 58
9	GOODS NOT CLASSD BY KIND		1.3		1.1		1.5		10.3	ART TRANSACT NON CLASSES
931	*SPECIAL TRANSACTIONS						0.1		10.1	TRANS.SPECIALES

1. HISTORICAL SERIES, 1962–1997 SPECIAL TRADE, IMPORTS C.I.F., EXPORTS F.O.B.
SERIES HISTORIQUES, 1962–1997 COMMERCE SPECIAL, IMPORTATIONS C.A.F., EXPORTATIONS F.O.B

YEAR ANNEE	VALUE IN MILLION FORINT / VALEUR EN MILLION FORINT: MERCHANDISE # 1 –MARCHANDISE IMPORTS	MERCHANDISE # 1 –MARCHANDISE EXPORTS	GOLD –OR IMPORTS	GOLD –OR EXPORTS	CONVERSION FACTORS U.S. CENTS PER FORINT / FACTEURS DE CONVERSION CENTS E.U. PAR FORINT: IMPORTS	CONVERSION FACTORS EXPORTS	INDEX NUMBERS –INDICES: QUANTUM IMPORTS	QUANTUM EXPORTS	UNIT VALUE / VALEUR UNITAIRE IMPORTS	UNIT VALUE / VALEUR UNITAIRE EXPORTS
1962	13485.00	12906.00			8.5200	8.5200				
1963	15327.00	14156.00			8.5200	8.5200				
1964	17546.00	15870.00			8.5200	8.5200				
1965	17849.00	17721.00			8.5200	8.5200				
1966	18379.00	18705.00			8.5200	8.5200				
1967	20841.00	19971.00			8.5200	8.5200				
1968	21163.00	21004.00			8.5200	8.5200				
1969	22631.00	24462.00			8.5200	8.5200				
1970	29410.00	27197.00			8.5200	8.5200				
1971	35098.00	29355.00			8.5200	8.5200				
1972	34093.00	35583.00			9.2507	9.2507				
1973	37299.00	42039.00			10.5063	10.5460				
1974	51010.00	46927.00			10.9315	10.9315				
1975	61537.00	52170.00			11.6611	11.6759				
1976	230056.00	204833.00			2.4030	2.4080				
1977	267309.00	238590.00			2.4401	2.4443				
1978	300933.00	240707.00			2.6258	2.6359				
1979	308905.00	282129.00			2.8079	2.8135				
1980	299899.00	281012.00			3.0793	3.0877	93	74	56	60
1981	314284.30	299405.30			2.9044	2.9099	94	77	59	62
1982	324818.70	324486.10			2.7134	2.7018	91	80	61	62
1983	364963.10	374107.90			2.3298	2.3244	92	86	66	66
1984	390511.10	413956.90			2.0720	2.0685	92	92	70	69
1985	410127.60	424600.60			2.0062	2.0118	99	96	73	71
1986	425005.00	406203.90			2.1864	2.1849	102	94	77	72
1987	443955.90	432609.00			2.1286	2.1277	104	97	78	74
1988	460893.90	492325.80			1.9822	1.9782	104	104	81	79
1989	523506.90	571322.80			1.6816	1.6775	105	104	91	91
1990	544900.10	603600.10			1.5912	1.5900	100	100	100	100
1991	855600.10	764300.00			1.3343	1.3345	105	95	146	131
1992	878599.90	843600.10			1.2640	1.2656	98	96	161	143
1993	1158099.00	819899.90			1.0811	1.0841	119	84	176	160
1994	1518299.00	1128699.00			0.9473	0.9470	136	97	203	189
1995	1894400.00	1576100.00			0.7942	0.7889	131	106	269	254
1996	2426400.00	1936400.00			0.6535	0.6531				
1997	3967491.00	3567415.00			0.5352	0.5354				

2. IMPORTS BY BROAD ECONOMIC CATEGORY AND EXPORTS BY INDUSTRIAL ORIGIN. (PERCENTAGE OF TOTAL VALUE)
IMPORTATIONS PAR CATEGORIES ECONOMIQUES ET EXPORTATIONS PAR BRANCHE D'ACTIVITE.(EN POURCENTAGE DE LA VALEUR TOTALE)

IMPORTS – IMPORTATIONS

	1991	1992	1993	1994	1995	1996	1997
TOTAL IMPORTS–IMPORTATIONS TOTALES	100.	100.	100.	100.	100.	100.	100.
1 FOOD BEV–ALIMENTATION BOISSONS	3.9	3.7	4.0	4.9	3.9	3.4	3.1
11 PRIMARY–PRODUITS DE BASE	2.0	1.6	1.7	2.6	2.0	1.6	1.4
111 FOR INDUSTRY–POUR L'INDUSTRIE	0.9	0.6	0.6	1.0	0.8	0.7	0.5
112 FOR HOUSEHOLDS–POUR LES MENAGES	1.0	1.0	1.1	1.6	1.2	0.9	0.8
12 PROCESSED–PRODUITS ELABORES	2.0	2.1	2.3	2.3	1.9	1.8	1.8
121 FOR INDUSTRY–POUR L'INDUSTRIE	0.4	0.2	0.5	0.4	0.3	0.4	0.3
122 FOR HOUSEHOLDS–POUR LES MENAGES	1.5	1.9	1.8	1.9	1.6	1.4	1.5
2 IND SUPPLIES–APPROV INDUSTRIELS	36.9	36.3	31.5	34.3	39.7	39.0	35.5
21 PRIMARY–PRODUITS DE BASE	4.3	2.5	1.9	2.5	2.4	2.4	1.7
22 PROCESSED–PRODUITS ELABORES	32.6	33.8	29.6	31.8	37.3	36.7	33.9
3 FUELS–COMBUSTIBLES	15.2	15.1	13.4	11.8	11.7	13.6	9.2
31 PRIMARY–PRODUITS DE BASE	11.6	12.0	10.0	8.2	8.9	10.8	7.8
32 PROCESSED–PRODUITS ELABORES	3.5	3.0	3.4	3.6	2.8	2.8	1.4
321 MOTOR SPIRIT–ESSENCE							
322 OTHER–AUTRES	3.5	3.0	3.4	3.6	2.8	2.8	1.4
4 MACHINERY–EQUIPEMENT	20.8	21.0	19.5	21.6	21.2	21.6	27.4
41 CAPITAL EQUIPMENT–MACHINES	17.4	17.8	16.5	18.4	17.8	18.2	17.8
42 PARTS–PIECES ACCESSOIRES	3.4	3.2	3.0	3.2	3.4	3.4	9.6
5 TRANSPORT–TRANSPORT	9.5	7.6	9.0	9.2	8.0	7.9	10.8
51 PASSENGER CARS–AUTOMOBILES	3.5	2.7	3.0	3.5	2.7	2.8	2.0
52 OTHER–AUTRES	3.7	2.6	2.5	2.4	2.8	2.6	1.8
521 INDUSTRIAL–INDUSTRIELS	3.5	2.4	2.3	2.3	2.7	2.5	1.8
522 NON INDUSTRIAL–NON INDUSTRIEL	0.2	0.1	0.1	0.1	0.1	0.0	0.1
53 PARTS–PIECES ACCESSOIRES	2.2	2.3	3.5	3.3	2.5	2.5	7.0
6 CONSUM GOODS–BIENS CONSOMMATION	13.7	14.5	13.4	14.1	13.6	13.5	12.4
61 DURABLE–DURABLES	3.8	3.7	3.3	3.3	3.0	2.8	2.8
62 SEMI DURABLE–SEMI DURABLES	6.9	7.0	6.1	6.1	6.3	6.5	6.0
63 NON DURABLE–NON DURABLES	3.0	3.7	4.0	4.6	4.3	4.2	3.6
7 GOODS NES–BIENS NDA	0.1	1.9	9.2	4.1	1.8	1.0	1.6

EXPORTS – EXPORTATIONS

	1991	1992	1993	1994	1995	1996	1997
TOTAL EXPORTS–EXPORTATIONS TOTALES		100.	100.	100.	100.	100.	100.
1 AGRICULTURE		9.6	6.2	6.7	8.1	5.6	4.4
2 MINING QUARRY–INDUS EXTRACTIVES		0.3	0.4	0.3	0.3	0.5	0.1
3 MANUFACTURING–IND MANUFACTUR		90.2	93.5	93.0	91.6	93.9	95.5
31 FOOD BEV TOBACCO–ALIM BOISS TAB		14.8	15.8	15.0	14.2	15.3	10.6
32 TEXTILES–INDUSTRIES TEXTILES		17.6	14.6	14.8	12.9	13.7	9.5
33 WOOD & PRODUCTS–BOIS & PRODUITS		1.5	1.4	1.5	1.6	1.7	1.3
34 PAPER & PRODUCTS–PAPIER & PRODT		1.2	1.0	1.4	1.6	2.0	1.5
35 CHEMICALS–INDUSTRIES CHIMIQUES		14.6	16.2	15.1	16.5	15.8	11.8
36 NON METAL MIN–MIN NON METAL		2.1	2.4	2.0	1.9	2.2	1.7
37 BASIC METAL–IND METAL BASE		4.8	4.4	5.0	6.3	5.5	3.9
38 METAL MANUF–MANUF METAL		26.8	29.5	29.7	32.9	33.1	51.4
39 OTH MANUF IND–AUTRES MANUF		6.7	8.1	8.4	3.7	4.5	3.7

3. TRADE BY PRINCIPAL COUNTRIES OF ORIGIN AND DESTINATION (VALUE IN MILLION U.S. DOLLARS)
ECHANGES SELON LES PRINCIPAUX PAYS D'ORIGINE ET DE DESTINATION (VALEUR EN MILLIONS DE DOLLARS EU)

COUNTRIES–PAYS	SPECIAL IMPORTS C.I.F. IMPORTATIONS SPECIALES C.A.F				
	1993	1994	1995	1996	1997
World	12530.3	14553.6	15466.2	16208.9	21234.0
Africa	58.8	90.2	154.2	147.3	111.7
Americas	701.4	685.5	751.0	863.8	1199.1
– Northern America	522.4	485.7	523.8	616.1	881.8
– LAIA	165.2	187.7	218.4	235.8	313.1
– CACM	9.8	8.3	7.4	6.9	3.1
– Caribbean	0.6	0.4	0.9	2.2	1.1
– Rest of America	3.4	3.4	0.6	2.9	0.1
Asia excl fmr USSR	802.5	960.7	1050.4	1207.9	2167.7
– Middle East	35.4	61.1	59.5	77.9	81.9
Asia former USSR	52.7	51.5	40.3	41.7	35.1
Europe excl fmr USSR	8087.1	10484.8	11218.7	11569.3	15264.5
– European Union	6816.2	8888.5	9514.9	9684.5	13256.4
– Eastern Europe	758.0	1038.9	1134.6	1334.2	1412.4
– Rest of Europe	512.9	557.4	569.1	550.6	595.7
Europe former USSR	2727.5	2141.1	2243.9	2363.8	2120.8
Oceania	5.8	5.5	7.4	15.0	17.3
Other	94.5	134.2	0.3	0.2	317.7
Germany/Allemagne	2704.3	3402.9	3628.2	3819.8	5694.9
Russian Federation	2446.8	1745.8	1839.8	2020.5	1833.5
Austria/Autriche	1455.8	1748.3	1663.7	1535.6	2213.9
Italy/Italie	750.3	1017.6	1220.4	1312.6	1553.7
France, Monaco	416.7	497.2	610.7	686.6	924.6
USA/Etats–Unis d'Amer	489.4	451.7	481.7	568.9	793.6
United Kingdom	319.2	571.1	476.5	528.8	723.3
Netherlands/Pays–Bas	337.5	443.2	483.7	513.3	546.9
Japan/Japon	343.5	392.9	339.2	361.5	690.4
Czech Republic	264.0	347.4	364.0	487.4	481.9
Belgium–Luxembourg	248.5	321.7	391.5	412.0	513.9
Switzerland,Liechtenst.	360.3	392.6	384.0	352.2	362.7
Slovakia/Slovaquie	238.0	355.6	369.7	382.2	399.6
Sweden/Suède	192.0	303.3	311.4	281.3	261.7
Ukraine	142.8	297.1	346.8	292.1	239.9
Poland/Pologne	148.2	193.3	248.5	298.4	355.2
Finland/Finlande	142.2	236.5	214.6	191.2	226.1
Spain/Espagne	106.1	144.6	220.6	162.8	271.9
China/Chine	71.6	99.2	126.3	192.2	288.0
Brazil/Brésil	123.2	139.0	140.7	173.7	180.8
Korea, Republic of	67.2	98.7	146.4	149.0	186.4
Romania/Roumanie	85.1	119.0	130.2	146.5	149.7
Areas n.e.s.	94.5	134.2	0.3	0.2	317.7
Denmark/Danemark	75.7	105.3	117.0	117.7	128.8
Other Asia n.e.s.	75.7	78.4	91.8	82.7	160.4
Slovenia/Slovénie	62.2	80.4	92.8	88.8	109.3
Singapore/Singapour	44.7	42.1	35.0	39.2	225.7
Ireland/Irlande	26.3	39.2	89.2	46.4	73.4
Croatia/Croatie	56.9	51.8	57.1	48.4	36.8
Thailand/Thaïlande	20.6	22.5	27.3	23.9	151.6
Malaysia/Malaisie	16.3	24.1	33.7	52.3	119.2
Canada	32.9	34.0	42.0	47.1	88.2
Turkey/Turquie	23.9	47.9	46.1	56.9	68.8
Greece/Grèce	34.4	40.3	54.0	52.7	52.4
China, Hong Kong SAR	21.6	27.2	46.6	58.5	55.5
Israel/Israël	29.8	33.4	47.4	50.9	44.3
India/Inde	33.4	25.5	32.5	45.9	44.4
Lithuania/Lituanie	108.5	43.9	10.1	8.3	5.0
Belarus/Bélarus	15.9	42.5	32.9	35.9	38.3
Indonesia/Indonésie	18.8	24.1	26.6	38.4	54.7

COUNTRIES–PAYS	SPECIAL EXPORTS F.O.B. EXPORTATIONS SPECIALES F.O.B.				
	1993	1994	1995	1996	1997
Monde	8906.2	10699.8	12865.5	13144.0	19099.2
Afrique	79.2	77.6	125.2	105.3	123.0
Amériques	450.5	531.3	498.6	555.7	702.8
– Amérique du Nord	401.7	466.1	435.5	487.2	626.6
– ALAI	40.4	50.0	58.3	61.4	65.4
– MCAC	2.2	1.6	0.9	1.6	0.7
– Caraïbes	5.2	5.8	3.6	4.9	8.8
– Autre Amérique	0.9	7.8	0.3	0.5	1.2
Asie anc. URSS exclus	650.1	511.6	540.0	553.2	542.1
– Moyen–Orient	313.2	190.1	232.8	241.8	215.4
Asie ancienne URSS	84.7	83.3	108.2	77.9	79.3
Europe anc. URSS exclus	6293.1	8215.8	9968.8	10376.2	15770.8
– Union Européenne	5178.8	6818.0	8079.4	8250.0	13341.1
– Europe de l'Est	673.3	796.7	1159.0	1250.9	1401.5
– Autre de l'Europe	441.1	601.1	730.4	875.4	1028.3
Europe ancienne URSS	1275.9	1158.0	1307.8	1162.1	1345.3
Océanie	20.2	22.3	22.9	23.3	22.7
Autre	52.6	99.9	294.1	290.2	513.2
Germany/Allemagne	2370.3	3017.5	3686.8	3814.8	7033.2
Austria/Autriche	897.5	1163.9	1303.3	1394.7	2138.2
Italy/Italie	713.4	906.1	1096.3	1055.0	1095.6
Russian Federation	952.8	807.0	822.8	776.6	947.4
France, Monaco	307.3	379.7	517.9	486.5	706.1
USA/Etats–Unis d'Amer	376.2	430.5	413.5	464.3	589.1
United Kingdom	203.2	464.7	391.5	383.8	630.1
Netherlands/Pays–Bas	210.4	270.7	374.9	351.7	532.3
Poland/Pologne	163.4	222.0	337.1	387.8	500.4
Belgium–Luxembourg	163.0	210.3	273.4	284.8	466.1
Romania/Roumanie	183.8	197.2	357.5	277.6	304.8
Areas n.e.s.	52.6	99.9	294.1	290.2	513.2
Czech Republic	170.1	197.7	207.4	289.7	302.9
Ukraine	160.0	229.8	317.7	219.8	240.1
Slovenia/Slovénie	139.9	195.8	255.2	220.0	277.4
Slovakia/Slovaquie	128.1	143.6	213.2	251.0	241.7
Switzerland,Liechtenst.	173.2	168.7	178.2	176.9	221.6
Croatia/Croatie	78.7	144.7	172.2	190.2	213.7
Spain/Espagne	65.6	94.9	122.3	141.6	278.7
Sweden/Suède	91.2	124.9	125.7	137.8	142.6
Japan/Japon	85.9	91.9	76.8	101.3	94.2
Yugoslavia/Yougoslavie	14.6	27.3	29.8	145.7	150.9
Finland/Finlande	49.3	72.8	57.0	62.9	87.0
Turkey/Turquie	95.2	32.4	52.5	56.9	78.4
Lithuania/Lituanie	107.9	52.7	39.8	60.6	53.0
Greece/Grèce	57.8	42.2	48.7	60.0	77.1
Denmark/Danemark	39.0	51.4	57.9	53.8	69.4
Bosnia and Herzegovina	2.8	18.2	40.0	97.6	107.1
Belarus/Bélarus	37.8	39.3	79.0	43.0	50.9
Israel/Israël	32.0	66.7	50.0	40.4	40.1
Uzbekistan/Ouzbékistan	27.7	50.4	71.4	19.8	25.6
Egypt/Egypte	31.8	26.0	25.0	40.9	45.0
Bulgaria/Bulgarie	23.3	32.1	38.3	32.5	40.3
Iran (Islamic Rep of)	57.8	26.5	33.4	23.3	20.4
Kazakhstan	37.3	24.2	23.5	32.2	31.8
Saudi Arabia	29.9	26.4	29.1	33.9	22.6
Canada	24.8	35.1	21.6	22.6	37.0
Lebanon/Liban	23.7	23.4	33.6	21.2	25.7
India/Inde	39.1	26.3	23.2	16.3	21.7
Syrian Arab Republic	33.2	22.2	18.4	26.2	18.6

(VALUE AS PERCENTAGE OF WORLD TOTAL)(VALEURS EN POURCENTAGE DU TOTAL MONDIAL)

	1988	1989	1990	1991	1992	1993	1994	1995	1996	1997
Africa	1.4	0.9	3.6	2.6	0.4	0.5	0.6	1.0	0.9	0.5
Americas	5.6	5.2	5.4	4.6	4.9	5.6	4.7	4.9	5.3	5.6
– Northern America	2.3	2.6	2.8	2.8	3.3	4.2	3.3	3.4	3.8	4.2
– LAIA	2.9	2.3	2.4	1.6	1.5	1.3	1.3	1.4	1.5	1.5
– CACM	0.2	0.1	0.2	0.2	0.1	0.1	0.1	0.0	0.0	0.0
– Caribbean	0.2	0.1	0.0	0.0	0.0	0.0	0.0	0.0	0.0	0.0
– Rest of America	0.0	0.0	0.0	0.0	0.0	0.0	0.0	0.0	0.0	0.0
Asia excl fmr USSR	6.9	6.3	7.2	7.4	5.7	6.4	6.6	6.8	7.5	10.2
– Middle East	0.8	0.4	0.7	1.0	0.3	0.3	0.4	0.4	0.5	0.4
Asia former USSR						0.4	0.4	0.3	0.3	0.2
Europe excl fmr USSR	60.9	65.4	64.6	68.5	71.3	64.5	72.0	72.5	71.4	71.9
– European Union	34.9	39.7	43.2	56.9	60.0	54.4	61.1	61.5	59.7	62.4
– Eastern Europe	18.8	17.2	14.7	7.0	6.7	6.0	7.1	7.3	8.2	6.7
– Rest of Europe	7.1	8.5	6.7	4.7	4.6	4.1	3.8	3.7	3.4	2.8
Europe former USSR	25.0	22.1	19.1	15.4	16.9	21.8	14.7	14.5	14.6	10.0
Oceania	0.2	0.1	0.1	0.1	0.1	0.0	0.0	0.0	0.1	0.1
Other			0.0	1.5	0.8	0.8	0.9	0.0	0.0	1.5
Germany/Allemagne				21.5	23.5	21.6	23.4	23.5	23.6	26.8
Russian Federation					16.9	19.5	12.0	11.9	12.5	8.6
Austria/Autriche	7.2	8.6	10.0	13.4	14.4	11.6	12.0	10.8	9.5	10.4
Italy/Italie	3.1	3.4	4.1	7.3	6.3	6.0	7.0	7.9	8.1	7.3
France, Monaco	2.0	2.2	2.1	2.7	3.1	3.3	3.4	3.9	4.2	4.4
USA/Etats–Unis d'Amer	2.2	2.5	2.6	2.6	2.9	3.9	3.1	3.1	3.5	3.7
United Kingdom	1.8	2.2	2.1	2.5	2.9	2.5	3.9	3.1	3.3	3.4
Netherlands/Pays–Bas	1.8	2.1	2.1	2.7	3.0	2.7	3.0	3.1	3.2	2.6
Japan/Japon	1.5	1.6	2.1	2.7	2.4	2.7	2.7	2.2	2.2	3.3
Czech Republic						2.1	2.4	2.4	3.0	2.3

	1988	1989	1990	1991	1992	1993	1994	1995	1996	1997
Afrique	2.5	2.0	2.1	1.4	0.9	0.9	0.7	1.0	0.8	0.6
Amériques	4.5	5.0	4.7	4.5	4.2	5.1	5.0	3.9	4.2	3.7
– Amérique du Nord	3.4	3.7	3.8	3.5	3.7	4.5	4.4	3.4	3.7	3.3
– ALAI	0.5	0.7	0.5	0.8	0.4	0.5	0.5	0.5	0.5	0.3
– MCAC	0.0	0.0	0.0	0.0	0.0	0.0	0.0	0.0	0.0	0.0
– Caraïbes	0.6	0.5	0.3	0.3	0.1	0.1	0.1	0.0	0.0	0.0
– Autre Amérique	0.1	0.1	0.0	0.0	0.0	0.0	0.1	0.0	0.0	0.0
Asie anc. URSS exclus	10.5	9.7	9.4	9.9	7.1	7.3	4.8	4.2	4.2	2.8
– Moyen–Orient	4.5	4.4	3.8	5.0	4.0	3.5	1.8	1.8	1.8	1.1
Asie ancienne URSS						1.0	0.8	0.8	0.6	0.4
Europe anc. URSS exclus	54.5	57.9	63.4	70.5	74.4	70.7	76.8	77.5	78.9	82.6
– Union Européenne	30.5	33.8	42.3	58.7	62.3	58.1	63.7	62.8	62.8	69.9
– Europe de l'Est	17.1	15.9	11.2	6.1	6.3	7.6	7.4	9.0	9.5	7.3
– Autre de l'Europe	7.0	8.1	9.9	5.8	5.7	5.0	5.6	5.7	6.7	5.4
Europe ancienne URSS	27.6	25.1	20.2	13.4	13.1	14.3	10.8	10.2	8.8	7.0
Océanie	0.3	0.2	0.2	0.2	0.2	0.2	0.2	0.2	0.2	0.1
Autre	0.0	0.0		0.1	0.1	0.6	0.9	2.3	2.2	2.7
Germany/Allemagne				26.9	27.7	26.6	28.2	28.7	29.0	36.8
Austria/Autriche	5.7	6.5	7.5	10.8	10.7	10.1	10.9	10.1	10.6	11.2
Italy/Italie	4.2	4.7	5.9	7.6	9.5	8.0	8.5	8.5	8.0	5.7
Russian Federation					13.1	10.7	7.5	6.4	5.9	5.0
France, Monaco	2.0	2.4	2.7	2.9	3.2	3.5	3.5	4.0	3.7	3.7
USA/Etats–Unis d'Amer	2.9	3.3	3.5	3.2	3.2	4.2	4.0	3.2	3.5	3.1
United Kingdom	1.9	1.8	2.0	2.0	2.0	2.3	4.3	3.0	2.9	3.3
Netherlands/Pays–Bas	1.2	1.3	1.5	2.1	2.2	2.4	2.5	2.9	2.7	2.8
Poland/Pologne	3.3	3.2	1.7	2.1	1.3	1.8	2.1	2.6	3.0	2.6
Belgium–Luxembourg	0.8	0.9	1.2	1.5	2.3	1.8	2.0	2.1	2.2	2.4

4. Special Imports C.I.F. by Commodities according to the S.I.T.C. (Rev. 2) in million U.S. Dollars
Importations Spéciales C.A.F. par Produits d'après la C.T.C.I. (Rév. 2) en millions de Dollars E.U.

SITC CTCI	COMMODITY	1994		1995		1996		1997		PRODUIT
		QUANTITY QUANTITE	VALUE VALEUR	QUANTITY QUANTITE	VALUE VALEUR	QUANTITY QUANTITE	VALUE VALEUR	QUANTITY QUANTITE	VALUE VALEUR	
	ALL COMMODITIES		14553.7		15466.3		16208.9		21234.1	TOUS PRODUITS
0	FOOD AND LIVE ANIMALS		809.8		714.7		688.9		772.0	ALIMENTS,ANIMAUX VIVANTS
01	MEAT AND PREPARATIONS		109.6		70.2		37.1		62.0	VIANDES ET PREPARATIONS
011	MEAT FRESH,CHILLD,FROZEN	W 85171	107.6	W 50802	69.2	W 27527	36.8	W 46880	61.1	VIANDES FRAICHES,REF,CONGE
0113	PIG MEAT FRESH,CHLD,FRZN	W 40079	51.8	W 30993	43.7	W 11824	17.8	W 20239	33.0	VIANDE DE PORC
04	CEREALS AND PREPARATIONS		87.5		50.5		62.3		61.0	CEREALES ET PRODUITS
05	VEGETABLES AND FRUIT		125.5		139.0		126.7		133.9	LEGUMES ET FRUITS
057	FRUIT,NUTS,FRESH,DRIED	W 177378	58.9	W 201765	60.9	W 170268	59.9	W 193141	59.6	FRUITS FRAIS OU SECS
07	COFFEE,TEA,COCOA,SPICES		143.7		156.9		152.5		148.1	CAFE,THE,CACAO,EPICES
071	COFFEE AND SUBSTITUTES	W 42911	86.1	W 29315	99.3	W 33032	81.9	W 36079	80.7	CAFE ET SUCCEDANES
0711	COFFEE GREEN,ROASTED,SUB	W 40415	71.4	W 27268	86.8	W 30374	65.8	W 32731	64.6	CAFE TORREFIE OU DECAFEINE
07111	COFFEE GREEN,HUSKS,SKINS	W 40318	71.1	W 27151	86.4	W 30272	65.4	W 32576	64.0	CAFE NON TORREFIE
081	*FEEDING STUFF FOR ANIML	W 573381	166.2	W 679313	186.8	W 662133	217.6	W 670885	235.9	NOURRITURE POUR ANIMAUX
0813	OILCAKE AND OTH RESIDUES	W 495239	119.5	W 588901	131.6	W 576129	164.7	W 584811	181.5	TOURTEAUX
08131	— OF SOYA BEANS	W 452900	114.3	W 539112	126.5	W 515065	157.7	W 530539	174.3	TOURTEAUX DE SOJA
09	MISC EDIBLE PRODUCTS		86.2		44.4		34.3		42.6	PREP ALIMENTAIRES DIVERSES
098	EDIBLE PRODCTS,PREPS NES	W 23579	78.6	W 15775	41.5	W 14922	31.5	W 25234	38.7	PREP ALIMENTAIRES NDA
09809	MISC FOOD PREPRTIONS NES	W 15779	66.6	W 8313	29.5	W 7423	21.2	W 17728	30.0	PREP ALIMENTAIRES NDA
1	BEVERAGES AND TOBACCO		92.3		79.1		99.7		103.5	BOISSONS ET TABACS
12	TOBACCO AND MANUFACTURES		59.7		49.0		71.3		77.0	TABACS BRUTS FABRIQUES
121	TOBACCO UNMNFCTRD,REFUSE	W 16138	56.0	W 13030	44.4	W 19431	58.5	W 19313	67.0	TABACS BRUTS,DECHETS
1212	TOBACCO STRIPPED OR PART	W 10614	44.1	W 9928	38.8	W 14666	51.1	W 14763	62.5	TABACS PART ECOTES
2	CRUDE MATERLS,EXCL FUELS		526.8		612.5		574.6		542.8	MAT BRUTES NON COMESTIBLES
23	RUBBER, CRUDE		35.2		52.9		52.0		35.4	CAOUTCHOUC BRUT
24	CORK AND WOOD		111.7		138.6		112.1		112.4	LIEGE ET BOIS
248	WOOD SHAPED,SLEEPERS	W 470536	98.9	W 525831	120.8	W 444181	96.2	W 458886	96.2	BOIS SIMPLEMENT TRAVAILLES
2482	LUMBER SHAPED CONIFER	W 423726	91.0	W 478600	111.5	W 416691	87.1	W 438947	86.6	CONIFERES SCIES,RABOTES
24821	LUMBER SAWN ETC CONIFER	W 418417	86.5	W 472628	106.4	W 410453	81.8	W 429681	80.7	CONIFERES SCIES LONGITUD
251	*PULP AND WASTE PAPER	W 178139	57.1	W 150347	82.5	W 208198	75.8	W 228910	80.7	PATES A PAPIER,DECHETS
26	TEXTILE FIBRES AND WASTE		83.0		87.6		90.6		99.6	FIBRES TEXTILES
27	CRUDE FERTLZR,MINRLS NES		50.8		54.7		63.7		60.8	ENGRAIS MINERAUX BRUTS
28	METALLIFEROUS ORES,SCRAP		61.9		74.1		70.1		33.8	MINERAIS METAL,DECHETS
281	IRON ORE,CONCENTRATES	W 2179368	56.7	W 2090676	59.0	W 1471522	53.1	W 378586	8.7	MINERAIS DE FER
2816	IRON ORE AGGLOMERATES	W 677243	16.1	W 1165957	40.6	W 1471522	53.1			MINERAIS AGGLOMERES
29	CRUDE ANIMAL,VEG MAT NES		68.4		64.8		61.7		65.3	MATIERES BRUTES ANIM,VEGET
292	CRUDE VEG MATERIALS NES	W 14885	49.8	W 10098	47.9	W 9096	42.4	W 10385	42.9	MAT BRUTES VEGETALES NDA
3	MINERAL FUELS ETC		1724.3		1812.4		2207.7		1961.8	COMBUSTIBLES MINERAUX LUB
32	COAL,COKE AND BRIQUETTES		206.5		202.3		216.9		164.2	HOUILLES,COKES,BRIQUETTES
322	COAL,LIGNITE AND PEAT	W 2586644	111.4	W 2150592	103.5	W 2448340	125.2	W 2205813	120.8	HOUILLES,LIGNITES,TOURBE
3222	OTH COAL,NOT AGGLOMERATD	W 1934751	90.9	W 1760751	91.1	W 1892707	106.3	W 1742300	104.9	AUTRES HOUILLES
323	BRIQUETS,COKE,SEMI–COKE	W 1013833	95.1	W 928951	98.8	W 995523	91.8	W 465141	43.5	BRIQUETTES
3232	COKE,SEMI–COKE,RTRT CRBN	W 959288	90.7	W 902172	96.4	W 976675	89.9	W 450416	42.2	COKES ET SEMI–COKES
33	PETROLEUM AND PRODUCTS		976.7		951.4		1048.8		954.3	PETROLE ET DERIVES
333	CRUDE PETROLEUM	W 5821385	590.7	W 5872242	678.8	W 5512325	766.7	W 5480450	688.4	HUILES BRUTES DE PETROLE
334	PETROLEUM PRODUCTS,REFIN	W 2487845	381.7	W 1675978	268.0	W 1651584	271.3	W 1546086	256.0	PRODUITS RAFFINES
341	*GAS,NATURAL AND MANUFCT	W 5628942	492.3	W 6105983	597.7	W 8254489	851.8	W 7629443	843.3	GAZ NATUREL,GAZ MANUFACT
3414	PETROLEUM GASES, GASEOUS	W 5619001	491.1	W 6082451	593.0	W 8170895	834.8	W 7526260	822.0	GAZ DE PETROLE GAZEUX
351	*ELECTRIC CURRENT		49.0		61.2		90.3			ENERGIE ELECTRIQUE
4	ANIMAL,VEGETABLE OIL,FAT		17.9		41.2		42.9		98.7	HUILES,GRAISSES ANIM,VEG
42	FIXED VEGETABLE OIL,FAT		5.8		19.5		20.9		74.2	HUILES VEGETALES FIXES
5	CHEMCLS,RELATED PROD NES		1768.2		2112.8		2148.6		2295.9	PRODUITS CHIMIQUES
51	ORGANIC CHEMICALS		355.6		490.1		400.6		442.5	PROD CHIMIQ ORGANIQUES
511	HYDROCARBONS NES,DERIVS	W 224145	115.0	W 234646	178.7	W 147721	101.1	W 243213	138.0	HYDROCARBURES NDA
5111	ACYCLIC HYDROCARBONS	W 85029	37.3	W 100245	63.5	W 54824	32.0	W 80925	43.2	HYDROCARBURES ACYCLIQUES
51111	ETHYLENE	W 73729	31.9	W 92359	57.2	W 50009	27.7	W 64783	37.4	ETHYLENE
5112	CYCLIC HYDROCARBONS	W 81259	49.1	W 88124	80.1	W 80134	54.8	W 81974	50.7	HYDROCARBURES CYCLIQUES
51125	STYRENE	W 74419	46.0	W 80925	75.1	W 75345	51.7	W 75589	47.2	STYRENE
512	ALCOHOLS,PHENOLS ETC	W 66474	28.5	W 88922	55.2	W 84154	40.0	W 71973	32.8	PHENOLS,PHENOLS–ALCOOLS
5121	ACYCLIC ALCOHOLS,DERIVS	W 62660	23.8	W 86405	47.2	W 80882	31.5	W 69172	26.2	ALCOOLS ACYCLIQUES
513	CARBOXYLIC ACIDS ETC	W 38169	49.4	W 36666	67.5	W 39434	61.1	W 40886	56.9	ACIDES CARBOXYLIQUES
514	NITROGEN–FNCTN COMPOUNDS	W 53407	89.4	W 50317	108.5	W 61496	120.1	W 73692	130.9	COMPOSES FONCT AZOTEES
5148	OTH NITROGN–FNCTN CMPNDS	W 25750	48.7	W 20529	54.9	W 30735	57.0	W 34569	59.2	AUTRES COMPOSES AZOTES
515	ORG–INORG COMPOUNDS ETC	W 8595	42.9	W 9036	47.6	W 9395	44.3	W 10788	51.8	COMPOSES ORGANO–MINERAUX
52	INORGANIC CHEMICALS		104.0		112.8		119.1		116.6	PROD CHIM INORGANIQUES
523	OTHR INORG CHEMICALS ETC		55.8		66.7		69.7		68.2	AUT PRODUITS CHIMIQUES INORG
53	DYES,TANNING,COLOUR PROD		124.8		143.7		151.5		171.8	PROD TEINTURE,COLORANTS
533	PIGMENTS,PAINTS,ETC	W 32707	93.5	W 31624	111.3	W 36461	117.3	W 51748	136.3	PIGMENTS,PEINTURES,VERNIS
541	*MEDICINAL,PHARM PRODUCT		446.3		441.8		464.9		485.8	PROD MEDICINAUX PHARMACEUT
5417	MEDICAMENTS	K 6050285	365.2	K 7742044	352.4	MK 9615	362.6	MK 9789	377.7	MEDICAMENTS
54171	— CONTAINNG ANTIBIOTICS	K 705033	54.0	K 883067	43.3	K 1272706	67.1	K 1406864	68.2	MED CONTN ANTIBIOTIQUES
54179	— CONTNG OTH SUBSTANCES	K 5198791	289.4	K 6600343	290.6	K 7942325	252.9	K 8046489	258.9	MED CONT AUT SUBSTANCES
55	PERFUME,CLEANING ETC PRD		174.8		200.1		222.0		238.5	PROD POUR PARFUM,TOILETTE
551	ESSENTL OILS,PERFUME,ETC	W 1907	21.6	W 3660	42.0	W 4506	51.7	W 4424	49.1	HUILES ESSENTIELLES
5514	MIXED PERFUME SUBSTANCES	W 1806	20.8	W 3527	40.8	W 4404	50.6	W 4241	47.3	MELANGES SUBSTAN ODORIFER
553	PERFUMERY,COSMETICS,ETC	W 23547	87.1	W 21522	84.0	W 23280	92.3	W 28042	107.4	PRODUITS DE PARFUMERIE
554	SOAP,CLEANSING ETC PREPS	W 64289	66.2	W 65547	74.2	W 72305	78.1	W 82964	82.2	SAVONS,PRODUITS DETERSIFS
5542	WASHING PREPARATIONS ETC	W 56571	55.1	W 57181	59.3	W 63829	64.9	W 72280	67.2	PROD ORG TENSIO–ACT NDA
562	*FERTILIZERS,MANUFACTURE	W 518806	44.7	W 436998	44.0	W 592113	76.5	W 496593	59.2	ENGRAIS MANUFACTURES
58	PLASTIC MATERIALS ETC		271.2		375.9		392.5		455.3	MAT PLAST ARTIFICIELLES
582	PROD OF CONDENSATION ETC	W 53659	81.4	W 57004	112.6	W 62732	112.8	W 88102	124.9	PROD CONDENS,POLYCOND
5823	ALKYDS,OTHER POLYESTERS	W 16819	35.2	W 19513	53.3	W 25151	51.4	W 29599	52.0	ALKYDES ET AUT POLYESTERS
583	POLYMERIZATION ETC PRODS	W 132110	182.0	W 134313	255.3	W 166568	272.2	W 200243	321.9	PROD POLYMERISATION
5831	POLYETHYLENE	W 50305	44.8	W 47377	63.7	W 54334	58.3	W 57763	67.2	POLYETHYLENE
5839	OTH POLYMRZTION ETC PROD	W 15243	52.4	W 16045	67.6	W 17687	72.0	W 29065	91.6	AUT PROD POLYMER COPOLYM
59	CHEMICAL MATERIALS NES		247.0		304.6		320.6		325.8	MAT PROD CHIMIQUES NDA
591	PESTICIDES,DISINFECTANTS	W 18318	87.0	W 21838	103.2	W 20962	118.7	W 18639	118.5	DESINF,INSECT,FONG,HERB
5913	HERBICIDES,FOR RETAIL	W 5438	42.5	W 5968	49.6	W 6235	58.2	W 7484	63.2	HERBICIDES VENTE AU DET
598	MISCEL CHEM PRODUCTS NES	W 71032	124.5	W 85767	155.9	W 94305	156.5	W 97528	162.6	PROD DIV INDUST CHIM NDA
5989	CHEM PRODUCTS,PREPS NES	W 41351	98.3	W 48928	120.0	W 50974	121.7	W 62851	129.8	PROD PREP CHIMIQUES NDA
59899	OTH CHEM PRODS,PREPS,NES	W 27654	65.6	W 35143	81.0	W 31881	82.5	W 38709	91.7	AUT PRODUITS CHIMIQUES NDA
6	BASIC MANUFACTURES		2959.8		3628.3		3705.6		4310.7	ART MANUFACTURES
61	LEATHER,DRESSED FUR,ETC		207.1		250.3		297.2		315.1	CUIRS,PELLETERIES
611	LEATHER	W 7182	133.4	W 7187	168.9	W 7695	200.7	W 9050	211.3	CUIRS,PEAUX PREPARES
6114	LEATHR BOVINE NES,EQUINE	W 4345	93.5	W 4927	124.2	W 5765	152.7	W 6200	158.1	CUIRS DE BOVINS
612	LEATHER ETC MANUFACTURES		65.3	W 6769	72.7	W 8226	84.5	W 9401	96.9	OUVRAGES EN CUIRS NDA
6123	PREPRD PARTS OF FOOTWEAR	W 6447	62.3	W 6531	68.1	W 8095	82.2	W 9181	92.7	PARTIES DE CHAUSSURES
62	RUBBER MANUFACTURES NES		135.6		143.9		154.4		200.8	CAOUTCHOUC MANUFACTURE
625	RUBBER TYRES, TUBES ETC	W 26937	67.0	W 23359	66.9	W 21599	70.6	W 24812	77.4	PNEUS CAOUTCHOUC VULCANISE
628	RUBBER ARTICLES NES	W 5040	50.8	W 4818	57.4	W 4902	58.2	W 6880	82.4	OUVRAGES CAOUTCHOUC NDA
63	WOOD,CORK MANUFACTRS NES		53.3		59.4		69.6		88.0	OUVRAGES LIEGE ET BOIS
64	PAPER,PAPERBOARD AND MFR		421.4		514.4		517.5		543.0	PAPIERS,CARTONS & OUVRAGES

4. Special Imports C.I.F. by Commodities according to the S.I.T.C. (Rev. 2) in million U.S. Dollars
Importations Spéciales C.A.F. par Produits d'après la C.T.C.I. (Rév. 2) en millions de Dollars E.U.

SITC CTCI	COMMODITY	1994 QUANTITY QUANTITE	1994 VALUE VALEUR	1995 QUANTITY QUANTITE	1995 VALUE VALEUR	1996 QUANTITY QUANTITE	1996 VALUE VALEUR	1997 QUANTITY QUANTITE	1997 VALUE VALEUR	PRODUIT
641	PAPER AND PAPERBOARD	W 317781	252.0	W 294476	312.0	W 320927	310.4	W 391465	312.8	PAPIERS ET CARTONS
6411	NEWSPRINT	W 106432	53.7	W 91589	69.5	W 84525	68.3	W 84813	48.3	PAPIER JOURNAL
6412	PRINTG,WRITING PAPER NES	W 67164	66.1	W 70573	85.3	W 79486	86.3	W 89684	79.5	PAPIERS POUR L'IMPRESSION
64122	— COATED,IMPREGNATD ETC	W 65472	63.1	W 66347	78.3	W 72177	75.7	W 81611	69.7	PAPIERS IMPRESSION COUCHES
6415	PAPER,PAPERBRD,BULK,NES	W 83181	60.6	W 80568	76.8	W 76768	55.7	W 90350	49.3	PAPIERS,CARTONS ROULEAUX
64159	OTHER PAPER ETC,BULK,NES	W 60260	47.5	W 72054	69.4	W 69869	50.4	W 73663	40.9	AUT PAPIER ROULEAUX FEUILLES
6418	COATED ETC PAPER NES BLK	W 21202	39.2	W 19414	47.0	W 33851	61.6	W 54025	82.5	PAP,CARTONS COUCHES,ENDUITS
642	PAPER,ETC,PRECUT,ARTS OF	W 105823	169.4	W 105034	202.5	W 113184	207.1	W 143421	230.2	PAP,CARTONS DECOUPES
6421	PAPER ETC CONTAINERS	W 64952	90.8	W 63282	103.9	W 66533	106.2	W 82486	113.2	BOITES,SACS EMBALLAGES
6428	PAPER ETC ARTICLES NES	W 23832	46.5	W 27439	63.7	W 28237	63.7	W 37614	76.9	OUVRAGES EN PATE A PAPIER
65	TEXTILE YARN,FABRICS,ETC		754.0		882.2		917.4		1017.6	FILS,TISSUS,ARTICLES TEXTILE
651	TEXTILE YARN		104.5		136.5	W 32537	136.7	W 35793	144.5	FILS TEXTILES
6514	SYN FIB YRN,BULK,MONOFIL	W 8300	43.7	W 10036	53.8	W 10675	55.6	W 12746	59.1	FILS CONT 85% FIB TEXT SYNTH
652	COTTON FABRICS,WOVEN	W 12823	96.8	W 13767	114.8	W 15682	127.3	W 16161	134.7	TISSUS DE COTON
6522	WOVEN COTTON BLEACHD,ETC	W 9168	78.1	W 10642	98.0	W 11997	110.8	W 13092	119.1	TISSUS COTON BLANCHIS ETC
65224	BLCHED COTTON FABRIC NES	W 7307	58.9	W 8413	70.4	W 9487	82.3	W 10786	94.0	AUT TIS PLUS 85% COT BLANCHI
653	WOVN MAN–MADE FIB FABRIC	W 16841	212.5	W 16175	223.6	W 16456	222.2	W 20656	248.8	TISSUS FIBRES SYNTH,ARTIF
6534	DISC SYN BLEND FABRC NES	W 4572	55.8	W 4370	57.3	W 4534	61.7	W 5732	77.3	TISSUS FIBRES SYNTH DISCONT
654	OTH WOVEN TEXTILE FABRIC	W 4078	103.3	W 4394	118.1	W 4195	119.6	W 4894	131.3	TISSUS AUT COTON SYNT,ARTIF
6542	WOVEN WOOL,HAIR NONPILE	W 2060	61.2	W 1997	68.2	W 1893	64.6	W 2264	73.7	TIS PLUS 85% LAINE,POILS
65422	WOVN COMB WOOL,FINE HAIR	W 1429	43.7	W 1304	48.3	W 1258	45.8	W 1522	52.7	TISSUS 85% LAINE,PLS PEIG
655	KNITTED,ETC FABRICS	W 4352	57.5	W 4854	72.3	W 5970	82.7	W 8178	98.8	ETOF BONNETERIE PIECES ETC
6552	OTHER KNIT ETC FAB NONEL	W 4352	57.5	W 4854	72.3	W 5970	82.7	W 8178	98.8	ETOF BON NON ELAS NON SYNT
656	LACE,RIBBONS,TULLE,ETC	W 10077	45.9	W 2228	59.4	W 2336	63.7	W 3169	66.8	TULLES,BRODERIE
657	SPECIAL TXTL FABRC,PRODS	W 11314	82.7	W 12416	104.0	W 11851	110.5	W 15597	132.7	TISSUS SPECIAUX
6573	COATED ETC TEXTILES NES	W 4319	39.1	W 5665	54.8	W 5301	57.5	W 6974	74.2	TISSUS,ART MATIERE TEXT NDA
66	NONMETAL MINERAL MFS NES		257.8		278.2		295.8		324.5	ART MIN NON METALLIQUES
662	CLAY,REFRACTORY BLDG PRD	W 152266	68.1	W 143638	68.9	W 137718	69.3	W 171909	72.0	MAT CONST REFRACTAIRES
6624	BRICKS ETC NONREFRACTORY	W 134365	53.0	W 121560	50.9	W 120019	51.0	W 153750	57.6	BRIQUES ETC CERAM NON REFR
663	MINERAL MANUFCTURES NES	W 51222	51.2	W 56938	56.3	W 70408	60.2	W 87478	68.9	ART MIN MANUF NDA
664	GLASS	W 31974	60.4	W 38824	67.7	W 36671	79.2	W 45172	83.8	VERRE
67	IRON AND STEEL		335.5		496.6		454.5		565.6	FER ET ACIER
672	IRON,STEEL PRIMARY FORMS	W 165172	40.2	W 355938	95.9	W 189258	53.5	W 321559	83.5	LINGOTS FER,ACIER
6725	IRN,STL BLOOMS,SLABS,ETC	W 139515	32.0	W 311737	78.7	W 168049	44.2	W 233860	56.6	BLOOMS,BILLETTES FER ACIER
67251	IRN,SMPLE STL BLOOMS,ETC	W 137019	29.8	W 311457	77.6	W 166405	42.2	W 232968	54.9	BLOOMS ETC NON ACIER FIN
673	IRON,STEEL SHAPES ETC	W 113381	51.2	W 132819	75.6	W 144926	86.3	W 232077	107.6	BARRES,PROFIL FER,ACIER
674	IRN,STL UNIV,PLATE,SHEET	W 166539	118.3	W 180771	172.7	W 175393	162.3	W 251740	203.7	LARGES PLATS,TOLES
6746	IRN,STL THIN PLATE,ROLLD	W 23751	27.8	W 30560	49.0	W 21145	32.6	W 48427	44.4	TOLES LAM MOINS 3MM
6749	OTH IRN,STL PLATES,SHEET	W 38738	28.8	W 46614	38.1	W 57104	49.3	W 71252	67.2	AUTRES TOLES FER,ACIER
678	IRON,STL TUBES,PIPES,ETC	W 66155	77.6	W 63916	89.9	W 62390	86.0	W 87762	105.4	TUBES,TUYAUX EN FONTE,FER
68	NON–FERROUS METALS		373.0		521.3		508.5		625.9	METAUX NON FERREUX
682	COPPER EXC CEMENT COPPER	W 30878	87.2	W 34796	123.9	W 45555	138.8	W 53033	158.7	CUIVRE
6822	COPPER,ALLOYS WORKED	W 13673	51.4	W 20357	85.7	W 33124	109.7	W 38483	126.0	CUIVRE,ALLIAGES OUVRES
68221	COPPER BARS,WIRE,ETC	W 6371	16.3	W 12283	38.3	W 25678	66.5	W 29813	79.0	BARRES,PROFILES ET FILS
684	ALUMINIUM	W 151420	246.3	W 160364	353.2	W 168127	319.2	W 207707	408.7	ALUMINIUM
6841	ALUMINIUM,ALLOYS,UNWRGHT	W 130669	179.9	W 134309	256.8	W 142687	229.2	W 170157	287.5	ALUMINIUM,ALLIAGES BRUTS
6842	ALUMINIUM,ALLOYS WORKED	W 20750	66.5	W 26054	96.5	W 25441	90.0	W 37549	121.3	ALUMINIUM,ALLIAGES OUVRE
69	METAL MANUFACTURES NES		422.7		482.4		491.1		630.6	ART MANUFACT EN METAL NDA
691	STRUCTURES AND PARTS NES	W 35974	76.0	W 36370	84.5	W 37364	82.7	W 40435	78.4	CONSTRUCT FER,ACIER,ALU
6911	STRUCTURES,PARTS IRN,STL	W 33367	59.5	W 33194	65.7	W 34502	64.7	W 37019	59.6	CONSTRUCT FER,ACIER,FONTE
692	METAL TANKS,BOXES,ETC	W 18769	43.7	W 18563	48.5	W 20591	55.6	W 27567	52.3	RECIPIENTS METALLIQUES
694	STL,COPPR NAILS,NUTS,ETC	W 9321	31.6	W 8821	41.5	W 7892	39.9	W 16508	90.0	CLOUS,VIS,ECROUS
69402	IRN,STL NUTS,BOLTS,ETC	W 7123	29.0	W 7017	37.9	W 7109	35.7	W 14916	83.6	BOULONS,VIS,ECROUS FER,AC
695	TOOLS	W 4849	57.2	W 4017	62.9	W 4233	67.4	W 5227	86.0	OUTILS A MAIN
697	BASE MTL HOUSEHOLD EQUIP	W 12108	54.9	W 11729	52.4	W 13001	45.9	W 11621	38.7	ART MENAGE MET COMMUNS
699	BASE METAL MFRS NES		130.7		160.9		172.2		256.3	ART MANUFACTURES MET NDA
6991	LOCKSMITHS WARES,ETC	W 6986	48.8	W 8234	56.5	W 9383	61.2	W 15650	81.8	ARTICLES DE SERRURERIE
6997	IRON,STEEL ARTICLES NES	W 4186	18.6	W 8549	27.5	W 9213	31.8	W 58175	71.5	OUV FONTE,FER,ACIER NDA
69979	IRN,STL MANUFACTURES NES	W 4178	18.5	W 8541	27.5	W 9206	31.7	W 58172	71.5	AUT OUVRAGES EN FER NDA
7	MACHINES,TRANSPORT EQUIP		4488.3		4553.9		4874.1		8769.6	MACHINES MATERIEL TRANSPORT
71	POWER GENERATING EQUIPMT		158.1		149.2		136.9		1031.6	MACHINES GENERATRICES
713	INTRNL COMBUS PSTN ENGIN		88.7		64.0	W 3921	39.3	W 90695	895.4	MOTEURS EXPL COMB INT, PIECE
7132	MOTOR VEHCL PISTN ENGINS	W 4377	62.0	W 2577	36.5	W 1541	9.0	W 6238	53.1	MOTEURS EXPL POUR VEHICULES
7139	PISTON ENGINE PARTS NES	W 1734	22.3	W 1872	23.1	W 1729	22.4	W 83915	837.1	PIECES POUR 713.2,3,8
716	ROTATING ELECTRIC PLANT	W 6000	46.3	W 5160	57.2	W 5248	52.9	W 11738	94.6	APP ELECTR ROTATIFS,PIECES
72	MACHS FOR SPCL INDUSTRYS		546.1		510.3		544.2		629.8	MAC SPECIALES POUR INDUST
721	AGRIC MACHY,EXC TRACTORS	W 35159	85.6	W 25310	97.7	W 23118	120.1	W 24361	128.9	MACHINES AGRICOLES
7212	HARVESTING ETC MACHINES	W 13629	46.4	W 15995	62.8	W 14373	81.1	W 14563	84.4	ENGINS POUR LA RECOLTE
72122	COMBINE HARVESTR–THRESHR	W 5932	18.8	W 9835	34.4	W 8468	50.9	W 9092	56.4	MOISSONNEUSES–BATTEUSES
722	TRACTORS NON–ROAD	W 43603	64.8	W 16307	32.5	W 15675	48.9	W 17674	65.5	TRACTEURS
7224	WHEELED TRACTORS NES	W 42831	63.9	W 15950	32.1	W 15388	48.5	W 17288	64.9	TRACTEURS A ROUES
723	CIVIL ENGNEERG EQUIP ETC	W 16903	67.0	W 11920	48.9	W 10892	41.5	W 14958	52.3	APPAREILS DE GENIE CIVIL
7234	CONST,MINING MACHNRY NES	W 14669	57.0	W 9890	39.7	W 9707	36.5	W 13373	45.0	MACH POUR LA CONST, MINES
724	TEXTILE,LEATHER MACHNRY	W 4888	49.9	W 3600	47.3		50.8	W 6366	58.3	MACH POUR INDUSTRIE TEXTILE
727	FOOD MACHRY NON–DOMESTIC	W 4052	69.7	W 3178	46.5	W 2651	38.2	W 3266	37.9	MACH INDUSTRIES ALIMENT
7272	OTH FOOD PROC MCHY,PARTS	W 3653	67.8	W 3039	45.1	W 2324	35.6	W 3140	36.6	AUT MACH IND ALIMENTAIRE
72722	INDUS FOOD PROC MACH NES	W 3440	63.6	W 2876	44.5	W 2308	35.5	W 3094	36.2	MACHINES BOULANGERIE
728	OTH MACHY FOR SPCL INDUS	W 11950	140.2	W 13404	175.0	W 18320	179.0	W 15774	202.9	AUT MACH IND PARTICULIERES
7284	MACHY FOR SPCL INDUS NES	W 6451	106.0	W 7655	137.1	W 12705	136.2	W 9618	160.5	MACH SPEC IND PARTICUL.
72842	RUBBER,PLASTICS WRKG MCH	W 2203	22.3	W 3378	47.3	W 4821	38.2	W 3967	40.7	MACH IND CAOUT MAT PLAST
72848	OTH MCHY WITH INDIV FNCT	W 2449	40.2	W 2083	40.2	W 2595	40.7	W 3079	65.2	AUTRES MACHINES NDA
73	METALWORKING MACHINERY		66.1		83.1		99.1		151.1	MACH TRAVAIL DES METAUX
736	METALWORKING MACH–TOOLS	W 5905	45.6	W 6479	58.1	W 10098	71.7	W 10775	110.5	MACH–OUTILS TRAVAIL METAUX
74	GENRL INDUSTRL MACHY NES		720.9		775.1		759.0		1111.2	MACH APP INDUSTRIE
741	HEATING,COOLING EQUIPMNT	W 15521	134.8	W 16209	153.4	W 17898	166.8	W 18724	170.3	MACH CHAUFFAGE,PIECES
7414	NONDOM REFRIG EQUIPT,PTS	W 6167	41.8	W 6997	46.8	W 7182	51.2	W 6697	44.5	MAT PRODUCTION DU FROID
7415	AIR–CONDITIONING MACHNRY	W 3268	38.8	W 3101	43.2	W 3807	49.5	W 3789	44.1	GROUPES CONDITION AIR
742	PUMPS FOR LIQUIDS ETC	W 3885	73.9	W 4001	75.0	W 3185	64.0	W 6286	117.3	POMPES MOTO–POMPES
7428	OTHER PUMPS FOR LIQUIDS	W 2147	40.4	W 1934	35.3	W 1263	27.2	W 3362	71.1	AUTRES POMPES POUR LIQ
74288	PUMPS FR LIQUIDS NES ETC	W 1379	22.9	W 1388	22.3	W 882	17.2	W 3043	63.8	POMPES POUR LIQUIDES NDA
743	PUMPS NES,CENTRFUGES ETC	W 11126	113.5	W 11994	127.5	W 11903	114.4	W 15505	140.5	POMPES COMPRES,VENT ETC
7436	GAS,LIQUID FILTERS ETC	W 2828	44.6	W 2868	44.6	W 2387	37.3	W 3519	46.6	APP POUR FILT DES LIQUIDES
744	MECHANICAL HANDLING EQU	W 13046	82.1	W 14905	88.7	W 14777	90.5	W 19072	89.8	EQUIP MANUTENTION PIECES
745	NONELEC MACHY,TOOLS NES	W 10390	148.0	W 9783	137.0	W 7201	124.0	W 6998	134.6	AUT MACH NON ELEC,PIECES
7452	OTH NONELEC MCHS,PTS NES	W 10080	139.6	W 9476	128.1	W 6942	115.2	W 6625	123.2	AUT MACH NON ELEC,PIECES
74522	PACKAGNG,BOTTLNG,ETC MCH	W 3589	79.9	W 3117	66.0	W 1992	57.7	W 1904	57.5	MACH NETT BOUTEILLES,ETC
749	NONELEC MACH PTS,ACC NES	W 11923	169.0	W 13067	193.8	W 12921	199.5	W 46281	458.9	PIECES MACH NON ELEC NDA
7492	COCKS,VALVES ETC NES	W 4669	77.3	W 5056	86.5	W 5022	85.4	W 6865	130.8	ART ROB,SIM POUR TUYAUX
7493	SHAFT,CRANK,PULLEY ETC	W 2214	31.2	W 3023	38.7	W 2606	35.5	W 33637	237.9	ARBRES TRANS,VILEBREQUINS
75	OFFICE MACHNES,ADP EQUIP		454.5		425.5		402.7		1281.5	MACH BUREAU TRAIT AUTOM
751	OFFICE MACHINES		63.4		63.5	W 2147	56.9	W 2092	50.8	MACH,APPAREILS DE BUREAU

4. Special Imports C.I.F. by Commodities according to the S.I.T.C. (Rev. 2) in million U.S. Dollars
Importations Spéciales C.A.F. par Produits d'après la C.T.C.I. (Rév. 2) en millions de Dollars E.U.

SITC CTCI	COMMODITY	1994		1995		1996		1997		PRODUIT
		QUANTITY QUANTITE	VALUE VALEUR	QUANTITY QUANTITE	VALUE VALEUR	QUANTITY QUANTITE	VALUE VALEUR	QUANTITY QUANTITE	VALUE VALEUR	
752	AUTOMTIC DATA PROC EQUIP	W 5050	284.3	W 4759	250.3	W 5080	249.9	W 7323	328.6	MACH TRAIT INFORMATION
7522	DIGITAL COMPUTERS	W 522	58.4	W 387	48.1	W 510	52.0	W 626	60.2	MACH DIGITALES COMPLETES
7523	DIGITL CENTRL PROCESSORS	W 728	69.1	W 559	55.7	W 320	46.5	W 505	55.2	UNITES CENTRALES
7525	ADP PERIPHERAL UNITS	W 3006	96.4	W 3117	99.0	W 2374	68.7	W 3070	70.8	UNITES PERIPHERIQUES
7528	OFF–LINE DATA PROC EQUIP	W 362	20.3	W 517	23.6	W 1517	41.4	W 2626	72.0	MACH AUXIL TRAIT INFORM
759	OFFICE,ADP MCH PTS,ACCES	W 1790	107.0	W 2073	111.9		96.0	W 6673	902.3	PIECES DU 751 ET 752
7599	ACCTG,ETC,ADP MCH PTS,AC	W 1350	88.1	W 1664	90.6	W 1743	72.9	W 5977	879.8	PIECES DU 751 ET 752
76	TELECOMM,SOUND EQUIPMENT		521.0		470.6		613.9		1144.8	EQUIPMENT DE TELECOM
763	SOUND RECORDRS,PHONOGRPH	W 1352	37.5	W 1059	30.9	W 985	32.8	W 2320	64.4	PHONO,APP ENREGISTREMENT
7638	OTHR SOUND APPARATUS ETC	W 1195	33.4	W 934	28.4	W 917	31.5	W 2290	64.0	AUT APP D'ENREGIS,REPROD
764	TELECOM EQPT,PTS,ACC NES	W 7489	437.6	W 7457	391.6	W 8369	527.9	W 26303	994.3	EQUIP TELECOM,PIECES
7641	LINE TELEPHONE,ETC EQUIP	W 942	92.8	W 967	76.4	W 1054	112.9	W 1406	106.6	APP TELEPHON PAR FIL
7643	TV,RADIO TRANSMITTRS ETC	W 482	105.0	W 357	81.6	W 1314	178.8	W 1130	174.9	APP EMET TELE RADIO
7649	PTS NES OF EQUIPMT OF 76	W 4367	215.8	W 4714	208.3	W 4436	208.9	W 19487	678.6	PIECES DE LA DIV 76
76491	PTS NES OF APPAR OF 7641	W 640	79.8	W 605	78.3	W 334	57.9	W 376	52.4	PIECES POUR 764.1
76493	TELECOMM EQUIPMT PTS NES	W 2019	70.5	W 2428	75.0	W 2202	65.7	W 4521	146.0	PIECES 761,762,764.3,8
76499	PARTS ETC OF SOUND EQUIP	W 1647	65.1	W 1602	54.3	W 1763	83.2	W 14260	475.7	PIECES NDA POUR 763
77	ELECTRIC MACHNRY NES ETC		897.0		1098.2		1218.5		2216.9	MACH APP ELECT NDA
771	ELECTRIC POWER MACHY NES	W 2740	43.9	W 3411	57.8	W 4104	61.3	W 10025	135.8	MACH PROD,TRANS ELECTR
7711	TRANSFORMERS,ELECTRICAL	W 843	14.2	W 1275	23.2	W 1642	22.1	W 5013	73.8	TRANSFO ELECTRIQUES
77118	OTHER ELEC TRANSFORMERS	W 665	13.3	W 1053	21.0	W 1306	20.3	W 4506	70.8	AUTRES TRANSFO ELECTRIQ
772	SWITCHGEAR ETC,PARTS NES	W 6885	225.1	W 9121	308.7	W 10023	333.7	W 16914	500.4	APP COUPURE,SECT ETC
7721	SWITCHGEAR ETC	W 5865	164.6	W 7648	227.1	W 8364	250.8	W 13046	338.1	APP COUPURE,SECTIONMNT
7722	PRINTED CIRCUITS,PTS NES	W 600	43.7	W 1022	60.6	W 1284	60.5	W 2825	103.9	CIRCUITS ET PIECES
773	ELECTR DISTRIBUTNG EQUIP	W 25047	166.5	W 29518	208.8	W 30842	267.6	W 44821	423.1	EQUIPMT DISTRIBUTION ELECT
7731	INSULATED WIRE,CABLE ETC	W 22996	138.1	W 26772	162.8	W 26775	186.8	W 39107	316.7	FILS,CABLES ISOLES ELECT
7732	ELECTRC INSULATING EQUIP	W 2051	28.4	W 2747	46.1	W 4067	80.9	W 5714	106.4	EQUIP ISOL ELECTRIQUE
77327	OTH ELEC INSUL FITTG NES	W 992	22.9	W 1596	37.8	W 2377	64.0	W 3563	89.9	PIECES ISOL EN AUT MATIERES
775	HOUSEHOLD TYPE EQUIP NES	W 22330	119.0	W 27177	132.7	W 23428	119.4	W 28877	143.7	MACH,APP USAGE DOMESTQUE
7758	ELECTRO–THERMIC APPL NES	W 6757	45.4	W 8551	49.8	W 7919	49.8	W 10689	60.4	APP ELECTROTHERMIQ NDA
776	TRANSISTORS,VALVES,ETC		104.0	W 4655	123.0	W 4603	156.0	W 27912	537.2	LAMPES,TUBES,VALVES
7761	TV PICTURE TUBES	W 2990	16.5	W 3845	23.2	W 3475	19.5	W 21663	200.2	TUBES CATHODIQUES
7762	OTH ELECTRONIC TUBES ETC		1.8	W 32	2.3	W 13	1.8	W 4438	81.1	AUT LAMPES ELECTRONIQUES
7763	DIODES,TRANSISTORS,ETC	W 285	22.8	W 425	33.2	W 400	41.0	W 793	92.4	DIODES,TRANSISTORS
7764	ELECTRONIC MICROCIRCUITS	W 309	55.0	W 229	54.6	W 342	79.5	W 480	135.1	MICROSTRUCTURES ELECTRON
778	ELECTRICAL MACHINERY NES	W 17154	199.0		236.9	W 16764	251.3	W 27050	452.8	AUTRES MACH ELECT NDA
7783	AUTOMOTIVE ELECTR EQUIP	W 3206	40.8	W 3581	41.6	W 2662	35.7	W 6716	86.5	EQUIP ELECT MOTEURS EXPL
77831	IGNITION,STARTING EQUIP	W 1977	22.6	W 2351	24.5	W 1630	17.8	W 5301	67.0	APP ELEC ALLUM,DEMARRAGE
7788	OTH ELEC MACHY,EQUIP NES	W 3788	83.2		119.0	W 3798	129.9	W 8160	262.0	AUT MACH APP ELEC NDA
77884	ELECTRICAL CONDENSERS	W 640	32.8	W 662	67.6	W 760	81.4	W 2060	155.2	CONDENSATEURS ELECTRIQUES
78	ROAD VEHICLES		1086.3		910.0		991.1		1144.9	VEHICULES ROUTIERS
781	PASS MOTOR VEH EXC BUSES	W 177233	511.6	W 99327	417.9	W 82661	456.8	W 67427	426.0	AUTO TRANSPORT PERSONNES
782	LORRIES,SPCL MTR VEH NES	W 68757	239.3	W 64858	215.6	W 59737	214.1	W 46273	252.6	VEHICULES SPECIAUX,MARCH
7821	LORRIES,TRUCKS	W 65964	221.0	W 62299	199.0	W 56339	200.2	W 44214	235.2	VEHICULES TRANSP MARCHAND
783	ROAD MOTOR VEHICLES NES	W 11975	42.3	W 10904	42.5	W 15405	83.8	W 13985	65.1	VEHICULES ROUTIERS NDA
7832	TRACTORS FOR TR–TRAILERS	W 6652	28.1	W 5824	33.2	W 9553	72.0	W 10606	58.0	TRACTEURS ROUTIERS
784	MOTOR VEH PRTS,ACCES NES	W 34607	214.6	W 23809	160.0	W 23381	162.9	W 50455	327.5	PIECES 722,781,782,783
7849	OTHER MOTOR VEHCL PARTS	W 32828	206.8	W 21865	153.4	W 22003	157.7	W 44636	285.5	PIECES 722,781,782,783
786	TRAILERS,NONMOTR VEH,NES	W 28803	49.5	W 19704	48.7	W 17137	49.1	W 18674	45.6	REMORQUES,CADRES,CONTAIN
79	OTHR TRANSPORT EQUIPMENT		38.7		132.2		109.0		58.2	AUTRE MATERIEL TRANSPORT
791	RAILWAY VEHICLES	W 10680	13.6	W 26099	127.1	W 16300	52.7	W 18176	39.8	VEHIC MAT CHEMINS DE FER
7914	RY COACHES NES NOT POWRD			W 4278	98.2	W 2218	7.2	W 1947	5.0	VOITURES A VOYAGEURS
792	AIRCRAFT ETC	W 409	23.1	W 48	3.7	W 387	53.5	W 102	16.1	APP NAVIGATION AERIENNE
8	MISC MANUFACTURED GOODS		1577.7		1630.2		1697.6		2047.0	ART MANUFACTURES DIVERS
812	*PLUMBG,HEATNG,LGHTNG EQ	W 13373	71.7	W 14679	76.7	W 16672	84.3	W 21496	95.3	APPAR SANITAIRES CHAUFFAGE
8124	LIGHTING EQUIPMENT NES	W 5093	44.1	W 5324	45.6	W 6114	49.6	W 7073	50.4	APPAREILS ECLAIRAGE ETC
821	*FURNITURE,PARTS THEREOF	W 55117	170.3	W 42748	155.5	W 40754	154.2	W 54553	201.0	MEUBLES ET PIECES
8211	CHAIRS,SEATS AND PARTS	W 13594	52.0	W 12161	59.9	W 11449	65.3	W 19152	104.2	SIEGES ET PIECES
82119	PTS NES OF CHAIRS ETC	W 2466	10.3	W 5071	30.5	W 4076	38.3	W 9073	70.0	PIECES DU 821.11
8219	FURNITURE AND PARTS NES	W 40494	106.7	W 29559	86.2	W 28119	80.1	W 34217	87.9	AUTRES MEUBLES ET PIECES
82192	WOOD FURNITURE NES	W 26002	61.3	W 18392	48.5	W 16536	43.3	W 21161	47.8	MEUBLES NDA EN BOIS
84	CLOTHING AND ACCESSORIES		339.3		376.4		393.5		386.4	VETEMENTS
843	WOMENS OUTERWEAR NONKNIT	W 6454	66.3	W 4187	61.8	W 3975	62.9	W 4425	57.5	VET DESSUS FEMMES MAT TEX
844	UNDER GARMENTS NOT KNIT	W 8685	33.1	W 11146	47.3	W 5591	43.5	W 4746	36.4	VETEMENT DESSOUS MAT TEX
845	OUTERWEAR KNIT NONELASTC	W 6886	47.4	W 3812	55.5	W 3587	57.7	W 3894	51.1	VET DESSOUS,ACCES BONNET
846	UNDER GARMENTS KNITTED	W 17570	114.0	W 10134	126.0	W 9471	135.6	W 10718	125.4	SOUS VETS DE BONNETERIE
8462	— OF COTTON NON ELASTIC	W 15251	70.0	W 8198	75.4	W 7384	84.0	W 8651	80.5	SOUS–VET BONNET COTON
84629	—— OTHER	W 15251	70.0	W 8198	75.4	W 7384	84.0	W 8651	80.5	AUT SOUS–VET BONNET COTON
851	*FOOTWEAR	W 31209	95.9	W 18425	85.1	W 18254	100.1	W 24319	99.8	CHAUSSURES
85102	FOOTWEAR LEATHER	W 20328	80.9	W 14700	74.4	W 11912	74.5	W 15187	75.8	CHAUS SEMELLES EN CUIR
87	PRECISION INSTRUMNTS NES		272.7		265.8		264.5		313.4	INSTRUM,APPAR SCIENT NDA
872	MEDICAL INSTRUMENTS NES	W 1843	99.0	W 1898	79.8	W 1807	70.6	W 2375	78.0	INSTR,APP MEDIC–CHIR NDA
87202	OTH MEDICAL INSTRUMENTS	W 1565	86.9	W 1697	71.4	W 1538	61.1	W 2075	69.4	INSTRUM,APP MEDECINE
874	MEASURNG,CONTROLNG INSTR		150.8	W 3566	161.9		161.3		203.5	INSTRUMENTS DE MESURE
8748	ELEC MEAS,CONTRL EQU NES	W 365	52.0	W 389	49.7	W 313	51.2	W 396	55.9	APP ELEC ELECTRO MESURE
87483	OTH ELCTRNC MEAS ETC EQU	W 309	47.3	W 283	45.7	W 240	45.7	W 321	49.8	AUT APP ELECTRO DE MESURE
88	PHOTO EQU,OPTICL GDS ETC		88.1		84.4		83.6		90.5	APP,FOURN PHOTO,OP,MONTR
89	MISC MANUFCTRD GOODS NES		518.7		568.3		597.6		839.5	ART MANUFACTURES DIVERS
892	PRINTED MATTER		102.8	W 18755	102.2	W 15930	90.3	W 22917	106.2	IMPRIMES
8928	PRINTED MATTER NES		52.7	W 7930	52.5	W 7262	53.6	W 9368	61.0	IMPRIMES NDA
893	ARTICLES OF PLASTIC NES		179.2		231.3		264.5		376.5	OUVRAGES EN MAT DIVIS 58
8931	PLSTC PACKG CONTNRS,LIDS	W 13760	40.1	W 14602	48.8	W 20834	65.0	W 30998	87.9	ART TRANSP EMBALLAGE ETC
8939	MISC PLASTIC ARTICLES	W 24174	135.0	W 23182	177.0	W 25409	191.2	W 38876	276.0	ART DIVERS EN MAT DIV 58
89399	OTHR PLASTC ARTICLES NES	W 20309	125.8	W 19563	167.6	W 22281	183.4	W 35311	267.5	AUT OUV MAT DIV 58
894	TOYS,SPORTING GOODS,ETC	W 13847	71.3	W 11447	62.1	W 10695	67.3	W 11775	74.3	VOITURES ENFANTS,JOUETS
8942	TOYS,INDOOR GAMES ETC	W 10727	51.8	W 8869	44.0	W 8132	45.0	W 8600	50.2	JOUETS,JEUX ETC
898	MUSICAL INSTRUMENTS,PTS	W 4768	48.7		57.3	W 4096	54.9		145.6	INSTRUMENTS DE MUSIQUE
8983	SOUND RECRDNG TAPE,DISCS	W 4216	43.2	W 5179	52.9	W 3910	50.5	W 4382	141.0	SUPPORTS SON POUR 763
89831	PREPD SND RECORDNG MEDIA	W 3259	25.4	W 4230	26.3	W 2734	26.5	W 3004	115.9	SUPPORTS PREPARES
899	OTHER MANUFACTURED GOODS		68.5		72.0		79.6		88.1	AUT ART MANUF DIVERS NDA
9	GOODS NOT CLASSD BY KIND		589.0		281.6		169.5		332.5	ART TRANSACT NON CLASSES
931	*SPECIAL TRANSACTIONS		587.6		280.7		166.3		315.7	TRANS.SPECIALES

5. Special Exports F.O.B. by Commodities according to the S.I.T.C. (Rev. 2) in million U.S. Dollars
Exportations Spéciales F.O.B. par Produits d'après la C.T.C.I. (Rév. 2) en millions de Dollars E.U.

SITC CTCI	COMMODITY	1994 QUANTITY QUANTITE	1994 VALUE VALEUR	1995 QUANTITY QUANTITE	1995 VALUE VALEUR	1996 QUANTITY QUANTITE	1996 VALUE VALEUR	1997 QUANTITY QUANTITE	1997 VALUE VALEUR	PRODUIT
	ALL COMMODITIES		10699.9		12865.5		13144.1		19099.2	TOUS PRODUITS
0	FOOD AND LIVE ANIMALS		1728.8		2254.2		2050.0		2193.0	ALIMENTS,ANIMAUX VIVANTS
001	*LIVE ANIMALS FOR FOOD	W 61295	125.8	W 54806	122.0	W 67080	135.9	W 62733	129.3	ANIMAUX VIVANTS
0011	BOVINE SPECIES,LIVE	W 31963	52.9	W 27850	49.5	W 33873	51.1	W 32508	46.8	ESPECE BOVINE
00119	— OTHR THAN FR BREEDING	W 27528	43.7	W 25471	43.2	W 32760	49.1	W 31744	45.3	BOVINS NON REPRODUCTEURS
0012	SHEEP AND GOATS,LIVE	W 20393	51.2	W 19306	50.5	W 18683	52.3	W 17998	49.6	ESPECES OVINE ET CAPRINE
00121	SHEEP,LIVE	W 20368	51.2	W 19269	50.4	W 18645	52.1	W 17946	49.4	ESPECE OVINE
01	MEAT AND PREPARATIONS		594.8		687.5		787.6		791.1	VIANDES ET PREPARATIONS
011	MEAT FRESH,CHILLD,FROZEN	W 149982	457.6	W 184589	543.1	W 237814	618.1	W 230787	589.9	VIANDES FRAICHES,REF,CONGE
0111	BOVINE MEAT FRESH,FROZEN	W 13447	33.0	W 8207	23.3	W 10506	28.2	W 10349	24.7	VIANDES BOVIN FRAI,REF
0113	PIG MEAT FRESH,CHLD,FRZN	W 41647	90.6	W 54052	124.5	W 103046	228.7	W 95810	218.6	VIANDE DE PORC
0114	POULTRY FRESH CHLLD,FRZN	W 76354	228.2	W 105530	295.2	W 107312	283.9	W 107215	261.1	VOLAILLES MORTES
0118	MEAT NES FRESH,CHLD,FRZN	W 12927	100.1	W 13553	96.9	W 11886	72.4	W 12453	80.8	AUTRES VIANDES,ABATS
01181	POULTRY LIVER FRESH,ETC	W 2282	60.4	W 2168	47.9	W 1372	35.4	W 1744	43.5	FOIES DE VOLAILLES
01189	OTHER MEAT NES FRESH,ETC	W 10645	39.8	W 11385	49.0	W 10514	37.0	W 10709	37.4	VIANDE,ABATS COMESTIBLES
014	MEAT PREPD,PRSVD,NES ETC	W 36034	134.0	W 32963	144.0	W 45633	158.6	W 77072	192.8	CONSERVES DE VIANDES
0142	SAUSAGES INCLDING TINNED	W 8189	60.7	W 9312	72.5	W 15324	92.4	W 29674	106.5	SAUCISSES,SAUCISSONS
0149	OTH PREPARD,PRESRVD MEAT	W 27845	73.3	W 23651	71.5	W 30309	66.3	W 47397	86.3	AUTRES PREP DE VIANDES
02	DAIRY PRODCTS,BIRDS'EGGS		40.1		51.3		60.8		60.6	PRODUITS LAITIERS,OEUFS
04	CEREALS AND PREPARATIONS		204.5		594.7		206.6		416.2	CEREALES ET PRODUITS
041	WHEAT ETC UNMILLED	W 759001	81.3	W 2764835	333.5	W 299463	54.5	W 970817	126.2	FROMENT,EPEAUTRE
0411	DURUM WHEAT UNMILLED	W 137863	14.5	W 647703	74.9	W 32537	6.3	W 37984	6.6	FROMENT DUR NON MOULU
0412	OTHER WHEAT ETC UNMILLED	W 621138	66.8	W 2117132	258.7	W 266925	48.2	W 932833	119.6	AUTRE FROMENT NON MOULU
044	MAIZE UNMILLED	W 180607	74.8	W 601031	109.4	W 129157	42.2	W 1192097	157.3	MAIS NON MOULU
046	WHEAT ETC MEAL OR FLOUR	W 57582	11.2	W 370315	76.0	W 66965	19.8	W 190050	47.6	SEMOULE FARINE,FROMENT
04601	FLOUR OF WHEAT OR MESLIN	W 57079	11.0	W 367949	75.5	W 57984	17.0	W 184319	46.0	FARINE DE FROMENT
048	CEREAL ETC PREPARATIONS	W 37117	24.9	W 82274	42.6	W 91466	56.4	W 86904	58.9	PREPTNS A BASE CEREALES
05	VEGETABLES AND FRUIT		534.8		511.1		522.5		462.8	LEGUMES ET FRUITS
054	VEG ETC FRSH,SMPLY PRSVD	W 290312	121.0	W 232318	127.7	W 419299	140.7	W 283191	122.4	LEGUMES FRAIS,CONG,SECS
0545	OTHER FRESH VEGETABLES	W 99416	59.7	W 118177	69.1	W 124687	64.6	W 86127	61.6	AUTRES LEGUMES FRAIS,REF
05459	FRESH VEGETABLES NES	W 58425	45.1	W 66440	52.4	W 61897	51.3	W 70213	55.9	LEGUMES FRAIS,REFRI NDA
0546	VEGETABLES SIMPLY PRESVD	W 58198	40.9	W 57814	42.0	W 82593	54.9	W 71374	47.9	LEGUMES CONG,CONSER
05461	VEGETABLES FROZEN	W 55700	39.3	W 57331	41.8	W 82479	54.9	W 71105	47.6	LEGUMES CONGELES
056	VEGTBLES ETC PRSVD,PREPD	W 131810	123.8	W 144789	144.3	W 138401	114.5	W 167921	132.5	CONSERVES DE LEGUMES
0565	VEGTBLES PRSVD,PREPD NES	W 124648	103.2	W 138009	120.6	W 130811	91.4	W 162406	117.0	LEGUMES PREPARES CONSERVE
05651	VEGTBLS,FRUIT IN VINEGAR	W 79252	62.3	W 92768	81.0	W 71501	47.5	W 85924	61.2	LEGUM CONSERV AU VINAIGRE
05659	OTH VEG PRESVD,PREPD NES	W 45396	40.9	W 45241	39.6	W 59310	43.9	W 76482	55.8	LEGUM PREPAP,CONSERV NDA
057	FRUIT,NUTS,FRESH,DRIED	W 189552	75.6	W 123241	48.7	W 201830	69.6	W 154755	66.4	FRUITS FRAIS OU SECS
0579	FRUIT FRESH OR DRIED NES	W 89057	41.3	W 86866	33.3	W 144566	49.2	W 121114	54.7	FRUITS FRAIS,SECS NDA
058	FRUIT PRESERVED,PREPARED	W 264324	214.6	W 289931	190.5	W 270299	197.9		141.7	CONSERVES DE FRUITS
0585	FRUIT OR VEGETABLE JUICE	W 192432	144.9	W 231706	128.6	W 212016	137.2	W 164817	86.8	JUS DE FRUITS
05857	JUICE OF OTHER FRUIT,VEG	W 136397	112.0	W 144303	85.1	W 146950	109.2	W 114531	64.9	JUS AUTRES FRUITS,LEGUMES
06	SUGAR AND PREPS,HONEY		26.9		54.2		57.1		55.3	SUCRES ET PRODUITS
061	SUGAR AND HONEY	W 20081	19.5	W 72456	46.0	W 68720	41.3	W 105014	36.2	SUCRES ET MIEL
07	COFFEE,TEA,COCOA,SPICES		72.0		78.1		83.0		72.4	CAFE,THE,CACAO,EPICES
073	CHOCOLATE AND PRODUCTS	W 13487	38.8	W 12675	38.5	W 15225	46.2	W 13857	40.3	CHOCOLAT
081	*FEEDING STUFF FOR ANIML	W 132017	30.4	W 213197	44.5	W 286604	70.3	W 184491	55.3	NOURRITURE POUR ANIMAUX
0819	FOOD WASTE AND FEED NES	W 92938	23.5	W 92669	27.9	W 148817	51.1	W 97684	42.6	DECHETS,ALIMENTS NDA
09	MISC EDIBLE PRODUCTS		92.1		103.2		118.5		144.8	PREP ALIMENTAIRES DIVERSES
098	EDIBLE PRODCTS,PREPS NES	W 71174	84.1	W 71314	97.7	W 97936	111.6	W 124189	139.6	PREP ALIMENTAIRES NDA
09809	MISC FOOD PREPRTIONS NES	W 55845	63.3	W 54369	71.5	W 80422	87.4	W 102212	113.4	PREP ALIMENTAIRES NDA
1	BEVERAGES AND TOBACCO		192.1		258.8		323.7		224.8	BOISSONS ET TABACS
11	BEVERAGES		178.1		257.6		235.2		179.5	BOISSONS
111	NON-ALCOHL BEVERAGES NES	W 27485	14.1	W 35908	15.2	W 189138	72.6	W 194659	72.7	BOISSONS NON ALCOOLIQUES
11102	FLAVORED WATERS NON-ALCO	W 26676	13.8	W 34501	14.9	W 185592	71.5	W 192702	72.1	LIMONADES,EAUX GAZEUSES
112	ALCOHOLIC BEVERAGES	W 223219	164.1	W 312009	242.4	W 216660	162.7	W 120585	106.9	BOISSONS ALCOOLIQUES
1121	WINE OF FRESH GRAPES ETC	W 104267	93.6	W 127413	124.4	W 108778	96.1	W 103136	96.5	VINS DE RAISINS FRAIS
11212	WINE OF FRESH GRAPES	W 102201	92.6	W 126893	124.2	W 106178	94.0	W 100641	94.2	VINS DE MOUTS DE RAISINS
1124	DISTILLED ALCOHOLIC BEVS	W 93349	61.7	W 168623	113.1	W 97450	61.8	W 9945	7.0	ALCOOLS,EAUX-DE-VIE
11249	OTH ALCOHOLC BEVS,CMPNDS	W 93122	61.5	W 168236	112.8	W 97386	61.7	W 9868	6.9	BOISSONS ALCOOLIQUES NDA
12	TOBACCO AND MANUFACTURES		14.0		1.3		88.5		45.4	TABACS BRUTS FABRIQUES
122	TOBACCO,MANUFACTURED	W 1786	11.2			W 13147	83.3	W 6264	43.9	TABACS FABRIQUES
1222	CIGARETTES	W 1786	11.2			W 7374	56.8	W 6264	43.9	CIGARETTES
2	CRUDE MATERLS,EXCL FUELS		523.2		595.9		573.3		523.7	MAT BRUTES NON COMESTIBLES
22	OIL SEEDS,OLEAGINOUS FRT		99.1		101.6		121.3		85.1	GRAINES,FRUITS OLEAGINEUX
222	SEEDS FOR'SOFT'FIXED OIL	W 304447	90.8	W 311750	92.6	W 344629	103.1	W 237229	66.3	GRAINES HUILES FIXES
2224	SUNFLOWER SEEDS	W 271384	82.3	W 249486	77.1	W 219900	70.1	W 155501	45.3	GRAINES DE TOURNESOL
24	CORK AND WOOD		115.7		130.2		122.9		129.4	LIEGE ET BOIS
247	OTH WOOD ROUGH,SQUARED	W 914758	53.3	W 928673	61.4	W 802481	52.6	W 1145586	56.2	BOIS BRUTS EQUARRIS
2472	SAW-,VENEER-LOGS NON-CON	W 771341	46.6	W 928673	61.4	W 645902	44.0	W 970629	49.5	NON CONIFERES SCIAGE,PLAC
24721	— IN THE ROUGH	W 771341	46.6	W 928673	61.4	W 645902	44.0	W 970629	49.5	BRUTS ECORCES DEGROSSIS
248	WOOD SHAPED,SLEEPERS	W 138431	52.1	W 141753	57.6	W 140891	56.5	W 184731	61.5	BOIS SIMPLEMENT TRAVAILLES
2483	LUMBER SHAPED NON-CONIFR	W 131508	49.1	W 133114	53.8	W 128920	52.5	W 172217	56.0	NON CONIFERES SCIES,RABOTES
24831	LUMBER SAWN ETC NON-CON	W 116672	37.7	W 120209	41.6	W 116194	40.7	W 157684	43.9	SCIES LONGITUDINALEMENT
28	METALLIFEROUS ORES,SCRAP		129.4		195.3		153.6		136.0	MINERAIS METAL,DECHETS
282	IRON AND STEEL SCRAP	W 637401	66.4	W 751557	90.1	W 611508	64.0	W 643823	65.7	FERRAILLES
28209	— OF OTHR IRON OR STEEL	W 611020	61.1	W 734242	84.3	W 590921	57.9	W 625476	58.6	FERRAILLES DE FER
287	BASE METAL ORES,CONC NES	W 76930	17.1	W 160817	36.5	W 176057	49.3	W 155002	28.1	MINERAIS METAUX COMMUNS
2873	ALUMINIUM ORES,ALUMINA	W 76930	17.1	W 160789	36.4	W 176057	49.3	W 154987	28.1	MINERAIS D'ALUMINIUM
28732	ALUMINA(ALUMINIUM OXIDE)	W 76930	17.1	W 141275	35.8	W 176057	49.3	W 95707	26.3	ALUMINE (OXYDE ALUMINIUM)
288	NONFERR METAL SCRAP NES	W 55562	46.1	W 64000	68.9	W 50768	40.5	W 37349	40.0	DECHETS NON FERREUX
2882	OTHER BASE MTL SCRAP NES	W 53360	45.1	W 61640	67.9	W 48826	40.1	W 34605	39.6	AUTRES DECHETS
28821	COPPER WASTE AND SCRAP	W 17833	26.0	W 22125	43.7	W 13233	20.6	W 13268	19.4	DECHETS DE CUIVRE
29	CRUDE ANIMAL,VEG MAT NES		124.9		109.3		118.9		105.7	MATIERES BRUTES ANIM,VEGET
291	CRUDE ANIMAL MTRIALS NES		97.1		70.2	W 12186	78.0	W 10951	71.7	MATIERES BRUTES ANIMALES
2919	OTH ANIMAL MATERIALS NES		76.1		49.1	W 8245	60.2	W 8353	56.6	MAT ORIGINE ANIMALE NDA
29196	BIRDS SKINS,FEATHERS,ETC	W 5403	69.5	W 3496	42.5	W 3963	53.6	W 4279	50.0	PLUMES,DUVETS BRUTS
292	CRUDE VEG MATERIALS NES	W 28379	27.9	W 32820	39.2	W 34712	41.0	W 42589	34.1	MAT BRUTES VEGETALES NDA
3	MINERAL FUELS ETC		367.7		384.2		427.5		433.2	COMBUSTIBLES MINERAUX LUB
33	PETROLEUM AND PRODUCTS		340.7		353.5		372.3		331.9	PETROLE ET DERIVES
334	PETROLEUM PRODUCTS,REFIN	W 1654608	302.9	W 1665610	316.6	W 1530032	340.2	W 1362104	306.5	PRODUITS RAFFINES
335	RESIDUAL PETRLM PROD NES	W 139980	37.9	W 93791	36.9	W 58108	32.2	W 41526	25.5	PRODUITS RESIDUELS NDA
351	*ELECTRIC CURRENT								95.1	ENERGIE ELECTRIQUE
4	ANIMAL,VEGETABLE OIL,FAT		85.1		48.3		49.4		166.4	HUILES,GRAISSES ANIM,VEG
42	FIXED VEGETABLE OIL,FAT		77.2		42.6		41.3		160.1	HUILES VEGETALES FIXES
423	FIXED VEG OILS,SOFT	W 111461	76.8	W 39870	42.3	W 45737	41.1	W 218018	157.9	HUILES VEGET DOUCES FIXES
4236	SUNFLOWER SEED OIL	W 111461	76.8	W 39870	42.3	W 45737	41.1	W 218018	157.9	HUILE DE TOURNESOL
5	CHEMCLS,RELATED PROD NES		1038.0		1420.6		1296.4		1452.7	PRODUITS CHIMIQUES
51	ORGANIC CHEMICALS		199.2		265.2		210.4		220.4	PROD CHIMIQ ORGANIQUES
511	HYDROCARBONS NES,DERIVS	W 194940	49.6	W 226553	93.7	W 115675	30.3	W 68026	21.1	HYDROCARBURES NDA
5112	CYCLIC HYDROCARBONS	W 105902	26.4	W 140937	54.5	W 96608	25.3	W 48392	15.9	HYDROCARBURES CYCLIQUES

5. Special Exports F.O.B. by Commodities according to the S.I.T.C. (Rev. 2) in million U.S. Dollars
Exportations Spéciales F.O.B. par Produits d'après la C.T.C.I. (Rév. 2) en millions de Dollars E.U.

SITC CTCI	COMMODITY	1994 QUANTITY QUANTITE	1994 VALUE VALEUR	1995 QUANTITY QUANTITE	1995 VALUE VALEUR	1996 QUANTITY QUANTITE	1996 VALUE VALEUR	1997 QUANTITY QUANTITE	1997 VALUE VALEUR	PRODUIT
513	CARBOXYLIC ACIDS ETC	W 23183	20.1	W 35685	45.0		22.7		28.4	ACIDES CARBOXYLIQUES
514	NITROGEN–FNCTN COMPOUNDS		82.5		80.0		80.2	W 13329	101.5	COMPOSES FONCT AZOTEES
5146	OXYGEN–FNCT AMINO–CMPNDS	W 8248	44.7	W 7079	36.6	W 6361	29.2	W 7576	33.8	COMP AMINES FONCT OXYGEN
515	ORG–INORG COMPOUNDS ETC		35.1	W 794	37.5	W 2655	66.0	W 2297	49.1	COMPOSES ORGANO–MINERAUX
5156	HETEROCYCLIC CMPDS ETC		32.8	W 702	33.9	W 1067	50.2	W 1013	38.8	COMPOSES HETEROCYCLIQUES
51569	OTH HETEROCYC CMPDS,ETC		32.8	W 702	33.9	W 1067	50.2	W 1013	38.8	AUT COMP HETEROCYCLIQUES
52	INORGANIC CHEMICALS		62.1		105.7		91.2		89.3	PROD CHIM INORGANIQUES
522	INORG ELEMNTS,OXIDES,ETC		61.1	W 392922	92.2	W 333156	80.5	W 329605	73.7	ELEMENTS INORGANIQUES
5225	INORGANIC BASES ETC NES	W 230782	44.5	W 278159	64.5	W 206701	49.9	W 212333	42.8	AUTRES BASES OXYDES METAL
541	*MEDICINAL,PHARM PRODUCT	K 7993742	249.5		276.7		281.4		357.3	PROD MEDICINAUX PHARMACEUT
5417	MEDICAMENTS	K 6561245	216.2	K 7836984	230.1	K 8152475	243.6	MK 10023	315.0	MEDICAMENTS
54173	— CONTAINING ALKALOIDS	K 244124	24.1	K 542917	39.4	K 347944	33.0	K 463303	44.4	MED CONTEN ALCALOIDES
54179	— CONTNG OTH SUBSTANCES	K 5483393	164.4	K 5672191	154.6	K 7328840	189.8	K 8820833	235.9	MED CONT AUT SUBSTANCES
55	PERFUME,CLEANING ETC PRD		17.4		24.6		52.1		64.4	PROD POUR PARFUM,TOILETTE
58	PLASTIC MATERIALS ETC		397.8		563.8		459.5		509.2	MAT PLAST ARTIFICIELLES
583	POLYMERIZATION ETC PRODS	W 510983	388.5	W 516430	548.9	W 495684	446.3	W 548890	498.8	PROD POLYMERISATION
5831	POLYETHYLENE	W 178268	116.2	W 193402	179.0	W 166161	134.6	W 189291	163.6	POLYETHYLENE
58311	— IN PRIMARY FORMS	W 167364	104.5	W 181976	161.4	W 157807	122.7	W 180804	150.1	POLYETHYLENE PRIMAIRES
5832	POLYPROPYLENE	W 101285	65.5	W 87729	83.6	W 81633	66.7	W 68963	59.1	POLYPROPYLENE
58321	— IN PRIMARY FORMS	W 94971	55.2	W 82716	68.7	W 76619	54.3	W 61999	45.0	POLYPROPYLENE PRIMAIRES
5833	POLYSTYRENE,ITS COPOLYMR	W 69589	66.8	W 73818	100.8	W 75870	78.9	W 74415	66.9	POLYPROPYLENE COPOLYMERES
58331	— IN PRIMARY FORMS	W 69280	66.1	W 73652	100.4	W 75236	77.7	W 73498	65.9	SOUS FORMES PRIMAIRES
5834	POLYVINYL CHLORIDE	W 148998	114.6	W 148981	147.1	W 154329	115.9	W 187410	149.0	CHLORURE DE POLYVINYLE
58341	— IN PRIMARY FORMS	W 138428	97.3	W 137256	124.6	W 139710	89.2	W 169889	119.4	SOUS FORMES PRIMAIRES
5839	OTH POLYMRZTION ETC PROD	W 10543	20.0	W 8991	29.8	W 12812	39.6	W 25928	53.9	AUT PROD POLYMER COPOLYM
59	CHEMICAL MATERIALS NES		83.4		141.6		150.2		157.6	MAT PROD CHIMIQUES NDA
591	PESTICIDES,DISINFECTANTS	W 10059	49.7	W 9567	68.5	W 13614	62.2	W 30107	59.0	DESINF,INSECT,FONG,HERB
598	MISCEL CHEM PRODUCTS NES		13.4		61.8		66.3		73.3	PROD DIV INDUST CHIM NDA
5989	CHEM PRODUCTS,PREPS NES	W 11134	11.2		59.0	W 36911	64.9	W 48376	70.6	PROD PREP CHIMIQUES NDA
59899	OTH CHEM PRODS,PREPS,NES	W 7278	6.8	W 27281	53.7	W 33146	59.9	W 43546	63.9	AUT PRODUITS CHIMIQUES NDA
6	BASIC MANUFACTURES		1724.0		2275.1		2405.3		2571.4	ART MANUFACTURES
61	LEATHER,DRESSED FUR,ETC		150.4		154.2		169.0		170.4	CUIRS,PELLETERIES
611	LEATHER		36.8		40.7	W 6796	44.6		47.2	CUIRS,PEAUX PREPARES
612	LEATHER ETC MANUFACTURES	W 3908	110.5	W 4109	109.7	W 4261	120.0	W 5706	120.3	OUVRAGES EN CUIRS NDA
6123	PREPRD PARTS OF FOOTWEAR	W 3783	109.3	W 3875	105.8	W 4135	118.6	W 5608	119.0	PARTIES DE CHAUSSURES
62	RUBBER MANUFACTURES NES		107.1		139.2		158.7		168.0	CAOUTCHOUC MANUFACTURE
625	RUBBER TYRES, TUBES ETC	W 25512	65.4	W 32995	84.5	W 32952	91.2	W 34357	84.6	PNEUS CAOUTCHOUC VULCANISE
6252	TYRES,NEW,BUS OR LORRY	W 11871	29.7	W 14926	40.9	W 14829	42.9	W 16565	43.1	PNEUS POUR AUTOBUS,CAMIONS
6259	OTH TYRES,TYRE CASES,ETC	W 13518	35.4	W 17761	42.8	W 17916	47.5	W 17694	41.1	AUTRES PNEUS RECHAPES FLAPS
62599	TYRES NES,TYRE CASES,ETC	W 12896	34.1	W 16877	40.5	W 17130	45.1	W 16925	38.7	PNEUS,FLAPS
628	RUBBER ARTICLES NES	W 5828	30.0	W 7897	41.1	W 8842	44.2	W 10676	50.8	OUVRAGES CAOUTCHOUC NDA
63	WOOD,CORK MANUFACTRS NES		111.2		146.3		168.3		190.4	OUVRAGES LIEGE ET BOIS
634	VENEERS,PLYWOOD,ETC	W 85877	30.5	W 82355	36.3	W 106536	44.0	W 120717	48.9	PLACAGES,CONTRE–PLAQUES
635	WOOD MANUFACTURES NES	W 129730	80.7	W 194069	110.0	W 194344	124.2	W 265573	141.0	ART MANUF EN BOIS NDA
6353	BUILDERS WOODWRK,PREFABS	W 25207	52.0	W 30701	68.9	W 35523	78.5	W 41526	82.7	OUVRAGES DE MENUISERIE
64	PAPER,PAPERBOARD AND MFR		120.1		162.9		228.9		266.6	PAPIERS,CARTONS & OUVRAGES
641	PAPER AND PAPERBOARD	W 106516	54.1	W 120484	72.9	W 171884	117.7	W 224440	137.9	PAPIERS ET CARTONS
6415	PAPER,PAPERBRD,BULK,NES	W 55051	23.5	W 53132	27.9	W 104559	67.4	W 133341	72.8	PAPIERS,CARTONS ROULEAUX
64159	OTHER PAPER ETC,BULK,NES	W 9644	7.9	W 12983	14.6	W 103040	65.6	W 130280	69.6	AUT PAPIER ROULEAUX FEUILLES
642	PAPER,ETC,PRECUT,ARTS OF	W 35431	66.0	W 42512	90.0	W 52674	111.2	W 70383	128.7	PAP,CARTONS DECOUPES
6428	PAPER ETC ARTICLES NES	W 15332	38.1	W 18520	51.9	W 22381	68.3	W 21734	63.6	OUVRAGES EN PATE A PAPIER
64285	PAPER ETC DIAPERS ETC	W 9534	33.2	W 11447	45.1	W 14568	59.8	W 12481	54.3	SERVIETTES HYGIENIQUES
65	TEXTILE YARN,FABRICS,ETC		235.0		273.1		280.1		271.7	FILS,TISSUS,ARTICLES TEXTILE
651	TEXTILE YARN	W 10489	49.7	W 11919	49.8	W 9630	48.9		46.8	FILS TEXTILES
658	TEXTILE ARTICLES NES		68.1		89.9	W 12149	91.0		87.5	ART FACONNES MAT TEXTILES
6584	LINENS ETC	W 2655	31.6	W 3665	48.2	W 4019	51.4	W 3655	39.4	LINGE DE MAISON
66	NONMETAL MINERAL MFS NES		205.0		230.6		265.4		296.2	ART MIN NON METALLIQUES
662	CLAY,REFRACTORY BLDG PRD	W 58594	27.2	W 60065	35.3	W 119838	39.7	W 237030	42.4	MAT CONST REFRACTAIRES
663	MINERAL MANUFCTURES NES		29.8		42.7		58.2	W 216884	63.9	ART MIN MANUF NDA
664	GLASS	W 146180	66.4	W 132956	72.6	W 139757	69.1	W 133400	83.3	VERRE
6644	GLASS SURFACE–GROUND ETC	W 108350	37.3	W 99036	41.4	W 107709	38.1	W 93329	30.7	VERRE COULE,LAMINE
665	GLASSWARE	W 5154	33.1	W 6013	34.6	W 22694	46.2	W 40089	51.7	OUVRAGES EN VERRE
67	IRON AND STEEL		268.9		385.8		373.8		312.9	FER ET ACIER
672	IRON,STEEL PRIMARY FORMS	W 116912	36.2	W 218654	84.1	W 355089	103.5	W 154896	44.9	LINGOTS FER,ACIER
6727	IRN,STL COIL FR REROLLNG	W 101224	29.4	W 193276	68.8	W 315180	89.5	W 131717	37.7	EBAUCHES POUR TOLES FER
67271	IRON,SIMPLE STEEL COILS	W 101159	29.4	W 193140	68.8	W 315180	89.5	W 131716	37.7	EBAUCHES NON EN ACIER
673	IRON,STEEL SHAPES ETC	W 161694	49.3	W 141378	54.1	W 91507	35.6	W 95729	33.5	BARRES,PROFIL FER,ACIER
6733	IRON,STEEL PROFILES ETC	W 126496	34.8	W 70293	23.9	W 52606	17.4	W 58256	17.6	PROFILES,PALPLAN FER,ACIER
674	IRN,STL UNIV,PLATE,SHEET		119.4	W 354887	166.6	W 397004	158.4	W 401948	157.5	LARGES PLATS,TOLES
6744	IRN,STL HVY PLATE,ROLLED	W 142271	44.4	W 151277	62.3	W 92393	31.1	W 112628	36.1	TOLES LAMINEES PLUS 4.75 MM
67441	— OF IRON OR SIMPLE STL	W 142227	44.3	W 151065	61.7	W 92299	30.8	W 112558	36.0	TOLES NON ACIER FIN CARB
6745	IRN,STL MED PLATE,ROLLED	W 49473	18.9	W 95061	39.3	W 166675	58.6	W 139729	49.3	TOLES 3 A 4.75 MM
67451	— OF IRON OR SIMPLE STL	W 46676	17.2	W 89714	34.9	W 161215	54.3	W 130138	44.3	TOLES AUT NON ACIER FIN
6746	IRN,STL THIN PLATE,ROLLD	W 135086	55.6	W 107319	63.7	W 132919	63.1	W 96322	43.0	TOLES LAM MOINS 3MM
67461	— OF IRON OR SIMPLE STL	W 132073	49.8	W 101898	50.5	W 129794	56.5	W 92992	37.0	TOL NON AC FIN MOINS 3 MM
678	IRON,STL TUBES,PIPES,ETC	W 91888	49.7	W 95971	65.1	W 87259	58.1	W 98980	56.4	TUBES,TUYAUX EN FONTE,FER
68	NON–FERROUS METALS		262.0		416.9		347.9		425.8	METAUX NON FERREUX
682	COPPER EXC CEMENT COPPER	W 13271	31.5	W 21591	62.2	W 14252	38.3	W 21303	56.8	CUIVRE
6822	COPPER,ALLOYS WORKED	W 13072	31.2	W 21139	61.1	W 14252	38.3	W 21301	56.8	CUIVRE,ALLIAGES OUVRES
684	ALUMINIUM	W 124529	227.5	W 142555	353.7	W 143359	309.4	W 166014	366.3	ALUMINIUM
6841	ALUMINIUM,ALLOYS,UNWRGHT	W 32369	47.1	W 48617	99.7	W 20416	36.0	W 19162	33.4	ALUMINIUM,ALLIAGES BRUTS
6842	ALUMINIUM,ALLOYS WORKED	W 92160	180.5	W 93939	254.0	W 122943	273.4	W 146852	332.9	ALUMINIUM,ALLIAGES OUVRE
68421	ALUMINIUM BARS,WIRE,ETC	W 28207	50.9	W 38099	96.1	W 63446	132.9	W 69761	147.7	BARRES,PROFILES FILS ALU
68422	ALUMNM PLATE,SHEET,STRIP	W 57701	113.9	W 49937	139.1	W 56570	130.3	W 74634	175.2	TOLES, PLANCHES EN ALU
69	METAL MANUFACTURES NES		264.8		366.4		413.6		469.8	ART MANUFACT EN METAL NDA
691	STRUCTURES AND PARTS NES	W 43919	82.3	W 52911	115.6	W 61995	125.3	W 68618	128.0	CONSTRUCT FER,ACIER,ALU
6911	STRUCTURES,PARTS IRN,STL	W 39230	54.7	W 46462	77.6	W 55907	89.8	W 59162	85.1	CONSTRUCT FER,ACIER,FONTE
692	METAL TANKS,BOXES,ETC	W 19360	41.7	W 15903	42.1	W 16475	48.5	W 37585	49.0	RECIPIENTS METALLIQUES
697	BASE MTL HOUSEHOLD EQUIP	W 14229	42.9	W 16856	54.1	W 19865	61.5	W 24870	64.2	ART MENAGE MET COMMUNS
6973	DMSTC HEATG,COOKG APPARA	W 10766	29.3	W 12867	36.7	W 15506	42.3	W 20838	47.5	APPS CHAUF NON ELECTRIQ
699	BASE METAL MFRS NES		64.7		103.5		132.5		161.5	ART MANUFACTURES MET NDA
6991	LOCKSMITHS WARES,ETC	W 6382	27.1	W 8203	34.6	W 9443	41.5	W 11668	50.6	ARTICLES DE SERRURERIE
6998	MFRS NES OF CPR,NIKL,ETC		12.0	W 4576	23.4	W 8812	41.3	W 11428	57.9	OUVRAGES EN CU,NI,AL,PB,ZN
7	MACHINES,TRANSPORT EQUIP		2433.1		3245.8		3284.1		8567.4	MACHINES MATERIEL TRANSPORT
71	POWER GENERATING EQUIPMT		94.4		106.5		135.6		1500.9	MACHINES GENERATRICES
713	INTRNL COMBUS PSTN ENGIN		22.1		21.0	W 2427	26.6	W 146589	1348.4	MOTEURS EXPL COMB INT, PIECE
7132	MOTOR VEHCL PISTN ENGINS	W 1078	11.3	W 824	6.9	W 952	9.3	W 135907	1240.9	MOTEURS EXPL POUR VEHICULES
7139	PISTON ENGINE PARTS NES	W 930	10.6	W 1107	13.5	W 1285	14.9	W 10622	107.2	PIECES POUR 713.2,3,8
716	ROTATING ELECTRIC PLANT		53.5	W 10896	52.8	W 13853	65.0		105.3	APP ELECTR ROTATIFS,PIECES
72	MACHS FOR SPCL INDUSTRYS		193.0		242.1		240.0		272.1	MAC SPECIALES POUR INDUST
721	AGRIC MACHY,EXC TRACTORS	W 18136	64.4		72.8	W 20091	77.3	W 33973	112.0	MACHINES AGRICOLES

5. Special Exports F.O.B. by Commodities according to the S.I.T.C. (Rev. 2) in million U.S. Dollars
Exportations Spéciales F.O.B. par Produits d'après la C.T.C.I. (Rév. 2) en millions de Dollars E.U.

SITC CTCI	COMMODITY	1994 QUANTITY QUANTITE	1994 VALUE VALEUR	1995 QUANTITY QUANTITE	1995 VALUE VALEUR	1996 QUANTITY QUANTITE	1996 VALUE VALEUR	1997 QUANTITY QUANTITE	1997 VALUE VALEUR	PRODUIT
7212	HARVESTING ETC MACHINES	W 12099	47.9	W 12159	50.4	W 12892	56.7	W 21548	81.5	ENGINS POUR LA RECOLTE
72129	PTS NES OF MACHY OF 7212	W 4974	16.0	W 5955	19.7	W 9398	40.5	W 15362	55.5	PIECES POUR MACH 721.2
723	CIVIL ENGNEERG EQUIP ETC	W 15728	35.8	W 17767	45.8	W 14206	36.7	W 17727	32.3	APPAREILS DE GENIE CIVIL
7239	CONSTR ETC MACHY PTS NES	W 14610	31.3	W 16043	40.9	W 12372	30.7	W 14414	30.1	PIECES 723.41–723.46
728	OTH MACHY FOR SPCL INDUS	W 8601	45.6	W 8484	72.0	W 11512	68.6	W 13264	74.6	AUT MACH IND PARTICULIERES
7284	MACHY FOR SPCL INDUS NES	W 4115	33.6	W 3971	56.1	W 6156	50.6	W 7109	54.1	MACH SPEC IND PARTICUL.
73	METALWORKING MACHINERY		36.7		49.6		55.7		45.5	MACH TRAVAIL DES METAUX
74	GENRL INDUSTRL MACHY NES		311.7		399.2		411.4		503.3	MACH APP INDUSTRIE
741	HEATING,COOLING EQUIPMNT	W 8015	45.2	W 8982	58.7	W 12893	76.7	W 15831	86.3	MACH CHAUFFAGE,PIECES
742	PUMPS FOR LIQUIDS ETC	W 2798	39.1	W 3280	59.4	W 2759	33.8	W 3658	70.6	POMPES MOTO–POMPES
7428	OTHER PUMPS FOR LIQUIDS	W 665	29.2	W 1151	45.3	W 697	19.3	W 926	46.4	AUTRES POMPES POUR LIQ
74288	PUMPS FR LIQUIDS NES ETC	W 635	28.9	W 1133	45.1	W 654	18.8	W 916	46.3	POMPES POUR LIQUIDES NDA
743	PUMPS NES,CENTRFUGES ETC	W 5032	41.6	W 5550	50.9	W 6120	57.2	W 7749	63.1	POMPES COMPRES,VENT ETC
744	MECHANICAL HANDLING EQU		51.0	W 27743	64.1		62.5	W 37441	81.7	EQUIP MANUTENTION PIECES
7449	PTS NES OF MACHY OF 7442	W 25298	39.8	W 22845	48.5	W 20470	44.6	W 28793	56.0	PIECES DU 744.2
749	NONELEC MACH PTS,ACC NES	W 13642	119.0	W 15658	143.0	W 14172	142.5		162.3	PIECES MACH NON ELEC NDA
7492	COCKS,VALVES ETC NES	W 5638	55.6	W 5436	60.9	W 4580	58.3	W 5557	68.4	ART ROB,SIM POUR TUYAUX
7499	OTH NONELEC MCHY PTS NES	W 2101	29.0	W 2207	32.1	W 3284	42.1		32.5	PIECES NON ELECT NDA
75	OFFICE MACHNES,ADP EQUIP		29.3		70.9		47.9		1690.0	MACH BUREAU TRAIT AUTOM
752	AUTOMTIC DATA PROC EQUIP		7.4		11.7	W 115	11.7		1349.9	MACH TRAIT INFORMATION
7524	DIGITL CENTRL STOR UNITS		0.8	W 19	2.3	W 12	2.5	W 2536	997.2	UNITES MEMOIRE CENTRALES
7525	ADP PERIPHERAL UNITS	W 74	1.9	W 141	4.0	W 36	1.6	W 6348	148.0	UNITES PERIPHERIQUES
7528	OFF–LINE DATA PROC EQUIP	W 26	1.6	W 23	1.3	W 36	2.6	W 15880	201.4	MACH AUXIL TRAIT INFORM
759	OFFICE,ADP MCH PTS,ACCES	W 1351	18.7	W 1213	52.6	W 1159	29.1	W 2849	333.8	PIECES DU 751 ET 752
7599	ACCTG,ETC,ADP MCH PTS,AC	W 972	16.4	W 929	50.3	W 843	23.3	W 2420	324.5	PIECES DU 751 ET 752
76	TELECOMM,SOUND EQUIPMENT		357.2		436.2		309.5		1226.1	EQUIPMENT DE TELECOM
761	TELEVISION RECEIVERS	W 2162	29.2	W 5844	84.5		31.1	W 27679	277.6	RECEPTEURS DE TELEVISION
7611	COLOUR TV RECEIVERS	W 2138	29.1	W 5837	84.4	W 2868	31.1	W 27678	277.6	RECEPTEURS COULEUR
762	RADIO BROADCAST RECEIVRS	W 1910	27.4	W 1392	20.4		30.2	W 3788	67.2	RECEPTEURS RADIODIFFUSION
763	SOUND RECORDRS,PHONOGRPH	W 322	10.1		49.9		6.3	W 19467	547.1	PHONO,APP ENREGISTREMENT
7638	OTHR SOUND APPARATUS ETC	W 322	10.1	W 1925	49.9		6.2	W 19454	546.9	AUT APP D'ENREGIS,REPROD
76381	TV IMAGE,SND RECRDRS ETC	W 6	0.5	W 1771	44.3		0.5	W 15331	462.0	APP ENREG,REPRO IMAG,SON
76388	DICTATING MACHINES ETC	W 316	9.7	W 154	5.7	W 233	5.8	W 4123	84.9	MACHINES A DICTER
764	TELECOM EQPT,PTS,ACC NES		290.6		281.5		242.0		334.3	EQUIP TELECOM,PIECES
7649	PTS NES OF EQUIPMT OF 76	W 10992	264.3	W 9204	264.3	W 9380	221.2	W 9324	299.0	PIECES DE LA DIV 76
76493	TELECOMM EQUIPMT PTS NES	W 3069	72.9	W 2955	86.5	W 4033	82.5	W 4605	95.4	PIECES 761,762,764.3,8
76499	PARTS ETC OF SOUND EQUIP	W 6738	183.2	W 5215	165.5	W 4265	129.2	W 3828	180.1	PIECES NDA POUR 763
77	ELECTRIC MACHNRY NES ETC		839.8		1246.7		1491.2		2186.5	MACH APP ELECT NDA
771	ELECTRIC POWER MACHY NES	W 3140	32.3	W 2643	46.1	W 6608	73.6	W 7418	84.9	MACH PROD,TRANS ELECTR
7711	TRANSFORMERS,ELECTRICAL	W 1530	11.4	W 1150	15.1	W 4263	40.2	W 4641	43.4	TRANSFO ELECTRIQUES
77118	OTHER ELEC TRANSFORMERS	W 1264	10.0	W 974	14.2	W 4256	40.2	W 4432	42.3	AUTRES TRANSFO ELECTRIQ
772	SWITCHGEAR ETC,PARTS NES	W 7200	152.0	W 10440	286.6	W 12525	294.3	W 20118	466.1	APP COUPURE,SECT ETC
7721	SWITCHGEAR ETC	W 6290	102.1	W 9193	206.3	W 10231	198.7	W 17334	352.1	APP COUPURE,SECTIONMNT
7722	PRINTED CIRCUITS,PTS NES	W 802	43.7	W 1073	72.2	W 2224	90.6	W 2555	91.2	CIRCUITS ET PIECES
773	ELECTR DISTRIBUTNG EQUIP	W 15496	161.0		250.7	W 46140	350.6	W 64048	602.5	EQUIPMT DISTRIBUTION ELECT
7731	INSULATED WIRE,CABLE ETC	W 13823	151.2	W 20602	237.3	W 43980	339.9	W 61797	590.6	FILS,CABLES ISOLES ELECT
775	HOUSEHOLD TYPE EQUIP NES		103.3	W 36108	154.1	W 41425	185.5		273.4	MACH,APP USAGE DOMESTQUE
7752	DOM REFRIGERATRS,FREEZRS	W 21794	77.2	W 28894	114.9	W 32571	135.7	W 44169	166.1	REFRIG,CONGEL MENAGER
77521	DOMESTIC REFRIGERATORS	W 17337	62.1	W 21516	86.5	W 22695	96.4	W 25747	95.5	REFRIGERATEURS
77522	DOMESTIC DEEP–FREEZERS	W 4457	15.2	W 7378	28.4	W 9875	39.4	W 18422	70.7	MEUBLES CONGELATEURS
778	ELECTRICAL MACHINERY NES	W 35305	362.8	W 40199	454.0	W 43462	530.7	W 65728	686.0	AUTRES MACH ELECT NDA
7782	ELECTRIC LAMPS,BULBS	W 25983	265.7	W 29900	302.5	W 32244	369.4	W 30814	367.3	LAMPES, TUBES ELECTRIQUES
77821	ELEC FILAMENT LAMPS NES	W 14921	145.0	W 16841	163.6	W 17830	189.6	W 17305	189.0	LAMPES NON INFRAROUGES
77822	ELEC DISCHARGE LAMPS NES	W 9274	107.7	W 10733	120.0	W 11570	148.8	W 9978	147.9	LAMPES NON ULTRA–VIOLETS
7783	AUTOMOTIVE ELECTR EQUIP	W 4549	63.3	W 5554	79.5	W 4580	65.5	W 10546	171.8	EQUIP ELECT MOTEURS EXPL
77831	IGNITION,STARTING EQUIP	W 2984	37.5	W 3928	50.4	W 2905	35.7	W 8631	141.2	APP ELEC ALLUM,DEMARRAGE
7788	OTH ELEC MACHY,EQUIP NES	W 677	26.0	W 1106	63.7	W 975	82.4	W 2536	131.4	AUT MACH APP ELEC NDA
77884	ELECTRICAL CONDENSERS	W 41	13.6	W 172	45.3	W 346	67.5	W 705	90.4	CONDENSATEURS ELECTRIQUES
78	ROAD VEHICLES		542.1		681.8		557.1		1089.4	VEHICULES ROUTIERS
781	PASS MOTOR VEH EXC BUSES	W 65714	130.1	W 97632	186.3	W 26695	52.6	W 43986	337.7	AUTO TRANSPORT PERSONNES
783	ROAD MOTOR VEHICLES NES	W 17461	110.8	W 21459	114.9	W 18142	113.5	W 26958	227.5	VEHICULES ROUTIERS NDA
7831	BUSES	W 17115	110.1	W 20701	111.9	W 17034	108.0	W 26150	223.4	VOITURES TRANSPORT COMMUN
784	MOTOR VEH PRTS,ACCES NES	W 54423	219.2	W 58188	249.6	W 63079	256.4	W 76824	370.4	PIECES 722,781,782,783
7849	OTHER MOTOR VEHCL PARTS	W 53424	212.5	W 57398	244.9	W 62407	253.5	W 73809	356.7	PIECES 722,781,782,783
786	TRAILERS,NONMOTR VEH,NES	W 23450	63.9	W 37491	104.1	W 40667	102.0	W 50102	125.9	REMORQUES,CADRES,CONTAIN
7868	OTH NONMOTR VEHICLES ETC	W 17855	46.9	W 28284	81.5	W 31034	73.2	W 40328	91.0	AUT VEHIC NON AUTO,PIECES
78689	PTS NES OF TRAILERS ETC	W 17182	44.8	W 27021	76.8	W 29539	67.6	W 38925	86.2	PIECES 786.11,12,786.81
8	MISC MANUFACTURED GOODS		1772.2		1959.3		2210.2		2441.4	ART MANUFACTURES DIVERS
812	*PLUMBG,HEATNG,LGHTNG EQ	W 14684	60.3		74.7		83.9	W 44154	121.0	APPAR SANITAIRES CHAUFFAGE
8124	LIGHTING EQUIPMENT NES	W 8953	49.2		58.7		64.7	W 13827	71.4	APPAREILS ECLAIRAGE ETC
81242	LAMPS,FITTINGS BASE METL	W 8330	43.7	W 9736	52.4	W 10722	56.3	W 12305	62.3	APPAREILS D'ECLAIRAGE
821	*FURNITURE,PARTS THEREOF	W 44796	161.3	W 49117	232.9	W 56674	283.5	W 70322	355.3	MEUBLES ET PIECES
8211	CHAIRS,SEATS AND PARTS	W 17184	79.0	W 21977	143.8	W 25622	182.8	W 34526	250.7	SIEGES ET PIECES
82111	CHAIRS AND OTHER SEATS	W 13300	63.2	W 15452	78.8	W 19416	87.6	W 17560	66.5	SIEGES
82119	PTS NES OF CHAIRS ETC	W 3884	15.8	W 6525	65.0	W 6206	95.3	W 16966	184.2	PIECES DU 821.11
8219	FURNITURE AND PARTS NES	W 25783	64.0	W 24552	66.8	W 27899	74.5	W 31799	75.1	AUTRES MEUBLES ET PIECES
82192	WOOD FURNITURE NES	W 17200	42.9	W 17808	45.3	W 17276	42.7	W 19309	41.7	MEUBLES NDA EN BOIS
831	*TRAVEL GOODS,HANDBAGS	W 3104	30.5	W 3462	29.3	W 4046	43.8	W 3530	36.8	ARTICLES DE VOYAGE ETC
84	CLOTHING AND ACCESSORIES		993.8		1034.7		1109.0		1122.5	VETEMENTS
842	MENS OUTERWEAR NOT KNIT	W 7553	220.4	W 7977	232.3	W 8758	252.1	W 10094	263.5	VET DESSUS POUR HOMMES
8422	— SUITS	W 923	39.0	W 989	43.2	W 1056	46.4	W 1383	52.7	COMPLETS HOMMES MAT TEXT
8423	— TROUSERS,BREECHES ETC	W 3671	79.0	W 4011	86.0	W 4689	99.4	W 4979	96.0	PANTALONS HOMMES MAT TEX
8424	— JACKETS,BLAZERS ETC	W 1477	58.6	W 1308	53.3	W 1437	55.7	W 1923	64.8	VESTES HOMMES MAT TEXTIL
843	WOMENS OUTERWEAR NONKNIT	W 8518	369.5	W 8113	347.8	W 8396	356.5	W 8659	346.7	VET DESSUS FEMMES MAT TEX
8431	— COATS AND JACKETS	W 2598	120.6	W 2377	102.7	W 2170	99.9	W 2493	103.3	MANT,VEST FEM MAT TEXTIL
8433	— DRESSES	W 778	39.3	W 972	46.3	W 1028	47.0	W 942	38.6	ROBES EN MAT–TEXTILES
8434	— SKIRTS	W 1096	43.5	W 1013	41.0	W 964	36.9	W 823	30.8	JUPES EN MAT TEXTILES
8435	— BLOUSES	W 1185	58.5	W 953	46.7	W 915	43.7	W 1004	44.7	BLOUSES FEM MAT TEXTILES
8439	— OTHER OUTER GARMENTS	W 2350	83.1	W 2145	82.1	W 2616	97.8	W 2837	105.0	AUT VET DES FEM MAT TEXT
845	OUTERWEAR KNIT NONELASTC	W 4847	118.9	W 5458	133.2	W 5741	140.0	W 6149	135.4	VET DESSOUS,ACCES BONNET
8451	— JERSEYS,PULLOVERS ETC	W 2195	48.3	W 2641	55.5	W 3001	61.6	W 3438	63.4	CHANDAILS,PULL–OVERS ETC
8459	— OTHER,CLTHG ACCESRYS	W 2396	61.4	W 2514	66.5	W 2427	67.1	W 2426	61.8	AUT VET DESSUS DE BONNE
846	UNDER GARMENTS KNITTED	W 7147	185.9	W 8785	216.8	W 9490	243.2	W 10986	241.1	SOUS VETS DE BONNETERIE
8462	— OF COTTON NON ELASTIC	W 5698	111.9	W 7215	136.6	W 7711	152.9	W 9156	162.2	SOUS–VET BONNET COTON
84629	—— OTHER	W 5698	111.9	W 7215	136.6	W 7711	152.9	W 9156	162.2	AUT SOUS–VET BONNET COTON
8465	CORSETS,GARTERS,ETC	W 853	63.9	W 1007	73.8	W 1100	81.9	W 988	68.1	CORSETS,GAINES ART SIM
84651	BRASSIERES	W 696	55.8	W 732	62.7	W 813	68.6	W 783	58.0	SOUTIENS–GORGE,BUSTIERS
847	TEXTILE CLTHNG ACCES NES	W 1346	32.2	W 1432	32.6		34.2	W 1553	30.3	ACCES VET MAT TEXT NDA
848	HEADGEAR,NONTXTL CLOTHNG		36.2		36.3		44.6		66.9	VET ACCES MAT AUT QUE TEX
851	*FOOTWEAR	W 9067	168.2	W 8607	160.8	W 9733	198.7	W 11734	213.8	CHAUSSURES
85102	FOOTWEAR LEATHER	W 8569	165.8	W 7985	157.4	W 8663	180.2	W 10213	191.6	CHAUS SEMELLES EN CUIR

5. Special Exports F.O.B. by Commodities according to the S.I.T.C. (Rev. 2) in million U.S. Dollars
Exportations Spéciales F.O.B. par Produits d'après la C.T.C.I. (Rév. 2) en millions de Dollars E.U.

SITC CTCI	COMMODITY	1994 QUANTITY QUANTITE	1994 VALUE VALEUR	1995 QUANTITY QUANTITE	1995 VALUE VALEUR	1996 QUANTITY QUANTITE	1996 VALUE VALEUR	1997 QUANTITY QUANTITE	1997 VALUE VALEUR	PRODUIT
87	PRECISION INSTRUMNTS NES		100.7		131.2		138.9		152.8	INSTRUM,APPAR SCIENT NDA
872	MEDICAL INSTRUMENTS NES	W 1748	26.1	W 2778	38.9		47.0		53.7	INSTR,APP MEDIC–CHIR NDA
87202	OTH MEDICAL INSTRUMENTS	W 1585	24.3	W 2593	36.7	W 3727	45.6	W 4944	50.3	INSTRUM,APP MEDECINE
874	MEASURNG,CONTROLNG INSTR		58.9		72.5		69.3		77.8	INSTRUMENTS DE MESURE
89	MISC MANUFCTRD GOODS NES		225.8		268.1		314.9		406.9	ART MANUFACTURES DIVERS
892	PRINTED MATTER		33.5	W 15826	41.5		41.9		37.3	IMPRIMES
893	ARTICLES OF PLASTIC NES		87.6		129.7		158.3		220.5	OUVRAGES EN MAT DIVIS 58
8931	PLSTC PACKG CONTNRS,LIDS	W 16022	29.7	W 17569	45.1	W 21848	62.7	W 37476	96.7	ART TRANSP EMBALLAGE ETC
8939	MISC PLASTIC ARTICLES	W 18365	56.5	W 23237	82.7	W 28368	93.5	W 41218	121.6	ART DIVERS EN MAT DIV 58
89399	OTHR PLASTC ARTICLES NES	W 13310	46.1	W 15473	63.7	W 20700	74.9	W 31939	101.4	AUT OUV MAT DIV 58
894	TOYS,SPORTING GOODS,ETC	W 7688	48.4	W 5993	38.7	W 7919	48.7	W 11007	68.9	VOITURES ENFANTS,JOUETS
8942	TOYS,INDOOR GAMES ETC	W 7081	43.7	W 4976	31.8	W 5926	37.9	W 8303	55.7	JOUETS,JEUX ETC
9	GOODS NOT CLASSD BY KIND		836.0		423.8		524.6		525.7	ART TRANSACT NON CLASSES
931	*SPECIAL TRANSACTIONS		824.5		413.5		511.3		513.2	TRANS.SPECIALES

FOOT NOTES – NOTES

TABLE 1 –
1 Prior to 1976, data are expressed in 'exchange forint s' and are not comparable with the later data, which are in 'forints'.
TABLEAU 1 –
1 Avant 1976 les données sont exprimé en 'forints c onvertibles', et ne sont pas comparables aux données ultérieures qui sont exprimées en 'forints'.

1. HISTORICAL SERIES, 1962–1997 GENERAL TRADE, IMPORTS C.I.F., EXPORTS F.O.B.
SERIES HISTORIQUES, 1962–1997 COMMERCE GENERAL, IMPORTATIONS C.A.F., EXPORTATIONS F.O.B

YEAR ANNEE	VALUE IN MILLION ICELANDIC KRONUR / VALEUR EN MILLION ICELANDIC KRONUR — MERCHANDISE # 1 –MARCHANDISE		GOLD –OR		CONVERSION FACTORS U.S. CENTS PER ICELANDIC KRONA FACTEURS DE CONVERSION CENTS E.U. PAR ICELANDIC KRONA		INDEX NUMBERS –INDICES — QUANTUM		UNIT VALUE VALEUR UNITAIRE	
	IMPORTS	EXPORTS	IMPORTS	EXPORTS	IMPORTS	EXPORTS	IMPORTS	EXPORTS	IMPORTS	EXPORTS
1962	3836.70	3628.00			2.3256	2.3256				
1963	4717.10	4042.80			2.3256	2.3256				
1964	5636.00	4776.00			2.3256	2.3256				
1965	5901.60	5563.20			2.3256	2.3256				
1966	6852.70	6041.50			2.3256	2.3256				
1967	7116.20	4303.10			2.2789	2.2575				
1968	8246.20	5097.70			1.6783	1.6125				
1969	10855.90	9466.40			1.1364	1.1364				
1970	13644.60	12915.00			1.1364	1.1364				
1971	18931.50	13177.90			1.1401	1.1393				
1972	20043.40	16701.00			1.1382	1.1404				
1973	31811.00	26020.00			1.1267	1.1163				
1974	52555.00	32880.00			0.9858	1.0062				
1975	75064.00	47435.00			0.6504	0.6482				
1976	85667.00	73498.00			0.5485	0.5497				
1977	120916.00	101880.00			0.5018	0.5031				
1978	184332.00	176286.00			0.3655	0.3636				
1979	292133.00	278450.00			0.2786	0.2802				
1980	480162.00	445953.00			0.2083	0.2088	83	81	6	6
1981	7484.70	6536.20			13.0873	13.1488	88	81	9	9
1982	11644.80	8478.80			8.0856	8.0817	85	67	14	14
1983	20606.00	18633.00			3.9590	4.0208	76	76	27	27
1984	26780.30	23557.00			3.1337	3.1421	81	78	34	33
1985	37600.30	33749.60			2.4044	2.4114	88	86	44	42
1986	45910.00	45093.01			2.4295	2.4366	95	95	49	51
1987	61237.01	53053.01			2.5960	2.5902	118	99	53	58
1988	68996.00	61674.00			2.3159	2.3087	112	98	63	68
1989	80284.00	79131.01			1.7460	1.7520	100	101	83	85
1990	97559.01	92624.00			1.7215	1.7177	100	100	100	100
1991	104129.00	91560.00			1.6910	1.6918	105	92	103	108
1992	96895.01	87833.01			1.7384	1.7400	97	91	104	104
1993	90775.01	94710.00			1.4779	1.4783	84	96	113	107
1994	102499.00	113279.00			1.4361	1.4327	90	108	118	113
1995	113388.00	116613.00			1.5478	1.5463	96	105	123	120
1996	135165.00	108977.00			1.5028	1.5029				
1997	141355.00	131228.00			1.4095	1.4113				

2. IMPORTS BY BROAD ECONOMIC CATEGORY AND EXPORTS BY INDUSTRIAL ORIGIN. (PERCENTAGE OF TOTAL VALUE)
IMPORTATIONS PAR CATEGORIES ECONOMIQUES ET EXPORTATIONS PAR BRANCHE D'ACTIVITE.(EN POURCENTAGE DE LA VALEUR TOTALE)

IMPORTS – IMPORTATIONS

	1991	1992	1993	1994	1995	1996	1997
TOTAL IMPORTS–IMPORTATIONS TOTALES	100.	100.	100.	100.	100.	100.	100.
1 FOOD BEV–ALIMENTATION BOISSONS	8.1	8.5	10.3	10.2	10.4	9.5	9.0
11 PRIMARY–PRODUITS DE BASE	2.6	2.6	3.8	3.8	4.4	4.0	3.5
111 FOR INDUSTRY–POUR L'INDUSTRIE	0.6	0.6	0.7	0.8	0.9	0.8	0.8
112 FOR HOUSEHOLDS–POUR LES MENAGES	2.1	2.0	3.1	3.0	3.5	3.2	2.7
12 PROCESSED–PRODUITS ELABORES	5.5	5.9	6.5	6.4	6.1	5.5	5.5
121 FOR INDUSTRY–POUR L'INDUSTRIE	0.7	0.7	0.9	0.9	0.8	0.7	0.7
122 FOR HOUSEHOLDS–POUR LES MENAGES	4.8	5.2	5.6	5.5	5.2	4.8	4.8
2 IND SUPPLIES–APPROV INDUSTRIELS	27.0	25.9	27.1	26.2	27.4	26.0	25.1
21 PRIMARY–PRODUITS DE BASE	1.1	1.1	1.2	1.2	1.2	1.2	1.3
22 PROCESSED–PRODUITS ELABORES	25.9	24.8	25.9	25.0	26.2	24.8	23.8
3 FUELS–COMBUSTIBLES	8.3	8.2	9.0	8.2	7.1	7.7	7.5
31 PRIMARY–PRODUITS DE BASE	0.4	0.3	0.4	0.4	0.4	0.3	0.3
32 PROCESSED–PRODUITS ELABORES	7.9	7.9	8.7	7.8	6.7	7.4	7.2
321 MOTOR SPIRIT–ESSENCE		1.9	1.8	1.8	1.4	1.6	1.5
322 OTHER–AUTRES	7.9	6.0	6.9	6.0	5.3	5.8	5.7
4 MACHINERY–EQUIPEMENT	19.4	18.2	18.7	19.5	20.5	21.7	24.0
41 CAPITAL EQUIPMENT–MACHINES	15.7	14.3	14.8	15.5	16.5	17.6	19.5
42 PARTS–PIECES ACCESSOIRES	3.7	3.9	3.9	4.1	4.0	4.1	4.5
5 TRANSPORT–TRANSPORT	14.6	16.1	10.6	12.2	12.0	14.2	13.5
51 PASSENGER CARS–AUTOMOBILES	4.8	3.8	3.8	3.5	4.3	5.2	6.3
52 OTHER–AUTRES	6.7	9.4	3.7	5.5	4.9	6.6	4.5
521 INDUSTRIAL–INDUSTRIELS	6.5	9.2	3.5	5.4	4.7	6.4	4.4
522 NON INDUSTRIAL–NON INDUSTRIEL	0.2	0.2	0.2	0.1	0.2	0.1	0.1
53 PARTS–PIECES ACCESSOIRES	3.1	2.9	3.1	3.2	2.8	2.5	2.8
6 CONSUM GOODS–BIENS CONSOMMATION	22.3	22.9	24.0	23.2	22.4	20.6	20.6
61 DURABLE–DURABLES	5.0	4.9	4.8	4.7	4.6	4.5	4.6
62 SEMI DURABLE–SEMI DURABLES	12.1	12.2	12.7	12.3	11.9	10.6	10.5
63 NON DURABLE–NON DURABLES	5.2	5.8	6.5	6.2	6.0	5.5	5.6
7 GOODS NES–BIENS NDA	0.2	0.2	0.3	0.4	0.2	0.3	0.2

EXPORTS – EXPORTATIONS

	1991	1992	1993	1994	1995	1996	1997
TOTAL EXPORTS–EXPORTATIONS TOTALES	100.	100.	100.	100.	100.	100.	100.
1 AGRICULTURE	78.4	73.8	64.9	61.4	55.3	54.0	51.5
2 MINING QUARRY–INDUS EXTRACTIVES	0.6	0.6	0.6	0.9	1.1	0.8	0.7
3 MANUFACTURING–IND MANUFACTUR	21.1	25.7	34.5	37.7	43.6	45.2	47.8
31 FOOD BEV TOBACCO–ALIM BOISS TAB	5.6	9.6	17.6	18.2	20.7	22.8	23.2
32 TEXTILES–INDUSTRIES TEXTILES	2.0	1.7	1.4	1.4	1.7	1.7	1.7
33 WOOD & PRODUCTS–BOIS & PRODUITS	0.0	0.0	0.0	0.2	0.1	0.0	0.0
34 PAPER & PRODUCTS–PAPIER & PRODT	0.1	0.1	0.2	0.2	0.2	0.2	0.2
35 CHEMICALS–INDUSTRIES CHIMIQUES	0.3	0.4	0.4	0.4	0.9	0.9	0.9
36 NON METAL MIN–MIN NON METAL	0.1	0.1	0.1	0.1	0.1	0.1	0.1
37 BASIC METAL–IND METAL BASE	10.9	11.1	11.2	12.0	13.4	12.7	14.4
38 METAL MANUF–MANUF METAL	1.6	2.1	3.2	5.0	6.1	5.8	6.7
39 OTH MANUF IND–AUTRES MANUF	0.5	0.6	0.5	0.3	0.4	1.0	0.5

3. TRADE BY PRINCIPAL COUNTRIES OF ORIGIN AND DESTINATION (VALUE IN MILLION U.S. DOLLARS)
ECHANGES SELON LES PRINCIPAUX PAYS D'ORIGINE ET DE DESTINATION (VALEUR EN MILLIONS DE DOLLARS EU)

COUNTRIES–PAYS	GENERAL IMPORTS C.I.F. IMPORTATIONS GENERALES C.A.F 1993	1994	1995	1996	1997
World	1349.4	1472.4	1751.4	2041.5	2019.5
Africa	3.8	4.3	4.1	4.2	5.0
Americas	149.6	157.3	181.4	224.8	227.8
– Northern America	138.3	146.8	169.3	212.6	215.7
– LAIA	7.2	7.2	7.3	6.3	6.7
– CACM	1.9	1.6	2.0	2.4	2.2
– Caribbean	0.1	0.3	1.0	1.8	1.7
– Rest of America	2.1	1.3	1.8	1.7	1.4
Asia excl fmr USSR	139.2	138.3	172.8	189.0	209.1
– Middle East	1.5	1.9	2.3	3.9	3.6
Asia former USSR	0.0	0.1	0.0		
Europe excl fmr USSR	987.2	1102.3	1285.2	1513.0	1480.7
– European Union	782.2	858.5	1047.4	1150.7	1172.9
– Eastern Europe	12.5	13.0	32.8	51.9	22.9
– Rest of Europe	192.5	230.8	205.1	310.5	284.9
Europe former USSR	36.1	36.1	52.1	58.6	60.3
Oceania	33.5	33.1	55.7	51.8	36.6
Other		1.0			
Norway,Svalbard and JM	167.0	210.7	178.3	276.2	232.7
Germany/Allemagne	160.8	165.3	200.0	222.2	237.5
United Kingdom	121.0	145.3	168.8	208.3	204.2
USA/Etats–Unis d'Amer	126.0	131.2	147.1	192.8	190.4
Denmark/Danemark	126.6	132.6	164.8	170.5	174.4
Sweden/Suède	91.4	103.3	122.3	137.1	135.1
Netherlands/Pays–Bas	80.9	92.3	119.8	121.8	130.6
Japan/Japon	74.8	59.2	76.9	81.9	99.2
France, Monaco	45.9	50.9	74.4	66.9	66.9
Italy/Italie	47.1	47.4	57.2	65.7	65.4
Russian Federation	34.1	32.8	40.9	50.6	50.1
Australia/Australie	32.6	32.2	54.4	50.5	35.3
Belgium–Luxembourg	26.1	29.6	35.3	40.0	41.6
Finland/Finlande	26.6	27.9	32.3	33.6	32.9
Switzerland,Liechtenst.	23.2	18.3	21.0	30.0	45.0
Spain/Espagne	18.7	20.4	28.2	35.4	33.3
China/Chine	13.8	19.5	23.6	26.6	27.6
Korea, Republic of	11.3	15.4	20.6	22.7	22.2
Ireland/Irlande	10.3	14.2	17.3	20.8	23.7
Poland/Pologne	6.5	5.4	22.5	39.9	11.6
Canada	8.4	15.4	16.8	18.6	20.9
Portugal	13.7	17.7	15.3	14.7	14.1
Other Asia n.e.s.	12.5	12.1	14.0	15.3	15.4
Austria/Autriche	11.1	9.9	10.0	12.6	12.1
China, Hong Kong SAR	7.8	7.7	9.4	10.4	10.6
Czech Republic	4.4	4.8	6.2	7.3	6.9
Thailand/Thaïlande	4.4	5.5	4.9	5.2	4.9
India/Inde	2.7	4.0	5.2	5.6	5.5
Malaysia/Malaisie	1.8	2.9	3.8	4.4	6.0
Singapore/Singapour	2.4	3.1	4.0	3.9	3.9
Brazil/Brésil	4.1	3.6	3.6	2.8	2.5
Faeroe Islds/Is Féroé	1.4	0.9	4.9	2.9	5.2
Greenland/Groenland	3.9	0.3	5.2	1.0	4.3
Estonia/Estonie	1.4	2.1	4.5	2.9	3.8
Indonesia/Indonésie	1.9	2.3	2.9	3.1	3.3
Latvia/Lettonie	0.3	0.7	2.8	3.3	5.1
Turkey/Turquie	1.2	1.4	2.0	3.1	3.1
So. African Customs Un	1.0	1.5	1.8	2.3	2.8
Costa Rica	1.5	1.3	1.3	2.0	2.0
Greece/Grèce	1.9	1.5	1.6	1.1	1.2

COUNTRIES–PAYS	GENERAL EXPORTS F.O.B. EXPORTATIONS GENERALES F.O.B. 1993	1994	1995	1996	1997
Monde	1399.3	1626.7	1802.5	1897.1	1851.4
Afrique	18.7	12.2	11.6	11.4	16.2
Amériques	237.2	263.6	280.2	327.5	306.2
– Amérique du Nord	230.8	258.9	271.1	257.2	288.1
– ALAI	5.3	4.5	8.9	13.7	17.3
– MCAC	0.0	0.0	0.0	0.0	
– Caraïbes	1.1	0.0	0.0	56.3	0.1
– Autre Amérique		0.2	0.2	0.3	0.7
Asie anc. URSS exclus	167.0	255.9	248.1	232.1	169.5
– Moyen–Orient	2.9	0.8	1.9	2.7	2.0
Asie ancienne URSS		0.1	0.1	0.0	0.0
Europe anc. URSS exclus	968.3	1082.4	1241.8	1302.3	1308.6
– Union Européenne	864.6	1001.6	1130.0	1178.0	1121.4
– Europe de l'Est	1.6	2.3	3.7	6.3	5.5
– Autre de l'Europe	102.2	78.6	108.2	118.0	181.6
Europe ancienne URSS	5.7	10.6	12.1	22.0	48.6
Océanie	2.3	1.8	8.6	1.7	2.4
Autre	0.1				
United Kingdom	302.6	331.0	347.4	359.7	350.0
USA/Etats–Unis d'Amer	222.2	235.8	223.4	234.0	263.9
Germany/Allemagne	154.5	208.8	246.1	243.8	242.1
Japan/Japon	129.8	229.2	204.6	185.8	122.7
France, Monaco	115.2	117.7	122.4	126.8	117.4
Denmark/Danemark	78.7	104.0	141.3	136.6	104.8
Spain/Espagne	68.3	75.5	66.0	73.3	80.6
Norway,Svalbard and JM	47.1	45.4	59.0	70.4	102.9
Netherlands/Pays–Bas	30.8	26.4	53.3	67.9	62.0
Switzerland,Liechtenst.	51.2	28.4	39.9	37.4	56.5
Portugal	22.9	20.4	32.8	48.6	48.9
Italy/Italie	28.6	37.8	36.9	36.1	32.6
Other Asia n.e.s.	27.3	19.8	28.7	29.6	28.8
Belgium–Luxembourg	22.4	29.4	32.0	25.7	24.4
Canada	7.4	21.6	30.3	22.0	22.4
Sweden/Suède	16.3	16.9	23.5	24.3	21.0
Russian Federation	5.5	9.8	10.5	19.3	33.3
Finland/Finlande	9.9	15.3	8.9	18.1	21.3
Greece/Grèce	11.5	13.5	14.3	12.6	11.2
Nigeria/Nigéria	12.6	9.8	8.1	8.7	12.8
Faeroe Islds/Is Féroé	3.7	4.4	8.7	8.0	20.7
Cayman Is/Is Caïmans	0.6			38.1	0.0
Brazil/Brésil	2.7	2.7	7.2	10.1	11.0
Korea, Republic of	3.3	2.5	7.4	7.1	3.6
Greenland/Groenland	1.2	1.5	17.4	1.2	1.8
Antigua and Barbuda				18.1	
Ireland/Irlande	1.4	2.7	3.0	2.5	3.4
Poland/Pologne	0.6	1.3	1.7	4.6	4.5
China/Chine	0.1	0.4	2.5	1.0	7.4
New Zealand	1.6	0.8	7.4	0.7	0.7
Lithuania/Lituanie	0.2	0.4	1.1	1.2	7.5
Austria/Autriche	1.4	2.2	2.1	1.9	1.8
Chile/Chili	1.5	0.4	0.7	1.8	4.3
So. African Customs Un	0.4	1.7	3.2	1.8	1.5
Latvia/Lettonie	0.0	0.1	0.0	0.7	5.6
Israel/Israël	1.9	0.6	0.5	1.2	1.9
Turkey/Turquie	0.2	0.2	1.2	2.1	1.4
Liberia/Libéria	4.6				
Australia/Australie	0.6	0.9	1.3	1.0	0.8
Cyprus/Chypre	2.4	0.3	0.4	0.4	0.4

(VALUE AS PERCENTAGE OF WORLD TOTAL)(VALEURS EN POURCENTAGE DU TOTAL MONDIAL)

	1988	1989	1990	1991	1992	1993	1994	1995	1996	1997
Africa	0.2	0.3	0.3	0.2	0.2	0.3	0.3	0.2	0.2	0.2
Americas	8.7	12.3	15.7	11.8	10.0	11.1	10.7	10.4	11.0	11.3
– Northern America	8.0	11.5	15.0	11.1	9.3	10.2	10.0	9.7	10.4	10.7
– LAIA	0.5	0.5	0.4	0.5	0.4	0.5	0.5	0.4	0.3	0.3
– CACM	0.1	0.1	0.1	0.1	0.1	0.1	0.1	0.1	0.1	0.1
– Caribbean	0.0	0.0	0.0	0.0	0.0	0.0	0.0	0.1	0.1	0.1
– Rest of America	0.1	0.2	0.2	0.1	0.2	0.2	0.1	0.1	0.1	0.1
Asia excl fmr USSR	9.7	7.8	8.5	11.0	10.0	10.3	9.4	9.9	9.3	10.4
– Middle East	0.1	0.1	0.1	0.1	0.1	0.1	0.1	0.1	0.2	0.2
Asia former USSR						0.0	0.0	0.0		
Europe excl fmr USSR	75.8	72.6	67.9	70.7	75.6	73.2	74.9	73.4	74.1	73.3
– European Union	63.5	62.1	59.8	62.5	57.8	58.0	58.3	59.8	56.4	58.1
– Eastern Europe	2.0	2.3	1.7	0.9	0.8	0.9	0.9	1.9	2.5	1.1
– Rest of Europe	10.2	8.2	6.4	7.3	17.0	14.3	15.7	11.7	15.2	14.1
Europe former USSR	3.5	4.2	5.0	3.3	1.6	2.7	2.5	3.0	2.9	3.0
Oceania	2.1	2.7	2.6	3.0	2.6	2.5	2.2	3.2	2.5	1.8
Other	0.0						0.1			
Norway,Svalbard and JM	9.0	6.6	5.0	5.5	14.6	12.4	14.3	10.2	13.5	11.5
Germany/Allemagne				13.0	12.4	11.9	11.2	11.4	10.9	11.8
United Kingdom	8.2	8.1	8.1	8.2	8.5	9.0	9.9	9.6	10.2	10.1
USA/Etats–Unis d'Amer	7.5	11.0	14.4	10.4	8.3	9.3	8.9	8.4	9.4	9.4
Denmark/Danemark	9.2	9.1	8.6	8.6	8.8	9.4	9.0	9.4	8.4	8.6
Sweden/Suède	8.8	8.2	7.6	7.6	6.8	6.8	7.0	7.0	6.7	6.7
Netherlands/Pays–Bas	8.2	10.4	10.4	10.0	7.4	6.0	6.3	6.8	6.0	6.5
Japan/Japon	6.9	4.9	5.6	7.4	5.8	5.5	4.0	4.4	4.0	4.9
France, Monaco	3.1	3.1	3.0	3.6	3.3	3.4	3.5	4.2	3.3	3.3
Italy/Italie	4.4	3.1	3.1	3.3	3.5	3.5	3.2	3.3	3.2	3.2

	1988	1989	1990	1991	1992	1993	1994	1995	1996	1997
Afrique	1.2	0.7	0.7	0.8	0.9	1.3	0.7	0.6	0.6	0.9
Amériques	14.6	16.1	10.8	13.4	12.3	17.0	16.2	15.5	17.3	16.5
– Amérique du Nord	14.3	14.8	10.4	13.0	11.9	16.5	15.9	15.0	13.6	15.6
– ALAI	0.1	0.5	0.2	0.3	0.2	0.4	0.3	0.5	0.7	0.9
– MCAC	0.0	0.0	0.0	0.0	0.0	0.0	0.0	0.0	0.0	
– Caraïbes	0.1	0.8	0.2	0.0	0.2	0.1	0.0	0.0	3.0	0.0
– Autre Amérique	0.1						0.0	0.0	0.0	0.0
Asie anc. URSS exclus	8.7	9.2	7.4	9.7	9.8	11.9	15.7	13.8	12.2	9.2
– Moyen–Orient	0.2	0.2	0.2	0.0	0.4	0.2	0.1	0.1	0.1	0.1
Asie ancienne URSS							0.0	0.0	0.0	0.0
Europe anc. URSS exclus	71.8	70.7	78.4	75.6	76.6	69.2	66.5	68.9	68.6	70.7
– Union Européenne	62.0	59.8	70.7	68.9	71.2	61.8	61.6	62.7	62.1	60.6
– Europe de l'Est	1.9	1.8	0.4	0.3	0.1	0.1	0.1	0.2	0.3	0.3
– Autre de l'Europe	7.9	9.1	7.3	6.5	5.3	7.3	4.8	6.0	6.2	9.8
Europe ancienne URSS	3.6	3.1	2.5	0.5	0.3	0.4	0.7	0.7	1.2	2.6
Océanie	0.1	0.2	0.1	0.1	0.1	0.2	0.1	0.5	0.1	0.1
Autre						0.0				
United Kingdom	23.3	20.8	25.3	23.4	25.1	21.6	20.3	19.3	19.0	18.9
USA/Etats–Unis d'Amer	13.6	14.3	9.9	12.6	11.4	15.9	14.5	12.4	12.3	14.3
Germany/Allemagne				12.1	12.5	11.0	12.8	13.7	12.8	13.1
Japan/Japon	7.6	7.1	6.0	7.9	7.5	9.3	14.1	11.3	9.8	6.6
France, Monaco	4.8	5.7	9.0	10.1	9.9	8.2	7.2	6.8	6.7	6.3
Denmark/Danemark	3.3	3.7	5.0	4.2	5.6	5.6	6.4	7.8	7.2	5.7
Spain/Espagne	3.4	3.4	5.0	4.8	5.1	4.9	4.6	3.7	3.9	4.4
Norway,Svalbard and JM	2.4	2.2	1.5	1.6	2.2	3.4	2.8	3.3	3.7	5.6
Netherlands/Pays–Bas	1.1	1.7	2.1	1.7	2.0	2.2	1.6	3.0	3.6	3.3
Switzerland,Liechtenst.	4.5	5.5	4.2	4.0	2.5	3.7	1.7	2.2	2.0	3.0

4. General Imports C.I.F. by Commodities according to the S.I.T.C. (Rev. 2) in million U.S. Dollars
Importations Générales C.A.F. par Produits d'après la C.T.C.I. (Rév. 2) en millions de Dollars E.U.

SITC CTCI	COMMODITY	1994 QUANTITY QUANTITE	1994 VALUE VALEUR	1995 QUANTITY QUANTITE	1995 VALUE VALEUR	1996 QUANTITY QUANTITE	1996 VALUE VALEUR	1997 QUANTITY QUANTITE	1997 VALUE VALEUR	PRODUIT
	ALL COMMODITIES		1472.4		1751.4		2041.6		2019.5	TOUS PRODUITS
0	FOOD AND LIVE ANIMALS		137.7		168.2		177.9		166.4	ALIMENTS,ANIMAUX VIVANTS
03	FISH AND PREPARATIONS		24.5		39.6		42.1		32.5	POISSONS ET PREPARATIONS
034	FISH,FRESH,CHILLED,FROZN	W 15918	18.2	W 19739	24.2	W 19824	28.4	W 11894	20.0	POISSON FRAIS, REFRIG,CONG
0341	FISH FRSH,CHLLD,EX FILLT	W 5145	4.0	W 7680	6.3	W 2516	3.0	W 837	1.3	POISSON FRAIS,REFRIGERE
0342	FISH FROZEN,EXCL FILLETS	W 10430	13.6	W 11905	17.4	W 16222	23.0	W 10708	17.1	POISSONS CONGELES
036	SHELL FISH FRESH,FROZEN	W 4156	4.8	W 6307	13.1	W 5469	8.1	W 6314	9.0	CRUSTACES,MOLLUSQUES
04	CEREALS AND PREPARATIONS		28.0		32.5		35.8		36.0	CEREALES ET PRODUITS
048	CEREAL ETC PREPARATIONS	W 19085	19.8	W 17977	21.6	W 8958	22.2	W 8809	22.7	PREPTNS A BASE CEREALES
0481	PREPD BREAKFAST FOOD ETC	W 13576	8.6	W 12521	9.0	W 2935	7.6	W 2750	8.0	CEREALES TRAVAILLEES
04812	CEREAL ROASTED, PUFFED	W 1867	6.5	W 1895	6.4	W 2013	6.7	W 1989	7.2	PRODTS BASE CEREALES
0484	BAKERY PRODUCTS	W 2581	7.2	W 2680	8.2	W 2933	9.3	W 3046	9.9	PRODUITS DE BOULANGERIE
05	VEGETABLES AND FRUIT		34.4		37.3		40.3		38.5	LEGUMES ET FRUITS
054	VEG ETC FRSH,SMPLY PRSVD	W 10640	8.8	W 7641	8.2	W 8865	9.5	W 8647	9.1	LEGUMES FRAIS,CONG,SECS
057	FRUIT,NUTS,FRESH,DRIED	W 12408	14.5	W 12822	16.7	W 12455	17.9	W 12509	17.3	FRUITS FRAIS OU SECS
058	FRUIT PRESERVED,PREPARED	W 4571	7.6	W 4162	8.1	W 4227	8.3	W 4777	8.1	CONSERVES DE FRUITS
06	SUGAR AND PREPS,HONEY		10.1		11.0		11.1		10.0	SUCRES ET PRODUITS
061	SUGAR AND HONEY	W 13270	7.0	W 12420	7.5	W 13103	7.3	W 12895	6.3	SUCRES ET MIEL
0612	REFINED SUGAR ETC	W 12696	6.4	W 11821	6.8	W 12469	6.5	W 12225	5.6	SUCRES RAFFINES
07	COFFEE,TEA,COCOA,SPICES		16.9		21.6		20.1		21.6	CAFE,THE,CACAO,EPICES
071	COFFEE AND SUBSTITUTES	W 2024	8.5	W 2067	11.7	W 2152	10.3	W 1960	10.5	CAFE ET SUCCEDANES
0711	COFFEE GREEN,ROASTED,SUB	W 1977	7.7	W 2017	10.7	W 2078	9.2	W 1916	9.6	CAFE TORREFIE OU DECAFEINE
07112	COFFEE ROASTED	W 1244	5.4	W 1210	7.4	W 1399	7.1	W 1352	7.3	CAFE TORREFIE
073	CHOCOLATE AND PRODUCTS	W 1210	5.5	W 1279	6.3	W 1301	6.5	W 1555	7.8	CHOCOLAT
081	*FEEDING STUFF FOR ANIML	W 9839	5.7	W 8199	6.9	W 8581	6.6	W 9835	6.2	NOURRITURE POUR ANIMAUX
0819	FOOD WASTE AND FEED NES	W 3662	4.2	W 3686	5.6	W 5200	5.4	W 3964	4.0	DECHETS,ALIMENTS NDA
08199	FODDER NES,INCL SWEETNED	W 3608	4.2	W 3624	5.6	W 3825	5.1	W 2804	3.8	PREPARATIONS FOURRAGERES
09	MISC EDIBLE PRODUCTS		17.9		18.8		20.8		20.1	PREP ALIMENTAIRES DIVERSES
098	EDIBLE PRODCTS,PREPS NES	W 3641	17.8	W 3846	18.6	W 4110	20.5	W 4171	19.8	PREP ALIMENTAIRES NDA
09809	MISC FOOD PREPRTIONS NES	W 1295	10.8	W 1366	10.4	W 1533	12.0	W 1489	11.4	PREP ALIMENTAIRES NDA
1	BEVERAGES AND TOBACCO		27.4		31.9		34.1		34.1	BOISSONS ET TABACS
11	BEVERAGES		14.1		17.9		19.3		19.4	BOISSONS
112	ALCOHOLIC BEVERAGES	W 7977	13.9	W 9259	17.4	W 10089	18.8	W 10503	18.1	BOISSONS ALCOOLIQUES
1121	WINE OF FRESH GRAPES ETC	W 2051	5.4	W 2166	6.1	W 2174	6.6	W 2036	6.1	VINS DE RAISINS FRAIS
11212	WINE OF FRESH GRAPES	W 1865	4.8	W 2043	5.7	W 2096	6.4	W 1999	6.1	VINS DE MOUTS DE RAISINS
1124	DISTILLED ALCOHOLIC BEVS	W 1275	5.3	W 1575	6.7	W 1475	6.8	W 1418	6.2	ALCOOLS,EAUX–DE–VIE
12	TOBACCO AND MANUFACTURES		13.3		14.0		14.9		14.7	TABACS BRUTS FABRIQUES
122	TOBACCO,MANUFACTURED	W 551	13.3	W 541	14.0	W 554	14.9	W 560	14.7	TABACS FABRIQUES
1222	CIGARETTES	W 469	11.4	W 470	12.0	W 497	12.9	W 496	12.8	CIGARETTES
2	CRUDE MATERLS,EXCL FUELS		66.5		93.4		92.5		77.3	MAT BRUTES NON COMESTIBLES
24	CORK AND WOOD		17.4		20.6		21.5		21.1	LIEGE ET BOIS
248	WOOD SHAPED,SLEEPERS	W 37983	16.4	W 45748	19.8	W 44980	20.4	W 43309	19.9	BOIS SIMPLEMENT TRAVAILLES
2482	LUMBER SHAPED CONIFER	W 36299	13.8	W 43892	16.6	W 42819	16.4	W 41302	16.5	CONIFERES SCIES,RABOTES
24821	LUMBER SAWN ETC CONIFER	W 35932	13.2	W 43757	16.2	W 42640	16.2	W 41128	16.1	CONIFERES SCIES LONGITUD
27	CRUDE FERTLZR,MINRLS NES		11.2		11.7		13.6		10.9	ENGRAIS MINERAUX BRUTS
278	OTHER CRUDE MINERALS		9.9	W 209292	10.5	W 223336	11.2	W 189296	8.8	AUTRES MINERAUX BRUTS
2783	COMMON SALT,ETC	W 89068	5.3	W 95194	5.9	W 90996	5.8	W 87194	5.0	SEL
28	METALLIFEROUS ORES,SCRAP		32.4		53.7		50.3		34.8	MINERAIS METAL,DECHETS
287	BASE METAL ORES,CONC NES	W 169692	31.6	W 229470	52.6	W 203152	49.0	W 155901	32.6	MINERAIS METAUX COMMUNS
2873	ALUMINIUM ORES,ALUMINA	W 169580	31.6	W 229470	52.6	W 203152	49.0	W 155811	32.5	MINERAIS D'ALUMINIUM
28732	ALUMINA(ALUMINIUM OXIDE)	W 169580	31.6	W 229470	52.6	W 203152	49.0	W 155801	32.5	ALUMINE (OXYDE ALUMINIUM)
29	CRUDE ANIMAL,VEG MAT NES		3.9		4.6		4.2		7.0	MATIERES BRUTES ANIM,VEGET
3	MINERAL FUELS ETC		122.9		127.6		161.3		154.4	COMBUSTIBLES MINERAUX LUB
32	COAL,COKE AND BRIQUETTES		9.1		7.8		9.4		8.8	HOUILLES,COKES,BRIQUETTES
322	COAL,LIGNITE AND PEAT	W 71395	5.6	W 65369	5.8	W 66069	5.9	W 58679	5.0	HOUILLES,LIGNITES,TOURBE
3221	ANTHRACITE,NOT AGGLOMRTD	W 52763	4.6	W 58106	5.3	W 59543	5.4	W 47288	4.3	ANTHRACITE
33	PETROLEUM AND PRODUCTS		113.4		119.3		151.5		144.8	PETROLE ET DERIVES
334	PETROLEUM PRODUCTS,REFIN	W 660476	110.4	W 676044	115.3	W 726076	147.0	W 732587	141.2	PRODUITS RAFFINES
3341	GASOLINE,OTH LIGHT OILS	W 144781	26.0	W 134428	25.0	W 153162	32.1	W 136149	29.7	ESSENCES POUR MOTEURS
33411	MOTOR,AVIATION SPIRIT	W 142385	25.3	W 132191	24.3	W 151165	31.3	W 132942	28.7	ESSENCES MOTEURS D'AVIONS
3342	KEROSENE,OTH MEDIUM OILS	W 102337	17.1	W 72284	12.7	W 96711	20.5	W 106261	21.7	PETR LAMPANTS,AUT HUIL
33421	KEROSENE INCL JET FUEL	W 73833	12.9	W 72283	12.7	W 96693	20.5	W 106260	21.7	PETROLES LAMPANTS
3343	GAS OILS	W 289483	46.2	W 296042	47.1	W 355160	68.8	W 336954	62.1	GAS OILS
3344	FUEL OILS,NES	W 116642	11.9	W 165227	19.8	W 113211	14.9	W 145862	18.4	FUEL OILS
3345	LUBS,PETROLEUM OILS NES	W 7234	9.4	W 8063	10.9	W 7830	10.9	W 7362	9.6	HUILES LUBRIFIANTES
33451	LUBS(HIGH PETR CONT) ETC	W 6926	8.5	W 7688	9.9	W 7479	9.7	W 7016	8.5	HUILES LUBRIF,H LOURDES
4	ANIMAL,VEGETABLE OIL,FAT		4.9		5.5		5.8		5.7	HUILES,GRAISSES ANIM,VEG
5	CHEMCLS,RELATED PROD NES		128.9		155.7		166.5		162.3	PRODUITS CHIMIQUES
51	ORGANIC CHEMICALS		6.6		8.6		9.4		8.1	PROD CHIMIQ ORGANIQUES
52	INORGANIC CHEMICALS		7.2		9.1		10.2		10.1	PROD CHIM INORGANIQUES
523	OTHR INORG CHEMICALS ETC	W 6822	3.9	W 6512	4.5	W 6752	5.1		6.2	AUT PRODUITS CHIMIQUES INORG
53	DYES,TANNING,COLOUR PROD		11.7		13.3		15.0		15.0	PROD TEINTURE,COLORANTS
533	PIGMENTS,PAINTS,ETC	W 3772	10.1	W 3710	11.5	W 4018	13.0	W 4686	13.1	PIGMENTS,PEINTURES,VERNIS
541	*MEDICINAL,PHARM PRODUCT		37.1	K 465327	44.9		49.5		47.9	PROD MEDICINAUX PHARMACEUT
5417	MEDICAMENTS	K 342694	31.1	K 345367	37.5	K 372708	42.0	K 376138	42.5	MEDICAMENTS
54172	— CONTAINING HORMONES	K 20117	4.7	K 23298	5.9	K 29274	7.1	K 26881	6.4	MED CONTENANT HORMONES
54179	— CONTNG OTH SUBSTANCES	K 293886	23.5	K 294492	28.7	K 315373	31.9	K 323418	33.4	MED CONT AUT SUBSTANCES
55	PERFUME,CLEANING ETC PRD		21.9		24.1		26.2		25.8	PROD POUR PARFUM,TOILETTE
553	PERFUMERY,COSMETICS,ETC	W 1312	12.7	W 1358	14.5	W 1416	15.4	W 1478	15.7	PRODUITS DE PARFUMERIE
554	SOAP,CLEANSING ETC PREPS	W 3586	8.5	W 3253	8.8	W 3780	9.7	W 3716	9.0	SAVONS,PRODUITS DETERSIFS
5542	WASHING PREPARATIONS ETC	W 2975	6.4	W 2617	6.4	W 2932	7.0	W 2968	6.5	PROD ORG TENSIO–ACT NDA
562	*FERTILIZERS,MANUFACTURE	W 19038	3.4	W 23391	5.5	W 21608	4.4	W 17041	4.0	ENGRAIS MANUFACTURES
58	PLASTIC MATERIALS ETC		26.5		34.3		33.6		31.6	MAT PLAST ARTIFICIELLES
582	PROD OF CONDENSATION ETC	W 2282	5.7	W 2433	6.7	W 2462	6.7	W 2744	6.0	PROD CONDENS,POLYCOND
583	POLYMERIZATION ETC PRODS	W 13024	20.1	W 12870	27.0	W 15227	26.4	W 15434	25.2	PROD POLYMERISATION
5831	POLYETHYLENE	W 7910	9.1	W 7397	12.3	W 9039	11.4	W 9081	11.5	POLYETHYLENE
58311	— IN PRIMARY FORMS	W 7055	7.1	W 6666	9.5	W 8220	9.1	W 8140	8.9	POLYETHYLENE PRIMAIRES
5839	OTH POLYMRZTION ETC PROD	W 952	3.8	W 1288	5.5	W 1422	5.9	W 1232	5.4	AUT PROD POLYMER COPOLYM
59	CHEMICAL MATERIALS NES		13.2		15.0		16.4		17.3	MAT PROD CHIMIQUES NDA
598	MISCEL CHEM PRODUCTS NES	W 7044	9.7	W 6429	10.9	W 7927	12.1	W 9914	13.4	PROD DIV INDUST CHIM NDA
5989	CHEM PRODUCTS,PREPS NES	W 1969	6.6	W 2117	8.0	W 2592	8.6	W 2851	9.3	PROD PREP CHIMIQUES NDA
59899	OTH CHEM PRODS,PREPS,NES	W 1613	5.5	W 1808	6.9	W 2227	7.3	W 2429	8.2	AUT PRODUITS CHIMIQUES NDA
6	BASIC MANUFACTURES		256.2		303.8		350.5		348.1	ART MANUFACTURES
62	RUBBER MANUFACTURES NES		16.3		19.5		20.5		21.3	CAOUTCHOUC MANUFACTURE
625	RUBBER TYRES, TUBES ETC	W 2730	8.5	W 2803	10.6	W 2735	11.0	W 3141	12.1	PNEUS CAOUTCHOUC VULCANISE
6251	TYRES NEW FOR MOTOR CARS	W 1128	4.7	W 1219	6.0	W 1352	6.4	W 1580	7.2	PNEUS POUR VOITURES
628	RUBBER ARTICLES NES	W 793	4.6	W 726	5.3	W 774	5.5	W 936	5.6	OUVRAGES CAOUTCHOUC NDA
63	WOOD,CORK MANUFACTRS NES		20.8		24.8		27.7		34.8	OUVRAGES LIEGE ET BOIS
634	VENEERS,PLYWOOD,ETC	W 12440	8.5	W 13306	10.5	W 13155	10.0	W 15385	10.4	PLACAGES,CONTRE–PLAQUES
6343	IMPROVED,RECONSTIT WOOD	W 9657	4.1	W 10338	5.3	W 10299	5.0	W 11713	5.2	BOIS AMELIORES,RECONST
635	WOOD MANUFACTURES NES	W 4377	12.2	W 4476	14.1	W 6099	17.5	W 10719	24.2	ART MANUF EN BOIS NDA

4. General Imports C.I.F. by Commodities according to the S.I.T.C. (Rev. 2) in million U.S. Dollars
Importations Générales C.A.F. par Produits d'après la C.T.C.I. (Rév. 2) en millions de Dollars E.U.

SITC CTCI	COMMODITY	1994 QUANTITY QUANTITE	1994 VALUE VALEUR	1995 QUANTITY QUANTITE	1995 VALUE VALEUR	1996 QUANTITY QUANTITE	1996 VALUE VALEUR	1997 QUANTITY QUANTITE	1997 VALUE VALEUR	PRODUIT
6353	BUILDERS WOODWRK,PREFABS	W 3748	10.0	W 3905	11.7	W 5213	14.2	W 9857	21.0	OUVRAGES DE MENUISERIE
64	PAPER,PAPERBOARD AND MFR		59.3		70.4		72.2		65.7	PAPIERS,CARTONS & OUVRAGES
641	PAPER AND PAPERBOARD	W 33172	32.2	W 31748	39.2	W 33181	39.8	W 34326	35.6	PAPIERS ET CARTONS
6412	PRINTG,WRITING PAPER NES	W 5373	6.4	W 5909	8.9	W 6085	8.7	W 7401	8.8	PAPIERS POUR L'IMPRESSION
64122	— COATED,IMPREGNATD ETC	W 4423	5.1	W 4700	6.7	W 4794	6.7	W 5666	6.5	PAPIERS IMPRESSION COUCHES
6415	PAPER,PAPERBRD,BULK,NES	W 6294	5.3	W 5858	6.6	W 5482	5.7	W 5523	4.9	PAPIERS,CARTONS ROULEAUX
6418	COATED ETC PAPER NES BLK	W 3924	8.9	W 3882	10.0	W 3989	10.2	W 3615	9.1	PAP,CARTONS COUCHES,ENDUITS
64181	PLASTIC COATED PAPER ETC	W 2895	5.5	W 2645	6.0	W 2769	6.1	W 2145	5.2	PAP,CARTONS ENDUITS,RESINES
642	PAPER,ETC,PRECUT,ARTS OF	W 10816	27.2	W 10671	31.3	W 12244	32.4	W 13176	30.1	PAP,CARTONS DECOUPES
6421	PAPER ETC CONTAINERS	W 6193	10.9	W 6241	12.7	W 7821	13.8	W 8775	13.3	BOITES,SACS EMBALLAGES
6428	PAPER ETC ARTICLES NES	W 2938	11.1	W 2800	12.7	W 2960	13.2	W 2785	11.3	OUVRAGES EN PATE A PAPIER
64285	PAPER ETC DIAPERS ETC	W 1229	6.4	W 1136	7.1	W 1098	6.7	W 940	5.3	SERVIETTES HYGIENIQUES
65	TEXTILE YARN,FABRICS,ETC		39.5		45.5		53.7		50.8	FILS,TISSUS,ARTICLES TEXTILE
657	SPECIAL TXTL FABRC,PRODS		15.4	W 2573	18.5		24.7		24.0	TISSUS SPECIAUX
6575	CORDAGE AND MANUFACTURES	W 2091	12.4	W 2143	14.7	W 2729	20.7	W 2530	19.9	FICELLES,CORDES,CORDAGES
65751	CORDAGE,CABLE,ROPE,TWINE	W 1207	5.1	W 1401	6.9	W 1489	7.3	W 1299	6.5	CORDAGES TRESSES OU NON
65752	NETTING OF ROPE,TWINE	W 835	6.9	W 712	7.5	W 1188	13.1	W 1193	13.1	FILETS MAT DU 657.51
658	TEXTILE ARTICLES NES	W 704	6.5	W 815	7.6	W 881	8.0	W 1017	7.9	ART FACONNES MAT TEXTILES
66	NONMETAL MINERAL MFS NES		22.7		24.7		26.7		27.1	ART MIN NON METALLIQUES
662	CLAY,REFRACTORY BLDG PRD	W 4430	3.2	W 4052	3.7	W 5795	5.5	W 7312	6.1	MAT CONST REFRACTAIRES
664	GLASS	W 3468	5.2	W 3509	5.9	W 3479	6.1	W 3768	6.4	VERRE
665	GLASSWARE	W 3142	5.5	W 2425	5.3	W 2483	5.2	W 2703	4.7	OUVRAGES EN VERRE
67	IRON AND STEEL		26.4		34.1		42.9		41.9	FER ET ACIER
673	IRON,STEEL SHAPES ETC	W 14414	7.6	W 13158	8.2	W 22550	13.2	W 23349	12.1	BARRES,PROFIL FER,ACIER
674	IRN,STL UNIV,PLATE,SHEET	W 9918	9.3	W 11288	12.7	W 13192	14.0	W 13400	12.5	LARGES PLATS,TOLES
6749	OTH IRN,STL PLATES,SHEET	W 4459	4.1	W 4634	5.1	W 6251	6.4	W 6917	6.3	AUTRES TOLES FER,ACIER
67491	— OF IRON OR SIMPLE STL	W 4241	3.9	W 4479	4.8	W 6101	6.2	W 6749	6.0	AUT TOLES AUTRES ACIER FIN
678	IRON,STL TUBES,PIPES,ETC	W 6025	8.2	W 6082	11.1	W 7279	12.6	W 9282	14.7	TUBES,TUYAUX EN FONTE,FER
6783	IRON,STL TUBES,PIPES NES	W 4055	3.6	W 3880	4.7	W 4255	4.5	W 5684	6.5	AUT TUBES,TUYAUX FER,ACIER
68	NON–FERROUS METALS		10.2		14.8		18.3		19.5	METAUX NON FERREUX
684	ALUMINIUM		7.4	W 2510	11.1	W 4094	13.8	W 4567	15.1	ALUMINIUM
6842	ALUMINIUM,ALLOYS WORKED	W 1165	6.2	W 1331	8.0	W 1977	10.3	W 1872	9.5	ALUMINIUM,ALLIAGES OUVRE
69	METAL MANUFACTURES NES		60.1		68.7		87.2		85.5	ART MANUFACT EN METAL NDA
691	STRUCTURES AND PARTS NES	W 3147	7.5	W 2851	8.3	W 7825	19.5	W 10395	22.3	CONSTRUCT FER,ACIER,ALU
6911	STRUCTURES,PARTS IRN,STL	W 2857	5.6	W 2592	6.2	W 7545	17.2	W 9908	18.9	CONSTRUCT FER,ACIER,FONTE
692	METAL TANKS,BOXES,ETC	W 1162	6.2	W 1167	6.0	W 1522	7.4	W 1252	7.3	RECIPIENTS METALLIQUES
6924	MTL TRANSPORT BOXES ETC	W 1110	5.9	W 1034	5.5	W 1254	6.2	W 1067	6.1	FUTS,TAMBOURS,BIDONS
693	WIRE PRODUCTS NON ELECTR	W 4226	8.4	W 4561	9.8	W 4664	10.1	W 4612	8.2	OUVRAGES FILS METALLIQUES
6931	WIRE CABLES, ROPES ETC	W 3641	7.6	W 4095	9.1	W 3981	9.0	W 3525	7.2	CORDAGES EN FILS DE FER
69311	IRN,STEEL CABLE,ROPE ETC	W 3576	7.4	W 3995	8.7	W 3838	8.5	W 3470	7.0	CORDAGES FILS FER,ACIER
694	STL,COPPR NAILS,NUTS,ETC	W 900	5.0	W 1011	6.1	W 1218	7.3	W 1276	6.8	CLOUS,VIS,ECROUS
695	TOOLS	W 395	6.6	W 410	7.5	W 454	8.9	W 566	9.6	OUTILS A MAIN
699	BASE METAL MFRS NES	W 3266	20.2	W 3585	23.8		26.5	W 3743	24.0	ART MANUFACTURES MET NDA
6991	LOCKSMITHS WARES,ETC	W 566	6.1	W 730	7.1	W 669	7.6	W 709	7.5	ARTICLES DE SERRURERIE
69913	BASE MTL DOOR,ETC FITTNG	W 488	4.6	W 643	5.3	W 560	5.7	W 590	5.5	GARNITURES POUR MEUBLES
6997	IRON,STEEL ARTICLES NES	W 1054	6.0	W 1122	6.8	W 1618	8.6	W 1239	6.7	OUV FONTE,FER,ACIER NDA
69979	IRN,STL MANUFACTURES NES	W 1047	5.9	W 1118	6.8	W 1615	8.6	W 1225	6.6	AUT OUVRAGES EN FER NDA
7	MACHINES,TRANSPORT EQUIP		462.9		564.3		729.2		752.7	MACHINES MATERIEL TRANSPORT
71	POWER GENERATING EQUIPMT		20.4		17.8		21.4		29.8	MACHINES GENERATRICES
713	INTRNL COMBUS PSTN ENGIN	W 265	6.7	W 287	8.0	W 332	9.4	W 420	10.6	MOTEURS EXPL COMB INT, PIECE
714	ENGINES AND MOTORS NES	W 38	8.7	W 26	3.9	W 48	3.7	W 40	6.0	MOTEURS NON ELECTRIQUES
7144	REACTION ENGINES	W 27	7.3	W 11	2.3	W 26	2.2	W 28	4.2	PROPULSEURS A REACTION
716	ROTATING ELECTRIC PLANT	W 245	3.7	W 280	4.1	W 302	5.4	W 419	7.0	APP ELECTR ROTATIFS,PIECES
72	MACHS FOR SPCL INDUSTRYS		37.4		53.2		65.7		74.2	MAC SPECIALES POUR INDUST
721	AGRIC MACHY,EXC TRACTORS	W 719	5.5	W 874	7.2	W 1006	7.8	W 1226	8.1	MACHINES AGRICOLES
722	TRACTORS NON–ROAD	W 587	3.7	W 790	6.0	W 1011	7.8	W 1190	9.4	TRACTEURS
7224	WHEELED TRACTORS NES	W 587	3.7	W 790	6.0	W 1011	7.8	W 1190	9.4	TRACTEURS A ROUES
723	CIVIL ENGNEERG EQUIP ETC	W 1455	7.9	W 1403	9.0	W 2484	14.2	W 3679	21.1	APPAREILS DE GENIE CIVIL
7234	CONST,MINING MACHNRY NES	W 1280	7.1	W 1248	7.9	W 2116	11.9	W 3384	18.6	MACH POUR LA CONST, MINES
72342	SLFPRP SHOVELS,EXCAVATRS	W 767	4.2	W 817	4.7	W 1425	7.6	W 2355	12.5	PELLES MECANIQUES
726	PRINTG,BKBINDG MACHY,PTS	W 48	2.3	W 129	4.7	W 117	3.6	W 222	6.9	MACHINES POUR IMPRIMERIE
727	FOOD MACHRY NON–DOMESTIC	W 347	8.1	W 476	15.1	W 650	13.5	W 528	12.1	MACH INDUSTRIES ALIMENT
7272	OTH FOOD PROC MCHY,PARTS	W 341	8.0	W 471	15.0	W 643	13.3	W 504	11.7	AUT MACH IND ALIMENTAIRE
72722	INDUS FOOD PROC MACH NES	W 340	8.0	W 470	14.9	W 642	13.3	W 497	11.6	MACHINES BOULANGERIE
728	OTH MACHY FOR SPCL INDUS	W 925	7.9	W 639	8.2	W 1064	15.7	W 1208	13.7	AUT MACH IND PARTICULIERES
7284	MACHY FOR SPCL INDUS NES	W 307	4.5	W 296	5.1	W 588	10.3	W 425	7.8	MACH SPEC IND PARTICUL.
73	METALWORKING MACHINERY		4.2		6.7		9.2		13.5	MACH TRAVAIL DES METAUX
736	METALWORKING MACH–TOOLS	W 157	1.6	W 219	2.3	W 443	5.4	W 526	6.2	MACH–OUTILS TRAVAIL METAUX
737	METALWORKING MACHNRY NES	W 404	2.7	W 455	4.5	W 876	3.8	W 1613	7.4	MACH TRAV METAUX PIECES
74	GENRL INDUSTRL MACHY NES		64.8		82.4		124.2		122.9	MACH APP INDUSTRIE
741	HEATING,COOLING EQUIPMNT	W 1183	12.7	W 1495	14.8	W 2531	31.1	W 3544	23.8	MACH CHAUFFAGE,PIECES
7414	NONDOM REFRIG EQUIPT,PTS	W 397	4.2	W 497	6.8	W 902	10.5	W 753	9.3	MAT PRODUCTION DU FROID
74141	REFRIG EQUIP NONDOMESTIC	W 313	3.2	W 386	4.9	W 687	8.0	W 688	8.3	REFIG INDUSTRIELS
7416	HEATING,COOLING EQU NES	W 652	7.5	W 893	6.5	W 1520	18.9	W 779	7.5	APP CHANGEMENT TEMP
742	PUMPS FOR LIQUIDS ETC	W 307	7.1	W 338	8.5	W 448	11.2	W 439	10.0	POMPES MOTO–POMPES
743	PUMPS NES,CENTRFUGES ETC	W 519	8.0	W 607	10.6	W 1377	17.8	W 1518	17.5	POMPES COMPRES,VENT ETC
7439	PTS NES OF APP OF 7435,6	W 29	1.0	W 41	1.5	W 704	5.3	W 792	6.5	PIECES 743.5 ET 743.6
744	MECHANICAL HANDLING EQU	W 1714	12.2	W 2189	18.5	W 3449	29.1	W 6622	36.0	EQUIP MANUTENTION PIECES
7441	FORK LIFT TRCKS,ETC,PTS	W 767	3.5	W 1014	6.2	W 1791	12.5	W 2014	10.5	CHARIOTS POUR USINES ETC
74411	FORK LIFT TRUCKS ETC	W 766	3.4	W 1013	6.2	W 1788	12.5	W 2012	10.5	CHARIOTS POUR LES GARES
7442	LIFTING,LOADING MACH NES	W 585	5.6	W 840	8.3	W 1278	12.0	W 3981	18.8	APP LEVAGE,MANUTENTION
74428	OTH HANDLING ETC MCH NES	W 319	3.0	W 440	4.2	W 563	6.2	W 1464	10.4	AUT APP LEVAGE ETC
7449	PTS NES OF MACHY OF 7442	W 362	3.3	W 335	4.0	W 380	4.7	W 627	6.8	PIECES DU 744.2
745	NONELEC MACHY,TOOLS NES	W 335	7.4	W 383	10.1	W 381	10.0	W 476	11.7	AUT MACH NON ELEC,PIECES
7452	OTH NONELEC MCHS,PTS NES	W 312	6.9	W 356	9.5	W 348	9.2	W 430	10.8	AUT MACH NON ELEC,PIECES
749	NONELEC MACH PTS,ACC NES	W 681	17.6	W 722	20.2	W 923	25.3	W 1187	24.2	PIECES MACH NON ELEC NDA
7492	COCKS,VALVES ETC NES	W 320	7.3	W 324	8.7	W 421	10.4	W 585	10.9	ART ROB,SIM POUR TUYAUX
7493	SHAFT,CRANK,PULLEY ETC	W 163	4.5	W 210	5.5	W 284	8.3	W 274	6.8	ARBRES TRANS,VILEBREQUINS
75	OFFICE MACHNES,ADP EQUIP		49.2		59.7		71.7		70.0	MACH BUREAU TRAIT AUTOM
752	AUTOMTIC DATA PROC EQUIP	W 422	36.4	W 480	44.7	W 572	55.4	W 650	53.6	MACH TRAIT INFORMATION
7522	DIGITAL COMPUTERS	W 163	14.1	W 170	14.0	W 180	18.2	W 205	15.8	MACH DIGITALES COMPLETES
7523	DIGITL CENTRL PROCESSORS	W 50	3.8	W 26	3.3	W 49	7.6	W 38	4.8	UNITES CENTRALES
7524	DIGITL CENTRL STOR UNITS	W 40	3.6	W 59	7.0	W 39	8.1	W 55	9.0	UNITES MEMOIRE CENTRALES
7525	ADP PERIPHERAL UNITS	W 116	11.2	W 148	14.1	W 159	12.0	W 202	14.3	UNITES PERIPHERIQUES
759	OFFICE,ADP MCH PTS,ACCES	W 77	9.3	W 100	11.6	W 117	11.9	W 164	12.9	PIECES DU 751 ET 752
7599	ACCTG,ETC,ADP MCH PTS,AC	W 58	8.3	W 78	10.1	W 90	10.5	W 134	11.6	PIECES DU 751 ET 752
76	TELECOMM,SOUND EQUIPMENT		53.4		60.4		64.0		67.9	EQUIPMENT DE TELECOM
761	TELEVISION RECEIVERS	W 422	9.8	W 434	11.2	W 650	14.7	W 687	15.0	RECEPTEURS DE TELEVISION
7611	COLOUR TV RECEIVERS	W 419	9.7	W 430	11.0	W 647	14.5	W 683	14.7	RECEPTEURS COULEUR
764	TELECOM EQPT,PTS,ACC NES	W 372	37.1	W 398	40.5	W 418	40.7	W 527	44.4	EQUIP TELECOM,PIECES
7641	LINE TELEPHONE,ETC EQUIP	W 70	4.8	W 90	7.7	W 95	8.5	W 111	10.2	APP TELEPHON PAR FIL

4. General Imports C.I.F. by Commodities according to the S.I.T.C. (Rev. 2) in million U.S. Dollars
Importations Générales C.A.F. par Produits d'après la C.T.C.I. (Rév. 2) en millions de Dollars E.U.

SITC CTCI	COMMODITY	1994		1995		1996		1997		PRODUIT
		QUANTITY QUANTITE	VALUE VALEUR	QUANTITY QUANTITE	VALUE VALEUR	QUANTITY QUANTITE	VALUE VALEUR	QUANTITY QUANTITE	VALUE VALEUR	
7643	TV,RADIO TRANSMITTRS ETC	W 35	6.2	W 56	11.0	W 86	13.6	W 77	14.3	APP EMET TELE RADIO
7649	PTS NES OF EQUIPMT OF 76	W 173	20.9	W 135	14.9	W 106	13.0	W 176	13.9	PIECES DE LA DIV 76
76491	PTS NES OF APPAR OF 7641	W 64	14.3	W 38	8.9	W 29	8.7	W 36	8.4	PIECES POUR 764.1
76493	TELECOMM EQUIPMT PTS NES	W 107	6.4	W 95	5.9	W 75	4.1	W 137	5.3	PIECES 761,762,764.3,8
77	ELECTRIC MACHNRY NES ETC		82.7		97.9		112.5		135.3	MACH APP ELECT NDA
771	ELECTRIC POWER MACHY NES	W 475	4.9	W 424	5.2	W 654	7.5	W 1429	13.8	MACH PROD,TRANS ELECTR
7712	OTH ELEC POWER MACHY NES	W 101	2.6	W 102	2.7	W 114	3.5	W 457	7.8	AUT APP PROD TRANSF ELEC
77121	STATIC CONVERTERS ETC	W 58	2.1	W 73	2.2	W 76	2.8	W 400	6.7	CONVERTISSEURS STATIQUES
772	SWITCHGEAR ETC,PARTS NES	W 438	11.1	W 560	15.6	W 571	15.5	W 942	25.5	APP COUPURE,SECT ETC
7721	SWITCHGEAR ETC	W 433	10.5	W 555	15.1	W 564	14.8	W 934	24.7	APP COUPURE,SECTIONMNT
773	ELECTR DISTRIBUTNG EQUIP	W 1995	8.2	W 1886	9.8	W 2675	13.0	W 3739	13.2	EQUIPMT DISTRIBUTION ELECT
7731	INSULATED WIRE,CABLE ETC	W 1952	7.8	W 1846	9.3	W 2611	12.2	W 3653	12.1	FILS,CABLES ISOLES ELECT
775	HOUSEHOLD TYPE EQUIP NES	W 1555	14.3	W 1584	16.1	W 1822	18.6	W 1816	16.1	MACH,APP USAGE DOMESTQUE
7758	ELECTRO–THERMIC APPL NES	W 489	5.3	W 493	5.9	W 559	6.4	W 515	5.5	APP ELECTROTHERMIQ NDA
776	TRANSISTORS,VALVES,ETC	W 12	2.0	W 9	2.1	W 16	3.7	W 16	6.7	LAMPES,TUBES,VALVES
778	ELECTRICAL MACHINERY NES	W 54644	40.0	W 54141	45.6	W 52731	52.2	W 70237	57.1	AUTRES MACH ELECT NDA
7788	OTH ELEC MACHY,EQUIP NES	W 53436	28.2	W 52885	32.0	W 51305	37.2	W 68842	42.5	AUT MACH APP ELEC NDA
77887	ELECTRICAL CARBONS	W 53355	24.6	W 52800	28.2	W 51212	33.0	W 68738	37.4	PIECES CHARBON,GRAPHITE
78	ROAD VEHICLES		83.3		118.9		157.8		186.7	VEHICULES ROUTIERS
781	PASS MOTOR VEH EXC BUSES	W 6307	51.7	W 8213	75.9	W 12031	105.5	W 15193	126.6	AUTO TRANSPORT PERSONNES
782	LORRIES,SPCL MTR VEH NES	W 1846	12.3	W 2512	20.8	W 3087	24.5	W 4570	29.9	VEHICULES SPECIAUX,MARCH
7821	LORRIES,TRUCKS	W 1711	12.1	W 2271	18.8	W 2995	23.9	W 3953	26.8	VEHICULES TRANSP MARCHAND
783	ROAD MOTOR VEHICLES NES	W 277	2.6	W 225	1.9	W 557	4.8	W 768	6.4	VEHICULES ROUTIERS NDA
784	MOTOR VEH PRTS,ACCES NES	W 1002	10.9	W 1174	13.6	W 1190	14.0	W 1428	15.1	PIECES 722,781,782,783
7849	OTHER MOTOR VEHCL PARTS	W 936	10.3	W 1117	13.2	W 1132	13.6	W 1363	14.8	PIECES 722,781,782,783
79	OTHR TRANSPORT EQUIPMENT		67.9		67.7		103.1		52.7	AUTRE MATERIEL TRANSPORT
792	AIRCRAFT ETC	W 36	9.2	W 202	20.4	W 48	7.6	W 39	8.8	APP NAVIGATION AERIENNE
7921	HELICOPTERS			W 10	12.2					HELICOPTERES
7929	AIRCRAFT PARTS NES	W 19	6.7	W 23	6.9	W 33	5.9	W 24	6.4	PIECES DU 792
793	SHIPS AND BOATS ETC	W 10045	58.7	W 19788	47.2	W 23905	95.5	W 8666	43.9	NAVIRES BATEAUX,ETC
7932	SHIPS AND BOATS NES	W 9656	57.6	W 13208	43.6	W 23774	95.1	W 8431	42.5	NAVIRES ET BATEAUX
79323	OTHER CARGO VESSELS			W 398	0.5	W 9850	24.7	W 10	0.1	AUT BATEAUX TRANS MARCH
79324	FISHING VESSELS ETC	W 9516	57.1	W 12793	42.7	W 13881	69.8	W 8390	42.0	BATEAUX DE PECHE
8	MISC MANUFACTURED GOODS		259.6		297.4		318.4		315.4	ART MANUFACTURES DIVERS
812	*PLUMBG,HEATNG,LGHTNG EQ	W 1516	9.6	W 1649	11.1	W 1749	12.5	W 1689	12.1	APPAR SANITAIRES CHAUFFAGE
8124	LIGHTING EQUIPMENT NES	W 626	7.2	W 694	8.3	W 742	9.1	W 764	9.1	APPAREILS ECLAIRAGE ETC
81242	LAMPS,FITTINGS BASE METL	W 577	6.6	W 639	7.5	W 688	8.3	W 691	8.1	APPAREILS D'ECLAIRAGE
821	*FURNITURE,PARTS THEREOF	W 6212	30.7	W 6417	35.1	W 6772	39.4	W 8274	42.7	MEUBLES ET PIECES
8211	CHAIRS,SEATS AND PARTS	W 1152	10.3	W 1325	11.6	W 1438	12.9	W 1712	14.2	SIEGES ET PIECES
82111	CHAIRS AND OTHER SEATS	W 1068	9.6	W 1246	10.8	W 1364	12.2	W 1623	13.4	SIEGES
8212	MED FURN,STUFFD FURNSHGS	W 682	5.4	W 728	6.2	W 894	6.5	W 1205	7.4	MOB MEDICO–CHIRUR,PIECES
8219	FURNITURE AND PARTS NES	W 4378	15.2	W 4364	17.3	W 4439	20.0	W 5357	21.2	AUTRES MEUBLES ET PIECES
82192	WOOD FURNITURE NES	W 2564	9.1	W 2516	9.8	W 2761	12.4	W 3267	13.0	MEUBLES NDA EN BOIS
84	CLOTHING AND ACCESSORIES		70.4		79.1		80.2		78.8	VETEMENTS
842	MENS OUTERWEAR NOT KNIT	W 309	11.6	W 412	14.9	W 384	15.0	W 386	14.7	VET DESSUS POUR HOMMES
843	WOMENS OUTERWEAR NONKNIT	W 477	21.8	W 482	23.2	W 488	23.6	W 531	23.0	VET DESSUS FEMMES MAT TEX
8439	— OTHER OUTER GARMENTS	W 285	10.7	W 298	11.6	W 283	11.7	W 321	11.7	AUT VET DES FEM MAT TEXT
845	OUTERWEAR KNIT NONELASTC	W 375	14.4	W 418	15.8	W 430	16.1	W 421	15.5	VET DESSOUS,ACCES BONNET
8451	— JERSEYS,PULLOVERS ETC	W 241	9.2	W 249	9.3	W 252	9.7	W 232	8.6	CHANDAILS,PULL–OVERS ETC
8459	— OTHER,CLTHG ACCESRYS	W 117	4.5	W 154	5.7	W 166	5.8	W 173	6.2	AUT VET DESSUS DE BONNE
846	UNDER GARMENTS KNITTED	W 310	9.7	W 296	11.3	W 299	11.7	W 347	11.7	SOUS VETS DE BONNETERIE
8462	— OF COTTON NON ELASTIC	W 244	6.4	W 211	7.1	W 229	7.6	W 264	8.2	SOUS–VET BONNET COTON
84629	—— OTHER	W 244	6.4	W 211	7.1	W 229	7.6	W 264	8.2	AUT SOUS–VET BONNET COTON
848	HEADGEAR,NONTXTL CLOTHNG	W 252	5.1	W 283	5.3	W 302	5.4	W 341	5.7	VET ACCES MAT AUT QUE TEX
851	*FOOTWEAR	W 609	15.2	W 636	17.7	W 595	17.3	W 635	17.7	CHAUSSURES
85102	FOOTWEAR LEATHER	W 429	12.0	W 462	14.3	W 425	13.9	W 451	14.1	CHAUS SEMELLES EN CUIR
87	PRECISION INSTRUMNTS NES		24.8		29.9		35.1		32.2	INSTRUM,APPAR SCIENT NDA
872	MEDICAL INSTRUMENTS NES	W 81	5.7	W 111	7.6	W 122	6.6	W 122	8.1	INSTR,APP MEDIC–CHIR NDA
87202	OTH MEDICAL INSTRUMENTS	W 66	4.7	W 100	6.7	W 103	5.3	W 103	6.8	INSTRUM,APP MEDECINE
874	MEASURNG,CONTROLNG INSTR	W 165	17.7	W 241	19.9	W 217	26.0	W 233	22.1	INSTRUMENTS DE MESURE
8741	SURVEYING INSTRUMENTS	W 20	4.9	W 34	4.9	W 31	8.3	W 37	6.2	INST GEODESIE,TOPO ETC
88	PHOTO EQU,OPTICL GDS ETC		14.9		17.0		18.4		19.3	APP,FOURN PHOTO,OP,MONTR
882	PHOTO,CINEMA SUPPLIES	W 537	7.6	W 511	8.3	W 521	8.4	W 497	8.9	PRODUITS PHOTO,CINEMA
8822	PHOTO FILM EXC DEV CINMA	W 368	5.5	W 359	5.7	W 363	5.7	W 332	6.2	PLAQUES,PELLICULES,FILMS
89	MISC MANUFCTRD GOODS NES		91.2		104.1		111.9		109.1	ART MANUFACTURES DIVERS
892	PRINTED MATTER	W 1258	14.2	W 1213	14.9	W 1176	15.2	W 1319	15.2	IMPRIMES
8921	PRINTED BOOKS,GLOBES,ETC	W 536	6.1	W 450	6.3	W 521	6.8	W 524	6.5	LIVRES,BROCHURES,CARTES
89211	PRINTED BOOKS,PAMPHLETS	W 515	5.9	W 414	5.9	W 502	6.6	W 492	6.2	LIVRES,BROCHURES
8928	PRINTED MATTER NES	W 379	4.9	W 369	4.5	W 343	4.6	W 461	4.9	IMPRIMES NDA
893	ARTICLES OF PLASTIC NES		34.1		39.9		43.5		39.4	OUVRAGES EN MAT DIVIS 58
8931	PLSTC PACKG CONTNRS,LIDS	W 3988	13.4	W 3927	16.1	W 4141	17.0	W 3382	12.9	ART TRANSP EMBALLAGE ETC
8939	MISC PLASTIC ARTICLES	W 2752	20.2	W 2959	23.3	W 3085	25.8	W 4343	25.8	ART DIVERS EN MAT DIV 58
89399	OTHR PLASTC ARTICLES NES	W 2200	17.7	W 2390	20.3	W 2461	22.6	W 3760	23.1	AUT OUV MAT DIV 58
894	TOYS,SPORTING GOODS,ETC	W 1227	14.0	W 1240	15.3	W 1410	17.5	W 1428	17.0	VOITURES ENFANTS,JOUETS
8942	TOYS,INDOOR GAMES ETC	W 721	8.7	W 768	9.7	W 892	11.3	W 987	10.9	JOUETS,JEUX ETC
8947	OTH SPORT GDS,FAIR AMUSM	W 379	4.5	W 327	4.6	W 379	5.1	W 324	5.1	AUT ART DE SPORT
898	MUSICAL INSTRUMENTS,PTS	W 378	15.0	W 393	18.1	W 408	19.0	W 448	19.9	INSTRUMENTS DE MUSIQUE
8983	SOUND RECRDNG TAPE,DISCS	W 300	13.4	W 314	15.8	W 327	16.5	W 373	17.7	SUPPORTS SON POUR 763
89832	RECORDED DISCS,TAPES ETC	W 155	11.1	W 167	13.2	W 194	13.9	W 223	15.0	DISQUES,PHONO,BANDES
899	OTHER MANUFACTURED GOODS		7.6		9.2		9.9		10.8	AUT ART MANUF DIVERS NDA
9	GOODS NOT CLASSD BY KIND		5.9		4.0		5.9		3.6	ART TRANSACT NON CLASSES
931	*SPECIAL TRANSACTIONS		5.1		3.2	W 956	5.0	W 564	3.0	TRANS.SPECIALES

5. General Exports F.O.B. by Commodities according to the S.I.T.C. (Rev. 2) in million U.S. Dollars
Exportations Générales F.O.B. par Produits d'après la C.T.C.I. (Rév. 2) en millions de Dollars E.U.

SITC CTCI	COMMODITY	1994 QUANTITY QUANTITE	1994 VALUE VALEUR	1995 QUANTITY QUANTITE	1995 VALUE VALEUR	1996 QUANTITY QUANTITE	1996 VALUE VALEUR	1997 QUANTITY QUANTITE	1997 VALUE VALEUR	PRODUIT
	ALL COMMODITIES		1626.7		1802.6		1897.1		1851.5	TOUS PRODUITS
0	FOOD AND LIVE ANIMALS		1246.8		1320.4		1385.3		1306.5	ALIMENTS,ANIMAUX VIVANTS
01	MEAT AND PREPARATIONS		5.2		5.2		8.2		4.2	VIANDES ET PREPARATIONS
011	MEAT FRESH,CHILLD,FROZEN	W 1571	5.1	W 1462	5.1	W 3261	8.0	W 1320	3.9	VIANDES FRAICHES,REF,CONGE
0112	MUTTON ETC FRSH,CHLD,FRN	W 1324	4.0	W 1140	3.4	W 3024	7.1	W 1047	3.3	VIANDE DE MOUTON
03	FISH AND PREPARATIONS		1157.7		1210.5		1217.6		1137.9	POISSONS ET PREPARATIONS
034	FISH,FRESH,CHILLED,FROZN	W 275270	717.5	W 242864	691.7	W 276678	670.9	W 291309	625.2	POISSON FRAIS, REFRIG,CONG
0341	FISH FRSH,CHLLD,EX FILLT	W 58195	91.6	W 42795	78.7	W 39618	69.2	W 46073	64.4	POISSON FRAIS,REFRIGERE
0342	FISH FROZEN,EXCL FILLETS	W 92394	188.8	W 85100	189.2	W 128074	215.7	W 145370	177.4	POISSONS CONGELES
0343	FISH FILLETS,FRESH,CHLLD	W 5620	28.2	W 6984	36.2	W 8497	42.3	W 9176	48.4	FILETS FRAIS,REFRIGERES
0344	FISH FILLETS,FROZEN	W 119061	409.0	W 107985	387.7	W 100488	343.8	W 90690	335.1	FILETS CONGELES
035	FISH SALTED,DRIED,SMOKED	W 67312	207.4	W 66741	231.1	W 74859	261.8	W 71882	245.1	POISSON SECHE,SALE,FUME
03502	COD(NOT IN FILLETS)DRIED	W 8086	19.2	W 8046	21.3	W 7956	22.8	W 10500	28.8	MORUE SECHEE,SALEE
03503	FISH(EX COD)DRIED,SALTED	W 58943	186.1	W 58605	208.9	W 66703	236.5	W 61131	213.4	POISSONS SECHES,SALES
036	SHELL FISH FRESH,FROZEN	W 12166	64.4	W 11365	64.9	W 17291	80.6	W 18675	74.9	CRUSTACES,MOLLUSQUES
037	FISH ETC PREPD,PRSVD NES	W 24735	168.6	W 24612	223.0	W 26617	204.5	W 28799	192.9	POIS,CRUST,MOL PREPARES
0371	FISH PREPARD,PRESRVD NES	W 1826	16.1	W 2225	20.6	W 2471	18.7	W 3071	20.7	CONSERVES DE POISSONS
0372	SHELL FISH PREPRD,PRESVD	W 22909	152.6	W 22388	202.5	W 24146	185.8	W 25728	172.2	CRUSTACES,COQUIL PREPARES
081	*FEEDING STUFF FOR ANIML	W 180871	79.7	W 185099	99.1	W 253565	154.1	W 255244	159.9	NOURRITURE POUR ANIMAUX
0814	MEAT OR FISH MEAL FODDER	W 175800	77.6	W 173752	90.9	W 248505	151.5	W 250379	157.7	FARINES DE VIANDES,POISSONS
08142	FISH MEAL FODDER	W 175800	77.6	W 173752	90.9	W 248505	151.5	W 250379	157.7	FARINES DE POISSONS
0819	FOOD WASTE AND FEED NES	W 4228	2.0	W 10210	8.0	W 4195	2.5	W 3427	1.9	DECHETS,ALIMENTS NDA
08199	FODDER NES,INCL SWEETNED	W 4228	2.0	W 10210	8.0	W 4195	2.5	W 3427	1.9	PREPARATIONS FOURRAGERES
1	BEVERAGES AND TOBACCO		7.6		3.5		2.6		2.2	BOISSONS ET TABACS
11	BEVERAGES		7.6		3.5		2.6		2.2	BOISSONS
111	NON–ALCOHL BEVERAGES NES	W 12190	7.0	W 5977	2.9	W 6103	2.6	W 4429	1.9	BOISSONS NON ALCOOLIQUES
2	CRUDE MATERLS,EXCL FUELS		30.4		36.6		32.8		29.1	MAT BRUTES NON COMESTIBLES
21	HIDES,SKINS,FURS UNDRSSD		6.8		5.0		6.8		4.9	CUIRS,PEAUX BRUTS
212	FURSKINS,RAW	W 34	5.7	W 20	4.1	W 25	6.1	W 24	4.1	PELLETERIES BRUTES
27	CRUDE FERTLZR,MINRLS NES		15.2		20.1		14.7		13.0	ENGRAIS MINERAUX BRUTS
277	NATURAL ABRASIVES NES	W 230458	7.0	W 303852	10.0	W 165033	5.3	W 148668	4.6	ABRASIFS NATURELS NDA
2772	OTHER NATURAL ABRASIVES	W 230458	7.0	W 303852	10.0	W 165033	5.3	W 148668	4.6	AUTR ABRASIFS NATURELS NDA
27722	OTHER NAT ABRASIVES NES	W 230458	7.0	W 303852	10.0	W 165033	5.3	W 148668	4.6	PIERRE PONCE,EMERI
278	OTHER CRUDE MINERALS	W 25365	8.0	W 28264	10.0	W 30353	9.4	W 30250	8.4	AUTRES MINERAUX BRUTS
2789	MINERALS CRUDE NES	W 24572	7.8	W 27740	9.9	W 26368	9.0	W 26935	8.1	MINERAUX BRUTS NDA
27895	SILICEOUS EARTHS	W 24560	7.8	W 27740	9.9	W 26358	9.0	W 26935	8.1	FARINES SILICEUSES FOSSILES
28	METALLIFEROUS ORES,SCRAP		5.2		6.7		5.4		6.7	MINERAIS METAL,DECHETS
4	ANIMAL,VEGETABLE OIL,FAT		31.7		37.6		58.7		65.8	HUILES,GRAISSES ANIM,VEG
411	*ANIMAL OILS AND FATS	W 89559	31.7	W 91359	37.6	W 139156	58.7	W 131652	65.8	HUILES,GRAISSES ANIMALES
4111	OILS OF FISH,WHALES ETC	W 89557	31.7	W 91357	37.6	W 139156	58.7	W 131652	65.8	GRAISSES,HUILES DE POISSONS
41112	OTHER FISH OILS AND FATS	W 88481	27.8	W 89993	33.6	W 137357	53.8	W 129970	61.3	AUTRES HUILES ET GRAISSES
5	CHEMCLS,RELATED PROD NES		1.9		12.0		9.8		8.3	PRODUITS CHIMIQUES
541	*MEDICINAL,PHARM PRODUCT	K 5376	0.6	K 104515	9.5		7.1	K 59018	5.9	PROD MEDICINAUX PHARMACEUT
5417	MEDICAMENTS	K 5312	0.5	K 104393	9.4	K 60282	6.8	K 58842	5.3	MEDICAMENTS
54179	— CONTNG OTH SUBSTANCES	K 2942	0.3	K 100126	9.0	K 59857	6.8	K 58731	5.2	MED CONT AUT SUBSTANCES
6	BASIC MANUFACTURES		222.7		278.8		281.3		309.5	ART MANUFACTURES
61	LEATHER,DRESSED FUR,ETC		12.1		15.5		18.5		17.5	CUIRS,PELLETERIES
613	FUR SKINS TANNED,DRESSED	W 307	12.1	W 315	15.2	W 399	18.0	W 354	17.0	PELLETERIES
65	TEXTILE YARN,FABRICS,ETC		5.3		10.0		10.0		10.5	FILS,TISSUS,ARTICLES TEXTILE
657	SPECIAL TXTL FABRC,PRODS	W 311	3.0	W 605	7.4	W 806	7.1	W 874	7.2	TISSUS SPECIAUX
6575	CORDAGE AND MANUFACTURES	W 311	3.0	W 605	7.4	W 806	7.1	W 874	7.2	FICELLES,CORDES,CORDAGES
65752	NETTING OF ROPE,TWINE	W 209	2.5	W 418	6.4	W 578	6.0	W 647	5.6	FILETS MAT DU 657.51
67	IRON AND STEEL		38.6		50.0		57.7		52.7	FER ET ACIER
671	PIG IRON ETC	W 70798	38.6	W 71518	49.7	W 68199	57.3	W 75610	52.4	FONTE,SPIEGEL,POUDRES
6716	FERRO–ALLOYS	W 70798	38.6	W 71518	49.7	W 68199	57.3	W 74996	52.4	FERRO–ALLIAGES
67162	FERRO–SILICON	W 70798	38.6	W 71453	49.7	W 68192	57.3	W 74993	52.4	FERRO–SILICIUM
68	NON–FERROUS METALS		155.3		190.3		181.9		214.7	METAUX NON FERREUX
684	ALUMINIUM	W 100570	155.2	W 99663	190.3	W 101126	181.9	W 119813	214.6	ALUMINIUM
6841	ALUMINIUM,ALLOYS,UNWRGHT	W 100567	155.2	W 99657	190.2	W 101125	181.9	W 119811	214.5	ALUMINIUM,ALLIAGES BRUTS
69	METAL MANUFACTURES NES		6.1		8.0		7.5		8.3	ART MANUFACT EN METAL NDA
7	MACHINES,TRANSPORT EQUIP		66.2		92.4		93.9		103.4	MACHINES MATERIEL TRANSPORT
72	MACHS FOR SPCL INDUSTRYS		6.1		10.4		6.6		5.8	MAC SPECIALES POUR INDUST
725	PAPER ETC MILL MACHINERY	W 86	2.3	W 146	5.8	W 98	2.3	W 70	2.6	MACHINES FABR PATE PAPIER
74	GENRL INDUSTRL MACHY NES		10.2		15.3		22.3		20.6	MACH APP INDUSTRIE
745	NONELEC MACHY,TOOLS NES	W 104	9.4	W 162	14.4	W 248	20.9	W 237	18.3	AUT MACH NON ELEC,PIECES
7452	OTH NONELEC MCHS,PTS NES	W 104	9.4	W 162	14.4	W 247	20.9	W 237	18.3	AUT MACH NON ELEC,PIECES
74525	WEIGHING MACHINERY	W 90	8.4	W 144	13.0	W 233	19.6	W 181	15.0	APP INSTRUMENTS PESAGE
79	OTHR TRANSPORT EQUIPMENT		48.5		63.9		62.7		74.9	AUTRE MATERIEL TRANSPORT
792	AIRCRAFT ETC	W 67	26.6	W 67	29.5	W 68	38.3	W 75	37.6	APP NAVIGATION AERIENNE
7924	AIRCRFT NES OVER 15000KG	W 67	26.6	W 67	29.5	W 65	38.2	W 65	37.3	AERODYNES PLUS 15000 KG
793	SHIPS AND BOATS ETC	W 5173	21.9	W 7650	34.5	W 16188	24.5	W 7584	37.3	NAVIRES BATEAUX,ETC
7932	SHIPS AND BOATS NES	W 5173	21.9	W 7642	34.4	W 16140	24.1	W 7308	36.9	NAVIRES ET BATEAUX
79323	OTHER CARGO VESSELS			W 5	0.1	W 13607	18.2			AUT BATEAUX TRANS MARCH
79324	FISHING VESSELS ETC	W 5173	21.9	W 7637	34.4	W 2523	6.0	W 7302	36.9	BATEAUX DE PECHE
8	MISC MANUFACTURED GOODS		14.6		15.9		15.2		18.4	ART MANUFACTURES DIVERS
89	MISC MANUFCTRD GOODS NES		10.2		10.8		10.7		13.3	ART MANUFACTURES DIVERS
893	ARTICLES OF PLASTIC NES	W 948	3.4	W 970	4.1	W 1284	5.1	W 1778	6.5	OUVRAGES EN MAT DIVIS 58
8931	PLSTC PACKG CONTNRS,LIDS	W 847	3.0	W 855	3.5	W 1200	4.8	W 1672	6.1	ART TRANSP EMBALLAGE ETC
9	GOODS NOT CLASSD BY KIND		4.0		4.9		16.7		7.5	ART TRANSACT NON CLASSES
931	*SPECIAL TRANSACTIONS		4.0		4.9	W 1011	7.4	W 652	7.5	TRANS.SPECIALES
961	*COIN NONGOLD,NONCURRENT		0.1	W 1	0.1	W 8	9.3			MONNAIES NON EMISES

FOOT NOTES – NOTES

TABLE 1 –

1 Beginning 1981, the new krona was introduced with a val ue of 100 old kronur.

TABLEAU 1 –

1 A partir de 1981, la nouvelle króna entrait en vigueu r avec une valeur de 100 anciennes krónur.

1. HISTORICAL SERIES, 1962–1997 GENERAL TRADE, IMPORTS C.I.F., EXPORTS F.O.B.
SERIES HISTORIQUES, 1962–1997 COMMERCE GENERAL, IMPORTATIONS C.A.F., EXPORTATIONS F.O.B

YEAR ANNEE	VALUE IN MILLION INDIAN RUPEES / VALEUR EN MILLION INDIAN RUPEES — MERCHANDISE – MARCHANDISE: IMPORTS	EXPORTS	GOLD – OR: IMPORTS	EXPORTS	CONVERSION FACTORS U.S. CENTS PER INDIAN RUPEE / FACTEURS DE CONVERSION CENTS E.U. PAR INDIAN RUPEE: IMPORTS	EXPORTS	INDEX NUMBERS – INDICES — QUANTUM: IMPORTS	EXPORTS	UNIT VALUE / VALEUR UNITAIRE: IMPORTS	EXPORTS
1962	11241.00	6682.00			21.0000	21.0000				
1963	11795.00	7741.00	13.90		21.0000	21.0000				
1964	13429.00	8128.00	7.60		21.0000	21.0000				
1965	13809.00	8030.00	4.20		21.0000	21.0000				
1966	20190.00	11552.00	4.70		15.4560	15.8970				
1967	20950.00	12097.00	3.60		13.3330	13.3330				
1968	19280.00	13207.00	6.80		13.3330	13.3330				
1969	16630.00	13763.00	3.50		13.3330	13.3330				
1970	15933.00	15198.00	9.00		13.3330	13.3330				
1971	18155.00	15256.00	265.30		13.3330	13.3330				
1972	16792.00	18227.00	10.60		13.2010	13.1730				
1973	24164.00	22730.00	8.30		12.9117	12.9036				
1974	40787.00	31786.00			12.3503	12.3527				
1975	53389.00	36412.00			11.9599	11.9606				
1976	50736.00	49698.00			11.1651	11.1641				
1977	57592.00	55516.00			11.4622	11.4470				
1978	64301.00	54443.00			12.2150	12.2138				
1979	82373.00	63801.00			12.3120	12.3036				
1980	110755.00	65908.00			12.7221	12.7117	46	76	52	34
1981	135441.50	72423.10			11.5581	11.5619	53	44	55	41
1982	135615.50	83091.00			10.5923	10.5988	56	48	55	44
1983	135682.30	88096.40			9.9013	9.8898	67	49	48	49
1984	175384.10	112077.90			8.8602	8.8096	57	54	61	57
1985	190780.80	107342.30			8.1688	8.1513	65	52	65	60
1986	194502.00	118524.00			7.9243	7.9232	85	59	54	58
1987	216134.00	146417.00			7.7166	7.7171	90	71	60	65
1988	266059.00	184099.00			7.1801	7.1889	96	74	69	78
1989	334010.80	257553.00			6.1525	6.1626	97	91	86	93
1990	413565.90	314394.10			5.7023	5.7159	100	100	100	100
1991	459379.90	401230.00			4.4505	4.4182	91	114	122	111
1992	611130.10	508709.80			3.8606	3.8609	120	116	125	142
1993	694459.90	656890.10			3.2816	3.2840	138	140	117	155
1994	842170.10	785029.80			3.1873	3.1874	168	154	122	168
1995	1127480.00	994550.00			3.0785	3.0796	261	189	110	167
1996	1328290.00	1169360.00			2.8231	2.8251	219	213	151	170
1997	1465449.00	1229890.00			2.7540	2.7563				

2. IMPORTS BY BROAD ECONOMIC CATEGORY AND EXPORTS BY INDUSTRIAL ORIGIN. (PERCENTAGE OF TOTAL VALUE)
IMPORTATIONS PAR CATEGORIES ECONOMIQUES ET EXPORTATIONS PAR BRANCHE D'ACTIVITE.(EN POURCENTAGE DE LA VALEUR TOTALE)

IMPORTS – IMPORTATIONS

	1990	1991	1992	1993	1994	1995	1996
TOTAL IMPORTS–IMPORTATIONS TOTALES	100.	100.	100.	100.	100.	100.	100.
1 FOOD BEV–ALIMENTATION BOISSONS	3.2	2.5	3.6	2.8	5.7	4.0	4.4
11 PRIMARY–PRODUITS DE BASE	1.8	1.4	2.6	1.9	1.8	1.5	1.8
111 FOR INDUSTRY–POUR L'INDUSTRIE	0.1	0.0	1.2	0.2	0.0	0.1	0.3
112 FOR HOUSEHOLDS–POUR LES MENAGES	1.7	1.3	1.4	1.7	1.7	1.5	1.5
12 PROCESSED–PRODUITS ELABORES	1.4	1.2	1.0	0.9	3.9	2.5	2.6
121 FOR INDUSTRY–POUR L'INDUSTRIE	0.9	0.7	0.4	0.4	1.1	1.9	2.0
122 FOR HOUSEHOLDS–POUR LES MENAGES	0.5	0.5	0.6	0.5	2.8	0.6	0.6
2 IND SUPPLIES–APPROV INDUSTRIELS	42.3	42.9	43.0	40.9	41.4	41.1	38.7
21 PRIMARY–PRODUITS DE BASE	16.6	16.6	18.5	16.6	12.6	11.8	12.6
22 PROCESSED–PRODUITS ELABORES	25.7	26.3	24.5	24.3	28.8	29.3	26.1
3 FUELS–COMBUSTIBLES	27.3	29.9	29.8	27.3	23.9	23.8	29.5
31 PRIMARY–PRODUITS DE BASE	16.1	18.4	19.2	17.0	14.3	12.1	16.7
32 PROCESSED–PRODUITS ELABORES	11.2	11.5	10.7	10.3	9.6	11.7	12.9
321 MOTOR SPIRIT–ESSENCE							
322 OTHER–AUTRES	11.2	11.5	10.7	10.3	9.6	11.7	12.9
4 MACHINERY–EQUIPEMENT	15.5	12.9	13.3	14.3	16.0	18.1	15.7
41 CAPITAL EQUIPMENT–MACHINES	10.8	8.7	9.4	10.6	12.3	14.0	12.4
42 PARTS–PIECES ACCESSOIRES	4.7	4.2	3.9	3.7	3.6	4.1	3.3
5 TRANSPORT–TRANSPORT	3.6	2.1	2.4	5.7	4.3	3.5	4.2
51 PASSENGER CARS–AUTOMOBILES	0.0	0.0	0.0	0.0	0.1	0.1	0.1
52 OTHER–AUTRES	1.2	0.2	0.6	3.8	1.6	0.8	1.9
521 INDUSTRIAL–INDUSTRIELS	1.2	0.2	0.6	3.8	1.6	0.8	1.9
522 NON INDUSTRIAL–NON INDUSTRIEL		0.0	0.0	0.0	0.0	0.0	0.0
53 PARTS–PIECES ACCESSOIRES	2.3	1.8	1.8	1.8	2.6	2.5	2.3
6 CONSUM GOODS–BIENS CONSOMMATION	1.9	1.7	1.6	1.7	1.9	2.3	1.6
61 DURABLE–DURABLES	0.3	0.2	0.3	0.4	0.4	0.4	0.4
62 SEMI DURABLE–SEMI DURABLES	0.4	0.4	0.4	0.4	0.6	1.1	0.6
63 NON DURABLE–NON DURABLES	1.3	1.1	0.9	0.9	0.9	0.9	0.6
7 GOODS NES–BIENS NDA	6.2	8.0	6.2	7.4	6.8	7.1	5.8

EXPORTS – EXPORTATIONS

	1990	1991	1992	1993	1994	1995	1996
TOTAL EXPORTS–EXPORTATIONS TOTALES	100.	100.	100.	100.	100.	100.	100.
1 AGRICULTURE	14.3	12.7	10.5	11.4	10.9	10.2	11.8
2 MINING QUARRY–INDUS EXTRACTIVES	19.6	18.3	18.5	20.0	18.5	17.9	15.1
3 MANUFACTURING–IND MANUFACTUR	66.1	69.0	71.0	68.7	70.6	71.9	73.1
31 FOOD BEV TOBACCO–ALIM BOISS TAB	5.0	5.9	7.1	7.3	5.7	9.6	9.1
32 TEXTILES–INDUSTRIES TEXTILES	32.8	33.9	34.3	31.1	33.5	31.1	31.1
33 WOOD & PRODUCTS–BOIS & PRODUITS	0.1	0.1	0.1	0.2	0.1	0.1	0.1
34 PAPER & PRODUCTS–PAPIER & PRODT	0.2	0.2	0.3	0.3	0.4	0.5	0.4
35 CHEMICALS–INDUSTRIES CHIMIQUES	12.1	12.1	11.3	11.2	12.0	11.7	12.3
36 NON METAL MIN–MIN NON METAL	0.5	0.7	0.9	1.2	1.3	1.2	1.2
37 BASIC METAL–IND METAL BASE	2.1	2.7	3.6	4.2	3.6	3.8	3.8
38 METAL MANUF–MANUF METAL	9.9	9.9	9.9	9.6	9.9	10.2	11.1
39 OTH MANUF IND–AUTRES MANUF	3.4	3.5	3.6	3.6	4.0	3.8	4.0

3. TRADE BY PRINCIPAL COUNTRIES OF CONSIGNMENT AND DESTINATION (VALUE IN MILLION U.S. DOLLARS)
ECHANGES SELON LES PRINCIPAUX PAYS DE CONSIGNATION ET DE DESTINATION (VALEUR EN MILLIONS DE DOLLARS EU)

COUNTRIES–PAYS	GENERAL IMPORTS C.I.F. IMPORTATIONS GENERALES C.A.F					COUNTRIES–PAYS	EXPORTS EXPORTATIONS ES F.O.B.				
	1992	1993	1994	1995	1996		1992	1993	1994	1995	1996
World	24452.4	23304.1	28654.8	36592.1	39112.8	Monde	20711.3	22236.9	26330.0	31698.6	33468.6
Africa	1529.1	1437.1	1487.4	1983.8	2871.0	Afrique	795.4	819.0	985.5	1659.6	1587.0
Americas	3081.9	3192.4	3928.9	4800.9	4501.4	Amériques	4324.5	4468.1	5648.5	6172.5	7388.7
– Northern America	2772.9	2917.2	3157.1	4210.1	3943.8	– Amérique du Nord	4142.8	4227.1	5289.8	5809.9	6912.8
– LAIA	302.7	266.4	759.5	579.3	544.4	– ALAI	141.4	202.6	295.8	302.5	414.2
– CACM	1.1	0.9	5.7	5.2	0.8	– MCAC	5.2	5.2	7.0	7.2	6.7
– Caribbean	4.8	7.6	6.5	5.5	9.5	– Caraïbes	10.5	13.8	20.0	21.3	24.5
– Rest of America	0.4	0.3	0.0	0.9	3.0	– Autre Amérique	24.7	19.4	35.9	31.7	30.5
Asia excl fmr USSR	7983.0	7456.7	10506.7	12385.0	13482.0	Asie anc. URSS exclus	7450.5	8957.5	10154.0	12571.7	13383.4
– Middle East	3860.9	3416.9	4280.5	4449.2	5445.8	– Moyen–Orient	2053.7	2391.9	2428.1	2798.1	3087.8
Asia former USSR		6.6	25.1	25.0	16.5	Asie ancienne URSS		7.3	16.2	23.6	17.7
Europe excl fmr USSR	8114.6	7752.9	8589.8	11391.4	11795.0	Europe anc. URSS exclus	6644.0	6518.7	7816.8	9259.5	9258.6
– European Union	7377.6	7048.9	7500.9	9981.1	10377.0	– Union Européenne	6125.2	6032.7	7336.7	8709.1	8684.0
– Eastern Europe	246.5	145.4	180.3	332.8	200.2	– Europe de l'Est	222.1	198.9	144.4	179.4	173.1
– Rest of Europe	490.5	558.7	908.7	1077.5	1217.8	– Autre de l'Europe	296.7	287.1	335.7	370.9	401.5
Europe former USSR	284.5	373.5	724.1	1163.5	659.3	Europe ancienne URSS	678.5	786.7	885.0	1117.7	894.6
Oceania	1005.5	739.2	997.2	1090.4	1401.3	Océanie	286.3	281.9	407.1	441.7	456.8
Other	2453.9	2345.6	2395.6	3752.2	4386.3	Autre	532.1	397.8	416.9	452.4	481.8
USA/Etats–Unis d'Amer	2325.5	2682.8	2891.6	3829.7	3615.3	USA/Etats–Unis d'Amer	3928.9	3999.1	5022.5	5505.0	6558.7
Areas n.e.s.	2453.9	2345.6	2395.6	3752.2	4386.3	Japan/Japon	1605.0	1740.8	2026.5	2208.9	2005.9
Germany/Allemagne	1837.2	1773.2	2185.2	3137.4	2828.9	Germany/Allemagne	1594.4	1539.1	1747.7	1971.4	1893.0
Japan/Japon	1587.6	1513.1	2036.5	2462.0	2186.4	United Kingdom	1356.2	1379.5	1690.9	2006.7	2049.5
Belgium–Luxembourg	2042.2	1873.5	1205.6	1690.8	2234.8	China, Hong Kong SAR	854.8	1249.5	1517.3	1815.9	1862.5
United Kingdom	1564.6	1508.3	1556.3	1901.8	2132.9	United Arab Emirates	909.8	1157.9	1265.8	1424.0	1476.0
Saudi Arabia	1374.6	1221.6	1273.1	1367.2	1818.7	Belgium–Luxembourg	764.4	843.9	992.5	1119.6	1095.9
United Arab Emirates	1021.7	841.4	1304.3	1247.2	1327.0	Italy/Italie	695.0	604.1	857.9	1010.9	933.7
Australia/Australie	931.7	657.1	915.1	1019.6	1316.5	Singapore/Singapour	657.6	751.9	770.3	898.9	977.4
Nigeria/Nigéria	646.5	827.3	423.8	768.0	1524.9	Russian Federation	677.5	649.3	807.1	1041.8	811.1
Switzerland,Liechtenst.	422.6	506.3	824.3	996.7	1126.8	Bangladesh	397.0	430.2	644.6	1045.9	868.9
Kuwait/Koweït	621.6	555.6	670.3	813.3	948.6	Netherlands/Pays–Bas	463.9	511.2	585.5	766.7	852.3
Italy/Italie	396.4	425.9	698.9	905.5	914.6	France, Monaco	526.8	504.3	582.1	744.7	719.0
Korea, Republic of	396.9	563.0	629.5	813.4	883.2	Saudi Arabia	455.2	510.8	435.7	480.8	577.2
France, Monaco	590.0	582.1	608.0	770.8	698.5	Areas n.e.s.	532.1	397.8	416.9	452.4	481.8
Singapore/Singapour	366.7	413.5	707.7	853.4	840.7	Thailand/Thaïlande	283.4	357.2	406.6	471.5	447.1
Malaysia/Malaisie	439.5	248.1	488.6	896.8	1102.7	Indonesia/Indonésie	154.7	234.9	277.7	660.4	591.8
Iran (Islamic Rep of)	444.4	378.7	534.4	582.1	860.0	Sri Lanka	277.1	288.0	366.6	400.5	477.4
China/Chine	140.8	299.4	757.3	810.1	756.5	Korea, Republic of	195.4	206.4	332.4	446.9	518.5
Russian Federation	284.5	257.0	504.4	822.8	527.6	Malaysia/Malaisie	212.1	247.3	286.5	392.0	531.1
Netherlands/Pays–Bas	398.1	352.6	373.3	551.7	415.2	China/Chine	157.9	279.1	254.2	331.7	614.8
Canada	447.3	234.4	265.5	380.4	313.2	Spain/Espagne	247.2	207.5	287.5	414.9	448.6
Indonesia/Indonésie	67.0	119.6	316.6	460.1	596.7	Australia/Australie	249.4	245.2	346.4	374.5	385.3
Other Asia n.e.s.	246.1	183.6	282.8	381.0	423.6	Other Asia n.e.s.	199.5	275.8	250.8	256.8	423.7
Morocco/Maroc	293.1	158.0	275.3	300.4	346.7	Canada	213.6	227.8	266.8	304.5	353.0
China, Hong Kong SAR	190.4	188.6	286.3	387.1	319.0	Switzerland,Liechtenst.	222.5	221.0	247.4	280.8	300.2
Brazil/Brésil	192.4	122.0	540.4	260.5	152.5	So. African Customs Un	11.1	37.4	160.8	337.8	320.8
Sweden/Suède	181.5	160.7	298.5	243.6	371.4	Israel/Israël	95.1	131.9	150.3	215.9	211.4
Israel/Israël	123.8	145.7	151.3	205.7	260.6	Iran (Islamic Rep of)	127.9	159.7	156.7	154.6	195.0
Denmark/Danemark	83.4	99.6	184.8	269.5	185.6	Turkey/Turquie	116.0	112.2	95.3	171.4	201.8
So. African Customs Un	1.9	37.3	152.6	244.6	328.0	Egypt/Egypte	127.6	121.0	119.8	163.8	157.5
Ukraine		106.9	199.9	332.3	121.8	Nigeria/Nigéria	161.6	119.3	109.1	150.4	146.4
Spain/Espagne	83.5	102.1	172.9	176.5	210.3	Kenya	64.4	70.8	122.7	244.3	168.5
Jordan/Jordanie	158.7	110.9	153.5	191.5	126.0	Sweden/Suède	112.3	107.4	146.9	145.9	151.5
Myanmar	129.6	121.3	126.8	162.0	177.1	Kuwait/Koweït	121.0	106.0	133.9	135.1	154.7
Thailand/Thaïlande	65.2	57.2	171.6	169.3	197.1	Nepal/Népal	81.0	98.1	120.1	159.6	165.7
Finland/Finlande	65.1	66.8	108.1	170.4	199.7	Denmark/Danemark	96.6	89.6	129.4	145.5	150.9
Qatar	111.9	132.1	114.6	107.5	122.8	Mauritius/Maurice	66.6	86.0	113.9	135.6	161.3
Egypt/Egypte	98.6	63.5	223.0	67.2	65.1	Philippines	61.1	58.2	99.5	143.8	183.6
Argentina/Argentine	25.1	38.3	73.0	130.8	201.2	Oman	83.4	83.7	88.4	109.2	117.0

(VALUE AS PERCENTAGE OF WORLD TOTAL)(VALEURS EN POURCENTAGE DU TOTAL MONDIAL)

	1987	1988	1989	1990	1991	1992	1993	1994	1995	1996
Africa	3.0	3.6	2.6	2.5	5.0	6.3	6.2	5.2	5.4	7.3
Americas	12.7	15.0	15.3	14.1	12.9	12.6	13.7	13.7	13.1	11.5
– Northern America	10.3	12.9	13.3	12.0	11.1	11.3	12.5	11.0	11.5	10.1
– LAIA	2.2	2.0	2.0	2.1	1.7	1.2	1.1	2.7	1.6	1.4
– CACM	0.0	0.0	0.0	0.0	0.0	0.0	0.0	0.0	0.0	0.0
– Caribbean	0.2	0.0	0.1	0.1	0.1	0.0	0.0	0.0	0.0	0.0
– Rest of America	0.0	0.0	0.0	0.0	0.0	0.0	0.0	0.0	0.0	0.0
Asia excl fmr USSR	33.1	33.7	30.6	32.3	33.3	32.6	32.0	36.7	33.8	34.5
– Middle East	12.8	12.8	12.1	14.5	16.8	15.8	14.7	14.9	12.2	13.9
Asia former USSR							0.0	0.1	0.1	0.0
Europe excl fmr USSR	39.1	36.6	37.8	33.0	32.1	33.2	33.3	30.0	31.1	30.2
– European Union	35.3	24.7	26.6	21.9	29.9	30.2	30.2	26.2	27.3	26.5
– Eastern Europe	1.6	10.1	9.5	9.5	1.0	1.0	0.6	0.6	0.9	0.5
– Rest of Europe	2.2	1.8	1.7	1.6	1.2	2.0	2.4	3.2	2.9	3.1
Europe former USSR	5.2	3.0	4.6	3.9	2.7	1.2	1.6	2.5	3.2	1.7
Oceania	2.5	2.8	2.7	3.5	3.3	4.1	3.2	3.5	3.0	3.6
Other	4.4	5.3	6.3	10.7	10.8	10.0	10.1	8.4	10.3	11.2
USA/Etats–Unis d'Amer	9.0	11.4	12.0	10.7	9.7	9.5	11.5	10.1	10.5	9.2
Areas n.e.s.	4.4	5.3	6.3	10.7	10.8	10.0	10.1	8.4	10.3	11.2
Germany/Allemagne					8.0	7.5	7.6	7.6	8.6	7.2
Japan/Japon	9.5	9.3	8.0	7.5	7.0	6.5	6.5	7.1	6.7	5.6
Belgium–Luxembourg	6.2	7.3	7.6	6.3	7.1	8.4	8.0	4.2	4.6	5.7
United Kingdom	8.2	8.5	8.3	6.4	6.1	6.4	6.5	5.4	5.2	5.5
Saudi Arabia	3.3	6.3	3.7	5.8	5.7	5.6	5.2	4.4	3.7	4.6
United Arab Emirates	3.4	3.0	3.3	3.2	5.1	4.2	3.6	4.6	3.4	3.4
Australia/Australie	2.2	2.5	2.5	3.1	2.9	3.8	2.8	3.2	2.8	3.4
Nigeria/Nigéria	0.0	0.0	0.0	0.1	0.6	2.6	3.6	1.5	2.1	3.9

	1987	1988	1989	1990	1991	1992	1993	1994	1995	1996
Afrique	2.4	2.3	2.3	2.5	3.1	3.8	3.7	3.7	5.2	4.7
Amériques	19.9	20.0	17.5	16.1	18.1	20.9	20.1	21.5	19.5	22.1
– Amérique du Nord	19.7	19.4	17.1	15.6	17.4	20.0	19.0	20.1	18.3	20.7
– ALAI	0.1	0.4	0.2	0.3	0.5	0.7	0.9	1.1	1.0	1.2
– MCAC	0.0	0.0	0.0	0.0	0.0	0.0	0.0	0.0	0.0	0.0
– Caraïbes	0.1	0.1	0.1	0.1	0.1	0.1	0.1	0.1	0.1	0.1
– Autre Amérique	0.0	0.0	0.0	0.1	0.1	0.1	0.1	0.1	0.1	0.1
Asie anc. URSS exclus	28.2	30.4	29.6	29.2	34.5	36.0	40.3	38.6	39.7	40.0
– Moyen–Orient	6.8	6.5	7.1	5.8	9.2	9.9	10.8	9.2	8.8	9.2
Asie ancienne URSS							0.0	0.1	0.1	0.1
Europe anc. URSS exclus	31.5	29.5	29.8	32.1	31.5	32.1	29.3	29.7	29.2	27.7
– Union Européenne	26.1	19.1	19.5	21.0	28.3	29.6	27.1	27.9	27.5	25.9
– Europe de l'Est	3.7	8.5	8.5	9.4	1.6	1.1	0.9	0.5	0.6	0.5
– Autre de l'Europe	1.8	1.9	1.8	1.7	1.7	1.4	1.3	1.3	1.2	1.2
Europe ancienne URSS	12.5	13.8	16.9	16.1	9.2	3.3	3.5	3.4	3.5	2.7
Océanie	1.3	1.5	1.4	1.1	1.3	1.4	1.3	1.5	1.4	1.4
Autre	4.1	2.5	2.5	2.9	2.3	2.6	1.8	1.6	1.4	1.4
USA/Etats–Unis d'Amer	18.6	18.4	16.2	14.7	16.4	19.0	18.0	19.1	17.4	19.6
Japan/Japon	10.3	10.6	9.9	9.3	9.2	7.7	7.8	7.7	7.0	6.0
Germany/Allemagne					7.1	7.7	6.9	6.6	6.2	5.7
United Kingdom	6.5	5.7	5.8	6.5	6.4	6.5	6.2	6.4	6.3	6.1
China, Hong Kong SAR	2.8	4.0	3.2	3.3	3.4	4.1	5.6	5.8	5.7	5.6
United Arab Emirates	2.0	2.1	2.6	2.4	4.1	4.4	5.2	4.8	4.5	4.4
Belgium–Luxembourg	3.1	4.4	4.4	3.9	3.7	3.7	3.8	3.8	3.5	3.3
Italy/Italie	3.2	2.7	2.7	3.1	3.2	3.4	2.7	3.3	3.2	2.8
Singapore/Singapour	1.7	1.6	1.7	2.1	2.2	3.2	3.4	2.9	2.8	2.9
Russian Federation						3.3	2.9	3.1	3.3	2.4

4. General Imports C.I.F. by Commodities according to the S.I.T.C. (Rev. 2) in million U.S. Dollars
Importations Générales C.A.F. par Produits d'après la C.T.C.I. (Rév. 2) en millions de Dollars E.U.

SITC CTCI	COMMODITY	1993 QUANTITY QUANTITE	1993 VALUE VALEUR	1994 QUANTITY QUANTITE	1994 VALUE VALEUR	1995 QUANTITY QUANTITE	1995 VALUE VALEUR	1996 QUANTITY QUANTITE	1996 VALUE VALEUR	PRODUIT
	ALL COMMODITIES		23304.1		28654.8		36592.1		39112.9	TOUS PRODUITS
0	FOOD AND LIVE ANIMALS		607.6		1423.8		768.9		861.8	ALIMENTS,ANIMAUX VIVANTS
04	CEREALS AND PREPARATIONS		92.7		29.5		24.1		137.7	CEREALES ET PRODUITS
05	VEGETABLES AND FRUIT		414.2		520.3		538.6		588.6	LEGUMES ET FRUITS
054	VEG ETC FRSH,SMPLY PRSVD	W 667466	190.8	W 583063	200.0	W 502833	212.2	W 694350	266.1	LEGUMES FRAIS,CONG,SECS
0542	LEGUMINOUS VEGETBLES DRY	W 652983	186.4	W 582124	198.8	W 502234	211.6	W 692430	264.8	LEGUMES A COSSE SECS
057	FRUIT,NUTS,FRESH,DRIED	W 92238	223.4	W 131390	320.0	W 129475	325.5	W 446740	322.0	FRUITS FRAIS OU SECS
0577	NUTS EDIBLE,FRESH,DRIED	W 15425	193.0	W 21505	275.8	W 23197	288.8	W 239706	268.7	FRUITS A COQUES
05773	CASHEW NUTS,FRESH,DRIED	W 191	153.9	W 228	220.1	W 223	226.8	W 212866	193.6	NOIX DE CAJOU
06	SUGAR AND PREPS,HONEY		6.1		732.0		69.8		7.0	SUCRES ET PRODUITS
061	SUGAR AND HONEY	W 22011	6.0	W 1787959	731.8	W 156324	69.1	W 10426	6.5	SUCRES ET MIEL
0612	REFINED SUGAR ETC	W 284	0.2	W 1669494	682.3	W 150632	64.4	W 1123	0.5	SUCRES RAFFINES
2	CRUDE MATERLS,EXCL FUELS		1513.5		2391.8		2709.5		2389.8	MAT BRUTES NON COMESTIBLES
23	RUBBER, CRUDE		109.1		118.4		214.6		177.7	CAOUTCHOUC BRUT
233	RUBBER,SYNTHTC,RECLAIMD	W 66886	91.6	W 76370	109.6	W 74742	131.5	W 94714	149.4	LATEX CAOUTCH SYNTH REGEN
2331	SYNTHETIC RUBBER ETC	W 66870	91.5	W 75904	109.3	W 74578	131.4	W 93734	149.0	LATEX CAOUTCH SYNTHETIQUE
24	CORK AND WOOD		139.6		212.6		232.7		256.2	LIEGE ET BOIS
247	OTH WOOD ROUGH,SQUARED	W 335639	134.5	W 467966	204.2	W 515279	225.4	W 651447	246.6	BOIS BRUTS EQUARRIS
2472	SAW–,VENEER–LOGS NON–CON	W 335622	134.5	W 465840	203.5	W 512828	224.7	W 649319	245.8	NON CONIFERES SCIAGE,PLAC
24721	— IN THE ROUGH	W 335622	134.5	W 465840	203.5	W 512828	224.7	W 649319	245.8	BRUTS ECORCES DEGROSSIS
251	*PULP AND WASTE PAPER	W 626139	158.6	W 596527	202.4	W 549777	274.7	W 759993	231.7	PATES A PAPIER,DECHETS
26	TEXTILE FIBRES AND WASTE		314.4		614.8		616.5		437.8	FIBRES TEXTILES
261	SILK	W 5004	86.3	W 6095	107.5	W 4289	92.0	W 3022	61.5	SOIE
2613	RAW SILK NOT THROWN	W 4892	85.7	W 5403	104.0	W 4150	90.4	W 2911	60.6	SOIE GREGE
263	COTTON	W 4070	6.0	W 80870	161.6	W 69620	155.6	W 2936	9.1	COTON
2631	RAW COTTON,EXCL LINTERS	W 3822	5.9	W 80503	161.4	W 69452	155.5	W 2850	8.9	COTON EN MASSE
266	SYNTHETIC FIBRES TO SPIN	W 25923	35.7	W 60888	100.4	W 55901	110.4	W 68972	93.0	FIBRES SYNTHETIQUES
268	WOOL(EXC TOPS),ANML HAIR	W 64710	128.5	W 44229	127.4	W 52481	159.8	W 67449	186.4	LAINES ET POILS
27	CRUDE FERTLZR,MINRLS NES		281.1		403.0		441.2		355.6	ENGRAIS MINERAUX BRUTS
271	FERTILIZERS,CRUDE	W 1922803	122.0		152.7	W 2443828	156.5	W 2038388	134.5	ENGRAIS BRUTS
2713	NAT CALCM PHOSPHATES ETC	W 1922739	122.0	W 2540138	149.2	W 2443753	156.4	W 2038153	134.4	PHOSPHATES DE CALCIUM
274	SULPHUR,UNRSTD IRN PYRTE	W 1264374	72.2	W 1600599	135.9	W 1543021	144.1	W 1543233	91.0	SOUFRE ET PYRITES
2741	SULPHUR,EX SULP IN 52215	W 1264367	72.2	W 1600570	135.9	W 1543002	144.1	W 1543187	91.0	SOUFRE
278	OTHER CRUDE MINERALS	W 235922	71.9	W 296875	93.9	W 320754	107.5	W 263540	86.7	AUTRES MINERAUX BRUTS
28	METALLIFEROUS ORES,SCRAP		442.4		748.2		820.8		819.4	MINERAIS METAL,DECHETS
282	IRON AND STEEL SCRAP	W 1096284	224.0	W 2171672	428.5	W 1948520	395.3	W 1917959	412.5	FERRAILLES
28209	— OF OTHR IRON OR STEEL	W 1046293	214.7	W 1993553	393.9	W 1858493	360.9	W 1852674	392.4	FERRAILLES DE FER
287	BASE METAL ORES,CONC NES	W 89097	40.1	W 142362	75.6	W 180079	101.7	W 213152	127.8	MINERAIS METAUX COMMUNS
288	NONFERR METAL SCRAP NES	W 220338	164.4	W 263900	176.1	W 289850	280.5	W 225693	243.7	DECHETS NON FERREUX
2882	OTHER BASE MTL SCRAP NES	W 148019	127.3	W 159089	123.9	W 183925	212.5	W 192091	223.2	AUTRES DECHETS
28821	COPPER WASTE AND SCRAP	W 97784	109.7	W 85071	95.3	W 110931	169.3	W 137262	180.7	DECHETS DE CUIVRE
3	MINERAL FUELS ETC		6338.8		6832.8		8677.8		11475.8	COMBUSTIBLES MINERAUX LUB
32	COAL,COKE AND BRIQUETTES		466.6		708.4		923.5		994.4	HOUILLES,COKES,BRIQUETTES
322	COAL,LIGNITE AND PEAT	W 7331163	451.3	MW 10740	648.4	MW 12512	802.7	W 3174961	874.5	HOUILLES,LIGNITES,TOURBE
3222	OTH COAL,NOT AGGLOMERATD	W 7329928	450.8	MW 10732	646.9	MW 12510	801.9	W 3173169	873.7	AUTRES HOUILLES
323	BRIQUETS,COKE,SEMI–COKE		15.3		60.1		120.8	W 1237368	120.0	BRIQUETTES
3232	COKE,SEMI–COKE,RTRT CRBN		15.3		60.1		120.8	W 1237359	120.0	COKES ET SEMI–COKES
33	PETROLEUM AND PRODUCTS		5816.7		6037.1		7618.9		10179.3	PETROLE ET DERIVES
333	CRUDE PETROLEUM	MW 30822	3407.5	MW 27349	3285.6	MW 27357	3442.1	MW 33710	5224.1	HUILES BRUTES DE PETROLE
334	PETROLEUM PRODUCTS,REFIN		2359.2		2656.6		4083.5	MW 19142	4824.2	PRODUITS RAFFINES
335	RESIDUAL PETRLM PROD NES	W 285671	50.1	W 513176	94.9	W 531103	93.5	W 712221	131.0	PRODUITS RESIDUELS NDA
3352	MINERAL TARS AND PRODCTS	W 280427	47.9	W 505946	92.0	W 522916	89.5	W 706111	128.3	GOUDRONS MINERAUX
33525	MINERAL TAR OILS ETC NES	W 274690	46.2	W 495414	88.5	W 516810	87.9	W 705763	127.9	AUTRES PRODUITS NDA
341	*GAS,NATURAL AND MANUFCT		55.7		87.4		135.5	W 950529	302.1	GAZ NATUREL,GAZ MANUFACT
3413	PETROLM GASES,LIQUEFIED		55.6		87.4		132.1	W 946368	301.1	GAZ DE PETROLE LIQUEFIE
34131	LIQUEFIED PROPANE,BUTANE		55.4		85.0		118.1	W 890139	284.6	PROPANE,BUTANE LIQUEFIES
4	ANIMAL,VEGETABLE OIL,FAT		104.6		264.5		757.0		934.1	HUILES,GRAISSES ANIM,VEG
42	FIXED VEGETABLE OIL,FAT		57.3		207.6		698.5		852.6	HUILES VEGETALES FIXES
423	FIXED VEG OILS,SOFT	W 30677	21.6	W 51871	39.7	W 226013	152.8	W 327262	186.0	HUILES VEGET DOUCES FIXES
4236	SUNFLOWER SEED OIL	W 1	0.1	W 11360	8.4	W 79367	52.9	W 272154	151.4	HUILE DE TOURNESOL
424	FIXED VEG OIL NONSOFT	W 88000	35.7	W 304032	168.0	W 866920	545.7	W 1133599	666.6	AUTRES HUILES VEG FIXES
4242	PALM OIL	W 73268	27.0	W 287498	155.1	W 850397	532.0	W 1113850	652.4	HUILE DE PALME
5	CHEMCLS,RELATED PROD NES		2979.4		4185.5		5582.1		4930.4	PRODUITS CHIMIQUES
51	ORGANIC CHEMICALS		883.1		1382.1		1699.8		1752.1	PROD CHIMIQ ORGANIQUES
511	HYDROCARBONS NES,DERIVS	W 867338	341.1	W 1136916	587.8	W 1312903	705.2	W 1373635	667.0	HYDROCARBURES NDA
5111	ACYCLIC HYDROCARBONS	W 231566	74.6	W 272735	131.6	W 355324	147.4	W 367401	196.5	HYDROCARBURES ACYCLIQUES
51111	ETHYLENE	W 215546	66.5	W 245641	117.5	W 326511	129.5	W 273345	139.4	ETHYLENE
5112	CYCLIC HYDROCARBONS	W 381581	151.0	W 550539	309.1	W 644959	415.6	W 647678	298.3	HYDROCARBURES CYCLIQUES
51124	XYLENES,CHEMICALLY PURE	W 158295	61.7	W 251241	145.4	W 245805	195.8	W 296912	135.0	XYLENES PURS
51125	STYRENE	W 72396	35.8	W 99521	80.4	W 139986	113.8	W 132607	72.3	STYRENE
5113	HALOG DERIV OF HYDROCARB	W 250423	109.5	W 306826	137.9	W 305756	133.4	W 350309	162.8	DERIVES HALOGENES HYDROCAR
51139	OTH HALOG HYDRCARB DERIV	W 204005	84.0	W 283191	122.0	W 295791	127.4	W 299821	133.0	AUTRE DERIVES HALOGENES
512	ALCOHOLS,PHENOLS ETC	W 74874	67.6	W 114410	123.7	W 149834	157.9		204.7	PHENOLS,PHENOLS–ALCOOLS
5121	ACYCLIC ALCOHOLS,DERIVS	W 51878	42.1	W 91994	86.8	W 111141	101.4		151.0	ALCOOLS ACYCLIQUES
513	CARBOXYLIC ACIDS ETC	W 127252	109.5	W 197095	197.2	W 188568	281.2	W 353427	305.6	ACIDES CARBOXYLIQUES
5138	POLYACIDS AND DERIVATIVS	W 85927	57.7	W 134373	122.1	W 137612	189.5	W 294423	210.6	ACIDES POLYCARBOXYLIQUES
51389	OTH POLYACIDS ETC,DERIVS	W 52624	38.6	W 74784	74.2	W 105659	153.8	W 275138	196.5	ACIDES POLYCARBOXYLIQUES
514	NITROGEN–FNCTN COMPOUNDS	W 65200	117.0	W 107401	186.9	W 105072	225.4	W 138184	255.8	COMPOSES FONCT AZOTEES
5148	OTH NITROGN–FNCTN CMPNDS	W 37065	55.7	W 63940	90.4	W 70773	124.1	W 96404	132.7	AUTRES COMPOSES AZOTES
515	ORG–INORG COMPOUNDS ETC	W 31205	79.0	W 34950	106.8	W 21703	99.4	W 22471	93.4	COMPOSES ORGANO–MINERAUX
516	OTHER ORGANIC CHEMICALS	W 35114	169.3	W 41576	179.9	W 62828	230.9	W 70986	225.9	AUTRES PROD ORGANIQUES
5169	ORGANIC CHEMICALS,NES	W 11695	124.1	W 9796	120.0	W 11550	142.2	W 10116	134.4	PROD CHIM ORGANIQUES NDA
51699	OTHER ORGANIC COMPOUNDS	W 11193	116.3	W 8968	110.2	W 10926	132.5	W 9356	126.1	AUTRES COMPOS ORGANIQUES
52	INORGANIC CHEMICALS		487.8		755.6		860.2		908.2	PROD CHIM INORGANIQUES
522	INORG ELEMNTS,OXIDES,ETC		451.5		704.0		790.6		831.9	ELEMENTS INORGANIQUES
5222	INORGANIC ACIDS ETC	W 1536142	282.6	W 2089995	453.6	W 2074581	500.0	W 2010849	521.6	ACIDES INORGANIQUES
52224	PHOSPHORIC ACIDS ETC	W 1533646	277.7	W 2083974	446.1	W 2071052	493.8	W 2006625	513.5	ACIDES PHOSPHORIQUES
5225	INORGANIC BASES ETC NES	W 677144	106.8	W 869286	189.4	W 873982	220.0	W 796330	207.3	AUTRES BASES OXYDES METAL
52251	AMMONIA,ANHYDROUS ETC	W 550059	77.7	W 753325	157.8	W 799190	183.1	W 721731	169.4	AMMONIAC LIQUEFIE
53	DYES,TANNING,COLOUR PROD		87.8		134.1		144.0		162.6	PROD TEINTURE,COLORANTS
541	*MEDICINAL,PHARM PRODUCT		257.9		298.5		405.1	MK 10429	306.7	PROD MEDICINAUX PHARMACEUT
5413	ANTIBIOTICS IN BULK	K 3149265	155.9	K 4454485	192.5	K 6126668	249.4	K 5526287	192.9	ANTIBIOTIQUES NDA
54131	PENICILLINS AND DERIVTVS	K 2229394	80.6	K 3435050	114.5	K 5167422	162.4	K 4733432	127.6	PENICILLINES ET DERIVES
54139	OTHER ANTIBIOTICS	K 648789	70.5	K 805770	72.0	K 780581	81.5	K 638698	60.3	AUTRES ANTIBIOTIQUES
562	*FERTILIZERS,MANUFACTURE	W 4634979	631.7	W 4630075	764.0	W 6595445	1378.4	W 3464132	685.4	ENGRAIS MANUFACTURES
5621	CHEM NITROGENOUS FERTLZR	W 2400234	300.8	W 2196209	409.1	W 3134929	768.9	W 2060831	435.0	ENGRAIS AZOTES
56216	UREA	W 2343136	293.3	W 2135672	399.1	W 3134822	768.8	W 2060724	435.0	UREE
5623	CHEM POTASSIC FERTILIZER	W 1117624	144.9	W 1717276	205.5	W 2026659	257.6	W 858042	113.1	ENGRAIS POTASSIQUES
56231	POTASSIUM CHLORIDE	W 1086248	139.8	W 1703423	202.5	W 1885667	238.2	W 830650	109.4	CHLORURE DE POTASSIUM
5629	FERTILIZERS NES	W 1117121	186.2	W 716590	149.4	W 1433857	352.0	W 545258	137.3	ENGRAIS NDA
56292	NITROG–PHOS FERTILZR NES	W 1112497	185.6	W 697822	147.3	W 1310406	322.7	W 544711	137.0	.ENGRAIS NDA CONT N P

4. General Imports C.I.F. by Commodities according to the S.I.T.C. (Rev. 2) in million U.S. Dollars
Importations Générales C.A.F. par Produits d'après la C.T.C.I. (Rév. 2) en millions de Dollars E.U.

SITC CTCI	COMMODITY	1993		1994		1995		1996		PRODUIT
		QUANTITY QUANTITE	VALUE VALEUR	QUANTITY QUANTITE	VALUE VALEUR	QUANTITY QUANTITE	VALUE VALEUR	QUANTITY QUANTITE	VALUE VALEUR	
58	PLASTIC MATERIALS ETC		424.3		590.2		779.8		778.2	MAT PLAST ARTIFICIELLES
582	PROD OF CONDENSATION ETC	W 20211	55.3	W 56743	120.0	W 53376	144.2	W 59813	128.1	PROD CONDENS,POLYCOND
583	POLYMERIZATION ETC PRODS	W 557918	360.9	W 579139	456.8	W 659047	623.0	W 720488	635.3	PROD POLYMERISATION
5831	POLYETHYLENE	W 230237	134.9	W 231638	151.0	W 290002	236.8	W 342042	271.9	POLYETHYLENE
58311	— IN PRIMARY FORMS	W 216734	131.7	W 221956	147.3	W 277012	230.9	W 338382	267.6	POLYETHYLENE PRIMAIRES
5832	POLYPROPYLENE	W 165625	96.4	W 181958	129.9	W 212435	191.8	W 225410	178.7	POLYPROPYLENE
58321	— IN PRIMARY FORMS	W 165071	92.8	W 180817	123.9	W 211107	185.0	W 223918	172.9	POLYPROPYLENE PRIMAIRES
59	CHEMICAL MATERIALS NES		169.0		205.3		249.0		269.0	MAT PROD CHIMIQUES NDA
598	MISCEL CHEM PRODUCTS NES		146.2		167.4		198.3	W 79344	211.0	PROD DIV INDUST CHIM NDA
5989	CHEM PRODUCTS,PREPS NES		86.5		109.8		133.4	W 39442	130.7	PROD PREP CHIMIQUES NDA
6	BASIC MANUFACTURES		4798.1		4868.9		6297.3		7227.8	ART MANUFACTURES
61	LEATHER,DRESSED FUR,ETC		105.0		99.1		113.6		100.9	CUIRS,PELLETERIES
611	LEATHER	A 3070	81.4	A 2475	71.9	A 3000	83.8	W 9426	77.6	CUIRS,PEAUX PREPARES
64	PAPER,PAPERBOARD AND MFR		219.7		243.0		467.4		494.1	PAPIERS,CARTONS & OUVRAGES
641	PAPER AND PAPERBOARD	W 345612	204.6	W 348465	218.4	W 420117	434.2	W 592114	468.2	PAPIERS ET CARTONS
6411	NEWSPRINT	W 315918	148.2	W 298375	155.1	W 347908	302.4	W 494037	308.7	PAPIER JOURNAL
65	TEXTILE YARN,FABRICS,ETC		228.1		330.9		358.4		348.2	FILS,TISSUS,ARTICLES TEXTILE
651	TEXTILE YARN		105.0		159.7		143.2	W 37129	116.1	FILS TEXTILES
6514	SYN FIB YRN,BULK,MONOFIL	W 30541	68.7	W 50210	108.9	W 30175	86.0	W 26482	63.8	FILS CONT 85% FIB TEXT SYNTH
65142	— NONTXT ETC CONT PAMID	W 27267	58.3	W 42254	87.6	W 25546	67.7	W 24338	53.7	FILS NON TEX FI CON POLYAMID
657	SPECIAL TXTL FABRC,PRODS		51.5		68.8		106.0	W 43458	134.4	TISSUS SPECIAUX
66	NONMETAL MINERAL MFS NES		2723.8		1771.0		2265.8		3057.9	ART MIN NON METALLIQUES
667	PEARL,PREC-,SEMI-P STONE		2635.8		1633.5		2110.0		2923.6	PERLES, PIERRES GEMMES
6672	DIAMONDS NONINDUST,UNSET		2582.8		1579.7		2050.4		2867.2	DIAMANTS BRUTS
66722	— SRTD,ROUGH,SIMPLY WKD		2532.0		1500.7		1951.9		2759.1	DIAMANTS TRIES BRUTS
67	IRON AND STEEL		797.0		1165.5		1444.4		1373.7	FER ET ACIER
672	IRON,STEEL PRIMARY FORMS	W 630129	209.9	W 886174	311.2	W 598340	277.2	W 633164	243.1	LINGOTS FER,ACIER
6725	IRN,STL BLOOMS,SLABS,ETC	W 54497	19.0	W 235038	64.5	W 323257	109.2	W 386172	141.9	BLOOMS,BILLETTES FER ACIER
6727	IRN,STL COIL FR REROLLNG	W 413156	155.9	W 608102	237.6	W 258113	164.1	W 205584	88.1	EBAUCHES POUR TOLES FER
67271	IRON,SIMPLE STEEL COILS	W 380379	123.0	W 544001	179.8	W 222974	95.1	W 192787	69.9	EBAUCHES NON EN ACIER
673	IRON,STEEL SHAPES ETC	W 64960	51.3	W 134778	96.1	W 164695	120.2	W 150798	109.1	BARRES,PROFIL FER,ACIER
674	IRN,STL UNIV,PLATE,SHEET	W 395601	240.5	W 825024	456.1	W 1157000	701.5	W 1189750	639.3	LARGES PLATS,TOLES
6744	IRN,STL HVY PLATE,ROLLED	W 119132	50.6	W 390368	162.2	W 621431	287.4	W 682019	250.2	TOLES LAMINEES PLUS 4.75 MM
67441	— OF IRON OR SIMPLE STL	W 115362	44.9	W 382758	152.4	W 612973	270.9	W 674208	237.8	TOLES NON ACIER FIN CARB
6745	IRN,STL MED PLATE,ROLLED	W 97289	76.9	W 154094	109.3	W 182246	140.0	W 127096	118.3	TOLES 3 A 4.75 MM
6749	OTH IRN,STL PLATES,SHEET	W 70963	48.4	W 102829	80.1	W 141074	131.8	W 206280	158.6	AUTRES TOLES FER,ACIER
678	IRON,STL TUBES,PIPES,ETC	W 248477	221.2	W 195000	184.3	W 141627	190.1	W 160324	248.3	TUBES,TUYAUX EN FONTE,FER
6782	IRON,STL SEAMLESS TUBES	W 180157	154.5	W 176320	154.4	W 115042	146.6	W 127279	183.4	TUBES,TUYAUX SANS SOUDURE
68	NON-FERROUS METALS		485.4		974.4		1241.0		1426.3	METAUX NON FERREUX
681	SILVER,PLATINUM,ETC		11.0		246.3		333.9		316.7	ARGENT ET PLATINE
6811	SILVER UNWKD,PARTLY WRKD		9.6		243.9		331.3		315.1	ARGENT BRUT MI-OUVRE
68113	SILVER UNWROUGHT		8.3		223.1		307.5		279.2	ARGENT ET ALLIAGES BRUTS
682	COPPER EXC CEMENT COPPER	W 135065	280.9	W 148260	373.6	W 138007	447.6	W 222503	559.4	CUIVRE
6821	COPPER NES,ALLOYS,UNWRT	W 88960	167.2	W 84758	193.5	W 83664	249.7	W 157915	367.3	CUIVRE BRUT
68212	COPPER REFINED,UNWROUGHT	W 87144	163.7	W 79995	182.0	W 82895	247.4	W 156697	364.2	CUIVRE AFFINE BRUT
6822	COPPER,ALLOYS WORKED	W 46104	113.8	W 63502	180.1	W 54343	198.0	W 64588	192.2	CUIVRE,ALLIAGES OUVRES
68221	COPPER BARS,WIRE,ETC	W 42604	92.5	W 58295	150.2	W 46783	149.9	W 56410	145.1	BARRES,PROFILES ET FILS
684	ALUMINIUM	W 50830	76.7	W 88425	171.2	W 102065	219.1	W 155707	280.0	ALUMINIUM
6841	ALUMINIUM,ALLOYS,UNWRGHT	W 43823	52.4	W 78903	136.7	W 92460	176.1	W 134603	217.4	ALUMINIUM,ALLIAGES BRUTS
69	METAL MANUFACTURES NES		175.3		204.2		271.9		311.7	ART MANUFACT EN METAL NDA
699	BASE METAL MFRS NES	W 6522	72.1	W 8337	85.4	W 12879	120.4	W 15105	129.5	ART MANUFACTURES MET NDA
7	MACHINES,TRANSPORT EQUIP		4332.4		5435.9		7366.8		7309.4	MACHINES MATERIEL TRANSPORT
71	POWER GENERATING EQUIPMT		325.2		537.6		785.0		580.1	MACHINES GENERATRICES
713	INTRNL COMBUS PSTN ENGIN		81.2		121.7		178.6		185.8	MOTEURS EXPL COMB INT, PIECE
7139	PISTON ENGINE PARTS NES	W 3212	57.5	W 4518	80.6	W 6035	107.8	W 8921	124.5	PIECES POUR 713.2,3,8
714	ENGINES AND MOTORS NES		132.6		142.9		112.8		39.8	MOTEURS NON ELECTRIQUES
7149	ENGINE & MOTOR PARTS NES	W 2573	125.9	W 4272	139.7	W 1527	74.8	W 1061	36.2	PIECES 714 ET 718.88
71499	PARTS NES,OF 71488,71888	W 2524	124.4	W 4207	138.4	W 1466	72.9	W 1051	35.9	PIECES 714.88 ET 718.88
716	ROTATING ELECTRIC PLANT		71.8		220.6		418.6		245.9	APP ELECTR ROTATIFS,PIECES
7169	PTS NES OF ROT ELEC PLNT	W 1753	31.7	W 6900	127.3	W 12861	234.9	W 4320	78.3	PIECES MAC APP ROTATIFS
72	MACHS FOR SPCL INDUSTRYS		843.7		1235.2		1720.6		1390.7	MAC SPECIALES POUR INDUST
724	TEXTILE,LEATHER MACHNRY		461.0		670.9		795.8		581.4	MACH POUR INDUSTRIE TEXTILE
7244	SPINNING,EXTRDNG,ETC MCH		208.6		284.2		337.3		249.8	MACH POUR LE FILAGE
72443	SPINNING,REELING,ETC MCH	N 858	69.3	N 1220	127.6	N 1170	163.3	N 987	117.7	MACH POUR LA FILATURE
72449	PTS NES OF MACHS OF 7244	W 3780	71.1	W 3113	73.2	W 4090	89.1	W 3522	64.1	PIECES DES MACH DU 724.4
7245	WEAVING,FELT MFG,ETC MCH		110.0		182.2		250.5		163.5	METIERS A TISSER,PIECES
72453	GIMPING,WARPING ETC MCHS	N 722	36.8	N 1249	90.3	N 1347	83.6	N 1133	71.4	METIERS A TULLE ETC
726	PRINTG,BKBINDG MACHY,PTS		48.1		84.7		155.5		90.7	MACHINES POUR IMPRIMERIE
728	OTH MACHY FOR SPCL INDUS		237.3		335.1		555.7		476.8	AUT MACH IND PARTICULIERES
7284	MACHY FOR SPCL INDUS NES		157.3		278.9		470.3		384.1	MACH SPEC IND PARTICUL.
72842	RUBBER,PLASTICS WRKG MCH	N 581	27.6	N 3032	71.0	N 2727	155.9	N 1416	88.4	MACH IND CAOUT MAT PLAST
72848	OTH MCHY WITH INDIV FNCT	N 6382	62.1	N 9371	111.6	N 15849	194.1	N 6963	175.9	AUTRES MACHINES NDA
73	METALWORKING MACHINERY		164.4		248.9		416.3		764.9	MACH TRAVAIL DES METAUX
736	METALWORKING MACH-TOOLS		119.4		182.8		319.9		499.2	MACH-OUTILS TRAVAIL METAUX
7361	METAL CUTTING MACH-TOOLS	N 1058	59.4	N 3646	75.8	N 4169	145.0	N 4766	243.2	MACH-OUT ENLEVEMENT METAL
7367	OTH METALWRKG MACH-TOOLS	N 649	14.6	N 617	20.7	N 1395	71.0	N 1305	137.5	AUT MACH-OUT POUR METAUX
737	METALWORKING MACHNRY NES		45.1		66.2		96.4		265.8	MACH TRAV METAUX PIECES
7372	ROLLING MILLS AND ROLLS		21.6		34.4		50.8		199.9	LAMINOIRS CYLINDRES PIEC
74	GENRL INDUSTRL MACHY NES		710.7		923.9		1377.8		1433.4	MACH APP INDUSTRIE
741	HEATING,COOLING EQUIPMNT		81.5		116.2		232.4		332.6	MACH CHAUFFAGE,PIECES
7413	INDUS FURNACES ETC,PARTS		12.3		24.7		56.0	N 829	125.0	FOURS IND,LABOR,PIECES
7416	HEATING,COOLING EQU NES		37.8		59.3		108.4		119.2	APP CHANGEMENT TEMP
743	PUMPS NES,CENTRFUGES ETC		98.8		122.3		197.2		164.3	POMPES COMPRES,VENT ETC
744	MECHANICAL HANDLING EQU		131.3		163.3		222.3		208.3	EQUIP MANUTENTION PIECES
7449	PTS NES OF MACHY OF 7442	W 6844	106.4	W 5172	112.6	W 7140	118.2	W 4413	83.7	PIECES DU 744.2
749	NONELEC MACH PTS,ACC NES		298.1		384.0		524.0		508.5	PIECES MACH NON ELEC NDA
7491	BALL,ROLLER,ETC BEARINGS	MN 12217	74.1	MN 12480	90.4	MN 27553	140.9	MN 24420	145.6	ROULEMENTS BILLES ETC
7493	SHAFT,CRANK,PULLEY ETC	N 1037118	104.4	N 2419902	126.1	N 3816260	161.1		147.2	ARBRES TRANS,VILEBREQUINS
7499	OTH NONELEC MCHY PTS NES	W 2308	55.0	W 3395	88.2	W 5435	112.8	W 4788	110.9	PIECES NON ELECT NDA
75	OFFICE MACHNES,ADP EQUIP		199.8		286.2		406.4		391.0	MACH BUREAU TRAIT AUTOM
752	AUTOMTIC DATA PROC EQUIP	N 133336	84.3	N 331213	127.2	N 479994	194.1	N 560157	188.3	MACH TRAIT INFORMATION
759	OFFICE,ADP MCH PTS,ACCES	W 1707	111.2	W 2704	143.4	W 3570	185.8	W 3567	184.3	PIECES DU 751 ET 752
7599	ACCTG,ETC,ADP MCH PTS,AC	W 1425	102.9	W 2231	131.8	W 3135	175.4	W 2879	171.1	PIECES DU 751 ET 752
76	TELECOMM,SOUND EQUIPMENT		173.4		260.9		352.2		321.0	EQUIPMENT DE TELECOM
764	TELECOM EQPT,PTS,ACC NES		169.1		250.0		327.0		310.7	EQUIP TELECOM,PIECES
7649	PTS NES OF EQUIPMT OF 76	W 2317	74.2	W 4626	134.0	W 7196	190.3	W 7142	184.8	PIECES DE LA DIV 76
77	ELECTRIC MACHNRY NES ETC		646.3		830.9		1214.0		946.3	MACH APP ELECT NDA
772	SWITCHGEAR ETC,PARTS NES		131.2		172.4		224.9	W 7481	180.4	APP COUPURE,SECT ETC
7721	SWITCHGEAR ETC	MN 105898	99.7		123.8	MN 176863	164.9	W 5544	131.8	APP COUPURE,SECTIONMNT
774	ELECTRO-MEDCL,XRAY EQUIP		58.3		94.5		106.5		83.2	APPAREILS MEDICAUX
776	TRANSISTORS,VALVES,ETC		211.7		269.3		440.1		299.5	LAMPES,TUBES,VALVES

4. General Imports C.I.F. by Commodities according to the S.I.T.C. (Rev. 2) in million U.S. Dollars
Importations Générales C.A.F. par Produits d'après la C.T.C.I. (Rév. 2) en millions de Dollars E.U.

SITC CTCI	COMMODITY	1993 QUANTITY QUANTITE	1993 VALUE VALEUR	1994 QUANTITY QUANTITE	1994 VALUE VALEUR	1995 QUANTITY QUANTITE	1995 VALUE VALEUR	1996 QUANTITY QUANTITE	1996 VALUE VALEUR	PRODUIT
7764	ELECTRONIC MICROCIRCUITS	MN 100091	99.3	MN 221567	120.2	MN 180966	214.7	MN 115134	127.1	MICROSTRUCTURES ELECTRON
778	ELECTRICAL MACHINERY NES		165.2		190.1		259.5		224.6	AUTRES MACH ELECT NDA
7788	OTH ELEC MACHY,EQUIP NES		133.4		147.3		190.3		164.0	AUT MACH APP ELEC NDA
78	ROAD VEHICLES		222.5		292.3		456.4		578.1	VEHICULES ROUTIERS
784	MOTOR VEH PRTS,ACCES NES		183.5		244.2		382.2		518.5	PIECES 722,781,782,783
7849	OTHER MOTOR VEHCL PARTS	W 20889	181.9	W 29951	239.4	W 37188	371.2	W 63679	517.7	PIECES 722,781,782,783
79	OTHR TRANSPORT EQUIPMENT		1046.8		820.4		638.5		904.3	AUTRE MATERIEL TRANSPORT
791	RAILWAY VEHICLES		30.5		15.7		48.2		132.8	VEHIC MAT CHEMINS DE FER
792	AIRCRAFT ETC		935.2		732.7		486.7		502.3	APP NAVIGATION AERIENNE
7924	AIRCRFT NES OVER 15000KG	N 25	787.4	N 9	318.4	N 6	132.9	N 6	440.0	AERODYNES PLUS 15000 KG
7929	AIRCRAFT PARTS NES	W 554	90.4	W 801	306.3	W 840	270.0	W 157	41.9	PIECES DU 792
793	SHIPS AND BOATS ETC		81.2	N 280	72.1	N 371	103.6	N 258	269.3	NAVIRES BATEAUX,ETC
7932	SHIPS AND BOATS NES	N 86	23.3	N 102	23.7	N 47	26.9	N 44	166.7	NAVIRES ET BATEAUX
79323	OTHER CARGO VESSELS	N 32	23.1	N 16	8.8	N 5	1.7	N 16	166.1	AUT BATEAUX TRANS MARCH
8	MISC MANUFACTURED GOODS		689.7		866.7		1310.1		1037.6	ART MANUFACTURES DIVERS
87	PRECISION INSTRUMNTS NES		348.3		372.3		545.0		422.6	INSTRUM,APPAR SCIENT NDA
874	MEASURNG,CONTROLNG INSTR		280.2		279.0		406.5		318.3	INSTRUMENTS DE MESURE
8749	INSTR PTS NES,ACCESSORYS	W 1325	88.5	W 2489	70.3	W 2044	105.0	W 1273	56.4	PIECES 873,874.3,54,874.8
88	PHOTO EQU,OPTICL GDS ETC		141.4		180.3		217.2		205.3	APP,FOURN PHOTO,OP,MONTR
882	PHOTO,CINEMA SUPPLIES		109.4		140.7		158.1		148.5	PRODUITS PHOTO,CINEMA
8822	PHOTO FILM EXC DEV CINMA		105.3		134.3		150.3		141.9	PLAQUES,PELLICULES,FILMS
89	MISC MANUFCTRD GOODS NES		191.5		302.5		523.4		380.8	ART MANUFACTURES DIVERS
893	ARTICLES OF PLASTIC NES		36.7		84.4	W 10864	167.6		56.0	OUVRAGES EN MAT DIVIS 58
8939	MISC PLASTIC ARTICLES	W 3243	30.1	W 4641	74.9	W 9030	156.3	W 5875	45.2	ART DIVERS EN MAT DIV 58
89399	OTHR PLASTC ARTICLES NES	W 3202	29.9	W 4593	74.4	W 8991	155.9	W 5770	44.6	AUT OUV MAT DIV 58
898	MUSICAL INSTRUMENTS,PTS		32.6		60.9		162.4		128.2	INSTRUMENTS DE MUSIQUE
8983	SOUND RECRDNG TAPE,DISCS	N 1197022	31.5	N 2252418	59.7	N 6294220	160.1	N 7796878	123.9	SUPPORTS SON POUR 763
89832	RECORDED DISCS,TAPES ETC	N 155430	28.1	N 439949	54.8	N 859167	147.2	N 940764	108.9	DISQUES,PHONO,BANDES
9	GOODS NOT CLASSD BY KIND		1935.3		2376.5		3107.6		2933.8	ART TRANSACT NON CLASSES
931	*SPECIAL TRANSACTIONS		1688.0		1905.5		2553.4		2234.4	TRANS.SPECIALES
971	*GOLD,NON MONETARY NES	K 19710	245.9	K 39055	470.1	K 45677	539.6	K 52468	688.6	OR NON MONETAIRE
97101	NONMON GLD UNWRT,SEMIMFD	K 19669	245.8	K 39038	470.1	K 45677	539.6	K 52425	688.5	OR,ALLIAGES D'OR BRUTS

5. General Exports F.O.B. by Commodities according to the S.I.T.C. (Rev. 2) in million U.S. Dollars
Exportations Générales F.O.B. par Produits d'après la C.T.C.I. (Rév. 2) en millions de Dollars E.U.

SITC CTCI	COMMODITY	1993 QUANTITY QUANTITE	1993 VALUE VALEUR	1994 QUANTITY QUANTITE	1994 VALUE VALEUR	1995 QUANTITY QUANTITE	1995 VALUE VALEUR	1996 QUANTITY QUANTITE	1996 VALUE VALEUR	PRODUIT
	ALL COMMODITIES		22237.0		26330.1		31698.7		33468.7	TOUS PRODUITS
0	FOOD AND LIVE ANIMALS		3384.2		3752.9		5351.2		5586.4	ALIMENTS,ANIMAUX VIVANTS
01	MEAT AND PREPARATIONS		110.1		126.2		184.9		196.5	VIANDES ET PREPARATIONS
011	MEAT FRESH,CHILLD,FROZEN	W 112861	109.5	W 127875	125.4	W 169352	183.2	W 166735	195.1	VIANDES FRAICHES,REF,CONGE
0111	BOVINE MEAT FRESH,FROZEN	W 101666	89.6	W 116138	103.4	W 159704	165.5	W 157574	174.4	VIANDES BOVIN FRAI,REF
01112	BOVINE MEAT BONELESS	W 82170	73.4	W 93590	86.5	W 131840	137.7	W 124575	141.3	VIANDES BOVIN DESOSSEES
03	FISH AND PREPARATIONS		807.1		1119.6		1000.3		1122.5	POISSONS ET PREPARATIONS
034	FISH,FRESH,CHILLED,FROZN	W 96490	102.6	W 144183	172.7	W 141405	196.1	W 217488	244.2	POISSON FRAIS, REFRIG,CONG
0342	FISH FROZEN,EXCL FILLETS	W 89107	86.0	W 133480	144.7	W 119092	143.4	W 201319	213.8	POISSONS CONGELES
036	SHELL FISH FRESH,FROZEN	W 154387	700.3	W 168914	938.8	W 158032	797.7	W 168956	867.1	CRUSTACES,MOLLUSQUES
04	CEREALS AND PREPARATIONS		441.9		429.7		1603.3		1285.5	CEREALES ET PRODUITS
041	WHEAT ETC UNMILLED	W 390	0.1	W 86628	13.5	W 632468	109.4	W 1145895	196.8	FROMENT,EPEAUTRE
0412	OTHER WHEAT ETC UNMILLED	W 350	0.1	W 86546	13.5	W 593176	102.2	W 920227	157.4	AUTRE FROMENT NON MOULU
042	RICE	W 767687	410.3	W 890613	384.1	W 4914011	1361.6	W 2511974	893.6	RIZ
0422	RICE SEMI-MILLED,MILLED	W 767671	410.3	W 890528	384.1	W 4911441	1361.0	W 2511887	893.6	RIZ POLI,GLACE INCL BRISURES
04221	RICE MILLED UNBROKEN	W 767660	410.2	W 890268	384.0	W 4893966	1357.4	W 2505167	891.8	RIZ POLI,GLACE EXCL BRISURES
046	WHEAT ETC MEAL OR FLOUR	W 3790	0.8	W 5545	1.3	W 460859	97.7	W 731607	148.3	SEMOULE FARINE,FROMENT
04601	FLOUR OF WHEAT OR MESLIN	W 3478	0.8	W 5543	1.3	W 459099	97.3	W 701868	142.8	FARINE DE FROMENT
05	VEGETABLES AND FRUIT		545.7		649.1		681.8		665.4	LEGUMES ET FRUITS
054	VEG ETC FRSH,SMPLY PRSVD	W 442306	95.3	W 524459	118.1	W 536670	153.9	W 582272	149.5	LEGUMES FRAIS,CONG,SECS
057	FRUIT,NUTS,FRESH,DRIED	W 88817	393.6	W 100637	459.3	W 116035	441.7	W 294233	435.0	FRUITS FRAIS OU SECS
0577	NUTS EDIBLE,FRESH,DRIED	W 7113	356.1	W 7519	417.7	W 7844	394.6	W 75630	386.3	FRUITS A COQUES
05773	CASHEW NUTS,FRESH,DRIED	W 70	333.3	W 77	396.4	W 70	368.4	W 68663	362.1	NOIX DE CAJOU
06	SUGAR AND PREPS,HONEY		58.9		22.9		159.5		309.6	SUCRES ET PRODUITS
061	SUGAR AND HONEY	W 206348	58.0	W 54197	21.7	W 740578	155.6	W 1723051	307.5	SUCRES ET MIEL
0612	REFINED SUGAR ETC	W 118992	35.6	W 39368	15.6	W 169621	75.6	W 390644	138.1	SUCRES RAFFINES
07	COFFEE,TEA,COCOA,SPICES		647.6		794.0		976.4		942.0	CAFE,THE,CACAO,EPICES
071	COFFEE AND SUBSTITUTES	W 120123	174.1	W 130090	335.5	W 157330	448.6	W 163255	401.9	CAFE ET SUCCEDANES
0711	COFFEE GREEN,ROASTED,SUB	W 114023	141.5	W 123923	289.5	W 148866	366.2	W 152618	323.3	CAFE TORREFIE OU DECAFEINE
07111	COFFEE GREEN,HUSKS,SKINS	W 112680	137.4	W 122122	282.8	W 144944	355.7	W 146772	310.8	CAFE NON TORREFIE
074	TEA AND MATE	W 153159	330.7	W 150874	307.0	W 158333	345.3	W 138360	284.3	THE ET MATE
0741	TEA	W 153159	330.7	W 150874	307.0	W 158333	345.3	W 138360	284.3	THE
075	SPICES	W 163468	142.1	W 137623	149.2	W 176847	180.0	W 200713	253.0	EPICES
0751	PEPPER AND PIMENTO	W 78161	81.8	W 56516	92.9	W 81134	115.7	W 95946	171.6	POIVRE,PIMENTS
081	*FEEDING STUFF FOR ANIML	W 4905737	748.2	W 3955107	582.4	W 4327302	706.4	W 4849342	997.2	NOURRITURE POUR ANIMAUX
0813	OILCAKE AND OTH RESIDUES	W 4302178	711.5	W 3576682	551.5	W 4020286	677.7	W 4478459	957.9	TOURTEAUX
08131	— OF SOYA BEANS	W 2755837	551.6	W 1929742	386.7	W 2591803	545.4	W 2981749	769.4	TOURTEAUX DE SOJA
08136	— OF RAPE OR COLZA SEED	W 778192	69.1	W 1040514	93.2	W 971707	74.6	W 1066624	115.7	TOURTEAUX DE NAVETTE,COLZA
1	BEVERAGES AND TOBACCO		159.5		96.0		145.4		226.2	BOISSONS ET TABACS
12	TOBACCO AND MANUFACTURES		147.1		81.2		133.2		213.2	TABACS BRUTS FABRIQUES
121	TOBACCO UNMNFCTRD,REFUSE	W 90493	117.5	W 42930	58.7	W 77678	112.9	W 106644	186.1	TABACS BRUTS,DECHETS
1211	TOBACCO,NOT STRIPPED	W 48673	47.8	W 25387	26.1	W 64341	85.7	W 90180	145.5	TABACS NON ECOTES
1212	TOBACCO STRIPPED OR PART	W 41820	69.7	W 17543	32.7	W 13337	27.3	W 15992	40.6	TABACS PART ECOTES
2	CRUDE MATERLS,EXCL FUELS		1298.7		1208.3		1544.2		2005.5	MAT BRUTES NON COMESTIBLES
22	OIL SEEDS,OLEAGINOUS FRT		84.6		83.1		157.7		187.6	GRAINES,FRUITS OLEAGINEUX
222	SEEDS FOR'SOFT'FIXED OIL	W 265058	72.2	W 103723	73.8	W 197156	140.9	W 244842	162.9	GRAINES HUILES FIXES
26	TEXTILE FIBRES AND WASTE		224.7		78.2		89.2		474.6	FIBRES TEXTILES
263	COTTON	W 193663	208.4	W 34801	44.6	W 36369	62.0	W 271705	444.5	COTON
2631	RAW COTTON,EXCL LINTERS	W 192197	206.3	W 29350	37.3	W 26676	49.0	W 253413	413.3	COTON EN MASSE
27	CRUDE FERTLZR,MINRLS NES		194.8		249.3		278.4		276.8	ENGRAIS MINERAUX BRUTS
273	STONE,SAND AND GRAVEL	W 1378784	154.3	W 1787520	197.3	W 2391998	214.0	W 2486774	212.2	PIERRES,SABLES,GRAVIERS
2731	BLDG,DIMENSION STONE	W 967680	149.5	W 1176458	189.5	W 1568326	202.3	W 1797491	196.4	PIERRES DE TAILLE
27313	GRANITE,SANDSTONE,ETC	W 881780	134.4	W 1076643	168.6	W 1442220	182.8	W 1698402	175.1	GYPSE,BASALTE,GRES
28	METALLIFEROUS ORES,SCRAP		582.4		563.0		699.0		695.4	MINERAIS METAL,DECHETS
281	IRON ORE,CONCENTRATES	MW 26857	438.0	MW 26058	413.3	MW 31720	513.0	MW 17628	480.7	MINERAIS DE FER
2815	IRON ORE,CONC,NOT AGGLOM	MW 25630	407.0	MW 24788	379.3	MW 29243	446.4	MW 15527	428.4	MINERAIS NON AGGLOMERES
287	BASE METAL ORES,CONC NES	W 1541920	143.6	W 1564150	148.7	W 1404981	183.9	W 1622210	203.9	MINERAIS METAUX COMMUNS
2873	ALUMINIUM ORES,ALUMINA	W 772370	89.7	W 576779	74.7	W 597956	98.5	W 664540	107.0	MINERAIS D'ALUMINIUM
28732	ALUMINA(ALUMINIUM OXIDE)	W 539947	86.9	W 479569	73.7	W 447988	97.1	W 560615	105.6	ALUMINE (OXYDE ALUMINIUM)
29	CRUDE ANIMAL,VEG MAT NES		207.5		224.7		309.7		356.1	MATIERES BRUTES ANIM,VEGET
292	CRUDE VEG MATERIALS NES		168.9		186.1		267.8		304.1	MAT BRUTES VEGETALES NDA
2929	OTH CRUDE VEG MATERIALS	W 91798	67.6	W 86762	74.0	W 104268	110.0	W 116875	149.4	MATIERES VEGETALES NDA
29291	VEGETABLE SAPS,EXTRACTS	W 75372	55.6	W 68933	59.8	W 85904	95.1	W 100471	135.3	SUCS,EXTRAITS VEGETAUX
3	MINERAL FUELS ETC		496.2		514.2		527.0		519.0	COMBUSTIBLES MINERAUX LUB
33	PETROLEUM AND PRODUCTS		399.8		424.8		465.7		492.9	PETROLE ET DERIVES
334	PETROLEUM PRODUCTS,REFIN		398.7		418.5	W 3	0.1	W 3029030	484.9	PRODUITS RAFFINES
341	*GAS,NATURAL AND MANUFCT		75.2		55.6		31.8	W 1187	1.7	GAZ NATUREL,GAZ MANUFACT
3413	PETROLM GASES,LIQUEFIED		74.6		52.5		27.1	W 109	0.2	GAZ DE PETROLE LIQUEFIE
34139	OTH HYDROCARBON GAS LQFD		74.6		52.5		27.0	W 57	0.1	HYDROCARBURES GAZEUX NDA
4	ANIMAL,VEGETABLE OIL,FAT		101.2		153.3		258.0		193.2	HUILES,GRAISSES ANIM,VEG
42	FIXED VEGETABLE OIL,FAT		89.9		126.5		216.2		162.8	HUILES VEGETALES FIXES
424	FIXED VEG OIL NONSOFT	W 135806	89.1	W 165673	126.0	W 271737	203.3	W 220208	160.9	AUTRES HUILES VEG FIXES
4245	CASTOR OIL	W 131351	85.9	W 159169	120.1	W 269892	200.4	W 216537	155.0	HUILE DE RICIN
5	CHEMCLS,RELATED PROD NES		1533.8		2134.0		2563.6		2992.5	PRODUITS CHIMIQUES
51	ORGANIC CHEMICALS		364.0		557.5		719.9		906.0	PROD CHIMIQ ORGANIQUES
511	HYDROCARBONS NES,DERIVS	W 23397	37.3	W 34332	62.0	W 57012	98.3	W 49123	105.5	HYDROCARBURES NDA
512	ALCOHOLS,PHENOLS ETC	W 23523	30.1	W 46754	50.9	W 25358	66.0		182.5	PHENOLS,PHENOLS-ALCOOLS
513	CARBOXYLIC ACIDS ETC	W 62004	44.0	W 79474	83.4	W 89932	117.1	W 104119	99.4	ACIDES CARBOXYLIQUES
514	NITROGEN-FNCTN COMPOUNDS	W 35746	133.3	W 47729	189.0	W 44282	205.1	W 48896	210.1	COMPOSES FONCT AZOTEES
5146	OXYGEN-FNCT AMINO-CMPNDS	W 16238	62.2	W 22444	97.8	W 19634	108.8	W 20706	107.3	COMP AMINES FONCT OXYGEN
516	OTHER ORGANIC CHEMICALS	W 11964	73.8	W 15569	103.8	W 23647	161.1	W 32893	233.2	AUTRES PROD ORGANIQUES
5169	ORGANIC CHEMICALS,NES	W 4178	57.8	W 4488	82.2	W 4105	116.3	W 8512	181.3	PROD CHIM ORGANIQUES NDA
51699	OTHER ORGANIC COMPOUNDS	W 3751	56.8	W 4042	80.1	W 3725	114.3	W 8055	179.0	AUTRES COMPOS ORGANIQUES
52	INORGANIC CHEMICALS		66.4		86.4		109.4		128.7	PROD CHIM INORGANIQUES
53	DYES,TANNING,COLOUR PROD		308.6		381.2		360.5		438.0	PROD TEINTURE,COLORANTS
531	SYNT DYE,NAT INDGO,LAKES	W 43575	289.8	W 51444	352.2	W 49017	336.5	W 64335	409.0	MAT COLOR ORGAN,LAQUES
5311	SYNTHIC ORGNIC DYESTUFFS	W 39236	267.7	W 46991	330.3	W 44720	313.0	W 57801	377.8	MAT COLOR ORGAN SYNTHET
541	*MEDICINAL,PHARM PRODUCT		482.9		585.8		724.2	MK 64398	814.0	PROD MEDICINAUX PHARMACEUT
5413	ANTIBIOTICS IN BULK	K 611886	30.2	K 931081	65.2	K 1268803	93.0	K 1648372	107.2	ANTIBIOTIQUES NDA
5417	MEDICAMENTS		409.9		484.3		583.0	MK 58852	639.8	MEDICAMENTS
54171	— CONTAINNG ANTIBIOTICS		85.5		118.5		165.0	K 6272025	160.9	MED CONTN ANTIBIOTIQUES
54179	— CONTNG OTH SUBSTANCES		310.1		340.3		395.3	MK 50863	447.9	MED CONT AUT SUBSTANCES
55	PERFUME,CLEANING ETC PRD		151.5		186.2		169.3		179.4	PROD POUR PARFUM,TOILETTE
553	PERFUMERY,COSMETICS,ETC	W 21655	68.7	W 26917	89.1	W 24421	82.0	W 26980	84.7	PRODUITS DE PARFUMERIE
58	PLASTIC MATERIALS ETC		57.9		163.6		224.9		224.1	MAT PLAST ARTIFICIELLES
582	PROD OF CONDENSATION ETC	W 11237	27.2	W 38047	70.8	W 53530	137.3	W 46738	115.4	PROD CONDENS,POLYCOND
5823	ALKYDS,OTHER POLYESTERS	W 9305	25.0	W 32734	63.7	W 50588	132.4	W 41551	108.5	ALKYDES ET AUT POLYESTERS
58232	— PLATES,FILM,STRIP ETC	W 7037	23.5	W 31187	61.4	W 48271	127.9	W 36220	96.2	SOUS FORME PLAQUES,FEUIL
583	POLYMERIZATION ETC PRODS	W 19240	27.7	W 79873	88.2	W 65594	80.9	W 91298	99.3	PROD POLYMERISATION
59	CHEMICAL MATERIALS NES		95.0		147.2		223.8		269.3	MAT PROD CHIMIQUES NDA
591	PESTICIDES,DISINFECTANTS	W 9683	58.8	W 12553	84.2	W 21994	156.0	W 27403	197.9	DESINF,INSECT,FONG,HERB

5. General Exports F.O.B. by Commodities according to the S.I.T.C. (Rev. 2) in million U.S. Dollars
Exportations Générales F.O.B. par Produits d'après la C.T.C.I. (Rév. 2) en millions de Dollars E.U.

SITC CTCI	COMMODITY	1993		1994		1995		1996		PRODUIT
		QUANTITY QUANTITE	VALUE VALEUR	QUANTITY QUANTITE	VALUE VALEUR	QUANTITY QUANTITE	VALUE VALEUR	QUANTITY QUANTITE	VALUE VALEUR	
5911	INSECTICIDES,FOR RETAIL	W 7729	48.6	W 10350	71.2	W 19856	142.2	W 25101	185.6	INSECTICIDES VENTE DET
6	BASIC MANUFACTURES		9098.8		10737.3		12382.5		12508.2	ART MANUFACTURES
61	LEATHER,DRESSED FUR,ETC		540.8		684.4		716.4		615.6	CUIRS,PELLETERIES
611	LEATHER	A 21635	269.4	A 27722	382.4	A 26303	370.0	W 13295	300.9	CUIRS,PEAUX PREPARES
6114	LEATHR BOVINE NES,EQUINE	A 5870	70.9	A 8409	112.6	A 8210	113.5	W 5127	83.1	CUIRS DE BOVINS
6116	LEATHER OF OTH HIDE,SKIN	A 9516	117.7	A 11752	157.9	A 12198	170.8	W 4869	139.9	PEAUX PREP D'AUTRES ANIMAUX
61161	LEATHER FROM GOAT,KID	A 9496	117.4	A 11736	157.7	A 12177	170.5	W 4820	139.4	PEAUX DE CAPRINS PREPAREES
612	LEATHER ETC MANUFACTURES	W 1	0.1		302.0	W 1	0.1	W 15347	314.8	OUVRAGES EN CUIRS NDA
6123	PREPRD PARTS OF FOOTWEAR	W 7071	217.9	W 6146	217.8	W 7141	247.2	W 6711	225.5	PARTIES DE CHAUSSURES
62	RUBBER MANUFACTURES NES		242.2		273.7		289.5		304.1	CAOUTCHOUC MANUFACTURE
625	RUBBER TYRES, TUBES ETC	MN 32601	204.6	MN 29256	237.6	MN 26093	235.9	N 3000	0.3	PNEUS CAOUTCHOUC VULCANISE
6252	TYRES,NEW,BUS OR LORRY	N 1924322	160.6	N 2380385	176.8	N 1806897	177.9	N 1725425	185.5	PNEUS POUR AUTOBUS,CAMIONS
64	PAPER,PAPERBOARD AND MFR		34.6		73.1		113.1		102.2	PAPIERS,CARTONS & OUVRAGES
65	TEXTILE YARN,FABRICS,ETC		2917.9		3829.9		4358.6		4936.9	FILS,TISSUS,ARTICLES TEXTILE
651	TEXTILE YARN		655.7		1051.2		1349.5	W 616099	1800.5	FILS TEXTILES
6513	COTTON YARN	W 161102	462.2	W 211635	755.2	W 260530	974.3	W 442960	1379.6	FILS DE COTON
6516	DISCON SYN FIB BLEND YRN	W 11772	35.0	W 15256	48.8	W 28745	98.8	W 40488	120.1	FILS FIBR TEX SYNT DIS MOINS
6517	REGEN FIBRE YARN,MONOFIL	W 15645	47.0	W 24387	77.3	W 28863	105.0	W 26120	84.8	FILS TEXT ART NON VENTE DT
652	COTTON FABRICS,WOVEN	A 854392	683.3	A 1018958	913.3	A 944519	959.8	W 208528	1008.2	TISSUS DE COTON
6521	GREY WOVEN COTTON FABRIC	A 482457	355.7	A 555124	449.6	A 473918	430.7	W 86176	406.0	TISSUS COT ECRUS NON MERCER
65214	GREY WOVEN COTTON NES	A 460272	343.5	A 511014	430.6	A 448039	413.6	W 83433	393.2	AUT TISSUS 85% COTON ECRUS
6522	WOVEN COTTON BLEACHD,ETC	A 371935	327.7	A 463834	463.8	A 470601	529.1	W 122352	602.2	TISSUS COTON BLANCHIS ETC
65224	BLCHED COTTON FABRIC NES	A 285072	250.3	A 360711	353.4	A 349369	376.3	W 86285	438.4	AUT TIS PLUS 85% COT BLANCHI
65225	BLCHD COTN BLEND FAB NES	A 81562	72.4	A 97338	104.2	A 115672	146.1	W 35331	159.8	AUT TIS MOINS 85% COT BLANCH
653	WOVN MAN–MADE FIB FABRIC		252.1		354.6		420.2	W 42764	351.7	TISSUS FIBRES SYNTH,ARTIF
6531	CONT SYNT WEAVES NONPILE	A 103874	144.7	A 155492	231.0	A 169962	236.2	W 20182	170.2	TISSUS FIBRES SYNTH CONTINUE
65315	CONT SYN TXTL FABRIC NES	A 83447	115.0	A 131714	195.4	A 138140	191.2	W 15336	128.5	TIS PLUS 85% TEXT SYNT CONT
6534	DISC SYN BLEND FABRC NES	A 41612	59.3	A 42813	66.1	A 77212	124.9	W 15878	119.3	TISSUS FIBRES SYNTH DISCONT
654	OTH WOVEN TEXTILE FABRIC		171.0		203.6		202.7	W 72587	203.4	TISSUS AUT COTON SYNT,ARTIF
6541	SILK FABRICS WOVEN	L 24122	112.5	L 22825	122.0	L 22029	121.6	W 2096	115.2	TISSUS DE SOIE
658	TEXTILE ARTICLES NES		424.6		543.3		646.1	W 168706	744.4	ART FACONNES MAT TEXTILES
6584	LINENS ETC	A 32124	30.2	A 40599	42.1	A 183272	187.3	W 32974	217.0	LINGE DE MAISON
65849	OTH FURN ART OF OTH FIBR	A 26144	25.2	A 33799	35.6	A 172763	177.2	W 30506	201.7	AUT ART AMEUBLEMENT AUT FIBR
6589	OTH TEXTILE ARTICLES NES		313.8		418.1		351.6	W 72069	437.5	AUT ART EN TEXTILES NDA
65898	KNITTED ETC ARTICLES NES	A 312384	277.7	A 399441	382.6	A 323515	309.4	W 61379	366.2	ART BONNET NON ELASTIQUE
659	FLOOR COVERINGS,ETC		604.5		610.9		624.9		656.3	COUVRE–PARQUETS,TAPIS ETC
6592	CARPETS ETC KNOTTED	A 3028	152.1	A 2502	136.7	A 2869	159.6	A 2242	120.6	TAPIS POINTS NOUES,ENROULES
65921	— OF WOOL OR FINE HAIR	A 2710	145.0	A 2288	133.3	A 2650	155.7	A 2035	116.1	TAP NOUES,ENROULES LAINE
6594	WOOL CARPETS ETC NES	A 8480	208.5	A 8359	205.9	A 7629	186.5	A 9816	263.1	TAPIS DE LAINE
65942	— WOVEN	A 8073	198.4	A 7929	194.8	A 6930	167.7	A 8652	229.8	TAPIS DE LAINE TISSES
6596	OTH TXTL CARPETS ETC NES		238.4		264.4		272.5	A 128761	264.4	TAPIS AUT MAT TEXT NDA
65962	— OTHR THAN KNOTTED ETC		237.3		260.2		268.6	A 127365	260.4	TAPIS AUT QUE NOUES TOUF
66	NONMETAL MINERAL MFS NES		3907.5		4389.7		5104.9		4572.4	ART MIN NON METALLIQUES
661	LIME,CEMENT,BLDG PRODS	W 1884860	172.1	W 1940277	230.5	W 1156610	225.5	W 1395551	258.4	CHAUX,CIMENTS MAT CONSTR
6612	CEMENT	W 1759508	72.4	W 1762251	77.4	W 943401	44.6	W 1153512	55.5	CIMENTS HYDRAULIQUES
6613	BUILDING STONE ETC WORKD	W 100809	96.2	W 154632	149.6	W 185030	176.7	W 229407	200.2	PIERRES A BATIR
66132	BUILDING STONE WORKED	W 94901	94.5	W 148298	147.4	W 176822	173.9	W 221587	197.0	OUVR EN PIERRES DE TAILLE
667	PEARL,PREC–,SEMI–P STONE		3667.6		4061.9		4752.6		4204.4	PERLES, PIERRES GEMMES
6672	DIAMONDS NONINDUST,UNSET		3573.7		3937.0		4589.0		4056.3	DIAMANTS BRUTS
66729	— CUT ETC NOT SET		3573.3		3935.6		4582.8		4028.1	DIAMANTS TAILLES
6673	PREC–,SEMI–PR STONES NES		86.1		116.3		153.2		142.4	AUTRES PIERRES NON SERTIES
67	IRON AND STEEL		804.5		775.4		1027.0		1059.0	FER ET ACIER
671	PIG IRON ETC	W 869454	171.3	W 874883	188.7	W 909400	246.0	W 597704	169.5	FONTE,SPIEGEL,POUDRES
6712	PIG IRN,SPIEGELEISEN ETC	W 689435	90.6	W 608651	84.3	W 511849	76.6	W 345481	59.2	FONTES BRUTES
6716	FERRO–ALLOYS	W 178906	80.3	W 199761	95.8	W 222518	144.1	W 182344	96.0	FERRO–ALLIAGES
67169	OTHER FERRO–ALLOYS	W 176784	79.4	W 189105	91.3	W 217759	142.0	W 176306	92.3	AUTRES FERRO–ALLIAGES
672	IRON,STEEL PRIMARY FORMS	W 511278	125.2	W 235397	81.5	W 315038	107.1	W 386552	119.6	LINGOTS FER,ACIER
6725	IRN,STL BLOOMS,SLABS,ETC	W 414882	98.9	W 141791	50.1	W 225260	69.9	W 232742	68.2	BLOOMS,BILLETTES FER ACIER
67255	OTH ALLOY STL BLOOMS ETC	W 367663	83.0	W 104900	25.6	W 105446	27.5	W 102438	29.3	BLOOMS ETC AUT AC ALLIES
673	IRON,STEEL SHAPES ETC	W 624322	202.9	W 418811	167.4	W 420559	217.1	W 592701	232.0	BARRES,PROFIL FER,ACIER
6732	IRON,STEEL BARS ETC	W 349683	117.4	W 247744	106.8	W 272298	146.2	W 420996	164.9	BARRES FER,ACIER
674	IRN,STL UNIV,PLATE,SHEET	W 396501	165.7	W 338542	147.7	W 340151	202.4	W 519818	279.3	LARGES PLATS,TOLES
6747	TINNED PLATES,SHEETS	W 180681	71.5	W 112098	57.9	W 69222	40.5	W 164931	95.6	TOLES ETAMEES EN ACIER
678	IRON,STL TUBES,PIPES,ETC	W 119597	71.6	W 114974	77.5	W 165576	95.1	W 183293	117.2	TUBES,TUYAUX EN FONTE,FER
68	NON–FERROUS METALS		131.6		175.6		159.1		225.7	METAUX NON FERREUX
684	ALUMINIUM	W 83118	115.4	W 88739	144.2	W 62584	127.2	W 107104	182.8	ALUMINIUM
6841	ALUMINIUM,ALLOYS,UNWRGHT	W 64487	75.7	W 66900	92.8	W 41298	68.3	W 86172	130.8	ALUMINIUM,ALLIAGES BRUTS
69	METAL MANUFACTURES NES		473.1		497.3		579.8		655.6	ART MANUFACT EN METAL NDA
695	TOOLS	N 1078	0.1	N 10000	0.1		119.1	W 39062	119.1	OUTILS A MAIN
6953	OTHER HAND TOOLS		75.7	N 10000	0.1		93.2	W 31355	90.1	AUTRES OUTILS A MAIN
697	BASE MTL HOUSEHOLD EQUIP		78.6		98.7	W 1	0.1		133.1	ART MENAGE MET COMMUNS
6974	BASE MTL DMSTC ARTIC NES		71.5		89.6	W 1	0.1	W 54218	119.8	ARTICLES NDA FONTE,FER,ETC
699	BASE METAL MFRS NES	W 127232	147.3	W 90928	148.1	W 69981	180.1	W 73950	206.1	ART MANUFACTURES MET NDA
7	MACHINES,TRANSPORT EQUIP		1509.0		1882.9		2370.9		2725.8	MACHINES MATERIEL TRANSPORT
71	POWER GENERATING EQUIPMT		171.8		149.7		173.0		221.2	MACHINES GENERATRICES
713	INTRNL COMBUS PSTN ENGIN		112.7		107.0		117.9	W 10	0.1	MOTEURS EXPL COMB INT, PIECE
72	MACHS FOR SPCL INDUSTRYS		155.8		212.5		241.0		279.0	MAC SPECIALES POUR INDUST
74	GENRL INDUSTRL MACHY NES		157.7		186.6		209.8		267.9	MACH APP INDUSTRIE
75	OFFICE MACHNES,ADP EQUIP		115.7		156.7		224.5		291.4	MACH BUREAU TRAIT AUTOM
752	AUTOMTIC DATA PROC EQUIP	N 1077336	59.5	N 1851192	83.4	N 1598521	94.0	N 1122922	158.0	MACH TRAIT INFORMATION
7524	DIGITL CENTRL STOR UNITS	N 46552	4.5	N 34355	3.0	N 133030	22.3	N 805218	127.9	UNITES MEMOIRE CENTRALES
759	OFFICE,ADP MCH PTS,ACCES	W 447	53.0	W 477	67.4	W 967	122.9	W 835	125.2	PIECES DU 751 ET 752
7599	ACCTG,ETC,ADP MCH PTS,AC	W 357	52.2	W 391	66.4	W 823	121.3	W 710	123.8	PIECES DU 751 ET 752
76	TELECOMM,SOUND EQUIPMENT		48.3		69.7		137.9		136.2	EQUIPMENT DE TELECOM
77	ELECTRIC MACHNRY NES ETC		228.5		299.2		430.5		534.9	MACH APP ELECT NDA
772	SWITCHGEAR ETC,PARTS NES	N 407	0.1	N 4101	0.1	N 5461	0.1	W 8538	103.0	APP COUPURE,SECT ETC
776	TRANSISTORS,VALVES,ETC	N 124943	0.3	N 283330	0.1		102.5	N 1	0.1	LAMPES,TUBES,VALVES
778	ELECTRICAL MACHINERY NES		72.6	W 18	0.4		106.2	N 244793	0.1	AUTRES MACH ELECT NDA
78	ROAD VEHICLES		568.1		717.4		876.9		871.8	VEHICULES ROUTIERS
781	PASS MOTOR VEH EXC BUSES	N 21022	89.7	N 26776	144.8	N 32255	181.4	N 38029	239.3	AUTO TRANSPORT PERSONNES
784	MOTOR VEH PRTS,ACCES NES		185.2		251.4	W 16	0.2		277.8	PIECES 722,781,782,783
7841	MOTOR VEHICLE CHASSIS	N 7588	66.9	N 11747	119.6	N 12384	108.4	N 10457	99.9	CHASSIS 722,781,782,783
7849	OTHER MOTOR VEHCL PARTS	W 43505	114.3	W 41807	127.2	W 47877	162.8	W 51967	176.2	PIECES 722,781,782,783
785	CYCLES,ETC MOTRZD OR NOT		227.9		229.4		323.0	N 2	0.1	MOTOCYCLES SCOOTERS
7853	INVAL CARR, PTS OF 785	W 90804	128.7	W 71331	111.6		189.1		111.7	FAUTEUILS INVALIDES,PIECES
78539	PARTS,ACCES NES OF 785	W 90804	128.7	W 71331	111.6	W 98060	189.1	W 66143	111.7	PIECES DU 785
8	MISC MANUFACTURED GOODS		4293.4		5406.3		6045.2		6124.6	ART MANUFACTURES DIVERS
831	*TRAVEL GOODS,HANDBAGS	MN 72194	198.8	MN 81384	253.7	MN 86914	309.3		245.2	ARTICLES DE VOYAGE ETC
83101	HANDBAGS NES	MN 42501	115.5	MN 41387	142.4	MN 42151	156.5	MN 895750	124.9	SACS A MAIN
83109	OTHER TRAVEL BAGS,CASES	MN 28890	71.5	MN 39075	98.4	MN 43861	133.9	W 3584	112.8	AUT CONTENANTS SIMILAIRES
84	CLOTHING AND ACCESSORIES		2977.0		3712.0		4124.1		4231.1	VETEMENTS

5. General Exports F.O.B. by Commodities according to the S.I.T.C. (Rev. 2) in million U.S. Dollars
Exportations Générales F.O.B. par Produits d'après la C.T.C.I. (Rév. 2) en millions de Dollars E.U.

SITC CTCI	COMMODITY	1993		1994		1995		1996		PRODUIT
		QUANTITY QUANTITE	VALUE VALEUR	QUANTITY QUANTITE	VALUE VALEUR	QUANTITY QUANTITE	VALUE VALEUR	QUANTITY QUANTITE	VALUE VALEUR	
842	MENS OUTERWEAR NOT KNIT	MN 19644	103.6	MN 27629	156.9	MN 33824	163.1	MN 36633	166.5	VET DESSUS POUR HOMMES
843	WOMENS OUTERWEAR NONKNIT	MN 217389	1076.8	MN 252102	1409.3	MN 306286	1568.8	N 1589	0.1	VET DESSUS FEMMES MAT TEX
8433	— DRESSES	MN 26628	199.9	MN 31850	286.0	MN 42433	374.1	MN 47205	399.1	ROBES EN MAT–TEXTILES
8434	— SKIRTS	MN 24093	123.2	MN 35323	194.0	MN 42479	202.4	MN 35122	173.1	JUPES EN MAT TEXTILES
8435	— BLOUSES	MN 110820	491.9	MN 126334	617.7	MN 151846	661.2	MN 152670	662.1	BLOUSES FEM MAT TEXTILES
8439	— OTHER OUTER GARMENTS	MN 47356	188.2	MN 49726	214.7	MN 61023	242.0		246.4	AUT VET DES FEM MAT TEXT
844	UNDER GARMENTS NOT KNIT	MN 123560	522.9	MN 155846	724.6	MN 170387	827.8	MN 182784	871.4	VETEMENT DESSOUS MAT TEX
8441	— MENS SHIRTS	MN 105115	464.3	MN 134461	659.0	MN 145663	755.1	MN 154151	797.3	CHEMISES HOMMES MAT TEXT
84411	—— OF COTTON	MN 88271	414.7	MN 113029	604.5	MN 130243	714.2	MN 146563	748.8	CHEMISES HOMMES DE COTON
845	OUTERWEAR KNIT NONELASTC	MN 103639	325.4	MN 98344	338.6	MN 106807	348.8	MN 107026	377.0	VET DESSOUS,ACCES BONNET
8451	— JERSEYS,PULLOVERS ETC	MN 27023	111.3	MN 25071	116.1	MN 26247	118.9	MN 32262	135.1	CHANDAILS,PULL–OVERS ETC
8459	— OTHER,CLTHG ACCESRYS	MN 66850	163.5	MN 65205	175.7	MN 73086	185.5	MN 67998	201.1	AUT VET DESSUS DE BONNE
846	UNDER GARMENTS KNITTED	MN 197268	417.1	MN 183614	480.3	MN 218878	608.3		636.9	SOUS VETS DE BONNETERIE
8462	— OF COTTON NON ELASTIC	MN 78996	149.4	MN 78179	167.2	MN 92832	213.7	MN 159853	410.0	SOUS–VET BONNET COTON
84629	—— OTHER	MN 78996	149.4	MN 78179	167.2	MN 92832	213.7	MN 159853	410.0	AUT SOUS–VET BONNET COTON
8463	— OF SYNTH FBR NONELAST	MN 117486	267.0	MN 104308	312.1	MN 124460	393.2		225.9	SOUS–VET BONNET FIB SYNT
84632	—— MENS SHIRTS	MN 114457	265.3	MN 101362	310.5	MN 118424	389.9	MN 187665	222.4	CHEMISES DE BON FIB SYNMT
847	TEXTILE CLTHNG ACCES NES		140.6		172.7		148.2		124.1	ACCES VET MAT TEXT NDA
8471	— NOT KNITTED		135.1		165.3		139.8		106.7	ACCES VET MAT TEX NON BON
84712	SHAWLS,VEILS ETC,NOT KNT	MN 86406	125.1	MN 105428	154.1	MN 88735	127.0	MN 66560	94.9	ECHARPES ETC MAT TEXT
848	HEADGEAR,NONTXTL CLOTHNG		390.9		429.9		459.5	W 1	0.1	VET ACCES MAT AUT QUE TEX
8481	LEATHER CLOTHES,ACCESSOR	MN 16892	369.2	MN 15191	407.4	MN 17217	435.3	W 10377	452.7	VET ACCES MAT CUIR ARTIF
851	*FOOTWEAR	MP 37688	280.0	MP 39773	345.8	MP 38285	345.1	MP 41774	347.2	CHAUSSURES
85102	FOOTWEAR LEATHER	MP 35346	273.0	MP 36688	336.5	MP 34689	339.2	MP 36816	341.1	CHAUS SEMELLES EN CUIR
89	MISC MANUFCTRD GOODS NES		737.0		971.5		1127.0		1132.4	ART MANUFACTURES DIVERS
893	ARTICLES OF PLASTIC NES		192.3		0.1	W 449	3.6	W 38	0.1	OUVRAGES EN MAT DIVIS 58
8931	PLSTC PACKG CONTNRS,LIDS	W 19998	82.5	W 18942	56.0	W 23147	46.8	W 29909	55.8	ART TRANSP EMBALLAGE ETC
8939	MISC PLASTIC ARTICLES	W 27355	108.7	W 36736	160.7	W 35603	190.7	W 35531	120.9	ART DIVERS EN MAT DIV 58
89399	OTHR PLASTC ARTICLES NES	W 20419	95.9	W 29107	143.3	W 26785	173.4	W 28828	104.6	AUT OUV MAT DIV 58
897	GOLD,SILVER WARE,JEWELRY		336.3		446.7		510.6		552.1	BIJOUTERIE,ORFEVRERIE
8973	PREC JEWLRY,GLD–SILVWARE		320.6		431.7		495.5		533.1	BIJOUX OR,ARGENT ORFEVRE
89731	PRECIOUS METAL JEWELLERY		317.9		429.9		493.6		530.3	ART BIJOUTERIE,JOAILLER
898	MUSICAL INSTRUMENTS,PTS	N 6209	5.2	N 6862	0.2		164.3		168.8	INSTRUMENTS DE MUSIQUE
8983	SOUND RECRDNG TAPE,DISCS	MN 35035	69.6	MN 47157	120.4	MN 32216	154.9	MN 16282	158.9	SUPPORTS SON POUR 763
89832	RECORDED DISCS,TAPES ETC	MN 13786	47.5	MN 20320	87.9	N 8263091	126.5	N 8079384	149.2	DISQUES,PHONO,BANDES
9	GOODS NOT CLASSD BY KIND		362.7		445.3		511.2		587.9	ART TRANSACT NON CLASSES
931	*SPECIAL TRANSACTIONS		362.3		445.0		511.0		587.4	TRANS.SPECIALES

1. HISTORICAL SERIES, 1962–1997 SPECIAL TRADE, IMPORTS C.I.F., EXPORTS F.O.B.
SERIES HISTORIQUES, 1962–1997 COMMERCE SPECIAL, IMPORTATIONS C.A.F., EXPORTATIONS F.O.B

YEAR ANNEE	VALUE IN MILLION U.S. DOLLARS VALEUR EN MILLION U.S. DOLLARS MERCHANDISE –MARCHANDISE		GOLD –OR		CONVERSION FACTORS FACTEURS DE CONVERSION CENTS E.U. PAR		INDEX NUMBERS –INDICES QUANTUM		UNIT VALUE VALEUR UNITAIRE	
	IMPORTS	EXPORTS	IMPORTS	EXPORTS	IMPORTS	EXPORTS	IMPORTS	EXPORTS	IMPORTS	EXPORTS
1962	647.00	663.70								
1963	521.40	697.90								
1964	679.90	724.20								
1965	694.70	707.70								
1966	526.70	678.70								
1967	649.20	665.40								
1968	715.80	730.70								
1969	780.70	853.70								
1970	1001.50	1108.10								
1971	1102.80	1233.60								
1972	1561.70	1777.70								
1973	2729.10	3210.80								
1974	3841.90	7426.30								
1975	4769.80	7102.50								
1976	5673.10	8546.50								
1977	6230.30	10852.60								
1978	6690.40	11643.20								
1979	7202.30	15590.10								
1980	10834.40	23950.40						92		157
1981	13272.20	25164.50						75		157
1982	16859.90	22328.30						72		153
1983	16351.80	21145.90						87		136
1984	13882.10	21887.90						81		133
1985	10259.10	18586.70						91		125
1986	10718.40	16075.00						98		87
1987	12890.70	17135.01						94		88
1988	13248.50	19465.01						93		82
1989	16360.00	22159.50						112		82
1990	21837.01	25673.90						100		100
1991	25868.80	29142.00						128		88
1992	27279.60	33966.90						141		84
1993	28327.81	36823.01						148		77
1994	31983.01	40055.01						163		50
1995	40630.00	45417.01						171		57
1996	42929.01	49814.00						179		60
1997	41693.30	53443.60								

2. IMPORTS BY BROAD ECONOMIC CATEGORY AND EXPORTS BY INDUSTRIAL ORIGIN. (PERCENTAGE OF TOTAL VALUE)
IMPORTATIONS PAR CATEGORIES ECONOMIQUES ET EXPORTATIONS PAR BRANCHE D'ACTIVITE.(EN POURCENTAGE DE LA VALEUR TOTALE)

IMPORTS – IMPORTATIONS

	1991	1992	1993	1994	1995	1996	1997
TOTAL IMPORTS–IMPORTATIONS TOTALES	100.	100.	100.	100.	100.	100.	100.
1 FOOD BEV–ALIMENTATION BOISSONS	4.1	5.2	4.7	5.5	6.9	8.6	6.4
11 PRIMARY–PRODUITS DE BASE	2.7	2.9	3.2	3.8	3.7	4.6	4.1
111 FOR INDUSTRY–POUR L'INDUSTRIE	2.3	2.4	2.6	3.1	3.0	3.9	3.3
112 FOR HOUSEHOLDS–POUR LES MENAGES	0.3	0.5	0.6	0.7	0.7	0.7	0.8
12 PROCESSED–PRODUITS ELABORES	1.5	2.4	1.5	1.8	3.2	4.0	2.3
121 FOR INDUSTRY–POUR L'INDUSTRIE	0.4	1.0	0.6	0.4	0.7	0.8	0.8
122 FOR HOUSEHOLDS–POUR LES MENAGES	1.1	1.3	0.9	1.3	2.5	3.3	1.5
2 IND SUPPLIES–APPROV INDUSTRIELS	38.9	40.9	41.9	41.9	42.4	39.0	38.8
21 PRIMARY–PRODUITS DE BASE	5.8	5.7	5.5	5.6	6.0	5.4	4.9
22 PROCESSED–PRODUITS ELABORES	33.1	35.2	36.4	36.3	36.4	33.6	33.9
3 FUELS–COMBUSTIBLES	8.7	7.5	7.5	7.5	7.3	8.5	9.5
31 PRIMARY–PRODUITS DE BASE	4.6	3.9	3.3	3.4	3.3	3.6	3.6
32 PROCESSED–PRODUITS ELABORES	4.1	3.6	4.1	4.1	4.0	4.9	5.9
321 MOTOR SPIRIT–ESSENCE	4.0	3.4	0.1	0.0	0.2	0.1	0.3
322 OTHER–AUTRES	0.1	0.2	4.0	4.0	3.8	4.8	5.6
4 MACHINERY–EQUIPEMENT	36.0	36.6	35.1	30.8	29.6	32.0	33.1
41 CAPITAL EQUIPMENT–MACHINES	32.8	33.1	31.4	27.1	26.4	28.8	29.8
42 PARTS–PIECES ACCESSOIRES	3.2	3.5	3.7	3.7	3.2	3.1	3.3
5 TRANSPORT–TRANSPORT	10.0	7.1	8.4	11.9	11.1	9.6	9.6
51 PASSENGER CARS–AUTOMOBILES	0.9	0.6	0.7	0.3	0.4	0.5	0.6
52 OTHER–AUTRES	3.2	1.9	1.8	2.5	1.8	1.5	1.3
521 INDUSTRIAL–INDUSTRIELS	3.2	1.9	1.8	2.5	1.8	1.5	1.3
522 NON INDUSTRIAL–NON INDUSTRIEL	0.0	0.0	0.0	0.0	0.0	0.0	0.0
53 PARTS–PIECES ACCESSOIRES	5.9	4.6	5.9	9.1	8.9	7.6	7.6
6 CONSUM GOODS–BIENS CONSOMMATION	2.0	2.0	2.1	2.1	2.3	2.1	2.4
61 DURABLE–DURABLES	0.7	0.7	0.6	0.6	0.7	0.6	0.7
62 SEMI DURABLE–SEMI DURABLES	0.7	0.8	0.9	0.8	0.8	0.8	0.8
63 NON DURABLE–NON DURABLES	0.5	0.6	0.7	0.7	0.7	0.7	0.9
7 GOODS NES–BIENS NDA	0.3	0.5	0.4	0.3	0.4	0.2	0.2

EXPORTS – EXPORTATIONS

	1991	1992	1993	1994	1995	1996	1997
TOTAL EXPORTS–EXPORTATIONS TOTALES	100.	100.	100.	100.	100.	100.	100.
1 AGRICULTURE	11.1	9.6	9.7	11.1	11.3	10.3	8.6
2 MINING QUARRY–INDUS EXTRACTIVES	37.2	32.3	28.2	26.6	26.3	26.7	25.4
3 MANUFACTURING–IND MANUFACTUR	51.7	58.1	62.1	62.3	62.5	63.1	66.0
31 FOOD BEV TOBACCO–ALIM BOISS TAB	3.9	4.1	4.2	5.2	4.8	5.1	5.8
32 TEXTILES–INDUSTRIES TEXTILES	17.1	21.5	20.9	18.6	17.5	16.7	12.2
33 WOOD & PRODUCTS–BOIS & PRODUITS	12.6	12.4	15.0	13.0	11.0	10.3	8.8
34 PAPER & PRODUCTS–PAPIER & PRODT	1.1	1.2	1.5	1.8	3.2	2.8	2.7
35 CHEMICALS–INDUSTRIES CHIMIQUES	7.7	7.5	6.5	6.7	8.3	8.9	7.8
36 NON METAL MIN–MIN NON METAL	0.8	1.0	0.9	0.8	0.8	0.8	0.6
37 BASIC METAL–IND METAL BASE	3.1	2.5	2.1	2.4	3.0	2.5	2.2
38 METAL MANUF–MANUF METAL	4.6	6.9	9.5	11.2	11.9	13.5	11.7
39 OTH MANUF IND–AUTRES MANUF	0.8	1.1	1.7	2.7	2.0	2.5	14.3

3. TRADE BY PRINCIPAL COUNTRIES OF ORIGIN AND DESTINATION (VALUE IN MILLION U.S. DOLLARS)
ECHANGES SELON LES PRINCIPAUX PAYS D'ORIGINE ET DE DESTINATION (VALEUR EN MILLIONS DE DOLLARS EU)

COUNTRIES–PAYS	SPECIAL IMPORTS C.I.F. IMPORTATIONS SPECIALES C.A.F				
	1993	1994	1995	1996	1997
World	28327.8	31983.5	40628.7	42928.5	41679.8
Africa	140.5	331.5	607.9	642.9	684.8
Americas	4289.9	4839.5	6654.4	6934.5	7047.6
– Northern America	3664.5	4084.6	5566.6	5845.4	6133.7
– LAIA	609.8	715.0	1071.7	1061.9	874.5
– CACM	4.6	18.8	1.9	2.8	2.6
– Caribbean	3.0	1.9	0.7	0.5	33.5
– Rest of America	7.9	19.2	13.4	23.9	3.3
Asia excl fmr USSR	14997.9	17725.7	21761.8	22239.9	21875.4
– Middle East	1056.7	1326.0	1642.4	1562.7	1605.9
Asia former USSR					28.3
Europe excl fmr USSR	7169.0	7091.3	8885.6	9879.8	8901.5
– European Union	6650.7	6612.1	8175.2	9233.6	8335.6
– Eastern Europe	100.8	132.6	207.8	142.5	142.6
– Rest of Europe	417.6	346.6	502.5	503.7	423.4
Europe former USSR	96.5	220.3	438.1	378.4	332.3
Oceania	1575.4	1732.8	2225.0	2782.6	2684.1
Other	58.6	42.4	56.0	70.3	125.8
Japan/Japon	6248.4	7740.1	9216.8	8504.0	8252.3
USA/Etats–Unis d'Amer	3254.5	3587.8	4755.9	5059.8	5444.3
Germany/Allemagne	2072.4	2472.7	2819.2	3001.4	2628.7
Singapore/Singapour	1793.3	1877.1	2367.5	2875.3	3410.9
Korea, Republic of	2103.1	2165.9	2451.3	2411.4	2321.8
Australia/Australie	1399.4	1542.0	2015.5	2535.1	2426.7
Other Asia n.e.s.	1317.9	1455.0	1828.2	1669.7	1590.7
China/Chine	936.0	1369.0	1495.2	1597.6	1518.0
France, Monaco	853.4	788.3	1063.6	1006.0	1019.4
United Kingdom	782.0	710.1	902.5	1117.8	1084.4
Italy/Italie	523.2	667.8	791.0	1212.1	917.9
Malaysia/Malaisie	517.4	578.8	767.0	823.7	864.8
Thailand/Thaïlande	235.3	406.2	737.1	1095.4	866.7
Saudi Arabia	351.1	680.2	943.3	664.6	587.7
Canada	410.0	496.8	810.7	785.6	682.4
Netherlands/Pays–Bas	626.0	563.7	842.1	493.0	565.9
India/Inde	335.4	318.3	478.8	866.2	697.4
Sweden/Suède	455.5	356.1	354.1	718.7	482.0
Iran (Islamic Rep of)	503.0	248.7	257.0	453.6	444.2
Brazil/Brésil	288.3	313.5	413.7	412.8	352.3
Belgium–Luxembourg	339.8	292.0	401.1	393.6	339.5
Switzerland,Liechtenst.	333.4	266.2	380.6	370.2	335.3
Finland/Finlande	265.5	241.3	252.0	330.8	373.3
Russian Federation	96.5	220.3	438.1	378.4	288.3
Spain/Espagne	261.8	174.1	219.3	345.3	370.4
Austria/Autriche	277.7	186.8	315.3	303.8	286.1
China, Hong Kong SAR	247.2	240.5	274.6	262.3	325.4
Chile/Chili	134.7	197.6	291.3	260.2	186.5
New Zealand	161.0	156.2	205.7	244.5	212.0
Kuwait/ Koweït	70.1	176.8	195.9	202.0	278.6
Argentina/Argentine	107.1	110.8	224.8	213.9	214.7
Denmark/Danemark	158.4	105.9	105.1	191.0	158.9
Viet Nam	39.1	78.8	156.8	204.4	117.3
Pakistan	59.3	32.3	102.6	189.0	128.9
Nigeria/Nigéria	0.7	26.2	172.9	149.3	141.8
Other Africa n.e.s.	22.4	116.2	206.0	109.9	
Norway,Svalbard and JM	78.1	73.8	108.3	107.3	67.2
Philippines	57.1	65.3	81.3	89.6	127.0
So. African Customs Un				153.9	255.0
Mexico/Mexique	58.2	41.6	92.5	113.9	62.7

COUNTRIES–PAYS	SPECIAL EXPORTS F.O.B. EXPORTATIONS SPECIALES F.O.B.				
	1993	1994	1995	1996	1997
Monde	36822.8	40053.4	45418.0	49814.7	53443.6
Afrique	460.8	582.9	621.3	639.2	771.9
Amériques	6002.1	6710.9	7440.0	7939.2	8499.1
– Amérique du Nord	5534.0	6150.3	6680.7	7162.7	7554.5
– ALAI	270.2	363.4	524.6	564.4	673.2
– MCAC	7.9	5.6	7.6	8.7	30.1
– Caraïbes	37.3	33.7	21.6	22.0	70.0
– Autre Amérique	152.7	157.9	205.4	181.4	171.3
Asie anc. URSS exclus	23772.8	25630.1	29060.9	31685.1	33969.4
– Moyen–Orient	1369.9	1241.2	1509.5	1625.0	1909.0
Asie ancienne URSS					6.7
Europe anc. URSS exclus	5585.4	6241.0	7067.1	8069.6	8426.2
– Union Européenne	5392.1	5949.4	6760.3	7723.3	8099.5
– Europe de l'Est	106.1	173.3	191.0	212.0	184.2
– Autre de l'Europe	87.2	118.3	115.8	134.4	142.4
Europe ancienne URSS	125.2	90.7	134.2	134.0	107.8
Océanie	875.4	796.3	1094.3	1347.5	1662.4
Autre	1.0	1.6	0.2	0.0	
Japan/Japon	11172.0	10929.0	12288.3	12885.2	12485.0
USA/Etats–Unis d'Amer	5229.8	5828.6	6321.7	6794.7	7154.5
Singapore/Singapour	3372.0	4149.7	3766.7	4564.6	5467.9
Korea, Republic of	2220.5	2593.0	2916.7	3281.0	3462.2
China/Chine	1249.5	1321.7	1741.7	2057.5	2229.3
Other Asia n.e.s.	1442.8	1646.9	1766.2	1627.3	1796.8
Netherlands/Pays–Bas	1086.4	1323.5	1452.4	1666.6	1842.4
China, Hong Kong SAR	900.4	1321.5	1657.1	1624.8	1785.1
Germany/Allemagne	1178.2	1263.4	1381.6	1489.0	1465.7
United Kingdom	1004.9	1038.2	1128.6	1192.9	1238.1
Australia/Australie	773.7	705.4	915.2	1201.5	1517.4
Malaysia/Malaisie	586.0	738.5	986.6	1109.7	1357.2
Italy/Italie	614.8	660.7	783.7	743.6	826.2
Thailand/Thaïlande	467.7	401.3	702.9	822.6	848.4
Spain/Espagne	332.7	453.9	534.6	812.7	888.1
United Arab Emirates	490.3	522.6	519.1	601.2	745.8
Belgium–Luxembourg	365.7	409.3	538.7	681.6	795.7
Philippines	285.0	365.1	590.3	688.4	794.1
France, Monaco	499.9	426.1	519.8	564.1	503.6
Saudi Arabia	556.3	413.1	448.2	515.6	579.3
India/Inde	99.9	277.7	381.0	531.0	689.5
Canada	304.2	321.7	359.0	368.1	399.7
Viet Nam	206.8	246.0	287.6	364.1	390.3
Egypt/Egypte	175.2	141.1	195.1	180.9	210.6
Brazil/Brésil	41.0	75.8	201.5	210.4	255.9
Panama	130.7	141.0	183.8	152.3	156.9
Pakistan	122.6	142.4	119.3	124.8	167.1
Mexico/Mexique	140.4	144.3	88.4	127.8	167.8
Denmark/Danemark	97.7	109.7	111.3	125.8	145.8
Russian Federation	125.2	90.7	134.2	134.0	86.7
Bangladesh	101.0	85.7	90.3	117.1	144.4
Sri Lanka	85.1	80.8	103.0	107.0	137.5
Turkey/Turquie	77.4	64.7	126.5	113.6	128.1
Poland/Pologne	60.8	98.7	105.4	117.1	87.2
New Zealand	61.3	51.6	129.8	100.7	84.8
Algeria/Algérie	64.6	186.4	83.2	27.8	42.0
Sweden/Suède	46.3	47.9	50.3	158.6	78.6
Iran (Islamic Rep of)	14.7	30.9	132.2	98.9	91.0
Myanmar	39.8	35.2	60.4	78.0	149.7
Greece/Grèce	45.4	63.1	78.9	85.6	88.6

(VALUE AS PERCENTAGE OF WORLD TOTAL)(VALEURS EN POURCENTAGE DU TOTAL MONDIAL)

	1988	1989	1990	1991	1992	1993	1994	1995	1996	1997
Africa	1.5	1.2	0.8	0.8	0.8	0.5	1.0	1.5	1.5	1.6
Americas	16.9	18.2	15.8	16.8	17.5	15.1	15.1	16.4	16.2	16.9
– Northern America	15.2	15.5	13.4	14.5	15.7	12.9	12.8	13.7	13.6	14.7
– LAIA	1.6	2.6	2.3	2.2	1.8	2.2	2.2	2.6	2.5	2.1
– CACM	0.0	0.0	0.1	0.0	0.0	0.0	0.1	0.0	0.0	0.0
– Caribbean	0.1	0.1	0.0	0.0	0.0	0.0	0.0	0.0	0.0	0.1
– Rest of America	0.0	0.0	0.0	0.0	0.0	0.0	0.1	0.0	0.1	0.0
Asia excl fmr USSR	53.2	53.7	54.8	54.6	52.3	52.9	55.4	53.6	51.8	52.5
– Middle East	5.1	5.0	5.8	4.3	4.0	3.7	4.1	4.0	3.6	3.9
Asia former USSR										0.1
Europe excl fmr USSR	22.7	19.5	22.1	21.7	23.3	25.3	22.2	21.9	23.0	21.4
– European Union	20.5	17.6	20.1	20.0	21.9	23.5	20.7	20.1	21.5	20.0
– Eastern Europe	0.5	0.7	0.5	0.4	0.3	0.4	0.4	0.5	0.3	0.3
– Rest of Europe	1.7	1.2	1.4	1.3	1.1	1.5	1.1	1.2	1.2	1.0
Europe former USSR	0.3	0.3	0.2	0.2	0.2	0.3	0.7	1.1	0.9	0.8
Oceania	5.1	6.3	6.0	5.8	5.7	5.6	5.4	5.5	6.5	6.4
Other	0.3	0.8	0.3	0.2	0.2	0.2	0.1	0.1	0.2	0.3
Japan/Japon	25.6	23.0	24.3	24.5	22.0	22.1	24.2	22.7	19.8	19.8
USA/Etats–Unis d'Amer	13.1	13.6	11.5	13.1	14.0	11.5	11.2	11.7	11.8	13.1
Germany/Allemagne				8.0	7.8	7.3	7.7	6.9	7.0	6.3
Singapore/Singapour	6.8	6.9	5.8	6.6	6.1	6.3	5.9	5.8	6.7	8.2
Korea, Republic of	2.8	3.4	4.5	5.6	6.9	7.4	6.8	6.0	5.6	5.6
Australia/Australie	4.4	5.7	5.4	5.3	5.2	4.9	4.8	5.0	5.9	5.8
Other Asia n.e.s.	4.7	6.0	6.2	5.1	4.8	4.7	4.5	4.5	3.9	3.8
China/Chine	3.3	3.2	3.0	3.2	2.8	3.3	4.3	3.7	3.7	3.6
France, Monaco	3.5	2.5	2.9	2.1	3.0	3.0	2.5	2.6	2.3	2.4
United Kingdom	2.6	2.2	2.0	2.3	2.6	2.8	2.2	2.2	2.6	2.6

	1988	1989	1990	1991	1992	1993	1994	1995	1996	1997
Afrique	1.4	1.0	0.8	1.4	1.2	1.3	1.5	1.4	1.3	1.4
Amériques	16.8	16.5	14.0	13.3	14.8	16.3	16.8	16.4	15.9	15.9
– Amérique du Nord	16.5	16.2	13.6	12.6	13.9	15.0	15.4	14.7	14.4	14.1
– ALAI	0.1	0.2	0.3	0.3	0.4	0.7	0.9	1.2	1.1	1.3
– MCAC	0.0	0.0	0.0	0.0	0.0	0.0	0.0	0.0	0.0	0.1
– Caraïbes	0.0	0.0	0.0	0.1	0.1	0.1	0.1	0.0	0.0	0.1
– Autre Amérique	0.1	0.1	0.1	0.3	0.4	0.4	0.4	0.5	0.4	0.3
Asie anc. URSS exclus	67.9	68.6	70.4	69.3	66.3	64.6	64.0	64.0	63.6	63.6
– Moyen–Orient	2.0	2.5	2.7	3.2	3.7	3.7	3.1	3.3	3.3	3.6
Asie ancienne URSS										0.0
Europe anc. URSS exclus	11.9	11.3	12.5	13.6	14.9	15.2	15.6	15.6	16.2	15.8
– Union Européenne	11.4	10.7	12.0	13.1	14.5	14.6	14.9	14.9	15.5	15.2
– Europe de l'Est	0.4	0.4	0.3	0.3	0.2	0.3	0.4	0.4	0.4	0.3
– Autre de l'Europe	0.1	0.2	0.2	0.2	0.2	0.2	0.3	0.3	0.3	0.3
Europe ancienne URSS	0.2	0.5	0.3	0.1	0.2	0.3	0.2	0.3	0.3	0.2
Océanie	1.7	2.0	1.9	2.3	2.4	2.4	2.0	2.4	2.7	3.1
Autre	0.0	0.2	0.0	0.0	0.0	0.0	0.0	0.0	0.0	
Japan/Japon	41.7	42.2	42.5	36.9	31.7	30.3	27.3	27.1	25.9	23.4
USA/Etats–Unis d'Amer	16.0	15.8	13.1	12.0	13.0	14.2	14.6	13.9	13.6	13.4
Singapore/Singapour	8.6	8.1	7.4	8.3	9.8	9.2	10.4	8.3	9.2	10.2
Korea, Republic of	4.4	4.2	5.3	6.7	6.1	6.0	6.5	6.4	6.6	6.5
China/Chine	2.6	2.6	3.2	4.1	4.1	3.4	3.3	3.8	4.1	4.2
Other Asia n.e.s.	2.5	2.6	3.3	3.6	3.8	3.9	4.1	3.9	3.3	3.4
Netherlands/Pays–Bas	3.4	3.1	2.8	2.9	3.2	3.0	3.3	3.2	3.3	3.4
China, Hong Kong SAR	2.9	2.5	2.4	2.4	2.6	2.4	3.3	3.6	3.3	3.3
Germany/Allemagne				3.1	2.9	3.2	3.2	3.0	3.0	2.7
United Kingdom	1.8	1.7	2.0	2.2	2.5	2.7	2.6	2.5	2.4	2.3

4. Special Imports C.I.F. by Commodities according to the S.I.T.C. (Rev. 2) in million U.S. Dollars
Importations Spéciales C.A.F. par Produits d'après la C.T.C.I. (Rév. 2) en millions de Dollars E.U.

SITC CTCI	COMMODITY	1994 QUANTITY QUANTITE	1994 VALUE VALEUR	1995 QUANTITY QUANTITE	1995 VALUE VALEUR	1996 QUANTITY QUANTITE	1996 VALUE VALEUR	1997 QUANTITY QUANTITE	1997 VALUE VALEUR	PRODUIT
	ALL COMMODITIES		31983.5		40628.8		42928.5		41679.8	TOUS PRODUITS
0	FOOD AND LIVE ANIMALS		1895.7		3020.1		3926.6		2979.8	ALIMENTS,ANIMAUX VIVANTS
001	*LIVE ANIMALS FOR FOOD	W 21709	56.1	W 78012	126.6	W 122770	204.5	W 132288	193.1	ANIMAUX VIVANTS
0011	BOVINE SPECIES,LIVE	W 21507	45.2	W 76346	112.4	W 122394	190.5	W 131571	180.4	ESPECE BOVINE
00119	— OTHR THAN FR BREEDING	W 21070	43.6	W 75042	109.2	W 121060	187.5	W 130118	177.3	BOVINS NON REPRODUCTEURS
02	DAIRY PRODCTS,BIRDS'EGGS		122.9		223.4		191.9		150.3	PRODUITS LAITIERS,OEUFS
022	MILK AND CREAM	W 63425	97.1	W 91290	178.9	W 75041	150.4	W 71845	125.5	LAIT ET CREME
0224	MILK,CREAM PRESERVED ETC	W 54360	84.5	W 77323	153.9	W 63011	127.6	W 57557	103.3	LAIT,CREME CONS,CONC
02242	MILK DRY,1.5% FAT OR LES	W 44060	74.2	W 60692	136.2	W 45916	104.8	W 41034	81.9	LAIT POUDRE INF 1.5%
04	CEREALS AND PREPARATIONS		926.6		1551.5		2002.5		1106.1	CEREALES ET PRODUITS
041	WHEAT ETC UNMILLED	W 3297139	579.7	W 4054202	803.5	W 4116261	1050.4	W 3611930	776.6	FROMENT,EPEAUTRE
0412	OTHER WHEAT ETC UNMILLED	W 3295022	579.1	W 4054202	803.5	W 4111842	1049.0	W 3611921	776.6	AUTRE FROMENT NON MOULU
042	RICE	W 633048	157.4	W 1807875	514.5	W 2149758	766.4	W 349681	109.0	RIZ
0422	RICE SEMI-MILLED,MILLED	W 622426	153.3	W 1778967	504.5	W 2130032	759.6	W 157472	42.6	RIZ POLI,GLACE INCL BRISURES
04221	RICE MILLED UNBROKEN	W 271802	69.8	W 1309510	375.2	W 2040203	731.1	W 10950	5.4	RIZ POLI,GLACE EXCL BRISURES
04222	RICE BROKEN	W 350624	83.6	W 469457	129.3	W 89828	28.6	W 146523	37.2	BRISURES DE RIZ
044	MAIZE UNMILLED	W 1118284	153.6	W 973968	154.2	W 617348	132.9	W 1098353	171.7	MAIS NON MOULU
05	VEGETABLES AND FRUIT		197.8		240.5		249.7		275.1	LEGUMES ET FRUITS
054	VEG ETC FRSH,SMPLY PRSVD	W 239221	102.2	W 242869	125.2	W 198928	123.1	W 219506	144.6	LEGUMES FRAIS,CONG,SECS
06	SUGAR AND PREPS,HONEY		62.0		279.9		513.4		463.7	SUCRES ET PRODUITS
061	SUGAR AND HONEY	W 151497	56.0	W 611775	272.1	W 1311381	505.5	W 1298302	453.9	SUCRES ET MIEL
0611	RAW BEET AND CANE SUGAR	W 15207	5.9	W 231051	104.9	W 422400	180.0	W 610254	199.7	SUCRES BRUTS
0612	REFINED SUGAR ETC	W 103633	37.5	W 323403	145.7	W 685338	288.5	W 578026	231.8	SUCRES RAFFINES
081	*FEEDING STUFF FOR ANIML	W 1408968	416.6	W 1557601	460.4	W 1763145	603.3	W 1625033	611.2	NOURRITURE POUR ANIMAUX
0813	OILCAKE AND OTH RESIDUES	W 806674	172.4	W 988840	209.6	W 1215572	320.1	W 1060156	317.1	TOURTEAUX
08131	— OF SOYA BEANS	W 498592	121.2	W 681875	163.8	W 942292	266.0	W 868790	281.8	TOURTEAUX DE SOJA
0814	MEAT OR FISH MEAL FODDER	W 437293	166.7	W 324526	141.0	W 175935	110.7	W 145451	91.8	FARINES DE VIANDES,POISSONS
08142	FISH MEAL FODDER	W 247918	102.7	W 136752	77.9	W 133612	92.3	W 120570	81.0	FARINES DE POISSONS
0819	FOOD WASTE AND FEED NES	W 153993	75.5	W 228375	107.5	W 357836	169.1	W 415218	201.3	DECHETS,ALIMENTS NDA
08199	FODDER NES,INCL SWEETNED	W 93864	50.5	W 162395	83.4	W 307820	145.9	W 317090	157.4	PREPARATIONS FOURRAGERES
1	BEVERAGES AND TOBACCO		141.8		178.1		220.2		250.2	BOISSONS ET TABACS
12	TOBACCO AND MANUFACTURES		125.3		156.2		181.5		206.6	TABACS BRUTS FABRIQUES
121	TOBACCO UNMNFCTRD,REFUSE	W 40322	100.3	W 47953	115.5	W 45060	134.2	W 47108	157.8	TABACS BRUTS,DECHETS
1212	TOBACCO STRIPPED OR PART	W 15944	40.2	W 26936	64.5	W 29720	89.2	W 37421	125.2	TABACS PART ECOTES
2	CRUDE MATERLS,EXCL FUELS		2723.7		3624.1		3441.3		2958.8	MAT BRUTES NON COMESTIBLES
22	OIL SEEDS,OLEAGINOUS FRT		339.6		287.1		383.4		329.9	GRAINES,FRUITS OLEAGINEUX
222	SEEDS FOR'SOFT'FIXED OIL	W 958586	336.3	W 759157	282.3	W 916456	373.7	W 795415	322.7	GRAINES HUILES FIXES
2222	SOYA BEANS	W 800461	243.8	W 607393	180.6	W 746329	251.7	W 616375	206.7	FEVES DE SOJA
23	RUBBER, CRUDE		137.7		215.5		203.1		160.2	CAOUTCHOUC BRUT
233	RUBBER,SYNTHTIC,RECLAIMD	W 115677	134.8	W 139803	204.1	W 133777	195.9	W 125048	153.0	LATEX CAOUTCH SYNTH REGEN
2331	SYNTHETIC RUBBER ETC	W 115167	134.5	W 138699	203.5	W 130925	191.1	W 123887	152.1	LATEX CAOUTCH SYNTHETIQUE
251	*PULP AND WASTE PAPER	W 1853578	614.2	W 1738800	882.3	W 2134901	704.6	W 2327951	616.5	PATES A PAPIER,DECHETS
2511	WASTE PAPER,PPRBOARD ETC	W 1009510	176.2	W 1054154	309.9	W 1296954	234.2	W 1382589	159.0	DECHETS DE PAPIER
2516	CHEM WOOD PULP DISSOLVNG	W 158145	111.3	W 172430	182.8	W 193435	157.6	W 167908	109.5	PATES CHIMIQUES DE BOIS
2517	SODA,SULPHATE WOOD PULP	W 566504	271.1	W 357534	281.0	W 441929	224.8	W 600582	278.3	PATES CHIMIQUES AU SULFATE
25172	— BLEACHED,NONDISSOLVNG	W 483236	231.7	W 290098	230.1	W 391798	202.8	W 529977	250.2	PATES BLANCHIES
26	TEXTILE FIBRES AND WASTE		948.3		1244.8		1261.3		1034.0	FIBRES TEXTILES
263	COTTON	W 441630	701.4	W 459570	923.2	W 492783	980.6	W 468163	818.9	COTON
2631	RAW COTTON,EXCL LINTERS	W 440726	700.7	W 458440	922.3	W 492166	980.1	W 465417	816.0	COTON EN MASSE
266	SYNTHETIC FIBRES TO SPIN	W 123286	197.7	W 133347	279.1	W 119090	207.0	W 115087	182.0	FIBRES SYNTHETIQUES
2665	DISCN SYNTH FIBRE UNCMBD	W 83428	133.8	W 90379	189.4	W 75621	134.8	W 77451	117.5	DISCONTINUES EN MASSE
27	CRUDE FERTLZR,MINRLS NES		242.3		303.6		344.0		309.7	ENGRAIS MINERAUX BRUTS
278	OTHER CRUDE MINERALS	W 1115340	127.1	W 1254699	172.0	W 1362123	177.5	W 1492149	163.0	AUTRES MINERAUX BRUTS
28	METALLIFEROUS ORES,SCRAP		344.7		541.4		395.8		361.7	MINERAIS METAL,DECHETS
281	IRON ORE,CONCENTRATES	W 1606401	84.9	W 2507146	142.1	W 2512637	148.5	W 1870634	96.5	MINERAIS DE FER
282	IRON AND STEEL SCRAP	W 1023999	175.3	W 1462330	269.0	W 788479	132.8	W 869725	137.7	FERRAILLES
28209	— OF OTHR IRON OR STEEL	W 759884	132.0	W 1180290	219.4	W 744035	125.4	W 773221	123.1	FERRAILLES DE FER
287	BASE METAL ORES,CONC NES	W 385037	73.8	W 631533	124.0	W 377891	108.7	W 416578	115.2	MINERAIS METAUX COMMUNS
3	MINERAL FUELS ETC		2487.6		3095.0		3775.0		4142.0	COMBUSTIBLES MINERAUX LUB
33	PETROLEUM AND PRODUCTS		2461.9		3045.2		3746.2		4094.9	PETROLE ET DERIVES
333	CRUDE PETROLEUM	MW 9473	1073.2	MW 9261	1317.7	MW 9350	1519.0	MW 9126	1467.1	HUILES BRUTES DE PETROLE
334	PETROLEUM PRODUCTS,REFIN	W 6408555	1290.6	W 7857043	1604.8	MW 9821	2086.2	MW 11429	2451.7	PRODUITS RAFFINES
3341	GASOLINE,OTH LIGHT OILS	W 1462778	276.7	W 365012	70.7	W 197132	45.1	W 590468	128.7	ESSENCES POUR MOTEURS
33411	MOTOR,AVIATION SPIRIT	W 42689	8.1	W 358049	66.7	W 190359	41.5	W 579377	126.4	ESSENCES MOTEURS D'AVIONS
33412	SPIRIT TYPE JET FUEL	W 1420089	268.6							CARBUREACTEURS
3342	KEROSENE,OTH MEDIUM OILS	W 175001	41.6	W 1568905	270.1	W 1868810	429.3	W 1539659	355.2	PETR LAMPANTS,AUT HUIL
33421	KEROSENE INCL JET FUEL	W 117728	21.7	W 1568905	270.1	W 1868810	429.3	W 1539659	355.2	PETROLES LAMPANTS
3343	GAS OILS	W 3498028	582.9	W 4515668	783.6	W 4738525	963.6	W 5726838	1173.1	GAS OILS
3344	FUEL OILS,NES	W 773483	82.2	W 918194	119.9	W 2581382	337.5	W 2226917	315.1	FUEL OILS
3345	LUBS,PETROLEUM OILS NES	W 499265	307.4	W 489264	360.6	W 434815	310.8	W 1344883	479.8	HUILES LUBRIFIANTES
33451	LUBS(HIGH PETR CONT) ETC	W 468961	244.7	W 437563	273.0	W 379311	205.7	W 1282612	384.8	HUILES LUBRIF,H LOURDES
335	RESIDUAL PETRLM PROD NES	W 419192	98.2	W 506882	122.8	W 575770	141.1	W 831205	176.2	PRODUITS RESIDUELS NDA
4	ANIMAL,VEGETABLE OIL,FAT		104.3		104.4		101.1		115.0	HUILES,GRAISSES ANIM,VEG
5	CHEMCLS,RELATED PROD NES		4757.3		6130.2		5876.9		5768.9	PRODUITS CHIMIQUES
51	ORGANIC CHEMICALS		1609.8		2328.0		2226.8		2222.9	PROD CHIMIQ ORGANIQUES
511	HYDROCARBONS NES,DERIVS	W 889028	455.3	W 1000285	636.9	W 1016870	544.5	W 1481864	729.5	HYDROCARBURES NDA
5111	ACYCLIC HYDROCARBONS	W 361324	163.8	W 402037	207.6	W 319279	159.9	W 440826	233.2	HYDROCARBURES ACYCLIQUES
51111	ETHYLENE	W 308098	132.6	W 354809	175.6	W 198430	85.8	W 333063	174.7	ETHYLENE
5112	CYCLIC HYDROCARBONS	W 369779	168.5	W 462438	310.3	W 511892	265.0	W 873347	391.7	HYDROCARBURES CYCLIQUES
51124	XYLENES,CHEMICALLY PURE	W 144184	73.0	W 216642	187.8	W 268581	174.9	W 607416	289.1	XYLENES PURS
5113	HALOG DERIV OF HYDROCARB	W 156160	120.2	W 133842	115.3	W 183397	115.7	W 165798	100.6	DERIVES HALOGENES HYDROCAR
512	ALCOHOLS,PHENOLS ETC		224.0	W 562063	366.6	W 603145	332.4	W 578424	366.7	PHENOLS,PHENOLS-ALCOOLS
5121	ACYCLIC ALCOHOLS,DERIVS		165.0	W 534308	326.0	W 571355	288.7	W 543230	321.8	ALCOOLS ACYCLIQUES
51215	ETHYLENE GLYCOL	W 143225	64.6	W 226014	155.4	W 252301	161.5	W 283531	187.2	ETHYLENE-GLYCOL
513	CARBOXYLIC ACIDS ETC	W 360927	350.1	W 445407	563.5	W 488566	538.3	W 450213	408.7	ACIDES CARBOXYLIQUES
5137	MONOACIDS AND DERIVATIVS	W 107634	138.1	W 151158	210.3	W 130353	196.9	W 163980	203.9	ACIDES MONOCARBOXYLIQUES
5138	POLYACIDS AND DERIVATIVS	W 241239	188.0	W 286236	332.0	W 351031	318.4	W 280910	188.8	ACIDES POLYCARBOXYLIQUES
51389	OTH POLYACIDS ETC,DERIVS	W 220124	170.0	W 262389	299.8	W 324912	296.2	W 263401	175.3	ACIDES POLYCARBOXYLIQUES
514	NITROGEN-FNCTN COMPOUNDS	W 93782	245.1	W 99473	301.2	W 101869	296.6	W 105154	267.7	COMPOSES FONCT AZOTEES
5148	OTH NITROGN-FNCTN CMPNDS	W 62531	138.0	W 59561	158.0	W 66065	174.4	W 62937	151.2	AUTRES COMPOSES AZOTES
515	ORG-INORG COMPOUNDS ETC	W 55127	208.1	W 69604	296.6	W 77993	351.0	W 65956	292.2	COMPOSES ORGANO-MINERAUX
5156	HETEROCYCLIC CMPDS ETC	W 36364	110.4	W 45709	160.9	W 48018	164.0	W 38949	139.6	COMPOSES HETEROCYCLIQUES
516	OTHER ORGANIC CHEMICALS	W 116203	127.4		163.5	W 152207	164.2	W 149505	158.3	AUTRES PROD ORGANIQUES
52	INORGANIC CHEMICALS		447.0		522.5		526.7		504.8	PROD CHIM INORGANIQUES
522	INORG ELEMNTS,OXIDES,ETC	W 746420	235.6	W 646945	263.8	W 376637	235.1	W 479223	235.2	ELEMENTS INORGANIQUES
523	OTHR INORG CHEMICALS ETC	W 724203	210.6	W 835318	257.8	W 933998	290.0	W 819172	267.7	AUT PRODUITS CHIMIQUES INORG
5232	OTH MTL CMPD OF INRG ACD	W 588722	153.4	W 693785	190.0	W 801650	218.2	W 648148	186.6	SELS METALLIQUES
53	DYES,TANNING,COLOUR PROD		430.8		504.8		505.2		527.5	PROD TEINTURE,COLORANTS
531	SYNT DYE,NAT INDGO,LAKES	W 30545	213.5	W 31918	238.4	W 32235	245.3	W 39973	238.9	MAT COLOR ORGAN,LAQUES
5311	SYNTHIC ORGNIC DYESTUFFS	W 27464	188.8	W 28091	212.0	W 26613	204.9	W 31470	194.0	MAT COLOR ORGAN SYNTHET
533	PIGMENTS,PAINTS,ETC	W 113680	202.0	W 135175	251.2	W 137670	248.7	W 161207	276.4	PIGMENTS,PEINTURES,VERNIS

4. Special Imports C.I.F. by Commodities according to the S.I.T.C. (Rev. 2) in million U.S. Dollars
Importations Spéciales C.A.F. par Produits d'après la C.T.C.I. (Rév. 2) en millions de Dollars E.U.

SITC CTCI	COMMODITY	1994 QUANTITY QUANTITE	1994 VALUE VALEUR	1995 QUANTITY QUANTITE	1995 VALUE VALEUR	1996 QUANTITY QUANTITE	1996 VALUE VALEUR	1997 QUANTITY QUANTITE	1997 VALUE VALEUR	PRODUIT
5335	GLAZES,DRIERS,PUTTY ETC	W 49518	57.3	W 74824	90.2	W 85196	100.8	W 100320	130.5	PREPTNS COLOR UTILISES CERAM
541	*MEDICINAL,PHARM PRODUCT	MK 11081	190.7		249.7	MK 11271	265.2	MK 14169	262.7	PROD MEDICINAUX PHARMACEUT
55	PERFUME,CLEANING ETC PRD		220.9		242.8		259.2		283.1	PROD POUR PARFUM,TOILETTE
551	ESSENTL OILS,PERFUME,ETC	W 13410	130.5	W 29073	148.4	W 13655	165.3	W 13149	150.4	HUILES ESSENTIELLES
5514	MIXED PERFUME SUBSTANCES	W 12722	124.2	W 28338	140.6	W 12941	156.5	W 12278	143.2	MELANGES SUBSTAN ODORIFER
562	*FERTILIZERS,MANUFACTURE	W 485798	75.2	W 764162	133.8	W 1111433	214.9	W 1172383	220.6	ENGRAIS MANUFACTURES
58	PLASTIC MATERIALS ETC		1145.3		1390.7		1166.4		1067.7	MAT PLAST ARTIFICIELLES
582	PROD OF CONDENSATION ETC	W 187153	325.7	W 193999	429.1	W 181407	362.3	W 187579	316.8	PROD CONDENS,POLYCOND
5823	ALKYDS,OTHER POLYESTERS	W 88747	128.6	W 93005	201.4	W 83567	140.1	W 79885	104.5	ALKYDES ET AUT POLYESTERS
58231	— IN PRIMARY FORMS	W 82152	112.2	W 86305	182.2	W 79023	125.0	W 76859	95.0	SOUS FORMES PRIMAIRES
583	POLYMERIZATION ETC PRODS	W 725043	754.2	W 665160	893.5	W 614361	740.8	W 605587	695.2	PROD POLYMERISATION
5831	POLYETHYLENE	W 278570	221.3	W 212261	241.6	W 203053	206.3	W 204103	200.1	POLYETHYLENE
58311	— IN PRIMARY FORMS	W 269638	206.0	W 200199	219.3	W 183764	174.8	W 186220	173.6	POLYETHYLENE PRIMAIRES
5832	POLYPROPYLENE	W 156099	134.9	W 143228	172.1	W 125333	127.6	W 108794	95.6	POLYPROPYLENE
58321	— IN PRIMARY FORMS	W 151808	128.4	W 136123	158.5	W 116261	108.8	W 103238	87.2	POLYPROPYLENE PRIMAIRES
5839	OTH POLYMRZTION ETC PROD	W 173674	237.9	W 177641	273.0	W 164708	236.7	W 190278	261.0	AUT PROD POLYMER COPOLYM
59	CHEMICAL MATERIALS NES		623.6		740.7		698.9		659.2	MAT PROD CHIMIQUES NDA
592	STARCH,INULIN,GLUTEN,ETC	W 207678	120.1	W 291146	192.8	W 107551	122.1	W 222892	143.7	AMIDONS,INUL,GLUT FROM
598	MISCEL CHEM PRODUCTS NES	W 216684	482.6	W 237830	523.7	W 224168	541.0	W 227169	485.5	PROD DIV INDUST CHIM NDA
5982	ANTI–KNOCK PREPARTNS ETC	W 41944	113.2	W 50341	137.3	W 30130	86.0	W 35320	79.4	PREPARAT ANTIDETONANTES
5989	CHEM PRODUCTS,PREPS NES	W 150531	334.0	W 159053	343.4	W 171458	420.8	W 167982	371.0	PROD PREP CHIMIQUES NDA
59899	OTH CHEM PRODS,PREPS,NES	W 86612	171.4	W 98359	200.4	W 114340	265.6	W 112701	209.3	AUT PRODUITS CHIMIQUES NDA
6	BASIC MANUFACTURES		5386.8		6855.2		6844.7		6715.4	ART MANUFACTURES
61	LEATHER,DRESSED FUR,ETC		468.5		442.8		415.3		368.0	CUIRS,PELLETERIES
611	LEATHER	W 27783	346.5	W 27044	320.6	W 32077	286.5	W 29326	246.4	CUIRS,PEAUX PREPARES
6114	LEATHR BOVINE NES,EQUINE	W 25648	319.8	W 24126	291.2	W 25907	248.2	W 20784	205.4	CUIRS DE BOVINS
612	LEATHER ETC MANUFACTURES	W 20926	121.7	W 19160	121.8	W 20577	128.1	W 20180	120.7	OUVRAGES EN CUIRS NDA
6123	PREPRD PARTS OF FOOTWEAR	W 20708	118.9	W 18991	117.9	W 19697	122.5	W 19725	116.4	PARTIES DE CHAUSSURES
62	RUBBER MANUFACTURES NES		117.0		155.4		193.8		210.9	CAOUTCHOUC MANUFACTURE
64	PAPER,PAPERBOARD AND MFR		253.9		326.2		299.7		355.0	PAPIERS,CARTONS & OUVRAGES
641	PAPER AND PAPERBOARD	W 186831	194.2	W 157024	244.3	W 210320	213.0	W 271480	255.5	PAPIERS ET CARTONS
65	TEXTILE YARN,FABRICS,ETC		1175.3		1327.2		1288.4		1172.9	FILS,TISSUS,ARTICLES TEXTILE
651	TEXTILE YARN	W 81841	279.7	W 87758	320.0	W 71098	297.2	W 71578	269.9	FILS TEXTILES
6514	SYN FIB YRN,BULK,MONOFIL	W 42914	133.4	W 40002	144.6	W 35084	138.9	W 29052	102.2	FILS CONT 85% FIB TEXT SYNTH
6517	REGEN FIBRE YARN,MONOFIL	W 25055	97.5	W 28595	115.8	W 22898	97.7	W 22770	92.7	FILS TEXT ART NON VENTE DT
652	COTTON FABRICS,WOVEN	W 14158	111.0	W 19924	139.5	W 16159	141.7	W 17946	147.8	TISSUS DE COTON
6522	WOVEN COTTON BLEACHD,ETC	W 12417	104.3	W 18808	134.2	W 14974	136.9	W 15674	137.9	TISSUS COTON BLANCHIS ETC
653	WOVN MAN–MADE FIB FABRIC	W 36423	237.8	W 35653	231.7	W 29559	186.8	W 27985	177.3	TISSUS FIBRES SYNTH,ARTIF
6531	CONT SYNT WEAVES NONPILE	W 18353	136.0	W 20177	142.5	W 18158	116.9	W 17992	110.9	TISSUS FIBRES SYNTH CONTINUE
65315	CONT SYN TXTL FABRIC NES	W 18226	134.7	W 19955	139.5	W 17886	113.7	W 17732	109.4	TIS PLUS 85% TEXT SYNT CONT
655	KNITTED,ETC FABRICS	W 19972	160.9	W 23867	210.5	W 22224	194.1	W 25761	152.5	ETOF BONNETERIE PIECES ETC
6552	OTHER KNIT ETC FAB NONEL	W 19972	160.9	W 23867	210.5	W 22224	194.1	W 25761	152.5	ETOF BON NON ELAS NON SYNT
657	SPECIAL TXTL FABRC,PRODS	W 44677	290.4	W 47496	325.3	W 51449	356.8	W 50524	318.6	TISSUS SPECIAUX
6573	COATED ETC TEXTILES NES	W 23085	138.7	W 24447	152.8	W 27142	160.1	W 26771	150.0	TISSUS,ART MATIERE TEXT NDA
65732	PLASTIC COATED TEXTILES	W 16442	109.8	W 16631	119.7	W 17266	113.1	W 15713	97.6	TISSUS IMPREGNES
66	NONMETAL MINERAL MFS NES		340.7		478.5		521.4		500.6	ART MIN NON METALLIQUES
661	LIME,CEMENT,BLDG PRODS	W 927997	59.8	W 1852069	118.8	W 2065438	133.5	W 1848914	108.9	CHAUX,CIMENTS MAT CONSTR
662	CLAY,REFRACTORY BLDG PRD	W 114261	102.7	W 164119	146.2	W 168041	144.5	W 151651	123.5	MAT CONST REFRACTAIRES
6623	REFRACTORY BUILDING PROD	W 91843	95.0	W 112753	126.9	W 108899	121.4	W 108057	106.8	BRIQUES REFRACTAIRES
664	GLASS	W 44429	58.2	W 62055	76.8	W 64098	104.4	W 69382	130.9	VERRE
67	IRON AND STEEL		1684.1		2451.1		2370.8		2286.4	FER ET ACIER
671	PIG IRON ETC	W 599841	115.2	W 1132090	218.1	W 633392	143.9	W 532955	123.2	FONTE,SPIEGEL,POUDRES
672	IRON,STEEL PRIMARY FORMS	W 1241317	382.8	W 1953028	670.5	W 1774657	568.3	W 2199061	642.3	LINGOTS FER,ACIER
6725	IRN,STL BLOOMS,SLABS,ETC	W 924911	238.2	W 1388143	391.6	W 1376311	395.7	W 1718072	442.4	BLOOMS,BILLETTES FER ACIER
67251	IRN,SMPLE STL BLOOMS,ETC	W 924511	236.1	W 1387769	391.3	W 1375831	395.3	W 1717416	439.9	BLOOMS ETC NON ACIER FIN
6727	IRN,STL COIL FR REROLLNG	W 315904	144.4	W 564421	278.5	W 398163	172.5	W 480473	197.7	EBAUCHES POUR TOLES FER
67271	IRON,SIMPLE STEEL COILS	W 242483	104.8	W 481236	223.9	W 356689	149.7	W 431143	170.4	EBAUCHES NON EN ACIER
673	IRON,STEEL SHAPES ETC	W 356039	205.2	W 469798	278.2	W 465753	265.7	W 465032	244.6	BARRES,PROFIL FER,ACIER
674	IRN,STL UNIV,PLATE,SHEET	W 850030	586.8	W 979927	796.3	W 928128	746.8	W 877473	650.2	LARGES PLATS,TOLES
6744	IRN,STL HVY PLATE,ROLLED	W 132313	91.7	W 173198	126.9	W 134822	115.8	W 139247	92.9	TOLES LAMINEES PLUS 4.75 MM
6746	IRN,STL THIN PLATE,ROLLD	W 485631	323.2	W 553620	448.3	W 533685	412.9	W 498549	352.3	TOLES LAM MOINS 3MM
67461	— OF IRON OR SIMPLE STL	W 442471	250.1	W 475936	304.9	W 469988	306.1	W 430626	254.2	TOL NON AC FIN MOINS 3 MM
67463	— OF STAINLESS ETC STL	W 36347	67.0	W 51911	124.6	W 43068	91.3	W 56613	88.7	TOL ACIER INOX MOINS 3 MM
678	IRON,STL TUBES,PIPES,ETC	W 190844	317.4	W 218832	379.6	W 330195	545.5	W 282692	505.3	TUBES,TUYAUX EN FONTE,FER
6782	IRON,STL SEAMLESS TUBES	W 110056	142.6	W 136851	167.5	W 195285	275.3	W 157909	227.9	TUBES,TUYAUX SANS SOUDURE
6783	IRON,STL TUBES,PIPES NES	W 54771	79.1	W 56616	126.6	W 107019	158.9	W 83551	133.7	AUT TUBES,TUYAUX FER,ACIER
6785	IRON,STEEL TUBE FITTINGS	W 19575	88.7	W 21911	81.5	W 25654	106.4	W 37613	134.6	ACCESSOIRES DE TUYAUTERIE
68	NON–FERROUS METALS		643.7		1018.8		905.4		825.0	METAUX NON FERREUX
682	COPPER EXC CEMENT COPPER	W 90636	234.7	W 122308	392.5	W 129989	358.8	W 87795	232.5	CUIVRE
6821	COPPER NES,ALLOYS,UNWRT	W 66341	154.2	W 94906	276.8	W 107396	270.0	W 60792	153.4	CUIVRE BRUT
68212	COPPER REFINED,UNWROUGHT	W 66246	153.9	W 94842	276.6	W 107372	269.9	W 60757	153.3	CUIVRE AFFINE BRUT
684	ALUMINIUM	W 131656	254.3	W 176497	432.4	W 152573	337.0	W 201050	382.8	ALUMINIUM
6841	ALUMINIUM,ALLOYS,UNWRGHT	W 100618	158.7	W 138381	301.4	W 118499	210.3	W 149790	254.3	ALUMINIUM,ALLIAGES BRUTS
6842	ALUMINIUM,ALLOYS WORKED	W 31038	95.7	W 38116	131.0	W 34074	126.8	W 51260	128.5	ALUMINIUM,ALLIAGES OUVRE
686	ZINC	W 93776	105.2	W 105905	129.2	W 96634	121.8	W 93640	122.1	ZINC
6861	ZINC,ALLOYS UNWROUGHT	W 91557	101.4	W 102488	124.0	W 94201	117.5	W 89400	116.7	ZINC ET ALLIAGES BRUTS
69	METAL MANUFACTURES NES		662.2		611.7		813.3		957.5	ART MANUFACT EN METAL NDA
691	STRUCTURES AND PARTS NES	W 77834	189.1	W 46121	103.3	W 57866	256.4	W 98179	348.3	CONSTRUCT FER,ACIER,ALU
6911	STRUCTURES,PARTS IRN,STL	W 77153	185.3	W 45535	99.1	W 56800	252.7	W 96835	343.4	CONSTRUCT FER,ACIER,FONTE
695	TOOLS	W 15874	105.4	W 19494	98.1	W 21918	143.3	W 29549	142.0	OUTILS A MAIN
699	BASE METAL MFRS NES	W 39738	173.8	MW 12077	196.8	W 48986	211.2	W 85456	232.0	ART MANUFACTURES MET NDA
7	MACHINES,TRANSPORT EQUIP		13426.3		16257.2		17458.6		17499.8	MACHINES MATERIEL TRANSPORT
71	POWER GENERATING EQUIPMT		1752.1		1827.7		1968.6		1877.0	MACHINES GENERATRICES
711	STEAM BOILERS & AUX PLNT	W 24593	173.4	W 19213	122.5	W 48707	241.3	W 32044	305.9	GENERATEURS VAPEUR EAU ETC
7111	STEAM BOILERS ETC	W 15776	84.1	W 8887	40.1	W 15828	107.7	W 14512	167.8	GENERATEURS VAPEUR EAU
712	STEAM ENGINES,TURBINES	W 14074	334.4	W 9371	244.5	W 10157	188.8	W 7428	237.5	MACHINES A VAPEUR D'EAU PIEC
7126	STEAM POWR UNITS,ENGINES	W 10345	255.8	W 7958	197.1	W 2344	67.9	W 2310	48.5	MACHINES A VAPEUR D EAU
7129	STM ENGINE ETC PARTS NES	W 3729	78.6	W 1413	47.5	W 7813	121.0	W 5118	189.0	PARTIES,PIECES DU 712.6
713	INTRNL COMBUS PSTN ENGIN	W 77391	717.9	W 92259	855.7	W 88662	727.5	W 101204	725.1	MOTEURS EXPL COMB INT, PIECE
7132	MOTOR VEHCL PISTN ENGINS	W 50359	548.3	W 52357	642.0	W 48053	517.2	W 56434	519.5	MOTEURS EXPL POUR VEHICULES
7139	PISTON ENGINE PARTS NES	W 19017	109.4	W 28526	127.6	W 28162	134.8	W 31008	139.7	PIECES POUR 713.2,3,8
714	ENGINES AND MOTORS NES	W 2790	138.9	W 1966	95.7	W 6067	311.5	W 3604	114.7	MOTEURS NON ELECTRIQUES
7148	GAS TURBINES NES	W 2122	90.9	W 1384	38.8	W 2729	145.0	W 1514	55.6	TURBINES A GAZ
71488	OTHER GAS TURBINES NES	W 2099	86.2	W 1302	34.0	W 2669	140.7	W 1497	54.1	AUTRES TURBINES A GAZ
7149	ENGINE & MOTOR PARTS NES	W 563	40.7	W 519	49.8	W 3219	152.7	W 897	43.1	PIECES 714 ET 718.88
716	ROTATING ELECTRIC PLANT	W 35105	367.8	W 42200	487.3	W 41133	459.7	W 43420	466.4	APP ELECTR ROTATIFS,PIECES
7162	AC MTRS,GENRTRS,GEN SETS	W 25790	263.4	W 31672	335.7	W 26429	312.9	W 32132	349.0	MOTEURS ELECTRIQUES
71623	GEN SETS WITH PISTN ENGN	W 13540	165.2	W 17844	222.6	W 11945	174.0	W 17393	246.0	GROUPES MOTEUR EXPLOSION
72	MACHS FOR SPCL INDUSTRYS		3014.8		3891.4		4118.4		3959.4	MAC SPECIALES POUR INDUST
723	CIVIL ENGNEERG EQUIP ETC	W 88739	520.9	W 79156	492.2	W 86886	483.2	W 109526	517.2	APPAREILS DE GENIE CIVIL
7234	CONST,MINING MACHNRY NES	W 74480	412.9	W 64209	379.2	W 72882	374.1	W 92211	396.5	MACH POUR LA CONST, MINES

4. Special Imports C.I.F. by Commodities according to the S.I.T.C. (Rev. 2) in million U.S. Dollars
Importations Spéciales C.A.F. par Produits d'après la C.T.C.I. (Rév. 2) en millions de Dollars E.U.

SITC CTCI	COMMODITY	1994 QUANTITY QUANTITE	1994 VALUE VALEUR	1995 QUANTITY QUANTITE	1995 VALUE VALEUR	1996 QUANTITY QUANTITE	1996 VALUE VALEUR	1997 QUANTITY QUANTITE	1997 VALUE VALEUR	PRODUIT
72341	SELF–PROPELLD DOZERS,ETC	W 23184	146.8	W 19296	126.9	W 14387	82.3	W 17954	111.7	BULLDOZERS
72342	SLFPRP SHOVELS,EXCAVATRS	W 45188	234.1	W 37406	202.4	W 47411	237.5	W 64569	226.5	PELLES MECANIQUES
724	TEXTILE,LEATHER MACHNRY	W 83821	837.0	W 103354	1051.4	W 63843	740.4	W 92095	783.9	MACH POUR INDUSTRIE TEXTILE
7244	SPINNING,EXTRDNG,ETC MCH	W 32409	370.9	W 54054	593.7	W 27149	382.7	W 33537	408.0	MACH POUR LE FILAGE
72441	TEXTILE EXTRUDING MACHS	W 4697	62.3	W 8186	152.9	W 3043	92.7	W 6259	93.2	MACH FILAGE TEXT SYNTH
72443	SPINNING,REELING,ETC MCH	W 19644	196.6	W 22579	213.8	W 14348	179.3	W 14639	171.2	MACH POUR LA FILATURE
7245	WEAVING,FELT MFG,ETC MCH	W 26881	234.5	W 24036	221.9	W 16746	173.2	W 14342	162.5	METIERS A TISSER,PIECES
72451	WEAVING MACHINES (LOOMS)	W 19261	145.6	W 14485	134.0	W 10810	97.5	W 7896	90.5	METIERS A TISSER
7247	TEXTILE MACHINERY NES	W 12593	135.5	W 11361	122.8	W 8515	94.6	W 8963	73.0	MACH LAVAGE,TEINTURE TEX
72474	OTH TEXTILE MACHNERY NES	W 10118	115.3	W 7437	100.3	W 5021	69.6	W 4414	48.4	MACH LAVAGE ETC MAT TEXT
725	PAPER ETC MILL MACHINERY	W 25581	387.6	W 55117	673.0	W 65792	806.8	W 52296	594.6	MACHINES FABR PATE PAPIER
7251	PAPER,PULP MAKING MACHRY	W 17093	297.2	W 25396	305.2	W 33595	406.3	W 11699	191.2	MACHINES FABR PATE CARTON
72511	CELLULOSE PULP MFG MACHY	W 13035	264.5	W 9993	97.9	W 17504	178.4	W 1592	13.8	MACH FABR PATE CELLULOSE
72512	PAPER ETC MAKING ETC MCH	W 4058	32.7	W 15402	207.3	W 16091	227.9	W 10107	177.5	MACH FABR FINITION DU PAP
7259	PTS NES OF MACHS OF 725	W 3758	49.4	W 23298	307.8	W 25570	313.9	W 34817	328.1	PIECES GROUPE 725
72591	PTS NES OF MACHS OF 7251	W 3541	47.6	W 23059	304.3	W 24899	302.1	W 33100	302.4	PIECES DU 725.1
726	PRINTG,BKBINDG MACHY,PTS	W 8501	156.9	W 8171	193.9	W 8076	168.2	W 10386	175.1	MACHINES POUR IMPRIMERIE
7264	PRINTING PRESSES	W 3831	79.7	W 4051	124.2	W 5033	111.6	W 5312	98.0	MACHINES A IMPRIMER
72641	ROTARY PRINTING PRESSES	W 3831	79.7	W 4051	124.2	W 5033	111.6	W 5312	98.0	MACH IMPRIMER ROTATIVES
727	FOOD MACHRY NON–DOMESTIC	W 13731	103.5	W 14009	124.5	W 19015	165.8	W 25854	178.7	MACH INDUSTRIES ALIMENT
7272	OTH FOOD PROC MCHY,PARTS	W 12145	96.3	W 12328	102.7	W 15481	147.0	W 21917	164.9	AUT MACH IND ALIMENTAIRE
728	OTH MACHY FOR SPCL INDUS	W 89994	952.7	W 111532	1268.8	W 135948	1641.2	W 162089	1588.8	AUT MACH IND PARTICULIERES
7281	MACH–TOOLS FR SPCL INDUS	W 24826	194.9	W 19059	166.7	W 18057	166.4	W 34167	299.3	MACH–OUTILS SPEC IND PART
72812	MACH–TOOLS TO WORK WOOD	W 19697	146.1	W 14871	114.7	W 12781	108.2	W 20345	161.7	MACH–OUT POUR TRAVAIL BOIS
7283	OTHR MINERAL WORKG MACHY	W 18288	123.3	W 37490	225.8	W 51543	455.0	W 58284	510.2	MACH TRIER,CRIBLER,BROYER
72839	PTS NES OF MACHY OF 7283	W 6977	41.5	W 14929	85.8	W 22511	208.4	W 29570	267.8	PIECES MACH DU 728.3
7284	MACHY FOR SPCL INDUS NES	W 46879	634.7	W 54983	876.4	W 66348	1019.9	W 69638	779.3	MACH SPEC IND PARTICUL.
72842	RUBBER,PLASTICS WRKG MCH	W 23774	292.2	W 24879	380.1	W 28053	311.7	W 38448	281.7	MACH IND CAOUT MAT PLAST
72848	OTH MCHY WITH INDIV FNCT	W 13738	194.4	W 19198	249.0	W 23818	409.9	W 16320	183.0	AUTRES MACHINES NDA
72849	PTS OF MACHS OF 7284 ETC	W 3158	49.7	W 3299	70.3	W 4654	85.8	W 8686	195.1	PIECES DU 728.4 ETC
73	METALWORKING MACHINERY		436.7		596.3		595.8		509.7	MACH TRAVAIL DES METAUX
736	METALWORKING MACH–TOOLS	W 51700	319.1	W 65619	453.3	W 58484	454.1	W 52326	368.3	MACH–OUTILS TRAVAIL METAUX
7361	METAL CUTTING MACH–TOOLS	W 21134	130.5	W 25502	178.5	W 21035	166.6	W 20628	145.4	MACH–OUT ENLEVEMENT METAL
7362	METAL FORMING MACH–TOOLS	W 19677	102.6	W 26841	162.1	W 21019	146.9	W 22783	121.8	MACH–OUTILS DEFORM METAL
737	METALWORKING MACHNRY NES	W 23470	117.7	W 41851	143.0	W 24794	141.8	W 28873	141.5	MACH TRAV METAUX PIECES
74	GENRL INDUSTRL MACHY NES		2393.0		3059.2		3629.2		3682.3	MACH APP INDUSTRIE
741	HEATING,COOLING EQUIPMNT	W 67315	643.1	W 81782	838.2	W 98840	944.1	W 101252	857.5	MACH CHAUFFAGE,PIECES
7413	INDUS FURNACES ETC,PARTS	W 13432	92.4	W 13865	126.5	W 20502	215.8	W 16972	145.4	FOURS IND,LABOR,PIECES
74132	INDUST FURNACES NONELECT	W 10395	72.1	W 11746	107.7	W 16541	173.5	W 13448	100.4	FOURS NON ELECTRIQUES
7415	AIR–CONDITIONING MACHNRY	W 10777	134.4	W 12587	143.7	W 11986	111.4	W 20492	146.8	GROUPES CONDITION AIR
7416	HEATING,COOLING EQU NES	W 29957	313.9	W 37717	423.7	W 45693	471.6	W 38326	408.8	APP CHANGEMENT TEMP
742	PUMPS FOR LIQUIDS ETC	W 19103	210.5	W 25560	250.4	W 26492	300.1	W 38915	391.5	POMPES MOTO–POMPES
7429	PTS NES OF PUMPS OF 742	W 4172	56.5	W 6274	77.7	W 6520	71.5	W 15535	160.6	PIECES POUR GROUPE 742
743	PUMPS NES,CENTRFUGES ETC	W 36039	375.9	W 49185	429.3	W 50361	528.2	W 60984	528.5	POMPES COMPRES,VENT ETC
7431	PUMPS FOR GASES ETC	W 19086	144.9	W 19587	185.0	W 22838	223.9	W 25713	210.7	POMPES AIR A VIDE,COMPRES
7436	GAS,LIQUID FILTERS ETC	W 8507	105.0	W 10676	102.4	W 14076	160.6	W 15530	153.8	APP POUR FILT DES LIQUIDES
744	MECHANICAL HANDLING EQU	W 87575	498.7	W 130342	796.1	W 146195	909.8	W 198706	905.7	EQUIP MANUTENTION PIECES
7442	LIFTING,LOADING MACH NES	W 33034	191.8	W 54134	304.4	W 64378	391.8	W 110089	413.9	APP LEVAGE,MANUTENTION
74428	OTH HANDLING ETC MCH NES	W 12362	88.0	W 23556	140.6	W 34929	217.9	W 56059	228.2	AUT APP LEVAGE ETC
7449	PTS NES OF MACHY OF 7442	W 42209	236.5	W 63210	409.8	W 64438	436.1	W 67868	416.9	PIECES DU 744.2
745	NONELEC MACHY,TOOLS NES	W 11549	163.0	W 12056	224.0	W 14946	324.1	W 20881	296.1	AUT MACH NON ELEC,PIECES
7452	OTH NONELEC MCHS,PTS NES	W 9032	138.3	W 9888	202.1	W 12182	293.2	W 17551	271.7	AUT MACH NON ELEC,PIECES
74522	PACKAGNG,BOTTLNG,ETC MCH	W 2830	73.6	W 4402	134.7	W 5029	203.1	W 5494	167.3	MACH NETT BOUTEILLES,ETC
749	NONELEC MACH PTS,ACC NES	W 46569	502.0	W 54538	521.5	W 59313	623.1	W 77471	703.2	PIECES MACH NON ELEC NDA
7492	COCKS,VALVES ETC NES	W 16718	247.9	W 17595	199.3	W 20899	260.4	W 26132	291.7	ART ROB,SIM POUR TUYAUX
7493	SHAFT,CRANK,PULLEY ETC	W 16212	101.1	W 17051	116.8	W 17875	121.5	W 18378	124.0	ARBRES TRANS,VILEBREQUINS
7499	OTH NONELEC MCHY PTS NES	W 9578	125.3	W 14247	169.8	W 15033	197.6	W 20758	223.6	PIECES NON ELECT NDA
74991	FOUNDRY MOULDS ETC NES	W 6288	92.5	W 9538	128.6	W 10315	157.4	W 14464	161.7	MOULES POUR METAUX
75	OFFICE MACHNES,ADP EQUIP		176.5		241.2		304.9		353.1	MACH BUREAU TRAIT AUTOM
752	AUTOMTIC DATA PROC EQUIP	W 2116	94.2	W 2533	121.7	W 5931	195.6	W 16358	235.2	MACH TRAIT INFORMATION
76	TELECOMM,SOUND EQUIPMENT		759.5		1086.2		1766.3		1778.8	EQUIPEMENT DE TELECOM
764	TELECOM EQPT,PTS,ACC NES	W 30446	741.2	W 35644	1061.0	W 32646	1724.3	W 42671	1707.2	EQUIP TELECOM,PIECES
7641	LINE TELEPHONE,ETC EQUIP	W 4531	300.2	W 4700	401.4	W 4599	454.7	W 11587	741.5	APP TELEPHON PAR FIL
7643	TV,RADIO TRANSMITTRS ETC	W 693	75.3	W 939	95.8	W 1956	367.4	W 2997	338.1	APP EMET TELE RADIO
7649	PTS NES OF EQUIPMT OF 76	W 22499	324.3	W 26093	492.3	W 21621	786.7	W 22863	583.5	PIECES DE LA DIV 76
76491	PTS NES OF APPAR OF 7641	W 1883	101.5	W 2613	171.4	W 4177	356.0	W 2954	314.7	PIECES POUR 764.1
76493	TELECOMM EQUIPMT PTS NES	W 12021	154.5	W 14664	275.2	W 11431	404.9	W 15025	245.7	PIECES 761,762,764.3,8
77	ELECTRIC MACHNRY NES ETC		1758.2		1965.7		1868.4		2110.7	MACH APP ELECT NDA
771	ELECTRIC POWER MACHY NES	W 20824	218.6	W 20466	206.3	W 26756	241.9	W 28876	374.3	MACH PROD,TRANS ELECTR
7711	TRANSFORMERS,ELECTRICAL	W 13662	160.5	W 13071	132.1	W 18951	174.0	W 16106	237.4	TRANSFO ELECTRIQUES
77118	OTHER ELEC TRANSFORMERS	W 6967	73.8	W 8199	90.4	W 11815	106.0	W 11151	170.8	AUTRES TRANSFO ELECTRIQ
7712	OTH ELEC POWER MACHY NES	W 7161	58.1	W 7395	74.2	W 7805	67.9	W 12770	137.0	AUT APP PROD TRANSF ELEC
772	SWITCHGEAR ETC,PARTS NES	W 27708	557.2	W 31727	559.3	W 27398	476.6	W 39187	587.6	APP COUPURE,SECT ETC
7721	SWITCHGEAR ETC	W 24836	502.5	W 29365	515.5	W 25388	439.6	W 34867	542.3	APP COUPURE,SECTIONMNT
773	ELECTR DISTRIBUTNG EQUIP	W 41474	220.6	W 56729	237.9	W 55193	270.6	W 52969	313.4	EQUIPMT DISTRIBUTION ELECT
7731	INSULATED WIRE,CABLE ETC	W 20764	167.1	W 32659	182.0	W 46059	235.2	W 33624	255.6	FILS,CABLES ISOLES ELECT
776	TRANSISTORS,VALVES,ETC	W 33886	327.9	W 41011	398.1	W 37435	333.7	W 29507	216.7	LAMPES,TUBES,VALVES
7761	TV PICTURE TUBES	W 28738	201.4	W 34911	250.8	W 30798	210.2	W 23047	118.8	TUBES CATHODIQUES
778	ELECTRICAL MACHINERY NES	W 54904	373.7	W 66049	436.9	W 57884	439.2	W 69847	483.7	AUTRES MACH ELECT NDA
7783	AUTOMOTIVE ELECTR EQUIP	W 10677	85.7	W 12056	102.3	W 9390	82.0	W 14895	148.6	EQUIP ELECT MOTEURS EXPL
7788	OTH ELEC MACHY,EQUIP NES	W 36090	227.6	W 43316	255.9	W 32608	185.6	W 32784	207.3	AUT MACH APP ELEC NDA
78	ROAD VEHICLES		2335.3		2983.8		2673.5		2593.0	VEHICULES ROUTIERS
781	PASS MOTOR VEH EXC BUSES	W 10469	85.8	W 17325	159.3	W 26679	227.0	W 30010	251.9	AUTO TRANSPORT PERSONNES
782	LORRIES,SPCL MTR VEH NES	W 34278	239.2	W 42630	303.7	W 51091	369.1	W 63371	333.2	VEHICULES SPECIAUX,MARCH
7821	LORRIES,TRUCKS	W 27832	209.5	W 36094	268.4	W 40687	297.5	W 51161	263.6	VEHICULES TRANSP MARCHAND
784	MOTOR VEH PRTS,ACCES NES	W 171194	1532.6	W 201365	1843.3	W 163265	1359.5	W 179008	1297.2	PIECES 722,781,782,783
7849	OTHER MOTOR VEHCL PARTS	W 170949	1530.6	W 200798	1835.8	W 162810	1354.5	W 178156	1294.2	PIECES 722,781,782,783
785	CYCLES,ETC MOTRZD OR NOT	W 40008	403.5	W 47223	557.8	W 52245	639.9	W 60357	646.2	MOTOCYCLES SCOOTERS
7853	INVAL CARR, PTS OF 785	W 39667	402.0	W 46367	556.3	W 51093	638.1	W 59554	645.0	FAUTEUILS INVALIDES,PIECES
78539	PARTS,ACCES NES OF 785	W 39370	401.5	W 46227	555.8	W 50977	637.7	W 59474	644.8	PIECES DU 785
79	OTHR TRANSPORT EQUIPMENT		800.7		606.2		533.9		636.2	AUTRE MATERIEL TRANSPORT
792	AIRCRAFT ETC	W 708	230.2	W 688	228.7	W 708	234.6	W 740	175.0	APP NAVIGATION AERIENNE
7924	AIRCRFT NES OVER 15000KG	W 269	131.8	W 215	116.0	W 57	15.1			AERODYNES PLUS 15000 KG
7929	AIRCRAFT PARTS NES	W 302	68.8	W 346	100.4	W 553	180.1	W 574	158.7	PIECES DU 792
793	SHIPS AND BOATS ETC	W 205760	514.4	W 94428	278.4	W 289355	243.7	W 367598	379.6	NAVIRES BATEAUX,ETC
7932	SHIPS AND BOATS NES	W 116027	314.2	W 64845	127.9	W 202634	124.4	W 273462	101.8	NAVIRES ET BATEAUX
79323	OTHER CARGO VESSELS	W 109206	295.4	W 61125	117.5	W 105062	41.5	W 147016	85.6	AUT BATEAUX TRANS MARCH
7938	TUGS,SPECIAL VESSELS ETC	W 88455	197.8	W 26971	95.9	W 86350	111.5	W 93640	270.6	REMORQUEURS,BATEAUX SPEC
79382	SPECL PURPOSE VESSLS ETC	W 83832	177.6	W 19510	79.4	W 68690	84.5	W 79972	232.7	BAT–PHARES,–POMPES,DRAGUES
8	MISC MANUFACTURED GOODS		1003.7		1282.6		1215.0		1164.8	ART MANUFACTURES DIVERS
87	PRECISION INSTRUMNTS NES		369.6		441.4		482.8		419.6	INSTRUM,APPAR SCIENT NDA

4. Special Imports C.I.F. by Commodities according to the S.I.T.C. (Rev. 2) in million U.S. Dollars
Importations Spéciales C.A.F. par Produits d'après la C.T.C.I. (Rév. 2) en millions de Dollars E.U.

SITC CTCI	COMMODITY	1994			1995			1996			1997			PRODUIT
		QUANTITY QUANTITE		VALUE VALEUR	QUANTITY QUANTITE		VALUE VALEUR	QUANTITY QUANTITE		VALUE VALEUR	QUANTITY QUANTITE		VALUE VALEUR	
874	MEASURNG,CONTROLNG INSTR	W	10605	322.8	W	11785	377.0	W	11650	433.0	W	17486	340.5	INSTRUMENTS DE MESURE
8743	GAS,LIQUID CONTROL INSTR	W	3422	85.6	W	3593	95.6	W	4011	147.8	W	4840	80.5	APP,INSTR MESURE FLUIDES
88	PHOTO EQU,OPTICL GDS ETC			222.2			263.7			194.0			199.3	APP,FOURN PHOTO,OP,MONTR
882	PHOTO,CINEMA SUPPLIES	W	18590	131.2	W	13741	134.7	W	13151	122.8	W	14481	127.0	PRODUITS PHOTO,CINEMA
8822	PHOTO FILM EXC DEV CINMA	W	8535	111.1	W	8288	115.5	W	8202	103.9	W	9040	109.3	PLAQUES,PELLICULES,FILMS
89	MISC MANUFCTRD GOODS NES			318.6			422.6			419.4			399.7	ART MANUFACTURES DIVERS
893	ARTICLES OF PLASTIC NES			101.5			120.0			122.9			141.5	OUVRAGES EN MAT DIVIS 58

5. Special Exports F.O.B. by Commodities according to the S.I.T.C. (Rev. 2) in million U.S. Dollars
Exportations Spéciales F.O.B. par Produits d'après la C.T.C.I. (Rév. 2) en millions de Dollars E.U.

SITC CTCI	COMMODITY	1994		1995		1996		1997		PRODUIT
		QUANTITY QUANTITE	VALUE VALEUR	QUANTITY QUANTITE	VALUE VALEUR	QUANTITY QUANTITE	VALUE VALEUR	QUANTITY QUANTITE	VALUE VALEUR	
	ALL COMMODITIES		40053.5		45418.0		49814.8		53443.7	TOUS PRODUITS
0	FOOD AND LIVE ANIMALS		3550.8		3579.9		3764.5		3531.5	ALIMENTS,ANIMAUX VIVANTS
03	FISH AND PREPARATIONS		1581.6		1665.3		1676.9		1619.4	POISSONS ET PREPARATIONS
034	FISH,FRESH,CHILLED,FROZN	W 313169	369.4	W 333513	417.9	W 351675	424.8	W 382683	430.6	POISSON FRAIS, REFRIG,CONG
0341	FISH FRSH,CHLLD,EX FILLT	W 114562	202.6	W 121846	222.8	W 121909	202.2	W 105680	181.1	POISSON FRAIS,REFRIGERE
0342	FISH FROZEN,EXCL FILLETS	W 189299	135.5	W 201011	160.6	W 217516	183.7	W 265801	212.3	POISSONS CONGELES
036	SHELL FISH FRESH,FROZEN	W 116991	1050.9	W 109959	1080.8	W 115110	1063.6	W 105298	1045.9	CRUSTACES,MOLLUSQUES
05	VEGETABLES AND FRUIT		303.9		299.5		376.1		246.4	LEGUMES ET FRUITS
07	COFFEE,TEA,COCOA,SPICES		1297.0		1250.5		1275.8		1285.1	CAFE,THE,CACAO,EPICES
071	COFFEE AND SUBSTITUTES	W 291152	753.7	W 231478	614.0	W 368626	606.0	W 316231	529.7	CAFE ET SUCCEDANES
0711	COFFEE GREEN,ROASTED,SUB	W 289304	745.9	W 230199	606.4	W 366603	595.3	W 313118	511.4	CAFE TORREFIE OU DECAFEINE
07111	COFFEE GREEN,HUSKS,SKINS	W 288974	744.8	W 230099	605.8	W 366472	595.0	W 312961	510.7	CAFE NON TORREFIE
072	COCOA	W 228679	273.2	W 230063	301.1	W 318704	365.4	W 261386	407.6	CACAO
0721	COCOA BEANS,RAW,ROASTED	W 200299	213.2	W 196443	224.5	W 274119	262.9	W 219782	294.9	CACAO EN FEVES
075	SPICES	W 108792	167.1	W 126279	240.5	W 110096	183.5	W 102068	246.5	EPICES
0751	PEPPER AND PIMENTO	W 36364	79.2	W 58373	157.0	W 37520	101.8	W 33776	164.7	POIVRE,PIMENTS
081	*FEEDING STUFF FOR ANIML	W 1495075	157.3	W 1388460	142.0	W 1557957	207.1	W 1510833	141.6	NOURRITURE POUR ANIMAUX
1	BEVERAGES AND TOBACCO		138.2		195.5		229.4		252.0	BOISSONS ET TABACS
12	TOBACCO AND MANUFACTURES		126.5		186.8		219.5		245.8	TABACS BRUTS FABRIQUES
2	CRUDE MATERLS,EXCL FUELS		3235.5		5033.7		5081.2		4357.9	MAT BRUTES NON COMESTIBLES
23	RUBBER, CRUDE		1274.7		1965.5		1922.9		1501.4	CAOUTCHOUC BRUT
232	NATURAL RUBBER,GUMS	W 1245537	1273.1	W 1324169	1963.9	W 1435365	1920.1	W 1421766	1498.9	LATEX CAOUTCHOUC NATUREL
23202	OTHER NATURAL RUBBER	W 1207547	1228.4	W 1296320	1919.4	W 1408098	1872.9	W 1382378	1467.0	CAOUTCHOUC NATUREL
24	CORK AND WOOD		388.9		363.2		326.0		279.2	LIEGE ET BOIS
248	WOOD SHAPED,SLEEPERS	W 354668	346.2	W 292870	315.0	W 294269	279.8	W 252289	242.7	BOIS SIMPLEMENT TRAVAILLES
2483	LUMBER SHAPED NON–CONIFR	W 346700	335.6	W 284350	304.2	W 266140	269.3	W 248389	237.6	NON CONIFERES SCIES,RABOTES
24831	LUMBER SAWN ETC NON–CON	W 166151	162.5	W 153974	161.2	W 143829	136.2	W 110860	105.9	SCIES LONGITUDINALEMENT
24832	LUMBER PLANED ETC NONCON	W 180548	173.1	W 130375	143.1	W 122311	133.1	W 137529	131.8	RABOTES,RAINES,LANGUETES
251	*PULP AND WASTE PAPER	W 236015	137.8	W 681802	513.4	W 1128457	431.8	W 1191877	489.8	PATES A PAPIER,DECHETS
2517	SODA,SULPHATE WOOD PULP	W 107047	63.1	W 574980	437.9	W 1126025	431.3	W 1185491	489.2	PATES CHIMIQUES AU SULFATE
25172	— BLEACHED,NONDISSOLVNG	W 102456	61.3	W 562899	430.7	W 1124024	430.6	W 1183975	488.6	PATES BLANCHIES
28	METALLIFEROUS ORES,SCRAP		1148.3		1883.6		2034.3		1737.5	MINERAIS METAL,DECHETS
287	BASE METAL ORES,CONC NES	W 3675552	1133.3	W 4002487	1870.3	W 4422937	2019.1	W 4420368	1718.2	MINERAIS METAUX COMMUNS
2871	CPR ORE ETC,CEMENT COPPR	W 1075634	857.7	W 1412139	1537.6	W 1860097	1747.7	W 1716828	1497.4	MINERAIS DE CUIVRE,MATTES
28711	COPPER ORES,EXCL MATTE	W 1075634	857.7	W 1412057	1537.5	W 1860070	1747.7	W 1716828	1497.4	MINERAIS DE CUIVRE
2872	NICKEL ORES,CONCENTRATES	W 1559626	252.0	W 1787978	321.8	W 1836563	260.2	W 1940317	210.3	MINERAIS DE NICKEL
28722	NICKEL MATTE,SINTERS,ETC	W 61766	224.7	W 54824	281.0	W 45373	217.3	W 41164	172.0	MATTES,SINTERS
3	MINERAL FUELS ETC		10523.5		11508.6		12860.9		13153.9	COMBUSTIBLES MINERAUX LUB
32	COAL,COKE AND BRIQUETTES		829.7		1043.8		1123.7		1491.4	HOUILLES,COKES,BRIQUETTES
322	COAL,LIGNITE AND PEAT	MW 25366	819.3	MW 31572	1033.2	MW 31957	1121.0	MW 42134	1485.1	HOUILLES,LIGNITES,TOURBE
3222	OTH COAL,NOT AGGLOMERATD	MW 24221	779.9	MW 29745	973.0	MW 30586	1072.8	MW 41038	1451.0	AUTRES HOUILLES
33	PETROLEUM AND PRODUCTS		6004.7		6442.9		7243.3		6822.4	PETROLE ET DERIVES
333	CRUDE PETROLEUM	MW 43677	5071.6	MW 40674	5145.8	MW 38255	5711.9	MW 38977	5480.0	HUILES BRUTES DE PETROLE
334	PETROLEUM PRODUCTS,REFIN	W 8625439	923.4	MW 10722	1276.5	MW 10385	1502.1	MW 9786	1283.1	PRODUITS RAFFINES
3341	GASOLINE,OTH LIGHT OILS	W 896974	133.9	W 1482395	322.9	W 1417719	336.9	W 1059750	219.0	ESSENCES POUR MOTEURS
33411	MOTOR,AVIATION SPIRIT	W 867878	128.0	W 1142780	182.3	W 1128358	211.8	W 828103	157.9	ESSENCES MOTEURS D'AVIONS
33419	OTH LIGHT PETROLEUM OILS			W 339615	140.6	W 289361	125.1	W 231647	61.2	AUTRES HUILES LEGERES
3342	KEROSENE,OTH MEDIUM OILS	W 877539	138.0					W 6102	0.1	PETR LAMPANTS,AUT HUIL
33429	OTH MEDIUM PETROLEUM OIL	W 877539	138.0							AUTRES HUILES MOYENNES
3344	FUEL OILS,NES	W 6760790	638.7	W 7948732	826.9	W 7893929	1021.8	W 7843804	970.8	FUEL OILS
341	*GAS,NATURAL AND MANUFCT	MW 29344	3689.2	MW 28190	4022.0	MW 29344	4494.0	MW 29016	4840.2	GAZ NATUREL,GAZ MANUFACT
3413	PETROLM GASES,LIQUEFIED	MW 29344	3689.2	MW 28190	4022.0	MW 29344	4494.0	MW 29016	4840.2	GAZ DE PETROLE LIQUEFIE
34131	LIQUEFIED PROPANE,BUTANE	W 2514541	305.8	W 2384200	407.0	W 2568849	467.9	W 1938528	420.3	PROPANE,BUTANE LIQUEFIES
34139	OTH HYDROCARBON GAS LQFD	MW 26829	3383.4	MW 25805	3615.1	MW 26775	4026.1	MW 27077	4419.9	HYDROCARBURES GAZEUX NDA
4	ANIMAL,VEGETABLE OIL,FAT		1374.5		1383.6		1567.8		2282.1	HUILES,GRAISSES ANIM,VEG
42	FIXED VEGETABLE OIL,FAT		1132.4		1040.9		1343.7		2196.0	HUILES VEGETALES FIXES
424	FIXED VEG OIL NONSOFT	W 2370637	1115.4	W 1728526	1034.8	W 2410601	1338.4	W 4178755	2174.9	AUTRES HUILES VEG FIXES
4242	PALM OIL	W 1631203	717.9	W 1265024	747.5	W 1671956	825.5	W 2967589	1446.2	HUILE DE PALME
4243	COCONUT (COPRA) OIL	W 392872	213.2	W 148280	93.6	W 378819	266.5	W 644252	401.7	HJUILE DE COPRAH
4244	PALM KERNEL OIL	W 340504	177.6	W 311399	187.3	W 341319	235.2	W 502979	294.3	HUILE DE PALMISTE
431	*PROCESD ANML VEG OIL,ET	W 585543	240.3	W 572641	341.8	W 467705	223.1	W 157594	85.4	HUILES,GRAISSES PREPAREES
4313	FATTY ACIDS ETC,RESIDUES	W 570670	229.9	W 549629	324.9	W 335525	161.6	W 63479	43.0	ACIDES GRAS INDUST,RESIDUS
43131	FATTY ACIDS,ACID OILS	W 570270	229.5	W 548462	324.8	W 335525	161.6	W 63369	42.4	ACIDES GRAS INDUSTRIELS
5	CHEMCLS,RELATED PROD NES		1001.2		1510.2		1723.6		1869.4	PRODUITS CHIMIQUES
51	ORGANIC CHEMICALS		334.6		489.0		514.2		645.1	PROD CHIMIQ ORGANIQUES
512	ALCOHOLS,PHENOLS ETC		78.9	W 88853	99.2	W 213010	164.3	W 229228	131.3	PHENOLS,PHENOLS–ALCOOLS
5121	ACYCLIC ALCOHOLS,DERIVS		76.0	W 88350	96.3	W 212439	161.2	W 228556	127.4	ALCOOLS ACYCLIQUES
513	CARBOXYLIC ACIDS ETC	W 130672	72.4	W 171291	154.7	W 202490	121.5	W 447015	222.6	ACIDES CARBOXYLIQUES
514	NITROGEN–FNCTN COMPOUNDS	W 109465	139.0	W 110405	154.9	W 110121	173.1	W 197342	217.8	COMPOSES FONCT AZOTEES
5146	OXYGEN–FNCT AMINO–CMPNDS	W 98640	123.0	W 94527	128.6	W 96111	144.3	W 180684	189.4	COMP AMINES FONCT OXYGEN
55	PERFUME,CLEANING ETC PRD		152.4		187.9		198.2		188.7	PROD POUR PARFUM,TOILETTE
562	*FERTILIZERS,MANUFACTURE	W 1372921	178.3	W 1329277	275.8	W 1260320	269.6	W 2097663	311.2	ENGRAIS MANUFACTURES
5621	CHEM NITROGENOUS FERTLZR	W 1187458	152.1	W 1052972	220.7	W 1260051	269.5	W 2087612	309.3	ENGRAIS AZOTES
56216	UREA	W 1187371	152.1	W 1052962	220.6	W 1260002	269.3	W 2087485	308.3	UREE
58	PLASTIC MATERIALS ETC		122.5		305.8		387.3		405.0	MAT PLAST ARTIFICIELLES
582	PROD OF CONDENSATION ETC	W 25234	26.4	W 89120	139.0	W 179201	186.9	W 226612	203.8	PROD CONDENS,POLYCOND
5823	ALKYDS,OTHER POLYESTERS	W 9707	15.6	W 66132	121.9	W 151793	162.2	W 205429	180.0	ALKYDES ET AUT POLYESTERS
58231	— IN PRIMARY FORMS	W 9133	12.8	W 65394	118.1	W 148625	152.5	W 199327	166.1	SOUS FORMES PRIMAIRES
583	POLYMERIZATION ETC PRODS	W 83329	95.9	W 129004	166.2	W 198131	199.7	W 226965	199.5	PROD POLYMERISATION
6	BASIC MANUFACTURES		9534.9		10527.2		10887.9		9778.8	ART MANUFACTURES
62	RUBBER MANUFACTURES NES		135.0		235.2		299.5		269.4	CAOUTCHOUC MANUFACTURE
625	RUBBER TYRES, TUBES ETC	W 49990	103.5	W 78735	182.0	W 105565	247.2	W 111299	232.7	PNEUS CAOUTCHOUC VULCANISE
63	WOOD,CORK MANUFACTRS NES		4832.4		4662.5		4839.8		4445.3	OUVRAGES LIEGE ET BOIS
634	VENEERS,PLYWOOD,ETC	W 6189650	4124.0	W 5736792	3825.5	W 5606114	3985.9	W 5272472	3729.2	PLACAGES,CONTRE–PLAQUES
6342	PLYWOOD OF WOOD SHEETS	W 5338355	3716.5	W 4909803	3462.0	W 4855086	3595.4	W 4611334	3410.6	BOIS CONTRE–PLAQUES
6343	IMPROVED,RECONSTIT WOOD	W 469781	387.9	W 471725	343.1	W 432036	371.2	W 361516	301.8	BOIS AMELIORES,RECONST
63431	IMPROVED WOOD	W 261734	339.8	W 241533	286.2	W 248245	329.2	W 215938	270.7	BOIS AMELIORES
635	WOOD MANUFACTURES NES	W 703622	708.5	W 638973	836.9	W 635175	853.9	W 577939	716.0	ART MANUF EN BOIS NDA
6353	BUILDERS WOODWRK,PREFABS	W 480032	534.1	W 527087	643.9	W 523958	663.3	W 476001	556.8	OUVRAGES DE MENUISERIE
64	PAPER,PAPERBOARD AND MFR		595.2		933.2		947.4		939.6	PAPIERS,CARTONS & OUVRAGES
641	PAPER AND PAPERBOARD	W 761950	486.2	W 909214	781.8	W 1997124	794.0	W 1534858	821.7	PAPIERS ET CARTONS
6412	PRINTG,WRITING PAPER NES	W 139313	120.1	W 183161	202.2	W 1110480	305.6	W 589932	368.4	PAPIERS POUR L'IMPRESSION
64122	— COATED,IMPREGNATD ETC	W 130707	112.5	W 144216	151.0	W 1010361	210.5	W 487513	275.1	PAPIERS IMPRESSION COUCHES
6415	PAPER,PAPERBRD,BULK,NES	W 300341	200.7	W 400827	376.5	W 521188	288.2	W 444183	235.7	PAPIERS,CARTONS ROULEAUX
64159	OTHER PAPER ETC,BULK,NES	W 262771	189.0	W 345784	352.9	W 356901	266.7	W 423608	229.2	AUT PAPIER ROULEAUX FEUILLES
642	PAPER,ETC,PRECUT,ARTS OF	W 93082	109.1	W 104696	151.5	W 108181	153.5	W 89497	118.0	PAP,CARTONS DECOUPES
65	TEXTILE YARN,FABRICS,ETC		2515.9		2738.2		2856.9		2268.9	FILS,TISSUS,ARTICLES TEXTILE
651	TEXTILE YARN	W 228580	678.8	W 254494	813.2	W 312882	912.6	W 271391	763.5	FILS TEXTILES
6513	COTTON YARN	W 60375	258.1	W 62725	244.4	W 78109	287.6	W 58471	212.1	FILS DE COTON
6514	SYN FIB YRN,BULK,MONOFIL	W 70439	133.6	W 84962	216.9	W 93825	193.8	W 105698	228.2	FILS CONT 85% FIB TEXT SYNTH
65144	— TEXTRD,CONT POLYESTER	W 48243	78.9	W 60741	143.2	W 61423	110.0	W 44267	93.8	FILS TEX FI CONT POLYESTERS

5. Special Exports F.O.B. by Commodities according to the S.I.T.C. (Rev. 2) in million U.S. Dollars
Exportations Spéciales F.O.B. par Produits d'après la C.T.C.I. (Rév. 2) en millions de Dollars E.U.

SITC CTCI	COMMODITY	1994 QUANTITY QUANTITE	1994 VALUE VALEUR	1995 QUANTITY QUANTITE	1995 VALUE VALEUR	1996 QUANTITY QUANTITE	1996 VALUE VALEUR	1997 QUANTITY QUANTITE	1997 VALUE VALEUR	PRODUIT
6516	DISCON SYN FIB BLEND YRN	W 78441	228.8	W 77492	247.5	W 102659	317.0	W 79847	235.8	FILS FIBR TEX SYNT DIS MOINS
65168	OTH DISC SYN BLEND YARN	W 48029	137.1	W 43477	134.2	W 50654	165.8	W 39783	125.3	FILS TEXT SYNT MELANGE AUT F
652	COTTON FABRICS,WOVEN	W 64175	318.5	W 56305	323.8	W 65768	347.8	W 56580	300.6	TISSUS DE COTON
6521	GREY WOVEN COTTON FABRIC	W 42714	184.0	W 36255	173.8	W 40163	180.8	W 36579	162.0	TISSUS COT ECRUS NON MERCER
65214	GREY WOVEN COTTON NES	W 31411	140.0	W 27189	135.1	W 31640	148.5	W 27959	130.6	AUT TISSUS 85% COTON ECRUS
6522	WOVEN COTTON BLEACHD,ETC	W 21461	134.5	W 20050	150.1	W 25606	167.0	W 20001	138.6	TISSUS COTON BLANCHIS ETC
653	WOVN MAN-MADE FIB FABRIC	W 147476	1115.7	W 145942	1180.0	W 162839	1150.7	W 124460	854.3	TISSUS FIBRES SYNTH,ARTIF
6531	CONT SYNT WEAVES NONPILE	W 68494	703.6	W 71396	763.5	W 80871	717.5	W 75776	606.6	TISSUS FIBRES SYNTH CONTINUE
65315	CONT SYN TXTL FABRIC NES	W 64829	688.2	W 69036	751.0	W 78209	703.6	W 73921	597.6	TIS PLUS 85% TEXT SYNT CONT
6534	DISC SYN BLEND FABRC NES	W 43605	227.1	W 42334	249.0	W 49721	273.0	W 35641	180.4	TISSUS FIBRES SYNTH DISCONT
65341	DISC SYN FIB-COTTN FABRC	W 35143	176.4	W 31403	185.1	W 37637	206.7	W 27433	139.4	TISSUS FIB SYNT DIS MEL COTO
6536	DISC REGN TXTL FABRC NES	W 26661	131.6	W 20714	97.1	W 21816	94.8	W 8275	39.8	TISSUS 85% TEXT ART DISC
658	TEXTILE ARTICLES NES	W 35758	175.1	W 43842	176.9	W 46082	194.9	W 30470	124.9	ART FACONNES MAT TEXTILES
66	NONMETAL MINERAL MFS NES		322.5		343.7		409.8		305.4	ART MIN NON METALLIQUES
67	IRON AND STEEL		311.2		379.6		338.3		330.0	FER ET ACIER
672	IRON,STEEL PRIMARY FORMS	W 411000	128.6	W 387974	155.2	W 203053	67.1	W 200168	63.4	LINGOTS FER,ACIER
6727	IRN,STL COIL FR REROLLNG	W 390759	123.1	W 364716	147.4	W 199503	65.1	W 117139	38.6	EBAUCHES POUR TOLES FER
67271	IRON,SIMPLE STEEL COILS	W 373796	117.7	W 362458	146.7	W 199502	65.1	W 117139	38.6	EBAUCHES NON EN ACIER
68	NON-FERROUS METALS		405.1		710.2		665.1		653.4	METAUX NON FERREUX
684	ALUMINIUM	W 177761	235.8	W 238460	369.3	W 204721	302.2	W 189600	303.5	ALUMINIUM
6841	ALUMINIUM,ALLOYS,UNWRGHT	W 148452	204.9	W 187985	332.7	W 180331	263.7	W 166194	268.8	ALUMINIUM,ALLIAGES BRUTS
687	TIN	W 22404	118.4	W 39712	239.4	W 46384	276.1	W 49973	274.6	ETAIN
6871	TIN,ALLOYS UNWROUGHT	W 22328	118.2	W 39667	239.3	W 46312	275.9	W 49908	274.2	ETAIN ET ALLIAGES BRUTS
69	METAL MANUFACTURES NES		330.7		423.0		434.5		476.8	ART MANUFACT EN METAL NDA
691	STRUCTURES AND PARTS NES	W 17202	44.2	W 17915	77.4	W 16621	69.0	W 19902	204.0	CONSTRUCT FER,ACIER,ALU
6911	STRUCTURES,PARTS IRN,STL	W 10237	20.6	W 10042	48.1	W 8329	39.5	W 9325	171.9	CONSTRUCT FER,ACIER,FONTE
697	BASE MTL HOUSEHOLD EQUIP	W 36159	125.9	W 38551	143.4	W 39085	152.4	W 23146	90.6	ART MENAGE MET COMMUNS
7	MACHINES,TRANSPORT EQUIP		3044.7		3823.6		4994.1		4620.1	MACHINES MATERIEL TRANSPORT
71	POWER GENERATING EQUIPMT		49.4		90.6		144.1		170.6	MACHINES GENERATRICES
72	MACHS FOR SPCL INDUSTRYS		33.9		160.9		126.4		87.0	MAC SPECIALES POUR INDUST
74	GENRL INDUSTRL MACHY NES		125.1		144.5		192.3		180.4	MACH APP INDUSTRIE
75	OFFICE MACHNES,ADP EQUIP		299.9		501.5		800.0		919.9	MACH BUREAU TRAIT AUTOM
752	AUTOMTIC DATA PROC EQUIP	W 2799	96.3	W 9373	170.0	W 21904	423.6	W 16157	264.7	MACH TRAIT INFORMATION
7525	ADP PERIPHERAL UNITS	W 1565	26.0	W 7953	124.4	W 7954	172.8	W 8631	134.3	UNITES PERIPHERIQUES
7528	OFF-LINE DATA PROC EQUIP	W 218	16.8	W 626	27.8	W 12530	222.0	W 5692	93.9	MACH AUXIL TRAIT INFORM
759	OFFICE,ADP MCH PTS,ACCES	W 12705	136.3	W 4777	252.9	W 2065	338.7	W 3932	619.4	PIECES DU 751 ET 752
7599	ACCTG,ETC,ADP MCH PTS,AC	W 2013	96.5	W 2874	220.3	W 1540	275.3	W 3649	607.2	PIECES DU 751 ET 752
76	TELECOMM,SOUND EQUIPMENT		1472.5		1634.3		2068.2		1752.8	EQUIPMENT DE TELECOM
761	TELEVISION RECEIVERS	W 7300	183.2	W 2401	33.2	W 3245	45.2	W 5368	64.9	RECEPTEURS DE TELEVISION
7611	COLOUR TV RECEIVERS	W 7212	181.4	W 1998	23.5	W 3179	43.5	W 5107	61.4	RECEPTEURS COULEUR
762	RADIO BROADCAST RECEIVRS	W 22124	268.9	W 34268	519.5	W 25245	460.8	W 11422	254.5	RECEPTEURS RADIODIFFUSION
7628	OTHER RADIO RECEIVERS	W 14245	131.5	W 26006	354.7	W 18008	222.8	W 4946	63.6	AUTRES RECEPT RADIO
763	SOUND RECORDRS,PHONOGRPH	W 21332	620.4	W 23554	692.7	W 30047	838.3	W 27603	803.8	PHONO,APP ENREGISTREMENT
7638	OTHR SOUND APPARATUS ETC	W 21292	619.6	W 23299	686.2	W 29911	831.4	W 27192	788.9	AUT APP D'ENREGIS,REPROD
76381	TV IMAGE,SND RECRDRS ETC	W 17758	510.5	W 17411	527.3	W 21689	648.8	W 20653	637.2	APP ENREG,REPRO IMAG,SON
76388	DICTATING MACHINES ETC	W 3534	109.2	W 5888	159.0	W 8222	182.6	W 6539	151.7	MACHINES A DICTER
764	TELECOM EQPT,PTS,ACC NES	W 32009	400.1	W 34441	389.1	W 42660	724.1	W 65933	629.8	EQUIP TELECOM,PIECES
7641	LINE TELEPHONE,ETC EQUIP	W 3604	80.5	W 3777	64.2	W 2984	231.0	W 3451	195.5	APP TELEPHON PAR FIL
7649	PTS NES OF EQUIPMT OF 76	W 13526	234.0	W 14646	229.8	W 17744	365.9	W 27185	274.3	PIECES DE LA DIV 76
76493	TELECOMM EQUIPMT PTS NES	W 9339	148.0	W 12458	149.7	W 12861	231.3	W 19379	173.9	PIECES 761,762,764.3,8
77	ELECTRIC MACHNRY NES ETC		613.7		808.5		1085.6		1084.3	MACH APP ELECT NDA
773	ELECTR DISTRIBUTNG EQUIP	W 4382	44.9	W 4934	72.1	W 7689	142.2	W 16286	182.1	EQUIPMT DISTRIBUTION ELECT
7731	INSULATED WIRE,CABLE ETC	W 4213	44.6	W 4838	71.5	W 7485	141.4	W 15893	180.7	FILS,CABLES ISOLES ELECT
776	TRANSISTORS,VALVES,ETC	W 2421	107.4	W 2769	145.4	W 8082	220.4	W 10731	220.8	LAMPES,TUBES,VALVES
778	ELECTRICAL MACHINERY NES	W 87891	317.9	W 101189	386.8	W 119246	466.5	W 330299	412.5	AUTRES MACH ELECT NDA
7781	BATTERIES,ACCUMULATORS	W 72225	182.4	W 81400	225.6	W 96574	279.8	W 213592	235.6	PILES ET ACCUMULATEURS
77811	PRIMARY BATTERIES,CELLS	W 45775	127.8	W 54346	151.8	W 51463	161.7	W 35454	127.2	PILES ELECTRIQUES,PIECES
78	ROAD VEHICLES		314.2		372.2		348.3		324.8	VEHICULES ROUTIERS
785	CYCLES,ETC MOTRZD OR NOT	W 39598	243.3	W 40745	246.9	W 31535	183.6	W 38953	171.3	MOTOCYCLES SCOOTERS
7853	INVAL CARR, PTS OF 785	W 26950	139.7	W 29387	157.8	W 24094	120.2	W 33277	121.9	FAUTEUILS INVALIDES,PIECES
78539	PARTS,ACCES NES OF 785	W 26950	139.7	W 29370	157.7	W 24094	120.2	W 33086	121.4	PIECES DU 785
79	OTHR TRANSPORT EQUIPMENT		133.9		108.0		223.6		95.3	AUTRE MATERIEL TRANSPORT
793	SHIPS AND BOATS ETC	W 34549	68.4	W 38982	91.1	W 64584	192.7	W 80968	71.2	NAVIRES BATEAUX,ETC
8	MISC MANUFACTURED GOODS		7499.9		7806.2		8613.8		6876.0	ART MANUFACTURES DIVERS
821	*FURNITURE,PARTS THEREOF	W 325814	784.5	W 355761	865.9	W 381786	952.7	W 400819	760.9	MEUBLES ET PIECES
8211	CHAIRS,SEATS AND PARTS	W 118627	322.6	W 125941	357.3	W 134911	404.9	W 165726	316.1	SIEGES ET PIECES
82111	CHAIRS AND OTHER SEATS	W 105458	303.8	W 112378	337.2	W 119234	383.2	W 156194	301.1	SIEGES
8219	FURNITURE AND PARTS NES	W 205625	457.2	W 227622	501.3	W 245653	542.0	W 233200	439.1	AUTRES MEUBLES ET PIECES
82192	WOOD FURNITURE NES	W 128976	265.0	W 152967	311.2	W 162904	354.1	W 168486	330.6	MEUBLES NDA EN BOIS
82199	OTHR FURN,FURN PARTS NES	W 74939	188.3	W 73643	187.9	W 81020	183.8	W 63697	106.3	MEUBLES NDA AUTRES MATIERES
84	CLOTHING AND ACCESSORIES		3272.9		3451.9		3654.7		2952.9	VETEMENTS
842	MENS OUTERWEAR NOT KNIT	W 46046	823.7	W 49697	728.0	W 54788	834.6	W 43149	650.3	VET DESSUS POUR HOMMES
8421	— OVERCOATS,OTHER COATS	W 6043	123.0	W 6715	116.0	W 5823	115.1	W 5092	85.6	MANTEAUX HOMMES MAT TEXT
8423	— TROUSERS,BREECHES ETC	W 17958	225.6	W 21370	263.8	W 24743	327.0	W 21090	282.6	PANTALONS HOMMES MAT TEX
8429	— OTHER OUTER GARMENTS	W 17659	401.9	W 17281	286.0	W 20119	330.1	W 13527	231.7	AUT VET DES HOM MAT TEX
843	WOMENS OUTERWEAR NONKNIT	W 54048	860.7	W 55560	887.8	W 60556	965.0	W 69865	854.4	VET DESSUS FEMMES MAT TEX
8433	— DRESSES	W 9758	148.2	W 10532	173.7	W 12716	213.7	W 23639	172.7	ROBES EN MAT-TEXTILES
8435	— BLOUSES	W 11511	209.8	W 9324	180.7	W 10841	194.3	W 9367	183.2	BLOUSES FEM MAT TEXTILES
8439	— OTHER OUTER GARMENTS	W 22145	324.9	W 23185	336.3	W 24903	374.0	W 25582	355.6	AUT VET DES FEM MAT TEXT
844	UNDER GARMENTS NOT KNIT	W 20439	314.0	W 27253	434.4	W 25746	408.5	W 22023	327.9	VETEMENT DESSOUS MAT TEX
8441	— MENS SHIRTS	W 15554	247.6	W 20593	330.3	W 19343	314.6	W 17488	259.0	CHEMISES HOMMES MAT TEXT
84411	—— OF COTTON	W 8805	147.6	W 11534	198.8	W 11539	203.6	W 9581	169.4	CHEMISES HOMMES DE COTON
845	OUTERWEAR KNIT NONELASTC	W 42968	578.0	W 44028	621.0	W 46280	654.8	W 43070	506.7	VET DESSOUS,ACCES BONNET
8451	— JERSEYS,PULLOVERS ETC	W 19329	243.4	W 20046	258.3	W 21543	290.8	W 19466	214.6	CHANDAILS,PULL-OVERS ETC
8459	— OTHER,CLTHG ACCESRYS	W 17528	252.8	W 18850	283.7	W 20053	296.2	W 19324	247.8	AUT VET DESSUS DE BONNE
846	UNDER GARMENTS KNITTED	W 29693	426.0	W 31843	489.7	W 33875	505.7	W 28408	393.7	SOUS VETS DE BONNETERIE
8462	— OF COTTON NON ELASTIC	W 18342	223.1	W 19292	246.0	W 20826	251.2	W 17356	186.7	SOUS-VET BONNET COTON
84629	—— OTHER	W 18342	223.1	W 19292	246.0	W 20826	251.2	W 17356	186.7	AUT SOUS-VET BONNET COTON
8463	— OF SYNTH FBR NONELAST	W 8850	135.6	W 9448	156.9	W 10180	169.2	W 8818	149.9	SOUS-VET BONNET FIB SYNT
84632	—— MENS SHIRTS	W 8770	134.8	W 9322	155.3	W 9943	166.1	W 8601	146.2	CHEMISES DE BON FIB SYNMT
848	HEADGEAR,NONTXTL CLOTHNG	W 16562	194.6	W 17187	210.2	W 22160	200.8	W 22486	167.9	VET ACCES MAT AUT QUE TEX
8481	LEATHER CLOTHES,ACCESSOR	W 3696	148.0	W 3472	146.5	W 3557	121.9	W 2863	90.9	VET ACCES MAT CUIR ARTIF
851	*FOOTWEAR	W 170935	1848.4	W 177373	1998.2	W 168460	2135.0	W 131258	1477.2	CHAUSSURES
85101	FOOTWEAR RUBBER,PLASTIC	W 41024	318.7	W 46267	375.7	W 52546	459.7	W 54696	329.7	CHAUS SEMELLES CAOUTCH
85102	FOOTWEAR LEATHER	W 127094	1511.5	W 128764	1602.0	W 114341	1662.4	W 76295	1145.6	CHAUS SEMELLES EN CUIR
88	PHOTO EQU,OPTICL GDS ETC		172.9		200.1		233.4		323.2	APP,FOURN PHOTO,OP,MONTR
881	PHOTO APPARAT,EQUIPT NES	W 1336	117.7	W 1499	123.6	W 1874	123.0	W 1795	203.7	APP,EQUIP PHOTO NDA
8811	CAMERAS STILL,FLASH APP	W 979	116.0	W 986	122.9	W 1218	122.4	W 1629	203.1	APPAREILS PHOTO,PIECES
88111	STILL CAMERAS	W 945	112.2	W 891	121.1	W 1181	119.0	W 1479	193.2	APPAREILS PHOTOGRAPHIQ
89	MISC MANUFCTRD GOODS NES		1282.7		1142.6		1478.5		1221.2	ART MANUFACTURES DIVERS
893	ARTICLES OF PLASTIC NES		141.5		185.2		203.8		141.3	OUVRAGES EN MAT DIVIS 58

5. Special Exports F.O.B. by Commodities according to the S.I.T.C. (Rev. 2) in million U.S. Dollars
Exportations Spéciales F.O.B. par Produits d'après la C.T.C.I. (Rév. 2) en millions de Dollars E.U.

SITC CTCI	COMMODITY	1994 QUANTITY QUANTITE	1994 VALUE VALEUR	1995 QUANTITY QUANTITE	1995 VALUE VALEUR	1996 QUANTITY QUANTITE	1996 VALUE VALEUR	1997 QUANTITY QUANTITE	1997 VALUE VALEUR	PRODUIT
894	TOYS,SPORTING GOODS,ETC	W 28301	181.4	W 34635	345.0	W 35079	405.1	W 18215	130.5	VOITURES ENFANTS,JOUETS
8942	TOYS,INDOOR GAMES ETC	W 24055	153.9	W 30661	310.8	W 31390	372.0	W 14178	96.3	JOUETS,JEUX ETC
89423	TOYS NES	W 17673	120.8	W 21224	138.8	W 17731	140.1	W 8285	65.4	JOUETS,MODELES REDUITS
89424	INDOOR GAME EQUIPMENT	W 2736	4.9	W 4765	130.9	W 6235	167.3	W 3390	8.4	ART,JEUX DE SOCIETE
897	GOLD,SILVER WARE,JEWELRY		726.3		334.9		528.2		703.4	BIJOUTERIE,ORFEVRERIE
8973	PREC JEWLRY,GLD-SILVWARE		721.8		331.1		524.8		700.8	BIJOUX OR,ARGENT ORFEVRE
89731	PRECIOUS METAL JEWELLERY		698.6		303.4		490.8		661.2	ART BIJOUTERIE,JOAILLER
9	GOODS NOT CLASSD BY KIND		150.7		50.0		92.1		6722.4	ART TRANSACT NON CLASSES
931	*SPECIAL TRANSACTIONS								6495.4	TRANS.SPECIALES
971	*GOLD,NON MONETARY NES	K 11821	146.4	K 3916	45.5	K 8737	88.0	K 33016	224.1	OR NON MONETAIRE
97101	NONMON GLD UNWRT,SEMIMFD	K 11607	146.3	K 3738	45.4	K 7689	88.0	K 26905	224.0	OR,ALLIAGES D'OR BRUTS

1. HISTORICAL SERIES, 1959–1995 GENERAL TRADE, IMPORTS C.I.F., EXPORTS F.O.B.
SERIES HISTORIQUES, 1959–1995 COMMERCE GENERAL, IMPORTATIONS C.A.F., EXPORTATIONS F.O.B

YEAR ANNEE	VALUE IN MILLION IRANIAN RIALS # 1 VALEUR EN MILLION IRANIAN RIALS # 1 MERCHANDISE –MARCHANDISE		GOLD –OR		CONVERSION FACTORS U.S. CENTS PER IRANIAN RIAL FACTEURS DE CONVERSION CENTS E.U. PAR IRANIAN RIAL		INDEX NUMBERS –INDICES QUANTUM		UNIT VALUE VALEUR UNITAIRE	
	IMPORTS	EXPORTS	IMPORTS	EXPORTS	IMPORTS	EXPORTS	IMPORTS	EXPORTS	IMPORTS	EXPORTS
1959	47.34	58.33			1.3201	1.3201				
1960	49.24	61.74			1.3201	1.3201				
1961	51.51	51.20			1.3201	1.3201				
1962	40.14	74.24			1.3201	1.3201				
1963	39.22	69.46			1.3201	1.3201				
1964	50.67	94.95			1.3201	1.3201				
1965	65.15	98.71			1.3201	1.3201				
1966	70.32	99.18			1.3201	1.3201				
1967	85.24	146.20			1.3201	1.3201				
1968	104.80	142.50			1.3201	1.3201				
1969	115.70	159.10			1.3201	1.3201				
1970	125.90	198.71			1.3201	1.3201				
1971	141.90	289.80			1.3201	1.3201				
1972	182.50	306.00			1.3201	1.3201				
1973	233.02	425.80			1.4560	1.4571				
1974	367.40	1458.80			1.4787	1.4787				
1975	700.30	1367.10			1.4770	1.4784				
1976	905.20	1651.60			1.4245	1.4231				
1977	1034.00	1713.10			1.4161	1.4161				
1978	954.90	1557.60			1.4189	1.4189				
1979	686.30	1407.80			1.4189	1.4189				
1980	863.30	994.39			1.4185	1.4219				
1981	985.30	980.79			1.2722	1.2840				
1982	1002.30	936.71			1.1961	1.1836				
1983	1582.70	1684.69			1.1568	1.1580				
1984	1332.67	1127.79			1.1145	1.1107				
1985	1058.34	1218.62			1.0997	1.1037				
1986	720.69	521.88			1.2654	1.2722				
1987	658.85	734.86			1.3992	1.4056				
1988	567.92	594.17			1.4577	1.4538				
1989	927.30	939.95			1.3910	1.3887				
1990	1261.70	1205.70			1.4756	1.4858				
1992	2009.95	1299.58			1.5262	1.5288				
1993	24457.35	14409.04			0.0973	0.0885				
1994	34520.00	17515.00			0.0572	0.0572				
1995	21522.73	32554.20			0.0572	0.0572				

2. IMPORTS BY BROAD ECONOMIC CATEGORY AND EXPORTS BY INDUSTRIAL ORIGIN. (PERCENTAGE OF TOTAL VALUE)
IMPORTATIONS PAR CATEGORIES ECONOMIQUES ET EXPORTATIONS PAR BRANCHE D'ACTIVITE.(EN POURCENTAGE DE LA VALEUR TOTALE)

IMPORTS – IMPORTATIONS

	1989	1990	1991	1992	1993	1994	1995
TOTAL IMPORTS–IMPORTATIONS TOTALES							
1 FOOD BEV–ALIMENTATION BOISSONS							
11 PRIMARY–PRODUITS DE BASE							
111 FOR INDUSTRY–POUR L'INDUSTRIE							
112 FOR HOUSEHOLDS–POUR LES MENAGES							
12 PROCESSED–PRODUITS ELABORES							
121 FOR INDUSTRY–POUR L'INDUSTRIE							
122 FOR HOUSEHOLDS–POUR LES MENAGES							
2 IND SUPPLIES–APPROV INDUSTRIELS							
21 PRIMARY–PRODUITS DE BASE							
22 PROCESSED–PRODUITS ELABORES							
3 FUELS–COMBUSTIBLES							
31 PRIMARY–PRODUITS DE BASE							
32 PROCESSED–PRODUITS ELABORES							
321 MOTOR SPIRIT–ESSENCE							
322 OTHER–AUTRES							
4 MACHINERY–EQUIPEMENT							
41 CAPITAL EQUIPMENT–MACHINES							
42 PARTS–PIECES ACCESSOIRES							
5 TRANSPORT–TRANSPORT							
51 PASSENGER CARS–AUTOMOBILES							
52 OTHER–AUTRES							
521 INDUSTRIAL–INDUSTRIELS							
522 NON INDUSTRIAL–NON INDUSTRIEL							
53 PARTS–PIECES ACCESSOIRES							
6 CONSUM GOODS–BIENS CONSOMMATION							
61 DURABLE–DURABLES							
62 SEMI DURABLE–SEMI DURABLES							
63 NON DURABLE–NON DURABLES							
7 GOODS NES–BIENS NDA							

EXPORTS – EXPORTATIONS

	1989	1990	1991	1992	1993	1994	1995
TOTAL EXPORTS–EXPORTATIONS TOTALES							
1 AGRICULTURE							
2 MINING QUARRY–INDUS EXTRACTIVES							
3 MANUFACTURING–IND MANUFACTUR							
31 FOOD BEV TOBACCO–ALIM BOISS TAB							
32 TEXTILES–INDUSTRIES TEXTILES							
33 WOOD & PRODUCTS–BOIS & PRODUITS							
34 PAPER & PRODUCTS–PAPIER & PRODT							
35 CHEMICALS–INDUSTRIES CHIMIQUES							
36 NON METAL MIN–MIN NON METAL							
37 BASIC METAL–IND METAL BASE							
38 METAL MANUF–MANUF METAL							
39 OTH MANUF IND–AUTRES MANUF							

3. TRADE BY PRINCIPAL COUNTRIES OF PURCHASE AND SALE (VALUE IN MILLION U.S. DOLLARS)
ECHANGES SELON LES PRINCIPAUX PAYS D'ACHAT ET DE VENTE (VALEUR EN MILLIONS DE DOLLARS EU)

COUNTRIES–PAYS	GENERAL IMPORTS C.I.F. IMPORTATIONS GENERALES C.A.F					COUNTRIES–PAYS	GENERAL EXPORTS F.O.B. # 1 EXPORTATIONS GENERALES F.O.B.				
	1991	1992	1993	1994	1995		1991	1992	1993	1994	1995
World		30712.1	23797.0	12061.0	12311.0	Monde		19868.0	18080.0	19164.0	18621.0
Africa		176.8				Afrique					
Americas		2441.4				Amériques					
– Northern America		1427.8				– Amérique du Nord					
– LAIA		972.8				– ALAI					
– CACM		13.8				– MCAC					
– Caribbean		26.1				– Caraïbes					
– Rest of America		1.0				– Autre Amérique					
Asia excl fmr USSR		8964.1				Asie anc. URSS exclus					
– Middle East		2847.0				– Moyen–Orient					
Asia former USSR		219.5				Asie ancienne URSS					
Europe excl fmr USSR		18114.8				Europe anc. URSS exclus					
– European Union		16521.9				– Union Européenne					
– Eastern Europe		604.3				– Europe de l'Est					
– Rest of Europe		988.7				– Autre de l'Europe					
Europe former USSR		333.9				Europe ancienne URSS					
Oceania		371.5				Océanie					
Other		89.9				Autre					
Germany/Allemagne		7524.1				Turkey/Turquie		356.6	692.0	689.0	627.0
United Arab Emirates		1520.2	1101.0	1069.0	971.0	Indonesia/Indonésie		1.4	457.0	444.0	202.0
Japan/Japon		3679.8				United Arab Emirates		335.4	225.0	219.0	260.0
Italy/Italie		2901.3				Germany/Allemagne		747.6			
United Kingdom		1677.2				Morocco/Maroc		0.0	156.0	160.0	157.0
Turkey/Turquie		668.3	318.0	294.0	292.0	Pakistan		36.1	135.0	118.0	171.0
Belgium–Luxembourg		1065.7				Azerbaijan/Azerbaïdjan		28.0	211.0	61.0	73.0
Saudi Arabia		80.1	272.0	264.0	239.0	Italy/Italie		221.7			
France, Monaco		823.4				Sudan/Soudan		37.4	41.0	42.0	48.0
USA/Etats–Unis d'Amer		820.6				Switzerland,Liechtenst.		160.9			
Switzerland,Liechtenst.		769.0				Saudi Arabia		4.2	32.0	65.0	54.0
Korea, Republic of		676.5				Turkmenistan/Turkménistn		20.8	42.0	63.0	27.0
Netherlands/Pays–Bas		673.3				China/Chine		147.1			
Azerbaijan/Azerbaïdjan		205.1		241.0	180.0	Malaysia/Malaisie		2.5	56.0	39.0	44.0
Canada		607.2				Belarus/Bélarus		139.0			
Oman		1.5	202.0	196.0	178.0	Kuwait/Koweït		51.0		80.0	
Austria/Autriche		564.2				Lebanon/Liban		27.6	30.0	31.0	35.0
Sweden/Suède		518.5				Bahrain/Bahreïn		22.5	25.0	25.0	29.0
Argentina/Argentine		437.4				France, Monaco		85.9			
Iraq		419.0				Japan/Japon		82.2			
Brazil/Brésil		404.3				Syrian Arab Republic		9.9	17.0	18.0	32.0
China/Chine		338.1				United Kingdom		74.1			
Russian Federation		331.8				Qatar		18.1	17.0	17.0	12.0
Spain/Espagne		317.5				Canada		50.6			
Malaysia/Malaisie		41.1	65.0	68.0	127.0	Austria/Autriche		37.7			
Pakistan		102.1	20.0	29.0	135.0	Jordan/Jordanie		3.5	10.0	10.0	8.0
Indonesia/Indonésie		200.7	16.0	16.0	24.0	Belgium–Luxembourg		28.8			
Thailand/Thaïlande		244.6				Netherlands/Pays–Bas		24.3			
India/Inde		244.5				Bangladesh		0.1	6.0	6.0	7.0
Denmark/Danemark		239.6				India/Inde		17.4			
Australia/Australie		237.2				Tunisia/Tunisie		3.9	7.0	3.0	3.0
Bangladesh		80.8	32.0	42.0	37.0	Spain/Espagne		16.6			
Singapore/Singapour		179.6				Oman		1.8	2.0	2.0	9.0
Senegal/Sénégal		108.4	24.0	26.0	10.0	USA/Etats–Unis d'Amer		14.3			
Former Czechoslovakia		168.1				Korea, Republic of		14.2			
Morocco/Maroc		12.3	61.0	66.0	25.0	Sweden/Suède		13.6			
Yugoslavia/Yougoslavie		153.4				Afghanistan		13.4			
Other Asia n.e.s.		151.4				Other Asia n.e.s.		10.2			
Romania/Roumanie		140.5				Finland/Finlande		9.7			
Finland/Finlande		137.5				China, Hong Kong SAR		8.1			

(VALUE AS PERCENTAGE OF WORLD TOTAL)(VALEURS EN POURCENTAGE DU TOTAL MONDIAL)

	1986	1987	1988	1989	1990	1991	1992	1993	1994	1995		1986	1987	1988	1989	1990	1991	1992	1993	1994	1995
Africa							0.6				Afrique										
Americas	6.1	11.0	7.1	8.6	8.6		7.9				Amériques	16.1	19.5	9.0							
– Northern America	0.7	1.1	1.0	2.2	2.2		4.6				– Amérique du Nord	12.7	16.7	5.9							
– LAIA	5.3	10.0	6.1	6.4	6.4		3.2				– ALAI	3.4	2.8	3.1							
– CACM							0.0				– MCAC										
– Caribbean							0.1				– Caraïbes										
– Rest of America							0.0				– Autre Amérique										
Asia excl fmr USSR	28.9	25.1	21.6	26.0	24.8		29.2				Asie anc. URSS exclus	36.8	26.7	26.7							
– Middle East	12.0	9.2	8.6	12.9	9.1		9.3				– Moyen–Orient	5.1	8.5	7.7							
Asia former USSR							0.7				Asie ancienne URSS										
Europe excl fmr USSR	48.3	46.5	51.4	45.3	52.7		59.0				Europe anc. URSS exclus	43.3	43.2	52.0							
– European Union	45.0	43.2	47.3	41.6	48.6		53.8				– Union Européenne	38.0	37.0	44.3							
– Eastern Europe							2.0				– Europe de l'Est	3.1	4.2	5.2							
– Rest of Europe	3.4	3.4	4.1	3.7	4.0		3.2				– Autre de l'Europe	2.2	2.0	2.5							
Europe former USSR	1.0	2.1	2.7	1.6	1.6		1.1				Europe ancienne URSS	0.3	1.1	0.7							
Oceania	2.6	3.5	2.6	3.5	3.7		1.2				Océanie										
Other	13.1	11.8	14.5	14.2	8.7		0.3				Autre	2.0	1.5	1.5							
Germany/Allemagne							24.5				Turkey/Turquie	2.8	7.0	6.0	1.5	0.6		1.8	3.8	3.6	3.4
United Arab Emirates	5.7	4.2	3.4	7.4	5.2		4.9	4.6	8.9	7.9	Indonesia/Indonésie							0.0	2.5	2.3	1.1
Japan/Japon	13.5	11.2	10.2	7.6	10.3		12.0				United Arab Emirates	2.4	1.5	1.7	1.1	0.9		1.7	1.2	1.1	1.4
Italy/Italie	6.5	6.1	5.1	6.3	8.0		9.4				Germany/Allemagne							3.8			
United Kingdom	6.8	5.9	6.8	4.4	5.4		5.5				Morocco/Maroc				0.1	0.0		0.0	0.9	0.8	0.8
Turkey/Turquie	6.3	5.1	5.2	5.5	3.9		2.2	1.3	2.4	2.4	Pakistan	0.7	0.0	0.0	0.0	0.0		0.2	0.7	0.6	0.9
Belgium–Luxembourg	3.6	3.4	4.8	3.8	4.3		3.5				Azerbaijan/Azerbaïdjan							0.1	1.2	0.3	0.4
Saudi Arabia							0.3	1.1	2.2	1.9	Italy/Italie	10.2	8.5	6.2	6.4	0.9		1.1			
France, Monaco	0.5	1.0	3.0	2.1	2.6		2.7				Sudan/Soudan							0.2	0.2	0.2	0.3
USA/Etats–Unis d'Amer							2.7				Switzerland,Liechtenst.	0.8	0.9	0.9	1.7	0.6		0.8			

4. General Imports C.I.F. by Commodities according to the S.I.T.C. (Rev. 2) in million U.S. Dollars
Importations Générales C.A.F. par Produits d'après la C.T.C.I. (Rév. 2) en millions de Dollars E.U.

SITC CTCI	COMMODITY	1992		1993		1994		1995		PRODUIT
		QUANTITY QUANTITE	VALUE VALEUR	QUANTITY QUANTITE	VALUE VALEUR	QUANTITY QUANTITE	VALUE VALEUR	QUANTITY QUANTITE	VALUE VALEUR	
	ALL COMMODITIES									TOUS PRODUITS

5. General Exports F.O.B. by Commodities according to the S.I.T.C. (Rev. 2) in million U.S. Dollars
Exportations Générales F.O.B. par Produits d'après la C.T.C.I. (Rév. 2) en millions de Dollars E.U.

SITC CTCI	COMMODITY	1992		1993		1994		1995		PRODUIT
		QUANTITY QUANTITE	VALUE VALEUR	QUANTITY QUANTITE	VALUE VALEUR	QUANTITY QUANTITE	VALUE VALEUR	QUANTITY QUANTITE	VALUE VALEUR	
	ALL COMMODITIES		19868.0							TOUS PRODUITS
057	FRUIT,NUTS,FRESH,DRIED		503.5							FRUITS FRAIS OU SECS
05779	NUTS EDIBLE,FRSH,DRY,NES		364.0							FRUITS A COQUES NDA
52	INORGANIC CHEMICALS		69.1							PROD CHIM INORGANIQUES
659	FLOOR COVERINGS,ETC		1133.4							COUVRE–PARQUETS,TAPIS ETC
68221	COPPER BARS,WIRE,ETC		157.1							BARRES,PROFILES ET FILS

FOOT NOTES – NOTES

TABLE 1 –
1 Values are in thousand million rials.
TABLE 3 –
1 Exports of petroleum products are included at the Worl d total level only.
TABLEAU 1 –
1 Les valeurs sont exprimées en milliards de rials.
TABLEAU 3 –
1 Les exportations des produits pétroliers sont comprise s seulement au niveau du monde.

1. HISTORICAL SERIES, 1962–1997 GENERAL TRADE, IMPORTS C.I.F., EXPORTS F.O.B.
SERIES HISTORIQUES, 1962–1997 COMMERCE GENERAL, IMPORTATIONS C.A.F., EXPORTATIONS F.O.B

YEAR ANNEE	VALUE IN MILLION IRISH POUNDS / VALEUR EN MILLION IRISH POUNDS: MERCHANDISE – MARCHANDISE IMPORTS	MERCHANDISE – MARCHANDISE EXPORTS	GOLD – OR IMPORTS	GOLD – OR EXPORTS	CONVERSION FACTORS U.S. CENTS PER IRISH POUND / FACTEURS DE CONVERSION CENTS E.U. PAR IRISH POUND: IMPORTS	EXPORTS	INDEX NUMBERS – INDICES: QUANTUM IMPORTS	QUANTUM EXPORTS	UNIT VALUE / VALEUR UNITAIRE IMPORTS	UNIT VALUE / VALEUR UNITAIRE EXPORTS
1962	273.70	174.40			280.0000	280.0000				
1963	307.90	197.20			280.0000	280.0000				
1964	349.60	222.60			280.0000	280.0000				
1965	372.00	221.30			280.0000	280.0000				
1966	373.30	244.80			280.0000	280.0000				
1967	392.40	285.80			275.1700	275.3200				
1968	496.60	333.40			240.0000	240.0000				
1969	590.30	371.90			240.0000	240.0000				
1970	655.50	433.10			240.0000	240.0000				
1971	754.90	538.70			243.0450	243.3800				
1972	838.10	647.50			249.4580	249.1080				
1973	1137.20	869.20			245.3610	245.2030				
1974	1626.80	1134.40			234.5720	234.3970				
1975	1704.10	1447.40			221.7360	220.5620				
1976	2337.90	1859.10			179.4800	178.3210				
1977	3090.90	2578.20			174.5100	174.8230				
1978	3713.10	2963.20			191.7710	192.0230				
1979	4827.90	3496.10			204.7030	205.1310				
1980	5420.70	4082.00			205.7530	205.7460	64	43	69	66
1981	6577.50	4776.70			161.2575	160.6862	65	44	82	76
1982	6890.20	6379.80			141.1912	140.2556	62	47	88	85
1983	7366.80	6943.80			124.7355	124.1352	64	53	92	92
1984	8912.90	8897.60			108.4137	108.2176	70	62	102	100
1985	9432.70	9743.20			106.2652	106.3493	72	65	105	104
1986	8621.00	9374.00			134.0769	134.2688	75	68	93	97
1987	9155.00	10723.00			148.9809	149.1719	79	78	93	97
1988	10215.00	12305.00			152.6120	152.6120	83	83	99	104
1989	12284.00	14597.00			141.8980	141.8980	94	92	105	110
1990	12469.00	14337.00			165.8646	165.6368	100	100	100	100
1991	12851.00	15019.00			161.5127	161.2822	101	106	102	99
1992	13195.00	16744.00			170.3880	170.3989	106	121	100	97
1993	14885.00	19830.00			146.4145	146.3525	113	133	105	104
1994	17283.01	22753.01			149.9185	150.1117	128	153	108	104
1995	20619.01	27825.01			160.3755	160.4223	146	184	113	106
1996	22459.01	30376.00			160.0381	160.0624	161	202	111	105
1997	25860.00	35027.01			151.6096	151.4810	185	230	112	106

2. IMPORTS BY BROAD ECONOMIC CATEGORY AND EXPORTS BY INDUSTRIAL ORIGIN. (PERCENTAGE OF TOTAL VALUE)
IMPORTATIONS PAR CATEGORIES ECONOMIQUES ET EXPORTATIONS PAR BRANCHE D'ACTIVITE.(EN POURCENTAGE DE LA VALEUR TOTALE)

IMPORTS – IMPORTATIONS

	1991	1992	1993	1994	1995	1996	1997
TOTAL IMPORTS–IMPORTATIONS TOTALES	100.	100.	100.	100.	100.	100.	100.
1 FOOD BEV–ALIMENTATION BOISSONS	8.9	9.1	7.7	7.5	6.6	6.6	6.2
11 PRIMARY–PRODUITS DE BASE	2.7	2.6	2.1	2.2	2.1	2.0	1.8
111 FOR INDUSTRY–POUR L'INDUSTRIE	0.7	0.6	0.5	0.5	0.4	0.4	0.3
112 FOR HOUSEHOLDS–POUR LES MENAGES	2.0	1.9	1.6	1.7	1.7	1.6	1.4
12 PROCESSED–PRODUITS ELABORES	6.2	6.6	5.7	5.4	4.6	4.7	4.4
121 FOR INDUSTRY–POUR L'INDUSTRIE	0.8	0.9	0.8	0.8	0.7	0.7	0.6
122 FOR HOUSEHOLDS–POUR LES MENAGES	5.4	5.7	4.9	4.6	3.8	4.0	3.9
2 IND SUPPLIES–APPROV INDUSTRIELS	28.8	27.9	24.8	25.2	24.5	23.2	22.5
21 PRIMARY–PRODUITS DE BASE	2.5	2.2	2.3	2.3	1.9	1.6	1.3
22 PROCESSED–PRODUITS ELABORES	26.3	25.7	22.5	22.9	22.6	21.6	21.2
3 FUELS–COMBUSTIBLES	5.7	5.1	4.7	3.8	3.2	3.6	3.4
31 PRIMARY–PRODUITS DE BASE	2.6	2.4	2.1	1.8	1.5	1.5	1.8
32 PROCESSED–PRODUITS ELABORES	3.1	2.7	2.6	2.0	1.7	2.1	1.5
321 MOTOR SPIRIT–ESSENCE	0.7	0.6	0.5	0.4	0.4	0.4	0.4
322 OTHER–AUTRES	2.4	2.0	2.1	1.6	1.4	1.6	1.1
4 MACHINERY–EQUIPEMENT	26.7	28.5	30.6	31.6	35.6	34.5	37.1
41 CAPITAL EQUIPMENT–MACHINES	16.4	17.0	18.1	19.1	20.3	22.2	25.1
42 PARTS–PIECES ACCESSOIRES	10.3	11.5	12.6	12.5	15.3	12.4	12.1
5 TRANSPORT–TRANSPORT	8.3	7.7	7.1	7.8	7.3	7.8	8.8
51 PASSENGER CARS–AUTOMOBILES	2.8	3.0	2.8	3.1	2.8	3.6	4.1
52 OTHER–AUTRES	2.7	1.9	1.6	1.6	1.8	1.6	2.1
521 INDUSTRIAL–INDUSTRIELS	2.6	1.8	1.4	1.5	1.7	1.6	2.0
522 NON INDUSTRIAL–NON INDUSTRIEL	0.1	0.1	0.1	0.1	0.1	0.1	0.1
53 PARTS–PIECES ACCESSOIRES	2.8	2.8	2.7	3.1	2.7	2.6	2.6
6 CONSUM GOODS–BIENS CONSOMMATION	18.4	18.5	15.9	15.0	13.4	15.7	14.5
61 DURABLE–DURABLES	3.6	3.2	2.4	2.3	2.2	3.0	2.8
62 SEMI DURABLE–SEMI DURABLES	10.4	10.8	9.8	9.0	7.7	9.4	8.3
63 NON DURABLE–NON DURABLES	4.3	4.4	3.7	3.7	3.4	3.3	3.4
7 GOODS NES–BIENS NDA	3.2	3.1	9.0	9.0	9.4	8.5	7.5

EXPORTS – EXPORTATIONS

	1991	1992	1993	1994	1995	1996	1997
TOTAL EXPORTS–EXPORTATIONS TOTALES	100.	100.	100.	100.	100.	100.	100.
1 AGRICULTURE	3.2	2.9	2.3	2.5	1.9	1.9	1.4
2 MINING QUARRY–INDUS EXTRACTIVES	0.8	0.8	0.7	0.6	0.5	0.4	0.4
3 MANUFACTURING–IND MANUFACTUR	95.9	96.3	97.0	96.9	97.7	97.7	98.2
31 FOOD BEV TOBACCO–ALIM BOISS TAB	20.4	22.5	20.3	21.4	18.1	15.1	10.9
32 TEXTILES–INDUSTRIES TEXTILES	4.7	4.3	3.5	3.7	2.8	2.8	2.2
33 WOOD & PRODUCTS–BOIS & PRODUITS	0.3	0.3	0.2	0.2	0.2	0.2	0.2
34 PAPER & PRODUCTS–PAPIER & PRODT	1.4	1.3	0.9	1.1	0.9	0.9	0.8
35 CHEMICALS–INDUSTRIES CHIMIQUES	21.3	22.7	22.3	26.5	20.9	25.9	27.4
36 NON METAL MIN–MIN NON METAL	1.1	1.0	0.8	0.8	0.6	0.7	0.7
37 BASIC METAL–IND METAL BASE	0.8	0.7	0.7	0.6	0.5	0.5	0.5
38 METAL MANUF–MANUF METAL	41.1	39.2	40.1	42.4	45.9	50.7	49.2
39 OTH MANUF IND–AUTRES MANUF	4.8	4.2	8.0	0.2	7.7	0.8	6.5

3. TRADE BY PRINCIPAL COUNTRIES OF ORIGIN AND DESTINATION (VALUE IN MILLION U.S. DOLLARS)
ECHANGES SELON LES PRINCIPAUX PAYS D'ORIGINE ET DE DESTINATION (VALEUR EN MILLIONS DE DOLLARS EU)

COUNTRIES–PAYS	GENERAL IMPORTS C.I.F. IMPORTATIONS GENERALES C.A.F				
	1993	1994	1995	1996	1997
World	21663.0	25763.8	32321.0	35764.7	39205.8
Africa	260.7	335.8	394.6	396.0	385.0
Americas	3986.9	5042.9	6181.6	6089.4	6451.6
– Northern America	3828.7	4868.2	5949.7	5786.9	6186.5
– LAIA	140.3	148.4	186.1	253.2	218.6
– CACM	9.7	8.8	18.7	16.8	25.5
– Caribbean	7.8	11.7	18.9	24.5	9.7
– Rest of America	0.5	5.8	8.1	8.0	11.2
Asia excl fmr USSR	3194.0	3362.6	5313.2	6202.1	7974.1
– Middle East	62.2	75.3	99.0	96.5	130.7
Asia former USSR	1.1	3.2	8.6	1.3	1.2
Europe excl fmr USSR	13330.9	15741.0	18985.1	21087.0	22605.4
– European Union	12680.4	14958.3	18141.1	20197.7	21453.7
– Eastern Europe	99.0	125.1	145.3	180.3	254.1
– Rest of Europe	551.5	657.5	698.8	708.9	897.6
Europe former USSR	52.5	38.0	50.2	80.6	37.4
Oceania	35.3	41.1	64.6	65.8	66.4
Other	801.5	1199.2	1323.1	1842.5	1684.8
United Kingdom	7846.2	9347.8	11498.3	12430.3	13216.4
USA/Etats–Unis d'Amer	3709.9	4709.9	5717.2	5537.3	5870.7
Germany/Allemagne	1568.6	1816.6	2256.2	2452.2	2328.2
Japan/Japon	1416.2	1233.6	1705.8	1929.9	2712.1
France, Monaco	845.8	981.0	1200.3	1395.6	1836.0
Areas n.e.s.	753.2	1134.0	1305.0	1478.8	1555.7
Singapore/Singapour	475.7	540.6	1292.7	1580.3	2151.6
Netherlands/Pays–Bas	680.9	727.3	871.3	1048.3	1260.5
Italy/Italie	440.8	568.0	637.7	750.4	704.9
Norway,Svalbard and JM	327.8	374.2	447.0	441.1	576.1
Belgium–Luxembourg	326.5	343.5	405.7	466.8	436.6
Malaysia/Malaisie	164.7	293.8	530.4	538.5	429.6
Other Asia n.e.s.	227.2	299.9	425.3	432.3	541.8
Sweden/Suède	300.0	370.1	346.1	481.6	426.1
China/Chine	306.7	307.2	346.7	407.1	478.4
Spain/Espagne	194.1	258.5	313.5	447.4	421.3
Korea, Republic of	130.6	126.8	268.9	392.6	531.6
Switzerland,Liechtenst.	202.0	258.6	215.7	235.5	276.4
Denmark/Danemark	166.1	186.7	227.2	261.6	285.9
Canada	118.7	158.2	232.1	249.3	315.6
Finland/Finlande	134.4	150.3	200.6	233.3	329.6
China, Hong Kong SAR	171.0	170.5	230.2	189.7	195.1
Thailand/Thaïlande	39.2	65.2	116.2	255.0	298.3
Free zones/Zone franches	48.4	65.2	18.1	363.7	129.2
Portugal	69.8	88.2	92.2	121.3	104.0
Guinea/Guinée	75.9	75.6	85.6	100.9	88.7
Austria/Autriche	90.4	97.6	71.0	83.8	78.5
Brazil/Brésil	85.0	91.1	92.2	75.7	74.9
Poland/Pologne	74.9	80.0	72.5	81.1	84.5
Israel/Israël	37.2	43.7	44.7	82.4	175.4
India/Inde	37.9	54.1	89.7	107.9	84.4
Indonesia/Indonésie	57.8	57.8	57.6	61.1	71.2
Turkey/Turquie	35.7	41.1	60.5	72.0	87.4
So. African Customs Un	34.0	64.8	69.6	54.5	57.3
Mexico/Mexique	11.6	12.4	54.6	103.1	79.0
Philippines	16.7	32.6	47.1	62.4	98.9
Morocco/Maroc	28.2	43.7	66.1	51.8	49.6
Ghana	28.0	38.4	40.9	44.1	52.2
Cote d'Ivoire	10.1	20.0	50.7	63.8	51.3
Hungary/Hongrie	6.8	10.6	20.2	29.2	97.8

COUNTRIES–PAYS	GENERAL EXPORTS F.O.B. EXPORTATIONS GENERALES F.O.B.				
	1993	1994	1995	1996	1997
Monde	28856.5	34395.1	43789.3	45565.4	53258.4
Afrique	483.0	602.2	695.7	738.5	879.4
Amériques	3281.0	3547.1	4427.0	5203.4	6966.8
– Amérique du Nord	2927.9	3179.1	3979.7	4683.9	6402.6
– ALAI	246.5	277.8	379.2	445.8	470.9
– MCAC	27.5	25.2	23.1	25.7	26.0
– Caraïbes	70.2	55.3	32.9	32.2	46.3
– Autre Amérique	8.9	9.7	12.1	15.8	20.9
Asie anc. URSS exclus	2281.7	2647.1	3452.0	4247.6	5236.9
– Moyen–Orient	471.9	490.9	634.2	638.4	773.3
Asie ancienne URSS	2.2	14.9	10.4	9.4	17.3
Europe anc. URSS exclus	21452.8	26167.3	33355.9	33764.5	37517.3
– Union Européenne	20520.2	24901.6	31649.2	31797.9	35450.3
– Europe de l'Est	115.0	174.7	365.8	429.7	471.7
– Autre de l'Europe	817.6	1091.0	1341.0	1537.0	1595.4
Europe ancienne URSS	100.0	225.6	397.5	439.4	423.9
Océanie	200.4	228.9	268.2	335.4	385.8
Autre	1055.4	962.0	1182.6	827.1	1830.9
United Kingdom	8204.0	9615.4	11140.1	11428.3	12946.7
Germany/Allemagne	3832.5	4837.0	6328.6	5844.8	6688.0
USA/Etats–Unis d'Amer	2621.7	2858.2	3641.8	4302.7	6052.5
France, Monaco	2640.2	3138.7	4143.4	3904.7	4185.8
Netherlands/Pays–Bas	1672.4	1900.6	3063.6	3234.8	3664.6
Belgium–Luxembourg	1165.6	1337.0	1908.6	2226.9	2657.1
Italy/Italie	1044.5	1334.1	1658.3	1645.3	1743.0
Japan/Japon	1063.4	1074.1	1307.4	1376.3	1702.8
Areas n.e.s.	1010.1	895.3	1158.7	827.1	1629.1
Spain/Espagne	636.0	841.8	1073.6	1092.3	1352.0
Switzerland,Liechtenst.	515.1	666.8	795.4	895.0	913.0
Sweden/Suède	499.8	757.4	809.5	857.5	799.6
Denmark/Danemark	263.0	329.2	546.4	609.8	572.4
Norway,Svalbard and JM	259.8	372.1	472.3	536.3	581.2
Canada	303.9	319.0	335.7	378.2	348.3
Malaysia/Malaisie	45.4	174.8	348.2	559.9	475.0
Korea, Republic of	54.9	124.9	158.8	328.6	757.8
Russian Federation	87.5	208.2	351.1	358.2	342.1
Australia/Australie	172.8	194.4	229.6	293.5	334.9
Singapore/Singapour	137.9	202.3	267.7	283.8	328.6
Saudi Arabia	202.9	187.6	241.5	234.8	279.6
Finland/Finlande	118.5	237.0	279.4	262.1	233.0
Austria/Autriche	162.9	251.2	263.5	229.7	213.8
Greece/Grèce	160.0	173.7	263.4	269.1	167.0
China, Hong Kong SAR	144.8	160.9	163.9	224.8	294.9
So. African Customs Un	87.4	143.4	166.2	246.0	344.6
Portugal	120.9	148.6	170.7	192.7	227.4
Egypt/Egypte	136.7	214.8	195.3	160.3	146.8
Mexico/Mexique	113.6	92.5	127.8	161.3	161.8
Philippines	31.2	39.6	82.3	231.6	243.0
Poland/Pologne	48.8	62.5	137.4	169.1	205.6
Other Asia n.e.s.	90.8	94.1	110.9	154.0	164.9
Israel/Israël	58.6	96.5	144.7	159.7	143.9
Turkey/Turquie	58.5	48.3	98.8	124.3	183.0
Brazil/Brésil	63.5	77.8	89.0	110.8	139.1
Czech Republic	34.8	56.9	108.6	130.4	131.0
United Arab Emirates	56.1	67.1	84.8	91.1	114.4
Thailand/Thaïlande	27.2	43.5	66.7	109.7	120.7
Free zones/Zone franches	45.4	66.7	23.8		201.8
Hungary/Hongrie	24.4	41.2	71.0	80.1	86.3

(VALUE AS PERCENTAGE OF WORLD TOTAL)(VALEURS EN POURCENTAGE DU TOTAL MONDIAL)

	1988	1989	1990	1991	1992	1993	1994	1995	1996	1997
Africa	1.2	1.3	1.3	1.2	1.2	1.2	1.3	1.2	1.1	1.0
Americas	17.8	17.9	16.3	16.7	15.3	18.4	19.6	19.1	17.0	16.5
– Northern America	17.1	17.1	15.6	16.0	14.6	17.7	18.9	18.4	16.2	15.8
– LAIA	0.7	0.7	0.7	0.7	0.6	0.6	0.6	0.6	0.7	0.6
– CACM	0.0	0.1	0.0	0.0	0.0	0.0	0.0	0.1	0.0	0.1
– Caribbean	0.0	0.0	0.0	0.0	0.0	0.0	0.0	0.1	0.1	0.0
– Rest of America	0.0	0.0	0.0	0.0	0.0	0.0	0.0	0.0	0.0	0.0
Asia excl fmr USSR	8.8	9.4	9.6	9.8	10.0	14.7	13.1	16.4	17.3	20.3
– Middle East	0.3	0.3	0.3	0.4	0.3	0.3	0.3	0.3	0.3	0.3
Asia former USSR					0.0	0.0	0.0	0.0	0.0	0.0
Europe excl fmr USSR	71.1	70.1	71.8	71.3	72.3	61.5	61.1	58.7	59.0	57.7
– European Union	69.1	68.3	69.4	68.3	69.1	58.5	58.1	56.1	56.5	54.7
– Eastern Europe	0.8	0.7	0.7	0.6	0.5	0.5	0.5	0.4	0.5	0.6
– Rest of Europe	1.2	1.1	1.7	2.4	2.7	2.5	2.6	2.2	2.0	2.3
Europe former USSR	0.3	0.4	0.3	0.4	0.2	0.2	0.1	0.2	0.2	0.1
Oceania	0.2	0.3	0.2	0.1	0.1	0.2	0.2	0.2	0.2	0.2
Other	0.5	0.5	0.5	0.5	0.7	3.7	4.7	4.1	5.2	4.3
United Kingdom	42.1	40.9	42.2	41.4	42.5	36.2	36.3	35.6	34.8	33.7
USA/Etats–Unis d'Amer	15.9	16.1	14.6	15.0	14.2	17.1	18.3	17.7	15.5	15.0
Germany/Allemagne				8.2	8.4	7.2	7.1	7.0	6.9	5.9
Japan/Japon	4.9	5.9	5.6	5.0	5.0	6.5	4.8	5.3	5.4	6.9
France, Monaco	4.1	4.1	4.6	4.4	4.4	3.9	3.8	3.7	3.9	4.7
Areas n.e.s.	0.3	0.3	0.3	0.3	0.5	3.5	4.4	4.0	4.1	4.0
Singapore/Singapour	0.4	0.3	0.5	0.7	0.8	2.2	2.1	4.0	4.4	5.5
Netherlands/Pays–Bas	4.0	4.1	4.1	4.4	4.4	3.1	2.8	2.7	2.9	3.2
Italy/Italie	2.5	2.6	2.6	2.5	2.4	2.0	2.2	2.0	2.1	1.8
Norway,Svalbard and JM	0.4	0.4	0.8	1.5	1.6	1.5	1.5	1.4	1.2	1.5

	1988	1989	1990	1991	1992	1993	1994	1995	1996	1997
Afrique	2.4	1.9	1.5	1.5	1.3	1.7	1.8	1.6	1.6	1.7
Amériques	10.1	10.1	10.4	11.1	10.5	11.4	10.3	10.1	11.4	13.1
– Amérique du Nord	9.1	9.0	9.4	10.1	9.3	10.1	9.2	9.1	10.3	12.0
– ALAI	0.8	1.0	0.8	0.7	0.9	0.9	0.8	0.9	1.0	0.9
– MCAC	0.0	0.0	0.0	0.1	0.1	0.1	0.1	0.1	0.1	0.0
– Caraïbes	0.1	0.1	0.2	0.2	0.1	0.2	0.2	0.1	0.1	0.1
– Autre Amérique	0.0	0.0	0.0	0.0	0.0	0.0	0.0	0.0	0.0	0.0
Asie anc. URSS exclus	5.8	5.9	5.2	5.4	6.2	7.9	7.7	7.9	9.3	9.8
– Moyen–Orient	2.0	2.0	1.5	1.3	1.3	1.6	1.4	1.4	1.4	1.5
Asie ancienne URSS						0.0	0.0	0.0	0.0	0.0
Europe anc. URSS exclus	80.2	80.5	81.0	80.4	79.9	74.3	76.1	76.2	74.1	70.4
– Union Européenne	77.1	77.3	78.0	77.4	77.1	71.1	72.4	72.3	69.8	66.6
– Europe de l'Est	0.4	0.3	0.3	0.3	0.3	0.4	0.5	0.8	0.9	0.9
– Autre de l'Europe	2.7	2.9	2.7	2.7	2.6	2.8	3.2	3.1	3.4	3.0
Europe ancienne URSS	0.1	0.3	0.6	0.5	0.7	0.3	0.7	0.9	1.0	0.8
Océanie	0.9	0.8	0.7	0.7	0.7	0.7	0.7	0.6	0.7	0.7
Autre	0.6	0.6	0.5	0.5	0.7	3.7	2.8	2.7	1.8	3.4
United Kingdom	35.4	33.5	33.7	31.9	31.5	28.4	28.0	25.4	25.1	24.3
Germany/Allemagne				12.7	12.8	13.3	14.1	14.5	12.8	12.6
USA/Etats–Unis d'Amer	7.7	7.9	8.2	8.7	8.2	9.1	8.3	8.3	9.4	11.4
France, Monaco	9.1	10.0	10.5	9.5	9.6	9.1	9.1	9.5	8.6	7.9
Netherlands/Pays–Bas	7.0	7.1	5.8	6.6	7.0	5.8	5.5	7.0	7.1	6.9
Belgium–Luxembourg	4.4	4.5	4.4	4.9	4.9	4.0	3.9	4.4	4.9	5.0
Italy/Italie	3.8	4.4	4.4	4.3	4.1	3.6	3.9	3.8	3.6	3.3
Japan/Japon	1.9	2.2	1.8	2.3	2.9	3.7	3.1	3.0	3.0	3.2
Areas n.e.s.	0.6	0.6	0.5	0.5	0.5	3.5	2.6	2.6	1.8	3.1
Spain/Espagne	1.9	2.1	2.3	2.5	2.5	2.2	2.4	2.5	2.4	2.5

4. General Imports C.I.F. by Commodities according to the S.I.T.C. (Rev. 2) in million U.S. Dollars
Importations Générales C.A.F. par Produits d'après la C.T.C.I. (Rév. 2) en millions de Dollars E.U.

SITC CTCI	COMMODITY	1994 QUANTITY QUANTITE	1994 VALUE VALEUR	1995 QUANTITY QUANTITE	1995 VALUE VALEUR	1996 QUANTITY QUANTITE	1996 VALUE VALEUR	1997 QUANTITY QUANTITE	1997 VALUE VALEUR	PRODUIT
	ALL COMMODITIES		25763.9		32321.1		35764.7		39205.8	TOUS PRODUITS
0	FOOD AND LIVE ANIMALS		2094.7		2298.7		2457.0		2500.9	ALIMENTS,ANIMAUX VIVANTS
001	*LIVE ANIMALS FOR FOOD	W 10912	56.7	W 10367	83.0	W 9703	89.0		163.0	ANIMAUX VIVANTS
0015	EQUINE SPECIES, LIVE	W 971	41.5	W 843	67.5	W 775	74.1	W 1099	152.4	CHEVAUX,ANES,MULETS
01	MEAT AND PREPARATIONS		169.5		221.7		226.0		233.7	VIANDES ET PREPARATIONS
011	MEAT FRESH,CHILLD,FROZEN	W 43387	85.2	W 53325	117.7	W 49495	105.8	W 42450	106.9	VIANDES FRAICHES,REF,CONGE
02	DAIRY PRODCTS,BIRDS'EGGS		140.2		193.5		216.2		229.8	PRODUITS LAITIERS,OEUFS
022	MILK AND CREAM	W 110832	79.5	W 197521	128.1	W 197056	128.3	W 247340	145.1	LAIT ET CREME
0223	MILK AND CREAM FRESH	W 98280	54.5	W 185741	107.4	W 183504	108.5	W 226812	115.6	LAIT,CREME FRAIS
04	CEREALS AND PREPARATIONS		385.2		415.2		424.9		426.9	CEREALES ET PRODUITS
048	CEREAL ETC PREPARATIONS	W 125572	264.8	W 133937	277.1	W 144226	296.4	W 140622	311.7	PREPTNS A BASE CEREALES
0484	BAKERY PRODUCTS	W 64474	144.9	W 69888	156.9	W 74565	170.3	W 74497	173.0	PRODUITS DE BOULANGERIE
04842	PASTRY, CAKES ETC	W 32334	86.4	W 28352	83.3	W 28671	83.9	W 26556	77.2	PATISSERIE ETC.
05	VEGETABLES AND FRUIT		402.3		436.5		489.3		444.6	LEGUMES ET FRUITS
054	VEG ETC FRSH,SMPLY PRSVD	W 289224	171.6	W 222840	187.6	W 268955	208.9	W 290474	186.5	LEGUMES FRAIS,CONG,SECS
057	FRUIT,NUTS,FRESH,DRIED	W 164866	139.2	W 159371	146.9	W 165516	161.4	W 165087	152.1	FRUITS FRAIS OU SECS
06	SUGAR AND PREPS,HONEY		119.3		136.7		150.7		166.1	SUCRES ET PRODUITS
07	COFFEE,TEA,COCOA,SPICES		195.6		202.4		210.9		227.3	CAFE,THE,CACAO,EPICES
073	CHOCOLATE AND PRODUCTS	W 29310	114.9	W 28722	119.6	W 28950	120.7	W 31124	128.5	CHOCOLAT
081	*FEEDING STUFF FOR ANIML	W 2465725	442.5	W 2160838	422.6	W 2049294	421.3	W 1696285	363.2	NOURRITURE POUR ANIMAUX
0813	OILCAKE AND OTH RESIDUES	W 836275	146.5	W 685705	120.4	W 669749	143.8	W 651242	137.3	TOURTEAUX
0819	FOOD WASTE AND FEED NES	W 1204948	225.0	W 1073504	226.7	W 986839	203.9	W 728856	171.9	DECHETS,ALIMENTS NDA
08193	BEET–PULP,BAGASSE,ETC	W 1002580	145.7	W 885539	136.9	W 485581	82.0	W 272312	40.9	PULPES,AUTRES DECHETS
08199	FODDER NES,INCL SWEETNED	W 202366	79.3	W 187965	89.8	W 501253	122.0	W 456527	131.1	PREPARATIONS FOURRAGERES
09	MISC EDIBLE PRODUCTS		121.4		119.7		145.8		163.7	PREP ALIMENTAIRES DIVERSES
098	EDIBLE PRODCTS,PREPS NES	W 55809	112.0	W 55222	109.1	W 109551	127.6	W 72398	146.5	PREP ALIMENTAIRES NDA
1	BEVERAGES AND TOBACCO		312.7		303.5		372.4		419.0	BOISSONS ET TABACS
11	BEVERAGES		248.6		234.3		296.2		342.0	BOISSONS
112	ALCOHOLIC BEVERAGES	W 116567	186.0	W 94436	180.7	W 115387	216.0	W 144648	244.7	BOISSONS ALCOOLIQUES
2	CRUDE MATERLS,EXCL FUELS		582.1		617.2		630.8		659.2	MAT BRUTES NON COMESTIBLES
24	CORK AND WOOD		154.3		144.7		160.5		208.5	LIEGE ET BOIS
248	WOOD SHAPED,SLEEPERS	W 253311	139.1	W 185615	128.4	W 214707	142.0	W 271319	174.8	BOIS SIMPLEMENT TRAVAILLES
2482	LUMBER SHAPED CONIFER	W 186526	82.8	W 130770	67.1	W 154096	77.7	W 193308	101.8	CONIFERES SCIES,RABOTES
24821	LUMBER SAWN ETC CONIFER	W 184972	79.7	W 128748	63.3	W 149116	70.1	W 185205	91.7	CONIFERES SCIES LONGITUD
26	TEXTILE FIBRES AND WASTE		80.6		94.9		89.2		66.4	FIBRES TEXTILES
27	CRUDE FERTLZR,MINRLS NES		104.3		89.8		82.9		106.2	ENGRAIS MINERAUX BRUTS
28	METALLIFEROUS ORES,SCRAP		117.4		134.9		128.2		119.3	MINERAIS METAL,DECHETS
287	BASE METAL ORES,CONC NES	W 2401105	80.5		93.1	W 2922711	107.1	W 2930456	95.4	MINERAIS METAUX COMMUNS
3	MINERAL FUELS ETC		999.3		1071.2		1326.6		1365.2	COMBUSTIBLES MINERAUX LUB
32	COAL,COKE AND BRIQUETTES		176.3		177.3		161.9		179.3	HOUILLES,COKES,BRIQUETTES
322	COAL,LIGNITE AND PEAT	W 4832345	171.0	W 2611269	172.9	W 2606239	156.8	W 3165719	174.8	HOUILLES,LIGNITES,TOURBE
3222	OTH COAL,NOT AGGLOMERATD	W 4733364	158.9	W 2538343	164.1	W 2487249	144.6	W 3053425	163.2	AUTRES HOUILLES
33	PETROLEUM AND PRODUCTS		804.6		871.7		1100.0		1066.5	PETROLE ET DERIVES
333	CRUDE PETROLEUM	W 2305205	270.7	W 1983871	277.7	W 2076881	326.0	W 2887604	425.4	HUILES BRUTES DE PETROLE
334	PETROLEUM PRODUCTS,REFIN	W 3086852	506.9	W 3456398	561.0	W 3871962	735.0	W 3222553	597.9	PRODUITS RAFFINES
3341	GASOLINE,OTH LIGHT OILS	W 551471	103.0	W 630222	123.0	W 720130	160.0	W 825623	171.3	ESSENCES POUR MOTEURS
33411	MOTOR,AVIATION SPIRIT	W 539004	99.2	W 618050	115.9	W 693222	150.6	W 789733	163.0	ESSENCES MOTEURS D'AVIONS
3342	KEROSENE,OTH MEDIUM OILS	W 448843	80.2	W 384339	72.9	W 505565	109.2	W 634562	121.0	PETR LAMPANTS,AUT HUIL
33421	KEROSENE INCL JET FUEL	W 439091	78.2	W 376270	71.3	W 451612	100.5	W 429773	84.9	PETROLES LAMPANTS
3343	GAS OILS	W 1198114	199.9	W 1162387	204.2	W 1570481	313.5	W 762652	132.4	GAS OILS
3344	FUEL OILS,NES	W 846395	88.7	W 1239102	128.0	W 1024391	114.5	W 955395	139.0	FUEL OILS
4	ANIMAL,VEGETABLE OIL,FAT		97.4		122.5		121.5		118.8	HUILES,GRAISSES ANIM,VEG
5	CHEMCLS,RELATED PROD NES		3255.1		4040.5		4259.2		4732.1	PRODUITS CHIMIQUES
51	ORGANIC CHEMICALS		772.2		1077.2		1038.7		1161.7	PROD CHIMIQ ORGANIQUES
513	CARBOXYLIC ACIDS ETC	W 65603	130.3	W 80642	368.4	W 102471	211.1	W 81118	246.8	ACIDES CARBOXYLIQUES
5139	OXY–FNCT ACIDS,DERIVATVS	W 7484	58.1	W 11616	260.2	W 8542	117.4	W 8499	153.1	ACIDES CARBOXYLIQUES
514	NITROGEN–FNCTN COMPOUNDS	W 24484	257.4	W 30646	327.6	W 26586	300.7	W 25797	358.5	COMPOSES FONCT AZOTEES
5147	AMIDE–FNCT CMPD,EXC UREA	W 7538	159.7	W 5088	146.6	W 4742	143.8	W 4464	134.7	COMPOSES CARBOXYAMIDE
5148	OTH NITROGN–FNCTN CMPNDS	W 7340	67.0	W 9685	127.5	W 10314	110.5	W 8869	164.9	AUTRES COMPOSES AZOTES
51482	IMIDE–,IMIDE–FNCT CMPNDS	W 2408	50.3	W 3517	105.4	W 3039	80.4	W 3519	134.7	COMPOSES A FONCTION IMIDE
515	ORG–INORG COMPOUNDS ETC	W 10452	206.0	W 16795	214.1	W 13135	334.5	W 13461	360.3	COMPOSES ORGANO–MINERAUX
5156	HETEROCYCLIC CMPDS ETC	W 7227	141.4	W 12466	178.7	W 7925	292.3	W 8627	304.5	COMPOSES HETEROCYCLIQUES
51569	OTH HETEROCYC CMPDS,ETC	W 7079	140.7	W 11759	172.9	W 7818	291.2	W 8492	302.8	AUT COMP HETEROCYCLIQUES
516	OTHER ORGANIC CHEMICALS	W 23137	113.9	W 21829	90.6	W 21381	115.5	W 24249	117.6	AUTRES PROD ORGANIQUES
52	INORGANIC CHEMICALS		140.4		182.0		209.5		183.3	PROD CHIM INORGANIQUES
522	INORG ELEMNTS,OXIDES,ETC	W 268525	81.0	W 340662	105.0	W 334864	110.0	W 246286	82.6	ELEMENTS INORGANIQUES
53	DYES,TANNING,COLOUR PROD		118.6		136.5		155.2		165.7	PROD TEINTURE,COLORANTS
533	PIGMENTS,PAINTS,ETC	W 33647	95.3	W 35258	106.2	W 37307	120.1	W 40626	127.4	PIGMENTS,PEINTURES,VERNIS
541	*MEDICINAL,PHARM PRODUCT	MK 22096	586.6	MK 26872	724.2	MK 24336	739.0	MK 28332	894.9	PROD MEDICINAUX PHARMACEUT
5417	MEDICAMENTS	MK 15312	381.1	MK 19435	464.6	MK 15230	459.1	MK 19803	572.2	MEDICAMENTS
54171	— CONTAINNG ANTIBIOTICS	K 2907911	56.4	K 3823848	89.3	K 1648463	138.4	K 1023803	160.8	MED CONTN ANTIBIOTIQUES
54179	— CONTNG OTH SUBSTANCES	MK 11697	295.8	MK 14763	338.6	MK 12132	278.6	MK 17636	352.1	MED CONT AUT SUBSTANCES
55	PERFUME,CLEANING ETC PRD		372.0		412.3		472.8		698.6	PROD POUR PARFUM,TOILETTE
551	ESSENTL OILS,PERFUME,ETC	W 7011	80.3	W 7690	96.1	W 13640	112.7	W 20046	298.1	HUILES ESSENTIELLES
5514	MIXED PERFUME SUBSTANCES	W 5475	55.2	W 5937	67.1	W 11819	80.7	W 18749	273.0	MELANGES SUBSTAN ODORIFER
553	PERFUMERY,COSMETICS,ETC	W 26805	167.2	W 24075	176.0	W 26947	202.2	W 30411	215.6	PRODUITS DE PARFUMERIE
554	SOAP,CLEANSING ETC PREPS	W 73366	124.6	W 67843	140.3	W 91596	158.0	W 77501	185.1	SAVONS,PRODUITS DETERSIFS
5542	WASHING PREPARATIONS ETC	W 61257	103.6	W 54851	116.4	W 77733	134.5	W 64546	161.4	PROD ORG TENSIO–ACT NDA
562	*FERTILIZERS,MANUFACTURE	W 1295747	195.4	W 1646150	289.7	W 1504675	273.2	W 1349281	214.6	ENGRAIS MANUFACTURES
5629	FERTILIZERS NES	W 588966	106.7	W 822823	164.1	W 656205	138.7	W 596296	115.8	ENGRAIS NDA
56291	NIT–PHOS–POT FERTLZR NES	W 341357	61.1	W 499412	97.2	W 421640	82.8	W 391304	72.5	ENGRAIS CONT N P K
58	PLASTIC MATERIALS ETC		564.0		740.3		710.5		728.3	MAT PLAST ARTIFICIELLES
582	PROD OF CONDENSATION ETC	W 72184	137.5	W 78389	198.1	W 105595	170.4	W 78077	169.1	PROD CONDENS,POLYCOND
5823	ALKYDS,OTHER POLYESTERS	W 35215	72.6	W 39463	113.5	W 27637	78.8	W 35966	83.3	ALKYDES ET AUT POLYESTERS
583	POLYMERIZATION ETC PRODS	W 313591	401.3	W 414575	514.9	W 343731	513.1	W 1086325	534.0	PROD POLYMERISATION
5831	POLYETHYLENE	W 78679	88.9	W 75573	95.8	W 85365	99.6	W 92058	105.6	POLYETHYLENE
5833	POLYSTYRENE,ITS COPOLYMR	W 58858	75.8	W 148900	107.8	W 56891	93.0	W 760611	96.2	POLYPROPYLENE COPOLYMERES
5839	OTH POLYMRZTION ETC PROD	W 79535	102.3	W 89034	136.3	W 89817	140.3	W 108273	138.9	AUT PROD POLYMER COPOLYM
59	CHEMICAL MATERIALS NES		503.9		476.3		658.3		678.5	MAT PROD CHIMIQUES NDA
592	STARCH,INULIN,GLUTEN,ETC	W 30879	122.2	W 33148	100.5	W 62922	233.5	W 45091	205.9	AMIDONS,INUL,GLUT FROM
5922	ALBUMINOID SUBSTAN,GLUES	W 18016	112.1	W 21650	91.7	W 50560	224.8	W 32841	198.0	MAT ALBUMIN,COLLES
59224	PROTEIN AND DERIVATS,ETC	W 1118	75.3	W 6479	47.7	W 11221	161.3	W 11113	121.1	PEPTONES
598	MISCEL CHEM PRODUCTS NES	W 140695	314.8	W 170133	301.2	W 170895	344.2	W 225398	394.0	PROD DIV INDUST CHIM NDA
5989	CHEM PRODUCTS,PREPS NES	W 116626	284.7	W 145595	273.5	W 153591	320.8	W 204035	366.0	PROD PREP CHIMIQUES NDA
59899	OTH CHEM PRODS,PREPS,NES	W 109333	262.3	W 138480	248.3	W 146497	288.3	W 197905	339.6	AUT PRODUITS CHIMIQUES NDA
6	BASIC MANUFACTURES		2996.5		3682.6		3897.5		4091.8	ART MANUFACTURES
62	RUBBER MANUFACTURES NES		158.5		177.4		207.9		199.8	CAOUTCHOUC MANUFACTURE
625	RUBBER TYRES, TUBES ETC	W 23784	78.7	W 24667	89.0	W 29228	109.4	W 28247	101.2	PNEUS CAOUTCHOUC VULCANISE
63	WOOD,CORK MANUFACTRS NES		98.9		112.2		138.9		159.5	OUVRAGES LIEGE ET BOIS
64	PAPER,PAPERBOARD AND MFR		647.4		852.8		834.0		865.4	PAPIERS,CARTONS & OUVRAGES
641	PAPER AND PAPERBOARD	W 463043	401.0	W 459970	528.0	W 428594	484.8	W 492251	480.3	PAPIERS ET CARTONS

4. General Imports C.I.F. by Commodities according to the S.I.T.C. (Rev. 2) in million U.S. Dollars
Importations Générales C.A.F. par Produits d'après la C.T.C.I. (Rév. 2) en millions de Dollars E.U.

SITC CTCI	COMMODITY	1994 QUANTITY QUANTITE	1994 VALUE VALEUR	1995 QUANTITY QUANTITE	1995 VALUE VALEUR	1996 QUANTITY QUANTITE	1996 VALUE VALEUR	1997 QUANTITY QUANTITE	1997 VALUE VALEUR	PRODUIT
6415	PAPER,PAPERBRD,BULK,NES	W 110839	83.7	W 128743	138.4	W 105422	97.8	W 109105	93.3	PAPIERS,CARTONS ROULEAUX
64159	OTHER PAPER ETC,BULK,NES	W 85607	71.9	W 108632	122.4	W 80452	86.9	W 83984	80.2	AUT PAPIER ROULEAUX FEUILLES
6418	COATED ETC PAPER NES BLK	W 55509	92.3	W 66643	129.5	W 65497	127.4	W 64683	121.5	PAP,CARTONS COUCHES,ENDUITS
64189	COATED PAPER ETC NES	W 43863	72.9	W 54175	99.4	W 52503	95.5	W 50145	89.5	PAPIERS,CARTONS COUCHES
642	PAPER,ETC,PRECUT,ARTS OF	W 115263	246.4	W 138254	324.8	W 300915	349.3	W 152428	385.1	PAP,CARTONS DECOUPES
6421	PAPER ETC CONTAINERS	W 58676	100.9	W 64320	129.7	W 225471	152.6	W 66157	174.2	BOITES,SACS EMBALLAGES
6428	PAPER ETC ARTICLES NES	W 28872	80.6	W 37303	104.6	W 38861	106.7	W 44338	116.2	OUVRAGES EN PATE A PAPIER
65	TEXTILE YARN,FABRICS,ETC		556.9		610.7		658.0		687.3	FILS,TISSUS,ARTICLES TEXTILE
651	TEXTILE YARN	W 47912	171.8	W 50142	188.6	W 53504	198.5	W 69015	215.7	FILS TEXTILES
653	WOVN MAN–MADE FIB FABRIC	W 8275	80.0	W 7930	82.2	W 7917	84.7	W 7264	74.3	TISSUS FIBRES SYNTH,ARTIF
66	NONMETAL MINERAL MFS NES		309.9		351.0		422.0		419.1	ART MIN NON METALLIQUES
663	MINERAL MANUFCTURES NES	W 194108	81.4	W 212187	86.7	W 307172	94.9	W 432230	106.9	ART MIN MANUF NDA
67	IRON AND STEEL		362.3		498.0		518.0		540.5	FER ET ACIER
673	IRON,STEEL SHAPES ETC	W 188996	85.8	W 213506	113.6	W 273047	130.9	W 283981	130.5	BARRES,PROFIL FER,ACIER
674	IRN,STL UNIV,PLATE,SHEET	W 179418	140.1	W 202373	191.7	W 235643	205.6	W 241366	211.9	LARGES PLATS,TOLES
6749	OTH IRN,STL PLATES,SHEET	W 81933	81.3	W 92674	100.4	W 113132	113.2	W 113550	122.7	AUTRES TOLES FER,ACIER
67491	— OF IRON OR SIMPLE STL	W 76194	70.4	W 90719	94.6	W 111483	108.6	W 112114	119.4	AUT TOLES AUTRES ACIER FIN
678	IRON,STL TUBES,PIPES,ETC	W 65425	70.7	W 93441	104.7	W 86088	94.6	W 100704	106.9	TUBES,TUYAUX EN FONTE,FER
68	NON–FERROUS METALS		336.1		460.0		427.2		432.7	METAUX NON FERREUX
682	COPPER EXC CEMENT COPPER	W 35095	96.9	W 38747	140.1		131.4	W 47026	145.5	CUIVRE
6822	COPPER,ALLOYS WORKED	W 34861	96.1	W 38495	139.2	W 37509	129.6	W 46627	143.1	CUIVRE,ALLIAGES OUVRES
684	ALUMINIUM	W 68970	173.6	W 67905	206.1	W 89832	196.9	W 73189	193.4	ALUMINIUM
6842	ALUMINIUM,ALLOYS WORKED	W 58734	156.0	W 62544	192.9	W 82562	183.6	W 62161	171.5	ALUMINIUM,ALLIAGES OUVRE
68422	ALUMNM PLATE,SHEET,STRIP	W 41023	89.5	W 44064	104.9	W 44772	90.9	W 40372	77.2	TOLES, PLANCHES EN ALU
69	METAL MANUFACTURES NES		512.0		598.8		675.0		772.4	ART MANUFACT EN METAL NDA
691	STRUCTURES AND PARTS NES	W 28930	52.1	W 32737	86.3	W 38531	86.8	W 73538	133.4	CONSTRUCT FER,ACIER,ALU
699	BASE METAL MFRS NES	W 37832	183.3	W 36649	194.9	W 40096	213.2	W 48337	221.4	ART MANUFACTURES MET NDA
7	MACHINES,TRANSPORT EQUIP		9923.9		13649.3		15045.8		17720.5	MACHINES MATERIEL TRANSPORT
71	POWER GENERATING EQUIPMT		410.8		420.4		416.3		459.1	MACHINES GENERATRICES
713	INTRNL COMBUS PSTN ENGIN	W 24099	85.1	W 5558	115.9	W 5413	121.3	W 5968	115.0	MOTEURS EXPL COMB INT, PIECE
714	ENGINES AND MOTORS NES	W 2315	217.6	W 2368	214.3	W 1625	175.7	W 2323	209.1	MOTEURS NON ELECTRIQUES
7144	REACTION ENGINES	W 616	84.7	W 397	70.5	W 279	55.3	W 269	46.3	PROPULSEURS A REACTION
7149	ENGINE & MOTOR PARTS NES	W 1439	94.2	W 1696	78.6	W 1246	100.5	W 1731	136.7	PIECES 714 ET 718.88
72	MACHS FOR SPCL INDUSTRYS		688.3		763.6		980.9		1065.6	MAC SPECIALES POUR INDUST
721	AGRIC MACHY,EXC TRACTORS	W 16211	111.8	W 17529	138.2	W 27522	148.7	W 20140	159.1	MACHINES AGRICOLES
728	OTH MACHY FOR SPCL INDUS	W 13087	258.5	W 16032	269.5	W 16131	425.1	W 12280	548.9	AUT MACH IND PARTICULIERES
7284	MACHY FOR SPCL INDUS NES	W 6852	196.9	W 7237	208.6	W 8767	350.6	W 6174	450.9	MACH SPEC IND PARTICUL.
72848	OTH MCHY WITH INDIV FNCT	W 1340	81.1	W 1714	60.4	W 2614	74.3	W 2156	207.2	AUTRES MACHINES NDA
72849	PTS OF MACHS OF 7284 ETC	W 2383	76.6	W 3908	110.5	W 3487	185.0	W 1864	192.4	PIECES DU 728.4 ETC
73	METALWORKING MACHINERY		88.7		87.0		103.0		131.1	MACH TRAVAIL DES METAUX
74	GENRL INDUSTRL MACHY NES		639.3		749.3		900.1		1050.2	MACH APP INDUSTRIE
741	HEATING,COOLING EQUIPMNT	W 14625	155.4	W 19288	207.8	W 19262	236.4	W 19071	263.6	MACH CHAUFFAGE,PIECES
743	PUMPS NES,CENTRFUGES ETC	W 6974	98.3	W 6690	98.6	W 7675	113.1	W 8893	164.9	POMPES COMPRES,VENT ETC
744	MECHANICAL HANDLING EQU	W 11569	88.9	W 14067	118.2	W 17773	167.8	W 20816	211.7	EQUIP MANUTENTION PIECES
745	NONELEC MACHY,TOOLS NES	W 4957	85.0	W 3603	76.6	W 5850	117.6	W 6232	122.5	AUT MACH NON ELEC,PIECES
749	NONELEC MACH PTS,ACC NES	W 7977	152.9	W 9282	174.2	W 12102	185.0	W 10918	209.1	PIECES MACH NON ELEC NDA
75	OFFICE MACHNES,ADP EQUIP		3329.8		5595.7		6113.6		7277.9	MACH BUREAU TRAIT AUTOM
752	AUTOMTIC DATA PROC EQUIP	W 17941	1704.0	W 33608	2769.7	W 53309	3492.4	W 59631	4530.0	MACH TRAIT INFORMATION
7522	DIGITAL COMPUTERS	W 2311	284.6	W 2273	287.0	W 5449	473.5	W 1815	363.2	MACH DIGITALES COMPLETES
7523	DIGITL CENTRL PROCESSORS	W 1044	89.6	W 2070	147.9	W 2541	198.9	W 1552	185.0	UNITES CENTRALES
7524	DIGITL CENTRL STOR UNITS	W 6140	1105.2	W 8519	1835.6	W 10472	2114.7	W 18255	3046.2	UNITES MEMOIRE CENTRALES
7525	ADP PERIPHERAL UNITS	W 5375	122.2	W 14515	311.7	W 29613	567.6	W 37044	825.4	UNITES PERIPHERIQUES
7528	OFF–LINE DATA PROC EQUIP	W 3016	96.4	W 6183	181.2	W 5040	124.6	W 778	93.5	MACH AUXIL TRAIT INFORM
759	OFFICE,ADP MCH PTS,ACCES	W 19874	1600.7	W 27279	2794.6	W 28906	2580.5	W 35334	2690.7	PIECES DU 751 ET 752
7599	ACCTG,ETC,ADP MCH PTS,AC	W 19077	1574.0	W 26243	2749.1	W 26619	2532.7	W 32990	2637.8	PIECES DU 751 ET 752
76	TELECOMM,SOUND EQUIPMENT		537.8		638.5		939.4		1010.7	EQUIPMENT DE TELECOM
763	SOUND RECORDRS,PHONOGRPH	W 1501	42.3	W 1753	79.9	W 4034	244.9	W 2567	125.7	PHONO,APP ENREGISTREMENT
7638	OTHR SOUND APPARATUS ETC	W 1209	35.7	W 1667	77.3	W 3978	243.2	W 2522	124.6	AUT APP D'ENREGIS,REPROD
76381	TV IMAGE,SND RECRDRS ETC	W 703	25.4	W 1065	61.5	W 3087	222.5	W 1866	107.3	APP ENREG,REPRO IMAG,SON
764	TELECOM EQPT,PTS,ACC NES	W 6647	407.9	W 8710	466.3	W 9009	579.4		771.7	EQUIP TELECOM,PIECES
7641	LINE TELEPHONE,ETC EQUIP	W 611	95.8	W 917	67.6	W 1238	108.6	W 9077	236.9	APP TELEPHON PAR FIL
7649	PTS NES OF EQUIPMT OF 76	W 4454	238.3	W 4670	288.8	W 4457	350.0	W 5195	352.5	PIECES DE LA DIV 76
76491	PTS NES OF APPAR OF 7641	W 1498	124.3	W 1736	142.1	W 1890	179.9	W 2295	207.4	PIECES POUR 764.1
76493	TELECOMM EQUIPMT PTS NES	W 944	79.6	W 1234	109.5	W 1532	141.3	W 1835	114.0	PIECES 761,762,764.3,8
77	ELECTRIC MACHNRY NES ETC		2691.9		3541.7		3265.3		3800.5	MACH APP ELECT NDA
771	ELECTRIC POWER MACHY NES	W 3920	113.5	W 6776	161.8	W 10786	269.2		383.0	MACH PROD,TRANS ELECTR
7712	OTH ELEC POWER MACHY NES	W 2070	72.7	W 2810	103.3	W 6635	200.7		292.2	AUT APP PROD TRANSF ELEC
77121	STATIC CONVERTERS ETC	W 719	35.7	W 1063	49.8	W 4360	127.0		205.5	CONVERTISSEURS STATIQUES
772	SWITCHGEAR ETC,PARTS NES	W 14698	591.9	W 14956	665.5	W 17083	678.4	W 20391	796.1	APP COUPURE,SECT ETC
7721	SWITCHGEAR ETC	W 12651	348.9	W 11933	346.9	W 13080	326.7	W 16440	399.2	APP COUPURE,SECTIONMNT
7722	PRINTED CIRCUITS,PTS NES	W 1697	213.9	W 2676	274.5	W 3692	314.6	W 3510	354.3	CIRCUITS ET PIECES
773	ELECTR DISTRIBUTNG EQUIP	W 17094	109.5	W 22140	150.9	W 22902	154.7	W 41436	195.4	EQUIPMT DISTRIBUTION ELECT
7731	INSULATED WIRE,CABLE ETC	W 14490	94.1	W 18225	131.5	W 18546	134.1	W 34451	170.4	FILS,CABLES ISOLES ELECT
775	HOUSEHOLD TYPE EQUIP NES	W 26102	189.0	W 31404	225.6	W 37117	257.4	W 40327	271.2	MACH,APP USAGE DOMESTQUE
7758	ELECTRO–THERMIC APPL NES	W 10794	90.0	W 11397	103.5	W 13842	104.2	W 11945	106.1	APP ELECTROTHERMIQ NDA
776	TRANSISTORS,VALVES,ETC		1317.2	W 2965	1774.1	W 2626	1400.4		1601.7	LAMPES,TUBES,VALVES
7764	ELECTRONIC MICROCIRCUITS		1260.3	W 2443	1690.2	W 1467	1205.8	W 1999	1315.1	MICROSTRUCTURES ELECTRON
7768	ELCTRNC COMP PTS,CRYSTLS	W 151	25.5	W 180	37.0	W 667	146.3	W 1731	228.3	CRIST PIEZO–ELEC,PCS 776
77689	ELECTRNIC COMPON PTS NES	W 115	9.8	W 129	14.1	W 628	121.8	W 1643	188.8	PIECES DU GROUPE 776
778	ELECTRICAL MACHINERY NES	W 15221	359.0	W 21491	550.3	W 54014	483.2		538.0	AUTRES MACH ELECT NDA
7781	BATTERIES,ACCUMULATORS	W 8313	133.5	W 12889	171.9	W 11970	117.6	W 17830	144.8	PILES ET ACCUMULATEURS
77812	ELECTRIC ACCUMULATORS	W 6370	114.7	W 7797	106.2	W 9963	78.9	W 15920	118.8	ACCUMULATEURS ELECTRIQ
7788	OTH ELEC MACHY,EQUIP NES	W 2412	153.1	W 3277	298.9	W 3738	281.4	W 7012	310.9	AUT MACH APP ELEC NDA
77883	ELEC SIGNALLING EQU NES	W 849	62.0	W 1016	100.6	W 1556	85.7	W 2112	145.1	APP ELECT SIGNAL ACOUS
78	ROAD VEHICLES		1271.2		1449.5		1932.9		2293.6	VEHICULES ROUTIERS
781	PASS MOTOR VEH EXC BUSES	W 93317	790.4	W 92674	907.1	W 140064	1286.5	W 207589	1618.0	AUTO TRANSPORT PERSONNES
782	LORRIES,SPCL MTR VEH NES	W 33330	205.6	W 30270	246.9	W 46014	319.8	W 41257	343.0	VEHICULES SPECIAUX,MARCH
7821	LORRIES,TRUCKS	W 32572	202.7	W 29781	244.6	W 45395	316.1	W 40670	340.0	VEHICULES TRANSP MARCHAND
784	MOTOR VEH PRTS,ACCES NES	W 20545	169.5	W 19031	181.1	W 21549	198.7	W 23845	211.6	PIECES 722,781,782,783
7849	OTHER MOTOR VEHCL PARTS	W 19416	161.7	W 18093	175.0	W 20279	186.2	W 21978	194.6	PIECES 722,781,782,783
79	OTHR TRANSPORT EQUIPMENT		266.5		403.9		394.6		632.1	AUTRE MATERIEL TRANSPORT
792	AIRCRAFT ETC	W 538	187.9	W 735	260.7	W 1086	338.1	W 1426	504.8	APP NAVIGATION AERIENNE
7929	AIRCRAFT PARTS NES	W 495	159.5	W 606	179.6	W 780	235.9	W 1006	255.9	PIECES DU 792
8	MISC MANUFACTURED GOODS		3222.7		3570.3		4676.2		4786.3	ART MANUFACTURES DIVERS
812	*PLUMBG,HEATNG,LGHTNG EQ	W 18161	74.8	W 20374	88.3	W 23161	115.6	W 29566	131.6	APPAR SANITAIRES CHAUFFAGE
821	*FURNITURE,PARTS THEREOF	W 24381	115.2	W 26662	139.7	W 86558	184.0	W 46321	227.9	MEUBLES ET PIECES
8219	FURNITURE AND PARTS NES	W 17630	73.8	W 18106	81.0	W 76537	117.1	W 33366	155.1	AUTRES MEUBLES ET PIECES
84	CLOTHING AND ACCESSORIES		783.2		842.7		1019.9		1082.5	VETEMENTS
842	MENS OUTERWEAR NOT KNIT	W 5002	123.1	W 5245	133.7	W 6184	162.2	W 5843	166.7	VET DESSUS POUR HOMMES
843	WOMENS OUTERWEAR NONKNIT	W 4965	192.5	W 5152	216.8	W 6518	265.4	W 7183	270.0	VET DESSUS FEMMES MAT TEX
845	OUTERWEAR KNIT NONELASTC	W 7751	214.3	W 8102	217.4	W 9952	262.3		300.6	VET DESSOUS,ACCES BONNET

4. General Imports C.I.F. by Commodities according to the S.I.T.C. (Rev. 2) in million U.S. Dollars
Importations Générales C.A.F. par Produits d'après la C.T.C.I. (Rév. 2) en millions de Dollars E.U.

SITC CTCI	COMMODITY	1994 QUANTITY QUANTITE	1994 VALUE VALEUR	1995 QUANTITY QUANTITE	1995 VALUE VALEUR	1996 QUANTITY QUANTITE	1996 VALUE VALEUR	1997 QUANTITY QUANTITE	1997 VALUE VALEUR	PRODUIT
8451	— JERSEYS,PULLOVERS ETC	W 3787	114.3	W 3909	116.4	W 5158	146.0		166.7	CHANDAILS,PULL–OVERS ETC
8459	— OTHER,CLTHG ACCESRYS	W 3514	84.0	W 3595	80.4	W 4263	95.7		109.6	AUT VET DESSUS DE BONNE
846	UNDER GARMENTS KNITTED	W 9827	129.1	W 6855	145.4		158.9		168.6	SOUS VETS DE BONNETERIE
851	*FOOTWEAR	W 19203	281.3	W 12926	246.0	W 14808	266.2	W 23377	245.8	CHAUSSURES
85102	FOOTWEAR LEATHER	W 13896	220.3	W 9737	201.5	W 10909	213.8	W 9338	198.0	CHAUS SEMELLES EN CUIR
87	PRECISION INSTRUMNTS NES		397.9		551.8		614.6		700.2	INSTRUM,APPAR SCIENT NDA
872	MEDICAL INSTRUMENTS NES	W 5125	169.8	W 5780	220.3	W 7020	281.2	W 7528	325.2	INSTR,APP MEDIC–CHIR NDA
87202	OTH MEDICAL INSTRUMENTS	W 4579	156.1	W 5002	199.9	W 6388	264.0	W 6804	304.4	INSTRUM,APP MEDECINE
874	MEASURNG,CONTROLNG INSTR	W 2419	194.2	W 5483	285.8	W 5842	291.7	W 4495	327.7	INSTRUMENTS DE MESURE
8748	ELEC MEAS,CONTRL EQU NES	W 416	61.0	W 727	109.7	W 799	94.4	W 705	97.6	APP ELEC ELECTRO MESURE
87483	OTH ELCTRNC MEAS ETC EQU	W 367	56.3	W 681	105.8	W 733	87.4	W 643	91.5	AUT APP ELECTRO DE MESURE
88	PHOTO EQU,OPTICL GDS ETC		209.0		206.0		229.1		233.5	APP,FOURN PHOTO,OP,MONTR
884	OPTICAL GOODS NES	W 617	78.4	W 692	87.6	W 852	107.3		94.8	ELEMENTS OPTIQ,ART LUNET
89	MISC MANUFCTRD GOODS NES		1329.4		1461.7		2205.3		2116.7	ART MANUFACTURES DIVERS
892	PRINTED MATTER	W 31636	227.5	W 25009	241.0	W 36400	277.7	W 39619	301.7	IMPRIMES
8921	PRINTED BOOKS,GLOBES,ETC	W 5908	80.7	W 5276	90.6	W 13347	123.1	W 7877	121.8	LIVRES,BROCHURES,CARTES
89211	PRINTED BOOKS,PAMPHLETS	W 5555	78.3	W 5020	88.3	W 13029	120.2	W 7348	118.2	LIVRES,BROCHURES
8922	NEWSPAPERS,PERIODICALS	W 16112	78.0	W 8723	78.2	W 9498	69.7	W 17042	91.7	JOURNAUX ET PERIODIQUES
893	ARTICLES OF PLASTIC NES		419.8		487.9		590.3		601.7	OUVRAGES EN MAT DIVIS 58
8931	PLSTC PACKG CONTNRS,LIDS	W 82346	195.1	W 106698	238.6	W 148573	251.4	W 114296	252.0	ART TRANSP EMBALLAGE ETC
8939	MISC PLASTIC ARTICLES	W 51352	215.4	W 50446	239.7	W 76481	326.9	W 71826	335.5	ART DIVERS EN MAT DIV 58
89399	OTHR PLASTC ARTICLES NES	W 45230	197.1	W 43633	217.8	W 69317	302.8	W 63562	310.3	AUT OUV MAT DIV 58
894	TOYS,SPORTING GOODS,ETC	W 21284	152.7	W 20265	170.9	W 22217	207.5	W 23059	219.5	VOITURES ENFANTS,JOUETS
8942	TOYS,INDOOR GAMES ETC	W 17908	125.1	W 16509	134.4	W 18263	156.1	W 18515	170.6	JOUETS,JEUX ETC
898	MUSICAL INSTRUMENTS,PTS	W 15254	392.5	W 12771	396.4	W 13691	870.1		641.5	INSTRUMENTS DE MUSIQUE
8983	SOUND RECRDNG TAPE,DISCS	W 14988	386.4	W 12503	389.8	W 13337	861.6	W 15649	633.0	SUPPORTS SON POUR 763
89831	PREPD SND RECORDNG MEDIA	W 7342	185.7	W 8038	173.4	W 8153	207.6	W 8414	261.2	SUPPORTS PREPARES
89832	RECORDED DISCS,TAPES ETC	W 7646	200.8	W 4465	216.5	W 5184	654.0	W 7235	371.8	DISQUES,PHONO,BANDES
899	OTHER MANUFACTURED GOODS		75.6		96.5		168.5		244.8	AUT ART MANUF DIVERS NDA
8996	HEARING,ORTHOPAEDIC AIDS		34.2		52.4		112.9		190.6	APPAREILS D'ORTHOPEDIE
89962	ORTHOPAEDIC ETC GOODS		32.9		50.4		111.2		187.8	APPAREILS D'ORTHOPEDIE
9	GOODS NOT CLASSD BY KIND		2280.0		2965.8		2978.3		2812.4	ART TRANSACT NON CLASSES
931	*SPECIAL TRANSACTIONS		2267.3		2950.2		2963.3		2797.7	TRANS.SPECIALES

5. General Exports F.O.B. by Commodities according to the S.I.T.C. (Rev. 2) in million U.S. Dollars
Exportations Générales F.O.B. par Produits d'après la C.T.C.I. (Rév. 2) en millions de Dollars E.U.

SITC CTCI	COMMODITY	1994 QUANTITY QUANTITE	1994 VALUE VALEUR	1995 QUANTITY QUANTITE	1995 VALUE VALEUR	1996 QUANTITY QUANTITE	1996 VALUE VALEUR	1997 QUANTITY QUANTITE	1997 VALUE VALEUR	PRODUIT
	ALL COMMODITIES		34395.2		43789.4		45565.4		53258.4	TOUS PRODUITS
0	FOOD AND LIVE ANIMALS		6365.8		7704.9		6625.8		5443.2	ALIMENTS,ANIMAUX VIVANTS
001	*LIVE ANIMALS FOR FOOD	W 182908	277.8	W 172552	257.7	W 114597	224.9		174.3	ANIMAUX VIVANTS
0011	BOVINE SPECIES,LIVE	W 171152	176.6	W 161657	175.9	W 86979	89.8	W 11690	20.2	ESPECE BOVINE
00119	— OTHR THAN FR BREEDING	W 169981	174.1	W 159221	170.7	W 86647	89.1	W 11394	19.6	BOVINS NON REPRODUCTEURS
01	MEAT AND PREPARATIONS		1805.9		1930.1		1737.5		1585.9	VIANDES ET PREPARATIONS
011	MEAT FRESH,CHILLD,FROZEN	W 593388	1598.2	W 595403	1695.3	W 524249	1481.7	W 528254	1350.5	VIANDES FRAICHES,REF,CONGE
0111	BOVINE MEAT FRESH,FROZEN	W 409449	1153.0	W 420311	1236.1	W 336717	914.8	W 332325	860.8	VIANDES BOVIN FRAI,REF
01111	BOVINE MEAT WITH BONE IN	W 74472	256.3	W 61725	235.6	W 49070	158.5	W 57178	165.8	VIANDES BOVIN NON DESOSS
01112	BOVINE MEAT BONELESS	W 334977	896.7	W 358587	1000.6	W 287648	756.4	W 275147	695.1	VIANDES BOVIN DESOSSEES
0112	MUTTON ETC FRSH,CHLD,FRN	W 64599	196.5	W 48711	153.1	W 61753	221.0	W 47078	175.3	VIANDE DE MOUTON
0113	PIG MEAT FRESH,CHLD,FRZN	W 69079	151.1	W 71765	191.5	W 64933	217.3	W 78700	196.0	VIANDE DE PORC
014	MEAT PREPD,PRSVD,NES ETC	W 51128	173.8	W 61388	204.2	W 59858	227.0	W 54854	220.4	CONSERVES DE VIANDES
0149	OTH PREPARD,PRESRVD MEAT	W 48827	166.7	W 59130	196.7	W 57601	218.9	W 53255	213.6	AUTRES PREP DE VIANDES
02	DAIRY PRODCTS,BIRDS'EGGS		1132.0		1571.4		1207.8		1246.7	PRODUITS LAITIERS,OEUFS
022	MILK AND CREAM	W 297040	408.4	W 404661	674.4	W 305944	383.7	W 333601	453.1	LAIT ET CREME
0224	MILK,CREAM PRESERVED ETC	W 165533	337.0	W 240242	569.0	W 139478	297.0	W 185398	365.6	LAIT,CREME CONS,CONC
02242	MILK DRY,1.5% FAT OR LES	W 79957	185.6	W 144806	380.1	W 58753	146.0	W 96411	211.1	LAIT POUDRE INF 1.5%
02243	MILK DRY,OVER 1.5% FAT	W 45608	112.6	W 40170	128.9	W 35716	103.2	W 39921	102.9	LAIT POUDRE SUP 1.5%
023	BUTTER	W 110324	393.8	W 137980	583.6	W 118716	439.4	W 138671	479.2	BEURRE
024	CHEESE AND CURD	W 89358	329.5	W 76953	313.0	W 94727	384.4	W 81690	313.7	FROMAGE ET CAILLEBOTTE
03	FISH AND PREPARATIONS		274.1		327.1		385.2		334.8	POISSONS ET PREPARATIONS
034	FISH,FRESH,CHILLED,FROZN	W 208315	183.3	W 241241	220.6	W 231148	260.9	W 463889	212.5	POISSON FRAIS, REFRIG,CONG
04	CEREALS AND PREPARATIONS		494.5		606.0		637.1		684.2	CEREALES ET PRODUITS
048	CEREAL ETC PREPARATIONS	W 183802	469.0	W 223865	586.8	W 231405	609.9	W 233187	632.6	PREPTNS A BASE CEREALES
0484	BAKERY PRODUCTS	W 40681	112.4	W 51340	152.9	W 63824	178.5	W 58236	194.3	PRODUITS DE BOULANGERIE
0488	OTH CEREAL PREPS,MALT EX	W 83544	333.5	W 105470	406.0	W 103783	398.4	W 117820	412.3	EXTRAITS DE MALT
05	VEGETABLES AND FRUIT		136.2		158.3		166.0		177.9	LEGUMES ET FRUITS
06	SUGAR AND PREPS,HONEY		95.4		130.5		139.1		147.0	SUCRES ET PRODUITS
07	COFFEE,TEA,COCOA,SPICES		222.1		210.6		220.4		194.4	CAFE,THE,CACAO,EPICES
073	CHOCOLATE AND PRODUCTS	W 76165	218.6	W 69665	206.8	W 75843	214.3	W 70705	188.1	CHOCOLAT
09	MISC EDIBLE PRODUCTS		1832.2		2395.1		1780.7		783.8	PREP ALIMENTAIRES DIVERSES
098	EDIBLE PRODCTS,PREPS NES	W 114675	1808.7	W 135393	2368.2	W 101641	1744.6	W 68257	753.9	PREP ALIMENTAIRES NDA
09809	MISC FOOD PREPRTIONS NES	W 107974	1776.3	W 128440	2348.1	W 94177	1720.7	W 61867	716.0	PREP ALIMENTAIRES NDA
1	BEVERAGES AND TOBACCO		679.0		747.0		824.4		831.7	BOISSONS ET TABACS
11	BEVERAGES		606.3		662.8		735.3		762.6	BOISSONS
112	ALCOHOLIC BEVERAGES	W 342827	569.0	W 395723	611.5	W 412245	681.1	W 436993	713.2	BOISSONS ALCOOLIQUES
1123	BEER,ALE,STOUT,PORTER	W 267630	141.2	W 308718	183.0	W 328566	197.9	W 349357	214.7	BIERES
1124	DISTILLED ALCOHOLIC BEVS	W 71400	421.5	W 84441	422.3	W 79957	477.6	W 84046	492.4	ALCOOLS,EAUX-DE-VIE
11249	OTH ALCOHOLC BEVS,CMPNDS	W 58618	369.8	W 66894	364.5	W 61185	407.9	W 63168	411.7	BOISSONS ALCOOLIQUES NDA
2	CRUDE MATERLS,EXCL FUELS		794.9		891.7		892.6		885.8	MAT BRUTES NON COMESTIBLES
21	HIDES,SKINS,FURS UNDRSSD		110.2		112.8		106.1		108.3	CUIRS,PEAUX BRUTS
211	HIDES,SKINS,EXC FURS,RAW	W 51466	108.0	W 48514	111.0	W 48413	103.3	W 51382	104.4	CUIRS ET PEAUX
26	TEXTILE FIBRES AND WASTE		151.2		192.1		162.8		149.5	FIBRES TEXTILES
266	SYNTHETIC FIBRES TO SPIN	W 70230	113.7	W 78691	147.5	W 54174	115.0	W 69294	117.5	FIBRES SYNTHETIQUES
2665	DISCN SYNTH FIBRE UNCMBD	W 70174	113.1	W 78629	146.4	W 54051	113.4	W 69234	116.2	DISCONTINUES EN MASSE
26652	— POLYESTER	W 65238	101.3	W 74444	135.0	W 50794	104.2	W 65650	106.4	FIBRES EN POLYESTERS
28	METALLIFEROUS ORES,SCRAP		341.1		373.3		370.8		404.5	MINERAIS METAL,DECHETS
287	BASE METAL ORES,CONC NES	W 1718139	299.3	W 1670863	329.0	W 1704817	331.8	W 1807277	363.5	MINERAIS METAUX COMMUNS
2873	ALUMINIUM ORES,ALUMINA	W 1227534	198.4	W 1251925	219.5	W 1346339	234.7	W 1407634	239.2	MINERAIS D'ALUMINIUM
28732	ALUMINA(ALUMINIUM OXIDE)	W 1213876	195.9	W 1197651	207.8	W 1346339	234.7	W 1407607	239.2	ALUMINE (OXYDE ALUMINIUM)
3	MINERAL FUELS ETC		167.3		194.1		190.2		231.5	COMBUSTIBLES MINERAUX LUB
33	PETROLEUM AND PRODUCTS		120.0		127.9		127.3		180.1	PETROLE ET DERIVES
334	PETROLEUM PRODUCTS,REFIN	W 970844	118.3	W 964551	124.8	W 884765	123.1	W 1257509	176.4	PRODUITS RAFFINES
5	CHEMCLS,RELATED PROD NES		7051.4		8042.4		10680.9		13377.7	PRODUITS CHIMIQUES
51	ORGANIC CHEMICALS		3634.5		4014.8		5045.4		6093.8	PROD CHIMIQ ORGANIQUES
513	CARBOXYLIC ACIDS ETC	W 20192	175.0	W 36572	155.6	W 24586	189.9	W 21778	199.6	ACIDES CARBOXYLIQUES
514	NITROGEN–FNCTN COMPOUNDS	W 17763	1415.6	W 19872	1651.7	W 27673	1861.2	W 49702	2276.2	COMPOSES FONCT AZOTEES
5146	OXYGEN–FNCT AMINO–CMPNDS	W 219	223.0	W 6394	291.7	W 13725	353.9	W 20671	379.8	COMP AMINES FONCT OXYGEN
5147	AMIDE–FNCT CMPD,EXC UREA	W 12806	229.5	W 12098	225.9	W 12022	207.7	W 15331	137.5	COMPOSES CARBOXYAMIDE
5148	OTH NITROGN–FNCTN CMPNDS	W 1635	885.7	W 966	1035.9	W 546	1166.9	W 13420	1610.0	AUTRES COMPOSES AZOTES
51482	IMIDE–,IMIDE–FNCT CMPNDS	W 1277	873.0	W 473	1027.9	W 371	1164.5	W 11656	1592.5	COMPOSES A FONCTION IMIDE
515	ORG–INORG COMPOUNDS ETC	W 39588	1974.3	W 37640	2120.8	W 30343	2897.7	W 138646	3546.2	COMPOSES ORGANO–MINERAUX
5155	OTH ORG–INORG COMPOUNDS	W 98	10.1	W 9896	82.7	W 22680	69.7	W 112840	186.3	AUTR COMP ORG–MINERAUX
5156	HETEROCYCLIC CMPDS ETC	W 39288	1936.1	W 26916	2021.3	W 6776	2811.4	W 25149	3334.6	COMPOSES HETEROCYCLIQUES
51569	OTH HETEROCYC CMPDS,ETC	W 39275	1934.7	W 26867	2016.7	W 6776	2811.3	W 25148	3333.3	AUT COMP HETEROCYCLIQUES
52	INORGANIC CHEMICALS		43.1		127.3		151.8		160.8	PROD CHIM INORGANIQUES
541	*MEDICINAL,PHARM PRODUCT	MK 71176	1847.6	MK 73762	2105.9	MK 93354	2782.9	MK 71659	3333.8	PROD MEDICINAUX PHARMACEUT
5413	ANTIBIOTICS IN BULK	K 243943	98.4	K 364100	170.7	K 491627	243.9	K 1201680	275.0	ANTIBIOTIQUES NDA
54139	OTHER ANTIBIOTICS	K 47491	56.6	K 118259	130.4	K 226470	207.1	K 997825	248.8	AUTRES ANTIBIOTIQUES
5417	MEDICAMENTS	MK 66712	1510.4	MK 69928	1646.4	MK 88197	2150.4	MK 65144	2586.6	MEDICAMENTS
54171	— CONTAINNG ANTIBIOTICS	K 3949354	136.9	K 4108027	178.3	K 5552334	260.8	K 3880233	296.9	MED CONTN ANTIBIOTIQUES
54172	— CONTAINING HORMONES	K 2947294	99.7	K 1436424	208.4	K 1561186	209.0	K 1438976	325.4	MED CONTENANT HORMONES
54173	— CONTAINING ALKALOIDS	K 865799	122.6	K 831053	133.9	K 66628	6.6	K 76716	5.0	MED CONTEN ALCALOIDES
54179	— CONTNG OTH SUBSTANCES	MK 58950	1151.3	MK 63553	1125.8	MK 81017	1674.2	MK 59748	1959.5	MED CONT AUT SUBSTANCES
5419	PHARMACEUTICAL GOODS NES	K 1617278	141.9	K 2154715	183.5	K 3110547	209.7	K 3237524	250.1	PREP,ART PHARMACEUTIQUES
54199	OTH PHARMACEUTICAL GOODS	K 641032	128.0	K 787065	159.7	K 1913887	184.9	K 1993686	220.5	AUT PREP PHARMACEUTIQUES
55	PERFUME,CLEANING ETC PRD		794.7		908.6		1362.6		2042.2	PROD POUR PARFUM,TOILETTE
551	ESSENTL OILS,PERFUME,ETC	W 12630	325.1	W 16756	416.6	W 30725	803.1	W 46626	1410.0	HUILES ESSENTIELLES
5514	MIXED PERFUME SUBSTANCES	W 11802	309.2	W 16033	400.5	W 29952	787.1	W 45993	1399.0	MELANGES SUBSTAN ODORIFER
553	PERFUMERY,COSMETICS,ETC	W 44458	430.1	W 49322	448.5	W 57134	517.2	W 69253	581.9	PRODUITS DE PARFUMERIE
58	PLASTIC MATERIALS ETC		205.8		231.6		239.9		255.5	MAT PLAST ARTIFICIELLES
583	POLYMERIZATION ETC PRODS	W 29887	123.2	W 385835	138.4	W 90679	142.3	W 826167	157.6	PROD POLYMERISATION
59	CHEMICAL MATERIALS NES		431.5		545.4		992.0		1368.3	MAT PROD CHIMIQUES NDA
592	STARCH,INULIN,GLUTEN,ETC	W 39025	248.3	W 68266	337.4	W 54386	288.1	W 36250	265.6	AMIDONS,INUL,GLUT FROM
5922	ALBUMINOID SUBSTAN,GLUES	W 34888	246.1	W 66415	337.0	W 54111	288.0	W 35797	265.1	MAT ALBUMIN,COLLES
59221	CASEIN AND DERIVATVS,ETC	W 30598	134.5	W 42155	220.0	W 32579	176.3	W 31743	153.7	CASEINES,CASEINATES
598	MISCEL CHEM PRODUCTS NES	W 26527	157.3	W 28200	175.5	W 33023	665.5	W 38729	1052.8	PROD DIV INDUST CHIM NDA
5989	CHEM PRODUCTS,PREPS NES	W 11333	123.7	W 14310	138.1	W 25507	646.9	W 28734	1030.6	PROD PREP CHIMIQUES NDA
59899	OTH CHEM PRODS,PREPS,NES	W 7905	108.1	W 8716	120.2	W 20928	631.9	W 25804	1017.8	AUT PRODUITS CHIMIQUES NDA
6	BASIC MANUFACTURES		1888.2		2105.8		2198.9		2101.2	ART MANUFACTURES
62	RUBBER MANUFACTURES NES		201.9		215.4		198.5		118.5	CAOUTCHOUC MANUFACTURE
625	RUBBER TYRES, TUBES ETC	W 21322	105.2	W 21640	102.3	W 17880	85.5	W 2022	9.7	PNEUS CAOUTCHOUC VULCANISE
6251	TYRES NEW FOR MOTOR CARS	W 21017	103.9	W 21039	100.0	W 16287	78.4	W 634	3.1	PNEUS POUR VOITURES
64	PAPER,PAPERBOARD AND MFR		161.5		215.9		229.8		233.2	PAPIERS,CARTONS & OUVRAGES
641	PAPER AND PAPERBOARD	W 158230	102.0	W 203203	140.3	W 216311	121.8	W 239380	133.9	PAPIERS ET CARTONS
65	TEXTILE YARN,FABRICS,ETC		522.8		586.6		598.6		539.4	FILS,TISSUS,ARTICLES TEXTILE
651	TEXTILE YARN	W 43128	167.3	W 54399	238.2	W 62858	267.7	W 58267	259.0	FILS TEXTILES
6514	SYN FIB YRN,BULK,MONOFIL	W 28441	83.4	W 38890	131.0	W 48478	164.7	W 43435	156.0	FILS CONT 85% FIB TEXT SYNTH
65144	— TEXTRD,CONT POLYESTER	W 27313	76.4	W 35402	114.4	W 46385	146.6	W 40641	132.7	FILS TEX FI CONT POLYESTERS
66	NONMETAL MINERAL MFS NES		326.1		312.2		370.5		379.4	ART MIN NON METALLIQUES

5. General Exports F.O.B. by Commodities according to the S.I.T.C. (Rev. 2) in million U.S. Dollars
Exportations Générales F.O.B. par Produits d'après la C.T.C.I. (Rév. 2) en millions de Dollars E.U.

SITC CTCI	COMMODITY	1994 QUANTITY QUANTITE	1994 VALUE VALEUR	1995 QUANTITY QUANTITE	1995 VALUE VALEUR	1996 QUANTITY QUANTITE	1996 VALUE VALEUR	1997 QUANTITY QUANTITE	1997 VALUE VALEUR	PRODUIT
67	IRON AND STEEL		128.3		152.3		149.7		151.5	FER ET ACIER
673	IRON,STEEL SHAPES ETC	W 253842	108.6	W 275987	124.6	W 291671	117.7	W 298287	117.5	BARRES,PROFIL FER,ACIER
6733	IRON,STEEL PROFILES ETC	W 245614	104.6	W 270167	121.0	W 284037	113.4	W 288132	112.5	PROFILES,PALPLAN FER,ACIER
69	METAL MANUFACTURES NES		414.1		452.2		464.2		469.0	ART MANUFACT EN METAL NDA
699	BASE METAL MFRS NES	W 38034	181.4	W 29550	187.3	W 26086	191.4	W 21536	149.6	ART MANUFACTURES MET NDA
6998	MFRS NES OF CPR,NIKL,ETC	W 26602	138.7	W 20250	138.9	W 19014	129.8	W 14087	96.3	OUVRAGES EN CU,NI,AL,PB,ZN
69983	ALUMINIUM MANUFACTS NES	W 26142	128.6	W 20054	130.3	W 18862	122.2	W 14027	93.6	OUVRAGES EN ALUMINIUM
7	MACHINES,TRANSPORT EQUIP		10293.8		15126.8		16749.1		20058.6	MACHINES MATERIEL TRANSPORT
71	POWER GENERATING EQUIPMT		222.6		301.0		365.8		399.5	MACHINES GENERATRICES
714	ENGINES AND MOTORS NES	W 489	112.7	W 755	178.5	W 801	182.0	W 464	181.7	MOTEURS NON ELECTRIQUES
72	MACHS FOR SPCL INDUSTRYS		237.1		239.3		266.2		273.6	MAC SPECIALES POUR INDUST
728	OTH MACHY FOR SPCL INDUS	W 6090	115.5	W 8509	110.4	W 6816	120.3	W 8033	136.3	AUT MACH IND PARTICULIERES
74	GENRL INDUSTRL MACHY NES		611.4		768.0		835.2		915.1	MACH APP INDUSTRIE
741	HEATING,COOLING EQUIPMNT	W 16901	242.9	W 24318	346.6	W 23889	350.5	W 22459	393.0	MACH CHAUFFAGE,PIECES
7414	NONDOM REFRIG EQUIPT,PTS	W 9637	205.9	W 16431	302.2	W 16087	288.5	W 16843	323.6	MAT PRODUCTION DU FROID
74141	REFRIG EQUIP NONDOMESTIC	W 7945	182.9	W 14999	283.9	W 14421	266.3	W 15665	297.9	REFIG INDUSTRIELS
75	OFFICE MACHNES,ADP EQUIP		6080.1		9346.8		10213.8		12239.6	MACH BUREAU TRAIT AUTOM
752	AUTOMTIC DATA PROC EQUIP	W 28581	3678.0	W 48703	5719.8	W 75895	6177.1		7984.0	MACH TRAIT INFORMATION
7522	DIGITAL COMPUTERS	W 2218	310.3	W 2270	525.7	W 16050	1615.7		1254.8	MACH DIGITALES COMPLETES
7523	DIGITL CENTRL PROCESSORS	W 10531	1585.3	W 22702	2885.1	W 25762	1569.6	W 19724	1722.0	UNITES CENTRALES
7524	DIGITL CENTRL STOR UNITS	W 3647	1037.0	W 4601	1447.9	W 8906	2151.2	W 12059	3187.0	UNITES MEMOIRE CENTRALES
7525	ADP PERIPHERAL UNITS	W 8623	486.4	W 3932	135.7	W 12900	451.7	W 29681	1399.7	UNITES PERIPHERIQUES
7528	OFF–LINE DATA PROC EQUIP	W 3493	253.8	W 15144	718.8	W 11517	294.0	W 28305	325.3	MACH AUXIL TRAIT INFORM
759	OFFICE,ADP MCH PTS,ACCES	W 20962	2397.0	W 23838	3620.1	W 29173	4007.4	W 28086	4246.3	PIECES DU 751 ET 752
7591	OFFICE MACHINE PARTS NES	W 1809	230.9	W 2650	449.3	W 3091	515.1	W 1670	520.1	PIECES DU 7511,7518
75915	OTH OFF MCH PTS,ACC NES	W 1190	191.3	W 1997	432.6	W 2401	490.9	W 1081	503.2	PIECES DU 751.18,81,88
7599	ACCTG,ETC,ADP MCH PTS,AC	W 19153	2166.1	W 21187	3170.8	W 26082	3492.4	W 26416	3726.2	PIECES DU 751 ET 752
76	TELECOMM,SOUND EQUIPMENT		735.1		851.3		999.5		1260.7	EQUIPMENT DE TELECOM
764	TELECOM EQPT,PTS,ACC NES	W 11607	729.7	W 10069	833.0	W 9936	972.5		1221.8	EQUIP TELECOM,PIECES
7641	LINE TELEPHONE,ETC EQUIP	W 1302	100.3	W 1101	163.5	W 1858	260.9	W 4030	602.9	APP TELEPHON PAR FIL
7643	TV,RADIO TRANSMITTRS ETC	W 636	112.2	W 595	176.3	W 596	184.0	W 680	128.3	APP EMET TELE RADIO
7648	TELECOMM EQUIPMENT NES	W 869	95.1	W 1011	137.1	W 540	185.0	W 375	71.8	APP TELECOM NDA
7649	PTS NES OF EQUIPMT OF 76	W 5442	369.2	W 4309	300.6	W 4716	305.3	W 9840	390.5	PIECES DE LA DIV 76
76491	PTS NES OF APPAR OF 7641	W 1535	235.4	W 1276	206.9	W 1096	243.6	W 2447	322.6	PIECES POUR 764.1
77	ELECTRIC MACHNRY NES ETC		2092.6		3261.3		3634.9		4425.5	MACH APP ELECT NDA
771	ELECTRIC POWER MACHY NES	W 5151	106.5	W 5523	121.2	W 6538	144.5		313.4	MACH PROD,TRANS ELECTR
7712	OTH ELEC POWER MACHY NES	W 723	66.6	W 868	86.8	W 943	94.2	W 1572	245.3	AUT APP PROD TRANSF ELEC
77121	STATIC CONVERTERS ETC	W 426	53.2	W 627	74.6	W 718	73.6	W 1222	216.6	CONVERTISSEURS STATIQUES
772	SWITCHGEAR ETC,PARTS NES	W 8047	376.0	W 9917	486.0	W 12132	650.6	W 17134	729.3	APP COUPURE,SECT ETC
7721	SWITCHGEAR ETC	W 7490	311.1	W 9311	369.4	W 10514	446.7	W 13597	503.3	APP COUPURE,SECTIONMNT
7722	PRINTED CIRCUITS,PTS NES	W 235	38.2	W 233	83.9	W 1188	135.0	W 3023	159.9	CIRCUITS ET PIECES
773	ELECTR DISTRIBUTNG EQUIP	W 32557	196.5	W 40474	243.7	W 64045	309.2	W 60692	317.5	EQUIPMT DISTRIBUTION ELECT
7731	INSULATED WIRE,CABLE ETC	W 32499	195.4	W 40257	241.6	W 63856	305.7	W 60508	309.6	FILS,CABLES ISOLES ELECT
775	HOUSEHOLD TYPE EQUIP NES	W 21093	279.0	W 23938	335.8	W 22342	316.6	W 28366	368.9	MACH,APP USAGE DOMESTQUE
7758	ELECTRO–THERMIC APPL NES	W 9099	127.5	W 8864	147.8	W 8615	129.5	W 13902	197.1	APP ELECTROTHERMIQ NDA
776	TRANSISTORS,VALVES,ETC	W 1284	750.3	W 2271	1509.8	W 4487	1780.4		2148.0	LAMPES,TUBES,VALVES
7764	ELECTRONIC MICROCIRCUITS	W 1003	678.0	W 2008	1393.4	W 3837	1532.7	W 1291	2023.3	MICROSTRUCTURES ELECTRON
7768	ELCTRNC COMP PTS,CRYSTLS	W 94	24.3	W 86	49.4	W 410	148.4	W 324	36.0	CRIST PIEZO–ELEC,PCS 776
77689	ELECTRNIC COMPON PTS NES	W 90	22.3	W 85	49.2	W 393	146.9	W 308	31.9	PIECES DU GROUPE 776
778	ELECTRICAL MACHINERY NES	W 7076	371.5	W 7647	549.0	W 7294	418.6		498.8	AUTRES MACH ELECT NDA
7781	BATTERIES,ACCUMULATORS	W 2001	143.9	W 1720	116.2	W 665	20.8	W 458	22.0	PILES ET ACCUMULATEURS
77812	ELECTRIC ACCUMULATORS	W 1841	133.9	W 1371	111.2	W 243	12.0	W 378	16.8	ACCUMULATEURS ELECTRIQ
7788	OTH ELEC MACHY,EQUIP NES	W 2611	160.6	W 3292	365.5	W 3973	330.6	W 5429	415.3	AUT MACH APP ELEC NDA
77889	ELEC PARTS OF MACHY NES	W 119	93.7	W 76	185.4	W 101	117.6	W 184	149.6	PIECES ELEC DE MACH NDA
78	ROAD VEHICLES		166.6		190.6		197.3		233.8	VEHICULES ROUTIERS
79	OTHR TRANSPORT EQUIPMENT		109.5		128.1		183.9		257.0	AUTRE MATERIEL TRANSPORT
792	AIRCRAFT ETC	W 418	90.7		103.4	W 716	160.1	W 744	238.0	APP NAVIGATION AERIENNE
7929	AIRCRAFT PARTS NES	W 353	76.6	W 379	89.6	W 417	93.4	W 592	160.7	PIECES DU 792
8	MISC MANUFACTURED GOODS		5058.1		5928.9		7361.0		7252.4	ART MANUFACTURES DIVERS
84	CLOTHING AND ACCESSORIES		475.3		505.0		532.2		492.9	VETEMENTS
845	OUTERWEAR KNIT NONELASTC	W 8082	115.4	W 7568	122.2	W 8519	131.8		125.0	VET DESSOUS,ACCES BONNET
846	UNDER GARMENTS KNITTED	W 12524	168.9	W 12019	176.5	W 8214	146.1		117.1	SOUS VETS DE BONNETERIE
8462	— OF COTTON NON ELASTIC	W 11083	132.9	W 11155	151.8	W 7827	122.6		93.6	SOUS–VET BONNET COTON
84629	—— OTHER	W 11083	132.9	W 11155	151.8	W 7827	122.6		93.6	AUT SOUS–VET BONNET COTON
87	PRECISION INSTRUMNTS NES		770.2		947.3		1299.8		1396.6	INSTRUM,APPAR SCIENT NDA
872	MEDICAL INSTRUMENTS NES	W 16065	514.2	W 15658	632.7	W 18090	919.0	W 18530	1060.3	INSTR,APP MEDIC–CHIR NDA
87202	OTH MEDICAL INSTRUMENTS	W 14975	457.2	W 14421	552.2	W 16368	779.4	W 16711	933.5	INSTRUM,APP MEDECINE
87203	MECHANO–THERAPY APPARAT	W 1089	57.0	W 1235	80.3	W 1722	139.6	W 1815	126.7	APP DE MECANOTHERAPIE
874	MEASURNG,CONTROLNG INSTR	W 5419	183.0	W 7597	215.9	W 8466	264.8	W 6490	223.7	INSTRUMENTS DE MESURE
88	PHOTO EQU,OPTICL GDS ETC		239.8		261.4		274.8		351.9	APP,FOURN PHOTO,OP,MONTR
884	OPTICAL GOODS NES	W 1059	192.5	W 1029	205.7	W 1536	231.4		315.3	ELEMENTS OPTIQ,ART LUNET
8841	OPTICAL ELEMENTS	W 570	77.0	W 526	73.5	W 956	97.9		183.8	LENTILLES,PRISMES,MIROIR
88411	OPTICAL ELMNTS UNMOUNTED	W 560	76.3	W 500	72.5	W 946	97.1		180.0	LENTIL,MIROIRS NON MONT
8842	SPECTACLES AND FRAMES	W 489	115.6	W 503	132.3	W 580	133.5		131.5	LUNETTES ET MONTURES
89	MISC MANUFCTRD GOODS NES		3339.3		3998.0		5001.7		4751.0	ART MANUFACTURES DIVERS
892	PRINTED MATTER	W 15518	157.6	W 13570	172.1	W 15240	194.4	W 13813	160.7	IMPRIMES
893	ARTICLES OF PLASTIC NES		285.7		324.3	W 85247	345.4		367.7	OUVRAGES EN MAT DIVIS 58
8939	MISC PLASTIC ARTICLES	W 54027	214.4	W 54609	237.6	W 59462	250.9	W 66777	267.1	ART DIVERS EN MAT DIV 58
89399	OTHR PLASTC ARTICLES NES	W 24918	132.4	W 28543	154.4	W 30214	164.4	W 32348	184.6	AUT OUV MAT DIV 58
894	TOYS,SPORTING GOODS,ETC	W 26390	166.9	W 25971	200.2	W 24791	200.5	W 25859	213.8	VOITURES ENFANTS,JOUETS
8942	TOYS,INDOOR GAMES ETC	W 22720	115.6	W 22211	141.4	W 21081	133.8	W 22409	148.1	JOUETS,JEUX ETC
895	OFFICE SUPPLIES NES		48.0	W 1517	52.0	W 1781	62.9	W 10402	222.8	ART PAPET NDA
898	MUSICAL INSTRUMENTS,PTS	W 45444	2508.7	W 38275	3009.7	W 55437	3921.5		3506.3	INSTRUMENTS DE MUSIQUE
8983	SOUND RECRDNG TAPE,DISCS	W 45399	2508.2	W 38238	3008.4	W 55376	3919.7	W 97412	3505.3	SUPPORTS SON POUR 763
89831	PREPD SND RECORDNG MEDIA	W 21182	228.4	W 22090	260.5	W 22703	270.3	W 33934	348.7	SUPPORTS PREPARES
89832	RECORDED DISCS,TAPES ETC	W 24218	2279.8	W 16148	2748.0	W 32673	3649.4	W 63478	3156.7	DISQUES,PHONO,BANDES
899	OTHER MANUFACTURED GOODS		124.6		181.4		226.8		233.9	AUT ART MANUF DIVERS NDA
8996	HEARING,ORTHOPAEDIC AIDS		72.4		121.0		158.5		163.4	APPAREILS D'ORTHOPEDIE
89962	ORTHOPAEDIC ETC GOODS		71.6		111.6		140.8		132.6	APPAREILS D'ORTHOPEDIE
9	GOODS NOT CLASSD BY KIND		2067.7		3010.8		0.6		3036.2	ART TRANSACT NON CLASSES
931	*SPECIAL TRANSACTIONS	W 164119	2066.3		3010.5				3035.0	TRANS.SPECIALES

1. HISTORICAL SERIES, 1962–1997 SPECIAL TRADE, IMPORTS C.I.F., EXPORTS F.O.B.
SERIES HISTORIQUES, 1962–1997 COMMERCE SPECIAL, IMPORTATIONS C.A.F., EXPORTATIONS F.O.B

YEAR ANNEE	VALUE IN MILLION U.S. DOLLARS VALEUR EN MILLION U.S. DOLLARS MERCHANDISE –MARCHANDISE		GOLD –OR		CONVERSION FACTORS FACTEURS DE CONVERSION CENTS E.U. PAR		INDEX NUMBERS –INDICES QUANTUM		UNIT VALUE VALEUR UNITAIRE	
	IMPORTS	EXPORTS	IMPORTS	EXPORTS	IMPORTS	EXPORTS	IMPORTS	EXPORTS	IMPORTS	EXPORTS
1962	625.80	271.40								
1963	660.30	338.30								
1964	814.90	351.80								
1965	814.30	406.10								
1966	816.10	476.90								
1967	756.30	517.30								
1968	1092.90	602.10								
1969	1302.10	688.70								
1970	1422.50	733.60								
1971	1780.00	915.10								
1972	1948.00	1099.80								
1973	2968.60	1391.80								
1974	4176.50	1737.40								
1975	4108.70	1834.60								
1976	4076.60	2305.80								
1977	4759.90	2963.10								
1978	5631.00	3716.10								
1979	7396.50	4313.40								
1980	9784.10	5538.00					59	57	89	80
1981	10235.10	5670.90					60	60	86	77
1982	9655.30	5255.00					67	59	79	73
1983	9574.00	5108.00					73	60	75	71
1984	9766.70	5566.00					73	69	75	70
1985	10009.55	6194.10					74	75	73	69
1986	10805.16	7154.00					86	83	73	71
1987	14359.20	8454.00					97	92	80	76
1988	15018.30	8198.00					97	95	87	87
1989	14347.10	10738.00					93	99	93	92
1990	16793.70	11576.00					100	100	100	100
1991	18621.37	11911.16					116	98	95	100
1992	20253.18	13074.99					130	107	95	101
1993	22623.56	14781.07					146	121	92	102
1994	25237.20	16881.38					166	140	94	100
1995	29578.95	19045.97					182	150	102	105
1996	31685.92	20610.09					193	163	101	105
1997	30782.94	22502.48					196	179	97	107

2. IMPORTS BY BROAD ECONOMIC CATEGORY AND EXPORTS BY INDUSTRIAL ORIGIN. (PERCENTAGE OF TOTAL VALUE)
IMPORTATIONS PAR CATEGORIES ECONOMIQUES ET EXPORTATIONS PAR BRANCHE D'ACTIVITE.(EN POURCENTAGE DE LA VALEUR TOTALE)

IMPORTS – IMPORTATIONS

	1991	1992	1993	1994	1995	1996	1997
TOTAL IMPORTS–IMPORTATIONS TOTALES	100.	100.	100.	100.	100.	100.	100.
1 FOOD BEV–ALIMENTATION BOISSONS	6.5	6.1	5.7	5.9	5.6	5.7	6.1
11 PRIMARY–PRODUITS DE BASE	3.9	3.4	3.2	3.3	2.9	3.0	3.3
111 FOR INDUSTRY–POUR L'INDUSTRIE	2.2	2.1	2.0	1.9	1.8	1.9	2.1
112 FOR HOUSEHOLDS–POUR LES MENAGES	1.7	1.3	1.2	1.3	1.1	1.1	1.3
12 PROCESSED–PRODUITS ELABORES	2.6	2.7	2.5	2.6	2.6	2.7	2.8
121 FOR INDUSTRY–POUR L'INDUSTRIE	0.4	0.5	0.4	0.4	0.4	0.3	0.4
122 FOR HOUSEHOLDS–POUR LES MENAGES	2.2	2.2	2.1	2.2	2.2	2.4	2.4
2 IND SUPPLIES–APPROV INDUSTRIELS	44.0	42.8	42.0	41.2	42.1	40.0	41.1
21 PRIMARY–PRODUITS DE BASE	18.0	18.3	19.0	18.8	18.0	18.5	18.8
22 PROCESSED–PRODUITS ELABORES	26.0	24.4	23.0	22.4	24.1	21.6	22.3
3 FUELS–COMBUSTIBLES	7.6	7.8	7.4	6.0	6.0	6.1	7.8
31 PRIMARY–PRODUITS DE BASE	6.2	7.1	6.6	5.3	4.8	5.0	6.6
32 PROCESSED–PRODUITS ELABORES	1.3	0.7	0.8	0.8	1.2	1.1	1.3
321 MOTOR SPIRIT–ESSENCE	1.3	0.6	0.4	0.7			
322 OTHER–AUTRES	0.0	0.1	0.0	0.0	1.2	1.1	1.3
4 MACHINERY–EQUIPEMENT	21.1	20.7	22.1	23.0	23.1	24.7	23.0
41 CAPITAL EQUIPMENT–MACHINES	17.0	16.6	17.6	18.3	18.2	19.2	17.8
42 PARTS–PIECES ACCESSOIRES	4.1	4.1	4.5	4.7	5.0	5.6	5.2
5 TRANSPORT–TRANSPORT	11.0	11.7	11.5	12.5	11.6	11.3	10.4
51 PASSENGER CARS–AUTOMOBILES	4.1	5.6	4.9	5.3	5.1	4.7	4.3
52 OTHER–AUTRES	4.1	3.2	3.6	4.6	3.7	3.4	2.9
521 INDUSTRIAL–INDUSTRIELS	4.0	3.1	3.4	4.4	3.6	3.3	2.8
522 NON INDUSTRIAL–NON INDUSTRIEL	0.1	0.1	0.1	0.2	0.1	0.1	0.1
53 PARTS–PIECES ACCESSOIRES	2.9	2.9	3.0	2.5	2.8	3.1	3.1
6 CONSUM GOODS–BIENS CONSOMMATION	8.5	9.3	9.9	10.1	10.0	10.7	11.1
61 DURABLE–DURABLES	3.1	3.3	3.4	3.4	3.3	3.4	3.4
62 SEMI DURABLE–SEMI DURABLES	3.3	3.7	4.1	4.2	4.4	4.7	5.0
63 NON DURABLE–NON DURABLES	2.1	2.3	2.4	2.4	2.4	2.6	2.8
7 GOODS NES–BIENS NDA	1.3	1.6	1.3	1.3	1.5	1.5	0.4

EXPORTS – EXPORTATIONS

	1991	1992	1993	1994	1995	1996	1997
TOTAL EXPORTS–EXPORTATIONS TOTALES	100.	100.	100.	100.	100.	100.	100.
1 AGRICULTURE	5.8	4.4	3.9	3.7	4.1	4.2	3.8
2 MINING QUARRY–INDUS EXTRACTIVES	30.0	29.8	29.0	30.4	30.7	31.2	30.7
3 MANUFACTURING–IND MANUFACTUR	64.3	65.8	67.1	65.9	65.2	64.7	65.5
31 FOOD BEV TOBACCO–ALIM BOISS TAB	4.3	4.0	3.4	3.1	2.8	2.7	2.1
32 TEXTILES–INDUSTRIES TEXTILES	6.9	7.2	6.1	5.9	5.7	5.2	4.8
33 WOOD & PRODUCTS–BOIS & PRODUITS	0.1	0.1	0.1	0.1	0.1	0.0	0.0
34 PAPER & PRODUCTS–PAPIER & PRODT	0.6	0.6	0.5	0.5	0.5	0.5	0.5
35 CHEMICALS–INDUSTRIES CHIMIQUES	16.6	16.4	16.7	16.6	17.2	16.8	17.4
36 NON METAL MIN–MIN NON METAL	0.3	0.2	0.2	0.3	0.4	0.4	0.3
37 BASIC METAL–IND METAL BASE	0.9	0.8	0.6	0.7	0.9	0.9	0.9
38 METAL MANUF–MANUF METAL	31.2	32.9	36.0	35.7	32.5	35.4	37.2
39 OTH MANUF IND–AUTRES MANUF	3.4	3.7	3.4	3.0	5.1	2.8	2.3

3. TRADE BY PRINCIPAL COUNTRIES OF PURCHASE AND SALE (VALUE IN MILLION U.S. DOLLARS)
ECHANGES SELON LES PRINCIPAUX PAYS D'ACHAT ET DE VENTE (VALEUR EN MILLIONS DE DOLLARS EU)

COUNTRIES–PAYS	SPECIAL IMPORTS C.I.F. IMPORTATIONS SPECIALES C.A.F					COUNTRIES–PAYS	SPECIAL EXPORTS F.O.B. EXPORTATIONS SPECIALES F.O.B.				
	1993	1994	1995	1996	1997		1993	1994	1995	1996	1997
World	20517.7	23778.8	28344.3	29948.5	29022.6	Monde	14825.3	16934.0	19047.4	20510.2	22503.0
Africa	326.0	329.6	413.6	389.5	387.7	Afrique	264.2	285.1	354.0	387.5	475.0
Americas	3977.5	4696.5	5764.4	6447.9	6061.7	Amériques	5122.0	5897.9	6410.0	7026.6	8155.1
– Northern America	3751.2	4426.6	5491.0	6149.5	5739.2	– Amérique du Nord	4724.7	5368.6	5850.1	6405.7	7365.9
– LAIA	206.6	253.4	245.1	262.6	311.8	– ALAI	355.7	478.5	494.6	556.4	693.9
– CACM	5.2	3.9	3.5	4.1	4.0	– MCAC	25.2	28.2	34.2	40.6	59.4
– Caribbean	0.5	0.3	1.2	0.5	1.0	– Caraïbes	7.8	8.4	16.0	15.3	25.4
– Rest of America	14.1	12.2	23.6	31.1	5.6	– Autre Amérique	8.7	14.1	15.1	8.6	10.4
Asia excl fmr USSR	2162.1	2483.3	3128.7	3338.6	3534.4	Asie anc. URSS exclus	2638.6	3320.4	4030.8	4349.9	4516.0
– Middle East	121.6	193.7	291.4	288.8	414.8	– Moyen–Orient	169.0	172.7	246.4	282.3	391.7
Asia former USSR	2.3	3.0	1.8	0.6	1.2	Asie ancienne URSS	42.5	33.3	43.7	39.8	51.1
Europe excl fmr USSR	12319.1	14591.8	16877.7	17489.3	16730.9	Europe anc. URSS exclus	5182.2	5566.2	6871.8	7324.9	7672.3
– European Union	10548.5	12719.0	14687.4	15357.0	14798.4	– Union Européenne	4538.0	4961.3	6150.1	6588.3	6778.2
– Eastern Europe	172.0	211.8	263.9	212.6	220.7	– Europe de l'Est	318.5	192.0	294.3	318.0	351.0
– Rest of Europe	1598.6	1661.0	1926.4	1919.8	1711.9	– Autre de l'Europe	325.7	412.8	427.4	418.5	543.2
Europe former USSR	73.0	116.1	274.8	236.8	210.0	Europe ancienne URSS	161.5	267.7	343.0	372.2	366.1
Oceania	55.6	63.0	78.2	91.2	92.1	Océanie	158.8	214.7	247.6	237.2	279.1
Other	1602.1	1495.6	1805.1	1954.7	2004.6	Autre	1255.6	1348.8	746.4	772.2	988.4
USA/Etats–Unis d'Amer	3643.2	4271.1	5263.6	5965.7	5444.8	USA/Etats–Unis d'Amer	4621.7	5262.4	5735.2	6281.2	7215.1
Belgium–Luxembourg	2504.9	3049.9	3433.4	3637.9	3618.3	United Kingdom	816.1	849.0	1160.1	1364.8	1401.7
Germany/Allemagne	2132.7	2467.5	2745.7	2801.2	2727.7	Japan/Japon	769.0	989.4	1322.5	1216.3	1029.9
United Kingdom	1773.6	2056.7	2324.8	2632.9	2424.9	Areas n.e.s.	1255.6	1348.8	746.4	772.2	988.4
Italy/Italie	1496.3	1849.1	2193.9	2258.1	1995.8	Belgium–Luxembourg	797.5	910.4	1019.8	1122.9	1116.6
Areas n.e.s.	1602.1	1495.6	1805.1	1954.7	2004.6	China, Hong Kong SAR	722.5	843.8	967.7	1066.1	1183.2
Switzerland,Liechtenst.	1533.8	1530.3	1680.5	1648.6	1598.4	Germany/Allemagne	786.6	850.3	1039.2	1037.1	977.3
France, Monaco	857.7	1058.2	1158.3	1165.4	1099.1	Netherlands/Pays–Bas	554.0	633.1	808.0	890.4	981.7
Japan/Japon	1047.7	963.6	931.4	1097.1	1033.6	France, Monaco	576.1	584.0	704.9	670.6	616.3
Netherlands/Pays–Bas	700.6	789.2	949.1	943.9	1094.8	Italy/Italie	437.3	505.2	567.4	553.1	623.7
Spain/Espagne	208.5	398.0	520.9	620.0	600.5	Switzerland,Liechtenst.	272.0	346.9	344.1	300.8	387.5
China, Hong Kong SAR	248.8	281.1	365.1	412.6	432.0	India/Inde	228.3	361.9	314.5	315.7	364.8
Other Asia n.e.s.	249.2	269.6	375.2	392.2	368.1	Spain/Espagne	199.2	236.3	313.8	352.3	344.4
Sweden/Suède	286.2	326.7	380.4	362.4	281.1	Korea, Republic of	138.2	147.8	301.9	364.4	414.4
Korea, Republic of	137.9	282.4	385.3	352.4	328.6	Thailand/Thaïlande	146.7	248.9	275.3	334.3	255.2
So. African Customs Un	253.9	236.7	295.1	300.9	306.7	Russian Federation	118.5	192.5	259.2	258.7	253.0
Turkey/Turquie	92.0	162.1	256.3	246.2	355.4	Australia/Australie	134.7	180.4	218.0	214.2	243.6
India/Inde	128.9	151.7	186.7	246.3	292.9	Singapore/Singapour	118.1	151.1	170.5	200.4	265.5
Canada	108.0	155.5	227.4	183.8	294.5	Turkey/Turquie	135.1	131.0	184.0	197.0	256.8
Finland/Finlande	104.3	124.0	233.5	211.4	263.8	Philippines	187.1	207.9	174.3	198.2	127.1
Singapore/Singapour	84.6	124.8	275.1	189.3	198.0	So. African Customs Un	122.6	128.6	173.9	179.7	220.6
Thailand/Thaïlande	99.5	118.5	159.1	173.8	215.6	Brazil/Brésil	80.4	128.3	132.0	186.7	265.2
Denmark/Danemark	139.3	140.2	167.1	153.0	141.7	Greece/Grèce	114.7	108.7	204.4	165.9	166.3
Austria/Autriche	115.1	128.7	155.1	148.2	138.9	Other Asia n.e.s.	89.1	121.8	118.1	159.3	225.0
Ireland/Irlande	71.3	105.6	159.1	171.6	177.6	Canada	102.9	106.2	114.8	124.2	150.8
Russian Federation	55.6	70.2	212.8	180.5	159.1	Romania/Roumanie	92.8	74.5	132.3	112.2	148.5
Greece/Grèce	84.5	115.9	150.9	136.9	127.0	Sweden/Suède	52.5	74.3	91.3	118.2	106.7
China/Chine	32.7	80.1	128.8	160.9	206.0	Argentina/Argentine	59.2	76.8	71.0	94.9	127.2
Portugal	73.4	109.2	115.3	114.2	107.0	Austria/Autriche	67.1	79.8	81.1	75.5	84.7
Romania/Roumanie	64.4	89.6	105.8	99.9	107.6	Chile/Chili	73.7	78.9	111.7	50.4	63.6
Other Europe n.e.s.	8.6	54.4	152.0	154.3	7.3	Ireland/Irlande	22.2	28.1	29.6	83.6	193.9
Norway,Svalbard and JM	41.3	56.6	76.8	87.6	67.5	China/Chine	54.7	59.5	84.5	82.7	71.3
Australia/Australie	52.7	60.3	73.2	47.2	88.6	Cyprus/Chypre	34.0	41.7	61.5	74.8	112.1
Uruguay	48.8	54.8	58.5	66.6	81.5	Poland/Pologne	39.7	39.1	63.8	80.2	83.5
Brazil/Brésil	74.3	80.3	36.2	48.2	48.9	Czech Republic	135.5	21.9	27.7	45.0	44.0
Colombia/Colombie	37.5	40.4	56.4	52.5	88.1	Mexico/Mexique	36.5	76.6	33.3	54.5	72.7
Argentina/Argentine	31.8	44.8	58.1	58.9	61.2	Ukraine	22.4	36.1	56.8	68.4	72.7
Czech Republic	36.3	51.7	44.9	24.8	30.7	Colombia/Colombie	25.3	40.4	65.6	56.7	61.8
Cyprus/Chypre	29.6	31.6	32.6	38.4	46.8	Denmark/Danemark	41.6	38.3	53.6	56.0	54.1
Hungary/Hongrie	34.7	24.5	40.0	39.9	39.8	Portugal	51.3	41.3	44.9	46.3	55.6

(VALUE AS PERCENTAGE OF WORLD TOTAL)(VALEURS EN POURCENTAGE DU TOTAL MONDIAL)

	1988	1989	1990	1991	1992	1993	1994	1995	1996	1997		1988	1989	1990	1991	1992	1993	1994	1995	1996	1997
Africa	1.9	1.9	1.8	1.8	1.8	1.6	1.4	1.5	1.3	1.3	Afrique	1.9	1.7	1.4	1.6	1.7	1.8	1.7	1.9	1.9	2.1
Americas	18.5	19.8	19.8	21.5	19.0	19.4	19.8	20.3	21.5	20.9	Amériques	34.1	34.1	32.3	33.5	33.6	34.5	34.8	33.7	34.3	36.2
– Northern America	17.3	18.5	18.6	20.1	17.8	18.3	18.6	19.4	20.5	19.8	– Amérique du Nord	31.6	31.9	29.7	31.0	31.2	31.9	31.7	30.7	31.2	32.7
– LAIA	1.1	1.2	1.1	1.2	1.1	1.0	1.1	0.9	0.9	1.1	– ALAI	2.1	1.8	2.5	2.2	2.1	2.4	2.8	2.6	2.7	3.1
– CACM	0.0	0.0	0.0	0.0	0.0	0.0	0.0	0.0	0.0	0.0	– MCAC	0.1	0.1	0.1	0.1	0.2	0.2	0.2	0.2	0.2	0.3
– Caribbean	0.0	0.0	0.0	0.0	0.0	0.0	0.0	0.0	0.0	0.0	– Caraïbes	0.1	0.3	0.1	0.1	0.0	0.1	0.0	0.1	0.1	0.1
– Rest of America	0.1	0.1	0.1	0.1	0.0	0.1	0.1	0.1	0.1	0.0	– Autre Amérique	0.1	0.0	0.0	0.1	0.0	0.1	0.1	0.1	0.0	0.0
Asia excl fmr USSR	7.2	6.1	7.2	8.6	9.9	10.5	10.4	11.0	11.1	12.2	Asie anc. URSS exclus	15.7	16.2	17.2	15.8	16.7	17.8	19.6	21.2	21.2	20.1
– Middle East	0.3	0.3	0.3	0.6	0.5	0.6	0.8	1.0	1.0	1.4	– Moyen–Orient	0.6	0.8	1.0	1.1	1.1	1.1	1.0	1.3	1.4	1.7
Asia former USSR					0.0	0.0	0.0	0.0	0.0	0.0	Asie ancienne URSS					0.0	0.3	0.2	0.2	0.2	0.2
Europe excl fmr USSR	64.1	62.6	61.6	59.5	60.6	60.0	61.4	59.5	58.4	57.6	Europe anc. URSS exclus	37.8	36.7	40.3	40.9	38.8	35.0	32.9	36.1	35.7	34.1
– European Union	54.3	52.5	51.3	49.8	52.3	51.4	53.5	51.8	51.3	51.0	– Union Européenne	34.4	32.9	36.6	37.2	35.6	30.6	29.3	32.3	32.1	30.1
– Eastern Europe	0.5	0.5	0.7	0.8	0.7	0.8	0.9	0.9	0.7	0.8	– Europe de l'Est	0.4	0.6	0.6	0.8	1.0	2.1	1.1	1.5	1.6	1.6
– Rest of Europe	9.3	9.6	9.5	8.9	7.6	7.8	7.0	6.8	6.4	5.9	– Autre de l'Europe	3.0	3.2	3.1	2.8	2.2	2.2	2.4	2.2	2.0	2.4
Europe former USSR	0.0	0.0	0.1	0.3	0.1	0.4	0.5	1.0	0.8	0.7	Europe ancienne URSS	0.0	0.1	0.0	0.1	0.6	1.1	1.6	1.8	1.8	1.6
Oceania	0.7	0.4	0.2	0.3	0.3	0.3	0.3	0.3	0.3	0.3	Océanie	1.2	1.2	0.9	1.0	1.1	1.1	1.3	1.3	1.2	1.2
Other	7.6	9.2	9.3	8.1	8.3	7.8	6.3	6.4	6.5	6.9	Autre	9.4	9.9	7.9	7.1	7.4	8.5	8.0	3.9	3.8	4.4
USA/Etats–Unis d'Amer	16.6	17.9	17.8	19.3	17.2	17.8	18.0	18.6	19.9	18.8	USA/Etats–Unis d'Amer	30.7	30.9	28.8	30.2	30.5	31.2	31.1	30.1	30.6	32.1
Belgium–Luxembourg	15.2	15.2	13.2	11.1	12.7	12.2	12.8	12.1	12.1	12.5	United Kingdom	7.9	6.8	7.0	6.7	7.7	5.5	5.0	6.1	6.7	6.2
Germany/Allemagne				11.9	11.9	10.4	10.4	9.7	9.4	9.4	Japan/Japon	6.7	7.0	7.2	6.1	5.3	5.2	5.8	6.9	5.9	4.6
United Kingdom	9.3	8.8	8.6	8.3	8.0	8.6	8.6	8.2	8.8	8.4	Areas n.e.s.	9.4	9.9	7.9	7.1	7.4	8.5	8.0	3.9	3.8	4.4
Italy/Italie	6.1	5.8	6.1	6.5	7.0	7.3	7.8	7.7	7.5	6.9	Belgium–Luxembourg	3.9	4.0	5.7	5.8	5.0	5.4	5.4	5.4	5.5	5.0
Areas n.e.s.	7.6	9.2	9.3	8.1	8.3	7.8	6.3	6.4	6.5	6.9	China, Hong Kong SAR	5.3	4.8	4.4	4.6	5.1	4.9	5.0	5.1	5.2	5.3
Switzerland,Liechtenst.	9.0	9.3	9.2	8.5	7.2	7.5	6.4	5.9	5.5	5.5	Germany/Allemagne				6.7	5.8	5.3	5.0	5.5	5.1	4.3
France, Monaco	4.2	4.1	3.9	4.2	4.5	4.2	4.5	4.1	3.9	3.8	Netherlands/Pays–Bas	4.7	4.6	4.5	4.5	4.2	3.7	3.7	4.2	4.3	4.4
Japan/Japon	3.7	2.7	3.6	4.3	5.3	5.1	4.1	3.3	3.7	3.6	France, Monaco	3.9	4.1	4.8	4.8	4.7	3.9	3.4	3.7	3.3	2.7
Netherlands/Pays–Bas	3.5	3.5	3.5	3.4	3.3	3.4	3.3	3.3	3.2	3.8	Italy/Italie	3.9	3.9	4.2	3.9	3.5	2.9	3.0	3.0	2.7	2.8

4. Special Imports C.I.F. by Commodities according to the S.I.T.C. (Rev. 2) in million U.S. Dollars
Importations Spéciales C.A.F. par Produits d'après la C.T.C.I. (Rév. 2) en millions de Dollars E.U.

SITC CTCI	COMMODITY	1994		1995		1996		1997		PRODUIT
		QUANTITY QUANTITE	VALUE VALEUR	QUANTITY QUANTITE	VALUE VALEUR	QUANTITY QUANTITE	VALUE VALEUR	QUANTITY QUANTITE	VALUE VALEUR	
	ALL COMMODITIES		23778.9		28344.3		29948.6		29022.7	TOUS PRODUITS
0	FOOD AND LIVE ANIMALS		1299.3		1503.2		1686.2		1646.9	ALIMENTS,ANIMAUX VIVANTS
01	MEAT AND PREPARATIONS		146.9		109.3		120.8		134.0	VIANDES ET PREPARATIONS
011	MEAT FRESH,CHILLD,FROZEN		146.7		109.3		120.3		134.0	VIANDES FRAICHES,REF,CONGE
0111	BOVINE MEAT FRESH,FROZEN		135.7		100.7		111.4		124.2	VIANDES BOVIN FRAI,REF
01112	BOVINE MEAT BONELESS		116.7		100.2	W 48057	110.0	W 52240	120.5	VIANDES BOVIN DESOSSEES
03	FISH AND PREPARATIONS		88.4		114.9		112.9		124.0	POISSONS ET PREPARATIONS
034	FISH,FRESH,CHILLED,FROZN		68.2		91.2		88.0		97.0	POISSON FRAIS, REFRIG,CONG
04	CEREALS AND PREPARATIONS		420.3		492.7		608.0		557.1	CEREALES ET PRODUITS
041	WHEAT ETC UNMILLED		173.4		145.5	W 852144	189.7		184.4	FROMENT,EPEAUTRE
0412	OTHER WHEAT ETC UNMILLED		132.3		112.6	W 674243	148.7	W 940541	156.4	AUTRE FROMENT NON MOULU
043	BARLEY UNMILLED		71.8		66.1	W 416987	72.9	W 368646	53.7	ORGE NON MONDEE
044	MAIZE UNMILLED		51.7		104.7	W 679286	120.5		84.9	MAIS NON MOULU
048	CEREAL ETC PREPARATIONS		69.0		83.9		90.4		97.3	PREPTNS A BASE CEREALES
05	VEGETABLES AND FRUIT		181.7		216.1		217.8		228.5	LEGUMES ET FRUITS
057	FRUIT,NUTS,FRESH,DRIED		63.9		79.5		81.2		97.5	FRUITS FRAIS OU SECS
06	SUGAR AND PREPS,HONEY		165.4		206.6		212.1		192.0	SUCRES ET PRODUITS
061	SUGAR AND HONEY		134.8		172.1		172.2		165.5	SUCRES ET MIEL
0612	REFINED SUGAR ETC		127.0		162.5	W 408476	162.8		155.9	SUCRES RAFFINES
07	COFFEE,TEA,COCOA,SPICES		125.3		164.7		153.3		152.4	CAFE,THE,CACAO,EPICES
071	COFFEE AND SUBSTITUTES		64.7		101.4		84.1		81.7	CAFE ET SUCCEDANES
09	MISC EDIBLE PRODUCTS		82.2		110.5		156.8		152.3	PREP ALIMENTAIRES DIVERSES
098	EDIBLE PRODCTS,PREPS NES		81.9		103.2		153.5		151.1	PREP ALIMENTAIRES NDA
09809	MISC FOOD PREPRTIONS NES		70.6		90.4		134.4		127.9	PREP ALIMENTAIRES NDA
1	BEVERAGES AND TOBACCO		104.8		110.9		114.5		122.7	BOISSONS ET TABACS
12	TOBACCO AND MANUFACTURES		84.9		90.0		91.4		97.0	TABACS BRUTS FABRIQUES
2	CRUDE MATERLS,EXCL FUELS		599.4		714.5		662.0		705.0	MAT BRUTES NON COMESTIBLES
22	OIL SEEDS,OLEAGINOUS FRT		133.9		161.3		180.0		222.3	GRAINES,FRUITS OLEAGINEUX
222	SEEDS FOR'SOFT'FIXED OIL		132.6		160.2		179.2		221.1	GRAINES HUILES FIXES
2222	SOYA BEANS		102.8		126.8	W 447182	139.4	W 579162	184.9	FEVES DE SOJA
24	CORK AND WOOD		178.1		179.8		159.6		164.2	LIEGE ET BOIS
248	WOOD SHAPED,SLEEPERS		125.6		140.8		132.2		140.6	BOIS SIMPLEMENT TRAVAILLES
2482	LUMBER SHAPED CONIFER		121.5		103.9		94.7		95.8	CONIFERES SCIES,RABOTES
24821	LUMBER SAWN ETC CONIFER		121.1		103.8		94.3	W 268718	95.5	CONIFERES SCIES LONGITUD
251	*PULP AND WASTE PAPER		55.6		92.5		55.0		62.9	PATES A PAPIER,DECHETS
27	CRUDE FERTLZR,MINRLS NES		81.8		110.8		100.8		114.9	ENGRAIS MINERAUX BRUTS
3	MINERAL FUELS ETC		1439.1		1686.2		1846.2		2280.9	COMBUSTIBLES MINERAUX LUB
32	COAL,COKE AND BRIQUETTES		3.5		3.6		8.7		384.6	HOUILLES,COKES,BRIQUETTES
322	COAL,LIGNITE AND PEAT		2.9		2.7		5.3		383.8	HOUILLES,LIGNITES,TOURBE
3222	OTH COAL,NOT AGGLOMERATD		0.1				3.0	W 8739176	381.0	AUTRES HOUILLES
33	PETROLEUM AND PRODUCTS		1434.5		1681.6		1836.7		1887.8	PETROLE ET DERIVES
333	CRUDE PETROLEUM		1242.1		1349.1	MW 10257	1490.4	W 3190110	1502.2	HUILES BRUTES DE PETROLE
334	PETROLEUM PRODUCTS,REFIN		179.1		318.3		307.2		354.2	PRODUITS RAFFINES
3341	GASOLINE,OTH LIGHT OILS		169.9							ESSENCES POUR MOTEURS
33419	OTH LIGHT PETROLEUM OILS		169.9							AUTRES HUILES LEGERES
4	ANIMAL,VEGETABLE OIL,FAT		86.9		88.9		68.8		69.8	HUILES,GRAISSES ANIM,VEG
5	CHEMCLS,RELATED PROD NES		2056.5		2565.6		2620.7		2655.1	PRODUITS CHIMIQUES
51	ORGANIC CHEMICALS		496.3		603.6		636.4		662.2	PROD CHIMIQ ORGANIQUES
511	HYDROCARBONS NES,DERIVS		91.5		102.7		95.7		94.9	HYDROCARBURES NDA
512	ALCOHOLS,PHENOLS ETC		59.3		71.0		79.2		95.6	PHENOLS,PHENOLS–ALCOOLS
513	CARBOXYLIC ACIDS ETC		76.6		104.3		103.1		105.8	ACIDES CARBOXYLIQUES
514	NITROGEN–FNCTN COMPOUNDS		149.5		188.8		207.3		200.5	COMPOSES FONCT AZOTEES
5148	OTH NITROGN–FNCTN CMPNDS		91.5		117.3		130.7		127.2	AUTRES COMPOSES AZOTES
515	ORG–INORG COMPOUNDS ETC		66.1		79.4		84.2		101.7	COMPOSES ORGANO–MINERAUX
52	INORGANIC CHEMICALS		131.5		148.0		142.4		132.8	PROD CHIM INORGANIQUES
53	DYES,TANNING,COLOUR PROD		141.1		165.3		168.3		166.7	PROD TEINTURE,COLORANTS
533	PIGMENTS,PAINTS,ETC		102.3		124.6		132.5		132.7	PIGMENTS,PEINTURES,VERNIS
541	*MEDICINAL,PHARM PRODUCT		347.1		419.2		477.1		486.7	PROD MEDICINAUX PHARMACEUT
5417	MEDICAMENTS		251.9		319.6		367.7		388.7	MEDICAMENTS
54179	— CONTNG OTH SUBSTANCES		228.7		296.2		343.4		366.1	MED CONT AUT SUBSTANCES
55	PERFUME,CLEANING ETC PRD		160.2		196.9		219.4		236.0	PROD POUR PARFUM,TOILETTE
553	PERFUMERY,COSMETICS,ETC		63.2		86.2		99.0		108.8	PRODUITS DE PARFUMERIE
554	SOAP,CLEANSING ETC PREPS		66.6		78.3		86.1		93.1	SAVONS,PRODUITS DETERSIFS
58	PLASTIC MATERIALS ETC		477.8		651.0		574.3		594.4	MAT PLAST ARTIFICIELLES
582	PROD OF CONDENSATION ETC		148.2		225.0		181.6		171.1	PROD CONDENS,POLYCOND
5823	ALKYDS,OTHER POLYESTERS		92.2		158.8		115.8		106.7	ALKYDES ET AUT POLYESTERS
58231	— IN PRIMARY FORMS		81.0		142.9		102.5		93.3	SOUS FORMES PRIMAIRES
583	POLYMERIZATION ETC PRODS		315.0		410.1		377.2		408.8	PROD POLYMERISATION
5831	POLYETHYLENE		95.8		128.7		116.5		135.8	POLYETHYLENE
58311	— IN PRIMARY FORMS		83.5		115.7		104.9		120.3	POLYETHYLENE PRIMAIRES
5839	OTH POLYMRZTION ETC PROD		81.3		82.7		82.6		82.2	AUT PROD POLYMER COPOLYM
59	CHEMICAL MATERIALS NES		290.0		360.6		385.3		356.1	MAT PROD CHIMIQUES NDA
598	MISCEL CHEM PRODUCTS NES		215.4		268.2		289.3		261.1	PROD DIV INDUST CHIM NDA
5989	CHEM PRODUCTS,PREPS NES		187.1		238.1		260.1		235.4	PROD PREP CHIMIQUES NDA
59899	OTH CHEM PRODS,PREPS,NES		149.2		195.7		208.9		196.3	AUT PRODUITS CHIMIQUES NDA
6	BASIC MANUFACTURES		7544.8		9104.5		9224.2		9217.8	ART MANUFACTURES
62	RUBBER MANUFACTURES NES		128.6		152.9		163.5		156.7	CAOUTCHOUC MANUFACTURE
63	WOOD,CORK MANUFACTRS NES		80.7		110.8		126.8		130.4	OUVRAGES LIEGE ET BOIS
64	PAPER,PAPERBOARD AND MFR		448.9		637.2		521.6		511.4	PAPIERS,CARTONS & OUVRAGES
641	PAPER AND PAPERBOARD		384.7		556.2		439.4		423.5	PAPIERS ET CARTONS
6411	NEWSPRINT		67.4		126.3	W 128314	103.1	W 132944	88.3	PAPIER JOURNAL
6413	KRAFT PAPER,PAPERBOARD		86.7		128.9		88.8		91.8	PAPIER ET CARTON KRAFT
6415	PAPER,PAPERBRD,BULK,NES		64.7		94.2		65.2		61.5	PAPIERS,CARTONS ROULEAUX
64159	OTHER PAPER ETC,BULK,NES		58.8		86.4		56.6		53.0	AUT PAPIER ROULEAUX FEUILLES
642	PAPER,ETC,PRECUT,ARTS OF		64.3		81.0		82.2		87.9	PAP,CARTONS DECOUPES
65	TEXTILE YARN,FABRICS,ETC		744.2		827.6		767.5		780.2	FILS,TISSUS,ARTICLES TEXTILE
651	TEXTILE YARN		246.3		270.7		228.4		234.6	FILS TEXTILES
6513	COTTON YARN		109.4		121.1		95.0		98.1	FILS DE COTON
6514	SYN FIB YRN,BULK,MONOFIL		72.3		81.1		74.0		74.5	FILS CONT 85% FIB TEXT SYNTH
652	COTTON FABRICS,WOVEN		74.9		88.3		75.0		81.6	TISSUS DE COTON
653	WOVN MAN–MADE FIB FABRIC		156.6		172.2		158.2		161.5	TISSUS FIBRES SYNTH,ARTIF
655	KNITTED,ETC FABRICS		80.4		90.1		91.3		86.7	ETOF BONNETERIE PIECES ETC
6552	OTHER KNIT ETC FAB NONEL		80.4		90.1		91.3		86.7	ETOF BON NON ELAS NON SYNT
657	SPECIAL TXTL FABRC,PRODS		73.8		95.3		103.6		95.7	TISSUS SPECIAUX
66	NONMETAL MINERAL MFS NES		4602.8		5261.6		5696.5		5638.1	ART MIN NON METALLIQUES
661	LIME,CEMENT,BLDG PRODS		154.4		200.6		174.0		163.5	CHAUX,CIMENTS MAT CONSTR
6612	CEMENT		98.4		128.7		95.4		77.6	CIMENTS HYDRAULIQUES
662	CLAY,REFRACTORY BLDG PRD		85.2		118.0		133.3		116.7	MAT CONST REFRACTAIRES
6624	BRICKS ETC NONREFRACTORY		74.3		102.5		119.7		108.9	BRIQUES ETC CERAM NON REFR
665	GLASSWARE		73.6		85.5		96.2		76.9	OUVRAGES EN VERRE
667	PEARL,PREC–,SEMI–P STONE		4152.4		4695.1		5122.3		5102.3	PERLES, PIERRES GEMMES

4. Special Imports C.I.F. by Commodities according to the S.I.T.C. (Rev. 2) in million U.S. Dollars
Importations Spéciales C.A.F. par Produits d'après la C.T.C.I. (Rév. 2) en millions de Dollars E.U.

SITC CTCI	COMMODITY	1994 QUANTITY QUANTITE	1994 VALUE VALEUR	1995 QUANTITY QUANTITE	1995 VALUE VALEUR	1996 QUANTITY QUANTITE	1996 VALUE VALEUR	1997 QUANTITY QUANTITE	1997 VALUE VALEUR	PRODUIT
6672	DIAMONDS NONINDUST,UNSET		4124.8		4656.4		5078.3		5068.5	DIAMANTS BRUTS
66722	— SRTD,ROUGH,SIMPLY WKD		3485.1		3932.8		4230.6		4142.5	DIAMANTS TRIES BRUTS
66729	— CUT ETC NOT SET		639.7		723.6		847.8		926.0	DIAMANTS TAILLES
67	IRON AND STEEL		607.5		930.1		751.1		768.8	FER ET ACIER
672	IRON,STEEL PRIMARY FORMS		129.7		190.5		134.7		163.9	LINGOTS FER,ACIER
6727	IRN,STL COIL FR REROLLNG		74.4		115.4		76.2		88.4	EBAUCHES POUR TOLES FER
67271	IRON,SIMPLE STEEL COILS		73.4		114.1		74.4		87.3	EBAUCHES NON EN ACIER
673	IRON,STEEL SHAPES ETC		184.6		280.8		241.2		217.9	BARRES,PROFIL FER,ACIER
6732	IRON,STEEL BARS ETC		79.6		146.7		126.2		101.2	BARRES FER,ACIER
67326	IRN,OTH STL BARS HOTROLD		54.6		110.0	W 282829	85.4	W 225431	66.2	BARRES PLEINES FER,ACIER
674	IRN,STL UNIV,PLATE,SHEET		194.3		314.3		238.6		261.9	LARGES PLATS,TOLES
6749	OTH IRN,STL PLATES,SHEET		95.7		161.2		120.2		145.5	AUTRES TOLES FER,ACIER
67491	— OF IRON OR SIMPLE STL		74.4		135.9		100.7	W 171744	124.4	AUT TOLES AUTRES ACIER FIN
678	IRON,STL TUBES,PIPES,ETC		66.0		90.7		97.4		90.8	TUBES,TUYAUX EN FONTE,FER
68	NON–FERROUS METALS		367.7		510.1		459.9		477.1	METAUX NON FERREUX
682	COPPER EXC CEMENT COPPER		141.8		198.4		170.2		181.0	CUIVRE
6822	COPPER,ALLOYS WORKED		140.9		195.9		167.7		179.6	CUIVRE,ALLIAGES OUVRES
68221	COPPER BARS,WIRE,ETC		95.4		124.7	W 36577	99.2		123.4	BARRES,PROFILES ET FILS
684	ALUMINIUM		164.2		230.7		216.2		202.7	ALUMINIUM
6841	ALUMINIUM,ALLOYS,UNWRGHT		66.0		95.3	W 42302	78.5	W 44698	82.4	ALUMINIUM,ALLIAGES BRUTS
6842	ALUMINIUM,ALLOYS WORKED		98.3		135.4		137.8		120.3	ALUMINIUM,ALLIAGES OUVRE
69	METAL MANUFACTURES NES		521.2		630.4		696.5		715.3	ART MANUFACT EN METAL NDA
691	STRUCTURES AND PARTS NES		43.8		57.3		88.1		108.2	CONSTRUCT FER,ACIER,ALU
695	TOOLS		76.3		99.2		105.4		97.9	OUTILS A MAIN
699	BASE METAL MFRS NES		230.5		252.4		261.2		268.8	ART MANUFACTURES MET NDA
6997	IRON,STEEL ARTICLES NES		101.7		94.8		84.5		84.7	OUV FONTE,FER,ACIER NDA
69979	IRN,STL MANUFACTURES NES		101.2		94.8		84.3		84.5	AUT OUVRAGES EN FER NDA
7	MACHINES,TRANSPORT EQUIP		8228.3		9611.0		10445.6		9427.1	MACHINES MATERIEL TRANSPORT
71	POWER GENERATING EQUIPMT		302.0		371.5		421.5		601.7	MACHINES GENERATRICES
714	ENGINES AND MOTORS NES		109.0		200.2		206.7		356.1	MOTEURS NON ELECTRIQUES
7148	GAS TURBINES NES		33.8		3.0		1.1		109.4	TURBINES A GAZ
71488	OTHER GAS TURBINES NES		33.7		2.5		0.6		108.3	AUTRES TURBINES A GAZ
7149	ENGINE & MOTOR PARTS NES		49.7		121.2		122.0		160.2	PIECES 714 ET 718.88
71491	PARTS NES OF 7144,71481		46.0		77.2		110.7		153.0	PIECES DES PROPULSEURS
716	ROTATING ELECTRIC PLANT		114.3		100.8		109.1		139.7	APP ELECTR ROTATIFS,PIECES
7162	AC MTRS,GENRTRS,GEN SETS		84.4		81.3		84.2		98.2	MOTEURS ELECTRIQUES
72	MACHS FOR SPCL INDUSTRYS		893.8		910.2		823.8		623.9	MAC SPECIALES POUR INDUST
723	CIVIL ENGNEERG EQUIP ETC		171.6		138.5		107.0		87.1	APPAREILS DE GENIE CIVIL
7234	CONST,MINING MACHNRY NES		133.2		118.9		95.7		77.7	MACH POUR LA CONST, MINES
72342	SLFPRP SHOVELS,EXCAVATRS		106.9		91.0		71.7		59.6	PELLES MECANIQUES
724	TEXTILE,LEATHER MACHNRY		115.2		100.6		97.5		75.9	MACH POUR INDUSTRIE TEXTILE
726	PRINTG,BKBINDG MACHY,PTS		105.1		120.4		72.8		67.0	MACHINES POUR IMPRIMERIE
728	OTH MACHY FOR SPCL INDUS		364.5		407.5		387.1		288.8	AUT MACH IND PARTICULIERES
7284	MACHY FOR SPCL INDUS NES		246.8		297.6		303.0		217.2	MACH SPEC IND PARTICUL.
72848	OTH MCHY WITH INDIV FNCT		130.6		174.3		169.5		109.9	AUTRES MACHINES NDA
73	METALWORKING MACHINERY		141.5		145.0		163.2		143.3	MACH TRAVAIL DES METAUX
736	METALWORKING MACH–TOOLS		113.1		119.8		132.1		119.7	MACH–OUTILS TRAVAIL METAUX
74	GENRL INDUSTRL MACHY NES		994.3		1265.3		1374.4		1220.7	MACH APP INDUSTRIE
741	HEATING,COOLING EQUIPMNT		193.0		234.9		302.3		234.6	MACH CHAUFFAGE,PIECES
7415	AIR–CONDITIONING MACHNRY		39.4		64.7		95.2		74.0	GROUPES CONDITION AIR
7416	HEATING,COOLING EQU NES		78.2		72.5		76.7		56.4	APP CHANGEMENT TEMP
742	PUMPS FOR LIQUIDS ETC		71.8		88.6		99.8		92.6	POMPES MOTO–POMPES
743	PUMPS NES,CENTRFUGES ETC		200.3		259.1		259.8		253.3	POMPES COMPRES,VENT ETC
7431	PUMPS FOR GASES ETC		88.2		115.6		114.8		94.3	POMPES AIR A VIDE,COMPRES
744	MECHANICAL HANDLING EQU		181.9		277.1		254.2		233.2	EQUIP MANUTENTION PIECES
7441	FORK LIFT TRCKS,ETC,PTS		45.5		85.6		59.0		44.4	CHARIOTS POUR USINES ETC
74411	FORK LIFT TRUCKS ETC		45.1		85.3		58.6		44.2	CHARIOTS POUR LES GARES
7442	LIFTING,LOADING MACH NES		93.4		132.2		124.7		120.8	APP LEVAGE,MANUTENTION
745	NONELEC MACHY,TOOLS NES		113.0		113.6		128.5		112.7	AUT MACH NON ELEC,PIECES
7452	OTH NONELEC MCHS,PTS NES		105.4		105.0		118.6		103.8	AUT MACH NON ELEC,PIECES
749	NONELEC MACH PTS,ACC NES		234.5		292.2		330.1		294.7	PIECES MACH NON ELEC NDA
7492	COCKS,VALVES ETC NES		89.2		105.9		123.5		109.9	ART ROB,SIM POUR TUYAUX
7499	OTH NONELEC MCHY PTS NES		78.9		98.6		112.3		103.9	PIECES NON ELECT NDA
75	OFFICE MACHNES,ADP EQUIP		743.7		941.6		1129.5		1163.7	MACH BUREAU TRAIT AUTOM
752	AUTOMTIC DATA PROC EQUIP		420.1		506.3		616.6		636.9	MACH TRAIT INFORMATION
7528	OFF–LINE DATA PROC EQUIP		315.4		399.3		464.5		435.1	MACH AUXIL TRAIT INFORM
759	OFFICE,ADP MCH PTS,ACCES		276.0		379.3		458.5		473.2	PIECES DU 751 ET 752
7599	ACCTG,ETC,ADP MCH PTS,AC		259.8		361.1		441.4		456.8	PIECES DU 751 ET 752
76	TELECOMM,SOUND EQUIPMENT		680.9		1008.6		1203.6		1072.4	EQUIPMENT DE TELECOM
761	TELEVISION RECEIVERS		86.1		88.7		98.0		94.7	RECEPTEURS DE TELEVISION
7611	COLOUR TV RECEIVERS		84.7		87.6	N 345608	95.5		92.5	RECEPTEURS COULEUR
762	RADIO BROADCAST RECEIVRS		76.1		69.3		65.6		58.4	RECEPTEURS RADIODIFFUSION
764	TELECOM EQPT,PTS,ACC NES		483.0		809.8		992.9		873.2	EQUIP TELECOM,PIECES
7641	LINE TELEPHONE,ETC EQUIP		81.8		104.7		141.8		121.0	APP TELEPHON PAR FIL
7643	TV,RADIO TRANSMITTRS ETC		182.9		366.7		473.4		386.5	APP EMET TELE RADIO
7648	TELECOMM EQUIPMENT NES		30.1		87.9		52.5		51.6	APP TELECOM NDA
7649	PTS NES OF EQUIPMT OF 76		169.3		218.7		288.5		279.2	PIECES DE LA DIV 76
76491	PTS NES OF APPAR OF 7641		82.4		104.4		147.2		119.4	PIECES POUR 764.1
76493	TELECOMM EQUIPMT PTS NES		81.8		109.2		134.8		153.5	PIECES 761,762,764.3,8
77	ELECTRIC MACHNRY NES ETC		1762.6		2038.3		2428.6		2057.5	MACH APP ELECT NDA
771	ELECTRIC POWER MACHY NES		114.4		132.7		166.3		134.1	MACH PROD,TRANS ELECTR
7712	OTH ELEC POWER MACHY NES		75.6		95.1		117.1		105.5	AUT APP PROD TRANSF ELEC
772	SWITCHGEAR ETC,PARTS NES		513.8		504.1		621.4		470.4	APP COUPURE,SECT ETC
7721	SWITCHGEAR ETC		422.6		400.1		498.1		363.5	APP COUPURE,SECTIONMNT
773	ELECTR DISTRIBUTNG EQUIP		78.8		119.6		117.2		130.8	EQUIPMT DISTRIBUTION ELECT
7731	INSULATED WIRE,CABLE ETC		65.0		94.1		95.9		120.0	FILS,CABLES ISOLES ELECT
775	HOUSEHOLD TYPE EQUIP NES		198.5		237.7		252.4		245.7	MACH,APP USAGE DOMESTQUE
776	TRANSISTORS,VALVES,ETC		502.1		606.4		721.9		603.0	LAMPES,TUBES,VALVES
7763	DIODES,TRANSISTORS,ETC		61.5		76.6		90.1		63.6	DIODES,TRANSISTORS
7764	ELECTRONIC MICROCIRCUITS		403.1		485.6		583.1		497.3	MICROSTRUCTURES ELECTRON
778	ELECTRICAL MACHINERY NES		298.2		382.8		480.1		411.3	AUTRES MACH ELECT NDA
7788	OTH ELEC MACHY,EQUIP NES		150.0		217.4		276.2		231.1	AUT MACH APP ELEC NDA
77884	ELECTRICAL CONDENSERS		56.7		87.0		105.5		78.5	CONDENSATEURS ELECTRIQUES
77886	OTH ELEC MACHINERY NES		74.5		83.1		119.1		98.1	AUT MACH APP ELECTRIQUES
78	ROAD VEHICLES		2177.1		2328.1		2332.1		1990.7	VEHICULES ROUTIERS
781	PASS MOTOR VEH EXC BUSES		1257.8		1439.6	N 152208	1410.1		1251.7	AUTO TRANSPORT PERSONNES
782	LORRIES,SPCL MTR VEH NES		588.4		538.5		583.6		437.3	VEHICULES SPECIAUX,MARCH
7821	LORRIES,TRUCKS		532.3		469.2		526.5		408.7	VEHICULES TRANSP MARCHAND
783	ROAD MOTOR VEHICLES NES		77.2		47.5	N 278	33.6		24.1	VEHICULES ROUTIERS NDA
7831	BUSES		75.2		45.9	N 258	31.9	N 232	23.1	VOITURES TRANSPORT COMMUN
784	MOTOR VEH PRTS,ACCES NES		172.5		214.7		211.4		193.9	PIECES 722,781,782,783

4. Special Imports C.I.F. by Commodities according to the S.I.T.C. (Rev. 2) in million U.S. Dollars
Importations Spéciales C.A.F. par Produits d'après la C.T.C.I. (Rév. 2) en millions de Dollars E.U.

SITC CTCI	COMMODITY	1994		1995		1996		1997		PRODUIT
		QUANTITY QUANTITE	VALUE VALEUR	QUANTITY QUANTITE	VALUE VALEUR	QUANTITY QUANTITE	VALUE VALEUR	QUANTITY QUANTITE	VALUE VALEUR	
7849	OTHER MOTOR VEHCL PARTS		118.5		156.8		157.0		142.3	PIECES 722,781,782,783
79	OTHR TRANSPORT EQUIPMENT		532.7		602.9		569.1		553.6	AUTRE MATERIEL TRANSPORT
792	AIRCRAFT ETC		503.9		504.8		294.1		265.3	APP NAVIGATION AERIENNE
7924	AIRCRFT NES OVER 15000KG		311.4		278.3		18.3		6.5	AERODYNES PLUS 15000 KG
7929	AIRCRAFT PARTS NES		183.0		212.1		245.6		240.6	PIECES DU 792
793	SHIPS AND BOATS ETC		14.1		62.9		230.8		258.4	NAVIRES BATEAUX,ETC
7932	SHIPS AND BOATS NES		11.5		60.2		227.0		257.2	NAVIRES ET BATEAUX
79323	OTHER CARGO VESSELS		7.9		0.2		220.2		249.4	AUT BATEAUX TRANS MARCH
8	MISC MANUFACTURED GOODS		1948.2		2376.3		2695.0		2643.6	ART MANUFACTURES DIVERS
821	*FURNITURE,PARTS THEREOF		193.1		236.0		273.8		292.4	MEUBLES ET PIECES
8219	FURNITURE AND PARTS NES		131.3		159.8		184.0		195.4	AUTRES MEUBLES ET PIECES
82192	WOOD FURNITURE NES		100.7		121.9		137.6		142.9	MEUBLES NDA EN BOIS
84	CLOTHING AND ACCESSORIES		211.4		269.6		331.8		341.1	VETEMENTS
843	WOMENS OUTERWEAR NONKNIT		75.8		103.2		131.7		129.5	VET DESSUS FEMMES MAT TEX
851	*FOOTWEAR		97.0		122.6		146.3		154.5	CHAUSSURES
85102	FOOTWEAR LEATHER		91.3		111.7		125.7		127.1	CHAUS SEMELLES EN CUIR
87	PRECISION INSTRUMNTS NES		443.3		525.5		629.3		595.5	INSTRUM,APPAR SCIENT NDA
872	MEDICAL INSTRUMENTS NES		105.8		117.5		136.3		142.3	INSTR,APP MEDIC–CHIR NDA
87202	OTH MEDICAL INSTRUMENTS		90.2		99.6		116.1		120.7	INSTRUM,APP MEDECINE
874	MEASURNG,CONTROLNG INSTR		268.0		330.5		392.4		359.2	INSTRUMENTS DE MESURE
8748	ELEC MEAS,CONTRL EQU NES		106.9		116.7		133.9		123.7	APP ELEC ELECTRO MESURE
87483	OTH ELCTRNC MEAS ETC EQU		103.6		112.5		130.0		118.4	AUT APP ELECTRO DE MESURE
88	PHOTO EQU,OPTICL GDS ETC		197.9		249.5		251.4		215.6	APP,FOURN PHOTO,OP,MONTR
882	PHOTO,CINEMA SUPPLIES		75.8		91.6		88.2		85.8	PRODUITS PHOTO,CINEMA
89	MISC MANUFCTRD GOODS NES		744.6		875.9		951.7		928.4	ART MANUFACTURES DIVERS
893	ARTICLES OF PLASTIC NES		199.0		262.1		263.5		267.3	OUVRAGES EN MAT DIVIS 58
8939	MISC PLASTIC ARTICLES		152.0		185.4		193.3		192.6	ART DIVERS EN MAT DIV 58
89399	OTHR PLASTC ARTICLES NES		143.5		175.7		183.5		182.9	AUT OUV MAT DIV 58
894	TOYS,SPORTING GOODS,ETC		110.1		108.1		102.2		114.4	VOITURES ENFANTS,JOUETS
8942	TOYS,INDOOR GAMES ETC		87.0		75.6		74.8		88.9	JOUETS,JEUX ETC
897	GOLD,SILVER WARE,JEWELRY		113.1		136.3		153.9		117.4	BIJOUTERIE,ORFEVRERIE
8973	PREC JEWLRY,GLD–SILVWARE		99.0		121.8		137.3		105.3	BIJOUX OR,ARGENT ORFEVRE
89731	PRECIOUS METAL JEWELLERY		94.6		117.2		133.3		100.5	ART BIJOUTERIE,JOAILLER
898	MUSICAL INSTRUMENTS,PTS		139.3		165.0		198.5		191.8	INSTRUMENTS DE MUSIQUE
8983	SOUND RECRDNG TAPE,DISCS		127.3		153.4		187.1		179.7	SUPPORTS SON POUR 763
89832	RECORDED DISCS,TAPES ETC		96.8		123.1		153.1		147.6	DISQUES,PHONO,BANDES
899	OTHER MANUFACTURED GOODS		77.3		86.0		92.8		98.0	AUT ART MANUF DIVERS NDA
9	GOODS NOT CLASSD BY KIND		472.1		583.7		586.0		254.2	ART TRANSACT NON CLASSES
931	*SPECIAL TRANSACTIONS		302.0		426.8		430.9		110.4	TRANS.SPECIALES
971	*GOLD,NON MONETARY NES		167.3		155.1		153.1		142.2	OR NON MONETAIRE
97101	NONMON GLD UNWRT,SEMIMFD		166.2		154.1		152.1		140.4	OR,ALLIAGES D'OR BRUTS

5. Special Exports F.O.B. by Commodities according to the S.I.T.C. (Rev. 2) in million U.S. Dollars
Exportations Spéciales F.O.B. par Produits d'après la C.T.C.I. (Rév. 2) en millions de Dollars E.U.

SITC CTCI	COMMODITY	1994 QUANTITY QUANTITE	1994 VALUE VALEUR	1995 QUANTITY QUANTITE	1995 VALUE VALEUR	1996 QUANTITY QUANTITE	1996 VALUE VALEUR	1997 QUANTITY QUANTITE	1997 VALUE VALEUR	PRODUIT
	ALL COMMODITIES		16934.0		19047.5		20510.3		22503.0	TOUS PRODUITS
0	FOOD AND LIVE ANIMALS		810.0		936.1		979.9		883.0	ALIMENTS,ANIMAUX VIVANTS
05	VEGETABLES AND FRUIT		516.2		674.4		631.8		571.8	LEGUMES ET FRUITS
054	VEG ETC FRSH,SMPLY PRSVD		85.6		116.4		131.4		132.2	LEGUMES FRAIS,CONG,SECS
057	FRUIT,NUTS,FRESH,DRIED		214.9		312.0		298.4		269.0	FRUITS FRAIS OU SECS
0571	ORANGES, MANDARINS ETC	W 156327	69.2		114.9		104.8		92.7	ORANGES,MAND,CLEMENTINES
05711	ORANGES,FRESH OR DRIED	W 134289	56.9		90.0	W 171098	80.0	W 160552	69.1	ORANGES FRAICHES,SECHEES
0572	LEMONS,GRAPEFRUIT ETC		57.4		86.5		75.9		73.7	AUTRES AGRUMES FRAIS,SECS
05722	GRAPEFRUITS,FRESH,DRIED	W 98673	54.5		83.0	W 122474	70.1	W 137986	69.0	PAMPLEMOUSSES,POMELOS
0579	FRUIT FRESH OR DRIED NES		74.5		90.2		96.9		90.6	FRUITS FRAIS,SECS NDA
058	FRUIT PRESERVED,PREPARED		195.6		223.0		170.1		136.7	CONSERVES DE FRUITS
0585	FRUIT OR VEGETABLE JUICE		107.1		109.2		96.6		75.3	JUS DE FRUITS
05851	ORANGE JUICE		52.2		47.5		39.8		31.1	JUS D'ORANGE
0589	FRUIT PREPRD,PRESRVD,NES		70.1		88.1		45.6		38.0	FRUITS PREPARES CONSERV
05899	FRUIT,NUTS NES,PRESERVED		69.6		87.8		45.4		37.8	FRUITS PREP CONSERV NDA
07	COFFEE,TEA,COCOA,SPICES		52.0		58.3		50.1		41.8	CAFE,THE,CACAO,EPICES
09	MISC EDIBLE PRODUCTS		115.4		89.0		182.9		170.6	PREP ALIMENTAIRES DIVERSES
098	EDIBLE PRODCTS,PREPS NES		115.1		88.5		182.6		170.3	PREP ALIMENTAIRES NDA
09809	MISC FOOD PREPRTIONS NES		94.6		68.0		165.5		155.5	PREP ALIMENTAIRES NDA
2	CRUDE MATERLS,EXCL FUELS		469.4		506.7		549.3		587.3	MAT BRUTES NON COMESTIBLES
26	TEXTILE FIBRES AND WASTE		71.8		50.9		61.3		88.1	FIBRES TEXTILES
263	COTTON		53.7		39.6		58.4		84.4	COTON
2631	RAW COTTON,EXCL LINTERS		53.7		39.5	W 26988	58.4	W 42587	84.3	COTON EN MASSE
27	CRUDE FERTLZR,MINRLS NES		102.4		99.3		104.5		99.8	ENGRAIS MINERAUX BRUTS
271	FERTILIZERS,CRUDE		73.6		70.6		80.1		71.7	ENGRAIS BRUTS
2713	NAT CALCM PHOSPHATES ETC		69.1		61.2	W 1935000	72.8		63.0	PHOSPHATES DE CALCIUM
27131	— UNGROUND		69.1		61.2	W 1935000	72.8	W 1417000	63.0	PHOSPHATES NON MOULUS
29	CRUDE ANIMAL,VEG MAT NES		230.2		274.3		307.1		309.8	MATIERES BRUTES ANIM,VEGET
292	CRUDE VEG MATERIALS NES		229.4		273.7		307.0		309.8	MAT BRUTES VEGETALES NDA
2927	CUT FLOWERS AND FOLIAGE		137.6		174.0	MN 15640697	194.8		184.4	FLEURS,FEUILLAGES COUPES
29271	CUT FLOWERS	MN 946451	129.6		163.8	MN 13639441	183.9	MN 1396645	169.1	FLEURS ET BOUTONS
3	MINERAL FUELS ETC		92.3		4.7		105.2		118.4	COMBUSTIBLES MINERAUX LUB
33	PETROLEUM AND PRODUCTS		91.7		4.1		104.5		116.8	PETROLE ET DERIVES
333	CRUDE PETROLEUM		85.4		0.2		0.4		0.4	HUILES BRUTES DE PETROLE
334	PETROLEUM PRODUCTS,REFIN		4.5		2.2		102.8		115.7	PRODUITS RAFFINES
5	CHEMCLS,RELATED PROD NES		2317.0		2626.6		2651.0		3062.0	PRODUITS CHIMIQUES
51	ORGANIC CHEMICALS		625.8		737.5		730.0		823.1	PROD CHIMIQ ORGANIQUES
511	HYDROCARBONS NES,DERIVS		128.3		172.1		149.3		175.6	HYDROCARBURES NDA
5112	CYCLIC HYDROCARBONS		59.2		94.2		54.2		73.7	HYDROCARBURES CYCLIQUES
51124	XYLENES,CHEMICALLY PURE		38.2		77.5	W 71811	36.6	W 97427	43.6	XYLENES PURS
5113	HALOG DERIV OF HYDROCARB		64.3		74.5		89.9		94.8	DERIVES HALOGENES HYDROCAR
51139	OTH HALOG HYDRCARB DERIV		64.2		74.3		89.9		94.8	AUTRE DERIVES HALOGENES
512	ALCOHOLS,PHENOLS ETC		104.6		115.0		121.2		166.3	PHENOLS,PHENOLS–ALCOOLS
5123	PHENOLS,PHEN ALCS,DERIVS		96.3		109.5		114.7		157.6	PHENOLS,PHENOLS–ALCOOLS
51237	DERIVATVS OF PHENOL ETC		94.1		107.7	W 44498	111.0	W 64194	153.6	DERIVES HALOGENES
513	CARBOXYLIC ACIDS ETC		70.6		91.7		82.8		76.6	ACIDES CARBOXYLIQUES
5139	OXY–FNCT ACIDS,DERIVATVS		49.5		57.3		58.0	W 41609	54.4	ACIDES CARBOXYLIQUES
514	NITROGEN–FNCTN COMPOUNDS		109.6		134.5		140.3		143.0	COMPOSES FONCT AZOTEES
5148	OTH NITROGN–FNCTN CMPNDS		56.3		76.7		67.6		87.4	AUTRES COMPOSES AZOTES
51482	IMIDE–,IMIDE–FNCT CMPNDS		46.1		66.8	W 11073	60.0	W 13115	73.4	COMPOSES A FONCTION IMIDE
515	ORG–INORG COMPOUNDS ETC		150.6		158.6		160.5		179.5	COMPOSES ORGANO–MINERAUX
5154	ORGANO–SULPHUR CMPNDS		61.9		62.6		69.3		72.2	THIOCOMPOSES ORGANIQUES
5156	HETEROCYCLIC CMPDS ETC		66.8		79.6		74.6		89.1	COMPOSES HETEROCYCLIQUES
51569	OTH HETEROCYC CMPDS,ETC		66.8		79.5		74.5		89.0	AUT COMP HETEROCYCLIQUES
516	OTHER ORGANIC CHEMICALS		62.2		65.9		76.1		82.5	AUTRES PROD ORGANIQUES
52	INORGANIC CHEMICALS		281.7		377.4		394.7		421.0	PROD CHIM INORGANIQUES
522	INORG ELEMNTS,OXIDES,ETC		114.9		151.6		169.3		204.8	ELEMENTS INORGANIQUES
5222	INORGANIC ACIDS ETC		52.2		64.7		89.2		110.7	ACIDES INORGANIQUES
52224	PHOSPHORIC ACIDS ETC		51.7		64.4	W 199079	89.0	W 264778	109.9	ACIDES PHOSPHORIQUES
523	OTHR INORG CHEMICALS ETC		165.2		224.3		224.1		215.0	AUT PRODUITS CHIMIQUES INORG
5231	METAL CMPD OF INORG ACID		58.7		60.3		65.9		72.1	SELS METALLIQUES
5232	OTH MTL CMPD OF INRG ACD		92.1		137.8		132.3		123.5	SELS METALLIQUES
52321	NITRITES AND NITRATES		57.4		102.3		101.3		90.0	NITRITES ET NITRATES
541	*MEDICINAL,PHARM PRODUCT		276.4		255.4		334.3		416.8	PROD MEDICINAUX PHARMACEUT
5417	MEDICAMENTS		239.3		217.7		289.1		360.7	MEDICAMENTS
54172	— CONTAINING HORMONES		60.6		55.5		47.0		61.3	MED CONTENANT HORMONES
54179	— CONTNG OTH SUBSTANCES		176.6		160.6		242.1		298.6	MED CONT AUT SUBSTANCES
55	PERFUME,CLEANING ETC PRD		73.6		101.0		106.1		112.1	PROD POUR PARFUM,TOILETTE
562	*FERTILIZERS,MANUFACTURE		288.2		341.4		324.5		382.5	ENGRAIS MANUFACTURES
5622	CHEM PHOSPHATIC FERTILZR		74.7		94.8		95.2		85.8	ENGRAIS PHOSPHATES
56222	SUPERPHOSPHATES		56.7		72.1		67.0		57.6	SUPERPHOSPHATES
5629	FERTILIZERS NES		208.8		242.5		224.9		295.1	ENGRAIS NDA
56299	OTHER FERTILIZERS NES		190.5		222.7	W 1533251	198.6	W 2680394	271.2	AUTRES ENGRAIS NDA
58	PLASTIC MATERIALS ETC		275.0		406.4		332.1		408.9	MAT PLAST ARTIFICIELLES
582	PROD OF CONDENSATION ETC		56.4		86.3		83.1		101.9	PROD CONDENS,POLYCOND
5823	ALKYDS,OTHER POLYESTERS		43.1		61.7		62.9		67.4	ALKYDES ET AUT POLYESTERS
58232	— PLATES,FILM,STRIP ETC		42.6		61.1	W 10742	62.0	W 12619	66.7	SOUS FORME PLAQUES,FEUIL
583	POLYMERIZATION ETC PRODS		218.5		319.7		248.8		306.8	PROD POLYMERISATION
5832	POLYPROPYLENE		31.5		59.5		36.4		74.5	POLYPROPYLENE
58321	— IN PRIMARY FORMS		30.1		57.1		34.9		71.3	POLYPROPYLENE PRIMAIRES
5834	POLYVINYL CHLORIDE		47.5		61.2		35.6		55.1	CHLORURE DE POLYVINYLE
5839	OTH POLYMRZTION ETC PROD		80.0		103.1		106.9		102.8	AUT PROD POLYMER COPOLYM
59	CHEMICAL MATERIALS NES		486.4		384.9		402.4		466.2	MAT PROD CHIMIQUES NDA
591	PESTICIDES,DISINFECTANTS		68.3		108.6	W 21071	105.7	W 23888	118.3	DESINF,INSECT,FONG,HERB
5914	DISINFECTANTS,ETC,FR RET		68.3		108.6	W 21071	105.7	W 23888	118.3	DESINFECTANTS VENTE DET
59149	RAT POISONS ETC FR RTAIL		68.3		108.6	W 21071	105.7	W 23888	118.3	ANTIPARASITES VENTE DET
598	MISCEL CHEM PRODUCTS NES		416.1		272.4		292.7		344.2	PROD DIV INDUST CHIM NDA
5989	CHEM PRODUCTS,PREPS NES		415.4		271.1		291.8		342.9	PROD PREP CHIMIQUES NDA
59899	OTH CHEM PRODS,PREPS,NES		399.2		248.3		276.2		325.8	AUT PRODUITS CHIMIQUES NDA
6	BASIC MANUFACTURES		6046.5		7061.3		7660.7		8309.2	ART MANUFACTURES
62	RUBBER MANUFACTURES NES		103.2		121.0		118.0		98.0	CAOUTCHOUC MANUFACTURE
625	RUBBER TYRES, TUBES ETC		79.9		94.1		90.5		71.4	PNEUS CAOUTCHOUC VULCANISE
6259	OTH TYRES,TYRE CASES,ETC		78.0		91.8		88.9		71.1	AUTRES PNEUS RECHAPES FLAPS
62599	TYRES NES,TYRE CASES,ETC		78.0		91.7		88.7		70.9	PNEUS,FLAPS
65	TEXTILE YARN,FABRICS,ETC		350.4		402.3		397.0		445.8	FILS,TISSUS,ARTICLES TEXTILE
651	TEXTILE YARN		72.7		91.2		96.2		106.6	FILS TEXTILES
6514	SYN FIB YRN,BULK,MONOFIL		67.1		83.7		92.3		101.9	FILS CONT 85% FIB TEXT SYNTH
657	SPECIAL TXTL FABRC,PRODS		72.6		75.2		80.6		100.9	TISSUS SPECIAUX
658	TEXTILE ARTICLES NES		89.7		99.4		87.9		100.8	ART FACONNES MAT TEXTILES
6584	LINENS ETC		76.6		91.8		77.8		86.9	LINGE DE MAISON
66	NONMETAL MINERAL MFS NES		5019.1		5821.3		6354.2		6878.0	ART MIN NON METALLIQUES

5. Special Exports F.O.B. by Commodities according to the S.I.T.C. (Rev. 2) in million U.S. Dollars
Exportations Spéciales F.O.B. par Produits d'après la C.T.C.I. (Rév. 2) en millions de Dollars E.U.

SITC CTCI	COMMODITY	1994 QUANTITY QUANTITE	1994 VALUE VALEUR	1995 QUANTITY QUANTITE	1995 VALUE VALEUR	1996 QUANTITY QUANTITE	1996 VALUE VALEUR	1997 QUANTITY QUANTITE	1997 VALUE VALEUR	PRODUIT
667	PEARL,PREC–,SEMI–P STONE		4967.6		5744.3		6284.5		6811.9	PERLES, PIERRES GEMMES
6672	DIAMONDS NONINDUST,UNSET		4892.3		5666.2		6202.5		6734.8	DIAMANTS BRUTS
66722	— SRTD,ROUGH,SIMPLY WKD		524.7		755.0		949.5		1049.8	DIAMANTS TRIES BRUTS
66729	— CUT ETC NOT SET		4367.2		4911.2		5253.1		5685.1	DIAMANTS TAILLES
6673	PREC–,SEMI–PR STONES NES		75.4		78.1		81.9		77.1	AUTRES PIERRES NON SERTIES
67	IRON AND STEEL		29.7		37.1		58.2		74.9	FER ET ACIER
68	NON–FERROUS METALS		81.7		125.8		114.3		121.6	METAUX NON FERREUX
684	ALUMINIUM		71.9		108.6		100.1		87.1	ALUMINIUM
6842	ALUMINIUM,ALLOYS WORKED		69.7		103.7		93.5		80.3	ALUMINIUM,ALLIAGES OUVRE
69	METAL MANUFACTURES NES		407.4		480.6		546.5		614.5	ART MANUFACT EN METAL NDA
695	TOOLS		215.6		268.5		316.2		356.1	OUTILS A MAIN
6954	BLADES,TIPS,ETC FR TOOLS		193.1		244.6		294.3		331.6	OUTILS POUR MACHINE–OUTIL
69541	PARTS TO INSERT IN TOOLS		41.4		50.4		59.4		70.3	OUTILS DE FORAGE
69543	CARBIDE TOOL TIPS ETC		148.1		189.5		231.2		257.8	PLAQUETTES,POINTES D'OUTILS
699	BASE METAL MFRS NES		100.9		101.5		105.0		123.3	ART MANUFACTURES MET NDA
7	MACHINES,TRANSPORT EQUIP		5182.8		5107.1		5980.2		6802.8	MACHINES MATERIEL TRANSPORT
71	POWER GENERATING EQUIPMT		97.7		155.2		180.0		229.6	MACHINES GENERATRICES
714	ENGINES AND MOTORS NES		70.6		111.4		121.6		154.0	MOTEURS NON ELECTRIQUES
7144	REACTION ENGINES		30.1		66.5		72.6		62.6	PROPULSEURS A REACTION
7149	ENGINE & MOTOR PARTS NES		40.5		44.7		49.0		91.5	PIECES 714 ET 718.88
71499	PARTS NES,OF 71488,71888		8.2		10.8		6.0		84.1	PIECES 714.88 ET 718.88
72	MACHS FOR SPCL INDUSTRYS		1382.4		709.9		539.0		522.7	MAC SPECIALES POUR INDUST
726	PRINTG,BKBINDG MACHY,PTS		411.3		479.9		338.2		289.8	MACHINES POUR IMPRIMERIE
7263	TYPESET ETC MCH,TYPE ETC		260.2		228.8		173.2		142.8	MACH COMPOSER,CLICHER
72631	TYPE SET,FOUND ETC MACHY		260.2		228.8		173.2		142.8	MACH COMPOSER CARACTERES
7267	OTH PRINTG & ANCILL MACH		53.1		116.7		103.7		89.5	AUT MACH IMPRIMERIE,PIEC
72671	PRINTING MACHINERY NES		53.0		116.7		103.6		89.3	AUT MACH IMPRIMERIE
7269	PTS OF 72631, 7264, 7267		95.6		121.0		59.6		55.3	PIECES 726.31 726.4 726.7
72691	PTS NES OF MCHS OF 72631		62.4		55.9		57.3		51.0	PIECES 726.31
72699	PTS NES OF MCH OF 7264,7		33.3		65.1		2.4		4.3	PIECES 726.4 ET 726.7
728	OTH MACHY FOR SPCL INDUS		900.0		156.1		127.9		159.2	AUT MACH IND PARTICULIERES
7284	MACHY FOR SPCL INDUS NES		888.0		141.8		113.0		132.1	MACH SPEC IND PARTICUL.
72848	OTH MCHY WITH INDIV FNCT		879.5		133.3		103.3		121.4	AUTRES MACHINES NDA
73	METALWORKING MACHINERY		41.9		53.3		58.2		73.2	MACH TRAVAIL DES METAUX
736	METALWORKING MACH–TOOLS		39.3		50.6		53.6		68.5	MACH–OUTILS TRAVAIL METAUX
74	GENRL INDUSTRL MACHY NES		549.8		551.9		724.4		622.7	MACH APP INDUSTRIE
741	HEATING,COOLING EQUIPMNT		140.9		199.8		247.2		165.1	MACH CHAUFFAGE,PIECES
7415	AIR–CONDITIONING MACHNRY		86.6		146.1		181.1		127.6	GROUPES CONDITION AIR
743	PUMPS NES,CENTRFUGES ETC		58.5		61.4		76.7		86.3	POMPES COMPRES,VENT ETC
745	NONELEC MACHY,TOOLS NES		54.8		83.0		135.8		120.3	AUT MACH NON ELEC,PIECES
7452	OTH NONELEC MCHS,PTS NES		54.4		82.6		135.1		119.2	AUT MACH NON ELEC,PIECES
74527	SPRAYING MACHINERY		48.6		76.7		126.4		108.3	APP PROJETER ETC LIQUID
749	NONELEC MACH PTS,ACC NES		291.8		203.2		259.9		243.7	PIECES MACH NON ELEC NDA
7499	OTH NONELEC MCHY PTS NES		242.2		147.2		200.7		174.0	PIECES NON ELECT NDA
74999	MACH PARTS NONELEC NES		238.6		144.2		197.5		167.3	PIECES MACHINES NDA
75	OFFICE MACHNES,ADP EQUIP		525.2		343.8		850.5		1042.0	MACH BUREAU TRAIT AUTOM
752	AUTOMTIC DATA PROC EQUIP		336.9		147.0		602.7		752.5	MACH TRAIT INFORMATION
7528	OFF–LINE DATA PROC EQUIP		319.1		132.0		586.3		736.6	MACH AUXIL TRAIT INFORM
759	OFFICE,ADP MCH PTS,ACCES		186.6		193.7		245.4		285.6	PIECES DU 751 ET 752
7591	OFFICE MACHINE PARTS NES		99.1		53.7		68.5		89.6	PIECES DU 7511,7518
75915	OTH OFF MCH PTS,ACC NES		98.9		53.4		67.1		89.3	PIECES DU 751.18,81,88
7599	ACCTG,ETC,ADP MCH PTS,AC		87.5		140.0		177.0		196.1	PIECES DU 751 ET 752
76	TELECOMM,SOUND EQUIPMENT		1197.9		1570.3		1803.0		2195.7	EQUIPMENT DE TELECOM
762	RADIO BROADCAST RECEIVRS		148.8		260.4		130.7		124.7	RECEPTEURS RADIODIFFUSION
7622	PORTABLE RADIO RECEIVERS		123.3		259.8		129.9		115.5	RECEPT PORTATIFS RADIO
764	TELECOM EQPT,PTS,ACC NES		1005.2		1281.2		1653.6		2047.1	EQUIP TELECOM,PIECES
7641	LINE TELEPHONE,ETC EQUIP		237.4		226.4		298.0		366.9	APP TELEPHON PAR FIL
7643	TV,RADIO TRANSMITTRS ETC		216.6		308.1		325.8		304.1	APP EMET TELE RADIO
7648	TELECOMM EQUIPMENT NES		7.0		46.2		39.7		92.3	APP TELECOM NDA
7649	PTS NES OF EQUIPMT OF 76		543.4		699.6		988.6		1282.8	PIECES DE LA DIV 76
76491	PTS NES OF APPAR OF 7641		437.6		600.7		916.7		1204.5	PIECES POUR 764.1
76493	TELECOMM EQUIPMT PTS NES		104.8		98.1		68.7		73.2	PIECES 761,762,764.3,8
77	ELECTRIC MACHNRY NES ETC		965.3		1197.9		1313.5		1525.9	MACH APP ELECT NDA
772	SWITCHGEAR ETC,PARTS NES		189.9		259.4		304.2		341.6	APP COUPURE,SECT ETC
7721	SWITCHGEAR ETC		51.8		55.5		86.1		84.0	APP COUPURE,SECTIONMNT
7723	FIXED,VARIABLE RESISTORS		124.5		183.2		195.1		239.6	POTENTIOMETRES PIECES
774	ELECTRO–MEDCL,XRAY EQUIP		157.4		188.7		217.8		298.1	APPAREILS MEDICAUX
7741	ELECTRO–MEDICAL EQUIPMNT		23.1		28.5		36.2		123.4	APP ELECTRICITE MEDICALE
7742	X–RAY APPARATUS ETC		134.3		160.3		181.7		174.8	APPAREILS A RAYONS X
776	TRANSISTORS,VALVES,ETC		407.3		454.9		411.2		492.0	LAMPES,TUBES,VALVES
7764	ELECTRONIC MICROCIRCUITS		397.6		441.6		398.3		478.5	MICROSTRUCTURES ELECTRON
778	ELECTRICAL MACHINERY NES		128.3		198.2		262.2		264.6	AUTRES MACH ELECT NDA
7784	ELECTRO–MECH HAND TOOLS		65.0		0.4		0.3		0.3	OUTILS ELECTROMEC,PIECES
7788	OTH ELEC MACHY,EQUIP NES		35.0		164.2		234.5		227.2	AUT MACH APP ELEC NDA
77883	ELEC SIGNALLING EQU NES		4.6		79.7		75.6		79.7	APP ELECT SIGNAL ACOUS
77884	ELECTRICAL CONDENSERS		12.9		41.0		52.2		77.9	CONDENSATEURS ELECTRIQUES
77886	OTH ELEC MACHINERY NES		10.1		28.5		83.9		40.9	AUT MACH APP ELECTRIQUES
79	OTHR TRANSPORT EQUIPMENT		374.2		486.0		462.4		551.5	AUTRE MATERIEL TRANSPORT
792	AIRCRAFT ETC		356.0		465.9		422.9		538.9	APP NAVIGATION AERIENNE
7929	AIRCRAFT PARTS NES		311.7		362.7		392.0		523.9	PIECES DU 792
8	MISC MANUFACTURED GOODS		1961.5		2309.2		2509.4		2680.1	ART MANUFACTURES DIVERS
84	CLOTHING AND ACCESSORIES		627.4		663.3		643.6		600.5	VETEMENTS
842	MENS OUTERWEAR NOT KNIT		96.0		85.2		85.2		82.4	VET DESSUS POUR HOMMES
843	WOMENS OUTERWEAR NONKNIT		105.3		104.4		101.2		82.0	VET DESSUS FEMMES MAT TEX
8439	— OTHER OUTER GARMENTS		71.6		67.2		70.7		55.1	AUT VET DES FEM MAT TEXT
845	OUTERWEAR KNIT NONELASTC		189.0		201.7		170.6		122.9	VET DESSOUS,ACCES BONNET
8459	— OTHER,CLTHG ACCESRYS		160.3		175.5	MN 11712	145.3	MN 11597	98.9	AUT VET DESSUS DE BONNE
846	UNDER GARMENTS KNITTED		165.1		187.0		196.7		216.1	SOUS VETS DE BONNETERIE
8462	— OF COTTON NON ELASTIC		148.3		172.4		176.3		189.2	SOUS–VET BONNET COTON
84629	—— OTHER		148.3		170.0		171.6		186.8	AUT SOUS–VET BONNET COTON
847	TEXTILE CLTHNG ACCES NES		63.6		76.3		80.1		76.6	ACCES VET MAT TEXT NDA
8472	CLTHNG ACCESRYS ETC KNIT		62.6		74.9		78.8		75.9	ACCES VET BONNE NDA
84722	KNIT SOCKS,ETC NONELASTC		62.6		74.9		78.7		75.9	CHAUSSETTES BON. NON ELAS
87	PRECISION INSTRUMNTS NES		321.9		439.6		574.1		752.3	INSTRUM,APPAR SCIENT NDA
871	OPTICAL INSTRUMENTS		21.8		59.1		69.0		82.4	APPAR,INSTRUM D'OPTIQUE
87109	OPTICAL INSTRUMENTS NES		16.6		54.5		63.0		79.4	APP,INSTRUM OPTIQUE NDA
872	MEDICAL INSTRUMENTS NES		108.6		129.5		176.2		247.3	INSTR,APP MEDIC–CHIR NDA
87202	OTH MEDICAL INSTRUMENTS		100.7		124.6		169.4		238.7	INSTRUM,APP MEDECINE
874	MEASURNG,CONTROLNG INSTR		182.0		240.8		317.3		413.0	INSTRUMENTS DE MESURE
8742	MEASUR,DRAW ETC INST,PTS		86.1		109.6		157.9		244.7	INST DESSIN,TRACAGE,PCS
87421	MEASURNG,DRAWNG ETC INST		62.4		81.6		133.1		206.8	INSTRUM DESSIN,TRACAGE

5. Special Exports F.O.B. by Commodities according to the S.I.T.C. (Rev. 2) in million U.S. Dollars
Exportations Spéciales F.O.B. par Produits d'après la C.T.C.I. (Rév. 2) en millions de Dollars E.U.

SITC CTCI	COMMODITY	1994		1995		1996		1997		PRODUIT
		QUANTITY QUANTITE	VALUE VALEUR	QUANTITY QUANTITE	VALUE VALEUR	QUANTITY QUANTITE	VALUE VALEUR	QUANTITY QUANTITE	VALUE VALEUR	
8748	ELEC MEAS,CONTRL EQU NES		44.8		60.9		57.0		56.0	APP ELEC ELECTRO MESURE
88	PHOTO EQU,OPTICL GDS ETC		59.0		61.0		71.9		74.8	APP,FOURN PHOTO,OP,MONTR
89	MISC MANUFCTRD GOODS NES		882.2		1065.2		1148.9		1175.6	ART MANUFACTURES DIVERS
893	ARTICLES OF PLASTIC NES		334.7		456.4		526.0		586.5	OUVRAGES EN MAT DIVIS 58
8931	PLSTC PACKG CONTNRS,LIDS		71.3		107.6		75.6		75.3	ART TRANSP EMBALLAGE ETC
8939	MISC PLASTIC ARTICLES		258.0		340.2		445.0		508.5	ART DIVERS EN MAT DIV 58
89399	OTHR PLASTC ARTICLES NES		253.6		334.6		440.4		502.4	AUT OUV MAT DIV 58
897	GOLD,SILVER WARE,JEWELRY		413.2		459.5		485.1		414.1	BIJOUTERIE,ORFEVRERIE
8973	PREC JEWLRY,GLD–SILVWARE		408.3		453.2		474.6		404.1	BIJOUX OR,ARGENT ORFEVRE
89731	PRECIOUS METAL JEWELLERY		379.7		430.4		466.9		402.4	ART BIJOUTERIE,JOAILLER
9	GOODS NOT CLASSD BY KIND		25.1		456.4		43.9		39.4	ART TRANSACT NON CLASSES
931	*SPECIAL TRANSACTIONS		23.4		453.1		34.8		35.5	TRANS.SPECIALES

Italy, including San Marino and Holy See

Italie y compris Saint–Martin et Saint–Siège

1. HISTORICAL SERIES, 1962–1997 SPECIAL TRADE, IMPORTS C.I.F., EXPORTS F.O.B.
SERIES HISTORIQUES, 1962–1997 COMMERCE SPECIAL, IMPORTATIONS C.A.F., EXPORTATIONS F.O.B

YEAR ANNEE	VALUE IN MILLION LIRE # 1 VALEUR EN MILLION LIRE # 1 MERCHANDISE –MARCHANDISE		GOLD –OR		CONVERSION FACTORS U.S. CENTS PER LIRA FACTEURS DE CONVERSION CENTS E.U. PAR LIRA		INDEX NUMBERS –INDICES QUANTUM		UNIT VALUE VALEUR UNITAIRE	
	IMPORTS	EXPORTS	IMPORTS	EXPORTS	IMPORTS	EXPORTS	IMPORTS	EXPORTS	IMPORTS	EXPORTS
1962	3797.10	2918.40	83.30		0.1600	0.1600				
1963	4744.70	3159.00	59.40		0.1600	0.1600				
1964	4532.80	3724.00	29.60		0.1600	0.1600				
1965	4611.40	4499.80	36.00		0.1600	0.1600				
1966	5367.90	5024.00	31.10	0.60	0.1600	0.1600				
1967	6141.60	5440.90	37.20	1.40	0.1600	0.1600				
1968	6428.70	6366.00	193.00	1.60	0.1600	0.1600				
1969	7791.80	7330.50	43.00	2.10	0.1600	0.1600				
1970	9355.90	8253.90	87.80	0.30	0.1600	0.1600				
1971	9901.30	9361.70	156.70	0.90	0.1614	0.1615				
1972	11243.60	10849.40	0.40	0.90	0.1715	0.1715				
1973	16343.40	12989.30	0.20	1.30	0.1713	0.1713				
1974	26715.00	19826.00	0.20	2.50	0.1538	0.1537				
1975	25199.60	22866.40			0.1529	0.1530				
1976	36730.60	31166.70			0.1196	0.1196				
1977	42429.10	39967.60			0.1134	0.1134				
1978	47857.90	47505.30			0.1180	0.1180				
1979	64597.20	59926.30			0.1206	0.1206				
1980	85564.30	66719.40			0.1164	0.1164	65	65	61	50
1981	103675.00	86040.00			0.0878	0.0874	60	68	79	62
1982	116212.00	99231.00			0.0742	0.0740	60	68	88	72
1983	122002.00	110537.00			0.0659	0.0658	60	71	93	77
1984	148162.00	129015.00			0.0568	0.0568	66	75	103	84
1985	172876.00	149701.00			0.0526	0.0527	72	81	111	91
1986	148195.90	145014.80			0.0671	0.0673	75	82	91	87
1987	162352.90	150440.90			0.0774	0.0774	83	84	90	88
1988	180013.90	166379.90			0.0770	0.0769	88	89	94	92
1989	209909.90	192887.90			0.0729	0.0729	96	97	101	98
1990	217703.90	203597.90			0.0836	0.0837	100	100	100	100
1991	225747.90	209738.90			0.0810	0.0808	105	100	99	103
1992	232110.90	219440.90			0.0812	0.0812	108	104	99	104
1993	232990.90	263966.90			0.0637	0.0635	96	112	110	115
1994	272381.90	308045.00			0.0621	0.0621	108	125	115	120
1995	335661.00	381174.90			0.0614	0.0614	119	141	129	131
1996	321285.90	386351.00			0.0648	0.0648	114	139	129	137
1997	354409.10	405870.00			0.0588	0.0587			130	134

2. IMPORTS BY BROAD ECONOMIC CATEGORY AND EXPORTS BY INDUSTRIAL ORIGIN. (PERCENTAGE OF TOTAL VALUE)
IMPORTATIONS PAR CATEGORIES ECONOMIQUES ET EXPORTATIONS PAR BRANCHE D'ACTIVITE.(EN POURCENTAGE DE LA VALEUR TOTALE)

IMPORTS – IMPORTATIONS

	1991	1992	1993	1994	1995	1996	1997
TOTAL IMPORTS–IMPORTATIONS TOTALES	100.	100.	100.	100.	100.	100.	100.
1 FOOD BEV–ALIMENTATION BOISSONS	11.6	11.2	11.8	11.1	10.1	10.2	9.6
11 PRIMARY–PRODUITS DE BASE	7.7	7.5	7.7	7.1	6.5	6.3	6.0
111 FOR INDUSTRY–POUR L'INDUSTRIE	2.6	2.5	2.6	2.3	2.3	2.2	2.0
112 FOR HOUSEHOLDS–POUR LES MENAGES	5.0	5.0	5.0	4.8	4.2	4.2	4.0
12 PROCESSED–PRODUITS ELABORES	3.9	3.7	4.1	4.0	3.7	3.8	3.5
121 FOR INDUSTRY–POUR L'INDUSTRIE	0.3	0.3	0.4	0.4	0.4	0.4	0.4
122 FOR HOUSEHOLDS–POUR LES MENAGES	3.6	3.3	3.7	3.6	3.2	3.4	3.2
2 IND SUPPLIES–APPROV INDUSTRIELS	32.2	31.9	33.0	35.9	37.6	34.7	34.6
21 PRIMARY–PRODUITS DE BASE	4.8	4.4	4.8	5.3	5.1	4.6	4.4
22 PROCESSED–PRODUITS ELABORES	27.3	27.5	28.2	30.6	32.5	30.1	30.2
3 FUELS–COMBUSTIBLES	9.4	8.5	9.4	8.3	7.3	8.4	7.9
31 PRIMARY–PRODUITS DE BASE	7.0	6.3	6.9	5.9	5.3	6.2	6.1
32 PROCESSED–PRODUITS ELABORES	2.5	2.3	2.5	2.3	2.0	2.2	1.8
321 MOTOR SPIRIT–ESSENCE	0.4	0.3	0.4		0.3	0.3	0.2
322 OTHER–AUTRES	2.1	2.0	2.0	2.3	1.8	1.9	1.5
4 MACHINERY–EQUIPEMENT	18.0	17.8	17.5	17.8	18.9	19.2	18.9
41 CAPITAL EQUIPMENT–MACHINES	13.6	13.3	12.7	12.7	13.6	14.0	14.2
42 PARTS–PIECES ACCESSOIRES	4.3	4.5	4.8	5.1	5.3	5.2	4.7
5 TRANSPORT–TRANSPORT	14.6	15.8	12.8	12.2	12.3	12.9	14.0
51 PASSENGER CARS–AUTOMOBILES	7.6	9.1	6.9	6.5	6.7	7.1	8.2
52 OTHER–AUTRES	3.4	3.1	2.3	2.2	2.0	2.2	2.0
521 INDUSTRIAL–INDUSTRIELS	3.1	2.8	2.0	1.9	1.7	2.0	1.8
522 NON INDUSTRIAL–NON INDUSTRIEL	0.3	0.3	0.3	0.3	0.2	0.3	0.3
53 PARTS–PIECES ACCESSOIRES	3.6	3.6	3.5	3.5	3.6	3.6	3.7
6 CONSUM GOODS–BIENS CONSOMMATION	11.4	12.1	12.4	11.9	11.2	11.8	12.1
61 DURABLE–DURABLES	3.4	3.2	3.0	2.8	2.5	2.5	2.5
62 SEMI DURABLE–SEMI DURABLES	5.4	5.9	6.2	6.0	5.7	6.0	6.3
63 NON DURABLE–NON DURABLES	2.7	3.0	3.2	3.2	3.0	3.3	3.3
7 GOODS NES–BIENS NDA	2.9	2.6	3.2	2.7	2.7	2.9	2.9

EXPORTS – EXPORTATIONS

	1991	1992	1993	1994	1995	1996	1997
TOTAL EXPORTS–EXPORTATIONS TOTALES	100.	100.	100.	100.	100.	100.	100.
1 AGRICULTURE	2.3	2.1	2.1	2.2	2.0	1.9	1.9
2 MINING QUARRY–INDUS EXTRACTIVES	0.3	0.3	0.3	0.3	0.3	0.3	0.3
3 MANUFACTURING–IND MANUFACTUR	97.4	97.6	97.6	97.5	97.7	97.8	97.9
31 FOOD BEV TOBACCO–ALIM BOISS TAB	4.9	5.3	5.1	4.9	4.9	5.0	4.9
32 TEXTILES–INDUSTRIES TEXTILES	17.7	17.6	17.5	17.8	16.9	17.1	16.9
33 WOOD & PRODUCTS–BOIS & PRODUITS	0.5	0.5	0.5	0.5	0.5	0.5	0.5
34 PAPER & PRODUCTS–PAPIER & PRODT	2.0	2.0	2.1	2.1	2.4	2.2	2.2
35 CHEMICALS–INDUSTRIES CHIMIQUES	11.9	12.5	12.4	12.0	12.1	11.9	12.5
36 NON METAL MIN–MIN NON METAL	3.9	4.0	4.0	4.1	4.0	3.8	3.8
37 BASIC METAL–IND METAL BASE	4.4	4.3	4.6	4.6	4.8	4.2	4.3
38 METAL MANUF–MANUF METAL	47.4	46.9	46.9	47.1	47.9	48.8	48.5
39 OTH MANUF IND–AUTRES MANUF	4.6	4.5	4.4	4.3	4.3	4.3	4.4

3. TRADE BY PRINCIPAL COUNTRIES OF ORIGIN AND CONSUMPTION (VALUE IN MILLION U.S. DOLLARS)
ECHANGES SELON LES PRINCIPAUX PAYS D'ORIGINE ET DE COMSOMMATION (VALEUR EN MILLIONS DE DOLLARS EU)

COUNTRIES–PAYS	SPECIAL IMPORTS C.I.F. IMPORTATIONS SPECIALES C.A.F				
	1993	1994	1995	1996	1997
World	147817.5	167975.1	204099.2	208145.0	208317.2
Africa	10843.9	11661.4	13875.5	15153.3	15197.0
Americas	12590.3	13487.7	17026.1	17109.3	17240.6
– Northern America	9090.0	9269.3	11694.9	12043.5	12136.3
– LAIA	3176.5	3841.1	4838.4	4587.6	4694.5
– CACM	129.3	167.3	163.7	173.1	200.2
– Caribbean	113.4	144.9	251.1	241.8	169.5
– Rest of America	81.0	65.0	78.1	63.3	40.1
Asia excl fmr USSR	17074.2	18105.5	22442.0	22552.6	23684.7
– Middle East	4591.4	4314.8	5699.1	6366.5	6626.4
Asia former USSR	279.7	378.0	516.1	502.7	482.6
Europe excl fmr USSR	101293.4	117253.9	142187.2	145547.2	144704.6
– European Union	87886.4	101418.7	123448.5	127132.6	126297.1
– Eastern Europe	3024.9	4246.8	5867.0	6080.4	6724.9
– Rest of Europe	10382.1	11588.5	12871.7	12334.2	11682.7
Europe former USSR	4486.7	5548.9	6339.1	5447.5	5099.2
Oceania	916.8	1121.7	1350.9	1447.5	1466.6
Other	332.5	417.9	362.3	384.9	442.0
Germany/Allemagne	28627.2	32310.9	38962.2	38555.7	37441.3
France, Monaco	20142.0	22781.1	28317.3	28245.2	27478.6
United Kingdom	8616.5	10265.8	12390.7	13761.9	13948.0
Netherlands/Pays–Bas	8417.0	9591.5	11229.2	12509.6	12816.4
USA/Etats–Unis d'Amer	7861.9	7803.3	9890.9	10170.7	10376.8
Belgium–Luxembourg	6885.6	7970.0	9761.8	9996.3	9724.9
Switzerland,Liechtenst.	7591.5	8254.9	9100.2	8853.4	8120.1
Spain/Espagne	4953.5	6517.8	8018.5	8682.9	9842.5
Russian Federation	3878.2	4801.6	5306.8	4696.6	4278.6
Austria/Autriche	3272.2	3761.8	4751.3	4803.3	4778.1
Japan/Japon	3811.4	3960.6	4491.3	3975.3	4219.9
Libyan Arab Jamahiriya	3338.9	3362.2	3742.6	4526.8	4462.1
China/Chine	2593.7	3128.3	3920.4	4033.1	4417.0
Sweden/Suède	1812.7	2114.4	2778.3	2886.2	2901.1
So. African Customs Un	2099.7	2206.3	2838.1	2454.7	2785.5
Algeria/Algérie	1935.5	1627.0	2289.3	2713.5	2969.7
Brazil/Brésil	1528.3	1847.8	2039.6	1894.2	1903.5
Saudi Arabia	1720.3	1481.5	1581.8	1888.7	2152.4
Ireland/Irlande	1162.2	1569.5	1884.8	2089.5	2085.6
Denmark/Danemark	1522.6	1660.8	1869.9	1923.7	1751.9
Canada	1219.8	1457.2	1803.8	1856.9	1734.4
Iran (Islamic Rep of)	1382.5	1023.2	1753.7	1938.4	1790.8
Greece/Grèce	1120.4	1322.8	1468.7	1556.4	1345.9
Turkey/Turquie	799.1	1122.4	1539.7	1574.2	1508.2
Romania/Roumanie	462.7	907.4	1370.5	1432.4	1701.5
Poland/Pologne	829.8	921.7	1227.6	1349.0	1531.2
India/Inde	815.5	1008.7	1341.3	1330.6	1332.7
Hungary/Hongrie	766.4	967.8	1271.6	1252.0	1305.3
Other Asia n.e.s.	928.7	934.3	1156.5	1238.9	1221.3
Finland/Finlande	886.6	966.4	1195.1	1111.5	1236.2
Egypt/Egypte	918.0	1206.9	1096.5	1156.1	877.7
Australia/Australie	752.5	914.0	1113.2	1180.4	1212.6
Slovenia/Slovénie	681.2	914.1	1169.0	1089.8	1211.4
Korea, Republic of	693.9	817.1	1086.5	1020.3	1270.7
Tunisia/Tunisie	607.4	872.3	1032.5	1173.6	1191.5
Indonesia/Indonésie	722.1	811.3	976.5	929.7	938.9
Croatia/Croatie	726.2	824.9	971.6	828.5	733.4
Norway,Svalbard and JM	769.1	747.0	781.7	908.0	841.2
Portugal	467.9	585.9	820.5	1010.5	946.5
Argentina/Argentine	534.2	696.6	862.5	850.5	833.3

COUNTRIES–PAYS	SPECIAL EXPORTS F.O.B. EXPORTATIONS SPECIALES F.O.B.				
	1993	1994	1995	1996	1997
Monde	168511.2	190004.6	231346.4	252106.4	238265.9
Afrique	7031.1	6943.2	8081.1	8299.9	8615.9
Amériques	20319.6	23633.5	27309.8	30072.8	31161.6
– Amérique du Nord	14453.5	16518.4	19066.9	20293.2	20814.7
– ALAI	4318.7	5759.0	7042.3	7741.3	8727.8
– MCAC	191.6	181.0	186.7	220.7	221.5
– Caraïbes	960.6	758.5	550.1	888.1	926.9
– Autre Amérique	395.2	416.7	463.8	929.6	470.8
Asie anc. URSS exclus	25539.4	27502.6	34731.8	39112.4	35053.0
– Moyen–Orient	9201.1	8148.0	9942.3	11760.7	11317.9
Asie ancienne URSS	234.7	222.4	136.8	200.6	243.2
Europe anc. URSS exclus	111199.5	126677.3	154574.9	166499.2	155166.8
– Union Européenne	96047.6	108717.6	131604.5	140496.5	130080.9
– Europe de l'Est	4468.8	5594.0	7790.6	9890.4	9889.2
– Autre de l'Europe	10683.1	12365.7	15179.8	16112.3	15196.6
Europe ancienne URSS	2100.4	2616.4	3536.2	4574.5	4880.7
Océanie	1248.4	1584.5	1896.0	2186.5	2046.9
Autre	838.1	824.7	1079.8	1160.7	1097.8
Germany/Allemagne	32819.8	36119.2	43248.4	44089.2	38960.2
France, Monaco	22135.6	24851.6	30018.9	32042.4	29010.6
USA/Etats–Unis d'Amer	13036.8	14744.6	16902.4	18450.8	18912.7
United Kingdom	10779.3	12337.4	14292.8	16325.5	16938.0
Spain/Espagne	7377.0	8920.8	11314.3	12628.1	12335.6
Switzerland,Liechtenst.	6621.9	7169.3	8771.2	9269.3	8215.0
Netherlands/Pays–Bas	4741.0	5440.6	6824.0	7437.8	6785.8
Belgium–Luxembourg	5019.8	5667.4	6637.6	6985.0	6428.6
Austria/Autriche	4201.3	4670.3	5487.4	5965.3	5403.3
Japan/Japon	3202.3	4055.1	5347.5	5584.1	4714.4
Greece/Grèce	2989.1	3404.7	4356.1	4782.1	4631.4
China, Hong Kong SAR	2509.2	3139.4	3905.4	4389.0	4003.6
Turkey/Turquie	2658.0	1911.6	3233.6	4284.3	4393.3
Portugal	2255.3	2560.7	3211.5	3352.0	3165.5
Russian Federation	1717.8	2172.9	2869.5	3717.9	3850.5
Poland/Pologne	1501.1	1769.3	2514.4	3427.6	3727.3
China/Chine	2468.6	2285.6	2695.5	2868.7	2528.5
Brazil/Brésil	1080.9	1846.0	3170.6	3113.3	3516.5
Korea, Republic of	1282.9	1780.3	2301.1	2829.6	2233.6
Sweden/Suède	1431.1	1731.2	2227.8	2530.3	2374.5
Israel/Israël	1512.2	1790.9	2191.7	2227.1	1942.1
Canada	1394.0	1741.5	2151.8	1820.2	1871.2
Denmark/Danemark	1218.8	1592.1	2004.4	2133.0	1968.0
Saudi Arabia	2024.8	1556.3	1524.3	1855.3	1713.9
Slovenia/Slovénie	1162.6	1423.0	1922.6	1956.0	1982.6
Singapore/Singapour	1121.5	1423.8	1747.4	2075.5	1594.6
Australia/Australie	940.9	1306.5	1543.6	1771.9	1719.5
Croatia/Croatie	792.4	1372.4	1675.6	1667.9	1759.3
United Arab Emirates	974.2	1462.7	1636.5	1580.8	1448.3
Argentina/Argentine	975.0	1405.4	1335.4	1622.8	1738.7
Other Asia n.e.s.	1205.1	1313.3	1508.0	1443.8	1447.9
Hungary/Hongrie	997.7	1181.0	1414.8	1522.8	1665.2
Egypt/Egypte	1209.9	1348.4	1204.6	1430.3	1428.9
Romania/Roumanie	636.8	877.3	1283.4	1670.5	1707.9
Tunisia/Tunisie	1036.9	965.2	1196.5	1422.5	1542.4
Czech Republic	629.3	859.1	1328.1	1740.8	1510.4
So. African Customs Un	701.0	866.4	1172.6	1243.9	1164.8
Norway,Svalbard and JM	750.6	778.3	961.0	1243.1	1364.8
Malta/Malte	957.5	1057.3	1234.8	867.4	753.8
Libyan Arab Jamahiriya	1122.2	754.5	956.5	1016.2	1010.9

(VALUE AS PERCENTAGE OF WORLD TOTAL)(VALEURS EN POURCENTAGE DU TOTAL MONDIAL)

	1988	1989	1990	1991	1992	1993	1994	1995	1996	1997
Africa	7.1	7.9	8.4	7.8	6.9	7.3	6.9	6.8	7.3	7.3
Americas	9.1	9.1	8.4	8.9	8.4	8.5	8.0	8.3	8.2	8.3
– Northern America	6.3	6.2	5.9	6.4	6.0	6.1	5.5	5.7	5.8	5.8
– LAIA	2.4	2.6	2.3	2.2	2.1	2.1	2.3	2.4	2.2	2.3
– CACM	0.2	0.1	0.1	0.1	0.1	0.1	0.1	0.1	0.1	0.1
– Caribbean	0.1	0.1	0.1	0.2	0.1	0.1	0.1	0.1	0.1	0.1
– Rest of America	0.1	0.1	0.1	0.1	0.1	0.1	0.0	0.0	0.0	0.0
Asia excl fmr USSR	10.4	10.2	10.0	10.3	10.4	11.6	10.8	11.0	10.8	11.4
– Middle East	3.3	3.4	3.5	3.2	2.9	3.1	2.6	2.8	3.1	3.2
Asia former USSR					0.1	0.2	0.2	0.3	0.2	0.2
Europe excl fmr USSR	70.1	69.4	70.1	69.7	71.0	68.5	69.8	69.7	69.9	69.5
– European Union	61.8	61.1	61.8	61.8	62.9	59.5	60.4	60.5	61.1	60.6
– Eastern Europe	1.8	1.8	1.5	1.4	1.7	2.0	2.5	2.9	2.9	3.2
– Rest of Europe	6.5	6.6	6.8	6.5	6.4	7.0	6.9	6.3	5.9	5.6
Europe former USSR	2.3	2.4	2.3	2.5	2.3	3.0	3.3	3.1	2.6	2.4
Oceania	0.9	0.8	0.7	0.6	0.6	0.6	0.7	0.7	0.7	0.7
Other	0.2	0.2	0.2	0.2	0.3	0.2	0.2	0.2	0.2	0.2
Germany/Allemagne				20.9	21.6	19.4	19.2	19.1	18.5	18.0
France, Monaco	14.8	14.7	14.2	14.2	14.5	13.6	13.6	13.9	13.6	13.2
United Kingdom	5.1	4.8	5.2	5.7	5.7	5.8	6.1	6.1	6.6	6.7
Netherlands/Pays–Bas	5.7	5.5	5.7	5.7	5.9	5.7	5.7	5.5	6.0	6.2
USA/Etats–Unis d'Amer	5.6	5.5	5.1	5.6	5.2	5.3	4.6	4.8	4.9	5.0
Belgium–Luxembourg	4.9	5.0	5.1	4.9	4.8	4.7	4.7	4.8	4.8	4.7
Switzerland,Liechtenst.	4.5	4.3	4.6	4.4	4.5	5.1	4.9	4.5	4.3	3.9
Spain/Espagne	2.4	2.4	3.0	3.5	3.4	3.4	3.9	3.9	4.2	4.7
Russian Federation					2.1	2.6	2.9	2.6	2.3	2.1
Austria/Autriche	2.4	2.3	2.3	2.2	2.2	2.2	2.2	2.3	2.3	2.3

	1988	1989	1990	1991	1992	1993	1994	1995	1996	1997
Afrique	4.8	4.8	4.5	4.4	4.1	4.2	3.7	3.5	3.3	3.6
Amériques	12.1	12.0	10.6	10.1	10.5	12.1	12.4	11.8	11.9	13.1
– Amérique du Nord	10.0	9.7	8.5	7.7	7.7	8.6	8.7	8.2	8.0	8.7
– ALAI	1.6	1.7	1.6	1.9	2.2	2.6	3.0	3.0	3.1	3.7
– MCAC	0.1	0.1	0.1	0.1	0.1	0.1	0.1	0.1	0.1	0.1
– Caraïbes	0.3	0.3	0.3	0.3	0.2	0.6	0.4	0.2	0.4	0.4
– Autre Amérique	0.1	0.1	0.1	0.2	0.2	0.2	0.2	0.2	0.4	0.2
Asie anc. URSS exclus	10.5	11.1	10.9	11.8	13.0	15.2	14.5	15.0	15.5	14.7
– Moyen–Orient	3.7	3.7	3.7	4.3	5.1	5.5	4.3	4.3	4.7	4.8
Asie ancienne URSS					0.0	0.1	0.1	0.1	0.1	0.1
Europe anc. URSS exclus	69.6	69.0	71.3	71.1	69.7	66.0	66.7	66.8	66.0	65.1
– Union Européenne	61.7	61.0	62.6	63.2	61.6	57.0	57.2	56.9	55.7	54.6
– Europe de l'Est	1.2	1.3	1.4	1.5	2.1	2.7	2.9	3.4	3.9	4.2
– Autre de l'Europe	6.8	6.7	7.2	6.4	6.1	6.3	6.5	6.6	6.4	6.4
Europe ancienne URSS	1.6	1.8	1.6	1.4	1.6	1.2	1.4	1.5	1.8	2.0
Océanie	0.9	1.0	0.8	0.7	0.6	0.7	0.8	0.8	0.9	0.9
Autre	0.4	0.4	0.4	0.4	0.4	0.5	0.4	0.5	0.5	0.5
Germany/Allemagne				21.0	20.4	19.5	19.0	18.7	17.5	16.4
France, Monaco	16.6	16.3	16.4	15.2	14.6	13.1	13.1	13.0	12.7	12.2
USA/Etats–Unis d'Amer	8.9	8.6	7.6	6.9	7.0	7.7	7.8	7.3	7.3	7.9
United Kingdom	8.0	7.9	7.1	6.7	6.6	6.4	6.5	6.2	6.5	7.1
Spain/Espagne	4.2	4.9	5.1	5.2	5.2	4.4	4.7	4.9	5.0	5.2
Switzerland,Liechtenst.	4.7	4.5	4.5	4.2	4.0	3.9	3.8	3.8	3.7	3.4
Netherlands/Pays–Bas	3.1	3.1	3.1	3.2	3.1	2.8	2.9	2.9	3.0	2.8
Belgium–Luxembourg	3.4	3.3	3.4	3.4	3.3	3.0	3.0	2.9	2.8	2.7
Austria/Autriche	2.5	2.4	2.4	2.5	2.5	2.5	2.5	2.4	2.4	2.3
Japan/Japon	1.9	2.3	2.3	2.2	1.9	1.9	2.1	2.3	2.2	2.0

Italy, including San Marino and Holy See

Italie y compris Saint–Martin et Saint–Siège

4. Special Imports C.I.F. by Commodities according to the S.I.T.C. (Rev. 2) in million U.S. Dollars
Importations Spéciales C.A.F. par Produits d'après la C.T.C.I. (Rév. 2) en millions de Dollars E.U.

SITC CTCI	COMMODITY	1994 QUANTITY QUANTITE	1994 VALUE VALEUR	1995 QUANTITY QUANTITE	1995 VALUE VALEUR	1996 QUANTITY QUANTITE	1996 VALUE VALEUR	1997 QUANTITY QUANTITE	1997 VALUE VALEUR	PRODUIT
	ALL COMMODITIES		167975.1		204099.2		208145.0		208317.2	TOUS PRODUITS
0	FOOD AND LIVE ANIMALS		17220.1		19380.3		19756.8		18362.3	ALIMENTS,ANIMAUX VIVANTS
001	*LIVE ANIMALS FOR FOOD	W 587002	1512.7	W 557948	1523.7	W 593017	1465.7	W 584881	1363.1	ANIMAUX VIVANTS
0011	BOVINE SPECIES,LIVE	W 373899	1103.5	W 360541	1117.7	W 379169	999.9	W 404564	998.6	ESPECE BOVINE
00119	— OTHR THAN FR BREEDING	W 359634	1066.0	W 351522	1092.7	W 365136	964.9	W 390416	966.0	BOVINS NON REPRODUCTEURS
01	MEAT AND PREPARATIONS		3551.7		3691.6		3639.5		3454.3	VIANDES ET PREPARATIONS
011	MEAT FRESH,CHILLD,FROZEN	W 1080047	3389.5	W 1055341	3518.1	W 1071062	3481.3	W 1096131	3306.9	VIANDES FRAICHES,REF,CONGE
0111	BOVINE MEAT FRESH,FROZEN	W 395098	1749.2	W 355851	1716.7	W 302618	1351.2	W 348373	1414.5	VIANDES BOVIN FRAI,REF
01111	BOVINE MEAT WITH BONE IN	W 345380	1540.8	W 312293	1483.9	W 260437	1136.1	W 300282	1188.2	VIANDES BOVIN NON DESOSS
0113	PIG MEAT FRESH,CHLD,FRZN	W 572052	1272.1	W 602100	1468.1	W 669538	1780.6	W 656099	1591.3	VIANDE DE PORC
02	DAIRY PRODCTS,BIRDS'EGGS		2794.0		3065.1		3008.7		2729.3	PRODUITS LAITIERS,OEUFS
022	MILK AND CREAM	W 2178524	1336.2	W 2182682	1480.5	W 2215983	1438.8	W 2410919	1376.0	LAIT ET CREME
0223	MILK AND CREAM FRESH	W 1923711	919.9	W 1951936	1032.0	W 1987775	1013.5	W 2205733	1011.1	LAIT,CREME FRAIS
024	CHEESE AND CURD	W 294453	1273.2	W 291507	1391.2	W 298423	1343.4	W 307409	1146.7	FROMAGE ET CAILLEBOTTE
03	FISH AND PREPARATIONS		2182.3		2374.8		2539.8		2498.8	POISSONS ET PREPARATIONS
034	FISH,FRESH,CHILLED,FROZN	W 264542	884.5	W 266227	941.4	W 270192	1036.2	W 253542	961.8	POISSON FRAIS, REFRIG,CONG
036	SHELL FISH FRESH,FROZEN	W 191906	672.0	W 207100	771.6	W 217996	810.3	W 233139	842.8	CRUSTACES,MOLLUSQUES
04	CEREALS AND PREPARATIONS		1665.7		2165.3		2405.3		2107.6	CEREALES ET PRODUITS
041	WHEAT ETC UNMILLED	W 4880480	962.4	W 5554036	1234.2	W 6447595	1438.4	W 6977048	1336.6	FROMENT,EPEAUTRE
0412	OTHER WHEAT ETC UNMILLED	W 4022046	789.4	W 4523037	971.6	W 5100860	1097.7	W 5378107	971.3	AUTRE FROMENT NON MOULU
05	VEGETABLES AND FRUIT		2428.4		2762.5		2822.6		2693.1	LEGUMES ET FRUITS
054	VEG ETC FRSH,SMPLY PRSVD	W 1639263	848.6	W 1639468	1005.5	W 1479216	911.2	W 1442796	805.4	LEGUMES FRAIS,CONG,SECS
057	FRUIT,NUTS,FRESH,DRIED	W 1138381	1090.1	W 1168058	1164.8	W 1229738	1278.8	W 1331968	1278.5	FRUITS FRAIS OU SECS
07	COFFEE,TEA,COCOA,SPICES		1132.7		1554.7		1320.2		1335.6	CAFE,THE,CACAO,EPICES
071	COFFEE AND SUBSTITUTES	W 326601	744.6	W 319067	1105.7	W 331121	877.2	W 339019	927.1	CAFE ET SUCCEDANES
0711	COFFEE GREEN,ROASTED,SUB	W 322399	710.0	W 316561	1073.5	W 328269	848.0	W 335908	894.7	CAFE TORREFIE OU DECAFEINE
07111	COFFEE GREEN,HUSKS,SKINS	W 320028	700.2	W 312905	1053.1	W 320664	812.3	W 327151	856.4	CAFE NON TORREFIE
081	*FEEDING STUFF FOR ANIML	W 3604979	1124.8	W 3982654	1242.9	W 3861481	1408.1	W 3634727	1285.2	NOURRITURE POUR ANIMAUX
0819	FOOD WASTE AND FEED NES	W 980681	597.3	W 1148776	701.4	W 1033032	706.0	W 916919	582.6	DECHETS,ALIMENTS NDA
08199	FODDER NES,INCL SWEETNED	W 471917	522.5	W 497068	603.5	W 649458	638.1	W 717700	551.0	PREPARATIONS FOURRAGERES
1	BEVERAGES AND TOBACCO		1803.7		1917.9		2128.8		2027.8	BOISSONS ET TABACS
11	BEVERAGES		697.1		757.1		802.7		760.6	BOISSONS
112	ALCOHOLIC BEVERAGES	W 422598	661.5	W 418160	716.9	W 424964	744.4	W 534760	715.7	BOISSONS ALCOOLIQUES
12	TOBACCO AND MANUFACTURES		1106.6		1160.9		1326.1		1267.2	TABACS BRUTS FABRIQUES
122	TOBACCO,MANUFACTURED	W 43643	994.6	W 41898	1022.9	W 42849	1191.2	W 44860	1096.1	TABACS FABRIQUES
1222	CIGARETTES	W 41625	968.5	W 38566	984.9	W 39372	1148.7	W 41479	1055.2	CIGARETTES
2	CRUDE MATERLS,EXCL FUELS		12909.4		15552.0		13557.0		13259.9	MAT BRUTES NON COMESTIBLES
21	HIDES,SKINS,FURS UNDRSSD		1462.8		1627.8		1546.7		1327.4	CUIRS,PEAUX BRUTS
211	HIDES,SKINS,EXC FURS,RAW	W 562270	1385.7	W 585806	1545.4	W 565834	1418.6	W 530756	1211.1	CUIRS ET PEAUX
2111	BOVINE,EQUINE HIDES,RAW	W 456215	900.2	W 488769	1013.2	W 477015	932.5	W 454528	855.1	PEAUX DE BOVINS
23	RUBBER, CRUDE		465.8		653.0		630.8		564.4	CAOUTCHOUC BRUT
24	CORK AND WOOD		2491.6		2845.2		2488.6		2440.8	LIEGE ET BOIS
247	OTH WOOD ROUGH,SQUARED	W 4239106	633.7	W 4411891	741.3	W 3914624	625.4	W 4421574	580.8	BOIS BRUTS EQUARRIS
248	WOOD SHAPED,SLEEPERS	W 4001518	1785.8	W 3990067	2027.4	W 3969952	1788.5	W 4284960	1783.5	BOIS SIMPLEMENT TRAVAILLES
2482	LUMBER SHAPED CONIFER	W 2668572	1016.1	W 2590244	1132.4	W 2697404	1047.2	W 2895770	1026.3	CONIFERES SCIES,RABOTES
24821	LUMBER SAWN ETC CONIFER	W 2625840	982.6	W 2549369	1094.9	W 2647262	1006.8	W 2827195	988.5	CONIFERES SCIES LONGITUD
2483	LUMBER SHAPED NON–CONIFR	W 1323935	767.9	W 1386425	891.3	W 1237699	732.3	W 1364526	750.5	NON CONIFERES SCIES,RABOTES
24831	LUMBER SAWN ETC NON–CON	W 1241122	651.0	W 1309196	769.5	W 1166871	629.4	W 1288174	646.8	SCIES LONGITUDINALEMENT
251	*PULP AND WASTE PAPER	W 3847980	1460.3	W 3882912	2466.6	W 3949102	1588.6	W 4139938	1576.5	PATES A PAPIER,DECHETS
2517	SODA,SULPHATE WOOD PULP	W 2209850	1062.3	W 2270028	1819.6	W 2362768	1200.5	W 2514909	1192.9	PATES CHIMIQUES AU SULFATE
25172	— BLEACHED,NONDISSOLVNG	W 2174511	1046.2	W 2229829	1790.5	W 2345674	1191.8	W 2495220	1184.2	PATES BLANCHIES
26	TEXTILE FIBRES AND WASTE		2363.3		2612.1		2404.3		2497.6	FIBRES TEXTILES
263	COTTON	W 412013	616.0	W 407448	812.4	W 403908	787.1	W 426694	745.0	COTON
2631	RAW COTTON,EXCL LINTERS	W 348290	560.8	W 345466	734.7	W 345716	721.1	W 354154	673.5	COTON EN MASSE
268	WOOL(EXC TOPS),ANML HAIR	W 190351	903.8	W 163256	908.2	W 161757	813.8	W 186335	902.6	LAINES ET POILS
27	CRUDE FERTLZR,MINRLS NES		1029.3		1185.4		1188.1		1157.5	ENGRAIS MINERAUX BRUTS
28	METALLIFEROUS ORES,SCRAP		2404.2		2896.3		2427.0		2487.8	MINERAIS METAL,DECHETS
282	IRON AND STEEL SCRAP	W 6264261	908.7	W 6315489	1091.3	W 4930854	719.8	W 4301575	626.0	FERRAILLES
28209	— OF OTHR IRON OR STEEL	W 5905078	819.8	W 5937211	960.7	W 4601922	605.5	W 3958437	501.4	FERRAILLES DE FER
288	NONFERR METAL SCRAP NES	W 643579	700.4	W 650139	813.3	W 692561	725.5	W 739161	854.9	DECHETS NON FERREUX
2882	OTHER BASE MTL SCRAP NES	W 502660	615.7	W 468495	718.4	W 526650	647.6	W 642617	799.9	AUTRES DECHETS
29	CRUDE ANIMAL,VEG MAT NES		794.3		828.4		881.6		851.5	MATIERES BRUTES ANIM,VEGET
292	CRUDE VEG MATERIALS NES	W 207930	652.7	W 193011	659.7	W 241911	704.3	W 215311	683.7	MAT BRUTES VEGETALES NDA
3	MINERAL FUELS ETC		13730.3		15060.6		17527.6		16624.0	COMBUSTIBLES MINERAUX LUB
32	COAL,COKE AND BRIQUETTES		892.8		1194.4		1044.4		967.3	HOUILLES,COKES,BRIQUETTES
322	COAL,LIGNITE AND PEAT	MW 16198	839.8	MW 19038	1063.1	MW 17133	965.1	MW 16358	903.4	HOUILLES,LIGNITES,TOURBE
3222	OTH COAL,NOT AGGLOMERATD	MW 15308	762.7	MW 18267	984.3	MW 16332	886.1	MW 15250	809.7	AUTRES HOUILLES
33	PETROLEUM AND PRODUCTS		12515.9		13436.2		15992.3		14966.2	PETROLE ET DERIVES
333	CRUDE PETROLEUM	MW 75626	8584.5	MW 73062	9103.3	MW 74542	11261.7	MW 78031	10950.2	HUILES BRUTES DE PETROLE
334	PETROLEUM PRODUCTS,REFIN	MW 31862	3618.2	MW 31302	3947.1	MW 30440	4382.1	MW 26901	3553.2	PRODUITS RAFFINES
3341	GASOLINE,OTH LIGHT OILS			W 3192958	568.3	W 3289879	673.3	W 2469982	501.6	ESSENCES POUR MOTEURS
3344	FUEL OILS,NES			MW 25922	2844.7	MW 25104	3088.8	MW 23324	2642.3	FUEL OILS
341	*GAS,NATURAL AND MANUFCT		321.7	W 1880843	430.1	W 1811344	491.1	W 3176587	690.7	GAZ NATUREL,GAZ MANUFACT
3413	PETROLM GASES,LIQUEFIED		319.5	W 1876691	429.6	W 1811067	490.8	W 3176547	690.5	GAZ DE PETROLE LIQUEFIE
4	ANIMAL,VEGETABLE OIL,FAT		1388.4		1382.7		1766.7		1810.5	HUILES,GRAISSES ANIM,VEG
42	FIXED VEGETABLE OIL,FAT		1231.6		1237.7		1619.0		1687.0	HUILES VEGETALES FIXES
423	FIXED VEG OILS,SOFT	W 526036	1005.8	W 452255	956.0	W 458538	1325.0	W 686558	1404.0	HUILES VEGET DOUCES FIXES
4235	OLIVE OIL	W 332661	862.2	W 248405	804.8	W 256087	1187.8	W 516411	1291.2	HUILE D'OLIVE
5	CHEMCLS,RELATED PROD NES		21041.3		25993.9		26581.5		26599.4	PRODUITS CHIMIQUES
51	ORGANIC CHEMICALS		5454.3		6800.0		6783.1		6776.2	PROD CHIMIQ ORGANIQUES
511	HYDROCARBONS NES,DERIVS	W 1034786	517.9	W 870009	610.2	W 989068	552.1	W 969238	543.4	HYDROCARBURES NDA
512	ALCOHOLS,PHENOLS ETC		653.4	W 1266153	909.8	W 1288535	770.0	W 1367315	781.1	PHENOLS,PHENOLS–ALCOOLS
5121	ACYCLIC ALCOHOLS,DERIVS		533.6	W 1187063	749.4	W 1216212	593.3	W 1291674	611.0	ALCOOLS ACYCLIQUES
513	CARBOXYLIC ACIDS ETC	W 795261	858.9	W 846100	1244.6	W 832484	1117.1	W 1033211	1135.6	ACIDES CARBOXYLIQUES
514	NITROGEN–FNCTN COMPOUNDS	W 422172	1692.6	W 455587	2060.3	W 460245	2119.7	W 459965	2074.2	COMPOSES FONCT AZOTEES
5148	OTH NITROGN–FNCTN CMPNDS	W 228711	1127.3	W 247410	1399.6	W 254013	1423.0	W 234023	1352.3	AUTRES COMPOSES AZOTES
51482	IMIDE–,IMIDE–FNCT CMPNDS	W 41012	840.1	W 47606	970.1	W 49926	991.5	W 47856	967.1	COMPOSES A FONCTION IMIDE
515	ORG–INORG COMPOUNDS ETC	W 175365	1220.5	W 178637	1349.6	W 170819	1620.0	W 182133	1659.7	COMPOSES ORGANO–MINERAUX
5156	HETEROCYCLIC CMPDS ETC	W 127148	944.8	W 130280	1039.7	W 117127	1203.0	W 129800	1231.0	COMPOSES HETEROCYCLIQUES
51569	OTH HETEROCYC CMPDS,ETC	W 21702	808.5	W 25820	850.0	W 25481	1024.3	W 24191	1058.4	AUT COMP HETEROCYCLIQUES
516	OTHER ORGANIC CHEMICALS	W 583638	511.4	W 540812	625.7	W 515061	604.3	W 528763	582.6	AUTRES PROD ORGANIQUES
52	INORGANIC CHEMICALS		1043.9		1224.2		1276.2		1202.7	PROD CHIM INORGANIQUES
522	INORG ELEMNTS,OXIDES,ETC	W 1297740	521.1	W 1313322	658.7	W 1341389	669.6	W 1479420	629.4	ELEMENTS INORGANIQUES
53	DYES,TANNING,COLOUR PROD		1502.5		1636.2		1689.8		1695.0	PROD TEINTURE,COLORANTS
531	SYNT DYE,NAT INDGO,LAKES	W 69791	663.5	W 69915	684.2	W 75778	714.1	W 84073	724.9	MAT COLOR ORGAN,LAQUES
5311	SYNTHIC ORGNIC DYESTUFFS	W 63007	628.3	W 62430	646.8	W 66321	670.1	W 74701	680.8	MAT COLOR ORGAN SYNTHET
533	PIGMENTS,PAINTS,ETC	W 300498	749.9	W 296181	863.6	W 300402	880.4	W 336195	875.8	PIGMENTS,PEINTURES,VERNIS
541	*MEDICINAL,PHARM PRODUCT		3262.5	MK 59793	3902.5		4624.1		4763.7	PROD MEDICINAUX PHARMACEUT
5413	ANTIBIOTICS IN BULK		539.6	K 3668437	683.1	K 4674133	747.7	K 4151933	655.8	ANTIBIOTIQUES NDA
5417	MEDICAMENTS		1730.2	MK 36680	2063.4	MK 40020	2590.8	MK 48115	2776.9	MEDICAMENTS
54179	— CONTNG OTH SUBSTANCES	MK 25323	1234.1	MK 32140	1573.1	MK 35914	1995.3	MK 43299	2145.7	MED CONT AUT SUBSTANCES

4. Special Imports C.I.F. by Commodities according to the S.I.T.C. (Rev. 2) in million U.S. Dollars
Importations Spéciales C.A.F. par Produits d'après la C.T.C.I. (Rév. 2) en millions de Dollars E.U.

SITC CTCI	COMMODITY	1994 QUANTITY QUANTITE	1994 VALUE VALEUR	1995 QUANTITY QUANTITE	1995 VALUE VALEUR	1996 QUANTITY QUANTITE	1996 VALUE VALEUR	1997 QUANTITY QUANTITE	1997 VALUE VALEUR	PRODUIT
55	PERFUME,CLEANING ETC PRD		1418.4		1593.8		1627.5		1665.1	PROD POUR PARFUM,TOILETTE
553	PERFUMERY,COSMETICS,ETC	W 91466	801.6	W 95792	909.4	W 98774	901.1	W 110593	895.7	PRODUITS DE PARFUMERIE
562	*FERTILIZERS,MANUFACTURE	W 3359673	543.8	W 3374589	657.3	W 3017504	636.0	W 3669830	644.4	ENGRAIS MANUFACTURES
58	PLASTIC MATERIALS ETC		5330.8		7256.2		6846.5		6826.7	MAT PLAST ARTIFICIELLES
582	PROD OF CONDENSATION ETC	W 666160	1388.4	W 782632	1964.3	W 773786	1913.6	W 921458	1905.6	PROD CONDENS,POLYCOND
5823	ALKYDS,OTHER POLYESTERS	W 261242	518.8	W 332961	827.3	W 338337	745.0	W 405365	733.7	ALKYDES ET AUT POLYESTERS
58231	— IN PRIMARY FORMS	W 232931	409.1	W 300822	674.9	W 306724	596.6	W 357137	565.3	SOUS FORMES PRIMAIRES
583	POLYMERIZATION ETC PRODS		3759.2	W 3701898	5071.9	W 3956591	4703.6	W 4228290	4702.1	PROD POLYMERISATION
5831	POLYETHYLENE	W 991099	740.0	W 952572	1023.9	W 1050293	968.9	W 1086617	1022.8	POLYETHYLENE
58311	— IN PRIMARY FORMS	W 908771	644.3	W 878554	911.4	W 971931	857.3	W 1005418	901.4	POLYETHYLENE PRIMAIRES
5832	POLYPROPYLENE	W 765515	607.7	W 701739	836.6	W 759955	740.9	W 815217	744.1	POLYPROPYLENE
58321	— IN PRIMARY FORMS	W 713571	475.6	W 646890	655.5	W 699861	570.2	W 757193	590.2	POLYPROPYLENE PRIMAIRES
5833	POLYSTYRENE,ITS COPOLYMR	W 589376	606.3	W 598555	845.3	W 644399	745.6	W 663261	652.7	POLYPROPYLENE COPOLYMERES
58331	— IN PRIMARY FORMS	W 569654	576.6	W 578652	810.4	W 624570	713.8	W 642397	624.6	SOUS FORMES PRIMAIRES
5834	POLYVINYL CHLORIDE	W 493828	476.0	W 519875	639.1	W 556711	520.3	W 551011	523.5	CHLORURE DE POLYVINYLE
5839	OTH POLYMRZTION ETC PROD		941.5	W 692218	1257.7	W 693778	1229.7	W 832550	1293.8	AUT PROD POLYMER COPOLYM
59	CHEMICAL MATERIALS NES		2450.8		2867.3		3028.0		2961.6	MAT PROD CHIMIQUES NDA
598	MISCEL CHEM PRODUCTS NES		1716.0	W 810800	2037.4	W 835187	2130.4	W 887123	2134.9	PROD DIV INDUST CHIM NDA
5989	CHEM PRODUCTS,PREPS NES		1449.6	W 624830	1710.6	W 646020	1786.8	W 694313	1789.7	PROD PREP CHIMIQUES NDA
59899	OTH CHEM PRODS,PREPS,NES		1100.4	W 460514	1312.5	W 452371	1355.6	W 483984	1376.4	AUT PRODUITS CHIMIQUES NDA
6	BASIC MANUFACTURES		28412.4		37232.3		34812.1		35009.3	ART MANUFACTURES
61	LEATHER,DRESSED FUR,ETC		2213.8		2495.2		2722.7		2688.4	CUIRS,PELLETERIES
611	LEATHER	W 335648	1616.9	W 335649	1784.1	W 368814	1861.6	W 392446	1822.2	CUIRS,PEAUX PREPARES
6114	LEATHR BOVINE NES,EQUINE	W 243088	913.6	W 253182	1015.4	W 270265	1004.4	W 298349	1041.4	CUIRS DE BOVINS
612	LEATHER ETC MANUFACTURES	W 28319	490.9	W 30479	588.3	W 34046	718.9	W 34879	724.3	OUVRAGES EN CUIRS NDA
6123	PREPRD PARTS OF FOOTWEAR	W 27077	473.4	W 29180	569.1	W 32795	699.4	W 33594	705.6	PARTIES DE CHAUSSURES
62	RUBBER MANUFACTURES NES		1485.8		1796.3		1931.4		1790.6	CAOUTCHOUC MANUFACTURE
625	RUBBER TYRES, TUBES ETC	W 270614	1071.1	W 303688	1252.3	W 306515	1331.5	W 320021	1217.2	PNEUS CAOUTCHOUC VULCANISE
6251	TYRES NEW FOR MOTOR CARS	W 115715	547.5	W 126339	616.4	W 130597	661.9	W 140628	616.9	PNEUS POUR VOITURES
63	WOOD,CORK MANUFACTRS NES		700.0		882.7		917.6		901.8	OUVRAGES LIEGE ET BOIS
64	PAPER,PAPERBOARD AND MFR		2971.4		4045.1		3478.5		3387.0	PAPIERS,CARTONS & OUVRAGES
641	PAPER AND PAPERBOARD	W 3813891	2624.4	W 3674959	3577.9	W 3511502	3010.8	W 4073984	2938.1	PAPIERS ET CARTONS
6412	PRINTG,WRITING PAPER NES	W 563956	482.0	W 568212	660.4	W 544535	543.7	W 769800	628.0	PAPIERS POUR L'IMPRESSION
6413	KRAFT PAPER,PAPERBOARD	W 949322	508.2	W 863656	717.9	W 897520	612.4	W 1060802	614.7	PAPIER ET CARTON KRAFT
6415	PAPER,PAPERBRD,BULK,NES	W 1164032	689.8	W 1124398	1010.9	W 1019868	742.7	W 1088302	667.8	PAPIERS,CARTONS ROULEAUX
64159	OTHER PAPER ETC,BULK,NES	W 874099	556.1	W 858385	814.6	W 774664	602.7	W 839341	543.9	AUT PAPIER ROULEAUX FEUILLES
6418	COATED ETC PAPER NES BLK	W 423997	588.4	W 400678	681.0	W 383367	623.9	W 384731	598.5	PAP,CARTONS COUCHES,ENDUITS
65	TEXTILE YARN,FABRICS,ETC		6004.4		6861.1		6555.9		6820.6	FILS,TISSUS,ARTICLES TEXTILE
651	TEXTILE YARN	W 557140	2567.2	W 546674	3029.6	W 513270	2853.9	W 621163	3006.6	FILS TEXTILES
6512	WOOL,HAIR YARN,INCL TOPS	W 84976	581.0	W 83025	708.5	W 73065	613.9	W 80258	627.2	FILS DE LAINE,DE POILS
6514	SYN FIB YRN,BULK,MONOFIL	W 169524	740.3	W 175747	941.3	W 184884	1055.1	W 226037	1117.4	FILS CONT 85% FIB TEXT SYNTH
65142	— NONTXT ETC CONT PAMID	W 117698	485.2	W 119461	619.9	W 122365	696.9	W 146202	733.1	FILS NON TEX FI CON POLYAMID
652	COTTON FABRICS,WOVEN	W 144947	832.3	W 140582	942.5	W 129528	879.2	W 129626	834.7	TISSUS DE COTON
653	WOVN MAN–MADE FIB FABRIC	W 92157	691.2	W 97549	815.4	W 94925	797.9	W 106118	856.8	TISSUS FIBRES SYNTH,ARTIF
657	SPECIAL TXTL FABRC,PRODS	W 69398	504.7	W 72307	594.9	W 79453	617.4	W 84167	609.3	TISSUS SPECIAUX
66	NONMETAL MINERAL MFS NES		2238.2		2582.7		2691.4		2578.3	ART MIN NON METALLIQUES
664	GLASS	W 729483	581.1	W 787799	728.3	W 715654	737.2	W 720547	670.1	VERRE
67	IRON AND STEEL		6205.3		9558.5		8142.0		8316.3	FER ET ACIER
671	PIG IRON ETC	W 1971550	678.4	W 2399738	965.4	W 1952787	812.1	W 2015538	805.7	FONTE,SPIEGEL,POUDRES
672	IRON,STEEL PRIMARY FORMS	W 4773979	1684.3	W 5990102	2611.5	W 4926761	1973.0	W 6282723	2198.5	LINGOTS FER,ACIER
6725	IRN,STL BLOOMS,SLABS,ETC	W 1251982	381.9	W 1982898	713.7	W 1119042	425.3	W 1575820	499.2	BLOOMS,BILLETTES FER ACIER
6727	IRN,STL COIL FR REROLLNG	W 3442285	1268.7	W 3931568	1864.3	W 3749179	1510.1	W 4631430	1665.4	EBAUCHES POUR TOLES FER
67271	IRON,SIMPLE STEEL COILS	W 3322873	1113.4	W 3769321	1559.9	W 3597993	1278.0	W 4383124	1377.7	EBAUCHES NON EN ACIER
673	IRON,STEEL SHAPES ETC	W 1401059	795.4	W 1727012	1207.4	W 1306239	983.5	W 1536551	953.0	BARRES,PROFIL FER,ACIER
674	IRN,STL UNIV,PLATE,SHEET	W 3685487	2302.1	W 4606614	3577.7	W 4167737	3115.8	W 5043526	3127.2	LARGES PLATS,TOLES
6746	IRN,STL THIN PLATE,ROLLD	W 1626716	1110.0	W 2071994	1773.0	W 1872908	1449.2	W 2328719	1479.5	TOLES LAM MOINS 3MM
67461	— OF IRON OR SIMPLE STL	W 1289331	577.6	W 1666925	906.0	W 1434742	694.6	W 1858725	768.5	TOL NON AC FIN MOINS 3 MM
67463	— OF STAINLESS ETC STL	W 262410	469.5	W 297443	763.9	W 309753	634.8	W 375123	625.2	TOL ACIER INOX MOINS 3 MM
6749	OTH IRN,STL PLATES,SHEET	W 973289	548.6	W 1171304	825.3	W 1097046	720.4	W 1322401	756.6	AUTRES TOLES FER,ACIER
67491	— OF IRON OR SIMPLE STL	W 961340	522.1	W 1154879	783.1	W 1051877	666.5	W 1241884	691.1	AUT TOLES AUTRES ACIER FIN
678	IRON,STL TUBES,PIPES,ETC		502.6	W 672346	828.1	W 670731	864.4	W 705604	813.9	TUBES,TUYAUX EN FONTE,FER
68	NON–FERROUS METALS		4304.3		6122.9		5305.8		5499.4	METAUX NON FERREUX
682	COPPER EXC CEMENT COPPER	W 697959	1758.3	W 736427	2453.3	W 777313	2193.4	W 783049	2113.5	CUIVRE
6821	COPPER NES,ALLOYS,UNWRT	W 429066	941.9	W 451613	1321.4	W 490153	1189.0	W 476605	1095.8	CUIVRE BRUT
68212	COPPER REFINED,UNWROUGHT	W 420520	918.1	W 435321	1269.9	W 463566	1131.7	W 469409	1078.6	CUIVRE AFFINE BRUT
6822	COPPER,ALLOYS WORKED	W 268893	816.4	W 284813	1131.9	W 287160	1004.4	W 306445	1017.8	CUIVRE,ALLIAGES OUVRES
684	ALUMINIUM		1723.9	W 946883	2413.8	W 851042	1984.0	W 1004015	2175.5	ALUMINIUM
6841	ALUMINIUM,ALLOYS,UNWRGHT	W 577593	898.4	W 574477	1203.6	W 487891	871.1	W 575081	1007.0	ALUMINIUM,ALLIAGES BRUTS
6842	ALUMINIUM,ALLOYS WORKED		825.6	W 372406	1210.3	W 363151	1112.9	W 428934	1168.6	ALUMINIUM,ALLIAGES OUVRE
68422	ALUMNM PLATE,SHEET,STRIP	W 232295	524.5	W 256203	771.3	W 237818	664.2	W 306614	773.6	TOLES, PLANCHES EN ALU
69	METAL MANUFACTURES NES		2289.6		2888.1		3067.1		3027.4	ART MANUFACT EN METAL NDA
695	TOOLS		597.4	W 39006	748.3	W 39858	811.8	W 42229	774.6	OUTILS A MAIN
699	BASE METAL MFRS NES		874.2	W 198861	1119.6	W 192755	1121.1	W 213836	1114.0	ART MANUFACTURES MET NDA
7	MACHINES,TRANSPORT EQUIP		47332.3		59736.8		62635.9		64387.1	MACHINES MATERIEL TRANSPORT
71	POWER GENERATING EQUIPMT		2243.3		3054.7		3123.7		3216.0	MACHINES GENERATRICES
713	INTRNL COMBUS PSTN ENGIN	W 77156	1050.1	W 100583	1435.0	W 90991	1436.5	W 101573	1467.4	MOTEURS EXPL COMB INT, PIECE
7139	PISTON ENGINE PARTS NES	W 31310	477.2	W 47467	668.9	W 36899	641.9	W 40250	655.3	PIECES POUR 713.2,3,8
714	ENGINES AND MOTORS NES		494.0	W 4386	653.2	W 6059	760.0	W 6663	800.3	MOTEURS NON ELECTRIQUES
716	ROTATING ELECTRIC PLANT	W 75022	585.8	W 95122	816.7	W 89238	738.9	W 101369	757.8	APP ELECTR ROTATIFS,PIECES
7162	AC MTRS,GENRTRS,GEN SETS	W 59623	432.3	W 78420	625.0	W 75419	581.2	W 80198	560.9	MOTEURS ELECTRIQUES
72	MACHS FOR SPCL INDUSTRYS		3170.2		4459.3		4665.7		4299.9	MAC SPECIALES POUR INDUST
724	TEXTILE,LEATHER MACHNRY		927.0	W 55077	1223.3	W 53086	1133.2	W 53704	1044.3	MACH POUR INDUSTRIE TEXTILE
728	OTH MACHY FOR SPCL INDUS		947.9	W 55962	1345.4	W 58185	1381.9	W 62403	1286.7	AUT MACH IND PARTICULIERES
7284	MACHY FOR SPCL INDUS NES	W 26089	770.5	W 36028	1111.7	W 37473	1129.1	W 39611	1046.2	MACH SPEC IND PARTICUL.
73	METALWORKING MACHINERY		1074.1		1620.6		1724.8		1532.7	MACH TRAVAIL DES METAUX
736	METALWORKING MACH–TOOLS		892.5	W 84085	1350.7	W 94576	1450.1	W 91812	1260.8	MACH–OUTILS TRAVAIL METAUX
7361	METAL CUTTING MACH–TOOLS		386.0	W 35276	614.9	W 41245	661.3	W 38119	555.0	MACH–OUT ENLEVEMENT METAL
74	GENRL INDUSTRL MACHY NES		5373.5		7192.0		7533.0		7171.6	MACH APP INDUSTRIE
741	HEATING,COOLING EQUIPMNT	W 51401	720.7	W 74024	1098.5	W 81884	1179.8	W 76943	1045.0	MACH CHAUFFAGE,PIECES
742	PUMPS FOR LIQUIDS ETC	W 29716	700.6	W 31618	864.0	W 33149	859.6	W 37176	848.9	POMPES MOTO–POMPES
743	PUMPS NES,CENTRFUGES ETC		912.5	W 105255	1256.0	W 103772	1238.8	W 109604	1172.1	POMPES COMPRES,VENT ETC
744	MECHANICAL HANDLING EQU	W 100589	600.3	W 138104	854.6	W 150852	922.8	W 162242	856.8	EQUIP MANUTENTION PIECES
745	NONELEC MACHY,TOOLS NES		581.5	W 31293	677.5	W 31354	716.7	W 35612	701.3	AUT MACH NON ELEC,PIECES
749	NONELEC MACH PTS,ACC NES		1858.2	W 158298	2441.6	W 161304	2615.6	W 172254	2547.7	PIECES MACH NON ELEC NDA
7491	BALL,ROLLER,ETC BEARINGS		558.5	W 58664	838.3	W 59719	888.1	W 55425	793.3	ROULEMENTS BILLES ETC
7492	COCKS,VALVES ETC NES		607.8	W 39585	753.1	W 40993	811.0	W 45886	834.5	ART ROB,SIM POUR TUYAUX
75	OFFICE MACHNES,ADP EQUIP		5374.0		6743.6		7494.9		7080.9	MACH BUREAU TRAIT AUTOM
752	AUTOMTIC DATA PROC EQUIP		2913.0	W 53194	3601.5	W 57779	4094.0	W 64237	4078.8	MACH TRAIT INFORMATION
7523	DIGITL CENTRL PROCESSORS	W 6703	651.6	W 8476	911.0	W 9347	1178.0	W 11405	1308.6	UNITES CENTRALES
7524	DIGITL CENTRL STOR UNITS	W 3279	689.1	W 3857	792.8	W 4326	961.0	W 5182	957.8	UNITES MEMOIRE CENTRALES
7525	ADP PERIPHERAL UNITS	W 27806	795.9	W 33155	1038.1	W 37783	1091.3	W 41204	1086.6	UNITES PERIPHERIQUES

4. Special Imports C.I.F. by Commodities according to the S.I.T.C. (Rev. 2) in million U.S. Dollars
Importations Spéciales C.A.F. par Produits d'après la C.T.C.I. (Rév. 2) en millions de Dollars E.U.

SITC CTCI	COMMODITY	1994 QUANTITY QUANTITE	1994 VALUE VALEUR	1995 QUANTITY QUANTITE	1995 VALUE VALEUR	1996 QUANTITY QUANTITE	1996 VALUE VALEUR	1997 QUANTITY QUANTITE	1997 VALUE VALEUR	PRODUIT
7528	OFF–LINE DATA PROC EQUIP		501.3	W 5862	544.2	W 4858	671.0	W 4856	516.1	MACH AUXIL TRAIT INFORM
759	OFFICE,ADP MCH PTS,ACCES		1971.2	W 27092	2597.9	W 35649	2956.7	W 36734	2560.2	PIECES DU 751 ET 752
7599	ACCTG,ETC,ADP MCH PTS,AC		1749.1	W 21572	2341.3	W 26124	2631.6	W 27081	2267.2	PIECES DU 751 ET 752
76	TELECOMM,SOUND EQUIPMENT		3571.3		4246.2		4543.8		5668.1	EQUIPMENT DE TELECOM
761	TELEVISION RECEIVERS	W 39113	594.2	W 41621	641.4	W 38454	645.9	W 45919	714.7	RECEPTEURS DE TELEVISION
7611	COLOUR TV RECEIVERS	W 38586	579.7	W 41062	625.2	W 38046	637.1	W 45414	703.9	RECEPTEURS COULEUR
764	TELECOM EQPT,PTS,ACC NES		2024.4	W 36651	2676.9	W 35518	2866.3	W 42907	3979.9	EQUIP TELECOM,PIECES
7641	LINE TELEPHONE,ETC EQUIP		379.4	W 7298	567.6	W 7807	662.9	W 8889	823.5	APP TELEPHON PAR FIL
7643	TV,RADIO TRANSMITTRS ETC		584.4	W 3923	932.1	W 3639	1036.0	W 5987	1688.4	APP EMET TELE RADIO
7649	PTS NES OF EQUIPMT OF 76		626.2	W 10654	706.2	W 9649	848.0	W 11518	1160.5	PIECES DE LA DIV 76
76491	PTS NES OF APPAR OF 7641	W 2637	298.5	W 2340	327.2	W 2924	434.1	W 3452	638.1	PIECES POUR 764.1
77	ELECTRIC MACHNRY NES ETC		9491.7		11689.3		11137.0		10697.0	MACH APP ELECT NDA
771	ELECTRIC POWER MACHY NES	W 29239	428.6	W 34575	579.6	W 37947	665.4	W 41315	691.3	MACH PROD,TRANS ELECTR
772	SWITCHGEAR ETC,PARTS NES		1937.3	W 61753	2528.2	W 60658	2487.3	W 64823	2476.1	APP COUPURE,SECT ETC
7721	SWITCHGEAR ETC		1648.8	W 57118	2151.2	W 56580	2145.8	W 60212	2103.8	APP COUPURE,SECTIONMNT
775	HOUSEHOLD TYPE EQUIP NES	W 92314	736.8	W 103903	869.1	W 100609	861.0	W 104077	825.2	MACH,APP USAGE DOMESTQUE
776	TRANSISTORS,VALVES,ETC		3682.0	W 47391	4390.3	W 51473	3887.8	W 43326	3429.9	LAMPES,TUBES,VALVES
7764	ELECTRONIC MICROCIRCUITS		2940.4	W 3084	3441.8	W 2960	2918.4	W 3571	2624.8	MICROSTRUCTURES ELECTRON
778	ELECTRICAL MACHINERY NES		2101.0	W 190906	2579.3	W 184300	2385.4	W 188345	2366.1	AUTRES MACH ELECT NDA
7788	OTH ELEC MACHY,EQUIP NES		838.7	W 40649	1070.7	W 42760	937.1	W 44970	957.6	AUT MACH APP ELEC NDA
78	ROAD VEHICLES		14908.9		18825.5		20418.6		22749.0	VEHICULES ROUTIERS
781	PASS MOTOR VEH EXC BUSES	W 1178456	10728.3	W 1317465	13299.3	W 1313554	14439.9	W 1830387	16804.2	AUTO TRANSPORT PERSONNES
782	LORRIES,SPCL MTR VEH NES	W 157718	1081.9	W 190663	1456.7	W 211326	1749.4	W 224487	1673.5	VEHICULES SPECIAUX,MARCH
7821	LORRIES,TRUCKS	W 152524	1035.2	W 185610	1405.9	W 201825	1652.3	W 215479	1589.4	VEHICULES TRANSP MARCHAND
783	ROAD MOTOR VEHICLES NES	W 34993	322.9	W 67739	666.3	W 69544	750.6	W 62133	627.9	VEHICULES ROUTIERS NDA
784	MOTOR VEH PRTS,ACCES NES	W 231735	1994.9	W 287162	2491.8	W 316794	2540.5	W 379087	2646.0	PIECES 722,781,782,783
7849	OTHER MOTOR VEHCL PARTS	W 228342	1963.1	W 282124	2433.5	W 312370	2482.8	W 373568	2583.3	PIECES 722,781,782,783
785	CYCLES,ETC MOTRZD OR NOT	W 49251	676.3	W 53812	772.9	W 52781	778.2	W 63390	832.2	MOTOCYCLES SCOOTERS
79	OTHR TRANSPORT EQUIPMENT		2125.6		1906.1		1994.7		1972.3	AUTRE MATERIEL TRANSPORT
792	AIRCRAFT ETC		1974.2	W 4286	1673.5	W 4067	1570.8	W 4133	1502.9	APP NAVIGATION AERIENNE
7924	AIRCRFT NES OVER 15000KG	W 3742	1275.4	W 2531	843.2	W 2540	896.1	W 2251	603.8	AERODYNES PLUS 15000 KG
7929	AIRCRAFT PARTS NES		443.1	W 1339	615.6	W 1280	524.7	W 1559	727.8	PIECES DU 792
8	MISC MANUFACTURED GOODS		15661.9		18335.6		19555.0		20258.8	ART MANUFACTURES DIVERS
821	*FURNITURE,PARTS THEREOF	W 141070	582.3	W 157231	698.9	W 171315	751.3	W 208784	787.1	MEUBLES ET PIECES
84	CLOTHING AND ACCESSORIES		3972.9		4659.0		5036.8		5319.5	VETEMENTS
842	MENS OUTERWEAR NOT KNIT	W 54907	1126.1	W 55934	1241.0	W 56789	1367.8	W 64702	1435.8	VET DESSUS POUR HOMMES
8423	— TROUSERS,BREECHES ETC	W 27539	464.2	W 26592	480.0	W 29621	586.9	W 33175	625.8	PANTALONS HOMMES MAT TEX
843	WOMENS OUTERWEAR NONKNIT		814.0	W 31579	936.4	W 33040	1010.1	W 37454	1021.8	VET DESSUS FEMMES MAT TEX
845	OUTERWEAR KNIT NONELASTC	W 33236	692.7	W 35895	799.0	W 39938	949.0	W 54138	1148.8	VET DESSOUS,ACCES BONNET
8451	— JERSEYS,PULLOVERS ETC	W 15376	385.0	W 16477	447.2	W 18197	508.1	W 26785	644.9	CHANDAILS,PULL–OVERS ETC
846	UNDER GARMENTS KNITTED		508.4	W 36081	652.3	W 35305	673.2	W 33854	681.5	SOUS VETS DE BONNETERIE
851	*FOOTWEAR	W 82648	987.6	W 85472	1111.1	W 82828	1195.6	W 104634	1456.4	CHAUSSURES
85102	FOOTWEAR LEATHER	W 66624	853.1	W 67456	935.3	W 63947	985.9	W 79018	1176.3	CHAUS SEMELLES EN CUIR
87	PRECISION INSTRUMNTS NES		2882.7		3440.1		3647.8		3701.9	INSTRUM,APPAR SCIENT NDA
872	MEDICAL INSTRUMENTS NES		719.5	W 15922	806.6	W 16657	917.0	W 18093	932.5	INSTR,APP MEDIC–CHIR NDA
87202	OTH MEDICAL INSTRUMENTS		664.3	W 14356	744.6	W 15112	840.8	W 16069	847.4	INSTRUM,APP MEDECINE
874	MEASURNG,CONTROLNG INSTR		1942.6	W 23111	2327.4	W 23879	2436.0	W 25694	2457.6	INSTRUMENTS DE MESURE
8742	MEASUR,DRAW ETC INST,PTS		571.8	W 6944	717.3	W 6891	720.0	W 7309	689.0	INST DESSIN,TRACAGE,PCS
8748	ELEC MEAS,CONTRL EQU NES		470.5	W 2859	568.8	W 3552	631.7	W 4066	714.7	APP ELEC ELECTRO MESURE
87483	OTH ELCTRNC MEAS ETC EQU		408.2	W 2206	495.7	W 3067	570.4	W 3665	662.4	AUT APP ELECTRO DE MESURE
88	PHOTO EQU,OPTICL GDS ETC		1943.8		2146.5		2174.3		2115.7	APP,FOURN PHOTO,OP,MONTR
882	PHOTO,CINEMA SUPPLIES		699.0	W 61124	746.0	W 56121	789.3	W 58892	723.9	PRODUITS PHOTO,CINEMA
8822	PHOTO FILM EXC DEV CINMA		525.6	W 41277	567.9	W 36733	608.6	W 38506	555.7	PLAQUES,PELLICULES,FILMS
885	WATCHES AND CLOCKS		769.7		845.5		782.7		789.4	HORLOGERIE
8851	WATCHES,MOVEMENTS,CASES		633.8		692.0		638.6		648.9	MONTRES,MOUVEMENTS,BOITES
88511	WATCHES		588.7		643.1		596.2		610.2	MONTRES POCHE,BRACELET
89	MISC MANUFCTRD GOODS NES		4556.3		5431.6		5822.1		5886.3	ART MANUFACTURES DIVERS
893	ARTICLES OF PLASTIC NES		1170.1		1409.2		1425.3		1427.5	OUVRAGES EN MAT DIVIS 58
8939	MISC PLASTIC ARTICLES	W 151610	839.7	W 156845	1004.9	W 156367	1024.1	W 179313	1049.0	ART DIVERS EN MAT DIV 58
89399	OTHR PLASTC ARTICLES NES	W 127076	775.0	W 133068	930.4	W 132293	944.8	W 155553	976.2	AUT OUV MAT DIV 58
894	TOYS,SPORTING GOODS,ETC	W 122620	1027.5	W 133135	1157.7	W 135780	1304.0	W 154728	1338.9	VOITURES ENFANTS,JOUETS
8942	TOYS,INDOOR GAMES ETC	W 96430	747.9	W 102410	813.2	W 100667	901.5	W 119289	975.9	JOUETS,JEUX ETC
898	MUSICAL INSTRUMENTS,PTS		725.3	W 43377	975.4	W 44237	1067.3	W 43210	1109.7	INSTRUMENTS DE MUSIQUE
8983	SOUND RECRDNG TAPE,DISCS		625.2	W 37198	863.4	W 38367	956.5	W 36565	1000.4	SUPPORTS SON POUR 763
89832	RECORDED DISCS,TAPES ETC		361.9	W 14699	597.0	W 15241	674.2	W 13338	754.4	DISQUES,PHONO,BANDES
899	OTHER MANUFACTURED GOODS		655.2		738.2		797.1		817.0	AUT ART MANUF DIVERS NDA
9	GOODS NOT CLASSD BY KIND		8475.9		9507.5		9824.1		9978.7	ART TRANSACT NON CLASSES
931	*SPECIAL TRANSACTIONS	MW 21947	4256.2	MW 25860	5123.1	MW 27626	5684.8	MW 27285	5703.7	TRANS.SPECIALES
971	*GOLD,NON MONETARY NES		4173.5	K 352873	4317.7	K 335405	4058.4	K 410917	4219.0	OR NON MONETAIRE
97101	NONMON GLD UNWRT,SEMIMFD		4170.6	K 346071	4313.9	K 331918	4056.3	K 407274	4217.1	OR,ALLIAGES D'OR BRUTS

5. Special Exports F.O.B. by Commodities according to the S.I.T.C. (Rev. 2) in million U.S. Dollars
Exportations Spéciales F.O.B. par Produits d'après la C.T.C.I. (Rév. 2) en millions de Dollars E.U.

SITC CTCI	COMMODITY	1994 QUANTITY QUANTITE	1994 VALUE VALEUR	1995 QUANTITY QUANTITE	1995 VALUE VALEUR	1996 QUANTITY QUANTITE	1996 VALUE VALEUR	1997 QUANTITY QUANTITE	1997 VALUE VALEUR	PRODUIT
	ALL COMMODITIES		190004.7		231346.5		252106.5		238265.9	TOUS PRODUITS
0	FOOD AND LIVE ANIMALS		9691.8		11226.3		12159.6		11228.3	ALIMENTS,ANIMAUX VIVANTS
01	MEAT AND PREPARATIONS		833.9		919.2		1093.1		1098.7	VIANDES ET PREPARATIONS
02	DAIRY PRODCTS,BIRDS'EGGS		742.3		865.0		948.0		886.3	PRODUITS LAITIERS,OEUFS
024	CHEESE AND CURD	W 113954	644.6	W 121096	762.5	W 132237	847.6	W 134240	765.6	FROMAGE ET CAILLEBOTTE
04	CEREALS AND PREPARATIONS		2229.3		2445.8		2847.5		2606.9	CEREALES ET PRODUITS
048	CEREAL ETC PREPARATIONS	W 1169697	1429.6	W 1272460	1737.3	W 1465929	2007.1	W 1558173	1879.6	PREPTNS A BASE CEREALES
0483	MACARONI,SPAGHETTI ETC	W 996570	876.5	W 1064197	1012.8	W 1240993	1207.4	W 1329773	1132.1	PATES ALMENTAIRES
0484	BAKERY PRODUCTS	W 149362	506.8	W 183762	675.4	W 203962	760.5	W 206482	710.2	PRODUITS DE BOULANGERIE
05	VEGETABLES AND FRUIT		4195.5		4835.8		4962.3		4439.9	LEGUMES ET FRUITS
054	VEG ETC FRSH,SMPLY PRSVD		1395.0	W 2348943	1730.9	W 2263313	1725.7	W 2217221	1491.5	LEGUMES FRAIS,CONG,SECS
0546	VEGETABLES SIMPLY PRESVD	W 1040265	688.7	W 1110305	804.4	W 1095655	814.3	W 1174623	748.4	LEGUMES CONG,CONSER
05461	VEGETABLES FROZEN	W 1036301	684.2	W 1107287	800.2	W 1093407	809.4	W 1171446	743.1	LEGUMES CONGELES
057	FRUIT,NUTS,FRESH,DRIED	W 2634500	2026.3	W 2385570	2132.2	W 2648830	2177.4	W 2365357	2018.7	FRUITS FRAIS OU SECS
0579	FRUIT FRESH OR DRIED NES	W 1213725	996.1	W 992927	1019.4	W 1159698	982.8	W 946898	882.4	FRUITS FRAIS,SECS NDA
058	FRUIT PRESERVED,PREPARED	W 639907	615.0	W 668997	774.4	W 670720	834.2	W 677911	712.6	CONSERVES DE FRUITS
07	COFFEE,TEA,COCOA,SPICES		558.2		789.1		830.5		702.3	CAFE,THE,CACAO,EPICES
1	BEVERAGES AND TOBACCO		2449.1		2935.8		3154.7		2955.6	BOISSONS ET TABACS
11	BEVERAGES		2286.9		2739.7		2893.5		2744.5	BOISSONS
112	ALCOHOLIC BEVERAGES	W 2055891	2156.9	W 2175674	2598.5	W 1771769	2750.9	W 1769828	2604.9	BOISSONS ALCOOLIQUES
1121	WINE OF FRESH GRAPES ETC	W 1890729	1808.6	W 1970602	2184.2	W 1595577	2372.4	W 1616250	2270.1	VINS DE RAISINS FRAIS
11212	WINE OF FRESH GRAPES	W 1698313	1635.7	W 1762699	1973.9	W 1399731	2139.8	W 1445006	2097.6	VINS DE MOUTS DE RAISINS
2	CRUDE MATERLS,EXCL FUELS		1810.3		2267.4		2337.6		2270.3	MAT BRUTES NON COMESTIBLES
29	CRUDE ANIMAL,VEG MAT NES		546.6		662.4		746.7		721.1	MATIERES BRUTES ANIM,VEGET
3	MINERAL FUELS ETC		3052.1		2932.6		3149.0		3451.6	COMBUSTIBLES MINERAUX LUB
33	PETROLEUM AND PRODUCTS		2981.2		2851.7		3078.9		3362.2	PETROLE ET DERIVES
334	PETROLEUM PRODUCTS,REFIN	MW 19477	2872.1	MW 17156	2755.2	MW 15897	2969.8	MW 19112	3256.4	PRODUITS RAFFINES
3341	GASOLINE,OTH LIGHT OILS			W 3708276	649.1	W 3393318	678.4	W 3981811	785.9	ESSENCES POUR MOTEURS
3343	GAS OILS			W 7092280	1085.9	W 7137267	1345.3	W 8721669	1508.2	GAS OILS
4	ANIMAL,VEGETABLE OIL,FAT		643.7		973.4		1205.5		980.9	HUILES,GRAISSES ANIM,VEG
42	FIXED VEGETABLE OIL,FAT		554.3		851.1		1070.0		869.0	HUILES VEGETALES FIXES
423	FIXED VEG OILS,SOFT	W 251076	499.5	W 272177	775.6	W 247066	984.3	W 303126	795.7	HUILES VEGET DOUCES FIXES
4235	OLIVE OIL	W 157358	424.5	W 187607	706.5	W 174781	928.0	W 215290	730.4	HUILE D'OLIVE
5	CHEMCLS,RELATED PROD NES		13649.5		17430.9		18743.0		18649.7	PRODUITS CHIMIQUES
51	ORGANIC CHEMICALS		2638.0		3340.2		3410.5		3219.7	PROD CHIMIQ ORGANIQUES
514	NITROGEN–FNCTN COMPOUNDS		1043.4	W 175101	1204.2	W 193273	1312.6	W 232927	1151.0	COMPOSES FONCT AZOTEES
53	DYES,TANNING,COLOUR PROD		897.1		1136.4		1294.7		1295.5	PROD TEINTURE,COLORANTS
533	PIGMENTS,PAINTS,ETC		642.9	W 399891	845.5	W 453765	964.5	W 478051	964.0	PIGMENTS,PEINTURES,VERNIS
541	*MEDICINAL,PHARM PRODUCT		2759.3	MK 80770	3630.0	MK 78220	4299.5	MK 78878	4430.4	PROD MEDICINAUX PHARMACEUT
5413	ANTIBIOTICS IN BULK		792.3	K 6096858	993.2	K 6145766	1066.6	K 6678049	851.7	ANTIBIOTIQUES NDA
54139	OTHER ANTIBIOTICS	K 2440721	640.2	K 3198343	789.1	K 3351027	867.1	K 4334419	704.1	AUTRES ANTIBIOTIQUES
5417	MEDICAMENTS	MK 48472	1549.6	MK 66033	2171.1	MK 63474	2718.0	MK 63091	3058.3	MEDICAMENTS
54171	— CONTAINNG ANTIBIOTICS	K 6763074	523.7	K 7820028	679.1	K 6934274	836.7	K 7754736	854.2	MED CONTN ANTIBIOTIQUES
54179	— CONTNG OTH SUBSTANCES	MK 38947	935.1	MK 55049	1373.6	MK 51990	1696.7	MK 49792	1921.2	MED CONT AUT SUBSTANCES
55	PERFUME,CLEANING ETC PRD		1233.8		1505.3		1789.4		1815.5	PROD POUR PARFUM,TOILETTE
553	PERFUMERY,COSMETICS,ETC	W 93182	643.3	W 112601	848.6	W 133281	1006.6	W 152734	1002.4	PRODUITS DE PARFUMERIE
554	SOAP,CLEANSING ETC PREPS	W 458314	512.9	W 473204	574.3	W 530637	687.5	W 655265	718.9	SAVONS,PRODUITS DETERSIFS
58	PLASTIC MATERIALS ETC		3916.0		5272.0		5141.5		5018.8	MAT PLAST ARTIFICIELLES
582	PROD OF CONDENSATION ETC	W 700741	1071.8	W 766273	1519.3	W 795786	1467.8	W 962023	1519.4	PROD CONDENS,POLYCOND
583	POLYMERIZATION ETC PRODS	W 1845227	2746.7	W 1848832	3633.4	W 2066326	3545.0	W 2133453	3376.2	PROD POLYMERISATION
5831	POLYETHYLENE	W 544271	492.0	W 548678	721.5	W 588245	663.2	W 575127	663.4	POLYETHYLENE
5834	POLYVINYL CHLORIDE	W 409979	585.8	W 376799	725.1	W 414012	677.5	W 440381	663.1	CHLORURE DE POLYVINYLE
5839	OTH POLYMRZTION ETC PROD	W 382517	882.5	W 384994	1100.9	W 458857	1169.9	W 496479	1095.8	AUT PROD POLYMER COPOLYM
59	CHEMICAL MATERIALS NES		1738.3		1965.7		2161.8		2222.3	MAT PROD CHIMIQUES NDA
598	MISCEL CHEM PRODUCTS NES	W 818935	1340.0	W 664427	1495.1	W 674734	1596.3	W 776171	1681.6	PROD DIV INDUST CHIM NDA
5989	CHEM PRODUCTS,PREPS NES	W 644330	1111.0	W 480413	1227.6	W 483732	1319.0	W 561773	1403.7	PROD PREP CHIMIQUES NDA
59899	OTH CHEM PRODS,PREPS,NES	W 522366	869.7	W 399056	920.9	W 388443	972.5	W 456507	1033.1	AUT PRODUITS CHIMIQUES NDA
6	BASIC MANUFACTURES		43399.6		52881.5		54817.5		52188.7	ART MANUFACTURES
61	LEATHER,DRESSED FUR,ETC		3446.3		3989.8		4540.9		4284.4	CUIRS,PELLETERIES
611	LEATHER	W 174322	2661.8	W 192076	3066.0	W 223411	3425.2	W 236480	3186.3	CUIRS,PEAUX PREPARES
6114	LEATHR BOVINE NES,EQUINE	W 123360	1595.8	W 143704	1931.0	W 163946	2142.1	W 187425	2048.4	CUIRS DE BOVINS
612	LEATHER ETC MANUFACTURES	W 87998	731.4	W 93806	849.1	W 107422	958.0	W 121916	943.3	OUVRAGES EN CUIRS NDA
6123	PREPRD PARTS OF FOOTWEAR	W 86559	683.0	W 92304	794.7	W 105886	900.4	W 120315	891.3	PARTIES DE CHAUSSURES
62	RUBBER MANUFACTURES NES		1992.2		2447.9		2642.0		2492.0	CAOUTCHOUC MANUFACTURE
625	RUBBER TYRES, TUBES ETC	W 234892	988.1	W 270347	1202.6	W 273733	1221.3	W 292318	1100.0	PNEUS CAOUTCHOUC VULCANISE
6251	TYRES NEW FOR MOTOR CARS	W 131649	630.9	W 141937	734.0	W 136539	711.8	W 143218	629.0	PNEUS POUR VOITURES
63	WOOD,CORK MANUFACTRS NES		804.7		951.1		1006.3		949.0	OUVRAGES LIEGE ET BOIS
64	PAPER,PAPERBOARD AND MFR		2817.4		3906.4		3981.8		3752.4	PAPIERS,CARTONS & OUVRAGES
641	PAPER AND PAPERBOARD		1815.1	W 1964908	2543.4	W 2059537	2382.5	W 2353711	2252.5	PAPIERS ET CARTONS
6412	PRINTG,WRITING PAPER NES	W 730514	674.8	W 755402	936.4	W 763716	804.5	W 843911	752.2	PAPIERS POUR L'IMPRESSION
64122	— COATED,IMPREGNATD ETC	W 724701	661.1	W 746737	914.3	W 745488	772.8	W 811720	710.8	PAPIERS IMPRESSION COUCHES
6418	COATED ETC PAPER NES BLK	W 456875	523.1	W 465181	744.1	W 498311	763.2	W 527668	683.2	PAP,CARTONS COUCHES,ENDUITS
642	PAPER,ETC,PRECUT,ARTS OF		1002.4	W 603168	1363.1	W 711229	1599.3	W 804941	1499.9	PAP,CARTONS DECOUPES
65	TEXTILE YARN,FABRICS,ETC		10874.9		12809.2		13219.7		12899.8	FILS,TISSUS,ARTICLES TEXTILE
651	TEXTILE YARN	W 367546	2222.9	W 394832	2602.1	W 431240	2736.7	W 458061	2672.4	FILS TEXTILES
6514	SYN FIB YRN,BULK,MONOFIL	W 158074	665.8	W 168286	803.9	W 171639	807.8	W 178702	737.7	FILS CONT 85% FIB TEXT SYNTH
652	COTTON FABRICS,WOVEN		1278.5	W 115939	1591.2	W 119116	1713.8	W 129881	1705.9	TISSUS DE COTON
6522	WOVEN COTTON BLEACHD,ETC		1160.1	W 106534	1476.2	W 110832	1600.8	W 120600	1593.3	TISSUS COTON BLANCHIS ETC
65224	BLCHED COTTON FABRIC NES		820.5	W 82491	1058.5	W 86083	1181.3	W 92167	1169.2	AUT TIS PLUS 85% COT BLANCHI
653	WOVN MAN–MADE FIB FABRIC		2260.6	W 131268	2643.3	W 130670	2543.2	W 141557	2420.4	TISSUS FIBRES SYNTH,ARTIF
6531	CONT SYNT WEAVES NONPILE	W 33705	583.8	W 35339	659.9	W 34827	637.8	W 40585	685.3	TISSUS FIBRES SYNTH CONTINUE
6534	DISC SYN BLEND FABRC NES		571.7	W 39443	555.3	W 40585	565.5	W 44720	515.7	TISSUS FIBRES SYNTH DISCONT
654	OTH WOVEN TEXTILE FABRIC	W 93191	2775.3	W 94105	3072.2	W 92128	3002.6	W 98366	2888.0	TISSUS AUT COTON SYNT,ARTIF
6542	WOVEN WOOL,HAIR NONPILE	W 29642	1140.6	W 29151	1306.0	W 32584	1375.2	W 34236	1328.6	TIS PLUS 85% LAINE,POILS
65422	WOVN COMB WOOL,FINE HAIR	W 20213	833.6	W 19856	972.0	W 21999	1020.4	W 21740	969.3	TISSUS 85% LAINE,PLS PEIG
6543	WOVEN WOOL ETC FABRC NES	W 42632	767.8	W 44836	921.6	W 45727	925.1	W 48741	887.0	TISSUS LAINE,POILS FINS NDA
65432	WOOL–DISC SYN FIBR FABRC	W 38911	643.6	W 39696	747.7	W 41864	787.1	W 45161	774.8	TISSUS LAINE MEL SYNT DISC
655	KNITTED,ETC FABRICS	W 43526	652.6	W 45735	763.9	W 49401	854.5	W 58957	889.1	ETOF BONNETERIE PIECES ETC
6552	OTHER KNIT ETC FAB NONEL	W 43526	652.6	W 45735	763.9	W 49401	854.5	W 58957	889.1	ETOF BON NON ELAS NON SYNT
657	SPECIAL TXTL FABRC,PRODS	W 167040	1075.0	W 189582	1362.7	W 208235	1504.6	W 232403	1499.8	TISSUS SPECIAUX
6573	COATED ETC TEXTILES NES	W 63678	546.7	W 66692	644.7	W 71620	725.5	W 76482	720.1	TISSUS,ART MATIERE TEXT NDA
66	NONMETAL MINERAL MFS NES		7486.0		8744.6		9035.3		8555.3	ART MIN NON METALLIQUES
661	LIME,CEMENT,BLDG PRODS	W 3512502	1910.8	W 4315553	2201.3	W 4715355	2342.8	W 4951002	2245.7	CHAUX,CIMENTS MAT CONSTR
6613	BUILDING STONE ETC WORKD	W 2522787	1709.3	W 2629778	1924.0	W 2652851	2030.2	W 2751401	1935.3	PIERRES A BATIR
66132	BUILDING STONE WORKED	W 2224988	1601.4	W 2360250	1821.2	W 2397463	1942.1	W 2501584	1857.7	OUVR EN PIERRES DE TAILLE
662	CLAY,REFRACTORY BLDG PRD	W 5477135	3131.0	W 5997553	3563.0	W 6135409	3648.6	W 6421130	3442.7	MAT CONST REFRACTAIRES
6624	BRICKS ETC NONREFRACTORY	W 5325927	3007.0	W 5812348	3399.4	W 5936216	3464.9	W 6219876	3276.3	BRIQUES ETC CERAM NON REFR
66244	UNGLAZD CERAMC SETTS ETC	W 598522	348.8	W 829474	487.6	W 1085151	628.8	W 1392186	732.5	CARREAUX, NON VERNIS
66245	GLAZED CERAMIC SETTS ETC	W 4556106	2629.4	W 4730920	2874.3	W 4583758	2798.5	W 4519875	2506.8	AUT CARREAUX CERAMIQUE
663	MINERAL MANUFCTURES NES	W 700675	623.3	W 857577	776.7	W 960997	863.0	W 985656	796.1	ART MIN MANUF NDA
664	GLASS	W 450783	739.1	W 416831	901.6	W 401064	797.4	W 437841	742.1	VERRE

Italy, including San Marino and Holy See

Italie y compris Saint–Martin et Saint–Siège

5. Special Exports F.O.B. by Commodities according to the S.I.T.C. (Rev. 2) in million U.S. Dollars
Exportations Spéciales F.O.B. par Produits d'après la C.T.C.I. (Rév. 2) en millions de Dollars E.U.

SITC CTCI	COMMODITY	1994 QUANTITY QUANTITE	1994 VALUE VALEUR	1995 QUANTITY QUANTITE	1995 VALUE VALEUR	1996 QUANTITY QUANTITE	1996 VALUE VALEUR	1997 QUANTITY QUANTITE	1997 VALUE VALEUR	PRODUIT
665	GLASSWARE	W 473250	691.6	W 548202	836.7	W 528140	899.0	W 564567	873.6	OUVRAGES EN VERRE
67	IRON AND STEEL		6754.0		8496.3		8028.9		7678.6	FER ET ACIER
672	IRON,STEEL PRIMARY FORMS	W 1774286	662.5	W 1798823	943.2	W 2553829	1030.6	W 1669173	746.8	LINGOTS FER,ACIER
6727	IRN,STL COIL FR REROLLNG	W 1140022	438.3	W 973444	577.4	W 1895829	785.7	W 1437048	597.4	EBAUCHES POUR TOLES FER
673	IRON,STEEL SHAPES ETC	W 4093247	1816.1	W 3711660	2209.4	W 3729098	1889.5	W 3772084	1824.4	BARRES,PROFIL FER,ACIER
6732	IRON,STEEL BARS ETC	W 2606144	1148.2	W 2333076	1412.2	W 2183154	1156.6	W 2092469	1078.7	BARRES FER,ACIER
67326	IRN,OTH STL BARS HOTROLD	W 2048965	660.7	W 1719037	670.1	W 1631048	533.1	W 1397623	442.5	BARRES PLEINES FER,ACIER
674	IRN,STL UNIV,PLATE,SHEET	W 2420597	1553.2	W 2167343	1904.1	W 1996865	1606.2	W 2193148	1574.9	LARGES PLATS,TOLES
6746	IRN,STL THIN PLATE,ROLLD	W 715277	512.2	W 682898	748.7	W 646861	572.5	W 609621	529.6	TOLES LAM MOINS 3MM
678	IRON,STL TUBES,PIPES,ETC	W 2073844	2091.2	W 1962837	2631.7	W 2205534	2774.5	W 2586965	2840.4	TUBES,TUYAUX EN FONTE,FER
6783	IRON,STL TUBES,PIPES NES	W 1368576	1056.4	W 1228267	1327.5	W 1445298	1295.1	W 1794176	1461.8	AUT TUBES,TUYAUX FER,ACIER
6785	IRON,STEEL TUBE FITTINGS	W 183523	531.7	W 192300	659.6	W 196303	743.2	W 212374	728.8	ACCESSOIRES DE TUYAUTERIE
68	NON–FERROUS METALS		1928.3		2537.0		2471.0		2332.3	METAUX NON FERREUX
682	COPPER EXC CEMENT COPPER	W 245575	857.1	W 235634	978.7	W 239473	894.9	W 269143	887.0	CUIVRE
6822	COPPER,ALLOYS WORKED	W 229592	816.1	W 212865	912.4	W 220273	846.2	W 250802	842.8	CUIVRE,ALLIAGES OUVRES
684	ALUMINIUM	W 298863	910.7	W 328406	1329.4	W 347077	1285.4	W 367740	1219.9	ALUMINIUM
6842	ALUMINIUM,ALLOYS WORKED	W 274072	872.3	W 291776	1254.1	W 305162	1216.9	W 330481	1157.3	ALUMINIUM,ALLIAGES OUVRE
69	METAL MANUFACTURES NES		7296.4		8999.6		9892.1		9245.4	ART MANUFACT EN METAL NDA
691	STRUCTURES AND PARTS NES	W 361420	744.8	W 443462	1013.0	W 406897	1069.7	W 398640	967.2	CONSTRUCT FER,ACIER,ALU
6911	STRUCTURES,PARTS IRN,STL	W 333488	558.1	W 405488	731.2	W 370227	774.8	W 360814	716.0	CONSTRUCT FER,ACIER,FONTE
694	STL,COPPR NAILS,NUTS,ETC	W 248556	599.8	W 263500	765.1	W 234011	716.0	W 265730	681.8	CLOUS,VIS,ECROUS
69402	IRN,STL NUTS,BOLTS,ETC	W 233712	563.2	W 248072	721.3	W 217945	667.5	W 246804	631.0	BOULONS,VIS,ECROUS FER,AC
695	TOOLS	W 96350	637.4	W 122764	886.2	W 116192	976.7	W 125676	924.6	OUTILS A MAIN
697	BASE MTL HOUSEHOLD EQUIP	W 243414	1313.5	W 256847	1503.2	W 275515	1738.0	W 292455	1624.8	ART MENAGE MET COMMUNS
6974	BASE MTL DMSTC ARTIC NES	W 99197	581.4	W 105672	685.8	W 116307	811.7	W 126577	733.3	ARTICLES NDA FONTE,FER,ETC
699	BASE METAL MFRS NES		3092.1	W 798042	3743.1	W 853152	4194.5	W 933262	4026.1	ART MANUFACTURES MET NDA
6991	LOCKSMITHS WARES,ETC	W 168942	1018.4	W 183485	1221.9	W 197647	1389.2	W 216651	1361.2	ARTICLES DE SERRURERIE
69913	BASE MTL DOOR,ETC FITTNG	W 142377	783.7	W 153561	939.4	W 165849	1077.5	W 184238	1063.7	GARNITURES POUR MEUBLES
6997	IRON,STEEL ARTICLES NES	W 280339	747.8	W 306312	907.5	W 312942	987.9	W 343188	946.5	OUV FONTE,FER,ACIER NDA
69979	IRN,STL MANUFACTURES NES	W 280092	747.1	W 306035	906.5	W 312521	986.1	W 342962	945.4	AUT OUVRAGES EN FER NDA
6998	MFRS NES OF CPR,NIKL,ETC	W 111648	613.8	W 116402	754.1	W 130324	833.1	W 141213	793.2	OUVRAGES EN CU,NI,AL,PB,ZN
7	MACHINES,TRANSPORT EQUIP		69730.7		86706.3		96370.7		90083.4	MACHINES MATERIEL TRANSPORT
71	POWER GENERATING EQUIPMT		3613.9		4616.8		5344.2		5185.7	MACHINES GENERATRICES
713	INTRNL COMBUS PSTN ENGIN	W 144599	1602.6	W 186508	2101.7	W 169669	2061.4	W 183186	2122.3	MOTEURS EXPL COMB INT, PIECE
7132	MOTOR VEHCL PISTN ENGINS	W 54464	609.4	W 77540	905.2	W 56238	717.7	W 68999	855.4	MOTEURS EXPL POUR VEHICULES
7139	PISTON ENGINE PARTS NES	W 66520	728.3	W 82426	880.3	W 83995	974.1	W 88417	976.1	PIECES POUR 713.2,3,8
714	ENGINES AND MOTORS NES		853.4	W 18089	1026.0	W 28020	1502.4	W 25759	1397.5	MOTEURS NON ELECTRIQUES
7149	ENGINE & MOTOR PARTS NES		466.6	W 13804	604.4	W 22089	1015.0	W 18548	933.0	PIECES 714 ET 718.88
716	ROTATING ELECTRIC PLANT	W 122220	905.6	W 138325	1100.1	W 162019	1295.7	W 172898	1199.1	APP ELECTR ROTATIFS,PIECES
7162	AC MTRS,GENRTRS,GEN SETS	W 90366	683.1	W 100052	815.9	W 115006	989.2	W 118175	897.9	MOTEURS ELECTRIQUES
72	MACHS FOR SPCL INDUSTRYS		13353.8		16140.5		17994.8		17297.8	MAC SPECIALES POUR INDUST
721	AGRIC MACHY,EXC TRACTORS		910.2	W 202201	1097.1	W 211299	1294.8	W 213629	1171.0	MACHINES AGRICOLES
722	TRACTORS NON–ROAD	W 123448	725.2	W 151171	974.2	W 172453	1221.6	W 199519	1283.7	TRACTEURS
7224	WHEELED TRACTORS NES	W 120958	714.7	W 148593	963.1	W 169079	1204.6	W 191967	1254.0	TRACTEURS A ROUES
723	CIVIL ENGNEERG EQUIP ETC	W 179885	809.9	W 197669	987.8	W 196864	1080.2	W 216497	1059.1	APPAREILS DE GENIE CIVIL
7234	CONST,MINING MACHNRY NES	W 153064	699.0	W 171264	865.5	W 166337	934.5	W 178574	896.0	MACH POUR LA CONST, MINES
724	TEXTILE,LEATHER MACHNRY	W 185540	2522.2	W 206736	2964.9	W 222509	3399.2	W 233714	3337.7	MACH POUR INDUSTRIE TEXTILE
7244	SPINNING,EXTRDNG,ETC MCH	W 42401	573.9	W 47739	713.7	W 47825	752.0	W 53126	759.4	MACH POUR LE FILAGE
7245	WEAVING,FELT MFG,ETC MCH	W 43841	649.4	W 53302	805.9	W 63165	1053.3	W 66878	1037.3	METIERS A TISSER,PIECES
7247	TEXTILE MACHINERY NES	W 50603	606.2	W 54472	693.1	W 57872	750.1	W 56758	705.9	MACH LAVAGE,TEINTURE TEX
725	PAPER ETC MILL MACHINERY	W 29708	480.8	W 41244	628.7	W 47126	747.0	W 42432	716.7	MACHINES FABR PATE PAPIER
726	PRINTG,BKBINDG MACHY,PTS	W 34641	605.0	W 38117	718.5	W 41793	847.1	W 40732	743.9	MACHINES POUR IMPRIMERIE
727	FOOD MACHRY NON–DOMESTIC	W 49151	855.2	W 54559	969.9	W 57906	1049.3	W 60731	1052.8	MACH INDUSTRIES ALIMENT
7272	OTH FOOD PROC MCHY,PARTS	W 41945	775.4	W 44328	855.3	W 47223	937.3	W 49008	938.2	AUT MACH IND ALIMENTAIRE
72722	INDUS FOOD PROC MACH NES	W 36707	701.4	W 41484	818.9	W 43738	886.3	W 46269	900.3	MACHINES BOULANGERIE
728	OTH MACHY FOR SPCL INDUS	W 551993	6445.8	W 644180	7799.7	W 629426	8355.9	W 629317	7933.3	AUT MACH IND PARTICULIERES
7281	MACH–TOOLS FR SPCL INDUS	W 175526	1779.2	W 193991	2060.6	W 185069	2098.9	W 183274	1970.8	MACH–OUTILS SPEC IND PART
72811	MACH–TOOLS TO WRK MINRLS	W 73561	621.3	W 79203	684.6	W 77944	725.1	W 75079	677.1	MACH POUR TRAVAIL PIERRE
72812	MACH–TOOLS TO WORK WOOD	W 88861	967.1	W 100788	1174.2	W 89657	1106.6	W 94582	1065.0	MACH–OUT POUR TRAVAIL BOIS
7283	OTHR MINERAL WORKG MACHY	W 92876	619.8	W 106857	728.9	W 103423	802.8	W 101351	715.2	MACH TRIER,CRIBLER,BROYER
7284	MACHY FOR SPCL INDUS NES	W 283591	4046.8	W 343332	5010.3	W 340934	5454.3	W 344692	5247.4	MACH SPEC IND PARTICUL.
72842	RUBBER,PLASTICS WRKG MCH	W 59225	931.0	W 70483	1085.7	W 82544	1359.5	W 81648	1301.8	MACH IND CAOUT MAT PLAST
72848	OTH MCHY WITH INDIV FNCT	W 140698	1663.0	W 169334	2176.6	W 135559	2030.3	W 152471	2129.9	AUTRES MACHINES NDA
72849	PTS OF MACHS OF 7284 ETC	W 67543	1144.9	W 80943	1342.8	W 98683	1588.2	W 84185	1357.1	PIECES DU 728.4 ETC
73	METALWORKING MACHINERY		2446.4		3212.3		3902.2		3757.9	MACH TRAVAIL DES METAUX
736	METALWORKING MACH–TOOLS	W 124471	1689.3	W 148102	2169.6	W 172245	2649.6	W 172571	2500.6	MACH–OUTILS TRAVAIL METAUX
7361	METAL CUTTING MACH–TOOLS	W 36494	517.5	W 42870	713.4	W 45426	812.0	W 45141	774.9	MACH–OUT ENLEVEMENT METAL
7362	METAL FORMING MACH–TOOLS	W 47811	475.8	W 55694	562.6	W 67775	713.9	W 70800	719.0	MACH–OUTILS DEFORM METAL
737	METALWORKING MACHNRY NES	W 85164	757.2	W 111178	1042.7	W 122520	1252.7	W 116984	1257.4	MACH TRAV METAUX PIECES
74	GENRL INDUSTRL MACHY NES		15050.0		18659.1		22084.2		20705.0	MACH APP INDUSTRIE
741	HEATING,COOLING EQUIPMNT	W 351213	3089.1	W 417490	3980.5	W 472994	4791.5	W 452394	4162.0	MACH CHAUFFAGE,PIECES
7414	NONDOM REFRIG EQUIPT,PTS	W 113050	850.6	W 135354	1106.6	W 138123	1255.9	W 149758	1171.4	MAT PRODUCTION DU FROID
74141	REFRIG EQUIP NONDOMESTIC	W 67429	609.0	W 87953	807.4	W 90310	931.5	W 91572	846.0	REFIG INDUSTRIELS
7415	AIR–CONDITIONING MACHNRY	W 34653	436.2	W 46972	668.0	W 58064	849.2	W 54848	708.3	GROUPES CONDITION AIR
7416	HEATING,COOLING EQU NES	W 121056	1161.7	W 136776	1420.4	W 156586	1706.4	W 146443	1454.8	APP CHANGEMENT TEMP
742	PUMPS FOR LIQUIDS ETC	W 109039	1118.8	W 127953	1374.1	W 135044	1570.9	W 138347	1499.1	POMPES MOTO–POMPES
7428	OTHER PUMPS FOR LIQUIDS	W 73217	692.9	W 87190	841.8	W 90954	933.5	W 94032	885.0	AUTRES POMPES POUR LIQ
74288	PUMPS FR LIQUIDS NES ETC	W 72676	686.1	W 86265	828.2	W 89292	903.7	W 92303	856.0	POMPES POUR LIQUIDES NDA
743	PUMPS NES,CENTRFUGES ETC	W 286827	2077.9	W 335563	2597.8	W 372704	3061.7	W 387782	2887.7	POMPES COMPRES,VENT ETC
7431	PUMPS FOR GASES ETC	W 129271	812.2	W 147607	976.0	W 158219	1101.2	W 160282	1092.6	POMPES AIR A VIDE,COMPRES
744	MECHANICAL HANDLING EQU	W 301326	1604.3	W 379664	2127.7	W 386338	2428.9	W 406868	2300.1	EQUIP MANUTENTION PIECES
7442	LIFTING,LOADING MACH NES	W 134635	798.1	W 167519	1040.9	W 168925	1187.5	W 169299	1090.2	APP LEVAGE,MANUTENTION
74428	OTH HANDLING ETC MCH NES	W 77715	520.2	W 90880	657.4	W 95711	755.7	W 102940	723.8	AUT APP LEVAGE ETC
7449	PTS NES OF MACHY OF 7442	W 129337	588.8	W 160402	775.0	W 164934	905.9	W 181287	891.8	PIECES DU 744.2
745	NONELEC MACHY,TOOLS NES		2785.8	W 163867	3378.8	W 192593	4095.6	W 184815	3848.3	AUT MACH NON ELEC,PIECES
7452	OTH NONELEC MCHS,PTS NES		2636.3	W 154807	3209.5	W 184066	3912.5	W 177807	3695.9	AUT MACH NON ELEC,PIECES
74522	PACKAGNG,BOTTLNG,ETC MCH		1652.7	W 55949	1925.3	W 65235	2281.9	W 66341	2170.9	MACH NETT BOUTEILLES,ETC
74527	SPRAYING MACHINERY	W 53201	464.6	W 68675	618.4	W 84269	805.5	W 73822	683.2	APP PROJETER ETC LIQUID
749	NONELEC MACH PTS,ACC NES		4374.2	W 425253	5200.4	W 472244	6135.7	W 509312	6008.1	PIECES MACH NON ELEC NDA
7491	BALL,ROLLER,ETC BEARINGS	W 48539	512.0	W 60157	765.5	W 61730	788.3	W 66929	745.3	ROULEMENTS BILLES ETC
7492	COCKS,VALVES ETC NES	W 217783	2411.1	W 233944	2704.1	W 263566	3189.0	W 293007	3277.4	ART ROB,SIM POUR TUYAUX
7493	SHAFT,CRANK,PULLEY ETC		688.4	W 94291	861.8	W 99986	997.4	W 102838	944.8	ARBRES TRANS,VILEBREQUINS
7499	OTH NONELEC MCHY PTS NES		763.0	W 36861	869.2	W 46962	1161.1	W 46538	1040.7	PIECES NON ELECT NDA
74991	FOUNDRY MOULDS ETC NES	W 20797	459.8	W 21756	559.8	W 31344	835.4	W 30170	742.6	MOULES POUR METAUX
75	OFFICE MACHNES,ADP EQUIP		4365.3		5285.9		4841.6		3829.3	MACH BUREAU TRAIT AUTOM
752	AUTOMTIC DATA PROC EQUIP		2169.8	W 31491	2313.0	W 25873	2200.8	W 21124	1647.3	MACH TRAIT INFORMATION
7523	DIGITL CENTRL PROCESSORS	W 9313	1108.3	W 10513	1173.6	W 9468	1176.5	W 8131	913.6	UNITES CENTRALES
7525	ADP PERIPHERAL UNITS	W 17930	604.0	W 18107	650.0	W 11781	410.7	W 8081	278.0	UNITES PERIPHERIQUES
759	OFFICE,ADP MCH PTS,ACCES	W 10308	1898.5	W 12800	2568.4	W 12590	2334.7	W 13426	1932.7	PIECES DU 751 ET 752
7599	ACCTG,ETC,ADP MCH PTS,AC	W 7382	1836.2	W 10203	2510.1	W 9378	2262.5	W 9945	1847.3	PIECES DU 751 ET 752
76	TELECOMM,SOUND EQUIPMENT		1950.9		2662.4		3022.3		3292.9	EQUIPMENT DE TELECOM

5. Special Exports F.O.B. by Commodities according to the S.I.T.C. (Rev. 2) in million U.S. Dollars
Exportations Spéciales F.O.B. par Produits d'après la C.T.C.I. (Rév. 2) en millions de Dollars E.U.

SITC CTCI	COMMODITY	1994 QUANTITY QUANTITE	1994 VALUE VALEUR	1995 QUANTITY QUANTITE	1995 VALUE VALEUR	1996 QUANTITY QUANTITE	1996 VALUE VALEUR	1997 QUANTITY QUANTITE	1997 VALUE VALEUR	PRODUIT
764	TELECOM EQPT,PTS,ACC NES		1448.0	W 45262	2082.3	W 48961	2431.9	W 51409	2916.5	EQUIP TELECOM,PIECES
7641	LINE TELEPHONE,ETC EQUIP	W 6046	342.4	W 6859	429.0	W 7051	531.6	W 6862	750.8	APP TELEPHON PAR FIL
7649	PTS NES OF EQUIPMT OF 76		722.6	W 26456	1058.8	W 29898	1332.0	W 32537	1588.6	PIECES DE LA DIV 76
76491	PTS NES OF APPAR OF 7641	W 3242	331.5	W 4137	549.4	W 5443	725.6	W 7063	913.8	PIECES POUR 764.1
77	ELECTRIC MACHNRY NES ETC		11593.5		14039.2		15058.2		14036.7	MACH APP ELECT NDA
771	ELECTRIC POWER MACHY NES		536.7	W 80896	683.8	W 92619	764.1	W 88732	749.6	MACH PROD,TRANS ELECTR
772	SWITCHGEAR ETC,PARTS NES		1496.2	W 77222	1866.4	W 91715	2173.0	W 96980	2033.2	APP COUPURE,SECT ETC
7721	SWITCHGEAR ETC		1293.6	W 73504	1592.7	W 87635	1906.5	W 91882	1780.1	APP COUPURE,SECTIONMNT
773	ELECTR DISTRIBUTNG EQUIP	W 201760	770.5	W 207613	969.6	W 228936	1038.2	W 248165	1007.7	EQUIPMT DISTRIBUTION ELECT
7731	INSULATED WIRE,CABLE ETC	W 189770	717.5	W 193135	910.2	W 215327	972.4	W 233899	941.9	FILS,CABLES ISOLES ELECT
775	HOUSEHOLD TYPE EQUIP NES	W 881298	4296.9	W 1007996	5131.1	W 1055180	5519.7	W 1117199	5250.8	MACH,APP USAGE DOMESTQUE
7751	HOUSEHOLD LDRY EQUIP NES	W 366881	1304.1	W 421545	1583.1	W 460300	1811.3	W 492484	1773.4	MACH A LAVER ET SECHOIRS
77511	DOMESTIC WASHING MACHNES	W 346141	1191.9	W 398759	1453.6	W 437826	1677.8	W 470015	1651.2	MACH LAVER LINGE MOINS 6 KG
7752	DOM REFRIGERATRS,FREEZRS	W 252759	1203.0	W 291152	1471.5	W 284979	1450.4	W 287867	1291.3	REFRIG,CONGEL MENAGER
77521	DOMESTIC REFRIGERATORS	W 187102	893.4	W 216473	1094.8	W 204618	1037.5	W 212082	950.7	REFRIGERATEURS
7758	ELECTRO–THERMIC APPL NES	W 181042	1212.5	W 200918	1355.6	W 211243	1464.9	W 228903	1444.3	APP ELECTROTHERMIQ NDA
77586	ELECTROTHERM DOM APP NES	W 86655	679.0	W 97003	762.0	W 97395	786.9	W 103851	749.9	APP ELECTRO THERMIQUES
776	TRANSISTORS,VALVES,ETC		2221.9	W 93010	2678.7	W 103107	2720.8	W 121307	2301.0	LAMPES,TUBES,VALVES
7764	ELECTRONIC MICROCIRCUITS		1568.3	W 676	1860.1	W 705	1816.2	W 827	1471.8	MICROSTRUCTURES ELECTRON
778	ELECTRICAL MACHINERY NES		2040.7	W 274652	2453.6	W 283874	2558.0	W 302923	2450.8	AUTRES MACH ELECT NDA
7788	OTH ELEC MACHY,EQUIP NES		953.7	W 97783	1077.8	W 95208	1048.6	W 92850	987.5	AUT MACH APP ELEC NDA
78	ROAD VEHICLES		14339.4		19058.4		20057.3		18485.5	VEHICULES ROUTIERS
781	PASS MOTOR VEH EXC BUSES	W 739747	5897.4	W 878280	8017.1	W 828493	7842.8	W 707176	6445.5	AUTO TRANSPORT PERSONNES
782	LORRIES,SPCL MTR VEH NES	W 302367	2030.5	W 357448	2646.0	W 363357	2783.9	W 381954	2644.0	VEHICULES SPECIAUX,MARCH
7821	LORRIES,TRUCKS	W 254707	1674.2	W 309407	2241.6	W 313527	2370.8	W 335018	2280.7	VEHICULES TRANSP MARCHAND
784	MOTOR VEH PRTS,ACCES NES	W 915391	4429.1	W 1139154	6053.1	W 1209245	6923.8	W 1335375	7021.1	PIECES 722,781,782,783
7849	OTHER MOTOR VEHCL PARTS	W 884053	4245.8	W 1113623	5814.5	W 1184555	6676.5	W 1289052	6603.0	PIECES 722,781,782,783
785	CYCLES,ETC MOTRZD OR NOT	W 154498	1553.5	W 156420	1847.6	W 153697	2010.8	W 152571	1926.1	MOTOCYCLES SCOOTERS
7851	MOTORCYCLES ETC	W 35113	647.0	W 38860	810.4	W 47690	983.1	W 51657	1017.2	MOTO VELO MOTEUR AUXIL
79	OTHR TRANSPORT EQUIPMENT		3017.9		3032.1		4066.2		3493.1	AUTRE MATERIEL TRANSPORT
792	AIRCRAFT ETC		2000.0	W 3687	1600.3	W 4406	1944.3	W 3652	1668.3	APP NAVIGATION AERIENNE
7924	AIRCRFT NES OVER 15000KG	W 4149	1167.9	W 1806	700.2	W 2342	841.0	W 1761	641.9	AERODYNES PLUS 15000 KG
7929	AIRCRAFT PARTS NES		525.3	W 1473	623.9	W 1713	827.2	W 1566	827.9	PIECES DU 792
793	SHIPS AND BOATS ETC	W 360001	722.4	W 378028	1237.4	W 539681	1772.9	W 466782	1505.6	NAVIRES BATEAUX,ETC
7932	SHIPS AND BOATS NES	W 352225	696.5	W 251797	875.8	W 433777	1583.9	W 359782	1359.2	NAVIRES ET BATEAUX
79323	OTHER CARGO VESSELS	W 305123	361.2	W 207270	503.7	W 216849	977.5	W 302001	805.0	AUT BATEAUX TRANS MARCH
8	MISC MANUFACTURED GOODS		43632.3		51839.1		57922.8		54099.0	ART MANUFACTURES DIVERS
812	*PLUMBG,HEATNG,LGHTNG EQ	W 380381	1921.8	W 399139	2213.8	W 423118	2487.4	W 436563	2372.8	APPAR SANITAIRES CHAUFFAGE
8121	CENTRAL HEATING EQUIPMNT	W 196187	589.5	W 201216	704.2	W 217345	819.9	W 232138	830.1	CHAUDIERES,RADIATEURS
8124	LIGHTING EQUIPMENT NES	W 125046	1142.5	W 137767	1299.3	W 137847	1428.7	W 131531	1324.5	APPAREILS ECLAIRAGE ETC
81242	LAMPS,FITTINGS BASE METL	W 93063	962.0	W 100641	1082.5	W 93475	1166.4	W 94373	1095.0	APPAREILS D'ECLAIRAGE
821	*FURNITURE,PARTS THEREOF	W 1411908	6735.4	W 1571245	8365.6	W 1632228	9095.7	W 1717730	8748.1	MEUBLES ET PIECES
8211	CHAIRS,SEATS AND PARTS	W 404354	2515.4	W 445622	3167.8	W 450328	3405.5	W 486519	3383.7	SIEGES ET PIECES
82111	CHAIRS AND OTHER SEATS	W 361842	2349.4	W 391749	2936.9	W 389482	3133.7	W 413930	3107.2	SIEGES
8219	FURNITURE AND PARTS NES	W 987288	4018.4	W 1097942	4934.3	W 1150640	5388.3	W 1199605	5085.6	AUTRES MEUBLES ET PIECES
82192	WOOD FURNITURE NES	W 540930	2490.2	W 616752	3088.5	W 638013	3372.2	W 665308	3161.5	MEUBLES NDA EN BOIS
82199	OTHR FURN,FURN PARTS NES	W 324224	1093.1	W 346292	1320.6	W 373249	1439.1	W 393068	1394.7	MEUBLES NDA AUTRES MATIERES
831	*TRAVEL GOODS,HANDBAGS	W 25617	1243.6	W 28031	1566.7	W 27266	1864.1	W 26616	1532.7	ARTICLES DE VOYAGE ETC
83101	HANDBAGS NES	W 14080	852.1	W 15456	1065.3	W 14324	1273.0	W 13333	1023.9	SACS A MAIN
84	CLOTHING AND ACCESSORIES		12528.2		14178.4		16177.9		14861.8	VETEMENTS
842	MENS OUTERWEAR NOT KNIT	W 49185	2144.2	W 50483	2514.0	W 52116	2815.3	W 50333	2471.8	VET DESSUS POUR HOMMES
8423	— TROUSERS,BREECHES ETC	W 31396	895.4	W 31416	977.2	W 32537	1085.1	W 31514	968.5	PANTALONS HOMMES MAT TEX
8429	— OTHER OUTER GARMENTS	W 10069	604.5	W 10786	768.8	W 11172	875.8	W 10025	682.4	AUT VET DES HOM MAT TEX
843	WOMENS OUTERWEAR NONKNIT	W 45455	3078.2	W 47815	3593.1	W 52071	4154.2	W 52193	3886.6	VET DESSUS FEMMES MAT TEX
8439	— OTHER OUTER GARMENTS	W 32148	1946.9	W 32927	2129.7	W 37295	2569.1	W 36972	2443.1	AUT VET DES FEM MAT TEXT
845	OUTERWEAR KNIT NONELASTC	W 83283	3740.9	W 76653	3969.3	W 81052	4378.7	W 80667	3970.2	VET DESSOUS,ACCES BONNET
8451	— JERSEYS,PULLOVERS ETC	W 63716	2788.0	W 57186	2908.7	W 57763	3120.8	W 58317	2858.6	CHANDAILS,PULL–OVERS ETC
8459	— OTHER,CLTHG ACCESRYS	W 17081	771.4	W 16661	833.2	W 20423	1030.2	W 19799	919.9	AUT VET DESSUS DE BONNE
846	UNDER GARMENTS KNITTED	W 40278	1181.9	W 45030	1390.7	W 48551	1689.2	W 49080	1584.6	SOUS VETS DE BONNETERIE
8463	— OF SYNTH FBR NONELAST	W 24954	581.3	W 27597	667.3	W 29242	873.2	W 30498	840.2	SOUS–VET BONNET FIB SYNT
84631	—— PANTY HOSE (TIGHTS)	W 23833	518.7	W 26161	582.2	W 27451	762.8	W 28694	744.6	COLLANTS BON FIBR SYNT
847	TEXTILE CLTHNG ACCES NES	W 34897	1189.0	W 32465	1306.9	W 36348	1514.9	W 37795	1421.7	ACCES VET MAT TEXT NDA
8471	— NOT KNITTED	W 9529	819.9	W 9932	933.6	W 10527	1052.8	W 11241	987.5	ACCES VET MAT TEX NON BON
848	HEADGEAR,NONTXTL CLOTHNG	W 15435	743.9	W 15548	828.9	W 17017	954.5	W 17181	881.3	VET ACCES MAT AUT QUE TEX
851	*FOOTWEAR	W 290725	6465.4	W 295826	7304.5	W 299666	8070.7	W 295976	7238.0	CHAUSSURES
85101	FOOTWEAR RUBBER,PLASTIC	W 68103	733.4	W 67887	801.4	W 63343	797.9	W 58810	689.0	CHAUS SEMELLES CAOUTCH
85102	FOOTWEAR LEATHER	W 215362	5620.8	W 220981	6392.2	W 229590	7148.9	W 230628	6431.6	CHAUS SEMELLES EN CUIR
87	PRECISION INSTRUMNTS NES		2035.7		2442.4		2803.0		2656.0	INSTRUM,APPAR SCIENT NDA
874	MEASURNG,CONTROLNG INSTR		1491.1	W 35305	1762.8	W 40616	2007.0	W 42731	1895.1	INSTRUMENTS DE MESURE
88	PHOTO EQU,OPTICL GDS ETC		1568.4		2004.8		2380.6		2315.6	APP,FOURN PHOTO,OP,MONTR
884	OPTICAL GOODS NES		782.8	W 4190	1047.8	W 4723	1269.3	W 5046	1179.1	ELEMENTS OPTIQ,ART LUNET
8842	SPECTACLES AND FRAMES	W 2897	753.2	W 3837	1015.1	W 4387	1236.3	W 4718	1145.8	LUNETTES ET MONTURES
88421	SPECTACLE FRAMES	W 1961	581.5	W 2406	702.8	W 2396	773.3	W 2683	723.3	MONTURES DE LUNETTES
89	MISC MANUFCTRD GOODS NES		11134.1		13763.2		15043.7		14374.2	ART MANUFACTURES DIVERS
892	PRINTED MATTER	W 354251	1208.2	W 391952	1521.8	W 412476	1607.3	W 416791	1428.1	IMPRIMES
893	ARTICLES OF PLASTIC NES		2856.4		3612.9		3893.2		3843.3	OUVRAGES EN MAT DIVIS 58
8931	PLSTC PACKG CONTNRS,LIDS	W 176828	512.5	W 197551	674.5	W 218279	734.4	W 261421	789.8	ART TRANSP EMBALLAGE ETC
8939	MISC PLASTIC ARTICLES	W 583909	2216.2	W 594484	2769.8	W 651386	2949.0	W 709959	2841.1	ART DIVERS EN MAT DIV 58
89399	OTHR PLASTC ARTICLES NES	W 577517	2194.3	W 587886	2742.1	W 641710	2897.3	W 696227	2766.0	AUT OUV MAT DIV 58
894	TOYS,SPORTING GOODS,ETC	W 182269	1454.3	W 202911	1805.6	W 201190	1934.2	W 209227	1764.8	VOITURES ENFANTS,JOUETS
8942	TOYS,INDOOR GAMES ETC	W 105243	725.0	W 116677	845.7	W 110060	845.6	W 113964	768.0	JOUETS,JEUX ETC
896	WORKS OF ART ETC		48.5		609.2		1092.0		1074.4	OBJETS D'ART
89603	ORIGINAL SCULPTURE ETC		17.2		578.3		1033.5		1028.9	PROD ORIG STATUAIRE
897	GOLD,SILVER WARE,JEWELRY		4297.6		4745.7		4954.9		4802.0	BIJOUTERIE,ORFEVRERIE
8973	PREC JEWLRY,GLD–SILVWARE		4200.6		4644.2		4849.2		4706.7	BIJOUX OR,ARGENT ORFEVRE
89731	PRECIOUS METAL JEWELLERY		4114.9		4542.0		4740.0		4608.4	ART BIJOUTERIE,JOAILLER
899	OTHER MANUFACTURED GOODS		648.6		739.8		823.9		805.4	AUT ART MANUF DIVERS NDA
9	GOODS NOT CLASSD BY KIND		1945.9		2153.7		2246.3		2359.0	ART TRANSACT NON CLASSES
931	*SPECIAL TRANSACTIONS	W 1754092	1727.1	W 1267509	1961.4	W 1382726	2037.0	W 1413546	2153.3	TRANS.SPECIALES

FOOT NOTES – NOTES

TABLE 1 –
1 Values are in thousand million lire.
TABLEAU 1 –
1 Les valeurs sont exprimées en milliards de lires.

1. HISTORICAL SERIES, 1962–1997 GENERAL TRADE, IMPORTS C.I.F., EXPORTS F.O.B.
SERIES HISTORIQUES, 1962–1997 COMMERCE GENERAL, IMPORTATIONS C.A.F., EXPORTATIONS F.O.B

YEAR ANNEE	VALUE IN MILLION JAMAICAN DOLLARS / VALEUR EN MILLION JAMAICAN DOLLARS — MERCHANDISE – MARCHANDISE: IMPORTS	MERCHANDISE – MARCHANDISE: EXPORTS	GOLD – OR: IMPORTS	GOLD – OR: EXPORTS	CONVERSION FACTORS U.S. CENTS PER JAMAICAN DOLLAR / FACTEURS DE CONVERSION CENTS E.U. PAR JAMAICAN DOLLAR: IMPORTS	CONVERSION FACTORS: EXPORTS	INDEX NUMBERS – INDICES — QUANTUM: IMPORTS	QUANTUM: EXPORTS	UNIT VALUE – VALEUR UNITAIRE: IMPORTS	UNIT VALUE – VALEUR UNITAIRE: EXPORTS
1962	159.20	129.70			140.0000	140.0000				
1963	161.10	144.20			140.0000	140.0000				
1964	206.70	154.50			140.0000	140.0000				
1965	206.50	153.10			140.0000	140.0000				
1966	233.70	162.90			140.0000	140.0000				
1967	252.60	163.30			138.1300	138.5750				
1968	320.40	183.00			120.0000	120.0000				
1969	363.30	211.80			120.0000	120.0000				
1970	437.80	284.80			120.0000	120.0000				
1971	459.80	282.70			120.0000	120.0000				
1972	489.30	300.20			125.7570	126.0920				
1973	615.10	354.60			110.6420	110.6420				
1974	850.80	549.10			110.0000	110.0000				
1975	1021.40	690.20			110.0000	110.0000				
1976	829.80	572.80			110.0000	110.0000				
1977	781.60	698.60			110.0000	110.0000				
1978	1260.00	1142.50			69.8794	68.9586				
1979	1754.40	1445.80			56.5432	56.5310				
1980	2086.60	1715.00			56.1349	56.1350				
1981	2623.40	1735.10			56.1349	56.1350				
1982	2460.30	1367.00			56.1350	56.1350				
1983	2841.00	1392.10			53.8694	52.6045				
1984	4509.50	2732.50			25.4151	25.7863				
1985	6146.70	3128.30			18.0641	18.0379				
1986	5322.40	3225.90			18.2520	18.2528				
1987	6790.50	3873.60			18.2241	18.2244				
1988	7983.20	4830.30			18.2197	18.2210				
1989	10668.30	5746.60			17.3702	17.3618				
1990	13923.00	8305.00			13.8168	13.9464				
1991	20830.00	13079.00			8.6926	8.3885				
1992	38267.01	24099.01			4.3765	4.3478				
1993	53737.01	26421.01			3.9684	4.0548				
1994	73631.01	40121.01			3.0159	3.0175				
1995	99418.00	49916.00			2.8245	2.8454				
1996	108464.00	51500.00			2.7034	2.6826				
1997	107129.00	47885.01			2.8203	2.8221				

2. IMPORTS BY BROAD ECONOMIC CATEGORY AND EXPORTS BY INDUSTRIAL ORIGIN. (PERCENTAGE OF TOTAL VALUE)
IMPORTATIONS PAR CATEGORIES ECONOMIQUES ET EXPORTATIONS PAR BRANCHE D'ACTIVITE.(EN POURCENTAGE DE LA VALEUR TOTALE)

IMPORTS – IMPORTATIONS

	1990	1991	1992	1993	1994	1995	1996
TOTAL IMPORTS–IMPORTATIONS TOTALES	100.	100.	100.	100.	100.	100.	100.
1 FOOD BEV–ALIMENTATION BOISSONS	12.9	12.5	12.9	12.1	11.8	11.9	12.1
11 PRIMARY–PRODUITS DE BASE	5.8	6.3	7.0	6.0	5.2	4.4	4.4
111 FOR INDUSTRY–POUR L'INDUSTRIE	2.7	3.6	4.3	3.0	2.3	1.5	1.3
112 FOR HOUSEHOLDS–POUR LES MENAGES	3.1	2.7	2.7	3.0	3.0	2.9	3.1
12 PROCESSED–PRODUITS ELABORES	7.1	6.2	5.9	6.1	6.5	7.5	7.8
121 FOR INDUSTRY–POUR L'INDUSTRIE	1.6	1.2	1.2	0.9	1.0	1.3	1.1
122 FOR HOUSEHOLDS–POUR LES MENAGES	5.5	4.9	4.7	5.2	5.6	6.2	6.7
2 IND SUPPLIES–APPROV INDUSTRIELS	28.3	29.4	30.5	26.1	26.8	27.6	24.4
21 PRIMARY–PRODUITS DE BASE	2.2	2.1	1.8	1.9	2.2	1.8	2.1
22 PROCESSED–PRODUITS ELABORES	26.1	27.4	28.7	24.3	24.7	25.7	22.4
3 FUELS–COMBUSTIBLES	19.7	17.8	17.8	15.6	14.8	12.6	15.2
31 PRIMARY–PRODUITS DE BASE	1.0	7.5	9.3	6.1	4.7	3.8	3.6
32 PROCESSED–PRODUITS ELABORES	18.8	10.2	8.5	9.5	10.0	8.8	11.6
321 MOTOR SPIRIT–ESSENCE	1.4	1.5	0.4	0.6	9.9	8.6	2.4
322 OTHER–AUTRES	17.4	8.7	8.1	8.9	0.1	0.2	9.2
4 MACHINERY–EQUIPEMENT	15.2	13.2	13.5	12.7	14.3	15.0	14.6
41 CAPITAL EQUIPMENT–MACHINES	12.9	10.6	10.9	10.5	12.0	13.1	12.4
42 PARTS–PIECES ACCESSOIRES	2.3	2.6	2.5	2.3	2.3	1.9	2.1
5 TRANSPORT–TRANSPORT	10.3	13.6	8.6	13.4	10.2	11.7	11.9
51 PASSENGER CARS–AUTOMOBILES	2.2	3.7	2.6	6.8	4.6	5.5	4.7
52 OTHER–AUTRES	5.8	6.9	2.7	4.1	3.0	3.4	4.4
521 INDUSTRIAL–INDUSTRIELS	5.7	6.8	2.6	4.0	2.9	3.3	4.3
522 NON INDUSTRIAL–NON INDUSTRIEL	0.2	0.1	0.1	0.1	0.1	0.1	0.1
53 PARTS–PIECES ACCESSOIRES	2.3	2.9	3.3	2.5	2.6	2.8	2.8
6 CONSUM GOODS–BIENS CONSOMMATION	11.9	12.3	15.1	17.3	19.9	18.2	18.9
61 DURABLE–DURABLES	2.1	2.3	3.2	3.5	4.0	4.0	4.1
62 SEMI DURABLE–SEMI DURABLES	6.4	7.1	8.8	10.8	12.5	10.9	11.0
63 NON DURABLE–NON DURABLES	3.4	3.0	3.0	3.0	3.3	3.3	3.8
7 GOODS NES–BIENS NDA	1.7	1.2	1.8	2.7	2.2	3.0	2.9

EXPORTS – EXPORTATIONS

	1990	1991	1992	1993	1994	1995	1996
TOTAL EXPORTS–EXPORTATIONS TOTALES	100.	100.	100.	100.	100.	100.	100.
1 AGRICULTURE	7.0	8.0	9.3	9.2	9.6	9.4	9.9
2 MINING QUARRY–INDUS EXTRACTIVES	9.2	9.9	8.6	8.0	6.2	5.3	5.8
3 MANUFACTURING–IND MANUFACTUR	83.8	82.0	82.0	82.7	84.3	85.3	84.3
31 FOOD BEV TOBACCO–ALIM BOISS TAB	12.2	12.9	14.0	16.0	11.6	12.4	13.8
32 TEXTILES–INDUSTRIES TEXTILES	7.7	8.3	15.0	18.9	20.8	20.4	18.3
33 WOOD & PRODUCTS–BOIS & PRODUITS	0.0	0.0	0.0	0.0	0.0	0.0	0.1
34 PAPER & PRODUCTS–PAPIER & PRODT	0.2	0.2	0.2	0.2	0.2	0.2	0.4
35 CHEMICALS–INDUSTRIES CHIMIQUES	59.1	51.1	49.2	44.7	47.5	47.8	48.3
36 NON METAL MIN–MIN NON METAL	0.3	0.3	0.4	0.3	0.3	0.3	0.1
37 BASIC METAL–IND METAL BASE	0.2	0.1	0.1	0.1	0.1	0.1	0.1
38 METAL MANUF–MANUF METAL	4.0	9.1	2.9	2.4	3.4	3.9	3.1
39 OTH MANUF IND–AUTRES MANUF	0.1	0.1	0.2	0.2	0.3	0.2	0.1

3. TRADE BY PRINCIPAL COUNTRIES OF ORIGIN AND DESTINATION (VALUE IN MILLION U.S. DOLLARS)
ECHANGES SELON LES PRINCIPAUX PAYS D'ORIGINE ET DE DESTINATION (VALEUR EN MILLIONS DE DOLLARS EU)

COUNTRIES–PAYS	GENERAL IMPORTS C.I.F. IMPORTATIONS GENERALES C.A.F					COUNTRIES–PAYS	EXPORTS EXPORTATIONS ES F.O.B.				
	1992	1993	1994	1995	1996		1992	1993	1994	1995	1996
World	1773.8	2189.2	2221.4	2772.9	2916.4	Monde	1050.4	1075.4	1210.7	1423.8	1386.9
Africa	0.7	0.9	1.2	1.7	2.0	Afrique	49.7	43.1	45.0	49.8	43.8
Americas	1373.4	1579.4	1670.0	1990.4	2167.3	Amériques	593.4	618.2	696.0	778.9	758.1
– Northern America	1028.6	1188.8	1277.0	1505.6	1614.3	– Amérique du Nord	512.2	532.0	588.2	679.4	678.4
– LAIA	214.9	205.0	187.3	195.0	207.9	– ALAI	8.9	12.2	35.4	23.2	10.2
– CACM	7.3	9.0	12.2	14.1	25.5	– MCAC	0.7	0.4	0.4	0.9	1.1
– Caribbean	95.2	159.6	178.1	256.6	293.5	– Caraïbes	59.4	62.4	59.9	61.2	54.6
– Rest of America	27.4	17.0	15.3	18.9	26.2	– Autre Amérique	12.0	11.2	12.2	14.2	13.8
Asia excl fmr USSR	142.6	266.1	230.6	325.1	257.9	Asie anc. URSS exclus	15.8	22.3	17.2	36.6	32.5
– Middle East	11.4	4.9	9.8	36.4	17.6	– Moyen–Orient	0.1	3.3	0.1	0.0	0.0
Asia former USSR		0.5	0.0	0.1	0.1	Asie ancienne URSS		0.0		0.0	0.0
Europe excl fmr USSR	194.5	235.4	241.5	332.8	359.6	Europe anc. URSS exclus	383.2	376.1	404.5	517.7	524.0
– European Union	175.3	204.5	211.9	296.7	326.5	– Union Européenne	268.8	278.0	302.8	408.9	432.7
– Eastern Europe	2.3	6.9	7.1	10.5	7.9	– Europe de l'Est	0.1	0.1	0.3	0.5	0.5
– Rest of Europe	16.9	24.0	22.5	25.6	25.2	– Autre de l'Europe	114.2	98.1	101.4	108.2	90.9
Europe former USSR	1.7	6.8	3.6	4.6	6.4	Europe ancienne URSS	4.2	8.6	42.4	37.5	25.6
Oceania	13.6	19.7	14.4	20.3	20.1	Océanie	2.6	2.3	2.4	2.7	2.6
Other	47.4	80.4	60.0	97.9	103.0	Autre	1.4	4.6	3.1	0.7	0.3
USA/Etats–Unis d'Amer	953.4	1099.6	1195.8	1406.5	1526.4	USA/Etats–Unis d'Amer	391.4	423.8	440.9	525.5	514.5
Japan/Japon	85.6	184.0	132.7	184.8	163.8	United Kingdom	177.0	147.9	162.0	191.8	183.6
Trinidad and Tobago	32.6	79.7	121.9	203.4	242.8	Canada	119.8	107.3	146.6	153.1	163.5
United Kingdom	86.0	94.7	96.5	112.5	116.1	Norway,Svalbard and JM	113.7	97.2	101.3	107.8	90.7
Canada	75.2	89.1	81.2	99.2	87.9	Netherlands/Pays–Bas	55.9	61.0	48.9	107.8	123.6
Mexico/Mexique	114.4	78.2	63.0	71.7	74.6	France, Monaco	3.3	58.4	62.9	85.1	80.0
Venezuela	70.1	90.8	70.8	56.7	66.8	Ghana	49.6	43.1	42.0	49.6	43.5
Areas n.e.s.	28.8	53.9	47.0	80.7	79.6	Russian Federation	4.2	8.4	42.4	37.4	25.6
Brazil/Brésil	24.3	27.2	35.8	42.5	51.2	Japan/Japon	15.1	18.5	15.6	27.3	31.3
Germany/Allemagne	23.2	32.5	25.3	37.7	34.1	Trinidad and Tobago	26.3	21.9	20.4	21.2	17.0
Netherlands Antilles	42.8	50.5	29.0	18.8	8.9	Brazil/Brésil	7.4	7.7	29.7	16.6	3.1
France, Monaco	13.8	17.6	20.2	34.3	63.4	Barbados/Barbade	12.5	13.3	12.7	12.2	12.0
Netherlands/Pays–Bas	11.1	15.6	19.2	20.3	34.5	Sweden/Suède	5.7	4.0	19.2	16.0	16.3
Free zones/Zone franches	18.7	26.6	13.0	17.2	23.4	Guyana	4.9	6.0	6.9	6.8	5.8
Italy/Italie	16.0	14.6	16.4	23.7	18.6	Germany/Allemagne	4.6	5.5	6.4	5.8	5.8
China/Chine	9.7	17.8	16.8	18.4	22.4	Finland/Finlande	20.4	0.0	0.1	0.5	3.5
Turkey/Turquie	10.5	4.3	8.8	35.5	16.9	Belize/Bélize	3.9	3.8	3.7	5.0	3.9
New Zealand	12.8	16.8	11.2	15.7	16.7	Saint Lucia/Ste–Lucie	3.5	4.2	4.2	3.7	3.1
Switzerland,Liechtenst.	10.9	15.6	12.4	16.6	16.6	Portugal	0.0				18.2
China, Hong Kong SAR	10.4	19.2	15.3	14.6	10.2	Cayman Is/Is Caïmans	2.5	2.8	3.0	3.7	3.7
Other Asia n.e.s.	9.6	14.2	13.2	17.3	15.0	Mexico/Mexique	1.0	3.4	3.2	3.5	3.2
Barbados/Barbade	5.9	14.8	11.9	15.4	19.5	Dominican Republic	2.5	3.0	2.2	2.7	3.7
Spain/Espagne	7.7	3.8	7.0	16.6	19.3	Antigua and Barbuda	2.8	3.4	2.8	2.4	2.5
Belgium–Luxembourg	6.2	6.2	8.2	14.0	16.8	New Zealand	2.3	2.1	2.2	2.1	2.4
Guyana	17.7	8.0	5.7	6.7	7.5	Free zones/Zone franches	1.4	4.6	3.1	0.7	0.3
Panama	7.8	5.9	7.2	9.9	14.2	St Vincent & Grenadines	1.5	1.9	1.7	2.0	1.6
Norway,Svalbard and JM	5.9	8.4	10.0	8.8	7.4	Dominica/Dominique	1.6	1.7	1.8	1.6	1.8
Costa Rica	4.3	5.5	8.9	9.3	10.8	Suriname/Surinam	2.6	1.1	1.1	1.2	2.4
Korea, Republic of			15.9	22.5		Saint Kitts and Nevis	1.4	1.6	1.6	1.5	1.7
Thailand/Thaïlande	6.4	8.1	6.5	9.6	6.8	Bahamas	1.0	0.9	2.0	1.4	2.1
Sweden/Suède	4.3	9.0	7.0	9.1	5.7	Grenada/Grenade	1.3	1.8	1.5	1.1	1.1
Dominica/Dominique	6.7	6.4	4.5	5.6	10.9	Belgium–Luxembourg	1.2	0.8	2.3	1.0	0.5
Colombia/Colombie	3.9	5.1	7.4	8.3	9.2	Guadeloupe	0.8	2.3	0.9	1.7	
Indonesia/Indonésie	2.5	3.6	6.4	5.4	6.7	Netherlands Antilles	0.6	1.2	1.1	1.2	1.5
Guatemala	1.2	1.3	1.8	4.1	13.9	Martinique	0.2	0.9	2.0	2.4	
Ireland/Irlande	3.1	3.3	2.8	4.9	7.3	Bangladesh			0.2	4.7	0.6
Finland/Finlande	0.7	1.6	4.6	10.4	3.8	Colombia/Colombie	0.2	0.8	1.6	1.5	1.0
Dominican Republic	2.9	3.3	3.5	3.5	5.7	Haiti/Haïti	0.1	0.3	1.0	1.6	1.2
Malaysia/Malaisie	1.9	3.0	3.0	5.0	5.4	Panama	0.5	0.3	0.4	1.1	1.7
Austria/Autriche	1.2	2.4	1.4	10.9	2.1	Bermuda/Bermudes	1.0	0.9	0.6	0.8	0.4

(VALUE AS PERCENTAGE OF WORLD TOTAL)(VALEURS EN POURCENTAGE DU TOTAL MONDIAL)

	1987	1988	1989	1990	1991	1992	1993	1994	1995	1996
Africa	0.6	0.0	0.0	0.0	0.0	0.0	0.0	0.1	0.1	0.1
Americas	72.7	71.9	74.0	76.4	73.4	77.4	72.1	75.2	71.8	74.3
– Northern America	55.0	56.1	56.6	55.4	56.0	58.0	54.3	57.5	54.3	55.4
– LAIA	11.9	10.5	10.5	14.6	9.9	12.1	9.4	8.4	7.0	7.1
– CACM	0.6	0.5	0.5	0.3	0.3	0.4	0.4	0.5	0.5	0.9
– Caribbean	4.4	4.1	5.5	5.4	6.5	5.4	7.3	8.0	9.3	10.1
– Rest of America	0.8	0.6	0.9	0.7	0.8	1.5	0.8	0.7	0.7	0.9
Asia excl fmr USSR	8.3	8.0	7.8	7.6	9.0	8.0	12.2	10.4	11.7	8.8
– Middle East	0.0	0.1	0.1	0.0	0.1	0.6	0.2	0.4	1.3	0.6
Asia former USSR							0.0	0.0	0.0	0.0
Europe excl fmr USSR	15.0	16.9	14.2	12.7	15.0	11.0	10.8	10.9	12.0	12.3
– European Union	14.1	15.8	12.9	11.3	14.0	9.9	9.3	9.5	10.7	11.2
– Eastern Europe	0.2	0.4	0.5	0.2	0.2	0.1	0.3	0.3	0.4	0.3
– Rest of Europe	0.6	0.7	0.9	1.3	0.8	1.0	1.1	1.0	0.9	0.9
Europe former USSR	0.6	0.4	0.5	0.3	0.1	0.1	0.3	0.2	0.2	0.2
Oceania	0.8	1.0	1.2	0.9	0.6	0.8	0.9	0.6	0.7	0.7
Other	2.0	1.7	2.2	2.1	1.8	2.7	3.7	2.7	3.5	3.5
USA/Etats–Unis d'Amer	49.4	48.8	50.9	49.1	51.8	53.7	50.2	53.8	50.7	52.3
Japan/Japon	4.1	3.4	4.0	4.8	6.9	4.8	8.4	6.0	6.7	5.6
Trinidad and Tobago	3.1	2.4	3.2	2.8	2.4	1.8	3.6	5.5	7.3	8.3
United Kingdom	6.9	6.9	6.2	5.3	5.6	4.9	4.3	4.3	4.1	4.0
Canada	5.6	7.3	5.7	6.3	4.2	4.2	4.1	3.7	3.6	3.0
Mexico/Mexique	4.6	3.6	2.1	5.0	3.6	6.4	3.6	2.8	2.6	2.6
Venezuela	4.0	4.3	5.5	5.1	5.0	4.0	4.1	3.2	2.0	2.3
Areas n.e.s.	1.7	1.4	1.7	1.7	1.0	1.6	2.5	2.1	2.9	2.7
Brazil/Brésil	1.8	2.2	1.9	3.8	0.8	1.4	1.2	1.6	1.5	1.8
Germany/Allemagne					1.2	1.3	1.5	1.1	1.4	1.2

	1987	1988	1989	1990	1991	1992	1993	1994	1995	1996
Afrique	0.0	0.5	2.6	4.6	3.6	4.7	4.0	3.7	3.5	3.2
Amériques	60.4	60.6	49.5	50.0	49.0	56.5	57.5	57.5	54.7	54.7
– Amérique du Nord	51.1	51.4	39.9	41.2	40.3	48.8	49.5	48.6	47.7	48.9
– ALAI	1.0	0.5	1.6	1.7	1.7	0.9	1.1	2.9	1.6	0.7
– MCAC	0.4	0.4	0.2	0.0	0.1	0.1	0.0	0.0	0.1	0.1
– Caraïbes	6.7	6.7	6.4	5.7	6.0	5.7	5.8	4.9	4.3	3.9
– Autre Amérique	1.3	1.5	1.3	1.4	0.9	1.1	1.0	1.0	1.0	1.0
Asie anc. URSS exclus	1.2	1.2	0.9	0.8	1.0	1.5	2.1	1.4	2.6	2.3
– Moyen–Orient	0.0	0.0	0.0	0.0	0.0	0.0	0.3	0.0	0.0	0.0
Asie ancienne URSS							0.0		0.0	0.0
Europe anc. URSS exclus	33.5	33.3	35.0	39.6	42.6	36.5	35.0	33.4	36.4	37.8
– Union Européenne	30.4	32.2	30.3	28.1	35.4	25.6	25.9	25.0	28.7	31.2
– Europe de l'Est	0.1	0.2	0.0	0.0		0.0	0.0	0.0	0.0	0.0
– Autre de l'Europe	3.1	1.0	4.8	11.5	7.2	10.9	9.1	8.4	7.6	6.6
Europe ancienne URSS	4.1	3.8	11.3	4.3	2.8	0.4	0.8	3.5	2.6	1.8
Océanie	0.2	0.3	0.3	0.2	0.8	0.3	0.2	0.2	0.2	0.2
Autre	0.5	0.4	0.4	0.4	0.2	0.1	0.4	0.3	0.1	0.0
USA/Etats–Unis d'Amer	37.3	36.8	26.2	29.8	29.9	37.3	39.4	36.4	36.9	37.1
United Kingdom	17.5	19.0	15.2	15.2	16.2	16.9	13.8	13.4	13.5	13.2
Canada	13.7	14.5	13.6	11.3	10.4	11.4	10.0	12.1	10.8	11.8
Norway,Svalbard and JM	3.0	0.9	4.5	11.5	7.2	10.8	9.0	8.4	7.6	6.5
Netherlands/Pays–Bas	11.6	10.7	11.7	9.6	8.9	5.3	5.7	4.0	7.6	8.9
France, Monaco	0.1	0.2	2.5	0.5	0.3	0.3	5.4	5.2	6.0	5.8
Ghana		0.5	2.6	4.6	3.6	4.7	4.0	3.5	3.5	3.1
Russian Federation						0.4	0.8	3.5	2.6	1.8
Japan/Japon	1.2	1.0	0.9	0.7	0.8	1.4	1.7	1.3	1.9	2.3
Trinidad and Tobago	2.5	3.0	3.1	2.8	2.7	2.5	2.0	1.7	1.5	1.2

4. General Imports C.I.F. by Commodities according to the S.I.T.C. (Rev. 2) in million U.S. Dollars
Importations Générales C.A.F. par Produits d'après la C.T.C.I. (Rév. 2) en millions de Dollars E.U.

SITC CTCI	COMMODITY	1993 QUANTITY QUANTITE	1993 VALUE VALEUR	1994 QUANTITY QUANTITE	1994 VALUE VALEUR	1995 QUANTITY QUANTITE	1995 VALUE VALEUR	1996 QUANTITY QUANTITE	1996 VALUE VALEUR	PRODUIT
	ALL COMMODITIES		2189.3		2221.4		2772.9		2916.4	TOUS PRODUITS
0	FOOD AND LIVE ANIMALS		259.9		248.7		336.7		365.7	ALIMENTS,ANIMAUX VIVANTS
01	MEAT AND PREPARATIONS		43.7		44.0		56.6		52.8	VIANDES ET PREPARATIONS
011	MEAT FRESH,CHILLD,FROZEN	W 47770	33.0	W 48092	33.2	W 52337	39.8	W 54031	42.0	VIANDES FRAICHES,REF,CONGE
0114	POULTRY FRESH CHLLD,FRZN	W 37282	21.6	W 38115	21.7	W 40784	25.1	W 42662	26.9	VOLAILLES MORTES
0116	EDIBLE OFFAL FRESH,CH,FR	W 8236	7.6	W 7174	6.9	W 7904	8.6	W 7805	9.0	ABATS COMESTIBLES
014	MEAT PREPD,PRSVD,NES ETC	W 4081	9.9	W 4063	10.0	W 4915	15.8	W 3477	9.6	CONSERVES DE VIANDES
0149	OTH PREPARD,PRESRVD MEAT	W 3823	9.3	W 3694	8.9	W 4425	14.5	W 2770	8.1	AUTRES PREP DE VIANDES
02	DAIRY PRODCTS,BIRDS'EGGS		40.9		31.9		45.0		44.6	PRODUITS LAITIERS,OEUFS
022	MILK AND CREAM	W 9994	18.0	W 8583	13.3	W 10086	20.5	W 9093	19.9	LAIT ET CREME
0224	MILK,CREAM PRESERVED ETC	W 9730	17.6	W 8431	13.0	W 9827	19.9	W 8789	19.3	LAIT,CREME CONS,CONC
02243	MILK DRY,OVER 1.5% FAT	W 6516	12.0	W 6683	10.5	W 7892	16.8	W 7169	16.5	LAIT POUDRE SUP 1.5%
024	CHEESE AND CURD	W 5164	12.0	W 3071	7.9	W 4699	12.4	W 3803	11.4	FROMAGE ET CAILLEBOTTE
025	EGGS,BIRDS,FRESH,PRSRVD	W 2355	6.5	W 2559	7.4	W 2614	7.5	W 3029	8.7	OEUFS
0251	— IN SHELL	W 2354	6.5	W 2558	7.4	W 2602	7.4	W 3013	8.7	OEUFS EN COQUILLE
03	FISH AND PREPARATIONS		31.3		28.6		37.2		39.1	POISSONS ET PREPARATIONS
034	FISH,FRESH,CHILLED,FROZN	W 5332	5.5	W 5692	5.6	W 6318	7.8	W 7659	11.0	POISSON FRAIS, REFRIG,CONG
0342	FISH FROZEN,EXCL FILLETS	W 5206	5.3	W 5620	5.4	W 6035	7.2	W 7336	10.1	POISSONS CONGELES
035	FISH SALTED,DRIED,SMOKED	W 3954	12.6	W 3524	10.5	W 3755	13.0	W 4314	15.3	POISSON SECHE,SALE,FUME
03503	FISH(EX COD)DRIED,SALTED	W 2469	8.1	W 2404	7.8	W 2382	8.9	W 2845	10.9	POISSONS SECHES,SALES
037	FISH ETC PREPD,PRSVD NES	W 5982	11.6	W 5782	10.7	W 8094	13.2	W 5674	10.5	POIS,CRUST,MOL PREPARES
0371	FISH PREPARD,PRESRVD NES	W 5978	11.6	W 5777	10.7	W 8084	13.2	W 5661	10.4	CONSERVES DE POISSONS
04	CEREALS AND PREPARATIONS		93.3		81.8		104.4		114.8	CEREALES ET PRODUITS
041	WHEAT ETC UNMILLED	W 146721	30.7	W 79930	11.6	W 88370	17.0	W 43192	13.8	FROMENT,EPEAUTRE
0411	DURUM WHEAT UNMILLED	W 51600	10.2	W 30000	4.2			W 1	0.1	FROMENT DUR NON MOULU
0412	OTHER WHEAT ETC UNMILLED	W 95121	20.6	W 49930	7.5	W 88370	17.0	W 43191	13.8	AUTRE FROMENT NON MOULU
042	RICE	W 80967	20.3	W 82221	24.3	W 121981	23.3	W 78705	29.9	RIZ
0421	RICE IN HUSK OR HUSKED	W 67917	15.4	W 67332	19.6	W 105912	18.8	W 53165	20.7	RIZ SANS AUTRE PREPARATION
04212	RICE HUSKED	W 67917	15.4	W 67319	19.6	W 105909	18.8	W 53164	20.7	RIZ CARGO
0422	RICE SEMI–MILLED,MILLED	W 13050	5.0	W 14889	4.8	W 16069	4.5	W 25540	9.2	RIZ POLI,GLACE INCL BRISURES
04221	RICE MILLED UNBROKEN	W 12978	5.0	W 11891	4.0	W 16069	4.5	W 25539	9.2	RIZ POLI,GLACE EXCL BRISURES
044	MAIZE UNMILLED	W 200137	22.0	W 200534	25.4	W 177668	27.1	W 157966	30.5	MAIS NON MOULU
048	CEREAL ETC PREPARATIONS	W 19920	17.4	W 16100	17.8	W 21690	29.1	W 24253	37.9	PREPTNS A BASE CEREALES
0482	MALT INCLUDING FLOUR	W 14690	6.8	W 11067	4.8	W 12789	5.9	W 12223	6.7	MALT MEME TORREFIE
0484	BAKERY PRODUCTS	W 510	1.2	W 1410	3.3	W 2566	6.6	W 3288	9.0	PRODUITS DE BOULANGERIE
0488	OTH CEREAL PREPS,MALT EX	W 3079	7.2	W 2363	6.4	W 3922	10.4	W 6095	14.7	EXTRAITS DE MALT
05	VEGETABLES AND FRUIT		13.1		14.8		19.3		23.1	LEGUMES ET FRUITS
054	VEG ETC FRSH,SMPLY PRSVD	W 7768	6.6	W 9471	7.1	W 12631	8.5	W 18482	9.7	LEGUMES FRAIS,CONG,SECS
06	SUGAR AND PREPS,HONEY		12.8		18.7		27.1		38.3	SUCRES ET PRODUITS
061	SUGAR AND HONEY	W 35095	12.0	W 45245	16.7	W 90560	23.9	W 290931	35.2	SUCRES ET MIEL
0612	REFINED SUGAR ETC	W 31729	10.3	W 39926	13.9	W 30909	14.3	W 282274	31.1	SUCRES RAFFINES
081	*FEEDING STUFF FOR ANIML	W 17084	8.4	W 20650	8.8	W 61842	23.2	W 65903	22.1	NOURRITURE POUR ANIMAUX
0813	OILCAKE AND OTH RESIDUES	W 11624	3.6	W 16056	4.1	W 52406	12.1	W 51483	15.7	TOURTEAUX
08131	— OF SOYA BEANS	W 7535	2.1	W 15263	3.9	W 52206	12.0	W 51483	15.7	TOURTEAUX DE SOJA
0819	FOOD WASTE AND FEED NES	W 2181	3.1	W 2674	3.9	W 6094	9.9	W 4751	3.6	DECHETS,ALIMENTS NDA
08199	FODDER NES,INCL SWEETNED	W 2181	3.1	W 2674	3.9	W 6094	9.9	W 4751	3.6	PREPARATIONS FOURRAGERES
09	MISC EDIBLE PRODUCTS		11.7		13.8		16.5		21.5	PREP ALIMENTAIRES DIVERSES
098	EDIBLE PRODCTS,PREPS NES	W 2971	9.0	W 4059	9.7	W 4047	11.3	W 5667	15.6	PREP ALIMENTAIRES NDA
09809	MISC FOOD PREPRTIONS NES	W 2016	6.9	W 3051	7.6	W 2622	8.3	W 4165	12.3	PREP ALIMENTAIRES NDA
1	BEVERAGES AND TOBACCO		16.8		26.8		36.2		35.9	BOISSONS ET TABACS
11	BEVERAGES		11.2		19.5		29.3		26.2	BOISSONS
111	NON–ALCOHL BEVERAGES NES	W 4310	3.1	W 8969	6.0	W 38719	22.2	W 42026	20.1	BOISSONS NON ALCOOLIQUES
11102	FLAVORED WATERS NON–ALCO	W 3995	2.9	W 8542	5.7	W 38196	21.9	W 41298	19.6	LIMONADES,EAUX GAZEUSES
112	ALCOHOLIC BEVERAGES	W 5446	8.1	W 16666	13.6	W 6994	7.1	W 3038	6.1	BOISSONS ALCOOLIQUES
1123	BEER,ALE,STOUT,PORTER	W 3998	3.5	W 15353	9.5	W 5376	2.4	W 1117	0.7	BIERES
12	TOBACCO AND MANUFACTURES		5.6		7.3		7.0		9.7	TABACS BRUTS FABRIQUES
121	TOBACCO UNMNFCTRD,REFUSE	W 753	5.4	W 1218	7.0	W 886	6.8	W 1226	9.2	TABACS BRUTS,DECHETS
1212	TOBACCO STRIPPED OR PART	W 712	5.0	W 1199	6.9	W 819	6.3	W 1219	9.1	TABACS PART ECOTES
2	CRUDE MATERLS,EXCL FUELS		63.3		64.9		53.0		51.4	MAT BRUTES NON COMESTIBLES
22	OIL SEEDS,OLEAGINOUS FRT		19.1		17.5		4.8		1.8	GRAINES,FRUITS OLEAGINEUX
222	SEEDS FOR'SOFT'FIXED OIL	W 68812	18.2	W 63581	17.4	W 17697	4.8	W 180	0.3	GRAINES HUILES FIXES
2222	SOYA BEANS	W 68666	18.1	W 63417	17.2	W 17593	4.6	W 23	0.1	FEVES DE SOJA
24	CORK AND WOOD		31.7		34.7		35.3		34.9	LIEGE ET BOIS
248	WOOD SHAPED,SLEEPERS	W 57478	28.0	W 59904	30.0	W 61888	30.9	W 60921	30.9	BOIS SIMPLEMENT TRAVAILLES
2482	LUMBER SHAPED CONIFER	W 53380	24.5	W 55688	26.5	W 56705	27.2	W 56421	27.3	CONIFERES SCIES,RABOTES
24821	LUMBER SAWN ETC CONIFER	W 49592	22.6	W 53371	25.2	W 54477	25.5	W 53832	25.8	CONIFERES SCIES LONGITUD
3	MINERAL FUELS ETC		344.1		330.1		351.3		444.7	COMBUSTIBLES MINERAUX LUB
33	PETROLEUM AND PRODUCTS		332.9		316.5		334.2		425.1	PETROLE ET DERIVES
333	CRUDE PETROLEUM	W 869347	124.1	W 832290	95.2	W 747315	93.5	W 622616	89.7	HUILES BRUTES DE PETROLE
334	PETROLEUM PRODUCTS,REFIN	W 1453309	207.1	W 1685675	219.6	W 1654248	239.0	W 1493687	333.8	PRODUITS RAFFINES
3341	GASOLINE,OTH LIGHT OILS	W 86313	13.6					W 345006	72.6	ESSENCES POUR MOTEURS
33411	MOTOR,AVIATION SPIRIT	W 84357	13.0					W 343429	69.5	ESSENCES MOTEURS D'AVIONS
3342	KEROSENE,OTH MEDIUM OILS	W 194518	32.2					W 170738	33.4	PETR LAMPANTS,AUT HUIL
33421	KEROSENE INCL JET FUEL	W 194432	32.2					W 166855	32.5	PETROLES LAMPANTS
3343	GAS OILS	W 253282	41.7					W 279242	54.1	GAS OILS
3344	FUEL OILS,NES	W 910894	114.4					W 610667	157.4	FUEL OILS
3345	LUBS,PETROLEUM OILS NES	W 8301	5.4					W 88034	16.6	HUILES LUBRIFIANTES
33451	LUBS(HIGH PETR CONT) ETC	W 8155	5.2					W 87869	16.2	HUILES LUBRIF,H LOURDES
341	*GAS,NATURAL AND MANUFCT	W 71358	10.1	W 72752	10.4	W 83587	12.7	W 87334	16.1	GAZ NATUREL,GAZ MANUFACT
3413	PETROLM GASES,LIQUEFIED	W 71354	10.1	W 72748	10.4	W 83583	12.7	W 87332	16.1	GAZ DE PETROLE LIQUEFIE
34131	LIQUEFIED PROPANE,BUTANE	W 71351	10.0	W 71654	10.2	W 83583	12.7	W 87331	16.1	PROPANE,BUTANE LIQUEFIES
4	ANIMAL,VEGETABLE OIL,FAT		11.5		18.2		20.0		23.4	HUILES,GRAISSES ANIM,VEG
42	FIXED VEGETABLE OIL,FAT		6.2		11.1		11.8		15.8	HUILES VEGETALES FIXES
423	FIXED VEG OILS,SOFT	W 1974	2.1	W 9593	7.5	W 7906	8.2	W 15604	12.4	HUILES VEGET DOUCES FIXES
4232	SOYA BEAN OIL	W 1925	1.9	W 6437	5.9	W 7790	7.9	W 15517	12.1	HUILE DE SOJA
5	CHEMCLS,RELATED PROD NES		200.8		212.4		264.6		286.6	PRODUITS CHIMIQUES
51	ORGANIC CHEMICALS		18.7		19.7		25.0		22.5	PROD CHIMIQ ORGANIQUES
512	ALCOHOLS,PHENOLS ETC	W 22247	5.3	W 32196	6.3	W 37886	10.1	W 22617	8.5	PHENOLS,PHENOLS–ALCOOLS
5121	ACYCLIC ALCOHOLS,DERIVS	W 22162	4.9	W 32138	6.1	W 37813	9.8	W 22520	8.1	ALCOOLS ACYCLIQUES
52	INORGANIC CHEMICALS		50.2		46.6		65.8		72.1	PROD CHIM INORGANIQUES
522	INORG ELEMNTS,OXIDES,ETC	W 244060	30.9	W 487096	26.2		48.9	W 340863	57.8	ELEMENTS INORGANIQUES
5225	INORGANIC BASES ETC NES	W 232842	23.3	W 477768	18.9	W 305267	40.2	W 335238	49.9	AUTRES BASES OXYDES METAL
52253	SODIUM HYDROXIDE, OTHER	W 201188	21.1	W 476979	18.3	W 304371	39.5	W 324450	48.0	HYDROXYDE SODIUM AQUEUX
523	OTHR INORG CHEMICALS ETC	W 48949	18.5	W 30965	20.0	W 38824	16.8	W 29271	13.8	AUT PRODUITS CHIMIQUES INORG
5232	OTH MTL CMPD OF INRG ACD	W 22655	6.7	W 12406	5.7	W 13542	6.5	W 11179	4.9	SELS METALLIQUES
5239	INORG CHEM PRODUCTS NES	W 4909	7.7	W 4895	10.0	W 3416	6.9	W 2378	4.6	PROD CHIM INORGANIQ NDA
52399	OTH INORG CMPNDS NES ETC	W 3772	7.0	W 4138	9.5	W 2335	6.3	W 1324	4.0	AUT COMP INORGANIQUES NDA
53	DYES,TANNING,COLOUR PROD		8.6		8.7		11.4		12.8	PROD TEINTURE,COLORANTS
533	PIGMENTS,PAINTS,ETC	W 4025	7.5	W 5380	7.8	W 7806	10.2	W 9896	11.3	PIGMENTS,PEINTURES,VERNIS
541	*MEDICINAL,PHARM PRODUCT	K 1136134	28.7		32.2	K 1663573	40.4	K 1482893	44.8	PROD MEDICINAUX PHARMACEUT
5417	MEDICAMENTS	K 927151	25.9	K 1007293	28.4	K 1381350	35.5	K 1288830	40.7	MEDICAMENTS

4. General Imports C.I.F. by Commodities according to the S.I.T.C. (Rev. 2) in million U.S. Dollars
Importations Générales C.A.F. par Produits d'après la C.T.C.I. (Rév. 2) en millions de Dollars E.U.

SITC CTCI	COMMODITY	1993 QUANTITY QUANTITE	1993 VALUE VALEUR	1994 QUANTITY QUANTITE	1994 VALUE VALEUR	1995 QUANTITY QUANTITE	1995 VALUE VALEUR	1996 QUANTITY QUANTITE	1996 VALUE VALEUR	PRODUIT
54179	— CONTNG OTH SUBSTANCES	K 815742	19.7	K 901263	22.4	K 1275125	28.7	K 1179632	33.7	MED CONT AUT SUBSTANCES
55	PERFUME,CLEANING ETC PRD		24.1		26.7		31.6		41.9	PROD POUR PARFUM,TOILETTE
553	PERFUMERY,COSMETICS,ETC	W 1114	8.0	W 893	7.4	W 1706	10.4	W 1711	10.9	PRODUITS DE PARFUMERIE
554	SOAP,CLEANSING ETC PREPS	W 9432	13.7	W 11726	16.8	W 13469	18.2	W 22685	28.2	SAVONS,PRODUITS DETERSIFS
5541	SOAPS	W 5745	8.3	W 6375	9.3	W 5974	8.9	W 9630	13.9	SAVONS,PROD TENSIO–ACTIFS
5542	WASHING PREPARATIONS ETC	W 3572	5.1	W 5115	6.9	W 7252	8.7	W 12368	12.5	PROD ORG TENSIO–ACT NDA
562	*FERTILIZERS,MANUFACTURE	W 63895	11.8	W 61650	9.7	W 55653	13.8	W 58567	11.8	ENGRAIS MANUFACTURES
5629	FERTILIZERS NES	W 34507	6.6	W 29789	5.2	W 23360	6.6	W 14186	3.9	ENGRAIS NDA
58	PLASTIC MATERIALS ETC		33.1		38.9		43.9		41.1	MAT PLAST ARTIFICIELLES
583	POLYMERIZATION ETC PRODS	W 20243	27.3	W 23885	33.3	W 22002	36.0	W 19789	32.5	PROD POLYMERISATION
5833	POLYSTYRENE,ITS COPOLYMR	W 853	0.9	W 8591	7.9	W 8735	10.6	W 781	0.8	POLYPROPYLENE COPOLYMERES
58331	— IN PRIMARY FORMS	W 853	0.9	W 8591	7.9	W 8735	10.6	W 781	0.8	SOUS FORMES PRIMAIRES
5839	OTH POLYMRZTION ETC PROD	W 19048	26.0	W 8085	15.2	W 7284	15.4	W 18520	30.9	AUT PROD POLYMER COPOLYM
59	CHEMICAL MATERIALS NES		25.4		29.8		32.7		39.5	MAT PROD CHIMIQUES NDA
591	PESTICIDES,DISINFECTANTS	W 2373	7.9	W 2778	8.6	W 2942	10.1	W 3590	11.9	DESINF,INSECT,FONG,HERB
598	MISCEL CHEM PRODUCTS NES	W 15095	15.2	W 21117	18.6	W 21386	20.3	W 24581	24.7	PROD DIV INDUST CHIM NDA
5982	ANTI–KNOCK PREPARTNS ETC	W 12123	8.1	W 18156	12.3	W 18341	12.3	W 19751	13.2	PREPARAT ANTIDETONANTES
5989	CHEM PRODUCTS,PREPS NES	W 2614	6.3	W 2508	5.5	W 2642	7.1	W 4400	10.7	PROD PREP CHIMIQUES NDA
6	BASIC MANUFACTURES		361.0		355.7		463.5		413.6	ART MANUFACTURES
62	RUBBER MANUFACTURES NES		25.0		24.8		36.8		38.2	CAOUTCHOUC MANUFACTURE
625	RUBBER TYRES, TUBES ETC	W 3961	14.2	W 3478	12.7	W 6571	24.9	W 5914	22.8	PNEUS CAOUTCHOUC VULCANISE
6251	TYRES NEW FOR MOTOR CARS	W 977	3.6	W 906	3.4	W 2799	10.8	W 2544	9.5	PNEUS POUR VOITURES
628	RUBBER ARTICLES NES	W 769	7.5	W 864	8.6	W 961	8.7	W 1100	11.1	OUVRAGES CAOUTCHOUC NDA
63	WOOD,CORK MANUFACTRS NES		14.8		15.7		18.2		22.0	OUVRAGES LIEGE ET BOIS
634	VENEERS,PLYWOOD,ETC	W 12459	8.7	W 25008	9.6	W 15086	10.5	W 14511	10.3	PLACAGES,CONTRE–PLAQUES
6342	PLYWOOD OF WOOD SHEETS	W 8535	6.1	W 21767	7.4	W 12195	8.6	W 11861	8.3	BOIS CONTRE–PLAQUES
635	WOOD MANUFACTURES NES	W 3762	6.0	W 3598	6.2	W 3646	7.6	W 5724	11.7	ART MANUF EN BOIS NDA
64	PAPER,PAPERBOARD AND MFR		67.8		71.7		94.4		87.9	PAPIERS,CARTONS & OUVRAGES
641	PAPER AND PAPERBOARD	W 61524	49.9	W 61730	49.3	W 66526	67.9	W 61434	56.9	PAPIERS ET CARTONS
6411	NEWSPRINT	W 9282	5.4	W 7462	4.0	W 11226	8.5	W 8886	7.5	PAPIER JOURNAL
6413	KRAFT PAPER,PAPERBOARD	W 14915	8.9	W 16929	11.3	W 15992	13.0	W 15056	10.1	PAPIER ET CARTON KRAFT
64131	KRAFT LINER IN BULK			W 16929	11.3	W 15992	13.0			PAP KRAFT POUR COUVERTURES
64139	KRAFT PAPER PAPERBD,NES	W 14915	8.9					W 15056	10.1	PAPIER,CARTON KRAFT NDA
6415	PAPER,PAPERBRD,BULK,NES	W 12785	11.4	W 7176	7.4	W 8609	12.0	W 8682	9.8	PAPIERS,CARTONS ROULEAUX
64159	OTHER PAPER ETC,BULK,NES	W 6508	7.2	W 7048	7.0	W 8481	11.7	W 7019	7.6	AUT PAPIER ROULEAUX FEUILLES
6417	CORRUGATED PAPER ETC,BLK	W 10107	7.5	W 13990	10.2	W 14449	13.9	W 11638	10.4	PAPIERS,CARTONS ONDULES
6418	COATED ETC PAPER NES BLK	W 10691	13.9	W 9216	10.9	W 10515	15.0	W 11498	15.0	PAP,CARTONS COUCHES,ENDUITS
64189	COATED PAPER ETC NES	W 7494	9.5	W 1032	1.9	W 1046	2.4	W 6737	8.3	PAPIERS,CARTONS COUCHES
642	PAPER,ETC,PRECUT,ARTS OF	W 7019	17.9	W 8750	22.5	W 9076	26.5	W 10467	31.1	PAP,CARTONS DECOUPES
6421	PAPER ETC CONTAINERS	W 3877	7.4	W 3785	7.2	W 3938	8.8	W 5216	11.3	BOITES,SACS EMBALLAGES
6428	PAPER ETC ARTICLES NES	W 1867	6.8	W 2549	9.0	W 2833	11.2	W 3228	13.6	OUVRAGES EN PATE A PAPIER
64285	PAPER ETC DIAPERS ETC	W 999	3.9	W 1412	5.5	W 1778	7.6	W 2202	9.5	SERVIETTES HYGIENIQUES
65	TEXTILE YARN,FABRICS,ETC		73.9		78.9		74.4		69.4	FILS,TISSUS,ARTICLES TEXTILE
651	TEXTILE YARN	W 954	5.5	W 1151	7.4	W 658	4.8	W 662	4.1	FILS TEXTILES
652	COTTON FABRICS,WOVEN	W 2039	10.7	W 3075	17.7	W 2622	14.2	W 1898	10.6	TISSUS DE COTON
6522	WOVEN COTTON BLEACHD,ETC	W 1831	9.5	W 2055	12.8	W 2423	13.1	W 1746	9.9	TISSUS COTON BLANCHIS ETC
65225	BLCHD COTN BLEND FAB NES	W 964	5.3	W 865	6.9	W 908	5.1	W 852	4.7	AUT TIS MOINS 85% COT BLANCH
653	WOVN MAN–MADE FIB FABRIC	W 4162	23.2	W 3664	20.4	W 3798	21.3	W 3854	22.1	TISSUS FIBRES SYNTH,ARTIF
6534	DISC SYN BLEND FABRC NES	W 2305	11.4	W 1959	9.9	W 2095	10.1	W 1771	8.7	TISSUS FIBRES SYNTH DISCONT
65341	DISC SYN FIB–COTTN FABRC	W 2003	8.5	W 1699	7.5	W 1803	7.9	W 1478	7.5	TISSUS FIB SYNT DIS MEL COTO
655	KNITTED,ETC FABRICS	W 1401	7.1	W 910	4.5	W 938	4.7	W 841	4.3	ETOF BONNETERIE PIECES ETC
6552	OTHER KNIT ETC FAB NONEL	W 1401	7.1	W 910	4.5	W 938	4.7	W 841	4.3	ETOF BON NON ELAS NON SYNT
656	LACE,RIBBONS,TULLE,ETC	W 461	6.1	W 568	7.9	W 728	7.2	W 592	5.7	TULLES,BRODERIE
657	SPECIAL TXTL FABRC,PRODS	W 1618	12.1	W 1588	12.3	W 1847	11.9	W 1576	10.9	TISSUS SPECIAUX
6573	COATED ETC TEXTILES NES	W 1147	9.2	W 1058	9.4	W 1030	8.0	W 896	6.6	TISSUS,ART MATIERE TEXT NDA
65733	RUBBERIZED TEXT NOT KNIT	W 760	7.5	W 752	8.0	W 726	6.5	W 688	5.2	TISSUS CAOUTCHOUTES
66	NONMETAL MINERAL MFS NES		31.9		37.3		47.6		46.1	ART MIN NON METALLIQUES
661	LIME,CEMENT,BLDG PRODS	W 21289	4.8	W 44531	6.7	W 124386	10.7	W 61304	8.6	CHAUX,CIMENTS MAT CONSTR
662	CLAY,REFRACTORY BLDG PRD	W 14232	9.6	W 18407	10.4	W 26991	15.0	W 30601	15.8	MAT CONST REFRACTAIRES
6624	BRICKS ETC NONREFRACTORY	W 12198	8.0	W 15350	8.2	W 24894	13.0	W 26755	12.9	BRIQUES ETC CERAM NON REFR
66245	GLAZED CERAMIC SETTS ETC	W 7767	5.2	W 11234	6.1	W 17800	9.3	W 20079	9.4	AUT CARREAUX CERAMIQUE
665	GLASSWARE	W 6847	6.9	W 11224	9.8	W 7882	8.7	W 4675	7.1	OUVRAGES EN VERRE
6651	BOTTLES ETC OF GLASS	W 4666	4.0	W 10233	7.5	W 6376	5.2	W 3238	3.7	RECIPIENTS EN VERRE
66511	GLASS BOTTLES ETC NONVAC	W 4665	4.0	W 10233	7.5	W 6376	5.2	W 3238	3.7	BONBONNES,BOUTEILLES,ETC
67	IRON AND STEEL		58.4		43.6		87.8		50.3	FER ET ACIER
673	IRON,STEEL SHAPES ETC	W 54624	22.9	W 52978	19.6	W 90770	38.3	W 49054	17.9	BARRES,PROFIL FER,ACIER
6732	IRON,STEEL BARS ETC	W 43575	16.9	W 45264	14.9	W 74851	25.9	W 43305	14.4	BARRES FER,ACIER
67325	OTH ALLOY STEEL BARS ETC	W 23899	10.2	W 34278	11.4	W 74066	25.3	W 41825	13.8	BARRES NON ACIERS ALLIES
6733	IRON,STEEL PROFILES ETC	W 8186	5.0	W 5644	3.9	W 13329	11.2	W 4455	3.0	PROFILES,PALPLAN FER,ACIER
674	IRN,STL UNIV,PLATE,SHEET	W 22490	13.8	W 13388	9.8	W 20235	14.9	W 18135	13.9	LARGES PLATS,TOLES
677	IRN,STL WIRE(EXCL W ROD)	W 13518	6.8	W 5623	2.7	W 3331	3.3	W 5926	2.9	FILS EN FER,ACIER
678	IRON,STL TUBES,PIPES,ETC	W 5448	11.9	W 3127	8.1	W 10506	24.9	W 7449	11.8	TUBES,TUYAUX EN FONTE,FER
6783	IRON,STL TUBES,PIPES NES	W 2325	4.2	W 1874	2.9	W 7001	15.2	W 5361	5.9	AUT TUBES,TUYAUX FER,ACIER
68	NON–FERROUS METALS		20.9		15.0		20.7		17.7	METAUX NON FERREUX
684	ALUMINIUM	W 4122	8.7	W 2083	6.3	W 2811	10.3	W 2729	9.1	ALUMINIUM
6842	ALUMINIUM,ALLOYS WORKED	W 3533	8.0	W 1402	4.9	W 1956	8.1	W 2040	7.6	ALUMINIUM,ALLIAGES OUVRE
687	TIN	W 6008	6.8	W 5114	5.0	W 4396	4.7	W 3238	3.6	ETAIN
6872	TIN,ALLOYS WORKED	W 6008	6.8	W 5114	5.0	W 4396	4.7	W 3238	3.6	ETAIN ET ALLIAGES OUVRES
68722	TIN SHEET,PLATE,STRIP	W 6006	6.8	W 5113	5.0	W 4396	4.7	W 3237	3.6	TABLES,PLANCHES ETAIN
69	METAL MANUFACTURES NES		67.1		67.8		82.4		81.1	ART MANUFACT EN METAL NDA
691	STRUCTURES AND PARTS NES	W 5382	7.9	W 3935	7.7	W 5078	10.6	W 5258	11.1	CONSTRUCT FER,ACIER,ALU
6911	STRUCTURES,PARTS IRN,STL	W 5165	6.9	W 3746	6.6	W 4807	9.4	W 4925	9.5	CONSTRUCT FER,ACIER,FONTE
692	METAL TANKS,BOXES,ETC	W 4841	13.8	W 4185	11.7	W 3982	10.7	W 3772	10.6	RECIPIENTS METALLIQUES
6924	MTL TRANSPORT BOXES ETC	W 4743	13.3	W 4042	10.9	W 3587	9.5	W 3500	9.4	FUTS,TAMBOURS,BIDONS
69241	STL TRANSPORT BOXES ETC	W 3220	8.7	W 2162	6.4	W 1870	4.7	W 1313	4.0	FUTS,TAMBOURS,BIDONS FER
693	WIRE PRODUCTS NON ELECTR	W 7789	8.5	W 5515	8.7	W 5050	9.6	W 3860	7.0	OUVRAGES FILS METALLIQUES
697	BASE MTL HOUSEHOLD EQUIP	W 1825	7.0	W 2350	8.4	W 2629	10.3	W 2766	11.1	ART MENAGE MET COMMUNS
699	BASE METAL MFRS NES	W 3621	17.9		18.7	W 6076	25.0		24.7	ART MANUFACTURES MET NDA
7	MACHINES,TRANSPORT EQUIP		563.5		547.5		759.1		776.2	MACHINES MATERIEL TRANSPORT
71	POWER GENERATING EQUIPMT		37.8		42.1		52.5		58.6	MACHINES GENERATRICES
712	STEAM ENGINES,TURBINES	W 90	2.1	W 260	12.5	W 83	8.7	W 109	10.5	MACHINES A VAPEUR D'EAU PIEC
7129	STM ENGINE ETC PARTS NES	W 83	1.8	W 212	10.7	W 62	4.3	W 74	4.2	PARTIES,PIECES DU 712.6
713	INTRNL COMBUS PSTN ENGIN	W 1841	10.6	W 1763	13.7	W 1825	19.5	W 1822	20.2	MOTEURS EXPL COMB INT, PIECE
7139	PISTON ENGINE PARTS NES	W 290	4.3	W 259	4.6	W 343	5.9	W 447	9.6	PIECES POUR 713.2,3,8
714	ENGINES AND MOTORS NES	W 258	10.4	W 24	0.4	W 24	0.8	W 8	2.5	MOTEURS NON ELECTRIQUES
7148	GAS TURBINES NES	W 70	7.0		0.1		0.1	W 6	2.4	TURBINES A GAZ
71488	OTHER GAS TURBINES NES	W 69	7.0		0.1		0.1	W 6	2.4	AUTRES TURBINES A GAZ
716	ROTATING ELECTRIC PLANT	W 586	12.3	W 865	12.5	W 800	14.1	W 1636	23.0	APP ELECTR ROTATIFS,PIECES
7161	DC MOTORS AND GENERATORS	W 71	2.4	W 243	5.6	W 150	4.9	W 884	13.0	MOTEURS COURANT CONTINU
7162	AC MTRS,GENRTRS,GEN SETS	W 462	9.1	W 541	5.8	W 603	6.9	W 523	6.9	MOTEURS ELECTRIQUES
72	MACHS FOR SPCL INDUSTRYS		37.9		42.4		46.9		57.2	MAC SPECIALES POUR INDUST

4. General Imports C.I.F. by Commodities according to the S.I.T.C. (Rev. 2) in million U.S. Dollars
Importations Générales C.A.F. par Produits d'après la C.T.C.I. (Rév. 2) en millions de Dollars E.U.

SITC CTCI	COMMODITY	1993 QUANTITY QUANTITE	1993 VALUE VALEUR	1994 QUANTITY QUANTITE	1994 VALUE VALEUR	1995 QUANTITY QUANTITE	1995 VALUE VALEUR	1996 QUANTITY QUANTITE	1996 VALUE VALEUR	PRODUIT
723	CIVIL ENGNEERG EQUIP ETC	W 2310	7.5	W 2111	5.7	W 3524	11.9	W 4801	23.9	APPAREILS DE GENIE CIVIL
7234	CONST,MINING MACHNRY NES	W 2153	7.1	W 1914	5.3	W 3200	11.5	W 4399	22.6	MACH POUR LA CONST, MINES
72342	SLFPRP SHOVELS,EXCAVATRS	W 1164	3.9	W 1410	4.1	W 2207	8.9	W 2198	8.7	PELLES MECANIQUES
724	TEXTILE,LEATHER MACHNRY		6.5	W 774	9.7	W 1163	6.4		6.3	MACH POUR INDUSTRIE TEXTILE
726	PRINTG,BKBINDG MACHY,PTS	W 287	4.4	W 356	7.2	W 174	4.2	W 112	2.4	MACHINES POUR IMPRIMERIE
728	OTH MACHY FOR SPCL INDUS	W 1091	9.3	W 1129	8.8	W 1071	8.7	W 1108	12.4	AUT MACH IND PARTICULIERES
74	GENRL INDUSTRL MACHY NES		90.0		95.2		105.8		144.2	MACH APP INDUSTRIE
741	HEATING,COOLING EQUIPMNT	W 1738	14.3	W 1734	16.8	W 2080	21.2	W 2424	22.8	MACH CHAUFFAGE,PIECES
7414	NONDOM REFRIG EQUIPT,PTS	W 402	4.2	W 649	6.0	W 882	8.4	W 1224	9.7	MAT PRODUCTION DU FROID
742	PUMPS FOR LIQUIDS ETC	W 618	11.0	W 600	10.8	W 512	10.8	W 1440	14.8	POMPES MOTO–POMPES
743	PUMPS NES,CENTRFUGES ETC	W 1159	12.3	W 1017	11.9	W 1138	13.7	W 1232	19.3	POMPES COMPRES,VENT ETC
7431	PUMPS FOR GASES ETC	W 628	5.8	W 342	3.3	W 480	4.2	W 493	9.1	POMPES AIR A VIDE,COMPRES
744	MECHANICAL HANDLING EQU	W 2107	11.4	W 1713	14.4	W 2763	18.9	W 2510	36.9	EQUIP MANUTENTION PIECES
7442	LIFTING,LOADING MACH NES	W 1174	5.3	W 755	4.7	W 1277	5.9	W 1019	23.6	APP LEVAGE,MANUTENTION
74422	SHIP DERRICKS,CRANES ETC	W 537	2.2	W 164	0.6	W 421	0.8	W 227	17.4	GRUES,PONTS ROULANTS
7449	PTS NES OF MACHY OF 7442	W 376	4.1	W 474	5.9	W 603	6.0	W 831	10.5	PIECES DU 744.2
745	NONELEC MACHY,TOOLS NES	W 537	9.9	W 578	10.4	W 657	9.5	W 1175	12.8	AUT MACH NON ELEC,PIECES
7452	OTH NONELEC MCHS,PTS NES	W 499	9.3	W 557	10.0	W 634	9.1	W 1144	12.3	AUT MACH NON ELEC,PIECES
749	NONELEC MACH PTS,ACC NES	W 2085	31.4	W 1821	31.1	W 1830	32.0	W 2168	37.8	PIECES MACH NON ELEC NDA
7492	COCKS,VALVES ETC NES	W 920	12.3	W 841	12.9	W 867	14.3	W 890	16.2	ART ROB,SIM POUR TUYAUX
7493	SHAFT,CRANK,PULLEY ETC	W 585	8.0	W 448	7.6	W 476	8.5	W 763	10.7	ARBRES TRANS,VILEBREQUINS
7499	OTH NONELEC MCHY PTS NES	W 344	7.2	W 342	6.7	W 309	5.7	W 319	6.6	PIECES NON ELECT NDA
75	OFFICE MACHNES,ADP EQUIP		31.8		33.3		46.1		54.7	MACH BUREAU TRAIT AUTOM
752	AUTOMTIC DATA PROC EQUIP	W 255	15.5	W 280	16.7	W 412	25.4	W 445	32.9	MACH TRAIT INFORMATION
7522	DIGITAL COMPUTERS	W 144	10.3	W 136	9.7	W 193	14.1	W 189	18.5	MACH DIGITALES COMPLETES
759	OFFICE,ADP MCH PTS,ACCES	W 227	11.4	W 202	12.8	W 214	14.3	W 222	16.7	PIECES DU 751 ET 752
7599	ACCTG,ETC,ADP MCH PTS,AC	W 167	9.7	W 160	11.3	W 151	11.8	W 184	14.9	PIECES DU 751 ET 752
76	TELECOMM,SOUND EQUIPMENT		38.8		51.6		67.2		69.5	EQUIPMENT DE TELECOM
761	TELEVISION RECEIVERS	W 428	4.3	W 554	5.7	W 993	9.4	W 1019	9.6	RECEPTEURS DE TELEVISION
7611	COLOUR TV RECEIVERS	W 402	4.1	W 527	5.5	W 949	9.2	W 978	9.4	RECEPTEURS COULEUR
764	TELECOM EQPT,PTS,ACC NES	W 789	29.8	W 873	41.2	W 959	51.3	W 860	52.0	EQUIP TELECOM,PIECES
7641	LINE TELEPHONE,ETC EQUIP	W 265	12.8	W 369	22.1	W 520	27.8	W 319	23.5	APP TELEPHON PAR FIL
7643	TV,RADIO TRANSMITTRS ETC	W 53	3.2	W 42	4.1	W 80	8.9	W 76	10.0	APP EMET TELE RADIO
7649	PTS NES OF EQUIPMT OF 76	W 393	12.2	W 340	13.0	W 255	12.2	W 375	15.9	PIECES DE LA DIV 76
76491	PTS NES OF APPAR OF 7641	W 105	9.1	W 117	7.8	W 114	9.8	W 55	9.5	PIECES POUR 764.1
77	ELECTRIC MACHNRY NES ETC		65.2		89.6		110.6		97.8	MACH APP ELECT NDA
771	ELECTRIC POWER MACHY NES	W 1383	8.0	W 2991	15.3	W 1380	9.2	W 1408	12.9	MACH PROD,TRANS ELECTR
7711	TRANSFORMERS,ELECTRICAL	W 1246	6.0	W 2381	10.7	W 1150	4.6	W 1147	8.3	TRANSFO ELECTRIQUES
77118	OTHER ELEC TRANSFORMERS	W 1213	5.8	W 2165	10.2	W 762	3.3	W 821	6.1	AUTRES TRANSFO ELECTRIQ
772	SWITCHGEAR ETC,PARTS NES	W 945	18.3	W 1064	22.0	W 1362	23.5	W 1111	19.8	APP COUPURE,SECT ETC
7721	SWITCHGEAR ETC	W 924	16.2	W 1051	19.9	W 1356	22.2	W 1107	19.0	APP COUPURE,SECTIONMNT
773	ELECTR DISTRIBUTNG EQUIP	W 1971	10.9	W 3117	18.4	W 5234	32.3	W 3043	17.4	EQUIPMT DISTRIBUTION ELECT
7731	INSULATED WIRE,CABLE ETC	W 1723	10.1	W 2800	17.3	W 4647	30.5	W 2784	16.2	FILS,CABLES ISOLES ELECT
775	HOUSEHOLD TYPE EQUIP NES	W 2693	12.3	W 3439	15.5	W 4698	22.6	W 4587	23.4	MACH,APP USAGE DOMESTQUE
7752	DOM REFRIGERATRS,FREEZRS	W 1991	8.1	W 2432	10.0	W 3407	15.1	W 3076	14.7	REFRIG,CONGEL MENAGER
77521	DOMESTIC REFRIGERATORS	W 1568	6.4	W 1899	7.4	W 2809	12.2	W 2527	12.0	REFRIGERATEURS
778	ELECTRICAL MACHINERY NES	W 2347	14.2	W 2380	16.2	W 3294	18.6	W 3077	20.9	AUTRES MACH ELECT NDA
78	ROAD VEHICLES		255.8		183.7		265.4		238.4	VEHICULES ROUTIERS
781	PASS MOTOR VEH EXC BUSES	W 17845	148.5	W 15031	101.4	W 27233	151.8	W 29099	136.0	AUTO TRANSPORT PERSONNES
782	LORRIES,SPCL MTR VEH NES	W 12722	54.9	W 12307	49.3	W 14591	65.2	W 14317	58.4	VEHICULES SPECIAUX,MARCH
7821	LORRIES,TRUCKS	W 12134	52.4	W 11959	48.0	W 13876	52.7	W 13653	55.4	VEHICULES TRANSP MARCHAND
7822	SPECIAL MOTOR VEHCLS NES	W 588	2.5	W 347	1.3	W 716	12.5	W 664	3.0	VEHICULES USAGES SPECIAUX
783	ROAD MOTOR VEHICLES NES	W 5082	28.2	W 3073	10.1	W 4671	19.8	W 4804	12.8	VEHICULES ROUTIERS NDA
7831	BUSES	W 3288	25.8	W 1032	7.1	W 1799	15.5	W 1176	7.5	VOITURES TRANSPORT COMMUN
784	MOTOR VEH PRTS,ACCES NES	W 3744	17.8	W 2537	16.7	W 3651	19.7	W 3289	21.8	PIECES 722,781,782,783
7849	OTHER MOTOR VEHCL PARTS	W 3307	16.7	W 2251	16.1	W 3155	19.0	W 3012	21.1	PIECES 722,781,782,783
79	OTHR TRANSPORT EQUIPMENT		4.5		7.2		62.8		53.5	AUTRE MATERIEL TRANSPORT
792	AIRCRAFT ETC	W 38	2.3	W 126	4.7	W 19	1.3	W 101	50.5	APP NAVIGATION AERIENNE
7924	AIRCRFT NES OVER 15000KG							W 60	45.1	AERODYNES PLUS 15000 KG
793	SHIPS AND BOATS ETC	W 177	1.4	W 446	1.7	W 20604	60.6	W 300	1.9	NAVIRES BATEAUX,ETC
7938	TUGS,SPECIAL VESSELS ETC	W 12	0.2	W 293	0.4	W 20409	59.2	W 10	0.3	REMORQUEURS,BATEAUX SPEC
79383	FLOATING STRUCTURES NES	W 1	0.1	W 2	0.1	W 20403	59.1	W 2	0.1	ENGINS FLOTTANTS DIVERS
8	MISC MANUFACTURED GOODS		315.1		369.1		407.0		439.0	ART MANUFACTURES DIVERS
812	*PLUMBG,HEATNG,LGHTNG EQ	W 2097	6.0	W 1785	6.4	W 2571	8.5	W 2279	8.9	APPAR SANITAIRES CHAUFFAGE
821	*FURNITURE,PARTS THEREOF	W 3033	10.3	W 3912	14.0	W 5191	19.3	W 6146	22.8	MEUBLES ET PIECES
8219	FURNITURE AND PARTS NES	W 1978	6.3	W 2161	7.7	W 3646	12.3	W 4156	14.7	AUTRES MEUBLES ET PIECES
82192	WOOD FURNITURE NES	W 1185	3.1	W 1244	4.6	W 2468	7.8	W 3039	9.0	MEUBLES NDA EN BOIS
84	CLOTHING AND ACCESSORIES		185.2		223.9		227.0		238.9	VETEMENTS
844	UNDER GARMENTS NOT KNIT	W 11271	84.9	W 113859	111.4	W 16655	118.6	W 21242	145.9	VETEMENT DESSOUS MAT TEX
8441	— MENS SHIRTS	W 11217	84.5	W 113797	110.9	W 16577	117.9	W 21149	145.1	CHEMISES HOMMES MAT TEXT
84412	—— OF SYNTHETIC FIBRES	W 11177	84.1	W 113763	110.4	W 16537	117.3	W 21098	144.1	CHEMISES HOMMES FIB SYNT
846	UNDER GARMENTS KNITTED	W 2596	92.6	W 3356	105.1	W 3594	97.0	W 3167	78.5	SOUS VETS DE BONNETERIE
8463	— OF SYNTH FBR NONELAST	W 1932	82.2	W 2348	90.3	W 2607	85.2	W 2188	66.6	SOUS–VET BONNET FIB SYNT
84631	—— PANTY HOSE (TIGHTS)	W 1924	82.0	W 2339	90.2	W 2572	84.4	W 2163	66.1	COLLANTS BON FIBR SYNT
8465	CORSETS,GARTERS,ETC	W 348	8.3	W 555	12.1	W 325	7.1	W 328	7.2	CORSETS,GAINES ART SIM
84651	BRASSIERES	W 265	6.4	W 335	6.8	W 208	3.9	W 120	2.0	SOUTIENS–GORGE,BUSTIERS
851	*FOOTWEAR	W 638	5.5	W 576	5.5	W 961	8.4	W 1319	10.9	CHAUSSURES
87	PRECISION INSTRUMNTS NES		14.0		16.2		16.6		21.7	INSTRUM,APPAR SCIENT NDA
874	MEASURNG,CONTROLNG INSTR	W 229	9.7	W 239	10.5	W 262	11.2	W 354	15.2	INSTRUMENTS DE MESURE
88	PHOTO EQU,OPTICL GDS ETC		15.6		16.6		20.4		21.4	APP,FOURN PHOTO,OP,MONTR
885	WATCHES AND CLOCKS		8.6		10.2		12.1		12.6	HORLOGERIE
8851	WATCHES,MOVEMENTS,CASES		8.3		9.6		11.5		12.0	MONTRES,MOUVEMENTS,BOITES
88511	WATCHES		8.2		9.6		11.4		12.0	MONTRES POCHE,BRACELET
89	MISC MANUFCTRD GOODS NES		77.4		85.1		104.8		112.0	ART MANUFACTURES DIVERS
892	PRINTED MATTER	W 2218	19.5	W 2503	20.0	W 3181	24.6	W 3798	29.3	IMPRIMES
8921	PRINTED BOOKS,GLOBES,ETC	W 1504	10.5	W 1659	13.4	W 2325	17.5	W 2640	17.7	LIVRES,BROCHURES,CARTES
89211	PRINTED BOOKS,PAMPHLETS	W 1473	10.3	W 1643	13.3	W 2295	17.3	W 2597	17.5	LIVRES,BROCHURES
8928	PRINTED MATTER NES	W 370	7.6	W 473	4.8	W 562	5.1	W 798	8.8	IMPRIMES NDA
893	ARTICLES OF PLASTIC NES		21.3		23.9		32.8		32.7	OUVRAGES EN MAT DIVIS 58
8931	PLSTC PACKG CONTNRS,LIDS	W 2243	9.5	W 2699	10.5	W 3574	12.8	W 4168	13.4	ART TRANSP EMBALLAGE ETC
8939	MISC PLASTIC ARTICLES	W 2776	11.5	W 3067	13.0	W 5011	19.3	W 4670	18.7	ART DIVERS EN MAT DIV 58
89399	OTHR PLASTC ARTICLES NES	W 2493	10.8	W 2703	12.2	W 4190	18.0	W 4108	17.7	AUT OUV MAT DIV 58
897	GOLD,SILVER WARE,JEWELRY		25.1		27.0		30.0		30.7	BIJOUTERIE,ORFEVRERIE
8973	PREC JEWLRY,GLD-SILVWARE		25.0		26.8		29.8		30.3	BIJOUX OR,ARGENT ORFEVRE
89731	PRECIOUS METAL JEWELLERY		24.3		26.4		29.2		29.6	ART BIJOUTERIE,JOAILLER
9	GOODS NOT CLASSD BY KIND		53.8		48.5		81.9		80.4	ART TRANSACT NON CLASSES
931	*SPECIAL TRANSACTIONS		53.4		47.5		81.0		79.7	TRANS.SPECIALES

5. General Exports F.O.B. by Commodities according to the S.I.T.C. (Rev. 2) in million U.S. Dollars
Exportations Générales F.O.B. par Produits d'après la C.T.C.I. (Rév. 2) en millions de Dollars E.U.

SITC CTCI	COMMODITY	1993 QUANTITY QUANTITE	1993 VALUE VALEUR	1994 QUANTITY QUANTITE	1994 VALUE VALEUR	1995 QUANTITY QUANTITE	1995 VALUE VALEUR	1996 QUANTITY QUANTITE	1996 VALUE VALEUR	PRODUIT
	ALL COMMODITIES		1075.4		1210.7		1423.8		1386.9	TOUS PRODUITS
0	FOOD AND LIVE ANIMALS		226.9		210.3		264.0		278.0	ALIMENTS,ANIMAUX VIVANTS
02	DAIRY PRODCTS,BIRDS'EGGS		3.6		3.6		4.7		4.0	PRODUITS LAITIERS,OEUFS
03	FISH AND PREPARATIONS		12.8		14.0		18.1		19.6	POISSONS ET PREPARATIONS
036	SHELL FISH FRESH,FROZEN	W 2322	11.5	W 2248	12.5	W 2411	15.6	W 3016	16.2	CRUSTACES,MOLLUSQUES
04	CEREALS AND PREPARATIONS		8.2		8.7		8.0		8.5	CEREALES ET PRODUITS
048	CEREAL ETC PREPARATIONS	W 3488	8.2	W 3114	7.0	W 3538	7.9	W 3710	8.5	PREPTNS A BASE CEREALES
0484	BAKERY PRODUCTS	W 1960	3.5	W 2263	4.0	W 2593	4.9	W 2642	4.9	PRODUITS DE BOULANGERIE
04841	BREAD,BISCUIT,COM WAFERS	W 1272	2.0	W 2263	4.0	W 2593	4.9	W 1725	2.9	PAINS,BISCUITS DE MER
0488	OTH CEREAL PREPS,MALT EX	W 1457	4.5	W 790	2.9	W 880	2.9	W 1018	3.5	EXTRAITS DE MALT
05	VEGETABLES AND FRUIT		66.1		77.4		85.3		82.0	LEGUMES ET FRUITS
054	VEG ETC FRSH,SMPLY PRSVD	W 18345	14.4	W 18834	16.1	W 18825	18.4	W 18379	16.3	LEGUMES FRAIS,CONG,SECS
0548	EDIBLE VEG NES FRESH,DRY	W 15081	12.2	W 14755	13.5	W 14958	15.7	W 15123	14.0	RACINES,TUBERCULES
05481	ROOTS,TUBERS FRESH,DRY	W 14967	12.1	W 14636	13.5	W 14858	15.6	W 15032	14.0	RACINES DE MANIOC ETC
057	FRUIT,NUTS,FRESH,DRIED	W 91564	44.3	W 90666	55.9	W 100268	59.0	W 103499	59.4	FRUITS FRAIS OU SECS
0571	ORANGES, MANDARINS ETC	W 10800	3.4	W 7669	2.7	W 9027	3.8	W 10149	4.9	ORANGES,MAND,CLEMENTINES
0573	BANANA,PLANTAIN,FRSH,DRY	W 74639	35.8	W 75680	46.0	W 83018	45.8	W 85746	45.3	BANANES FRAICHES,SECHEES
0579	FRUIT FRESH OR DRIED NES	W 4816	4.6	W 5949	6.4	W 7109	8.7	W 6246	8.4	FRUITS FRAIS,SECS NDA
05798	OTHER FRESH FRUIT	W 3968	3.9	W 4981	5.5	W 5721	7.4	W 5306	7.3	AUTRES FRUITS FRAIS
058	FRUIT PRESERVED,PREPARED	W 4932	7.1	W 2869	5.1	W 4252	7.5	W 2508	5.7	CONSERVES DE FRUITS
0589	FRUIT PREPRD,PRESRVD,NES	W 1550	3.7	W 1136	3.2	W 1118	3.6	W 1263	4.1	FRUITS PREPARES CONSERV
05899	FRUIT,NUTS NES,PRESERVED	W 1549	3.6					W 1263	4.1	FRUITS PREP CONSERV NDA
06	SUGAR AND PREPS,HONEY		97.7		68.2		96.2		109.4	SUCRES ET PRODUITS
061	SUGAR AND HONEY	W 149715	97.6	W 126224	68.0	W 145004	96.1	W 181488	109.3	SUCRES ET MIEL
0611	RAW BEET AND CANE SUGAR	W 149708	97.5	W 126106	68.0	W 144986	96.1	W 181473	109.3	SUCRES BRUTS
07	COFFEE,TEA,COCOA,SPICES		27.9		27.1		38.8		40.6	CAFE,THE,CACAO,EPICES
071	COFFEE AND SUBSTITUTES	W 1418	19.8	W 982	16.7	W 1549	28.3	W 1660	32.3	CAFE ET SUCCEDANES
0711	COFFEE GREEN,ROASTED,SUB	W 1395	19.5	W 972	16.6	W 1544	28.2	W 1651	32.1	CAFE TORREFIE OU DECAFEINE
07111	COFFEE GREEN,HUSKS,SKINS	W 1375	19.1	W 948	16.1	W 1525	27.7	W 1631	31.5	CAFE NON TORREFIE
072	COCOA	W 1750	2.7	W 2874	4.2	W 2286	4.0	W 1607	2.7	CACAO
075	SPICES	W 1971	4.0	W 2412	4.7	W 2330	5.3	W 2013	4.8	EPICES
0751	PEPPER AND PIMENTO	W 1744	3.3	W 2143	3.9	W 2065	4.4	W 1731	3.9	POIVRE,PIMENTS
09	MISC EDIBLE PRODUCTS		8.8		9.4		11.0		11.8	PREP ALIMENTAIRES DIVERSES
098	EDIBLE PRODCTS,PREPS NES	W 3689	8.8	W 3875	9.4	W 4362	11.0	W 4617	11.8	PREP ALIMENTAIRES NDA
09804	SAUCES,MIXED SEASONINGS	W 1286	3.3	W 1324	3.6	W 1371	4.5	W 1187	4.0	SAUCES,ASSAISONNEMENTS
09809	MISC FOOD PREPRTIONS NES	W 1908	4.2	W 2010	4.3	W 2392	4.8	W 2864	5.8	PREP ALIMENTAIRES NDA
1	BEVERAGES AND TOBACCO		40.7		40.2		43.5		47.6	BOISSONS ET TABACS
11	BEVERAGES		35.1		33.8		34.8		37.4	BOISSONS
112	ALCOHOLIC BEVERAGES	W 25953	34.0	W 26297	32.8	W 25921	33.8	W 17037	36.4	BOISSONS ALCOOLIQUES
1123	BEER,ALE,STOUT,PORTER	W 8576	8.0	W 8685	7.6	W 9326	8.1	W 8848	7.9	BIERES
1124	DISTILLED ALCOHOLIC BEVS	W 16813	24.9	W 17079	24.0	W 16048	24.5	W 7477	26.9	ALCOOLS,EAUX-DE-VIE
11249	OTH ALCOHOLC BEVS,CMPNDS	W 16805	24.8	W 17073	24.0	W 16041	24.5	W 7469	26.9	BOISSONS ALCOOLIQUES NDA
12	TOBACCO AND MANUFACTURES		5.6		6.5		8.7		10.3	TABACS BRUTS FABRIQUES
122	TOBACCO,MANUFACTURED	W 110	5.3	W 145	6.3	W 175	8.4	W 186	9.9	TABACS FABRIQUES
1221	CIGARS,CHEROOTS,ETC	W 98	5.1	W 133	6.0	W 161	8.2	W 170	9.6	CIGARES
2	CRUDE MATERLS,EXCL FUELS		532.0		615.3		706.5		692.6	MAT BRUTES NON COMESTIBLES
28	METALLIFEROUS ORES,SCRAP		527.0		608.8		699.9		687.1	MINERAIS METAL,DECHETS
287	BASE METAL ORES,CONC NES	W 3827004	524.0	W 3939046	606.5	W 3593957	697.9	W 7139451	685.4	MINERAIS METAUX COMMUNS
2873	ALUMINIUM ORES,ALUMINA	W 3827004	524.0	W 3939046	606.5	W 3593907	697.8	W 7139451	685.4	MINERAIS D'ALUMINIUM
28731	ALUMINIUM ORE,CONCNTRATE	W 916723	84.3	W 649419	73.0	W 609095	72.2	W 3917478	78.4	MINERAIS D'ALUMINIUM
28732	ALUMINA(ALUMINIUM OXIDE)	W 2910281	439.8	W 3289627	533.5	W 2984812	625.6	W 3221973	607.1	ALUMINE (OXYDE ALUMINIUM)
29	CRUDE ANIMAL,VEG MAT NES		2.7		4.1		3.0		2.6	MATIERES BRUTES ANIM,VEGET
292	CRUDE VEG MATERIALS NES			W 46334	4.1	W 11695	3.0		0.1	MAT BRUTES VEGETALES NDA
3	MINERAL FUELS ETC		6.6		6.0		7.7		6.0	COMBUSTIBLES MINERAUX LUB
33	PETROLEUM AND PRODUCTS		6.6		6.0		7.7		6.0	PETROLE ET DERIVES
334	PETROLEUM PRODUCTS,REFIN	W 16992	6.6	W 14525	6.0	W 17706	7.7	W 12886	6.0	PRODUITS RAFFINES
3345	LUBS,PETROLEUM OILS NES	W 7148	5.4					W 4525	3.9	HUILES LUBRIFIANTES
33451	LUBS(HIGH PETR CONT) ETC	W 7147	5.4					W 4523	3.9	HUILES LUBRIF,H LOURDES
5	CHEMCLS,RELATED PROD NES		25.1		24.6		37.5		46.6	PRODUITS CHIMIQUES
51	ORGANIC CHEMICALS		0.2		0.7		9.3		18.6	PROD CHIMIQ ORGANIQUES
512	ALCOHOLS,PHENOLS ETC	W 165	0.1	W 103	0.1	W 25907	9.1	W 31151	13.8	PHENOLS,PHENOLS-ALCOOLS
5121	ACYCLIC ALCOHOLS,DERIVS	W 165	0.1	W 103	0.1	W 25907	9.1	W 31151	13.8	ALCOOLS ACYCLIQUES
51216	ETHYL ALC,DENATRD SPIRIT	W 3	0.1			W 25752	9.0	W 30694	12.2	ALCOOL ETHYLIQUE NON DENAT
516	OTHER ORGANIC CHEMICALS	W 5	0.1	W 30	0.1	W 19	0.1	W 10979	4.3	AUTRES PROD ORGANIQUES
5161	ETHERS,EPOXIDES,ACETALS	W 1	0.1	W 1	0.1	W 11	0.1	W 10976	4.3	ETHERS-OXYDES,ALCOOLS
51611	ETHERS,ETHER-ALCOHOL,ETC	W 1	0.1	W 1	0.1	W 11	0.1	W 10976	4.3	ETHERS-OXYDES
52	INORGANIC CHEMICALS		5.7		7.3		11.1		10.3	PROD CHIM INORGANIQUES
522	INORG ELEMNTS,OXIDES,ETC	W 40694	4.0	W 60242	6.0	W 79124	9.9	W 53000	9.0	ELEMENTS INORGANIQUES
5225	INORGANIC BASES ETC NES	W 39989	3.8	W 59425	5.8	W 76834	8.9	W 49009	6.6	AUTRES BASES OXYDES METAL
52256	ALUMINIUM HYDROXIDE	W 39989	3.8	W 59406	5.7	W 76834	8.9	W 49009	6.6	HYDROXYDE D'ALUMINIUM
541	*MEDICINAL,PHARM PRODUCT	K 2744	0.3	K 151519	2.3	K 98222	1.7	K 70327	2.6	PROD MEDICINAUX PHARMACEUT
5417	MEDICAMENTS	K 269761	4.0	K 149463	2.3	K 93227	1.6	K 66832	2.5	MEDICAMENTS
54179	— CONTNG OTH SUBSTANCES	K 267873	4.0	K 148305	2.3	K 89042	1.5	K 61388	2.2	MED CONT AUT SUBSTANCES
55	PERFUME,CLEANING ETC PRD		13.0		12.4		13.3		12.3	PROD POUR PARFUM,TOILETTE
551	ESSENTL OILS,PERFUME,ETC	W 563	3.3	W 759	3.4	W 773	3.7	W 2190	5.2	HUILES ESSENTIELLES
553	PERFUMERY,COSMETICS,ETC	W 1320	7.0	W 1149	6.0	W 1157	6.2	W 1043	5.3	PRODUITS DE PARFUMERIE
6	BASIC MANUFACTURES		16.1		21.4		19.4		19.5	ART MANUFACTURES
62	RUBBER MANUFACTURES NES		5.5		7.2		5.2		5.6	CAOUTCHOUC MANUFACTURE
625	RUBBER TYRES, TUBES ETC	W 1419	5.5	W 2205	7.2	W 1273	4.5	W 1541	5.6	PNEUS CAOUTCHOUC VULCANISE
66	NONMETAL MINERAL MFS NES		3.2		4.0		4.1		2.0	ART MIN NON METALLIQUES
69	METAL MANUFACTURES NES		3.9		5.4		4.8		4.4	ART MANUFACT EN METAL NDA
7	MACHINES,TRANSPORT EQUIP		14.4		27.8		43.7		31.6	MACHINES MATERIEL TRANSPORT
71	POWER GENERATING EQUIPMT		2.5		11.1		15.5		6.3	MACHINES GENERATRICES
713	INTRNL COMBUS PSTN ENGIN	W 18	2.3	W 32	11.0	W 53	15.4	W 44	6.0	MOTEURS EXPL COMB INT, PIECE
7131	AIRCRAFT PSTN ENGINS,PTS	W 17	2.3	W 28	10.9	W 49	15.4	W 32	5.7	MOTEURS EXPL P.AVIATION, PIE
71311	AIRCRAFT PISTON ENGINES	W 13	1.7	W 28	10.9	W 47	14.8	W 31	5.6	MOTEURS EXPL P.AVIATION
72	MACHS FOR SPCL INDUSTRYS		0.5		0.9		5.0		2.4	MAC SPECIALES POUR INDUST
724	TEXTILE,LEATHER MACHNRY	W 9	0.1	W 41	0.6	W 243	4.7	W 105	1.3	MACH POUR INDUSTRIE TEXTILE
7245	WEAVING,FELT MFG,ETC MCH					W 185	4.5		0.1	METIERS A TISSER,PIECES
72453	GIMPING,WARPING ETC MCHS					W 185	4.5		0.1	METIERS A TULLE ETC
77	ELECTRIC MACHNRY NES ETC		2.3		2.6		5.1		4.0	MACH APP ELECT NDA
79	OTHR TRANSPORT EQUIPMENT		4.5		9.0		11.2		13.1	AUTRE MATERIEL TRANSPORT
792	AIRCRAFT ETC	W 31	4.5	W 56	9.0	W 71	11.1	W 47	12.7	APP NAVIGATION AERIENNE
7929	AIRCRAFT PARTS NES	W 30	4.4	W 56	9.0	W 56	11.1	W 47	12.7	PIECES DU 792
8	MISC MANUFACTURED GOODS		212.4		263.9		301.1		265.2	ART MANUFACTURES DIVERS
821	*FURNITURE,PARTS THEREOF	W 605	3.6	W 755	4.5	W 561	3.5	W 433	3.4	MEUBLES ET PIECES
84	CLOTHING AND ACCESSORIES		200.3		249.1		287.4		250.4	VETEMENTS
842	MENS OUTERWEAR NOT KNIT	W 326	4.4	W 410	6.0	W 456	6.5	W 520	7.7	VET DESSUS POUR HOMMES
8423	— TROUSERS,BREECHES ETC	W 275	3.3	W 341	4.7	W 394	5.5	W 429	5.9	PANTALONS HOMMES MAT TEX
843	WOMENS OUTERWEAR NONKNIT	W 1165	15.9	W 998	15.1	W 844	13.8	W 760	14.0	VET DESSUS FEMMES MAT TEX
8439	— OTHER OUTER GARMENTS	W 990	13.1	W 894	12.6	W 788	11.7	W 751	13.8	AUT VET DES FEM MAT TEXT

5. General Exports F.O.B. by Commodities according to the S.I.T.C. (Rev. 2) in million U.S. Dollars
Exportations Générales F.O.B. par Produits d'après la C.T.C.I. (Rév. 2) en millions de Dollars E.U.

SITC CTCI	COMMODITY	1993		1994		1995		1996		PRODUIT
		QUANTITY QUANTITE	VALUE VALEUR	QUANTITY QUANTITE	VALUE VALEUR	QUANTITY QUANTITE	VALUE VALEUR	QUANTITY QUANTITE	VALUE VALEUR	
844	UNDER GARMENTS NOT KNIT	W 522	10.7	W 665	9.2	W 578	10.8	W 410	8.8	VETEMENT DESSOUS MAT TEX
8441	— MENS SHIRTS	W 446	10.0	W 293	6.5	W 404	8.2	W 318	7.5	CHEMISES HOMMES MAT TEXT
84412	—— OF SYNTHETIC FIBRES	W 439	9.9	W 229	5.3	W 372	7.8	W 316	7.4	CHEMISES HOMMES FIB SYNT
845	OUTERWEAR KNIT NONELASTC	W 645	10.3	W 688	10.1	W 515	8.5	W 227	3.9	VET DESSOUS,ACCES BONNET
8459	— OTHER,CLTHG ACCESRYS	W 499	8.0	W 548	7.9	W 384	6.9	W 217	3.7	AUT VET DESSUS DE BONNE
846	UNDER GARMENTS KNITTED	W 8244	156.5	W 10500	206.8	W 14601	245.3	W 13902	214.9	SOUS VETS DE BONNETERIE
8462	— OF COTTON NON ELASTIC	W 6112	60.0	W 7576	74.1	W 11819	110.9	W 12098	128.0	SOUS–VET BONNET COTON
84629	—— OTHER	W 6112	60.0	W 7576	74.1	W 11819	110.9	W 12098	128.0	AUT SOUS–VET BONNET COTON
8463	— OF SYNTH FBR NONELAST	W 1620	80.7	W 2220	114.0	W 2214	117.8	W 1369	74.7	SOUS–VET BONNET FIB SYNT
84631	—— PANTY HOSE (TIGHTS)	W 1592	80.1	W 2176	113.3	W 2097	116.1	W 1366	74.6	COLLANTS BON FIBR SYNT
8465	CORSETS,GARTERS,ETC	W 512	15.8	W 704	18.8	W 567	16.7	W 435	12.4	CORSETS,GAINES ART SIM
84651	BRASSIERES	W 338	12.2	W 322	12.0	W 275	10.6	W 141	5.6	SOUTIENS–GORGE,BUSTIERS
84652	CORSETS,BRACES ETC	W 174	3.7	W 382	6.9	W 292	6.2	W 294	6.9	CORSETS,GAINES,JARRETEL
89	MISC MANUFCTRD GOODS NES		6.3		8.1		7.5		8.0	ART MANUFACTURES DIVERS

1. HISTORICAL SERIES, 1962–1997 GENERAL TRADE, IMPORTS C.I.F., EXPORTS F.O.B.
SERIES HISTORIQUES, 1962–1997 COMMERCE GENERAL, IMPORTATIONS C.A.F., EXPORTATIONS F.O.B

YEAR ANNEE	VALUE IN MILLION YEN VALEUR EN MILLION YEN MERCHANDISE –MARCHANDISE IMPORTS	EXPORTS	GOLD –OR IMPORTS	EXPORTS	CONVERSION FACTORS U.S. CENTS PER YEN FACTEURS DE CONVERSION CENTS E.U. PAR YEN IMPORTS	EXPORTS	INDEX NUMBERS –INDICES QUANTUM IMPORTS	EXPORTS	UNIT VALUE VALEUR UNITAIRE IMPORTS	EXPORTS
1962	2029158.00	1769618.00	50.40	842.30	0.2778	0.2778				
1963	2424766.00	1962563.00	86.39	878.30	0.2778	0.2778				
1964	2857451.00	2402088.00	50.40	914.30	0.2778	0.2778				
1965	2940605.00	3042477.00	50.40	806.30	0.2778	0.2778				
1966	3428006.00	3519078.00		1526.00	0.2778	0.2778				
1967	4198711.00	3758966.00	50.40	1418.00	0.2778	0.2778				
1968	4675407.00	4669796.00	4082.00	986.30	0.2778	0.2778				
1969	5408473.00	5756403.00	18877.00	1706.00	0.2778	0.2778				
1970	6797221.00	6954369.00	30360.00	1166.00	0.2778	0.2778				
1971	6909956.00	8392769.00	31209.00	782.70	0.2853	0.2862				
1972	7228977.00	8806072.00	27114.00	628.30	0.3247	0.3247				
1973	10404356.00	10031427.00	95600.00	1641.00	0.3682	0.3681				
1974	18076381.00	16207880.00			0.3436	0.3426				
1975	17170026.00	16545312.00			0.3371	0.3375				
1976	19229167.00	19934617.00			0.3370	0.3372				
1977	19131781.00	21648068.00			0.3700	0.3718				
1978	16727625.00	20555841.00			0.4743	0.4745				
1979	24245350.00	22531538.00			0.4565	0.4573				
1980	31994998.00	29382000.00			0.4392	0.4418	57	62	164	115
1981	31464001.00	33469001.00			0.4554	0.4542	56	68	164	119
1982	32655998.00	34432999.00			0.4029	0.4021	56	67	171	125
1983	30015000.00	34909999.00			0.4213	0.4210	57	72	156	117
1984	32319999.00	40325001.00			0.4214	0.4208	63	84	152	117
1985	31075999.00	41958998.00			0.4200	0.4223	63	88	146	116
1986	21551001.00	35291000.00			0.5920	0.5974	69	87	92	98
1987	21738999.00	33315999.00			0.6950	0.6944	75	87	85	92
1988	24007000.00	33927999.00			0.7807	0.7808	87	91	81	90
1989	28980998.00	37823000.00			0.7238	0.7244	94	95	90	97
1990	33854001.00	41457000.00			0.6954	0.6938	100	100	100	100
1991	31900000.00	42359001.00			0.7439	0.7440	104	103	91	100
1992	29526999.00	43010998.00			0.7900	0.7903	104	104	84	100
1993	26823999.00	40199999.00			0.9009	0.9012	107	102	75	96
1994	28051001.00	40470000.00			0.9813	0.9811	121	103	69	95
1995	31533998.00	41531998.00			1.0655	1.0673	136	107	68	94
1996	37992002.00	44729000.00			0.9191	0.9187	141	107	80	101
1997	40955998.00	50937999.00			0.8273	0.8266	145	117	84	105

2. IMPORTS BY BROAD ECONOMIC CATEGORY AND EXPORTS BY INDUSTRIAL ORIGIN. (PERCENTAGE OF TOTAL VALUE)
IMPORTATIONS PAR CATEGORIES ECONOMIQUES ET EXPORTATIONS PAR BRANCHE D'ACTIVITE.(EN POURCENTAGE DE LA VALEUR TOTALE)

IMPORTS – IMPORTATIONS

	1991	1992	1993	1994	1995	1996	1997
TOTAL IMPORTS–IMPORTATIONS TOTALES	100.	100.	100.	100.	100.	100.	100.
1 FOOD BEV–ALIMENTATION BOISSONS	13.2	14.5	14.8	15.6	13.8	13.2	12.4
11 PRIMARY–PRODUITS DE BASE	9.8	10.7	11.1	11.5	10.1	9.5	8.7
111 FOR INDUSTRY–POUR L'INDUSTRIE	2.0	2.1	2.1	2.5	1.8	2.0	2.0
112 FOR HOUSEHOLDS–POUR LES MENAGES	7.8	8.6	9.0	9.0	8.3	7.5	6.8
12 PROCESSED–PRODUITS ELABORES	3.4	3.7	3.8	4.1	3.7	3.6	3.7
121 FOR INDUSTRY–POUR L'INDUSTRIE	0.6	0.7	0.6	0.6	0.6	0.5	0.5
122 FOR HOUSEHOLDS–POUR LES MENAGES	2.8	3.1	3.2	3.5	3.2	3.1	3.1
2 IND SUPPLIES–APPROV INDUSTRIELS	32.5	30.1	30.2	29.1	29.0	26.3	26.5
21 PRIMARY–PRODUITS DE BASE	11.1	10.5	10.2	9.3	8.5	7.7	7.2
22 PROCESSED–PRODUITS ELABORES	21.4	19.6	20.0	19.8	20.5	18.6	19.3
3 FUELS–COMBUSTIBLES	23.3	22.7	20.5	17.5	16.0	17.3	18.4
31 PRIMARY–PRODUITS DE BASE	19.9	19.9	18.2	15.6	14.2	15.0	16.3
32 PROCESSED–PRODUITS ELABORES	3.4	2.9	2.3	1.9	1.8	2.3	2.1
321 MOTOR SPIRIT–ESSENCE		1.5	1.2	1.0	1.1	1.2	1.4
322 OTHER–AUTRES	3.4	1.3	1.1	0.9	0.7	1.1	0.7
4 MACHINERY–EQUIPEMENT	11.7	11.7	12.6	14.1	17.4	19.4	20.0
41 CAPITAL EQUIPMENT–MACHINES	8.1	8.0	8.5	9.4	11.4	12.9	13.3
42 PARTS–PIECES ACCESSOIRES	3.5	3.7	4.1	4.7	6.0	6.5	6.7
5 TRANSPORT–TRANSPORT	5.2	5.2	5.1	5.6	5.4	5.3	5.2
51 PASSENGER CARS–AUTOMOBILES	2.2	2.2	2.1	2.6	3.0	2.9	2.3
52 OTHER–AUTRES	1.6	1.5	1.4	1.6	1.0	0.9	1.2
521 INDUSTRIAL–INDUSTRIELS	1.5	1.4	1.3	1.5	0.8	0.8	1.1
522 NON INDUSTRIAL–NON INDUSTRIEL	0.1	0.1	0.1	0.1	0.1	0.1	0.1
53 PARTS–PIECES ACCESSOIRES	1.4	1.5	1.5	1.4	1.4	1.5	1.7
6 CONSUM GOODS–BIENS CONSOMMATION	12.8	14.3	15.4	16.7	17.0	17.0	16.1
61 DURABLE–DURABLES	3.1	3.0	3.2	3.7	3.9	3.9	3.8
62 SEMI DURABLE–SEMI DURABLES	7.8	9.1	9.9	10.6	10.8	10.9	10.1
63 NON DURABLE–NON DURABLES	1.9	2.2	2.3	2.4	2.4	2.2	2.2
7 GOODS NES–BIENS NDA	1.4	1.5	1.4	1.5	1.4	1.4	1.4

EXPORTS – EXPORTATIONS

	1991	1992	1993	1994	1995	1996	1997
TOTAL EXPORTS–EXPORTATIONS TOTALES	100.	100.	100.	100.	100.	100.	100.
1 AGRICULTURE	0.3	0.3	0.2	0.2	0.2	0.3	0.3
2 MINING QUARRY–INDUS EXTRACTIVES	0.1	0.1	0.1	0.1	0.1	0.1	0.1
3 MANUFACTURING–IND MANUFACTUR	99.6	99.6	99.6	99.6	99.7	99.6	99.6
31 FOOD BEV TOBACCO–ALIM BOISS TAB	0.4	0.4	0.4	0.4	0.4	0.4	0.4
32 TEXTILES–INDUSTRIES TEXTILES	2.4	2.4	2.1	1.9	1.8	1.9	1.8
33 WOOD & PRODUCTS–BOIS & PRODUITS	0.0	0.0	0.0	0.0	0.0	0.0	0.0
34 PAPER & PRODUCTS–PAPIER & PRODT	0.8	0.8	0.7	0.7	0.7	0.6	0.6
35 CHEMICALS–INDUSTRIES CHIMIQUES	8.7	8.8	8.8	9.3	10.2	10.4	10.4
36 NON METAL MIN–MIN NON METAL	1.1	1.1	1.1	1.2	1.3	1.3	1.2
37 BASIC METAL–IND METAL BASE	5.1	4.7	4.8	4.6	5.0	4.7	4.8
38 METAL MANUF–MANUF METAL	77.8	78.2	78.6	78.5	77.0	76.6	76.3
39 OTH MANUF IND–AUTRES MANUF	3.2	3.2	3.1	3.1	3.3	3.7	4.1

3. TRADE BY PRINCIPAL COUNTRIES OF ORIGIN AND DESTINATION (VALUE IN MILLION U.S. DOLLARS)
ECHANGES SELON LES PRINCIPAUX PAYS D'ORIGINE ET DE DESTINATION (VALEUR EN MILLIONS DE DOLLARS EU)

COUNTRIES–PAYS	GENERAL IMPORTS C.I.F. IMPORTATIONS GENERALES C.A.F				
	1993	1994	1995	1996	1997
World	240670.2	274741.8	336094.0	349186.0	338842.4
Africa	3781.4	4017.7	4624.5	4968.8	4835.8
Americas	71866.2	81395.2	98142.9	101048.3	97092.4
– Northern America	63981.2	72304.5	86784.4	90003.4	85890.4
– LAIA	7368.6	8532.4	10714.3	10422.3	10516.4
– CACM	143.1	226.5	282.4	263.5	312.3
– Caribbean	201.6	177.9	219.0	208.6	224.0
– Rest of America	171.7	153.9	142.8	150.5	149.3
Asia excl fmr USSR	109693.7	125111.8	155076.5	166166.2	163892.0
– Middle East	26591.5	27043.0	30564.6	34195.7	37413.4
Asia former USSR	96.8	85.8	172.1	196.8	239.3
Europe excl fmr USSR	37195.4	43413.1	54647.6	54748.4	50577.8
– European Union	32913.1	38839.9	48871.9	49381.8	45027.2
– Eastern Europe	423.0	377.4	443.2	479.6	613.4
– Rest of Europe	3859.2	4195.9	5332.5	4887.0	4937.2
Europe former USSR	2930.5	3645.1	4937.0	4140.7	4189.6
Oceania	15103.1	17068.4	18491.5	17912.9	18013.5
Other	3.2	4.8	2.1	3.9	1.8
USA/Etats–Unis d'Amer	55764.5	63288.2	75900.5	79771.0	76009.1
China/Chine	20437.1	27483.6	36017.1	40436.1	41876.7
Korea, Republic of	11638.8	13488.9	17281.3	15948.9	14583.8
Indonesia/Indonésie	12499.5	12923.6	14225.7	15193.8	14638.6
Australia/Australie	12216.8	13641.6	14558.4	14229.4	14588.2
Other Asia n.e.s.	9669.5	10753.1	14350.2	14959.3	12500.4
Germany/Allemagne	9787.6	11121.0	13725.6	14161.7	12421.0
United Arab Emirates	9005.0	9144.0	10203.3	11516.1	12339.5
Saudi Arabia	8937.5	8387.1	9730.3	10664.7	11942.4
Malaysia/Malaisie	7639.7	8228.4	10564.4	11750.4	11376.5
Canada	8091.3	8917.4	10777.7	10114.7	9800.4
Thailand/Thaïlande	6488.3	8192.1	10120.0	10212.3	9574.9
United Kingdom	4945.3	5907.8	7133.7	7168.2	7191.9
France, Monaco	5127.4	5668.1	6679.2	6265.0	5779.8
Singapore/Singapour	3600.6	4645.1	6864.3	7322.6	5874.7
Italy/Italie	3824.1	4932.1	6362.0	6759.4	5922.8
Russian Federation	2756.0	3473.7	4738.3	3937.0	3997.1
Philippines	2373.7	2652.0	3476.1	4522.1	5017.6
Brazil/Brésil	2841.5	3245.7	3942.1	3754.1	3744.0
Switzerland,Liechtenst.	2839.2	3068.7	4053.7	3563.4	3431.5
Iran (Islamic Rep of)	2439.3	2758.9	2823.7	3279.9	3551.0
Kuwait/ Koweït	1676.7	2093.0	2779.1	3175.0	3727.7
India/Inde	2283.3	2665.4	2924.1	2842.8	2665.0
Chile/Chili	1820.7	2163.8	3166.3	2762.7	2981.2
So. African Customs Un	1920.4	2220.8	2567.5	2852.9	2823.3
Qatar	2121.5	1972.5	2177.2	2467.0	3029.4
China, Hong Kong SAR	1986.5	2144.2	2738.3	2574.3	2251.5
Sweden/Suède	1538.4	1832.4	2584.9	2798.4	2559.5
New Zealand	1750.6	2067.9	2542.2	2458.1	2337.2
Belgium–Luxembourg	1393.3	1840.6	2393.6	2358.0	1844.0
Netherlands/Pays–Bas	1334.5	1602.6	2186.7	2103.0	1956.1
Ireland/Irlande	1301.7	1415.3	1978.6	2104.7	2280.6
Oman	1558.9	1858.0	1869.4	1955.4	1835.1
Denmark/Danemark	1555.7	1637.9	1922.5	1702.7	1694.3
Viet Nam	1064.5	1348.1	1720.4	2017.8	2188.0
Mexico/Mexique	1074.1	1341.7	1495.5	1889.6	1613.1
Brunei Darussalam	1416.2	1204.8	1356.3	1392.4	1405.9
Spain/Espagne	727.5	1134.7	1510.1	1552.2	1346.7
Israel/Israël	776.3	980.1	1296.2	1231.6	1028.7
Norway,Svalbard and JM	803.5	864.3	994.9	1004.9	1247.5

COUNTRIES–PAYS	GENERAL EXPORTS F.O.B. EXPORTATIONS GENERALES F.O.B.				
	1993	1994	1995	1996	1997
Monde	360911.1	395599.9	442937.3	410946.8	421052.9
Afrique	7295.7	6869.9	7381.7	5700.1	5340.7
Amériques	128595.4	142270.2	146365.8	134836.0	144298.7
– Amérique du Nord	112712.9	124651.9	127886.6	118138.2	124559.7
– ALAI	9604.8	10159.5	10109.5	9147.1	11337.4
– MCAC	536.2	443.9	479.5	353.5	458.8
– Caraïbes	1083.4	1072.2	648.2	1217.9	1184.8
– Autre Amérique	4658.1	5942.7	7242.0	5979.3	6758.0
Asie anc. URSS exclus	148788.8	168455.7	202745.6	191806.2	189116.8
– Moyen–Orient	12569.1	9820.7	8892.3	9853.0	11355.9
Asie ancienne URSS	95.2	83.7	124.6	163.9	117.3
Europe anc. URSS exclus	64776.3	65733.0	74668.3	67346.7	70741.6
– Union Européenne	60222.0	61384.1	70515.6	63136.9	65814.4
– Europe de l'Est	622.3	561.8	734.4	867.8	1181.6
– Autre de l'Europe	3932.0	3787.1	3418.3	3342.0	3745.6
Europe ancienne URSS	1580.6	1297.7	1214.8	1107.0	1129.9
Océanie	9778.5	10889.4	10436.4	9987.0	10307.7
Autre	0.5	0.4	0.2		0.1
USA/Etats–Unis d'Amer	106353.3	118706.2	122024.1	112990.8	118412.5
Korea, Republic of	19066.8	24317.7	31226.0	29328.0	26064.6
China, Hong Kong SAR	22666.7	25712.9	27725.1	25355.8	27259.3
Other Asia n.e.s.	22051.9	23780.2	28898.4	25954.5	27568.4
China/Chine	17158.4	18694.0	21991.3	21886.8	21745.5
Singapore/Singapour	16557.3	19596.3	23011.4	20758.8	20248.6
Germany/Allemagne	18146.9	17812.8	20348.9	18198.3	18000.4
Thailand/Thaïlande	12256.8	14676.8	19730.0	18263.5	14584.2
Malaysia/Malaisie	9603.2	12333.1	16777.0	15327.8	14511.2
United Kingdom	12047.9	12747.6	14113.5	12476.3	13711.5
Netherlands/Pays–Bas	7450.5	8379.3	9941.7	9251.2	9803.8
Indonesia/Indonésie	5986.1	7652.7	9968.2	9058.5	10168.6
Australia/Australie	7702.2	8693.9	8099.2	7404.9	7954.8
Philippines	4812.3	5896.7	7118.1	8403.7	8689.6
Panama	4608.0	5887.4	7179.0	5910.2	6682.9
Canada	6328.1	5913.5	5819.6	5120.8	6101.1
France, Monaco	5488.7	5261.7	6083.9	5500.0	5725.6
Belgium–Luxembourg	4274.3	4108.5	4879.4	4318.9	4148.5
Mexico/Mexique	3960.1	4198.8	3575.7	3653.0	3876.7
Italy/Italie	3242.1	3355.9	4081.8	3383.9	3792.8
Saudi Arabia	4102.3	3261.5	2712.1	3011.4	3076.7
United Arab Emirates	2551.7	2262.0	2110.6	2309.8	2537.9
Brazil/Brésil	1613.3	1875.6	2584.5	2217.6	2929.6
Spain/Espagne	2209.4	2109.8	2394.7	2186.3	2227.7
Switzerland,Liechtenst.	2151.7	2267.5	2337.1	2027.5	2118.2
India/Inde	1521.2	2041.2	2538.3	2431.6	2213.1
So. African Customs Un	2032.4	2054.6	2469.6	2075.2	1882.2
Ireland/Irlande	1486.2	1685.7	2089.6	1911.4	2176.8
Sweden/Suède	1292.8	1484.0	1698.6	1438.2	1631.6
New Zealand	1272.3	1535.2	1623.9	1676.1	1411.9
Liberia/Libéria	2157.1	2046.2	1806.4	809.0	466.6
Norway,Svalbard and JM	1580.3	1359.5	900.7	1094.6	1378.7
Russian Federation	1496.6	1174.4	1153.5	1023.0	1013.9
Austria/Autriche	1331.8	1249.7	1197.7	967.4	993.9
Turkey/Turquie	1286.8	621.8	912.7	1113.7	1749.6
Finland/Finlande	687.7	985.1	1387.7	1149.3	1339.3
Pakistan	1375.3	853.2	1230.8	1155.8	762.7
Israel/Israël	989.8	871.9	1012.1	1108.4	1034.3
Colombia/Colombie	929.8	1031.8	1091.3	887.9	998.7
Iran (Islamic Rep of)	1459.7	929.1	660.6	716.2	881.0

(VALUE AS PERCENTAGE OF WORLD TOTAL)(VALEURS EN POURCENTAGE DU TOTAL MONDIAL)

	1988	1989	1990	1991	1992	1993	1994	1995	1996	1997
Africa	2.2	2.0	1.6	1.6	1.5	1.6	1.5	1.4	1.4	1.4
Americas	31.4	31.3	30.1	30.0	29.5	29.9	29.6	29.2	28.9	28.7
– Northern America	27.1	27.2	26.1	26.0	26.0	26.6	26.3	25.8	25.8	25.3
– LAIA	4.0	3.8	3.8	3.7	3.3	3.1	3.1	3.2	3.0	3.1
– CACM	0.1	0.1	0.1	0.1	0.1	0.1	0.1	0.1	0.1	0.1
– Caribbean	0.2	0.1	0.1	0.1	0.1	0.1	0.1	0.1	0.1	0.1
– Rest of America	0.1	0.1	0.1	0.1	0.1	0.1	0.1	0.0	0.0	0.0
Asia excl fmr USSR	41.5	41.6	42.1	43.7	45.0	45.6	45.5	46.1	47.6	48.4
– Middle East	10.0	10.6	13.0	12.1	12.3	11.0	9.8	9.1	9.8	11.0
Asia former USSR					0.0	0.0	0.0	0.1	0.1	0.1
Europe excl fmr USSR	16.6	17.0	18.4	16.8	16.5	15.5	15.8	16.3	15.7	14.9
– European Union	13.9	14.4	16.0	14.5	14.5	13.7	14.1	14.5	14.1	13.3
– Eastern Europe	0.4	0.4	0.3	0.3	0.2	0.2	0.1	0.1	0.1	0.2
– Rest of Europe	2.3	2.2	2.1	2.0	1.8	1.6	1.5	1.6	1.4	1.5
Europe former USSR	1.5	1.4	1.4	1.4	1.1	1.2	1.3	1.5	1.2	1.2
Oceania	6.8	6.7	6.3	6.6	6.4	6.3	6.2	5.5	5.1	5.3
Other	0.0	0.0	0.0	0.0	0.0	0.0	0.0	0.0	0.0	0.0
USA/Etats–Unis d'Amer	22.6	23.0	22.5	22.7	22.6	23.2	23.0	22.6	22.8	22.4
China/Chine	5.3	5.3	5.1	6.0	7.3	8.5	10.0	10.7	11.6	12.4
Korea, Republic of	6.3	6.2	5.0	5.2	5.0	4.8	4.9	5.1	4.6	4.3
Indonesia/Indonésie	5.1	5.2	5.4	5.4	5.2	5.2	4.7	4.2	4.4	4.3
Australia/Australie	5.5	5.5	5.3	5.5	5.3	5.1	5.0	4.3	4.1	4.3
Other Asia n.e.s.	4.7	4.3	3.6	4.0	4.1	4.0	3.9	4.3	4.3	3.7
Germany/Allemagne				4.5	4.6	4.1	4.0	4.1	4.1	3.7
United Arab Emirates	2.8	2.9	3.9	4.4	4.2	3.7	3.3	3.0	3.3	3.6
Saudi Arabia	3.4	3.3	4.5	4.3	4.4	3.7	3.1	2.9	3.1	3.5
Malaysia/Malaisie	2.5	2.4	2.3	2.7	2.8	3.2	3.0	3.1	3.4	3.4

	1988	1989	1990	1991	1992	1993	1994	1995	1996	1997
Afrique	2.2	1.9	1.9	1.8	1.9	2.0	1.7	1.7	1.4	1.3
Amériques	39.8	39.7	37.4	35.5	34.9	35.6	36.0	33.0	32.8	34.3
– Amérique du Nord	36.5	36.6	34.1	31.7	30.6	31.2	31.5	28.9	28.7	29.6
– ALAI	1.9	1.9	1.9	2.2	2.6	2.7	2.6	2.3	2.2	2.7
– MCAC	0.1	0.1	0.1	0.1	0.2	0.1	0.1	0.1	0.1	0.1
– Caraïbes	0.3	0.3	0.3	0.3	0.3	0.3	0.3	0.1	0.3	0.3
– Autre Amérique	1.0	0.9	1.0	1.3	1.3	1.3	1.5	1.6	1.5	1.6
Asie anc. URSS exclus	32.3	32.9	34.6	37.4	38.9	41.2	42.6	45.8	46.7	44.9
– Moyen–Orient	3.1	2.8	3.3	3.7	4.2	3.5	2.5	2.0	2.4	2.7
Asie ancienne URSS					0.0	0.0	0.0	0.0	0.0	0.0
Europe anc. URSS exclus	21.4	20.7	22.1	22.0	21.3	17.9	16.6	16.9	16.4	16.8
– Union Européenne	19.7	19.2	20.4	20.4	19.8	16.7	15.5	15.9	15.4	15.6
– Europe de l'Est	0.3	0.2	0.3	0.2	0.2	0.2	0.1	0.2	0.2	0.3
– Autre de l'Europe	1.4	1.3	1.5	1.4	1.3	1.1	1.0	0.8	0.8	0.9
Europe ancienne URSS	1.2	1.1	0.9	0.7	0.3	0.4	0.3	0.3	0.3	0.3
Océanie	3.2	3.6	3.1	2.7	2.6	2.7	2.8	2.4	2.4	2.4
Autre	0.0	0.0	0.0	0.0	0.0	0.0	0.0	0.0		0.0
USA/Etats–Unis d'Amer	34.1	34.1	31.7	29.3	28.4	29.5	30.0	27.5	27.5	28.1
Korea, Republic of	5.8	6.0	6.1	6.4	5.2	5.3	6.1	7.0	7.1	6.2
China, Hong Kong SAR	4.4	4.2	4.6	5.2	6.1	6.3	6.5	6.3	6.2	6.5
Other Asia n.e.s.	5.4	5.6	5.4	5.8	6.2	6.1	6.0	6.5	6.3	6.5
China/Chine	3.6	3.1	2.1	2.7	3.5	4.8	4.7	5.0	5.3	5.2
Singapore/Singapour	3.1	3.4	3.7	3.9	3.8	4.6	5.0	5.2	5.1	4.8
Germany/Allemagne				6.6	6.0	5.0	4.5	4.6	4.4	4.3
Thailand/Thaïlande	1.9	2.5	3.2	3.0	3.1	3.4	3.7	4.5	4.4	3.5
Malaysia/Malaisie	1.2	1.5	1.9	2.4	2.4	2.7	3.1	3.8	3.7	3.4
United Kingdom	4.0	3.9	3.8	3.5	3.6	3.3	3.2	3.2	3.0	3.3

4. General Imports C.I.F. by Commodities according to the S.I.T.C. (Rev. 2) in million U.S. Dollars
Importations Générales C.A.F. par Produits d'après la C.T.C.I. (Rév. 2) en millions de Dollars E.U.

SITC CTCI	COMMODITY	1994 QUANTITY QUANTITE	1994 VALUE VALEUR	1995 QUANTITY QUANTITE	1995 VALUE VALEUR	1996 QUANTITY QUANTITE	1996 VALUE VALEUR	1997 QUANTITY QUANTITE	1997 VALUE VALEUR	PRODUIT
	ALL COMMODITIES		274742.0		336094.3		349186.2		338842.4	TOUS PRODUITS
0	FOOD AND LIVE ANIMALS		41701.0		45748.2		46101.3		41568.3	ALIMENTS,ANIMAUX VIVANTS
01	MEAT AND PREPARATIONS		7764.3		9652.8		9373.0		7584.8	VIANDES ET PREPARATIONS
011	MEAT FRESH,CHILLD,FROZEN	W 1727115	7381.7	W 1984455	9114.9	W 2035349	8689.0	W 1839809	6942.5	VIANDES FRAICHES,REF,CONGE
0111	BOVINE MEAT FRESH,FROZEN	W 588609	2855.3	W 648739	3246.8	W 629639	2715.9	W 647312	2614.2	VIANDES BOVIN FRAI,REF
01112	BOVINE MEAT BONELESS	W 575095	2795.1	W 636108	3176.0	W 614419	2644.7	W 636137	2565.0	VIANDES BOVIN DESOSSEES
0113	PIG MEAT FRESH,CHLD,FRZN	W 493903	2920.7	W 580675	3723.8	W 653293	3827.1	W 511956	2695.9	VIANDE DE PORC
0114	POULTRY FRESH CHLLD,FRZN	W 454727	987.0	W 549252	1305.7	W 560643	1287.9	W 509018	1016.6	VOLAILLES MORTES
03	FISH AND PREPARATIONS		15866.8		17378.2		·16666.5		15188.5	POISSONS ET PREPARATIONS
034	FISH,FRESH,CHILLED,FROZN	W 1716601	6746.2	W 1755951	7242.4	W 1757164	7116.9	W 1751181	6640.9	POISSON FRAIS, REFRIG,CONG
0341	FISH FRSH,CHLLD,EX FILLT	W 159386	1605.1	W 166716	1719.7	W 167600	1513.5	W 166650	1453.5	POISSON FRAIS,REFRIGERE
0342	FISH FROZEN,EXCL FILLETS	W 1427056	4206.7	W 1420084	4225.0	W 1417770	4424.3	W 1398419	4049.4	POISSONS CONGELES
0344	FISH FILLETS,FROZEN	W 124760	879.0	W 162993	1231.7	W 165717	1117.7	W 180251	1084.6	FILETS CONGELES
036	SHELL FISH FRESH,FROZEN	W 830948	6773.1	W 798573	7363.2	W 821450	6686.5	W 754933	5852.7	CRUSTACES,MOLLUSQUES
037	FISH ETC PREPD,PRSVD NES	W 190954	1960.4	W 220956	2336.2	W 243784	2418.8	W 268832	2381.9	POIS,CRUST,MOL PREPARES
0371	FISH PREPARD,PRESRVD NES	W 113366	1318.5	W 128739	1534.3	W 148385	1617.0	W 168494	1605.5	CONSERVES DE POISSONS
04	CEREALS AND PREPARATIONS		6525.4		5435.7		6907.2		5935.4	CEREALES ET PRODUITS
041	WHEAT ETC UNMILLED	W 6352435	1352.5	W 5965296	1342.5	W 5927749	1560.7	W 6315254	1362.8	FROMENT,EPEAUTRE
0412	OTHER WHEAT ETC UNMILLED	W 6179028	1304.6	W 5792466	1293.2	W 5728434	1502.1	W 6131198	1317.3	AUTRE FROMENT NON MOULU
042	RICE	W 2536319	1436.7	W 28971	22.3	W 444992	267.0	W 568730	331.1	RIZ
0421	RICE IN HUSK OR HUSKED	W 1741365	993.9	W 22831	18.4	W 300924	201.0	W 157968	97.2	RIZ SANS AUTRE PREPARATION
04212	RICE HUSKED	W 1741365	993.9	W 22831	18.4	W 300924	201.0	W 157965	97.2	RIZ CARGO
044	MAIZE UNMILLED	MW 15930	2261.9	MW 16584	2395.4	MW 16004	3048.4	MW 16097	2447.7	MAIS NON MOULU
048	CEREAL ETC PREPARATIONS	W 1174268	772.8	W 1215973	950.9	W 1292145	1115.7	W 1292692	1026.9	PREPTNS A BASE CEREALES
05	VEGETABLES AND FRUIT		5775.2		6277.6		6093.8		5653.5	LEGUMES ET FRUITS
054	VEG ETC FRSH,SMPLY PRSVD	W 1703801	2015.6	W 1696152	2159.9	W 1716564	2157.1	W 1659564	2021.6	LEGUMES FRAIS,CONG,SECS
0545	OTHER FRESH VEGETABLES	W 581498	866.1	W 632952	984.7	W 562966	840.3	W 530379	773.1	AUTRES LEGUMES FRAIS,REF
057	FRUIT,NUTS,FRESH,DRIED	W 1877888	1844.2	W 1815376	1946.3	W 1695885	1862.4	W 1777929	1794.2	FRUITS FRAIS OU SECS
058	FRUIT PRESERVED,PREPARED	W 739090	1223.7	W 837268	1407.5	W 766160	1295.6	W 695783	1100.9	CONSERVES DE FRUITS
07	COFFEE,TEA,COCOA,SPICES		1752.4		2084.9		2051.4		2150.8	CAFE,THE,CACAO,EPICES
071	COFFEE AND SUBSTITUTES	W 371590	1064.9	W 326110	1264.7	W 355404	1073.5	W 353900	1230.0	CAFE ET SUCCEDANES
0711	COFFEE GREEN,ROASTED,SUB	W 347622	958.7	W 302720	1115.0	W 330307	932.5	W 327076	1095.1	CAFE TORREFIE OU DECAFEINE
07111	COFFEE GREEN,HUSKS,SKINS	W 345280	941.8	W 300563	1092.1	W 326914	900.3	W 325233	1072.9	CAFE NON TORREFIE
081	*FEEDING STUFF FOR ANIML	W 5955199	1851.7	W 6311549	2208.6	W 6249320	2287.2	W 6352842	2373.7	NOURRITURE POUR ANIMAUX
1	BEVERAGES AND TOBACCO		4791.0		5027.8		4483.0		4400.6	BOISSONS ET TABACS
11	BEVERAGES		2193.0		2271.9		1972.0		1901.6	BOISSONS
112	ALCOHOLIC BEVERAGES	W 550290	1948.3	W 534132	1955.9	W 455441	1748.5	W 459665	1725.4	BOISSONS ALCOOLIQUES
1124	DISTILLED ALCOHOLIC BEVS	W 121744	1251.3	W 118782	1173.1	W 123264	1016.2	W 131752	896.1	ALCOOLS,EAUX–DE–VIE
12	TOBACCO AND MANUFACTURES		2598.0		2756.0		2511.0		2499.0	TABACS BRUTS FABRIQUES
122	TOBACCO,MANUFACTURED	W 67217	1912.1	W 72296	2173.7	W 77450	2037.2	W 77890	1947.5	TABACS FABRIQUES
1222	CIGARETTES	W 66908	1906.5	W 71912	2168.0	W 77192	2032.2	W 77581	1939.7	CIGARETTES
2	CRUDE MATERLS,EXCL FUELS		29659.5		34267.9		31611.8		30557.1	MAT BRUTES NON COMESTIBLES
22	OIL SEEDS,OLEAGINOUS FRT		2282.6		2297.2		2629.1		2764.8	GRAINES,FRUITS OLEAGINEUX
222	SEEDS FOR'SOFT'FIXED OIL	W 7011717	2211.9	W 7061468	2224.5	W 7157237	2561.4	W 7494834	2686.3	GRAINES HUILES FIXES
2222	SOYA BEANS	W 4731319	1405.3	W 4813489	1372.4	W 4870324	1652.8	W 5056935	1752.2	FEVES DE SOJA
23	RUBBER, CRUDE		869.5		1317.0		1245.8		1086.3	CAOUTCHOUC BRUT
232	NATURAL RUBBER,GUMS	W 654067	666.7	W 703967	1096.1	W 732835	1063.9	W 740443	890.2	LATEX CAOUTCHOUC NATUREL
24	CORK AND WOOD		11401.7		12247.3		11654.9		10842.8	LIEGE ET BOIS
246	PULPWOOD,CHIPS,WOODWASTE	MW 11973	1795.6	MW 13684	2337.5	MW 13693	2225.1	MW 13889	2103.7	BOIS DE TRITURATION
24602	PULPWOOD CHIPS,PARTICLES	MW 11968	1793.1	MW 13679	2334.6	MW 13687	2222.2	MW 13883	2100.6	EN FORME DE PLAQUETTES
247	OTH WOOD ROUGH,SQUARED	MW 16068	4990.7	MW 15713	4740.7	MW 15270	4435.9	MW 14607	3732.3	BOIS BRUTS EQUARRIS
2471	SAW–,VENEER–LOGS CONIFER	MW 10107	3026.0	MW 10431	3161.1	MW 10256	2962.8	MW 9773	2401.3	CONIFERES POUR SCIAGE,PLACAG
24711	— IN THE ROUGH	MW 10107	3026.0	MW 10431	3161.1	MW 10256	2962.8	MW 9773	2401.3	ECORCES OU DEGROSSIS
2472	SAW–,VENEER–LOGS NON–CON	W 5960920	1964.7	W 5281714	1579.7	W 5013985	1473.1	W 4834212	1331.1	NON CONIFERES SCIAGE,PLAC
24721	— IN THE ROUGH	W 5960920	1964.7	W 5281714	1579.7	W 5013985	1473.1	W 4834212	1331.1	BRUTS ECORCES DEGROSSIS
248	WOOD SHAPED,SLEEPERS	W 6641851	4574.0	W 7283370	5122.4	W 7322308	4941.9	W 7695622	4946.3	BOIS SIMPLEMENT TRAVAILLES
2482	LUMBER SHAPED CONIFER	W 5450747	3412.5	W 6008962	3790.1	W 6172622	3725.3	W 6471557	3709.4	CONIFERES SCIES,RABOTES
24821	LUMBER SAWN ETC CONIFER	W 5348250	3340.5	W 5889195	3703.4	W 6068674	3628.2	W 6409274	3624.4	CONIFERES SCIES LONGITUD
2483	LUMBER SHAPED NON–CONIFR	W 1158959	1144.2	W 1241002	1312.7	W 1117641	1198.5	W 1191038	1219.2	NON CONIFERES SCIES,RABOTES
24831	LUMBER SAWN ETC NON–CON	W 1021175	956.0	W 1078383	1078.4	W 989363	950.0	W 1054442	969.3	SCIES LONGITUDINALEMENT
251	*PULP AND WASTE PAPER	W 4117268	1963.3	W 4061440	2984.2	W 3850644	2010.0	W 3812221	1859.0	PATES A PAPIER,DECHETS
2517	SODA,SULPHATE WOOD PULP	W 2977404	1487.5	W 2803730	2280.5	W 2658478	1459.1	W 2692720	1354.0	PATES CHIMIQUES AU SULFATE
25172	— BLEACHED,NONDISSOLVNG	W 2857310	1432.0	W 2669369	2180.0	W 2537938	1396.0	W 2572331	1299.2	PATES BLANCHIES
26	TEXTILE FIBRES AND WASTE		1663.3		1594.8		1500.7		1286.1	FIBRES TEXTILES
27	CRUDE FERTLZR,MINRLS NES		1797.6		1912.9		1843.1		1866.8	ENGRAIS MINERAUX BRUTS
278	OTHER CRUDE MINERALS	MW 14109	1057.7	MW 15599	1205.4	MW 15255	1208.4	MW 16013	1242.3	AUTRES MINERAUX BRUTS
28	METALLIFEROUS ORES,SCRAP		7491.8		9418.9		8299.5		8650.1	MINERAIS METAL,DECHETS
281	IRON ORE,CONCENTRATES	MW 116090	2904.2	MW 120435	3127.0	MW 119205	3117.8	MW 126600	3271.7	MINERAIS DE FER
2815	IRON ORE,CONC,NOT AGGLOM	MW 106360	2523.6	MW 111247	2740.8	MW 110426	2751.7	MW 117086	2886.3	MINERAIS NON AGGLOMERES
287	BASE METAL ORES,CONC NES	MW 11992	3417.9	MW 13428	4805.7	MW 13680	3965.2		3992.8	MINERAIS METAUX COMMUNS
2871	CPR ORE ETC,CEMENT COPPR	W 3459011	2247.8	W 3828506	3093.0	W 3848021	2476.3	W 3849808	2457.2	MINERAIS DE CUIVRE,MATTES
28711	COPPER ORES,EXCL MATTE	W 3457066	2245.9	W 3825212	3088.1	W 3840935	2467.0	W 3837455	2436.5	MINERAIS DE CUIVRE
288	NONFERR METAL SCRAP NES	W 456370	825.6	W 423410	1011.7		723.3	W 408299	763.8	DECHETS NON FERREUX
29	CRUDE ANIMAL,VEG MAT NES		1745.5		1987.1		2026.5		1840.6	MATIERES BRUTES ANIM,VEGET
292	CRUDE VEG MATERIALS NES		1126.8		1284.2		1287.2		1150.7	MAT BRUTES VEGETALES NDA
3	MINERAL FUELS ETC		48195.8		53976.4		60931.3		62901.2	COMBUSTIBLES MINERAUX LUB
32	COAL,COKE AND BRIQUETTES		5795.3		6704.6		7024.0		6981.6	HOUILLES,COKES,BRIQUETTES
322	COAL,LIGNITE AND PEAT	MW 117273	5752.2	MW 126319	6636.9	MW 129605	6947.1	MW 133727	6853.1	HOUILLES,LIGNITES,TOURBE
3222	OTH COAL,NOT AGGLOMERATD	MW 114689	5606.3	MW 123398	6462.4	MW 126183	6749.2	MW 130109	6650.8	AUTRES HOUILLES
33	PETROLEUM AND PRODUCTS		32982.9		36249.7		41697.6		42322.3	PETROLE ET DERIVES
333	CRUDE PETROLEUM	MW 226364	27233.3	MW 223793	29627.2	MW 219943	33089.3	MW 226880	34562.4	HUILES BRUTES DE PETROLE
334	PETROLEUM PRODUCTS,REFIN	MW 33440	5125.9	MW 35237	5864.8	MW 39689	7903.3	MW 31505	6943.4	PRODUITS RAFFINES
3341	GASOLINE,OTH LIGHT OILS	MW 18623	2806.7	MW 21866	3645.4	MW 21885	4259.2	MW 21339	4784.3	ESSENCES POUR MOTEURS
33419	OTH LIGHT PETROLEUM OILS	MW 18534	2789.1	MW 21827	3637.9	MW 21757	4229.8	MW 21249	4760.8	AUTRES HUILES LEGERES
3342	KEROSENE,OTH MEDIUM OILS	W 4598839	893.5	W 4089084	841.3	W 7269123	1801.9	W 4217475	1019.0	PETR LAMPANTS,AUT HUIL
341	*GAS,NATURAL AND MANUFCT		9417.7		11022.2		12209.7		13597.3	GAZ NATUREL,GAZ MANUFACT
3413	PETROLM GASES,LIQUEFIED	MW 56945	9417.7	MW 57894	11022.1	MW 61288	12209.7	MW 62836	13597.2	GAZ DE PETROLE LIQUEFIE
34131	LIQUEFIED PROPANE,BUTANE	MW 14828	2477.4	MW 14971	3343.0	MW 15403	3566.7	MW 15175	4036.5	PROPANE,BUTANE LIQUEFIES
34139	OTH HYDROCARBON GAS LQFD	MW 42117	6940.4	MW 42923	7679.2	MW 45886	8643.0	MW 47661	9560.8	HYDROCARBURES GAZEUX NDA
5	CHEMCLS,RELATED PROD NES		19606.3		23862.4		22570.4		22699.8	PRODUITS CHIMIQUES
51	ORGANIC CHEMICALS		5830.4		7633.4		6799.5		6992.0	PROD CHIMIQ ORGANIQUES
512	ALCOHOLS,PHENOLS ETC		1112.1		1483.7	W 2813004	1093.1		1274.7	PHENOLS,PHENOLS–ALCOOLS
5121	ACYCLIC ALCOHOLS,DERIVS		937.1		1257.4	W 2700971	883.5		1079.9	ALCOOLS ACYCLIQUES
514	NITROGEN–FNCTN COMPOUNDS	W 350792	1797.5	W 397042	2335.6	W 420723	1999.8	W 438836	1995.1	COMPOSES FONCT AZOTEES
5148	OTH NITROGN–FNCTN CMPNDS	W 170947	861.9	W 179674	1169.5	W 197591	911.7	W 203058	915.1	AUTRES COMPOSES AZOTES
515	ORG–INORG COMPOUNDS ETC	W 76408	1543.3	W 97756	2036.6	W 100687	2038.0	W 106625	1986.7	COMPOSES ORGANO–MINERAUX
5156	HETEROCYCLIC CMPDS ETC	W 46503	1196.1	W 57614	1552.4	W 56482	1564.5	W 58708	1583.7	COMPOSES HETEROCYCLIQUES
51569	OTH HETEROCYC CMPDS,ETC	W 43196	1159.0	W 54136	1511.3	W 51637	1518.9	W 51817	1527.5	AUT COMP HETEROCYCLIQUES
52	INORGANIC CHEMICALS		2889.9		3424.0		3175.6		3209.6	PROD CHIM INORGANIQUES
522	INORG ELEMNTS,OXIDES,ETC	W 673447	902.4	W 880731	1259.2	W 889694	1310.9	W 877713	1284.5	ELEMENTS INORGANIQUES
524	RADIOACTIVE ETC MATERIAL		1446.9		1505.6		1214.3		1275.7	MATIERES RADIOACTIVES

4. General Imports C.I.F. by Commodities according to the S.I.T.C. (Rev. 2) in million U.S. Dollars
Importations Générales C.A.F. par Produits d'après la C.T.C.I. (Rév. 2) en millions de Dollars E.U.

SITC CTCI	COMMODITY	1994 QUANTITY QUANTITE	1994 VALUE VALEUR	1995 QUANTITY QUANTITE	1995 VALUE VALEUR	1996 QUANTITY QUANTITE	1996 VALUE VALEUR	1997 QUANTITY QUANTITE	1997 VALUE VALEUR	PRODUIT
5241	RADIOACTIVE ELEMENTS ETC		1349.6		1366.8		1057.8		1132.1	RADIOELEMENTS,ISOTOPES
541	*MEDICINAL,PHARM PRODUCT	MK 34828	4222.0	MK 39561	4916.7	MK 42924	4501.9	MK 46788	4243.2	PROD MEDICINAUX PHARMACEUT
5417	MEDICAMENTS	MK 15765	2050.7	MK 18691	2496.2	MK 21760	2186.7	MK 23657	2190.6	MEDICAMENTS
54179	— CONTNG OTH SUBSTANCES	MK 13432	1169.4	MK 16229	1459.5	MK 19441	1291.7	MK 20573	1323.8	MED CONT AUT SUBSTANCES
55	PERFUME,CLEANING ETC PRD		1187.0		1502.5		1574.4		1625.4	PROD POUR PARFUM,TOILETTE
58	PLASTIC MATERIALS ETC		1725.7		2028.1		2034.3		2201.3	MAT PLAST ARTIFICIELLES
583	POLYMERIZATION ETC PRODS	W 447743	926.7	W 418746	1099.0	W 453339	1112.5	W 523811	1175.8	PROD POLYMERISATION
59	CHEMICAL MATERIALS NES		2445.7		2884.1		3029.2		2945.6	MAT PROD CHIMIQUES NDA
598	MISCEL CHEM PRODUCTS NES	W 703068	1676.6	W 776773	1983.2	W 856904	2093.7	W 911952	2090.6	PROD DIV INDUST CHIM NDA
5989	CHEM PRODUCTS,PREPS NES	W 316163	1247.9	W 353259	1483.4	W 417218	1587.2	W 460127	1586.8	PROD PREP CHIMIQUES NDA
59899	OTH CHEM PRODS,PREPS,NES	W 222149	852.0	W 258461	1031.6	W 306424	1128.1	W 344212	1152.6	AUT PRODUITS CHIMIQUES NDA
6	BASIC MANUFACTURES		31294.4		39846.7		38048.8		37216.9	ART MANUFACTURES
62	RUBBER MANUFACTURES NES		906.3		1030.5		983.7		1049.6	CAOUTCHOUC MANUFACTURE
63	WOOD,CORK MANUFACTRS NES		3089.9		3688.9		4472.1		4374.2	OUVRAGES LIEGE ET BOIS
634	VENEERS,PLYWOOD,ETC		2217.2		2415.3		2954.7		2950.7	PLACAGES,CONTRE–PLAQUES
6342	PLYWOOD OF WOOD SHEETS	A 517756	1922.0	A 623395	2103.6	V 5380471	2601.5	A 703626	2595.3	BOIS CONTRE–PLAQUES
635	WOOD MANUFACTURES NES		851.9		1249.3	W 686149	1495.0	W 683957	1399.4	ART MANUF EN BOIS NDA
64	PAPER,PAPERBOARD AND MFR		1735.0		2215.0		2434.3		2008.0	PAPIERS,CARTONS & OUVRAGES
641	PAPER AND PAPERBOARD	W 1742664	1515.3	W 1868720	1924.8	W 2239417	2136.1	W 2053859	1710.0	PAPIERS ET CARTONS
65	TEXTILE YARN,FABRICS,ETC		5519.4		6350.7		6531.6		6240.8	FILS,TISSUS,ARTICLES TEXTILE
651	TEXTILE YARN	W 376191	1486.1	W 361460	1619.9	W 399875	1718.1	W 461112	1854.1	FILS TEXTILES
658	TEXTILE ARTICLES NES	W 170425	1102.4	W 200636	1423.3	W 200552	1414.9	W 204513	1372.7	ART FACONNES MAT TEXTILES
66	NONMETAL MINERAL MFS NES		5207.5		6177.1		5953.8		5166.0	ART MIN NON METALLIQUES
664	GLASS		532.6		766.5		828.0		1018.1	VERRE
667	PEARL,PREC–,SEMI–P STONE		3058.1		3364.8		2986.1		2066.0	PERLES, PIERRES GEMMES
6672	DIAMONDS NONINDUST,UNSET		2201.6		2577.0		2191.9		1455.7	DIAMANTS BRUTS
66729	— CUT ETC NOT SET		2181.3		2560.9		2171.2		1438.0	DIAMANTS TAILLES
67	IRON AND STEEL		4100.9		5907.9		4543.2		4520.2	FER ET ACIER
671	PIG IRON ETC	W 3285052	1259.0	W 4646015	2030.6	W 2632418	1594.6	W 3099254	1553.0	FONTE,SPIEGEL,POUDRES
6716	FERRO–ALLOYS	W 1474386	926.4	W 1869476	1486.3	W 1677432	1372.5	W 1814040	1270.8	FERRO–ALLIAGES
67169	OTHER FERRO–ALLOYS	W 904092	602.7	W 1188404	1028.0	W 1048897	889.7	W 1162069	834.3	AUTRES FERRO–ALLIAGES
672	IRON,STEEL PRIMARY FORMS		894.6	W 3112259	1326.6	W 2702474	924.9	W 2942276	963.8	LINGOTS FER,ACIER
6727	IRN,STL COIL FR REROLLNG		794.5	W 2540376	1106.2	W 2402383	835.5	W 2668142	890.7	EBAUCHES POUR TOLES FER
67271	IRON,SIMPLE STEEL COILS	W 2015008	780.0	W 2531025	1089.3	W 2392109	820.2	W 2652131	870.5	EBAUCHES NON EN ACIER
674	IRN,STL UNIV,PLATE,SHEET	W 2462890	1218.9	W 2854307	1574.4	W 2411117	1152.8	W 2732573	1204.5	LARGES PLATS,TOLES
68	NON–FERROUS METALS		7771.4		10662.6		9080.6		9872.3	METAUX NON FERREUX
681	SILVER,PLATINUM,ETC		1554.8		1716.7		1457.8		1668.2	ARGENT ET PLATINE
6812	METALS OF PLATINUM GROUP		1387.0		1519.5		1274.4		1448.6	PLATINE
68123	PLATINUM,ALLOYS UNWRGHT		903.0		918.5		870.6		780.7	PLATINE,ALLIAGES BRUTS
682	COPPER EXC CEMENT COPPER	W 462720	1108.4	W 477189	1549.3	W 427834	1203.2	W 428485	1161.4	CUIVRE
6821	COPPER NES,ALLOYS,UNWRT	W 412398	871.9	W 419829	1230.0	W 372151	925.1	W 365058	870.6	CUIVRE BRUT
68212	COPPER REFINED,UNWROUGHT	W 363860	761.7	W 397575	1159.0	W 365302	907.9	W 358635	852.1	CUIVRE AFFINE BRUT
684	ALUMINIUM	W 2712102	3937.8	W 2901878	5620.1	W 2862265	4820.5	W 3083956	5297.3	ALUMINIUM
6841	ALUMINIUM,ALLOYS,UNWRGHT	W 2639423	3691.7	W 2802785	5217.5	W 2758858	4375.9	W 2986016	4866.0	ALUMINIUM,ALLIAGES BRUTS
69	METAL MANUFACTURES NES		2530.7		3282.5		3487.4		3481.4	ART MANUFACT EN METAL NDA
699	BASE METAL MFRS NES	W 149120	867.4	W 200808	1157.2	W 239836	1281.9	W 254502	1292.2	ART MANUFACTURES MET NDA
7	MACHINES,TRANSPORT EQUIP		52582.0		75721.9		85058.4		83420.1	MACHINES MATERIEL TRANSPORT
71	POWER GENERATING EQUIPMT		2794.6		3585.6		3694.9		4237.3	MACHINES GENERATRICES
714	ENGINES AND MOTORS NES	W 4261	1162.6	W 5903	1487.0	W 5994	1575.6	W 8268	2004.7	MOTEURS NON ELECTRIQUES
7149	ENGINE & MOTOR PARTS NES	W 2607	674.8	W 2848	785.7	W 4541	1006.2	W 6349	1284.9	PIECES 714 ET 718.88
716	ROTATING ELECTRIC PLANT	W 55765	870.4	W 77040	1180.9	W 91990	1290.7	W 106036	1367.8	APP ELECTR ROTATIFS,PIECES
7162	AC MTRS,GENRTRS,GEN SETS	W 41716	740.1	W 55956	995.1	W 66213	1066.5	W 74477	1099.3	MOTEURS ELECTRIQUES
72	MACHS FOR SPCL INDUSTRYS		2641.2		3447.1		4181.8		4335.9	MAC SPECIALES POUR INDUST
728	OTH MACHY FOR SPCL INDUS	W 47209	1257.6	W 65041	1709.0		2233.9		2458.1	AUT MACH IND PARTICULIERES
7284	MACHY FOR SPCL INDUS NES	W 33971	1107.0	W 45924	1515.2		2004.5		2224.6	MACH SPEC IND PARTICUL.
72848	OTH MCHY WITH INDIV FNCT	W 21152	644.4	W 26865	861.3	W 33123	1203.5	W 37327	1324.6	AUTRES MACHINES NDA
73	METALWORKING MACHINERY		609.8		912.0		1168.4		1142.9	MACH TRAVAIL DES METAUX
74	GENRL INDUSTRL MACHY NES		3907.2		5246.8		6075.6		6070.3	MACH APP INDUSTRIE
741	HEATING,COOLING EQUIPMNT		847.0		1183.8		1299.3		1237.1	MACH CHAUFFAGE,PIECES
743	PUMPS NES,CENTRFUGES ETC	W 41359	755.0	W 68596	1026.5	W 79970	1213.7	W 83843	1196.6	POMPES COMPRES,VENT ETC
749	NONELEC MACH PTS,ACC NES	W 76103	1191.8	W 101488	1553.1	W 121202	1787.9	W 141604	1920.5	PIECES MACH NON ELEC NDA
75	OFFICE MACHNES,ADP EQUIP		9358.5		16273.5		19479.2		19369.9	MACH BUREAU TRAIT AUTOM
752	AUTOMTIC DATA PROC EQUIP	W 40101	5472.1	W 96086	10429.1	MN 48723	12405.7	MN 61349	11986.6	MACH TRAIT INFORMATION
7522	DIGITAL COMPUTERS	W 2715	470.6	W 7638	1233.6	N 1229621	1023.1	N 624053	872.9	MACH DIGITALES COMPLETES
7523	DIGITL CENTRL PROCESSORS	W 11554	2554.5	W 23396	4308.8	N 2269429	4845.8	N 1771093	4357.7	UNITES CENTRALES
7524	DIGITL CENTRL STOR UNITS	W 5184	1339.2	W 9679	2716.5	MN 21351	3571.1	MN 26350	3590.4	UNITES MEMOIRE CENTRALES
7525	ADP PERIPHERAL UNITS	W 18263	653.2	W 50536	1461.6	MN 21959	1949.3	MN 29659	1952.3	UNITES PERIPHERIQUES
7528	OFF–LINE DATA PROC EQUIP	W 2378	453.8	W 4815	707.3	N 1913106	1013.6	N 2941688	1210.6	MACH AUXIL TRAIT INFORM
759	OFFICE,ADP MCH PTS,ACCES	W 32906	3570.7	W 49460	5305.3	W 64425	6439.2	W 67057	6782.6	PIECES DU 751 ET 752
7599	ACCTG,ETC,ADP MCH PTS,AC	W 17691	3329.7	W 29556	4969.3	W 41049	5996.3	W 40908	6290.7	PIECES DU 751 ET 752
76	TELECOMM,SOUND EQUIPMENT		6213.1		9144.1		10634.0		9659.0	EQUIPEMENT DE TELECOM
761	TELEVISION RECEIVERS	W 76669	1007.9	W 102978	1390.9	N 7699822	1484.3	N 7488201	1303.0	RECEPTEURS DE TELEVISION
7611	COLOUR TV RECEIVERS	W 76363	999.6	W 102679	1382.7	N 7610085	1471.9	N 7392874	1291.0	RECEPTEURS COULEUR
763	SOUND RECORDRS,PHONOGRPH	W 15306	531.0	W 24949	936.5		1141.4		984.6	PHONO,APP ENREGISTREMENT
7638	OTHR SOUND APPARATUS ETC	W 15017	526.1	W 24586	928.1		1130.8		976.0	AUT APP D'ENREGIS,REPROD
764	TELECOM EQPT,PTS,ACC NES	W 95043	4019.1	W 109468	5814.0		7097.6		6571.2	EQUIP TELECOM,PIECES
7641	LINE TELEPHONE,ETC EQUIP	W 7636	674.0	W 11829	1189.8	MN 10739	1826.3	MN 10607	1699.7	APP TELEPHON PAR FIL
7643	TV,RADIO TRANSMITTRS ETC	W 1911	582.4	W 2765	1216.0	W 2251	1126.1	W 1583	667.2	APP EMET TELE RADIO
7649	PTS NES OF EQUIPMT OF 76	W 49247	2125.5	W 49401	2613.1	W 52168	3265.7	W 51636	3272.8	PIECES DE LA DIV 76
76491	PTS NES OF APPAR OF 7641	W 6947	501.4	W 6923	616.2	W 8576	894.2	W 9706	1019.0	PIECES POUR 764.1
76493	TELECOMM EQUIPMT PTS NES	W 14656	816.4	W 15506	1010.1	W 20530	1526.4	W 21443	1450.8	PIECES 761,762,764.3,8
77	ELECTRIC MACHNRY NES ETC		13877.5		21476.3		23902.4		23898.1	MACH APP ELECT NDA
771	ELECTRIC POWER MACHY NES	W 56902	1009.0	W 73302	1426.4	W 86443	1693.0	W 92016	1743.0	MACH PROD,TRANS ELECTR
7712	OTH ELEC POWER MACHY NES	W 27879	638.6	W 35525	971.2	W 46187	1257.6	W 50298	1286.0	AUT APP PROD TRANSF ELEC
772	SWITCHGEAR ETC,PARTS NES	W 21830	1219.6	W 30160	1738.7	W 39212	2012.8	W 48775	2262.9	APP COUPURE,SECT ETC
7721	SWITCHGEAR ETC	W 18756	1049.7	W 25808	1472.3	W 33875	1670.4	W 42912	1874.9	APP COUPURE,SECTIONMNT
773	ELECTR DISTRIBUTNG EQUIP	W 44071	680.2	W 60257	987.5	W 89754	1324.4	W 108945	1516.6	EQUIPMT DISTRIBUTION ELECT
7731	INSULATED WIRE,CABLE ETC	W 42987	659.7	W 57966	959.0	W 86273	1290.7	W 106730	1482.6	FILS,CABLES ISOLES ELECT
775	HOUSEHOLD TYPE EQUIP NES	W 76997	828.3	W 121734	1268.8	W 150096	1353.9	W 148032	1243.3	MACH,APP USAGE DOMESTQUE
776	TRANSISTORS,VALVES,ETC		7306.2		12260.4		13239.7		12871.1	LAMPES,TUBES,VALVES
7764	ELECTRONIC MICROCIRCUITS	MN 4148359	6067.3	MN 5570746	10843.8	MN 5387991	11726.8	MN 6674362	11067.5	MICROSTRUCTURES ELECTRON
778	ELECTRICAL MACHINERY NES	W 83140	2186.9	W 110998	2987.0		3320.7		3401.2	AUTRES MACH ELECT NDA
7788	OTH ELEC MACHY,EQUIP NES	W 32081	1630.9	W 45910	2234.8		2455.8		2478.2	AUT MACH APP ELEC NDA
77886	OTH ELEC MACHINERY NES	W 6421	1199.6	W 9048	1682.4	MN 74239	1742.4	MN 84487	1696.2	AUT MACH APP ELECTRIQUES
78	ROAD VEHICLES		8967.6		12540.8		13019.9		10664.4	VEHICULES ROUTIERS
781	PASS MOTOR VEH EXC BUSES	N 295476	6951.4	N 401836	9992.6	N 439638	10245.3	N 371113	7835.5	AUTO TRANSPORT PERSONNES
784	MOTOR VEH PRTS,ACCES NES	W 140229	1136.9	W 161502	1454.5	W 181973	1633.3	W 212026	1785.6	PIECES 722,781,782,783
7849	OTHER MOTOR VEHCL PARTS	W 139856	1130.7	W 160979	1444.6	W 181253	1624.4	W 211420	1777.8	PIECES 722,781,782,783
79	OTHR TRANSPORT EQUIPMENT		4212.9		3096.1		2902.6		4042.6	AUTRE MATERIEL TRANSPORT
792	AIRCRAFT ETC	W 4844	3891.4	W 3839	2768.1	W 3737	2528.4	W 4915	3752.5	APP NAVIGATION AERIENNE
7924	AIRCRFT NES OVER 15000KG	W 3209	3142.9	W 1825	1846.1	W 1542	1531.6	W 2526	2789.9	AERODYNES PLUS 15000 KG

4. General Imports C.I.F. by Commodities according to the S.I.T.C. (Rev. 2) in million U.S. Dollars
Importations Générales C.A.F. par Produits d'après la C.T.C.I. (Rév. 2) en millions de Dollars E.U.

SITC CTCI	COMMODITY	1994		1995		1996		1997		PRODUIT
		QUANTITY QUANTITE	VALUE VALEUR	QUANTITY QUANTITE	VALUE VALEUR	QUANTITY QUANTITE	VALUE VALEUR	QUANTITY QUANTITE	VALUE VALEUR	
8	MISC MANUFACTURED GOODS		39978.1		49364.7		53215.2		49561.3	ART MANUFACTURES DIVERS
821	*FURNITURE,PARTS THEREOF	W 519747	2676.6	W 624003	3155.5	W 709990	3453.1	W 769840	3339.8	MEUBLES ET PIECES
8211	CHAIRS,SEATS AND PARTS	W 152830	949.3	W 171953	1071.7	W 185148	1166.6	W 200273	1157.7	SIEGES ET PIECES
8219	FURNITURE AND PARTS NES	W 312880	1113.9	W 392550	1414.4	W 467007	1631.6	W 516173	1615.8	AUTRES MEUBLES ET PIECES
831	*TRAVEL GOODS,HANDBAGS	W 83043	2373.3	W 106831	2953.1	W 108502	3023.3	W 104199	2709.9	ARTICLES DE VOYAGE ETC
83109	OTHER TRAVEL BAGS,CASES	W 63121	1514.3	W 83640	2070.0	W 83492	2107.3	W 77729	1831.5	AUT CONTENANTS SIMILAIRES
84	CLOTHING AND ACCESSORIES		15294.6		18787.4		19700.0		16753.0	VETEMENTS
842	MENS OUTERWEAR NOT KNIT	W 108730	2624.1	W 117722	3244.7	W 136659	3736.1	W 122038	3179.4	VET DESSUS POUR HOMMES
8423	— TROUSERS,BREECHES ETC	W 40116	751.1	W 50135	1068.5	W 56703	1161.9	W 55397	1092.2	PANTALONS HOMMES MAT TEX
8429	— OTHER OUTER GARMENTS	W 43426	968.6	W 44310	1157.5	W 57815	1535.7	W 45362	1111.8	AUT VET DES HOM MAT TEX
843	WOMENS OUTERWEAR NONKNIT	W 114085	3526.1	W 129726	4556.0	W 141958	4971.9	W 119751	4033.9	VET DESSUS FEMMES MAT TEX
8431	— COATS AND JACKETS	W 18559	892.3	W 21866	1137.1	W 26826	1326.7	W 21417	1076.7	MANT,VEST FEM MAT TEXTIL
8439	— OTHER OUTER GARMENTS	W 60310	1301.0	W 66058	1679.7	W 73595	1922.6	W 61914	1508.6	AUT VET DES FEM MAT TEXT
844	UNDER GARMENTS NOT KNIT	W 62857	1113.0	W 61814	1287.3	W 59183	1267.7	W 53483	1081.6	VETEMENT DESSOUS MAT TEX
845	OUTERWEAR KNIT NONELASTC	W 181593	4241.4	W 191271	5053.3	W 193468	5069.1	W 186084	4716.8	VET DESSOUS,ACCES BONNET
8451	— JERSEYS,PULLOVERS ETC	W 112023	2964.6	W 114820	3438.5	W 117029	3390.9	W 115086	3101.8	CHANDAILS,PULL–OVERS ETC
8459	— OTHER,CLTHG ACCESRYS	W 64781	1113.0	W 69482	1357.4	W 69769	1420.5	W 62201	1308.5	AUT VET DESSUS DE BONNE
846	UNDER GARMENTS KNITTED	W 91127	1848.0	W 111866	2512.0	W 112140	2586.0	W 95469	2090.7	SOUS VETS DE BONNETERIE
8462	— OF COTTON NON ELASTIC	W 67836	1124.6	W 87986	1615.1	W 85954	1631.3	W 72709	1264.4	SOUS–VET BONNET COTON
84629	—— OTHER	W 67836	1124.6	W 87986	1615.1	W 85954	1631.3	W 72709	1264.4	AUT SOUS–VET BONNET COTON
847	TEXTILE CLTHNG ACCES NES	W 35908	864.4	W 43239	1003.3	W 47032	992.7	W 50645	882.7	ACCES VET MAT TEXT NDA
848	HEADGEAR,NONTXTL CLOTHNG	W 47960	1077.9	W 50669	1131.2	W 54665	1076.9	W 53966	768.1	VET ACCES MAT AUT QUE TEX
851	*FOOTWEAR	W 178221	2191.0	W 200053	2746.9	W 213325	3118.0	W 203805	2959.5	CHAUSSURES
85101	FOOTWEAR RUBBER,PLASTIC	W 80953	889.9	W 92083	1146.0	W 100216	1296.9	W 94701	1189.7	CHAUS SEMELLES CAOUTCH
85102	FOOTWEAR LEATHER	W 94622	1276.4	W 106599	1586.6	W 111553	1805.2	W 107904	1758.8	CHAUS SEMELLES EN CUIR
87	PRECISION INSTRUMNTS NES		4506.6		5666.1		6822.7		7224.6	INSTRUM,APPAR SCIENT NDA
871	OPTICAL INSTRUMENTS	W 2716	373.5	W 3452	508.1	W 4132	780.2	W 4831	1074.1	APPAR,INSTRUM D'OPTIQUE
872	MEDICAL INSTRUMENTS NES	W 13971	1280.4	W 16946	1734.5	W 22442	1961.1	W 24928	2019.9	INSTR,APP MEDIC–CHIR NDA
87202	OTH MEDICAL INSTRUMENTS	W 12557	1196.6	W 14116	1597.9	W 17488	1780.6	W 20307	1840.9	INSTRUM,APP MEDECINE
874	MEASURNG,CONTROLNG INSTR	W 14854	2822.8	W 20060	3391.1		4042.1		4081.0	INSTRUMENTS DE MESURE
8742	MEASUR,DRAW ETC INST,PTS	W 4286	690.5	W 6383	863.7		1126.0		1162.0	INST DESSIN,TRACAGE,PCS
8748	ELEC MEAS,CONTRL EQU NES	W 3004	939.5	W 3520	1163.7	W 4179	1362.4	W 4310	1372.1	APP ELEC ELECTRO MESURE
87483	OTH ELCTRNC MEAS ETC EQU	W 2919	920.7	W 3411	1139.0	W 4009	1329.1	W 4202	1347.0	AUT APP ELECTRO DE MESURE
88	PHOTO EQU,OPTICL GDS ETC		3169.7		3887.8		4146.1		4049.4	APP,FOURN PHOTO,OP,MONTR
881	PHOTO APPARAT,EQUIPT NES		654.9		876.6		1024.9		1083.0	APP,EQUIP PHOTO NDA
885	WATCHES AND CLOCKS		1438.8		1762.2		1782.1		1698.5	HORLOGERIE
8851	WATCHES,MOVEMENTS,CASES		1194.8		1444.2		1446.0		1368.7	MONTRES,MOUVEMENTS,BOITES
88511	WATCHES		1113.6		1365.2		1354.5		1275.8	MONTRES POCHE,BRACELET
89	MISC MANUFCTRD GOODS NES		9521.6		11785.5		12520.6		12151.7	ART MANUFACTURES DIVERS
893	ARTICLES OF PLASTIC NES		1277.9		1740.5		1980.1		2081.4	OUVRAGES EN MAT DIVIS 58
8939	MISC PLASTIC ARTICLES	W 148165	871.6	W 195040	1192.1	W 226846	1370.6	W 243391	1395.4	ART DIVERS EN MAT DIV 58
89399	OTHR PLASTC ARTICLES NES	W 127298	786.6	W 166196	1071.1	W 191291	1240.9	W 206757	1266.9	AUT OUV MAT DIV 58
894	TOYS,SPORTING GOODS,ETC	W 175169	2605.6	W 225648	3509.7	W 246092	3744.1	W 221006	3668.5	VOITURES ENFANTS,JOUETS
8942	TOYS,INDOOR GAMES ETC	W 117966	1019.3	W 157595	1404.7	W 181764	1668.9	W 167807	1979.7	JOUETS,JEUX ETC
8947	OTH SPORT GDS,FAIR AMUSM	W 53105	1545.4	W 62527	2049.6	W 59008	2003.8	W 47196	1632.1	AUT ART DE SPORT
89472	OTH OUTDOOR SPORT GOODS	W 44438	1276.8	W 48828	1652.7	W 43960	1488.4	W 35315	1209.8	ART POUR JEUX PLEIN AIR
897	GOLD,SILVER WARE,JEWELRY		1274.6		1414.7		1308.2		1076.8	BIJOUTERIE,ORFEVRERIE
8973	PREC JEWLRY,GLD–SILVWARE		1056.9		1203.4		1142.2		942.4	BIJOUX OR,ARGENT ORFEVRE
89731	PRECIOUS METAL JEWELLERY		997.4		1141.2		1093.3		889.2	ART BIJOUTERIE,JOAILLER
898	MUSICAL INSTRUMENTS,PTS		1422.3		1837.4		2033.6		1903.7	INSTRUMENTS DE MUSIQUE
8983	SOUND RECRDNG TAPE,DISCS		1111.5		1488.3		1667.9		1513.5	SUPPORTS SON POUR 763
89832	RECORDED DISCS,TAPES ETC		765.4		1048.3	MN 134949	1086.7	MN 162995	928.1	DISQUES,PHONO,BANDES
899	OTHER MANUFACTURED GOODS		1436.3		1609.4		1700.4		1644.3	AUT ART MANUF DIVERS NDA
9	GOODS NOT CLASSD BY KIND		6370.2		7518.3		6395.9		5763.9	ART TRANSACT NON CLASSES
931	*SPECIAL TRANSACTIONS	W 227234	3507.8	W 213762	3902.2		4452.1	W 201957	4195.2	TRANS.SPECIALES
971	*GOLD,NON MONETARY NES	K 201164	2434.2	K 278144	3250.4		1690.6	K 183542	1341.5	OR NON MONETAIRE
97101	NONMON GLD UNWRT,SEMIMFD	K 197349	2403.0	K 271332	3201.7	K 135667	1631.4	K 119358	1262.8	OR,ALLIAGES D'OR BRUTS

5. General Exports F.O.B. by Commodities according to the S.I.T.C. (Rev. 2) in million U.S. Dollars
Exportations Générales F.O.B. par Produits d'après la C.T.C.I. (Rév. 2) en millions de Dollars E.U.

SITC CTCI	COMMODITY	1994 QUANTITY QUANTITE	1994 VALUE VALEUR	1995 QUANTITY QUANTITE	1995 VALUE VALEUR	1996 QUANTITY QUANTITE	1996 VALUE VALEUR	1997 QUANTITY QUANTITE	1997 VALUE VALEUR	PRODUIT
	ALL COMMODITIES		395600.0		442937.5		410947.1		421053.0	TOUS PRODUITS
0	FOOD AND LIVE ANIMALS		1644.2		1611.7		1558.1		1746.3	ALIMENTS,ANIMAUX VIVANTS
2	CRUDE MATERLS,EXCL FUELS		2567.6		3085.7		3033.2		3006.8	MAT BRUTES NON COMESTIBLES
3	MINERAL FUELS ETC		2517.9		2735.8		2197.1		2181.3	COMBUSTIBLES MINERAUX LUB
33	PETROLEUM AND PRODUCTS		2212.6		2387.8		1900.2		1921.3	PETROLE ET DERIVES
334	PETROLEUM PRODUCTS,REFIN	W 7561858	2066.5	MW 9072	2200.2	W 8160078	1695.1	W 8741296	1718.4	PRODUITS RAFFINES
5	CHEMCLS,RELATED PROD NES		22863.2		29253.6		27922.3		28979.4	PRODUITS CHIMIQUES
51	ORGANIC CHEMICALS		8040.5		11133.1		10290.4		10249.9	PROD CHIMIQ ORGANIQUES
511	HYDROCARBONS NES,DERIVS	W 2474343	1482.1	W 3527642	2735.1	W 3427432	1982.4	W 4057198	2053.4	HYDROCARBURES NDA
5112	CYCLIC HYDROCARBONS	W 1995075	1072.5	W 2571311	2064.1	W 2434968	1349.3	W 3072459	1394.0	HYDROCARBURES CYCLIQUES
513	CARBOXYLIC ACIDS ETC	W 1382635	1797.4	W 1442272	2559.5	W 1484518	2476.3	W 1492172	2126.1	ACIDES CARBOXYLIQUES
514	NITROGEN-FNCTN COMPOUNDS	W 534117	1922.5	W 567798	2342.8	W 592474	2238.0	W 605851	2254.4	COMPOSES FONCT AZOTEES
5148	OTH NITROGN-FNCTN CMPNDS	W 317017	1038.7	W 375593	1425.5	W 389973	1368.8	W 406462	1393.4	AUTRES COMPOSES AZOTES
515	ORG-INORG COMPOUNDS ETC	W 300060	1509.0	W 328448	1806.2	W 355249	1946.4	W 339433	2096.7	COMPOSES ORGANO-MINERAUX
5156	HETEROCYCLIC CMPDS ETC	W 229343	1108.9	W 260227	1358.0	W 276175	1373.0	W 257753	1502.1	COMPOSES HETEROCYCLIQUES
52	INORGANIC CHEMICALS		1390.3		1676.8		1656.8		1664.0	PROD CHIM INORGANIQUES
53	DYES,TANNING,COLOUR PROD		1792.9		1934.3		1913.7		2256.6	PROD TEINTURE,COLORANTS
533	PIGMENTS,PAINTS,ETC	W 166384	1113.9	W 163273	1263.1	W 173763	1300.8	W 207738	1606.5	PIGMENTS,PEINTURES,VERNIS
541	*MEDICINAL,PHARM PRODUCT		1547.9		1843.7		1889.4		1952.5	PROD MEDICINAUX PHARMACEUT
58	PLASTIC MATERIALS ETC		6135.3		7975.1		7434.1		7651.3	MAT PLAST ARTIFICIELLES
582	PROD OF CONDENSATION ETC	W 640214	2041.4	W 759939	2824.5	W 722676	2609.3	W 804624	2630.3	PROD CONDENS,POLYCOND
583	POLYMERIZATION ETC PRODS	W 2349102	3912.9	W 2722629	4952.5	W 2949574	4606.9	W 3163954	4800.8	PROD POLYMERISATION
5839	OTH POLYMRZTION ETC PROD	W 535024	1628.9	W 591426	1994.0	W 670013	1915.2	W 687660	1974.0	AUT PROD POLYMER COPOLYM
59	CHEMICAL MATERIALS NES		3020.1		3672.6		3729.9		4134.7	MAT PROD CHIMIQUES NDA
598	MISCEL CHEM PRODUCTS NES	W 480252	2479.9	W 478795	3085.4	W 419622	3219.5	W 426533	3617.0	PROD DIV INDUST CHIM NDA
5989	CHEM PRODUCTS,PREPS NES	W 434895	2328.4	W 435696	2919.3	W 370394	3034.1	W 377080	3429.2	PROD PREP CHIMIQUES NDA
59899	OTH CHEM PRODS,PREPS,NES	W 325068	1742.6	W 334756	2229.1	W 273176	2387.1	W 271654	2708.7	AUT PRODUITS CHIMIQUES NDA
6	BASIC MANUFACTURES		42851.4		49847.6		45733.4		46598.2	ART MANUFACTURES
62	RUBBER MANUFACTURES NES		4452.1		5283.3		5273.3		5139.4	CAOUTCHOUC MANUFACTURE
625	RUBBER TYRES, TUBES ETC	W 891214	2602.1	W 1016385	3184.1	W 1083846	3377.7	W 1135976	3345.3	PNEUS CAOUTCHOUC VULCANISE
6252	TYRES,NEW,BUS OR LORRY	W 334647	935.3	W 406123	1189.1	W 442367	1295.6	W 442014	1226.5	PNEUS POUR AUTOBUS,CAMIONS
628	RUBBER ARTICLES NES	W 60741	1284.8	W 60552	1463.8	W 59802	1336.7	W 66211	1275.5	OUVRAGES CAOUTCHOUC NDA
64	PAPER,PAPERBOARD AND MFR		2145.7		2405.0		1944.0		2112.8	PAPIERS,CARTONS & OUVRAGES
641	PAPER AND PAPERBOARD	W 1032739	1470.9	W 1058948	1729.1	W 861459	1414.8	W 1159411	1627.1	PAPIERS ET CARTONS
65	TEXTILE YARN,FABRICS,ETC		6777.6		7174.1		6927.1		6753.1	FILS,TISSUS,ARTICLES TEXTILE
653	WOVN MAN-MADE FIB FABRIC	W 136393	2621.9	W 131066	2731.3	W 143204	2686.2	W 141046	2485.1	TISSUS FIBRES SYNTH,ARTIF
6531	CONT SYNT WEAVES NONPILE	W 79710	1542.7	W 78506	1623.1	W 89887	1649.8	W 89731	1548.2	TISSUS FIBRES SYNTH CONTINUE
65315	CONT SYN TXTL FABRIC NES	W 77087	1485.8	W 74622	1536.3	W 84597	1547.9	W 83500	1436.0	TIS PLUS 85% TEXT SYNT CONT
66	NONMETAL MINERAL MFS NES		4834.2		5868.4		5748.6		5493.5	ART MIN NON METALLIQUES
663	MINERAL MANUFCTURES NES	W 123582	1519.2	W 134958	1885.6	W 131533	1862.8	W 138265	1849.6	ART MIN MANUF NDA
664	GLASS	W 584090	1755.5	W 652893	2387.2	W 562875	2125.8	W 483856	1974.2	VERRE
6649	GLASS NES	W 426768	1131.6	W 466949	1425.5	W 445647	1384.3	W 362471	1149.4	VERRE NDA
67	IRON AND STEEL		14915.4		17608.0		15284.1		16015.2	FER ET ACIER
672	IRON,STEEL PRIMARY FORMS	W 4196914	1553.3	W 3974816	2184.5	W 2718737	1368.5	W 4476277	1745.7	LINGOTS FER,ACIER
6727	IRN,STL COIL FR REROLLNG	W 2637222	1150.3	W 3340933	1939.7	W 2290434	1210.2	W 3899418	1579.2	EBAUCHES POUR TOLES FER
673	IRON,STEEL SHAPES ETC	W 3288876	1807.6	W 2788033	1899.8	W 2783640	1705.2	W 3468086	1852.8	BARRES,PROFIL FER,ACIER
674	IRN,STL UNIV,PLATE,SHEET	MW 11359	7598.3	MW 12410	9670.7	MW 11072	8403.2	MW 11693	8380.3	LARGES PLATS,TOLES
6744	IRN,STL HVY PLATE,ROLLED	W 1994682	1104.2	W 2188862	1437.9	W 1997575	1235.4	W 2004021	1169.0	TOLES LAMINEES PLUS 4.75 MM
6746	IRN,STL THIN PLATE,ROLLD	W 4406711	3076.9	W 4931705	3998.7	W 4336683	3458.4	W 4177316	3152.0	TOLES LAM MOINS 3MM
67461	— OF IRON OR SIMPLE STL	W 3767677	1945.2	W 4266496	2505.6	W 3693498	2232.8	W 3511093	2002.4	TOL NON AC FIN MOINS 3 MM
67463	— OF STAINLESS ETC STL	W 508566	1018.1	W 524650	1346.8	W 493569	1085.4	W 542976	1031.8	TOL ACIER INOX MOINS 3 MM
6749	OTH IRN,STL PLATES,SHEET	W 3535911	2310.0	W 3742330	2887.2	W 3367210	2487.1	W 4051378	2833.4	AUTRES TOLES FER,ACIER
67491	— OF IRON OR SIMPLE STL	W 2855927	1790.6	W 2987546	2230.4	W 2728526	1942.5	W 3081147	2099.4	AUT TOLES AUTRES ACIER FIN
678	IRON,STL TUBES,PIPES,ETC	W 3216595	3152.8	W 2589350	3023.1	W 2372349	2989.2	W 2803272	3247.5	TUBES,TUYAUX EN FONTE,FER
6782	IRON,STL SEAMLESS TUBES	W 1726879	1734.2	W 1448730	1738.5	W 1267700	1760.2	W 1384463	1755.0	TUBES,TUYAUX SANS SOUDURE
68	NON-FERROUS METALS		2925.1		4042.2		3732.8		4045.0	METAUX NON FERREUX
682	COPPER EXC CEMENT COPPER		1632.9	W 485747	2310.8	W 497114	2005.0	W 511764	2049.0	CUIVRE
6822	COPPER,ALLOYS WORKED	W 300588	1352.4	W 314903	1793.9	W 310555	1573.3	W 318710	1585.2	CUIVRE,ALLIAGES OUVRES
684	ALUMINIUM	W 225784	913.6	W 249945	1259.2	W 247056	1185.9	W 287844	1299.2	ALUMINIUM
6842	ALUMINIUM,ALLOYS WORKED	W 214049	888.1	W 237081	1225.0	W 235033	1159.0	W 277583	1275.8	ALUMINIUM,ALLIAGES OUVRE
69	METAL MANUFACTURES NES		6430.9		7145.1		6527.8		6775.4	ART MANUFACT EN METAL NDA
695	TOOLS		1867.4		2215.2	W 77513	1969.5	W 102046	2273.5	OUTILS A MAIN
6954	BLADES,TIPS,ETC FR TOOLS	W 57056	1517.0	W 66130	1832.6	W 58178	1639.6	W 82690	1962.0	OUTILS POUR MACHINE-OUTIL
69541	PARTS TO INSERT IN TOOLS	W 51202	1257.9	W 60065	1501.1	W 51924	1331.6	W 75879	1642.1	OUTILS DE FORAGE
699	BASE METAL MFRS NES		2128.2		2377.0	W 223657	2161.2	W 222158	2172.5	ART MANUFACTURES MET NDA
7	MACHINES,TRANSPORT EQUIP		284160.3		310708.3		285090.1		290458.0	MACHINES MATERIEL TRANSPORT
71	POWER GENERATING EQUIPMT		17348.7		19145.3		17285.3		16023.9	MACHINES GENERATRICES
713	INTRNL COMBUS PSTN ENGIN	W 1127761	11657.2	W 1129811	13119.3	W 1065134	11748.7	W 1038853	10520.5	MOTEURS EXPL COMB INT, PIECE
7132	MOTOR VEHCL PISTN ENGINS	W 704648	5523.5	W 672749	5988.9	W 621330	5127.8	W 576174	4222.8	MOTEURS EXPL POUR VEHICULES
7138	PISTON ENGINES NES	W 113014	1351.5	W 124459	1596.9	W 112892	1298.2	W 117157	1235.7	MOTEURS A PISTONS NDA
7139	PISTON ENGINE PARTS NES	W 267022	3982.2	W 276786	4573.9	W 280313	4491.4	W 289313	4199.6	PIECES POUR 713.2,3,8
716	ROTATING ELECTRIC PLANT	W 155910	3335.1	W 156526	3678.4	W 152684	3198.7	W 161023	3085.3	APP ELECTR ROTATIFS,PIECES
7162	AC MTRS,GENRTRS,GEN SETS	W 101496	2208.7	W 105181	2446.8	W 106702	2146.5	W 111094	2009.2	MOTEURS ELECTRIQUES
71621	AC MTRS,INC UNIVRSL MTRS	W 48824	1557.8	W 50842	1755.0	W 51974	1529.9	W 49437	1406.2	MOT ELEC NON COUR CONTINU
72	MACHS FOR SPCL INDUSTRYS		19666.2		23356.0		22070.0		22233.4	MAC SPECIALES POUR INDUST
723	CIVIL ENGNEERG EQUIP ETC	W 888909	3534.2	W 940403	3845.2	W 1039331	3707.6	W 1096598	3823.2	APPAREILS DE GENIE CIVIL
7234	CONST,MINING MACHNRY NES	W 858310	3417.0	W 912274	3722.3	W 1011440	3595.6	W 1062751	3681.8	MACH POUR LA CONST, MINES
72342	SLFPRP SHOVELS,EXCAVATRS	W 724842	2648.5	W 775464	2933.5	W 857815	2815.8	W 910614	2939.4	PELLES MECANIQUES
724	TEXTILE,LEATHER MACHNRY		4510.6		4685.4		3919.2		3898.8	MACH POUR INDUSTRIE TEXTILE
7243	SEWING MACHS,NEEDLES ETC	W 37170	1209.1	W 35927	1250.9	W 31788	1015.9	W 33070	1002.8	MACHINES A COUDRE,PIECES
7244	SPINNING,EXTRDNG,ETC MCH	W 67246	1268.7	W 81502	1424.4	W 63969	1062.7	W 64133	1092.9	MACH POUR LE FILAGE
7245	WEAVING,FELT MFG,ETC MCH	W 78967	1491.2	W 72385	1467.3	W 71485	1381.8	W 79644	1424.2	METIERS A TISSER,PIECES
726	PRINTG,BKBINDG MACHY,PTS	W 61189	1402.3	W 66652	1709.7	W 72797	1664.8	W 85690	1765.9	MACHINES POUR IMPRIMERIE
728	OTH MACHY FOR SPCL INDUS	W 281396	8527.7	W 313964	11259.9		10933.4		11121.4	AUT MACH IND PARTICULIERES
7284	MACHY FOR SPCL INDUS NES	W 225610	7659.9	W 256710	10177.5		9840.3		9952.7	MACH SPEC IND PARTICUL.
72842	RUBBER,PLASTICS WRKG MCH	W 115463	1519.6	W 123158	1711.5	W 138302	1810.9	W 140972	1746.6	MACH IND CAOUT MAT PLAST
72848	OTH MCHY WITH INDIV FNCT	W 87299	4849.3	W 105240	6761.0	W 111935	6357.7	W 122604	6593.1	AUTRES MACHINES NDA
73	METALWORKING MACHINERY		6142.9		8978.0		9410.1		9066.7	MACH TRAVAIL DES METAUX
736	METALWORKING MACH-TOOLS	W 245747	4707.3	W 331391	7103.8	W 390175	7523.5	W 398615	7322.6	MACH-OUTILS TRAVAIL METAUX
7361	METAL CUTTING MACH-TOOLS	W 88950	2137.2	W 124272	3499.7	W 137339	3598.0	W 136461	3431.2	MACH-OUT ENLEVEMENT METAL
73613	LATHES,METALWORKING	W 40363	801.3	W 61633	1381.0	W 64707	1311.6	W 65852	1229.3	TOURS A METAUX
7362	METAL FORMING MACH-TOOLS	W 85744	948.7	W 109298	1270.7	W 131495	1331.5	W 120210	1138.8	MACH-OUTILS DEFORM METAL
7367	OTH METALWRKG MACH-TOOLS	W 55844	1101.0	W 79727	1621.4	W 95556	1839.4	W 109888	1890.4	AUT MACH-OUT POUR METAUX
737	METALWORKING MACHNRY NES	W 80622	1435.7	W 94919	1874.3	W 136102	1886.7	W 116770	1744.1	MACH TRAV METAUX PIECES
74	GENRL INDUSTRL MACHY NES		24870.9		29444.7		27893.5		25719.1	MACH APP INDUSTRIE
741	HEATING,COOLING EQUIPMNT		4668.9		5618.4		5386.8		4707.0	MACH CHAUFFAGE,PIECES
7415	AIR-CONDITIONING MACHNRY		2052.7		1996.6		1728.2		1547.2	GROUPES CONDITION AIR
7416	HEATING,COOLING EQU NES	W 66259	1478.2	W 105796	2131.9	W 86211	2209.1	W 92454	1851.0	APP CHANGEMENT TEMP
742	PUMPS FOR LIQUIDS ETC	W 78233	2146.1	W 87146	2411.8	W 90185	2157.4	W 94382	1947.1	POMPES MOTO-POMPES
743	PUMPS NES,CENTRFUGES ETC	W 246593	4230.8	W 254828	4866.6	W 247370	4479.4	W 242070	4030.9	POMPES COMPRES,VENT ETC
7431	PUMPS FOR GASES ETC	W 150951	2199.4	W 157016	2589.9	W 149285	2422.6	W 141955	2076.4	POMPES AIR A VIDE,COMPRES

5. General Exports F.O.B. by Commodities according to the S.I.T.C. (Rev. 2) in million U.S. Dollars
Exportations Générales F.O.B. par Produits d'après la C.T.C.I. (Rév. 2) en millions de Dollars E.U.

SITC CTCI	COMMODITY	1994 QUANTITY QUANTITE	1994 VALUE VALEUR	1995 QUANTITY QUANTITE	1995 VALUE VALEUR	1996 QUANTITY QUANTITE	1996 VALUE VALEUR	1997 QUANTITY QUANTITE	1997 VALUE VALEUR	PRODUIT
744	MECHANICAL HANDLING EQU	W 584331	4167.4	W 645259	4850.4	W 685784	4800.0	W 730649	4528.6	EQUIP MANUTENTION PIECES
7441	FORK LIFT TRCKS,ETC,PTS	W 294779	1197.2	W 325046	1369.2	W 361496	1374.3	W 381504	1316.3	CHARIOTS POUR USINES ETC
74411	FORK LIFT TRUCKS ETC	W 294651	1196.3	W 325001	1368.2	W 361376	1372.3	W 381343	1314.1	CHARIOTS POUR LES GARES
7442	LIFTING,LOADING MACH NES	W 145732	1832.6	W 163744	2146.8	W 190281	2284.9	W 196955	2071.8	APP LEVAGE,MANUTENTION
7449	PTS NES OF MACHY OF 7442	W 143821	1137.7	W 156469	1334.5	W 134008	1140.8	W 152190	1140.5	PIECES DU 744.2
745	NONELEC MACHY,TOOLS NES	W 40445	1501.1	W 44717	1718.3	W 45475	1622.5	W 44248	1485.7	AUT MACH NON ELEC,PIECES
749	NONELEC MACH PTS,ACC NES	W 445673	8156.9	W 497182	9979.4	W 494192	9447.7	W 502762	9020.1	PIECES MACH NON ELEC NDA
7491	BALL,ROLLER,ETC BEARINGS	W 139522	1898.2	W 164611	2510.8	W 163539	2360.3	W 158821	2175.1	ROULEMENTS BILLES ETC
7492	COCKS,VALVES ETC NES	W 59553	1757.2	W 66450	2110.3	W 65530	1975.9	W 70491	1874.6	ART ROB,SIM POUR TUYAUX
7493	SHAFT,CRANK,PULLEY ETC	W 204466	2539.7	W 217918	3025.7	W 213719	2832.9	W 220064	2729.4	ARBRES TRANS,VILEBREQUINS
7499	OTH NONELEC MCHY PTS NES	W 42133	1962.0	W 48202	2332.7	W 51404	2278.8	W 53386	2241.2	PIECES NON ELECT NDA
74991	FOUNDRY MOULDS ETC NES	W 27462	1373.3	W 31384	1614.9	W 33879	1592.6	W 35507	1586.4	MOULES POUR METAUX
75	OFFICE MACHNES,ADP EQUIP		35170.2		37452.4		35054.0		37919.2	MACH BUREAU TRAIT AUTOM
751	OFFICE MACHINES		3908.8		3940.5		3432.7		3793.3	MACH,APPAREILS DE BUREAU
7518	OFFICE MACHINES NES	W 109980	3420.5	W 103990	3565.3	W 97389	3137.0	W 116256	3513.4	MACH,APP DE BUREAU NDA
75182	PHOTO,THERMOCOPY APPARAT	W 102049	3027.5	W 96287	3165.4	W 90693	2812.9	W 110368	3261.5	APPAREILS DE PHOTOCOPIE
752	AUTOMTIC DATA PROC EQUIP	W 227492	15975.3	W 237365	17162.6	MN 65665	15848.8	MN 83109	18434.8	MACH TRAIT INFORMATION
7522	DIGITAL COMPUTERS	W 7298	1593.6	W 7576	2015.3	N 2254211	2228.2	N 2455292	2909.1	MACH DIGITALES COMPLETES
7523	DIGITL CENTRL PROCESSORS	W 4280	881.3	W 4920	992.3	N 3777956	1225.4	MN 11401	2223.4	UNITES CENTRALES
7524	DIGITL CENTRL STOR UNITS	W 22177	4843.4	W 24913	5137.8	MN 38176	5298.7	MN 47919	6126.8	UNITES MEMOIRE CENTRALES
7525	ADP PERIPHERAL UNITS	W 187409	7868.7	W 189873	7920.6	MN 18408	6678.8	MN 19228	6852.6	UNITES PERIPHERIQUES
759	OFFICE,ADP MCH PTS,ACCES	W 191818	15286.1	W 197943	16349.5	W 211387	15772.7	W 245558	15691.2	PIECES DU 751 ET 752
7591	OFFICE MACHINE PARTS NES	W 92895	3211.2	W 97881	3693.8	W 94750	3408.0	W 105495	3465.4	PIECES DU 7511,7518
75919	COPY MACH PRTS,ACCES NES	W 89348	3042.3	W 94872	3473.3	W 89731	2948.3	W 100222	3035.3	PIECES DU 751.82
7599	ACCTG,ETC,ADP MCH PTS,AC	W 98923	12075.0	W 100062	12655.7	W 116637	12364.7	W 140063	12225.8	PIECES DU 751 ET 752
76	TELECOMM,SOUND EQUIPMENT		30083.3		28311.4		23221.9		23556.9	EQUIPMENT DE TELECOM
761	TELEVISION RECEIVERS	N 5121991	2449.9	N 4182319	2256.1	N 3653027	2031.6	N 4575638	2219.1	RECEPTEURS DE TELEVISION
7611	COLOUR TV RECEIVERS	N 4870588	2410.1	N 3981210	2218.2	N 3438892	2002.9	N 4358125	2196.7	RECEPTEURS COULEUR
762	RADIO BROADCAST RECEIVRS	MN 14771	2327.2	MN 13860	2284.0	MN 9866	1518.9	N 8399812	1330.8	RECEPTEURS RADIODIFFUSION
7621	MTR VEHC RADIO RECEIVERS	N 8345024	1252.7	MN 9049	1386.7	N 6314167	962.5	N 4764725	821.3	RECEPTEURS RADIO AUTO
763	SOUND RECORDRS,PHONOGRPH		6482.6		5558.9		4730.9		4842.0	PHONO,APP ENREGISTREMENT
7638	OTHR SOUND APPARATUS ETC		6444.3		5511.5		4697.1		4812.6	AUT APP D'ENREGIS,REPROD
76381	TV IMAGE,SND RECRDRS ETC	W 80134	4140.3	W 58326	3323.9	W 46382	2826.2		2987.0	APP ENREG,REPRO IMAG,SON
76388	DICTATING MACHINES ETC	MN 25190	2304.0	MN 21874	2187.6		1870.9		1825.6	MACHINES A DICTER
764	TELECOM EQPT,PTS,ACC NES		18823.8		18212.5		14940.6		15165.2	EQUIP TELECOM,PIECES
7641	LINE TELEPHONE,ETC EQUIP	W 55176	3922.8	W 42552	2945.8	N 8115128	2430.4	MN 9578	2434.5	APP TELEPHON PAR FIL
7643	TV,RADIO TRANSMITTRS ETC	W 13550	2330.5	W 9949	1643.8		903.4	W 7095	1146.8	APP EMET TELE RADIO
7648	TELECOMM EQUIPMENT NES		4942.3		5432.2		4666.6		4386.2	APP TELECOM NDA
76482	TELEVISION CAMERAS	W 12939	4171.3	W 14130	4692.5	W 12723	4078.2	W 12647	3839.9	APP PRISE DE VUES TELE
7649	PTS NES OF EQUIPMT OF 76	W 114591	6450.2	W 104281	7160.1	W 90954	6267.1	W 88635	6626.1	PIECES DE LA DIV 76
76491	PTS NES OF APPAR OF 7641	W 13483	1547.7	W 17074	2024.1	W 16689	2004.0	W 20028	2259.7	PIECES POUR 764.1
76493	TELECOMM EQUIPMT PTS NES	W 27887	2035.3	W 26027	2258.5	W 21554	2104.2	W 23228	2496.3	PIECES 761,762,764.3,8
76499	PARTS ETC OF SOUND EQUIP	W 64126	2744.7	W 51915	2745.4	W 43409	2037.1	W 37806	1749.8	PIECES NDA POUR 763
77	ELECTRIC MACHNRY NES ETC		58101.4		74160.5		66229.6		65302.2	MACH APP ELECT NDA
771	ELECTRIC POWER MACHY NES	W 67893	2203.1	W 71117	2532.3	W 74620	2320.5	W 94745	2508.0	MACH PROD,TRANS ELECTR
7712	OTH ELEC POWER MACHY NES	W 41019	1717.2	W 43600	2002.1	W 45214	1892.0	W 50478	1924.7	AUT APP PROD TRANSF ELEC
772	SWITCHGEAR ETC,PARTS NES	W 148966	9729.3	W 155244	11435.0	W 170279	10422.8	W 173104	10664.4	APP COUPURE,SECT ETC
7721	SWITCHGEAR ETC	W 121326	7449.9	W 127289	8620.5	W 144720	7930.2	W 145900	7874.4	APP COUPURE,SECTIONMNT
7722	PRINTED CIRCUITS,PTS NES	W 14031	1100.4	W 13827	1434.1	W 12909	1368.5	W 13899	1697.2	CIRCUITS ET PIECES
7723	FIXED,VARIABLE RESISTORS	W 13610	1179.0	W 14129	1380.5	W 12650	1124.2	W 13306	1092.9	POTENTIOMETRES PIECES
773	ELECTR DISTRIBUTNG EQUIP	W 144299	1878.7	W 151712	2086.4	W 170427	2011.3	W 173708	2011.9	EQUIPMT DISTRIBUTION ELECT
7731	INSULATED WIRE,CABLE ETC	W 99784	1291.6	W 100528	1418.8	W 107510	1358.4	W 112926	1340.1	FILS,CABLES ISOLES ELECT
774	ELECTRO–MEDCL,XRAY EQUIP	W 12955	1688.6	W 13124	1809.5		1778.8		1828.8	APPAREILS MEDICAUX
776	TRANSISTORS,VALVES,ETC		29263.6		40847.0		35656.6		33606.6	LAMPES,TUBES,VALVES
7762	OTH ELECTRONIC TUBES ETC	W 137990	2751.3	W 173909	3902.0	MN 34458	3704.5	MN 35028	3495.5	AUT LAMPES ELECTRONIQUES
7763	DIODES,TRANSISTORS,ETC	MN 72702997	2928.4	MN 91252086	3883.9	MN 84234941	3754.0	MN 100577698	3935.2	DIODES,TRANSISTORS
7764	ELECTRONIC MICROCIRCUITS	MN 13438717	18460.4	MN 15805403	26470.4	MN 15635535	22283.4	MN 18924926	20297.2	MICROSTRUCTURES ELECTRON
7768	ELCTRNC COMP PTS,CRYSTLS		4287.5		5661.5		5428.5		5383.0	CRIST PIEZO–ELEC,PCS 776
77681	PIEZO–ELEC CRYSTALS,MNTD	MN 4595677	1152.5	MN 4817019	1353.1	MN 5804700	1095.4	MN 6174415	1138.9	CRISTAUX PIEZO–ELECTRIQ
77689	ELECTRNIC COMPON PTS NES	W 54551	3135.1	W 51403	4308.4	W 46448	4333.1	W 47958	4244.1	PIECES DU GROUPE 776
778	ELECTRICAL MACHINERY NES		12185.3		14430.7		13156.4		13876.9	AUTRES MACH ELECT NDA
7781	BATTERIES,ACCUMULATORS	W 93478	2283.6	W 91243	2690.8		2630.6		3043.7	PILES ET ACCUMULATEURS
77812	ELECTRIC ACCUMULATORS	W 62504	1787.0	W 60568	2156.1	W 57218	2153.0	W 65332	2513.2	ACCUMULATEURS ELECTRIQ
7783	AUTOMOTIVE ELECTR EQUIP	W 142607	2369.0	W 142218	2613.0	W 138535	2344.6	W 138682	2133.7	EQUIP ELECT MOTEURS EXPL
77831	IGNITION,STARTING EQUIP	W 111206	1573.7	W 113378	1826.5	W 111659	1663.7	W 112571	1551.0	APP ELEC ALLUM,DEMARRAGE
7788	OTH ELEC MACHY,EQUIP NES		6411.9		7951.2		7163.5		7633.4	AUT MACH APP ELEC NDA
77884	ELECTRICAL CONDENSERS	MN 82631148	2489.3	MN 138097091	3221.6	W 37287	2764.7	W 39707	2912.9	CONDENSATEURS ELECTRIQUES
77886	OTH ELEC MACHINERY NES	W 13735	2127.7	W 16981	2509.3	MN 301986	2374.6	MN 460711	2620.6	AUT MACH APP ELECTRIQUES
78	ROAD VEHICLES		80294.3		78071.4		73258.7		79246.6	VEHICULES ROUTIERS
781	PASS MOTOR VEH EXC BUSES	N 3385363	44920.7	N 2981754	41673.8	N 3232330	39973.7	N 3867845	47656.1	AUTO TRANSPORT PERSONNES
782	LORRIES,SPCL MTR VEH NES		9976.3		9616.0		8989.7		9420.8	VEHICULES SPECIAUX,MARCH
7821	LORRIES,TRUCKS		9718.0		9273.1	N 901775	8613.1		9025.9	VEHICULES TRANSP MARCHAND
783	ROAD MOTOR VEHICLES NES		1563.7		1161.6		1152.0		1210.7	VEHICULES ROUTIERS NDA
7831	BUSES	N 81281	1391.1	N 57132	1005.7	N 61847	1006.7	N 69670	1047.5	VOITURES TRANSPORT COMMUN
784	MOTOR VEH PRTS,ACCES NES		18118.4		19656.4		17446.0		15292.8	PIECES 722,781,782,783
7849	OTHER MOTOR VEHCL PARTS	W 1868465	17377.8	W 1829420	18745.1	W 1735388	16629.7	W 1662942	14571.7	PIECES 722,781,782,783
785	CYCLES,ETC MOTRZD OR NOT		5509.6		5803.9		5591.2		5553.4	MOTOCYCLES SCOOTERS
7851	MOTORCYCLES ETC	N 2028153	3867.4		3947.6	N 2158714	4004.5	N 2182318	3979.9	MOTO VELO MOTEUR AUXIL
7853	INVAL CARR, PTS OF 785		1622.4		1839.4	W 93595	1576.9	W 82700	1564.9	FAUTEUILS INVALIDES,PIECES
78539	PARTS,ACCES NES OF 785		1618.3		1836.0	W 93497	1574.0	W 82624	1562.8	PIECES DU 785
79	OTHR TRANSPORT EQUIPMENT		12482.7		11789.0		10667.4		11390.3	AUTRE MATERIEL TRANSPORT
792	AIRCRAFT ETC	W 1671	661.8	W 1584	605.9	W 2311	873.7	W 3521	1362.3	APP NAVIGATION AERIENNE
7929	AIRCRAFT PARTS NES	W 1415	558.0	W 1379	573.0	W 2018	848.4	W 3323	1343.9	PIECES DU 792
793	SHIPS AND BOATS ETC	W 8886267	11615.4	MW 9343	10932.2		9612.4	MW 9675	9852.2	NAVIRES BATEAUX,ETC
7932	SHIPS AND BOATS NES	W 8802479	11204.5	MW 9288	10865.1		9309.5	MW 9414	9417.5	NAVIRES ET BATEAUX
79322	TANKERS OF ALL KINDS	W 2551188	3394.0	W 2705738	2975.6		3046.0	W 1900092	1956.7	BATEAUX–CITERNES
79323	OTHER CARGO VESSELS	W 6208723	7559.6	W 6541424	7633.4		6057.2	W 7493938	7322.2	AUT BATEAUX TRANS MARCH
8	MISC MANUFACTURED GOODS		30892.3		35661.0		34562.6		35824.5	ART MANUFACTURES DIVERS
87	PRECISION INSTRUMNTS NES		9341.8		11503.4		11358.0		12233.3	INSTRUM,APPAR SCIENT NDA
871	OPTICAL INSTRUMENTS	W 11037	1763.1	W 11167	2150.2	W 13004	2225.3	W 16033	2801.7	APPAR,INSTRUM D'OPTIQUE
87109	OPTICAL INSTRUMENTS NES	W 7184	1295.4	W 7656	1540.4	W 8683	1605.0	W 12140	2204.1	APP,INSTRUM OPTIQUE NDA
872	MEDICAL INSTRUMENTS NES	W 23089	1352.5	W 22396	1417.3	W 22383	1307.7	W 24564	1394.9	INSTR,APP MEDIC–CHIR NDA
87202	OTH MEDICAL INSTRUMENTS	W 18502	1187.6	W 18016	1258.5	W 18845	1204.7	W 21264	1308.1	INSTRUM,APP MEDECINE
874	MEASURNG,CONTROLNG INSTR	W 46029	5939.5	W 52419	7628.7	W 57167	7563.8	W 60238	7793.6	INSTRUMENTS DE MESURE
8742	MEASUR,DRAW ETC INST,PTS	W 12139	1192.6	W 15271	1603.6	W 18524	1705.9	W 20213	1744.6	INST DESSIN,TRACAGE,PCS
87421	MEASURNG,DRAWNG ETC INST	W 11078	1060.3	W 13688	1413.8	W 17124	1498.8	W 18584	1513.8	INSTRUM DESSIN,TRACAGE
8743	GAS,LIQUID CONTROL INSTR	W 15921	1830.1	W 16296	2062.1	W 16522	1891.9	W 16267	1701.7	APP,INSTR MESURE FLUIDES
8748	ELEC MEAS,CONTRL EQU NES	W 7142	1596.4	W 8951	2286.5	W 9121	2197.0	W 9992	2556.2	APP ELEC ELECTRO MESURE
87483	OTH ELCTRNC MEAS ETC EQU	W 7053	1584.1	W 8865	2273.0	W 9021	2179.5	W 9809	2536.9	AUT APP ELECTRO DE MESURE
88	PHOTO EQU,OPTICL GDS ETC		10785.8		12290.3		11750.9		11363.1	APP,FOURN PHOTO,OP,MONTR
881	PHOTO APPARAT,EQUIPT NES		3592.5		4421.4		4481.3		4142.8	APP,EQUIP PHOTO NDA

5. General Exports F.O.B. by Commodities according to the S.I.T.C. (Rev. 2) in million U.S. Dollars
Exportations Générales F.O.B. par Produits d'après la C.T.C.I. (Rév. 2) en millions de Dollars E.U.

SITC CTCI	COMMODITY	1994		1995		1996		1997		PRODUIT
		QUANTITY QUANTITE	VALUE VALEUR	QUANTITY QUANTITE	VALUE VALEUR	QUANTITY QUANTITE	VALUE VALEUR	QUANTITY QUANTITE	VALUE VALEUR	
8811	CAMERAS STILL,FLASH APP		1791.4		1818.0		1714.4		1525.1	APPAREILS PHOTO,PIECES
88111	STILL CAMERAS	MN 39310	1241.3	MN 44854	1180.6	MN 36690	1128.3	MN 49980	946.4	APPAREILS PHOTOGRAPHIQ
8813	OTH PHOTO,CINE EQUIP NES	W 16333	1794.9	W 17531	2598.4		2762.9		2612.0	APP,MAT PHOTO,CINEMA
88139	PHOTO,CINE LAB EQUIP NES	W 13132	1649.2	W 14579	2451.9	N 177088	2637.9	N 221212	2500.2	APP TYPES UTIL LABOR
882	PHOTO,CINEMA SUPPLIES		3674.0		4188.2		4024.8		4007.8	PRODUITS PHOTO,CINEMA
8821	CHEM PHOTO GOODS,RETAIL	W 61941	1446.9	W 68492	1768.1	W 71003	1653.6	W 76884	1722.8	PROD CHIMIQ USAGES PHOTO
8822	PHOTO FILM EXC DEV CINMA	A 452601	2227.1	A 471065	2420.2		2371.2		2285.0	PLAQUES,PELLICULES,FILMS
884	OPTICAL GOODS NES		1319.8		1482.5		1403.7		1426.4	ELEMENTS OPTIQ,ART LUNET
885	WATCHES AND CLOCKS		2195.8		2195.7		1837.6		1784.4	HORLOGERIE
8851	WATCHES,MOVEMENTS,CASES		1686.8		1659.6		1414.5		1405.4	MONTRES,MOUVEMENTS,BOITES
89	MISC MANUFCTRD GOODS NES		9296.7		10507.4		10178.0		11066.9	ART MANUFACTURES DIVERS
893	ARTICLES OF PLASTIC NES		1493.3		1756.7		1650.0		1768.6	OUVRAGES EN MAT DIVIS 58
8939	MISC PLASTIC ARTICLES	W 81151	1201.6	W 81823	1391.2	W 87751	1294.8	W 101539	1408.8	ART DIVERS EN MAT DIV 58
89399	OTHR PLASTC ARTICLES NES	W 65844	1148.3	W 68656	1340.9	W 73001	1244.4	W 83331	1352.4	AUT OUV MAT DIV 58
894	TOYS,SPORTING GOODS,ETC		1583.9		2096.6		2280.6		2839.5	VOITURES ENFANTS,JOUETS
8942	TOYS,INDOOR GAMES ETC	W 22188	1150.7	W 26719	1623.7	W 35395	1784.4	W 54870	2356.4	JOUETS,JEUX ETC
89424	INDOOR GAME EQUIPMENT	W 16118	976.7	W 21830	1466.3	W 30704	1640.9	W 49280	2207.1	ART,JEUX DE SOCIETE
898	MUSICAL INSTRUMENTS,PTS		3501.9	W 122985	3696.9		3792.8		3915.1	INSTRUMENTS DE MUSIQUE
8983	SOUND RECRDNG TAPE,DISCS	W 97391	2458.8	W 85784	2680.1		2926.3		3018.1	SUPPORTS SON POUR 763
89831	PREPD SND RECORDNG MEDIA	W 92996	2160.3	W 81650	2357.6	W 81047	2599.5	W 79666	2692.6	SUPPORTS PREPARES
9	GOODS NOT CLASSD BY KIND		7675.0		9476.8		10389.4		11755.2	ART TRANSACT NON CLASSES
931	*SPECIAL TRANSACTIONS	W 383411	7316.4	W 642197	9066.3	W 545995	9884.9	W 571485	11160.8	TRANS.SPECIALES

1. HISTORICAL SERIES, 1961–1996 GENERAL TRADE, IMPORTS C.I.F., EXPORTS F.O.B. # 1
SERIES HISTORIQUES, 1961–1996 COMMERCE GENERAL, IMPORTATIONS C.A.F., EXPORTATIONS F.O.B

YEAR ANNEE	VALUE IN MILLION JORDANIAN DINARS / VALEUR EN MILLION JORDANIAN DINARS: MERCHANDISE –MARCHANDISE IMPORTS	MERCHANDISE –MARCHANDISE EXPORTS	GOLD –OR IMPORTS	GOLD –OR EXPORTS	CONVERSION FACTORS U.S. CENTS PER JORDANIAN DINAR / FACTEURS DE CONVERSION CENTS E.U. PAR JORDANIAN DINAR: IMPORTS	EXPORTS	INDEX NUMBERS –INDICES: QUANTUM IMPORTS	QUANTUM EXPORTS	UNIT VALUE / VALEUR UNITAIRE IMPORTS	UNIT VALUE / VALEUR UNITAIRE EXPORTS
1961	41.90	5.30			280.0000	280.0000				
1962	45.60	5.90			280.0000	280.0000				
1963	50.90	6.60			280.0000	280.0000				
1964	53.60	8.70			280.0000	280.0000				
1965	56.00	9.90			280.0000	280.0000				
1966	68.20	10.40			280.0000	280.0000				
1967	55.10	11.30			280.0000	280.0000				
1968	57.50	14.30			280.0000	280.0000				
1969	67.80	14.80			280.0000	280.0000				
1970	65.90	12.20			280.0000	280.0000				
1971	76.60	11.40			280.0000	280.0000				
1972	95.30	17.00			280.0000	280.0000				
1973	107.80	19.00			305.7830	305.5860				
1974	155.70	49.80			311.9310	312.1340				
1975	232.90	48.90			312.3910	313.0160				
1976	338.70	68.70			301.0650	301.1060				
1977	454.40	82.10			303.9140	303.6550				
1978	458.80	90.90			326.6470	326.3450				
1979	589.50	120.90			332.7870	332.7430				
1980	716.00	171.60			334.4050	334.2840	85	40	59	49
1981	1047.50	242.60			300.6278	301.5760	81	21	50	39
1982	1142.50	264.50			283.6940	284.5715	89	22	51	43
1983	1103.30	210.60			274.6308	274.8350	90	22	46	39
1984	1071.30	290.70			259.8862	258.7057	84	31	49	43
1985	1074.40	310.90			254.2936	254.1612	101	72	62	58
1986	850.20	256.00			286.0511	286.1834	106	74	47	50
1987	915.50	315.70			295.2200	295.2200	110	88	48	46
1988	1022.50	381.50			264.5387	262.1128	116	102	51	53
1989	1230.00	637.60			172.8350	173.6358	96	104	74	84
1990	1725.80	706.10			150.8096	150.5477	100	100	100	100
1991	1710.50	770.70			146.6166	146.5649	99	88	100	111
1992	2214.00	829.30			147.0031	147.0345	136	97	95	107
1993	2453.60	864.70			144.2223	144.0789	148	104	96	108
1994	2362.60	995.20			143.1500	143.1154	144	112	94	114
1995	2590.30	1241.00			142.7040	142.5193	152	137	99	117
1996	3043.60	1288.20			141.0439	141.0439	172	135	110	126

2. IMPORTS BY BROAD ECONOMIC CATEGORY AND EXPORTS BY INDUSTRIAL ORIGIN. (PERCENTAGE OF TOTAL VALUE)
IMPORTATIONS PAR CATEGORIES ECONOMIQUES ET EXPORTATIONS PAR BRANCHE D'ACTIVITE.(EN POURCENTAGE DE LA VALEUR TOTALE)

IMPORTS – IMPORTATIONS

	1989	1990	1991	1992	1993	1994	1995
TOTAL IMPORTS–IMPORTATIONS TOTALES	100.	100.	100.	100.	100.	100.	100.
1 FOOD BEV–ALIMENTATION BOISSONS	12.4	21.4	22.9	16.7	17.0	18.1	17.2
11 PRIMARY–PRODUITS DE BASE	8.6	13.4	15.1	10.6	11.0	9.0	8.4
111 FOR INDUSTRY–POUR L'INDUSTRIE	3.9	9.2	9.2	6.1	6.9	5.3	5.0
112 FOR HOUSEHOLDS–POUR LES MENAGES	4.7	4.2	5.9	4.5	4.1	3.6	3.4
12 PROCESSED–PRODUITS ELABORES	3.8	8.0	7.8	6.1	6.1	9.1	8.8
121 FOR INDUSTRY–POUR L'INDUSTRIE	0.9	1.0	1.5	1.4	1.9	3.0	3.7
122 FOR HOUSEHOLDS–POUR LES MENAGES	2.9	7.1	6.3	4.8	4.2	6.1	5.1
2 IND SUPPLIES–APPROV INDUSTRIELS	30.7	30.5	34.4	32.2	31.0	32.0	33.4
21 PRIMARY–PRODUITS DE BASE	5.0	4.3	4.4	4.2	3.2	3.3	3.4
22 PROCESSED–PRODUITS ELABORES	25.7	26.2	30.0	28.0	27.8	28.7	30.0
3 FUELS–COMBUSTIBLES	18.6	18.1	14.5	13.7	12.8	12.6	13.0
31 PRIMARY–PRODUITS DE BASE	15.7	13.9	12.0	10.6	9.9	10.2	10.3
32 PROCESSED–PRODUITS ELABORES	2.9	4.2	2.5	3.1	2.9	2.5	2.7
321 MOTOR SPIRIT–ESSENCE	0.9	0.0	0.1	0.8	0.7	2.4	2.7
322 OTHER–AUTRES	2.0	4.2	2.4	2.3	2.3	0.0	0.0
4 MACHINERY–EQUIPEMENT	11.8	9.6	9.3	13.4	16.1	15.7	14.0
41 CAPITAL EQUIPMENT–MACHINES	10.1	7.5	6.9	11.0	13.4	13.6	12.3
42 PARTS–PIECES ACCESSOIRES	1.7	2.1	2.4	2.4	2.6	2.1	1.8
5 TRANSPORT–TRANSPORT	10.5	11.4	10.1	13.5	12.8	11.6	12.1
51 PASSENGER CARS–AUTOMOBILES	0.9	0.9	1.3	1.5	1.5	1.6	2.0
52 OTHER–AUTRES	1.2	2.5	1.6	4.2	4.1	3.5	4.0
521 INDUSTRIAL–INDUSTRIELS	1.1	2.5	1.6	4.2	4.0	3.5	4.0
522 NON INDUSTRIAL–NON INDUSTRIEL	0.0	0.0	0.0	0.0	0.0	0.0	0.0
53 PARTS–PIECES ACCESSOIRES	8.4	8.0	7.3	7.9	7.3	6.5	6.0
6 CONSUM GOODS–BIENS CONSOMMATION	9.9	7.9	8.0	9.7	9.1	9.5	9.7
61 DURABLE–DURABLES	2.4	1.8	1.6	2.0	2.0	2.0	1.9
62 SEMI DURABLE–SEMI DURABLES	3.9	3.2	3.5	4.2	3.8	3.9	3.9
63 NON DURABLE–NON DURABLES	3.5	2.9	2.9	3.6	3.3	3.5	3.9
7 GOODS NES–BIENS NDA	6.2	1.1	0.7	0.6	1.1	0.5	0.6

EXPORTS – EXPORTATIONS

	1989	1990	1991	1992	1993	1994	1995
TOTAL EXPORTS–EXPORTATIONS TOTALES	100.	100.	100.	100.	100.	100.	100.
1 AGRICULTURE	6.5	8.3	10.1	9.9	10.2	8.9	7.5
2 MINING QUARRY–INDUS EXTRACTIVES	35.0	32.4	29.2	26.4	22.0	19.7	18.4
3 MANUFACTURING–IND MANUFACTUR	58.5	59.2	60.7	63.7	67.8	71.4	74.1
31 FOOD BEV TOBACCO–ALIM BOISS TAB	3.0	2.1	8.1	6.3	9.0	9.5	16.4
32 TEXTILES–INDUSTRIES TEXTILES	3.6	4.4	4.8	4.4	5.0	4.4	4.7
33 WOOD & PRODUCTS–BOIS & PRODUITS	0.1	0.8	0.2	0.1	0.1	0.2	0.0
34 PAPER & PRODUCTS–PAPIER & PRODT	1.7	1.3	1.2	2.2	3.6	2.0	2.2
35 CHEMICALS–INDUSTRIES CHIMIQUES	25.8	28.5	28.1	30.4	27.8	30.4	28.6
36 NON METAL MIN–MIN NON METAL	2.1	4.2	4.1	3.5	2.8	3.5	3.5
37 BASIC METAL–IND METAL BASE	1.5	0.7	0.7	1.2	1.2	0.6	0.9
38 METAL MANUF–MANUF METAL	15.3	15.2	12.5	14.7	17.5	19.9	16.0
39 OTH MANUF IND–AUTRES MANUF	5.3	2.1	0.9	0.9	0.7	0.9	1.7

3. TRADE BY PRINCIPAL COUNTRIES OF ORIGIN AND DESTINATION (VALUE IN MILLION U.S. DOLLARS)
ECHANGES SELON LES PRINCIPAUX PAYS D'ORIGINE ET DE DESTINATION (VALEUR EN MILLIONS DE DOLLARS EU)

GENERAL IMPORTS C.I.F. IMPORTATIONS GENERALES C.A.F

COUNTRIES–PAYS	1991	1992	1993	1994	1995
World	2507.8	3254.7	3538.7	3382.3	3696.4
Africa	102.9	139.3	115.8	98.9	103.4
Americas	336.4	435.2	535.6	408.2	462.0
– Northern America	284.3	377.1	460.6	348.5	354.7
– LAIA	45.0	56.2	73.0	56.7	104.8
– CACM	1.6	1.3	1.9	2.8	2.2
– Caribbean	5.4	0.6	0.2	0.2	0.2
– Rest of America				0.0	
Asia excl fmr USSR	991.4	1367.6	1375.0	1381.7	1603.7
– Middle East	570.6	748.8	734.2	767.2	931.9
Asia former USSR		0.3	3.1	1.5	1.9
Europe excl fmr USSR	936.2	1204.1	1328.2	1336.4	1362.9
– European Union	810.1	1027.1	1174.5	1199.9	1226.2
– Eastern Europe	83.4	128.7	111.8	93.9	71.2
– Rest of Europe	42.7	48.2	41.9	42.6	65.5
Europe former USSR	27.4	52.6	92.9	95.7	99.5
Oceania	72.3	43.5	81.9	48.5	53.1
Other	41.3	12.0	6.2	11.4	9.9
Iraq	275.3	434.3	442.8	417.1	451.3
USA/Etats–Unis d'Amer	261.1	361.9	449.2	332.9	343.2
Germany/Allemagne	195.3	274.5	292.5	263.9	311.6
Italy/Italie	107.9	163.1	194.6	199.2	198.0
United Kingdom	113.7	159.4	184.5	172.9	177.7
Japan/Japon	89.6	194.3	178.3	134.0	130.5
France, Monaco	107.9	114.8	142.1	159.0	170.0
Turkey/Turquie	83.8	143.2	84.3	90.0	127.0
Netherlands/Pays–Bas	84.6	77.3	90.3	129.0	102.1
Saudi Arabia	40.6	57.8	70.2	102.4	130.4
Belgium–Luxembourg	65.2	72.9	84.1	100.6	74.2
Korea, Republic of	36.3	68.7	88.4	83.4	109.6
China/Chine	42.7	76.7	73.0	89.5	84.2
India/Inde	78.4	45.9	62.7	55.7	69.5
Malaysia/Malaisie	16.3	29.0	57.7	94.8	107.8
Other Asia n.e.s.	58.8	77.5	63.0	56.1	47.3
Syrian Arab Republic	57.2	31.4	47.1	69.1	78.4
Spain/Espagne	26.5	53.7	44.1	54.4	58.1
Egypt/Egypte	33.6	55.2	41.3	43.0	46.2
Brazil/Brésil	25.6	32.2	58.3	37.7	52.6
Thailand/Thaïlande	38.6	60.4	44.7	22.4	26.8
Romania/Roumanie	32.7	46.8	40.9	39.4	30.7
Switzerland,Liechtenst.	22.8	37.3	29.0	34.8	57.7
Ukraine		8.8	45.0	71.2	55.4
Australia/Australie	37.2	22.5	50.0	29.8	40.1
Lebanon/Liban	30.9	44.6	34.9	25.8	42.5
Indonesia/Indonésie	15.4	22.7	31.9	35.2	54.8
Russian Federation		43.9	47.6	24.3	43.9
Sweden/Suède	26.6	30.9	36.3	30.4	34.3
Austria/Autriche	25.7	33.4	35.3	24.0	23.9
Bulgaria/Bulgarie	14.2	40.3	30.9	27.0	16.0
Zimbabwe	44.4	46.3	26.5	7.6	1.2
New Zealand	35.1	21.0	31.9	18.7	13.0
Argentina/Argentine	11.8	21.7	11.8	16.1	48.0
Denmark/Danemark	18.5	17.3	20.6	28.3	22.3
Bahrain/Bahreïn	15.8	4.4	16.5	22.3	40.4
Libyan Arab Jamahiriya	9.9	13.2	29.8	22.3	17.0
Greece/Grèce	23.4	13.8	21.9	13.4	11.7
Canada	23.2	15.3	11.3	15.5	11.5
Areas n.e.s.	39.2	10.2	4.1	10.0	9.1

EXPORTS EXPORTATIONS ES F.O.B.

COUNTRIES–PAYS	1991	1992	1993	1994	1995
Monde	1129.6	1219.4	1245.8	1424.3	1768.9
Afrique	64.5	77.1	43.1	79.2	93.2
Amériques	16.4	26.3	46.3	57.8	77.5
– Amérique du Nord	13.0	19.2	39.2	48.0	70.2
– ALAI	3.4	6.8	6.4	9.5	6.8
– MCAC	0.0		0.0	0.0	0.3
– Caraïbes				0.0	0.2
– Autre Amérique		0.3	0.6	0.3	
Asie anc. URSS exclus	698.1	711.1	723.6	797.2	1065.5
– Moyen–Orient	347.5	394.5	466.3	499.5	707.2
Asie ancienne URSS		0.3	0.3	0.8	3.5
Europe anc. URSS exclus	87.2	135.6	124.5	136.1	158.0
– Union Européenne	51.7	61.0	108.9	123.8	142.0
– Europe de l'Est	8.8	13.1	10.5	7.7	12.3
– Autre de l'Europe	26.7	61.5	5.1	4.5	3.7
Europe ancienne URSS	24.8	2.1	37.2	9.4	11.4
Océanie	1.4	6.7	13.9	25.8	13.9
Autre	237.1	260.3	256.8	318.2	345.7
Areas n.e.s.	186.7	199.8	192.4	239.8	237.4
Iraq	131.7	102.4	139.1	165.0	301.7
India/Inde	161.5	142.1	95.1	126.5	162.9
Saudi Arabia	18.0	110.2	123.7	110.5	108.2
Free zones/Zone franches	50.4	60.4	64.4	78.4	108.3
United Arab Emirates	43.6	41.4	48.1	68.8	67.2
Indonesia/Indonésie	35.6	43.5	54.4	40.0	39.2
Syrian Arab Republic	16.6	22.6	36.1	49.8	63.2
USA/Etats–Unis d'Amer	12.8	19.1	38.3	47.5	68.3
Lebanon/Liban	19.2	18.0	27.7	29.2	39.0
Iran (Islamic Rep of)	49.2	29.2	14.4	6.4	27.9
China/Chine	47.7	20.6	24.1	12.0	19.5
France, Monaco	16.0	12.3	21.2	35.5	30.3
Turkey/Turquie	20.8	24.2	20.3	15.7	30.4
United Kingdom	5.0	8.1	44.0	27.1	20.6
Bahrain/Bahreïn	17.2	11.8	20.6	23.0	21.5
Japan/Japon	15.8	17.8	14.2	18.3	19.1
Netherlands/Pays–Bas	10.0	11.7	16.4	19.1	25.9
Korea, Republic of	14.9	17.8	10.9	20.8	18.6
Malaysia/Malaisie	11.1	13.6	16.2	18.9	21.2
Other Asia n.e.s.	15.7	15.4	14.8	14.3	18.8
Libyan Arab Jamahiriya	21.4	15.2	11.3	14.0	17.0
Yemen/Yémen	12.7	17.7	17.2	11.1	15.8
Switzerland,Liechtenst.	18.8	52.0	1.2	0.9	0.4
Qatar	15.7	12.8	14.7	13.3	14.7
Italy/Italie	6.0	7.1	10.6	16.4	28.9
Sudan/Soudan	9.1	12.6	8.9	15.1	18.4
Pakistan	6.9	8.8	5.9	24.0	16.0
Egypt/Egypte	7.5	8.3	8.6	16.2	17.0
Russian Federation		2.0	37.1	8.8	8.2
Germany/Allemagne	7.5	15.1	5.7	8.7	8.8
Ethiopia, incl Eritrea	14.1	29.1			
Australia/Australie	1.2	4.6	8.1	18.0	11.1
Thailand/Thaïlande	16.2	13.1	5.8	2.0	5.8
Philippines	4.8	5.7	4.6	5.6	21.5
Algeria/Algérie	1.0	2.3	0.9	15.2	10.9
Tunisia/Tunisie	6.6	4.8	5.7	6.1	6.1
Brazil/Brésil	3.4	6.8	6.3	5.9	6.3
Greece/Grèce	3.5	2.7	5.3	6.7	9.8
Romania/Roumanie	2.9	5.5	6.0	4.1	7.6

(VALUE AS PERCENTAGE OF WORLD TOTAL)(VALEURS EN POURCENTAGE DU TOTAL MONDIAL)

	1986	1987	1988	1989	1990	1991	1992	1993	1994	1995
Africa	2.9	2.4	2.4	3.6	2.9	4.1	4.3	3.3	2.9	2.8
Americas	10.6	12.0	14.9	16.0	19.1	13.4	13.4	15.1	12.1	12.5
– Northern America	9.2	10.5	13.3	14.5	17.6	11.3	11.6	13.0	10.3	9.6
– LAIA	1.2	1.3	1.4	1.3	1.2	1.8	1.7	2.1	1.7	2.8
– CACM	0.1	0.1	0.2	0.1	0.1	0.1	0.0	0.1	0.1	0.1
– Caribbean	0.0	0.0	0.0	0.0	0.2	0.2	0.0	0.0	0.0	0.0
– Rest of America	0.0	0.0	0.0	0.0					0.0	
Asia excl fmr USSR	41.5	44.0	41.5	40.3	39.0	39.5	42.0	38.9	40.8	43.4
– Middle East	26.0	30.3	28.2	28.5	27.0	22.8	23.0	20.7	22.7	25.2
Asia former USSR							0.0	0.1	0.0	0.1
Europe excl fmr USSR	43.7	40.9	39.9	38.7	35.7	37.3	37.0	37.5	39.5	36.9
– European Union	37.4	33.9	31.8	32.3	29.9	32.3	31.6	33.2	35.5	33.2
– Eastern Europe	4.5	4.9	5.5	3.8	3.7	3.3	4.0	3.2	2.8	1.9
– Rest of Europe	1.9	2.0	2.7	2.6	2.0	1.7	1.5	1.2	1.3	1.8
Europe former USSR	0.7	0.4	0.4	0.4	0.7	1.1	1.6	2.6	2.8	2.7
Oceania	0.6	0.4	0.9	0.7	1.4	2.9	1.3	2.3	1.4	1.4
Other				0.2	1.1	1.6	0.4	0.2	0.3	0.3
Iraq	9.5	11.0	11.5	17.3	15.8	11.0	13.3	12.5	12.3	12.2
USA/Etats–Unis d'Amer	8.8	10.2	12.6	13.8	17.0	10.4	11.1	12.7	9.8	9.3
Germany/Allemagne						7.8	8.4	8.3	7.8	8.4
Italy/Italie	5.9	5.1	4.5	4.2	3.9	4.3	5.0	5.5	5.9	5.4
United Kingdom	8.0	6.4	6.3	6.0	4.8	4.5	4.9	5.2	5.1	4.8
Japan/Japon	7.8	6.1	5.3	3.7	3.1	3.6	6.0	5.0	4.0	3.5
France, Monaco	3.9	3.7	3.9	5.9	5.7	4.3	3.5	4.0	4.7	4.6
Turkey/Turquie	3.2	3.8	2.9	2.3	2.7	3.3	4.4	2.4	2.7	3.4
Netherlands/Pays–Bas	3.2	3.0	3.2	2.8	2.8	3.4	2.4	2.6	3.8	2.8
Saudi Arabia	7.4	8.9	7.5	2.8	4.6	1.6	1.8	2.0	3.0	3.5

	1986	1987	1988	1989	1990	1991	1992	1993	1994	1995
Afrique	4.3	5.7	6.1	5.1	7.5	5.7	6.3	3.5	5.6	5.3
Amériques	2.3	3.1	1.3	2.5	4.7	1.5	2.2	3.7	4.1	4.4
– Amérique du Nord	0.8	1.9	1.1	2.4	4.6	1.1	1.6	3.1	3.4	4.0
– ALAI	1.5	0.9	0.1	0.0	0.1	0.3	0.6	0.5	0.7	0.4
– MCAC		0.3	0.2	0.1		0.0		0.0	0.0	0.0
– Caraïbes									0.0	0.0
– Autre Amérique							0.0	0.1	0.0	
Asie anc. URSS exclus	69.8	64.1	70.8	73.2	77.4	61.8	58.3	58.1	56.0	60.2
– Moyen–Orient	41.6	41.4	39.1	42.2	40.5	30.8	32.4	37.4	35.1	40.0
Asie ancienne URSS							0.0	0.0	0.1	0.2
Europe anc. URSS exclus	23.2	19.9	21.8	18.8	8.2	7.7	11.1	10.0	9.6	8.9
– Union Européenne	11.7	8.4	9.9	10.4	5.9	4.6	5.0	8.7	8.7	8.0
– Europe de l'Est	6.0	5.5	3.8	5.2	1.0	0.8	1.1	0.8	0.5	0.7
– Autre de l'Europe	5.5	6.0	8.1	3.2	1.3	2.4	5.0	0.4	0.3	0.2
Europe ancienne URSS	0.0	0.0	0.0	0.0	1.4	2.2	0.2	3.0	0.7	0.6
Océanie	0.4	7.2	0.0	0.3	0.0	0.1	0.6	1.1	1.8	0.8
Autre				0.0	0.7	21.0	21.3	20.6	22.3	19.5
Areas n.e.s.				0.0	0.7	16.5	16.4	15.4	16.8	13.4
Iraq	17.7	19.7	18.4	20.9	18.6	11.7	8.4	11.2	11.6	17.1
India/Inde	13.4	7.1	14.6	15.0	18.3	14.3	11.7	7.6	8.9	9.2
Saudi Arabia	11.4	9.4	9.4	8.5	7.1	1.6	9.0	9.9	7.8	6.1
Free zones/Zone franches						4.5	5.0	5.2	5.5	6.1
United Arab Emirates	2.0	1.6	2.2	2.5	3.5	3.9	3.4	3.9	4.8	3.8
Indonesia/Indonésie	3.0	2.5	2.9	4.3	4.3	3.1	3.6	4.4	2.8	2.2
Syrian Arab Republic	2.2	2.8	1.5	2.6	1.5	1.5	1.9	2.9	3.5	3.6
USA/Etats–Unis d'Amer	0.6	1.9	1.0	2.2	4.6	1.1	1.6	3.1	3.3	3.9
Lebanon/Liban	0.6	0.7	0.6	0.7	1.5	1.7	1.5	2.2	2.0	2.2

4. General Imports C.I.F. by Commodities according to the S.I.T.C. (Rev. 2) in million U.S. Dollars
Importations Générales C.A.F. par Produits d'après la C.T.C.I. (Rév. 2) en millions de Dollars E.U.

SITC CTCI	COMMODITY	1992 QUANTITY QUANTITE	1992 VALUE VALEUR	1993 QUANTITY QUANTITE	1993 VALUE VALEUR	1994 QUANTITY QUANTITE	1994 VALUE VALEUR	1995 QUANTITY QUANTITE	1995 VALUE VALEUR	PRODUIT
	ALL COMMODITIES		3254.7		3538.7		3382.4		3696.4	TOUS PRODUITS
0	FOOD AND LIVE ANIMALS		615.6		631.8		586.0		598.1	ALIMENTS,ANIMAUX VIVANTS
001	*LIVE ANIMALS FOR FOOD		38.1		39.9	W 630	43.8	W 580	42.5	ANIMAUX VIVANTS
0011	BOVINE SPECIES,LIVE	N 21015	13.8	N 13602	9.2	W 24	16.4	W 23	14.5	ESPECE BOVINE
00119	— OTHR THAN FR BREEDING	N 21015	13.8	N 13602	9.2	W 24	16.4	W 23	13.8	BOVINS NON REPRODUCTEURS
0012	SHEEP AND GOATS,LIVE	N 515159	21.2	N 675548	28.9	W 567	25.1	W 522	25.4	ESPECES OVINE ET CAPRINE
00121	SHEEP,LIVE	N 497814	20.0	N 633580	27.2	W 504	22.5	W 522	25.3	ESPECE OVINE
01	MEAT AND PREPARATIONS		74.5		84.6		67.6		50.0	VIANDES ET PREPARATIONS
011	MEAT FRESH,CHILLD,FROZEN	W 45333	73.9	W 53262	84.4	W 38391	61.9	W 25098	42.0	VIANDES FRAICHES,REF,CONGE
0111	BOVINE MEAT FRESH,FROZEN	W 18851	24.4	W 23289	31.2	W 19035	26.0	W 14189	23.1	VIANDES BOVIN FRAI,REF
01111	BOVINE MEAT WITH BONE IN	W 18851	24.4	W 23289	31.2	W 13581	21.2	W 10483	17.7	VIANDES BOVIN NON DESOSS
0112	MUTTON ETC FRSH,CHLD,FRN	W 17670	38.6	W 19782	41.0	W 13402	29.7	W 8808	16.2	VIANDE DE MOUTON
0114	POULTRY FRESH CHLLD,FRZN	W 7628	9.1	W 9569	11.5	W 5211	5.1	W 1677	2.1	VOLAILLES MORTES
02	DAIRY PRODCTS,BIRDS'EGGS		50.9		59.7		44.1		55.9	PRODUITS LAITIERS,OEUFS
022	MILK AND CREAM	W 15410	34.5	W 19072	42.4	W 12291	24.7	W 15064	33.6	LAIT ET CREME
0224	MILK,CREAM PRESERVED ETC	W 15167	34.0	W 18691	41.5	W 9172	21.5	W 11914	30.2	LAIT,CREME CONS,CONC
02242	MILK DRY,1.5% FAT OR LES	W 12663	31.1	W 15462	38.4	W 7369	17.2	W 10652	26.6	LAIT POUDRE INF 1.5%
024	CHEESE AND CURD	W 4854	12.3	W 4748	12.1	W 5712	14.8	W 5559	15.6	FROMAGE ET CAILLEBOTTE
03	FISH AND PREPARATIONS		16.4		19.7		19.4		23.8	POISSONS ET PREPARATIONS
034	FISH,FRESH,CHILLED,FROZN	W 7661	9.3	W 8932	10.9	W 7714	9.2	W 9575	12.1	POISSON FRAIS, REFRIG,CONG
0342	FISH FROZEN,EXCL FILLETS	W 7656	9.3	W 8927	10.9	W 5920	5.6	W 8749	8.9	POISSONS CONGELES
04	CEREALS AND PREPARATIONS		228.5		248.6		187.9		201.1	CEREALES ET PRODUITS
041	WHEAT ETC UNMILLED					W 508126	74.3	W 335435	56.9	FROMENT,EPEAUTRE
0411	DURUM WHEAT UNMILLED					W 248424	38.6	W 335435	56.9	FROMENT DUR NON MOULU
0412	OTHER WHEAT ETC UNMILLED					W 259702	35.7			AUTRE FROMENT NON MOULU
042	RICE	W 81725	30.8	W 84535	29.6	W 62064	22.9	W 76283	31.0	RIZ
0421	RICE IN HUSK OR HUSKED	W 81725	30.8	W 84535	29.6					RIZ SANS AUTRE PREPARATION
04212	RICE HUSKED	W 81725	30.8	W 84535	29.6					RIZ CARGO
0422	RICE SEMI–MILLED,MILLED					W 62064	22.9	W 76283	31.0	RIZ POLI,GLACE INCL BRISURES
04221	RICE MILLED UNBROKEN					W 62064	22.9	W 76283	31.0	RIZ POLI,GLACE EXCL BRISURES
043	BARLEY UNMILLED	W 293481	33.1	W 482996	51.4	W 471864	43.8	W 487930	54.0	ORGE NON MONDEE
044	MAIZE UNMILLED	W 1129677	157.0	W 1017086	159.9	W 298905	40.8	W 348308	50.7	MAIS NON MOULU
05	VEGETABLES AND FRUIT		64.5		41.7		40.7		61.5	LEGUMES ET FRUITS
054	VEG ETC FRSH,SMPLY PRSVD	W 54268	25.6	W 44437	20.2	W 54576	23.5	W 57054	29.8	LEGUMES FRAIS,CONG,SECS
0542	LEGUMINOUS VEGETBLES DRY	W 28187	14.2	W 20488	9.0	W 24997	10.6	W 26677	14.4	LEGUMES A COSSE SECS
057	FRUIT,NUTS,FRESH,DRIED	W 71572	31.5	W 19072	14.6	W 13040	10.7	W 36269	24.8	FRUITS FRAIS OU SECS
0571	ORANGES, MANDARINS ETC	W 34510	9.9	W 117	0.1	W 844	0.1	W 11407	4.6	ORANGES,MAND,CLEMENTINES
05711	ORANGES,FRESH OR DRIED	W 34510	9.9	W 117	0.1	W 844	0.1	W 11407	4.6	ORANGES FRAICHES,SECHEES
0579	FRUIT FRESH OR DRIED NES	W 27846	11.5	W 8796	4.2	W 6068	3.8	W 5279	3.5	FRUITS FRAIS,SECS NDA
06	SUGAR AND PREPS,HONEY		47.0		52.9		85.5		49.2	SUCRES ET PRODUITS
061	SUGAR AND HONEY	W 139453	45.0	W 162011	51.1	W 214563	83.5	W 100783	46.6	SUCRES ET MIEL
0612	REFINED SUGAR ETC	W 135422	42.4	W 156660	47.8	W 212050	80.5	W 94581	42.4	SUCRES RAFFINES
07	COFFEE,TEA,COCOA,SPICES		26.1		21.3		28.9		35.0	CAFE,THE,CACAO,EPICES
071	COFFEE AND SUBSTITUTES	W 6231	8.3	W 2654	4.3	W 2635	7.6	W 4440	14.9	CAFE ET SUCCEDANES
0711	COFFEE GREEN,ROASTED,SUB	W 6163	7.6	W 2548	3.4	W 2523	6.5	W 4289	13.4	CAFE TORREFIE OU DECAFEINE
07111	COFFEE GREEN,HUSKS,SKINS	W 6023	7.3	W 2520	3.2	W 2432	6.2	W 4288	13.4	CAFE NON TORREFIE
074	TEA AND MATE	W 4618	11.8	W 4520	11.2	W 5626	13.8	W 5153	12.1	THE ET MATE
0741	TEA	W 4618	11.8	W 4520	11.2	W 5624	13.8	W 5153	12.1	THE
081	*FEEDING STUFF FOR ANIML	W 161940	50.7		45.0	W 169928	50.9	W 204494	57.8	NOURRITURE POUR ANIMAUX
0813	OILCAKE AND OTH RESIDUES	W 116430	30.7	W 89477	22.8	W 116971	28.5	W 140437	32.2	TOURTEAUX
08131	— OF SOYA BEANS					W 116971	28.5	W 139910	32.1	TOURTEAUX DE SOJA
08139	— OF OTHER OILSEEDS ETC	W 116430	30.7	W 89477	22.8					TOURTEAUX D'AUTRES OLEAGINEU
0819	FOOD WASTE AND FEED NES	W 37685	18.4	W 44497	20.8	W 38908	19.5	W 38321	20.6	DECHETS,ALIMENTS NDA
08199	FODDER NES,INCL SWEETNED	W 37685	18.4	W 44497	20.8	W 37608	19.4	W 38321	20.6	PREPARATIONS FOURRAGERES
09	MISC EDIBLE PRODUCTS		19.2		18.7		17.7		21.7	PREP ALIMENTAIRES DIVERSES
098	EDIBLE PRODCTS,PREPS NES	W 7151	19.1	W 7090	18.6	W 3949	17.7	W 4615	21.4	PREP ALIMENTAIRES NDA
09809	MISC FOOD PREPRTIONS NES	W 6112	16.5	W 4864	15.3	W 2481	14.1	W 2958	17.8	PREP ALIMENTAIRES NDA
1	BEVERAGES AND TOBACCO		13.8		14.0		19.9		14.2	BOISSONS ET TABACS
12	TOBACCO AND MANUFACTURES		10.5		10.3		17.8		11.7	TABACS BRUTS FABRIQUES
122	TOBACCO,MANUFACTURED	W 146	4.6	W 358	7.1	W 1447	10.5	W 1323	10.0	TABACS FABRIQUES
2	CRUDE MATERLS,EXCL FUELS		94.4		111.3		101.8		130.1	MAT BRUTES NON COMESTIBLES
22	OIL SEEDS,OLEAGINOUS FRT		10.1		10.8		8.1		13.6	GRAINES,FRUITS OLEAGINEUX
222	SEEDS FOR'SOFT'FIXED OIL	W 12926	10.1	W 17598	10.7	W 12476	8.0	W 15661	13.6	GRAINES HUILES FIXES
24	CORK AND WOOD		31.8		30.0		24.4		27.5	LIEGE ET BOIS
248	WOOD SHAPED,SLEEPERS	MW 77698	29.1	MW 79937	28.7	W 6999	21.8	W 6450	26.8	BOIS SIMPLEMENT TRAVAILLES
2483	LUMBER SHAPED NON–CONIFR	MW 57027	20.5	MW 53323	18.6	W 4750	20.8	W 4204	26.1	NON CONIFERES SCIES,RABOTES
24831	LUMBER SAWN ETC NON–CON	MW 57027	20.5	MW 53323	18.6	W 4725	20.8	W 4186	26.0	SCIES LONGITUDINALEMENT
251	*PULP AND WASTE PAPER	W 7578	4.9	W 14911	7.8	W 13915	7.8	W 16899	14.6	PATES A PAPIER,DECHETS
26	TEXTILE FIBRES AND WASTE		15.8		20.7		20.3		23.8	FIBRES TEXTILES
269	WASTE OF TEXTILE FABRICS	W 8491	11.3	W 10411	12.9	W 9600	12.2	W 10768	13.8	FRIPERIE DRILLES,CHIFFONS
26901	BULK TEXT WSTE,OLD CLTHG	W 8431	11.2	W 10374	12.9	W 9535	12.1	W 10480	13.6	ART ET ACCESS D'HABILLEMENT
27	CRUDE FERTLZR,MINRLS NES		11.1		16.6		27.4		36.5	ENGRAIS MINERAUX BRUTS
274	SULPHUR,UNRSTD IRN PYRTE	W 65080	4.8	W 183275	9.8	W 305911	20.5	W 301549	27.8	SOUFRE ET PYRITES
2741	SULPHUR,EX SULP IN 52215	W 64811	4.7	W 182153	9.6	W 305911	20.5	W 301508	27.7	SOUFRE
28	METALLIFEROUS ORES,SCRAP		7.9		14.7		2.4		2.5	MINERAIS METAL,DECHETS
288	NONFERR METAL SCRAP NES	W 4399	6.1	W 9046	11.8	W 1982	2.0	W 1676	2.2	DECHETS NON FERREUX
2882	OTHER BASE MTL SCRAP NES	W 4399	6.1	W 9046	11.8	W 1982	2.0	W 1666	2.2	AUTRES DECHETS
29	CRUDE ANIMAL,VEG MAT NES		10.3		9.0		9.0		8.8	MATIERES BRUTES ANIM,VEGET
3	MINERAL FUELS ETC		446.1		454.0		426.3		477.6	COMBUSTIBLES MINERAUX LUB
33	PETROLEUM AND PRODUCTS		437.7		445.9		415.9		454.7	PETROLE ET DERIVES
333	CRUDE PETROLEUM	W 2974858	336.5	W 2899533	341.6	W 2977092	332.7	W 3162859	355.8	HUILES BRUTES DE PETROLE
334	PETROLEUM PRODUCTS,REFIN	W 842298	100.3	W 885730	103.8	W 893537	82.2	W 942344	98.4	PRODUITS RAFFINES
3342	KEROSENE,OTH MEDIUM OILS	W 800892	78.9	W 862786	89.2					PETR LAMPANTS,AUT HUIL
33421	KEROSENE INCL JET FUEL	W 159564	27.6	W 157742	27.1					PETROLES LAMPANTS
33429	OTH MEDIUM PETROLEUM OIL	W 641328	51.3	W 705044	62.2					AUTRES HUILES MOYENNES
3345	LUBS,PETROLEUM OILS NES	W 41406	21.4	W 22945	14.7					HUILES LUBRIFIANTES
33451	LUBS(HIGH PETR CONT) ETC	W 41068	21.1	W 22425	14.2					HUILES LUBRIF,H LOURDES
341	*GAS,NATURAL AND MANUFCT	W 34168	7.2	W 42280	7.0	W 52399	9.5	W 82103	21.9	GAZ NATUREL,GAZ MANUFACT
3413	PETROLM GASES,LIQUEFIED	W 34168	7.2	W 42280	7.0	W 52399	9.5	W 82102	21.9	GAZ DE PETROLE LIQUEFIE
34139	OTH HYDROCARBON GAS LQFD	W 34168	7.2	W 42280	7.0	W 52399	9.5	W 82102	21.9	HYDROCARBURES GAZEUX NDA
4	ANIMAL,VEGETABLE OIL,FAT		55.4		61.6		118.2		135.2	HUILES,GRAISSES ANIM,VEG
42	FIXED VEGETABLE OIL,FAT		52.8		59.0		111.7		125.0	HUILES VEGETALES FIXES
423	FIXED VEG OILS,SOFT	W 18707	26.2	W 17328	10.7	W 17346	19.8	W 15376	11.9	HUILES VEGET DOUCES FIXES
4232	SOYA BEAN OIL	W 9969	5.9	W 16135	8.7	W 9555	6.6	W 14959	11.4	HUILE DE SOJA
4235	OLIVE OIL	W 8285	19.9	W 1112	2.1	W 6996	12.3	W 88	0.1	HUILE D'OLIVE
424	FIXED VEG OIL NONSOFT	W 57589	26.6	W 111257	48.3	W 185705	92.0	W 166532	113.2	AUTRES HUILES VEG FIXES
4242	PALM OIL	W 50758	21.2	W 103931	43.8	W 173487	82.3	W 156062	104.9	HUILE DE PALME
5	CHEMCLS,RELATED PROD NES		357.1		355.0		401.6		443.7	PRODUITS CHIMIQUES
51	ORGANIC CHEMICALS		47.3		37.4		44.5		51.3	PROD CHIMIQ ORGANIQUES
513	CARBOXYLIC ACIDS ETC	W 8995	8.7	W 8381	7.7	W 8869	9.4	W 9543	14.1	ACIDES CARBOXYLIQUES

4. General Imports C.I.F. by Commodities according to the S.I.T.C. (Rev. 2) in million U.S. Dollars
Importations Générales C.A.F. par Produits d'après la C.T.C.I. (Rév. 2) en millions de Dollars E.U.

SITC CTCI	COMMODITY	1992 QUANTITY QUANTITE	1992 VALUE VALEUR	1993 QUANTITY QUANTITE	1993 VALUE VALEUR	1994 QUANTITY QUANTITE	1994 VALUE VALEUR	1995 QUANTITY QUANTITE	1995 VALUE VALEUR	PRODUIT
516	OTHER ORGANIC CHEMICALS	W 2792	19.6		8.6	W 3709	17.0	W 3422	15.0	AUTRES PROD ORGANIQUES
5169	ORGANIC CHEMICALS,NES	W 458	15.3		6.8	W 839	14.2	W 571	11.4	PROD CHIM ORGANIQUES NDA
51699	OTHER ORGANIC COMPOUNDS	W 426	14.9	W 608	6.5	W 770	13.8	W 522	11.0	AUTRES COMPOS ORGANIQUES
52	INORGANIC CHEMICALS		41.2		42.7		65.9		67.8	PROD CHIM INORGANIQUES
522	INORG ELEMNTS,OXIDES,ETC	W 158722	29.0	W 145159	26.2	W 203262	43.3	W 197966	50.8	ELEMENTS INORGANIQUES
5225	INORGANIC BASES ETC NES	W 88474	15.8	W 137002	19.2	W 194572	34.0	W 189174	42.1	AUTRES BASES OXYDES METAL
52251	AMMONIA,ANHYDROUS ETC	W 57711	7.2	W 119014	13.6	W 177463	31.0	W 160045	36.7	AMMONIAC LIQUEFIE
523	OTHR INORG CHEMICALS ETC	W 30499	11.9	W 41749	16.1	W 55426	22.4	W 42984	16.6	AUT PRODUITS CHIMIQUES INORG
5232	OTH MTL CMPD OF INRG ACD	W 16417	7.7	W 21453	10.2	W 33755	17.8	W 25764	12.8	SELS METALLIQUES
52322	PHOSPHITES,PHOSPHATES	W 6901	4.8	W 12493	7.6	W 27270	15.6	W 17932	9.8	PHOSPHITES,PHOSPHATES
53	DYES,TANNING,COLOUR PROD		12.3		12.3		15.3		15.9	PROD TEINTURE,COLORANTS
533	PIGMENTS,PAINTS,ETC	W 5737	9.8	W 6370	9.8	W 7077	12.7	W 7772	13.6	PIGMENTS,PEINTURES,VERNIS
541	*MEDICINAL,PHARM PRODUCT	K 4831789	86.8	K 5299586	99.6	K 5087046	101.4	K 5979880	128.1	PROD MEDICINAUX PHARMACEUT
5413	ANTIBIOTICS IN BULK	K 967169	16.4	K 1329213	31.1	K 556245	21.3	K 859338	21.2	ANTIBIOTIQUES NDA
54139	OTHER ANTIBIOTICS	K 967167	16.4	K 1329213	31.1	K 482502	19.2	K 807756	18.4	AUTRES ANTIBIOTIQUES
5417	MEDICAMENTS	K 3285655	62.2	K 3542291	60.7	K 3790690	68.1	K 4489677	93.0	MEDICAMENTS
54171	— CONTAINNG ANTIBIOTICS	K 2690952	54.0	K 2784320	52.3	K 860466	14.2	K 488648	14.7	MED CONTN ANTIBIOTIQUES
54179	— CONTNG OTH SUBSTANCES					K 2592649	48.6	K 3687939	75.0	MED CONT AUT SUBSTANCES
55	PERFUME,CLEANING ETC PRD		25.2		30.3		22.1		25.4	PROD POUR PARFUM,TOILETTE
554	SOAP,CLEANSING ETC PREPS	W 15508	14.2	W 23979	18.7	W 11063	10.9	W 9893	11.9	SAVONS,PRODUITS DETERSIFS
5541	SOAPS	W 7334	5.5	W 17984	11.6	W 7605	5.5	W 6922	6.5	SAVONS,PROD TENSIO–ACTIFS
562	*FERTILIZERS,MANUFACTURE	W 81364	18.0	W 48871	11.0	W 31690	8.8	W 42718	11.5	ENGRAIS MANUFACTURES
5621	CHEM NITROGENOUS FERTLZR	W 75209	13.5	W 44364	8.2	W 25767	5.0	W 32828	6.2	ENGRAIS AZOTES
56211	AMMONIUM NITRATE	W 72862	12.1	W 16363	3.7	W 5368	1.2	W 6968	1.6	NITRATE D'AMMONIUM
58	PLASTIC MATERIALS ETC		90.0		89.5		100.5		102.9	MAT PLAST ARTIFICIELLES
582	PROD OF CONDENSATION ETC	W 4770	8.9	W 6756	11.4	W 7288	12.3	W 5266	10.7	PROD CONDENS,POLYCOND
583	POLYMERIZATION ETC PRODS	W 79438	78.2	W 85538	76.1	W 97607	85.4	W 73281	89.0	PROD POLYMERISATION
5831	POLYETHYLENE	W 77250	75.3	W 82927	73.0	W 41262	31.1	W 33514	35.2	POLYETHYLENE
58311	— IN PRIMARY FORMS	W 68184	57.3	W 74048	55.7	W 40165	29.2	W 32364	32.8	POLYETHYLENE PRIMAIRES
58313	— PLATES,FILM,STRIP,ETC	W 8528	17.2	W 8675	16.3	W 1052	1.8	W 1108	2.4	POLYETHYLENE PLAQUES
5832	POLYPROPYLENE	W 90	0.1	W 292	0.3	W 17666	14.9	W 14982	20.0	POLYPROPYLENE
58321	— IN PRIMARY FORMS	W 90	0.1	W 292	0.3	W 15493	11.1	W 12338	13.3	POLYPROPYLENE PRIMAIRES
5833	POLYSTYRENE,ITS COPOLYMR					W 10572	10.6	W 5838	7.9	POLYPROPYLENE COPOLYMERES
58331	— IN PRIMARY FORMS					W 10500	10.4	W 5744	7.7	SOUS FORMES PRIMAIRES
5834	POLYVINYL CHLORIDE					W 17350	13.8	W 10755	11.6	CHLORURE DE POLYVINYLE
58341	— IN PRIMARY FORMS					W 16833	12.8	W 9923	10.1	SOUS FORMES PRIMAIRES
5839	OTH POLYMRZTION ETC PROD					W 7734	11.2	W 6313	11.4	AUT PROD POLYMER COPOLYM
59	CHEMICAL MATERIALS NES		35.0		31.6		42.4		41.0	MAT PROD CHIMIQUES NDA
591	PESTICIDES,DISINFECTANTS	W 2298	11.6	W 1739	8.8	W 1969	9.6	W 1778	9.5	DESINF,INSECT,FONG,HERB
5912	FUNGICIDES,FOR RETAIL	W 2286	11.5	W 1725	8.8	W 458	1.9	W 605	3.1	FONGICIDES VENTE AU DET
598	MISCEL CHEM PRODUCTS NES	W 8293	19.0	W 9287	17.4	W 24810	28.2	W 21909	27.4	PROD DIV INDUST CHIM NDA
5989	CHEM PRODUCTS,PREPS NES	W 7433	17.3	W 8555	16.0	W 21149	21.8	W 20307	23.6	PROD PREP CHIMIQUES NDA
59899	OTH CHEM PRODS,PREPS,NES	W 6258	15.5	W 6692	14.1	W 18620	18.9	W 19003	21.1	AUT PRODUITS CHIMIQUES NDA
6	BASIC MANUFACTURES		622.9		695.6		620.6		720.1	ART MANUFACTURES
62	RUBBER MANUFACTURES NES		45.9		44.6		38.2		44.9	CAOUTCHOUC MANUFACTURE
625	RUBBER TYRES, TUBES ETC	W 15050	37.3	W 16428	36.1	W 13738	30.1	W 16249	37.2	PNEUS CAOUTCHOUC VULCANISE
6251	TYRES NEW FOR MOTOR CARS					W 8330	20.8	W 12435	30.5	PNEUS POUR VOITURES
6252	TYRES,NEW,BUS OR LORRY	W 14919	37.0	W 16233	35.6	W 1369	3.4	W 1578	4.4	PNEUS POUR AUTOBUS,CAMIONS
63	WOOD,CORK MANUFACTRS NES		28.6		34.5		33.2		27.4	OUVRAGES LIEGE ET BOIS
634	VENEERS,PLYWOOD,ETC		22.0		27.3	W 53059	25.9	W 30825	22.8	PLACAGES,CONTRE–PLAQUES
6342	PLYWOOD OF WOOD SHEETS	MV 22459	7.8	MV 22315	7.1	W 41682	22.9	W 22604	20.0	BOIS CONTRE–PLAQUES
6344	WOOD–BASED PANELS NES	W 30648	13.8	W 35619	19.8					PANNEAUX SUPPORT BOIS NDA
63441	BLOCKBOARD,LAMINBRD, ETC	W 30648	13.8	W 35619	19.8					BOIS CONTRE–PLAQUES
64	PAPER,PAPERBOARD AND MFR		74.7		84.2		69.0		107.6	PAPIERS,CARTONS & OUVRAGES
641	PAPER AND PAPERBOARD	W 83624	60.4	W 111915	72.8	W 85376	58.2	W 96351	92.5	PAPIERS ET CARTONS
6412	PRINTG,WRITING PAPER NES	W 23777	19.2	W 36953	26.7	W 2029	2.1	W 1864	2.6	PAPIERS POUR L'IMPRESSION
64121	— UNCOATED	W 21546	16.3	W 33954	23.4	W 113	0.2	W 67	0.2	PAPIERS IMPRES NON COUCHES
6413	KRAFT PAPER,PAPERBOARD	W 21574	12.5	W 24903	13.6	W 19731	10.5	W 24239	19.5	PAPIER ET CARTON KRAFT
64131	KRAFT LINER IN BULK	W 21574	12.5	W 24903	13.6	W 7052	2.8	W 8534	5.8	PAP KRAFT POUR COUVERTURES
6415	PAPER,PAPERBRD,BULK,NES	W 4630	7.3	W 6310	6.7	W 22145	16.8	W 29010	34.6	PAPIERS,CARTONS ROULEAUX
64159	OTHER PAPER ETC,BULK,NES	W 931	2.7	W 776	1.3	W 20666	15.7	W 28901	34.4	AUT PAPIER ROULEAUX FEUILLES
6418	COATED ETC PAPER NES BLK	W 17664	14.7	W 20301	16.4	W 13690	13.3	W 14595	17.1	PAP,CARTONS COUCHES,ENDUITS
64189	COATED PAPER ETC NES	W 3005	5.2	W 3826	6.2	W 13330	12.6	W 14210	16.4	PAPIERS,CARTONS COUCHES
642	PAPER,ETC,PRECUT,ARTS OF	W 6467	14.3	W 5591	11.4	W 5370	10.8	W 8198	15.2	PAP,CARTONS DECOUPES
65	TEXTILE YARN,FABRICS,ETC		139.4		137.6		125.5		127.5	FILS,TISSUS,ARTICLES TEXTILE
651	TEXTILE YARN	W 12201	45.0		44.3	W 9638	34.9	W 9378	37.2	FILS TEXTILES
6512	WOOL,HAIR YARN,INCL TOPS	W 71	0.9	W 92	1.0	W 1572	10.1	W 1205	13.8	FILS DE LAINE,DE POILS
6514	SYN FIB YRN,BULK,MONOFIL	W 8944	34.0	W 10104	32.5	W 3040	9.7	W 3304	9.9	FILS CONT 85% FIB TEXT SYNTH
65141	— TEXTRD,CONT POLYAMIDE	W 3025	10.7	W 3585	11.8	W 496	1.9	W 531	1.8	FILS TEXT FIB CONT POLYAMID
65142	— NONTXT ETC CONT PAMID	W 5715	21.5	W 6386	20.0	W 1217	3.9	W 1538	4.4	FILS NON TEX FI CON POLYAMID
653	WOVN MAN–MADE FIB FABRIC	W 10056	59.7	W 10779	61.3	W 9628	56.3	W 9157	56.8	TISSUS FIBRES SYNTH,ARTIF
6531	CONT SYNT WEAVES NONPILE	W 10011	59.5	W 10745	61.2	W 8236	48.3	W 7933	49.3	TISSUS FIBRES SYNTH CONTINUE
65314	CONT SYN TYRE CORD FABRC	W 8656	52.1	W 9252	54.2	W 792	3.8	W 516	2.2	TIS ARMATURE PNEUMATIQUES
65315	CONT SYN TXTL FABRIC NES	W 1356	7.5	W 1493	7.0	W 7444	44.6	W 7417	47.1	TIS PLUS 85% TEXT SYNT CONT
657	SPECIAL TXTL FABRC,PRODS	W 4193	9.5	W 4197	10.0	W 4551	10.8	W 4082	11.7	TISSUS SPECIAUX
66	NONMETAL MINERAL MFS NES		40.5		43.7		47.5		48.6	ART MIN NON METALLIQUES
662	CLAY,REFRACTORY BLDG PRD	W 23107	8.2		11.0	W 25223	8.6	W 25720	10.2	MAT CONST REFRACTAIRES
665	GLASSWARE	W 20173	17.1	W 16251	14.6	W 27290	20.1	W 23625	18.7	OUVRAGES EN VERRE
6651	BOTTLES ETC OF GLASS	W 14777	8.8	W 10074	6.6	W 21238	11.2	W 16702	9.7	RECIPIENTS EN VERRE
66511	GLASS BOTTLES ETC NONVAC	W 14777	8.8	W 10069	6.6	W 21226	11.2	W 16698	9.7	BONBONNES,BOUTEILLES,ETC
67	IRON AND STEEL		196.4		227.9		190.1		210.9	FER ET ACIER
672	IRON,STEEL PRIMARY FORMS	W 292041	76.7	W 211349	61.8	W 217558	58.9	W 257277	77.1	LINGOTS FER,ACIER
6725	IRN,STL BLOOMS,SLABS,ETC	W 256801	62.1	W 164140	42.2	W 158309	37.6	W 210726	57.3	BLOOMS,BILLETTES FER ACIER
67251	IRN,SMPLE STL BLOOMS,ETC	W 256801	62.1	W 164140	42.2	W 157783	37.1	W 210291	56.8	BLOOMS ETC NON ACIER FIN
6727	IRN,STL COIL FR REROLLNG	W 32088	11.3	W 42697	15.6	W 46381	18.3	W 46486	19.8	EBAUCHES POUR TOLES FER
67271	IRON,SIMPLE STEEL COILS	W 32088	11.3	W 42697	15.6	W 39392	14.1	W 38346	15.4	EBAUCHES NON EN ACIER
673	IRON,STEEL SHAPES ETC	W 156499	51.1	W 268423	77.9	W 196195	58.4	W 195263	59.9	BARRES,PROFIL FER,ACIER
6731	IRON,STEEL WIRE ROD	W 13937	4.4	W 947	0.5	W 115026	31.6	W 67687	19.2	FIL MACHINE FER,ACIER
67311	IRON,SIMPLE STL WIRE ROD	W 13937	4.4	W 947	0.5	W 103699	28.5	W 53775	15.1	FIL MACH AUT ACIER FIN
6732	IRON,STEEL BARS ETC	W 109679	34.9	W 219837	58.9	W 44720	12.7	W 95789	27.9	BARRES FER,ACIER
67325	OTH ALLOY STEEL BARS ETC					W 12680	3.6	W 41746	12.1	BARRES NON ACIERS ALLIES
67327	IRN, OTH STL BARS FORGED	W 97131	30.8	W 207550	55.9	W 10475	3.2	W 10769	2.9	BARRES FORGEES CREUSES
6733	IRON,STEEL PROFILES ETC	W 32883	11.9	W 47640	18.6	W 36449	14.2	W 31787	12.9	PROFILES,PALPLAN FER,ACIER
67331	SMALL U,I,H SECTIONS ETC	W 32883	11.9	W 47640	18.6	W 15634	5.7	W 11222	4.2	PROFILES MOINS 80MM
674	IRN,STL UNIV,PLATE,SHEET	W 66267	35.1	W 113321	57.4	W 80157	44.4	W 77271	46.0	LARGES PLATS,TOLES
6744	IRN,STL HVY PLATE,ROLLED	W 12936	10.1	W 17780	13.4	W 15954	8.0	W 9117	4.2	TOLES LAMINEES PLUS 4.75 MM
67441	— OF IRON OR SIMPLE STL	W 12936	10.1	W 17780	13.4	W 15571	7.9	W 9089	4.2	TOLES NON ACIER FIN CARB
6745	IRN,STL MED PLATE,ROLLED	W 45340	21.4	W 81314	38.0	W 14227	7.4	W 10769	6.6	TOLES 3 A 4.75 MM
67451	— OF IRON OR SIMPLE STL	W 45340	21.4	W 81314	38.0	W 13832	7.1	W 10607	6.4	TOLES AUT NON ACIER FIN
6746	IRN,STL THIN PLATE,ROLLD					W 15140	7.8	W 24979	13.0	TOLES LAM MOINS 3MM
67461	— OF IRON OR SIMPLE STL					W 14804	7.3	W 24234	12.2	TOL NON AC FIN MOINS 3 MM

4. General Imports C.I.F. by Commodities according to the S.I.T.C. (Rev. 2) in million U.S. Dollars
Importations Générales C.A.F. par Produits d'après la C.T.C.I. (Rév. 2) en millions de Dollars E.U.

SITC CTCI	COMMODITY	1992 QUANTITY QUANTITE	1992 VALUE VALEUR	1993 QUANTITY QUANTITE	1993 VALUE VALEUR	1994 QUANTITY QUANTITE	1994 VALUE VALEUR	1995 QUANTITY QUANTITE	1995 VALUE VALEUR	PRODUIT
6749	OTH IRN,STL PLATES,SHEET					W 25677	15.3	W 18700	12.0	AUTRES TOLES FER,ACIER
67491	— OF IRON OR SIMPLE STL					W 25040	14.3	W 17949	10.9	AUT TOLES AUTRES ACIER FIN
678	IRON,STL TUBES,PIPES,ETC	W 33385	26.3	W 23261	25.1	W 25058	21.3	W 24317	22.5	TUBES,TUYAUX EN FONTE,FER
6782	IRON,STL SEAMLESS TUBES	W 26163	17.9	W 19652	17.2	W 2940	2.2	W 5535	4.3	TUBES,TUYAUX SANS SOUDURE
6783	IRON,STL TUBES,PIPES NES	W 1447	1.0	W 225	0.2	W 18664	13.7	W 15790	13.2	AUT TUBES,TUYAUX FER,ACIER
68	NON–FERROUS METALS		23.2		26.6		35.6		53.5	METAUX NON FERREUX
682	COPPER EXC CEMENT COPPER		11.1		14.0	W 4721	12.9	W 6681	22.8	CUIVRE
6822	COPPER,ALLOYS WORKED		10.3		13.7	W 4482	12.5	W 6499	22.4	CUIVRE,ALLIAGES OUVRES
68221	COPPER BARS,WIRE,ETC	W 2212	5.9	W 4076	8.9	W 3469	8.5	W 5505	17.2	BARRES,PROFILES ET FILS
684	ALUMINIUM	W 4530	11.4	W 5310	11.5	W 10201	19.4	W 10189	26.0	ALUMINIUM
6841	ALUMINIUM,ALLOYS,UNWRGHT	W 1118	1.0	W 1043	1.0	W 7086	10.3	W 6250	13.4	ALUMINIUM,ALLIAGES BRUTS
6842	ALUMINIUM,ALLOYS WORKED	W 3413	10.4	W 4267	10.6	W 3114	9.1	W 3939	12.6	ALUMINIUM,ALLIAGES OUVRE
69	METAL MANUFACTURES NES		73.5		95.5		81.0		98.6	ART MANUFACT EN METAL NDA
691	STRUCTURES AND PARTS NES	W 1517	4.5	W 10252	15.0	W 10854	9.8	W 9700	27.1	CONSTRUCT FER,ACIER,ALU
6911	STRUCTURES,PARTS IRN,STL	W 1445	4.4	W 10166	14.6	W 10656	8.9	W 9627	26.8	CONSTRUCT FER,ACIER,FONTE
692	METAL TANKS,BOXES,ETC	W 2444	8.0	W 4223	14.6	W 5413	15.1	W 4339	12.8	RECIPIENTS METALLIQUES
6924	MTL TRANSPORT BOXES ETC	W 2177	7.3	W 3356	12.3	W 4391	14.0	W 3628	12.2	FUTS,TAMBOURS,BIDONS
69242	ALUMNM TRNSPRT BOXES ETC	W 540	4.7	W 1447	9.8	W 2310	11.3	W 1547	8.8	FUTS,TAMBOURS,BIDONS ALU
697	BASE MTL HOUSEHOLD EQUIP		21.8		22.6	W 5229	19.4	W 5049	19.4	ART MENAGE MET COMMUNS
6973	DMSTC HEATG,COOKG APPARA		8.7		12.6	W 2304	9.5	W 2245	8.8	APPS CHAUF NON ELECTRIQ
69734	COPPER DOMSTC STOVES,ETC	W 1685	7.7	W 2534	11.0	W 105	0.4	W 68	0.4	APP NON ELEC CUISSON CUIVRE
699	BASE METAL MFRS NES	W 7602	20.6		22.6	W 6745	18.5	W 7722	18.8	ART MANUFACTURES MET NDA
6991	LOCKSMITHS WARES,ETC	W 2754	10.2	W 3086	11.2	W 2991	10.4	W 2510	8.6	ARTICLES DE SERRURERIE
7	MACHINES,TRANSPORT EQUIP		802.4		957.1		858.9		905.5	MACHINES MATERIEL TRANSPORT
71	POWER GENERATING EQUIPMT		56.3		87.2		58.9		33.1	MACHINES GENERATRICES
714	ENGINES AND MOTORS NES		0.1	W 2	0.1	W 663	13.2	W 324	13.6	MOTEURS NON ELECTRIQUES
7144	REACTION ENGINES		0.1	W 1	0.1	W 603	11.9	W 305	12.3	PROPULSEURS A REACTION
716	ROTATING ELECTRIC PLANT	W 3611	14.8	W 4637	20.7	W 3674	38.6	W 2735	11.3	APP ELECTR ROTATIFS,PIECES
7162	AC MTRS,GENRTRS,GEN SETS	W 3048	12.2	W 4429	19.7	W 3129	36.2	W 2559	9.8	MOTEURS ELECTRIQUES
71621	AC MTRS,INC UNIVRSL MTRS	W 3048	12.2	W 4429	19.7	W 2660	34.1	W 2377	8.2	MOT ELEC NON COUR CONTINU
718	OTH POWER GENERATG MACHY	W 3969	38.7	W 5498	63.7	W 139	1.6	W 55	0.7	AUTRES MOTEURS PARTIES
7187	NUCLEAR REACTORS,PTS NES	W 3967	38.6	W 5492	63.5		0.1	W 17	0.1	REACTEURS NUCLEAIRES
72	MACHS FOR SPCL INDUSTRYS		98.8		132.1		141.5		127.9	MAC SPECIALES POUR INDUST
723	CIVIL ENGNEERG EQUIP ETC		32.5		56.0	W 289	21.0	W 124	23.7	APPAREILS DE GENIE CIVIL
7234	CONST,MINING MACHNRY NES		31.5		54.1	W 135	19.4	W 53	22.4	MACH POUR LA CONST, MINES
72341	SELF–PROPELLD DOZERS,ETC	N 423	25.7	N 600	43.0		14.5		13.5	BULLDOZERS
724	TEXTILE,LEATHER MACHNRY		24.5		24.5	W 2020	20.4	W 1275	14.2	MACH POUR INDUSTRIE TEXTILE
726	PRINTG,BKBINDG MACHY,PTS	W 716	13.8	W 1117	15.3	W 854	9.5	W 544	8.0	MACHINES POUR IMPRIMERIE
727	FOOD MACHRY NON–DOMESTIC	W 359	4.6	W 1170	8.7	W 1425	13.7	W 1430	16.6	MACH INDUSTRIES ALIMENT
7272	OTH FOOD PROC MCHY,PARTS	W 321	3.8	W 1150	8.4	W 1338	13.0	W 1157	14.5	AUT MACH IND ALIMENTAIRE
72722	INDUS FOOD PROC MACH NES	W 308	3.7	W 1099	7.7	W 1227	11.3	W 1051	14.1	MACHINES BOULANGERIE
728	OTH MACHY FOR SPCL INDUS	W 2131	9.6	W 2228	13.2	W 7609	61.9	W 5125	51.2	AUT MACH IND PARTICULIERES
7284	MACHY FOR SPCL INDUS NES	W 1	0.1	W 1	0.1	W 4964	48.9	W 3508	44.3	MACH SPEC IND PARTICUL.
72845	MTL ETC TREATNG MACH NES					W 1122	11.8	W 333	6.2	MACH TRAITEMENT METAUX
72848	OTH MCHY WITH INDIV FNCT					W 2394	23.6	W 1574	21.7	AUTRES MACHINES NDA
73	METALWORKING MACHINERY		15.9		22.3		25.2		26.4	MACH TRAVAIL DES METAUX
736	METALWORKING MACH–TOOLS	W 4986	14.8	W 6989	21.2	W 6189	20.3	W 5843	23.0	MACH–OUTILS TRAVAIL METAUX
7361	METAL CUTTING MACH–TOOLS	W 4964	14.3	W 6760	20.3	W 2468	5.5	W 1689	5.0	MACH–OUT ENLEVEMENT METAL
73611	ULTRASNC ETC MTLWKG MCHS	W 4964	14.3	W 6760	20.3	W 25	0.2	W 3	0.1	MACH–OUT ELECTRO–EROSION
7367	OTH METALWRKG MACH–TOOLS					W 2099	10.8	W 2738	12.7	AUT MACH–OUT POUR METAUX
74	GENRL INDUSTRL MACHY NES		118.4		152.9		129.6		134.5	MACH APP INDUSTRIE
741	HEATING,COOLING EQUIPMNT		19.6		24.7	W 2653	25.8	W 3539	28.3	MACH CHAUFFAGE,PIECES
7414	NONDOM REFRIG EQUIPT,PTS		5.2		7.8	W 1077	11.7	W 1326	7.7	MAT PRODUCTION DU FROID
742	PUMPS FOR LIQUIDS ETC	W 1606	16.2	W 1549	15.4	W 1770	12.8	W 1425	14.2	POMPES MOTO–POMPES
7422	CENTRIFUGAL PUMPS NES	W 1050	10.7	W 989	9.3	W 80	0.4	W 38	0.5	POMPES CENTRIF NON 742.81
7428	OTHER PUMPS FOR LIQUIDS	W 556	5.5	W 560	6.2	W 1562	10.6	W 1140	10.2	AUTRES POMPES POUR LIQ
74288	PUMPS FR LIQUIDS NES ETC					W 1538	10.5	W 1138	10.1	POMPES POUR LIQUIDES NDA
743	PUMPS NES,CENTRFUGES ETC	W 1539	11.1	W 3314	19.1	W 2334	14.4	W 1849	15.3	POMPES COMPRES,VENT ETC
744	MECHANICAL HANDLING EQU		5.5		10.0	W 1796	9.9	W 1809	11.8	EQUIP MANUTENTION PIECES
745	NONELEC MACHY,TOOLS NES	W 785	10.0	W 1307	14.1	W 1221	16.0	W 1682	20.5	AUT MACH NON ELEC,PIECES
7452	OTH NONELEC MCHS,PTS NES	W 709	9.1	W 1255	13.7	W 1145	15.3	W 1627	20.1	AUT MACH NON ELEC,PIECES
749	NONELEC MACH PTS,ACC NES	W 4004	56.3	W 6347	69.8	W 5164	51.0	W 3393	44.6	PIECES MACH NON ELEC NDA
7492	COCKS,VALVES ETC NES	W 1396	13.4	W 2313	18.5	W 1925	14.7	W 1398	14.5	ART ROB,SIM POUR TUYAUX
7493	SHAFT,CRANK,PULLEY ETC	W 1727	31.8	W 2994	39.6	W 1771	22.4	W 1027	17.6	ARBRES TRANS,VILEBREQUINS
7499	OTH NONELEC MCHY PTS NES	W 562	8.5	W 760	9.8	W 1113	10.5	W 539	9.5	PIECES NON ELECT NDA
75	OFFICE MACHNES,ADP EQUIP		34.6		35.4		37.5		36.2	MACH BUREAU TRAIT AUTOM
752	AUTOMTIC DATA PROC EQUIP	N 15864	18.7	N 18840	20.3	W 21	23.0	W 21	19.3	MACH TRAIT INFORMATION
7521	ANALOG,HYBRID COMPUTERS	N 15864	18.7	N 18840	20.3	W 3	3.7	W 4	4.6	MACH POUR TRAIT INFORMAT
7522	DIGITAL COMPUTERS					W 14	16.0	W 10	10.5	MACH DIGITALES COMPLETES
76	TELECOMM,SOUND EQUIPMENT		32.5		40.2		36.7		68.2	EQUIPMENT DE TELECOM
761	TELEVISION RECEIVERS		17.0		20.0	W 121	6.0	W 153	6.3	RECEPTEURS DE TELEVISION
7611	COLOUR TV RECEIVERS		12.1		14.1	W 94	5.5	W 134	5.6	RECEPTEURS COULEUR
764	TELECOM EQPT,PTS,ACC NES	W 233	11.7	W 332	16.0	W 1264	26.6	W 1994	57.8	EQUIP TELECOM,PIECES
7641	LINE TELEPHONE,ETC EQUIP	W 159	10.8	W 248	15.2	W 151	6.6	W 385	29.4	APP TELEPHON PAR FIL
7649	PTS NES OF EQUIPMT OF 76	W 13	0.6	W 11	0.3	W 1034	16.4	W 1539	26.9	PIECES DE LA DIV 76
76493	TELECOMM EQUIPMT PTS NES					W 915	11.1	W 1329	16.1	PIECES 761,762,764.3,8
77	ELECTRIC MACHNRY NES ETC		50.6		75.7		87.6		91.3	MACH APP ELECT NDA
772	SWITCHGEAR ETC,PARTS NES	W 942	11.8	W 2190	20.3	W 1639	14.7	W 1259	16.2	APP COUPURE,SECT ETC
7721	SWITCHGEAR ETC	W 109	2.0	W 219	2.0	W 1592	14.0	W 1244	16.1	APP COUPURE,SECTIONMNT
7722	PRINTED CIRCUITS,PTS NES	W 833	9.9	W 1971	18.4		0.1		0.1	CIRCUITS ET PIECES
773	ELECTR DISTRIBUTNG EQUIP	W 2417	7.2	W 6892	18.2	W 4913	13.9	W 6149	18.9	EQUIPMT DISTRIBUTION ELECT
7731	INSULATED WIRE,CABLE ETC	W 2267	6.8	W 5735	15.5	W 4775	13.3	W 5467	15.0	FILS,CABLES ISOLES ELECT
774	ELECTRO–MEDCL,XRAY EQUIP	W 63	2.8	W 67	3.8	W 154	12.8	W 143	8.9	APPAREILS MEDICAUX
775	HOUSEHOLD TYPE EQUIP NES		12.4		15.6	W 1405	21.6	W 1671	22.5	MACH,APP USAGE DOMESTQUE
778	ELECTRICAL MACHINERY NES	W 3560	14.2	W 3319	15.9	W 3654	18.0	W 3724	17.0	AUTRES MACH ELECT NDA
78	ROAD VEHICLES		259.3		282.4		249.3		300.3	VEHICULES ROUTIERS
781	PASS MOTOR VEH EXC BUSES	N 7481	61.6	N 7367	63.8	W 6	52.9	W 8	74.4	AUTO TRANSPORT PERSONNES
782	LORRIES,SPCL MTR VEH NES	N 5707	72.6	N 6136	91.1	W 7	93.9	W 7	109.8	VEHICULES SPECIAUX,MARCH
7821	LORRIES,TRUCKS	N 5514	61.9	N 5928	80.5	W 7	87.5	W 6	101.9	VEHICULES TRANSP MARCHAND
7822	SPECIAL MOTOR VEHCLS NES	N 193	10.8	N 208	10.7		6.5		7.9	VEHICULES USAGES SPECIAUX
783	ROAD MOTOR VEHICLES NES	N 961	20.0	N 1036	25.7	W 1	15.5	W 1	32.4	VEHICULES ROUTIERS NDA
7831	BUSES	N 958	19.6	N 1035	25.6	W 1	15.5	W 1	32.1	VOITURES TRANSPORT COMMUN
784	MOTOR VEH PRTS,ACCES NES		96.9		91.9	W 15147	77.8	W 15416	79.4	PIECES 722,781,782,783
7849	OTHER MOTOR VEHCL PARTS	W 17080	93.1	W 17290	89.1	W 15146	70.8	W 15415	70.7	PIECES 722,781,782,783
79	OTHR TRANSPORT EQUIPMENT		136.6		129.4		93.0		88.1	AUTRE MATERIEL TRANSPORT
792	AIRCRAFT ETC		135.2	W 499	121.8	W 425	92.1	W 391	84.5	APP NAVIGATION AERIENNE
7928	AIRCRAFT NES,ASSOC EQUIP		22.1				0.1		0.1	APP NAVIG AERIENNE NDA
79281	GLIDERS,KITES,ROTOCHUTES	N 4	22.1							ROTOCHUTES
7929	AIRCRAFT PARTS NES	W 464	113.2	W 499	121.8	W 425	92.1	W 391	84.5	PIECES DU 792
8	MISC MANUFACTURED GOODS		221.0		214.5		218.2		220.4	ART MANUFACTURES DIVERS
812	*PLUMBG,HEATNG,LGHTNG EQ	W 8798	12.1	W 9621	14.9	W 6850	12.0	W 6375	11.9	APPAR SANITAIRES CHAUFFAGE

4. General Imports C.I.F. by Commodities according to the S.I.T.C. (Rev. 2) in million U.S. Dollars
Importations Générales C.A.F. par Produits d'après la C.T.C.I. (Rév. 2) en millions de Dollars E.U.

SITC CTCI	COMMODITY	1992			1993			1994			1995			PRODUIT
		QUANTITY QUANTITE		VALUE VALEUR	QUANTITY QUANTITE		VALUE VALEUR	QUANTITY QUANTITE		VALUE VALEUR	QUANTITY QUANTITE		VALUE VALEUR	
821	*FURNITURE,PARTS THEREOF	W	1214	5.4	W	1578	5.9	W	1732	11.4	W	2040	8.6	MEUBLES ET PIECES
84	CLOTHING AND ACCESSORIES			53.3			53.2			52.7			56.3	VETEMENTS
842	MENS OUTERWEAR NOT KNIT	W	2536	13.9	W	2503	12.9	W	1675	11.2	W	3152	20.0	VET DESSUS POUR HOMMES
8422	— SUITS	W	2513	13.7	W	2493	12.9	W	447	3.2	W	1746	11.6	COMPLETS HOMMES MAT TEXT
84223	—— OF MAN–MADE FIBRES	W	2513	13.7	W	2493	12.9	W	130	1.0	W	226	1.7	COMPLETS HOMMES FIB SYNT
843	WOMENS OUTERWEAR NONKNIT	W	5391	34.2	W	5404	34.0	W	2527	16.5	W	2671	17.5	VET DESSUS FEMMES MAT TEX
8431	— COATS AND JACKETS	W	5391	34.2	W	5404	34.0	W	334	2.2	W	397	3.3	MANT,VEST FEM MAT TEXTIL
84319	—— OF OTHER FIBRES	W	5382	34.1	W	5399	34.0							MANT,VEST FEM AUT FIBRES
845	OUTERWEAR KNIT NONELASTC							W	1690	13.5	W	1125	10.1	VET DESSOUS,ACCES BONNET
8459	— OTHER,CLTHG ACCESRYS							W	1466	11.9	W	984	8.9	AUT VET DESSUS DE BONNE
87	PRECISION INSTRUMNTS NES			52.1			48.7			52.3			47.0	INSTRUM,APPAR SCIENT NDA
872	MEDICAL INSTRUMENTS NES	W	1905	33.3	W	784	27.7	W	846	28.2	W	855	28.0	INSTR,APP MEDIC–CHIR NDA
87202	OTH MEDICAL INSTRUMENTS	W	1855	31.1	W	741	26.5	W	787	25.7	W	764	25.2	INSTRUM,APP MEDECINE
874	MEASURNG,CONTROLNG INSTR	W	343	11.3	W	618	18.9	W	460	18.7	W	485	16.2	INSTRUMENTS DE MESURE
88	PHOTO EQU,OPTICL GDS ETC			19.0			15.7			15.4			16.9	APP,FOURN PHOTO,OP,MONTR
89	MISC MANUFCTRD GOODS NES			69.6			67.7			65.2			71.8	ART MANUFACTURES DIVERS
892	PRINTED MATTER	W	2433	12.4	W	2809	13.1	W	1862	11.6	W	1712	10.3	IMPRIMES
893	ARTICLES OF PLASTIC NES	W	4053	15.3	W	3371	17.0			18.7			27.1	OUVRAGES EN MAT DIVIS 58
8939	MISC PLASTIC ARTICLES	W	3417	12.2	W	2653	13.7	W	4622	14.2	W	6700	22.1	ART DIVERS EN MAT DIV 58
89399	OTHR PLASTC ARTICLES NES	W	3352	11.9	W	2590	13.4	W	3165	12.6	W	5647	20.9	AUT OUV MAT DIV 58
897	GOLD,SILVER WARE,JEWELRY			11.3			9.3			7.5			9.2	BIJOUTERIE,ORFEVRERIE
9	GOODS NOT CLASSD BY KIND			26.5			44.2			31.3			52.0	ART TRANSACT NON CLASSES
931	*SPECIAL TRANSACTIONS	W	3258	20.3	W	6021	38.0	W	4062	17.1	W	1387	19.8	TRANS.SPECIALES
971	*GOLD,NON MONETARY NES	K	535	6.0	K	502	5.8	K	1174	13.8	K	2550	32.0	OR NON MONETAIRE
97101	NONMON GLD UNWRT,SEMIMFD	K	535	6.0	K	502	5.8	K	1174	13.8	K	2550	32.0	OR,ALLIAGES D'OR BRUTS

5. General Exports F.O.B. by Commodities according to the S.I.T.C. (Rev. 2) in million U.S. Dollars
Exportations Générales F.O.B. par Produits d'après la C.T.C.I. (Rév. 2) en millions de Dollars E.U.

SITC CTCI	COMMODITY	1992 QUANTITY QUANTITE	1992 VALUE VALEUR	1993 QUANTITY QUANTITE	1993 VALUE VALEUR	1994 QUANTITY QUANTITE	1994 VALUE VALEUR	1995 QUANTITY QUANTITE	1995 VALUE VALEUR	PRODUIT
	ALL COMMODITIES		1219.4		1245.8		1424.4		1768.9	TOUS PRODUITS
0	FOOD AND LIVE ANIMALS		167.4		218.8		148.4		169.5	ALIMENTS,ANIMAUX VIVANTS
001	*LIVE ANIMALS FOR FOOD		22.5	N 4	0.1	W 907	18.9	W 340	22.1	ANIMAUX VIVANTS
0012	SHEEP AND GOATS,LIVE	N 552092	17.5	N 790178	22.0	W 410	16.3	W 298	21.5	ESPECES OVINE ET CAPRINE
00121	SHEEP,LIVE	N 549112	17.4	N 789571	22.0	W 409	16.3	W 298	21.4	ESPECE OVINE
0014	LIVE POULTRY	W 954	5.0	W 1115	4.6	W 498	2.6	W 41	0.6	VOLAILLES VIVANTES
00141	LIVE PLTRY 185 GR OR LES	W 954	5.0	W 1115	4.6	W 153	1.2	W 40	0.6	VOL VIVANTES MOINS 185 GR.
01	MEAT AND PREPARATIONS		13.8		10.8		7.0		8.6	VIANDES ET PREPARATIONS
011	MEAT FRESH,CHILLD,FROZEN	W 17775	13.8	W 3211	5.4	W 2358	3.8	W 3565	6.2	VIANDES FRAICHES,REF,CONGE
0111	BOVINE MEAT FRESH,FROZEN	W 16915	13.0	W 2439	2.2	W 1317	1.7	W 465	0.7	VIANDES BOVIN FRAI,REF
01111	BOVINE MEAT WITH BONE IN	W 16915	13.0	W 2439	2.2	W 584	0.8	W 221	0.3	VIANDES BOVIN NON DESOSS
0114	POULTRY FRESH CHLLD,FRZN	W 139	0.2	W 5606	8.2	W 1020	2.0	W 2845	5.2	VOLAILLES MORTES
02	DAIRY PRODCTS,BIRDS'EGGS		25.3		57.0		6.2		9.0	PRODUITS LAITIERS,OEUFS
023	BUTTER	W 13053	11.1	W 63992	48.8	W 185	0.4	W 114	0.3	BEURRE
025	EGGS,BIRDS,FRESH,PRSRVD	W 6604	10.7	W 3653	5.7	W 42098	3.5	W 14530	3.1	OEUFS
0251	— IN SHELL	W 6604	10.7	W 3653	5.7	W 42098	3.5	W 14530	3.1	OEUFS EN COQUILLE
04	CEREALS AND PREPARATIONS		3.4		2.6		3.3		7.7	CEREALES ET PRODUITS
05	VEGETABLES AND FRUIT		77.5		101.0		96.3		99.7	LEGUMES ET FRUITS
054	VEG ETC FRSH,SMPLY PRSVD	W 268064	57.7	W 214710	54.8	W 188412	63.3	W 276084	76.9	LEGUMES FRAIS,CONG,SECS
0541	POTATOES FRSH EXCL SWEET	W 2636	0.7	W 2819	0.8	W 4625	1.7	W 11972	5.6	POMMES DE TERRE
0544	TOMATOES FRESH	W 488	0.1	W 265	0.2	W 100924	26.8	W 135745	24.7	TOMATES FRAICHES
0545	OTHER FRESH VEGETABLES	W 262277	55.6	W 210950	53.5	W 76815	29.9	W 119521	38.4	AUTRES LEGUMES FRAIS,REF
05459	FRESH VEGETABLES NES	W 261634	55.5	W 210899	53.4	W 76214	29.7	W 119400	38.4	LEGUMES FRAIS,REFRI NDA
0546	VEGETABLES SIMPLY PRESVD	W 55	0.1	W 40	0.1	W 5405	4.6	W 7949	7.6	LEGUMES CONG,CONSER
05461	VEGETABLES FROZEN	W 55	0.1	W 40	0.1	W 5373	4.6	W 7949	7.6	LEGUMES CONGELES
056	VEGTBLES ETC PRSVD,PREPD	W 3660	2.7	W 21723	14.6	W 1108	0.8	W 858	0.7	CONSERVES DE LEGUMES
0565	VEGTBLES PRSVD,PREPD NES	W 3465	2.6	W 21719	14.6	W 1101	0.8	W 855	0.7	LEGUMES PREPARES CONSERVE
05659	OTH VEG PRESVD,PREPD NES	W 3417	2.5	W 21702	14.6	W 1094	0.7	W 855	0.7	LEGUM PREPAP,CONSERV NDA
057	FRUIT,NUTS,FRESH,DRIED	W 77119	16.9	W 86196	31.3	W 90646	31.7	W 62817	21.9	FRUITS FRAIS OU SECS
0571	ORANGES, MANDARINS ETC	W 38827	8.6	W 57123	22.3	W 51625	19.7	W 23597	9.0	ORANGES,MAND,CLEMENTINES
05711	ORANGES,FRESH OR DRIED	W 25090	6.9	W 38085	17.9	W 33569	14.1	W 6425	3.8	ORANGES FRAICHES,SECHEES
05712	MANDARINS ETC FRESH, DRY	W 13736	1.7	W 19038	4.5	W 18056	5.7	W 17171	5.3	MANDARINES,CLEMENTINES
0572	LEMONS,GRAPEFRUIT ETC	W 10458	1.9	W 13492	4.2	W 18368	5.1	W 13683	4.4	AUTRES AGRUMES FRAIS,SECS
0579	FRUIT FRESH OR DRIED NES	W 26441	4.9	W 14187	3.5	W 18869	5.2	W 23406	6.5	FRUITS FRAIS,SECS NDA
05798	OTHER FRESH FRUIT	W 25903	4.7	W 13818	3.3	W 17760	4.5	W 22667	6.0	AUTRES FRUITS FRAIS
07	COFFEE,TEA,COCOA,SPICES		2.7		1.8		4.1		9.5	CAFE,THE,CACAO,EPICES
071	COFFEE AND SUBSTITUTES	W 706	0.9	W 287	0.5	W 423	1.7	W 1892	6.2	CAFE ET SUCCEDANES
0711	COFFEE GREEN,ROASTED,SUB	W 698	0.9	W 270	0.4	W 423	1.7	W 1892	6.2	CAFE TORREFIE OU DECAFEINE
07111	COFFEE GREEN,HUSKS,SKINS	W 698	0.9	W 270	0.4	W 423	1.7	W 1838	6.1	CAFE NON TORREFIE
081	*FEEDING STUFF FOR ANIML	W 37829	13.1	W 33831	12.1	W 16244	5.6	W 12576	4.9	NOURRITURE POUR ANIMAUX
0819	FOOD WASTE AND FEED NES	W 34303	12.2	W 32152	11.5	W 10526	4.2	W 5898	3.0	DECHETS,ALIMENTS NDA
08199	FODDER NES,INCL SWEETNED	W 34303	12.2	W 32152	11.5	W 10526	4.2	W 5898	3.0	PREPARATIONS FOURRAGERES
09	MISC EDIBLE PRODUCTS		5.8		5.8		4.2		5.0	PREP ALIMENTAIRES DIVERSES
098	EDIBLE PRODCTS,PREPS NES	W 3318	5.8	W 3140	5.8	W 2524	4.2	W 2631	4.9	PREP ALIMENTAIRES NDA
1	BEVERAGES AND TOBACCO		8.9		5.7		6.2		8.2	BOISSONS ET TABACS
11	BEVERAGES		3.8		4.6		4.7		7.6	BOISSONS
112	ALCOHOLIC BEVERAGES	W 2277	3.6	W 2823	4.1	W 1976	2.4	W 3470	4.1	BOISSONS ALCOOLIQUES
1124	DISTILLED ALCOHOLIC BEVS	W 1856	3.3	W 2800	4.1	W 1761	2.3	W 3025	3.9	ALCOOLS,EAUX–DE–VIE
12	TOBACCO AND MANUFACTURES		5.2		1.2		1.5		0.6	TABACS BRUTS FABRIQUES
122	TOBACCO,MANUFACTURED	W 1319	5.2	W 104	1.2	W 106	1.5	W 20	0.4	TABACS FABRIQUES
2	CRUDE MATERLS,EXCL FUELS		321.1		277.8		306.4		375.3	MAT BRUTES NON COMESTIBLES
21	HIDES,SKINS,FURS UNDRSSD		4.2		2.5		5.8		20.0	CUIRS,PEAUX BRUTS
211	HIDES,SKINS,EXC FURS,RAW	W 3185	4.2	W 2347	2.5	W 2284	5.8	W 6670	20.0	CUIRS ET PEAUX
2116	SHEEP SKIN WITH WOOL	W 2874	3.6	W 2126	2.4	W 1749	4.6	W 1419	4.4	PEAUX LAINEES D'OVINS
2117	SHEEP SKIN WITHOUT WOOL					W 124	0.8	W 2388	13.8	PEAUX EPILEES D'OVINS
26	TEXTILE FIBRES AND WASTE		1.8		2.4		2.2		6.7	FIBRES TEXTILES
27	CRUDE FERTLZR,MINRLS NES		308.4		267.5		277.6		325.7	ENGRAIS MINERAUX BRUTS
271	FERTILIZERS,CRUDE	W 5499076	306.9		265.0		276.2	W 1	0.1	ENGRAIS BRUTS
2713	NAT CALCM PHOSPHATES ETC	W 4263880	180.1		141.1		143.7		150.4	PHOSPHATES DE CALCIUM
27131	— UNGROUND	W 4263880	180.1		141.1		143.7		150.4	PHOSPHATES NON MOULUS
2714	NTRL POTASSIC SALTS,CRDE	W 1235196	126.8		124.0		132.5		173.4	SELS DE POTASSIUM
28	METALLIFEROUS ORES,SCRAP		3.7		3.1		10.6		17.8	MINERAIS METAL,DECHETS
288	NONFERR METAL SCRAP NES	W 2887	3.5	W 2033	2.6	W 9024	10.0	W 11117	15.1	DECHETS NON FERREUX
2882	OTHER BASE MTL SCRAP NES	W 2887	3.5	W 2033	2.6	W 8924	10.0	W 11117	15.1	AUTRES DECHETS
28821	COPPER WASTE AND SCRAP	W 2866	3.5	W 2033	2.6	W 2207	3.4	W 2906	5.6	DECHETS DE CUIVRE
28823	ALUMINIUM WSTE AND SCRAP	W 21	0.1			W 4680	6.0	W 4818	8.0	DECHETS D'ALUMINIUM
29	CRUDE ANIMAL,VEG MAT NES		2.1		1.6		9.1		4.5	MATIERES BRUTES ANIM,VEGET
292	CRUDE VEG MATERIALS NES	W 1089	1.4	W 263	0.6	W 7586	8.5	W 1256	2.7	MAT BRUTES VEGETALES NDA
2925	SEEDS,ETC FOR PLANTING	W 73	0.8	W 46	0.5	W 6388	7.1	W 156	1.8	SEMENCES NDA
4	ANIMAL,VEGETABLE OIL,FAT		4.0		2.7		89.9		216.8	HUILES,GRAISSES ANIM,VEG
42	FIXED VEGETABLE OIL,FAT		3.8		2.6		1.4		9.5	HUILES VEGETALES FIXES
424	FIXED VEG OIL NONSOFT	W 869	1.0	W 358	0.3	W 752	0.6	W 10100	8.7	AUTRES HUILES VEG FIXES
4242	PALM OIL	W 99	0.1	W 307	0.3	W 173	0.2	W 8115	6.1	HUILE DE PALME
431	*PROCESD ANML VEG OIL,ET	W 300	0.3	W 374	0.2	W 123115	88.6	W 203414	207.4	HUILES,GRAISSES PREPAREES
4312	HYDROGENATED OIL,FAT					W 122260	88.2	W 195654	200.4	HUILES HYDROGENEES
4313	FATTY ACIDS ETC,RESIDUES	W 101	0.1	W 204	0.1	W 854	0.4	W 7732	7.0	ACIDES GRAS INDUST,RESIDUS
43131	FATTY ACIDS,ACID OILS	W 101	0.1	W 204	0.1	W 834	0.4	W 7732	7.0	ACIDES GRAS INDUSTRIELS
5	CHEMCLS,RELATED PROD NES		328.1		310.2		393.0		467.7	PRODUITS CHIMIQUES
51	ORGANIC CHEMICALS		1.9		2.0		2.2		6.1	PROD CHIMIQ ORGANIQUES
52	INORGANIC CHEMICALS		30.2		16.2		22.3		38.3	PROD CHIM INORGANIQUES
522	INORG ELEMNTS,OXIDES,ETC	W 23982	9.2	W 3586	2.6	W 16838	8.7	W 16294	9.7	ELEMENTS INORGANIQUES
5222	INORGANIC ACIDS ETC	W 19261	7.0	W 2571	2.0	W 14889	7.7	W 15535	9.1	ACIDES INORGANIQUES
52222	SULPHURIC ACID;OLEUM		0.1			W 6609	4.2	W 13998	8.8	ACIDE SULFURIQUE,OLEUM
52224	PHOSPHORIC ACIDS ETC	W 18165	6.0	W 23	0.1	W 5820	1.7	W 1536	0.4	ACIDES PHOSPHORIQUES
523	OTHR INORG CHEMICALS ETC	W 107478	20.7	W 108001	13.5	W 96386	13.4	W 137144	28.3	AUT PRODUITS CHIMIQUES INORG
5231	METAL CMPD OF INORG ACID	W 14613	13.3	W 10416	7.0	W 9935	6.5	W 22427	14.9	SELS METALLIQUES
52311	FLUORIDES ETC	W 13292	12.9	W 10329	7.0	W 9697	6.4	W 21700	14.6	FLUORURES
5232	OTH MTL CMPD OF INRG ACD	W 92707	7.4	W 96683	6.2	W 86390	7.0	W 114526	13.3	SELS METALLIQUES
52324	CARBONATE NES,PERCBONATE	W 91961	7.0	W 96484	6.1	W 85406	6.7	W 114227	12.9	CARBONATES,PERCARBONATES
53	DYES,TANNING,COLOUR PROD		4.0		8.5		6.8		12.1	PROD TEINTURE,COLORANTS
533	PIGMENTS,PAINTS,ETC	W 3055	3.6	W 4634	8.3	W 4062	6.3	W 5676	11.4	PIGMENTS,PEINTURES,VERNIS
5334	VARNISHES,DISTEMPERS ETC	W 2264	2.8	W 3540	6.3	W 2823	4.7	W 5130	10.5	PEINTURES A L'EAU
53341	WATER–THINNED PAINTS		0.1	W 23	0.1	W 1518	2.8	W 5041	10.2	PEINTURES DILUEES
53344	DISTEMPERS,DYES NES ETC	W 2260	2.7	W 3516	6.3	W 1236	1.8	W 39	0.2	PEINTURES A L'EAU
541	*MEDICINAL,PHARM PRODUCT	K 7720992	88.4	K 5960449	119.2	K 7134121	139.0	K 6759753	147.5	PROD MEDICINAUX PHARMACEUT
5417	MEDICAMENTS	K 7649766	87.1	K 5913885	116.7	K 7033713	136.9	K 6611713	140.0	MEDICAMENTS
54171	— CONTAINNG ANTIBIOTICS	K 7038453	80.3	K 5161842	105.4	K 4025	0.2	K 7125	0.5	MED CONTN ANTIBIOTIQUES
54172	— CONTAINING HORMONES	K 611313	6.8	K 752043	11.3	K 1481680	14.9	K 924697	12.4	MED CONTENANT HORMONES
54179	— CONTNG OTH SUBSTANCES					K 5548008	121.9	K 5679891	127.2	MED CONT AUT SUBSTANCES
55	PERFUME,CLEANING ETC PRD		55.3		58.4		43.4		53.3	PROD POUR PARFUM,TOILETTE
553	PERFUMERY,COSMETICS,ETC	W 1863	3.3	W 3579	6.6	W 1973	4.9	W 1750	5.1	PRODUITS DE PARFUMERIE

5. General Exports F.O.B. by Commodities according to the S.I.T.C. (Rev. 2) in million U.S. Dollars
Exportations Générales F.O.B. par Produits d'après la C.T.C.I. (Rév. 2) en millions de Dollars E.U.

SITC CTCI	COMMODITY	1992 QUANTITY QUANTITE	1992 VALUE VALEUR	1993 QUANTITY QUANTITE	1993 VALUE VALEUR	1994 QUANTITY QUANTITE	1994 VALUE VALEUR	1995 QUANTITY QUANTITE	1995 VALUE VALEUR	PRODUIT
554	SOAP,CLEANSING ETC PREPS	W 54194	51.7	W 57893	51.6	W 54179	38.3	W 60762	47.6	SAVONS,PRODUITS DETERSIFS
5541	SOAPS	W 16502	19.1	W 22791	24.6	W 9513	9.9	W 10344	10.0	SAVONS,PROD TENSIO–ACTIFS
5542	WASHING PREPARATIONS ETC	W 37292	32.4	W 33761	25.3	W 44104	28.0	W 50079	37.2	PROD ORG TENSIO–ACT NDA
562	*FERTILIZERS,MANUFACTURE	W 597918	106.7	W 9713	1.8	W 379	0.2	W 1404	0.4	ENGRAIS MANUFACTURES
5621	CHEM NITROGENOUS FERTLZR	W 594386	105.2	W 2	0.1		124.1		156.7	ENGRAIS AZOTES
56219	CHEM NITROG FERTILZR NES	W 594186	105.1	W 2	0.1		124.1		156.7	ENGRAIS AZOTES NDA
58	PLASTIC MATERIALS ETC		14.4		9.6		8.0		18.6	MAT PLAST ARTIFICIELLES
582	PROD OF CONDENSATION ETC	W 5153	4.8	W 3373	2.0	W 6620	4.0	W 13128	13.2	PROD CONDENS,POLYCOND
5823	ALKYDS,OTHER POLYESTERS					W 6602	4.0	W 12667	12.6	ALKYDES ET AUT POLYESTERS
58231	— IN PRIMARY FORMS					W 6602	4.0	W 12667	12.6	SOUS FORMES PRIMAIRES
5828	ION EXCH,CONDEN ETC TYPE	W 5153	4.8	W 3208	1.9					ECHANGEURS D'IONS
583	POLYMERIZATION ETC PRODS	W 8328	9.3	W 7375	7.5	W 3780	3.8	W 4339	5.0	PROD POLYMERISATION
5831	POLYETHYLENE	W 6724	8.1	W 5965	6.8	W 497	0.5	W 199	0.3	POLYETHYLENE
58311	— IN PRIMARY FORMS	W 4985	5.1	W 4013	3.3	W 361	0.3	W 71	0.2	POLYETHYLENE PRIMAIRES
59	CHEMICAL MATERIALS NES		27.5		14.5		43.7		30.6	MAT PROD CHIMIQUES NDA
591	PESTICIDES,DISINFECTANTS	W 3760	17.7	W 2298	8.0	W 7774	38.3	W 5220	20.4	DESINF,INSECT,FONG,HERB
5912	FUNGICIDES,FOR RETAIL	W 3760	17.7	W 2298	8.0	W 3	0.1	W 11	0.2	FONGICIDES VENTE AU DET
5913	HERBICIDES,FOR RETAIL					W 6998	37.7	W 2667	15.1	HERBICIDES VENTE AU DET
592	STARCH,INULIN,GLUTEN,ETC	W 1888	4.0	W 654	2.8	W 997	2.6	W 893	2.7	AMIDONS,INUL,GLUT FROM
598	MISCEL CHEM PRODUCTS NES	W 4476	6.0	W 750	0.9	W 1725	2.9	W 3694	7.7	PROD DIV INDUST CHIM NDA
5989	CHEM PRODUCTS,PREPS NES	W 4440	5.9	W 1721	3.9	W 1703	2.7	W 3193	6.6	PROD PREP CHIMIQUES NDA
59899	OTH CHEM PRODS,PREPS,NES	W 3248	5.4	W 1338	3.6	W 639	2.0	W 1319	5.1	AUT PRODUITS CHIMIQUES NDA
6	BASIC MANUFACTURES		132.3		148.3		154.1		182.6	ART MANUFACTURES
61	LEATHER,DRESSED FUR,ETC		2.0		1.8		1.6		8.2	CUIRS,PELLETERIES
62	RUBBER MANUFACTURES NES		2.3		1.4		8.3		11.4	CAOUTCHOUC MANUFACTURE
625	RUBBER TYRES, TUBES ETC	W 722	1.9	W 415	1.1	W 1697	6.4	W 2240	10.5	PNEUS CAOUTCHOUC VULCANISE
6251	TYRES NEW FOR MOTOR CARS					W 1226	5.5	W 2137	10.0	PNEUS POUR VOITURES
64	PAPER,PAPERBOARD AND MFR		14.3		22.8		20.7		22.1	PAPIERS,CARTONS & OUVRAGES
641	PAPER AND PAPERBOARD	W 5660	8.5	W 10230	10.5	W 10153	11.9	W 7653	10.9	PAPIERS ET CARTONS
6412	PRINTG,WRITING PAPER NES	W 2260	4.4	W 7466	6.5	W 629	2.2	W 540	2.3	PAPIERS POUR L'IMPRESSION
64121	— UNCOATED	W 2246	4.4	W 7284	6.4	W 492	2.1	W 494	2.2	PAPIERS IMPRES NON COUCHES
6415	PAPER,PAPERBRD,BULK,NES	W 244	0.4	W 125	0.7	W 5558	5.0	W 2165	3.0	PAPIERS,CARTONS ROULEAUX
64159	OTHER PAPER ETC,BULK,NES	W 37	0.2	W 30	0.2	W 5550	5.0	W 598	0.8	AUT PAPIER ROULEAUX FEUILLES
642	PAPER,ETC,PRECUT,ARTS OF	W 3539	5.8	W 8482	12.4	W 8095	8.9	W 8085	11.3	PAP,CARTONS DECOUPES
6421	PAPER ETC CONTAINERS	W 1840	2.8	W 4109	6.5	W 2161	2.1	W 2897	3.9	BOITES,SACS EMBALLAGES
65	TEXTILE YARN,FABRICS,ETC		30.3		35.3		38.0		44.1	FILS,TISSUS,ARTICLES TEXTILE
651	TEXTILE YARN	W 2616	8.5	W 3934	10.0	W 4660	15.0	W 2429	10.5	FILS TEXTILES
6513	COTTON YARN	W 762	3.1	W 655	2.1	W 1660	6.0	W 965	4.2	FILS DE COTON
6514	SYN FIB YRN,BULK,MONOFIL	W 845	2.0	W 1589	3.4	W 1583	5.1	W 800	3.9	FILS CONT 85% FIB TEXT SYNTH
652	COTTON FABRICS,WOVEN	W 604	4.7	W 409	3.2	W 73	0.4	W 90	0.8	TISSUS DE COTON
6522	WOVEN COTTON BLEACHD,ETC	W 604	4.7	W 409	3.2	W 73	0.4	W 80	0.8	TISSUS COTON BLANCHIS ETC
65224	BLCHED COTTON FABRIC NES	W 604	4.7	W 409	3.2	W 7	0.1	W 58	0.7	AUT TIS PLUS 85% COT BLANCHI
653	WOVN MAN–MADE FIB FABRIC	W 1357	8.7	W 1411	9.7	W 1580	11.3	W 1479	14.8	TISSUS FIBRES SYNTH,ARTIF
6531	CONT SYNT WEAVES NONPILE	W 1357	8.7	W 1387	9.6	W 858	4.4	W 595	4.5	TISSUS FIBRES SYNTH CONTINUE
65314	CONT SYN TYRE CORD FABRC	W 1297	7.9	W 1357	9.5	W 283	1.4			TIS ARMATURE PNEUMATIQUES
6534	DISC SYN BLEND FABRC NES	W 1	0.1	W 24	0.1	W 695	6.8	W 670	9.0	TISSUS FIBRES SYNTH DISCONT
65349	OTH DISC SYN BLEND FABRC					W 647	6.6	W 623	8.3	TISSUS FIB SYNT MEL MAT AUT
657	SPECIAL TXTL FABRC,PRODS	W 879	3.2	W 700	2.2	W 1202	3.3	W 1646	7.9	TISSUS SPECIAUX
659	FLOOR COVERINGS,ETC	W 1327	4.1	W 1418	6.5	W 1731	5.9	W 1846	6.0	COUVRE–PARQUETS,TAPIS ETC
6594	WOOL CARPETS ETC NES	W 970	3.5	W 1265	6.0	W 2	0.1	W 27	0.2	TAPIS DE LAINE
65941	— TUFTED	W 970	3.5	W 1265	6.0					TAPIS DE LAINE TOUFFETES
6596	OTH TXTL CARPETS ETC NES				0.1	W 1394	4.6	W 1721	5.3	TAPIS AUT MAT TEXT NDA
65962	— OTHR THAN KNOTTED ETC					W 1394	4.6	W 1721	5.2	TAPIS AUT QUE NOUES TOUF
66	NONMETAL MINERAL MFS NES		40.8		33.6		49.2		61.3	ART MIN NON METALLIQUES
661	LIME,CEMENT,BLDG PRODS	W 1093295	34.8	W 909542	27.3	W 1063911	43.9	W 934369	56.2	CHAUX,CIMENTS MAT CONSTR
6612	CEMENT	W 1045352	32.7	W 823299	25.1	W 923210	39.2	W 753908	42.2	CIMENTS HYDRAULIQUES
6613	BUILDING STONE ETC WORKD	W 18586	0.9	W 43812	0.9	W 74170	2.4	W 120008	10.8	PIERRES A BATIR
66132	BUILDING STONE WORKED	W 18586	0.9	W 43812	0.9	W 74167	2.4	W 120008	10.8	OUVR EN PIERRES DE TAILLE
67	IRON AND STEEL		10.7		12.8		6.3		9.4	FER ET ACIER
674	IRN,STL UNIV,PLATE,SHEET	W 3094	2.2	W 7612	4.5	W 1607	1.6	W 2174	2.3	LARGES PLATS,TOLES
678	IRON,STL TUBES,PIPES,ETC	W 9427	6.7	W 8856	6.5	W 3714	3.4	W 7366	4.8	TUBES,TUYAUX EN FONTE,FER
6782	IRON,STL SEAMLESS TUBES	W 5204	3.9	W 2286	2.2	W 2155	1.7	W 3	0.1	TUBES,TUYAUX SANS SOUDURE
6783	IRON,STL TUBES,PIPES NES	W 3964	2.6	W 6562	4.3	W 1528	1.6	W 7340	4.6	AUT TUBES,TUYAUX FER,ACIER
68	NON–FERROUS METALS		5.2		4.6		2.2		6.4	METAUX NON FERREUX
684	ALUMINIUM	W 2716	4.8	W 2752	3.7	W 584	1.9	W 746	5.7	ALUMINIUM
6842	ALUMINIUM,ALLOYS WORKED	W 346	2.6	W 265	1.2	W 584	1.9	W 746	5.7	ALUMINIUM,ALLIAGES OUVRE
69	METAL MANUFACTURES NES		25.6		33.4		25.6		19.5	ART MANUFACT EN METAL NDA
691	STRUCTURES AND PARTS NES	W 3101	9.4	W 5689	15.4	W 8242	17.8	W 3723	4.2	CONSTRUCT FER,ACIER,ALU
6911	STRUCTURES,PARTS IRN,STL	W 2689	7.9	W 5489	14.9	W 8138	17.5	W 3548	3.5	CONSTRUCT FER,ACIER,FONTE
692	METAL TANKS,BOXES,ETC	W 1445	1.3	W 2432	5.4	W 1565	0.9	W 1533	1.2	RECIPIENTS METALLIQUES
697	BASE MTL HOUSEHOLD EQUIP		10.1		9.7	W 869	4.8	W 770	7.7	ART MENAGE MET COMMUNS
6973	DMSTC HEATG,COOKG APPARA		9.3		8.6	W 516	4.3	W 448	6.4	APPS CHAUF NON ELECTRIQ
69732	IRN,STL DOM HEATG APPARA	N 32911	4.0	N 40694	7.0	W 75	0.5	W 128	1.0	POELES,RECHAUDS NON ELECTRS
69735	DMSTC WATERHEATRS NONELE	W 771	4.3	W 10	0.1					CHAUFFE–EAU NON ELECTR.
7	MACHINES,TRANSPORT EQUIP		126.3		155.9		224.7		231.0	MACHINES MATERIEL TRANSPORT
71	POWER GENERATING EQUIPMT		2.9		5.2		2.5		3.2	MACHINES GENERATRICES
72	MACHS FOR SPCL INDUSTRYS		11.5		15.8		25.3		17.3	MAC SPECIALES POUR INDUST
723	CIVIL ENGNEERG EQUIP ETC	W 22	0.1	W 4	0.1	W 1146	12.8	W 175	5.5	APPAREILS DE GENIE CIVIL
7234	CONST,MINING MACHNRY NES	W 22	0.1	W 4	0.1	W 51	10.1	W 131	4.9	MACH POUR LA CONST, MINES
72341	SELF–PROPELLD DOZERS,ETC	N 165	4.5	N 84	2.9		3.6		3.3	BULLDOZERS
72343	SLFPRP CONST ETC MCH NES						4.7		0.2	AUT MACH EXTR,TERRASSEM
728	OTH MACHY FOR SPCL INDUS	W 1112	2.8	W 2193	6.7	W 1490	8.3	W 1394	7.7	AUT MACH IND PARTICULIERES
7281	MACH–TOOLS FR SPCL INDUS	W 544	1.1	W 1094	4.7	W 570	3.0	W 505	1.4	MACH–OUTILS SPEC IND PART
72811	MACH–TOOLS TO WRK MINRLS	W 345	1.0	W 1055	4.6	W 428	2.1	W 463	1.3	MACH POUR TRAVAIL PIERRE
74	GENRL INDUSTRL MACHY NES		14.3		17.3		32.5		36.2	MACH APP INDUSTRIE
741	HEATING,COOLING EQUIPMNT		2.2	W 456	1.4	W 1622	15.5	W 1152	11.7	MACH CHAUFFAGE,PIECES
7414	NONDOM REFRIG EQUIPT,PTS		0.4	W 274	0.6	W 400	6.3	W 504	6.1	MAT PRODUCTION DU FROID
74149	PTS NES OF REFRIG EQUIPT	W 18	0.3	W 468	0.9	W 387	5.6	W 482	6.0	PIECES POUR MACH FROID
7415	AIR–CONDITIONING MACHNRY	W 145	1.3	W 360	2.7	W 624	4.8	W 350	3.0	GROUPES CONDITION AIR
743	PUMPS NES,CENTRFUGES ETC	W 228	1.7	W 238	1.4	W 592	3.9	W 815	5.5	POMPES COMPRES,VENT ETC
749	NONELEC MACH PTS,ACC NES	W 541	5.0	W 534	5.7	W 620	4.6	W 774	8.5	PIECES MACH NON ELEC NDA
75	OFFICE MACHNES,ADP EQUIP		1.6		3.0		3.8		6.5	MACH BUREAU TRAIT AUTOM
76	TELECOMM,SOUND EQUIPMENT		3.5		3.6		4.0		5.5	EQUIPMENT DE TELECOM
77	ELECTRIC MACHNRY NES ETC		9.5		13.6		13.4		21.3	MACH APP ELECT NDA
772	SWITCHGEAR ETC,PARTS NES	W 159	2.4	W 318	5.1	W 161	4.2	W 129	2.4	APP COUPURE,SECT ETC
7722	PRINTED CIRCUITS,PTS NES	W 110	1.9	W 263	4.0				0.1	CIRCUITS ET PIECES
773	ELECTR DISTRIBUTNG EQUIP	W 1096	2.7	W 1751	4.1	W 1057	2.9	W 2743	10.5	EQUIPMT DISTRIBUTION ELECT
7731	INSULATED WIRE,CABLE ETC	W 1081	2.6	W 1663	3.9	W 1055	2.8	W 2739	10.5	FILS,CABLES ISOLES ELECT
78	ROAD VEHICLES		42.3		48.5		69.3		74.5	VEHICULES ROUTIERS
781	PASS MOTOR VEH EXC BUSES	N 2832	20.9	N 1101	8.9	W 1	13.8	W 1	13.5	AUTO TRANSPORT PERSONNES
782	LORRIES,SPCL MTR VEH NES	N 321	6.2	N 627	14.0		12.0	W 1	14.2	VEHICULES SPECIAUX,MARCH

5. General Exports F.O.B. by Commodities according to the S.I.T.C. (Rev. 2) in million U.S. Dollars
Exportations Générales F.O.B. par Produits d'après la C.T.C.I. (Rév. 2) en millions de Dollars E.U.

SITC CTCI	COMMODITY	1992 QUANTITY QUANTITE	1992 VALUE VALEUR	1993 QUANTITY QUANTITE	1993 VALUE VALEUR	1994 QUANTITY QUANTITE	1994 VALUE VALEUR	1995 QUANTITY QUANTITE	1995 VALUE VALEUR	PRODUIT
7821	LORRIES,TRUCKS	N 295	5.3	N 580	12.9		8.2	W 1	13.1	VEHICULES TRANSP MARCHAND
783	ROAD MOTOR VEHICLES NES	N 175	3.4	N 343	14.1		29.7	W 1	29.9	VEHICULES ROUTIERS NDA
7831	BUSES	N 175	3.4	N 343	14.1		29.7	W 1	29.9	VOITURES TRANSPORT COMMUN
784	MOTOR VEH PRTS,ACCES NES	W 1227	9.4		9.7	W 2369	13.2	W 1858	14.2	PIECES 722,781,782,783
7849	OTHER MOTOR VEHCL PARTS	W 1559	10.7	W 1432	9.7	W 2369	13.1	W 1858	14.2	PIECES 722,781,782,783
79	OTHR TRANSPORT EQUIPMENT		40.4		47.9		72.2		64.0	AUTRE MATERIEL TRANSPORT
792	AIRCRAFT ETC		40.3	W 29	47.8	W 68	72.0	W 38	63.0	APP NAVIGATION AERIENNE
7924	AIRCRFT NES OVER 15000KG						5.1			AERODYNES PLUS 15000 KG
7928	AIRCRAFT NES,ASSOC EQUIP		8.2		2.4		0.1			APP NAVIG AERIENNE NDA
79281	GLIDERS,KITES,ROTOCHUTES	N 6	8.2							ROTOCHUTES
7929	AIRCRAFT PARTS NES	W 31	32.1	W 29	45.5	W 68	66.9	W 38	61.2	PIECES DU 792
8	MISC MANUFACTURED GOODS		77.9		95.9		82.8		96.6	ART MANUFACTURES DIVERS
821	*FURNITURE,PARTS THEREOF	W 2074	5.3	W 1769	3.4	W 1652	4.2	W 1700	4.7	MEUBLES ET PIECES
8219	FURNITURE AND PARTS NES	W 2035	5.2	W 1758	3.3	W 1215	3.2	W 1334	4.0	AUTRES MEUBLES ET PIECES
82199	OTHR FURN,FURN PARTS NES	W 2035	5.2	W 1758	3.3	W 17	0.1	W 17	0.2	MEUBLES NDA AUTRES MATIERES
84	CLOTHING AND ACCESSORIES		17.7		21.4		20.4		28.8	VETEMENTS
842	MENS OUTERWEAR NOT KNIT	W 572	6.5	W 759	9.3	W 502	6.2	W 355	5.0	VET DESSUS POUR HOMMES
8422	— SUITS	W 558	6.4	W 736	8.8	W 67	0.5	W 34	0.4	COMPLETS HOMMES MAT TEXT
84223	—— OF MAN–MADE FIBRES	W 553	6.2	W 726	8.6	W 63	0.5	W 29	0.4	COMPLETS HOMMES FIB SYNT
8423	— TROUSERS,BREECHES ETC					W 366	4.7	W 277	4.1	PANTALONS HOMMES MAT TEX
843	WOMENS OUTERWEAR NONKNIT	W 1044	10.2	W 1040	10.4	W 820	8.3	W 1584	16.4	VET DESSUS FEMMES MAT TEX
8431	— COATS AND JACKETS	W 1044	10.2	W 1040	10.4	W 24	0.2	W 42	0.7	MANT,VEST FEM MAT TEXTIL
84319	—— OF OTHER FIBRES	W 982	10.1	W 1033	10.3					MANT,VEST FEM AUT FIBRES
8433	— DRESSES					W 184	1.9	W 521	5.9	ROBES EN MAT–TEXTILES
8435	— BLOUSES					W 171	1.4	W 584	5.6	BLOUSES FEM MAT TEXTILES
8439	— OTHER OUTER GARMENTS					W 401	4.7	W 385	4.0	AUT VET DES FEM MAT TEXT
851	*FOOTWEAR	W 2508	5.1	W 2297	4.8	W 1606	4.0	W 2041	5.9	CHAUSSURES
87	PRECISION INSTRUMNTS NES		5.5		10.4		12.3		6.3	INSTRUM,APPAR SCIENT NDA
872	MEDICAL INSTRUMENTS NES	W 343	3.8	W 247	4.5	W 415	8.2	W 151	3.7	INSTR,APP MEDIC–CHIR NDA
87202	OTH MEDICAL INSTRUMENTS	W 343	3.8	W 247	4.5	W 414	8.2	W 148	3.5	INSTRUM,APP MEDECINE
874	MEASURNG,CONTROLNG INSTR	W 21	1.7	W 88	5.9	W 87	3.4	W 27	2.1	INSTRUMENTS DE MESURE
88	PHOTO EQU,OPTICL GDS ETC		5.1		4.6		3.5		2.9	APP,FOURN PHOTO,OP,MONTR
89	MISC MANUFCTRD GOODS NES		38.8		50.5		37.4		46.4	ART MANUFACTURES DIVERS
892	PRINTED MATTER	W 4490	11.1	W 7432	19.0	W 3390	7.5	W 6978	16.4	IMPRIMES
8921	PRINTED BOOKS,GLOBES,ETC	W 4338	10.6	W 7368	18.7	W 3253	6.8	W 6784	15.8	LIVRES,BROCHURES,CARTES
89211	PRINTED BOOKS,PAMPHLETS	W 4338	10.6	W 7368	18.7	W 3253	6.8	W 6784	15.8	LIVRES,BROCHURES
893	ARTICLES OF PLASTIC NES	W 7670	15.5	W 9387	22.6		20.8		20.6	OUVRAGES EN MAT DIVIS 58
8931	PLSTC PACKG CONTNRS,LIDS	W 105	0.9	W 1	0.1	W 5272	11.1	W 4443	8.9	ART TRANSP EMBALLAGE ETC
8932	PLSTC SANITRY,TOILET ART	W 675	1.4	W 903	4.8	W 1	0.1	W 30	0.2	OBJETS HYGIEN MAT DU 58
8939	MISC PLASTIC ARTICLES	W 6820	13.1	W 8389	17.7	W 4129	9.6	W 4458	11.5	ART DIVERS EN MAT DIV 58
89399	OTHR PLASTC ARTICLES NES	W 6770	12.8	W 8269	17.1	W 4109	9.5	W 4429	11.5	AUT OUV MAT DIV 58
897	GOLD,SILVER WARE,JEWELRY		7.7		5.6		4.9		5.7	BIJOUTERIE,ORFEVRERIE
8973	PREC JEWLRY,GLD–SILVWARE		7.6		5.6		4.9		5.4	BIJOUX OR,ARGENT ORFEVRE
89731	PRECIOUS METAL JEWELLERY		7.6		5.6		4.9		5.4	ART BIJOUTERIE,JOAILLER
9	GOODS NOT CLASSD BY KIND		52.7		30.7		17.8		21.0	ART TRANSACT NON CLASSES
931	*SPECIAL TRANSACTIONS		0.1	W 81	0.3	W 1223	4.5	W 1454	21.0	TRANS.SPECIALES
971	*GOLD,NON MONETARY NES	K 5282	52.6	K 4106	30.4	K 1579	13.3	K 1	0.1	OR NON MONETAIRE
97101	NONMON GLD UNWRT,SEMIMFD	K 5282	52.6	K 4106	30.4	K 1579	13.3	K 1	0.1	OR,ALLIAGES D'OR BRUTS

FOOT NOTES – NOTES

TABLE 1 –
1 Prior to 1981, special trade.
TABLEAU 1 –
1 Avant 1981, commerce spécial.

1. HISTORICAL SERIES, 1992–1997 GENERAL TRADE, IMPORTS C.I.F., EXPORTS F.O.B.
SERIES HISTORIQUES, 1992–1997 COMMERCE GENERAL, IMPORTATIONS C.A.F., EXPORTATIONS F.O.B

YEAR ANNEE	VALUE IN MILLION U.S. DOLLARS / VALEUR EN MILLION U.S. DOLLARS: MERCHANDISE – MARCHANDISE		GOLD – OR		CONVERSION FACTORS FACTEURS DE CONVERSION CENTS E.U. PAR		INDEX NUMBERS – INDICES: QUANTUM		UNIT VALUE / VALEUR UNITAIRE	
	IMPORTS	EXPORTS	IMPORTS	EXPORTS	IMPORTS	EXPORTS	IMPORTS	EXPORTS	IMPORTS	EXPORTS
1992	468.80	1398.40								
1993	494.00	1501.00								
1994	4499.00	3231.00								
1995	3882.00	5064.00								
1996	4261.30	6112.50								
1997	4275.00	6366.40								

2. IMPORTS BY BROAD ECONOMIC CATEGORY AND EXPORTS BY INDUSTRIAL ORIGIN. (PERCENTAGE OF TOTAL VALUE)
IMPORTATIONS PAR CATEGORIES ECONOMIQUES ET EXPORTATIONS PAR BRANCHE D'ACTIVITE. (EN POURCENTAGE DE LA VALEUR TOTALE)

IMPORTS – IMPORTATIONS

	1990	1991	1992	1993	1994	1995	1996
TOTAL IMPORTS–IMPORTATIONS TOTALES							
1 FOOD BEV–ALIMENTATION BOISSONS							
11 PRIMARY–PRODUITS DE BASE							
111 FOR INDUSTRY–POUR L'INDUSTRIE							
112 FOR HOUSEHOLDS–POUR LES MENAGES							
12 PROCESSED–PRODUITS ELABORES							
121 FOR INDUSTRY–POUR L'INDUSTRIE							
122 FOR HOUSEHOLDS–POUR LES MENAGES							
2 IND SUPPLIES–APPROV INDUSTRIELS							
21 PRIMARY–PRODUITS DE BASE							
22 PROCESSED–PRODUITS ELABORES							
3 FUELS–COMBUSTIBLES							
31 PRIMARY–PRODUITS DE BASE							
32 PROCESSED–PRODUITS ELABORES							
321 MOTOR SPIRIT–ESSENCE							
322 OTHER–AUTRES							
4 MACHINERY–EQUIPEMENT							
41 CAPITAL EQUIPMENT–MACHINES							
42 PARTS–PIECES ACCESSOIRES							
5 TRANSPORT–TRANSPORT							
51 PASSENGER CARS–AUTOMOBILES							
52 OTHER–AUTRES							
521 INDUSTRIAL–INDUSTRIELS							
522 NON INDUSTRIAL–NON INDUSTRIEL							
53 PARTS–PIECES ACCESSOIRES							
6 CONSUM GOODS–BIENS CONSOMMATION							
61 DURABLE–DURABLES							
62 SEMI DURABLE–SEMI DURABLES							
63 NON DURABLE–NON DURABLES							
7 GOODS NES–BIENS NDA							

EXPORTS – EXPORTATIONS

	1990	1991	1992	1993	1994	1995	1996
TOTAL EXPORTS–EXPORTATIONS TOTALES							
1 AGRICULTURE							
2 MINING QUARRY–INDUS EXTRACTIVES							
3 MANUFACTURING–IND MANUFACTUR							
31 FOOD BEV TOBACCO–ALIM BOISS TAB							
32 TEXTILES–INDUSTRIES TEXTILES							
33 WOOD & PRODUCTS–BOIS & PRODUITS							
34 PAPER & PRODUCTS–PAPIER & PRODT							
35 CHEMICALS–INDUSTRIES CHIMIQUES							
36 NON METAL MIN–MIN NON METAL							
37 BASIC METAL–IND METAL BASE							
38 METAL MANUF–MANUF METAL							
39 OTH MANUF IND–AUTRES MANUF							

3. TRADE BY PRINCIPAL COUNTRIES OF PURCHASE AND SALE (VALUE IN MILLION U.S. DOLLARS)
ECHANGES SELON LES PRINCIPAUX PAYS D'ACHAT ET DE VENTE (VALEUR EN MILLIONS DE DOLLARS EU)

COUNTRIES–PAYS	GENERAL IMPORTS C.I.F. IMPORTATIONS GENERALES C.A.F 1992	1993	1994	1995	1996
World			3561.2	3781.0	4261.3
Africa					
Americas			126.8	116.6	77.5
– Northern America			124.3	80.4	72.7
– LAIA			2.5	36.2	4.8
– CACM					
– Caribbean					
– Rest of America					
Asia excl fmr USSR			392.4	336.4	394.2
– Middle East			105.0	147.0	175.8
Asia former USSR			690.7	579.5	399.6
Europe excl fmr USSR			776.7	660.1	726.3
– European Union			584.7	519.5	551.6
– Eastern Europe			121.8	81.4	126.5
– Rest of Europe			70.2	59.2	48.2
Europe former USSR			1515.0	2062.8	2612.0
Oceania			7.5	2.9	4.9
Other					
Russian Federation			1292.8	1854.4	2342.3
Turkmenistan/Turkménistn			277.6	241.3	176.3
Germany/Allemagne			293.6	201.5	197.7
Uzbekistan/Ouzbékistan			276.6	268.2	89.3
Turkey/Turquie			87.2	123.9	151.3
Ukraine			119.8	86.7	92.4
Belarus/Bélarus			64.1	79.8	120.8
USA/Etats–Unis d'Amer			109.3	72.5	66.3
Kyrgyzstan/Kirghizistan			104.0	30.8	91.0
United Kingdom			66.4	82.8	76.6
Korea, Republic of			67.0	43.2	87.8
Switzerland,Liechtenst.			65.3	57.3	45.8
China/Chine			69.8	34.2	36.1
Italy/Italie			60.7	30.1	42.2
Mongolia/Mongolie			22.4	60.7	30.8
France, Monaco			30.6	48.9	34.1
Netherlands/Pays–Bas			31.1	30.9	49.0
Austria/Autriche			39.4	51.6	19.7
Finland/Finlande			15.9	31.3	56.1
Hungary/Hongrie			31.2	21.4	34.8
Poland/Pologne			23.4	20.8	42.2
Japan/Japon			53.2	8.4	18.1
Czech Republic			29.5	22.4	26.3
India/Inde			33.5	14.2	17.4
Lithuania/Lituanie			16.5	18.0	26.7
Azerbaijan/Azerbaïdjan			11.7	24.9	22.6
Israel/Israël			26.4	15.4	16.3
Belgium–Luxembourg			12.8	7.0	32.0
Tajikistan/Tadjikistan			17.9	12.1	17.5
Chile/Chili			2.5	36.2	4.8
Sweden/Suède			11.7	16.5	11.0
Latvia/Lettonie			10.3	11.5	12.3
Singapore/Singapour			14.0	13.0	6.4
Bulgaria/Bulgarie			16.5	7.4	7.3
Iran (Islamic Rep of)			10.6	14.0	6.0
Canada			15.0	7.9	6.4
United Arab Emirates			4.4	4.9	16.0
Romania/Roumanie			17.0	2.3	5.4
Ireland/Irlande			7.0	7.8	7.6
Greece/Grèce			4.6	2.2	15.3

COUNTRIES–PAYS	GENERAL EXPORTS F.O.B. EXPORTATIONS GENERALES F.O.B. 1992	1993	1994	1995	1996
Monde			3231.2	4974.4	6230.4
Afrique			0.1	0.2	4.7
Amériques			75.1	45.0	78.2
– Amérique du Nord			75.1	44.7	59.4
– ALAI					
– MCAC					
– Caraïbes				0.3	18.8
– Autre Amérique					
Asie anc. URSS exclus			327.0	678.9	1004.5
– Moyen–Orient			61.2	120.2	140.2
Asie ancienne URSS			259.4	347.4	438.5
Europe anc. URSS exclus			817.6	1377.0	1436.5
– Union Européenne			486.4	1090.6	1144.8
– Europe de l'Est			201.2	99.7	71.2
– Autre de l'Europe			130.0	186.7	220.5
Europe ancienne URSS			1644.9	2453.6	3233.0
Océanie					
Autre					
Russian Federation			1438.3	2102.6	2770.6
Netherlands/Pays–Bas			247.8	492.8	323.2
China/Chine			148.9	294.2	461.4
Switzerland,Liechtenst.			130.0	186.7	211.4
Uzbekistan/Ouzbékistan			117.2	159.5	204.2
Ukraine			128.0	121.3	212.9
Germany/Allemagne			73.2	170.4	183.3
United Kingdom			64.9	111.7	230.9
Italy/Italie			42.3	142.6	197.1
Korea, Republic of			60.1	91.6	178.2
Lithuania/Lituanie			13.4	120.8	167.0
Kyrgyzstan/Kirghizistan			59.8	73.3	112.6
USA/Etats–Unis d'Amer			75.1	44.7	59.4
Finland/Finlande			16.6	50.5	111.8
Turkey/Turquie			49.1	70.8	51.7
Japan/Japon			27.1	45.0	87.2
Belarus/Bélarus			43.9	57.5	47.0
Iran (Islamic Rep of)			11.8	48.5	63.2
Czech Republic			70.5	26.7	23.7
Turkmenistan/Turkménistn			25.3	51.1	39.4
Poland/Pologne			55.7	38.0	22.0
Tajikistan/Tadjikistan			9.5	40.8	61.6
Thailand/Thaïlande			16.5	39.9	55.2
Ireland/Irlande			1.9	71.6	20.5
Azerbaijan/Azerbaïdjan			46.3	22.4	10.6
Hungary/Hongrie			49.0	8.4	11.3
Bahamas				55.3	11.8
France, Monaco			10.8	17.4	37.9
Latvia/Lettonie			14.5	33.2	18.0
Austria/Autriche			12.5	15.7	14.2
Other Asia n.e.s.			4.6	19.3	17.0
Slovakia/Slovaquie			13.7	20.9	5.1
Estonia/Estonie			3.6	15.7	14.3
Sweden/Suède			10.0	2.8	19.3
Belgium–Luxembourg			6.4	15.1	6.6
Bulgaria/Bulgarie			12.3	5.7	9.1
Pakistan			4.9	3.2	12.2
British Virgin Islds				0.3	18.8
Saudi Arabia			0.1	0.6	14.0
Philippines			0.4	0.4	13.7

(VALUE AS PERCENTAGE OF WORLD TOTAL)(VALEURS EN POURCENTAGE DU TOTAL MONDIAL)

	1987	1988	1989	1990	1991	1992	1993	1994	1995	1996
Africa										
Americas								3.6	3.1	1.8
– Northern America								3.5	2.1	1.7
– LAIA								0.1	1.0	0.1
– CACM										
– Caribbean										
– Rest of America										
Asia excl fmr USSR								11.0	8.9	9.3
– Middle East								2.9	3.9	4.1
Asia former USSR								19.4	15.3	9.4
Europe excl fmr USSR								21.8	17.5	17.0
– European Union								16.4	13.7	12.9
– Eastern Europe								3.4	2.2	3.0
– Rest of Europe								2.0	1.6	1.1
Europe former USSR								42.5	54.6	61.3
Oceania								0.2	0.1	0.1
Other										
Russian Federation								36.3	49.0	55.0
Turkmenistan/Turkménistn								7.8	6.4	4.1
Germany/Allemagne								8.2	5.3	4.6
Uzbekistan/Ouzbékistan								7.8	7.1	2.1
Turkey/Turquie								2.4	3.3	3.6
Ukraine								3.4	2.3	2.2
Belarus/Bélarus								1.8	2.1	2.8
USA/Etats–Unis d'Amer								3.1	1.9	1.6
Kyrgyzstan/Kirghizistan								2.9	0.8	2.1
United Kingdom								1.9	2.2	1.8

	1987	1988	1989	1990	1991	1992	1993	1994	1995	1996
Afrique								0.0	0.0	0.1
Amériques								2.3	0.9	1.3
– Amérique du Nord								2.3	0.9	1.0
– ALAI										
– MCAC										
– Caraïbes									0.0	0.3
– Autre Amérique										
Asie anc. URSS exclus								10.1	13.6	16.1
– Moyen–Orient								1.9	2.4	2.3
Asie ancienne URSS								8.0	7.0	7.0
Europe anc. URSS exclus								25.3	27.7	23.1
– Union Européenne								15.1	21.9	18.4
– Europe de l'Est								6.2	2.0	1.1
– Autre de l'Europe								4.0	3.8	3.5
Europe ancienne URSS								50.9	49.3	51.9
Océanie										
Autre										
Russian Federation								44.5	42.3	44.5
Netherlands/Pays–Bas								7.7	9.9	5.2
China/Chine								4.6	5.9	7.4
Switzerland,Liechtenst.								4.0	3.8	3.4
Uzbekistan/Ouzbékistan								3.6	3.2	3.3
Ukraine								4.0	2.4	3.4
Germany/Allemagne								2.3	3.4	2.9
United Kingdom								2.0	2.2	3.7
Italy/Italie								1.3	2.9	3.2
Korea, Republic of								1.9	1.8	2.9

Kazakhstan

4. General Imports C.I.F. by Commodities according to the S.I.T.C. (Rev. 2) in million U.S. Dollars
Importations Générales C.A.F. par Produits d'après la C.T.C.I. (Rév. 2) en millions de Dollars E.U.

SITC CTCI	COMMODITY	1993		1994		1995		1996		PRODUIT
		QUANTITY QUANTITE	VALUE VALEUR	QUANTITY QUANTITE	VALUE VALEUR	QUANTITY QUANTITE	VALUE VALEUR	QUANTITY QUANTITE	VALUE VALEUR	
	ALL COMMODITIES				3561.2		3781.0		4261.3	TOUS PRODUITS
0	FOOD AND LIVE ANIMALS				99.6					ALIMENTS,ANIMAUX VIVANTS
01	MEAT AND PREPARATIONS						8.1		24.1	VIANDES ET PREPARATIONS
02	DAIRY PRODCTS,BIRDS'EGGS						16.1		29.1	PRODUITS LAITIERS,OEUFS
06	SUGAR AND PREPS,HONEY						125.0		139.0	SUCRES ET PRODUITS
07	COFFEE,TEA,COCOA,SPICES						34.1		28.1	CAFE,THE,CACAO,EPICES
11	BEVERAGES						44.1		107.1	BOISSONS
12	TOBACCO AND MANUFACTURES						39.1		78.1	TABACS BRUTS FABRIQUES
24	CORK AND WOOD						62.1		57.1	LIEGE ET BOIS
27	CRUDE FERTLZR,MINRLS NES						29.1		44.1	ENGRAIS MINERAUX BRUTS
28	METALLIFEROUS ORES,SCRAP						110.1		51.1	MINERAIS METAL,DECHETS
3	MINERAL FUELS ETC				1103.7		966.0		808.0	COMBUSTIBLES MINERAUX LUB
4	ANIMAL,VEGETABLE OIL,FAT				30.0		21.1		35.1	HUILES,GRAISSES ANIM,VEG
5	CHEMCLS,RELATED PROD NES				272.5					PRODUITS CHIMIQUES
51	ORGANIC CHEMICALS						56.1		49.1	PROD CHIMIQ ORGANIQUES
52	INORGANIC CHEMICALS						87.1		102.1	PROD CHIM INORGANIQUES
53	DYES,TANNING,COLOUR PROD						23.1		28.1	PROD TEINTURE,COLORANTS
541	*MEDICINAL,PHARM PRODUCT						26.1		39.1	PROD MEDICINAUX PHARMACEUT
572	*EXPLOSIVES,PYROTECH PRO						35.1		59.1	EXPLOSIFS
6	BASIC MANUFACTURES				303.8					ART MANUFACTURES
62	RUBBER MANUFACTURES NES						90.1		172.0	CAOUTCHOUC MANUFACTURE
64	PAPER,PAPERBOARD AND MFR						71.1		92.1	PAPIERS,CARTONS & OUVRAGES
66	NONMETAL MINERAL MFS NES						48.1		67.1	ART MIN NON METALLIQUES
67	IRON AND STEEL						77.1		123.0	FER ET ACIER
682	COPPER EXC CEMENT COPPER						13.1		8.1	CUIVRE
684	ALUMINIUM						17.1		23.1	ALUMINIUM
69	METAL MANUFACTURES NES						165.0		265.0	ART MANUFACT EN METAL NDA
7	MACHINES,TRANSPORT EQUIP				993.7		928.0		1068.0	MACHINES MATERIEL TRANSPORT
78	ROAD VEHICLES						216.0		303.0	VEHICULES ROUTIERS
8	MISC MANUFACTURED GOODS				133.8					ART MANUFACTURES DIVERS
821	*FURNITURE,PARTS THEREOF						46.1		65.1	MEUBLES ET PIECES
84	CLOTHING AND ACCESSORIES						38.1		22.1	VETEMENTS
851	*FOOTWEAR						33.1		18.1	CHAUSSURES

Kazakhstan

5. General Exports F.O.B. by Commodities according to the S.I.T.C. (Rev. 2) in million U.S. Dollars
Exportations Générales F.O.B. par Produits d'après la C.T.C.I. (Rév. 2) en millions de Dollars E.U.

SITC CTCI	COMMODITY	1993 QUANTITY QUANTITE	1993 VALUE VALEUR	1994 QUANTITY QUANTITE	1994 VALUE VALEUR	1995 QUANTITY QUANTITE	1995 VALUE VALEUR	1996 QUANTITY QUANTITE	1996 VALUE VALEUR	PRODUIT
	ALL COMMODITIES				3231.2		4974.4		6230.4	TOUS PRODUITS
0	FOOD AND LIVE ANIMALS				155.6					ALIMENTS,ANIMAUX VIVANTS
01	MEAT AND PREPARATIONS						60.1		44.1	VIANDES ET PREPARATIONS
02	DAIRY PRODCTS,BIRDS'EGGS						22.1		9.1	PRODUITS LAITIERS,OEUFS
04	CEREALS AND PREPARATIONS						375.0		515.0	CEREALES ET PRODUITS
06	SUGAR AND PREPS,HONEY						5.1		27.1	SUCRES ET PRODUITS
11	BEVERAGES						7.1		19.1	BOISSONS
12	TOBACCO AND MANUFACTURES						5.1		40.1	TABACS BRUTS FABRIQUES
263	COTTON						46.1		103.1	COTON
27	CRUDE FERTLZR,MINRLS NES						82.1		107.1	ENGRAIS MINERAUX BRUTS
28	METALLIFEROUS ORES,SCRAP						119.0		158.0	MINERAIS METAL,DECHETS
3	MINERAL FUELS ETC				1091.1		1184.0		2057.0	COMBUSTIBLES MINERAUX LUB
5	CHEMCLS,RELATED PROD NES				319.9					PRODUITS CHIMIQUES
51	ORGANIC CHEMICALS						15.1		11.1	PROD CHIMIQ ORGANIQUES
52	INORGANIC CHEMICALS						365.0		425.0	PROD CHIM INORGANIQUES
572	*EXPLOSIVES,PYROTECH PRO						43.1		42.1	EXPLOSIFS
6	BASIC MANUFACTURES				1314.4					ART MANUFACTURES
611	LEATHER						37.1		60.1	CUIRS,PEAUX PREPARES
67	IRON AND STEEL						959.0		983.0	FER ET ACIER
682	COPPER EXC CEMENT COPPER						612.0		619.0	CUIVRE
684	ALUMINIUM						29.1		24.1	ALUMINIUM
685	LEAD						33.1		48.1	PLOMB
686	ZINC						145.0		146.0	ZINC
689	NON–FER BASE METALS NES						55.1		71.1	AUT METAUX NON FERREUX
69	METAL MANUFACTURES NES						67.1		54.1	ART MANUFACT EN METAL NDA
7	MACHINES,TRANSPORT EQUIP				119.0		189.0		288.0	MACHINES MATERIEL TRANSPORT
78	ROAD VEHICLES						50.1		83.1	VEHICULES ROUTIERS
8	MISC MANUFACTURED GOODS				12.8					ART MANUFACTURES DIVERS
951	*WAR FIREARMS,AMMUNITION				12.4					VEHIC BLINDES ARMES

1. HISTORICAL SERIES, 1962–1997 GENERAL TRADE, IMPORTS C.I.F., EXPORTS F.O.B.
SERIES HISTORIQUES, 1962–1997 COMMERCE GENERAL, IMPORTATIONS C.A.F., EXPORTATIONS F.O.B

YEAR ANNEE	VALUE IN MILLION KENYA SHILLINGS VALEUR EN MILLION KENYA SHILLINGS MERCHANDISE –MARCHANDISE		GOLD –OR		CONVERSION FACTORS U.S. CENTS PER KENYA SHILLING FACTEURS DE CONVERSION CENTS E.U. PAR KENYA SHILLING		INDEX NUMBERS –INDICES QUANTUM		UNIT VALUE VALEUR UNITAIRE	
	IMPORTS	EXPORTS	IMPORTS	EXPORTS	IMPORTS	EXPORTS	IMPORTS	EXPORTS	IMPORTS	EXPORTS
1962	1536.70	1249.30			14.0000	14.0000				
1963	1657.00	1415.40			14.0000	14.0000				
1964	1759.00	1558.60			14.0000	14.0000				
1965	2014.80	1629.40			14.0000	14.0000				
1966	2470.00	1824.20			14.0000	14.0000				
1967	2401.00	1715.30			14.0000	14.0000				
1968	2542.10	1785.30			14.0000	14.0000				
1969	2582.30	1962.00			14.0000	14.0000				
1970	3160.20	2178.00			14.0000	14.0000				
1971	4015.30	2232.20			14.0000	14.0000				
1972	3956.90	2654.30			14.0000	14.0000				
1973	4571.00	3614.30			14.3340	14.2860				
1974	7678.70	4718.00			14.0000	14.0000				
1975	7256.90	4761.70			13.5000	13.5160				
1976	8139.90	6901.20			11.9480	11.9500				
1977	10625.70	9892.90			12.0840	12.0840				
1978	13223.10	7915.00			12.9300	12.9160				
1979	12386.00	8269.00			13.3800	13.3820				
1980	15747.00	9248.00			13.4570	13.4220	127	89	29	49
1981	17413.00	10243.00			11.1790	11.1610	99	84	37	54
1982	17809.00	11109.00			9.2335	9.1937	84	82	42	59
1983	18112.40	13101.40			7.4914	7.5065	66	79	54	71
1984	21180.00	15507.00			6.9360	6.9687	78	78	55	85
1985	23589.00	15725.00			6.0878	6.0892	72	81	65	84
1986	26163.01	19460.00			6.1658	6.1643	85	93	62	90
1987	28904.00	15790.00			6.0730	6.0838	89	90	63	75
1988	35072.00	19012.00			5.6300	5.6350	100	95	69	86
1989	44235.01	19904.00			4.8552	4.8749	105	94	83	92
1990	48661.01	23677.01			4.3658	4.3551	100	100	100	100
1991	52918.00	32589.01			3.6610	3.6458	93	105	111	128
1992	59097.01	34845.01			3.1184	3.0609	90	121	129	144
1993	101128.00	73565.01			1.7543	1.7631	97	133	208	259
1994	115080.00	85643.01			1.8162	1.8277	121	153	187	266
1995	155168.00	97339.01			1.9372	1.9417	141	183	216	289
1996	168486.00	118199.00			1.7501	1.7487	140	164	235	307
1997	190357.00	119961.00			1.7194	1.7119				

2. IMPORTS BY BROAD ECONOMIC CATEGORY AND EXPORTS BY INDUSTRIAL ORIGIN. (PERCENTAGE OF TOTAL VALUE)
IMPORTATIONS PAR CATEGORIES ECONOMIQUES ET EXPORTATIONS PAR BRANCHE D'ACTIVITE.(EN POURCENTAGE DE LA VALEUR TOTALE)

IMPORTS – IMPORTATIONS

	1991	1992	1993	1994	1995	1996	1997
TOTAL IMPORTS–IMPORTATIONS TOTALES	100.	100.	100.	100.	100.	100.	
1 FOOD BEV–ALIMENTATION BOISSONS	9.4	12.7	12.1	14.8	9.3	11.2	
11 PRIMARY–PRODUITS DE BASE	2.5	1.9	5.0	3.1	2.2	4.4	
111 FOR INDUSTRY–POUR L'INDUSTRIE	2.4	1.7	4.4	2.7	1.9	3.8	
112 FOR HOUSEHOLDS–POUR LES MENAGES	0.0	0.2	0.7	0.4	0.3	0.5	
12 PROCESSED–PRODUITS ELABORES	6.9	10.8	7.1	11.7	7.0	6.8	
121 FOR INDUSTRY–POUR L'INDUSTRIE	5.0	8.6	5.7	9.5	5.6	5.2	
122 FOR HOUSEHOLDS–POUR LES MENAGES	1.9	2.2	1.4	2.2	1.4	1.6	
2 IND SUPPLIES–APPROV INDUSTRIELS	32.5	36.8	35.9	36.2	31.9	32.6	
21 PRIMARY–PRODUITS DE BASE	1.7	6.0	2.7	6.0	1.5	1.2	
22 PROCESSED–PRODUITS ELABORES	30.8	30.8	33.2	30.2	30.4	31.4	
3 FUELS–COMBUSTIBLES	17.9	19.2	14.5	12.3	14.4	16.1	
31 PRIMARY–PRODUITS DE BASE	0.6	0.9	0.7	9.8	8.5	8.3	
32 PROCESSED–PRODUITS ELABORES	17.3	18.3	13.8	2.5	6.0	7.8	
321 MOTOR SPIRIT–ESSENCE	5.8	5.7	4.2	0.3	1.5	1.6	
322 OTHER–AUTRES	11.6	12.6	9.6	2.1	4.5	6.2	
4 MACHINERY–EQUIPEMENT	24.7	19.1	16.5	15.2	18.2	17.9	
41 CAPITAL EQUIPMENT–MACHINES	22.1	16.7	14.1	13.0	16.0	15.3	
42 PARTS–PIECES ACCESSOIRES	2.6	2.4	2.4	2.2	2.2	2.6	
5 TRANSPORT–TRANSPORT	8.6	5.3	10.8	13.3	15.5	14.4	
51 PASSENGER CARS–AUTOMOBILES	2.3	1.9	3.3	3.9	4.7	3.5	
52 OTHER–AUTRES	2.1	1.1	4.1	6.2	7.3	6.9	
521 INDUSTRIAL–INDUSTRIELS	1.9	0.9	3.9	6.0	7.0	6.6	
522 NON INDUSTRIAL–NON INDUSTRIEL	0.2	0.2	0.2	0.3	0.3	0.3	
53 PARTS–PIECES ACCESSOIRES	4.2	2.2	3.4	3.1	3.5	4.0	
6 CONSUM GOODS–BIENS CONSOMMATION	6.2	6.1	8.7	6.9	10.0	7.7	
61 DURABLE–DURABLES	1.2	0.9	1.2	1.2	1.3	1.1	
62 SEMI DURABLE–SEMI DURABLES	1.4	1.7	1.7	2.1	4.8	2.5	
63 NON DURABLE–NON DURABLES	3.6	3.5	5.8	3.6	3.9	4.1	
7 GOODS NES–BIENS NDA	0.7	0.8	1.5	1.3	0.6	0.2	

EXPORTS – EXPORTATIONS

	1991	1992	1993	1994	1995	1996	1997
TOTAL EXPORTS–EXPORTATIONS TOTALES	100.	100.	100.	100.	100.	100.	
1 AGRICULTURE	50.9	42.0	49.8	51.7	50.2	50.0	
2 MINING QUARRY–INDUS EXTRACTIVES	3.1	2.1	2.6	2.2	2.4	2.6	
3 MANUFACTURING–IND MANUFACTUR	46.0	56.0	47.6	46.1	47.5	47.4	
31 FOOD BEV TOBACCO–ALIM BOISS TAB	7.4	7.0	8.8	12.6	13.2	13.7	
32 TEXTILES–INDUSTRIES TEXTILES	4.0	3.4	4.3	4.9	3.7	3.2	
33 WOOD & PRODUCTS–BOIS & PRODUITS	0.2	0.3	0.6	0.6	0.6	0.6	
34 PAPER & PRODUCTS–PAPIER & PRODT	1.7	0.7	1.5	2.2	2.0	2.5	
35 CHEMICALS–INDUSTRIES CHIMIQUES	21.4	15.3	14.9	13.0	14.7	15.6	
36 NON METAL MIN–MIN NON METAL	1.4	1.4	2.8	3.0	2.7	3.1	
37 BASIC METAL–IND METAL BASE	1.9	2.4	4.8	5.1	5.7	5.1	
38 METAL MANUF–MANUF METAL	2.4	3.0	3.2	4.0	4.3	3.1	
39 OTH MANUF IND–AUTRES MANUF	5.6	22.5	6.7	0.7	0.6	0.5	

3. TRADE BY PRINCIPAL COUNTRIES OF ORIGIN AND DESTINATION (VALUE IN MILLION U.S. DOLLARS)
ECHANGES SELON LES PRINCIPAUX PAYS D'ORIGINE ET DE DESTINATION (VALEUR EN MILLIONS DE DOLLARS EU)

COUNTRIES–PAYS	GENERAL IMPORTS C.I.F. IMPORTATIONS GENERALES C.A.F				
	1993	1994	1995	1996	1997
World	1695.9	2142.5	2817.9	2749.6	3278.4
Africa	106.6	303.2	248.2	263.2	479.5
Americas	180.0	187.1	187.0	204.8	313.0
– Northern America	159.2	166.3	128.2	176.5	270.0
– LAIA	20.6	20.4	57.2	27.9	42.9
– CACM	0.2	0.3	1.5	0.4	
– Caribbean	0.1	0.1	0.1	0.1	0.1
– Rest of America					
Asia excl fmr USSR	415.2	813.9	1140.5	1123.9	1284.6
– Middle East	40.1	236.9	367.2	425.0	544.9
Asia former USSR					
Europe excl fmr USSR	749.8	820.8	1211.4	1118.1	1116.8
– European Union	711.4	764.6	1148.2	1040.2	1050.1
– Eastern Europe	8.0	14.5	23.8	18.1	18.4
– Rest of Europe	30.5	41.7	39.5	59.8	48.3
Europe former USSR	4.4	9.7	16.2	12.3	18.3
Oceania	5.1	7.0	9.7	25.3	37.6
Other	234.7	0.8	4.9	2.0	
United Kingdom	243.1	261.8	349.0	358.9	370.6
Japan/Japon	142.1	194.9	289.5	205.3	246.9
So. African Customs Un	58.8	221.8	209.8	209.4	374.8
United Arab Emirates	5.9	171.8	225.5	223.7	326.9
Germany/Allemagne	126.3	138.6	191.6	166.7	218.8
USA/Etats–Unis d'Amer	140.0	156.2	114.8	147.0	242.6
India/Inde	54.4	88.1	154.1	161.1	141.2
France, Monaco	74.9	88.6	143.7	137.4	122.3
Saudi Arabia	28.3	39.8	99.6	138.7	175.7
Italy/Italie	88.7	68.5	141.5	90.9	79.7
Belgium–Luxembourg	49.1	57.5	151.4	90.0	62.2
Netherlands/Pays–Bas	48.7	63.5	83.7	78.6	81.8
Indonesia/Indonésie	13.9	48.7	70.6	107.6	108.6
Areas n.e.s.	232.3	0.2	3.8	0.8	
China/Chine	29.1	29.4	59.8	46.1	63.9
Switzerland,Liechtenst.	21.6	34.2	32.2	44.7	42.4
Malaysia/Malaisie	38.3	30.7	54.9	18.1	17.7
Singapore/Singapour	20.6	30.4	30.1	35.6	34.0
Korea, Republic of	12.4	18.6	30.4	38.6	30.9
Zimbabwe	14.8	29.9	4.0	4.6	56.7
Argentina/Argentine	17.6	2.8	37.5	20.7	31.0
Israel/Israël	14.2	21.0	24.1	21.3	27.9
Sweden/Suède	14.0	15.8	22.0	26.7	27.7
Canada	19.1	10.2	13.4	29.4	27.4
Spain/Espagne	12.7	17.4	16.1	21.1	29.4
Pakistan	8.3	53.4	7.2	7.3	17.3
Denmark/Danemark	23.0	18.8	13.6	17.4	19.2
China, Hong Kong SAR	17.8	29.1	18.7	10.9	11.4
Finland/Finlande	17.2	16.1	16.5	15.8	17.4
Australia/Australie	4.8	6.2	8.9	24.5	35.4
Other Asia n.e.s.	8.9	12.8	19.0	19.0	18.2
United Rep of Tanzania	8.8	21.1	10.9	14.3	14.9
Thailand/Thaïlande	9.7	11.7	9.2	19.7	12.6
Russian Federation	4.4	9.7	16.2	12.3	18.3
Brazil/Brésil	1.7	17.4	19.0	5.7	8.1
Austria/Autriche	7.5	9.1	10.2	14.4	8.0
Bahrain/Bahreïn	4.9	0.7	6.1	21.3	14.5
Iran (Islamic Rep of)	0.1	18.5	10.4	2.0	11.9
Norway,Svalbard and JM	7.4	6.6	5.2	13.7	4.5
Kuwait/ Koweït	0.1	0.1	22.8	9.4	0.7

COUNTRIES–PAYS	EXPORTS EXPORTATIONS ES F.O.B.				
	1993	1994	1995	1996	1997
Monde	1391.9	1618.6	1826.0	1992.2	2061.9
Afrique	456.4	641.3	826.7	892.0	897.8
Amériques	60.0	75.4	63.5	68.2	69.6
– Amérique du Nord	59.0	73.8	61.6	66.8	68.4
– ALAI	0.7	1.3	0.5	1.0	1.2
– MCAC	0.3	0.3	0.2	0.3	
– Caraïbes	0.0	0.0	1.1	0.1	
– Autre Amérique					
Asie anc. URSS exclus	282.5	230.0	237.7	275.1	271.2
– Moyen–Orient	110.0	21.6	41.7	57.6	54.3
Asie ancienne URSS					
Europe anc. URSS exclus	516.4	645.6	675.4	712.9	690.5
– Union Européenne	503.3	628.7	649.5	687.4	661.5
– Europe de l'Est	0.7	2.6	2.2	4.4	5.3
– Autre de l'Europe	12.3	14.3	23.7	21.1	23.6
Europe ancienne URSS	1.3	0.5	0.9	0.4	0.5
Océanie	5.8	8.3	5.5	8.6	8.0
Autre	69.6	17.5	16.3	35.0	
Uganda/Ouganda	118.1	208.0	277.1	306.0	311.5
United Kingdom	211.4	237.2	197.6	215.6	237.7
United Rep of Tanzania	95.5	171.9	216.1	238.7	281.8
Germany/Allemagne	94.4	137.8	155.2	154.2	131.0
Pakistan	97.6	118.4	110.6	91.5	88.5
Netherlands/Pays–Bas	51.5	76.8	86.1	111.6	97.5
Egypt/Egypte	55.2	50.7	58.0	75.1	52.4
USA/Etats–Unis d'Amer	48.5	63.1	49.6	55.5	58.2
France, Monaco	25.7	36.0	46.4	39.3	44.0
Somalia/Somalie	41.4	37.7	31.6	40.3	34.2
Rwanda	24.0	26.3	34.2	35.4	64.7
Belgium–Luxembourg	30.3	31.7	43.4	39.0	32.7
Ethiopia/Ethiopie	29.9	37.8	53.3	40.1	
Italy/Italie	23.4	30.4	31.8	35.9	38.6
Dem Rep of the Congo	10.2	21.8	41.0	33.4	42.3
Sudan/Soudan	29.0	27.4	21.5	23.5	33.8
United Arab Emirates	89.1	5.6	9.7	9.2	15.6
So. African Customs Un	7.5	9.6	51.1	41.9	19.0
Bunkers, ship stores	68.7	15.4	13.2	28.0	
Sweden/Suède	21.9	19.0	29.4	20.8	31.0
Spain/Espagne	16.8	18.3	16.6	24.0	15.3
Switzerland,Liechtenst.	11.4	12.3	19.5	17.7	20.5
Finland/Finlande	12.1	12.6	15.8	17.0	19.8
Singapore/Singapour	10.4	20.2	6.1	27.3	13.1
Japan/Japon	11.9	14.0	13.1	16.6	15.2
India/Inde	10.6	12.4	13.4	12.7	20.3
Canada	10.5	10.6	12.0	11.3	10.1
Israel/Israël	11.1	8.7	8.6	11.8	13.9
Other Asia n.e.s.	1.4	3.9	11.5	25.4	1.0
Saudi Arabia	9.6	6.8	10.9	7.6	6.2
Iran (Islamic Rep of)	0.0	0.1	5.1	22.1	12.9
Yemen/Yémen	6.8	4.0	6.3	7.8	14.0
Mauritius/Maurice	9.8	9.7	8.9	10.0	0.0
Burundi	7.8	10.3	7.7	6.2	5.4
Thailand/Thaïlande	7.3	6.0	6.9	8.1	8.3
Afghanistan					35.0
Ireland/Irlande	7.3	8.6	9.1	9.1	
China, Hong Kong SAR	2.7	7.3	8.7	6.4	6.2
Greece/Grèce	2.9	11.7	4.5	6.4	5.2
Australia/Australie	4.5	6.4	4.7	7.2	6.5

(VALUE AS PERCENTAGE OF WORLD TOTAL)(VALEURS EN POURCENTAGE DU TOTAL MONDIAL)

	1988	1989	1990	1991	1992	1993	1994	1995	1996	1997
Africa	3.0	3.3	6.6	3.2	5.3	6.3	14.2	8.8	9.6	14.6
Americas	5.9	7.6	9.8	6.9	11.1	10.6	8.7	6.6	7.4	9.5
– Northern America	5.5	7.6	8.6	6.0	9.2	9.4	7.8	4.6	6.4	8.2
– LAIA	0.4		0.7	1.0	1.9	1.2	1.0	2.0	1.0	1.3
– CACM	0.0		0.5	0.0	0.0	0.0	0.0	0.1	0.0	
– Caribbean	0.0		0.0	0.0	0.0	0.0	0.0	0.0	0.0	0.0
– Rest of America										
Asia excl fmr USSR	36.2	29.3	30.3	23.7	23.4	24.5	38.0	40.5	40.9	39.2
– Middle East	13.8	15.6	11.1	2.3	1.8	2.4	11.1	13.0	15.5	16.6
Asia former USSR										
Europe excl fmr USSR	54.2	51.8	44.1	48.1	35.8	44.2	38.3	43.0	40.7	34.1
– European Union	51.3	50.6	42.2	45.2	33.2	41.9	35.7	40.7	37.8	32.0
– Eastern Europe	0.7	1.1	0.6	0.7	0.4	0.5	0.7	0.8	0.7	0.6
– Rest of Europe	2.2		1.3	2.2	2.2	1.8	1.9	1.4	2.2	1.5
Europe former USSR	0.1		0.0	0.0	0.1	0.3	0.5	0.6	0.4	0.6
Oceania	0.6	0.5	0.3	0.2	0.3	0.3	0.3	0.3	0.9	1.1
Other	0.0	7.5	8.8	17.8	24.1	13.8	0.0	0.2	0.1	
United Kingdom	18.9	15.7	14.4	17.3	10.9	14.3	12.2	12.4	13.1	11.3
Japan/Japon	12.3	11.0	11.4	9.0	7.1	8.4	9.1	10.3	7.5	7.5
So. African Customs Un	0.3	0.3	0.4	0.6	2.7	3.5	10.4	7.4	7.6	11.4
United Arab Emirates	11.4	11.3	7.2	0.2	0.3	0.4	8.0	8.0	8.1	10.0
Germany/Allemagne				8.7	6.2	7.4	6.5	6.8	6.1	6.7
USA/Etats–Unis d'Amer	5.0	7.3	8.1	5.1	8.2	8.3	7.3	4.1	5.3	7.4
India/Inde	1.6	1.9	1.6	1.9	2.8	3.2	4.1	5.5	5.9	4.3
France, Monaco	6.2	8.8	5.5	5.1	3.8	4.4	4.1	5.1	5.0	3.7
Saudi Arabia	0.9	1.9	2.8	2.0	1.0	1.7	1.9	3.5	5.0	5.4
Italy/Italie	3.6	4.5	4.5	3.3	2.7	5.2	3.2	5.0	3.3	2.4

	1988	1989	1990	1991	1992	1993	1994	1995	1996	1997
Afrique	25.6	22.3	43.0	23.6	21.0	32.8	39.6	45.3	44.8	43.5
Amériques	5.8	5.8	3.0	4.3	3.5	4.3	4.7	3.5	3.4	3.4
– Amérique du Nord	5.8	5.8	2.9	4.1	3.4	4.2	4.6	3.4	3.4	3.3
– ALAI	0.1		0.0	0.0	0.0	0.1	0.1	0.0	0.0	0.1
– MCAC	0.0		0.0	0.2	0.0	0.0	0.0	0.0	0.0	
– Caraïbes	0.0			0.0	0.0	0.0	0.0	0.1	0.0	
– Autre Amérique										
Asie anc. URSS exclus	10.0	14.7	12.8	13.3	31.2	20.3	14.2	13.0	13.8	13.2
– Moyen–Orient	2.0	2.9	1.8	2.0	20.1	7.9	1.3	2.3	2.9	2.6
Asie ancienne URSS										
Europe anc. URSS exclus	52.6	50.0	34.9	47.1	37.0	37.1	39.9	37.0	35.8	33.5
– Union Européenne	51.0	48.0	33.6	41.1	33.4	36.2	38.8	35.6	34.5	32.1
– Europe de l'Est	0.3	2.0	0.4	0.1	0.0	0.1	0.2	0.1	0.2	0.3
– Autre de l'Europe	1.3		0.9	5.9	3.6	0.9	0.9	1.3	1.1	1.1
Europe ancienne URSS	0.2		0.9	0.0	0.0	0.1	0.0	0.0	0.0	0.0
Océanie	0.6	0.6	0.3	0.5	0.4	0.4	0.5	0.3	0.4	0.4
Autre	5.2	6.6	5.1	11.2	7.0	5.0	1.1	0.9	1.8	
Uganda/Ouganda	8.8	6.5	18.5	6.6	5.5	8.5	12.9	15.2	15.4	15.1
United Kingdom	19.6	19.5	13.3	16.3	14.4	15.2	14.7	10.8	10.8	11.5
United Rep of Tanzania	2.6	2.7	2.2	3.4	3.6	6.9	10.6	11.8	12.0	13.7
Germany/Allemagne				7.6	5.3	6.8	8.5	8.5	7.7	6.4
Pakistan	2.8		5.8	6.4	6.2	7.0	7.3	6.1	4.6	4.3
Netherlands/Pays–Bas	5.1	4.9	3.9	3.9	3.3	3.7	4.7	4.7	5.6	4.7
Egypt/Egypte	1.1	1.1	1.5	2.9	3.0	4.0	3.1	3.2	3.8	2.5
USA/Etats–Unis d'Amer	4.9	4.8	2.4	3.4	2.9	3.5	3.9	2.7	2.8	2.8
France, Monaco	1.8	2.1	1.7	2.4	2.1	1.8	2.2	2.5	2.0	2.1
Somalia/Somalie	0.7	0.8	1.6	1.1	2.2	3.0	2.3	1.7	2.0	1.7

4. General Imports C.I.F. by Commodities according to the S.I.T.C. (Rev. 2) in million U.S. Dollars
Importations Générales C.A.F. par Produits d'après la C.T.C.I. (Rév. 2) en millions de Dollars E.U.

SITC CTCI	COMMODITY	1994 QUANTITY QUANTITE	1994 VALUE VALEUR	1995 QUANTITY QUANTITE	1995 VALUE VALEUR	1996 QUANTITY QUANTITE	1996 VALUE VALEUR	1997 QUANTITY QUANTITE	1997 VALUE VALEUR	PRODUIT
	ALL COMMODITIES		2142.5		2818.0		2749.6			TOUS PRODUITS
0	FOOD AND LIVE ANIMALS		317.0		121.9		185.0			ALIMENTS,ANIMAUX VIVANTS
03	FISH AND PREPARATIONS		5.3		3.2		10.1			POISSONS ET PREPARATIONS
034	FISH,FRESH,CHILLED,FROZN	W 4884	5.2	W 2867	3.0	W 6121	8.6			POISSON FRAIS, REFRIG,CONG
04	CEREALS AND PREPARATIONS		180.5		69.0		122.5			CEREALES ET PRODUITS
041	WHEAT ETC UNMILLED	W 311492	52.8	W 206434	45.1	W 486917	103.6			FROMENT,EPEAUTRE
0411	DURUM WHEAT UNMILLED	W 106586	20.4			W 50530	9.0			FROMENT DUR NON MOULU
0412	OTHER WHEAT ETC UNMILLED	W 204905	32.4	W 206434	45.1	W 436387	94.6			AUTRE FROMENT NON MOULU
042	RICE	W 95622	24.8	W 27129	8.5	W 39159	10.1			RIZ
0422	RICE SEMI-MILLED,MILLED	W 95530	24.8	W 27004	8.4	W 38976	10.0			RIZ POLI,GLACE INCL BRISURES
04221	RICE MILLED UNBROKEN	W 69609	18.4	W 16797	6.1	W 33418	8.3			RIZ POLI,GLACE EXCL BRISURES
044	MAIZE UNMILLED	W 909102	94.6	W 14557	2.9	W 10759	0.8			MAIS NON MOULU
05	VEGETABLES AND FRUIT		9.4		8.8		7.9			LEGUMES ET FRUITS
06	SUGAR AND PREPS,HONEY		108.5		25.6		29.3			SUCRES ET PRODUITS
061	SUGAR AND HONEY	W 212798	108.1	W 58494	25.3	W 68498	29.1			SUCRES ET MIEL
0611	RAW BEET AND CANE SUGAR	W 208490	106.5	W 50781	21.7	W 36983	15.4			SUCRES BRUTS
0612	REFINED SUGAR ETC	W 30	0.1	W 3046	1.2	W 26710	11.3			SUCRES RAFFINES
1	BEVERAGES AND TOBACCO		9.0		11.6		9.3			BOISSONS ET TABACS
2	CRUDE MATERLS,EXCL FUELS		55.3		65.5		59.6			MAT BRUTES NON COMESTIBLES
23	RUBBER, CRUDE		9.0		14.4		13.3			CAOUTCHOUC BRUT
26	TEXTILE FIBRES AND WASTE		25.1		22.2		25.5			FIBRES TEXTILES
266	SYNTHETIC FIBRES TO SPIN	W 93968	15.1	W 9071	15.2	W 10191	16.2			FIBRES SYNTHETIQUES
2665	DISCN SYNTH FIBRE UNCMBD	W 11293	8.3	W 5740	6.6	W 5256	6.1			DISCONTINUES EN MASSE
2666	CONTIN FILAMNT TOW SYNTH	W 82290	6.2	W 3038	7.9	W 4516	9.2			CABLES POUR DISCONTINUS
27	CRUDE FERTLZR,MINRLS NES		5.0		10.1		6.0			ENGRAIS MINERAUX BRUTS
29	CRUDE ANIMAL,VEG MAT NES		10.0		12.8		11.0			MATIERES BRUTES ANIM,VEGET
292	CRUDE VEG MATERIALS NES	W 1858	10.0		12.5	W 1537	10.7			MAT BRUTES VEGETALES NDA
3	MINERAL FUELS ETC		269.2		414.1		452.1			COMBUSTIBLES MINERAUX LUB
33	PETROLEUM AND PRODUCTS		264.5		408.2		444.2			PETROLE ET DERIVES
333	CRUDE PETROLEUM	W 1598067	206.9	W 1356907	232.9	W 1412947	221.3			HUILES BRUTES DE PETROLE
334	PETROLEUM PRODUCTS,REFIN	W 226794	52.1	W 833870	168.1	W 1010789	213.7			PRODUITS RAFFINES
3341	GASOLINE,OTH LIGHT OILS	W 39562	6.9	W 240284	42.1	W 207882	44.4			ESSENCES POUR MOTEURS
33411	MOTOR,AVIATION SPIRIT	W 39561	6.9	W 240284	42.1	W 207817	44.3			ESSENCES MOTEURS D'AVIONS
3342	KEROSENE,OTH MEDIUM OILS	W 96951	19.4	W 272332	50.7	W 451007	80.0			PETR LAMPANTS,AUT HUIL
33421	KEROSENE INCL JET FUEL	W 96938	19.4	W 272293	50.7	W 450991	79.9			PETROLES LAMPANTS
3343	GAS OILS	W 70876	11.0	W 267080	45.5	W 308826	67.2			GAS OILS
3345	LUBS,PETROLEUM OILS NES	W 19378	14.9	W 49479	29.0	W 43074	22.2			HUILES LUBRIFIANTES
33451	LUBS(HIGH PETR CONT) ETC	W 19032	14.2	W 49204	28.4	W 42834	21.6			HUILES LUBRIF,H LOURDES
335	RESIDUAL PETRLM PROD NES	W 11593	5.6	W 9406	7.3	W 22426	9.3			PRODUITS RESIDUELS NDA
4	ANIMAL,VEGETABLE OIL,FAT		95.8		150.5		136.2			HUILES,GRAISSES ANIM,VEG
411	*ANIMAL OILS AND FATS	W 5155	2.6	W 11116	7.8	W 12888	9.3			HUILES,GRAISSES ANIMALES
4113	ANIML OIL,FAT,GREASE NES	W 5131	2.5	W 11093	7.6	W 12850	9.2			HUILES,GRAISSES ANIMALES NDA
41132	FATS OF BOVINE,SHEEP,ETC	W 5102	2.5	W 11077	7.5	W 12843	9.2			SUIFS BRUTS FONDUS
42	FIXED VEGETABLE OIL,FAT		91.2		139.7		120.5			HUILES VEGETALES FIXES
423	FIXED VEG OILS,SOFT	W 7082	4.9	W 15439	12.8	W 2228	2.2			HUILES VEGET DOUCES FIXES
4236	SUNFLOWER SEED OIL	W 4085	2.4	W 14199	10.5	W 328	0.3			HUILE DE TOURNESOL
424	FIXED VEG OIL NONSOFT	W 225928	86.3	W 185447	127.0	W 212359	118.4			AUTRES HUILES VEG FIXES
4242	PALM OIL	W 221302	83.2	W 177194	117.8	W 201904	112.0			HUILE DE PALME
5	CHEMCLS,RELATED PROD NES		370.8		428.6		465.2			PRODUITS CHIMIQUES
51	ORGANIC CHEMICALS		37.1		63.9		46.6			PROD CHIMIQ ORGANIQUES
511	HYDROCARBONS NES,DERIVS	W 65830	7.3	W 6767	6.2	W 6852	5.4			HYDROCARBURES NDA
513	CARBOXYLIC ACIDS ETC	W 8513	6.9	W 10699	24.3	W 9237	12.1			ACIDES CARBOXYLIQUES
5138	POLYACIDS AND DERIVATIVS	W 2058	1.6	W 7197	18.6	W 5318	5.1			ACIDES POLYCARBOXYLIQUES
51389	OTH POLYACIDS ETC,DERIVS	W 1050	0.7	W 5661	16.7	W 3206	3.1			ACIDES POLYCARBOXYLIQUES
514	NITROGEN-FNCTN COMPOUNDS	W 1444	5.2	W 3457	11.1	W 3658	12.1			COMPOSES FONCT AZOTEES
5148	OTH NITROGN-FNCTN CMPNDS	W 1002	2.9	W 2844	8.5	W 2905	8.8			AUTRES COMPOSES AZOTES
516	OTHER ORGANIC CHEMICALS	W 2372	11.5	W 4547	11.8	W 5222	8.0			AUTRES PROD ORGANIQUES
5169	ORGANIC CHEMICALS,NES	W 377	9.5	W 465	6.3	W 213	2.3			PROD CHIM ORGANIQUES NDA
52	INORGANIC CHEMICALS		26.3		32.3		35.9			PROD CHIM INORGANIQUES
522	INORG ELEMNTS,OXIDES,ETC	W 28507	12.6	W 109768	16.7	W 34391	20.0			ELEMENTS INORGANIQUES
5225	INORGANIC BASES ETC NES	W 20497	4.9	W 13084	6.8	W 22760	9.1			AUTRES BASES OXYDES METAL
523	OTHR INORG CHEMICALS ETC	W 26956	13.3	W 26605	15.5	W 31751	15.8			AUT PRODUITS CHIMIQUES INORG
53	DYES,TANNING,COLOUR PROD		18.9		15.2		19.8			PROD TEINTURE,COLORANTS
531	SYNT DYE,NAT INDGO,LAKES	W 1613	7.4	W 903	7.3	W 3788	9.5			MAT COLOR ORGAN,LAQUES
533	PIGMENTS,PAINTS,ETC	W 3517	9.0	W 3100	7.0	W 4240	9.4			PIGMENTS,PEINTURES,VERNIS
541	*MEDICINAL,PHARM PRODUCT	MK 46795	68.7	MK 32512	84.7	MK 12355	84.7			PROD MEDICINAUX PHARMACEUT
5417	MEDICAMENTS	MK 31437	52.1	MK 31434	62.7	K 5644605	62.7			MEDICAMENTS
54171	— CONTAINNG ANTIBIOTICS	MK 28286	22.5	K 1621308	23.4	K 1517264	20.8			MED CONTN ANTIBIOTIQUES
54172	— CONTAINING HORMONES	K 747571	12.5	MK 26682	13.3	K 555448	12.2			MED CONTENANT HORMONES
54179	— CONTNG OTH SUBSTANCES	K 2360972	16.2	K 2996340	25.3	K 3497089	28.9			MED CONT AUT SUBSTANCES
5419	PHARMACEUTICAL GOODS NES	MK 14777	4.8	K 738918	7.5	K 5807224	8.8			PREP,ART PHARMACEUTIQUES
55	PERFUME,CLEANING ETC PRD		8.4		15.5		17.0			PROD POUR PARFUM,TOILETTE
562	*FERTILIZERS,MANUFACTURE	W 320704	79.9	W 147004	44.4	W 295374	83.0			ENGRAIS MANUFACTURES
5621	CHEM NITROGENOUS FERTLZR	W 57113	17.4	W 36185	8.7	W 65209	17.2			ENGRAIS AZOTES
56219	CHEM NITROG FERTLZR NES	W 34442	10.7	W 18344	4.0	W 35042	8.6			ENGRAIS AZOTES NDA
5629	FERTILIZERS NES	W 251463	60.0	W 101897	33.8	W 225527	65.0			ENGRAIS NDA
56291	NIT-PHOS-POT FERTLZR NES	W 73861	16.6	W 48004	19.9	W 118767	32.1			ENGRAIS CONT N P K
56292	NITROG-PHOS FERTILZR NES	W 177454	43.3	W 52904	12.8	W 105774	32.3			ENGRAIS NDA CONT N P
58	PLASTIC MATERIALS ETC		79.6		108.9		111.8			MAT PLAST ARTIFICIELLES
582	PROD OF CONDENSATION ETC	W 17080	17.8	W 20387	23.8	W 15473	22.9			PROD CONDENS,POLYCOND
5823	ALKYDS,OTHER POLYESTERS	W 10736	8.4	W 6725	11.1	W 7924	10.5			ALKYDES ET AUT POLYESTERS
58231	— IN PRIMARY FORMS	W 10614	8.1	W 6641	10.6	W 7805	10.0			SOUS FORMES PRIMAIRES
5829	OTH CONDNSATION,ETC PROD	W 4702	6.4	W 6432	9.4	W 5453	9.2			AUT PROD CONDENSATION
583	POLYMERIZATION ETC PRODS	W 88114	59.7	W 235905	83.1	W 126676	85.8			PROD POLYMERISATION
5831	POLYETHYLENE	W 49903	28.3	W 202651	40.7	W 53813	43.5			POLYETHYLENE
58311	— IN PRIMARY FORMS	W 49268	27.3	W 200726	39.4	W 53468	42.2			POLYETHYLENE PRIMAIRES
5832	POLYPROPYLENE	W 10241	7.0	W 10123	12.3	W 12573	12.0			POLYPROPYLENE
58321	— IN PRIMARY FORMS	W 9605	5.5	W 9429	10.1	W 11662	10.1			POLYPROPYLENE PRIMAIRES
5834	POLYVINYL CHLORIDE	W 14484	12.9	W 14689	12.3	W 45149	13.1			CHLORURE DE POLYVINYLE
58341	— IN PRIMARY FORMS	W 13867	12.2	W 11266	11.4	W 44101	11.2			SOUS FORMES PRIMAIRES
5839	OTH POLYMRZTION ETC PROD	W 6495	8.5	W 6897	13.3	W 9174	13.2			AUT PROD POLYMER COPOLYM
59	CHEMICAL MATERIALS NES		51.3		63.1		65.9			MAT PROD CHIMIQUES NDA
591	PESTICIDES,DISINFECTANTS	W 5057	26.6	W 26631	33.1	W 8247	36.2			DESINF,INSECT,FONG,HERB
5911	INSECTICIDES,FOR RETAIL	W 1059	8.5	W 20864	7.0	W 1835	8.2			INSECTICIDES VENTE DET
5912	FUNGICIDES,FOR RETAIL	W 1698	9.6	W 3261	14.4	W 3000	14.1			FONGICIDES VENTE AU DET
5914	DISINFECTANTS,ETC,FR RET	W 1576	4.5	W 1583	6.3	W 1921	8.8			DESINFECTANTS VENTE DET
598	MISCEL CHEM PRODUCTS NES	W 9430	23.0		27.6	W 14879	26.8			PROD DIV INDUST CHIM NDA
5982	ANTI-KNOCK PREPARTNS ETC	W 3111	10.0	W 3447	9.0	W 4644	10.4			PREPARAT ANTIDETONANTES
5989	CHEM PRODUCTS,PREPS NES	W 5599	10.3	W 22027	15.3	W 9182	13.8			PROD PREP CHIMIQUES NDA
59899	OTH CHEM PRODS,PREPS,NES	W 3466	6.7	W 16929	11.3	W 5811	9.7			AUT PRODUITS CHIMIQUES NDA
6	BASIC MANUFACTURES		312.7		477.9		435.8			ART MANUFACTURES

4. General Imports C.I.F. by Commodities according to the S.I.T.C. (Rev. 2) in million U.S. Dollars
Importations Générales C.A.F. par Produits d'après la C.T.C.I. (Rév. 2) en millions de Dollars E.U.

SITC CTCI	COMMODITY	1994 QUANTITY QUANTITE	1994 VALUE VALEUR	1995 QUANTITY QUANTITE	1995 VALUE VALEUR	1996 QUANTITY QUANTITE	1996 VALUE VALEUR	1997 QUANTITY QUANTITE	1997 VALUE VALEUR	PRODUIT
62	RUBBER MANUFACTURES NES		17.6		26.7		25.0			CAOUTCHOUC MANUFACTURE
625	RUBBER TYRES, TUBES ETC	N 590796	5.9	N 970168	13.3	N 2225407	11.7			PNEUS CAOUTCHOUC VULCANISE
628	RUBBER ARTICLES NES		7.5		8.7		7.9			OUVRAGES CAOUTCHOUC NDA
63	WOOD,CORK MANUFACTRS NES		6.8		7.3		7.0			OUVRAGES LIEGE ET BOIS
64	PAPER,PAPERBOARD AND MFR		28.8		53.1		65.4			PAPIERS,CARTONS & OUVRAGES
641	PAPER AND PAPERBOARD	W 38954	25.5	W 40364	42.9	W 53188	44.0			PAPIERS ET CARTONS
6412	PRINTG,WRITING PAPER NES	W 8701	7.0	W 10087	12.0	W 10774	10.2			PAPIERS POUR L'IMPRESSION
64122	— COATED,IMPREGNATD ETC	W 8425	6.7	W 9468	11.1	W 8488	8.2			PAPIERS IMPRESSION COUCHES
6415	PAPER,PAPERBRD,BULK,NES	W 7495	5.2	W 7017	7.9	W 17511	12.7			PAPIERS,CARTONS ROULEAUX
64159	OTHER PAPER ETC,BULK,NES	W 3583	2.9	W 5349	6.4	W 9410	8.3			AUT PAPIER ROULEAUX FEUILLES
642	PAPER,ETC,PRECUT,ARTS OF		3.3		10.3		21.4			PAP,CARTONS DECOUPES
6428	PAPER ETC ARTICLES NES	W 244	0.6	W 757	1.1	W 1595	9.7			OUVRAGES EN PATE A PAPIER
65	TEXTILE YARN,FABRICS,ETC		46.1		42.0		40.4			FILS,TISSUS,ARTICLES TEXTILE
652	COTTON FABRICS,WOVEN	A 20576	19.8	A 11544	12.4	A 8008	6.8			TISSUS DE COTON
6522	WOVEN COTTON BLEACHD,ETC	A 19268	18.5	A 10530	11.1	A 5747	5.6			TISSUS COTON BLANCHIS ETC
65225	BLCHD COTN BLEND FAB NES	A 11807	13.8	A 7301	8.6	A 2212	2.2			AUT TIS MOINS 85% COT BLANCH
657	SPECIAL TXTL FABRC,PRODS		12.0		9.6		13.2			TISSUS SPECIAUX
658	TEXTILE ARTICLES NES		7.1		6.1		6.1			ART FACONNES MAT TEXTILES
66	NONMETAL MINERAL MFS NES		19.1		44.5		36.6			ART MIN NON METALLIQUES
661	LIME,CEMENT,BLDG PRODS		0.7		3.3		8.5			CHAUX,CIMENTS MAT CONSTR
662	CLAY,REFRACTORY BLDG PRD	W 9971	5.6	W 9546	17.0	W 16837	9.1			MAT CONST REFRACTAIRES
6624	BRICKS ETC NONREFRACTORY	W 2728	0.9	W 5146	12.2	W 9327	4.1			BRIQUES ETC CERAM NON REFR
66245	GLAZED CERAMIC SETTS ETC	W 2249	0.7	W 4002	11.3	W 6315	2.9			AUT CARREAUX CERAMIQUE
664	GLASS	W 13312	6.1	W 14758	8.8	W 12444	6.2			VERRE
67	IRON AND STEEL		126.9		202.4		159.8			FER ET ACIER
672	IRON,STEEL PRIMARY FORMS	W 206312	73.0	W 237698	112.9	W 231820	83.9			LINGOTS FER,ACIER
6725	IRN,STL BLOOMS,SLABS,ETC	W 65687	17.3	W 57793	18.7	W 83296	21.3			BLOOMS,BILLETTES FER ACIER
67251	IRN,SMPLE STL BLOOMS,ETC	W 65682	17.3	W 57775	18.6	W 83296	21.3			BLOOMS ETC NON ACIER FIN
6727	IRN,STL COIL FR REROLLNG	W 124738	55.0	W 178905	94.0	W 145715	62.0			EBAUCHES POUR TOLES FER
67271	IRON,SIMPLE STEEL COILS	W 124514	54.9	W 178324	93.7	W 145696	62.0			EBAUCHES NON EN ACIER
673	IRON,STEEL SHAPES ETC	W 36241	15.8	W 52040	21.9	W 49160	18.9			BARRES,PROFIL FER,ACIER
6731	IRON,STEEL WIRE ROD	W 26891	10.1	W 32040	11.7	W 30564	10.3			FIL MACHINE FER,ACIER
67311	IRON,SIMPLE STL WIRE ROD	W 26600	9.9	W 27879	10.0	W 30384	10.3			FIL MACH AUT ACIER FIN
674	IRN,STL UNIV,PLATE,SHEET	W 36999	30.2	W 80659	53.3	W 61959	46.9			LARGES PLATS,TOLES
6746	IRN,STL THIN PLATE,ROLLD	W 11354	7.1	W 23734	18.5	W 23472	13.3			TOLES LAM MOINS 3MM
67461	— OF IRON OR SIMPLE STL	W 10978	6.7	W 23349	17.4	W 22901	12.5			TOL NON AC FIN MOINS 3 MM
6747	TINNED PLATES,SHEETS	W 18073	18.2	W 16223	14.7	W 19919	19.0			TOLES ETAMEES EN ACIER
6749	OTH IRN,STL PLATES,SHEET	W 2872	2.1	W 31905	15.4	W 13933	11.9			AUTRES TOLES FER,ACIER
67491	— OF IRON OR SIMPLE STL	W 2768	2.0	W 31769	15.3	W 13793	11.5			AUT TOLES AUTRES ACIER FIN
678	IRON,STL TUBES,PIPES,ETC	W 2906	5.1	W 28108	12.2	W 3254	7.2			TUBES,TUYAUX EN FONTE,FER
68	NON-FERROUS METALS		31.4		45.1		41.3			METAUX NON FERREUX
684	ALUMINIUM	W 6436	14.1	W 6419	16.9	W 7329	16.4			ALUMINIUM
6841	ALUMINIUM,ALLOYS,UNWRGHT	W 4444	8.0	W 2686	7.1	W 4855	8.7			ALUMINIUM,ALLIAGES BRUTS
6842	ALUMINIUM,ALLOYS WORKED	W 1992	6.2	W 3733	9.9	W 2474	7.7			ALUMINIUM,ALLIAGES OUVRE
686	ZINC		11.8	W 12999	18.7	W 13263	15.9			ZINC
6861	ZINC,ALLOYS UNWROUGHT	W 12889	11.7	W 12984	18.6	W 13237	15.7			ZINC ET ALLIAGES BRUTS
69	METAL MANUFACTURES NES		36.0		57.0		59.9			ART MANUFACT EN METAL NDA
691	STRUCTURES AND PARTS NES	W 956	2.0	W 1888	5.5	W 1427	9.4			CONSTRUCT FER,ACIER,ALU
6911	STRUCTURES,PARTS IRN,STL	W 734	1.5	W 1811	5.0	W 1349	8.6			CONSTRUCT FER,ACIER,FONTE
695	TOOLS	N 7783499	8.5	MN 10090	15.0	MN 11753	13.1			OUTILS A MAIN
6953	OTHER HAND TOOLS	N 6251831	5.4	N 5379456	7.0	N 7886736	8.6			AUTRES OUTILS A MAIN
699	BASE METAL MFRS NES		12.1		15.3		17.4			ART MANUFACTURES MET NDA
7	MACHINES,TRANSPORT EQUIP		593.7		942.9		864.5			MACHINES MATERIEL TRANSPORT
71	POWER GENERATING EQUIPMT		39.7		46.5		61.7			MACHINES GENERATRICES
713	INTRNL COMBUS PSTN ENGIN		18.6		20.2		24.3			MOTEURS EXPL COMB INT, PIECE
7131	AIRCRAFT PSTN ENGINS,PTS		10.9		7.3		10.1			MOTEURS EXPL P.AVIATION, PIE
71311	AIRCRAFT PISTON ENGINES	N 623	9.4	N 41896	5.4	N 675	7.4			MOTEURS EXPL P.AVIATION
7139	PISTON ENGINE PARTS NES	W 390	5.7	W 800	9.3	W 875	8.2			PIECES POUR 713.2,3,8
716	ROTATING ELECTRIC PLANT		14.6		17.7		25.2			APP ELECTR ROTATIFS,PIECES
7162	AC MTRS,GENRTRS,GEN SETS	N 37004	12.4	N 55138	12.0	N 499364	20.6			MOTEURS ELECTRIQUES
71623	GEN SETS WITH PISTN ENGN	N 10334	6.7	N 40739	9.1	N 107185	14.8			GROUPES MOTEUR EXPLOSION
72	MACHS FOR SPCL INDUSTRYS		80.6		157.4		144.5			MAC SPECIALES POUR INDUST
721	AGRIC MACHY,EXC TRACTORS		6.3		10.6		12.9			MACHINES AGRICOLES
722	TRACTORS NON-ROAD	N 856	14.1	N 61783	24.9	N 982	16.9			TRACTEURS
7224	WHEELED TRACTORS NES	N 852	14.1	N 61776	24.6	N 977	16.5			TRACTEURS A ROUES
723	CIVIL ENGNEERG EQUIP ETC		6.6		12.8		15.8			APPAREILS DE GENIE CIVIL
7234	CONST,MINING MACHNRY NES	N 2663	4.6	N 13412	10.0	N 35514	13.4			MACH POUR LA CONST, MINES
724	TEXTILE,LEATHER MACHNRY		13.7		12.0		11.1			MACH POUR INDUSTRIE TEXTILE
725	PAPER ETC MILL MACHINERY		4.1		18.2		11.4			MACHINES FABR PATE PAPIER
7251	PAPER,PULP MAKING MACHRY	N 25	0.2	N 5799	12.7	N 18868	5.9			MACHINES FABR PATE CARTON
72512	PAPER ETC MAKING ETC MCH	N 22	0.1	N 5747	12.6	N 18540	5.7			MACH FABR FINITION DU PAP
726	PRINTG,BKBINDG MACHY,PTS		3.6		9.3		11.3			MACHINES POUR IMPRIMERIE
727	FOOD MACHRY NON-DOMESTIC		12.8		13.8		26.1			MACH INDUSTRIES ALIMENT
7272	OTH FOOD PROC MCHY,PARTS		11.5		12.1		19.9			AUT MACH IND ALIMENTAIRE
72721	ANML,VEGTBL OIL,FAT MACH	N 396	0.5	N 15086	6.1	N 257727	9.8			MACH IND HUILES,GRAISSES
72722	INDUS FOOD PROC MACH NES		11.0		6.1		10.1			MACHINES BOULANGERIE
728	OTH MACHY FOR SPCL INDUS		19.8		56.2		39.2			AUT MACH IND PARTICULIERES
7281	MACH-TOOLS FR SPCL INDUS		2.1		11.8		12.7			MACH-OUTILS SPEC IND PART
72812	MACH-TOOLS TO WORK WOOD	N 11849	1.4	N 12799	10.5	N 4421	11.9			MACH-OUT POUR TRAVAIL BOIS
7283	OTHR MINERAL WORKG MACHY		3.7		17.8		3.4			MACH TRIER,CRIBLER,BROYER
72834	MINRL MOULDING ETC MACHY	N 497	0.8	N 284	10.4	N 61	0.2			MACH AGGLO CIMENT ETC
7284	MACHY FOR SPCL INDUS NES		14.0		26.7		23.2			MACH SPEC IND PARTICUL.
72842	RUBBER,PLASTICS WRKG MCH	N 31606	8.5	N 64321	16.3	N 24079	13.9			MACH IND CAOUT MAT PLAST
73	METALWORKING MACHINERY		8.3		17.5		11.2			MACH TRAVAIL DES METAUX
736	METALWORKING MACH-TOOLS		5.6		11.8		6.5			MACH-OUTILS TRAVAIL METAUX
74	GENRL INDUSTRL MACHY NES		95.7		153.5		137.1			MACH APP INDUSTRIE
741	HEATING,COOLING EQUIPMNT		12.0		30.4		15.5			MACH CHAUFFAGE,PIECES
7416	HEATING,COOLING EQU NES	N 15726	4.5	N 169914	15.9	N 231353	4.8			APP CHANGEMENT TEMP
742	PUMPS FOR LIQUIDS ETC		11.4		14.8		17.3			POMPES MOTO-POMPES
7428	OTHER PUMPS FOR LIQUIDS	N 80428	5.5	N 79571	7.9	N 63951	9.1			AUTRES POMPES POUR LIQ
743	PUMPS NES,CENTRFUGES ETC		15.0		15.7		16.6			POMPES COMPRES,VENT ETC
7436	GAS,LIQUID FILTERS ETC	MN 132551	8.0	N 577420	5.3	N 943379	7.7			APP POUR FILT DES LIQUIDES
744	MECHANICAL HANDLING EQU		14.7		26.7		19.4			EQUIP MANUTENTION PIECES
7442	LIFTING,LOADING MACH NES	N 44233	3.8	N 58201	14.0	N 86010	10.3			APP LEVAGE,MANUTENTION
745	NONELEC MACHY,TOOLS NES		11.9		26.1		23.1			AUT MACH NON ELEC,PIECES
7452	OTH NONELEC MCHS,PTS NES		11.4		25.3		21.7			AUT MACH NON ELEC,PIECES
74522	PACKAGNG,BOTTLNG,ETC MCH	N 44832	4.7	N 17226	11.4	N 41136	9.0			MACH NETT BOUTEILLES,ETC
74527	SPRAYING MACHINERY	N 327566	5.0	N 843060	8.0	N 388706	8.5			APP PROJETER ETC LIQUID
749	NONELEC MACH PTS,ACC NES		31.0		40.0		45.3			PIECES MACH NON ELEC NDA
7491	BALL,ROLLER,ETC BEARINGS	W 530	6.4	W 575	8.2	W 3589	9.3			ROULEMENTS BILLES ETC
7492	COCKS,VALVES ETC NES	W 798	8.7	W 1461	8.8	W 1485	12.7			ART ROB,SIM POUR TUYAUX

4. General Imports C.I.F. by Commodities according to the S.I.T.C. (Rev. 2) in million U.S. Dollars
Importations Générales C.A.F. par Produits d'après la C.T.C.I. (Rév. 2) en millions de Dollars E.U.

SITC CTCI	COMMODITY	1994		1995		1996		1997		PRODUIT
		QUANTITY QUANTITE	VALUE VALEUR	QUANTITY QUANTITE	VALUE VALEUR	QUANTITY QUANTITE	VALUE VALEUR	QUANTITY QUANTITE	VALUE VALEUR	
7493	SHAFT,CRANK,PULLEY ETC	W 565	9.9	W 991	13.8	W 10100	14.3			ARBRES TRANS,VILEBREQUINS
7499	OTH NONELEC MCHY PTS NES		6.1		9.4		9.1			PIECES NON ELECT NDA
75	OFFICE MACHINES,ADP EQUIP		18.3		38.4		44.9			MACH BUREAU TRAIT AUTOM
751	OFFICE MACHINES	N 149139	3.4	N 193883	7.8	N 152203	10.0			MACH,APPAREILS DE BUREAU
7518	OFFICE MACHINES NES	N 27219	2.6	N 78409	6.5	N 65562	8.4			MACH,APP DE BUREAU NDA
752	AUTOMTIC DATA PROC EQUIP	N 25821	11.4	N 50172	23.9	N 49232	23.3			MACH TRAIT INFORMATION
7523	DIGITL CENTRL PROCESSORS	N 7507	3.8	N 8348	8.8	N 6381	3.8			UNITES CENTRALES
7528	OFF-LINE DATA PROC EQUIP	N 8181	3.2	N 17212	4.8	N 21681	9.2			MACH AUXIL TRAIT INFORM
759	OFFICE,ADP MCH PTS,ACCES	W 151	3.7	W 186	6.8	W 211	11.8			PIECES DU 751 ET 752
7599	ACCTG,ETC,ADP MCH PTS,AC	W 115	2.8	W 147	5.3	W 150	9.5			PIECES DU 751 ET 752
76	TELECOMM,SOUND EQUIPMENT		44.5		43.0		35.7			EQUIPMENT DE TELECOM
764	TELECOM EQPT,PTS,ACC NES		37.8		32.6		28.5			EQUIP TELECOM,PIECES
7641	LINE TELEPHONE,ETC EQUIP	N 122832	19.3	N 162159	12.7	N 53560	6.9			APP TELEPHON PAR FIL
7648	TELECOMM EQUIPMENT NES	N 2366	3.1	N 5592	2.5	N 9733	8.4			APP TELECOM NDA
7649	PTS NES OF EQUIPMT OF 76	W 261	9.7	W 159	9.2	W 134	6.3			PIECES DE LA DIV 76
77	ELECTRIC MACHNRY NES ETC		53.6		92.9		80.5			MACH APP ELECT NDA
771	ELECTRIC POWER MACHY NES		6.7		6.1		9.1			MACH PROD,TRANS ELECTR
772	SWITCHGEAR ETC,PARTS NES		11.7		27.2		21.3			APP COUPURE,SECT ETC
7721	SWITCHGEAR ETC		11.3		26.7		20.8			APP COUPURE,SECTIONMNT
773	ELECTR DISTRIBUTNG EQUIP	W 1180	4.2	W 2384	8.6	W 2090	6.5			EQUIPMT DISTRIBUTION ELECT
774	ELECTRO-MEDCL,XRAY EQUIP	N 8719658	7.1	N 2526984	4.0	N 351045	6.9			APPAREILS MEDICAUX
775	HOUSEHOLD TYPE EQUIP NES		5.9		10.9		10.1			MACH,APP USAGE DOMESTQUE
778	ELECTRICAL MACHINERY NES		16.1		32.3		24.9			AUTRES MACH ELECT NDA
7788	OTH ELEC MACHY,EQUIP NES		5.0		13.8		5.6			AUT MACH APP ELEC NDA
78	ROAD VEHICLES		214.0		351.7		305.8			VEHICULES ROUTIERS
781	PASS MOTOR VEH EXC BUSES	N 13097	83.3	N 691630	133.0	N 16456	97.1			AUTO TRANSPORT PERSONNES
782	LORRIES,SPCL MTR VEH NES	N 4933	73.3	N 1510308	125.8	N 15348	125.5			VEHICULES SPECIAUX,MARCH
7821	LORRIES,TRUCKS	N 4859	69.6	N 1510227	117.5	N 15271	111.3			VEHICULES TRANSP MARCHAND
7822	SPECIAL MOTOR VEHCLS NES	N 74	3.8	N 81	8.3	N 77	14.3			VEHICULES USAGES SPECIAUX
783	ROAD MOTOR VEHICLES NES	N 4584	19.5	N 12969	32.9	N 11331	29.6			VEHICULES ROUTIERS NDA
7831	BUSES	N 4556	19.1	N 12863	30.2	N 10650	25.4			VOITURES TRANSPORT COMMUN
784	MOTOR VEH PRTS,ACCES NES		23.8		41.8		38.4			PIECES 722,781,782,783
7849	OTHER MOTOR VEHCL PARTS	W 3105	20.8	W 5050	34.4	W 3607	31.9			PIECES 722,781,782,783
785	CYCLES,ETC MOTRZD OR NOT		8.2		12.1		10.0			MOTOCYCLES SCOOTERS
79	OTHR TRANSPORT EQUIPMENT		39.4		42.3		43.6			AUTRE MATERIEL TRANSPORT
791	RAILWAY VEHICLES		10.2		1.7	W 427	1.7			VEHIC MAT CHEMINS DE FER
7912	OTH RAIL LOCOMOTIVES ETC	N 10	7.5							AUTRES LOCOMOTIVES
792	AIRCRAFT ETC		26.8		39.9		41.6			APP NAVIGATION AERIENNE
7923	AIRCRFT NES2000-15000KG	N 36	13.4	N 833	20.1	N 46	8.3			AERODYNES 2000 A 15000 KG
7924	AIRCRFT NES OVER 15000KG	N 3	0.3	N 7	7.6	N 10	11.6			AERODYNES PLUS 15000 KG
7929	AIRCRAFT PARTS NES	W 101	7.3	W 87	8.5	W 88	20.5			PIECES DU 792
8	MISC MANUFACTURED GOODS		116.0		202.0		139.3			ART MANUFACTURES DIVERS
812	*PLUMBG,HEATNG,LGHTNG EQ		5.8		8.5		10.6			APPAR SANITAIRES CHAUFFAGE
84	CLOTHING AND ACCESSORIES		12.9		15.3		8.6			VETEMENTS
846	UNDER GARMENTS KNITTED	N 141001	7.4	N 205957	0.6	N 230142	0.5			SOUS VETS DE BONNETERIE
8462	— OF COTTON NON ELASTIC	N 78514	7.3	N 169235	0.4	N 144865	0.3			SOUS-VET BONNET COTON
84629	—— OTHER	N 78514	7.3	N 169235	0.4	N 144865	0.3			AUT SOUS-VET BONNET COTON
87	PRECISION INSTRUMNTS NES		22.4		22.9		29.7			INSTRUM,APPAR SCIENT NDA
872	MEDICAL INSTRUMENTS NES	MN 47195	10.9	MN 64433	7.5	MN 69961	8.8			INSTR,APP MEDIC-CHIR NDA
87202	OTH MEDICAL INSTRUMENTS	MN 45807	8.0	MN 64059	7.2	MN 69469	8.3			INSTRUM,APP MEDECINE
874	MEASURNG,CONTROLNG INSTR		9.5		12.6		15.9			INSTRUMENTS DE MESURE
88	PHOTO EQU,OPTICL GDS ETC		11.1		13.3		18.2			APP,FOURN PHOTO,OP,MONTR
881	PHOTO APPARAT,EQUIPT NES		6.6		2.5		2.2			APP,EQUIP PHOTO NDA
882	PHOTO,CINEMA SUPPLIES		3.7		9.3		13.4			PRODUITS PHOTO,CINEMA
8822	PHOTO FILM EXC DEV CINMA		3.0		8.1		11.8			PLAQUES,PELLICULES,FILMS
89	MISC MANUFCTRD GOODS NES		58.0		130.7		60.0			ART MANUFACTURES DIVERS
892	PRINTED MATTER		36.3		31.5		23.9			IMPRIMES
8921	PRINTED BOOKS,GLOBES,ETC		6.6		9.5		12.7			LIVRES,BROCHURES,CARTES
89211	PRINTED BOOKS,PAMPHLETS	W 38696	6.2	W 1584	9.1	W 2491	12.3			LIVRES,BROCHURES
8928	PRINTED MATTER NES		26.9		19.7		8.1			IMPRIMES NDA
89283	UNISSUED BANKNOTES ETC	W 3292	24.3	W 25	13.8	W 47	3.1			TIMBRES-POSTE FISCAUX
893	ARTICLES OF PLASTIC NES		9.7		77.0		18.4			OUVRAGES EN MAT DIVIS 58
8939	MISC PLASTIC ARTICLES	W 2736	6.4	W 3429	71.4	W 4443	12.4			ART DIVERS EN MAT DIV 58
89399	OTHR PLASTC ARTICLES NES	W 2264	5.6	W 2324	70.1	W 3363	11.1			AUT OUV MAT DIV 58
894	TOYS,SPORTING GOODS,ETC		3.9		9.9		4.2			VOITURES ENFANTS,JOUETS

5. General Exports F.O.B. by Commodities according to the S.I.T.C. (Rev. 2) in million U.S. Dollars
Exportations Générales F.O.B. par Produits d'après la C.T.C.I. (Rév. 2) en millions de Dollars E.U.

SITC CTCI	COMMODITY	1994		1995		1996		1997		PRODUIT
		QUANTITY QUANTITE	VALUE VALEUR	QUANTITY QUANTITE	VALUE VALEUR	QUANTITY QUANTITE	VALUE VALEUR	QUANTITY QUANTITE	VALUE VALEUR	
	ALL COMMODITIES		1618.7		1826.1		1992.2			TOUS PRODUITS
0	FOOD AND LIVE ANIMALS		828.3		933.8		1042.7			ALIMENTS,ANIMAUX VIVANTS
02	DAIRY PRODCTS,BIRDS'EGGS		2.3		3.1		8.8			PRODUITS LAITIERS,OEUFS
022	MILK AND CREAM	W 2538	1.8	W 1338	2.5	W 3746	6.6			LAIT ET CREME
0224	MILK,CREAM PRESERVED ETC	W 1925	1.4	W 1108	2.3	W 3691	6.5			LAIT,CREME CONS,CONC
02243	MILK DRY,OVER 1.5% FAT	W 1798	1.1	W 973	2.1	W 3599	6.3			LAIT POUDRE SUP 1.5%
03	FISH AND PREPARATIONS		38.6		35.3		57.6			POISSONS ET PREPARATIONS
034	FISH,FRESH,CHILLED,FROZN	W 20063	35.7	W 18514	33.0	W 17263	52.1			POISSON FRAIS, REFRIG,CONG
0344	FISH FILLETS,FROZEN	W 19615	34.8	W 17279	29.7	W 15427	46.6			FILETS CONGELES
04	CEREALS AND PREPARATIONS		11.0		71.1		69.2			CEREALES ET PRODUITS
044	MAIZE UNMILLED	W 8785	0.5	W 139658	36.4	W 221478	35.0			MAIS NON MOULU
046	WHEAT ETC MEAL OR FLOUR	W 980	0.4	W 51848	23.5	W 36577	18.0			SEMOULE FARINE,FROMENT
04601	FLOUR OF WHEAT OR MESLIN	W 980	0.4	W 51846	23.5	W 36561	18.0			FARINE DE FROMENT
048	CEREAL ETC PREPARATIONS	W 14543	9.7	W 9725	10.5	W 49505	14.2			PREPTNS A BASE CEREALES
0484	BAKERY PRODUCTS	W 3928	4.9	W 5415	6.3	W 6512	8.0			PRODUITS DE BOULANGERIE
05	VEGETABLES AND FRUIT		109.8		130.9		156.9			LEGUMES ET FRUITS
054	VEG ETC FRSH,SMPLY PRSVD	W 189332	31.4	W 34779	39.3	W 46863	46.2			LEGUMES FRAIS,CONG,SECS
0545	OTHER FRESH VEGETABLES	W 186878	29.7	W 29962	36.5	W 43832	45.4			AUTRES LEGUMES FRAIS,REF
05459	FRESH VEGETABLES NES	W 186685	29.5	W 29517	35.8	W 43523	44.7			LEGUMES FRAIS,REFRI NDA
056	VEGTBLES ETC PRSVD,PREPD	W 6559	9.9	W 8706	17.1	W 11698	17.9			CONSERVES DE LEGUMES
0565	VEGTBLES PRSVD,PREPD NES	W 6543	9.0	W 8701	17.0	W 11655	17.9			LEGUMES PREPARES CONSERVE
05659	OTH VEG PRESVD,PREPD NES	W 6526	8.9	W 8700	17.0	W 11655	17.9			LEGUM PREPAP,CONSERV NDA
057	FRUIT,NUTS,FRESH,DRIED	W 18982	16.9	W 15455	15.9	W 117161	19.1			FRUITS FRAIS OU SECS
0577	NUTS EDIBLE,FRESH,DRIED	W 2663	6.8	W 879	5.1	W 1723	7.1			FRUITS A COQUES
05779	NUTS EDIBLE,FRSH,DRY,NES	W 727	4.8	W 727	4.7	W 924	6.5			FRUITS A COQUES NDA
0579	FRUIT FRESH OR DRIED NES	W 15767	9.6	W 14274	10.5	W 114982	11.8			FRUITS FRAIS,SECS NDA
05797	OTH TROP FRUIT,FRESH,DRY	W 13238	7.1	W 12746	8.5	W 113406	10.0			AVOCATS,MANGUES,GOYAVES
058	FRUIT PRESERVED,PREPARED	W 511352	51.8	W 97355	58.8	W 94308	73.8			CONSERVES DE FRUITS
0585	FRUIT OR VEGETABLE JUICE	W 123452	12.5	W 8083	4.8	W 598	1.2			JUS DE FRUITS
05854	PINEAPPLE JUICE	W 121397	10.5	W 7685	4.3	W 122	0.2			JUS D'ANANAS
0589	FRUIT PREPRD,PRESRVD,NES	W 387686	39.0	W 89088	53.7	W 93605	72.5			FRUITS PREPARES CONSERV
05899	FRUIT,NUTS NES,PRESERVED	W 386492	34.8	W 88545	52.5	W 92454	67.8			FRUITS PREP CONSERV NDA
06	SUGAR AND PREPS,HONEY		10.8		22.4		42.8			SUCRES ET PRODUITS
061	SUGAR AND HONEY	W 23103	1.2	W 29378	10.0	W 71525	31.6			SUCRES ET MIEL
0611	RAW BEET AND CANE SUGAR	W 172	0.2	W 12814	9.6	W 54398	30.4			SUCRES BRUTS
062	SUGAR CANDY NON-CHOCLATE	W 7739	9.6	W 9024	12.4	W 7549	11.3			SUCRERIES
07	COFFEE,TEA,COCOA,SPICES		640.5		655.8		687.4			CAFE,THE,CACAO,EPICES
071	COFFEE AND SUBSTITUTES	W 85752	258.9	W 108898	291.9	W 116731	288.4			CAFE ET SUCCEDANES
0711	COFFEE GREEN,ROASTED,SUB	W 85739	258.8	W 108876	291.6	W 115400	287.6			CAFE TORREFIE OU DECAFEINE
07111	COFFEE GREEN,HUSKS,SKINS	W 85712	258.7	W 108684	291.0	W 115300	287.3			CAFE NON TORREFIE
074	TEA AND MATE	W 229827	375.6	W 258564	362.4	W 262146	397.1			THE ET MATE
0741	TEA	W 229827	375.6	W 258564	362.4	W 262146	397.1			THE
09	MISC EDIBLE PRODUCTS		11.1		11.3		17.6			PREP ALIMENTAIRES DIVERSES
091	MARGARINE AND SHORTENING	W 4198	5.6	W 4566	6.5	W 9500	11.4			MARGARINE ET GRAISSES
0914	MARGARINE,EDIBLE FAT NES	W 4197	5.6	W 4566	6.5	W 9500	11.4			MARGARINES,SIMILI SAINDOUX
09141	MARGARINE	W 4176	5.6	W 4529	6.5	W 4963	6.1			MARGARINE
098	EDIBLE PRODCTS,PREPS NES	W 4099	5.5	W 3622	4.8	W 4438	6.2			PREP ALIMENTAIRES NDA
1	BEVERAGES AND TOBACCO		56.7		47.5		47.6			BOISSONS ET TABACS
11	BEVERAGES		42.1		27.3		16.6			BOISSONS
112	ALCOHOLIC BEVERAGES		41.0		27.1		16.5			BOISSONS ALCOOLIQUES
1123	BEER,ALE,STOUT,PORTER	W 108357	40.5	W 51605	25.9	W 36790	15.7			BIERES
12	TOBACCO AND MANUFACTURES		14.7		20.2		31.1			TABACS BRUTS FABRIQUES
121	TOBACCO UNMNFCTRD,REFUSE	W 491	1.3	W 2988	4.8	W 11376	16.2			TABACS BRUTS,DECHETS
1212	TOBACCO STRIPPED OR PART	W 76	0.1	W 408	0.7	W 10481	14.8			TABACS PART ECOTES
122	TOBACCO,MANUFACTURED	W 2884	13.5	W 5077	15.5	W 1988	14.9			TABACS FABRIQUES
1222	CIGARETTES	W 2342	13.2	W 5046	15.5	W 1963	14.9			CIGARETTES
2	CRUDE MATERLS,EXCL FUELS		164.6		180.3		189.1			MAT BRUTES NON COMESTIBLES
21	HIDES,SKINS,FURS UNDRSSD		15.0		6.2		4.1			CUIRS,PEAUX BRUTS
211	HIDES,SKINS,EXC FURS,RAW	W 4326	15.0	W 2254	6.1	W 2301	4.1			CUIRS ET PEAUX
2112	CALF AND KIP SKINS,RAW	W 1347	10.3	W 729	1.4	W 1634	2.9			PEAUX DE VEAUX
26	TEXTILE FIBRES AND WASTE		15.9		16.1		15.8			FIBRES TEXTILES
265	VEG FIBRE,EXCL COTN,JUTE	W 27886	14.1	W 25198	13.0	W 21672	14.3			FIBRES VEGETALES
2654	SISAL,AGAVE FIBRES,WASTE	W 27886	14.1	W 25188	12.9	W 21672	14.3			SISAL,AUTRES AGAVES
27	CRUDE FERTLZR,MINRLS NES		32.4		38.9		42.8			ENGRAIS MINERAUX BRUTS
278	OTHER CRUDE MINERALS	W 393640	31.9	W 369697	38.1	W 378704	39.1			AUTRES MINERAUX BRUTS
2783	COMMON SALT,ETC	W 92694	6.8	W 100334	12.1	W 109474	11.5			SEL
2785	QUARTZ,MICA,FELSPAR,ETC	W 62346	5.3	W 56330	4.8	W 59185	6.3			QUARTZ,MICA,FELDSPATH
27854	FELSPAR,FLOURSPAR,ETC	W 62341	5.3	W 56315	4.8	W 59175	6.3			FELDSPATH,LEUCITE ETC.
2789	MINERALS CRUDE NES	W 238508	19.9	W 212615	21.3	W 209081	21.2			MINERAUX BRUTS NDA
27899	MINERAL SUBSTANCES NES	W 237113	19.4	W 210805	20.8	W 207062	20.7			MATIERES MINERALES NDA
29	CRUDE ANIMAL,VEG MAT NES		95.5		109.5		118.6			MATIERES BRUTES ANIM,VEGET
292	CRUDE VEG MATERIALS NES	W 46197	93.7	W 37607	108.0	W 41314	115.9			MAT BRUTES VEGETALES NDA
2926	LIVE PLANTS,BULBS,ETC	W 422	4.2	W 952	6.8	W 676	7.4			BULBES,TUBERCULES
29269	LIVE PLANTS NES	W 421	4.2	W 945	6.6	W 674	7.4			AUTRES PLANTES VIVANTES
2927	CUT FLOWERS AND FOLIAGE	W 40522	55.5	W 30660	67.7	W 34205	73.2			FLEURS,FEUILLAGES COUPES
29271	CUT FLOWERS	W 34640	53.4	W 28372	64.9	W 33247	72.2			FLEURS ET BOUTONS
2929	OTH CRUDE VEG MATERIALS	W 3077	30.1	W 3898	29.2	W 4045	31.0			MATIERES VEGETALES NDA
29291	VEGETABLE SAPS,EXTRACTS	W 528	29.0	W 476	27.4	W 441	28.2			SUCS,EXTRAITS VEGETAUX
3	MINERAL FUELS ETC		66.9		112.3		139.6			COMBUSTIBLES MINERAUX LUB
33	PETROLEUM AND PRODUCTS		66.6		111.8		139.1			PETROLE ET DERIVES
334	PETROLEUM PRODUCTS,REFIN	W 472467	57.3	W 374599	102.3	W 471610	131.8			PRODUITS RAFFINES
3341	GASOLINE,OTH LIGHT OILS	W 53972	14.0	W 108386	40.7	W 127422	41.8			ESSENCES POUR MOTEURS
33411	MOTOR,AVIATION SPIRIT	W 53971	14.0	W 108366	40.7	W 119833	39.3			ESSENCES MOTEURS D'AVIONS
3342	KEROSENE,OTH MEDIUM OILS	W 184872	11.1	W 53095	15.4	W 111895	34.5			PETR LAMPANTS,AUT HUIL
33421	KEROSENE INCL JET FUEL	W 184825	11.1	W 53042	15.4	W 111895	34.5			PETROLES LAMPANTS
3343	GAS OILS	W 90907	12.6	W 82907	19.0	W 139312	35.8			GAS OILS
3344	FUEL OILS,NES	W 132900	13.5	W 115051	14.4	W 82524	10.9			FUEL OILS
3345	LUBS,PETROLEUM OILS NES	W 9816	6.3	W 15159	12.9	W 10457	9.1			HUILES LUBRIFIANTES
33451	LUBS(HIGH PETR CONT) ETC	W 9742	6.2	W 15078	12.8	W 10366	8.9			HUILES LUBRIF,H LOURDES
335	RESIDUAL PETRLM PROD NES	W 14821	9.4	W 12280	9.6	W 6231	7.3			PRODUITS RESIDUELS NDA
3351	PETRLM JELLY,MINERAL WAX	W 5159	8.0	W 4820	8.1	W 4351	6.6			VASELINE,CIRES MINERALES
33511	PETROLATUM	W 5108	8.0	W 4722	8.1	W 4277	6.5			VASELINE (PETROLATUM)
4	ANIMAL,VEGETABLE OIL,FAT		26.4		38.5		34.6			HUILES,GRAISSES ANIM,VEG
42	FIXED VEGETABLE OIL,FAT		20.4		27.2		22.2			HUILES VEGETALES FIXES
424	FIXED VEG OIL NONSOFT	W 170990	19.3	W 22552	22.6	W 16135	18.2			AUTRES HUILES VEG FIXES
4242	PALM OIL	W 163458	12.2	W 13381	12.0	W 10558	12.7			HUILE DE PALME
4244	PALM KERNEL OIL	W 6642	6.1	W 7941	9.5	W 2386	2.9			HUILE DE PALMISTE
431	*PROCESD ANML VEG OIL,ET	W 5253	6.0	W 10336	11.4	W 10371	12.4			HUILES,GRAISSES PREPAREES
4312	HYDROGENATED OIL,FAT	W 5040	5.8	W 10163	11.2	W 10125	12.1			HUILES HYDROGENEES
5	CHEMCLS,RELATED PROD NES		109.3		119.4		126.6			PRODUITS CHIMIQUES
52	INORGANIC CHEMICALS		6.6		3.5		4.1			PROD CHIM INORGANIQUES

5. General Exports F.O.B. by Commodities according to the S.I.T.C. (Rev. 2) in million U.S. Dollars
Exportations Générales F.O.B. par Produits d'après la C.T.C.I. (Rév. 2) en millions de Dollars E.U.

SITC CTCI	COMMODITY	1994		1995		1996		1997		PRODUIT
		QUANTITY QUANTITE	VALUE VALEUR	QUANTITY QUANTITE	VALUE VALEUR	QUANTITY QUANTITE	VALUE VALEUR	QUANTITY QUANTITE	VALUE VALEUR	
522	INORG ELEMNTS,OXIDES,ETC	W 1733	5.2	W 3774	1.8	W 4726	2.1			ELEMENTS INORGANIQUES
53	DYES,TANNING,COLOUR PROD		9.0		10.0		9.9			PROD TEINTURE,COLORANTS
532	DYES NES,TANNING PROD	W 8390	6.5	W 6550	4.6	W 7600	5.3			EXTRAITS TEINTURE,TANNAGE
5322	DYE,TANN EXTRCTS,TANNINS	W 8368	6.5	W 6528	4.6	W 7520	5.2			EXT TAN ORIG VEG,TANNINS
53221	VEG TANN EXTRCTS,TANNINS	W 8366	6.5	W 6523	4.6	W 7470	5.2			EXTR TANNANTS ORIG VEGET
541	*MEDICINAL,PHARM PRODUCT	K 3291322	30.8		21.6	K 2228257	28.5			PROD MEDICINAUX PHARMACEUT
5417	MEDICAMENTS	K 2990092	28.1		19.8	K 1850393	25.6			MEDICAMENTS
54173	— CONTAINING ALKALOIDS	K 356791	9.0	K 810994	7.9	K 719510	9.5			MED CONTEN ALCALOIDES
54179	— CONTNG OTH SUBSTANCES	K 1108541	12.2	K 1080927	6.2	K 1786	8.3			MED CONT AUT SUBSTANCES
55	PERFUME,CLEANING ETC PRD		45.2		53.5		57.8			PROD POUR PARFUM,TOILETTE
553	PERFUMERY,COSMETICS,ETC	W 3979	9.2	W 1960	11.2	W 3436	11.3			PRODUITS DE PARFUMERIE
554	SOAP,CLEANSING ETC PREPS	W 40011	33.0	W 46203	39.8	W 40898	45.0			SAVONS,PRODUITS DETERSIFS
5541	SOAPS	W 38244	27.5	W 43146	30.8	W 38075	35.5			SAVONS,PROD TENSIO–ACTIFS
5543	POLISHES,CREAMS,ETC	W 1497	4.3	W 2680	7.8	W 2161	8.7			CIRAGES,ENCAUSTIQUES
58	PLASTIC MATERIALS ETC		4.7		9.7		7.6			MAT PLAST ARTIFICIELLES
583	POLYMERIZATION ETC PRODS	W 2778	4.3	W 3386	5.8	W 4472	6.3			PROD POLYMERISATION
59	CHEMICAL MATERIALS NES		10.3		15.7		13.9			MAT PROD CHIMIQUES NDA
591	PESTICIDES,DISINFECTANTS	W 2689	7.1	W 2481	9.8	W 3696	10.7			DESINF,INSECT,FONG,HERB
5911	INSECTICIDES,FOR RETAIL	W 2207	5.2	W 1224	6.3	W 2771	6.7			INSECTICIDES VENTE DET
6	BASIC MANUFACTURES		255.2		280.5		290.5			ART MANUFACTURES
61	LEATHER,DRESSED FUR,ETC		31.5		19.0		11.9			CUIRS,PELLETERIES
611	LEATHER	W 17891	31.0	W 6801	18.5	W 5414	11.6			CUIRS,PEAUX PREPARES
6113	CALF LEATHER	W 11754	10.0	W 2296	3.5	W 1063	2.1			CUIRS,PEAUX DE VEAUX
6114	LEATHR BOVINE NES,EQUINE	W 2525	11.6	W 2106	8.6	W 1136	1.8			CUIRS DE BOVINS
6116	LEATHER OF OTH HIDE,SKIN	W 2546	6.8	W 1874	5.1	W 2536	5.9			PEAUX PREP D'AUTRES ANIMAUX
61161	LEATHER FROM GOAT,KID	W 2546	6.8	W 1874	5.1	W 2528	5.9			PEAUX DE CAPRINS PREPAREES
62	RUBBER MANUFACTURES NES		5.3		4.4		5.9			CAOUTCHOUC MANUFACTURE
63	WOOD,CORK MANUFACTRS NES		9.6		10.8		11.0			OUVRAGES LIEGE ET BOIS
635	WOOD MANUFACTURES NES		5.8		5.7		5.5			ART MANUF EN BOIS NDA
64	PAPER,PAPERBOARD AND MFR		18.2		27.1		25.3			PAPIERS,CARTONS & OUVRAGES
641	PAPER AND PAPERBOARD	W 29328	5.0	W 12028	10.1	W 8949	6.8			PAPIERS ET CARTONS
6413	KRAFT PAPER,PAPERBOARD	W 5255	2.5	W 7884	6.9	W 4717	3.2			PAPIER ET CARTON KRAFT
642	PAPER,ETC,PRECUT,ARTS OF		13.3		17.0		18.5			PAP,CARTONS DECOUPES
6421	PAPER ETC CONTAINERS	MN 56439	9.0	MN 51353	10.4	MN 77297	11.2			BOITES,SACS EMBALLAGES
65	TEXTILE YARN,FABRICS,ETC		30.0		34.2		35.6			FILS,TISSUS,ARTICLES TEXTILE
651	TEXTILE YARN	W 3566	7.4	W 4045	5.8	W 6219	7.4			FILS TEXTILES
652	COTTON FABRICS,WOVEN	A 5770	3.0	A 9180	8.7	A 13251	8.5			TISSUS DE COTON
6522	WOVEN COTTON BLEACHD,ETC	A 2271	2.2	A 6986	7.2	A 8162	8.2			TISSUS COTON BLANCHIS ETC
653	WOVN MAN–MADE FIB FABRIC		3.3		4.4		7.1			TISSUS FIBRES SYNTH,ARTIF
658	TEXTILE ARTICLES NES		13.3		9.3		9.5			ART FACONNES MAT TEXTILES
6583	BLANKETS ETC NON ELECTRC	N 2990343	10.1	N 1596779	5.8	N 1825816	5.9			COUVERTURES
65833	SYN FIB BLANKETS ETC NES	N 1608659	5.1	N 943212	3.0	N 1229328	3.2			COUVERTURES FIBRES SYNTHET
66	NONMETAL MINERAL MFS NES		51.4		52.9		69.9			ART MIN NON METALLIQUES
661	LIME,CEMENT,BLDG PRODS		41.4		35.3		45.4			CHAUX,CIMENTS MAT CONSTR
6612	CEMENT	W 2031678	40.8	W 472981	34.4	W 662116	44.6			CIMENTS HYDRAULIQUES
665	GLASSWARE	W 8105	3.9	W 25666	11.3	W 25945	11.9			OUVRAGES EN VERRE
6651	BOTTLES ETC OF GLASS	W 8086	3.9	W 25635	11.1	W 25398	11.6			RECIPIENTS EN VERRE
66511	GLASS BOTTLES ETC NONVAC	W 8079	3.8	W 25633	11.1	W 25356	11.6			BONBONNES,BOUTEILLES,ETC
667	PEARL,PREC–,SEMI–P STONE		3.0		3.8		7.9			PERLES, PIERRES GEMMES
6673	PREC–,SEMI–PR STONES NES		2.9		3.7		7.7			AUTRES PIERRES NON SERTIES
67	IRON AND STEEL		76.5		95.5		92.3			FER ET ACIER
673	IRON,STEEL SHAPES ETC	W 27095	10.1	W 26677	13.3	W 32405	15.5			BARRES,PROFIL FER,ACIER
6732	IRON,STEEL BARS ETC	W 17652	6.6	W 16419	7.7	W 18590	8.4			BARRES FER,ACIER
67326	IRN,OTH STL BARS HOTROLD	W 16934	6.2	W 15104	7.0	W 11660	5.3			BARRES PLEINES FER,ACIER
6733	IRON,STEEL PROFILES ETC	W 8466	3.1	W 8612	4.8	W 12521	6.5			PROFILES,PALPLAN FER,ACIER
674	IRN,STL UNIV,PLATE,SHEET	W 88270	60.8		75.1	W 88624	67.0			LARGES PLATS,TOLES
6746	IRN,STL THIN PLATE,ROLLD	W 2370	1.3	W 27703	6.5	W 11298	6.8			TOLES LAM MOINS 3MM
67461	— OF IRON OR SIMPLE STL	W 2369	1.3	W 27273	6.3	W 11289	6.8			TOL NON AC FIN MOINS 3 MM
6749	OTH IRN,STL PLATES,SHEET	W 72888	57.7	W 151845	66.3	W 71320	56.3			AUTRES TOLES FER,ACIER
67491	— OF IRON OR SIMPLE STL	W 72888	57.7	W 151816	66.2	W 71253	56.3			AUT TOLES AUTRES ACIER FIN
678	IRON,STL TUBES,PIPES,ETC	W 4950	3.6	W 7623	5.6	W 40378	6.5			TUBES,TUYAUX EN FONTE,FER
68	NON–FERROUS METALS		7.0		8.8		8.8			METAUX NON FERREUX
684	ALUMINIUM	W 1701	5.6	W 1931	6.8	W 2047	7.0			ALUMINIUM
6842	ALUMINIUM,ALLOYS WORKED	W 1701	5.6	W 1931	6.8	W 2047	7.0			ALUMINIUM,ALLIAGES OUVRE
68422	ALUMNM PLATE,SHEET,STRIP	W 1524	4.9	W 1717	5.8	W 1821	6.2			TOLES, PLANCHES EN ALU
69	METAL MANUFACTURES NES		26.2		28.2		30.1			ART MANUFACT EN METAL NDA
697	BASE MTL HOUSEHOLD EQUIP		9.5		8.6		9.6			ART MENAGE MET COMMUNS
6974	BASE MTL DMSTC ARTIC NES		9.1		8.4		9.1			ARTICLES NDA FONTE,FER,ETC
69743	— OF ALUMINIUM		7.6		6.4		6.5			ARTICLES NDA EN ALUMINIUM
699	BASE METAL MFRS NES		4.9		6.4		9.2			ART MANUFACTURES MET NDA
6996	BASE MTL MISC ARTICLES	W 2915	4.1	W 2518	5.3	W 2852	7.5			ART DIVERS METAUX COMMUNS
69963	BASE METAL STOPPERS,ETC	W 2759	3.5	W 2360	4.8	W 2716	6.9			BOUCHONS METALLIQUES
7	MACHINES,TRANSPORT EQUIP		15.6		28.7		14.8			MACHINES MATERIEL TRANSPORT
78	ROAD VEHICLES		4.8		6.1		3.3			VEHICULES ROUTIERS
8	MISC MANUFACTURED GOODS		94.1		84.0		101.8			ART MANUFACTURES DIVERS
821	*FURNITURE,PARTS THEREOF		14.9		12.8		8.0			MEUBLES ET PIECES
8212	MED FURN,STUFFD FURNSHGS	N 1767219	13.0	N 773162	10.9	N 365092	5.5			MOB MEDICO–CHIRUR,PIECES
82122	MATTRESSES ETC	N 1764751	13.0	N 771477	10.8	N 361894	5.5			SOMMIERS,ARTICLES DE LITERIE
84	CLOTHING AND ACCESSORIES		9.2		9.9		9.6			VETEMENTS
851	*FOOTWEAR		15.4		12.0		14.2			CHAUSSURES
85101	FOOTWEAR RUBBER,PLASTIC		8.1		8.4		9.0			CHAUS SEMELLES CAOUTCH
89	MISC MANUFCTRD GOODS NES		52.6		45.9		66.0			ART MANUFACTURES DIVERS
892	PRINTED MATTER		18.8		10.6		24.4			IMPRIMES
8928	PRINTED MATTER NES		17.7		7.4		21.9			IMPRIMES NDA
89283	UNISSUED BANKNOTES ETC	W 1	17.2	W 1	6.4	W 1	19.1			TIMBRES–POSTE FISCAUX
893	ARTICLES OF PLASTIC NES		21.7		25.2		31.4			OUVRAGES EN MAT DIVIS 58
8931	PLSTC PACKG CONTNRS,LIDS	W 4839	8.7	W 8985	12.5	W 8847	12.9			ART TRANSP EMBALLAGE ETC
8939	MISC PLASTIC ARTICLES	W 10761	12.5	W 8741	11.1	W 8609	14.3			ART DIVERS EN MAT DIV 58
89399	OTHR PLASTC ARTICLES NES	W 10351	12.3	W 8582	11.0	W 8424	14.2			AUT OUV MAT DIV 58

1. HISTORICAL SERIES, 1960–1995 GENERAL TRADE, IMPORTS F.O.B., EXPORTS F.O.B.
SERIES HISTORIQUES, 1960–1995 COMMERCE GENERAL, IMPORTATIONS F.O.B., EXPORTATIONS F.O.B

YEAR ANNEE	VALUE IN MILLION ASTL. DOLLARS VALEUR EN MILLION ASTL. DOLLARS MERCHANDISE –MARCHANDISE IMPORTS	EXPORTS	GOLD –OR IMPORTS	EXPORTS	CONVERSION FACTORS U.S. CENTS PER ASTL. DOLLAR FACTEURS DE CONVERSION CENTS E.U. PAR ASTL. DOLLAR IMPORTS	EXPORTS	INDEX NUMBERS –INDICES QUANTUM IMPORTS	EXPORTS	UNIT VALUE VALEUR UNITAIRE IMPORTS	EXPORTS
1960	2.59	1.88			112.0000	112.0000				
1961	3.48	1.96			112.0000	112.0000				
1962	3.84	1.79			112.0000	112.0000				
1963	3.57	2.68			112.0000	112.0000				
1964	3.25	2.64			112.0000	112.0000				
1965	3.65	3.73			112.0000	112.0000				
1966	2.70	4.80			112.0000	112.0000				
1967	3.94	6.20			112.0000	112.0000				
1968	4.13	6.80			112.0000	112.0000				
1969	3.15	7.31			112.0000	112.0000				
1970	3.92	6.97			112.0000	112.0000				
1971	4.73	8.69			113.4000	113.4000				
1972	5.42	6.60			119.1000	119.1000				
1973	6.82	11.69			142.2680	142.2690				
1974	7.55	24.05			142.9070	140.9340				
1975	9.28	27.73			131.0470	131.4290				
1976	10.06	18.15			122.4040	122.5440				
1977	11.69	18.21			110.9040	110.9040				
1978	14.11	21.40			114.4730	114.4680				
1979	15.55	21.21			111.7760	111.7760				
1980	16.62	2.54			114.9420	114.9420				
1981	19.91	3.58			114.9300	114.9300				
1982	22.77	2.35			110.1740	110.1740				
1983	19.61	4.00			94.4800	94.4800				
1984	20.88	8.80			87.9600	87.9600				
1985	21.58	6.06			70.0800	70.0800				
1986	21.45	2.50			67.0900	67.0900				
1987	25.14	2.87			70.0900	70.0900				
1988	28.18	6.67			78.4200	78.4200				
1989	28.60	6.44			79.2500	79.2500				
1990	34.45	3.68			79.3110	79.3110				
1991	33.23	3.70			77.9100	77.9100				
1992	50.53	6.51			73.5298	73.5298				
1993	40.87	5.07			67.9312	67.9312				
1994	36.11	7.11			73.3267	73.3267				
1995	47.55	10.03			71.6932	71.6932				

2. IMPORTS BY BROAD ECONOMIC CATEGORY AND EXPORTS BY INDUSTRIAL ORIGIN. (PERCENTAGE OF TOTAL VALUE)
IMPORTATIONS PAR CATEGORIES ECONOMIQUES ET EXPORTATIONS PAR BRANCHE D'ACTIVITE.(EN POURCENTAGE DE LA VALEUR TOTALE)

IMPORTS – IMPORTATIONS

	1989	1990	1991	1992	1993	1994	1995
TOTAL IMPORTS–IMPORTATIONS TOTALES	100.	100.	100.	100.	100.	100.	100.
1 FOOD BEV–ALIMENTATION BOISSONS	32.6	28.6	33.4	23.1	32.1	34.9	35.2
11 PRIMARY–PRODUITS DE BASE	3.1	2.7	3.7	2.3	4.0	4.0	5.4
111 FOR INDUSTRY–POUR L'INDUSTRIE	0.5	0.4	0.5	0.3	0.5	0.3	1.9
112 FOR HOUSEHOLDS–POUR LES MENAGES	2.7	2.3	3.1	2.1	3.5	3.7	3.5
12 PROCESSED–PRODUITS ELABORES	29.5	25.9	29.7	20.8	28.1	30.9	29.7
121 FOR INDUSTRY–POUR L'INDUSTRIE	6.4	5.5	6.5	4.4	6.4	6.8	5.9
122 FOR HOUSEHOLDS–POUR LES MENAGES	23.2	20.4	23.1	16.3	21.7	24.1	23.8
2 IND SUPPLIES–APPROV INDUSTRIELS	12.7	18.9	14.5	9.6	16.7	14.7	22.8
21 PRIMARY–PRODUITS DE BASE	0.8	0.8	0.6	0.3	1.3	1.0	0.9
22 PROCESSED–PRODUITS ELABORES	11.9	18.1	13.9	9.3	15.4	13.7	21.9
3 FUELS–COMBUSTIBLES	11.2	10.6	10.9	7.8	7.4	9.2	10.0
31 PRIMARY–PRODUITS DE BASE	0.0	0.1	0.1	0.1	0.1	0.2	0.1
32 PROCESSED–PRODUITS ELABORES	11.1	10.6	10.8	7.7	7.4	9.1	10.0
321 MOTOR SPIRIT–ESSENCE	2.8	2.6	2.7	1.9	1.5	1.7	7.7
322 OTHER–AUTRES	8.3	8.0	8.1	5.9	5.9	7.4	2.3
4 MACHINERY–EQUIPEMENT	9.5	21.1	12.6	26.5	14.0	12.2	9.3
41 CAPITAL EQUIPMENT–MACHINES	8.7	20.2	12.0	25.5	13.5	11.5	8.8
42 PARTS–PIECES ACCESSOIRES	0.8	0.9	0.6	1.0	0.4	0.7	0.5
5 TRANSPORT–TRANSPORT	13.3	7.1	11.1	21.3	9.6	7.1	6.2
51 PASSENGER CARS–AUTOMOBILES					3.7	1.7	0.5
52 OTHER–AUTRES	9.1	4.7	6.5	19.5	3.4	3.1	3.1
521 INDUSTRIAL–INDUSTRIELS	8.1	3.8	5.8	18.7	2.7	2.1	2.3
522 NON INDUSTRIAL–NON INDUSTRIEL	1.0	0.9	0.7	0.8	0.7	1.0	0.8
53 PARTS–PIECES ACCESSOIRES	4.2	2.4	4.6	1.8	2.5	2.3	2.6
6 CONSUM GOODS–BIENS CONSOMMATION	19.6	12.9	16.9	11.3	19.7	21.1	15.3
61 DURABLE–DURABLES	2.7	1.9	2.1	1.2	5.0	2.4	2.2
62 SEMI DURABLE–SEMI DURABLES	9.7	5.8	6.5	3.7	4.4	6.0	4.4
63 NON DURABLE–NON DURABLES	7.2	5.2	8.3	6.4	10.4	12.6	8.7
7 GOODS NES–BIENS NDA	1.1	0.7	0.6	0.4	0.6	0.8	1.3

EXPORTS – EXPORTATIONS

	1989	1990	1991	1992	1993	1994	1995
TOTAL EXPORTS–EXPORTATIONS TOTALES	100.	100.	100.	100.	100.	100.	100.
1 AGRICULTURE	91.0	74.5	79.4	82.5	86.2	86.7	86.8
2 MINING QUARRY–INDUS EXTRACTIVES							0.1
3 MANUFACTURING–IND MANUFACTUR	9.0	25.5	20.5	17.4	13.8	13.2	13.1
31 FOOD BEV TOBACCO–ALIM BOISS TAB							
32 TEXTILES–INDUSTRIES TEXTILES							
33 WOOD & PRODUCTS–BOIS & PRODUITS							
34 PAPER & PRODUCTS–PAPIER & PRODT							
35 CHEMICALS–INDUSTRIES CHIMIQUES	0.2			0.0			
36 NON METAL MIN–MIN NON METAL							
37 BASIC METAL–IND METAL BASE		1.2		1.5			
38 METAL MANUF–MANUF METAL	0.4		9.7		0.2	0.7	1.0
39 OTH MANUF IND–AUTRES MANUF	8.5	24.2	10.8	15.9	13.6	12.6	12.1

3. TRADE BY PRINCIPAL COUNTRIES OF ORIGIN AND DESTINATION (VALUE IN MILLION U.S. DOLLARS)
ECHANGES SELON LES PRINCIPAUX PAYS D'ORIGINE ET DE DESTINATION (VALEUR EN MILLIONS DE DOLLARS EU)

COUNTRIES–PAYS	GENERAL IMPORTS F.O.B. IMPORTATIONS GENERALES F.O.B.				
	1991	1992	1993	1994	1995
World	25.9	36.7	27.8	26.5	34.1
Africa	0.0		0.0		
Americas	0.9	1.1	0.8	2.6	1.0
– Northern America	0.9	1.1	0.8	2.6	1.0
– LAIA	0.0	0.0	0.0	0.0	0.0
– CACM					
– Caribbean					
– Rest of America					
Asia excl fmr USSR	7.8	10.8	7.3	4.8	6.4
– Middle East					
Asia former USSR					
Europe excl fmr USSR	0.5	3.9	2.1	0.2	0.4
– European Union	0.4	3.9	2.0	0.2	0.4
– Eastern Europe	0.0	0.0	0.0		
– Rest of Europe	0.1	0.1	0.0	0.0	0.0
Europe former USSR					
Oceania	16.6	20.9	17.6	18.9	26.2
Other					
Australia/Australie	10.4	14.1	11.9	12.1	16.2
Fiji/Fidji	4.4	4.2	3.2	4.6	6.5
Japan/Japon	4.8	8.3	4.1	1.8	2.6
New Zealand	1.7	2.0	1.8	1.7	3.0
China/Chine	1.4	1.2	1.6	1.5	1.8
USA/Etats–Unis d'Amer	0.9	1.1	0.8	2.6	1.0
France, Monaco	0.0	3.5	1.6	0.0	0.0
Papua New Guinea	0.0	0.6	0.8	0.4	0.2
Singapore/Singapour	0.4	0.2	0.3	0.2	0.4
Other Asia n.e.s.	0.3	0.2	0.3	0.3	0.4
China, Hong Kong SAR	0.4	0.4	0.2	0.3	0.2
Korea, Republic of	0.1	0.1	0.4	0.2	0.6
United Kingdom	0.3	0.2	0.1	0.2	0.3
Germany/Allemagne	0.1	0.2	0.3	0.0	0.1
Malaysia/Malaisie	0.0	0.1	0.1	0.1	0.2
Thailand/Thaïlande	0.1	0.1	0.1	0.1	0.1
India/Inde	0.1	0.1	0.1	0.1	0.0
Indonesia/Indonésie	0.0	0.0	0.0	0.0	0.2
US Misc Pacific Islands		0.0			0.1
Bangladesh	0.0	0.0	0.0	0.1	
Nauru	0.0	0.0	0.0	0.0	0.0
Netherlands/Pays–Bas	0.0	0.0	0.0	0.0	0.0
Denmark/Danemark	0.0	0.0	0.0	0.0	
Tuvalu	0.0	0.0	0.0	0.0	0.0
Samoa					0.0
Tonga	0.0		0.0		
Palau	0.0				
Sweden/Suède	0.0	0.0	0.0	0.0	

COUNTRIES–PAYS	EXPORTS EXPORTATIONS ES F.O.B.				
	1991	1992	1993	1994	1995
Monde	2.9	4.7	3.0	5.6	7.2
Afrique					
Amériques	0.6	0.6	0.6	0.7	0.7
– Amérique du Nord	0.6	0.6	0.6	0.7	0.7
– ALAI					
– MCAC					
– Caraïbes					
– Autre Amérique					
Asie anc. URSS exclus	1.1	3.3	0.6	3.9	5.2
– Moyen–Orient					
Asie ancienne URSS					
Europe anc. URSS exclus	0.6	0.3	1.4	0.3	0.2
– Union Européenne	0.6	0.3	1.4	0.3	0.2
– Europe de l'Est					
– Autre de l'Europe			0.0		
Europe ancienne URSS					
Océanie	0.5	0.6	0.4	0.7	1.1
Autre			0.0		0.0
Bangladesh	1.1	3.2	0.0	3.3	4.5
USA/Etats–Unis d'Amer	0.6	0.6	0.6	0.7	0.7
China, Hong Kong SAR	0.0	0.0	0.5	0.6	0.4
Australia/Australie	0.2	0.2	0.1	0.2	0.5
Denmark/Danemark	0.5	0.2	0.1	0.2	0.1
Netherlands/Pays–Bas			1.2		
Fiji/Fidji	0.1	0.2	0.1	0.1	0.1
New Zealand	0.0	0.1	0.0	0.2	0.1
Singapore/Singapour		0.1	0.0	0.0	0.2
Tuvalu	0.0	0.0	0.0	0.1	0.1
Oceania n.e.s.					0.2
United Kingdom	0.0	0.0	0.0	0.0	0.0
Samoa	0.2			0.0	0.0
Nauru	0.0	0.1	0.0	0.1	0.0
Japan/Japon	0.0	0.0	0.0	0.0	0.0
Germany/Allemagne	0.0	0.0	0.0	0.0	0.0
France, Monaco			0.0	0.0	0.0
Palau	0.0				
US Misc Pacific Islands				0.0	
India/Inde		0.0			
Korea, Republic of		0.0	0.0	0.0	
Thailand/Thaïlande		0.0			
Tonga		0.0			
Papua New Guinea	0.0				

(VALUE AS PERCENTAGE OF WORLD TOTAL)(VALEURS EN POURCENTAGE DU TOTAL MONDIAL)

	1986	1987	1988	1989	1990	1991	1992	1993	1994	1995
Africa		0.0		0.0		0.0		0.0		
Americas	3.7	4.8	4.9	6.5	6.7	3.6	2.9	2.8	9.7	3.1
– Northern America	3.4	4.4	4.8	6.4	6.6	3.6	2.9	2.8	9.6	3.1
– LAIA	0.3	0.5	0.1	0.0	0.1	0.1	0.1	0.0	0.0	0.0
– CACM										
– Caribbean				0.0						
– Rest of America										
Asia excl fmr USSR	26.2	23.4	22.1	26.2	32.6	30.2	29.5	26.3	18.2	18.9
– Middle East										
Asia former USSR										
Europe excl fmr USSR	4.0	4.6	3.4	2.2	1.9	1.9	10.7	7.4	0.9	1.1
– European Union	3.5	4.5	3.3	2.1	1.7	1.5	10.5	7.3	0.8	1.1
– Eastern Europe	0.0		0.0	0.0	0.0	0.0	0.0	0.0		
– Rest of Europe	0.4	0.1	0.0	0.1	0.1	0.5	0.2	0.1	0.1	0.0
Europe former USSR	0.0									
Oceania	66.1	67.2	69.6	65.1	58.9	64.3	56.8	63.5	71.2	76.9
Other			0.1							
Australia/Australie	40.5	43.7	43.8	45.9	33.4	40.3	38.4	42.7	45.9	47.6
Fiji/Fidji	11.9	7.3	15.3	12.7	19.3	17.2	11.3	11.4	17.2	19.1
Japan/Japon	19.4	11.9	10.9	15.3	23.6	18.4	22.7	14.7	6.7	7.6
New Zealand	5.0	7.2	4.9	4.9	5.6	6.5	5.4	6.4	6.6	8.9
China/Chine	2.8	4.5	5.2	4.8	4.4	5.2	3.3	5.8	5.8	5.4
USA/Etats–Unis d'Amer	3.3	4.3	4.8	6.4	6.6	3.6	2.9	2.7	9.6	3.1
France, Monaco	0.0	0.2	0.0	0.1	0.0	0.0	9.4	5.6	0.1	0.0
Papua New Guinea	1.6	0.2	0.0	0.0	0.3	0.0	1.6	2.8	1.4	0.6
Singapore/Singapour	0.3	0.3	0.4	0.7	0.6	1.6	0.7	1.2	0.7	1.3
Other Asia n.e.s.	1.0	1.5	0.6	0.7	0.9	1.2	0.5	1.0	1.2	1.2

	1986	1987	1988	1989	1990	1991	1992	1993	1994	1995
Afrique		0.1	0.9							
Amériques	19.5	11.6	3.8	5.2	15.4	22.3	12.3	19.7	13.2	10.4
– Amérique du Nord	19.5	11.6	3.8	5.2	15.4	22.3	12.3	19.7	13.2	10.4
– ALAI										
– MCAC										
– Caraïbes										
– Autre Amérique										
Asie anc. URSS exclus	1.3	2.1	1.6	0.1	1.5	39.7	69.4	20.2	70.1	71.9
– Moyen–Orient										
Asie ancienne URSS										
Europe anc. URSS exclus	17.9	38.2	62.6	45.7	42.8	19.7	5.9	45.6	4.9	2.2
– Union Européenne	17.9	38.2	62.6	45.7	42.8	19.7	5.9	45.6	4.9	2.2
– Europe de l'Est										
– Autre de l'Europe					0.0			0.0		
Europe ancienne URSS										
Océanie	61.3	47.9	29.8	48.9	40.3	18.3	12.4	14.2	11.7	15.5
Autre			1.2					0.3		0.1
Bangladesh						38.4	66.8	0.2	58.9	62.5
USA/Etats–Unis d'Amer	19.5	11.6	3.8	5.2	15.4	22.3	12.3	19.7	13.2	10.4
China, Hong Kong SAR	0.0			0.0		1.2	0.7	17.2	9.9	6.2
Australia/Australie	3.1	20.8	2.4	3.1	10.8	5.5	4.8	4.1	3.3	7.2
Denmark/Danemark				1.3	19.7	18.3	4.5	4.1	4.2	1.5
Netherlands/Pays–Bas	6.4	36.1	60.8	43.0	21.1			39.2		
Fiji/Fidji	46.2	16.1	22.5	38.1	18.7	3.7	4.1	4.8	1.1	1.6
New Zealand	3.0	3.3	1.3	0.6	1.1	1.7	1.6	1.1	2.9	1.2
Singapore/Singapour	0.0		1.5		0.1		1.7	1.4	0.6	2.7
Tuvalu	1.0	1.5	1.0	0.4	1.0	0.5	0.2	1.0	2.2	0.8

4. General Imports F.O.B. by Commodities according to the S.I.T.C. (Rev. 2) in million U.S. Dollars
Importations Générales F.O.B. par Produits d'après la C.T.C.I. (Rév. 2) en millions de Dollars E.U.

SITC CTCI	COMMODITY	1992 QUANTITY QUANTITE	1992 VALUE VALEUR	1993 QUANTITY QUANTITE	1993 VALUE VALEUR	1994 QUANTITY QUANTITE	1994 VALUE VALEUR	1995 QUANTITY QUANTITE	1995 VALUE VALEUR	PRODUIT
	ALL COMMODITIES		36.8		27.8		26.5		34.1	TOUS PRODUITS
0	FOOD AND LIVE ANIMALS		7.8		8.1		8.4		11.0	ALIMENTS,ANIMAUX VIVANTS
01	MEAT AND PREPARATIONS		1.6		1.6		1.7		2.5	VIANDES ET PREPARATIONS
011	MEAT FRESH,CHILLD,FROZEN	W 186	0.4	W 300	0.5	W 264	0.5	W 471	0.7	VIANDES FRAICHES,REF,CONGE
0114	POULTRY FRESH CHLLD,FRZN	W 160	0.3	W 257	0.4	W 230	0.4	W 440	0.6	VOLAILLES MORTES
014	MEAT PREPD,PRSVD,NES ETC	W 413	1.2	W 393	1.1	W 366	1.2	W 600	1.9	CONSERVES DE VIANDES
0142	SAUSAGES INCLDING TINNED	W 8	0.1	W 24	0.1	W 37	0.2	W 35	0.2	SAUCISSES,SAUCISSONS
0149	OTH PREPARD,PRESRVD MEAT	W 405	1.2	W 369	1.0	W 329	1.0	W 564	1.8	AUTRES PREP DE VIANDES
02	DAIRY PRODCTS,BIRDS'EGGS		0.6		0.6		0.7		0.8	PRODUITS LAITIERS,OEUFS
022	MILK AND CREAM	W 170	0.5		0.5	W 181	0.6	W 238	0.7	LAIT ET CREME
0224	MILK,CREAM PRESERVED ETC	W 164	0.5		0.5	W 174	0.6	W 230	0.7	LAIT,CREME CONS,CONC
02242	MILK DRY,1.5% FAT OR LES	W 73	0.4	W 86	0.4	W 79	0.4	W 81	0.4	LAIT POUDRE INF 1.5%
02243	MILK DRY,OVER 1.5% FAT							W 38	0.2	LAIT POUDRE SUP 1.5%
02249	MILK(EX DRY) PRSVD,SWEET	W 91	0.2	W 62	0.1	W 89	0.2	W 110	0.2	LAIT CONS,CONC SUCRE
03	FISH AND PREPARATIONS		0.3		0.4		0.4		0.5	POISSONS ET PREPARATIONS
037	FISH ETC PREPD,PRSVD NES	W 371	0.3	W 334	0.4	W 256	0.4	W 372	0.4	POIS,CRUST,MOL PREPARES
0371	FISH PREPARD,PRESRVD NES	W 371	0.3	W 318	0.3	W 249	0.4	W 371	0.4	CONSERVES DE POISSONS
04	CEREALS AND PREPARATIONS		3.4		3.2		3.2		4.5	CEREALES ET PRODUITS
042	RICE	W 5191	2.0	W 5220	1.9	W 4952	2.0	W 6945	2.8	RIZ
0421	RICE IN HUSK OR HUSKED							W 1116	0.5	RIZ SANS AUTRE PREPARATION
04211	RICE IN THE HUSK							W 514	0.3	RIZ PADDY
04212	RICE HUSKED							W 602	0.3	RIZ CARGO
0422	RICE SEMI–MILLED,MILLED							W 5829	2.3	RIZ POLI,GLACE INCL BRISURES
04221	RICE MILLED UNBROKEN							W 4775	1.9	RIZ POLI,GLACE EXCL BRISURES
04222	RICE BROKEN							W 1054	0.5	BRISURES DE RIZ
046	WHEAT ETC MEAL OR FLOUR	W 2751	0.9	W 2098	0.7	W 1515	0.5	W 1868	0.7	SEMOULE FARINE,FROMENT
04601	FLOUR OF WHEAT OR MESLIN							W 1868	0.7	FARINE DE FROMENT
047	OTHER CEREAL MEALS,FLOUR			W 1122	0.4	W 861	0.3	W 939	0.4	AUTRES SEMOULES,FARINES
04701	CEREAL FLOUR(NON–WHEAT)							W 939	0.4	FARINES DE CEREALES
048	CEREAL ETC PREPARATIONS	W 304	0.6	W 189	0.3	W 102	0.5	W 350	0.7	PREPTNS A BASE CEREALES
0481	PREPD BREAKFAST FOOD ETC	W 40	0.2	W 49	0.1	W 27	0.2	W 28	0.1	CEREALES TRAVAILLEES
0483	MACARONI,SPAGHETTI ETC							W 118	0.2	PATES ALMENTAIRES
0484	BAKERY PRODUCTS	W 161	0.3	W 139	0.2	W 74	0.3	W 146	0.3	PRODUITS DE BOULANGERIE
04841	BREAD,BISCUIT,COM WAFERS	W 140	0.2	W 101	0.2	W 46	0.3	W 117	0.2	PAINS,BISCUITS DE MER
04842	PASTRY, CAKES ETC	W 22	0.1	W 38	0.1	W 27	0.1	W 29	0.1	PATISSERIE ETC.
0488	OTH CEREAL PREPS,MALT EX	W 101	0.3					W 58	0.2	EXTRAITS DE MALT
05	VEGETABLES AND FRUIT		0.4		0.4		0.6		0.5	LEGUMES ET FRUITS
054	VEG ETC FRSH,SMPLY PRSVD	W 223	0.2	W 227	0.2	W 314	0.2	W 230	0.3	LEGUMES FRAIS,CONG,SECS
0545	OTHER FRESH VEGETABLES	W 160	0.2	W 169	0.2	W 257	0.2	W 135	0.2	AUTRES LEGUMES FRAIS,REF
05459	FRESH VEGETABLES NES	W 64	0.1	W 85	0.1	W 176	0.1	W 40	0.1	LEGUMES FRAIS,REFRI NDA
056	VEGTBLES ETC PRSVD,PREPD	W 63	0.1	W 87	0.2	W 291	0.2	W 79	0.1	CONSERVES DE LEGUMES
058	FRUIT PRESERVED,PREPARED	W 98	0.2	W 49	0.1	W 62	0.2	W 72	0.1	CONSERVES DE FRUITS
06	SUGAR AND PREPS,HONEY		0.9		0.9		1.1		1.2	SUCRES ET PRODUITS
061	SUGAR AND HONEY	W 2770	0.8	W 2850	0.8	W 2914	1.0	W 2944	1.0	SUCRES ET MIEL
0611	RAW BEET AND CANE SUGAR	W 2744	0.8	W 2789	0.8	W 2907	0.9	W 2700	0.9	SUCRES BRUTS
062	SUGAR CANDY NON–CHOCLATE	W 42	0.2	W 34	0.2	W 30	0.2	W 72	0.2	SUCRERIES
07	COFFEE,TEA,COCOA,SPICES		0.4		0.5		0.4		0.5	CAFE,THE,CACAO,EPICES
071	COFFEE AND SUBSTITUTES	W 8	0.2	W 10	0.2	W 7	0.1	W 12	0.2	CAFE ET SUCCEDANES
0711	COFFEE GREEN,ROASTED,SUB							W 12	0.2	CAFE TORREFIE OU DECAFEINE
074	TEA AND MATE	W 32	0.2	W 49	0.3	W 35	0.2	W 52	0.3	THE ET MATE
0741	TEA							W 52	0.3	THE
081	*FEEDING STUFF FOR ANIML	W 148	0.1	W 189	0.1	W 149	0.1	W 327	0.2	NOURRITURE POUR ANIMAUX
0819	FOOD WASTE AND FEED NES							W 327	0.2	DECHETS,ALIMENTS NDA
08199	FODDER NES,INCL SWEETNED							W 327	0.2	PREPARATIONS FOURRAGERES
09	MISC EDIBLE PRODUCTS		0.4		0.9		0.8		0.8	PREP ALIMENTAIRES DIVERSES
091	MARGARINE AND SHORTENING	W 295	0.2	W 112	0.2	W 111	0.2	W 78	0.2	MARGARINE ET GRAISSES
0914	MARGARINE,EDIBLE FAT NES			W 112	0.2	W 111	0.2	W 70	0.2	MARGARINES,SIMILI SAINDOUX
09141	MARGARINE							W 63	0.2	MARGARINE
098	EDIBLE PRODCTS,PREPS NES	W 159	0.3		0.8		0.7		0.7	PREP ALIMENTAIRES NDA
09804	SAUCES,MIXED SEASONINGS	W 69	0.1	W 252	0.4	W 64	0.2	W 205	0.2	SAUCES,ASSAISONNEMENTS
09809	MISC FOOD PREPRTIONS NES	W 18	0.1	W 172	0.4	W 149	0.4		0.3	PREP ALIMENTAIRES NDA
1	BEVERAGES AND TOBACCO		1.9		1.8		2.4		2.3	BOISSONS ET TABACS
11	BEVERAGES		0.8		0.9		0.9		1.1	BOISSONS
111	NON–ALCOHL BEVERAGES NES	W 159	0.2	W 223	0.2	W 223	0.2	W 269	0.2	BOISSONS NON ALCOOLIQUES
11102	FLAVORED WATERS NON–ALCO	W 158	0.2	W 218	0.2	W 217	0.2	W 238	0.2	LIMONADES,EAUX GAZEUSES
112	ALCOHOLIC BEVERAGES	W 808	0.7	W 861	0.7	W 791	0.8		0.9	BOISSONS ALCOOLIQUES
1123	BEER,ALE,STOUT,PORTER	W 796	0.6	W 849	0.6	W 781	0.7	W 1026	0.9	BIERES
12	TOBACCO AND MANUFACTURES		1.1		1.0		1.5		1.2	TABACS BRUTS FABRIQUES
122	TOBACCO,MANUFACTURED	W 57	1.1	W 70	1.0	W 62	1.5		1.2	TABACS FABRIQUES
1222	CIGARETTES	W 15	0.4	W 28	0.3	W 21	0.7		0.3	CIGARETTES
1223	OTH MANUFACTURED TOBACCO	W 43	0.8	W 40	0.7	W 40	0.8	W 51	1.0	TABACS FUMER,CHIQUER,PRISER
2	CRUDE MATERLS,EXCL FUELS		0.5		0.7		0.6		0.5	MAT BRUTES NON COMESTIBLES
24	CORK AND WOOD		0.4		0.5		0.4		0.3	LIEGE ET BOIS
247	OTH WOOD ROUGH,SQUARED	W 33	0.1	W 419	0.2	W 158	0.1	W 186	0.1	BOIS BRUTS EQUARRIS
248	WOOD SHAPED,SLEEPERS	W 822	0.4	W 2322	0.3	W 480	0.3		0.3	BOIS SIMPLEMENT TRAVAILLES
2482	LUMBER SHAPED CONIFER							W 321	0.3	CONIFERES SCIES,RABOTES
24821	LUMBER SAWN ETC CONIFER							W 321	0.3	CONIFERES SCIES LONGITUD
26	TEXTILE FIBRES AND WASTE		0.1		0.1		0.1		0.2	FIBRES TEXTILES
269	WASTE OF TEXTILE FABRICS	W 659	0.1	W 369	0.1	W 1113	0.1		0.2	FRIPERIE DRILLES,CHIFFONS
26901	BULK TEXT WSTE,OLD CLTHG							N 1143	0.2	ART ET ACCESS D'HABILLEMENT
27	CRUDE FERTLZR,MINRLS NES		0.1		0.2		0.1		0.1	ENGRAIS MINERAUX BRUTS
278	OTHER CRUDE MINERALS	W 226	0.1	W 349	0.2	W 201	0.1	W 392	0.1	AUTRES MINERAUX BRUTS
2789	MINERALS CRUDE NES	W 8	0.1	W 121	0.1	W 17	0.1			MINERAUX BRUTS NDA
3	MINERAL FUELS ETC		2.9		2.1		2.5		3.5	COMBUSTIBLES MINERAUX LUB
33	PETROLEUM AND PRODUCTS		2.9		2.1		2.5		3.5	PETROLE ET DERIVES
334	PETROLEUM PRODUCTS,REFIN	W 10584	2.9	W 9504	2.1	W 8315	2.5		3.4	PRODUITS RAFFINES
3341	GASOLINE,OTH LIGHT OILS	W 4207	1.3	W 2377	0.6	W 2605	1.0		2.7	ESSENCES POUR MOTEURS
33411	MOTOR,AVIATION SPIRIT	W 2402	0.7	W 1650	0.5	W 1659	0.5	W 2585	1.0	ESSENCES MOTEURS D'AVIONS
33412	SPIRIT TYPE JET FUEL	W 1805	0.6	W 727	0.2	W 946	0.6	W 270	0.1	CARBUREACTEURS
33419	OTH LIGHT PETROLEUM OILS								1.7	AUTRES HUILES LEGERES
3342	KEROSENE,OTH MEDIUM OILS	W 686	0.2	W 1041	0.3	W 787	0.3	W 1141	0.6	PETR LAMPANTS,AUT HUIL
33421	KEROSENE INCL JET FUEL	W 686	0.2	W 1041	0.3	W 787	0.3	W 1141	0.6	PETROLES LAMPANTS
3343	GAS OILS	W 5579	1.4	W 5961	1.1	W 4752	1.1			GAS OILS
3345	LUBS,PETROLEUM OILS NES	W 112	0.1	W 126	0.1	W 172	0.2		0.2	HUILES LUBRIFIANTES
33451	LUBS(HIGH PETR CONT) ETC	W 112	0.1	W 126	0.1	W 172	0.2	W 123	0.2	HUILES LUBRIF,H LOURDES
4	ANIMAL,VEGETABLE OIL,FAT		0.1		0.1		0.1		0.3	HUILES,GRAISSES ANIM,VEG
5	CHEMCLS,RELATED PROD NES		1.2		1.7		1.5		2.4	PRODUITS CHIMIQUES
53	DYES,TANNING,COLOUR PROD		0.2		0.2		0.2		0.3	PROD TEINTURE,COLORANTS
533	PIGMENTS,PAINTS,ETC		0.2		0.2		0.2		0.3	PIGMENTS,PEINTURES,VERNIS
5334	VARNISHES,DISTEMPERS ETC	W 22	0.2	V 51	0.2	V 42	0.2	V 48	0.2	PEINTURES A L'EAU
541	*MEDICINAL,PHARM PRODUCT		0.4		0.7		0.5		0.4	PROD MEDICINAUX PHARMACEUT

4. General Imports F.O.B. by Commodities according to the S.I.T.C. (Rev. 2) in million U.S. Dollars
Importations Générales F.O.B. par Produits d'après la C.T.C.I. (Rév. 2) en millions de Dollars E.U.

SITC CTCI	COMMODITY	1992 QUANTITY QUANTITE	1992 VALUE VALEUR	1993 QUANTITY QUANTITE	1993 VALUE VALEUR	1994 QUANTITY QUANTITE	1994 VALUE VALEUR	1995 QUANTITY QUANTITE	1995 VALUE VALEUR	PRODUIT
5419	PHARMACEUTICAL GOODS NES		0.3		0.6		0.5		0.4	PREP,ART PHARMACEUTIQUES
54191	BANDAGES PREPARED ETC						0.5		0.1	OUATES,GAZES,BANDES
54199	OTH PHARMACEUTICAL GOODS		0.3		0.6		0.1		0.3	AUT PREP PHARMACEUTIQUES
55	PERFUME,CLEANING ETC PRD		0.5		0.6		0.7		0.8	PROD POUR PARFUM,TOILETTE
553	PERFUMERY,COSMETICS,ETC		0.2		0.3		0.2		0.3	PRODUITS DE PARFUMERIE
554	SOAP,CLEANSING ETC PREPS		0.4		0.4		0.5		0.6	SAVONS,PRODUITS DETERSIFS
5541	SOAPS	W 291	0.4	W 365	0.4	W 303	0.5	W 374	0.5	SAVONS,PROD TENSIO–ACTIFS
5542	WASHING PREPARATIONS ETC							W 77	0.2	PROD ORG TENSIO–ACT NDA
572	*EXPLOSIVES,PYROTECH PRO		0.1				0.1		0.5	EXPLOSIFS
5723	PYROTECHNIC ARTICLES								0.5	ARTICLES DE PYROTECHNIE
59	CHEMICAL MATERIALS NES		0.1		0.2		0.2		0.6	MAT PROD CHIMIQUES NDA
591	PESTICIDES,DISINFECTANTS		0.1		0.1		0.1		0.5	DESINF,INSECT,FONG,HERB
5912	FUNGICIDES,FOR RETAIL								0.4	FONGICIDES VENTE AU DET
6	BASIC MANUFACTURES		3.0		3.5		3.6		6.6	ART MANUFACTURES
62	RUBBER MANUFACTURES NES		0.2		0.3		0.3		0.2	CAOUTCHOUC MANUFACTURE
625	RUBBER TYRES, TUBES ETC	N 12875	0.2	N 14334	0.2	N 10757	0.3	N 17938	0.2	PNEUS CAOUTCHOUC VULCANISE
6251	TYRES NEW FOR MOTOR CARS	N 4840	0.2	N 7371	0.2	N 6257	0.3	N 1173	0.1	PNEUS POUR VOITURES
63	WOOD,CORK MANUFACTRS NES		0.4		0.4		0.4		0.6	OUVRAGES LIEGE ET BOIS
634	VENEERS,PLYWOOD,ETC		0.3	A 1	0.3	A 1	0.3	V 1268	0.6	PLACAGES,CONTRE–PLAQUES
6341	VENEER SHEETS ETC							V 541	0.2	BOIS SIMPLEMENT SCIES
6342	PLYWOOD OF WOOD SHEETS							V 338	0.2	BOIS CONTRE–PLAQUES
6349	WOOD SIMPLY SHAPED NES							V 293	0.2	BOIS SIMPL TRAVAILLES NDA
63491	HOOPWOOD,SPLIT POLES ETC							V 293	0.2	BOIS ETC
635	WOOD MANUFACTURES NES		0.1		0.1		0.2		0.1	ART MANUF EN BOIS NDA
64	PAPER,PAPERBOARD AND MFR		0.5		0.4		0.4		0.8	PAPIERS,CARTONS & OUVRAGES
641	PAPER AND PAPERBOARD		0.1		0.2		0.2		0.2	PAPIERS ET CARTONS
6419	CONVERTED PAPER ETC NES		0.1		0.1		0.2		0.1	PAP,CART TRANSFORMES NDA
64192	COMPOSITE PAPER ETC,BULK				0.1		0.2		0.1	PAP,CART SIMPL ASSEMBLE
642	PAPER,ETC,PRECUT,ARTS OF		0.4		0.3		0.3		0.6	PAP,CARTONS DECOUPES
6422	CORRESPONDENCE STATIONRY		0.4		0.3		0.3		0.1	ARTICLES CORRESPONDANCE
6423	EXERCISE BOOKS ETC								0.3	REGISTRES,CAHIERS,CARNETS
6424	PAPER ETC CT TO SIZE NES		0.1		0.1		0.1		0.2	PAP,CARTONS DECOUPES
64243	TOILET PAPER CUT TO SIZE								0.2	PAPIER HYGIENIQUE
65	TEXTILE YARN,FABRICS,ETC		0.7		0.7		1.0		1.0	FILS,TISSUS,ARTICLES TEXTILE
651	TEXTILE YARN		0.1		0.1		0.1		0.2	FILS TEXTILES
652	COTTON FABRICS,WOVEN	A 268	0.3	A 272	0.3	A 240	0.3		0.4	TISSUS DE COTON
6521	GREY WOVEN COTTON FABRIC							A 281	0.4	TISSUS COT ECRUS NON MERCER
65215	GREY WOVN COTN BLEND NES							A 266	0.4	AUT TIS MOINS 85% COT ECRUS
653	WOVN MAN–MADE FIB FABRIC		0.1	A 168	0.2	A 62	0.2	A 95	0.2	TISSUS FIBRES SYNTH,ARTIF
657	SPECIAL TXTL FABRC,PRODS		0.2		0.1		0.3		0.2	TISSUS SPECIAUX
6575	CORDAGE AND MANUFACTURES	W 27	0.2	W 11	0.1	W 18	0.2		0.2	FICELLES,CORDES,CORDAGES
65751	CORDAGE,CABLE,ROPE,TWINE	W 14	0.1	W 7	0.1	W 7	0.1	W 4	0.1	CORDAGES TRESSES OU NON
65752	NETTING OF ROPE,TWINE	W 13	0.1	W 3	0.1	W 12	0.2	W 9	0.1	FILETS MAT DU 657.51
658	TEXTILE ARTICLES NES		0.2		0.1		0.3		0.2	ART FACONNES MAT TEXTILES
6581	BAGS,SACKS OF TEXTILES	W 86	0.1			W 79	0.1	W 24	0.1	SACS EMBALLAGE TEXTILES
6584	LINENS ETC		0.1		0.1		0.1		0.1	LINGE DE MAISON
66	NONMETAL MINERAL MFS NES		0.3		0.5		0.4		0.6	ART MIN NON METALLIQUES
661	LIME,CEMENT,BLDG PRODS	W 1369	0.2	W 2813	0.4	W 2164	0.3	W 3267	0.4	CHAUX,CIMENTS MAT CONSTR
6612	CEMENT	W 1369	0.2	W 2813	0.4	W 2164	0.3	W 3267	0.4	CIMENTS HYDRAULIQUES
662	CLAY,REFRACTORY BLDG PRD		0.1		0.1		0.1		0.1	MAT CONST REFRACTAIRES
67	IRON AND STEEL		0.3		0.3		0.2		0.2	FER ET ACIER
673	IRON,STEEL SHAPES ETC	W 28	0.1	W 128	0.2	W 29	0.1	W 26	0.1	BARRES,PROFIL FER,ACIER
677	IRN,STL WIRE(EXCL W ROD)	W 98	0.2	W 43	0.1	W 12	0.1		0.1	FILS EN FER,ACIER
68	NON–FERROUS METALS		0.2		0.1		0.1		0.2	METAUX NON FERREUX
684	ALUMINIUM	W 56	0.2	W 34	0.1	W 66	0.1	W 5	0.2	ALUMINIUM
6842	ALUMINIUM,ALLOYS WORKED							W 5	0.2	ALUMINIUM,ALLIAGES OUVRE
69	METAL MANUFACTURES NES		0.8		1.0		1.0		3.4	ART MANUFACT EN METAL NDA
691	STRUCTURES AND PARTS NES	W 102	0.2	W 205	0.3	W 94	0.3		0.5	CONSTRUCT FER,ACIER,ALU
6911	STRUCTURES,PARTS IRN,STL								0.3	CONSTRUCT FER,ACIER,FONTE
6912	STRUCTURES,PARTS ALUMNM							N 251	0.2	CONSTRUCT ALUMINIUM
692	METAL TANKS,BOXES,ETC		0.1		0.1		0.1		0.7	RECIPIENTS METALLIQUES
6924	MTL TRANSPORT BOXES ETC		0.1		0.1		0.1		0.6	FUTS,TAMBOURS,BIDONS
69241	STL TRANSPORT BOXES ETC								0.6	FUTS,TAMBOURS,BIDONS FER
693	WIRE PRODUCTS NON ELECTR		0.2	W 108039	0.2	W 93	0.1	W 1	0.2	OUVRAGES FILS METALLIQUES
6931	WIRE CABLES, ROPES ETC	W 4	0.1	W 42838	0.1	W 5	0.1	W 1	0.1	CORDAGES EN FILS DE FER
6935	METAL FENCING,GAUZE,ETC	W 63	0.2	W 64329	0.2	W 86	0.1		0.2	TOILES EN FER,ACIER,CUIVRE
69351	IRN,STL FENCNG,GAUZE ETC								0.2	TOILES EN FER,ACIER
694	STL,COPPR NAILS,NUTS,ETC		0.1		0.1		0.2	W 10	0.1	CLOUS,VIS,ECROUS
69401	IRON,STEEL NAILS ETC		0.1		0.1		0.2	W 7	0.1	CLOUS,POINTES FER,ACIER
695	TOOLS		0.2		0.2		0.2		0.2	OUTILS A MAIN
697	BASE MTL HOUSEHOLD EQUIP		0.2		0.1		0.2		0.2	ART MENAGE MET COMMUNS
699	BASE METAL MFRS NES		0.2		0.2		0.2		1.7	ART MANUFACTURES MET NDA
6991	LOCKSMITHS WARES,ETC		0.1		0.1		0.1		0.1	ARTICLES DE SERRURERIE
69911	LOCKS,KEYS AND PARTS				0.1		0.1		0.1	SERRURES,VERROUS,CADENAS
6996	BASE MTL MISC ARTICLES								1.4	ART DIVERS METAUX COMMUNS
69965	BASE MTL SOLDERING RODS								1.4	FILS,BAGUETTES POUR SOUDURE
7	MACHINES,TRANSPORT EQUIP		17.4		6.9		4.6		5.1	MACHINES MATERIEL TRANSPORT
71	POWER GENERATING EQUIPMT		1.3		0.5		0.6		0.8	MACHINES GENERATRICES
713	INTRNL COMBUS PSTN ENGIN		0.3		0.3		0.2		0.4	MOTEURS EXPL COMB INT, PIECE
7133	MARINE PISTON ENGINES	N 180	0.2	N 631	0.3	N 170	0.2	N 218	0.3	MOTEURS EXPL POUR BATEAUX
71331	—— OUTBOARD	N 180	0.2					N 212	0.3	MOTEURS BATEAUX HORSBORD
716	ROTATING ELECTRIC PLANT		1.0		0.2	N 477	0.3		0.3	APP ELECTR ROTATIFS,PIECES
7161	DC MOTORS AND GENERATORS							N 222	0.2	MOTEURS COURANT CONTINU
72	MACHS FOR SPCL INDUSTRYS		0.3		0.4		0.2		0.4	MAC SPECIALES POUR INDUST
723	CIVIL ENGNEERG EQUIP ETC	N 4	0.2	N 6	0.3	N 6	0.1	N 1	0.1	APPAREILS DE GENIE CIVIL
74	GENRL INDUSTRL MACHY NES		0.8		0.6		0.5		0.9	MACH APP INDUSTRIE
741	HEATING,COOLING EQUIPMNT		0.3		0.2		0.2		0.2	MACH CHAUFFAGE,PIECES
7414	NONDOM REFRIG EQUIPT,PTS		0.2		0.1	N 189682	0.1		0.1	MAT PRODUCTION DU FROID
74141	REFRIG EQUIP NONDOMESTIC		0.2					N 23	0.1	REFIG INDUSTRIELS
7415	AIR–CONDITIONING MACHNRY	N 144	0.1	N 141	0.1	N 203	0.1	N 286	0.2	GROUPES CONDITION AIR
742	PUMPS FOR LIQUIDS ETC		0.2		0.1		0.1		0.2	POMPES MOTO–POMPES
7428	OTHER PUMPS FOR LIQUIDS	N 1045	0.2	N 218	0.1	N 514	0.1	N 3135	0.2	AUTRES POMPES POUR LIQ
74288	PUMPS FR LIQUIDS NES ETC			N 218	0.1	N 514	0.1	N 3135	0.2	POMPES POUR LIQUIDES NDA
743	PUMPS NES,CENTRFUGES ETC		0.2		0.1		0.1		0.1	POMPES COMPRES,VENT ETC
7431	PUMPS FOR GASES ETC		0.2	N 1285	0.1	N 4911	0.1	N 2144	0.1	POMPES AIR A VIDE,COMPRES
744	MECHANICAL HANDLING EQU		0.1		0.2		0.1		0.5	EQUIP MANUTENTION PIECES
7441	FORK LIFT TRCKS,ETC,PTS		0.1	N 5	0.1	N 5	0.1		0.2	CHARIOTS POUR USINES ETC
74419	PTS NES OF VEHC OF 74411								0.2	PIECES POUR 744.11
7442	LIFTING,LOADING MACH NES		0.1		0.1		0.1	N 25021	0.2	APP LEVAGE,MANUTENTION
74428	OTH HANDLING ETC MCH NES							N 25014	0.2	AUT APP LEVAGE ETC
7449	PTS NES OF MACHY OF 7442		0.1		0.1		0.1		0.1	PIECES DU 744.2

4. General Imports F.O.B. by Commodities according to the S.I.T.C. (Rev. 2) in million U.S. Dollars
Importations Générales F.O.B. par Produits d'après la C.T.C.I. (Rév. 2) en millions de Dollars E.U.

SITC CTCI	COMMODITY	1992		1993		1994		1995		PRODUIT
		QUANTITY QUANTITE	VALUE VALEUR	QUANTITY QUANTITE	VALUE VALEUR	QUANTITY QUANTITE	VALUE VALEUR	QUANTITY QUANTITE	VALUE VALEUR	
75	OFFICE MACHNES,ADP EQUIP		0.3		0.3		0.3		0.3	MACH BUREAU TRAIT AUTOM
752	AUTOMTIC DATA PROC EQUIP	N 93	0.2	N 183	0.2	N 173	0.2	N 106	0.2	MACH TRAIT INFORMATION
76	TELECOMM,SOUND EQUIPMENT		6.4		1.2		1.2		0.4	EQUIPMENT DE TELECOM
764	TELECOM EQPT,PTS,ACC NES	N 2801	6.3	N 1761	1.1	N 4271	1.1		0.3	EQUIP TELECOM,PIECES
77	ELECTRIC MACHNRY NES ETC		1.1		1.9		0.7		0.9	MACH APP ELECT NDA
772	SWITCHGEAR ETC,PARTS NES		0.4		0.6		0.1		0.2	APP COUPURE,SECT ETC
7721	SWITCHGEAR ETC								0.2	APP COUPURE,SECTIONMNT
775	HOUSEHOLD TYPE EQUIP NES		0.1		0.2		0.2		0.2	MACH,APP USAGE DOMESTQUE
7752	DOM REFRIGERATRS,FREEZRS	N 169	0.1	N 662	0.1	N 632	0.1	N 200	0.1	REFRIG,CONGEL MENAGER
776	TRANSISTORS,VALVES,ETC		0.3		0.1		0.2		0.1	LAMPES,TUBES,VALVES
778	ELECTRICAL MACHINERY NES		0.4		1.0		0.3		0.5	AUTRES MACH ELECT NDA
7781	BATTERIES,ACCUMULATORS	N 1038961	0.2	N 944559	0.3	N 746508	0.2	N 1090975	0.3	PILES ET ACCUMULATEURS
77811	PRIMARY BATTERIES,CELLS	N 1038243	0.2	N 943916	0.3	N 746030	0.2	N 1090702	0.3	PILES ELECTRIQUES,PIECES
7788	OTH ELEC MACHY,EQUIP NES		0.1		0.6		0.1		0.1	AUT MACH APP ELEC NDA
77886	OTH ELEC MACHINERY NES				0.6		0.1		0.1	AUT MACH APP ELECTRIQUES
78	ROAD VEHICLES		1.5		2.2		1.4		1.4	VEHICULES ROUTIERS
781	PASS MOTOR VEH EXC BUSES			N 1402	1.1	N 84	0.5	N 63	0.2	AUTO TRANSPORT PERSONNES
782	LORRIES,SPCL MTR VEH NES	N 116	0.9	N 27	0.5	N 27	0.4	N 42	0.5	VEHICULES SPECIAUX,MARCH
7821	LORRIES,TRUCKS	N 116	0.9	N 27	0.5	N 27	0.4	N 41	0.5	VEHICULES TRANSP MARCHAND
783	ROAD MOTOR VEHICLES NES	N 17	0.2	N 35	0.3	N 18	0.2	N 14	0.3	VEHICULES ROUTIERS NDA
7831	BUSES	N 17	0.2	N 23	0.3	N 18	0.2	N 14	0.3	VOITURES TRANSPORT COMMUN
784	MOTOR VEH PRTS,ACCES NES		0.2		0.2		0.1		0.2	PIECES 722,781,782,783
7849	OTHER MOTOR VEHCL PARTS								0.2	PIECES 722,781,782,783
785	CYCLES,ETC MOTRZD OR NOT		0.4		0.3		0.3		0.4	MOTOCYCLES SCOOTERS
7852	CYCLES, ETC NON–MOTOR	N 3751	0.3	N 1995	0.2	N 2248	0.2	N 3490	0.3	VELOCIPEDES SANS MOTEUR
79	OTHR TRANSPORT EQUIPMENT		6.1		0.1		0.2		0.3	AUTRE MATERIEL TRANSPORT
792	AIRCRAFT ETC		0.1		0.1		0.1		0.2	APP NAVIGATION AERIENNE
7929	AIRCRAFT PARTS NES		0.1		0.1		0.1		0.2	PIECES DU 792
793	SHIPS AND BOATS ETC		6.1		0.1		0.1		0.2	NAVIRES BATEAUX,ETC
7932	SHIPS AND BOATS NES	N 9	6.0	N 17	0.1	N 9	0.1	N 42	0.1	NAVIRES ET BATEAUX
7938	TUGS,SPECIAL VESSELS ETC		0.2		0.1		0.1		0.1	REMORQUEURS,BATEAUX SPEC
8	MISC MANUFACTURED GOODS		2.2		3.1		2.9		2.6	ART MANUFACTURES DIVERS
812	*PLUMBG,HEATNG,LGHTNG EQ		0.2		0.1		0.2		0.2	APPAR SANITAIRES CHAUFFAGE
8124	LIGHTING EQUIPMENT NES		0.1		0.1		0.1		0.2	APPAREILS ECLAIRAGE ETC
821	*FURNITURE,PARTS THEREOF		0.2		1.0		0.3		0.3	MEUBLES ET PIECES
8219	FURNITURE AND PARTS NES								0.3	AUTRES MEUBLES ET PIECES
82191	METAL FURNITURE NES								0.2	MEUBLES NDA EN METAL
84	CLOTHING AND ACCESSORIES		0.4		0.3		0.4		0.4	VETEMENTS
846	UNDER GARMENTS KNITTED		0.1		0.1		0.1		0.1	SOUS VETS DE BONNETERIE
8462	— OF COTTON NON ELASTIC		0.1		0.1		0.1		0.1	SOUS–VET BONNET COTON
84629	—— OTHER		0.1		0.1		0.1		0.1	AUT SOUS–VET BONNET COTON
87	PRECISION INSTRUMNTS NES		0.5		0.2		0.7		0.2	INSTRUM,APPAR SCIENT NDA
874	MEASURNG,CONTROLNG INSTR		0.4		0.2		0.7		0.1	INSTRUMENTS DE MESURE
8742	MEASUR,DRAW ETC INST,PTS				0.2		0.7		0.1	INST DESSIN,TRACAGE,PCS
89	MISC MANUFCTRD GOODS NES		1.1		1.5		1.4		1.6	ART MANUFACTURES DIVERS
892	PRINTED MATTER		0.3		0.6		0.4		0.7	IMPRIMES
8921	PRINTED BOOKS,GLOBES,ETC								0.4	LIVRES,BROCHURES,CARTES
89211	PRINTED BOOKS,PAMPHLETS								0.4	LIVRES,BROCHURES
8928	PRINTED MATTER NES								0.3	IMPRIMES NDA
89283	UNISSUED BANKNOTES ETC								0.2	TIMBRES–POSTE FISCAUX
893	ARTICLES OF PLASTIC NES		0.4		0.4		0.6		0.4	OUVRAGES EN MAT DIVIS 58
8931	PLSTC PACKG CONTNRS,LIDS		0.3						0.1	ART TRANSP EMBALLAGE ETC
8939	MISC PLASTIC ARTICLES		0.2		0.4		0.6		0.3	ART DIVERS EN MAT DIV 58
89399	OTHR PLASTC ARTICLES NES		0.2		0.4		0.6		0.3	AUT OUV MAT DIV 58
894	TOYS,SPORTING GOODS,ETC		0.2		0.2		0.2		0.2	VOITURES ENFANTS,JOUETS
8947	OTH SPORT GDS,FAIR AMUSM		0.2		0.2		0.2		0.1	AUT ART DE SPORT
89471	FISHNG,HUNTNG EQUIP NES		0.2		0.1		0.1		0.1	HAMECONS ET EPUISETTES
895	OFFICE SUPPLIES NES		0.1		0.2		0.1		0.2	ART PAPET NDA
899	OTHER MANUFACTURED GOODS		0.2		0.3		0.2		0.3	AUT ART MANUF DIVERS NDA
8993	COMBUSTIBLE PRODUCTS ETC		0.1		0.1		0.1		0.2	BOUGIES,ALLUMETTES ETC
8998	SMALLWARES,TOILETRYS ETC		0.1		0.2		0.1		0.1	ART MERCERIE,TOILETTE
89983	BUTTONS,STUDS,ETC				0.2		0.1			BOUTONS,BOUTONS–PRESSION
9	GOODS NOT CLASSD BY KIND		0.2		0.2		0.3		0.3	ART TRANSACT NON CLASSES
931	*SPECIAL TRANSACTIONS		0.2		0.2		0.2		0.3	TRANS.SPECIALES

5. General Exports F.O.B. by Commodities according to the S.I.T.C. (Rev. 2) in million U.S. Dollars
Exportations Générales F.O.B. par Produits d'après la C.T.C.I. (Rév. 2) en millions de Dollars E.U.

SITC CTCI	COMMODITY	1992 QUANTITY QUANTITE	1992 VALUE VALEUR	1993 QUANTITY QUANTITE	1993 VALUE VALEUR	1994 QUANTITY QUANTITE	1994 VALUE VALEUR	1995 QUANTITY QUANTITE	1995 VALUE VALEUR	PRODUIT
	ALL COMMODITIES		4.8		3.1		5.6		7.2	TOUS PRODUITS
0	FOOD AND LIVE ANIMALS		0.6		1.3		1.4		1.6	ALIMENTS,ANIMAUX VIVANTS
03	FISH AND PREPARATIONS		0.6		1.3		1.4		1.6	POISSONS ET PREPARATIONS
034	FISH,FRESH,CHILLED,FROZN		0.5	W 354	0.8	W 90	0.6	W 123	0.8	POISSON FRAIS, REFRIG,CONG
0341	FISH FRSH,CHLLD,EX FILLT			W 354	0.8	W 90	0.6	W 123	0.8	POISSON FRAIS,REFRIGERE
035	FISH SALTED,DRIED,SMOKED	W 6	0.1	W 2	0.1	W 3	0.2	W 17	0.5	POISSON SECHE,SALE,FUME
03503	FISH(EX COD)DRIED,SALTED			W 2	0.1	W 3	0.2	W 17	0.5	POISSONS SECHES,SALES
036	SHELL FISH FRESH,FROZEN			W 97	0.5	W 47	0.7	W 45	0.4	CRUSTACES,MOLLUSQUES
2	CRUDE MATERLS,EXCL FUELS		3.4		1.4		3.6		4.7	MAT BRUTES NON COMESTIBLES
22	OIL SEEDS,OLEAGINOUS FRT		3.2		1.2		3.3		4.6	GRAINES,FRUITS OLEAGINEUX
223	SEEDS FOR OTH FIXED OILS	W 9907	3.2	W 6352	1.2	W 10317	3.3	W 13159	4.6	GRAINES AUTRES HUILES FIXES
2231	COPRA	W 9907	3.2	W 6352	1.2	W 10317	3.3	W 13159	4.6	COPRAH
29	CRUDE ANIMAL,VEG MAT NES		0.3		0.2		0.3		0.2	MATIERES BRUTES ANIM,VEGET
292	CRUDE VEG MATERIALS NES	W 388	0.3	W 373	0.2	W 374	0.3	W 178	0.2	MAT BRUTES VEGETALES NDA
2929	OTH CRUDE VEG MATERIALS	W 388	0.3	W 373	0.2	W 374	0.3	W 178	0.2	MATIERES VEGETALES NDA
29298	OTH CRD VEG MATERIAL NES			W 373	0.2	W 374	0.3	W 178	0.2	PRODUITS ORIGINE VEGET NDA
6	BASIC MANUFACTURES		0.1				0.1		0.1	ART MANUFACTURES
68	NON-FERROUS METALS		0.1							METAUX NON FERREUX
684	ALUMINIUM	W 79	0.1							ALUMINIUM
69	METAL MANUFACTURES NES						0.1		0.1	ART MANUFACT EN METAL NDA
692	METAL TANKS,BOXES,ETC					N 591	0.1	W 3	0.1	RECIPIENTS METALLIQUES
6924	MTL TRANSPORT BOXES ETC					N 591	0.1	W 3	0.1	FUTS,TAMBOURS,BIDONS
69243	IRN,STL COMP GAS CYLINDR					N 591	0.1	W 3	0.1	RECIP FER,ACIER GAZ COMP
8	MISC MANUFACTURED GOODS		0.1		0.1		0.1		0.1	ART MANUFACTURES DIVERS
88	PHOTO EQU,OPTICL GDS ETC		0.1		0.1		0.1		0.1	APP,FOURN PHOTO,OP,MONTR
883	DEVELOPED CINEMA FILM			N 44	0.1	N 55	0.1		0.1	FILMS CINE IMPRES NEG,POS
9	GOODS NOT CLASSD BY KIND		0.8		0.4		0.7		0.9	ART TRANSACT NON CLASSES
931	*SPECIAL TRANSACTIONS		0.8		0.4		0.7	W 36	0.9	TRANS.SPECIALES

1. HISTORICAL SERIES, 1962–1997 SPECIAL TRADE, IMPORTS C.I.F., EXPORTS F.O.B.
SERIES HISTORIQUES, 1962–1997 COMMERCE SPECIAL, IMPORTATIONS C.A.F., EXPORTATIONS F.O.B

YEAR ANNEE	VALUE IN MILLION U.S. DOLLARS / VALEUR EN MILLION U.S. DOLLARS — MERCHANDISE –MARCHANDISE IMPORTS	EXPORTS	GOLD –OR IMPORTS	EXPORTS	CONVERSION FACTORS FACTEURS DE CONVERSION CENTS E.U. PAR IMPORTS	EXPORTS	INDEX NUMBERS –INDICES — QUANTUM IMPORTS	EXPORTS	UNIT VALUE / VALEUR UNITAIRE IMPORTS	EXPORTS
1962	421.80	54.80								
1963	560.30	86.80								
1964	404.40	119.10								
1965	463.40	175.10								
1966	716.40	250.30								
1967	996.20	320.20								
1968	1462.50	455.40								
1969	1822.80	622.50								
1970	1983.30	835.20								
1971	2393.60	1067.60								
1972	2522.00	1624.10								
1973	4240.30	3225.00								
1974	6851.80	4460.40								
1975	7274.40	5081.00								
1976	8773.60	7715.10								
1977	10810.50	10046.50								
1978	14971.90	12710.60								
1979	20338.60	15055.50								
1980	22291.60	17504.90					33	33	82	70
1981	26131.40	21253.80					37	39	97	81
1982	24250.80	21853.30					37	41	97	85
1983	26192.00	24445.10					42	48	98	86
1984	30631.40	29244.90					49	55	103	93
1985	31135.70	30283.10					52	60	106	96
1986	31598.64	34747.24					56	67	101	100
1987	41157.03	47358.22					67	83	101	102
1988	51968.66	60993.43					77	93	100	103
1989	61476.98	62384.04					89	94	93	97
1990	69739.79	64879.61					100	100	100	100
1991	81525.01	71870.00					117	110	104	104
1992	81775.01	76632.00					119	119	109	109
1993	83800.00	82236.00					127	127	107	111
1994	102348.00	96013.01					154	146	108	115
1995	135119.00	125058.00					187	181	113	116
1996	150339.00	129715.00					210	217	117	105
1997	144614.90	136740.90					213	271		105

2. IMPORTS BY BROAD ECONOMIC CATEGORY AND EXPORTS BY INDUSTRIAL ORIGIN. (PERCENTAGE OF TOTAL VALUE)
IMPORTATIONS PAR CATEGORIES ECONOMIQUES ET EXPORTATIONS PAR BRANCHE D'ACTIVITE.(EN POURCENTAGE DE LA VALEUR TOTALE)

IMPORTS – IMPORTATIONS

	1990	1991	1992	1993	1994	1995	1996
TOTAL IMPORTS–IMPORTATIONS TOTALES	100.	100.	100.	100.	100.	100.	100.
1 FOOD BEV–ALIMENTATION BOISSONS	3.7	4.3	4.3	4.1	4.3	3.7	4.1
11 PRIMARY–PRODUITS DE BASE	2.4	3.0	2.8	2.6	2.8	2.3	2.6
111 FOR INDUSTRY–POUR L'INDUSTRIE	1.3	1.3	1.4	1.4	1.4	1.0	1.3
112 FOR HOUSEHOLDS–POUR LES MENAGES	1.1	1.7	1.4	1.2	1.4	1.2	1.3
12 PROCESSED–PRODUITS ELABORES	1.3	1.3	1.5	1.5	1.5	1.5	1.5
121 FOR INDUSTRY–POUR L'INDUSTRIE	0.8	0.7	0.7	0.7	0.7	0.6	0.6
122 FOR HOUSEHOLDS–POUR LES MENAGES	0.5	0.6	0.8	0.8	0.8	0.8	0.9
2 IND SUPPLIES–APPROV INDUSTRIELS	39.9	38.9	35.7	36.4	35.5	36.2	32.7
21 PRIMARY–PRODUITS DE BASE	11.2	9.7	8.9	9.1	7.7	7.5	6.7
22 PROCESSED–PRODUITS ELABORES	28.7	29.2	26.8	27.4	27.8	28.7	26.0
3 FUELS–COMBUSTIBLES	15.8	15.7	18.0	18.0	15.2	14.3	16.7
31 PRIMARY–PRODUITS DE BASE	12.2	13.1	15.1	14.7	12.0	11.4	13.6
32 PROCESSED–PRODUITS ELABORES	3.6	2.6	2.8	3.3	3.2	3.0	3.2
321 MOTOR SPIRIT–ESSENCE	0.7		1.4	1.6			
322 OTHER–AUTRES	2.9	2.6	1.4	1.8	3.2	3.0	3.2
4 MACHINERY–EQUIPEMENT	30.9	31.1	31.2	30.3	32.5	34.0	34.6
41 CAPITAL EQUIPMENT–MACHINES	21.2	21.4	20.8	20.5	22.6	23.5	23.6
42 PARTS–PIECES ACCESSOIRES	9.7	9.7	10.4	9.7	9.9	10.5	11.0
5 TRANSPORT–TRANSPORT	5.4	5.8	6.4	6.0	7.1	6.3	6.0
51 PASSENGER CARS–AUTOMOBILES	0.1	0.0	0.1	0.1	0.1	0.2	0.3
52 OTHER–AUTRES	2.5	2.7	3.2	2.5	3.1	2.6	2.9
521 INDUSTRIAL–INDUSTRIELS	2.5	2.7	3.2	2.5	3.1	2.6	2.9
522 NON INDUSTRIAL–NON INDUSTRIEL	0.0	0.0	0.0	0.0	0.0	0.0	0.0
53 PARTS–PIECES ACCESSOIRES	2.8	3.0	3.1	3.4	3.9	3.5	2.8
6 CONSUM GOODS–BIENS CONSOMMATION	3.8	3.7	3.9	4.5	4.9	5.1	5.6
61 DURABLE–DURABLES	1.3	1.1	1.0	1.2	1.2	1.2	1.3
62 SEMI DURABLE–SEMI DURABLES	1.6	1.7	1.9	2.2	2.5	2.7	3.1
63 NON DURABLE–NON DURABLES	0.9	0.9	1.0	1.1	1.1	1.1	1.3
7 GOODS NES–BIENS NDA	0.5	0.6	0.5	0.7	0.5	0.3	0.3

EXPORTS – EXPORTATIONS

	1990	1991	1992	1993	1994	1995	1996
TOTAL EXPORTS–EXPORTATIONS TOTALES	100.	100.	100.	100.	100.	100.	100.
1 AGRICULTURE	2.6	2.5	2.1	1.7	1.6	1.4	1.3
2 MINING QUARRY–INDUS EXTRACTIVES	0.2	0.2	0.2	0.2	0.2	0.1	0.1
3 MANUFACTURING–IND MANUFACTUR	97.2	97.3	97.7	98.1	98.2	98.5	98.6
31 FOOD BEV TOBACCO–ALIM BOISS TAB	1.3	1.2	1.2	1.2	1.2	1.2	1.4
32 TEXTILES–INDUSTRIES TEXTILES	30.0	27.7	25.6	23.0	20.8	16.8	16.1
33 WOOD & PRODUCTS–BOIS & PRODUITS	0.2	0.2	0.1	0.1	0.1	0.1	0.1
34 PAPER & PRODUCTS–PAPIER & PRODT	0.8	0.7	0.8	0.8	1.0	1.1	1.1
35 CHEMICALS–INDUSTRIES CHIMIQUES	8.6	9.8	11.6	11.8	11.8	12.4	13.6
36 NON METAL MIN–MIN NON METAL	1.0	0.9	0.8	0.8	0.7	0.6	0.6
37 BASIC METAL–IND METAL BASE	6.4	6.1	6.7	6.7	5.8	5.4	5.1
38 METAL MANUF–MANUF METAL	45.2	47.3	48.0	51.1	54.5	58.9	58.8
39 OTH MANUF IND–AUTRES MANUF	3.7	3.4	3.0	2.5	2.1	1.9	1.8

3. TRADE BY PRINCIPAL COUNTRIES OF ORIGIN AND DESTINATION (VALUE IN MILLION U.S. DOLLARS)
ECHANGES SELON LES PRINCIPAUX PAYS D'ORIGINE ET DE DESTINATION (VALEUR EN MILLIONS DE DOLLARS EU)

COUNTRIES–PAYS	SPECIAL IMPORTS C.I.F. IMPORTATIONS SPECIALES C.A.F				
	1992	1993	1994	1995	1996
World	81758.4	83794.0	102342.5	135112.9	150334.3
Africa	1080.2	954.0	1428.0	2271.7	2865.8
Americas	22376.4	22004.7	26860.3	36969.8	40419.1
– Northern America	19888.4	19644.5	23604.2	33022.8	36043.9
– LAIA	2034.9	2006.4	2547.5	3435.3	3703.5
– CACM	22.4	26.8	36.8	50.2	43.3
– Caribbean	57.0	44.0	62.6	45.7	74.2
– Rest of America	373.7	283.0	609.2	415.7	554.2
Asia excl fmr USSR	42019.5	43111.3	51220.2	66345.7	72164.2
– Middle East	8775.2	8627.8	9025.0	11349.9	14506.2
Asia former USSR	9.8	65.2	169.1	216.9	333.5
Europe excl fmr USSR	11493.1	11995.3	15852.8	20265.0	24111.7
– European Union	10473.8	11124.1	14537.9	18192.8	21206.6
– Eastern Europe	170.1	117.3	251.9	300.6	329.6
– Rest of Europe	849.2	753.9	1063.0	1771.6	2575.5
Europe former USSR	576.4	1055.0	1352.4	2069.8	1966.7
Oceania	3807.4	4357.5	4787.7	6050.5	7405.6
Other	395.6	251.0	671.9	923.5	1067.6
Japan/Japon	19457.6	20015.2	25388.5	32604.1	31447.7
USA/Etats–Unis d'Amer	18319.0	17951.6	21598.6	30418.7	33319.8
China/Chine	3724.7	3928.6	5462.7	7400.9	8538.2
Germany/Allemagne	3742.5	3954.7	5159.4	6583.8	7239.2
Saudi Arabia	3797.4	3734.7	3815.5	5432.1	6666.9
Australia/Australie	3077.4	3344.3	3780.9	4897.1	6271.7
Indonesia/Indonésie	2292.0	2588.4	2842.9	3325.2	4013.0
Malaysia/Malaisie	1758.2	1946.5	1876.0	2515.2	3006.5
Canada	1568.5	1692.5	2004.3	2603.5	2723.3
Italy/Italie	1348.5	1397.6	1954.4	2425.4	3070.2
Other Asia n.e.s.	1315.2	1407.1	1799.5	2563.7	2725.4
United Kingdom	1354.9	1400.8	1662.0	2387.2	2994.3
Singapore/Singapour	1788.3	1539.9	1659.8	2168.0	2527.2
France, Monaco	1381.2	1486.1	1819.9	1948.6	2208.2
United Arab Emirates	1282.9	1233.1	1080.8	1558.1	2259.2
Russian Federation	569.3	974.8	1229.6	1892.9	1810.3
Iran (Islamic Rep of)	1062.0	1092.9	1280.2	1258.4	1634.4
Switzerland,Liechtenst.	671.8	608.2	869.8	1474.4	2251.7
Oman	1329.4	1117.1	787.9	927.9	1221.6
Brazil/Brésil	796.9	779.3	1019.1	1388.2	1324.6
So. African Customs Un	651.7	549.8	764.2	1240.9	1723.9
Netherlands/Pays–Bas	628.6	770.2	815.7	1112.8	1207.9
Kuwait/ Koweït	340.6	713.5	864.3	1068.0	1444.5
China, Hong Kong SAR	793.9	934.8	660.0	837.4	1142.6
Thailand/Thaïlande	637.8	538.5	619.8	935.5	1218.8
Chile/Chili	365.5	538.0	705.4	1020.9	1102.5
India/Inde	477.5	523.4	584.6	798.3	975.7
New Zealand	488.1	570.7	662.9	817.2	816.2
Sweden/Suède	476.0	418.4	614.4	755.6	795.7
Belgium–Luxembourg	474.1	416.2	532.4	742.3	728.6
Spain/Espagne	266.0	345.2	691.4	562.3	698.8
Panama	370.1	278.9	599.9	406.2	547.7
Philippines	264.9	317.5	411.8	610.8	581.3
Finland/Finlande	203.4	303.0	393.9	538.3	653.8
Denmark/Danemark	223.1	225.0	368.0	425.7	551.8
Brunei Darussalam	313.6	273.4	311.6	376.0	474.8
Austria/Autriche	211.3	231.3	290.9	430.0	579.4
Ecuador/Equateur	393.7	310.1	327.6	311.9	346.1
Free zones/Zone franches		212.0	611.0	863.0	
Areas n.e.s.	395.6	39.0	60.9	60.5	1067.6

COUNTRIES–PAYS	SPECIAL EXPORTS F.O.B. EXPORTATIONS SPECIALES F.O.B.				
	1992	1993	1994	1995	1996
Monde	76631.5	82232.1	96007.7	125056.5	129714.6
Afrique	2577.3	2004.1	3146.1	3060.2	3356.1
Amériques	24660.6	24429.6	28367.6	33291.0	31797.2
– Amérique du Nord	19762.9	19736.1	22094.8	26182.8	23131.0
– ALAI	2564.6	3162.5	3785.7	4280.2	4568.9
– MCAC	218.1	251.3	287.7	324.9	356.9
– Caraïbes	261.9	186.1	221.1	244.9	537.1
– Autre Amérique	1853.1	1093.6	1978.3	2258.3	3203.3
Asie anc. URSS exclus	36572.5	42457.2	49119.5	66037.2	70635.1
– Moyen–Orient	3569.0	3813.6	3491.4	4367.6	5181.5
Asie ancienne URSS	5.7	143.0	270.3	318.7	618.6
Europe anc. URSS exclus	10758.0	10928.7	12339.1	18648.6	18362.4
– Union Européenne	9832.5	9941.9	11248.6	16304.3	15377.0
– Europe de l'Est	309.9	557.8	586.7	1132.4	1786.0
– Autre de l'Europe	615.6	429.1	503.8	1211.9	1199.4
Europe ancienne URSS	488.0	631.9	993.5	1468.4	2162.3
Océanie	1346.6	1404.4	1508.0	1897.0	2443.1
Autre	222.8	233.2	263.7	335.3	339.9
USA/Etats–Unis d'Amer	18153.1	18218.6	20703.4	24343.7	21925.6
Japan/Japon	11599.5	11564.4	13522.9	17048.8	15766.8
China, Hong Kong SAR	5909.0	6430.8	8014.7	10682.0	11131.0
China/Chine	2653.6	5151.0	6203.0	9143.6	11377.1
Singapore/Singapour	3221.8	3109.5	4151.8	6689.4	6438.8
Germany/Allemagne	2877.0	3592.8	4313.5	5965.2	4705.2
Other Asia n.e.s.	2262.3	2296.3	2731.7	3881.5	4004.9
Indonesia/Indonésie	1934.7	2094.8	2539.7	2957.9	3198.1
Malaysia/Malaisie	1135.9	1430.0	1651.7	2950.9	4333.0
United Kingdom	1829.7	1661.1	1782.6	2874.0	3221.7
Panama	1841.8	1081.7	1968.5	2246.3	3195.2
Thailand/Thaïlande	1532.3	1760.6	1835.1	2427.5	2664.1
Canada	1608.3	1374.0	1389.7	1790.4	1203.3
Australia/Australie	1094.5	1184.7	1231.9	1569.3	1807.7
Netherlands/Pays–Bas	1014.3	950.0	1121.4	1542.3	1675.6
Philippines	745.9	934.9	1212.4	1493.1	1905.5
Liberia/Libéria	1340.6	782.1	1779.4	998.4	875.3
United Arab Emirates	803.4	1053.3	1171.2	1321.1	1377.9
India/Inde	438.3	1803.7	1160.0	1125.8	1177.0
France, Monaco	982.5	895.0	1003.0	1469.7	1249.1
Russian Federation	482.7	601.2	961.9	1415.9	1967.5
Mexico/Mexique	905.4	997.1	1289.2	941.1	1191.0
Viet Nam	436.2	728.3	1027.4	1351.0	1599.1
Saudi Arabia	940.8	944.0	878.0	1106.9	1096.9
Brazil/Brésil	164.5	448.5	844.2	1518.6	1497.2
Italy/Italie	869.2	606.3	756.2	1031.2	921.8
Spain/Espagne	574.2	526.3	631.7	847.5	899.9
Turkey/Turquie	399.1	610.2	276.0	574.7	745.9
Iran (Islamic Rep of)	560.1	430.7	260.7	352.1	883.9
Belgium–Luxembourg	480.1	443.1	418.7	573.8	561.6
Chile/Chili	326.0	372.9	408.5	636.5	640.2
So. African Customs Un	294.9	285.6	364.4	606.1	724.9
Bangladesh	332.6	366.8	452.4	567.7	517.6
Argentina/Argentine	463.3	531.3	472.2	303.8	443.1
Pakistan	371.6	462.2	363.3	358.4	358.1
Poland/Pologne	119.6	240.5	275.9	411.3	782.0
Egypt/Egypte	187.6	251.4	354.4	468.9	473.6
Switzerland,Liechtenst.	242.3	207.2	225.1	368.6	643.1
Greece/Grèce	171.8	221.2	171.0	404.9	520.6
Sweden/Suède	283.6	231.0	350.8	307.0	311.6

(VALUE AS PERCENTAGE OF WORLD TOTAL)(VALEURS EN POURCENTAGE DU TOTAL MONDIAL)

	1987	1988	1989	1990	1991	1992	1993	1994	1995	1996
Africa	0.9	0.9	0.8	0.9	0.2	1.3	1.1	1.4	1.7	1.9
Americas	26.5	29.7	31.1	28.8	28.3	27.4	26.3	26.2	27.4	26.9
– Northern America	23.7	26.9	28.6	26.4	25.5	24.3	23.4	23.1	24.4	24.0
– LAIA	2.3	2.6	2.3	2.2	2.6	2.5	2.4	2.5	2.5	2.5
– CACM	0.0	0.0	0.0	0.0	0.1	0.0	0.0	0.0	0.0	0.0
– Caribbean	0.0	0.0	0.1	0.0	0.1	0.1	0.1	0.1	0.0	0.0
– Rest of America	0.6	0.2	0.1	0.1	0.0	0.5	0.3	0.6	0.3	0.4
Asia excl fmr USSR	49.7	46.2	45.0	46.0	50.5	51.4	51.4	50.0	49.1	48.0
– Middle East	5.8	5.1	6.0	7.5	9.0	10.7	10.3	8.8	8.4	9.6
Asia former USSR						0.0	0.1	0.2	0.2	0.2
Europe excl fmr USSR	13.3	13.5	12.4	14.0	14.5	14.1	14.3	15.5	15.0	16.0
– European Union	12.3	12.6	11.4	13.0	13.1	12.8	13.3	14.2	13.5	14.1
– Eastern Europe					0.4	0.2	0.1	0.2	0.2	0.2
– Rest of Europe	1.0	0.9	0.9	1.0	1.0	1.0	0.9	1.0	1.3	1.7
Europe former USSR					0.7	0.7	1.3	1.3	1.5	1.3
Oceania	4.0	4.2	4.5	4.6	4.6	4.7	5.2	4.7	4.5	4.9
Other	5.4	5.5	6.2	5.8	1.1	0.5	0.3	0.7	0.7	0.7
Japan/Japon	33.3	30.7	28.4	26.6	25.9	23.8	23.9	24.8	24.1	20.9
USA/Etats–Unis d'Amer	21.4	24.6	25.9	24.3	23.2	22.4	21.4	21.1	22.5	22.2
China/Chine			2.2	2.1	4.2	4.6	4.7	5.3	5.5	5.7
Germany/Allemagne					4.5	4.6	4.7	5.0	4.9	4.8
Saudi Arabia	2.6	1.6	1.7	2.5	4.0	4.6	4.5	3.7	4.0	4.4
Australia/Australie	3.1	3.5	3.6	3.7	3.7	3.8	4.0	3.7	3.6	4.2
Indonesia/Indonésie	2.0	1.7	1.8	2.3	2.5	2.8	3.1	2.8	2.5	2.7
Malaysia/Malaisie	2.6	2.6	2.4	2.3	2.3	2.2	2.3	1.8	1.9	2.0
Canada	2.3	2.3	2.7	2.1	2.3	1.9	2.0	2.0	1.9	1.8
Italy/Italie	1.3	1.2	1.4	1.7	1.8	1.6	1.7	1.9	1.8	2.0

	1987	1988	1989	1990	1991	1992	1993	1994	1995	1996
Afrique	1.8	2.0	2.0	1.9	3.9	3.4	2.4	3.3	2.4	2.6
Amériques	44.4	40.8	38.9	35.7	32.1	32.2	29.7	29.5	26.6	24.5
– Amérique du Nord	42.0	38.3	36.3	32.6	28.2	25.8	24.0	23.0	20.9	17.8
– ALAI	1.0	1.1	1.5	1.7	2.4	3.3	3.8	3.9	3.4	3.5
– MCAC	0.2	0.1	0.2	0.2	0.4	0.3	0.3	0.3	0.3	0.3
– Caraïbes	0.2	0.3	0.2	0.3	0.2	0.3	0.2	0.2	0.2	0.4
– Autre Amérique	1.1	0.9	0.7	0.9	0.9	2.4	1.3	2.1	1.8	2.5
Asie anc. URSS exclus	33.8	38.0	40.5	40.6	44.2	47.7	51.6	51.2	52.8	54.5
– Moyen–Orient	3.9	3.9	3.0	3.3	4.6	4.7	4.6	3.6	3.5	4.0
Asie ancienne URSS						0.0	0.2	0.3	0.3	0.5
Europe anc. URSS exclus	16.4	15.6	13.9	16.2	16.3	14.0	13.3	12.9	14.9	14.2
– Union Européenne	15.6	14.7	13.2	15.4	14.7	12.8	12.1	11.7	13.0	11.9
– Europe de l'Est					0.7	0.4	0.7	0.6	0.9	1.4
– Autre de l'Europe	0.8	0.9	0.8	0.8	1.0	0.8	0.5	0.5	1.0	0.9
Europe ancienne URSS					0.9	0.6	0.8	1.0	1.2	1.7
Océanie	1.7	1.8	2.1	1.9	1.7	1.8	1.7	1.6	1.5	1.9
Autre	1.8	1.8	2.5	3.8	0.8	0.3	0.3	0.3	0.3	0.3
USA/Etats–Unis d'Amer	38.9	35.4	33.2	29.9	25.9	23.7	22.2	21.6	19.5	16.9
Japan/Japon	17.8	19.8	21.6	19.4	17.2	15.1	14.1	14.1	13.6	12.2
China, Hong Kong SAR	4.7	5.9	5.4	5.8	6.6	7.7	7.8	8.3	8.5	8.6
China/Chine			2.1	2.1	1.4	3.5	6.3	6.5	7.3	8.8
Singapore/Singapour	2.0	2.2	2.5	2.8	3.8	4.2	3.8	4.3	5.3	5.0
Germany/Allemagne					4.4	3.8	4.4	4.5	4.8	3.6
Other Asia n.e.s.	1.2	1.6			2.2	3.0	2.8	2.8	3.1	3.1
Indonesia/Indonésie	0.5	0.7	1.1	1.7	1.9	2.5	2.5	2.6	2.4	2.5
Malaysia/Malaisie	0.6	0.7	0.9	1.1	1.4	1.5	1.7	1.7	2.4	3.3
United Kingdom	3.2	3.2	3.0	2.7	2.5	2.4	2.0	1.9	2.3	2.5

4. Special Imports C.I.F. by Commodities according to the S.I.T.C. (Rev. 2) in million U.S. Dollars
Importations Spéciales C.A.F. par Produits d'après la C.T.C.I. (Rév. 2) en millions de Dollars E.U.

SITC CTCI	COMMODITY	1993 QUANTITY QUANTITE	1993 VALUE VALEUR	1994 QUANTITY QUANTITE	1994 VALUE VALEUR	1995 QUANTITY QUANTITE	1995 VALUE VALEUR	1996 QUANTITY QUANTITE	1996 VALUE VALEUR	PRODUIT
	ALL COMMODITIES		83794.0		102342.6		135113.0		150334.4	TOUS PRODUITS
0	FOOD AND LIVE ANIMALS		3989.7		4749.3		5912.4		7249.4	ALIMENTS,ANIMAUX VIVANTS
01	MEAT AND PREPARATIONS		408.3		594.7		766.2		769.4	VIANDES ET PREPARATIONS
011	MEAT FRESH,CHILLD,FROZEN		385.6	W 214167	572.6	W 269556	737.6	W 266042	736.2	VIANDES FRAICHES,REF,CONGE
0111	BOVINE MEAT FRESH,FROZEN		329.7	W 142496	429.5	W 168367	537.7	W 163191	496.5	VIANDES BOVIN FRAI,REF
03	FISH AND PREPARATIONS		508.0		681.0		784.3		1008.8	POISSONS ET PREPARATIONS
034	FISH,FRESH,CHILLED,FROZN	W 242702	360.4	W 232159	431.9	W 261265	505.3	W 332771	614.7	POISSON FRAIS, REFRIG,CONG
0342	FISH FROZEN,EXCL FILLETS	W 231496	260.3	W 205420	259.7	W 225141	299.1	W 287892	365.4	POISSONS CONGELES
04	CEREALS AND PREPARATIONS		1458.4		1576.1		1983.0		2688.8	CEREALES ET PRODUITS
041	WHEAT ETC UNMILLED	W 4938837	674.0	W 6056524	783.5		467.1	W 3222977	723.9	FROMENT,EPEAUTRE
0412	OTHER WHEAT ETC UNMILLED	W 4938837	674.0	W 6056524	783.5	W 2341779	467.1	W 3222975	723.9	AUTRE FROMENT NON MOULU
044	MAIZE UNMILLED		702.4	W 5748702	696.2	MW 9035	1265.5	W 8704563	1571.9	MAIS NON MOULU
05	VEGETABLES AND FRUIT		396.1		493.7		533.9		675.1	LEGUMES ET FRUITS
06	SUGAR AND PREPS,HONEY		387.0		452.5		555.6		581.9	SUCRES ET PRODUITS
061	SUGAR AND HONEY		363.0	W 1864447	425.4	W 1969612	521.3	W 2138783	546.3	SUCRES ET MIEL
0611	RAW BEET AND CANE SUGAR		315.2	W 1274410	367.0	W 1305791	440.5	W 1399928	443.1	SUCRES BRUTS
081	*FEEDING STUFF FOR ANIML		396.4	W 2231402	391.4	W 3179180	551.9	W 3613241	765.7	NOURRITURE POUR ANIMAUX
0813	OILCAKE AND OTH RESIDUES		271.7	W 1372652	230.9	W 2206276	348.2	W 2544302	503.8	TOURTEAUX
1	BEVERAGES AND TOBACCO		262.8		348.7		534.6		664.8	BOISSONS ET TABACS
2	CRUDE MATERLS,EXCL FUELS		8772.2		9269.9		11550.1		10820.4	MAT BRUTES NON COMESTIBLES
21	HIDES,SKINS,FURS UNDRSSD		973.4		1092.1		1189.4		1175.5	CUIRS,PEAUX BRUTS
211	HIDES,SKINS,EXC FURS,RAW	W 389043	881.1	W 370822	922.0	W 353757	991.1	W 353301	890.7	CUIRS ET PEAUX
2111	BOVINE,EQUINE HIDES,RAW	W 371741	799.5	W 356058	837.8	W 341908	914.4	W 340553	802.5	PEAUX DE BOVINS
22	OIL SEEDS,OLEAGINOUS FRT		346.2		447.1		483.0		577.8	GRAINES,FRUITS OLEAGINEUX
222	SEEDS FOR'SOFT'FIXED OIL	W 1170179	332.0	W 1341213	429.1	W 1551363	462.2	W 1588616	561.0	GRAINES HUILES FIXES
2222	SOYA BEANS	W 1087995	290.4	W 1228408	351.5	W 1467706	401.9	W 1469619	473.3	FEVES DE SOJA
23	RUBBER, CRUDE		447.3		551.8		728.6		702.7	CAOUTCHOUC BRUT
232	NATURAL RUBBER,GUMS	W 292692	251.8	W 321199	332.4	W 307664	476.7	W 321440	460.5	LATEX CAOUTCHOUC NATUREL
24	CORK AND WOOD		1777.0		1570.3		1694.7		1696.8	LIEGE ET BOIS
247	OTH WOOD ROUGH,SQUARED	W 6856299	1182.6	W 6934653	1011.6	W 7369760	1047.4	W 7239492	963.2	BOIS BRUTS EQUARRIS
2471	SAW–,VENEER–LOGS CONIFER	W 4871935	710.2	W 5141971	616.5	W 5796477	728.0	W 5987727	705.4	CONIFERES POUR SCIAGE,PLACAG
24711	— IN THE ROUGH	W 4871935	710.2	W 5141971	616.5	W 5796477	728.0	W 5987727	705.4	ECORCES OU DEGROSSIS
2472	SAW–,VENEER–LOGS NON–CON	W 1984364	472.4	W 1792682	395.2	W 1573283	319.5	W 1251765	257.9	NON CONIFERES SCIAGE,PLAC
24721	— IN THE ROUGH	W 1984364	472.4	W 1792682	395.2	W 1573283	319.5	W 1251765	257.9	BRUTS ECORCES DEGROSSIS
248	WOOD SHAPED,SLEEPERS		515.1	W 765457	462.7	W 773714	522.8	W 791904	607.6	BOIS SIMPLEMENT TRAVAILLES
2483	LUMBER SHAPED NON–CONIFR		447.8	W 649122	408.4	W 620990	420.8	W 562454	436.0	NON CONIFERES SCIES,RABOTES
24831	LUMBER SAWN ETC NON–CON		386.8	W 564487	321.0	W 523193	310.4	W 449314	299.9	SCIES LONGITUDINALEMENT
251	*PULP AND WASTE PAPER		839.5	W 3251698	1044.1	W 3231572	1858.0	W 3683038	1473.4	PATES A PAPIER,DECHETS
2517	SODA,SULPHATE WOOD PULP	W 1497959	585.4	W 1723127	766.1	W 1749647	1334.8	W 2045202	1096.2	PATES CHIMIQUES AU SULFATE
25172	— BLEACHED,NONDISSOLVNG	W 1251446	493.8	W 1451678	657.4	W 1479126	1146.1	W 1773674	959.6	PATES BLANCHIES
26	TEXTILE FIBRES AND WASTE		1043.6		1143.5		1387.8		1221.8	FIBRES TEXTILES
263	COTTON	W 371013	539.5	W 373157	593.1	W 372042	774.7	W 351625	717.3	COTON
2631	RAW COTTON,EXCL LINTERS	W 366251	534.7	W 370666	589.9	W 369046	771.6	W 347094	713.6	COTON EN MASSE
27	CRUDE FERTLZR,MINRLS NES		487.7		523.2		604.6		599.5	ENGRAIS MINERAUX BRUTS
28	METALLIFEROUS ORES,SCRAP		2572.4		2585.8		3237.7		2981.4	MINERAIS METAL,DECHETS
281	IRON ORE,CONCENTRATES		887.6	MW 34250	797.0	MW 35075	850.7	MW 34824	918.3	MINERAIS DE FER
2815	IRON ORE,CONC,NOT AGGLOM		865.3	MW 33883	786.1	MW 34372	820.8	MW 33280	853.8	MINERAIS NON AGGLOMERES
282	IRON AND STEEL SCRAP		775.8	W 4969623	846.9	W 5003108	996.2	W 5209919	940.1	FERRAILLES
28209	— OF OTHR IRON OR STEEL		709.3	W 4761020	758.6	W 4717685	831.9	W 5061170	830.5	FERRAILLES DE FER
287	BASE METAL ORES,CONC NES		630.6	W 1816659	661.9	W 1952971	908.1		773.4	MINERAIS METAUX COMMUNS
2871	CPR ORE ETC,CEMENT COPPR	W 573932	342.7	W 428869	302.0	W 468714	464.6	W 439732	315.5	MINERAIS DE CUIVRE,MATTES
28711	COPPER ORES,EXCL MATTE	W 571187	341.0	W 426421	300.6	W 468714	464.6	W 439732	315.5	MINERAIS DE CUIVRE
288	NONFERR METAL SCRAP NES		278.1	W 170144	280.0	W 215514	481.7	W 193007	349.6	DECHETS NON FERREUX
2882	OTHER BASE MTL SCRAP NES		270.3	W 161629	273.7	W 209034	476.3	W 185826	343.8	AUTRES DECHETS
29	CRUDE ANIMAL,VEG MAT NES		285.6		312.4		366.8		392.1	MATIERES BRUTES ANIM,VEGET
3	MINERAL FUELS ETC		15155.3		15532.3		19150.2		24423.1	COMBUSTIBLES MINERAUX LUB
32	COAL,COKE AND BRIQUETTES		1732.9		1776.6		2081.4		2337.1	HOUILLES,COKES,BRIQUETTES
322	COAL,LIGNITE AND PEAT		1712.2		1753.2	MW 43848	2057.3	MW 46289	2310.4	HOUILLES,LIGNITES,TOURBE
3222	OTH COAL,NOT AGGLOMERATD		1670.7	MW 38507	1718.1	MW 43113	2018.6	MW 45398	2260.0	AUTRES HOUILLES
33	PETROLEUM AND PRODUCTS		12039.9		12194.2		14897.0		19188.9	PETROLE ET DERIVES
333	CRUDE PETROLEUM	MW 74153	9151.0	MW 77693	8878.3	MW 84282	10809.2	MW 94103	14431.6	HUILES BRUTES DE PETROLE
334	PETROLEUM PRODUCTS,REFIN		2752.8	MW 19768	3140.8	MW 21829	3864.6	MW 21462	4460.0	PRODUITS RAFFINES
3341	GASOLINE,OTH LIGHT OILS		1324.4							ESSENCES POUR MOTEURS
33419	OTH LIGHT PETROLEUM OILS		1319.0							AUTRES HUILES LEGERES
3342	KEROSENE,OTH MEDIUM OILS		437.2							PETR LAMPANTS,AUT HUIL
33421	KEROSENE INCL JET FUEL	W 2033936	427.5							PETROLES LAMPANTS
3343	GAS OILS	W 1501006	285.8							GAS OILS
3344	FUEL OILS,NES	W 5203321	570.8							FUEL OILS
341	*GAS,NATURAL AND MANUFCT		1382.6		1561.6		2171.9	MW 13835	2897.2	GAZ NATUREL,GAZ MANUFACT
3413	PETROLM GASES,LIQUEFIED		1382.5	MW 10042	1561.6	MW 11161	2171.9	MW 13835	2897.1	GAZ DE PETROLE LIQUEFIE
34131	LIQUEFIED PROPANE,BUTANE		601.1	W 4045425	600.1	W 4405815	896.4	W 4577041	1018.6	PROPANE,BUTANE LIQUEFIES
34139	OTH HYDROCARBON GAS LQFD		781.5	W 5996546	961.5	W 6755683	1275.5	MW 9258	1878.6	HYDROCARBURES GAZEUX NDA
4	ANIMAL,VEGETABLE OIL,FAT		258.1		322.6		392.1		368.7	HUILES,GRAISSES ANIM,VEG
5	CHEMCLS,RELATED PROD NES		8030.0		9510.8		12840.2		12917.2	PRODUITS CHIMIQUES
51	ORGANIC CHEMICALS		2917.0		3489.5		5365.9		4882.3	PROD CHIMIQ ORGANIQUES
511	HYDROCARBONS NES,DERIVS		655.2	W 1625476	747.8	W 2386940	1634.9	W 2532177	1310.1	HYDROCARBURES NDA
5112	CYCLIC HYDROCARBONS		360.8	W 995156	447.3	W 1478128	1096.0	W 1576650	816.6	HYDROCARBURES CYCLIQUES
51124	XYLENES,CHEMICALLY PURE	W 551241	206.5	W 525064	235.5	W 904803	765.6	W 905631	532.9	XYLENES PURS
512	ALCOHOLS,PHENOLS ETC	W 1157008	437.3	W 1321678	643.6	W 1541136	1003.3	W 1822201	971.3	PHENOLS,PHENOLS–ALCOOLS
5121	ACYCLIC ALCOHOLS,DERIVS	W 1107803	349.0	W 1259353	534.0	W 1469700	864.2	W 1741478	813.4	ALCOOLS ACYCLIQUES
513	CARBOXYLIC ACIDS ETC		427.5	W 511066	512.7	W 429175	620.3	W 435891	559.1	ACIDES CARBOXYLIQUES
514	NITROGEN–FNCTN COMPOUNDS		598.8	W 325686	647.3	W 372487	932.1	W 366612	832.6	COMPOSES FONCT AZOTEES
5148	OTH NITROGN–FNCTN CMPNDS		356.7	W 252030	386.8	W 285989	623.2	W 267680	492.2	AUTRES COMPOSES AZOTES
515	ORG–INORG COMPOUNDS ETC		555.4	W 252639	631.8	W 265961	762.5	W 273232	813.6	COMPOSES ORGANO–MINERAUX
5156	HETEROCYCLIC CMPDS ETC		420.2	W 228382	478.8	W 241631	592.6	W 246519	614.0	COMPOSES HETEROCYCLIQUES
516	OTHER ORGANIC CHEMICALS	W 165974	243.1	W 249734	306.6	W 381605	413.0	W 358614	395.8	AUTRES PROD ORGANIQUES
52	INORGANIC CHEMICALS		870.2		1034.4		1253.4		1404.3	PROD CHIM INORGANIQUES
522	INORG ELEMNTS,OXIDES,ETC		437.0	W 1262074	501.5	W 1323180	646.3	W 1485506	704.2	ELEMENTS INORGANIQUES
523	OTHR INORG CHEMICALS ETC		279.7	W 827154	321.7	W 852556	379.2	W 847890	387.9	AUT PRODUITS CHIMIQUES INORG
53	DYES,TANNING,COLOUR PROD		690.7		807.0		906.9		914.9	PROD TEINTURE,COLORANTS
531	SYNT DYE,NAT INDGO,LAKES	W 22225	329.4	W 26055	348.9	W 27209	352.6	W 29352	353.7	MAT COLOR ORGAN,LAQUES
5311	SYNTHIC ORGNIC DYESTUFFS	W 21315	311.8	W 25087	329.8	W 26173	332.4	W 28374	334.0	MAT COLOR ORGAN SYNTHET
533	PIGMENTS,PAINTS,ETC		307.9	W 131016	404.6	W 137950	496.4	W 137494	503.0	PIGMENTS,PEINTURES,VERNIS
541	*MEDICINAL,PHARM PRODUCT		470.2		546.5		659.9	MK 104005	764.5	PROD MEDICINAUX PHARMACEUT
55	PERFUME,CLEANING ETC PRD		330.0		427.7		528.3		679.3	PROD POUR PARFUM,TOILETTE
58	PLASTIC MATERIALS ETC		1414.9		1629.3		1973.7		1984.0	MAT PLAST ARTIFICIELLES
582	PROD OF CONDENSATION ETC		595.5	W 211334	720.3	W 246140	931.9	W 243634	927.3	PROD CONDENS,POLYCOND
583	POLYMERIZATION ETC PRODS		714.1	W 339162	801.9	W 326343	923.3	W 358556	942.0	PROD POLYMERISATION
5839	OTH POLYMRZTION ETC PROD		395.8	W 127019	443.7	W 121633	513.3	W 121514	519.1	AUT PROD POLYMER COPOLYM
59	CHEMICAL MATERIALS NES		1213.2		1468.7		1995.4		2150.7	MAT PROD CHIMIQUES NDA
598	MISCEL CHEM PRODUCTS NES		1005.9	W 396942	1220.7	W 465815	1715.1	W 490457	1869.9	PROD DIV INDUST CHIM NDA

4. Special Imports C.I.F. by Commodities according to the S.I.T.C. (Rev. 2) in million U.S. Dollars
Importations Spéciales C.A.F. par Produits d'après la C.T.C.I. (Rév. 2) en millions de Dollars E.U.

SITC CTCI	COMMODITY	1993 QUANTITY QUANTITE	1993 VALUE VALEUR	1994 QUANTITY QUANTITE	1994 VALUE VALEUR	1995 QUANTITY QUANTITE	1995 VALUE VALEUR	1996 QUANTITY QUANTITE	1996 VALUE VALEUR	PRODUIT
5989	CHEM PRODUCTS,PREPS NES		816.3	W 250398	1012.4	W 304673	1471.7	W 312414	1599.0	PROD PREP CHIMIQUES NDA
59899	OTH CHEM PRODS,PREPS,NES		609.6	W 193840	772.9	W 226108	1069.3	W 222335	1181.7	AUT PRODUITS CHIMIQUES NDA
6	BASIC MANUFACTURES		12328.0		16276.3		21708.0		21428.6	ART MANUFACTURES
61	LEATHER,DRESSED FUR,ETC		792.3		998.8		1090.5		1156.8	CUIRS,PELLETERIES
611	LEATHER		468.7	W 75009	576.9	W 79019	540.2	W 71712	498.1	CUIRS,PEAUX PREPARES
613	FUR SKINS TANNED,DRESSED	W 3929	213.0	W 5137	279.8	W 5217	368.2	W 5882	473.9	PELLETERIES
63	WOOD,CORK MANUFACTRS NES		783.0		804.5		915.2		911.5	OUVRAGES LIEGE ET BOIS
634	VENEERS,PLYWOOD,ETC		682.8	W 965813	667.0	W 1571190	738.7	W 1037622	678.5	PLACAGES,CONTRE–PLAQUES
6342	PLYWOOD OF WOOD SHEETS		552.0	W 651148	536.0	W 848583	593.9	W 695755	531.5	BOIS CONTRE–PLAQUES
64	PAPER,PAPERBOARD AND MFR		588.4		675.6		929.3		881.9	PAPIERS,CARTONS & OUVRAGES
641	PAPER AND PAPERBOARD	W 632138	509.2	W 709177	591.2	W 771910	825.9	W 729576	756.1	PAPIERS ET CARTONS
65	TEXTILE YARN,FABRICS,ETC		2706.1		3481.7		4142.9		4001.1	FILS,TISSUS,ARTICLES TEXTILE
651	TEXTILE YARN		1068.8	W 458889	1456.1	W 454686	1765.1	W 459072	1701.2	FILS TEXTILES
6514	SYN FIB YRN,BULK,MONOFIL	W 108814	275.5	W 168272	411.7	W 166358	513.7	W 155786	433.6	FILS CONT 85% FIB TEXT SYNTH
652	COTTON FABRICS,WOVEN		260.7	W 68969	319.0	W 70045	363.9	W 68731	372.4	TISSUS DE COTON
653	WOVN MAN–MADE FIB FABRIC		594.2	W 164341	843.9	W 164222	968.0	W 138227	848.1	TISSUS FIBRES SYNTH,ARTIF
654	OTH WOVEN TEXTILE FABRIC	W 23014	400.3	W 22354	407.8	W 24735	472.2	W 23501	483.3	TISSUS AUT COTON SYNT,ARTIF
66	NONMETAL MINERAL MFS NES		816.7		1093.7		1563.3		1673.9	ART MIN NON METALLIQUES
664	GLASS		269.6	W 310352	401.4	W 532233	641.8	W 331183	558.7	VERRE
67	IRON AND STEEL		3161.4		4566.0		6630.6		6679.5	FER ET ACIER
671	PIG IRON ETC		592.5	W 2754151	692.4	W 3328883	967.9	W 3969470	1123.9	FONTE,SPIEGEL,POUDRES
6716	FERRO–ALLOYS		295.8	W 427130	310.7	W 496311	467.0	W 571445	553.6	FERRO–ALLIAGES
672	IRON,STEEL PRIMARY FORMS		1134.3	W 4673753	1614.1	W 5636960	2386.0	W 6369234	2220.5	LINGOTS FER,ACIER
6725	IRN,STL BLOOMS,SLABS,ETC		612.1	W 3027144	786.5	W 3187115	989.9	W 4186345	1153.0	BLOOMS,BILLETTES FER ACIER
67251	IRN,SMPLE STL BLOOMS,ETC		541.8	W 2928952	703.3	W 3099519	852.2	W 4113201	1079.0	BLOOMS ETC NON ACIER FIN
6727	IRN,STL COIL FR REROLLNG		512.4	W 1598764	814.8	W 2385175	1363.3	W 2175661	1041.7	EBAUCHES POUR TOLES FER
67271	IRON,SIMPLE STEEL COILS		223.7	W 1333567	455.8	W 2090468	826.2	W 1924571	653.5	EBAUCHES NON EN ACIER
67274	STNLESS STEEL ETC COILS		282.6	W 262781	356.9	W 285613	532.3	W 244193	383.4	EBAUCHES ACIER INOXYDBLE
673	IRON,STEEL SHAPES ETC		468.2	W 1616056	702.1	W 2022077	945.1	W 1695821	826.7	BARRES,PROFIL FER,ACIER
6733	IRON,STEEL PROFILES ETC		141.8	W 802991	316.7	W 989051	423.8	W 887164	373.7	PROFILES,PALPLAN FER,ACIER
674	IRN,STL UNIV,PLATE,SHEET		608.5	W 1695088	1025.5	W 2470861	1573.7	W 2552854	1629.5	LARGES PLATS,TOLES
6744	IRN,STL HVY PLATE,ROLLED		226.8	W 1000750	453.5	W 1611181	785.5	W 1580957	786.8	TOLES LAMINEES PLUS 4.75 MM
67441	— OF IRON OR SIMPLE STL		195.6	W 981358	419.3	W 1591207	733.9	W 1565939	742.2	TOLES NON ACIER FIN CARB
678	IRON,STL TUBES,PIPES,ETC		277.3	W 215417	392.0	W 373500	599.1	W 436581	671.7	TUBES,TUYAUX EN FONTE,FER
68	NON–FERROUS METALS		2226.4		3066.4		4617.4		4141.3	METAUX NON FERREUX
682	COPPER EXC CEMENT COPPER		751.3	W 405139	1052.7	W 484684	1697.9	W 535535	1554.4	CUIVRE
6821	COPPER NES,ALLOYS,UNWRT		526.9	W 351857	767.1	W 406877	1235.6	W 433788	1098.2	CUIVRE BRUT
68212	COPPER REFINED,UNWROUGHT		365.6	W 264376	576.3	W 326716	978.4	W 346163	865.8	CUIVRE AFFINE BRUT
6822	COPPER,ALLOYS WORKED		224.5	W 53282	285.6	W 77807	462.3	W 101747	456.2	CUIVRE,ALLIAGES OUVRES
684	ALUMINIUM		1102.5	W 822510	1459.5	W 915328	2140.8	W 838221	1728.4	ALUMINIUM
6841	ALUMINIUM,ALLOYS,UNWRGHT	W 579343	718.6	W 689328	1013.6	W 783423	1569.9	W 724458	1209.5	ALUMINIUM,ALLIAGES BRUTS
6842	ALUMINIUM,ALLOYS WORKED		384.0	W 133181	445.9	W 131905	571.0	W 113763	518.9	ALUMINIUM,ALLIAGES OUVRE
68422	ALUMNM PLATE,SHEET,STRIP	W 99662	252.4	W 113178	279.7	W 107114	349.1	W 88649	302.7	TOLES, PLANCHES EN ALU
69	METAL MANUFACTURES NES		1030.0		1318.7		1489.9		1642.8	ART MANUFACT EN METAL NDA
695	TOOLS		279.7	W 20661	323.4	W 22711	370.4	W 26571	445.4	OUTILS A MAIN
699	BASE METAL MFRS NES		393.4	W 63672	516.1	W 74711	584.2	W 78996	591.1	ART MANUFACTURES MET NDA
7	MACHINES,TRANSPORT EQUIP		28397.9		37381.9		49403.9		54654.6	MACHINES MATERIEL TRANSPORT
71	POWER GENERATING EQUIPMT		2492.9		2767.9		3891.4		3666.0	MACHINES GENERATRICES
713	INTRNL COMBUS PSTN ENGIN		748.4	W 70134	1047.7	W 85232	1218.4	W 89336	1174.0	MOTEURS EXPL COMB INT, PIECE
7139	PISTON ENGINE PARTS NES		386.4	W 31379	534.3	W 30675	597.6	W 43422	597.3	PIECES POUR 713.2,3,8
714	ENGINES AND MOTORS NES		751.8	W 2651	772.3	W 12165	1154.9	W 12765	742.8	MOTEURS NON ELECTRIQUES
7144	REACTION ENGINES	W 414	405.7	W 411	389.5	W 327	315.4	W 173	140.3	PROPULSEURS A REACTION
7149	ENGINE & MOTOR PARTS NES		308.5	W 1283	318.7	W 7957	555.3	W 9432	404.2	PIECES 714 ET 718.88
716	ROTATING ELECTRIC PLANT		590.5	W 29949	646.2	W 38691	812.8	W 50709	924.7	APP ELECTR ROTATIFS,PIECES
7162	AC MTRS,GENRTRS,GEN SETS	W 15377	265.8	W 19632	376.5	W 29248	553.3	W 36923	684.5	MOTEURS ELECTRIQUES
72	MACHS FOR SPCL INDUSTRYS		4379.1		5924.3		8078.7		8003.5	MAC SPECIALES POUR INDUST
724	TEXTILE,LEATHER MACHNRY		1006.2	W 61313	1315.8	W 52304	1180.2	W 35081	825.6	MACH POUR INDUSTRIE TEXTILE
7244	SPINNING,EXTRDNG,ETC MCH	W 17489	446.8	W 17750	421.0	W 21218	489.6	W 12992	311.7	MACH POUR LE FILAGE
7245	WEAVING,FELT MFG,ETC MCH	W 15662	318.8	W 30632	572.6	W 19627	403.6	W 11269	256.3	METIERS A TISSER,PIECES
72451	WEAVING MACHINES (LOOMS)	W 9801	152.2	W 21552	321.0	W 13817	230.8	W 6380	93.0	METIERS A TISSER
725	PAPER ETC MILL MACHINERY		246.9	W 6299	170.6	W 23833	444.0	W 20251	430.5	MACHINES FABR PATE PAPIER
726	PRINTG,BKBINDG MACHY,PTS		327.8	W 19413	544.8	W 17699	536.5	W 20897	500.0	MACHINES POUR IMPRIMERIE
7264	PRINTING PRESSES		222.9	W 14881	368.7	W 13999	353.4	W 17705	369.0	MACHINES A IMPRIMER
72641	ROTARY PRINTING PRESSES		222.9	W 14881	368.7	W 13999	353.4	W 17705	369.0	MACH IMPRIMER ROTATIVES
728	OTH MACHY FOR SPCL INDUS		2191.0	W 67448	3301.8	W 89979	5215.4	W 109988	5409.5	AUT MACH IND PARTICULIERES
7284	MACHY FOR SPCL INDUS NES		1980.3	W 51028	3015.0	W 73061	4857.1	W 94321	5063.3	MACH SPEC IND PARTICUL.
72848	OTH MCHY WITH INDIV FNCT		1397.1	W 30925	2221.4	W 43283	3544.0	W 58423	3668.2	AUTRES MACHINES NDA
72849	PTS OF MACHS OF 7284 ETC	W 4759	248.2	W 6609	406.7	W 7220	663.2	W 9299	729.6	PIECES DU 728.4 ETC
73	METALWORKING MACHINERY		1154.4		1741.0		2270.7		3109.3	MACH TRAVAIL DES METAUX
736	METALWORKING MACH–TOOLS		789.0	W 54958	1102.7	W 72579	1580.7	W 104024	2056.7	MACH–OUTILS TRAVAIL METAUX
7361	METAL CUTTING MACH–TOOLS		321.4	W 23337	476.3	W 28550	789.2	W 32741	968.3	MACH–OUT ENLEVEMENT METAL
7362	METAL FORMING MACH–TOOLS		202.8	W 17490	224.9	W 30480	421.9	W 48646	490.2	MACH–OUTILS DEFORM METAL
737	METALWORKING MACHNRY NES		365.5	W 36464	638.3	W 45210	690.0	W 71794	1052.6	MACH TRAV METAUX PIECES
7372	ROLLING MILLS AND ROLLS		145.7	W 22350	295.0	W 31466	235.8	W 55970	542.6	LAMINOIRS CYLINDRES PIEC
74	GENRL INDUSTRL MACHY NES		4266.2		5775.5		7751.4		8797.3	MACH APP INDUSTRIE
741	HEATING,COOLING EQUIPMNT		794.9	W 76260	1337.4	W 92434	1783.8	W 111636	2160.0	MACH CHAUFFAGE,PIECES
7413	INDUS FURNACES ETC,PARTS		227.0	W 15230	393.3	W 15614	558.6	W 31706	813.3	FOURS IND,LABOR,PIECES
74131	INDUS FURNACES ETC ELCTR	W 5143	126.4	W 7333	299.8	W 7466	421.5	W 9707	391.4	FOURS ELECTRIQUES
7416	HEATING,COOLING EQU NES		275.5	W 38674	545.2	W 47389	706.0	W 51458	856.3	APP CHANGEMENT TEMP
742	PUMPS FOR LIQUIDS ETC		481.6	W 25774	617.4	W 32510	781.3	W 34473	800.7	POMPES MOTO–POMPES
743	PUMPS NES,CENTRFUGES ETC		710.1	W 54771	956.5	W 79297	1315.8	W 89974	1521.5	POMPES COMPRES,VENT ETC
7431	PUMPS FOR GASES ETC	W 19618	273.1	W 31284	353.0	W 48531	581.3	W 57211	696.8	POMPES AIR A VIDE,COMPRES
744	MECHANICAL HANDLING EQU		647.8	W 79700	903.1	W 113792	1241.9	W 155353	1578.9	EQUIP MANUTENTION PIECES
7442	LIFTING,LOADING MACH NES		335.3	W 34989	517.0	W 42971	686.8	W 68223	960.1	APP LEVAGE,MANUTENTION
74428	OTH HANDLING ETC MCH NES		237.7	W 20001	329.4	W 25012	485.5	W 38937	672.1	AUT APP LEVAGE ETC
745	NONELEC MACHY,TOOLS NES		377.0	W 12353	411.6	W 17815	611.7	W 18800	620.8	AUT MACH NON ELEC,PIECES
7452	OTH NONELEC MCHS,PTS NES	W 11335	331.7	W 10885	354.5	W 16396	550.0	W 17269	557.3	AUT MACH NON ELEC,PIECES
749	NONELEC MACH PTS,ACC NES		1255.1	W 80075	1549.8	W 103216	2017.3	W 120690	2115.7	PIECES MACH NON ELEC NDA
7491	BALL,ROLLER,ETC BEARINGS		312.8	W 24295	400.4	W 29964	517.0	W 32293	495.8	ROULEMENTS BILLES ETC
7492	COCKS,VALVES ETC NES	W 17757	465.7	W 23642	603.2	W 27371	805.5	W 32488	828.8	ART ROB,SIM POUR TUYAUX
7493	SHAFT,CRANK,PULLEY ETC		292.1	W 25190	340.0	W 35423	427.9	W 42259	460.8	ARBRES TRANS,VILEBREQUINS
75	OFFICE MACHNES,ADP EQUIP		2000.6		2615.1		3569.9		3998.2	MACH BUREAU TRAIT AUTOM
752	AUTOMTIC DATA PROC EQUIP		1185.1	W 15104	1602.7	W 19327	2164.8	W 23698	2525.9	MACH TRAIT INFORMATION
7523	DIGITL CENTRL PROCESSORS	W 1836	406.1	W 2395	517.0	W 3364	728.3	W 3421	734.2	UNITES CENTRALES
7524	DIGITL CENTRL STOR UNITS	W 1502	329.6	W 1950	449.7	W 2702	572.5	W 2799	712.3	UNITES MEMOIRE CENTRALES
7525	ADP PERIPHERAL UNITS	W 5658	275.8	W 9412	395.2	W 11906	576.9	W 15205	612.2	UNITES PERIPHERIQUES
759	OFFICE,ADP MCH PTS,ACCES	W 7028	633.7	W 7423	813.8	W 8595	1142.5	W 10916	1300.7	PIECES DU 751 ET 752
7599	ACCTG,ETC,ADP MCH PTS,AC	W 4112	538.3	W 4311	679.2	W 5523	971.8	W 7612	1130.7	PIECES DU 751 ET 752
76	TELECOMM,SOUND EQUIPMENT		1872.3		2520.4		3058.8		3505.3	EQUIPMENT DE TELECOM
764	TELECOM EQPT,PTS,ACC NES		1645.1	W 23618	2221.1	W 27796	2658.5	W 31550	3070.2	EQUIP TELECOM,PIECES
7641	LINE TELEPHONE,ETC EQUIP		117.9	W 1812	230.9	W 2395	375.6	W 3604	485.4	APP TELEPHON PAR FIL

4. Special Imports C.I.F. by Commodities according to the S.I.T.C. (Rev. 2) in million U.S. Dollars
Importations Spéciales C.A.F. par Produits d'après la C.T.C.I. (Rév. 2) en millions de Dollars E.U.

SITC CTCI	COMMODITY	1993		1994		1995		1996		PRODUIT
		QUANTITY QUANTITE	VALUE VALEUR	QUANTITY QUANTITE	VALUE VALEUR	QUANTITY QUANTITE	VALUE VALEUR	QUANTITY QUANTITE	VALUE VALEUR	
7643	TV,RADIO TRANSMITTRS ETC	W 1421	302.6	W 2726	636.1	W 2415	575.3	W 2229	640.8	APP EMET TELE RADIO
7649	PTS NES OF EQUIPMT OF 76	W 11627	1008.8	W 11947	1070.6	W 13867	1339.4	W 17285	1603.3	PIECES DE LA DIV 76
76493	TELECOMM EQUIPMT PTS NES	W 4311	460.8	W 4867	465.3	W 5094	574.5	W 5992	801.2	PIECES 761,762,764.3,8
76499	PARTS ETC OF SOUND EQUIP	W 3460	396.8	W 3442	391.3	W 4029	454.9	W 4833	458.2	PIECES NDA POUR 763
77	ELECTRIC MACHNRY NES ETC		8557.9		10722.9		14550.1		16571.1	MACH APP ELECT NDA
771	ELECTRIC POWER MACHY NES	W 13252	360.3	W 16315	417.4	W 19693	483.2	W 22349	576.1	MACH PROD,TRANS ELECTR
7712	OTH ELEC POWER MACHY NES	W 7276	259.3	W 9164	316.6	W 11761	357.7	W 14501	458.6	AUT APP PROD TRANSF ELEC
772	SWITCHGEAR ETC,PARTS NES		1076.7	W 19359	1319.9	W 23885	1697.5	W 26482	1725.2	APP COUPURE,SECT ETC
7721	SWITCHGEAR ETC		866.6	W 16339	1049.0	W 20152	1370.3	W 22408	1394.9	APP COUPURE,SECTIONMNT
774	ELECTRO–MEDCL,XRAY EQUIP		198.0	W 2514	319.7	W 2643	355.1	W 3264	385.8	APPAREILS MEDICAUX
776	TRANSISTORS,VALVES,ETC		5649.7	W 52822	6982.6	W 66485	9838.2	W 92133	11460.1	LAMPES,TUBES,VALVES
7762	OTH ELECTRONIC TUBES ETC		347.5	W 16064	340.5	W 25633	584.1	W 24722	584.8	AUT LAMPES ELECTRONIQUES
7763	DIODES,TRANSISTORS,ETC		457.3	W 3033	632.7	W 3437	785.4	W 3620	832.7	DIODES,TRANSISTORS
7764	ELECTRONIC MICROCIRCUITS		3344.3	W 4075	4231.0	W 5029	6773.2	W 5819	8206.9	MICROSTRUCTURES ELECTRON
7768	ELCTRNC COMP PTS,CRYSTLS		1274.2	W 12275	1606.3	W 12986	1492.7	W 12574	1427.8	CRIST PIEZO–ELEC,PCS 776
77689	ELECTRNIC COMPON PTS NES		1146.3	W 11760	1397.3	W 12490	1210.7	W 11976	1160.7	PIECES DU GROUPE 776
778	ELECTRICAL MACHINERY NES		938.7	W 67827	1267.3	W 79825	1580.7	W 91575	1681.1	AUTRES MACH ELECT NDA
7788	OTH ELEC MACHY,EQUIP NES		630.5	W 48360	863.8	W 56642	1088.3	W 62085	1118.1	AUT MACH APP ELEC NDA
77884	ELECTRICAL CONDENSERS		219.5	W 3043	308.3	W 3186	362.5	W 4469	332.8	CONDENSATEURS ELECTRIQUES
78	ROAD VEHICLES		984.3		1467.4		1910.4		2067.8	VEHICULES ROUTIERS
784	MOTOR VEH PRTS,ACCES NES		774.4	W 74745	1118.3	W 80215	1303.7	W 84070	1245.3	PIECES 722,781,782,783
7849	OTHER MOTOR VEHCL PARTS		770.0	W 73780	1111.1	W 80118	1301.2	W 83946	1240.3	PIECES 722,781,782,783
79	OTHR TRANSPORT EQUIPMENT		2690.6		3847.8		4322.9		4936.4	AUTRE MATERIEL TRANSPORT
792	AIRCRAFT ETC		1846.5		2207.5		2479.4	W 4560	2765.8	APP NAVIGATION AERIENNE
7924	AIRCRFT NES OVER 15000KG	W 1611	1292.8	W 1802	1377.7	W 2048	1603.1	W 2499	1928.7	AERODYNES PLUS 15000 KG
7929	AIRCRAFT PARTS NES	W 1448	376.8	W 2210	676.3	W 1819	741.5	W 1837	698.2	PIECES DU 792
793	SHIPS AND BOATS ETC		718.8		1467.5	W 1430133	1556.3	W 1346445	1934.4	NAVIRES BATEAUX,ETC
7932	SHIPS AND BOATS NES		475.5	W 1263006	1433.7	W 1373137	1448.0	W 1190060	1740.1	NAVIRES ET BATEAUX
79322	TANKERS OF ALL KINDS	W 117318	57.9	W 433048	604.4	W 611253	426.1	W 388084	579.2	BATEAUX–CITERNES
79323	OTHER CARGO VESSELS	W 444907	415.5	W 818356	772.5	W 736506	960.7	W 783822	1124.9	AUT BATEAUX TRANS MARCH
8	MISC MANUFACTURED GOODS		5870.3		7805.5		10551.1		11844.1	ART MANUFACTURES DIVERS
84	CLOTHING AND ACCESSORIES		361.3		699.8		1081.3		1516.8	VETEMENTS
87	PRECISION INSTRUMNTS NES		2456.7		3248.9		4292.7		4565.1	INSTRUM,APPAR SCIENT NDA
871	OPTICAL INSTRUMENTS		225.8	W 1731	328.2	W 2164	416.7	W 2356	389.8	APPAR,INSTRUM D'OPTIQUE
874	MEASURNG,CONTROLNG INSTR		2010.1	W 18584	2618.8	W 22021	3559.0	W 26324	3846.3	INSTRUMENTS DE MESURE
8742	MEASUR,DRAW ETC INST,PTS	W 5844	642.2	W 6858	703.2	W 8140	933.9	W 10511	1101.9	INST DESSIN,TRACAGE,PCS
87421	MEASURNG,DRAWNG ETC INST	W 5528	594.1	W 6512	628.5	W 7603	830.4	W 9759	967.5	INSTRUM DESSIN,TRACAGE
8743	GAS,LIQUID CONTROL INSTR	W 3687	428.8	W 4777	515.1	W 5011	629.2	W 5439	562.6	APP,INSTR MESURE FLUIDES
8748	ELEC MEAS,CONTRL EQU NES		615.1	W 3563	928.1	W 5022	1436.2	W 5406	1559.1	APP ELEC ELECTRO MESURE
87483	OTH ELCTRNC MEAS ETC EQU		587.7	W 3279	901.9	W 4729	1406.1	W 5168	1530.5	AUT APP ELECTRO DE MESURE
88	PHOTO EQU,OPTICL GDS ETC		1135.4		1470.3		2017.0		2072.0	APP,FOURN PHOTO,OP,MONTR
881	PHOTO APPARAT,EQUIPT NES		383.6	W 3841	606.5	W 4718	958.7	W 5391	952.6	APP,EQUIP PHOTO NDA
8813	OTH PHOTO,CINE EQUIP NES		234.0	W 2425	439.0	W 2932	755.5	W 3244	753.6	APP,MAT PHOTO,CINEMA
88139	PHOTO,CINE LAB EQUIP NES	W 1379	224.0	W 2055	423.1	W 2515	736.5	W 2781	734.0	APP TYPES UTIL LABOR
882	PHOTO,CINEMA SUPPLIES		400.3	W 33129	468.7	W 39144	593.4	W 41354	663.9	PRODUITS PHOTO,CINEMA
8822	PHOTO FILM EXC DEV CINMA		299.9	W 18451	337.2	W 21283	396.9	W 21893	441.1	PLAQUES,PELLICULES,FILMS
89	MISC MANUFCTRD GOODS NES		1644.4		1986.3		2524.3		2800.4	ART MANUFACTURES DIVERS
893	ARTICLES OF PLASTIC NES		298.5		371.5		491.8		533.3	OUVRAGES EN MAT DIVIS 58
894	TOYS,SPORTING GOODS,ETC		406.1	W 45182	446.7	W 48936	604.8	W 55771	715.1	VOITURES ENFANTS,JOUETS
898	MUSICAL INSTRUMENTS,PTS		424.0	W 18382	565.4	W 23854	701.2	W 18257	735.0	INSTRUMENTS DE MUSIQUE
8983	SOUND RECRDNG TAPE,DISCS		351.2	W 8761	479.8	W 8680	598.7	W 7527	643.6	SUPPORTS SON POUR 763
89832	RECORDED DISCS,TAPES ETC		245.1	W 1265	341.0	W 1209	431.1	W 1255	499.1	DISQUES,PHONO,BANDES
9	GOODS NOT CLASSD BY KIND		730.3		1145.8		3071.0		5963.9	ART TRANSACT NON CLASSES
951	*WAR FIREARMS,AMMUNITION	W 2694	243.3	W 2502	322.7	W 2211	198.7	W 2225	222.1	VEHIC BLINDES ARMES
971	*GOLD,NON MONETARY NES		396.4	K 58545	713.8	K 217180	2737.5	K 446807	5610.2	OR NON MONETAIRE
97101	NONMON GLD UNWRT,SEMIMFD		396.2	K 58324	713.5	K 217118	2737.3	K 446755	5610.0	OR,ALLIAGES D'OR BRUTS

5. Special Exports F.O.B. by Commodities according to the S.I.T.C. (Rev. 2) in million U.S. Dollars
Exportations Spéciales F.O.B. par Produits d'après la C.T.C.I. (Rév. 2) en millions de Dollars E.U.

SITC CTCI	COMMODITY	1993 QUANTITY QUANTITE	1993 VALUE VALEUR	1994 QUANTITY QUANTITE	1994 VALUE VALEUR	1995 QUANTITY QUANTITE	1995 VALUE VALEUR	1996 QUANTITY QUANTITE	1996 VALUE VALEUR	PRODUIT
	ALL COMMODITIES		82232.2		96007.8		125056.5		129714.6	TOUS PRODUITS
0	FOOD AND LIVE ANIMALS		2042.2		2280.3		2645.4		2717.3	ALIMENTS,ANIMAUX VIVANTS
03	FISH AND PREPARATIONS		1325.3		1400.5		1550.6		1493.8	POISSONS ET PREPARATIONS
034	FISH,FRESH,CHILLED,FROZN	W 216426	636.1	W 200373	697.4	W 220400	745.0	W 227180	694.1	POISSON FRAIS, REFRIG,CONG
0342	FISH FROZEN,EXCL FILLETS	W 178388	385.4	W 161461	376.2	W 178055	395.7	W 194932	431.7	POISSONS CONGELES
036	SHELL FISH FRESH,FROZEN	W 43359	327.9	W 43159	327.3	W 93017	398.9	W 90116	372.5	CRUSTACES,MOLLUSQUES
037	FISH ETC PREPD,PRSVD NES	W 57897	344.2	W 64374	362.4	W 66539	395.4	W 77769	416.9	POIS,CRUST,MOL PREPARES
2	CRUDE MATERLS,EXCL FUELS		1156.8		1426.3		1785.3		1604.5	MAT BRUTES NON COMESTIBLES
26	TEXTILE FIBRES AND WASTE		565.3		773.6		1056.7		923.6	FIBRES TEXTILES
266	SYNTHETIC FIBRES TO SPIN	W 453287	521.1	W 541248	718.4	W 559659	974.5	W 690303	835.3	FIBRES SYNTHETIQUES
2665	DISCN SYNTH FIBRE UNCMBD	W 412972	461.9	W 486676	632.8	W 510393	875.3	W 637695	749.2	DISCONTINUES EN MASSE
26652	— POLYESTER	W 357579	386.9	W 405194	509.3	W 434585	724.4	W 564444	639.5	FIBRES EN POLYESTERS
29	CRUDE ANIMAL,VEG MAT NES		299.3		315.6		341.8		289.3	MATIERES BRUTES ANIM,VEGET
292	CRUDE VEG MATERIALS NES		281.7	W 33918	296.4	W 30957	316.2	W 26681	252.5	MAT BRUTES VEGETALES NDA
3	MINERAL FUELS ETC		1858.8		1756.4		2486.8		3893.3	COMBUSTIBLES MINERAUX LUB
33	PETROLEUM AND PRODUCTS		1838.3		1723.7		2432.4		3820.1	PETROLE ET DERIVES
334	PETROLEUM PRODUCTS,REFIN		1739.0	MW 12627	1618.7	MW 15878	2306.0	MW 20507	3705.1	PRODUITS RAFFINES
3343	GAS OILS	W 4501946	806.7							GAS OILS
3344	FUEL OILS,NES	MW 9084	625.9							FUEL OILS
5	CHEMCLS,RELATED PROD NES		4850.2		6248.6		8827.1		9009.6	PRODUITS CHIMIQUES
51	ORGANIC CHEMICALS		1462.0		1892.3		2668.4		2664.7	PROD CHIMIQ ORGANIQUES
511	HYDROCARBONS NES,DERIVS	W 2007944	641.3	W 2518217	965.7	W 2684507	1214.0	W 3214124	1216.8	HYDROCARBURES NDA
5112	CYCLIC HYDROCARBONS	W 1317984	435.2	W 1625813	661.4	W 1804028	861.5	W 2269381	857.6	HYDROCARBURES CYCLIQUES
513	CARBOXYLIC ACIDS ETC	W 468923	272.0	W 396403	301.3	W 617761	693.7	W 796562	578.8	ACIDES CARBOXYLIQUES
5138	POLYACIDS AND DERIVATIVS	W 331579	187.2	W 242058	192.6	W 472049	543.7	W 642341	440.9	ACIDES POLYCARBOXYLIQUES
514	NITROGEN–FNCTN COMPOUNDS	W 137702	305.2	W 174739	370.2	W 182315	437.5	W 224469	503.4	COMPOSES FONCT AZOTEES
53	DYES,TANNING,COLOUR PROD		271.8		342.9		417.8		465.9	PROD TEINTURE,COLORANTS
58	PLASTIC MATERIALS ETC		2257.3		2915.8		4399.9		4267.3	MAT PLAST ARTIFICIELLES
582	PROD OF CONDENSATION ETC	W 400514	578.3	W 502970	764.8	W 578614	1245.0	W 763939	1161.3	PROD CONDENS,POLYCOND
5823	ALKYDS,OTHER POLYESTERS	W 325768	451.4	W 401004	585.0	W 454086	985.0	W 631688	892.6	ALKYDES ET AUT POLYESTERS
58231	— IN PRIMARY FORMS	W 264623	276.3	W 336971	396.5	W 379776	697.7	W 540540	540.9	SOUS FORMES PRIMAIRES
583	POLYMERIZATION ETC PRODS		1676.1	W 2533251	2147.2	W 2944547	3146.8	W 3298347	3095.9	PROD POLYMERISATION
5831	POLYETHYLENE	W 949785	538.1	W 935633	649.2	W 1110070	977.2	W 1153620	936.5	POLYETHYLENE
58311	— IN PRIMARY FORMS	W 936894	516.5	W 918167	617.6	W 1085689	928.7	W 1127488	883.9	POLYETHYLENE PRIMAIRES
5832	POLYPROPYLENE	W 780354	437.5	W 841722	617.4	W 857593	855.7	W 943660	787.4	POLYPROPYLENE
58321	— IN PRIMARY FORMS	W 746642	375.9	W 805497	550.3	W 810844	751.1	W 898671	698.0	POLYPROPYLENE PRIMAIRES
5833	POLYSTYRENE,ITS COPOLYMR	W 471212	389.1	W 472765	474.1	W 605559	742.5	W 721445	698.3	POLYPROPYLENE COPOLYMERES
58331	— IN PRIMARY FORMS	W 468783	385.8	W 470407	470.7	W 603261	737.9	W 720014	695.3	SOUS FORMES PRIMAIRES
59	CHEMICAL MATERIALS NES		222.6		298.8		400.6		568.0	MAT PROD CHIMIQUES NDA
598	MISCEL CHEM PRODUCTS NES	W 155645	174.5	W 198139	231.5	W 220727	311.9	W 222473	458.9	PROD DIV INDUST CHIM NDA
5989	CHEM PRODUCTS,PREPS NES	W 152215	168.9	W 193982	223.6	W 213952	300.9	W 215668	448.8	PROD PREP CHIMIQUES NDA
59899	OTH CHEM PRODS,PREPS,NES	W 143754	152.0	W 182201	196.4	W 192347	265.9	W 194289	404.6	AUT PRODUITS CHIMIQUES NDA
6	BASIC MANUFACTURES		20901.4		23216.6		27899.7		27373.2	ART MANUFACTURES
61	LEATHER,DRESSED FUR,ETC		1167.6		1553.5		1808.2		1986.6	CUIRS,PELLETERIES
611	LEATHER	W 86936	970.7	W 107753	1302.5	W 116694	1525.6	W 118588	1599.4	CUIRS,PEAUX PREPARES
6114	LEATHR BOVINE NES,EQUINE	W 60006	670.6	W 74054	878.6	W 83352	1047.8	W 88786	1123.4	CUIRS DE BOVINS
62	RUBBER MANUFACTURES NES		1279.7		1391.2		1518.1		1763.7	CAOUTCHOUC MANUFACTURE
625	RUBBER TYRES, TUBES ETC	W 448426	1132.1	W 507928	1233.0	W 502871	1329.8	W 553783	1548.7	PNEUS CAOUTCHOUC VULCANISE
6251	TYRES NEW FOR MOTOR CARS	W 174785	480.3	W 220300	583.3	W 227744	656.5	W 244157	738.8	PNEUS POUR VOITURES
6252	TYRES,NEW,BUS OR LORRY	W 182850	437.3	W 186762	432.4	W 166117	421.9	W 194453	529.2	PNEUS POUR AUTOBUS,CAMIONS
64	PAPER,PAPERBOARD AND MFR		572.9		832.2		1178.1		1239.2	PAPIERS,CARTONS & OUVRAGES
641	PAPER AND PAPERBOARD		416.9	W 952538	633.8	W 1013294	884.9	W 1416259	937.9	PAPIERS ET CARTONS
6412	PRINTG,WRITING PAPER NES	W 593059	336.7	W 727310	498.6	W 700884	626.3	W 958741	675.5	PAPIERS POUR L'IMPRESSION
64122	— COATED,IMPREGNATD ETC	W 592640	333.3	W 726856	495.1	W 700113	622.4	W 958106	671.8	PAPIERS IMPRESSION COUCHES
65	TEXTILE YARN,FABRICS,ETC		8963.3		10702.3		12320.0		12717.4	FILS,TISSUS,ARTICLES TEXTILE
651	TEXTILE YARN		948.0	W 262317	1059.4	W 311592	1335.9	W 454080	1473.8	FILS TEXTILES
6514	SYN FIB YRN,BULK,MONOFIL	W 143819	513.0	W 164643	552.2	W 220202	828.6	W 365569	1000.0	FILS CONT 85% FIB TEXT SYNTH
65142	— NONTXT ETC CONT PAMID	W 125405	416.1	W 137598	419.5	W 190774	659.1	W 328298	832.1	FILS NON TEX FI CON POLYAMID
652	COTTON FABRICS,WOVEN	W 47533	392.2	W 53342	469.6	W 52392	520.5	W 53856	557.5	TISSUS DE COTON
6522	WOVEN COTTON BLEACHD,ETC	W 35692	338.2	W 45134	426.5	W 47089	488.7	W 49629	531.6	TISSUS COTON BLANCHIS ETC
653	WOVN MAN–MADE FIB FABRIC	W 472404	4724.8	W 591791	5781.7	W 655051	6561.5	W 693707	6274.0	TISSUS FIBRES SYNTH,ARTIF
6531	CONT SYNT WEAVES NONPILE	W 342657	3531.7	W 437663	4341.1	W 505274	5038.4	W 559849	4925.3	TISSUS FIBRES SYNTH CONTINUE
65315	CONT SYN TXTL FABRIC NES	W 338599	3479.8	W 433382	4282.9	W 500533	4968.9	W 554937	4862.7	TIS PLUS 85% TEXT SYNT CONT
6534	DISC SYN BLEND FABRC NES	W 45282	350.5	W 46385	355.4	W 40048	317.8	W 37734	298.3	TISSUS FIBRES SYNTH DISCONT
65341	DISC SYN FIB–COTTN FABRC	W 37472	274.6	W 39594	284.2	W 33755	247.5	W 31656	228.9	TISSUS FIB SYNT DIS MEL COTO
6535	CONT REGN WEAVES NONPILE	W 25230	262.3	W 25481	270.6	W 27254	315.1	W 28245	328.9	TISSUS FIB TEXT ART CONTINU
6536	DISC REGN TXTL FABRC NES	W 31808	247.7	W 47106	388.7	W 43528	366.8	W 29690	236.0	TISSUS 85% TEXT ART DISC
654	OTH WOVEN TEXTILE FABRIC	W 16460	497.2	W 14639	476.6	W 14049	436.4	W 11283	439.1	TISSUS AUT COTON SYNT,ARTIF
6541	SILK FABRICS WOVEN	W 3155	306.3	W 3144	297.6	W 2966	266.3	W 3401	297.2	TISSUS DE SOIE
655	KNITTED,ETC FABRICS	W 111084	840.0	W 141801	1121.6	W 152420	1227.4	W 172119	1447.5	ETOF BONNETERIE PIECES ETC
6552	OTHER KNIT ETC FAB NONEL	W 111084	840.0	W 141801	1121.6	W 152420	1227.4	W 172119	1447.5	ETOF BON NON ELAS NON SYNT
656	LACE,RIBBONS,TULLE,ETC	W 23608	269.1	W 23442	298.1	W 26359	369.1	W 30601	449.9	TULLES,BRODERIE
657	SPECIAL TXTL FABRC,PRODS	W 194319	923.9	W 230850	1114.2	W 269530	1438.8	W 292335	1695.1	TISSUS SPECIAUX
6573	COATED ETC TEXTILES NES	W 130858	654.4	W 158730	787.4	W 185949	1000.4	W 202038	1172.9	TISSUS,ART MATIERE TEXT NDA
65732	PLASTIC COATED TEXTILES	W 93532	491.2	W 117902	609.1	W 144678	801.0	W 160161	973.0	TISSUS IMPREGNES
658	TEXTILE ARTICLES NES	W 61489	344.4	W 55319	353.7	W 58154	397.2	W 52298	339.1	ART FACONNES MAT TEXTILES
66	NONMETAL MINERAL MFS NES		648.2		661.2		690.1		660.4	ART MIN NON METALLIQUES
661	LIME,CEMENT,BLDG PRODS		358.3	W 4455209	339.2	W 3598534	290.7	W 2407191	213.2	CHAUX,CIMENTS MAT CONSTR
67	IRON AND STEEL		5022.5		4787.7		5558.0		5372.9	FER ET ACIER
672	IRON,STEEL PRIMARY FORMS		1246.4	W 3110158	1119.1	W 3152589	1289.4	W 3606147	1267.5	LINGOTS FER,ACIER
6727	IRN,STL COIL FR REROLLNG		1168.2	W 2924588	1067.6	W 2711069	1157.7	W 3171887	1161.7	EBAUCHES POUR TOLES FER
67271	IRON,SIMPLE STEEL COILS	W 3309636	1112.1	W 2885564	1013.5	W 2666736	1079.2	W 3109424	1066.6	EBAUCHES NON EN ACIER
673	IRON,STEEL SHAPES ETC		674.0	W 1494614	669.0	W 962086	574.2	W 1321889	609.2	BARRES,PROFIL FER,ACIER
6732	IRON,STEEL BARS ETC		271.5	W 871524	300.8	W 291890	170.2	W 453612	203.7	BARRES FER,ACIER
6733	IRON,STEEL PROFILES ETC		270.0	W 446132	250.8	W 509020	281.3	W 706982	299.6	PROFILES,PALPLAN FER,ACIER
674	IRN,STL UNIV,PLATE,SHEET		2269.1	W 3897800	2142.5	W 3951012	2633.5	W 4021732	2487.4	LARGES PLATS,TOLES
6744	IRN,STL HVY PLATE,ROLLED		326.2	W 593923	252.8	W 615139	310.9	W 510944	224.8	TOLES LAMINEES PLUS 4.75 MM
67441	— OF IRON OR SIMPLE STL		321.6	W 591311	248.2	W 609716	297.3	W 499297	201.3	TOLES NON ACIER FIN CARB
6746	IRN,STL THIN PLATE,ROLLD		1080.3	W 1890817	1043.0	W 1902334	1285.2	W 1991183	1252.5	TOLES LAM MOINS 3MM
67461	— OF IRON OR SIMPLE STL		819.5	W 1738600	760.7	W 1752675	923.7	W 1773298	858.3	TOL NON AC FIN MOINS 3 MM
67463	— OF STAINLESS ETC STL		257.7	W 152209	282.4	W 135808	353.3	W 189412	378.9	TOL ACIER INOX MOINS 3 MM
6749	OTH IRN,STL PLATES,SHEET		652.9	W 1025520	625.4	W 1047445	794.5	W 1078236	735.3	AUTRES TOLES FER,ACIER
67491	— OF IRON OR SIMPLE STL		642.0	W 1019258	612.3	W 1040524	774.2	W 1069153	718.1	AUT TOLES AUTRES ACIER FIN
678	IRON,STL TUBES,PIPES,ETC		554.7	W 884850	525.1	W 895539	610.5	W 856883	572.5	TUBES,TUYAUX EN FONTE,FER
6783	IRON,STL TUBES,PIPES NES		463.7	W 823860	414.8	W 826320	466.4	W 806335	441.5	AUT TUBES,TUYAUX FER,ACIER
68	NON–FERROUS METALS		476.0		751.0		1099.8		1010.1	METAUX NON FERREUX
682	COPPER EXC CEMENT COPPER		243.7	W 106057	318.4	W 115663	430.4	W 148724	448.1	CUIVRE
6822	COPPER,ALLOYS WORKED	W 79707	231.2	W 98790	301.7	W 111047	416.7	W 140080	427.4	CUIVRE,ALLIAGES OUVRES
684	ALUMINIUM		153.5	W 121215	283.4	W 185381	522.9	W 141616	395.3	ALUMINIUM
69	METAL MANUFACTURES NES		2692.7		2423.0		3581.3		2491.0	ART MANUFACT EN METAL NDA
691	STRUCTURES AND PARTS NES		1026.2	W 227729	534.7	W 607109	1352.9	W 196022	405.2	CONSTRUCT FER,ACIER,ALU

5. Special Exports F.O.B. by Commodities according to the S.I.T.C. (Rev. 2) in million U.S. Dollars
Exportations Spéciales F.O.B. par Produits d'après la C.T.C.I. (Rév. 2) en millions de Dollars E.U.

SITC CTCI	COMMODITY	1993		1994		1995		1996		PRODUIT
		QUANTITY QUANTITE	VALUE VALEUR	QUANTITY QUANTITE	VALUE VALEUR	QUANTITY QUANTITE	VALUE VALEUR	QUANTITY QUANTITE	VALUE VALEUR	
6911	STRUCTURES,PARTS IRN,STL		989.1	W 220286	493.9	W 595521	1286.3	W 185583	328.9	CONSTRUCT FER,ACIER,FONTE
697	BASE MTL HOUSEHOLD EQUIP	W 66953	464.3	W 73402	488.4	W 68674	488.0	W 62751	436.3	ART MENAGE MET COMMUNS
6974	BASE MTL DMSTC ARTIC NES	W 47751	352.5	W 55356	388.7	W 49931	387.5	W 46950	345.7	ARTICLES NDA FONTE,FER,ETC
69741	— OF IRON OR STEEL	W 33769	249.0	W 35987	258.6	W 33417	267.4	W 29147	229.0	ART NDA EN FONTE,FER
699	BASE METAL MFRS NES		316.6	W 119406	377.6	W 147101	507.4	W 136082	475.0	ART MANUFACTURES MET NDA
7	MACHINES,TRANSPORT EQUIP		36934.8		47037.3		65624.7		67550.6	MACHINES MATERIEL TRANSPORT
71	POWER GENERATING EQUIPMT		845.3		1002.3		1212.2		692.8	MACHINES GENERATRICES
714	ENGINES AND MOTORS NES	W 832	520.9	W 1254	541.9	W 1565	608.1	W 684	141.6	MOTEURS NON ELECTRIQUES
7144	REACTION ENGINES	W 337	326.2	W 297	290.1	W 231	246.6	W 100	72.5	PROPULSEURS A REACTION
72	MACHS FOR SPCL INDUSTRYS		1210.1		1729.5		2588.4		3047.6	MAC SPECIALES POUR INDUST
723	CIVIL ENGNEERG EQUIP ETC	W 79004	240.8	W 134062	430.0	W 194079	672.9	W 206559	723.6	APPAREILS DE GENIE CIVIL
7234	CONST,MINING MACHNRY NES	W 64795	210.6	W 117707	392.6	W 168387	604.8	W 180182	665.3	MACH POUR LA CONST, MINES
72342	SLFPRP SHOVELS,EXCAVATRS	W 62651	199.1	W 114617	377.8	W 163211	579.5	W 175819	632.4	PELLES MECANIQUES
724	TEXTILE,LEATHER MACHNRY		462.9	W 92119	612.9	W 97375	745.1	W 115100	816.9	MACH POUR INDUSTRIE TEXTILE
728	OTH MACHY FOR SPCL INDUS		392.0	W 59107	550.7	W 72350	1001.7	W 87783	1315.5	AUT MACH IND PARTICULIERES
7284	MACHY FOR SPCL INDUS NES		334.6	W 38118	461.7	W 52895	881.6	W 65611	1167.8	MACH SPEC IND PARTICUL.
72848	OTH MCHY WITH INDIV FNCT	W 10622	132.7	W 15768	211.2	W 22791	430.1	W 27453	558.7	AUTRES MACHINES NDA
73	METALWORKING MACHINERY		171.9		329.2		472.5		614.6	MACH TRAVAIL DES METAUX
736	METALWORKING MACH–TOOLS	W 16018	123.9	W 20049	199.1	W 35223	356.1	W 47837	510.0	MACH–OUTILS TRAVAIL METAUX
74	GENRL INDUSTRL MACHY NES		1715.3		2199.6		2953.3		3150.7	MACH APP INDUSTRIE
741	HEATING,COOLING EQUIPMNT	W 68489	472.8	W 78207	564.7	W 104006	783.7	W 97326	759.2	MACH CHAUFFAGE,PIECES
7415	AIR–CONDITIONING MACHNRY	W 26430	206.2	W 32291	244.1	W 46845	396.8	W 53057	450.8	GROUPES CONDITION AIR
743	PUMPS NES,CENTRFUGES ETC		254.3	W 44327	277.8	W 68696	455.5	W 75919	528.5	POMPES COMPRES,VENT ETC
7431	PUMPS FOR GASES ETC	W 29489	171.8	W 33177	193.0	W 54374	333.6	W 57371	390.9	POMPES AIR A VIDE,COMPRES
744	MECHANICAL HANDLING EQU	W 93296	470.6	W 134431	679.0	W 159850	836.0	W 186590	890.8	EQUIP MANUTENTION PIECES
7442	LIFTING,LOADING MACH NES	W 38881	220.7	W 70109	371.4	W 66738	424.1	W 71135	426.9	APP LEVAGE,MANUTENTION
74428	OTH HANDLING ETC MCH NES	W 27797	156.1	W 57291	306.2	W 43706	300.5	W 48664	305.1	AUT APP LEVAGE ETC
749	NONELEC MACH PTS,ACC NES		404.3	W 46613	459.9	W 56753	653.9	W 62676	774.0	PIECES MACH NON ELEC NDA
7499	OTH NONELEC MCHY PTS NES		168.0	W 13253	200.9	W 16825	296.3	W 22281	447.1	PIECES NON ELECT NDA
74991	FOUNDRY MOULDS ETC NES	W 9949	158.5	W 11801	190.6	W 14853	279.6	W 19633	408.1	MOULES POUR METAUX
75	OFFICE MACHNES,ADP EQUIP		3474.4		3607.3		4967.0		5673.4	MACH BUREAU TRAIT AUTOM
752	AUTOMTIC DATA PROC EQUIP	W 134097	2584.8	W 145438	2799.9	W 190097	3956.1	W 206123	4706.9	MACH TRAIT INFORMATION
7522	DIGITAL COMPUTERS	W 7247	344.9	W 4013	257.0	W 3136	169.4	W 526	74.3	MACH DIGITALES COMPLETES
7524	DIGITL CENTRL STOR UNITS	W 881	116.6	W 1459	222.1	W 2628	375.0	W 5657	684.6	UNITES MEMOIRE CENTRALES
7525	ADP PERIPHERAL UNITS	W 123868	1990.9	W 138487	2229.6	W 181995	3239.7	W 197783	3745.5	UNITES PERIPHERIQUES
759	OFFICE,ADP MCH PTS,ACCES		739.9	W 5803	624.5	W 7265	805.6	W 9272	733.5	PIECES DU 751 ET 752
7599	ACCTG,ETC,ADP MCH PTS,AC		722.9	W 4164	595.7	W 4961	768.2	W 8072	716.9	PIECES DU 751 ET 752
76	TELECOMM,SOUND EQUIPMENT		7093.0		8234.4		8877.5		8887.3	EQUIPMENT DE TELECOM
761	TELEVISION RECEIVERS	W 140758	1462.8	W 160385	1698.3	W 173061	1900.8	W 201018	2206.5	RECEPTEURS DE TELEVISION
7611	COLOUR TV RECEIVERS	W 134982	1406.3	W 156845	1648.8	W 169778	1844.0	W 198679	2157.1	RECEPTEURS COULEUR
762	RADIO BROADCAST RECEIVRS	W 55752	1126.0	W 52689	1092.4	W 41420	908.9	W 18577	530.1	RECEPTEURS RADIODIFFUSION
7621	MTR VEHC RADIO RECEIVERS	W 14399	469.0	W 14237	464.9	W 12163	424.1	W 8640	333.1	RECEPTEURS RADIO AUTO
7628	OTHER RADIO RECEIVERS	W 36761	567.3	W 32032	500.9	W 25383	409.8	W 8423	156.7	AUTRES RECEPT RADIO
763	SOUND RECORDRS,PHONOGRPH	W 56125	1581.9	W 62696	1756.8	W 58595	1824.3	W 47293	1747.1	PHONO,APP ENREGISTREMENT
7638	OTHR SOUND APPARATUS ETC	W 51425	1524.4	W 59255	1715.8	W 56547	1797.8	W 45515	1724.0	AUT APP D'ENREGIS,REPROD
76381	TV IMAGE,SND RECRDRS ETC	W 43174	1310.0	W 49056	1479.7	W 45354	1498.6	W 36691	1434.8	APP ENREG,REPRO IMAG,SON
764	TELECOM EQPT,PTS,ACC NES	W 127621	2922.4	W 144787	3687.1	W 149975	4243.7	W 168243	4403.7	EQUIP TELECOM,PIECES
7641	LINE TELEPHONE,ETC EQUIP	W 12973	591.7	W 14256	669.7	W 16788	792.4	W 17094	766.5	APP TELEPHON PAR FIL
7642	MICROPH,LOUDSPKR,AMPLIFR	W 43130	348.8	W 45316	399.9	W 46811	447.6	W 42585	458.1	MICRO,HAUT–PARLEUR,AMPLI
7643	TV,RADIO TRANSMITTRS ETC	W 2033	277.7	W 2135	453.6	W 2533	584.5	W 2052	529.3	APP EMET TELE RADIO
7648	TELECOMM EQUIPMENT NES	W 9259	411.5	W 9274	485.3	W 9241	551.4	W 9759	398.2	APP TELECOM NDA
7649	PTS NES OF EQUIPMT OF 76	W 60227	1292.8	W 73807	1678.8	W 74602	1867.9	W 96754	2251.8	PIECES DE LA DIV 76
76493	TELECOMM EQUIPMT PTS NES	W 44159	765.5	W 56081	1026.5	W 51836	1040.5	W 67249	1354.9	PIECES 761,762,764.3,8
76499	PARTS ETC OF SOUND EQUIP	W 8937	410.4	W 9423	500.8	W 12292	613.0	W 18201	644.1	PIECES NDA POUR 763
77	ELECTRIC MACHNRY NES ETC		12340.8		18114.4		28499.1		25498.7	MACH APP ELECT NDA
771	ELECTRIC POWER MACHY NES		406.2	W 62737	442.7	W 78470	565.0	W 86304	711.9	MACH PROD,TRANS ELECTR
7712	OTH ELEC POWER MACHY NES		201.4	W 21941	211.8	W 31261	310.0	W 37437	426.8	AUT APP PROD TRANSF ELEC
772	SWITCHGEAR ETC,PARTS NES		469.6	W 23556	662.1	W 25663	757.0	W 32127	909.0	APP COUPURE,SECT ETC
7721	SWITCHGEAR ETC		250.3	W 15915	331.8	W 16553	374.0	W 21437	453.5	APP COUPURE,SECTIONMNT
773	ELECTR DISTRIBUTNG EQUIP	W 115921	394.9	W 100136	360.1	W 129107	490.0	W 158150	620.3	EQUIPMT DISTRIBUTION ELECT
7731	INSULATED WIRE,CABLE ETC	W 112020	386.0	W 98086	352.4	W 125656	478.9	W 155835	601.5	FILS,CABLES ISOLES ELECT
775	HOUSEHOLD TYPE EQUIP NES		1217.8	W 273308	1487.7	W 302994	1691.3	W 336126	1921.7	MACH,APP USAGE DOMESTQUE
7752	DOM REFRIGERATRS,FREEZRS	W 74584	338.8	W 79765	368.0	W 84210	393.2	W 102479	480.5	REFRIG,CONGEL MENAGER
77521	DOMESTIC REFRIGERATORS	W 74073	336.2	W 78943	363.3	W 83168	386.3	W 101598	475.6	REFRIGERATEURS
7758	ELECTRO–THERMIC APPL NES		743.3	W 158754	925.2	W 168703	1007.8	W 171467	1059.6	APP ELECTROTHERMIQ NDA
77586	ELECTROTHERM DOM APP NES	W 117379	680.8	W 146491	816.9	W 145059	837.5	W 143565	864.3	APP ELECTRO THERMIQUES
776	TRANSISTORS,VALVES,ETC		8078.4	W 199742	11848.0	W 245138	19372.9	W 291802	17305.2	LAMPES,TUBES,VALVES
7761	TV PICTURE TUBES	W 151167	889.1	W 159850	913.5	W 181016	1087.6	W 192271	1098.2	TUBES CATHODIQUES
7762	OTH ELECTRONIC TUBES ETC		124.4	W 20748	239.0	W 36747	506.4	W 60895	876.6	AUT LAMPES ELECTRONIQUES
7763	DIODES,TRANSISTORS,ETC		438.9	W 2542	511.1	W 2989	669.6	W 3407	673.9	DIODES,TRANSISTORS
7764	ELECTRONIC MICROCIRCUITS		6425.8	W 8714	9917.9	W 10433	16734.6	W 11262	14161.2	MICROSTRUCTURES ELECTRON
7768	ELCTRNC COMP PTS,CRYSTLS		200.5	W 7888	266.8	W 13954	374.9	W 23967	495.4	CRIST PIEZO–ELEC,PCS 776
77689	ELECTRNIC COMPON PTS NES		133.3	W 7575	181.9	W 13547	255.8	W 23585	396.3	PIECES DU GROUPE 776
778	ELECTRICAL MACHINERY NES		1734.0	W 148151	3258.5	W 181803	5556.2	W 206354	3954.3	AUTRES MACH ELECT NDA
7788	OTH ELEC MACHY,EQUIP NES		1336.5	W 30187	2788.6	W 34668	5015.4	W 36961	3399.5	AUT MACH APP ELEC NDA
77889	ELEC PARTS OF MACHY NES	W 315	1002.0	W 503	2347.6	W 691	4419.8	W 678	2605.3	PIECES ELEC DE MACH NDA
78	ROAD VEHICLES		5725.1		6631.7		10121.9		12350.6	VEHICULES ROUTIERS
781	PASS MOTOR VEH EXC BUSES	W 588214	3884.0	W 670197	4470.5	W 1015619	7242.0	W 1277117	9087.7	AUTO TRANSPORT PERSONNES
782	LORRIES,SPCL MTR VEH NES	W 91250	334.5	W 144222	507.8	W 239859	796.5	W 257232	872.5	VEHICULES SPECIAUX,MARCH
7821	LORRIES,TRUCKS	W 87800	323.4	W 133524	463.0	W 217418	698.7	W 241994	814.2	VEHICULES TRANSP MARCHAND
783	ROAD MOTOR VEHICLES NES	W 57019	256.1	W 77359	279.1	W 91622	363.7	W 102286	465.2	VEHICULES ROUTIERS NDA
7831	BUSES	W 56801	255.3	W 77131	279.0	W 91500	363.6	W 102174	465.1	VOITURES TRANSPORT COMMUN
784	MOTOR VEH PRTS,ACCES NES	W 70202	385.1	W 82003	500.9	W 113604	667.4	W 166235	1036.9	PIECES 722,781,782,783
7849	OTHER MOTOR VEHCL PARTS	W 69452	382.3	W 81166	497.1	W 109507	653.0	W 161545	1008.8	PIECES 722,781,782,783
786	TRAILERS,NONMOTR VEH,NES	W 193603	725.7	W 297621	711.8	W 295856	874.1	W 194407	700.5	REMORQUES,CADRES,CONTAIN
7861	TRAILERS,TRANSP CONTAINR	W 176872	689.0	W 275774	665.4	W 272841	823.5	W 175739	659.8	REMORQUES TOUS VEHICULES
78613	CONTAINERS INC ROAD–RAIL	W 176439	687.9	W 275027	663.7	W 272050	821.6	W 174932	657.8	CADRES ET CONTAINERS
79	OTHR TRANSPORT EQUIPMENT		4359.4		5189.3		5933.1		7635.3	AUTRE MATERIEL TRANSPORT
792	AIRCRAFT ETC		286.4		224.9		282.0	W 1268	236.8	APP NAVIGATION AERIENNE
793	SHIPS AND BOATS ETC		4060.7	MW 13943	4944.9		5532.8	MW 16153	7127.4	NAVIRES BATEAUX,ETC
7932	SHIPS AND BOATS NES		3583.8	MW 13925	4888.7	MW 16431	5427.1	MW 16050	7009.5	NAVIRES ET BATEAUX
79322	TANKERS OF ALL KINDS		1467.9	W 2500999	2086.5	W 2696805	1896.8	W 2613019	2290.9	BATEAUX–CITERNES
79323	OTHER CARGO VESSELS		2084.4	MW 11421	2790.8	MW 13727	3512.7	MW 13428	4697.6	AUT BATEAUX TRANS MARCH
7938	TUGS,SPECIAL VESSELS ETC		473.9	W 12831	53.5		103.1	W 94491	86.6	REMORQUEURS,BATEAUX SPEC
79382	SPECL PURPOSE VESSLS ETC	W 64731	471.9	W 11971	49.2	W 35966	82.8	W 88629	48.0	BAT–PHARES,–POMPES,DRAGUES
8	MISC MANUFACTURED GOODS		14068.3		13293.6		13135.9		11978.3	ART MANUFACTURES DIVERS
831	*TRAVEL GOODS,HANDBAGS	W 51438	796.4	W 45773	706.2	W 42408	681.4	W 30882	540.9	ARTICLES DE VOYAGE ETC
83102	TRAVEL GDS,TOILET–CASES	W 23107	306.4	W 21139	277.9	W 19762	260.2	W 12954	192.0	ARTICLES DE VOYAGE
83109	OTHER TRAVEL BAGS,CASES	W 20469	303.2	W 18439	280.7	W 18917	309.2	W 15858	278.1	AUT CONTENANTS SIMILAIRES
84	CLOTHING AND ACCESSORIES		6229.2		5692.7		4981.7		4237.4	VETEMENTS
842	MENS OUTERWEAR NOT KNIT	W 30222	748.5	W 32763	667.3	W 23417	543.4	W 20087	463.9	VET DESSUS POUR HOMMES

5. Special Exports F.O.B. by Commodities according to the S.I.T.C. (Rev. 2) in million U.S. Dollars
Exportations Spéciales F.O.B. par Produits d'après la C.T.C.I. (Rév. 2) en millions de Dollars E.U.

SITC CTCI	COMMODITY	1993		1994		1995		1996		PRODUIT
		QUANTITY QUANTITE	VALUE VALEUR	QUANTITY QUANTITE	VALUE VALEUR	QUANTITY QUANTITE	VALUE VALEUR	QUANTITY QUANTITE	VALUE VALEUR	
8429	— OTHER OUTER GARMENTS	W 16481	367.7	W 16274	347.7	W 14006	294.6	W 12260	259.5	AUT VET DES HOM MAT TEX
843	WOMENS OUTERWEAR NONKNIT		1059.8	W 42410	1035.0	W 33893	887.9	W 29976	733.5	VET DESSUS FEMMES MAT TEX
8431	— COATS AND JACKETS	W 8508	249.4	W 7216	235.4	W 5346	199.8	W 4131	160.9	MANT,VEST FEM MAT TEXTIL
8435	— BLOUSES	W 15904	267.1	W 14136	250.2	W 8062	199.0	W 7010	148.7	BLOUSES FEM MAT TEXTILES
8439	— OTHER OUTER GARMENTS		301.4	W 12184	280.8	W 12707	279.1	W 10622	226.7	AUT VET DES FEM MAT TEXT
844	UNDER GARMENTS NOT KNIT	W 29969	565.4	W 28604	517.5	W 24566	465.4	W 20473	367.0	VETEMENT DESSOUS MAT TEX
8441	— MENS SHIRTS	W 27653	510.1	W 27622	484.5	W 23892	440.0	W 19776	350.2	CHEMISES HOMMES MAT TEXT
84412	—— OF SYNTHETIC FIBRES	W 18867	313.1	W 19898	308.9	W 16807	273.4	W 14223	226.2	CHEMISES HOMMES FIB SYNT
845	OUTERWEAR KNIT NONELASTC		1412.4	W 81983	1468.4	W 63438	1275.5	W 52326	1062.7	VET DESSOUS,ACCES BONNET
8451	— JERSEYS,PULLOVERS ETC		744.4	W 39700	660.9	W 26981	498.9	W 22576	413.0	CHANDAILS,PULL–OVERS ETC
8459	— OTHER,CLTHG ACCESRYS	W 33847	602.2	W 38751	728.5	W 32627	682.4	W 26433	574.2	AUT VET DESSUS DE BONNE
846	UNDER GARMENTS KNITTED		650.3	W 35544	652.9	W 39797	741.1	W 37384	668.0	SOUS VETS DE BONNETERIE
8463	— OF SYNTH FBR NONELAST	W 20514	346.3	W 18131	327.7	W 15286	310.4	W 13706	284.4	SOUS–VET BONNET FIB SYNT
84632	—— MENS SHIRTS	W 18872	317.5	W 16792	303.1	W 14162	284.9	W 12419	254.2	CHEMISES DE BON FIB SYNMT
847	TEXTILE CLTHNG ACCES NES		561.2	W 26723	547.5	W 26887	539.9	W 28314	548.1	ACCES VET MAT TEXT NDA
8471	— NOT KNITTED		258.0	W 6197	232.4	W 5137	197.8	W 6565	219.8	ACCES VET MAT TEX NON BON
8472	CLTHNG ACCESRYS ETC KNIT		303.3	W 20526	315.2	W 21750	342.1	W 21749	328.3	ACCES VET BONNE NDA
84722	KNIT SOCKS,ETC NONELASTC		277.6	W 17178	288.0	W 18185	314.3	W 17868	301.3	CHAUSSETTES BON. NON ELAS
848	HEADGEAR,NONTXTL CLOTHNG		1231.9	W 20813	804.3	W 14689	528.9	W 11853	394.5	VET ACCES MAT AUT QUE TEX
8481	LEATHER CLOTHES,ACCESSOR	W 19554	1003.1	W 11015	602.8	W 5871	335.8	W 4011	221.0	VET ACCES MAT CUIR ARTIF
851	*FOOTWEAR	W 110290	2128.1	W 85870	1556.7	W 65335	1245.8	W 48399	890.5	CHAUSSURES
85101	FOOTWEAR RUBBER,PLASTIC	W 20263	388.5	W 17209	265.0	W 16153	297.8	W 11899	227.9	CHAUS SEMELLES CAOUTCH
85102	FOOTWEAR LEATHER	W 89038	1719.3	W 67717	1278.2	W 48761	943.3	W 36122	659.3	CHAUS SEMELLES EN CUIR
87	PRECISION INSTRUMNTS NES		521.4		612.8		806.1		778.9	INSTRUM,APPAR SCIENT NDA
871	OPTICAL INSTRUMENTS	W 2049	142.8	W 2125	176.6	W 2500	246.1	W 3692	392.7	APPAR,INSTRUM D'OPTIQUE
874	MEASURNG,CONTROLNG INSTR		322.7	W 6916	362.8	W 7738	474.5	W 8104	302.5	INSTRUMENTS DE MESURE
88	PHOTO EQU,OPTICL GDS ETC		657.9		748.7		891.5		887.7	APP,FOURN PHOTO,OP,MONTR
89	MISC MANUFCTRD GOODS NES		3499.4		3675.4		4217.8		4324.4	ART MANUFACTURES DIVERS
893	ARTICLES OF PLASTIC NES		521.4		623.2		756.2		763.7	OUVRAGES EN MAT DIVIS 58
8939	MISC PLASTIC ARTICLES		435.7	W 243922	517.1	W 258267	622.4	W 258017	601.3	ART DIVERS EN MAT DIV 58
89399	OTHR PLASTC ARTICLES NES		347.7	W 153602	401.9	W 161161	480.2	W 160373	462.3	AUT OUV MAT DIV 58
894	TOYS,SPORTING GOODS,ETC		715.4	W 46041	660.9	W 51083	774.7	W 50729	846.0	VOITURES ENFANTS,JOUETS
8942	TOYS,INDOOR GAMES ETC		332.5	W 25190	238.2	W 25881	272.0	W 25502	296.1	JOUETS,JEUX ETC
8947	OTH SPORT GDS,FAIR AMUSM	W 17702	366.3	W 19994	408.8	W 24648	496.8	W 24792	543.7	AUT ART DE SPORT
89471	FISHNG,HUNTNG EQUIP NES	W 10154	287.0	W 11396	312.4	W 13961	384.1	W 12869	423.3	HAMECONS ET EPUISETTES
897	GOLD,SILVER WARE,JEWELRY		337.1		338.5		328.3		328.1	BIJOUTERIE,ORFEVRERIE
8972	IMITATION JEWELLERY		290.3		293.6		272.7		273.3	BIJOUTERIE DE FANTAISIE
898	MUSICAL INSTRUMENTS,PTS	W 169859	1133.3	W 182224	1198.6	W 184717	1385.4	W 184945	1451.1	INSTRUMENTS DE MUSIQUE
8983	SOUND RECRDNG TAPE,DISCS	W 146671	844.0	W 159621	897.6	W 160304	1021.6	W 165046	1115.0	SUPPORTS SON POUR 763
89831	PREPD SND RECORDNG MEDIA	W 146324	824.2	W 159131	872.4	W 159699	987.7	W 164373	1073.8	SUPPORTS PREPARES
899	OTHER MANUFACTURED GOODS		556.0		580.5		642.8		597.1	AUT ART MANUF DIVERS NDA
9	GOODS NOT CLASSD BY KIND		342.1		639.8		2483.9		5372.3	ART TRANSACT NON CLASSES
971	*GOLD,NON MONETARY NES		290.5		567.8	K 197821	2431.1	K 429320	5310.9	OR NON MONETAIRE
97101	NONMON GLD UNWRT,SEMIMFD		290.2	K 48357	567.4	K 197671	2430.9	K 427268	5310.3	OR,ALLIAGES D'OR BRUTS

1. HISTORICAL SERIES, 1961–1996 SPECIAL TRADE, IMPORTS C.I.F., EXPORTS F.O.B.
SERIES HISTORIQUES, 1961–1996 COMMERCE SPECIAL, IMPORTATIONS C.A.F., EXPORTATIONS F.O.B

YEAR ANNEE	VALUE IN MILLION KUWAITI DINARS / VALEUR EN MILLION KUWAITI DINARS — MERCHANDISE – MARCHANDISE IMPORTS	EXPORTS	GOLD – OR IMPORTS	EXPORTS	CONVERSION FACTORS U.S. CENTS PER KUWAITI DINAR / FACTEURS DE CONVERSION CENTS E.U. PAR KUWAITI DINAR IMPORTS	EXPORTS	INDEX NUMBERS – INDICES: QUANTUM IMPORTS	EXPORTS	UNIT VALUE / VALEUR UNITAIRE IMPORTS	EXPORTS
1961	89.10	336.80			280.0000	280.0000				
1962	101.90	375.30			280.0000	280.0000				
1963	115.70	395.30			280.0000	280.0000				
1964	115.10	434.80			280.0000	280.0000				
1965	134.70	444.10			280.0000	280.0000				
1966	165.30	479.40			280.0000	280.0000				
1967	211.90	484.40			280.0000	280.0000				
1968	218.30	513.20			280.0000	280.0000				
1969	230.80	550.00			280.0000	280.0000				
1970	223.30	679.10			280.0000	280.0000				
1971	232.30	918.80			280.0000	280.0000				
1972	262.20	1005.40			304.0000	304.0000				
1973	310.60	1129.70			338.7460	338.7080				
1974	455.10	3214.70			341.4810	340.9120				
1975	693.20	2663.00			344.5620	344.8930				
1976	972.00	2875.80			342.2760	342.5400				
1977	1387.00	2796.60			349.3440	349.2760				
1978	1263.90	2868.20			363.7790	364.0810				
1979	1437.00	5172.90			362.1230	361.2400				
1980	1765.00	5369.00			370.0710	369.7990				
1981	1945.40	4553.50			358.2264	359.7197				
1982	2384.60	3156.40			347.3700	347.1835				
1983	2149.10	3373.60			343.1681	343.0791				
1984	2041.70	3631.00			338.0041	337.9205				
1985	1784.70	3151.90			342.6100	332.4677				
1986	1661.20	2105.00			342.3271	343.0552				
1987	1530.70	2304.40			359.0400	358.6852				
1988	1714.20	2166.00			358.5079	358.2112				
1989	1849.40	3378.00			340.4900	340.4900				
1990	1145.70	2031.40			342.4096	342.4343				
1991	1353.30	309.40			351.7800	351.7800				
1992	2129.20	1931.10			340.5632	340.0697				
1993	2123.80	3091.20			331.5726	331.4038				
1994	1988.20	3341.60			335.9886	336.0161				
1995	2323.10	3814.50			335.4347	335.1575				
1996	2507.20	4458.00			333.9900	333.9900				

2. IMPORTS BY BROAD ECONOMIC CATEGORY AND EXPORTS BY INDUSTRIAL ORIGIN. (PERCENTAGE OF TOTAL VALUE)
IMPORTATIONS PAR CATEGORIES ECONOMIQUES ET EXPORTATIONS PAR BRANCHE D'ACTIVITE.(EN POURCENTAGE DE LA VALEUR TOTALE)

IMPORTS – IMPORTATIONS

	1990	1991	1992	1993	1994	1995	1996
TOTAL IMPORTS–IMPORTATIONS TOTALES	100.	100.	100.	100.	100.	100.	100.
1 FOOD BEV–ALIMENTATION BOISSONS	15.3	9.5	12.3	13.6	15.2	13.8	14.2
11 PRIMARY–PRODUITS DE BASE	9.7	5.3	7.5	8.5	9.3	8.4	8.5
111 FOR INDUSTRY–POUR L'INDUSTRIE	3.7	2.3	3.1	3.4	3.9	3.3	3.6
112 FOR HOUSEHOLDS–POUR LES MENAGES	6.0	3.0	4.4	5.1	5.3	5.1	4.9
12 PROCESSED–PRODUITS ELABORES	5.6	4.2	4.7	5.0	5.9	5.5	5.7
121 FOR INDUSTRY–POUR L'INDUSTRIE	1.0	0.3	0.5	0.5	0.7	0.6	0.6
122 FOR HOUSEHOLDS–POUR LES MENAGES	4.6	3.9	4.3	4.6	5.2	4.8	5.1
2 IND SUPPLIES–APPROV INDUSTRIELS	26.8	11.0	18.7	22.0	24.6	24.5	24.5
21 PRIMARY–PRODUITS DE BASE	1.3	0.4	0.7	1.0	1.2	1.1	1.0
22 PROCESSED–PRODUITS ELABORES	25.5	10.7	18.1	21.0	23.4	23.4	23.5
3 FUELS–COMBUSTIBLES	0.6	0.7	0.4	0.3	0.5	0.4	0.4
31 PRIMARY–PRODUITS DE BASE	0.1	0.0	0.1	0.1	0.0	0.1	0.1
32 PROCESSED–PRODUITS ELABORES	0.5	0.7	0.4	0.3	0.4	0.3	0.4
321 MOTOR SPIRIT–ESSENCE							
322 OTHER–AUTRES	0.5	0.7	0.4	0.3	0.4	0.3	0.4
4 MACHINERY–EQUIPEMENT	14.6	23.6	19.5	18.8	17.6	15.3	24.8
41 CAPITAL EQUIPMENT–MACHINES	13.8	22.1	18.0	17.2	16.1	13.9	23.3
42 PARTS–PIECES ACCESSOIRES	0.8	1.5	1.4	1.6	1.5	1.4	1.5
5 TRANSPORT–TRANSPORT	17.2	34.3	23.6	23.2	19.1	24.9	16.2
51 PASSENGER CARS–AUTOMOBILES	8.5	23.6	12.7	8.0	8.4	8.4	8.8
52 OTHER–AUTRES	4.2	6.8	6.3	10.6	6.5	11.9	3.3
521 INDUSTRIAL–INDUSTRIELS	4.1	6.7	6.2	10.5	6.4	11.8	3.2
522 NON INDUSTRIAL–NON INDUSTRIEL	0.1	0.0	0.1	0.1	0.1	0.1	0.1
53 PARTS–PIECES ACCESSOIRES	4.5	3.9	4.5	4.6	4.2	4.6	4.1
6 CONSUM GOODS–BIENS CONSOMMATION	25.3	20.4	25.4	22.1	23.0	21.1	19.8
61 DURABLE–DURABLES	8.2	10.4	12.1	8.3	8.2	7.2	6.3
62 SEMI DURABLE–SEMI DURABLES	12.0	7.0	9.6	9.2	9.7	9.1	8.9
63 NON DURABLE–NON DURABLES	5.0	2.9	3.7	4.6	5.1	4.8	4.7
7 GOODS NES–BIENS NDA	0.2	0.5	0.1	0.1	0.2	0.1	0.1

EXPORTS – EXPORTATIONS

	1990	1991	1992	1993	1994	1995	1996
TOTAL EXPORTS–EXPORTATIONS TOTALES	100.	100.	100.	100.	100.	100.	100.
1 AGRICULTURE	0.3	0.3	0.1	0.1	0.1	0.1	0.1
2 MINING QUARRY–INDUS EXTRACTIVES	92.4	80.4	94.5	94.9	93.6	94.4	94.9
3 MANUFACTURING–IND MANUFACTUR	7.3	19.3	5.4	5.0	6.3	5.5	5.0
31 FOOD BEV TOBACCO–ALIM BOISS TAB	0.5	0.2	0.3	0.2	0.2	0.2	0.4
32 TEXTILES–INDUSTRIES TEXTILES	0.7	0.5	0.2	0.2	0.2	0.2	0.2
33 WOOD & PRODUCTS–BOIS & PRODUITS	0.1	0.0	0.0	0.0	0.0	0.0	0.0
34 PAPER & PRODUCTS–PAPIER & PRODT	0.2	0.1	0.2	0.2	0.3	0.3	0.2
35 CHEMICALS–INDUSTRIES CHIMIQUES	2.3	1.0	1.0	1.2	1.7	2.4	2.0
36 NON METAL MIN–MIN NON METAL	0.2	0.2	0.3	0.3	0.3	0.3	0.3
37 BASIC METAL–IND METAL BASE	0.2	0.0	0.0	0.0	0.0	0.0	0.0
38 METAL MANUF–MANUF METAL	3.1	17.1	3.2	2.7	3.6	2.1	1.8
39 OTH MANUF IND–AUTRES MANUF	0.1	0.1	0.0	0.1	0.1	0.0	0.1

3. TRADE BY PRINCIPAL COUNTRIES OF ORIGIN AND DESTINATION (VALUE IN MILLION U.S. DOLLARS)
ECHANGES SELON LES PRINCIPAUX PAYS D'ORIGINE ET DE DESTINATION (VALEUR EN MILLIONS DE DOLLARS EU)

COUNTRIES–PAYS	SPECIAL IMPORTS C.I.F. IMPORTATIONS SPECIALES C.A.F				
	1992	1993	1994	1995	1996
World	7251.4	7042.1	6680.4	7789.8	8373.7
Africa	82.3	88.4	104.5	110.9	154.9
Americas	1641.6	1218.1	1110.4	1487.6	1664.8
– Northern America	1530.2	1106.7	1030.9	1362.6	1533.5
– LAIA	105.1	107.5	74.4	119.1	125.3
– CACM	6.1	3.9	5.0	5.5	5.5
– Caribbean	0.2	0.0	0.1	0.4	0.5
– Rest of America	0.0	0.0	0.0	0.0	0.0
Asia excl fmr USSR	2789.5	2689.1	2753.3	2941.6	3442.3
– Middle East	956.3	886.4	985.8	1105.0	1165.8
Asia former USSR			0.0	0.7	0.5
Europe excl fmr USSR	2608.0	2927.9	2582.0	3122.1	2920.9
– European Union	2428.4	2745.9	2421.9	2964.1	2676.4
– Eastern Europe	37.3	48.6	52.8	50.7	77.7
– Rest of Europe	142.4	133.4	107.2	107.3	166.8
Europe former USSR	12.3	9.7	7.3	21.4	3.9
Oceania	116.3	108.7	122.6	104.2	184.9
Other	1.5	0.3	0.4	1.3	1.5
USA/Etats–Unis d'Amer	1476.3	1048.7	971.2	1255.2	1398.5
Japan/Japon	917.8	892.4	783.1	728.7	1011.8
Germany/Allemagne	668.3	556.3	549.5	564.7	586.5
France, Monaco	369.9	775.9	424.1	868.0	336.3
United Kingdom	445.0	472.1	463.5	466.9	513.3
Italy/Italie	418.7	420.0	399.7	459.6	581.8
Saudi Arabia	318.7	347.1	383.7	475.3	557.4
India/Inde	167.9	162.6	193.9	225.0	269.0
United Arab Emirates	215.2	121.0	134.8	171.8	156.6
China/Chine	124.2	134.4	153.9	179.3	206.5
Korea, Republic of	134.8	132.9	134.4	152.3	181.7
Turkey/Turquie	88.7	114.1	162.3	140.7	152.2
Netherlands/Pays–Bas	108.6	125.3	158.2	115.1	142.2
Other Asia n.e.s.	141.1	126.1	105.0	114.7	126.1
Switzerland,Liechtenst.	128.0	120.8	96.7	94.8	155.1
Australia/Australie	103.4	88.9	104.1	89.5	164.0
Spain/Espagne	79.9	67.9	78.0	113.8	113.7
Thailand/Thaïlande	71.7	76.2	88.7	101.9	105.6
Belgium–Luxembourg	97.9	76.8	75.9	75.4	89.7
Canada	53.9	57.9	59.7	107.3	135.0
Malaysia/Malaisie	66.6	54.0	78.5	101.7	103.6
Syrian Arab Republic	95.1	84.7	64.9	71.6	67.8
Sweden/Suède	72.9	82.3	83.8	77.3	62.3
Indonesia/Indonésie	53.2	68.9	78.4	75.5	90.8
Egypt/Egypte	72.6	73.0	65.2	65.8	76.6
Singapore/Singapour	64.1	72.4	75.6	68.7	61.9
Iran (Islamic Rep of)	37.6	50.7	87.7	82.6	66.2
Bahrain/Bahreïn	92.5	60.5	56.0	66.4	48.1
Brazil/Brésil	51.7	70.5	45.1	78.0	59.6
Lebanon/Liban	78.2	64.1	53.9	48.7	44.4
Denmark/Danemark	60.9	50.7	57.1	59.4	54.8
Austria/Autriche	34.4	33.7	41.9	68.6	89.9
Pakistan	50.5	41.1	31.8	33.3	38.0
Ireland/Irlande	22.7	28.9	38.2	39.1	51.3
Finland/Finlande	25.2	23.8	20.4	26.4	22.4
So. African Customs Un	3.8	7.8	20.4	27.7	56.1
Qatar	11.6	22.2	19.7	25.5	26.7
Hungary/Hongrie	11.6	15.8	21.3	16.2	38.6
Philippines	12.0	15.1	15.5	18.9	40.2
Mexico/Mexique	10.0	6.8	19.0	18.5	44.1

COUNTRIES–PAYS	SPECIAL EXPORTS F.O.B. EXPORTATIONS SPECIALES F.O.B.				
	1992	1993	1994	1995	1996
Monde	6585.3	10519.0	11964.5	12944.4	14855.7
Afrique	11.8	22.2	33.5	45.9	34.0
Amériques	10.0	15.1	15.4	35.7	44.0
– Amérique du Nord	9.9	13.7	15.1	32.5	43.9
– ALAI	0.1	1.3	0.3	3.3	0.1
– MCAC		0.0	0.0		
– Caraïbes		0.0	0.0		
– Autre Amérique	0.0	0.0			
Asie anc. URSS exclus	316.7	471.5	556.2	618.3	642.7
– Moyen–Orient	245.6	291.2	292.9	284.6	354.8
Asie ancienne URSS				0.2	1.8
Europe anc. URSS exclus	22.0	23.5	161.1	26.9	32.4
– Union Européenne	20.4	21.5	159.9	25.5	29.9
– Europe de l'Est	0.4	1.0	0.4	0.7	0.5
– Autre de l'Europe	1.2	1.0	0.8	0.8	2.0
Europe ancienne URSS	0.5	0.5	0.8	0.7	1.6
Océanie	0.3	0.3	0.5	0.7	0.5
Autre	6224.1	9986.0	11197.0	12216.0	14098.7
Areas n.e.s.	6224.1	9986.0	11197.0	12216.0	14098.7
Saudi Arabia	93.1	111.1	111.3	113.0	128.1
United Arab Emirates	91.7	96.2	105.7	75.8	113.7
India/Inde	17.3	67.9	103.4	119.3	140.8
China, Hong Kong SAR	8.0	43.4	63.5	30.8	25.0
China/Chine	0.0	5.6	25.1	87.0	37.4
France, Monaco	1.2	1.5	120.3	1.4	2.3
USA/Etats–Unis d'Amer	9.5	13.0	14.5	30.6	43.2
Bahrain/Bahreïn	11.7	18.7	15.0	17.2	17.7
Philippines	7.0	9.8	15.4	26.3	19.9
Egypt/Egypte	8.9	15.2	16.8	19.4	17.5
Pakistan	14.0	10.4	21.8	12.6	12.7
Singapore/Singapour	10.1	13.0	14.0	17.3	15.4
Syrian Arab Republic	8.6	14.3	9.3	16.1	19.9
Iran (Islamic Rep of)	16.7	10.7	8.7	13.7	15.7
Qatar	8.3	11.2	12.9	14.9	16.7
Lebanon/Liban	7.7	10.9	10.6	13.9	9.9
Oman	6.3	12.6	9.1	10.9	12.6
Japan/Japon	3.5	12.3	9.3	12.0	9.8
Sri Lanka	1.6	8.1	2.3	9.9	15.0
United Kingdom	6.5	5.5	8.5	5.8	7.3
Italy/Italie	3.2	2.3	15.7	7.4	4.6
Germany/Allemagne	4.4	6.9	5.8	6.7	6.6
Morocco/Maroc	0.2	1.1	10.6	10.5	4.4
Turkey/Turquie	1.4	5.0	5.6	4.1	8.6
Tunisia/Tunisie	0.3	1.4	3.3	7.1	10.5
Viet Nam		2.3	2.2	8.8	1.7
Jordan/Jordanie			3.4	4.1	6.5
Other Asia n.e.s.	2.6	5.2	0.3	4.3	0.6
Netherlands/Pays–Bas	1.5	1.6	3.6	1.9	2.2
Korea, Republic of	4.9	0.2	0.4	0.5	4.8
Libyan Arab Jamahiriya	1.0	1.2	0.0	7.5	0.1
Bangladesh	0.8	1.0	2.7	2.1	2.5
Belgium–Luxembourg	0.1	0.9	1.6	0.7	4.9
Sweden/Suède	2.2	1.0	1.4	0.6	0.7
Malaysia/Malaisie	0.2	0.2	2.1	1.8	0.2
Canada	0.4	0.7	0.6	1.9	0.7
Cyprus/Chypre	0.3	0.4	0.9	0.1	2.3
Russian Federation	0.5	0.5	0.8	0.6	1.6
Switzerland,Liechtenst.	1.1	0.7	0.7	0.7	0.7

(VALUE AS PERCENTAGE OF WORLD TOTAL)(VALEURS EN POURCENTAGE DU TOTAL MONDIAL)

	1987	1988	1989	1990	1991	1992	1993	1994	1995	1996
Africa	0.8	0.8	0.9	0.9	0.8	1.1	1.3	1.6	1.4	1.8
Americas	11.9	14.8	15.3	15.6	31.3	22.6	17.3	16.6	19.1	19.9
– Northern America	10.7	13.0	13.8	13.9	30.6	21.1	15.7	15.4	17.5	18.3
– LAIA	0.9	1.6	1.4	1.6	0.7	1.4	1.5	1.1	1.5	1.5
– CACM	0.2	0.1	0.1	0.1	0.0	0.1	0.1	0.1	0.1	0.1
– Caribbean	0.0	0.0	0.0	0.0	0.0	0.0	0.0	0.0	0.0	0.0
– Rest of America	0.0	0.0	0.0	0.0	0.0	0.0	0.0	0.0	0.0	0.0
Asia excl fmr USSR	49.0	47.2	46.4	43.5	34.6	38.5	38.2	41.2	37.8	41.1
– Middle East	13.9	16.5	15.5	14.8	9.1	13.2	12.6	14.8	14.2	13.9
Asia former USSR								0.0	0.0	0.0
Europe excl fmr USSR	36.1	35.1	35.6	37.8	31.8	36.0	41.6	38.6	40.1	34.9
– European Union	32.1	29.5	31.7	33.6	30.1	33.5	39.0	36.3	38.1	32.0
– Eastern Europe	1.1	1.4	1.5	1.2	0.6	0.5	0.7	0.8	0.7	0.9
– Rest of Europe	2.9	4.1	2.5	3.0	1.1	2.0	1.9	1.6	1.4	2.0
Europe former USSR	0.1	0.2	0.2	0.2	0.1	0.2	0.1	0.1	0.3	0.0
Oceania	2.1	2.0	1.6	2.0	1.2	1.6	1.5	1.8	1.3	2.2
Other	0.0	0.0	0.0	0.0	0.3	0.0	0.0	0.0	0.0	0.0
USA/Etats–Unis d'Amer	10.4	12.3	13.2	13.0	29.4	20.4	14.9	14.5	16.1	16.7
Japan/Japon	19.2	13.5	12.9	12.2	16.2	12.7	12.7	11.7	9.4	12.1
Germany/Allemagne					9.1	9.2	7.9	8.2	7.2	7.0
France, Monaco	4.0	3.1	3.4	3.3	2.5	5.1	11.0	6.3	11.1	4.0
United Kingdom	6.8	6.1	6.6	6.0	7.0	6.1	6.7	6.9	6.0	6.1
Italy/Italie	5.0	4.7	5.4	5.5	4.4	5.8	6.0	6.0	5.9	6.9
Saudi Arabia	3.0	3.7	4.5	5.1	5.4	4.4	4.9	5.7	6.1	6.7
India/Inde	2.2	1.8	2.8	2.2	1.3	2.3	2.3	2.9	2.9	3.2
United Arab Emirates	1.9	2.5	1.6	1.6	1.5	3.0	1.7	2.0	2.2	1.9
China/Chine	2.2	3.0	3.5	3.2	1.0	1.7	1.9	2.3	2.3	2.5

	1987	1988	1989	1990	1991	1992	1993	1994	1995	1996
Afrique	7.4	3.6	6.9	0.6	0.5	0.2	0.2	0.3	0.4	0.2
Amériques	3.7	1.1	2.5	0.1	0.1	0.2	0.1	0.1	0.3	0.3
– Amérique du Nord	3.7	1.0	2.4	0.1	0.1	0.2	0.1	0.1	0.3	0.3
– ALAI	0.0	0.1	0.1	0.0	0.0	0.0	0.0	0.0	0.0	0.0
– MCAC				0.0	0.0		0.0	0.0		
– Caraïbes	0.0	0.0	0.0	0.0			0.0	0.0		
– Autre Amérique	0.0	0.0			0.0	0.0	0.0			
Asie anc. URSS exclus	80.0	89.4	84.2	6.5	13.3	4.8	4.5	4.6	4.8	4.3
– Moyen–Orient	62.4	73.3	67.6	5.3	12.4	3.7	2.8	2.4	2.2	2.4
Asie ancienne URSS									0.0	0.0
Europe anc. URSS exclus	8.8	4.9	6.5	0.8	5.5	0.3	0.2	1.3	0.2	0.2
– Union Européenne	5.7	3.8	5.5	0.6	0.7	0.3	0.2	1.3	0.2	0.2
– Europe de l'Est	0.4	0.3	0.2	0.0	4.8	0.0	0.0	0.0	0.0	0.0
– Autre de l'Europe	2.6	0.8	0.8	0.2	0.0	0.0	0.0	0.0	0.0	0.0
Europe ancienne URSS	0.0	0.0	0.0	0.0	0.1	0.0	0.0	0.0	0.0	0.0
Océanie	0.1	0.1	0.0	0.0	0.0	0.0	0.0	0.0	0.0	0.0
Autre	0.0	0.9	0.0	92.1	80.4	94.5	94.9	93.6	94.4	94.9
Areas n.e.s.	0.0	0.9	0.0	92.1	80.4	94.5	94.9	93.6	94.4	94.9
Saudi Arabia	26.0	18.4	15.6	1.2	2.3	1.4	1.1	0.9	0.9	0.9
United Arab Emirates	7.0	6.6	6.4	0.6	2.9	1.4	0.9	0.9	0.6	0.8
India/Inde	5.7	3.3	3.4	0.2	0.0	0.3	0.6	0.9	0.9	0.9
China, Hong Kong SAR	0.5	0.4	1.1	0.0	0.0	0.1	0.4	0.5	0.2	0.2
China/Chine	4.7	5.7	4.1	0.3	0.0	0.0	0.1	0.2	0.7	0.3
France, Monaco	0.6	0.5	0.3	0.0	0.3	0.0	0.0	1.0	0.0	0.0
USA/Etats–Unis d'Amer	3.7	1.0	2.3	0.1	0.1	0.1	0.1	0.1	0.2	0.3
Bahrain/Bahreïn	1.3	1.9	2.2	0.2	0.2	0.2	0.2	0.1	0.1	0.1
Philippines	1.8	2.2	1.2	0.2	0.4	0.1	0.1	0.1	0.2	0.1

4. Special Imports C.I.F. by Commodities according to the S.I.T.C. (Rev. 2) in million U.S. Dollars
Importations Spéciales C.A.F. par Produits d'après la C.T.C.I. (Rév. 2) en millions de Dollars E.U.

SITC CTCI	COMMODITY	1993 QUANTITY QUANTITE	1993 VALUE VALEUR	1994 QUANTITY QUANTITE	1994 VALUE VALEUR	1995 QUANTITY QUANTITE	1995 VALUE VALEUR	1996 QUANTITY QUANTITE	1996 VALUE VALEUR	PRODUIT
	ALL COMMODITIES		7042.1		6680.4		7789.8		8373.7	TOUS PRODUITS
0	FOOD AND LIVE ANIMALS		933.6		991.0		1061.2		1171.2	ALIMENTS,ANIMAUX VIVANTS
001	*LIVE ANIMALS FOR FOOD		132.1		137.2		98.3		110.6	ANIMAUX VIVANTS
0012	SHEEP AND GOATS,LIVE	W 99129	126.7	W 113445	128.2	W 84518	92.4	W 94667	103.4	ESPECES OVINE ET CAPRINE
00121	SHEEP,LIVE	W 99038	126.2	W 112503	126.7	W 84422	92.2	W 94665	103.4	ESPECE OVINE
01	MEAT AND PREPARATIONS		116.0		105.9		126.6		132.9	VIANDES ET PREPARATIONS
011	MEAT FRESH,CHILLD,FROZEN	W 68232	105.1	W 59811	93.7	W 70341	114.4	W 68675	120.7	VIANDES FRAICHES,REF,CONGE
0111	BOVINE MEAT FRESH,FROZEN	W 13177	27.1	W 11138	22.8	W 11802	23.6	W 11368	24.5	VIANDES BOVIN FRAI,REF
01111	BOVINE MEAT WITH BONE IN	W 13177	27.1	W 11138	22.8	W 11802	23.6	W 11368	24.5	VIANDES BOVIN NON DESOSS
0114	POULTRY FRESH CHLLD,FRZN	W 50158	65.6	W 43958	59.9	W 54692	81.8	W 53112	87.1	VOLAILLES MORTES
02	DAIRY PRODCTS,BIRDS'EGGS		147.1		147.8		152.3		179.9	PRODUITS LAITIERS,OEUFS
022	MILK AND CREAM	W 50584	79.7	W 48129	81.2	W 46978	82.9	W 51956	104.4	LAIT ET CREME
0223	MILK AND CREAM FRESH	W 25142	24.4	W 21362	25.3	W 21666	28.1	W 22247	30.6	LAIT,CREME FRAIS
0224	MILK,CREAM PRESERVED ETC	W 25442	55.3	W 26767	55.9	W 25312	54.9	W 29708	73.8	LAIT,CREME CONS,CONC
02242	MILK DRY,1.5% FAT OR LES	W 14120	39.0	W 15773	39.6	W 13847	37.4	W 17932	55.3	LAIT POUDRE INF 1.5%
024	CHEESE AND CURD	W 11611	36.7	W 13173	41.2	W 12461	42.2	W 13481	47.7	FROMAGE ET CAILLEBOTTE
025	EGGS,BIRDS,FRESH,PRSRVD	W 17585	22.8	W 11419	15.5	W 11788	17.1	W 11197	16.7	OEUFS
0251	— IN SHELL	W 17585	22.8	W 11413	15.5	W 11718	16.9	W 11116	16.5	OEUFS EN COQUILLE
04	CEREALS AND PREPARATIONS		132.8		146.5		184.3		215.2	CEREALES ET PRODUITS
041	WHEAT ETC UNMILLED	W 211213	28.2	W 123437	17.1	W 182728	34.6	W 278825	64.1	FROMENT,EPEAUTRE
0411	DURUM WHEAT UNMILLED	W 211213	28.2	W 123437	17.1	W 182728	34.6	W 278825	64.1	FROMENT DUR NON MOULU
042	RICE	W 83366	55.4	W 102835	66.5	W 88612	60.7	W 103800	67.5	RIZ
0421	RICE IN HUSK OR HUSKED	W 83354	55.4	W 102817	66.5	W 88562	60.6	W 103726	67.4	RIZ SANS AUTRE PREPARATION
04211	RICE IN THE HUSK	W 83354	55.4	W 102817	66.5	W 88562	60.6	W 103726	67.4	RIZ PADDY
043	BARLEY UNMILLED	W 57942	7.0	W 169035	16.6	W 157985	25.6	W 154321	26.3	ORGE NON MONDEE
048	CEREAL ETC PREPARATIONS	W 11409	32.8	W 11909	36.6	W 13577	47.9	W 13031	45.3	PREPTNS A BASE CEREALES
05	VEGETABLES AND FRUIT		219.7		241.8		255.8		263.0	LEGUMES ET FRUITS
054	VEG ETC FRSH,SMPLY PRSVD	W 204959	97.7	W 202621	105.6	W 204923	114.9	W 202460	111.7	LEGUMES FRAIS,CONG,SECS
0545	OTHER FRESH VEGETABLES	W 87872	34.8	W 83842	40.3	W 83601	42.2	W 78909	40.7	AUTRES LEGUMES FRAIS,REF
05459	FRESH VEGETABLES NES	W 52773	23.7	W 45381	28.2	W 40655	29.4	W 37538	28.3	LEGUMES FRAIS,REFRI NDA
0546	VEGETABLES SIMPLY PRESVD	W 22790	23.8	W 29041	29.4	W 32004	35.7	W 29819	32.6	LEGUMES CONG,CONSER
057	FRUIT,NUTS,FRESH,DRIED	W 160406	98.0	W 185607	109.6	W 194174	109.6	W 201565	118.4	FRUITS FRAIS OU SECS
0579	FRUIT FRESH OR DRIED NES	W 68351	44.5	W 77746	45.4	W 75593	44.7	W 81619	49.0	FRUITS FRAIS,SECS NDA
05798	OTHER FRESH FRUIT	W 50932	23.0	W 56919	24.0	W 53157	22.8	W 57313	25.3	AUTRES FRUITS FRAIS
06	SUGAR AND PREPS,HONEY		32.2		45.1		48.4		58.1	SUCRES ET PRODUITS
061	SUGAR AND HONEY	W 48576	20.2	W 68411	31.2	W 57279	32.7	W 75408	41.2	SUCRES ET MIEL
0611	RAW BEET AND CANE SUGAR	W 46679	15.7	W 66376	26.2	W 54535	25.7	W 72147	33.0	SUCRES BRUTS
07	COFFEE,TEA,COCOA,SPICES		69.8		73.5		89.6		95.3	CAFE,THE,CACAO,EPICES
073	CHOCOLATE AND PRODUCTS	W 7052	37.8	W 6211	33.5	W 7470	40.7	W 7577	50.2	CHOCOLAT
074	TEA AND MATE	W 3551	16.6	W 4433	22.8	W 5050	26.3	W 4278	24.1	THE ET MATE
0741	TEA	W 3548	16.6	W 4433	22.8	W 5050	26.3	W 4269	24.1	THE
081	*FEEDING STUFF FOR ANIML	W 54001	17.3	W 72285	24.2	W 84354	27.8	W 102437	34.7	NOURRITURE POUR ANIMAUX
09	MISC EDIBLE PRODUCTS		51.3		54.1		58.1		61.4	PREP ALIMENTAIRES DIVERSES
098	EDIBLE PRODCTS,PREPS NES	W 16120	48.6	W 15268	51.3	W 16522	54.7	W 17992	58.4	PREP ALIMENTAIRES NDA
09809	MISC FOOD PREPRTIONS NES	W 9992	35.6	W 8801	37.4	W 9136	38.7	W 9549	40.5	PREP ALIMENTAIRES NDA
1	BEVERAGES AND TOBACCO		96.6		106.9		93.7		93.1	BOISSONS ET TABACS
11	BEVERAGES		26.3		31.4		28.6		29.4	BOISSONS
111	NON–ALCOHL BEVERAGES NES	W 62099	26.3	W 71719	31.4	W 73192	28.6	W 76486	29.4	BOISSONS NON ALCOOLIQUES
12	TOBACCO AND MANUFACTURES		70.4		75.6		65.2		63.8	TABACS BRUTS FABRIQUES
122	TOBACCO,MANUFACTURED	W 3566	70.4	W 4060	75.6	W 3671	65.1	W 3688	63.8	TABACS FABRIQUES
1222	CIGARETTES	W 3531	69.5	W 4052	75.2	W 3667	64.9	W 3687	63.8	CIGARETTES
2	CRUDE MATERLS,EXCL FUELS		90.1		103.8		121.0		115.0	MAT BRUTES NON COMESTIBLES
24	CORK AND WOOD		34.6		40.2		53.2		49.8	LIEGE ET BOIS
248	WOOD SHAPED,SLEEPERS	W 60210	26.2	W 69401	35.7	W 82218	45.0	W 77891	40.5	BOIS SIMPLEMENT TRAVAILLES
2481	RAILWAY SLEEPERS,TIES	W 60210	26.2	W 69401	35.7	W 82218	45.0	W 77891	40.5	TRAVERSES VOIES FERREES
27	CRUDE FERTLZR,MINRLS NES		26.5		33.0		30.6		34.2	ENGRAIS MINERAUX BRUTS
273	STONE,SAND AND GRAVEL	W 728492	21.6	W 949601	26.8	W 672102	25.0	W 952719	28.5	PIERRES,SABLES,GRAVIERS
3	MINERAL FUELS ETC		31.6		43.6		41.2		49.9	COMBUSTIBLES MINERAUX LUB
33	PETROLEUM AND PRODUCTS		30.3		42.3		40.2		48.8	PETROLE ET DERIVES
334	PETROLEUM PRODUCTS,REFIN	W 15422	17.1	W 21956	25.7	W 21668	23.4	W 34760	29.6	PRODUITS RAFFINES
3345	LUBS,PETROLEUM OILS NES	W 15422	17.1	W 21956	25.7	W 21668	23.4	W 34760	29.6	HUILES LUBRIFIANTES
33451	LUBS(HIGH PETR CONT) ETC	W 15422	17.1	W 21956	25.7	W 21668	23.4	W 34760	29.6	HUILES LUBRIF,H LOURDES
4	ANIMAL,VEGETABLE OIL,FAT		26.3		29.5		47.7		41.0	HUILES,GRAISSES ANIM,VEG
42	FIXED VEGETABLE OIL,FAT		26.1		29.2		47.0		40.2	HUILES VEGETALES FIXES
424	FIXED VEG OIL NONSOFT	W 19718	18.9	W 20101	19.6	W 34348	34.5	W 27235	26.9	AUTRES HUILES VEG FIXES
4249	FIXED VEGETABLE OILS NES	W 11410	13.8	W 12054	14.1	W 23964	24.8	W 17445	19.0	HUILES VEGET FIXES NDA
5	CHEMCLS,RELATED PROD NES		429.7		492.3		550.5		584.8	PRODUITS CHIMIQUES
52	INORGANIC CHEMICALS		63.4		68.0		62.3		57.1	PROD CHIM INORGANIQUES
523	OTHR INORG CHEMICALS ETC	W 51161	56.5	W 39218	60.1	W 56436	52.0	W 43744	49.5	AUT PRODUITS CHIMIQUES INORG
5239	INORG CHEM PRODUCTS NES	W 20920	47.5	W 17979	54.3	W 33099	46.4	W 17772	43.2	PROD CHIM INORGANIQ NDA
52399	OTH INORG CMPNDS NES ETC	W 20674	47.3	W 17370	54.1	W 32119	46.0	W 17068	42.8	AUT COMP INORGANIQUES NDA
53	DYES,TANNING,COLOUR PROD		29.6		31.0		31.7		39.9	PROD TEINTURE,COLORANTS
533	PIGMENTS,PAINTS,ETC	W 12311	27.1	W 11171	27.0	W 11466	28.4	W 14796	36.7	PIGMENTS,PEINTURES,VERNIS
541	*MEDICINAL,PHARM PRODUCT	K 5432404	107.1	K 5552036	105.7	K 6303820	124.8	K 5358059	129.3	PROD MEDICINAUX PHARMACEUT
5417	MEDICAMENTS	K 3357181	85.8	K 3294190	82.1	K 4543348	102.2	K 4145868	111.4	MEDICAMENTS
54171	— CONTAINNG ANTIBIOTICS	K 3357181	85.8	K 3294190	82.1	K 4543348	102.2	K 4145868	111.4	MED CONTN ANTIBIOTIQUES
5419	PHARMACEUTICAL GOODS NES	K 2071917	21.3	K 2248864	23.5	K 1758091	22.5	K 1180355	17.7	PREP,ART PHARMACEUTIQUES
54191	BANDAGES PREPARED ETC	K 2071917	21.3	K 2248864	23.5	K 1758091	22.5	K 1180355	17.7	OUATES,GAZES,BANDES
55	PERFUME,CLEANING ETC PRD		122.5		135.3		158.4		167.0	PROD POUR PARFUM,TOILETTE
553	PERFUMERY,COSMETICS,ETC	W 7438	78.9	W 8652	86.1	W 9730	104.7	W 10254	111.2	PRODUITS DE PARFUMERIE
554	SOAP,CLEANSING ETC PREPS	W 26363	39.8	W 30039	45.0	W 31899	48.6	W 31790	48.8	SAVONS,PRODUITS DETERSIFS
5542	WASHING PREPARATIONS ETC	W 21545	27.6	W 24417	30.9	W 26173	34.1	W 25714	32.3	PROD ORG TENSIO–ACT NDA
58	PLASTIC MATERIALS ETC		57.1		74.0		87.6		83.2	MAT PLAST ARTIFICIELLES
583	POLYMERIZATION ETC PRODS	W 40206	35.3	W 57158	55.5	W 46609	56.6	W 52232	53.2	PROD POLYMERISATION
5832	POLYPROPYLENE	W 14514	14.4	W 21822	23.1	W 15096	22.9	W 11915	16.9	POLYPROPYLENE
58321	— IN PRIMARY FORMS	W 14514	14.4	W 21822	23.1	W 15096	22.9	W 11915	16.9	POLYPROPYLENE PRIMAIRES
59	CHEMICAL MATERIALS NES		47.6		76.0		82.6		103.0	MAT PROD CHIMIQUES NDA
598	MISCEL CHEM PRODUCTS NES	W 19694	36.2	W 25597	61.6	W 27179	65.1	W 29764	85.4	PROD DIV INDUST CHIM NDA
5982	ANTI–KNOCK PREPARTNS ETC	W 2749	12.6	W 6372	35.6	W 4985	29.3	W 4535	28.6	PREPARAT ANTIDETONANTES
5989	CHEM PRODUCTS,PREPS NES	W 16849	23.6	W 19033	25.8	W 22084	35.8	W 25127	56.6	PROD PREP CHIMIQUES NDA
59899	OTH CHEM PRODS,PREPS,NES	W 10916	17.5	W 11606	18.6	W 13110	25.4	W 17662	49.6	AUT PRODUITS CHIMIQUES NDA
6	BASIC MANUFACTURES		1317.6		1288.8		1523.6		1659.5	ART MANUFACTURES
62	RUBBER MANUFACTURES NES		84.6		65.4		76.7		93.2	CAOUTCHOUC MANUFACTURE
625	RUBBER TYRES, TUBES ETC	W 24127	75.2	W 18763	58.2	W 20835	68.8	W 24731	83.5	PNEUS CAOUTCHOUC VULCANISE
6251	TYRES NEW FOR MOTOR CARS	W 22329	69.8	W 17273	54.0	W 19894	66.0	W 23172	78.5	PNEUS POUR VOITURES
63	WOOD,CORK MANUFACTRS NES		56.2		61.3		51.3		56.5	OUVRAGES LIEGE ET BOIS
634	VENEERS,PLYWOOD,ETC	W 57467	46.8	W 65487	49.8	W 45666	37.1	W 55349	45.2	PLACAGES,CONTRE–PLAQUES
6342	PLYWOOD OF WOOD SHEETS	W 55267	45.5	W 62217	47.6	W 40664	33.7	W 48520	42.1	BOIS CONTRE–PLAQUES
64	PAPER,PAPERBOARD AND MFR		121.1		143.0		171.6		144.9	PAPIERS,CARTONS & OUVRAGES
641	PAPER AND PAPERBOARD	W 76157	68.6	W 92051	88.8	W 88274	108.5	W 69118	82.4	PAPIERS ET CARTONS
6412	PRINTG,WRITING PAPER NES	W 45005	34.7	W 42746	35.4	W 40033	45.8	W 27604	27.0	PAPIERS POUR L'IMPRESSION

4. Special Imports C.I.F. by Commodities according to the S.I.T.C. (Rev. 2) in million U.S. Dollars
Importations Spéciales C.A.F. par Produits d'après la C.T.C.I. (Rév. 2) en millions de Dollars E.U.

SITC CTCI	COMMODITY	1993 QUANTITY QUANTITE	1993 VALUE VALEUR	1994 QUANTITY QUANTITE	1994 VALUE VALEUR	1995 QUANTITY QUANTITE	1995 VALUE VALEUR	1996 QUANTITY QUANTITE	1996 VALUE VALEUR	PRODUIT
64121	— UNCOATED	W 45005	34.7	W 42746	35.4	W 40033	45.8	W 27604	27.0	PAPIERS IMPRES NON COUCHES
642	PAPER,ETC,PRECUT,ARTS OF	W 17335	52.6	W 18091	54.3	W 20726	63.2	W 21415	62.6	PAP,CARTONS DECOUPES
6428	PAPER ETC ARTICLES NES	W 8257	31.5	W 9271	35.4	W 10989	41.6	W 10680	40.0	OUVRAGES EN PATE A PAPIER
64285	PAPER ETC DIAPERS ETC	W 5334	24.2	W 6949	29.0	W 8082	33.9	W 7562	32.0	SERVIETTES HYGIENIQUES
65	TEXTILE YARN,FABRICS,ETC		254.4		244.2		263.1		251.8	FILS,TISSUS,ARTICLES TEXTILE
653	WOVN MAN-MADE FIB FABRIC	W 10918	117.8	W 11069	110.0	W 11905	128.5	W 12375	129.8	TISSUS FIBRES SYNTH,ARTIF
6531	CONT SYNT WEAVES NONPILE	W 10528	111.6	W 10761	104.7	W 11612	122.3	W 11988	123.1	TISSUS FIBRES SYNTH CONTINUE
65315	CONT SYN TXTL FABRIC NES	W 10528	111.6	W 10761	104.7	W 11612	122.3	W 11988	123.1	TIS PLUS 85% TEXT SYNT CONT
658	TEXTILE ARTICLES NES	W 7239	36.6	W 5694	28.0	W 6517	30.5	W 7549	33.5	ART FACONNES MAT TEXTILES
6583	BLANKETS ETC NON ELECTRC	W 3349	23.3	W 2457	15.0	W 2758	15.9	W 3011	16.3	COUVERTURES
65831	WOOL BLANKETS ETC NES	W 3349	23.3	W 2457	15.0	W 2758	15.9	W 3011	16.3	COUVERTURES DE LAINE
659	FLOOR COVERINGS,ETC	W 17154	62.3	W 18858	65.3	W 17825	64.6	W 15863	53.8	COUVRE-PARQUETS,TAPIS ETC
6594	WOOL CARPETS ETC NES	W 16738	55.7	W 18488	58.4	W 17433	59.3	W 15456	48.6	TAPIS DE LAINE
65941	— TUFTED	W 7378	32.0	W 5865	27.0	W 5120	24.6	W 3035	15.5	TAPIS DE LAINE TOUFFETES
65942	— WOVEN	W 9359	23.7	W 12623	31.4	W 12313	34.7	W 12421	33.2	TAPIS DE LAINE TISSES
66	NONMETAL MINERAL MFS NES		213.1		250.9		345.7		358.9	ART MIN NON METALLIQUES
661	LIME,CEMENT,BLDG PRODS	W 1755869	132.2	W 1891664	153.0	W 2722196	221.7	W 3246096	237.8	CHAUX,CIMENTS MAT CONSTR
6612	CEMENT	W 1642243	88.4	W 1714180	89.3	W 2502978	138.7	W 3025406	163.3	CIMENTS HYDRAULIQUES
6613	BUILDING STONE ETC WORKD	W 112115	43.4	W 175415	63.2	W 216126	82.3	W 218411	74.1	PIERRES A BATIR
66132	BUILDING STONE WORKED	W 112115	43.4	W 175415	63.2	W 216126	82.3	W 218411	74.1	OUVR EN PIERRES DE TAILLE
662	CLAY,REFRACTORY BLDG PRD	W 52256	29.6	W 67722	36.6	W 94226	49.5	W 101959	51.9	MAT CONST REFRACTAIRES
6624	BRICKS ETC NONREFRACTORY	W 51768	29.3	W 66914	35.3	W 93044	48.8	W 101675	51.6	BRIQUES ETC CERAM NON REFR
66245	GLAZED CERAMIC SETTS ETC	W 41502	25.6	W 58036	31.9	W 77048	42.5	W 89185	46.6	AUT CARREAUX CERAMIQUE
664	GLASS	W 16896	21.7	W 24003	24.5	W 25720	30.9	W 22100	24.8	VERRE
67	IRON AND STEEL		316.6		246.6		299.4		399.5	FER ET ACIER
673	IRON,STEEL SHAPES ETC	W 258697	97.3	W 387184	131.0	W 345804	119.6	W 430338	146.6	BARRES,PROFIL FER,ACIER
6731	IRON,STEEL WIRE ROD	W 204154	70.6	W 326584	103.6	W 288352	93.3	W 366504	116.0	FIL MACHINE FER,ACIER
67311	IRON,SIMPLE STL WIRE ROD	W 204154	70.6	W 326584	103.6	W 288352	93.3	W 366504	116.0	FIL MACH AUT ACIER FIN
6733	IRON,STEEL PROFILES ETC	W 47034	23.5	W 45969	21.3	W 44702	20.9	W 54560	26.6	PROFILES,PALPLAN FER,ACIER
67331	SMALL U,I,H SECTIONS ETC	W 47034	23.5	W 45969	21.3	W 44702	20.9	W 54560	26.6	PROFILES MOINS 80MM
674	IRN,STL UNIV,PLATE,SHEET	W 58487	43.5	W 51579	40.2	W 76531	66.4	W 88377	68.5	LARGES PLATS,TOLES
6749	OTH IRN,STL PLATES,SHEET	W 56903	39.4	W 49776	36.2	W 74974	61.6	W 86704	63.1	AUTRES TOLES FER,ACIER
67491	— OF IRON OR SIMPLE STL	W 56903	39.4	W 49776	36.2	W 74974	61.6	W 86704	63.1	AUT TOLES AUTRES ACIER FIN
678	IRON,STL TUBES,PIPES,ETC	W 160273	153.0	W 52851	56.8	W 96366	92.4	W 102435	151.9	TUBES,TUYAUX EN FONTE,FER
6783	IRON,STL TUBES,PIPES NES	W 135093	130.0	W 44671	41.8	W 85441	68.2	W 86946	96.4	AUT TUBES,TUYAUX FER,ACIER
6785	IRON,STEEL TUBE FITTINGS	W 24851	23.0	W 7788	14.7	W 10925	24.3	W 15333	55.4	ACCESSOIRES DE TUYAUTERIE
68	NON-FERROUS METALS		72.7		79.6		99.4		100.6	METAUX NON FERREUX
682	COPPER EXC CEMENT COPPER	W 9928	28.4	W 10673	31.1	W 9223	35.4	W 14651	46.5	CUIVRE
6821	COPPER NES,ALLOYS,UNWRT	W 9928	28.4	W 10673	31.1	W 9223	35.4	W 14651	46.5	CUIVRE BRUT
68211	COPPER UNREF,EXC CEMENT	W 9928	28.4	W 10673	31.1	W 9223	35.4	W 14651	46.5	CUIVRE POUR AFFINAGE
684	ALUMINIUM	W 21147	44.0	W 21602	48.2	W 23632	63.1	W 19433	52.9	ALUMINIUM
6842	ALUMINIUM,ALLOYS WORKED	W 21147	44.0	W 21602	48.2	W 23632	63.1	W 19433	52.9	ALUMINIUM,ALLIAGES OUVRE
68421	ALUMINIUM BARS,WIRE,ETC	W 13402	23.4	W 13790	25.3	W 17091	40.5	W 12237	28.3	BARRES,PROFILES FILS ALU
69	METAL MANUFACTURES NES		197.5		196.3		214.9		252.5	ART MANUFACT EN METAL NDA
691	STRUCTURES AND PARTS NES	W 11508	23.5	W 12402	27.9	W 29885	49.9	W 46009	67.7	CONSTRUCT FER,ACIER,ALU
6911	STRUCTURES,PARTS IRN,STL	W 10077	16.5	W 10300	18.5	W 26544	34.9	W 43640	57.9	CONSTRUCT FER,ACIER,FONTE
697	BASE MTL HOUSEHOLD EQUIP	W 14546	75.9	W 11111	66.3	W 9612	61.4	W 9861	65.7	ART MENAGE MET COMMUNS
6974	BASE MTL DMSTC ARTIC NES	W 4237	24.3	W 3487	19.0	W 2425	14.2	W 2594	15.8	ARTICLES NDA FONTE,FER,ETC
69741	— OF IRON OR STEEL	W 3556	21.5	W 2674	16.1	W 1809	11.6	W 2064	13.3	ART NDA EN FONTE,FER
6975	BASE MTL INDR SANIT WARE	W 7481	35.0	W 4925	31.8	W 3899	27.7	W 4168	30.8	ART HYG NDA FER,AC,CU,ALU
69751	IRON,STL INDR SANIT WARE	W 7481	35.0	W 4925	31.8	W 3899	27.7	W 4168	30.8	ART HYGIENE NDA FER,ACIER
699	BASE METAL MFRS NES	W 14213	51.3	W 13931	54.2	W 12003	50.7	W 13353	53.3	ART MANUFACTURES MET NDA
6991	LOCKSMITHS WARES,ETC	W 5219	26.3	W 4987	27.1	W 5765	29.6	W 6133	31.2	ARTICLES DE SERRURERIE
69913	BASE MTL DOOR,ETC FITTNG	W 3240	17.7	W 3711	20.7	W 4667	23.6	W 4799	25.8	GARNITURES POUR MEUBLES
6996	BASE MTL MISC ARTICLES	W 5195	18.1	W 5877	20.2	W 5427	18.3	W 5772	17.9	ART DIVERS METAUX COMMUNS
69961	BASE MTL FLEXIBLE TUBING	W 5195	18.1	W 5877	20.2	W 5427	18.3	W 5772	17.9	TUYAUX FLEXIBLES
7	MACHINES,TRANSPORT EQUIP		2992.5		2548.0		3212.6		3481.2	MACHINES MATERIEL TRANSPORT
71	POWER GENERATING EQUIPMT		131.4		127.2		179.3		514.3	MACHINES GENERATRICES
716	ROTATING ELECTRIC PLANT	W 1986	30.7	W 1636	24.9	W 2277	29.7	W 3109	37.6	APP ELECTR ROTATIFS,PIECES
718	OTH POWER GENERATG MACHY	W 2864	70.7	W 3392	86.7	W 4467	130.0	W 19932	438.8	AUTRES MOTEURS PARTIES
7188	WIND,WATER,ETC ENGINES	W 2864	70.7	W 3392	86.7	W 4467	130.0	W 19932	438.8	MOT MACHINES MOTRICES NDA
71889	PARTS NES OF 71881,71882	W 2857	70.7	W 3388	86.6	W 4467	130.0	W 19932	438.7	PARTIES DES POS 718.81,82
72	MACHS FOR SPCL INDUSTRYS		333.4		239.7		188.3		635.8	MAC SPECIALES POUR INDUST
723	CIVIL ENGNEERG EQUIP ETC	W 14680	134.6	W 10170	85.8	W 7042	70.1	W 8174	99.9	APPAREILS DE GENIE CIVIL
7234	CONST,MINING MACHNRY NES	W 13303	119.8	W 8782	70.8	W 5715	56.0	W 6857	84.3	MACH POUR LA CONST, MINES
72343	SLFPRP CONST ETC MCH NES	W 7048	91.2	W 4215	49.7	W 3199	42.8	W 4233	70.5	AUT MACH EXTR,TERRASSEM
728	OTH MACHY FOR SPCL INDUS	W 9295	138.9	W 7672	92.4	W 5789	76.7	W 53069	499.9	AUT MACH IND PARTICULIERES
7284	MACHY FOR SPCL INDUS NES	W 6381	116.0	W 5027	74.6	W 2870	52.6	W 50334	479.7	MACH SPEC IND PARTICUL.
72848	OTH MCHY WITH INDIV FNCT	W 6317	114.6	W 4967	73.0	W 2775	49.8	W 50250	477.2	AUTRES MACHINES NDA
74	GENRL INDUSTRL MACHY NES		346.3		297.7		328.5		370.3	MACH APP INDUSTRIE
741	HEATING,COOLING EQUIPMNT	W 20206	186.9	W 18148	160.7	W 20476	171.1	W 20289	163.5	MACH CHAUFFAGE,PIECES
7415	AIR-CONDITIONING MACHNRY	W 16599	127.8	W 14594	119.8	W 17560	134.8	W 16912	129.1	GROUPES CONDITION AIR
7416	HEATING,COOLING EQU NES	W 1838	44.2	W 1238	22.5	W 794	17.7	W 1132	17.1	APP CHANGEMENT TEMP
742	PUMPS FOR LIQUIDS ETC	W 1803	42.0	W 1505	34.9	W 1879	35.7	W 2521	38.9	POMPES MOTO-POMPES
7429	PTS NES OF PUMPS OF 742	W 477	22.7	W 567	22.7	W 569	19.4	W 1041	20.8	PIECES POUR GROUPE 742
743	PUMPS NES,CENTRFUGES ETC	W 2294	34.3	W 2363	31.8	W 1944	38.7	W 4507	65.0	POMPES COMPRES,VENT ETC
7436	GAS,LIQUID FILTERS ETC	W 886	12.7	W 883	11.4	W 871	24.1	W 2665	38.8	APP POUR FILT DES LIQUIDES
744	MECHANICAL HANDLING EQU	W 6867	38.0	W 6343	35.6	W 9088	46.6	W 12135	56.1	EQUIP MANUTENTION PIECES
7442	LIFTING,LOADING MACH NES	W 5680	27.5	W 4919	23.8	W 7573	30.5	W 9546	37.1	APP LEVAGE,MANUTENTION
749	NONELEC MACH PTS,ACC NES	W 3536	33.3	W 2290	18.6	W 2696	21.6	W 3233	32.8	PIECES MACH NON ELEC NDA
7492	COCKS,VALVES ETC NES	W 3519	33.2	W 2186	17.4	W 2583	19.9	W 3092	31.1	ART ROB,SIM POUR TUYAUX
75	OFFICE MACHNES,ADP EQUIP		113.4		115.3		116.1		121.7	MACH BUREAU TRAIT AUTOM
752	AUTOMTIC DATA PROC EQUIP	W 577	43.7	W 516	36.8	W 442	27.0	W 749	37.2	MACH TRAIT INFORMATION
7522	DIGITAL COMPUTERS	W 574	43.5	W 512	36.6	W 441	26.9	W 747	37.1	MACH DIGITALES COMPLETES
759	OFFICE,ADP MCH PTS,ACCES	W 782	51.6	W 773	62.5	W 779	74.5	W 998	67.7	PIECES DU 751 ET 752
7591	OFFICE MACHINE PARTS NES	W 782	51.6	W 773	62.5	W 779	74.5	W 998	67.7	PIECES DU 7511,7518
75911	TYPEWRTR PARTS,ACCES NES	W 782	51.6	W 773	62.5	W 779	74.5	W 998	67.7	PIECES DU 7511
76	TELECOMM,SOUND EQUIPMENT		214.5		196.4		222.7		232.8	EQUIPMENT DE TELECOM
761	TELEVISION RECEIVERS	W 2105	30.2	W 2239	32.5	W 2789	41.2	W 2620	37.8	RECEPTEURS DE TELEVISION
7611	COLOUR TV RECEIVERS	W 2105	30.2	W 2228	32.5	W 2779	41.1	W 2618	37.8	RECEPTEURS COULEUR
762	RADIO BROADCAST RECEIVRS	W 1210	21.2	W 1302	22.9	W 1543	26.8	W 1398	24.2	RECEPTEURS RADIODIFFUSION
7622	PORTABLE RADIO RECEIVERS	W 1171	20.1	W 1213	20.7	W 1489	25.0	W 1345	22.9	RECEPT PORTATIFS RADIO
763	SOUND RECORDRS,PHONOGRPH	W 409	17.9	W 536	20.8	W 507	20.1	W 538	18.1	PHONO,APP ENREGISTREMENT
7638	OTHR SOUND APPARATUS ETC	W 409	17.9	W 536	20.8	W 507	20.1	W 538	18.1	AUT APP D'ENREGIS,REPROD
764	TELECOM EQPT,PTS,ACC NES	W 3579	145.5	W 3615	120.3	W 4209	134.7	W 5601	152.8	EQUIP TELECOM,PIECES
7641	LINE TELEPHONE,ETC EQUIP	W 273	21.7	W 335	30.6	W 329	35.5	W 285	27.8	APP TELEPHON PAR FIL
7648	TELECOMM EQUIPMENT NES	W 510	44.5	W 289	22.6	W 105	17.4	W 142	19.8	APP TELECOM NDA
76481	RADIOTELEPHONE ETC RCVRS	W 510	44.5	W 289	22.6	W 105	17.4	W 142	19.8	RECEP RADIOTELEPHONIE
7649	PTS NES OF EQUIPMT OF 76	W 2420	66.3	W 2719	58.6	W 3486	75.0	W 4875	97.3	PIECES DE LA DIV 76
76491	PTS NES OF APPAR OF 7641	W 2420	66.3	W 2719	58.6	W 3486	75.0	W 4875	97.3	PIECES POUR 764.1
77	ELECTRIC MACHNRY NES ETC		311.7		341.8		291.3		358.7	MACH APP ELECT NDA

4. Special Imports C.I.F. by Commodities according to the S.I.T.C. (Rev. 2) in million U.S. Dollars
Importations Spéciales C.A.F. par Produits d'après la C.T.C.I. (Rév. 2) en millions de Dollars E.U.

SITC CTCI	COMMODITY	1993 QUANTITY QUANTITE	1993 VALUE VALEUR	1994 QUANTITY QUANTITE	1994 VALUE VALEUR	1995 QUANTITY QUANTITE	1995 VALUE VALEUR	1996 QUANTITY QUANTITE	1996 VALUE VALEUR	PRODUIT
771	ELECTRIC POWER MACHY NES	W 2561	23.0	W 5408	30.2	W 2008	12.8	W 2716	23.9	MACH PROD,TRANS ELECTR
7711	TRANSFORMERS,ELECTRICAL	W 2561	23.0	W 5408	30.2	W 2008	12.8	W 2716	23.9	TRANSFO ELECTRIQUES
77111	LIQUID DIELEC TRANSFRMRS	W 2561	23.0	W 5408	30.2	W 2008	12.8	W 2716	23.9	TRANSFO DIELEC LIQUIDE
772	SWITCHGEAR ETC,PARTS NES	W 5341	55.4	W 5482	71.1	W 5377	60.4	W 6643	103.5	APP COUPURE,SECT ETC
7722	PRINTED CIRCUITS,PTS NES	W 5341	55.4	W 5482	71.1	W 5377	60.4	W 6643	103.5	CIRCUITS ET PIECES
773	ELECTR DISTRIBUTNG EQUIP	W 11778	51.7	W 14067	72.3	W 12271	55.8	W 13023	65.2	EQUIPMT DISTRIBUTION ELECT
7731	INSULATED WIRE,CABLE ETC	W 11622	50.0	W 13970	71.5	W 9598	41.4	W 12368	59.1	FILS,CABLES ISOLES ELECT
774	ELECTRO-MEDCL,XRAY EQUIP	W 258	23.9	W 265	27.1	W 186	19.2	W 201	20.0	APPAREILS MEDICAUX
7741	ELECTRO-MEDICAL EQUIPMNT	W 228	21.8	W 205	21.9	W 132	16.3	W 159	15.3	APP ELECTRICITE MEDICALE
775	HOUSEHOLD TYPE EQUIP NES	W 12469	89.4	W 11930	80.8	W 12237	81.2	W 12675	83.3	MACH,APP USAGE DOMESTQUE
7757	DOMESTIC ELECTRC EQU NES	W 2756	30.9	W 2434	26.9	W 2588	26.6	W 2832	25.9	APP ELECTR DOMEST NDA
7758	ELECTRO-THERMIC APPL NES	W 4625	28.9	W 4226	23.3	W 4159	23.2	W 3993	22.6	APP ELECTROTHERMIQ NDA
778	ELECTRICAL MACHINERY NES	W 8013	65.8	W 8634	58.8	W 8527	60.1	W 9619	62.0	AUTRES MACH ELECT NDA
7788	OTH ELEC MACHY,EQUIP NES	W 803	26.8	W 533	20.6	W 439	18.9	W 490	21.8	AUT MACH APP ELEC NDA
78	ROAD VEHICLES		933.4		916.2		1007.7		1180.3	VEHICULES ROUTIERS
781	PASS MOTOR VEH EXC BUSES	W 53479	560.8	W 53612	557.9	W 59540	650.5	W 70480	727.9	AUTO TRANSPORT PERSONNES
782	LORRIES,SPCL MTR VEH NES	W 21425	150.7	W 22285	152.5	W 20756	138.7	W 29052	219.1	VEHICULES SPECIAUX,MARCH
7821	LORRIES,TRUCKS	W 20074	140.7	W 21198	144.5	W 19858	133.0	W 27273	209.9	VEHICULES TRANSP MARCHAND
783	ROAD MOTOR VEHICLES NES	W 7563	48.8	W 5085	42.6	W 4782	34.0	W 5858	36.3	VEHICULES ROUTIERS NDA
7831	BUSES	W 6567	45.1	W 3946	37.9	W 3961	31.8	W 3542	28.1	VOITURES TRANSPORT COMMUN
784	MOTOR VEH PRTS,ACCES NES	W 16325	162.4	W 15747	154.2	W 16717	175.7	W 18327	186.0	PIECES 722,781,782,783
7849	OTHER MOTOR VEHCL PARTS	W 16024	161.1	W 15582	153.8	W 16587	175.4	W 18170	185.6	PIECES 722,781,782,783
79	OTHR TRANSPORT EQUIPMENT		595.2		301.8		861.1		49.0	AUTRE MATERIEL TRANSPORT
792	AIRCRAFT ETC	W 168	552.8	W 148	212.6	W 165	809.2	W 84	32.2	APP NAVIGATION AERIENNE
7922	AIRCRFT NES 2000KG OR LS	W 1	509.0		169.8	W 1	723.8			AERODYNES MOINS 2000 KG
7929	AIRCRAFT PARTS NES	W 167	43.8	W 147	42.9	W 164	85.5	W 84	32.2	PIECES DU 792
793	SHIPS AND BOATS ETC		42.5		89.2		51.9		16.8	NAVIRES BATEAUX,ETC
7938	TUGS,SPECIAL VESSELS ETC		24.0		63.7		34.8	W 295	7.4	REMORQUEURS,BATEAUX SPEC
79381	TUGS				41.8					BATEAUX REMORQUEURS
79383	FLOATING STRUCTURES NES	W 2418	17.7	W 473	10.9	W 1976	33.2	W 295	7.4	ENGINS FLOTTANTS DIVERS
8	MISC MANUFACTURED GOODS		1067.8		1042.9		1107.2		1098.7	ART MANUFACTURES DIVERS
812	*PLUMBG,HEATNG,LGHTNG EQ	W 7133	36.1	W 9984	47.7	W 9676	51.1	W 9352	43.3	APPAR SANITAIRES CHAUFFAGE
8124	LIGHTING EQUIPMENT NES	W 2621	24.7	W 3040	29.5	W 2497	29.7	W 2385	23.3	APPAREILS ECLAIRAGE ETC
81242	LAMPS,FITTINGS BASE METL	W 2194	19.3	W 2549	25.4	W 2172	26.4	W 1979	20.1	APPAREILS D'ECLAIRAGE
821	*FURNITURE,PARTS THEREOF	W 37497	145.0	W 30189	120.9	W 29870	132.8	W 30158	124.0	MEUBLES ET PIECES
8219	FURNITURE AND PARTS NES	W 34550	126.4	W 27719	104.2	W 27048	112.7	W 27379	107.1	AUTRES MEUBLES ET PIECES
82191	METAL FURNITURE NES	W 10307	30.1	W 7388	23.4	W 6799	22.4	W 6931	22.7	MEUBLES NDA EN METAL
82192	WOOD FURNITURE NES	W 23010	92.6	W 18514	74.3	W 18161	81.8	W 18826	78.1	MEUBLES NDA EN BOIS
831	*TRAVEL GOODS,HANDBAGS	W 4066	26.1	W 4154	27.0	W 4432	34.0	W 4452	36.4	ARTICLES DE VOYAGE ETC
84	CLOTHING AND ACCESSORIES		287.8		291.4		319.0		322.4	VETEMENTS
842	MENS OUTERWEAR NOT KNIT	W 5234	71.3	W 4753	60.1	W 4859	59.7	W 5192	66.2	VET DESSUS POUR HOMMES
8421	— OVERCOATS,OTHER COATS	W 5234	71.3	W 4753	60.1	W 4859	59.7	W 5192	66.2	MANTEAUX HOMMES MAT TEXT
84211	—— OF WOOL,FINE HAIR	W 5234	71.3	W 4753	60.1	W 4859	59.7	W 5192	66.2	MANTEAUX HOMMES DE LAINE
843	WOMENS OUTERWEAR NONKNIT	W 6728	132.0	W 6525	140.5	W 6726	153.0	W 6361	150.8	VET DESSUS FEMMES MAT TEX
8431	— COATS AND JACKETS	W 4240	95.5	W 3887	94.5	W 4385	111.9	W 4052	108.8	MANT,VEST FEM MAT TEXTIL
8439	— OTHER OUTER GARMENTS	W 2488	36.5	W 2638	46.1	W 2341	41.2	W 2309	42.0	AUT VET DES FEM MAT TEXT
844	UNDER GARMENTS NOT KNIT	W 4081	54.7	W 4409	62.4	W 4708	70.6	W 5235	70.5	VETEMENT DESSOUS MAT TEXT
8443	— WOMENS	W 1891	32.6	W 2076	35.7	W 2216	39.9	W 2493	38.7	VET DESSOUS FEM MAT TEXT
851	*FOOTWEAR	W 4372	64.7	W 4685	62.3	W 4792	69.6	W 5260	75.3	CHAUSSURES
85102	FOOTWEAR LEATHER	W 3512	56.0	W 3882	54.0	W 3619	58.3	W 4206	64.8	CHAUS SEMELLES EN CUIR
87	PRECISION INSTRUMNTS NES		75.8		71.3		63.1		55.7	INSTRUM,APPAR SCIENT NDA
874	MEASURNG,CONTROLNG INSTR	W 969	59.8	W 918	56.6	W 785	47.7	W 962	40.6	INSTRUMENTS DE MESURE
8748	ELEC MEAS,CONTRL EQU NES	W 734	43.0	W 606	48.1	W 442	32.0	W 666	29.6	APP ELEC ELECTRO MESURE
87483	OTH ELCTRNC MEAS ETC EQU	W 734	43.0	W 606	48.1	W 442	32.0	W 666	29.6	AUT APP ELECTRO DE MESURE
88	PHOTO EQU,OPTICL GDS ETC		78.4		83.1		78.7		84.4	APP,FOURN PHOTO,OP,MONTR
885	WATCHES AND CLOCKS		42.1		43.7		37.6		39.3	HORLOGERIE
8851	WATCHES,MOVEMENTS,CASES		33.5		37.8		32.4		33.1	MONTRES,MOUVEMENTS,BOITES
88511	WATCHES		33.5		37.8		32.4		33.1	MONTRES POCHE,BRACELET
89	MISC MANUFCTRD GOODS NES		354.1		339.5		359.1		357.6	ART MANUFACTURES DIVERS
892	PRINTED MATTER	W 4683	31.2	W 5426	28.1	W 4887	29.4	W 4583	28.8	IMPRIMES
893	ARTICLES OF PLASTIC NES	W 15608	42.6	W 17960	51.4	W 18592	64.4	W 21539	71.8	OUVRAGES EN MAT DIVIS 58
8939	MISC PLASTIC ARTICLES	W 7865	23.7	W 9698	29.1	W 10165	36.9	W 12395	43.1	ART DIVERS EN MAT DIV 58
894	TOYS,SPORTING GOODS,ETC	W 8867	56.4	W 8901	54.4	W 8406	60.1	W 8440	57.6	VOITURES ENFANTS,JOUETS
8942	TOYS,INDOOR GAMES ETC	W 6647	37.7	W 6099	34.8	W 5301	35.2	W 5783	38.3	JOUETS,JEUX ETC
89421	LARGE SIZE WHEELED TOYS	W 5898	26.9	W 5482	26.2	W 4716	27.5	W 5044	28.3	VOITURES AMUSEM ENFANTS
897	GOLD,SILVER WARE,JEWELRY		155.2		140.5		140.7		132.8	BIJOUTERIE,ORFEVRERIE
8973	PREC JEWLRY,GLD-SILVWARE		149.4		135.2		133.4		126.2	BIJOUX OR,ARGENT ORFEVRE
89731	PRECIOUS METAL JEWELLERY		149.0		134.8		133.2		125.9	ART BIJOUTERIE,JOAILLER
898	MUSICAL INSTRUMENTS,PTS	W 2391	28.1	W 2450	22.8	W 1592	17.7	W 1759	20.9	INSTRUMENTS DE MUSIQUE
8983	SOUND RECRDNG TAPE,DISCS	W 2179	24.1	W 2289	19.6	W 1459	14.9	W 1640	18.5	SUPPORTS SON POUR 763
899	OTHER MANUFACTURED GOODS		20.7		19.8		24.2		24.9	AUT ART MANUF DIVERS NDA
9	GOODS NOT CLASSD BY KIND		56.9		34.1		31.6		79.7	ART TRANSACT NON CLASSES
971	*GOLD,NON MONETARY NES	K 4588	52.8	K 9991	30.3	K 2254	28.2	K 5967252	75.3	OR NON MONETAIRE
97101	NONMON GLD UNWRT,SEMIMFD	K 4588	52.8	K 2491	30.3	K 2254	28.2	K 5967252	75.3	OR,ALLIAGES D'OR BRUTS

5. Special Exports F.O.B. by Commodities according to the S.I.T.C. (Rev. 2) in million U.S. Dollars
Exportations Spéciales F.O.B. par Produits d'après la C.T.C.I. (Rév. 2) en millions de Dollars E.U.

SITC CTCI	COMMODITY	1993 QUANTITY QUANTITE	1993 VALUE VALEUR	1994 QUANTITY QUANTITE	1994 VALUE VALEUR	1995 QUANTITY QUANTITE	1995 VALUE VALEUR	1996 QUANTITY QUANTITE	1996 VALUE VALEUR	PRODUIT
	ALL COMMODITIES		10519.1		11964.6		12944.5		14855.8	TOUS PRODUITS
0	FOOD AND LIVE ANIMALS		25.5		25.4		27.4		65.0	ALIMENTS,ANIMAUX VIVANTS
2	CRUDE MATERLS,EXCL FUELS		36.1		44.6		42.5		39.9	MAT BRUTES NON COMESTIBLES
28	METALLIFEROUS ORES,SCRAP		32.4		40.7		36.5		31.7	MINERAIS METAL,DECHETS
3	MINERAL FUELS ETC		10000.2		11231.0		12255.2		14145.9	COMBUSTIBLES MINERAUX LUB
33	PETROLEUM AND PRODUCTS		10000.1		11230.9		12255.2		14145.9	PETROLE ET DERIVES
333	CRUDE PETROLEUM		9986.0		11197.0		12216.0		14098.7	HUILES BRUTES DE PETROLE
335	RESIDUAL PETRLM PROD NES	W 357214	12.5	W 830365	33.0	W 792208	37.9	W 837468	45.5	PRODUITS RESIDUELS NDA
3354	PETROLM BITUMEN,COKE ETC	W 357214	12.5	W 830365	33.0	W 792208	37.9	W 837468	45.5	BITUME,COKE DE PETROLE
33542	PETROLEUM COKE	W 357150	12.5	W 830350	33.0	W 792200	37.9	W 837450	45.5	COKE DE PETROLE
5	CHEMCLS,RELATED PROD NES		100.8		150.9		260.2		224.3	PRODUITS CHIMIQUES
52	INORGANIC CHEMICALS		11.7		38.1		58.7		49.1	PROD CHIM INORGANIQUES
522	INORG ELEMNTS,OXIDES,ETC	W 241020	10.7	W 539029	37.4	W 635405	58.4	W 707825	48.0	ELEMENTS INORGANIQUES
5221	CHEMICAL ELEMENTS	W 227639	7.9	W 470298	24.2	W 555288	41.0	W 633065	31.6	ELEMENTS CHIMIQUES
52215	SULPHUR,PURIFIED	W 225095	7.0	W 467924	23.4	W 553000	40.5	W 630739	31.0	SOUFRE SUBLIME,PRECIPITE
562	*FERTILIZERS,MANUFACTURE	W 673580	70.0	W 716573	94.6	W 945183	180.3	W 781540	148.7	ENGRAIS MANUFACTURES
5621	CHEM NITROGENOUS FERTLZR	W 673540	70.0	W 716573	94.6	W 945183	180.3	W 781540	148.7	ENGRAIS AZOTES
56216	UREA	W 673540	70.0	W 716573	94.6	W 945183	180.3	W 781540	148.7	UREE
6	BASIC MANUFACTURES		91.6		113.8		133.6		126.1	ART MANUFACTURES
66	NONMETAL MINERAL MFS NES		28.4		32.5		41.5		38.7	ART MIN NON METALLIQUES
7	MACHINES,TRANSPORT EQUIP		216.6		343.8		182.3		191.8	MACHINES MATERIEL TRANSPORT
77	ELECTRIC MACHNRY NES ETC		40.2		36.6		31.2		45.3	MACH APP ELECT NDA
78	ROAD VEHICLES		115.5		117.7		109.9		98.7	VEHICULES ROUTIERS
781	PASS MOTOR VEH EXC BUSES	W 5093	44.6	W 4398	42.4	W 3643	32.1	W 3599	22.9	AUTO TRANSPORT PERSONNES
782	LORRIES,SPCL MTR VEH NES	W 7643	34.6	W 6079	36.4	W 6328	27.0	W 4872	24.4	VEHICULES SPECIAUX,MARCH
7821	LORRIES,TRUCKS	W 7492	34.1	W 5988	35.7	W 6155	26.0	W 4654	23.5	VEHICULES TRANSP MARCHAND
79	OTHR TRANSPORT EQUIPMENT		1.0		123.8		1.1		1.1	AUTRE MATERIEL TRANSPORT
792	AIRCRAFT ETC			W 1	122.1			W 15	0.5	APP NAVIGATION AERIENNE
7922	AIRCRFT NES 2000KG OR LS			W 1	122.1					AERODYNES MOINS 2000 KG
8	MISC MANUFACTURED GOODS		42.3		49.6		37.5		44.2	ART MANUFACTURES DIVERS

1. HISTORICAL SERIES, 1992–1997 GENERAL TRADE, IMPORTS F.O.B., EXPORTS F.O.B.
SERIES HISTORIQUES, 1992–1997 COMMERCE GENERAL, IMPORTATIONS F.O.B., EXPORTATIONS F.O.B

YEAR ANNEE	VALUE IN MILLION U.S. DOLLARS VALEUR EN MILLION U.S. DOLLARS MERCHANDISE –MARCHANDISE		GOLD –OR		CONVERSION FACTORS FACTEURS DE CONVERSION CENTS E.U. PAR		INDEX NUMBERS –INDICES QUANTUM		UNIT VALUE VALEUR UNITAIRE	
	IMPORTS	EXPORTS	IMPORTS	EXPORTS	IMPORTS	EXPORTS	IMPORTS	EXPORTS	IMPORTS	EXPORTS
1992	70.47	76.45								
1993	112.00	112.10								
1994	369.00	340.00								
1995	439.00	380.00								
1996	837.93	507.07								
1997	709.30	603.80								

2. IMPORTS BY BROAD ECONOMIC CATEGORY AND EXPORTS BY INDUSTRIAL ORIGIN. (PERCENTAGE OF TOTAL VALUE)
IMPORTATIONS PAR CATEGORIES ECONOMIQUES ET EXPORTATIONS PAR BRANCHE D'ACTIVITE.(EN POURCENTAGE DE LA VALEUR TOTALE)

IMPORTS – IMPORTATIONS

	1991	1992	1993	1994	1995	1996	1997
TOTAL IMPORTS–IMPORTATIONS TOTALES					100.	100.	
1 FOOD BEV–ALIMENTATION BOISSONS					17.5	20.3	
11 PRIMARY–PRODUITS DE BASE					3.6	4.0	
111 FOR INDUSTRY–POUR L'INDUSTRIE					2.8	2.9	
112 FOR HOUSEHOLDS–POUR LES MENAGES					0.8	1.1	
12 PROCESSED–PRODUITS ELABORES					13.9	16.3	
121 FOR INDUSTRY–POUR L'INDUSTRIE					8.3	12.3	
122 FOR HOUSEHOLDS–POUR LES MENAGES					5.6	4.1	
2 IND SUPPLIES–APPROV INDUSTRIELS					21.2	18.7	
21 PRIMARY–PRODUITS DE BASE					4.0	1.8	
22 PROCESSED–PRODUITS ELABORES					17.3	16.9	
3 FUELS–COMBUSTIBLES					36.0	28.4	
31 PRIMARY–PRODUITS DE BASE					14.7	13.2	
32 PROCESSED–PRODUITS ELABORES					21.3	15.2	
321 MOTOR SPIRIT–ESSENCE					19.6	11.9	
322 OTHER–AUTRES					1.7	3.3	
4 MACHINERY–EQUIPEMENT					12.8	20.6	
41 CAPITAL EQUIPMENT–MACHINES					10.0	13.4	
42 PARTS–PIECES ACCESSOIRES					2.8	7.2	
5 TRANSPORT–TRANSPORT					6.1	6.2	
51 PASSENGER CARS–AUTOMOBILES					0.1	0.0	
52 OTHER–AUTRES					3.0	2.3	
521 INDUSTRIAL–INDUSTRIELS					3.0	2.3	
522 NON INDUSTRIAL–NON INDUSTRIEL					0.0	0.0	
53 PARTS–PIECES ACCESSOIRES					3.0	3.9	
6 CONSUM GOODS–BIENS CONSOMMATION					6.4	5.6	
61 DURABLE–DURABLES					1.3	1.2	
62 SEMI DURABLE–SEMI DURABLES					2.1	1.2	
63 NON DURABLE–NON DURABLES					2.9	3.2	
7 GOODS NES–BIENS NDA					0.0	0.1	

EXPORTS – EXPORTATIONS

	1991	1992	1993	1994	1995	1996	1997
TOTAL EXPORTS–EXPORTATIONS TOTALES					100.	100.	
1 AGRICULTURE					19.3	17.9	
2 MINING QUARRY–INDUS EXTRACTIVES					1.2	1.1	
3 MANUFACTURING–IND MANUFACTUR					79.5	81.0	
31 FOOD BEV TOBACCO–ALIM BOISS TAB					12.3	20.5	
32 TEXTILES–INDUSTRIES TEXTILES					12.4	7.8	
33 WOOD & PRODUCTS–BOIS & PRODUITS					0.1	0.1	
34 PAPER & PRODUCTS–PAPIER & PRODT					0.2	0.3	
35 CHEMICALS–INDUSTRIES CHIMIQUES					14.2	14.4	
36 NON METAL MIN–MIN NON METAL					2.7	4.1	
37 BASIC METAL–IND METAL BASE					10.8	4.8	
38 METAL MANUF–MANUF METAL					16.0	14.0	
39 OTH MANUF IND–AUTRES MANUF					10.8	15.0	

3. TRADE BY PRINCIPAL COUNTRIES OF CONSIGNMENT AND DESTINATION (VALUE IN MILLION U.S. DOLLARS)
ECHANGES SELON LES PRINCIPAUX PAYS DE CONSIGNATION ET DE DESTINATION (VALEUR EN MILLIONS DE DOLLARS EU)

COUNTRIES–PAYS	GENERAL IMPORTS F.O.B. IMPORTATIONS GENERALES F.O.B.				
	1993	1994	1995	1996	1997
World		317.0	522.4	837.9	709.3
Africa				0.1	
Americas		48.2	47.7	132.7	
– Northern America		36.6	25.0	78.2	
– LAIA				32.3	
– CACM					
– Caribbean		11.6	22.7	22.1	
– Rest of America				0.0	
Asia excl fmr USSR		35.6	65.9	88.5	
– Middle East		16.1	41.8	53.3	
Asia former USSR		134.3	229.1	294.1	
Europe excl fmr USSR		21.3	43.6	115.9	
– European Union		17.0	34.1	93.2	
– Eastern Europe		1.5	6.5	6.4	
– Rest of Europe		2.8	3.0	16.4	
Europe former USSR		76.9	128.1	203.6	
Oceania				0.1	
Other			8.0	3.0	
Russian Federation		69.3	114.3	174.5	138.2
Kazakhstan		58.3	112.5	139.7	48.7
Uzbekistan/Ouzbékistan		63.7	88.9	131.6	32.9
USA/Etats–Unis d'Amer		35.0	19.1	35.7	76.7
Turkey/Turquie		15.0	38.3	47.6	11.7
Germany/Allemagne		6.8	18.7	31.8	28.6
Cuba		11.6	22.7	22.1	
Canada		1.6	5.9	42.5	
Turkmenistan/Turkménistn		10.4	18.6	13.6	6.0
China/Chine		10.6	6.3	7.8	15.9
France, Monaco		1.8	1.8	19.1	10.7
Brazil/Brésil				32.3	
Japan/Japon		2.7	7.2	12.5	
Belarus/Bélarus		2.6	5.0	6.1	7.2
Belgium–Luxembourg		0.4	3.8	8.7	7.7
Ukraine		3.2	4.9	12.3	
Tajikistan/Tadjikistan		1.1	4.8	6.3	4.3
Switzerland,Liechtenst.		2.5	1.2	12.5	
Italy/Italie		0.9	1.7	5.8	4.9
Pakistan			3.0	4.1	4.8
Austria/Autriche		0.5	1.3	9.8	
Korea, Republic of		3.6	2.5	5.1	
Areas n.e.s.			8.0	3.0	
United Arab Emirates		0.1	0.7	1.7	6.9
Latvia/Lettonie		0.6	1.5	6.4	
Denmark/Danemark		0.7	1.9	4.2	
Netherlands/Pays–Bas		1.8	1.5	3.4	
Iran (Islamic Rep of)		0.7	2.3	3.4	
United Kingdom		1.0	1.7	3.6	
Lithuania/Lituanie		1.2	1.7	2.9	
Norway,Svalbard and JM		0.3	1.7	3.7	
Azerbaijan/Azerbaïdjan		0.6	3.3	1.4	
Sweden/Suède		2.6	0.1	2.4	
Finland/Finlande		0.5	1.3	3.1	
Bulgaria/Bulgarie		0.4	3.0	0.9	
India/Inde		0.7	0.6	2.9	
Poland/Pologne		0.6	1.9	1.6	
Hungary/Hongrie		0.5	1.0	1.8	
Afghanistan			3.0	0.0	
Georgia/Géorgie		0.2	0.3	1.6	

COUNTRIES–PAYS	GENERAL EXPORTS F.O.B. EXPORTATIONS GENERALES F.O.B.				
	1993	1994	1995	1996	1997
Monde		340.1	412.0	507.1	603.8
Afrique					
Amériques		4.6	5.4	17.9	17.9
– Amérique du Nord		4.6	5.4	17.9	17.9
– ALAI					
– MCAC					
– Caraïbes					
– Autre Amérique					
Asie anc. URSS exclus		67.1	84.3	61.0	49.9
– Moyen–Orient		6.4	8.9	13.8	14.2
Asie ancienne URSS		150.9	151.4	244.6	201.3
Europe anc. URSS exclus		43.8	47.2	32.3	194.5
– Union Européenne		41.4	38.9	19.9	22.5
– Europe de l'Est		2.1	6.5	11.5	9.6
– Autre de l'Europe		0.3	1.8	0.9	162.3
Europe ancienne URSS		73.0	123.7	151.4	112.1
Océanie			0.0	0.0	
Autre				0.0	
Russian Federation		58.5	106.6	134.7	98.8
Kazakhstan		95.2	67.2	113.0	87.1
Uzbekistan/Ouzbékistan		43.6	70.8	116.8	101.5
China/Chine		56.1	68.5	36.4	31.6
Switzerland,Liechtenst.		0.3	1.8	0.9	162.3
United Kingdom		29.5	27.4	5.3	
USA/Etats–Unis d'Amer		0.6	4.0	17.6	17.9
Tajikistan/Tadjikistan		3.0	8.3	8.3	12.7
Ukraine		9.1	8.3	9.4	4.6
Germany/Allemagne		6.6	2.1	2.9	18.1
Belarus/Bélarus		3.8	5.0	5.6	8.6
Turkey/Turquie		3.9	3.2	5.3	8.0
Czech Republic			1.2	8.2	9.6
Iran (Islamic Rep of)		0.2	4.1	6.3	6.2
Afghanistan		2.0	3.0	6.5	4.1
Turkmenistan/Turkménistn		7.3	2.2	3.2	
Belgium–Luxembourg			0.2	3.7	4.5
France, Monaco		2.2	3.6	1.8	
Italy/Italie		1.8	2.9	2.5	
Azerbaijan/Azerbaïdjan		1.6	2.1	3.2	
Canada		4.0	1.4	0.2	
Cyprus/Chypre		2.2	1.4	1.3	
Bulgaria/Bulgarie		0.3	2.9	0.7	
Netherlands/Pays–Bas		0.6	0.9	2.1	
Austria/Autriche		0.2	1.7	1.2	
Mongolia/Mongolie		0.7	0.9	1.4	
Latvia/Lettonie		0.3	2.3	0.3	
Poland/Pologne		0.6	1.3	0.5	
Republic of Moldova		0.5	1.0	0.8	
India/Inde		0.6	0.5	1.0	
Hungary/Hongrie		0.6	0.2	1.0	
Japan/Japon			0.6	1.0	
Lithuania/Lituanie		0.6	0.4	0.5	
Romania/Roumanie		0.3	0.2	1.0	
Korea Dem People's Rp		0.6	0.5	0.3	
Korea, Republic of		0.5	0.8	0.1	
Slovakia/Slovaquie		0.3	0.8	0.2	
Pakistan		0.2	0.6	0.4	
United Arab Emirates		0.1	0.1	1.0	
Georgia/Géorgie		0.2	0.7	0.1	

(VALUE AS PERCENTAGE OF WORLD TOTAL)(VALEURS EN POURCENTAGE DU TOTAL MONDIAL)

	1988	1989	1990	1991	1992	1993	1994	1995	1996	1997
Africa									0.0	
Americas							15.2	9.1	15.8	
– Northern America							11.5	4.8	9.3	
– LAIA									3.9	
– CACM										
– Caribbean							3.7	4.4	2.6	
– Rest of America									0.0	
Asia excl fmr USSR							11.2	12.6	10.6	
– Middle East							5.1	8.0	6.4	
Asia former USSR							42.4	43.9	35.1	
Europe excl fmr USSR							6.7	8.3	13.8	
– European Union							5.4	6.5	11.1	
– Eastern Europe							0.5	1.2	0.8	
– Rest of Europe							0.9	0.6	2.0	
Europe former USSR							24.3	24.5	24.3	
Oceania									0.0	
Other								1.5	0.4	
Russian Federation							21.9	21.9	20.8	19.5
Kazakhstan							18.4	21.5	16.7	6.9
Uzbekistan/Ouzbékistan							20.1	17.0	15.7	4.6
USA/Etats–Unis d'Amer							11.0	3.7	4.3	10.8
Turkey/Turquie							4.7	7.3	5.7	1.6
Germany/Allemagne							2.1	3.6	3.8	4.0
Cuba							3.7	4.4	2.6	
Canada							0.5	1.1	5.1	
Turkmenistan/Turkménistn							3.3	3.6	1.6	0.9
China/Chine							3.3	1.2	0.9	2.2

	1988	1989	1990	1991	1992	1993	1994	1995	1996	1997
Afrique										
Amériques							1.4	1.3	3.5	3.0
– Amérique du Nord							1.4	1.3	3.5	3.0
– ALAI										
– MCAC										
– Caraïbes										
– Autre Amérique										
Asie anc. URSS exclus							19.7	20.5	12.0	8.3
– Moyen–Orient							1.9	2.2	2.7	2.4
Asie ancienne URSS							44.4	36.7	48.2	33.3
Europe anc. URSS exclus							12.9	11.5	6.4	32.2
– Union Européenne							12.2	9.4	3.9	3.7
– Europe de l'Est							0.6	1.6	2.3	1.6
– Autre de l'Europe							0.1	0.4	0.2	26.9
Europe ancienne URSS							21.5	30.0	29.9	18.6
Océanie								0.0	0.0	
Autre									0.0	
Russian Federation							17.2	25.9	26.6	16.4
Kazakhstan							28.0	16.3	22.3	14.4
Uzbekistan/Ouzbékistan							12.8	17.2	23.0	16.8
China/Chine							16.5	16.6	7.2	5.2
Switzerland,Liechtenst.							0.1	0.4	0.2	26.9
United Kingdom							8.7	6.6	1.1	
USA/Etats–Unis d'Amer							0.2	1.0	3.5	3.0
Tajikistan/Tadjikistan							0.9	2.0	1.6	2.1
Ukraine							2.7	2.0	1.9	0.8
Germany/Allemagne							1.9	0.5	0.6	3.0

4. General Imports F.O.B. by Commodities according to the S.I.T.C. (Rev. 2) in million U.S. Dollars
Importations Générales F.O.B. par Produits d'après la C.T.C.I. (Rév. 2) en millions de Dollars E.U.

SITC CTCI	COMMODITY	1994 QUANTITY QUANTITE	1994 VALUE VALEUR	1995 QUANTITY QUANTITE	1995 VALUE VALEUR	1996 QUANTITY QUANTITE	1996 VALUE VALEUR	1997 QUANTITY QUANTITE	1997 VALUE VALEUR	PRODUIT
	ALL COMMODITIES				522.4		838.0			TOUS PRODUITS
0	FOOD AND LIVE ANIMALS				77.8		149.8			ALIMENTS,ANIMAUX VIVANTS
02	DAIRY PRODCTS,BIRDS'EGGS				1.1		4.3			PRODUITS LAITIERS,OEUFS
022	MILK AND CREAM			W 1126	0.7	W 1714	3.8			LAIT ET CREME
0223	MILK AND CREAM FRESH			W 1126	0.7	W 1714	3.8			LAIT,CREME FRAIS
04	CEREALS AND PREPARATIONS				28.6		39.6			CEREALES ET PRODUITS
041	WHEAT ETC UNMILLED			W 84116	12.5	W 109377	22.4			FROMENT,EPEAUTRE
0411	DURUM WHEAT UNMILLED			W 84116	12.5	W 109377	22.4			FROMENT DUR NON MOULU
042	RICE			W 3505	1.9	W 3560	1.6			RIZ
0421	RICE IN HUSK OR HUSKED			W 3505	1.9	W 3560	1.6			RIZ SANS AUTRE PREPARATION
04211	RICE IN THE HUSK			W 3505	1.9	W 3560	1.6			RIZ PADDY
046	WHEAT ETC MEAL OR FLOUR			W 56324	10.6	W 30115	11.6			SEMOULE FARINE,FROMENT
04601	FLOUR OF WHEAT OR MESLIN			W 56324	10.6	W 30115	11.6			FARINE DE FROMENT
048	CEREAL ETC PREPARATIONS				2.1		2.4			PREPTNS A BASE CEREALES
05	VEGETABLES AND FRUIT				1.4		3.4			LEGUMES ET FRUITS
06	SUGAR AND PREPS,HONEY				36.4		92.7			SUCRES ET PRODUITS
061	SUGAR AND HONEY			W 144140	34.7	W 241765	91.6			SUCRES ET MIEL
0611	RAW BEET AND CANE SUGAR			W 72316	25.8	W 197558	83.7			SUCRES BRUTS
0612	REFINED SUGAR ETC			W 8304	3.3	W 4760	2.8			SUCRES RAFFINES
0615	MOLASSES			W 63518	5.7	W 39447	5.2			MELASSES
062	SUGAR CANDY NON-CHOCLATE				1.8		1.2			SUCRERIES
07	COFFEE,TEA,COCOA,SPICES				4.7		3.7			CAFE,THE,CACAO,EPICES
073	CHOCOLATE AND PRODUCTS			W 1699	3.8	W 1263	1.9			CHOCOLAT
09	MISC EDIBLE PRODUCTS				4.9		3.6			PREP ALIMENTAIRES DIVERSES
098	EDIBLE PRODCTS,PREPS NES				4.2		3.0			PREP ALIMENTAIRES NDA
09809	MISC FOOD PREPRTIONS NES				2.4		1.5			PREP ALIMENTAIRES NDA
1	BEVERAGES AND TOBACCO				12.6		20.4			BOISSONS ET TABACS
11	BEVERAGES				11.6		17.8			BOISSONS
111	NON-ALCOHL BEVERAGES NES			W 28533	2.3	W 5273	0.6			BOISSONS NON ALCOOLIQUES
11102	FLAVORED WATERS NON-ALCO			W 28533	2.3	W 5273	0.6			LIMONADES,EAUX GAZEUSES
112	ALCOHOLIC BEVERAGES			W 53232	9.4	W 148857	17.2			BOISSONS ALCOOLIQUES
1121	WINE OF FRESH GRAPES ETC			W 13690	2.6	W 48783	6.0			VINS DE RAISINS FRAIS
11212	WINE OF FRESH GRAPES			W 13690	2.6	W 48783	6.0			VINS DE MOUTS DE RAISINS
1123	BEER,ALE,STOUT,PORTER			W 26559	2.9	W 36565	3.2			BIERES
1124	DISTILLED ALCOHOLIC BEVS			W 10809	3.7	W 32363	6.0			ALCOOLS,EAUX-DE-VIE
11249	OTH ALCOHOLC BEVS,CMPNDS			W 10809	3.7	W 32363	6.0			BOISSONS ALCOOLIQUES NDA
12	TOBACCO AND MANUFACTURES				1.0		2.6			TABACS BRUTS FABRIQUES
122	TOBACCO,MANUFACTURED			W 204	0.9	W 1385	2.6			TABACS FABRIQUES
1222	CIGARETTES			W 204	0.9	W 1385	2.6			CIGARETTES
2	CRUDE MATERLS,EXCL FUELS				24.0		21.3			MAT BRUTES NON COMESTIBLES
24	CORK AND WOOD				3.9		5.3			LIEGE ET BOIS
248	WOOD SHAPED,SLEEPERS			W 16161	2.7	W 27297	4.4			BOIS SIMPLEMENT TRAVAILLES
2482	LUMBER SHAPED CONIFER			W 14955	2.3	W 26135	4.2			CONIFERES SCIES,RABOTES
24822	LUMBER PLANED ETC CONIFR			W 14955	2.3	W 26135	4.2			CONIFER RABOTES,RAINES
26	TEXTILE FIBRES AND WASTE				9.9		6.9			FIBRES TEXTILES
263	COTTON			W 5689	4.9	W 1575	0.5			COTON
2631	RAW COTTON,EXCL LINTERS			W 2746	4.0	W 94	0.2			COTON EN MASSE
268	WOOL(EXC TOPS),ANML HAIR			W 1269	1.7	W 1049	1.6			LAINES ET POILS
27	CRUDE FERTLZR,MINRLS NES				4.5		5.7			ENGRAIS MINERAUX BRUTS
278	OTHER CRUDE MINERALS				3.5		5.0			AUTRES MINERAUX BRUTS
2784	ASBESTOS CRDE,SMPLY WRKD			W 11446	2.1	W 12542	2.5			AMIANTE (ASBESTE)
28	METALLIFEROUS ORES,SCRAP				5.6		2.9			MINERAIS METAL,DECHETS
287	BASE METAL ORES,CONC NES			W 2178	2.3	W 1197	1.5			MINERAIS METAUX COMMUNS
2879	OTH NONFER ORE,CONCNTRTE			W 2178	2.3	W 1197	1.5			MINERAIS D'AUTRES METAUX
28799	OTH BASE MTL ORE,CON NES			W 2178	2.3	W 1197	1.5			AUTRES MINERAIS
288	NONFERR METAL SCRAP NES			W 6113	3.1	W 2121	1.4			DECHETS NON FERREUX
2882	OTHER BASE MTL SCRAP NES			W 6113	3.1	W 2121	1.4			AUTRES DECHETS
28821	COPPER WASTE AND SCRAP			W 5080	2.8	W 1781	1.4			DECHETS DE CUIVRE
3	MINERAL FUELS ETC				188.5		240.1			COMBUSTIBLES MINERAUX LUB
32	COAL,COKE AND BRIQUETTES				17.1		25.8			HOUILLES,COKES,BRIQUETTES
322	COAL,LIGNITE AND PEAT			W 4099709	17.1	W 7144500	25.2			HOUILLES,LIGNITES,TOURBE
3222	OTH COAL,NOT AGGLOMERATD			W 4092267	16.9	W 7092911	23.9			AUTRES HOUILLES
33	PETROLEUM AND PRODUCTS				103.3		103.2			PETROLE ET DERIVES
334	PETROLEUM PRODUCTS,REFIN			W 1440853	102.5	W 3276155	99.7			PRODUITS RAFFINES
341	*GAS,NATURAL AND MANUFCT				59.6		84.4			GAZ NATUREL,GAZ MANUFACT
3413	PETROLM GASES,LIQUEFIED				55.6		71.8			GAZ DE PETROLE LIQUEFIE
34139	OTH HYDROCARBON GAS LQFD				55.6		71.8			HYDROCARBURES GAZEUX NDA
3414	PETROLEUM GASES, GASEOUS				4.1		12.6			GAZ DE PETROLE GAZEUX
351	*ELECTRIC CURRENT			H 254400	8.6	H 815100	26.8			ENERGIE ELECTRIQUE
4	ANIMAL,VEGETABLE OIL,FAT				5.4		4.6			HUILES,GRAISSES ANIM,VEG
42	FIXED VEGETABLE OIL,FAT				5.2		4.5			HUILES VEGETALES FIXES
423	FIXED VEG OILS,SOFT			W 7758	3.2	W 5239	3.8			HUILES VEGET DOUCES FIXES
4236	SUNFLOWER SEED OIL			W 7007	2.6	W 4643	3.4			HUILE DE TOURNESOL
424	FIXED VEG OIL NONSOFT			W 1662	2.0	W 741	0.8			AUTRES HUILES VEG FIXES
4249	FIXED VEGETABLE OILS NES			W 1625	1.9	W 711	0.7			HUILES VEGET FIXES NDA
5	CHEMCLS,RELATED PROD NES				32.0		64.5			PRODUITS CHIMIQUES
51	ORGANIC CHEMICALS				3.6		13.9			PROD CHIMIQ ORGANIQUES
512	ALCOHOLS,PHENOLS ETC				2.1		12.3			PHENOLS,PHENOLS-ALCOOLS
5121	ACYCLIC ALCOHOLS,DERIVS				2.1		12.2			ALCOOLS ACYCLIQUES
51216	ETHYL ALC,DENATRD SPIRIT			V 12549	2.1	V 109540	12.2			ALCOOL ETHYLIQUE NON DENAT
52	INORGANIC CHEMICALS				6.3		9.8			PROD CHIM INORGANIQUES
522	INORG ELEMNTS,OXIDES,ETC			W 15680	3.3	W 13970	3.8			ELEMENTS INORGANIQUES
5225	INORGANIC BASES ETC NES			W 11580	2.5	W 11727	3.0			AUTRES BASES OXYDES METAL
523	OTHR INORG CHEMICALS ETC				3.0		6.0			AUT PRODUITS CHIMIQUES INORG
5239	INORG CHEM PRODUCTS NES				2.0		4.3			PROD CHIM INORGANIQ NDA
52399	OTH INORG CMPNDS NES ETC				2.0		3.7			AUT COMP INORGANIQUES NDA
53	DYES,TANNING,COLOUR PROD				2.5		2.0			PROD TEINTURE,COLORANTS
531	SYNT DYE,NAT INDGO,LAKES			W 1011	2.4	W 699	1.9			MAT COLOR ORGAN,LAQUES
541	*MEDICINAL,PHARM PRODUCT				8.9		17.8			PROD MEDICINAUX PHARMACEUT
5417	MEDICAMENTS				7.7		15.9			MEDICAMENTS
54171	— CONTAINNG ANTIBIOTICS				7.7		15.9			MED CONTN ANTIBIOTIQUES
55	PERFUME,CLEANING ETC PRD				3.7		2.5			PROD POUR PARFUM,TOILETTE
554	SOAP,CLEANSING ETC PREPS			W 3765	2.6	W 1583	1.5			SAVONS,PRODUITS DETERSIFS
562	*FERTILIZERS,MANUFACTURE			W 22517	3.8	W 89763	10.8			ENGRAIS MANUFACTURES
5621	CHEM NITROGENOUS FERTLZR			W 16415	3.3	W 62899	8.8			ENGRAIS AZOTES
56216	UREA			W 16415	3.3	W 62899	8.8			UREE
58	PLASTIC MATERIALS ETC				1.6		3.9			MAT PLAST ARTIFICIELLES
583	POLYMERIZATION ETC PRODS			W 1287	1.6	W 2713	3.9			PROD POLYMERISATION
59	CHEMICAL MATERIALS NES				1.0		3.5			MAT PROD CHIMIQUES NDA
6	BASIC MANUFACTURES				67.1		94.0			ART MANUFACTURES
62	RUBBER MANUFACTURES NES				4.7		10.8			CAOUTCHOUC MANUFACTURE

4. General Imports F.O.B. by Commodities according to the S.I.T.C. (Rev. 2) in million U.S. Dollars
Importations Générales F.O.B. par Produits d'après la C.T.C.I. (Rév. 2) en millions de Dollars E.U.

SITC CTCI	COMMODITY	1994 QUANTITY QUANTITE	1994 VALUE VALEUR	1995 QUANTITY QUANTITE	1995 VALUE VALEUR	1996 QUANTITY QUANTITE	1996 VALUE VALEUR	1997 QUANTITY QUANTITE	1997 VALUE VALEUR	PRODUIT
625	RUBBER TYRES, TUBES ETC			N 78670	4.0	N 60932	7.1			PNEUS CAOUTCHOUC VULCANISE
6252	TYRES,NEW,BUS OR LORRY			N 26137	2.2	N 18767	4.3			PNEUS POUR AUTOBUS,CAMIONS
628	RUBBER ARTICLES NES				0.7		3.6			OUVRAGES CAOUTCHOUC NDA
6289	OTH RUBBER ARTICLES NES				0.5		3.3			AUT OUVR CAOUTCHOUC NDA
62898	UNHARD RUBBER PRODS NES				0.5		3.3			OUV CAOUT VULC NON DURCI
63	WOOD,CORK MANUFACTRS NES				6.8		6.1			OUVRAGES LIEGE ET BOIS
635	WOOD MANUFACTURES NES				5.6		4.2			ART MANUF EN BOIS NDA
6353	BUILDERS WOODWRK,PREFABS				5.5		3.5			OUVRAGES DE MENUISERIE
64	PAPER,PAPERBOARD AND MFR				5.8		11.1			PAPIERS,CARTONS & OUVRAGES
641	PAPER AND PAPERBOARD				3.5		7.6			PAPIERS ET CARTONS
642	PAPER,ETC,PRECUT,ARTS OF				2.3		3.5			PAP,CARTONS DECOUPES
6423	EXERCISE BOOKS ETC				1.9		2.0			REGISTRES,CAHIERS,CARNETS
65	TEXTILE YARN,FABRICS,ETC				10.1		8.9			FILS,TISSUS,ARTICLES TEXTILE
651	TEXTILE YARN			W 1566	3.4		2.2			FILS TEXTILES
6513	COTTON YARN			W 875	1.8	W 398	0.7			FILS DE COTON
652	COTTON FABRICS,WOVEN				1.9		0.8			TISSUS DE COTON
657	SPECIAL TXTL FABRC,PRODS				1.3		2.8			TISSUS SPECIAUX
66	NONMETAL MINERAL MFS NES				6.2		12.2			ART MIN NON METALLIQUES
661	LIME,CEMENT,BLDG PRODS				1.7		2.4			CHAUX,CIMENTS MAT CONSTR
663	MINERAL MANUFCTURES NES				2.8		3.1			ART MIN MANUF NDA
6633	MINRL MFS NES NONCERAMIC				2.3		1.9			OUVR MAT MINERALE NDA
66332	CEMENT,ARTFCL STONE PROD				1.8		0.8			OUVRAGES EN CIMENT
665	GLASSWARE				1.1		5.1			OUVRAGES EN VERRE
6658	GLASS ARTICLES NES				1.0		4.9			ARTICLES FAB EN VERRE NDA
66581	LABORATORY ETC GLASS			MN 37255	0.8	MN 241451	4.7			VERRERIE LABOR,HYG,PHAR ETC
67	IRON AND STEEL				16.7		12.6			FER ET ACIER
672	IRON,STEEL PRIMARY FORMS			W 21745	7.1	W 9296	4.2			LINGOTS FER,ACIER
6727	IRN,STL COIL FR REROLLNG			W 21111	6.6	W 8636	3.8			EBAUCHES POUR TOLES FER
67271	IRON,SIMPLE STEEL COILS			W 21111	6.6	W 8636	3.8			EBAUCHES NON EN ACIER
673	IRON,STEEL SHAPES ETC			W 8053	2.8	W 6325	2.3			BARRES,PROFIL FER,ACIER
6731	IRON,STEEL WIRE ROD			W 8053	2.8	W 6325	2.3			FIL MACHINE FER,ACIER
67311	IRON,SIMPLE STL WIRE ROD			W 8053	2.8	W 6325	2.3			FIL MACH AUT ACIER FIN
674	IRN,STL UNIV,PLATE,SHEET			W 6706	2.4	W 2231	1.4			LARGES PLATS,TOLES
678	IRON,STL TUBES,PIPES,ETC			W 5458	3.6	W 5834	3.7			TUBES,TUYAUX EN FONTE,FER
6782	IRON,STL SEAMLESS TUBES			W 1986	1.6	W 4422	2.9			TUBES,TUYAUX SANS SOUDURE
6783	IRON,STL TUBES,PIPES NES			W 3329	2.0	W 1171	0.6			AUT TUBES,TUYAUX FER,ACIER
68	NON–FERROUS METALS				3.4		1.8			METAUX NON FERREUX
682	COPPER EXC CEMENT COPPER			W 2395	2.8	W 316	1.1			CUIVRE
6821	COPPER NES,ALLOYS,UNWRT			W 1915	1.9	W 143	0.6			CUIVRE BRUT
69	METAL MANUFACTURES NES				12.9		30.1			ART MANUFACT EN METAL NDA
691	STRUCTURES AND PARTS NES			W 810	0.3	W 3762	6.2			CONSTRUCT FER,ACIER,ALU
6911	STRUCTURES,PARTS IRN,STL			W 810	0.3	W 3762	6.2			CONSTRUCT FER,ACIER,FONTE
693	WIRE PRODUCTS NON ELECTR			W 2198	4.0	W 1410	3.2			OUVRAGES FILS METALLIQUES
6931	WIRE CABLES, ROPES ETC			W 2198	4.0	W 1410	3.2			CORDAGES EN FILS DE FER
69312	COPPER CABLES, ROPES ETC			W 1476	2.9	W 673	1.9			CORDAGES DE CUIVRE
699	BASE METAL MFRS NES				6.3		14.3			ART MANUFACTURES MET NDA
6997	IRON,STEEL ARTICLES NES				2.8		7.4			OUV FONTE,FER,ACIER NDA
69979	IRN,STL MANUFACTURES NES				2.8		7.4			AUT OUVRAGES EN FER NDA
6998	MFRS NES OF CPR,NIKL,ETC				1.9		3.3			OUVRAGES EN CU,NI,AL,PB,ZN
7	MACHINES,TRANSPORT EQUIP				96.2		219.0			MACHINES MATERIEL TRANSPORT
72	MACHS FOR SPCL INDUSTRYS				32.3		59.6			MAC SPECIALES POUR INDUST
721	AGRIC MACHY,EXC TRACTORS				0.5		5.3			MACHINES AGRICOLES
7212	HARVESTING ETC MACHINES			N 38	0.1	N 301	4.0			ENGINS POUR LA RECOLTE
72123	OTH HARVSTER,MOWRS,BALER			N 10	0.1	N 93	3.9			AUT MACH POUR LA RECOLTE
723	CIVIL ENGNEERG EQUIP ETC				20.2		34.2			APPAREILS DE GENIE CIVIL
7234	CONST,MINING MACHNRY NES				20.2		34.2			MACH POUR LA CONST, MINES
72345	PILE DRIVERS,ETC			N 1893	16.0	N 5608	28.1			CHASSE–NEIGE
72348	PUBLIC WORKS MACHNRY NES				3.1		5.4			MACHINES TRAVAUX PUBLICS
724	TEXTILE,LEATHER MACHNRY				5.9		6.7			MACH POUR INDUSTRIE TEXTILE
7244	SPINNING,EXTRDNG,ETC MCH				5.9		4.5			MACH POUR LE FILAGE
72442	FIBRE PROCESSNG MACH NES				5.9		4.5			MACH PREP MAT TEXTILES
727	FOOD MACHRY NON–DOMESTIC				4.1		3.6			MACH INDUSTRIES ALIMENT
7272	OTH FOOD PROC MCHY,PARTS				4.1		3.6			AUT MACH IND ALIMENTAIRE
72722	INDUS FOOD PROC MACH NES				4.1		3.6			MACHINES BOULANGERIE
728	OTH MACHY FOR SPCL INDUS				0.7		6.8			AUT MACH IND PARTICULIERES
7281	MACH–TOOLS FR SPCL INDUS					N 1223	4.0			MACH–OUTILS SPEC IND PART
72811	MACH–TOOLS TO WRK MINRLS					N 832	3.8			MACH POUR TRAVAIL PIERRE
73	METALWORKING MACHINERY				3.6		2.4			MACH TRAVAIL DES METAUX
737	METALWORKING MACHNRY NES				2.8		2.1			MACH TRAV METAUX PIECES
7373	WELDING,BRAZING,ETC MCHS				2.8		2.1			MACH SOUDAGE ETC PIECES
73732	ELECTRIC WELDERS,ETC				2.8		2.1			MACH ELECT POUR SOUDER
74	GENRL INDUSTRL MACHY NES				14.3		32.8			MACH APP INDUSTRIE
749	NONELEC MACH PTS,ACC NES				10.0		28.7			PIECES MACH NON ELEC NDA
7499	OTH NONELEC MCHY PTS NES				9.6		28.5			PIECES NON ELECT NDA
74999	MACH PARTS NONELEC NES				9.6		28.5			PIECES MACHINES NDA
75	OFFICE MACHNES,ADP EQUIP				2.1		7.7			MACH BUREAU TRAIT AUTOM
752	AUTOMTIC DATA PROC EQUIP				1.8		7.2			MACH TRAIT INFORMATION
7528	OFF–LINE DATA PROC EQUIP				1.3		5.5			MACH AUXIL TRAIT INFORM
76	TELECOMM,SOUND EQUIPMENT				2.9		11.2			EQUIPMENT DE TELECOM
764	TELECOM EQPT,PTS,ACC NES				2.2		10.1			EQUIP TELECOM,PIECES
7641	LINE TELEPHONE,ETC EQUIP				0.4		3.5			APP TELEPHON PAR FIL
7643	TV,RADIO TRANSMITTRS ETC				1.8		6.7			APP EMET TELE RADIO
77	ELECTRIC MACHNRY NES ETC				11.5		60.8			MACH APP ELECT NDA
771	ELECTRIC POWER MACHY NES			N 260	0.6	N 2520	7.3			MACH PROD,TRANS ELECTR
7711	TRANSFORMERS,ELECTRICAL			N 260	0.6	N 2520	7.3			TRANSFO ELECTRIQUES
77111	LIQUID DIELEC TRANSFRMRS			N 260	0.6	N 2520	7.3			TRANSFO DIELEC LIQUIDE
773	ELECTR DISTRIBUTNG EQUIP				3.8		10.0			EQUIPMT DISTRIBUTION ELECT
7731	INSULATED WIRE,CABLE ETC				2.9	W 342	9.0			FILS,CABLES ISOLES ELECT
774	ELECTRO–MEDCL,XRAY EQUIP				2.7		12.2			APPAREILS MEDICAUX
7741	ELECTRO–MEDICAL EQUIPMNT				2.7		12.2			APP ELECTRICITE MEDICALE
776	TRANSISTORS,VALVES,ETC				0.4		8.7			LAMPES,TUBES,VALVES
7768	ELCTRNC COMP PTS,CRYSTLS				0.2		8.6			CRIST PIEZO–ELEC,PCS 776
77689	ELECTRNIC COMPON PTS NES				0.2		8.6			PIECES DU GROUPE 776
778	ELECTRICAL MACHINERY NES				2.5		18.9			AUTRES MACH ELECT NDA
7788	OTH ELEC MACHY,EQUIP NES				2.0		15.8			AUT MACH APP ELEC NDA
77886	OTH ELEC MACHINERY NES				1.0		3.2			AUT MACH APP ELECTRIQUES
77889	ELEC PARTS OF MACHY NES				0.7		12.3			PIECES ELEC DE MACH NDA
78	ROAD VEHICLES				27.6		41.8			VEHICULES ROUTIERS
782	LORRIES,SPCL MTR VEH NES			N 1192	12.5	N 1421	16.1			VEHICULES SPECIAUX,MARCH
7821	LORRIES,TRUCKS			N 1153	11.0	N 1313	13.8			VEHICULES TRANSP MARCHAND
783	ROAD MOTOR VEHICLES NES			N 110	2.4	N 55	1.6			VEHICULES ROUTIERS NDA

4. General Imports F.O.B. by Commodities according to the S.I.T.C. (Rev. 2) in million U.S. Dollars
Importations Générales F.O.B. par Produits d'après la C.T.C.I. (Rév. 2) en millions de Dollars E.U.

SITC CTCI	COMMODITY	1994		1995		1996		1997		PRODUIT
		QUANTITY QUANTITE	VALUE VALEUR	QUANTITY QUANTITE	VALUE VALEUR	QUANTITY QUANTITE	VALUE VALEUR	QUANTITY QUANTITE	VALUE VALEUR	
7831	BUSES			N 110	2.4	N 55	1.6			VOITURES TRANSPORT COMMUN
784	MOTOR VEH PRTS,ACCES NES				11.2		22.3			PIECES 722,781,782,783
7849	OTHER MOTOR VEHCL PARTS				10.3		22.2			PIECES 722,781,782,783
79	OTHR TRANSPORT EQUIPMENT				1.7		1.9			AUTRE MATERIEL TRANSPORT
8	MISC MANUFACTURED GOODS				19.2		24.1			ART MANUFACTURES DIVERS
821	*FURNITURE,PARTS THEREOF				3.1		3.7			MEUBLES ET PIECES
8211	CHAIRS,SEATS AND PARTS				3.1		3.6			SIEGES ET PIECES
82111	CHAIRS AND OTHER SEATS				3.1		3.6			SIEGES
84	CLOTHING AND ACCESSORIES				4.3		2.2			VETEMENTS
842	MENS OUTERWEAR NOT KNIT				2.0		1.4			VET DESSUS POUR HOMMES
8421	— OVERCOATS,OTHER COATS				2.0		1.4			MANTEAUX HOMMES MAT TEXT
84219	—— OF OTHER FIBRES				2.0		1.4			MANTEAUX HOMMES AUT FIBR
851	*FOOTWEAR				2.7		1.9			CHAUSSURES
87	PRECISION INSTRUMNTS NES				1.2		6.7			INSTRUM,APPAR SCIENT NDA
874	MEASURNG,CONTROLNG INSTR				0.9		6.3			INSTRUMENTS DE MESURE
8749	INSTR PTS NES,ACCESSORYS				0.7		6.0			PIECES 873,874.3,54,874.8
89	MISC MANUFCTRD GOODS NES				6.3		7.9			ART MANUFACTURES DIVERS
893	ARTICLES OF PLASTIC NES				1.7		3.9			OUVRAGES EN MAT DIVIS 58
8939	MISC PLASTIC ARTICLES				1.3		3.4			ART DIVERS EN MAT DIV 58
89399	OTHR PLASTC ARTICLES NES				1.3		3.4			AUT OUV MAT DIV 58

5. General Exports F.O.B. by Commodities according to the S.I.T.C. (Rev. 2) in million U.S. Dollars
Exportations Générales F.O.B. par Produits d'après la C.T.C.I. (Rév. 2) en millions de Dollars E.U.

SITC CTCI	COMMODITY	1994 QUANTITY QUANTITE	1994 VALUE VALEUR	1995 QUANTITY QUANTITE	1995 VALUE VALEUR	1996 QUANTITY QUANTITE	1996 VALUE VALEUR	1997 QUANTITY QUANTITE	1997 VALUE VALEUR	PRODUIT
	ALL COMMODITIES				412.1		507.1			TOUS PRODUITS
0	FOOD AND LIVE ANIMALS				60.3		112.6			ALIMENTS,ANIMAUX VIVANTS
01	MEAT AND PREPARATIONS				5.3		6.4			VIANDES ET PREPARATIONS
011	MEAT FRESH,CHILLD,FROZEN			W 3333	2.9	W 1996	2.2			VIANDES FRAICHES,REF,CONGE
0111	BOVINE MEAT FRESH,FROZEN			W 3333	2.9	W 1996	2.2			VIANDES BOVIN FRAI,REF
01111	BOVINE MEAT WITH BONE IN			W 3333	2.9	W 1996	2.2			VIANDES BOVIN NON DESOSS
014	MEAT PREPD,PRSVD,NES ETC				2.4		4.3			CONSERVES DE VIANDES
0149	OTH PREPARD,PRESRVD MEAT				2.4		4.2			AUTRES PREP DE VIANDES
02	DAIRY PRODCTS,BIRDS'EGGS				3.0		1.5			PRODUITS LAITIERS,OEUFS
022	MILK AND CREAM			W 1166	1.4	W 801	0.7			LAIT ET CREME
0223	MILK AND CREAM FRESH			W 1166	1.4	W 801	0.7			LAIT,CREME FRAIS
023	BUTTER			W 889	1.4	W 165	0.5			BEURRE
04	CEREALS AND PREPARATIONS				2.5		13.6			CEREALES ET PRODUITS
041	WHEAT ETC UNMILLED			W 52	0.1	W 6152	3.6			FROMENT,EPEAUTRE
0411	DURUM WHEAT UNMILLED			W 52	0.1	W 6152	3.6			FROMENT DUR NON MOULU
044	MAIZE UNMILLED			W 132	0.1	W 5469	3.6			MAIS NON MOULU
046	WHEAT ETC MEAL OR FLOUR			W 3357	0.8	W 11053	4.4			SEMOULE FARINE,FROMENT
04601	FLOUR OF WHEAT OR MESLIN			W 3357	0.8	W 11053	4.4			FARINE DE FROMENT
048	CEREAL ETC PREPARATIONS				1.2		1.7			PREPTNS A BASE CEREALES
05	VEGETABLES AND FRUIT				24.9		27.3			LEGUMES ET FRUITS
054	VEG ETC FRSH,SMPLY PRSVD				12.9		12.9			LEGUMES FRAIS,CONG,SECS
0544	TOMATOES FRESH			W 10970	2.1	W 11985	1.9			TOMATES FRAICHES
0545	OTHER FRESH VEGETABLES			W 72981	9.6	W 77368	9.8			AUTRES LEGUMES FRAIS,REF
05451	ALLIACEOUS VEGTBLS,FRESH			W 60517	7.6	W 64300	7.3			OIGNONS,ECHALOTES,AULX
05459	FRESH VEGETABLES NES			W 12465	2.1	W 13068	2.5			LEGUMES FRAIS,REFRI NDA
056	VEGTBLES ETC PRSVD,PREPD				1.4		1.1			CONSERVES DE LEGUMES
0565	VEGTBLES PRSVD,PREPD NES				1.3		1.0			LEGUMES PREPARES CONSERVE
05651	VEGTBLS,FRUIT IN VINEGAR				1.3		1.0			LEGUM CONSERV AU VINAIGRE
057	FRUIT,NUTS,FRESH,DRIED			W 49003	10.3	W 68353	13.0			FRUITS FRAIS OU SECS
0574	APPLES FRESH			W 36588	7.2	W 47300	8.1			POMMES FRAICHES
0579	FRUIT FRESH OR DRIED NES			W 9478	2.4	W 12773	3.1			FRUITS FRAIS,SECS NDA
05799	OTHER DRIED FRUIT			W 3898	1.7	W 6756	2.3			AUTRES FRUITS SECHES
06	SUGAR AND PREPS,HONEY				21.6		56.9			SUCRES ET PRODUITS
061	SUGAR AND HONEY			W 32203	18.8	W 106247	56.6			SUCRES ET MIEL
0612	REFINED SUGAR ETC			W 26346	15.4	W 96763	52.1			SUCRES RAFFINES
0615	MOLASSES			W 5598	3.1	W 9208	4.2			MELASSES
062	SUGAR CANDY NON–CHOCLATE			W 3129	2.9		0.4			SUCRERIES
09	MISC EDIBLE PRODUCTS				1.1		4.3			PREP ALIMENTAIRES DIVERSES
098	EDIBLE PRODCTS,PREPS NES				1.0		4.1			PREP ALIMENTAIRES NDA
09807	VINEGAR AND SUBSTITUTES			V 1136	0.5	V 15103	3.4			VINAIGRES COMESTIBLES
1	BEVERAGES AND TOBACCO				32.1		27.9			BOISSONS ET TABACS
11	BEVERAGES				9.5		8.4			BOISSONS
112	ALCOHOLIC BEVERAGES			W 44821	9.2	W 45242	8.2			BOISSONS ALCOOLIQUES
1121	WINE OF FRESH GRAPES ETC			W 11323	3.0	W 9254	2.0			VINS DE RAISINS FRAIS
11212	WINE OF FRESH GRAPES			W 11323	3.0	W 9254	2.0			VINS DE MOUTS DE RAISINS
1124	DISTILLED ALCOHOLIC BEVS			W 28297	5.6	W 28851	5.5			ALCOOLS,EAUX–DE–VIE
11249	OTH ALCOHOLC BEVS,CMPNDS			W 28297	5.6	W 28851	5.5			BOISSONS ALCOOLIQUES NDA
12	TOBACCO AND MANUFACTURES				22.7		19.5			TABACS BRUTS FABRIQUES
121	TOBACCO UNMNFCTRD,REFUSE			W 36527	21.7	W 19113	16.3			TABACS BRUTS,DECHETS
1211	TOBACCO,NOT STRIPPED			W 22840	13.0	W 10675	9.5			TABACS NON ECOTES
1212	TOBACCO STRIPPED OR PART			W 13678	8.8	W 8363	6.9			TABACS PART ECOTES
122	TOBACCO,MANUFACTURED				1.0		3.2			TABACS FABRIQUES
1222	CIGARETTES				1.0		3.2			CIGARETTES
2	CRUDE MATERLS,EXCL FUELS				70.1		73.4			MAT BRUTES NON COMESTIBLES
21	HIDES,SKINS,FURS UNDRSSD				4.0		15.2			CUIRS,PEAUX BRUTS
211	HIDES,SKINS,EXC FURS,RAW				4.0		15.2			CUIRS ET PEAUX
2112	CALF AND KIP SKINS,RAW			N 4064674	2.2	MN 17060	10.9			PEAUX DE VEAUX
2116	SHEEP SKIN WITH WOOL			MN 13214	1.9	MN 19222	4.3			PEAUX LAINEES D'OVINS
22	OIL SEEDS,OLEAGINOUS FRT				1.0		3.2			GRAINES,FRUITS OLEAGINEUX
223	SEEDS FOR OTH FIXED OILS			W 704	1.0	W 8434	3.2			GRAINES AUTRES HUILES FIXES
2234	LINSEED			W 704	1.0	W 8434	3.2			GRAINES DE LIN
26	TEXTILE FIBRES AND WASTE				47.2		41.5			FIBRES TEXTILES
261	SILK			W 2015	1.9	W 1847	1.8			SOIE
2614	SILK WORM COCOONS,WASTE			W 2001	1.7	W 1798	1.3			COCONS ET DECHETS
26142	SILK WASTE			W 1858	1.4	W 1704	1.2			DECHETS DE SOIE
263	COTTON			W 27383	25.6	W 26139	34.4			COTON
2631	RAW COTTON,EXCL LINTERS			W 17799	21.7	W 22180	32.1			COTON EN MASSE
2634	COTTON,CARDED OR COMBED			W 1487	2.1	W 626	0.9			COTON CARDE OU PEIGNE
268	WOOL(EXC TOPS),ANML HAIR			W 14895	19.8	W 4340	5.1			LAINES ET POILS
2681	WOOL GREASY,FLEECE–WSHED			W 9161	8.2	W 2439	1.9			LAINE EN SUINT
2682	WOOL DEGREASED,UNCOMBED			W 5194	11.1	W 1721	3.0			LAINE DEGRAISSEE
28	METALLIFEROUS ORES,SCRAP				16.5		12.0			MINERAIS METAL,DECHETS
288	NONFERR METAL SCRAP NES			W 29955	15.8	W 13392	10.3			DECHETS NON FERREUX
2882	OTHER BASE MTL SCRAP NES			W 29955	15.8	W 13392	10.3			AUTRES DECHETS
28821	COPPER WASTE AND SCRAP			W 17485	11.8	W 9262	8.7			DECHETS DE CUIVRE
28823	ALUMINIUM WSTE AND SCRAP			W 12460	4.0	W 3832	1.6			DECHETS D'ALUMINIUM
3	MINERAL FUELS ETC				45.6		77.7			COMBUSTIBLES MINERAUX LUB
32	COAL,COKE AND BRIQUETTES				3.2		2.1			HOUILLES,COKES,BRIQUETTES
322	COAL,LIGNITE AND PEAT			W 170638	3.2	W 100377	2.1			HOUILLES,LIGNITES,TOURBE
3222	OTH COAL,NOT AGGLOMERATD			W 170638	3.2	W 92277	1.9			AUTRES HOUILLES
33	PETROLEUM AND PRODUCTS				1.4		2.1			PETROLE ET DERIVES
333	CRUDE PETROLEUM			W 24600	0.9	W 21103	1.7			HUILES BRUTES DE PETROLE
351	*ELECTRIC CURRENT			H 1622000	41.0	H 2880800	73.6			ENERGIE ELECTRIQUE
5	CHEMCLS,RELATED PROD NES				48.7		65.4			PRODUITS CHIMIQUES
51	ORGANIC CHEMICALS				23.8		30.3			PROD CHIMIQ ORGANIQUES
512	ALCOHOLS,PHENOLS ETC			V 183393	23.8		30.3			PHENOLS,PHENOLS–ALCOOLS
5121	ACYCLIC ALCOHOLS,DERIVS			V 183393	23.8		30.3			ALCOOLS ACYCLIQUES
51216	ETHYL ALC,DENATRD SPIRIT			V 183393	23.8	V 237199	30.3			ALCOOL ETHYLIQUE NON DENAT
52	INORGANIC CHEMICALS				20.4		32.3			PROD CHIM INORGANIQUES
522	INORG ELEMNTS,OXIDES,ETC			W 418	1.5	W 830	5.2			ELEMENTS INORGANIQUES
5221	CHEMICAL ELEMENTS			W 342	1.5	W 780	5.1			ELEMENTS CHIMIQUES
52216	MERCURY			W 261	1.0	W 628	2.6			MERCURE
52217	ALKALI,RARE EARTH METALS			W 65	0.3	W 137	1.8			METAUX ALCALINS
523	OTHR INORG CHEMICALS ETC				9.9		5.9			AUT PRODUITS CHIMIQUES INORG
5231	METAL CMPD OF INORG ACID			W 749	1.5	W 152	0.9			SELS METALLIQUES
52319	OTH SULPHATES,PERSLPHTES			W 749	1.5	W 152	0.9			AUTRE SULFATES,ALUNS
5239	INORG CHEM PRODUCTS NES				8.5		5.1			PROD CHIM INORGANIQ NDA
52399	OTH INORG CMPNDS NES ETC				8.5		5.0			AUT COMP INORGANIQUES NDA
524	RADIOACTIVE ETC MATERIAL				9.1		21.3			MATIERES RADIOACTIVES
5241	RADIOACTIVE ELEMENTS ETC				9.1		21.3			RADIOELEMENTS,ISOTOPES
541	*MEDICINAL,PHARM PRODUCT				2.6		1.6			PROD MEDICINAUX PHARMACEUT

5. General Exports F.O.B. by Commodities according to the S.I.T.C. (Rev. 2) in million U.S. Dollars
Exportations Générales F.O.B. par Produits d'après la C.T.C.I. (Rév. 2) en millions de Dollars E.U.

SITC CTCI	COMMODITY	1994 QUANTITY QUANTITE	1994 VALUE VALEUR	1995 QUANTITY QUANTITE	1995 VALUE VALEUR	1996 QUANTITY QUANTITE	1996 VALUE VALEUR	1997 QUANTITY QUANTITE	1997 VALUE VALEUR	PRODUIT
5417	MEDICAMENTS				1.4		0.9			MEDICAMENTS
54171	— CONTAINNG ANTIBIOTICS				1.4		0.9			MED CONTN ANTIBIOTIQUES
6	BASIC MANUFACTURES				92.3		78.8			ART MANUFACTURES
62	RUBBER MANUFACTURES NES				1.3		1.1			CAOUTCHOUC MANUFACTURE
65	TEXTILE YARN,FABRICS,ETC				25.7		22.2			FILS,TISSUS,ARTICLES TEXTILE
651	TEXTILE YARN			W 3020	6.6		2.9			FILS TEXTILES
6512	WOOL,HAIR YARN,INCL TOPS			W 802	4.1	W 330	2.0			FILS DE LAINE,DE POILS
65122	CARDED WOOL YARN IN BULK			W 802	4.1	W 330	2.0			FILS CONT 85% LAINE CARDEE
6513	COTTON YARN			W 2181	2.5	W 399	0.9			FILS DE COTON
652	COTTON FABRICS,WOVEN				6.5		4.8			TISSUS DE COTON
6521	GREY WOVEN COTTON FABRIC				6.4		4.8			TISSUS COT ECRUS NON MERCER
65214	GREY WOVEN COTTON NES				6.3		4.7			AUT TISSUS 85% COTON ECRUS
654	OTH WOVEN TEXTILE FABRIC				4.1		3.6			TISSUS AUT COTON SYNT,ARTIF
6542	WOVEN WOOL,HAIR NONPILE				2.8		2.3			TIS PLUS 85% LAINE,POILS
65421	WOVN CARD WOOL,FINE HAIR				2.8		2.3			TISSUS 85% LAINE,PLS CARD
657	SPECIAL TXTL FABRC,PRODS				3.8		4.5			TISSUS SPECIAUX
6577	TEXTILES FOR MACHINERY				3.0		3.4			OUATES,MECHES ART TEXT
65773	TEXTLS FOR MACHINES NES				2.4		3.2			TISSUS USAGE TECH MAT TEX
658	TEXTILE ARTICLES NES				1.3		3.1			ART FACONNES MAT TEXTILES
6589	OTH TEXTILE ARTICLES NES				1.0		2.4			AUT ART EN TEXTILES NDA
65898	KNITTED ETC ARTICLES NES				0.9		2.3			ART BONNET NON ELASTIQUE
659	FLOOR COVERINGS,ETC				3.4		3.3			COUVRE–PARQUETS,TAPIS ETC
6592	CARPETS ETC KNOTTED			A 1154	2.9	A 1143	2.8			TAPIS POINTS NOUES,ENROULES
65921	— OF WOOL OR FINE HAIR			A 1154	2.9	A 1143	2.8			TAP NOUES,ENROULES LAINE
66	NONMETAL MINERAL MFS NES				11.3		21.0			ART MIN NON METALLIQUES
661	LIME,CEMENT,BLDG PRODS				4.2		9.7			CHAUX,CIMENTS MAT CONSTR
6612	CEMENT			W 82042	2.1	W 1142603	6.1			CIMENTS HYDRAULIQUES
6618	MNRL BLDG PRD UNFIRD NES				1.8		3.1			MAT CONST AMIANTE–CIMENT
66183	ASBESTOS–,FIBRE–CMNT PRD				1.8		3.1			OUVRAGES AMIANTE–CIMENT
663	MINERAL MANUFCTURES NES				1.9		2.7			ART MIN MANUF NDA
6633	MINRL MFS NES NONCERAMIC				1.5		1.4			OUVR MAT MINERALE NDA
664	GLASS				4.8		7.9			VERRE
6645	CAST,ROLLED GLASS UNWRKD			A 14189	4.2	A 20157	7.4			VERRE COULE NON TRAVAILLE
67	IRON AND STEEL				9.6		5.8			FER ET ACIER
672	IRON,STEEL PRIMARY FORMS			W 22966	5.8	W 2960	1.1			LINGOTS FER,ACIER
6727	IRN,STL COIL FR REROLLNG			W 22601	5.6	W 2890	1.0			EBAUCHES POUR TOLES FER
67271	IRON,SIMPLE STEEL COILS			W 22601	5.6	W 2890	1.0			EBAUCHES NON EN ACIER
677	IRN,STL WIRE(EXCL W ROD)				2.0		0.1			FILS EN FER,ACIER
67705	OTHER ALLOY STEEL WIRE				2.0		0.1			FILS ACIER AUT ACIERS ALLIES
678	IRON,STL TUBES,PIPES,ETC			W 851	0.8	W 5995	3.6			TUBES,TUYAUX EN FONTE,FER
6782	IRON,STL SEAMLESS TUBES			W 259	0.2	W 3701	2.1			TUBES,TUYAUX SANS SOUDURE
68	NON–FERROUS METALS				31.1		18.6			METAUX NON FERREUX
682	COPPER EXC CEMENT COPPER			W 6191	4.8	W 138	0.2			CUIVRE
6821	COPPER NES,ALLOYS,UNWRT			W 5392	4.0					CUIVRE BRUT
68212	COPPER REFINED,UNWROUGHT			W 5392	4.0					CUIVRE AFFINE BRUT
689	NON–FER BASE METALS NES			W 6363	25.1	W 4733	18.1			AUT METAUX NON FERREUX
6899	BASE METALS NES,CERMETS			W 6354	25.1	W 4733	18.1			METAUX COMMUNS NDA
68999	BASE MTL NES UNWRT,WASTE			W 6354	25.1	W 4733	18.1			AUT METAUX COM BRUTS NDA
69	METAL MANUFACTURES NES				11.9		7.4			ART MANUFACT EN METAL NDA
693	WIRE PRODUCTS NON ELECTR			W 2708	2.9	W 97	0.1			OUVRAGES FILS METALLIQUES
6931	WIRE CABLES, ROPES ETC			W 2708	2.9	W 97	0.1			CORDAGES EN FILS DE FER
69312	COPPER CABLES, ROPES ETC			W 2556	2.8	W 61	0.1			CORDAGES DE CUIVRE
695	TOOLS				2.1		2.6			OUTILS A MAIN
6954	BLADES,TIPS,ETC FR TOOLS				1.7		2.5			OUTILS POUR MACHINE–OUTIL
69541	PARTS TO INSERT IN TOOLS				1.7		2.5			OUTILS DE FORAGE
699	BASE METAL MFRS NES				6.6		4.2			ART MANUFACTURES MET NDA
6997	IRON,STEEL ARTICLES NES				1.5		2.5			OUV FONTE,FER,ACIER NDA
69979	IRN,STL MANUFACTURES NES				1.5		2.5			AUT OUVRAGES EN FER NDA
6999	OTHR BASE METAL MFRS ETC			W 190	3.9		0.1			OUVRAGES EN TUNGST,MOLYB
69995	BERYLLIUM WRGHT,MFRS NES			W 190	3.9		0.1			BERYLLIUM OUVRE NDA
7	MACHINES,TRANSPORT EQUIP				38.5		49.7			MACHINES MATERIEL TRANSPORT
71	POWER GENERATING EQUIPMT				2.2		2.9			MACHINES GENERATRICES
716	ROTATING ELECTRIC PLANT			N 114699	2.1	N 92538	2.8			APP ELECTR ROTATIFS,PIECES
7162	AC MTRS,GENRTRS,GEN SETS			N 114699	2.1	N 92538	2.8			MOTEURS ELECTRIQUES
71621	AC MTRS,INC UNIVRSL MTRS			N 114101	1.9	N 91513	2.7			MOT ELEC NON COUR CONTINU
72	MACHS FOR SPCL INDUSTRYS				3.5		5.3			MAC SPECIALES POUR INDUST
723	CIVIL ENGNEERG EQUIP ETC				2.2		2.2			APPAREILS DE GENIE CIVIL
7234	CONST,MINING MACHNRY NES				2.2		2.2			MACH POUR LA CONST, MINES
72348	PUBLIC WORKS MACHNRY NES				2.2		1.3			MACHINES TRAVAUX PUBLICS
73	METALWORKING MACHINERY				1.5		2.7			MACH TRAVAIL DES METAUX
736	METALWORKING MACH–TOOLS				1.1		2.3			MACH–OUTILS TRAVAIL METAUX
74	GENRL INDUSTRL MACHY NES				7.4		7.2			MACH APP INDUSTRIE
742	PUMPS FOR LIQUIDS ETC			N 8772	1.5	N 8710	1.5			POMPES MOTO–POMPES
7422	CENTRIFUGAL PUMPS NES			N 8772	1.5	N 8710	1.5			POMPES CENTRIF NON 742.81
743	PUMPS NES,CENTRFUGES ETC			N 9148	1.6	N 7303	1.2			POMPES COMPRES,VENT ETC
7439	PTS NES OF APP OF 7435,6			N 8801	1.5	N 7040	1.1			PIECES 743.5 ET 743.6
744	MECHANICAL HANDLING EQU				1.4		2.1			EQUIP MANUTENTION PIECES
749	NONELEC MACH PTS,ACC NES				2.9		2.4			PIECES MACH NON ELEC NDA
7499	OTH NONELEC MCHY PTS NES				2.7		2.0			PIECES NON ELECT NDA
74999	MACH PARTS NONELEC NES				2.7		2.0			PIECES MACHINES NDA
76	TELECOMM,SOUND EQUIPMENT				0.7		3.5			EQUIPMENT DE TELECOM
764	TELECOM EQPT,PTS,ACC NES				0.2		3.4			EQUIP TELECOM,PIECES
7643	TV,RADIO TRANSMITTRS ETC				0.2		3.4			APP EMET TELE RADIO
77	ELECTRIC MACHNRY NES ETC				16.0		21.0			MACH APP ELECT NDA
773	ELECTR DISTRIBUTNG EQUIP				1.9		2.0			EQUIPMT DISTRIBUTION ELECT
7731	INSULATED WIRE,CABLE ETC			W 449	1.8		1.7			FILS,CABLES ISOLES ELECT
778	ELECTRICAL MACHINERY NES				11.3		16.2			AUTRES MACH ELECT NDA
7782	ELECTRIC LAMPS,BULBS			MN 1238645	10.1	MN 1419510	14.2			LAMPES, TUBES ELECTRIQUES
77821	ELEC FILAMENT LAMPS NES			MN 1238645	10.1	MN 1419510	14.2			LAMPES NON INFRAROUGES
7788	OTH ELEC MACHY,EQUIP NES				1.0		1.8			AUT MACH APP ELEC NDA
78	ROAD VEHICLES				7.0		6.7			VEHICULES ROUTIERS
782	LORRIES,SPCL MTR VEH NES			N 216	1.6	N 148	1.9			VEHICULES SPECIAUX,MARCH
7821	LORRIES,TRUCKS			N 212	1.5	N 130	1.5			VEHICULES TRANSP MARCHAND
784	MOTOR VEH PRTS,ACCES NES				4.5		4.0			PIECES 722,781,782,783
7849	OTHER MOTOR VEHCL PARTS				4.4		4.0			PIECES 722,781,782,783
8	MISC MANUFACTURED GOODS				20.9		19.5			ART MANUFACTURES DIVERS
84	CLOTHING AND ACCESSORIES				7.8		8.4			VETEMENTS
842	MENS OUTERWEAR NOT KNIT				4.6		4.4			VET DESSUS POUR HOMMES
8421	— OVERCOATS,OTHER COATS				4.6		4.4			MANTEAUX HOMMES MAT TEXT
84219	—— OF OTHER FIBRES				4.6		4.4			MANTEAUX HOMMES AUT FIBR
851	*FOOTWEAR				1.6		1.5			CHAUSSURES

5. General Exports F.O.B. by Commodities according to the S.I.T.C. (Rev. 2) in million U.S. Dollars
Exportations Générales F.O.B. par Produits d'après la C.T.C.I. (Rév. 2) en millions de Dollars E.U.

SITC CTCI	COMMODITY	1994 QUANTITY QUANTITE	1994 VALUE VALEUR	1995 QUANTITY QUANTITE	1995 VALUE VALEUR	1996 QUANTITY QUANTITE	1996 VALUE VALEUR	1997 QUANTITY QUANTITE	1997 VALUE VALEUR	PRODUIT
89	MISC MANUFCTRD GOODS NES				9.9		7.5			ART MANUFACTURES DIVERS
894	TOYS,SPORTING GOODS,ETC				8.3		5.2			VOITURES ENFANTS,JOUETS
8946	NON–MILITARY ARMS,AMMO				7.9		4.6			ARMES NON MILITAIRES
89463	HUNTNG,SPORTNG AMMUNTION				7.9		4.6			MUNITIONS
9	GOODS NOT CLASSD BY KIND				3.2		2.0			ART TRANSACT NON CLASSES
931	*SPECIAL TRANSACTIONS				3.1		1.7			TRANS.SPECIALES

1. HISTORICAL SERIES, 1993–1997 SPECIAL TRADE, IMPORTS C.I.F., EXPORTS F.O.B.
SERIES HISTORIQUES, 1993–1997 COMMERCE SPECIAL, IMPORTATIONS C.A.F., EXPORTATIONS F.O.B

YEAR ANNEE	VALUE IN MILLION U.S. DOLLARS VALEUR EN MILLION U.S. DOLLARS MERCHANDISE –MARCHANDISE IMPORTS	EXPORTS	GOLD –OR IMPORTS	EXPORTS	CONVERSION FACTORS FACTEURS DE CONVERSION CENTS E.U. PAR IMPORTS	EXPORTS	INDEX NUMBERS –INDICES QUANTUM IMPORTS	EXPORTS	UNIT VALUE VALEUR UNITAIRE IMPORTS	EXPORTS
1993	960.97	1003.62								
1994	1244.41	990.73								
1995	1818.76	1304.23								
1996	2319.22	1442.99								
1997	2720.35	1672.04								

2. IMPORTS BY BROAD ECONOMIC CATEGORY AND EXPORTS BY INDUSTRIAL ORIGIN. (PERCENTAGE OF TOTAL VALUE)
IMPORTATIONS PAR CATEGORIES ECONOMIQUES ET EXPORTATIONS PAR BRANCHE D'ACTIVITE.(EN POURCENTAGE DE LA VALEUR TOTALE)

IMPORTS – IMPORTATIONS

	1991	1992	1993	1994	1995	1996	1997
TOTAL IMPORTS–IMPORTATIONS TOTALES				100.	100.	100.	100.
1 FOOD BEV–ALIMENTATION BOISSONS				9.8	9.7	11.8	12.1
11 PRIMARY–PRODUITS DE BASE				4.2	3.8	5.3	4.8
111 FOR INDUSTRY–POUR L'INDUSTRIE				1.5	1.1	2.4	1.3
112 FOR HOUSEHOLDS–POUR LES MENAGES				2.8	2.7	2.9	3.5
12 PROCESSED–PRODUITS ELABORES				5.6	5.9	6.5	7.3
121 FOR INDUSTRY–POUR L'INDUSTRIE				2.2	1.8	1.9	1.7
122 FOR HOUSEHOLDS–POUR LES MENAGES				3.4	4.1	4.6	5.5
2 IND SUPPLIES–APPROV INDUSTRIELS				21.3	27.9	28.1	29.4
21 PRIMARY–PRODUITS DE BASE				1.3	2.0	2.3	2.7
22 PROCESSED–PRODUITS ELABORES				20.0	25.9	25.8	26.8
3 FUELS–COMBUSTIBLES				28.8	21.1	21.6	13.5
31 PRIMARY–PRODUITS DE BASE				7.8	5.7	4.1	4.3
32 PROCESSED–PRODUITS ELABORES				21.0	15.5	17.4	9.3
321 MOTOR SPIRIT–ESSENCE							
322 OTHER–AUTRES				21.0	15.5	17.4	9.3
4 MACHINERY–EQUIPEMENT				16.5	16.7	16.8	19.3
41 CAPITAL EQUIPMENT–MACHINES				14.8	14.9	14.3	16.6
42 PARTS–PIECES ACCESSOIRES				1.7	1.8	2.5	2.7
5 TRANSPORT–TRANSPORT				7.5	8.9	6.7	9.0
51 PASSENGER CARS–AUTOMOBILES				2.1	2.8	1.7	2.5
52 OTHER–AUTRES				2.2	2.7	2.3	3.8
521 INDUSTRIAL–INDUSTRIELS				2.1	2.7	2.3	3.8
522 NON INDUSTRIAL–NON INDUSTRIEL				0.0	0.0	0.0	0.0
53 PARTS–PIECES ACCESSOIRES				3.2	3.4	2.6	2.6
6 CONSUM GOODS–BIENS CONSOMMATION				13.4	15.4	14.8	16.3
61 DURABLE–DURABLES				2.4	2.7	2.4	2.8
62 SEMI DURABLE–SEMI DURABLES				5.4	7.1	6.7	7.2
63 NON DURABLE–NON DURABLES				5.5	5.6	5.7	6.4
7 GOODS NES–BIENS NDA				2.7	0.2	0.2	0.4

EXPORTS – EXPORTATIONS

	1991	1992	1993	1994	1995	1996	1997
TOTAL EXPORTS–EXPORTATIONS TOTALES				100.	100.	100.	100.
1 AGRICULTURE				9.0	13.2	6.3	7.2
2 MINING QUARRY–INDUS EXTRACTIVES				0.9	0.7	0.7	0.5
3 MANUFACTURING–IND MANUFACTUR				90.2	86.1	93.0	92.3
31 FOOD BEV TOBACCO–ALIM BOISS TAB				10.5	12.8	13.9	13.0
32 TEXTILES–INDUSTRIES TEXTILES				15.2	15.7	18.5	17.8
33 WOOD & PRODUCTS–BOIS & PRODUITS				13.9	15.4	19.8	23.9
34 PAPER & PRODUCTS–PAPIER & PRODT				1.1	1.5	2.5	2.9
35 CHEMICALS–INDUSTRIES CHIMIQUES				10.4	9.5	10.0	8.5
36 NON METAL MIN–MIN NON METAL				1.0	1.0	1.2	1.0
37 BASIC METAL–IND METAL BASE				7.6	5.1	4.0	4.8
38 METAL MANUF–MANUF METAL				26.5	22.5	20.7	19.0
39 OTH MANUF IND–AUTRES MANUF				4.0	2.5	2.2	1.4

3. TRADE BY PRINCIPAL COUNTRIES OF ORIGIN AND DESTINATION (VALUE IN MILLION U.S. DOLLARS)
ECHANGES SELON LES PRINCIPAUX PAYS D'ORIGINE ET DE DESTINATION (VALEUR EN MILLIONS DE DOLLARS EU)

COUNTRIES–PAYS	SPECIAL IMPORTS C.I.F. IMPORTATIONS SPECIALES C.A.F					COUNTRIES–PAYS	SPECIAL EXPORTS F.O.B. EXPORTATIONS SPECIALES F.O.B.				
	1993	1994	1995	1996	1997		1993	1994	1995	1996	1997
World	961.3	1241.5	1818.0	2319.5	2721.0	Monde	1003.0	989.7	1305.0	1443.3	1671.6
Africa	0.5	3.8	1.9	3.1	3.3	Afrique	8.7	5.8	7.2	21.9	13.1
Americas	16.9	46.2	49.4	88.1	101.6	Amériques	12.9	17.6	18.4	11.6	32.0
– Northern America	12.3	25.8	38.2	54.9	72.6	– Amérique du Nord	7.0	12.8	18.0	10.3	25.3
– LAIA	1.3	5.6	10.0	12.1	13.7	– ALAI	2.5	2.2	0.2	0.2	2.6
– CACM		0.5	0.9	6.1	7.2	– MCAC	0.0	0.4	0.0	0.0	0.0
– Caribbean	3.4	14.2	0.1	14.9	8.0	– Caraïbes	2.7	1.9	0.0	1.0	2.0
– Rest of America		0.1	0.2	0.1	0.1	– Autre Amérique	0.6	0.3	0.2	0.2	2.1
Asia excl fmr USSR	18.9	37.6	36.4	36.0	52.4	Asie anc. URSS exclus	52.4	24.3	16.0	32.9	54.5
– Middle East	7.1	3.8	3.6	4.8	13.6	– Moyen–Orient	9.3	6.1	7.2	10.1	11.5
Asia former USSR	21.1	6.3	12.8	21.4	20.9	Asie ancienne URSS	64.6	39.2	36.1	30.3	22.5
Europe excl fmr USSR	290.1	564.8	1008.5	1318.9	1688.5	Europe anc. URSS exclus	388.8	438.9	650.6	699.4	882.5
– European Union	263.1	505.3	906.8	1142.3	1446.5	– Union Européenne	334.6	389.2	574.8	645.2	816.8
– Eastern Europe	17.8	44.2	67.9	109.6	156.8	– Europe de l'Est	45.6	27.1	46.5	34.3	34.9
– Rest of Europe	9.3	15.4	33.9	67.0	85.2	– Autre de l'Europe	8.6	22.6	29.3	19.9	30.8
Europe former USSR	476.5	488.3	693.1	849.2	852.1	Europe ancienne URSS	475.1	463.6	576.4	646.8	666.3
Oceania	0.0	2.4	16.0	2.9	2.2	Océanie	0.4	0.2	0.2	0.4	0.7
Other	44.3	91.9			0.0	Autre					
Russian Federation	273.6	292.1	394.7	469.0	424.6	Russian Federation	297.1	278.3	330.6	329.6	350.2
Germany/Allemagne	95.8	168.8	280.1	321.0	435.4	Germany/Allemagne	66.1	104.4	177.6	198.9	230.2
Finland/Finlande	40.5	106.1	189.6	213.7	263.8	United Kingdom	47.0	96.1	118.2	160.2	239.7
Sweden/Suède	50.8	79.8	145.8	182.6	208.9	Sweden/Suède	65.0	68.4	121.5	94.6	138.7
Lithuania/Lituanie	92.1	73.9	100.9	146.3	173.3	Lithuania/Lituanie	42.9	54.7	72.3	107.4	125.6
Estonia/Estonie	38.0	43.7	91.9	132.1	162.8	Ukraine	59.5	58.4	71.5	89.1	65.0
Denmark/Danemark	17.7	28.6	52.6	91.3	95.0	Belarus/Bélarus	51.1	42.7	56.7	64.1	52.7
Netherlands/Pays–Bas	9.9	19.4	55.4	81.5	102.4	Estonia/Estonie	19.4	25.8	40.6	52.8	69.8
United Kingdom	17.9	29.7	49.5	63.9	88.8	Netherlands/Pays–Bas	81.8	18.7	25.7	27.7	40.3
Ukraine	28.7	37.6	41.8	59.3	55.6	Denmark/Danemark	8.9	15.5	26.3	52.8	64.8
Italy/Italie	7.3	22.3	42.1	61.5	84.1	Finland/Finlande	20.2	23.9	42.1	34.3	25.9
Poland/Pologne	9.4	19.9	34.5	59.5	87.3	Poland/Pologne	29.6	16.0	32.6	19.9	20.3
Belarus/Bélarus	39.8	37.9	57.4	39.7	33.5	France, Monaco	10.4	14.1	16.8	18.7	21.4
USA/Etats–Unis d'Amer	11.5	24.6	35.2	49.1	63.9	Kazakhstan	22.7	19.1	15.4	8.3	9.9
France, Monaco	7.8	18.9	28.3	35.9	56.8	Italy/Italie	13.4	9.4	14.9	15.8	15.2
Belgium–Luxembourg	6.6	13.3	25.1	41.6	51.1	USA/Etats–Unis d'Amer	6.4	12.0	17.0	9.3	23.9
Areas n.e.s.	44.3	91.9			0.0	Belgium–Luxembourg	15.9	4.6	11.9	15.0	20.0
Switzerland,Liechtenst.	6.3	6.5	16.8	27.7	38.3	Uzbekistan/Ouzbékistan	8.7	10.0	13.8	16.1	8.0
Norway,Svalbard and JM	1.3	6.8	13.9	31.7	40.8	Norway,Svalbard and JM	2.9	6.4	22.5	9.6	9.8
Austria/Autriche	5.3	9.1	21.5	22.0	22.3	Switzerland,Liechtenst.	4.0	13.6	4.1	5.4	13.8
Czech Republic	4.0	9.8	14.4	20.6	26.0	Ireland/Irlande	1.0	10.0	14.0	4.6	8.4
Hungary/Hongrie	2.6	7.9	8.3	14.4	20.6	Austria/Autriche	2.3	20.5	3.6	6.0	5.3
Spain/Espagne	2.3	5.7	7.9	14.4	19.7	Czech Republic	4.3	3.7	6.8	6.9	5.9
Japan/Japon	4.2	15.4	10.4	5.6	8.1	Azerbaijan/Azerbaïdjan	15.3	5.6	2.1	1.8	1.8
Kazakhstan	9.6	2.7	8.0	10.4	12.1	Thailand/Thaïlande	18.4	6.4	0.0	0.2	0.6
Ireland/Irlande	0.6	2.9	5.8	8.8	12.9	Spain/Espagne	1.5	0.9	1.6	15.6	5.7
Slovakia/Slovaquie		2.2	6.4	8.3	13.9	Japan/Japon	6.6	3.8	3.8	4.4	4.7
Cuba	0.3	14.1	0.0	10.7	4.4	Singapore/Singapour	0.0	0.3	0.6	4.7	17.6
Turkey/Turquie	7.0	2.3	1.8	2.4	11.1	Republic of Moldova	5.2	3.7	4.7	3.8	3.0
Bulgaria/Bulgarie	1.5	4.1	3.9	6.4	8.3	Egypt/Egypte	0.0	0.3	2.2	13.1	3.6
Israel/Israël	1.1	3.9	6.3	6.2	5.5	China/Chine	10.5	4.8	0.1	1.2	2.0
Australia/Australie	0.0	1.7	15.6	2.7	2.0	Hungary/Hongrie	6.3	4.6	2.5	3.0	1.8
Canada	0.8	1.2	2.9	5.8	8.7	Lebanon/Liban	3.7	4.0	2.1	3.2	2.8
Republic of Moldova	4.3	3.2	6.5	2.7	2.2	Turkmenistan/Turkménistn	11.7	2.0	1.2	0.3	0.5
Brazil/Brésil	0.5	0.5	5.1	6.9	4.6	Mauritania/Mauritanie	4.5	5.0	3.9	1.8	
Uzbekistan/Ouzbékistan	1.1	0.7	2.3	7.7	5.4	Algeria/Algérie		0.0		6.3	7.7
India/Inde	2.9	3.4	3.3	3.6	3.4	Bulgaria/Bulgarie	4.6	1.3	1.9	1.0	2.6
Other Asia n.e.s.	0.5	2.1	2.9	4.0	6.2	Slovakia/Slovaquie		1.1	2.4	3.4	4.2
China/Chine	0.4	1.4	1.8	3.4	6.1	Philippines	0.1	0.0	0.0	3.2	5.9
Azerbaijan/Azerbaïdjan	8.1	1.1	0.6	1.1	1.9	Cyprus/Chypre	0.0	0.1	1.9	0.6	5.7

(VALUE AS PERCENTAGE OF WORLD TOTAL)(VALEURS EN POURCENTAGE DU TOTAL MONDIAL)

	1988	1989	1990	1991	1992	1993	1994	1995	1996	1997
Africa					0.4	0.1	0.3	0.1	0.1	0.1
Americas					3.9	1.8	3.7	2.7	3.8	3.7
– Northern America					3.4	1.3	2.1	2.1	2.4	2.7
– LAIA					0.1	0.1	0.4	0.5	0.5	0.5
– CACM					0.0		0.0	0.1	0.3	0.3
– Caribbean					0.4	0.4	1.1	0.0	0.6	0.3
– Rest of America					0.0		0.0	0.0	0.0	0.0
Asia excl fmr USSR					0.8	2.0	3.0	2.0	1.6	1.9
– Middle East						0.7	0.3	0.2	0.2	0.5
Asia former USSR					2.0	2.2	0.5	0.7	0.9	0.8
Europe excl fmr USSR					33.9	30.2	45.5	55.5	56.9	62.1
– European Union					29.4	27.4	40.7	49.9	49.2	53.2
– Eastern Europe					2.8	1.8	3.6	3.7	4.7	5.8
– Rest of Europe					1.7	1.0	1.2	1.9	2.9	3.1
Europe former USSR					44.9	49.6	39.3	38.1	36.6	31.3
Oceania						0.0	0.2	0.9	0.1	0.1
Other						4.6	7.4			0.0
Russian Federation					27.8	28.5	23.5	21.7	20.2	15.6
Germany/Allemagne					14.9	10.0	13.6	15.4	13.8	16.0
Finland/Finlande					2.6	4.2	8.5	10.4	9.2	9.7
Sweden/Suède					3.8	5.3	6.4	8.0	7.9	7.7
Lithuania/Lituanie					3.1	9.6	5.9	5.5	6.3	6.4
Estonia/Estonie					6.4	3.9	3.5	5.1	5.7	6.0
Denmark/Danemark					0.8	1.8	2.3	2.9	3.9	3.5
Netherlands/Pays–Bas					3.5	1.0	1.6	3.0	3.5	3.8
United Kingdom					0.6	1.9	2.4	2.7	2.8	3.3
Ukraine					3.6	3.0	3.0	2.3	2.6	2.0

	1988	1989	1990	1991	1992	1993	1994	1995	1996	1997
Afrique					0.5	0.9	0.6	0.6	1.5	0.8
Amériques					1.0	1.3	1.8	1.4	0.8	1.9
– Amérique du Nord					0.4	0.7	1.3	1.4	0.7	1.5
– ALAI					0.0	0.3	0.2	0.0	0.0	0.2
– MCAC					0.0	0.0	0.0	0.0	0.0	0.0
– Caraïbes					0.5	0.3	0.2	0.0	0.1	0.1
– Autre Amérique					0.0	0.1	0.0	0.0	0.0	0.1
Asie anc. URSS exclus					0.7	5.2	2.5	1.2	2.3	3.3
– Moyen–Orient						0.9	0.6	0.6	0.7	0.7
Asie ancienne URSS					4.8	6.4	4.0	2.8	2.1	1.3
Europe anc. URSS exclus					44.6	38.8	44.4	49.9	48.5	52.8
– Union Européenne					39.6	33.4	39.3	44.0	44.7	48.9
– Europe de l'Est					4.2	4.5	2.7	3.6	2.4	2.1
– Autre de l'Europe					0.8	0.9	2.3	2.2	1.4	1.8
Europe ancienne URSS					44.2	47.4	46.8	44.2	44.8	39.9
Océanie					0.1	0.0	0.0	0.0	0.0	0.0
Autre										
Russian Federation					25.8	29.6	28.1	25.3	22.8	21.0
Germany/Allemagne					7.9	6.6	10.5	13.6	13.8	13.8
United Kingdom					3.5	4.7	9.7	9.1	11.1	14.3
Sweden/Suède					7.5	6.5	6.9	9.3	6.6	8.3
Lithuania/Lituanie					3.6	4.3	5.5	5.5	7.4	7.5
Ukraine					8.2	5.9	5.9	5.5	6.2	3.9
Belarus/Bélarus					4.7	5.1	4.3	4.3	4.4	3.2
Estonia/Estonie					1.3	1.9	2.6	3.1	3.7	4.2
Netherlands/Pays–Bas					7.4	8.2	1.9	2.0	1.9	2.4
Denmark/Danemark					0.8	0.9	1.6	2.0	3.7	3.9

4. Special Imports C.I.F. by Commodities according to the S.I.T.C. (Rev. 2) in million U.S. Dollars
Importations Spéciales C.A.F. par Produits d'après la C.T.C.I. (Rév. 2) en millions de Dollars E.U.

SITC CTCI	COMMODITY	1994 QUANTITY QUANTITE	1994 VALUE VALEUR	1995 QUANTITY QUANTITE	1995 VALUE VALEUR	1996 QUANTITY QUANTITE	1996 VALUE VALEUR	1997 QUANTITY QUANTITE	1997 VALUE VALEUR	PRODUIT
	ALL COMMODITIES		1241.5		1818.1		2319.6		2721.0	TOUS PRODUITS
0	FOOD AND LIVE ANIMALS		101.5		138.2		226.9		273.7	ALIMENTS,ANIMAUX VIVANTS
001	*LIVE ANIMALS FOR FOOD	W 11783	9.3	W 1920	3.2	W 384	1.5	W 1798	3.0	ANIMAUX VIVANTS
0013	SWINE,LIVE	W 4426	4.5	W 531	0.6	W 111	0.2	W 978	1.6	ESPECE PORCINE
01	MEAT AND PREPARATIONS		7.0		4.8		12.0		17.5	VIANDES ET PREPARATIONS
011	MEAT FRESH,CHILLD,FROZEN	W 5294	5.1	W 4338	4.4	W 11092	11.1	W 16875	15.0	VIANDES FRAICHES,REF,CONGE
03	FISH AND PREPARATIONS		11.1		17.5		26.8		37.7	POISSONS ET PREPARATIONS
034	FISH,FRESH,CHILLED,FROZN	W 29621	10.0	W 31772	16.2	W 43808	25.0	W 56754	35.4	POISSON FRAIS, REFRIG,CONG
0342	FISH FROZEN,EXCL FILLETS	W 27867	9.1	W 29707	14.9	W 40128	22.2	W 51815	31.6	POISSONS CONGELES
04	CEREALS AND PREPARATIONS		13.1		17.7		55.0		27.1	CEREALES ET PRODUITS
041	WHEAT ETC UNMILLED	W 34070	2.3	W 35984	4.9	W 123472	25.1	W 26438	4.6	FROMENT,EPEAUTRE
0412	OTHER WHEAT ETC UNMILLED	W 32054	2.2	W 28731	3.9	W 116382	23.9	W 26438	4.6	AUTRE FROMENT NON MOULU
045	CEREALS NES UNMILLED	W 3011	0.5	W 2221	0.4	W 50157	7.9	W 20712	3.1	AUTRES CEREALES NON MOULUES
0451	RYE UNMILLED			W 12	0.1	W 46193	7.3	W 17927	2.7	SEIGLE NON MOULU
048	CEREAL ETC PREPARATIONS	W 15987	5.6	W 18395	9.3	W 16993	11.1	W 19764	12.4	PREPTNS A BASE CEREALES
05	VEGETABLES AND FRUIT		22.3		33.6		40.4		59.6	LEGUMES ET FRUITS
054	VEG ETC FRSH,SMPLY PRSVD	W 14440	3.9	W 16548	6.6	W 18939	7.5	W 71004	18.8	LEGUMES FRAIS,CONG,SECS
057	FRUIT,NUTS,FRESH,DRIED	W 33969	13.6	W 53680	19.2	W 55873	21.4	W 80419	24.3	FRUITS FRAIS OU SECS
0573	BANANA,PLANTAIN,FRSH,DRY	W 14013	4.0	W 17118	6.0	W 16989	5.6	W 17295	5.4	BANANES FRAICHES,SECHEES
058	FRUIT PRESERVED,PREPARED	W 11895	3.4	W 8085	6.1	W 9913	9.5	W 11728	13.1	CONSERVES DE FRUITS
0585	FRUIT OR VEGETABLE JUICE	W 8192	1.9	W 3792	1.4	W 4370	2.7	W 9815	11.1	JUS DE FRUITS
06	SUGAR AND PREPS,HONEY		16.9		22.4		32.3		27.8	SUCRES ET PRODUITS
061	SUGAR AND HONEY	W 52384	14.9	W 184828	20.5	W 82208	29.3	W 73022	24.0	SUCRES ET MIEL
0611	RAW BEET AND CANE SUGAR	W 47900	14.2	W 179785	18.6	W 65647	22.6	W 49500	15.0	SUCRES BRUTS
07	COFFEE,TEA,COCOA,SPICES		8.1		15.0		27.2		44.2	CAFE,THE,CACAO,EPICES
071	COFFEE AND SUBSTITUTES	W 1289	2.7	W 1613	7.2	W 2937	12.8	W 5468	23.7	CAFE ET SUCCEDANES
0711	COFFEE GREEN,ROASTED,SUB	W 1128	2.3	W 1506	6.4	W 2408	8.8	W 3708	14.7	CAFE TORREFIE OU DECAFEINE
07112	COFFEE ROASTED	W 436	1.4	W 389	2.6	W 889	5.0	W 1849	10.4	CAFE TORREFIE
0712	COFFEE EXTRACTS,ESSENCES	W 161	0.4	W 108	0.8	W 529	4.0	W 1761	9.0	EXTRAITS DE CAFE
081	*FEEDING STUFF FOR ANIML	W 11844	2.6	W 22209	6.6	W 34892	8.5	W 27072	12.4	NOURRITURE POUR ANIMAUX
09	MISC EDIBLE PRODUCTS		9.4		14.0		20.9		38.5	PREP ALIMENTAIRES DIVERSES
098	EDIBLE PRODCTS,PREPS NES	W 15736	7.9	W 13076	11.0	W 15776	16.9	W 17113	31.2	PREP ALIMENTAIRES NDA
09809	MISC FOOD PREPRTIONS NES	W 9485	5.4	W 10636	9.0	W 13173	12.6	W 13574	25.0	PREP ALIMENTAIRES NDA
1	BEVERAGES AND TOBACCO		21.9		37.4		50.2		62.5	BOISSONS ET TABACS
11	BEVERAGES		16.6		32.7		38.7		42.0	BOISSONS
111	NON-ALCOHL BEVERAGES NES	W 22079	6.4	W 30943	9.8	W 29548	11.9	W 41498	13.9	BOISSONS NON ALCOOLIQUES
11102	FLAVORED WATERS NON-ALCO	W 16128	5.0	W 23075	7.6	W 24691	10.3	W 34346	12.0	LIMONADES,EAUX GAZEUSES
112	ALCOHOLIC BEVERAGES	W 18192	10.3	W 24741	22.9	W 27110	26.9	W 27211	28.2	BOISSONS ALCOOLIQUES
1121	WINE OF FRESH GRAPES ETC	W 12521	4.7	W 19473	13.5	W 21161	15.7	W 20093	15.3	VINS DE RAISINS FRAIS
11212	WINE OF FRESH GRAPES	W 5092	2.5	W 16470	10.8	W 19329	12.9	W 12883	10.9	VINS DE MOUTS DE RAISINS
1124	DISTILLED ALCOHOLIC BEVS	W 1655	3.8	W 2056	7.0	W 2657	8.8	W 3584	10.8	ALCOOLS,EAUX-DE-VIE
12	TOBACCO AND MANUFACTURES		5.3		4.8		11.5		20.6	TABACS BRUTS FABRIQUES
122	TOBACCO,MANUFACTURED	W 1149	3.3	W 281	3.1	W 733	7.9	W 1793	19.3	TABACS FABRIQUES
1222	CIGARETTES	W 156	2.2	W 185	2.6	W 624	7.3	W 1747	19.0	CIGARETTES
2	CRUDE MATERLS,EXCL FUELS		20.2		43.1		59.8		88.1	MAT BRUTES NON COMESTIBLES
22	OIL SEEDS,OLEAGINOUS FRT		3.9		4.1		4.7		6.4	GRAINES,FRUITS OLEAGINEUX
24	CORK AND WOOD		1.7		7.0		4.2		7.4	LIEGE ET BOIS
26	TEXTILE FIBRES AND WASTE		7.3		15.3		24.1		27.7	FIBRES TEXTILES
263	COTTON	W 1269	1.2	W 3760	4.7	W 6986	9.3	W 7428	10.9	COTON
2631	RAW COTTON,EXCL LINTERS	W 1195	1.2	W 3750	4.7	W 6370	7.6	W 6450	8.6	COTON EN MASSE
268	WOOL(EXC TOPS),ANML HAIR	W 1274	3.8	W 2374	7.2	W 1836	7.5	W 1706	6.7	LAINES ET POILS
2682	WOOL DEGREASED,UNCOMBED	W 1113	3.0	W 2127	5.7	W 1671	6.6	W 1677	6.5	LAINE DEGRAISSEE
27	CRUDE FERTLZR,MINRLS NES		4.1		6.8		10.0		12.0	ENGRAIS MINERAUX BRUTS
278	OTHER CRUDE MINERALS	W 103178	3.1	W 106672	4.8	W 145594	7.1	W 147031	6.0	AUTRES MINERAUX BRUTS
28	METALLIFEROUS ORES,SCRAP		0.6		0.7		5.1		20.4	MINERAIS METAL,DECHETS
282	IRON AND STEEL SCRAP	W 6532	0.4	W 5882	0.4	W 65650	4.6	W 280169	20.2	FERRAILLES
28209	— OF OTHR IRON OR STEEL	W 4382	0.2	W 5823	0.4	W 62396	4.4	W 267134	19.5	FERRAILLES DE FER
29	CRUDE ANIMAL,VEG MAT NES		1.6		6.5		8.7		11.9	MATIERES BRUTES ANIM,VEGET
3	MINERAL FUELS ETC		358.5		385.9		501.8		369.4	COMBUSTIBLES MINERAUX LUB
32	COAL,COKE AND BRIQUETTES		11.4		6.5		9.8		7.8	HOUILLES,COKES,BRIQUETTES
322	COAL,LIGNITE AND PEAT	W 465858	10.9	W 160065	5.9	W 207396	9.2	W 143475	6.8	HOUILLES,LIGNITES,TOURBE
3222	OTH COAL,NOT AGGLOMERATD	W 380487	8.9	W 115698	4.2	W 164152	7.2	W 138929	6.6	AUTRES HOUILLES
33	PETROLEUM AND PRODUCTS		225.9		231.6		325.9		210.5	PETROLE ET DERIVES
334	PETROLEUM PRODUCTS,REFIN	W 2395709	223.1	W 1764752	225.9	W 2203001	320.2	W 1469344	201.5	PRODUITS RAFFINES
335	RESIDUAL PETRLM PROD NES	W 21838	2.9	W 45075	5.3	W 42922	5.7	W 72829	9.0	PRODUITS RESIDUELS NDA
341	*GAS,NATURAL AND MANUFCT		85.9		96.8		87.1		109.7	GAZ NATUREL,GAZ MANUFACT
3413	PETROLM GASES,LIQUEFIED	W 44694	5.7	W 38308	5.4	W 31043	5.1	W 39000	6.4	GAZ DE PETROLE LIQUEFIE
3414	PETROLEUM GASES, GASEOUS		80.3		91.5		82.0		103.3	GAZ DE PETROLE GAZEUX
351	*ELECTRIC CURRENT		35.3		51.1		79.1		41.7	ENERGIE ELECTRIQUE
4	ANIMAL,VEGETABLE OIL,FAT		3.7		10.7		18.6		22.5	HUILES,GRAISSES ANIM,VEG
42	FIXED VEGETABLE OIL,FAT		2.7		9.3		15.9		19.1	HUILES VEGETALES FIXES
423	FIXED VEG OILS,SOFT	W 4867	2.3	W 11729	8.1	W 20954	13.1	W 28694	16.4	HUILES VEGET DOUCES FIXES
4239	OTH FIXED VEG OILS,SOFT	W 413	0.2	W 5254	3.1	W 13644	7.1	W 18895	9.2	AUTRES HUILES FIXES
42391	RAPE,COLZA,MUSTARD OILS	W 413	0.2	W 5254	3.1	W 13644	7.1	W 18895	9.2	H NAVETTE COLZA MOUTARDE
5	CHEMCLS,RELATED PROD NES		136.0		221.8		275.6		322.5	PRODUITS CHIMIQUES
51	ORGANIC CHEMICALS		29.8		47.0		39.9		44.9	PROD CHIMIQ ORGANIQUES
515	ORG-INORG COMPOUNDS ETC		22.1	W 24954	35.1	W 17342	24.8	W 16755	23.8	COMPOSES ORGANO-MINERAUX
5156	HETEROCYCLIC CMPDS ETC	W 23588	22.0	W 24899	34.8	W 17273	24.5	W 16687	23.3	COMPOSES HETEROCYCLIQUES
51561	LACTAMS	W 23562	21.9	W 24790	34.6	W 17213	24.2	W 16656	22.9	LACTAMES .
52	INORGANIC CHEMICALS		6.2		7.8		10.9		10.6	PROD CHIM INORGANIQUES
523	OTHR INORG CHEMICALS ETC	W 22032	3.8	W 18961	3.5	W 21827	5.9	W 22343	5.8	AUT PRODUITS CHIMIQUES INORG
53	DYES,TANNING,COLOUR PROD		12.9		20.0		23.2		29.5	PROD TEINTURE,COLORANTS
533	PIGMENTS,PAINTS,ETC	W 7176	10.1	W 9167	18.1	W 11417	20.1	W 20538	26.0	PIGMENTS,PEINTURES,VERNIS
5334	VARNISHES,DISTEMPERS ETC	W 4314	6.9	W 5281	12.3	W 4958	12.0	W 6164	13.6	PEINTURES A L'EAU
53342	OTH PAINTS,VARNISHES ETC	W 2812	5.0	W 3491	8.8	W 2723	8.2	W 3326	9.5	AUTRES PEINTURES,VERNIS
541	*MEDICINAL,PHARM PRODUCT	MK 9464	52.2	K 7950581	66.4	K 7537077	79.6	K 8241866	98.5	PROD MEDICINAUX PHARMACEUT
5417	MEDICAMENTS	K 4640558	43.9	K 4436181	54.7	K 5145625	67.0	K 4611667	82.8	MEDICAMENTS
54171	— CONTAINNG ANTIBIOTICS	K 1028382	14.1	K 415814	9.4	K 408966	7.1	K 363014	7.3	MED CONTN ANTIBIOTIQUES
54172	— CONTAINING HORMONES	K 402858	4.9	K 594445	8.8	K 323519	5.1	K 167779	4.2	MED CONTENANT HORMONES
54179	— CONTNG OTH SUBSTANCES	K 3123641	24.0	K 3396264	36.2	K 4348302	53.8	K 3967571	70.3	MED CONT AUT SUBSTANCES
5419	PHARMACEUTICAL GOODS NES	K 1229720	5.8	K 1316260	7.5	K 673192	7.2	K 577841	8.0	PREP,ART PHARMACEUTIQUES
54191	BANDAGES PREPARED ETC	K 1168628	4.3	K 1219044	4.4	K 578500	3.0	K 484248	3.8	OUATES,GAZES,BANDES
55	PERFUME,CLEANING ETC PRD		14.2		31.9		43.4		52.8	PROD POUR PARFUM,TOILETTE
553	PERFUMERY,COSMETICS,ETC	W 1530	7.0	W 3261	19.8	W 4292	27.8	W 5349	32.0	PRODUITS DE PARFUMERIE
554	SOAP,CLEANSING ETC PREPS	W 6359	6.7	W 7444	11.1	W 10900	14.5	W 17430	19.1	SAVONS,PRODUITS DETERSIFS
5542	WASHING PREPARATIONS ETC	W 5690	5.4	W 6353	8.3	W 9131	10.7	W 14414	14.0	PROD ORG TENSIO-ACT NDA
562	*FERTILIZERS,MANUFACTURE	W 45855	3.0	W 86609	9.2	W 205862	26.3	W 132088	17.2	ENGRAIS MANUFACTURES
5621	CHEM NITROGENOUS FERTLZR	W 33085	2.2	W 51781	5.2	W 127810	14.6	W 75527	7.9	ENGRAIS AZOTES
56211	AMMONIUM NITRATE	W 25077	1.6	W 42169	3.9	W 110878	12.3	W 61853	6.0	NITRATE D'AMMONIUM
5629	FERTILIZERS NES	W 6020	0.5	W 13805	2.5	W 42036	8.3	W 40228	7.8	ENGRAIS NDA
56291	NIT-PHOS-POT FERTLZR NES	W 2694	0.3	W 11959	2.3	W 36338	7.2	W 35294	6.8	ENGRAIS CONT N P K

4. Special Imports C.I.F. by Commodities according to the S.I.T.C. (Rev. 2) in million U.S. Dollars
Importations Spéciales C.A.F. par Produits d'après la C.T.C.I. (Rév. 2) en millions de Dollars E.U.

SITC CTCI	COMMODITY	1994 QUANTITY QUANTITE	1994 VALUE VALEUR	1995 QUANTITY QUANTITE	1995 VALUE VALEUR	1996 QUANTITY QUANTITE	1996 VALUE VALEUR	1997 QUANTITY QUANTITE	1997 VALUE VALEUR	PRODUIT
58	PLASTIC MATERIALS ETC		11.4		21.2		27.0		36.9	MAT PLAST ARTIFICIELLES
582	PROD OF CONDENSATION ETC	W 12476	4.9	W 10464	8.1	W 14587	10.0	W 15555	12.2	PROD CONDENS,POLYCOND
583	POLYMERIZATION ETC PRODS	W 6506	6.0	W 8643	12.8	W 10648	16.4	W 14624	24.1	PROD POLYMERISATION
59	CHEMICAL MATERIALS NES		6.7		18.4		25.4		32.1	MAT PROD CHIMIQUES NDA
591	PESTICIDES,DISINFECTANTS	W 673	1.1	W 714	3.1	W 1120	5.6	W 1701	9.7	DESINF,INSECT,FONG,HERB
592	STARCH,INULIN,GLUTEN,ETC	W 5439	3.0	W 6531	7.6	W 8024	10.4	W 7691	13.0	AMIDONS,INUL,GLUT FROM
5922	ALBUMINOID SUBSTAN,GLUES	W 2010	2.1	W 3471	6.6	W 4598	8.9	W 5824	12.3	MAT ALBUMIN,COLLES
598	MISCEL CHEM PRODUCTS NES		2.8	W 8029	7.8	W 6986	9.4	W 7310	9.4	PROD DIV INDUST CHIM NDA
5989	CHEM PRODUCTS,PREPS NES		2.4	W 6227	7.0	W 5523	7.9	W 5905	8.0	PROD PREP CHIMIQUES NDA
6	BASIC MANUFACTURES		164.4		321.9		418.2		523.9	ART MANUFACTURES
61	LEATHER,DRESSED FUR,ETC		4.2		5.9		7.3		9.2	CUIRS,PELLETERIES
62	RUBBER MANUFACTURES NES		9.8		17.5		23.3		29.5	CAOUTCHOUC MANUFACTURE
625	RUBBER TYRES, TUBES ETC	W 4010	6.7	W 5365	11.8	W 5603	16.9	W 7339	21.5	PNEUS CAOUTCHOUC VULCANISE
6251	TYRES NEW FOR MOTOR CARS	W 1521	3.7	W 2275	5.5	W 1417	6.4	W 1778	7.9	PNEUS POUR VOITURES
6252	TYRES,NEW,BUS OR LORRY	W 1419	1.9	W 1539	4.1	W 2254	7.2	W 2673	7.8	PNEUS POUR AUTOBUS,CAMIONS
63	WOOD,CORK MANUFACTRS NES		5.2		16.3		13.0		14.9	OUVRAGES LIEGE ET BOIS
635	WOOD MANUFACTURES NES	W 2186	3.5	W 3557	11.8	W 9252	8.2	W 4511	8.5	ART MANUF EN BOIS NDA
6353	BUILDERS WOODWRK,PREFABS	W 1731	3.2	W 2961	11.1	W 8034	7.3	W 2603	7.5	OUVRAGES DE MENUISERIE
64	PAPER,PAPERBOARD AND MFR		29.4		71.3		93.8		103.0	PAPIERS,CARTONS & OUVRAGES
641	PAPER AND PAPERBOARD	W 43089	19.1	W 44088	44.8	W 55243	61.6	W 70944	69.0	PAPIERS ET CARTONS
6411	NEWSPRINT	W 11641	2.8	W 14317	8.7	W 10909	7.5	W 12500	6.3	PAPIER JOURNAL
6412	PRINTG,WRITING PAPER NES	W 4740	4.1	W 8222	8.8	W 12147	11.7	W 12433	12.3	PAPIERS POUR L'IMPRESSION
64122	— COATED,IMPREGNATD ETC	W 2666	2.2	W 7007	7.1	W 9378	8.7	W 9685	9.4	PAPIERS IMPRESSION COUCHES
6415	PAPER,PAPERBRD,BULK,NES	W 11665	4.0	W 6360	5.8	W 9224	7.2	W 13195	9.5	PAPIERS,CARTONS ROULEAUX
64159	OTHER PAPER ETC,BULK,NES	W 10945	3.0	W 5948	5.1	W 8540	6.2	W 12302	8.6	AUT PAPIER ROULEAUX FEUILLES
6418	COATED ETC PAPER NES BLK	W 8087	3.9	W 8583	14.5	W 13013	25.5	W 15107	27.5	PAP,CARTONS COUCHES,ENDUITS
64181	PLASTIC COATED PAPER ETC	W 985	1.7	W 2896	7.5	W 4967	16.1	W 5424	16.6	PAP,CARTONS ENDUITS,RESINES
64189	COATED PAPER ETC NES	W 1296	1.7	W 3446	6.5	W 5360	8.6	W 8228	10.3	PAPIERS,CARTONS COUCHES
642	PAPER,ETC,PRECUT,ARTS OF	W 11201	10.3	W 15445	26.5	W 18753	32.3	W 18492	34.0	PAP,CARTONS DECOUPES
6421	PAPER ETC CONTAINERS	W 8611	5.4	W 10209	12.2	W 11409	13.5	W 9447	11.7	BOITES,SACS EMBALLAGES
6428	PAPER ETC ARTICLES NES	W 1670	2.9	W 3680	10.3	W 4658	12.8	W 5708	15.1	OUVRAGES EN PATE A PAPIER
64285	PAPER ETC DIAPERS ETC	W 490	1.5	W 1336	6.4	W 1632	7.1	W 2342	8.5	SERVIETTES HYGIENIQUES
65	TEXTILE YARN,FABRICS,ETC		36.9		62.3		92.8		107.9	FILS,TISSUS,ARTICLES TEXTILE
651	TEXTILE YARN	W 3035	10.2	W 2822	15.1	W 3339	21.1	W 4782	26.8	FILS TEXTILES
6514	SYN FIB YRN,BULK,MONOFIL	W 1770	6.6	W 1979	11.1	W 2157	15.7	W 3008	18.9	FILS CONT 85% FIB TEXT SYNTH
65142	— NONTXT ETC CONT PAMID	W 961	2.1	W 1012	5.1	W 1213	7.0	W 1749	8.1	FILS NON TEX FI CON POLYAMID
652	COTTON FABRICS,WOVEN	W 537	3.7	W 655	5.9	W 844	8.1	W 1683	13.3	TISSUS DE COTON
6522	WOVEN COTTON BLEACHD,ETC	W 363	2.2	W 505	4.5	W 607	7.0	W 1109	11.3	TISSUS COTON BLANCHIS ETC
653	WOVN MAN-MADE FIB FABRIC	W 767	8.3	W 1206	17.7	W 1859	30.9	W 1827	29.5	TISSUS FIBRES SYNTH,ARTIF
6531	CONT SYNT WEAVES NONPILE	W 221	3.1	W 457	6.4	W 707	10.2	W 404	5.3	TISSUS FIBRES SYNTH CONTINUE
65315	CONT SYN TXTL FABRIC NES	W 196	2.9	W 451	6.2	W 662	9.4	W 344	4.5	TIS PLUS 85% TEXT SYNT CONT
6534	DISC SYN BLEND FABRC NES	W 246	2.3	W 259	3.5	W 595	10.4	W 861	13.0	TISSUS FIBRES SYNTH DISCONT
65341	DISC SYN FIB-COTTN FABRC	W 41	0.3	W 109	1.2	W 308	4.8	W 549	8.5	TISSUS FIB SYNT DIS MEL COTO
655	KNITTED,ETC FABRICS	W 311	2.7	W 524	5.5	W 839	10.8	W 1133	14.0	ETOF BONNETERIE PIECES ETC
6552	OTHER KNIT ETC FAB NONEL	W 311	2.7	W 524	5.5	W 839	10.8	W 1133	14.0	ETOF BON NON ELAS NON SYNT
657	SPECIAL TXTL FABRC,PRODS	W 1725	5.3	W 1802	9.8	W 1939	10.6	W 1977	10.9	TISSUS SPECIAUX
6577	TEXTILES FOR MACHINERY	W 839	3.0	W 833	6.0	W 689	4.8	W 613	3.4	OUATES,MECHES ART TEXT
65771	TEXTILE WADDING NES ETC	W 814	2.9	W 798	5.7	W 605	4.3	W 447	2.9	OUATES,ARTICLES EN OUATE
66	NONMETAL MINERAL MFS NES		18.5		33.6		45.6		65.5	ART MIN NON METALLIQUES
661	LIME,CEMENT,BLDG PRODS	W 66224	2.3	W 74894	5.3	W 108640	7.2	W 102448	8.3	CHAUX,CIMENTS MAT CONSTR
662	CLAY,REFRACTORY BLDG PRD	W 25770	3.7	W 51033	6.4	W 43316	8.6	W 46043	11.5	MAT CONST REFRACTAIRES
663	MINERAL MANUFCTURES NES	W 30441	4.5	W 41492	7.7	W 56188	11.8	W 87220	17.5	ART MIN MANUF NDA
6633	MINRL MFS NES NONCERAMIC	W 26352	1.9	W 37320	3.2	W 49919	5.4	W 75777	8.3	OUVR MAT MINERALE NDA
664	GLASS	W 11470	4.6	W 13386	5.7	W 11279	7.3	W 15048	13.2	VERRE
665	GLASSWARE	W 10836	3.3	W 17141	8.3	W 18656	10.4	W 28056	14.4	OUVRAGES EN VERRE
6651	BOTTLES ETC OF GLASS	W 9393	1.8	W 16565	7.1	W 18051	8.7	W 26760	10.6	RECIPIENTS EN VERRE
66511	GLASS BOTTLES ETC NONVAC	W 9393	1.8	W 16565	7.1	W 18051	8.7	W 26754	10.6	BONBONNES,BOUTEILLES,ETC
67	IRON AND STEEL		30.5		54.4		71.3		97.8	FER ET ACIER
671	PIG IRON ETC	W 36827	5.9	W 12179	4.0	W 5918	3.8	W 12303	5.1	FONTE,SPIEGEL,POUDRES
673	IRON,STEEL SHAPES ETC	W 13212	2.2	W 19970	5.8	W 28513	9.5	W 40798	13.8	BARRES,PROFIL FER,ACIER
6733	IRON,STEEL PROFILES ETC	W 7695	1.3	W 13848	3.5	W 22109	6.6	W 31347	10.0	PROFILES,PALPLAN FER,ACIER
674	IRN,STL UNIV,PLATE,SHEET	W 55469	10.6	W 59140	25.2	W 56677	32.3	W 91415	53.2	LARGES PLATS,TOLES
6746	IRN,STL THIN PLATE,ROLLD	W 21884	4.6	W 16231	7.2	W 10651	4.6	W 13320	6.1	TOLES LAM MOINS 3MM
67461	— OF IRON OR SIMPLE STL	W 21757	4.6	W 15937	6.8	W 10227	4.1	W 12525	5.5	TOL NON AC FIN MOINS 3 MM
6747	TINNED PLATES,SHEETS	W 9320	2.8	W 16282	8.8	W 19183	12.9	W 22191	14.2	TOLES ETAMEES EN ACIER
6749	OTH IRN,STL PLATES,SHEET	W 6160	1.3	W 9421	4.0	W 11867	10.2	W 26221	22.3	AUTRES TOLES FER,ACIER
67491	— OF IRON OR SIMPLE STL	W 3990	1.0	W 7400	2.9	W 11491	9.6	W 25902	21.7	AUT TOLES AUTRES ACIER FIN
678	IRON,STL TUBES,PIPES,ETC	W 13348	5.4	W 13024	10.7	W 15852	15.2	W 20533	15.3	TUBES,TUYAUX EN FONTE,FER
6783	IRON,STL TUBES,PIPES NES	W 6239	1.6	W 6095	3.5	W 10208	8.9	W 12659	7.9	AUT TUBES,TUYAUX FER,ACIER
68	NON-FERROUS METALS		6.2		11.3		11.5		16.4	METAUX NON FERREUX
684	ALUMINIUM	W 1718	4.8	W 2003	7.8	W 2076	7.9	W 2837	11.4	ALUMINIUM
6842	ALUMINIUM,ALLOYS WORKED	W 1265	4.5	W 1352	6.9	W 1765	7.5	W 2642	11.1	ALUMINIUM,ALLIAGES OUVRE
69	METAL MANUFACTURES NES		24.3		49.8		59.8		80.1	ART MANUFACT EN METAL NDA
691	STRUCTURES AND PARTS NES	W 2520	6.5	W 3338	13.6	W 5712	11.1	W 8794	16.8	CONSTRUCT FER,ACIER,ALU
6911	STRUCTURES,PARTS IRN,STL	W 2061	4.2	W 3088	11.6	W 5506	9.6	W 8451	14.4	CONSTRUCT FER,ACIER,FONTE
692	METAL TANKS,BOXES,ETC	W 4295	3.2	W 5164	7.4	W 4264	7.9	W 5389	10.5	RECIPIENTS METALLIQUES
695	TOOLS	W 833	3.1	W 772	5.2	W 876	6.3	W 1159	8.8	OUTILS A MAIN
697	BASE MTL HOUSEHOLD EQUIP	W 1229	2.8	W 1282	5.0	W 1839	10.2	W 2333	11.8	ART MENAGE MET COMMUNS
699	BASE METAL MFRS NES	W 7430	6.1	W 6114	13.3	W 7533	18.5	W 6534	23.9	ART MANUFACTURES MET NDA
6991	LOCKSMITHS WARES,ETC	W 763	2.1	W 881	5.5	W 1145	7.6	W 1526	9.0	ARTICLES DE SERRURERIE
7	MACHINES,TRANSPORT EQUIP		283.1		460.9		522.4		743.6	MACHINES MATERIEL TRANSPORT
71	POWER GENERATING EQUIPMT		11.0		22.1		14.1		17.4	MACHINES GENERATRICES
713	INTRNL COMBUS PSTN ENGIN	W 2176	5.7	W 1478	7.9	W 659	5.5	W 758	4.9	MOTEURS EXPL COMB INT, PIECE
716	ROTATING ELECTRIC PLANT	W 1104	2.9	W 1342	7.3	W 805	3.1	W 2224	4.3	APP ELECTR ROTATIFS,PIECES
72	MACHS FOR SPCL INDUSTRYS		50.6		67.4		72.2		105.6	MAC SPECIALES POUR INDUST
721	AGRIC MACHY,EXC TRACTORS	W 2054	5.5	W 2018	6.3	W 2076	7.6	W 3439	14.2	MACHINES AGRICOLES
722	TRACTORS NON-ROAD	W 2147	4.3	W 2494	5.3	W 1154	6.9	W 2067	11.8	TRACTEURS
7224	WHEELED TRACTORS NES	W 2130	4.3	W 2492	5.3	W 1128	6.8	W 2062	11.8	TRACTEURS A ROUES
723	CIVIL ENGNEERG EQUIP ETC	W 499	3.6	W 599	2.9	W 916	4.2	W 1613	10.2	APPAREILS DE GENIE CIVIL
7234	CONST,MINING MACHNRY NES	W 423	3.3	W 526	2.5	W 809	3.8	W 1429	9.1	MACH POUR LA CONST, MINES
724	TEXTILE,LEATHER MACHNRY	W 592	7.7	W 599	9.9	W 686	6.7	W 1242	10.4	MACH POUR INDUSTRIE TEXTILE
7244	SPINNING,EXTRDNG,ETC MCH	W 219	4.6	W 216	5.1	W 280	1.1	W 486	1.6	MACH POUR LE FILAGE
72443	SPINNING,REELING,ETC MCH	W 76	4.1	W 180	4.5	W 40	0.2	W 41	0.2	MACH POUR LA FILATURE
726	PRINTG,BKBINDG MACHY,PTS	W 282	2.6	W 358	7.3	W 355	5.0	W 648	16.6	MACHINES POUR IMPRIMERIE
7264	PRINTING PRESSES	W 117	1.2	W 152	4.8	W 110	2.1	W 411	13.0	MACHINES A IMPRIMER
72641	ROTARY PRINTING PRESSES	W 117	1.2	W 152	4.8	W 110	2.1	W 411	13.0	MACH IMPRIMER ROTATIVES
727	FOOD MACHRY NON-DOMESTIC	W 1315	9.8	W 972	12.7	W 1242	16.6	W 975	13.3	MACH INDUSTRIES ALIMENT
7272	OTH FOOD PROC MCHY,PARTS	W 1179	9.6	W 810	11.8	W 1188	16.1	W 917	12.5	AUT MACH IND ALIMENTAIRE
72722	INDUS FOOD PROC MACH NES	W 1080	8.5	W 803	11.8	W 1140	15.9	W 916	12.4	MACHINES BOULANGERIE
728	OTH MACHY FOR SPCL INDUS	W 4682	17.2	W 2347	21.4	W 3161	22.7	W 4201	27.7	AUT MACH IND PARTICULIERES
7281	MACH-TOOLS FR SPCL INDUS	W 3823	10.7	W 1506	11.1	W 2347	15.7	W 1754	13.3	MACH-OUTILS SPEC IND PART

4. Special Imports C.I.F. by Commodities according to the S.I.T.C. (Rev. 2) in million U.S. Dollars
Importations Spéciales C.A.F. par Produits d'après la C.T.C.I. (Rév. 2) en millions de Dollars E.U.

SITC CTCI	COMMODITY	1994 QUANTITY QUANTITE	1994 VALUE VALEUR	1995 QUANTITY QUANTITE	1995 VALUE VALEUR	1996 QUANTITY QUANTITE	1996 VALUE VALEUR	1997 QUANTITY QUANTITE	1997 VALUE VALEUR	PRODUIT
72812	MACH–TOOLS TO WORK WOOD	W 3385	8.6	W 1330	7.4	W 2114	13.4	W 1400	10.2	MACH–OUT POUR TRAVAIL BOIS
7284	MACHY FOR SPCL INDUS NES	W 551	4.8	W 429	8.7	W 484	6.4	W 1678	11.8	MACH SPEC IND PARTICUL.
73	METALWORKING MACHINERY		4.3		5.1		6.0		8.4	MACH TRAVAIL DES METAUX
74	GENRL INDUSTRL MACHY NES		34.2		61.9		83.6		106.6	MACH APP INDUSTRIE
741	HEATING,COOLING EQUIPMNT	W 2139	7.9	W 2308	17.5	W 1860	19.7	W 4027	29.9	MACH CHAUFFAGE,PIECES
7414	NONDOM REFRIG EQUIPT,PTS	W 958	3.2	W 934	5.8	W 732	6.2	W 1161	9.4	MAT PRODUCTION DU FROID
7416	HEATING,COOLING EQU NES	W 663	2.8	W 948	8.0	W 659	8.2	W 1648	13.1	APP CHANGEMENT TEMP
742	PUMPS FOR LIQUIDS ETC	W 648	2.8	W 558	5.6	W 694	8.6	W 829	9.8	POMPES MOTO–POMPES
743	PUMPS NES,CENTRFUGES ETC	W 649	3.5	W 576	6.2	W 887	8.8	W 1108	12.7	POMPES COMPRES,VENT ETC
744	MECHANICAL HANDLING EQU	W 3169	9.2	W 3374	10.2	W 3926	14.1	W 3077	18.9	EQUIP MANUTENTION PIECES
7441	FORK LIFT TRCKS,ETC,PTS	W 923	3.8	W 719	2.8	W 878	3.7	W 1334	6.8	CHARIOTS POUR USINES ETC
74411	FORK LIFT TRUCKS ETC	W 902	3.8	W 695	2.7	W 725	3.1	W 1286	6.0	CHARIOTS POUR LES GARES
7442	LIFTING,LOADING MACH NES	W 1762	3.4	W 2479	6.0	W 2744	7.5	W 1355	8.7	APP LEVAGE,MANUTENTION
745	NONELEC MACHY,TOOLS NES	W 661	6.8	W 628	14.7	W 889	18.1	W 932	19.7	AUT MACH NON ELEC,PIECES
7451	POWER TOOLS NONELEC, PTS	W 122	2.9	W 199	7.1	W 132	3.9	W 227	6.1	OUT MACH PNEUM A MOTEUR
7452	OTH NONELEC MCHS,PTS NES	W 538	3.9	W 429	7.7	W 757	14.2	W 705	13.6	AUT MACH NON ELEC,PIECES
74522	PACKAGNG,BOTTLNG,ETC MCH	W 182	2.7	W 179	5.1	W 378	10.1	W 275	8.4	MACH NETT BOUTEILLES,ETC
749	NONELEC MACH PTS,ACC NES	W 947	4.3	W 804	8.0	W 1429	14.7	W 1809	15.9	PIECES MACH NON ELEC NDA
7492	COCKS,VALVES ETC NES	W 472	1.9	W 349	3.8	W 900	8.5	W 1232	10.1	ART ROB,SIM POUR TUYAUX
75	OFFICE MACHNES,ADP EQUIP		29.0		39.6		61.0		85.8	MACH BUREAU TRAIT AUTOM
751	OFFICE MACHINES	W 243	8.4	W 263	7.7	W 195	6.6	W 325	10.1	MACH,APPAREILS DE BUREAU
7518	OFFICE MACHINES NES	W 98	4.5	W 152	4.8	W 128	4.2	W 257	7.7	MACH,APP DE BUREAU NDA
752	AUTOMTIC DATA PROC EQUIP	W 195	9.2	W 215	16.1	W 283	21.5	W 657	35.7	MACH TRAIT INFORMATION
7525	ADP PERIPHERAL UNITS	W 79	2.8	W 100	4.3	W 124	6.3	W 328	9.4	UNITES PERIPHERIQUES
759	OFFICE,ADP MCH PTS,ACCES	W 348	11.4	W 326	15.9	W 512	33.0	W 797	40.1	PIECES DU 751 ET 752
7599	ACCTG,ETC,ADP MCH PTS,AC	W 309	10.2	W 263	13.6	W 443	30.0	W 657	34.3	PIECES DU 751 ET 752
76	TELECOMM,SOUND EQUIPMENT		34.1		45.2		64.0		81.3	EQUIPMENT DE TELECOM
761	TELEVISION RECEIVERS	W 215	2.7	W 445	5.1	W 521	7.1	W 454	5.5	RECEPTEURS DE TELEVISION
764	TELECOM EQPT,PTS,ACC NES	W 1398	28.0	W 1038	35.3	W 1067	52.9	W 835	66.2	EQUIP TELECOM,PIECES
7641	LINE TELEPHONE,ETC EQUIP	W 181	8.7	W 223	7.8	W 96	10.9	W 267	28.1	APP TELEPHON PAR FIL
7643	TV,RADIO TRANSMITTRS ETC	W 43	4.6	W 49	10.2	W 84	14.1	W 100	17.5	APP EMET TELE RADIO
7648	TELECOMM EQUIPMENT NES	W 41	5.1	W 26	2.9	W 36	5.0	W 35	4.3	APP TELECOM NDA
76481	RADIOTELEPHONE ETC RCVRS	W 28	4.0	W 4	2.0	W 5	2.8	W 12	2.7	RECEP RADIOTELEPHONIE
7649	PTS NES OF EQUIPMT OF 76	W 1092	9.4	W 701	13.8	W 810	22.5	W 340	15.0	PIECES DE LA DIV 76
76491	PTS NES OF APPAR OF 7641	W 976	6.9	W 458	5.1	W 600	15.5	W 104	8.0	PIECES POUR 764.1
76493	TELECOMM EQUIPMT PTS NES	W 102	2.3	W 218	8.2	W 175	6.1	W 210	6.3	PIECES 761,762,764.3,8
77	ELECTRIC MACHNRY NES ETC		41.2		79.2		92.5		124.7	MACH APP ELECT NDA
771	ELECTRIC POWER MACHY NES	W 687	2.5	W 683	7.3	W 496	11.6	W 910	22.0	MACH PROD,TRANS ELECTR
7712	OTH ELEC POWER MACHY NES	W 393	1.3	W 343	5.0	W 221	7.5	W 601	20.0	AUT APP PROD TRANSF ELEC
77121	STATIC CONVERTERS ETC	W 14	0.2	W 41	1.0	W 60	2.1	W 509	19.2	CONVERTISSEURS STATIQUES
772	SWITCHGEAR ETC,PARTS NES	W 727	6.8	W 979	16.0	W 901	19.9	W 1594	23.0	APP COUPURE,SECT ETC
7721	SWITCHGEAR ETC	W 722	6.7	W 876	14.8	W 875	18.4	W 1586	22.7	APP COUPURE,SECTIONMNT
773	ELECTR DISTRIBUTNG EQUIP	W 4390	8.0	W 4704	18.0	W 3589	14.2	W 5863	21.9	EQUIPMT DISTRIBUTION ELECT
7731	INSULATED WIRE,CABLE ETC	W 3992	7.3	W 4287	16.4	W 3395	13.1	W 5647	20.6	FILS,CABLES ISOLES ELECT
774	ELECTRO–MEDCL,XRAY EQUIP	W 121	4.6	W 159	5.9	W 143	8.1	W 134	6.9	APPAREILS MEDICAUX
775	HOUSEHOLD TYPE EQUIP NES	W 1851	6.7	W 2775	14.3	W 2754	15.5	W 4201	21.5	MACH,APP USAGE DOMESTQUE
7758	ELECTRO–THERMIC APPL NES	W 617	2.9	W 1125	6.8	W 1302	7.8	W 1519	8.9	APP ELECTROTHERMIQ NDA
778	ELECTRICAL MACHINERY NES	W 3116	11.9	W 3164	16.1	W 3720	22.1	W 4256	23.4	AUTRES MACH ELECT NDA
7788	OTH ELEC MACHY,EQUIP NES	W 426	3.6	W 309	4.5	W 387	6.8	W 370	8.6	AUT MACH APP ELEC NDA
78	ROAD VEHICLES		70.1		119.0		112.8		193.7	VEHICULES ROUTIERS
781	PASS MOTOR VEH EXC BUSES	W 4427	26.3	W 13741	51.6	W 8959	39.0	W 13106	69.1	AUTO TRANSPORT PERSONNES
782	LORRIES,SPCL MTR VEH NES	W 7807	19.0	W 6518	27.1	W 7082	36.4	W 14611	61.0	VEHICULES SPECIAUX,MARCH
7821	LORRIES,TRUCKS	W 6756	14.3	W 5209	20.2	W 6310	33.5	W 13489	53.5	VEHICULES TRANSP MARCHAND
7822	SPECIAL MOTOR VEHCLS NES	W 1051	4.8	W 1309	6.9	W 772	3.0	W 1123	7.5	VEHICULES USAGES SPECIAUX
783	ROAD MOTOR VEHICLES NES	W 1312	3.5	W 1078	5.6	W 828	3.5	W 2617	14.6	VEHICULES ROUTIERS NDA
7831	BUSES	W 413	1.7	W 914	4.5	W 723	3.0	W 2404	13.6	VOITURES TRANSPORT COMMUN
784	MOTOR VEH PRTS,ACCES NES	W 5130	18.0	W 4174	27.7	W 2622	24.2	W 3039	29.6	PIECES 722,781,782,783
7849	OTHER MOTOR VEHCL PARTS	W 5015	17.8	W 4053	27.6	W 2591	24.1	W 2978	29.5	PIECES 722,781,782,783
786	TRAILERS,NONMOTR VEH,NES	W 4181	2.8	W 3352	6.3	W 3790	8.8	W 8805	17.7	REMORQUES,CADRES,CONTAIN
7861	TRAILERS,TRANSP CONTAINR	W 2609	2.1	W 2198	4.6	W 2679	5.8	W 7220	13.0	REMORQUES TOUS VEHICULES
78612	OTHER TRAILERS	W 2252	1.8	W 1601	3.1	W 2362	5.2	W 6707	12.1	REMORQUES TRANSP MARCH
79	OTHR TRANSPORT EQUIPMENT		9.0		21.8		16.6		20.5	AUTRE MATERIEL TRANSPORT
791	RAILWAY VEHICLES	W 17973	8.6	W 24179	18.8	W 46816	11.5	W 75509	14.0	VEHIC MAT CHEMINS DE FER
7915	FRT,MAINT CARS NOT POWRD	W 2225	1.0	W 2132	7.7	W 4035	0.5	W 7657	0.8	WAGONS DE SERVICE
79151	RY SERV CARS NOT POWERED	W 1023	0.9	W 266	7.7	W 28	0.2	W 595	0.5	WAGONS–ATELIERS,–GRUES
7919	RY TRACK FIXT,ETC,PARTS	W 9818	7.5	W 11077	10.1	W 7238	9.0	W 8188	7.9	MATER FIXE VOIES FERREES
79199	PARTS NES OF 7911–7915	W 9306	6.3	W 9190	9.1	W 6545	8.1	W 5513	6.3	PIECES 791.1 ET 5
8	MISC MANUFACTURED GOODS		119.0		196.6		243.7		311.2	ART MANUFACTURES DIVERS
812	*PLUMBG,HEATNG,LGHTNG EQ	W 3426	8.5	W 2429	11.5	W 3140	15.6	W 4481	20.2	APPAR SANITAIRES CHAUFFAGE
8124	LIGHTING EQUIPMENT NES	W 517	3.0	W 635	6.2	W 712	8.0	W 1084	10.9	APPAREILS ECLAIRAGE ETC
81242	LAMPS,FITTINGS BASE METL	W 415	2.6	W 509	5.2	W 523	5.8	W 862	9.1	APPAREILS D'ECLAIRAGE
821	*FURNITURE,PARTS THEREOF	W 4763	14.1	W 5306	20.0	W 5236	21.1	W 6792	26.1	MEUBLES ET PIECES
8219	FURNITURE AND PARTS NES	W 3781	9.6	W 4394	14.1	W 4138	14.1	W 4963	16.5	AUTRES MEUBLES ET PIECES
82192	WOOD FURNITURE NES	W 2824	7.1	W 3228	9.2	W 2734	8.0	W 2967	8.6	MEUBLES NDA EN BOIS
84	CLOTHING AND ACCESSORIES		31.0		67.0		72.7		82.0	VETEMENTS
842	MENS OUTERWEAR NOT KNIT	W 168	3.8	W 132	3.8	W 215	5.8	W 248	5.7	VET DESSUS POUR HOMMES
843	WOMENS OUTERWEAR NONKNIT	W 327	4.4	W 167	5.2	W 253	7.3	W 204	5.9	VET DESSUS FEMMES MAT TEX
844	UNDER GARMENTS NOT KNIT	W 673	13.1	W 1858	44.2	W 1397	34.1	W 1781	39.2	VETEMENT DESSOUS MAT TEX
8441	— MENS SHIRTS	W 662	13.0	W 1844	44.0	W 1387	33.9	W 1775	39.1	CHEMISES HOMMES MAT TEXT
84412	—— OF SYNTHETIC FIBRES	W 639	12.8	W 1824	43.7	W 1364	33.3	W 1736	38.1	CHEMISES HOMMES FIB SYNT
846	UNDER GARMENTS KNITTED	W 242	4.0	W 288	7.1	W 320	9.5	W 371	11.4	SOUS VETS DE BONNETERIE
847	TEXTILE CLTHNG ACCES NES	W 226	2.6	W 162	2.8	W 391	8.8	W 486	9.9	ACCES VET MAT TEXT NDA
8471	— NOT KNITTED	W 78	1.6	W 84	1.9	W 288	7.5	W 381	8.1	ACCES VET MAT TEX NON BON
851	*FOOTWEAR	W 954	8.4	W 794	10.2	W 833	12.6	W 1064	16.4	CHAUSSURES
85102	FOOTWEAR LEATHER	W 846	7.9	W 617	8.9	W 705	11.4	W 899	15.0	CHAUS SEMELLES EN CUIR
87	PRECISION INSTRUMNTS NES		19.1		23.8		33.1		36.4	INSTRUM,APPAR SCIENT NDA
872	MEDICAL INSTRUMENTS NES	W 382	9.1	W 456	10.5	W 522	12.1	W 499	12.4	INSTR,APP MEDIC–CHIR NDA
87202	OTH MEDICAL INSTRUMENTS	W 305	6.9	W 349	8.5	W 407	9.7	W 373	10.0	INSTRUM,APP MEDECINE
873	METERS AND COUNTERS NES	W 292	4.8	W 227	4.4	W 296	7.2	W 298	7.3	COMPTEURS,INST DE MESURE
8731	GAS SUPPLY METERS ETC	W 292	4.8	W 225	4.2	W 295	7.0	W 297	7.3	COMPTEURS GAZ,LIQ ELECT
874	MEASURNG,CONTROLNG INSTR	W 184	4.2	W 188	8.4	W 290	13.1	W 291	15.9	INSTRUMENTS DE MESURE
88	PHOTO EQU,OPTICL GDS ETC		4.1		6.9		11.5		14.2	APP,FOURN PHOTO,OP,MONTR
89	MISC MANUFCTRD GOODS NES		33.5		56.4		76.2		113.8	ART MANUFACTURES DIVERS
892	PRINTED MATTER	W 2890	7.9	W 2223	9.4	W 2039	11.3	W 3218	19.6	IMPRIMES
8928	PRINTED MATTER NES	W 1187	4.4	W 532	4.1	W 563	5.7	W 1153	12.2	IMPRIMES NDA
893	ARTICLES OF PLASTIC NES		14.5		29.3		37.4		49.6	OUVRAGES EN MAT DIVIS 58
8931	PLSTC PACKG CONTNRS,LIDS	W 1381	2.9	W 2073	6.5	W 3198	10.1	W 4074	12.0	ART TRANSP EMBALLAGE ETC
8939	MISC PLASTIC ARTICLES	W 3545	11.0	W 5121	21.9	W 5978	25.9	W 10019	35.9	ART DIVERS EN MAT DIV 58
89399	OTHR PLASTC ARTICLES NES	W 2500	8.1	W 3620	16.0	W 3969	18.8	W 7612	28.5	AUT OUV MAT DIV 58
894	TOYS,SPORTING GOODS,ETC	W 1107	4.8	W 1305	8.5	W 1305	9.4	W 1765	14.0	VOITURES ENFANTS,JOUETS
8942	TOYS,INDOOR GAMES ETC	W 851	3.1	W 923	5.4	W 896	6.2	W 1256	9.2	JOUETS,JEUX ETC

4. Special Imports C.I.F. by Commodities according to the S.I.T.C. (Rev. 2) in million U.S. Dollars
Importations Spéciales C.A.F. par Produits d'après la C.T.C.I. (Rév. 2) en millions de Dollars E.U.

SITC CTCI	COMMODITY	1994		1995		1996		1997		PRODUIT
		QUANTITY QUANTITE	VALUE VALEUR	QUANTITY QUANTITE	VALUE VALEUR	QUANTITY QUANTITE	VALUE VALEUR	QUANTITY QUANTITE	VALUE VALEUR	
897	GOLD,SILVER WARE,JEWELRY		0.7		1.2		1.7		9.2	BIJOUTERIE,ORFEVRERIE
899	OTHER MANUFACTURED GOODS		3.1		4.2		7.2		9.8	AUT ART MANUF DIVERS NDA
9	GOODS NOT CLASSD BY KIND		33.7		2.0		2.9		4.0	ART TRANSACT NON CLASSES
931	*SPECIAL TRANSACTIONS	W 58657	32.5	W 75	0.3	W 198	1.1	W 79	0.4	TRANS.SPECIALES

5. Special Exports F.O.B. by Commodities according to the S.I.T.C. (Rev. 2) in million U.S. Dollars
Exportations Spéciales F.O.B. par Produits d'après la C.T.C.I. (Rév. 2) en millions de Dollars E.U.

SITC CTCI	COMMODITY	1994 QUANTITY QUANTITE	1994 VALUE VALEUR	1995 QUANTITY QUANTITE	1995 VALUE VALEUR	1996 QUANTITY QUANTITE	1996 VALUE VALEUR	1997 QUANTITY QUANTITE	1997 VALUE VALEUR	PRODUIT
	ALL COMMODITIES		989.7		1305.1		1443.4		1671.7	TOUS PRODUITS
0	FOOD AND LIVE ANIMALS		104.1		162.6		204.7		212.4	ALIMENTS,ANIMAUX VIVANTS
01	MEAT AND PREPARATIONS		4.5		4.7		6.9		13.3	VIANDES ET PREPARATIONS
014	MEAT PREPD,PRSVD,NES ETC	W 1458	2.2	W 1870	3.4	W 3609	6.1	W 5006	10.1	CONSERVES DE VIANDES
0142	SAUSAGES INCLDING TINNED	W 1158	1.8	W 1286	1.8	W 3453	5.6	W 3992	8.1	SAUCISSES,SAUCISSONS
02	DAIRY PRODCTS,BIRDS'EGGS		12.5		16.4		26.7		37.6	PRODUITS LAITIERS,OEUFS
022	MILK AND CREAM	W 19906	5.7	W 17788	8.2	W 30497	11.1	W 30337	20.4	LAIT ET CREME
0224	MILK,CREAM PRESERVED ETC	W 10982	5.2	W 5939	6.6	W 6772	7.9	W 16440	17.0	LAIT,CREME CONS,CONC
02249	MILK(EX DRY) PRSVD,SWEET	W 10698	4.8	W 5361	5.7	W 5526	6.1	W 13416	12.1	LAIT CONS,CONC SUCRE
023	BUTTER	W 2320	3.2	W 1084	2.3	W 3182	6.9	W 2981	5.3	BEURRE
024	CHEESE AND CURD	W 2124	3.5	W 2399	5.9	W 3322	8.5	W 4823	11.2	FROMAGE ET CAILLEBOTTE
03	FISH AND PREPARATIONS		53.1		87.3		111.0		81.6	POISSONS ET PREPARATIONS
034	FISH,FRESH,CHILLED,FROZN	W 17513	10.4	W 26233	15.3	W 22399	13.0	W 13538	8.7	POISSON FRAIS, REFRIG,CONG
0342	FISH FROZEN,EXCL FILLETS	W 15322	7.8	W 22131	12.2	W 15996	8.6	W 10008	5.3	POISSONS CONGELES
035	FISH SALTED,DRIED,SMOKED	W 2603	2.3	W 3367	3.3	W 5895	5.2	W 6466	3.1	POISSON SECHE,SALE,FUME
037	FISH ETC PREPD,PRSVD NES	W 24978	40.4	W 34510	68.7	W 52653	93.0	W 85506	69.8	POIS,CRUST,MOL PREPARES
0371	FISH PREPARD,PRESRVD NES	W 24968	40.4	W 34508	68.7	W 52652	93.0	W 85487	69.8	CONSERVES DE POISSONS
04	CEREALS AND PREPARATIONS		5.8		5.2		4.8		9.4	CEREALES ET PRODUITS
045	CEREALS NES UNMILLED	W 67405	3.1	W 23057	1.0					AUTRES CEREALES NON MOULUES
0451	RYE UNMILLED	W 67385	3.1	W 23043	1.0					SEIGLE NON MOULU
048	CEREAL ETC PREPARATIONS	W 1494	2.6	W 1900	4.0	W 2440	4.7	W 3826	6.5	PREPTNS A BASE CEREALES
05	VEGETABLES AND FRUIT		5.5		14.1		13.8		21.1	LEGUMES ET FRUITS
058	FRUIT PRESERVED,PREPARED	W 4132	2.4	W 18125	11.2	W 17097	10.0	W 37742	16.6	CONSERVES DE FRUITS
0585	FRUIT OR VEGETABLE JUICE	W 2850	1.6	W 17926	10.8	W 16450	9.1	W 37222	16.4	JUS DE FRUITS
05857	JUICE OF OTHER FRUIT,VEG	W 1752	1.1	W 7727	5.3	W 3199	2.0	W 6855	4.3	JUS AUTRES FRUITS,LEGUMES
05858	MIXTURES OF DIFF JUICES	W 14	0.1	W 704	0.4	W 8333	4.5	W 18196	7.1	MELANGES JUS FRUITS,LEGUMES
06	SUGAR AND PREPS,HONEY		7.4		20.1		21.1		17.7	SUCRES ET PRODUITS
061	SUGAR AND HONEY	W 4636	0.8	W 28857	10.0	W 27992	6.8	W 11868	2.5	SUCRES ET MIEL
0612	REFINED SUGAR ETC	W 940	0.6	W 22184	9.5	W 15815	5.8	W 3805	1.9	SUCRES RAFFINES
062	SUGAR CANDY NON–CHOCLATE	W 5202	6.6	W 8200	10.1	W 11241	14.3	W 14236	15.2	SUCRERIES
07	COFFEE,TEA,COCOA,SPICES		10.5		9.4		13.0		16.5	CAFE,THE,CACAO,EPICES
071	COFFEE AND SUBSTITUTES	W 554	2.9	W 456	3.1	W 452	4.0	W 834	7.1	CAFE ET SUCCEDANES
0712	COFFEE EXTRACTS,ESSENCES	W 310	2.1	W 286	2.3	W 323	3.3	W 531	5.5	EXTRAITS DE CAFE
073	CHOCOLATE AND PRODUCTS	W 2126	6.9	W 1592	5.6	W 3237	8.3	W 3790	8.8	CHOCOLAT
09	MISC EDIBLE PRODUCTS		1.6		2.0		4.5		12.6	PREP ALIMENTAIRES DIVERSES
098	EDIBLE PRODCTS,PREPS NES	W 1081	1.3	W 1509	1.6	W 6463	4.4	W 13677	12.6	PREP ALIMENTAIRES NDA
09804	SAUCES,MIXED SEASONINGS	W 404	0.5	W 972	0.8	W 5496	3.0	W 10055	5.4	SAUCES,ASSAISONNEMENTS
09809	MISC FOOD PREPRTIONS NES	W 62	0.1	W 392	0.6	W 755	1.2	W 3126	6.8	PREP ALIMENTAIRES NDA
1	BEVERAGES AND TOBACCO		18.1		24.0		16.4		18.6	BOISSONS ET TABACS
11	BEVERAGES		11.2		15.6		12.7		17.4	BOISSONS
111	NON–ALCOHL BEVERAGES NES	W 12097	3.4	W 18004	4.6	W 5408	1.5	W 5949	1.6	BOISSONS NON ALCOOLIQUES
11102	FLAVORED WATERS NON–ALCO	W 10948	3.1	W 12000	3.2	W 2634	0.8	W 3067	0.9	LIMONADES,EAUX GAZEUSES
112	ALCOHOLIC BEVERAGES	W 8246	7.8	W 12364	11.0	W 13335	11.3	W 21585	15.9	BOISSONS ALCOOLIQUES
1121	WINE OF FRESH GRAPES ETC	W 4747	4.6	W 7552	7.7	W 8216	7.7	W 15509	11.7	VINS DE RAISINS FRAIS
11212	WINE OF FRESH GRAPES	W 4747	4.6	W 7552	7.7	W 8216	7.7	W 15496	11.7	VINS DE MOUTS DE RAISINS
12	TOBACCO AND MANUFACTURES		7.0		8.4		3.7		1.2	TABACS BRUTS FABRIQUES
122	TOBACCO,MANUFACTURED	W 2210	6.9	W 2146	8.4	W 887	3.7		1.2	TABACS FABRIQUES
1222	CIGARETTES	W 2210	6.9	W 2146	8.4	W 875	3.7	W 193	1.1	CIGARETTES
2	CRUDE MATERLS,EXCL FUELS		175.5		307.9		289.8		435.1	MAT BRUTES NON COMESTIBLES
21	HIDES,SKINS,FURS UNDRSSD		2.7		4.6		4.0		5.8	CUIRS,PEAUX BRUTS
24	CORK AND WOOD		161.7		285.1		269.2		392.5	LIEGE ET BOIS
245	FUEL WOOD NES, CHARCOAL	W 108099	2.2	W 322384	10.4	W 397564	13.8	W 843370	30.0	BOIS DE CHAUFFAGE
24501	FUEL WOOD IN LOGS,ETC	W 107964	2.2	W 322246	10.3	W 394852	12.9	W 837266	27.8	RONDINS,BUCHES ETC.
247	OTH WOOD ROUGH,SQUARED	W 1793956	60.1	W 3048171	132.3	W 1288520	49.1	W 1774563	64.7	BOIS BRUTS EQUARRIS
2471	SAW–,VENEER–LOGS CONIFER	W 1088089	37.9	W 1615041	72.9	W 674957	28.4	W 886416	32.8	CONIFERES POUR SCIAGE,PLACAG
24711	— IN THE ROUGH	W 1088089	37.9	W 1615041	72.9	W 674957	28.4	W 886416	32.8	ECORCES OU DEGROSSIS
2472	SAW–,VENEER–LOGS NON–CON	W 705868	22.3	W 1433130	59.5	W 613563	20.7	W 888148	31.9	NON CONIFERES SCIAGE,PLAC
24721	— IN THE ROUGH	W 705868	22.3	W 1433130	59.5	W 613563	20.7	W 888148	31.9	BRUTS ECORCES DEGROSSIS
248	WOOD SHAPED,SLEEPERS	W 629855	97.8	W 780751	141.2	W 1172875	204.1	W 1623770	293.6	BOIS SIMPLEMENT TRAVAILLES
2481	RAILWAY SLEEPERS,TIES	W 18969	2.6	W 20375	3.3	W 56285	11.1	W 17552	4.0	TRAVERSES VOIES FERREES
2482	LUMBER SHAPED CONIFER	W 397637	65.3	W 695174	127.1	W 1043543	180.0	W 1503535	272.2	CONIFERES SCIES,RABOTES
24821	LUMBER SAWN ETC CONIFER	W 396320	64.9	W 693063	126.2	W 1039781	179.0	W 1496146	270.5	CONIFERES SCIES LONGITUD
2483	LUMBER SHAPED NON–CONIFR	W 213249	29.9	W 65203	10.9	W 73047	13.2	W 102682	17.4	NON CONIFERES SCIES,RABOTES
24831	LUMBER SAWN ETC NON–CON	W 212958	29.8	W 63772	10.3	W 71427	12.3	W 100585	16.6	SCIES LONGITUDINALEMENT
26	TEXTILE FIBRES AND WASTE		4.4		5.6		3.3		2.9	FIBRES TEXTILES
28	METALLIFEROUS ORES,SCRAP		2.8		7.0		7.9		27.5	MINERAIS METAL,DECHETS
282	IRON AND STEEL SCRAP	W 19172	0.8	W 35663	2.1	W 56513	3.4	W 157731	12.6	FERRAILLES
28209	— OF OTHR IRON OR STEEL	W 15016	0.6	W 23355	1.2	W 42931	2.7	W 123258	9.7	FERRAILLES DE FER
288	NONFERR METAL SCRAP NES	W 5094	1.5	W 14408	4.7	W 9330	3.0	W 14771	7.8	DECHETS NON FERREUX
2882	OTHER BASE MTL SCRAP NES	W 4985	1.5	W 14314	4.6	W 8891	3.0	W 14562	7.8	AUTRES DECHETS
289	PREC MTAL ORES,WASTE NES	K 13083	0.6	K 13224	0.3	K 132626	1.5	K 56043	7.2	MINERAIS,DECHETS MET PREC
28902	PREC METAL SCRAP, WASTE	K 13083	0.6	K 13224	0.3	K 132626	1.5	K 56043	7.2	CENDRES D'ORFEVRERIE
3	MINERAL FUELS ETC		17.6		23.0		29.4		17.7	COMBUSTIBLES MINERAUX LUB
32	COAL,COKE AND BRIQUETTES		6.5		4.5		4.3		4.8	HOUILLES,COKES,BRIQUETTES
322	COAL,LIGNITE AND PEAT	W 223923	6.5	W 134922	4.5	W 132885	4.3	W 151425	4.8	HOUILLES,LIGNITES,TOURBE
3224	PEAT,NOT AGGLOMERATED	W 130129	4.1	W 126581	4.2	W 128267	4.0	W 149587	4.7	TOURBE
33	PETROLEUM AND PRODUCTS		4.4		12.5		21.4		13.0	PETROLE ET DERIVES
334	PETROLEUM PRODUCTS,REFIN	W 21195	3.7	W 51444	9.3	W 109701	17.3	W 63799	12.3	PRODUITS RAFFINES
351	*ELECTRIC CURRENT		6.7		6.1		3.8		0.1	ENERGIE ELECTRIQUE
5	CHEMCLS,RELATED PROD NES		77.5		89.4		96.1		111.8	PRODUITS CHIMIQUES
51	ORGANIC CHEMICALS		6.4		7.8		7.1		8.6	PROD CHIMIQ ORGANIQUES
53	DYES,TANNING,COLOUR PROD		6.5		10.8		13.8		16.4	PROD TEINTURE,COLORANTS
533	PIGMENTS,PAINTS,ETC	W 5987	6.4	W 5717	10.8	W 7501	13.7	W 9117	16.1	PIGMENTS,PEINTURES,VERNIS
5334	VARNISHES,DISTEMPERS ETC	W 5484	6.0	W 5531	10.4	W 6685	12.7	W 7724	13.9	PEINTURES A L'EAU
53342	OTH PAINTS,VARNISHES ETC	W 4804	5.1	W 4745	8.9	W 5795	10.9	W 6821	12.3	AUTRES PEINTURES,VERNIS
541	*MEDICINAL,PHARM PRODUCT		28.3	K 3189533	38.6	K 3768407	41.1		47.3	PROD MEDICINAUX PHARMACEUT
5417	MEDICAMENTS	K 1856549	25.1	K 2115051	33.3	K 2723550	36.6	K 2737392	43.9	MEDICAMENTS
54171	— CONTAINNG ANTIBIOTICS	K 489600	6.3	K 406712	6.2	K 188115	2.1	K 40451	0.4	MED CONTN ANTIBIOTIQUES
54179	— CONTNG OTH SUBSTANCES	K 1333880	18.3	K 1427984	23.6	K 2395451	32.8	K 2647622	42.4	MED CONT AUT SUBSTANCES
5419	PHARMACEUTICAL GOODS NES	K 702453	2.5	K 762450	4.0	K 518444	3.5	K 338511	3.0	PREP,ART PHARMACEUTIQUES
55	PERFUME,CLEANING ETC PRD		21.8		11.6		10.3		14.9	PROD POUR PARFUM,TOILETTE
553	PERFUMERY,COSMETICS,ETC	W 2937	19.7	W 2129	9.9	W 1119	6.6	W 1115	10.4	PRODUITS DE PARFUMERIE
562	*FERTILIZERS,MANUFACTURE	W 14130	1.2	W 24913	2.6	W 62040	7.7	W 26196	3.2	ENGRAIS MANUFACTURES
58	PLASTIC MATERIALS ETC		4.8		6.7		3.4		5.3	MAT PLAST ARTIFICIELLES
582	PROD OF CONDENSATION ETC	W 3733	4.0	W 3205	5.2	W 648	1.2	W 1260	2.5	PROD CONDENS,POLYCOND
5824	POLYAMIDES	W 3518	3.8	W 3126	5.0	W 619	1.1	W 637	1.2	POLYAMIDES
58241	— IN PRIMARY FORMS	W 3518	3.8	W 3126	5.0	W 619	1.1	W 637	1.2	POLYAMIDES PRIMAIRES
59	CHEMICAL MATERIALS NES		7.3		10.9		12.3		15.6	MAT PROD CHIMIQUES NDA
592	STARCH,INULIN,GLUTEN,ETC	W 3575	6.1	W 2297	7.9	W 3390	8.4	W 5125	11.1	AMIDONS,INUL,GLUT FROM
5922	ALBUMINOID SUBSTAN,GLUES	W 2864	6.0	W 2050	7.7	W 2757	8.0	W 3087	10.0	MAT ALBUMIN,COLLES
59221	CASEIN AND DERIVATVS,ETC	W 1953	5.3	W 1672	7.0	W 2427	7.4	W 2505	8.5	CASEINES,CASEINATES

5. Special Exports F.O.B. by Commodities according to the S.I.T.C. (Rev. 2) in million U.S. Dollars
Exportations Spéciales F.O.B. par Produits d'après la C.T.C.I. (Rév. 2) en millions de Dollars E.U.

SITC CTCI	COMMODITY	1994 QUANTITY QUANTITE	1994 VALUE VALEUR	1995 QUANTITY QUANTITE	1995 VALUE VALEUR	1996 QUANTITY QUANTITE	1996 VALUE VALEUR	1997 QUANTITY QUANTITE	1997 VALUE VALEUR	PRODUIT
6	BASIC MANUFACTURES		251.7		323.2		372.0		413.2	ART MANUFACTURES
61	LEATHER,DRESSED FUR,ETC		14.5		16.4		16.9		16.9	CUIRS,PELLETERIES
611	LEATHER	W 2962	5.6	W 2182	6.7	W 1342	4.1	W 568	1.9	CUIRS,PEAUX PREPARES
613	FUR SKINS TANNED,DRESSED	W 73	7.9	W 90	8.6	W 79	11.0	W 52	10.3	PELLETERIES
63	WOOD,CORK MANUFACTRS NES		39.0		59.0		81.2		102.9	OUVRAGES LIEGE ET BOIS
634	VENEERS,PLYWOOD,ETC	W 112376	34.6	W 110350	50.4	W 144482	70.1	W 171250	83.2	PLACAGES,CONTRE–PLAQUES
6341	VENEER SHEETS ETC	W 3918	3.7	W 4199	7.7	W 3297	8.1	W 3619	7.9	BOIS SIMPLEMENT SCIES
6342	PLYWOOD OF WOOD SHEETS	W 35589	21.9	W 39851	30.9	W 61431	47.2	W 73012	55.8	BOIS CONTRE–PLAQUES
6343	IMPROVED,RECONSTIT WOOD	W 71384	8.9	W 65976	11.8	W 78559	14.7	W 85636	18.2	BOIS AMELIORES,RECONST
63432	RECONSTITUTED WOOD	W 71383	8.9	W 65549	11.7	W 77518	13.8	W 82491	15.9	BOIS RECONSTITUES
635	WOOD MANUFACTURES NES	W 12177	4.5	W 24724	8.6	W 33254	11.2	W 46286	19.8	ART MANUF EN BOIS NDA
6353	BUILDERS WOODWRK,PREFABS	W 4720	1.9	W 11561	4.0	W 12243	4.1	W 10549	9.0	OUVRAGES DE MENUISERIE
6359	OTHER WOOD MANUFACTURES	W 4669	1.9	W 6346	3.0	W 8459	4.2	W 15274	7.3	OUVRAGES EN BOIS NDA
63599	OTHER WOOD ARTICLES NES	W 4634	1.8	W 6289	2.9	W 8177	4.0	W 15008	7.0	AUTRES OUVRAGES EN BOIS NDA
64	PAPER,PAPERBOARD AND MFR		8.6		15.4		26.2		30.0	PAPIERS,CARTONS & OUVRAGES
641	PAPER AND PAPERBOARD	W 18986	6.5	W 25711	11.2	W 26249	16.2	W 26189	14.2	PAPIERS ET CARTONS
6416	FIBRE BUILDING BOARD	W 13477	2.2	W 17963	4.0	W 18593	5.0	W 19806	5.2	PLAQUES CONSTRUCT EN PATE
64161	HARDBOARD	W 11571	1.9	W 17645	4.0	W 17773	4.6	W 19406	5.1	PLAQUES CONSTR COMPRIMES
6418	COATED ETC PAPER NES BLK	W 270	0.4	W 944	2.3	W 1936	6.6	W 1387	3.8	PAP,CARTONS COUCHES,ENDUITS
64181	PLASTIC COATED PAPER ETC	W 79	0.1	W 228	0.8	W 1138	4.6	W 795	2.8	PAP,CARTONS ENDUITS,RESINES
642	PAPER,ETC,PRECUT,ARTS OF	W 1768	2.2	W 2641	4.2	W 5783	10.1	W 7574	15.9	PAP,CARTONS DECOUPES
6421	PAPER ETC CONTAINERS	W 547	1.1	W 1148	2.3	W 2061	5.0	W 3501	7.6	BOITES,SACS EMBALLAGES
6428	PAPER ETC ARTICLES NES	W 993	0.8	W 1125	1.4	W 3248	4.5	W 3725	7.4	OUVRAGES EN PATE A PAPIER
65	TEXTILE YARN,FABRICS,ETC		80.9		121.3		131.2		122.5	FILS,TISSUS,ARTICLES TEXTILE
651	TEXTILE YARN	W 15441	34.9	W 18508	53.0	W 17535	55.7	W 17957	50.9	FILS TEXTILES
6512	WOOL,HAIR YARN,INCL TOPS	W 686	2.9	W 1298	6.5	W 786	5.5	W 636	4.5	FILS DE LAINE,DE POILS
6513	COTTON YARN	W 1577	3.8	W 1435	4.7	W 2221	7.5	W 2743	8.7	FILS DE COTON
6514	SYN FIB YRN,BULK,MONOFIL	W 11311	23.3	W 11653	31.0	W 10224	31.6	W 8487	22.2	FILS CONT 85% FIB TEXT SYNTH
65141	— TEXTRD,CONT POLYAMIDE	W 7129	14.9	W 8759	22.5	W 7292	21.4	W 7668	19.7	FILS TEXT FIB CONT POLYAMID
65142	— NONTXT ETC CONT PAMID	W 4030	8.1	W 2735	8.1	W 2731	9.8	W 599	2.0	FILS NON TEX FI CON POLYAMID
6515	YARN OF 6514 FOR RETAIL			W 38	0.1	W 28	0.2	W 1537	6.3	FILS CONT 85% FI SYNTHETIQ
65151	— OF CONTINUOUS FIBRES			W 38	0.1	W 28	0.2	W 1537	6.3	FILS FI TEX SYNT CONT
6519	TEXTILE FIBRE YARN NES	W 1256	3.1	W 3411	8.8	W 3216	7.2	W 4055	7.7	FILS TEXT NDA FILE FIB VER
65195	YARN ETC OF GLASS FIBRE	W 1088	2.6	W 3137	8.2	W 3079	6.9	W 3314	6.3	FILS DE FIBRES DE VERRE
652	COTTON FABRICS,WOVEN	W 707	2.2	W 458	2.8	W 1101	4.8	W 1705	6.7	TISSUS DE COTON
654	OTH WOVEN TEXTILE FABRIC	W 1742	6.3	W 2567	9.6	W 2435	10.6	W 3018	12.1	TISSUS AUT COTON SYNT,ARTIF
6546	GLASS FIBRE FABRIC ETC	W 1015	3.7	W 2180	8.1	W 2178	9.6	W 2827	11.0	TISSUS DE FIBRES DE VERRE
655	KNITTED,ETC FABRICS	W 1125	8.6	W 1348	12.8	W 1722	18.5	W 1972	23.2	ETOF BONNETERIE PIECES ETC
6552	OTHER KNIT ETC FAB NONEL	W 1125	8.6	W 1348	12.8	W 1722	18.5	W 1972	23.2	ETOF BON NON ELAS NON SYNT
656	LACE,RIBBONS,TULLE,ETC	W 392	3.1	W 380	4.5	W 375	5.2	W 390	5.5	TULLES,BRODERIE
657	SPECIAL TXTL FABRC,PRODS	W 5392	13.6	W 5347	17.7	W 4555	17.0	W 977	3.6	TISSUS SPECIAUX
6573	COATED ETC TEXTILES NES	W 4848	12.8	W 4524	15.1	W 4074	15.4	W 602	2.3	TISSUS,ART MATIERE TEXT NDA
65733	RUBBERIZED TEXT NOT KNIT	W 4821	12.7	W 4496	14.9	W 4037	15.1	W 496	1.9	TISSUS CAOUTCHOUTES
658	TEXTILE ARTICLES NES	W 2213	10.4	W 2839	19.0	W 2776	17.7	W 2818	19.3	ART FACONNES MAT TEXTILES
6584	LINENS ETC	W 1818	8.5	W 2373	15.3	W 2246	12.9	W 2439	16.3	LINGE DE MAISON
65845	OTHER LINEN OF COTTON	W 1296	6.0	W 1987	12.1	W 2174	12.1	W 1990	11.5	LINGE DE TOILETTE COTON
66	NONMETAL MINERAL MFS NES		9.8		13.1		18.3		15.3	ART MIN NON METALLIQUES
661	LIME,CEMENT,BLDG PRODS	W 108944	3.3	W 96856	3.6	W 163962	6.4	W 106331	4.2	CHAUX,CIMENTS MAT CONSTR
6612	CEMENT	W 88933	2.7	W 88708	3.1	W 151558	5.7	W 102048	3.5	CIMENTS HYDRAULIQUES
665	GLASSWARE	W 2428	1.3	W 13117	3.0	W 25743	4.5	W 19575	4.1	OUVRAGES EN VERRE
67	IRON AND STEEL		73.6		63.8		54.6		75.3	FER ET ACIER
673	IRON,STEEL SHAPES ETC	W 293358	61.2	W 252599	52.8	W 232148	44.7	W 363584	63.6	BARRES,PROFIL FER,ACIER
6731	IRON,STEEL WIRE ROD	W 243238	51.1	W 230105	48.1	W 198765	37.4	W 20607	3.5	FIL MACHINE FER,ACIER
67311	IRON,SIMPLE STL WIRE ROD	W 196151	41.2	W 229994	48.0	W 198627	37.3	W 20580	3.5	FIL MACH AUT ACIER FIN
67312	HIGH CARBON STL WIRE ROD	W 47088	9.9			W 5	0.1	W 27	0.1	FIL MACH ACIER FIN CARBONE
6732	IRON,STEEL BARS ETC	W 48438	9.9	W 16300	3.3	W 31981	6.9	W 340660	59.1	BARRES FER,ACIER
67326	IRN,OTH STL BARS HOTROLD	W 47673	9.8	W 11727	2.3	W 30802	6.6	W 340505	59.1	BARRES PLEINES FER,ACIER
674	IRN,STL UNIV,PLATE,SHEET	W 22816	4.7	W 9533	2.9	W 6697	2.8	W 9749	5.1	LARGES PLATS,TOLES
677	IRN,STL WIRE(EXCL W ROD)	W 21503	5.0	W 20501	4.9	W 14431	3.8	W 17458	4.3	FILS EN FER,ACIER
67701	IRON, SIMPLE STEEL WIRE	W 21461	5.0	W 20427	4.9	W 14359	3.8	W 17431	4.3	FILS NON ACIER FIN CARBONE
69	METAL MANUFACTURES NES		22.7		29.8		37.1		42.3	ART MANUFACT EN METAL NDA
692	METAL TANKS,BOXES,ETC	W 2188	2.0	W 3619	2.9	W 4177	6.4	W 4456	7.0	RECIPIENTS METALLIQUES
6924	MTL TRANSPORT BOXES ETC	W 1897	1.8	W 3190	2.7	W 3805	6.1	W 4198	6.6	FUTS,TAMBOURS,BIDONS
69241	STL TRANSPORT BOXES ETC	W 1635	1.5	W 2864	2.2	W 3447	5.6	W 3897	5.8	FUTS,TAMBOURS,BIDONS FER
699	BASE METAL MFRS NES	W 10222	16.7	W 8801	21.3	W 5731	19.6	W 6700	24.9	ART MANUFACTURES MET NDA
6991	LOCKSMITHS WARES,ETC	W 362	0.7	W 271	0.8	W 550	1.7	W 915	7.3	ARTICLES DE SERRURERIE
69911	LOCKS,KEYS AND PARTS	W 172	0.4	W 199	0.6	W 419	1.5	W 741	6.0	SERRURES,VERROUS,CADENAS
6992	IRON,STL CHAIN AND PARTS	W 4173	12.1	W 5337	17.4	W 3902	14.5	W 4221	14.0	CHAINES EN FONTE,FER
7	MACHINES,TRANSPORT EQUIP		189.3		195.9		187.6		175.5	MACHINES MATERIEL TRANSPORT
71	POWER GENERATING EQUIPMT		11.9		6.9		6.1		6.9	MACHINES GENERATRICES
713	INTRNL COMBUS PSTN ENGIN	W 2369	3.8	W 419	1.5	W 329	1.2	W 161	0.9	MOTEURS EXPL COMB INT, PIECE
716	ROTATING ELECTRIC PLANT	W 5826	7.6	W 1038	5.0	W 672	4.0	W 618	3.7	APP ELECTR ROTATIFS,PIECES
7161	DC MOTORS AND GENERATORS	W 4386	4.2	W 495	2.4	W 197	0.8	W 337	1.5	MOTEURS COURANT CONTINU
72	MACHS FOR SPCL INDUSTRYS		12.0		13.0		12.8		13.0	MAC SPECIALES POUR INDUST
721	AGRIC MACHY,EXC TRACTORS	W 6249	5.5	W 3158	4.7	W 2010	4.2	W 1600	3.6	MACHINES AGRICOLES
728	OTH MACHY FOR SPCL INDUS	W 2458	2.5	W 1170	4.5	W 1420	5.8	W 2895	5.9	AUT MACH IND PARTICULIERES
73	METALWORKING MACHINERY		1.5		2.8		6.4		2.5	MACH TRAVAIL DES METAUX
736	METALWORKING MACH–TOOLS	W 855	0.9	W 547	1.4	W 1135	5.3	W 4472	0.9	MACH–OUTILS TRAVAIL METAUX
74	GENRL INDUSTRL MACHY NES		7.7		11.2		10.1		12.4	MACH APP INDUSTRIE
75	OFFICE MACHNES,ADP EQUIP		4.8		4.4		8.5		11.7	MACH BUREAU TRAIT AUTOM
759	OFFICE,ADP MCH PTS,ACCES	W 37	1.3	W 24	1.3	W 82	5.2	W 101	7.0	PIECES DU 751 ET 752
7599	ACCTG,ETC,ADP MCH PTS,AC	W 25	1.2	W 14	1.0	W 81	5.1	W 96	6.6	PIECES DU 751 ET 752
76	TELECOMM,SOUND EQUIPMENT		20.1		17.5		15.5		12.1	EQUIPMENT DE TELECOM
764	TELECOM EQPT,PTS,ACC NES	W 3611	18.7	W 3061	16.5	W 1977	13.1	W 1303	10.4	EQUIP TELECOM,PIECES
7641	LINE TELEPHONE,ETC EQUIP	W 1997	14.8	W 1620	12.3	W 974	8.9	W 368	4.5	APP TELEPHON PAR FIL
77	ELECTRIC MACHNRY NES ETC		34.6		58.1		69.4		84.2	MACH APP ELECT NDA
771	ELECTRIC POWER MACHY NES	W 554	1.4	W 435	7.1	W 266	10.2	W 607	18.4	MACH PROD,TRANS ELECTR
7712	OTH ELEC POWER MACHY NES	W 538	1.4	W 434	7.1	W 265	10.2	W 577	18.3	AUT APP PROD TRANSF ELEC
77129	PTS NES OF MACHY OF 771	W 14	0.3	W 385	6.0	W 254	9.9	W 429	18.1	PIECES MACH DU 771
772	SWITCHGEAR ETC,PARTS NES	W 820	2.9	W 713	4.1	W 463	3.2	W 644	8.4	APP COUPURE,SECT ETC
7721	SWITCHGEAR ETC	W 816	2.9	W 713	4.0	W 462	3.2	W 642	8.3	APP COUPURE,SECTIONMNT
778	ELECTRICAL MACHINERY NES	W 5259	26.5	W 7272	43.4	W 7251	51.6	W 8908	50.6	AUTRES MACH ELECT NDA
7784	ELECTRO–MECH HAND TOOLS	W 3650	20.9	W 4478	30.8	W 4356	35.6	W 3987	30.8	OUTILS ELECTROMEC,PIECES
7788	OTH ELEC MACHY,EQUIP NES	W 664	3.5	W 1755	10.0	W 1659	12.3	W 1920	15.3	AUT MACH APP ELEC NDA
77886	OTH ELEC MACHINERY NES	W 41	0.2	W 5	0.1	W 60	0.6	W 1891	14.9	AUT MACH APP ELECTRIQUES
77889	ELEC PARTS OF MACHY NES	W 577	2.9	W 1740	9.5	W 1584	10.7	W 19	0.2	PIECES ELEC DE MACH NDA
78	ROAD VEHICLES		57.7		49.0		30.6		25.2	VEHICULES ROUTIERS
782	LORRIES,SPCL MTR VEH NES	W 4233	13.3	W 1724	6.1	W 753	3.3	W 817	2.7	VEHICULES SPECIAUX,MARCH
7822	SPECIAL MOTOR VEHCLS NES	W 3424	12.5	W 1429	5.4	W 437	2.9	W 334	1.8	VEHICULES USAGES SPECIAUX
783	ROAD MOTOR VEHICLES NES	W 8620	31.6	W 6568	25.2	W 1926	7.9	W 183	0.7	VEHICULES ROUTIERS NDA
7831	BUSES	W 8538	31.3	W 6518	25.1	W 1820	7.5	W 146	0.7	VOITURES TRANSPORT COMMUN

5. Special Exports F.O.B. by Commodities according to the S.I.T.C. (Rev. 2) in million U.S. Dollars
Exportations Spéciales F.O.B. par Produits d'après la C.T.C.I. (Rév. 2) en millions de Dollars E.U.

SITC CTCI	COMMODITY	1994 QUANTITY QUANTITE	1994 VALUE VALEUR	1995 QUANTITY QUANTITE	1995 VALUE VALEUR	1996 QUANTITY QUANTITE	1996 VALUE VALEUR	1997 QUANTITY QUANTITE	1997 VALUE VALEUR	PRODUIT
784	MOTOR VEH PRTS,ACCES NES	W 1772	6.4	W 1922	8.3	W 1137	8.8	W 1349	12.0	PIECES 722,781,782,783
7849	OTHER MOTOR VEHCL PARTS	W 1663	6.2	W 1817	8.0	W 1065	8.6	W 1281	11.7	PIECES 722,781,782,783
786	TRAILERS,NONMOTR VEH,NES	W 1263	1.2	W 3555	3.3	W 6386	5.7	W 6819	7.3	REMORQUES,CADRES,CONTAIN
79	OTHR TRANSPORT EQUIPMENT		39.6		33.5		28.6		8.0	AUTRE MATERIEL TRANSPORT
791	RAILWAY VEHICLES	W 71789	35.7	W 12143	31.6	W 11521	24.3	W 14433	4.9	VEHIC MAT CHEMINS DE FER
7912	OTH RAIL LOCOMOTIVES ETC	W 45577	7.5	W 17	0.4	W 2631	1.0	W 2532	0.3	AUTRES LOCOMOTIVES
7913	MECHAN–PROPELLED RY CARS	W 17536	23.3	W 7452	25.3	W 3992	18.2	W 224	2.1	AUTOMOTRICES,DRAISINES
7919	RY TRACK FIXT,ETC,PARTS	W 3907	3.4	W 2076	3.1	W 1912	3.4	W 3004	2.3	MATER FIXE VOIES FERREES
79199	PARTS NES OF 7911–7915	W 3791	3.2	W 2044	3.1	W 1228	3.2	W 2017	1.1	PIECES 791.1 ET 5
8	MISC MANUFACTURED GOODS		128.2		155.3		225.9		275.6	ART MANUFACTURES DIVERS
812	*PLUMBG,HEATNG,LGHTNG EQ	W 2066	4.4	W 1474	4.4	W 788	3.3	W 854	2.8	APPAR SANITAIRES CHAUFFAGE
8124	LIGHTING EQUIPMENT NES	W 1949	4.2	W 1289	4.1	W 736	3.1	W 536	1.8	APPAREILS ECLAIRAGE ETC
81242	LAMPS,FITTINGS BASE METL	W 1813	3.9	W 1001	3.5	W 483	2.5	W 138	0.6	APPAREILS D'ECLAIRAGE
821	*FURNITURE,PARTS THEREOF	W 29810	35.6	W 27740	46.9	W 27361	45.0	W 35246	57.5	MEUBLES ET PIECES
8211	CHAIRS,SEATS AND PARTS	W 5152	8.0	W 2048	5.1	W 1391	5.1	W 2667	8.3	SIEGES ET PIECES
82111	CHAIRS AND OTHER SEATS	W 4928	7.7	W 2038	5.0	W 1332	4.8	W 2628	7.8	SIEGES
8219	FURNITURE AND PARTS NES	W 24211	26.7	W 24787	39.9	W 25819	39.4	W 32513	49.1	AUTRES MEUBLES ET PIECES
82192	WOOD FURNITURE NES	W 16208	19.2	W 13449	23.4	W 9523	18.3	W 10476	21.5	MEUBLES NDA EN BOIS
82199	OTHR FURN,FURN PARTS NES	W 7949	7.5	W 11070	16.2	W 16218	20.9	W 21754	26.8	MEUBLES NDA AUTRES MATIERES
84	CLOTHING AND ACCESSORIES		52.9		73.1		127.0		152.9	VETEMENTS
842	MENS OUTERWEAR NOT KNIT	W 1059	7.5	W 1502	10.9	W 1443	21.0	W 1971	30.6	VET DESSUS POUR HOMMES
8423	— TROUSERS,BREECHES ETC	W 226	1.9	W 462	3.7	W 567	8.9	W 607	9.7	PANTALONS HOMMES MAT TEX
8429	— OTHER OUTER GARMENTS	W 430	1.9	W 610	3.4	W 471	6.2	W 831	12.4	AUT VET DES HOM MAT TEX
843	WOMENS OUTERWEAR NONKNIT	W 1092	6.4	W 1167	10.9	W 1975	35.6	W 2455	43.8	VET DESSUS FEMMES MAT TEX
8431	— COATS AND JACKETS	W 103	0.6	W 247	2.3	W 395	6.2	W 494	9.2	MANT,VEST FEM MAT TEXTIL
8433	— DRESSES	W 52	0.4	W 113	1.5	W 312	7.7	W 255	5.4	ROBES EN MAT–TEXTILES
8434	— SKIRTS	W 133	0.7	W 84	0.8	W 246	5.0	W 257	4.4	JUPES EN MAT TEXTILES
8435	— BLOUSES	W 109	0.8	W 100	1.3	W 221	5.0	W 396	7.8	BLOUSES FEM MAT TEXTILES
8439	— OTHER OUTER GARMENTS	W 515	3.4	W 524	4.2	W 712	10.5	W 1014	16.6	AUT VET DES FEM MAT TEXT
845	OUTERWEAR KNIT NONELASTC	W 1921	15.4	W 1265	15.7	W 1420	26.9	W 1402	27.3	VET DESSOUS,ACCES BONNET
8451	— JERSEYS,PULLOVERS ETC	W 377	4.6	W 317	6.2	W 658	12.6	W 823	16.0	CHANDAILS,PULL–OVERS ETC
8452	— WOMENS DRESSES ETC	W 441	5.0	W 261	4.3	W 336	8.4	W 252	6.1	ROBES,JUPES BONNETERIE
8459	— OTHER,CLTHG ACCESRYS	W 1103	5.9	W 686	5.3	W 426	6.0	W 328	5.3	AUT VET DESSUS DE BONNE
846	UNDER GARMENTS KNITTED	W 1323	18.9	W 1479	29.9	W 1760	37.6	W 1901	46.5	SOUS VETS DE BONNETERIE
8462	— OF COTTON NON ELASTIC	W 214	1.5	W 310	3.1	W 486	6.1	W 626	7.7	SOUS–VET BONNET COTON
84629	—— OTHER	W 212	1.4	W 310	3.1	W 486	6.1	W 626	7.7	AUT SOUS–VET BONNET COTON
8463	— OF SYNTH FBR NONELAST	W 744	5.3	W 830	8.4	W 950	9.9	W 954	11.2	SOUS–VET BONNET FIB SYNT
84631	—— PANTY HOSE (TIGHTS)	W 721	5.2	W 816	8.2	W 930	9.6	W 901	10.4	COLLANTS BON FIBR SYNT
8465	CORSETS,GARTERS,ETC	W 364	12.3	W 339	18.4	W 323	21.6	W 321	27.7	CORSETS,GAINES ART SIM
84651	BRASSIERES	W 205	7.7	W 175	9.9	W 206	11.3	W 175	13.5	SOUTIENS–GORGE,BUSTIERS
84652	CORSETS,BRACES ETC	W 159	4.6	W 164	8.5	W 117	10.4	W 146	14.2	CORSETS,GAINES,JARRETEL
847	TEXTILE CLTHNG ACCES NES	W 498	3.1	W 324	3.7	W 324	3.5	W 327	3.0	ACCES VET MAT TEXT NDA
851	*FOOTWEAR	W 3700	16.2	W 1966	7.8	W 2449	7.6	W 1429	9.1	CHAUSSURES
85101	FOOTWEAR RUBBER,PLASTIC	W 2193	3.5	W 1460	2.3	W 1848	2.6	W 921	3.0	CHAUS SEMELLES CAOUTCH
85102	FOOTWEAR LEATHER	W 1281	10.7	W 274	3.2	W 165	1.8	W 246	2.3	CHAUS SEMELLES EN CUIR
89	MISC MANUFCTRD GOODS NES		13.3		18.0		38.2		46.8	ART MANUFACTURES DIVERS
892	PRINTED MATTER	W 1231	1.6	W 784	2.7		8.5	W 2185	16.9	IMPRIMES
8928	PRINTED MATTER NES	W 412	0.9	W 373	1.8		7.1	W 1226	13.8	IMPRIMES NDA
89283	UNISSUED BANKNOTES ETC		0.1		0.1		3.4	W 11	9.2	TIMBRES–POSTE FISCAUX
893	ARTICLES OF PLASTIC NES		3.1		5.5		5.7		8.2	OUVRAGES EN MAT DIVIS 58
894	TOYS,SPORTING GOODS,ETC	W 745	3.0	W 683	3.4	W 775	5.4	W 547	4.6	VOITURES ENFANTS,JOUETS
898	MUSICAL INSTRUMENTS,PTS	W 174	1.2	W 64	1.4		11.9	W 30	10.1	INSTRUMENTS DE MUSIQUE
8983	SOUND RECRDNG TAPE,DISCS	W 110	1.0	W 21	1.3		11.9	W 20	10.0	SUPPORTS SON POUR 763
89832	RECORDED DISCS,TAPES ETC	W 90	0.9	W 12	1.2		11.8	W 5	9.8	DISQUES,PHONO,BANDES
899	OTHER MANUFACTURED GOODS		3.3		4.4		5.9		6.5	AUT ART MANUF DIVERS NDA
8993	COMBUSTIBLE PRODUCTS ETC	W 1933	1.8	W 2969	3.1	W 4105	4.5	W 3968	4.1	BOUGIES,ALLUMETTES ETC
9	GOODS NOT CLASSD BY KIND		27.2		23.1		21.2		11.1	ART TRANSACT NON CLASSES
931	*SPECIAL TRANSACTIONS	W 62616	26.8	W 60807	21.9	W 54221	20.5	W 19906	9.1	TRANS.SPECIALES

1. HISTORICAL SERIES, 1961–1997 GENERAL TRADE, IMPORTS C.I.F., EXPORTS F.O.B.
SERIES HISTORIQUES, 1961–1997 COMMERCE GENERAL, IMPORTATIONS C.A.F., EXPORTATIONS F.O.B

YEAR ANNEE	VALUE IN MILLION U.S. DOLLARS VALEUR EN MILLION U.S. DOLLARS MERCHANDISE –MARCHANDISE IMPORTS	EXPORTS	GOLD –OR IMPORTS	EXPORTS	CONVERSION FACTORS FACTEURS DE CONVERSION CENTS E.U. PAR IMPORTS	EXPORTS	INDEX NUMBERS –INDICES QUANTUM IMPORTS	EXPORTS	UNIT VALUE VALEUR UNITAIRE IMPORTS	EXPORTS
1961	331.71	40.38								
1962	355.93	55.17								
1963	384.73	57.28								
1964	428.24	62.32								
1965	481.72	85.37								
1966	518.20	102.66								
1967	471.03	119.27								
1968	521.14	146.05								
1969	531.98	170.48								
1970	567.44	197.80								
1971	677.06	255.93								
1972	849.28	350.47								
1973	1292.03	618.30								
1975	2330.90	1121.00								
1976	838.30	496.00								
1977	1692.29	394.32								
1978	2049.85	755.00								
1979	2938.72	773.00								
1980	3650.00	868.18								
1981	3499.00	836.36								
1982	3391.00	727.27								
1983	3661.00	690.91								
1984	2948.00	581.82								
1985	2203.00	481.82								
1986	2203.00	500.00								
1987	1879.00	590.91								
1988	2457.09	709.15								
1989	2234.56	485.36								
1990	2524.34	494.04								
1991	3744.37	539.07								
1992	4202.38	560.12								
1993	2215.09	451.67								
1994	2856.22	572.71								
1995	5334.71	732.71								
1996	7568.57	1014.41								
1997	7469.37	717.24								

2. IMPORTS BY BROAD ECONOMIC CATEGORY AND EXPORTS BY INDUSTRIAL ORIGIN. (PERCENTAGE OF TOTAL VALUE)
IMPORTATIONS PAR CATEGORIES ECONOMIQUES ET EXPORTATIONS PAR BRANCHE D'ACTIVITE.(EN POURCENTAGE DE LA VALEUR TOTALE)

IMPORTS – IMPORTATIONS

	1990	1991	1992	1993	1994	1995	1996
TOTAL IMPORTS–IMPORTATIONS TOTALES							
1 FOOD BEV–ALIMENTATION BOISSONS							
11 PRIMARY–PRODUITS DE BASE							
111 FOR INDUSTRY–POUR L'INDUSTRIE							
112 FOR HOUSEHOLDS–POUR LES MENAGES							
12 PROCESSED–PRODUITS ELABORES							
121 FOR INDUSTRY–POUR L'INDUSTRIE							
122 FOR HOUSEHOLDS–POUR LES MENAGES							
2 IND SUPPLIES–APPROV INDUSTRIELS							
21 PRIMARY–PRODUITS DE BASE							
22 PROCESSED–PRODUITS ELABORES							
3 FUELS–COMBUSTIBLES							
31 PRIMARY–PRODUITS DE BASE							
32 PROCESSED–PRODUITS ELABORES							
321 MOTOR SPIRIT–ESSENCE							
322 OTHER–AUTRES							
4 MACHINERY–EQUIPEMENT							
41 CAPITAL EQUIPMENT–MACHINES							
42 PARTS–PIECES ACCESSOIRES							
5 TRANSPORT–TRANSPORT							
51 PASSENGER CARS–AUTOMOBILES							
52 OTHER–AUTRES							
521 INDUSTRIAL–INDUSTRIELS							
522 NON INDUSTRIAL–NON INDUSTRIEL							
53 PARTS–PIECES ACCESSOIRES							
6 CONSUM GOODS–BIENS CONSOMMATION							
61 DURABLE–DURABLES							
62 SEMI DURABLE–SEMI DURABLES							
63 NON DURABLE–NON DURABLES							
7 GOODS NES–BIENS NDA							

EXPORTS – EXPORTATIONS

	1990	1991	1992	1993	1994	1995	1996
TOTAL EXPORTS–EXPORTATIONS TOTALES							
1 AGRICULTURE							
2 MINING QUARRY–INDUS EXTRACTIVES							
3 MANUFACTURING–IND MANUFACTUR							
31 FOOD BEV TOBACCO–ALIM BOISS TAB							
32 TEXTILES–INDUSTRIES TEXTILES							
33 WOOD & PRODUCTS–BOIS & PRODUITS							
34 PAPER & PRODUCTS–PAPIER & PRODT							
35 CHEMICALS–INDUSTRIES CHIMIQUES							
36 NON METAL MIN–MIN NON METAL							
37 BASIC METAL–IND METAL BASE							
38 METAL MANUF–MANUF METAL							
39 OTH MANUF IND–AUTRES MANUF							

3. TRADE BY PRINCIPAL COUNTRIES OF ORIGIN AND DESTINATION (VALUE IN MILLION U.S. DOLLARS)
ECHANGES SELON LES PRINCIPAUX PAYS D'ORIGINE ET DE DESTINATION (VALEUR EN MILLIONS DE DOLLARS EU)

COUNTRIES–PAYS	GENERAL IMPORTS C.I.F. IMPORTATIONS GENERALES C.A.F					COUNTRIES–PAYS	GENERAL EXPORTS F.O.B. EXPORTATIONS GENERALES F.O.B.				
	1992	1993	1994	1995	1996		1992	1993	1994	1995	1996
World		2215.0	2861.0	7295.3	7570.8	Monde		452.0	572.7	826.2	1019.4
Africa			55.5	141.8	133.0	Afrique		70.0	42.0	44.7	50.8
Americas			342.1	911.0	957.9	Amériques			27.5	37.9	38.9
– Northern America			282.7	814.6	881.1	– Amérique du Nord			24.3	35.2	35.0
– LAIA			52.4	96.5	76.8	– ALAI			3.0	2.7	3.8
– CACM			1.6			– MCAC			0.0		
– Caribbean			5.0			– Caraïbes			0.1		
– Rest of America			0.5			– Autre Amérique			0.2		
Asia excl fmr USSR			673.0	1411.6	1509.8	Asie anc. URSS exclus		301.0	355.1	516.5	634.6
– Middle East			281.5	630.1	692.6	– Moyen–Orient		301.0	345.2	504.3	626.4
Asia former USSR			0.6			Asie ancienne URSS			0.7		
Europe excl fmr USSR			1619.5	3714.9	3684.9	Europe anc. URSS exclus			118.6	157.5	193.0
– European Union			1389.7	3322.3	3317.1	– Union Européenne			86.5	130.2	165.4
– Eastern Europe			118.8	59.2	109.4	– Europe de l'Est			17.8	17.9	12.9
– Rest of Europe			111.0	333.4	258.5	– Autre de l'Europe			14.3	9.3	14.8
Europe former USSR			108.2	249.1	279.1	Europe ancienne URSS			14.8	15.4	11.4
Oceania			5.1			Océanie			2.7	3.8	4.1
Other			2.6			Autre			11.2		
Italy/Italie			384.9	945.3	916.1	United Arab Emirates		76.0	102.9	236.9	238.9
USA/Etats–Unis d'Amer			266.9	771.3	825.8	Saudi Arabia		99.0	87.3	91.4	139.1
Germany/Allemagne			288.5	611.0	645.0	Syrian Arab Republic		59.0	63.1	69.2	70.2
France, Monaco			256.7	555.6	589.6	Kuwait/ Koweït			32.3	32.5	77.9
Syrian Arab Republic		284.0	124.7	234.8	308.0	Jordan/Jordanie		32.0	22.9	29.6	50.0
United Kingdom			119.8	284.7	305.2	France, Monaco			26.5	49.5	47.0
Japan/Japon			121.5	287.4	293.0	USA/Etats–Unis d'Amer			20.7	31.0	30.7
Switzerland,Liechtenst.			99.8	333.4	258.5	Egypt/Egypte		18.0	11.9	15.9	16.9
China/Chine			88.9	239.6	220.4	Italy/Italie			11.1	12.2	38.6
Greece/Grèce			69.8	224.4	190.8	Libyan Arab Jamahiriya		24.0	7.2	11.2	13.6
Ukraine			66.2	184.5	190.7	Germany/Allemagne			9.6	18.3	22.9
Turkey/Turquie		110.0	63.1	88.1	173.3	United Kingdom			11.0	13.9	16.0
Spain/Espagne			62.6	144.9	142.2	Turkey/Turquie		5.0	5.1	15.4	12.7
Korea, Republic of			54.9	144.8	134.4	Switzerland,Liechtenst.			13.1	9.3	14.8
Saudi Arabia		47.0	40.0	126.1	112.7	Netherlands/Pays–Bas			9.4	12.4	14.4
Belgium–Luxembourg			52.6	138.0	111.7	Bahrain/Bahreïn		11.0	6.0	6.0	11.3
Netherlands/Pays–Bas			50.0	121.0	114.5	Qatar		12.0	6.3	7.3	6.9
Sweden/Suède			31.3	101.1	93.9	Romania/Roumanie			10.6	12.6	9.2
Brazil/Brésil			40.1	96.5	76.8	Russian Federation			12.1	11.7	7.9
Jordan/Jordanie		28.0	13.5	119.1	35.6	Cyprus/Chypre			12.3	10.8	8.3
Russian Federation			39.4	64.7	88.4	Belgium–Luxembourg			5.9	7.1	11.3
Other Asia n.e.s.			39.7	41.9	91.5	Greece/Grèce			5.7	4.5	7.7
Egypt/Egypte			21.5	63.4	54.7	Bulgaria/Bulgarie			6.3	5.3	3.7
Denmark/Danemark			23.4	58.3	50.2	Algeria/Algérie		14.0	1.3		
Bulgaria/Bulgarie			22.3	59.2	47.7	Oman		2.0	2.7	3.0	6.6
Canada			15.8	43.2	55.3	Japan/Japon			3.7	5.9	4.3
Finland/Finlande			16.1	48.3	47.5	Spain/Espagne			3.6	8.0	2.3
Austria/Autriche			17.0	42.4	52.0	Canada			3.5	4.2	4.4
Romania/Roumanie			45.2		61.6	Australia/Australie			2.6	3.8	4.1
Indonesia/Indonésie		16.0	10.2	30.9	40.8	Ukraine			2.5	3.7	3.5
Libyan Arab Jamahiriya			12.1	37.0	39.3	Morocco/Maroc		5.0	1.9	1.9	0.7
Singapore/Singapour			11.0	32.7	32.2	Bunkers, ship stores			9.2		
Ireland/Irlande			10.4	29.5	30.3	Guinea/Guinée			2.7	3.4	2.5
Cyprus/Chypre			10.9	29.2	28.1	Sudan/Soudan		2.0	1.7	1.9	2.8
United Arab Emirates			5.9	23.8	27.7	Brazil/Brésil			1.8	2.7	3.8
Portugal			6.5	18.0	28.0	Yemen/Yémen		3.0	1.5	1.0	2.9
Sudan/Soudan		11.0	5.7	18.2	15.9	Cote d'Ivoire			1.2	3.0	4.0
Morocco/Maroc		4.0	3.2	8.5	13.1	Sweden/Suède			1.8	2.4	3.1
Malaysia/Malaisie		11.0	13.6			Ghana			1.0	2.4	3.6
Czech Republic			23.6			Iran (Islamic Rep of)		2.0	2.1	1.2	1.6

(VALUE AS PERCENTAGE OF WORLD TOTAL)(VALEURS EN POURCENTAGE DU TOTAL MONDIAL)

	1987	1988	1989	1990	1991	1992	1993	1994	1995	1996		1987	1988	1989	1990	1991	1992	1993	1994	1995	1996
Africa								1.9	1.9	1.8	Afrique							15.5	7.3	5.4	5.0
Americas								12.0	12.5	12.7	Amériques								4.8	4.6	3.8
– Northern America								9.9	11.2	11.6	– Amérique du Nord								4.2	4.3	3.4
– LAIA								1.8	1.3	1.0	– ALAI								0.5	0.3	0.4
– CACM								0.1			– MCAC								0.0		
– Caribbean								0.2			– Caraïbes								0.0		
– Rest of America								0.0			– Autre Amérique								0.0		
Asia excl fmr USSR								23.5	19.3	19.9	Asie anc. URSS exclus							66.6	62.0	62.5	62.2
– Middle East								9.8	8.6	9.1	– Moyen–Orient							66.6	60.3	61.0	61.4
Asia former USSR								0.0			Asie ancienne URSS								0.1		
Europe excl fmr USSR								56.6	50.9	48.7	Europe anc. URSS exclus								20.7	19.1	18.9
– European Union								48.6	45.5	43.8	– Union Européenne								15.1	15.8	16.2
– Eastern Europe								4.2	0.8	1.4	– Europe de l'Est								3.1	2.2	1.3
– Rest of Europe								3.9	4.6	3.4	– Autre de l'Europe								2.5	1.1	1.5
Europe former USSR								3.8	3.4	3.7	Europe ancienne URSS								2.6	1.9	1.1
Oceania								0.2			Océanie								0.5	0.5	0.4
Other								0.1			Autre								2.0		
Italy/Italie								13.5	13.0	12.1	United Arab Emirates							16.8	18.0	28.7	23.4
USA/Etats–Unis d'Amer								9.3	10.6	10.9	Saudi Arabia							21.9	15.2	11.1	13.6
Germany/Allemagne								10.1	8.4	8.5	Syrian Arab Republic							13.1	11.0	8.4	6.9
France, Monaco								9.0	7.6	7.8	Kuwait/ Koweït								5.6	3.9	7.6
Syrian Arab Republic							12.8	4.4	3.2	4.1	Jordan/Jordanie							7.1	4.0	3.6	4.9
United Kingdom								4.2	3.9	4.0	France, Monaco								4.6	6.0	4.6
Japan/Japon								4.2	3.9	3.9	USA/Etats–Unis d'Amer								3.6	3.7	3.0
Switzerland,Liechtenst.								3.5	4.6	3.4	Egypt/Egypte							4.0	2.1	1.9	1.7
China/Chine								3.1	3.3	2.9	Italy/Italie								1.9	1.5	3.8
Greece/Grèce								2.4	3.1	2.5	Libyan Arab Jamahiriya							5.3	1.3	1.4	1.3

4. General Imports C.I.F. by Commodities according to the S.I.T.C. (Rev. 2) in million U.S. Dollars
Importations Générales C.A.F. par Produits d'après la C.T.C.I. (Rév. 2) en millions de Dollars E.U.

SITC CTCI	COMMODITY	1993		1994		1995		1996		PRODUIT
		QUANTITY QUANTITE	VALUE VALEUR	QUANTITY QUANTITE	VALUE VALEUR	QUANTITY QUANTITE	VALUE VALEUR	QUANTITY QUANTITE	VALUE VALEUR	
	ALL COMMODITIES						7295.3		7570.8	TOUS PRODUITS
001	*LIVE ANIMALS FOR FOOD						290.8		385.1	ANIMAUX VIVANTS
1	BEVERAGES AND TOBACCO						573.3		573.6	BOISSONS ET TABACS
3	MINERAL FUELS ETC						642.3		727.1	COMBUSTIBLES MINERAUX LUB
4	ANIMAL,VEGETABLE OIL,FAT						67.1		65.5	HUILES,GRAISSES ANIM,VEG
5	CHEMCLS,RELATED PROD NES						486.8		520.2	PRODUITS CHIMIQUES
61	LEATHER,DRESSED FUR,ETC						26.3		26.8	CUIRS,PELLETERIES
63	WOOD,CORK MANUFACTRS NES						115.1		123.0	OUVRAGES LIEGE ET BOIS
66	NONMETAL MINERAL MFS NES						203.1		185.6	ART MIN NON METALLIQUES
77	ELECTRIC MACHNRY NES ETC						1140.4		1337.6	MACH APP ELECT NDA
78	ROAD VEHICLES						828.7		892.6	VEHICULES ROUTIERS
897	GOLD,SILVER WARE,JEWELRY						367.9		324.2	BIJOUTERIE,ORFEVRERIE
931	*SPECIAL TRANSACTIONS						131.9		159.7	TRANS.SPECIALES

5. General Exports F.O.B. by Commodities according to the S.I.T.C. (Rev. 2) in million U.S. Dollars
Exportations Générales F.O.B. par Produits d'après la C.T.C.I. (Rév. 2) en millions de Dollars E.U.

SITC CTCI	COMMODITY	1993		1994		1995		1996		PRODUIT
		QUANTITY QUANTITE	VALUE VALEUR	QUANTITY QUANTITE	VALUE VALEUR	QUANTITY QUANTITE	VALUE VALEUR	QUANTITY QUANTITE	VALUE VALEUR	
	ALL COMMODITIES						826.3		1019.5	TOUS PRODUITS
001	*LIVE ANIMALS FOR FOOD						5.9		5.6	ANIMAUX VIVANTS
1	BEVERAGES AND TOBACCO						58.8		61.4	BOISSONS ET TABACS
3	MINERAL FUELS ETC						7.6		6.8	COMBUSTIBLES MINERAUX LUB
4	ANIMAL,VEGETABLE OIL,FAT						9.3		17.6	HUILES,GRAISSES ANIM,VEG
5	CHEMCLS,RELATED PROD NES						47.7		34.8	PRODUITS CHIMIQUES
61	LEATHER,DRESSED FUR,ETC						9.2		8.0	CUIRS,PELLETERIES
66	NONMETAL MINERAL MFS NES						32.1		23.2	ART MIN NON METALLIQUES
77	ELECTRIC MACHNRY NES ETC						65.3		78.0	MACH APP ELECT NDA
78	ROAD VEHICLES						29.0		52.2	VEHICULES ROUTIERS
897	GOLD,SILVER WARE,JEWELRY						69.5		81.8	BIJOUTERIE,ORFEVRERIE
931	*SPECIAL TRANSACTIONS						15.5		14.1	TRANS.SPECIALES

1. HISTORICAL SERIES, 1959–1995 GENERAL TRADE, IMPORTS C.I.F., EXPORTS F.O.B.
SERIES HISTORIQUES, 1959–1995 COMMERCE GENERAL, IMPORTATIONS C.A.F., EXPORTATIONS F.O.B

YEAR ANNEE	VALUE IN MILLION LIBYAN DINARS / VALEUR EN MILLION LIBYAN DINARS: MERCHANDISE – MARCHANDISE IMPORTS	MERCHANDISE – MARCHANDISE EXPORTS	GOLD – OR IMPORTS	GOLD – OR EXPORTS	CONVERSION FACTORS U.S. CENTS PER LIBYAN DINAR / FACTEURS DE CONVERSION CENTS E.U. PAR LIBYAN DINAR: IMPORTS	EXPORTS	INDEX NUMBERS – INDICES: QUANTUM IMPORTS	QUANTUM EXPORTS	UNIT VALUE / VALEUR UNITAIRE IMPORTS	UNIT VALUE / VALEUR UNITAIRE EXPORTS
1959	40.60	4.30			280.0000	280.0000				
1960	60.40	4.00			280.0000	280.0000				
1961	53.30	7.90			280.0000	280.0000				
1962	73.40	50.50			280.0000	280.0000				
1963	85.30	119.90			280.0000	280.0000				
1964	104.40	221.40			280.0000	280.0000				
1965	114.40	284.30			280.0000	280.0000				
1966	144.70	360.90			280.0000	280.0000				
1967	170.20	420.00			280.0000	280.0000				
1968	230.20	669.90			280.0000	280.0000				
1969	241.30	773.90			280.0000	280.0000				
1970	198.00	844.90			280.0000	280.0000				
1971	250.40	962.50			282.5560	282.0500				
1972	343.20	968.10			304.0000	304.0000				
1973	539.90	1197.10			335.7970	335.5820				
1974	817.80	2446.20			337.7800	337.7800				
1975	1048.70	2025.10			337.7810	337.7810				
1976	950.80	2830.70			337.7810	337.7810				
1977	1117.10	3381.80			337.7800	337.7800				
1978	1362.60	2933.00			337.7800	337.7800				
1979	1572.40	4761.90			337.7800	337.7800				
1980	2006.20	6489.20			337.7800	337.7800				
1981	2481.40	4611.20			337.7800	337.7800				
1982	2124.30	3908.80			337.7800	337.7800				
1983	1784.80	3616.60			337.7800	337.7800				
1984	1841.70	3300.40			337.7800	337.7800				
1985	1214.40	3645.60			337.7800	337.7800				
1986	1316.00	2432.00			318.6000	318.6000				
1987	1278.00	2372.00			369.5100	369.5100				
1988	1677.00	1907.00			350.5100	350.5100				
1989	1475.00	2407.00			342.2900	342.2900				
1990	1511.00	3745.00			370.5500	370.5500				
1991	1505.00	3154.00			355.8743	355.5068				
1993	1575.90	3248.55			324.2721	324.2368				
1994	1618.28	3456.85			310.5776	310.4849				
1995	1672.48	2996.33			291.1849	290.6220				

2. IMPORTS BY BROAD ECONOMIC CATEGORY AND EXPORTS BY INDUSTRIAL ORIGIN. (PERCENTAGE OF TOTAL VALUE)
IMPORTATIONS PAR CATEGORIES ECONOMIQUES ET EXPORTATIONS PAR BRANCHE D'ACTIVITE.(EN POURCENTAGE DE LA VALEUR TOTALE)

IMPORTS – IMPORTATIONS

	1989	1990	1991	1992	1993	1994	1995
TOTAL IMPORTS–IMPORTATIONS TOTALES	100.	100.	100.				
1 FOOD BEV–ALIMENTATION BOISSONS	17.7	18.5	19.7				
11 PRIMARY–PRODUITS DE BASE	8.3	7.5	7.6				
111 FOR INDUSTRY–POUR L'INDUSTRIE	6.4	5.7	6.0				
112 FOR HOUSEHOLDS–POUR LES MENAGES	1.9	1.8	1.6				
12 PROCESSED–PRODUITS ELABORES	9.4	11.0	12.1				
121 FOR INDUSTRY–POUR L'INDUSTRIE	2.6	4.7	4.6				
122 FOR HOUSEHOLDS–POUR LES MENAGES	6.8	6.3	7.5				
2 IND SUPPLIES–APPROV INDUSTRIELS	33.0	35.0	33.9				
21 PRIMARY–PRODUITS DE BASE	2.6	3.4	2.3				
22 PROCESSED–PRODUITS ELABORES	30.4	31.7	31.6				
3 FUELS–COMBUSTIBLES	0.3	0.3	0.2				
31 PRIMARY–PRODUITS DE BASE	0.0	0.0	0.0				
32 PROCESSED–PRODUITS ELABORES	0.3	0.2	0.2				
321 MOTOR SPIRIT–ESSENCE	0.0						
322 OTHER–AUTRES	0.3	0.2	0.2				
4 MACHINERY–EQUIPEMENT	24.8	24.6	23.8				
41 CAPITAL EQUIPMENT–MACHINES	18.5	19.5	18.3				
42 PARTS–PIECES ACCESSOIRES	6.3	5.1	5.5				
5 TRANSPORT–TRANSPORT	12.3	12.3	11.5				
51 PASSENGER CARS–AUTOMOBILES	2.2	2.8	2.9				
52 OTHER–AUTRES	3.4	2.8	2.8				
521 INDUSTRIAL–INDUSTRIELS	3.3	2.8	2.7				
522 NON INDUSTRIAL–NON INDUSTRIEL	0.1	0.0	0.1				
53 PARTS–PIECES ACCESSOIRES	6.7	6.7	5.9				
6 CONSUM GOODS–BIENS CONSOMMATION	11.9	9.2	10.7				
61 DURABLE–DURABLES	3.3	3.0	2.5				
62 SEMI DURABLE–SEMI DURABLES	5.6	4.1	5.5				
63 NON DURABLE–NON DURABLES	3.0	2.2	2.7				
7 GOODS NES–BIENS NDA	0.0	0.0	0.0				

EXPORTS – EXPORTATIONS

	1989	1990	1991	1992	1993	1994	1995
TOTAL EXPORTS–EXPORTATIONS TOTALES	100.	100.	100.				
1 AGRICULTURE	0.0	0.4	0.6				
2 MINING QUARRY–INDUS EXTRACTIVES	83.6	83.6	85.9				
3 MANUFACTURING–IND MANUFACTUR	16.4	16.0	13.5				
31 FOOD BEV TOBACCO–ALIM BOISS TAB	0.0	0.2	0.1				
32 TEXTILES–INDUSTRIES TEXTILES		0.0	0.0				
33 WOOD & PRODUCTS–BOIS & PRODUITS							
34 PAPER & PRODUCTS–PAPIER & PRODT		0.0	0.0				
35 CHEMICALS–INDUSTRIES CHIMIQUES	16.4	15.0	12.9				
36 NON METAL MIN–MIN NON METAL		0.2	0.0				
37 BASIC METAL–IND METAL BASE		0.6	0.4				
38 METAL MANUF–MANUF METAL	0.0	0.0	0.0				
39 OTH MANUF IND–AUTRES MANUF		0.0	0.0				

3. TRADE BY PRINCIPAL COUNTRIES OF ORIGIN AND DESTINATION (VALUE IN MILLION U.S. DOLLARS)
ECHANGES SELON LES PRINCIPAUX PAYS D'ORIGINE ET DE DESTINATION (VALEUR EN MILLIONS DE DOLLARS EU)

COUNTRIES–PAYS	GENERAL IMPORTS C.I.F. IMPORTATIONS GENERALES C.A.F				
	1991	1992	1993	1994	1995
World	5357.5		5110.2	5026.0	4870.0
Africa	401.7				
Americas	272.0				
– Northern America	132.8				
– LAIA	110.5				
– CACM	0.3				
– Caribbean	28.5				
– Rest of America					
Asia excl fmr USSR	1016.2				
– Middle East	429.9				
Asia former USSR					
Europe excl fmr USSR	3642.6				
– European Union	3355.3				
– Eastern Europe	39.9				
– Rest of Europe	247.4				
Europe former USSR	6.5				
Oceania	18.5				
Other					
Italy/Italie	1160.5				
Turkey/Turquie	340.3		270.0	226.0	262.0
Tunisia/Tunisie	114.6		207.0	174.0	212.0
Germany/Allemagne	701.0				
Morocco/Maroc	191.0		155.0	167.0	133.0
United Kingdom	441.9				
France, Monaco	333.2				
Egypt/Egypte	73.3		65.0	70.0	
Netherlands/Pays–Bas	207.0				
Japan/Japon	178.6				
Korea, Republic of	170.4				
Austria/Autriche	155.2				
Switzerland,Liechtenst.	126.3				
Belgium–Luxembourg	110.5				
Malaysia/Malaisie	3.4		26.0	31.0	30.0
Lebanon/Liban	23.6		26.0	28.0	
Brazil/Brésil	75.0				
USA/Etats–Unis d'Amer	69.6				
Sweden/Suède	69.1				
Malta/Malte	69.1				
Syrian Arab Republic	24.1		21.0	23.0	
Greece/Grèce	65.2				
Canada	63.1				
China/Chine	62.2				
Other Asia n.e.s.	54.0				
Benin/Bénin			16.0	17.0	17.0
Spain/Espagne	47.9				
Former SFR Yugoslavia	45.9				
Thailand/Thaïlande	40.4				
Jordan/Jordanie	12.1		11.0	12.0	
Cuba	28.5				
Ireland/Irlande	25.2				
Algeria/Algérie	8.4		3.0	3.0	9.0
Denmark/Danemark	23.4				
China, Hong Kong SAR	22.5				
Sudan/Soudan	4.7		5.0	6.0	6.0
India/Inde	21.3				
Poland/Pologne	20.2				
Pakistan	1.4		6.0	2.0	9.0
Cyprus/Chypre	16.2				

COUNTRIES–PAYS	GENERAL EXPORTS F.O.B. EXPORTATIONS GENERALES F.O.B.				
	1991	1992	1993	1994	1995
Monde	11211.7		10533.0	10733.0	8708.0
Afrique	392.4				
Amériques	30.1				
– Amérique du Nord	0.0				
– ALAI	30.1				
– MCAC					
– Caraïbes					
– Autre Amérique					
Asie anc. URSS exclus	351.6				
– Moyen–Orient	275.8				
Asie ancienne URSS					
Europe anc. URSS exclus	10437.6				
– Union Européenne	9668.3				
– Europe de l'Est	180.0				
– Autre de l'Europe	589.3				
Europe ancienne URSS					
Océanie					
Autre					
Italy/Italie	4565.2				
Germany/Allemagne	1869.9				
Spain/Espagne	1077.7				
Turkey/Turquie	246.2		120.0	258.0	326.0
France, Monaco	865.3				
Sudan/Soudan	153.0		184.0	188.0	214.0
Greece/Grèce	582.0				
Tunisia/Tunisie	96.1		47.0	111.0	160.0
Former SFR Yugoslavia	347.2				
Belgium–Luxembourg	308.3				
Switzerland,Liechtenst.	215.0				
Morocco/Maroc	122.4		16.0	17.0	47.0
Netherlands/Pays–Bas	194.6				
United Kingdom	144.9				
Egypt/Egypte	19.2		47.0	48.0	
Romania/Roumanie	87.1				
Bulgaria/Bulgarie	84.4				
Jordan/Jordanie	14.7		27.0	28.0	
Indonesia/Indonésie	0.7		13.0	13.0	38.0
Portugal	51.2				
China/Chine	38.5				
Malta/Malte	26.5				
Malaysia/Malaisie			13.0	1.0	8.0
Brazil/Brésil	20.7				
Syrian Arab Republic	3.3		7.0	7.0	
Algeria/Algérie	0.9		2.0	2.0	5.0
Thailand/Thaïlande	9.4				
Korea, Republic of	9.3				
Sweden/Suède	8.4				
Poland/Pologne	8.3				
India/Inde	8.3				
Lebanon/Liban	7.3				
United Arab Emirates	3.3		2.0	2.0	
Singapore/Singapour	6.4				
Argentina/Argentine	4.1				
Mauritania/Mauritanie	0.5		1.0	1.0	1.0
Venezuela	3.2				
Pakistan					3.0
Other Asia n.e.s.	2.9				
Colombia/Colombie	2.1				

(VALUE AS PERCENTAGE OF WORLD TOTAL)(VALEURS EN POURCENTAGE DU TOTAL MONDIAL)

	1986	1987	1988	1989	1990	1991	1992	1993	1994	1995
Africa	1.3	2.3	2.9	2.8	5.3	7.5				
Americas	5.3	2.6	2.7	3.9	5.0	5.1				
– Northern America	4.4	1.7	1.9	2.6	2.3	2.5				
– LAIA	0.6	0.6	0.7	1.2	1.8	2.1				
– CACM	0.0			0.0	0.0	0.0				
– Caribbean	0.3	0.3	0.0	0.1	1.0	0.5				
– Rest of America			0.0		0.0					
Asia excl fmr USSR	18.5	18.6	25.4	17.4	16.6	19.0				
– Middle East	4.1	5.1	5.4	6.2	6.2	8.0				
Asia former USSR										
Europe excl fmr USSR	73.9	75.8	68.8	75.6	72.8	68.0				
– European Union	66.2	64.7	59.1	67.6	65.3	62.6				
– Eastern Europe	2.1	3.3	4.0	3.0	1.1	0.7				
– Rest of Europe	5.6	7.7	5.7	4.9	6.4	4.6				
Europe former USSR	0.1	0.1	0.0	0.0	0.0	0.1				
Oceania	0.8	0.7	0.2	0.3	0.2	0.3				
Other										
Italy/Italie	22.8	23.4	21.4	24.2	18.5	21.7				
Turkey/Turquie	3.7	3.4	3.6	4.8	5.2	6.4		5.3	4.5	5.4
Tunisia/Tunisie	0.1	0.1	0.9	0.9	2.2	2.1		4.1	3.5	4.4
Germany/Allemagne						13.1				
Morocco/Maroc	0.9	1.8	1.6	1.6	2.2	3.6		3.0	3.3	2.7
United Kingdom	10.1	10.0	8.5	8.3	8.4	8.2				
France, Monaco	4.9	5.4	4.7	6.8	7.4	6.2				
Egypt/Egypte		0.0	0.0	0.0	0.7	1.4		1.3	1.4	
Netherlands/Pays–Bas	4.4	2.8	3.3	3.3	5.6	3.9				
Japan/Japon	4.8	5.9	11.7	4.6	4.4	3.3				

	1986	1987	1988	1989	1990	1991	1992	1993	1994	1995
Afrique	1.1	0.6	1.5	1.6	3.3	3.5				
Amériques	0.2	0.1	0.4	0.1	0.1	0.3				
– Amérique du Nord			0.1	0.1	0.0	0.0				
– ALAI	0.0	0.1	0.3	0.0	0.1	0.3				
– MCAC										
– Caraïbes	0.2									
– Autre Amérique										
Asie anc. URSS exclus	7.2	7.6	2.5	3.9	4.2	3.1				
– Moyen–Orient	6.2	5.8	1.3	3.4	4.0	2.5				
Asie ancienne URSS										
Europe anc. URSS exclus	90.1	90.4	94.0	92.8	90.9	93.1				
– Union Européenne	77.2	80.6	88.0	88.4	84.4	86.2				
– Europe de l'Est	9.2	7.5	2.7	2.4	3.5	1.6				
– Autre de l'Europe	3.8	2.2	3.3	2.1	3.0	5.3				
Europe ancienne URSS	1.4	1.2	1.7	1.6	1.5					
Océanie										
Autre										
Italy/Italie	32.8	40.5	41.9	48.6	47.9	40.7				
Germany/Allemagne						16.7				
Spain/Espagne	12.7	7.0	6.7	8.7	9.2	9.6				
Turkey/Turquie	4.5	4.1	1.2	3.2	3.7	2.2		1.1	2.4	3.7
France, Monaco	8.6	9.2	13.1	9.8	8.6	7.7				
Sudan/Soudan	0.4		1.0	0.8	1.1	1.4		1.7	1.8	2.5
Greece/Grèce	5.3	5.2	7.6	5.8	4.4	5.2				
Tunisia/Tunisie	0.0		0.2	0.2	0.5	0.9		0.4	1.0	1.8
Former SFR Yugoslavia	1.8	1.8	2.3	1.8	2.7	3.1				
Belgium–Luxembourg	3.2	5.4	2.6	2.3	2.2	2.7				

4. General Imports C.I.F. by Commodities according to the S.I.T.C. (Rev. 2) in million U.S. Dollars
Importations Générales C.A.F. par Produits d'après la C.T.C.I. (Rév. 2) en millions de Dollars E.U.

SITC CTCI	COMMODITY	1992		1993		1994		1995		PRODUIT
		QUANTITY QUANTITE	VALUE VALEUR	QUANTITY QUANTITE	VALUE VALEUR	QUANTITY QUANTITE	VALUE VALEUR	QUANTITY QUANTITE	VALUE VALEUR	
	ALL COMMODITIES									TOUS PRODUITS

5. General Exports F.O.B. by Commodities according to the S.I.T.C. (Rev. 2) in million U.S. Dollars
Exportations Générales F.O.B. par Produits d'après la C.T.C.I. (Rév. 2) en millions de Dollars E.U.

SITC CTCI	COMMODITY	1992		1993		1994		1995		PRODUIT
		QUANTITY QUANTITE	VALUE VALEUR	QUANTITY QUANTITE	VALUE VALEUR	QUANTITY QUANTITE	VALUE VALEUR	QUANTITY QUANTITE	VALUE VALEUR	
	ALL COMMODITIES									TOUS PRODUITS

1. HISTORICAL SERIES, 1992–1997 GENERAL TRADE, IMPORTS C.I.F., EXPORTS F.O.B.
SERIES HISTORIQUES, 1992–1997 COMMERCE GENERAL, IMPORTATIONS C.A.F., EXPORTATIONS F.O.B

YEAR ANNEE	VALUE IN MILLION U.S. DOLLARS VALEUR EN MILLION U.S. DOLLARS MERCHANDISE –MARCHANDISE IMPORTS	EXPORTS	GOLD –OR IMPORTS	EXPORTS	CONVERSION FACTORS FACTEURS DE CONVERSION CENTS E.U. PAR IMPORTS	EXPORTS	INDEX NUMBERS –INDICES QUANTUM IMPORTS	EXPORTS	UNIT VALUE VALEUR UNITAIRE IMPORTS	EXPORTS
1992	601.90	852.30								
1993	2283.50	2029.12								
1994	2353.25	2028.58								
1995	3648.50	2705.00								
1996	4558.75	3355.00								
1997	5644.25	3860.25								

2. IMPORTS BY BROAD ECONOMIC CATEGORY AND EXPORTS BY INDUSTRIAL ORIGIN. (PERCENTAGE OF TOTAL VALUE)
IMPORTATIONS PAR CATEGORIES ECONOMIQUES ET EXPORTATIONS PAR BRANCHE D'ACTIVITE.(EN POURCENTAGE DE LA VALEUR TOTALE)

IMPORTS – IMPORTATIONS

	1991	1992	1993	1994	1995	1996	1997
TOTAL IMPORTS–IMPORTATIONS TOTALES				100.	100.	100.	100.
1 FOOD BEV–ALIMENTATION BOISSONS				8.5	11.5	10.8	9.1
11 PRIMARY–PRODUITS DE BASE				3.6	4.6	4.4	3.7
111 FOR INDUSTRY–POUR L'INDUSTRIE				0.8	1.3	1.5	1.0
112 FOR HOUSEHOLDS–POUR LES MENAGES				2.8	3.3	2.9	2.7
12 PROCESSED–PRODUITS ELABORES				4.9	6.8	6.4	5.4
121 FOR INDUSTRY–POUR L'INDUSTRIE				1.5	1.0	1.0	0.7
122 FOR HOUSEHOLDS–POUR LES MENAGES				3.5	5.9	5.4	4.7
2 IND SUPPLIES–APPROV INDUSTRIELS				25.7	34.4	31.1	30.9
21 PRIMARY–PRODUITS DE BASE				3.5	6.0	4.1	3.6
22 PROCESSED–PRODUITS ELABORES				22.2	28.5	27.0	27.3
3 FUELS–COMBUSTIBLES				31.4	19.3	17.9	14.2
31 PRIMARY–PRODUITS DE BASE				6.7	13.6	13.4	14.1
32 PROCESSED–PRODUITS ELABORES				24.7	5.7	4.5	0.1
321 MOTOR SPIRIT–ESSENCE				23.7	5.6	4.5	0.1
322 OTHER–AUTRES				1.0	0.0	0.0	0.1
4 MACHINERY–EQUIPEMENT				15.8	12.7	14.1	17.1
41 CAPITAL EQUIPMENT–MACHINES				13.9	11.2	12.3	15.2
42 PARTS–PIECES ACCESSOIRES				1.9	1.5	1.8	1.9
5 TRANSPORT–TRANSPORT				6.7	9.1	11.0	12.7
51 PASSENGER CARS–AUTOMOBILES				1.7	3.9	5.9	6.5
52 OTHER–AUTRES				2.6	2.6	2.4	3.7
521 INDUSTRIAL–INDUSTRIELS				2.6	2.6	2.4	3.6
522 NON INDUSTRIAL–NON INDUSTRIEL				0.0	0.0	0.0	0.0
53 PARTS–PIECES ACCESSOIRES				2.4	2.6	2.7	2.5
6 CONSUM GOODS–BIENS CONSOMMATION				10.7	11.2	12.5	14.5
61 DURABLE–DURABLES				2.2	2.4	3.2	3.6
62 SEMI DURABLE–SEMI DURABLES				3.8	4.1	4.0	4.7
63 NON DURABLE–NON DURABLES				4.8	4.6	5.3	6.3
7 GOODS NES–BIENS NDA				1.1	1.8	2.7	1.4

EXPORTS – EXPORTATIONS

	1991	1992	1993	1994	1995	1996	1997
TOTAL EXPORTS–EXPORTATIONS TOTALES				100.	100.	100.	100.
1 AGRICULTURE				7.0	7.8	4.9	5.6
2 MINING QUARRY–INDUS EXTRACTIVES				2.3	1.0	1.6	2.1
3 MANUFACTURING–IND MANUFACTUR				90.7	91.3	93.5	92.2
31 FOOD BEV TOBACCO–ALIM BOISS TAB				18.6	14.0	13.3	13.7
32 TEXTILES–INDUSTRIES TEXTILES				13.0	15.4	17.0	20.4
33 WOOD & PRODUCTS–BOIS & PRODUITS				2.7	4.3	5.1	5.1
34 PAPER & PRODUCTS–PAPIER & PRODT				1.7	2.0	2.0	2.5
35 CHEMICALS–INDUSTRIES CHIMIQUES				26.8	24.3	25.2	14.4
36 NON METAL MIN–MIN NON METAL				1.7	1.7	1.8	1.8
37 BASIC METAL–IND METAL BASE				3.6	3.4	1.4	1.6
38 METAL MANUF–MANUF METAL				21.2	23.9	24.9	29.8
39 OTH MANUF IND–AUTRES MANUF				1.5	2.2	2.9	2.9

3. TRADE BY PRINCIPAL COUNTRIES OF PURCHASE AND CONSUMPTION (VALUE IN MILLION U.S. DOLLARS)
ECHANGES SELON LES PRINCIPAUX PAYS D'ACHAT ET DE COMSOMMATION (VALEUR EN MILLIONS DE DOLLARS EU)

COUNTRIES–PAYS	GENERAL IMPORTS C.I.F. IMPORTATIONS GENERALES C.A.F				
	1993	1994	1995	1996	1997
World	2274.5	2589.0	3648.6	4558.5	5469.5
Africa	0.9	3.9	6.3	1.1	0.8
Americas	34.7	59.0	123.3	158.7	162.8
– Northern America	31.7	53.8	84.8	133.4	141.9
– LAIA	2.0	4.2	31.5	6.1	5.5
– CACM	0.7	0.4	0.4	0.3	0.2
– Caribbean	0.3	0.4	5.5	17.2	14.2
– Rest of America		0.2	1.2	1.7	1.0
Asia excl fmr USSR	29.3	26.6	58.9	132.7	146.8
– Middle East	17.5	8.7	21.0	30.6	33.9
Asia former USSR	88.3	50.4	116.8	52.9	27.4
Europe excl fmr USSR	620.9	1072.0	1740.1	2492.1	3299.7
– European Union	499.6	828.4	1354.3	1935.7	2609.4
– Eastern Europe	85.7	187.9	288.7	416.5	535.3
– Rest of Europe	35.6	55.6	97.1	139.9	155.0
Europe former USSR	1498.4	1337.9	1534.3	1696.7	1802.2
Oceania	1.4	1.8	2.7	5.5	5.7
Other		37.3	66.1	18.9	24.0
Russian Federation	1220.2	995.2	1076.3	1181.2	1263.7
Germany/Allemagne	219.4	353.9	521.8	720.1	1053.3
Poland/Pologne	49.8	102.5	154.5	231.0	324.0
Denmark/Danemark	55.6	66.6	127.3	172.7	241.6
Ukraine	141.4	128.7	134.2	148.4	109.5
Finland/Finlande	29.1	74.8	120.8	168.3	188.8
Latvia/Lettonie	33.3	69.8	114.8	148.3	178.1
Belarus/Bélarus	75.6	97.9	133.1	108.2	115.4
United Kingdom	21.2	35.9	112.8	178.5	179.4
Netherlands/Pays–Bas	52.0	69.5	94.0	126.0	184.8
Italy/Italie	41.7	70.6	86.3	142.4	175.8
Sweden/Suède	24.9	60.9	103.0	143.4	179.3
USA/Etats–Unis d'Amer	26.8	50.8	69.8	106.9	133.4
France, Monaco	15.9	45.3	59.6	96.6	143.0
Estonia/Estonie	18.1	40.7	65.5	102.0	129.0
Czech Republic	15.6	37.3	61.1	83.1	104.0
Switzerland,Liechtenst.	30.0	30.9	55.8	84.0	93.1
Belgium–Luxembourg	15.0	19.5	54.7	79.4	109.7
Hungary/Hongrie	11.0	21.4	40.5	63.1	67.2
Austria/Autriche	19.4	15.5	36.7	46.1	57.2
Kazakhstan	46.7	16.6	65.6	24.6	15.1
Areas n.e.s.		37.3	66.1	18.9	24.0
Norway,Svalbard and JM	2.9	17.2	31.0	38.8	38.9
Korea, Republic of	1.3	2.4	7.3	51.1	53.9
Spain/Espagne	2.8	6.8	14.0	24.1	41.0
Slovakia/Slovaquie	3.9	14.5	20.1	23.9	25.3
Uzbekistan/Ouzbékistan	10.1	18.8	27.2	17.0	7.6
Ireland/Irlande	0.9	2.1	6.6	30.2	28.9
Turkey/Turquie	16.5	4.0	9.7	12.8	18.3
Canada	4.9	3.1	15.0	26.5	8.5
Bulgaria/Bulgarie	5.0	9.7	11.4	13.4	11.9
Slovenia/Slovénie	2.3	6.3	8.8	11.3	15.5
Tajikistan/Tadjikistan	16.7	7.4	10.1	7.3	0.9
Republic of Moldova	9.7	5.6	10.4	8.6	6.5
Japan/Japon	5.5	5.5	8.9	11.4	8.4
China, Hong Kong SAR	0.3	0.3	4.5	13.4	12.3
Greece/Grèce	1.8	1.3	2.4	2.7	22.2
Portugal		5.7	14.5	5.1	4.5
Ecuador/Equateur	0.8	2.5	20.8	3.1	0.7
United Arab Emirates	0.8	2.1	4.4	9.8	10.1

COUNTRIES–PAYS	GENERAL EXPORTS F.O.B. EXPORTATIONS GENERALES F.O.B.				
	1993	1994	1995	1996	1997
Monde	2024.7	2029.0	2705.7	3356.4	3343.0
Afrique	6.6	22.2	3.6	2.0	9.2
Amériques	13.9	23.8	32.3	43.3	89.2
– Amérique du Nord	9.3	17.8	22.1	33.9	65.2
– ALAI	1.2	4.7	7.5	5.0	7.9
– MCAC	0.0	0.1	0.0	0.1	0.4
– Caraïbes	3.2	1.0	2.4	3.4	11.6
– Autre Amérique	0.2	0.2	0.2	0.9	4.3
Asie anc. URSS exclus	45.3	33.1	56.8	81.2	88.7
– Moyen–Orient	6.3	6.0	27.3	30.2	31.4
Asie ancienne URSS	95.6	104.2	84.6	108.8	94.9
Europe anc. URSS exclus	603.2	772.1	1216.7	1307.6	1406.3
– Union Européenne	398.5	605.9	983.5	1103.4	1227.0
– Europe de l'Est	190.0	144.7	145.3	146.7	119.8
– Autre de l'Europe	14.7	21.5	88.0	57.5	59.5
Europe ancienne URSS	1259.0	1059.1	1310.9	1809.9	1651.3
Océanie	1.0	0.6	0.2	0.6	0.8
Autre		13.9	0.6	3.0	2.7
Russian Federation	670.8	569.0	551.9	806.9	765.7
Germany/Allemagne	137.7	229.2	389.2	430.6	438.6
Belarus/Bélarus	149.1	131.7	291.0	342.0	394.4
Latvia/Lettonie	147.8	170.6	191.2	309.1	224.6
Ukraine	227.3	124.0	202.8	257.1	160.0
Poland/Pologne	141.4	101.5	104.8	106.7	82.2
Netherlands/Pays–Bas	56.7	106.1	132.4	109.2	108.4
United Kingdom	31.7	46.7	84.4	93.3	122.1
Estonia/Estonie	50.9	51.2	60.4	84.1	96.0
Italy/Italie	43.7	38.3	52.4	90.6	117.3
Denmark/Danemark	30.3	35.1	72.0	86.9	102.8
Sweden/Suède	35.5	62.7	68.8	57.8	75.1
France, Monaco	16.8	24.1	45.8	53.3	83.9
Kazakhstan	38.9	42.2	34.2	30.9	43.8
Switzerland,Liechtenst.	9.3	6.9	66.4	37.5	25.9
Belgium–Luxembourg	13.7	15.7	28.4	34.9	51.0
Uzbekistan/Ouzbékistan	16.2	17.3	26.5	45.9	24.7
Finland/Finlande	17.6	19.4	29.1	32.8	28.6
USA/Etats–Unis d'Amer	5.2	12.9	20.2	27.6	59.2
Spain/Espagne	8.4	17.8	22.4	33.3	35.0
Ireland/Irlande	1.0	1.8	30.5	41.4	29.8
Turkey/Turquie	5.0	3.6	25.7	28.0	29.7
Hungary/Hongrie	18.5	17.4	13.6	14.6	9.7
Norway,Svalbard and JM	3.9	12.1	16.6	15.5	17.9
Korea, Republic of	1.6	1.6	14.8	19.6	26.2
Austria/Autriche	4.0	5.6	13.6	17.9	21.3
Republic of Moldova	13.1	12.6	13.5	10.7	10.7
Czech Republic	8.4	12.2	10.0	14.2	15.8
Portugal	0.6	1.8	12.9	19.7	10.6
Azerbaijan/Azerbaïdjan	17.3	9.3	5.2	6.0	7.4
Bulgaria/Bulgarie	12.0	7.6	11.1	7.7	5.4
Turkmenistan/Turkménistn	13.2	11.5	4.3	7.8	3.3
Viet Nam	26.3	6.5	1.2	1.0	0.7
Georgia/Géorgie	1.3	14.4	7.8	7.7	4.5
Japan/Japon	0.7	2.9	2.1	15.5	13.8
Nigeria/Nigéria	2.4	20.7	0.1		0.1
Canada	4.1	4.9	1.9	6.3	6.0
Areas n.e.s.		13.9	0.6	3.0	2.7
Tajikistan/Tadjikistan	4.5	4.3	2.6	2.5	6.1
Romania/Roumanie	6.1	3.8	3.7	1.9	3.9

(VALUE AS PERCENTAGE OF WORLD TOTAL)(VALEURS EN POURCENTAGE DU TOTAL MONDIAL)

	1988	1989	1990	1991	1992	1993	1994	1995	1996	1997
Africa					0.1	0.0	0.2	0.2	0.0	0.0
Americas					2.8	1.5	2.3	3.4	3.5	3.0
– Northern America					2.8	1.4	2.1	2.3	2.9	2.6
– LAIA						0.1	0.2	0.9	0.1	0.1
– CACM						0.0	0.0	0.0	0.0	0.0
– Caribbean					0.0	0.0	0.0	0.1	0.4	0.3
– Rest of America					0.0		0.0	0.0	0.0	0.0
Asia excl fmr USSR					0.4	1.3	1.0	1.6	2.9	2.7
– Middle East					0.3	0.8	0.3	0.6	0.7	0.6
Asia former USSR					7.5	3.9	1.9	3.2	1.2	0.5
Europe excl fmr USSR					11.0	27.3	41.4	47.7	54.7	60.3
– European Union					9.0	22.0	32.0	37.1	42.5	47.7
– Eastern Europe					1.5	3.8	7.3	7.9	9.1	9.8
– Rest of Europe					0.5	1.6	2.1	2.7	3.1	2.8
Europe former USSR					76.3	65.9	51.7	42.1	37.2	32.9
Oceania					0.0	0.1	0.1	0.1	0.1	0.1
Other							1.4	1.8	0.4	0.4
Russian Federation					57.7	53.6	38.4	29.5	25.9	23.1
Germany/Allemagne					4.7	9.6	13.7	14.3	15.8	19.3
Poland/Pologne					1.1	2.2	4.0	4.2	5.1	5.9
Denmark/Danemark					0.2	2.4	2.6	3.5	3.8	4.4
Ukraine					7.7	6.2	5.0	3.7	3.3	2.0
Finland/Finlande					0.9	1.3	2.9	3.3	3.7	3.5
Latvia/Lettonie					2.3	1.5	2.7	3.1	3.3	3.3
Belarus/Bélarus					5.8	3.3	3.8	3.6	2.4	2.1
United Kingdom					0.6	0.9	1.4	3.1	3.9	3.3
Netherlands/Pays–Bas					0.3	2.3	2.7	2.6	2.8	3.4

	1988	1989	1990	1991	1992	1993	1994	1995	1996	1997
Afrique					0.0	0.3	1.1	0.1	0.1	0.3
Amériques					0.6	0.7	1.2	1.2	1.3	2.7
– Amérique du Nord					0.6	0.5	0.9	0.8	1.0	1.9
– ALAI					0.0	0.1	0.2	0.3	0.1	0.2
– MCAC						0.0	0.0	0.0	0.0	0.0
– Caraïbes					0.0	0.2	0.0	0.1	0.1	0.3
– Autre Amérique						0.0	0.0	0.0	0.0	0.1
Asie anc. URSS exclus					1.0	2.2	1.6	2.1	2.4	2.7
– Moyen–Orient					0.7	0.3	0.3	1.0	0.9	0.9
Asie ancienne URSS					6.3	4.7	5.1	3.1	3.2	2.8
Europe anc. URSS exclus					28.4	29.8	38.1	45.0	39.0	42.1
– Union Européenne					21.1	19.7	29.9	36.3	32.9	36.7
– Europe de l'Est					6.3	9.4	7.1	5.4	4.4	3.6
– Autre de l'Europe					1.1	0.7	1.1	3.3	1.7	1.8
Europe ancienne URSS					63.5	62.2	52.2	48.4	53.9	49.4
Océanie					0.0	0.0	0.0	0.0	0.0	0.0
Autre							0.7	0.0	0.1	0.1
Russian Federation					28.3	33.1	28.0	20.4	24.0	22.9
Germany/Allemagne					4.6	6.8	11.3	14.4	12.8	13.1
Belarus/Bélarus					12.1	7.4	6.5	10.8	10.2	11.8
Latvia/Lettonie					4.8	7.3	8.4	7.1	9.2	6.7
Ukraine					15.6	11.2	6.1	7.5	7.7	4.8
Poland/Pologne					4.2	7.0	5.0	3.9	3.2	2.5
Netherlands/Pays–Bas					2.3	2.8	5.2	4.9	3.3	3.2
United Kingdom					3.5	1.6	2.3	3.1	2.8	3.7
Estonia/Estonie					1.5	2.5	2.5	2.2	2.5	2.9
Italy/Italie					1.0	2.2	1.9	1.9	2.7	3.5

4. General Imports C.I.F. by Commodities according to the S.I.T.C. (Rev. 2) in million U.S. Dollars
Importations Générales C.A.F. par Produits d'après la C.T.C.I. (Rév. 2) en millions de Dollars E.U.

SITC CTCI	COMMODITY	1994		1995		1996		1997		PRODUIT
		QUANTITY QUANTITE	VALUE VALEUR	QUANTITY QUANTITE	VALUE VALEUR	QUANTITY QUANTITE	VALUE VALEUR	QUANTITY QUANTITE	VALUE VALEUR	
	ALL COMMODITIES		2589.1		3648.6		4558.6		5469.6	TOUS PRODUITS
0	FOOD AND LIVE ANIMALS		168.8		389.0		475.3		463.6	ALIMENTS,ANIMAUX VIVANTS
01	MEAT AND PREPARATIONS		15.6		10.4		16.0		21.0	VIANDES ET PREPARATIONS
011	MEAT FRESH,CHILLD,FROZEN	W 12837	12.9	W 9677	9.7	W 13004	15.8	W 15800	19.5	VIANDES FRAICHES,REF,CONGE
0113	PIG MEAT FRESH,CHLD,FRZN	W 6898	8.4	W 1352	2.1	W 1097	1.6	W 1815	3.3	VIANDE DE PORC
02	DAIRY PRODCTS,BIRDS'EGGS		5.8		61.4		53.1		32.4	PRODUITS LAITIERS,OEUFS
022	MILK AND CREAM	W 5713	3.9	W 45045	53.1	W 42207	52.3	W 23929	29.9	LAIT ET CREME
0224	MILK,CREAM PRESERVED ETC	W 4399	2.4	W 42805	50.7	W 38550	47.9	W 19414	25.4	LAIT,CREME CONS,CONC
02242	MILK DRY,1.5% FAT OR LES	W 3904	1.9	W 41207	48.7	W 37295	46.1	W 17044	22.5	LAIT POUDRE INF 1.5%
03	FISH AND PREPARATIONS		22.3		38.8		67.5		66.9	POISSONS ET PREPARATIONS
034	FISH,FRESH,CHILLED,FROZN		15.6	W 52110	33.1	W 67886	52.5	W 78794	56.5	POISSON FRAIS, REFRIG,CONG
0342	FISH FROZEN,EXCL FILLETS	W 20504	11.0	W 44243	26.1	W 49017	37.0	W 49297	33.5	POISSONS CONGELES
04	CEREALS AND PREPARATIONS		13.3		39.2		65.0		50.8	CEREALES ET PRODUITS
043	BARLEY UNMILLED	W 386	0.1	W 97959	6.8	W 104212	13.9	W 3507	0.6	ORGE NON MONDEE
048	CEREAL ETC PREPARATIONS	W 21697	8.9	W 26918	16.2	W 30725	22.5	W 33944	21.9	PREPTNS A BASE CEREALES
05	VEGETABLES AND FRUIT		51.9		89.2		72.0		85.6	LEGUMES ET FRUITS
054	VEG ETC FRSH,SMPLY PRSVD	W 30702	9.4	W 47576	14.3	W 25379	11.3	W 32863	14.6	LEGUMES FRAIS,CONG,SECS
057	FRUIT,NUTS,FRESH,DRIED		29.9	W 133319	58.7	W 102134	37.9	W 114522	45.9	FRUITS FRAIS OU SECS
0573	BANANA,PLANTAIN,FRSH,DRY	W 22329	11.7	W 91619	36.7	W 53080	15.6	W 47274	14.5	BANANES FRAICHES,SECHEES
058	FRUIT PRESERVED,PREPARED	W 17657	9.4	W 17483	11.2	W 18589	13.7	W 17875	13.0	CONSERVES DE FRUITS
06	SUGAR AND PREPS,HONEY		6.4		28.4		38.6		24.6	SUCRES ET PRODUITS
061	SUGAR AND HONEY	W 11163	1.9	W 44536	14.4	W 82803	24.0	W 33279	9.5	SUCRES ET MIEL
0611	RAW BEET AND CANE SUGAR	W 234	0.1	W 30602	11.0	W 50008	16.9	W 430	0.2	SUCRES BRUTS
062	SUGAR CANDY NON–CHOCLATE	W 2033	4.5	W 4090	14.1	W 4856	14.6	W 7087	15.1	SUCRERIES
07	COFFEE,TEA,COCOA,SPICES		23.1		58.0		69.5		83.4	CAFE,THE,CACAO,EPICES
071	COFFEE AND SUBSTITUTES	W 2541	8.8	W 4750	26.4	W 6218	32.5	W 7691	47.3	CAFE ET SUCCEDANES
0711	COFFEE GREEN,ROASTED,SUB	W 2149	7.0	W 3753	18.8	W 4824	19.3	W 5822	25.7	CAFE TORREFIE OU DECAFEINE
07112	COFFEE ROASTED	W 1580	5.2	W 2741	14.5	W 4094	16.5	W 5540	24.9	CAFE TORREFIE
0712	COFFEE EXTRACTS,ESSENCES	W 392	1.9	W 998	7.7	W 1394	13.3	W 1869	21.6	EXTRAITS DE CAFE
073	CHOCOLATE AND PRODUCTS	W 2192	5.7	W 4501	19.8	W 5202	22.7	W 5607	18.6	CHOCOLAT
081	*FEEDING STUFF FOR ANIML	W 43644	8.2	W 122741	24.5	W 209859	37.7	W 89507	29.2	NOURRITURE POUR ANIMAUX
0813	OILCAKE AND OTH RESIDUES	W 21038	2.7	W 76949	14.6	W 101980	18.8	W 43379	9.3	TOURTEAUX
08131	— OF SOYA BEANS	W 2800	0.8	W 47062	11.6	W 37138	12.3	W 21533	6.8	TOURTEAUX DE SOJA
09	MISC EDIBLE PRODUCTS		21.3		38.8		55.3		68.1	PREP ALIMENTAIRES DIVERSES
091	MARGARINE AND SHORTENING	W 6423	6.8	W 20674	22.2	W 28414	26.9	W 37693	26.5	MARGARINE ET GRAISSES
0914	MARGARINE,EDIBLE FAT NES	W 5012	4.2	W 19975	21.7	W 27416	25.9	W 37075	26.1	MARGARINES,SIMILI SAINDOUX
09141	MARGARINE	W 4190	3.6	W 12624	13.8	W 14654	15.7	W 17025	15.9	MARGARINE
098	EDIBLE PRODCTS,PREPS NES		14.6		16.6		28.4	W 18430	41.6	PREP ALIMENTAIRES NDA
09809	MISC FOOD PREPRTIONS NES	W 3340	7.6	W 3093	10.8	W 5742	18.4	W 7382	27.2	PREP ALIMENTAIRES NDA
1	BEVERAGES AND TOBACCO		43.8		62.3		75.1		106.6	BOISSONS ET TABACS
11	BEVERAGES		22.6		31.7		33.8		42.0	BOISSONS
111	NON–ALCOHL BEVERAGES NES	W 84526	8.4	W 35590	12.0	W 41821	13.6	W 45255	14.1	BOISSONS NON ALCOOLIQUES
112	ALCOHOLIC BEVERAGES	W 17428	14.3	W 33431	19.7	W 25793	20.2	W 25926	28.0	BOISSONS ALCOOLIQUES
1121	WINE OF FRESH GRAPES ETC	W 8142	4.7	W 22487	9.6	W 16461	12.0	W 18268	18.4	VINS DE RAISINS FRAIS
11212	WINE OF FRESH GRAPES	W 7604	4.3	W 22159	9.0	W 15554	10.6	W 17084	16.8	VINS DE MOUTS DE RAISINS
12	TOBACCO AND MANUFACTURES		21.2		30.7		41.4		64.6	TABACS BRUTS FABRIQUES
121	TOBACCO UNMNFCTRD,REFUSE	W 3598	6.1	W 6523	13.1	W 4370	7.3	W 10228	18.6	TABACS BRUTS,DECHETS
1211	TOBACCO,NOT STRIPPED	W 2700	4.5	W 6523	13.1	W 2576	4.5	W 5767	12.2	TABACS NON ECOTES
122	TOBACCO,MANUFACTURED	W 1920	15.2	W 2124	17.7	W 4118	34.2	W 5791	46.1	TABACS FABRIQUES
1222	CIGARETTES	W 1916	15.1	W 1806	16.1	W 2694	27.2	W 3271	32.5	CIGARETTES
2	CRUDE MATERLS,EXCL FUELS		123.8		255.2		225.0		239.4	MAT BRUTES NON COMESTIBLES
21	HIDES,SKINS,FURS UNDRSSD		6.0		20.3		18.1		14.6	CUIRS,PEAUX BRUTS
211	HIDES,SKINS,EXC FURS,RAW	W 7409	5.1	W 14880	13.9	W 9747	11.4	W 7469	10.1	CUIRS ET PEAUX
22	OIL SEEDS,OLEAGINOUS FRT		29.6		8.1		15.7		15.3	GRAINES,FRUITS OLEAGINEUX
223	SEEDS FOR OTH FIXED OILS	W 113436	24.4	W 8802	2.2	W 17060	3.5	W 35538	8.4	GRAINES AUTRES HUILES FIXES
2239	OIL SEED FLOUR AND MEAL	W 110898	23.2	W 8060	1.2	W 14631	2.2	W 33912	7.2	FARINES GRAINES OLEAG
23	RUBBER, CRUDE		1.3		14.1		7.9		12.1	CAOUTCHOUC BRUT
233	RUBBER,SYNTHTIC,RECLAIMD	W 1293	1.3	W 8282	14.0	W 5160	7.9	W 9548	12.1	LATEX CAOUTCH SYNTH REGEN
2331	SYNTHETIC RUBBER ETC	W 1122	1.1	W 8217	13.9	W 4965	7.7	W 9450	12.0	LATEX CAOUTCH SYNTHETIQUE
24	CORK AND WOOD		2.3		3.5		7.1		19.9	LIEGE ET BOIS
26	TEXTILE FIBRES AND WASTE		50.8		82.9		70.0		71.4	FIBRES TEXTILES
263	COTTON	W 19379	23.4	W 22978	39.6	W 15533	23.4	W 13640	24.5	COTON
2631	RAW COTTON,EXCL LINTERS	W 17973	22.2	W 22605	39.1	W 14732	22.2	W 13107	22.9	COTON EN MASSE
266	SYNTHETIC FIBRES TO SPIN	W 6145	8.9	W 10322	18.5		18.0	W 11613	18.3	FIBRES SYNTHETIQUES
2665	DISCN SYNTH FIBRE UNCMBD	W 5879	8.5	W 8621	14.5	W 8209	13.7	W 9912	15.5	DISCONTINUES EN MASSE
268	WOOL(EXC TOPS),ANML HAIR	W 3089	9.4	W 3019	9.9	W 3140	12.9	W 2660	9.4	LAINES ET POILS
27	CRUDE FERTLZR,MINRLS NES		26.1		39.4		53.6		59.5	ENGRAIS MINERAUX BRUTS
271	FERTILIZERS,CRUDE	W 296338	12.9	W 413463	23.4	W 472631	30.4	W 543238	34.6	ENGRAIS BRUTS
2713	NAT CALCM PHOSPHATES ETC	W 295644	12.8	W 412196	23.3	W 468682	30.1	W 539771	34.3	PHOSPHATES DE CALCIUM
27132	— GROUND	W 295644	12.8	W 403540	23.2	W 464688	30.0	W 539771	34.3	PHOSPHATES MOULUS
278	OTHER CRUDE MINERALS	W 180160	8.5	W 172262	7.2	W 255850	11.4	W 293255	13.0	AUTRES MINERAUX BRUTS
28	METALLIFEROUS ORES,SCRAP		0.5		67.5		31.0		20.3	MINERAIS METAL,DECHETS
288	NONFERR METAL SCRAP NES	W 210	0.1	W 39387	59.9	W 21671	22.8	W 12413	11.8	DECHETS NON FERREUX
2882	OTHER BASE MTL SCRAP NES			W 39148	59.8	W 21250	22.8	W 12314	11.8	AUTRES DECHETS
28821	COPPER WASTE AND SCRAP			W 28056	49.1	W 15329	19.2	W 6409	7.1	DECHETS DE CUIVRE
29	CRUDE ANIMAL,VEG MAT NES		6.4		8.8		14.0		18.4	MATIERES BRUTES ANIM,VEGET
3	MINERAL FUELS ETC		818.0		709.4		823.6		787.8	COMBUSTIBLES MINERAUX LUB
32	COAL,COKE AND BRIQUETTES		19.1		12.3		22.1		15.6	HOUILLES,COKES,BRIQUETTES
322	COAL,LIGNITE AND PEAT	W 355238	18.4	W 265778	11.1	W 417065	21.1	W 329469	14.4	HOUILLES,LIGNITES,TOURBE
3222	OTH COAL,NOT AGGLOMERATD	W 319438	13.4	W 216684	9.5	W 341278	18.0	W 314299	13.7	AUTRES HOUILLES
33	PETROLEUM AND PRODUCTS		624.2		506.3		604.3		583.8	PETROLE ET DERIVES
333	CRUDE PETROLEUM	W 911539	8.8	W 3014528	295.9	W 3672207	393.4	W 5033453	569.9	HUILES BRUTES DE PETROLE
334	PETROLEUM PRODUCTS,REFIN	W 6868701	613.3	W 1847820	205.4	W 1646264	203.1	W 1699	4.2	PRODUITS RAFFINES
341	*GAS,NATURAL AND MANUFCT	W 1143032	150.6	W 1868064	190.9	W 1805108	197.3	W 1663950	186.5	GAZ NATUREL,GAZ MANUFACT
3414	PETROLEUM GASES, GASEOUS	W 1088300	144.2	W 1833506	186.5	W 1783589	194.1	W 1632724	181.9	GAZ DE PETROLE GAZEUX
351	*ELECTRIC CURRENT	H 1482100	24.3						2.0	ENERGIE ELECTRIQUE
4	ANIMAL,VEGETABLE OIL,FAT		9.7		18.4		16.8		20.7	HUILES,GRAISSES ANIM,VEG
42	FIXED VEGETABLE OIL,FAT		6.2		15.8		12.4		14.8	HUILES VEGETALES FIXES
423	FIXED VEG OILS,SOFT	W 7897	5.7	W 15374	14.5	W 13964	10.8	W 16747	12.8	HUILES VEGET DOUCES FIXES
5	CHEMCLS,RELATED PROD NES		262.0		442.1		535.0		663.6	PRODUITS CHIMIQUES
51	ORGANIC CHEMICALS		9.5		42.6		52.5		24.2	PROD CHIMIQ ORGANIQUES
512	ALCOHOLS,PHENOLS ETC		1.2		24.8		20.5	W 10918	6.2	PHENOLS,PHENOLS–ALCOOLS
5121	ACYCLIC ALCOHOLS,DERIVS		1.0		24.0		19.7	W 10010	5.4	ALCOOLS ACYCLIQUES
51215	ETHYLENE GLYCOL	W 47	0.1	W 38588	22.4	W 37965	17.8	W 8932	4.8	ETHYLENE–GLYCOL
52	INORGANIC CHEMICALS		31.5		21.8		23.9		24.9	PROD CHIM INORGANIQUES
522	INORG ELEMNTS,OXIDES,ETC		9.6	W 54814	11.3		11.2	W 64864	13.2	ELEMENTS INORGANIQUES
524	RADIOACTIVE ETC MATERIAL		16.2		0.5		0.8		0.7	MATIERES RADIOACTIVES
5241	RADIOACTIVE ELEMENTS ETC		16.0		0.1		0.3		0.3	RADIOELEMENTS,ISOTOPES
53	DYES,TANNING,COLOUR PROD		26.7		43.5		54.8		70.5	PROD TEINTURE,COLORANTS
533	PIGMENTS,PAINTS,ETC	W 15201	20.8	W 20573	36.9	W 26658	46.8	W 42845	61.9	PIGMENTS,PEINTURES,VERNIS
5334	VARNISHES,DISTEMPERS ETC	W 11107	15.8	W 13076	25.7	W 14535	29.6	W 17685	38.3	PEINTURES A L'EAU

4. General Imports C.I.F. by Commodities according to the S.I.T.C. (Rev. 2) in million U.S. Dollars
Importations Générales C.A.F. par Produits d'après la C.T.C.I. (Rév. 2) en millions de Dollars E.U.

SITC CTCI	COMMODITY	1994 QUANTITY QUANTITE	1994 VALUE VALEUR	1995 QUANTITY QUANTITE	1995 VALUE VALEUR	1996 QUANTITY QUANTITE	1996 VALUE VALEUR	1997 QUANTITY QUANTITE	1997 VALUE VALEUR	PRODUIT
53342	OTH PAINTS,VARNISHES ETC	W 7784	11.4	W 10021	20.7	W 10764	25.2	W 13017	31.4	AUTRES PEINTURES,VERNIS
5335	GLAZES,DRIERS,PUTTY ETC	W 3545	3.3	W 7033	6.0	W 11366	10.3	W 23995	17.7	PREPTNS COLOR UTILISES CERAM
541	*MEDICINAL,PHARM PRODUCT		88.3	MK 9045	109.1	K 7693321	137.2	K 7373286	180.7	PROD MEDICINAUX PHARMACEUT
5417	MEDICAMENTS	K 4155122	73.7	K 5103477	90.9	K 5978069	114.7	K 5976515	160.7	MEDICAMENTS
54171	— CONTAINNG ANTIBIOTICS	K 1629935	29.1	K 1041325	24.8	K 823335	22.0	K 509712	13.2	MED CONTN ANTIBIOTIQUES
54172	— CONTAINING HORMONES	K 675787	12.7	K 454069	10.1	K 559929	12.1	K 282156	12.1	MED CONTENANT HORMONES
54179	— CONTNG OTH SUBSTANCES	K 1767841	30.9	K 3436456	54.0	K 4384666	78.9	K 5061408	132.9	MED CONT AUT SUBSTANCES
55	PERFUME,CLEANING ETC PRD		26.9		45.3		67.4		110.9	PROD POUR PARFUM,TOILETTE
553	PERFUMERY,COSMETICS,ETC	W 3799	15.9	W 6837	30.4	W 9545	45.7	W 16573	74.8	PRODUITS DE PARFUMERIE
554	SOAP,CLEANSING ETC PREPS	W 8663	10.3	W 11293	13.6	W 17616	19.8	W 32552	33.0	SAVONS,PRODUITS DETERSIFS
5542	WASHING PREPARATIONS ETC	W 7955	8.9	W 10008	11.1	W 15803	15.9	W 26665	22.6	PROD ORG TENSIO–ACT NDA
562	*FERTILIZERS,MANUFACTURE		13.6	W 260848	16.8	W 213248	20.9	W 286956	25.0	ENGRAIS MANUFACTURES
5621	CHEM NITROGENOUS FERTLZR	W 120207	9.2	W 95820	7.1	W 133561	13.6	W 177027	14.1	ENGRAIS AZOTES
58	PLASTIC MATERIALS ETC		41.5		109.5		120.3		155.9	MAT PLAST ARTIFICIELLES
582	PROD OF CONDENSATION ETC	W 8492	7.2	W 7995	13.0	W 10878	14.7	W 18488	16.9	PROD CONDENS,POLYCOND
583	POLYMERIZATION ETC PRODS	W 28102	23.7	W 89250	78.7	W 70539	70.9	W 101153	106.3	PROD POLYMERISATION
5831	POLYETHYLENE	W 13484	6.8	W 63154	44.0	W 46334	31.7	W 64568	44.9	POLYETHYLENE
58311	— IN PRIMARY FORMS	W 11875	5.3	W 60408	41.9	W 44667	28.7	W 62441	41.7	POLYETHYLENE PRIMAIRES
5833	POLYSTYRENE,ITS COPOLYMR	W 6348	6.1	W 14655	14.7	W 9015	10.1	W 7159	9.0	POLYPROPYLENE COPOLYMERES
58331	— IN PRIMARY FORMS	W 6173	5.7	W 14290	13.8	W 8620	9.0	W 6221	7.2	SOUS FORMES PRIMAIRES
5834	POLYVINYL CHLORIDE	W 3518	5.3	W 5362	10.1	W 5478	13.3	W 9670	20.8	CHLORURE DE POLYVINYLE
5839	OTH POLYMRZTION ETC PROD	W 4002	4.5	W 4668	6.8	W 8103	9.9	W 15903	22.7	AUT PROD POLYMER COPOLYM
584	CELLULOSE DERIVATIVS ETC	W 4757	10.6	W 7976	17.9	W 13115	34.5	W 12743	32.6	CEL REGEN NIT ACETATE
5843	CELLULOSE ACETATES	W 4646	10.3	W 7864	17.5	W 12669	32.5	W 12251	30.4	ACETATES DE CELLULOSE
58431	— NON–PLASTICIZED	W 197	0.4	W 469	1.1	W 12458	32.0	W 12250	30.4	ACETAT CELLULOSE NON PLAST
58432	— PLASTICIZED	W 4449	10.0	W 7396	16.5	W 211	0.6	W 1	0.1	ACETAT CELLULOSE PLASTIF
59	CHEMICAL MATERIALS NES		24.2		54.0		57.9		71.3	MAT PROD CHIMIQUES NDA
592	STARCH,INULIN,GLUTEN,ETC	W 8232	7.2	W 18293	31.2	W 19783	25.6	W 30322	25.9	AMIDONS,INUL,GLUT FROM
5922	ALBUMINOID SUBSTAN,GLUES	W 7222	7.0	W 16316	30.2	W 18427	24.9	W 28479	25.0	MAT ALBUMIN,COLLES
59221	CASEIN AND DERIVATVS,ETC	W 2114	2.8	W 8372	24.3	W 5285	15.9	W 4058	12.4	CASEINES,CASEINATES
598	MISCEL CHEM PRODUCTS NES	W 7605	14.1	W 9546	15.6	W 12090	22.3	W 13802	29.3	PROD DIV INDUST CHIM NDA
5989	CHEM PRODUCTS,PREPS NES	W 5821	13.1	W 7452	12.2	W 8976	17.0	W 9974	22.1	PROD PREP CHIMIQUES NDA
6	BASIC MANUFACTURES		390.2		645.7		789.0		996.0	ART MANUFACTURES
61	LEATHER,DRESSED FUR,ETC		5.8		14.2		23.3		23.9	CUIRS,PELLETERIES
613	FUR SKINS TANNED,DRESSED	W 31	1.8	W 122	8.7	W 225	14.0	W 308	16.7	PELLETERIES
62	RUBBER MANUFACTURES NES		15.1		29.4		41.7		54.9	CAOUTCHOUC MANUFACTURE
625	RUBBER TYRES, TUBES ETC	N 917150	10.1	N 1305796	20.7	N 1891196	28.2	W 14818	37.2	PNEUS CAOUTCHOUC VULCANISE
63	WOOD,CORK MANUFACTRS NES		18.0		24.1		28.7		34.9	OUVRAGES LIEGE ET BOIS
634	VENEERS,PLYWOOD,ETC		9.2		16.0		18.6	W 33369	20.3	PLACAGES,CONTRE–PLAQUES
635	WOOD MANUFACTURES NES		8.7	W 6278	7.9		9.8	W 13404	14.0	ART MANUF EN BOIS NDA
6353	BUILDERS WOODWRK,PREFABS	W 4211	7.9	W 3742	7.0	W 5708	7.9	W 4413	11.1	OUVRAGES DE MENUISERIE
64	PAPER,PAPERBOARD AND MFR		45.9		83.7		105.3		138.4	PAPIERS,CARTONS & OUVRAGES
641	PAPER AND PAPERBOARD	W 53114	32.0	W 56591	50.4	W 52295	57.2	W 87811	75.6	PAPIERS ET CARTONS
642	PAPER,ETC,PRECUT,ARTS OF	W 9128	13.9	W 15000	33.3	W 22342	48.2	W 27824	62.8	PAP,CARTONS DECOUPES
6421	PAPER ETC CONTAINERS	W 5877	5.1	W 10156	16.1	W 13697	20.1	W 15193	18.4	BOITES,SACS EMBALLAGES
6428	PAPER ETC ARTICLES NES	W 2107	5.6	W 3006	11.7	W 5731	20.7	W 8812	34.5	OUVRAGES EN PATE A PAPIER
64285	PAPER ETC DIAPERS ETC	W 1444	4.2	W 2327	9.7	W 4200	17.3	W 6913	29.6	SERVIETTES HYGIENIQUES
65	TEXTILE YARN,FABRICS,ETC		105.6		190.8		248.4		320.1	FILS,TISSUS,ARTICLES TEXTILE
651	TEXTILE YARN		28.3	W 9276	50.3	W 12752	54.8	W 13957	63.2	FILS TEXTILES
6513	COTTON YARN	W 3117	8.7	W 2875	9.4	W 3169	11.0	W 2796	10.6	FILS DE COTON
6514	SYN FIB YRN,BULK,MONOFIL	W 4714	11.5	W 3562	15.5	W 4646	22.3	W 6473	30.6	FILS CONT 85% FIB TEXT SYNTH
65141	— TEXTRD,CONT POLYAMIDE	W 3222	6.6	W 1639	8.2	W 2420	13.0	W 3730	18.7	FILS TEXT FIB CONT POLYAMID
6517	REGEN FIBRE YARN,MONOFIL	W 638	2.1	W 381	13.0	W 556	3.3	W 1079	6.1	FILS TEXT ART NON VENTE DT
65171	CONT VISCOSE RAYON YARN	W 398	1.3	W 243	12.6	W 307	2.4	W 632	4.8	FILS RAY,VIS NON VENTE DET
652	COTTON FABRICS,WOVEN	W 2795	12.5	W 4379	22.9	W 3610	27.9	W 6091	38.8	TISSUS DE COTON
6522	WOVEN COTTON BLEACHD,ETC	W 1568	10.0	W 1580	14.7	W 1742	21.2	W 2349	25.8	TISSUS COTON BLANCHIS ETC
65224	BLCHED COTTON FABRIC NES	W 1288	7.2	W 1150	9.5	W 1344	15.2	W 1726	18.5	AUT TIS PLUS 85% COT BLANCHI
653	WOVN MAN–MADE FIB FABRIC	W 2325	27.5	W 4250	50.9	W 7304	73.5	W 10319	92.6	TISSUS FIBRES SYNTH,ARTIF
6534	DISC SYN BLEND FABRC NES	W 747	8.2	W 1198	14.3	W 2745	25.2	W 3810	31.9	TISSUS FIBRES SYNTH DISCONT
654	OTH WOVEN TEXTILE FABRIC		10.4	W 1174	17.6		26.5	W 2585	39.7	TISSUS AUT COTON SYNT,ARTIF
6542	WOVEN WOOL,HAIR NONPILE	W 76	1.6	W 209	4.7	W 591	11.4	W 845	19.2	TIS PLUS 85% LAINE,POILS
655	KNITTED,ETC FABRICS	W 1727	7.4	W 14301	12.4	W 2328	19.1	W 3640	25.6	ETOF BONNETERIE PIECES ETC
6552	OTHER KNIT ETC FAB NONEL	W 1727	7.4	W 14301	12.4	W 2328	19.1	W 3640	25.6	ETOF BON NON ELAS NON SYNT
657	SPECIAL TXTL FABRC,PRODS	W 1739	9.1	W 2914	14.5	W 4213	19.1	W 5907	28.5	TISSUS SPECIAUX
658	TEXTILE ARTICLES NES	W 663	2.5	W 949	7.9		15.0	W 2115	14.6	ART FACONNES MAT TEXTILES
66	NONMETAL MINERAL MFS NES		33.8		51.5		68.3		97.2	ART MIN NON METALLIQUES
661	LIME,CEMENT,BLDG PRODS	W 259394	7.7	W 225767	9.9	W 236873	11.7	W 304846	17.1	CHAUX,CIMENTS MAT CONSTR
662	CLAY,REFRACTORY BLDG PRD		8.3		13.8		15.4	W 45915	22.4	MAT CONST REFRACTAIRES
6624	BRICKS ETC NONREFRACTORY		6.4		12.8		14.5	W 40673	20.3	BRIQUES ETC CERAM NON REFR
66245	GLAZED CERAMIC SETTS ETC		5.5	A 1918	11.0	A 1926	13.1	W 33293	17.1	AUT CARREAUX CERAMIQUE
663	MINERAL MANUFCTURES NES	W 37984	6.2	W 36205	10.7		17.8	W 75446	21.8	ART MIN MANUF NDA
664	GLASS	W 30628	6.5		9.5		12.8	W 24560	20.1	VERRE
67	IRON AND STEEL		96.4		146.3		135.2		160.2	FER ET ACIER
672	IRON,STEEL PRIMARY FORMS	W 33806	5.9	W 234490	44.9	W 21717	6.9	W 10666	4.6	LINGOTS FER,ACIER
6727	IRN,STL COIL FR REROLLNG	W 18557	3.1	W 218860	41.0	W 7651	2.5	W 8260	3.0	EBAUCHES POUR TOLES FER
67271	IRON,SIMPLE STEEL COILS	W 16660	2.6	W 210544	38.6	W 5637	1.7	W 7982	2.4	EBAUCHES NON EN ACIER
673	IRON,STEEL SHAPES ETC	W 55780	43.4	W 58668	17.0	W 70298	25.6	W 75639	25.9	BARRES,PROFIL FER,ACIER
6732	IRON,STEEL BARS ETC	W 19997	36.4	W 24013	6.9	W 25397	9.2	W 23886	8.5	BARRES FER,ACIER
67326	IRN,OTH STL BARS HOTROLD	W 10400	34.0	W 10406	2.7	W 18738	4.7	W 16429	4.4	BARRES PLEINES FER,ACIER
6733	IRON,STEEL PROFILES ETC	W 20722	4.9	W 28982	8.8	W 38930	14.6	W 37700	13.7	PROFILES,PALPLAN FER,ACIER
674	IRN,STL UNIV,PLATE,SHEET	W 54613	16.3	W 139101	53.8	W 116406	61.1	W 128686	66.7	LARGES PLATS,TOLES
6744	IRN,STL HVY PLATE,ROLLED	W 13720	4.3	W 37027	11.2	W 37459	16.0	W 26082	13.0	TOLES LAMINEES PLUS 4.75 MM
67441	— OF IRON OR SIMPLE STL	W 13487	3.8	W 36800	10.1	W 37045	14.2	W 25348	10.4	TOLES NON ACIER FIN CARB
6747	TINNED PLATES,SHEETS	W 5874	2.1	W 22457	14.0	W 24905	16.4	W 24669	16.1	TOLES ETAMEES EN ACIER
6749	OTH IRN,STL PLATES,SHEET	W 10584	3.4	W 16416	8.0	W 14340	11.0	W 31016	17.9	AUTRES TOLES FER,ACIER
67491	— OF IRON OR SIMPLE STL	W 10316	3.1	W 16165	7.4	W 14139	10.5	W 30620	17.5	AUT TOLES AUTRES ACIER FIN
678	IRON,STL TUBES,PIPES,ETC	W 25525	14.8	W 26725	21.6	W 26616	25.5	W 54440	48.2	TUBES,TUYAUX EN FONTE,FER
6783	IRON,STL TUBES,PIPES NES	W 7063	5.6	W 12768	10.5	W 15257	12.8	W 39012	30.4	AUT TUBES,TUYAUX FER,ACIER
68	NON–FERROUS METALS		24.4		37.0		33.6		35.5	METAUX NON FERREUX
682	COPPER EXC CEMENT COPPER	W 4173	10.1	W 3876	10.7	W 3927	11.2		8.5	CUIVRE
684	ALUMINIUM	W 3707	11.3	W 8704	22.1	W 4701	17.4	W 4746	20.4	ALUMINIUM
6842	ALUMINIUM,ALLOYS WORKED	W 2759	10.6	W 3603	15.5	W 3277	15.4	W 3784	18.8	ALUMINIUM,ALLIAGES OUVRE
69	METAL MANUFACTURES NES		45.7		69.2		104.9		131.3	ART MANUFACT EN METAL NDA
691	STRUCTURES AND PARTS NES	W 7281	9.7	W 9274	16.5	W 13476	20.5	W 17704	25.8	CONSTRUCT FER,ACIER,ALU
6911	STRUCTURES,PARTS IRN,STL	W 6665	5.6	W 8601	11.2	W 13002	16.7	W 17012	22.2	CONSTRUCT FER,ACIER,FONTE
697	BASE MTL HOUSEHOLD EQUIP		6.4		11.0		15.3	W 5740	21.9	ART MENAGE MET COMMUNS
699	BASE METAL MFRS NES	W 8546	12.9	W 6704	20.6		32.5	W 13856	43.9	ART MANUFACTURES MET NDA
6991	LOCKSMITHS WARES,ETC	W 3083	5.8	W 1661	9.2	W 2452	15.0	W 3813	20.9	ARTICLES DE SERRURERIE
7	MACHINES,TRANSPORT EQUIP		567.1		791.7		1175.6		1677.7	MACHINES MATERIEL TRANSPORT
71	POWER GENERATING EQUIPMT		19.6		23.7		31.9		116.1	MACHINES GENERATRICES
713	INTRNL COMBUS PSTN ENGIN		8.6		14.9		17.0	W 3900	17.0	MOTEURS EXPL COMB INT, PIECE

4. General Imports C.I.F. by Commodities according to the S.I.T.C. (Rev. 2) in million U.S. Dollars
Importations Générales C.A.F. par Produits d'après la C.T.C.I. (Rév. 2) en millions de Dollars E.U.

SITC CTCI	COMMODITY	1994 QUANTITY QUANTITE	1994 VALUE VALEUR	1995 QUANTITY QUANTITE	1995 VALUE VALEUR	1996 QUANTITY QUANTITE	1996 VALUE VALEUR	1997 QUANTITY QUANTITE	1997 VALUE VALEUR	PRODUIT
718	OTH POWER GENERATG MACHY		0.3		1.2		5.0		81.9	AUTRES MOTEURS PARTIES
7187	NUCLEAR REACTORS,PTS NES					W 32	4.0		81.0	REACTEURS NUCLEAIRES
72	MACHS FOR SPCL INDUSTRYS		122.6		116.0		131.5		161.3	MAC SPECIALES POUR INDUST
721	AGRIC MACHY,EXC TRACTORS		10.4		12.0		16.2	W 8596	24.1	MACHINES AGRICOLES
722	TRACTORS NON–ROAD	N 3259	9.6	N 1759	10.4	N 915	8.7	W 7292	17.6	TRACTEURS
7224	WHEELED TRACTORS NES	N 3256	9.4	N 1743	10.3	N 899	8.5	W 7178	17.5	TRACTEURS A ROUES
724	TEXTILE,LEATHER MACHNRY		25.5		22.4		28.5	W 3565	29.8	MACH POUR INDUSTRIE TEXTILE
7247	TEXTILE MACHINERY NES		8.3		5.8		6.7	W 948	9.2	MACH LAVAGE,TEINTURE TEX
726	PRINTG,BKBINDG MACHY,PTS		8.4		5.7		5.7	W 570	8.9	MACHINES POUR IMPRIMERIE
727	FOOD MACHRY NON–DOMESTIC		13.4		22.9		16.9	W 1789	21.2	MACH INDUSTRIES ALIMENT
7272	OTH FOOD PROC MCHY,PARTS		12.9		21.8		15.7	W 1492	19.6	AUT MACH IND ALIMENTAIRE
72722	INDUS FOOD PROC MACH NES		10.7	N 99162	14.6	N 151952	11.9	W 1144	14.4	MACHINES BOULANGERIE
728	OTH MACHY FOR SPCL INDUS		43.6		37.5		42.9	W 4712	40.7	AUT MACH IND PARTICULIERES
7281	MACH–TOOLS FR SPCL INDUS		20.9		14.0		11.2	W 1516	10.0	MACH–OUTILS SPEC IND PART
72812	MACH–TOOLS TO WORK WOOD		19.2	N 2430	11.4	N 6438	9.3	W 1001	7.9	MACH–OUT POUR TRAVAIL BOIS
7284	MACHY FOR SPCL INDUS NES		19.5		22.8		23.9	W 2229	25.6	MACH SPEC IND PARTICUL.
72848	OTH MCHY WITH INDIV FNCT		5.0	N 11707	11.3	N 4892	3.8	W 763	9.6	AUTRES MACHINES NDA
72849	PTS OF MACHS OF 7284 ETC	W 129	1.2	W 110	3.8	W 932	14.2	W 838	5.2	PIECES DU 728.4 ETC
74	GENRL INDUSTRL MACHY NES		92.7		100.8		148.3		192.7	MACH APP INDUSTRIE
741	HEATING,COOLING EQUIPMNT		50.5		27.3		32.0	W 6100	46.5	MACH CHAUFFAGE,PIECES
7414	NONDOM REFRIG EQUIPT,PTS		8.4		13.6		14.9	W 3938	23.5	MAT PRODUCTION DU FROID
74141	REFRIG EQUIP NONDOMESTIC	N 225103	7.5	N 23556	11.3	N 22515	13.0	W 3164	19.7	REFIG INDUSTRIELS
7416	HEATING,COOLING EQU NES		33.7	N 73724	8.6	N 2988188	9.5	W 1113	11.8	APP CHANGEMENT TEMP
742	PUMPS FOR LIQUIDS ETC		7.6		11.2		17.1	W 1468	22.5	POMPES MOTO–POMPES
743	PUMPS NES,CENTRFUGES ETC		9.1		18.0		28.3	W 5260	35.6	POMPES COMPRES,VENT ETC
744	MECHANICAL HANDLING EQU		8.1		14.5		14.6	W 6956	21.2	EQUIP MANUTENTION PIECES
745	NONELEC MACHY,TOOLS NES		10.5		17.1		27.6	W 1602	25.7	AUT MACH NON ELEC,PIECES
7452	OTH NONELEC MCHS,PTS NES		7.7		11.7		23.6	W 1446	20.2	AUT MACH NON ELEC,PIECES
749	NONELEC MACH PTS,ACC NES		7.1		13.0		29.0	W 4943	41.4	PIECES MACH NON ELEC NDA
7492	COCKS,VALVES ETC NES	W 1049	4.2	W 1121	7.6	W 2092	18.0	W 2604	24.4	ART ROB,SIM POUR TUYAUX
75	OFFICE MACHNES,ADP EQUIP		58.9		56.7		72.6		107.6	MACH BUREAU TRAIT AUTOM
751	OFFICE MACHINES		16.2	N 166696	13.7	N 530321	10.1	W 612	14.3	MACH,APPAREILS DE BUREAU
7512	CALCULATNG,ACCTG,ETC MCH		8.1	N 112847	6.2	N 477437	5.1	W 264	5.3	MACHINE A CALCULER ETC
752	AUTOMTIC DATA PROC EQUIP		18.6	N 116294	23.0	N 153799	40.7	W 1563	66.1	MACH TRAIT INFORMATION
7525	ADP PERIPHERAL UNITS		3.0	N 57673	5.5	N 75529	13.9	W 1003	24.1	UNITES PERIPHERIQUES
759	OFFICE,ADP MCH PTS,ACCES	W 535	24.2	W 478	20.1	W 470	21.9	W 577	27.3	PIECES DU 751 ET 752
7599	ACCTG,ETC,ADP MCH PTS,AC	W 429	20.5	W 398	17.2	W 391	18.7	W 453	22.7	PIECES DU 751 ET 752
76	TELECOMM,SOUND EQUIPMENT		44.2		80.5		149.6		204.1	EQUIPMENT DE TELECOM
761	TELEVISION RECEIVERS		2.0	N 66601	14.1	N 201869	37.0	W 4416	40.0	RECEPTEURS DE TELEVISION
7611	COLOUR TV RECEIVERS	N 7694	1.9	N 65732	13.9	N 195118	36.7	W 4399	39.9	RECEPTEURS COULEUR
764	TELECOM EQPT,PTS,ACC NES		35.6		58.2		97.3	W 2390	142.7	EQUIP TELECOM,PIECES
7641	LINE TELEPHONE,ETC EQUIP		8.9	N 131674	16.9	N 220418	24.6	W 700	48.6	APP TELEPHON PAR FIL
7643	TV,RADIO TRANSMITTRS ETC		10.3	N 36275	20.1	N 68406	34.8	W 197	41.6	APP EMET TELE RADIO
7648	TELECOMM EQUIPMENT NES		9.9	N 5020	1.6	N 51823	7.9	W 49	7.3	APP TELECOM NDA
76483	RADAR APPARATUS ETC		8.9	N 2695	0.5	N 32317	4.7	W 12	1.3	APP DE RADIOGUIDAGE ETC
7649	PTS NES OF EQUIPMT OF 76	W 206	5.4	W 486	18.7	W 1149	28.0	W 1148	42.0	PIECES DE LA DIV 76
76493	TELECOMM EQUIPMT PTS NES	W 134	2.4	W 376	10.5	W 990	18.7	W 981	26.3	PIECES 761,762,764.3,8
77	ELECTRIC MACHNRY NES ETC		77.1		123.0		188.1		259.1	MACH APP ELECT NDA
772	SWITCHGEAR ETC,PARTS NES	W 1132	9.8	W 1359	11.6		18.3	W 1811	35.5	APP COUPURE,SECT ETC
7721	SWITCHGEAR ETC	W 1096	9.3	W 1341	11.4	W 1063	17.9	W 1798	34.8	APP COUPURE,SECTIONMNT
773	ELECTR DISTRIBUTNG EQUIP	W 6324	15.4	W 7123	38.7	W 7906	51.1	W 12371	58.2	EQUIPMT DISTRIBUTION ELECT
7731	INSULATED WIRE,CABLE ETC	W 5933	14.8	W 6700	37.8	W 7439	49.0	W 11792	54.0	FILS,CABLES ISOLES ELECT
774	ELECTRO–MEDCL,XRAY EQUIP		4.4	N 53583	8.9	N 104585	16.3	W 140	16.7	APPAREILS MEDICAUX
775	HOUSEHOLD TYPE EQUIP NES		13.0		20.8		38.6	W 14849	71.5	MACH,APP USAGE DOMESTQUE
7751	HOUSEHOLD LDRY EQUIP NES		2.7	N 32046	5.8	N 51379	11.0	W 7651	28.7	MACH A LAVER ET SECHOIRS
77511	DOMESTIC WASHING MACHNES	N 53011	2.6	N 31782	5.8	N 51075	10.9	W 7627	28.5	MACH LAVER LINGE MOINS 6 KG
7758	ELECTRO–THERMIC APPL NES		8.3		10.5		18.5	W 4057	24.7	APP ELECTROTHERMIQ NDA
776	TRANSISTORS,VALVES,ETC		13.3		13.6		18.4	W 1096	19.2	LAMPES,TUBES,VALVES
778	ELECTRICAL MACHINERY NES		18.2		25.6		38.3	W 8209	46.3	AUTRES MACH ELECT NDA
78	ROAD VEHICLES		125.0		240.8		405.7		575.9	VEHICULES ROUTIERS
781	PASS MOTOR VEH EXC BUSES	N 37773	43.1	N 117860	141.1	N 204117	268.2	W 109333	356.4	AUTO TRANSPORT PERSONNES
782	LORRIES,SPCL MTR VEH NES		30.1	N 178650	34.3	N 10656	51.4	W 37650	61.4	VEHICULES SPECIAUX,MARCH
7821	LORRIES,TRUCKS		25.6	N 3955	25.2	N 10472	41.6	W 36070	54.9	VEHICULES TRANSP MARCHAND
783	ROAD MOTOR VEHICLES NES		11.4	N 1005	10.7	N 1437	22.9	W 18520	73.8	VEHICULES ROUTIERS NDA
7831	BUSES		6.1	N 405	5.6	N 901	19.2	W 6334	22.5	VOITURES TRANSPORT COMMUN
7832	TRACTORS FOR TR–TRAILERS		5.3	N 600	5.1	N 536	3.8	W 12185	51.3	TRACTEURS ROUTIERS
784	MOTOR VEH PRTS,ACCES NES		20.5		32.8		41.6	W 14181	44.4	PIECES 722,781,782,783
7849	OTHER MOTOR VEHCL PARTS	W 8346	19.5	W 10285	32.1	W 10880	40.1	W 9735	42.7	PIECES 722,781,782,783
786	TRAILERS,NONMOTR VEH,NES		12.5		12.6		12.4	W 19798	28.0	REMORQUES,CADRES,CONTAIN
7861	TRAILERS,TRANSP CONTAINR		8.9	N 47221	9.6	N 12577	8.8	W 14776	21.4	REMORQUES TOUS VEHICULES
78612	OTHER TRAILERS	N 15183	8.1	N 13506	8.9	N 11069	8.4	W 13631	20.9	REMORQUES TRANSP MARCH
79	OTHR TRANSPORT EQUIPMENT		20.7		44.9		35.3		48.7	AUTRE MATERIEL TRANSPORT
791	RAILWAY VEHICLES		14.0		14.8		27.1	W 82994	26.8	VEHIC MAT CHEMINS DE FER
792	AIRCRAFT ETC		5.8		22.8		5.7	W 218	12.2	APP NAVIGATION AERIENNE
7924	AIRCRFT NES OVER 15000KG			N 5	19.3			W 7	0.1	AERODYNES PLUS 15000 KG
8	MISC MANUFACTURED GOODS		176.9		268.4		322.9		440.2	ART MANUFACTURES DIVERS
812	*PLUMBG,HEATNG,LGHTNG EQ		11.9		16.6		22.4	W 9280	30.8	APPAR SANITAIRES CHAUFFAGE
821	*FURNITURE,PARTS THEREOF		17.5		24.8		25.8	W 9937	29.8	MEUBLES ET PIECES
8219	FURNITURE AND PARTS NES		11.9		17.1		17.7	W 7953	19.7	AUTRES MEUBLES ET PIECES
82192	WOOD FURNITURE NES	N 114835	8.4	N 142451	12.4	N 97892	11.9	W 5630	11.7	MEUBLES NDA EN BOIS
84	CLOTHING AND ACCESSORIES		39.8		50.3		47.8		65.1	VETEMENTS
844	UNDER GARMENTS NOT KNIT		14.0		12.0		4.8	W 762	6.4	VETEMENT DESSOUS MAT TEX
8441	— MENS SHIRTS		13.4		11.8		4.5	W 536	5.9	CHEMISES HOMMES MAT TEXT
84412	—— OF SYNTHETIC FIBRES	W 739	12.5	W 521	11.1	W 164	3.6	W 384	4.9	CHEMISES HOMMES FIB SYNT
851	*FOOTWEAR	P 1344176	10.9	P 1539403	12.0	P 2813306	13.9	W 2973	20.4	CHAUSSURES
85102	FOOTWEAR LEATHER	P 834100	7.1	P 1121030	8.8	P 2165809	10.9	W 2016	17.7	CHAUS SEMELLES EN CUIR
87	PRECISION INSTRUMNTS NES		29.0		49.6		55.3		79.7	INSTRUM,APPAR SCIENT NDA
872	MEDICAL INSTRUMENTS NES		5.0		17.4		18.1	W 957	18.1	INSTR,APP MEDIC–CHIR NDA
87202	OTH MEDICAL INSTRUMENTS	MN 185189	3.2	MN 62783	10.6	MN 60038	14.4	W 574	12.3	INSTRUM,APP MEDECINE
873	METERS AND COUNTERS NES		9.7	N 317223	8.4	N 152301	4.7	W 306	6.6	COMPTEURS,INST DE MESURE
8731	GAS SUPPLY METERS ETC	N 495884	9.6	N 310483	7.6	N 148675	4.5	W 303	6.4	COMPTEURS GAZ,LIQ ELECT
874	MEASURNG,CONTROLNG INSTR		13.8		22.6		30.3	W 1152	52.5	INSTRUMENTS DE MESURE
88	PHOTO EQU,OPTICL GDS ETC		12.7		20.5		27.0		32.7	APP,FOURN PHOTO,OP,MONTR
89	MISC MANUFCTRD GOODS NES		54.1		93.0		128.8		178.6	ART MANUFACTURES DIVERS
892	PRINTED MATTER	W 2581	10.0	W 3331	19.1	W 3650	26.4	W 3905	29.1	IMPRIMES
8928	PRINTED MATTER NES	W 1590	6.4	W 2250	11.6	W 2251	14.5	W 2130	16.1	IMPRIMES NDA
893	ARTICLES OF PLASTIC NES		21.0		39.3		54.5		71.8	OUVRAGES EN MAT DIVIS 58
8931	PLSTC PACKG CONTNRS,LIDS	W 3260	6.8	W 7418	16.7	W 9206	23.1	W 11481	26.3	ART TRANSP EMBALLAGE ETC
8939	MISC PLASTIC ARTICLES	W 3206	13.8	W 4629	21.8	W 6646	30.0	W 10951	43.4	ART DIVERS EN MAT DIV 58
89399	OTHR PLASTC ARTICLES NES	W 2893	12.9	W 4054	20.1	W 5356	26.8	W 8358	36.7	AUT OUV MAT DIV 58
894	TOYS,SPORTING GOODS,ETC		7.5		9.4		13.5	W 4359	22.2	VOITURES ENFANTS,JOUETS

4. General Imports C.I.F. by Commodities according to the S.I.T.C. (Rev. 2) in million U.S. Dollars
Importations Générales C.A.F. par Produits d'après la C.T.C.I. (Rév. 2) en millions de Dollars E.U.

SITC CTCI	COMMODITY	1994 QUANTITY QUANTITE	1994 VALUE VALEUR	1995 QUANTITY QUANTITE	1995 VALUE VALEUR	1996 QUANTITY QUANTITE	1996 VALUE VALEUR	1997 QUANTITY QUANTITE	1997 VALUE VALEUR	PRODUIT
899	OTHER MANUFACTURED GOODS		4.9		11.0		16.6		28.5	AUT ART MANUF DIVERS NDA
9	GOODS NOT CLASSD BY KIND		29.1		66.8		120.6		74.4	ART TRANSACT NON CLASSES
931	*SPECIAL TRANSACTIONS		28.8		66.5		120.1		73.4	TRANS.SPECIALES

5. General Exports F.O.B. by Commodities according to the S.I.T.C. (Rev. 2) in million U.S. Dollars
Exportations Générales F.O.B. par Produits d'après la C.T.C.I. (Rév. 2) en millions de Dollars E.U.

SITC CTCI	COMMODITY	1994 QUANTITY QUANTITE	1994 VALUE VALEUR	1995 QUANTITY QUANTITE	1995 VALUE VALEUR	1996 QUANTITY QUANTITE	1996 VALUE VALEUR	1997 QUANTITY QUANTITE	1997 VALUE VALEUR	PRODUIT
	ALL COMMODITIES		2029.1		2705.7		3356.4		3343.1	TOUS PRODUITS
0	FOOD AND LIVE ANIMALS		326.9		452.5		521.6		566.1	ALIMENTS,ANIMAUX VIVANTS
001	*LIVE ANIMALS FOR FOOD	N 982883	26.7	N 569309	6.2	N 414130	3.9	W 4763	5.0	ANIMAUX VIVANTS
0011	BOVINE SPECIES,LIVE	N 129498	21.6	N 10213	2.0	N 1956	0.6	W 995	0.7	ESPECE BOVINE
00119	— OTHR THAN FR BREEDING	N 128933	21.5	N 9181	1.8	N 1780	0.5	W 785	0.5	BOVINS NON REPRODUCTEURS
01	MEAT AND PREPARATIONS		37.4		34.0		30.6		44.4	VIANDES ET PREPARATIONS
011	MEAT FRESH,CHILLD,FROZEN	W 21831	30.4	W 14148	22.1	W 9740	15.0	W 18835	27.3	VIANDES FRAICHES,REF,CONGE
0111	BOVINE MEAT FRESH,FROZEN	W 17229	22.8	W 8268	13.5	W 5375	9.7	W 17051	24.1	VIANDES BOVIN FRAI,REF
01111	BOVINE MEAT WITH BONE IN	W 13901	16.4	W 5657	7.7	W 4126	6.8	W 15487	21.0	VIANDES BOVIN NON DESOSS
01112	BOVINE MEAT BONELESS	W 3328	6.5	W 2612	5.8	W 1249	3.0	W 1564	3.2	VIANDES BOVIN DESOSSEES
014	MEAT PREPD,PRSVD,NES ETC	W 4043	6.9	W 5792	11.9	W 5939	15.3	W 6674	16.7	CONSERVES DE VIANDES
0149	OTH PREPARD,PRESRVD MEAT	W 3317	5.4	W 5222	10.5	W 3881	9.5	W 3486	7.7	AUTRES PREP DE VIANDES
02	DAIRY PRODCTS,BIRDS'EGGS		109.6		167.8		193.8		201.0	PRODUITS LAITIERS,OEUFS
022	MILK AND CREAM	W 87263	68.4	W 83357	104.8	W 79780	101.8	W 88053	105.1	LAIT ET CREME
0224	MILK,CREAM PRESERVED ETC	W 81665	64.4	W 77389	100.8	W 68823	93.7	W 71077	96.1	LAIT,CREME CONS,CONC
02242	MILK DRY,1.5% FAT OR LES	W 67229	52.4	W 59892	84.3	W 57038	77.7	W 47581	66.9	LAIT POUDRE INF 1.5%
02243	MILK DRY,OVER 1.5% FAT	W 10651	8.9	W 7221	5.5	W 2931	5.2	W 5710	10.3	LAIT POUDRE SUP 1.5%
02249	MILK(EX DRY) PRSVD,SWEET	W 3184	2.6	W 9982	10.8	W 8053	10.0	W 16686	17.7	LAIT CONS,CONC SUCRE
023	BUTTER	W 17879	21.8	W 20005	36.0	W 27494	54.2	W 23061	44.0	BEURRE
024	CHEESE AND CURD	W 11991	18.9	W 11661	24.7	W 14170	35.1	W 19594	47.6	FROMAGE ET CAILLEBOTTE
03	FISH AND PREPARATIONS		18.0		39.2		59.6		68.1	POISSONS ET PREPARATIONS
034	FISH,FRESH,CHILLED,FROZN	W 12077	8.9	W 31788	23.2	W 41937	35.5	W 41228	46.2	POISSON FRAIS, REFRIG,CONG
0342	FISH FROZEN,EXCL FILLETS	W 7737	6.0	W 28300	19.5	W 34788	27.8	W 30523	36.6	POISSONS CONGELES
037	FISH ETC PREPD,PRSVD NES	W 5038	6.7	W 5677	8.9	W 8938	13.3	W 10569	17.7	POIS,CRUST,MOL PREPARES
0371	FISH PREPARD,PRESRVD NES	W 4988	6.4	W 5644	8.7	W 8929	13.2	W 10434	17.3	CONSERVES DE POISSONS
04	CEREALS AND PREPARATIONS		14.2		14.8		18.7		39.2	CEREALES ET PRODUITS
041	WHEAT ETC UNMILLED	W 68801	6.0	W 3440	0.4	W 14068	3.1	W 122666	22.2	FROMENT,EPEAUTRE
0412	OTHER WHEAT ETC UNMILLED	W 25701	1.8	W 2978	0.4	W 14068	3.1	W 111131	20.3	AUTRE FROMENT NON MOULU
048	CEREAL ETC PREPARATIONS	W 7719	4.0	W 9619	7.9	W 11528	12.4	W 6301	6.0	PREPTNS A BASE CEREALES
05	VEGETABLES AND FRUIT		46.3		82.1		60.1		47.9	LEGUMES ET FRUITS
054	VEG ETC FRSH,SMPLY PRSVD	W 35187	14.7	W 55836	22.2	W 20241	14.0	W 65713	18.6	LEGUMES FRAIS,CONG,SECS
0545	OTHER FRESH VEGETABLES	W 19631	8.9	W 25349	13.4	W 12628	8.8	W 12775	9.7	AUTRES LEGUMES FRAIS,REF
05459	FRESH VEGETABLES NES	W 16144	7.9	W 24527	13.1	W 11739	8.6	W 12147	9.6	LEGUMES FRAIS,REFRI NDA
057	FRUIT,NUTS,FRESH,DRIED	W 38902	21.4	W 91555	39.0	W 40558	15.7	W 57346	15.2	FRUITS FRAIS OU SECS
0573	BANANA,PLANTAIN,FRSH,DRY	W 21762	10.7	W 60490	26.8	W 27049	8.2	W 22929	7.1	BANANES FRAICHES,SECHEES
058	FRUIT PRESERVED,PREPARED	W 16373	8.8	W 24362	18.4	W 44214	26.9	W 17770	11.8	CONSERVES DE FRUITS
0585	FRUIT OR VEGETABLE JUICE	W 14430	6.7	W 23156	17.0	W 42171	24.9	W 13717	7.1	JUS DE FRUITS
05857	JUICE OF OTHER FRUIT,VEG	W 6360	3.1	W 8159	9.0	W 7944	6.8	W 4185	2.6	JUS AUTRES FRUITS,LEGUMES
06	SUGAR AND PREPS,HONEY		16.0		22.8		30.6		20.0	SUCRES ET PRODUITS
062	SUGAR CANDY NON-CHOCLATE	W 8596	11.3	W 9544	19.5	W 11265	24.6	W 7808	15.9	SUCRERIES
07	COFFEE,TEA,COCOA,SPICES		24.9		48.7		71.5		72.6	CAFE,THE,CACAO,EPICES
071	COFFEE AND SUBSTITUTES	W 547	2.6	W 1709	11.6	W 3344	21.5	W 2627	25.7	CAFE ET SUCCEDANES
0711	COFFEE GREEN,ROASTED,SUB	W 424	2.0	W 1152	6.6	W 2282	10.7	W 1423	7.0	CAFE TORREFIE OU DECAFEINE
0712	COFFEE EXTRACTS,ESSENCES	W 123	0.7	W 557	5.0	W 1062	10.9	W 1204	18.8	EXTRAITS DE CAFE
073	CHOCOLATE AND PRODUCTS	W 9980	21.1	W 12957	35.2	W 16020	46.7	W 17685	41.0	CHOCOLAT
081	*FEEDING STUFF FOR ANIML	W 78707	22.3	W 45427	10.2	W 95962	22.1	W 143386	44.5	NOURRITURE POUR ANIMAUX
0811	HAY, FODDER, GREEN, DRY	W 29706	3.6	W 13880	2.6	W 25105	6.3	W 59107	13.4	FOIN ET FOURRAGE
08112	FODDER ROOTS,HAY,ETC	W 29400	3.6	W 12221	2.4	W 22986	6.0	W 43353	10.6	RACINES FOURRAGERES
0812	BRAN,POLLARD,SHARPS,ETC	W 2383	14.1	W 998	0.2	W 1001	0.1	W 671	0.2	SONS
08121	BRAN, ETC OF MAIZE, RICE	W 528	14.0	W 15	0.1			W 66	0.1	SONS DE MAIS OU DE RIZ
0819	FOOD WASTE AND FEED NES	W 8486	1.4	W 12857	5.2	W 19711	9.6	W 48665	26.9	DECHETS,ALIMENTS NDA
08199	FODDER NES,INCL SWEETNED	W 1988	0.9	W 5753	4.5	W 12003	8.7	W 38500	25.9	PREPARATIONS FOURRAGERES
09	MISC EDIBLE PRODUCTS		12.0		27.1		31.1		24.0	PREP ALIMENTAIRES DIVERSES
091	MARGARINE AND SHORTENING	W 2363	2.0	W 14654	16.6	W 13078	13.9	W 4003	4.4	MARGARINE ET GRAISSES
0914	MARGARINE,EDIBLE FAT NES	W 2215	1.8	W 14378	16.4	W 12612	13.4	W 3924	4.3	MARGARINES,SIMILI SAINDOUX
09141	MARGARINE	W 1833	1.5	W 8652	10.5	W 6633	7.8	W 2838	3.3	MARGARINE
098	EDIBLE PRODCTS,PREPS NES		10.1		10.6		17.3	W 10013	19.6	PREP ALIMENTAIRES NDA
09809	MISC FOOD PREPRTIONS NES	W 12711	6.0	W 5615	5.6	W 4695	10.0	W 4450	13.9	PREP ALIMENTAIRES NDA
1	BEVERAGES AND TOBACCO		122.8		16.5		14.9		27.6	BOISSONS ET TABACS
11	BEVERAGES		81.6		14.0		10.9		14.7	BOISSONS
111	NON-ALCOHL BEVERAGES NES	W 42780	10.4	W 26819	8.7	W 14664	5.1	W 26950	10.6	BOISSONS NON ALCOOLIQUES
11102	FLAVORED WATERS NON-ALCO	W 41304	10.0	W 24372	8.1	W 12768	4.6	W 22019	10.1	LIMONADES,EAUX GAZEUSES
112	ALCOHOLIC BEVERAGES	W 69749	71.3	W 3662	5.3	W 5668	5.9	W 10102	4.1	BOISSONS ALCOOLIQUES
1121	WINE OF FRESH GRAPES ETC	W 15399	14.7	W 296	0.6	W 64	0.2	W 48	0.2	VINS DE RAISINS FRAIS
11212	WINE OF FRESH GRAPES	W 14804	14.3	W 296	0.6	W 64	0.2	W 46	0.1	VINS DE MOUTS DE RAISINS
1123	BEER,ALE,STOUT,PORTER	W 16893	9.3	W 22	0.1	W 2854	1.2	W 9049	2.1	BIERES
1124	DISTILLED ALCOHOLIC BEVS	W 36814	47.0	W 3343	4.8	W 2679	4.5	W 1004	1.9	ALCOOLS,EAUX-DE-VIE
11249	OTH ALCOHOLC BEVS,CMPNDS	W 35440	45.5	W 3319	4.7	W 2549	4.0	W 977	1.8	BOISSONS ALCOOLIQUES NDA
12	TOBACCO AND MANUFACTURES		41.3		2.6		4.0		12.9	TABACS BRUTS FABRIQUES
121	TOBACCO UNMNFCTRD,REFUSE	W 770	1.0	W 1412	1.6	W 2419	3.8	W 5896	12.5	TABACS BRUTS,DECHETS
122	TOBACCO,MANUFACTURED	W 6064	40.3	W 194	1.0	W 30	0.3	W 48	0.5	TABACS FABRIQUES
1222	CIGARETTES	W 6063	40.3	W 146	1.0	W 30	0.3	W 48	0.5	CIGARETTES
2	CRUDE MATERLS,EXCL FUELS		133.0		341.1		284.2		254.4	MAT BRUTES NON COMESTIBLES
21	HIDES,SKINS,FURS UNDRSSD		6.2		11.9		7.4		5.7	CUIRS,PEAUX BRUTS
22	OIL SEEDS,OLEAGINOUS FRT		5.3		7.8		15.9		9.4	GRAINES,FRUITS OLEAGINEUX
222	SEEDS FOR'SOFT'FIXED OIL	W 18127	4.2	W 23773	6.1	W 41180	12.7	W 28489	7.4	GRAINES HUILES FIXES
23	RUBBER, CRUDE		0.4		11.8		11.1		12.6	CAOUTCHOUC BRUT
233	RUBBER,SYNTHTIC,RECLAIMD	W 275	0.4	W 7668	11.8	W 5802	11.1	W 9068	12.6	LATEX CAOUTCH SYNTH REGEN
2331	SYNTHETIC RUBBER ETC	W 275	0.4	W 7650	11.8	W 5742	11.0	W 9067	12.6	LATEX CAOUTCH SYNTHETIQUE
24	CORK AND WOOD		53.6		137.8		143.4		134.1	LIEGE ET BOIS
247	OTH WOOD ROUGH,SQUARED		21.2	W 1231863	53.5	W 677787	23.2	W 602983	21.8	BOIS BRUTS EQUARRIS
2471	SAW-,VENEER-LOGS CONIFER		12.4	W 934930	39.8	W 505834	16.9	W 322717	11.6	CONIFERES POUR SCIAGE,PLACAG
24711	— IN THE ROUGH		12.4	W 934930	39.8	W 505834	16.9	W 322717	11.6	ECORCES OU DEGROSSIS
2472	SAW-,VENEER-LOGS NON-CON		8.9	W 296933	13.8	W 171953	6.3	W 280267	10.3	NON CONIFERES SCIAGE,PLAC
24721	— IN THE ROUGH		8.9	W 296933	13.8	W 171953	6.3	W 280267	10.3	BRUTS ECORCES DEGROSSIS
248	WOOD SHAPED,SLEEPERS		32.3	W 467944	84.2	W 672588	120.2	W 666493	112.0	BOIS SIMPLEMENT TRAVAILLES
2482	LUMBER SHAPED CONIFER	W 685058	27.5	W 436915	77.6	W 613480	106.2	W 557838	92.7	CONIFERES SCIES,RABOTES
24821	LUMBER SAWN ETC CONIFER	W 680821	26.7	W 425657	74.9	W 609283	104.9	W 552302	90.5	CONIFERES SCIES LONGITUD
2483	LUMBER SHAPED NON-CONIFR	W 55964	3.7	W 26535	5.9	W 36487	8.7	W 93977	15.1	NON CONIFERES SCIES,RABOTES
24831	LUMBER SAWN ETC NON-CON	W 54839	3.5	W 25149	5.5	W 35936	8.2	W 92030	14.2	SCIES LONGITUDINALEMENT
251	*PULP AND WASTE PAPER	W 5644	0.6	W 76839	9.3	W 18697	6.2	W 14500	5.7	PATES A PAPIER,DECHETS
26	TEXTILE FIBRES AND WASTE		30.2		38.1		22.6		14.4	FIBRES TEXTILES
263	COTTON	W 18273	22.1	W 16518	25.6	W 7641	12.6	W 1342	1.7	COTON
2631	RAW COTTON,EXCL LINTERS	W 17531	21.6	W 15107	24.7	W 7129	12.2	W 908	1.5	COTON EN MASSE
28	METALLIFEROUS ORES,SCRAP		29.5		118.3		70.4		63.7	MINERAIS METAL,DECHETS
282	IRON AND STEEL SCRAP	W 503726	25.8	W 584090	51.1	W 447898	39.7	W 459301	40.3	FERRAILLES
28202	— OF ALLOY STEEL	W 185560	9.9	W 88079	12.5	W 80580	11.9	W 66498	9.5	FERRAILLES D'ACIERS ALLIES
28209	— OF OTHR IRON OR STEEL	W 280348	13.7	W 443611	34.7	W 358761	27.2	W 388505	30.5	FERRAILLES DE FER
288	NONFERR METAL SCRAP NES	W 1492	0.6	W 42600	66.0	W 29334	28.6	W 29952	21.1	DECHETS NON FERREUX
2882	OTHER BASE MTL SCRAP NES	W 1413	0.5	W 42503	65.9	W 27843	28.3	W 27944	20.9	AUTRES DECHETS
28821	COPPER WASTE AND SCRAP			W 29152	53.5	W 18177	23.6	W 12301	12.4	DECHETS DE CUIVRE

5. General Exports F.O.B. by Commodities according to the S.I.T.C. (Rev. 2) in million U.S. Dollars
Exportations Générales F.O.B. par Produits d'après la C.T.C.I. (Rév. 2) en millions de Dollars E.U.

SITC CTCI	COMMODITY	1994 QUANTITY QUANTITE	1994 VALUE VALEUR	1995 QUANTITY QUANTITE	1995 VALUE VALEUR	1996 QUANTITY QUANTITE	1996 VALUE VALEUR	1997 QUANTITY QUANTITE	1997 VALUE VALEUR	PRODUIT
28823	ALUMINIUM WSTE AND SCRAP	W 1009	0.5	W 11031	10.1	W 6704	3.8	W 12350	7.6	DECHETS D'ALUMINIUM
3	MINERAL FUELS ETC		322.1		308.3		499.4		146.7	COMBUSTIBLES MINERAUX LUB
32	COAL,COKE AND BRIQUETTES		34.2		8.9		10.8		16.1	HOUILLES,COKES,BRIQUETTES
322	COAL,LIGNITE AND PEAT	W 146785	34.2	W 170076	8.9	W 211714	10.8	W 358290	16.1	HOUILLES,LIGNITES,TOURBE
3224	PEAT,NOT AGGLOMERATED	W 137400	33.7	W 168163	8.8	W 206327	10.5	W 240276	9.9	TOURBE
33	PETROLEUM AND PRODUCTS		272.8		236.9		385.6		29.7	PETROLE ET DERIVES
333	CRUDE PETROLEUM	W 1100	0.2	W 7722	0.9	W 122963	18.4	W 201316	27.1	HUILES BRUTES DE PETROLE
334	PETROLEUM PRODUCTS,REFIN	W 6005258	270.4	W 1491938	234.2	W 2118410	365.1	W 234	0.5	PRODUITS RAFFINES
341	*GAS,NATURAL AND MANUFCT	W 3123565	7.3	W 100793	12.6	W 170772	19.7	W 190434	23.8	GAZ NATUREL,GAZ MANUFACT
3413	PETROLM GASES,LIQUEFIED	W 3123500	7.3	W 100792	12.6	W 170772	19.7	W 190434	23.8	GAZ DE PETROLE LIQUEFIE
34131	LIQUEFIED PROPANE,BUTANE	W 3123500	7.3	W 98034	12.2	W 170772	19.7	W 190196	23.8	PROPANE,BUTANE LIQUEFIES
351	*ELECTRIC CURRENT	H 506300	8.1	H 2886900	50.2	H 4550373	83.4		77.2	ENERGIE ELECTRIQUE
4	ANIMAL,VEGETABLE OIL,FAT		7.4		12.2		7.5		4.6	HUILES,GRAISSES ANIM,VEG
42	FIXED VEGETABLE OIL,FAT		6.3		11.4		6.5		3.6	HUILES VEGETALES FIXES
423	FIXED VEG OILS,SOFT	W 7183	6.2	W 9906	11.1	W 6997	6.1	W 3754	3.3	HUILES VEGET DOUCES FIXES
5	CHEMCLS,RELATED PROD NES		257.2		384.3		425.0		414.7	PRODUITS CHIMIQUES
51	ORGANIC CHEMICALS		43.3		53.4		57.3		24.7	PROD CHIMIQ ORGANIQUES
511	HYDROCARBONS NES,DERIVS	W 1068	0.4	W 2401	1.7		12.6	W 3744	2.7	HYDROCARBURES NDA
5112	CYCLIC HYDROCARBONS	W 48	0.1	W 2257	1.7		12.5	W 3665	2.3	HYDROCARBURES CYCLIQUES
51124	XYLENES,CHEMICALLY PURE					W 25431	12.0	W 3475	2.1	XYLENES PURS
512	ALCOHOLS,PHENOLS ETC		33.9		42.4		31.7	W 16269	12.5	PHENOLS,PHENOLS–ALCOOLS
5121	ACYCLIC ALCOHOLS,DERIVS		33.9		41.7		31.0	W 15745	12.0	ALCOOLS ACYCLIQUES
51211	METHYL ALCOHOL(METHANOL)	W 25200	8.8	W 29631	12.5	W 2526	0.6	W 2536	0.6	ALCOOLS METHYLIQUES
51215	ETHYLENE GLYCOL	W 4002	1.6	W 38713	23.6	W 37676	18.6	W 8374	4.5	ETHYLENE–GLYCOL
51216	ETHYL ALC,DENATRD SPIRIT	V 22744	23.6	V 5523	4.0	V 11501	10.7	W 4612	6.7	ALCOOL ETHYLIQUE NON DENAT
52	INORGANIC CHEMICALS		13.2		33.2		29.4		16.8	PROD CHIM INORGANIQUES
522	INORG ELEMNTS,OXIDES,ETC	W 51418	8.0	W 146092	29.7		25.4	W 81577	11.6	ELEMENTS INORGANIQUES
5225	INORGANIC BASES ETC NES	W 49817	7.2	W 144127	21.2	W 163559	24.1	W 78926	10.4	AUTRES BASES OXYDES METAL
52251	AMMONIA,ANHYDROUS ETC	W 47807	7.0	W 140267	20.4	W 162554	23.8	W 78469	10.2	AMMONIAC LIQUEFIE
53	DYES,TANNING,COLOUR PROD		4.3		6.4		9.4		15.0	PROD TEINTURE,COLORANTS
533	PIGMENTS,PAINTS,ETC	W 3804	3.7	W 2887	5.5		8.5	W 12477	13.6	PIGMENTS,PEINTURES,VERNIS
541	*MEDICINAL,PHARM PRODUCT	MK 16292	38.6	K 5910567	52.0	K 4405242	55.3		67.3	PROD MEDICINAUX PHARMACEUT
5417	MEDICAMENTS	K 3445639	31.2	K 3602504	47.0	K 4121451	49.8	K 4414555	60.8	MEDICAMENTS
54171	— CONTAINNG ANTIBIOTICS	K 967518	9.8	K 562797	9.7	K 336010	6.8	K 124254	2.3	MED CONTN ANTIBIOTIQUES
54179	— CONTNG OTH SUBSTANCES	K 2137521	15.9	K 2644835	30.6	K 3447720	37.8	K 4109903	54.3	MED CONT AUT SUBSTANCES
55	PERFUME,CLEANING ETC PRD		8.4		14.8		22.8		47.3	PROD POUR PARFUM,TOILETTE
553	PERFUMERY,COSMETICS,ETC	W 1594	4.6	W 1339	9.1	W 2369	13.7	W 5355	28.6	PRODUITS DE PARFUMERIE
554	SOAP,CLEANSING ETC PREPS	W 4068	3.7	W 4696	5.4	W 7290	8.3	W 13833	18.0	SAVONS,PRODUITS DETERSIFS
5541	SOAPS	W 2571	1.8	W 3241	3.6	W 3300	4.1	W 5608	10.1	SAVONS,PROD TENSIO–ACTIFS
562	*FERTILIZERS,MANUFACTURE	W 723592	90.9	W 906503	120.9	W 1088320	156.8	W 1103443	145.4	ENGRAIS MANUFACTURES
5621	CHEM NITROGENOUS FERTLZR	W 470733	44.0	W 539945	67.8	W 741719	94.2	W 726278	76.7	ENGRAIS AZOTES
56211	AMMONIUM NITRATE	W 299543	22.7	W 222036	23.8	W 241082	32.7	W 323781	35.7	NITRATE D'AMMONIUM
56216	UREA	W 147145	16.6	W 224858	35.0	W 249914	35.6	W 162529	21.3	UREE
56219	CHEM NITROG FERTILZR NES	W 22000	1.9	W 79071	8.0	W 236665	24.9	W 237372	19.7	ENGRAIS AZOTES NDA
5629	FERTILIZERS NES	W 165757	40.1	W 251603	44.4	W 291687	58.2	W 353111	66.6	ENGRAIS NDA
56291	NIT–PHOS–POT FERTLZR NES	W 42208	20.3	W 20645	2.2	W 24377	3.1	W 17532	2.5	ENGRAIS CONT N P K
56292	NITROG–PHOS FERTILZR NES	W 121777	19.8	W 223805	41.5	W 263592	54.8	W 326787	62.4	ENGRAIS NDA CONT N P
58	PLASTIC MATERIALS ETC		19.0		53.6		52.4		62.8	MAT PLAST ARTIFICIELLES
583	POLYMERIZATION ETC PRODS	W 28661	17.1	W 55363	51.1	W 55937	45.9	W 66265	58.8	PROD POLYMERISATION
5831	POLYETHYLENE	W 18452	9.8	W 43614	36.4	W 50056	36.1	W 54095	40.2	POLYETHYLENE
58311	— IN PRIMARY FORMS	W 15625	8.0	W 39515	31.8	W 45065	31.2	W 47424	33.9	POLYETHYLENE PRIMAIRES
5833	POLYSTYRENE,ITS COPOLYMR	W 4641	3.8	W 8460	9.2	W 2528	3.3	W 3747	2.7	POLYPROPYLENE COPOLYMERES
58331	— IN PRIMARY FORMS	W 4637	3.8	W 8443	9.2	W 2465	3.1	W 3698	2.6	SOUS FORMES PRIMAIRES
59	CHEMICAL MATERIALS NES		39.9		50.3		41.7		35.9	MAT PROD CHIMIQUES NDA
592	STARCH,INULIN,GLUTEN,ETC	W 18636	34.1	W 15964	44.7	W 15308	35.8	W 20047	29.9	AMIDONS,INUL,GLUT FROM
5922	ALBUMINOID SUBSTAN,GLUES	W 18600	34.1	W 15482	44.4	W 14961	35.5	W 19864	29.9	MAT ALBUMIN,COLLES
59221	CASEIN AND DERIVATVS,ETC	W 14033	28.5	W 10915	38.1	W 7391	25.3	W 6210	20.1	CASEINES,CASEINATES
6	BASIC MANUFACTURES		315.9		429.3		491.7		574.9	ART MANUFACTURES
61	LEATHER,DRESSED FUR,ETC		17.6		25.8		34.0		35.6	CUIRS,PELLETERIES
611	LEATHER	W 8176	14.5	W 7146	15.6		18.0	W 7364	23.3	CUIRS,PEAUX PREPARES
6113	CALF LEATHER	W 6038	9.9	W 5021	10.1	W 4285	6.9	W 4657	9.4	CUIRS,PEAUX DE VEAUX
6114	LEATHR BOVINE NES,EQUINE	W 186	0.6	W 1022	3.4	W 2373	10.5	W 2531	13.4	CUIRS DE BOVINS
613	FUR SKINS TANNED,DRESSED	W 73	2.5	W 177	9.0	W 175	13.5	W 124	10.5	PELLETERIES
63	WOOD,CORK MANUFACTRS NES		21.9		32.7		50.2		58.0	OUVRAGES LIEGE ET BOIS
634	VENEERS,PLYWOOD,ETC		11.3		13.8		22.1	W 109029	27.4	PLACAGES,CONTRE–PLAQUES
6342	PLYWOOD OF WOOD SHEETS		7.9	V 18334	6.5	V 21483	9.0	W 12981	6.0	BOIS CONTRE–PLAQUES
6343	IMPROVED,RECONSTIT WOOD	W 107392	2.7	W 24403	4.8	W 46554	9.5	W 89172	17.3	BOIS AMELIORES,RECONST
63432	RECONSTITUTED WOOD	W 107048	2.6	W 23642	4.5	W 46495	9.5	W 88824	16.9	BOIS RECONSTITUES
635	WOOD MANUFACTURES NES	W 73321	10.7	W 53587	19.0		28.2	W 69214	30.6	ART MANUF EN BOIS NDA
6353	BUILDERS WOODWRK,PREFABS	W 49154	6.4	W 28824	9.7	W 15852	14.5	W 16273	15.1	OUVRAGES DE MENUISERIE
64	PAPER,PAPERBOARD AND MFR		31.2		38.6		46.0		61.3	PAPIERS,CARTONS & OUVRAGES
641	PAPER AND PAPERBOARD	W 73626	24.3	W 64780	25.7	W 63118	27.9	W 71175	30.0	PAPIERS ET CARTONS
6416	FIBRE BUILDING BOARD	W 56041	9.7	W 44819	10.3	W 42537	11.1	W 39162	10.2	PLAQUES CONSTRUCT EN PATE
64161	HARDBOARD	W 51968	8.5	W 41567	8.9	W 38323	9.1	W 35343	8.0	PLAQUES CONSTR COMPRIMES
642	PAPER,ETC,PRECUT,ARTS OF	W 11355	6.9	W 12060	13.0	W 13259	18.2	W 17605	31.4	PAP,CARTONS DECOUPES
6428	PAPER ETC ARTICLES NES	W 3851	3.1	W 1455	1.6	W 2160	3.9	W 5058	16.8	OUVRAGES EN PATE A PAPIER
64285	PAPER ETC DIAPERS ETC	W 1671	1.6	W 416	0.9	W 630	2.6	W 3120	15.3	SERVIETTES HYGIENIQUES
65	TEXTILE YARN,FABRICS,ETC		114.8		163.4		215.2		255.5	FILS,TISSUS,ARTICLES TEXTILE
651	TEXTILE YARN	W 8769	26.5	W 12125	45.5		74.9	W 18182	77.6	FILS TEXTILES
6516	DISCON SYN FIB BLEND YRN	W 467	1.4	W 2182	8.3	W 3717	13.9	W 3188	12.4	FILS FIBR TEX SYNT DIS MOINS
65168	OTH DISC SYN BLEND YARN	W 457	1.3	W 2140	8.0	W 3435	12.8	W 3065	11.7	FILS TEXT SYNT MELANGE AUT F
6517	REGEN FIBRE YARN,MONOFIL	W 5481	17.0	W 7549	28.7	W 10762	48.5	W 10586	47.0	FILS TEXT ART NON VENTE DT
65171	CONT VISCOSE RAYON YARN	W 3629	12.3	W 7092	27.4	W 10752	48.5	W 10536	46.8	FILS RAY,VIS NON VENTE DET
652	COTTON FABRICS,WOVEN	W 5775	17.8	W 5548	24.0	W 4757	20.7	W 9222	35.4	TISSUS DE COTON
6521	GREY WOVEN COTTON FABRIC	W 2727	6.2	W 3934	13.2	W 3563	12.3	W 8148	28.0	TISSUS COT ECRUS NON MERCER
65214	GREY WOVEN COTTON NES	W 2686	6.1	W 3831	12.7	W 3528	12.1	W 8130	27.9	AUT TISSUS 85% COTON ECRUS
6522	WOVEN COTTON BLEACHD,ETC	W 3049	11.6	W 1614	10.8	W 1194	8.5	W 1074	7.5	TISSUS COTON BLANCHIS ETC
65224	BLCHED COTTON FABRIC NES	W 2672	10.0	W 1298	7.9	W 1007	7.0	W 866	5.6	AUT TIS PLUS 85% COT BLANCHI
653	WOVN MAN–MADE FIB FABRIC	W 2174	11.7	W 3498	29.8	W 5041	46.0	W 5546	48.1	TISSUS FIBRES SYNTH,ARTIF
6534	DISC SYN BLEND FABRC NES	W 279	0.9	W 1595	17.2	W 2234	27.4	W 1899	22.9	TISSUS FIBRES SYNTH DISCONT
65342	DISC SYN FIB–WOOL FABRIC		0.1	W 844	12.9	W 1320	21.2	W 1401	18.5	TISSUS FIB SYNT MEL LAINE
6535	CONT REGN WEAVES NONPILE	W 1558	9.0	W 1445	9.4	W 2034	13.4	W 2767	18.5	TISSUS FIB TEXT ART CONTINU
65356	CONT REG BLEND FABRC NES	W 828	5.0	W 1340	8.4	W 2004	13.2	W 2726	17.9	TIS MOINS 85% TEXT ART CONT
654	OTH WOVEN TEXTILE FABRIC	W 4035	29.1	W 2489	22.2	W 2385	26.2	W 3423	37.9	TISSUS AUT COTON SYNT,ARTIF
6542	WOVEN WOOL,HAIR NONPILE	W 912	7.7	W 850	10.6	W 979	14.1	W 1065	15.5	TIS PLUS 85% LAINE,POILS
65421	WOVN CARD WOOL,FINE HAIR	W 866	7.3	W 840	10.4	W 911	12.9	W 921	12.9	TISSUS 85% LAINE,PLS CARD
6543	WOVEN WOOL ETC FABRC NES	W 1183	10.5	W 548	4.8	W 187	2.2	W 274	4.0	TISSUS LAINE,POILS FINS NDA
65432	WOOL–DISC SYN FIBR FABRC	W 1180	10.5	W 537	4.7	W 186	2.2	W 252	3.7	TISSUS LAINE MEL SYNT DISC
6544	WOVEN FLAX,RAMIE FABRICS	W 1845	10.6	W 1023	6.7	W 1209	10.0	W 1936	17.8	TISSUS DE LIN,RAMIE
657	SPECIAL TXTL FABRC,PRODS		3.6	W 3966	10.7		13.8	W 5702	20.5	TISSUS SPECIAUX
658	TEXTILE ARTICLES NES	W 3505	14.6	W 3235	21.1		25.2	W 3424	26.5	ART FACONNES MAT TEXTILES

5. General Exports F.O.B. by Commodities according to the S.I.T.C. (Rev. 2) in million U.S. Dollars
Exportations Générales F.O.B. par Produits d'après la C.T.C.I. (Rév. 2) en millions de Dollars E.U.

SITC CTCI	COMMODITY	1994 QUANTITY QUANTITE	1994 VALUE VALEUR	1995 QUANTITY QUANTITE	1995 VALUE VALEUR	1996 QUANTITY QUANTITE	1996 VALUE VALEUR	1997 QUANTITY QUANTITE	1997 VALUE VALEUR	PRODUIT
6584	LINENS ETC	W 2113	11.4	W 1985	15.2	W 2061	17.9	W 2163	18.7	LINGE DE MAISON
659	FLOOR COVERINGS,ETC		7.6		5.3		3.6	W 877	2.5	COUVRE-PARQUETS,TAPIS ETC
66	NONMETAL MINERAL MFS NES		33.3		44.7		58.1		59.3	ART MIN NON METALLIQUES
661	LIME,CEMENT,BLDG PRODS	W 452523	13.0	W 313467	11.9	W 422059	16.8	W 469877	19.5	CHAUX,CIMENTS MAT CONSTR
6612	CEMENT	W 435836	12.1	W 290838	10.0	W 402390	14.6	W 453157	16.7	CIMENTS HYDRAULIQUES
663	MINERAL MANUFCTURES NES	W 306000	8.8	W 170867	7.0	W 93686	6.1	W 83372	8.8	ART MIN MANUF NDA
6633	MINRL MFS NES NONCERAMIC	W 302383	7.5	W 168406	5.8	W 90503	4.0	W 77983	4.4	OUVR MAT MINERALE NDA
66332	CEMENT,ARTFCL STONE PROD	W 302193	7.5	W 168046	5.6	W 88952	3.1	W 75891	3.4	OUVRAGES EN CIMENT
664	GLASS	W 6661	2.2		6.6		10.6	W 30554	12.1	VERRE
665	GLASSWARE	W 18246	4.1	W 37890	11.0		17.1	W 19563	9.5	OUVRAGES EN VERRE
6651	BOTTLES ETC OF GLASS	W 17282	3.0	W 36812	8.5		14.0	W 18322	6.9	RECIPIENTS EN VERRE
66511	GLASS BOTTLES ETC NONVAC	W 17282	3.0	W 36812	8.5	W 53729	14.0	W 18322	6.9	BONBONNES,BOUTEILLES,ETC
67	IRON AND STEEL		56.2		80.2		37.9		44.3	FER ET ACIER
672	IRON,STEEL PRIMARY FORMS	W 34627	5.3	W 203333	36.0	W 3868	0.9	W 10776	2.0	LINGOTS FER,ACIER
6727	IRN,STL COIL FR REROLLNG	W 31250	4.9	W 199228	35.0	W 1819	0.6	W 2326	1.0	EBAUCHES POUR TOLES FER
67271	IRON,SIMPLE STEEL COILS	W 22968	3.5	W 194158	34.0	W 1147	0.4	W 2291	0.9	EBAUCHES NON EN ACIER
673	IRON,STEEL SHAPES ETC	W 151988	13.0	W 13015	3.5	W 10637	4.2	W 6950	3.0	BARRES,PROFIL FER,ACIER
674	IRN,STL UNIV,PLATE,SHEET	W 109700	17.0	W 91678	28.1	W 39004	22.2	W 45003	26.5	LARGES PLATS,TOLES
6747	TINNED PLATES,SHEETS	W 9192	2.5	W 15732	9.5	W 16267	11.1	W 8599	6.2	TOLES ETAMEES EN ACIER
6749	OTH IRN,STL PLATES,SHEET	W 17932	3.6	W 5409	2.5	W 3204	2.5	W 19086	12.6	AUTRES TOLES FER,ACIER
67491	— OF IRON OR SIMPLE STL	W 17862	3.5	W 5338	2.4	W 3204	2.5	W 19076	12.6	AUT TOLES AUTRES ACIER FIN
677	IRN,STL WIRE(EXCL W ROD)	W 45691	8.6	W 8445	2.7	W 4886	2.4	W 4872	2.4	FILS EN FER,ACIER
67701	IRON, SIMPLE STEEL WIRE	W 45030	8.6	W 8287	2.6	W 4604	2.1	W 4725	2.2	FILS NON ACIER FIN CARBONE
68	NON-FERROUS METALS		15.6		12.8		9.2		9.5	METAUX NON FERREUX
682	COPPER EXC CEMENT COPPER	W 6996	11.0	W 1298	2.3	W 1329	2.2	W 303	0.7	CUIVRE
6821	COPPER NES,ALLOYS,UNWRT	W 5938	9.6	W 954	1.3	W 585	0.7	W 127	0.1	CUIVRE BRUT
68212	COPPER REFINED,UNWROUGHT	W 5906	9.5	W 953	1.3	W 585	0.7	W 127	0.1	CUIVRE AFFINE BRUT
69	METAL MANUFACTURES NES		22.4		25.0		31.5		42.6	ART MANUFACT EN METAL NDA
699	BASE METAL MFRS NES	W 5261	5.6	W 6133	8.4		11.6	W 7170	15.7	ART MANUFACTURES MET NDA
7	MACHINES,TRANSPORT EQUIP		315.4		425.1		637.1		774.2	MACHINES MATERIEL TRANSPORT
71	POWER GENERATING EQUIPMT		19.6		16.3		24.2		24.2	MACHINES GENERATRICES
713	INTRNL COMBUS PSTN ENGIN		6.8		7.0		14.0	W 1998	12.8	MOTEURS EXPL COMB INT, PIECE
716	ROTATING ELECTRIC PLANT		9.6		8.0		9.1	W 2320	7.1	APP ELECTR ROTATIFS,PIECES
7162	AC MTRS,GENRTRS,GEN SETS		9.4	N 418389	7.3	N 349832	7.9	W 1773	5.8	MOTEURS ELECTRIQUES
71621	AC MTRS,INC UNIVRSL MTRS	N 1307519	9.2	N 417088	7.0	N 349755	7.8	W 1746	5.7	MOT ELEC NON COUR CONTINU
72	MACHS FOR SPCL INDUSTRYS		14.3		19.2		24.9		29.9	MAC SPECIALES POUR INDUST
73	METALWORKING MACHINERY		12.4		10.9		12.9		11.3	MACH TRAVAIL DES METAUX
737	METALWORKING MACHNRY NES		7.9		7.4		8.7	W 1770	7.5	MACH TRAV METAUX PIECES
7373	WELDING,BRAZING,ETC MCHS		7.9	N 14007	7.2	N 18878	8.1	W 1676	7.4	MACH SOUDAGE ETC PIECES
73732	ELECTRIC WELDERS,ETC		7.9	N 13504	7.2	N 18161	8.1	W 1673	7.4	MACH ELECT POUR SOUDER
74	GENRL INDUSTRL MACHY NES		47.8		47.8		60.5		67.9	MACH APP INDUSTRIE
741	HEATING,COOLING EQUIPMNT		3.8		7.4		11.1	W 2636	16.4	MACH CHAUFFAGE,PIECES
7414	NONDOM REFRIG EQUIPT,PTS		1.5		4.4		7.4	W 2078	12.0	MAT PRODUCTION DU FROID
74141	REFRIG EQUIP NONDOMESTIC	N 4821	1.2	N 7503	4.1	N 20361	7.0	W 1942	11.4	REFIG INDUSTRIELS
742	PUMPS FOR LIQUIDS ETC		18.6		15.2		17.4	W 677	12.3	POMPES MOTO-POMPES
7428	OTHER PUMPS FOR LIQUIDS		11.3	N 72748	6.5	N 82182	9.2	W 369	5.4	AUTRES POMPES POUR LIQ
74288	PUMPS FR LIQUIDS NES ETC		11.3	N 72718	6.5	N 82081	9.0	W 334	4.7	POMPES POUR LIQUIDES NDA
7429	PTS NES OF PUMPS OF 742	W 552	7.0	W 344	8.2	W 268	7.1	W 270	6.5	PIECES POUR GROUPE 742
743	PUMPS NES,CENTRFUGES ETC		18.2		15.8		15.2	W 2813	15.0	POMPES COMPRES,VENT ETC
7431	PUMPS FOR GASES ETC	N 881656	15.5	N 236373	11.8	N 151024	10.7	W 1904	7.9	POMPES AIR A VIDE,COMPRES
749	NONELEC MACH PTS,ACC NES		1.9		3.5		8.6	W 1178	12.8	PIECES MACH NON ELEC NDA
75	OFFICE MACHNES,ADP EQUIP		9.5		8.0		11.5		19.2	MACH BUREAU TRAIT AUTOM
752	AUTOMTIC DATA PROC EQUIP		3.8	N 38590	2.2	N 28800	4.9	W 404	10.7	MACH TRAIT INFORMATION
76	TELECOMM,SOUND EQUIPMENT		46.1		35.0		72.0		80.3	EQUIPMENT DE TELECOM
761	TELEVISION RECEIVERS		27.0	N 90046	17.3	N 194548	39.5	W 3909	40.7	RECEPTEURS DE TELEVISION
7611	COLOUR TV RECEIVERS	N 139200	25.6	N 74163	16.4	N 188613	39.1	W 3906	40.7	RECEPTEURS COULEUR
764	TELECOM EQPT,PTS,ACC NES		13.5		12.4		21.5	W 1315	26.6	EQUIP TELECOM,PIECES
7649	PTS NES OF EQUIPMT OF 76	W 903	10.2	W 575	6.6	W 884	13.3	W 1062	14.4	PIECES DE LA DIV 76
76493	TELECOMM EQUIPMT PTS NES	W 870	9.7	W 556	6.2	W 852	12.4	W 1037	12.7	PIECES 761,762,764.3,8
77	ELECTRIC MACHNRY NES ETC		95.2		152.9		189.9		236.7	MACH APP ELECT NDA
773	ELECTR DISTRIBUTNG EQUIP	W 3223	6.8	W 3704	22.0		39.4	W 4516	66.3	EQUIPMT DISTRIBUTION ELECT
7731	INSULATED WIRE,CABLE ETC	W 3143	6.8	W 3646	21.9	W 3939	39.2	W 4485	65.4	FILS,CABLES ISOLES ELECT
775	HOUSEHOLD TYPE EQUIP NES		36.4		45.5		47.2	W 18484	72.1	MACH,APP USAGE DOMESTQUE
7751	HOUSEHOLD LDRY EQUIP NES		1.7	N 12598	2.8	N 24064	7.0	W 3818	19.4	MACH A LAVER ET SECHOIRS
77511	DOMESTIC WASHING MACHNES	N 12173	1.6	N 12532	2.8	N 23941	6.8	W 3786	18.9	MACH LAVER LINGE MOINS 6 KG
7752	DOM REFRIGERATRS,FREEZRS	N 228539	31.9	N 250663	39.3	N 172252	31.3	W 13037	38.9	REFRIG,CONGEL MENAGER
77521	DOMESTIC REFRIGERATORS	N 161288	22.0	N 171621	26.7	N 129957	23.8	W 10297	31.2	REFRIGERATEURS
77522	DOMESTIC DEEP-FREEZERS	N 67251	9.9	N 79042	12.7	N 42295	7.6	W 2740	7.8	MEUBLES CONGELATEURS
776	TRANSISTORS,VALVES,ETC		41.9		72.6		88.0	W 17911	84.3	LAMPES,TUBES,VALVES
7761	TV PICTURE TUBES		37.9	N 1560012	70.7	N 1703321	82.9	W 17285	75.4	TUBES CATHODIQUES
78	ROAD VEHICLES		55.8		99.5		205.9		263.2	VEHICULES ROUTIERS
781	PASS MOTOR VEH EXC BUSES	N 8665	33.5	N 15067	71.4	N 88555	157.6	W 99320	206.4	AUTO TRANSPORT PERSONNES
784	MOTOR VEH PRTS,ACCES NES		4.9		10.9		22.8	W 6054	20.3	PIECES 722,781,782,783
7849	OTHER MOTOR VEHCL PARTS	W 2667	4.8	W 3840	10.7	W 6671	22.2	W 5733	19.5	PIECES 722,781,782,783
785	CYCLES,ETC MOTRZD OR NOT		9.3		11.9		16.7	W 2818	19.1	MOTOCYCLES SCOOTERS
7852	CYCLES, ETC NON-MOTOR	N 116000	8.0	N 97146	10.1	N 141124	14.0	W 2564	17.1	VELOCIPEDES SANS MOTEUR
79	OTHR TRANSPORT EQUIPMENT		15.2		35.9		35.9		41.9	AUTRE MATERIEL TRANSPORT
791	RAILWAY VEHICLES		4.4		5.9		9.9	W 27670	11.0	VEHIC MAT CHEMINS DE FER
792	AIRCRAFT ETC		5.7		8.3		6.3	W 262	12.2	APP NAVIGATION AERIENNE
793	SHIPS AND BOATS ETC		5.2	N 120	21.7	N 1590	19.8	W 37990	18.8	NAVIRES BATEAUX,ETC
7932	SHIPS AND BOATS NES	N 8	0.7	N 94	13.2	N 1218	17.0	W 4736	11.0	NAVIRES ET BATEAUX
79323	OTHER CARGO VESSELS	N 2	0.1	N 10	8.8	N 8	14.6	W 4508	10.6	AUT BATEAUX TRANS MARCH
8	MISC MANUFACTURED GOODS		219.9		335.8		473.9		576.6	ART MANUFACTURES DIVERS
821	*FURNITURE,PARTS THEREOF		36.2		46.2		55.8	W 36152	63.6	MEUBLES ET PIECES
8211	CHAIRS,SEATS AND PARTS		7.4		8.0		9.1	W 3558	9.4	SIEGES ET PIECES
82111	CHAIRS AND OTHER SEATS	N 303329	7.3	N 222633	7.9	N 208597	9.0	W 3494	9.2	SIEGES
8219	FURNITURE AND PARTS NES		27.5		35.9		43.1	W 31973	50.6	AUTRES MEUBLES ET PIECES
82192	WOOD FURNITURE NES	N 675447	24.8	N 700359	31.4	N 789180	34.4	W 19230	34.8	MEUBLES NDA EN BOIS
82199	OTHR FURN,FURN PARTS NES	W 970	1.2	W 2773	4.0	W 4988	7.5	W 12319	14.5	MEUBLES NDA AUTRES MATIERES
84	CLOTHING AND ACCESSORIES		109.6		204.9		299.8		373.4	VETEMENTS
842	MENS OUTERWEAR NOT KNIT		32.7		47.5		78.4	W 3854	85.6	VET DESSUS POUR HOMMES
8423	— TROUSERS,BREECHES ETC	N 2090200	7.9	N 1940389	17.3	N 2524689	31.3	W 1890	33.5	PANTALONS HOMMES MAT TEX
8424	— JACKETS,BLAZERS ETC	N 1061431	15.8	N 5490280	21.9	N 1071317	31.7	W 924	29.1	VESTES HOMMES MAT TEXTIL
8429	— OTHER OUTER GARMENTS		2.3		4.5		7.9	W 656	14.0	AUT VET DES HOM MAT TEX
843	WOMENS OUTERWEAR NONKNIT	N 5939080	22.3	N 8692031	68.3	MN 10890	104.8	W 6922	148.5	VET DESSUS FEMMES MAT TEX
8431	— COATS AND JACKETS	N 561502	4.0	N 865647	15.4	N 1171635	21.9	W 1558	41.0	MANT,VEST FEM MAT TEXTIL
8434	— SKIRTS	N 870600	2.3	N 1256663	7.9	N 1535218	11.0	W 894	17.6	JUPES EN MAT TEXTILES
8435	— BLOUSES	N 2034421	4.4	N 2585619	16.2	N 3355230	25.0	W 1234	30.3	BLOUSES FEM MAT TEXTILES
8439	— OTHER OUTER GARMENTS	N 1948757	9.5	N 3127730	22.2	N 3874555	38.6	W 2566	48.4	AUT VET DES FEM MAT TEXT
844	UNDER GARMENTS NOT KNIT	N 4094991	6.1	N 3229794	8.9	N 3250117	9.2	W 1015	13.2	VETEMENT DESSOUS MAT TEXT
8441	— MENS SHIRTS	N 2160922	4.5	N 2059422	7.4	N 2224801	7.9	W 870	11.6	CHEMISES HOMMES MAT TEXT

5. General Exports F.O.B. by Commodities according to the S.I.T.C. (Rev. 2) in million U.S. Dollars
Exportations Générales F.O.B. par Produits d'après la C.T.C.I. (Rév. 2) en millions de Dollars E.U.

SITC CTCI	COMMODITY	1994 QUANTITY QUANTITE	1994 VALUE VALEUR	1995 QUANTITY QUANTITE	1995 VALUE VALEUR	1996 QUANTITY QUANTITE	1996 VALUE VALEUR	1997 QUANTITY QUANTITE	1997 VALUE VALEUR	PRODUIT
845	OUTERWEAR KNIT NONELASTC	MN 10471	28.9	MN 10126	36.9	MN 12290	52.5	W 5722	68.2	VET DESSOUS,ACCES BONNET
8451	— JERSEYS,PULLOVERS ETC	N 3909500	9.4	N 3280256	13.8	N 3692101	19.1	W 2584	28.8	CHANDAILS,PULL–OVERS ETC
8459	— OTHER,CLTHG ACCESRYS	N 5700500	16.1	N 5647600	19.8	N 7380259	28.2	W 2280	29.5	AUT VET DESSUS DE BONNE
846	UNDER GARMENTS KNITTED		9.7		24.0		32.6	W 3102	37.1	SOUS VETS DE BONNETERIE
8462	— OF COTTON NON ELASTIC	N 4812200	3.9	N 8086471	16.4	MN 11946	24.9	W 1675	24.7	SOUS–VET BONNET COTON
84629	—— OTHER	N 4585000	3.6	N 7848666	16.0	MN 11844	24.7	W 1643	24.4	AUT SOUS–VET BONNET COTON
8463	— OF SYNTH FBR NONELAST		5.8		6.9		7.1	W 1391	11.2	SOUS–VET BONNET FIB SYNT
84631	—— PANTY HOSE (TIGHTS)	W 2165	5.6	W 666	6.9	W 407	6.7	W 1298	10.1	COLLANTS BON FIBR SYNT
847	TEXTILE CLTHNG ACCES NES		6.0		11.4		9.6	W 566	6.8	ACCES VET MAT TEXT NDA
8472	CLTHNG ACCESRYS ETC KNIT	W 1451	5.7	W 1218	10.9	W 661	9.2	W 527	6.2	ACCES VET BONNE NDA
84722	KNIT SOCKS,ETC NONELASTC	W 1397	5.5	W 1193	10.7	W 650	9.1	W 516	6.0	CHAUSSETTES BON. NON ELAS
848	HEADGEAR,NONTXTL CLOTHNG		4.3		8.1		12.9	W 247	14.3	VET ACCES MAT AUT QUE TEX
8483	FUR ETC,CLOTHES,PRODUCTS	W 102	2.7	W 50	6.5	W 174	11.6	W 157	12.3	VETEMENTS DE FOURRURE
84831	ARTICLES OF FURSKIN,NES	W 73	2.4	W 48	6.3	W 106	11.1	W 75	11.0	PELLETERIES OUVREES NDA
851	*FOOTWEAR	P 2777131	19.5	P 2142196	19.4	P 2951332	23.1	W 2362	21.4	CHAUSSURES
85102	FOOTWEAR LEATHER	P 2300989	16.1	P 1777905	16.9	P 2224609	17.9	W 1242	12.1	CHAUS SEMELLES EN CUIR
87	PRECISION INSTRUMNTS NES		19.7		20.3		23.8		33.4	INSTRUM,APPAR SCIENT NDA
873	METERS AND COUNTERS NES	N 1069284	8.7	N 716132	9.0	N 427200	7.9	W 860	11.5	COMPTEURS,INST DE MESURE
8731	GAS SUPPLY METERS ETC	N 1069282	8.7	N 714489	8.9	N 426977	7.9	W 860	11.4	COMPTEURS GAZ,LIQ ELECT
874	MEASURNG,CONTROLNG INSTR		5.5		5.7		9.2	W 668	12.7	INSTRUMENTS DE MESURE
88	PHOTO EQU,OPTICL GDS ETC		3.6		8.7		15.9		16.6	APP,FOURN PHOTO,OP,MONTR
89	MISC MANUFCTRD GOODS NES		28.2		32.7		50.1		60.1	ART MANUFACTURES DIVERS
892	PRINTED MATTER		2.3	W 1141	6.7		13.4	W 2793	17.0	IMPRIMES
8928	PRINTED MATTER NES	W 894	1.1	W 473	4.8		10.3	W 454	12.3	IMPRIMES NDA
893	ARTICLES OF PLASTIC NES		9.1		12.2		21.1		24.3	OUVRAGES EN MAT DIVIS 58
8931	PLSTC PACKG CONTNRS,LIDS	W 83045	4.6	W 3993	6.5	W 6133	11.2	W 8987	13.3	ART TRANSP EMBALLAGE ETC
8939	MISC PLASTIC ARTICLES	W 2514	4.3	W 2332	5.4	W 3178	9.4	W 3355	10.3	ART DIVERS EN MAT DIV 58
9	GOODS NOT CLASSD BY KIND		8.8		1.0		1.6		3.7	ART TRANSACT NON CLASSES
931	*SPECIAL TRANSACTIONS		8.6		0.9	W 816	1.5		3.5	TRANS.SPECIALES

1. HISTORICAL SERIES, 1962–1997 GENERAL TRADE, IMPORTS C.I.F., EXPORTS F.O.B.
SERIES HISTORIQUES, 1962–1997 COMMERCE GENERAL, IMPORTATIONS C.A.F., EXPORTATIONS F.O.B

YEAR ANNEE	VALUE IN MILLION PATACAS / VALEUR EN MILLION PATACAS MERCHANDISE – MARCHANDISE IMPORTS	EXPORTS	GOLD – OR IMPORTS	EXPORTS	CONVERSION FACTORS U.S. CENTS PER PATACA / FACTEURS DE CONVERSION CENTS E.U. PAR PATACA IMPORTS	EXPORTS	INDEX NUMBERS – INDICES QUANTUM IMPORTS	EXPORTS	UNIT VALUE / VALEUR UNITAIRE IMPORTS	EXPORTS
1962	196.80	86.70			19.1290	19.1290				
1963	218.50	108.90			19.1290	19.1290				
1964	252.40	114.80			19.1290	19.1290				
1965	269.90	122.90			19.1290	19.1290				
1966	293.80	138.20			19.1290	19.1290				
1967	245.50	143.20			19.1290	19.1290				
1968	303.20	170.60			19.1290	19.1290				
1969	360.10	225.80			16.3185	16.5289				
1970	393.20	255.80			16.3908	16.5892				
1971	447.20	291.10			16.7001	16.9147				
1972	592.50	409.70			17.6667	17.8724				
1973	750.30	497.10			19.1567	19.5207				
1974	648.70	551.20			19.5564	20.0153				
1975	791.30	683.90			18.7112	18.7043				
1976	977.10	1146.20			18.6654	18.9789				
1977	1102.40	1221.50			19.6927	20.0260				
1978	1252.40	1302.90			19.7420	20.0944				
1979	1817.90	2291.60			19.2611	19.2264				
1980	2779.90	2742.00			19.5321	19.5710				
1981	4141.20	4015.30			17.4487	17.0836				
1982	4475.40	4521.10			15.8143	15.8753				
1983	5423.30	5673.00			13.5434	13.5220				
1984	6399.20	7324.70			12.4695	12.4669				
1985	6200.00	7207.00			12.5653	12.5722				
1986	7326.67	8653.25			12.1449	12.0869				
1987	9028.09	11245.69			12.4187	12.4189				
1988	10380.58	12007.06			12.4224	12.4224				
1989	11873.42	13208.65			12.4471	12.4456				
1990	12343.09	13638.19			12.4241	12.4239				
1991	14832.42	13326.06			12.4224	12.4224				
1992	15684.72	14080.16			12.4224	12.4224				
1993	16137.99	14236.22			12.3898	12.3869				
1994	16925.12	14853.89			12.3457	12.3457				
1995	16267.10	15913.45			12.4525	12.4603				
1996	15930.66	15898.51			12.5111	12.5121				
1997	16603.39	17129.17			12.5207	12.5205				

2. IMPORTS BY BROAD ECONOMIC CATEGORY AND EXPORTS BY INDUSTRIAL ORIGIN. (PERCENTAGE OF TOTAL VALUE)
IMPORTATIONS PAR CATEGORIES ECONOMIQUES ET EXPORTATIONS PAR BRANCHE D'ACTIVITE.(EN POURCENTAGE DE LA VALEUR TOTALE)

IMPORTS – IMPORTATIONS

	1991	1992	1993	1994	1995	1996	1997
TOTAL IMPORTS–IMPORTATIONS TOTALES	100.	100.	100.	100.	100.	100.	100.
1 FOOD BEV–ALIMENTATION BOISSONS	8.4	8.9	9.3	10.3	10.1	10.0	9.3
11 PRIMARY–PRODUITS DE BASE	3.3	3.3	3.2	3.2	3.4	3.5	3.2
111 FOR INDUSTRY–POUR L'INDUSTRIE	1.1	1.1	1.2	1.3	1.3	1.3	1.2
112 FOR HOUSEHOLDS–POUR LES MENAGES	2.2	2.1	2.0	1.9	2.1	2.2	2.0
12 PROCESSED–PRODUITS ELABORES	5.1	5.7	6.1	7.1	6.7	6.4	6.1
121 FOR INDUSTRY–POUR L'INDUSTRIE	0.4	0.4	0.4	0.5	0.5	0.5	0.5
122 FOR HOUSEHOLDS–POUR LES MENAGES	4.6	5.2	5.7	6.7	6.1	5.9	5.6
2 IND SUPPLIES–APPROV INDUSTRIELS	52.4	50.7	52.3	50.5	50.1	52.8	52.7
21 PRIMARY–PRODUITS DE BASE	3.9	3.7	6.9	3.1	2.5	3.0	2.0
22 PROCESSED–PRODUITS ELABORES	48.5	47.0	45.4	47.4	47.7	49.9	50.7
3 FUELS–COMBUSTIBLES	4.5	4.3	4.6	4.7	5.1	6.4	6.5
31 PRIMARY–PRODUITS DE BASE	0.4	0.4	0.5	0.5	0.7	0.8	0.7
32 PROCESSED–PRODUITS ELABORES	4.1	3.8	4.1	4.2	4.5	5.6	5.8
321 MOTOR SPIRIT–ESSENCE	0.4	0.5	0.6	0.6	0.6	0.8	0.8
322 OTHER–AUTRES	3.6	3.3	3.5	3.6	3.8	4.8	5.0
4 MACHINERY–EQUIPEMENT	12.5	11.7	10.7	12.2	12.2	9.1	9.5
41 CAPITAL EQUIPMENT–MACHINES	11.5	10.9	9.9	11.1	11.0	8.2	8.7
42 PARTS–PIECES ACCESSOIRES	1.0	0.8	0.8	1.1	1.2	0.9	0.8
5 TRANSPORT–TRANSPORT	2.4	3.5	3.7	4.2	4.0	4.7	6.2
51 PASSENGER CARS–AUTOMOBILES	1.1	2.1	2.3	2.3	1.5	1.8	2.5
52 OTHER–AUTRES	0.8	1.0	1.1	1.0	1.8	1.3	2.2
521 INDUSTRIAL–INDUSTRIELS	0.4	0.6	0.6	0.6	1.5	0.7	1.6
522 NON INDUSTRIAL–NON INDUSTRIEL	0.4	0.4	0.4	0.4	0.3	0.5	0.6
53 PARTS–PIECES ACCESSOIRES	0.5	0.5	0.4	0.9	0.7	1.5	1.6
6 CONSUM GOODS–BIENS CONSOMMATION	19.4	20.5	19.0	17.8	18.0	16.7	15.3
61 DURABLE–DURABLES	6.8	7.4	6.8	5.0	4.1	3.2	2.6
62 SEMI DURABLE–SEMI DURABLES	9.1	9.5	7.7	7.8	7.9	7.9	7.7
63 NON DURABLE–NON DURABLES	3.4	3.5	4.5	5.1	6.0	5.5	5.0
7 GOODS NES–BIENS NDA	0.4	0.4	0.4	0.3	0.4	0.4	0.5

EXPORTS – EXPORTATIONS

	1991	1992	1993	1994	1995	1996	1997
TOTAL EXPORTS–EXPORTATIONS TOTALES	100.	100.	100.	100.	100.	100.	100.
1 AGRICULTURE	0.8	0.9	1.7	1.7	1.6	1.8	0.6
2 MINING QUARRY–INDUS EXTRACTIVES	0.0	0.0	0.0	0.0	0.0	0.0	0.0
3 MANUFACTURING–IND MANUFACTUR	99.2	99.1	98.3	98.3	98.4	98.2	99.4
31 FOOD BEV TOBACCO–ALIM BOISS TAB	0.8	1.5	3.6	3.4	1.5	1.4	1.3
32 TEXTILES–INDUSTRIES TEXTILES	79.7	79.7	76.3	76.9	80.8	84.3	88.3
33 WOOD & PRODUCTS–BOIS & PRODUITS	0.2	0.1	0.1	0.2	0.1	0.1	0.0
34 PAPER & PRODUCTS–PAPIER & PRODT	0.2	0.2	0.2	0.2	0.2	1.5	0.2
35 CHEMICALS–INDUSTRIES CHIMIQUES	2.8	2.6	2.8	2.6	2.3	2.3	2.2
36 NON METAL MIN–MIN NON METAL	0.9	1.0	1.2	0.9	0.9	1.1	0.9
37 BASIC METAL–IND METAL BASE	0.1	0.1	0.3	0.2	0.1	0.1	0.2
38 METAL MANUF–MANUF METAL	6.9	7.5	8.3	8.4	7.4	5.2	5.1
39 OTH MANUF IND–AUTRES MANUF	7.6	6.4	5.5	5.7	5.1	2.2	1.1

3. TRADE BY PRINCIPAL COUNTRIES OF ORIGIN AND DESTINATION (VALUE IN MILLION U.S. DOLLARS)
ECHANGES SELON LES PRINCIPAUX PAYS D'ORIGINE ET DE DESTINATION (VALEUR EN MILLIONS DE DOLLARS EU)

COUNTRIES–PAYS	GENERAL IMPORTS C.I.F. IMPORTATIONS GENERALES C.A.F					COUNTRIES–PAYS	EXPORTS EXPORTATIONS ES F.O.B.				
	1993	1994	1995	1996	1997		1993	1994	1995	1996	1997
World	1996.4	2089.2	2025.3	1992.0	2076.6	Monde	1796.8	1872.2	2024.7	2100.0	2282.1
Africa	4.4	17.5	7.7	4.8	11.0	Afrique	0.6	1.0	1.9	1.3	1.3
Americas	131.2	154.2	176.7	131.6	140.4	Amériques	633.7	721.9	874.5	836.7	1015.1
– Northern America	124.8	146.5	173.7	125.5	135.5	– Amérique du Nord	616.2	707.2	864.1	830.4	1005.6
– LAIA	6.2	7.7	2.9	5.9	3.8	– ALAI	16.0	13.9	8.7	4.8	7.9
– CACM	0.1	0.0		0.0	0.0	– MCAC	0.5	0.1	0.1	0.1	
– Caribbean	0.0	0.1	0.1	0.2	1.1	– Caraïbes	0.0		0.1	0.2	0.0
– Rest of America						– Autre Amérique	1.0	0.8	1.6	1.2	1.4
Asia excl fmr USSR	1577.0	1556.9	1512.6	1549.1	1641.1	Asie anc. URSS exclus	523.8	524.8	490.5	560.7	524.4
– Middle East	14.1	11.4	12.9	13.8	14.8	– Moyen–Orient	1.8	2.6	2.2	1.7	1.2
Asia former USSR			0.0			Asie ancienne URSS			0.0		
Europe excl fmr USSR	252.4	334.3	306.7	284.0	264.0	Europe anc. URSS exclus	625.4	612.8	647.4	684.9	723.1
– European Union	242.5	323.1	298.2	272.7	255.9	– Union Européenne	608.1	598.0	635.7	672.8	711.3
– Eastern Europe	2.0	1.6	0.3	1.2	0.2	– Europe de l'Est	0.5	0.6	0.7	0.7	1.1
– Rest of Europe	7.9	9.6	8.3	10.0	7.9	– Autre de l'Europe	16.8	14.3	11.0	11.4	10.8
Europe former USSR	4.1	6.8	5.3	0.3	0.0	Europe ancienne URSS	0.5	0.5	0.1	0.1	0.2
Oceania	27.3	19.5	16.2	22.2	20.1	Océanie	12.7	11.2	10.2	8.5	8.9
Other						Autre				7.7	9.0
China, Hong Kong SAR	597.0	634.2	585.2	578.8	522.9	USA/Etats–Unis d'Amer	590.0	681.8	834.2	802.2	970.5
China/Chine	424.9	393.4	440.7	477.0	592.9	China/Chine	241.9	241.3	212.6	264.1	266.4
Japan/Japon	315.8	267.2	213.1	179.0	177.5	China, Hong Kong SAR	232.5	222.6	205.1	212.7	167.8
Other Asia n.e.s.	130.5	141.9	146.6	175.6	192.5	Germany/Allemagne	203.3	189.0	197.6	213.4	211.5
USA/Etats–Unis d'Amer	115.7	142.8	150.2	117.5	130.5	United Kingdom	111.5	130.7	142.2	151.7	168.5
United Kingdom	70.5	88.2	84.3	77.0	76.1	France, Monaco	148.8	131.7	137.8	136.1	144.6
Korea, Republic of	45.3	51.2	47.7	52.5	53.1	Netherlands/Pays–Bas	47.2	45.8	46.6	56.2	59.2
France, Monaco	40.5	62.1	41.4	35.4	32.0	Canada	26.0	25.3	29.8	28.1	34.9
Germany/Allemagne	37.2	48.0	42.9	31.9	44.5	Japan/Japon	26.0	25.1	26.2	27.8	23.8
Denmark/Danemark	26.2	39.4	34.6	22.9	13.8	Denmark/Danemark	19.4	20.6	24.1	29.4	29.1
Portugal	16.6	25.1	23.5	30.5	20.8	Other Asia n.e.s.	15.5	21.3	22.8	23.3	30.8
Italy/Italie	15.4	20.3	26.6	25.3	24.3	Italy/Italie	21.7	19.1	18.4	15.8	17.5
Australia/Australie	22.9	15.7	13.6	18.2	15.3	Sweden/Suède	7.4	7.7	18.6	23.0	26.0
Singapore/Singapour	9.6	11.3	17.7	17.0	24.1	Spain/Espagne	8.2	16.4	10.8	12.5	16.1
Indonesia/Indonésie	13.1	14.9	12.6	12.6	13.1	Belgium–Luxembourg	13.0	13.3	10.9	8.1	8.6
Finland/Finlande	11.7	11.9	15.4	18.7	7.1	Austria/Autriche	8.8	10.4	8.3	12.0	9.7
Thailand/Thaïlande	11.8	9.8	10.2	15.5	17.1	Portugal	10.4	6.5	12.5	5.9	4.5
Malaysia/Malaisie	7.7	11.1	14.1	14.1	16.1	Australia/Australie	10.5	9.3	7.7	6.0	6.2
Sweden/Suède	8.9	8.0	7.5	11.9	16.8	Switzerland,Liechtenst.	10.5	7.0	5.8	6.5	5.1
Saudi Arabia	10.7	8.9	9.5	11.4	12.6	Singapore/Singapour	2.1	3.0	7.7	12.1	6.2
Canada	9.1	3.7	23.5	7.9	5.0	Mexico/Mexique	13.0	10.0	4.3	1.1	2.5
So. African Customs Un	4.4	17.5	7.0	2.5	10.0	Norway,Svalbard and JM	5.1	6.3	4.7	4.7	5.4
Netherlands/Pays–Bas	7.2	5.8	6.4	8.5	11.5	Ireland/Irlande	3.7	3.3	4.4	4.8	10.1
Spain/Espagne	2.6	11.5	10.3	3.8	3.8	Korea, Republic of	1.2	3.8	4.3	5.2	9.2
Switzerland,Liechtenst.	6.3	4.5	5.1	6.2	6.9	Viet Nam	0.1	1.4	4.9	3.9	6.8
India/Inde	1.1	3.9	5.0	6.0	6.3	Finland/Finlande	4.4	2.7	2.5	2.9	4.6
New Zealand	4.4	3.8	2.6	4.0	4.7	Chile/Chili	2.3	2.9	3.5	2.9	3.7
Brazil/Brésil	5.5	6.1	1.8	2.7	2.3	Bunkers, ship stores					9.0
Russian Federation	4.1	6.8	5.3	0.3	0.0	Philippines	0.0	0.3	0.2	3.0	4.7
Norway,Svalbard and JM	1.2	5.1	3.2	3.8	1.1	Malaysia/Malaisie	0.5	0.6	1.0	2.1	3.6
Belgium–Luxembourg	1.9	1.7	2.8	4.3	2.5	Areas n.e.s.				7.7	
Turkey/Turquie	3.1	2.1	3.1	2.2	1.9	Panama	1.0	0.8	1.6	1.2	1.4
Pakistan	1.6	2.7	4.5	2.5	1.1	Thailand/Thaïlande	0.7	0.9	1.0	2.0	0.8
Philippines	3.2	2.2	1.6	2.0	2.3	New Zealand	0.8	0.7	1.2	1.2	1.1
Korea Dem People's Rp	0.1	0.0	0.0	0.0	5.6	So. African Customs Un	0.2	1.0	1.3	1.1	1.2
Austria/Autriche	0.9	0.5	1.4	0.9	1.5	Lao People's Dem Rep	0.5	1.2	1.0	0.6	1.2
Ireland/Irlande	0.2	0.5	0.7	1.6	0.9	Greece/Grèce	0.4	0.6	1.0	1.1	1.3
Greece/Grèce	2.8	0.2	0.1	0.2	0.1	Northern Mariana Isls			1.1	1.2	1.4
Czech Republic	1.4	1.0	0.0	0.1	0.1	Saudi Arabia	0.4	1.3	1.0	0.3	0.0
Mauritius/Maurice	0.0		0.7	1.2	0.4	US Misc Pacific Islands	1.4	1.2	0.2	0.1	0.1

(VALUE AS PERCENTAGE OF WORLD TOTAL)(VALEURS EN POURCENTAGE DU TOTAL MONDIAL)

	1988	1989	1990	1991	1992	1993	1994	1995	1996	1997		1988	1989	1990	1991	1992	1993	1994	1995	1996	1997
Africa	0.6	0.5	0.3	0.3	0.2	0.2	0.8	0.4	0.2	0.5	Afrique	0.3	0.3	0.4	0.1	0.1	0.0	0.1	0.1	0.1	0.1
Americas	5.8	6.4	5.5	5.0	5.6	6.6	7.4	8.7	6.6	6.8	Amériques	35.4	39.2	37.8	33.0	36.4	35.3	38.6	43.2	39.8	44.5
– Northern America	5.6	6.1	5.3	4.8	5.4	6.3	7.0	8.6	6.3	6.5	– Amérique du Nord	35.2	39.0	37.5	32.7	36.2	34.3	37.8	42.7	39.5	44.1
– LAIA	0.2	0.2	0.2	0.1	0.2	0.3	0.4	0.1	0.3	0.2	– ALAI	0.1	0.1	0.1	0.1	0.2	0.9	0.7	0.4	0.2	0.3
– CACM				0.0		0.0	0.0		0.0	0.0	– MCAC	0.0	0.0	0.0	0.0	0.0	0.0	0.0	0.0	0.0	
– Caribbean	0.0	0.0	0.0	0.0	0.0	0.0	0.0	0.0	0.0	0.1	– Caraïbes	0.0	0.0	0.0	0.0	0.0	0.0		0.0	0.0	0.0
– Rest of America		0.0			0.0						– Autre Amérique	0.1	0.1	0.1	0.1	0.1	0.1	0.0	0.1	0.1	0.1
Asia excl fmr USSR	82.1	82.5	83.1	84.0	82.7	79.0	74.5	74.7	77.8	79.0	Asie anc. URSS exclus	22.8	23.4	21.7	24.8	25.9	29.2	28.0	24.2	26.7	23.0
– Middle East	0.2	0.2	0.2	0.3	0.4	0.7	0.5	0.6	0.7	0.7	– Moyen–Orient	0.3	0.2	0.2	0.2	0.2	0.1	0.1	0.1	0.1	0.1
Asia former USSR								0.0			Asie ancienne URSS								0.0		
Europe excl fmr USSR	8.2	7.6	9.5	9.0	9.9	12.6	16.0	15.1	14.3	12.7	Europe anc. URSS exclus	39.5	35.1	38.5	40.8	36.5	34.8	32.7	32.0	32.6	31.7
– European Union	7.9	7.4	9.3	8.7	9.5	12.1	15.5	14.7	13.7	12.3	– Union Européenne	37.9	33.7	36.8	39.6	35.5	33.8	31.9	31.4	32.0	31.2
– Eastern Europe	0.0	0.0	0.0	0.1	0.0	0.1	0.1	0.0	0.1	0.0	– Europe de l'Est	0.3	0.3	0.4	0.2	0.0	0.0	0.0	0.0	0.0	0.0
– Rest of Europe	0.3	0.2	0.2	0.2	0.4	0.4	0.5	0.4	0.5	0.4	– Autre de l'Europe	1.3	1.1	1.3	1.0	1.0	0.9	0.8	0.5	0.5	0.5
Europe former USSR	0.5	0.4	0.4	0.2	0.2	0.2	0.3	0.3	0.0	0.0	Europe ancienne URSS	0.1	0.1	0.0	0.0	0.0	0.0	0.0	0.0	0.0	0.0
Oceania	1.7	2.6	1.2	1.6	1.5	1.4	0.9	0.8	1.1	1.0	Océanie	2.0	1.9	1.6	1.3	0.9	0.7	0.6	0.5	0.4	0.4
Other	1.0	0.0		0.0							Autre									0.4	0.4
China, Hong Kong SAR	42.9	42.3	42.2	34.9	32.9	29.9	30.4	28.9	29.1	25.2	USA/Etats–Unis d'Amer	33.8	37.5	36.0	31.2	34.7	32.8	36.4	41.2	38.2	42.5
China/Chine	19.9	19.6	17.8	21.6	20.4	21.3	18.8	21.8	23.9	28.6	China/Chine	4.5	3.4	4.5	8.6	10.3	13.5	12.9	10.5	12.6	11.7
Japan/Japon	10.5	10.2	11.5	17.4	18.0	15.8	12.8	10.5	9.0	8.5	China, Hong Kong SAR	14.0	14.7	13.1	13.2	12.9	12.9	11.9	10.1	10.1	7.4
Other Asia n.e.s.	5.2	6.7	7.1	6.1	6.4	6.5	6.8	7.2	8.8	9.3	Germany/Allemagne				13.6	11.9	11.3	10.1	9.8	10.2	9.3
USA/Etats–Unis d'Amer	4.5	5.5	5.1	4.6	5.2	5.8	6.8	7.4	5.9	6.3	United Kingdom	7.6	7.3	7.7	7.3	6.6	6.2	7.0	7.0	7.2	7.4
United Kingdom	2.6	2.4	2.9	2.5	2.5	3.5	4.2	4.2	3.9	3.7	France, Monaco	8.8	7.5	8.0	8.8	8.7	8.3	7.0	6.8	6.5	6.3
Korea, Republic of	1.7	1.6	2.0	2.0	2.2	2.3	2.5	2.4	2.6	2.6	Netherlands/Pays–Bas	2.3	2.0	2.1	2.5	2.2	2.6	2.4	2.3	2.7	2.6
France, Monaco	0.9	0.8	1.0	0.9	1.5	2.0	3.0	2.0	1.8	1.5	Canada	1.4	1.5	1.5	1.5	1.5	1.4	1.4	1.5	1.3	1.5
Germany/Allemagne				1.4	1.6	1.9	2.3	2.1	1.6	2.1	Japan/Japon	3.5	4.5	3.1	1.8	1.6	1.4	1.3	1.3	1.3	1.0
Denmark/Danemark	1.0	0.6	1.7	1.5	1.0	1.3	1.9	1.7	1.1	0.7	Denmark/Danemark	1.0	0.9	0.8	1.0	0.8	1.1	1.1	1.2	1.4	1.3

4. General Imports C.I.F. by Commodities according to the S.I.T.C. (Rev. 2) in million U.S. Dollars
Importations Générales C.A.F. par Produits d'après la C.T.C.I. (Rév. 2) en millions de Dollars E.U.

SITC CTCI	COMMODITY	1994		1995		1996		1997		PRODUIT
		QUANTITY QUANTITE	VALUE VALEUR	QUANTITY QUANTITE	VALUE VALEUR	QUANTITY QUANTITE	VALUE VALEUR	QUANTITY QUANTITE	VALUE VALEUR	
	ALL COMMODITIES		2089.3		2025.4		1992.0		2076.7	TOUS PRODUITS
0	FOOD AND LIVE ANIMALS		139.5		144.3		148.6		144.8	ALIMENTS,ANIMAUX VIVANTS
001	*LIVE ANIMALS FOR FOOD	W 23800	28.3	W 23587	28.5	W 23437	29.2	W 22069	29.5	ANIMAUX VIVANTS
0013	SWINE,LIVE	W 14760	15.1	W 15030	15.1	W 14785	14.9	W 14297	14.5	ESPECE PORCINE
0014	LIVE POULTRY	W 6734	8.2	W 6615	8.3	W 6719	8.7	W 6264	8.1	VOLAILLES VIVANTES
00149	LIVE POULTRY OVER 185 GR	W 6715	8.2	W 6592	8.2	W 6708	8.7	W 6229	8.0	VOL VIVANTES PLUS 185 GR.
01	MEAT AND PREPARATIONS		10.6		11.2		10.7		10.4	VIANDES ET PREPARATIONS
02	DAIRY PRODCTS,BIRDS'EGGS		14.2		14.8		16.5		16.3	PRODUITS LAITIERS,OEUFS
022	MILK AND CREAM	W 6990	10.2	W 7337	11.4	W 6275	12.4	W 6162	12.7	LAIT ET CREME
0224	MILK,CREAM PRESERVED ETC	W 4126	7.3	W 4384	8.3	W 3527	9.1	W 3228	9.0	LAIT,CREME CONS,CONC
03	FISH AND PREPARATIONS		16.3		19.2		18.3		16.5	POISSONS ET PREPARATIONS
034	FISH,FRESH,CHILLED,FROZN	W 5869	5.8	W 6740	7.8	W 7106	7.5	W 7019	7.6	POISSON FRAIS, REFRIG,CONG
0341	FISH FRSH,CHLLD,EX FILLT	W 4910	4.6	W 5714	6.4	W 6423	6.4	W 6647	7.1	POISSON FRAIS,REFRIGERE
036	SHELL FISH FRESH,FROZEN	W 3351	5.9	W 3056	6.4	W 2456	5.7	W 1868	4.5	CRUSTACES,MOLLUSQUES
04	CEREALS AND PREPARATIONS		18.0		18.5		19.4		20.3	CEREALES ET PRODUITS
048	CEREAL ETC PREPARATIONS	W 7680	10.7	W 7624	11.3	W 8090	12.2	W 8169	13.1	PREPTNS A BASE CEREALES
0484	BAKERY PRODUCTS	W 2980	5.4	W 2814	5.3	W 2706	5.8	W 3118	6.5	PRODUITS DE BOULANGERIE
05	VEGETABLES AND FRUIT		26.1		25.8		26.3		23.7	LEGUMES ET FRUITS
054	VEG ETC FRSH,SMPLY PRSVD	W 29758	5.4	W 30232	5.3	W 33479	6.1	W 32920	5.8	LEGUMES FRAIS,CONG,SECS
057	FRUIT,NUTS,FRESH,DRIED	W 24120	11.8	W 24059	11.6	W 25171	11.1	W 22791	10.0	FRUITS FRAIS OU SECS
06	SUGAR AND PREPS,HONEY		6.4		6.7		6.6		6.6	SUCRES ET PRODUITS
07	COFFEE,TEA,COCOA,SPICES		6.5		6.1		7.8		8.3	CAFE,THE,CACAO,EPICES
09	MISC EDIBLE PRODUCTS		12.4		12.3		12.3		11.5	PREP ALIMENTAIRES DIVERSES
098	EDIBLE PRODCTS,PREPS NES	W 8954	11.1	W 7516	11.6	W 6816	11.6	W 6660	11.0	PREP ALIMENTAIRES NDA
1	BEVERAGES AND TOBACCO		137.3		130.6		104.2		102.4	BOISSONS ET TABACS
11	BEVERAGES		74.2		59.3		50.0		50.3	BOISSONS
111	NON–ALCOHL BEVERAGES NES	MW 50891	16.1	MW 53039	17.6	MW 54407	19.3	MW 53072	20.2	BOISSONS NON ALCOOLIQUES
11101	WATERS,ICE AND SNOW	MW 50880	7.7	MW 53027	8.1	MW 54395	9.0	MW 53060	9.2	EAU,EAUX MINERALES
11102	FLAVORED WATERS NON–ALCO	W 11594	8.4	W 12140	9.6	W 11777	10.3	W 12445	11.1	LIMONADES,EAUX GAZEUSES
112	ALCOHOLIC BEVERAGES	W 23550	58.2	W 22017	41.7	W 21230	30.8	W 21227	30.2	BOISSONS ALCOOLIQUES
1121	WINE OF FRESH GRAPES ETC	W 837	2.4	W 974	3.0	W 1927	7.2	W 2616	9.3	VINS DE RAISINS FRAIS
11212	WINE OF FRESH GRAPES	W 834	2.4	W 972	2.9	W 1918	7.1	W 2608	9.2	VINS DE MOUTS DE RAISINS
1123	BEER,ALE,STOUT,PORTER	W 20575	9.9	W 19103	11.9	W 17189	10.7	W 16840	10.2	BIERES
1124	DISTILLED ALCOHOLIC BEVS	W 2048	45.8	W 1175	26.0	W 617	10.9	W 530	8.8	ALCOOLS,EAUX–DE–VIE
11242	DISTILLD WINE,GRAPE MARC	W 1213	43.0	W 792	24.4	W 334	8.8	W 314	6.8	EAUX–DE–VIE NATURELLES
12	TOBACCO AND MANUFACTURES		63.2		71.4		54.2		52.1	TABACS BRUTS FABRIQUES
122	TOBACCO,MANUFACTURED	W 5151	63.1	W 4917	71.3	W 3080	54.0	W 2738	51.9	TABACS FABRIQUES
1222	CIGARETTES	W 4407	59.0	W 4096	66.4	W 2227	46.8	W 1774	41.5	CIGARETTES
1223	OTH MANUFACTURED TOBACCO	W 739	3.9	W 813	4.4	W 839	6.3	W 944	8.1	TABACS FUMER,CHIQUER,PRISER
2	CRUDE MATERLS,EXCL FUELS		74.3		58.3		65.9		46.9	MAT BRUTES NON COMESTIBLES
21	HIDES,SKINS,FURS UNDRSSD		26.9		28.4		36.5		14.7	CUIRS,PEAUX BRUTS
212	FURSKINS,RAW	W 127	26.9	W 157	28.4	W 189	36.5	W 326	14.7	PELLETERIES BRUTES
21201	MINK SKINS,RAW	W 93	21.6	W 85	16.7	W 71	23.9	W 78	7.6	PEAUX DE VISON BRUTES
21209	OTHER FURSKINS,RAW	W 33	5.3	W 71	11.8	W 118	12.7	W 248	7.1	AUTRES PELLETERIES BRUTES
24	CORK AND WOOD		7.5		6.8		4.5		4.2	LIEGE ET BOIS
26	TEXTILE FIBRES AND WASTE		19.7		15.3		20.4		21.5	FIBRES TEXTILES
268	WOOL(EXC TOPS),ANML HAIR	W 3855	14.9	W 3490	13.1	W 4675	16.6	W 4806	19.2	LAINES ET POILS
2682	WOOL DEGREASED,UNCOMBED	W 3360	12.4	W 2870	10.2	W 4082	13.3	W 4256	16.0	LAINE DEGRAISSEE
27	CRUDE FERTLZR,MINRLS NES		17.8		4.4		1.9		3.6	ENGRAIS MINERAUX BRUTS
273	STONE,SAND AND GRAVEL	MW 12699	17.0	W 1021069	3.5	W 141802	1.3	W 261556	2.2	PIERRES,SABLES,GRAVIERS
2733	SAND,EXCL METAL–BEARING	MW 11621	11.5	W 737671	1.2	W 48537	0.2	W 142475	0.4	SABLES NATURELS
3	MINERAL FUELS ETC		98.9		104.8		129.5		138.0	COMBUSTIBLES MINERAUX LUB
33	PETROLEUM AND PRODUCTS		77.9		79.3		101.9		110.5	PETROLE ET DERIVES
334	PETROLEUM PRODUCTS,REFIN	W 410525	76.7	W 384767	78.0	W 442708	99.3	W 466058	106.3	PRODUITS RAFFINES
3341	GASOLINE,OTH LIGHT OILS	W 25568	11.9	W 25857	13.0	W 29817	15.7	W 32059	17.4	ESSENCES POUR MOTEURS
33411	MOTOR,AVIATION SPIRIT	W 25426	11.9	W 25672	12.9	W 29670	15.7	W 31795	17.4	ESSENCES MOTEURS D'AVIONS
3342	KEROSENE,OTH MEDIUM OILS	W 10851	3.1	W 15122	6.9	W 57613	17.2	W 84359	21.0	PETR LAMPANTS,AUT HUIL
33421	KEROSENE INCL JET FUEL			W 6478	4.0	W 57613	17.2	W 84359	21.0	PETROLES LAMPANTS
3343	GAS OILS	W 95714	29.0	W 76332	24.3	W 79666	27.2	W 80272	28.8	GAS OILS
3344	FUEL OILS,NES	W 273944	28.4	W 262741	29.4	W 270282	34.6	W 262901	33.4	FUEL OILS
341	*GAS,NATURAL AND MANUFCT	W 18588	10.6	W 20879	12.6	W 22744	14.5	W 20503	13.7	GAZ NATUREL,GAZ MANUFACT
3413	PETROLM GASES,LIQUEFIED	W 18588	10.6	W 20879	12.6	W 22744	14.5	W 20503	13.7	GAZ DE PETROLE LIQUEFIE
34131	LIQUEFIED PROPANE,BUTANE	W 18588	10.6	W 20879	12.6	W 22744	14.5	W 20503	13.7	PROPANE,BUTANE LIQUEFIES
351	*ELECTRIC CURRENT		10.4		12.3		12.3	H 175284	13.9	ENERGIE ELECTRIQUE
4	ANIMAL,VEGETABLE OIL,FAT		5.8		6.6		7.1		6.6	HUILES,GRAISSES ANIM,VEG
42	FIXED VEGETABLE OIL,FAT		5.8		6.6		7.0		6.6	HUILES VEGETALES FIXES
5	CHEMCLS,RELATED PROD NES		90.0		87.5		87.6		84.9	PRODUITS CHIMIQUES
53	DYES,TANNING,COLOUR PROD		9.6		9.2		7.5		9.0	PROD TEINTURE,COLORANTS
541	*MEDICINAL,PHARM PRODUCT	K 1469828	15.6	K 1660827	18.4	K 1957219	21.2	K 1887280	18.2	PROD MEDICINAUX PHARMACEUT
5417	MEDICAMENTS	K 1395770	13.2	K 1551979	15.7	K 1870454	17.4	K 1765881	15.0	MEDICAMENTS
54179	— CONTNG OTH SUBSTANCES	K 1174444	9.8	K 1376544	10.3	K 1501036	12.4	K 1263512	11.2	MED CONT AUT SUBSTANCES
55	PERFUME,CLEANING ETC PRD		23.3		27.2		33.9		32.5	PROD POUR PARFUM,TOILETTE
553	PERFUMERY,COSMETICS,ETC	W 9798	13.4	W 11141	15.7	W 10731	20.9	W 9859	21.8	PRODUITS DE PARFUMERIE
554	SOAP,CLEANSING ETC PREPS	W 13959	9.0	W 12416	10.6	W 16635	12.2	W 9752	10.0	SAVONS,PRODUITS DETERSIFS
5541	SOAPS	W 6713	3.8	W 5382	5.2	W 9917	6.5	W 2855	3.9	SAVONS,PROD TENSIO–ACTIFS
58	PLASTIC MATERIALS ETC		24.9		18.5		12.8		13.5	MAT PLAST ARTIFICIELLES
583	POLYMERIZATION ETC PRODS	W 18505	19.1	W 13661	17.0	W 12516	11.5	W 13514	11.6	PROD POLYMERISATION
5833	POLYSTYRENE,ITS COPOLYMR	W 6721	7.3	W 5571	7.7	W 3722	3.8	W 4894	3.8	POLYPROPYLENE COPOLYMERES
58331	— IN PRIMARY FORMS	W 6504	6.9	W 5391	7.3	W 3527	3.6	W 4677	3.7	SOUS FORMES PRIMAIRES
5834	POLYVINYL CHLORIDE	W 5146	6.4	W 3291	4.7	W 2561	3.6	W 2525	3.5	CHLORURE DE POLYVINYLE
59	CHEMICAL MATERIALS NES		8.0		8.4		8.2		7.6	MAT PROD CHIMIQUES NDA
6	BASIC MANUFACTURES		889.0		882.8		918.0		971.4	ART MANUFACTURES
61	LEATHER,DRESSED FUR,ETC		39.8		43.1		24.0		15.0	CUIRS,PELLETERIES
611	LEATHER	W 914	8.3	W 1147	6.7	W 1224	4.8	W 1256	4.2	CUIRS,PEAUX PREPARES
612	LEATHER ETC MANUFACTURES	W 1849	4.5	W 3217	9.5	W 1874	6.9	W 2122	6.3	OUVRAGES EN CUIRS NDA
6123	PREPRD PARTS OF FOOTWEAR	W 1844	4.4	W 3214	9.4	W 1865	6.7	W 2115	6.1	PARTIES DE CHAUSSURES
613	FUR SKINS TANNED,DRESSED	W 88	27.2	W 103	27.0	W 42	12.4	W 45	4.7	PELLETERIES
63	WOOD,CORK MANUFACTRS NES		11.4		8.0		6.9		7.6	OUVRAGES LIEGE ET BOIS
634	VENEERS,PLYWOOD,ETC	W 22196	7.6	W 15522	4.6	W 16115	4.6	W 15585	5.1	PLACAGES,CONTRE–PLAQUES
6342	PLYWOOD OF WOOD SHEETS	W 22101	7.5	W 15435	4.5	W 16094	4.6	W 15561	5.1	BOIS CONTRE–PLAQUES
64	PAPER,PAPERBOARD AND MFR		28.0		26.1		24.7		24.6	PAPIERS,CARTONS & OUVRAGES
641	PAPER AND PAPERBOARD	W 19258	8.7	W 17497	9.0	W 16422	8.5	W 15926	8.6	PAPIERS ET CARTONS
642	PAPER,ETC,PRECUT,ARTS OF	W 14863	19.3	W 12540	17.1	W 9849	16.3	W 8615	16.0	PAP,CARTONS DECOUPES
6421	PAPER ETC CONTAINERS	W 7098	6.6	W 6014	5.5	W 3815	4.1	W 2605	3.1	BOITES,SACS EMBALLAGES
6428	PAPER ETC ARTICLES NES	W 4633	10.3	W 3879	9.0	W 3590	9.1	W 3747	10.0	OUVRAGES EN PATE A PAPIER
65	TEXTILE YARN,FABRICS,ETC		666.9		698.2		769.1		839.5	FILS,TISSUS,ARTICLES TEXTILE
651	TEXTILE YARN	W 26238	133.2	W 24360	124.8	W 23808	131.9	W 24663	140.2	FILS TEXTILES
6512	WOOL,HAIR YARN,INCL TOPS	W 6868	64.8	W 5926	60.7	W 5334	57.2	W 6406	66.1	FILS DE LAINE,DE POILS
65122	CARDED WOOL YARN IN BULK	W 4595	41.4	W 4170	42.1	W 3812	40.1	W 5150	53.2	FILS CONT 85% LAINE CARDEE
65123	COMBED WOOL YARN IN BULK	W 685	8.1	W 547	5.4	W 481	5.1	W 475	4.4	FILS CONT 85% LAINE PEIGNEE
65127	CARDED WOOL BLEND YARN	W 774	7.6	W 712	7.5	W 720	7.7	W 503	4.6	LAINE CARD MOINS 85% LAINE

4. General Imports C.I.F. by Commodities according to the S.I.T.C. (Rev. 2) in million U.S. Dollars
Importations Générales C.A.F. par Produits d'après la C.T.C.I. (Rév. 2) en millions de Dollars E.U.

SITC CTCI	COMMODITY	1994 QUANTITY QUANTITE	1994 VALUE VALEUR	1995 QUANTITY QUANTITE	1995 VALUE VALEUR	1996 QUANTITY QUANTITE	1996 VALUE VALEUR	1997 QUANTITY QUANTITE	1997 VALUE VALEUR	PRODUIT
6513	COTTON YARN	W 10033	31.6	W 9190	32.3	W 10018	39.5	W 9752	36.5	FILS DE COTON
6514	SYN FIB YRN,BULK,MONOFIL	W 4644	14.5	W 5106	15.2	W 4527	16.7	W 4277	19.5	FILS CONT 85% FIB TEXT SYNTH
65142	— NONTXT ETC CONT PAMID	W 2789	9.0	W 2629	9.2	W 2297	10.3	W 2807	13.4	FILS NON TEX FI CON POLYAMID
6516	DISCON SYN FIB BLEND YRN	W 3162	10.3	W 3244	8.7	W 2814	8.8	W 2412	7.4	FILS FIBR TEX SYNT DIS MOINS
652	COTTON FABRICS,WOVEN	W 23343	157.0	W 24701	180.5	W 25251	214.2	W 22021	209.6	TISSUS DE COTON
6522	WOVEN COTTON BLEACHD,ETC	W 23184	156.3	W 24608	180.0	W 25217	214.0	W 21958	209.3	TISSUS COTON BLANCHIS ETC
65223	PILE ETC COTTON FABRICS	W 1146	6.8	W 1591	12.2	W 2130	19.5	W 1719	16.9	VELOURS TISSUS BOUCLES
65224	BLCHED COTTON FABRIC NES	W 20897	143.6	W 21853	160.0	W 22481	186.2	W 19039	182.4	AUT TIS PLUS 85% COT BLANCHI
65225	BLCHD COTN BLEND FAB NES	W 568	5.5	W 737	7.6	W 587	8.3	W 657	10.0	AUT TIS MOINS 85% COT BLANCH
653	WOVN MAN–MADE FIB FABRIC	W 42848	98.9	W 47575	102.7	W 46125	100.7	W 46286	117.6	TISSUS FIBRES SYNTH,ARTIF
6531	CONT SYNT WEAVES NONPILE	W 37788	66.2	W 41353	63.0	W 41717	64.6	W 42302	83.3	TISSUS FIBRES SYNTH CONTINUE
65314	CONT SYN TYRE CORD FABRC	W 4141	14.4	W 4301	12.4	W 3450	11.6	W 3317	11.2	TIS ARMATURE PNEUMATIQUES
65315	CONT SYN TXTL FABRIC NES	W 33647	51.8	W 37052	50.6	W 38267	53.1	W 38985	72.2	TIS PLUS 85% TEXT SYNT CONT
6532	DISC SYN TXTL FABRIC NES	W 686	6.3	W 750	9.7	W 843	12.9	W 918	10.1	TIS DISC MOINS 85% FIBR TEXT
6534	DISC SYN BLEND FABRC NES	W 3646	18.0	W 4662	19.9	W 2880	14.8	W 2371	14.3	TISSUS FIBRES SYNTH DISCONT
65341	DISC SYN FIB–COTTN FABRC	W 3505	17.4	W 4456	19.0	W 2760	14.4	W 2223	13.8	TISSUS FIB SYNT DIS MEL COTO
654	OTH WOVEN TEXTILE FABRIC	W 760	10.6	W 554	7.5	W 365	6.1	W 409	4.6	TISSUS AUT COTON SYNT,ARTIF
6544	WOVEN FLAX,RAMIE FABRICS	W 497	7.3	W 387	5.2	W 266	5.0	W 270	3.1	TISSUS DE LIN,RAMIE
655	KNITTED,ETC FABRICS	W 40361	236.2	W 43969	249.9	W 48166	282.9	W 47582	328.9	ETOF BONNETERIE PIECES ETC
6552	OTHER KNIT ETC FAB NONEL	W 40361	236.2	W 43969	249.9	W 48166	282.9	W 47582	328.9	ETOF BON NON ELAS NON SYNT
656	LACE,RIBBONS,TULLE,ETC	W 2057	12.6	W 1985	15.0	W 1777	17.8	W 1888	22.9	TULLES,BRODERIE
65601	NARROW FABRICS NES	W 1479	4.3	W 1496	5.3	W 1247	6.8	W 1215	7.3	RUBANS SANS TRAME EN FILS
657	SPECIAL TXTL FABRC,PRODS	W 3482	12.8	W 3774	12.1	W 3833	10.8	W 3226	11.5	TISSUS SPECIAUX
6573	COATED ETC TEXTILES NES	W 1922	7.4	W 2282	6.3	W 2350	5.4	W 1923	6.2	TISSUS,ART MATIERE TEXT NDA
65732	PLASTIC COATED TEXTILES	W 1808	6.8	W 2187	5.7	W 2118	4.8	W 1711	4.4	TISSUS IMPREGNES
66	NONMETAL MINERAL MFS NES		58.7		43.3		39.4		31.9	ART MIN NON METALLIQUES
661	LIME,CEMENT,BLDG PRODS	W 720718	26.8	W 512264	21.6	W 587693	24.5	W 500300	18.5	CHAUX,CIMENTS MAT CONSTR
6612	CEMENT	W 712842	23.8	W 492461	16.7	W 578490	21.5	W 490580	15.9	CIMENTS HYDRAULIQUES
662	CLAY,REFRACTORY BLDG PRD	W 29939	8.1	W 37609	10.4	W 21230	6.7	W 20826	5.1	MAT CONST REFRACTAIRES
6624	BRICKS ETC NONREFRACTORY	W 29688	8.0	W 37565	10.4	W 21094	6.7	W 20813	5.1	BRIQUES ETC CERAM NON REFR
66245	GLAZED CERAMIC SETTS ETC	W 17836	5.7	W 23273	7.9	W 12362	4.3	W 13021	3.9	AUT CARREAUX CERAMIQUE
663	MINERAL MANUFCTURES NES	W 206849	17.2	W 67494	4.7	W 21562	2.6	W 27671	3.3	ART MIN MANUF NDA
6633	MINRL MFS NES NONCERAMIC	W 206267	16.5	W 67262	4.3	W 21342	2.3	W 27458	3.0	OUVR MAT MINERALE NDA
66332	CEMENT,ARTFCL STONE PROD	W 206003	16.4	W 66941	4.1	W 21113	2.2	W 27046	2.8	OUVRAGES EN CIMENT
67	IRON AND STEEL		45.1		22.7		18.5		19.6	FER ET ACIER
673	IRON,STEEL SHAPES ETC	W 157595	31.7	W 76138	13.9	W 69334	11.9	W 61992	11.6	BARRES,PROFIL FER,ACIER
6732	IRON,STEEL BARS ETC	W 132448	25.2	W 65387	11.2	W 62720	9.8	W 52840	8.5	BARRES FER,ACIER
67326	IRN,OTH STL BARS HOTROLD	W 119324	21.5	W 64843	11.0	W 61951	9.5	W 52572	8.4	BARRES PLEINES FER,ACIER
6733	IRON,STEEL PROFILES ETC	W 25147	6.5	W 10750	2.8	W 6609	2.2	W 9152	3.2	PROFILES,PALPLAN FER,ACIER
678	IRON,STL TUBES,PIPES,ETC	W 15023	9.9	W 10229	5.7	W 7248	3.6	W 8542	3.7	TUBES,TUYAUX EN FONTE,FER
68	NON–FERROUS METALS		5.1		7.5		9.4		8.2	METAUX NON FERREUX
69	METAL MANUFACTURES NES		30.4		30.4		22.0		21.3	ART MANUFACT EN METAL NDA
691	STRUCTURES AND PARTS NES	W 6547	8.8	W 3786	8.9	W 2613	3.9	W 3348	4.4	CONSTRUCT FER,ACIER,ALU
6911	STRUCTURES,PARTS IRN,STL	W 5677	7.5	W 2462	5.0	W 1586	2.9	W 2671	3.2	CONSTRUCT FER,ACIER,FONTE
699	BASE METAL MFRS NES	W 4712	9.7		9.5	W 3147	8.3	W 3188	7.7	ART MANUFACTURES MET NDA
7	MACHINES,TRANSPORT EQUIP		423.7		382.7		312.8		351.8	MACHINES MATERIEL TRANSPORT
71	POWER GENERATING EQUIPMT		26.5		39.5		8.4		13.9	MACHINES GENERATRICES
713	INTRNL COMBUS PSTN ENGIN	W 3454	6.3	W 2143	3.0	W 1867	2.4	W 1635	8.7	MOTEURS EXPL COMB INT, PIECE
716	ROTATING ELECTRIC PLANT	W 1982	19.8	W 3452	34.7	W 925	5.4	W 646	4.2	APP ELECTR ROTATIFS,PIECES
7162	AC MTRS,GENRTRS,GEN SETS	W 1275	12.8	W 3139	28.5	W 698	2.7	W 535	2.4	MOTEURS ELECTRIQUES
71622	AC GENERATORS	W 599	7.0	W 602	7.0	W 26	0.1	W 13	0.1	GENER COURANT ALTERNATIF
71623	GEN SETS WITH PISTN ENGN	W 306	4.6	W 2173	20.5	W 129	0.9	W 103	1.0	GROUPES MOTEUR EXPLOSION
7169	PTS NES OF ROT ELEC PLNT	W 707	7.0	W 313	6.2	W 224	2.8	W 111	1.8	PIECES MAC APP ROTATIFS
72	MACHS FOR SPCL INDUSTRYS		22.4		16.7		12.3		36.4	MAC SPECIALES POUR INDUST
724	TEXTILE,LEATHER MACHNRY	W 733	7.6	W 526	5.8	W 458	4.9	W 2224	14.2	MACH POUR INDUSTRIE TEXTILE
7245	WEAVING,FELT MFG,ETC MCH	W 123	1.4	W 101	2.4	W 120	1.7	W 1672	9.5	METIERS A TISSER,PIECES
728	OTH MACHY FOR SPCL INDUS	W 968	7.3	W 686	5.4	W 678	4.5	W 796	18.1	AUT MACH IND PARTICULIERES
7284	MACHY FOR SPCL INDUS NES	W 587	6.0	W 325	3.2	W 562	4.2	W 672	17.7	MACH SPEC IND PARTICUL.
72848	OTH MCHY WITH INDIV FNCT	W 231	3.8	W 227	1.6	W 263	2.4	W 390	12.5	AUTRES MACHINES NDA
74	GENRL INDUSTRL MACHY NES		83.4		66.2		52.5		47.8	MACH APP INDUSTRIE
741	HEATING,COOLING EQUIPMNT	W 4341	30.5	W 4037	26.3	W 3100	24.0	W 2961	21.4	MACH CHAUFFAGE,PIECES
7415	AIR–CONDITIONING MACHNRY	W 3740	23.9	W 3440	22.4	W 2679	20.9	W 2259	16.9	GROUPES CONDITION AIR
743	PUMPS NES,CENTRFUGES ETC	W 1173	10.7	W 634	3.1	W 658	2.8	W 488	2.9	POMPES COMPRES,VENT ETC
744	MECHANICAL HANDLING EQU	W 6984	24.2	W 5226	24.1	W 3088	16.0	W 3278	15.2	EQUIP MANUTENTION PIECES
7442	LIFTING,LOADING MACH NES	W 3851	14.6	W 2751	13.1	W 1604	9.4	W 1623	8.7	APP LEVAGE,MANUTENTION
74424	LIFTS AND SKIP HOISTS	W 1693	6.3	W 1679	6.9	W 942	4.3	W 886	4.1	ASCENSEURS,MONTE–CHARGE
7449	PTS NES OF MACHY OF 7442	W 2947	9.3	W 2160	8.7	W 1135	5.7	W 1510	5.9	PIECES DU 744.2
749	NONELEC MACH PTS,ACC NES	W 1554	12.4	W 1434	8.8	W 1308	6.3	W 1640	5.4	PIECES MACH NON ELEC NDA
7499	OTH NONELEC MCHY PTS NES	W 818	8.0	W 426	3.9	W 235	2.3	W 244	1.9	PIECES NON ELECT NDA
74991	FOUNDRY MOULDS ETC NES	W 722	7.2	W 353	3.7	W 181	2.1	W 206	1.8	MOULES POUR METAUX
75	OFFICE MACHNES,ADP EQUIP		21.9		26.7		19.5		17.8	MACH BUREAU TRAIT AUTOM
752	AUTOMTIC DATA PROC EQUIP	W 237	11.4	W 239	14.0	W 217	10.4	W 309	9.1	MACH TRAIT INFORMATION
7523	DIGITL CENTRL PROCESSORS	W 74	7.4	W 80	6.4	W 2	0.1	W 10	0.3	UNITES CENTRALES
7525	ADP PERIPHERAL UNITS	W 122	2.9	W 150	6.2	W 142	3.6	W 189	3.6	UNITES PERIPHERIQUES
759	OFFICE,ADP MCH PTS,ACCES	W 106	4.4	W 177	7.1	W 255	5.5	W 273	5.6	PIECES DU 751 ET 752
7599	ACCTG,ETC,ADP MCH PTS,AC	W 80	3.8	W 151	6.5	W 203	4.8	W 219	4.9	PIECES DU 751 ET 752
76	TELECOMM,SOUND EQUIPMENT		97.0		76.8		60.6		46.1	EQUIPMENT DE TELECOM
761	TELEVISION RECEIVERS	W 1240	15.1	W 1244	19.8	W 1340	14.6	W 762	7.6	RECEPTEURS DE TELEVISION
7611	COLOUR TV RECEIVERS	W 1238	15.1	W 1242	19.7	W 1338	14.6	W 758	7.5	RECEPTEURS COULEUR
762	RADIO BROADCAST RECEIVRS	W 4624	29.8	W 1990	11.6	W 238	2.7	W 124	1.6	RECEPTEURS RADIODIFFUSION
7628	OTHER RADIO RECEIVERS	W 4576	28.9	W 1965	11.2	W 219	1.9	W 107	1.4	AUTRES RECEPT RADIO
763	SOUND RECORDRS,PHONOGRPH	W 512	8.7	W 352	6.9	W 303	8.3	W 205	7.8	PHONO,APP ENREGISTREMENT
7638	OTHR SOUND APPARATUS ETC	W 511	8.7	W 350	6.9	W 303	8.3	W 205	7.8	AUT APP D'ENREGIS,REPROD
76381	TV IMAGE,SND RECRDRS ETC	W 367	6.6	W 298	6.0	W 265	7.5	W 183	7.1	APP ENREG,REPRO IMAG,SON
764	TELECOM EQPT,PTS,ACC NES	W 921	43.5	W 756	38.7	W 945	35.1	W 446	29.3	EQUIP TELECOM,PIECES
7641	LINE TELEPHONE,ETC EQUIP	W 93	6.8	W 58	3.9	W 66	5.7	W 55	3.3	APP TELEPHON PAR FIL
7643	TV,RADIO TRANSMITTRS ETC	W 21	12.0	W 37	17.1	W 34	15.0	W 41	18.5	APP EMET TELE RADIO
7648	TELECOMM EQUIPMENT NES	W 27	12.3	W 27	9.1	W 9	5.0	W 2	1.6	APP TELECOM NDA
76481	RADIOTELEPHONE ETC RCVRS	W 5	4.8	W 7	6.9	W 3	3.0	W 1	1.3	RECEP RADIOTELEPHONIE
76483	RADAR APPARATUS ETC	W 10	6.3	W 1	0.4		0.2		0.1	APP DE RADIOGUIDAGE ETC
7649	PTS NES OF EQUIPMT OF 76	W 134	7.9	W 199	6.4	W 250	6.2	W 128	4.2	PIECES DE LA DIV 76
77	ELECTRIC MACHNRY NES ETC		99.8		83.3		75.7		75.7	MACH APP ELECT NDA
771	ELECTRIC POWER MACHY NES	W 794	10.4	W 834	16.9	W 1842	20.8	W 12232	29.2	MACH PROD,TRANS ELECTR
7711	TRANSFORMERS,ELECTRICAL	W 361	3.6	W 347	1.7	W 930	6.0	W 11690	18.7	TRANSFO ELECTRIQUES
77118	OTHER ELEC TRANSFORMERS	W 70	0.9	W 59	0.3	W 560	4.9	W 11535	18.0	AUTRES TRANSFO ELECTRIQ
7712	OTH ELEC POWER MACHY NES	W 433	6.9	W 487	15.3	W 913	14.9	W 541	10.5	AUT APP PROD TRANSF ELEC
77122	INDUCTORS	W 60	1.5	W 132	6.1	W 122	4.0	W 230	5.0	BOBINES REACTANCE,SELFS
77129	PTS NES OF MACHY OF 771	W 345	4.8	W 302	6.2	W 653	10.0	W 247	4.7	PIECES MACH DU 771
772	SWITCHGEAR ETC,PARTS NES	W 919	20.3	W 694	14.3	W 852	8.5	W 566	7.7	APP COUPURE,SECT ETC
7721	SWITCHGEAR ETC	W 894	18.9	W 675	12.8	W 823	7.0	W 544	5.8	APP COUPURE,SECTIONMNT
773	ELECTR DISTRIBUTNG EQUIP	W 4063	13.9	W 2532	7.5	W 2220	6.6	W 1897	5.8	EQUIPMT DISTRIBUTION ELECT

4. General Imports C.I.F. by Commodities according to the S.I.T.C. (Rev. 2) in million U.S. Dollars
Importations Générales C.A.F. par Produits d'après la C.T.C.I. (Rév. 2) en millions de Dollars E.U.

SITC CTCI	COMMODITY	1994		1995		1996		1997		PRODUIT
		QUANTITY QUANTITE	VALUE VALEUR	QUANTITY QUANTITE	VALUE VALEUR	QUANTITY QUANTITE	VALUE VALEUR	QUANTITY QUANTITE	VALUE VALEUR	
7731	INSULATED WIRE,CABLE ETC	W 4059	13.8	W 2526	7.5	W 2217	6.5	W 1894	5.8	FILS,CABLES ISOLES ELECT
775	HOUSEHOLD TYPE EQUIP NES	W 4419	25.1		17.2	W 2944	16.6	W 2228	11.8	MACH,APP USAGE DOMESTQUE
7752	DOM REFRIGERATRS,FREEZRS	W 2011	10.7	W 1202	6.4	W 1329	6.5	W 891	3.9	REFRIG,CONGEL MENAGER
77521	DOMESTIC REFRIGERATORS	W 2002	10.6	W 1196	6.3	W 1323	6.4	W 880	3.8	REFRIGERATEURS
7758	ELECTRO–THERMIC APPL NES	W 956	7.1		5.2	W 709	5.2	W 543	3.8	APP ELECTROTHERMIQ NDA
776	TRANSISTORS,VALVES,ETC	W 34	6.6	W 55	9.3	W 35	6.4	W 46	5.1	LAMPES,TUBES,VALVES
7764	ELECTRONIC MICROCIRCUITS	W 19	4.2	W 40	6.4	W 16	4.4	W 29	3.2	MICROSTRUCTURES ELECTRON
778	ELECTRICAL MACHINERY NES	W 1994	23.3	W 1571	17.0	W 1334	15.3	W 1284	13.3	AUTRES MACH ELECT NDA
7781	BATTERIES,ACCUMULATORS	W 1276	10.0	W 945	6.9	W 681	6.7	W 741	6.0	PILES ET ACCUMULATEURS
77812	ELECTRIC ACCUMULATORS	W 373	7.8	W 329	4.4	W 408	5.4	W 464	4.9	ACCUMULATEURS ELECTRIQ
7788	OTH ELEC MACHY,EQUIP NES	W 165	10.1	W 186	7.2	W 315	6.1	W 241	5.0	AUT MACH APP ELEC NDA
78	ROAD VEHICLES		70.4		51.2		62.8		77.6	VEHICULES ROUTIERS
781	PASS MOTOR VEH EXC BUSES	W 5581	47.3	W 3600	31.3	W 5730	36.7	W 4729	51.4	AUTO TRANSPORT PERSONNES
782	LORRIES,SPCL MTR VEH NES	W 1106	8.7	W 655	7.2	W 492	4.3	W 558	5.0	VEHICULES SPECIAUX,MARCH
783	ROAD MOTOR VEHICLES NES	W 400	3.5	W 400	4.6	W 721	7.9	W 636	7.7	VEHICULES ROUTIERS NDA
7831	BUSES	W 259	2.4	W 380	4.5	W 607	7.4	W 629	7.6	VOITURES TRANSPORT COMMUN
785	CYCLES,ETC MOTRZD OR NOT	W 1010	9.6	W 461	5.8	W 935	10.9	W 821	12.1	MOTOCYCLES SCOOTERS
7851	MOTORCYCLES ETC	W 549	8.8	W 366	5.4	W 838	10.5	W 761	11.8	MOTO VELO MOTEUR AUXIL
79	OTHR TRANSPORT EQUIPMENT		0.7		21.6		20.0		35.5	AUTRE MATERIEL TRANSPORT
792	AIRCRAFT ETC	W 1	0.4	W 18	20.8	W 56	19.6	W 87	35.1	APP NAVIGATION AERIENNE
7921	HELICOPTERS					W 6	1.9	W 24	19.6	HELICOPTERES
7923	AIRCRFT NES2000–15000KG			W 14	18.0					AERODYNES 2000 A 15000 KG
7929	AIRCRAFT PARTS NES	W 1	0.4	W 4	2.9	W 50	17.7	W 64	15.6	PIECES DU 792
8	MISC MANUFACTURED GOODS		214.5		220.1		215.8		218.0	ART MANUFACTURES DIVERS
821	*FURNITURE,PARTS THEREOF	W 7589	13.4	W 7718	14.8	W 7213	12.8	W 6655	13.3	MEUBLES ET PIECES
8219	FURNITURE AND PARTS NES	W 5098	7.9	W 5480	9.8	W 5186	7.9	W 4769	8.9	AUTRES MEUBLES ET PIECES
82192	WOOD FURNITURE NES	W 4253	6.3	W 4476	7.7	W 4323	6.4	W 3732	6.4	MEUBLES NDA EN BOIS
84	CLOTHING AND ACCESSORIES		87.0		88.9		101.6		106.7	VETEMENTS
843	WOMENS OUTERWEAR NONKNIT	W 168	2.9	W 174	3.9	W 147	4.3	W 292	7.6	VET DESSUS FEMMES MAT TEX
845	OUTERWEAR KNIT NONELASTC	W 5521	68.6	W 5192	68.9	W 5632	74.1	W 5332	71.9	VET DESSOUS,ACCES BONNET
8451	— JERSEYS,PULLOVERS ETC	W 5308	65.1	W 5015	65.6	W 5268	68.3	W 4738	64.3	CHANDAILS,PULL–OVERS ETC
846	UNDER GARMENTS KNITTED	W 184	3.5	W 181	3.6	W 281	5.3	W 362	7.2	SOUS VETS DE BONNETERIE
847	TEXTILE CLTHNG ACCES NES	W 549	4.9	W 561	5.6	W 673	8.8	W 749	10.3	ACCES VET MAT TEXT NDA
8471	— NOT KNITTED	W 459	4.7	W 495	5.3	W 637	8.4	W 711	10.1	ACCES VET MAT TEX NON BON
84719	MADE–UP CLTHG ACCESS NES	W 422	4.1	W 448	4.6	W 600	7.5	W 701	9.3	AUT ACCES VET MAT TEXTIL
851	*FOOTWEAR	W 1087	7.2	W 1406	8.8	W 1991	9.4	W 1106	7.1	CHAUSSURES
85102	FOOTWEAR LEATHER	W 628	5.9	W 938	7.3	W 1584	8.3	W 902	6.5	CHAUS SEMELLES EN CUIR
87	PRECISION INSTRUMNTS NES		7.1		7.8		8.0		6.2	INSTRUM,APPAR SCIENT NDA
89	MISC MANUFCTRD GOODS NES		86.7		87.6		70.9		72.9	ART MANUFACTURES DIVERS
892	PRINTED MATTER	W 1608	7.3	W 1366	9.7	W 1278	10.3	W 1439	9.6	IMPRIMES
8928	PRINTED MATTER NES	W 1274	6.0	W 1063	8.3	W 992	8.7	W 1009	7.3	IMPRIMES NDA
89281	LABELS PAPER,PAPERBOARD	W 678	4.5	W 619	5.4	W 594	5.9	W 601	6.3	ETIQUETTES TOUS GENRES
893	ARTICLES OF PLASTIC NES		31.2		27.0	W 8336	17.4		17.1	OUVRAGES EN MAT DIVIS 58
8931	PLSTC PACKG CONTNRS,LIDS	W 8102	10.0	W 6837	9.6	W 4101	6.1	W 3261	5.6	ART TRANSP EMBALLAGE ETC
8939	MISC PLASTIC ARTICLES	W 8012	21.0	W 6684	17.2	W 4147	11.1	W 4031	11.3	ART DIVERS EN MAT DIV 58
89399	OTHR PLASTC ARTICLES NES	W 7756	20.6	W 6383	16.6	W 3907	10.6	W 3529	10.5	AUT OUV MAT DIV 58
894	TOYS,SPORTING GOODS,ETC	W 3375	12.1	W 1392	11.4	W 1321	11.3	W 789	8.5	VOITURES ENFANTS,JOUETS
8942	TOYS,INDOOR GAMES ETC	W 3313	11.6	W 1295	10.8	W 1102	9.8	W 633	7.7	JOUETS,JEUX ETC
89424	INDOOR GAME EQUIPMENT	W 265	6.0	W 275	5.0	W 462	6.2	W 264	5.3	ART,JEUX DE SOCIETE
897	GOLD,SILVER WARE,JEWELRY		7.4		6.8		4.4		6.8	BIJOUTERIE,ORFEVRERIE
898	MUSICAL INSTRUMENTS,PTS	W 1754	9.2	W 1222	7.4	W 827	3.5	W 1029	4.4	INSTRUMENTS DE MUSIQUE
8983	SOUND RECRDNG TAPE,DISCS	W 1123	6.8	W 739	5.5	W 304	1.8	W 554	2.9	SUPPORTS SON POUR 763
899	OTHER MANUFACTURED GOODS		18.2		21.2		22.1		23.6	AUT ART MANUF DIVERS NDA
8998	SMALLWARES,TOILETRYS ETC	W 1677	15.1	W 1789	16.4	W 2092	18.2	W 1529	18.9	ART MERCERIE,TOILETTE
89983	BUTTONS,STUDS,ETC	W 845	7.3	W 815	8.0	W 754	8.0	W 693	8.8	BOUTONS,BOUTONS–PRESSION
89984	SLIDE FASTENERS,PARTS	W 774	7.7	W 910	8.3	W 1281	10.0	W 781	10.0	FERMETURES A GLISSIERE
9	GOODS NOT CLASSD BY KIND		16.7		8.1		3.0		12.3	ART TRANSACT NON CLASSES
971	*GOLD,NON MONETARY NES	K 1157	13.8	K 4407	5.1	K 18	0.2	K 769	8.2	OR NON MONETAIRE
97101	NONMON GLD UNWRT,SEMIMFD	K 1117	13.8	K 420	5.1	K 15	0.2	K 769	8.2	OR,ALLIAGES D'OR BRUTS

5. General Exports F.O.B. by Commodities according to the S.I.T.C. (Rev. 2) in million U.S. Dollars
Exportations Générales F.O.B. par Produits d'après la C.T.C.I. (Rév. 2) en millions de Dollars E.U.

SITC CTCI	COMMODITY	1994		1995		1996		1997		PRODUIT
		QUANTITY QUANTITE	VALUE VALEUR	QUANTITY QUANTITE	VALUE VALEUR	QUANTITY QUANTITE	VALUE VALEUR	QUANTITY QUANTITE	VALUE VALEUR	
	ALL COMMODITIES		1872.2		2024.7		2100.1		2282.1	TOUS PRODUITS
0	FOOD AND LIVE ANIMALS		15.2		9.1		7.3		6.7	ALIMENTS,ANIMAUX VIVANTS
1	BEVERAGES AND TOBACCO		52.5		24.3		25.4		26.0	BOISSONS ET TABACS
11	BEVERAGES		33.4		10.9		9.1		8.6	BOISSONS
112	ALCOHOLIC BEVERAGES	W 2420	29.9	W 3313	7.5	W 2319	7.5	W 3053	6.9	BOISSONS ALCOOLIQUES
1124	DISTILLED ALCOHOLIC BEVS	W 989	28.7	W 318	4.6	W 281	4.9	W 181	3.5	ALCOOLS,EAUX–DE–VIE
11242	DISTILLD WINE,GRAPE MARC	W 723	27.2	W 126	4.1	W 129	4.5	W 128	3.0	EAUX–DE–VIE NATURELLES
12	TOBACCO AND MANUFACTURES		19.1		13.5		16.3		17.5	TABACS BRUTS FABRIQUES
122	TOBACCO,MANUFACTURED	W 2318	19.1	W 1308	13.5	W 1544	16.3	W 1590	17.5	TABACS FABRIQUES
1222	CIGARETTES	W 2261	18.9	W 1258	13.3	W 1496	16.0	W 1543	17.2	CIGARETTES
2	CRUDE MATERLS,EXCL FUELS		43.1		48.5		48.3		23.8	MAT BRUTES NON COMESTIBLES
21	HIDES,SKINS,FURS UNDRSSD		25.8		27.9		33.1		11.1	CUIRS,PEAUX BRUTS
212	FURSKINS,RAW	W 122	25.8	W 148	27.9	W 187	33.1	W 325	11.0	PELLETERIES BRUTES
21201	MINK SKINS,RAW	W 98	22.0	W 80	16.6	W 69	20.9	W 88	5.5	PEAUX DE VISON BRUTES
21209	OTHER FURSKINS,RAW	W 24	3.8	W 68	11.3	W 118	12.2	W 237	5.5	AUTRES PELLETERIES BRUTES
26	TEXTILE FIBRES AND WASTE		14.8		17.9		13.0		11.1	FIBRES TEXTILES
268	WOOL(EXC TOPS),ANML HAIR	W 2651	14.6	W 2959	17.6	W 3452	12.8	W 2959	10.8	LAINES ET POILS
2682	WOOL DEGREASED,UNCOMBED	W 2526	14.1	W 2782	16.5	W 3191	11.2	W 2737	10.2	LAINE DEGRAISSEE
3	MINERAL FUELS ETC		0.4		0.3		8.1		9.2	COMBUSTIBLES MINERAUX LUB
33	PETROLEUM AND PRODUCTS		0.3		0.3		8.1		9.2	PETROLE ET DERIVES
334	PETROLEUM PRODUCTS,REFIN	W 217	0.2	W 177	0.2	W 28986	8.1	W 36508	9.2	PRODUITS RAFFINES
3342	KEROSENE,OTH MEDIUM OILS					W 28744	7.8	W 36306	9.1	PETR LAMPANTS,AUT HUIL
33421	KEROSENE INCL JET FUEL					W 28744	7.8	W 36306	9.1	PETROLES LAMPANTS
5	CHEMCLS,RELATED PROD NES		22.5		21.1		18.7		21.0	PRODUITS CHIMIQUES
541	*MEDICINAL,PHARM PRODUCT	K 304354	6.1	K 196627	9.0	K 2500	0.1	K 148648	11.7	PROD MEDICINAUX PHARMACEUT
5413	ANTIBIOTICS IN BULK	K 23287	3.6	K 42851	7.1	K 31729	5.4	K 56071	9.9	ANTIBIOTIQUES NDA
54133	TETRACYCLINES AND DERIVS	K 23287	3.6	K 42251	7.1	K 31729	5.4	K 55933	9.9	TETRACYCLINES ET DERIVES
6	BASIC MANUFACTURES		232.8		244.6		215.0		189.2	ART MANUFACTURES
61	LEATHER,DRESSED FUR,ETC		39.7		41.0		23.9		6.6	CUIRS,PELLETERIES
611	LEATHER	W 532	7.0	W 360	3.5	W 425	1.9	W 370	1.1	CUIRS,PEAUX PREPARES
6116	LEATHER OF OTH HIDE,SKIN	W 276	5.9	W 110	2.2	W 18	0.4	W 15	0.3	PEAUX PREP D'AUTRES ANIMAUX
61161	LEATHER FROM GOAT,KID	W 272	5.8	W 106	2.2	W 11	0.3	W 13	0.3	PEAUX DE CAPRINS PREPAREES
613	FUR SKINS TANNED,DRESSED	W 94	28.0	W 106	32.0	W 61	16.5	W 2	0.2	PELLETERIES
65	TEXTILE YARN,FABRICS,ETC		158.6		169.0		154.6		148.3	FILS,TISSUS,ARTICLES TEXTILE
651	TEXTILE YARN	W 9369	70.5	W 9025	63.6	W 9062	71.6	W 8500	70.3	FILS TEXTILES
6512	WOOL,HAIR YARN,INCL TOPS	W 4704	50.5	W 4290	44.5	W 4286	47.5	W 4699	49.7	FILS DE LAINE,DE POILS
65122	CARDED WOOL YARN IN BULK	W 3387	35.1	W 3037	30.8	W 3169	34.5	W 3884	40.6	FILS CONT 85% LAINE CARDEE
65127	CARDED WOOL BLEND YARN	W 699	7.8	W 809	8.7	W 642	7.2	W 350	4.0	LAINE CARD MOINS 85% LAINE
6513	COTTON YARN	W 1434	7.2	W 1153	6.5	W 2141	13.9	W 1789	10.7	FILS DE COTON
652	COTTON FABRICS,WOVEN	W 8250	33.8	W 7738	35.4	W 7065	33.5	W 5943	30.5	TISSUS DE COTON
6522	WOVEN COTTON BLEACHD,ETC	W 8136	33.3	W 7724	35.3	W 7055	33.4	W 5936	30.5	TISSUS COTON BLANCHIS ETC
65224	BLCHED COTTON FABRIC NES	W 8022	32.7	W 7510	34.0	W 6822	31.7	W 5847	29.5	AUT TIS PLUS 85% COT BLANCHI
653	WOVN MAN–MADE FIB FABRIC	W 4541	14.4	W 5944	14.0	W 7533	12.7	W 9345	12.4	TISSUS FIBRES SYNTH,ARTIF
6531	CONT SYNT WEAVES NONPILE	W 4040	11.1	W 5498	11.8	W 6935	10.8	W 8730	9.7	TISSUS FIBRES SYNTH CONTINUE
65315	CONT SYN TXTL FABRIC NES	W 3540	9.6	W 5150	11.2	W 6639	10.2	W 8328	9.2	TIS PLUS 85% TEXT SYNT CONT
654	OTH WOVEN TEXTILE FABRIC	W 157	6.4	W 166	5.9	W 125	5.0	W 249	3.1	TISSUS AUT COTON SYNT,ARTIF
6541	SILK FABRICS WOVEN	W 101	5.8	W 99	5.3	W 86	4.6	W 45	2.2	TISSUS DE SOIE
655	KNITTED,ETC FABRICS	W 4796	22.8	W 6589	35.6	W 6310	25.7	W 5796	27.7	ETOF BONNETERIE PIECES ETC
6552	OTHER KNIT ETC FAB NONEL	W 4796	22.8	W 6589	35.6	W 6310	25.7	W 5796	27.7	ETOF BON NON ELAS NON SYNT
658	TEXTILE ARTICLES NES	W 552	4.7	W 694	7.2	W 170	2.0	W 88	1.1	ART FACONNES MAT TEXTILES
66	NONMETAL MINERAL MFS NES		16.6		18.8		23.6		21.0	ART MIN NON METALLIQUES
661	LIME,CEMENT,BLDG PRODS	W 270449	14.9	W 307449	17.2	W 404356	22.2	W 337528	18.5	CHAUX,CIMENTS MAT CONSTR
6612	CEMENT	W 269348	14.7	W 306400	16.9	W 403600	22.0	W 337001	18.4	CIMENTS HYDRAULIQUES
69	METAL MANUFACTURES NES		9.7		9.8		8.3		5.7	ART MANUFACT EN METAL NDA
692	METAL TANKS,BOXES,ETC	W 18610	5.8	W 17816	6.1	W 12343	4.7	W 4929	2.8	RECIPIENTS METALLIQUES
6924	MTL TRANSPORT BOXES ETC	W 18579	5.7	W 17739	6.1	W 12290	4.6	W 4904	2.8	FUTS,TAMBOURS,BIDONS
7	MACHINES,TRANSPORT EQUIP		78.4		88.7		76.9		89.9	MACHINES MATERIEL TRANSPORT
71	POWER GENERATING EQUIPMT		1.8		1.5		4.5		7.9	MACHINES GENERATRICES
72	MACHS FOR SPCL INDUSTRYS		8.8		14.8		6.2		2.3	MAC SPECIALES POUR INDUST
723	CIVIL ENGNEERG EQUIP ETC	W 869	3.0	W 1876	6.4	W 615	0.7	W 545	0.6	APPAREILS DE GENIE CIVIL
74	GENRL INDUSTRL MACHY NES		17.2		12.1		3.8		3.0	MACH APP INDUSTRIE
744	MECHANICAL HANDLING EQU	W 2623	8.7	W 1759	5.0	W 339	1.0	W 237	0.4	EQUIP MANUTENTION PIECES
7441	FORK LIFT TRCKS,ETC,PTS	W 1760	6.7	W 848	2.7	W 103	0.4	W 69	0.2	CHARIOTS POUR USINES ETC
74411	FORK LIFT TRUCKS ETC	W 1760	6.7	W 848	2.7	W 103	0.4	W 69	0.2	CHARIOTS POUR LES GARES
75	OFFICE MACHNES,ADP EQUIP		9.1		20.0		18.7		14.4	MACH BUREAU TRAIT AUTOM
759	OFFICE,ADP MCH PTS,ACCES	W 65	7.0	W 140	18.2	W 138	17.8	W 87	13.2	PIECES DU 751 ET 752
7599	ACCTG,ETC,ADP MCH PTS,AC	W 43	6.9	W 93	18.1	W 99	17.8	W 67	13.1	PIECES DU 751 ET 752
76	TELECOMM,SOUND EQUIPMENT		19.1		9.3		4.5		4.0	EQUIPMENT DE TELECOM
762	RADIO BROADCAST RECEIVRS	W 916	6.8	W 421	1.9	W 22	0.3	W 25	0.3	RECEPTEURS RADIODIFFUSION
7628	OTHER RADIO RECEIVERS	W 897	6.6	W 420	1.9	W 17	0.3	W 23	0.2	AUTRES RECEPT RADIO
764	TELECOM EQPT,PTS,ACC NES	W 829	9.5	W 529	4.3	W 206	2.2	W 47	2.0	EQUIP TELECOM,PIECES
77	ELECTRIC MACHNRY NES ETC		15.1		23.8		27.8		45.3	MACH APP ELECT NDA
771	ELECTRIC POWER MACHY NES	W 378	3.4	W 774	10.6	W 1267	12.6	W 729	24.8	MACH PROD,TRANS ELECTR
7711	TRANSFORMERS,ELECTRICAL	W 220	0.8	W 484	1.5	W 910	3.9	W 529	11.4	TRANSFO ELECTRIQUES
77118	OTHER ELEC TRANSFORMERS	W 51	0.3	W 22	0.1	W 276	1.5	W 134	10.1	AUTRES TRANSFO ELECTRIQ
7712	OTH ELEC POWER MACHY NES	W 158	2.6	W 290	9.1	W 357	8.8	W 200	13.4	AUT APP PROD TRANSF ELEC
77122	INDUCTORS	W 58	0.9	W 166	7.3	W 143	7.0	W 63	3.2	BOBINES REACTANCE,SELFS
77129	PTS NES OF MACHY OF 771	W 99	1.5	W 121	1.9	W 158	1.4	W 127	10.1	PIECES MACH DU 771
778	ELECTRICAL MACHINERY NES	W 1121	9.2	W 4	0.5	W 474	8.0	W 467	9.2	AUTRES MACH ELECT NDA
7781	BATTERIES,ACCUMULATORS	W 948	8.2	W 574	7.2	W 323	7.1	W 274	6.4	PILES ET ACCUMULATEURS
77812	ELECTRIC ACCUMULATORS	W 179	6.4	W 141	6.0	W 232	6.5	W 209	6.1	ACCUMULATEURS ELECTRIQ
78	ROAD VEHICLES		6.8		6.9		2.6		3.2	VEHICULES ROUTIERS
79	OTHR TRANSPORT EQUIPMENT		0.4		0.1		8.7		9.8	AUTRE MATERIEL TRANSPORT
792	AIRCRAFT ETC		0.2			W 33	8.4	W 56	9.6	APP NAVIGATION AERIENNE
7929	AIRCRAFT PARTS NES		0.2			W 33	8.4	W 56	9.6	PIECES DU 792
8	MISC MANUFACTURED GOODS		1427.3		1587.5		1700.3		1910.6	ART MANUFACTURES DIVERS
812	*PLUMBG,HEATNG,LGHTNG EQ	W 2054	13.0	W 2700	21.3	W 2814	20.2	W 1960	16.4	APPAR SANITAIRES CHAUFFAGE
8124	LIGHTING EQUIPMENT NES	W 1941	12.8	W 2645	21.2	W 2746	20.1	W 1900	16.4	APPAREILS ECLAIRAGE ETC
81242	LAMPS,FITTINGS BASE METL	W 264	2.6	W 297	2.9	W 804	5.9	W 555	7.0	APPAREILS D'ECLAIRAGE
81243	PORTABLE BATTERY LAMPS	W 1643	10.2	W 2331	18.4	W 1934	14.2	W 1344	9.4	LAMPES ELECT PORTATIVES
84	CLOTHING AND ACCESSORIES		1203.9		1377.4		1547.0		1805.1	VETEMENTS
842	MENS OUTERWEAR NOT KNIT	W 13437	182.9	W 13104	188.4	W 14779	207.2	W 14233	231.3	VET DESSUS POUR HOMMES
8421	— OVERCOATS,OTHER COATS	W 1689	25.8	W 1289	21.4	W 720	12.4	W 804	13.4	MANTEAUX HOMMES MAT TEXT
84219	—— OF OTHER FIBRES	W 1679	25.5	W 1273	20.8	W 720	12.4	W 803	13.3	MANTEAUX HOMMES AUT FIBR
8423	— TROUSERS,BREECHES ETC	W 8298	101.2	W 8270	108.3	W 9668	119.3	W 8015	116.3	PANTALONS HOMMES MAT TEX
8429	— OTHER OUTER GARMENTS	W 3268	52.9	W 3369	56.2	W 4324	74.7	W 5337	100.6	AUT VET DES HOM MAT TEX
843	WOMENS OUTERWEAR NONKNIT	W 11698	199.8	W 12581	238.6	W 14768	282.8	W 16479	341.0	VET DESSUS FEMMES MAT TEX
8431	— COATS AND JACKETS	W 1097	18.2	W 608	10.8	W 559	10.5	W 750	16.8	MANT,VEST FEM MAT TEXTIL
8433	— DRESSES	W 367	10.0	W 1227	32.0	W 967	26.8	W 916	28.8	ROBES EN MAT–TEXTILES
8434	— SKIRTS	W 513	10.9	W 682	15.5	W 581	15.0	W 656	15.6	JUPES EN MAT TEXTILES
8435	— BLOUSES	W 1437	38.6	W 1780	44.6	W 1736	47.6	W 1951	53.3	BLOUSES FEM MAT TEXTILES

5. General Exports F.O.B. by Commodities according to the S.I.T.C. (Rev. 2) in million U.S. Dollars
Exportations Générales F.O.B. par Produits d'après la C.T.C.I. (Rév. 2) en millions de Dollars E.U.

SITC CTCI	COMMODITY	1994 QUANTITY QUANTITE	1994 VALUE VALEUR	1995 QUANTITY QUANTITE	1995 VALUE VALEUR	1996 QUANTITY QUANTITE	1996 VALUE VALEUR	1997 QUANTITY QUANTITE	1997 VALUE VALEUR	PRODUIT
8439	— OTHER OUTER GARMENTS	W 8273	122.2	W 8273	135.7	W 10913	182.9	W 12197	226.7	AUT VET DES FEM MAT TEXT
844	UNDER GARMENTS NOT KNIT	W 6505	129.7	W 6412	137.9	W 6174	137.8	W 6164	143.9	VETEMENT DESSOUS MAT TEX
8441	— MENS SHIRTS	W 3912	82.4	W 4061	89.1	W 3794	85.3	W 3950	96.1	CHEMISES HOMMES MAT TEXT
84411	—— OF COTTON	W 3102	66.8	W 3284	72.3	W 3290	74.3	W 3347	82.4	CHEMISES HOMMES DE COTON
84412	—— OF SYNTHETIC FIBRES	W 810	15.6	W 777	16.8	W 504	11.1	W 602	13.8	CHEMISES HOMMES FIB SYNT
8442	— MENS,OTHR THAN SHIRTS	W 1247	17.6	W 1125	20.7	W 1099	21.9	W 912	18.0	SOUS–VET HOMMES MAT TEXT
8443	— WOMENS	W 1346	29.9	W 1226	28.2	W 1281	30.8	W 1302	29.9	VET DESSOUS FEM MAT TEXT
845	OUTERWEAR KNIT NONELASTC	W 22548	507.7	W 24954	594.0	W 31533	688.0	W 35948	819.7	VET DESSOUS,ACCES BONNET
8451	— JERSEYS,PULLOVERS ETC	W 10801	263.4	W 10494	275.2	W 15723	336.1	W 17710	390.6	CHANDAILS,PULL–OVERS ETC
8452	— WOMENS DRESSES ETC	W 1020	24.9	W 1430	37.2	W 1522	35.5	W 1293	34.5	ROBES,JUPES BONNETERIE
8459	— OTHER,CLTHG ACCESRYS	W 10727	219.5	W 13030	281.7	W 14289	316.5	W 16944	394.7	AUT VET DESSUS DE BONNE
846	UNDER GARMENTS KNITTED	W 8304	169.4	W 9070	199.2	W 8855	203.9	W 11123	245.3	SOUS VETS DE BONNETERIE
8462	— OF COTTON NON ELASTIC	W 4720	89.4	W 5234	105.3	W 5278	112.8	W 6653	137.5	SOUS–VET BONNET COTON
84629	—— OTHER	W 4720	89.4	W 5234	105.3	W 5278	112.8	W 6653	137.5	AUT SOUS–VET BONNET COTON
8463	— OF SYNTH FBR NONELAST	W 2905	58.1	W 2939	61.7	W 2807	61.1	W 3574	74.1	SOUS–VET BONNET FIB SYNT
84632	—— MENS SHIRTS	W 2897	58.1	W 2939	61.7	W 2807	61.1	W 3574	74.1	CHEMISES DE BON FIB SYNMT
8465	CORSETS,GARTERS,ETC	W 678	22.1	W 897	32.2	W 914	32.0	W 896	33.7	CORSETS,GAINES ART SIM
84651	BRASSIERES	W 652	21.3	W 880	31.4	W 903	31.3	W 885	33.0	SOUTIENS–GORGE,BUSTIERS
847	TEXTILE CLTHNG ACCES NES	W 905	7.3	W 986	7.9	W 578	3.9	W 1113	13.7	ACCES VET MAT TEXT NDA
8471	— NOT KNITTED	W 442	4.2	W 391	3.5	W 951	12.2	W 1029	12.8	ACCES VET MAT TEX NON BON
84719	MADE–UP CLTHG ACCESS NES	W 186	1.3	W 201	1.7	W 886	11.6	W 997	12.2	AUT ACCES VET MAT TEXTIL
848	HEADGEAR,NONTXTL CLOTHNG	W 1091	7.2	W 765	11.7	W 721	11.2	W 780	10.5	VET ACCES MAT AUT QUE TEX
8484	HEADGEAR	W 116	2.6	W 506	9.2	W 586	9.3	W 700	9.9	COIFFURES ET PARTIES NDA
84843	HEADGEAR TEXTILE NONFELT	W 99	2.3	W 503	9.2	W 582	9.3	W 700	9.9	CHAPEAUX EN BONNETERIE
851	*FOOTWEAR	W 4313	33.3	W 4684	40.3	W 4260	37.6	W 5085	40.4	CHAUSSURES
85101	FOOTWEAR RUBBER,PLASTIC	W 1658	10.9	W 1163	8.3	W 732	4.8	W 815	4.2	CHAUS SEMELLES CAOUTCH
85102	FOOTWEAR LEATHER	W 2647	22.4	W 3516	32.0	W 3526	32.8	W 4269	36.3	CHAUS SEMELLES EN CUIR
88	PHOTO EQU,OPTICL GDS ETC		7.0		7.0		6.9		6.2	APP,FOURN PHOTO,OP,MONTR
882	PHOTO,CINEMA SUPPLIES	W 886	4.6	W 1699	6.3	W 1251	6.5	W 1187	6.0	PRODUITS PHOTO,CINEMA
89	MISC MANUFCTRD GOODS NES		163.9		135.1		84.4		36.6	ART MANUFACTURES DIVERS
892	PRINTED MATTER	W 150	0.5	W 165	0.5	W 114	28.8	W 152	0.9	IMPRIMES
8928	PRINTED MATTER NES	W 99	0.4	W 126	0.4	W 77	28.8	W 96	0.5	IMPRIMES NDA
89283	UNISSUED BANKNOTES ETC					W 1	28.4		0.1	TIMBRES–POSTE FISCAUX
894	TOYS,SPORTING GOODS,ETC	W 16202	96.0	W 11456	73.0	W 5591	34.1	W 2494	12.4	VOITURES ENFANTS,JOUETS
8942	TOYS,INDOOR GAMES ETC	W 16093	95.1	W 11338	72.5	W 5478	33.4	W 2425	11.9	JOUETS,JEUX ETC
89422	DOLLS	W 3135	26.0	W 1246	9.7	W 128	0.6	W 92	0.5	POUPEES
89423	TOYS NES	W 11725	64.0	W 9971	62.5	W 5257	32.4	W 2209	11.1	JOUETS,MODELES REDUITS
896	WORKS OF ART ETC		1.5		17.9		0.5		0.4	OBJETS D'ART
89601	HAND PAINTINGS ETC NES		0.2		6.6		0.4		0.1	TABLEAUX,PEINTURES
89606	ANTIQUES NES		1.3		9.0		0.1			OBJETS D'ANTIQUITE
898	MUSICAL INSTRUMENTS,PTS	W 7399	49.7	W 3360	25.5	W 503	2.1	W 597	2.5	INSTRUMENTS DE MUSIQUE
8983	SOUND RECRDNG TAPE,DISCS	W 6893	47.9	W 2900	23.4	W 94	0.6	W 108	0.6	SUPPORTS SON POUR 763
89831	PREPD SND RECORDNG MEDIA	W 6889	47.8	W 2877	23.2	W 70	0.4	W 3	0.1	SUPPORTS PREPARES
899	OTHER MANUFACTURED GOODS			W 1	0.1		11.1		12.4	AUT ART MANUF DIVERS NDA
8993	COMBUSTIBLE PRODUCTS ETC	W 2777	4.0	W 3213	6.0	W 4088	9.0	W 4677	10.3	BOUGIES,ALLUMETTES ETC

1. HISTORICAL SERIES, 1962–1997 SPECIAL TRADE, IMPORTS C.I.F., EXPORTS F.O.B.
SERIES HISTORIQUES, 1962–1997 COMMERCE SPECIAL, IMPORTATIONS C.A.F., EXPORTATIONS F.O.B

YEAR ANNEE	VALUE IN MILLION MALAGASY FRANCS VALEUR EN MILLION MALAGASY FRANCS MERCHANDISE –MARCHANDISE		GOLD –OR		CONVERSION FACTORS U.S. CENTS PER MALAGASY FRANC FACTEURS DE CONVERSION CENTS E.U. PAR MALAGASY FRANC		INDEX NUMBERS –INDICES QUANTUM		UNIT VALUE VALEUR UNITAIRE	
	IMPORTS	EXPORTS	IMPORTS	EXPORTS	IMPORTS	EXPORTS	IMPORTS	EXPORTS	IMPORTS	EXPORTS
1962	30000.00	23286.00	28.00		0.4051	0.4051				
1963	31459.00	20262.00	21.10		0.4051	0.4051				
1964	33429.00	22654.00	22.60		0.4051	0.4051				
1965	34089.00	22632.00	22.40		0.4051	0.4051				
1966	35004.00	24132.00	21.80		0.4051	0.4051				
1967	35847.00	25711.00	26.00		0.4051	0.4051				
1968	41937.00	28608.00	45.70		0.4051	0.4051				
1969	47198.00	29154.00	24.50		0.3881	0.3831				
1970	47320.00	40222.00	26.20		0.3601	0.3601				
1971	59228.00	40807.00	33.50		0.3601	0.3601				
1972	51754.00	41864.00	52.60		0.3967	0.3966				
1973	45089.00	44751.00	66.20		0.4495	0.4532				
1974	67257.00	58504.00			0.4180	0.4177				
1975	78047.00	63044.00			0.4702	0.4668				
1976	68434.00	66035.00			0.4168	0.4165				
1977	85217.00	82927.00			0.4075	0.4080				
1978	99632.00	87214.00			0.4450	0.4432				
1979	135319.00	83826.00			0.4736	0.4706				
1980	126775.00	84781.00			0.4730	0.4736				
1981	147977.00	85741.60			0.3646	0.3690				
1982	148601.00	108347.00			0.2860	0.2860				
1983	166750.00	127249.40			0.2319	0.2325				
1984	213531.00	192332.00			0.1715	0.1730				
1985	265916.00	181630.40			0.1511	0.1509				
1986	238458.00	212736.00			0.1479	0.1479				
1987	323046.90	353975.00			0.0935	0.0941				
1988	538361.00	385095.90			0.0711	0.0711				
1989	595640.00	514845.90			0.0624	0.0624				
1990	969540.10	476681.90			0.0672	0.0670				
1991	785690.10	559073.00			0.0555	0.0546				
1992	833773.00	516822.00			0.0537	0.0538				
1993	895687.90	498995.90			0.0523	0.0523				
1994	1408620.00	1246720.00			0.0318	0.0301				
1995	2333890.00	1569390.00			0.0233	0.0235				
1996	2056110.00	1215709.00			0.0247	0.0246				
1997	2429600.00	1142519.00			0.0197	0.0195				

2. IMPORTS BY BROAD ECONOMIC CATEGORY AND EXPORTS BY INDUSTRIAL ORIGIN. (PERCENTAGE OF TOTAL VALUE)
IMPORTATIONS PAR CATEGORIES ECONOMIQUES ET EXPORTATIONS PAR BRANCHE D'ACTIVITE.(EN POURCENTAGE DE LA VALEUR TOTALE)

IMPORTS – IMPORTATIONS

	1991	1992	1993	1994	1995	1996	1997
TOTAL IMPORTS–IMPORTATIONS TOTALES	100.	100.	100.	100.	100.	100.	100.
1 FOOD BEV–ALIMENTATION BOISSONS	9.7	11.6	11.8	14.1	14.6	10.2	13.7
11 PRIMARY–PRODUITS DE BASE	2.4	3.5	3.7	2.8	4.0	3.4	1.4
111 FOR INDUSTRY–POUR L'INDUSTRIE	1.4	0.9	2.0	1.7	2.4	2.6	1.3
112 FOR HOUSEHOLDS–POUR LES MENAGES	1.0	2.6	1.7	1.1	1.6	0.8	0.1
12 PROCESSED–PRODUITS ELABORES	7.3	8.1	8.1	11.4	10.6	6.9	12.3
121 FOR INDUSTRY–POUR L'INDUSTRIE	3.1	2.5	5.5	2.4	5.2	3.5	7.3
122 FOR HOUSEHOLDS–POUR LES MENAGES	4.2	5.6	2.6	8.9	5.4	3.3	4.9
2 IND SUPPLIES–APPROV INDUSTRIELS	26.3	27.2	28.5	26.8	31.9	24.1	25.8
21 PRIMARY–PRODUITS DE BASE	0.9	1.7	1.6	0.9	1.5	1.0	1.4
22 PROCESSED–PRODUITS ELABORES	25.4	25.5	26.9	26.0	30.4	23.1	24.4
3 FUELS–COMBUSTIBLES	11.8	19.1	18.1	14.4	13.7	26.8	20.7
31 PRIMARY–PRODUITS DE BASE	6.8	13.2	13.2	7.5	11.3	15.7	13.9
32 PROCESSED–PRODUITS ELABORES	5.1	6.0	4.9	6.9	2.4	11.1	6.8
321 MOTOR SPIRIT–ESSENCE	5.1	6.0	4.8	6.9	2.4	1.4	1.1
322 OTHER–AUTRES	0.0	0.0	0.0		0.0	9.7	5.7
4 MACHINERY–EQUIPEMENT	23.4	16.0	16.8	17.2	14.2	15.6	12.7
41 CAPITAL EQUIPMENT–MACHINES	20.3	13.8	14.5	14.7	12.0	13.7	10.9
42 PARTS–PIECES ACCESSOIRES	3.1	2.3	2.3	2.5	2.2	1.9	1.8
5 TRANSPORT–TRANSPORT	19.8	13.6	14.4	14.5	13.1	12.0	13.6
51 PASSENGER CARS–AUTOMOBILES	3.3	2.8	2.4	2.0	2.4	2.2	2.6
52 OTHER–AUTRES	11.1	5.9	7.5	7.7	5.9	4.8	6.6
521 INDUSTRIAL–INDUSTRIELS	10.7	5.7	7.0	7.3	5.5	4.5	6.2
522 NON INDUSTRIAL–NON INDUSTRIEL	0.4	0.2	0.4	0.4	0.4	0.3	0.3
53 PARTS–PIECES ACCESSOIRES	5.3	5.0	4.5	4.8	4.8	5.0	4.4
6 CONSUM GOODS–BIENS CONSOMMATION	7.7	8.7	8.8	9.3	8.7	9.5	12.3
61 DURABLE–DURABLES	1.6	2.2	1.9	1.7	1.4	2.0	2.4
62 SEMI DURABLE–SEMI DURABLES	2.3	2.0	2.5	3.3	2.9	3.4	4.3
63 NON DURABLE–NON DURABLES	3.9	4.5	4.3	4.4	4.4	4.1	5.6
7 GOODS NES–BIENS NDA	1.3	3.7	1.6	3.6	3.8	1.8	1.3

EXPORTS – EXPORTATIONS

	1991	1992	1993	1994	1995	1996	1997
TOTAL EXPORTS–EXPORTATIONS TOTALES	100.	100.	100.	100.	100.	100.	100.
1 AGRICULTURE	65.0	64.6	64.1	75.0	66.3	59.0	56.6
2 MINING QUARRY–INDUS EXTRACTIVES	7.9	7.6	7.2	4.6	7.8	17.0	9.4
3 MANUFACTURING–IND MANUFACTUR	27.1	27.8	28.7	20.4	25.9	24.0	33.9
31 FOOD BEV TOBACCO–ALIM BOISS TAB	5.8	6.1	5.6	6.6	6.4	4.7	2.8
32 TEXTILES–INDUSTRIES TEXTILES	11.2	9.9	9.8	6.2	6.9	7.8	20.1
33 WOOD & PRODUCTS–BOIS & PRODUITS	0.6	1.2	1.0	0.6	1.4	1.6	1.9
34 PAPER & PRODUCTS–PAPIER & PRODT	0.1	0.1	0.1	2.9	1.2	0.8	0.2
35 CHEMICALS–INDUSTRIES CHIMIQUES	3.4	4.9	5.0	1.9	6.2	5.3	5.1
36 NON METAL MIN–MIN NON METAL	0.0	0.0	0.0	0.0	0.0	0.0	0.1
37 BASIC METAL–IND METAL BASE	0.1	0.0	0.4	0.0	0.0	0.0	0.0
38 METAL MANUF–MANUF METAL	2.6	2.2	4.2	0.5	1.3	1.3	1.2
39 OTH MANUF IND–AUTRES MANUF	3.1	3.4	2.5	1.6	2.5	2.4	2.5

3. TRADE BY PRINCIPAL COUNTRIES OF ORIGIN AND CONSUMPTION (VALUE IN MILLION U.S. DOLLARS)
ECHANGES SELON LES PRINCIPAUX PAYS D'ORIGINE ET DE COMSOMMATION (VALEUR EN MILLIONS DE DOLLARS EU)

COUNTRIES–PAYS	SPECIAL IMPORTS C.I.F. IMPORTATIONS SPECIALES C.A.F				
	1993	1994	1995	1996	1997
World	468.6	431.7	549.5	602.1	573.1
Africa	52.7	55.3	42.1	86.8	65.7
Americas	37.7	21.4	29.0	29.5	44.4
– Northern America	31.2	19.9	21.6	26.8	27.3
– LAIA	4.7	1.3	7.3	2.6	17.0
– CACM	0.0	0.0	0.0		0.0
– Caribbean	1.8	0.1	0.1	0.0	0.0
– Rest of America	0.0	0.0	0.0	0.1	0.1
Asia excl fmr USSR	156.3	140.0	172.1	209.6	210.6
– Middle East	64.7	30.0	63.5	100.7	88.9
Asia former USSR					
Europe excl fmr USSR	218.3	213.5	288.6	252.2	220.9
– European Union	208.7	202.1	277.8	243.1	214.6
– Eastern Europe	4.5	5.3	2.7	5.2	2.4
– Rest of Europe	5.1	6.1	8.0	3.9	3.9
Europe former USSR	2.8	0.8	1.0	0.7	0.4
Oceania	0.8	0.8	1.8	3.8	5.4
Other	0.0	0.0	15.0	19.5	25.6
France, Monaco	127.1	131.6	163.0	158.1	131.7
Iran (Islamic Rep of)	55.6	22.0	55.3	84.3	50.6
So. African Customs Un	24.5	44.9	34.6	75.0	55.3
Japan/Japon	41.1	42.6	32.8	29.2	34.8
Germany/Allemagne	32.1	24.9	55.5	29.9	24.9
USA/Etats–Unis d'Amer	29.4	19.3	20.8	25.4	25.6
China/Chine	13.5	14.1	18.1	23.3	25.3
United Kingdom	9.5	12.7	13.0	21.2	13.3
Saudi Arabia	8.6	7.1	7.2	14.3	23.8
Free zones/Zone franches			14.4	19.3	25.5
Italy/Italie	10.4	8.6	12.7	10.0	14.1
Belgium–Luxembourg	10.0	7.8	13.0	8.8	12.0
Singapore/Singapour	11.9	6.7	9.0	11.7	7.2
India/Inde	6.3	5.8	7.1	8.7	10.1
Malaysia/Malaisie	5.0	6.6	8.5	8.3	5.8
Netherlands/Pays–Bas	5.7	5.1	7.0	5.7	6.9
Mauritius/Maurice	14.8	2.3	2.6	4.5	5.2
Pakistan	0.5	8.4	7.8	0.6	11.6
Korea, Republic of	2.2	4.3	5.4	6.6	7.5
Other Asia n.e.s.	4.0	6.5	4.9	5.0	4.5
Switzerland,Liechtenst.	4.3	5.3	7.3	3.6	3.3
Brazil/Brésil	3.4	0.7	6.2	1.2	12.1
Spain/Espagne	5.5	5.4	4.0	3.6	4.2
Thailand/Thaïlande	3.3	1.8	4.5	4.3	3.9
Romania/Roumanie	3.8	4.7	1.4	4.3	0.9
China, Hong Kong SAR	2.3	1.5	4.1	4.2	2.2
Indonesia/Indonésie				5.2	7.4
United Arab Emirates	0.0	0.0	0.4	1.3	10.7
Denmark/Danemark	3.9	1.8	2.7	1.2	2.6
Sweden/Suède	1.5	1.4	3.8	1.4	1.5
Myanmar		7.1	2.3		
Nigeria/Nigéria	8.0	1.1	0.0	0.0	0.0
Australia/Australie	0.5	0.5	1.7	2.8	3.1
Ireland/Irlande	1.1	1.4	1.1	2.1	1.9
Viet Nam	0.9	4.5	0.0	0.9	0.4
Canada	1.8	0.7	0.8	1.4	1.7
Russian Federation	2.8	0.8	1.0	0.7	0.4
United Rep of Tanzania	0.0	2.1	0.6	2.2	0.5
Argentina/Argentine	0.2	0.0	0.1	0.6	4.1
Kenya	0.8	1.0	0.6	0.9	1.4

COUNTRIES–PAYS	SPECIAL EXPORTS F.O.B. EXPORTATIONS SPECIALES F.O.B.				
	1993	1994	1995	1996	1997
Monde	261.7	326.6	359.9	299.1	277.8
Afrique	32.8	37.0	55.1	20.5	18.4
Amériques	20.9	29.9	24.6	13.7	11.9
– Amérique du Nord	20.2	29.5	23.9	13.3	11.1
– ALAI	0.1	0.1	0.3	0.2	0.5
– MCAC	0.0		0.0	0.0	0.0
– Caraïbes	0.5	0.3	0.3	0.1	0.1
– Autre Amérique	0.2	0.0	0.0	0.0	0.2
Asie anc. URSS exclus	34.6	41.4	41.5	60.9	46.1
– Moyen–Orient	2.6	0.7	1.2	0.3	0.2
Asie ancienne URSS					
Europe anc. URSS exclus	167.6	217.8	226.4	192.1	184.8
– Union Européenne	162.8	211.6	215.7	189.1	182.8
– Europe de l'Est	2.9	5.1	2.7	2.1	1.3
– Autre de l'Europe	1.9	1.1	8.0	0.9	0.7
Europe ancienne URSS	5.8	0.3	0.7	0.3	0.2
Océanie	0.1	0.2	0.3	0.4	0.2
Autre			11.5	11.2	16.1
France, Monaco	87.2	111.8	102.2	112.3	125.6
Japan/Japon	17.9	26.4	22.3	47.4	25.0
Germany/Allemagne	32.9	37.1	29.9	19.1	13.5
USA/Etats–Unis d'Amer	19.3	26.0	23.7	12.5	10.5
Italy/Italie	8.8	15.1	18.9	13.3	8.2
Reunion/Réunion	16.2	20.8	21.4		
Belgium–Luxembourg	8.6	9.7	17.6	13.1	8.5
United Kingdom	9.6	16.1	13.6	9.1	8.9
Mauritius/Maurice	9.7	6.3	14.0	11.7	10.9
Singapore/Singapour	10.2	7.1	8.4	4.7	8.4
Spain/Espagne	4.1	8.2	12.5	6.8	6.4
Free zones/Zone franches			6.7	11.2	15.9
Netherlands/Pays–Bas	4.9	9.1	7.5	4.8	2.9
Sweden/Suède	1.9	1.7	8.4	6.5	7.4
Portugal	2.9	2.3	4.2	4.1	0.9
China, Hong Kong SAR	2.2	2.6	3.0	2.3	2.5
Poland/Pologne	2.3	4.8	2.2	1.9	1.0
Algeria/Algérie		1.2	5.0	3.5	2.1
So. African Customs Un	1.6	1.6	2.7	1.9	3.3
Switzerland,Liechtenst.	1.8	1.1	5.8	0.6	0.5
India/Inde	0.7	1.7	2.9	2.2	2.3
Comoros/Comores	1.5	1.5	4.5	1.5	0.7
Tunisia/Tunisie	1.7	4.1	1.4	0.1	0.1
Russian Federation	5.8	0.3	0.7	0.3	0.2
Thailand/Thaïlande	0.1	0.4	0.6	0.9	4.3
Canada	0.9	3.5	0.3	0.8	0.6
Areas n.e.s.			4.7	0.0	0.2
Other Asia n.e.s.	0.3	1.3	0.7	1.1	0.7
United Arab Emirates	2.2	0.4	1.0	0.0	0.1
Greece/Grèce	1.9	0.2	0.6	0.1	0.2
China/Chine	0.0	0.4	1.7	0.4	0.4
Gibraltar			2.1	0.3	0.2
Kenya	0.5	0.1	1.6	0.0	0.1
Zimbabwe	0.0	0.0	1.2	0.7	0.2
Seychelles	0.6	0.6	0.4	0.1	0.2
Pakistan	0.4	0.3	0.3	0.3	0.2
Korea, Republic of	0.0	0.3	0.2	0.3	0.7
Morocco/Maroc	0.3	0.1	0.4	0.3	0.1
Mozambique	0.0	0.2	0.7	0.0	0.2
Israel/Israël	0.1	0.0	0.2	0.6	0.2

(VALUE AS PERCENTAGE OF WORLD TOTAL)(VALEURS EN POURCENTAGE DU TOTAL MONDIAL)

	1988	1989	1990	1991	1992	1993	1994	1995	1996	1997
Africa	1.4	2.3	7.5	7.2	9.6	11.2	12.8	7.7	14.4	11.5
Americas	4.2	5.7	5.8	7.9	6.0	8.0	4.9	5.3	4.9	7.7
– Northern America	3.9	4.8	4.4	6.4	5.0	6.7	4.6	3.9	4.4	4.8
– LAIA	0.4	0.9	1.4	1.5	0.7	1.0	0.3	1.3	0.4	3.0
– CACM			0.0	0.0	0.0	0.0	0.0	0.0		0.0
– Caribbean			0.0	0.0	0.1	0.4	0.0	0.0	0.0	0.0
– Rest of America			0.0	0.0	0.2	0.0	0.0	0.0	0.0	0.0
Asia excl fmr USSR	18.5	20.1	31.7	24.1	29.9	33.3	32.4	31.3	34.8	36.7
– Middle East	5.5	6.5	12.8	8.6	15.0	13.8	6.9	11.5	16.7	15.5
Asia former USSR										
Europe excl fmr USSR	56.8	55.5	54.3	60.3	53.7	46.6	49.4	52.5	41.9	38.6
– European Union	54.8	52.5	50.9	57.9	51.1	44.5	46.8	50.6	40.4	37.5
– Eastern Europe	0.8	0.7	1.6	1.0	1.0	1.0	1.2	0.5	0.9	0.4
– Rest of Europe	1.3	2.4	1.7	1.4	1.5	1.1	1.4	1.5	0.6	0.7
Europe former USSR	9.0	0.7	0.4	0.2	0.3	0.6	0.2	0.2	0.1	0.1
Oceania			0.4	0.3	0.5	0.2	0.2	0.3	0.6	0.9
Other	1.0	0.5	0.0		0.0	0.0	0.0	2.7	3.2	4.5
France, Monaco	34.3	34.7	30.6	33.6	30.1	27.1	30.5	29.7	26.3	23.0
Iran (Islamic Rep of)	1.5	6.4	5.7	6.5	3.4	11.9	5.1	10.1	14.0	8.8
So. African Customs Un			1.5	4.3	5.6	5.2	10.4	6.3	12.5	9.7
Japan/Japon	6.4	6.3	6.3	7.1	5.9	8.8	9.9	6.0	4.9	6.1
Germany/Allemagne				9.0	6.2	6.9	5.8	10.1	5.0	4.3
USA/Etats–Unis d'Amer	3.6	4.6	4.1	6.3	4.9	6.3	4.5	3.8	4.2	4.5
China/Chine	1.8	1.5	2.3	1.9	2.3	2.9	3.3	3.3	3.9	4.4
United Kingdom	2.9	2.7	4.7	2.9	5.2	2.0	2.9	2.4	3.5	2.3
Saudi Arabia	4.0	0.0	0.5	0.4	10.7	1.8	1.6	1.3	2.4	4.1
Free zones/Zone franches								2.6	3.2	4.5

	1988	1989	1990	1991	1992	1993	1994	1995	1996	1997
Afrique	8.1	10.4	12.0	10.0	11.2	12.5	11.3	15.3	6.9	6.6
Amériques	12.5	12.7	18.1	14.7	16.0	8.0	9.2	6.8	4.6	4.3
– Amérique du Nord	12.5	12.7	17.9	14.6	15.8	7.7	9.0	6.6	4.4	4.0
– ALAI	0.0	0.0	0.0	0.0	0.0	0.0	0.0	0.1	0.1	0.2
– MCAC			0.0		0.0	0.0		0.0	0.0	0.0
– Caraïbes			0.0	0.0	0.0	0.2	0.1	0.1	0.0	0.0
– Autre Amérique			0.1	0.1	0.1	0.1	0.0	0.0	0.0	0.1
Asie anc. URSS exclus	13.3	14.7	14.6	16.5	15.2	13.2	12.7	11.5	20.4	16.6
– Moyen–Orient	0.1	0.0	0.1	0.5	2.3	1.0	0.2	0.3	0.1	0.1
Asie ancienne URSS										
Europe anc. URSS exclus	55.4	48.0	54.3	53.2	52.8	64.0	66.7	62.9	64.2	66.5
– Union Européenne	53.9	46.4	52.2	51.1	49.9	62.2	64.8	59.9	63.2	65.8
– Europe de l'Est	0.7	0.9	0.9	0.5	1.6	1.1	1.6	0.7	0.7	0.5
– Autre de l'Europe	0.7	0.7	1.2	1.6	1.3	0.7	0.3	2.2	0.3	0.3
Europe ancienne URSS	2.7	2.6	0.8	5.6	4.8	2.2	0.1	0.2	0.1	0.1
Océanie			0.1	0.1	0.1	0.1	0.0	0.1	0.1	0.1
Autre		0.0						3.2	3.7	5.8
France, Monaco	34.9	28.5	28.9	26.5	26.6	33.3	34.2	28.4	37.5	45.2
Japan/Japon	11.5	10.8	6.9	8.8	8.6	6.8	8.1	6.2	15.8	9.0
Germany/Allemagne				10.3	9.9	12.6	11.4	8.3	6.4	4.8
USA/Etats–Unis d'Amer	12.3	12.5	17.8	14.4	15.5	7.4	8.0	6.6	4.2	3.8
Italy/Italie	3.9	3.2	2.7	2.9	3.1	3.3	4.6	5.2	4.4	3.0
Reunion/Réunion	6.3	4.2	5.2	5.2	5.0	6.2	6.4	5.9		
Belgium–Luxembourg	2.9	3.2	4.9	3.0	3.3	3.3	3.0	4.9	4.4	3.0
United Kingdom	3.3	2.2	1.6	3.2	2.6	3.7	4.9	3.8	3.0	3.2
Mauritius/Maurice	1.4	2.2	2.4	3.0	3.2	3.7	1.9	3.9	3.9	3.9
Singapore/Singapour			6.1	5.7	1.9	3.9	2.2	2.3	1.6	3.0

4. Special Imports C.I.F. by Commodities according to the S.I.T.C. (Rev. 2) in million U.S. Dollars
Importations Spéciales C.A.F. par Produits d'après la C.T.C.I. (Rév. 2) en millions de Dollars E.U.

SITC CTCI	COMMODITY	1994 QUANTITY QUANTITE	1994 VALUE VALEUR	1995 QUANTITY QUANTITE	1995 VALUE VALEUR	1996 QUANTITY QUANTITE	1996 VALUE VALEUR	1997 QUANTITY QUANTITE	1997 VALUE VALEUR	PRODUIT
	ALL COMMODITIES		431.8		549.6		602.2		573.1	TOUS PRODUITS
0	FOOD AND LIVE ANIMALS		53.3		68.1		48.5		56.4	ALIMENTS,ANIMAUX VIVANTS
02	DAIRY PRODCTS,BIRDS'EGGS		3.5		5.2		6.2		6.0	PRODUITS LAITIERS,OEUFS
022	MILK AND CREAM	W 1488	2.6	W 1675	4.2	W 2476	4.8	W 2495	4.6	LAIT ET CREME
0224	MILK,CREAM PRESERVED ETC	W 1304	2.4	W 1440	4.0	W 2169	4.5	W 2282	4.4	LAIT,CREME CONS,CONC
02243	MILK DRY,OVER 1.5% FAT	W 716	1.3	W 902	2.7	W 842	2.1	W 1223	2.9	LAIT POUDRE SUP 1.5%
03	FISH AND PREPARATIONS		5.1		8.8		4.6		0.5	POISSONS ET PREPARATIONS
034	FISH,FRESH,CHILLED,FROZN	W 7746	4.4	W 10533	8.6	W 5859	4.0	W 8	0.1	POISSON FRAIS, REFRIG,CONG
0342	FISH FROZEN,EXCL FILLETS	W 7744	4.4	W 10533	8.6	W 5858	4.0	W 8	0.1	POISSONS CONGELES
04	CEREALS AND PREPARATIONS		37.4		41.3		30.6		35.7	CEREALES ET PRODUITS
041	WHEAT ETC UNMILLED	W 53444	6.8	W 70133	12.7	W 57673	14.4	W 17460	3.5	FROMENT,EPEAUTRE
0412	OTHER WHEAT ETC UNMILLED	W 53444	6.8	W 70133	12.7	W 57673	14.4	W 17460	3.5	AUTRE FROMENT NON MOULU
042	RICE	W 79847	26.8	W 125061	17.2	W 20605	8.6	W 57823	16.8	RIZ
0421	RICE IN HUSK OR HUSKED	W 3	0.1	W 712	0.3	W 1524	1.1	W 11790	3.8	RIZ SANS AUTRE PREPARATION
04212	RICE HUSKED	W 3	0.1	W 712	0.3	W 1524	1.1	W 11790	3.8	RIZ CARGO
0422	RICE SEMI-MILLED,MILLED	W 79844	26.8	W 124349	17.0	W 19081	7.5	W 46033	13.1	RIZ POLI,GLACE INCL BRISURES
04221	RICE MILLED UNBROKEN	W 78575	26.4	W 122038	16.4	W 13477	5.7	W 44150	12.3	RIZ POLI,GLACE EXCL BRISURES
04222	RICE BROKEN	W 1269	0.4	W 2312	0.6	W 5603	1.9	W 1883	0.9	BRISURES DE RIZ
046	WHEAT ETC MEAL OR FLOUR	W 3621	0.9	W 14112	6.5	W 6491	2.6	W 33472	10.5	SEMOULE FARINE,FROMENT
04601	FLOUR OF WHEAT OR MESLIN	W 3512	0.8	W 14111	6.5	W 6489	2.6	W 33472	10.5	FARINE DE FROMENT
048	CEREAL ETC PREPARATIONS	W 2598	1.9	W 6586	4.7	W 4570	3.8	W 4596	3.8	PREPTNS A BASE CEREALES
0482	MALT INCLUDING FLOUR	W 1600	0.9	W 3300	2.7	W 2800	2.2	W 3427	2.3	MALT MEME TORREFIE
06	SUGAR AND PREPS,HONEY		4.3		8.4		2.7		8.2	SUCRES ET PRODUITS
061	SUGAR AND HONEY	W 15348	4.2	W 21219	8.3	W 5738	2.4	W 23717	7.6	SUCRES ET MIEL
0611	RAW BEET AND CANE SUGAR	W 1522	0.5	W 20617	7.9	W 4815	1.9	W 19660	6.0	SUCRES BRUTS
0612	REFINED SUGAR ETC	W 13585	3.6	W 59	0.1	W 658	0.4	W 3178	1.2	SUCRES RAFFINES
09	MISC EDIBLE PRODUCTS		1.9		3.0		3.2		3.5	PREP ALIMENTAIRES DIVERSES
098	EDIBLE PRODCTS,PREPS NES	W 525	1.9	W 715	2.8	W 631	3.0	W 1087	3.4	PREP ALIMENTAIRES NDA
09809	MISC FOOD PREPRTIONS NES	W 173	1.2	W 165	1.6	W 204	1.9	W 390	2.3	PREP ALIMENTAIRES NDA
1	BEVERAGES AND TOBACCO		1.4		2.1		1.6		2.5	BOISSONS ET TABACS
2	CRUDE MATERLS,EXCL FUELS		5.9		11.6		8.7		8.3	MAT BRUTES NON COMESTIBLES
251	*PULP AND WASTE PAPER	W 5412	1.4	W 6905	1.7	W 2756	0.8	W 4623	0.7	PATES A PAPIER,DECHETS
26	TEXTILE FIBRES AND WASTE		2.5		6.5		6.2		6.4	FIBRES TEXTILES
266	SYNTHETIC FIBRES TO SPIN	W 827	1.4	W 681	1.8	W 603	1.2	W 93	0.3	FIBRES SYNTHETIQUES
2665	DISCN SYNTH FIBRE UNCMBD	W 668	1.2	W 679	1.8	W 602	1.2	W 93	0.3	DISCONTINUES EN MASSE
267	OTHER MAN-MADE FIBRES	W 460	0.9	W 776	2.3	W 386	1.4	W 292	1.0	AUTR FIBR TEXT ARTIF SYNTH
2671	REGENERATD FIBRE TO SPIN	W 302	0.8	W 408	1.8	W 267	1.2	W 152	0.8	FIBRES TEXT ARTIFIC
26711	DISCN REGEN FIBRE UNCMBD	W 302	0.8	W 408	1.8	W 267	1.2	W 152	0.8	FIBRES TEX ARTIF DISCONT
269	WASTE OF TEXTILE FABRICS	W 481	0.3	W 1944	2.1	W 2931	3.4	W 4513	4.8	FRIPERIE DRILLES,CHIFFONS
26901	BULK TEXT WSTE,OLD CLTHG	W 480	0.3	W 1944	2.1	W 2931	3.4	W 4508	4.8	ART ET ACCESS D'HABILLEMENT
29	CRUDE ANIMAL,VEG MAT NES		1.6		1.8		0.4		0.5	MATIERES BRUTES ANIM,VEGET
292	CRUDE VEG MATERIALS NES	W 556	1.6	W 572	1.7	W 70	0.4	W 98	0.5	MAT BRUTES VEGETALES NDA
3	MINERAL FUELS ETC		64.4		77.2		164.9		120.9	COMBUSTIBLES MINERAUX LUB
32	COAL,COKE AND BRIQUETTES				0.7		2.9		1.3	HOUILLES,COKES,BRIQUETTES
322	COAL,LIGNITE AND PEAT			W 8345	0.7	W 36283	2.8	W 13688	1.3	HOUILLES,LIGNITES,TOURBE
3222	OTH COAL,NOT AGGLOMERATD			W 4495	0.3	W 26889	1.9	W 4725	0.4	AUTRES HOUILLES
33	PETROLEUM AND PRODUCTS		64.0		76.5		162.1		119.6	PETROLE ET DERIVES
333	CRUDE PETROLEUM	W 235208	32.0	W 435754	61.7	W 545007	91.6	W 477449	78.2	HUILES BRUTES DE PETROLE
334	PETROLEUM PRODUCTS,REFIN	W 183188	30.0	W 57870	13.1	W 253123	66.8	W 177336	38.9	PRODUITS RAFFINES
3341	GASOLINE,OTH LIGHT OILS					W 33758	8.2	W 26696	6.2	ESSENCES POUR MOTEURS
33411	MOTOR,AVIATION SPIRIT					W 33755	8.2	W 26691	6.2	ESSENCES MOTEURS D'AVIONS
3342	KEROSENE,OTH MEDIUM OILS					W 26148	6.7	W 11898	2.7	PETR LAMPANTS,AUT HUIL
33421	KEROSENE INCL JET FUEL					W 26147	6.7	W 11898	2.7	PETROLES LAMPANTS
3343	GAS OILS					W 184806	46.4	W 134186	26.4	GAS OILS
3345	LUBS,PETROLEUM OILS NES					W 8412	5.5	W 4557	3.8	HUILES LUBRIFIANTES
33451	LUBS(HIGH PETR CONT) ETC					W 8299	5.1	W 4458	3.5	HUILES LUBRIF,H LOURDES
335	RESIDUAL PETRLM PROD NES	W 3802	2.1	W 5511	1.8	W 13601	3.8	W 5705	2.5	PRODUITS RESIDUELS NDA
3351	PETRLM JELLY,MINERAL WAX	W 2249	1.8	W 889	0.7	W 1240	1.0	W 2255	1.8	VASELINE,CIRES MINERALES
33512	MINERAL WAXES	W 2232	1.7	W 805	0.5	W 1199	0.9	W 2115	1.7	PARAFFINES,CIRES DE PETROLE
3354	PETROLM BITUMEN,COKE ETC	W 1553	0.4	W 4622	1.2	W 12361	2.9	W 3450	0.8	BITUME,COKE DE PETROLE
33541	PETROLEUM BITUMEN, ETC	W 1225	0.2	W 4575	1.1	W 12349	2.9	W 3427	0.8	BITUME DE PETROLE
4	ANIMAL,VEGETABLE OIL,FAT		11.5		19.3		18.8		28.3	HUILES,GRAISSES ANIM,VEG
411	*ANIMAL OILS AND FATS	W 119	0.2	W 3809	2.2	W 2200	1.4	W 5340	3.2	HUILES,GRAISSES ANIMALES
4113	ANIML OIL,FAT,GREASE NES	W 118	0.1	W 3809	2.2	W 2199	1.4	W 5339	3.2	HUILES,GRAISSES ANIMALES NDA
41132	FATS OF BOVINE,SHEEP,ETC	W 100	0.1	W 3698	2.1	W 2194	1.3	W 5337	3.1	SUIFS BRUTS FONDUS
42	FIXED VEGETABLE OIL,FAT		6.9		10.6		12.0		20.1	HUILES VEGETALES FIXES
423	FIXED VEG OILS,SOFT	W 2719	2.1	W 5998	5.0	W 5294	5.2	W 26130	17.8	HUILES VEGET DOUCES FIXES
4232	SOYA BEAN OIL	W 2387	1.7	W 2949	3.1	W 4080	4.1	W 24639	16.6	HUILE DE SOJA
424	FIXED VEG OIL NONSOFT	W 7776	4.9	W 8413	5.6	W 12326	6.9	W 4064	2.3	AUTRES HUILES VEG FIXES
4242	PALM OIL	W 7284	4.6	W 7344	4.9	W 11850	6.3	W 3862	2.2	HUILE DE PALME
431	*PROCESD ANML VEG OIL,ET	W 10333	4.6	W 9812	6.6	W 8280	5.6	W 7490	5.2	HUILES,GRAISSES PREPAREES
4312	HYDROGENATED OIL,FAT	W 373	0.5	W 546	0.9	W 476	0.6	W 1420	1.8	HUILES HYDROGENEES
4313	FATTY ACIDS ETC,RESIDUES	W 9906	4.1	W 9258	5.8	W 7784	5.0	W 6071	3.4	ACIDES GRAS INDUST,RESIDUS
43131	FATTY ACIDS,ACID OILS	W 9906	4.1	W 9258	5.8	W 7784	5.0	W 6071	3.4	ACIDES GRAS INDUSTRIELS
5	CHEMCLS,RELATED PROD NES		56.3		69.8		66.9		72.7	PRODUITS CHIMIQUES
51	ORGANIC CHEMICALS		3.8		4.3		5.3		4.4	PROD CHIMIQ ORGANIQUES
511	HYDROCARBONS NES,DERIVS	W 463	1.7	W 495	1.1	W 683	1.9	W 328	0.7	HYDROCARBURES NDA
5113	HALOG DERIV OF HYDROCARB	W 446	1.7	W 421	0.9	W 663	1.8	W 255	0.6	DERIVES HALOGENES HYDROCAR
51139	OTH HALOG HYDRCARB DERIV	W 442	1.7	W 393	0.9	W 660	1.8	W 226	0.6	AUTRE DERIVES HALOGENES
52	INORGANIC CHEMICALS		4.9		6.4		5.1		5.1	PROD CHIM INORGANIQUES
522	INORG ELEMNTS,OXIDES,ETC	W 4971	2.9		3.9	W 3499	2.7	W 4032	3.2	ELEMENTS INORGANIQUES
5225	INORGANIC BASES ETC NES	W 4186	1.7	W 3182	1.9	W 2339	1.3	W 2729	1.3	AUTRES BASES OXYDES METAL
52252	SODIUM HYDROXIDE, SOLID	W 3213	1.4	W 2623	1.5	W 2063	1.2	W 2399	1.2	HYDROXYDE DE SODIUM
523	OTHR INORG CHEMICALS ETC	W 3488	2.1	W 2410	2.5	W 2623	2.4	W 3510	2.0	AUT PRODUITS CHIMIQUES INORG
53	DYES,TANNING,COLOUR PROD		5.8		4.5		3.9		4.7	PROD TEINTURE,COLORANTS
531	SYNT DYE,NAT INDGO,LAKES	W 275	4.2	W 137	2.4	W 182	2.0	W 222	2.2	MAT COLOR ORGAN,LAQUES
5311	SYNTHIC ORGNIC DYESTUFFS	W 202	3.7	W 122	2.2	W 120	1.7	W 151	1.8	MAT COLOR ORGAN SYNTHET
533	PIGMENTS,PAINTS,ETC	W 707	1.5	W 857	2.0	W 603	1.9	W 1169	2.4	PIGMENTS,PEINTURES,VERNIS
541	*MEDICINAL,PHARM PRODUCT	K 884885	13.5	K 1021357	16.2	K 972932	16.3	K 1456653	23.9	PROD MEDICINAUX PHARMACEUT
5416	GLYCOSIDES,GLANDS,SERA	K 26203	0.3	K 64823	1.7	K 32331	1.4	K 53812	2.4	HETEROSIDES
54164	ANTISERA,MICROB VACCINES	K 22127	0.2	K 63107	1.6	K 29608	1.3	K 45715	2.4	SERUMS,VACCINS
5417	MEDICAMENTS	K 776543	11.7	K 878740	13.4	K 868771	13.5	K 1223957	19.4	MEDICAMENTS
54171	— CONTAINNG ANTIBIOTICS	K 125119	2.8	K 165072	2.8	K 139823	2.7	K 214835	3.6	MED CONTN ANTIBIOTIQUES
54179	— CONTNG OTH SUBSTANCES	K 615005	7.7	K 673487	9.6	K 694730	9.7	K 914242	14.0	MED CONT AUT SUBSTANCES
55	PERFUME,CLEANING ETC PRD		2.8		4.4		4.9		7.5	PROD POUR PARFUM,TOILETTE
551	ESSENTL OILS,PERFUME,ETC	W 102	0.8	W 127	1.2	W 122	1.1	W 162	2.0	HUILES ESSENTIELLES
5514	MIXED PERFUME SUBSTANCES	W 92	0.8	W 124	1.2	W 120	1.1	W 159	2.0	MELANGES SUBSTAN ODORIFER
553	PERFUMERY,COSMETICS,ETC	W 338	0.7	W 646	1.6	W 403	1.4	W 830	2.2	PRODUITS DE PARFUMERIE
554	SOAP,CLEANSING ETC PREPS	W 1536	1.4	W 1369	1.6	W 1923	2.5	W 3201	3.4	SAVONS,PRODUITS DETERSIFS
5542	WASHING PREPARATIONS ETC	W 1160	1.2	W 627	1.1	W 910	1.3	W 2119	2.3	PROD ORG TENSIO-ACT NDA
562	*FERTILIZERS,MANUFACTURE	W 17506	6.0	W 18914	7.1	W 25757	8.2	W 11291	3.6	ENGRAIS MANUFACTURES

4. Special Imports C.I.F. by Commodities according to the S.I.T.C. (Rev. 2) in million U.S. Dollars
Importations Spéciales C.A.F. par Produits d'après la C.T.C.I. (Rév. 2) en millions de Dollars E.U.

SITC CTCI	COMMODITY	1994 QUANTITY QUANTITE	1994 VALUE VALEUR	1995 QUANTITY QUANTITE	1995 VALUE VALEUR	1996 QUANTITY QUANTITE	1996 VALUE VALEUR	1997 QUANTITY QUANTITE	1997 VALUE VALEUR	PRODUIT
5621	CHEM NITROGENOUS FERTLZR	W 7235	1.9	W 6650	2.3	W 7504	2.4	W 3295	1.0	ENGRAIS AZOTES
56216	UREA	W 6929	1.8	W 6445	2.2	W 7241	2.3	W 3030	0.9	UREE
5623	CHEM POTASSIC FERTILIZER	W 1275	0.4	W 7908	3.4	W 6090	1.8	W 1400	0.4	ENGRAIS POTASSIQUES
56239	CHEM POTASS FERTILZR NES	W 1	0.1	W 3854	2.2	W 2950	0.9	W 675	0.2	ENGRAIS POTASSIQUES NDA
5629	FERTILIZERS NES	W 8597	3.6	W 4037	1.5	W 11939	3.9	W 6548	2.2	ENGRAIS NDA
56291	NIT-PHOS-POT FERTLZR NES	W 8139	3.4	W 3446	1.2	W 11737	3.8	W 5619	1.8	ENGRAIS CONT N P K
58	PLASTIC MATERIALS ETC		9.9		16.3		9.9		12.5	MAT PLAST ARTIFICIELLES
582	PROD OF CONDENSATION ETC	W 783	1.6	W 850	1.9	W 698	1.7	W 1099	2.2	PROD CONDENS,POLYCOND
583	POLYMERIZATION ETC PRODS	W 6475	7.9	W 8703	14.0	W 5612	7.8	W 8053	10.1	PROD POLYMERISATION
5831	POLYETHYLENE	W 2040	1.9	W 2866	4.1	W 1811	1.8	W 2712	2.8	POLYETHYLENE
58311	— IN PRIMARY FORMS	W 2023	1.8	W 2857	4.1	W 1809	1.8	W 2707	2.8	POLYETHYLENE PRIMAIRES
5832	POLYPROPYLENE	W 1932	1.8	W 2148	2.5	W 1399	1.4	W 1703	1.5	POLYPROPYLENE
58321	— IN PRIMARY FORMS	W 1926	1.7	W 2147	2.5	W 1397	1.4	W 1701	1.5	POLYPROPYLENE PRIMAIRES
5834	POLYVINYL CHLORIDE	W 900	1.3	W 1500	2.3	W 1088	1.8	W 1555	2.6	CHLORURE DE POLYVINYLE
58341	— IN PRIMARY FORMS	W 770	1.0	W 1258	1.8	W 950	1.5	W 1389	1.8	SOUS FORMES PRIMAIRES
5839	OTH POLYMRZTION ETC PROD	W 492	1.2	W 813	2.6	W 559	1.6	W 832	1.6	AUT PROD POLYMER COPOLYM
59	CHEMICAL MATERIALS NES		9.9		10.6		13.1		11.2	MAT PROD CHIMIQUES NDA
591	PESTICIDES,DISINFECTANTS	W 1230	4.9	W 1020	4.7	W 1498	6.9	W 1134	5.6	DESINF,INSECT,FONG,HERB
5911	INSECTICIDES,FOR RETAIL	W 1032	3.9	W 812	3.5	W 1285	5.3	W 862	4.1	INSECTICIDES VENTE DET
598	MISCEL CHEM PRODUCTS NES	W 1080	4.2	W 1374	4.6	W 1613	5.2	W 1463	4.4	PROD DIV INDUST CHIM NDA
5982	ANTI-KNOCK PREPARTNS ETC	W 311	1.1	W 709	2.3	W 893	2.6	W 629	2.0	PREPARAT ANTIDETONANTES
5989	CHEM PRODUCTS,PREPS NES	W 752	3.0	W 644	2.3	W 709	2.6	W 803	2.4	PROD PREP CHIMIQUES NDA
59899	OTH CHEM PRODS,PREPS,NES	W 359	1.5	W 356	1.3	W 398	1.5	W 387	1.1	AUT PRODUITS CHIMIQUES NDA
6	BASIC MANUFACTURES		67.5		111.2		90.6		90.9	ART MANUFACTURES
62	RUBBER MANUFACTURES NES		8.6		12.5		16.4		12.4	CAOUTCHOUC MANUFACTURE
625	RUBBER TYRES, TUBES ETC	W 2535	6.2	W 3614	8.7	W 4445	12.8	W 3649	9.2	PNEUS CAOUTCHOUC VULCANISE
6251	TYRES NEW FOR MOTOR CARS	W 416	1.4	W 562	1.8	W 680	2.3	W 712	2.1	PNEUS POUR VOITURES
6252	TYRES,NEW,BUS OR LORRY	W 1189	3.1	W 1741	4.4	W 2613	8.2	W 1824	5.2	PNEUS POUR AUTOBUS,CAMIONS
6259	OTH TYRES,TYRE CASES,ETC	W 849	1.4	W 1169	2.2	W 1025	1.9	W 959	1.6	AUTRES PNEUS RECHAPES FLAPS
62599	TYRES NES,TYRE CASES,ETC	W 710	1.1	W 1082	1.9	W 872	1.4	W 777	1.2	PNEUS,FLAPS
628	RUBBER ARTICLES NES	W 102	1.7	W 142	2.2	W 165	2.0	W 187	2.1	OUVRAGES CAOUTCHOUC NDA
64	PAPER,PAPERBOARD AND MFR		6.4		11.9		10.5		10.7	PAPIERS,CARTONS & OUVRAGES
641	PAPER AND PAPERBOARD	W 4292	4.1	W 5313	7.7	W 4957	5.7	W 5499	6.3	PAPIERS ET CARTONS
6412	PRINTG,WRITING PAPER NES	W 1319	1.5	W 1741	2.8	W 1333	2.1	W 2207	2.8	PAPIERS POUR L'IMPRESSION
64122	— COATED,IMPREGNATD ETC	W 741	0.8	W 978	1.6	W 827	1.3	W 1742	2.1	PAPIERS IMPRESSION COUCHES
642	PAPER,ETC,PRECUT,ARTS OF	W 986	2.4	W 1523	4.2	W 2302	4.9	W 2620	4.5	PAP,CARTONS DECOUPES
65	TEXTILE YARN,FABRICS,ETC		7.2		8.6		11.4		16.0	FILS,TISSUS,ARTICLES TEXTILE
651	TEXTILE YARN	W 409	1.2	W 450	1.5	W 568	1.9	W 1161	3.3	FILS TEXTILES
6514	SYN FIB YRN,BULK,MONOFIL	W 335	1.0	W 323	1.1	W 446	1.4	W 769	2.1	FILS CONT 85% FIB TEXT SYNTH
652	COTTON FABRICS,WOVEN	W 869	1.2	W 1216	1.4	W 1069	2.4	W 1463	4.4	TISSUS DE COTON
6522	WOVEN COTTON BLEACHD,ETC	W 790	1.0	W 933	1.1	W 699	1.8	W 983	2.9	TISSUS COTON BLANCHIS ETC
65224	BLCHED COTTON FABRIC NES	W 591	0.7	W 733	0.8	W 511	1.5	W 755	2.5	AUT TIS PLUS 85% COT BLANCHI
653	WOVN MAN-MADE FIB FABRIC	W 1977	2.7	W 2667	2.6	W 2462	3.6	W 1915	3.3	TISSUS FIBRES SYNTH,ARTIF
6531	CONT SYNT WEAVES NONPILE	W 761	0.6	W 1207	0.9	W 1244	1.5	W 1318	2.1	TISSUS FIBRES SYNTH CONTINUE
6534	DISC SYN BLEND FABRC NES	W 1023	2.0	W 994	1.2	W 776	1.4	W 530	1.1	TISSUS FIBRES SYNTH DISCONT
65341	DISC SYN FIB-COTTN FABRC	W 815	1.5	W 535	0.4	W 716	1.0	W 358	0.8	TISSUS FIB SYNT DIS MEL COTO
658	TEXTILE ARTICLES NES	W 302	0.4	W 374	0.6	W 363	1.3	W 689	2.1	ART FACONNES MAT TEXTILES
66	NONMETAL MINERAL MFS NES		11.8		15.2		11.7		12.3	ART MIN NON METALLIQUES
661	LIME,CEMENT,BLDG PRODS	W 96451	7.3	W 86305	7.5	W 30664	3.0	W 39424	2.9	CHAUX,CIMENTS MAT CONSTR
6612	CEMENT	W 96122	6.9	W 85967	7.1	W 30493	2.8	W 39104	2.6	CIMENTS HYDRAULIQUES
662	CLAY,REFRACTORY BLDG PRD	W 2443	0.9	W 2400	1.0	W 3400	1.7	W 6780	2.1	MAT CONST REFRACTAIRES
6624	BRICKS ETC NONREFRACTORY	W 2408	0.8	W 2329	0.9	W 3039	1.4	W 5351	1.9	BRIQUES ETC CERAM NON REFR
665	GLASSWARE	W 2077	1.6	W 4536	3.8	W 5059	3.6	W 6093	4.2	OUVRAGES EN VERRE
6651	BOTTLES ETC OF GLASS	W 966	0.8	W 3491	2.7	W 3598	2.3	W 4356	2.7	RECIPIENTS EN VERRE
66511	GLASS BOTTLES ETC NONVAC	W 961	0.8	W 3491	2.7	W 3596	2.3	W 4356	2.7	BONBONNES,BOUTEILLES,ETC
67	IRON AND STEEL		17.5		44.1		21.2		20.3	FER ET ACIER
673	IRON,STEEL SHAPES ETC	W 12158	5.1	W 43337	28.0	W 13762	6.2	W 16797	6.7	BARRES,PROFIL FER,ACIER
6732	IRON,STEEL BARS ETC	W 6848	2.7	W 38772	25.4	W 8345	3.6	W 11275	4.1	BARRES FER,ACIER
67322	HIGH CARBON STL BARS ETC	W 666	0.3	W 31828	22.1	W 183	0.2	W 1218	0.5	BARRES ACIER FIN CARBONE
67326	IRN,OTH STL BARS HOTROLD	W 5805	2.4	W 6741	3.2	W 7923	3.3	W 9955	3.6	BARRES PLEINES FER,ACIER
674	IRN,STL UNIV,PLATE,SHEET	W 12527	9.5	W 13177	12.7	W 12305	11.1	W 14152	10.3	LARGES PLATS,TOLES
6749	OTH IRN,STL PLATES,SHEET	W 8426	7.2	W 9385	9.8	W 7790	8.2	W 9181	7.3	AUTRES TOLES FER,ACIER
67491	— OF IRON OR SIMPLE STL	W 8412	7.2	W 9367	9.8	W 7782	8.2	W 9173	7.3	AUT TOLES AUTRES ACIER FIN
678	IRON,STL TUBES,PIPES,ETC	W 1489	1.9	W 998	1.7	W 1370	2.5	W 1594	2.4	TUBES,TUYAUX EN FONTE,FER
68	NON-FERROUS METALS		1.8		2.2		2.3		2.0	METAUX NON FERREUX
684	ALUMINIUM	W 465	1.5	W 324	1.7	W 332	1.9	W 416	1.6	ALUMINIUM
6842	ALUMINIUM,ALLOYS WORKED	W 465	1.5	W 324	1.7	W 328	1.9	W 375	1.6	ALUMINIUM,ALLIAGES OUVRE
69	METAL MANUFACTURES NES		14.0		16.5		16.4		16.3	ART MANUFACT EN METAL NDA
691	STRUCTURES AND PARTS NES	W 1489	3.4	W 1440	3.0	W 894	2.4	W 681	1.2	CONSTRUCT FER,ACIER,ALU
6911	STRUCTURES,PARTS IRN,STL	W 1440	3.3	W 1424	2.9	W 838	2.2	W 589	1.0	CONSTRUCT FER,ACIER,FONTE
694	STL,COPPR NAILS,NUTS,ETC	W 441	1.3	W 441	1.8	W 722	1.8	W 721	1.4	CLOUS,VIS,ECROUS
695	TOOLS	W 507	2.7	W 293	2.1	W 284	2.0	W 368	2.7	OUTILS A MAIN
6954	BLADES,TIPS,ETC FR TOOLS	W 78	1.6	W 36	0.8	W 43	0.7	W 48	1.0	OUTILS POUR MACHINE-OUTIL
69541	PARTS TO INSERT IN TOOLS	W 71	1.5	W 30	0.6	W 37	0.6	W 36	0.7	OUTILS DE FORAGE
697	BASE MTL HOUSEHOLD EQUIP	W 448	1.0	W 644	1.9	W 638	1.6	W 1022	2.1	ART MENAGE MET COMMUNS
699	BASE METAL MFRS NES	W 1952	4.1	W 1925	5.8	W 2296	7.0	W 2351	7.3	ART MANUFACTURES MET NDA
6991	LOCKSMITHS WARES,ETC	W 398	0.9	W 371	1.2	W 456	1.6	W 725	2.1	ARTICLES DE SERRURERIE
6997	IRON,STEEL ARTICLES NES	W 456	1.0	W 420	1.3	W 793	2.4	W 411	1.2	OUV FONTE,FER,ACIER NDA
69979	IRN,STL MANUFACTURES NES	W 456	1.0	W 419	1.3	W 784	2.4	W 408	1.2	AUT OUVRAGES EN FER NDA
7	MACHINES,TRANSPORT EQUIP		129.9		140.9		152.4		147.0	MACHINES MATERIEL TRANSPORT
71	POWER GENERATING EQUIPMT		7.5		8.8		10.1		7.6	MACHINES GENERATRICES
713	INTRNL COMBUS PSTN ENGIN	W 428	3.8	W 639	5.6	W 517	5.2	W 517	4.2	MOTEURS EXPL COMB INT, PIECE
7139	PISTON ENGINE PARTS NES	W 106	2.6	W 204	4.1	W 113	3.6	W 143	2.7	PIECES POUR 713.2,3,8
714	ENGINES AND MOTORS NES	W 32	1.8	W 3	0.7	W 2	1.2	W 4	0.9	MOTEURS NON ELECTRIQUES
716	ROTATING ELECTRIC PLANT	W 269	1.8	W 164	2.3	W 374	3.7	W 292	2.5	APP ELECTR ROTATIFS,PIECES
7162	AC MTRS,GENRTRS,GEN SETS	W 156	1.3	W 130	1.7	W 307	3.0	W 241	1.8	MOTEURS ELECTRIQUES
71623	GEN SETS WITH PISTN ENGN	W 104	0.7	W 98	1.3	W 272	2.3	W 179	1.0	GROUPES MOTEUR EXPLOSION
72	MACHS FOR SPCL INDUSTRYS		16.1		18.1		18.7		15.7	MAC SPECIALES POUR INDUST
721	AGRIC MACHY,EXC TRACTORS	W 116	1.1	W 154	2.0	W 156	1.4	W 123	1.5	MACHINES AGRICOLES
722	TRACTORS NON-ROAD	W 174	0.8	W 346	1.8	W 316	1.9	W 319	1.5	TRACTEURS
7224	WHEELED TRACTORS NES	W 166	0.8	W 326	1.7	W 308	1.8	W 278	1.4	TRACTEURS A ROUES
723	CIVIL ENGNEERG EQUIP ETC	W 505	1.1	W 963	2.6		4.5	W 1576	2.9	APPAREILS DE GENIE CIVIL
7234	CONST,MINING MACHNRY NES	W 404	0.7	W 814	2.1		4.2	W 1400	2.5	MACH POUR LA CONST, MINES
724	TEXTILE,LEATHER MACHNRY	W 424	2.8	W 484	3.8	W 582	3.1	W 756	4.0	MACH POUR INDUSTRIE TEXTILE
7244	SPINNING,EXTRDNG,ETC MCH	W 50	0.7	W 94	1.1	W 118	1.0	W 436	1.8	MACH POUR LE FILAGE
726	PRINTG,BKBINDG MACHY,PTS	W 100	1.6	W 80	1.3		0.6	W 81	0.8	MACHINES POUR IMPRIMERIE
727	FOOD MACHRY NON-DOMESTIC	W 322	2.3	W 216	2.0	W 241	1.8	W 414	2.0	MACH INDUSTRIES ALIMENT
728	OTH MACHY FOR SPCL INDUS	W 916	6.3	W 728	4.4		4.9	W 788	3.2	AUT MACH IND PARTICULIERES
7284	MACHY FOR SPCL INDUS NES	W 251	4.7	W 202	2.5		3.2	W 188	1.2	MACH SPEC IND PARTICUL.
72848	OTH MCHY WITH INDIV FNCT	W 158	3.6	W 42	0.6	W 69	1.1	W 63	0.4	AUTRES MACHINES NDA
74	GENRL INDUSTRL MACHY NES		16.2		23.9		20.2		16.9	MACH APP INDUSTRIE

4. Special Imports C.I.F. by Commodities according to the S.I.T.C. (Rev. 2) in million U.S. Dollars
Importations Spéciales C.A.F. par Produits d'après la C.T.C.I. (Rév. 2) en millions de Dollars E.U.

SITC CTCI	COMMODITY	1994 QUANTITY QUANTITE	1994 VALUE VALEUR	1995 QUANTITY QUANTITE	1995 VALUE VALEUR	1996 QUANTITY QUANTITE	1996 VALUE VALEUR	1997 QUANTITY QUANTITE	1997 VALUE VALEUR	PRODUIT
741	HEATING,COOLING EQUIPMNT	W 273	2.4	W 269	2.4	W 201	2.7	W 207	1.7	MACH CHAUFFAGE,PIECES
742	PUMPS FOR LIQUIDS ETC	W 101	1.9	W 134	2.4	W 249	2.8	W 136	2.2	POMPES MOTO-POMPES
7428	OTHER PUMPS FOR LIQUIDS	W 73	1.2	W 86	1.4	W 102	2.0	W 107	1.4	AUTRES POMPES POUR LIQ
74288	PUMPS FR LIQUIDS NES ETC	W 73	1.2	W 85	1.4	W 100	2.0	W 106	1.4	POMPES POUR LIQUIDES NDA
743	PUMPS NES,CENTRFUGES ETC	W 207	2.7	W 257	3.9	W 302	2.7	W 242	2.5	POMPES COMPRES,VENT ETC
7436	GAS,LIQUID FILTERS ETC	W 113	1.4	W 98	1.4	W 139	1.1	W 81	1.1	APP POUR FILT DES LIQUIDES
744	MECHANICAL HANDLING EQU	W 1085	2.3	W 899	5.6	W 313	2.0	W 521	2.6	EQUIP MANUTENTION PIECES
7441	FORK LIFT TRCKS,ETC,PTS	W 237	0.7	W 478	3.0	W 99	0.5	W 75	0.5	CHARIOTS POUR USINES ETC
74411	FORK LIFT TRUCKS ETC	W 236	0.6	W 476	2.9	W 98	0.5	W 72	0.4	CHARIOTS POUR LES GARES
745	NONELEC MACHY,TOOLS NES	W 194	1.5	W 203	2.6	W 233	2.9	W 214	2.2	AUT MACH NON ELEC,PIECES
7452	OTH NONELEC MCHS,PTS NES	W 170	1.3	W 195	2.4	W 208	2.6	W 205	2.0	AUT MACH NON ELEC,PIECES
749	NONELEC MACH PTS,ACC NES	W 447	5.7	W 469	7.2	W 397	7.3	W 630	6.0	PIECES MACH NON ELEC NDA
7491	BALL,ROLLER,ETC BEARINGS	W 75	1.4	W 70	1.5	W 71	1.5	W 130	1.6	ROULEMENTS BILLES ETC
7493	SHAFT,CRANK,PULLEY ETC	W 108	2.4	W 129	3.1	W 129	3.2	W 184	2.1	ARBRES TRANS,VILEBREQUINS
75	OFFICE MACHNES,ADP EQUIP		6.9		7.2		8.2		7.0	MACH BUREAU TRAIT AUTOM
751	OFFICE MACHINES	W 147	1.2	W 112	2.3	W 94	2.0	W 123	1.7	MACH,APPAREILS DE BUREAU
7518	OFFICE MACHINES NES	W 112	0.9	W 68	1.9	W 65	1.6	W 73	1.2	MACH,APP DE BUREAU NDA
752	AUTOMTIC DATA PROC EQUIP	W 80	4.8	W 86	4.0	W 107	5.0	W 135	4.3	MACH TRAIT INFORMATION
7522	DIGITAL COMPUTERS	W 32	2.5	W 34	1.8	W 37	2.0	W 35	1.4	MACH DIGITALES COMPLETES
7525	ADP PERIPHERAL UNITS	W 22	1.4	W 28	1.3	W 35	1.8	W 53	1.6	UNITES PERIPHERIQUES
76	TELECOMM,SOUND EQUIPMENT		17.9		10.4		24.4		17.3	EQUIPMENT DE TELECOM
761	TELEVISION RECEIVERS	W 293	0.7	W 227	0.6	W 341	1.9	W 511	2.1	RECEPTEURS DE TELEVISION
762	RADIO BROADCAST RECEIVRS	W 594	1.0	W 432	0.9	W 599	2.4	W 501	1.5	RECEPTEURS RADIODIFFUSION
764	TELECOM EQPT,PTS,ACC NES	W 813	16.0	W 205	8.5	W 412	19.3	W 288	13.3	EQUIP TELECOM,PIECES
7641	LINE TELEPHONE,ETC EQUIP	W 110	4.3	W 32	2.6	W 71	8.3	W 89	7.1	APP TELEPHON PAR FIL
7643	TV,RADIO TRANSMITTRS ETC	W 19	2.6	W 14	1.5	W 47	2.4	W 36	1.2	APP EMET TELE RADIO
7649	PTS NES OF EQUIPMT OF 76	W 605	8.6	W 115	3.8	W 194	7.9	W 98	4.2	PIECES DE LA DIV 76
76491	PTS NES OF APPAR OF 7641	W 14	1.5	W 14	2.4	W 45	5.5	W 23	2.9	PIECES POUR 764.1
76493	TELECOMM EQUIPMT PTS NES	W 585	7.1	W 71	1.3	W 145	2.4	W 66	1.3	PIECES 761,762,764.3,8
77	ELECTRIC MACHNRY NES ETC		15.8		16.4		18.5		21.0	MACH APP ELECT NDA
771	ELECTRIC POWER MACHY NES	W 127	1.9	W 101	1.5	W 124	2.1	W 190	1.8	MACH PROD,TRANS ELECTR
772	SWITCHGEAR ETC,PARTS NES	W 233	3.7	W 199	4.0	W 229	3.7	W 275	4.2	APP COUPURE,SECT ETC
7721	SWITCHGEAR ETC	W 232	3.6	W 196	3.9	W 223	3.6	W 273	4.1	APP COUPURE,SECTIONMNT
773	ELECTR DISTRIBUTNG EQUIP	W 559	1.9	W 451	2.2	W 851	3.4	W 1048	4.3	EQUIPMT DISTRIBUTION ELECT
7731	INSULATED WIRE,CABLE ETC	W 547	1.9	W 441	2.1	W 836	3.2	W 1000	4.0	FILS,CABLES ISOLES ELECT
775	HOUSEHOLD TYPE EQUIP NES	W 624	2.5	W 593	2.1	W 541	2.4	W 858	3.6	MACH,APP USAGE DOMESTQUE
7752	DOM REFRIGERATRS,FREEZRS	W 341	1.3	W 278	0.8	W 206	0.8	W 555	2.0	REFRIG,CONGEL MENAGER
778	ELECTRICAL MACHINERY NES	W 1763	4.5	W 2344	5.7	W 1721	6.1	W 2195	6.0	AUTRES MACH ELECT NDA
7781	BATTERIES,ACCUMULATORS	W 1364	1.3	W 1744	2.0	W 1177	2.6	W 1615	2.2	PILES ET ACCUMULATEURS
78	ROAD VEHICLES		45.0		50.7		47.8		55.3	VEHICULES ROUTIERS
781	PASS MOTOR VEH EXC BUSES	W 1965	8.7	W 2359	13.2	W 3390	13.4	W 4434	14.8	AUTO TRANSPORT PERSONNES
782	LORRIES,SPCL MTR VEH NES	W 5981	18.4	W 6135	21.5	W 6494	19.2	W 8727	22.0	VEHICULES SPECIAUX,MARCH
7821	LORRIES,TRUCKS	W 5758	17.0	W 5903	18.9	W 6422	19.2	W 8341	19.5	VEHICULES TRANSP MARCHAND
7822	SPECIAL MOTOR VEHCLS NES	W 223	1.5	W 233	2.6	W 72	0.1	W 386	2.5	VEHICULES USAGES SPECIAUX
783	ROAD MOTOR VEHICLES NES	W 1639	8.6	W 1039	6.1	W 1107	5.5	W 1916	9.0	VEHICULES ROUTIERS NDA
7831	BUSES	W 923	6.3	W 491	4.9	W 700	4.7	W 1202	8.1	VOITURES TRANSPORT COMMUN
7832	TRACTORS FOR TR-TRAILERS	W 716	2.3	W 547	1.3	W 406	0.8	W 714	1.0	TRACTEURS ROUTIERS
784	MOTOR VEH PRTS,ACCES NES	W 1104	5.4	W 1215	6.5	W 1071	6.3	W 2301	6.3	PIECES 722,781,782,783
7849	OTHER MOTOR VEHCL PARTS	W 957	5.3	W 1013	6.4	W 995	6.3	W 2245	6.3	PIECES 722,781,782,783
785	CYCLES,ETC MOTRZD OR NOT	W 586	2.1	W 704	2.9	W 691	2.3	W 872	2.5	MOTOCYCLES SCOOTERS
7851	MOTORCYCLES ETC	W 115	1.2	W 162	1.8	W 106	1.1	W 144	1.1	MOTO VELO MOTEUR AUXIL
786	TRAILERS,NONMOTR VEH,NES	W 1072	2.0	W 907	0.8	W 822	1.2	W 880	1.0	REMORQUES,CADRES,CONTAIN
7861	TRAILERS,TRANSP CONTAINR	W 820	1.7	W 563	0.5	W 509	0.7	W 595	0.7	REMORQUES TOUS VEHICULES
78612	OTHER TRAILERS	W 407	1.5	W 266	0.3	W 260	0.5	W 434	0.5	REMORQUES TRANSP MARCH
79	OTHR TRANSPORT EQUIPMENT		3.9		4.6		3.5		5.6	AUTRE MATERIEL TRANSPORT
792	AIRCRAFT ETC	W 108	2.3	W 47	2.0	W 8	1.2	W 20	1.7	APP NAVIGATION AERIENNE
7929	AIRCRAFT PARTS NES	W 5	1.4	W 8	1.6	W 4	1.1	W 8	1.6	PIECES DU 792
793	SHIPS AND BOATS ETC	W 786	0.8	W 1131	2.5	W 141	2.3	W 153	3.9	NAVIRES BATEAUX,ETC
7932	SHIPS AND BOATS NES	W 763	0.3	W 1063	1.8	W 109	1.3	W 136	3.9	NAVIRES ET BATEAUX
79324	FISHING VESSELS ETC	W 712	0.2	W 699	1.5	W 67	0.8	W 128	3.9	BATEAUX DE PECHE
8	MISC MANUFACTURED GOODS		35.1		37.7		44.6		41.4	ART MANUFACTURES DIVERS
812	*PLUMBG,HEATNG,LGHTNG EQ	W 456	1.1	W 454	1.7	W 832	2.2	W 714	2.0	APPAR SANITAIRES CHAUFFAGE
821	*FURNITURE,PARTS THEREOF	W 524	1.6	W 434	1.8	W 557	2.2	W 1171	4.3	MEUBLES ET PIECES
8219	FURNITURE AND PARTS NES	W 351	1.0	W 294	1.0	W 363	1.4	W 868	3.0	AUTRES MEUBLES ET PIECES
82192	WOOD FURNITURE NES	W 169	0.4	W 181	0.5	W 189	0.8	W 568	2.1	MEUBLES NDA EN BOIS
84	CLOTHING AND ACCESSORIES		1.5		1.5		2.0		2.3	VETEMENTS
851	*FOOTWEAR	W 1089	1.4	W 1440	2.3	W 1386	3.1	W 2313	4.3	CHAUSSURES
85101	FOOTWEAR RUBBER,PLASTIC	W 477	0.5	W 707	1.0	W 727	1.6	W 1588	2.8	CHAUS SEMELLES CAOUTCH
87	PRECISION INSTRUMNTS NES		4.9		6.4		13.2		6.0	INSTRUM,APPAR SCIENT NDA
872	MEDICAL INSTRUMENTS NES	W 177	1.6	W 132	1.5	W 181	6.4	W 151	1.2	INSTR,APP MEDIC-CHIR NDA
87202	OTH MEDICAL INSTRUMENTS	W 173	1.6	W 126	1.3	W 171	6.2	W 146	1.2	INSTRUM,APP MEDECINE
874	MEASURNG,CONTROLNG INSTR	W 138	2.7	W 89	4.0	W 115	5.2	W 127	4.2	INSTRUMENTS DE MESURE
8748	ELEC MEAS,CONTRL EQU NES	W 8	0.7	W 24	1.0	W 22	1.8	W 14	1.8	APP ELEC ELECTRO MESURE
88	PHOTO EQU,OPTICL GDS ETC		2.8		2.6		2.4		2.5	APP,FOURN PHOTO,OP,MONTR
882	PHOTO,CINEMA SUPPLIES	W 176	1.6	W 137	1.3	W 98	1.1	W 171	1.6	PRODUITS PHOTO,CINEMA
8822	PHOTO FILM EXC DEV CINMA	W 136	1.3	W 105	0.9	W 61	0.9	W 118	1.3	PLAQUES,PELLICULES,FILMS
89	MISC MANUFCTRD GOODS NES		21.8		21.2		19.0		19.2	ART MANUFACTURES DIVERS
892	PRINTED MATTER	W 771	12.6	W 814	12.3	W 759	8.5	W 1019	7.3	IMPRIMES
8921	PRINTED BOOKS,GLOBES,ETC	W 441	2.2	W 506	2.6	W 367	1.7	W 617	3.2	LIVRES,BROCHURES,CARTES
89211	PRINTED BOOKS,PAMPHLETS	W 432	2.2	W 488	2.5	W 351	1.6	W 598	3.2	LIVRES,BROCHURES
8928	PRINTED MATTER NES	W 251	9.6	W 191	8.6	W 275	5.7	W 208	2.9	IMPRIMES NDA
89283	UNISSUED BANKNOTES ETC	W 133	8.9	W 99	8.2	W 70	4.3	W 68	2.1	TIMBRES-POSTE FISCAUX
893	ARTICLES OF PLASTIC NES		4.7		3.9		4.2		4.7	OUVRAGES EN MAT DIVIS 58
8939	MISC PLASTIC ARTICLES	W 1081	4.1	W 911	2.8	W 916	3.1	W 960	2.9	ART DIVERS EN MAT DIV 58
89399	OTHR PLASTC ARTICLES NES	W 1026	3.9	W 756	2.6	W 733	2.8	W 736	2.6	AUT OUV MAT DIV 58
894	TOYS,SPORTING GOODS,ETC	W 253	0.9	W 371	1.2	W 387	1.7	W 536	2.1	VOITURES ENFANTS,JOUETS
898	MUSICAL INSTRUMENTS,PTS	W 332	1.6	W 121	1.2	W 196	1.8	W 217	2.0	INSTRUMENTS DE MUSIQUE
8983	SOUND RECRDNG TAPE,DISCS	W 322	1.5	W 109	1.1	W 177	1.6	W 193	1.8	SUPPORTS SON POUR 763
9	GOODS NOT CLASSD BY KIND		6.9		12.1		5.6		5.2	ART TRANSACT NON CLASSES
931	*SPECIAL TRANSACTIONS		6.9		12.1	W 1128	5.6	W 1011	5.2	TRANS.SPECIALES

5. Special Exports F.O.B. by Commodities according to the S.I.T.C. (Rev. 2) in million U.S. Dollars
Exportations Spéciales F.O.B. par Produits d'après la C.T.C.I. (Rév. 2) en millions de Dollars E.U.

SITC CTCI	COMMODITY	1994		1995		1996		1997		PRODUIT
		QUANTITY QUANTITE	VALUE VALEUR	QUANTITY QUANTITE	VALUE VALEUR	QUANTITY QUANTITE	VALUE VALEUR	QUANTITY QUANTITE	VALUE VALEUR	
	ALL COMMODITIES		326.7		359.9		299.1		277.8	TOUS PRODUITS
0	FOOD AND LIVE ANIMALS		254.3		241.2		170.7		150.5	ALIMENTS,ANIMAUX VIVANTS
01	MEAT AND PREPARATIONS		4.5		9.1		4.4		1.3	VIANDES ET PREPARATIONS
011	MEAT FRESH,CHILLD,FROZEN	W 2357	4.4	W 3841	9.0	W 1947	4.3	W 670	1.3	VIANDES FRAICHES,REF,CONGE
0111	BOVINE MEAT FRESH,FROZEN	W 2311	4.2	W 3774	8.9	W 1840	4.1	W 610	1.2	VIANDES BOVIN FRAI,REF
01112	BOVINE MEAT BONELESS	W 2296	4.2	W 3740	8.8	W 1785	4.0	W 578	1.2	VIANDES BOVIN DESOSSEES
03	FISH AND PREPARATIONS		60.9		56.7		51.6		69.1	POISSONS ET PREPARATIONS
034	FISH,FRESH,CHILLED,FROZN	W 541	1.1	W 428	1.0	W 398	1.1	W 275	0.5	POISSON FRAIS, REFRIG,CONG
036	SHELL FISH FRESH,FROZEN	W 9282	59.2	W 7927	55.1	W 7423	50.2	W 9075	68.5	CRUSTACES,MOLLUSQUES
04	CEREALS AND PREPARATIONS		2.8		1.3		1.3		2.3	CEREALES ET PRODUITS
042	RICE	W 1288	0.8	W 598	0.4	W 1558	0.9	W 2156	1.1	RIZ
044	MAIZE UNMILLED	W 18827	2.0	W 6620	1.0	W 2700	0.5	W 9250	1.2	MAIS NON MOULU
05	VEGETABLES AND FRUIT		22.3		29.9		26.9		17.4	LEGUMES ET FRUITS
054	VEG ETC FRSH,SMPLY PRSVD	W 19800	4.9	W 23160	9.1	W 12124	6.4	W 8173	4.2	LEGUMES FRAIS,CONG,SECS
0542	LEGUMINOUS VEGETBLES DRY	W 7835	3.2	W 12723	5.9	W 9086	3.9	W 5894	2.3	LEGUMES A COSSE SECS
0545	OTHER FRESH VEGETABLES	W 2502	1.3	W 2713	2.4	W 2744	1.9	W 1845	0.9	AUTRES LEGUMES FRAIS,REF
05459	FRESH VEGETABLES NES	W 415	0.7	W 843	1.4	W 475	1.3	W 333	0.6	LEGUMES FRAIS,REFRI NDA
0546	VEGETABLES SIMPLY PRESVD	W 75	0.1	W 892	0.5	W 217	0.7	W 429	1.1	LEGUMES CONG,CONSER
05461	VEGETABLES FROZEN	W 60	0.1	W 858	0.3	W 187	0.6	W 423	1.1	LEGUMES CONGELES
056	VEGTBLES ETC PRSVD,PREPD	W 1383	1.7	W 1480	1.9	W 1189	1.9	W 709	1.0	CONSERVES DE LEGUMES
0565	VEGTBLES PRSVD,PREPD NES	W 800	1.5	W 882	1.8	W 1003	1.8	W 552	0.9	LEGUMES PREPARES CONSERVE
05651	VEGTBLS,FRUIT IN VINEGAR	W 763	1.4	W 830	1.5	W 872	1.5	W 489	0.7	LEGUM CONSERV AU VINAIGRE
057	FRUIT,NUTS,FRESH,DRIED	W 6729	8.5	W 8166	9.2	W 6836	8.8	W 4230	3.6	FRUITS FRAIS OU SECS
0577	NUTS EDIBLE,FRESH,DRIED	W 3528	1.6	W 3278	2.1	W 2223	1.7	W 1282	0.3	FRUITS A COQUES
05773	CASHEW NUTS,FRESH,DRIED	W 3366	1.5	W 3142	2.0	W 2131	1.7	W 1200	0.2	NOIX DE CAJOU
0579	FRUIT FRESH OR DRIED NES	W 3192	7.0	W 4876	7.1	W 4596	7.1	W 2929	3.4	FRUITS FRAIS,SECS NDA
05798	OTHER FRESH FRUIT	W 3182	6.9	W 4855	7.1	W 4520	7.0	W 2928	3.4	AUTRES FRUITS FRAIS
058	FRUIT PRESERVED,PREPARED	W 2847	7.4	W 6434	9.9	W 6627	9.9	W 7156	8.8	CONSERVES DE FRUITS
0586	FRUIT TEMPORARILY PRESVD	W 2819	7.3	W 6397	9.9	W 6493	9.8	W 6577	7.9	FRUITS CONSERV TEMPORAIRE
05863	FRUIT TEMP PRSVD,UNFROZN	W 2808	7.3	W 6391	9.9	W 6492	9.8	W 6569	7.9	FRUITS CONSERVES PROVIS
06	SUGAR AND PREPS,HONEY		13.4		9.2		5.3		1.1	SUCRES ET PRODUITS
061	SUGAR AND HONEY	W 23560	13.3	W 15075	9.1	W 7427	5.2	W 1368	1.1	SUCRES ET MIEL
0611	RAW BEET AND CANE SUGAR	W 23558	13.3	W 14802	9.0	W 7424	5.2	W 1345	1.1	SUCRES BRUTS
07	COFFEE,TEA,COCOA,SPICES		150.4		134.7		81.1		59.3	CAFE,THE,CACAO,EPICES
071	COFFEE AND SUBSTITUTES	W 36526	79.1	W 35244	82.8	W 40118	57.2	W 25896	32.9	CAFE ET SUCCEDANES
0711	COFFEE GREEN,ROASTED,SUB	W 36526	79.1	W 35242	82.8	W 40115	57.2	W 25896	32.9	CAFE TORREFIE OU DECAFEINE
07111	COFFEE GREEN,HUSKS,SKINS	W 36509	79.0	W 35240	82.8	W 40112	57.2	W 25896	32.9	CAFE NON TORREFIE
072	COCOA	W 2838	3.4	W 2464	2.9	W 2133	2.4	W 656	0.8	CACAO
0721	COCOA BEANS,RAW,ROASTED	W 2838	3.4	W 2464	2.9	W 2133	2.4	W 656	0.8	CACAO EN FEVES
075	SPICES	W 18377	67.8	W 19825	48.9	W 9903	21.4	W 17899	25.2	EPICES
0751	PEPPER AND PIMENTO	W 2086	3.1	W 1291	2.7	W 1587	3.5	W 912	2.9	POIVRE,PIMENTS
0752	SPICES,EX PEPPER,PIMENTO	W 16291	64.8	W 18534	46.3	W 8316	17.9	W 16987	22.3	AUTRES EPICES
07521	VANILLA	W 934	56.3	W 602	34.1	W 640	11.9	W 653	9.6	VANILLE
07523	CLOVES	W 14117	7.5	W 17128	11.3	W 7268	5.7	W 15839	12.3	GIROFLES
1	BEVERAGES AND TOBACCO		0.2		0.7		1.0		0.3	BOISSONS ET TABACS
2	CRUDE MATERLS,EXCL FUELS		24.1		45.6		66.4		36.1	MAT BRUTES NON COMESTIBLES
21	HIDES,SKINS,FURS UNDRSSD		1.1		1.9		1.2		1.2	CUIRS,PEAUX BRUTS
211	HIDES,SKINS,EXC FURS,RAW	W 1059	1.1	W 1482	1.9	W 1012	1.2	W 1215	1.2	CUIRS ET PEAUX
2111	BOVINE,EQUINE HIDES,RAW	W 795	0.7	W 989	1.2	W 682	0.7	W 885	0.6	PEAUX DE BOVINS
24	CORK AND WOOD		1.2		3.2		2.9		4.5	LIEGE ET BOIS
248	WOOD SHAPED,SLEEPERS	W 4429	1.1	W 8228	2.6	W 18079	2.8	W 20428	3.8	BOIS SIMPLEMENT TRAVAILLES
2482	LUMBER SHAPED CONIFER	W 1986	0.3	W 1545	0.3	W 13811	1.0	W 15678	1.9	CONIFERES SCIES,RABOTES
24822	LUMBER PLANED ETC CONIFR	W 174	0.1	W 250	0.1	W 12750	0.7	W 13654	1.5	CONIFER RABOTES,RAINES
2483	LUMBER SHAPED NON–CONIFR	W 2443	0.8	W 6644	2.4	W 4224	1.9	W 4685	1.9	NON CONIFERES SCIES,RABOTES
24831	LUMBER SAWN ETC NON–CON	W 2179	0.7	W 5797	1.9	W 3164	1.3	W 4179	1.5	SCIES LONGITUDINALEMENT
26	TEXTILE FIBRES AND WASTE		3.1		6.4		7.1		3.1	FIBRES TEXTILES
263	COTTON	W 537	0.8	W 1200	2.3	W 1400	2.3	W 795	1.2	COTON
2631	RAW COTTON,EXCL LINTERS	W 537	0.8	W 1200	2.3	W 1400	2.3	W 200	0.3	COTON EN MASSE
2634	COTTON,CARDED OR COMBED							W 595	0.9	COTON CARDE OU PEIGNE
265	VEG FIBRE,EXCL COTN,JUTE	W 7836	2.4	W 10482	4.1	W 10486	4.9	W 3815	2.0	FIBRES VEGETALES
2654	SISAL,AGAVE FIBRES,WASTE	W 7815	2.4	W 10482	4.1	W 10486	4.9	W 3815	2.0	SISAL,AUTRES AGAVES
27	CRUDE FERTLZR,MINRLS NES		7.9		11.6		9.0		7.7	ENGRAIS MINERAUX BRUTS
278	OTHER CRUDE MINERALS	W 27071	7.6	W 28460	11.4	W 17921	8.9	W 15452	7.4	AUTRES MINERAUX BRUTS
2782	REFRACTORY MINERALS NES	W 12716	6.3	W 16523	9.8	W 14630	8.2	W 13987	7.0	ARGILE MINERAUX REFRACTAIRES
27822	NATURAL GRAPHITE	W 12715	6.3	W 16522	9.8	W 14629	8.2	W 13975	7.0	GRAPHITE NATUREL
2783	COMMON SALT,ETC	W 13666	1.0	W 10814	1.0	W 2331	0.2	W 827	0.1	SEL
28	METALLIFEROUS ORES,SCRAP		3.9		12.8		37.5		10.8	MINERAIS METAL,DECHETS
287	BASE METAL ORES,CONC NES	W 74191	3.8	W 128544	12.5	W 157157	37.4	W 117772	9.0	MINERAIS METAUX COMMUNS
2879	OTH NONFER ORE,CONCNTRTE	W 74191	3.8	W 128543	12.5	W 157157	37.3	W 117760	9.0	MINERAIS D'AUTRES METAUX
28791	CHROMIUM ORE,CONCENTRATE	W 74191	3.8	W 128543	12.5	W 157157	37.3	W 117760	9.0	MINERAIS DE CHROME
289	PREC MTAL ORES,WASTE NES							MK 23000	1.7	MINERAIS,DECHETS MET PREC
28901	PRECIOUS METAL ORES,CONC							MK 23000	1.7	MINERAIS METAUX PRECIEUX
29	CRUDE ANIMAL,VEG MAT NES		6.8		9.7		8.8		8.7	MATIERES BRUTES ANIM,VEGET
292	CRUDE VEG MATERIALS NES	W 3318	6.6	W 4611	9.3	W 3237	8.6	W 2271	7.9	MAT BRUTES VEGETALES NDA
2923	VEG PLAITING MATERIALS	W 2520	3.3	W 3215	5.2	W 2601	4.7	W 1462	2.6	MAT VEGET POUR VANNERIE
2924	VEG USED IN PHARMACY ETC	W 196	0.4	W 371	0.8	W 335	0.8	W 496	1.2	PLANTES MEDICINALES
2929	OTH CRUDE VEG MATERIALS	W 569	2.8	W 975	3.2	W 266	3.1	W 297	4.1	MATIERES VEGETALES NDA
29291	VEGETABLE SAPS,EXTRACTS	W 56	2.4	W 95	2.5	W 34	2.8	W 85	3.8	SUCS,EXTRAITS VEGETAUX
3	MINERAL FUELS ETC		2.1		14.6		9.7		8.0	COMBUSTIBLES MINERAUX LUB
33	PETROLEUM AND PRODUCTS		2.1		14.6		9.7		8.0	PETROLE ET DERIVES
334	PETROLEUM PRODUCTS,REFIN	W 22217	2.1	W 128911	14.5	W 57248	9.7	W 47985	8.0	PRODUITS RAFFINES
3342	KEROSENE,OTH MEDIUM OILS					W 3913	1.4	W 8972	3.4	PETR LAMPANTS,AUT HUIL
33421	KEROSENE INCL JET FUEL					W 3913	1.4	W 8972	3.4	PETROLES LAMPANTS
3343	GAS OILS					W 53116	8.0	W 38954	4.5	GAS OILS
5	CHEMCLS,RELATED PROD NES		4.2		7.5		6.0		5.9	PRODUITS CHIMIQUES
55	PERFUME,CLEANING ETC PRD		4.0		7.3		5.9		5.8	PROD POUR PARFUM,TOILETTE
551	ESSENTL OILS,PERFUME,ETC	W 1142	3.9	W 1657	7.3	W 1164	5.9	W 1398	5.8	HUILES ESSENTIELLES
5513	ESSENTL OIL,RESINOID,ETC	W 1142	3.9	W 1657	7.3	W 1142	5.8	W 1398	5.8	HUILES ESSENTIELLES,RESIN
6	BASIC MANUFACTURES		16.6		26.6		27.5		63.2	ART MANUFACTURES
61	LEATHER,DRESSED FUR,ETC		2.1		1.3		1.0		1.6	CUIRS,PELLETERIES
611	LEATHER	W 830	2.1	W 441	1.3	W 229	1.0	W 336	1.6	CUIRS,PEAUX PREPARES
6114	LEATHR BOVINE NES,EQUINE	W 349	1.3	W 225	1.0	W 210	1.0	W 318	1.6	CUIRS DE BOVINS
63	WOOD,CORK MANUFACTRS NES		1.0		2.4		2.2		1.7	OUVRAGES LIEGE ET BOIS
634	VENEERS,PLYWOOD,ETC	W 1480	0.3	W 5073	1.3	W 2956	0.8	W 2200	0.6	PLACAGES,CONTRE–PLAQUES
6343	IMPROVED,RECONSTIT WOOD	W 1449	0.3	W 5041	1.3	W 2930	0.7	W 2136	0.6	BOIS AMELIORES,RECONST
63431	IMPROVED WOOD	W 1449	0.3	W 5026	1.3	W 2929	0.7	W 2108	0.6	BOIS AMELIORES
635	WOOD MANUFACTURES NES	W 594	0.8	W 1172	1.1	W 1803	1.5	W 1055	1.2	ART MANUF EN BOIS NDA
65	TEXTILE YARN,FABRICS,ETC		10.1		18.1		19.2		50.9	FILS,TISSUS,ARTICLES TEXTILE
651	TEXTILE YARN	W 357	1.4	W 810	3.4	W 900	3.8	W 1322	6.0	FILS TEXTILES
6512	WOOL,HAIR YARN,INCL TOPS			W 8	0.1	W 7	0.1	W 154	1.6	FILS DE LAINE,DE POILS
65122	CARDED WOOL YARN IN BULK			W 8	0.1	W 6	0.1	W 144	1.5	FILS CONT 85% LAINE CARDEE

5. Special Exports F.O.B. by Commodities according to the S.I.T.C. (Rev. 2) in million U.S. Dollars
Exportations Spéciales F.O.B. par Produits d'après la C.T.C.I. (Rév. 2) en millions de Dollars E.U.

SITC CTCI	COMMODITY	1994 QUANTITY QUANTITE	1994 VALUE VALEUR	1995 QUANTITY QUANTITE	1995 VALUE VALEUR	1996 QUANTITY QUANTITE	1996 VALUE VALEUR	1997 QUANTITY QUANTITE	1997 VALUE VALEUR	PRODUIT
6513	COTTON YARN	W 357	1.4	W 801	3.4	W 869	3.6	W 1098	4.3	FILS DE COTON
652	COTTON FABRICS,WOVEN	W 1927	6.9	W 2038	11.7	W 1557	11.1	W 2456	17.6	TISSUS DE COTON
6521	GREY WOVEN COTTON FABRIC	W 1808	5.6	W 1489	5.2	W 781	3.3	W 982	3.5	TISSUS COT ECRUS NON MERCER
65214	GREY WOVEN COTTON NES	W 1808	5.6	W 1489	5.2	W 780	3.3	W 982	3.5	AUT TISSUS 85% COTON ECRUS
6522	WOVEN COTTON BLEACHD,ETC	W 119	1.4	W 549	6.6	W 776	7.9	W 1475	14.2	TISSUS COTON BLANCHIS ETC
65224	BLCHED COTTON FABRIC NES	W 117	1.4	W 536	6.6	W 714	7.5	W 1466	14.1	AUT TIS PLUS 85% COT BLANCHI
654	OTH WOVEN TEXTILE FABRIC		0.1		0.1	W 2	0.1	W 51	20.4	TISSUS AUT COTON SYNT,ARTIF
6541	SILK FABRICS WOVEN		0.1		0.1		0.1	W 47	20.4	TISSUS DE SOIE
655	KNITTED,ETC FABRICS					W 184	1.5	W 184	1.3	ETOF BONNETERIE PIECES ETC
6552	OTHER KNIT ETC FAB NONEL					W 184	1.5	W 184	1.3	ETOF BON NON ELAS NON SYNT
656	LACE,RIBBONS,TULLE,ETC	W 1	0.1		0.1	W 11	0.3	W 32	1.8	TULLES,BRODERIE
65601	NARROW FABRICS NES				0.1	W 6	0.2	W 20	1.4	RUBANS SANS TRAME EN FILS
657	SPECIAL TXTL FABRC,PRODS	W 927	0.5	W 1807	1.2	W 1286	1.1	W 573	0.6	TISSUS SPECIAUX
6575	CORDAGE AND MANUFACTURES	W 927	0.5	W 1806	1.2	W 1270	1.0	W 567	0.5	FICELLES,CORDES,CORDAGES
65751	CORDAGE,CABLE,ROPE,TWINE	W 927	0.5	W 1806	1.2	W 1269	1.0	W 566	0.4	CORDAGES TRESSES OU NON
658	TEXTILE ARTICLES NES	W 208	1.0	W 234	1.5	W 165	1.0	W 154	3.1	ART FACONNES MAT TEXTILES
6584	LINENS ETC	W 135	0.8	W 153	1.3	W 112	0.8	W 105	2.9	LINGE DE MAISON
65843	TABLE LINEN OF COTTON	W 126	0.7	W 135	1.1	W 103	0.7	W 90	2.8	LINGE DE TABLE DE COTON
66	NONMETAL MINERAL MFS NES		3.3		4.2		4.7		8.2	ART MIN NON METALLIQUES
667	PEARL,PREC–,SEMI–P STONE		3.2		4.2		4.6		8.1	PERLES, PIERRES GEMMES
6673	PREC–,SEMI–PR STONES NES		3.2		4.2		4.5		8.0	AUTRES PIERRES NON SERTIES
7	MACHINES,TRANSPORT EQUIP		1.2		3.3		2.3		2.0	MACHINES MATERIEL TRANSPORT
71	POWER GENERATING EQUIPMT		0.1		1.0		1.0		0.3	MACHINES GENERATRICES
8	MISC MANUFACTURED GOODS		20.0		13.5		9.6		6.5	ART MANUFACTURES DIVERS
84	CLOTHING AND ACCESSORIES		7.7		5.2		3.3		2.5	VETEMENTS
842	MENS OUTERWEAR NOT KNIT	W 70	1.2	W 80	1.3	W 30	0.2	W 9	0.1	VET DESSUS POUR HOMMES
8423	— TROUSERS,BREECHES ETC	W 57	1.1	W 72	1.2	W 28	0.1	W 6	0.1	PANTALONS HOMMES MAT TEX
843	WOMENS OUTERWEAR NONKNIT	W 256	4.2	W 102	2.2	W 69	1.5	W 52	1.0	VET DESSUS FEMMES MAT TEX
8435	— BLOUSES	W 76	1.1	W 27	0.6	W 16	0.4	W 8	0.2	BLOUSES FEM MAT TEXTILES
8439	— OTHER OUTER GARMENTS	W 134	2.4	W 44	0.9	W 31	0.5	W 24	0.5	AUT VET DES FEM MAT TEXT
844	UNDER GARMENTS NOT KNIT	W 83	1.2	W 31	0.7	W 16	0.4	W 8	0.2	VETEMENT DESSOUS MAT TEX
8443	— WOMENS	W 72	1.0	W 21	0.5	W 9	0.3	W 3	0.1	VET DESSOUS FEM MAT TEXT
89	MISC MANUFCTRD GOODS NES		11.4		7.2		5.0		3.4	ART MANUFACTURES DIVERS
892	PRINTED MATTER	W 6	9.4	W 115	4.2	W 7	1.9	W 12	0.4	IMPRIMES
8928	PRINTED MATTER NES	W 1	9.3	W 111	4.1	W 4	1.9	W 9	0.3	IMPRIMES NDA
89283	UNISSUED BANKNOTES ETC		9.3		1.2		1.8			TIMBRES–POSTE FISCAUX
89284	CALENDARS ON PAPER			W 111	3.0		0.1		0.1	CALENDRIERS,BLOCS
899	OTHER MANUFACTURED GOODS	W 286	0.9	W 365	1.9	W 300	1.8	W 340	1.7	AUT ART MANUF DIVERS NDA
8997	BASKETWORK,BROOMS ETC	W 163	0.5	W 206	1.1	W 181	1.0	W 264	1.2	OUVRAGES VANNERIE NDA
89971	BASKETWORK,WICKERWRK,ETC	W 161	0.5	W 201	1.1	W 180	1.0	W 263	1.2	OUVRAGES DE VANNERIE
9	GOODS NOT CLASSD BY KIND		3.9		7.2		5.9		5.7	ART TRANSACT NON CLASSES
931	*SPECIAL TRANSACTIONS		3.3		6.1	W 603	4.4		4.2	TRANS.SPECIALES
941	*ZOO ANIMALS,PETS ETC	W 8	0.7	W 6	1.2	W 8	1.5	W 8	1.5	ANIMAUX DE ZOO ETC

1. HISTORICAL SERIES, 1961–1996 GENERAL TRADE, IMPORTS C.I.F., EXPORTS F.O.B.
SERIES HISTORIQUES, 1961–1996 COMMERCE GENERAL, IMPORTATIONS C.A.F., EXPORTATIONS F.O.B

YEAR ANNEE	VALUE IN MILLION MALAWI KWACHAS VALEUR EN MILLION MALAWI KWACHAS MERCHANDISE –MARCHANDISE		GOLD –OR		CONVERSION FACTORS U.S. CENTS PER MALAWI KWACHA FACTEURS DE CONVERSION CENTS E.U. PAR MALAWI KWACHA		INDEX NUMBERS –INDICES QUANTUM		UNIT VALUE VALEUR UNITAIRE	
	IMPORTS	EXPORTS	IMPORTS	EXPORTS	IMPORTS	EXPORTS	IMPORTS	EXPORTS	IMPORTS	EXPORTS
1961		18.60				140.0000				
1962		20.40				140.0000				
1963		21.60				140.0000				
1964	28.60	25.00			140.0000	140.0000				
1965	40.80	28.80			140.0000	140.0000				
1966	54.30	34.80			140.0000	140.0000				
1967	50.90	40.90			138.4000	138.0300				
1968	58.20	40.00			120.0000	120.0000				
1969	61.50	44.00			120.0000	120.0000				
1970	71.40	49.70			120.0000	120.0000				
1971	89.80	59.30			121.5500	120.3500				
1972	102.90	64.50			124.2850	122.8440				
1973	114.70	79.90			122.7160	122.7600				
1974	157.70	101.30			119.1280	119.0470				
1975	218.70	122.10			114.6350	113.9270				
1976	188.50	151.60			109.2000	109.1800				
1977	209.80	180.30			110.8790	110.8370				
1978	284.80	155.70			118.8050	119.0260				
1979	324.80	189.80			122.4960	122.5730				
1980	357.20	231.00			123.2430	123.4380				23
1981	313.00	243.70			111.8494	110.6412				27
1982	322.10	256.60			96.6153	95.7387				30
1983	363.80	270.60			85.5543	84.4785				29
1984	381.70	440.70			70.5320	70.1519				44
1985	492.60	429.70			58.3389	58.9372				40
1986	477.97	462.10			54.0515	53.0795				45
1987	653.94	615.06			45.1839	44.9795				59
1988	1080.15	751.69			38.8453	38.3223				71
1989	1398.80	743.22			36.2398	35.9122				
1990	1572.47	1123.52			36.5942	37.1076				
1991	1975.81	1326.36			35.5787	35.3779				
1992	2653.83	1488.90			27.7121	26.6120				
1993	2404.86	1410.91			22.6722	22.6326				
1994	4264.01	2805.75			11.6071	11.5844				
1995	7255.00	6193.40			6.5435	6.5447				
1996	9544.90	7358.70			6.5321	6.5317				

2. IMPORTS BY BROAD ECONOMIC CATEGORY AND EXPORTS BY INDUSTRIAL ORIGIN. (PERCENTAGE OF TOTAL VALUE)
IMPORTATIONS PAR CATEGORIES ECONOMIQUES ET EXPORTATIONS PAR BRANCHE D'ACTIVITE.(EN POURCENTAGE DE LA VALEUR TOTALE)

IMPORTS – IMPORTATIONS

	1989	1990	1991	1992	1993	1994	1995
TOTAL IMPORTS–IMPORTATIONS TOTALES	100.	100.	100.			100.	100.
1 FOOD BEV–ALIMENTATION BOISSONS	5.8	7.3	6.6			8.4	7.7
11 PRIMARY–PRODUITS DE BASE	1.0	1.3	1.7			2.4	2.1
111 FOR INDUSTRY–POUR L'INDUSTRIE	0.9	1.2	1.5			1.8	1.6
112 FOR HOUSEHOLDS–POUR LES MENAGES	0.1	0.1	0.2			0.5	0.6
12 PROCESSED–PRODUITS ELABORES	4.7	6.0	4.9			6.0	5.5
121 FOR INDUSTRY–POUR L'INDUSTRIE	2.0	4.3	2.8			3.9	4.2
122 FOR HOUSEHOLDS–POUR LES MENAGES	2.7	1.7	2.1			2.2	1.4
2 IND SUPPLIES–APPROV INDUSTRIELS	44.5	37.2	40.7			40.8	39.2
21 PRIMARY–PRODUITS DE BASE	5.9	2.4	2.2			8.3	6.4
22 PROCESSED–PRODUITS ELABORES	38.6	34.8	38.5			32.5	32.8
3 FUELS–COMBUSTIBLES	10.6	10.3	10.4			7.6	11.1
31 PRIMARY–PRODUITS DE BASE	0.2	0.3	0.2			0.3	0.5
32 PROCESSED–PRODUITS ELABORES	10.4	10.0	10.2			7.3	10.6
321 MOTOR SPIRIT–ESSENCE	3.8	10.0	10.2				
322 OTHER–AUTRES	6.6	0.0	0.0			7.3	10.6
4 MACHINERY–EQUIPEMENT	18.9	16.8	16.4			18.3	13.7
41 CAPITAL EQUIPMENT–MACHINES	16.6	14.3	14.2			16.1	12.3
42 PARTS–PIECES ACCESSOIRES	2.3	2.4	2.1			2.1	1.5
5 TRANSPORT–TRANSPORT	13.0	20.2	16.6			16.3	15.0
51 PASSENGER CARS–AUTOMOBILES	3.6	3.2	2.4			2.8	2.9
52 OTHER–AUTRES	2.5	9.9	7.6			7.4	8.9
521 INDUSTRIAL–INDUSTRIELS	2.2	9.6	7.1			6.0	8.2
522 NON INDUSTRIAL–NON INDUSTRIEL	0.3	0.4	0.5			1.4	0.7
53 PARTS–PIECES ACCESSOIRES	6.9	7.1	6.5			6.1	3.2
6 CONSUM GOODS–BIENS CONSOMMATION	6.2	7.0	7.8			8.2	12.5
61 DURABLE–DURABLES	1.0	1.3	1.7			1.5	0.9
62 SEMI DURABLE–SEMI DURABLES	2.4	2.9	3.2			3.2	2.3
63 NON DURABLE–NON DURABLES	2.8	2.8	2.9			3.5	9.3
7 GOODS NES–BIENS NDA	1.0	1.2	1.6			0.4	0.8

EXPORTS – EXPORTATIONS

	1989	1990	1991	1992	1993	1994	1995
TOTAL EXPORTS–EXPORTATIONS TOTALES	100.	100.	100.			100.	100.
1 AGRICULTURE	80.5	84.7	87.5			75.0	82.0
2 MINING QUARRY–INDUS EXTRACTIVES	0.0	0.0	0.0			0.0	0.0
3 MANUFACTURING–IND MANUFACTUR	19.5	15.3	12.4			25.0	18.0
31 FOOD BEV TOBACCO–ALIM BOISS TAB	10.0	7.8	6.0			9.3	6.8
32 TEXTILES–INDUSTRIES TEXTILES	5.4	2.5	2.8			8.8	6.8
33 WOOD & PRODUCTS–BOIS & PRODUITS	0.8	1.0	0.4			0.9	0.6
34 PAPER & PRODUCTS–PAPIER & PRODT	0.1	0.0	0.0			0.0	0.0
35 CHEMICALS–INDUSTRIES CHIMIQUES	0.6	0.5	0.5			0.9	0.9
36 NON METAL MIN–MIN NON METAL	0.0	0.0	0.0			0.1	0.1
37 BASIC METAL–IND METAL BASE	0.0	0.0	0.1			0.2	0.1
38 METAL MANUF–MANUF METAL	2.1	3.1	2.3			4.4	2.6
39 OTH MANUF IND–AUTRES MANUF	0.4	0.3	0.3			0.4	0.2

3. TRADE BY PRINCIPAL COUNTRIES OF ORIGIN AND DESTINATION (VALUE IN MILLION U.S. DOLLARS)
ECHANGES SELON LES PRINCIPAUX PAYS D'ORIGINE ET DE DESTINATION (VALEUR EN MILLIONS DE DOLLARS EU)

COUNTRIES–PAYS	GENERAL IMPORTS C.I.F. IMPORTATIONS GENERALES C.A.F				
	1991	1992	1993	1994	1995
World	647.4			539.3	500.4
Africa	270.2			252.7	226.6
Americas	36.1			23.1	21.4
– Northern America	31.0			18.7	17.0
– LAIA	5.1			4.3	4.1
– CACM				0.0	0.0
– Caribbean	0.0			0.1	0.1
– Rest of America				0.0	0.1
Asia excl fmr USSR	89.5			101.5	84.2
– Middle East	0.4			1.0	3.0
Asia former USSR					0.0
Europe excl fmr USSR	242.9			160.9	166.3
– European Union	230.2			156.1	159.8
– Eastern Europe	0.4			1.1	2.2
– Rest of Europe	12.3			3.7	4.4
Europe former USSR				0.2	0.1
Oceania	6.6			1.0	1.8
Other	2.1			0.0	0.0
So. African Customs Un	229.4			174.1	159.8
United Kingdom	132.7			82.2	78.9
Zimbabwe	30.5			55.0	39.9
Japan/Japon	47.7			35.1	24.9
Germany/Allemagne	27.6			21.7	46.6
USA/Etats–Unis d'Amer	21.6			18.4	13.1
India/Inde	6.6			21.7	15.9
France, Monaco	16.9			12.7	8.4
China/Chine	0.2			17.6	15.8
Zambia/Zambie	5.4			13.4	6.1
Italy/Italie	9.2			9.2	5.0
Austria/Autriche	2.1			11.0	8.0
Mozambique	1.7			4.4	15.1
Netherlands/Pays–Bas	9.3			4.5	3.8
Switzerland,Liechtenst.	10.6			3.0	3.8
China, Hong Kong SAR	8.6			5.1	3.5
Korea, Republic of	3.1			6.9	5.6
Malaysia/Malaisie	3.5			4.0	6.8
Other Asia n.e.s.	14.2				
Denmark/Danemark	10.3			2.0	1.3
Canada	9.4			0.2	3.9
Belgium–Luxembourg	4.5			4.2	1.7
Finland/Finlande	3.8			3.1	2.8
Brazil/Brésil	4.1			2.1	2.7
Sweden/Suède	3.2			2.5	2.4
Portugal	6.4			0.9	0.2
Kenya	2.0			2.4	2.4
Australia/Australie	4.7			0.8	0.8
Pakistan	0.3			2.0	3.8
Thailand/Thaïlande	0.5			4.1	0.4
Spain/Espagne	3.7			0.8	0.4
Singapore/Singapour	2.2			0.8	1.5
Indonesia/Indonésie	0.0			2.3	2.1
Argentina/Argentine	0.9			2.1	1.1
United Rep of Tanzania	0.5			1.4	2.1
New Zealand	1.9			0.2	1.0
Mauritius/Maurice	0.1			1.8	1.0
Norway,Svalbard and JM	1.7			0.6	0.3
Saudi Arabia				0.0	2.3
Romania/Roumanie	0.0			0.2	2.1

COUNTRIES–PAYS	EXPORTS EXPORTATIONS ES F.O.B.				
	1991	1992	1993	1994	1995
Monde	483.0			337.1	433.3
Afrique	63.0			74.7	82.0
Amériques	76.6			35.0	63.7
– Amérique du Nord	71.9			33.5	57.8
– ALAI	4.6			1.1	5.9
– MCAC				0.0	0.0
– Caraïbes				0.2	0.0
– Autre Amérique				0.1	0.0
Asie anc. URSS exclus	70.3			34.6	32.7
– Moyen–Orient	0.1			0.1	1.6
Asie ancienne URSS					
Europe anc. URSS exclus	261.7			182.3	243.3
– Union Européenne	229.5			154.7	206.9
– Europe de l'Est	0.0			8.5	13.7
– Autre de l'Europe	32.2			19.0	22.7
Europe ancienne URSS				0.0	1.5
Océanie	7.7			8.2	8.8
Autre	3.7			2.4	1.3
Germany/Allemagne	71.5			51.7	58.9
USA/Etats–Unis d'Amer	71.1			32.6	57.0
So. African Customs Un	43.4			45.5	44.8
United Kingdom	54.2			41.2	30.0
Netherlands/Pays–Bas	43.3			26.0	39.4
Japan/Japon	56.7			27.5	21.8
France, Monaco	15.5			10.4	43.3
Switzerland,Liechtenst.	31.0			15.9	17.5
Spain/Espagne	15.0			4.3	12.6
Belgium–Luxembourg	14.2			8.2	6.5
Mozambique	1.6			7.6	9.9
Zimbabwe	3.4			8.0	7.1
Australia/Australie	6.4			4.2	5.6
Zambia/Zambie	3.2			4.1	5.1
Hungary/Hongrie	0.0			4.8	6.4
United Rep of Tanzania	2.1			2.2	6.5
Denmark/Danemark	4.9			2.2	3.5
Austria/Autriche	3.4			3.4	3.6
Pakistan	4.0			2.1	2.1
New Zealand	1.2			3.4	2.5
Czech Republic				1.9	4.7
Egypt/Egypte	3.8			0.3	2.4
Other Asia n.e.s.	6.2				
Portugal	2.4			1.2	2.6
Sweden/Suède	3.2			2.1	0.9
Croatia/Croatie				2.4	3.8
China/Chine	0.0			4.1	1.5
Brazil/Brésil	0.3			1.1	3.5
India/Inde	0.0			0.0	4.7
Poland/Pologne				1.8	2.4
Special Categories	3.6			0.3	
Mexico/Mexique	3.9				
Finland/Finlande	0.7			1.6	1.4
Italy/Italie	0.7			0.9	2.1
Uganda/Ouganda	0.1			2.3	1.2
Areas n.e.s.	0.1			2.0	1.3
Greece/Grèce	0.4			1.2	1.8
Burundi	2.1			0.6	0.5
Norway,Svalbard and JM	1.2			0.6	1.4
Kenya	0.3			1.6	0.8

(VALUE AS PERCENTAGE OF WORLD TOTAL)(VALEURS EN POURCENTAGE DU TOTAL MONDIAL)

	1986	1987	1988	1989	1990	1991	1992	1993	1994	1995
Africa	36.3	44.8	40.1	47.3	38.5	41.7			46.9	45.3
Americas	4.3	4.7	6.3	5.7	3.4	5.6			4.3	4.3
– Northern America	4.0	4.6	5.8	4.7	2.6	4.8			3.5	3.4
– LAIA	0.3	0.2	0.5	0.9	0.8	0.8			0.8	0.8
– CACM		0.0							0.0	0.0
– Caribbean		0.0		0.2	0.0	0.0			0.0	0.0
– Rest of America			0.0						0.0	0.0
Asia excl fmr USSR	14.6	9.4	13.8	11.4	14.2	13.8			18.8	16.8
– Middle East	0.0	0.1	0.1	0.0	0.1	0.1			0.2	0.6
Asia former USSR										0.0
Europe excl fmr USSR	43.3	40.1	39.2	34.5	42.8	37.5			29.8	33.2
– European Union	41.1	38.3	36.9	33.3	41.2	35.6			28.9	31.9
– Eastern Europe	0.0	0.4	0.6	0.2	0.1	0.1			0.2	0.4
– Rest of Europe	2.2	1.4	1.7	1.0	1.4	1.9			0.7	0.9
Europe former USSR				0.0					0.0	0.0
Oceania	1.6	1.0	0.7	1.1	0.5	1.0			0.2	0.4
Other				0.0	0.6	0.3			0.0	0.0
So. African Customs Un	29.6	36.2	32.2	37.6	31.7	35.4			32.3	31.9
United Kingdom	24.5	20.1	22.0	17.0	22.9	20.5			15.2	15.8
Zimbabwe	4.6	5.6	5.0	5.8	4.6	4.7			10.2	8.0
Japan/Japon	9.2	5.6	9.2	6.3	7.5	7.4			6.5	5.0
Germany/Allemagne						4.3			4.0	9.3
USA/Etats–Unis d'Amer	3.6	3.1	5.1	3.4	2.1	3.3			3.4	2.6
India/Inde	0.7	0.3	0.4	1.0	0.8	1.0			4.0	3.2
France, Monaco	2.4	2.4	2.8	1.2	2.9	2.6			2.4	1.7
China/Chine	0.0	0.0	0.0	0.0		0.0			3.3	3.2
Zambia/Zambie	1.5	2.4	1.9	3.2	1.6	0.8			2.5	1.2

	1986	1987	1988	1989	1990	1991	1992	1993	1994	1995
Afrique	22.0	17.8	18.6	16.3	15.7	13.0			22.1	18.9
Amériques	8.8	11.0	11.6	12.9	13.1	15.9			10.4	14.7
– Amérique du Nord	8.8	10.9	11.6	12.7	11.9	14.9			9.9	13.3
– ALAI	0.1	0.1	0.0	0.2	1.2	1.0			0.3	1.4
– MCAC		0.0							0.0	0.0
– Caraïbes	0.0		0.0	0.0					0.1	0.0
– Autre Amérique									0.0	0.0
Asie anc. URSS exclus	7.2	12.2	14.7	15.2	15.9	14.6			10.3	7.5
– Moyen–Orient	0.0	0.0	0.2	0.0	0.0	0.0			0.0	0.4
Asie ancienne URSS										
Europe anc. URSS exclus	56.1	56.1	52.6	52.3	52.9	54.2			54.1	56.2
– Union Européenne	54.1	55.2	50.8	50.7	50.1	47.5			45.9	47.7
– Europe de l'Est			0.0	0.0		0.0			2.5	3.2
– Autre de l'Europe	2.0	0.9	1.7	1.6	2.8	6.7			5.6	5.2
Europe ancienne URSS									0.0	0.3
Océanie	2.9	2.9	2.5	3.3	1.9	1.6			2.4	2.0
Autre	3.0			0.0	0.5	0.8			0.7	0.3
Germany/Allemagne						14.8			15.3	13.6
USA/Etats–Unis d'Amer	8.5	10.8	11.0	12.6	11.7	14.7			9.7	13.1
So. African Customs Un	8.1	11.2	11.3	10.5	8.0	9.0			13.5	10.3
United Kingdom	25.6	23.6	18.1	20.9	15.5	11.2			12.2	6.9
Netherlands/Pays–Bas	6.1	10.0	8.3	7.7	6.8	9.0			7.7	9.1
Japan/Japon	6.0	9.3	11.7	12.6	13.2	11.7			8.1	5.0
France, Monaco	3.5	3.3	3.6	3.7	3.4	3.2			3.1	10.0
Switzerland,Liechtenst.	1.7	0.5	1.4	1.3	1.8	6.4			4.7	4.0
Spain/Espagne	0.5	0.8	1.3	2.2	2.1	3.1			1.3	2.9
Belgium–Luxembourg	5.3	4.2	3.4	2.1	3.1	2.9			2.4	1.5

4. General Imports C.I.F. by Commodities according to the S.I.T.C. (Rev. 2) in million U.S. Dollars
Importations Générales C.A.F. par Produits d'après la C.T.C.I. (Rév. 2) en millions de Dollars E.U.

SITC CTCI	COMMODITY	1992 QUANTITY QUANTITE	1992 VALUE VALEUR	1993 QUANTITY QUANTITE	1993 VALUE VALEUR	1994 QUANTITY QUANTITE	1994 VALUE VALEUR	1995 QUANTITY QUANTITE	1995 VALUE VALEUR	PRODUIT
	ALL COMMODITIES		735.0		545.3		539.3		500.5	TOUS PRODUITS
0	FOOD AND LIVE ANIMALS						75.9		52.9	ALIMENTS,ANIMAUX VIVANTS
02	DAIRY PRODCTS,BIRDS'EGGS						6.2		3.8	PRODUITS LAITIERS,OEUFS
022	MILK AND CREAM					W 2974	5.5	W 1208	2.8	LAIT ET CREME
0224	MILK,CREAM PRESERVED ETC					W 2877	5.2	W 1075	2.5	LAIT,CREME CONS,CONC
02243	MILK DRY,OVER 1.5% FAT					W 1446	2.9	W 705	1.8	LAIT POUDRE SUP 1.5%
02249	MILK(EX DRY) PRSVD,SWEET					W 1000	1.9	W 205	0.3	LAIT CONS,CONC SUCRE
04	CEREALS AND PREPARATIONS						57.6		42.1	CEREALES ET PRODUITS
041	WHEAT ETC UNMILLED							W 14875	2.7	FROMENT,EPEAUTRE
0412	OTHER WHEAT ETC UNMILLED							W 14875	2.7	AUTRE FROMENT NON MOULU
044	MAIZE UNMILLED					W 259890	37.8	W 154336	25.8	MAIS NON MOULU
045	CEREALS NES UNMILLED					W 438816	8.8	W 15875	4.4	AUTRES CEREALES NON MOULUES
0459	OTHER CEREALS UNMILLED					W 438816	8.8	W 15875	4.4	SARRASIN,MILLET,SORGHO
04599	OTH CEREALS UNMILLED NES					W 438815	8.8	W 15825	3.3	AUTRES CEREALES NDA
046	WHEAT ETC MEAL OR FLOUR					W 25026	8.8	W 19129	7.8	SEMOULE FARINE,FROMENT
04601	FLOUR OF WHEAT OR MESLIN					W 25026	8.8	W 19119	7.8	FARINE DE FROMENT
048	CEREAL ETC PREPARATIONS					W 3508	2.2	W 1838	1.2	PREPTNS A BASE CEREALES
05	VEGETABLES AND FRUIT						1.9		1.6	LEGUMES ET FRUITS
06	SUGAR AND PREPS,HONEY						4.1		0.3	SUCRES ET PRODUITS
061	SUGAR AND HONEY					W 12680	3.9	W 457	0.3	SUCRES ET MIEL
0611	RAW BEET AND CANE SUGAR					W 11897	3.5			SUCRES BRUTS
081	*FEEDING STUFF FOR ANIML					W 3131	1.6	W 3211	1.8	NOURRITURE POUR ANIMAUX
09	MISC EDIBLE PRODUCTS						3.0		1.9	PREP ALIMENTAIRES DIVERSES
098	EDIBLE PRODCTS,PREPS NES					W 1047	3.0	W 466	1.8	PREP ALIMENTAIRES NDA
09806	YEASTS,BAKING POWDERS					W 764	1.9	W 202	0.5	LEVURES
1	BEVERAGES AND TOBACCO						2.4		1.5	BOISSONS ET TABACS
2	CRUDE MATERLS,EXCL FUELS						8.1		6.3	MAT BRUTES NON COMESTIBLES
26	TEXTILE FIBRES AND WASTE						2.4		2.7	FIBRES TEXTILES
27	CRUDE FERTLZR,MINRLS NES						3.6		3.2	ENGRAIS MINERAUX BRUTS
278	OTHER CRUDE MINERALS					W 26914	3.0	W 26159	2.8	AUTRES MINERAUX BRUTS
2783	COMMON SALT,ETC					W 24744	2.0	W 25392	2.4	SEL
3	MINERAL FUELS ETC						41.2		55.8	COMBUSTIBLES MINERAUX LUB
32	COAL,COKE AND BRIQUETTES						1.3		2.0	HOUILLES,COKES,BRIQUETTES
322	COAL,LIGNITE AND PEAT					W 26870	1.3	W 135238	1.9	HOUILLES,LIGNITES,TOURBE
3222	OTH COAL,NOT AGGLOMERATD					W 26869	1.2	W 135238	1.9	AUTRES HOUILLES
33	PETROLEUM AND PRODUCTS						39.7		53.4	PETROLE ET DERIVES
334	PETROLEUM PRODUCTS,REFIN					W 215916	37.5	W 645200	51.1	PRODUITS RAFFINES
33411	MOTOR,AVIATION SPIRIT	W 55870	19.4	W 55500	17.5					ESSENCES MOTEURS D'AVIONS
3343	GAS OILS	W 93873	25.0	W 94221	21.5					GAS OILS
335	RESIDUAL PETRLM PROD NES					W 3817	2.3	W 3630	2.3	PRODUITS RESIDUELS NDA
3351	PETRLM JELLY,MINERAL WAX					W 2146	1.7	W 1658	1.7	VASELINE,CIRES MINERALES
4	ANIMAL,VEGETABLE OIL,FAT						11.0		15.3	HUILES,GRAISSES ANIM,VEG
42	FIXED VEGETABLE OIL,FAT						9.7		14.7	HUILES VEGETALES FIXES
423	FIXED VEG OILS,SOFT					W 8638	5.9	W 8270	6.6	HUILES VEGET DOUCES FIXES
4232	SOYA BEAN OIL					W 6122	3.7	W 6600	5.3	HUILE DE SOJA
4236	SUNFLOWER SEED OIL					W 2511	2.2	W 1461	1.3	HUILE DE TOURNESOL
424	FIXED VEG OIL NONSOFT					W 9913	3.9	W 10998	8.1	AUTRES HUILES VEG FIXES
4242	PALM OIL					W 26	0.1	W 3130	2.3	HUILE DE PALME
4244	PALM KERNEL OIL					W 486	0.3	W 4646	3.6	HUILE DE PALMISTE
4249	FIXED VEGETABLE OILS NES					W 9396	3.5	W 2865	2.0	HUILES VEGET FIXES NDA
5	CHEMCLS,RELATED PROD NES						81.6		112.6	PRODUITS CHIMIQUES
51	ORGANIC CHEMICALS						4.5		2.6	PROD CHIMIQ ORGANIQUES
52	INORGANIC CHEMICALS						4.6		3.7	PROD CHIM INORGANIQUES
522	INORG ELEMNTS,OXIDES,ETC					W 2993	2.3	W 4698	2.4	ELEMENTS INORGANIQUES
5225	INORGANIC BASES ETC NES					W 1390	0.8	W 3777	1.6	AUTRES BASES OXYDES METAL
523	OTHR INORG CHEMICALS ETC					W 4710	2.4	W 2112	1.3	AUT PRODUITS CHIMIQUES INORG
53	DYES,TANNING,COLOUR PROD						3.6		2.0	PROD TEINTURE,COLORANTS
533	PIGMENTS,PAINTS,ETC					W 977	1.9	W 1520	1.3	PIGMENTS,PEINTURES,VERNIS
541	*MEDICINAL,PHARM PRODUCT					K 1719613	11.3	K 1581757	39.7	PROD MEDICINAUX PHARMACEUT
5417	MEDICAMENTS					K 1180209	8.0	K 1039724	36.7	MEDICAMENTS
54171	— CONTAINNG ANTIBIOTICS					K 174921	2.4	K 126711	3.1	MED CONTN ANTIBIOTIQUES
54172	— CONTAINING HORMONES					K 366497	1.3	K 145667	30.0	MED CONTENANT HORMONES
54179	— CONTNG OTH SUBSTANCES					K 565220	3.9	K 616849	2.6	MED CONT AUT SUBSTANCES
5419	PHARMACEUTICAL GOODS NES					K 268459	2.1	K 448762	1.6	PREP,ART PHARMACEUTIQUES
54199	OTH PHARMACEUTICAL GOODS					K 61706	1.7	K 171606	1.2	AUT PREP PHARMACEUTIQUES
55	PERFUME,CLEANING ETC PRD						6.7		6.6	PROD POUR PARFUM,TOILETTE
551	ESSENTL OILS,PERFUME,ETC					W 505	3.4	W 480	3.7	HUILES ESSENTIELLES
5514	MIXED PERFUME SUBSTANCES					W 476	3.3	W 452	3.1	MELANGES SUBSTAN ODORIFER
554	SOAP,CLEANSING ETC PREPS					W 2642	2.3	W 3074	2.5	SAVONS,PRODUITS DETERSIFS
562	*FERTILIZERS,MANUFACTURE	W 194400	58.6	W 201000	61.5	W 92289	26.7	W 132355	37.7	ENGRAIS MANUFACTURES
5621	CHEM NITROGENOUS FERTLZR					W 59185	17.7	W 82270	21.6	ENGRAIS AZOTES
56212	AMMONIUM SULPHONITRATE					W 9813	4.6	W 2757	0.4	SULFONITRATE D'AMMONIUM
56213	AMMONIUM SULPHATE					W 8355	3.2	W 7562	1.9	SULFATE D'AMMONIUM
56216	UREA					W 33459	7.2	W 34674	10.5	UREE
56219	CHEM NITROG FERTILZR NES					W 4958	2.2	W 37201	8.9	ENGRAIS AZOTES NDA
5623	CHEM POTASSIC FERTILIZER					W 2301	0.7	W 7152	2.3	ENGRAIS POTASSIQUES
5629	FERTILIZERS NES					W 29178	7.8	W 42541	13.6	ENGRAIS NDA
56291	NIT–PHOS–POT FERTLZR NES					W 4443	1.1	W 7753	2.3	ENGRAIS CONT N P K
56292	NITROG–PHOS FERTILZR NES					W 24734	6.1	W 34784	10.1	ENGRAIS NDA CONT N P
58	PLASTIC MATERIALS ETC						13.5		12.2	MAT PLAST ARTIFICIELLES
583	POLYMERIZATION ETC PRODS					W 11797	11.7	W 7786	11.1	PROD POLYMERISATION
5834	POLYVINYL CHLORIDE					W 2553	2.9	W 1439	2.0	CHLORURE DE POLYVINYLE
58341	— IN PRIMARY FORMS					W 2445	2.7	W 1349	1.9	SOUS FORMES PRIMAIRES
5839	OTH POLYMRZTION ETC PROD					W 5397	5.8	W 3933	5.7	AUT PROD POLYMER COPOLYM
59	CHEMICAL MATERIALS NES						10.7		8.3	MAT PROD CHIMIQUES NDA
591	PESTICIDES,DISINFECTANTS					W 1712	6.8	W 1420	5.7	DESINF,INSECT,FONG,HERB
5911	INSECTICIDES,FOR RETAIL					W 1087	4.5	W 723	3.2	INSECTICIDES VENTE DET
598	MISCEL CHEM PRODUCTS NES					W 1215	2.7	W 811	1.8	PROD DIV INDUST CHIM NDA
5989	CHEM PRODUCTS,PREPS NES					W 910	2.4	W 796	1.7	PROD PREP CHIMIQUES NDA
59899	OTH CHEM PRODS,PREPS,NES					W 563	2.0	W 497	1.3	AUT PRODUITS CHIMIQUES NDA
6	BASIC MANUFACTURES						112.4		90.8	ART MANUFACTURES
62	RUBBER MANUFACTURES NES						15.0		8.3	CAOUTCHOUC MANUFACTURE
625	RUBBER TYRES, TUBES ETC					W 812	11.6	W 635	5.4	PNEUS CAOUTCHOUC VULCANISE
6251	TYRES NEW FOR MOTOR CARS					W 110	4.2	W 43	1.6	PNEUS POUR VOITURES
6252	TYRES,NEW,BUS OR LORRY					W 58	5.3	W 20	1.4	PNEUS POUR AUTOBUS,CAMIONS
628	RUBBER ARTICLES NES					W 304	1.8	W 1316	1.9	OUVRAGES CAOUTCHOUC NDA
64	PAPER,PAPERBOARD AND MFR						18.6		15.9	PAPIERS,CARTONS & OUVRAGES
641	PAPER AND PAPERBOARD					W 14320	13.3	W 12579	12.9	PAPIERS ET CARTONS
6413	KRAFT PAPER,PAPERBOARD					W 3964	3.1	W 4670	4.5	PAPIER ET CARTON KRAFT
64131	KRAFT LINER IN BULK					W 2395	1.8	W 3806	3.3	PAP KRAFT POUR COUVERTURES
6415	PAPER,PAPERBRD,BULK,NES					W 5890	4.4	W 3600	2.7	PAPIERS,CARTONS ROULEAUX

Malawi

4. General Imports C.I.F. by Commodities according to the S.I.T.C. (Rev. 2) in million U.S. Dollars
Importations Générales C.A.F. par Produits d'après la C.T.C.I. (Rév. 2) en millions de Dollars E.U.

SITC CTCI	COMMODITY	1992 QUANTITY QUANTITE	1992 VALUE VALEUR	1993 QUANTITY QUANTITE	1993 VALUE VALEUR	1994 QUANTITY QUANTITE	1994 VALUE VALEUR	1995 QUANTITY QUANTITE	1995 VALUE VALEUR	PRODUIT
64159	OTHER PAPER ETC,BULK,NES					W 4957	4.0	W 2296	1.9	AUT PAPIER ROULEAUX FEUILLES
6418	COATED ETC PAPER NES BLK					W 2873	3.7	W 2772	3.5	PAP,CARTONS COUCHES,ENDUITS
64181	PLASTIC COATED PAPER ETC					W 2396	3.1	W 2282	2.9	PAP,CARTONS ENDUITS,RESINES
642	PAPER,ETC,PRECUT,ARTS OF					W 6146	5.3	W 2038	3.0	PAP,CARTONS DECOUPES
6423	EXERCISE BOOKS ETC					W 513	1.9	W 365	0.7	REGISTRES,CAHIERS,CARNETS
65	TEXTILE YARN,FABRICS,ETC						24.8		25.6	FILS,TISSUS,ARTICLES TEXTILE
651	TEXTILE YARN					W 1596	3.6	W 505	2.2	FILS TEXTILES
652	COTTON FABRICS,WOVEN					W 7450	8.5	W 10207	9.4	TISSUS DE COTON
6522	WOVEN COTTON BLEACHD,ETC					W 6818	8.2	W 8744	8.8	TISSUS COTON BLANCHIS ETC
65224	BLCHED COTTON FABRIC NES					W 2386	3.1	W 4392	2.9	AUT TIS PLUS 85% COT BLANCHI
65225	BLCHD COTN BLEND FAB NES					W 4408	5.1	W 4238	5.6	AUT TIS MOINS 85% COT BLANCH
653	WOVN MAN-MADE FIB FABRIC					W 17772	7.3	W 16572	9.7	TISSUS FIBRES SYNTH,ARTIF
6531	CONT SYNT WEAVES NONPILE					W 9099	1.8	W 1181	1.2	TISSUS FIBRES SYNTH CONTINUE
6534	DISC SYN BLEND FABRC NES					W 8054	4.9	W 13797	6.9	TISSUS FIBRES SYNTH DISCONT
65341	DISC SYN FIB-COTTN FABRC					W 7901	4.8	W 12833	6.0	TISSUS FIB SYNT DIS MEL COTO
658	TEXTILE ARTICLES NES					W 1200	1.5	W 3386	1.9	ART FACONNES MAT TEXTILES
66	NONMETAL MINERAL MFS NES						7.3		7.7	ART MIN NON METALLIQUES
661	LIME,CEMENT,BLDG PRODS					W 12787	1.8	W 88314	3.9	CHAUX,CIMENTS MAT CONSTR
6612	CEMENT					W 12358	1.1	W 84695	1.6	CIMENTS HYDRAULIQUES
6618	MNRL BLDG PRD UNFIRD NES					W 384	0.3	W 3557	1.6	MAT CONST AMIANTE-CIMENT
67	IRON AND STEEL						19.5		15.1	FER ET ACIER
673	IRON,STEEL SHAPES ETC					W 7908	4.6	W 30625	4.2	BARRES,PROFIL FER,ACIER
6732	IRON,STEEL BARS ETC					W 5504	2.2	W 29671	1.9	BARRES FER,ACIER
674	IRN,STL UNIV,PLATE,SHEET					W 10404	11.1	W 36132	6.1	LARGES PLATS,TOLES
6749	OTH IRN,STL PLATES,SHEET					W 9616	9.1	W 35587	5.0	AUTRES TOLES FER,ACIER
67491	— OF IRON OR SIMPLE STL					W 9601	9.1	W 35540	4.9	AUT TOLES AUTRES ACIER FIN
678	IRON,STL TUBES,PIPES,ETC					W 1837	2.2	W 5491	4.0	TUBES,TUYAUX EN FONTE,FER
6783	IRON,STL TUBES,PIPES NES					W 1820	1.1	W 5415	2.0	AUT TUBES,TUYAUX FER,ACIER
68	NON-FERROUS METALS						1.9		1.2	METAUX NON FERREUX
684	ALUMINIUM					W 706	1.7	W 347	1.1	ALUMINIUM
6842	ALUMINIUM,ALLOYS WORKED					W 706	1.7	W 347	1.1	ALUMINIUM,ALLIAGES OUVRE
69	METAL MANUFACTURES NES						24.3		16.8	ART MANUFACT EN METAL NDA
691	STRUCTURES AND PARTS NES					W 895	9.5	W 76	7.0	CONSTRUCT FER,ACIER,ALU
6911	STRUCTURES,PARTS IRN,STL					W 827	9.2	W 40	6.8	CONSTRUCT FER,ACIER,FONTE
692	METAL TANKS,BOXES,ETC					W 255	2.0	W 55	0.6	RECIPIENTS METALLIQUES
695	TOOLS					W 701	2.3	W 168	1.9	OUTILS A MAIN
699	BASE METAL MFRS NES					W 2699	6.1	W 1300	4.7	ART MANUFACTURES MET NDA
6991	LOCKSMITHS WARES,ETC					W 524	2.0	W 283	1.2	ARTICLES DE SERRURERIE
6996	BASE MTL MISC ARTICLES					W 995	2.4	W 603	1.8	ART DIVERS METAUX COMMUNS
7	MACHINES,TRANSPORT EQUIP						175.3		138.0	MACHINES MATERIEL TRANSPORT
71	POWER GENERATING EQUIPMT						7.6		7.7	MACHINES GENERATRICES
713	INTRNL COMBUS PSTN ENGIN					W 151	4.3	W 67	1.8	MOTEURS EXPL COMB INT, PIECE
716	ROTATING ELECTRIC PLANT					W 1107	2.9	W 209	3.4	APP ELECTR ROTATIFS,PIECES
7162	AC MTRS,GENRTRS,GEN SETS					W 1074	2.1	W 81	1.1	MOTEURS ELECTRIQUES
72	MACHS FOR SPCL INDUSTRYS						36.0		21.4	MAC SPECIALES POUR INDUST
723	CIVIL ENGNEERG EQUIP ETC					W 22	7.5	W 27	5.3	APPAREILS DE GENIE CIVIL
7234	CONST,MINING MACHNRY NES					W 21	6.0	W 27	5.0	MACH POUR LA CONST, MINES
72341	SELF-PROPELLD DOZERS,ETC						1.6		2.4	BULLDOZERS
72342	SLFPRP SHOVELS,EXCAVATRS					W 8	3.0	W 20	1.9	PELLES MECANIQUES
724	TEXTILE,LEATHER MACHNRY					W 237	3.0	W 194	6.8	MACH POUR INDUSTRIE TEXTILE
7244	SPINNING,EXTRDNG,ETC MCH					W 167	1.8	W 118	5.7	MACH POUR LE FILAGE
72443	SPINNING,REELING,ETC MCH					W 100	0.7	W 50	4.8	MACH POUR LA FILATURE
726	PRINTG,BKBINDG MACHY,PTS					W 131	8.6	W 78	0.8	MACHINES POUR IMPRIMERIE
7264	PRINTING PRESSES					W 63	7.4	W 53	0.4	MACHINES A IMPRIMER
72641	ROTARY PRINTING PRESSES					W 63	7.4	W 53	0.4	MACH IMPRIMER ROTATIVES
727	FOOD MACHRY NON-DOMESTIC					W 776	4.5	W 376	2.9	MACH INDUSTRIES ALIMENT
7272	OTH FOOD PROC MCHY,PARTS					W 290	3.4	W 234	2.1	AUT MACH IND ALIMENTAIRE
72722	INDUS FOOD PROC MACH NES					W 290	3.4	W 231	2.1	MACHINES BOULANGERIE
728	OTH MACHY FOR SPCL INDUS					W 1377	10.0	W 322	3.0	AUT MACH IND PARTICULIERES
7283	OTHR MINERAL WORKG MACHY					W 302	1.7	W 114	0.5	MACH TRIER,CRIBLER,BROYER
7284	MACHY FOR SPCL INDUS NES					W 948	7.8	W 145	2.2	MACH SPEC IND PARTICUL.
72842	RUBBER,PLASTICS WRKG MCH					W 152	1.8	W 11	0.2	MACH IND CAOUT MAT PLAST
72848	OTH MCHY WITH INDIV FNCT					W 332	2.1	W 50	0.5	AUTRES MACHINES NDA
73	METALWORKING MACHINERY						1.8		0.8	MACH TRAVAIL DES METAUX
74	GENRL INDUSTRL MACHY NES						18.8		14.1	MACH APP INDUSTRIE
741	HEATING,COOLING EQUIPMNT					W 166	2.1	W 86	1.4	MACH CHAUFFAGE,PIECES
742	PUMPS FOR LIQUIDS ETC					W 455	2.7	W 290	2.1	POMPES MOTO-POMPES
7428	OTHER PUMPS FOR LIQUIDS					W 348	1.8	W 240	1.6	AUTRES POMPES POUR LIQ
74288	PUMPS FR LIQUIDS NES ETC					W 346	1.8	W 237	1.6	POMPES POUR LIQUIDES NDA
743	PUMPS NES,CENTRFUGES ETC					W 337	2.2	W 319	2.1	POMPES COMPRES,VENT ETC
744	MECHANICAL HANDLING EQU					W 585	3.9	W 474	3.7	EQUIP MANUTENTION PIECES
7449	PTS NES OF MACHY OF 7442					W 221	2.5	W 237	2.1	PIECES DU 744.2
745	NONELEC MACHY,TOOLS NES					W 221	2.3	W 232	1.2	AUT MACH NON ELEC,PIECES
7452	OTH NONELEC MCHS,PTS NES					W 207	2.2	W 217	1.1	AUT MACH NON ELEC,PIECES
749	NONELEC MACH PTS,ACC NES					W 552	5.9	W 344	3.8	PIECES MACH NON ELEC NDA
7492	COCKS,VALVES ETC NES					W 143	1.7	W 74	0.9	ART ROB,SIM POUR TUYAUX
7493	SHAFT,CRANK,PULLEY ETC					W 198	2.3	W 143	1.5	ARBRES TRANS,VILEBREQUINS
75	OFFICE MACHNES,ADP EQUIP						8.3		7.4	MACH BUREAU TRAIT AUTOM
751	OFFICE MACHINES					W 12	2.0	W 35	3.1	MACH,APPAREILS DE BUREAU
7518	OFFICE MACHINES NES					W 7	0.8	W 23	2.3	MACH,APP DE BUREAU NDA
75188	OTHR OFFICE MACHINES NES					W 3	0.1	W 17	1.8	AUTRES MACH DE BUREAU
752	AUTOMTIC DATA PROC EQUIP					W 10	4.0	W 46	3.3	MACH TRAIT INFORMATION
759	OFFICE,ADP MCH PTS,ACCES					W 33	2.4	W 21	1.2	PIECES DU 751 ET 752
7599	ACCTG,ETC,ADP MCH PTS,AC					W 22	2.1	W 16	1.0	PIECES DU 751 ET 752
76	TELECOMM,SOUND EQUIPMENT						15.6		4.5	EQUIPMENT DE TELECOM
764	TELECOM EQPT,PTS,ACC NES					W 159	13.1	W 84	3.3	EQUIP TELECOM,PIECES
7641	LINE TELEPHONE,ETC EQUIP					W 43	2.5	W 20	1.1	APP TELEPHON PAR FIL
7649	PTS NES OF EQUIPMT OF 76					W 104	9.8	W 36	0.9	PIECES DE LA DIV 76
76491	PTS NES OF APPAR OF 7641					W 67	9.3	W 7	0.2	PIECES POUR 764.1
77	ELECTRIC MACHNRY NES ETC						17.3		15.9	MACH APP ELECT NDA
771	ELECTRIC POWER MACHY NES					W 106	1.9	W 224	2.7	MACH PROD,TRANS ELECTR
7711	TRANSFORMERS,ELECTRICAL					W 91	1.6	W 157	2.0	TRANSFO ELECTRIQUES
77118	OTHER ELEC TRANSFORMERS					W 91	1.5	W 153	1.7	AUTRES TRANSFO ELECTRIQ
772	SWITCHGEAR ETC,PARTS NES					W 273	3.5	W 351	4.3	APP COUPURE,SECT ETC
7721	SWITCHGEAR ETC					W 272	3.5	W 351	4.3	APP COUPURE,SECTIONMNT
773	ELECTR DISTRIBUTNG EQUIP					W 1273	2.7	W 965	3.4	EQUIPMT DISTRIBUTION ELECT
7731	INSULATED WIRE,CABLE ETC					W 1109	2.0	W 746	3.0	FILS,CABLES ISOLES ELECT
775	HOUSEHOLD TYPE EQUIP NES					W 766	2.6	W 1781	1.5	MACH,APP USAGE DOMESTQUE
778	ELECTRICAL MACHINERY NES					W 11104	5.4	W 7258	3.9	AUTRES MACH ELECT NDA
7781	BATTERIES,ACCUMULATORS					W 10555	2.1	W 7046	1.5	PILES ET ACCUMULATEURS
78	ROAD VEHICLES						66.3		64.9	VEHICULES ROUTIERS

Malawi

4. General Imports C.I.F. by Commodities according to the S.I.T.C. (Rev. 2) in million U.S. Dollars
Importations Générales C.A.F. par Produits d'après la C.T.C.I. (Rév. 2) en millions de Dollars E.U.

SITC CTCI	COMMODITY	1992 QUANTITY QUANTITE	1992 VALUE VALEUR	1993 QUANTITY QUANTITE	1993 VALUE VALEUR	1994 QUANTITY QUANTITE	1994 VALUE VALEUR	1995 QUANTITY QUANTITE	1995 VALUE VALEUR	PRODUIT
781	PASS MOTOR VEH EXC BUSES					W 1152	15.3	W 1057	14.7	AUTO TRANSPORT PERSONNES
782	LORRIES,SPCL MTR VEH NES					W 2658	26.1	W 1361	30.1	VEHICULES SPECIAUX,MARCH
7821	LORRIES,TRUCKS					W 2658	22.9	W 1361	29.1	VEHICULES TRANSP MARCHAND
7822	SPECIAL MOTOR VEHCLS NES						3.2		1.0	VEHICULES USAGES SPECIAUX
783	ROAD MOTOR VEHICLES NES						5.6		9.6	VEHICULES ROUTIERS NDA
7831	BUSES						4.0		5.3	VOITURES TRANSPORT COMMUN
7832	TRACTORS FOR TR–TRAILERS						1.6		4.3	TRACTEURS ROUTIERS
784	MOTOR VEH PRTS,ACCES NES					W 432	8.5	W 264	4.2	PIECES 722,781,782,783
7841	MOTOR VEHICLE CHASSIS						2.6		0.8	CHASSIS 722,781,782,783
7849	OTHER MOTOR VEHCL PARTS					W 422	5.2	W 257	3.4	PIECES 722,781,782,783
785	CYCLES,ETC MOTRZD OR NOT					W 1912	10.2	W 1295	5.3	MOTOCYCLES SCOOTERS
7852	CYCLES, ETC NON–MOTOR					W 249	6.3	W 311	2.5	VELOCIPEDES SANS MOTEUR
7853	INVAL CARR, PTS OF 785					W 1662	2.7	W 983	1.9	FAUTEUILS INVALIDES,PIECES
78539	PARTS,ACCES NES OF 785					W 1662	2.7	W 982	1.9	PIECES DU 785
79	OTHR TRANSPORT EQUIPMENT						3.9		1.6	AUTRE MATERIEL TRANSPORT
791	RAILWAY VEHICLES					W 158	2.5	W 63	0.9	VEHIC MAT CHEMINS DE FER
7919	RY TRACK FIXT,ETC,PARTS					W 158	2.5	W 63	0.9	MATER FIXE VOIES FERREES
79199	PARTS NES OF 7911–7915					W 158	2.5	W 63	0.9	PIECES 791.1 ET 5
8	MISC MANUFACTURED GOODS						31.6		27.2	ART MANUFACTURES DIVERS
812	*PLUMBG,HEATNG,LGHTNG EQ					W 916	1.8	W 616	1.6	APPAR SANITAIRES CHAUFFAGE
821	*FURNITURE,PARTS THEREOF					W 836	2.0	W 351	2.1	MEUBLES ET PIECES
84	CLOTHING AND ACCESSORIES						5.4		2.1	VETEMENTS
851	*FOOTWEAR					W 1044	2.9	W 1218	1.9	CHAUSSURES
87	PRECISION INSTRUMNTS NES						5.0		3.8	INSTRUM,APPAR SCIENT NDA
872	MEDICAL INSTRUMENTS NES					W 105	1.5	W 166	1.8	INSTR,APP MEDIC–CHIR NDA
87202	OTH MEDICAL INSTRUMENTS					W 87	1.4	W 164	1.7	INSTRUM,APP MEDECINE
874	MEASURNG,CONTROLNG INSTR					W 145	2.4	W 121	1.8	INSTRUMENTS DE MESURE
89	MISC MANUFCTRD GOODS NES						13.2		14.7	ART MANUFACTURES DIVERS
892	PRINTED MATTER					W 799	6.6	W 1071	9.8	IMPRIMES
8921	PRINTED BOOKS,GLOBES,ETC					W 436	3.0	W 826	4.8	LIVRES,BROCHURES,CARTES
89211	PRINTED BOOKS,PAMPHLETS					W 435	3.0	W 800	4.4	LIVRES,BROCHURES
8928	PRINTED MATTER NES					W 202	2.9	W 137	4.4	IMPRIMES NDA
89283	UNISSUED BANKNOTES ETC					W 68	1.9	W 51	3.6	TIMBRES–POSTE FISCAUX
893	ARTICLES OF PLASTIC NES						3.5		2.2	OUVRAGES EN MAT DIVIS 58

5. General Exports F.O.B. by Commodities according to the S.I.T.C. (Rev. 2) in million U.S. Dollars
Exportations Générales F.O.B. par Produits d'après la C.T.C.I. (Rév. 2) en millions de Dollars E.U.

SITC CTCI	COMMODITY	1992 QUANTITY QUANTITE	1992 VALUE VALEUR	1993 QUANTITY QUANTITE	1993 VALUE VALEUR	1994 QUANTITY QUANTITE	1994 VALUE VALEUR	1995 QUANTITY QUANTITE	1995 VALUE VALEUR	PRODUIT
	ALL COMMODITIES		396.0		319.1		337.1		433.4	TOUS PRODUITS
0	FOOD AND LIVE ANIMALS						79.9		79.6	ALIMENTS,ANIMAUX VIVANTS
04	CEREALS AND PREPARATIONS						4.2		4.0	CEREALES ET PRODUITS
042	RICE			W 100	0.1	W 5908	2.8	W 4712	1.5	RIZ
0422	RICE SEMI–MILLED,MILLED					W 5883	2.8	W 4712	1.5	RIZ POLI,GLACE INCL BRISURES
04221	RICE MILLED UNBROKEN					W 5882	2.8	W 4712	1.5	RIZ POLI,GLACE EXCL BRISURES
044	MAIZE UNMILLED					W 1259	0.9	W 31260	2.0	MAIS NON MOULU
05	VEGETABLES AND FRUIT						4.9		10.9	LEGUMES ET FRUITS
054	VEG ETC FRSH,SMPLY PRSVD					W 10336	3.5	W 29426	8.3	LEGUMES FRAIS,CONG,SECS
0542	LEGUMINOUS VEGETBLES DRY	W 5700	1.9	W 3500	1.4	W 9979	3.4	W 29093	8.2	LEGUMES A COSSE SECS
057	FRUIT,NUTS,FRESH,DRIED					W 361	1.3	W 635	2.5	FRUITS FRAIS OU SECS
0577	NUTS EDIBLE,FRESH,DRIED					W 301	1.3	W 635	2.5	FRUITS A COQUES
05779	NUTS EDIBLE,FRSH,DRY,NES					W 220	1.3	W 337	2.5	FRUITS A COQUES NDA
06	SUGAR AND PREPS,HONEY						24.8		19.7	SUCRES ET PRODUITS
061	SUGAR AND HONEY		25.3	W 26800	15.6	W 33520	24.8	W 66025	19.7	SUCRES ET MIEL
0611	RAW BEET AND CANE SUGAR					W 25373	17.6	W 56479	16.2	SUCRES BRUTS
0612	REFINED SUGAR ETC					W 8110	7.3	W 8414	3.5	SUCRES RAFFINES
07	COFFEE,TEA,COCOA,SPICES						45.3		44.2	CAFE,THE,CACAO,EPICES
071	COFFEE AND SUBSTITUTES					W 4586	14.8	W 5246	15.5	CAFE ET SUCCEDANES
0711	COFFEE GREEN,ROASTED,SUB	W 8300	8.1	W 5700	8.0	W 4586	14.8	W 5246	15.5	CAFE TORREFIE OU DECAFEINE
07111	COFFEE GREEN,HUSKS,SKINS	W 8300	8.1	W 5700	8.0	W 4586	14.8	W 5228	15.5	CAFE NON TORREFIE
074	TEA AND MATE		27.6	W 35300	35.5	W 35138	30.0	W 32387	26.6	THE ET MATE
0741	TEA		27.6	W 35300	35.5	W 35138	30.0	W 32387	26.6	THE
075	SPICES					W 361	0.6	W 1187	2.1	EPICES
0751	PEPPER AND PIMENTO					W 343	0.6	W 1086	1.6	POIVRE,PIMENTS
1	BEVERAGES AND TOBACCO						198.7		300.0	BOISSONS ET TABACS
11	BEVERAGES						0.6		4.4	BOISSONS
112	ALCOHOLIC BEVERAGES					W 290	0.6	W 829	4.3	BOISSONS ALCOOLIQUES
1124	DISTILLED ALCOHOLIC BEVS					W 44	0.4	W 697	4.2	ALCOOLS,EAUX–DE–VIE
11249	OTH ALCOHOLC BEVS,CMPNDS					W 29	0.2	W 685	4.1	BOISSONS ALCOOLIQUES NDA
12	TOBACCO AND MANUFACTURES				212.3		198.2		295.7	TABACS BRUTS FABRIQUES
121	TOBACCO UNMNFCTRD,REFUSE		265.8	W 95700	212.3	W 98313	196.7	W 97955	293.8	TABACS BRUTS,DECHETS
1211	TOBACCO,NOT STRIPPED					W 32808	67.9	W 24756	70.8	TABACS NON ECOTES
1212	TOBACCO STRIPPED OR PART					W 65505	128.9	W 73198	223.1	TABACS PART ECOTES
122	TOBACCO,MANUFACTURED					W 396	1.5	W 158	1.9	TABACS FABRIQUES
1222	CIGARETTES					W 353	1.3	W 3	0.1	CIGARETTES
1223	OTH MANUFACTURED TOBACCO					W 6	0.1	W 136	1.7	TABACS FUMER,CHIQUER,PRISER
2	CRUDE MATERLS,EXCL FUELS						10.5		11.3	MAT BRUTES NON COMESTIBLES
22	OIL SEEDS,OLEAGINOUS FRT						0.7		1.8	GRAINES,FRUITS OLEAGINEUX
222	SEEDS FOR'SOFT'FIXED OIL					W 2555	0.7	W 7378	1.7	GRAINES HUILES FIXES
23	RUBBER, CRUDE						2.6		1.6	CAOUTCHOUC BRUT
232	NATURAL RUBBER,GUMS					W 2312	2.6	W 979	1.6	LATEX CAOUTCHOUC NATUREL
23203	BALATA,GUTTA–PERCHA, ETC					W 2312	2.6	W 939	1.6	BALATA,GUTTA–PERCHA
26	TEXTILE FIBRES AND WASTE						4.0		4.6	FIBRES TEXTILES
263	COTTON			W 1900	2.1	W 2219	3.2	W 3044	3.8	COTON
2631	RAW COTTON,EXCL LINTERS		4.3	W 1900	2.1					COTON EN MASSE
2634	COTTON,CARDED OR COMBED					W 2208	3.2	W 3044	3.8	COTON CARDE OU PEIGNE
29	CRUDE ANIMAL,VEG MAT NES						1.7		1.7	MATIERES BRUTES ANIM,VEGET
292	CRUDE VEG MATERIALS NES					W 581	1.7	W 995	1.7	MAT BRUTES VEGETALES NDA
2927	CUT FLOWERS AND FOLIAGE					W 352	1.5	W 742	1.6	FLEURS,FEUILLAGES COUPES
29271	CUT FLOWERS					W 352	1.5	W 742	1.6	FLEURS ET BOUTONS
5	CHEMCLS,RELATED PROD NES						2.2		1.7	PRODUITS CHIMIQUES
6	BASIC MANUFACTURES						20.0		17.0	ART MANUFACTURES
62	RUBBER MANUFACTURES NES						0.5		1.4	CAOUTCHOUC MANUFACTURE
625	RUBBER TYRES, TUBES ETC					W 101	0.5	W 154	1.4	PNEUS CAOUTCHOUC VULCANISE
63	WOOD,CORK MANUFACTRS NES						2.6		2.1	OUVRAGES LIEGE ET BOIS
634	VENEERS,PLYWOOD,ETC					W 3494	2.1	W 15565	1.9	PLACAGES,CONTRE–PLAQUES
6342	PLYWOOD OF WOOD SHEETS					W 3017	1.9	W 15489	1.8	BOIS CONTRE–PLAQUES
65	TEXTILE YARN,FABRICS,ETC						15.1		11.1	FILS,TISSUS,ARTICLES TEXTILE
652	COTTON FABRICS,WOVEN					W 19297	12.0	W 14541	7.1	TISSUS DE COTON
6521	GREY WOVEN COTTON FABRIC					W 17741	10.8	W 10841	6.5	TISSUS COT ECRUS NON MERCER
65214	GREY WOVEN COTTON NES					W 17741	10.8	W 10841	6.5	AUT TISSUS 85% COTON ECRUS
6522	WOVEN COTTON BLEACHD,ETC					W 1556	1.3	W 3701	0.6	TISSUS COTON BLANCHIS ETC
653	WOVN MAN–MADE FIB FABRIC					W 3462	2.3	W 4011	1.9	TISSUS FIBRES SYNTH,ARTIF
6534	DISC SYN BLEND FABRC NES					W 3440	2.2	W 3789	1.3	TISSUS FIBRES SYNTH DISCONT
65341	DISC SYN FIB–COTTN FABRC					W 3440	2.2	W 3789	1.3	TISSUS FIB SYNT DIS MEL COTO
658	TEXTILE ARTICLES NES					W 358	0.7	W 963	2.1	ART FACONNES MAT TEXTILES
6584	LINENS ETC					W 50	0.3	W 194	1.6	LINGE DE MAISON
69	METAL MANUFACTURES NES						0.9		1.8	ART MANUFACT EN METAL NDA
7	MACHINES,TRANSPORT EQUIP						13.3		8.6	MACHINES MATERIEL TRANSPORT
72	MACHS FOR SPCL INDUSTRYS						3.3		1.9	MAC SPECIALES POUR INDUST
724	TEXTILE,LEATHER MACHNRY					W 205	1.5	W 12	0.1	MACH POUR INDUSTRIE TEXTILE
7245	WEAVING,FELT MFG,ETC MCH					W 201	1.5	W 1	0.1	METIERS A TISSER,PIECES
72453	GIMPING,WARPING ETC MCHS					W 201	1.5	W 1	0.1	METIERS A TULLE ETC
76	TELECOMM,SOUND EQUIPMENT						2.0		0.8	EQUIPMENT DE TELECOM
763	SOUND RECORDRS,PHONOGRPH					W 6	1.1	W 3	0.5	PHONO,APP ENREGISTREMENT
7638	OTHR SOUND APPARATUS ETC					W 6	1.1	W 3	0.5	AUT APP D'ENREGIS,REPROD
76381	TV IMAGE,SND RECRDRS ETC					W 6	1.1	W 3	0.5	APP ENREG,REPRO IMAG,SON
78	ROAD VEHICLES						5.6		3.8	VEHICULES ROUTIERS
781	PASS MOTOR VEH EXC BUSES						1.3		1.3	AUTO TRANSPORT PERSONNES
782	LORRIES,SPCL MTR VEH NES						1.3		1.3	VEHICULES SPECIAUX,MARCH
7821	LORRIES,TRUCKS						1.1		0.9	VEHICULES TRANSP MARCHAND
786	TRAILERS,NONMOTR VEH,NES					W 1	1.5	W 11	0.2	REMORQUES,CADRES,CONTAIN
7861	TRAILERS,TRANSP CONTAINR						1.4	W 10	0.2	REMORQUES TOUS VEHICULES
78611	HOUSING,CAMPING TRAILERS						1.4	W 1	0.1	REMORQUES POUR CAMPING
8	MISC MANUFACTURED GOODS						12.6		15.0	ART MANUFACTURES DIVERS
84	CLOTHING AND ACCESSORIES						11.2		13.4	VETEMENTS
842	MENS OUTERWEAR NOT KNIT					W 382	1.9	W 486	2.3	VET DESSUS POUR HOMMES
8423	— TROUSERS,BREECHES ETC					W 313	1.7	W 476	2.3	PANTALONS HOMMES MAT TEX
844	UNDER GARMENTS NOT KNIT					W 1636	2.1	W 1463	2.8	VETEMENT DESSOUS MAT TEX
8441	— MENS SHIRTS					W 1401	1.9	W 1065	2.6	CHEMISES HOMMES MAT TEXT
84411	—— OF COTTON					W 535	1.3	W 849	2.2	CHEMISES HOMMES DE COTON
845	OUTERWEAR KNIT NONELASTC					W 1181	1.7	W 1127	2.5	VET DESSOUS,ACCES BONNET
8459	— OTHER,CLTHG ACCESRYS					W 1102	1.6	W 1004	2.3	AUT VET DESSUS DE BONNE
846	UNDER GARMENTS KNITTED					W 2777	5.1	W 2922	4.8	SOUS VETS DE BONNETERIE
8462	— OF COTTON NON ELASTIC					W 1864	1.4	W 1853	1.6	SOUS–VET BONNET COTON
84629	—— OTHER					W 1864	1.4	W 1853	1.6	AUT SOUS–VET BONNET COTON
8463	— OF SYNTH FBR NONELAST					W 912	3.7	W 1057	3.1	SOUS–VET BONNET FIB SYNT
84632	—— MENS SHIRTS					W 912	3.7	W 1057	3.1	CHEMISES DE BON FIB SYNMT

1. HISTORICAL SERIES, 1964–1996 GENERAL TRADE, IMPORTS C.I.F., EXPORTS F.O.B.
SERIES HISTORIQUES, 1964–1996 COMMERCE GENERAL, IMPORTATIONS C.A.F., EXPORTATIONS F.O.B

YEAR ANNEE	VALUE IN MILLION RINGGIT VALEUR EN MILLION RINGGIT: MERCHANDISE –MARCHANDISE IMPORTS	EXPORTS	GOLD –OR IMPORTS	EXPORTS	CONVERSION FACTORS U.S. CENTS PER RINGGIT FACTEURS DE CONVERSION CENTS E.U. PAR RINGGIT IMPORTS	EXPORTS	INDEX NUMBERS –INDICES: QUANTUM IMPORTS	EXPORTS	UNIT VALUE VALEUR UNITAIRE IMPORTS	EXPORTS
1964	3227.20	3387.50			32.6667	32.6667				
1965	3356.20	3782.60	5.01	0.20	32.6667	32.6667				
1966	3378.70	3845.80	7.21		32.6667	32.6667				
1967	3319.00	3722.80	3.31		32.6667	32.6667				
1968	3524.10	4122.50	4.35		32.6667	32.6667				
1969	3581.90	5051.60	18.78		32.6667	32.6667				
1970	4288.40	5163.10	12.77		32.6667	32.6667				
1971	4416.20	5016.80	18.81		32.6667	32.6667				
1972	4543.20	4854.20	7.91		35.4667	35.4667				
1973	5933.90	7372.10	4.34		41.3055	41.3771				
1974	9891.20	10194.70			41.5950	41.5582				
1975	8530.40	9230.90			41.6313	41.5423				
1976	9713.30	13442.90			39.3754	39.3769				
1977	11164.70	14959.20			40.6500	40.6500				
1978	13645.90	17073.90			43.3084	43.3634				
1979	17161.10	24218.90			45.7101	45.7436				
1980	23451.00	28171.60			45.9652	45.9499		65		126
1981	26603.80	27109.40			43.4004	43.4004		63		122
1982	29023.80	28108.20			42.8030	42.7872		67		114
1983	30795.20	32771.20			43.0760	43.0474		74		109
1984	32925.90	38646.90			42.5711	42.5688		72		114
1985	30437.80	38016.70			41.4037	41.4662		76		103
1986	27921.01	35319.01			38.7020	38.7552		82		77
1987	31934.00	45225.01			39.7100	39.7079		86		90
1988	43293.01	55260.00			38.1279	38.1505		70		102
1989	60858.00	67824.00			36.9400	36.9313		75		104
1990	79119.01	79646.00			36.9808	36.9800		100		100
1991	100831.00	94497.01			36.3466	36.3506		97		103
1992	101441.00	103657.00			39.2875	39.3331		96		
1993	117422.00	121238.00			38.8828	38.8749		86		
1994	155871.00	153688.00			38.2245	38.2300		84		
1995	194517.00	184827.00			39.9007	39.8834		84		
1996	197305.00	196862.00			39.7445	39.7500				

2. IMPORTS BY BROAD ECONOMIC CATEGORY AND EXPORTS BY INDUSTRIAL ORIGIN. (PERCENTAGE OF TOTAL VALUE)
IMPORTATIONS PAR CATEGORIES ECONOMIQUES ET EXPORTATIONS PAR BRANCHE D'ACTIVITE.(EN POURCENTAGE DE LA VALEUR TOTALE)

IMPORTS – IMPORTATIONS

	1990	1991	1992	1993	1994	1995	1996
TOTAL IMPORTS–IMPORTATIONS TOTALES	100.	100.	100.	100.	100.	100.	100.
1 FOOD BEV–ALIMENTATION BOISSONS	6.0	5.5	5.4	5.0	4.5	3.9	4.3
11 PRIMARY–PRODUITS DE BASE	2.6	2.4	2.4	2.3	2.0	1.8	2.0
111 FOR INDUSTRY–POUR L'INDUSTRIE	1.1	1.1	0.9	0.9	0.8	0.7	0.7
112 FOR HOUSEHOLDS–POUR LES MENAGES	1.5	1.3	1.5	1.4	1.2	1.1	1.2
12 PROCESSED–PRODUITS ELABORES	3.4	3.1	3.0	2.7	2.4	2.1	2.3
121 FOR INDUSTRY–POUR L'INDUSTRIE	1.1	1.1	0.9	0.9	0.8	0.6	0.6
122 FOR HOUSEHOLDS–POUR LES MENAGES	2.3	2.0	2.0	1.8	1.6	1.5	1.7
2 IND SUPPLIES–APPROV INDUSTRIELS	30.3	28.7	28.8	28.2	26.0	25.8	24.8
21 PRIMARY–PRODUITS DE BASE	3.7	3.1	2.9	3.0	2.5	2.5	2.7
22 PROCESSED–PRODUITS ELABORES	26.6	25.7	26.0	25.2	23.4	23.2	22.1
3 FUELS–COMBUSTIBLES	5.2	4.3	4.2	3.7	2.6	2.3	2.7
31 PRIMARY–PRODUITS DE BASE	1.0	0.8	0.8	0.8	0.6	0.5	0.6
32 PROCESSED–PRODUITS ELABORES	4.2	3.5	3.4	2.8	2.0	1.8	2.1
321 MOTOR SPIRIT–ESSENCE		1.2	1.1	0.9	0.8	0.8	0.8
322 OTHER–AUTRES	4.2	2.3	2.3	1.9	1.2	1.1	1.3
4 MACHINERY–EQUIPEMENT	42.0	45.8	45.4	47.3	50.3	51.6	52.9
41 CAPITAL EQUIPMENT–MACHINES	24.4	28.4	26.7	26.5	26.9	26.1	25.1
42 PARTS–PIECES ACCESSOIRES	17.6	17.4	18.7	20.8	23.4	25.5	27.8
5 TRANSPORT–TRANSPORT	10.1	9.2	9.3	8.4	9.6	9.0	8.1
51 PASSENGER CARS–AUTOMOBILES	2.8	2.6	1.7	1.7	1.9	2.2	2.2
52 OTHER–AUTRES	4.6	4.2	5.0	4.6	6.0	5.1	3.8
521 INDUSTRIAL–INDUSTRIELS	4.5	4.0	4.9	4.5	5.8	4.9	3.7
522 NON INDUSTRIAL–NON INDUSTRIEL	0.1	0.1	0.1	0.2	0.1	0.1	0.1
53 PARTS–PIECES ACCESSOIRES	2.6	2.4	2.6	2.0	1.7	1.7	2.1
6 CONSUM GOODS–BIENS CONSOMMATION	6.1	5.9	6.2	5.9	5.7	4.8	4.7
61 DURABLE–DURABLES	2.1	2.0	1.9	1.8	1.8	1.5	1.3
62 SEMI DURABLE–SEMI DURABLES	2.3	2.2	2.5	2.5	2.5	2.1	2.1
63 NON DURABLE–NON DURABLES	1.7	1.6	1.8	1.5	1.4	1.3	1.3
7 GOODS NES–BIENS NDA	0.4	0.6	0.7	1.6	1.4	2.6	2.5

EXPORTS – EXPORTATIONS

	1990	1991	1992	1993	1994	1995	1996
TOTAL EXPORTS–EXPORTATIONS TOTALES	100.	100.	100.	100.	100.	100.	100.
1 AGRICULTURE	11.3	9.2	7.9	5.8	4.9	4.5	4.0
2 MINING QUARRY–INDUS EXTRACTIVES	17.5	14.9	12.2	9.6	6.6	6.0	7.0
3 MANUFACTURING–IND MANUFACTUR	71.3	75.8	79.9	84.6	88.5	89.6	89.0
31 FOOD BEV TOBACCO–ALIM BOISS TAB	9.4	8.8	8.8	7.9	8.6	8.5	7.7
32 TEXTILES–INDUSTRIES TEXTILES	6.1	6.2	6.4	5.9	5.3	4.9	5.1
33 WOOD & PRODUCTS–BOIS & PRODUITS	6.2	5.5	6.1	7.5	6.3	5.1	4.9
34 PAPER & PRODUCTS–PAPIER & PRODT	0.6	0.6	0.6	0.6	0.6	0.6	0.6
35 CHEMICALS–INDUSTRIES CHIMIQUES	4.5	4.5	4.8	4.7	5.1	5.7	5.7
36 NON METAL MIN–MIN NON METAL	0.8	0.7	0.7	0.7	0.8	0.8	0.8
37 BASIC METAL–IND METAL BASE	2.3	1.7	2.0	1.9	1.7	1.7	1.8
38 METAL MANUF–MANUF METAL	38.6	44.7	47.6	52.6	57.7	59.4	59.8
39 OTH MANUF IND–AUTRES MANUF	2.7	3.1	2.9	2.7	2.4	2.8	2.7

3. TRADE BY PRINCIPAL COUNTRIES OF ORIGIN AND DESTINATION (VALUE IN MILLION U.S. DOLLARS)
ECHANGES SELON LES PRINCIPAUX PAYS D'ORIGINE ET DE DESTINATION (VALEUR EN MILLIONS DE DOLLARS EU)

COUNTRIES–PAYS	GENERAL IMPORTS C.I.F. IMPORTATIONS GENERALES C.A.F				
	1992	1993	1994	1995	1996
World	39788.4	45390.0	59086.0	77045.6	77904.7
Africa	147.2	170.3	295.5	408.8	562.1
Americas	7127.8	8485.0	10788.2	13876.9	13601.7
– Northern America	6590.1	7959.5	10190.6	12956.7	12624.7
– LAIA	484.5	522.4	567.9	889.8	956.4
– CACM	3.2	0.7	4.9	9.8	0.5
– Caribbean	1.6	1.6	11.1	7.6	4.2
– Rest of America	48.5	0.7	13.7	13.1	15.9
Asia excl fmr USSR	24830.5	28507.7	35776.3	46466.6	47890.4
– Middle East	369.5	469.4	524.2	587.2	678.5
Asia former USSR		5.5	0.8	6.9	5.0
Europe excl fmr USSR	6111.8	6528.0	9966.1	13565.7	12745.8
– European Union	5420.8	5819.0	8807.6	11952.4	11294.8
– Eastern Europe	76.7	66.2	92.4	130.5	147.3
– Rest of Europe	614.3	642.8	1066.1	1482.8	1303.7
Europe former USSR	77.4	99.3	129.0	229.0	394.6
Oceania	1365.4	1592.9	2129.1	2489.5	2644.8
Other	128.2	1.3	0.9	2.3	60.3
Japan/Japon	10358.5	12541.8	15911.8	21183.2	19225.2
USA/Etats–Unis d'Amer	6301.4	7726.1	9955.2	12546.3	12152.3
Singapore/Singapour	6273.0	6949.0	8402.6	9607.8	10471.8
Other Asia n.e.s.	2263.1	2448.4	3042.7	3955.6	3901.9
Germany/Allemagne	1677.8	1750.6	2500.2	3434.9	3351.5
Korea, Republic of	1219.1	1399.3	1903.0	3178.3	4071.3
United Kingdom	1360.4	1428.0	1910.4	2186.4	2042.6
Australia/Australie	1058.3	1292.4	1765.5	2109.6	2209.6
Thailand/Thaïlande	988.3	1133.8	1474.2	2047.6	2593.3
China/Chine	975.0	1096.9	1367.4	1715.1	1876.1
France, Monaco	519.4	651.3	1555.3	2361.2	1575.1
China, Hong Kong SAR	904.3	921.9	1187.2	1673.3	1818.7
Indonesia/Indonésie	637.0	717.0	940.8	1219.9	1424.9
Switzerland,Liechtenst.	568.3	584.7	978.8	1392.0	1158.4
Italy/Italie	525.6	585.7	807.9	982.6	1089.1
India/Inde	354.4	397.8	412.5	549.8	735.1
Netherlands/Pays–Bas	337.7	358.1	404.0	524.0	690.7
Sweden/Suède	260.4	294.7	475.8	653.6	619.9
Philippines	240.1	219.1	321.5	460.3	800.3
Belgium–Luxembourg	294.2	258.3	366.4	460.3	466.1
Canada	288.7	233.4	235.3	410.4	472.3
Ireland/Irlande	47.8	51.3	281.0	547.7	710.1
New Zealand	262.9	242.5	275.8	319.6	365.9
Brazil/Brésil	271.9	285.6	281.6	308.5	298.4
Saudi Arabia	206.7	259.8	217.4	227.0	328.0
Finland/Finlande	102.6	136.1	171.4	257.8	196.5
Argentina/Argentine	84.3	105.2	80.0	259.2	275.2
Spain/Espagne	49.9	76.1	94.6	262.4	228.9
Russian Federation	77.4	60.4	73.8	175.1	265.3
Viet Nam	126.8	92.8	111.7	125.9	150.4
Chile/Chili	60.8	80.6	118.5	164.2	180.4
So. African Customs Un	1.3	7.6	120.9	204.7	257.1
Denmark/Danemark	121.2	106.7	96.1	109.9	145.7
Austria/Autriche	91.4	86.9	102.3	114.4	118.4
Turkey/Turquie	29.7	55.3	144.1	123.7	127.4
Norway,Svalbard and JM	36.4	51.4	82.0	83.1	131.2
Zambia/Zambie	86.3	88.2	85.5	52.4	33.1
Peru/Pérou	34.2	28.0	67.1	89.5	87.8
Pakistan	67.2	59.7	63.3	66.6	48.8
Iran (Islamic Rep of)	26.2	59.1	42.0	46.4	48.7

COUNTRIES–PAYS	GENERAL EXPORTS F.O.B. EXPORTATIONS GENERALES F.O.B.				
	1992	1993	1994	1995	1996
Monde	40768.5	47127.2	58842.7	73778.2	78314.9
Afrique	356.8	454.0	572.7	803.8	810.6
Amériques	8413.1	10690.5	13898.3	17021.3	15847.1
– Amérique du Nord	7937.6	10038.2	12982.2	15878.9	14798.7
– ALAI	350.2	484.2	750.4	927.1	844.8
– MCAC	10.1	23.7	18.7	15.7	21.7
– Caraïbes	35.6	37.4	37.2	37.0	45.4
– Autre Amérique	79.6	106.9	109.7	162.5	136.5
Asie anc. URSS exclus	24574.4	27810.5	34416.2	43687.0	48922.9
– Moyen–Orient	965.3	1150.6	1406.2	1828.2	1736.9
Asie ancienne URSS		3.3	6.1	8.2	18.0
Europe anc. URSS exclus	6398.5	7226.1	8648.9	10765.0	11062.9
– Union Européenne	6236.1	7018.0	8407.9	10478.9	10737.2
– Europe de l'Est	35.2	28.2	85.8	132.5	142.9
– Autre de l'Europe	127.2	179.9	155.2	153.7	182.9
Europe ancienne URSS	35.8	43.0	61.9	106.1	121.8
Océanie	936.8	899.6	1238.4	1379.2	1522.6
Autre	53.2	0.1	0.2	7.6	8.9
Singapore/Singapour	9384.8	10208.3	12173.3	14990.0	16013.7
USA/Etats–Unis d'Amer	7585.1	9582.3	12438.5	15278.6	14251.2
Japan/Japon	5475.6	6119.4	7091.8	9352.2	10564.9
China, Hong Kong SAR	1543.8	1944.4	2714.7	3947.8	4605.7
United Kingdom	1642.6	1990.7	2233.0	2984.7	2694.3
Thailand/Thaïlande	1488.7	1695.0	2218.2	2894.7	3202.7
Other Asia n.e.s.	1269.6	1511.5	1754.9	2318.5	3212.4
Germany/Allemagne	1634.6	1723.0	1944.8	2363.7	2376.5
Korea, Republic of	1396.0	1628.6	1648.1	2058.8	2407.5
China/Chine	771.3	1203.1	1935.5	1956.0	1908.7
Netherlands/Pays–Bas	992.6	1147.7	1355.1	1796.8	2324.9
Australia/Australie	681.3	628.6	921.4	1126.6	1215.8
Indonesia/Indonésie	506.8	543.4	714.2	973.6	1217.8
Belgium–Luxembourg	482.3	567.3	756.0	793.3	855.7
France, Monaco	565.6	666.0	800.6	738.9	642.9
India/Inde	430.6	209.7	527.6	831.2	1205.7
Philippines	478.0	479.7	608.0	674.9	937.5
Pakistan	369.5	426.0	662.0	714.0	644.6
United Arab Emirates	276.6	352.9	506.2	685.3	735.1
Canada	352.2	455.7	543.3	600.1	547.2
Italy/Italie	369.6	341.0	430.9	565.7	610.2
Saudi Arabia	266.6	279.8	271.2	337.8	318.7
Mexico/Mexique	135.9	244.6	388.8	324.9	199.4
Spain/Espagne	170.1	157.2	258.7	368.1	328.9
Brunei Darussalam	149.9	188.0	263.3	296.2	324.2
Brazil/Brésil	73.5	124.0	207.4	373.2	404.0
New Zealand	219.4	200.5	265.3	194.6	240.6
Egypt/Egypte	151.3	183.3	201.7	271.3	240.8
Ireland/Irlande	51.1	84.2	213.8	326.5	338.7
Viet Nam	49.8	137.6	159.3	268.3	323.1
Turkey/Turquie	116.3	135.6	195.7	224.9	213.7
Myanmar	89.7	103.8	220.3	230.2	220.8
Sri Lanka	110.3	159.8	148.6	186.0	157.6
So. African Customs Un	0.2	10.4	176.4	272.0	287.6
Sweden/Suède	98.3	95.2	126.3	172.7	164.0
Panama	72.3	101.0	107.5	153.7	135.9
Denmark/Danemark	80.6	75.9	110.9	134.0	130.3
Switzerland,Liechtenst.	89.0	75.5	81.5	103.2	119.3
Jordan/Jordanie	54.0	82.2	91.4	134.0	72.0
Yemen/Yémen	84.4	99.6	49.1	81.9	69.4

(VALUE AS PERCENTAGE OF WORLD TOTAL)(VALEURS EN POURCENTAGE DU TOTAL MONDIAL)

	1987	1988	1989	1990	1991	1992	1993	1994	1995	1996
Africa	0.4	0.5	0.6	0.5	0.5	0.4	0.4	0.5	0.5	0.7
Americas	21.1	20.7	19.9	19.5	17.6	17.9	18.7	18.3	18.0	17.5
– Northern America	19.8	18.9	17.8	17.8	16.2	16.6	17.5	17.2	16.8	16.2
– LAIA	1.3	1.7	1.6	1.7	1.3	1.2	1.2	1.0	1.2	1.2
– CACM				0.0	0.0	0.0	0.0	0.0	0.0	0.0
– Caribbean	0.0	0.1	0.1	0.0	0.0	0.0	0.0	0.0	0.0	0.0
– Rest of America	0.0	0.0	0.4	0.1	0.1	0.1	0.0	0.0	0.0	0.0
Asia excl fmr USSR	57.3	57.5	57.8	57.5	60.6	62.4	62.8	60.5	60.3	61.5
– Middle East	2.1	1.6	1.3	1.2	0.9	0.9	1.0	0.9	0.8	0.9
Asia former USSR							0.0	0.0	0.0	0.0
Europe excl fmr USSR	15.7	15.7	16.6	17.6	17.0	15.4	14.4	16.9	17.6	16.4
– European Union	14.5	14.4	15.2	15.9	15.3	13.6	12.8	14.9	15.5	14.5
– Eastern Europe	0.2	0.2	0.2	0.2	0.2	0.2	0.1	0.2	0.2	0.2
– Rest of Europe	1.0	1.0	1.2	1.5	1.5	1.5	1.4	1.8	1.9	1.7
Europe former USSR	0.2	0.3	0.3	0.3	0.2	0.2	0.2	0.2	0.3	0.5
Oceania	5.2	5.2	4.7	4.5	3.8	3.4	3.5	3.6	3.2	3.4
Other	0.1	0.1	0.1	0.1	0.3	0.3	0.0	0.0	0.0	0.1
Japan/Japon	21.7	23.5	24.2	24.1	26.1	26.0	27.6	26.9	27.5	24.7
USA/Etats–Unis d'Amer	18.7	17.7	16.9	16.8	15.4	15.8	17.0	16.8	16.3	15.6
Singapore/Singapour	14.7	13.2	13.6	15.0	15.6	15.8	15.3	14.2	12.5	13.4
Other Asia n.e.s.	3.8	4.6	5.0	5.5	5.5	5.7	5.4	5.1	5.1	5.0
Germany/Allemagne					4.4	4.2	3.9	4.2	4.5	4.3
Korea, Republic of	2.6	2.6	2.5	2.6	2.7	3.1	3.1	3.2	4.1	5.2
United Kingdom	4.3	4.9	5.4	5.5	4.6	3.4	3.1	3.2	2.8	2.6
Australia/Australie	4.2	4.1	3.8	3.7	3.1	2.7	2.8	3.0	2.7	2.8
Thailand/Thaïlande	3.5	3.1	3.0	2.4	2.4	2.5	2.5	2.5	2.7	3.3
China/Chine	3.0	2.9	2.7	1.9	2.2	2.5	2.4	2.3	2.2	2.4

	1987	1988	1989	1990	1991	1992	1993	1994	1995	1996
Afrique	0.6	0.7	0.9	0.8	0.8	0.9	1.0	1.0	1.1	1.0
Amériques	18.1	19.0	20.2	18.4	18.8	20.6	22.7	23.6	23.1	20.2
– Amérique du Nord	17.4	18.1	19.4	17.7	17.7	19.5	21.3	22.1	21.5	18.9
– ALAI	0.7	0.8	0.6	0.5	0.8	0.9	1.0	1.3	1.3	1.1
– MCAC				0.0	0.0	0.0	0.1	0.0	0.0	0.0
– Caraïbes	0.0	0.0	0.0	0.1	0.1	0.1	0.1	0.1	0.1	0.1
– Autre Amérique	0.1	0.1	0.1	0.1	0.1	0.2	0.2	0.2	0.2	0.2
Asie anc. URSS exclus	62.5	61.5	58.9	62.5	62.3	60.3	59.0	58.5	59.2	62.5
– Moyen–Orient	1.9	2.5	2.3	2.4	2.3	2.4	2.4	2.4	2.5	2.2
Asie ancienne URSS							0.0	0.0	0.0	0.0
Europe anc. URSS exclus	15.4	15.6	16.5	15.9	15.7	15.7	15.3	14.7	14.6	14.1
– Union Européenne	14.7	14.9	15.8	15.3	15.2	15.3	14.9	14.3	14.2	13.7
– Europe de l'Est	0.3	0.2	0.2	0.2	0.1	0.1	0.1	0.1	0.2	0.2
– Autre de l'Europe	0.5	0.5	0.5	0.4	0.4	0.3	0.4	0.3	0.2	0.2
Europe ancienne URSS	0.8	0.6	1.0	0.5	0.2	0.1	0.1	0.1	0.1	0.2
Océanie	2.5	2.7	2.5	1.9	2.0	2.3	1.9	2.1	1.9	1.9
Autre	0.0	0.0	0.0	0.0	0.1	0.1	0.0	0.0	0.0	0.0
Singapore/Singapour	18.2	19.3	19.7	22.8	23.3	23.0	21.7	20.7	20.3	20.4
USA/Etats–Unis d'Amer	16.6	17.4	18.7	16.9	16.9	18.6	20.3	21.1	20.7	18.2
Japan/Japon	19.5	16.9	16.1	15.8	15.7	13.4	13.0	12.1	12.7	13.5
China, Hong Kong SAR	2.8	3.5	3.1	3.2	3.4	3.8	4.1	4.6	5.4	5.9
United Kingdom	3.2	3.5	3.7	3.9	4.4	4.0	4.2	3.8	4.0	3.4
Thailand/Thaïlande	2.9	2.0	2.5	3.5	3.2	3.7	3.6	3.8	3.9	4.1
Other Asia n.e.s.	2.8	3.0	2.3	2.2	2.7	3.1	3.2	3.0	3.1	4.1
Germany/Allemagne					3.6	4.0	3.7	3.3	3.2	3.0
Korea, Republic of	5.3	5.0	5.0	4.6	4.4	3.4	3.5	2.8	2.8	3.1
China/Chine	1.6	2.0	1.9	2.1	1.9	1.9	2.6	3.3	2.7	2.4

4. General Imports C.I.F. by Commodities according to the S.I.T.C. (Rev. 2) in million U.S. Dollars
Importations Générales C.A.F. par Produits d'après la C.T.C.I. (Rév. 2) en millions de Dollars E.U.

SITC CTCI	COMMODITY	1993 QUANTITY QUANTITE	1993 VALUE VALEUR	1994 QUANTITY QUANTITE	1994 VALUE VALEUR	1995 QUANTITY QUANTITE	1995 VALUE VALEUR	1996 QUANTITY QUANTITE	1996 VALUE VALEUR	PRODUIT
	ALL COMMODITIES		45390.0		59086.1		77045.7		77904.8	TOUS PRODUITS
0	FOOD AND LIVE ANIMALS		2258.4		2544.9		3129.0		3607.5	ALIMENTS,ANIMAUX VIVANTS
02	DAIRY PRODCTS,BIRDS'EGGS		274.8		270.5		370.0		381.2	PRODUITS LAITIERS,OEUFS
022	MILK AND CREAM	W 132799	247.7	W 142554	240.2	W 164242	333.2	W 196086	345.3	LAIT ET CREME
0224	MILK,CREAM PRESERVED ETC	W 127382	241.9	W 134749	233.0	W 156434	321.4	W 179419	316.1	LAIT,CREME CONS,CONC
03	FISH AND PREPARATIONS		254.2		290.2		307.3		331.5	POISSONS ET PREPARATIONS
034	FISH,FRESH,CHILLED,FROZN		159.5	W 176197	180.5		185.3	W 222794	220.0	POISSON FRAIS, REFRIG,CONG
04	CEREALS AND PREPARATIONS		673.8		726.0		924.5		1143.1	CEREALES ET PRODUITS
041	WHEAT ETC UNMILLED	W 1094185	184.7	W 1176223	214.8	W 1117646	239.5	W 1096170	270.0	FROMENT,EPEAUTRE
0412	OTHER WHEAT ETC UNMILLED	W 1094181	184.7	W 1176133	214.8	W 1111930	238.1	W 1046965	258.1	AUTRE FROMENT NON MOULU
044	MAIZE UNMILLED	W 1799607	222.9	W 1730884	227.0	W 2084387	332.0	W 1964049	372.7	MAIS NON MOULU
048	CEREAL ETC PREPARATIONS	W 334723	142.6	W 341104	157.9	W 405453	197.8	W 466944	265.9	PREPTNS A BASE CEREALES
05	VEGETABLES AND FRUIT		334.1		377.4		451.4		506.6	LEGUMES ET FRUITS
054	VEG ETC FRSH,SMPLY PRSVD		168.0	W 494127	179.0		233.3	W 653160	271.0	LEGUMES FRAIS,CONG,SECS
06	SUGAR AND PREPS,HONEY		235.7		279.1		339.2		344.8	SUCRES ET PRODUITS
061	SUGAR AND HONEY	W 892068	225.6	W 970966	266.2	W 1057603	323.1	W 1111531	326.1	SUCRES ET MIEL
0611	RAW BEET AND CANE SUGAR	W 877550	215.6	W 959502	253.9	W 1033099	308.0	W 1090054	310.5	SUCRES BRUTS
081	*FEEDING STUFF FOR ANIML	W 657041	175.8	W 747535	206.9	W 821386	232.5	W 1004603	337.2	NOURRITURE POUR ANIMAUX
1	BEVERAGES AND TOBACCO		150.5		163.7		221.2		197.6	BOISSONS ET TABACS
2	CRUDE MATERLS,EXCL FUELS		1267.2		1435.3		1850.9		1970.3	MAT BRUTES NON COMESTIBLES
22	OIL SEEDS,OLEAGINOUS FRT		154.4		166.5		166.0		172.3	GRAINES,FRUITS OLEAGINEUX
222	SEEDS FOR'SOFT'FIXED OIL	W 533807	149.7	W 530745	160.1	W 540502	159.5	W 465196	163.3	GRAINES HUILES FIXES
23	RUBBER, CRUDE		172.0		227.7		325.5		371.5	CAOUTCHOUC BRUT
232	NATURAL RUBBER,GUMS	W 167375	98.1	W 235313	159.1		229.4	W 270933	276.2	LATEX CAOUTCHOUC NATUREL
26	TEXTILE FIBRES AND WASTE		189.8		258.0		347.4		412.8	FIBRES TEXTILES
27	CRUDE FERTLZR,MINRLS NES		148.3		160.9		202.0		222.1	ENGRAIS MINERAUX BRUTS
28	METALLIFEROUS ORES,SCRAP		440.5		407.9		537.0		498.8	MINERAIS METAL,DECHETS
282	IRON AND STEEL SCRAP	W 1417058	219.3	W 869436	143.8	W 1064477	174.9	W 1040684	168.3	FERRAILLES
28202	— OF ALLOY STEEL	W 959659	152.5	W 615887	103.7	W 480108	79.8	W 652650	109.9	FERRAILLES D'ACIERS ALLIES
287	BASE METAL ORES,CONC NES		127.7	W 142073	178.3		206.8	W 188917	201.9	MINERAIS METAUX COMMUNS
3	MINERAL FUELS ETC		1673.8		1558.3		1778.5		2111.0	COMBUSTIBLES MINERAUX LUB
33	PETROLEUM AND PRODUCTS		1473.9		1379.6		1570.4		1816.2	PETROLE ET DERIVES
333	CRUDE PETROLEUM	W 1672456	173.3	W 1539983	176.5	W 1276588	150.8	W 1398010	185.0	HUILES BRUTES DE PETROLE
334	PETROLEUM PRODUCTS,REFIN	W 7071127	1252.3	W 6806536	1150.4	W 7439278	1372.1	W 8201772	1577.7	PRODUITS RAFFINES
3341	GASOLINE,OTH LIGHT OILS	W 1761874	415.3	W 2166979	449.8	W 2724713	574.4	W 2929219	626.4	ESSENCES POUR MOTEURS
33411	MOTOR,AVIATION SPIRIT	W 1710907	403.4	W 1832647	389.1	W 1533586	348.1	W 2396928	538.5	ESSENCES MOTEURS D'AVIONS
3343	GAS OILS	W 1933155	379.4	W 1677333	296.1	W 1604230	287.3	W 1703233	348.7	GAS OILS
3344	FUEL OILS,NES	W 2736024	240.2	W 2581895	235.7	W 2782869	310.3	W 3194356	382.5	FUEL OILS
4	ANIMAL,VEGETABLE OIL,FAT		157.1		213.7		151.5		108.8	HUILES,GRAISSES ANIM,VEG
42	FIXED VEGETABLE OIL,FAT		149.1		203.6		132.9		88.9	HUILES VEGETALES FIXES
5	CHEMCLS,RELATED PROD NES		3328.0		3910.2		5322.9		5123.4	PRODUITS CHIMIQUES
51	ORGANIC CHEMICALS		562.9		660.5		1230.8		1060.1	PROD CHIMIQ ORGANIQUES
511	HYDROCARBONS NES,DERIVS		178.0		195.5		416.5		267.8	HYDROCARBURES NDA
5112	CYCLIC HYDROCARBONS		54.3		115.5		274.7		182.1	HYDROCARBURES CYCLIQUES
51125	STYRENE	V 70059	33.1	V 124322	90.2	V 262793	249.8	V 153280	82.4	STYRENE
513	CARBOXYLIC ACIDS ETC	W 116365	104.8	W 140897	136.8	W 222522	281.5	W 253959	261.7	ACIDES CARBOXYLIQUES
52	INORGANIC CHEMICALS		331.9		413.9		545.4		590.0	PROD CHIM INORGANIQUES
522	INORG ELEMNTS,OXIDES,ETC		178.9		240.7		307.0		320.9	ELEMENTS INORGANIQUES
523	OTHR INORG CHEMICALS ETC	W 549497	146.6	W 588020	166.3		227.3	W 792228	262.0	AUT PRODUITS CHIMIQUES INORG
53	DYES,TANNING,COLOUR PROD		245.5		308.9		355.7		368.3	PROD TEINTURE,COLORANTS
533	PIGMENTS,PAINTS,ETC		162.1		206.5		239.3		259.4	PIGMENTS,PEINTURES,VERNIS
541	*MEDICINAL,PHARM PRODUCT		232.0		271.5		318.5		333.1	PROD MEDICINAUX PHARMACEUT
5417	MEDICAMENTS		179.7		212.2		246.8		249.2	MEDICAMENTS
54179	— CONTNG OTH SUBSTANCES		143.3		175.5		204.1		200.6	MED CONT AUT SUBSTANCES
55	PERFUME,CLEANING ETC PRD		245.0		295.9		345.4		368.4	PROD POUR PARFUM,TOILETTE
562	*FERTILIZERS,MANUFACTURE	W 1900893	246.1	W 2114472	270.1	W 2286279	339.3	W 2039241	335.1	ENGRAIS MANUFACTURES
58	PLASTIC MATERIALS ETC		1087.1		1230.7		1628.7		1476.7	MAT PLAST ARTIFICIELLES
582	PROD OF CONDENSATION ETC	W 191696	341.4	W 266096	461.7	W 414262	622.2	W 248119	532.0	PROD CONDENS,POLYCOND
5823	ALKYDS,OTHER POLYESTERS	W 60536	108.7	W 116069	183.9	W 105242	243.9	W 93925	179.6	ALKYDES ET AUT POLYESTERS
583	POLYMERIZATION ETC PRODS		727.9	W 666457	746.4		980.2	W 696192	919.2	PROD POLYMERISATION
5831	POLYETHYLENE	W 277478	228.0	W 202797	181.4	W 213836	245.0	W 218722	233.8	POLYETHYLENE
58311	— IN PRIMARY FORMS	W 272123	202.4	W 196335	157.7	W 205520	218.8	W 209388	204.4	POLYETHYLENE PRIMAIRES
5833	POLYSTYRENE,ITS COPOLYMR	W 141115	171.6	W 156030	210.5	W 189577	314.2	W 181865	263.9	POLYPROPYLENE COPOLYMERES
58331	— IN PRIMARY FORMS	W 140038	169.1	W 154643	207.9	W 187852	309.9	W 178132	253.4	SOUS FORMES PRIMAIRES
5839	OTH POLYMRZTION ETC PROD		163.0	W 55702	149.5		166.4	W 87568	173.7	AUT PROD POLYMER COPOLYM
59	CHEMICAL MATERIALS NES		369.3		448.3		550.3		580.3	MAT PROD CHIMIQUES NDA
598	MISCEL CHEM PRODUCTS NES		260.5		321.7		380.5		401.6	PROD DIV INDUST CHIM NDA
5989	CHEM PRODUCTS,PREPS NES		202.5		258.4		300.6		312.6	PROD PREP CHIMIQUES NDA
59899	OTH CHEM PRODS,PREPS,NES		126.1		178.3		198.2	W 101148	188.2	AUT PRODUITS CHIMIQUES NDA
6	BASIC MANUFACTURES		6925.5		8319.4		10844.4		10582.2	ART MANUFACTURES
62	RUBBER MANUFACTURES NES		144.8		171.0		183.0		191.7	CAOUTCHOUC MANUFACTURE
64	PAPER,PAPERBOARD AND MFR		736.9		900.3		1343.1		1088.2	PAPIERS,CARTONS & OUVRAGES
641	PAPER AND PAPERBOARD		625.1		752.3		1164.3		909.9	PAPIERS ET CARTONS
6411	NEWSPRINT	W 218655	101.8	W 253532	119.7	W 322162	285.3	W 237724	176.3	PAPIER JOURNAL
6413	KRAFT PAPER,PAPERBOARD	W 257366	136.9	W 299977	146.5	W 299044	224.8	W 419250	177.4	PAPIER ET CARTON KRAFT
6415	PAPER,PAPERBRD,BULK,NES	W 226796	162.5	W 491918	212.8	W 290940	302.6	W 1517541	247.1	PAPIERS,CARTONS ROULEAUX
64159	OTHER PAPER ETC,BULK,NES	W 195847	149.7	W 406470	190.6	W 244984	273.2	W 542503	220.8	AUT PAPIER ROULEAUX FEUILLES
65	TEXTILE YARN,FABRICS,ETC		1194.3		1393.2		1539.3		1367.0	FILS,TISSUS,ARTICLES TEXTILE
651	TEXTILE YARN		246.6		325.4		405.1		296.6	FILS TEXTILES
652	COTTON FABRICS,WOVEN		256.4	A 38255	258.4		252.5	A 139474	229.5	TISSUS DE COTON
6522	WOVEN COTTON BLEACHD,ETC		163.7	A 36493	161.3		169.1	A 89304	138.8	TISSUS COTON BLANCHIS ETC
65224	BLCHED COTTON FABRIC NES		139.7	A 20032	140.6		149.6	A 76676	120.3	AUT TIS PLUS 85% COT BLANCHI
653	WOVN MAN-MADE FIB FABRIC		278.1	A 177644	304.1		317.1		294.6	TISSUS FIBRES SYNTH,ARTIF
6531	CONT SYNT WEAVES NONPILE		150.2	A 1092	156.7		161.0		154.0	TISSUS FIBRES SYNTH CONTINUE
655	KNITTED,ETC FABRICS	A 164641	204.1	A 177155	231.7	A 200612	225.7		222.6	ETOF BONNETERIE PIECES ETC
6552	OTHER KNIT ETC FAB NONEL	A 164641	204.1	A 177155	231.7	A 200612	225.7		222.6	ETOF BON NON ELAS NON SYNT
66	NONMETAL MINERAL MFS NES		683.0		863.5		1203.7		1145.0	ART MIN NON METALLIQUES
661	LIME,CEMENT,BLDG PRODS	W 1996079	111.7	W 1630823	101.4	W 2942430	184.0	W 5956117	340.2	CHAUX,CIMENTS MAT CONSTR
6612	CEMENT	W 1957706	89.5	W 1583667	75.4	W 2882861	153.3	W 5180780	301.1	CIMENTS HYDRAULIQUES
663	MINERAL MANUFCTURES NES		152.8		181.4		295.3		205.8	ART MIN MANUF NDA
664	GLASS		182.3		287.8		375.9		296.0	VERRE
6649	GLASS NES		135.7		207.6		252.4		170.0	VERRE NDA
66492	LAMP ETC ENVELOPES GLASS	MN 72297	116.5	MN 127383	183.6	MN 627929	207.8	MN 143062	141.0	AMPOULES EN VERRE
67	IRON AND STEEL		2111.5		2449.5		3320.6		3536.2	FER ET ACIER
672	IRON,STEEL PRIMARY FORMS	W 1669987	546.9	W 1656653	544.8	W 1896015	754.9	W 2135594	726.6	LINGOTS FER,ACIER
6725	IRN,STL BLOOMS,SLABS,ETC	W 687412	187.2	W 715738	194.9	W 580958	167.8	W 890740	245.0	BLOOMS,BILLETTES FER ACIER
67251	IRN,SMPLE STL BLOOMS,ETC	W 686590	185.5	W 712484	188.5	W 580114	164.3	W 889414	240.9	BLOOMS ETC NON ACIER FIN
6727	IRN,STL COIL FR REROLLNG	W 981060	358.8	W 939566	348.4	W 1313870	586.5	W 1243917	480.7	EBAUCHES POUR TOLES FER
67271	IRON,SIMPLE STEEL COILS	W 958077	327.3	W 915244	320.3	W 1282134	541.6	W 1150133	418.6	EBAUCHES NON EN ACIER
673	IRON,STEEL SHAPES ETC	W 527374	249.3	W 646916	308.4	W 1003365	511.0	W 1137502	531.1	BARRES,PROFIL FER,ACIER
6733	IRON,STEEL PROFILES ETC	W 322871	127.5	W 418469	164.8	W 599067	267.9	W 677614	276.0	PROFILES,PALPLAN FER,ACIER

4. General Imports C.I.F. by Commodities according to the S.I.T.C. (Rev. 2) in million U.S. Dollars
Importations Générales C.A.F. par Produits d'après la C.T.C.I. (Rév. 2) en millions de Dollars E.U.

SITC CTCI	COMMODITY	1993 QUANTITY QUANTITE	1993 VALUE VALEUR	1994 QUANTITY QUANTITE	1994 VALUE VALEUR	1995 QUANTITY QUANTITE	1995 VALUE VALEUR	1996 QUANTITY QUANTITE	1996 VALUE VALEUR	PRODUIT
674	IRN,STL UNIV,PLATE,SHEET	W 1412924	799.7	W 1589966	933.5	W 2348897	1507.7	W 2596119	1502.9	LARGES PLATS,TOLES
6744	IRN,STL HVY PLATE,ROLLED	W 324630	128.3	W 388169	152.4	W 592490	254.2	W 750405	295.8	TOLES LAMINEES PLUS 4.75 MM
67441	— OF IRON OR SIMPLE STL	W 318952	121.0	W 380687	140.6	W 583162	236.5	W 739791	278.8	TOLES NON ACIER FIN CARB
6745	IRN,STL MED PLATE,ROLLED	W 137917	84.9	W 195885	119.5	W 317454	190.3	W 506072	249.2	TOLES 3 A 4.75 MM
6746	IRN,STL THIN PLATE,ROLLD	W 541668	309.2	W 535871	322.2	W 734988	498.3	W 581083	408.2	TOLES LAM MOINS 3MM
67461	— OF IRON OR SIMPLE STL	W 524110	274.9	W 511326	272.5	W 690395	410.1	W 538705	322.4	TOL NON AC FIN MOINS 3 MM
6749	OTH IRN,STL PLATES,SHEET	W 395527	268.5	W 440738	320.2	W 679671	547.3	W 730297	528.1	AUTRES TOLES FER,ACIER
67491	— OF IRON OR SIMPLE STL	W 388951	258.0	W 433897	308.8	W 672724	531.4	W 713961	502.4	AUT TOLES AUTRES ACIER FIN
678	IRON,STL TUBES,PIPES,ETC	W 226928	341.3	W 438406	457.8	W 266487	283.7	W 480093	499.0	TUBES,TUYAUX EN FONTE,FER
6783	IRON,STL TUBES,PIPES NES	W 91796	119.8	W 280959	263.1	W 114563	118.6	W 262554	233.6	AUT TUBES,TUYAUX FER,ACIER
68	NON-FERROUS METALS		963.8		1240.2		1725.9		1703.5	METAUX NON FERREUX
682	COPPER EXC CEMENT COPPER	W 186743	507.1	W 290616	661.8	W 320839	874.7	W 269603	855.6	CUIVRE
6821	COPPER NES,ALLOYS,UNWRT	W 94489	191.1	W 110242	254.9	W 116290	331.3	W 145401	332.2	CUIVRE BRUT
68212	COPPER REFINED,UNWROUGHT	W 94290	190.3	W 109556	253.2	W 115360	328.5	W 145298	331.4	CUIVRE AFFINE BRUT
6822	COPPER,ALLOYS WORKED	W 92254	316.0	W 180374	406.9	W 204549	543.4	W 124202	523.5	CUIVRE,ALLIAGES OUVRES
684	ALUMINIUM	W 125630	262.1	W 186026	384.7	W 306401	605.1	W 290896	576.3	ALUMINIUM
6841	ALUMINIUM,ALLOYS,UNWRGHT	W 88592	118.3	W 105479	164.3	W 202282	310.4	W 177050	267.4	ALUMINIUM,ALLIAGES BRUTS
6842	ALUMINIUM,ALLOYS WORKED	W 37038	143.8	W 80547	220.4	W 104119	294.7	W 113846	309.0	ALUMINIUM,ALLIAGES OUVRE
69	METAL MANUFACTURES NES		1002.2		1180.9		1314.8		1376.9	ART MANUFACT EN METAL NDA
694	STL,COPPR NAILS,NUTS,ETC	W 53419	128.1	W 583927	183.0	W 76087	166.4	W 123167	160.3	CLOUS,VIS,ECROUS
695	TOOLS		184.9		205.4		247.0		234.9	OUTILS A MAIN
699	BASE METAL MFRS NES		462.7		533.8		634.6		651.0	ART MANUFACTURES MET NDA
6997	IRON,STEEL ARTICLES NES		160.4		189.0		246.0		247.0	OUV FONTE,FER,ACIER NDA
69979	IRN,STL MANUFACTURES NES		159.2		187.3		243.5		244.3	AUT OUVRAGES EN FER NDA
7	MACHINES,TRANSPORT EQUIP		25386.5		35338.6		46078.0		46631.2	MACHINES MATERIEL TRANSPORT
71	POWER GENERATING EQUIPMT		1204.4		1779.9		2052.9		2018.0	MACHINES GENERATRICES
712	STEAM ENGINES,TURBINES		10.1		31.3		325.4		233.3	MACHINES A VAPEUR D'EAU PIEC
7126	STEAM POWR UNITS,ENGINES	N 1142	2.3	N 623	20.8	N 14402	252.5		56.7	MACHINES A VAPEUR D EAU
713	INTRNL COMBUS PSTN ENGIN		384.2		422.2		507.9		639.6	MOTEURS EXPL COMB INT, PIECE
7131	AIRCRAFT PSTN ENGINS,PTS		139.7		130.8		128.2		249.4	MOTEURS EXPL P.AVIATION, PIE
714	ENGINES AND MOTORS NES	N 130352	349.4	N 1245127	530.2	N 3599154	401.6	N 868881	307.0	MOTEURS NON ELECTRIQUES
7148	GAS TURBINES NES	N 102	242.2	N 1464	336.5	N 2049	275.2	N 581	108.8	TURBINES A GAZ
71488	OTHER GAS TURBINES NES	N 72	242.1	N 1406	336.1	N 1951	274.9	N 543	107.2	AUTRES TURBINES A GAZ
7149	ENGINE & MOTOR PARTS NES	N 130177	107.2	N 1243516	193.6	N 3596993	125.7	N 868160	196.5	PIECES 714 ET 718.88
71499	PARTS NES,OF 71488,71888	N 130132	107.1	N 1190834	190.0	N 3595439	124.8	N 867230	195.3	PIECES 714.88 ET 718.88
716	ROTATING ELECTRIC PLANT		426.3		747.2		763.6		746.1	APP ELECTR ROTATIFS,PIECES
7161	DC MOTORS AND GENERATORS	MN 16024	85.5	MN 51047	185.3	MN 60410	227.5	MN 69105	146.3	MOTEURS COURANT CONTINU
7162	AC MTRS,GENRTRS,GEN SETS	MN 145953	274.7	MN 599373	448.5	MN 223789	345.0	MN 262509	446.2	MOTEURS ELECTRIQUES
71621	AC MTRS,INC UNIVRSL MTRS	MN 145930	216.6	MN 598926	302.9	MN 223148	298.6	MN 262466	362.5	MOT ELEC NON COUR CONTINU
72	MACHS FOR SPCL INDUSTRYS		2416.0		3102.9		4461.3		4413.9	MAC SPECIALES POUR INDUST
723	CIVIL ENGNEERG EQUIP ETC		265.5		345.6		859.9		955.1	APPAREILS DE GENIE CIVIL
7234	CONST,MINING MACHNRY NES	N 6200	155.9	N 10020	247.9	N 19549	727.7	N 21058	811.3	MACH POUR LA CONST, MINES
72342	SLFPRP SHOVELS,EXCAVATRS	N 3580	115.3	N 5132	174.0	N 9953	417.6	N 12941	505.1	PELLES MECANIQUES
724	TEXTILE,LEATHER MACHNRY		265.3		277.0		476.4		359.3	MACH POUR INDUSTRIE TEXTILE
726	PRINTG,BKBINDG MACHY,PTS		154.7		177.2		182.9		254.2	MACHINES POUR IMPRIMERIE
728	OTH MACHY FOR SPCL INDUS		1549.2		2114.0		2688.6		2559.2	AUT MACH IND PARTICULIERES
7281	MACH-TOOLS FR SPCL INDUS		323.2		524.4		492.8		432.3	MACH-OUTILS SPEC IND PART
72812	MACH-TOOLS TO WORK WOOD	N 26147	278.3	N 186541	418.6	N 68649	376.0	N 56526	346.5	MACH-OUT POUR TRAVAIL BOIS
7283	OTHR MINERAL WORKG MACHY	N 141759	110.3	N 1138983	159.5	N 1537585	206.9	N 1645020	311.5	MACH TRIER,CRIBLER,BROYER
7284	MACHY FOR SPCL INDUS NES		1115.9		1430.2		1989.0		1815.5	MACH SPEC IND PARTICUL.
72842	RUBBER,PLASTICS WRKG MCH	N 14687	259.2	N 160702	323.3	N 77657	417.4	N 76302	386.0	MACH IND CAOUT MAT PLAST
72848	OTH MCHY WITH INDIV FNCT	N 62091	515.9	N 542977	722.1	N 408516	958.4	N 245338	902.1	AUTRES MACHINES NDA
72849	PTS OF MACHS OF 7284 ETC		197.3		251.3		362.6		359.6	PIECES DU 728.4 ETC
73	METALWORKING MACHINERY		708.2		952.9		1689.4		1138.1	MACH TRAVAIL DES METAUX
736	METALWORKING MACH-TOOLS		537.8		715.3		785.0		865.1	MACH-OUTILS TRAVAIL METAUX
7361	METAL CUTTING MACH-TOOLS	N 41519	205.9	N 81817	212.4	N 89581	253.9	N 53516	277.5	MACH-OUT ENLEVEMENT METAL
7362	METAL FORMING MACH-TOOLS	N 19827	168.8	N 204291	259.1	N 126135	250.3	N 81943	291.8	MACH-OUTILS DEFORM METAL
737	METALWORKING MACHNRY NES		170.5		237.6		904.4		273.1	MACH TRAV METAUX PIECES
7371	FOUNDRY EQUIPMNT,PTS NES		19.2		39.6		342.9		62.0	CONVERTISSEURS ACIERIE,PIEC
73711	FOUNDRY EQUIPMENT NES	N 1379	9.2	N 7596	30.3	N 19587	321.6	N 2381	57.1	CONVERTISSEURS ACIERIE
7372	ROLLING MILLS AND ROLLS		59.4		71.6		312.0		53.4	LAMINOIRS CYLINDRES PIEC
73721	ROLLING MILLS	N 340	49.6	N 2556	61.3	N 43058	287.3	N 1792	28.2	LAMINOIRS ET TRAINS
7373	WELDING,BRAZING,ETC MCHS		92.0	MN 117971	126.5		249.5		157.8	MACH SOUDAGE ETC PIECES
73732	ELECTRIC WELDERS,ETC		88.3	MN 117894	121.2		244.8		153.1	MACH ELECT POUR SOUDER
74	GENRL INDUSTRL MACHY NES		2797.6		3172.3		3474.7		3743.8	MACH APP INDUSTRIE
741	HEATING,COOLING EQUIPMNT		687.2		740.9		778.1		597.9	MACH CHAUFFAGE,PIECES
7413	INDUS FURNACES ETC,PARTS		155.7		127.7		238.7		183.9	FOURS IND,LABOR,PIECES
7416	HEATING,COOLING EQU NES		398.4	N 2205039	479.7		345.0	N 293488	232.8	APP CHANGEMENT TEMP
742	PUMPS FOR LIQUIDS ETC		148.6		131.7		163.7		198.6	POMPES MOTO-POMPES
743	PUMPS NES,CENTRFUGES ETC		524.0		512.9		501.5		592.7	POMPES COMPRES,VENT ETC
7431	PUMPS FOR GASES ETC		319.9	N 1783830	226.3		219.6		251.5	POMPES AIR A VIDE,COMPRES
744	MECHANICAL HANDLING EQU		507.2		622.3		843.0		1048.9	EQUIP MANUTENTION PIECES
7442	LIFTING,LOADING MACH NES	N 319523	327.3	N 1325541	361.2	N 1385933	562.9	N 780167	673.8	APP LEVAGE,MANUTENTION
74428	OTH HANDLING ETC MCH NES	N 288760	155.8	N 1133154	165.6	N 1333433	282.1	N 687614	301.8	AUT APP LEVAGE ETC
745	NONELEC MACHY,TOOLS NES		192.2		231.4		290.3		337.2	AUT MACH NON ELEC,PIECES
7452	OTH NONELEC MCHS,PTS NES		154.0		186.9		232.9		278.2	AUT MACH NON ELEC,PIECES
749	NONELEC MACH PTS,ACC NES		738.7		933.3		898.3		968.8	PIECES MACH NON ELEC NDA
7492	COCKS,VALVES ETC NES		245.2	MN 64864	300.1		177.3	MN 145340	240.3	ART ROB,SIM POUR TUYAUX
7499	OTH NONELEC MCHY PTS NES		310.7		377.9		434.5		429.2	PIECES NON ELECT NDA
74991	FOUNDRY MOULDS ETC NES	N 495984	246.0	N 621675	299.5	N 1135020	360.2	N 5546693	351.5	MOULES POUR METAUX
75	OFFICE MACHNES,ADP EQUIP		1376.6		1893.6		2790.5		3904.3	MACH BUREAU TRAIT AUTOM
752	AUTOMTIC DATA PROC EQUIP	N 203920	312.2	N 1483629	405.9	N 1363074	566.9	N 3626333	936.0	MACH TRAIT INFORMATION
7528	OFF-LINE DATA PROC EQUIP	N 43726	81.5	N 168043	83.8	N 529784	111.2	N 1688654	298.1	MACH AUXIL TRAIT INFORM
759	OFFICE,ADP MCH PTS,ACCES		1002.0		1406.0		2123.7		2883.5	PIECES DU 751 ET 752
7599	ACCTG,ETC,ADP MCH PTS,AC		978.9		1376.9		2075.7		2835.6	PIECES DU 751 ET 752
76	TELECOMM,SOUND EQUIPMENT		2485.4		3173.9		3857.1		3208.1	EQUIPMENT DE TELECOM
764	TELECOM EQPT,PTS,ACC NES		2284.9		2908.2		3577.0		3024.2	EQUIP TELECOM,PIECES
7641	LINE TELEPHONE,ETC EQUIP	MN 19576	91.9	MN 27332	119.1	MN 22430	263.9	MN 16436	170.0	APP TELEPHON PAR FIL
7643	TV,RADIO TRANSMITTRS ETC	N 441461	331.0	N 837434	313.5	N 1064046	499.5	N 1044349	380.4	APP EMET TELE RADIO
7649	PTS NES OF EQUIPMT OF 76		1734.1		2288.1		2622.4		2266.8	PIECES DE LA DIV 76
76491	PTS NES OF APPAR OF 7641		161.5		208.3		303.3		306.2	PIECES POUR 764.1
76493	TELECOMM EQUIPMT PTS NES		732.0		964.6		1229.9		1042.2	PIECES 761,762,764.3,8
76499	PARTS ETC OF SOUND EQUIP		799.7		1055.3		1011.2		849.2	PIECES NDA POUR 763
77	ELECTRIC MACHNRY NES ETC		11021.3		16059.0		21472.5		22742.4	MACH APP ELECT NDA
771	ELECTRIC POWER MACHY NES		475.1		679.6		685.6		813.7	MACH PROD,TRANS ELECTR
7711	TRANSFORMERS,ELECTRICAL		158.8		246.5		221.0	MN 211578	338.8	TRANSFO ELECTRIQUES
77118	OTHER ELEC TRANSFORMERS		140.4		219.0		207.8	MN 211577	319.6	AUTRES TRANSFO ELECTRIQ
7712	OTH ELEC POWER MACHY NES		316.4		433.1		464.6		474.9	AUT APP PROD TRANSF ELEC
77129	PTS NES OF MACHY OF 771		131.3		199.5		196.6		219.9	PIECES MACH DU 771
772	SWITCHGEAR ETC,PARTS NES		1769.0		2530.1		2675.4		2653.5	APP COUPURE,SECT ETC
7721	SWITCHGEAR ETC		893.1	MN 11649	1168.3		1307.0		1324.8	APP COUPURE,SECTIONMNT

4. General Imports C.I.F. by Commodities according to the S.I.T.C. (Rev. 2) in million U.S. Dollars
Importations Générales C.A.F. par Produits d'après la C.T.C.I. (Rév. 2) en millions de Dollars E.U.

SITC CTCI	COMMODITY	1993 QUANTITY QUANTITE	1993 VALUE VALEUR	1994 QUANTITY QUANTITE	1994 VALUE VALEUR	1995 QUANTITY QUANTITE	1995 VALUE VALEUR	1996 QUANTITY QUANTITE	1996 VALUE VALEUR	PRODUIT
7722	PRINTED CIRCUITS,PTS NES		597.8		841.8		1012.5		994.9	CIRCUITS ET PIECES
7723	FIXED,VARIABLE RESISTORS		278.2		520.0		355.9		333.9	POTENTIOMETRES PIECES
773	ELECTR DISTRIBUTNG EQUIP		430.3		482.0		534.6		509.0	EQUIPMT DISTRIBUTION ELECT
7731	INSULATED WIRE,CABLE ETC	W 61883	349.9	W 49269	387.3	W 50203	441.9	W 105334	400.0	FILS,CABLES ISOLES ELECT
776	TRANSISTORS,VALVES,ETC		7122.5	MN 50666974	10616.4		15516.7	MN 59656516	16710.4	LAMPES,TUBES,VALVES
7761	TV PICTURE TUBES	N 6706872	466.6	N 7249417	430.6	MN 10272	828.0	MN 9775	894.9	TUBES CATHODIQUES
7762	OTH ELECTRONIC TUBES ETC		127.3	N 6551598	246.5	N 6897587	319.8	N 8352876	482.8	AUT LAMPES ELECTRONIQUES
7763	DIODES,TRANSISTORS,ETC	MN 11485908	648.2	MN 12225466	1002.8	MN 16649698	1183.3	MN 21125004	1457.5	DIODES,TRANSISTORS
7764	ELECTRONIC MICROCIRCUITS	MN 3864993	2117.8	MN 8157722	3691.3	MN 9949087	5611.5	MN 8591415	6647.2	MICROSTRUCTURES ELECTRON
7768	ELCTRNC COMP PTS,CRYSTLS		3762.8	MN 30269985	5245.3		7574.3	MN 29921968	7228.2	CRIST PIEZO–ELEC,PCS 776
77689	ELECTRNIC COMPON PTS NES		3731.5	MN 30049067	5175.2		7482.0	MN 29545904	7133.0	PIECES DU GROUPE 776
778	ELECTRICAL MACHINERY NES		1065.4		1552.0		1828.4		1838.5	AUTRES MACH ELECT NDA
7788	OTH ELEC MACHY,EQUIP NES		858.2		1255.2		1459.8		1440.6	AUT MACH APP ELEC NDA
77884	ELECTRICAL CONDENSERS		551.7	MN 23216409	817.7		997.2	MN 24716099	940.9	CONDENSATEURS ELECTRIQUES
78	ROAD VEHICLES		1340.7		1767.8		2735.7		3057.0	VEHICULES ROUTIERS
781	PASS MOTOR VEH EXC BUSES	N 173308	770.5	N 222879	1077.3	N 310200	1674.1	N 352900	1697.8	AUTO TRANSPORT PERSONNES
782	LORRIES,SPCL MTR VEH NES	N 19683	178.7	N 24710	253.1	N 41561	480.2	N 66129	670.9	VEHICULES SPECIAUX,MARCH
7821	LORRIES,TRUCKS	N 18368	165.9	N 23267	237.8	N 39633	445.7	N 56911	637.5	VEHICULES TRANSP MARCHAND
784	MOTOR VEH PRTS,ACCES NES	MN 101436	172.4	MN 107670	230.4	MN 128902	301.0	MN 145034	380.9	PIECES 722,781,782,783
7849	OTHER MOTOR VEHCL PARTS	MN 101433	157.8	MN 107666	212.3	MN 128897	259.5	MN 145024	347.1	PIECES 722,781,782,783
785	CYCLES,ETC MOTRZD OR NOT		164.3	N 804293	147.5		173.2		154.0	MOTOCYCLES SCOOTERS
79	OTHR TRANSPORT EQUIPMENT		2036.7		3436.7		3544.2		2405.9	AUTRE MATERIEL TRANSPORT
792	AIRCRAFT ETC		1698.5		2061.4		2523.6		1397.8	APP NAVIGATION AERIENNE
7924	AIRCRFT NES OVER 15000KG		1549.9	N 36	1859.7		2342.6	N 45	1080.4	AERODYNES PLUS 15000 KG
793	SHIPS AND BOATS ETC	N 15561	325.4	N 30691	1328.1	N 117201	906.6	N 8323	931.9	NAVIRES BATEAUX,ETC
7932	SHIPS AND BOATS NES	N 1091	171.6	N 3207	1033.7	N 2085	613.7	N 3395	745.7	NAVIRES ET BATEAUX
79322	TANKERS OF ALL KINDS	N 8	105.3	N 17	410.5	N 7	5.2	N 7	120.5	BATEAUX–CITERNES
79323	OTHER CARGO VESSELS	N 140	58.0	N 167	611.5	N 71	595.5	N 1231	609.4	AUT BATEAUX TRANS MARCH
7938	TUGS,SPECIAL VESSELS ETC	N 1764	150.2	N 3546	291.9	N 18307	278.9	N 3993	185.0	REMORQUEURS,BATEAUX SPEC
79382	SPECL PURPOSE VESSLS ETC	N 83	144.6	N 83	279.1	N 85	270.2	N 73	174.7	BAT–PHARES,–POMPES,DRAGUES
8	MISC MANUFACTURED GOODS		2604.1		3280.5		3862.5		3846.5	ART MANUFACTURES DIVERS
87	PRECISION INSTRUMNTS NES		715.5		938.9		1216.8		1181.8	INSTRUM,APPAR SCIENT NDA
874	MEASURNG,CONTROLNG INSTR		609.7		791.6		1041.7		988.2	INSTRUMENTS DE MESURE
8742	MEASUR,DRAW ETC INST,PTS		229.7	MN 24758	331.5		457.1	MN 29661	462.4	INST DESSIN,TRACAGE,PCS
87421	MEASURNG,DRAWNG ETC INST		185.4	N 149326	265.8		350.1	N 428516	349.4	INSTRUM DESSIN,TRACAGE
8748	ELEC MEAS,CONTRL EQU NES		120.8		172.4		235.8		224.3	APP ELEC ELECTRO MESURE
88	PHOTO EQU,OPTICL GDS ETC		587.3		725.8		824.5		783.0	APP,FOURN PHOTO,OP,MONTR
881	PHOTO APPARAT,EQUIPT NES		221.6		288.1		312.9		280.0	APP,EQUIP PHOTO NDA
8811	CAMERAS STILL,FLASH APP	MN 684615	203.2	MN 640267	265.4	MN 714606	287.8	MN 370289	230.1	APPAREILS PHOTO,PIECES
88119	PTS NES OF APPAR OF 8811	MN 683161	162.3	MN 637282	209.7	MN 706187	192.1	MN 364647	149.4	PIECES POUR 881.1
885	WATCHES AND CLOCKS		227.7		276.8		321.2		306.7	HORLOGERIE
89	MISC MANUFCTRD GOODS NES		1017.9		1266.3		1414.6		1436.8	ART MANUFACTURES DIVERS
893	ARTICLES OF PLASTIC NES		443.8		573.2		607.5		575.3	OUVRAGES EN MAT DIVIS 58
8939	MISC PLASTIC ARTICLES		338.1	W 46924	436.6		448.9	W 249135	430.4	ART DIVERS EN MAT DIV 58
89399	OTHR PLASTC ARTICLES NES		328.5	W 26259	424.2		436.9	W 242270	419.2	AUT OUV MAT DIV 58
898	MUSICAL INSTRUMENTS,PTS		195.7		247.1		285.6		250.2	INSTRUMENTS DE MUSIQUE
8983	SOUND RECRDNG TAPE,DISCS	MN 69668	174.5	MN 115352	224.8	MN 179149	264.2	MN 241098	234.1	SUPPORTS SON POUR 763
9	GOODS NOT CLASSD BY KIND		1639.6		2321.9		3807.3		3726.6	ART TRANSACT NON CLASSES
931	*SPECIAL TRANSACTIONS		650.3		785.1		1890.8		1869.0	TRANS.SPECIALES
971	*GOLD,NON MONETARY NES	K 81733	973.5	K 121919	1515.5	K 159855	1884.7	K 244205	1841.9	OR NON MONETAIRE
97101	NONMON GLD UNWRT,SEMIMFD	K 81579	972.2	K 121795	1514.1	K 159806	1884.1	K 243445	1839.3	OR,ALLIAGES D'OR BRUTS

5. General Exports F.O.B. by Commodities according to the S.I.T.C. (Rev. 2) in million U.S. Dollars
Exportations Générales F.O.B. par Produits d'après la C.T.C.I. (Rév. 2) en millions de Dollars E.U.

SITC CTCI	COMMODITY	1993		1994		1995		1996		PRODUIT
		QUANTITY QUANTITE	VALUE VALEUR	QUANTITY QUANTITE	VALUE VALEUR	QUANTITY QUANTITE	VALUE VALEUR	QUANTITY QUANTITE	VALUE VALEUR	
	ALL COMMODITIES		47127.2		58842.7		73778.2		78314.9	TOUS PRODUITS
0	FOOD AND LIVE ANIMALS		1544.3		1711.2		1799.4		1876.4	ALIMENTS,ANIMAUX VIVANTS
001	*LIVE ANIMALS FOR FOOD	MN 51747	195.1	MN 49083	207.4	MN 48833	219.0	MN 63679	243.1	ANIMAUX VIVANTS
03	FISH AND PREPARATIONS		304.1		323.9		328.9		320.1	POISSONS ET PREPARATIONS
04	CEREALS AND PREPARATIONS		133.7		183.2		228.1		233.4	CEREALES ET PRODUITS
05	VEGETABLES AND FRUIT		215.4		205.2		199.0		208.0	LEGUMES ET FRUITS
07	COFFEE,TEA,COCOA,SPICES		298.9		334.6		311.0		311.9	CAFE,THE,CACAO,EPICES
072	COCOA	W 202767	242.7	W 157989	251.1	W 127707	226.0	W 110368	209.7	CACAO
2	CRUDE MATERLS,EXCL FUELS		4241.2		4367.6		4737.7		4222.7	MAT BRUTES NON COMESTIBLES
23	RUBBER, CRUDE		834.4		1125.8		1619.0		1404.3	CAOUTCHOUC BRUT
232	NATURAL RUBBER,GUMS	W 937348	830.0	W 1017725	1120.6	W 1013456	1613.0	W 981742	1398.0	LATEX CAOUTCHOUC NATUREL
23201	NATURAL RUBBER LATEX	W 120986	146.7	W 120231	157.9	W 109188	206.3	W 115760	210.8	LATEX NATUREL
23202	OTHER NATURAL RUBBER	W 816356	683.4	W 854854	920.9	W 860451	1343.8	W 821868	1130.8	CAOUTCHOUC NATUREL
24	CORK AND WOOD		3160.1		2920.9		2753.3		2467.0	LIEGE ET BOIS
247	OTH WOOD ROUGH,SQUARED	W 7069479	1137.9	W 6417893	977.1	W 5894434	907.3	W 5312114	911.4	BOIS BRUTS EQUARRIS
2472	SAW–,VENEER–LOGS NON–CON	W 7033337	1130.9	W 6344009	961.6	W 5828534	893.5	W 5253515	897.9	NON CONIFERES SCIAGE,PLAC
24721	— IN THE ROUGH	W 7033337	1130.9	W 6344009	961.6	W 5828534	893.5	W 5253515	897.9	BRUTS ECORCES DEGROSSIS
248	WOOD SHAPED,SLEEPERS		2011.9		1934.6		1833.3		1538.7	BOIS SIMPLEMENT TRAVAILLES
2483	LUMBER SHAPED NON–CONIFR		1954.9		1882.9		1784.9		1507.8	NON CONIFERES SCIES,RABOTES
24831	LUMBER SAWN ETC NON–CON	W 3807943	1741.1	W 3309464	1642.7	W 3085931	1552.2	W 2695091	1286.3	SCIES LONGITUDINALEMENT
24832	LUMBER PLANED ETC NONCON		213.9		240.3		232.8		221.5	RABOTES,RAINES,LANGUETES
3	MINERAL FUELS ETC		4848.9		4336.1		5159.1		6315.6	COMBUSTIBLES MINERAUX LUB
33	PETROLEUM AND PRODUCTS		3673.4		3220.9		3669.9		4135.8	PETROLE ET DERIVES
333	CRUDE PETROLEUM	MW 21589	3166.2	MW 19371	2540.8	MW 19247	2684.6	MW 18699	3073.5	HUILES BRUTES DE PETROLE
334	PETROLEUM PRODUCTS,REFIN	W 3433522	503.1	W 4963823	670.4	W 6557438	958.4	W 6179899	1029.4	PRODUITS RAFFINES
3341	GASOLINE,OTH LIGHT OILS	W 636253	105.5	W 1534342	239.8	W 2129448	355.7	W 1762307	327.2	ESSENCES POUR MOTEURS
33419	OTH LIGHT PETROLEUM OILS	W 636159	105.5	W 1534325	239.8	W 2128911	355.6	W 1757189	326.1	AUTRES HUILES LEGERES
3344	FUEL OILS,NES	W 1580998	169.9	W 1938867	185.2	W 2367317	239.7	W 2631559	319.4	FUEL OILS
341	*GAS,NATURAL AND MANUFCT	MW 9147	1174.4	MW 9377	1113.5	MW 11526	1487.0	MW 14591	2179.3	GAZ NATUREL,GAZ MANUFACT
3413	PETROLM GASES,LIQUEFIED	W 8096357	1070.1	W 8114171	977.9	MW 10257	1326.2	MW 13494	2017.9	GAZ DE PETROLE LIQUEFIE
34139	OTH HYDROCARBON GAS LQFD	W 7840708	1032.1	W 8092963	974.9	MW 9727	1224.0	MW 12908	1886.5	HYDROCARBURES GAZEUX NDA
4	ANIMAL,VEGETABLE OIL,FAT		2815.4		4008.4		5038.9		4699.5	HUILES,GRAISSES ANIM,VEG
42	FIXED VEGETABLE OIL,FAT		2269.3		3178.3		3947.4		3702.8	HUILES VEGETALES FIXES
424	FIXED VEG OIL NONSOFT		2227.3		3106.2		3833.7		3603.7	AUTRES HUILES VEG FIXES
4242	PALM OIL	W 5105852	2001.2	W 5665842	2844.5	W 5495599	3588.7	W 6132972	3298.9	HUILE DE PALME
4244	PALM KERNEL OIL	W 484104	192.5	W 375803	211.5	W 299330	194.9	W 384216	266.2	HUILE DE PALMISTE
431	*PROCESD ANML VEG OIL,ET		546.1		830.0		1091.3	W 1848125	988.9	HUILES,GRAISSES PREPAREES
4312	HYDROGENATED OIL,FAT		338.4	W 130	468.8		598.2	W 1059595	535.4	HUILES HYDROGENEES
4313	FATTY ACIDS ETC,RESIDUES	W 582745	207.6	W 676605	360.5	W 766810	492.4	W 786644	451.3	ACIDES GRAS INDUST,RESIDUS
43131	FATTY ACIDS,ACID OILS	W 563365	203.2	W 658908	356.5	W 748058	488.5	W 756745	445.3	ACIDES GRAS INDUSTRIELS
5	CHEMCLS,RELATED PROD NES		1003.0		1536.2		2210.6		2415.3	PRODUITS CHIMIQUES
51	ORGANIC CHEMICALS		276.4		438.6		493.7		496.2	PROD CHIMIQ ORGANIQUES
512	ALCOHOLS,PHENOLS ETC		171.2		286.1		303.4		234.0	PHENOLS,PHENOLS–ALCOOLS
5121	ACYCLIC ALCOHOLS,DERIVS		168.1		282.7		291.2		227.2	ALCOOLS ACYCLIQUES
55	PERFUME,CLEANING ETC PRD		152.1		177.3		193.5		207.6	PROD POUR PARFUM,TOILETTE
58	PLASTIC MATERIALS ETC		208.3		306.5		545.3		591.8	MAT PLAST ARTIFICIELLES
583	POLYMERIZATION ETC PRODS		178.6	W 220361	259.0		449.4	W 463938	478.6	PROD POLYMERISATION
59	CHEMICAL MATERIALS NES		119.0		309.1		602.8		707.8	MAT PROD CHIMIQUES NDA
598	MISCEL CHEM PRODUCTS NES		80.3		254.8		527.3		613.6	PROD DIV INDUST CHIM NDA
5989	CHEM PRODUCTS,PREPS NES		71.5		241.7		505.5		593.0	PROD PREP CHIMIQUES NDA
59899	OTH CHEM PRODS,PREPS,NES		53.2		215.6		475.4	W 281456	561.0	AUT PRODUITS CHIMIQUES NDA
6	BASIC MANUFACTURES		4543.2		5370.1		6574.7		7348.4	ART MANUFACTURES
62	RUBBER MANUFACTURES NES		311.4		346.7		399.3		407.0	CAOUTCHOUC MANUFACTURE
621	MATERIALS OF RUBBER		163.1		192.9		218.0		207.4	PRODUITS EN CAOUTCHOUC
63	WOOD,CORK MANUFACTRS NES		1537.4		1766.3		1904.4		2330.3	OUVRAGES LIEGE ET BOIS
634	VENEERS,PLYWOOD,ETC		1364.3		1563.1		1687.3		2085.9	PLACAGES,CONTRE–PLAQUES
6341	VENEER SHEETS ETC	V 772953	298.4	V 621999	257.3	V 589983	230.8	V 650358	251.4	BOIS SIMPLEMENT SCIES
6342	PLYWOOD OF WOOD SHEETS	V 2475213	1055.5	V 3114019	1295.7	V 3562097	1438.7	V 4218162	1804.5	BOIS CONTRE–PLAQUES
635	WOOD MANUFACTURES NES		173.1		203.1		217.0		244.4	ART MANUF EN BOIS NDA
64	PAPER,PAPERBOARD AND MFR		226.1		288.5		364.1		353.5	PAPIERS,CARTONS & OUVRAGES
65	TEXTILE YARN,FABRICS,ETC		698.2		868.9		1174.7		1357.4	FILS,TISSUS,ARTICLES TEXTILE
651	TEXTILE YARN		225.0		303.0		538.6		688.3	FILS TEXTILES
6514	SYN FIB YRN,BULK,MONOFIL	W 53695	90.1	W 76499	136.8	W 121392	268.1	W 195658	373.1	FILS CONT 85% FIB TEXT SYNTH
65144	— TEXTRD,CONT POLYESTER	W 52155	84.6	W 74329	130.1	W 116689	255.7	W 148023	285.4	FILS TEX FI CONT POLYESTERS
653	WOVN MAN–MADE FIB FABRIC		179.6	A 149704	238.3		265.3		306.6	TISSUS FIBRES SYNTH,ARTIF
66	NONMETAL MINERAL MFS NES		406.4		547.4		660.3		655.8	ART MIN NON METALLIQUES
663	MINERAL MANUFCTURES NES		116.0		171.9		230.9		209.7	ART MIN MANUF NDA
67	IRON AND STEEL		465.5		419.6		498.1		597.4	FER ET ACIER
678	IRON,STL TUBES,PIPES,ETC	W 356384	146.1	W 189549	114.0	W 156103	128.0	W 348227	211.7	TUBES,TUYAUX EN FONTE,FER
68	NON–FERROUS METALS		448.3		565.9		783.2		771.5	METAUX NON FERREUX
682	COPPER EXC CEMENT COPPER	W 49366	176.6	W 67567	224.8	W 99402	359.4	W 111346	369.5	CUIVRE
6822	COPPER,ALLOYS WORKED	W 49252	176.2	W 67434	224.6	W 97437	354.1	W 111142	369.1	CUIVRE,ALLIAGES OUVRES
687	TIN	W 39386	198.6	W 41160	204.5	W 39224	231.8	W 40331	232.8	ETAIN
6871	TIN,ALLOYS UNWROUGHT	W 36906	194.7	W 38935	199.9	W 37567	225.3	W 37310	221.9	ETAIN ET ALLIAGES BRUTS
69	METAL MANUFACTURES NES		438.7		550.8		739.0		796.0	ART MANUFACT EN METAL NDA
699	BASE METAL MFRS NES		194.8		252.2		314.0		371.2	ART MANUFACTURES MET NDA
7	MACHINES,TRANSPORT EQUIP		22854.5		31420.6		40673.2		43291.2	MACHINES MATERIEL TRANSPORT
71	POWER GENERATING EQUIPMT		466.7		549.1		655.0		789.7	MACHINES GENERATRICES
713	INTRNL COMBUS PSTN ENGIN		160.3		176.8		137.2		283.9	MOTEURS EXPL COMB INT, PIECE
7131	AIRCRAFT PSTN ENGINS,PTS		146.9		165.6		119.0		257.9	MOTEURS EXPL P.AVIATION, PIE
716	ROTATING ELECTRIC PLANT		268.8		332.3		489.5		458.3	APP ELECTR ROTATIFS,PIECES
7162	AC MTRS,GENRTRS,GEN SETS	MN 160491	221.8	MN 175056	293.8	MN 245668	441.5	MN 246982	417.6	MOTEURS ELECTRIQUES
71621	AC MTRS,INC UNIVRSL MTRS	MN 160490	219.5	MN 175053	289.6	MN 245497	434.3	MN 246978	408.4	MOT ELEC NON COUR CONTINU
72	MACHS FOR SPCL INDUSTRYS		262.5		285.3		421.1		564.6	MAC SPECIALES POUR INDUST
728	OTH MACHY FOR SPCL INDUS		114.4		129.2		211.6		301.8	AUT MACH IND PARTICULIERES
7284	MACHY FOR SPCL INDUS NES		90.3		101.7		173.6		236.5	MACH SPEC IND PARTICUL.
74	GENRL INDUSTRL MACHY NES		953.3		1264.5		1648.6		1506.8	MACH APP INDUSTRIE
741	HEATING,COOLING EQUIPMNT		655.8		821.8		1061.7		915.7	MACH CHAUFFAGE,PIECES
7415	AIR–CONDITIONING MACHNRY		622.6	N 2894554	785.6		998.8	N 2849901	818.6	GROUPES CONDITION AIR
743	PUMPS NES,CENTRFUGES ETC		117.1		189.6		242.6		219.4	POMPES COMPRES,VENT ETC
75	OFFICE MACHNES,ADP EQUIP		3316.5		5032.0		7180.6		9003.2	MACH BUREAU TRAIT AUTOM
751	OFFICE MACHINES	MN 29197	209.0	MN 22196	207.5	MN 21022	227.6	MN 14109	204.5	MACH,APPAREILS DE BUREAU
7512	CALCULATNG,ACCTG,ETC MCH	MN 29158	194.7	MN 22050	188.3	MN 20487	189.1	MN 13197	159.7	MACHINE A CALCULER ETC
75121	CALCULATING MACHINES	MN 28945	177.5	MN 21803	161.6	MN 20148	153.5	MN 12738	126.9	MACHINES A CALCULER
752	AUTOMTIC DATA PROC EQUIP	N 1437007	448.4	N 5927122	1181.6	MN 28582	2185.2	MN 27661	3924.9	MACH TRAIT INFORMATION
7524	DIGITL CENTRL STOR UNITS	N 169	0.7	N 554887	60.6	N 3641605	431.6	N 158292	109.2	UNITES MEMOIRE CENTRALES
7525	ADP PERIPHERAL UNITS	N 120892	112.9	N 4905305	935.9	MN 17237	1474.0	MN 12052	1715.7	UNITES PERIPHERIQUES
7528	OFF–LINE DATA PROC EQUIP	N 1315015	331.3	N 412467	97.8	N 6641692	175.1	MN 14852	1839.8	MACH AUXIL TRAIT INFORM
759	OFFICE,ADP MCH PTS,ACCES		2659.2		3643.0		4767.9		4873.9	PIECES DU 751 ET 752
7599	ACCTG,ETC,ADP MCH PTS,AC		2615.6		3540.9		4690.8		4808.9	PIECES DU 751 ET 752
76	TELECOMM,SOUND EQUIPMENT		7113.0		10046.8		12300.7		11885.9	EQUIPMENT DE TELECOM

5. General Exports F.O.B. by Commodities according to the S.I.T.C. (Rev. 2) in million U.S. Dollars
Exportations Générales F.O.B. par Produits d'après la C.T.C.I. (Rév. 2) en millions de Dollars E.U.

SITC CTCI	COMMODITY	1993 QUANTITY QUANTITE	1993 VALUE VALEUR	1994 QUANTITY QUANTITE	1994 VALUE VALEUR	1995 QUANTITY QUANTITE	1995 VALUE VALEUR	1996 QUANTITY QUANTITE	1996 VALUE VALEUR	PRODUIT
761	TELEVISION RECEIVERS	N 7742739	1236.2	MN 19402	1731.7	MN 24650	2239.2	MN 16894	2083.6	RECEPTEURS DE TELEVISION
7611	COLOUR TV RECEIVERS	N 7332613	1216.8	MN 18050	1716.7	MN 24132	2227.9	MN 16450	2074.3	RECEPTEURS COULEUR
762	RADIO BROADCAST RECEIVRS	MN 42787	2090.1	MN 70052	2840.4	MN 86882	3485.1	MN 51264	3065.8	RECEPTEURS RADIODIFFUSION
7621	MTR VEHC RADIO RECEIVERS	N 4467556	358.9	N 6709822	443.9	MN 13244	508.9	N 5109433	452.4	RECEPTEURS RADIO AUTO
7622	PORTABLE RADIO RECEIVERS	MN 24606	933.1	MN 37469	1246.5	MN 39203	1589.2	MN 22341	1164.8	RECEPT PORTATIFS RADIO
7628	OTHER RADIO RECEIVERS	MN 13713	798.2	MN 25873	1150.2	MN 34435	1387.2	MN 23814	1448.7	AUTRES RECEPT RADIO
763	SOUND RECORDRS,PHONOGRPH	MN 23889	1574.6	MN 48555	2298.9	MN 38109	2792.1	MN 38577	2768.8	PHONO,APP ENREGISTREMENT
7631	ELECTRIC GRAMOPHONES ETC	N 3312695	162.3	N 6571098	290.6	N 7957406	474.7	N 6469372	369.2	ELECTROPHON,TOURNE–DISQ
76318	OTH ELEC GRAMOPHONES ETC	N 3291318	160.8	N 6474958	281.4	N 7790267	463.5	N 6366073	359.3	AUT ELECTRO,TOURNE–DISQ
7638	OTHR SOUND APPARATUS ETC	MN 20576	1412.4	MN 41984	2008.4	MN 30151	2317.4	MN 32108	2399.7	AUT APP D'ENREGIS,REPROD
76381	TV IMAGE,SND RECRDRS ETC	N 6285492	1027.5	MN 14936	1407.8	MN 15761	1646.3	MN 16614	1714.1	APP ENREG,REPRO IMAG,SON
76388	DICTATING MACHINES ETC	MN 14290	384.9	MN 27048	600.7	MN 14391	671.2	MN 15494	685.6	MACHINES A DICTER
764	TELECOM EQPT,PTS,ACC NES		2212.2		3175.8		3784.4		3967.7	EQUIP TELECOM,PIECES
7641	LINE TELEPHONE,ETC EQUIP	MN 24355	505.4	MN 39229	748.8	MN 43231	875.8	MN 42466	946.5	APP TELEPHON PAR FIL
7642	MICROPH,LOUDSPKR,AMPLIFR	MN 58346	178.0	MN 137130	270.3	MN 125780	303.9	MN 73736	324.9	MICRO,HAUT–PARLEUR,AMPLI
7643	TV,RADIO TRANSMITTRS ETC	N 2367726	196.1	N 6762902	180.3	N 2974116	142.6	N 1990782	122.3	APP EMET TELE RADIO
7649	PTS NES OF EQUIPMT OF 76		1237.3		1868.8		2329.1		2355.5	PIECES DE LA DIV 76
76491	PTS NES OF APPAR OF 7641		90.3		167.8		180.9		262.7	PIECES POUR 764.1
76493	TELECOMM EQUIPMT PTS NES		645.5		871.0		1107.1		1151.0	PIECES 761,762,764.3,8
76499	PARTS ETC OF SOUND EQUIP		472.4		785.0		1000.5		898.1	PIECES NDA POUR 763
77	ELECTRIC MACHNRY NES ETC		9270.7		11948.3		16287.1		17591.8	MACH APP ELECT NDA
771	ELECTRIC POWER MACHY NES		455.2		508.9		538.9		530.3	MACH PROD,TRANS ELECTR
7711	TRANSFORMERS,ELECTRICAL		191.0		208.3		218.0		207.2	TRANSFO ELECTRIQUES
77118	OTHER ELEC TRANSFORMERS		190.7		207.3		216.7		206.3	AUTRES TRANSFO ELECTRIQ
7712	OTH ELEC POWER MACHY NES		264.2		300.7		321.0		323.1	AUT APP PROD TRANSF ELEC
77122	INDUCTORS	MN 511010	154.6	MN 518691	155.6	MN 690039	156.3	MN 319082	74.9	BOBINES REACTANCE,SELFS
772	SWITCHGEAR ETC,PARTS NES		771.4		887.6		1201.1		1583.3	APP COUPURE,SECT ETC
7721	SWITCHGEAR ETC		362.1	N 282248	445.8		478.0		556.2	APP COUPURE,SECTIONMNT
7722	PRINTED CIRCUITS,PTS NES		305.6		292.8		559.8		870.8	CIRCUITS ET PIECES
773	ELECTR DISTRIBUTNG EQUIP		211.5		271.7		351.9		424.2	EQUIPMT DISTRIBUTION ELECT
7731	INSULATED WIRE,CABLE ETC	W 38304	202.8	W 83567	255.5	W 73013	328.9	W 73148	350.6	FILS,CABLES ISOLES ELECT
775	HOUSEHOLD TYPE EQUIP NES		174.8		198.9		236.8		267.4	MACH,APP USAGE DOMESTQUE
776	TRANSISTORS,VALVES,ETC		7289.3	MN 39561757	9512.1		13240.1	MN 43484514	14114.9	LAMPES,TUBES,VALVES
7761	TV PICTURE TUBES	N 5280088	320.5	MN 413656	465.4	MN 13928	677.2	MN 14965	848.9	TUBES CATHODIQUES
7762	OTH ELECTRONIC TUBES ETC	N 682924	53.3	N 5430910	235.8	MN 15937	398.3	MN 13886	613.9	AUT LAMPES ELECTRONIQUES
7763	DIODES,TRANSISTORS,ETC	MN 19567227	1056.2	MN 22034936	1311.4	MN 26105842	1630.6	MN 25684955	1647.3	DIODES,TRANSISTORS
7764	ELECTRONIC MICROCIRCUITS	MN 9231615	5262.1	MN 10567871	6893.1	MN 12443281	9845.6	MN 10852117	10125.9	MICROSTRUCTURES ELECTRON
7768	ELCTRNC COMP PTS,CRYSTLS		597.4	MN 6539863	606.5		688.5	MN 6918591	879.1	CRIST PIEZO–ELEC,PCS 776
77689	ELECTRNIC COMPON PTS NES		525.6	MN 6126266	506.1		553.5	MN 6368218	761.4	PIECES DU GROUPE 776
778	ELECTRICAL MACHINERY NES		366.5		566.9		713.0		664.6	AUTRES MACH ELECT NDA
7788	OTH ELEC MACHY,EQUIP NES		288.2		451.1		566.4		491.0	AUT MACH APP ELEC NDA
77884	ELECTRICAL CONDENSERS		124.9	MN 10925491	184.2		244.0	MN 11877478	296.4	CONDENSATEURS ELECTRIQUES
78	ROAD VEHICLES		381.7		387.6		466.3		518.8	VEHICULES ROUTIERS
781	PASS MOTOR VEH EXC BUSES	N 20438	157.9	N 15299	123.8	N 21002	168.7	N 22859	190.0	AUTO TRANSPORT PERSONNES
79	OTHR TRANSPORT EQUIPMENT		1044.3		1842.2		1626.6		1332.8	AUTRE MATERIEL TRANSPORT
792	AIRCRAFT ETC		873.1		1558.7		1287.3		978.7	APP NAVIGATION AERIENNE
7924	AIRCRFT NES OVER 15000KG	N 35	709.7	N 33	1445.5	N 41	1164.1	N 221	774.6	AERODYNES PLUS 15000 KG
7929	AIRCRAFT PARTS NES		158.0		104.0		99.7		198.5	PIECES DU 792
793	SHIPS AND BOATS ETC	N 5744	170.3	N 18444	282.9	N 39385	338.6	N 19332	350.6	NAVIRES BATEAUX,ETC
7938	TUGS,SPECIAL VESSELS ETC	N 3370	141.8	N 7408	231.7	N 22601	302.7	N 15879	340.1	REMORQUEURS,BATEAUX SPEC
79382	SPECL PURPOSE VESSLS ETC	N 403	138.0	N 262	224.9	N 442	299.3	N 2414	336.9	BAT–PHARES,–POMPES,DRAGUES
8	MISC MANUFACTURED GOODS		4885.0		5589.9		6455.4		7054.9	ART MANUFACTURES DIVERS
821	*FURNITURE,PARTS THEREOF		566.3		768.6		916.0		1119.9	MEUBLES ET PIECES
8211	CHAIRS,SEATS AND PARTS	MN 17725	118.1	MN 22283	165.6	MN 19911	196.1	MN 13539	256.5	SIEGES ET PIECES
82111	CHAIRS AND OTHER SEATS	N 4576181	109.6	N 6643656	155.1	N 7359515	184.6	N 8573949	239.7	SIEGES
8219	FURNITURE AND PARTS NES		432.2		585.9		703.3		841.3	AUTRES MEUBLES ET PIECES
82192	WOOD FURNITURE NES		297.4		432.0		528.2		647.5	MEUBLES NDA EN BOIS
84	CLOTHING AND ACCESSORIES		1959.1		2076.1		2270.0		2378.5	VETEMENTS
842	MENS OUTERWEAR NOT KNIT		184.0	MN 23782	197.5		199.2	MN 36995	196.6	VET DESSUS POUR HOMMES
843	WOMENS OUTERWEAR NONKNIT		216.8	MN 28477	221.3		204.5		186.1	VET DESSUS FEMMES MAT TEX
844	UNDER GARMENTS NOT KNIT		195.9	MN 49563	214.3		212.7	MN 50022	185.4	VETEMENT DESSOUS MAT TEX
8441	— MENS SHIRTS		178.1	MN 41171	192.7		190.6	MN 38504	162.2	CHEMISES HOMMES MAT TEXT
84411	—— OF COTTON	MN 21415	158.3	MN 21556	152.7	MN 18933	151.3	MN 30583	146.4	CHEMISES HOMMES DE COTON
845	OUTERWEAR KNIT NONELASTC		407.9	MN 66190	398.0		393.6		390.6	VET DESSOUS,ACCES BONNET
8459	— OTHER,CLTHG ACCESRYS		274.1	MN 34906	255.9		270.2		257.7	AUT VET DESSUS DE BONNE
846	UNDER GARMENTS KNITTED		224.6		243.1		249.3		281.9	SOUS VETS DE BONNETERIE
8462	— OF COTTON NON ELASTIC		172.4	MN 76059	115.6	MN 58932	129.0	MN 80700	127.5	SOUS–VET BONNET COTON
848	HEADGEAR,NONTXTL CLOTHNG		688.2		755.1		953.6		1070.3	VET ACCES MAT AUT QUE TEX
8482	PLASTC,RUBBR CLTHG,ACCES		654.5		724.5		924.6		1041.9	VET ACCES MAT PLAS ARTIF
84822	RUBBER CLOTHING,ACCESRYS	MN 13471601	654.1	MN 16055069	724.1	MN 18317515	924.1	MN 19942414	1040.9	VET ACCES CAOUT VULCAN
87	PRECISION INSTRUMNTS NES		314.3		371.2		426.5		503.3	INSTRUM,APPAR SCIENT NDA
874	MEASURNG,CONTROLNG INSTR		141.2		169.4		205.3		272.1	INSTRUMENTS DE MESURE
88	PHOTO EQU,OPTICL GDS ETC		456.8		591.2		723.7		731.6	APP,FOURN PHOTO,OP,MONTR
881	PHOTO APPARAT,EQUIPT NES		268.1		314.8		426.6		410.3	APP,EQUIP PHOTO NDA
8811	CAMERAS STILL,FLASH APP	MN 68007	265.8	MN 66045	312.0	MN 112755	424.0	MN 78283	397.8	APPAREILS PHOTO,PIECES
88111	STILL CAMERAS	N 4957172	222.9	N 4783701	272.8	N 7251103	357.5	N 5827708	331.8	APPAREILS PHOTOGRAPHIQ
885	WATCHES AND CLOCKS		139.7		225.3		242.4		244.5	HORLOGERIE
89	MISC MANUFCTRD GOODS NES		1397.2		1581.4		1905.0		2102.5	ART MANUFACTURES DIVERS
893	ARTICLES OF PLASTIC NES		274.7		335.7		462.0		469.6	OUVRAGES EN MAT DIVIS 58
8931	PLSTC PACKG CONTNRS,LIDS	W 82400	130.4	W 108637	163.7	W 197047	227.7	W 274632	237.7	ART TRANSP EMBALLAGE ETC
8939	MISC PLASTIC ARTICLES		137.8	W 25452	165.3		229.1	W 123264	226.2	ART DIVERS EN MAT DIV 58
894	TOYS,SPORTING GOODS,ETC		359.8		364.7		436.1		554.8	VOITURES ENFANTS,JOUETS
8942	TOYS,INDOOR GAMES ETC		307.7		302.5		337.2		444.6	JOUETS,JEUX ETC
897	GOLD,SILVER WARE,JEWELRY		465.3		461.3		475.9		438.1	BIJOUTERIE,ORFEVRERIE
8973	PREC JEWLRY,GLD–SILVWARE		463.8		458.7		470.3		421.6	BIJOUX OR,ARGENT ORFEVRE
89731	PRECIOUS METAL JEWELLERY		460.5		456.1		466.5		419.5	ART BIJOUTERIE,JOAILLER
898	MUSICAL INSTRUMENTS,PTS		117.5		208.4		306.0		393.6	INSTRUMENTS DE MUSIQUE
8983	SOUND RECRDNG TAPE,DISCS	MN 176015	107.8	MN 539192	203.1	MN 278451	287.5	MN 246673	370.7	SUPPORTS SON POUR 763
89831	PREPD SND RECORDNG MEDIA	MN 160125	97.4	MN 419423	162.4	MN 236769	203.9	MN 214852	322.3	SUPPORTS PREPARES
9	GOODS NOT CLASSD BY KIND		321.2		422.6		971.1		862.0	ART TRANSACT NON CLASSES
931	*SPECIAL TRANSACTIONS		295.0		391.4		924.0		823.0	TRANS.SPECIALES

1. HISTORICAL SERIES, 1962–1997 GENERAL TRADE, IMPORTS C.I.F., EXPORTS F.O.B.
SERIES HISTORIQUES, 1962–1997 COMMERCE GENERAL, IMPORTATIONS C.A.F., EXPORTATIONS F.O.B

YEAR ANNEE	VALUE IN MILLION U.S. DOLLARS VALEUR EN MILLION U.S. DOLLARS MERCHANDISE –MARCHANDISE IMPORTS	EXPORTS	GOLD –OR IMPORTS	EXPORTS	CONVERSION FACTORS U.S. CENTS PER RUFIYAA FACTEURS DE CONVERSION CENTS E.U. PAR RUFIYAA IMPORTS	EXPORTS	INDEX NUMBERS –INDICES QUANTUM IMPORTS	EXPORTS	UNIT VALUE VALEUR UNITAIRE IMPORTS	EXPORTS
1962	0.30	2.09								
1963	1.73	1.83								
1964	1.68	1.89								
1965	1.65	2.49								
1966	2.06	2.21								
1967	2.39	2.43								
1968	1.97	2.37								
1969	3.12	2.84								
1970	1.98	3.86								
1971	3.45	4.29								
1972	2.62	3.19								
1973	3.66	2.30								
1974	6.79	3.97								
1975	6.75	2.63								
1976	5.47	2.97								
1977	9.11	4.77								
1978	12.34	6.89								
1979	19.52	4.59								
1980	28.60	7.80								
1981	30.60	8.60								
1982	43.20	9.80								
1983	56.90	13.40								
1984	53.30	17.60								
1985	52.70	23.00								
1986	44.60	24.50								
1987	81.00	30.80								
1988	90.10	40.20								
1989	112.60	44.70								
1990	137.80	52.10								
1991	161.20	53.70								
1992	189.30	40.00								
1993	185.10	34.60								
1994	221.60	45.90								
1995	267.90	49.50								
1996	301.80	59.30								
1997	348.90	73.20								

2. IMPORTS BY BROAD ECONOMIC CATEGORY AND EXPORTS BY INDUSTRIAL ORIGIN. (PERCENTAGE OF TOTAL VALUE)
IMPORTATIONS PAR CATEGORIES ECONOMIQUES ET EXPORTATIONS PAR BRANCHE D'ACTIVITE.(EN POURCENTAGE DE LA VALEUR TOTALE)

IMPORTS – IMPORTATIONS

	1989	1990	1991	1992	1993	1994	1995
TOTAL IMPORTS–IMPORTATIONS TOTALES							
1 FOOD BEV–ALIMENTATION BOISSONS							
11 PRIMARY–PRODUITS DE BASE							
111 FOR INDUSTRY–POUR L'INDUSTRIE							
112 FOR HOUSEHOLDS–POUR LES MENAGES							
12 PROCESSED–PRODUITS ELABORES							
121 FOR INDUSTRY–POUR L'INDUSTRIE							
122 FOR HOUSEHOLDS–POUR LES MENAGES							
2 IND SUPPLIES–APPROV INDUSTRIELS							
21 PRIMARY–PRODUITS DE BASE							
22 PROCESSED–PRODUITS ELABORES							
3 FUELS–COMBUSTIBLES							
31 PRIMARY–PRODUITS DE BASE							
32 PROCESSED–PRODUITS ELABORES							
321 MOTOR SPIRIT–ESSENCE							
322 OTHER–AUTRES							
4 MACHINERY–EQUIPEMENT							
41 CAPITAL EQUIPMENT–MACHINES							
42 PARTS–PIECES ACCESSOIRES							
5 TRANSPORT–TRANSPORT							
51 PASSENGER CARS–AUTOMOBILES							
52 OTHER–AUTRES							
521 INDUSTRIAL–INDUSTRIELS							
522 NON INDUSTRIAL–NON INDUSTRIEL							
53 PARTS–PIECES ACCESSOIRES							
6 CONSUM GOODS–BIENS CONSOMMATION							
61 DURABLE–DURABLES							
62 SEMI DURABLE–SEMI DURABLES							
63 NON DURABLE–NON DURABLES							
7 GOODS NES–BIENS NDA							

EXPORTS – EXPORTATIONS

	1989	1990	1991	1992	1993	1994	1995
TOTAL EXPORTS–EXPORTATIONS TOTALES							
1 AGRICULTURE							
2 MINING QUARRY–INDUS EXTRACTIVES							
3 MANUFACTURING–IND MANUFACTUR							
31 FOOD BEV TOBACCO–ALIM BOISS TAB							
32 TEXTILES–INDUSTRIES TEXTILES							
33 WOOD & PRODUCTS–BOIS & PRODUITS							
34 PAPER & PRODUCTS–PAPIER & PRODT							
35 CHEMICALS–INDUSTRIES CHIMIQUES							
36 NON METAL MIN–MIN NON METAL							
37 BASIC METAL–IND METAL BASE							
38 METAL MANUF–MANUF METAL							
39 OTH MANUF IND–AUTRES MANUF							

3. TRADE BY PRINCIPAL COUNTRIES OF CONSIGNMENT AND DESTINATION (VALUE IN MILLION U.S. DOLLARS)
ECHANGES SELON LES PRINCIPAUX PAYS DE CONSIGNATION ET DE DESTINATION (VALEUR EN MILLIONS DE DOLLARS EU)

GENERAL IMPORTS C.I.F. IMPORTATIONS GENERALES C.A.F

COUNTRIES–PAYS	1991	1992	1993	1994	1995
World	161.3	189.4	191.4	222.0	266.8
Africa	0.0	0.1	0.1		1.4
Americas	1.4	1.9	1.9		2.2
– Northern America	1.2	1.9	1.9		2.1
– LAIA	0.0	0.0	0.0		0.1
– CACM					
– Caribbean		0.0			
– Rest of America	0.2	0.0	0.0		
Asia excl fmr USSR	142.1	170.4	171.4		217.1
– Middle East	3.3	4.0	12.6		25.8
Asia former USSR					
Europe excl fmr USSR	16.5	15.4	16.6		41.8
– European Union	15.5	14.6	15.1		39.2
– Eastern Europe	0.1	0.3	0.7		0.2
– Rest of Europe	1.0	0.5	0.8		2.4
Europe former USSR	0.0	0.0	0.0		
Oceania	1.2	1.6	1.4		4.2
Other					
Singapore/Singapour	92.0	110.1	99.1		97.3
India/Inde	12.5	13.9	16.4		30.9
Sri Lanka	12.3	12.3	12.8		15.2
United Arab Emirates	3.2	3.9	12.5	13.0	19.7
Japan/Japon	6.5	7.2	7.4		13.7
United Kingdom	9.3	7.3	5.7		11.0
Malaysia/Malaisie	2.4	4.7	4.3	6.0	10.5
China, Hong Kong SAR	3.6	5.2	5.6		9.6
Thailand/Thaïlande	4.5	6.2	6.3		6.8
Germany/Allemagne	2.8	3.5	3.8		10.0
Netherlands/Pays–Bas	0.9	1.2	2.5		7.4
Indonesia/Indonésie	0.3	1.9	2.4	3.0	3.9
Myanmar	2.7	2.2	2.6		0.5
Denmark/Danemark	0.5	0.3	0.7		6.3
USA/Etats–Unis d'Amer	1.2	1.9	1.9		1.5
Australia/Australie	1.0	1.6	1.1		2.1
Pakistan	0.6	1.2	0.8	1.0	0.7
Italy/Italie	0.9	0.8	0.6		1.6
Switzerland,Liechtenst.	0.5	0.5	0.6		1.4
Bahrain/Bahreïn	0.1	0.0	0.0		3.0
China/Chine	0.6	0.6	0.5		1.0
New Zealand	0.2	0.1	0.2		2.1
Sweden/Suède	0.2	0.4	0.5		1.0
Other Asia n.e.s.	0.5	0.3	0.2		1.1
Saudi Arabia	0.0	0.0	0.0		1.9
France, Monaco	0.2	0.3	0.5		0.7
Belgium–Luxembourg	0.5	0.3	0.6		0.2
Norway,Svalbard and JM	0.4	0.1	0.1		1.0
So. African Customs Un					1.4
Bulgaria/Bulgarie	0.1	0.3	0.7		0.2
Yemen/Yémen					1.1
Finland/Finlande		0.3	0.2		0.7
Oman				1.0	
Korea, Republic of	0.5	0.1	0.2		0.0
Canada	0.0	0.0	0.0		0.6
Bangladesh		0.4	0.0		
Austria/Autriche	0.1	0.0	0.0		0.1
Ireland/Irlande	0.0	0.0	0.0		0.2
Panama	0.2	0.0	0.0		
Other Africa n.e.s.			0.1		

GENERAL EXPORTS F.O.B. EXPORTATIONS GENERALES F.O.B.

COUNTRIES–PAYS	1991	1992	1993	1994	1995
Monde	53.1	39.7	34.4		49.6
Afrique			0.8		0.0
Amériques	13.2	5.5	4.0		9.6
– Amérique du Nord	13.2	5.5	4.0		9.6
– ALAI					
– MCAC					
– Caraïbes					
– Autre Amérique					
Asie anc. URSS exclus	21.7	16.8	18.8		20.8
– Moyen–Orient	0.0		0.5		0.2
Asie ancienne URSS					
Europe anc. URSS exclus	18.2	17.4	10.8		19.2
– Union Européenne	18.2	17.4	10.8		18.9
– Europe de l'Est					0.1
– Autre de l'Europe		0.0	0.1		0.1
Europe ancienne URSS					
Océanie	0.0		0.1		0.0
Autre					
United Kingdom	13.2	11.7	8.4		12.9
Sri Lanka	10.1	10.3	10.4		11.1
USA/Etats–Unis d'Amer	12.3	5.5	3.9		9.5
Germany/Allemagne	3.5	4.9	2.0		5.2
Thailand/Thaïlande	5.8	2.6	4.8		0.5
Japan/Japon	2.1	1.3	1.4		2.8
Singapore/Singapour	2.7	2.1	1.2		1.1
China, Hong Kong SAR	1.0	0.4	0.4		2.7
Other Asia n.e.s.		0.0			2.2
Netherlands/Pays–Bas	1.1	0.3	0.2		0.5
Canada	0.9	0.1	0.1		0.1
Tunisia/Tunisie			0.8		
Turkey/Turquie			0.4		
Ireland/Irlande	0.1	0.2	0.0		
United Arab Emirates			0.0		0.2
India/Inde	0.0	0.0	0.1		0.1
Italy/Italie	0.0	0.2	0.0		0.0
France, Monaco	0.1	0.0	0.1		0.0
Switzerland,Liechtenst.		0.0	0.1		0.1
Belgium–Luxembourg	0.0	0.0	0.0		0.1
Denmark/Danemark	0.1	0.0			
Poland/Pologne					0.1
Austria/Autriche	0.0		0.0		0.1
Australia/Australie	0.0		0.1		0.0
Malaysia/Malaisie					0.0
Saudi Arabia					0.0
New Zealand	0.0				
Pakistan	0.0				0.0
So. African Customs Un					0.0
Korea, Republic of	0.0				

(VALUE AS PERCENTAGE OF WORLD TOTAL)(VALEURS EN POURCENTAGE DU TOTAL MONDIAL)

	1986	1987	1988	1989	1990	1991	1992	1993	1994	1995
Africa						0.0	0.0	0.1		0.5
Americas						0.9	1.0	1.0		0.8
– Northern America						0.8	1.0	1.0		0.8
– LAIA						0.0	0.0	0.0		0.0
– CACM										
– Caribbean							0.0			
– Rest of America						0.1	0.0	0.0		
Asia excl fmr USSR						88.1	90.0	89.6		81.4
– Middle East						2.0	2.1	6.6		9.7
Asia former USSR										
Europe excl fmr USSR						10.2	8.1	8.7		15.7
– European Union						9.6	7.7	7.9		14.7
– Eastern Europe						0.0	0.2	0.4		0.1
– Rest of Europe						0.6	0.3	0.4		0.9
Europe former USSR						0.0	0.0	0.0		
Oceania						0.7	0.9	0.7		1.6
Other										
Singapore/Singapour						57.0	58.2	51.8		36.5
India/Inde						7.7	7.3	8.6		11.6
Sri Lanka						7.6	6.5	6.7		5.7
United Arab Emirates						2.0	2.0	6.5	5.9	7.4
Japan/Japon						4.0	3.8	3.9		5.1
United Kingdom						5.8	3.9	3.0		4.1
Malaysia/Malaisie						1.5	2.5	2.3	2.7	3.9
China, Hong Kong SAR						2.2	2.7	2.9		3.6
Thailand/Thaïlande						2.8	3.3	3.3		2.6
Germany/Allemagne						1.7	1.8	2.0		3.8

	1986	1987	1988	1989	1990	1991	1992	1993	1994	1995
Afrique								2.2		0.0
Amériques				21.2		24.8	13.9	11.6		19.3
– Amérique du Nord				21.2		24.8	13.9	11.6		19.3
– ALAI										
– MCAC										
– Caraïbes										
– Autre Amérique										
Asie anc. URSS exclus				52.3		41.0	42.3	54.5		42.0
– Moyen–Orient				1.3		0.0		1.4		0.5
Asie ancienne URSS										
Europe anc. URSS exclus				26.3		34.2	43.8	31.4		38.7
– Union Européenne				25.5		34.2	43.8	31.3		38.1
– Europe de l'Est										0.3
– Autre de l'Europe				0.9			0.1	0.1		0.3
Europe ancienne URSS										
Océanie						0.0		0.2		0.0
Autre				0.1						
United Kingdom				18.5		24.9	29.3	24.5		26.1
Sri Lanka				13.0		19.1	25.9	30.3		22.4
USA/Etats–Unis d'Amer				19.7		23.1	13.8	11.3		19.2
Germany/Allemagne						6.5	12.4	5.9		10.6
Thailand/Thaïlande				30.1		10.9	6.5	13.9		1.0
Japan/Japon				2.3		3.9	3.4	4.1		5.7
Singapore/Singapour				3.6		5.1	5.4	3.5		2.2
China, Hong Kong SAR				2.0		1.8	1.0	1.0		5.5
Other Asia n.e.s.				0.0			0.0			4.4
Netherlands/Pays–Bas				0.2		2.1	0.9	0.4		1.0

4. General Imports C.I.F. by Commodities according to the S.I.T.C. (Rev. 2) in million U.S. Dollars
Importations Générales C.A.F. par Produits d'après la C.T.C.I. (Rév. 2) en millions de Dollars E.U.

SITC CTCI	COMMODITY	1992		1993		1994		1995		PRODUIT
		QUANTITY QUANTITE	VALUE VALEUR	QUANTITY QUANTITE	VALUE VALEUR	QUANTITY QUANTITE	VALUE VALEUR	QUANTITY QUANTITE	VALUE VALEUR	
	ALL COMMODITIES									TOUS PRODUITS

Maldives

5. General Exports F.O.B. by Commodities according to the S.I.T.C. (Rev. 2) in million U.S. Dollars
Exportations Générales F.O.B. par Produits d'après la C.T.C.I. (Rév. 2) en millions de Dollars E.U.

SITC CTCI	COMMODITY	1992		1993		1994		1995		PRODUIT
		QUANTITY QUANTITE	VALUE VALEUR	QUANTITY QUANTITE	VALUE VALEUR	QUANTITY QUANTITE	VALUE VALEUR	QUANTITY QUANTITE	VALUE VALEUR	
	ALL COMMODITIES									TOUS PRODUITS

1. HISTORICAL SERIES, 1962–1997 GENERAL TRADE, IMPORTS C.I.F., EXPORTS F.O.B.
SERIES HISTORIQUES, 1962–1997 COMMERCE GENERAL, IMPORTATIONS C.A.F., EXPORTATIONS F.O.B

YEAR ANNEE	VALUE IN MILLION MALTESE LIRI / VALEUR EN MILLION MALTESE LIRI: MERCHANDISE –MARCHANDISE IMPORTS	MERCHANDISE –MARCHANDISE EXPORTS	GOLD –OR IMPORTS	GOLD –OR EXPORTS	CONVERSION FACTORS U.S. CENTS PER MALTESE LIRA / FACTEURS DE CONVERSION CENTS E.U. PAR MALTESE LIRA: IMPORTS	CONVERSION FACTORS EXPORTS	INDEX NUMBERS –INDICES: QUANTUM IMPORTS	QUANTUM EXPORTS	UNIT VALUE / VALEUR UNITAIRE IMPORTS	UNIT VALUE / VALEUR UNITAIRE EXPORTS
1962	28.50	4.30			280.0000	280.0000				
1963	30.20	5.30			280.0000	280.0000				
1964	34.50	6.90			280.0000	280.0000				
1965	35.00	8.70			280.0000	280.0000				
1966	38.70	10.80			280.0000	280.0000				
1967	40.30	9.90			276.0000	275.0000				
1968	51.20	14.10			240.0000	240.0000				
1969	61.30	16.00			240.0000	240.0000				
1970	66.90	16.10			240.0000	240.0000				
1971	65.10	18.80			240.0000	240.0000				
1972	66.90	25.70			260.5410	261.2830				
1973	87.90	36.00			272.5280	272.8710				
1974	137.40	51.60			259.8310	259.7420				
1975	144.50	63.90			261.2910	261.2280				
1976	179.90	97.40			235.0410	234.5430				
1977	217.70	121.80			236.8720	236.9740				
1978	221.50	132.00			259.7050	259.6030				
1979	272.00	152.20			279.2560	278.9150				
1980	323.70	166.70			289.7520	289.5700			88	80
1981	332.30	173.70			257.2947	257.6450			96	86
1982	325.10	169.00			242.6453	243.0725			96	89
1983	316.60	156.70			231.3645	231.3670			98	83
1984	330.50	181.40			216.8977	217.4057			96	85
1985	354.10	187.10			214.1725	213.4865			95	85
1986	348.10	194.70			254.9532	255.2462			91	87
1987	392.90	208.60			290.0488	290.0625			92	91
1988	447.40	235.90			302.3064	302.4701			93	101
1989	515.80	294.40			286.8896	286.7454				
1990	620.50	357.90			316.0878	315.8176				
1991	684.00	405.50			309.0511	308.7928				
1992	747.80	490.90			314.0854	314.3505				
1993	830.92	518.32			261.6693	261.4783				
1994	918.80	592.40			265.6647	265.3693				
1995	1037.70	674.90			283.5303	283.4626				
1996	1007.80	624.10			277.3894	277.3931				
1997	985.30	632.80			259.4296	259.2305				

2. IMPORTS BY BROAD ECONOMIC CATEGORY AND EXPORTS BY INDUSTRIAL ORIGIN. (PERCENTAGE OF TOTAL VALUE)
IMPORTATIONS PAR CATEGORIES ECONOMIQUES ET EXPORTATIONS PAR BRANCHE D'ACTIVITE.(EN POURCENTAGE DE LA VALEUR TOTALE)

IMPORTS – IMPORTATIONS

	1991	1992	1993	1994	1995	1996	1997
TOTAL IMPORTS–IMPORTATIONS TOTALES	100.	100.	100.	100.	100.	100.	
1 FOOD BEV–ALIMENTATION BOISSONS	9.2	9.0	8.5	7.4	8.6	9.2	
11 PRIMARY–PRODUITS DE BASE	3.3	3.3	3.0	2.4	2.7	3.1	
111 FOR INDUSTRY–POUR L'INDUSTRIE	0.5	0.7	0.6	0.6	0.7	1.0	
112 FOR HOUSEHOLDS–POUR LES MENAGES	2.8	2.6	2.4	1.8	2.0	2.2	
12 PROCESSED–PRODUITS ELABORES	5.9	5.7	5.5	5.0	5.9	6.0	
121 FOR INDUSTRY–POUR L'INDUSTRIE	0.4	0.4	0.5	0.5	0.4	0.5	
122 FOR HOUSEHOLDS–POUR LES MENAGES	5.5	5.2	5.1	4.5	5.5	5.5	
2 IND SUPPLIES–APPROV INDUSTRIELS	25.2	24.0	22.6	21.2	19.8	20.4	
21 PRIMARY–PRODUITS DE BASE	1.4	1.2	1.2	1.1	0.8	1.1	
22 PROCESSED–PRODUITS ELABORES	23.8	22.8	21.5	20.0	18.9	19.3	
3 FUELS–COMBUSTIBLES	5.0	4.6	4.6	4.5	4.0	5.5	
31 PRIMARY–PRODUITS DE BASE	0.7	0.6	0.5	0.4	0.2	0.2	
32 PROCESSED–PRODUITS ELABORES	4.3	4.0	4.1	4.1	3.8	5.3	
321 MOTOR SPIRIT–ESSENCE	4.3	4.0	0.6				
322 OTHER–AUTRES	0.0	0.0	3.5	4.1	3.8	5.3	
4 MACHINERY–EQUIPEMENT	39.7	40.5	40.0	44.9	44.5	41.4	
41 CAPITAL EQUIPMENT–MACHINES	14.7	12.0	12.0	11.7	13.3	12.5	
42 PARTS–PIECES ACCESSOIRES	25.0	28.5	28.0	33.2	31.3	29.0	
5 TRANSPORT–TRANSPORT	8.0	8.7	10.6	9.5	8.6	8.3	
51 PASSENGER CARS–AUTOMOBILES	3.1	3.4	2.7	3.3	3.7	3.8	
52 OTHER–AUTRES	1.3	3.1	5.3	4.0	2.6	2.2	
521 INDUSTRIAL–INDUSTRIELS	1.3	3.0	5.2	4.0	2.5	2.1	
522 NON INDUSTRIAL–NON INDUSTRIEL	0.1	0.1	0.0	0.1	0.1	0.1	
53 PARTS–PIECES ACCESSOIRES	3.6	2.2	2.6	2.1	2.3	2.4	
6 CONSUM GOODS–BIENS CONSOMMATION	12.2	12.7	13.0	12.5	14.3	15.0	
61 DURABLE–DURABLES	2.7	3.4	3.6	3.0	3.7	3.3	
62 SEMI DURABLE–SEMI DURABLES	6.1	5.9	6.0	5.7	6.7	7.2	
63 NON DURABLE–NON DURABLES	3.4	3.3	3.4	3.9	4.0	4.4	
7 GOODS NES–BIENS NDA	0.7	0.5	0.5	0.1	0.1	0.1	

EXPORTS – EXPORTATIONS

	1991	1992	1993	1994	1995	1996	1997
TOTAL EXPORTS–EXPORTATIONS TOTALES	100.	100.	100.	100.	100.	100.	
1 AGRICULTURE	0.7	0.5	1.0	0.7	0.5	0.6	
2 MINING QUARRY–INDUS EXTRACTIVES	0.2	0.1	0.0	0.0	0.1	0.0	
3 MANUFACTURING–IND MANUFACTUR	99.1	99.4	99.0	99.2	99.4	99.4	
31 FOOD BEV TOBACCO–ALIM BOISS TAB	2.6	2.4	2.3	1.8	1.7	2.8	
32 TEXTILES–INDUSTRIES TEXTILES	17.2	15.5	15.1	12.3	11.8	13.2	
33 WOOD & PRODUCTS–BOIS & PRODUITS	0.1	0.1	0.1	0.0	0.0	0.0	
34 PAPER & PRODUCTS–PAPIER & PRODT	4.3	3.8	4.9	3.7	2.7	3.6	
35 CHEMICALS–INDUSTRIES CHIMIQUES	7.3	7.3	7.9	7.0	6.5	8.8	
36 NON METAL MIN–MIN NON METAL	0.2	0.1	0.2	0.1	0.1	0.2	
37 BASIC METAL–IND METAL BASE	0.7	0.4	0.3	0.3	0.3	0.2	
38 METAL MANUF–MANUF METAL	62.5	65.4	62.6	69.7	72.0	66.3	
39 OTH MANUF IND–AUTRES MANUF	4.2	4.4	5.7	4.4	4.4	4.4	

3. TRADE BY PRINCIPAL COUNTRIES OF ORIGIN AND DESTINATION (VALUE IN MILLION U.S. DOLLARS)
ECHANGES SELON LES PRINCIPAUX PAYS D'ORIGINE ET DE DESTINATION (VALEUR EN MILLIONS DE DOLLARS EU)

COUNTRIES–PAYS	GENERAL IMPORTS C.I.F. IMPORTATIONS GENERALES C.A.F				
	1993	1994	1995	1996	1997
World	2173.4	2440.7	2941.8	2802.3	2554.7
Africa	56.2	64.3	106.1	133.5	64.7
Americas	210.3	144.4	204.9	215.4	229.7
– Northern America	192.5	127.8	180.6	197.8	208.9
– LAIA	16.5	15.5	22.9	14.2	18.2
– CACM	1.2	0.9	1.1	2.4	2.2
– Caribbean	0.1	0.2	0.1	0.9	0.5
– Rest of America	0.0	0.1	0.2	0.2	0.0
Asia excl fmr USSR	257.6	263.1	416.0	426.8	351.6
– Middle East	21.2	22.6	24.9	29.3	25.6
Asia former USSR	0.0	0.4	0.0	0.6	0.0
Europe excl fmr USSR	1630.8	1951.2	2192.1	1993.7	1884.8
– European Union	1576.1	1871.4	2138.3	1920.3	1823.7
– Eastern Europe	14.8	18.4	17.8	17.3	15.5
– Rest of Europe	39.9	61.4	36.0	56.1	45.5
Europe former USSR	12.8	9.9	14.6	19.7	11.8
Oceania	5.7	7.5	8.0	12.6	
Other		0.0	0.0		
Italy/Italie	591.0	646.0	807.5	548.3	516.8
United Kingdom	291.4	373.8	457.8	398.9	377.1
Germany/Allemagne	310.5	429.1	357.9	262.9	254.7
France, Monaco	182.5	205.2	245.6	443.4	422.9
USA/Etats–Unis d'Amer	189.7	124.7	176.9	193.6	202.4
Singapore/Singapour	70.0	87.4	166.8	161.7	109.5
Japan/Japon	58.4	55.8	74.8	89.1	87.7
Libyan Arab Jamahiriya	46.7	50.8	88.2	119.4	50.7
Netherlands/Pays–Bas	57.4	57.5	67.5	74.8	66.7
Spain/Espagne	31.7	42.6	59.9	52.8	56.3
Switzerland,Liechtenst.	25.8	51.9	29.6	40.0	33.4
Belgium–Luxembourg	29.7	28.7	36.5	41.0	32.3
Korea, Republic of	27.9	19.7	40.1	36.8	22.4
China/Chine	21.6	17.0	30.2	34.3	30.8
Ireland/Irlande	21.5	18.2	24.7	23.9	25.1
Turkey/Turquie	14.7	16.9	22.7	25.3	21.5
Other Asia n.e.s.	16.7	15.9	22.3	21.9	22.7
Denmark/Danemark	17.4	17.9	21.9	19.6	20.3
Greece/Grèce	16.5	20.6	20.5	19.0	18.2
China, Hong Kong SAR	14.0	12.9	14.3	13.8	11.8
Austria/Autriche	10.3	11.6	14.5	12.6	13.8
India/Inde	10.3	9.1	13.2	11.3	12.1
Russian Federation	12.6	7.6	11.5	14.4	9.8
Sweden/Suède	7.6	9.3	10.9	11.0	7.7
Brazil/Brésil	8.4	8.0	12.0	6.5	7.8
Portugal	6.0	7.7	10.0	7.9	8.5
Thailand/Thaïlande	4.8	7.3	8.5	9.1	9.6
Norway,Svalbard and JM	11.0	5.3	2.7	10.4	9.2
Malaysia/Malaisie	2.8	5.8	10.8	8.2	10.1
Czech Republic	8.5	8.3	7.2	7.4	4.5
Canada	2.8	3.0	3.7	4.1	6.3
Australia/Australie	2.4	4.6	4.5	8.0	
Argentina/Argentine	4.9	3.7	5.1	2.3	3.5
Israel/Israël	2.1	3.4	4.1	4.2	3.6
Hungary/Hongrie	2.8	1.9	4.0	3.1	4.7
Finland/Finlande	2.7	3.3	3.1	4.1	3.2
Tunisia/Tunisie	1.7	2.4	3.6	3.9	3.4
So. African Customs Un	2.2	3.4	3.6	2.1	3.7
New Zealand	3.2	2.9	3.6	4.3	
Slovenia/Slovénie	2.4	2.5	3.0	3.5	1.4

COUNTRIES–PAYS	GENERAL EXPORTS F.O.B. EXPORTATIONS GENERALES F.O.B.				
	1993	1994	1995	1996	1997
Monde	1355.4	1557.7	1913.2	1747.9	1644.6
Afrique	82.8	90.9	57.7	53.7	77.2
Amériques	109.4	134.6	198.1	273.5	287.1
– Amérique du Nord	108.0	133.7	192.6	262.1	283.4
– ALAI	0.7	0.4	5.4	2.2	3.5
– MCAC	0.4	0.0	0.1	0.1	0.0
– Caraïbes	0.3	0.4	0.1	9.2	0.0
– Autre Amérique		0.0	0.0	0.0	0.2
Asie anc. URSS exclus	105.4	106.2	209.2	319.8	288.1
– Moyen–Orient	21.9	13.8	16.7	30.1	41.6
Asie ancienne URSS	4.6	0.5	3.0	0.7	0.2
Europe anc. URSS exclus	986.5	1172.1	1397.9	1030.9	911.3
– Union Européenne	976.2	1157.5	1367.0	997.6	886.7
– Europe de l'Est	4.4	9.2	3.3	15.2	13.4
– Autre de l'Europe	5.9	5.5	27.6	18.2	11.3
Europe ancienne URSS	20.6	4.0	2.3	2.6	1.5
Océanie	0.6	5.4	1.6	1.5	
Autre	45.4	43.9	43.4	65.1	
Italy/Italie	437.1	583.5	581.1	223.4	92.9
Germany/Allemagne	211.8	220.8	287.1	250.8	220.4
France, Monaco	141.1	153.4	233.6	260.1	315.4
USA/Etats–Unis d'Amer	101.7	116.7	182.8	234.0	247.2
Singapore/Singapour	67.2	75.5	142.9	209.6	169.1
United Kingdom	109.4	115.2	143.6	146.8	133.6
Libyan Arab Jamahiriya	65.7	52.8	40.7	44.0	65.0
Belgium–Luxembourg	26.1	34.2	67.2	62.6	63.0
Bunkers, ship stores	45.4	43.9	43.4	65.1	
Netherlands/Pays–Bas	33.9	29.9	29.5	31.9	37.5
Japan/Japon	7.5	11.6	16.8	49.9	57.0
Canada	6.3	17.0	9.8	28.0	36.1
Nigeria/Nigéria	2.2	30.1	6.1	0.5	0.1
Switzerland,Liechtenst.	3.8	4.0	9.6	12.6	7.1
Saudi Arabia	5.8	4.4	6.9	9.9	9.6
Other Asia n.e.s.	1.5	2.2	2.0	17.3	13.2
United Arab Emirates	6.4	4.5	4.9	9.1	7.6
Norway,Svalbard and JM	1.6	1.3	17.9	3.1	3.0
China/Chine	0.7	0.6	23.1	0.8	0.8
Spain/Espagne	4.1	6.7	5.6	2.4	5.0
Turkey/Turquie	3.2	0.5	0.3	2.0	17.9
Poland/Pologne	0.4	5.7	0.8	10.8	4.5
Russian Federation	12.0	3.8	2.0	1.8	0.9
Denmark/Danemark	3.2	3.5	3.0	2.9	3.6
Ireland/Irlande	2.5	1.9	2.1	4.2	5.1
Austria/Autriche	1.4	2.1	2.6	3.3	3.0
Sweden/Suède	2.4	2.3	3.0	2.4	2.4
Portugal	1.1	1.8	4.8	2.4	1.9
Greece/Grèce	1.8	1.7	3.7	2.8	1.6
Egypt/Egypte	2.0	1.4	1.9	1.9	3.1
Ukraine	8.7	0.1	0.3	0.6	0.4
Bahamas	0.3	0.0		8.9	
Kuwait/ Koweït	2.1	1.3	1.2	2.1	1.7
Afghanistan			4.3	3.8	
Angola	4.4		3.0		0.0
China, Hong Kong SAR	3.3	0.7	0.4	0.7	1.8
Korea, Republic of	0.3	0.2	1.1	2.6	2.5
Slovakia/Slovaquie	2.7	0.4	0.6	0.9	1.9
Albania/Albanie	0.2	2.4	0.1	0.7	3.0
Colombia/Colombie	0.2	0.2	4.1	1.6	0.2

(VALUE AS PERCENTAGE OF WORLD TOTAL)(VALEURS EN POURCENTAGE DU TOTAL MONDIAL)

	1988	1989	1990	1991	1992	1993	1994	1995	1996	1997
Africa	3.3	0.5	3.6	2.7	2.7	2.6	2.6	3.6	4.8	2.5
Americas	11.4	5.7	4.7	5.6	4.0	9.7	5.9	7.0	7.7	9.0
– Northern America	9.8	4.2	3.5	4.2	3.3	8.9	5.2	6.1	7.1	8.2
– LAIA	1.5	1.4	1.1	1.3	0.7	0.8	0.6	0.8	0.5	0.7
– CACM	0.1	0.1	0.1	0.0	0.0	0.1	0.0	0.0	0.1	0.1
– Caribbean	0.0	0.0	0.0	0.0	0.0	0.0	0.0	0.0	0.0	0.0
– Rest of America	0.0	0.0	0.0	0.0	0.0	0.0	0.0	0.0	0.0	0.0
Asia excl fmr USSR	8.5	9.6	9.7	10.9	12.0	11.8	10.8	14.1	15.2	13.8
– Middle East	0.9	1.1	0.9	1.0	1.2	1.0	0.9	0.8	1.0	1.0
Asia former USSR					0.0	0.0	0.0	0.0	0.0	0.0
Europe excl fmr USSR	75.2	78.3	80.0	78.9	80.0	75.0	79.9	74.5	71.1	73.8
– European Union	71.4	75.6	77.5	76.6	77.9	72.5	76.7	72.7	68.5	71.4
– Eastern Europe	2.3	1.4	1.0	1.0	0.7	0.7	0.8	0.6	0.6	0.6
– Rest of Europe	1.4	1.4	1.5	1.2	1.4	1.8	2.5	1.2	2.0	1.8
Europe former USSR	1.2	0.8	1.6	1.6	1.1	0.6	0.4	0.5	0.7	0.5
Oceania	0.4	0.3	0.3	0.3	0.2	0.3	0.3	0.3	0.4	
Other	0.0	4.8					0.0	0.0		
Italy/Italie	22.6	30.3	32.6	36.3	37.7	27.2	26.5	27.4	19.6	20.2
United Kingdom	16.9	15.3	14.9	14.7	12.9	13.4	15.3	15.6	14.2	14.8
Germany/Allemagne				11.1	10.7	14.3	17.6	12.2	9.4	10.0
France, Monaco	5.0	5.6	7.2	4.6	6.3	8.4	8.4	8.3	15.8	16.6
USA/Etats–Unis d'Amer	9.7	3.9	3.3	4.1	3.2	8.7	5.1	6.0	6.9	7.9
Singapore/Singapour	0.7	1.0	1.5	1.4	2.0	3.2	3.6	5.7	5.8	4.3
Japan/Japon	2.8	3.1	3.7	3.9	4.1	2.7	2.3	2.5	3.2	3.4
Libyan Arab Jamahiriya	2.5	0.0	3.1	2.1	2.1	2.1	2.1	3.0	4.3	2.0
Netherlands/Pays–Bas	2.9	2.9	2.8	2.9	3.2	2.6	2.4	2.3	2.7	2.6
Spain/Espagne	2.1	2.3	1.6	1.5	1.6	1.5	1.7	2.0	1.9	2.2

	1988	1989	1990	1991	1992	1993	1994	1995	1996	1997
Afrique	7.1	5.4	6.4	7.4	5.7	6.1	5.8	3.0	3.1	4.7
Amériques	11.5	5.7	4.0	4.4	6.1	8.1	8.6	10.4	15.6	17.5
– Amérique du Nord	11.5	5.6	3.9	4.3	5.9	8.0	8.6	10.1	15.0	17.2
– ALAI	0.0	0.0	0.0	0.1	0.2	0.1	0.0	0.3	0.1	0.2
– MCAC			0.0	0.0	0.0	0.0	0.0	0.0	0.0	0.0
– Caraïbes	0.0	0.0	0.0	0.0	0.0	0.0	0.0	0.0	0.5	0.0
– Autre Amérique							0.0	0.0	0.0	0.0
Asie anc. URSS exclus	6.4	6.0	5.3	5.0	6.3	7.8	6.8	10.9	18.3	17.5
– Moyen–Orient	2.6	1.9	1.7	2.4	1.9	1.6	0.9	0.9	1.7	2.5
Asie ancienne URSS						0.3	0.0	0.2	0.0	0.0
Europe anc. URSS exclus	71.1	75.8	78.0	78.8	76.8	72.8	75.3	73.1	59.0	55.4
– Union Européenne	69.3	74.3	76.9	78.2	75.6	72.0	74.3	71.4	57.1	53.9
– Europe de l'Est	1.2	0.8	0.6	0.2	0.2	0.3	0.6	0.2	0.9	0.8
– Autre de l'Europe	0.6	0.7	0.5	0.5	1.0	0.4	0.4	1.4	1.0	0.7
Europe ancienne URSS	0.8	1.0	3.0	1.0	2.1	1.5	0.3	0.1	0.1	0.1
Océanie	0.1	0.1	0.1	0.1	0.1	0.0	0.3	0.1	0.1	
Autre	3.0	6.1	3.3	3.3	3.0	3.3	2.8	2.3	3.7	
Italy/Italie	17.5	29.5	34.6	38.6	40.8	32.2	37.5	30.4	12.8	5.6
Germany/Allemagne				17.8	14.2	15.6	14.2	15.0	14.3	13.4
France, Monaco	4.2	5.3	7.1	9.1	9.1	10.4	9.9	12.2	14.9	19.2
USA/Etats–Unis d'Amer	11.2	5.4	3.8	4.2	5.8	7.5	7.5	9.6	13.4	15.0
Singapore/Singapour	3.3	4.0	3.3	2.5	4.1	5.0	4.8	7.5	12.0	10.3
United Kingdom	13.2	10.7	8.9	7.3	6.5	8.1	7.4	7.5	8.4	8.1
Libyan Arab Jamahiriya	6.2	4.9	5.1	5.5	4.2	4.8	3.4	2.1	2.5	4.0
Belgium–Luxembourg	3.1	2.4	2.4	2.2	1.7	1.9	2.2	3.5	3.6	3.8
Bunkers, ship stores	3.0	1.3	3.3	3.3	3.0	3.3	2.8	2.3	3.7	
Netherlands/Pays–Bas	2.1	2.1	1.8	1.8	1.8	2.5	1.9	1.5	1.8	2.3

4. General Imports C.I.F. by Commodities according to the S.I.T.C. (Rev. 2) in million U.S. Dollars
Importations Générales C.A.F. par Produits d'après la C.T.C.I. (Rév. 2) en millions de Dollars E.U.

SITC CTCI	COMMODITY	1994		1995		1996		1997		PRODUIT
		QUANTITY QUANTITE	VALUE VALEUR	QUANTITY QUANTITE	VALUE VALEUR	QUANTITY QUANTITE	VALUE VALEUR	QUANTITY QUANTITE	VALUE VALEUR	
	ALL COMMODITIES		2440.8		2941.8		2802.4			TOUS PRODUITS
0	FOOD AND LIVE ANIMALS		171.7		247.9		254.7			ALIMENTS,ANIMAUX VIVANTS
01	MEAT AND PREPARATIONS		21.7		36.5		33.0			VIANDES ET PREPARATIONS
011	MEAT FRESH,CHILLD,FROZEN	W 5689	14.8	W 8711	24.2	W 7837	21.4			VIANDES FRAICHES,REF,CONGE
0111	BOVINE MEAT FRESH,FROZEN	W 4691	12.1	W 6528	18.3	W 5846	15.7			VIANDES BOVIN FRAI,REF
01112	BOVINE MEAT BONELESS	W 4580	11.8	W 6508	18.3	W 5844	15.7			VIANDES BOVIN DESOSSEES
014	MEAT PREPD,PRSVD,NES ETC		6.8	W 3884	12.3	W 3604	11.6			CONSERVES DE VIANDES
0149	OTH PREPARD,PRESRVD MEAT	W 1953	4.9	W 2993	9.7	W 2894	9.0			AUTRES PREP DE VIANDES
02	DAIRY PRODCTS,BIRDS'EGGS		21.9		28.9		30.3			PRODUITS LAITIERS,OEUFS
022	MILK AND CREAM		8.0	W 4676	7.1	W 4272	6.8			LAIT ET CREME
024	CHEESE AND CURD	W 3972	11.5	W 5491	18.0	W 5171	19.4			FROMAGE ET CAILLEBOTTE
03	FISH AND PREPARATIONS		13.2		16.2		17.2			POISSONS ET PREPARATIONS
04	CEREALS AND PREPARATIONS		32.9		51.4		61.6			CEREALES ET PRODUITS
041	WHEAT ETC UNMILLED	W 40048	5.6	W 54315	10.1	W 47153	11.6			FROMENT,EPEAUTRE
0412	OTHER WHEAT ETC UNMILLED	W 40048	5.6	W 44685	7.8	W 47153	11.6			AUTRE FROMENT NON MOULU
043	BARLEY UNMILLED	W 50740	4.3	W 48488	5.7	W 57826	11.2			ORGE NON MONDEE
044	MAIZE UNMILLED	W 29577	5.6	W 46580	8.6	W 41255	10.1			MAIS NON MOULU
048	CEREAL ETC PREPARATIONS		13.5	W 9263	22.3	W 9821	23.9			PREPTNS A BASE CEREALES
0484	BAKERY PRODUCTS		4.6	W 2695	10.5	W 2765	10.9			PRODUITS DE BOULANGERIE
05	VEGETABLES AND FRUIT		29.8		39.6		41.5			LEGUMES ET FRUITS
057	FRUIT,NUTS,FRESH,DRIED	W 24653	15.8	W 29165	21.3	W 28219	22.5			FRUITS FRAIS OU SECS
06	SUGAR AND PREPS,HONEY		12.8		15.1		12.6			SUCRES ET PRODUITS
061	SUGAR AND HONEY		10.9	W 23315	10.2	W 16578	7.4			SUCRES ET MIEL
0612	REFINED SUGAR ETC	W 24863	9.4	W 21966	9.3	W 13422	5.7			SUCRES RAFFINES
07	COFFEE,TEA,COCOA,SPICES		13.8		27.4		20.9			CAFE,THE,CACAO,EPICES
071	COFFEE AND SUBSTITUTES	W 459	4.8	W 612	9.0	W 388	4.5			CAFE ET SUCCEDANES
073	CHOCOLATE AND PRODUCTS	W 1537	7.0	W 3171	15.9	W 2616	13.7			CHOCOLAT
081	*FEEDING STUFF FOR ANIML		13.1	W 33361	14.9	W 36101	18.2			NOURRITURE POUR ANIMAUX
0819	FOOD WASTE AND FEED NES		6.1	W 7697	7.6	W 9337	8.9			DECHETS,ALIMENTS NDA
08199	FODDER NES,INCL SWEETNED		6.1	W 7678	7.3	W 9337	8.9			PREPARATIONS FOURRAGERES
09	MISC EDIBLE PRODUCTS		11.7		16.6		19.0			PREP ALIMENTAIRES DIVERSES
098	EDIBLE PRODCTS,PREPS NES		10.7		14.9		16.2			PREP ALIMENTAIRES NDA
09809	MISC FOOD PREPRTIONS NES		6.4		9.1		10.5			PREP ALIMENTAIRES NDA
1	BEVERAGES AND TOBACCO		38.6		40.0		37.9			BOISSONS ET TABACS
11	BEVERAGES		17.4		20.4		18.5			BOISSONS
112	ALCOHOLIC BEVERAGES	W 3675	14.3	W 4426	16.2	W 4047	15.3			BOISSONS ALCOOLIQUES
1124	DISTILLED ALCOHOLIC BEVS	W 1477	9.5	W 1857	10.2	W 1391	9.1			ALCOOLS,EAUX–DE–VIE
12	TOBACCO AND MANUFACTURES		21.3		19.7		19.5			TABACS BRUTS FABRIQUES
122	TOBACCO,MANUFACTURED	W 1565	21.2	W 1440	19.6	W 1251	19.4			TABACS FABRIQUES
1222	CIGARETTES	W 208	5.6	W 163	5.4	W 357	8.5			CIGARETTES
1223	OTH MANUFACTURED TOBACCO	W 1342	15.0	W 1157	13.3	W 874	10.2			TABACS FUMER,CHIQUER,PRISER
2	CRUDE MATERLS,EXCL FUELS		37.6		33.3		31.8			MAT BRUTES NON COMESTIBLES
24	CORK AND WOOD		12.3		13.3		10.2			LIEGE ET BOIS
248	WOOD SHAPED,SLEEPERS		10.5		12.4		5.3			BOIS SIMPLEMENT TRAVAILLES
27	CRUDE FERTLZR,MINRLS NES		12.4		8.0		10.2			ENGRAIS MINERAUX BRUTS
3	MINERAL FUELS ETC		109.0		116.6		152.5			COMBUSTIBLES MINERAUX LUB
33	PETROLEUM AND PRODUCTS		99.1		110.5		147.8			PETROLE ET DERIVES
334	PETROLEUM PRODUCTS,REFIN		97.6	W 381295	109.2	W 407667	147.2			PRODUITS RAFFINES
4	ANIMAL,VEGETABLE OIL,FAT		6.7		7.8		8.6			HUILES,GRAISSES ANIM,VEG
5	CHEMCLS,RELATED PROD NES		162.6		193.9		199.4			PRODUITS CHIMIQUES
51	ORGANIC CHEMICALS		14.2		16.0		19.8			PROD CHIMIQ ORGANIQUES
52	INORGANIC CHEMICALS		8.2		7.3		7.8			PROD CHIM INORGANIQUES
53	DYES,TANNING,COLOUR PROD		20.5		18.9		18.5			PROD TEINTURE,COLORANTS
533	PIGMENTS,PAINTS,ETC		19.8		18.2		18.0			PIGMENTS,PEINTURES,VERNIS
5332	PRINTING INKS	W 696	9.8	W 447	6.2	W 555	7.3			ENCRES D'IMPRIMERIE
541	*MEDICINAL,PHARM PRODUCT		32.7		36.8		38.7			PROD MEDICINAUX PHARMACEUT
5417	MEDICAMENTS		26.4		29.3	MK 59507	30.5			MEDICAMENTS
54179	— CONTNG OTH SUBSTANCES		20.7		20.7	MK 50288	22.7			MED CONT AUT SUBSTANCES
55	PERFUME,CLEANING ETC PRD		24.5		39.9		41.3			PROD POUR PARFUM,TOILETTE
553	PERFUMERY,COSMETICS,ETC		14.7	MN 16344	26.8	MN 16089	26.9			PRODUITS DE PARFUMERIE
554	SOAP,CLEANSING ETC PREPS		6.7		9.2		10.3			SAVONS,PRODUITS DETERSIFS
58	PLASTIC MATERIALS ETC		47.0		55.9		54.1			MAT PLAST ARTIFICIELLES
582	PROD OF CONDENSATION ETC		14.4	W 6171	20.3	W 6416	22.2			PROD CONDENS,POLYCOND
5826	EPOXIDE RESINS	W 380	4.3	W 583	7.1	W 686	9.7			RESINES EPOXYDES
58261	— IN PRIMARY FORMS	W 380	4.3	W 583	7.1	W 686	9.7			EPOXYDES PRIMAIRES
583	POLYMERIZATION ETC PRODS		30.3	W 14096	34.1	W 13547	30.4			PROD POLYMERISATION
5833	POLYSTYRENE,ITS COPOLYMR		8.3	W 3523	9.8	W 3194	7.6			POLYPROPYLENE COPOLYMERES
58331	— IN PRIMARY FORMS	W 4149	8.1	W 3500	9.6	W 2998	7.2			SOUS FORMES PRIMAIRES
5839	OTH POLYMRZTION ETC PROD	W 2800	10.9	W 2319	9.8	W 2815	10.3			AUT PROD POLYMER COPOLYM
59	CHEMICAL MATERIALS NES		14.5		17.9		18.3			MAT PROD CHIMIQUES NDA
598	MISCEL CHEM PRODUCTS NES		8.0		11.3		10.6			PROD DIV INDUST CHIM NDA
5989	CHEM PRODUCTS,PREPS NES		7.0		9.4		9.2			PROD PREP CHIMIQUES NDA
6	BASIC MANUFACTURES		355.4		413.9		394.1			ART MANUFACTURES
61	LEATHER,DRESSED FUR,ETC		23.2		22.5		22.1			CUIRS,PELLETERIES
611	LEATHER		16.7	A 626	17.0	A 1173	17.1			CUIRS,PEAUX PREPARES
6114	LEATHR BOVINE NES,EQUINE		13.7	A 450	15.0	A 1045	16.3			CUIRS DE BOVINS
62	RUBBER MANUFACTURES NES		8.1		12.0		12.9			CAOUTCHOUC MANUFACTURE
63	WOOD,CORK MANUFACTRS NES		12.4		13.2		13.3			OUVRAGES LIEGE ET BOIS
634	VENEERS,PLYWOOD,ETC		9.5		9.5		8.9			PLACAGES,CONTRE–PLAQUES
64	PAPER,PAPERBOARD AND MFR		53.2		69.5		60.3			PAPIERS,CARTONS & OUVRAGES
641	PAPER AND PAPERBOARD		39.5		50.2		40.9			PAPIERS ET CARTONS
6415	PAPER,PAPERBRD,BULK,NES		21.4	W 9234	25.1	W 7864	21.2			PAPIERS,CARTONS ROULEAUX
64159	OTHER PAPER ETC,BULK,NES	W 8861	20.9	W 7506	23.7	W 6053	20.0			AUT PAPIER ROULEAUX FEUILLES
642	PAPER,ETC,PRECUT,ARTS OF		13.7		19.3		19.5			PAP,CARTONS DECOUPES
65	TEXTILE YARN,FABRICS,ETC		107.8		123.9		124.8			FILS,TISSUS,ARTICLES TEXTILE
652	COTTON FABRICS,WOVEN		33.4	A 10848	42.4		52.8			TISSUS DE COTON
6522	WOVEN COTTON BLEACHD,ETC		30.2	A 9987	39.1		47.4			TISSUS COTON BLANCHIS ETC
65224	BLCHED COTTON FABRIC NES		28.7	A 9174	37.1	A 14226	45.2			AUT TIS PLUS 85% COT BLANCHI
653	WOVN MAN–MADE FIB FABRIC		26.9	A 6282	22.4	A 9670	16.0			TISSUS FIBRES SYNTH,ARTIF
6534	DISC SYN BLEND FABRC NES		14.8	A 1711	7.6	A 4803	6.8			TISSUS FIBRES SYNTH DISCONT
65341	DISC SYN FIB–COTTN FABRC		10.8	A 1300	5.5	A 4525	5.8			TISSUS FIB SYNT DIS MEL COTO
6535	CONT REGN WEAVES NONPILE		6.2	A 2370	9.0	A 2730	3.9			TISSUS FIB TEXT ART CONTINU
654	OTH WOVEN TEXTILE FABRIC		10.3		18.2		17.7			TISSUS AUT COTON SYNT,ARTIF
6542	WOVEN WOOL,HAIR NONPILE		7.7	A 2069	16.6	A 3333	16.8			TIS PLUS 85% LAINE,POILS
65422	WOVN COMB WOOL,FINE HAIR		6.3	A 2005	15.9	A 3311	16.6			TISSUS 85% LAINE,PLS PEIG
656	LACE,RIBBONS,TULLE,ETC		7.6		8.8		8.1			TULLES,BRODERIE
657	SPECIAL TXTL FABRC,PRODS		10.0		9.1		8.6			TISSUS SPECIAUX
66	NONMETAL MINERAL MFS NES		45.9		52.3		50.9			ART MIN NON METALLIQUES
661	LIME,CEMENT,BLDG PRODS		12.7		12.9		14.4			CHAUX,CIMENTS MAT CONSTR
6612	CEMENT	W 212558	10.9	W 195634	10.7	W 246836	11.8			CIMENTS HYDRAULIQUES
662	CLAY,REFRACTORY BLDG PRD		13.8		14.9		13.8			MAT CONST REFRACTAIRES

4. General Imports C.I.F. by Commodities according to the S.I.T.C. (Rev. 2) in million U.S. Dollars
Importations Générales C.A.F. par Produits d'après la C.T.C.I. (Rév. 2) en millions de Dollars E.U.

SITC CTCI	COMMODITY	1994 QUANTITY QUANTITE	1994 VALUE VALEUR	1995 QUANTITY QUANTITE	1995 VALUE VALEUR	1996 QUANTITY QUANTITE	1996 VALUE VALEUR	1997 QUANTITY QUANTITE	1997 VALUE VALEUR	PRODUIT
6624	BRICKS ETC NONREFRACTORY		13.6		14.8		13.6			BRIQUES ETC CERAM NON REFR
66245	GLAZED CERAMIC SETTS ETC		12.6	A 1755	13.9	A 22587	12.9			AUT CARREAUX CERAMIQUE
67	IRON AND STEEL		29.8		36.3		34.5			FER ET ACIER
673	IRON,STEEL SHAPES ETC		8.5		10.8		11.7			BARRES,PROFIL FER,ACIER
674	IRN,STL UNIV,PLATE,SHEET		7.0	W 10935	11.4	W 13828	12.3			LARGES PLATS,TOLES
678	IRON,STL TUBES,PIPES,ETC		8.0		10.5		7.0			TUBES,TUYAUX EN FONTE,FER
68	NON-FERROUS METALS		21.3		21.8		16.6			METAUX NON FERREUX
684	ALUMINIUM		13.3		14.4		10.6			ALUMINIUM
6842	ALUMINIUM,ALLOYS WORKED		11.9		11.4		8.9			ALUMINIUM,ALLIAGES OUVRE
68421	ALUMINIUM BARS,WIRE,ETC	W 3014	9.7	W 1604	9.6	W 1970	7.1			BARRES,PROFILES FILS ALU
69	METAL MANUFACTURES NES		54.2		62.7		59.2			ART MANUFACT EN METAL NDA
695	TOOLS		10.4		8.9	N 7479640	8.6			OUTILS A MAIN
6954	BLADES,TIPS,ETC FR TOOLS		7.7	N 4607110	5.7	N 6040160	5.1			OUTILS POUR MACHINE-OUTIL
697	BASE MTL HOUSEHOLD EQUIP		5.1		9.1		8.0			ART MENAGE MET COMMUNS
699	BASE METAL MFRS NES		16.4		21.8		19.9			ART MANUFACTURES MET NDA
7	MACHINES,TRANSPORT EQUIP		1284.1		1526.3		1355.2			MACHINES MATERIEL TRANSPORT
71	POWER GENERATING EQUIPMT		27.3		47.5		33.6			MACHINES GENERATRICES
713	INTRNL COMBUS PSTN ENGIN		7.5		5.3		5.6			MOTEURS EXPL COMB INT, PIECE
714	ENGINES AND MOTORS NES		9.4		15.3		15.5			MOTEURS NON ELECTRIQUES
716	ROTATING ELECTRIC PLANT		9.3		26.0		6.0			APP ELECTR ROTATIFS,PIECES
7162	AC MTRS,GENRTRS,GEN SETS		8.1	N 129658	25.0	N 15201	4.7			MOTEURS ELECTRIQUES
71623	GEN SETS WITH PISTN ENGN		0.9	N 2894	20.4	N 255	1.6			GROUPES MOTEUR EXPLOSION
72	MACHS FOR SPCL INDUSTRYS		57.4		59.7		60.4			MAC SPECIALES POUR INDUST
724	TEXTILE,LEATHER MACHNRY		8.6		8.3		6.6			MACH POUR INDUSTRIE TEXTILE
726	PRINTG,BKBINDG MACHY,PTS		12.7		9.1		16.3			MACHINES POUR IMPRIMERIE
7264	PRINTING PRESSES		3.4	N 46	2.6	N 64	11.2			MACHINES A IMPRIMER
72641	ROTARY PRINTING PRESSES		3.4	N 46	2.6	N 64	11.2			MACH IMPRIMER ROTATIVES
728	OTH MACHY FOR SPCL INDUS		23.1		27.8		18.2			AUT MACH IND PARTICULIERES
7281	MACH-TOOLS FR SPCL INDUS		5.3	N 22263	10.6	N 109360	5.3			MACH-OUTILS SPEC IND PART
7284	MACHY FOR SPCL INDUS NES		14.9		14.8		10.3			MACH SPEC IND PARTICUL.
73	METALWORKING MACHINERY		19.4		27.7		31.1			MACH TRAVAIL DES METAUX
736	METALWORKING MACH-TOOLS		12.1		8.9	N 236939	10.9			MACH-OUTILS TRAVAIL METAUX
7362	METAL FORMING MACH-TOOLS		8.2		4.0	N 71164	7.7			MACH-OUTILS DEFORM METAL
73621	FORGING ETC MCHS,MTLWRKG	N 962	7.4		0.3	N 9200	0.2			MACH FORGER OU ESTAMPER
737	METALWORKING MACHNRY NES		7.4		18.8		20.3			MACH TRAV METAUX PIECES
7373	WELDING,BRAZING,ETC MCHS		6.1		18.5		20.2			MACH SOUDAGE ETC PIECES
73732	ELECTRIC WELDERS,ETC		6.0		18.4		20.1			MACH ELECT POUR SOUDER
74	GENRL INDUSTRL MACHY NES		85.3		97.6		97.5			MACH APP INDUSTRIE
741	HEATING,COOLING EQUIPMNT		23.1		32.3		31.8			MACH CHAUFFAGE,PIECES
7415	AIR-CONDITIONING MACHNRY	N 19840	11.8	N 18941	17.2		19.6			GROUPES CONDITION AIR
742	PUMPS FOR LIQUIDS ETC		10.7		12.4		7.5			POMPES MOTO-POMPES
743	PUMPS NES,CENTRFUGES ETC		10.9		8.9		9.7			POMPES COMPRES,VENT ETC
744	MECHANICAL HANDLING EQU		14.1		13.4		15.4			EQUIP MANUTENTION PIECES
7442	LIFTING,LOADING MACH NES		9.2		7.9	N 18309	9.2			APP LEVAGE,MANUTENTION
745	NONELEC MACHY,TOOLS NES		9.5		10.7		7.5			AUT MACH NON ELEC,PIECES
7452	OTH NONELEC MCHS,PTS NES		8.8		10.3		6.9			AUT MACH NON ELEC,PIECES
749	NONELEC MACH PTS,ACC NES		17.4	N 2217684	20.1	MN 71971	25.8			PIECES MACH NON ELEC NDA
7499	OTH NONELEC MCHY PTS NES		7.9	N 1179694	9.7	MN 68608	16.6			PIECES NON ELECT NDA
74991	FOUNDRY MOULDS ETC NES	N 25861	6.7	N 26127	8.2	N 46381	15.2			MOULES POUR METAUX
75	OFFICE MACHNES,ADP EQUIP		46.6		68.0		63.4			MACH BUREAU TRAIT AUTOM
751	OFFICE MACHINES		4.2		10.1	N 133477	3.7			MACH,APPAREILS DE BUREAU
752	AUTOMTIC DATA PROC EQUIP	N 71006	23.2	N 78298	29.5	N 266855	28.7			MACH TRAIT INFORMATION
7522	DIGITAL COMPUTERS	N 7357	10.0	N 5926	11.9	N 4750	5.5			MACH DIGITALES COMPLETES
7528	OFF-LINE DATA PROC EQUIP	N 50782	7.5	N 28723	5.0	N 204067	5.6			MACH AUXIL TRAIT INFORM
759	OFFICE,ADP MCH PTS,ACCES		19.2	W 287	28.5	W 292	31.1			PIECES DU 751 ET 752
7599	ACCTG,ETC,ADP MCH PTS,AC		18.2	W 235	26.7	W 251	28.3			PIECES DU 751 ET 752
76	TELECOMM,SOUND EQUIPMENT		36.1		48.2		40.9			EQUIPMENT DE TELECOM
761	TELEVISION RECEIVERS	N 5915	2.0	N 18361	9.4	N 27180	7.8			RECEPTEURS DE TELEVISION
7611	COLOUR TV RECEIVERS	N 5583	1.9	N 17626	9.2	N 26642	7.8			RECEPTEURS COULEUR
764	TELECOM EQPT,PTS,ACC NES		28.8		29.4		24.8			EQUIP TELECOM,PIECES
7641	LINE TELEPHONE,ETC EQUIP		5.8	N 134670	7.4	N 345696	10.5			APP TELEPHON PAR FIL
7649	PTS NES OF EQUIPMT OF 76		14.1		9.7		5.9			PIECES DE LA DIV 76
76493	TELECOMM EQUIPMT PTS NES		12.6	N 730612	7.3	N 397122	4.4			PIECES 761,762,764.3,8
77	ELECTRIC MACHNRY NES ETC		804.2		950.7		823.5			MACH APP ELECT NDA
771	ELECTRIC POWER MACHY NES		8.3		9.9		10.1			MACH PROD,TRANS ELECTR
772	SWITCHGEAR ETC,PARTS NES		25.2	MN 153398	34.8	MN 197550	30.0			APP COUPURE,SECT ETC
7721	SWITCHGEAR ETC		23.5	MN 149718	31.1	MN 192613	26.8			APP COUPURE,SECTIONMNT
773	ELECTR DISTRIBUTNG EQUIP		10.9		13.1		11.8			EQUIPMT DISTRIBUTION ELECT
7731	INSULATED WIRE,CABLE ETC		9.9	L 15644	11.9	L 26924	10.9			FILS,CABLES ISOLES ELECT
775	HOUSEHOLD TYPE EQUIP NES		14.3		24.5		24.0			MACH,APP USAGE DOMESTQUE
7758	ELECTRO-THERMIC APPL NES		4.4		8.1		8.8			APP ELECTROTHERMIQ NDA
776	TRANSISTORS,VALVES,ETC		732.5		848.0		729.3			LAMPES,TUBES,VALVES
7764	ELECTRONIC MICROCIRCUITS	MN 42570	72.5	MN 175010	808.0	MN 295644	695.7			MICROSTRUCTURES ELECTRON
7768	ELCTRNC COMP PTS,CRYSTLS		651.1		31.7		31.4			CRIST PIEZO-ELEC,PCS 776
77689	ELECTRNIC COMPON PTS NES	W 175	651.1	W 348	31.7	W 527	31.4			PIECES DU GROUPE 776
778	ELECTRICAL MACHINERY NES		11.6		18.1		17.5			AUTRES MACH ELECT NDA
78	ROAD VEHICLES		108.6		169.1		162.5			VEHICULES ROUTIERS
781	PASS MOTOR VEH EXC BUSES	N 10554	81.0	N 11149	109.1	N 12113	104.8			AUTO TRANSPORT PERSONNES
782	LORRIES,SPCL MTR VEH NES	N 3574	11.8	N 3148	24.9	N 3913	30.8			VEHICULES SPECIAUX,MARCH
7821	LORRIES,TRUCKS	N 3483	9.1	N 2968	21.4	N 3769	26.7			VEHICULES TRANSP MARCHAND
783	ROAD MOTOR VEHICLES NES	N 161	2.5	N 243	13.1	N 210	2.8			VEHICULES ROUTIERS NDA
7831	BUSES	N 67	1.7	N 111	11.5	N 62	1.5			VOITURES TRANSPORT COMMUN
784	MOTOR VEH PRTS,ACCES NES		10.0		16.8	N 1386565	18.9			PIECES 722,781,782,783
7849	OTHER MOTOR VEHCL PARTS		9.8	N 993698	16.6	N 1384722	18.6			PIECES 722,781,782,783
79	OTHR TRANSPORT EQUIPMENT		99.5		58.2		42.7			AUTRE MATERIEL TRANSPORT
792	AIRCRAFT ETC		93.1		48.5		19.0			APP NAVIGATION AERIENNE
7923	AIRCRFT NES2000-15000KG		74.9							AERODYNES 2000 A 15000 KG
7924	AIRCRFT NES OVER 15000KG				26.7					AERODYNES PLUS 15000 KG
7929	AIRCRAFT PARTS NES		18.2		21.8		19.0			PIECES DU 792
793	SHIPS AND BOATS ETC		6.5		9.6		23.7			NAVIRES BATEAUX,ETC
7932	SHIPS AND BOATS NES		5.3		6.8		20.1			NAVIRES ET BATEAUX
79321	YACHTS,SPORTS VESSLS ETC		2.8		6.0		11.4			BATEAUX DE PLAISANCE
8	MISC MANUFACTURED GOODS		249.5		337.6		335.9			ART MANUFACTURES DIVERS
812	*PLUMBG,HEATNG,LGHTNG EQ		8.6		13.9	N 2742778	12.0			APPAR SANITAIRES CHAUFFAGE
8124	LIGHTING EQUIPMENT NES		4.7		9.4	N 2625087	8.3			APPAREILS ECLAIRAGE ETC
821	*FURNITURE,PARTS THEREOF		6.6	N 2987292	10.9	N 714511	11.5			MEUBLES ET PIECES
84	CLOTHING AND ACCESSORIES		36.4		60.5		62.2			VETEMENTS
843	WOMENS OUTERWEAR NONKNIT		8.3	N 1243733	16.2	N 1889601	18.8			VET DESSUS FEMMES MAT TEX
845	OUTERWEAR KNIT NONELASTC		11.8	N 2111328	21.3	N 2440763	18.8			VET DESSOUS,ACCES BONNET
8451	— JERSEYS,PULLOVERS ETC	N 801181	5.4	N 916512	9.4	N 1337275	10.0			CHANDAILS,PULL-OVERS ETC
846	UNDER GARMENTS KNITTED		4.9	N 2199100	8.3	N 2582202	8.5			SOUS VETS DE BONNETERIE

4. General Imports C.I.F. by Commodities according to the S.I.T.C. (Rev. 2) in million U.S. Dollars
Importations Générales C.A.F. par Produits d'après la C.T.C.I. (Rév. 2) en millions de Dollars E.U.

SITC CTCI	COMMODITY	1994		1995		1996		1997		PRODUIT
		QUANTITY QUANTITE	VALUE VALEUR	QUANTITY QUANTITE	VALUE VALEUR	QUANTITY QUANTITE	VALUE VALEUR	QUANTITY QUANTITE	VALUE VALEUR	
851	*FOOTWEAR		7.6	P 1315013	14.3	P 8045692	15.5			CHAUSSURES
85102	FOOTWEAR LEATHER		5.1	P 834727	10.3	P 1029371	10.4			CHAUS SEMELLES EN CUIR
87	PRECISION INSTRUMNTS NES		46.2		65.3		59.5			INSTRUM,APPAR SCIENT NDA
874	MEASURNG,CONTROLNG INSTR		39.2		54.2		51.2			INSTRUMENTS DE MESURE
8743	GAS,LIQUID CONTROL INSTR		8.1	N 97231	3.4	N 118725	2.0			APP,INSTR MESURE FLUIDES
8745	MEAS,CONTRL,SCI INST NES		7.2	N 97177	39.1	N 85920	36.1			APP SCIENT MESURE NDA
87453	MECHANCL TESTING APPARAT		6.8	N 3324	38.7	N 1316	35.5			MACH NON ELEC ESSAIS MEC
8749	INSTR PTS NES,ACCESSORYS		19.0	N 2444050	6.0	MN 63403	8.4			PIECES 873,874.3,54,874.8
88	PHOTO EQU,OPTICL GDS ETC		24.8		28.0		25.9			APP,FOURN PHOTO,OP,MONTR
884	OPTICAL GOODS NES		13.6		11.5		11.4			ELEMENTS OPTIQ,ART LUNET
8842	SPECTACLES AND FRAMES		12.8		10.3		9.6			LUNETTES ET MONTURES
88421	SPECTACLE FRAMES	MN 98439	11.9	W 179	9.0	W 42	7.9			MONTURES DE LUNETTES
89	MISC MANUFCTRD GOODS NES		118.0		140.9		145.2			ART MANUFACTURES DIVERS
892	PRINTED MATTER		19.4		22.7		28.2			IMPRIMES
8922	NEWSPAPERS,PERIODICALS		7.3	N 6980506	6.9	N 6585695	8.9			JOURNAUX ET PERIODIQUES
8928	PRINTED MATTER NES		5.2		7.1		10.1			IMPRIMES NDA
893	ARTICLES OF PLASTIC NES		36.7		41.8		48.3			OUVRAGES EN MAT DIVIS 58
8931	PLSTC PACKG CONTNRS,LIDS		6.0	MN 104332	7.1	MN 104694	9.7			ART TRANSP EMBALLAGE ETC
8939	MISC PLASTIC ARTICLES		29.1		32.4		36.3			ART DIVERS EN MAT DIV 58
89399	OTHR PLASTC ARTICLES NES		28.3	MN 166468	31.1	MN 313251	35.0			AUT OUV MAT DIV 58
894	TOYS,SPORTING GOODS,ETC		10.0		16.0		16.9			VOITURES ENFANTS,JOUETS
8942	TOYS,INDOOR GAMES ETC		7.9		12.0		12.3			JOUETS,JEUX ETC
897	GOLD,SILVER WARE,JEWELRY		29.2		33.2		24.9			BIJOUTERIE,ORFEVRERIE
8973	PREC JEWLRY,GLD–SILVWARE		28.6		32.3		24.1			BIJOUX OR,ARGENT ORFEVRE
89732	GOLD,SILVER,ETC WARE		25.4		24.8		15.8			ORFEVRERIE MET PRECIEUX
898	MUSICAL INSTRUMENTS,PTS		9.7		11.3		11.4			INSTRUMENTS DE MUSIQUE
8983	SOUND RECRDNG TAPE,DISCS		8.8	N 1183673	9.5	N 2017545	9.7			SUPPORTS SON POUR 763
89832	RECORDED DISCS,TAPES ETC	N 853353	7.9	N 549273	8.0	N 953256	8.1			DISQUES,PHONO,BANDES
899	OTHER MANUFACTURED GOODS		8.1		10.5		10.1			AUT ART MANUF DIVERS NDA
9	GOODS NOT CLASSD BY KIND		26.0		24.9		32.8			ART TRANSACT NON CLASSES
971	*GOLD,NON MONETARY NES		23.6	K 1626	22.6		31.0			OR NON MONETAIRE
97101	NONMON GLD UNWRT,SEMIMFD		23.6	K 1626	22.6	K 13759	31.0			OR,ALLIAGES D'OR BRUTS

5. General Exports F.O.B. by Commodities according to the S.I.T.C. (Rev. 2) in million U.S. Dollars
Exportations Générales F.O.B. par Produits d'après la C.T.C.I. (Rév. 2) en millions de Dollars E.U.

SITC CTCI	COMMODITY	1994 QUANTITY QUANTITE	1994 VALUE VALEUR	1995 QUANTITY QUANTITE	1995 VALUE VALEUR	1996 QUANTITY QUANTITE	1996 VALUE VALEUR	1997 QUANTITY QUANTITE	1997 VALUE VALEUR	PRODUIT
	ALL COMMODITIES		1557.7		1913.3		1747.9			TOUS PRODUITS
0	FOOD AND LIVE ANIMALS		24.1		26.4		32.6			ALIMENTS,ANIMAUX VIVANTS
03	FISH AND PREPARATIONS		6.7		4.4		6.1			POISSONS ET PREPARATIONS
034	FISH,FRESH,CHILLED,FROZN		6.5	W 1025	4.0	W 1252	5.3			POISSON FRAIS, REFRIG,CONG
0341	FISH FRSH,CHLLD,EX FILLT		6.4	W 1024	4.0	W 567	2.4			POISSON FRAIS,REFRIGERE
09	MISC EDIBLE PRODUCTS		9.9		12.9		16.8			PREP ALIMENTAIRES DIVERSES
098	EDIBLE PRODCTS,PREPS NES		9.9		12.6		16.1			PREP ALIMENTAIRES NDA
09809	MISC FOOD PREPRTIONS NES		8.0	N 5210576	10.7	N 16376	0.1			PREP ALIMENTAIRES NDA
1	BEVERAGES AND TOBACCO		12.4		14.5		24.5			BOISSONS ET TABACS
11	BEVERAGES		6.5		6.5		6.5			BOISSONS
112	ALCOHOLIC BEVERAGES	W 1852	1.0	W 2164	1.1		6.1			BOISSONS ALCOOLIQUES
1124	DISTILLED ALCOHOLIC BEVS	W 431	4.8	W 380	4.6	W 447	4.7			ALCOOLS,EAUX-DE-VIE
12	TOBACCO AND MANUFACTURES		5.9		8.0		18.0			TABACS BRUTS FABRIQUES
122	TOBACCO,MANUFACTURED	W 161	5.9	W 292	8.0	W 757	18.0			TABACS FABRIQUES
1222	CIGARETTES	W 133	5.2	W 186	6.7	W 599	16.3			CIGARETTES
2	CRUDE MATERLS,EXCL FUELS		6.4		6.3		4.5			MAT BRUTES NON COMESTIBLES
3	MINERAL FUELS ETC		29.7		29.7		47.0			COMBUSTIBLES MINERAUX LUB
33	PETROLEUM AND PRODUCTS		29.7		29.7		47.0			PETROLE ET DERIVES
334	PETROLEUM PRODUCTS,REFIN		29.7	W 114334	29.7	W 173613	47.0			PRODUITS RAFFINES
5	CHEMCLS,RELATED PROD NES		35.8		41.1		50.8			PRODUITS CHIMIQUES
51	ORGANIC CHEMICALS		0.6		0.8		5.9			PROD CHIMIQ ORGANIQUES
541	*MEDICINAL,PHARM PRODUCT		19.5		22.8	K 2682671	22.2			PROD MEDICINAUX PHARMACEUT
5417	MEDICAMENTS		18.6		21.0	K 2018344	22.0			MEDICAMENTS
54179	— CONTNG OTH SUBSTANCES		17.6		20.4	K 1374333	21.5			MED CONT AUT SUBSTANCES
55	PERFUME,CLEANING ETC PRD		13.5		14.4		17.8			PROD POUR PARFUM,TOILETTE
553	PERFUMERY,COSMETICS,ETC	W 120	6.5	N 6855556	12.0	N 6601917	14.5			PRODUITS DE PARFUMERIE
6	BASIC MANUFACTURES		97.2		116.3		131.9			ART MANUFACTURES
61	LEATHER,DRESSED FUR,ETC		27.2		31.8		34.8			CUIRS,PELLETERIES
612	LEATHER ETC MANUFACTURES		25.3		31.3		34.1			OUVRAGES EN CUIRS NDA
6123	PREPRD PARTS OF FOOTWEAR		24.1	P 2083097	29.8	P 2917941	32.9			PARTIES DE CHAUSSURES
62	RUBBER MANUFACTURES NES		30.4		38.8		38.4			CAOUTCHOUC MANUFACTURE
628	RUBBER ARTICLES NES		30.1	MN 943364	38.6	MN 874465	37.9			OUVRAGES CAOUTCHOUC NDA
6289	OTH RUBBER ARTICLES NES		30.1	MN 943364	38.6	MN 874467	38.0			AUT OUVR CAOUTCHOUC NDA
62898	UNHARD RUBBER PRODS NES	W 1	0.1	MN 943364	38.6	MN 874465	38.0			OUV CAOUT VULC NON DURCI
64	PAPER,PAPERBOARD AND MFR		4.8		1.9		8.8			PAPIERS,CARTONS & OUVRAGES
65	TEXTILE YARN,FABRICS,ETC		14.9		22.7		21.8			FILS,TISSUS,ARTICLES TEXTILE
651	TEXTILE YARN		8.3	W 3492	15.9	W 2918	14.1			FILS TEXTILES
6514	SYN FIB YRN,BULK,MONOFIL	W 2189	8.3	W 3462	15.7	W 2846	13.6			FILS CONT 85% FIB TEXT SYNTH
65142	— NONTXT ETC CONT PAMID	W 2037	7.5	W 3067	14.0	W 2024	10.1			FILS NON TEX FI CON POLYAMID
69	METAL MANUFACTURES NES		13.5		13.8		21.3			ART MANUFACT EN METAL NDA
691	STRUCTURES AND PARTS NES	W 766	1.5		0.1	N 485	0.1			CONSTRUCT FER,ACIER,ALU
6911	STRUCTURES,PARTS IRN,STL	W 737	1.5		0.1	N 181	0.1			CONSTRUCT FER,ACIER,FONTE
697	BASE MTL HOUSEHOLD EQUIP		6.1	N 258729	6.4	N 229421	5.7			ART MENAGE MET COMMUNS
6975	BASE MTL INDR SANIT WARE		6.0	N 232917	6.3	N 220008	5.5			ART HYG NDA FER,AC,CU,ALU
69751	IRON,STL INDR SANIT WARE		6.0	N 232917	6.3	N 220008	5.5			ART HYGIENE NDA FER,ACIER
7	MACHINES,TRANSPORT EQUIP		1004.5		1269.3		1050.6			MACHINES MATERIEL TRANSPORT
71	POWER GENERATING EQUIPMT		14.9		24.7		21.3			MACHINES GENERATRICES
714	ENGINES AND MOTORS NES		14.3		19.8		18.6			MOTEURS NON ELECTRIQUES
7144	REACTION ENGINES	N 52	4.2	N 49	7.1	N 72	11.2			PROPULSEURS A REACTION
7148	GAS TURBINES NES		2.5	N 38	6.9	N 67	3.6			TURBINES A GAZ
7149	ENGINE & MOTOR PARTS NES		5.7	W 9	5.9	W 3	4.0			PIECES 714 ET 718.88
71491	PARTS NES OF 7144,71481		5.7	W 3	5.9	W 3	4.0			PIECES DES PROPULSEURS
72	MACHS FOR SPCL INDUSTRYS		9.6		3.2		13.3			MAC SPECIALES POUR INDUST
726	PRINTG,BKBINDG MACHY,PTS		6.1	W 3	0.1		7.8			MACHINES POUR IMPRIMERIE
7269	PTS OF 72631, 7264, 7267		5.6	W 13	0.9	W 85	7.4			PIECES 726.31 726.4 726.7
72699	PTS NES OF MCH OF 7264,7		5.6	W 13	0.8	W 85	7.4			PIECES 726.4 ET 726.7
74	GENRL INDUSTRL MACHY NES		23.6		17.3		23.4			MACH APP INDUSTRIE
741	HEATING,COOLING EQUIPMNT		3.8		4.8		9.5			MACH CHAUFFAGE,PIECES
7416	HEATING,COOLING EQU NES	N 7	0.1		0.1	N 35628	5.3			APP CHANGEMENT TEMP
742	PUMPS FOR LIQUIDS ETC		13.6		5.5		4.8			POMPES MOTO-POMPES
7428	OTHER PUMPS FOR LIQUIDS	N 8212	8.8		0.3	N 416	0.1			AUTRES POMPES POUR LIQ
74288	PUMPS FR LIQUIDS NES ETC	N 8233	8.9		0.3	N 173	0.1			POMPES POUR LIQUIDES NDA
7429	PTS NES OF PUMPS OF 742	W 167	4.8	W 41	3.8	W 192	4.7			PIECES POUR GROUPE 742
749	NONELEC MACH PTS,ACC NES		4.3		5.1		5.8			PIECES MACH NON ELEC NDA
75	OFFICE MACHNES,ADP EQUIP		20.1		29.9		18.6			MACH BUREAU TRAIT AUTOM
759	OFFICE,ADP MCH PTS,ACCES		17.9	W 313	27.9	W 21	13.8			PIECES DU 751 ET 752
7599	ACCTG,ETC,ADP MCH PTS,AC		17.8	W 311	27.8	W 16	13.5			PIECES DU 751 ET 752
76	TELECOMM,SOUND EQUIPMENT		26.2		25.3		27.8			EQUIPMENT DE TELECOM
761	TELEVISION RECEIVERS	N 152926	23.0	N 73833	14.7	N 558	0.2			RECEPTEURS DE TELEVISION
7611	COLOUR TV RECEIVERS	N 152919	23.0	N 74547	14.9	N 555	0.2			RECEPTEURS COULEUR
764	TELECOM EQPT,PTS,ACC NES		3.0		10.4		26.7			EQUIP TELECOM,PIECES
7643	TV,RADIO TRANSMITTRS ETC		0.1	N 275	4.2	N 10638	22.1			APP EMET TELE RADIO
77	ELECTRIC MACHNRY NES ETC		877.6		1094.9		919.7			MACH APP ELECT NDA
771	ELECTRIC POWER MACHY NES		5.3		5.8		5.4			MACH PROD,TRANS ELECTR
772	SWITCHGEAR ETC,PARTS NES		62.5	MN 15110	65.4	N 3004382	3.4			APP COUPURE,SECT ETC
7721	SWITCHGEAR ETC		48.6	MN 15197	55.8	MN 42742	48.4			APP COUPURE,SECTIONMNT
7722	PRINTED CIRCUITS,PTS NES		13.9	N 60885	10.7	N 4105	0.6			CIRCUITS ET PIECES
775	HOUSEHOLD TYPE EQUIP NES		4.2		5.6	N 1218199	7.0			MACH,APP USAGE DOMESTQUE
7758	ELECTRO-THERMIC APPL NES		4.0		5.5	N 1218196	7.0			APP ELECTROTHERMIQ NDA
77582	ELEC SOIL,SPACE HEATERS		0.1		0.1	N 1065345	5.7			APP ELECT CHAUF LOCAUX
776	TRANSISTORS,VALVES,ETC		804.4		1009.2		851.9			LAMPES,TUBES,VALVES
7763	DIODES,TRANSISTORS,ETC		804.0	MN 89122	404.6	N 385176	32.6			DIODES,TRANSISTORS
7764	ELECTRONIC MICROCIRCUITS		0.1	N 3883672	407.0	MN 169851	818.5			MICROSTRUCTURES ELECTRON
7768	ELCTRNC COMP PTS,CRYSTLS		0.3	W 535	197.7	W 38	0.6			CRIST PIEZO-ELEC,PCS 776
77689	ELECTRNIC COMPON PTS NES		0.3	W 535	197.7	W 38	0.6			PIECES DU GROUPE 776
778	ELECTRICAL MACHINERY NES		0.2		6.2		3.5			AUTRES MACH ELECT NDA
78	ROAD VEHICLES		3.2		4.9		6.5			VEHICULES ROUTIERS
79	OTHR TRANSPORT EQUIPMENT		28.1		66.7		17.2			AUTRE MATERIEL TRANSPORT
792	AIRCRAFT ETC		27.6		27.3		16.6			APP NAVIGATION AERIENNE
7923	AIRCRFT NES2000-15000KG		4.9							AERODYNES 2000 A 15000 KG
7929	AIRCRAFT PARTS NES		22.7		27.3		16.6			PIECES DU 792
793	SHIPS AND BOATS ETC		0.6		39.3		0.5			NAVIRES BATEAUX,ETC
7932	SHIPS AND BOATS NES		0.5		39.3		0.5			NAVIRES ET BATEAUX
79322	TANKERS OF ALL KINDS				16.0		0.2			BATEAUX-CITERNES
79323	OTHER CARGO VESSELS		0.1		22.9		0.1			AUT BATEAUX TRANS MARCH
8	MISC MANUFACTURED GOODS		347.4		407.1		405.1			ART MANUFACTURES DIVERS
831	*TRAVEL GOODS,HANDBAGS		5.6	N 2999580	8.0	N 3300002	8.3			ARTICLES DE VOYAGE ETC
84	CLOTHING AND ACCESSORIES		141.6		161.6		163.4			VETEMENTS
842	MENS OUTERWEAR NOT KNIT		96.5		119.8	N 7302232	124.9			VET DESSUS POUR HOMMES
8422	— SUITS	N 118830	8.1		14.8	N 172641	14.5			COMPLETS HOMMES MAT TEXT
84221	—— OF WOOL,FINE HAIR	N 201	0.1		0.4	N 84121	8.2			COMPLETS HOMMES LAINE

5. General Exports F.O.B. by Commodities according to the S.I.T.C. (Rev. 2) in million U.S. Dollars
Exportations Générales F.O.B. par Produits d'après la C.T.C.I. (Rév. 2) en millions de Dollars E.U.

SITC CTCI	COMMODITY	1994 QUANTITY QUANTITE	1994 VALUE VALEUR	1995 QUANTITY QUANTITE	1995 VALUE VALEUR	1996 QUANTITY QUANTITE	1996 VALUE VALEUR	1997 QUANTITY QUANTITE	1997 VALUE VALEUR	PRODUIT
84223	—— OF MAN–MADE FIBRES	N 118629	8.0	N 215895	14.5	N 88520	6.3			COMPLETS HOMMES FIB SYNT
8423	— TROUSERS,BREECHES ETC	N 5223550	66.7	N 4841078	81.4	N 6706623	92.0			PANTALONS HOMMES MAT TEX
8424	— JACKETS,BLAZERS ETC	N 412782	18.3	N 319108	20.7	N 298315	16.6			VESTES HOMMES MAT TEXTIL
843	WOMENS OUTERWEAR NONKNIT	N 1369295	26.8	N 1201089	24.8	N 1961182	24.3			VET DESSUS FEMMES MAT TEX
8431	— COATS AND JACKETS	N 140754	8.8	N 44064	2.5	N 42970	2.1			MANT,VEST FEM MAT TEXTIL
8439	— OTHER OUTER GARMENTS	N 496706	9.4	N 715079	13.7	N 1674558	17.9			AUT VET DES FEM MAT TEXT
846	UNDER GARMENTS KNITTED		11.6	N 1797587	7.9	N 2397605	6.8			SOUS VETS DE BONNETERIE
8462	— OF COTTON NON ELASTIC		4.8	N 1197032	3.4	N 2054152	5.3			SOUS–VET BONNET COTON
84629	—— OTHER		4.8	N 1197032	3.4	N 2054152	5.3			AUT SOUS–VET BONNET COTON
8465	CORSETS,GARTERS,ETC		6.5	N 593577	4.5	N 275079	1.3			CORSETS,GAINES ART SIM
84651	BRASSIERES	N 1169792	6.1	N 501264	3.9	N 53764	0.3			SOUTIENS–GORGE,BUSTIERS
87	PRECISION INSTRUMNTS NES		25.5		43.3		44.3			INSTRUM,APPAR SCIENT NDA
872	MEDICAL INSTRUMENTS NES		21.9	MN 28429	38.0	MN 35872	36.9			INSTR,APP MEDIC–CHIR NDA
87202	OTH MEDICAL INSTRUMENTS	W 4	0.3	MN 28429	38.0	MN 36584	37.2			INSTRUM,APP MEDECINE
874	MEASURNG,CONTROLNG INSTR		3.0		4.2		6.9			INSTRUMENTS DE MESURE
88	PHOTO EQU,OPTICL GDS ETC		34.0		41.0		33.7			APP,FOURN PHOTO,OP,MONTR
884	OPTICAL GOODS NES		27.5	MN 13437	36.0	N 1478740	29.5			ELEMENTS OPTIQ,ART LUNET
8842	SPECTACLES AND FRAMES		27.5	MN 13437	36.0	N 1470271	29.3			LUNETTES ET MONTURES
88421	SPECTACLE FRAMES		26.4	MW 3	0.4	N 1215247	24.2			MONTURES DE LUNETTES
885	WATCHES AND CLOCKS		6.3		3.9		3.1			HORLOGERIE
8852	CLOCKS,CLOCK,WATCH PARTS		6.3		3.8		3.0			HORLOGES,MOUV,PARTIES
88524	TIME SWITCHES		6.1		3.6		3.0			APP DECLENC MECANISME
89	MISC MANUFCTRD GOODS NES		133.9		145.9		148.6			ART MANUFACTURES DIVERS
892	PRINTED MATTER		53.7		50.2		54.5			IMPRIMES
8928	PRINTED MATTER NES		51.3		47.7		51.3			IMPRIMES NDA
89283	UNISSUED BANKNOTES ETC		51.1	W 1555	47.5	W 1913	51.0			TIMBRES–POSTE FISCAUX
893	ARTICLES OF PLASTIC NES		12.6		12.9		16.8			OUVRAGES EN MAT DIVIS 58
8931	PLSTC PACKG CONTNRS,LIDS		11.6	MN 31623	11.6	MN 46278	15.6			ART TRANSP EMBALLAGE ETC
894	TOYS,SPORTING GOODS,ETC		32.3		44.6		39.8			VOITURES ENFANTS,JOUETS
8942	TOYS,INDOOR GAMES ETC		32.3		44.5	MN 61056	39.5			JOUETS,JEUX ETC
89422	DOLLS		12.4	MN 29153	16.6	MN 28974	13.1			POUPEES
89423	TOYS NES		19.9	MN 39497	27.9	MN 32077	26.4			JOUETS,MODELES REDUITS
896	WORKS OF ART ETC		0.3		2.0		5.8			OBJETS D'ART
89606	ANTIQUES NES		0.1		0.4		5.6			OBJETS D'ANTIQUITE
897	GOLD,SILVER WARE,JEWELRY		34.4		35.2		30.0			BIJOUTERIE,ORFEVRERIE
8973	PREC JEWLRY,GLD–SILVWARE		33.6		35.1		30.0			BIJOUX OR,ARGENT ORFEVRE
89731	PRECIOUS METAL JEWELLERY		33.3		33.6		29.9			ART BIJOUTERIE,JOAILLER

1. HISTORICAL SERIES, 1961–1996 GENERAL TRADE, IMPORTS C.I.F., EXPORTS F.O.B.
SERIES HISTORIQUES, 1961–1996 COMMERCE GENERAL, IMPORTATIONS C.A.F., EXPORTATIONS F.O.B

YEAR ANNEE	VALUE IN MILLION MAUR. RUPEES / VALEUR EN MILLION MAUR. RUPEES — MERCHANDISE –MARCHANDISE IMPORTS	EXPORTS	GOLD –OR IMPORTS	EXPORTS	CONVERSION FACTORS U.S. CENTS PER MAUR. RUPEE FACTEURS DE CONVERSION CENTS E.U. PAR MAUR. RUPEE IMPORTS	EXPORTS	INDEX NUMBERS –INDICES — QUANTUM IMPORTS	EXPORTS	UNIT VALUE / VALEUR UNITAIRE IMPORTS	EXPORTS
1961	324.00	294.20	0.14		21.0000	21.0000				
1962	322.70	305.90	0.03		21.0000	21.0000				
1963	333.10	427.80	0.37		21.0000	21.0000				
1964	388.90	366.90	0.39		21.0000	21.0000				
1965	367.30	313.40	0.42		21.0000	21.0000				
1966	333.20	337.60	0.48		21.0000	21.0000				
1967	371.10	306.80	0.77		21.0000	21.0000				
1968	421.10	354.00	0.87		18.0000	18.0000				
1969	376.00	365.20	0.44		18.0000	18.0000				
1970	419.90	383.40	0.25		18.0000	18.0000				
1971	461.60	360.80	1.03		18.0000	18.0000				
1972	635.80	573.80	1.82		18.8495	18.6417				
1973	915.80	748.40			18.3641	18.2525				
1974	1759.80	1787.50	7.10		17.5784	17.4854				
1975	1995.30	1838.90			16.6315	16.2095				
1976	2397.90	1769.80			14.9559	14.9756				
1977	2950.80	2041.50		379.00	15.1551	15.1766				
1978	3076.40	1987.10			16.2961	16.3937				
1979	3634.40	2432.70			15.5665	15.4642				
1980	4721.40	3341.30			13.1176	12.8877			44	28
1981	4976.80	2999.20			11.1325	10.8052			47	31
1982	5048.20	3988.70			9.1971	9.1971			59	34
1983	5175.00	4311.40			8.4120	8.3780			57	37
1984	6494.00	5180.30			7.2750	7.2016			64	41
1985	8119.00	6644.00			6.5143	6.5491			71	47
1986	9199.00	9062.00			7.4383	7.4582			57	49
1987	13037.00	11336.00			7.7676	7.7636			59	55
1988	17242.00	13455.00			7.4743	7.4113			79	80
1989	20217.01	15049.00			6.5570	6.5570			96	89
1990	24019.01	17677.01			6.7347	6.7517			100	100
1991	24383.01	18700.00			6.3942	6.3882			105	106
1992	25280.00	20244.00			6.4255	6.4255			107	114
1993	30319.01	22992.00			5.6584	5.6495			119	124
1994	34548.00	24097.01			5.5871	5.5895			127	130
1995	34071.01	26742.00			5.7511	5.7492			135	138
1996	40892.00	31391.01			5.5718	5.5765			144	153

2. IMPORTS BY BROAD ECONOMIC CATEGORY AND EXPORTS BY INDUSTRIAL ORIGIN. (PERCENTAGE OF TOTAL VALUE)
IMPORTATIONS PAR CATEGORIES ECONOMIQUES ET EXPORTATIONS PAR BRANCHE D'ACTIVITE.(EN POURCENTAGE DE LA VALEUR TOTALE)

IMPORTS – IMPORTATIONS

	1990	1991	1992	1993	1994	1995	1996
TOTAL IMPORTS–IMPORTATIONS TOTALES	100.	100.	100.	100.	100.	100.	100.
1 FOOD BEV–ALIMENTATION BOISSONS	11.6	11.5	12.2	12.8	13.3	15.5	15.1
11 PRIMARY–PRODUITS DE BASE	4.5	4.3	4.8	4.8	5.3	5.8	6.1
111 FOR INDUSTRY–POUR L'INDUSTRIE	1.1	0.7	1.1	1.5	1.7	1.7	1.9
112 FOR HOUSEHOLDS–POUR LES MENAGES	3.4	3.6	3.6	3.3	3.6	4.1	4.2
12 PROCESSED–PRODUITS ELABORES	7.1	7.2	7.5	8.0	8.0	9.7	9.0
121 FOR INDUSTRY–POUR L'INDUSTRIE	1.0	1.3	1.3	1.2	1.2	1.6	1.4
122 FOR HOUSEHOLDS–POUR LES MENAGES	6.0	5.9	6.2	6.8	6.8	8.1	7.6
2 IND SUPPLIES–APPROV INDUSTRIELS	44.3	42.3	42.9	46.9	44.8	47.8	45.6
21 PRIMARY–PRODUITS DE BASE	3.6	3.6	3.3	3.8	3.4	4.1	4.4
22 PROCESSED–PRODUITS ELABORES	40.8	38.8	39.6	43.1	41.3	43.7	41.1
3 FUELS–COMBUSTIBLES	7.7	10.2	8.5	6.7	5.9	6.7	7.8
31 PRIMARY–PRODUITS DE BASE	0.6	0.7	0.8	0.8	0.7	0.9	0.8
32 PROCESSED–PRODUITS ELABORES	7.1	9.5	7.7	5.9	5.2	5.9	7.0
321 MOTOR SPIRIT–ESSENCE	1.0	1.8					1.0
322 OTHER–AUTRES	6.1	7.7	7.7	5.9	5.2	5.9	6.1
4 MACHINERY–EQUIPEMENT	12.5	14.3	12.7	13.5	12.5	12.0	13.8
41 CAPITAL EQUIPMENT–MACHINES	11.4	13.0	11.3	12.3	11.4	10.7	12.6
42 PARTS–PIECES ACCESSOIRES	1.1	1.3	1.4	1.2	1.1	1.3	1.2
5 TRANSPORT–TRANSPORT	13.7	9.6	10.6	7.0	11.8	6.4	6.4
51 PASSENGER CARS–AUTOMOBILES	2.9	2.3	2.8	1.8	1.9	1.9	2.0
52 OTHER–AUTRES	7.5	3.9	3.9	3.3	8.3	2.2	2.0
521 INDUSTRIAL–INDUSTRIELS	6.9	3.2	3.3	2.8	8.0	2.0	1.8
522 NON INDUSTRIAL–NON INDUSTRIEL	0.6	0.7	0.6	0.5	0.3	0.2	0.2
53 PARTS–PIECES ACCESSOIRES	3.3	3.5	4.0	1.9	1.6	2.2	2.4
6 CONSUM GOODS–BIENS CONSOMMATION	9.9	11.7	12.7	12.9	11.6	11.6	10.6
61 DURABLE–DURABLES	3.6	5.0	4.8	4.4	3.8	3.7	3.5
62 SEMI DURABLE–SEMI DURABLES	3.8	4.0	4.8	5.3	4.7	4.6	4.0
63 NON DURABLE–NON DURABLES	2.4	2.7	3.1	3.2	3.1	3.2	3.2
7 GOODS NES–BIENS NDA	0.3	0.3	0.3	0.3	0.0	0.1	0.7

EXPORTS – EXPORTATIONS

	1990	1991	1992	1993	1994	1995	1996
TOTAL EXPORTS–EXPORTATIONS TOTALES	100.	100.	100.	100.	100.	100.	100.
1 AGRICULTURE	1.4	1.6	1.4	1.4	1.4	1.4	1.2
2 MINING QUARRY–INDUS EXTRACTIVES	2.1	2.1	1.6	1.8	1.9	1.7	1.6
3 MANUFACTURING–IND MANUFACTUR	96.5	96.3	96.9	96.7	96.7	97.0	97.2
31 FOOD BEV TOBACCO–ALIM BOISS TAB	31.0	30.2	30.1	28.4	28.0	28.1	30.5
32 TEXTILES–INDUSTRIES TEXTILES	54.2	54.5	54.5	59.5	58.7	58.1	59.7
33 WOOD & PRODUCTS–BOIS & PRODUITS	0.3	0.2	0.2	0.1	0.2	0.1	0.1
34 PAPER & PRODUCTS–PAPIER & PRODT	0.2	0.1	0.3	0.1	0.2	0.2	0.3
35 CHEMICALS–INDUSTRIES CHIMIQUES	2.4	2.9	3.0	1.1	0.9	1.0	0.8
36 NON METAL MIN–MIN NON METAL	0.1	0.0	0.2	0.3	0.3	0.4	0.3
37 BASIC METAL–IND METAL BASE	0.1	0.0	0.1	0.0	0.0	0.0	0.0
38 METAL MANUF–MANUF METAL	4.5	4.8	4.4	3.6	5.0	5.1	2.7
39 OTH MANUF IND–AUTRES MANUF	3.8	3.6	4.2	3.5	3.5	3.8	2.8

3. TRADE BY PRINCIPAL COUNTRIES OF ORIGIN AND DESTINATION (VALUE IN MILLION U.S. DOLLARS)
ECHANGES SELON LES PRINCIPAUX PAYS D'ORIGINE ET DE DESTINATION (VALEUR EN MILLIONS DE DOLLARS EU)

COUNTRIES–PAYS	GENERAL IMPORTS C.I.F. IMPORTATIONS GENERALES C.A.F					COUNTRIES–PAYS	GENERAL EXPORTS F.O.B. EXPORTATIONS GENERALES F.O.B.				
	1992	1993	1994	1995	1996		1992	1993	1994	1995	1996
World	1782.9	1919.1	1923.9	2000.5	2276.9	Monde	1335.5	1467.1	1348.0	1538.3	1699.4
Africa	295.0	336.9	291.7	302.8	349.3	Afrique	73.7	94.4	83.8	94.5	79.6
Americas	82.7	69.7	72.0	95.7	107.0	Amériques	175.6	271.2	272.8	261.5	242.2
– Northern America	54.9	48.0	45.4	54.8	59.9	– Amérique du Nord	171.3	270.3	255.9	242.3	239.0
– LAIA	27.5	21.5	22.3	39.0	45.5	– ALAI	0.4	0.5	16.0	0.8	1.8
– CACM	0.0	0.1	0.0	0.0	0.1	– MCAC	0.5	0.1	0.0		0.0
– Caribbean	0.2	0.1	4.1	1.9	0.8	– Caraïbes	1.0	0.3	0.7	18.4	0.7
– Rest of America	0.1	0.1	0.1	0.1	0.7	– Autre Amérique	2.5	0.0	0.1	0.1	0.7
Asia excl fmr USSR	701.4	739.8	731.3	776.3	880.3	Asie anc. URSS exclus	35.5	27.8	31.3	40.0	33.0
– Middle East	48.4	27.9	64.2	83.8	108.9	– Moyen–Orient	1.5	0.7	0.4	0.6	0.9
Asia former USSR				0.7	0.4	Asie ancienne URSS				0.1	0.0
Europe excl fmr USSR	605.3	688.6	751.9	729.8	807.9	Europe anc. URSS exclus	1025.5	1069.9	956.8	1136.8	1338.6
– European Union	571.3	652.0	709.2	672.3	751.8	– Union Européenne	1008.4	1049.1	938.0	1114.6	1315.6
– Eastern Europe	1.6	1.3	3.0	7.5	3.1	– Europe de l'Est	0.2	0.2	0.3	0.4	0.4
– Rest of Europe	32.4	35.2	39.8	50.1	53.0	– Autre de l'Europe	16.9	20.6	18.5	21.8	22.6
Europe former USSR	4.6	4.4	0.3	2.0	2.6	Europe ancienne URSS	1.6	0.3	1.2	1.0	0.3
Oceania	75.4	79.6	76.5	88.6	125.7	Océanie	4.0	3.4	1.9	3.4	5.4
Other	18.5	0.1	0.1	4.5	3.7	Autre	19.6	0.1	0.2	1.0	0.2
France, Monaco	231.4	242.4	356.6	278.9	255.4	United Kingdom	449.8	476.8	430.9	527.4	600.3
So. African Customs Un	232.2	275.4	234.4	225.7	277.5	France, Monaco	272.1	300.0	270.9	325.5	362.6
India/Inde	84.0	112.2	128.2	166.8	201.6	USA/Etats–Unis d'Amer	160.7	262.5	244.3	228.0	227.5
United Kingdom	123.4	135.7	128.8	131.5	146.2	Germany/Allemagne	114.6	104.0	79.7	89.7	93.6
Japan/Japon	168.8	113.4	97.8	94.4	100.3	Italy/Italie	60.3	58.5	56.1	63.1	70.5
Germany/Allemagne	83.8	92.3	88.8	89.4	106.0	Netherlands/Pays–Bas	23.6	30.5	28.5	33.3	42.3
China, Hong Kong SAR	70.2	88.2	99.1	94.4	82.2	Madagascar	15.2	29.6	31.7	39.8	39.0
China/Chine	55.1	80.8	69.3	57.8	97.0	Belgium–Luxembourg	23.0	31.6	28.6	29.4	39.9
Other Asia n.e.s.	62.8	79.9	67.6	62.3	62.5	Spain/Espagne	30.9	36.4	24.9	21.1	36.2
Australia/Australie	52.8	56.8	57.2	63.8	100.9	Reunion/Réunion	29.1	30.7	27.2	28.2	
Italy/Italie	53.7	64.9	55.2	63.8	77.6	Portugal	20.8	4.4	12.2	14.1	56.3
Singapore/Singapour	55.7	56.5	55.4	52.3	48.4	Switzerland,Liechtenst.	15.5	19.1	16.9	20.8	21.1
Malaysia/Malaisie	48.1	52.8	45.2	64.5	53.7	Canada	10.5	7.8	11.6	14.3	11.5
USA/Etats–Unis d'Amer	52.9	45.8	43.1	51.3	57.0	China, Hong Kong SAR	5.3	7.9	12.5	13.5	10.1
Switzerland,Liechtenst.	28.8	34.5	38.9	46.6	49.0	So. African Customs Un	12.3	7.6	5.2	6.8	12.0
Belgium–Luxembourg	24.0	47.6	30.3	32.1	38.4	Japan/Japon	3.1	5.8	5.5	9.8	10.4
Pakistan	19.6	29.3	27.8	21.0	35.9	Zimbabwe	3.6	5.4	4.6	6.6	8.7
Korea, Republic of	25.9	28.4	26.5	25.1	27.5	Singapore/Singapour	6.3	6.1	3.4	3.4	2.0
Kuwait/Koweït	0.0		16.3	44.6	69.5	Sweden/Suède	4.5	1.0	1.9	3.9	6.7
New Zealand	22.5	22.8	19.3	24.7	24.8	Areas n.e.s.	16.1	0.1	0.2	1.0	0.2
Kenya	25.0	22.5	20.5	21.4	14.3	Bahamas	0.3	0.0		17.3	0.0
Denmark/Danemark	4.8	24.2	5.4	12.7	54.4	Other Asia n.e.s.	11.3	1.6	1.5	1.3	1.4
Indonesia/Indonésie	15.0	25.5	16.5	16.8	24.9	Brazil/Brésil	0.2	0.2	15.7	0.1	0.7
Thailand/Thaïlande	22.1	23.3	17.2	15.8	15.0	Australia/Australie	3.6	3.1	1.5	3.0	4.8
Spain/Espagne	9.2	11.5	14.1	21.7	33.7	India/Inde	1.0	1.0	3.5	7.1	3.0
Madagascar	15.6	16.0	11.7	20.3	25.9	Seychelles	2.7	3.2	2.9	2.6	1.9
Argentina/Argentine	17.1	14.8	17.8	16.5	15.2	Kenya	1.6	3.8	2.1	1.8	3.5
Saudi Arabia	4.7	3.8	25.6	21.7	11.9	Denmark/Danemark	2.8	2.6	1.1	2.1	2.6
Netherlands/Pays–Bas	12.4	13.8	12.6	12.9	12.3	Comoros/Comores	2.1	2.1	2.5	2.4	1.2
Brazil/Brésil	9.9	5.2	3.3	20.6	11.5	Austria/Autriche	2.2	1.7	1.3	2.1	2.2
Bahrain/Bahreïn	24.9	0.8	3.6	4.4	12.3	United Rep of Tanzania	0.6	2.1	0.1	0.9	4.6
Turkey/Turquie	3.6	4.9	10.2	6.7	10.1	Ireland/Irlande	2.4	0.9	1.3	1.8	1.2
Ireland/Irlande	4.4	5.5	6.0	8.9	9.4	Mozambique	1.1	4.8	1.0	0.2	0.0
Burkina Faso	2.0	5.5	7.2	4.4	12.6	Pakistan	2.7	2.2	1.6	0.4	0.2
Zimbabwe	4.1	6.4	8.3	9.0	3.4	Rwanda	2.1	1.3	1.1	0.9	1.2
Israel/Israël	8.7	5.2	6.1	4.4	6.7	Malawi	0.1	0.6	1.2	0.5	3.8
Areas n.e.s.	18.0	0.1	0.1	4.5	3.7	Thailand/Thaïlande	0.4	0.1	0.7	1.0	2.3
Philippines	4.4	9.9	3.0	4.4	3.0	Burundi	0.2	0.6	2.2	0.4	0.5
Jordan/Jordanie	2.6	11.2	4.6	2.1	2.0	Uganda/Ouganda	0.1	0.8	0.7	1.6	0.8
United Arab Emirates	9.1	6.7	1.4	3.5	1.7	Israel/Israël	2.0	0.8	0.5	0.1	0.2

(VALUE AS PERCENTAGE OF WORLD TOTAL)(VALEURS EN POURCENTAGE DU TOTAL MONDIAL)

	1987	1988	1989	1990	1991	1992	1993	1994	1995	1996
Africa	2.3	9.6	10.2	12.1	15.8	16.5	17.6	15.2	15.1	15.3
Americas	1.0	12.8	2.9	5.6	4.4	4.6	3.6	3.7	4.8	4.7
– Northern America	0.8	12.1	1.7	4.5	2.8	3.1	2.5	2.4	2.7	2.6
– LAIA	0.2	0.7	1.1	1.0	1.5	1.5	1.1	1.2	1.9	2.0
– CACM				0.0	0.0	0.0	0.0	0.0	0.0	0.0
– Caribbean				0.0	0.0	0.0	0.0	0.2	0.1	0.0
– Rest of America				0.1	0.0	0.0	0.0	0.0	0.0	0.0
Asia excl fmr USSR	31.6	40.1	45.8	39.5	41.0	39.3	38.5	38.0	38.8	38.7
– Middle East	6.4	4.7	6.8	5.5	5.8	2.7	1.5	3.3	4.2	4.8
Asia former USSR									0.0	0.0
Europe excl fmr USSR	13.5	33.2	36.6	38.6	33.4	33.9	35.9	39.1	36.5	35.5
– European Union	13.0	31.2	34.6	36.7	31.9	32.0	34.0	36.9	33.6	33.0
– Eastern Europe		0.1	0.1	0.1	0.1	0.1	0.1	0.2	0.4	0.1
– Rest of Europe	0.5	1.9	1.9	1.8	1.4	1.8	1.8	2.1	2.5	2.3
Europe former USSR		0.0		0.0	0.3	0.3	0.2	0.0	0.1	0.1
Oceania	2.6	3.8	4.0	3.7	4.4	4.2	4.1	4.0	4.4	5.5
Other	48.9	0.4	0.6	0.5	0.9	1.0	0.0	0.0	0.2	0.2
France, Monaco	7.2	12.4	13.6	14.5	12.6	13.0	12.6	18.5	13.9	11.2
So. African Customs Un	2.0	8.6	9.0	8.8	11.6	13.0	14.3	12.2	11.3	12.2
India/Inde	1.9	3.7	3.8	4.1	4.3	4.7	5.8	6.7	8.3	8.9
United Kingdom	2.1	7.3	6.4	7.1	6.5	6.9	7.1	6.7	6.6	6.4
Japan/Japon	5.5	7.4	9.1	7.4	8.7	9.5	5.9	5.1	4.7	4.4
Germany/Allemagne					5.2	4.7	4.8	4.6	4.5	4.7
China, Hong Kong SAR	4.3	5.5	4.8	3.7	4.0	3.9	4.6	5.1	4.7	3.6
China/Chine	3.6	3.9	4.9	3.3	3.6	3.1	4.2	3.6	2.9	4.3
Other Asia n.e.s.	3.7	4.4	5.3	4.6	4.2	3.5	4.2	3.5	3.1	2.7
Australia/Australie	1.4	2.6	2.5	2.4	3.1	3.0	3.0	3.0	3.2	4.4

	1987	1988	1989	1990	1991	1992	1993	1994	1995	1996
Afrique	0.4	3.4	3.7	4.2	4.9	5.5	6.4	6.2	6.1	4.7
Amériques	14.5	15.1	15.7	13.5	12.4	13.2	18.5	20.2	17.0	14.3
– Amérique du Nord	14.5	15.1	14.8	13.2	12.1	12.8	18.4	19.0	15.7	14.1
– ALAI				0.0	0.0	0.0	0.0	1.2	0.1	0.1
– MCAC				0.0	0.0	0.0	0.0	0.0		0.0
– Caraïbes			0.9	0.0	0.1	0.1	0.0	0.1	1.2	0.0
– Autre Amérique				0.2	0.2	0.2	0.0	0.0	0.0	0.0
Asie anc. URSS exclus	0.3	2.5	1.9	2.4	3.0	2.7	1.9	2.3	2.6	1.9
– Moyen–Orient			0.2	0.1	0.1	0.1	0.0	0.0	0.0	0.1
Asie ancienne URSS									0.0	0.0
Europe anc. URSS exclus	66.8	78.1	76.1	78.1	79.0	76.8	72.9	71.0	73.9	78.8
– Union Européenne	66.8	77.4	75.3	77.0	77.6	75.5	71.5	69.6	72.5	77.4
– Europe de l'Est				0.0	0.0	0.0	0.0	0.0	0.0	0.0
– Autre de l'Europe		0.7	0.8	1.1	1.3	1.3	1.4	1.4	1.4	1.3
Europe ancienne URSS	0.3	0.0	1.3	0.1	0.1	0.1	0.0	0.1	0.1	0.0
Océanie	0.4	0.2	0.2	0.2	0.3	0.3	0.2	0.1	0.2	0.3
Autre	17.4	0.7	1.1	1.4	0.4	1.5	0.0	0.0	0.1	0.0
United Kingdom	33.1	35.7	35.8	35.3	35.4	33.7	32.5	32.0	34.3	35.3
France, Monaco	21.4	22.5	19.8	22.1	19.6	20.4	20.4	20.1	21.2	21.3
USA/Etats–Unis d'Amer	12.6	13.3	13.8	12.7	11.6	12.0	17.9	18.1	14.8	13.4
Germany/Allemagne					10.8	8.6	7.1	5.9	5.8	5.5
Italy/Italie	1.9	3.8	3.8	4.4	4.8	4.5	4.0	4.2	4.1	4.1
Netherlands/Pays–Bas	1.2	1.2	2.3	1.7	1.9	1.8	2.1	2.1	2.2	2.5
Madagascar		0.2	0.3	0.8	0.6	1.1	2.0	2.4	2.6	2.3
Belgium–Luxembourg	1.3	2.3	2.0	2.3	1.8	1.7	2.2	2.1	1.9	2.3
Spain/Espagne				0.5	1.6	2.3	2.5	1.8	1.4	2.1
Reunion/Réunion	0.3	2.1	1.9	1.8	1.9	2.2	2.1	2.0	1.8	

4. General Imports C.I.F. by Commodities according to the S.I.T.C. (Rev. 2) in million U.S. Dollars
Importations Générales C.A.F. par Produits d'après la C.T.C.I. (Rév. 2) en millions de Dollars E.U.

SITC CTCI	COMMODITY	1993 QUANTITY QUANTITE	1993 VALUE VALEUR	1994 QUANTITY QUANTITE	1994 VALUE VALEUR	1995 QUANTITY QUANTITE	1995 VALUE VALEUR	1996 QUANTITY QUANTITE	1996 VALUE VALEUR	PRODUIT
	ALL COMMODITIES		1919.2		1923.9		2000.5		2277.0	TOUS PRODUITS
0	FOOD AND LIVE ANIMALS		236.9		237.0		293.1		329.9	ALIMENTS,ANIMAUX VIVANTS
001	*LIVE ANIMALS FOR FOOD	N 182269	9.8	N 332303	10.5	N 198468	10.6	N 160529	7.7	ANIMAUX VIVANTS
0011	BOVINE SPECIES,LIVE	N 10641	8.6	N 11171	8.6	N 10063	9.4	N 8971	6.6	ESPECE BOVINE
00119	— OTHR THAN FR BREEDING	N 8896	7.3	N 9873	7.9	N 8801	8.4	N 6018	4.5	BOVINS NON REPRODUCTEURS
01	MEAT AND PREPARATIONS		26.6		31.3		31.1		32.2	VIANDES ET PREPARATIONS
011	MEAT FRESH,CHILLD,FROZEN	W 14584	21.2	W 17818	25.3	W 16442	26.0	W 14713	26.4	VIANDES FRAICHES,REF,CONGE
0111	BOVINE MEAT FRESH,FROZEN	W 7340	11.2	W 10584	14.8	W 9780	15.4	W 7719	13.4	VIANDES BOVIN FRAI,REF
01112	BOVINE MEAT BONELESS	W 7238	11.0	W 10413	14.3	W 9607	14.8	W 7130	12.6	VIANDES BOVIN DESOSSEES
0112	MUTTON ETC FRSH,CHLD,FRN	W 4489	7.1	W 5098	8.0	W 4643	8.1	W 5099	10.2	VIANDE DE MOUTON
014	MEAT PREPD,PRSVD,NES ETC	W 1952	5.5	W 2341	6.0	W 1632	5.1	W 1761	5.8	CONSERVES DE VIANDES
02	DAIRY PRODCTS,BIRDS'EGGS		42.0		42.5		72.8		52.5	PRODUITS LAITIERS,OEUFS
022	MILK AND CREAM	W 14048	32.4	W 15965	32.6	W 16240	62.5	W 15241	40.1	LAIT ET CREME
0224	MILK,CREAM PRESERVED ETC	W 12119	30.8	W 13792	31.1	W 13653	60.7	W 12634	38.1	LAIT,CREME CONS,CONC
02243	MILK DRY,OVER 1.5% FAT	W 10876	28.1	W 12264	27.9	W 12518	57.9	W 11769	36.1	LAIT POUDRE SUP 1.5%
024	CHEESE AND CURD	W 1731	7.2	W 1742	7.3	W 1818	7.8	W 1964	9.4	FROMAGE ET CAILLEBOTTE
03	FISH AND PREPARATIONS		23.8		27.3		36.6		42.2	POISSONS ET PREPARATIONS
034	FISH,FRESH,CHILLED,FROZN	W 12819	13.6	W 16216	17.7	W 25000	25.5	W 26798	30.9	POISSON FRAIS, REFRIG,CONG
0342	FISH FROZEN,EXCL FILLETS	W 12715	13.1	W 15986	17.0	W 24826	24.8	W 26619	30.1	POISSONS CONGELES
037	FISH ETC PREPD,PRSVD NES	W 3049	6.3	W 3358	6.1	W 3007	6.1	W 3168	6.4	POIS,CRUST,MOL PREPARES
0371	FISH PREPARD,PRESRVD NES	W 3041	6.2	W 3340	6.0	W 2992	6.0	W 3163	6.4	CONSERVES DE POISSONS
04	CEREALS AND PREPARATIONS		71.1		63.7		65.9		103.4	CEREALES ET PRODUITS
041	WHEAT ETC UNMILLED	W 124050	18.2	W 134686	20.1	W 112365	21.9	W 123739	33.4	FROMENT,EPEAUTRE
0411	DURUM WHEAT UNMILLED	W 52650	8.2	W 110274	17.1	W 55156	9.3	W 5970	1.5	FROMENT DUR NON MOULU
0412	OTHER WHEAT ETC UNMILLED	W 71400	10.1	W 24412	3.1	W 57209	12.6	W 117769	31.9	AUTRE FROMENT NON MOULU
042	RICE	W 90417	29.4	W 79567	22.2	W 56921	19.0	W 88557	37.3	RIZ
0422	RICE SEMI–MILLED,MILLED	W 90147	29.3	W 79495	22.2	W 56891	19.0	W 88551	37.2	RIZ POLI,GLACE INCL BRISURES
04221	RICE MILLED UNBROKEN	W 89968	29.2	W 79429	22.2	W 56868	19.0	W 88534	37.2	RIZ POLI,GLACE EXCL BRISURES
044	MAIZE UNMILLED	W 42584	7.4	W 36574	5.9	W 60293	10.2	W 50277	12.2	MAIS NON MOULU
048	CEREAL ETC PREPARATIONS	W 7753	12.9	W 9442	14.3	W 9011	14.3	W 9236	15.4	PREPTNS A BASE CEREALES
05	VEGETABLES AND FRUIT		29.8		29.2		30.6		38.7	LEGUMES ET FRUITS
054	VEG ETC FRSH,SMPLY PRSVD	W 25277	12.3	W 23936	10.8	W 26448	12.2	W 30171	16.5	LEGUMES FRAIS,CONG,SECS
0542	LEGUMINOUS VEGETBLES DRY	W 10433	6.1	W 10523	5.3	W 10515	5.5	W 10862	6.8	LEGUMES A COSSE SECS
057	FRUIT,NUTS,FRESH,DRIED		10.2		10.7	W 12268	10.6	W 14405	14.7	FRUITS FRAIS OU SECS
06	SUGAR AND PREPS,HONEY		3.7		3.5		12.4		18.0	SUCRES ET PRODUITS
061	SUGAR AND HONEY	W 696	1.8	W 1008	1.7	W 21355	10.6	W 31751	16.4	SUCRES ET MIEL
0611	RAW BEET AND CANE SUGAR	W 3	0.1			W 17535	7.9			SUCRES BRUTS
0612	REFINED SUGAR ETC	W 2	0.1	W 1	0.1	W 2458	1.2	W 30986	14.7	SUCRES RAFFINES
07	COFFEE,TEA,COCOA,SPICES		6.7		6.2		6.7		8.1	CAFE,THE,CACAO,EPICES
081	*FEEDING STUFF FOR ANIML	W 21614	8.5	W 18051	7.8	W 27270	10.3	W 23672	10.6	NOURRITURE POUR ANIMAUX
09	MISC EDIBLE PRODUCTS		15.4		15.4		16.5		17.0	PREP ALIMENTAIRES DIVERSES
098	EDIBLE PRODCTS,PREPS NES		12.0		12.7		13.4		13.0	PREP ALIMENTAIRES NDA
09809	MISC FOOD PREPRTIONS NES	W 2489	8.9	W 2919	9.7	W 2671	10.3	W 2294	9.2	PREP ALIMENTAIRES NDA
1	BEVERAGES AND TOBACCO		9.6		11.2		12.8		11.9	BOISSONS ET TABACS
11	BEVERAGES		8.4		9.9		11.3		10.7	BOISSONS
112	ALCOHOLIC BEVERAGES	W 1754	6.8		8.4	W 2836	9.5	W 2661	9.4	BOISSONS ALCOOLIQUES
2	CRUDE MATERLS,EXCL FUELS		57.8		54.7		66.9		86.0	MAT BRUTES NON COMESTIBLES
24	CORK AND WOOD		20.8		17.4		17.9		18.5	LIEGE ET BOIS
248	WOOD SHAPED,SLEEPERS	W 23055	16.8	W 20545	14.4	W 25223	16.4	W 19820	15.2	BOIS SIMPLEMENT TRAVAILLES
2483	LUMBER SHAPED NON–CONIFR	W 21503	16.0	W 18498	13.2	W 23189	15.1	W 18911	14.3	NON CONIFERES SCIES,RABOTES
24831	LUMBER SAWN ETC NON–CON	W 21446	15.9	W 18483	13.1	W 23134	15.0	W 18778	14.1	SCIES LONGITUDINALEMENT
26	TEXTILE FIBRES AND WASTE		27.0		28.0		37.5		46.1	FIBRES TEXTILES
263	COTTON	W 6565	9.7	W 7048	10.2	W 10311	20.2	W 12120	27.6	COTON
2631	RAW COTTON,EXCL LINTERS	W 6481	9.4	W 6862	9.6	W 10243	20.0	W 11995	27.0	COTON EN MASSE
268	WOOL(EXC TOPS),ANML HAIR	W 3106	15.5	W 3263	15.8	W 2801	15.1	W 3117	16.0	LAINES ET POILS
2682	WOOL DEGREASED,UNCOMBED	W 2325	10.2	W 2252	9.2	W 1857	9.7	W 2060	9.8	LAINE DEGRAISSEE
27	CRUDE FERTLZR,MINRLS NES		3.9		3.5		6.0		15.1	ENGRAIS MINERAUX BRUTS
277	NATURAL ABRASIVES NES		1.2		1.2		3.4		12.0	ABRASIFS NATURELS NDA
2771	INDUSTRIAL DIAMONDS		0.3		0.2		2.3		10.6	DIAMANTS INDUSTRIELS
3	MINERAL FUELS ETC		134.0		119.9		138.9		180.0	COMBUSTIBLES MINERAUX LUB
33	PETROLEUM AND PRODUCTS		118.6		106.9		122.0		162.9	PETROLE ET DERIVES
334	PETROLEUM PRODUCTS,REFIN	W 612325	112.6	W 655393	100.1	W 696652	117.0	W 710163	158.3	PRODUITS RAFFINES
3341	GASOLINE,OTH LIGHT OILS							W 88695	21.5	ESSENCES POUR MOTEURS
33411	MOTOR,AVIATION SPIRIT							W 88041	21.3	ESSENCES MOTEURS D'AVIONS
3342	KEROSENE,OTH MEDIUM OILS							W 196021	50.5	PETR LAMPANTS,AUT HUIL
33421	KEROSENE INCL JET FUEL							W 195988	50.4	PETROLES LAMPANTS
3343	GAS OILS							W 416357	76.0	GAS OILS
3345	LUBS,PETROLEUM OILS NES							W 9090	10.4	HUILES LUBRIFIANTES
33451	LUBS(HIGH PETR CONT) ETC							W 8715	9.4	HUILES LUBRIF,H LOURDES
335	RESIDUAL PETRLM PROD NES	W 22912	6.1		6.8	W 18185	5.0	W 15761	4.6	PRODUITS RESIDUELS NDA
341	*GAS,NATURAL AND MANUFCT	W 29545	11.5	W 32678	11.0	W 36223	13.2	W 36585	14.7	GAZ NATUREL,GAZ MANUFACT
3413	PETROLM GASES,LIQUEFIED	W 29544	11.5	W 32677	11.0	W 36223	13.2	W 36585	14.7	GAZ DE PETROLE LIQUEFIE
34131	LIQUEFIED PROPANE,BUTANE	W 29386	11.4	W 32676	11.0	W 36223	13.2	W 36585	14.7	PROPANE,BUTANE LIQUEFIES
4	ANIMAL,VEGETABLE OIL,FAT		18.4		23.2		25.4		25.9	HUILES,GRAISSES ANIM,VEG
42	FIXED VEGETABLE OIL,FAT		12.9		19.1		20.8		19.0	HUILES VEGETALES FIXES
423	FIXED VEG OILS,SOFT	W 19275	11.1	W 28096	17.6	W 26112	18.5	W 26468	18.1	HUILES VEGET DOUCES FIXES
4232	SOYA BEAN OIL	W 18191	10.1	W 23669	14.4	W 20604	14.2	W 22954	15.3	HUILE DE SOJA
5	CHEMCLS,RELATED PROD NES		134.7		131.4		149.4		170.7	PRODUITS CHIMIQUES
51	ORGANIC CHEMICALS		9.3		8.0		8.9		9.7	PROD CHIMIQ ORGANIQUES
52	INORGANIC CHEMICALS		11.5		11.1		15.0		16.4	PROD CHIM INORGANIQUES
522	INORG ELEMNTS,OXIDES,ETC	W 24398	6.1	W 16925	5.3	W 24415	7.8	W 23482	7.6	ELEMENTS INORGANIQUES
5225	INORGANIC BASES ETC NES	W 22907	4.7	W 15251	3.9	W 22885	6.5	W 21703	6.3	AUTRES BASES OXYDES METAL
523	OTHR INORG CHEMICALS ETC	W 10521	5.4	W 13353	5.8	W 16554	7.2	W 19580	8.9	AUT PRODUITS CHIMIQUES INORG
53	DYES,TANNING,COLOUR PROD		18.7		17.8		18.8		23.2	PROD TEINTURE,COLORANTS
531	SYNT DYE,NAT INDGO,LAKES	W 723	11.3	W 779	10.5	W 991	11.6	W 1693	15.3	MAT COLOR ORGAN,LAQUES
5311	SYNTHIC ORGNIC DYESTUFFS	W 658	10.8	W 695	10.0	W 904	11.2	W 1576	14.3	MAT COLOR ORGAN SYNTHET
533	PIGMENTS,PAINTS,ETC	W 3162	6.8	W 3729	6.7	W 2032	6.1	W 3064	7.6	PIGMENTS,PEINTURES,VERNIS
541	*MEDICINAL,PHARM PRODUCT	K 1731230	30.0	K 1584028	27.3	K 1825980	33.1	K 1980037	37.4	PROD MEDICINAUX PHARMACEUT
5417	MEDICAMENTS	K 1231218	25.1	K 1298901	24.2	K 1379463	28.8	K 1767005	34.1	MEDICAMENTS
54179	— CONTNG OTH SUBSTANCES	K 1192170	24.0	K 1271779	23.4	K 1355764	27.7	K 1719393	32.7	MED CONT AUT SUBSTANCES
55	PERFUME,CLEANING ETC PRD		13.2		14.1		15.4		18.2	PROD POUR PARFUM,TOILETTE
553	PERFUMERY,COSMETICS,ETC	W 733	7.4	W 1031	7.8	W 856	8.6	W 1198	10.4	PRODUITS DE PARFUMERIE
562	*FERTILIZERS,MANUFACTURE	W 63253	9.9	W 54947	7.8	W 46774	8.4	W 55768	10.6	ENGRAIS MANUFACTURES
58	PLASTIC MATERIALS ETC		21.5		23.7		26.0		26.6	MAT PLAST ARTIFICIELLES
583	POLYMERIZATION ETC PRODS	W 12055	16.9	W 14322	19.3	W 12446	21.4	W 13746	21.5	PROD POLYMERISATION
5839	OTH POLYMRZTION ETC PROD	W 5573	8.5	W 6355	9.4	W 5709	10.4	W 5932	9.7	AUT PROD POLYMER COPOLYM
59	CHEMICAL MATERIALS NES		20.6		21.4		23.8		28.4	MAT PROD CHIMIQUES NDA
591	PESTICIDES,DISINFECTANTS	W 1523	8.8	W 1595	8.8	W 1731	9.5	W 1592	10.5	DESINF,INSECT,FONG,HERB
598	MISCEL CHEM PRODUCTS NES	W 3466	9.6	W 4258	10.6	W 4556	11.9	W 6525	15.4	PROD DIV INDUST CHIM NDA
5989	CHEM PRODUCTS,PREPS NES	W 3342	9.0	W 4128	10.3	W 4441	11.5	W 6197	14.8	PROD PREP CHIMIQUES NDA
59891	PREPD GLAZINGS,DRESSINGS	W 1858	4.8	W 2372	6.3	W 2550	6.0	W 3064	7.8	PAREMENTS,APPRETS

4. General Imports C.I.F. by Commodities according to the S.I.T.C. (Rev. 2) in million U.S. Dollars
Importations Générales C.A.F. par Produits d'après la C.T.C.I. (Rév. 2) en millions de Dollars E.U.

SITC CTCI	COMMODITY	1993 QUANTITY QUANTITE		1993 VALUE VALEUR	1994 QUANTITY QUANTITE		1994 VALUE VALEUR	1995 QUANTITY QUANTITE		1995 VALUE VALEUR	1996 QUANTITY QUANTITE		1996 VALUE VALEUR	PRODUIT
6	BASIC MANUFACTURES			705.0			665.3			730.7			770.7	ART MANUFACTURES
61	LEATHER,DRESSED FUR,ETC			11.8			8.6			11.5			10.3	CUIRS,PELLETERIES
611	LEATHER	W	255	8.6	W	386	6.1	W	318	8.7	W	250	7.5	CUIRS,PEAUX PREPARES
62	RUBBER MANUFACTURES NES			15.2			14.7			15.4			16.3	CAOUTCHOUC MANUFACTURE
625	RUBBER TYRES, TUBES ETC			9.3	N	625242	8.7	N	561864	9.2	N	560274	9.9	PNEUS CAOUTCHOUC VULCANISE
63	WOOD,CORK MANUFACTRS NES			13.1			10.9			11.3			10.9	OUVRAGES LIEGE ET BOIS
634	VENEERS,PLYWOOD,ETC	W	7413	10.1			7.9			7.9			8.6	PLACAGES,CONTRE–PLAQUES
6342	PLYWOOD OF WOOD SHEETS	W	6235	9.5			7.1	V	10897	6.5	V	8710	7.0	BOIS CONTRE–PLAQUES
64	PAPER,PAPERBOARD AND MFR			29.8			30.9			43.7			39.5	PAPIERS,CARTONS & OUVRAGES
641	PAPER AND PAPERBOARD	W	26264	20.5	W	28223	21.3	W	29835	31.4	W	31077	28.3	PAPIERS ET CARTONS
6413	KRAFT PAPER,PAPERBOARD	W	8811	5.8	W	9139	5.1	W	7828	6.1	W	8692	5.4	PAPIER ET CARTON KRAFT
6415	PAPER,PAPERBRD,BULK,NES	W	9807	7.1	W	8896	6.7	W	9519	10.2	W	11083	10.4	PAPIERS,CARTONS ROULEAUX
64159	OTHER PAPER ETC,BULK,NES	W	5412	5.1	W	6285	5.5	W	6451	8.2	W	7435	8.6	AUT PAPIER ROULEAUX FEUILLES
642	PAPER,ETC,PRECUT,ARTS OF	W	3487	9.4	W	3626	9.6	W	3810	12.3	W	3544	11.3	PAP,CARTONS DECOUPES
65	TEXTILE YARN,FABRICS,ETC			421.9			402.9			444.7			461.0	FILS,TISSUS,ARTICLES TEXTILE
651	TEXTILE YARN			145.1	W	29609	129.7	W	31297	155.4	W	40026	194.6	FILS TEXTILES
6512	WOOL,HAIR YARN,INCL TOPS	W	3081	37.3	W	1460	15.9	W	1231	13.9	W	1666	17.2	FILS DE LAINE,DE POILS
65122	CARDED WOOL YARN IN BULK	W	2132	26.6	W	591	6.7	W	298	3.8	W	449	5.3	FILS CONT 85% LAINE CARDEE
6513	COTTON YARN	W	22037	89.6	W	25799	99.5	W	27882	125.8	W	36237	158.5	FILS DE COTON
6514	SYN FIB YRN,BULK,MONOFIL			9.3	W	1211	8.0	W	1090	8.4	W	1080	9.7	FILS CONT 85% FIB TEXT SYNTH
6516	DISCON SYN FIB BLEND YRN	W	822	7.0	W	848	5.0	W	837	5.6	W	724	5.9	FILS FIBR TEX SYNT DIS MOINS
652	COTTON FABRICS,WOVEN	A	71860	112.0			118.1	W	24894	123.7	W	11192	112.1	TISSUS DE COTON
6521	GREY WOVEN COTTON FABRIC	A	7390	7.5			4.9	W	955	6.8	W	940	7.4	TISSUS COT ECRUS NON MERCER
65214	GREY WOVEN COTTON NES	A	6471	6.4			4.2	W	873	6.0	W	832	6.7	AUT TISSUS 85% COTON ECRUS
6522	WOVEN COTTON BLEACHD,ETC	A	64470	104.6			113.2	W	23938	117.0	W	10252	104.7	TISSUS COTON BLANCHIS ETC
65224	BLCHED COTTON FABRIC NES	A	27333	49.0			54.5	W	5389	50.2	W	5675	58.1	AUT TIS PLUS 85% COT BLANCHI
65225	BLCHD COTN BLEND FAB NES	A	34637	51.4			55.6	W	18228	63.9	W	3882	40.5	AUT TIS MOINS 85% COT BLANCH
653	WOVN MAN–MADE FIB FABRIC			59.5			50.7	W	5222	49.4	W	5587	52.0	TISSUS FIBRES SYNTH,ARTIF
6531	CONT SYNT WEAVES NONPILE	A	17704	19.6			16.6	W	1628	15.8	W	1485	15.6	TISSUS FIBRES SYNTH CONTINUE
65314	CONT SYN TYRE CORD FABRC	A	5266	5.9			4.9	W	497	4.5	W	382	4.2	TIS ARMATURE PNEUMATIQUES
65315	CONT SYN TXTL FABRIC NES	A	12439	13.8			11.7	W	1131	11.3	W	1102	11.4	TIS PLUS 85% TEXT SYNT CONT
6532	DISC SYN TXTL FABRIC NES	A	5390	6.4			4.7	W	452	4.4	W	602	5.6	TIS DISC MOINS 85% FIBR TEXT
6534	DISC SYN BLEND FABRC NES	A	14942	18.9			19.7	W	1887	17.9	W	2101	19.3	TISSUS FIBRES SYNTH DISCONT
65341	DISC SYN FIB–COTTN FABRC	A	10612	10.8			12.5	W	1289	10.6	W	1271	11.0	TISSUS FIB SYNT DIS MEL COTO
65349	OTH DISC SYN BLEND FABRC	A	3825	6.1			5.4	W	444	4.6	W	693	6.1	TISSUS FIB SYNT MEL MAT AUT
6538	DISC REG BLEND FABRC NES			7.1			3.8	W	427	3.6	W	369	2.9	TIS MOINS 85% TEXT ART DISC
654	OTH WOVEN TEXTILE FABRIC			25.6			24.3	W	794	27.7	W	428	19.6	TISSUS AUT COTON SYNT,ARTIF
6541	SILK FABRICS WOVEN	A	633	14.9			13.7	W	338	15.9	W	31	9.6	TISSUS DE SOIE
6542	WOVEN WOOL,HAIR NONPILE	A	941	7.2			5.1	W	152	6.8	W	129	5.8	TIS PLUS 85% LAINE,POILS
65421	WOVN CARD WOOL,FINE HAIR	A	892	6.8			4.7	W	140	6.3	W	121	5.5	TISSUS 85% LAINE,PLS CARD
655	KNITTED,ETC FABRICS	A	31690	48.8			49.0	W	7857	55.9	W	4817	48.1	ETOF BONNETERIE PIECES ETC
6552	OTHER KNIT ETC FAB NONEL	A	31690	48.8			49.0	W	7857	55.9	W	4817	48.1	ETOF BON NON ELAS NON SYNT
656	LACE,RIBBONS,TULLE,ETC			14.3			13.1	W	918	15.0	W	908	16.6	TULLES,BRODERIE
65601	NARROW FABRICS NES			6.4			5.8	W	501	8.1	W	513	7.2	RUBANS SANS TRAME EN FILS
657	SPECIAL TXTL FABRC,PRODS			13.6			14.9	W	1498	14.3	W	1661	14.9	TISSUS SPECIAUX
6573	COATED ETC TEXTILES NES	A	6382	8.8			8.9	W	871	7.9	W	983	7.9	TISSUS,ART MATIERE TEXT NDA
65732	PLASTIC COATED TEXTILES	A	6323	8.7			8.6	W	831	7.6	W	902	7.3	TISSUS IMPREGNES
66	NONMETAL MINERAL MFS NES			104.6			96.9			101.8			106.5	ART MIN NON METALLIQUES
661	LIME,CEMENT,BLDG PRODS	W	551988	43.3	W	564279	40.7	W	583985	42.0	W	606806	45.9	CHAUX,CIMENTS MAT CONSTR
6612	CEMENT	W	548276	39.9	W	560504	36.6	W	580660	39.6	W	600815	42.2	CIMENTS HYDRAULIQUES
662	CLAY,REFRACTORY BLDG PRD	W	22600	12.8	W	24960	12.4	W	24438	12.4			16.4	MAT CONST REFRACTAIRES
6624	BRICKS ETC NONREFRACTORY	W	22171	12.6	W	24584	12.3	W	24117	12.2			16.1	BRIQUES ETC CERAM NON REFR
66245	GLAZED CERAMIC SETTS ETC	W	19484	11.3	W	22168	11.1	W	21046	10.8	W	25582	13.5	AUT CARREAUX CERAMIQUE
664	GLASS			4.5			4.4			6.2			5.1	VERRE
665	GLASSWARE			8.9			7.7			7.6			8.0	OUVRAGES EN VERRE
667	PEARL,PREC–,SEMI–P STONE			30.5			27.9			29.7			26.4	PERLES, PIERRES GEMMES
6672	DIAMONDS NONINDUST,UNSET			26.8			24.7			23.9			21.1	DIAMANTS BRUTS
66722	— SRTD,ROUGH,SIMPLY WKD			21.8			20.9			20.3			13.7	DIAMANTS TRIES BRUTS
67	IRON AND STEEL			50.3			52.1			51.7			71.0	FER ET ACIER
672	IRON,STEEL PRIMARY FORMS	W	43505	14.0	W	39421	13.2	W	41151	14.8	W	41008	16.0	LINGOTS FER,ACIER
6725	IRN,STL BLOOMS,SLABS,ETC	W	43103	13.8	W	37201	11.9	W	39393	13.5	W	39486	14.8	BLOOMS,BILLETTES FER ACIER
67251	IRN,SMPLE STL BLOOMS,ETC	W	43102	13.8	W	37199	11.9	W	39390	13.5	W	39479	14.8	BLOOMS ETC NON ACIER FIN
673	IRON,STEEL SHAPES ETC	W	21457	9.1	W	32749	13.1			9.5	W	28374	15.5	BARRES,PROFIL FER,ACIER
6733	IRON,STEEL PROFILES ETC	W	9891	4.6	W	15059	6.5	W	11478	5.5	W	14595	8.8	PROFILES,PALPLAN FER,ACIER
674	IRN,STL UNIV,PLATE,SHEET	W	15742	13.4	W	18277	14.1	W	12603	13.1	W	14678	16.8	LARGES PLATS,TOLES
6749	OTH IRN,STL PLATES,SHEET	W	9636	10.1	W	11331	11.0	W	9779	11.5	W	11407	15.0	AUTRES TOLES FER,ACIER
67491	— OF IRON OR SIMPLE STL	W	9172	9.6	W	10378	10.3	W	9546	11.3	W	10717	14.6	AUT TOLES AUTRES ACIER FIN
678	IRON,STL TUBES,PIPES,ETC	W	11782	11.0	W	11410	9.2	W	13135	12.6	W	16296	20.2	TUBES,TUYAUX EN FONTE,FER
6783	IRON,STL TUBES,PIPES NES	W	6092	4.8	W	4255	3.1	W	5291	4.6	W	6288	7.9	AUT TUBES,TUYAUX FER,ACIER
68	NON–FERROUS METALS			10.5			9.0			10.8			11.1	METAUX NON FERREUX
684	ALUMINIUM	W	1331	6.0	W	1447	5.3	W	1396	6.8	W	1061	4.8	ALUMINIUM
6842	ALUMINIUM,ALLOYS WORKED	W	1331	6.0	W	1447	5.3	W	1396	6.8	W	1061	4.8	ALUMINIUM,ALLIAGES OUVRE
69	METAL MANUFACTURES NES			48.3			39.6			40.3			44.3	ART MANUFACT EN METAL NDA
691	STRUCTURES AND PARTS NES	W	4727	7.8	W	1836	5.2	W	1518	3.0	W	1744	5.1	CONSTRUCT FER,ACIER,ALU
6911	STRUCTURES,PARTS IRN,STL	W	4331	6.1	W	1629	4.1	W	1459	2.7	W	1648	4.8	CONSTRUCT FER,ACIER,FONTE
697	BASE MTL HOUSEHOLD EQUIP			9.1			7.2			7.1			7.2	ART MENAGE MET COMMUNS
699	BASE METAL MFRS NES			14.4			12.6	W	2805	14.1	W	2568	15.1	ART MANUFACTURES MET NDA
7	MACHINES,TRANSPORT EQUIP			430.3			494.7			381.9			496.9	MACHINES MATERIEL TRANSPORT
71	POWER GENERATING EQUIPMT			11.4			22.8			18.4			42.8	MACHINES GENERATRICES
713	INTRNL COMBUS PSTN ENGIN			5.3			5.6			6.8			8.5	MOTEURS EXPL COMB INT, PIECE
716	ROTATING ELECTRIC PLANT			3.5			14.4			9.2			30.8	APP ELECTR ROTATIFS,PIECES
7161	DC MOTORS AND GENERATORS	N	1600	0.8	N	5693	9.9	N	2678	2.2	N	2770	19.5	MOTEURS COURANT CONTINU
72	MACHS FOR SPCL INDUSTRYS			100.7			81.0			71.8			81.9	MAC SPECIALES POUR INDUST
722	TRACTORS NON–ROAD	N	100	6.9	N	91	3.6	N	92	3.4	N	67	2.3	TRACTEURS
7224	WHEELED TRACTORS NES	N	93	6.5	N	87	2.4	N	84	3.0	N	65	1.9	TRACTEURS A ROUES
723	CIVIL ENGNEERG EQUIP ETC			9.6			7.1			3.8			9.6	APPAREILS DE GENIE CIVIL
7234	CONST,MINING MACHNRY NES	N	206	8.2	N	1055	6.2	N	159	3.3	N	1029	9.1	MACH POUR LA CONST, MINES
72342	SLFPRP SHOVELS,EXCAVATRS	N	121	6.3	N	100	5.2	N	52	2.1	N	64	4.6	PELLES MECANIQUES
724	TEXTILE,LEATHER MACHNRY			52.3			41.2			39.3			42.1	MACH POUR INDUSTRIE TEXTILE
7243	SEWING MACHS,NEEDLES ETC			11.1			10.3			10.4			11.2	MACHINES A COUDRE,PIECES
72431	SEWING MACHINES	N	17033	8.7	N	14951	7.3	N	11351	7.6	N	11232	8.3	MACHINES A COUDRE
7244	SPINNING,EXTRDNG,ETC MCH			9.6			4.4			2.8			3.0	MACH POUR LE FILAGE
7245	WEAVING,FELT MFG,ETC MCH	N	650	15.4	N	1017	12.6	N	727	9.4	N	791	10.0	METIERS A TISSER,PIECES
72453	GIMPING,WARPING ETC MCHS	N	412	7.0	N	781	5.2	N	424	3.5	N	593	5.0	METIERS A TULLE ETC
7247	TEXTILE MACHINERY NES			11.7			10.2			10.9			12.1	MACH LAVAGE,TEINTURE TEX
72474	OTH TEXTILE MACHNERY NES	N	2413	10.0	N	723	7.7	N	677	7.8	N	1167	8.3	MACH LAVAGE ETC MAT TEXT
726	PRINTG,BKBINDG MACHY,PTS			6.5			5.7			3.7			7.0	MACHINES POUR IMPRIMERIE
728	OTH MACHY FOR SPCL INDUS			15.2			15.5			12.4			15.7	AUT MACH IND PARTICULIERES
7284	MACHY FOR SPCL INDUS NES			7.6			10.0			6.2			8.4	MACH SPEC IND PARTICUL.
73	METALWORKING MACHINERY			5.9			4.7			3.9			5.6	MACH TRAVAIL DES METAUX
74	GENRL INDUSTRL MACHY NES			57.5			55.5			53.8			67.6	MACH APP INDUSTRIE

4. General Imports C.I.F. by Commodities according to the S.I.T.C. (Rev. 2) in million U.S. Dollars
Importations Générales C.A.F. par Produits d'après la C.T.C.I. (Rév. 2) en millions de Dollars E.U.

SITC CTCI	COMMODITY	1993 QUANTITY QUANTITE	1993 VALUE VALEUR	1994 QUANTITY QUANTITE	1994 VALUE VALEUR	1995 QUANTITY QUANTITE	1995 VALUE VALEUR	1996 QUANTITY QUANTITE	1996 VALUE VALEUR	PRODUIT
741	HEATING,COOLING EQUIPMNT		12.2		14.0		12.5		14.3	MACH CHAUFFAGE,PIECES
743	PUMPS NES,CENTRFUGES ETC		9.0		9.8		7.1		10.5	POMPES COMPRES,VENT ETC
744	MECHANICAL HANDLING EQU		13.6		9.7		10.5		15.8	EQUIP MANUTENTION PIECES
7442	LIFTING,LOADING MACH NES	N 4998	9.9	N 11012	6.4	N 9550	6.2	N 3764	6.1	APP LEVAGE,MANUTENTION
745	NONELEC MACHY,TOOLS NES		8.9		7.9		7.8		11.2	AUT MACH NON ELEC,PIECES
7452	OTH NONELEC MCHS,PTS NES		8.3		7.3		7.2		10.5	AUT MACH NON ELEC,PIECES
749	NONELEC MACH PTS,ACC NES		10.7		10.8		12.3		12.0	PIECES MACH NON ELEC NDA
7492	COCKS,VALVES ETC NES		5.8		4.8	W 423	5.7	W 617	5.9	ART ROB,SIM POUR TUYAUX
75	OFFICE MACHNES,ADP EQUIP		25.7		26.3		26.1		34.7	MACH BUREAU TRAIT AUTOM
752	AUTOMTIC DATA PROC EQUIP	N 21908	16.3	N 28742	16.2	N 37742	16.4	N 19745	21.9	MACH TRAIT INFORMATION
7528	OFF–LINE DATA PROC EQUIP	N 14119	6.3	N 16877	7.1	N 20132	7.4	N 10663	9.4	MACH AUXIL TRAIT INFORM
759	OFFICE,ADP MCH PTS,ACCES	W 102	6.6		5.9	W 79	6.4	W 107	8.7	PIECES DU 751 ET 752
7599	ACCTG,ETC,ADP MCH PTS,AC	W 94	6.0		5.4	W 68	5.7	W 98	8.0	PIECES DU 751 ET 752
76	TELECOMM,SOUND EQUIPMENT		41.0		37.1		42.2		56.5	EQUIPMENT DE TELECOM
761	TELEVISION RECEIVERS		7.9		6.5	N 22426	5.1	N 21349	5.7	RECEPTEURS DE TELEVISION
7611	COLOUR TV RECEIVERS	N 34311	7.9	N 29690	6.5	N 22136	5.1	N 20352	5.7	RECEPTEURS COULEUR
763	SOUND RECORDRS,PHONOGRPH	N 30880	6.0	N 47019	7.2	N 38408	5.2	N 37396	5.7	PHONO,APP ENREGISTREMENT
7638	OTHR SOUND APPARATUS ETC	N 28980	5.9	N 44243	7.1	N 35731	4.9	N 36549	5.6	AUT APP D'ENREGIS,REPROD
764	TELECOM EQPT,PTS,ACC NES		23.7		21.1		29.8		42.8	EQUIP TELECOM,PIECES
7641	LINE TELEPHONE,ETC EQUIP	N 106145	14.6	N 264377	14.7	N 173042	14.7	N 151483	28.7	APP TELEPHON PAR FIL
7643	TV,RADIO TRANSMITTRS ETC	N 2779	1.6	N 1545	1.6	N 2852	8.9	N 2092	8.7	APP EMET TELE RADIO
77	ELECTRIC MACHNRY NES ETC		68.6		57.9		58.9		79.0	MACH APP ELECT NDA
772	SWITCHGEAR ETC,PARTS NES	W 605	13.5	W 663	13.5	W 463	11.6	W 666	15.3	APP COUPURE,SECT ETC
7721	SWITCHGEAR ETC	W 600	11.8	W 652	11.6	W 446	9.2	W 650	13.2	APP COUPURE,SECTIONMNT
773	ELECTR DISTRIBUTNG EQUIP	W 1564	9.3	W 2599	9.8	W 1890	7.8	W 3220	13.5	EQUIPMT DISTRIBUTION ELECT
7731	INSULATED WIRE,CABLE ETC	W 1488	9.0	W 2417	8.8	W 1876	7.6	W 3114	12.9	FILS,CABLES ISOLES ELECT
775	HOUSEHOLD TYPE EQUIP NES		28.5		18.3		18.1		22.3	MACH,APP USAGE DOMESTQUE
7751	HOUSEHOLD LDRY EQUIP NES	N 14698	9.3	N 13725	4.0	N 12499	3.7	N 16978	5.6	MACH A LAVER ET SECHOIRS
77511	DOMESTIC WASHING MACHNES	N 14654	9.3	N 13664	4.0	N 12313	3.6	N 16755	5.5	MACH LAVER LINGE MOINS 6 KG
7752	DOM REFRIGERATRS,FREEZRS	N 23377	8.6	N 20866	6.6	N 22576	7.4	N 21542	7.5	REFRIG,CONGEL MENAGER
77521	DOMESTIC REFRIGERATORS	N 20433	7.5	N 19071	5.9	N 20190	6.6	N 18913	6.3	REFRIGERATEURS
7758	ELECTRO–THERMIC APPL NES		6.3		5.4		4.7		7.2	APP ELECTROTHERMIQ NDA
778	ELECTRICAL MACHINERY NES		10.5		10.1		13.5		19.5	AUTRES MACH ELECT NDA
7783	AUTOMOTIVE ELECTR EQUIP		2.2		2.1		2.4		9.2	EQUIP ELECT MOTEURS EXPL
77831	IGNITION,STARTING EQUIP		1.3		1.1		1.4		8.2	APP ELEC ALLUM,DEMARRAGE
78	ROAD VEHICLES		88.3		86.4		85.6		95.4	VEHICULES ROUTIERS
781	PASS MOTOR VEH EXC BUSES	N 4036	34.4	N 4198	35.9	N 3844	37.3	N 4019	44.3	AUTO TRANSPORT PERSONNES
782	LORRIES,SPCL MTR VEH NES	N 1948	23.2	N 2090	26.0	N 1826	24.3	N 2087	25.9	VEHICULES SPECIAUX,MARCH
7821	LORRIES,TRUCKS	N 1943	22.5	N 2076	24.7	N 1809	22.7	N 2068	24.7	VEHICULES TRANSP MARCHAND
783	ROAD MOTOR VEHICLES NES	N 252	6.5	N 255	5.4	N 163	4.0	N 241	6.0	VEHICULES ROUTIERS NDA
7831	BUSES	N 249	6.3	N 234	5.1	N 150	3.4	N 232	5.7	VOITURES TRANSPORT COMMUN
784	MOTOR VEH PRTS,ACCES NES		11.2		9.9		13.1		12.5	PIECES 722,781,782,783
7849	OTHER MOTOR VEHCL PARTS	W 1344	8.9	W 1276	7.7	W 1213	8.0		10.7	PIECES 722,781,782,783
785	CYCLES,ETC MOTRZD OR NOT		10.9		8.0		5.6		6.0	MOTOCYCLES SCOOTERS
7851	MOTORCYCLES ETC	N 9083	7.4	N 8048	4.5	N 4350	2.9	N 3626	3.0	MOTO VELO MOTEUR AUXIL
79	OTHR TRANSPORT EQUIPMENT		31.6		123.4		21.7		33.8	AUTRE MATERIEL TRANSPORT
792	AIRCRAFT ETC		5.6		114.6		13.7		14.8	APP NAVIGATION AERIENNE
7924	AIRCRFT NES OVER 15000KG			N 1	111.8					AERODYNES PLUS 15000 KG
7929	AIRCRAFT PARTS NES	W 4	5.6		2.8		10.7		10.6	PIECES DU 792
793	SHIPS AND BOATS ETC	N 3577	25.8	N 470	8.8	N 1229	8.0		19.0	NAVIRES BATEAUX,ETC
7931	WARSHIPS	N 2	3.5	N 1	0.1			N 3	15.4	NAVIRES DE GUERRE
7932	SHIPS AND BOATS NES	N 95	21.1	N 81	0.8	N 131	7.7		3.5	NAVIRES ET BATEAUX
79324	FISHING VESSELS ETC	N 4	20.1			N 7	7.3	N 1	0.4	BATEAUX DE PECHE
7938	TUGS,SPECIAL VESSELS ETC	N 3479	1.3	N 388	8.1	N 1098	0.3	N 4589	0.3	REMORQUEURS,BATEAUX SPEC
79381	TUGS	N 1	0.2	N 2	7.3					BATEAUX REMORQUEURS
8	MISC MANUFACTURED GOODS		181.2		174.4		186.2		183.3	ART MANUFACTURES DIVERS
812	*PLUMBG,HEATNG,LGHTNG EQ		8.9		7.5		7.0		8.9	APPAR SANITAIRES CHAUFFAGE
821	*FURNITURE,PARTS THEREOF		6.5		8.7		6.4		5.4	MEUBLES ET PIECES
8219	FURNITURE AND PARTS NES		4.4		6.7		4.7		3.7	AUTRES MEUBLES ET PIECES
84	CLOTHING AND ACCESSORIES		26.9		22.4		20.3		19.7	VETEMENTS
843	WOMENS OUTERWEAR NONKNIT	N 1890167	10.5		10.4		11.4		10.7	VET DESSUS FEMMES MAT TEX
8439	— OTHER OUTER GARMENTS	N 1520375	9.3		9.3	W 410	9.8	W 418	9.3	AUT VET DES FEM MAT TEXT
845	OUTERWEAR KNIT NONELASTC	N 1147705	6.9	N 1065208	4.8	N 805439	2.3	N 622719	1.6	VET DESSOUS,ACCES BONNET
8451	— JERSEYS,PULLOVERS ETC	N 858459	5.9	N 886972	3.9	N 554065	1.5	N 402882	1.0	CHANDAILS,PULL–OVERS ETC
87	PRECISION INSTRUMNTS NES		12.0		11.2		14.6		15.9	INSTRUM,APPAR SCIENT NDA
874	MEASURNG,CONTROLNG INSTR		5.3		5.1		7.2		8.4	INSTRUMENTS DE MESURE
88	PHOTO EQU,OPTICL GDS ETC		38.4		33.2		36.9		28.3	APP,FOURN PHOTO,OP,MONTR
884	OPTICAL GOODS NES		8.9		3.1		3.8		2.7	ELEMENTS OPTIQ,ART LUNET
8842	SPECTACLES AND FRAMES		8.5		2.7		3.4		2.3	LUNETTES ET MONTURES
88421	SPECTACLE FRAMES	W 17	8.3		2.5	W 26	3.2		2.2	MONTURES DE LUNETTES
885	WATCHES AND CLOCKS		23.3		23.3		27.0		19.3	HORLOGERIE
8851	WATCHES,MOVEMENTS,CASES		5.7		7.7		11.3		4.3	MONTRES,MOUVEMENTS,BOITES
88511	WATCHES		5.7		4.5		8.8		4.2	MONTRES POCHE,BRACELET
8852	CLOCKS,CLOCK,WATCH PARTS		17.6		15.7		15.8		15.1	HORLOGES,MOUV,PARTIES
88529	CLOCK,WATCH PARTS NES		16.8		15.2		15.2		14.7	FOURNIT D HORLOG NDA
89	MISC MANUFCTRD GOODS NES		82.4		84.9		94.3		98.8	ART MANUFACTURES DIVERS
892	PRINTED MATTER	W 1718	17.3	W 1851	17.3	W 1890	19.9	W 1946	20.1	IMPRIMES
8921	PRINTED BOOKS,GLOBES,ETC	W 988	8.7	W 1048	9.2	W 1078	9.9	W 1080	9.8	LIVRES,BROCHURES,CARTES
89211	PRINTED BOOKS,PAMPHLETS	W 982	8.6	W 1032	9.1	W 1061	9.6	W 1067	9.7	LIVRES,BROCHURES
893	ARTICLES OF PLASTIC NES		27.3		27.8		32.7		30.6	OUVRAGES EN MAT DIVIS 58
8931	PLSTC PACKG CONTNRS,LIDS		6.6		8.1	W 1723	8.7	W 1475	8.0	ART TRANSP EMBALLAGE ETC
8939	MISC PLASTIC ARTICLES	W 6450	19.0	W 6622	19.0	W 7301	23.1	W 6916	21.4	ART DIVERS EN MAT DIV 58
89399	OTHR PLASTC ARTICLES NES	W 3224	15.7	W 3973	16.6	W 4746	20.7	W 4773	19.3	AUT OUV MAT DIV 58
894	TOYS,SPORTING GOODS,ETC		7.7		6.5		5.6		7.0	VOITURES ENFANTS,JOUETS
897	GOLD,SILVER WARE,JEWELRY		9.8		10.4		13.6		17.5	BIJOUTERIE,ORFEVRERIE
8973	PREC JEWLRY,GLD–SILVWARE		8.4		9.0		11.7		15.4	BIJOUX OR,ARGENT ORFEVRE
89731	PRECIOUS METAL JEWELLERY		8.3		8.2		10.7		15.1	ART BIJOUTERIE,JOAILLER
899	OTHER MANUFACTURED GOODS		12.3		14.7		14.3		15.9	AUT ART MANUF DIVERS NDA
8998	SMALLWARES,TOILETRYS ETC		9.2		11.3		11.4		12.9	ART MERCERIE,TOILETTE
89983	BUTTONS,STUDS,ETC	W 263	5.2	W 362	6.6	W 305	7.1	W 312	7.1	BOUTONS,BOUTONS–PRESSION
9	GOODS NOT CLASSD BY KIND		11.6		12.5		15.6		22.2	ART TRANSACT NON CLASSES
971	*GOLD,NON MONETARY NES		10.2		12.3	K 405656	14.7	K 4256	21.7	OR NON MONETAIRE
97101	NONMON GLD UNWRT,SEMIMFD		10.2		12.3	K 1656	14.6	K 4151	21.7	OR,ALLIAGES D'OR BRUTS

5. General Exports F.O.B. by Commodities according to the S.I.T.C. (Rev. 2) in million U.S. Dollars
Exportations Générales F.O.B. par Produits d'après la C.T.C.I. (Rév. 2) en millions de Dollars E.U.

SITC CTCI	COMMODITY	1993 QUANTITY QUANTITE	1993 VALUE VALEUR	1994 QUANTITY QUANTITE	1994 VALUE VALEUR	1995 QUANTITY QUANTITE	1995 VALUE VALEUR	1996 QUANTITY QUANTITE	1996 VALUE VALEUR	PRODUIT
	ALL COMMODITIES		1467.1		1348.1		1538.3		1699.4	TOUS PRODUITS
0	FOOD AND LIVE ANIMALS		426.0		384.5		437.7		523.5	ALIMENTS,ANIMAUX VIVANTS
01	MEAT AND PREPARATIONS		6.9		12.4		14.5		9.6	VIANDES ET PREPARATIONS
014	MEAT PREPD,PRSVD,NES ETC	W 2391	6.8	W 4820	12.4	W 5122	14.4	W 3335	9.6	CONSERVES DE VIANDES
0149	OTH PREPARD,PRESRVD MEAT	W 2391	6.8	W 4820	12.4	W 5122	14.4	W 3335	9.6	AUTRES PREP DE VIANDES
03	FISH AND PREPARATIONS		25.9		30.4		37.9		41.9	POISSONS ET PREPARATIONS
037	FISH ETC PREPD,PRSVD NES	W 7830	24.2	W 9319	28.5	W 13241	36.1	W 13264	39.9	POIS,CRUST,MOL PREPARES
0371	FISH PREPARD,PRESRVD NES	W 7797	24.1	W 9302	28.5	W 13241	36.1	W 13247	39.8	CONSERVES DE POISSONS
04	CEREALS AND PREPARATIONS		4.1		4.0		3.6		9.5	CEREALES ET PRODUITS
046	WHEAT ETC MEAL OR FLOUR	W 14645	3.6	W 16232	3.7	W 16264	3.4	W 28901	9.4	SEMOULE FARINE,FROMENT
04601	FLOUR OF WHEAT OR MESLIN	W 14644	3.6	W 16231	3.7	W 8640	2.5	W 26111	9.0	FARINE DE FROMENT
06	SUGAR AND PREPS,HONEY		377.2		328.2		371.9		454.8	SUCRES ET PRODUITS
061	SUGAR AND HONEY	W 665325	376.9	W 641962	328.0	W 640659	371.6	W 870498	454.6	SUCRES ET MIEL
0611	RAW BEET AND CANE SUGAR	W 539984	371.0	W 518782	321.5	W 523889	363.7	W 772524	447.6	SUCRES BRUTS
0615	MOLASSES	W 125335	6.0	W 123179	6.5	W 116766	7.9	W 97972	7.1	MELASSES
07	COFFEE,TEA,COCOA,SPICES		7.5		5.5		4.4		2.5	CAFE,THE,CACAO,EPICES
074	TEA AND MATE	W 4367	6.6	W 4029	4.7	W 2898	3.0	W 1397	1.6	THE ET MATE
0741	TEA	W 4367	6.6	W 4029	4.7	W 2898	3.0	W 1397	1.6	THE
2	CRUDE MATERLS,EXCL FUELS		10.3		9.9		13.2		12.8	MAT BRUTES NON COMESTIBLES
29	CRUDE ANIMAL,VEG MAT NES		7.5		6.6		8.0		7.8	MATIERES BRUTES ANIM,VEGET
292	CRUDE VEG MATERIALS NES	W 612	7.3		6.4		7.9		7.6	MAT BRUTES VEGETALES NDA
2927	CUT FLOWERS AND FOLIAGE	W 587	7.2	W 575	6.4	W 601	7.8	W 589	7.6	FLEURS,FEUILLAGES COUPES
29271	CUT FLOWERS	W 583	7.2	W 569	6.3	W 596	7.8	W 579	7.5	FLEURS ET BOUTONS
5	CHEMCLS,RELATED PROD NES		14.3		10.1		11.9		8.5	PRODUITS CHIMIQUES
562	*FERTILIZERS,MANUFACTURE	W 31007	7.9	W 21752	5.2	W 22736	6.0	W 25805	7.0	ENGRAIS MANUFACTURES
5629	FERTILIZERS NES	W 27493	7.2	W 19352	4.8	W 19993	5.3	W 25739	7.0	ENGRAIS NDA
56291	NIT–PHOS–POT FERTLZR NES	W 27413	7.2	W 15752	4.1	W 19993	5.3	W 25739	7.0	ENGRAIS CONT N P K
6	BASIC MANUFACTURES		87.4		90.1		117.5		127.7	ART MANUFACTURES
65	TEXTILE YARN,FABRICS,ETC		48.7		54.1		76.9		87.9	FILS,TISSUS,ARTICLES TEXTILE
651	TEXTILE YARN	W 1342	12.1	W 1458	12.3	W 1509	12.5	W 1280	11.3	FILS TEXTILES
6512	WOOL,HAIR YARN,INCL TOPS	W 887	9.5	W 837	8.9	W 854	8.9	W 658	8.4	FILS DE LAINE,DE POILS
65123	COMBED WOOL YARN IN BULK	W 644	6.9	W 620	6.8	W 644	6.6	W 561	7.3	FILS CONT 85% LAINE PEIGNEE
652	COTTON FABRICS,WOVEN	A 13713	23.3		26.7	W 8789	42.2	W 10485	49.7	TISSUS DE COTON
6522	WOVEN COTTON BLEACHD,ETC	A 13683	23.3		25.1	W 8610	40.3	W 10442	49.2	TISSUS COTON BLANCHIS ETC
65224	BLCHED COTTON FABRIC NES	A 11358	19.8		18.5	W 8079	35.3	W 10114	43.9	AUT TIS PLUS 85% COT BLANCHI
65225	BLCHD COTN BLEND FAB NES	A 2301	3.5		6.7	W 527	5.0	W 328	5.3	AUT TIS MOINS 85% COT BLANCH
655	KNITTED,ETC FABRICS	A 2658	3.9		4.7	W 888	7.8	W 1547	14.2	ETOF BONNETERIE PIECES ETC
6552	OTHER KNIT ETC FAB NONEL	A 2658	3.9		4.7	W 888	7.8	W 1547	14.2	ETOF BON NON ELAS NON SYNT
658	TEXTILE ARTICLES NES		5.1		7.0	W 1111	10.7	W 1099	11.9	ART FACONNES MAT TEXTILES
6584	LINENS ETC	N 1639358	4.8		6.7	W 1064	10.4	W 1073	11.7	LINGE DE MAISON
65845	OTHER LINEN OF COTTON	N 800705	1.0		3.7	W 887	9.0	W 893	10.3	LINGE DE TOILETTE COTON
66	NONMETAL MINERAL MFS NES		31.6		29.6		33.2		34.2	ART MIN NON METALLIQUES
664	GLASS		3.3		3.3	W 10	5.5		5.7	VERRE
6649	GLASS NES		3.3	W 4	3.3	W 7	5.5	W 8	5.6	VERRE NDA
66493	CLOCK,WATCH GLASSES ETC	W 4	3.3	W 3	3.3	W 4	5.5	W 8	5.6	VERRES D'HORLOGERIE
667	PEARL,PREC–,SEMI–P STONE		27.9		26.0		27.3		28.5	PERLES, PIERRES GEMMES
6672	DIAMONDS NONINDUST,UNSET		26.7		24.9		25.8		26.6	DIAMANTS BRUTS
66729	— CUT ETC NOT SET		26.1		24.6		24.6		26.3	DIAMANTS TAILLES
7	MACHINES,TRANSPORT EQUIP		15.4		30.1		35.3		6.3	MACHINES MATERIEL TRANSPORT
72	MACHS FOR SPCL INDUSTRYS		7.6		5.0		7.7		0.9	MAC SPECIALES POUR INDUST
724	TEXTILE,LEATHER MACHNRY		3.1		3.0		5.8		0.1	MACH POUR INDUSTRIE TEXTILE
74	GENRL INDUSTRL MACHY NES		1.8		2.8		4.9		4.4	MACH APP INDUSTRIE
79	OTHR TRANSPORT EQUIPMENT		0.6		15.9		18.1		0.1	AUTRE MATERIEL TRANSPORT
793	SHIPS AND BOATS ETC	N 36	0.6	N 9	15.9		17.3	N 2	0.1	NAVIRES BATEAUX,ETC
7932	SHIPS AND BOATS NES	N 36	0.6	N 9	15.9		17.3	N 1	0.1	NAVIRES ET BATEAUX
79323	OTHER CARGO VESSELS			N 1	15.7					AUT BATEAUX TRANS MARCH
79324	FISHING VESSELS ETC						17.3			BATEAUX DE PECHE
8	MISC MANUFACTURED GOODS		910.3		817.6		914.8		1012.2	ART MANUFACTURES DIVERS
831	*TRAVEL GOODS,HANDBAGS	N 1697170	3.3		3.5	N 3010389	4.7	N 2272121	4.0	ARTICLES DE VOYAGE ETC
84	CLOTHING AND ACCESSORIES		818.1		731.1		808.3		918.7	VETEMENTS
842	MENS OUTERWEAR NOT KNIT	MN 12652	105.1	MN 12026	94.8	MN 12058	104.8	MN 16088	150.4	VET DESSUS POUR HOMMES
8422	— SUITS	N 35768	2.1	N 86212	6.1	N 32494	2.4	N 45767	3.4	COMPLETS HOMMES MAT TEXT
84221	—— OF WOOL,FINE HAIR	N 20800	1.8	N 78194	5.8	N 22994	2.2	N 16801	1.5	COMPLETS HOMMES LAINE
8423	— TROUSERS,BREECHES ETC	MN 12075	92.3	MN 11417	79.7	MN 11360	88.7	MN 15501	135.9	PANTALONS HOMMES MAT TEX
8424	— JACKETS,BLAZERS ETC	N 412704	10.0	N 378231	7.6	N 412030	11.9	N 407998	9.7	VESTES HOMMES MAT TEXTIL
843	WOMENS OUTERWEAR NONKNIT	MN 10880	66.5	N 8911886	54.1	MN 9140	68.7	MN 9277	73.9	VET DESSUS FEMMES MAT TEX
8433	— DRESSES	N 498509	4.0	N 520176	3.5	N 766901	5.2	N 760675	6.3	ROBES EN MAT–TEXTILES
8434	— SKIRTS	N 367357	2.9	N 304408	2.1	N 857709	6.0	N 1691412	12.3	JUPES EN MAT TEXTILES
8435	— BLOUSES	N 2721947	19.1	N 2157303	12.8	N 1719798	15.8	N 1517749	14.0	BLOUSES FEM MAT TEXTILES
8439	— OTHER OUTER GARMENTS	N 7012166	38.0	N 5844556	34.5	N 5671720	40.1	N 5168377	40.1	AUT VET DES FEM MAT TEXT
844	UNDER GARMENTS NOT KNIT		162.6	MN 15874	154.5		143.4	MN 13166	147.2	VETEMENT DESSOUS MAT TEX
8441	— MENS SHIRTS		160.2	MN 14984	150.3	MN 12855	137.6	MN 12317	142.0	CHEMISES HOMMES MAT TEXT
84411	—— OF COTTON	MN 13221	141.5	MN 12839	133.8	MN 10842	123.1	MN 10995	131.6	CHEMISES HOMMES DE COTON
84412	—— OF SYNTHETIC FIBRES		18.8	N 2144772	16.6	N 2012802	14.6	N 1321469	10.5	CHEMISES HOMMES FIB SYNT
845	OUTERWEAR KNIT NONELASTC	MN 26877	240.8		207.9	MN 25806	217.0	MN 24013	224.4	VET DESSOUS,ACCES BONNET
8451	— JERSEYS,PULLOVERS ETC	MN 15891	187.4		154.7	MN 15531	161.6	MN 15364	178.7	CHANDAILS,PULL–OVERS ETC
8452	— WOMENS DRESSES ETC	N 1948415	14.4	N 1869246	12.1	N 2071149	14.2	N 1051335	6.5	ROBES,JUPES BONNETERIE
8459	— OTHER,CLTHG ACCESRYS	MN 9038	39.0	MN 9250	41.1	N 8204187	41.3	N 7597959	39.3	AUT VET DESSUS DE BONNE
846	UNDER GARMENTS KNITTED	MN 77903	222.2		214.2		270.6		318.5	SOUS VETS DE BONNETERIE
8462	— OF COTTON NON ELASTIC	MN 71643	203.5	MN 69001	190.8	MN 75599	242.6	MN 75242	293.5	SOUS–VET BONNET COTON
84629	—— OTHER	MN 71643	203.5	MN 69001	190.8	MN 75599	242.6	MN 75242	293.5	AUT SOUS–VET BONNET COTON
8463	— OF SYNTH FBR NONELAST	N 2641116	11.7		16.2		18.0		14.5	SOUS–VET BONNET FIB SYNT
84632	—— MENS SHIRTS	N 2620326	11.7	N 3837420	16.1	N 3231816	17.9	N 2495440	14.5	CHEMISES DE BON FIB SYNMT
8465	CORSETS,GARTERS,ETC	N 3618606	7.1		7.3	W 227	10.0	W 236	10.6	CORSETS,GAINES ART SIM
84651	BRASSIERES	N 3129486	5.8		5.9	W 192	8.4	W 197	8.6	SOUTIENS–GORGE,BUSTIERS
847	TEXTILE CLTHNG ACCES NES		19.2		4.1		2.1		3.0	ACCES VET MAT TEXT NDA
8471	— NOT KNITTED	N 986266	17.8		3.3		1.2		1.8	ACCES VET MAT TEX NON BON
84712	SHAWLS,VEILS ETC,NOT KNT	N 656108	16.3	N 482288	2.6		1.1	N 496871	1.7	ECHARPES ETC MAT TEXT
87	PRECISION INSTRUMNTS NES		4.1		5.5		7.5		7.2	INSTRUM,APPAR SCIENT NDA
874	MEASURNG,CONTROLNG INSTR		3.5		4.9		6.6		6.3	INSTRUMENTS DE MESURE
8748	ELEC MEAS,CONTRL EQU NES	N 437845	2.8	N 500683	4.8	N 709960	5.5	N 1024824	6.3	APP ELEC ELECTRO MESURE
87483	OTH ELCTRNC MEAS ETC EQU	N 334110	2.4	N 495190	4.6	N 709809	5.5	N 1007456	6.1	AUT APP ELECTRO DE MESURE
88	PHOTO EQU,OPTICL GDS ETC		38.1		36.3		41.8		31.5	APP,FOURN PHOTO,OP,MONTR
884	OPTICAL GOODS NES		11.6		10.9		13.9		11.9	ELEMENTS OPTIQ,ART LUNET
8842	SPECTACLES AND FRAMES		10.5		9.2	N 6042070	12.4	N 5444805	10.8	LUNETTES ET MONTURES
88422	SPECTACLES ETC	P 4133863	8.8		7.2	N 5238881	9.3	N 4800799	8.5	LUNETTES
885	WATCHES AND CLOCKS		26.0		25.1		27.7		19.6	HORLOGERIE
8851	WATCHES,MOVEMENTS,CASES		13.0		13.5		15.0		13.6	MONTRES,MOUVEMENTS,BOITES
88513	WATCH MOVEMENTS ASSEMBLD		12.8		10.6		11.0		11.6	MOUVEMENTS TERMINES
8852	CLOCKS,CLOCK,WATCH PARTS		13.1		11.7		12.7		6.0	HORLOGES,MOUV,PARTIES
88529	CLOCK,WATCH PARTS NES		12.1		11.7		12.6		6.0	FOURNIT D HORLOG NDA

5. General Exports F.O.B. by Commodities according to the S.I.T.C. (Rev. 2) in million U.S. Dollars
Exportations Générales F.O.B. par Produits d'après la C.T.C.I. (Rév. 2) en millions de Dollars E.U.

SITC CTCI	COMMODITY	1993 QUANTITY QUANTITE	1993 VALUE VALEUR	1994 QUANTITY QUANTITE	1994 VALUE VALEUR	1995 QUANTITY QUANTITE	1995 VALUE VALEUR	1996 QUANTITY QUANTITE	1996 VALUE VALEUR	PRODUIT
89	MISC MANUFCTRD GOODS NES		44.2		39.4		50.5		48.5	ART MANUFACTURES DIVERS
894	TOYS,SPORTING GOODS,ETC		10.7		9.3		12.2		11.0	VOITURES ENFANTS,JOUETS
8942	TOYS,INDOOR GAMES ETC		9.5		8.7		11.2		10.7	JOUETS,JEUX ETC
89423	TOYS NES	N 2107765	7.9	N 1743297	7.2	N 2234128	9.2	N 2025195	9.1	JOUETS,MODELES REDUITS
897	GOLD,SILVER WARE,JEWELRY		26.3		22.6		29.7		27.4	BIJOUTERIE,ORFEVRERIE
8973	PREC JEWLRY,GLD–SILVWARE		25.3		21.4		26.5		24.2	BIJOUX OR,ARGENT ORFEVRE
89731	PRECIOUS METAL JEWELLERY		7.0		7.4		8.2		9.3	ART BIJOUTERIE,JOAILLER
89733	JEWELLERY NES		14.4		11.0		15.4		11.3	OUV PERLES,PIERRES
899	OTHER MANUFACTURED GOODS		3.5		4.3		4.6		4.5	AUT ART MANUF DIVERS NDA
9	GOODS NOT CLASSD BY KIND		3.0		4.7		5.8		7.5	ART TRANSACT NON CLASSES
941	*ZOO ANIMALS,PETS ETC	N 3847	3.0	N 5508	4.5	N 5627	5.2	N 7037	7.4	ANIMAUX DE ZOO ETC

1. HISTORICAL SERIES, 1962–1997 GENERAL TRADE, IMPORTS F.O.B., EXPORTS F.O.B.
SERIES HISTORIQUES, 1962–1997 COMMERCE GENERAL, IMPORTATIONS F.O.B., EXPORTATIONS F.O.B

YEAR ANNEE	VALUE IN MILLION U.S. DOLLARS VALEUR EN MILLION U.S. DOLLARS MERCHANDISE –MARCHANDISE IMPORTS	EXPORTS	GOLD –OR IMPORTS	EXPORTS	CONVERSION FACTORS U.S. CENTS PER MEXICAN PESO FACTEURS DE CONVERSION CENTS E.U. PAR MEXICAN PESO IMPORTS	EXPORTS	INDEX NUMBERS –INDICES QUANTUM IMPORTS	EXPORTS	UNIT VALUE VALEUR UNITAIRE IMPORTS	EXPORTS
1962	1142.96	882.33								
1963	1239.68	920.31	0.03							
1964	1492.56	999.37	0.04							
1965	1559.68	1088.78								
1966	1605.12	1162.76								
1967	1745.92	1103.81								
1968	1960.11	1180.71	0.01							
1969	2077.92	1384.95	0.01							
1970	2319.51	1310.89	0.02							
1971	2250.41	1395.46	0.02							
1972	2718.48	1693.90	0.03							
1973	3813.44	2256.79	0.0							
1974	6056.71	2961.66	0.01	0.01						
1975	6570.15	2992.27								
1976	6032.15	3431.00								
1977	5589.31	4285.18								
1978	7918.00	6063.00								
1979	11980.00	8816.00								
1980	19431.00	15307.48								
1981	25053.62	19419.62								
1982	15056.73	21229.66								
1983	9005.76	22312.05								
1984	11788.19	24196.03								
1985	13762.49	21663.81								
1986	11918.16	16031.00								
1987	12760.76	20656.19								
1988	18954.40	20657.60								
1989	23633.44	22818.59								
1990	29968.80	27130.70							100	100
1991	38138.73	27286.24							100	92
1992	48135.91	27729.64							101	92
1993	49622.91	30188.01							102	89
1994	60980.02	34531.99								
1995	45976.89	47056.02								
1996	61178.62	59072.36								
1997	111974.10	110046.90								

2. IMPORTS BY BROAD ECONOMIC CATEGORY AND EXPORTS BY INDUSTRIAL ORIGIN. (PERCENTAGE OF TOTAL VALUE)
IMPORTATIONS PAR CATEGORIES ECONOMIQUES ET EXPORTATIONS PAR BRANCHE D'ACTIVITE.(EN POURCENTAGE DE LA VALEUR TOTALE)

IMPORTS – IMPORTATIONS

	1991	1992	1993	1994	1995	1996	1997
TOTAL IMPORTS–IMPORTATIONS TOTALES	100.	100.	100.	100.	100.	100.	100.
1 FOOD BEV–ALIMENTATION BOISSONS	9.5	7.9	7.3	7.2	5.2	5.9	5.3
11 PRIMARY–PRODUITS DE BASE	5.7	4.6	4.0	4.0	2.9	3.7	3.4
111 FOR INDUSTRY–POUR L'INDUSTRIE	3.2	2.8	2.3	2.2	1.9	2.6	2.2
112 FOR HOUSEHOLDS–POUR LES MENAGES	2.5	1.9	1.7	1.8	1.0	1.1	1.2
12 PROCESSED–PRODUITS ELABORES	3.8	3.3	3.3	3.2	2.3	2.2	2.0
121 FOR INDUSTRY–POUR L'INDUSTRIE	0.8	0.5	0.4	0.5	0.4	0.6	0.4
122 FOR HOUSEHOLDS–POUR LES MENAGES	2.9	2.8	2.9	2.7	1.9	1.7	1.5
2 IND SUPPLIES–APPROV INDUSTRIELS	28.1	29.5	29.8	29.5	32.0	32.1	30.7
21 PRIMARY–PRODUITS DE BASE	3.5	2.4	2.1	2.3	2.7	3.2	2.6
22 PROCESSED–PRODUITS ELABORES	24.6	27.1	27.7	27.2	29.3	28.8	28.1
3 FUELS–COMBUSTIBLES	3.4	2.7	2.3	1.8	2.0	1.9	2.5
31 PRIMARY–PRODUITS DE BASE	0.5	0.6	0.5	0.4	0.5	0.5	0.6
32 PROCESSED–PRODUITS ELABORES	2.9	2.1	1.8	1.4	1.4	1.4	1.9
321 MOTOR SPIRIT–ESSENCE	1.8	1.2	1.0	0.6	0.7	0.0	1.0
322 OTHER–AUTRES	1.1	0.9	0.8	0.8	0.8	1.3	0.9
4 MACHINERY–EQUIPEMENT	25.8	29.9	30.2	29.6	31.7	32.0	32.1
41 CAPITAL EQUIPMENT–MACHINES	21.4	22.6	22.3	22.4	21.5	21.9	22.4
42 PARTS–PIECES ACCESSOIRES	4.5	7.3	7.8	7.3	10.1	10.1	9.7
5 TRANSPORT–TRANSPORT	6.6	16.1	15.6	6.7	8.3	12.1	12.3
51 PASSENGER CARS–AUTOMOBILES	0.8	0.6	0.6	1.6	0.6	1.0	1.4
52 OTHER–AUTRES	2.0	2.0	1.3	1.4	0.5	0.6	1.0
521 INDUSTRIAL–INDUSTRIELS	1.8	1.8	1.2	1.3	0.5	0.6	1.0
522 NON INDUSTRIAL–NON INDUSTRIEL	0.2	0.2	0.1	0.1	0.0	0.0	0.0
53 PARTS–PIECES ACCESSOIRES	3.8	13.5	13.7	3.7	7.2	10.5	9.8
6 CONSUM GOODS–BIENS CONSOMMATION	10.8	13.6	14.3	14.8	14.0	13.4	13.7
61 DURABLE–DURABLES	3.9	3.6	3.8	4.0	3.2	2.8	2.6
62 SEMI DURABLE–SEMI DURABLES	4.8	7.7	8.1	8.3	8.4	8.3	8.7
63 NON DURABLE–NON DURABLES	2.0	2.2	2.5	2.4	2.4	2.3	2.3
7 GOODS NES–BIENS NDA	15.8	0.3	0.3	10.4	6.9	2.5	3.5

EXPORTS – EXPORTATIONS

	1991	1992	1993	1994	1995	1996	1997
TOTAL EXPORTS–EXPORTATIONS TOTALES	100.	100.	100.	100.	100.	100.	100.
1 AGRICULTURE	10.0	5.2	5.5	5.1	5.8	4.4	4.1
2 MINING QUARRY–INDUS EXTRACTIVES	29.6	17.1	13.2	11.6	10.2	11.8	9.9
3 MANUFACTURING–IND MANUFACTUR	60.4	77.6	81.2	83.3	84.0	83.8	86.0
31 FOOD BEV TOBACCO–ALIM BOISS TAB	3.3	2.2	2.1	2.2	2.3	2.4	2.3
32 TEXTILES–INDUSTRIES TEXTILES	2.5	4.9	4.8	5.1	5.9	6.4	7.8
33 WOOD & PRODUCTS–BOIS & PRODUITS	0.5	0.6	0.7	0.6	0.5	0.5	0.5
34 PAPER & PRODUCTS–PAPIER & PRODT	0.9	1.4	1.3	0.9	1.1	0.9	1.0
35 CHEMICALS–INDUSTRIES CHIMIQUES	10.7	8.3	8.0	7.5	7.8	6.5	6.5
36 NON METAL MIN–MIN NON METAL	2.2	1.7	1.8	1.6	1.5	1.5	1.5
37 BASIC METAL–IND METAL BASE	5.5	3.3	3.5	3.2	4.9	3.7	3.6
38 METAL MANUF–MANUF METAL	33.4	53.3	57.1	60.2	58.2	60.2	61.3
39 OTH MANUF IND–AUTRES MANUF	1.3	1.8	1.9	1.9	1.9	1.7	1.7

3. TRADE BY PRINCIPAL COUNTRIES OF ORIGIN AND CONSUMPTION (VALUE IN MILLION U.S. DOLLARS)
ECHANGES SELON LES PRINCIPAUX PAYS D'ORIGINE ET DE COMSOMMATION (VALEUR EN MILLIONS DE DOLLARS EU)

COUNTRIES–PAYS	GENERAL IMPORTS F.O.B. IMPORTATIONS GENERALES F.O.B.				
	1993	1994	1995	1996	1997
World	65272.0	79335.0	72453.0	89355.1	111974.1
Africa	60.0	149.3	128.6	219.9	301.2
Americas	51716.0	59344.3	56972.7	71667.2	88019.1
– Northern America	49360.3	56450.7	55347.8	69360.1	85225.9
– LAIA	1800.4	2585.8	1414.1	2027.5	2409.9
– CACM	102.2	144.4	86.5	170.7	206.9
– Caribbean	78.2	130.7	112.4	100.8	152.9
– Rest of America	375.0	32.7	11.9	8.1	23.5
Asia excl fmr USSR	4995.3	9498.8	7707.1	8706.9	11671.6
– Middle East	9.6	68.9	27.5	106.5	89.9
Asia former USSR			0.7	26.7	0.7
Europe excl fmr USSR	8091.2	9746.8	7265.5	8351.0	11287.6
– European Union	7333.4	9054.3	6748.9	7741.6	10427.6
– Eastern Europe	54.8	159.1	96.8	110.9	206.1
– Rest of Europe	702.9	533.3	419.8	498.5	654.0
Europe former USSR	35.5	147.6	74.3	86.0	265.0
Oceania	213.8	316.7	177.6	261.0	340.3
Other	160.1	131.5	126.5	36.4	88.6
USA/Etats–Unis d'Amer	48321.2	54812.8	53973.1	67615.4	83205.8
Japan/Japon	3056.5	4778.3	3951.0	3836.8	4465.9
Germany/Allemagne	2652.4	3099.7	2686.3	3173.6	3996.7
Canada	988.2	1620.1	1373.9	1743.5	2020.0
France, Monaco	1012.0	1526.9	980.5	1020.1	1230.0
Italy/Italie	734.8	1020.8	771.0	999.1	1530.8
Spain/Espagne	1172.3	1337.7	693.7	629.5	1056.4
Korea, Republic of	475.8	938.0	770.6	1059.4	1641.2
Brazil/Brésil	1077.3	1224.6	565.1	690.0	932.8
Other Asia n.e.s.		1027.8	715.3	890.9	1167.5
China/Chine	454.5	499.4	520.1	759.7	1289.5
United Kingdom	543.8	706.0	531.2	679.4	942.6
Switzerland,Liechtenst.	678.9	490.4	389.4	458.0	572.7
Malaysia/Malaisie	28.7	448.3	435.9	533.6	748.2
Singapore/Singapour	219.4	289.9	289.1	382.9	431.3
Belgium–Luxembourg	225.4	346.6	217.9	247.3	359.3
Venezuela	205.1	297.4	214.0	234.0	440.9
Chile/Chili	109.6	230.0	154.2	466.1	394.5
Sweden/Suède	245.8	276.9	200.6	228.8	368.0
Netherlands/Pays–Bas	362.4	240.0	217.8	225.1	272.5
China, Hong Kong SAR	494.4	286.7	159.3	129.2	194.3
Argentina/Argentine	160.8	332.5	190.7	299.6	248.2
Thailand/Thaïlande	49.3	235.8	166.4	244.1	383.0
Indonesia/Indonésie	55.5	251.8	167.4	250.0	310.7
Ireland/Irlande	144.0	137.7	181.1	239.1	269.5
Korea Dem People's Rp	18.3	270.3	203.2	118.2	248.0
Peru/Pérou	79.8	210.9	98.7	116.7	150.5
New Zealand	138.5	146.2	75.8	132.1	162.2
India/Inde	49.3	137.0	120.5	124.5	215.4
Australia/Australie	52.7	166.9	99.2	128.4	176.4
Philippines	8.9	83.3	68.5	137.8	281.3
Austria/Autriche	84.6	120.6	87.4	113.1	143.9
Areas n.e.s.	160.1	131.5	126.5	36.4	88.6
Colombia/Colombie	74.1	120.9	97.4	97.0	129.8
Russian Federation	35.1	140.7	63.6	59.4	190.1
Denmark/Danemark	103.1	130.8	70.8	70.7	100.1
Panama	355.3	25.1	8.9	6.5	21.0
Israel/Israël	42.4	85.0	46.6	79.1	115.9
Finland/Finlande	33.9	66.1	63.4	84.7	104.0
Guatemala	53.4	83.3	51.0	76.8	82.2

COUNTRIES–PAYS	GENERAL EXPORTS F.O.B. EXPORTATIONS GENERALES F.O.B.				
	1993	1994	1995	1996	1997
Monde	51886.4	60618.6	79540.6	95661.2	110046.9
Afrique	14.6	38.6	46.9	117.8	225.7
Amériques	47552.0	55920.2	73272.6	88366.6	102495.2
– Amérique du Nord	44637.3	52753.5	68372.0	82034.7	95343.4
– ALAI	1597.8	1817.8	2853.0	3813.5	4361.6
– MCAC	474.1	553.1	691.1	904.8	1231.2
– Caraïbes	656.1	603.9	1102.4	1347.5	1242.1
– Autre Amérique	186.6	192.0	254.0	266.2	316.8
Asie anc. URSS exclus	1309.8	1661.2	2063.5	3079.1	2993.3
– Moyen–Orient	71.0	99.8	121.7	318.1	411.3
Asie ancienne URSS			0.2	15.2	0.6
Europe anc. URSS exclus	2839.5	2900.9	3996.9	3722.5	4126.6
– Union Européenne	2680.0	2809.0	3351.7	3470.0	3899.5
– Europe de l'Est	6.9	6.1	10.0	46.7	84.7
– Autre de l'Europe	152.6	85.8	635.2	205.8	142.5
Europe ancienne URSS	11.7	21.2	18.0	217.1	55.1
Océanie	55.8	59.0	75.1	92.8	119.3
Autre	102.9	17.4	67.5	50.1	31.1
USA/Etats–Unis d'Amer	42935.4	51198.2	66338.8	79771.4	93018.8
Canada	1562.0	1530.8	1985.8	2232.8	2302.9
Japan/Japon	705.0	923.3	979.3	1242.4	1014.5
Spain/Espagne	876.2	869.8	788.9	952.7	947.2
Brazil/Brésil	292.2	404.5	800.2	974.4	877.6
Chile/Chili	198.5	260.6	489.7	755.9	968.6
Germany/Allemagne	425.6	400.8	515.4	595.8	623.6
Venezuela	227.4	228.9	379.6	524.8	812.1
France, Monaco	444.0	426.2	483.6	375.4	367.3
Colombia/Colombie	238.7	319.5	453.4	466.7	558.9
Belgium–Luxembourg	279.7	361.9	488.8	473.7	419.6
Argentina/Argentine	282.3	276.6	312.9	536.5	576.5
United Kingdom	219.8	275.7	487.6	433.6	555.7
Guatemala	203.5	223.0	303.0	365.1	535.9
Cuba	188.1	269.4	394.1	369.1	326.8
Netherlands/Pays–Bas	124.0	232.6	177.1	261.5	373.3
Dominican Republic	203.1	163.5	167.0	292.7	327.8
China, Hong Kong SAR	94.4	103.8	504.3	221.8	197.0
Switzerland,Liechtenst.	140.9	70.5	617.8	153.0	114.5
Panama	158.4	167.2	229.0	231.4	278.8
Singapore/Singapour	130.9	45.8	173.5	248.8	388.6
Peru/Pérou	93.8	133.8	178.8	228.3	285.2
Netherlands Antilles	26.4	10.1	63.6	464.7	336.6
Italy/Italie	75.7	98.6	197.4	183.0	343.7
Korea, Republic of	26.9	142.0	88.3	337.7	213.0
El Salvador	113.2	134.6	146.5	172.7	237.9
Costa Rica	99.1	99.1	141.8	204.4	243.7
Ecuador/Equateur	56.1	140.0	116.0	165.2	169.8
China/Chine	23.6	100.4	37.0	202.6	141.6
Cayman Is/Is Caïmans	116.0	43.1	253.0	45.4	32.9
Uruguay	179.4	33.8	76.7	102.6	61.9
Honduras	37.7	75.3	68.7	103.2	125.8
Portugal	70.3	61.7	81.4	62.5	101.2
Other Asia n.e.s.		60.4	44.0	110.1	137.8
Thailand/Thaïlande	10.9	66.8	30.8	91.7	144.6
Jamaica/Jamaïque	44.6	60.0	50.0	85.8	81.7
Australia/Australie	48.0	45.1	63.3	70.5	92.1
Russian Federation	11.6	16.2	17.3	211.3	53.9
Areas n.e.s.	102.9	17.4	67.5	50.1	31.1
Bermuda/Bermudes	140.0	24.5	47.5	30.5	21.8

(VALUE AS PERCENTAGE OF WORLD TOTAL)(VALEURS EN POURCENTAGE DU TOTAL MONDIAL)

	1988	1989	1990	1991	1992	1993	1994	1995	1996	1997
Africa	0.4	0.3	0.2	0.2	0.1	0.1	0.2	0.2	0.2	0.3
Americas	72.5	74.2	73.0	74.6	78.9	79.2	74.8	78.6	80.2	78.6
– Northern America	68.5	69.8	68.5	70.4	75.2	75.6	71.2	76.4	77.6	76.1
– LAIA	3.1	2.9	3.4	3.1	2.7	2.8	3.3	2.0	2.3	2.2
– CACM	0.2	0.3	0.3	0.3	0.2	0.2	0.2	0.1	0.2	0.2
– Caribbean	0.2	0.3	0.3	0.2	0.2	0.1	0.2	0.2	0.1	0.1
– Rest of America	0.4	0.8	0.5	0.7	0.7	0.6	0.0	0.0	0.0	0.0
Asia excl fmr USSR	8.7	6.4	7.3	7.4	7.6	7.7	12.0	10.6	9.7	10.4
– Middle East	0.1	0.1	0.2	0.0	0.0	0.0	0.1	0.0	0.1	0.1
Asia former USSR								0.0	0.0	0.0
Europe excl fmr USSR	17.4	15.0	18.6	17.2	12.9	12.4	12.3	10.0	9.3	10.1
– European Union	15.8	13.1	16.8	15.4	11.7	11.2	11.4	9.3	8.7	9.3
– Eastern Europe	0.3	0.4	0.3	0.2	0.1	0.1	0.2	0.1	0.1	0.2
– Rest of Europe	1.3	1.4	1.5	1.6	1.1	1.1	0.7	0.6	0.6	0.6
Europe former USSR	0.0	0.0	0.0	0.0	0.0	0.1	0.2	0.1	0.1	0.2
Oceania	0.6	0.5	0.8	0.3	0.3	0.3	0.4	0.2	0.3	0.3
Other	0.5	3.6	0.0	0.3	0.2	0.2	0.2	0.2	0.0	0.1
USA/Etats–Unis d'Amer	66.7	68.3	67.1	68.6	73.8	74.0	69.1	74.5	75.7	74.3
Japan/Japon	6.0	3.6	4.3	4.1	4.6	4.7	6.0	5.5	4.3	4.0
Germany/Allemagne				5.8	3.7	4.1	3.9	3.7	3.6	3.6
Canada	1.8	1.6	1.3	1.8	1.3	1.5	2.0	1.9	2.0	1.8
France, Monaco	2.3	2.1	2.4	2.2	2.0	1.6	1.9	1.4	1.1	1.1
Italy/Italie	1.4	1.5	1.5	1.5	1.5	1.1	1.3	1.1	1.1	1.4
Spain/Espagne	1.1	1.4	1.7	1.4	1.3	1.8	1.7	1.0	0.7	0.9
Korea, Republic of	0.6	0.7	0.6	0.9	0.7	0.7	1.2	1.1	1.2	1.5
Brazil/Brésil	1.6	1.3	1.2	1.7	1.7	1.7	1.5	0.8	0.8	0.8
Other Asia n.e.s.				0.8			1.3	1.0	1.0	1.0

	1988	1989	1990	1991	1992	1993	1994	1995	1996	1997
Afrique	0.7	0.4	0.3	0.5	0.1	0.0	0.1	0.1	0.1	0.2
Amériques	75.3	78.9	78.1	79.4	88.8	91.6	92.2	92.1	92.4	93.1
– Amérique du Nord	67.3	71.3	71.0	72.2	83.2	86.0	87.0	86.0	85.8	86.6
– ALAI	4.1	3.2	3.3	3.6	3.0	3.1	3.0	3.6	4.0	4.0
– MCAC	1.6	1.9	1.6	1.2	1.0	0.9	0.9	0.9	0.9	1.1
– Caraïbes	2.0	2.0	1.9	2.0	1.3	1.3	1.0	1.4	1.4	1.1
– Autre Amérique	0.4	0.5	0.3	0.5	0.3	0.4	0.3	0.3	0.3	0.3
Asie anc. URSS exclus	9.4	8.0	7.7	6.6	3.1	2.5	2.7	2.6	3.2	2.7
– Moyen–Orient	0.1	0.1	0.2	0.2	0.1	0.1	0.2	0.2	0.3	0.4
Asie ancienne URSS								0.0	0.0	0.0
Europe anc. URSS exclus	13.9	12.1	13.6	12.9	7.8	5.5	4.8	5.0	3.9	3.7
– Union Européenne	13.3	11.7	12.8	12.2	7.4	5.2	4.6	4.2	3.6	3.5
– Europe de l'Est	0.2	0.1	0.0	0.1	0.0	0.0	0.0	0.0	0.0	0.1
– Autre de l'Europe	0.4	0.3	0.8	0.6	0.3	0.3	0.1	0.8	0.2	0.1
Europe ancienne URSS	0.5	0.2	0.1	0.1	0.0	0.0	0.0	0.0	0.2	0.1
Océanie	0.2	0.2	0.2	0.3	0.1	0.1	0.1	0.1	0.1	0.1
Autre	0.0	0.1	0.0	0.3	0.1	0.2	0.0	0.1	0.1	0.0
USA/Etats–Unis d'Amer	65.9	70.1	70.2	67.9	80.7	82.7	84.5	83.4	83.4	84.5
Canada	1.3	1.2	0.8	4.1	2.2	3.0	2.5	2.5	2.3	2.1
Japan/Japon	6.0	5.7	5.5	4.6	1.8	1.4	1.5	1.2	1.3	0.9
Spain/Espagne	4.8	4.9	5.5	4.2	2.7	1.7	1.4	1.0	1.0	0.9
Brazil/Brésil	0.6	0.8	0.6	0.7	0.9	0.6	0.7	1.0	1.0	0.8
Chile/Chili	0.6	0.4	0.3	0.5	0.3	0.4	0.4	0.6	0.8	0.9
Germany/Allemagne				1.9	1.1	0.8	0.7	0.6	0.6	0.6
Venezuela	0.4	0.3	0.5	0.5	0.4	0.4	0.4	0.5	0.5	0.7
France, Monaco	2.7	2.1	2.1	2.2	1.3	0.9	0.7	0.6	0.4	0.3
Colombia/Colombie	0.9	0.5	0.4	0.6	0.5	0.5	0.5	0.6	0.5	0.5

4. General Imports F.O.B. by Commodities according to the S.I.T.C. (Rev. 2) in million U.S. Dollars
Importations Générales F.O.B. par Produits d'après la C.T.C.I. (Rév. 2) en millions de Dollars E.U.

SITC CTCI	COMMODITY	1994 QUANTITY QUANTITE	1994 VALUE VALEUR	1995 QUANTITY QUANTITE	1995 VALUE VALEUR	1996 QUANTITY QUANTITE	1996 VALUE VALEUR	1997 QUANTITY QUANTITE	1997 VALUE VALEUR	PRODUIT
	ALL COMMODITIES		79335.0		72453.0		89355.1		111974.2	TOUS PRODUITS
0	FOOD AND LIVE ANIMALS		4884.0		3095.4		4897.2		4633.9	ALIMENTS,ANIMAUX VIVANTS
01	MEAT AND PREPARATIONS		992.5		504.0		652.3		934.5	VIANDES ET PREPARATIONS
011	MEAT FRESH,CHILLD,FROZEN	W 616158	825.3	W 415784	428.5		574.5	W 705593	840.2	VIANDES FRAICHES,REF,CONGE
0111	BOVINE MEAT FRESH,FROZEN	W 119328	336.9	W 41115	107.1	W 87235	183.4	W 160378	355.8	VIANDES BOVIN FRAI,REF
01112	BOVINE MEAT BONELESS	W 97760	286.1	W 35364	94.8	W 69766	156.9	W 129672	305.3	VIANDES BOVIN DESOSSEES
02	DAIRY PRODCTS,BIRDS'EGGS		545.1		423.8		560.1		588.4	PRODUITS LAITIERS,OEUFS
022	MILK AND CREAM	W 339105	371.8	W 230224	320.7	W 288490	434.6	W 293959	428.0	LAIT ET CREME
0224	MILK,CREAM PRESERVED ETC	W 195125	289.4	W 160718	285.1	W 223370	403.5	W 229333	393.2	LAIT,CREME CONS,CONC
02242	MILK DRY,1.5% FAT OR LES	W 118319	194.8	W 106400	211.5	W 140896	299.6	W 135141	268.9	LAIT POUDRE INF 1.5%
04	CEREALS AND PREPARATIONS		1419.0		1127.0		2281.8		1438.4	CEREALES ET PRODUITS
041	WHEAT ETC UNMILLED	W 1413743	189.3	W 1222652	217.2	W 1969329	427.2	W 1794674	323.0	FROMENT,EPEAUTRE
0412	OTHER WHEAT ETC UNMILLED	W 1372688	184.5	W 1199329	212.9	W 1839567	397.8	W 1738107	309.7	AUTRE FROMENT NON MOULU
044	MAIZE UNMILLED	W 2746639	369.6	W 2686920	376.2	W 5872159	1063.5	W 2473569	379.6	MAIS NON MOULU
045	CEREALS NES UNMILLED	W 3554859	417.0	W 2162632	272.8	W 2157509	360.9	W 2288319	303.7	AUTRES CEREALES NON MOULUES
0459	OTHER CEREALS UNMILLED	W 3511674	411.4	W 2132029	267.6	W 2114565	352.5	W 2235273	294.5	SARRASIN,MILLET,SORGHO
04592	SORGHUM UNMILLED	W 3473258	394.9	W 2092492	254.4	W 2066392	331.3	W 2189028	280.3	SORGHO NON MOULU
048	CEREAL ETC PREPARATIONS	W 560694	308.8	W 252907	150.0	W 342721	200.7	W 363384	226.0	PREPTNS A BASE CEREALES
05	VEGETABLES AND FRUIT		660.8		310.5		432.2		505.2	LEGUMES ET FRUITS
057	FRUIT,NUTS,FRESH,DRIED	W 381815	331.3	W 193809	150.7		169.0		224.4	FRUITS FRAIS OU SECS
081	*FEEDING STUFF FOR ANIML	W 1189558	327.8		219.2	W 711825	238.5		234.9	NOURRITURE POUR ANIMAUX
09	MISC EDIBLE PRODUCTS		309.1		215.4		240.2		308.3	PREP ALIMENTAIRES DIVERSES
098	EDIBLE PRODCTS,PREPS NES		274.1		176.7	W 182920	194.0	W 204523	262.4	PREP ALIMENTAIRES NDA
1	BEVERAGES AND TOBACCO		342.6		139.4		146.8		208.1	BOISSONS ET TABACS
11	BEVERAGES		324.5		131.2		134.1		166.6	BOISSONS
2	CRUDE MATERLS,EXCL FUELS		3030.5		3034.2		3641.7		4518.3	MAT BRUTES NON COMESTIBLES
22	OIL SEEDS,OLEAGINOUS FRT		870.3		769.7		1239.5		1382.1	GRAINES,FRUITS OLEAGINEUX
222	SEEDS FOR'SOFT'FIXED OIL	W 3245671	862.3	W 2923357	765.9	W 3988145	1228.1	W 4251123	1372.2	GRAINES HUILES FIXES
2222	SOYA BEANS	W 2496565	640.5	W 2232453	542.4	W 3057345	897.6	W 3380868	1077.6	FEVES DE SOJA
24	CORK AND WOOD		302.6		172.9		162.3		205.7	LIEGE ET BOIS
248	WOOD SHAPED,SLEEPERS		277.3		162.7	W 269412	153.8	W 274098	186.2	BOIS SIMPLEMENT TRAVAILLES
251	*PULP AND WASTE PAPER	W 1704123	483.8	W 1629024	677.1		405.9		512.9	PATES A PAPIER,DECHETS
2511	WASTE PAPER,PPRBOARD ETC	W 1091364	177.8	W 1109907	267.0	W 1261524	155.1	W 1406598	208.8	DECHETS DE PAPIER
2517	SODA,SULPHATE WOOD PULP	W 490321	242.6	W 425169	340.3	W 380758	190.5	W 452995	229.0	PATES CHIMIQUES AU SULFATE
25172	— BLEACHED,NONDISSOLVNG	W 487144	240.9	W 422469	338.3	W 375163	187.8	W 448202	226.5	PATES BLANCHIES
26	TEXTILE FIBRES AND WASTE		383.1		342.6		480.0		585.5	FIBRES TEXTILES
263	COTTON	W 184080	231.2	W 142506	231.4	W 213363	358.4	W 299662	455.1	COTON
2631	RAW COTTON,EXCL LINTERS	W 148488	222.7	W 114784	219.8	W 186245	346.2	W 262357	442.6	COTON EN MASSE
27	CRUDE FERTLZR,MINRLS NES		216.6		259.5		307.8		382.8	ENGRAIS MINERAUX BRUTS
28	METALLIFEROUS ORES,SCRAP		236.7		315.2		386.2		680.3	MINERAIS METAL,DECHETS
29	CRUDE ANIMAL,VEG MAT NES		245.6		226.2		269.1		323.0	MATIERES BRUTES ANIM,VEGET
3	MINERAL FUELS ETC		1507.3		1540.1		1808.9		2986.3	COMBUSTIBLES MINERAUX LUB
33	PETROLEUM AND PRODUCTS		1120.6		1053.5		1223.0		2119.7	PETROLE ET DERIVES
334	PETROLEUM PRODUCTS,REFIN	W 7618328	1015.8	W 6929627	931.5	W 6015170	1096.1	MW 10894	1953.3	PRODUITS RAFFINES
3341	GASOLINE,OTH LIGHT OILS	W 2517132	450.3	W 2500805	471.3	W 131735	42.7	W 4822010	1072.8	ESSENCES POUR MOTEURS
33411	MOTOR,AVIATION SPIRIT	W 2517132	450.3	W 2500805	471.3	W 131735	42.7	W 4822010	1072.8	ESSENCES MOTEURS D'AVIONS
3342	KEROSENE,OTH MEDIUM OILS	W 809	0.4	W 2445	0.9	W 2745835	601.0	W 4438	1.0	PETR LAMPANTS,AUT HUIL
33421	KEROSENE INCL JET FUEL	W 809	0.4	W 2445	0.9	W 2745835	601.0			PETROLES LAMPANTS
3344	FUEL OILS,NES	W 3669538	311.3	W 3163524	244.4	W 1888	0.8	W 349751	103.0	FUEL OILS
3345	LUBS,PETROLEUM OILS NES	W 1430848	254.0	W 1262853	215.1	W 2883246	366.2	W 4923988	620.6	HUILES LUBRIFIANTES
33451	LUBS(HIGH PETR CONT) ETC	W 1415080	211.4	W 1250029	177.1	W 2780037	321.9	W 4781280	556.4	HUILES LUBRIF,H LOURDES
341	*GAS,NATURAL AND MANUFCT	MV 66076	271.4	MV 127114	328.7		393.8	W 3246220	602.2	GAZ NATUREL,GAZ MANUFACT
3413	PETROLM GASES,LIQUEFIED	V 2466587	198.7	V 2702433	222.8	W 1443195	334.5	W 2045448	493.9	GAZ DE PETROLE LIQUEFIE
4	ANIMAL,VEGETABLE OIL,FAT		496.3		550.4		521.5		560.1	HUILES,GRAISSES ANIM,VEG
42	FIXED VEGETABLE OIL,FAT		337.5		344.2		318.1		343.3	HUILES VEGETALES FIXES
423	FIXED VEG OILS,SOFT	W 388253	228.6	W 392033	243.8	W 368035	210.6	W 387080	223.4	HUILES VEGET DOUCES FIXES
5	CHEMCLS,RELATED PROD NES		6762.4		6702.9		8134.7		10054.1	PRODUITS CHIMIQUES
51	ORGANIC CHEMICALS		1794.3		2022.6		2139.5		2687.1	PROD CHIMIQ ORGANIQUES
511	HYDROCARBONS NES,DERIVS		406.7		586.7		504.8	W 1339584	665.2	HYDROCARBURES NDA
5112	CYCLIC HYDROCARBONS		171.0		318.1		220.2	W 715387	335.3	HYDROCARBURES CYCLIQUES
51124	XYLENES,CHEMICALLY PURE	V 353793	134.5	V 402021	275.7	W 304694	158.1	W 460937	209.8	XYLENES PURS
512	ALCOHOLS,PHENOLS ETC		187.5		228.5	W 511812	255.1	W 802149	316.3	PHENOLS,PHENOLS–ALCOOLS
513	CARBOXYLIC ACIDS ETC	W 112625	220.2	W 89475	234.0		299.4		378.7	ACIDES CARBOXYLIQUES
514	NITROGEN–FNCTN COMPOUNDS	W 72520	410.2	W 73946	386.2	W 114496	454.4	W 147219	564.7	COMPOSES FONCT AZOTEES
515	ORG–INORG COMPOUNDS ETC	W 41655	299.2	W 29851	279.8	W 40605	359.1	W 48277	398.9	COMPOSES ORGANO–MINERAUX
516	OTHER ORGANIC CHEMICALS	W 444857	270.8	W 1399335	307.6		267.0	W 556719	363.6	AUTRES PROD ORGANIQUES
52	INORGANIC CHEMICALS		425.4		443.2		539.3		616.2	PROD CHIM INORGANIQUES
523	OTHR INORG CHEMICALS ETC	W 672623	236.2	W 674544	266.5	W 735600	290.6	W 955230	372.7	AUT PRODUITS CHIMIQUES INORG
53	DYES,TANNING,COLOUR PROD		449.5		403.3		539.7		699.8	PROD TEINTURE,COLORANTS
533	PIGMENTS,PAINTS,ETC	W 112476	296.3	W 88689	258.7	W 1394967	334.6	W 1456354	441.0	PIGMENTS,PEINTURES,VERNIS
541	*MEDICINAL,PHARM PRODUCT		676.0	MK 13574	585.0	MK 72724	803.0	MK 81599	898.8	PROD MEDICINAUX PHARMACEUT
5417	MEDICAMENTS	K 5085488	233.8	K 5953928	209.1	MK 15927	264.1	MK 23408	388.9	MEDICAMENTS
55	PERFUME,CLEANING ETC PRD		489.6		371.9		435.3		535.0	PROD POUR PARFUM,TOILETTE
553	PERFUMERY,COSMETICS,ETC	W 71301	277.8		183.4	W 79273	204.2	W 86591	256.0	PRODUITS DE PARFUMERIE
58	PLASTIC MATERIALS ETC		1809.1		1948.1		2350.5		2953.0	MAT PLAST ARTIFICIELLES
582	PROD OF CONDENSATION ETC	W 135671	415.7	W 154913	501.6	W 393244	589.9	W 422642	701.7	PROD CONDENS,POLYCOND
5823	ALKYDS,OTHER POLYESTERS	W 69141	191.8	W 78621	248.9	W 148526	270.7	W 181178	336.9	ALKYDES ET AUT POLYESTERS
583	POLYMERIZATION ETC PRODS		1280.0		1344.0	W 1477361	1655.0	W 1807395	2126.3	PROD POLYMERISATION
5831	POLYETHYLENE	W 398988	373.3	W 288123	321.6	W 480780	421.1	W 627739	590.9	POLYETHYLENE
58311	— IN PRIMARY FORMS	W 364609	293.1	W 255413	244.4	W 364682	321.1	W 501198	461.8	POLYETHYLENE PRIMAIRES
5839	OTH POLYMRZTION ETC PROD	W 132373	392.4	W 226688	448.6	W 426372	535.0	W 477418	644.0	AUT PROD POLYMER COPOLYM
59	CHEMICAL MATERIALS NES		888.8		825.7		1099.7		1383.4	MAT PROD CHIMIQUES NDA
598	MISCEL CHEM PRODUCTS NES		556.3		512.5	W 817068	718.0	W 829579	890.1	PROD DIV INDUST CHIM NDA
5989	CHEM PRODUCTS,PREPS NES	W 318660	487.4	W 331481	443.0	W 714812	625.1	W 721047	806.0	PROD PREP CHIMIQUES NDA
59899	OTH CHEM PRODS,PREPS,NES	W 277159	338.2	W 290757	306.2	W 452187	384.9	W 413946	532.2	AUT PRODUITS CHIMIQUES NDA
6	BASIC MANUFACTURES		12950.6		12024.5		15373.0		18900.4	ART MANUFACTURES
61	LEATHER,DRESSED FUR,ETC		279.9		325.2		457.1		634.1	CUIRS,PELLETERIES
611	LEATHER		161.0		180.7	W 28360	260.5	W 51361	366.6	CUIRS,PEAUX PREPARES
62	RUBBER MANUFACTURES NES		747.0		785.9		1174.6		1469.6	CAOUTCHOUC MANUFACTURE
625	RUBBER TYRES, TUBES ETC	MN 29739	328.0		245.9	W 785660	418.4	W 326131	561.6	PNEUS CAOUTCHOUC VULCANISE
628	RUBBER ARTICLES NES	W 27892	272.0	W 30442	358.3	W 274452	500.4	W 789366	605.5	OUVRAGES CAOUTCHOUC NDA
6289	OTH RUBBER ARTICLES NES	W 22429	230.0	W 25887	319.1	W 110928	446.5	W 595330	539.9	AUT OUVR CAOUTCHOUC NDA
62898	UNHARD RUBBER PRODS NES	W 21991	225.8	W 25138	311.8	W 101885	439.6	W 585272	533.6	OUV CAOUT VULC NON DURCI
63	WOOD,CORK MANUFACTRS NES		390.1		185.4		226.6		259.5	OUVRAGES LIEGE ET BOIS
64	PAPER,PAPERBOARD AND MFR		1980.7		1810.0		2052.4		2359.5	PAPIERS,CARTONS & OUVRAGES
641	PAPER AND PAPERBOARD	W 1126911	877.3	W 744541	751.1	W 1010374	868.4	W 1294708	1111.2	PAPIERS ET CARTONS
642	PAPER,ETC,PRECUT,ARTS OF	W 654892	1103.5	W 619804	1059.0	W 1605206	1184.1	W 1229671	1248.4	PAP,CARTONS DECOUPES
6421	PAPER ETC CONTAINERS	W 450308	596.2	W 457896	668.3	W 728211	757.6	W 738066	815.4	BOITES,SACS EMBALLAGES
6428	PAPER ETC ARTICLES NES	W 142087	366.4	W 115925	285.9	W 745282	302.6	W 377205	286.9	OUVRAGES EN PATE A PAPIER
65	TEXTILE YARN,FABRICS,ETC		2147.0		1768.9		2241.5		2897.0	FILS,TISSUS,ARTICLES TEXTILE
651	TEXTILE YARN		178.6	W 33557	171.9		321.7		441.1	FILS TEXTILES

4. General Imports F.O.B. by Commodities according to the S.I.T.C. (Rev. 2) in million U.S. Dollars
Importations Générales F.O.B. par Produits d'après la C.T.C.I. (Rév. 2) en millions de Dollars E.U.

SITC CTCI	COMMODITY	1994 QUANTITY QUANTITE	1994 VALUE VALEUR	1995 QUANTITY QUANTITE	1995 VALUE VALEUR	1996 QUANTITY QUANTITE	1996 VALUE VALEUR	1997 QUANTITY QUANTITE	1997 VALUE VALEUR	PRODUIT
652	COTTON FABRICS,WOVEN		227.7	A 115928	178.6		263.9		338.8	TISSUS DE COTON
653	WOVN MAN–MADE FIB FABRIC	A 528813	829.5	A 337599	590.6	W 122570	709.4	W 133199	814.1	TISSUS FIBRES SYNTH,ARTIF
6531	CONT SYNT WEAVES NONPILE	A 271494	270.4	A 187476	217.0	W 74616	284.1	W 86215	376.0	TISSUS FIBRES SYNTH CONTINUE
65315	CONT SYN TXTL FABRIC NES	A 223935	247.8	A 177210	201.4	W 47775	255.6	W 68780	345.2	TIS PLUS 85% TEXT SYNT CONT
657	SPECIAL TXTL FABRC,PRODS		416.0		427.9	W 444177	392.5	W 269476	526.4	TISSUS SPECIAUX
66	NONMETAL MINERAL MFS NES		815.2		659.6		1020.0		1233.3	ART MIN NON METALLIQUES
664	GLASS	W 172322	264.2	W 165623	270.8		508.9		593.9	VERRE
67	IRON AND STEEL		2163.9		1938.4		2519.8		3106.2	FER ET ACIER
672	IRON,STEEL PRIMARY FORMS	W 1124934	468.1	W 429462	313.9	W 695903	356.7	W 914657	468.6	LINGOTS FER,ACIER
6727	IRN,STL COIL FR REROLLNG	W 890752	400.6	W 292029	268.9	W 289926	249.2	W 514974	344.9	EBAUCHES POUR TOLES FER
67271	IRON,SIMPLE STEEL COILS	W 735786	244.1	W 169960	74.8	W 140080	65.9	W 307094	129.6	EBAUCHES NON EN ACIER
673	IRON,STEEL SHAPES ETC	W 621923	324.7	W 338448	227.8	W 592886	328.3	W 749151	416.0	BARRES,PROFIL FER,ACIER
674	IRN,STL UNIV,PLATE,SHEET	W 1149538	747.9	W 1015722	717.8	W 1453541	964.7	W 1535497	1121.6	LARGES PLATS,TOLES
6746	IRN,STL THIN PLATE,ROLLD	W 399676	230.7	W 249677	172.9	W 488395	288.7	W 561579	331.5	TOLES LAM MOINS 3MM
6749	OTH IRN,STL PLATES,SHEET	W 299863	215.0	W 278382	214.5	W 486564	278.2	W 396083	318.7	AUTRES TOLES FER,ACIER
678	IRON,STL TUBES,PIPES,ETC	W 182470	305.6	W 145228	270.4	W 846662	380.3	W 517962	537.0	TUBES,TUYAUX EN FONTE,FER
68	NON–FERROUS METALS		1028.5		1026.6		1248.0		1542.9	METAUX NON FERREUX
682	COPPER EXC CEMENT COPPER	W 105174	341.5	W 72398	296.7	W 216052	429.6	W 188765	501.5	CUIVRE
6822	COPPER,ALLOYS WORKED	W 65122	243.2	W 53218	238.1	W 170663	310.7	W 122375	342.7	CUIVRE,ALLIAGES OUVRES
684	ALUMINIUM	W 272761	611.5	W 230671	654.0	W 397692	690.8	W 372185	866.0	ALUMINIUM
6842	ALUMINIUM,ALLOYS WORKED	W 155381	420.2	W 153212	498.5	W 291073	512.6	W 243588	633.1	ALUMINIUM,ALLIAGES OUVRE
68422	ALUMNM PLATE,SHEET,STRIP	W 95680	216.8	W 97844	299.0	W 118259	282.5	W 134845	337.5	TOLES, PLANCHES EN ALU
69	METAL MANUFACTURES NES		3398.6		3524.9		4433.4		5398.9	ART MANUFACT EN METAL NDA
694	STL,COPPR NAILS,NUTS,ETC	W 172025	396.6	W 113402	463.9	W 528609	639.9	W 449485	782.2	CLOUS,VIS,ECROUS
69402	IRN,STL NUTS,BOLTS,ETC	W 163567	367.2	W 105793	431.1	W 431503	598.1	W 389477	724.2	BOULONS,VIS,ECROUS FER,AC
695	TOOLS		365.0		280.5	W 424329	367.0	W 191307	509.2	OUTILS A MAIN
6954	BLADES,TIPS,ETC FR TOOLS		237.1		202.5	W 53569	269.6	W 48276	362.7	OUTILS POUR MACHINE–OUTIL
699	BASE METAL MFRS NES		2125.0		2453.4		3077.9		3635.2	ART MANUFACTURES MET NDA
6991	LOCKSMITHS WARES,ETC		293.8		349.1	W 1079163	483.4	W 566223	560.7	ARTICLES DE SERRURERIE
69913	BASE MTL DOOR,ETC FITTNG	W 35289	173.1	W 44066	210.7	W 86426	303.6	W 348229	355.5	GARNITURES POUR MEUBLES
6997	IRON,STEEL ARTICLES NES	W 329488	1074.2	W 334002	1160.3	W 1164469	1325.2	W 629696	1540.3	OUV FONTE,FER,ACIER NDA
69979	IRN,STL MANUFACTURES NES	W 329405	1074.0	W 333972	1160.2	W 1164415	1325.1	W 629518	1540.1	AUT OUVRAGES EN FER NDA
6998	MFRS NES OF CPR,NIKL,ETC	W 43464	362.6	W 145849	494.7	W 324372	701.0	W 221191	809.5	OUVRAGES EN CU,NI,AL,PB,ZN
69981	COPPER MANUFACTURES NES	W 10162	148.2	W 35080	215.8	W 100573	358.3	W 57111	355.4	OUVRAGES EN CUIVRE
69983	ALUMINIUM MANUFACTS NES	W 28274	196.4	W 104966	256.7	W 195689	312.3	W 145929	411.8	OUVRAGES EN ALUMINIUM
7	MACHINES,TRANSPORT EQUIP		30899.7		31247.0		41391.9		51783.5	MACHINES MATERIEL TRANSPORT
71	POWER GENERATING EQUIPMT		1535.0		1915.5		3461.7		4002.2	MACHINES GENERATRICES
713	INTRNL COMBUS PSTN ENGIN		647.3		1098.5		2391.1		2526.5	MOTEURS EXPL COMB INT, PIECE
7132	MOTOR VEHCL PISTN ENGINS	N 5102489	198.7	W 35509	381.4	W 551063	1293.4	W 193554	1348.1	MOTEURS EXPL POUR VEHICULES
7139	PISTON ENGINE PARTS NES	W 56363	376.8	W 63681	665.7		1013.6		1065.1	PIECES POUR 713.2,3,8
716	ROTATING ELECTRIC PLANT		641.5		571.7	W 528661	757.4		1040.8	APP ELECTR ROTATIFS,PIECES
7161	DC MOTORS AND GENERATORS	N 6713284	89.6	MN 14499	101.5	W 340950	143.8	W 139620	354.4	MOTEURS COURANT CONTINU
7162	AC MTRS,GENRTRS,GEN SETS	MN 30079	252.6	MN 50928	167.2	W 64541	212.6	W 44202	251.4	MOTEURS ELECTRIQUES
7169	PTS NES OF ROT ELEC PLNT	W 92762	298.0	W 110902	302.4	W 123149	400.7	W 93252	434.1	PIECES MAC APP ROTATIFS
72	MACHS FOR SPCL INDUSTRYS		3235.8		2445.9		2891.9		4055.7	MAC SPECIALES POUR INDUST
723	CIVIL ENGNEERG EQUIP ETC		526.0		160.7	W 41791	220.3	W 74125	351.2	APPAREILS DE GENIE CIVIL
7234	CONST,MINING MACHNRY NES		438.3		116.3	W 31487	160.8	W 59557	262.1	MACH POUR LA CONST, MINES
724	TEXTILE,LEATHER MACHNRY		527.4		477.0	W 47086	589.6	W 92709	960.8	MACH POUR INDUSTRIE TEXTILE
726	PRINTG,BKBINDG MACHY,PTS		238.9		128.7		142.7	W 12796	228.5	MACHINES POUR IMPRIMERIE
728	OTH MACHY FOR SPCL INDUS		1448.9		1295.1	W 119573	1583.3	W 131126	2018.9	AUT MACH IND PARTICULIERES
7284	MACHY FOR SPCL INDUS NES		1240.0		1146.5	W 92347	1390.4	W 94299	1756.4	MACH SPEC IND PARTICUL.
72842	RUBBER,PLASTICS WRKG MCH		325.6		314.5	W 24658	309.5	W 32188	439.7	MACH IND CAOUT MAT PLAST
72848	OTH MCHY WITH INDIV FNCT	N 3250538	716.4	N 1933429	498.8	W 35282	745.4	W 36063	885.7	AUTRES MACHINES NDA
73	METALWORKING MACHINERY		918.9		754.4		992.8		1195.2	MACH TRAVAIL DES METAUX
736	METALWORKING MACH–TOOLS		527.4		530.0		743.4	W 95677	815.5	MACH–OUTILS TRAVAIL METAUX
737	METALWORKING MACHNRY NES		391.6		224.5	W 28576	249.5	W 34669	379.8	MACH TRAV METAUX PIECES
74	GENRL INDUSTRL MACHY NES		4301.1		3882.6		4837.3		5957.2	MACH APP INDUSTRIE
741	HEATING,COOLING EQUIPMNT		671.9		619.3		790.3	W 234083	976.5	MACH CHAUFFAGE,PIECES
7416	HEATING,COOLING EQU NES	N 1725507	218.0	N 1182997	276.5	W 34375	230.0	W 30818	218.8	APP CHANGEMENT TEMP
742	PUMPS FOR LIQUIDS ETC		261.8		241.4	W 828220	319.1	W 268551	415.3	POMPES MOTO–POMPES
743	PUMPS NES,CENTRFUGES ETC		916.6		864.4	W 303142	1009.0	W 536895	1109.1	POMPES COMPRES,VENT ETC
7431	PUMPS FOR GASES ETC	N 5624137	248.9	MN 33809	247.7	W 42165	387.5	W 139665	402.3	POMPES AIR A VIDE,COMPRES
7436	GAS,LIQUID FILTERS ETC	W 29831	380.0	W 29953	352.8	W 105983	334.4	W 356304	372.5	APP POUR FILT DES LIQUIDES
7439	PTS NES OF APP OF 7435,6	W 37068	240.8	W 36193	211.8	W 130534	221.0	W 28965	248.7	PIECES 743.5 ET 743.6
744	MECHANICAL HANDLING EQU		478.4		360.9	W 555105	437.3	W 213305	573.4	EQUIP MANUTENTION PIECES
7442	LIFTING,LOADING MACH NES	N 1463979	315.3	N 545454	221.5	W 266019	259.2	W 119689	307.1	APP LEVAGE,MANUTENTION
74428	OTH HANDLING ETC MCH NES	N 1160789	239.9	N 454727	174.3	W 258071	210.2	W 110247	247.1	AUT APP LEVAGE ETC
745	NONELEC MACHY,TOOLS NES		709.2		516.3	W 85973	525.2	W 72539	679.3	AUT MACH NON ELEC,PIECES
7452	OTH NONELEC MCHS,PTS NES		607.2		438.6	W 80202	431.2	W 64673	552.3	AUT MACH NON ELEC,PIECES
74522	PACKAGNG,BOTTLNG,ETC MCH	N 706800	314.4	N 130541	209.1	W 9678	169.2	W 8254	201.1	MACH NETT BOUTEILLES,ETC
749	NONELEC MACH PTS,ACC NES	W 146450	1263.4	W 112827	1280.6	W 1201190	1756.7	W 1538417	2203.8	PIECES MACH NON ELEC NDA
7492	COCKS,VALVES ETC NES	W 28943	370.4	W 22320	340.3	W 48837	508.3	W 355533	656.8	ART ROB,SIM POUR TUYAUX
7493	SHAFT,CRANK,PULLEY ETC	W 76606	329.3	W 56899	369.3	W 209802	514.2	W 683371	619.7	ARBRES TRANS,VILEBREQUINS
7499	OTH NONELEC MCHY PTS NES	W 19817	370.3	W 19486	389.8	W 869757	486.1	W 250628	609.8	PIECES NON ELECT NDA
74991	FOUNDRY MOULDS ETC NES	W 12360	279.7	W 13045	292.9	W 12356	352.6	W 14497	456.3	MOULES POUR METAUX
75	OFFICE MACHNES,ADP EQUIP		2280.5		1891.2		2344.7		2913.6	MACH BUREAU TRAIT AUTOM
751	OFFICE MACHINES	N 7115911	320.9	N 4455494	200.8	W 22990	223.4	W 24495	269.0	MACH,APPAREILS DE BUREAU
752	AUTOMTIC DATA PROC EQUIP	MN 12809	1303.0	N 6292701	979.5	W 55658	1291.0	W 57635	1632.4	MACH TRAIT INFORMATION
7523	DIGITL CENTRL PROCESSORS	N 280031	318.9	N 113067	204.7	W 4818	296.0	W 5972	386.9	UNITES CENTRALES
7525	ADP PERIPHERAL UNITS	MN 10730	544.5	N 4356003	452.5	W 34684	577.6	W 38210	661.8	UNITES PERIPHERIQUES
759	OFFICE,ADP MCH PTS,ACCES	W 16905	656.7	W 32127	711.1	W 67220	830.4	W 54974	1012.3	PIECES DU 751 ET 752
7599	ACCTG,ETC,ADP MCH PTS,AC	W 9093	521.0	W 23924	581.2	W 57588	685.8	W 42785	821.5	PIECES DU 751 ET 752
76	TELECOMM,SOUND EQUIPMENT		3938.7		3161.9		3583.4		4775.3	EQUIPMENT DE TELECOM
761	TELEVISION RECEIVERS	N 7289885	319.3	N 1453810	165.7	W 29722	161.1	W 35627	263.3	RECEPTEURS DE TELEVISION
7611	COLOUR TV RECEIVERS	N 6926730	309.1	N 1336233	161.4	W 28605	157.5	W 34458	257.9	RECEPTEURS COULEUR
762	RADIO BROADCAST RECEIVRS	MN 10764	354.5	N 7354323	320.5		411.8	W 209384	485.3	RECEPTEURS RADIODIFFUSION
7628	OTHER RADIO RECEIVERS	N 7489933	298.6	N 4748168	216.4	W 19215	219.0	W 28697	267.0	AUTRES RECEPT RADIO
763	SOUND RECORDRS,PHONOGRPH	MN 13975	821.5	MN 12582	745.6		613.1		497.7	PHONO,APP ENREGISTREMENT
7638	OTHR SOUND APPARATUS ETC	MN 12088	676.9	MN 11002	598.3		587.8	W 48002	482.7	AUT APP D'ENREGIS,REPROD
76381	TV IMAGE,SND RECRDRS ETC	N 6018951	425.0	N 4131670	316.4	W 9005	303.2	W 7826	237.0	APP ENREG,REPRO IMAG,SON
76388	DICTATING MACHINES ETC	N 6068987	252.0	N 6870040	281.9		284.6	W 40176	245.8	MACHINES A DICTER
764	TELECOM EQPT,PTS,ACC NES		2443.5		1930.3	W 928553	2397.5	W 661665	3529.2	EQUIP TELECOM,PIECES
7641	LINE TELEPHONE,ETC EQUIP	N 7816383	500.6	MN 9234	357.5	W 21712	641.7	W 18735	783.4	APP TELEPHON PAR FIL
7643	TV,RADIO TRANSMITTRS ETC		507.8		242.4	W 8667	226.1	W 10138	508.3	APP EMET TELE RADIO
7649	PTS NES OF EQUIPMT OF 76		1127.5		1092.0	W 122629	1184.3	W 314484	1692.9	PIECES DE LA DIV 76
76493	TELECOMM EQUIPMT PTS NES	W 56280	752.0	W 58703	737.5	W 48155	700.5	W 244813	894.4	PIECES 761,762,764.3,8
76499	PARTS ETC OF SOUND EQUIP		130.4	W 2669	167.7	W 8770	250.2	W 29259	423.2	PIECES NDA POUR 763
77	ELECTRIC MACHNRY NES ETC		10764.0		13134.7		16141.3		19356.1	MACH APP ELECT NDA
771	ELECTRIC POWER MACHY NES		612.7		742.3	W 312778	905.8	W 241042	1301.1	MACH PROD,TRANS ELECTR
7711	TRANSFORMERS,ELECTRICAL	MN 478530	254.7	MN 684505	291.2	W 113967	315.2	W 87855	393.5	TRANSFO ELECTRIQUES
7712	OTH ELEC POWER MACHY NES		358.0		451.2	W 198811	590.6	W 153187	907.7	AUT APP PROD TRANSF ELEC

4. General Imports F.O.B. by Commodities according to the S.I.T.C. (Rev. 2) in million U.S. Dollars
Importations Générales F.O.B. par Produits d'après la C.T.C.I. (Rév. 2) en millions de Dollars E.U.

SITC CTCI	COMMODITY	1994 QUANTITY QUANTITE	1994 VALUE VALEUR	1995 QUANTITY QUANTITE	1995 VALUE VALEUR	1996 QUANTITY QUANTITE	1996 VALUE VALEUR	1997 QUANTITY QUANTITE	1997 VALUE VALEUR	PRODUIT
772	SWITCHGEAR ETC,PARTS NES		2469.2		2804.8	W 542104	3743.7	W 1401099	4476.4	APP COUPURE,SECT ETC
7721	SWITCHGEAR ETC	W 72586	1707.6	W 76712	1856.2	W 145760	2468.2	W 1141256	3039.7	APP COUPURE,SECTIONMNT
7722	PRINTED CIRCUITS,PTS NES	MN 314854	464.9	MN 381497	655.9	W 87373	882.1	W 74687	947.2	CIRCUITS ET PIECES
7723	FIXED,VARIABLE RESISTORS	W 11801	296.8		292.8	W 308971	393.5	W 185156	489.7	POTENTIOMETRES PIECES
773	ELECTR DISTRIBUTNG EQUIP	W 277666	1961.2	W 319252	2315.2	W 653038	2550.8	W 594814	3038.2	EQUIPMT DISTRIBUTION ELECT
7731	INSULATED WIRE,CABLE ETC	W 256530	1597.0	W 299152	1883.6	W 504794	2087.6	W 486549	2455.3	FILS,CABLES ISOLES ELECT
7732	ELECTRC INSULATING EQUIP	W 21136	364.2	W 20100	431.6	W 148243	463.3	W 108266	583.0	EQUIP ISOL ELECTRIQUE
775	HOUSEHOLD TYPE EQUIP NES		440.1		240.8	W 507368	293.2		372.1	MACH,APP USAGE DOMESTQUE
776	TRANSISTORS,VALVES,ETC		3117.3		4510.4		5577.1		6505.1	LAMPES,TUBES,VALVES
7761	TV PICTURE TUBES	MN 34409	864.3	MN 53560	1245.7	W 333719	1577.6	W 100535	1679.8	TUBES CATHODIQUES
7763	DIODES,TRANSISTORS,ETC	W 10198	467.3	W 12508	615.0	W 42482	726.7	W 288144	835.0	DIODES,TRANSISTORS
7764	ELECTRONIC MICROCIRCUITS		1535.6		2299.3	W 100753	2896.0	W 106338	3275.5	MICROSTRUCTURES ELECTRON
7768	ELCTRNC COMP PTS,CRYSTLS	W 14693	240.3	W 14487	332.9	W 62382	341.1	W 129651	425.6	CRIST PIEZO–ELEC,PCS 776
77689	ELECTRNIC COMPON PTS NES	W 14401	196.6	W 13837	267.9	W 11880	252.2	W 89239	285.1	PIECES DU GROUPE 776
778	ELECTRICAL MACHINERY NES		1969.0		2422.3	W 3099847	2983.7	W 1921908	3547.5	AUTRES MACH ELECT NDA
7781	BATTERIES,ACCUMULATORS		255.4		331.1	W 317903	436.1	W 190856	621.0	PILES ET ACCUMULATEURS
7783	AUTOMOTIVE ELECTR EQUIP		268.7		357.4	W 2026614	527.4	W 1042849	541.6	EQUIP ELECT MOTEURS EXPL
77831	IGNITION,STARTING EQUIP		141.8		225.7	W 152244	323.1	W 546907	307.3	APP ELEC ALLUM,DEMARRAGE
7788	OTH ELEC MACHY,EQUIP NES		1204.4		1504.0	W 318187	1736.5	W 483896	2055.6	AUT MACH APP ELEC NDA
77884	ELECTRICAL CONDENSERS	MN 8865516	500.3	MN 10443350	704.2	W 30340	895.9	W 190169	1114.7	CONDENSATEURS ELECTRIQUES
77886	OTH ELEC MACHINERY NES	MN 28904	222.4		175.0	W 28148	286.2	W 93901	274.0	AUT MACH APP ELECTRIQUES
77889	ELEC PARTS OF MACHY NES	W 3825	285.5	W 6983	422.8	W 31953	295.5	W 31310	322.9	PIECES ELEC DE MACH NDA
78	ROAD VEHICLES		3179.9		3831.7		6990.9		9274.5	VEHICULES ROUTIERS
781	PASS MOTOR VEH EXC BUSES	N 140313	1239.9	N 66554	438.6	W 279853	920.6	W 542967	1554.3	AUTO TRANSPORT PERSONNES
782	LORRIES,SPCL MTR VEH NES	N 56426	175.0	N 32296	122.6	W 147695	332.5	W 1112798	801.0	VEHICULES SPECIAUX,MARCH
7821	LORRIES,TRUCKS	N 55839	130.0	N 31982	104.1	W 144034	307.4	W 1107703	768.1	VEHICULES TRANSP MARCHAND
784	MOTOR VEH PRTS,ACCES NES	MN 347424	1343.0	MN 1207116	3103.9		5578.9	W 1998944	6638.4	PIECES 722,781,782,783
7849	OTHER MOTOR VEHCL PARTS	MN 347374	1289.2	MN 1207109	3081.5	W 6088295	5526.1	W 1955217	6499.6	PIECES 722,781,782,783
79	OTHR TRANSPORT EQUIPMENT		746.1		229.4		148.2		254.1	AUTRE MATERIEL TRANSPORT
792	AIRCRAFT ETC		536.7		85.4		87.8	W 2206	163.8	APP NAVIGATION AERIENNE
8	MISC MANUFACTURED GOODS		10122.8		9100.3		11139.1		14293.7	ART MANUFACTURES DIVERS
821	*FURNITURE,PARTS THEREOF		611.6		428.9	W 420029	484.3	W 194489	623.5	MEUBLES ET PIECES
8211	CHAIRS,SEATS AND PARTS		231.7		238.0	W 340587	312.7	W 111054	392.7	SIEGES ET PIECES
8219	FURNITURE AND PARTS NES		326.8		166.3	W 67520	147.2	W 74347	196.0	AUTRES MEUBLES ET PIECES
84	CLOTHING AND ACCESSORIES		1823.6		1912.5		2394.6		3355.2	VETEMENTS
842	MENS OUTERWEAR NOT KNIT	MN 98547	423.8	MN 150505	455.5		489.4	W 43874	606.2	VET DESSUS POUR HOMMES
8423	— TROUSERS,BREECHES ETC	MN 77520	328.0	MN 119038	390.7	W 34043	424.7	W 36924	506.0	PANTALONS HOMMES MAT TEX
843	WOMENS OUTERWEAR NONKNIT	MN 139544	491.8		435.4	W 58464	586.9	W 60442	684.9	VET DESSUS FEMMES MAT TEX
8439	— OTHER OUTER GARMENTS	MN 111370	323.5	MN 143738	303.1	W 42405	446.3	W 45352	538.0	AUT VET DES FEM MAT TEXT
844	UNDER GARMENTS NOT KNIT	MN 317889	163.3	MN 474034	203.7	W 53105	262.6	W 50864	368.7	VETEMENT DESSOUS MAT TEX
845	OUTERWEAR KNIT NONELASTC	MN 71018	275.0	MN 95980	309.8	W 37837	366.7	W 36784	586.7	VET DESSOUS,ACCES BONNET
8459	— OTHER,CLTHG ACCESRYS	MN 45996	158.2	MN .52547	154.3	W 25794	227.6	W 27536	354.0	AUT VET DESSUS DE BONNE
846	UNDER GARMENTS KNITTED	MN 262878	282.9	MN 373433	325.2	W 36915	453.8	W 32344	667.1	SOUS VETS DE BONNETERIE
8462	— OF COTTON NON ELASTIC	MN 133011	171.4	MN 170576	189.1	W 26091	263.8	W 18822	384.5	SOUS–VET BONNET COTON
84629	—— OTHER	MN 133011	171.4	MN 170576	189.1	W 26091	263.8	W 18822	384.5	AUT SOUS–VET BONNET COTON
87	PRECISION INSTRUMNTS NES		1457.9		1387.6		1884.5		2222.3	INSTRUM,APPAR SCIENT NDA
874	MEASURNG,CONTROLNG INSTR		1044.8		1007.9	W 358254	1426.1	W 772283	1702.7	INSTRUMENTS DE MESURE
8742	MEASUR,DRAW ETC INST,PTS		232.9		245.4	W 18566	318.8	W 160503	428.2	INST DESSIN,TRACAGE,PCS
87421	MEASURNG,DRAWNG ETC INST	MN 10758	216.8	N 6748722	226.5	W 17290	292.0	W 159075	377.2	INSTRUM DESSIN,TRACAGE
8743	GAS,LIQUID CONTROL INSTR	MN 96662	278.4	MN 87080	326.1	W 15284	523.6	W 428796	546.7	APP,INSTR MESURE FLUIDES
8748	ELEC MEAS,CONTRL EQU NES	N 3739777	293.2	N 5406423	248.9	W 3968	310.6	W 11089	364.0	APP ELEC ELECTRO MESURE
87483	OTH ELCTRNC MEAS ETC EQU	N 3112914	274.0	N 4521252	224.3	W 2436	283.2	W 9700	328.3	AUT APP ELECTRO DE MESURE
88	PHOTO EQU,OPTICL GDS ETC		704.0		503.6		627.8		798.3	APP,FOURN PHOTO,OP,MONTR
882	PHOTO,CINEMA SUPPLIES	W 27192	279.8	W 19798	257.1	W 48700	316.7	W 56140	390.2	PRODUITS PHOTO,CINEMA
89	MISC MANUFCTRD GOODS NES		5100.9		4643.0		5528.4		6980.7	ART MANUFACTURES DIVERS
892	PRINTED MATTER		728.8		581.7	W 1434676	639.8	W 997514	762.0	IMPRIMES
8921	PRINTED BOOKS,GLOBES,ETC		330.4		204.9	W 417038	211.3	W 209989	252.0	LIVRES,BROCHURES,CARTES
89211	PRINTED BOOKS,PAMPHLETS	MN 224817	324.9	MN 203625	202.9	W 414795	209.9	W 206710	247.5	LIVRES,BROCHURES
8928	PRINTED MATTER NES		256.6		265.6	W 997078	326.8	W 621175	395.8	IMPRIMES NDA
893	ARTICLES OF PLASTIC NES		2567.7		2817.5		3469.8		4349.5	OUVRAGES EN MAT DIVIS 58
8931	PLSTC PACKG CONTNRS,LIDS	W 199629	479.8	W 195062	566.3	W 1453768	664.5	W 914288	909.2	ART TRANSP EMBALLAGE ETC
8939	MISC PLASTIC ARTICLES	W 389914	2070.5	W 447365	2239.3	W 4089759	2790.6	W 2296304	3424.6	ART DIVERS EN MAT DIV 58
89399	OTHR PLASTC ARTICLES NES	W 378678	2044.6	W 441811	2224.1	W 4073802	2773.9	W 2275324	3401.0	AUT OUV MAT DIV 58
894	TOYS,SPORTING GOODS,ETC		641.6		357.8	W 130010	389.0		563.0	VOITURES ENFANTS,JOUETS
8942	TOYS,INDOOR GAMES ETC		477.9		240.7	W 108609	253.9	W 91151	315.6	JOUETS,JEUX ETC
895	OFFICE SUPPLIES NES		184.5		145.1	W 169339	197.7	W 170193	340.3	ART PAPET NDA
898	MUSICAL INSTRUMENTS,PTS		604.4		464.0		522.3		555.3	INSTRUMENTS DE MUSIQUE
8983	SOUND RECRDNG TAPE,DISCS	W 30354	547.6	W 26763	416.7	W 39146	487.2	W 47103	519.2	SUPPORTS SON POUR 763
89831	PREPD SND RECORDNG MEDIA	W 24944	290.3	W 23703	263.3	W 29497	255.4	W 32888	246.3	SUPPORTS PREPARES
89832	RECORDED DISCS,TAPES ETC	W 5410	257.4	W 3060	153.5	W 9649	231.9	W 14215	272.9	DISQUES,PHONO,BANDES
9	GOODS NOT CLASSD BY KIND		8339.5		5019.3		2300.9		4036.2	ART TRANSACT NON CLASSES
931	*SPECIAL TRANSACTIONS	W 1422786	8105.6	W 799954	4955.9	MW 90125	2201.9	W 189480	3870.1	TRANS.SPECIALES

5. General Exports F.O.B. by Commodities according to the S.I.T.C. (Rev. 2) in million U.S. Dollars
Exportations Générales F.O.B. par Produits d'après la C.T.C.I. (Rév. 2) en millions de Dollars E.U.

SITC CTCI	COMMODITY	1994		1995		1996		1997		PRODUIT
		QUANTITY QUANTITE	VALUE VALEUR	QUANTITY QUANTITE	VALUE VALEUR	QUANTITY QUANTITE	VALUE VALEUR	QUANTITY QUANTITE	VALUE VALEUR	
	ALL COMMODITIES		60618.6		79540.7		95661.2		110047.0	TOUS PRODUITS
0	FOOD AND LIVE ANIMALS		3736.6		5445.4		5311.4		5813.5	ALIMENTS,ANIMAUX VIVANTS
001	*LIVE ANIMALS FOR FOOD	W 195908	362.3	N 1679984	540.3		130.6	W 134571	199.6	ANIMAUX VIVANTS
0011	BOVINE SPECIES,LIVE	W 195304	361.7	N 1658153	536.2	W 89212	127.6	W 133794	198.3	ESPECE BOVINE
00119	— OTHR THAN FR BREEDING	W 195174	361.4	N 1656663	535.7	W 89156	127.5	W 133535	198.0	BOVINS NON REPRODUCTEURS
03	FISH AND PREPARATIONS		455.5		689.3		776.3		801.6	POISSONS ET PREPARATIONS
036	SHELL FISH FRESH,FROZEN	W 39512	376.3	W 57904	537.3	W 88398	574.5	W 87298	609.3	CRUSTACES,MOLLUSQUES
05	VEGETABLES AND FRUIT		2044.8		2680.5		2601.8		2651.2	LEGUMES ET FRUITS
054	VEG ETC FRSH,SMPLY PRSVD	W 1978848	1333.2	W 2471445	1795.4	W 3072819	1686.1	W 4330031	1725.1	LEGUMES FRAIS,CONG,SECS
0544	TOMATOES FRESH	W 516065	394.6	W 717287	585.7	W 979016	539.9	W 848001	523.5	TOMATES FRAICHES
0545	OTHER FRESH VEGETABLES	W 1037779	703.3	W 1299782	949.4	W 1663347	863.1	W 3078768	945.5	AUTRES LEGUMES FRAIS,REF
05459	FRESH VEGETABLES NES	W 792248	549.3	W 1062773	759.2	W 1355065	657.6	W 2752427	766.5	LEGUMES FRAIS,REFRI NDA
057	FRUIT,NUTS,FRESH,DRIED		476.3	W 1030875	572.8		615.7		603.3	FRUITS FRAIS OU SECS
0579	FRUIT FRESH OR DRIED NES		267.0	W 555116	318.4	W 813647	392.9		365.2	FRUITS FRAIS,SECS NDA
06	SUGAR AND PREPS,HONEY		119.6		258.6		455.1		447.4	SUCRES ET PRODUITS
061	SUGAR AND HONEY	W 322084	52.3	W 1052875	156.1	W 1303776	321.4	W 1852375	273.8	SUCRES ET MIEL
07	COFFEE,TEA,COCOA,SPICES		470.8		875.0		858.0		1035.8	CAFE,THE,CACAO,EPICES
071	COFFEE AND SUBSTITUTES	W 184970	436.0	W 196058	818.9	W 282529	795.3	W 259138	965.5	CAFE ET SUCCEDANES
0711	COFFEE GREEN,ROASTED,SUB	W 178900	414.2	W 188027	771.1	W 269114	749.8	W 247155	923.9	CAFE TORREFIE OU DECAFEINE
07111	COFFEE GREEN,HUSKS,SKINS	W 171084	396.0	W 187174	766.7	W 266111	743.9	W 245086	913.7	CAFE NON TORREFIE
1	BEVERAGES AND TOBACCO		479.7		590.1		720.6		877.5	BOISSONS ET TABACS
11	BEVERAGES		423.4		528.7		623.0		772.8	BOISSONS
112	ALCOHOLIC BEVERAGES	W 606980	396.8	W 792207	493.1		572.2	W 1353694	706.1	BOISSONS ALCOOLIQUES
1123	BEER,ALE,STOUT,PORTER	W 531081	230.1	W 687692	309.7	W 887574	371.6	W 1244278	486.1	BIERES
2	CRUDE MATERLS,EXCL FUELS		1364.4		2017.9		1902.5		1920.2	MAT BRUTES NON COMESTIBLES
24	CORK AND WOOD		182.1		168.1		229.1		243.1	LIEGE ET BOIS
26	TEXTILE FIBRES AND WASTE		346.9		616.3		570.7		533.7	FIBRES TEXTILES
266	SYNTHETIC FIBRES TO SPIN		213.0	W 182372	320.6		256.6		245.1	FIBRES SYNTHETIQUES
27	CRUDE FERTLZR,MINRLS NES		224.4		287.6		247.9		253.1	ENGRAIS MINERAUX BRUTS
28	METALLIFEROUS ORES,SCRAP		354.1		640.5		513.4		531.7	MINERAIS METAL,DECHETS
288	NONFERR METAL SCRAP NES	W 129070	167.9	W 239483	340.0	W 214241	262.8	W 205631	236.9	DECHETS NON FERREUX
2882	OTHER BASE MTL SCRAP NES	W 121013	156.8	W 213281	323.9	W 208950	251.6	W 196402	225.1	AUTRES DECHETS
3	MINERAL FUELS ETC		7208.6		8157.3		11442.0		11036.4	COMBUSTIBLES MINERAUX LUB
33	PETROLEUM AND PRODUCTS		6997.5		7929.9		11219.3		10970.4	PETROLE ET DERIVES
333	CRUDE PETROLEUM	MW 65627	6572.3	MW 64572	7419.7	MW 76278	10705.4	MW 83375	10332.7	HUILES BRUTES DE PETROLE
334	PETROLEUM PRODUCTS,REFIN	MW 15502	415.9	W 5300533	502.5	W 2859102	505.4	W 3523863	616.8	PRODUITS RAFFINES
3345	LUBS,PETROLEUM OILS NES	W 1117545	177.4	W 1109072	188.9	W 1342615	252.4	W 2298044	427.4	HUILES LUBRIFIANTES
33451	LUBS(HIGH PETR CONT) ETC	W 1115374	175.4	W 1107689	187.1	W 1338039	249.5	W 2288370	425.8	HUILES LUBRIF,H LOURDES
5	CHEMCLS,RELATED PROD NES		2688.4		3928.9		3808.1		4190.6	PRODUITS CHIMIQUES
51	ORGANIC CHEMICALS		825.9		1219.3		916.8		890.8	PROD CHIMIQ ORGANIQUES
513	CARBOXYLIC ACIDS ETC		415.4	W 723589	740.7	W 687704	477.6	W 640498	447.8	ACIDES CARBOXYLIQUES
5138	POLYACIDS AND DERIVATIVS	W 423203	267.8	W 538232	528.4	W 430381	273.4	W 401985	215.6	ACIDES POLYCARBOXYLIQUES
51384	TEREPHTHALIC ACID ESTERS	W 245148	151.6	W 302337	277.7	W 266082	157.7	W 246974	125.8	ESTERS DE L'ACIDE TEREPHTALI
52	INORGANIC CHEMICALS		358.1		425.6		461.9		554.2	PROD CHIM INORGANIQUES
522	INORG ELEMNTS,OXIDES,ETC		203.6	W 1162942	228.3		235.9		302.8	ELEMENTS INORGANIQUES
53	DYES,TANNING,COLOUR PROD		178.8		241.7		252.9		215.2	PROD TEINTURE,COLORANTS
541	*MEDICINAL,PHARM PRODUCT		296.8		399.5		552.5		636.9	PROD MEDICINAUX PHARMACEUT
55	PERFUME,CLEANING ETC PRD		183.3		289.2		307.0		418.7	PROD POUR PARFUM,TOILETTE
562	*FERTILIZERS,MANUFACTURE		111.7	W 1456539	263.4		270.0	W 1195903	183.6	ENGRAIS MANUFACTURES
58	PLASTIC MATERIALS ETC		554.6		842.2		759.4		907.4	MAT PLAST ARTIFICIELLES
583	POLYMERIZATION ETC PRODS		378.7	W 762470	598.6	W 843860	483.0	W 881553	592.3	PROD POLYMERISATION
59	CHEMICAL MATERIALS NES		172.7		239.4		276.4		371.8	MAT PROD CHIMIQUES NDA
6	BASIC MANUFACTURES		5960.2		9034.7		9833.1		11634.4	ART MANUFACTURES
61	LEATHER,DRESSED FUR,ETC		160.5		242.6		262.1		290.9	CUIRS,PELLETERIES
62	RUBBER MANUFACTURES NES		144.6		236.8		271.1		330.3	CAOUTCHOUC MANUFACTURE
63	WOOD,CORK MANUFACTRS NES		189.5		201.8		272.5		309.6	OUVRAGES LIEGE ET BOIS
64	PAPER,PAPERBOARD AND MFR		373.5		641.4		641.7		749.3	PAPIERS,CARTONS & OUVRAGES
641	PAPER AND PAPERBOARD		86.9	W 396900	295.3		160.0		153.1	PAPIERS ET CARTONS
642	PAPER,ETC,PRECUT,ARTS OF		286.6	W 157530	346.2	W 459905	481.8	W 478929	596.3	PAP,CARTONS DECOUPES
65	TEXTILE YARN,FABRICS,ETC		940.1		1285.4		1549.1		1910.4	FILS,TISSUS,ARTICLES TEXTILE
651	TEXTILE YARN		189.2	W 108158	346.9		331.5		368.1	FILS TEXTILES
652	COTTON FABRICS,WOVEN		72.2	W 43786	215.5		283.3	W 79018	377.0	TISSUS DE COTON
6522	WOVEN COTTON BLEACHD,ETC		53.6	W 34612	182.5		250.8	W 69518	341.2	TISSUS COTON BLANCHIS ETC
658	TEXTILE ARTICLES NES		333.9	W 59036	303.0	W 69689	396.1	W 64680	557.6	ART FACONNES MAT TEXTILES
6589	OTH TEXTILE ARTICLES NES	W 9144	201.5	W 15080	135.4	W 17799	172.1	W 20971	286.3	AUT ART EN TEXTILES NDA
66	NONMETAL MINERAL MFS NES		860.2		1062.9		1235.1		1456.6	ART MIN NON METALLIQUES
664	GLASS		300.7	W 232255	339.4	W 278875	386.8	W 284784	473.9	VERRE
6647	SAFETY GLASS CUT OR NOT	W 75032	207.8	W 75279	200.1	W 93752	213.5	W 87077	230.5	GLACES DE SECURITE
665	GLASSWARE	W 279497	184.5	W 293616	212.3	W 346957	222.3	W 388857	260.9	OUVRAGES EN VERRE
67	IRON AND STEEL		1058.5		2517.8		2337.4		2667.8	FER ET ACIER
672	IRON,STEEL PRIMARY FORMS		335.3	W 3067103	968.5		756.6		780.9	LINGOTS FER,ACIER
6725	IRN,STL BLOOMS,SLABS,ETC		324.9	W 2003532	594.1		526.0	W 2271458	624.0	BLOOMS,BILLETTES FER ACIER
67251	IRN,SMPLE STL BLOOMS,ETC	W 1226752	323.9	W 1997710	590.8	W 2007982	520.7	W 2251136	610.3	BLOOMS ETC NON ACIER FIN
6727	IRN,STL COIL FR REROLLNG	W 21134	9.9	W 1062746	374.0		230.2	W 470913	156.9	EBAUCHES POUR TOLES FER
67271	IRON,SIMPLE STEEL COILS	W 20163	9.2	W 1047715	369.0	W 803677	230.2	W 470739	156.7	EBAUCHES NON EN ACIER
673	IRON,STEEL SHAPES ETC		79.5	W 1415054	449.1	W 1095459	326.0		276.6	BARRES,PROFIL FER,ACIER
674	IRN,STL UNIV,PLATE,SHEET		245.1	W 824756	575.1		560.8		752.5	LARGES PLATS,TOLES
6746	IRN,STL THIN PLATE,ROLLD	W 126318	136.3	W 258350	244.9	W 330356	242.7	W 404340	296.1	TOLES LAM MOINS 3MM
6749	OTH IRN,STL PLATES,SHEET	W 114977	81.7	W 293014	215.2	W 448011	271.7	W 658680	406.3	AUTRES TOLES FER,ACIER
67491	— OF IRON OR SIMPLE STL	W 114327	81.4	W 292733	214.6	W 444729	269.3	W 650929	404.3	AUT TOLES AUTRES ACIER FIN
678	IRON,STL TUBES,PIPES,ETC	W 511553	329.2	W 634518	427.9	W 761765	578.4	W 880692	693.0	TUBES,TUYAUX EN FONTE,FER
6782	IRON,STL SEAMLESS TUBES	W 320968	209.0	W 421772	293.7	W 478488	387.8	W 500236	408.1	TUBES,TUYAUX SANS SOUDURE
68	NON–FERROUS METALS		833.0		1359.2		1177.6		1287.6	METAUX NON FERREUX
681	SILVER,PLATINUM,ETC		214.9		301.3		328.0		323.4	ARGENT ET PLATINE
6811	SILVER UNWKD,PARTLY WRKD		214.4		300.9		327.7		322.1	ARGENT BRUT MI–OUVRE
68113	SILVER UNWROUGHT		212.7		299.7		321.4		320.8	ARGENT ET ALLIAGES BRUTS
682	COPPER EXC CEMENT COPPER	W 173457	445.2	W 250568	776.4	W 234128	590.5	W 256126	647.2	CUIVRE
6821	COPPER NES,ALLOYS,UNWRT	W 142354	334.8	W 194647	572.1	W 157810	392.2	W 198049	504.0	CUIVRE BRUT
68211	COPPER UNREF,EXC CEMENT	W 120476	287.0	W 124429	369.9	W 117047	296.2	W 120914	313.0	CUIVRE POUR AFFINAGE
69	METAL MANUFACTURES NES		1400.7		1487.1		2086.7		2632.3	ART MANUFACT EN METAL NDA
697	BASE MTL HOUSEHOLD EQUIP		306.6	W 106861	332.3		390.5	W 129676	412.0	ART MENAGE MET COMMUNS
6973	DMSTC HEATG,COOKG APPARA		236.0	W 83320	251.8		294.3	W 91073	282.9	APPS CHAUF NON ELECTRIQ
69731	IRN,STL DOM COOKG APPARA	W 80263	226.9	W 79635	242.5	W 93170	285.1	W 84569	263.6	APPS CUISSON FER,ACIER
699	BASE METAL MFRS NES		821.4	W 381665	784.0		1160.7		1457.7	ART MANUFACTURES MET NDA
6991	LOCKSMITHS WARES,ETC	W 44906	311.8	W 44802	192.1	W 103240	311.6	W 70279	359.2	ARTICLES DE SERRURERIE
6997	IRON,STEEL ARTICLES NES	W 76367	231.7	W 195619	255.9	W 413326	397.5		535.5	OUV FONTE,FER,ACIER NDA
69979	IRN,STL MANUFACTURES NES	W 75344	230.8	W 195316	255.5	W 413105	397.3	W 433441	535.3	AUT OUVRAGES EN FER NDA
7	MACHINES,TRANSPORT EQUIP		32255.8		41563.9		51166.8		59445.7	MACHINES MATERIEL TRANSPORT
71	POWER GENERATING EQUIPMT		3283.4		3876.4		4215.8		4416.2	MACHINES GENERATRICES
713	INTRNL COMBUS PSTN ENGIN	W 195136	2201.0		2822.4	W 331936	2820.1	W 258530	2808.9	MOTEURS EXPL COMB INT, PIECE
7132	MOTOR VEHCL PISTN ENGINS	W 119526	1763.0	N 1850155	2123.3	W 223852	2214.6	W 130479	2167.3	MOTEURS EXPL POUR VEHICULES

5. General Exports F.O.B. by Commodities according to the S.I.T.C. (Rev. 2) in million U.S. Dollars
Exportations Générales F.O.B. par Produits d'après la C.T.C.I. (Rév. 2) en millions de Dollars E.U.

SITC CTCI	COMMODITY	1994 QUANTITY QUANTITE	1994 VALUE VALEUR	1995 QUANTITY QUANTITE	1995 VALUE VALEUR	1996 QUANTITY QUANTITE	1996 VALUE VALEUR	1997 QUANTITY QUANTITE	1997 VALUE VALEUR	PRODUIT
7139	PISTON ENGINE PARTS NES	W 72071	399.0	W 68552	463.8	W 99134	549.3	W 123417	607.4	PIECES POUR 713.2,3,8
714	ENGINES AND MOTORS NES	W 1395	302.5	W 1629	227.1	W 2354	257.1	W 2796	339.1	MOTEURS NON ELECTRIQUES
716	ROTATING ELECTRIC PLANT	W 138580	742.5	W 220447	781.8	W 150107	1077.0	W 127435	1183.4	APP ELECTR ROTATIFS,PIECES
7162	AC MTRS,GENRTRS,GEN SETS	W 109126	488.1	W 152407	494.5	W 62056	684.4	W 49656	662.7	MOTEURS ELECTRIQUES
71621	AC MTRS,INC UNIVRSL MTRS	W 108033	464.4	W 151871	486.1	W 60804	667.4	W 47228	626.0	MOT ELEC NON COUR CONTINU
72	MACHS FOR SPCL INDUSTRYS		327.8		659.9		629.2		781.8	MAC SPECIALES POUR INDUST
728	OTH MACHY FOR SPCL INDUS		86.4	W 43262	224.4	W 55248	295.0		336.3	AUT MACH IND PARTICULIERES
74	GENRL INDUSTRL MACHY NES		1938.5		2175.4		2520.1		3191.7	MACH APP INDUSTRIE
741	HEATING,COOLING EQUIPMNT	W 74230	447.8	W 108273	597.7	W 131359	800.6	W 102656	754.8	MACH CHAUFFAGE,PIECES
7415	AIR–CONDITIONING MACHNRY	W 28220	250.7	W 38165	319.7	W 33421	483.6	W 24505	416.0	GROUPES CONDITION AIR
743	PUMPS NES,CENTRFUGES ETC	W 81376	490.3	W 63777	515.1	W 68520	455.0	W 79216	523.7	POMPES COMPRES,VENT ETC
7436	GAS,LIQUID FILTERS ETC	W 71600	330.5	W 40307	315.0	W 31388	245.8	W 33617	189.3	APP POUR FILT DES LIQUIDES
744	MECHANICAL HANDLING EQU		154.1	W 82172	193.3	W 158908	269.7		403.5	EQUIP MANUTENTION PIECES
749	NONELEC MACH PTS,ACC NES	W 53815	698.8	W 74966	715.3	W 157623	763.6	W 129416	1148.9	PIECES MACH NON ELEC NDA
7492	COCKS,VALVES ETC NES	W 12680	387.3	W 40034	387.2	W 65190	485.8	W 57806	772.0	ART ROB,SIM POUR TUYAUX
75	OFFICE MACHNES,ADP EQUIP		2280.3		2924.1		4241.5		6044.1	MACH BUREAU TRAIT AUTOM
751	OFFICE MACHINES		387.6	W 19663	385.1		387.0	W 32403	379.2	MACH,APPAREILS DE BUREAU
7511	TYPEWRITERS,CHEQUE–WRTRS	W 9131	191.8	W 7769	116.3	W 9029	85.7	W 14710	67.1	MACHINES A ECRIRE
7518	OFFICE MACHINES NES	W 10686	187.2	W 11501	253.3		283.7	W 17138	293.6	MACH,APP DE BUREAU NDA
75182	PHOTO,THERMOCOPY APPARAT	W 10041	182.4	W 10605	241.4	W 14802	273.5	W 16225	277.8	APPAREILS DE PHOTOCOPIE
752	AUTOMTIC DATA PROC EQUIP	W 18783	1241.3	W 51757	1734.1	W 149719	2700.4	W 143465	3767.2	MACH TRAIT INFORMATION
7522	DIGITAL COMPUTERS	W 2422	309.9	W 1874	396.7	W 6342	1277.0	W 9904	1859.6	MACH DIGITALES COMPLETES
7523	DIGITL CENTRL PROCESSORS	W 4901	400.8	W 6717	464.0	W 11500	354.4	W 7784	423.5	UNITES CENTRALES
7525	ADP PERIPHERAL UNITS	W 9409	410.9	W 39050	782.6	W 125777	864.4	W 118382	1269.4	UNITES PERIPHERIQUES
759	OFFICE,ADP MCH PTS,ACCES	W 7231	651.6	W 13226	804.9	W 26493	1154.3	W 22533	1897.7	PIECES DU 751 ET 752
7599	ACCTG,ETC,ADP MCH PTS,AC	W 3090	599.5	W 9230	757.1	W 19192	1081.6	W 16861	1817.5	PIECES DU 751 ET 752
76	TELECOMM,SOUND EQUIPMENT		6274.5		7560.1		8260.6		10003.7	EQUIPMENT DE TELECOM
761	TELEVISION RECEIVERS	W 139310	2678.3	W 537398	2977.6	W 578300	3331.0		3852.7	RECEPTEURS DE TELEVISION
7611	COLOUR TV RECEIVERS	W 139310	2678.1	W 537360	2977.2	W 578143	3330.8	W 412294	3852.5	RECEPTEURS COULEUR
762	RADIO BROADCAST RECEIVRS	W 12056	909.1	W 27847	1048.9	W 15930	1104.6	W 12287	1358.1	RECEPTEURS RADIODIFFUSION
7621	MTR VEHC RADIO RECEIVERS	W 5251	270.6	W 7101	413.2	W 7327	689.9	W 8421	1303.8	RECEPTEURS RADIO AUTO
7628	OTHER RADIO RECEIVERS	W 6795	628.9	W 19024	617.1	W 7169	403.5	W 2529	47.0	AUTRES RECEPT RADIO
763	SOUND RECORDRS,PHONOGRPH	W 23747	354.1	W 25791	529.7	W 14147	414.5	W 17505	456.8	PHONO,APP ENREGISTREMENT
7638	OTHR SOUND APPARATUS ETC	W 23497	338.5	W 23386	466.7	W 13044	387.5	W 15041	401.2	AUT APP D'ENREGIS,REPROD
76388	DICTATING MACHINES ETC	W 23482	247.7	W 12646	235.8	W 7906	202.1	W 8101	218.0	MACHINES A DICTER
764	TELECOM EQPT,PTS,ACC NES		2333.1	W 143886	3004.0	W 259485	3410.7		4336.2	EQUIP TELECOM,PIECES
7641	LINE TELEPHONE,ETC EQUIP	W 12125	451.0	W 18520	504.1	W 25172	661.4	W 20820	987.2	APP TELEPHON PAR FIL
7642	MICROPH,LOUDSPKR,AMPLIFR	W 48332	193.8	W 42742	238.4	W 63561	348.1	W 48720	429.7	MICRO,HAUT–PARLEUR,AMPLI
7643	TV,RADIO TRANSMITTRS ETC	W 2249	270.0	W 9841	516.1	W 14864	509.9	W 22772	482.7	APP EMET TELE RADIO
7648	TELECOMM EQUIPMENT NES		117.8	W 11916	274.1	W 21697	336.2		681.9	APP TELECOM NDA
76481	RADIOTELEPHONE ETC RCVRS	W 37	26.5	W 7472	176.0	W 16426	249.2	W 13219	573.1	RECEP RADIOTELEPHONIE
7649	PTS NES OF EQUIPMT OF 76	W 20902	1300.6	W 60867	1471.5	W 134191	1555.3	W 155914	1754.9	PIECES DE LA DIV 76
76493	TELECOMM EQUIPMT PTS NES	W 17765	1168.8	W 56065	1276.9	W 118952	1349.7	W 140570	1413.5	PIECES 761,762,764.3,8
77	ELECTRIC MACHNRY NES ETC		9552.3		11685.9		14344.0		16986.8	MACH APP ELECT NDA
771	ELECTRIC POWER MACHY NES	W 113743	819.1	W 154054	955.5	W 295517	1309.5	W 262461	1606.7	MACH PROD,TRANS ELECTR
7711	TRANSFORMERS,ELECTRICAL	W 46635	222.6	W 44841	207.0	W 148373	287.6	W 153389	405.2	TRANSFO ELECTRIQUES
77118	OTHER ELEC TRANSFORMERS	W 43607	178.5	W 41588	169.0	W 131235	246.7	W 133375	372.3	AUTRES TRANSFO ELECTRIQ
7712	OTH ELEC POWER MACHY NES	W 67108	596.6	W 109213	748.5	W 147143	1021.9	W 109072	1201.5	AUT APP PROD TRANSF ELEC
77121	STATIC CONVERTERS ETC	W 8560	311.3	W 17393	349.9	W 23560	463.4	W 30275	669.3	CONVERTISSEURS STATIQUES
77122	INDUCTORS	W 57232	248.8	W 89468	357.4	W 100929	473.8	W 61797	480.2	BOBINES REACTANCE,SELFS
772	SWITCHGEAR ETC,PARTS NES	W 57433	1809.9	W 115927	2095.8	W 267977	2451.5	W 301003	2727.8	APP COUPURE,SECT ETC
7721	SWITCHGEAR ETC	W 50934	1322.7	W 109809	1374.3	W 238120	2017.6	W 248304	2294.5	APP COUPURE,SECTIONMNT
7722	PRINTED CIRCUITS,PTS NES	W 3778	408.2	W 2849	631.0	W 2019	329.8	W 25126	295.5	CIRCUITS ET PIECES
773	ELECTR DISTRIBUTNG EQUIP		2939.7	W 404602	3427.2		4472.8	W 411972	4959.1	EQUIPMT DISTRIBUTION ELECT
7731	INSULATED WIRE,CABLE ETC	W 247279	2923.0	W 401570	3410.4	W 422269	4454.7	W 378011	4936.2	FILS,CABLES ISOLES ELECT
775	HOUSEHOLD TYPE EQUIP NES		600.5	W 241884	771.6		933.3	W 169392	1116.5	MACH,APP USAGE DOMESTQUE
7757	DOMESTIC ELECTRC EQU NES		198.9	W 44309	234.3	W 31794	256.2	W 44079	295.7	APP ELECTR DOMEST NDA
7758	ELECTRO–THERMIC APPL NES		244.2	W 64575	331.3		384.5	W 50453	474.7	APP ELECTROTHERMIQ NDA
776	TRANSISTORS,VALVES,ETC		916.1	W 26576	1132.2	W 128011	1875.1	W 188780	1869.4	LAMPES,TUBES,VALVES
7763	DIODES,TRANSISTORS,ETC	W 3778	310.6	W 6881	346.5	W 33874	407.4	W 34035	543.8	DIODES,TRANSISTORS
7764	ELECTRONIC MICROCIRCUITS	W 1459	453.5	W 2943	603.5	W 26083	1195.7	W 82575	1015.7	MICROSTRUCTURES ELECTRON
778	ELECTRICAL MACHINERY NES	W 115213	2413.6	W 229919	3265.6	W 337431	3224.3	W 360354	4546.1	AUTRES MACH ELECT NDA
7781	BATTERIES,ACCUMULATORS	W 47109	324.8	W 70085	386.8	W 123823	532.1	W 160416	792.9	PILES ET ACCUMULATEURS
77811	PRIMARY BATTERIES,CELLS	W 7270	230.4	W 20371	175.0	W 34827	163.4	W 27808	248.3	PILES ELECTRIQUES,PIECES
77812	ELECTRIC ACCUMULATORS	W 31847	83.0	W 47538	206.9	W 87106	364.3	W 129939	538.7	ACCUMULATEURS ELECTRIQ
7783	AUTOMOTIVE ELECTR EQUIP	W 9559	283.4	W 40312	287.1	W 82585	383.3	W 45460	445.2	EQUIP ELECT MOTEURS EXPL
77832	ELECT VEHICLE LGHTNG EQU	W 5173	212.6	W 27204	196.1	W 54903	278.2	W 16399	274.0	APP ELEC ECLAIR,SIGNAL AUTO
7788	OTH ELEC MACHY,EQUIP NES	W 46970	1586.0	W 95833	2355.7	W 99073	1990.9	W 120530	2937.2	AUT MACH APP ELEC NDA
77883	ELEC SIGNALLING EQU NES	W 14221	385.6	W 22946	427.3	W 13700	546.2	W 12424	517.1	APP ELECT SIGNAL ACOUS
77884	ELECTRICAL CONDENSERS	W 5561	417.0	W 29871	946.3	W 33211	588.1	W 52074	1361.4	CONDENSATEURS ELECTRIQUES
77886	OTH ELEC MACHINERY NES	W 6000	231.2	W 20177	312.7	W 15373	525.6	W 13512	694.2	AUT MACH APP ELECTRIQUES
77889	ELEC PARTS OF MACHY NES	W 5878	503.2	W 9041	616.7	W 17206	255.6	W 20160	253.9	PIECES ELEC DE MACH NDA
78	ROAD VEHICLES		8385.4		12156.8		16495.0		17704.0	VEHICULES ROUTIERS
781	PASS MOTOR VEH EXC BUSES	W 384988	5050.9	N 645012	7521.8	W 1184632	9673.0	W 939426	9700.1	AUTO TRANSPORT PERSONNES
782	LORRIES,SPCL MTR VEH NES	W 65479	817.1	N 120509	1850.2	W 592776	3426.9	W 509429	3995.3	VEHICULES SPECIAUX,MARCH
7821	LORRIES,TRUCKS	W 65479	817.1	N 120509	1850.2	W 590595	3422.4	W 507564	3985.2	VEHICULES TRANSP MARCHAND
784	MOTOR VEH PRTS,ACCES NES	W 329021	2307.5		2498.9	W 643628	2976.1	W 465822	3462.1	PIECES 722,781,782,783
7841	MOTOR VEHICLE CHASSIS	W 21393	212.4	N 15298	217.3	W 47686	265.4	W 36164	187.2	CHASSIS 722,781,782,783
7849	OTHER MOTOR VEHCL PARTS	W 274931	2056.3	W 494744	2236.1	W 594857	2706.5	W 428633	3270.1	PIECES 722,781,782,783
79	OTHR TRANSPORT EQUIPMENT		169.9		418.7		294.5		254.1	AUTRE MATERIEL TRANSPORT
792	AIRCRAFT ETC	W 1951	143.0		339.1	W 1227	195.1	W 2771	183.8	APP NAVIGATION AERIENNE
8	MISC MANUFACTURED GOODS		6771.4		8469.8		11071.3		14840.8	ART MANUFACTURES DIVERS
812	*PLUMBG,HEATNG,LGHTNG EQ	W 109196	339.4	W 151976	326.8	W 258105	446.3	W 247314	564.0	APPAR SANITAIRES CHAUFFAGE
8124	LIGHTING EQUIPMENT NES	W 36204	251.0	W 56498	220.9	W 135745	313.4	W 115938	405.4	APPAREILS ECLAIRAGE ETC
81242	LAMPS,FITTINGS BASE METL	W 32878	177.8	W 50483	189.4	W 115028	280.6	W 101205	365.6	APPAREILS D'ECLAIRAGE
821	*FURNITURE,PARTS THEREOF		850.6	W 295878	894.8	W 343620	1364.6	W 379354	1770.2	MEUBLES ET PIECES
8211	CHAIRS,SEATS AND PARTS		511.8	W 117828	518.5	W 107297	827.9	W 114715	1047.3	SIEGES ET PIECES
82119	PTS NES OF CHAIRS ETC	W 16492	377.4	W 78429	414.0	W 54492	674.2	W 46730	802.4	PIECES DU 821.11
8219	FURNITURE AND PARTS NES	W 128163	305.4	W 172749	336.9	W 230173	487.1	W 257336	655.3	AUTRES MEUBLES ET PIECES
82192	WOOD FURNITURE NES	W 79278	170.7	W 103054	197.6	W 133529	289.4	W 141277	386.9	MEUBLES NDA EN BOIS
84	CLOTHING AND ACCESSORIES		1701.3		2731.6		3754.1		5637.1	VETEMENTS
842	MENS OUTERWEAR NOT KNIT	W 45527	386.9	W 68833	603.4		838.5	W 119215	1286.6	VET DESSUS POUR HOMMES
8423	— TROUSERS,BREECHES ETC	W 39681	313.8	W 61904	507.5	W 79480	717.1	W 107945	1075.8	PANTALONS HOMMES MAT TEX
843	WOMENS OUTERWEAR NONKNIT	W 42268	504.9	W 73087	725.9	W 107926	1077.8	W 123776	1553.9	VET DESSUS FEMMES MAT TEX
8439	— OTHER OUTER GARMENTS	W 31657	371.5	W 61656	550.3	W 86297	830.3	W 99497	1213.2	AUT VET DES FEM MAT TEXT
845	OUTERWEAR KNIT NONELASTC	W 24033	216.5	W 53609	456.3	W 62074	577.7	W 86030	1035.7	VET DESSOUS,ACCES BONNET
8459	— OTHER,CLTHG ACCESRYS	W 12730	129.4	W 23112	215.3	W 40653	334.7	W 70213	679.9	AUT VET DESSUS DE BONNE
846	UNDER GARMENTS KNITTED	W 22118	284.6	W 50897	564.3	W 76780	847.4	W 100541	1174.7	SOUS VETS DE BONNETERIE
8462	— OF COTTON NON ELASTIC	W 16076	153.4	W 38062	329.5	W 60134	546.0	W 78608	726.3	SOUS–VET BONNET COTON
84629	—— OTHER	W 16076	153.4	W 38062	329.5	W 60134	546.0	W 78608	726.3	AUT SOUS–VET BONNET COTON
848	HEADGEAR,NONTXTL CLOTHNG	W 22981	202.2	W 34718	211.3	W 39729	200.8		226.5	VET ACCES MAT AUT QUE TEX

5. General Exports F.O.B. by Commodities according to the S.I.T.C. (Rev. 2) in million U.S. Dollars
Exportations Générales F.O.B. par Produits d'après la C.T.C.I. (Rév. 2) en millions de Dollars E.U.

SITC CTCI	COMMODITY	1994		1995		1996		1997		PRODUIT
		QUANTITY QUANTITE	VALUE VALEUR	QUANTITY QUANTITE	VALUE VALEUR	QUANTITY QUANTITE	VALUE VALEUR	QUANTITY QUANTITE	VALUE VALEUR	
851	*FOOTWEAR	W 11921	149.8	W 19132	190.9	W 25571	274.6	W 28263	365.2	CHAUSSURES
87	PRECISION INSTRUMNTS NES		870.8		961.0		1372.5		1901.9	INSTRUM,APPAR SCIENT NDA
872	MEDICAL INSTRUMENTS NES		352.6	W 48288	422.5	W 63996	589.7	W 53247	747.5	INSTR,APP MEDIC–CHIR NDA
87202	OTH MEDICAL INSTRUMENTS	W 19050	315.7	W 36665	368.8	W 56351	525.1	W 46923	677.5	INSTRUM,APP MEDECINE
874	MEASURNG,CONTROLNG INSTR	W 18197	457.2	W 25770	477.0	W 66690	685.3		937.7	INSTRUMENTS DE MESURE
8743	GAS,LIQUID CONTROL INSTR	W 13719	264.7	W 14641	229.1	W 45209	367.5	W 43797	519.7	APP,INSTR MESURE FLUIDES
88	PHOTO EQU,OPTICL GDS ETC		312.0		363.0		420.3		537.0	APP,FOURN PHOTO,OP,MONTR
882	PHOTO,CINEMA SUPPLIES		191.7	W 9002	235.6	W 13658	237.4	W 16031	300.8	PRODUITS PHOTO,CINEMA
89	MISC MANUFCTRD GOODS NES		2456.2		2906.6		3295.8		3861.0	ART MANUFACTURES DIVERS
893	ARTICLES OF PLASTIC NES		779.9		833.4		1025.7		1252.7	OUVRAGES EN MAT DIVIS 58
8931	PLSTC PACKG CONTNRS,LIDS	W 180090	238.6	W 95159	290.6	W 550703	422.6	W 553776	516.7	ART TRANSP EMBALLAGE ETC
8939	MISC PLASTIC ARTICLES	W 395107	528.0	W 171364	525.8	W 869198	581.4	W 843738	710.0	ART DIVERS EN MAT DIV 58
89399	OTHR PLASTC ARTICLES NES	W 385216	500.5	W 158556	498.7	W 853421	547.5	W 818312	665.8	AUT OUV MAT DIV 58
894	TOYS,SPORTING GOODS,ETC		559.5	W 130000	796.7		882.9		1005.1	VOITURES ENFANTS,JOUETS
8942	TOYS,INDOOR GAMES ETC	W 85755	414.9	W 115724	616.5	W 112719	602.1	W 111082	629.1	JOUETS,JEUX ETC
89423	TOYS NES	W 66544	284.7	W 80072	336.0	W 83256	369.7	W 81566	419.4	JOUETS,MODELES REDUITS
8947	OTH SPORT GDS,FAIR AMUSM	W 10614	140.5	W 13611	176.2	W 18747	277.7	W 14826	369.4	AUT ART DE SPORT
89472	OTH OUTDOOR SPORT GOODS	W 9240	125.2	W 11564	158.1	W 12514	254.0	W 12314	350.4	ART POUR JEUX PLEIN AIR
898	MUSICAL INSTRUMENTS,PTS		570.4	W 66542	607.2	W 57563	599.5		537.5	INSTRUMENTS DE MUSIQUE
8983	SOUND RECRDNG TAPE,DISCS	W 54280	497.3	W 57547	516.9	W 49978	521.7	W 49977	451.6	SUPPORTS SON POUR 763
89831	PREPD SND RECORDNG MEDIA	W 50667	447.0	W 52334	424.2	W 43454	432.4	W 42100	366.0	SUPPORTS PREPARES
9	GOODS NOT CLASSD BY KIND		113.5		272.6		342.2		240.6	ART TRANSACT NON CLASSES

1. HISTORICAL SERIES, 1992–1994 GENERAL TRADE, IMPORTS C.I.F., EXPORTS F.O.B.
SERIES HISTORIQUES, 1992–1994 COMMERCE GENERAL, IMPORTATIONS C.A.F., EXPORTATIONS F.O.B

YEAR ANNEE	VALUE IN MILLION U.S. DOLLARS / VALEUR EN MILLION U.S. DOLLARS — MERCHANDISE–MARCHANDISE IMPORTS	MERCHANDISE–MARCHANDISE EXPORTS	GOLD–OR IMPORTS	GOLD–OR EXPORTS	CONVERSION FACTORS FACTEURS DE CONVERSION CENTS E.U. PAR IMPORTS	CONVERSION FACTORS EXPORTS	INDEX NUMBERS–INDICES QUANTUM IMPORTS	QUANTUM EXPORTS	UNIT VALUE VALEUR UNITAIRE IMPORTS	UNIT VALUE EXPORTS
1992	98.80	23.30								
1993		29.20								
1994	129.10	78.20								

2. IMPORTS BY BROAD ECONOMIC CATEGORY AND EXPORTS BY INDUSTRIAL ORIGIN. (PERCENTAGE OF TOTAL VALUE)
IMPORTATIONS PAR CATEGORIES ECONOMIQUES ET EXPORTATIONS PAR BRANCHE D'ACTIVITE.(EN POURCENTAGE DE LA VALEUR TOTALE)

IMPORTS – IMPORTATIONS

	1988	1989	1990	1991	1992	1993	1994
TOTAL IMPORTS–IMPORTATIONS TOTALES							
1 FOOD BEV–ALIMENTATION BOISSONS							
11 PRIMARY–PRODUITS DE BASE							
111 FOR INDUSTRY–POUR L'INDUSTRIE							
112 FOR HOUSEHOLDS–POUR LES MENAGES							
12 PROCESSED–PRODUITS ELABORES							
121 FOR INDUSTRY–POUR L'INDUSTRIE							
122 FOR HOUSEHOLDS–POUR LES MENAGES							
2 IND SUPPLIES–APPROV INDUSTRIELS							
21 PRIMARY–PRODUITS DE BASE							
22 PROCESSED–PRODUITS ELABORES							
3 FUELS–COMBUSTIBLES							
31 PRIMARY–PRODUITS DE BASE							
32 PROCESSED–PRODUITS ELABORES							
321 MOTOR SPIRIT–ESSENCE							
322 OTHER–AUTRES							
4 MACHINERY–EQUIPEMENT							
41 CAPITAL EQUIPMENT–MACHINES							
42 PARTS–PIECES ACCESSOIRES							
5 TRANSPORT–TRANSPORT							
51 PASSENGER CARS–AUTOMOBILES							
52 OTHER–AUTRES							
521 INDUSTRIAL–INDUSTRIELS							
522 NON INDUSTRIAL–NON INDUSTRIEL							
53 PARTS–PIECES ACCESSOIRES							
6 CONSUM GOODS–BIENS CONSOMMATION							
61 DURABLE–DURABLES							
62 SEMI DURABLE–SEMI DURABLES							
63 NON DURABLE–NON DURABLES							
7 GOODS NES–BIENS NDA							

EXPORTS – EXPORTATIONS

	1988	1989	1990	1991	1992	1993	1994
TOTAL EXPORTS–EXPORTATIONS TOTALES							
1 AGRICULTURE							
2 MINING QUARRY–INDUS EXTRACTIVES							
3 MANUFACTURING–IND MANUFACTUR							
31 FOOD BEV TOBACCO–ALIM BOISS TAB							
32 TEXTILES–INDUSTRIES TEXTILES							
33 WOOD & PRODUCTS–BOIS & PRODUITS							
34 PAPER & PRODUCTS–PAPIER & PRODT							
35 CHEMICALS–INDUSTRIES CHIMIQUES							
36 NON METAL MIN–MIN NON METAL							
37 BASIC METAL–IND METAL BASE							
38 METAL MANUF–MANUF METAL							
39 OTH MANUF IND–AUTRES MANUF							

3. TRADE BY PRINCIPAL COUNTRIES OF CONSIGNMENT AND DESTINATION (VALUE IN MILLION U.S. DOLLARS)
ECHANGES SELON LES PRINCIPAUX PAYS DE CONSIGNATION ET DE DESTINATION (VALEUR EN MILLIONS DE DOLLARS EU)

COUNTRIES–PAYS	GENERAL IMPORTS C.I.F. IMPORTATIONS GENERALES C.A.F				
	1990	1991	1992	1993	1994
World			98.8		129.1
Africa					
Americas			39.8		42.4
– Northern America			39.8		42.4
– LAIA					
– CACM					
– Caribbean					
– Rest of America					
Asia excl fmr USSR			20.2		41.3
– Middle East					
Asia former USSR					
Europe excl fmr USSR					
– European Union					
– Eastern Europe					
– Rest of Europe					
Europe former USSR					
Oceania			32.0		34.5
Other			6.7		10.8
USA/Etats–Unis d'Amer			39.8		42.4
Japan/Japon			20.2		41.3
US Misc Pacific Islands			28.9		30.0
Areas n.e.s.			6.7		10.8
Australia/Australie			3.2		4.6

COUNTRIES–PAYS	GENERAL EXPORTS F.O.B. EXPORTATIONS GENERALES F.O.B.				
	1990	1991	1992	1993	1994
Monde			23.3	29.2	78.2
Afrique					
Amériques			2.2	2.7	2.8
– Amérique du Nord			2.2	2.7	2.8
– ALAI					
– MCAC					
– Caraïbes					
– Autre Amérique					
Asie anc. URSS exclus			18.7	22.4	56.8
– Moyen–Orient					
Asie ancienne URSS					
Europe anc. URSS exclus					
– Union Européenne					
– Europe de l'Est					
– Autre de l'Europe					
Europe ancienne URSS					
Océanie			2.2	4.0	4.2
Autre			0.2	0.1	13.9
Japan/Japon			18.7	22.4	56.8
Areas n.e.s.			0.2	0.1	13.9
US Misc Pacific Islands			1.9	3.7	4.0
USA/Etats–Unis d'Amer			2.2	2.7	2.8
Palau			0.3	0.3	0.3

(VALUE AS PERCENTAGE OF WORLD TOTAL)(VALEURS EN POURCENTAGE DU TOTAL MONDIAL)

	1985	1986	1987	1988	1989	1990	1991	1992	1993	1994
Africa										
Americas								40.3		32.9
– Northern America								40.3		32.9
– LAIA										
– CACM										
– Caribbean										
– Rest of America										
Asia excl fmr USSR								20.5		32.0
– Middle East										
Asia former USSR										
Europe excl fmr USSR										
– European Union										
– Eastern Europe										
– Rest of Europe										
Europe former USSR										
Oceania								32.4		26.8
Other								6.8		8.4
USA/Etats–Unis d'Amer								40.3		32.9
Japan/Japon								20.5		32.0
US Misc Pacific Islands								29.2		23.2
Areas n.e.s.								6.8		8.4
Australia/Australie								3.2		3.5

	1985	1986	1987	1988	1989	1990	1991	1992	1993	1994
Afrique										
Amériques								9.3	9.2	3.5
– Amérique du Nord								9.3	9.2	3.5
– ALAI										
– MCAC										
– Caraïbes										
– Autre Amérique										
Asie anc. URSS exclus								80.0	76.7	72.7
– Moyen–Orient										
Asie ancienne URSS										
Europe anc. URSS exclus										
– Union Européenne										
– Europe de l'Est										
– Autre de l'Europe										
Europe ancienne URSS										
Océanie								9.6	13.8	5.4
Autre								1.0	0.3	17.8
Japan/Japon								80.0	76.7	72.7
Areas n.e.s.								1.0	0.3	17.8
US Misc Pacific Islands								8.3	12.6	5.1
USA/Etats–Unis d'Amer								9.3	9.2	3.5
Palau								1.1	0.9	0.3

4. General Imports C.I.F. by Commodities according to the S.I.T.C. (Rev. 2) in million U.S. Dollars
Importations Générales C.A.F. par Produits d'après la C.T.C.I. (Rév. 2) en millions de Dollars E.U.

SITC CTCI	COMMODITY	1991		1992		1993		1994		PRODUIT
		QUANTITY QUANTITE	VALUE VALEUR	QUANTITY QUANTITE	VALUE VALEUR	QUANTITY QUANTITE	VALUE VALEUR	QUANTITY QUANTITE	VALUE VALEUR	
	ALL COMMODITIES				98.8		109.5		129.1	TOUS PRODUITS
0	FOOD AND LIVE ANIMALS				19.8		31.2		25.4	ALIMENTS,ANIMAUX VIVANTS
011	MEAT FRESH,CHILLD,FROZEN				2.2		2.2			VIANDES FRAICHES,REF,CONGE
012	MEAT DRIED,SALTED,SMOKED				1.3		1.6			VIANDE,ABATS SALES,SECHES
014	MEAT PREPD,PRSVD,NES ETC				1.9		2.3			CONSERVES DE VIANDES
037	FISH ETC PREPD,PRSVD NES				1.7		5.5			POIS,CRUST,MOL PREPARES
042	RICE				3.3		4.1			RIZ
045	CEREALS NES UNMILLED				0.7		1.0			AUTRES CEREALES NON MOULUES
046	WHEAT ETC MEAL OR FLOUR				0.6		0.6			SEMOULE FARINE,FROMENT
05	VEGETABLES AND FRUIT				1.1					LEGUMES ET FRUITS
061	SUGAR AND HONEY				0.9		0.7			SUCRES ET MIEL
062	SUGAR CANDY NON–CHOCLATE				0.5		0.5			SUCRERIES
071	COFFEE AND SUBSTITUTES				0.4		0.5			CAFE ET SUCCEDANES
098	EDIBLE PRODCTS,PREPS NES				0.6		0.6			PREP ALIMENTAIRES NDA
1	BEVERAGES AND TOBACCO				8.1		7.1		6.1	BOISSONS ET TABACS
111	NON–ALCOHL BEVERAGES NES						1.9			BOISSONS NON ALCOOLIQUES
11102	FLAVORED WATERS NON–ALCO				2.0					LIMONADES,EAUX GAZEUSES
1123	BEER,ALE,STOUT,PORTER				3.0		2.4			BIERES
1222	CIGARETTES				2.5		2.3			CIGARETTES
2	CRUDE MATERLS,EXCL FUELS				1.7		2.2		0.5	MAT BRUTES NON COMESTIBLES
248	WOOD SHAPED,SLEEPERS				1.6		2.2			BOIS SIMPLEMENT TRAVAILLES
3	MINERAL FUELS ETC				16.9		11.3		18.5	COMBUSTIBLES MINERAUX LUB
5	CHEMCLS,RELATED PROD NES				4.5		4.3		5.7	PRODUITS CHIMIQUES
553	PERFUMERY,COSMETICS,ETC				0.5		0.8			PRODUITS DE PARFUMERIE
554	SOAP,CLEANSING ETC PREPS				0.8					SAVONS,PRODUITS DETERSIFS
5541	SOAPS						0.7			SAVONS,PROD TENSIO–ACTIFS
6	BASIC MANUFACTURES				12.4		16.5		40.8	ART MANUFACTURES
6342	PLYWOOD OF WOOD SHEETS				0.9		1.0			BOIS CONTRE–PLAQUES
6612	CEMENT				1.4		1.6			CIMENTS HYDRAULIQUES
7	MACHINES,TRANSPORT EQUIP				16.8		22.1		17.5	MACHINES MATERIEL TRANSPORT
71331	—— OUTBOARD				0.8		1.0			MOTEURS BATEAUX HORSBORD
781	PASS MOTOR VEH EXC BUSES				4.4		6.4			AUTO TRANSPORT PERSONNES
8	MISC MANUFACTURED GOODS				7.7		13.0		13.4	ART MANUFACTURES DIVERS
821	*FURNITURE,PARTS THEREOF				0.6		0.5			MEUBLES ET PIECES
851	*FOOTWEAR				0.7		0.8			CHAUSSURES
8932	PLSTC SANITRY,TOILET ART				0.6		0.5			OBJETS HYGIEN MAT DU 58
89471	FISHNG,HUNTNG EQUIP NES				0.4		0.4			HAMECONS ET EPUISETTES
9	GOODS NOT CLASSD BY KIND				11.4		2.2		1.5	ART TRANSACT NON CLASSES

5. General Exports F.O.B. by Commodities according to the S.I.T.C. (Rev. 2) in million U.S. Dollars
Exportations Générales F.O.B. par Produits d'après la C.T.C.I. (Rév. 2) en millions de Dollars E.U.

SITC CTCI	COMMODITY	1991		1992		1993		1994		PRODUIT
		QUANTITY QUANTITE	VALUE VALEUR	QUANTITY QUANTITE	VALUE VALEUR	QUANTITY QUANTITE	VALUE VALEUR	QUANTITY QUANTITE	VALUE VALEUR	
	ALL COMMODITIES				23.4		29.2		78.2	TOUS PRODUITS
0	FOOD AND LIVE ANIMALS				21.1		27.1		75.8	ALIMENTS,ANIMAUX VIVANTS
03	FISH AND PREPARATIONS				20.2		25.4			POISSONS ET PREPARATIONS
034	FISH,FRESH,CHILLED,FROZN				19.5		25.3		73.6	POISSON FRAIS, REFRIG,CONG
037	FISH ETC PREPD,PRSVD NES				0.6		0.1		0.5	POIS,CRUST,MOL PREPARES
05	VEGETABLES AND FRUIT				0.5		1.2		0.9	LEGUMES ET FRUITS
057	FRUIT,NUTS,FRESH,DRIED				0.4		1.1		0.8	FRUITS FRAIS OU SECS
0573	BANANA,PLANTAIN,FRSH,DRY				0.3		0.8		0.5	BANANES FRAICHES,SECHEES
0577	NUTS EDIBLE,FRESH,DRIED						0.3		0.3	FRUITS A COQUES
081	*FEEDING STUFF FOR ANIML				0.3				0.4	NOURRITURE POUR ANIMAUX
8	MISC MANUFACTURED GOODS				2.3		2.2		2.5	ART MANUFACTURES DIVERS
84	CLOTHING AND ACCESSORIES				2.1		2.1		2.2	VETEMENTS
899	OTHER MANUFACTURED GOODS				0.2					AUT ART MANUF DIVERS NDA

1. HISTORICAL SERIES, 1957–1996 SPECIAL TRADE, IMPORTS C.I.F., EXPORTS F.O.B.
SERIES HISTORIQUES, 1957–1996 COMMERCE SPECIAL, IMPORTATIONS C.A.F., EXPORTATIONS F.O.B

YEAR ANNEE	VALUE IN MILLION U.S. DOLLARS / VALEUR EN MILLION U.S. DOLLARS — MERCHANDISE – MARCHANDISE: IMPORTS	MERCHANDISE – MARCHANDISE: EXPORTS	GOLD – OR: IMPORTS	GOLD – OR: EXPORTS	CONVERSION FACTORS FACTEURS DE CONVERSION CENTS E.U. PAR: IMPORTS	CONVERSION FACTORS: EXPORTS	INDEX NUMBERS – INDICES — QUANTUM: IMPORTS	QUANTUM: EXPORTS	UNIT VALUE VALEUR UNITAIRE: IMPORTS	UNIT VALUE: EXPORTS
1957	75.00	57.00								
1958	77.00	55.00								
1959	83.00	62.00								
1960	97.00	72.00								
1962	97.00	72.00								
1963	125.00	70.00								
1965	98.00	81.00								
1966	109.00	82.00								
1967	116.00	86.00								
1968	116.00	77.00								
1969	110.00	77.00								
1970	121.00	84.00								
1971	128.00	101.70								
1972	157.00	130.00								
1973	230.00	167.00								
1974	225.00	200.00								
1975	266.00	218.00								
1976	301.00	232.00								
1977	375.00	232.00								
1978	417.00	280.00								
1979	498.00	343.00								
1980	547.80	402.80								
1985	1095.50	689.10								
1986	1139.70	716.10								
1987	1104.60	717.90								
1988	1113.60	739.10								
1989	963.00	721.50								
1990	924.00	660.70								
1991	360.90	348.00								
1992	418.30	388.50								
1993	361.50	380.90								
1994	222.70	324.20								
1995	415.30	473.30								
1996	438.50	423.00								

2. IMPORTS BY BROAD ECONOMIC CATEGORY AND EXPORTS BY INDUSTRIAL ORIGIN. (PERCENTAGE OF TOTAL VALUE)
IMPORTATIONS PAR CATEGORIES ECONOMIQUES ET EXPORTATIONS PAR BRANCHE D'ACTIVITE.(EN POURCENTAGE DE LA VALEUR TOTALE)

IMPORTS – IMPORTATIONS

	1990	1991	1992	1993	1994	1995	1996
TOTAL IMPORTS–IMPORTATIONS TOTALES							100.
1 FOOD BEV–ALIMENTATION BOISSONS							13.5
11 PRIMARY–PRODUITS DE BASE							1.0
111 FOR INDUSTRY–POUR L'INDUSTRIE							0.1
112 FOR HOUSEHOLDS–POUR LES MENAGES							0.8
12 PROCESSED–PRODUITS ELABORES							12.6
121 FOR INDUSTRY–POUR L'INDUSTRIE							7.4
122 FOR HOUSEHOLDS–POUR LES MENAGES							5.2
2 IND SUPPLIES–APPROV INDUSTRIELS							19.3
21 PRIMARY–PRODUITS DE BASE							0.8
22 PROCESSED–PRODUITS ELABORES							18.5
3 FUELS–COMBUSTIBLES							19.3
31 PRIMARY–PRODUITS DE BASE							0.2
32 PROCESSED–PRODUITS ELABORES							19.2
321 MOTOR SPIRIT–ESSENCE							
322 OTHER–AUTRES							19.2
4 MACHINERY–EQUIPEMENT							23.3
41 CAPITAL EQUIPMENT–MACHINES							21.7
42 PARTS–PIECES ACCESSOIRES							1.6
5 TRANSPORT–TRANSPORT							17.3
51 PASSENGER CARS–AUTOMOBILES							3.6
52 OTHER–AUTRES							10.2
521 INDUSTRIAL–INDUSTRIELS							9.9
522 NON INDUSTRIAL–NON INDUSTRIEL							0.3
53 PARTS–PIECES ACCESSOIRES							3.5
6 CONSUM GOODS–BIENS CONSOMMATION							7.3
61 DURABLE–DURABLES							3.1
62 SEMI DURABLE–SEMI DURABLES							1.6
63 NON DURABLE–NON DURABLES							2.6
7 GOODS NES–BIENS NDA							0.0

EXPORTS – EXPORTATIONS

	1990	1991	1992	1993	1994	1995	1996
TOTAL EXPORTS–EXPORTATIONS TOTALES							100.
1 AGRICULTURE							5.4
2 MINING QUARRY–INDUS EXTRACTIVES							57.2
3 MANUFACTURING–IND MANUFACTUR							37.4
31 FOOD BEV TOBACCO–ALIM BOISS TAB							8.8
32 TEXTILES–INDUSTRIES TEXTILES							19.7
33 WOOD & PRODUCTS–BOIS & PRODUITS							2.4
34 PAPER & PRODUCTS–PAPIER & PRODT							0.0
35 CHEMICALS–INDUSTRIES CHIMIQUES							0.9
36 NON METAL MIN–MIN NON METAL							0.0
37 BASIC METAL–IND METAL BASE							1.0
38 METAL MANUF–MANUF METAL							4.5
39 OTH MANUF IND–AUTRES MANUF							0.0

3. TRADE BY PRINCIPAL COUNTRIES OF ORIGIN AND DESTINATION (VALUE IN MILLION U.S. DOLLARS)
ECHANGES SELON LES PRINCIPAUX PAYS D'ORIGINE ET DE DESTINATION (VALEUR EN MILLIONS DE DOLLARS EU)

COUNTRIES–PAYS	SPECIAL IMPORTS C.I.F. IMPORTATIONS SPECIALES C.A.F				
	1992	1993	1994	1995	1996
World	418.3				450.9
Africa					0.0
Americas					10.9
– Northern America					10.8
– LAIA					0.1
– CACM					
– Caribbean					0.0
– Rest of America					
Asia excl fmr USSR	121.9				162.8
– Middle East					0.1
Asia former USSR					2.3
Europe excl fmr USSR	74.3				81.3
– European Union	54.7				66.4
– Eastern Europe	12.1				8.7
– Rest of Europe	7.5				6.1
Europe former USSR	214.3				167.2
Oceania					0.4
Other					26.0
Russian Federation	214.3				164.0
China/Chine	57.5				69.5
Japan/Japon	40.1				52.8
Germany/Allemagne	22.1				33.4
Areas n.e.s.					26.0
Korea, Republic of	8.1				17.7
Italy/Italie	1.2				23.2
Singapore/Singapour	6.3				13.9
Austria/Autriche	19.4				0.6
China, Hong Kong SAR	9.6				3.6
USA/Etats–Unis d'Amer					10.6
France, Monaco	7.3				1.1
Hungary/Hongrie	4.9				2.3
Switzerland,Liechtenst.	5.1				1.1
Former Czechoslovakia	5.4				
Denmark/Danemark	3.0				2.0
Norway,Svalbard and JM					4.9
Poland/Pologne	1.2				3.5
United Kingdom	1.5				2.4
Ukraine					2.8
Viet Nam					2.7
Bulgaria/Bulgarie	0.5				2.1
Yugoslavia/Yougoslavie	2.4				0.1
Netherlands/Pays–Bas	0.2				1.6
Malaysia/Malaisie					1.4
Belgium–Luxembourg					1.0
Finland/Finlande					0.8
Kyrgyzstan/Kirghizistan					0.8
Kazakhstan					0.6
Uzbekistan/Ouzbékistan					0.5
Australia/Australie					0.4
India/Inde					0.4
Czech Republic					0.4
Korea Dem People's Rp	0.3				0.1
Canada					0.3
Romania/Roumanie	0.1				0.2
Turkmenistan/Turkménistn					0.3
Slovakia/Slovaquie					0.3
Thailand/Thaïlande					0.2
Latvia/Lettonie					0.2

COUNTRIES–PAYS	SPECIAL EXPORTS F.O.B. EXPORTATIONS SPECIALES F.O.B.				
	1992	1993	1994	1995	1996
Monde	388.5				424.3
Afrique					
Amériques	4.4				1.3
– Amérique du Nord	4.4				1.3
– ALAI					
– MCAC					
– Caraïbes					
– Autre Amérique					0.0
Asie anc. URSS exclus	94.4				93.9
– Moyen–Orient					
Asie ancienne URSS					0.2
Europe anc. URSS exclus	60.1				58.4
– Union Européenne	27.0				57.9
– Europe de l'Est	14.9				0.0
– Autre de l'Europe	18.2				0.5
Europe ancienne URSS	219.7				267.5
Océanie					
Autre					2.8
Russian Federation	219.7				267.5
China/Chine	69.4				76.0
United Kingdom	3.9				53.9
Japan/Japon	18.7				2.2
Switzerland,Liechtenst.	16.4				0.1
Germany/Allemagne	12.1				0.5
China, Hong Kong SAR	3.8				6.1
Korea, Republic of					9.2
Italy/Italie	8.2				0.0
Bulgaria/Bulgarie	7.3				0.0
USA/Etats–Unis d'Amer	4.4				0.9
Netherlands/Pays–Bas	1.7				3.3
Former Czechoslovakia	4.2				
Hungary/Hongrie	3.0				0.0
Areas n.e.s.					2.8
Yugoslavia/Yougoslavie	1.8				
Korea Dem People's Rp	1.2				
France, Monaco	0.8				0.0
Singapore/Singapour	0.6				0.2
Afghanistan	0.7				
Poland/Pologne	0.4				0.0
Canada					0.4
Croatia/Croatie					0.3
Austria/Autriche	0.3				0.0
Other Asia n.e.s.					0.3
Belgium–Luxembourg					0.2
Kazakhstan					0.2
Uzbekistan/Ouzbékistan					0.0
Georgia/Géorgie					0.0
Romania/Roumanie	0.0				

(VALUE AS PERCENTAGE OF WORLD TOTAL)(VALEURS EN POURCENTAGE DU TOTAL MONDIAL)

	1987	1988	1989	1990	1991	1992	1993	1994	1995	1996
Africa										0.0
Americas										2.4
– Northern America										2.4
– LAIA										0.0
– CACM										
– Caribbean										0.0
– Rest of America										
Asia excl fmr USSR	2.7	2.5	3.5	4.5	8.1	29.1				36.1
– Middle East										0.0
Asia former USSR										0.5
Europe excl fmr USSR	9.4	11.1	13.2	17.5	15.7	17.8				18.0
– European Union	2.8	3.0	4.8	6.1	9.4	13.1				14.7
– Eastern Europe	6.3	7.7	7.6	9.8	4.2	2.9				1.9
– Rest of Europe	0.3	0.5	0.8	1.6	2.1	1.8				1.4
Europe former USSR	87.2	86.0	82.8	77.5	66.0	51.2				37.1
Oceania										0.1
Other										5.8
Russian Federation						51.2				36.4
China/Chine	1.4	1.2	2.1	2.4	4.5	13.7				15.4
Japan/Japon	0.2	0.4	0.7	1.1	0.8	9.6				11.7
Germany/Allemagne					3.5	5.3				7.4
Areas n.e.s.										5.8
Korea, Republic of				0.1	2.0	1.9				3.9
Italy/Italie	0.1	0.1	0.5	0.4	0.6	0.3				5.1
Singapore/Singapour		0.0	0.0	0.1	0.2	1.5				3.1
Austria/Autriche	0.3	0.4	1.0	1.1	4.8	4.6				0.1
China, Hong Kong SAR		0.0		0.3	0.2	2.3				0.8

	1987	1988	1989	1990	1991	1992	1993	1994	1995	1996
Afrique										
Amériques	0.0	0.2	0.0	0.1	0.1	1.1				0.3
– Amérique du Nord	0.0	0.2	0.0	0.1	0.1	1.1				0.3
– ALAI										
– MCAC										
– Caraïbes										
– Autre Amérique										0.0
Asie anc. URSS exclus	2.8	4.2	4.8	4.3	20.9	24.3				22.1
– Moyen–Orient										
Asie ancienne URSS										0.0
Europe anc. URSS exclus	18.4	18.0	21.2	17.0	10.5	15.5				13.8
– Union Européenne	4.7	3.7	5.1	4.0	5.3	6.9				13.6
– Europe de l'Est	12.0	13.0	13.6	12.4	4.4	3.8				0.0
– Autre de l'Europe	1.7	1.3	2.4	0.6	0.8	4.7				0.1
Europe ancienne URSS	78.0	75.6	73.2	78.3	67.6	56.6				63.1
Océanie										
Autre										0.7
Russian Federation						56.6				63.1
China/Chine	0.5	0.4	0.6	1.7	15.2	17.9				17.9
United Kingdom	0.5	0.2	0.7	0.5	0.5	1.0				12.7
Japan/Japon	1.2	3.0	3.4	1.2	3.4	4.8				0.5
Switzerland,Liechtenst.	1.2	1.1	1.1	0.2	0.3	4.2				0.0
Germany/Allemagne					2.9	3.1				0.1
China, Hong Kong SAR					1.1	1.0				1.4
Korea, Republic of										2.2
Italy/Italie	0.0	0.0	0.2	0.8	1.4	2.1				0.0
Bulgaria/Bulgarie	2.1	2.0	3.0	2.5	0.4	1.9				0.0

4. Special Imports C.I.F. by Commodities according to the S.I.T.C. (Rev. 2) in million U.S. Dollars
Importations Spéciales C.A.F. par Produits d'après la C.T.C.I. (Rév. 2) en millions de Dollars E.U.

SITC CTCI	COMMODITY	1993 QUANTITY QUANTITE	1993 VALUE VALEUR	1994 QUANTITY QUANTITE	1994 VALUE VALEUR	1995 QUANTITY QUANTITE	1995 VALUE VALEUR	1996 QUANTITY QUANTITE	1996 VALUE VALEUR	PRODUIT
	ALL COMMODITIES								451.0	TOUS PRODUITS
0	FOOD AND LIVE ANIMALS								54.0	ALIMENTS,ANIMAUX VIVANTS
04	CEREALS AND PREPARATIONS								33.7	CEREALES ET PRODUITS
042	RICE							W 7900	3.3	RIZ
0422	RICE SEMI-MILLED,MILLED							W 7900	3.3	RIZ POLI,GLACE INCL BRISURES
04221	RICE MILLED UNBROKEN							W 7900	3.3	RIZ POLI,GLACE EXCL BRISURES
046	WHEAT ETC MEAL OR FLOUR							W 100277	27.3	SEMOULE FARINE,FROMENT
04601	FLOUR OF WHEAT OR MESLIN							W 100232	27.2	FARINE DE FROMENT
048	CEREAL ETC PREPARATIONS							W 2589	2.9	PREPTNS A BASE CEREALES
0484	BAKERY PRODUCTS							W 1761	2.3	PRODUITS DE BOULANGERIE
04842	PASTRY, CAKES ETC							W 1430	1.7	PATISSERIE ETC.
05	VEGETABLES AND FRUIT								6.9	LEGUMES ET FRUITS
054	VEG ETC FRSH,SMPLY PRSVD								1.7	LEGUMES FRAIS,CONG,SECS
057	FRUIT,NUTS,FRESH,DRIED								1.6	FRUITS FRAIS OU SECS
058	FRUIT PRESERVED,PREPARED							W 2523	2.3	CONSERVES DE FRUITS
0582	FRUIT PRESERVED BY SUGAR							W 1899	1.7	FRUITS CONFITS AU SUCRE
06	SUGAR AND PREPS,HONEY								7.4	SUCRES ET PRODUITS
061	SUGAR AND HONEY							W 10943	4.2	SUCRES ET MIEL
0611	RAW BEET AND CANE SUGAR							W 10920	4.1	SUCRES BRUTS
062	SUGAR CANDY NON-CHOCLATE							W 3067	3.3	SUCRERIES
07	COFFEE,TEA,COCOA,SPICES								2.0	CAFE,THE,CACAO,EPICES
09	MISC EDIBLE PRODUCTS								3.2	PREP ALIMENTAIRES DIVERSES
098	EDIBLE PRODCTS,PREPS NES								2.2	PREP ALIMENTAIRES NDA
1	BEVERAGES AND TOBACCO								7.4	BOISSONS ET TABACS
11	BEVERAGES								4.4	BOISSONS
111	NON-ALCOHL BEVERAGES NES							W 2666	1.5	BOISSONS NON ALCOOLIQUES
11102	FLAVORED WATERS NON-ALCO							W 2503	1.4	LIMONADES,EAUX GAZEUSES
112	ALCOHOLIC BEVERAGES							W 2876	3.0	BOISSONS ALCOOLIQUES
12	TOBACCO AND MANUFACTURES								3.0	TABACS BRUTS FABRIQUES
122	TOBACCO,MANUFACTURED								3.0	TABACS FABRIQUES
1222	CIGARETTES							MN 672630	2.2	CIGARETTES
2	CRUDE MATERLS,EXCL FUELS								4.3	MAT BRUTES NON COMESTIBLES
26	TEXTILE FIBRES AND WASTE								2.3	FIBRES TEXTILES
269	WASTE OF TEXTILE FABRICS							W 377	1.4	FRIPERIE DRILLES,CHIFFONS
26901	BULK TEXT WSTE,OLD CLTHG							W 376	1.4	ART ET ACCESS D'HABILLEMENT
3	MINERAL FUELS ETC								87.2	COMBUSTIBLES MINERAUX LUB
33	PETROLEUM AND PRODUCTS								70.6	PETROLE ET DERIVES
334	PETROLEUM PRODUCTS,REFIN							W 380321	70.3	PRODUITS RAFFINES
351	*ELECTRIC CURRENT							H 374769	15.8	ENERGIE ELECTRIQUE
4	ANIMAL,VEGETABLE OIL,FAT								3.1	HUILES,GRAISSES ANIM,VEG
42	FIXED VEGETABLE OIL,FAT								1.9	HUILES VEGETALES FIXES
423	FIXED VEG OILS,SOFT								1.7	HUILES VEGET DOUCES FIXES
4236	SUNFLOWER SEED OIL							W 1721	1.7	HUILE DE TOURNESOL
5	CHEMCLS,RELATED PROD NES								22.1	PRODUITS CHIMIQUES
51	ORGANIC CHEMICALS								2.4	PROD CHIMIQ ORGANIQUES
52	INORGANIC CHEMICALS								3.8	PROD CHIM INORGANIQUES
523	OTHR INORG CHEMICALS ETC								2.7	AUT PRODUITS CHIMIQUES INORG
5231	METAL CMPD OF INORG ACID								2.0	SELS METALLIQUES
52317	SULPHITES,THIOSULPHATES							W 3801	1.5	SULFITES,HYPOSULFITES
541	*MEDICINAL,PHARM PRODUCT							MK 782047	6.2	PROD MEDICINAUX PHARMACEUT
5417	MEDICAMENTS							MK 477601	3.0	MEDICAMENTS
54179	— CONTNG OTH SUBSTANCES							MK 420240	2.3	MED CONT AUT SUBSTANCES
55	PERFUME,CLEANING ETC PRD								4.6	PROD POUR PARFUM,TOILETTE
554	SOAP,CLEANSING ETC PREPS							W 4113	3.1	SAVONS,PRODUITS DETERSIFS
5541	SOAPS							W 3277	1.9	SAVONS,PROD TENSIO-ACTIFS
562	*FERTILIZERS,MANUFACTURE								2.1	ENGRAIS MANUFACTURES
5621	CHEM NITROGENOUS FERTLZR								1.6	ENGRAIS AZOTES
56211	AMMONIUM NITRATE							W 5989	1.5	NITRATE D'AMMONIUM
6	BASIC MANUFACTURES								74.8	ART MANUFACTURES
62	RUBBER MANUFACTURES NES								9.5	CAOUTCHOUC MANUFACTURE
625	RUBBER TYRES, TUBES ETC							N 82475	5.4	PNEUS CAOUTCHOUC VULCANISE
6252	TYRES,NEW,BUS OR LORRY							N 15693	4.1	PNEUS POUR AUTOBUS,CAMIONS
628	RUBBER ARTICLES NES								3.5	OUVRAGES CAOUTCHOUC NDA
6282	VULCANIZD RUBBER BELTING							W 122	3.4	COURROIES EN CAOUTCHOUC
64	PAPER,PAPERBOARD AND MFR								4.0	PAPIERS,CARTONS & OUVRAGES
641	PAPER AND PAPERBOARD								2.3	PAPIERS ET CARTONS
642	PAPER,ETC,PRECUT,ARTS OF								1.7	PAP,CARTONS DECOUPES
65	TEXTILE YARN,FABRICS,ETC								14.0	FILS,TISSUS,ARTICLES TEXTILE
651	TEXTILE YARN								1.7	FILS TEXTILES
652	COTTON FABRICS,WOVEN							L 3706	4.0	TISSUS DE COTON
6521	GREY WOVEN COTTON FABRIC							L 3018	3.4	TISSUS COT ECRUS NON MERCER
65214	GREY WOVEN COTTON NES							L 3018	3.4	AUT TISSUS 85% COTON ECRUS
653	WOVN MAN-MADE FIB FABRIC							L 3818	3.6	TISSUS FIBRES SYNTH,ARTIF
6531	CONT SYNT WEAVES NONPILE							L 3763	3.6	TISSUS FIBRES SYNTH CONTINUE
65315	CONT SYN TXTL FABRIC NES							L 3677	3.5	TIS PLUS 85% TEXT SYNT CONT
657	SPECIAL TXTL FABRC,PRODS								1.6	TISSUS SPECIAUX
658	TEXTILE ARTICLES NES							N 686847	1.6	ART FACONNES MAT TEXTILES
66	NONMETAL MINERAL MFS NES								12.4	ART MIN NON METALLIQUES
661	LIME,CEMENT,BLDG PRODS							W 10508	1.9	CHAUX,CIMENTS MAT CONSTR
6618	MNRL BLDG PRD UNFIRD NES							W 7092	1.4	MAT CONST AMIANTE-CIMENT
662	CLAY,REFRACTORY BLDG PRD								2.6	MAT CONST REFRACTAIRES
6623	REFRACTORY BUILDING PROD							W 1825	2.2	BRIQUES REFRACTAIRES
66233	REFRACTORY CEMENT,MORTAR							W 408	1.7	CIMENTS REFRACTAIRES
663	MINERAL MANUFCTURES NES								6.2	ART MIN MANUF NDA
6633	MINRL MFS NES NONCERAMIC							W 4187	5.6	OUVR MAT MINERALE NDA
66332	CEMENT,ARTFCL STONE PROD							W 3896	5.5	OUVRAGES EN CIMENT
67	IRON AND STEEL								27.3	FER ET ACIER
671	PIG IRON ETC								5.0	FONTE,SPIEGEL,POUDRES
6713	IRON,STL POWDER,SHOT,ETC								3.4	POUDRES,GREN FER,ACIER
67131	IRON,STEEL SHOT,GRIT,ETC							W 9745	3.4	GRENAILLE FER,ACIER
6716	FERRO-ALLOYS							W 1562	1.6	FERRO-ALLIAGES
674	IRN,STL UNIV,PLATE,SHEET								4.2	LARGES PLATS,TOLES
6749	OTH IRN,STL PLATES,SHEET							W 9628	2.7	AUTRES TOLES FER,ACIER
678	IRON,STL TUBES,PIPES,ETC							W 5730	9.8	TUBES,TUYAUX EN FONTE,FER
6782	IRON,STL SEAMLESS TUBES							W 4040	8.6	TUBES,TUYAUX SANS SOUDURE
679	IRN,STL CASTINGS UNWORKD								6.0	OUVRAGES EN FONTE,FER,ACIER
6793	IRON,STL FORGINGS ROUGH							N 3651	1.4	OUVRAGES FORGES,ESTAMPES
6794	IRON,STL CASTINGS ROUGH								4.6	OUVRAGES COULES,MOULES
67941	IRON CASTINGS ROUGH								4.6	OUVRAGES A L'ETAT BRUT
68	NON-FERROUS METALS								1.8	METAUX NON FERREUX
69	METAL MANUFACTURES NES								5.1	ART MANUFACT EN METAL NDA

4. Special Imports C.I.F. by Commodities according to the S.I.T.C. (Rev. 2) in million U.S. Dollars
Importations Spéciales C.A.F. par Produits d'après la C.T.C.I. (Rév. 2) en millions de Dollars E.U.

SITC CTCI	COMMODITY	1993 QUANTITY QUANTITE	1993 VALUE VALEUR	1994 QUANTITY QUANTITE	1994 VALUE VALEUR	1995 QUANTITY QUANTITE	1995 VALUE VALEUR	1996 QUANTITY QUANTITE	1996 VALUE VALEUR	PRODUIT
7	MACHINES,TRANSPORT EQUIP								179.2	MACHINES MATERIEL TRANSPORT
71	POWER GENERATING EQUIPMT								5.7	MACHINES GENERATRICES
716	ROTATING ELECTRIC PLANT							N 7557	3.5	APP ELECTR ROTATIFS,PIECES
72	MACHS FOR SPCL INDUSTRYS								46.2	MAC SPECIALES POUR INDUST
722	TRACTORS NON–ROAD							N 38	2.6	TRACTEURS
7223	TRACK–LAYING TRACTORS							N 27	1.9	TRACTEURS A CHENILLES
723	CIVIL ENGNEERG EQUIP ETC							N 4329	8.3	APPAREILS DE GENIE CIVIL
7234	CONST,MINING MACHNRY NES							N 1301	7.5	MACH POUR LA CONST, MINES
72341	SELF–PROPELLD DOZERS,ETC							N 99	2.7	BULLDOZERS
72342	SLFPRP SHOVELS,EXCAVATRS							N 57	3.4	PELLES MECANIQUES
724	TEXTILE,LEATHER MACHNRY							N 179445	14.5	MACH POUR INDUSTRIE TEXTILE
7244	SPINNING,EXTRDNG,ETC MCH							N 4705	4.6	MACH POUR LE FILAGE
72442	FIBRE PROCESSNG MACH NES							N 69	2.4	MACH PREP MAT TEXTILES
72443	SPINNING,REELING,ETC MCH							N 12	2.1	MACH POUR LA FILATURE
7245	WEAVING,FELT MFG,ETC MCH							N 212	4.4	METIERS A TISSER,PIECES
72453	GIMPING,WARPING ETC MCHS							N 90	3.5	METIERS A TULLE ETC
7248	SKIN,LEATHER WORKNG MACH							N 36442	3.3	MACHINES TRAVAIL DES CUIRS
727	FOOD MACHRY NON–DOMESTIC							N 10747	5.5	MACH INDUSTRIES ALIMENT
7272	OTH FOOD PROC MCHY,PARTS							N 3574	5.0	AUT MACH IND ALIMENTAIRE
72722	INDUS FOOD PROC MACH NES							N 1549	3.6	MACHINES BOULANGERIE
72729	PTS NES OF MCHY OF 72722							N 2025	1.4	PIECES MACH DU 727.22
728	OTH MACHY FOR SPCL INDUS							N 25256	12.8	AUT MACH IND PARTICULIERES
7283	OTHR MINERAL WORKG MACHY							N 8600	4.1	MACH TRIER,CRIBLER,BROYER
72839	PTS NES OF MACHY OF 7283							N 5892	2.2	PIECES MACH DU 728.3
7284	MACHY FOR SPCL INDUS NES							N 16462	8.3	MACH SPEC IND PARTICUL.
72842	RUBBER,PLASTICS WRKG MCH							N 1456	3.6	MACH IND CAOUT MAT PLAST
72848	OTH MCHY WITH INDIV FNCT							N 109	2.9	AUTRES MACHINES NDA
72849	PTS OF MACHS OF 7284 ETC							N 14761	1.8	PIECES DU 728.4 ETC
73	METALWORKING MACHINERY								2.0	MACH TRAVAIL DES METAUX
74	GENRL INDUSTRL MACHY NES								19.6	MACH APP INDUSTRIE
741	HEATING,COOLING EQUIPMNT							N 7895	2.4	MACH CHAUFFAGE,PIECES
742	PUMPS FOR LIQUIDS ETC							N 5433	1.5	POMPES MOTO–POMPES
743	PUMPS NES,CENTRFUGES ETC							N 4920	1.5	POMPES COMPRES,VENT ETC
744	MECHANICAL HANDLING EQU							N 51139	11.8	EQUIP MANUTENTION PIECES
7442	LIFTING,LOADING MACH NES							N 2544	8.3	APP LEVAGE,MANUTENTION
74422	SHIP DERRICKS,CRANES ETC							N 24	5.9	GRUES,PONTS ROULANTS
74428	OTH HANDLING ETC MCH NES							N 2394	1.9	AUT APP LEVAGE ETC
7449	PTS NES OF MACHY OF 7442							N 48467	3.3	PIECES DU 744.2
749	NONELEC MACH PTS,ACC NES							N 22997	2.0	PIECES MACH NON ELEC NDA
75	OFFICE MACHNES,ADP EQUIP								3.8	MACH BUREAU TRAIT AUTOM
752	AUTOMTIC DATA PROC EQUIP							N 49334	2.1	MACH TRAIT INFORMATION
76	TELECOMM,SOUND EQUIPMENT								14.2	EQUIPMENT DE TELECOM
761	TELEVISION RECEIVERS							N 34660	2.9	RECEPTEURS DE TELEVISION
7611	COLOUR TV RECEIVERS							N 34377	2.8	RECEPTEURS COULEUR
764	TELECOM EQPT,PTS,ACC NES							N 139173	10.7	EQUIP TELECOM,PIECES
7641	LINE TELEPHONE,ETC EQUIP							N 99735	8.8	APP TELEPHON PAR FIL
7649	PTS NES OF EQUIPMT OF 76							N 33883	1.6	PIECES DE LA DIV 76
77	ELECTRIC MACHNRY NES ETC								13.6	MACH APP ELECT NDA
771	ELECTRIC POWER MACHY NES							N 4018	1.7	MACH PROD,TRANS ELECTR
772	SWITCHGEAR ETC,PARTS NES							N 2334497	1.5	APP COUPURE,SECT ETC
7721	SWITCHGEAR ETC							N 2334454	1.5	APP COUPURE,SECTIONMNT
773	ELECTR DISTRIBUTNG EQUIP								1.9	EQUIPMT DISTRIBUTION ELECT
7731	INSULATED WIRE,CABLE ETC							L 488	1.6	FILS,CABLES ISOLES ELECT
775	HOUSEHOLD TYPE EQUIP NES							N 48215	3.4	MACH,APP USAGE DOMESTQUE
7758	ELECTRO–THERMIC APPL NES							N 34045	1.8	APP ELECTROTHERMIQ NDA
778	ELECTRICAL MACHINERY NES								5.0	AUTRES MACH ELECT NDA
7781	BATTERIES,ACCUMULATORS								1.6	PILES ET ACCUMULATEURS
7788	OTH ELEC MACHY,EQUIP NES								2.4	AUT MACH APP ELEC NDA
78	ROAD VEHICLES								49.6	VEHICULES ROUTIERS
781	PASS MOTOR VEH EXC BUSES							N 2994	16.3	AUTO TRANSPORT PERSONNES
782	LORRIES,SPCL MTR VEH NES							N 340	14.7	VEHICULES SPECIAUX,MARCH
7821	LORRIES,TRUCKS							N 299	14.0	VEHICULES TRANSP MARCHAND
783	ROAD MOTOR VEHICLES NES							N 245	9.2	VEHICULES ROUTIERS NDA
7831	BUSES							N 194	8.0	VOITURES TRANSPORT COMMUN
784	MOTOR VEH PRTS,ACCES NES							N 261153	6.8	PIECES 722,781,782,783
7849	OTHER MOTOR VEHCL PARTS							N 260287	6.7	PIECES 722,781,782,783
785	CYCLES,ETC MOTRZD OR NOT							N 24682	2.3	MOTOCYCLES SCOOTERS
79	OTHR TRANSPORT EQUIPMENT								25.0	AUTRE MATERIEL TRANSPORT
791	RAILWAY VEHICLES							N 44811	24.8	VEHIC MAT CHEMINS DE FER
7913	MECHAN–PROPELLED RY CARS							N 24	11.2	AUTOMOTRICES,DRAISINES
7914	RY COACHES NES NOT POWRD							N 340	6.2	VOITURES A VOYAGEURS
7915	FRT,MAINT CARS NOT POWRD							N 227	2.9	WAGONS DE SERVICE
79152	RAILWAY FREIGHT CARS NES							N 227	2.9	WAGONS MARCHANDISES
7919	RY TRACK FIXT,ETC,PARTS							N 44108	4.6	MATER FIXE VOIES FERREES
79191	RY TRACK FIXTURES ETC							N 10738	3.5	APP DE SIGNALISATION
8	MISC MANUFACTURED GOODS								19.2	ART MANUFACTURES DIVERS
821	*FURNITURE,PARTS THEREOF							N 109182	5.4	MEUBLES ET PIECES
8219	FURNITURE AND PARTS NES							N 61765	4.7	AUTRES MEUBLES ET PIECES
82192	WOOD FURNITURE NES							N 37810	4.3	MEUBLES NDA EN BOIS
87	PRECISION INSTRUMNTS NES								4.5	INSTRUM,APPAR SCIENT NDA
872	MEDICAL INSTRUMENTS NES							N 21361	2.0	INSTR,APP MEDIC–CHIR NDA
87202	OTH MEDICAL INSTRUMENTS							N 7241	1.8	INSTRUM,APP MEDECINE
874	MEASURNG,CONTROLNG INSTR							N 21824	2.5	INSTRUMENTS DE MESURE
89	MISC MANUFCTRD GOODS NES								5.8	ART MANUFACTURES DIVERS
893	ARTICLES OF PLASTIC NES								2.9	OUVRAGES EN MAT DIVIS 58
8939	MISC PLASTIC ARTICLES								1.6	ART DIVERS EN MAT DIV 58
899	OTHER MANUFACTURED GOODS								1.7	AUT ART MANUF DIVERS NDA

5. Special Exports F.O.B. by Commodities according to the S.I.T.C. (Rev. 2) in million U.S. Dollars
Exportations Spéciales F.O.B. par Produits d'après la C.T.C.I. (Rév. 2) en millions de Dollars E.U.

SITC CTCI	COMMODITY	1993		1994		1995		1996		PRODUIT
		QUANTITY QUANTITE	VALUE VALEUR	QUANTITY QUANTITE	VALUE VALEUR	QUANTITY QUANTITE	VALUE VALEUR	QUANTITY QUANTITE	VALUE VALEUR	
	ALL COMMODITIES								424.3	TOUS PRODUITS
0	FOOD AND LIVE ANIMALS								8.8	ALIMENTS,ANIMAUX VIVANTS
01	MEAT AND PREPARATIONS								6.2	VIANDES ET PREPARATIONS
011	MEAT FRESH,CHILLD,FROZEN							W 5553	6.0	VIANDES FRAICHES,REF,CONGE
0111	BOVINE MEAT FRESH,FROZEN							W 3356	4.8	VIANDES BOVIN FRAI,REF
01111	BOVINE MEAT WITH BONE IN							W 3296	4.7	VIANDES BOVIN NON DESOSS
081	*FEEDING STUFF FOR ANIML							W 6962084	2.1	NOURRITURE POUR ANIMAUX
0811	HAY, FODDER, GREEN, DRY							W 23146	1.7	FOIN ET FOURRAGE
08112	FODDER ROOTS,HAY,ETC							W 23146	1.7	RACINES FOURRAGERES
2	CRUDE MATERLS,EXCL FUELS								371.4	MAT BRUTES NON COMESTIBLES
21	HIDES,SKINS,FURS UNDRSSD								22.3	CUIRS,PEAUX BRUTS
211	HIDES,SKINS,EXC FURS,RAW								22.2	CUIRS ET PEAUX
2111	BOVINE,EQUINE HIDES,RAW							N 207924	3.7	PEAUX DE BOVINS
2112	CALF AND KIP SKINS,RAW							N 123646	2.4	PEAUX DE VEAUX
2114	GOAT AND KID SKINS,RAW							N 387986	2.3	PEAUX DE CAPRINS
2116	SHEEP SKIN WITH WOOL							N 1950081	13.7	PEAUX LAINEES D'OVINS
24	CORK AND WOOD								10.2	LIEGE ET BOIS
248	WOOD SHAPED,SLEEPERS							W 62808	10.0	BOIS SIMPLEMENT TRAVAILLES
2482	LUMBER SHAPED CONIFER							W 62773	10.0	CONIFERES SCIES,RABOTES
24821	LUMBER SAWN ETC CONIFER							W 62773	10.0	CONIFERES SCIES LONGITUD
26	TEXTILE FIBRES AND WASTE								78.6	FIBRES TEXTILES
268	WOOL(EXC TOPS),ANML HAIR							W 13430	78.6	LAINES ET POILS
2681	WOOL GREASY,FLEECE–WSHED							W 6794	5.9	LAINE EN SUINT
2683	FINE ANIMAL HAIR,UNCOMBD							W 1559	11.9	POILS FINS EN MASSE
2685	COARSE HAIR UNCOMBED							W 3094	4.7	CRINS EN MASSE
26851	HORSEHAIR AND ITS WASTE							W 997	1.8	CRINS ET DECHETS
26859	COARSE HAIR NES UNCOMBED							W 2097	2.9	AUTRES POILS EN MASSE
2687	WOOL OR HAIR COMBED ETC							W 773	54.0	LAINE CARDEE PEIGNEE
27	CRUDE FERTLZR,MINRLS NES								23.2	ENGRAIS MINERAUX BRUTS
278	OTHER CRUDE MINERALS								23.2	AUTRES MINERAUX BRUTS
2785	QUARTZ,MICA,FELSPAR,ETC								23.2	QUARTZ,MICA,FELDSPATH
27854	FELSPAR,FLOURSPAR,ETC							W 159424	23.2	FELDSPATH,LEUCITE ETC.
28	METALLIFEROUS ORES,SCRAP								230.9	MINERAIS METAL,DECHETS
282	IRON AND STEEL SCRAP							W 71913	8.2	FERRAILLES
28209	— OF OTHR IRON OR STEEL							W 71082	8.1	FERRAILLES DE FER
287	BASE METAL ORES,CONC NES								219.5	MINERAIS METAUX COMMUNS
2871	CPR ORE ETC,CEMENT COPPR							W 473578	205.2	MINERAIS DE CUIVRE,MATTES
28711	COPPER ORES,EXCL MATTE							W 473578	205.2	MINERAIS DE CUIVRE
2879	OTH NONFER ORE,CONCNTRTE							W 5109	14.2	MINERAIS D'AUTRES METAUX
28793	MOLYBD, NIOBIUM ETC ORES							W 5095	14.2	MINERAIS DE MOLYBDENE,TITANE
288	NONFERR METAL SCRAP NES							W 3709	3.2	DECHETS NON FERREUX
2882	OTHER BASE MTL SCRAP NES							W 3709	3.2	AUTRES DECHETS
28823	ALUMINIUM WSTE AND SCRAP							W 2331	2.2	DECHETS D'ALUMINIUM
29	CRUDE ANIMAL,VEG MAT NES								6.3	MATIERES BRUTES ANIM,VEGET
291	CRUDE ANIMAL MTRIALS NES								6.3	MATIERES BRUTES ANIMALES
2911	BONES,IVORY,HORNS,ETC							W 3753	3.0	OS,CORNES,SABOTS
29116	IVORY,TORTOISE–SHELL ETC							W 772	2.7	IVOIRE ECAILLE
2919	OTH ANIMAL MATERIALS NES								3.3	MAT ORIGINE ANIMALE NDA
29193	GUT,BLADDERS,ETC NONFISH								3.3	BOYAUX,VESSIES
5	CHEMCLS,RELATED PROD NES								2.8	PRODUITS CHIMIQUES
562	*FERTILIZERS,MANUFACTURE								2.0	ENGRAIS MANUFACTURES
5629	FERTILIZERS NES								1.7	ENGRAIS NDA
56291	NIT–PHOS–POT FERTLZR NES							W 7994	1.7	ENGRAIS CONT N P K
6	BASIC MANUFACTURES								6.4	ART MANUFACTURES
67	IRON AND STEEL								4.3	FER ET ACIER
672	IRON,STEEL PRIMARY FORMS							W 15894	2.9	LINGOTS FER,ACIER
6724	IRN,STL INGOTS,LUMPS,ETC							W 15872	2.9	FER,ACIER LINGOTS,MASSES
67241	IRON,SIMPLE STEEL INGOTS							W 15872	2.9	LINGOTS EN FER ET ACIER
7	MACHINES,TRANSPORT EQUIP								7.4	MACHINES MATERIEL TRANSPORT
78	ROAD VEHICLES								6.1	VEHICULES ROUTIERS
781	PASS MOTOR VEH EXC BUSES							N 1682	5.8	AUTO TRANSPORT PERSONNES
8	MISC MANUFACTURED GOODS								27.0	ART MANUFACTURES DIVERS
84	CLOTHING AND ACCESSORIES								26.6	VETEMENTS
842	MENS OUTERWEAR NOT KNIT							N 1021329	8.9	VET DESSUS POUR HOMMES
8421	— OVERCOATS,OTHER COATS							N 510277	4.7	MANTEAUX HOMMES MAT TEXT
84219	—— OF OTHER FIBRES							N 510277	4.7	MANTEAUX HOMMES AUT FIBR
8429	— OTHER OUTER GARMENTS							N 371561	3.7	AUT VET DES HOM MAT TEX
843	WOMENS OUTERWEAR NONKNIT							N 688564	4.3	VET DESSUS FEMMES MAT TEX
8431	— COATS AND JACKETS							N 194653	2.2	MANT,VEST FEM MAT TEXTIL
8439	— OTHER OUTER GARMENTS							N 457478	2.0	AUT VET DES FEM MAT TEXT
844	UNDER GARMENTS NOT KNIT							N 986555	3.3	VETEMENT DESSOUS MAT TEX
8441	— MENS SHIRTS							N 986517	3.2	CHEMISES HOMMES MAT TEXT
84411	—— OF COTTON							N 919309	3.0	CHEMISES HOMMES DE COTON
845	OUTERWEAR KNIT NONELASTC							N 349382	9.4	VET DESSOUS,ACCES BONNET
8451	— JERSEYS,PULLOVERS ETC							N 192273	8.7	CHANDAILS,PULL–OVERS ETC

1. HISTORICAL SERIES, 1958–1993 SPECIAL TRADE, IMPORTS C.I.F., EXPORTS F.O.B.
SERIES HISTORIQUES, 1958–1993 COMMERCE SPECIAL, IMPORTATIONS C.A.F., EXPORTATIONS F.O.B

YEAR ANNEE	VALUE IN MILLION E.C. DOLLARS VALEUR EN MILLION E.C. DOLLARS MERCHANDISE –MARCHANDISE		GOLD –OR		CONVERSION FACTORS U.S. CENTS PER E.C. DOLLAR FACTEURS DE CONVERSION CENTS E.U. PAR E.C. DOLLAR		INDEX NUMBERS –INDICES QUANTUM		UNIT VALUE VALEUR UNITAIRE	
	IMPORTS	EXPORTS	IMPORTS	EXPORTS	IMPORTS	EXPORTS	IMPORTS	EXPORTS	IMPORTS	EXPORTS
1958	1.54	0.38			58.3300	58.3300				
1959	8.50				58.3300					
1960	1.98	0.27			58.3300	58.3300				
1961	2.14	0.31			58.3300	58.3300				
1962	2.54	0.55			58.3300	58.3300				
1963	2.76	0.33			58.3300	58.3300				
1964	4.02	0.32			58.3300	58.3300				
1965	4.89	0.27			58.3300	58.3300				
1967	6.92	0.23			57.6500	57.6500				
1968	7.73	0.24			50.0000	50.0000				
1970	8.81	0.45			50.0000	50.0000				
1971	8.86	0.30			50.7166	50.7166				
1972	12.08	0.37			52.1216	52.1216				
1973	12.15	0.69			51.0860	51.0860				
1974	15.97	1.05			48.7301	48.7301				
1975	16.54	1.02			46.2878	46.2878				
1976	20.80	1.12			38.0480	38.0480				
1977	18.93	1.64			37.0370	37.0370				
1978	26.93	3.71			37.0370	37.0370				
1979	32.32	2.09			37.0370	37.0370				
1980	44.55	3.20			37.0370	37.0370				
1981	51.00	5.97			37.0370	37.0370				
1982	54.87	6.98			37.0370	37.0370				
1983	53.80	12.33			37.0370	37.0370				
1984	47.26	8.51			37.0370	37.0370				
1985	49.59	7.82			37.0370	37.0370				
1987	68.20	9.50			37.0370	37.0370				
1988	71.70	6.20			37.0370	37.0370				
1989	100.00	3.40			37.0370	37.0370				
1990	130.00	4.00			37.0370	37.0370				
1991	95.00	2.78			37.0370	37.0370				
1992	91.52	4.52			37.0370	37.0370				
1993	75.59	1.55			37.0370	37.0370				

2. IMPORTS BY BROAD ECONOMIC CATEGORY AND EXPORTS BY INDUSTRIAL ORIGIN. (PERCENTAGE OF TOTAL VALUE)
IMPORTATIONS PAR CATEGORIES ECONOMIQUES ET EXPORTATIONS PAR BRANCHE D'ACTIVITE.(EN POURCENTAGE DE LA VALEUR TOTALE)

IMPORTS – IMPORTATIONS

	1987	1988	1989	1990	1991	1992	1993
TOTAL IMPORTS–IMPORTATIONS TOTALES							
1 FOOD BEV–ALIMENTATION BOISSONS							
11 PRIMARY–PRODUITS DE BASE							
111 FOR INDUSTRY–POUR L'INDUSTRIE							
112 FOR HOUSEHOLDS–POUR LES MENAGES							
12 PROCESSED–PRODUITS ELABORES							
121 FOR INDUSTRY–POUR L'INDUSTRIE							
122 FOR HOUSEHOLDS–POUR LES MENAGES							
2 IND SUPPLIES–APPROV INDUSTRIELS							
21 PRIMARY–PRODUITS DE BASE							
22 PROCESSED–PRODUITS ELABORES							
3 FUELS–COMBUSTIBLES							
31 PRIMARY–PRODUITS DE BASE							
32 PROCESSED–PRODUITS ELABORES							
321 MOTOR SPIRIT–ESSENCE							
322 OTHER–AUTRES							
4 MACHINERY–EQUIPEMENT							
41 CAPITAL EQUIPMENT–MACHINES							
42 PARTS–PIECES ACCESSOIRES							
5 TRANSPORT–TRANSPORT							
51 PASSENGER CARS–AUTOMOBILES							
52 OTHER–AUTRES							
521 INDUSTRIAL–INDUSTRIELS							
522 NON INDUSTRIAL–NON INDUSTRIEL							
53 PARTS–PIECES ACCESSOIRES							
6 CONSUM GOODS–BIENS CONSOMMATION							
61 DURABLE–DURABLES							
62 SEMI DURABLE–SEMI DURABLES							
63 NON DURABLE–NON DURABLES							
7 GOODS NES–BIENS NDA							

EXPORTS – EXPORTATIONS

	1987	1988	1989	1990	1991	1992	1993
TOTAL EXPORTS–EXPORTATIONS TOTALES							100.
1 AGRICULTURE							0.3
2 MINING QUARRY–INDUS EXTRACTIVES							
3 MANUFACTURING–IND MANUFACTUR							99.1
31 FOOD BEV TOBACCO–ALIM BOISS TAB							8.7
32 TEXTILES–INDUSTRIES TEXTILES							3.8
33 WOOD & PRODUCTS–BOIS & PRODUITS							1.4
34 PAPER & PRODUCTS–PAPIER & PRODT							0.5
35 CHEMICALS–INDUSTRIES CHIMIQUES							9.6
36 NON METAL MIN–MIN NON METAL							1.2
37 BASIC METAL–IND METAL BASE							
38 METAL MANUF–MANUF METAL							73.9
39 OTH MANUF IND–AUTRES MANUF							

3. TRADE BY PRINCIPAL COUNTRIES OF ORIGIN AND DESTINATION (VALUE IN MILLION U.S. DOLLARS) ECHANGES SELON LES PRINCIPAUX PAYS D'ORIGINE ET DE DESTINATION (VALEUR EN MILLIONS DE DOLLARS EU)

COUNTRIES–PAYS	SPECIAL IMPORTS C.I.F. IMPORTATIONS SPECIALES C.A.F				
	1989	1990	1991	1992	1993
World	31.5	44.0	38.8		28.0
Africa					0.0
Americas	5.6	7.6			21.5
– Northern America					13.8
– LAIA					0.6
– CACM					0.0
– Caribbean	5.6	7.6			6.7
– Rest of America	0.0	0.0			0.4
Asia excl fmr USSR					1.0
– Middle East					0.0
Asia former USSR					
Europe excl fmr USSR					4.7
– European Union					4.7
– Eastern Europe					0.0
– Rest of Europe					0.0
Europe former USSR					
Oceania					0.0
Other	26.0	36.3			0.3
Areas n.e.s.	26.0	36.3	7.0		0.3
Trinidad and Tobago	2.8	3.8	6.4		4.5
USA/Etats–Unis d'Amer					13.3
United Kingdom					4.0
Barbados/Barbade	0.8	0.9	0.7		0.4
Saint Lucia/Ste–Lucie	0.5	0.7	0.7		0.3
St Vincent & Grenadines	0.4	0.6	0.4		0.5
Jamaica/Jamaïque	0.5	0.4	0.4		0.4
Saint Kitts and Nevis	0.3	0.3	0.4		0.3
Antigua and Barbuda	0.2	0.7	0.2		0.1
Japan/Japon					0.8
Canada					0.5
Dominica/Dominique	0.0	0.1	0.2		0.1
Colombia/Colombie					0.3
Suriname/Surinam					0.2
Netherlands/Pays–Bas					0.2
Venezuela					0.2
Germany/Allemagne					0.2
Denmark/Danemark					0.1
France, Monaco					0.1
Italy/Italie					0.0

COUNTRIES–PAYS	SPECIAL EXPORTS F.O.B. EXPORTATIONS SPECIALES F.O.B.				
	1989	1990	1991	1992	1993
Monde	1.6	1.9	1.5		0.6
Afrique					
Amériques	0.5	0.2	0.2		0.6
– Amérique du Nord	0.4	0.1	0.2		0.4
– ALAI					
– MCAC					
– Caraïbes	0.1	0.0	0.1		0.2
– Autre Amérique					
Asie anc. URSS exclus					0.0
– Moyen–Orient					
Asie ancienne URSS					
Europe anc. URSS exclus	0.0	0.0			
– Union Européenne	0.0	0.0			
– Europe de l'Est					
– Autre de l'Europe					
Europe ancienne URSS					
Océanie					
Autre	1.2	1.7	1.3		
Areas n.e.s.	1.2	1.7	1.3		
USA/Etats–Unis d'Amer	0.4	0.1	0.1		0.4
Antigua and Barbuda	0.0	0.0	0.0		0.1
Saint Kitts and Nevis	0.0	0.0	0.1		0.1
Canada		0.0	0.0		
Barbados/Barbade	0.0				0.0
St Vincent & Grenadines	0.0	0.0			0.0
Dominica/Dominique	0.0	0.0			0.0
Saint Lucia/Ste–Lucie	0.0	0.0	0.0		0.0
United Kingdom	0.0	0.0			

(VALUE AS PERCENTAGE OF WORLD TOTAL)(VALEURS EN POURCENTAGE DU TOTAL MONDIAL)

	1984	1985	1986	1987	1988	1989	1990	1991	1992	1993
Africa										0.0
Americas	63.7	62.2	57.6	61.3	18.0	17.6	17.4			76.9
– Northern America	42.1	41.1	40.2	42.3						49.4
– LAIA										2.2
– CACM										0.0
– Caribbean	21.2	20.9	17.1	18.4	17.9	17.6	17.3			23.9
– Rest of America	0.3	0.3	0.2	0.6	0.0	0.0	0.1			1.4
Asia excl fmr USSR										3.4
– Middle East										0.1
Asia former USSR										
Europe excl fmr USSR	19.7	19.4	25.8	23.0						16.7
– European Union	19.7	19.4	25.8	23.0						16.7
– Eastern Europe										0.0
– Rest of Europe										0.0
Europe former USSR										
Oceania										0.0
Other	16.5	18.4	16.6	15.7	82.0	82.4	82.6			1.2
Areas n.e.s.	16.5	18.4	16.6	15.7	82.0	82.4	82.6	18.0		1.2
Trinidad and Tobago	11.5	11.7	7.9	9.9	8.9	8.8	8.7	16.6		16.0
USA/Etats–Unis d'Amer	38.5	35.7	37.1	31.0						47.7
United Kingdom	15.2	15.1	19.9	18.6						14.5
Barbados/Barbade	2.5	2.2	3.2	2.5	2.7	2.7	2.0	1.7		1.5
Saint Lucia/Ste–Lucie	0.3	0.3	0.3	1.2	1.7	1.6	1.7	1.9		1.2
St Vincent & Grenadines	1.9	1.8	1.5	1.4	1.3	1.3	1.3	1.0		1.6
Jamaica/Jamaïque	1.8	1.6	1.2	1.3	1.6	1.6	0.9	1.0		1.3
Saint Kitts and Nevis	1.6	1.7	1.5	1.1	1.0	0.9	0.7	1.1		1.0
Antigua and Barbuda	1.4	1.1	0.9	0.7	0.6	0.6	1.6	0.6		0.5

	1984	1985	1986	1987	1988	1989	1990	1991	1992	1993
Afrique										
Amériques	44.6	29.7	78.5	83.6	72.4	27.7	9.5	15.8		99.7
– Amérique du Nord	19.1	20.0	68.2	77.9	67.1	22.5	7.0	10.5		64.9
– ALAI										
– MCAC										
– Caraïbes	25.5	9.8	10.3	5.7	5.3	5.1	2.5	5.3		34.8
– Autre Amérique	0.0									
Asie anc. URSS exclus										0.3
– Moyen–Orient										
Asie ancienne URSS										
Europe anc. URSS exclus	2.3	2.3	3.0	1.3		0.5	0.2			
– Union Européenne	2.3	2.3	3.0	1.3		0.5	0.2			
– Europe de l'Est										
– Autre de l'Europe										
Europe ancienne URSS										
Océanie										
Autre	53.2	67.9	18.6	15.0	27.6	71.8	90.4	84.1		
Areas n.e.s.	53.2	67.9	18.6	15.0	27.6	71.8	90.4	84.1		
USA/Etats–Unis d'Amer	18.8	19.6	68.1	77.9	67.1	22.5	5.7	9.7		64.9
Antigua and Barbuda	6.3	4.1	5.9	2.0	2.6	2.0	1.2	1.9		18.3
Saint Kitts and Nevis	1.4	1.4	1.2	1.0	1.4	1.2	1.0	3.4		10.1
Canada	0.3	0.3	0.0		0.0		1.4	0.7		
Barbados/Barbade	0.9	2.0	0.7	0.4	0.6	0.6				2.2
St Vincent & Grenadines	5.9	0.3	0.8	0.6	0.4	0.9	0.1			0.4
Dominica/Dominique	0.4	0.6	1.1	0.5	0.3	0.3	0.1			1.2
Saint Lucia/Ste–Lucie	0.4	0.9	0.3	0.6	0.0	0.1	0.1	0.1		1.6
United Kingdom	2.3	2.3	3.0	1.3		0.5	0.2			

4. Special Imports C.I.F. by Commodities according to the S.I.T.C. (Rev. 2) in million U.S. Dollars
Importations Spéciales C.A.F. par Produits d'après la C.T.C.I. (Rév. 2) en millions de Dollars E.U.

SITC CTCI	COMMODITY	1990 QUANTITY QUANTITE	1990 VALUE VALEUR	1991 QUANTITY QUANTITE	1991 VALUE VALEUR	1992 QUANTITY QUANTITE	1992 VALUE VALEUR	1993 QUANTITY QUANTITE	1993 VALUE VALEUR	PRODUIT
	ALL COMMODITIES		44.0		38.8				28.1	TOUS PRODUITS
0	FOOD AND LIVE ANIMALS		6.9		6.3				5.3	ALIMENTS,ANIMAUX VIVANTS
1	BEVERAGES AND TOBACCO		3.2		3.0				2.4	BOISSONS ET TABACS
2	CRUDE MATERLS,EXCL FUELS		1.7		0.8				0.5	MAT BRUTES NON COMESTIBLES
3	MINERAL FUELS ETC		4.7		5.9				4.9	COMBUSTIBLES MINERAUX LUB
4	ANIMAL,VEGETABLE OIL,FAT		0.2		0.2				0.2	HUILES,GRAISSES ANIM,VEG
5	CHEMCLS,RELATED PROD NES		2.6		2.5				1.9	PRODUITS CHIMIQUES
6	BASIC MANUFACTURES		9.1		7.3				4.6	ART MANUFACTURES
7	MACHINES,TRANSPORT EQUIP		11.5		9.4				4.1	MACHINES MATERIEL TRANSPORT
8	MISC MANUFACTURED GOODS		4.0		3.7				2.4	ART MANUFACTURES DIVERS
9	GOODS NOT CLASSD BY KIND		0.4		0.3				2.4	ART TRANSACT NON CLASSES

5. Special Exports F.O.B. by Commodities according to the S.I.T.C. (Rev. 2) in million U.S. Dollars
Exportations Spéciales F.O.B. par Produits d'après la C.T.C.I. (Rév. 2) en millions de Dollars E.U.

SITC CTCI	COMMODITY	1990 QUANTITY QUANTITE	1990 VALUE VALEUR	1991 QUANTITY QUANTITE	1991 VALUE VALEUR	1992 QUANTITY QUANTITE	1992 VALUE VALEUR	1993 QUANTITY QUANTITE	1993 VALUE VALEUR	PRODUIT
	ALL COMMODITIES		2.0		1.5				0.6	TOUS PRODUITS
0	FOOD AND LIVE ANIMALS		0.1		0.1				0.1	ALIMENTS,ANIMAUX VIVANTS
01	MEAT AND PREPARATIONS								0.1	VIANDES ET PREPARATIONS
011	MEAT FRESH,CHILLD,FROZEN							W 1	0.1	VIANDES FRAICHES,REF,CONGE
0114	POULTRY FRESH CHLLD,FRZN							W 1	0.1	VOLAILLES MORTES
1	BEVERAGES AND TOBACCO		0.1		0.1				0.1	BOISSONS ET TABACS
11	BEVERAGES								0.1	BOISSONS
112	ALCOHOLIC BEVERAGES							W 18	0.1	BOISSONS ALCOOLIQUES
1124	DISTILLED ALCOHOLIC BEVS							W 18	0.1	ALCOOLS,EAUX-DE-VIE
11249	OTH ALCOHOLC BEVS,CMPNDS							W 18	0.1	BOISSONS ALCOOLIQUES NDA
2	CRUDE MATERLS,EXCL FUELS		0.1		0.1					MAT BRUTES NON COMESTIBLES
3	MINERAL FUELS ETC		0.1							COMBUSTIBLES MINERAUX LUB
5	CHEMCLS,RELATED PROD NES		0.1		0.1				0.1	PRODUITS CHIMIQUES
55	PERFUME,CLEANING ETC PRD								0.1	PROD POUR PARFUM,TOILETTE
551	ESSENTL OILS,PERFUME,ETC							W 2	0.1	HUILES ESSENTIELLES
5513	ESSENTL OIL,RESINOID,ETC							W 2	0.1	HUILES ESSENTIELLES,RESIN
6	BASIC MANUFACTURES		0.2		0.1				0.1	ART MANUFACTURES
63	WOOD,CORK MANUFACTRS NES								0.1	OUVRAGES LIEGE ET BOIS
635	WOOD MANUFACTURES NES								0.1	ART MANUF EN BOIS NDA
6359	OTHER WOOD MANUFACTURES								0.1	OUVRAGES EN BOIS NDA
63591	TOOLS,HANDLES ETC WOOD								0.1	OUTILS MANCHES D'OUTILS
66	NONMETAL MINERAL MFS NES								0.1	ART MIN NON METALLIQUES
663	MINERAL MANUFCTURES NES							W 1	0.1	ART MIN MANUF NDA
666	POTTERY								0.1	POTERIE
6666	CERAMIC ORNAMENTS ETC								0.1	OBJETS PORCELAINE,CERAM
7	MACHINES,TRANSPORT EQUIP		0.7		0.5				0.4	MACHINES MATERIEL TRANSPORT
74	GENRL INDUSTRL MACHY NES								0.1	MACH APP INDUSTRIE
741	HEATING,COOLING EQUIPMNT								0.1	MACH CHAUFFAGE,PIECES
7415	AIR-CONDITIONING MACHNRY								0.1	GROUPES CONDITION AIR
77	ELECTRIC MACHNRY NES ETC								0.4	MACH APP ELECT NDA
778	ELECTRICAL MACHINERY NES							W 7	0.4	AUTRES MACH ELECT NDA
7782	ELECTRIC LAMPS,BULBS								0.1	LAMPES, TUBES ELECTRIQUES
77822	ELEC DISCHARGE LAMPS NES								0.1	LAMPES NON ULTRA-VIOLETS
7783	AUTOMOTIVE ELECTR EQUIP							W 7	0.4	EQUIP ELECT MOTEURS EXPL
78	ROAD VEHICLES								0.1	VEHICULES ROUTIERS
784	MOTOR VEH PRTS,ACCES NES							W 3	0.1	PIECES 722,781,782,783
7849	OTHER MOTOR VEHCL PARTS							W 3	0.1	PIECES 722,781,782,783
8	MISC MANUFACTURED GOODS		0.8		0.5				0.2	ART MANUFACTURES DIVERS
812	*PLUMBG,HEATNG,LGHTNG EQ							W 2	0.1	APPAR SANITAIRES CHAUFFAGE
8124	LIGHTING EQUIPMENT NES							W 2	0.1	APPAREILS ECLAIRAGE ETC
81242	LAMPS,FITTINGS BASE METL							W 2	0.1	APPAREILS D'ECLAIRAGE
84	CLOTHING AND ACCESSORIES								0.1	VETEMENTS
846	UNDER GARMENTS KNITTED								0.1	SOUS VETS DE BONNETERIE
8462	— OF COTTON NON ELASTIC								0.1	SOUS-VET BONNET COTON
84629	—— OTHER								0.1	AUT SOUS-VET BONNET COTON
89	MISC MANUFCTRD GOODS NES								0.1	ART MANUFACTURES DIVERS
892	PRINTED MATTER								0.1	IMPRIMES
8921	PRINTED BOOKS,GLOBES,ETC								0.1	LIVRES,BROCHURES,CARTES
89211	PRINTED BOOKS,PAMPHLETS								0.1	LIVRES,BROCHURES
893	ARTICLES OF PLASTIC NES							W 10	0.1	OUVRAGES EN MAT DIVIS 58
8931	PLSTC PACKG CONTNRS,LIDS							W 10	0.1	ART TRANSP EMBALLAGE ETC
9	GOODS NOT CLASSD BY KIND		0.4		0.6					ART TRANSACT NON CLASSES

1. HISTORICAL SERIES, 1962–1997 SPECIAL TRADE, IMPORTS C.I.F., EXPORTS F.O.B.
SERIES HISTORIQUES, 1962–1997 COMMERCE SPECIAL, IMPORTATIONS C.A.F., EXPORTATIONS F.O.B

YEAR ANNEE	VALUE IN MILLION MOR. DIRHAMS VALEUR EN MILLION MOR. DIRHAMS MERCHANDISE – MARCHANDISE		GOLD – OR		CONVERSION FACTORS U.S. CENTS PER MOR. DIRHAM FACTEURS DE CONVERSION CENTS E.U. PAR MOR. DIRHAM		INDEX NUMBERS – INDICES QUANTUM		UNIT VALUE VALEUR UNITAIRE	
	IMPORTS	EXPORTS	IMPORTS	EXPORTS	IMPORTS	EXPORTS	IMPORTS	EXPORTS	IMPORTS	EXPORTS
1962	2139.30	1762.50	6.80		19.7600	19.7600				
1963	2235.60	1942.80	7.00		19.7600	19.7600				
1964	2308.40	2185.80	14.40		19.7600	19.7600				
1965	2250.80	2176.30	10.40		19.7600	19.7600				
1966	2406.30	2168.10	6.10		19.7600	19.7600				
1967	2616.50	2146.40	3.30		19.7600	19.7600				
1968	2778.40	2278.00	4.70		19.7600	19.7600				
1969	2835.20	2455.00	1.80		19.7600	19.7600				
1970	3463.10	2471.10	7.70		19.7600	19.7600				
1971	3537.10	2532.80	4.70		19.8140	19.8298				
1972	3577.40	2952.90	10.60		21.7647	21.7547				
1973	4683.60	3745.90			24.4186	24.2819				
1974	8258.00	7439.90			22.9421	22.9355				
1975	10399.00	6536.00			24.6947	24.7377				
1976	11553.00	5579.30			22.6556	22.6214				
1977	14400.00	5859.00			22.1783	22.1843				
1978	12362.00	6261.10			24.0263	24.1392				
1979	14327.70	7622.00			25.6726	25.6996				
1980	16792.60	9645.00			24.9190	24.9190	69	44	21	18
1981	22455.00	12002.60			19.3984	19.3314	61	56	63	59
1982	25990.20	12439.70			16.6059	16.5491	68	55	66	61
1983	25591.20	14724.20			14.0632	14.0048	58	61	75	65
1984	34395.50	19109.50			11.3583	11.3655	65	64	91	81
1985	38674.90	21740.00			9.9534	9.9586	66	66	102	90
1986	34604.00	22103.01			10.9912	11.0080	66	66	91	91
1987	35271.01	23390.00			11.9914	12.0020	68	72	89	88
1988	39133.01	29751.01			12.1962	12.1867	74	84	91	97
1989	46594.00	28271.01			11.7883	11.8023	87	92	91	96
1990	57021.01	35135.01			12.1455	12.1395	100	100	100	100
1991	59720.00	37283.01			11.5440	11.4938	112	108	96	100
1992	62804.00	33954.00			11.7120	11.7120	128	101	92	95
1993	66576.00	31839.01			10.7583	10.7657	120	105	101	95
1994	66119.01	36815.01			10.8712	10.8800	96	115	114	94
1995	72869.01	40240.00			11.7226	11.7309				128
1996	84612.00	60013.01			11.4689	11.4661				
1997	90549.01	66603.01			10.5033	10.4910				

2. IMPORTS BY BROAD ECONOMIC CATEGORY AND EXPORTS BY INDUSTRIAL ORIGIN. (PERCENTAGE OF TOTAL VALUE)
IMPORTATIONS PAR CATEGORIES ECONOMIQUES ET EXPORTATIONS PAR BRANCHE D'ACTIVITE.(EN POURCENTAGE DE LA VALEUR TOTALE)

IMPORTS – IMPORTATIONS

	1990	1991	1992	1993	1994	1995	1996
TOTAL IMPORTS–IMPORTATIONS TOTALES	100.	100.	100.	100.	100.	100.	100.
1 FOOD BEV–ALIMENTATION BOISSONS	8.7	8.7	12.2	14.2	12.3	16.7	16.1
11 PRIMARY–PRODUITS DE BASE	4.7	4.7	7.5	9.1	6.5	10.8	9.9
111 FOR INDUSTRY–POUR L'INDUSTRIE	3.1	3.3	5.9	7.3	4.8	8.5	8.3
112 FOR HOUSEHOLDS–POUR LES MENAGES	1.6	1.4	1.6	1.9	1.8	2.4	1.6
12 PROCESSED–PRODUITS ELABORES	4.0	4.0	4.8	5.1	5.7	5.9	6.2
121 FOR INDUSTRY–POUR L'INDUSTRIE	2.5	2.5	2.7	3.3	3.9	4.0	4.3
122 FOR HOUSEHOLDS–POUR LES MENAGES	1.5	1.4	2.1	1.8	1.8	1.9	1.9
2 IND SUPPLIES–APPROV INDUSTRIELS	39.8	41.6	38.6	36.5	39.2	40.6	38.4
21 PRIMARY–PRODUITS DE BASE	7.8	7.6	6.9	6.0	5.7	7.5	6.5
22 PROCESSED–PRODUITS ELABORES	32.1	33.9	31.6	30.5	33.5	33.2	31.9
3 FUELS–COMBUSTIBLES	16.7	14.3	15.1	14.1	15.2	13.5	15.2
31 PRIMARY–PRODUITS DE BASE	16.2	13.4	14.3	12.7	12.7	12.1	13.5
32 PROCESSED–PRODUITS ELABORES	0.5	0.9	0.9	1.4	2.5	1.4	1.7
321 MOTOR SPIRIT–ESSENCE	0.0	0.0	0.0	0.6	1.6	0.7	0.3
322 OTHER–AUTRES	0.5	0.8	0.8	0.8	0.8	0.7	1.4
4 MACHINERY–EQUIPEMENT	19.2	20.1	20.4	21.8	18.3	16.5	16.9
41 CAPITAL EQUIPMENT–MACHINES	15.9	16.8	17.8	19.9	16.5	14.7	14.6
42 PARTS–PIECES ACCESSOIRES	3.3	3.3	2.6	1.9	1.8	1.8	2.3
5 TRANSPORT–TRANSPORT	10.4	9.8	8.1	7.0	8.7	6.6	6.8
51 PASSENGER CARS–AUTOMOBILES	1.6	1.9	1.3	1.2	1.2	1.1	2.2
52 OTHER–AUTRES	6.3	4.9	3.8	3.7	5.2	3.4	2.2
521 INDUSTRIAL–INDUSTRIELS	6.2	4.8	3.7	3.6	5.1	3.4	2.1
522 NON INDUSTRIAL–NON INDUSTRIEL	0.1	0.1	0.1	0.1	0.1	0.0	0.1
53 PARTS–PIECES ACCESSOIRES	2.5	3.0	3.0	2.2	2.3	2.1	2.4
6 CONSUM GOODS–BIENS CONSOMMATION	5.0	5.4	5.4	6.1	6.2	6.0	6.7
61 DURABLE–DURABLES	1.3	1.3	1.1	1.2	1.2	1.5	1.9
62 SEMI DURABLE–SEMI DURABLES	1.5	1.7	1.8	2.0	1.9	2.1	2.1
63 NON DURABLE–NON DURABLES	2.2	2.4	2.5	2.9	3.0	2.5	2.8
7 GOODS NES–BIENS NDA	0.1	0.1	0.1	0.2	0.1	0.1	0.0

EXPORTS – EXPORTATIONS

	1990	1991	1992	1993	1994	1995	1996
TOTAL EXPORTS–EXPORTATIONS TOTALES	100.	100.	100.	100.	100.	100.	100.
1 AGRICULTURE	17.8	21.1	19.8	20.1	20.9	23.1	24.2
2 MINING QUARRY–INDUS EXTRACTIVES	12.9	10.6	10.3	9.5	10.4	9.3	10.5
3 MANUFACTURING–IND MANUFACTUR	69.3	68.3	69.9	70.5	68.8	67.7	65.2
31 FOOD BEV TOBACCO–ALIM BOISS TAB	10.0	9.0	9.0	8.5	9.5	10.3	10.5
32 TEXTILES–INDUSTRIES TEXTILES	24.7	25.2	27.4	27.9	25.0	23.2	22.7
33 WOOD & PRODUCTS–BOIS & PRODUITS	0.7	0.5	0.7	0.9	0.9	0.8	0.8
34 PAPER & PRODUCTS–PAPIER & PRODT	1.4	1.0	1.3	0.9	1.7	1.8	1.0
35 CHEMICALS–INDUSTRIES CHIMIQUES	23.6	23.1	22.3	22.9	23.2	23.9	22.7
36 NON METAL MIN–MIN NON METAL	0.6	0.6	0.6	0.7	0.9	0.9	1.0
37 BASIC METAL–IND METAL BASE	2.0	1.6	1.4	1.6	1.7	1.8	2.0
38 METAL MANUF–MANUF METAL	6.0	6.9	6.9	6.8	5.4	4.6	4.1
39 OTH MANUF IND–AUTRES MANUF	0.2	0.2	0.3	0.3	0.4	0.4	0.4

3. TRADE BY PRINCIPAL COUNTRIES OF ORIGIN AND DESTINATION (VALUE IN MILLION U.S. DOLLARS)
ECHANGES SELON LES PRINCIPAUX PAYS D'ORIGINE ET DE DESTINATION (VALEUR EN MILLIONS DE DOLLARS EU)

COUNTRIES–PAYS	SPECIAL IMPORTS C.I.F. IMPORTATIONS SPECIALES C.A.F				
	1992	1993	1994	1995	1996
World	7355.6	6658.9	7193.7	8540.5	8253.5
Africa	428.0	331.2	507.1	500.7	661.3
Americas	842.5	1021.5	1021.0	1080.7	1242.4
– Northern America	591.8	774.9	683.7	721.9	793.2
– LAIA	223.6	217.1	251.8	344.7	423.5
– CACM	4.7	8.5	12.2	10.0	9.7
– Caribbean	21.4	20.3	73.0	2.9	7.0
– Rest of America	0.9	0.7	0.3	1.2	9.1
Asia excl fmr USSR	1468.4	1188.1	1167.3	1342.1	1248.0
– Middle East	993.5	770.8	753.5	824.7	657.0
Asia former USSR		0.1	0.6	3.1	1.4
Europe excl fmr USSR	4470.7	4008.7	4328.0	5209.6	4746.6
– European Union	4176.5	3793.3	4063.5	4789.6	4467.5
– Eastern Europe	150.0	117.9	151.0	292.3	150.9
– Rest of Europe	144.2	97.5	113.6	127.7	128.1
Europe former USSR	102.6	85.5	129.3	375.0	291.0
Oceania	37.8	22.9	39.7	28.3	62.7
Other	5.7	0.9	0.7	1.0	0.1
France, Monaco	1750.7	1528.8	1626.8	1865.6	1720.7
Spain/Espagne	627.9	699.3	631.4	728.5	723.2
USA/Etats–Unis d'Amer	434.9	672.3	620.4	559.1	612.0
Italy/Italie	457.0	417.9	485.7	489.3	590.4
Germany/Allemagne	436.5	395.3	506.7	534.9	501.7
Saudi Arabia	405.1	373.8	385.0	449.0	491.2
United Kingdom	201.5	180.7	202.1	311.5	231.9
Belgium–Luxembourg	199.4	154.3	166.0	238.3	186.5
Brazil/Brésil	152.2	143.6	150.6	241.6	248.8
Netherlands/Pays–Bas	179.2	145.6	156.2	207.1	163.7
Russian Federation	102.6	83.3	110.1	284.8	234.3
Iran (Islamic Rep of)	171.9	166.9	195.2	207.7	57.9
China/Chine	146.0	125.7	123.6	166.3	145.7
Sweden/Suède	132.9	119.2	126.1	175.5	119.0
Japan/Japon	154.2	114.1	122.4	124.3	152.3
Canada	156.9	102.6	63.3	162.7	179.4
Algeria/Algérie	91.2	107.9	119.3	111.3	102.2
United Arab Emirates	259.8	110.9	86.5	17.3	3.3
Switzerland,Liechtenst.	102.8	75.0	89.2	92.8	92.6
Poland/Pologne	84.1	69.1	85.8	134.5	66.2
Libyan Arab Jamahiriya	101.9	17.3	82.6	55.6	139.1
Argentina/Argentine	37.7	50.4	74.4	44.3	134.1
Portugal	53.0	51.3	59.2	68.1	85.2
Nigeria/Nigéria	4.1	21.3	10.5	61.9	216.6
Turkey/Turquie	86.8	23.6	42.2	82.3	57.2
Korea, Republic of	42.4	37.2	27.2	44.6	59.7
Finland/Finlande	48.4	30.2	33.7	51.6	45.9
Gabon	22.2	24.4	85.4	53.3	20.5
Other Asia n.e.s.	33.5	34.6	34.4	45.2	54.6
Tunisia/Tunisie	50.8	36.5	29.1	32.9	42.2
Romania/Roumanie	26.1	24.7	33.9	51.9	50.2
Denmark/Danemark	33.6	25.5	23.0	46.2	38.0
Cameroon/Cameroun	69.6	39.9	34.4	8.3	8.5
Kuwait/ Koweït	35.9	80.4	16.0	10.3	7.1
New Zealand	33.2	19.9	22.2	26.1	39.2
Cote d'Ivoire	26.7	23.8	29.8	32.8	25.9
Ukraine		2.1	15.3	71.3	46.6
India/Inde	18.4	20.3	16.0	25.4	52.3
Austria/Autriche	31.0	16.7	20.8	27.9	27.1
Indonesia/Indonésie	16.3	20.5	30.9	28.8	25.7

COUNTRIES–PAYS	SPECIAL EXPORTS F.O.B. EXPORTATIONS SPECIALES F.O.B.				
	1992	1993	1994	1995	1996
Monde	3977.2	3695.9	4034.6	4718.9	4742.0
Afrique	352.7	372.6	308.1	379.3	346.2
Amériques	248.1	232.8	239.1	286.9	314.4
– Amérique du Nord	172.8	148.9	160.6	189.5	201.4
– ALAI	65.1	81.1	75.0	94.4	111.3
– MCAC	0.7	0.3	0.6	0.5	1.0
– Caraïbes	3.9	2.2	2.4	1.9	0.8
– Autre Amérique	5.7	0.4	0.6	0.5	0.0
Asie anc. URSS exclus	668.8	620.8	759.4	933.1	963.1
– Moyen–Orient	133.2	164.2	168.8	168.8	226.3
Asie ancienne URSS		0.2	0.2	0.0	0.4
Europe anc. URSS exclus	2670.7	2433.1	2673.5	3047.2	3031.3
– Union Européenne	2582.4	2344.3	2580.5	2928.6	2915.7
– Europe de l'Est	29.4	35.6	36.5	48.3	52.3
– Autre de l'Europe	58.9	53.2	56.5	70.4	63.3
Europe ancienne URSS	0.8	3.3	13.2	22.8	34.5
Océanie	13.4	18.7	23.3	23.2	39.0
Autre	22.7	14.4	17.8	26.4	13.0
France, Monaco	1303.5	1227.5	1279.2	1400.2	1344.0
Spain/Espagne	359.1	326.6	373.8	443.1	468.9
Japan/Japon	196.5	217.3	268.1	361.8	329.6
India/Inde	237.0	143.6	258.2	309.6	299.0
Italy/Italie	221.8	193.2	231.1	268.7	298.9
Germany/Allemagne	188.0	163.4	172.6	193.9	185.1
United Kingdom	133.2	133.8	155.4	211.4	183.5
USA/Etats–Unis d'Amer	149.0	126.0	141.7	159.7	164.2
Belgium–Luxembourg	137.7	110.3	135.3	146.6	167.0
Libyan Arab Jamahiriya	131.2	136.9	99.0	161.5	125.2
Netherlands/Pays–Bas	124.4	96.6	118.2	114.1	127.4
Algeria/Algérie	71.7	77.8	96.6	56.0	35.4
Saudi Arabia	65.4	48.3	54.7	60.6	62.0
Tunisia/Tunisie	49.6	39.3	41.9	53.0	59.3
Turkey/Turquie	29.8	41.5	33.7	47.2	77.0
Mexico/Mexique	31.0	39.0	34.1	37.7	56.7
Portugal	34.8	25.8	38.9	49.6	43.7
Iran (Islamic Rep of)	25.4	54.0	49.5	22.5	36.0
Brazil/Brésil	22.2	28.6	30.5	43.0	28.3
Ireland/Irlande	26.2	17.4	29.0	39.5	31.0
Canada	23.8	22.9	18.8	29.8	37.2
Indonesia/Indonésie	32.2	28.8	31.5	16.6	20.0
Switzerland,Liechtenst.	18.0	19.4	26.0	38.5	27.1
China/Chine	30.7	24.1	14.5	38.5	16.6
Poland/Pologne	16.7	15.5	22.9	31.9	33.2
Pakistan	4.2	24.3	3.1	21.3	52.6
Norway,Svalbard and JM	23.4	18.7	15.9	17.5	20.4
Bunkers, ship stores	21.1	13.9	17.0	25.7	11.8
Greece/Grèce	13.4	11.1	13.8	20.4	23.9
New Zealand	9.6	10.4	12.5	14.2	29.6
Sweden/Suède	16.9	14.5	10.4	16.6	16.5
Russian Federation	0.8	2.8	11.9	16.0	30.4
Cote d'Ivoire	5.9	7.2	7.2	19.3	19.6
Finland/Finlande	9.2	13.5	8.6	13.4	11.6
Croatia/Croatie		10.7	13.3	12.0	14.6
Korea, Republic of	9.9	6.8	10.3	10.6	11.2
Nigeria/Nigéria	12.1	9.0	10.1	7.9	9.5
Austria/Autriche	9.2	8.7	11.1	7.4	10.6
Romania/Roumanie	10.7	13.8	6.5	7.2	7.3
Liberia/Libéria	0.1	41.8	0.2	0.1	0.2

(VALUE AS PERCENTAGE OF WORLD TOTAL)(VALEURS EN POURCENTAGE DU TOTAL MONDIAL)

	1987	1988	1989	1990	1991	1992	1993	1994	1995	1996
Africa	3.2	2.1	2.6	5.8	6.0	5.8	5.0	7.0	5.9	8.0
Americas	17.2	17.7	13.0	11.8	12.6	11.5	15.3	14.2	12.7	15.1
– Northern America	13.6	12.1	9.6	8.6	9.1	8.0	11.6	9.5	8.5	9.6
– LAIA	3.2	5.0	2.8	2.8	3.2	3.0	3.3	3.5	4.0	5.1
– CACM	0.0	0.1	0.1	0.0	0.0	0.1	0.1	0.2	0.1	0.1
– Caribbean	0.3	0.4	0.3	0.3	0.2	0.3	0.3	1.0	0.0	0.1
– Rest of America	0.0	0.1	0.2	0.1	0.0	0.0	0.0	0.0	0.0	0.1
Asia excl fmr USSR	17.4	17.1	17.9	17.7	16.4	20.0	17.8	16.2	15.7	15.1
– Middle East	12.3	11.0	11.9	12.2	9.9	13.5	11.6	10.5	9.7	8.0
Asia former USSR							0.0	0.0	0.0	0.0
Europe excl fmr USSR	59.1	60.4	62.8	61.8	62.6	60.8	60.2	60.2	61.0	57.5
– European Union	55.1	55.0	57.9	57.2	58.6	56.8	57.0	56.5	56.1	54.1
– Eastern Europe	2.2	3.1	2.5	2.6	2.1	2.0	1.8	2.1	3.4	1.8
– Rest of Europe	1.8	2.4	2.4	2.0	1.9	2.0	1.5	1.6	1.5	1.6
Europe former USSR	2.9	2.4	3.5	2.7	2.1	1.4	1.3	1.8	4.4	3.5
Oceania	0.2	0.2	0.1	0.1	0.1	0.5	0.3	0.6	0.3	0.8
Other	0.0	0.0	0.1	0.1	0.1	0.1	0.0	0.0	0.0	0.0
France, Monaco	21.8	22.2	24.4	22.9	24.2	23.8	23.0	22.6	21.8	20.8
Spain/Espagne	8.8	7.8	8.7	8.4	8.3	8.5	10.5	8.8	8.5	8.8
USA/Etats–Unis d'Amer	9.1	7.0	6.8	6.3	5.8	5.9	10.1	8.6	6.5	7.4
Italy/Italie	5.5	5.5	6.3	6.8	6.9	6.2	6.3	6.8	5.7	7.2
Germany/Allemagne					5.9	5.9	5.9	7.0	6.3	6.1
Saudi Arabia	0.2	0.8	0.7	2.7	4.9	5.5	5.6	5.4	5.3	6.0
United Kingdom	3.0	3.0	2.6	3.5	3.4	2.7	2.7	2.8	3.6	2.8
Belgium–Luxembourg	3.0	3.1	2.8	2.6	2.9	2.7	2.3	2.3	2.8	2.3
Brazil/Brésil	1.5	1.9	1.7	1.8	2.4	2.1	2.2	2.1	2.8	3.0
Netherlands/Pays–Bas	2.4	2.4	2.4	2.2	2.6	2.4	2.2	2.2	2.4	2.0

	1987	1988	1989	1990	1991	1992	1993	1994	1995	1996
Afrique	6.9	7.2	8.1	7.8	9.9	8.9	10.1	7.6	8.0	7.3
Amériques	5.6	5.2	4.6	3.9	4.5	6.2	6.3	5.9	6.1	6.6
– Amérique du Nord	2.2	2.6	2.6	2.3	3.1	4.3	4.0	4.0	4.0	4.2
– ALAI	3.3	2.3	1.7	1.4	1.3	1.6	2.2	1.9	2.0	2.3
– MCAC	0.0	0.1	0.0	0.0	0.0	0.0	0.0	0.0	0.0	0.0
– Caraïbes	0.0	0.1	0.1	0.1	0.1	0.1	0.1	0.1	0.0	0.0
– Autre Amérique	0.1	0.1	0.2	0.1	0.0	0.1	0.0	0.0	0.0	0.0
Asie anc. URSS exclus	16.3	21.6	14.2	18.0	20.0	16.8	16.8	18.8	19.8	20.3
– Moyen–Orient	3.9	4.4	4.1	6.7	5.1	3.3	4.4	4.2	3.6	4.8
Asie ancienne URSS							0.0	0.0	0.0	0.0
Europe anc. URSS exclus	68.2	64.3	71.5	69.4	65.2	67.1	65.8	66.3	64.6	63.9
– Union Européenne	62.9	57.9	65.7	65.9	63.2	64.9	63.4	64.0	62.1	61.5
– Europe de l'Est	3.4	4.7	3.6	1.9	0.7	0.7	1.0	0.9	1.0	1.1
– Autre de l'Europe	1.9	1.7	2.2	1.6	1.3	1.5	1.4	1.4	1.5	1.3
Europe ancienne URSS	1.6	0.2	0.3	0.2	0.0	0.0	0.1	0.3	0.5	0.7
Océanie	0.8	1.0	0.8	0.3	0.2	0.3	0.5	0.6	0.5	0.8
Autre	0.6	0.5	0.6	0.5	0.1	0.6	0.4	0.4	0.6	0.3
France, Monaco	29.5	26.0	29.3	31.5	31.8	32.8	33.2	31.7	29.7	28.3
Spain/Espagne	6.8	7.2	8.3	9.2	8.8	9.0	8.8	9.3	9.4	9.9
Japan/Japon	4.3	4.6	4.6	3.9	5.2	4.9	5.9	6.6	7.7	6.9
India/Inde	5.4	9.2	2.0	4.6	7.0	6.0	3.9	6.4	6.6	6.3
Italy/Italie	5.5	5.6	6.3	6.9	6.2	5.6	5.2	5.7	5.7	6.3
Germany/Allemagne					4.9	4.7	4.4	4.3	4.1	3.9
United Kingdom	2.7	2.9	3.9	3.3	2.7	3.3	3.6	3.9	4.5	3.9
USA/Etats–Unis d'Amer	1.6	2.1	2.2	1.9	2.5	3.7	3.4	3.5	3.4	3.5
Belgium–Luxembourg	4.0	3.7	5.7	3.9	3.4	3.5	3.0	3.4	3.1	3.5
Libyan Arab Jamahiriya	3.3	2.7	2.5	2.8	4.6	3.3	3.7	2.5	3.4	2.6

4. Special Imports C.I.F. by Commodities according to the S.I.T.C. (Rev. 2) in million U.S. Dollars
Importations Spéciales C.A.F. par Produits d'après la C.T.C.I. (Rév. 2) en millions de Dollars E.U.

SITC CTCI	COMMODITY	1993 QUANTITY QUANTITE	1993 VALUE VALEUR	1994 QUANTITY QUANTITE	1994 VALUE VALEUR	1995 QUANTITY QUANTITE	1995 VALUE VALEUR	1996 QUANTITY QUANTITE	1996 VALUE VALEUR	PRODUIT
	ALL COMMODITIES		6658.9		7193.7		8540.5		8253.5	TOUS PRODUITS
0	FOOD AND LIVE ANIMALS		889.7		699.5		1303.5		1196.4	ALIMENTS,ANIMAUX VIVANTS
001	*LIVE ANIMALS FOR FOOD	W 5163	16.2	W 23804	53.6	W 11389	38.0	W 21114	61.5	ANIMAUX VIVANTS
0011	BOVINE SPECIES,LIVE	W 4515	9.5	W 22986	45.9	W 10518	29.1	W 20397	52.7	ESPECE BOVINE
00111	— PURE BRED FR BREEDING	W 4515	9.5	W 13956	31.9	W 10479	29.0	W 20396	52.7	BOVINS REPRODUCTEURS
02	DAIRY PRODCTS,BIRDS'EGGS		73.3		83.9		96.3		84.1	PRODUITS LAITIERS,OEUFS
022	MILK AND CREAM	W 13202	21.8	W 15798	25.5	W 22215	45.6	W 11594	21.9	LAIT ET CREME
0224	MILK,CREAM PRESERVED ETC	W 13098	21.6	W 15701	25.4	W 22046	45.4	W 11394	21.7	LAIT,CREME CONS,CONC
02242	MILK DRY,1.5% FAT OR LES	W 6916	11.9	W 12267	21.0	W 18476	41.0	W 9330	19.2	LAIT POUDRE INF 1.5%
023	BUTTER	W 25904	48.1	W 29034	53.4	W 21500	45.9	W 28050	56.5	BEURRE
04	CEREALS AND PREPARATIONS		473.8		228.4		628.9		623.5	CEREALES ET PRODUITS
041	WHEAT ETC UNMILLED	W 2694919	351.6	W 1191452	162.6	W 2549113	468.6	W 2240101	474.5	FROMENT,EPEAUTRE
0411	DURUM WHEAT UNMILLED	W 390392	55.7	W 95454	24.3	W 260932	64.7	W 322624	77.6	FROMENT DUR NON MOULU
0412	OTHER WHEAT ETC UNMILLED	W 2304527	295.9	W 1095998	138.4	W 2288181	404.0	W 1917476	396.9	AUTRE FROMENT NON MOULU
043	BARLEY UNMILLED	W 579305	65.4	W 115090	9.8	W 465029	62.9	W 29684	5.6	ORGE NON MONDEE
044	MAIZE UNMILLED	W 354250	45.1	W 364025	46.4	W 548610	82.9	W 542963	102.5	MAIS NON MOULU
05	VEGETABLES AND FRUIT		44.9		44.1		102.7		57.8	LEGUMES ET FRUITS
054	VEG ETC FRSH,SMPLY PRSVD	W 138282	37.6	W 86498	36.8	W 131544	86.8	W 58527	37.4	LEGUMES FRAIS,CONG,SECS
0541	POTATOES FRSH EXCL SWEET	W 41293	11.4	W 51276	20.7	W 54387	36.5	W 20066	12.8	POMMES DE TERRE
0542	LEGUMINOUS VEGETBLES DRY	W 41218	18.6	W 19836	8.4	W 72995	39.3	W 32559	19.4	LEGUMES A COSSE SECS
06	SUGAR AND PREPS,HONEY		95.1		129.3		158.5		159.3	SUCRES ET PRODUITS
061	SUGAR AND HONEY	W 416793	93.8	W 455453	127.9	W 479158	156.7	W 514099	157.0	SUCRES ET MIEL
0611	RAW BEET AND CANE SUGAR	W 416002	92.9	W 454615	127.0	W 477250	154.5	W 512290	154.5	SUCRES BRUTS
07	COFFEE,TEA,COCOA,SPICES		109.8		125.3		158.3		119.1	CAFE,THE,CACAO,EPICES
071	COFFEE AND SUBSTITUTES	W 20415	23.7	W 21889	38.6	W 20068	60.7	W 22564	44.4	CAFE ET SUCCEDANES
0711	COFFEE GREEN,ROASTED,SUB	W 20295	21.8	W 21833	38.1	W 20042	60.3	W 22520	43.9	CAFE TORREFIE OU DECAFEINE
07111	COFFEE GREEN,HUSKS,SKINS	W 20271	21.6	W 21809	38.1	W 20015	60.1	W 22478	43.6	CAFE NON TORREFIE
074	TEA AND MATE	W 27142	71.0	W 34027	74.3	W 37628	81.5	W 28399	57.5	THE ET MATE
0741	TEA	W 27142	71.0	W 34027	74.3	W 37628	81.5	W 28399	57.5	THE
081	*FEEDING STUFF FOR ANIML	W 408426	60.1	W 33205	11.8	W 519850	83.7	W 226056	51.1	NOURRITURE POUR ANIMAUX
0812	BRAN,POLLARD,SHARPS,ETC	W 219657	24.9	W 20829	2.1	W 291482	36.2	W 98022	12.3	SONS
08122	BRAN,ETC OF OTHR CEREALS	W 219157	24.9	W 20829	2.1	W 291482	36.2	W 98022	12.3	SONS D'AUTRES CEREALES
0819	FOOD WASTE AND FEED NES	W 80097	15.7	W 2873	5.1	W 120509	29.2	W 57682	17.3	DECHETS,ALIMENTS NDA
1	BEVERAGES AND TOBACCO		90.6		107.7		82.5		92.5	BOISSONS ET TABACS
11	BEVERAGES		12.5		17.3		22.8		26.3	BOISSONS
112	ALCOHOLIC BEVERAGES	W 3387	11.3	W 13453	16.2	W 19020	21.6	W 26143	25.3	BOISSONS ALCOOLIQUES
12	TOBACCO AND MANUFACTURES		78.1		90.4		59.7		66.2	TABACS BRUTS FABRIQUES
122	TOBACCO,MANUFACTURED	W 3885	64.0	W 4111	73.8	W 1990	45.6	W 1950	41.9	TABACS FABRIQUES
1222	CIGARETTES	W 3830	62.6	W 3970	72.1	W 1953	44.3	W 1780	40.5	CIGARETTES
2	CRUDE MATERLS,EXCL FUELS		510.3		645.6		843.9		681.4	MAT BRUTES NON COMESTIBLES
22	OIL SEEDS,OLEAGINOUS FRT		22.9		71.8		84.0		70.8	GRAINES,FRUITS OLEAGINEUX
222	SEEDS FOR'SOFT'FIXED OIL	W 76621	20.9		70.4	W 249063	82.4	W 199058	68.5	GRAINES HUILES FIXES
2222	SOYA BEANS	W 31672	7.9	W 38093	9.8	W 55977	14.5	W 78813	25.1	FEVES DE SOJA
2224	SUNFLOWER SEEDS	W 970	0.6	W 144843	48.7	W 142985	49.3	W 75479	26.5	GRAINES DE TOURNESOL
23	RUBBER, CRUDE		16.2		19.5		28.6		23.9	CAOUTCHOUC BRUT
24	CORK AND WOOD		150.3		188.6		230.0		176.9	LIEGE ET BOIS
247	OTH WOOD ROUGH,SQUARED	W 230431	45.0	W 341251	60.9	W 419958	66.5	W 277440	51.2	BOIS BRUTS EQUARRIS
2472	SAW–,VENEER–LOGS NON–CON	W 205764	39.5	W 306878	53.2	W 391508	59.4	W 216932	37.8	NON CONIFERES SCIAGE,PLAC
24721	— IN THE ROUGH	W 205764	39.5	W 306878	53.2	W 391508	59.4	W 216932	37.8	BRUTS ECORCES DEGROSSIS
248	WOOD SHAPED,SLEEPERS	W 299050	105.3	W 322801	127.8	W 372143	163.4	W 306133	125.8	BOIS SIMPLEMENT TRAVAILLES
2482	LUMBER SHAPED CONIFER	W 252522	81.5	W 268124	96.6	W 321362	132.2	W 257049	99.5	CONIFERES SCIES,RABOTES
24821	LUMBER SAWN ETC CONIFER	W 252494	81.4	W 268052	96.6	W 321269	132.2	W 256921	99.4	CONIFERES SCIES LONGITUD
2483	LUMBER SHAPED NON–CONIFR	W 45882	23.6	W 54152	30.9	W 49899	31.0	W 48952	26.3	NON CONIFERES SCIES,RABOTES
24831	LUMBER SAWN ETC NON–CON	W 44721	23.0	W 53870	30.8	W 49395	30.7	W 48577	26.1	SCIES LONGITUDINALEMENT
251	*PULP AND WASTE PAPER	W 49224	16.2	W 40049	15.7	W 56024	35.3	W 50478	19.3	PATES A PAPIER,DECHETS
26	TEXTILE FIBRES AND WASTE		132.2		171.4		203.5		170.1	FIBRES TEXTILES
263	COTTON	W 41510	54.8	W 46946	76.9	W 45864	96.0	W 40513	81.7	COTON
2631	RAW COTTON,EXCL LINTERS	W 40211	53.7	W 45330	75.4	W 44167	93.5	W 38968	78.8	COTON EN MASSE
266	SYNTHETIC FIBRES TO SPIN	W 32626	54.1	W 35762	64.3	W 31531	74.9	W 33249	60.8	FIBRES SYNTHETIQUES
2665	DISCN SYNTH FIBRE UNCMBD	W 17297	24.7	W 17799	28.1	W 17287	37.5	W 18232	29.9	DISCONTINUES EN MASSE
27	CRUDE FERTLZR,MINRLS NES		136.8		143.5		211.5		167.2	ENGRAIS MINERAUX BRUTS
274	SULPHUR,UNRSTD IRN PYRTE	W 2588177	115.5	W 2653784	123.1	W 2806822	186.3	W 2600810	141.9	SOUFRE ET PYRITES
2741	SULPHUR,EX SULP IN 52215	W 2588171	115.5	W 2653772	123.1	W 2806820	186.3	W 2600662	141.8	SOUFRE
29	CRUDE ANIMAL,VEG MAT NES		27.2		25.4		32.0		33.7	MATIERES BRUTES ANIM,VEGET
292	CRUDE VEG MATERIALS NES	W 6367	27.0	W 4748	25.2	W 5628	31.6	W 5651	33.3	MAT BRUTES VEGETALES NDA
3	MINERAL FUELS ETC		957.3		1116.8		1178.8		1289.9	COMBUSTIBLES MINERAUX LUB
32	COAL,COKE AND BRIQUETTES		53.2		63.2		98.2		109.9	HOUILLES,COKES,BRIQUETTES
322	COAL,LIGNITE AND PEAT	W 986369	47.7	W 1268110	56.5	W 1894970	92.4	W 2222414	104.5	HOUILLES,LIGNITES,TOURBE
3222	OTH COAL,NOT AGGLOMERATD	W 973533	46.2	W 1207486	50.5	W 1852278	87.3	W 2185560	99.7	AUTRES HOUILLES
33	PETROLEUM AND PRODUCTS		776.9		895.9		916.0		1004.5	PETROLE ET DERIVES
333	CRUDE PETROLEUM	W 6122630	720.1	W 6855120	752.8	W 6751486	787.9	W 5743317	848.4	HUILES BRUTES DE PETROLE
334	PETROLEUM PRODUCTS,REFIN	W 179907	42.6	W 677329	123.6	W 500508	102.2	W 517375	119.8	PRODUITS RAFFINES
3341	GASOLINE,OTH LIGHT OILS	W 177817	38.7	W 674410	117.9	W 310206	60.1	W 76620	21.2	ESSENCES POUR MOTEURS
33419	OTH LIGHT PETROLEUM OILS	W 177817	38.7	W 674410	117.9	W 306128	58.8	W 56761	16.6	AUTRES HUILES LEGERES
3343	GAS OILS					W 185277	34.2	W 432856	91.5	GAS OILS
335	RESIDUAL PETRLM PROD NES	W 204464	14.4	W 370804	19.7	W 436875	26.0	W 632180	36.4	PRODUITS RESIDUELS NDA
3354	PETROLM BITUMEN,COKE ETC	W 190380	6.0	W 358646	12.3	W 422698	16.5	W 617794	27.1	BITUME,COKE DE PETROLE
33542	PETROLEUM COKE	W 190320	5.9	W 358572	12.2	W 417339	15.9	W 617616	26.9	COKE DE PETROLE
341	*GAS,NATURAL AND MANUFCT	W 420465	80.6	W 636443	109.3	W 686428	154.8		163.4	GAZ NATUREL,GAZ MANUFACT
3413	PETROLM GASES,LIQUEFIED	W 420465	80.6	W 636388	109.3	W 686427	154.8		163.4	GAZ DE PETROLE LIQUEFIE
34131	LIQUEFIED PROPANE,BUTANE	W 420465	80.6	W 636388	109.3	W 686427	154.8	W 687899	163.4	PROPANE,BUTANE LIQUEFIES
351	*ELECTRIC CURRENT		46.7		48.6		9.8		12.3	ENERGIE ELECTRIQUE
4	ANIMAL,VEGETABLE OIL,FAT		136.9		162.8		197.3		198.7	HUILES,GRAISSES ANIM,VEG
42	FIXED VEGETABLE OIL,FAT		115.0		140.3		166.3		166.9	HUILES VEGETALES FIXES
423	FIXED VEG OILS,SOFT		109.0	W 219211	135.4	W 242067	160.8	W 283184	161.7	HUILES VEGET DOUCES FIXES
4232	SOYA BEAN OIL	W 157439	73.6	W 177790	105.8	W 114849	77.1	W 197682	108.8	HUILE DE SOJA
4239	OTH FIXED VEG OILS,SOFT	W 68872	31.6	W 37417	23.7	W 124476	78.1	W 75904	45.3	AUTRES HUILES FIXES
42391	RAPE,COLZA,MUSTARD OILS	W 68870	31.6	W 37413	23.7	W 124476	78.1	W 75904	45.3	H NAVETTE COLZA MOUTARDE
5	CHEMCLS,RELATED PROD NES		720.3		859.9		998.7		1023.8	PRODUITS CHIMIQUES
51	ORGANIC CHEMICALS		96.3		115.9		134.8		128.7	PROD CHIMIQ ORGANIQUES
513	CARBOXYLIC ACIDS ETC	W 19738	21.1	W 21836	28.0	W 15368	28.0	W 21844	28.2	ACIDES CARBOXYLIQUES
514	NITROGEN–FNCTN COMPOUNDS	W 7344	26.0	W 8365	29.3	W 8258	34.8	W 9017	35.1	COMPOSES FONCT AZOTEES
515	ORG–INORG COMPOUNDS ETC	W 2102	24.2	W 1652	25.8	W 1621	30.6	W 2161	30.0	COMPOSES ORGANO–MINERAUX
52	INORGANIC CHEMICALS		120.5		122.1		150.6		150.7	PROD CHIM INORGANIQUES
522	INORG ELEMNTS,OXIDES,ETC	W 551120	81.1	W 383158	82.9	W 380144	102.3	W 404375	94.5	ELEMENTS INORGANIQUES
5225	INORGANIC BASES ETC NES	W 530558	66.8	W 359927	67.4	W 350165	81.8	W 354160	75.7	AUTRES BASES OXYDES METAL
52251	AMMONIA,ANHYDROUS ETC	W 520165	62.8	W 342325	62.3	W 334580	76.2	W 333856	70.3	AMMONIAC LIQUEFIE
523	OTHR INORG CHEMICALS ETC	W 81935	39.0	W 84206	38.6	W 93467	47.6		55.7	AUT PRODUITS CHIMIQUES INORG
5232	OTH MTL CMPD OF INRG ACD	W 55170	28.0	W 53306	25.8	W 62249	32.4	W 71305	37.8	SELS METALLIQUES
53	DYES,TANNING,COLOUR PROD		69.0		74.8		84.3		79.0	PROD TEINTURE,COLORANTS
531	SYNT DYE,NAT INDGO,LAKES	W 2859	24.2	W 3062	24.0	W 3499	27.2	W 3473	25.7	MAT COLOR ORGAN,LAQUES

4. Special Imports C.I.F. by Commodities according to the S.I.T.C. (Rev. 2) in million U.S. Dollars
Importations Spéciales C.A.F. par Produits d'après la C.T.C.I. (Rév. 2) en millions de Dollars E.U.

SITC CTCI	COMMODITY	1993 QUANTITY QUANTITE	1993 VALUE VALEUR	1994 QUANTITY QUANTITE	1994 VALUE VALEUR	1995 QUANTITY QUANTITE	1995 VALUE VALEUR	1996 QUANTITY QUANTITE	1996 VALUE VALEUR	PRODUIT
5311	SYNTHIC ORGNIC DYESTUFFS	W 2307	20.4	W 2381	20.0	W 2532	22.6	W 2575	21.7	MAT COLOR ORGAN SYNTHET
533	PIGMENTS,PAINTS,ETC	W 27341	40.7	W 30924	47.2	W 33222	53.4	W 28105	48.9	PIGMENTS,PEINTURES,VERNIS
541	*MEDICINAL,PHARM PRODUCT		98.5		114.2		129.9		130.3	PROD MEDICINAUX PHARMACEUT
5413	ANTIBIOTICS IN BULK		20.0		27.1		26.0		22.4	ANTIBIOTIQUES NDA
5417	MEDICAMENTS	K 1879211	55.1	K 1900518	59.1	K 2034641	71.9	K 2150063	74.9	MEDICAMENTS
54179	— CONTNG OTH SUBSTANCES	K 1368351	33.5	K 1401552	35.5	K 1491745	42.3	K 1613330	44.8	MED CONT AUT SUBSTANCES
55	PERFUME,CLEANING ETC PRD		35.1		40.1		48.1		49.7	PROD POUR PARFUM,TOILETTE
562	*FERTILIZERS,MANUFACTURE	W 342296	48.3	W 525414	67.5	W 378327	62.5		106.7	ENGRAIS MANUFACTURES
5621	CHEM NITROGENOUS FERTLZR	W 288000	34.9	W 418431	48.8	W 290098	45.5	W 488598	88.0	ENGRAIS AZOTES
56211	AMMONIUM NITRATE	W 115890	15.3	W 160100	21.0	W 135929	22.0	W 211685	37.1	NITRATE D'AMMONIUM
56216	UREA	W 114010	15.4	W 137727	19.2	W 91226	17.4	W 185679	41.0	UREE
58	PLASTIC MATERIALS ETC		148.5		198.7		251.3		232.9	MAT PLAST ARTIFICIELLES
582	PROD OF CONDENSATION ETC	W 21934	30.7	W 33163	45.1	W 36071	63.3	W 32780	53.6	PROD CONDENS,POLYCOND
5823	ALKYDS,OTHER POLYESTERS	W 12992	16.6	W 17233	22.6	W 18503	35.7	W 16782	26.2	ALKYDES ET AUT POLYESTERS
58231	— IN PRIMARY FORMS	W 12832	15.8	W 17067	21.7	W 18308	34.4	W 16616	25.0	SOUS FORMES PRIMAIRES
583	POLYMERIZATION ETC PRODS	W 126839	111.9	W 159259	147.1	W 138405	180.1	W 157707	173.3	PROD POLYMERISATION
5831	POLYETHYLENE	W 77890	58.1	W 96438	78.7	W 84275	97.1	W 94757	90.7	POLYETHYLENE
58311	— IN PRIMARY FORMS	W 77488	57.1	W 94772	75.0	W 82238	92.0	W 92567	85.7	POLYETHYLENE PRIMAIRES
5832	POLYPROPYLENE	W 23082	14.7	W 32376	24.0	W 29867	33.3	W 36710	35.3	POLYPROPYLENE
58321	— IN PRIMARY FORMS	W 22354	12.7	W 31349	21.4	W 28704	29.4	W 34993	29.3	POLYPROPYLENE PRIMAIRES
59	CHEMICAL MATERIALS NES		102.5		125.1		136.1		144.4	MAT PROD CHIMIQUES NDA
591	PESTICIDES,DISINFECTANTS	W 7261	30.1	W 9968	42.9	W 9958	44.8	W 11670	54.5	DESINF,INSECT,FONG,HERB
598	MISCEL CHEM PRODUCTS NES	W 40290	64.2	W 43017	70.9	W 44546	80.4	W 44172	77.7	PROD DIV INDUST CHIM NDA
5989	CHEM PRODUCTS,PREPS NES	W 33228	48.3	W 34377	51.3	W 36775	62.2	W 36578	60.8	PROD PREP CHIMIQUES NDA
59899	OTH CHEM PRODS,PREPS,NES	W 25822	37.9	W 27116	41.6	W 30384	51.8	W 28733	47.6	AUT PRODUITS CHIMIQUES NDA
6	BASIC MANUFACTURES		1159.1		1355.8		1589.3		1458.5	ART MANUFACTURES
61	LEATHER,DRESSED FUR,ETC		27.5		31.3		30.5		27.8	CUIRS,PELLETERIES
62	RUBBER MANUFACTURES NES		47.8		47.2		55.0		91.4	CAOUTCHOUC MANUFACTURE
625	RUBBER TYRES, TUBES ETC	W 2837	11.1	W 3452	12.8	W 4680	19.1	W 9508	35.8	PNEUS CAOUTCHOUC VULCANISE
628	RUBBER ARTICLES NES	W 4030	27.7	W 3163	25.9	W 3089	26.0	W 6720	43.5	OUVRAGES CAOUTCHOUC NDA
6282	VULCANIZD RUBBER BELTING	W 3062	15.4	W 2140	12.2	W 1897	11.0	W 5389	25.8	COURROIES EN CAOUTCHOUC
64	PAPER,PAPERBOARD AND MFR		128.4		132.5		183.2		162.4	PAPIERS,CARTONS & OUVRAGES
641	PAPER AND PAPERBOARD	W 171485	108.0	W 176749	117.3	W 177841	156.9	W 164336	138.2	PAPIERS ET CARTONS
6413	KRAFT PAPER,PAPERBOARD	W 63272	34.6	W 62950	34.5	W 67992	54.1	W 54871	42.9	PAPIER ET CARTON KRAFT
64139	KRAFT PAPER PAPERBD,NES	W 58913	32.2	W 54015	29.8	W 59243	47.3	W 46879	37.5	PAPIER,CARTON KRAFT NDA
6415	PAPER,PAPERBRD,BULK,NES	W 40059	20.7	W 40897	23.9	W 39996	35.2	W 34375	24.4	PAPIERS,CARTONS ROULEAUX
6418	COATED ETC PAPER NES BLK	W 15530	26.2	W 18722	29.3	W 16802	29.6	W 20620	33.3	PAP,CARTONS COUCHES,ENDUITS
64189	COATED PAPER ETC NES	W 13488	22.7	W 16974	25.8	W 15272	26.2	W 19452	30.0	PAPIERS,CARTONS COUCHES
642	PAPER,ETC,PRECUT,ARTS OF	W 13261	20.5	W 7527	15.3	W 13073	26.4	W 10529	24.2	PAP,CARTONS DECOUPES
65	TEXTILE YARN,FABRICS,ETC		309.6		346.1		404.5		404.7	FILS,TISSUS,ARTICLES TEXTILE
651	TEXTILE YARN	W 26987	94.0	W 30770	110.2	W 25464	112.4	W 30751	113.1	FILS TEXTILES
6514	SYN FIB YRN,BULK,MONOFIL	W 12365	34.1	W 13477	37.4	W 11074	41.9	W 16446	46.3	FILS CONT 85% FIB TEXT SYNTH
65142	— NONTXT ETC CONT PAMID	W 9781	22.7	W 10334	24.9	W 8419	27.0	W 14629	35.6	FILS NON TEX FI CON POLYAMID
6516	DISCON SYN FIB BLEND YRN	W 6560	27.5	W 7960	34.2	W 6402	33.4	W 6439	30.2	FILS FIBR TEX SYNT DIS MOINS
65166	DISCON SYN FIB–COTTN YRN	W 5946	24.9	W 7409	31.5	W 6163	32.0	W 6069	28.2	FILS TEXT SYNT MELANGE COTON
652	COTTON FABRICS,WOVEN	W 15283	98.6	W 17005	112.4	W 15931	132.2	W 18036	140.6	TISSUS DE COTON
6522	WOVEN COTTON BLEACHD,ETC	W 14383	94.3	W 16004	107.0	W 14894	126.0	W 17175	134.4	TISSUS COTON BLANCHIS ETC
65224	BLCHED COTTON FABRIC NES	W 13088	78.9	W 14685	89.8	W 12952	101.7	W 15488	114.8	AUT TIS PLUS 85% COT BLANCHI
653	WOVN MAN–MADE FIB FABRIC	W 3714	47.0	W 3588	42.4	W 4010	51.1	W 3142	41.3	TISSUS FIBRES SYNTH,ARTIF
657	SPECIAL TXTL FABRC,PRODS	W 8687	46.2	W 11126	51.9	W 11002	63.3	W 10292	59.2	TISSUS SPECIAUX
6573	COATED ETC TEXTILES NES	W 3136	20.5	W 3175	21.4	W 3266	24.5	W 3499	24.4	TISSUS,ART MATIERE TEXT NDA
66	NONMETAL MINERAL MFS NES		78.5		79.9		101.8		86.5	ART MIN NON METALLIQUES
664	GLASS	W 34298	18.8	W 37444	25.4	W 39994	34.1	W 39668	27.9	VERRE
67	IRON AND STEEL		323.9		475.5		491.8		366.9	FER ET ACIER
672	IRON,STEEL PRIMARY FORMS	W 386908	105.0	W 476179	124.6	W 691994	205.8	W 575578	147.9	LINGOTS FER,ACIER
6725	IRN,STL BLOOMS,SLABS,ETC	W 315451	81.9	W 411442	103.3	W 536670	140.7	W 523065	130.7	BLOOMS,BILLETTES FER ACIER
67251	IRN,SMPLE STL BLOOMS,ETC	W 315293	81.8	W 411285	103.2	W 536452	140.6	W 523064	130.7	BLOOMS ETC NON ACIER FIN
6727	IRN,STL COIL FR REROLLNG	W 71457	23.2	W 64737	21.4	W 155324	65.1	W 52514	17.2	EBAUCHES POUR TOLES FER
67271	IRON,SIMPLE STEEL COILS	W 69866	22.6	W 64708	21.3	W 155279	65.0	W 52502	17.2	EBAUCHES NON EN ACIER
673	IRON,STEEL SHAPES ETC	W 257542	85.9	W 198229	72.6	W 196601	79.4	W 161240	63.2	BARRES,PROFIL FER,ACIER
6732	IRON,STEEL BARS ETC	W 144462	47.8	W 75423	29.1	W 73916	33.1	W 58274	26.9	BARRES FER,ACIER
67326	IRN,OTH STL BARS HOTROLD	W 130451	39.6	W 65942	21.9	W 63444	22.7	W 47716	16.5	BARRES PLEINES FER,ACIER
6733	IRON,STEEL PROFILES ETC	W 64834	22.6	W 89153	31.9	W 83204	31.9	W 70586	25.5	PROFILES,PALPLAN FER,ACIER
674	IRN,STL UNIV,PLATE,SHEET	W 158495	90.8	W 152989	91.6	W 237018	150.6	W 173681	113.0	LARGES PLATS,TOLES
6746	IRN,STL THIN PLATE,ROLLD	W 74173	34.1	W 56893	28.1	W 136305	70.2	W 83006	43.2	TOLES LAM MOINS 3MM
67461	— OF IRON OR SIMPLE STL	W 71617	29.3	W 54334	23.3	W 133655	64.7	W 78869	36.6	TOL NON AC FIN MOINS 3 MM
6747	TINNED PLATES,SHEETS	W 30168	26.2	W 36964	31.0	W 40958	39.3	W 38838	36.9	TOLES ETAMEES EN ACIER
678	IRON,STL TUBES,PIPES,ETC	W 20426	26.1	W 256788	168.0	W 26331	34.6	W 14940	23.8	TUBES,TUYAUX EN FONTE,FER
6783	IRON,STL TUBES,PIPES NES	W 8953	7.9	W 244596	152.1	W 12738	12.2	W 3961	5.2	AUT TUBES,TUYAUX FER,ACIER
68	NON–FERROUS METALS		95.9		97.5		120.2		109.9	METAUX NON FERREUX
682	COPPER EXC CEMENT COPPER	W 19511	49.1	W 17529	46.7	W 16230	57.7		55.1	CUIVRE
6822	COPPER,ALLOYS WORKED	W 18933	48.0	W 16720	45.3	W 15643	56.2	W 17898	53.9	CUIVRE,ALLIAGES OUVRES
68221	COPPER BARS,WIRE,ETC	W 14658	34.2	W 13339	33.4	W 12114	39.5	W 14112	37.9	BARRES,PROFILES ET FILS
684	ALUMINIUM	W 15797	35.7	W 15397	38.9	W 16114	48.5	W 15770	43.5	ALUMINIUM
6842	ALUMINIUM,ALLOYS WORKED	W 12952	31.4	W 12937	34.6	W 12880	40.4	W 14171	40.1	ALUMINIUM,ALLIAGES OUVRE
69	METAL MANUFACTURES NES		136.4		131.8		184.8		188.6	ART MANUFACT EN METAL NDA
692	METAL TANKS,BOXES,ETC	W 4656	17.2	W 4982	12.3	W 12786	31.5	W 9638	35.3	RECIPIENTS METALLIQUES
6924	MTL TRANSPORT BOXES ETC	W 3816	13.5	W 4027	10.0	W 8149	27.5	W 8448	31.1	FUTS,TAMBOURS,BIDONS
699	BASE METAL MFRS NES		51.4		54.8	W 27599	71.1	W 15975	71.0	ART MANUFACTURES MET NDA
7	MACHINES,TRANSPORT EQUIP		1907.1		1944.1		1975.0		1942.9	MACHINES MATERIEL TRANSPORT
71	POWER GENERATING EQUIPMT		438.9		177.3		100.9		103.9	MACHINES GENERATRICES
711	STEAM BOILERS & AUX PLNT	W 26523	262.2	W 2587	19.5	W 474	3.4	W 1583	5.8	GENERATEURS VAPEUR EAU ETC
7111	STEAM BOILERS ETC	W 26388	261.0	W 2377	17.8	W 242	1.7	W 348	1.3	GENERATEURS VAPEUR EAU
713	INTRNL COMBUS PSTN ENGIN	W 9651	46.4	W 9392	47.0	W 11102	61.2	W 10324	61.8	MOTEURS EXPL COMB INT, PIECE
7139	PISTON ENGINE PARTS NES	W 1725	24.6	W 1771	26.0	W 1923	32.1	W 2578	37.1	PIECES POUR 713.2,3,8
714	ENGINES AND MOTORS NES	W 2316	46.5	W 2816	80.7		2.0	W 3	1.0	MOTEURS NON ELECTRIQUES
7148	GAS TURBINES NES	W 2298	45.1	W 2807	78.5	W 80	1.4		0.1	TURBINES A GAZ
71488	OTHER GAS TURBINES NES	W 2298	45.1	W 2807	78.5	W 80	1.4		0.1	AUTRES TURBINES A GAZ
716	ROTATING ELECTRIC PLANT	W 7069	71.2	W 2337	27.7	W 3351	27.5	W 3487	26.7	APP ELECTR ROTATIFS,PIECES
7162	AC MTRS,GENRTRS,GEN SETS	W 6600	63.9	W 2074	23.0	W 2993	23.2	W 3156	22.7	MOTEURS ELECTRIQUES
71622	AC GENERATORS	W 1990	30.1	W 276	8.2	W 723	4.7	W 1445	9.8	GENER COURANT ALTERNATIF
71623	GEN SETS WITH PISTN ENGN	W 3918	28.5	W 1010	8.8	W 1494	12.1	W 684	4.7	GROUPES MOTEUR EXPLOSION
72	MACHS FOR SPCL INDUSTRYS		327.7		375.5		505.2		445.6	MAC SPECIALES POUR INDUST
721	AGRIC MACHY,EXC TRACTORS	W 3629	18.7	W 8421	36.3	W 4853	28.4	W 14399	52.0	MACHINES AGRICOLES
7212	HARVESTING ETC MACHINES	W 917	7.1	W 6017	27.7	W 1519	9.0	W 11153	38.1	ENGINS POUR LA RECOLTE
722	TRACTORS NON–ROAD	W 3297	14.0	W 9910	51.2	W 5485	23.2	W 9539	38.6	TRACTEURS
7224	WHEELED TRACTORS NES	W 3229	13.8	W 9810	51.1	W 5462	23.1	W 9498	38.6	TRACTEURS A ROUES
723	CIVIL ENGNEERG EQUIP ETC	W 13065	44.0	W 9559	28.0	W 16744	91.8	W 16169	57.5	APPAREILS DE GENIE CIVIL
7234	CONST,MINING MACHNRY NES	W 12293	41.5	W 8618	25.1	W 15612	87.7	W 14658	52.7	MACH POUR LA CONST, MINES
72342	SLFPRP SHOVELS,EXCAVATRS	W 7674	30.4	W 5369	14.0	W 10238	68.2	W 9191	34.8	PELLES MECANIQUES
724	TEXTILE,LEATHER MACHNRY	W 9976	80.1	W 7865	83.8	W 8331	100.4	W 9009	120.0	MACH POUR INDUSTRIE TEXTILE

4. Special Imports C.I.F. by Commodities according to the S.I.T.C. (Rev. 2) in million U.S. Dollars
Importations Spéciales C.A.F. par Produits d'après la C.T.C.I. (Rév. 2) en millions de Dollars E.U.

SITC CTCI	COMMODITY	1993 QUANTITY QUANTITE	1993 VALUE VALEUR	1994 QUANTITY QUANTITE	1994 VALUE VALEUR	1995 QUANTITY QUANTITE	1995 VALUE VALEUR	1996 QUANTITY QUANTITE	1996 VALUE VALEUR	PRODUIT
7243	SEWING MACHS,NEEDLES ETC	W 4437	27.2	W 2017	21.4	W 1877	29.3	W 1610	31.9	MACHINES A COUDRE,PIECES
72431	SEWING MACHINES	W 3860	23.8	W 1796	18.8	W 1712	25.9	W 1319	26.0	MACHINES A COUDRE
7245	WEAVING,FELT MFG,ETC MCH	W 1507	16.4	W 1973	21.2	W 1829	27.6	W 3214	36.3	METIERS A TISSER,PIECES
725	PAPER ETC MILL MACHINERY	W 1282	9.2	W 1905	14.7	W 3320	47.6	W 576	8.6	MACHINES FABR PATE PAPIER
7251	PAPER,PULP MAKING MACHRY	W 476	1.3	W 1241	6.0	W 2795	41.4	W 122	2.5	MACHINES FABR PATE CARTON
72511	CELLULOSE PULP MFG MACHY	W 24	0.3	W 24	1.2	W 2460	39.4	W 19	0.7	MACH FABR PATE CELLULOSE
727	FOOD MACHRY NON-DOMESTIC	W 2688	26.5	W 2852	25.5	W 4254	50.4	W 3780	41.8	MACH INDUSTRIES ALIMENT
7272	OTH FOOD PROC MCHY,PARTS	W 1989	17.4	W 2245	21.2	W 2801	33.9	W 2577	28.1	AUT MACH IND ALIMENTAIRE
72722	INDUS FOOD PROC MACH NES	W 1578	14.2	W 1514	20.2	W 2207	31.1	W 1672	24.4	MACHINES BOULANGERIE
728	OTH MACHY FOR SPCL INDUS	W 19948	123.6	W 15229	116.6	W 21686	142.3	W 12226	113.7	AUT MACH IND PARTICULIERES
7283	OTHR MINERAL WORKG MACHY	W 12179	40.3	W 7270	25.4	W 11142	43.8	W 5393	24.6	MACH TRIER,CRIBLER,BROYER
72834	MINRL MOULDING ETC MACHY	W 8178	27.4	W 3863	14.1	W 7988	29.7	W 1741	8.0	MACH AGGLO CIMENT ETC
7284	MACHY FOR SPCL INDUS NES	W 6394	76.4	W 6634	84.1	W 8699	88.4	W 5547	81.6	MACH SPEC IND PARTICUL.
72842	RUBBER,PLASTICS WRKG MCH	W 2125	21.6	W 1862	17.5	W 2171	23.8	W 2428	27.5	MACH IND CAOUT MAT PLAST
72843	TOBACCO WORKING MACH NES	W 827	21.4	W 435	12.7	W 54	7.7	W 251	12.5	MACH POUR IND DU TABAC
72848	OTH MCHY WITH INDIV FNCT	W 2092	21.2	W 3415	43.6	W 5658	46.4	W 2247	32.6	AUTRES MACHINES NDA
73	METALWORKING MACHINERY		28.3		27.2		34.5		36.9	MACH TRAVAIL DES METAUX
736	METALWORKING MACH-TOOLS	W 4048	24.3	W 4558	22.9	W 4189	23.6	W 4047	28.7	MACH-OUTILS TRAVAIL METAUX
74	GENRL INDUSTRL MACHY NES		310.0		334.2		380.8		405.1	MACH APP INDUSTRIE
741	HEATING,COOLING EQUIPMNT	W 4867	47.5	W 6571	67.3	W 8776	80.9	W 8861	83.7	MACH CHAUFFAGE,PIECES
7415	AIR-CONDITIONING MACHNRY	W 756	9.3	W 1428	23.6	W 1328	21.8	W 1181	18.7	GROUPES CONDITION AIR
742	PUMPS FOR LIQUIDS ETC	W 2657	31.2	W 2706	27.5	W 4443	37.1	W 3559	43.3	POMPES MOTO-POMPES
743	PUMPS NES,CENTRFUGES ETC	W 3993	38.9	W 3916	43.3	W 5490	53.9	W 4927	50.0	POMPES COMPRES,VENT ETC
7436	GAS,LIQUID FILTERS ETC	W 1025	17.8	W 1009	22.4	W 1668	24.3	W 1162	17.3	APP POUR FILT DES LIQUIDES
744	MECHANICAL HANDLING EQU	W 14084	78.4	W 14004	86.9	W 10552	71.2	W 11518	65.9	EQUIP MANUTENTION PIECES
7442	LIFTING,LOADING MACH NES	W 10058	57.3	W 10720	70.4	W 7704	56.3	W 7151	44.2	APP LEVAGE,MANUTENTION
74428	OTH HANDLING ETC MCH NES	W 7542	43.2	W 7773	54.9	W 3473	25.4	W 2868	23.7	AUT APP LEVAGE ETC
745	NONELEC MACHY,TOOLS NES	W 2493	45.3	W 2413	36.1	W 3282	42.2	W 2745	57.7	AUT MACH NON ELEC,PIECES
7452	OTH NONELEC MCHS,PTS NES	W 2438	43.9	W 2352	34.8	W 3228	40.6	W 2661	55.6	AUT MACH NON ELEC,PIECES
74522	PACKAGNG,BOTTLNG,ETC MCH	W 920	30.8	W 883	22.6	W 1311	22.5	W 1097	37.3	MACH NETT BOUTEILLES,ETC
749	NONELEC MACH PTS,ACC NES	W 4542	69.0	W 5254	73.4	W 17220	95.7	W 6319	104.8	PIECES MACH NON ELEC NDA
7492	COCKS,VALVES ETC NES	W 2229	24.8	W 2528	25.5	W 14324	42.9	W 2522	32.5	ART ROB,SIM POUR TUYAUX
7493	SHAFT,CRANK,PULLEY ETC	W 873	18.3	W 1063	19.4	W 1116	20.5	W 1529	28.6	ARBRES TRANS,VILEBREQUINS
7499	OTH NONELEC MCHY PTS NES	W 779	15.8	W 947	17.4	W 1078	20.3	W 1247	25.7	PIECES NON ELECT NDA
75	OFFICE MACHNES,ADP EQUIP		82.8		87.2		95.7		118.3	MACH BUREAU TRAIT AUTOM
752	AUTOMTIC DATA PROC EQUIP	W 837	56.7	W 964	62.3	W 976	68.1	W 1310	81.1	MACH TRAIT INFORMATION
7522	DIGITAL COMPUTERS	W 201	14.1	W 161	11.0	W 246	20.6	W 369	27.0	MACH DIGITALES COMPLETES
76	TELECOMM,SOUND EQUIPMENT		105.9		160.6		134.8		158.1	EQUIPMENT DE TELECOM
761	TELEVISION RECEIVERS	W 1488	16.3	W 1524	17.5	W 2695	31.2	W 4314	49.6	RECEPTEURS DE TELEVISION
7611	COLOUR TV RECEIVERS	W 1241	15.2	W 1386	16.9	W 2452	29.7	W 3760	46.3	RECEPTEURS COULEUR
764	TELECOM EQPT,PTS,ACC NES	W 1738	84.5	W 2247	137.2	W 2495	92.3	W 2538	90.7	EQUIP TELECOM,PIECES
7641	LINE TELEPHONE,ETC EQUIP	W 574	37.9	W 1009	64.2	W 713	45.7	W 563	47.6	APP TELEPHON PAR FIL
7643	TV,RADIO TRANSMITTRS ETC	W 573	23.9	W 646	46.3	W 315	25.6	W 92	17.6	APP EMET TELE RADIO
77	ELECTRIC MACHNRY NES ETC		209.9		235.0		257.3		233.9	MACH APP ELECT NDA
771	ELECTRIC POWER MACHY NES	W 1750	25.8	W 2379	26.3	W 3536	32.9	W 4004	22.3	MACH PROD,TRANS ELECTR
7711	TRANSFORMERS,ELECTRICAL	W 1051	21.9	W 1349	20.4	W 2283	22.8	W 3079	15.9	TRANSFO ELECTRIQUES
772	SWITCHGEAR ETC,PARTS NES	W 3250	63.0	W 3005	62.5	W 2766	57.9	W 1954	52.9	APP COUPURE,SECT ETC
7721	SWITCHGEAR ETC	W 3205	61.0	W 2988	59.8	W 2733	54.5	W 1915	49.9	APP COUPURE,SECTIONMNT
773	ELECTR DISTRIBUTNG EQUIP	W 6766	43.3	W 8561	53.0	W 11210	73.2	W 6461	56.4	EQUIPMT DISTRIBUTION ELECT
7731	INSULATED WIRE,CABLE ETC	W 5955	37.4	W 5832	42.2	W 8418	58.1	W 5067	46.1	FILS,CABLES ISOLES ELECT
775	HOUSEHOLD TYPE EQUIP NES	W 2197	13.1	W 3838	19.3	W 3572	23.2	W 3649	25.0	MACH,APP USAGE DOMESTQUE
778	ELECTRICAL MACHINERY NES	W 5516	48.7	W 6058	46.9	W 5571	48.8	W 6709	59.2	AUTRES MACH ELECT NDA
78	ROAD VEHICLES		222.8		273.6		310.8		389.7	VEHICULES ROUTIERS
781	PASS MOTOR VEH EXC BUSES	W 8907	76.8	W 9348	83.9	W 10210	89.8	W 22083	183.1	AUTO TRANSPORT PERSONNES
782	LORRIES,SPCL MTR VEH NES	W 13749	78.6	W 16392	102.3	W 14438	106.2	W 17520	106.9	VEHICULES SPECIAUX,MARCH
7821	LORRIES,TRUCKS	W 10940	68.9	W 12986	91.9	W 12304	88.7	W 14047	95.1	VEHICULES TRANSP MARCHAND
783	ROAD MOTOR VEHICLES NES	W 3851	19.3	W 4193	31.8	W 5986	55.1	W 4643	37.3	VEHICULES ROUTIERS NDA
7831	BUSES	W 3144	14.2	W 2862	22.4	W 3218	32.1	W 2510	20.8	VOITURES TRANSPORT COMMUN
784	MOTOR VEH PRTS,ACCES NES	W 8008	35.0	W 8711	39.9	W 8771	42.1	W 8882	44.3	PIECES 722,781,782,783
7849	OTHER MOTOR VEHCL PARTS	W 7658	34.2	W 8286	38.8	W 8290	40.8	W 8407	43.0	PIECES 722,781,782,783
79	OTHR TRANSPORT EQUIPMENT		181.3		273.9		155.7		51.7	AUTRE MATERIEL TRANSPORT
791	RAILWAY VEHICLES	W 693	7.2	W 2023	3.6	W 2452	36.3	W 2847	3.5	VEHIC MAT CHEMINS DE FER
7913	MECHAN-PROPELLED RY CARS					W 915	33.7			AUTOMOTRICES,DRAISINES
792	AIRCRAFT ETC	W 312	104.5	W 484	249.7		109.8	W 165	25.7	APP NAVIGATION AERIENNE
7924	AIRCRFT NES OVER 15000KG	W 67	67.7	W 220	208.6	W 67	69.9			AERODYNES PLUS 15000 KG
7929	AIRCRAFT PARTS NES	W 196	25.7	W 254	40.8	W 220	31.9	W 165	25.6	PIECES DU 792
793	SHIPS AND BOATS ETC	W 11513	69.7		20.8		9.6		22.7	NAVIRES BATEAUX,ETC
7932	SHIPS AND BOATS NES	W 11434	68.8	W 67	0.6	W 4566	7.3	W 5626	18.3	NAVIRES ET BATEAUX
79323	OTHER CARGO VESSELS	W 3920	54.5			W 4499	6.4	W 4531	11.8	AUT BATEAUX TRANS MARCH
8	MISC MANUFACTURED GOODS		287.0		299.6		370.9		369.1	ART MANUFACTURES DIVERS
821	*FURNITURE,PARTS THEREOF	W 2887	14.4	W 3984	18.2	W 6038	27.6	W 6040	24.1	MEUBLES ET PIECES
87	PRECISION INSTRUMNTS NES		65.5		64.9		84.2		78.7	INSTRUM,APPAR SCIENT NDA
874	MEASURNG,CONTROLNG INSTR	W 1064	46.9	W 1148	45.1	W 1482	59.8	W 1132	52.2	INSTRUMENTS DE MESURE
88	PHOTO EQU,OPTICL GDS ETC		32.6		33.5		37.0		38.3	APP,FOURN PHOTO,OP,MONTR
882	PHOTO,CINEMA SUPPLIES	W 1959	19.3	W 2097	22.0	W 1911	21.2	W 2261	22.7	PRODUITS PHOTO,CINEMA
89	MISC MANUFCTRD GOODS NES		140.7		152.0		193.7		198.2	ART MANUFACTURES DIVERS
892	PRINTED MATTER	W 8617	38.0	W 8472	42.7	W 7564	43.8	W 9214	52.2	IMPRIMES
8921	PRINTED BOOKS,GLOBES,ETC	W 6480	24.0	W 5885	25.0	W 5239	24.4	W 5255	24.7	LIVRES,BROCHURES,CARTES
89211	PRINTED BOOKS,PAMPHLETS	W 6136	23.3	W 5233	23.9	W 4282	22.6	W 4612	23.8	LIVRES,BROCHURES
893	ARTICLES OF PLASTIC NES		49.2		54.2		79.6		67.4	OUVRAGES EN MAT DIVIS 58
8939	MISC PLASTIC ARTICLES	W 7182	38.2	W 7506	41.0	W 9289	55.7	W 8873	50.7	ART DIVERS EN MAT DIV 58
89399	OTHR PLASTC ARTICLES NES	W 6754	37.1	W 7003	39.6	W 8458	53.3	W 8469	49.3	AUT OUV MAT DIV 58
899	OTHER MANUFACTURED GOODS		17.3		20.6		23.1		27.7	AUT ART MANUF DIVERS NDA

5. Special Exports F.O.B. by Commodities according to the S.I.T.C. (Rev. 2) in million U.S. Dollars
Exportations Spéciales F.O.B. par Produits d'après la C.T.C.I. (Rév. 2) en millions de Dollars E.U.

SITC CTCI	COMMODITY	1993 QUANTITY QUANTITE	1993 VALUE VALEUR	1994 QUANTITY QUANTITE	1994 VALUE VALEUR	1995 QUANTITY QUANTITE	1995 VALUE VALEUR	1996 QUANTITY QUANTITE	1996 VALUE VALEUR	PRODUIT
	ALL COMMODITIES		3696.0		4034.6		4718.9		4742.1	TOUS PRODUITS
0	FOOD AND LIVE ANIMALS		977.7		1127.9		1444.3		1497.3	ALIMENTS,ANIMAUX VIVANTS
03	FISH AND PREPARATIONS		538.4		620.6		773.9		737.1	POISSONS ET PREPARATIONS
034	FISH,FRESH,CHILLED,FROZN	W 31542	78.6	W 31319	79.6	W 28339	88.1	W 29517	91.4	POISSON FRAIS, REFRIG,CONG
0341	FISH FRSH,CHLLD,EX FILLT	W 19438	61.2	W 17116	58.1	W 15024	70.1	W 17875	74.3	POISSON FRAIS,REFRIGERE
0342	FISH FROZEN,EXCL FILLETS	W 11266	16.3	W 13566	20.0	W 12692	16.7	W 11259	16.3	POISSONS CONGELES
036	SHELL FISH FRESH,FROZEN	W 105395	313.0	W 107872	382.0	W 108044	503.4	W 91651	468.0	CRUSTACES,MOLLUSQUES
037	FISH ETC PREPD,PRSVD NES	W 56397	146.1	W 59517	157.8	W 68064	181.1	W 61625	176.1	POIS,CRUST,MOL PREPARES
0371	FISH PREPARD,PRESRVD NES	W 56294	145.7	W 59381	157.0	W 68028	180.9	W 61613	176.1	CONSERVES DE POISSONS
05	VEGETABLES AND FRUIT		406.5		451.6		585.6		671.7	LEGUMES ET FRUITS
054	VEG ETC FRSH,SMPLY PRSVD	W 267564	127.4	W 293040	135.5	W 297730	182.6	W 247434	167.5	LEGUMES FRAIS,CONG,SECS
0541	POTATOES FRSH EXCL SWEET	W 60974	20.0	W 86871	26.8	W 96853	48.7	W 52934	25.7	POMMES DE TERRE
0544	TOMATOES FRESH	W 162355	52.9	W 150876	44.1	W 156221	71.9	W 153046	82.4	TOMATES FRAICHES
0545	OTHER FRESH VEGETABLES	W 17137	11.7	W 18901	14.8	W 14356	13.0	W 16745	18.4	AUTRES LEGUMES FRAIS,REF
05459	FRESH VEGETABLES NES	W 15615	10.9	W 16301	14.1	W 13517	12.3	W 16409	18.0	LEGUMES FRAIS,REFRI NDA
0546	VEGETABLES SIMPLY PRESVD	W 12547	29.1	W 14436	32.1	W 13013	35.6	W 9891	26.4	LEGUMES CONG,CONSER
05461	VEGETABLES FROZEN	W 8773	18.9	W 8624	19.4	W 7603	19.8	W 4403	10.6	LEGUMES CONGELES
05462	VEG PRSVD UNFRZN UNTINND	W 3773	10.2	W 5812	12.8	W 5410	15.9	W 5489	15.9	LEGUMES CONSER PROVISOIR
0548	EDIBLE VEG NES FRESH,DRY	W 12860	12.7	W 14988	13.6	W 11273	6.9	W 9698	9.0	RACINES,TUBERCULES
05488	VEG PRODTS NES FRESH,DRY	W 12860	12.7	W 14986	13.6	W 11273	6.9	W 9697	9.0	PROD VEGET ALIM HUMAINE
056	VEGTBLES ETC PRSVD,PREPD	W 61403	82.9	W 71742	100.0	W 86136	132.4	W 77242	130.3	CONSERVES DE LEGUMES
0561	VEG DRIED EXC LEGUMINOUS	W 9402	13.7	W 7471	9.4	W 3607	4.3	W 1331	3.3	LEGUM DESSECH,DESHYDRAT
0565	VEGTBLES PRSVD,PREPD NES	W 52001	69.3	W 64271	90.7	W 82528	128.2	W 75911	127.1	LEGUMES PREPARES CONSERVE
05651	VEGTBLS,FRUIT IN VINEGAR	W 6196	11.7	W 5558	11.6	W 6086	14.8	W 5471	12.5	LEGUM CONSERV AU VINAIGRE
05659	OTH VEG PRESVD,PREPD NES	W 45806	57.6	W 58712	79.1	W 76442	113.5	W 70440	114.6	LEGUM PREPAP,CONSERV NDA
057	FRUIT,NUTS,FRESH,DRIED	W 525656	170.2	W 518691	171.1		226.6	W 654814	333.1	FRUITS FRAIS OU SECS
0571	ORANGES, MANDARINS ETC	W 508161	153.8	W 498321	150.7	W 414282	201.2	W 631054	309.0	ORANGES,MAND,CLEMENTINES
05711	ORANGES,FRESH OR DRIED	W 314741	89.6	W 314217	84.1	W 253618	112.9	W 428042	177.4	ORANGES FRAICHES,SECHEES
05712	MANDARINS ETC FRESH, DRY	W 193419	64.3	W 184104	66.6	W 160664	88.4	W 203012	131.6	MANDARINES,CLEMENTINES
0579	FRUIT FRESH OR DRIED NES	W 13372	10.6	W 17911	16.0	W 24069	19.9	W 21380	18.6	FRUITS FRAIS,SECS NDA
058	FRUIT PRESERVED,PREPARED		26.1	W 50797	45.2		44.2	W 34961	40.9	CONSERVES DE FRUITS
0585	FRUIT OR VEGETABLE JUICE	W 11608	9.7	W 27912	24.6	W 10231	10.5	W 13196	16.9	JUS DE FRUITS
05851	ORANGE JUICE	W 10632	8.8	W 27112	24.0	W 10000	10.3	W 12754	16.5	JUS D'ORANGE
0589	FRUIT PREPRD,PRESRVD,NES		14.6	W 15205	14.6		24.8	W 15978	20.5	FRUITS PREPARES CONSERV
05899	FRUIT,NUTS NES,PRESERVED	W 16292	14.6	W 15205	14.6	W 17676	24.8	W 15978	20.5	FRUITS PREP CONSERV NDA
07	COFFEE,TEA,COCOA,SPICES		9.9		18.2		31.8		34.8	CAFE,THE,CACAO,EPICES
071	COFFEE AND SUBSTITUTES	W 104	0.7		7.1	W 816	14.0	W 1321	16.6	CAFE ET SUCCEDANES
0712	COFFEE EXTRACTS,ESSENCES	W 72	0.6	W 576	7.0	W 800	14.0	W 1320	16.6	EXTRAITS DE CAFE
075	SPICES	W 7844	9.2	W 9340	10.5		17.3	W 15935	18.2	EPICES
09	MISC EDIBLE PRODUCTS		15.6		12.0		19.9		12.1	PREP ALIMENTAIRES DIVERSES
098	EDIBLE PRODCTS,PREPS NES	W 2950	8.4	W 1587	9.3	W 2957	19.8	W 1363	12.0	PREP ALIMENTAIRES NDA
09809	MISC FOOD PREPRTIONS NES	W 571	5.3	W 549	7.0	W 1938	17.3	W 1000	10.8	PREP ALIMENTAIRES NDA
1	BEVERAGES AND TOBACCO		7.7		13.1		14.2		9.8	BOISSONS ET TABACS
2	CRUDE MATERLS,EXCL FUELS		466.9		586.4		634.0		642.5	MAT BRUTES NON COMESTIBLES
251	*PULP AND WASTE PAPER	W 62951	21.3	W 112357	54.9	W 74183	66.8	W 68282	32.7	PATES A PAPIER,DECHETS
2516	CHEM WOOD PULP DISSOLVNG	W 62951	21.3	W 3134	1.0	W 1435	1.2			PATES CHIMIQUES DE BOIS
2517	SODA,SULPHATE WOOD PULP			W 109199	54.0	W 72748	65.6	W 68282	32.7	PATES CHIMIQUES AU SULFATE
25172	— BLEACHED,NONDISSOLVNG			W 109199	54.0	W 72748	65.6	W 68282	32.7	PATES BLANCHIES
27	CRUDE FERTLZR,MINRLS NES		290.9		322.2		326.7		389.4	ENGRAIS MINERAUX BRUTS
271	FERTILIZERS,CRUDE	W 8399144	260.0	MW 9527	281.8	MW 9420	284.6	MW 10140	347.5	ENGRAIS BRUTS
2713	NAT CALCM PHOSPHATES ETC	W 8398409	259.9	MW 9527	281.8	MW 9420	284.6	MW 10140	347.5	PHOSPHATES DE CALCIUM
27131	— UNGROUND	W 8398409	259.9	MW 9527	281.8	MW 9420	284.6	MW 10140	347.5	PHOSPHATES NON MOULUS
273	STONE,SAND AND GRAVEL	W 1195848	11.1	W 2038890	16.6	W 1052399	9.0	W 868584	8.8	PIERRES,SABLES,GRAVIERS
278	OTHER CRUDE MINERALS	W 426800	19.9	W 519490	23.9	W 601395	33.2	W 535376	33.1	AUTRES MINERAUX BRUTS
2789	MINERALS CRUDE NES	W 311121	12.4	W 334473	13.9	W 381593	18.6	W 326237	17.8	MINERAUX BRUTS NDA
27892	NAT BARIUM SULPHATE,CARB	W 306647	12.2	W 333863	13.6	W 371308	16.6	W 321520	15.7	SULFATE DE BARYUM NATUREL
28	METALLIFEROUS ORES,SCRAP		85.4		125.9		146.1		133.1	MINERAIS METAL,DECHETS
282	IRON AND STEEL SCRAP	W 153150	12.8	W 108104	10.9	W 120747	13.7	W 90590	10.2	FERRAILLES
287	BASE METAL ORES,CONC NES	W 229160	58.9	W 285615	99.1	W 282981	111.7	W 300648	110.0	MINERAIS METAUX COMMUNS
2871	CPR ORE ETC,CEMENT COPPR	W 46045	22.4	W 44057	31.0	W 42194	33.3	W 41993	22.5	MINERAIS DE CUIVRE,MATTES
28711	COPPER ORES,EXCL MATTE	W 44342	21.7	W 41831	27.0	W 40080	31.4	W 40650	22.0	MINERAIS DE CUIVRE
2874	LEAD ORES,CONCENTRATES	W 32543	4.4	W 55423	15.7	W 36905	13.0	W 45720	18.4	MINERAIS DE PLOMB
2875	ZINC ORES,CONCENTRATES	W 111780	23.3	W 151161	36.8	W 171466	44.3	W 178175	45.1	MINERAIS DE ZINC
2879	OTH NONFER ORE,CONCNTRTE	W 3663	0.6	W 4208	8.9	W 4544	14.1	W 4890	16.2	MINERAIS D'AUTRES METAUX
28799	OTH BASE MTL ORE,CON NES	W 3663	0.6	W 4208	8.9	W 4544	14.1	W 4890	16.2	AUTRES MINERAIS
288	NONFERR METAL SCRAP NES	W 9611	11.1	W 12809	14.8	W 12196	19.8	W 9927	12.8	DECHETS NON FERREUX
2882	OTHER BASE MTL SCRAP NES	W 8939	11.0	W 11804	14.5	W 11612	19.6	W 8804	12.5	AUTRES DECHETS
28821	COPPER WASTE AND SCRAP	W 6920	9.9	W 6632	10.1	W 7158	14.6	W 5526	9.8	DECHETS DE CUIVRE
29	CRUDE ANIMAL,VEG MAT NES		55.4		69.3		86.3		81.8	MATIERES BRUTES ANIM,VEGET
292	CRUDE VEG MATERIALS NES	W 16484	51.3	W 19623	64.7		81.3		74.8	MAT BRUTES VEGETALES NDA
2924	VEG USED IN PHARMACY ETC	W 5510	10.6	W 7199	13.0	W 7753	15.1	W 8028	16.5	PLANTES MEDICINALES
2927	CUT FLOWERS AND FOLIAGE	W 2496	13.9	W 3018	16.4	W 3780	18.8	W 3144	15.8	FLEURS,FEUILLAGES COUPES
29271	CUT FLOWERS	W 2475	13.8	W 2980	16.3	W 3737	18.6	W 3138	15.8	FLEURS ET BOUTONS
2929	OTH CRUDE VEG MATERIALS	W 6566	23.4	W 7400	32.7	W 5235	44.1	W 6522	39.9	MATIERES VEGETALES NDA
29291	VEGETABLE SAPS,EXTRACTS	W 3954	21.9	W 4494	30.5	W 2995	42.2	W 3747	36.4	SUCS,EXTRAITS VEGETAUX
3	MINERAL FUELS ETC		98.4		84.0		104.0		77.2	COMBUSTIBLES MINERAUX LUB
33	PETROLEUM AND PRODUCTS		98.4		84.0		104.0		77.2	PETROLE ET DERIVES
334	PETROLEUM PRODUCTS,REFIN	W 535579	98.3	W 514543	84.0	W 555809	104.0	W 364385	77.2	PRODUITS RAFFINES
3341	GASOLINE,OTH LIGHT OILS	W 535574	98.3	W 514542	84.0	W 553335	103.4	W 268971	50.7	ESSENCES POUR MOTEURS
33411	MOTOR,AVIATION SPIRIT					W 63506	10.0	W 119630	21.5	ESSENCES MOTEURS D'AVIONS
33419	OTH LIGHT PETROLEUM OILS	W 535574	98.3	W 514542	84.0	W 489829	93.5	W 149341	29.2	AUTRES HUILES LEGERES
3345	LUBS,PETROLEUM OILS NES	W 4	0.1	W 1	0.1	W 8	0.1	W 73354	21.5	HUILES LUBRIFIANTES
33451	LUBS(HIGH PETR CONT) ETC			W 1	0.1	W 2	0.1	W 73351	21.5	HUILES LUBRIF,H LOURDES
4	ANIMAL,VEGETABLE OIL,FAT		1.1		4.3		23.1		50.7	HUILES,GRAISSES ANIM,VEG
42	FIXED VEGETABLE OIL,FAT		0.8		2.8		17.2		47.7	HUILES VEGETALES FIXES
423	FIXED VEG OILS,SOFT	W 425	0.8	W 2520	2.8	W 6449	17.2	W 14661	47.6	HUILES VEGET DOUCES FIXES
4235	OLIVE OIL	W 422	0.8	W 250	0.7	W 6449	17.2	W 14660	47.6	HUILE D'OLIVE
5	CHEMCLS,RELATED PROD NES		721.5		813.3		980.2		954.6	PRODUITS CHIMIQUES
52	INORGANIC CHEMICALS		351.3		472.3		551.5		527.7	PROD CHIM INORGANIQUES
522	INORG ELEMNTS,OXIDES,ETC	W 1434523	350.7	W 1675561	471.8	W 1723014	551.2	W 1618463	527.4	ELEMENTS INORGANIQUES
5222	INORGANIC ACIDS ETC	W 1434104	350.5	W 1675503	471.7	W 1722959	551.1	W 1618433	527.3	ACIDES INORGANIQUES
52224	PHOSPHORIC ACIDS ETC	W 1433916	350.2	W 1675496	471.7	W 1722958	551.1	W 1618433	527.3	ACIDES PHOSPHORIQUES
541	*MEDICINAL,PHARM PRODUCT		24.4		29.7		18.7		10.1	PROD MEDICINAUX PHARMACEUT
5417	MEDICAMENTS	K 2047407	22.1	K 2686333	27.2	K 653996	15.1	K 337065	6.7	MEDICAMENTS
54179	— CONTNG OTH SUBSTANCES	K 1804555	16.8	K 2619966	24.0	K 556675	10.1	K 299211	4.9	MED CONT AUT SUBSTANCES
55	PERFUME,CLEANING ETC PRD		21.2		24.6		32.5		26.2	PROD POUR PARFUM,TOILETTE
551	ESSENTL OILS,PERFUME,ETC	W 698	16.1	W 1484	16.1	W 1075	22.1	W 810	17.9	HUILES ESSENTIELLES
5513	ESSENTL OIL,RESINOID,ETC	W 487	14.6	W 1403	15.6	W 826	20.1	W 606	15.5	HUILES ESSENTIELLES,RESIN
562	*FERTILIZERS,MANUFACTURE	W 2408486	311.3	W 1674075	272.1	W 1784150	360.7	W 1884573	380.9	ENGRAIS MANUFACTURES
5622	CHEM PHOSPHATIC FERTILZR	W 2247642	290.3	W 1623355	263.3	W 1761162	355.6	W 1749647	351.1	ENGRAIS PHOSPHATES
56222	SUPERPHOSPHATES	W 473771	52.5	W 445141	57.4	W 491908	76.3	W 660486	112.3	SUPERPHOSPHATES

5. Special Exports F.O.B. by Commodities according to the S.I.T.C. (Rev. 2) in million U.S. Dollars
Exportations Spéciales F.O.B. par Produits d'après la C.T.C.I. (Rév. 2) en millions de Dollars E.U.

SITC CTCI	COMMODITY	1993 QUANTITY QUANTITE	1993 VALUE VALEUR	1994 QUANTITY QUANTITE	1994 VALUE VALEUR	1995 QUANTITY QUANTITE	1995 VALUE VALEUR	1996 QUANTITY QUANTITE	1996 VALUE VALEUR	PRODUIT
56229	CHEM PHOSPH FERTILZR NES	W 1773871	237.8	W 1178214	205.9	W 1269254	279.3	W 1089161	238.8	ENGRAIS PHOSPHATES NDA
5629	FERTILIZERS NES	W 160820	21.1	W 50577	8.8	W 22988	5.2	W 134926	29.9	ENGRAIS NDA
56292	NITROG–PHOS FERTILZR NES	W 160737	21.0	W 50577	8.8	W 22988	5.2	W 134925	29.8	ENGRAIS NDA CONT N P
6	BASIC MANUFACTURES		328.9		373.3		432.0		445.4	ART MANUFACTURES
61	LEATHER,DRESSED FUR,ETC		21.2		45.1		44.5		66.4	CUIRS,PELLETERIES
611	LEATHER	W 1254	9.5	W 4361	33.7	W 1875	37.3	W 2761	58.6	CUIRS,PEAUX PREPARES
6115	LEATHER FROM SHEEP,LAMBS	W 479	3.9	W 2591	23.5	W 1370	31.5	W 2498	51.9	PEAUX D'OVINS PREPAREES
612	LEATHER ETC MANUFACTURES	W 1043	11.8	W 1139	11.4	W 862	7.3	W 561	7.8	OUVRAGES EN CUIRS NDA
62	RUBBER MANUFACTURES NES		10.8		21.0		22.6		20.4	CAOUTCHOUC MANUFACTURE
625	RUBBER TYRES, TUBES ETC	W 3231	10.5	W 6374	20.4	W 6592	22.3	W 6019	20.2	PNEUS CAOUTCHOUC VULCANISE
63	WOOD,CORK MANUFACTRS NES		32.2		34.2		36.2		36.2	OUVRAGES LIEGE ET BOIS
634	VENEERS,PLYWOOD,ETC	W 18581	19.1	W 15682	20.1	W 16856	21.8	W 16329	21.2	PLACAGES,CONTRE–PLAQUES
6342	PLYWOOD OF WOOD SHEETS	W 13349	15.8	W 15186	19.0	W 14195	20.1	W 15175	20.2	BOIS CONTRE–PLAQUES
64	PAPER,PAPERBOARD AND MFR		8.4		8.1		15.0		13.4	PAPIERS,CARTONS & OUVRAGES
65	TEXTILE YARN,FABRICS,ETC		165.6		155.5		177.5		158.5	FILS,TISSUS,ARTICLES TEXTILE
651	TEXTILE YARN	W 9937	44.9	W 12115	55.6	W 10908	57.6	W 7457	39.7	FILS TEXTILES
6513	COTTON YARN	W 5795	25.0	W 6913	31.1	W 6829	34.1	W 5158	25.0	FILS DE COTON
6516	DISCON SYN FIB BLEND YRN	W 2510	13.5	W 3154	18.2	W 2408	15.8	W 1326	9.1	FILS FIBR TEX SYNT DIS MOINS
652	COTTON FABRICS,WOVEN	W 2891	14.2	W 1584	9.4	W 1841	11.2	W 573	5.1	TISSUS DE COTON
653	WOVN MAN–MADE FIB FABRIC	W 3328	29.0	W 3103	26.4	W 3478	34.0	W 2962	34.2	TISSUS FIBRES SYNTH,ARTIF
658	TEXTILE ARTICLES NES	W 4246	21.7	W 1994	12.3	W 4097	24.7	W 6684	33.3	ART FACONNES MAT TEXTILES
659	FLOOR COVERINGS,ETC	W 7551	39.2	W 6890	38.7	W 4120	35.6	W 3515	30.0	COUVRE–PARQUETS,TAPIS ETC
6592	CARPETS ETC KNOTTED	W 3753	29.9	W 3953	30.7	W 3575	32.0	W 3121	27.3	TAPIS POINTS NOUES,ENROULES
65921	— OF WOOL OR FINE HAIR	W 3747	29.8	W 3939	30.6	W 3570	31.9	W 3120	27.3	TAP NOUES,ENROULES LAINE
66	NONMETAL MINERAL MFS NES		17.5		27.7		34.6		37.3	ART MIN NON METALLIQUES
661	LIME,CEMENT,BLDG PRODS	W 5291	1.5		9.4	W 451924	15.1	W 244942	11.9	CHAUX,CIMENTS MAT CONSTR
67	IRON AND STEEL		13.0		6.0		11.6		16.6	FER ET ACIER
68	NON–FERROUS METALS		46.5		59.3		72.2		77.9	METAUX NON FERREUX
681	SILVER,PLATINUM,ETC		19.6		28.4		37.5		31.7	ARGENT ET PLATINE
6811	SILVER UNWKD,PARTLY WRKD		19.6		28.4		37.5		31.7	ARGENT BRUT MI–OUVRE
68113	SILVER UNWROUGHT		19.3		28.4		37.1		31.5	ARGENT ET ALLIAGES BRUTS
685	LEAD		24.1	W 58212	28.1	W 63922	33.8	W 54522	42.5	PLOMB
6851	LEAD,ALLOYS UNWROUGHT		24.1	W 58212	28.1	W 63922	33.8	W 54522	42.5	PLOMB,ALLIAGES BRUTS
68511	UNREFINED LEAD	W 74939	24.1	W 58212	28.1	W 63922	33.8	W 54454	42.4	PLOMB POUR AFFINAGE
69	METAL MANUFACTURES NES		13.9		16.9		18.2		19.1	ART MANUFACT EN METAL NDA
7	MACHINES,TRANSPORT EQUIP		204.0		167.3		152.8		138.2	MACHINES MATERIEL TRANSPORT
74	GENRL INDUSTRL MACHY NES		11.4		9.3		26.8		26.3	MACH APP INDUSTRIE
741	HEATING,COOLING EQUIPMNT	W 92	0.6		0.5		19.7	W 1455	21.3	MACH CHAUFFAGE,PIECES
7413	INDUS FURNACES ETC,PARTS	W 29	0.2	W 2	0.1	W 560	19.1	W 1442	21.1	FOURS IND,LABOR,PIECES
74132	INDUST FURNACES NONELECT	W 9	0.1	W 1	0.1	W 560	19.1	W 1442	21.1	FOURS NON ELECTRIQUES
77	ELECTRIC MACHNRY NES ETC		103.3		125.2		90.2		80.7	MACH APP ELECT NDA
773	ELECTR DISTRIBUTNG EQUIP	W 3175	51.2	W 3753	59.9	W 4199	72.6	W 5148	71.8	EQUIPMT DISTRIBUTION ELECT
7731	INSULATED WIRE,CABLE ETC	W 3171	51.1	W 3746	59.7	W 4195	72.5	W 5140	71.6	FILS,CABLES ISOLES ELECT
775	HOUSEHOLD TYPE EQUIP NES		2.1		16.7		5.3		0.2	MACH,APP USAGE DOMESTQUE
7752	DOM REFRIGERATRS,FREEZRS	W 330	1.8	W 2819	15.9	W 832	5.0	W 2	0.1	REFRIG,CONGEL MENAGER
776	TRANSISTORS,VALVES,ETC	W 1202	36.7		36.1	W 21	0.6	W 1	0.1	LAMPES,TUBES,VALVES
7763	DIODES,TRANSISTORS,ETC	W 999	35.1	W 1085	31.7	W 21	0.6	W 1	0.1	DIODES,TRANSISTORS
78	ROAD VEHICLES		18.5		20.4		23.2		20.2	VEHICULES ROUTIERS
784	MOTOR VEH PRTS,ACCES NES	W 2041	17.1	W 2322	18.4	W 2345	19.5	W 2333	17.0	PIECES 722,781,782,783
7849	OTHER MOTOR VEHCL PARTS	W 2035	17.1	W 2322	18.4	W 2345	19.5	W 2333	17.0	PIECES 722,781,782,783
79	OTHR TRANSPORT EQUIPMENT		53.4		0.8		3.3		0.8	AUTRE MATERIEL TRANSPORT
793	SHIPS AND BOATS ETC	W 82320	53.1	W 3659	0.8	W 2022	1.8	W 842	0.8	NAVIRES BATEAUX,ETC
7932	SHIPS AND BOATS NES	W 82319	53.1	W 3659	0.8	W 2022	1.8	W 842	0.8	NAVIRES ET BATEAUX
79323	OTHER CARGO VESSELS	W 82314	52.7	W 3651	0.7			W 842	0.8	AUT BATEAUX TRANS MARCH
8	MISC MANUFACTURED GOODS		889.7		864.0		933.2		925.1	ART MANUFACTURES DIVERS
812	*PLUMBG,HEATNG,LGHTNG EQ	W 2710	11.9	W 2329	12.1	W 3377	12.3	W 6642	16.0	APPAR SANITAIRES CHAUFFAGE
831	*TRAVEL GOODS,HANDBAGS	W 1569	18.1	W 1253	16.7	W 830	16.2	W 528	12.9	ARTICLES DE VOYAGE ETC
84	CLOTHING AND ACCESSORIES		760.3		739.0		796.9		779.1	VETEMENTS
842	MENS OUTERWEAR NOT KNIT	W 24108	259.3	W 22348	255.0	W 19899	281.3	W 16770	257.0	VET DESSUS POUR HOMMES
8421	— OVERCOATS,OTHER COATS	W 1606	18.3	W 1477	17.9	W 859	13.5	W 291	7.3	MANTEAUX HOMMES MAT TEXT
84219	—— OF OTHER FIBRES	W 1578	17.7	W 1439	17.4	W 847	13.1	W 291	7.3	MANTEAUX HOMMES AUT FIBR
8423	— TROUSERS,BREECHES ETC	W 17218	178.6	W 16329	166.9	W 15277	202.7	W 14489	208.5	PANTALONS HOMMES MAT TEX
8429	— OTHER OUTER GARMENTS	W 5039	57.4	W 4144	56.8	W 3593	59.6	W 1864	34.3	AUT VET DES HOM MAT TEX
843	WOMENS OUTERWEAR NONKNIT	W 7282	97.1	W 5911	89.1	W 4500	81.8	W 4621	83.1	VET DESSUS FEMMES MAT TEX
8439	— OTHER OUTER GARMENTS	W 5299	68.0	W 4320	60.9	W 3516	56.7	W 3905	63.0	AUT VET DES FEM MAT TEXT
844	UNDER GARMENTS NOT KNIT	W 3780	80.6	W 3312	75.8	W 2448	69.4	W 1926	53.4	VETEMENT DESSOUS MAT TEX
8441	— MENS SHIRTS	W 3436	75.5	W 3001	69.9	W 2283	64.8	W 1779	50.2	CHEMISES HOMMES MAT TEXT
84411	—— OF COTTON	W 2161	48.2	W 1904	44.4	W 1348	39.9	W 1026	31.3	CHEMISES HOMMES DE COTON
84412	—— OF SYNTHETIC FIBRES	W 1275	27.4	W 1097	25.5	W 935	24.9	W 753	18.9	CHEMISES HOMMES FIB SYNT
845	OUTERWEAR KNIT NONELASTC	W 15668	210.8	W 16231	221.2	W 14833	249.0	W 14242	265.7	VET DESSOUS,ACCES BONNET
8451	— JERSEYS,PULLOVERS ETC	W 7061	100.2	W 7518	109.4	W 7038	125.1	W 7198	139.4	CHANDAILS,PULL–OVERS ETC
8459	— OTHER,CLTHG ACCESRYS	W 8242	105.4	W 8457	107.0	W 7541	117.4	W 6832	120.7	AUT VET DESSUS DE BONNE
846	UNDER GARMENTS KNITTED	W 4593	90.3	W 3892	77.7	W 3990	92.9	W 3679	95.8	SOUS VETS DE BONNETERIE
8462	— OF COTTON NON ELASTIC	W 4250	75.3	W 3605	66.0	W 3475	72.2	W 3274	72.2	SOUS–VET BONNET COTON
84629	—— OTHER	W 4250	75.3	W 3605	66.0	W 3475	72.2	W 3274	72.2	AUT SOUS–VET BONNET COTON
8465	CORSETS,GARTERS,ETC	W 214	12.6	W 148	8.8	W 331	16.4	W 245	19.6	CORSETS,GAINES ART SIM
84652	CORSETS,BRACES ETC	W 151	10.4	W 125	7.9	W 327	16.1	W 232	18.9	CORSETS,GAINES,JARRETEL
848	HEADGEAR,NONTXTL CLOTHNG	W 603	20.8	W 498	18.5		14.8	W 502	13.9	VET ACCES MAT AUT QUE TEX
8481	LEATHER CLOTHES,ACCESSOR	W 530	20.0	W 448	17.7	W 345	14.2	W 322	12.9	VET ACCES MAT CUIR ARTIF
851	*FOOTWEAR	W 5407	71.8	W 4718	61.6	W 4626	71.4	W 4375	72.0	CHAUSSURES
85102	FOOTWEAR LEATHER	W 3487	57.6	W 3109	50.7	W 2887	57.5	W 2880	58.8	CHAUS SEMELLES EN CUIR
89	MISC MANUFCTRD GOODS NES		20.9		29.0		29.0		37.8	ART MANUFACTURES DIVERS

1. HISTORICAL SERIES, 1961–1996 SPECIAL TRADE, IMPORTS C.I.F., EXPORTS F.O.B.
SERIES HISTORIQUES, 1961–1996 COMMERCE SPECIAL, IMPORTATIONS C.A.F., EXPORTATIONS F.O.B

YEAR ANNEE	VALUE IN MILLION U.S. DOLLARS VALEUR EN MILLION U.S. DOLLARS MERCHANDISE –MARCHANDISE		GOLD –OR		CONVERSION FACTORS FACTEURS DE CONVERSION CENTS E.U. PAR		INDEX NUMBERS –INDICES QUANTUM		UNIT VALUE VALEUR UNITAIRE	
	IMPORTS	EXPORTS	IMPORTS	EXPORTS	IMPORTS	EXPORTS	IMPORTS	EXPORTS	IMPORTS	EXPORTS
1961	137.27	95.09	112.60	399.70						
1962	135.91	90.98	113.20	229.00						
1963	141.71	100.73	112.50	398.50						
1964	156.19	105.84								
1965	173.24	108.02	135.30	325.30						
1966	207.91	112.12	271.80	299.30						
1967	199.20	121.78	301.10	301.10						
1968	234.29	155.10	299.90	298.30						
1969	260.20	141.90								
1970	323.53	156.40								
1971	340.91	163.34								
1972	330.02	176.64								
1973	467.08	226.55								
1974	468.08	301.39								
1975	427.61	200.97								
1976	288.38	150.00								
1977	330.79	150.00								
1978	523.09	162.53								
1979	567.87	254.08								
1980	800.00	281.00								
1981	801.00	281.00								
1982	836.00	229.00								
1983	636.00	132.00								
1984	540.00	96.00								
1985	424.00	77.00								
1986	543.00	79.00								
1987	642.00	97.00								
1988	736.00	103.00								
1989	808.00	105.00								
1990	878.00	126.00								
1991	899.00	162.00								
1992	855.00	139.00								
1993	955.00	132.00								
1994	1019.00	150.00								
1995	784.00	168.00								
1996	782.64	226.09								

2. IMPORTS BY BROAD ECONOMIC CATEGORY AND EXPORTS BY INDUSTRIAL ORIGIN. (PERCENTAGE OF TOTAL VALUE)
IMPORTATIONS PAR CATEGORIES ECONOMIQUES ET EXPORTATIONS PAR BRANCHE D'ACTIVITE.(EN POURCENTAGE DE LA VALEUR TOTALE)

IMPORTS – IMPORTATIONS

	1990	1991	1992	1993	1994	1995	1996
TOTAL IMPORTS–IMPORTATIONS TOTALES					100.	100.	100.
1 FOOD BEV–ALIMENTATION BOISSONS					16.3	19.2	19.6
11 PRIMARY–PRODUITS DE BASE					6.7	10.0	10.4
111 FOR INDUSTRY–POUR L'INDUSTRIE					5.7	8.1	9.3
112 FOR HOUSEHOLDS–POUR LES MENAGES					1.0	1.9	1.1
12 PROCESSED–PRODUITS ELABORES					9.6	9.3	9.2
121 FOR INDUSTRY–POUR L'INDUSTRIE					5.1	4.8	6.2
122 FOR HOUSEHOLDS–POUR LES MENAGES					4.6	4.5	3.0
2 IND SUPPLIES–APPROV INDUSTRIELS					21.5	27.0	27.5
21 PRIMARY–PRODUITS DE BASE					2.2	3.5	3.4
22 PROCESSED–PRODUITS ELABORES					19.4	23.5	24.1
3 FUELS–COMBUSTIBLES					13.9	9.8	11.3
31 PRIMARY–PRODUITS DE BASE					0.0	0.0	0.1
32 PROCESSED–PRODUITS ELABORES					13.8	9.8	11.2
321 MOTOR SPIRIT–ESSENCE					10.8	8.0	9.5
322 OTHER–AUTRES					3.1	1.8	1.7
4 MACHINERY–EQUIPEMENT					17.9	15.7	18.1
41 CAPITAL EQUIPMENT–MACHINES					16.7	14.8	17.0
42 PARTS–PIECES ACCESSOIRES					1.3	0.9	1.1
5 TRANSPORT–TRANSPORT					17.5	17.9	13.1
51 PASSENGER CARS–AUTOMOBILES							
52 OTHER–AUTRES					14.3	15.1	10.2
521 INDUSTRIAL–INDUSTRIELS					13.4	14.5	9.2
522 NON INDUSTRIAL–NON INDUSTRIEL					0.9	0.6	1.0
53 PARTS–PIECES ACCESSOIRES					3.2	2.7	2.9
6 CONSUM GOODS–BIENS CONSOMMATION					10.8	8.6	9.1
61 DURABLE–DURABLES					1.9	1.7	2.1
62 SEMI DURABLE–SEMI DURABLES					2.4	2.3	2.8
63 NON DURABLE–NON DURABLES					6.5	4.7	4.1
7 GOODS NES–BIENS NDA					2.0	1.8	1.3

EXPORTS – EXPORTATIONS

	1990	1991	1992	1993	1994	1995	1996
TOTAL EXPORTS–EXPORTATIONS TOTALES					100.	100.	100.
1 AGRICULTURE					64.8	67.6	62.8
2 MINING QUARRY–INDUS EXTRACTIVES					1.3	1.4	1.4
3 MANUFACTURING–IND MANUFACTUR					33.9	31.0	35.8
31 FOOD BEV TOBACCO–ALIM BOISS TAB					8.6	6.2	8.1
32 TEXTILES–INDUSTRIES TEXTILES					5.2	8.7	5.3
33 WOOD & PRODUCTS–BOIS & PRODUITS					1.5	2.3	3.3
34 PAPER & PRODUCTS–PAPIER & PRODT					0.7	0.5	1.0
35 CHEMICALS–INDUSTRIES CHIMIQUES					12.1	4.2	3.0
36 NON METAL MIN–MIN NON METAL					0.2	0.2	0.0
37 BASIC METAL–IND METAL BASE					0.2	1.9	0.4
38 METAL MANUF–MANUF METAL					4.7	6.8	14.7
39 OTH MANUF IND–AUTRES MANUF					0.7	0.2	0.1

Mozambique

3. TRADE BY PRINCIPAL COUNTRIES OF ORIGIN AND DESTINATION (VALUE IN MILLION U.S. DOLLARS)
ECHANGES SELON LES PRINCIPAUX PAYS D'ORIGINE ET DE DESTINATION (VALEUR EN MILLIONS DE DOLLARS EU)

COUNTRIES–PAYS	SPECIAL IMPORTS C.I.F. IMPORTATIONS SPECIALES C.A.F				
	1992	1993	1994	1995	1996
World			544.0	727.0	782.6
Africa			186.6	246.3	314.1
Americas			27.3	71.8	58.7
– Northern America			26.4	61.9	43.2
– LAIA			0.9	9.9	15.4
– CACM					
– Caribbean					
– Rest of America					
Asia excl fmr USSR			75.5	107.3	102.6
– Middle East			2.2	5.4	11.9
Asia former USSR					
Europe excl fmr USSR			191.3	242.7	228.2
– European Union			179.4	233.7	212.0
– Eastern Europe					0.1
– Rest of Europe			11.9	9.0	16.0
Europe former USSR					0.2
Oceania			3.6	1.7	10.3
Other			59.7	57.2	68.5
So. African Customs Un			163.5	213.2	270.3
Areas n.e.s.			59.7	57.2	68.5
Portugal			25.2	65.7	49.3
Japan/Japon			45.7	36.8	31.0
USA/Etats–Unis d'Amer			22.4	49.9	32.6
Zimbabwe			21.2	30.7	30.6
United Kingdom			36.1	26.5	18.2
France, Monaco			21.5	23.8	34.7
Italy/Italie			16.9	24.1	32.7
Germany/Allemagne			23.0	24.1	20.7
India/Inde			5.6	23.7	35.8
Netherlands/Pays–Bas			12.7	17.1	15.9
Denmark/Danemark			21.1	11.5	11.9
Spain/Espagne			10.1	23.7	9.9
Canada			4.0	12.0	10.6
Sweden/Suède			5.2	9.9	8.1
China, Hong Kong SAR			6.0	10.6	5.4
Brazil/Brésil			0.7	5.9	13.6
Norway,Svalbard and JM			3.2	4.8	12.0
United Arab Emirates			2.2	5.2	11.4
Switzerland,Liechtenst.			8.6	4.2	4.0
Australia/Australie			3.5	1.7	10.3
Pakistan			5.3	8.0	1.9
Thailand/Thaïlande			2.4	6.8	5.8
Belgium–Luxembourg			3.5	3.6	7.8
Malawi			0.8	0.7	10.7
China/Chine			0.8	4.8	4.5
Singapore/Singapour			0.6	4.8	2.8
Argentina/Argentine				3.9	1.8
Other Asia n.e.s.			0.8	3.8	0.7
Finland/Finlande			2.1	1.4	1.4
Austria/Autriche			1.1	2.3	1.1
Indonesia/Indonésie			2.1	1.1	0.9
Korea, Republic of			1.3	1.0	1.4
Kenya			0.3	1.1	1.8
Myanmar			1.8		
Ireland/Irlande			0.7		0.2
Mauritius/Maurice			0.6	0.2	
Bangladesh			0.1	0.3	0.2
Zambia/Zambie			0.1	0.4	0.2

COUNTRIES–PAYS	SPECIAL EXPORTS F.O.B. EXPORTATIONS SPECIALES F.O.B.				
	1992	1993	1994	1995	1996
Monde			164.0	174.3	226.1
Afrique			40.5	52.5	59.8
Amériques			13.9	12.8	28.8
– Amérique du Nord			13.9	12.7	26.5
– ALAI				0.1	1.4
– MCAC					
– Caraïbes				0.1	0.8
– Autre Amérique				0.0	0.0
Asie anc. URSS exclus			37.9	33.5	50.2
– Moyen–Orient			0.1	0.1	0.0
Asie ancienne URSS					
Europe anc. URSS exclus			57.0	71.7	79.1
– Union Européenne			57.0	71.4	78.4
– Europe de l'Est				0.1	0.2
– Autre de l'Europe				0.2	0.5
Europe ancienne URSS				0.0	0.4
Océanie				0.0	0.0
Autre			14.8	3.7	7.8
Spain/Espagne			31.6	36.4	47.6
So. African Customs Un			29.0	41.2	43.9
Japan/Japon			24.1	24.8	17.2
USA/Etats–Unis d'Amer			13.8	9.5	25.8
Portugal			14.6	14.6	17.5
India/Inde			11.6	4.5	26.8
Areas n.e.s.			14.8	3.7	7.8
Zimbabwe			7.3	7.9	9.8
Belgium–Luxembourg			3.7	2.9	3.5
France, Monaco			0.3	7.5	1.3
Netherlands/Pays–Bas			1.1	3.2	3.5
United Kingdom			3.1	0.8	3.0
United Rep of Tanzania			1.1	0.1	4.0
Malawi			0.8	2.6	1.4
China, Hong Kong SAR			0.3	1.8	2.0
Canada			0.1	3.1	0.7
Indonesia/Indonésie				0.8	3.1
Ireland/Irlande			0.4	3.0	
Italy/Italie			0.9	1.1	1.4
Germany/Allemagne			0.9	1.5	0.3
Mexico/Mexique				0.0	1.4
Angola			0.7	0.1	0.5
Singapore/Singapour			0.6	0.1	0.4
Thailand/Thaïlande			0.2	0.8	
Cuba				0.1	0.8
Other Asia n.e.s.			0.5	0.3	0.0
Rwanda			0.7	0.1	
Malaysia/Malaisie			0.6		0.3
Sweden/Suède			0.2	0.5	0.2
Norway,Svalbard and JM				0.1	0.5
Kenya			0.4	0.1	0.0
Dem Rep of the Congo			0.3	0.0	0.1
Russian Federation				0.0	0.4
Sri Lanka					0.3
Hungary/Hongrie				0.1	0.2
Zambia/Zambie			0.1	0.0	0.1
China/Chine			0.1	0.2	0.0
United Arab Emirates			0.1	0.1	
Denmark/Danemark			0.1	0.1	0.0
Switzerland,Liechtenst.				0.1	0.0

(VALUE AS PERCENTAGE OF WORLD TOTAL)(VALEURS EN POURCENTAGE DU TOTAL MONDIAL)

	1987	1988	1989	1990	1991	1992	1993	1994	1995	1996
Africa	18.1	23.3	33.4					34.3	33.9	40.1
Americas	0.8	3.4	8.5					5.0	9.9	7.5
– Northern America	0.8	3.4	8.5					4.9	8.5	5.5
– LAIA								0.2	1.4	2.0
– CACM										
– Caribbean										
– Rest of America										
Asia excl fmr USSR	15.7	11.9	5.6					13.9	14.8	13.1
– Middle East	10.1	7.9						0.4	0.7	1.5
Asia former USSR										
Europe excl fmr USSR	51.9	46.4	35.8					35.2	33.4	29.2
– European Union	43.3	38.8	31.5					33.0	32.1	27.1
– Eastern Europe	1.5	2.3	3.8							0.0
– Rest of Europe	7.1	5.2	0.6					2.2	1.2	2.1
Europe former USSR	8.8	10.2	9.9							0.0
Oceania								0.7	0.2	1.3
Other	4.7	4.8	6.7					11.0	7.9	8.8
So. African Customs Un	12.2	13.7	23.3					30.1	29.3	34.5
Areas n.e.s.	4.7	4.8	6.7					11.0	7.9	8.8
Portugal	4.7	5.7	6.8					4.6	9.0	6.3
Japan/Japon	5.5	3.4	5.6					8.4	5.1	4.0
USA/Etats–Unis d'Amer			7.1					4.1	6.9	4.2
Zimbabwe	2.5	4.4	2.8					3.9	4.2	3.9
United Kingdom	4.7	5.6	4.8					6.6	3.6	2.3
France, Monaco	5.7	4.1	4.1					4.0	3.3	4.4
Italy/Italie	13.6	9.5	6.0					3.1	3.3	4.2
Germany/Allemagne								4.2	3.3	2.6

	1987	1988	1989	1990	1991	1992	1993	1994	1995	1996
Afrique	9.8	17.5	6.5					24.7	30.1	26.5
Amériques			11.0					8.5	7.4	12.7
– Amérique du Nord			11.0					8.5	7.3	11.7
– ALAI									0.0	0.6
– MCAC										
– Caraïbes									0.1	0.4
– Autre Amérique									0.0	0.0
Asie anc. URSS exclus	39.1	32.0	10.7					23.1	19.2	22.2
– Moyen–Orient	20.8	15.5						0.0	0.1	0.0
Asie ancienne URSS										
Europe anc. URSS exclus	44.7	45.0	41.3					34.7	41.1	35.0
– Union Européenne	32.4	36.1	32.0					34.7	41.0	34.7
– Europe de l'Est	11.2	7.5	9.4						0.0	0.1
– Autre de l'Europe	1.1	1.4							0.1	0.2
Europe ancienne URSS	6.4	5.4	4.1						0.0	0.2
Océanie									0.0	0.0
Autre			26.4					9.0	2.1	3.4
Spain/Espagne	18.2	20.9	19.8					19.2	20.9	21.1
So. African Customs Un	4.3	6.5	4.7					17.7	23.6	19.4
Japan/Japon	18.3	16.6	10.7					14.7	14.2	7.6
USA/Etats–Unis d'Amer			11.0					8.4	5.5	11.4
Portugal	7.0	7.8	8.8					8.9	8.4	7.7
India/Inde								7.1	2.6	11.8
Areas n.e.s.			26.4					9.0	2.1	3.4
Zimbabwe	0.6	0.8	1.0					4.4	4.6	4.3
Belgium–Luxembourg								2.3	1.7	1.5
France, Monaco	1.7	3.0	0.9					0.2	4.3	0.6

4. Special Imports C.I.F. by Commodities according to the S.I.T.C. (Rev. 2) in million U.S. Dollars
Importations Spéciales C.A.F. par Produits d'après la C.T.C.I. (Rév. 2) en millions de Dollars E.U.

SITC CTCI	COMMODITY	1993		1994		1995		1996		PRODUIT
		QUANTITY QUANTITE	VALUE VALEUR	QUANTITY QUANTITE	VALUE VALEUR	QUANTITY QUANTITE	VALUE VALEUR	QUANTITY QUANTITE	VALUE VALEUR	
	ALL COMMODITIES				544.1		727.0		782.7	TOUS PRODUITS
0	FOOD AND LIVE ANIMALS				78.7		130.9		137.0	ALIMENTS,ANIMAUX VIVANTS
01	MEAT AND PREPARATIONS				1.5		2.9		1.3	VIANDES ET PREPARATIONS
02	DAIRY PRODCTS,BIRDS'EGGS				4.4		3.7		4.6	PRODUITS LAITIERS,OEUFS
022	MILK AND CREAM				3.3		2.6		2.3	LAIT ET CREME
0224	MILK,CREAM PRESERVED ETC				2.5		1.5		1.4	LAIT,CREME CONS,CONC
03	FISH AND PREPARATIONS				2.3		2.2		1.7	POISSONS ET PREPARATIONS
04	CEREALS AND PREPARATIONS				52.7		89.0		95.9	CEREALES ET PRODUITS
041	WHEAT ETC UNMILLED				8.7		15.0		31.7	FROMENT,EPEAUTRE
0411	DURUM WHEAT UNMILLED				8.7		15.0		31.7	FROMENT DUR NON MOULU
042	RICE				19.7		40.1		38.4	RIZ
0421	RICE IN HUSK OR HUSKED				19.7		40.1		38.4	RIZ SANS AUTRE PREPARATION
04211	RICE IN THE HUSK				19.7		40.1		38.4	RIZ PADDY
044	MAIZE UNMILLED				3.3		11.5		4.1	MAIS NON MOULU
046	WHEAT ETC MEAL OR FLOUR				12.0		9.1		15.2	SEMOULE FARINE,FROMENT
04601	FLOUR OF WHEAT OR MESLIN				11.8		9.0		15.2	FARINE DE FROMENT
047	OTHER CEREAL MEALS,FLOUR				0.4		0.8		2.8	AUTRES SEMOULES,FARINES
04701	CEREAL FLOUR(NON-WHEAT)				0.4		0.8		2.8	FARINES DE CEREALES
048	CEREAL ETC PREPARATIONS				8.9		12.8		3.6	PREPTNS A BASE CEREALES
0481	PREPD BREAKFAST FOOD ETC				6.8		9.8		0.5	CEREALES TRAVAILLEES
05	VEGETABLES AND FRUIT				2.2		9.5		3.9	LEGUMES ET FRUITS
054	VEG ETC FRSH,SMPLY PRSVD				1.5		8.8		3.3	LEGUMES FRAIS,CONG,SECS
0542	LEGUMINOUS VEGETBLES DRY				0.4		7.3		1.4	LEGUMES A COSSE SECS
06	SUGAR AND PREPS,HONEY				9.8		15.7		20.1	SUCRES ET PRODUITS
061	SUGAR AND HONEY				9.6		15.5		19.9	SUCRES ET MIEL
0611	RAW BEET AND CANE SUGAR				8.1		15.0		19.9	SUCRES BRUTS
081	*FEEDING STUFF FOR ANIML				2.7		3.4		3.9	NOURRITURE POUR ANIMAUX
0819	FOOD WASTE AND FEED NES				2.0		2.4		2.9	DECHETS,ALIMENTS NDA
08199	FODDER NES,INCL SWEETNED				2.0		2.4		2.9	PREPARATIONS FOURRAGERES
09	MISC EDIBLE PRODUCTS				2.6		3.7		4.2	PREP ALIMENTAIRES DIVERSES
098	EDIBLE PRODCTS,PREPS NES				2.3		3.3		3.9	PREP ALIMENTAIRES NDA
09809	MISC FOOD PREPRTIONS NES				1.5		2.0		2.9	PREP ALIMENTAIRES NDA
1	BEVERAGES AND TOBACCO				8.4		6.6		14.1	BOISSONS ET TABACS
11	BEVERAGES				7.2		5.7		6.3	BOISSONS
111	NON-ALCOHL BEVERAGES NES				3.2		2.3		2.9	BOISSONS NON ALCOOLIQUES
11102	FLAVORED WATERS NON-ALCO				2.8		1.9		1.9	LIMONADES,EAUX GAZEUSES
112	ALCOHOLIC BEVERAGES				4.1		3.4		3.5	BOISSONS ALCOOLIQUES
1121	WINE OF FRESH GRAPES ETC				2.6		2.3		1.9	VINS DE RAISINS FRAIS
12	TOBACCO AND MANUFACTURES				1.3		1.0		7.8	TABACS BRUTS FABRIQUES
121	TOBACCO UNMNFCTRD,REFUSE				1.0		0.7		7.4	TABACS BRUTS,DECHETS
2	CRUDE MATERLS,EXCL FUELS				10.4		29.5		18.4	MAT BRUTES NON COMESTIBLES
22	OIL SEEDS,OLEAGINOUS FRT				1.8		3.2		1.3	GRAINES,FRUITS OLEAGINEUX
222	SEEDS FOR'SOFT'FIXED OIL				1.7		1.4		1.1	GRAINES HUILES FIXES
2221	GROUNDNUTS,GREEN				1.7		1.3		1.1	ARACHIDES NON GRILLEES
251	*PULP AND WASTE PAPER				0.1		11.9		0.3	PATES A PAPIER,DECHETS
2516	CHEM WOOD PULP DISSOLVNG						11.7			PATES CHIMIQUES DE BOIS
26	TEXTILE FIBRES AND WASTE				4.2		7.3		7.5	FIBRES TEXTILES
269	WASTE OF TEXTILE FABRICS				3.9		7.1		6.9	FRIPERIE DRILLES,CHIFFONS
26901	BULK TEXT WSTE,OLD CLTHG				3.9		7.1		6.8	ART ET ACCESS D'HABILLEMENT
27	CRUDE FERTLZR,MINRLS NES				1.6		2.4		3.3	ENGRAIS MINERAUX BRUTS
278	OTHER CRUDE MINERALS				1.4		1.8		2.7	AUTRES MINERAUX BRUTS
2789	MINERALS CRUDE NES				1.3		1.5		2.6	MINERAUX BRUTS NDA
29	CRUDE ANIMAL,VEG MAT NES				0.8		2.4		1.2	MATIERES BRUTES ANIM,VEGET
292	CRUDE VEG MATERIALS NES				0.8		2.3		1.2	MAT BRUTES VEGETALES NDA
3	MINERAL FUELS ETC				76.5		72.0		90.0	COMBUSTIBLES MINERAUX LUB
33	PETROLEUM AND PRODUCTS				59.6		58.8		75.3	PETROLE ET DERIVES
334	PETROLEUM PRODUCTS,REFIN				58.6		57.9		74.1	PRODUITS RAFFINES
351	*ELECTRIC CURRENT				16.8		13.2		13.3	ENERGIE ELECTRIQUE
4	ANIMAL,VEGETABLE OIL,FAT				8.8		21.7		20.3	HUILES,GRAISSES ANIM,VEG
42	FIXED VEGETABLE OIL,FAT				5.4		17.5		15.2	HUILES VEGETALES FIXES
423	FIXED VEG OILS,SOFT				3.6		9.7		12.1	HUILES VEGET DOUCES FIXES
4236	SUNFLOWER SEED OIL				2.5		7.7		8.4	HUILE DE TOURNESOL
4239	OTH FIXED VEG OILS,SOFT				0.3		0.1		2.4	AUTRES HUILES FIXES
42391	RAPE,COLZA,MUSTARD OILS				0.3		0.1		2.4	H NAVETTE COLZA MOUTARDE
424	FIXED VEG OIL NONSOFT				1.8		7.8		3.2	AUTRES HUILES VEG FIXES
4241	LINSEED OIL				0.2		3.5		1.4	HUILE DE LIN
4242	PALM OIL				1.6		4.3		1.1	HUILE DE PALME
431	*PROCESD ANML VEG OIL,ET				2.0		2.7		3.3	HUILES,GRAISSES PREPAREES
4312	HYDROGENATED OIL,FAT				1.9		1.1		3.1	HUILES HYDROGENEES
5	CHEMCLS,RELATED PROD NES				70.8		72.9		62.0	PRODUITS CHIMIQUES
52	INORGANIC CHEMICALS				3.1		3.7		5.4	PROD CHIM INORGANIQUES
522	INORG ELEMNTS,OXIDES,ETC				1.5		2.4		3.9	ELEMENTS INORGANIQUES
53	DYES,TANNING,COLOUR PROD				2.4		2.9		2.8	PROD TEINTURE,COLORANTS
533	PIGMENTS,PAINTS,ETC				2.1		2.5		2.5	PIGMENTS,PEINTURES,VERNIS
541	*MEDICINAL,PHARM PRODUCT				33.2		42.6		22.7	PROD MEDICINAUX PHARMACEUT
5413	ANTIBIOTICS IN BULK				1.2		16.0		1.6	ANTIBIOTIQUES NDA
5417	MEDICAMENTS				29.1		19.4		19.4	MEDICAMENTS
54171	— CONTAINNG ANTIBIOTICS				29.1		19.4		19.4	MED CONTN ANTIBIOTIQUES
5419	PHARMACEUTICAL GOODS NES				1.4		6.1		1.2	PREP,ART PHARMACEUTIQUES
55	PERFUME,CLEANING ETC PRD				2.7		5.0		4.8	PROD POUR PARFUM,TOILETTE
554	SOAP,CLEANSING ETC PREPS				1.7		4.3		3.9	SAVONS,PRODUITS DETERSIFS
5541	SOAPS				1.2		3.3		2.5	SAVONS,PROD TENSIO-ACTIFS
562	*FERTILIZERS,MANUFACTURE				1.2		1.1		3.1	ENGRAIS MANUFACTURES
58	PLASTIC MATERIALS ETC				3.4		4.3		4.7	MAT PLAST ARTIFICIELLES
583	POLYMERIZATION ETC PRODS				2.8		3.2		3.9	PROD POLYMERISATION
59	CHEMICAL MATERIALS NES				24.3		12.5		16.3	MAT PROD CHIMIQUES NDA
591	PESTICIDES,DISINFECTANTS				20.9		9.4		11.7	DESINF,INSECT,FONG,HERB
598	MISCEL CHEM PRODUCTS NES				3.2		2.8		4.2	PROD DIV INDUST CHIM NDA
5989	CHEM PRODUCTS,PREPS NES				1.7		1.7		2.5	PROD PREP CHIMIQUES NDA
6	BASIC MANUFACTURES				65.4		91.5		136.2	ART MANUFACTURES
62	RUBBER MANUFACTURES NES				4.0		5.2		8.1	CAOUTCHOUC MANUFACTURE
625	RUBBER TYRES, TUBES ETC				2.6		3.8		5.8	PNEUS CAOUTCHOUC VULCANISE
6251	TYRES NEW FOR MOTOR CARS				2.1		3.0		4.9	PNEUS POUR VOITURES
63	WOOD,CORK MANUFACTRS NES				2.3		3.4		3.3	OUVRAGES LIEGE ET BOIS
635	WOOD MANUFACTURES NES				1.7		2.9		2.6	ART MANUF EN BOIS NDA
6353	BUILDERS WOODWRK,PREFABS				1.5		2.6		2.2	OUVRAGES DE MENUISERIE
64	PAPER,PAPERBOARD AND MFR				7.8		10.5		11.7	PAPIERS,CARTONS & OUVRAGES
641	PAPER AND PAPERBOARD				4.7		5.1		5.4	PAPIERS ET CARTONS
6411	NEWSPRINT				1.7		1.6		0.6	PAPIER JOURNAL
6412	PRINTG,WRITING PAPER NES				1.9		1.6		1.9	PAPIERS POUR L'IMPRESSION
64121	— UNCOATED				1.9		1.6		1.9	PAPIERS IMPRES NON COUCHES

4. Special Imports C.I.F. by Commodities according to the S.I.T.C. (Rev. 2) in million U.S. Dollars
Importations Spéciales C.A.F. par Produits d'après la C.T.C.I. (Rév. 2) en millions de Dollars E.U.

SITC CTCI	COMMODITY	1993 QUANTITY QUANTITE	1993 VALUE VALEUR	1994 QUANTITY QUANTITE	1994 VALUE VALEUR	1995 QUANTITY QUANTITE	1995 VALUE VALEUR	1996 QUANTITY QUANTITE	1996 VALUE VALEUR	PRODUIT
642	PAPER,ETC,PRECUT,ARTS OF				3.2		5.5		6.4	PAP,CARTONS DECOUPES
6421	PAPER ETC CONTAINERS				1.8		3.4		3.6	BOITES,SACS EMBALLAGES
65	TEXTILE YARN,FABRICS,ETC				12.0		11.6		13.8	FILS,TISSUS,ARTICLES TEXTILE
652	COTTON FABRICS,WOVEN				2.4		2.0		7.0	TISSUS DE COTON
6521	GREY WOVEN COTTON FABRIC				2.4		1.9		7.0	TISSUS COT ECRUS NON MERCER
65214	GREY WOVEN COTTON NES				2.1		1.5		3.6	AUT TISSUS 85% COTON ECRUS
65215	GREY WOVN COTN BLEND NES				0.3		0.5		3.4	AUT TIS MOINS 85% COT ECRUS
655	KNITTED,ETC FABRICS				4.0		0.1		0.3	ETOF BONNETERIE PIECES ETC
6552	OTHER KNIT ETC FAB NONEL				4.0		0.1		0.3	ETOF BON NON ELAS NON SYNT
658	TEXTILE ARTICLES NES				2.2		3.9		4.0	ART FACONNES MAT TEXTILES
6581	BAGS,SACKS OF TEXTILES				1.7		2.9		3.4	SACS EMBALLAGE TEXTILES
66	NONMETAL MINERAL MFS NES				11.1		16.8		26.5	ART MIN NON METALLIQUES
661	LIME,CEMENT,BLDG PRODS				6.0		11.1		17.3	CHAUX,CIMENTS MAT CONSTR
6612	CEMENT				4.6		9.8		16.8	CIMENTS HYDRAULIQUES
662	CLAY,REFRACTORY BLDG PRD				1.6		1.6		3.2	MAT CONST REFRACTAIRES
665	GLASSWARE				2.1		2.3		3.2	OUVRAGES EN VERRE
6658	GLASS ARTICLES NES				1.6		1.7		2.6	ARTICLES FAB EN VERRE NDA
66581	LABORATORY ETC GLASS				1.6		1.6		2.5	VERRERIE LABOR,HYG,PHAR ETC
67	IRON AND STEEL				7.9		8.0		10.6	FER ET ACIER
673	IRON,STEEL SHAPES ETC				2.5		3.1		4.1	BARRES,PROFIL FER,ACIER
6732	IRON,STEEL BARS ETC				1.5		1.7		3.2	BARRES FER,ACIER
678	IRON,STL TUBES,PIPES,ETC				3.1		3.2		2.6	TUBES,TUYAUX EN FONTE,FER
6785	IRON,STEEL TUBE FITTINGS				2.0		1.4		0.6	ACCESSOIRES DE TUYAUTERIE
68	NON-FERROUS METALS				3.3		2.1		5.8	METAUX NON FERREUX
686	ZINC				1.7		0.9		4.2	ZINC
6863	ZINC,ALLOYS WKD,INC DUST				1.5		0.4		3.0	ZINC ET ALLIAGES OUVRES
68632	ZINC SHEETS,STRIP,FOIL				1.1		0.4		3.0	PLANCHES,FEUILLES EN ZINC
69	METAL MANUFACTURES NES				17.1		34.1		56.7	ART MANUFACT EN METAL NDA
691	STRUCTURES AND PARTS NES				6.9		16.5		30.5	CONSTRUCT FER,ACIER,ALU
6911	STRUCTURES,PARTS IRN,STL				6.7		16.2		29.9	CONSTRUCT FER,ACIER,FONTE
693	WIRE PRODUCTS NON ELECTR				1.5		8.1		12.9	OUVRAGES FILS METALLIQUES
6931	WIRE CABLES, ROPES ETC				0.7		2.4		11.7	CORDAGES EN FILS DE FER
69313	ALUMNM CABLES, ROPES ETC				0.4		1.7		11.3	CORDAGES D'ALUMINIUM
6932	IRON,STEEL FENCING WIRE				0.4		4.7		0.4	RONCES DE FER OU ACIER
694	STL,COPPR NAILS,NUTS,ETC				0.9		1.2		2.8	CLOUS,VIS,ECROUS
69402	IRN,STL NUTS,BOLTS,ETC				0.8		1.0		2.7	BOULONS,VIS,ECROUS FER,AC
695	TOOLS				3.1		2.7		2.8	OUTILS A MAIN
699	BASE METAL MFRS NES				3.0		3.4		4.9	ART MANUFACTURES MET NDA
7	MACHINES,TRANSPORT EQUIP				192.9		259.9		252.5	MACHINES MATERIEL TRANSPORT
71	POWER GENERATING EQUIPMT				5.5		6.0		6.8	MACHINES GENERATRICES
713	INTRNL COMBUS PSTN ENGIN				2.8		2.4		2.1	MOTEURS EXPL COMB INT, PIECE
7131	AIRCRAFT PSTN ENGINS,PTS				2.4		2.0		1.8	MOTEURS EXPL P.AVIATION, PIE
71319	PTS NES OF ENGN OF 71311				2.3		1.8		1.3	PIECES POUR 713.11
716	ROTATING ELECTRIC PLANT				2.2		2.7		2.9	APP ELECTR ROTATIFS,PIECES
7162	AC MTRS,GENRTRS,GEN SETS				1.9		2.3		2.9	MOTEURS ELECTRIQUES
72	MACHS FOR SPCL INDUSTRYS				21.7		32.1		47.5	MAC SPECIALES POUR INDUST
721	AGRIC MACHY,EXC TRACTORS				5.3		4.2		10.3	MACHINES AGRICOLES
7212	HARVESTING ETC MACHINES				4.8		3.2		9.5	ENGINS POUR LA RECOLTE
722	TRACTORS NON-ROAD				5.6		7.6		6.1	TRACTEURS
7224	WHEELED TRACTORS NES				5.6		7.6		6.1	TRACTEURS A ROUES
723	CIVIL ENGNEERG EQUIP ETC				5.6		10.6		18.7	APPAREILS DE GENIE CIVIL
7234	CONST,MINING MACHNRY NES				5.6		10.6		18.7	MACH POUR LA CONST, MINES
72341	SELF-PROPELLD DOZERS,ETC				4.1		6.2		11.4	BULLDOZERS
72345	PILE DRIVERS,ETC				1.5		4.5		7.3	CHASSE-NEIGE
727	FOOD MACHRY NON-DOMESTIC				1.5		1.6		4.0	MACH INDUSTRIES ALIMENT
7272	OTH FOOD PROC MCHY,PARTS				1.5		1.6		4.0	AUT MACH IND ALIMENTAIRE
72722	INDUS FOOD PROC MACH NES				1.5		1.6		4.0	MACHINES BOULANGERIE
728	OTH MACHY FOR SPCL INDUS				2.4		6.7		5.3	AUT MACH IND PARTICULIERES
7283	OTHR MINERAL WORKG MACHY				1.0		3.0		3.0	MACH TRIER,CRIBLER,BROYER
7284	MACHY FOR SPCL INDUS NES				0.9		2.7		1.3	MACH SPEC IND PARTICUL.
73	METALWORKING MACHINERY				9.7		3.2		4.5	MACH TRAVAIL DES METAUX
736	METALWORKING MACH-TOOLS				5.8		2.3		1.8	MACH-OUTILS TRAVAIL METAUX
7362	METAL FORMING MACH-TOOLS				1.8		0.8		0.9	MACH-OUTILS DEFORM METAL
7367	OTH METALWRKG MACH-TOOLS				3.3		0.8		0.3	AUT MACH-OUT POUR METAUX
737	METALWORKING MACHNRY NES				4.0		0.9		2.8	MACH TRAV METAUX PIECES
7371	FOUNDRY EQUIPMNT,PTS NES				2.1					CONVERTISSEURS ACIERIE,PIEC
7373	WELDING,BRAZING,ETC MCHS				1.9		0.9		0.6	MACH SOUDAGE ETC PIECES
73732	ELECTRIC WELDERS,ETC				1.7		0.7		0.5	MACH ELECT POUR SOUDER
74	GENRL INDUSTRL MACHY NES				27.0		27.3		33.6	MACH APP INDUSTRIE
741	HEATING,COOLING EQUIPMNT				7.8		4.8		4.0	MACH CHAUFFAGE,PIECES
7413	INDUS FURNACES ETC,PARTS				3.0		0.7		0.9	FOURS IND,LABOR,PIECES
742	PUMPS FOR LIQUIDS ETC				5.4		5.3		6.2	POMPES MOTO-POMPES
7428	OTHER PUMPS FOR LIQUIDS				5.4		5.3		6.2	AUTRES POMPES POUR LIQ
743	PUMPS NES,CENTRFUGES ETC				3.2		3.7		3.2	POMPES COMPRES,VENT ETC
7431	PUMPS FOR GASES ETC				1.8		1.8		2.0	POMPES AIR A VIDE,COMPRES
744	MECHANICAL HANDLING EQU				6.3		8.6		14.6	EQUIP MANUTENTION PIECES
7441	FORK LIFT TRCKS,ETC,PTS				2.5		2.7		0.9	CHARIOTS POUR USINES ETC
7442	LIFTING,LOADING MACH NES				2.0		2.3		4.2	APP LEVAGE,MANUTENTION
7449	PTS NES OF MACHY OF 7442				1.9		3.7		9.6	PIECES DU 744.2
749	NONELEC MACH PTS,ACC NES				3.2		3.8		3.9	PIECES MACH NON ELEC NDA
75	OFFICE MACHNES,ADP EQUIP				5.7		7.2		8.8	MACH BUREAU TRAIT AUTOM
752	AUTOMTIC DATA PROC EQUIP				2.8		4.4		5.1	MACH TRAIT INFORMATION
7521	ANALOG,HYBRID COMPUTERS				2.8		4.4		5.1	MACH POUR TRAIT INFORMAT
76	TELECOMM,SOUND EQUIPMENT				13.3		14.6		8.6	EQUIPMENT DE TELECOM
763	SOUND RECORDRS,PHONOGRPH				2.9		1.2		1.0	PHONO,APP ENREGISTREMENT
7631	ELECTRIC GRAMOPHONES ETC				2.6		0.1		0.3	ELECTROPHON,TOURNE-DISQ
764	TELECOM EQPT,PTS,ACC NES				9.9		12.3		6.3	EQUIP TELECOM,PIECES
7641	LINE TELEPHONE,ETC EQUIP				5.0		9.1		3.6	APP TELEPHON PAR FIL
7643	TV,RADIO TRANSMITTRS ETC				3.8		2.0		1.9	APP EMET TELE RADIO
77	ELECTRIC MACHNRY NES ETC				23.8		48.0		53.5	MACH APP ELECT NDA
771	ELECTRIC POWER MACHY NES				0.9		2.6		4.9	MACH PROD,TRANS ELECTR
7712	OTH ELEC POWER MACHY NES				0.9		2.6		4.9	AUT APP PROD TRANSF ELEC
772	SWITCHGEAR ETC,PARTS NES				5.5		6.5		14.5	APP COUPURE,SECT ETC
7721	SWITCHGEAR ETC				5.5		6.5		14.5	APP COUPURE,SECTIONMNT
773	ELECTR DISTRIBUTNG EQUIP				2.6		21.6		17.4	EQUIPMT DISTRIBUTION ELECT
7731	INSULATED WIRE,CABLE ETC				2.4		16.8		11.0	FILS,CABLES ISOLES ELECT
7732	ELECTRC INSULATING EQUIP				0.2		4.8		6.5	EQUIP ISOL ELECTRIQUE
774	ELECTRO-MEDCL,XRAY EQUIP				5.1		7.9		5.7	APPAREILS MEDICAUX
7741	ELECTRO-MEDICAL EQUIPMNT				5.1		7.4		4.5	APP ELECTRICITE MEDICALE
775	HOUSEHOLD TYPE EQUIP NES				3.9		5.4		4.2	MACH,APP USAGE DOMESTQUE
7753	DOMSTC DISHWASHING MACHS				1.4		2.8		1.3	MACH A LAVER VAISSELLE

4. Special Imports C.I.F. by Commodities according to the S.I.T.C. (Rev. 2) in million U.S. Dollars
Importations Spéciales C.A.F. par Produits d'après la C.T.C.I. (Rév. 2) en millions de Dollars E.U.

SITC CTCI	COMMODITY	1993		1994		1995		1996		PRODUIT
		QUANTITY QUANTITE	VALUE VALEUR	QUANTITY QUANTITE	VALUE VALEUR	QUANTITY QUANTITE	VALUE VALEUR	QUANTITY QUANTITE	VALUE VALEUR	
778	ELECTRICAL MACHINERY NES				4.9		4.1		6.6	AUTRES MACH ELECT NDA
7781	BATTERIES,ACCUMULATORS				2.3		1.6		2.8	PILES ET ACCUMULATEURS
78	ROAD VEHICLES				80.7		100.0		84.7	VEHICULES ROUTIERS
782	LORRIES,SPCL MTR VEH NES				57.9		65.3		57.4	VEHICULES SPECIAUX,MARCH
7821	LORRIES,TRUCKS				56.2		62.3		53.2	VEHICULES TRANSP MARCHAND
7822	SPECIAL MOTOR VEHCLS NES				1.7		3.1		4.2	VEHICULES USAGES SPECIAUX
783	ROAD MOTOR VEHICLES NES				10.3		21.1		9.5	VEHICULES ROUTIERS NDA
7831	BUSES				10.3		21.1		9.5	VOITURES TRANSPORT COMMUN
784	MOTOR VEH PRTS,ACCES NES				6.3		7.0		7.6	PIECES 722,781,782,783
7849	OTHER MOTOR VEHCL PARTS				4.7		5.8		6.0	PIECES 722,781,782,783
785	CYCLES,ETC MOTRZD OR NOT				4.8		4.4		7.6	MOTOCYCLES SCOOTERS
7851	MOTORCYCLES ETC				4.1		2.2		1.7	MOTO VELO MOTEUR AUXIL
7852	CYCLES, ETC NON-MOTOR				0.5		1.3		5.1	VELOCIPEDES SANS MOTEUR
786	TRAILERS,NONMOTR VEH,NES				1.6		2.3		2.8	REMORQUES,CADRES,CONTAIN
7861	TRAILERS,TRANSP CONTAINR				1.6		2.3		2.8	REMORQUES TOUS VEHICULES
78611	HOUSING,CAMPING TRAILERS				1.6		2.2		2.8	REMORQUES POUR CAMPING
79	OTHR TRANSPORT EQUIPMENT				5.8		21.9		4.9	AUTRE MATERIEL TRANSPORT
791	RAILWAY VEHICLES				3.8		3.9		2.1	VEHIC MAT CHEMINS DE FER
7919	RY TRACK FIXT,ETC,PARTS				1.5		3.9		2.0	MATER FIXE VOIES FERREES
79199	PARTS NES OF 7911-7915				1.2		3.8		1.9	PIECES 791.1 ET 5
793	SHIPS AND BOATS ETC				1.4		18.0		2.4	NAVIRES BATEAUX,ETC
7932	SHIPS AND BOATS NES				1.1		17.2		2.4	NAVIRES ET BATEAUX
79322	TANKERS OF ALL KINDS				0.3		16.7		2.4	BATEAUX-CITERNES
8	MISC MANUFACTURED GOODS				21.9		30.2		42.8	ART MANUFACTURES DIVERS
812	*PLUMBG,HEATNG,LGHTNG EQ				1.4		1.9		2.6	APPAR SANITAIRES CHAUFFAGE
821	*FURNITURE,PARTS THEREOF				4.4		6.4		9.8	MEUBLES ET PIECES
8219	FURNITURE AND PARTS NES				3.5		5.2		8.4	AUTRES MEUBLES ET PIECES
82191	METAL FURNITURE NES				3.5		5.2		8.4	MEUBLES NDA EN METAL
84	CLOTHING AND ACCESSORIES				2.7		1.7		2.9	VETEMENTS
851	*FOOTWEAR				1.5		1.7		2.5	CHAUSSURES
87	PRECISION INSTRUMNTS NES				3.1		4.0		2.9	INSTRUM,APPAR SCIENT NDA
874	MEASURNG,CONTROLNG INSTR				2.1		2.7		2.5	INSTRUMENTS DE MESURE
89	MISC MANUFCTRD GOODS NES				7.9		13.0		19.9	ART MANUFACTURES DIVERS
892	PRINTED MATTER				1.9		2.6		7.7	IMPRIMES
8921	PRINTED BOOKS,GLOBES,ETC				1.1		1.5		6.2	LIVRES,BROCHURES,CARTES
893	ARTICLES OF PLASTIC NES				4.4		8.1		9.6	OUVRAGES EN MAT DIVIS 58
8931	PLSTC PACKG CONTNRS,LIDS				0.9		2.0		6.5	ART TRANSP EMBALLAGE ETC
8939	MISC PLASTIC ARTICLES				3.6		6.1		3.0	ART DIVERS EN MAT DIV 58
89399	OTHR PLASTC ARTICLES NES				3.2		5.5		2.4	AUT OUV MAT DIV 58
9	GOODS NOT CLASSD BY KIND				10.7		12.2		9.8	ART TRANSACT NON CLASSES
931	*SPECIAL TRANSACTIONS				10.6		10.9		9.8	TRANS.SPECIALES

5. Special Exports F.O.B. by Commodities according to the S.I.T.C. (Rev. 2) in million U.S. Dollars
Exportations Spéciales F.O.B. par Produits d'après la C.T.C.I. (Rév. 2) en millions de Dollars E.U.

SITC CTCI	COMMODITY	1993 QUANTITY QUANTITE	1993 VALUE VALEUR	1994 QUANTITY QUANTITE	1994 VALUE VALEUR	1995 QUANTITY QUANTITE	1995 VALUE VALEUR	1996 QUANTITY QUANTITE	1996 VALUE VALEUR	PRODUIT
	ALL COMMODITIES				164.0		174.3		226.1	TOUS PRODUITS
0	FOOD AND LIVE ANIMALS				100.8		106.2		150.1	ALIMENTS,ANIMAUX VIVANTS
02	DAIRY PRODCTS,BIRDS'EGGS				0.7		0.1		0.1	PRODUITS LAITIERS,OEUFS
022	MILK AND CREAM				0.7		0.1		0.1	LAIT ET CREME
0224	MILK,CREAM PRESERVED ETC				0.7		0.1		0.1	LAIT,CREME CONS,CONC
03	FISH AND PREPARATIONS				68.6		81.4		86.3	POISSONS ET PREPARATIONS
034	FISH,FRESH,CHILLED,FROZN				0.6		1.0			POISSON FRAIS, REFRIG,CONG
0341	FISH FRSH,CHLLD,EX FILLT				0.4		0.7			POISSON FRAIS,REFRIGERE
035	FISH SALTED,DRIED,SMOKED				0.1		0.9		0.1	POISSON SECHE,SALE,FUME
03502	COD(NOT IN FILLETS)DRIED				0.1		0.9		0.1	MORUE SECHEE,SALEE
036	SHELL FISH FRESH,FROZEN				68.1		79.5		86.2	CRUSTACES,MOLLUSQUES
04	CEREALS AND PREPARATIONS				1.1		0.7		2.2	CEREALES ET PRODUITS
044	MAIZE UNMILLED				0.7		0.7		2.2	MAIS NON MOULU
05	VEGETABLES AND FRUIT				17.9		14.7		46.0	LEGUMES ET FRUITS
054	VEG ETC FRSH,SMPLY PRSVD						0.1		1.2	LEGUMES FRAIS,CONG,SECS
0542	LEGUMINOUS VEGETBLES DRY						0.1		1.0	LEGUMES A COSSE SECS
057	FRUIT,NUTS,FRESH,DRIED				17.7		14.0		44.5	FRUITS FRAIS OU SECS
0571	ORANGES, MANDARINS ETC				1.3		1.2		0.9	ORANGES,MAND,CLEMENTINES
0577	NUTS EDIBLE,FRESH,DRIED				16.5		12.8		43.5	FRUITS A COQUES
058	FRUIT PRESERVED,PREPARED				0.2		0.6		0.4	CONSERVES DE FRUITS
0589	FRUIT PREPRD,PRESRVD,NES				0.2		0.6		0.4	FRUITS PREPARES CONSERV
06	SUGAR AND PREPS,HONEY				11.2		7.4		12.9	SUCRES ET PRODUITS
061	SUGAR AND HONEY				11.2		7.4		12.9	SUCRES ET MIEL
0611	RAW BEET AND CANE SUGAR				11.2		7.4		12.9	SUCRES BRUTS
07	COFFEE,TEA,COCOA,SPICES				0.6		0.1		0.1	CAFE,THE,CACAO,EPICES
074	TEA AND MATE				0.6		0.1		0.1	THE ET MATE
0741	TEA				0.6		0.1		0.1	THE
081	*FEEDING STUFF FOR ANIML				0.9		2.2		2.3	NOURRITURE POUR ANIMAUX
0812	BRAN,POLLARD,SHARPS,ETC				0.3		1.1		1.9	SONS
0813	OILCAKE AND OTH RESIDUES				0.7		1.1		0.5	TOURTEAUX
1	BEVERAGES AND TOBACCO				1.1		1.3		1.8	BOISSONS ET TABACS
12	TOBACCO AND MANUFACTURES				1.1		1.3		1.7	TABACS BRUTS FABRIQUES
121	TOBACCO UNMNFCTRD,REFUSE				1.1		1.2		0.9	TABACS BRUTS,DECHETS
122	TOBACCO,MANUFACTURED						0.1		0.9	TABACS FABRIQUES
2	CRUDE MATERLS,EXCL FUELS				24.9		37.8		31.5	MAT BRUTES NON COMESTIBLES
22	OIL SEEDS,OLEAGINOUS FRT				5.1		6.7		2.6	GRAINES,FRUITS OLEAGINEUX
223	SEEDS FOR OTH FIXED OILS				5.1		6.3		2.6	GRAINES AUTRES HUILES FIXES
24	CORK AND WOOD				2.8		8.1		7.4	LIEGE ET BOIS
247	OTH WOOD ROUGH,SQUARED				1.6		5.5		0.7	BOIS BRUTS EQUARRIS
2471	SAW–,VENEER–LOGS CONIFER				1.6		5.5		0.7	CONIFERES POUR SCIAGE,PLACAG
24711	— IN THE ROUGH				1.6		5.5		0.7	ECORCES OU DEGROSSIS
248	WOOD SHAPED,SLEEPERS				1.3		2.7		6.8	BOIS SIMPLEMENT TRAVAILLES
2481	RAILWAY SLEEPERS,TIES				0.3		0.5		4.9	TRAVERSES VOIES FERREES
2482	LUMBER SHAPED CONIFER				1.1		2.2		1.9	CONIFERES SCIES,RABOTES
24821	LUMBER SAWN ETC CONIFER				1.1		2.2		0.1	CONIFERES SCIES LONGITUD
24822	LUMBER PLANED ETC CONIFR						0.1		1.9	CONIFER RABOTES,RAINES
26	TEXTILE FIBRES AND WASTE				14.0		19.2		13.1	FIBRES TEXTILES
263	COTTON				13.9		18.9		12.8	COTON
2631	RAW COTTON,EXCL LINTERS				9.3		6.9		3.4	COTON EN MASSE
2633	COTTON WASTE,UNCOMBED				0.9					DECHETS DE COTON
2634	COTTON,CARDED OR COMBED				3.8		12.1		9.5	COTON CARDE OU PEIGNE
27	CRUDE FERTLZR,MINRLS NES				0.5		2.0		2.3	ENGRAIS MINERAUX BRUTS
278	OTHER CRUDE MINERALS				0.5		1.9		2.3	AUTRES MINERAUX BRUTS
2782	REFRACTORY MINERALS NES				0.2		1.7		1.0	ARGILE MINERAUX REFRACTAIRES
2783	COMMON SALT,ETC				0.3		0.2		1.4	SEL
28	METALLIFEROUS ORES,SCRAP				2.5		1.7		6.1	MINERAIS METAL,DECHETS
282	IRON AND STEEL SCRAP				0.9		1.5		2.8	FERRAILLES
28201	— OF PIG OR CAST IRON				0.9		1.5		2.8	FERRAILLES DE FONTE
287	BASE METAL ORES,CONC NES				1.5				0.6	MINERAIS METAUX COMMUNS
2873	ALUMINIUM ORES,ALUMINA				1.5				0.6	MINERAIS D'ALUMINIUM
28731	ALUMINIUM ORE,CONCNTRATE				1.5				0.6	MINERAIS D'ALUMINIUM
288	NONFERR METAL SCRAP NES				0.2		0.2		2.8	DECHETS NON FERREUX
2882	OTHER BASE MTL SCRAP NES				0.2		0.2		2.8	AUTRES DECHETS
28823	ALUMINIUM WSTE AND SCRAP				0.1		0.1		2.7	DECHETS D'ALUMINIUM
3	MINERAL FUELS ETC				14.8		3.6		2.9	COMBUSTIBLES MINERAUX LUB
33	PETROLEUM AND PRODUCTS				14.6		3.2		2.6	PETROLE ET DERIVES
334	PETROLEUM PRODUCTS,REFIN				14.6		3.2		2.6	PRODUITS RAFFINES
4	ANIMAL,VEGETABLE OIL,FAT				0.7		0.2		1.1	HUILES,GRAISSES ANIM,VEG
42	FIXED VEGETABLE OIL,FAT				0.6		0.2		1.1	HUILES VEGETALES FIXES
424	FIXED VEG OIL NONSOFT				0.6		0.2		1.1	AUTRES HUILES VEG FIXES
4241	LINSEED OIL				0.6		0.1		0.2	HUILE DE LIN
4243	COCONUT (COPRA) OIL						0.1		1.0	HJUILE DE COPRAH
5	CHEMCLS,RELATED PROD NES				0.2		0.6		0.9	PRODUITS CHIMIQUES
6	BASIC MANUFACTURES				10.9		11.4		5.8	ART MANUFACTURES
62	RUBBER MANUFACTURES NES				2.8		2.6		1.4	CAOUTCHOUC MANUFACTURE
625	RUBBER TYRES, TUBES ETC				2.8		2.5		1.3	PNEUS CAOUTCHOUC VULCANISE
6251	TYRES NEW FOR MOTOR CARS				2.6		2.1		1.2	PNEUS POUR VOITURES
63	WOOD,CORK MANUFACTRS NES				1.2		1.4		0.7	OUVRAGES LIEGE ET BOIS
634	VENEERS,PLYWOOD,ETC				1.1		1.2		0.4	PLACAGES,CONTRE–PLAQUES
6341	VENEER SHEETS ETC				1.0		0.6			BOIS SIMPLEMENT SCIES
6342	PLYWOOD OF WOOD SHEETS				0.1		0.6		0.4	BOIS CONTRE–PLAQUES
64	PAPER,PAPERBOARD AND MFR				1.1		0.9		0.5	PAPIERS,CARTONS & OUVRAGES
642	PAPER,ETC,PRECUT,ARTS OF				1.1		0.9		0.4	PAP,CARTONS DECOUPES
6421	PAPER ETC CONTAINERS				1.1		0.9		0.4	BOITES,SACS EMBALLAGES
65	TEXTILE YARN,FABRICS,ETC				4.2		1.5		1.6	FILS,TISSUS,ARTICLES TEXTILE
651	TEXTILE YARN				1.7		0.1		0.1	FILS TEXTILES
6513	COTTON YARN				1.7					FILS DE COTON
657	SPECIAL TXTL FABRC,PRODS				2.4		1.4		1.5	TISSUS SPECIAUX
6573	COATED ETC TEXTILES NES				2.0		0.9		1.3	TISSUS,ART MATIERE TEXT NDA
65733	RUBBERIZED TEXT NOT KNIT				1.9		0.7		1.3	TISSUS CAOUTCHOUTES
67	IRON AND STEEL				0.4		3.0		0.3	FER ET ACIER
676	RAILWY RAILS ETC IRN,STL						2.3			RAILS,ELEMENTS VOIES FERREE
67601	RAILWAY RAILS IRN,STL						2.3			RAILS,ELEMENTS FER,ACIER
69	METAL MANUFACTURES NES				0.9		1.5		0.9	ART MANUFACT EN METAL NDA
699	BASE METAL MFRS NES				0.2		1.0		0.1	ART MANUFACTURES MET NDA
6997	IRON,STEEL ARTICLES NES				0.1		0.9		0.1	OUV FONTE,FER,ACIER NDA
7	MACHINES,TRANSPORT EQUIP				5.4		8.4		26.1	MACHINES MATERIEL TRANSPORT
71	POWER GENERATING EQUIPMT				0.7		1.2		1.0	MACHINES GENERATRICES
713	INTRNL COMBUS PSTN ENGIN				0.4		0.9		0.6	MOTEURS EXPL COMB INT, PIECE
7131	AIRCRAFT PSTN ENGINS,PTS				0.4		0.8		0.6	MOTEURS EXPL P.AVIATION, PIE
71319	PTS NES OF ENGN OF 71311				0.2		0.8		0.3	PIECES POUR 713.11

5. Special Exports F.O.B. by Commodities according to the S.I.T.C. (Rev. 2) in million U.S. Dollars
Exportations Spéciales F.O.B. par Produits d'après la C.T.C.I. (Rév. 2) en millions de Dollars E.U.

SITC CTCI	COMMODITY	1993		1994		1995		1996		PRODUIT
		QUANTITY QUANTITE	VALUE VALEUR	QUANTITY QUANTITE	VALUE VALEUR	QUANTITY QUANTITE	VALUE VALEUR	QUANTITY QUANTITE	VALUE VALEUR	
72	MACHS FOR SPCL INDUSTRYS				1.2		1.1		9.6	MAC SPECIALES POUR INDUST
721	AGRIC MACHY,EXC TRACTORS				0.1		0.1		7.2	MACHINES AGRICOLES
7212	HARVESTING ETC MACHINES						0.1		7.2	ENGINS POUR LA RECOLTE
723	CIVIL ENGNEERG EQUIP ETC				0.8		0.8		0.6	APPAREILS DE GENIE CIVIL
7234	CONST,MINING MACHNRY NES				0.8		0.8		0.6	MACH POUR LA CONST, MINES
72341	SELF-PROPELLD DOZERS,ETC				0.7		0.5		0.4	BULLDOZERS
728	OTH MACHY FOR SPCL INDUS				0.2		0.2		1.5	AUT MACH IND PARTICULIERES
7283	OTHR MINERAL WORKG MACHY				0.1		0.1		1.2	MACH TRIER,CRIBLER,BROYER
73	METALWORKING MACHINERY				0.1		0.1		1.2	MACH TRAVAIL DES METAUX
736	METALWORKING MACH-TOOLS						0.1		1.0	MACH-OUTILS TRAVAIL METAUX
7368	WORK,TOOL HOLDERS ETC								1.0	PORTE-PIECES DIVISEURS
74	GENRL INDUSTRL MACHY NES				1.3		1.9		5.5	MACH APP INDUSTRIE
743	PUMPS NES,CENTRFUGES ETC				0.3		0.3		2.2	POMPES COMPRES,VENT ETC
7431	PUMPS FOR GASES ETC				0.3		0.3		1.1	POMPES AIR A VIDE,COMPRES
7435	CENTRIFUGES						0.1		1.1	CENTRIF,ESSOREUSES
744	MECHANICAL HANDLING EQU				0.4		0.8		0.5	EQUIP MANUTENTION PIECES
7442	LIFTING,LOADING MACH NES				0.3		0.6		0.1	APP LEVAGE,MANUTENTION
745	NONELEC MACHY,TOOLS NES				0.1		0.2		2.5	AUT MACH NON ELEC,PIECES
7452	OTH NONELEC MCHS,PTS NES				0.1		0.2		2.5	AUT MACH NON ELEC,PIECES
74521	CALENDERING MACHINES ETC								2.5	CALANDRES,LAMINOIRS ETC
76	TELECOMM,SOUND EQUIPMENT				0.1		0.3		1.3	EQUIPMENT DE TELECOM
764	TELECOM EQPT,PTS,ACC NES				0.1		0.2		1.3	EQUIP TELECOM,PIECES
7641	LINE TELEPHONE,ETC EQUIP				0.1		0.1		1.0	APP TELEPHON PAR FIL
78	ROAD VEHICLES				1.9		2.7		2.4	VEHICULES ROUTIERS
782	LORRIES,SPCL MTR VEH NES				1.8		2.6		1.2	VEHICULES SPECIAUX,MARCH
7821	LORRIES,TRUCKS				1.7		2.1		1.2	VEHICULES TRANSP MARCHAND
784	MOTOR VEH PRTS,ACCES NES				0.1		0.1		1.0	PIECES 722,781,782,783
7849	OTHER MOTOR VEHCL PARTS				0.1		0.1		1.0	PIECES 722,781,782,783
79	OTHR TRANSPORT EQUIPMENT				0.2		0.8		5.0	AUTRE MATERIEL TRANSPORT
791	RAILWAY VEHICLES				0.1		0.2		3.4	VEHIC MAT CHEMINS DE FER
7915	FRT,MAINT CARS NOT POWRD						0.1		3.4	WAGONS DE SERVICE
79152	RAILWAY FREIGHT CARS NES						0.1		3.4	WAGONS MARCHANDISES
792	AIRCRAFT ETC				0.1		0.6		0.1	APP NAVIGATION AERIENNE
793	SHIPS AND BOATS ETC				0.1		0.1		1.6	NAVIRES BATEAUX,ETC
7932	SHIPS AND BOATS NES						0.1		1.6	NAVIRES ET BATEAUX
79322	TANKERS OF ALL KINDS						0.1		1.6	BATEAUX-CITERNES
8	MISC MANUFACTURED GOODS				2.1		3.0		5.6	ART MANUFACTURES DIVERS
84	CLOTHING AND ACCESSORIES				1.4		2.0		2.1	VETEMENTS
843	WOMENS OUTERWEAR NONKNIT				0.7		0.7		0.1	VET DESSUS FEMMES MAT TEX
8432	— SUITS AND COSTUMES				0.6		0.2		0.1	COSTUMES-TAIL MAT TEXIL
844	UNDER GARMENTS NOT KNIT				0.1		0.8		1.3	VETEMENT DESSOUS MAT TEX
8441	— MENS SHIRTS				0.1		0.8		1.3	CHEMISES HOMMES MAT TEXT
846	UNDER GARMENTS KNITTED				0.1		0.3		0.8	SOUS VETS DE BONNETERIE
8462	— OF COTTON NON ELASTIC				0.1		0.3		0.8	SOUS-VET BONNET COTON
84621	—— MENS SHIRTS						0.1		0.8	CHEMISES DE COTON
89	MISC MANUFCTRD GOODS NES				0.4		0.7		2.8	ART MANUFACTURES DIVERS
892	PRINTED MATTER						0.1		1.9	IMPRIMES
8928	PRINTED MATTER NES						0.1		1.9	IMPRIMES NDA
89283	UNISSUED BANKNOTES ETC						0.1		1.9	TIMBRES-POSTE FISCAUX
893	ARTICLES OF PLASTIC NES				0.2		0.4		0.8	OUVRAGES EN MAT DIVIS 58
8939	MISC PLASTIC ARTICLES				0.1		0.3		0.8	ART DIVERS EN MAT DIV 58
89394	PLASTC OFFICE,SCHOOL SUP				0.1		0.2		0.7	ART BUREAU MAT DIV 58
9	GOODS NOT CLASSD BY KIND				3.7		2.3		0.7	ART TRANSACT NON CLASSES
931	*SPECIAL TRANSACTIONS				1.1		0.2		0.1	TRANS.SPECIALES
971	*GOLD,NON MONETARY NES				2.6		2.1		0.6	OR NON MONETAIRE
97101	NONMON GLD UNWRT,SEMIMFD				2.6		2.1		0.6	OR,ALLIAGES D'OR BRUTS

1. HISTORICAL SERIES, 1962–1997 GENERAL TRADE, IMPORTS C.I.F., EXPORTS F.O.B.
SERIES HISTORIQUES, 1962–1997 COMMERCE GENERAL, IMPORTATIONS C.A.F., EXPORTATIONS F.O.B

YEAR ANNEE	VALUE IN MILLION KYATS VALEUR EN MILLION KYATS MERCHANDISE –MARCHANDISE		GOLD –OR		CONVERSION FACTORS U.S. CENTS PER KYAT FACTEURS DE CONVERSION CENTS E.U. PAR KYAT		INDEX NUMBERS –INDICES QUANTUM		UNIT VALUE VALEUR UNITAIRE	
	IMPORTS	EXPORTS	IMPORTS	EXPORTS	IMPORTS	EXPORTS	IMPORTS	EXPORTS	IMPORTS	EXPORTS
1962	1042.00	1263.00			21.0000	21.0000				
1963	1115.30	1288.00			21.0000	21.0000				
1964	1292.70	1126.00			21.0000	21.0000				
1965	1177.90	1076.00			21.0000	21.0000				
1966	751.90	934.00			21.0000	21.0000				
1967	741.20	590.30			21.0000	21.0000				
1968	858.70	529.40			21.0000	21.0000				
1969	784.80	629.10			21.0000	21.0000				
1970	807.00	515.80			21.0000	21.0000				
1971	933.30	609.60			21.0000	21.0000				
1972	866.63	654.70			18.3404	18.3379				
1973	702.70	698.60			20.3605	20.4048				
1974	1047.20	958.40			20.6012	20.5788				
1975	1612.60	1104.60			15.4769	15.5273				
1976	1311.11	1304.39			14.7860	14.7724				
1977	1946.50	1474.70			14.0539	14.0574				
1978	2240.40	1608.40			14.6056	14.5567				
1979	2116.00	2548.80			15.0679	15.0664				
1980	2337.30	3122.70			15.1222	15.1234		100		136
1981	2702.50	3352.70			13.8019	13.7660		99		151
1982	3178.10	3040.00			12.8610	12.8609		114		126
1983	2150.80	3039.40			12.4487	12.4396		124		123
1984	2016.20	2512.00			11.8483	11.9676		118		130
1985	2401.50	2575.90			11.8251	11.8041		100		133
1986	2245.20	2116.50			13.5609	13.5967		113		112
1987	1785.60	1449.80			15.0338	15.0782		82		94
1988	1538.00	1051.40			15.8628	15.7500		53		92
1989	1280.50	1410.40			14.9257	14.9048		72		112
1990	1709.40	2037.00			15.7995	15.9544		100		100
1991	4058.80	2633.00			15.9192	15.9275		97		101
1992	3971.00	3241.10			16.4040	16.3974		108		88
1993	5007.00	3609.40			16.2624	16.2390		149		81
1994	5285.90	4776.70			16.6127	16.5859		145		87
1995	7564.20	4825.80			17.6448	17.6383		151		136
1996	8032.00	4419.50			16.8741	16.8441		104		131
1997	14142.30	5415.80			15.9886	15.9969		110		132

2. IMPORTS BY BROAD ECONOMIC CATEGORY AND EXPORTS BY INDUSTRIAL ORIGIN. (PERCENTAGE OF TOTAL VALUE)
IMPORTATIONS PAR CATEGORIES ECONOMIQUES ET EXPORTATIONS PAR BRANCHE D'ACTIVITE.(EN POURCENTAGE DE LA VALEUR TOTALE)

IMPORTS – IMPORTATIONS

	1990	1991	1992	1993	1994	1995	1996
TOTAL IMPORTS–IMPORTATIONS TOTALES		100.	100.				
1 FOOD BEV–ALIMENTATION BOISSONS		12.2	14.2				
11 PRIMARY–PRODUITS DE BASE		0.6	2.2				
111 FOR INDUSTRY–POUR L'INDUSTRIE		0.0	0.1				
112 FOR HOUSEHOLDS–POUR LES MENAGES		0.5	2.1				
12 PROCESSED–PRODUITS ELABORES		11.6	12.0				
121 FOR INDUSTRY–POUR L'INDUSTRIE		7.3	10.2				
122 FOR HOUSEHOLDS–POUR LES MENAGES		4.3	1.8				
2 IND SUPPLIES–APPROV INDUSTRIELS		31.9	34.4				
21 PRIMARY–PRODUITS DE BASE		0.4	0.4				
22 PROCESSED–PRODUITS ELABORES		31.5	34.0				
3 FUELS–COMBUSTIBLES		3.3	2.2				
31 PRIMARY–PRODUITS DE BASE		1.5	0.0				
32 PROCESSED–PRODUITS ELABORES		1.8	2.2				
321 MOTOR SPIRIT–ESSENCE		0.1	2.2				
322 OTHER–AUTRES		1.7	0.0				
4 MACHINERY–EQUIPEMENT		16.7	12.7				
41 CAPITAL EQUIPMENT–MACHINES		15.1	10.9				
42 PARTS–PIECES ACCESSOIRES		1.7	1.8				
5 TRANSPORT–TRANSPORT		19.0	25.5				
51 PASSENGER CARS–AUTOMOBILES		3.2	2.1				
52 OTHER–AUTRES		9.2	10.4				
521 INDUSTRIAL–INDUSTRIELS		6.9	8.5				
522 NON INDUSTRIAL–NON INDUSTRIEL		2.3	1.9				
53 PARTS–PIECES ACCESSOIRES		6.7	13.1				
6 CONSUM GOODS–BIENS CONSOMMATION		15.8	10.9				
61 DURABLE–DURABLES		4.0	5.4				
62 SEMI DURABLE–SEMI DURABLES		6.9	2.7				
63 NON DURABLE–NON DURABLES		4.9	2.7				
7 GOODS NES–BIENS NDA		1.0	0.1				

EXPORTS – EXPORTATIONS

	1990	1991	1992	1993	1994	1995	1996
TOTAL EXPORTS–EXPORTATIONS TOTALES		100.	100.				
1 AGRICULTURE		71.1	72.9				
2 MINING QUARRY–INDUS EXTRACTIVES		3.2	4.3				
3 MANUFACTURING–IND MANUFACTUR		25.7	22.8				
31 FOOD BEV TOBACCO–ALIM BOISS TAB		13.9	10.4				
32 TEXTILES–INDUSTRIES TEXTILES		3.6	3.6				
33 WOOD & PRODUCTS–BOIS & PRODUITS		2.6	4.5				
34 PAPER & PRODUCTS–PAPIER & PRODT		0.0	0.1				
35 CHEMICALS–INDUSTRIES CHIMIQUES		1.0	0.3				
36 NON METAL MIN–MIN NON METAL		0.2	0.0				
37 BASIC METAL–IND METAL BASE		0.3	0.3				
38 METAL MANUF–MANUF METAL		2.6	2.7				
39 OTH MANUF IND–AUTRES MANUF		1.5	0.7				

3. TRADE BY PRINCIPAL COUNTRIES OF ORIGIN AND DESTINATION (VALUE IN MILLION U.S. DOLLARS)
ECHANGES SELON LES PRINCIPAUX PAYS D'ORIGINE ET DE DESTINATION (VALEUR EN MILLIONS DE DOLLARS EU)

COUNTRIES–PAYS	GENERAL IMPORTS C.I.F. IMPORTATIONS GENERALES C.A.F				
	1992	1993	1994	1995	1996
World	618.4	1288.5	1384.2	1817.7	1914.0
Africa	11.8	3.4	1.2	22.1	
Americas	38.5	48.7	19.5	24.3	94.6
– Northern America	37.2	48.6	18.5	19.7	94.6
– LAIA	0.3	0.1	0.9	4.6	
– CACM	0.3				
– Caribbean	0.7				
– Rest of America	0.0				
Asia excl fmr USSR	513.4	1105.0	1186.1	1286.2	1543.4
– Middle East	15.2	1.8	1.0	1.5	
Asia former USSR					
Europe excl fmr USSR	51.0	87.1	79.2	86.1	71.4
– European Union	40.4	76.6	61.1	66.5	50.2
– Eastern Europe	5.3	2.8	1.5	1.1	
– Rest of Europe	5.3	7.8	16.6	18.5	21.1
Europe former USSR	1.9		0.6	2.7	
Oceania	1.3	9.2	15.9	18.9	5.1
Other	0.5			30.0	
Japan/Japon	247.0	328.5	326.1	346.3	430.9
Singapore/Singapour	92.5	133.4	202.0	214.5	358.2
China/Chine	16.7	205.1	169.3	179.9	180.1
Thailand/Thaïlande	11.6	140.7	137.9	146.5	182.2
Malaysia/Malaisie	53.4	92.3	129.9	138.0	143.0
Korea, Republic of	28.2	47.6	65.6	69.7	65.1
India/Inde	12.1	45.8	51.3	54.5	98.8
Indonesia/Indonésie	19.0	52.3	53.2	56.5	49.9
USA/Etats–Unis d'Amer	35.4	46.0	17.0	18.0	94.6
China, Hong Kong SAR	6.4	21.9	42.0	44.6	25.2
Germany/Allemagne	18.5	40.3	22.2	23.5	18.8
Switzerland,Liechtenst.	5.0	7.6	7.9	8.4	21.1
France, Monaco	4.4	10.4	7.7	8.2	17.8
Australia/Australie	1.0	9.2	15.9	16.9	5.1
Bangladesh	4.8	29.8	2.3	2.4	8.6
United Kingdom	7.9	8.4	7.2	7.7	5.4
Areas n.e.s.	0.5			30.0	
Other Asia n.e.s.	3.0			26.0	
Netherlands/Pays–Bas	3.8	5.7	8.1	8.6	2.0
Northern Africa n.e.s.				20.9	
Yugoslavia/Yougoslavie	0.0	0.1	8.6	9.1	
Italy/Italie	0.8	6.1	2.5	2.7	2.5
Turkey/Turquie	10.4	1.6			
Belgium–Luxembourg	2.2	0.7	2.9	3.0	1.6
Pakistan	0.2	4.9	1.5	1.6	0.6
Sweden/Suède	0.8	2.1	2.5	2.7	0.4
Denmark/Danemark	0.9	0.7	2.7	2.9	1.0
Canada	1.7	2.6	1.6	1.7	
Israel/Israël	2.6	0.5	1.8	1.9	
Morocco/Maroc	0.0	3.4	1.1	1.2	
Philippines	0.0	0.4	2.2	2.3	0.8
Ireland/Irlande	0.7	1.1	1.4	1.5	0.5
Russian Federation	1.9		0.6	2.7	
Mali	5.1				
Iran (Islamic Rep of)	2.3	0.1	1.0	1.1	
Portugal			1.8	1.9	
LAIA n.e.s.				3.6	
Poland/Pologne	2.5	0.0	0.1	0.1	
Austria/Autriche	0.1	0.3	1.1	1.1	
Greece/Grèce	0.2	0.4	0.9	1.0	

COUNTRIES–PAYS	GENERAL EXPORTS F.O.B. EXPORTATIONS GENERALES F.O.B.				
	1992	1993	1994	1995	1996
Monde	449.4	686.6	896.5	953.8	883.0
Afrique	24.0	4.6	1.7	51.4	3.9
Amériques	12.4	26.1	47.1	50.2	44.9
– Amérique du Nord	12.3	26.1	47.1	50.2	44.9
– ALAI	0.0				
– MCAC	0.0				
– Caraïbes					
– Autre Amérique				0.1	
Asie anc. URSS exclus	389.5	573.2	684.6	728.7	724.3
– Moyen–Orient	7.7	2.4	2.7	3.1	1.3
Asie ancienne URSS					
Europe anc. URSS exclus	19.6	25.6	19.2	17.9	38.8
– Union Européenne	18.2	23.8	19.0	17.7	38.2
– Europe de l'Est	0.0				
– Autre de l'Europe	1.4	1.7	0.2	0.2	0.7
Europe ancienne URSS				7.0	0.1
Océanie	2.6	1.8	1.8	2.2	5.0
Autre	1.3			96.3	
Singapore/Singapour	105.9	133.1	146.5	155.9	159.1
India/Inde	100.6	103.1	115.3	122.7	160.7
Thailand/Thaïlande	22.7	119.7	90.0	95.8	93.7
Indonesia/Indonésie	2.3	11.5	139.8	148.7	23.9
China, Hong Kong SAR	56.1	73.6	44.6	47.5	60.9
Japan/Japon	33.2	30.5	43.4	46.2	64.4
China/Chine	1.3	34.1	46.0	49.0	47.5
USA/Etats–Unis d'Amer	12.1	24.8	45.3	48.2	43.4
Malaysia/Malaisie	9.7	16.0	16.9	18.0	51.5
Areas n.e.s.	1.3			96.3	
Pakistan	28.4	18.5	13.5	14.4	18.2
Other Africa n.e.s.	7.5			49.5	
Bangladesh	1.7	15.3	6.1	6.5	18.3
Sri Lanka	12.9	7.3	11.0	11.8	0.3
Korea, Republic of	4.5	5.7	6.6	7.0	8.9
Germany/Allemagne	11.2	8.3	3.4	3.7	5.2
United Kingdom	1.7	3.3	4.5	4.8	10.4
Netherlands/Pays–Bas	3.2	2.7	1.4	1.5	6.5
France, Monaco	0.3	0.8	2.7	2.9	8.6
Cote d'Ivoire	5.6	4.6	1.7	1.8	
Australia/Australie	2.6	1.8	1.8	1.9	5.0
Philippines	0.1	0.4	0.4	0.4	10.7
Maldives	2.1	2.1	1.4	1.5	4.9
Italy/Italie	0.4	3.5	2.6	1.6	3.1
Russian Federation				7.0	0.1
Canada	0.3	1.3	1.9	2.0	1.5
Kuwait/ Koweït		2.0	2.3	2.4	
Mauritius/Maurice	4.4				2.2
Yemen/Yémen	5.6				
Belgium–Luxembourg	0.9	0.8	0.8	0.8	2.2
Sweden/Suède	0.2	1.3	1.8	1.9	0.1
Spain/Espagne	0.0	1.8	1.5	0.3	1.0
Kenya	3.6				
Switzerland,Liechtenst.	1.4	1.7	0.2	0.2	0.1
Denmark/Danemark	0.0	1.3	0.3	0.3	0.9
Sierra Leone		0.0	0.0	0.0	1.6
Oman	1.4				
United Arab Emirates	0.7	0.4	0.1	0.0	0.1
Iran (Islamic Rep of)					1.1
Ghana	0.9				

(VALUE AS PERCENTAGE OF WORLD TOTAL)(VALEURS EN POURCENTAGE DU TOTAL MONDIAL)

	1987	1988	1989	1990	1991	1992	1993	1994	1995	1996
Africa		0.3	0.1	0.4	0.6	1.9	0.3	0.1	1.2	
Americas		1.5	2.1	12.6	3.3	6.2	3.8	1.4	1.3	4.9
– Northern America		1.5	1.9	12.5	3.2	6.0	3.8	1.3	1.1	4.9
– LAIA		0.0	0.1	0.1	0.1	0.0	0.0	0.1	0.3	
– CACM					0.0	0.1				
– Caribbean					0.0	0.1				
– Rest of America						0.0				
Asia excl fmr USSR		71.3	73.7	70.6	81.0	83.0	85.8	85.7	70.8	80.6
– Middle East		0.1	0.0	0.1	0.1	2.5	0.1	0.1	0.1	
Asia former USSR										
Europe excl fmr USSR		21.9	23.9	13.8	13.4	8.2	6.8	5.7	4.7	3.7
– European Union		18.9	21.8	11.2	11.3	6.5	5.9	4.4	3.7	2.6
– Eastern Europe		0.0	1.0	0.3	0.8	0.9	0.2	0.1	0.1	
– Rest of Europe		3.0	1.1	2.3	1.2	0.9	0.6	1.2	1.0	1.1
Europe former USSR		0.0	0.0	0.0	0.0	0.3		0.0	0.1	
Oceania		0.8	0.2	2.6	1.7	0.2	0.7	1.1	1.0	0.3
Other		0.0				0.1			1.7	
Japan/Japon		33.2	23.8	16.3	21.9	39.9	25.5	23.6	19.1	22.5
Singapore/Singapour		5.7	9.3	9.6	12.4	15.0	10.4	14.6	11.8	18.7
China/Chine		27.0	15.3	21.8	16.8	2.7	15.9	12.2	9.9	9.4
Thailand/Thaïlande			16.5	10.0	14.9	1.9	10.9	10.0	8.1	9.5
Malaysia/Malaisie		0.9	2.4	6.9	7.2	8.6	7.2	9.4	7.6	7.5
Korea, Republic of		2.8	3.4	3.6	2.6	4.6	3.7	4.7	3.8	3.4
India/Inde		0.6	1.4	0.7	2.8	2.0	3.6	3.7	3.0	5.2
Indonesia/Indonésie		0.2	0.3	0.3	1.0	3.1	4.1	3.8	3.1	2.6
USA/Etats–Unis d'Amer		1.4	1.8	12.3	3.1	5.7	3.6	1.2	1.0	4.9
China, Hong Kong SAR		0.4	0.3	0.6	0.5	1.0	1.7	3.0	2.5	1.3

	1987	1988	1989	1990	1991	1992	1993	1994	1995	1996
Afrique		1.5	2.8	1.8	3.1	5.3	0.7	0.2	5.4	0.4
Amériques		0.5	0.4	0.7	1.1	2.8	3.8	5.3	5.3	5.1
– Amérique du Nord		0.5	0.4	0.2	0.5	2.7	3.8	5.3	5.3	5.1
– ALAI				0.5	0.7	0.0				
– MCAC						0.0				
– Caraïbes										
– Autre Amérique									0.0	
Asie anc. URSS exclus		86.7	85.4	94.1	93.3	86.7	83.5	76.4	76.4	82.0
– Moyen–Orient		0.7	1.8	0.4	0.5	1.7	0.4	0.3	0.3	0.1
Asie ancienne URSS										
Europe anc. URSS exclus		3.5	5.8	3.1	2.4	4.4	3.7	2.1	1.9	4.4
– Union Européenne		3.5	5.2	3.1	2.2	4.0	3.5	2.1	1.9	4.3
– Europe de l'Est			0.0			0.0				
– Autre de l'Europe		0.0	0.6	0.0	0.3	0.3	0.3	0.0	0.0	0.1
Europe ancienne URSS		0.0							0.7	0.0
Océanie		0.0	0.0	0.0	0.0	0.6	0.3	0.2	0.2	0.6
Autre		7.8	5.5	0.4	0.0	0.3			10.1	
Singapore/Singapour		6.1	9.1	28.6	23.3	23.6	19.4	16.3	16.3	18.0
India/Inde		16.9	12.9	17.7	11.0	22.4	15.0	12.9	12.9	18.2
Thailand/Thaïlande		10.2	14.9	13.1	19.6	5.1	17.4	10.0	10.0	10.6
Indonesia/Indonésie			0.1		1.8	0.5	1.7	15.6	15.6	2.7
China, Hong Kong SAR		3.9	6.4	8.4	7.4	12.5	10.7	5.0	5.0	6.9
Japan/Japon		3.5	4.6	7.5	6.5	7.4	4.4	4.8	4.8	7.3
China/Chine		43.0	28.1	13.4	15.0	0.3	5.0	5.1	5.1	5.4
USA/Etats–Unis d'Amer		0.5	0.4	0.1	0.4	2.7	3.6	5.1	5.1	4.9
Malaysia/Malaisie		0.3	0.5	1.4	1.3	2.2	2.3	1.9	1.9	5.8
Areas n.e.s.		7.7	5.5	0.2	0.0	0.3			10.1	

4. General Imports C.I.F. by Commodities according to the S.I.T.C. (Rev. 2) in million U.S. Dollars
Importations Générales C.A.F. par Produits d'après la C.T.C.I. (Rév. 2) en millions de Dollars E.U.

SITC CTCI	COMMODITY	1993		1994		1995		1996		PRODUIT
		QUANTITY QUANTITE	VALUE VALEUR	QUANTITY QUANTITE	VALUE VALEUR	QUANTITY QUANTITE	VALUE VALEUR	QUANTITY QUANTITE	VALUE VALEUR	
	ALL COMMODITIES		1288.6		1384.3		1817.7		1914.0	TOUS PRODUITS
0	FOOD AND LIVE ANIMALS		26.8		77.0		62.8		42.2	ALIMENTS,ANIMAUX VIVANTS
0224	MILK,CREAM PRESERVED ETC						23.8		11.2	LAIT,CREME CONS,CONC
02249	MILK(EX DRY) PRSVD,SWEET		11.6		17.3					LAIT CONS,CONC SUCRE
04601	FLOUR OF WHEAT OR MESLIN	W 24	0.8	W 61	17.7		16.2		9.3	FARINE DE FROMENT
1	BEVERAGES AND TOBACCO		5.9		5.8		13.7		18.0	BOISSONS ET TABACS
12	TOBACCO AND MANUFACTURES		0.6		0.5		8.0		4.1	TABACS BRUTS FABRIQUES
2	CRUDE MATERLS,EXCL FUELS		4.2		8.4		8.3		38.6	MAT BRUTES NON COMESTIBLES
3	MINERAL FUELS ETC		53.4		47.2		37.9		83.7	COMBUSTIBLES MINERAUX LUB
32	COAL,COKE AND BRIQUETTES		5.4		0.7		1.4		0.5	HOUILLES,COKES,BRIQUETTES
334	PETROLEUM PRODUCTS,REFIN						5.7		77.2	PRODUITS RAFFINES
33525	MINERAL TAR OILS ETC NES				37.6					AUTRES PRODUITS NDA
4	ANIMAL,VEGETABLE OIL,FAT		86.1		133.8		210.8		67.7	HUILES,GRAISSES ANIM,VEG
42	FIXED VEGETABLE OIL,FAT						208.9		66.1	HUILES VEGETALES FIXES
5	CHEMCLS,RELATED PROD NES		171.3		100.8		352.2		164.2	PRODUITS CHIMIQUES
5146	OXYGEN–FNCT AMINO–CMPNDS		25.1		26.0					COMP AMINES FONCT OXYGEN
53	DYES,TANNING,COLOUR PROD		7.7		7.6					PROD TEINTURE,COLORANTS
532	DYES NES,TANNING PROD						17.1		12.5	EXTRAITS TEINTURE,TANNAGE
541	*MEDICINAL,PHARM PRODUCT		14.0		13.3		19.1		22.1	PROD MEDICINAUX PHARMACEUT
5541	SOAPS		3.7		4.9					SAVONS,PROD TENSIO–ACTIFS
562	*FERTILIZERS,MANUFACTURE	W 4	21.0	W 4	4.9		23.1		12.1	ENGRAIS MANUFACTURES
6	BASIC MANUFACTURES		220.2		242.1		285.1		382.9	ART MANUFACTURES
62	RUBBER MANUFACTURES NES		13.9		12.6		15.5		21.4	CAOUTCHOUC MANUFACTURE
64	PAPER,PAPERBOARD AND MFR		13.6		7.8		27.0		22.7	PAPIERS,CARTONS & OUVRAGES
652	COTTON FABRICS,WOVEN		13.5		23.5		18.0		11.4	TISSUS DE COTON
653	WOVN MAN–MADE FIB FABRIC		1.9		4.7		8.1		8.7	TISSUS FIBRES SYNTH,ARTIF
661	LIME,CEMENT,BLDG PRODS						23.9		44.3	CHAUX,CIMENTS MAT CONSTR
6612	CEMENT		11.4		17.8					CIMENTS HYDRAULIQUES
699	BASE METAL MFRS NES		110.3		74.2					ART MANUFACTURES MET NDA
7	MACHINES,TRANSPORT EQUIP		405.2		440.8		529.4		517.7	MACHINES MATERIEL TRANSPORT
77	ELECTRIC MACHNRY NES ETC		71.0		93.3		105.6		100.2	MACH APP ELECT NDA
8	MISC MANUFACTURED GOODS		51.1		59.2		43.8		39.7	ART MANUFACTURES DIVERS
87	PRECISION INSTRUMNTS NES						16.6		14.9	INSTRUM,APPAR SCIENT NDA
8745	MEAS,CONTRL,SCI INST NES		6.9		8.3					APP SCIENT MESURE NDA
9	GOODS NOT CLASSD BY KIND		264.8		269.7		274.2		559.4	ART TRANSACT NON CLASSES

5. General Exports F.O.B. by Commodities according to the S.I.T.C. (Rev. 2) in million U.S. Dollars
Exportations Générales F.O.B. par Produits d'après la C.T.C.I. (Rév. 2) en millions de Dollars E.U.

SITC CTCI	COMMODITY	1993 QUANTITY QUANTITE	1993 VALUE VALEUR	1994 QUANTITY QUANTITE	1994 VALUE VALEUR	1995 QUANTITY QUANTITE	1995 VALUE VALEUR	1996 QUANTITY QUANTITE	1996 VALUE VALEUR	PRODUIT
	ALL COMMODITIES		686.6		896.5		953.8		883.1	TOUS PRODUITS
0	FOOD AND LIVE ANIMALS		237.1		454.0		452.6		408.3	ALIMENTS,ANIMAUX VIVANTS
042	RICE	W 261	43.6	W 1025	193.4		77.7		21.3	RIZ
044	MAIZE UNMILLED	W 40	4.6	W 69	8.2		8.2		18.2	MAIS NON MOULU
054	VEG ETC FRSH,SMPLY PRSVD						239.6		213.6	LEGUMES FRAIS,CONG,SECS
0542	LEGUMINOUS VEGETBLES DRY	W 514	117.6	W 418	132.6					LEGUMES A COSSE SECS
081	*FEEDING STUFF FOR ANIML	W 35	4.3	W 14	2.0					NOURRITURE POUR ANIMAUX
0813	OILCAKE AND OTH RESIDUES	W 35	4.3	W 14	2.0		2.2		0.7	TOURTEAUX
2	CRUDE MATERLS,EXCL FUELS		252.5		252.8		266.6		273.4	MAT BRUTES NON COMESTIBLES
23	RUBBER, CRUDE						31.8		28.5	CAOUTCHOUC BRUT
232	NATURAL RUBBER,GUMS	W 23	14.8	W 24	20.3					LATEX CAOUTCHOUC NATUREL
23202	OTHER NATURAL RUBBER	W 23	14.8	W 24	20.3					CAOUTCHOUC NATUREL
247	OTH WOOD ROUGH,SQUARED		120.4		158.1					BOIS BRUTS EQUARRIS
2472	SAW-,VENEER-LOGS NON-CON						159.3		166.5	NON CONIFERES SCIAGE,PLAC
248	WOOD SHAPED,SLEEPERS		81.2		18.0					BOIS SIMPLEMENT TRAVAILLES
287	BASE METAL ORES,CONC NES		4.8		10.2					MINERAIS METAUX COMMUNS
3	MINERAL FUELS ETC		1.4		8.3		5.1		4.9	COMBUSTIBLES MINERAUX LUB
6	BASIC MANUFACTURES		32.4		41.1		56.3		28.1	ART MANUFACTURES
7	MACHINES,TRANSPORT EQUIP		3.5		4.1		8.7		9.9	MACHINES MATERIEL TRANSPORT
8	MISC MANUFACTURED GOODS		40.1		60.9		57.4		71.7	ART MANUFACTURES DIVERS
9	GOODS NOT CLASSD BY KIND		119.6		75.1		35.7		86.3	ART TRANSACT NON CLASSES

1. HISTORICAL SERIES, 1961–1996 SPECIAL TRADE, IMPORTS C.I.F., EXPORTS F.O.B. #1
SERIES HISTORIQUES, 1961–1996 COMMERCE SPECIAL, IMPORTATIONS C.A.F., EXPORTATIONS F.O.B

YEAR ANNEE	VALUE IN MILLION U.S. DOLLARS VALEUR EN MILLION U.S. DOLLARS MERCHANDISE –MARCHANDISE		GOLD –OR		CONVERSION FACTORS FACTEURS DE CONVERSION CENTS E.U. PAR		INDEX NUMBERS –INDICES QUANTUM		UNIT VALUE VALEUR UNITAIRE	
	IMPORTS	EXPORTS	IMPORTS	EXPORTS	IMPORTS	EXPORTS	IMPORTS	EXPORTS	IMPORTS	EXPORTS
1961	55.30	31.20								
1962	68.80	36.30								
1963	79.30	38.00								
1964	98.40	43.40								
1965	107.55	57.03								
1966	77.80	57.00								
1967	61.10	56.90								
1968	65.50	40.10								
1969	84.00	53.90								
1970	84.40	48.30								
1971	63.90	45.60								
1972	79.10	41.20								
1973	80.90	46.10								
1974	83.00	60.00								
1975	171.48	99.99								
1976	163.24	96.90								
1977	168.78	83.79								
1978	221.75	91.08								
1979	254.43	108.81								
1980	342.27	80.35								
1981	369.20	140.89								
1982	395.41	87.72								
1983	464.18	93.35								
1984	415.51	127.11								
1985	455.43	160.66								
1986	459.69	141.61								
1987	570.57	150.74								
1988	678.90	191.48								
1989	581.63	159.04								
1990	671.92	203.90								
1991	737.26	256.77								
1992	776.19	367.64								
1993	890.22	383.79								
1994	1155.40	362.34								
1995	1333.41	345.51								
1996	1442.15	384.96								

2. IMPORTS BY BROAD ECONOMIC CATEGORY AND EXPORTS BY INDUSTRIAL ORIGIN. (PERCENTAGE OF TOTAL VALUE)
IMPORTATIONS PAR CATEGORIES ECONOMIQUES ET EXPORTATIONS PAR BRANCHE D'ACTIVITE.(EN POURCENTAGE DE LA VALEUR TOTALE)

IMPORTS – IMPORTATIONS

	1989	1990	1991	1992	1993	1994	1995
TOTAL IMPORTS–IMPORTATIONS TOTALES	100.	100.	100.	100.	100.		100.
1 FOOD BEV–ALIMENTATION BOISSONS	9.5	12.9	8.6	10.3	8.0		15.0
11 PRIMARY–PRODUITS DE BASE	6.1	6.0	4.2	6.0	2.8		5.1
111 FOR INDUSTRY–POUR L'INDUSTRIE	3.2	2.5	1.8	3.5	1.2		1.3
112 FOR HOUSEHOLDS–POUR LES MENAGES	2.9	3.6	2.4	2.5	1.6		3.8
12 PROCESSED–PRODUITS ELABORES	3.4	6.8	4.3	4.3	5.2		9.9
121 FOR INDUSTRY–POUR L'INDUSTRIE	2.6	3.5	3.5	3.4	4.1		6.9
122 FOR HOUSEHOLDS–POUR LES MENAGES	0.8	3.3	0.9	0.9	1.1		3.0
2 IND SUPPLIES–APPROV INDUSTRIELS	37.2	47.4	40.6	40.9	39.4		30.8
21 PRIMARY–PRODUITS DE BASE	5.4	8.8	9.0	12.8	11.9		5.4
22 PROCESSED–PRODUITS ELABORES	31.9	38.5	31.6	28.1	27.5		25.3
3 FUELS–COMBUSTIBLES	8.5	8.6	8.8	12.4	11.5		19.5
31 PRIMARY–PRODUITS DE BASE	0.6	0.0	1.1	12.2	0.8		0.0
32 PROCESSED–PRODUITS ELABORES	7.9	8.6	7.6	0.2	10.7		19.5
321 MOTOR SPIRIT–ESSENCE	7.7	0.4					
322 OTHER–AUTRES	0.2	8.1	7.6	0.2	10.7		19.5
4 MACHINERY–EQUIPEMENT	10.9	13.8	17.7	10.7	8.7		12.8
41 CAPITAL EQUIPMENT–MACHINES	10.8	11.8	16.7	10.6	8.6		11.8
42 PARTS–PIECES ACCESSOIRES	0.1	2.0	1.0	0.1	0.1		1.0
5 TRANSPORT–TRANSPORT	9.1	4.4	5.7	6.8	6.9		5.1
51 PASSENGER CARS–AUTOMOBILES	4.6	1.0	1.0	1.1	1.7		
52 OTHER–AUTRES	3.4	0.9	3.3	4.3	4.1		1.5
521 INDUSTRIAL–INDUSTRIELS	3.1	0.6	2.9	4.0	4.0		1.5
522 NON INDUSTRIAL–NON INDUSTRIEL	0.3	0.3	0.2	0.3	0.1		
53 PARTS–PIECES ACCESSOIRES	1.1	2.5	1.4	1.4	1.1		3.6
6 CONSUM GOODS–BIENS CONSOMMATION	10.7	12.5	9.3	8.4	9.6		8.7
61 DURABLE–DURABLES	4.2	1.5	1.5	1.4	2.0		2.2
62 SEMI DURABLE–SEMI DURABLES	2.2	4.0	2.6	2.4	2.8		4.0
63 NON DURABLE–NON DURABLES	4.3	7.0	5.1	4.7	4.8		2.5
7 GOODS NES–BIENS NDA	14.1	0.4	9.3	10.6	15.9		8.1

EXPORTS – EXPORTATIONS

	1989	1990	1991	1992	1993	1994	1995
TOTAL EXPORTS–EXPORTATIONS TOTALES	100.	100.	100.	100.	100.		100.
1 AGRICULTURE	9.4	12.7	14.4	14.3	11.2		1.1
2 MINING QUARRY–INDUS EXTRACTIVES	0.9	0.2	0.2	0.2	0.1		
3 MANUFACTURING–IND MANUFACTUR	89.7	87.0	85.4	85.6	88.7		98.9
31 FOOD BEV TOBACCO–ALIM BOISS TAB	7.0	3.5	2.5	1.2	1.0		0.0
32 TEXTILES–INDUSTRIES TEXTILES	72.6	79.3	77.1	79.8	82.3		96.6
33 WOOD & PRODUCTS–BOIS & PRODUITS		0.1	0.1	0.1	0.0		0.1
34 PAPER & PRODUCTS–PAPIER & PRODT	0.0	0.0	0.1	0.2	0.1		0.3
35 CHEMICALS–INDUSTRIES CHIMIQUES	0.1	0.5	2.1	1.6	0.6		0.1
36 NON METAL MIN–MIN NON METAL	0.0	0.0	0.0				
37 BASIC METAL–IND METAL BASE		0.0					
38 METAL MANUF–MANUF METAL	0.7	0.3	0.7	0.5	0.8		1.1
39 OTH MANUF IND–AUTRES MANUF	9.2	3.2	2.8	2.2	3.7		0.8

3. TRADE BY PRINCIPAL COUNTRIES OF ORIGIN AND DESTINATION (VALUE IN MILLION U.S. DOLLARS)
ECHANGES SELON LES PRINCIPAUX PAYS D'ORIGINE ET DE DESTINATION (VALEUR EN MILLIONS DE DOLLARS EU)

COUNTRIES–PAYS	SPECIAL IMPORTS C.I.F. IMPORTATIONS SPECIALES C.A.F				
	1991	1992	1993	1994	1995
World	592.1	695.2	696.0	1047.0	1272.5
Africa	6.2	5.0	7.8	0.2	0.3
Americas	8.1	18.3	18.5	23.5	26.7
– Northern America	5.3	9.7	9.9	11.2	11.5
– LAIA	2.7	8.6	8.6	12.2	15.1
– CACM				0.0	0.0
– Caribbean	0.0				
– Rest of America					
Asia excl fmr USSR	465.3	541.7	534.6	883.3	1108.6
– Middle East	9.5	9.0	8.8	19.1	59.4
Asia former USSR					
Europe excl fmr USSR	76.1	78.0	71.3	65.5	99.5
– European Union	53.9	52.0	50.7	54.9	91.1
– Eastern Europe	13.3	21.7	17.8	5.8	3.8
– Rest of Europe	8.9	4.3	2.7	4.8	4.6
Europe former USSR	0.4	0.2	3.4	0.5	4.4
Oceania	36.0	52.0	60.5	44.8	33.1
Other	0.0	0.0	0.0		
India/Inde	198.4	263.3	265.0	362.8	416.6
Singapore/Singapour	91.5	137.3	128.6	190.9	218.1
China, Hong Kong SAR	9.1	9.6	15.1	149.3	218.3
Japan/Japon	84.8	67.3	55.8	55.6	64.0
New Zealand	32.9	47.4	55.1	36.7	27.9
China/Chine	29.9	16.2	20.4	37.0	46.0
Germany/Allemagne	13.4	18.5	17.6	16.0	35.0
Korea, Republic of	14.0	16.0	14.4	16.9	16.4
France, Monaco	19.7	10.9	13.6	4.2	11.6
United Kingdom	4.1	7.7	10.1	11.9	16.5
Thailand/Thaïlande	5.6	7.1	7.2	12.5	12.8
Bangladesh	7.3	0.8	4.3	14.9	17.6
Other Asia n.e.s.	10.5	9.7	9.0		15.6
Poland/Pologne	9.9	13.6	8.7	5.3	2.6
USA/Etats–Unis d'Amer	4.4	8.5	5.0	7.7	8.6
Brazil/Brésil	2.5	5.0	7.0	9.8	8.2
United Arab Emirates	1.0	0.7	1.6	7.7	19.7
Australia/Australie	3.1	4.6	5.4	8.0	5.1
Saudi Arabia	0.5	4.8	2.1	7.3	9.3
Bahrain/Bahreïn	0.0	0.1	0.1	1.4	20.7
Indonesia/Indonésie	2.5	3.2	3.1	6.8	6.5
Belgium–Luxembourg	2.1	3.0	2.2	8.0	5.7
Switzerland,Liechtenst.	8.6	4.1	1.8	3.1	2.9
Denmark/Danemark	0.8	2.0	1.4	5.2	9.4
Madagascar	6.2	4.9	7.3		
Malaysia/Malaisie				6.6	9.9
Finland/Finlande	4.5	5.2	0.6	1.5	3.1
Argentina/Argentine		3.5	1.3	2.1	6.7
Canada	0.9	1.2	4.9	3.5	3.0
Jordan/Jordanie		3.1	4.6	1.1	2.9
Romania/Roumanie	2.3	5.3	3.5		
Spain/Espagne	3.5	0.7	2.1	1.1	1.8
Italy/Italie	2.0	1.4	0.5	1.7	3.1
Brunei Darussalam	0.5	0.2	0.2	4.2	3.6
Netherlands/Pays–Bas	1.9	0.9	1.3	1.8	2.7
Pakistan	0.4	0.9	0.9	4.2	2.3
Russian Federation		0.2	3.4	0.4	4.3
Kuwait/ Koweït	6.4			0.6	0.6
Oman	0.0	0.0	0.0	0.5	5.9
Ireland/Irlande	0.8	1.1	1.1	0.8	1.3

COUNTRIES–PAYS	SPECIAL EXPORTS F.O.B. EXPORTATIONS SPECIALES F.O.B.				
	1991	1992	1993	1994	1995
Monde	192.9	319.2	354.6	390.8	353.8
Afrique	0.0	0.1	0.0	0.1	0.1
Amériques	38.8	76.8	81.2	117.3	106.8
– Amérique du Nord	38.8	76.7	81.1	116.3	106.2
– ALAI	0.0	0.1	0.1	1.0	0.5
– MCAC					
– Caraïbes					0.1
– Autre Amérique			0.0		0.0
Asie anc. URSS exclus	48.0	63.4	60.3	59.3	72.8
– Moyen–Orient	0.0	0.2	0.9	0.8	0.1
Asie ancienne URSS					
Europe anc. URSS exclus	105.8	178.1	210.3	209.2	173.4
– Union Européenne	91.8	163.0	194.5	193.0	163.6
– Europe de l'Est	0.6	0.0	0.2	0.2	0.3
– Autre de l'Europe	13.4	15.0	15.6	16.0	9.5
Europe ancienne URSS	0.1	0.0	0.0	0.2	0.1
Océanie	0.2	0.8	2.7	0.9	0.7
Autre					
Germany/Allemagne	72.9	139.8	172.5	165.7	131.2
USA/Etats–Unis d'Amer	37.4	74.0	75.8	113.4	103.0
India/Inde	41.5	33.9	34.8	52.4	67.5
Switzerland,Liechtenst.	13.3	14.9	15.5	16.0	9.3
Sri Lanka	2.7	20.0	16.4	2.9	0.9
Belgium–Luxembourg	4.7	6.4	5.9	6.8	5.5
United Kingdom	4.5	4.2	4.3	7.1	6.6
Italy/Italie	3.9	3.9	3.8	3.4	7.2
Canada	1.4	2.7	5.2	2.8	3.2
Austria/Autriche	0.9	2.0	1.9	4.2	4.0
Netherlands/Pays–Bas	2.0	2.3	1.7	2.4	2.7
France, Monaco	1.6	1.6	2.7	1.8	2.8
Singapore/Singapour	0.8	3.6	2.6	0.2	0.5
Japan/Japon	0.8	1.2	1.7	1.6	1.5
Australia/Australie	0.1	0.7	2.6	0.7	0.6
Spain/Espagne	0.2	0.4	0.8	0.7	2.3
China, Hong Kong SAR	0.2	1.1	0.8	0.6	1.1
Pakistan	0.2	2.4	0.6	0.0	0.1
Sweden/Suède	0.6	1.0	0.5	0.4	0.5
Bangladesh	0.1	0.6	1.2	0.4	0.1
Korea, Republic of	1.5	0.1	0.1	0.1	0.3
Ireland/Irlande	0.2	0.8	0.2	0.1	0.1
United Arab Emirates	0.0	0.2	0.8	0.3	0.0
Other Asia n.e.s.	0.1	0.3	0.6		0.3
Denmark/Danemark	0.2	0.3	0.2	0.3	0.3
Mexico/Mexique		0.0	0.0	0.7	0.2
Thailand/Thaïlande	0.0	0.0	0.5	0.1	0.2
Norway,Svalbard and JM	0.2	0.1	0.1	0.2	0.2
Iran (Islamic Rep of)	0.0	0.1	0.1	0.5	0.0
Former Czechoslovakia	0.5	0.0			
New Zealand	0.0	0.1	0.1	0.1	0.1
Finland/Finlande	0.0	0.1	0.1	0.1	0.1
Brazil/Brésil	0.0	0.1	0.0	0.1	0.2
Russian Federation		0.0	0.0	0.2	0.1
Portugal	0.0	0.2	0.1	0.0	0.1
Hungary/Hongrie	0.0	0.0	0.1	0.1	0.2
Czech Republic			0.1	0.1	0.1
Argentina/Argentine	0.0	0.0	0.0	0.0	0.1
Poland/Pologne	0.1	0.0	0.0	0.0	0.0
Venezuela				0.1	

(VALUE AS PERCENTAGE OF WORLD TOTAL)(VALEURS EN POURCENTAGE DU TOTAL MONDIAL)

	1986	1987	1988	1989	1990	1991	1992	1993	1994	1995
Africa	0.5	0.4	0.7	1.4	1.1	1.1	0.7	1.1	0.0	0.0
Americas	1.9	1.0	1.6	1.6	1.4	1.4	2.6	2.7	2.2	2.1
– Northern America	1.8	1.0	1.5	1.5	1.3	0.9	1.4	1.4	1.1	0.9
– LAIA	0.1	0.0	0.1	0.1	0.1	0.5	1.2	1.2	1.2	1.2
– CACM				0.0	0.0				0.0	0.0
– Caribbean	0.0				0.0	0.0				
– Rest of America	0.0				0.0					
Asia excl fmr USSR	88.1	83.3	76.7	73.6	78.8	78.6	77.9	76.8	84.4	87.1
– Middle East	0.0	8.4	6.3	4.5	1.1	1.6	1.3	1.3	1.8	4.7
Asia former USSR										
Europe excl fmr USSR	8.7	13.6	12.9	19.3	14.2	12.9	11.2	10.2	6.3	7.8
– European Union	6.7	11.3	11.5	14.9	11.5	9.1	7.5	7.3	5.2	7.2
– Eastern Europe	1.1	1.9	0.9	4.1	2.0	2.2	3.1	2.6	0.6	0.3
– Rest of Europe	0.9	0.4	0.5	0.4	0.7	1.5	0.6	0.4	0.5	0.4
Europe former USSR	0.1	0.0	2.9	0.9	0.0	0.1	0.0	0.5	0.0	0.3
Oceania	0.7	1.6	4.8	3.1	4.4	6.1	7.5	8.7	4.3	2.6
Other	0.0	0.0	0.4	0.0		0.0	0.0	0.0		
India/Inde	53.4	40.4	37.3	31.0	27.6	33.5	37.9	38.1	34.6	32.7
Singapore/Singapour	3.2	7.4	8.2	10.7	16.2	15.4	19.8	18.5	18.2	17.1
China, Hong Kong SAR	2.4	1.9	1.5	1.9	5.0	1.5	1.4	2.2	14.3	17.2
Japan/Japon	15.7	13.6	13.1	12.7	8.1	14.3	9.7	8.0	5.3	5.0
New Zealand	0.3	1.3	4.1	2.5	4.0	5.6	6.8	7.9	3.5	2.2
China/Chine	5.5	2.6	3.4	3.2	7.5	5.0	2.3	2.9	3.5	3.6
Germany/Allemagne						2.3	2.7	2.5	1.5	2.8
Korea, Republic of	5.0	5.5	4.3	4.4	4.6	2.4	2.3	2.1	1.6	1.3
France, Monaco	0.6	0.3	1.1	2.1	3.3	3.3	1.6	2.0	0.4	0.9
United Kingdom	1.0	1.8	1.9	2.7	1.1	0.7	1.1	1.4	1.1	1.3

	1986	1987	1988	1989	1990	1991	1992	1993	1994	1995
Afrique	0.0	0.0	0.0	0.0	0.0	0.0	0.0	0.0	0.0	0.0
Amériques	29.4	21.0	23.2	29.3	34.4	20.1	24.1	22.9	30.0	30.2
– Amérique du Nord	29.0	20.9	23.1	29.3	34.3	20.1	24.0	22.9	29.8	30.0
– ALAI	0.2	0.1	0.1	0.0	0.0	0.0	0.0	0.0	0.3	0.1
– MCAC	0.1				0.0					
– Caraïbes										0.0
– Autre Amérique	0.1				0.1			0.0		0.0
Asie anc. URSS exclus	49.0	50.2	40.3	29.1	21.4	24.9	19.9	17.0	15.2	20.6
– Moyen–Orient	0.1	0.3	0.0	1.3	2.1	0.0	0.1	0.3	0.2	0.0
Asie ancienne URSS										
Europe anc. URSS exclus	19.1	27.2	35.5	41.5	42.5	54.8	55.8	59.3	53.5	49.0
– Union Européenne	15.7	20.5	27.3	33.0	35.0	47.6	51.1	54.9	49.4	46.2
– Europe de l'Est	1.4	1.0	1.3	0.7	0.7	0.3	0.0	0.0	0.0	0.1
– Autre de l'Europe	2.0	5.8	6.9	7.9	6.9	7.0	4.7	4.4	4.1	2.7
Europe ancienne URSS	2.3	1.5	1.0		1.1	0.1	0.0	0.0	0.0	0.0
Océanie	0.2	0.1	0.1	0.1	0.4	0.1	0.2	0.8	0.2	0.2
Autre		0.0	0.0	0.0						
Germany/Allemagne						37.8	43.8	48.6	42.4	37.1
USA/Etats–Unis d'Amer	28.5	20.4	22.8	28.7	33.8	19.4	23.2	21.4	29.0	29.1
India/Inde	33.8	44.0	38.6	25.4	12.1	21.5	10.6	9.8	13.4	19.1
Switzerland,Liechtenst.	2.0	5.4	6.6	7.7	6.5	6.9	4.7	4.4	4.1	2.6
Sri Lanka	5.3	0.7	0.0		0.0	1.4	6.3	4.6	0.7	0.3
Belgium–Luxembourg	0.7	0.9	1.4	2.3	3.1	2.4	2.0	1.7	1.7	1.6
United Kingdom	3.7	5.7	6.1	5.9	4.4	2.3	1.3	1.2	1.8	1.9
Italy/Italie	3.2	2.5	1.7	1.7	1.9	2.0	1.2	1.1	0.9	2.0
Canada	0.5	0.4	0.3	0.5	0.6	0.7	0.9	1.5	0.7	0.9
Austria/Autriche	0.0	0.0	0.1	0.1	0.1	0.5	0.6	0.5	1.1	1.1

4. Special Imports C.I.F. by Commodities according to the S.I.T.C. (Rev. 2) in million U.S. Dollars
Importations Spéciales C.A.F. par Produits d'après la C.T.C.I. (Rév. 2) en millions de Dollars E.U.

SITC CTCI	COMMODITY	1992 QUANTITY QUANTITE	1992 VALUE VALEUR	1993 QUANTITY QUANTITE	1993 VALUE VALEUR	1994 QUANTITY QUANTITE	1994 VALUE VALEUR	1995 QUANTITY QUANTITE	1995 VALUE VALEUR	PRODUIT
	ALL COMMODITIES		695.2		696.0				1272.6	TOUS PRODUITS
0	FOOD AND LIVE ANIMALS		46.7		30.8				70.3	ALIMENTS,ANIMAUX VIVANTS
001	*LIVE ANIMALS FOR FOOD		12.6		0.6				0.8	ANIMAUX VIVANTS
0019	LIVE ANIMALS FR FOOD NES		12.6		0.6					ANIMAUX VIVANTS NDA
02	DAIRY PRODCTS,BIRDS'EGGS		9.1		5.4				6.8	PRODUITS LAITIERS,OEUFS
022	MILK AND CREAM		8.2		5.4				6.6	LAIT ET CREME
0223	MILK AND CREAM FRESH		4.0		0.9					LAIT,CREME FRAIS
04	CEREALS AND PREPARATIONS		11.1		8.2				12.5	CEREALES ET PRODUITS
041	WHEAT ETC UNMILLED		4.7		1.2					FROMENT,EPEAUTRE
0411	DURUM WHEAT UNMILLED		4.7		1.2					FROMENT DUR NON MOULU
042	RICE		5.7		6.2				9.1	RIZ
0421	RICE IN HUSK OR HUSKED		5.7		5.7					RIZ SANS AUTRE PREPARATION
0422	RICE SEMI–MILLED,MILLED		0.1		0.5				9.1	RIZ POLI,GLACE INCL BRISURES
04221	RICE MILLED UNBROKEN								9.1	RIZ POLI,GLACE EXCL BRISURES
05	VEGETABLES AND FRUIT		6.3		4.7				29.4	LEGUMES ET FRUITS
054	VEG ETC FRSH,SMPLY PRSVD		3.3		3.3				10.2	LEGUMES FRAIS,CONG,SECS
0548	EDIBLE VEG NES FRESH,DRY								5.5	RACINES,TUBERCULES
057	FRUIT,NUTS,FRESH,DRIED		2.8		1.5				12.6	FRUITS FRAIS OU SECS
0577	NUTS EDIBLE,FRESH,DRIED		0.4		0.3				11.7	FRUITS A COQUES
05779	NUTS EDIBLE,FRSH,DRY,NES		0.3						11.1	FRUITS A COQUES NDA
058	FRUIT PRESERVED,PREPARED								4.9	CONSERVES DE FRUITS
0582	FRUIT PRESERVED BY SUGAR								4.9	FRUITS CONFITS AU SUCRE
06	SUGAR AND PREPS,HONEY		0.7		5.1				7.1	SUCRES ET PRODUITS
061	SUGAR AND HONEY		0.7		5.1				7.0	SUCRES ET MIEL
0611	RAW BEET AND CANE SUGAR		0.7		5.0					SUCRES BRUTS
0612	REFINED SUGAR ETC								7.0	SUCRES RAFFINES
07	COFFEE,TEA,COCOA,SPICES		6.7		5.8				12.9	CAFE,THE,CACAO,EPICES
075	SPICES		4.9		4.5				10.7	EPICES
0751	PEPPER AND PIMENTO		0.4		0.4				4.1	POIVRE,PIMENTS
0752	SPICES,EX PEPPER,PIMENTO		4.6		4.1				6.6	AUTRES EPICES
07525	SEEDS OF ANISE,CUMIN,ETC		2.6							GRAINES ANIS,FENOUIL
1	BEVERAGES AND TOBACCO		7.1		6.3				8.4	BOISSONS ET TABACS
12	TOBACCO AND MANUFACTURES		6.1		5.3				7.0	TABACS BRUTS FABRIQUES
121	TOBACCO UNMNFCTRD,REFUSE		5.9		5.2				6.3	TABACS BRUTS,DECHETS
2	CRUDE MATERLS,EXCL FUELS		85.3		81.6				43.6	MAT BRUTES NON COMESTIBLES
22	OIL SEEDS,OLEAGINOUS FRT		1.5		3.6				7.4	GRAINES,FRUITS OLEAGINEUX
223	SEEDS FOR OTH FIXED OILS		1.5		3.6				6.1	GRAINES AUTRES HUILES FIXES
2234	LINSEED				2.2					GRAINES DE LIN
2238	OIL SEEDS AND FRUITS NES		1.5		1.1				6.1	GRAINES D'OLEAGINEUX NDA
23	RUBBER, CRUDE		0.9		2.6				0.6	CAOUTCHOUC BRUT
233	RUBBER,SYNTHTIC,RECLAIMD		0.9		2.6					LATEX CAOUTCH SYNTH REGEN
2331	SYNTHETIC RUBBER ETC		0.9		2.6					LATEX CAOUTCH SYNTHETIQUE
26	TEXTILE FIBRES AND WASTE		50.5		58.0				29.6	FIBRES TEXTILES
263	COTTON		3.1		3.3				0.5	COTON
2631	RAW COTTON,EXCL LINTERS		3.1		3.3					COTON EN MASSE
268	WOOL(EXC TOPS),ANML HAIR		47.4		54.7				27.3	LAINES ET POILS
2681	WOOL GREASY,FLEECE–WSHED		47.4		54.7					LAINE EN SUINT
2682	WOOL DEGREASED,UNCOMBED								27.3	LAINE DEGRAISSEE
28	METALLIFEROUS ORES,SCRAP		31.5		16.3				4.7	MINERAIS METAL,DECHETS
287	BASE METAL ORES,CONC NES		22.9		11.6					MINERAIS METAUX COMMUNS
288	NONFERR METAL SCRAP NES		8.6		4.7				4.0	DECHETS NON FERREUX
2882	OTHER BASE MTL SCRAP NES		8.6		4.7				4.0	AUTRES DECHETS
28821	COPPER WASTE AND SCRAP		6.5		2.7				3.8	DECHETS DE CUIVRE
3	MINERAL FUELS ETC		88.3		82.1				123.0	COMBUSTIBLES MINERAUX LUB
32	COAL,COKE AND BRIQUETTES		6.8		5.7				4.4	HOUILLES,COKES,BRIQUETTES
322	COAL,LIGNITE AND PEAT		6.8		5.7				4.4	HOUILLES,LIGNITES,TOURBE
3222	OTH COAL,NOT AGGLOMERATD								4.4	AUTRES HOUILLES
33	PETROLEUM AND PRODUCTS		81.6		76.4				118.7	PETROLE ET DERIVES
333	CRUDE PETROLEUM		78.3							HUILES BRUTES DE PETROLE
334	PETROLEUM PRODUCTS,REFIN		1.6		74.8				116.8	PRODUITS RAFFINES
3341	GASOLINE,OTH LIGHT OILS								112.4	ESSENCES POUR MOTEURS
3345	LUBS,PETROLEUM OILS NES		1.6		3.2				4.4	HUILES LUBRIFIANTES
4	ANIMAL,VEGETABLE OIL,FAT		22.9		23.3				40.7	HUILES,GRAISSES ANIM,VEG
42	FIXED VEGETABLE OIL,FAT		22.4		22.6				40.7	HUILES VEGETALES FIXES
423	FIXED VEG OILS,SOFT		13.6		12.3				28.4	HUILES VEGET DOUCES FIXES
4232	SOYA BEAN OIL		13.4		12.1				11.1	HUILE DE SOJA
4239	OTH FIXED VEG OILS,SOFT								17.0	AUTRES HUILES FIXES
42391	RAPE,COLZA,MUSTARD OILS								17.0	H NAVETTE COLZA MOUTARDE
424	FIXED VEG OIL NONSOFT		8.8		10.4				12.4	AUTRES HUILES VEG FIXES
4242	PALM OIL		7.1		7.5				9.6	HUILE DE PALME
4243	COCONUT (COPRA) OIL		1.1		2.5				2.7	HJUILE DE COPRAH
5	CHEMCLS,RELATED PROD NES		84.7		83.3				111.6	PRODUITS CHIMIQUES
51	ORGANIC CHEMICALS		0.1		5.8				12.2	PROD CHIMIQ ORGANIQUES
514	NITROGEN–FNCTN COMPOUNDS								7.2	COMPOSES FONCT AZOTEES
516	OTHER ORGANIC CHEMICALS								4.3	AUTRES PROD ORGANIQUES
53	DYES,TANNING,COLOUR PROD		2.6		1.8				2.7	PROD TEINTURE,COLORANTS
541	*MEDICINAL,PHARM PRODUCT		27.8		29.0				44.1	PROD MEDICINAUX PHARMACEUT
562	*FERTILIZERS,MANUFACTURE		36.5		27.7				29.4	ENGRAIS MANUFACTURES
5629	FERTILIZERS NES				27.5					ENGRAIS NDA
56299	OTHER FERTILIZERS NES				27.5					AUTRES ENGRAIS NDA
58	PLASTIC MATERIALS ETC		13.1		12.3				16.8	MAT PLAST ARTIFICIELLES
582	PROD OF CONDENSATION ETC		2.8		2.2					PROD CONDENS,POLYCOND
583	POLYMERIZATION ETC PRODS		10.0		10.2				16.7	PROD POLYMERISATION
5831	POLYETHYLENE								13.7	POLYETHYLENE
59	CHEMICAL MATERIALS NES		2.7		5.3				2.9	MAT PROD CHIMIQUES NDA
6	BASIC MANUFACTURES		139.0		131.1				155.1	ART MANUFACTURES
62	RUBBER MANUFACTURES NES		28.1		25.2				7.1	CAOUTCHOUC MANUFACTURE
621	MATERIALS OF RUBBER		23.7		21.7				2.8	PRODUITS EN CAOUTCHOUC
625	RUBBER TYRES, TUBES ETC		4.4		3.3				3.0	PNEUS CAOUTCHOUC VULCANISE
63	WOOD,CORK MANUFACTRS NES		0.6		2.7				0.4	OUVRAGES LIEGE ET BOIS
635	WOOD MANUFACTURES NES		0.1		2.4					ART MANUF EN BOIS NDA
6351	BOXES,CASES,CRATES,ETC				2.2					CAISSES EMBALLAGES BOIS
64	PAPER,PAPERBOARD AND MFR		5.8		6.2				6.5	PAPIERS,CARTONS & OUVRAGES
641	PAPER AND PAPERBOARD		5.5		5.8				6.4	PAPIERS ET CARTONS
6415	PAPER,PAPERBRD,BULK,NES		0.4		0.3				5.4	PAPIERS,CARTONS ROULEAUX
64159	OTHER PAPER ETC,BULK,NES		0.4		0.3				5.4	AUT PAPIER ROULEAUX FEUILLES
65	TEXTILE YARN,FABRICS,ETC		29.3		31.7				70.2	FILS,TISSUS,ARTICLES TEXTILE
651	TEXTILE YARN		1.0		3.7				29.1	FILS TEXTILES
6511	SILK YARN, SILKWORM GUT								6.5	FILS DE SOIE
6512	WOOL,HAIR YARN,INCL TOPS								12.0	FILS DE LAINE,DE POILS
6519	TEXTILE FIBRE YARN NES								10.7	FILS TEXT NDA FILE FIB VER

4. Special Imports C.I.F. by Commodities according to the S.I.T.C. (Rev. 2) in million U.S. Dollars
Importations Spéciales C.A.F. par Produits d'après la C.T.C.I. (Rév. 2) en millions de Dollars E.U.

SITC CTCI	COMMODITY	1992 QUANTITY QUANTITE	1992 VALUE VALEUR	1993 QUANTITY QUANTITE	1993 VALUE VALEUR	1994 QUANTITY QUANTITE	1994 VALUE VALEUR	1995 QUANTITY QUANTITE	1995 VALUE VALEUR	PRODUIT
652	COTTON FABRICS,WOVEN		27.3		24.9				34.2	TISSUS DE COTON
66	NONMETAL MINERAL MFS NES		26.4		19.0				16.2	ART MIN NON METALLIQUES
661	LIME,CEMENT,BLDG PRODS		15.3		11.6				10.7	CHAUX,CIMENTS MAT CONSTR
6612	CEMENT		13.6		10.3				10.6	CIMENTS HYDRAULIQUES
662	CLAY,REFRACTORY BLDG PRD		9.6		5.6				1.8	MAT CONST REFRACTAIRES
6623	REFRACTORY BUILDING PROD		9.6		5.6				1.8	BRIQUES REFRACTAIRES
67	IRON AND STEEL		40.3		26.5				15.9	FER ET ACIER
672	IRON,STEEL PRIMARY FORMS		16.3		10.7				2.1	LINGOTS FER,ACIER
673	IRON,STEEL SHAPES ETC		3.7		3.4				5.9	BARRES,PROFIL FER,ACIER
6733	IRON,STEEL PROFILES ETC				0.1				5.8	PROFILES,PALPLAN FER,ACIER
67334	OTH PRFILES COLDFRMD ETC								5.8	PROFILES OBTENUS A FROID
674	IRN,STL UNIV,PLATE,SHEET		10.2		7.5				7.9	LARGES PLATS,TOLES
6747	TINNED PLATES,SHEETS								7.8	TOLES ETAMEES EN ACIER
677	IRN,STL WIRE(EXCL W ROD)		3.3		1.8				0.1	FILS EN FER,ACIER
678	IRON,STL TUBES,PIPES,ETC		7.1		3.2				0.2	TUBES,TUYAUX EN FONTE,FER
6783	IRON,STL TUBES,PIPES NES		3.5		1.1				0.2	AUT TUBES,TUYAUX FER,ACIER
68	NON–FERROUS METALS		7.1		17.3				28.5	METAUX NON FERREUX
681	SILVER,PLATINUM,ETC		0.4		0.4				16.2	ARGENT ET PLATINE
682	COPPER EXC CEMENT COPPER		3.3		8.3				5.9	CUIVRE
6821	COPPER NES,ALLOYS,UNWRT		0.2		2.3				0.6	CUIVRE BRUT
68212	COPPER REFINED,UNWROUGHT		0.2		2.3					CUIVRE AFFINE BRUT
6822	COPPER,ALLOYS WORKED		1.3		1.3				5.3	CUIVRE,ALLIAGES OUVRES
684	ALUMINIUM		1.2		2.9				1.5	ALUMINIUM
686	ZINC		0.2		1.9				4.2	ZINC
69	METAL MANUFACTURES NES		1.6		3.0				10.4	ART MANUFACT EN METAL NDA
7	MACHINES,TRANSPORT EQUIP		118.9		115.7				193.7	MACHINES MATERIEL TRANSPORT
71	POWER GENERATING EQUIPMT								13.6	MACHINES GENERATRICES
716	ROTATING ELECTRIC PLANT								13.6	APP ELECTR ROTATIFS,PIECES
7162	AC MTRS,GENRTRS,GEN SETS								13.6	MOTEURS ELECTRIQUES
72	MACHS FOR SPCL INDUSTRYS		22.2		20.0				32.6	MAC SPECIALES POUR INDUST
721	AGRIC MACHY,EXC TRACTORS				2.5					MACHINES AGRICOLES
722	TRACTORS NON–ROAD								6.2	TRACTEURS
7223	TRACK–LAYING TRACTORS								6.0	TRACTEURS A CHENILLES
728	OTH MACHY FOR SPCL INDUS		22.0		16.8				25.2	AUT MACH IND PARTICULIERES
74	GENRL INDUSTRL MACHY NES		26.0		3.0				8.4	MACH APP INDUSTRIE
741	HEATING,COOLING EQUIPMNT		20.1							MACH CHAUFFAGE,PIECES
742	PUMPS FOR LIQUIDS ETC		4.5		1.0				0.5	POMPES MOTO–POMPES
7421	RECIPROCATING PUMPS NES		4.5		0.5					POMPES ALTERN NON 742.81
749	NONELEC MACH PTS,ACC NES		0.7		0.4				6.0	PIECES MACH NON ELEC NDA
75	OFFICE MACHNES,ADP EQUIP		5.8		12.0				25.7	MACH BUREAU TRAIT AUTOM
752	AUTOMTIC DATA PROC EQUIP		5.4		9.9				23.2	MACH TRAIT INFORMATION
76	TELECOMM,SOUND EQUIPMENT		6.0		11.4				31.3	EQUIPMENT DE TELECOM
761	TELEVISION RECEIVERS		1.6		2.4				4.4	RECEPTEURS DE TELEVISION
7611	COLOUR TV RECEIVERS		1.6		2.4					RECEPTEURS COULEUR
764	TELECOM EQPT,PTS,ACC NES		4.2		8.7				26.6	EQUIP TELECOM,PIECES
7648	TELECOMM EQUIPMENT NES		4.2							APP TELECOM NDA
77	ELECTRIC MACHNRY NES ETC		13.3		21.5				18.1	MACH APP ELECT NDA
771	ELECTRIC POWER MACHY NES		0.4		0.2				5.2	MACH PROD,TRANS ELECTR
7711	TRANSFORMERS,ELECTRICAL		0.4		0.2				5.2	TRANSFO ELECTRIQUES
774	ELECTRO–MEDCL,XRAY EQUIP								5.1	APPAREILS MEDICAUX
775	HOUSEHOLD TYPE EQUIP NES		6.1		9.1				4.1	MACH,APP USAGE DOMESTQUE
7758	ELECTRO–THERMIC APPL NES		4.7		7.9				0.3	APP ELECTROTHERMIQ NDA
77586	ELECTROTHERM DOM APP NES		4.6		7.8				0.2	APP ELECTRO THERMIQUES
778	ELECTRICAL MACHINERY NES		2.5		4.8				3.7	AUTRES MACH ELECT NDA
7783	AUTOMOTIVE ELECTR EQUIP		0.4		3.4					EQUIP ELECT MOTEURS EXPL
78	ROAD VEHICLES		40.6		39.2				55.3	VEHICULES ROUTIERS
781	PASS MOTOR VEH EXC BUSES		7.9		11.7				52.3	AUTO TRANSPORT PERSONNES
783	ROAD MOTOR VEHICLES NES		3.0		2.4					VEHICULES ROUTIERS NDA
7831	BUSES		2.7		2.3					VOITURES TRANSPORT COMMUN
79	OTHR TRANSPORT EQUIPMENT		4.9		8.6				9.2	AUTRE MATERIEL TRANSPORT
792	AIRCRAFT ETC		4.9		8.5				9.2	APP NAVIGATION AERIENNE
7922	AIRCRFT NES 2000KG OR LS				8.5					AERODYNES MOINS 2000 KG
7929	AIRCRAFT PARTS NES		4.9							PIECES DU 792
8	MISC MANUFACTURED GOODS		29.0		31.6				44.7	ART MANUFACTURES DIVERS
812	*PLUMBG,HEATNG,LGHTNG EQ		1.8		2.7				0.8	APPAR SANITAIRES CHAUFFAGE
84	CLOTHING AND ACCESSORIES		8.5		8.8				9.1	VETEMENTS
842	MENS OUTERWEAR NOT KNIT		7.8		7.7				8.8	VET DESSUS POUR HOMMES
851	*FOOTWEAR		1.9						4.0	CHAUSSURES
87	PRECISION INSTRUMNTS NES		6.5		7.8				0.6	INSTRUM,APPAR SCIENT NDA
871	OPTICAL INSTRUMENTS		1.4		2.7				0.1	APPAR,INSTRUM D'OPTIQUE
872	MEDICAL INSTRUMENTS NES		4.3		4.2					INSTR,APP MEDIC–CHIR NDA
87202	OTH MEDICAL INSTRUMENTS		4.3		4.2					INSTRUM,APP MEDECINE
88	PHOTO EQU,OPTICL GDS ETC		2.3		3.2				16.2	APP,FOURN PHOTO,OP,MONTR
882	PHOTO,CINEMA SUPPLIES		1.4		2.3				14.0	PRODUITS PHOTO,CINEMA
8822	PHOTO FILM EXC DEV CINMA		1.4		2.3					PLAQUES,PELLICULES,FILMS
89	MISC MANUFCTRD GOODS NES		7.7		8.3				13.8	ART MANUFACTURES DIVERS
892	PRINTED MATTER		2.8		2.9				3.8	IMPRIMES
895	OFFICE SUPPLIES NES		1.1		2.3				3.3	ART PAPET NDA
9	GOODS NOT CLASSD BY KIND		73.6		110.8				481.9	ART TRANSACT NON CLASSES
931	*SPECIAL TRANSACTIONS		70.1		107.8				225.1	TRANS.SPECIALES
951	*WAR FIREARMS,AMMUNITION		3.6		2.3				2.4	VEHIC BLINDES ARMES
971	*GOLD,NON MONETARY NES								254.3	OR NON MONETAIRE

5. Special Exports F.O.B. by Commodities according to the S.I.T.C. (Rev. 2) in million U.S. Dollars
Exportations Spéciales F.O.B. par Produits d'après la C.T.C.I. (Rév. 2) en millions de Dollars E.U.

SITC CTCI	COMMODITY	1992 QUANTITY QUANTITE	1992 VALUE VALEUR	1993 QUANTITY QUANTITE	1993 VALUE VALEUR	1994 QUANTITY QUANTITE	1994 VALUE VALEUR	1995 QUANTITY QUANTITE	1995 VALUE VALEUR	PRODUIT
	ALL COMMODITIES		319.2		354.7				353.9	TOUS PRODUITS
0	FOOD AND LIVE ANIMALS		40.5		31.8				20.7	ALIMENTS,ANIMAUX VIVANTS
001	*LIVE ANIMALS FOR FOOD		3.8		1.4			N 112	1.4	ANIMAUX VIVANTS
0019	LIVE ANIMALS FR FOOD NES		3.8		1.4					ANIMAUX VIVANTS NDA
04	CEREALS AND PREPARATIONS		0.4		0.5				1.3	CEREALES ET PRODUITS
048	CEREAL ETC PREPARATIONS		0.4		0.5				1.3	PREPTNS A BASE CEREALES
05	VEGETABLES AND FRUIT		27.5		22.6				9.3	LEGUMES ET FRUITS
054	VEG ETC FRSH,SMPLY PRSVD		27.4		22.6			W 2117	9.3	LEGUMES FRAIS,CONG,SECS
0542	LEGUMINOUS VEGETBLES DRY		27.3		22.6			W 19917	9.1	LEGUMES A COSSE SECS
07	COFFEE,TEA,COCOA,SPICES		5.4		4.3				5.5	CAFE,THE,CACAO,EPICES
075	SPICES		5.4		4.2				5.2	EPICES
0752	SPICES,EX PEPPER,PIMENTO		5.4		4.2				5.2	AUTRES EPICES
07524	NUTMEG,MACE,CARDAMOMS		2.7					W 2214	2.2	NOIX MUSCADES
07526	GINGER (EXCPT SWEETENED)		2.0					W 19300	3.0	GINGEMBRE
081	*FEEDING STUFF FOR ANIML		3.0		2.9				3.3	NOURRITURE POUR ANIMAUX
0812	BRAN,POLLARD,SHARPS,ETC		1.4		1.1				0.6	SONS
0813	OILCAKE AND OTH RESIDUES		1.6		1.9				2.1	TOURTEAUX
08139	— OF OTHER OILSEEDS ETC								2.1	TOURTEAUX D'AUTRES OLEAGINEU
2	CRUDE MATERLS,EXCL FUELS		9.6		12.1				7.8	MAT BRUTES NON COMESTIBLES
21	HIDES,SKINS,FURS UNDRSSD		1.3		2.3					CUIRS,PEAUX BRUTS
211	HIDES,SKINS,EXC FURS,RAW		1.3		2.3					CUIRS ET PEAUX
2119	SKIN NES,WASTE,USED LTHR		1.3		2.3					CUIRS ET PEAUX NDA
22	OIL SEEDS,OLEAGINOUS FRT		7.2		8.2				3.3	GRAINES,FRUITS OLEAGINEUX
223	SEEDS FOR OTH FIXED OILS		7.2		8.2			W 8847	3.0	GRAINES AUTRES HUILES FIXES
2234	LINSEED							W 5000	1.3	GRAINES DE LIN
2238	OIL SEEDS AND FRUITS NES		5.0	W 7672	5.6			W 3847	1.8	GRAINES D'OLEAGINEUX NDA
2239	OIL SEED FLOUR AND MEAL		2.3		2.6					FARINES GRAINES OLEAG
26	TEXTILE FIBRES AND WASTE		0.1		0.9				1.8	FIBRES TEXTILES
264	JUTE,OTH TEX BAST FIBRES		0.1		0.9				1.8	JUTE
29	CRUDE ANIMAL,VEG MAT NES		0.6		0.4				2.3	MATIERES BRUTES ANIM,VEGET
292	CRUDE VEG MATERIALS NES		0.6		0.4				2.3	MAT BRUTES VEGETALES NDA
2922	NAT GUMS,RESINS,LACS,ETC								1.7	GOMME LAQUE
4	ANIMAL,VEGETABLE OIL,FAT								4.3	HUILES,GRAISSES ANIM,VEG
42	FIXED VEGETABLE OIL,FAT								4.3	HUILES VEGETALES FIXES
424	FIXED VEG OIL NONSOFT								4.3	AUTRES HUILES VEG FIXES
4249	FIXED VEGETABLE OILS NES								3.3	HUILES VEGET FIXES NDA
5	CHEMCLS,RELATED PROD NES		5.1		2.2				4.4	PRODUITS CHIMIQUES
53	DYES,TANNING,COLOUR PROD		2.4		1.0				0.2	PROD TEINTURE,COLORANTS
532	DYES NES,TANNING PROD		2.4		1.0			W 20	0.2	EXTRAITS TEINTURE,TANNAGE
5322	DYE,TANN EXTRCTS,TANNINS		2.4		1.0			W 20	0.2	EXT TAN ORIG VEG,TANNINS
55	PERFUME,CLEANING ETC PRD		0.1		0.2				4.2	PROD POUR PARFUM,TOILETTE
553	PERFUMERY,COSMETICS,ETC		0.1		0.1			W 1600	4.1	PRODUITS DE PARFUMERIE
59	CHEMICAL MATERIALS NES		2.6		1.2				0.2	MAT PROD CHIMIQUES NDA
598	MISCEL CHEM PRODUCTS NES		2.6		1.2				0.2	PROD DIV INDUST CHIM NDA
5981	CHEMCLS FROM WOOD,RESIN		2.6		1.2				0.2	PROD CHIM BASE BOIS RESIN
6	BASIC MANUFACTURES		179.5		210.4				181.4	ART MANUFACTURES
61	LEATHER,DRESSED FUR,ETC		5.5		5.6				11.8	CUIRS,PELLETERIES
611	LEATHER		5.1	A 663	5.0			A 1317	11.7	CUIRS,PEAUX PREPARES
6114	LEATHR BOVINE NES,EQUINE	A 50	0.4	A 86	0.7			A 167	1.4	CUIRS DE BOVINS
6116	LEATHER OF OTH HIDE,SKIN		4.7	A 577	4.4			A 1150	10.4	PEAUX PREP D'AUTRES ANIMAUX
61161	LEATHER FROM GOAT,KID			A 284	2.0			A 1150	10.4	PEAUX DE CAPRINS PREPAREES
61169	LEATHER NES			A 293	2.5					PEAUX PREPAREES NDA
65	TEXTILE YARN,FABRICS,ETC		171.5		201.5				165.8	FILS,TISSUS,ARTICLES TEXTILE
651	TEXTILE YARN				0.5				5.1	FILS TEXTILES
6514	SYN FIB YRN,BULK,MONOFIL			W 42	0.1				5.1	FILS CONT 85% FIB TEXT SYNTH
65144	— TEXTRD,CONT POLYESTER								5.1	FILS TEX FI CONT POLYESTERS
654	OTH WOVEN TEXTILE FABRIC		1.7		1.5				0.4	TISSUS AUT COTON SYNT,ARTIF
6545	WEAVES OF FIBRES OF 2640		1.7		1.4				0.4	TISSUS DE JUTE
657	SPECIAL TXTL FABRC,PRODS		2.1		2.1				4.4	TISSUS SPECIAUX
6575	CORDAGE AND MANUFACTURES		2.1		2.1				4.4	FICELLES,CORDES,CORDAGES
658	TEXTILE ARTICLES NES		0.7		0.6				1.7	ART FACONNES MAT TEXTILES
6584	LINENS ETC				0.1				1.4	LINGE DE MAISON
659	FLOOR COVERINGS,ETC	A 2371	167.0	A 3126	196.7				154.4	COUVRE–PARQUETS,TAPIS ETC
6592	CARPETS ETC KNOTTED	A 2371	167.0	A 3126	196.7				154.4	TAPIS POINTS NOUES,ENROULES
65921	— OF WOOL OR FINE HAIR	A 2371	167.0	A 3126	196.7				154.4	TAP NOUES,ENROULES LAINE
69	METAL MANUFACTURES NES		1.8		2.7				2.6	ART MANUFACT EN METAL NDA
697	BASE MTL HOUSEHOLD EQUIP		1.8		2.7				2.6	ART MENAGE MET COMMUNS
6978	BASE MTL HOUSE EQUIP NES		1.8		2.7					ART MENAGE MET COMMUNS
69782	BASE MTL DECOR ARTICLES		1.8		2.7					AUT OBJETS ORNEM INTERIEUR
8	MISC MANUFACTURED GOODS		79.9		86.3				114.5	ART MANUFACTURES DIVERS
84	CLOTHING AND ACCESSORIES		77.9		85.0				111.4	VETEMENTS
842	MENS OUTERWEAR NOT KNIT		12.9		10.6				10.0	VET DESSUS POUR HOMMES
8423	— TROUSERS,BREECHES ETC		12.0		8.7					PANTALONS HOMMES MAT TEX
843	WOMENS OUTERWEAR NONKNIT		34.6		48.9				51.8	VET DESSUS FEMMES MAT TEX
8433	— DRESSES		1.3		4.0				13.8	ROBES EN MAT–TEXTILES
8434	— SKIRTS		0.6		0.8				4.8	JUPES EN MAT TEXTILES
8435	— BLOUSES		19.3		33.1				21.4	BLOUSES FEM MAT TEXTILES
8439	— OTHER OUTER GARMENTS		12.4		9.8				10.8	AUT VET DES FEM MAT TEXT
844	UNDER GARMENTS NOT KNIT		25.5		17.2				32.8	VETEMENT DESSOUS MAT TEX
8441	— MENS SHIRTS		21.5		15.0				32.8	CHEMISES HOMMES MAT TEXT
8442	— MENS,OTHR THAN SHIRTS		1.1		0.6					SOUS–VET HOMMES MAT TEXT
8443	— WOMENS		3.0		1.7					VET DESSOUS FEM MAT TEXT
845	OUTERWEAR KNIT NONELASTC		4.4		7.1				13.7	VET DESSOUS,ACCES BONNET
8451	— JERSEYS,PULLOVERS ETC		4.4		6.6					CHANDAILS,PULL–OVERS ETC
847	TEXTILE CLTHNG ACCES NES		0.6		0.6				1.8	ACCES VET MAT TEXT NDA
89	MISC MANUFCTRD GOODS NES		2.1		1.4				2.4	ART MANUFACTURES DIVERS
897	GOLD,SILVER WARE,JEWELRY		2.0		1.4				2.1	BIJOUTERIE,ORFEVRERIE
8973	PREC JEWLRY,GLD–SILVWARE		1.5		1.4				2.1	BIJOUX OR,ARGENT ORFEVRE
9	GOODS NOT CLASSD BY KIND		4.9		12.0				20.6	ART TRANSACT NON CLASSES
931	*SPECIAL TRANSACTIONS		4.9		12.0				20.6	TRANS.SPECIALES

FOOT NOTES – NOTES

TABLE 1 –
1 Prior to 1986, general trade.
TABLEAU 1 –
1 Avant 1986, commerce général.

1. HISTORICAL SERIES, 1962–1997 SPECIAL TRADE, IMPORTS C.I.F., EXPORTS F.O.B.
SERIES HISTORIQUES, 1962–1997 COMMERCE SPECIAL, IMPORTATIONS C.A.F., EXPORTATIONS F.O.B

YEAR ANNEE	VALUE IN MILLION NETH. GUILDERS VALEUR EN MILLION NETH. GUILDERS MERCHANDISE –MARCHANDISE IMPORTS	EXPORTS	GOLD # 1 –OR IMPORTS	EXPORTS	CONVERSION FACTORS U.S. CENTS PER NETH. GUILDER FACTEURS DE CONVERSION CENTS E.U. PAR NETH. GUILDER IMPORTS	EXPORTS	INDEX NUMBERS –INDICES QUANTUM IMPORTS	EXPORTS	UNIT VALUE VALEUR UNITAIRE IMPORTS	EXPORTS
1962	19358.00	16596.00	27.40	13.00	27.6243	27.6243				
1963	21602.00	17962.00	21.60	6.00	27.6243	27.6243				
1964	25548.00	21025.00	26.60	8.00	27.6243	27.6243				
1965	27010.00	23144.00	35.90	15.00	27.6243	27.6243				
1966	29024.00	24443.00	40.10	28.00	27.6243	27.6243				
1967	30181.00	26380.00	124.80	95.00	27.6243	27.6243				
1968	33638.00	30197.00	166.40	121.00	27.6243	27.6243				
1969	39797.00	36074.00	155.80	131.00	27.6243	27.6243				
1970	48603.00	42622.00	114.80	54.00	27.6243	27.6243				
1971	52294.00	49775.00	117.40	27.00	28.5600	28.5840				
1972	55422.00	53879.00	60.00	17.00	31.1517	31.1488				
1973	66560.00	66873.00	141.20	89.00	36.0457	35.9656				
1974	87821.00	87993.00	278.00	162.00	37.3230	37.3154				
1975	88010.00	88655.00			39.5815	39.5903				
1976	104250.00	106017.00			37.9621	37.9328				
1977	111974.00	107195.00			40.7577	40.7690				
1978	114372.00	108205.00			46.3722	46.3483				
1979	134885.00	127689.00			49.9034	49.8842				
1980	152279.00	146967.00			50.3142	50.3185	70	66	96	92
1981	163999.00	170772.00			40.1962	40.2479	65	67	111	107
1982	167346.00	176761.00			37.4489	37.5014	66	66	113	111
1983	175456.00	186745.00			35.1295	35.1697	67	69	114	111
1984	198921.50	210691.30			31.2365	31.2690	72	74	120	119
1985	216008.00	226017.00			30.2682	30.2713	77	77	122	122
1986	185053.00	197286.00			40.9016	40.8096	80	79	100	103
1987	184844.00	188017.00			49.4987	49.5146	85	83	94	94
1988	195801.00	203778.00			50.8281	50.8326	91	91	94	94
1989	221412.00	229409.00			47.1823	47.2017	95	95	103	101
1990	229708.00	239181.00			55.0632	55.0994	100	100	100	100
1991	237118.00	249051.00			53.6658	53.6725	104	105	100	98
1992	236597.00	246541.00			56.9194	56.9301	106	108	97	95
1993	231637.00	258343.00			53.8524	53.8534	110	116	92	92
1994	256442.00	282209.00			55.1067	55.1202	121	129	92	92
1995	283537.90	314693.10			62.3809	62.3706	136	140	92	94
1996	304557.00	332920.00			59.3127	59.2996	144	147	93	94
1997	345784.00	378245.10			51.2968	51.2925				

2. IMPORTS BY BROAD ECONOMIC CATEGORY AND EXPORTS BY INDUSTRIAL ORIGIN. (PERCENTAGE OF TOTAL VALUE)
IMPORTATIONS PAR CATEGORIES ECONOMIQUES ET EXPORTATIONS PAR BRANCHE D'ACTIVITE.(EN POURCENTAGE DE LA VALEUR TOTALE)

IMPORTS – IMPORTATIONS

	1991	1992	1993	1994	1995	1996	1997
TOTAL IMPORTS–IMPORTATIONS TOTALES	100.	100.	100.	100.	100.	100.	100.
1 FOOD BEV–ALIMENTATION BOISSONS	11.0	11.7	12.1	12.4	11.7	11.3	9.3
11 PRIMARY–PRODUITS DE BASE	5.8	6.0	6.2	6.8	6.0	6.2	5.1
111 FOR INDUSTRY–POUR L'INDUSTRIE	2.9	2.9	3.0	3.4	2.9	3.1	2.3
112 FOR HOUSEHOLDS–POUR LES MENAGES	3.0	3.0	3.2	3.4	3.2	3.1	2.7
12 PROCESSED–PRODUITS ELABORES	5.1	5.7	5.9	5.7	5.6	5.1	4.3
121 FOR INDUSTRY–POUR L'INDUSTRIE	0.9	0.9	1.1	1.2	1.1	1.1	0.8
122 FOR HOUSEHOLDS–POUR LES MENAGES	4.3	4.8	4.8	4.5	4.6	4.1	3.5
2 IND SUPPLIES–APPROV INDUSTRIELS	29.6	29.2	28.8	30.2	31.2	28.5	26.5
21 PRIMARY–PRODUITS DE BASE	3.4	3.3	3.4	3.3	3.3	2.9	2.7
22 PROCESSED–PRODUITS ELABORES	26.2	25.9	25.4	26.9	27.9	25.7	23.8
3 FUELS–COMBUSTIBLES	9.0	8.2	9.2	7.8	7.4	8.5	8.4
31 PRIMARY–PRODUITS DE BASE	7.2	6.8	6.8	5.9	5.8	6.8	6.4
32 PROCESSED–PRODUITS ELABORES	1.8	1.4	2.4	1.9	1.6	1.8	2.0
321 MOTOR SPIRIT–ESSENCE	0.6	0.6	0.7	0.6	0.5	0.5	0.7
322 OTHER–AUTRES	1.2	0.8	1.7	1.3	1.1	1.2	1.3
4 MACHINERY–EQUIPEMENT	20.7	20.9	20.4	21.0	22.3	23.9	27.2
41 CAPITAL EQUIPMENT–MACHINES	15.9	16.1	15.3	15.8	16.6	17.8	18.3
42 PARTS–PIECES ACCESSOIRES	4.8	4.8	5.1	5.2	5.7	6.1	8.9
5 TRANSPORT–TRANSPORT	11.3	11.2	10.9	10.7	11.1	10.9	10.6
51 PASSENGER CARS–AUTOMOBILES	4.0	3.7	4.2	4.0	4.2	4.3	4.0
52 OTHER–AUTRES	2.6	3.0	2.4	2.7	2.6	2.4	2.3
521 INDUSTRIAL–INDUSTRIELS	2.4	2.7	2.1	2.4	2.4	2.0	2.0
522 NON INDUSTRIAL–NON INDUSTRIEL	0.3	0.3	0.3	0.3	0.2	0.4	0.3
53 PARTS–PIECES ACCESSOIRES	4.6	4.5	4.2	4.0	4.3	4.2	4.3
6 CONSUM GOODS–BIENS CONSOMMATION	17.8	18.1	18.0	17.2	15.8	16.1	17.7
61 DURABLE–DURABLES	4.7	4.5	4.3	4.0	3.8	4.1	4.4
62 SEMI DURABLE–SEMI DURABLES	9.6	9.9	9.7	9.1	7.9	8.3	9.3
63 NON DURABLE–NON DURABLES	3.4	3.7	4.0	4.2	4.1	3.8	4.0
7 GOODS NES–BIENS NDA	0.6	0.7	0.6	0.6	0.5	0.8	0.2

EXPORTS – EXPORTATIONS

	1991	1992	1993	1994	1995	1996	1997
TOTAL EXPORTS–EXPORTATIONS TOTALES	100.	100.	100.	100.	100.	100.	100.
1 AGRICULTURE	8.6	8.6	8.1	8.5	7.6	7.3	5.9
2 MINING QUARRY–INDUS EXTRACTIVES	3.9	3.5	3.5	2.9	2.9	3.3	2.8
3 MANUFACTURING–IND MANUFACTUR	87.5	87.8	88.4	88.5	89.5	89.4	91.3
31 FOOD BEV TOBACCO–ALIM BOISS TAB	15.7	16.7	17.1	16.4	15.7	15.0	12.9
32 TEXTILES–INDUSTRIES TEXTILES	4.5	4.6	4.3	4.2	4.1	4.0	7.9
33 WOOD & PRODUCTS–BOIS & PRODUITS	0.6	0.6	0.6	0.6	0.5	0.5	0.4
34 PAPER & PRODUCTS–PAPIER & PRODT	3.1	3.2	2.6	2.9	3.1	2.7	2.4
35 CHEMICALS–INDUSTRIES CHIMIQUES	23.3	22.2	22.4	22.7	23.1	23.0	23.0
36 NON METAL MIN–MIN NON METAL	1.1	1.2	1.1	1.0	0.9	0.8	0.9
37 BASIC METAL–IND METAL BASE	3.9	3.6	3.4	3.8	4.1	3.6	3.5
38 METAL MANUF–MANUF METAL	30.7	31.1	32.3	31.8	33.2	35.1	39.1
39 OTH MANUF IND–AUTRES MANUF	4.6	4.7	4.7	5.1	4.7	4.6	1.2

3. TRADE BY PRINCIPAL COUNTRIES OF ORIGIN AND DESTINATION (VALUE IN MILLION U.S. DOLLARS)
ECHANGES SELON LES PRINCIPAUX PAYS D'ORIGINE ET DE DESTINATION (VALEUR EN MILLIONS DE DOLLARS EU)

COUNTRIES–PAYS	SPECIAL IMPORTS C.I.F. IMPORTATIONS SPECIALES C.A.F				
	1993	1994	1995	1996	1997
World	115667.7	130511.7	157929.4	160896.3	162359.7
Africa	2772.6	2916.1	3471.7	3869.2	3309.2
Americas	13539.5	15433.6	18869.2	18894.8	21225.0
– Northern America	10508.3	11013.6	14252.0	14421.2	17010.2
– LAIA	2643.3	3870.3	3974.4	3805.4	3429.1
– CACM	153.7	200.5	216.0	261.2	230.8
– Caribbean	147.5	259.2	325.4	308.2	440.7
– Rest of America	86.7	90.0	101.5	98.8	114.3
Asia excl fmr USSR	19403.9	20041.5	23932.5	27013.6	30672.3
– Middle East	4824.6	4280.7	4771.7	5171.3	5138.0
Asia former USSR	22.0	9.4	13.2	16.5	27.5
Europe excl fmr USSR	75479.8	86972.7	104861.0	103097.3	104035.5
– European Union	70426.8	80924.1	97063.2	94569.5	95468.3
– Eastern Europe	1311.3	1594.4	2226.2	2267.5	2591.7
– Rest of Europe	3741.7	4454.2	5571.6	6260.3	5975.5
Europe former USSR	1434.2	1472.5	2049.9	2374.4	2654.4
Oceania	447.5	505.0	458.0	427.8	397.1
Other	2568.2	3160.8	4274.0	5202.7	38.8
Germany/Allemagne	25124.1	28787.7	34168.2	32896.0	29075.8
Belgium–Luxembourg	12614.9	14690.3	17247.0	16563.6	15285.0
United Kingdom	10056.7	11379.5	14614.3	14365.0	16240.4
USA/Etats–Unis d'Amer	9833.4	10268.0	13292.0	13497.4	16121.4
France, Monaco	8081.9	9395.4	10937.1	10925.0	11244.6
Japan/Japon	4701.5	4754.3	5626.5	6176.5	6310.1
Italy/Italie	4068.0	4669.2	5323.3	5312.2	5641.2
Sweden/Suède	2412.1	3017.9	4054.7	4078.4	4544.5
Spain/Espagne	2212.3	2457.3	3112.1	3363.5	4081.2
Special Categories	2558.3	3156.1	4265.1	5183.5	
Norway,Svalbard and JM	1838.0	2357.0	3086.3	3853.5	3689.5
China/Chine	1442.6	1746.8	2168.9	2456.3	2973.0
Other Asia n.e.s.	1418.1	1414.0	1829.0	2195.9	2958.2
Switzerland,Liechtenst.	1608.8	1818.2	2137.1	2061.9	1919.4
China, Hong Kong SAR	1518.5	1581.6	1958.3	2118.7	2338.3
Saudi Arabia	1565.5	1616.6	1936.6	2063.9	2213.9
Ireland/Irlande	1425.1	1536.8	2041.0	1654.1	2325.9
Brazil/Brésil	1226.0	1848.5	1709.7	1713.1	1560.7
Denmark/Danemark	1357.1	1483.0	1663.6	1624.0	1924.8
Finland/Finlande	1194.6	1490.6	1544.7	1346.2	1854.1
Russian Federation	928.1	940.1	1296.7	1573.8	1824.1
Singapore/Singapour	706.8	1107.1	1421.2	1637.3	1567.8
Malaysia/Malaisie	773.8	851.6	1085.0	1307.5	2206.6
Austria/Autriche	1080.0	1137.0	1245.9	1252.3	1420.3
Kuwait/ Koweït	1291.3	922.8	1148.3	1384.4	1069.2
Thailand/Thaïlande	903.7	818.8	958.6	1261.9	1320.5
Indonesia/Indonésie	814.8	1009.7	1084.4	1181.9	1038.4
Portugal	587.5	673.7	894.3	953.8	1238.3
Iran (Islamic Rep of)	1185.0	991.2	751.5	739.9	645.4
Poland/Pologne	624.2	727.5	934.7	975.5	962.9
Canada	668.7	741.3	925.7	873.2	865.7
Algeria/Algérie	821.7	625.1	893.1	864.6	842.5
Korea, Republic of	634.8	644.3	801.5	922.2	991.0
Turkey/Turquie	598.7	601.5	739.5	788.2	815.9
Israel/Israël	492.0	524.2	636.4	778.1	816.3
India/Inde	479.7	543.0	680.7	747.7	756.5
Argentina/Argentine	495.2	810.9	732.9	725.4	426.1
Nigeria/Nigéria	542.6	669.3	407.0	620.8	364.7
Philippines	226.1	218.8	280.9	372.3	1505.3
Hungary/Hongrie	218.7	254.2	402.8	463.4	784.0

COUNTRIES–PAYS	SPECIAL EXPORTS F.O.B. EXPORTATIONS SPECIALES F.O.B.				
	1993	1994	1995	1996	1997
Monde	131143.3	145825.3	177626.3	177369.4	184433.3
Afrique	2617.2	2352.6	3082.8	2762.7	3063.7
Amériques	7519.5	7815.6	8830.3	8232.6	10426.8
– Amérique du Nord	5357.8	5927.8	6297.7	6021.1	7716.0
– ALAI	1465.6	1208.1	1714.9	1576.9	1976.5
– MCAC	76.5	103.2	135.1	125.1	95.5
– Caraïbes	507.6	476.0	555.5	396.9	503.3
– Autre Amérique	112.0	100.5	127.1	112.6	135.5
Asie anc. URSS exclus	9292.7	9568.9	12155.1	12139.2	14328.3
– Moyen–Orient	2887.2	2576.8	3070.6	3053.1	3734.9
Asie ancienne URSS	116.1	92.8	103.2	148.1	153.6
Europe anc. URSS exclus	97277.0	109384.1	134431.1	133655.8	151944.2
– Union Européenne	91910.6	103211.0	126783.8	126464.1	143492.0
– Europe de l'Est	1829.8	2150.3	2732.9	2807.3	3583.6
– Autre de l'Europe	3536.6	4022.8	4914.3	4384.3	4868.6
Europe ancienne URSS	1226.0	1553.5	2111.4	2202.7	2643.4
Océanie	531.5	663.9	598.5	574.5	766.0
Autre	12563.3	14393.9	16313.9	17653.9	1107.2
Germany/Allemagne	34730.9	38267.2	46123.3	45896.3	46095.0
Belgium–Luxembourg	15526.1	18050.7	21162.6	21240.8	20995.5
France, Monaco	12409.9	13978.9	17636.6	17478.6	19215.8
United Kingdom	10918.6	12533.9	15183.0	14846.8	17810.6
Special Categories	11428.0	13282.9	15174.0	16630.5	
Italy/Italie	6689.8	7104.0	8754.8	9235.2	11137.0
USA/Etats–Unis d'Amer	4883.0	5360.5	5680.5	5469.9	7109.3
Spain/Espagne	2911.4	3345.3	4609.3	4492.8	6053.0
Sweden/Suède	1885.2	2133.3	3233.4	3481.2	5309.0
Denmark/Danemark	1749.1	2164.3	2664.3	2622.6	3781.3
Switzerland,Liechtenst.	2121.6	2375.9	2887.2	2525.0	2637.7
Austria/Autriche	1446.9	1637.0	2376.2	2383.8	3250.9
Greece/Grèce	1249.1	1411.5	1586.3	1389.2	2773.0
Japan/Japon	1096.7	1335.7	1698.0	1759.6	1881.4
Russian Federation	1018.9	1243.0	1576.7	1589.3	1921.0
Portugal	1059.1	986.4	1173.9	1119.5	2149.3
Ireland/Irlande	685.3	768.8	1018.9	975.6	2766.5
Finland/Finlande	649.3	829.6	1261.2	1301.5	2155.1
Poland/Pologne	846.5	975.4	1240.6	1281.4	1674.3
Norway,Svalbard and JM	810.7	977.0	1284.2	1116.3	1365.5
Bunkers, ship stores	1117.8	1094.7	1127.7	996.0	1062.1
Turkey/Turquie	818.0	644.3	990.8	1128.3	1504.3
Other Asia n.e.s.	728.3	801.7	890.7	1020.4	1548.5
China, Hong Kong SAR	615.7	788.4	1021.2	963.8	1098.6
Singapore/Singapour	720.1	693.0	992.6	875.9	939.0
Korea, Republic of	487.0	592.8	762.0	910.7	1079.3
China/Chine	609.6	562.7	722.6	645.2	813.4
Saudi Arabia	684.6	591.7	629.3	595.5	653.8
Brazil/Brésil	453.9	343.8	799.9	617.2	691.2
Canada	454.6	541.7	611.0	540.7	593.5
Czech Republic	341.4	412.6	554.1	637.4	704.1
Indonesia/Indonésie	539.5	369.7	733.5	398.2	528.4
Israel/Israël	381.1	439.6	513.9	514.9	618.0
Australia/Australie	418.7	535.7	445.2	430.8	604.1
Hungary/Hongrie	332.2	411.7	458.4	444.4	640.6
So. African Customs Un	360.3	388.7	478.6	449.0	567.9
Thailand/Thaïlande	266.1	407.7	498.7	498.7	554.7
United Arab Emirates	375.9	385.0	435.5	405.1	470.8
India/Inde	257.5	262.4	367.9	451.0	480.6
Egypt/Egypte	292.3	315.4	334.5	299.0	406.3

(VALUE AS PERCENTAGE OF WORLD TOTAL)(VALEURS EN POURCENTAGE DU TOTAL MONDIAL)

	1988	1989	1990	1991	1992	1993	1994	1995	1996	1997
Africa	2.7	2.6	2.7	2.7	2.4	2.4	2.2	2.2	2.4	2.0
Americas	11.0	11.5	10.9	10.7	10.3	11.7	11.8	11.9	11.7	13.1
– Northern America	8.3	9.0	8.4	8.4	8.1	9.1	8.4	9.0	9.0	10.5
– LAIA	2.3	2.2	2.2	2.0	1.9	2.3	3.0	2.5	2.4	2.1
– CACM	0.1	0.1	0.1	0.1	0.1	0.1	0.2	0.1	0.2	0.1
– Caribbean	0.1	0.1	0.1	0.1	0.1	0.1	0.2	0.2	0.2	0.3
– Rest of America	0.2	0.2	0.2	0.1	0.1	0.1	0.1	0.1	0.1	0.1
Asia excl fmr USSR	12.0	12.5	12.4	13.1	13.2	16.8	15.4	15.2	16.8	18.9
– Middle East	3.4	4.3	4.0	3.6	3.5	4.2	3.3	3.0	3.2	3.2
Asia former USSR					0.0	0.0	0.0	0.0	0.0	0.0
Europe excl fmr USSR	71.5	70.3	71.1	71.1	71.4	65.3	66.6	66.4	64.1	64.1
– European Union	67.6	66.4	67.0	67.6	67.5	60.9	62.0	61.5	58.8	58.8
– Eastern Europe	0.9	1.0	1.0	0.9	1.0	1.1	1.2	1.4	1.4	1.6
– Rest of Europe	2.9	2.9	3.0	2.7	2.9	3.2	3.4	3.5	3.9	3.7
Europe former USSR	1.1	1.3	1.2	0.9	0.9	1.2	1.1	1.3	1.5	1.6
Oceania	0.5	0.4	0.4	0.4	0.4	0.4	0.4	0.3	0.3	0.2
Other	1.3	1.5	1.3	1.2	1.5	2.2	2.4	2.7	3.2	0.0
Germany/Allemagne				25.4	24.9	21.7	22.1	21.6	20.4	17.9
Belgium–Luxembourg	14.5	13.9	13.7	14.0	14.1	10.9	11.3	10.9	10.3	9.4
United Kingdom	7.6	7.8	8.1	8.6	8.5	8.7	8.7	9.3	8.9	10.0
USA/Etats–Unis d'Amer	7.5	8.2	7.7	7.7	7.6	8.5	7.9	8.4	8.4	9.9
France, Monaco	7.6	7.5	7.7	7.5	7.8	7.0	7.2	6.9	6.8	6.9
Japan/Japon	3.2	3.0	3.1	3.6	3.5	4.1	3.6	3.6	3.8	3.9
Italy/Italie	3.7	3.6	3.7	3.7	3.6	3.5	3.6	3.4	3.3	3.5
Sweden/Suède	2.2	2.2	2.1	2.0	2.0	2.1	2.3	2.6	2.5	2.8
Spain/Espagne	1.4	1.3	1.5	1.5	1.6	1.9	1.9	2.0	2.1	2.5
Special Categories	1.2	1.5	1.3	1.2	1.5	2.2	2.4	2.7	3.2	

	1988	1989	1990	1991	1992	1993	1994	1995	1996	1997
Afrique	2.5	2.3	2.0	1.8	1.8	2.0	1.6	1.7	1.6	1.7
Amériques	5.4	5.8	4.9	4.8	5.2	5.7	5.4	5.0	4.6	5.7
– Amérique du Nord	4.4	4.7	4.0	3.8	4.0	4.1	4.1	3.5	3.4	4.2
– ALAI	0.6	0.6	0.5	0.6	0.8	1.1	0.8	1.0	0.9	1.1
– MCAC	0.1	0.1	0.1	0.0	0.0	0.1	0.1	0.1	0.1	0.1
– Caraïbes	0.3	0.3	0.3	0.3	0.3	0.4	0.3	0.3	0.2	0.3
– Autre Amérique	0.1	0.1	0.1	0.1	0.1	0.1	0.1	0.1	0.1	0.1
Asie anc. URSS exclus	5.7	5.0	5.0	5.2	5.7	7.1	6.6	6.8	6.8	7.8
– Moyen–Orient	1.8	1.7	1.7	1.8	1.9	2.2	1.8	1.7	1.7	2.0
Asie ancienne URSS					0.0	0.1	0.1	0.1	0.1	0.1
Europe anc. URSS exclus	77.9	77.9	79.1	79.2	78.3	74.2	75.0	75.7	75.4	82.4
– Union Européenne	74.0	74.3	75.3	75.0	74.2	70.1	70.8	71.4	71.3	77.8
– Europe de l'Est	0.8	0.9	0.9	1.0	1.2	1.4	1.5	1.5	1.6	1.9
– Autre de l'Europe	3.1	2.7	2.9	3.2	2.9	2.7	2.8	2.8	2.5	2.6
Europe ancienne URSS	0.4	0.5	0.4	0.4	0.5	0.9	1.1	1.2	1.2	1.4
Océanie	0.5	0.5	0.4	0.4	0.4	0.4	0.5	0.3	0.3	0.4
Autre	7.6	8.1	8.3	8.2	8.1	9.6	9.9	9.2	10.0	0.6
Germany/Allemagne				27.8	27.1	26.5	26.2	26.0	25.9	25.0
Belgium–Luxembourg	14.1	13.9	13.9	13.6	13.6	11.8	12.4	11.9	12.0	11.4
France, Monaco	10.2	10.2	10.4	9.9	9.8	9.5	9.6	9.9	9.9	10.4
United Kingdom	10.1	10.4	9.5	8.6	8.5	8.3	8.6	8.5	8.4	9.7
Special Categories	6.9	7.3	7.5	7.4	7.4	8.7	9.1	8.5	9.4	
Italy/Italie	5.9	6.0	6.1	5.9	6.0	5.1	4.9	4.9	5.2	6.0
USA/Etats–Unis d'Amer	3.9	4.1	3.6	3.4	3.7	3.7	3.7	3.2	3.1	3.9
Spain/Espagne	1.8	2.2	2.4	2.4	2.5	2.2	2.3	2.6	2.5	3.3
Sweden/Suède	1.7	1.8	1.6	1.5	1.4	1.4	1.5	1.8	2.0	2.9
Denmark/Danemark	1.5	1.5	1.5	1.5	1.4	1.3	1.5	1.5	1.5	2.1

4. Special Imports C.I.F. by Commodities according to the S.I.T.C. (Rev. 2) in million U.S. Dollars
Importations Spéciales C.A.F. par Produits d'après la C.T.C.I. (Rév. 2) en millions de Dollars E.U.

SITC CTCI	COMMODITY	1994 QUANTITY QUANTITE	1994 VALUE VALEUR	1995 QUANTITY QUANTITE	1995 VALUE VALEUR	1996 QUANTITY QUANTITE	1996 VALUE VALEUR	1997 QUANTITY QUANTITE	1997 VALUE VALEUR	PRODUIT
	ALL COMMODITIES		130511.8		157929.5		160896.4		162359.7	TOUS PRODUITS
0	FOOD AND LIVE ANIMALS		14832.4		16837.1		16619.0		13415.6	ALIMENTS,ANIMAUX VIVANTS
001	*LIVE ANIMALS FOR FOOD	W 271980	529.2	W 267708	514.5	W 264845	450.2	W 97155	408.2	ANIMAUX VIVANTS
0011	BOVINE SPECIES,LIVE	W 153970	399.5	W 111910	327.7	W 93680	240.2		232.4	ESPECE BOVINE
01	MEAT AND PREPARATIONS		1168.3		1277.5		1313.6		1214.9	VIANDES ET PREPARATIONS
011	MEAT FRESH,CHILLD,FROZEN	W 346920	891.6	W 344197	976.8	W 362799	1002.9	W 377015	933.0	VIANDES FRAICHES,REF,CONGE
0111	BOVINE MEAT FRESH,FROZEN	W 107393	422.0	W 112430	480.1	W 118549	435.2	W 127513	400.7	VIANDES BOVIN FRAI,REF
02	DAIRY PRODCTS,BIRDS'EGGS		2004.2		2963.9		2283.2		1970.0	PRODUITS LAITIERS,OEUFS
022	MILK AND CREAM	W 1549622	1348.9	W 1760799	2136.8	W 1764392	1611.0	W 1613593	1368.9	LAIT ET CREME
0224	MILK,CREAM PRESERVED ETC	W 923094	1008.3	W 1089819	1718.5	W 1028555	1203.8	W 907754	1033.8	LAIT,CREME CONS,CONC
02242	MILK DRY,1.5% FAT OR LES	W 229584	532.9	W 294223	823.1	W 221808	532.4	W 234180	508.4	LAIT POUDRE INF 1.5%
02243	MILK DRY,OVER 1.5% FAT	W 69484	197.8	W 136761	488.9	W 94378	298.0	W 80859	226.2	LAIT POUDRE SUP 1.5%
03	FISH AND PREPARATIONS		786.9		948.2		943.4		835.7	POISSONS ET PREPARATIONS
034	FISH,FRESH,CHILLED,FROZN	W 299004	425.5	W 294802	499.2	W 246896	497.0	W 268899	437.9	POISSON FRAIS, REFRIG,CONG
04	CEREALS AND PREPARATIONS		1936.6		2100.8		2135.8		1784.7	CEREALES ET PRODUITS
041	WHEAT ETC UNMILLED	W 2490034	451.5	W 2720648	540.4	W 2930358	578.0	W 2877940	467.8	FROMENT,EPEAUTRE
0412	OTHER WHEAT ETC UNMILLED	W 2481665	449.8	W 2711274	538.4	W 2904028	571.3	W 2807554	454.9	AUTRE FROMENT NON MOULU
044	MAIZE UNMILLED	W 1987326	410.3	W 1721684	430.9	W 1597742	376.2	W 2049999	362.4	MAIS NON MOULU
048	CEREAL ETC PREPARATIONS	W 475890	540.2	W 492708	601.7	W 484522	579.6	W 483163	518.0	PREPTNS A BASE CEREALES
05	VEGETABLES AND FRUIT		4039.2		4348.5		4494.6		3663.0	LEGUMES ET FRUITS
054	VEG ETC FRSH,SMPLY PRSVD	W 5866245	1490.5	W 4327969	1517.0	W 5177909	1545.8	W 3796362	1193.7	LEGUMES FRAIS,CONG,SECS
057	FRUIT,NUTS,FRESH,DRIED	W 1862932	1511.3	W 1826406	1610.1	W 1806011	1642.7	W 1735850	1456.7	FRUITS FRAIS OU SECS
0579	FRUIT FRESH OR DRIED NES	W 417242	415.4	W 406958	441.5	W 462287	468.2	W 443211	424.6	FRUITS FRAIS,SECS NDA
058	FRUIT PRESERVED,PREPARED	W 833207	802.1	W 908661	975.8	W 913393	1032.1	W 792085	783.2	CONSERVES DE FRUITS
0585	FRUIT OR VEGETABLE JUICE	W 555772	501.3	W 646333	667.7	W 617836	706.7	W 499587	467.9	JUS DE FRUITS
06	SUGAR AND PREPS,HONEY		426.9		466.2		451.9		360.2	SUCRES ET PRODUITS
07	COFFEE,TEA,COCOA,SPICES		1559.4		1961.1		2053.7		1652.2	CAFE,THE,CACAO,EPICES
071	COFFEE AND SUBSTITUTES	W 168762	493.5	W 166658	725.2	W 183202	599.5	W 163978	619.0	CAFE ET SUCCEDANES
0711	COFFEE GREEN,ROASTED,SUB	W 162800	440.7	W 160678	660.5	W 175359	533.3	W 156581	553.8	CAFE TORREFIE OU DECAFEINE
07111	COFFEE GREEN,HUSKS,SKINS	W 137446	324.2	W 137918	519.3	W 152338	415.9	W 132828	431.2	CAFE NON TORREFIE
072	COCOA	W 439357	678.2	W 462622	799.8	W 626544	1015.7	W 357280	589.2	CACAO
0721	COCOA BEANS,RAW,ROASTED	W 363965	492.5	W 399182	621.4	W 556841	819.8	W 288080	426.0	CACAO EN FEVES
081	*FEEDING STUFF FOR ANIML	MW 11085	1831.0	MW 10252	1657.8	MW 10877	1960.5	W 5773994	1071.1	NOURRITURE POUR ANIMAUX
0813	OILCAKE AND OTH RESIDUES	W 4550473	717.2	W 4063243	588.4	W 4150794	729.8	W 1625722	300.4	TOURTEAUX
0819	FOOD WASTE AND FEED NES	W 3804258	687.1	W 3908209	716.7	W 4202053	828.2	W 2683649	539.0	DECHETS,ALIMENTS NDA
08199	FODDER NES,INCL SWEETNED	W 659685	355.4	W 613398	349.6	W 2101333	589.5	W 1830107	487.0	PREPARATIONS FOURRAGERES
09	MISC EDIBLE PRODUCTS		551.2		599.0		532.5		456.1	PREP ALIMENTAIRES DIVERSES
098	EDIBLE PRODCTS,PREPS NES	W 246653	472.7	W 237695	504.4	W 248655	461.4	W 243226	388.5	PREP ALIMENTAIRES NDA
1	BEVERAGES AND TOBACCO		1849.5		2085.5		2083.6		2045.8	BOISSONS ET TABACS
11	BEVERAGES		977.2		1084.1		1111.7		1048.3	BOISSONS
112	ALCOHOLIC BEVERAGES	W 417126	763.7	W 428191	841.1	W 425969	850.4	W 460732	766.4	BOISSONS ALCOOLIQUES
1121	WINE OF FRESH GRAPES ETC	W 237446	513.3	W 219301	539.7	W 229183	568.8	W 244057	532.2	VINS DE RAISINS FRAIS
11212	WINE OF FRESH GRAPES	W 233903	508.4	W 213183	528.7	W 222992	557.5	W 240041	525.9	VINS DE MOUTS DE RAISINS
12	TOBACCO AND MANUFACTURES		872.3		1001.4		972.0		997.5	TABACS BRUTS FABRIQUES
121	TOBACCO UNMNFCTRD,REFUSE	W 87683	433.4	W 89087	478.2	W 97651	465.5	W 118772	538.3	TABACS BRUTS,DECHETS
122	TOBACCO,MANUFACTURED	W 38593	438.9	W 38132	523.3	W 39106	506.6	W 40113	459.2	TABACS FABRIQUES
2	CRUDE MATERLS,EXCL FUELS		7002.4		7930.2		7655.4		7286.9	MAT BRUTES NON COMESTIBLES
22	OIL SEEDS,OLEAGINOUS FRT		1909.4		1695.7		1908.3		1520.9	GRAINES,FRUITS OLEAGINEUX
222	SEEDS FOR'SOFT'FIXED OIL	W 6354151	1854.0	W 5969008	1639.8	W 5852693	1839.7	W 4513492	1460.2	GRAINES HUILES FIXES
2222	SOYA BEANS	W 5232517	1377.2	W 4880370	1191.9	W 4736947	1378.9	W 3501153	1050.3	FEVES DE SOJA
24	CORK AND WOOD		1171.3		1109.6		1037.7		1022.6	LIEGE ET BOIS
248	WOOD SHAPED,SLEEPERS	W 2168819	1092.3	W 1843118	1028.4	W 1899509	963.7	W 1929973	963.4	BOIS SIMPLEMENT TRAVAILLES
2482	LUMBER SHAPED CONIFER	W 1591602	659.6	W 1371317	615.0	W 1442323	565.4	W 1466482	580.2	CONIFERES SCIES,RABOTES
24821	LUMBER SAWN ETC CONIFER	W 1582766	651.2	W 1363259	603.7	W 1435730	559.1	W 1461698	574.0	CONIFERES SCIES LONGITUD
2483	LUMBER SHAPED NON–CONIFR	W 559786	429.1	W 462745	411.6	W 450938	397.2	W 457401	382.3	NON CONIFERES SCIES,RABOTES
251	*PULP AND WASTE PAPER	W 2007156	547.5	W 2345070	970.0	W 2348380	718.0	W 2290071	684.7	PATES A PAPIER,DECHETS
2517	SODA,SULPHATE WOOD PULP	W 734312	349.0	W 714129	545.3	W 862540	488.5	W 960774	513.8	PATES CHIMIQUES AU SULFATE
25172	— BLEACHED,NONDISSOLVNG	W 731947	347.9	W 709286	541.7	W 856077	485.0	W 951294	509.2	PATES BLANCHIES
27	CRUDE FERTLZR,MINRLS NES		679.3		814.3		840.4		700.8	ENGRAIS MINERAUX BRUTS
28	METALLIFEROUS ORES,SCRAP		1235.9		1679.1		1412.9		1606.1	MINERAIS METAL,DECHETS
282	IRON AND STEEL SCRAP	W 2933386	424.6	W 3042422	545.0	W 2810018	431.4	W 2070167	325.1	FERRAILLES
287	BASE METAL ORES,CONC NES	W 1270534	334.4	W 1301185	437.1	W 1380546	397.6	W 1268044	648.7	MINERAIS METAUX COMMUNS
288	NONFERR METAL SCRAP NES	W 297389	298.2	W 364210	504.4	W 340773	394.1	W 394482	455.1	DECHETS NON FERREUX
2882	OTHER BASE MTL SCRAP NES	W 268821	281.3	W 329756	478.7	W 302231	371.4	W 348850	431.2	AUTRES DECHETS
29	CRUDE ANIMAL,VEG MAT NES		893.1		992.0		1155.0		1172.5	MATIERES BRUTES ANIM,VEGET
292	CRUDE VEG MATERIALS NES	W 475617	785.0	W 344962	854.6	W 560214	991.1		1025.1	MAT BRUTES VEGETALES NDA
2927	CUT FLOWERS AND FOLIAGE	W 101734	375.6	W 107621	442.8	W 137387	533.9	W 152750	542.8	FLEURS,FEUILLAGES COUPES
3	MINERAL FUELS ETC		10691.5		12161.8		14326.3		14142.2	COMBUSTIBLES MINERAUX LUB
32	COAL,COKE AND BRIQUETTES		886.6		987.4		920.0		950.3	HOUILLES,COKES,BRIQUETTES
322	COAL,LIGNITE AND PEAT	MW 18886	833.3	MW 19127	905.8	MW 19600	882.7	MW 20883	914.3	HOUILLES,LIGNITES,TOURBE
3222	OTH COAL,NOT AGGLOMERATD	MW 16792	728.9	MW 17438	815.1	MW 17528	776.8	MW 18997	830.1	AUTRES HOUILLES
33	PETROLEUM AND PRODUCTS		9005.9		10290.2		12463.8		11892.3	PETROLE ET DERIVES
333	CRUDE PETROLEUM	MW 56594	6400.5	MW 59800	7635.9	MW 61489	9371.9	MW 61200	8485.1	HUILES BRUTES DE PETROLE
334	PETROLEUM PRODUCTS,REFIN	MW 15041	2179.3	MW 13451	2158.0	MW 13538	2553.7	MW 16432	2881.5	PRODUITS RAFFINES
3341	GASOLINE,OTH LIGHT OILS	W 4266901	730.8	W 4404792	806.8	W 4256214	874.4	W 5771585	1130.1	ESSENCES POUR MOTEURS
33419	OTH LIGHT PETROLEUM OILS	W 3865607	660.2	W 3971972	724.9	W 4120151	848.5	W 5658337	1108.2	AUTRES HUILES LEGERES
3343	GAS OILS	W 4887910	747.5	W 3700448	592.4	W 5178276	1016.6	W 6176682	1093.0	GAS OILS
3344	FUEL OILS,NES	W 5163773	443.5	W 4748568	463.6	W 3523912	370.6	W 3657530	357.9	FUEL OILS
335	RESIDUAL PETRLM PROD NES	W 2624670	426.2	W 2773432	496.4	W 3007343	538.2	W 3136156	525.8	PRODUITS RESIDUELS NDA
341	*GAS,NATURAL AND MANUFCT	W 4915370	576.5	W 4705458	631.6	W 4933480	724.4		1053.3	GAZ NATUREL,GAZ MANUFACT
3414	PETROLEUM GASES, GASEOUS	W 2967678	291.2	W 3117800	350.6	W 3262571	374.4	W 5257513	741.5	GAZ DE PETROLE GAZEUX
4	ANIMAL,VEGETABLE OIL,FAT		1089.2		1354.0		1227.5		878.1	HUILES,GRAISSES ANIM,VEG
42	FIXED VEGETABLE OIL,FAT		698.7		840.1		822.5		563.6	HUILES VEGETALES FIXES
424	FIXED VEG OIL NONSOFT	W 773456	396.2	W 764769	526.1	W 829031	545.9	W 428037	279.6	AUTRES HUILES VEG FIXES
5	CHEMCLS,RELATED PROD NES		15805.1		20218.0		18497.8		18177.6	PRODUITS CHIMIQUES
51	ORGANIC CHEMICALS		4475.3		5687.7		5074.8		5394.2	PROD CHIMIQ ORGANIQUES
511	HYDROCARBONS NES,DERIVS	W 1920678	765.1	W 2047218	1064.4	W 2334745	983.2	W 2886327	1252.1	HYDROCARBURES NDA
5111	ACYCLIC HYDROCARBONS	W 746065	231.7	W 832753	399.8	W 1154367	439.4	W 1277184	537.0	HYDROCARBURES ACYCLIQUES
5112	CYCLIC HYDROCARBONS	W 949473	378.1	W 1050879	491.4	W 971846	353.1	W 1196165	433.4	HYDROCARBURES CYCLIQUES
512	ALCOHOLS,PHENOLS ETC	W 1319675	694.5	W 1632878	947.8	W 1977640	948.4	W 2218190	933.0	PHENOLS,PHENOLS–ALCOOLS
5121	ACYCLIC ALCOHOLS,DERIVS	W 1095540	518.9	W 1335076	697.7	W 1534034	624.6	W 1827854	641.1	ALCOOLS ACYCLIQUES
513	CARBOXYLIC ACIDS ETC	W 833854	803.6	W 899743	1179.3	W 812318	924.2	W 888161	861.2	ACIDES CARBOXYLIQUES
5137	MONOACIDS AND DERIVATIVS	W 446572	449.5	W 527772	708.8	W 520718	595.6	W 572509	560.4	ACIDES MONOCARBOXYLIQUES
514	NITROGEN–FNCTN COMPOUNDS	W 318397	1135.9	W 370071	1127.2	W 375591	1040.0	W 423626	1001.7	COMPOSES FONCT AZOTEES
5148	OTH NITROGN–FNCTN CMPNDS	W 130987	509.5	W 175648	562.5	W 175994	445.2	W 166688	487.0	AUTRES COMPOSES AZOTES
515	ORG–INORG COMPOUNDS ETC	W 120417	552.9	W 131900	699.1	W 77103	555.6	W 101617	675.6	COMPOSES ORGANO–MINERAUX
5156	HETEROCYCLIC CMPDS ETC	W 74155	357.2	W 87215	481.9	W 41514	348.7	W 64621	470.6	COMPOSES HETEROCYCLIQUES
516	OTHER ORGANIC CHEMICALS	W 740526	523.5	W 637147	670.1	W 585917	623.7	W 633020	670.8	AUTRES PROD ORGANIQUES
52	INORGANIC CHEMICALS		891.9		1019.0		1048.1		1215.9	PROD CHIM INORGANIQUES
522	INORG ELEMNTS,OXIDES,ETC	W 2717587	466.4	W 2957553	586.9	W 3259496	583.8	W 3209109	616.2	ELEMENTS INORGANIQUES
53	DYES,TANNING,COLOUR PROD		903.5		1083.9		1011.8		965.8	PROD TEINTURE,COLORANTS

4. Special Imports C.I.F. by Commodities according to the S.I.T.C. (Rev. 2) in million U.S. Dollars
Importations Spéciales C.A.F. par Produits d'après la C.T.C.I. (Rév. 2) en millions de Dollars E.U.

SITC CTCI	COMMODITY	1994 QUANTITY QUANTITE	1994 VALUE VALEUR	1995 QUANTITY QUANTITE	1995 VALUE VALEUR	1996 QUANTITY QUANTITE	1996 VALUE VALEUR	1997 QUANTITY QUANTITE	1997 VALUE VALEUR	PRODUIT
533	PIGMENTS,PAINTS,ETC	W 231462	583.5	W 252882	710.8	W 248046	659.1	W 247268	604.6	PIGMENTS,PEINTURES,VERNIS
541	*MEDICINAL,PHARM PRODUCT	MK 55525	2805.0	MK 77907	3894.2	MK 77269	3431.0		3478.2	PROD MEDICINAUX PHARMACEUT
5413	ANTIBIOTICS IN BULK	K 3492731	209.4	MK 10751	514.0	MK 10621	446.5	MK 13246	383.3	ANTIBIOTIQUES NDA
54139	OTHER ANTIBIOTICS	K 2615807	183.4	MK 9623	474.6	K 8677063	368.8	MK 10959	307.3	AUTRES ANTIBIOTIQUES
5417	MEDICAMENTS	MK 24288	2013.9	MK 24139	2529.0	MK 22290	2081.6		2258.4	MEDICAMENTS
54179	— CONTNG OTH SUBSTANCES	MK 20794	1648.5	MK 20138	2015.5	MK 17592	1504.2	MK 19402	1646.6	MED CONT AUT SUBSTANCES
55	PERFUME,CLEANING ETC PRD		1239.8		1481.7		1378.7		1222.5	PROD POUR PARFUM,TOILETTE
553	PERFUMERY,COSMETICS,ETC	W 68884	513.4	W 77910	693.2	W 80896	654.7	W 90391	574.6	PRODUITS DE PARFUMERIE
554	SOAP,CLEANSING ETC PREPS	W 344247	529.9	W 319309	555.1	W 313048	488.1	W 304509	421.4	SAVONS,PRODUITS DETERSIFS
5542	WASHING PREPARATIONS ETC	W 300378	434.3	W 284961	465.7	W 281070	411.9	W 268466	351.3	PROD ORG TENSIO–ACT NDA
58	PLASTIC MATERIALS ETC		3430.9		4494.8		4060.4		3699.1	MAT PLAST ARTIFICIELLES
582	PROD OF CONDENSATION ETC	W 530864	1022.8	W 590833	1390.3	W 562447	1245.4	W 559993	1062.4	PROD CONDENS,POLYCOND
5823	ALKYDS,OTHER POLYESTERS	W 232834	480.9	W 265104	655.7	W 246764	585.5	W 250578	483.2	ALKYDES ET AUT POLYESTERS
58231	— IN PRIMARY FORMS	W 214911	365.6	W 243638	513.4	W 229390	463.0	W 232285	368.7	SOUS FORMES PRIMAIRES
583	POLYMERIZATION ETC PRODS	W 1712338	2268.6	W 1666674	2930.5	W 1724876	2596.7	W 1860426	2418.9	PROD POLYMERISATION
5831	POLYETHYLENE	W 478205	403.9	W 485658	573.2	W 461829	449.1	W 537703	477.3	POLYETHYLENE
5839	OTH POLYMRZTION ETC PROD	W 330381	670.9	W 333886	864.6	W 322450	806.1	W 432539	795.3	AUT PROD POLYMER COPOLYM
59	CHEMICAL MATERIALS NES		1786.1		2210.5		2163.9		1954.9	MAT PROD CHIMIQUES NDA
598	MISCEL CHEM PRODUCTS NES	W 1030235	1167.2	W 1073039	1482.6	W 1124052	1462.2	W 1019553	1345.2	PROD DIV INDUST CHIM NDA
5989	CHEM PRODUCTS,PREPS NES	W 816510	894.5	W 854768	1173.1	W 882463	1137.0	W 771895	1035.3	PROD PREP CHIMIQUES NDA
59899	OTH CHEM PRODS,PREPS,NES	W 738534	704.5	W 769072	980.6	W 792400	881.0	W 638300	787.0	AUT PRODUITS CHIMIQUES NDA
6	BASIC MANUFACTURES		19944.1		25296.2		23387.0		22046.0	ART MANUFACTURES
62	RUBBER MANUFACTURES NES		1329.5		1612.7		1627.8		1422.8	CAOUTCHOUC MANUFACTURE
625	RUBBER TYRES, TUBES ETC	W 230306	906.3	W 253141	1114.0	W 257944	1099.6	W 256911	949.3	PNEUS CAOUTCHOUC VULCANISE
6251	TYRES NEW FOR MOTOR CARS	W 100621	501.6	W 101964	560.9	W 107353	552.5	W 116673	506.0	PNEUS POUR VOITURES
63	WOOD,CORK MANUFACTRS NES		1019.9		1081.2		1065.1		969.0	OUVRAGES LIEGE ET BOIS
634	VENEERS,PLYWOOD,ETC	W 802592	556.5	W 829447	594.8	W 775978	538.4	W 769859	501.1	PLACAGES,CONTRE–PLAQUES
635	WOOD MANUFACTURES NES	W 394554	449.1	W 359012	469.8	W 374638	510.0	W 384841	454.8	ART MANUF EN BOIS NDA
64	PAPER,PAPERBOARD AND MFR		3595.2		4543.3		4269.7		3779.6	PAPIERS,CARTONS & OUVRAGES
641	PAPER AND PAPERBOARD	W 3066362	2417.4	W 3094798	3161.5	W 3168472	2990.2	W 3387556	2720.9	PAPIERS ET CARTONS
6412	PRINTG,WRITING PAPER NES	W 619348	585.1	W 553679	706.1	W 621606	693.3	W 722950	672.3	PAPIERS POUR L'IMPRESSION
64122	— COATED,IMPREGNATD ETC	W 566921	517.1	W 465774	568.5	W 528112	568.8	W 629836	559.4	PAPIERS IMPRESSION COUCHES
6415	PAPER,PAPERBRD,BULK,NES	W 903407	645.9	W 787916	766.8	W 831077	700.4	W 850517	610.2	PAPIERS,CARTONS ROULEAUX
64159	OTHER PAPER ETC,BULK,NES	W 839615	600.2	W 724030	704.3	W 766668	650.7	W 800829	573.8	AUT PAPIER ROULEAUX FEUILLES
6418	COATED ETC PAPER NES BLK	W 352572	463.2	W 519110	737.9	W 560896	733.5	W 526546	649.7	PAP,CARTONS COUCHES,ENDUITS
642	PAPER,ETC,PRECUT,ARTS OF	W 591989	1177.8	W 595832	1381.9	W 593696	1279.5	W 592604	1058.7	PAP,CARTONS DECOUPES
6421	PAPER ETC CONTAINERS	W 306787	455.9	W 327628	580.7	W 339887	529.2	W 317738	413.7	BOITES,SACS EMBALLAGES
6428	PAPER ETC ARTICLES NES	W 171861	437.4	W 172779	501.1	W 155447	451.9	W 163313	387.7	OUVRAGES EN PATE A PAPIER
65	TEXTILE YARN,FABRICS,ETC		3050.0		3508.0		3441.6		3806.5	FILS,TISSUS,ARTICLES TEXTILE
651	TEXTILE YARN	W 163631	774.4	W 157405	844.8	W 160397	910.9		858.4	FILS TEXTILES
6514	SYN FIB YRN,BULK,MONOFIL	W 88415	506.7	W 80538	553.3	W 90850	652.7	W 116532	620.4	FILS CONT 85% FIB TEXT SYNTH
653	WOVN MAN–MADE FIB FABRIC	W 48273	510.0	W 51906	624.6	W 56445	554.7	W 47194	452.2	TISSUS FIBRES SYNTH,ARTIF
658	TEXTILE ARTICLES NES	W 72271	446.2	W 74252	484.9	W 80614	475.5		426.3	ART FACONNES MAT TEXTILES
659	FLOOR COVERINGS,ETC	W 74758	310.3	W 84651	430.0	W 85459	390.0		1104.1	COUVRE–PARQUETS,TAPIS ETC
6595	MAN–MADE TXTL CARPTS NES	W 48993	196.4	W 55409	289.7	W 53543	250.6		582.8	TAPIS MAT TEXT SYNT ARTIF
66	NONMETAL MINERAL MFS NES		1986.6		2202.9		2108.9		1907.3	ART MIN NON METALLIQUES
661	LIME,CEMENT,BLDG PRODS	W 4483271	419.0	W 4448264	474.6	W 4143679	446.4	W 3886126	380.6	CHAUX,CIMENTS MAT CONSTR
664	GLASS	W 458381	451.6	W 489539	523.5	W 451625	458.3	W 592774	408.4	VERRE
67	IRON AND STEEL		3557.3		5166.5		4350.0		3860.0	FER ET ACIER
673	IRON,STEEL SHAPES ETC	W 1865421	778.4	W 1963862	1029.2	W 1943430	854.1	W 2015347	790.9	BARRES,PROFIL FER,ACIER
674	IRN,STL UNIV,PLATE,SHEET	W 1938340	1477.2	W 2170228	2232.0	W 2132607	1754.5	W 2107322	1567.5	LARGES PLATS,TOLES
6746	IRN,STL THIN PLATE,ROLLD	W 593755	577.5	W 674140	955.6	W 612742	670.4	W 587896	609.5	TOLES LAM MOINS 3MM
67463	— OF STAINLESS ETC STL	W 192879	351.0	W 256842	661.8	W 226452	437.1	W 252059	430.3	TOL ACIER INOX MOINS 3 MM
6749	OTH IRN,STL PLATES,SHEET	W 464358	344.0	W 543928	474.2	W 542244	428.2	W 513849	342.2	AUTRES TOLES FER,ACIER
678	IRON,STL TUBES,PIPES,ETC	W 642237	683.9	W 658173	917.7	W 677466	889.6	W 595132	680.1	TUBES,TUYAUX EN FONTE,FER
68	NON–FERROUS METALS		2015.2		3099.4		2419.1		2628.6	METAUX NON FERREUX
682	COPPER EXC CEMENT COPPER	W 142986	418.5	W 154491	575.1	W 164763	496.5	W 182546	481.7	CUIVRE
684	ALUMINIUM	W 652214	1209.3	W 821356	1912.5	W 666104	1454.7	W 771033	1538.5	ALUMINIUM
6841	ALUMINIUM,ALLOYS,UNWRGHT	W 458322	632.0	W 622326	1164.5	W 464298	775.8	W 536513	837.8	ALUMINIUM,ALLIAGES BRUTS
6842	ALUMINIUM,ALLOYS WORKED	W 193893	577.4	W 199030	748.0	W 201806	678.9	W 234521	700.8	ALUMINIUM,ALLIAGES OUVRE
69	METAL MANUFACTURES NES		3136.0		3811.9		3841.4		3451.1	ART MANUFACT EN METAL NDA
691	STRUCTURES AND PARTS NES	W 207724	384.8	W 232440	497.4	W 218789	436.3	W 184824	400.7	CONSTRUCT FER,ACIER,ALU
692	METAL TANKS,BOXES,ETC	W 184037	427.4	W 173384	469.7	W 228467	512.3	W 169952	367.0	RECIPIENTS METALLIQUES
6924	MTL TRANSPORT BOXES ETC	W 170620	397.9	W 160618	431.2	W 214249	477.4	W 158783	343.8	FUTS,TAMBOURS,BIDONS
695	TOOLS	W 53063	558.7	W 50425	786.6	W 62037	819.4	W 54070	786.1	OUTILS A MAIN
6954	BLADES,TIPS,ETC FR TOOLS	W 10030	318.6	W 9548	481.9	W 13174	450.9	W 11687	467.6	OUTILS POUR MACHINE–OUTIL
699	BASE METAL MFRS NES	W 242800	1016.9	W 257472	1171.9	W 315406	1215.0		1105.2	ART MANUFACTURES MET NDA
7	MACHINES,TRANSPORT EQUIP		40800.4		51947.3		55316.2		61322.7	MACHINES MATERIEL TRANSPORT
71	POWER GENERATING EQUIPMT		1971.1		2429.8		2463.1		2674.3	MACHINES GENERATRICES
713	INTRNL COMBUS PSTN ENGIN	W 50815	626.7	W 67019	873.7	W 78706	1004.1	W 92953	1168.5	MOTEURS EXPL COMB INT, PIECE
7132	MOTOR VEHCL PSTN ENGINS	W 10632	105.7	W 16297	198.4	W 27134	357.9	W 45651	644.3	MOTEURS EXPL POUR VEHICULES
7139	PISTON ENGINE PARTS NES	W 27969	358.7	W 38642	496.3	W 39458	464.8	W 37951	393.2	PIECES POUR 713.2,3,8
714	ENGINES AND MOTORS NES	W 5692	919.9	W 5428	1027.4	W 5067	965.4	W 6545	1039.3	MOTEURS NON ELECTRIQUES
7149	ENGINE & MOTOR PARTS NES	W 5149	632.1	W 4538	737.3	W 4648	764.3	W 5980	863.8	PIECES 714 ET 718.88
71491	PARTS NES OF 7144,71481	W 536	382.9	W 605	463.7	W 577	490.8	W 639	581.9	PIECES DES PROPULSEURS
72	MACHS FOR SPCL INDUSTRYS		2379.1		2659.1		2715.7		2276.0	MAC SPECIALES POUR INDUST
723	CIVIL ENGNEERG EQUIP ETC	W 68741	414.5	W 80463	515.5	W 86212	508.0	W 76543	435.8	APPAREILS DE GENIE CIVIL
728	OTH MACHY FOR SPCL INDUS	W 46907	759.6	W 48781	886.1	W 52639	911.3	W 63882	794.4	AUT MACH IND PARTICULIERES
7284	MACHY FOR SPCL INDUS NES	W 29569	617.3	W 30926	722.8	W 31779	724.5	W 33114	629.6	MACH SPEC IND PARTICUL.
73	METALWORKING MACHINERY		445.1		464.9		587.9		401.9	MACH TRAVAIL DES METAUX
74	GENRL INDUSTRL MACHY NES		4074.9		4885.4		5325.5		4460.2	MACH APP INDUSTRIE
741	HEATING,COOLING EQUIPMNT	W 47866	580.2	W 50230	716.0	W 57810	933.6	W 57316	703.2	MACH CHAUFFAGE,PIECES
743	PUMPS NES,CENTRFUGES ETC	W 45440	667.2	W 49805	721.1	W 62490	787.5	W 61646	692.8	POMPES COMPRES,VENT ETC
744	MECHANICAL HANDLING EQU	W 110872	845.5	W 130034	953.8	W 142907	982.3	W 143143	826.5	EQUIP MANUTENTION PIECES
7449	PTS NES OF MACHY OF 7442	W 44319	358.1	W 55932	489.9	W 47410	423.1	W 47516	350.8	PIECES DU 744.2
745	NONELEC MACHY,TOOLS NES	W 24631	496.7	W 23024	522.5	W 31691	592.4	W 39499	551.9	AUT MACH NON ELEC,PIECES
7452	OTH NONELEC MCHS,PTS NES	W 23102	446.7	W 21453	467.4	W 28996	524.1	W 35434	469.5	AUT MACH NON ELEC,PIECES
749	NONELEC MACH PTS,ACC NES	W 70297	1116.5	W 93475	1546.1	W 105718	1596.5	W 115185	1294.8	PIECES MACH NON ELEC NDA
7492	COCKS,VALVES ETC NES	W 26670	497.2	W 30831	619.0	W 38506	659.5	W 45280	572.7	ART ROB,SIM POUR TUYAUX
75	OFFICE MACHNES,ADP EQUIP		10364.3		13694.7		15741.2		19544.6	MACH BUREAU TRAIT AUTOM
751	OFFICE MACHINES	W 35467	1061.9	W 44935	1448.5	W 40270	1176.1		1016.5	MACH,APPAREILS DE BUREAU
7518	OFFICE MACHINES NES	W 32179	956.3	W 41000	1330.1	W 37250	1082.8	W 33443	902.3	MACH,APP DE BUREAU NDA
75182	PHOTO,THERMOCOPY APPARAT	W 23964	639.9	W 31544	933.7	W 29735	818.8	W 26711	692.3	APPAREILS DE PHOTOCOPIE
752	AUTOMTIC DATA PROC EQUIP	W 97856	5961.8	W 130416	8230.6	W 150718	9889.0	W 193045	11577.1	MACH TRAIT INFORMATION
7522	DIGITAL COMPUTERS	W 2420	481.4	W 3474	852.4	W 4066	992.2	W 4819	1063.8	MACH DIGITALES COMPLETES
7523	DIGITL CENTRL PROCESSORS	W 17086	1685.2	W 22963	2590.2	W 26002	2588.8	W 37539	3212.5	UNITES CENTRALES
7524	DIGITL CENTRL STOR UNITS	W 7354	1360.4	W 11647	1952.1	W 12950	2891.5	W 18660	4042.6	UNITES MEMOIRE CENTRALES
7525	ADP PERIPHERAL UNITS	W 65915	1904.7	W 84718	2364.5	W 97693	2730.0	W 125596	2683.5	UNITES PERIPHERIQUES
7528	OFF–LINE DATA PROC EQUIP	W 5061	526.9	W 7585	464.5	W 9812	667.1	W 6189	534.1	MACH AUXIL TRAIT INFORM
759	OFFICE,ADP MCH PTS,ACCES	W 54053	3340.7	W 58663	4015.7	W 70274	4676.2		6951.1	PIECES DU 751 ET 752
7591	OFFICE MACHINE PARTS NES	W 16530	577.7	W 14038	584.8	W 17629	631.2		551.1	PIECES DU 7511,7518

4. Special Imports C.I.F. by Commodities according to the S.I.T.C. (Rev. 2) in million U.S. Dollars
Importations Spéciales C.A.F. par Produits d'après la C.T.C.I. (Rév. 2) en millions de Dollars E.U.

SITC CTCI	COMMODITY	1994		1995		1996		1997		PRODUIT
		QUANTITY QUANTITE	VALUE VALEUR	QUANTITY QUANTITE	VALUE VALEUR	QUANTITY QUANTITE	VALUE VALEUR	QUANTITY QUANTITE	VALUE VALEUR	
75919	COPY MACH PRTS,ACCES NES	W 14279	439.1	W 12025	440.8	W 15214	487.4	W 16379	441.5	PIECES DU 751.82
7599	ACCTG,ETC,ADP MCH PTS,AC	W 37523	2763.0	W 44625	3431.0	W 52645	4045.0	W 63524	6400.0	PIECES DU 751 ET 752
76	TELECOMM,SOUND EQUIPMENT		3115.5		4190.4		4454.9		4614.6	EQUIPMENT DE TELECOM
761	TELEVISION RECEIVERS	W 32136	508.5	W 39190	640.1	W 48094	771.3	W 69118	933.7	RECEPTEURS DE TELEVISION
7611	COLOUR TV RECEIVERS	W 31476	498.2	W 38695	629.4	W 47395	756.1	W 68490	916.8	RECEPTEURS COULEUR
762	RADIO BROADCAST RECEIVRS	W 22605	506.8	W 27298	652.7	W 30480	659.9	W 33871	651.9	RECEPTEURS RADIODIFFUSION
763	SOUND RECORDRS,PHONOGRPH	W 11481	522.1	W 11126	563.3	W 13415	780.1	W 12784	596.7	PHONO,APP ENREGISTREMENT
7638	OTHR SOUND APPARATUS ETC	W 11151	517.9	W 10732	558.8	W 13116	776.5	W 12522	593.9	AUT APP D'ENREGIS,REPROD
76381	TV IMAGE,SND RECRDRS ETC	W 5402	301.7	W 5441	337.6	W 7900	596.9	W 6371	398.4	APP ENREG,REPRO IMAG,SON
764	TELECOM EQPT,PTS,ACC NES	W 31817	1578.2	W 38330	2334.5	W 43303	2243.7		2432.5	EQUIP TELECOM,PIECES
7641	LINE TELEPHONE,ETC EQUIP	W 6202	421.9	W 8015	606.2	W 8620	726.4	W 9992	957.3	APP TELEPHON PAR FIL
7649	PTS NES OF EQUIPMT OF 76	W 6764	566.2	W 9539	975.7	W 10898	1038.4	W 10332	830.7	PIECES DE LA DIV 76
76491	PTS NES OF APPAR OF 7641	W 1556	255.0	W 2592	591.6	W 4181	685.9	W 2873	484.3	PIECES POUR 764.1
77	ELECTRIC MACHNRY NES ETC		7009.6		9125.4		9693.7		13414.9	MACH APP ELECT NDA
771	ELECTRIC POWER MACHY NES	W 16884	275.4	W 16031	336.9	W 27026	404.6		1065.3	MACH PROD,TRANS ELECTR
7712	OTH ELEC POWER MACHY NES	W 11522	203.8	W 9883	255.9	W 22276	334.7	W 28602	696.8	AUT APP PROD TRANSF ELEC
772	SWITCHGEAR ETC,PARTS NES	W 32943	1041.2	W 42483	1472.4	W 50321	1530.6	W 49805	1440.4	APP COUPURE,SECT ETC
7721	SWITCHGEAR ETC	W 31532	931.9	W 41002	1327.0	W 48762	1407.9	W 47578	1307.3	APP COUPURE,SECTIONMNT
773	ELECTR DISTRIBUTNG EQUIP	W 56023	419.9	W 64811	541.3	W 69128	565.5	W 68305	568.7	EQUIPMT DISTRIBUTION ELECT
7731	INSULATED WIRE,CABLE ETC	W 52763	381.2	W 61118	500.7	W 65794	532.9	W 64556	535.9	FILS,CABLES ISOLES ELECT
774	ELECTRO–MEDCL,XRAY EQUIP	W 3458	403.2	W 4237	495.4	W 5363	580.2	W 5016	492.6	APPAREILS MEDICAUX
775	HOUSEHOLD TYPE EQUIP NES	W 157278	1212.2	W 165400	1379.4	W 182837	1437.6	W 185471	1380.4	MACH,APP USAGE DOMESTQUE
7758	ELECTRO–THERMIC APPL NES	W 40270	405.3	W 40218	440.4	W 44533	460.6	W 48866	451.3	APP ELECTROTHERMIQ NDA
776	TRANSISTORS,VALVES,ETC	W 10072	1980.3	W 10168	2873.6	W 9526	3075.6		5771.5	LAMPES,TUBES,VALVES
7764	ELECTRONIC MICROCIRCUITS	W 2802	1630.3	W 4423	2410.0	W 5357	2729.8	W 6650	4727.3	MICROSTRUCTURES ELECTRON
778	ELECTRICAL MACHINERY NES	W 120465	1677.8	W 139630	2026.7	W 156700	2099.9		2696.4	AUTRES MACH ELECT NDA
7782	ELECTRIC LAMPS,BULBS	W 20510	379.7	W 20890	387.7	W 21093	408.6		1023.4	LAMPES, TUBES ELECTRIQUES
7788	OTH ELEC MACHY,EQUIP NES	W 25913	588.0	W 34939	798.0	W 34395	781.7	W 40352	780.5	AUT MACH APP ELEC NDA
78	ROAD VEHICLES		9285.3		12045.9		13009.2		12365.3	VEHICULES ROUTIERS
781	PASS MOTOR VEH EXC BUSES	W 529785	5248.5	W 585552	6693.8	W 625439	6889.5	W 688932	6515.7	AUTO TRANSPORT PERSONNES
782	LORRIES,SPCL MTR VEH NES	W 140462	966.8	W 149028	1241.7	W 196326	1585.1	W 216054	1512.6	VEHICULES SPECIAUX,MARCH
7821	LORRIES,TRUCKS	W 128856	904.2	W 134535	1146.0	W 175695	1453.2	W 197375	1401.3	VEHICULES TRANSP MARCHAND
784	MOTOR VEH PRTS,ACCES NES	W 246218	1907.7	W 310332	2593.0	W 360923	2857.0	W 391204	2810.7	PIECES 722,781,782,783
7849	OTHER MOTOR VEHCL PARTS	W 232216	1743.9	W 292210	2358.5	W 341933	2580.9	W 368810	2497.1	PIECES 722,781,782,783
785	CYCLES,ETC MOTRZD OR NOT	W 48720	591.9	W 47117	636.6	W 58001	849.1	W 71074	862.9	MOTOCYCLES SCOOTERS
786	TRAILERS,NONMOTR VEH,NES	W 104941	413.9	W 104480	472.2	W 125045	475.1	W 102559	389.8	REMORQUES,CADRES,CONTAIN
79	OTHR TRANSPORT EQUIPMENT		2155.9		2451.9		1325.4		1571.3	AUTRE MATERIEL TRANSPORT
792	AIRCRAFT ETC	W 2738	1709.1	W 3307	1955.8	W 2007	860.4		1117.4	APP NAVIGATION AERIENNE
7924	AIRCRFT NES OVER 15000KG	W 1133	1159.6	W 937	1148.0	W 347	364.6	W 669	510.0	AERODYNES PLUS 15000 KG
7929	AIRCRAFT PARTS NES	W 1469	517.3	W 2160	740.0	W 1535	450.5	W 1333	544.7	PIECES DU 792
8	MISC MANUFACTURED GOODS		17462.5		19042.9		20344.0		22498.3	ART MANUFACTURES DIVERS
812	*PLUMBG,HEATNG,LGHTNG EQ	W 106335	632.9	W 101792	718.1	W 117715	742.8	W 125137	662.1	APPAR SANITAIRES CHAUFFAGE
821	*FURNITURE,PARTS THEREOF	W 398547	1611.2	W 374811	1740.7	W 388854	1841.1	W 437858	1708.0	MEUBLES ET PIECES
8211	CHAIRS,SEATS AND PARTS	W 90510	504.8	W 84019	537.3	W 93722	615.6	W 105303	587.5	SIEGES ET PIECES
82111	CHAIRS AND OTHER SEATS	W 77173	444.1	W 69626	456.8	W 76937	486.7	W 84552	438.2	SIEGES
8219	FURNITURE AND PARTS NES	W 289672	931.1	W 270318	1005.6	W 274527	1020.3	W 311770	945.8	AUTRES MEUBLES ET PIECES
82192	WOOD FURNITURE NES	W 192876	637.0	W 184052	686.6	W 188563	703.7	W 211661	651.9	MEUBLES NDA EN BOIS
84	CLOTHING AND ACCESSORIES		5029.1		5014.8		5439.3		7631.4	VETEMENTS
842	MENS OUTERWEAR NOT KNIT	W 43677	1035.6	W 41111	1059.5	W 42659	1113.0	W 44063	1234.9	VET DESSUS POUR HOMMES
8423	— TROUSERS,BREECHES ETC	W 22494	466.4	W 20677	459.3	W 23091	527.8	W 23544	470.0	PANTALONS HOMMES MAT TEX
8429	— OTHER OUTER GARMENTS	W 14229	311.9	W 13905	329.6	W 13355	324.9	W 13500	532.2	AUT VET DES HOM MAT TEX
843	WOMENS OUTERWEAR NONKNIT	W 46762	1386.5	W 44497	1419.4	W 50809	1461.1		1457.3	VET DESSUS FEMMES MAT TEX
8439	— OTHER OUTER GARMENTS	W 26094	614.2	W 23628	599.2	W 27799	687.4		826.2	AUT VET DES FEM MAT TEXT
845	OUTERWEAR KNIT NONELASTC	W 44445	1051.5	W 36656	978.0	W 44719	1094.1		2832.1	VET DESSOUS,ACCES BONNET
8451	— JERSEYS,PULLOVERS ETC	W 23618	583.3	W 19976	550.9	W 25569	631.6		868.4	CHANDAILS,PULL–OVERS ETC
8459	— OTHER,CLTHG ACCESRYS	W 17658	385.0	W 14361	354.7	W 16828	396.5		1612.3	AUT VET DESSUS DE BONNE
846	UNDER GARMENTS KNITTED	W 35874	752.4	W 32819	778.5	W 40155	913.7		1265.1	SOUS VETS DE BONNETERIE
8462	— OF COTTON NON ELASTIC	W 28867	516.3	W 25856	520.5	W 31690	618.7		785.7	SOUS–VET BONNET COTON
84629	—— OTHER	W 28867	516.3	W 25856	520.5	W 31690	618.7		785.7	AUT SOUS–VET BONNET COTON
851	*FOOTWEAR	W 70206	999.3	W 65348	1020.3	W 72603	1142.3	W 68248	1022.0	CHAUSSURES
85102	FOOTWEAR LEATHER	W 57346	882.2	W 51358	872.6	W 55650	963.4	W 50024	862.4	CHAUS SEMELLES EN CUIR
87	PRECISION INSTRUMNTS NES		2001.4		2541.3		2761.0		3030.7	INSTRUM,APPAR SCIENT NDA
872	MEDICAL INSTRUMENTS NES	W 11215	537.0	W 11386	654.1	W 12957	733.7	W 15537	878.5	INSTR,APP MEDIC–CHIR NDA
87202	OTH MEDICAL INSTRUMENTS	W 9416	491.9	W 9275	597.6	W 10686	676.3	W 12995	817.7	INSTRUM,APP MEDECINE
874	MEASURNG,CONTROLNG INSTR	W 13392	1296.8	W 15706	1675.9	W 19093	1783.6		1714.3	INSTRUMENTS DE MESURE
8748	ELEC MEAS,CONTRL EQU NES	W 1426	261.5	W 1722	366.7	W 2571	489.6	W 3074	559.6	APP ELEC ELECTRO MESURE
87483	OTH ELCTRNC MEAS ETC EQU	W 1234	224.5	W 1557	335.9	W 2314	449.5	W 2762	513.4	AUT APP ELECTRO DE MESURE
88	PHOTO EQU,OPTICL GDS ETC		1264.7		1408.5		1568.5		1795.7	APP,FOURN PHOTO,OP,MONTR
882	PHOTO,CINEMA SUPPLIES	W 38597	627.0	W 36443	705.6	W 39638	745.4	W 40886	719.8	PRODUITS PHOTO,CINEMA
8822	PHOTO FILM EXC DEV CINMA	W 23005	458.6	W 18806	489.8	W 18683	492.2	W 18832	461.9	PLAQUES,PELLICULES,FILMS
884	OPTICAL GOODS NES	W 1801	206.7	W 2265	215.6	W 3170	350.1	W 2756	598.2	ELEMENTS OPTIQ,ART LUNET
89	MISC MANUFCTRD GOODS NES		5699.7		6312.9		6522.7		6361.5	ART MANUFACTURES DIVERS
892	PRINTED MATTER	W 144851	779.4	W 127317	754.9	W 123278	751.8		604.9	IMPRIMES
893	ARTICLES OF PLASTIC NES		1880.2		2101.5		2135.4		1842.1	OUVRAGES EN MAT DIVIS 58
8931	PLSTC PACKG CONTNRS,LIDS	W 246210	661.4	W 222209	731.5	W 230580	745.8	W 251603	623.9	ART TRANSP EMBALLAGE ETC
8939	MISC PLASTIC ARTICLES	W 234278	1145.9	W 241353	1281.5	W 264558	1305.9	W 267144	1142.7	ART DIVERS EN MAT DIV 58
89399	OTHR PLASTC ARTICLES NES	W 207367	1046.1	W 211926	1166.0	W 235102	1197.5	W 236013	1054.6	AUT OUV MAT DIV 58
894	TOYS,SPORTING GOODS,ETC	W 118356	920.5	W 112754	1046.2	W 118446	1174.5		1564.0	VOITURES ENFANTS,JOUETS
8942	TOYS,INDOOR GAMES ETC	W 98449	754.8	W 91551	870.2	W 93567	969.6	W 111090	1352.5	JOUETS,JEUX ETC
89424	INDOOR GAME EQUIPMENT	W 27127	264.9	W 24729	392.4	W 24554	481.4	W 35769	829.4	ART,JEUX DE SOCIETE
898	MUSICAL INSTRUMENTS,PTS	W 46657	1111.7	W 53819	1249.9	W 44153	1247.0	W 41551	1211.2	INSTRUMENTS DE MUSIQUE
8983	SOUND RECRDNG TAPE,DISCS	W 41467	1038.9	W 49154	1179.9	W 40387	1173.5	W 36115	957.3	SUPPORTS SON POUR 763
89831	PREPD SND RECORDNG MEDIA	W 26310	389.2	W 33606	514.9	W 24998	425.3	W 23674	431.2	SUPPORTS PREPARES
89832	RECORDED DISCS,TAPES ETC	W 15156	649.7	W 15547	665.1	W 15390	748.2	W 12441	526.2	DISQUES,PHONO,BANDES
899	OTHER MANUFACTURED GOODS		609.5		743.8		813.3		716.9	AUT ART MANUF DIVERS NDA
9	GOODS NOT CLASSD BY KIND		1035.2		1057.0		1440.1		547.1	ART TRANSACT NON CLASSES
931	*SPECIAL TRANSACTIONS	W 665970	548.6	W 670856	671.2	W 838954	1007.9	W 7208	28.4	TRANS.SPECIALES

5. Special Exports F.O.B. by Commodities according to the S.I.T.C. (Rev. 2) in million U.S. Dollars
Exportations Spéciales F.O.B. par Produits d'après la C.T.C.I. (Rév. 2) en millions de Dollars E.U.

SITC CTCI	COMMODITY	1994		1995		1996		1997		PRODUIT
		QUANTITY QUANTITE	VALUE VALEUR	QUANTITY QUANTITE	VALUE VALEUR	QUANTITY QUANTITE	VALUE VALEUR	QUANTITY QUANTITE	VALUE VALEUR	
	ALL COMMODITIES		145825.3		177626.4		177369.4		184433.3	TOUS PRODUITS
0	FOOD AND LIVE ANIMALS		25172.4		28729.8		27057.6		23168.5	ALIMENTS,ANIMAUX VIVANTS
001	*LIVE ANIMALS FOR FOOD	W 472719	797.9	W 492846	943.7	W 499395	1039.5	W 127473	375.0	ANIMAUX VIVANTS
0013	SWINE,LIVE	W 340200	494.8	W 359269	638.7	W 371744	739.4	W 62882	105.1	ESPECE PORCINE
01	MEAT AND PREPARATIONS		5103.8		5421.7		5303.5		4645.2	VIANDES ET PREPARATIONS
011	MEAT FRESH,CHILLD,FROZEN	W 1791329	4428.4	W 1746935	4637.1	W 1706363	4387.7	W 1705505	3874.8	VIANDES FRAICHES,REF,CONGE
0111	BOVINE MEAT FRESH,FROZEN	W 364756	1569.8	W 343271	1604.1	W 330053	1324.9	W 372178	1357.9	VIANDES BOVIN FRAI,REF
01111	BOVINE MEAT WITH BONE IN	W 241675	1026.5	W 209269	988.2	W 180637	730.3	W 192658	734.3	VIANDES BOVIN NON DESOSS
01112	BOVINE MEAT BONELESS	W 123082	543.3	W 134002	616.0	W 149417	594.7	W 179521	623.7	VIANDES BOVIN DESOSSEES
0113	PIG MEAT FRESH,CHLD,FRZN	W 844929	1689.0	W 767944	1773.1	W 703193	1786.7	W 569259	1273.2	VIANDE DE PORC
0114	POULTRY FRESH CHLLD,FRZN	W 407259	880.3	W 465833	993.3	W 499726	1042.9	W 556928	986.7	VOLAILLES MORTES
02	DAIRY PRODCTS,BIRDS'EGGS		4269.9		5049.1		4839.6		3883.9	PRODUITS LAITIERS,OEUFS
022	MILK AND CREAM	W 857758	1277.3	W 975889	1686.8	W 902227	1460.5	W 829082	1210.5	LAIT ET CREME
0224	MILK,CREAM PRESERVED ETC	W 652972	1058.8	W 750779	1425.7	W 656953	1180.9	W 621964	992.1	LAIT,CREME CONS,CONC
02243	MILK DRY,OVER 1.5% FAT	W 192234	463.8	W 234069	622.6	W 198557	529.1	W 172015	420.4	LAIT POUDRE SUP 1.5%
023	BUTTER	W 168284	524.1	W 186670	652.1	W 163243	565.5	W 156857	491.9	BEURRE
024	CHEESE AND CURD	W 486133	2028.5	W 502057	2272.7	W 525291	2288.5	W 455184	1747.5	FROMAGE ET CAILLEBOTTE
025	EGGS,BIRDS,FRESH,PRSRVD	W 383494	440.0	W 380288	437.7	W 376537	525.2	W 374158	434.1	OEUFS
03	FISH AND PREPARATIONS		1308.7		1473.7		1395.8		1233.4	POISSONS ET PREPARATIONS
034	FISH,FRESH,CHILLED,FROZN	W 440984	695.3	W 442657	807.9	W 423492	770.0	W 467050	697.3	POISSON FRAIS, REFRIG,CONG
04	CEREALS AND PREPARATIONS		1570.5		1739.6		1670.2		1577.7	CEREALES ET PRODUITS
048	CEREAL ETC PREPARATIONS	W 636585	1204.9	W 684872	1398.7	W 645535	1271.3	W 675142	1181.2	PREPTNS A BASE CEREALES
0484	BAKERY PRODUCTS	W 230697	600.5	W 230151	657.7	W 211165	590.2	W 216119	506.7	PRODUITS DE BOULANGERIE
0488	OTH CEREAL PREPS,MALT EX	W 166751	464.6	W 182143	559.1	W 166803	508.8	W 176050	503.8	EXTRAITS DE MALT
05	VEGETABLES AND FRUIT		6651.5		7719.1		6800.7		5722.3	LEGUMES ET FRUITS
054	VEG ETC FRSH,SMPLY PRSVD	W 6329538	3840.3	W 5808254	4551.6	W 5162041	3883.4	W 5420921	3350.1	LEGUMES FRAIS,CONG,SECS
0541	POTATOES FRSH EXCL SWEET	W 2107264	474.1	W 1835817	681.7	W 1353561	406.1	W 1515144	309.3	POMMES DE TERRE
0544	TOMATOES FRESH	W 701825	792.1	W 747956	824.5	W 660669	833.8	W 633670	688.5	TOMATES FRAICHES
0545	OTHER FRESH VEGETABLES	W 2138431	1751.8	W 2021854	1947.3	W 1940134	1766.7	W 1898474	1512.9	AUTRES LEGUMES FRAIS,REF
05459	FRESH VEGETABLES NES	W 1459791	1514.7	W 1454210	1673.1	W 1434159	1583.1	W 1276323	1308.1	LEGUMES FRAIS,REFRI NDA
0546	VEGETABLES SIMPLY PRESVD	W 916155	688.4	W 960283	988.9	W 969137	782.2	W 1145184	748.5	LEGUMES CONG,CONSER
05461	VEGETABLES FROZEN	W 897293	669.7	W 943821	973.2	W 950463	764.6	W 1125408	733.6	LEGUMES CONGELES
056	VEGTBLES ETC PRSVD,PREPD	W 754029	823.2	W 751813	991.0	W 649789	758.6	W 666523	633.9	CONSERVES DE LEGUMES
0565	VEGTBLES PRSVD,PREPD NES	W 676816	727.7	W 681168	872.7	W 578118	642.9	W 586602	524.7	LEGUMES PREPARES CONSERVE
05659	OTH VEG PRESVD,PREPD NES	W 622701	642.7	W 632842	788.7	W 547649	604.0	W 552666	488.8	LEGUM PREPAP,CONSERV NDA
057	FRUIT,NUTS,FRESH,DRIED	W 1292853	1166.6	W 1298705	1256.4	W 1298007	1275.7	W 1222121	1089.1	FRUITS FRAIS OU SECS
058	FRUIT PRESERVED,PREPARED	W 597700	821.5	W 607255	920.1	W 576850	883.3	W 548551	649.4	CONSERVES DE FRUITS
0585	FRUIT OR VEGETABLE JUICE	W 395857	543.9	W 387064	592.9	W 346197	556.4	W 307338	385.3	JUS DE FRUITS
06	SUGAR AND PREPS,HONEY		597.1		679.1		577.7		593.3	SUCRES ET PRODUITS
07	COFFEE,TEA,COCOA,SPICES		1716.6		2002.2		1909.6		1898.1	CAFE,THE,CACAO,EPICES
072	COCOA	W 352773	819.8	W 365632	951.8	W 402002	985.5	W 421926	1000.0	CACAO
0723	COCOA BUTTER AND PASTE	W 166272	560.5	W 172539	665.6	W 189678	699.5	W 202002	737.8	BEURRE ET PATE DE CACAO
07232	COCOA BUTTER	W 143327	514.8	W 146823	606.7	W 153429	623.6	W 162240	655.5	BEURRE DE CACAO
073	CHOCOLATE AND PRODUCTS	W 217160	648.3	W 215988	741.8	W 213389	655.2	W 200161	571.8	CHOCOLAT
081	*FEEDING STUFF FOR ANIML	W 7325816	2042.9	W 7756875	2319.3	W 6903344	2233.4	W 6907482	2083.0	NOURRITURE POUR ANIMAUX
0813	OILCAKE AND OTH RESIDUES	W 2818858	569.7	W 3218500	641.1	W 2728413	659.0	W 2840347	737.6	TOURTEAUX
08131	— OF SOYA BEANS	W 2232015	490.4	W 2489025	550.2	W 2089493	567.0	W 2216732	657.3	TOURTEAUX DE SOJA
0819	FOOD WASTE AND FEED NES	W 3225096	1247.0	W 3373262	1470.5	W 3090337	1376.8	W 3051290	1185.0	DECHETS,ALIMENTS NDA
08199	FODDER NES,INCL SWEETNED	W 1749818	1044.4	W 1790191	1245.1	W 1877396	1195.4	W 2465073	1104.6	PREPARATIONS FOURRAGERES
09	MISC EDIBLE PRODUCTS		1113.9		1382.7		1287.9		1157.0	PREP ALIMENTAIRES DIVERSES
098	EDIBLE PRODCTS,PREPS NES	W 425503	924.3	W 451237	1101.9	W 427933	1015.9	W 465695	911.0	PREP ALIMENTAIRES NDA
09809	MISC FOOD PREPRTIONS NES	W 182385	501.5	W 189817	551.3	W 194116	554.8	W 221268	528.0	PREP ALIMENTAIRES NDA
1	BEVERAGES AND TOBACCO		3788.9		4619.3		4909.4		4478.4	BOISSONS ET TABACS
11	BEVERAGES		1471.6		1788.6		1863.0		1596.1	BOISSONS
112	ALCOHOLIC BEVERAGES	W 1059663	1128.0	W 1213249	1397.4	W 1353694	1489.1		1245.6	BOISSONS ALCOOLIQUES
1123	BEER,ALE,STOUT,PORTER	W 940530	833.8	W 1083982	1075.8	W 1203143	1160.9	W 1195988	991.7	BIERES
12	TOBACCO AND MANUFACTURES		2317.4		2830.7		3046.5		2882.4	TABACS BRUTS FABRIQUES
122	TOBACCO,MANUFACTURED	W 118827	2259.1	W 124989	2769.3	W 138264	2988.6	W 144246	2818.5	TABACS FABRIQUES
1222	CIGARETTES	W 86373	1775.5	W 89198	2186.1	W 104837	2457.6	W 112881	2321.3	CIGARETTES
2	CRUDE MATERLS,EXCL FUELS		8188.2		9133.8		8397.5		7881.4	MAT BRUTES NON COMESTIBLES
22	OIL SEEDS,OLEAGINOUS FRT		464.3		264.4		241.8		335.0	GRAINES,FRUITS OLEAGINEUX
28	METALLIFEROUS ORES,SCRAP		1119.1		1428.1		1110.8		1204.0	MINERAIS METAL,DECHETS
282	IRON AND STEEL SCRAP	W 3658302	608.7	W 3617656	747.3	W 3046591	562.6	W 3365824	560.7	FERRAILLES
28209	— OF OTHR IRON OR STEEL	W 3316269	438.9	W 3238211	462.3	W 2742176	393.1	W 2979954	358.1	FERRAILLES DE FER
29	CRUDE ANIMAL,VEG MAT NES		4931.1		5399.8		5289.8		4546.9	MATIERES BRUTES ANIM,VEGET
292	CRUDE VEG MATERIALS NES	W 1282365	4740.8	W 1162220	5179.1	W 1268146	5056.1		4356.8	MAT BRUTES VEGETALES NDA
2926	LIVE PLANTS,BULBS,ETC	W 734680	2107.5	W 701645	2261.1	W 737697	2183.7	W 648579	1837.6	BULBES,TUBERCULES
29261	BULBS,TUBERS,CORMS,ETC	W 167165	680.4	W 156918	751.5	W 159383	694.2	W 151646	558.6	BULBES,OIGNONS
29269	LIVE PLANTS NES	W 567514	1427.1	W 544728	1509.6	W 578314	1489.5	W 496933	1279.0	AUTRES PLANTES VIVANTES
2927	CUT FLOWERS AND FOLIAGE	W 391795	2195.9	W 366262	2425.9	W 389989	2382.2	W 390305	2066.5	FLEURS,FEUILLAGES COUPES
29271	CUT FLOWERS	W 381831	2139.6	W 355814	2363.9	W 375999	2306.4	W 376688	2001.3	FLEURS ET BOUTONS
3	MINERAL FUELS ETC		11143.4		12745.1		14701.4		13434.8	COMBUSTIBLES MINERAUX LUB
33	PETROLEUM AND PRODUCTS		7502.1		8269.3		9552.1		8818.4	PETROLE ET DERIVES
334	PETROLEUM PRODUCTS,REFIN	MW 49275	7043.9	MW 49742	7792.4	MW 49367	9101.6	MW 49710	8358.1	PRODUITS RAFFINES
3341	GASOLINE,OTH LIGHT OILS	MW 12574	2118.9	MW 13214	2346.7	MW 13043	2743.7	MW 13114	2612.7	ESSENCES POUR MOTEURS
33411	MOTOR,AVIATION SPIRIT	W 2644435	469.4	W 1694768	316.8	W 1280515	276.1	W 1074870	227.8	ESSENCES MOTEURS D'AVIONS
33419	OTH LIGHT PETROLEUM OILS	MW 9930	1649.5	MW 11519	2029.9	MW 11762	2467.7	MW 12040	2384.9	AUTRES HUILES LEGERES
3342	KEROSENE,OTH MEDIUM OILS	W 3765649	653.4	W 4122974	732.6	W 4392590	895.7	W 3994101	743.6	PETR LAMPANTS,AUT HUIL
33421	KEROSENE INCL JET FUEL	W 3689547	631.0	W 4063645	713.4	W 4299721	865.9	W 3895276	708.1	PETROLES LAMPANTS
3343	GAS OILS	MW 16037	2386.8	MW 17667	2760.6	MW 18377	3504.6	MW 17509	3094.8	GAS OILS
3344	FUEL OILS,NES	MW 16085	1410.7	MW 13973	1427.1	MW 12665	1383.7	MW 14223	1434.4	FUEL OILS
3345	LUBS,PETROLEUM OILS NES	W 813686	474.4	W 763946	525.5	W 889136	574.0	W 869338	472.8	HUILES LUBRIFIANTES
341	*GAS,NATURAL AND MANUFCT	MW 31454	3351.3		4079.9		4836.0		4343.4	GAZ NATUREL,GAZ MANUFACT
3414	PETROLEUM GASES, GASEOUS	MW 30387	3173.1	MW 30225	3839.2	MW 36004	4561.9	MW 30943	4074.6	GAZ DE PETROLE GAZEUX
4	ANIMAL,VEGETABLE OIL,FAT		1294.5		1575.8		1492.2		1491.6	HUILES,GRAISSES ANIM,VEG
42	FIXED VEGETABLE OIL,FAT		830.7		1018.1		971.6		1006.2	HUILES VEGETALES FIXES
423	FIXED VEG OILS,SOFT	W 1007799	635.9	W 1010976	748.3	W 957639	641.3	W 1017743	629.9	HUILES VEGET DOUCES FIXES
5	CHEMCLS,RELATED PROD NES		21797.1		28502.3		26942.3		28642.9	PRODUITS CHIMIQUES
51	ORGANIC CHEMICALS		5114.7		7513.3		6942.2		8025.6	PROD CHIMIQ ORGANIQUES
511	HYDROCARBONS NES,DERIVS	W 3879557	1660.1	W 4678308	2763.1	W 5093639	2373.9	W 4411349	2079.6	HYDROCARBURES NDA
5111	ACYCLIC HYDROCARBONS	W 1497473	519.9	W 1646831	864.3	W 1846164	788.1	W 1458994	676.3	HYDROCARBURES ACYCLIQUES
5112	CYCLIC HYDROCARBONS	W 2254141	1027.5	W 2865559	1677.7	W 3068795	1362.5	W 2782528	1157.9	HYDROCARBURES CYCLIQUES
51125	STYRENE	W 940921	558.2	W 979248	850.9	W 1267195	696.0	W 1073757	544.1	STYRENE
512	ALCOHOLS,PHENOLS ETC	W 1376195	585.6	W 1445081	789.3	W 1721211	745.2	W 2227500	1018.8	PHENOLS,PHENOLS–ALCOOLS
5121	ACYCLIC ALCOHOLS,DERIVS	W 1320445	486.5	W 1380257	640.9	W 1652420	600.6	W 2088842	820.8	ALCOOLS ACYCLIQUES
513	CARBOXYLIC ACIDS ETC	W 591677	732.8	W 648376	1009.3	W 648861	891.7	W 1067279	1182.1	ACIDES CARBOXYLIQUES
5137	MONOACIDS AND DERIVATIVS	W 412152	499.4	W 476366	712.8	W 518169	655.7	W 562097	627.7	ACIDES MONOCARBOXYLIQUES
514	NITROGEN–FNCTN COMPOUNDS	W 463439	1027.7	W 485670	1175.6	W 532947	1070.7	W 728625	1536.8	COMPOSES FONCT AZOTEES
5148	OTH NITROGN–FNCTN CMPNDS	W 303996	622.5	W 294777	755.7	W 347601	689.1	W 437823	789.0	AUTRES COMPOSES AZOTES
515	ORG–INORG COMPOUNDS ETC	W 56620	516.2	W 221023	891.2	W 264913	997.1	W 192909	954.3	COMPOSES ORGANO–MINERAUX
5156	HETEROCYCLIC CMPDS ETC	W 24438	348.9	W 187302	699.8	W 239084	823.2	W 155768	756.2	COMPOSES HETEROCYCLIQUES

5. Special Exports F.O.B. by Commodities according to the S.I.T.C. (Rev. 2) in million U.S. Dollars
Exportations Spéciales F.O.B. par Produits d'après la C.T.C.I. (Rév. 2) en millions de Dollars E.U.

SITC CTCI	COMMODITY	1994			1995			1996			1997			PRODUIT
		QUANTITY QUANTITE		VALUE VALEUR	QUANTITY QUANTITE		VALUE VALEUR	QUANTITY QUANTITE		VALUE VALEUR	QUANTITY QUANTITE		VALUE VALEUR	
51569	OTH HETEROCYC CMPDS,ETC	W	24438	348.9	W	14935	403.8	W	18057	513.9	W	15495	558.6	AUT COMP HETEROCYCLIQUES
516	OTHER ORGANIC CHEMICALS	W	986807	592.7	W	1395897	885.0	W	1461146	863.9			1254.3	AUTRES PROD ORGANIQUES
5161	ETHERS,EPOXIDES,ACETALS	W	805498	313.2	W	1118186	514.3	W	1124096	487.8	W	1242835	793.6	ETHERS–OXYDES,ALCOOLS
52	INORGANIC CHEMICALS			1044.0			1112.7			1179.0			1720.3	PROD CHIM INORGANIQUES
522	INORG ELEMNTS,OXIDES,ETC	W	2544553	490.8	W	2368747	619.2	W	3080266	647.2	W	3836330	832.2	ELEMENTS INORGANIQUES
523	OTHR INORG CHEMICALS ETC	W	906559	315.3	W	884548	308.1	W	807710	331.9			631.9	AUT PRODUITS CHIMIQUES INORG
53	DYES,TANNING,COLOUR PROD			1231.9			1479.4			1659.2			1745.8	PROD TEINTURE,COLORANTS
533	PIGMENTS,PAINTS,ETC	W	308477	973.9	W	285627	1112.2	W	309325	1241.8	W	682989	1277.9	PIGMENTS,PEINTURES,VERNIS
5334	VARNISHES,DISTEMPERS ETC	W	170398	534.2	W	139399	573.1	W	152327	655.8	W	412224	524.1	PEINTURES A L'EAU
53342	OTH PAINTS,VARNISHES ETC	W	125588	439.5	W	103917	478.4	W	115946	554.9	W	367471	427.5	AUTRES PEINTURES,VERNIS
541	*MEDICINAL,PHARM PRODUCT	MK	155578	2780.7	MK	89627	3973.8	MK	80110	3438.0			3770.6	PROD MEDICINAUX PHARMACEUT
5417	MEDICAMENTS	MK	32791	1998.9	MK	47693	2636.2	MK	30306	2016.7	MK	28963	2104.7	MEDICAMENTS
54179	— CONTNG OTH SUBSTANCES	MK	27952	1614.5	MK	43259	2138.7	MK	26345	1490.8	MK	24341	1572.0	MED CONT AUT SUBSTANCES
55	PERFUME,CLEANING ETC PRD			1346.5			1394.0			1453.0			1295.9	PROD POUR PARFUM,TOILETTE
554	SOAP,CLEANSING ETC PREPS	W	543008	658.2	W	487914	647.7	W	534885	647.4	W	517448	545.8	SAVONS,PRODUITS DETERSIFS
562	*FERTILIZERS,MANUFACTURE	W	7056992	848.2	W	6604331	1080.4	W	6079681	1013.6	W	6124848	823.1	ENGRAIS MANUFACTURES
5621	CHEM NITROGENOUS FERTLZR	W	5032713	514.5	W	4666261	669.2	W	4456480	661.9	W	4330688	492.6	ENGRAIS AZOTES
58	PLASTIC MATERIALS ETC			6516.7			8635.7			8018.5			8253.8	MAT PLAST ARTIFICIELLES
582	PROD OF CONDENSATION ETC	W	1161834	2152.2	W	1228695	2849.8	W	1320584	2856.2	W	1652569	3233.1	PROD CONDENS,POLYCOND
5823	ALKYDS,OTHER POLYESTERS	W	415390	1026.9	W	478691	1400.5	W	506839	1379.0	W	601401	1375.6	ALKYDES ET AUT POLYESTERS
58231	— IN PRIMARY FORMS	W	388582	871.6	W	447619	1198.8	W	473470	1173.7	W	565971	1162.7	SOUS FORMES PRIMAIRES
5829	OTH CONDNSATION,ETC PROD	W	297526	351.8	W	320375	490.6	W	351974	527.2	W	547022	943.0	AUT PROD CONDENSATION
583	POLYMERIZATION ETC PRODS	W	3873870	4281.9	W	3691169	5682.0	W	3795256	5041.2	W	4119770	4657.7	PROD POLYMERISATION
5831	POLYETHYLENE	W	1394198	979.1	W	1262011	1303.4	W	1244194	1120.0	W	1389702	1096.8	POLYETHYLENE
58311	— IN PRIMARY FORMS	W	1189131	848.4	W	1152479	1170.4	W	1133300	992.6	W	1259161	959.6	POLYETHYLENE PRIMAIRES
5832	POLYPROPYLENE	W	591051	500.0	W	560212	745.5	W	593554	631.3	W	519877	536.5	POLYPROPYLENE
58321	— IN PRIMARY FORMS	W	542794	397.9	W	508560	584.2	W	535026	483.3	W	450642	378.5	POLYPROPYLENE PRIMAIRES
5833	POLYSTYRENE,ITS COPOLYMR	W	520426	656.8	W	476846	844.4	W	503722	760.7	W	600853	697.5	POLYPROPYLENE COPOLYMERES
58331	— IN PRIMARY FORMS	W	481079	636.1	W	459883	816.6	W	488316	735.5	W	583869	674.6	SOUS FORMES PRIMAIRES
5834	POLYVINYL CHLORIDE	W	509298	513.0	W	476991	698.4	W	498352	509.9	W	492278	486.4	CHLORURE DE POLYVINYLE
5839	OTH POLYMRZTION ETC PROD	W	665063	1235.9	W	720322	1603.6	W	777862	1570.7	W	882201	1373.1	AUT PROD POLYMER COPOLYM
59	CHEMICAL MATERIALS NES			2904.7			3303.1			3227.0			3004.3	MAT PROD CHIMIQUES NDA
591	PESTICIDES,DISINFECTANTS	W	103763	488.5	W	89531	486.6	W	79813	435.5	W	76668	376.5	DESINF,INSECT,FONG,HERB
592	STARCH,INULIN,GLUTEN,ETC	W	1013319	807.7	W	1038994	909.6	W	1052421	940.0	W	1020486	907.1	AMIDONS,INUL,GLUT FROM
5922	ALBUMINOID SUBSTAN,GLUES	W	539357	581.5	W	580307	661.6	W	604125	693.4	W	683262	750.7	MAT ALBUMIN,COLLES
598	MISCEL CHEM PRODUCTS NES	W	1099829	1608.6	W	1057996	1907.0	W	1322308	1851.6			1720.8	PROD DIV INDUST CHIM NDA
5989	CHEM PRODUCTS,PREPS NES	W	1017390	1414.8	W	961806	1681.5	W	1220033	1655.7	W	979453	1489.8	PROD PREP CHIMIQUES NDA
59899	OTH CHEM PRODS,PREPS,NES	W	861285	1027.8	W	820496	1286.9	W	1065186	1269.5	W	776779	1128.8	AUT PRODUITS CHIMIQUES NDA
6	BASIC MANUFACTURES			17803.0			22421.3			20268.2			21808.3	ART MANUFACTURES
62	RUBBER MANUFACTURES NES			1098.6			1320.9			1272.4			1163.0	CAOUTCHOUC MANUFACTURE
625	RUBBER TYRES, TUBES ETC	W	189574	712.5	W	216074	851.8	W	204080	822.9	W	188060	721.4	PNEUS CAOUTCHOUC VULCANISE
63	WOOD,CORK MANUFACTRS NES			701.2			731.6			661.4			608.9	OUVRAGES LIEGE ET BOIS
635	WOOD MANUFACTURES NES	W	414852	540.8	W	383591	594.4	W	378998	550.7	W	411786	499.6	ART MANUF EN BOIS NDA
64	PAPER,PAPERBOARD AND MFR			3156.7			4065.4			3724.2			3507.1	PAPIERS,CARTONS & OUVRAGES
641	PAPER AND PAPERBOARD	W	2677681	2139.7	W	2687693	2844.4	W	2686107	2517.8	W	3028280	2436.2	PAPIERS ET CARTONS
6412	PRINTG,WRITING PAPER NES	W	635005	564.7	W	609202	753.5	W	627196	640.1	W	771811	678.7	PAPIERS POUR L'IMPRESSION
64122	— COATED,IMPREGNATD ETC	W	586190	508.8	W	543783	644.8	W	518043	504.9	W	652790	552.1	PAPIERS IMPRESSION COUCHES
6415	PAPER,PAPERBRD,BULK,NES	W	886230	537.8	W	866219	733.7	W	821699	535.1	W	853868	482.9	PAPIERS,CARTONS ROULEAUX
64159	OTHER PAPER ETC,BULK,NES	W	869916	526.1	W	852593	718.9	W	809733	524.2	W	840419	472.5	AUT PAPIER ROULEAUX FEUILLES
6418	COATED ETC PAPER NES BLK	W	211847	414.6	W	247248	505.8	W	279388	548.7	W	314686	547.9	PAP,CARTONS COUCHES,ENDUITS
642	PAPER,ETC,PRECUT,ARTS OF	W	486000	1017.1	W	502608	1221.1	W	541850	1206.5	W	566038	1071.0	PAP,CARTONS DECOUPES
6428	PAPER ETC ARTICLES NES	W	173931	466.4	W	177150	554.8	W	203683	558.2	W	231913	521.4	OUVRAGES EN PATE A PAPIER
65	TEXTILE YARN,FABRICS,ETC			2700.5			3532.1			3243.0			5196.0	FILS,TISSUS,ARTICLES TEXTILE
651	TEXTILE YARN	W	73050	233.3	W	105591	470.4	W	93700	367.3			1088.7	FILS TEXTILES
6514	SYN FIB YRN,BULK,MONOFIL	W	12425	79.5	W	36580	259.8	W	28424	182.8	W	107901	895.4	FILS CONT 85% FIB TEXT SYNTH
65142	— NONTXT ETC CONT PAMID	W	4345	22.2	W	4091	23.8	W	6875	48.7	W	72425	560.0	FILS NON TEX FI CON POLYAMID
653	WOVN MAN–MADE FIB FABRIC	W	34913	418.2	W	42759	562.4	W	46039	475.1	W	41220	435.9	TISSUS FIBRES SYNTH,ARTIF
657	SPECIAL TXTL FABRC,PRODS	W	76580	564.4	W	81831	666.8	W	80773	617.8			615.7	TISSUS SPECIAUX
659	FLOOR COVERINGS,ETC	W	138782	481.4	W	185018	680.8	W	193485	680.4			2063.3	COUVRE–PARQUETS,TAPIS ETC
6595	MAN–MADE TXTL CARPTS NES	W	109008	359.5	W	145961	521.5	W	156566	529.0			676.4	TAPIS MAT TEXT SYNT ARTIF
65951	— TUFTED	W	107948	349.1	W	144820	509.0	W	155206	517.0			554.6	TAPIS MAT TEXT SYNT TOUFFT
6596	OTH TXTL CARPETS ETC NES	W	23834	75.4	W	30507	99.4	W	31259	104.6			736.3	TAPIS AUT MAT TEXT NDA
66	NONMETAL MINERAL MFS NES			1409.8			1514.5			1429.7			1488.3	ART MIN NON METALLIQUES
67	IRON AND STEEL			3459.5			4313.3			3742.8			3683.5	FER ET ACIER
672	IRON,STEEL PRIMARY FORMS	W	2811612	861.2	W	2514247	956.4	W	2773652	827.6			792.1	LINGOTS FER,ACIER
6727	IRN,STL COIL FR REROLLNG	W	1270129	466.4	W	1300262	558.1	W	1261276	439.9	W	1414979	452.6	EBAUCHES POUR TOLES FER
67271	IRON,SIMPLE STEEL COILS	W	1264361	460.0	W	1292287	544.3	W	1258470	434.5	W	1364980	429.0	EBAUCHES NON EN ACIER
674	IRN,STL UNIV,PLATE,SHEET	W	2480537	1528.8	W	2515319	1973.7	W	2578416	1771.9	W	2817703	1714.2	LARGES PLATS,TOLES
6746	IRN,STL THIN PLATE,ROLLD	W	1045951	644.2	W	986428	798.7	W	1040256	718.7	W	1093512	656.6	TOLES LAM MOINS 3MM
678	IRON,STL TUBES,PIPES,ETC	W	523864	487.3	W	479401	619.0	W	446389	555.1	W	462016	496.5	TUBES,TUYAUX EN FONTE,FER
68	NON–FERROUS METALS			2003.1			2937.9			2479.8			2637.5	METAUX NON FERREUX
684	ALUMINIUM	W	652796	1371.3	W	809463	2141.6	W	702617	1669.2	W	689215	1555.4	ALUMINIUM
6841	ALUMINIUM,ALLOYS,UNWRGHT	W	443871	676.8	W	576826	1189.4	W	483772	836.9	W	454494	780.2	ALUMINIUM,ALLIAGES BRUTS
6842	ALUMINIUM,ALLOYS WORKED	W	208926	694.5	W	232638	952.3	W	218845	832.4	W	234721	775.3	ALUMINIUM,ALLIAGES OUVRE
69	METAL MANUFACTURES NES			3051.0			3773.5			3501.7			3299.7	ART MANUFACT EN METAL NDA
691	STRUCTURES AND PARTS NES	W	321996	714.6	W	327050	1093.4	W	325955	785.4	W	301140	649.2	CONSTRUCT FER,ACIER,ALU
6911	STRUCTURES,PARTS IRN,STL	W	302812	571.6	W	301121	903.5	W	303552	611.1	W	278170	499.0	CONSTRUCT FER,ACIER,FONTE
695	TOOLS	W	30756	453.3	W	29432	595.1	W	34978	671.3	W	34504	714.9	OUTILS A MAIN
699	BASE METAL MFRS NES	W	186431	945.2	W	178200	1091.6	W	359271	1067.8			989.3	ART MANUFACTURES MET NDA
7	MACHINES,TRANSPORT EQUIP			36255.1			47165.6			50488.7			59190.7	MACHINES MATERIEL TRANSPORT
71	POWER GENERATING EQUIPMT			1526.2			1787.5			1822.6			1880.9	MACHINES GENERATRICES
713	INTRNL COMBUS PSTN ENGIN	W	33031	429.6	W	35040	582.1	W	41583	611.3			653.7	MOTEURS EXPL COMB INT, PIECE
714	ENGINES AND MOTORS NES	W	8295	742.4	W	9910	862.7	W	9081	873.9	W	11507	886.8	MOTEURS NON ELECTRIQUES
7149	ENGINE & MOTOR PARTS NES	W	7690	552.6	W	9238	705.8	W	8682	726.6	W	10525	697.9	PIECES 714 ET 718.88
72	MACHS FOR SPCL INDUSTRYS			3156.4			3602.0			3645.7			3453.0	MAC SPECIALES POUR INDUST
721	AGRIC MACHY,EXC TRACTORS	W	60221	499.3	W	61729	578.8	W	61069	513.3			493.3	MACHINES AGRICOLES
727	FOOD MACHRY NON–DOMESTIC	W	26977	560.0	W	29638	628.0	W	25478	595.8	W	27335	588.3	MACH INDUSTRIES ALIMENT
7272	OTH FOOD PROC MCHY,PARTS	W	21310	525.6	W	22871	587.1	W	17618	560.3	W	19987	551.9	AUT MACH IND ALIMENTAIRE
72722	INDUS FOOD PROC MACH NES	W	21058	522.4	W	22787	585.1	W	17108	557.3	W	19425	550.1	MACHINES BOULANGERIE
728	OTH MACHY FOR SPCL INDUS	W	51622	1063.3	W	58362	1265.2	W	54863	1344.9	W	63058	1296.2	AUT MACH IND PARTICULIERES
7284	MACHY FOR SPCL INDUS NES	W	38318	940.4	W	43353	1111.5	W	38998	1199.6	W	44197	1173.6	MACH SPEC IND PARTICUL.
72849	PTS OF MACHS OF 7284 ETC	W	13287	407.1	W	17150	474.6	W	16390	575.2	W	17964	481.2	PIECES DU 728.4 ETC
74	GENRL INDUSTRL MACHY NES			3898.8			4586.6			4747.6			4384.9	MACH APP INDUSTRIE
741	HEATING,COOLING EQUIPMNT	W	54444	694.8	W	50178	813.6	W	51143	911.9	W	51411	721.3	MACH CHAUFFAGE,PIECES
743	PUMPS NES,CENTRFUGES ETC	W	30853	538.4	W	32843	607.7	W	42639	766.6	W	46611	698.1	POMPES COMPRES,VENT ETC
744	MECHANICAL HANDLING EQU	W	141165	1016.3	W	168963	1278.9	W	157769	1220.4	W	175772	1142.8	EQUIP MANUTENTION PIECES
745	NONELEC MACHY,TOOLS NES	W	1208184	495.0	W	19916	543.8			534.3			572.6	AUT MACH NON ELEC,PIECES
7452	OTH NONELEC MCHS,PTS NES	W	1206873	451.5	W	18789	492.5			477.0			521.9	AUT MACH NON ELEC,PIECES
749	NONELEC MACH PTS,ACC NES	W	49924	791.9	W	54819	977.7	W	59776	960.1	W	76932	911.4	PIECES MACH NON ELEC NDA
75	OFFICE MACHINES,ADP EQUIP			10144.8			13355.6			15372.7			18637.3	MACH BUREAU TRAIT AUTOM
751	OFFICE MACHINES	W	54178	1555.8	W	53347	1796.2	W	66126	1561.8			1501.7	MACH,APPAREILS DE BUREAU

5. Special Exports F.O.B. by Commodities according to the S.I.T.C. (Rev. 2) in million U.S. Dollars
Exportations Spéciales F.O.B. par Produits d'après la C.T.C.I. (Rév. 2) en millions de Dollars E.U.

SITC CTCI	COMMODITY	1994		1995		1996		1997		PRODUIT
		QUANTITY QUANTITE	VALUE VALEUR	QUANTITY QUANTITE	VALUE VALEUR	QUANTITY QUANTITE	VALUE VALEUR	QUANTITY QUANTITE	VALUE VALEUR	
7518	OFFICE MACHINES NES	W 52310	1498.6	W 51333	1735.2	W 63954	1496.0	W 52874	1446.6	MACH,APP DE BUREAU NDA
75182	PHOTO,THERMOCOPY APPARAT	W 44444	1232.9	W 44099	1419.2	W 39928	1198.4	W 45001	1200.7	APPAREILS DE PHOTOCOPIE
752	AUTOMTIC DATA PROC EQUIP	W 74824	5586.7	W 96841	7697.2	W 120938	9764.4		11466.5	MACH TRAIT INFORMATION
7522	DIGITAL COMPUTERS	W 1988	479.1	W 2785	840.7	W 3879	936.2	W 4346	1022.9	MACH DIGITALES COMPLETES
7523	DIGITL CENTRL PROCESSORS	W 16771	1642.1	W 17949	2187.6	W 20162	2427.2	W 28061	2603.1	UNITES CENTRALES
7524	DIGITL CENTRL STOR UNITS	W 5045	986.9	W 8080	1872.8	W 12331	2849.4	W 19230	4172.9	UNITES MEMOIRE CENTRALES
7525	ADP PERIPHERAL UNITS	W 46728	2005.8	W 63338	2432.7	W 77963	2966.9	W 94561	3108.4	UNITES PERIPHERIQUES
7528	OFF–LINE DATA PROC EQUIP	W 4255	469.2	W 4578	355.2	W 6412	562.9	W 11823	547.1	MACH AUXIL TRAIT INFORM
759	OFFICE,ADP MCH PTS,ACCES	W 45067	3002.4	W 47627	3862.3	W 49892	4046.5	W 57397	5669.3	PIECES DU 751 ET 752
7591	OFFICE MACHINE PARTS NES	W 26111	1039.6	W 23363	1087.5	W 16823	689.5	W 27490	895.4	PIECES DU 7511,7518
75919	COPY MACH PRTS,ACCES NES	W 23949	853.1	W 20944	867.1	W 14914	534.7	W 24510	739.8	PIECES DU 751.82
7599	ACCTG,ETC,ADP MCH PTS,AC	W 18955	1962.8	W 24264	2774.8	W 33069	3357.1	W 29907	4773.9	PIECES DU 751 ET 752
76	TELECOMM,SOUND EQUIPMENT		2398.5		3121.8		3482.8		3232.5	EQUIPMENT DE TELECOM
762	RADIO BROADCAST RECEIVRS	W 16793	388.2	W 20272	527.5	W 23172	592.7	W 24363	504.3	RECEPTEURS RADIODIFFUSION
764	TELECOM EQPT,PTS,ACC NES	W 24454	1547.4	W 26336	2030.9	W 27370	2096.0		2034.5	EQUIP TELECOM,PIECES
7641	LINE TELEPHONE,ETC EQUIP	W 2545	181.9	W 3626	303.9	W 4118	433.6	W 6569	732.2	APP TELEPHON PAR FIL
7649	PTS NES OF EQUIPMT OF 76	W 9859	938.2	W 10749	1245.5	W 9755	1265.3	W 9530	925.3	PIECES DE LA DIV 76
76491	PTS NES OF APPAR OF 7641	W 2840	469.5	W 4193	840.7	W 4016	794.3	W 2832	496.7	PIECES POUR 764.1
77	ELECTRIC MACHNRY NES ETC		7883.5		10264.4		11502.5		17425.3	MACH APP ELECT NDA
771	ELECTRIC POWER MACHY NES	W 21760	334.0	W 21300	369.1	W 27961	467.0		1580.8	MACH PROD,TRANS ELECTR
7711	TRANSFORMERS,ELECTRICAL	W 5476	61.8	W 4594	59.8	W 4911	57.6		903.3	TRANSFO ELECTRIQUES
7712	OTH ELEC POWER MACHY NES	W 16283	272.3	W 16706	309.4	W 23050	409.4		677.6	AUT APP PROD TRANSF ELEC
772	SWITCHGEAR ETC,PARTS NES	W 32801	975.8	W 29274	1423.3	W 29536	1391.6	W 40228	1551.7	APP COUPURE,SECT ETC
7721	SWITCHGEAR ETC	W 31076	781.1	W 27429	1204.6	W 27124	1167.1	W 36930	1333.3	APP COUPURE,SECTIONMNT
774	ELECTRO–MEDCL,XRAY EQUIP	W 4754	963.5	W 5197	1134.2	W 5818	1069.6	W 6234	1110.5	APPAREILS MEDICAUX
7742	X–RAY APPARATUS ETC	W 3885	729.5	W 3991	770.4	W 4478	770.7	W 4302	748.6	APPAREILS A RAYONS X
775	HOUSEHOLD TYPE EQUIP NES	W 42826	736.4	W 50073	887.6	W 56638	768.6	W 65098	749.7	MACH,APP USAGE DOMESTQUE
776	TRANSISTORS,VALVES,ETC	W 15492	2820.0	W 17606	3946.5	W 20045	5322.9		9099.6	LAMPES,TUBES,VALVES
7761	TV PICTURE TUBES	W 2219	26.8	W 1061	17.6	W 503	8.1	W 32334	618.3	TUBES CATHODIQUES
7762	OTH ELECTRONIC TUBES ETC	W 273	61.0	W 520	59.9	W 869	64.6		1390.2	AUT LAMPES ELECTRONIQUES
7763	DIODES,TRANSISTORS,ETC	W 1605	399.9	W 1877	576.7	W 1869	515.7	W 2373	593.6	DIODES,TRANSISTORS
7764	ELECTRONIC MICROCIRCUITS	W 2811	2054.5	W 3246	2923.8	W 4622	4352.5		6141.4	MICROSTRUCTURES ELECTRON
778	ELECTRICAL MACHINERY NES	W 102618	1700.2	W 111982	2101.2		2084.4		2905.8	AUTRES MACH ELECT NDA
7782	ELECTRIC LAMPS,BULBS	W 49021	708.5	W 53259	803.2	W 52782	721.5		1388.2	LAMPES, TUBES ELECTRIQUES
77822	ELEC DISCHARGE LAMPS NES	W 23896	362.5	W 26610	417.6	W 26155	379.3		635.6	LAMPES NON ULTRA–VIOLETS
7788	OTH ELEC MACHY,EQUIP NES	W 15991	624.4	W 16476	809.5		877.4	W 314306	945.7	AUT MACH APP ELEC NDA
78	ROAD VEHICLES		5007.1		7382.2		8328.4		8457.1	VEHICULES ROUTIERS
781	PASS MOTOR VEH EXC BUSES	W 189123	1474.6	W 247307	2624.9	W 303534	3325.7	W 375824	3652.3	AUTO TRANSPORT PERSONNES
782	LORRIES,SPCL MTR VEH NES	W 158160	777.9	W 175126	1124.2	W 192830	1164.0	W 218666	1094.3	VEHICULES SPECIAUX,MARCH
7821	LORRIES,TRUCKS	W 147018	720.3	W 163012	1054.5	W 175394	1062.0	W 193625	976.6	VEHICULES TRANSP MARCHAND
783	ROAD MOTOR VEHICLES NES	W 104690	865.1	W 143036	1381.7	W 153087	1399.2	W 178042	1431.7	VEHICULES ROUTIERS NDA
7832	TRACTORS FOR TR–TRAILERS	W 92180	723.1	W 130860	1239.6	W 140278	1257.4	W 163225	1296.4	TRACTEURS ROUTIERS
784	MOTOR VEH PRTS,ACCES NES	W 200784	1236.6	W 222976	1575.4	W 238535	1586.6	W 255285	1395.3	PIECES 722,781,782,783
7849	OTHER MOTOR VEHCL PARTS	W 192487	1166.3	W 216903	1511.3	W 232094	1529.7	W 247241	1332.0	PIECES 722,781,782,783
785	CYCLES,ETC MOTRZD OR NOT	W 21838	350.9	W 16263	340.5	W 25432	539.2	W 32181	593.3	MOTOCYCLES SCOOTERS
79	OTHR TRANSPORT EQUIPMENT		1886.7		2684.3		1204.9		1328.3	AUTRE MATERIEL TRANSPORT
792	AIRCRAFT ETC	W 2046	1191.8	W 2757	2008.4	W 1885	847.1		434.1	APP NAVIGATION AERIENNE
7924	AIRCRFT NES OVER 15000KG	W 530	533.8	W 1187	1160.0	W 693	384.4	W 148	96.7	AERODYNES PLUS 15000 KG
793	SHIPS AND BOATS ETC	W 87702	642.5	W 46289	612.5	W 1043253	309.3		858.2	NAVIRES BATEAUX,ETC
7932	SHIPS AND BOATS NES	W 34173	333.6	W 21934	341.0	W 1035636	242.9	W 1151133	735.0	NAVIRES ET BATEAUX
8	MISC MANUFACTURED GOODS		13793.2		15545.9		15886.5		23576.6	ART MANUFACTURES DIVERS
812	*PLUMBG,HEATNG,LGHTNG EQ	W 90879	495.0	W 81698	518.7	W 81498	492.5	W 94632	540.7	APPAR SANITAIRES CHAUFFAGE
821	*FURNITURE,PARTS THEREOF	W 283565	878.5	W 172742	960.1	W 166020	971.5	W 167723	795.4	MEUBLES ET PIECES
8219	FURNITURE AND PARTS NES	W 223746	524.8	W 120071	567.0	W 111062	563.1	W 113332	467.2	AUTRES MEUBLES ET PIECES
84	CLOTHING AND ACCESSORIES		2623.5		2772.1		3054.1		8518.8	VETEMENTS
842	MENS OUTERWEAR NOT KNIT	W 14132	474.2	W 14156	542.0	W 16206	572.3		1564.6	VET DESSUS POUR HOMMES
8429	— OTHER OUTER GARMENTS	W 5904	193.9	W 5871	215.3	W 5608	214.1		1177.3	AUT VET DES HOM MAT TEX
843	WOMENS OUTERWEAR NONKNIT	W 19506	766.5	W 19210	792.6	W 21382	793.7	W 25599	943.4	VET DESSUS FEMMES MAT TEX
8439	— OTHER OUTER GARMENTS	W 10917	353.5	W 10150	352.1	W 11571	367.2	W 16189	594.7	AUT VET DES FEM MAT TEXT
845	OUTERWEAR KNIT NONELASTC	W 18851	562.8	W 16183	531.0	W 22541	645.2		4013.3	VET DESSOUS,ACCES BONNET
8451	— JERSEYS,PULLOVERS ETC	W 9312	310.7	W 7721	277.0	W 10975	345.8		672.1	CHANDAILS,PULL–OVERS ETC
8452	— WOMENS DRESSES ETC	W 1454	39.9	W 1104	37.9	W 1210	38.2	W 26890	782.5	ROBES,JUPES BONNETERIE
8459	— OTHER,CLTHG ACCESRYS	W 8084	212.3	W 7358	216.3	W 10356	261.2		2558.8	AUT VET DESSUS DE BONNE
846	UNDER GARMENTS KNITTED	W 13603	390.2	W 14223	459.8	W 18664	533.9		1570.3	SOUS VETS DE BONNETERIE
8462	— OF COTTON NON ELASTIC	W 11105	268.5	W 11292	300.9	W 14812	352.8		1109.8	SOUS–VET BONNET COTON
84629	—— OTHER	W 11105	268.5	W 11292	300.9	W 14812	352.8		1109.8	AUT SOUS–VET BONNET COTON
851	*FOOTWEAR	W 33804	489.0	W 32614	564.1	W 34141	559.3	W 33551	545.3	CHAUSSURES
87	PRECISION INSTRUMNTS NES		1975.8		2356.5		2649.3		3145.8	INSTRUM,APPAR SCIENT NDA
872	MEDICAL INSTRUMENTS NES	W 7832	580.3	W 7547	704.3	W 9571	833.6		1020.6	INSTR,APP MEDIC–CHIR NDA
87202	OTH MEDICAL INSTRUMENTS	W 7022	555.2	W 6575	672.0	W 8566	788.9	W 10074	976.9	INSTRUM,APP MEDECINE
874	MEASURNG,CONTROLNG INSTR	W 12756	1264.8	W 12356	1498.7	W 17497	1654.4		1740.9	INSTRUMENTS DE MESURE
8748	ELEC MEAS,CONTRL EQU NES	W 1449	320.3	W 1501	378.6	W 3071	533.3		585.3	APP ELEC ELECTRO MESURE
88	PHOTO EQU,OPTICL GDS ETC		1419.9		1477.6		1803.1		3389.1	APP,FOURN PHOTO,OP,MONTR
881	PHOTO APPARAT,EQUIPT NES	W 3885	459.4	W 3674	504.8	W 4303	800.3		1204.3	APP,EQUIP PHOTO NDA
8813	OTH PHOTO,CINE EQUIP NES	W 1871	336.0	W 1924	398.3	W 2394	688.6	W 3056	964.1	APP,MAT PHOTO,CINEMA
88139	PHOTO,CINE LAB EQUIP NES	W 1236	314.5	W 1333	375.6	W 1720	666.1	W 2185	943.1	APP TYPES UTIL LABOR
882	PHOTO,CINEMA SUPPLIES	W 41377	821.2	W 40359	801.4	W 37930	830.8		1455.2	PRODUITS PHOTO,CINEMA
8822	PHOTO FILM EXC DEV CINMA	W 34501	732.3	W 30479	686.2	W 30084	719.4		1050.0	PLAQUES,PELLICULES,FILMS
88221	PHOTO FILM FLAT UNEXPOSD	W 29953	601.0	W 26189	555.4	W 25279	595.5	W 19522	433.4	PLAQUES PHOTO,FILMS SENS
884	OPTICAL GOODS NES	W 764	75.0	W 902	109.1	W 1586	116.2		670.3	ELEMENTS OPTIQ,ART LUNET
89	MISC MANUFCTRD GOODS NES		5770.5		6707.3		6172.1		6472.7	ART MANUFACTURES DIVERS
892	PRINTED MATTER	W 167537	863.1	W 181258	989.5	W 173507	884.5		707.6	IMPRIMES
893	ARTICLES OF PLASTIC NES		1727.2		1985.6		1898.1		1832.7	OUVRAGES EN MAT DIVIS 58
8931	PLSTC PACKG CONTNRS,LIDS	W 174381	539.4	W 174048	639.0	W 173614	589.0	W 197329	552.6	ART TRANSP EMBALLAGE ETC
8939	MISC PLASTIC ARTICLES	W 220081	1138.9	W 222455	1290.5	W 221858	1247.9	W 250679	1224.2	ART DIVERS EN MAT DIV 58
89399	OTHR PLASTC ARTICLES NES	W 212136	1076.6	W 214284	1225.3	W 214293	1195.2	W 211139	1077.4	AUT OUV MAT DIV 58
894	TOYS,SPORTING GOODS,ETC	W 72593	686.5	W 62759	941.4	W 65554	807.4		932.9	VOITURES ENFANTS,JOUETS
8942	TOYS,INDOOR GAMES ETC	W 59404	561.3	W 50285	814.5	W 50883	659.8	W 60414	804.1	JOUETS,JEUX ETC
898	MUSICAL INSTRUMENTS,PTS	W 71273	1581.5	W 78800	1772.1	W 65751	1504.9		1914.3	INSTRUMENTS DE MUSIQUE
8983	SOUND RECRDNG TAPE,DISCS	W 69356	1542.1	W 77148	1733.0	W 64235	1474.6	W 68185	1540.0	SUPPORTS SON POUR 763
89831	PREPD SND RECORDNG MEDIA	W 33211	560.0	W 35789	660.4	W 22185	340.9	W 21243	307.6	SUPPORTS PREPARES
89832	RECORDED DISCS,TAPES ETC	W 36145	982.2	W 41358	1072.6	W 42050	1133.8	W 46942	1232.4	DISQUES,PHONO,BANDES
899	OTHER MANUFACTURED GOODS		639.6		719.7		820.6		791.3	AUT ART MANUF DIVERS NDA
9	GOODS NOT CLASSD BY KIND		6589.9		7187.8		7226.0		760.4	ART TRANSACT NON CLASSES
931	*SPECIAL TRANSACTIONS	W 4598731	6225.0	W 4363002	6813.1	W 4353344	6742.3	W 118767	443.4	TRANS.SPECIALES

FOOT NOTES – NOTES

TABLE 1 –
1 The gold trade includes gold bullion, bars, dust, concentrates, scrap, sweepings, specie and partly–worked gold.
TABLEAU 1 –
1 Le commerce d'or comprend l'or en lingots, les barres, la poussière, les concentrés, les déchets, les balayures, les pièces de monnaie et l'or partiellement travaillé.

1. HISTORICAL SERIES, 1988–1995 SPECIAL TRADE, IMPORTS C.I.F., EXPORTS F.O.B.
SERIES HISTORIQUES, 1988–1995 COMMERCE SPECIAL, IMPORTATIONS C.A.F., EXPORTATIONS F.O.B

YEAR ANNEE	VALUE IN MILLION N.A. GUILDERS / VALEUR EN MILLION N.A. GUILDERS — MERCHANDISE –MARCHANDISE IMPORTS	EXPORTS	GOLD –OR IMPORTS	EXPORTS	CONVERSION FACTORS U.S. CENTS PER N.A. GUILDER FACTEURS DE CONVERSION CENTS E.U. PAR N.A. GUILDER IMPORTS	EXPORTS	INDEX NUMBERS –INDICES QUANTUM IMPORTS	EXPORTS	UNIT VALUE VALEUR UNITAIRE IMPORTS	EXPORTS
1988	2526.00	2041.00			55.5500	55.5500				
1989	2888.00	2608.00			55.7633	55.7633				
1990	3833.00	3204.00			55.8700	55.8700				
1991	3828.00	2862.00			55.8700	55.8700				
1992	3344.00	2790.00			55.8700	55.8700				
1993	3485.00	2297.00			55.8700	55.8700				
1994	3146.00	2462.00			55.8700	55.8700				
1995	3408.00	2534.00								

2. IMPORTS BY BROAD ECONOMIC CATEGORY AND EXPORTS BY INDUSTRIAL ORIGIN. (PERCENTAGE OF TOTAL VALUE)
IMPORTATIONS PAR CATEGORIES ECONOMIQUES ET EXPORTATIONS PAR BRANCHE D'ACTIVITE.(EN POURCENTAGE DE LA VALEUR TOTALE)

IMPORTS – IMPORTATIONS

	1989	1990	1991	1992	1993	1994	1995
TOTAL IMPORTS–IMPORTATIONS TOTALES	100.	100.	100.	100.			100.
1 FOOD BEV–ALIMENTATION BOISSONS	6.6	5.5	5.4	8.3			12.0
11 PRIMARY–PRODUITS DE BASE	2.8	2.2	2.2	3.4			4.7
111 FOR INDUSTRY–POUR L'INDUSTRIE	0.2	0.2	0.2	1.0			1.7
112 FOR HOUSEHOLDS–POUR LES MENAGES	2.6	2.0	2.0	2.4			3.0
12 PROCESSED–PRODUITS ELABORES	3.9	3.3	3.1	5.0			7.3
121 FOR INDUSTRY–POUR L'INDUSTRIE	0.2	0.1	0.1	0.2			0.5
122 FOR HOUSEHOLDS–POUR LES MENAGES	3.7	3.2	3.0	4.7			6.8
2 IND SUPPLIES–APPROV INDUSTRIELS	8.6	7.4	7.5	8.8			10.3
21 PRIMARY–PRODUITS DE BASE	0.8	0.4	0.3	0.5			0.5
22 PROCESSED–PRODUITS ELABORES	7.8	7.0	7.1	8.3			9.8
3 FUELS–COMBUSTIBLES	67.1	70.4	70.7	58.8			55.2
31 PRIMARY–PRODUITS DE BASE	59.9	64.4	64.3	52.8			49.1
32 PROCESSED–PRODUITS ELABORES	7.2	6.0	6.4	6.0			6.1
321 MOTOR SPIRIT–ESSENCE	0.5	0.4	0.1	0.0			0.3
322 OTHER–AUTRES	6.7	5.6	6.2	6.0			5.7
4 MACHINERY–EQUIPEMENT	5.5	5.4	5.0	6.6			7.2
41 CAPITAL EQUIPMENT–MACHINES	5.0	5.0	4.5	5.9			6.5
42 PARTS–PIECES ACCESSOIRES	0.5	0.5	0.5	0.7			0.7
5 TRANSPORT–TRANSPORT	3.6	3.9	3.7	6.4			4.8
51 PASSENGER CARS–AUTOMOBILES	1.5	1.3	1.6	2.1			2.4
52 OTHER–AUTRES	0.8	1.5	0.8	2.3			0.9
521 INDUSTRIAL–INDUSTRIELS	0.8	1.4	0.8	2.3			0.9
522 NON INDUSTRIAL–NON INDUSTRIEL	0.0	0.0	0.0	0.0			0.1
53 PARTS–PIECES ACCESSOIRES	1.3	1.1	1.3	2.0			1.5
6 CONSUM GOODS–BIENS CONSOMMATION	8.6	7.4	7.8	11.1			10.5
61 DURABLE–DURABLES	2.0	1.8	1.8	2.9			2.4
62 SEMI DURABLE–SEMI DURABLES	3.7	3.5	4.0	5.2			4.6
63 NON DURABLE–NON DURABLES	2.9	2.1	2.1	3.0			3.5
7 GOODS NES–BIENS NDA	0.0	0.0	0.0	0.0			0.0

EXPORTS – EXPORTATIONS

	1989	1990	1991	1992	1993	1994	1995
TOTAL EXPORTS–EXPORTATIONS TOTALES	100.	100.	100.	100.			100.
1 AGRICULTURE	0.1	0.0	0.1	2.6			5.8
2 MINING QUARRY–INDUS EXTRACTIVES	14.3	12.0	9.6	7.3			3.5
3 MANUFACTURING–IND MANUFACTUR	85.6	88.0	90.4	90.2			90.7
31 FOOD BEV TOBACCO–ALIM BOISS TAB	0.6	0.5	0.5	0.5			1.1
32 TEXTILES–INDUSTRIES TEXTILES	0.1	0.1	0.1	0.1			0.1
33 WOOD & PRODUCTS–BOIS & PRODUITS	0.0	0.0	0.0	0.0			0.0
34 PAPER & PRODUCTS–PAPIER & PRODT	0.2	0.2	0.1	0.2			1.0
35 CHEMICALS–INDUSTRIES CHIMIQUES	83.6	86.2	88.3	85.6			84.7
36 NON METAL MIN–MIN NON METAL	0.0	0.0	0.0	0.0			0.0
37 BASIC METAL–IND METAL BASE	0.1	0.1	0.0	0.1			0.1
38 METAL MANUF–MANUF METAL	1.1	0.9	1.2	3.6			2.1
39 OTH MANUF IND–AUTRES MANUF	0.0	0.0	0.1	0.1			1.5

3. TRADE BY PRINCIPAL COUNTRIES OF CONSIGNMENT AND DESTINATION (VALUE IN MILLION U.S. DOLLARS)
ECHANGES SELON LES PRINCIPAUX PAYS DE CONSIGNATION ET DE DESTINATION (VALEUR EN MILLIONS DE DOLLARS EU)

COUNTRIES–PAYS	SPECIAL IMPORTS C.I.F. IMPORTATIONS SPECIALES C.A.F					COUNTRIES–PAYS	SPECIAL EXPORTS F.O.B. EXPORTATIONS SPECIALES F.O.B.				
	1991	1992	1993	1994	1995		1991	1992	1993	1994	1995
World	2188.9	1868.3	1946.9	1464.9	1832.5	Monde	1599.2	1558.9	1398.9		1355.7
Africa	0.1	0.1			0.2	Afrique	51.7	68.4			12.9
Americas	1908.4	1539.8			1515.7	Amériques	1359.9	1231.3			1030.3
– Northern America	324.0	349.6			373.5	– Amérique du Nord	482.3	480.0			223.7
– LAIA	1545.9	1106.3			1052.9	– ALAI	282.1	215.7			172.5
– CACM	1.8	2.2			2.9	– MCAC	83.1	99.1			230.4
– Caribbean	24.6	45.8			14.8	– Caraïbes	414.6	351.3			259.4
– Rest of America	12.1	35.8			71.5	– Autre Amérique	97.8	85.2			144.3
Asia excl fmr USSR	48.6	56.7			50.6	Asie anc. URSS exclus	85.7	101.6			24.3
– Middle East	0.0	0.1			0.0	– Moyen–Orient		0.3			
Asia former USSR						Asie ancienne URSS					
Europe excl fmr USSR	198.3	235.3			245.5	Europe anc. URSS exclus	74.2	154.3			217.8
– European Union	183.0	218.3			239.5	– Union Européenne	73.6	126.9			194.2
– Eastern Europe	2.4	2.2			0.2	– Europe de l'Est					
– Rest of Europe	12.9	14.8			5.9	– Autre de l'Europe	0.6	27.3			23.6
Europe former USSR	0.4	0.1			0.0	Europe ancienne URSS					
Oceania	1.3	1.1			0.7	Océanie	1.1	0.8			1.5
Other	31.8	35.1			19.8	Autre	26.6	2.7			68.9
Venezuela	1522.4	1075.7			1006.2	USA/Etats–Unis d'Amer	453.5	389.6	14.5		188.5
USA/Etats–Unis d'Amer	316.4	317.4	334.6	284.9	363.8	Colombia/Colombie	80.8	111.7			71.3
Netherlands/Pays–Bas	130.1	152.0	169.8	163.7	195.3	Dominican Republic	78.0	109.5			73.4
Japan/Japon	38.1	41.0	42.5	32.4	30.4	Netherlands/Pays–Bas	16.9	50.1	68.3		98.0
Free zones/Zone franches	31.7	35.1			19.0	Costa Rica	44.5	56.2			63.3
United Kingdom	16.9	18.3	15.6	12.3	13.1	Guadeloupe	53.8	51.4			47.7
Trinidad and Tobago	16.0	34.3			4.5	Honduras	30.4	30.7			87.9
Canada	7.3	32.0			9.3	Venezuela	77.7	28.5			42.6
Guyana	0.0	9.1			32.5	Jamaica/Jamaïque	67.7	39.9			29.6
Germany/Allemagne	13.9	13.9			11.6	Bahamas	50.7	43.2			41.0
Panama	11.4	13.3			11.7	Canada	16.1	83.4			33.3
Suriname/Surinam	0.7	13.3			21.6	Guyana	35.7	46.8			48.2
Italy/Italie	9.2	15.2			4.7	Singapore/Singapour	32.7	52.7			18.0
Colombia/Colombie	7.9	10.6			9.6	Japan/Japon	47.2	48.0			3.1
Brazil/Brésil	6.2	9.4			7.9	Brazil/Brésil	64.2	18.4			8.5
Aruba	7.0	8.5			6.5	Aruba	39.5	25.8			20.9
Switzerland,Liechtenst.	4.5	12.0			4.5	Areas n.e.s.	24.3	0.7			60.1
Mexico/Mexique	5.0	6.4			7.0	Dominica/Dominique	29.7	26.3			23.2
Ecuador/Equateur	0.0	0.1			16.8	Chile/Chili	25.7	37.0			13.4
France, Monaco	4.2	4.8			5.6	Germany/Allemagne	30.2	36.4			8.2
China, Hong Kong SAR	4.3	5.3			2.9	Guatemala	4.4	6.8			55.5
Argentina/Argentine	3.8	3.5			3.3	Panama	27.9	6.9			28.3
Korea, Republic of	2.0	2.3			5.6	Belgium–Luxembourg	1.2	9.5			44.7
Sweden/Suède	2.5	3.8			2.0	Cuba	25.9	12.2			13.8
Other Europe n.e.s.	6.7	0.7			0.2	Suriname/Surinam	18.7	18.3			13.1
Belgium–Luxembourg	2.0	4.0			1.5	United Kingdom	13.1	8.6	2.1		22.0
Spain/Espagne	1.6	2.3			2.6	Barbados/Barbade	29.3	12.3			2.5
Other Asia n.e.s.	2.0	2.8			1.3	Rest of America n.e.s.					41.5
Korea Dem People's Rp					6.1	Belize/Bélize	14.2	13.1			13.0
Denmark/Danemark	1.5	2.0			2.3	Trinidad and Tobago	7.1	28.9			3.1
Rest of America n.e.s.					5.7	Senegal/Sénégal	12.7	23.6			
Singapore/Singapour	0.7	2.8			1.4	Peru/Pérou	10.0	10.5			15.7
Norway,Svalbard and JM	1.6	1.8			1.2	Haiti/Haïti	31.9	0.5			3.7
Costa Rica	1.3	1.4			1.3	Ecuador/Equateur	10.4	6.6			15.6
Hungary/Hongrie	2.0	1.8			0.0	Spain/Espagne	8.1	16.9			4.9
Dominican Republic	0.6	1.3			1.2	Nigeria/Nigéria	6.4	17.8			5.2
Thailand/Thaïlande	0.6	0.9			0.8	Yugoslavia/Yougoslavie		26.8			
Israel/Israël	0.3	0.6			1.3	Bermuda/Bermudes	12.7	7.0			1.9
Portugal	0.8	0.9			0.3	Switzerland,Liechtenst.	0.5	0.4			20.2
Barbados/Barbade	0.5	0.6			0.8	Nicaragua	3.7	3.5			10.3

(VALUE AS PERCENTAGE OF WORLD TOTAL)(VALEURS EN POURCENTAGE DU TOTAL MONDIAL)

	1986	1987	1988	1989	1990	1991	1992	1993	1994	1995		1986	1987	1988	1989	1990	1991	1992	1993	1994	1995
Africa			0.0	0.0	0.0	0.0	0.0			0.0	Afrique			0.2	2.2	3.7	3.2	4.4			1.0
Americas			84.5	85.6	84.2	87.2	82.4			82.7	Amériques			83.4	81.8	87.6	85.0	79.0			76.0
– Northern America			14.1	13.6	13.6	14.8	18.7			20.4	– Amérique du Nord			31.2	36.1	35.4	30.2	30.8			16.5
– LAIA			68.6	69.2	68.2	70.6	59.2			57.5	– ALAI			16.5	10.1	13.8	17.6	13.8			12.7
– CACM			0.1	0.1	0.1	0.1	0.1			0.2	– MCAC			5.3	5.6	6.6	5.2	6.4			17.0
– Caribbean			1.0	2.0	1.9	1.1	2.5			0.8	– Caraïbes			24.1	24.0	27.2	25.9	22.5			19.1
– Rest of America			0.7	0.7	0.5	0.6	1.9			3.9	– Autre Amérique			6.2	6.1	4.6	6.1	5.5			10.6
Asia excl fmr USSR			3.3	2.8	4.6	2.2	3.0			2.8	Asie anc. URSS exclus			4.3	4.3	2.9	5.4	6.5			1.8
– Middle East			0.0	0.2	1.8	0.0	0.0			0.0	– Moyen–Orient			0.0	0.1			0.0			
Asia former USSR											Asie ancienne URSS										
Europe excl fmr USSR			11.5	10.8	9.7	9.1	12.6			13.4	Europe anc. URSS exclus			5.1	9.7	4.1	4.6	9.9			16.1
– European Union			10.5	10.1	8.8	8.4	11.7			13.1	– Union Européenne			5.1	9.6	4.1	4.6	8.1			14.3
– Eastern Europe			0.1	0.1	0.1	0.1	0.1			0.0	– Europe de l'Est										
– Rest of Europe			0.8	0.5	0.8	0.6	0.8			0.3	– Autre de l'Europe			0.0	0.0	0.0	0.0	1.8			1.7
Europe former USSR			0.1	0.0	0.0	0.0	0.0			0.0	Europe ancienne URSS										
Oceania			0.1	0.1	0.1	0.1	0.1			0.0	Océanie			0.3	0.2	0.1	0.1	0.1			0.1
Other			0.6	0.8	1.4	1.5	1.9			1.1	Autre			6.8	1.8	1.6	1.7	0.2			5.1
Venezuela			57.5	67.8	59.2	69.5	57.6			54.9	USA/Etats–Unis d'Amer			28.1	33.8	33.4	28.4	25.0	1.0		13.9
USA/Etats–Unis d'Amer			13.6	13.2	12.7	14.5	17.0	17.2	19.5	19.9	Colombia/Colombie			1.8	1.2	3.2	5.1	7.2			5.3
Netherlands/Pays–Bas			7.1	6.6	5.7	5.9	8.1	8.7	11.2	10.7	Dominican Republic			5.1	6.3	7.4	4.9	7.0			5.4
Japan/Japon			1.9	1.7	2.2	1.7	2.2	2.2	2.2	1.7	Netherlands/Pays–Bas			1.0	2.0	0.9	1.1	3.2	4.9		7.2
Free zones/Zone franches			0.5	0.8	1.4	1.4	1.9			1.0	Costa Rica			1.1	1.9	3.3	2.8	3.6			4.7
United Kingdom			1.0	0.9	1.0	0.8	1.0	0.8	0.8	0.7	Guadeloupe			2.6	3.2	3.1	3.4	3.3			3.5
Trinidad and Tobago			0.1	0.1	1.2	0.7	1.8			0.2	Honduras			2.8	2.8	2.4	1.9	2.0			6.5
Canada			0.5	0.4	0.8	0.3	1.7			0.5	Venezuela			6.0	4.2	4.6	4.9	1.8			3.1
Guyana			0.0	0.0	0.0	0.0	0.5			1.8	Jamaica/Jamaïque			2.0	2.0	1.8	4.2	2.6			2.2
Germany/Allemagne						0.6	0.7			0.6	Bahamas			2.4	2.8	3.0	3.2	2.8			3.0

4. Special Imports C.I.F. by Commodities according to the S.I.T.C. (Rev. 2) in million U.S. Dollars
Importations Spéciales C.A.F. par Produits d'après la C.T.C.I. (Rév. 2) en millions de Dollars E.U.

SITC CTCI	COMMODITY	1992 QUANTITY QUANTITE	1992 VALUE VALEUR	1993 QUANTITY QUANTITE	1993 VALUE VALEUR	1994 QUANTITY QUANTITE	1994 VALUE VALEUR	1995 QUANTITY QUANTITE	1995 VALUE VALEUR	PRODUIT
	ALL COMMODITIES		1868.4		1947.0		1465.0		1832.5	TOUS PRODUITS
0	FOOD AND LIVE ANIMALS		145.0		197.3		186.1		205.6	ALIMENTS,ANIMAUX VIVANTS
01	MEAT AND PREPARATIONS		30.3						36.7	VIANDES ET PREPARATIONS
011	MEAT FRESH,CHILLD,FROZEN	W 10934	21.4						26.9	VIANDES FRAICHES,REF,CONGE
0111	BOVINE MEAT FRESH,FROZEN	W 2344	7.0					W 2985	8.4	VIANDES BOVIN FRAI,REF
0113	PIG MEAT FRESH,CHLD,FRZN	W 1975	5.5					W 2099	6.2	VIANDE DE PORC
0114	POULTRY FRESH CHLLD,FRZN	W 5632	7.1					W 7096	10.7	VOLAILLES MORTES
014	MEAT PREPD,PRSVD,NES ETC	W 1877	5.6					W 2093	6.6	CONSERVES DE VIANDES
02	DAIRY PRODCTS,BIRDS'EGGS		15.5						25.5	PRODUITS LAITIERS,OEUFS
022	MILK AND CREAM	W 4578	7.5					W 8544	16.6	LAIT ET CREME
0224	MILK,CREAM PRESERVED ETC	W 3400	6.2					W 7015	14.3	LAIT,CREME CONS,CONC
02242	MILK DRY,1.5% FAT OR LES	W 1171	3.7					W 4245	10.7	LAIT POUDRE INF 1.5%
024	CHEESE AND CURD	W 2372	7.3					W 2399	8.1	FROMAGE ET CAILLEBOTTE
03	FISH AND PREPARATIONS		8.3						10.6	POISSONS ET PREPARATIONS
04	CEREALS AND PREPARATIONS		36.5				76.6		66.2	CEREALES ET PRODUITS
042	RICE	W 54639	24.0					W 123372	53.3	RIZ
0421	RICE IN HUSK OR HUSKED	W 31165	13.0					W 62953	26.1	RIZ SANS AUTRE PREPARATION
0422	RICE SEMI-MILLED,MILLED	W 23474	11.1					W 60419	27.2	RIZ POLI,GLACE INCL BRISURES
048	CEREAL ETC PREPARATIONS	W 3161	6.6					W 4591	8.3	PREPTNS A BASE CEREALES
05	VEGETABLES AND FRUIT		29.8				27.4		32.2	LEGUMES ET FRUITS
054	VEG ETC FRSH,SMPLY PRSVD		10.3					W 17220	12.1	LEGUMES FRAIS,CONG,SECS
057	FRUIT,NUTS,FRESH,DRIED		7.3						6.3	FRUITS FRAIS OU SECS
058	FRUIT PRESERVED,PREPARED		8.5					W 9909	9.9	CONSERVES DE FRUITS
0585	FRUIT OR VEGETABLE JUICE	W 5807	6.1					W 8553	7.4	JUS DE FRUITS
06	SUGAR AND PREPS,HONEY		4.8						9.2	SUCRES ET PRODUITS
061	SUGAR AND HONEY		1.7						6.3	SUCRES ET MIEL
07	COFFEE,TEA,COCOA,SPICES		5.5						6.6	CAFE,THE,CACAO,EPICES
09	MISC EDIBLE PRODUCTS		11.2						14.5	PREP ALIMENTAIRES DIVERSES
098	EDIBLE PRODCTS,PREPS NES	W 4480	9.7						12.4	PREP ALIMENTAIRES NDA
09809	MISC FOOD PREPRTIONS NES	W 2050	5.0					W 2541	7.2	PREP ALIMENTAIRES NDA
1	BEVERAGES AND TOBACCO		16.0		18.5		15.7		18.8	BOISSONS ET TABACS
11	BEVERAGES		14.9						16.7	BOISSONS
112	ALCOHOLIC BEVERAGES	W 5026	13.5						14.6	BOISSONS ALCOOLIQUES
1123	BEER,ALE,STOUT,PORTER	W 3191	5.0					W 4327	6.5	BIERES
2	CRUDE MATERLS,EXCL FUELS		9.5		12.3		11.8		10.6	MAT BRUTES NON COMESTIBLES
24	CORK AND WOOD		5.9						6.4	LIEGE ET BOIS
248	WOOD SHAPED,SLEEPERS	W 7310763	4.5						5.9	BOIS SIMPLEMENT TRAVAILLES
3	MINERAL FUELS ETC		1097.9		1117.4				1011.8	COMBUSTIBLES MINERAUX LUB
33	PETROLEUM AND PRODUCTS		1088.0				727.5		1000.9	PETROLE ET DERIVES
333	CRUDE PETROLEUM	MW 9205	976.6					MW 9137	889.6	HUILES BRUTES DE PETROLE
334	PETROLEUM PRODUCTS,REFIN		111.2					W 1021716	110.8	PRODUITS RAFFINES
3341	GASOLINE,OTH LIGHT OILS		24.4					W 86360	14.7	ESSENCES POUR MOTEURS
33411	MOTOR,AVIATION SPIRIT		0.1					W 34053	6.2	ESSENCES MOTEURS D'AVIONS
33412	SPIRIT TYPE JET FUEL	W 123103	24.4					W 52308	8.6	CARBUREACTEURS
3343	GAS OILS	W 195001	32.4					W 109019	16.1	GAS OILS
3344	FUEL OILS,NES	W 636000	47.2					W 824000	77.1	FUEL OILS
3345	LUBS,PETROLEUM OILS NES	W 14052	7.4					W 2336	3.0	HUILES LUBRIFIANTES
33451	LUBS(HIGH PETR CONT) ETC	W 14052	7.4					W 2336	3.0	HUILES LUBRIF,H LOURDES
341	*GAS,NATURAL AND MANUFCT	W 38403	9.9					W 38141	10.9	GAZ NATUREL,GAZ MANUFACT
3413	PETROLM GASES,LIQUEFIED	W 38000	9.8					W 37000	10.4	GAZ DE PETROLE LIQUEFIE
5	CHEMCLS,RELATED PROD NES		68.5		85.0		67.7		81.9	PRODUITS CHIMIQUES
53	DYES,TANNING,COLOUR PROD		2.1						6.0	PROD TEINTURE,COLORANTS
533	PIGMENTS,PAINTS,ETC		2.0					W 2107	5.6	PIGMENTS,PEINTURES,VERNIS
541	*MEDICINAL,PHARM PRODUCT	W 993953	19.3					K 1027084	24.4	PROD MEDICINAUX PHARMACEUT
55	PERFUME,CLEANING ETC PRD		17.9						19.1	PROD POUR PARFUM,TOILETTE
553	PERFUMERY,COSMETICS,ETC	W 1400	15.3					W 1793	15.7	PRODUITS DE PARFUMERIE
58	PLASTIC MATERIALS ETC		3.7						7.2	MAT PLAST ARTIFICIELLES
59	CHEMICAL MATERIALS NES		22.3						18.9	MAT PROD CHIMIQUES NDA
598	MISCEL CHEM PRODUCTS NES		18.0						13.6	PROD DIV INDUST CHIM NDA
5989	CHEM PRODUCTS,PREPS NES	W 13766	17.5					W 6693	13.2	PROD PREP CHIMIQUES NDA
59899	OTH CHEM PRODS,PREPS,NES	W 13692	17.3					W 6548	12.9	AUT PRODUITS CHIMIQUES NDA
6	BASIC MANUFACTURES		124.6		133.0		117.9		137.7	ART MANUFACTURES
62	RUBBER MANUFACTURES NES		6.9						5.9	CAOUTCHOUC MANUFACTURE
63	WOOD,CORK MANUFACTRS NES		9.9						9.8	OUVRAGES LIEGE ET BOIS
64	PAPER,PAPERBOARD AND MFR		18.8						26.9	PAPIERS,CARTONS & OUVRAGES
641	PAPER AND PAPERBOARD	W 5017	6.6					W 5846	7.9	PAPIERS ET CARTONS
642	PAPER,ETC,PRECUT,ARTS OF	W 3925	12.3					W 7984	19.0	PAP,CARTONS DECOUPES
6428	PAPER ETC ARTICLES NES	W 1238	4.1					W 3249	7.7	OUVRAGES EN PATE A PAPIER
64282	PUNCHED CARD MACH CARDS	W 1238	4.1					W 3249	7.7	CARTES POUR MACHINES
65	TEXTILE YARN,FABRICS,ETC		13.4						11.6	FILS,TISSUS,ARTICLES TEXTILE
658	TEXTILE ARTICLES NES		6.1						4.6	ART FACONNES MAT TEXTILES
66	NONMETAL MINERAL MFS NES		23.7						24.1	ART MIN NON METALLIQUES
661	LIME,CEMENT,BLDG PRODS		8.8						9.3	CHAUX,CIMENTS MAT CONSTR
6612	CEMENT	W 75141	6.5					W 84071	6.8	CIMENTS HYDRAULIQUES
662	CLAY,REFRACTORY BLDG PRD		5.7						6.2	MAT CONST REFRACTAIRES
6624	BRICKS ETC NONREFRACTORY		5.1						5.7	BRIQUES ETC CERAM NON REFR
67	IRON AND STEEL		15.4		14.0		12.9		16.7	FER ET ACIER
678	IRON,STL TUBES,PIPES,ETC	W 3995	9.3					W 3759	9.7	TUBES,TUYAUX EN FONTE,FER
69	METAL MANUFACTURES NES		32.4						38.1	ART MANUFACT EN METAL NDA
691	STRUCTURES AND PARTS NES	W 2844	7.4					W 3761	11.8	CONSTRUCT FER,ACIER,ALU
6912	STRUCTURES,PARTS ALUMNM	W 479	2.4					W 2189	7.9	CONSTRUCT ALUMINIUM
699	BASE METAL MFRS NES		9.4						10.9	ART MANUFACTURES MET NDA
7	MACHINES,TRANSPORT EQUIP		258.4		238.6		211.2		232.6	MACHINES MATERIEL TRANSPORT
71	POWER GENERATING EQUIPMT		34.0						21.9	MACHINES GENERATRICES
713	INTRNL COMBUS PSTN ENGIN	W 293	21.4					W 232	7.6	MOTEURS EXPL COMB INT, PIECE
7131	AIRCRAFT PSTN ENGINS,PTS	W 26	18.2					W 16	5.5	MOTEURS EXPL P.AVIATION, PIE
716	ROTATING ELECTRIC PLANT	W 360	7.0					W 664	6.6	APP ELECTR ROTATIFS,PIECES
72	MACHS FOR SPCL INDUSTRYS		10.1						11.5	MAC SPECIALES POUR INDUST
728	OTH MACHY FOR SPCL INDUS	W 278	4.3					W 576	6.7	AUT MACH IND PARTICULIERES
74	GENRL INDUSTRL MACHY NES		41.2						41.5	MACH APP INDUSTRIE
741	HEATING,COOLING EQUIPMNT		7.2						18.1	MACH CHAUFFAGE,PIECES
7416	HEATING,COOLING EQU NES	W 75	1.2					W 717	10.1	APP CHANGEMENT TEMP
742	PUMPS FOR LIQUIDS ETC	W 551	11.1					W 191	5.7	POMPES MOTO-POMPES
743	PUMPS NES,CENTRFUGES ETC	W 212	6.0					W 190	2.5	POMPES COMPRES,VENT ETC
7431	PUMPS FOR GASES ETC	W 212	6.0					W 190	2.5	POMPES AIR A VIDE,COMPRES
744	MECHANICAL HANDLING EQU	W 710	6.5					W 468	2.8	EQUIP MANUTENTION PIECES
749	NONELEC MACH PTS,ACC NES	W 851	10.7					W 743	12.7	PIECES MACH NON ELEC NDA
7499	OTH NONELEC MCHY PTS NES	W 824	9.7					W 722	11.7	PIECES NON ELECT NDA
75	OFFICE MACHNES,ADP EQUIP		16.8						22.3	MACH BUREAU TRAIT AUTOM
752	AUTOMTIC DATA PROC EQUIP		13.4						19.5	MACH TRAIT INFORMATION
76	TELECOMM,SOUND EQUIPMENT		28.3						21.5	EQUIPMENT DE TELECOM

4. Special Imports C.I.F. by Commodities according to the S.I.T.C. (Rev. 2) in million U.S. Dollars
Importations Spéciales C.A.F. par Produits d'après la C.T.C.I. (Rév. 2) en millions de Dollars E.U.

SITC CTCI	COMMODITY	1992 QUANTITY QUANTITE	1992 VALUE VALEUR	1993 QUANTITY QUANTITE	1993 VALUE VALEUR	1994 QUANTITY QUANTITE	1994 VALUE VALEUR	1995 QUANTITY QUANTITE	1995 VALUE VALEUR	PRODUIT
764	TELECOM EQPT,PTS,ACC NES		17.4					W 230	11.7	EQUIP TELECOM,PIECES
7641	LINE TELEPHONE,ETC EQUIP	W 98	12.5					W 95	6.9	APP TELEPHON PAR FIL
77	ELECTRIC MACHNRY NES ETC		33.8						36.5	MACH APP ELECT NDA
773	ELECTR DISTRIBUTNG EQUIP	W 1778	11.0					W 1826	11.2	EQUIPMT DISTRIBUTION ELECT
7731	INSULATED WIRE,CABLE ETC	W 1402	7.5					W 1293	6.7	FILS,CABLES ISOLES ELECT
775	HOUSEHOLD TYPE EQUIP NES		7.8						8.4	MACH,APP USAGE DOMESTQUE
778	ELECTRICAL MACHINERY NES		10.3						11.5	AUTRES MACH ELECT NDA
7788	OTH ELEC MACHY,EQUIP NES	W 287	6.6					W 283	7.3	AUT MACH APP ELEC NDA
78	ROAD VEHICLES		62.2		63.7		58.7		69.7	VEHICULES ROUTIERS
781	PASS MOTOR VEH EXC BUSES	N 4294	38.7					N 4332	43.9	AUTO TRANSPORT PERSONNES
782	LORRIES,SPCL MTR VEH NES	N 955	11.1					N 937	10.2	VEHICULES SPECIAUX,MARCH
7821	LORRIES,TRUCKS	N 937	9.4					N 922	9.7	VEHICULES TRANSP MARCHAND
784	MOTOR VEH PRTS,ACCES NES		9.0						11.9	PIECES 722,781,782,783
7849	OTHER MOTOR VEHCL PARTS	W 1537	9.0					W 860	11.8	PIECES 722,781,782,783
79	OTHR TRANSPORT EQUIPMENT		31.3						6.1	AUTRE MATERIEL TRANSPORT
792	AIRCRAFT ETC		26.4						3.4	APP NAVIGATION AERIENNE
7921	HELICOPTERS	N 2	24.7					N 5	0.2	HELICOPTERES
8	MISC MANUFACTURED GOODS		147.0						130.0	ART MANUFACTURES DIVERS
821	*FURNITURE,PARTS THEREOF		13.7		17.4		14.0	W 3336	13.0	MEUBLES ET PIECES
8219	FURNITURE AND PARTS NES	W 3122	12.9					W 3268	12.2	AUTRES MEUBLES ET PIECES
84	CLOTHING AND ACCESSORIES		41.6						32.9	VETEMENTS
842	MENS OUTERWEAR NOT KNIT		15.6						8.5	VET DESSUS POUR HOMMES
843	WOMENS OUTERWEAR NONKNIT		15.2						9.8	VET DESSUS FEMMES MAT TEX
847	TEXTILE CLTHNG ACCES NES		3.4						9.7	ACCES VET MAT TEXT NDA
8471	— NOT KNITTED		1.7						8.5	ACCES VET MAT TEX NON BON
84719	MADE-UP CLTHG ACCESS NES		1.2					W 261	8.2	AUT ACCES VET MAT TEXTIL
851	*FOOTWEAR		8.9						8.0	CHAUSSURES
87	PRECISION INSTRUMNTS NES		9.8						10.3	INSTRUM,APPAR SCIENT NDA
874	MEASURNG,CONTROLNG INSTR	W 81	6.3					W 140	7.3	INSTRUMENTS DE MESURE
88	PHOTO EQU,OPTICL GDS ETC		11.3						12.4	APP,FOURN PHOTO,OP,MONTR
89	MISC MANUFCTRD GOODS NES		54.9						46.8	ART MANUFACTURES DIVERS
892	PRINTED MATTER		10.4						11.6	IMPRIMES
893	ARTICLES OF PLASTIC NES		12.9					W 3037	13.6	OUVRAGES EN MAT DIVIS 58
894	TOYS,SPORTING GOODS,ETC		7.1						6.6	VOITURES ENFANTS,JOUETS
897	GOLD,SILVER WARE,JEWELRY		14.3						4.4	BIJOUTERIE,ORFEVRERIE
8973	PREC JEWLRY,GLD-SILVWARE		13.7						3.9	BIJOUX OR,ARGENT ORFEVRE

5. Special Exports F.O.B. by Commodities according to the S.I.T.C. (Rev. 2) in million U.S. Dollars
Exportations Spéciales F.O.B. par Produits d'après la C.T.C.I. (Rév. 2) en millions de Dollars E.U.

SITC CTCI	COMMODITY	1992 QUANTITY QUANTITE	1992 VALUE VALEUR	1993 QUANTITY QUANTITE	1993 VALUE VALEUR	1994 QUANTITY QUANTITE	1994 VALUE VALEUR	1995 QUANTITY QUANTITE	1995 VALUE VALEUR	PRODUIT
	ALL COMMODITIES		1558.9		1398.9		1375.6		1355.8	TOUS PRODUITS
0	FOOD AND LIVE ANIMALS		43.4		91.1		100.8		91.7	ALIMENTS,ANIMAUX VIVANTS
04	CEREALS AND PREPARATIONS		40.0						85.5	CEREALES ET PRODUITS
042	RICE	W 61092	39.4					W 136547	78.8	RIZ
048	CEREAL ETC PREPARATIONS		0.1					W 1679	4.5	PREPTNS A BASE CEREALES
2	CRUDE MATERLS,EXCL FUELS		10.7		12.5		13.0		2.0	MAT BRUTES NON COMESTIBLES
27	CRUDE FERTLZR,MINRLS NES		10.2						1.4	ENGRAIS MINERAUX BRUTS
278	OTHER CRUDE MINERALS	W 370629	7.6					W 63	0.1	AUTRES MINERAUX BRUTS
2783	COMMON SALT,ETC	W 370503	7.6							SEL
3	MINERAL FUELS ETC		1421.9		1245.3				1153.3	COMBUSTIBLES MINERAUX LUB
33	PETROLEUM AND PRODUCTS		1410.1				829.2		1143.3	PETROLE ET DERIVES
333	CRUDE PETROLEUM	W 956000	90.4					W 114000	10.4	HUILES BRUTES DE PETROLE
334	PETROLEUM PRODUCTS,REFIN	MW 11206	1285.6					W 8225927	1086.8	PRODUITS RAFFINES
3341	GASOLINE,OTH LIGHT OILS	W 2908705	551.1					W 2471338	428.1	ESSENCES POUR MOTEURS
33411	MOTOR,AVIATION SPIRIT	W 2191690	419.0					W 1902317	335.7	ESSENCES MOTEURS D'AVIONS
33412	SPIRIT TYPE JET FUEL	W 717015	132.2					W 569021	92.5	CARBUREACTEURS
3343	GAS OILS	W 2534000	249.1					W 1587554	235.2	GAS OILS
3344	FUEL OILS,NES	W 5465000	394.7					W 3828000	318.8	FUEL OILS
3345	LUBS,PETROLEUM OILS NES	W 298032	90.9					W 339035	104.7	HUILES LUBRIFIANTES
33451	LUBS(HIGH PETR CONT) ETC	W 298032	90.9					W 339035	104.7	HUILES LUBRIF,H LOURDES
335	RESIDUAL PETRLM PROD NES	W 507713	34.2						46.3	PRODUITS RESIDUELS NDA
3354	PETROLM BITUMEN,COKE ETC	W 507713	34.2					W 447805	46.3	BITUME,COKE DE PETROLE
33541	PETROLEUM BITUMEN, ETC	W 507713	34.2					W 447805	46.3	BITUME DE PETROLE
341	*GAS,NATURAL AND MANUFCT	W 49593	11.8					W 49588	10.1	GAZ NATUREL,GAZ MANUFACT
3413	PETROLM GASES,LIQUEFIED	W 49593	11.8					W 49588	10.1	GAZ DE PETROLE LIQUEFIE
5	CHEMCLS,RELATED PROD NES		13.8		9.3		6.4		13.8	PRODUITS CHIMIQUES
51	ORGANIC CHEMICALS		4.7						7.9	PROD CHIMIQ ORGANIQUES
516	OTHER ORGANIC CHEMICALS							W 2461	7.9	AUTRES PROD ORGANIQUES
5169	ORGANIC CHEMICALS,NES							W 2461	7.9	PROD CHIM ORGANIQUES NDA
6	BASIC MANUFACTURES		9.0		8.7		48.8		33.9	ART MANUFACTURES
66	NONMETAL MINERAL MFS NES		1.7						25.6	ART MIN NON METALLIQUES
667	PEARL,PREC–,SEMI–P STONE		1.4						25.4	PERLES, PIERRES GEMMES
7	MACHINES,TRANSPORT EQUIP		49.5		21.4		18.7		22.5	MACHINES MATERIEL TRANSPORT
71	POWER GENERATING EQUIPMT		4.4						4.2	MACHINES GENERATRICES
72	MACHS FOR SPCL INDUSTRYS		1.3						5.5	MAC SPECIALES POUR INDUST
79	OTHR TRANSPORT EQUIPMENT		34.5						5.3	AUTRE MATERIEL TRANSPORT
792	AIRCRAFT ETC	W 73	31.8						4.4	APP NAVIGATION AERIENNE
7921	HELICOPTERS								4.4	HELICOPTERES
8	MISC MANUFACTURED GOODS		7.2						36.1	ART MANUFACTURES DIVERS
89	MISC MANUFCTRD GOODS NES		4.4						33.0	ART MANUFACTURES DIVERS
892	PRINTED MATTER	W 84	1.0						10.7	IMPRIMES
8921	PRINTED BOOKS,GLOBES,ETC								10.7	LIVRES,BROCHURES,CARTES
89211	PRINTED BOOKS,PAMPHLETS								10.7	LIVRES,BROCHURES
897	GOLD,SILVER WARE,JEWELRY		1.1						19.5	BIJOUTERIE,ORFEVRERIE
8973	PREC JEWLRY,GLD–SILVWARE								19.5	BIJOUX OR,ARGENT ORFEVRE

1. HISTORICAL SERIES, 1962–1997 SPECIAL TRADE, IMPORTS C.I.F., EXPORTS F.O.B.
SERIES HISTORIQUES, 1962–1997 COMMERCE SPECIAL, IMPORTATIONS C.A.F., EXPORTATIONS F.O.B

YEAR ANNEE	VALUE IN MILLION C.F.P. FRANCS VALEUR EN MILLION C.F.P. FRANCS MERCHANDISE –MARCHANDISE		GOLD –OR		CONVERSION FACTORS U.S. CENTS PER C.F.P. FRANC FACTEURS DE CONVERSION CENTS E.U. PAR C.F.P. FRANC		INDEX NUMBERS –INDICES QUANTUM		UNIT VALUE VALEUR UNITAIRE	
	IMPORTS	EXPORTS	IMPORTS	EXPORTS	IMPORTS	EXPORTS	IMPORTS	EXPORTS	IMPORTS	EXPORTS
1962	3683.00	3088.00			1.1140	1.1140				
1963	3451.00	4147.00			1.1140	1.1140				
1964	4888.00	5596.00			1.1140	1.1140				
1965	6885.00	5848.00			1.1140	1.1140				
1966	6037.00	6970.00			1.1140	1.1140				
1967	7068.00	6748.00			1.1140	1.1140				
1968	8350.00	10164.00			1.1140	1.1140				
1969	12098.00	12733.00			1.0510	1.0540				
1970	23271.00	19362.00			0.9902	0.9902				
1971	23529.00	20178.00			0.9902	0.9902				
1972	19144.00	17415.00			1.0907	1.0908				
1973	17748.00	15677.00			1.2335	1.2460				
1974	24635.00	24857.00			1.1489	1.1409				
1975	27049.00	25494.00			1.2849	1.2916				
1976	24074.00	26612.00			1.1422	1.1489				
1977	26032.00	27799.00			1.1183	1.1157				
1978	23926.00	17500.00			1.2208	1.2353				
1979	27791.00	27905.00			1.2973	1.2916				
1980	35041.00	31340.00			1.3055	1.2933				
1981	40480.00	34295.80			1.0081	0.9989				
1982	43735.00	32055.00			0.8393	0.8283				
1983	42201.00	21271.70			0.7201	0.7225				
1984	49605.00	33098.00			0.6273	0.6241				
1985	55931.00	43864.00			0.6228	0.6171				
1986	62938.99	26248.99			0.7281	0.7262				
1987	68532.98	24478.99			0.9139	0.9207				
1988	65386.98	50804.99			0.9233	0.9142				
1989	88607.98	77900.00			0.8644	0.8668				
1990	86929.98	43930.99			1.0162	1.0224				
1991	88748.00	45915.98			0.9730	0.9665				
1992	88120.98	39447.98			1.0401	1.0381				
1993	87419.98	36611.98			0.9809	0.9812				
1994	87304.98	36208.99			1.0035	1.0103				
1995	81933.97	46188.99			1.1133	1.1140				
1996	93086.99	50224.99			1.0866	1.0871				
1997	97699.97	55912.01			0.9459	0.9467				

2. IMPORTS BY BROAD ECONOMIC CATEGORY AND EXPORTS BY INDUSTRIAL ORIGIN. (PERCENTAGE OF TOTAL VALUE)
IMPORTATIONS PAR CATEGORIES ECONOMIQUES ET EXPORTATIONS PAR BRANCHE D'ACTIVITE.(EN POURCENTAGE DE LA VALEUR TOTALE)

IMPORTS – IMPORTATIONS

	1991	1992	1993	1994	1995	1996	1997
TOTAL IMPORTS–IMPORTATIONS TOTALES							
1 FOOD BEV–ALIMENTATION BOISSONS							
11 PRIMARY–PRODUITS DE BASE							
111 FOR INDUSTRY–POUR L'INDUSTRIE							
112 FOR HOUSEHOLDS–POUR LES MENAGES							
12 PROCESSED–PRODUITS ELABORES							
121 FOR INDUSTRY–POUR L'INDUSTRIE							
122 FOR HOUSEHOLDS–POUR LES MENAGES							
2 IND SUPPLIES–APPROV INDUSTRIELS							
21 PRIMARY–PRODUITS DE BASE							
22 PROCESSED–PRODUITS ELABORES							
3 FUELS–COMBUSTIBLES							
31 PRIMARY–PRODUITS DE BASE							
32 PROCESSED–PRODUITS ELABORES							
321 MOTOR SPIRIT–ESSENCE							
322 OTHER–AUTRES							
4 MACHINERY–EQUIPEMENT							
41 CAPITAL EQUIPMENT–MACHINES							
42 PARTS–PIECES ACCESSOIRES							
5 TRANSPORT–TRANSPORT							
51 PASSENGER CARS–AUTOMOBILES							
52 OTHER–AUTRES							
521 INDUSTRIAL–INDUSTRIELS							
522 NON INDUSTRIAL–NON INDUSTRIEL							
53 PARTS–PIECES ACCESSOIRES							
6 CONSUM GOODS–BIENS CONSOMMATION							
61 DURABLE–DURABLES							
62 SEMI DURABLE–SEMI DURABLES							
63 NON DURABLE–NON DURABLES							
7 GOODS NES–BIENS NDA							

EXPORTS – EXPORTATIONS

	1991	1992	1993	1994	1995	1996	1997
TOTAL EXPORTS–EXPORTATIONS TOTALES	100.	100.	100.	100.	100.	100.	100.
1 AGRICULTURE							
2 MINING QUARRY–INDUS EXTRACTIVES	21.2	22.2	20.3	18.7	23.9	24.1	26.5
3 MANUFACTURING–IND MANUFACTUR	78.8	77.8	79.7	81.3	76.1	75.9	73.5
31 FOOD BEV TOBACCO–ALIM BOISS TAB							
32 TEXTILES–INDUSTRIES TEXTILES							
33 WOOD & PRODUCTS–BOIS & PRODUITS							
34 PAPER & PRODUCTS–PAPIER & PRODT							
35 CHEMICALS–INDUSTRIES CHIMIQUES							
36 NON METAL MIN–MIN NON METAL							
37 BASIC METAL–IND METAL BASE	68.8	63.9	68.7	71.3	69.0	69.8	65.4
38 METAL MANUF–MANUF METAL							
39 OTH MANUF IND–AUTRES MANUF	10.0	13.9	11.0	10.1	7.1	6.1	8.1

3. TRADE BY PRINCIPAL COUNTRIES OF ORIGIN AND DESTINATION (VALUE IN MILLION U.S. DOLLARS)
ECHANGES SELON LES PRINCIPAUX PAYS D'ORIGINE ET DE DESTINATION (VALEUR EN MILLIONS DE DOLLARS EU)

COUNTRIES–PAYS	SPECIAL IMPORTS C.I.F. IMPORTATIONS SPECIALES C.A.F				
	1993	1994	1995	1996	1997
World	855.3	842.2	841.3	1007.9	924.1
Africa					
Americas	46.2	38.4	35.4	46.4	49.0
– Northern America	46.2	38.4	35.4	46.4	49.0
– LAIA					
– CACM					
– Caribbean					
– Rest of America					
Asia excl fmr USSR	45.0	40.3	36.3	46.2	39.6
– Middle East					
Asia former USSR					
Europe excl fmr USSR	503.3	496.9	492.7	566.9	387.1
– European Union	380.9	368.0	375.4	417.5	387.1
– Eastern Europe					
– Rest of Europe	122.4	128.9	117.3	149.4	
Europe former USSR					
Oceania	148.6	147.6	156.7	199.4	171.3
Other	112.2	119.0	120.3	149.0	277.2
France, Monaco	380.9	368.0	375.4	417.5	387.1
Areas n.e.s.	112.2	119.0	120.3	149.0	277.2
Australia/Australie	105.4	99.8	107.2	132.8	122.8
Other Europe n.e.s.	122.4	128.9	117.3	149.4	
New Zealand	43.1	47.7	49.5	66.6	48.5
USA/Etats–Unis d'Amer	46.2	38.4	35.4	46.4	49.0
Japan/Japon	45.0	40.3	36.3	46.2	39.6

COUNTRIES–PAYS	SPECIAL EXPORTS F.O.B. EXPORTATIONS SPECIALES F.O.B.				
	1993	1994	1995	1996	1997
Monde	376.7	354.8			
Afrique					
Amériques	28.2	17.1			
– Amérique du Nord	28.2	17.1			
– ALAI					
– MCAC					
– Caraïbes					
– Autre Amérique					
Asie anc. URSS exclus	134.3	127.9			
– Moyen–Orient					
Asie ancienne URSS					
Europe anc. URSS exclus	177.0	164.1			
– Union Européenne	177.0	164.1			
– Europe de l'Est					
– Autre de l'Europe					
Europe ancienne URSS					
Océanie	33.1	36.8			
Autre	4.0	8.8			
Areas n.e.s.	4.0	8.8			
France, Monaco	121.3	98.3			
Japan/Japon	101.1	96.0			
Australia/Australie	25.7	29.9			
Korea, Republic of	25.0	26.9			
USA/Etats–Unis d'Amer	28.2	17.1			
Germany/Allemagne	11.8	26.9			
Spain/Espagne	15.8	14.8			
United Kingdom	12.3	12.5			
Belgium–Luxembourg	8.5	6.4			
India/Inde	7.0	4.8			
Wallis and Futuna Is	5.5	4.3			
Sweden/Suède	2.5	4.3			
Italy/Italie	4.7	1.0			
French Polynesia	1.1	1.7			
Vanuatu	0.9	0.9			
China, Hong Kong SAR	1.3	0.3			

(VALUE AS PERCENTAGE OF WORLD TOTAL)(VALEURS EN POURCENTAGE DU TOTAL MONDIAL)

	1988	1989	1990	1991	1992	1993	1994	1995	1996	1997
Africa										
Americas	6.6	10.4	6.0	7.0	5.3	5.4	4.6	4.2	4.6	5.3
– Northern America	6.6	10.4	6.0	7.0	5.3	5.4	4.6	4.2	4.6	5.3
– LAIA										
– CACM										
– Caribbean										
– Rest of America										
Asia excl fmr USSR	5.2	5.3	4.9	5.8	6.3	5.3	4.8	4.3	4.6	4.3
– Middle East										
Asia former USSR										
Europe excl fmr USSR	63.5	60.3	64.1	60.8	61.2	58.8	59.0	58.6	56.2	41.9
– European Union	50.2	44.1	47.5	45.7	61.2	44.5	43.7	44.6	41.4	41.9
– Eastern Europe										
– Rest of Europe	13.2	16.2	16.6	15.1		14.3	15.3	13.9	14.8	
Europe former USSR										
Oceania	13.9	12.4	11.8	13.4	14.6	17.4	17.5	18.6	19.8	18.5
Other	10.8	11.6	13.2	13.0	12.6	13.1	14.1	14.3	14.8	30.0
France, Monaco	47.9	44.1	47.5	45.7	46.3	44.5	43.7	44.6	41.4	41.9
Areas n.e.s.	10.8	11.6	13.2	13.0	12.6	13.1	14.1	14.3	14.8	30.0
Australia/Australie	10.3	9.1	8.5	9.7	10.2	12.3	11.9	12.7	13.2	13.3
Other Europe n.e.s.	13.2	16.2	16.6	15.1		14.3	15.3	13.9	14.8	
New Zealand	3.6	3.3	3.3	3.7	4.4	5.0	5.7	5.9	6.6	5.2
USA/Etats–Unis d'Amer	6.6	10.4	6.0	7.0	5.3	5.4	4.6	4.2	4.6	5.3
Japan/Japon	5.2	5.3	4.9	5.8	6.3	5.3	4.8	4.3	4.6	4.3

	1988	1989	1990	1991	1992	1993	1994	1995	1996	1997
Afrique				0.0	0.0					
Amériques	4.9			4.8	3.6	7.5	4.8			
– Amérique du Nord	4.9			4.8	3.6	7.5	4.8			
– ALAI										
– MCAC										
– Caraïbes				0.0	0.0					
– Autre Amérique										
Asie anc. URSS exclus	29.4			39.3	33.0	35.7	36.1			
– Moyen–Orient										
Asie ancienne URSS										
Europe anc. URSS exclus	62.0			48.8	52.3	47.0	46.3			
– Union Européenne	40.8			48.7	52.3	47.0	46.3			
– Europe de l'Est				0.1						
– Autre de l'Europe	21.1									
Europe ancienne URSS										
Océanie	3.1			6.8	10.9	8.8	10.4			
Autre	0.6			0.2	0.1	1.1	2.5			
Areas n.e.s.	0.6			0.2	0.1	1.1	2.5			
France, Monaco	38.4			27.8	32.2	32.2	27.7			
Japan/Japon	23.1			29.5	23.5	26.8	27.1			
Australia/Australie	0.9			4.3	8.1	6.8	8.4			
Korea, Republic of				8.0	7.5	6.6	7.6			
USA/Etats–Unis d'Amer	4.9			4.8	3.6	7.5	4.8			
Germany/Allemagne				6.9	6.7	3.1	7.6			
Spain/Espagne				4.7	4.7	4.2	4.2			
United Kingdom	2.4			2.5	2.4	3.3	3.5			
Belgium–Luxembourg				1.3	1.1	2.3	1.8			

4. Special Imports C.I.F. by Commodities according to the S.I.T.C. (Rev. 2) in million U.S. Dollars
Importations Spéciales C.A.F. par Produits d'après la C.T.C.I. (Rév. 2) en millions de Dollars E.U.

SITC CTCI	COMMODITY	1994 QUANTITY QUANTITE	1994 VALUE VALEUR	1995 QUANTITY QUANTITE	1995 VALUE VALEUR	1996 QUANTITY QUANTITE	1996 VALUE VALEUR	1997 QUANTITY QUANTITE	1997 VALUE VALEUR	PRODUIT
	ALL COMMODITIES		842.3		841.4		1008.0		924.2	TOUS PRODUITS
0	FOOD AND LIVE ANIMALS		159.2		156.2		181.0		167.9	ALIMENTS,ANIMAUX VIVANTS
01	MEAT AND PREPARATIONS		13.3		7.1		7.1		5.4	VIANDES ET PREPARATIONS
011	MEAT FRESH,CHILLD,FROZEN	W 4280	9.3	W 839	3.4	W 769	2.9		2.2	VIANDES FRAICHES,REF,CONGE
0114	POULTRY FRESH CHLLD,FRZN	W 3632	6.5	W 241	0.6	W 219	0.5			VOLAILLES MORTES
014	MEAT PREPD,PRSVD,NES ETC	W 920	4.0	W 849	3.7	W 871	4.3		3.3	CONSERVES DE VIANDES
0149	OTH PREPARD,PRESRVD MEAT	W 920	4.0	W 849	3.7	W 871	4.3		3.3	AUTRES PREP DE VIANDES
02	DAIRY PRODCTS,BIRDS'EGGS		16.4		15.3		17.7		17.2	PRODUITS LAITIERS,OEUFS
022	MILK AND CREAM	W 5756	7.9	W 5052	6.8	W 2060	8.0		8.3	LAIT ET CREME
0224	MILK,CREAM PRESERVED ETC	W 1669	5.6	W 1427	4.8	W 633	5.6		6.2	LAIT,CREME CONS,CONC
02243	MILK DRY,OVER 1.5% FAT	W 1669	5.6	W 1427	4.8				6.2	LAIT POUDRE SUP 1.5%
024	CHEESE AND CURD	W 1392	7.0	W 1246	6.9	W 352	7.8		7.3	FROMAGE ET CAILLEBOTTE
03	FISH AND PREPARATIONS		5.0		4.4		5.8		5.2	POISSONS ET PREPARATIONS
037	FISH ETC PREPD,PRSVD NES	W 936	3.2	W 857	2.8	W 1006	3.7		3.5	POIS,CRUST,MOL PREPARES
0371	FISH PREPARD,PRESRVD NES	W 936	3.2	W 857	2.8	W 1006	3.7		3.5	CONSERVES DE POISSONS
04	CEREALS AND PREPARATIONS		8.1		10.1		10.6		4.0	CEREALES ET PRODUITS
041	WHEAT ETC UNMILLED			W 26954	5.8	W 17527	5.7			FROMENT,EPEAUTRE
042	RICE	W 8171	3.6	W 9929	4.2	W 8593	4.5		0.2	RIZ
0421	RICE IN HUSK OR HUSKED					W 8593	4.5			RIZ SANS AUTRE PREPARATION
048	CEREAL ETC PREPARATIONS	W 21631	4.4			W 162	0.4		3.5	PREPTNS A BASE CEREALES
0481	PREPD BREAKFAST FOOD ETC	W 21631	4.4						3.5	CEREALES TRAVAILLEES
05	VEGETABLES AND FRUIT		10.6		10.1		12.6		8.2	LEGUMES ET FRUITS
054	VEG ETC FRSH,SMPLY PRSVD	W 2787	3.7	W 2776	3.4	W 3565	4.6		3.9	LEGUMES FRAIS,CONG,SECS
0545	OTHER FRESH VEGETABLES	W 2561	3.5	W 2356	3.1	W 3495	4.0		3.5	AUTRES LEGUMES FRAIS,REF
05459	FRESH VEGETABLES NES	W 1550	2.7	W 1188	2.2	W 2780	3.0		2.5	LEGUMES FRAIS,REFRI NDA
056	VEGTBLES ETC PRSVD,PREPD	W 2597	4.1	W 2804	3.9	W 4073	4.2		1.3	CONSERVES DE LEGUMES
0565	VEGTBLES PRSVD,PREPD NES					W 2755	4.1			LEGUMES PREPARES CONSERVE
057	FRUIT,NUTS,FRESH,DRIED	W 1840	2.9	W 1973	2.8	W 20257	3.9		3.2	FRUITS FRAIS OU SECS
06	SUGAR AND PREPS,HONEY		3.6		3.4		3.9		0.4	SUCRES ET PRODUITS
061	SUGAR AND HONEY	W 6737	3.6	W 6738	3.4	W 7032	3.9		0.4	SUCRES ET MIEL
0611	RAW BEET AND CANE SUGAR					W 7032	3.9			SUCRES BRUTS
09	MISC EDIBLE PRODUCTS		1.7		1.9		1.9		6.6	PREP ALIMENTAIRES DIVERSES
091	MARGARINE AND SHORTENING	W 810	1.5	W 870	1.6	W 846	1.9		3.2	MARGARINE ET GRAISSES
0914	MARGARINE,EDIBLE FAT NES	W 810	1.5	W 870	1.6	W 846	1.9		3.2	MARGARINES,SIMILI SAINDOUX
098	EDIBLE PRODCTS,PREPS NES	W 65	0.2	W 134	0.3				3.5	PREP ALIMENTAIRES NDA
1	BEVERAGES AND TOBACCO		18.0		18.1		19.0		15.9	BOISSONS ET TABACS
11	BEVERAGES		18.0		18.1		19.0		15.9	BOISSONS
111	NON–ALCOHL BEVERAGES NES	W 3435	2.2	W 3153	1.8	W 2996	1.9		3.3	BOISSONS NON ALCOOLIQUES
11102	FLAVORED WATERS NON–ALCO	W 329	0.4	W 305	0.3	W 282	0.3		3.1	LIMONADES,EAUX GAZEUSES
112	ALCOHOLIC BEVERAGES	W 82460	15.9	W 80898	16.3	W 73463	17.1		12.7	BOISSONS ALCOOLIQUES
1121	WINE OF FRESH GRAPES ETC	W 43262	10.3	W 42467	10.7	W 44058	11.9			VINS DE RAISINS FRAIS
1123	BEER,ALE,STOUT,PORTER	W 37559	3.5	W 36590	3.3	W 27798	3.0		10.4	BIERES
3	MINERAL FUELS ETC		86.4		82.5		98.7		107.9	COMBUSTIBLES MINERAUX LUB
32	COAL,COKE AND BRIQUETTES		6.7		5.0		7.6		8.4	HOUILLES,COKES,BRIQUETTES
322	COAL,LIGNITE AND PEAT	W 175132	6.7	W 135096	5.0	W 177176	7.6		8.4	HOUILLES,LIGNITES,TOURBE
3221	ANTHRACITE,NOT AGGLOMRTD	W 175132	6.7	W 135096	5.0	W 177176	7.6		8.4	ANTHRACITE
33	PETROLEUM AND PRODUCTS		30.4		32.6		37.8		42.8	PETROLE ET DERIVES
334	PETROLEUM PRODUCTS,REFIN	W 167817	30.4	W 187617	32.6	W 171817	37.8		42.8	PRODUITS RAFFINES
3341	GASOLINE,OTH LIGHT OILS	W 81729	12.2	W 82798	12.5	W 74995	13.0		15.3	ESSENCES POUR MOTEURS
33411	MOTOR,AVIATION SPIRIT	W 81729	12.2	W 82798	12.5	W 74995	13.0		15.3	ESSENCES MOTEURS D'AVIONS
3343	GAS OILS	W 75022	13.6	W 92945	15.5	W 84447	18.7		21.6	GAS OILS
3345	LUBS,PETROLEUM OILS NES	W 2525	3.4	W 2694	3.6	W 3709	4.7		4.3	HUILES LUBRIFIANTES
341	*GAS,NATURAL AND MANUFCT	W 6401	2.4	W 6930	2.7	W 5983	2.7		4.5	GAZ NATUREL,GAZ MANUFACT
4	ANIMAL,VEGETABLE OIL,FAT		2.5		2.8		2.6		4.1	HUILES,GRAISSES ANIM,VEG
42	FIXED VEGETABLE OIL,FAT		2.5		2.8		2.6		4.1	HUILES VEGETALES FIXES
423	FIXED VEG OILS,SOFT	W 1891	2.5	W 2059	2.8	W 1904	2.6		4.1	HUILES VEGET DOUCES FIXES
5	CHEMCLS,RELATED PROD NES		62.7		85.7		76.7		71.4	PRODUITS CHIMIQUES
541	*MEDICINAL,PHARM PRODUCT	K 806000	21.7	K 799000	24.7	K 831000	29.3		29.1	PROD MEDICINAUX PHARMACEUT
5417	MEDICAMENTS	K 806000	21.7	K 799000	24.7	K 831000	29.3		29.1	MEDICAMENTS
55	PERFUME,CLEANING ETC PRD		4.0		3.6		3.6			PROD POUR PARFUM,TOILETTE
554	SOAP,CLEANSING ETC PREPS	W 2155	4.0	W 2244	3.6	W 2115	3.6			SAVONS,PRODUITS DETERSIFS
5542	WASHING PREPARATIONS ETC	W 2155	4.0	W 2244	3.6	W 2115	3.6			PROD ORG TENSIO–ACT NDA
6	BASIC MANUFACTURES		144.6		148.1		206.0		190.1	ART MANUFACTURES
62	RUBBER MANUFACTURES NES		7.3		7.5		46.0		39.9	CAOUTCHOUC MANUFACTURE
625	RUBBER TYRES, TUBES ETC	N 147448	7.3	N 124752	7.5	W 147954	10.3		9.4	PNEUS CAOUTCHOUC VULCANISE
6252	TYRES,NEW,BUS OR LORRY	N 147448	7.3	N 124752	7.5	W 147954	10.3		9.4	PNEUS POUR AUTOBUS,CAMIONS
63	WOOD,CORK MANUFACTRS NES		14.7		13.4		13.9		16.5	OUVRAGES LIEGE ET BOIS
64	PAPER,PAPERBOARD AND MFR		28.3		29.4		31.5		29.4	PAPIERS,CARTONS & OUVRAGES
65	TEXTILE YARN,FABRICS,ETC		34.9		34.2		39.2		33.1	FILS,TISSUS,ARTICLES TEXTILE
66	NONMETAL MINERAL MFS NES		4.3		4.1		4.0		4.9	ART MIN NON METALLIQUES
661	LIME,CEMENT,BLDG PRODS	W 80710	4.3	W 83691	4.1	W 68206	4.0		4.9	CHAUX,CIMENTS MAT CONSTR
6612	CEMENT	W 80710	4.3	W 83691	4.1	W 68206	4.0		4.9	CIMENTS HYDRAULIQUES
69	METAL MANUFACTURES NES		53.4		57.3		69.5		64.4	ART MANUFACT EN METAL NDA
7	MACHINES,TRANSPORT EQUIP		277.8		278.8		359.1		307.3	MACHINES MATERIEL TRANSPORT
76	TELECOMM,SOUND EQUIPMENT		2.3		2.0		3.2		2.0	EQUIPMENT DE TELECOM
761	TELEVISION RECEIVERS	N 8315	2.3	N 6918	2.0	W 12233	3.2		2.0	RECEPTEURS DE TELEVISION
7611	COLOUR TV RECEIVERS	N 8315	2.3	N 6918	2.0	W 12233	3.2		2.0	RECEPTEURS COULEUR
77	ELECTRIC MACHNRY NES ETC		139.2		141.9		181.6		157.4	MACH APP ELECT NDA
78	ROAD VEHICLES		134.0		132.4		172.0		145.5	VEHICULES ROUTIERS
781	PASS MOTOR VEH EXC BUSES	N 4391	53.9	N 5360	53.5	W 4897	65.8		57.8	AUTO TRANSPORT PERSONNES
782	LORRIES,SPCL MTR VEH NES	N 1521	24.8	N 1488	30.6	W 1584	34.3		26.5	VEHICULES SPECIAUX,MARCH
7821	LORRIES,TRUCKS	N 1521	24.8	N 1488	30.6	W 1584	34.3		26.5	VEHICULES TRANSP MARCHAND
79	OTHR TRANSPORT EQUIPMENT		2.4		2.6		2.5		2.4	AUTRE MATERIEL TRANSPORT
793	SHIPS AND BOATS ETC	N 186	2.4	N 173	2.6	W 196	2.5		2.4	NAVIRES BATEAUX,ETC
7932	SHIPS AND BOATS NES	N 186	2.4	N 173	2.6	W 196	2.5		2.4	NAVIRES ET BATEAUX
9	GOODS NOT CLASSD BY KIND		91.1		69.0		64.8		59.5	ART TRANSACT NON CLASSES
931	*SPECIAL TRANSACTIONS	W 31700	91.1		69.0		64.8		59.5	TRANS.SPECIALES

5. Special Exports F.O.B. by Commodities according to the S.I.T.C. (Rev. 2) in million U.S. Dollars
Exportations Spéciales F.O.B. par Produits d'après la C.T.C.I. (Rév. 2) en millions de Dollars E.U.

SITC CTCI	COMMODITY	1994		1995		1996		1997		PRODUIT
		QUANTITY QUANTITE	VALUE VALEUR	QUANTITY QUANTITE	VALUE VALEUR	QUANTITY QUANTITE	VALUE VALEUR	QUANTITY QUANTITE	VALUE VALEUR	
	ALL COMMODITIES		354.9		465.8		543.9		529.4	TOUS PRODUITS
2	CRUDE MATERLS,EXCL FUELS		110.6		175.4		207.6		208.9	MAT BRUTES NON COMESTIBLES
28	METALLIFEROUS ORES,SCRAP		110.6		175.4		207.6		208.9	MINERAIS METAL,DECHETS
287	BASE METAL ORES,CONC NES	W 3181400	110.6		175.4		207.6		208.9	MINERAIS METAUX COMMUNS
2872	NICKEL ORES,CONCENTRATES	W 3181400	110.6	W 4531500	175.2		207.6		208.9	MINERAIS DE NICKEL
28721	NICKEL ORES,EXCL MATTE	W 3169000	66.3	W 4517000	111.2		131.1		140.5	MINERAIS DE NICKEL
28722	NICKEL MATTE,SINTERS,ETC	W 12400	44.3	W 14500	64.0		76.6		68.4	MATTES,SINTERS
6	BASIC MANUFACTURES		208.7		257.3		303.2		277.7	ART MANUFACTURES
67	IRON AND STEEL		208.7		257.3		303.2		277.7	FER ET ACIER
671	PIG IRON ETC	W 133000	208.7	W 144700	257.3		303.2		277.7	FONTE,SPIEGEL,POUDRES
6716	FERRO–ALLOYS	W 133000	208.7	W 144700	257.3		303.2		277.7	FERRO–ALLIAGES
67169	OTHER FERRO–ALLOYS	W 133000	208.7	W 144700	257.3		303.2		277.7	AUTRES FERRO–ALLIAGES
9	GOODS NOT CLASSD BY KIND		35.7		33.3		33.3		42.8	ART TRANSACT NON CLASSES
931	*SPECIAL TRANSACTIONS		35.7		33.3		33.3		42.8	TRANS.SPECIALES

1. HISTORICAL SERIES, 1962–1997 GENERAL TRADE, IMPORTS C.I.F., EXPORTS F.O.B.
SERIES HISTORIQUES, 1962–1997 COMMERCE GENERAL, IMPORTATIONS C.A.F., EXPORTATIONS F.O.B

YEAR ANNEE	VALUE IN MILLION N.Z. DOLLARS / VALEUR EN MILLION N.Z. DOLLARS — MERCHANDISE – MARCHANDISE		GOLD – OR		CONVERSION FACTORS U.S. CENTS PER N.Z. DOLLAR / FACTEURS DE CONVERSION CENTS E.U. PAR N.Z. DOLLAR		INDEX NUMBERS – INDICES — QUANTUM		UNIT VALUE / VALEUR UNITAIRE	
	IMPORTS	EXPORTS	IMPORTS	EXPORTS	IMPORTS	EXPORTS	IMPORTS	EXPORTS	IMPORTS	EXPORTS
1962	541.60	573.80	0.22	0.44	139.0000	139.0000				
1963	650.60	664.10	0.19	0.30	139.0000	139.0000				
1964	701.50	773.80	0.27	0.18	139.0000	139.0000				
1965	756.70	723.90	0.27	0.16	139.0000	139.0000				
1966	787.50	780.00	0.24	0.09	139.0000	139.0000				
1967	695.60	725.40	0.27	0.07	137.0000	136.0000				
1968	799.10	920.90	0.17	0.05	112.0000	112.0000				
1969	895.60	1080.90	0.25	0.03	112.0000	112.0000				
1970	1111.80	1093.70	0.36	0.06	112.0000	112.0000				
1971	1186.10	1199.80			113.6170	113.4520				
1972	1273.90	1499.40	0.56		119.5000	119.5000				
1973	1591.50	1913.10	0.90	0.20	136.8690	135.7620				
1974	2615.00	1733.80	1.03	0.20	139.7100	140.4810				
1975	2613.50	1796.40			120.1640	119.7570				
1976	3270.80	2815.50			99.2790	99.1790				
1977	3464.00	3294.90			97.0810	97.0440				
1978	3359.40	3603.50			104.1680	103.9370				
1979	4466.10	4606.70			101.5700	101.8250				
1980	5615.90	5568.80			97.3950	97.2950	62	73	57	50
1981	6635.60	6465.90			85.6608	86.0289	64	74	65	56
1982	7800.30	7408.40			74.6812	74.7677	68	76	73	62
1983	7991.70	7907.50			66.7289	66.8189	63	80	79	66
1984	10933.50	9582.30			54.9687	55.9120	76	84	90	74
1985	12473.00	11316.00			49.6737	49.4017	76	93	100	81
1986	11622.10	11225.10			52.1817	52.3969	75	91	97	79
1987	12242.50	12149.70			59.4362	59.2258	85	94	93	84
1988	11216.90	13488.20			65.4549	65.6077	77	97	92	89
1989	14710.10	14819.50			59.7138	59.8900	93	95	99	101
1990	15895.50	15760.00			59.7719	59.6056	100	100	100	100
1991	14526.80	16671.00			57.8770	57.8791	90	110	101	96
1992	17132.00	18208.00			53.8042	53.8184	100	113	108	104
1993	17781.01	19492.00			54.1936	54.0815	104	118	107	106
1994	19981.01	20519.01			59.6236	59.3825	122	130	104	102
1995	21252.40	20787.01			65.6801	65.6434	129	134	103	100
1996	21400.00	20876.00			68.8086	68.7984	134	140	101	97
1997	21966.00	21189.01			66.1014	66.3152	139	145	100	94

2. IMPORTS BY BROAD ECONOMIC CATEGORY AND EXPORTS BY INDUSTRIAL ORIGIN. (PERCENTAGE OF TOTAL VALUE)
IMPORTATIONS PAR CATEGORIES ECONOMIQUES ET EXPORTATIONS PAR BRANCHE D'ACTIVITE.(EN POURCENTAGE DE LA VALEUR TOTALE)

IMPORTS – IMPORTATIONS

	1990	1991	1992	1993	1994	1995	1996
TOTAL IMPORTS–IMPORTATIONS TOTALES	100.	100.	100.	100.	100.	100.	100.
1 FOOD BEV–ALIMENTATION BOISSONS	6.1	7.1	6.6	7.1	6.8	6.7	6.9
11 PRIMARY–PRODUITS DE BASE	1.7	1.9	1.9	2.0	1.9	1.9	1.9
111 FOR INDUSTRY–POUR L'INDUSTRIE	0.6	0.7	0.7	0.7	0.7	0.7	0.7
112 FOR HOUSEHOLDS–POUR LES MENAGES	1.1	1.2	1.2	1.3	1.2	1.2	1.2
12 PROCESSED–PRODUITS ELABORES	4.4	5.2	4.7	5.0	4.9	4.9	5.0
121 FOR INDUSTRY–POUR L'INDUSTRIE	1.2	1.4	1.3	1.3	1.2	1.2	1.1
122 FOR HOUSEHOLDS–POUR LES MENAGES	3.3	3.7	3.5	3.8	3.8	3.7	3.9
2 IND SUPPLIES–APPROV INDUSTRIELS	27.6	29.9	28.8	29.1	27.8	27.9	26.6
21 PRIMARY–PRODUITS DE BASE	1.7	1.7	1.9	2.1	1.8	1.8	1.6
22 PROCESSED–PRODUITS ELABORES	25.8	28.1	26.9	27.0	25.9	26.1	25.0
3 FUELS–COMBUSTIBLES	7.3	7.3	6.4	6.2	5.3	5.2	6.1
31 PRIMARY–PRODUITS DE BASE	5.7	5.6	4.9	4.8	4.0	3.7	3.8
32 PROCESSED–PRODUITS ELABORES	1.6	1.7	1.5	1.4	1.3	1.5	2.3
321 MOTOR SPIRIT–ESSENCE			0.7	0.8	0.8	0.9	1.1
322 OTHER–AUTRES	1.6	1.7	0.8	0.6	0.6	0.6	1.2
4 MACHINERY–EQUIPEMENT	22.9	21.4	21.9	22.5	23.2	24.2	24.6
41 CAPITAL EQUIPMENT–MACHINES	19.9	18.1	18.4	18.8	19.5	20.5	21.1
42 PARTS–PIECES ACCESSOIRES	3.1	3.3	3.4	3.6	3.6	3.7	3.5
5 TRANSPORT–TRANSPORT	19.0	15.1	17.2	15.9	18.2	17.6	17.2
51 PASSENGER CARS–AUTOMOBILES	7.5	6.1	6.4	7.1	8.1	8.2	9.6
52 OTHER–AUTRES	7.5	5.2	6.9	4.7	6.4	5.9	4.4
521 INDUSTRIAL–INDUSTRIELS	7.2	4.9	6.6	4.5	6.2	5.7	4.1
522 NON INDUSTRIAL–NON INDUSTRIEL	0.3	0.3	0.3	0.3	0.2	0.3	0.3
53 PARTS–PIECES ACCESSOIRES	4.0	3.9	4.0	4.1	3.7	3.5	3.3
6 CONSUM GOODS–BIENS CONSOMMATION	16.7	18.7	18.7	19.0	18.5	18.0	18.3
61 DURABLE–DURABLES	4.7	4.8	4.8	4.6	4.6	4.3	4.3
62 SEMI DURABLE–SEMI DURABLES	6.7	7.9	7.9	8.2	8.2	8.3	8.6
63 NON DURABLE–NON DURABLES	5.3	6.0	6.0	6.1	5.7	5.3	5.5
7 GOODS NES–BIENS NDA	0.4	0.5	0.4	0.3	0.3	0.4	0.2

EXPORTS – EXPORTATIONS

	1990	1991	1992	1993	1994	1995	1996
TOTAL EXPORTS–EXPORTATIONS TOTALES	100.	100.	100.	100.	100.	100.	100.
1 AGRICULTURE	17.4	16.8	17.6	17.6	16.7	17.2	16.1
2 MINING QUARRY–INDUS EXTRACTIVES	1.9	2.4	2.3	2.3	2.0	1.8	2.4
3 MANUFACTURING–IND MANUFACTUR	80.7	80.8	80.1	80.1	81.3	80.9	81.5
31 FOOD BEV TOBACCO–ALIM BOISS TAB	36.9	37.4	38.0	37.8	35.9	34.6	38.0
32 TEXTILES–INDUSTRIES TEXTILES	8.3	7.8	8.0	7.6	8.3	8.1	7.8
33 WOOD & PRODUCTS–BOIS & PRODUITS	2.0	2.5	2.8	3.6	3.8	3.8	3.4
34 PAPER & PRODUCTS–PAPIER & PRODT	6.2	5.8	5.5	5.2	5.4	6.1	5.4
35 CHEMICALS–INDUSTRIES CHIMIQUES	8.2	8.0	7.3	7.7	9.3	8.9	8.6
36 NON METAL MIN–MIN NON METAL	0.3	0.4	0.4	0.4	0.4	0.3	0.3
37 BASIC METAL–IND METAL BASE	6.8	6.5	5.8	5.4	5.2	6.0	5.3
38 METAL MANUF–MANUF METAL	9.3	9.9	10.2	10.3	11.4	11.6	10.9
39 OTH MANUF IND–AUTRES MANUF	2.6	2.5	2.1	2.1	1.7	1.7	1.9

3. TRADE BY PRINCIPAL COUNTRIES OF ORIGIN AND DESTINATION (VALUE IN MILLION U.S. DOLLARS)
ECHANGES SELON LES PRINCIPAUX PAYS D'ORIGINE ET DE DESTINATION (VALEUR EN MILLIONS DE DOLLARS EU)

COUNTRIES–PAYS	GENERAL IMPORTS C.I.F. IMPORTATIONS GENERALES C.A.F				
	1992	1993	1994	1995	1996
World	9205.0	9654.8	11901.4	13957.7	14724.2
Africa	37.5	44.5	69.4	88.0	97.4
Americas	2064.7	2004.7	2571.7	3002.9	2904.4
– Northern America	1948.4	1894.7	2451.9	2854.1	2746.4
– LAIA	91.1	92.4	101.8	140.2	149.6
– CACM	0.8	0.9	1.7	1.5	1.4
– Caribbean	16.9	4.0	5.3	6.0	7.0
– Rest of America	7.6	12.7	11.0	1.1	0.0
Asia excl fmr USSR	3063.8	3357.7	3942.9	4479.6	4793.1
– Middle East	401.9	403.7	387.3	313.3	334.4
Asia former USSR	0.0	0.1	0.2	0.1	0.6
Europe excl fmr USSR	1975.6	2058.3	2563.1	3195.3	3183.7
– European Union	1830.2	1917.4	2393.4	3011.1	2978.7
– Eastern Europe	8.9	11.4	18.2	15.1	14.7
– Rest of Europe	136.5	129.6	151.5	169.0	190.4
Europe former USSR	2.5	7.7	4.5	4.1	3.0
Oceania	2018.0	2134.5	2695.7	3124.1	3673.1
Other	42.9	47.2	53.9	63.6	68.9
Australia/Australie	1946.2	2060.7	2558.4	3010.8	3569.9
USA/Etats–Unis d'Amer	1800.2	1733.6	2279.9	2610.4	2458.2
Japan/Japon	1353.2	1565.8	1826.4	1936.0	2103.3
United Kingdom	581.6	562.5	737.6	818.1	770.6
Germany/Allemagne	383.6	416.6	542.6	664.5	689.7
China/Chine	242.9	292.6	388.3	493.9	548.2
Other Asia n.e.s.	244.8	274.4	320.2	363.4	373.9
Italy/Italie	215.6	243.0	260.7	345.9	361.4
France, Monaco	159.7	161.3	205.6	318.9	259.3
Singapore/Singapour	200.2	137.2	211.0	270.5	270.7
Saudi Arabia	255.1	227.2	181.0	180.7	239.9
Canada	148.1	156.0	171.8	243.0	287.2
Korea, Republic of	141.3	154.2	191.8	238.5	272.0
Sweden/Suède	114.7	156.7	193.7	239.3	245.7
Malaysia/Malaisie	107.7	126.2	144.9	245.6	285.6
Netherlands/Pays–Bas	100.5	113.2	127.3	166.7	155.2
China, Hong Kong SAR	119.2	121.4	130.1	149.6	114.7
Switzerland,Liechtenst.	98.0	110.9	119.9	133.9	138.9
Indonesia/Indonésie	61.6	77.0	84.2	171.3	142.4
United Arab Emirates	113.5	140.9	136.6	53.6	34.2
Thailand/Thaïlande	75.6	77.1	89.6	105.2	117.5
Belgium–Luxembourg	68.3	73.7	84.6	115.5	113.3
Finland/Finlande	37.8	45.6	51.9	78.9	108.0
Denmark/Danemark	44.7	45.4	62.3	87.9	75.4
India/Inde	39.9	44.9	62.1	75.5	85.8
Special Categories	42.9	47.2	53.9	63.6	68.9
Spain/Espagne	30.7	30.5	47.3	55.7	69.9
Brazil/Brésil	35.0	40.3	43.6	58.4	51.6
Papua New Guinea	11.3	15.8	82.8	51.2	42.9
Austria/Autriche	30.8	24.8	30.2	59.8	58.2
Ireland/Irlande	46.7	29.4	34.3	42.4	48.5
So. African Customs Un	12.1	20.0	35.9	54.6	47.6
Norway,Svalbard and JM	36.7	16.0	26.7	28.3	46.7
Fiji/Fidji	30.5	24.3	30.2	33.9	31.4
Pakistan	22.4	26.9	31.2	29.1	29.5
Israel/Israël	24.6	23.0	28.7	28.9	29.2
Philippines	15.7	19.8	30.7	35.6	30.5
Oman	9.1	5.4	17.5	46.9	29.2
Ecuador/Equateur	24.5	18.4	13.2	21.8	29.2
Nauru	22.5	24.5	18.1	19.7	18.2

COUNTRIES–PAYS	EXPORTS EXPORTATIONS ES F.O.B.				
	1992	1993	1994	1995	1996
Monde	9830.0	10558.2	12185.5	13745.4	14354.3
Afrique	151.4	185.6	174.1	175.5	215.1
Amériques	1702.5	1871.8	1943.4	2045.8	2081.8
– Amérique du Nord	1358.0	1409.7	1555.0	1606.0	1527.3
– ALAI	247.0	385.8	298.9	319.0	408.1
– MCAC	17.0	14.7	24.1	34.4	63.6
– Caraïbes	70.4	51.2	55.9	63.9	67.4
– Autre Amérique	10.1	10.4	9.5	22.4	15.4
Asie anc. URSS exclus	3824.8	4031.2	4748.1	5732.8	5950.2
– Moyen–Orient	368.3	336.7	315.6	371.0	469.2
Asie ancienne URSS		1.2	0.3	0.0	0.0
Europe anc. URSS exclus	1673.5	1681.9	1997.0	2263.0	2391.7
– Union Européenne	1631.0	1633.5	1944.8	2196.8	2313.4
– Europe de l'Est	3.9	3.7	6.2	7.4	7.9
– Autre de l'Europe	38.6	44.7	45.9	58.7	70.4
Europe ancienne URSS	16.0	96.9	112.9	115.3	130.6
Océanie	2327.2	2542.7	3068.1	3245.1	3387.2
Autre	134.7	146.9	141.7	167.9	197.5
Australia/Australie	1938.3	2106.3	2606.6	2806.6	2933.3
Japan/Japon	1468.0	1540.9	1867.6	2229.5	2208.9
USA/Etats–Unis d'Amer	1212.9	1226.9	1343.6	1376.1	1317.0
United Kingdom	629.1	641.3	734.9	832.3	922.3
Korea, Republic of	403.2	502.9	585.7	708.7	677.3
China, Hong Kong SAR	220.8	241.7	320.2	417.1	456.3
Other Asia n.e.s.	238.8	278.8	334.3	397.9	389.7
Germany/Allemagne	240.2	249.3	314.2	329.6	347.1
China/Chine	192.8	212.3	337.8	348.2	367.3
Malaysia/Malaisie	267.0	210.1	235.0	287.3	327.6
European Union n.e.s.	174.0	161.7	192.3	258.5	220.0
Canada	142.6	180.2	209.0	223.1	208.4
Singapore/Singapour	163.0	145.8	163.8	192.1	202.8
Indonesia/Indonésie	141.8	126.2	146.5	199.3	232.7
Italy/Italie	110.0	120.1	171.1	197.2	237.0
Thailand/Thaïlande	111.4	107.6	129.7	183.9	186.2
Belgium–Luxembourg	133.3	124.3	137.0	152.9	168.1
France, Monaco	117.5	122.6	134.4	145.9	151.2
Philippines	92.2	118.6	115.2	137.7	170.2
Saudi Arabia	125.0	130.4	120.5	107.3	129.3
Fiji/Fidji	102.4	118.6	126.6	120.6	128.5
Mexico/Mexique	110.5	166.6	114.6	73.1	106.0
Bunkers, ship stores	101.3	101.7	88.8	94.7	106.3
Russian Federation	16.0	89.2	75.0	113.9	130.0
India/Inde	61.7	88.7	76.6	79.9	79.6
Turkey/Turquie	39.1	51.4	72.1	102.2	92.8
Iran (Islamic Rep of)	107.3	50.0	29.1	53.7	116.9
Netherlands/Pays–Bas	49.0	59.4	74.5	69.9	85.8
Areas n.e.s.	33.4	45.2	52.8	73.2	91.2
Papua New Guinea	52.9	62.9	59.5	50.3	65.4
Algeria/Algérie	56.1	85.7	63.5	40.7	41.1
French Polynesia	41.6	57.9	65.0	54.9	56.1
Spain/Espagne	46.4	37.4	52.4	65.0	46.4
Peru/Pérou	29.4	46.7	47.5	59.2	61.7
Venezuela	36.0	45.8	53.3	46.8	61.8
Samoa	54.5	50.2	47.8	46.1	35.6
Sri Lanka	29.8	36.8	43.4	59.9	63.2
New Caledonia	34.7	38.9	41.5	50.8	58.6
Brazil/Brésil	7.3	64.6	14.4	42.4	75.9
Switzerland,Liechtenst.	31.9	37.2	35.9	44.5	51.0

(VALUE AS PERCENTAGE OF WORLD TOTAL)(VALEURS EN POURCENTAGE DU TOTAL MONDIAL)

	1987	1988	1989	1990	1991	1992	1993	1994	1995	1996
Africa	0.4	0.3	0.4	0.3	0.4	0.4	0.5	0.6	0.6	0.7
Americas	18.9	20.0	20.1	21.0	19.8	22.4	20.8	21.6	21.5	19.7
– Northern America	17.8	18.7	18.8	19.8	18.4	21.2	19.6	20.6	20.4	18.7
– LAIA	1.0	1.2	1.3	1.1	1.1	1.0	1.0	0.9	1.0	1.0
– CACM	0.0	0.0	0.0	0.0	0.0	0.0	0.0	0.0	0.0	0.0
– Caribbean	0.1	0.0	0.0	0.0	0.2	0.2	0.0	0.0	0.0	0.0
– Rest of America	0.0	0.0	0.0	0.0	0.1	0.1	0.1	0.1	0.0	0.0
Asia excl fmr USSR	33.1	32.8	34.4	32.0	33.1	33.3	34.8	33.1	32.1	32.6
– Middle East	3.0	3.4	4.0	5.2	5.2	4.4	4.2	3.3	2.2	2.3
Asia former USSR						0.0	0.0	0.0	0.0	0.0
Europe excl fmr USSR	26.3	23.5	22.8	24.6	23.2	21.5	21.3	21.5	22.9	21.6
– European Union	24.9	22.2	21.4	22.6	20.8	19.9	19.9	20.1	21.6	20.2
– Eastern Europe	0.2	0.2	0.2	0.1	0.1	0.1	0.1	0.2	0.1	0.1
– Rest of Europe	1.2	1.2	1.2	1.9	2.4	1.5	1.3	1.3	1.2	1.3
Europe former USSR	0.1	0.2	0.2	0.1	0.0	0.0	0.1	0.0	0.0	0.0
Oceania	20.7	22.4	21.7	21.4	23.0	21.9	22.1	22.7	22.4	24.9
Other	0.5	0.7	0.5	0.7	0.5	0.5	0.5	0.5	0.5	0.5
Australia/Australie	20.0	21.6	20.7	20.3	22.1	21.1	21.3	21.5	21.6	24.2
USA/Etats–Unis d'Amer	16.1	16.7	16.8	17.9	16.8	19.6	18.0	19.2	18.7	16.7
Japan/Japon	18.8	17.0	18.4	15.5	15.6	14.7	16.2	15.3	13.9	14.3
United Kingdom	9.8	8.6	8.8	7.3	6.4	6.3	5.8	6.2	5.9	5.2
Germany/Allemagne					4.2	4.2	4.3	4.6	4.8	4.7
China/Chine	1.0	1.2	1.1	1.2	1.9	2.6	3.0	3.3	3.5	3.7
Other Asia n.e.s.	2.9	3.4	3.0	2.5	2.7	2.7	2.8	2.7	2.6	2.5
Italy/Italie	2.1	1.8	1.8	2.2	2.4	2.3	2.5	2.2	2.5	2.5
France, Monaco	1.7	1.6	1.5	1.8	2.2	1.7	1.7	1.7	2.3	1.8
Singapore/Singapour	1.4	1.2	1.3	1.4	1.4	2.2	1.4	1.8	1.9	1.8

	1987	1988	1989	1990	1991	1992	1993	1994	1995	1996
Afrique	0.9	0.9	0.8	1.4	1.7	1.5	1.8	1.4	1.3	1.5
Amériques	19.7	18.5	17.7	18.0	17.5	17.3	17.7	15.9	14.9	14.5
– Amérique du Nord	16.8	15.8	14.9	14.9	14.2	13.8	13.4	12.8	11.7	10.6
– ALAI	2.1	2.1	2.0	2.3	2.3	2.5	3.7	2.5	2.3	2.8
– MCAC	0.1	0.1	0.1	0.1	0.1	0.2	0.1	0.2	0.3	0.4
– Caraïbes	0.5	0.5	0.6	0.7	0.9	0.7	0.5	0.5	0.5	0.5
– Autre Amérique	0.1	0.1	0.1	0.1	0.1	0.1	0.1	0.1	0.2	0.1
Asie anc. URSS exclus	33.6	36.8	36.4	34.5	37.3	38.9	38.2	39.0	41.7	41.5
– Moyen–Orient	3.7	3.0	3.0	2.7	3.1	3.7	3.2	2.6	2.7	3.3
Asie ancienne URSS							0.0	0.0	0.0	0.0
Europe anc. URSS exclus	23.5	19.7	19.5	19.2	17.5	17.0	15.9	16.4	16.5	16.7
– Union Européenne	22.7	18.8	19.0	18.6	17.0	16.6	15.5	16.0	16.0	16.1
– Europe de l'Est	0.4	0.4	0.2	0.3	0.1	0.0	0.0	0.1	0.1	0.1
– Autre de l'Europe	0.4	0.5	0.3	0.4	0.4	0.4	0.4	0.4	0.4	0.5
Europe ancienne URSS	1.5	1.9	2.0	1.8	1.4	0.2	0.9	0.9	0.8	0.9
Océanie	19.0	20.4	22.3	22.9	22.8	23.7	24.1	25.2	23.6	23.6
Autre	1.9	1.8	1.4	2.1	1.9	1.4	1.4	1.2	1.2	1.4
Australia/Australie	15.7	17.4	18.9	19.0	18.8	19.7	19.9	21.4	20.4	20.4
Japan/Japon	16.1	17.7	17.4	16.1	16.0	14.9	14.6	15.3	16.2	15.4
USA/Etats–Unis d'Amer	15.2	13.6	13.2	13.1	12.8	12.3	11.6	11.0	10.0	9.2
United Kingdom	9.5	7.2	7.1	7.0	6.2	6.4	6.1	6.0	6.1	6.4
Korea, Republic of	2.2	2.3	3.3	4.2	4.3	4.1	4.8	4.8	5.2	4.7
China, Hong Kong SAR	1.4	1.4	1.7	1.5	1.6	2.2	2.3	2.6	3.0	3.2
Other Asia n.e.s.	1.7	1.6	1.9	1.7	2.3	2.4	2.6	2.7	2.9	2.7
Germany/Allemagne					2.4	2.4	2.4	2.6	2.4	2.4
China/Chine	2.7	4.6	2.0	1.0	1.7	2.0	2.0	2.8	2.5	2.6
Malaysia/Malaisie	1.1	1.5	1.6	1.7	2.5	2.7	2.0	1.9	2.1	2.3

4. General Imports C.I.F. by Commodities according to the S.I.T.C. (Rev. 2) in million U.S. Dollars
Importations Générales C.A.F. par Produits d'après la C.T.C.I. (Rév. 2) en millions de Dollars E.U.

SITC CTCI	COMMODITY	1993 QUANTITY QUANTITE	1993 VALUE VALEUR	1994 QUANTITY QUANTITE	1994 VALUE VALEUR	1995 QUANTITY QUANTITE	1995 VALUE VALEUR	1996 QUANTITY QUANTITE	1996 VALUE VALEUR	PRODUIT
	ALL COMMODITIES		9654.8		11901.5		13957.7		14724.3	TOUS PRODUITS
0	FOOD AND LIVE ANIMALS		584.4		696.3		810.4		888.8	ALIMENTS,ANIMAUX VIVANTS
03	FISH AND PREPARATIONS		35.5		39.7		52.6		44.0	POISSONS ET PREPARATIONS
04	CEREALS AND PREPARATIONS		103.5		116.5		135.1		159.9	CEREALES ET PRODUITS
041	WHEAT ETC UNMILLED	W 229034	42.0	W 242884	44.6	W 169540	36.0	W 214368	55.6	FROMENT,EPEAUTRE
0412	OTHER WHEAT ETC UNMILLED	W 227660	41.7	W 242884	44.6	W 169530	36.0	W 214295	55.6	AUTRE FROMENT NON MOULU
048	CEREAL ETC PREPARATIONS	W 24746	42.9	W 25367	50.1		60.2		77.8	PREPTNS A BASE CEREALES
05	VEGETABLES AND FRUIT		155.5		165.0		203.0		209.8	LEGUMES ET FRUITS
057	FRUIT,NUTS,FRESH,DRIED	W 106058	81.3	W 118340	86.7	W 118016	92.8	W 119921	107.1	FRUITS FRAIS OU SECS
0573	BANANA,PLANTAIN,FRSH,DRY	W 65168	30.9	W 73395	28.4	W 71733	29.6	W 70525	32.9	BANANES FRAICHES,SECHEES
058	FRUIT PRESERVED,PREPARED	W 12147	35.9	W 13208	39.7	W 37736	55.6	W 33718	52.3	CONSERVES DE FRUITS
06	SUGAR AND PREPS,HONEY		72.9		89.5		97.4		112.0	SUCRES ET PRODUITS
061	SUGAR AND HONEY	W 193707	56.3	W 231032	69.5		75.8	W 288000	87.9	SUCRES ET MIEL
0611	RAW BEET AND CANE SUGAR	W 158813	39.5	W 174101	49.4	W 175659	55.1	W 170734	50.5	SUCRES BRUTS
07	COFFEE,TEA,COCOA,SPICES		61.9		78.1		95.8		95.1	CAFE,THE,CACAO,EPICES
081	*FEEDING STUFF FOR ANIML		27.6		42.1		44.2		52.2	NOURRITURE POUR ANIMAUX
09	MISC EDIBLE PRODUCTS		76.8		107.5		116.7		140.9	PREP ALIMENTAIRES DIVERSES
098	EDIBLE PRODCTS,PREPS NES		74.6		104.9		112.3		129.0	PREP ALIMENTAIRES NDA
09809	MISC FOOD PREPRTIONS NES		50.5	W 1	77.6		84.1		95.5	PREP ALIMENTAIRES NDA
1	BEVERAGES AND TOBACCO		103.2		128.4		135.8		145.7	BOISSONS ET TABACS
11	BEVERAGES		86.8		110.5		117.7		122.8	BOISSONS
112	ALCOHOLIC BEVERAGES	W 37202	82.2	W 54590	101.3	W 27087	105.7	W 28476	111.0	BOISSONS ALCOOLIQUES
1121	WINE OF FRESH GRAPES ETC	W 24756	37.1	W 34547	47.6	W 20978	45.1	W 22553	51.9	VINS DE RAISINS FRAIS
11212	WINE OF FRESH GRAPES	W 24682	36.8	W 34488	47.4	W 20904	44.8	W 22482	51.6	VINS DE MOUTS DE RAISINS
1124	DISTILLED ALCOHOLIC BEVS	W 3659	35.7	W 4594	43.2	W 4170	48.7	W 4352	47.8	ALCOOLS,EAUX–DE–VIE
2	CRUDE MATERLS,EXCL FUELS		361.2		388.1		440.2		453.8	MAT BRUTES NON COMESTIBLES
27	CRUDE FERTLZR,MINRLS NES		90.2		91.5		104.3		96.1	ENGRAIS MINERAUX BRUTS
271	FERTILIZERS,CRUDE	W 835418	57.3	W 794377	53.8	W 792623	55.6	W 720604	51.7	ENGRAIS BRUTS
2713	NAT CALCM PHOSPHATES ETC	W 835228	57.1	W 793855	52.5	W 792245	54.8	W 720381	51.1	PHOSPHATES DE CALCIUM
27131	— UNGROUND	W 604425	42.5	W 231013	15.0	W 223612	15.0	W 165676	10.4	PHOSPHATES NON MOULUS
27132	— GROUND	W 230803	14.6	W 562842	37.6	W 568634	39.9	W 554704	40.8	PHOSPHATES MOULUS
28	METALLIFEROUS ORES,SCRAP		139.1		141.3		147.2		179.9	MINERAIS METAL,DECHETS
287	BASE METAL ORES,CONC NES	W 544024	118.3	W 537550	126.4	W 492650	129.0	W 617844	164.6	MINERAIS METAUX COMMUNS
2873	ALUMINIUM ORES,ALUMINA	W 543144	117.9	W 536810	126.1	W 491730	128.6	W 616961	164.1	MINERAIS D'ALUMINIUM
28732	ALUMINA(ALUMINIUM OXIDE)	W 538489	117.0	W 534692	125.6	W 489303	128.0	W 616958	164.1	ALUMINE (OXYDE ALUMINIUM)
29	CRUDE ANIMAL,VEG MAT NES		33.2		38.9		45.3		41.7	MATIERES BRUTES ANIM,VEGET
3	MINERAL FUELS ETC		624.2		670.9		752.5		937.7	COMBUSTIBLES MINERAUX LUB
33	PETROLEUM AND PRODUCTS		622.2		669.0		751.4		935.3	PETROLE ET DERIVES
333	CRUDE PETROLEUM	W 3432510	464.6	W 3774686	473.1	W 3670356	514.8	W 3576302	559.0	HUILES BRUTES DE PETROLE
334	PETROLEUM PRODUCTS,REFIN		131.6		158.9		203.6		336.8	PRODUITS RAFFINES
3341	GASOLINE,OTH LIGHT OILS	W 325513	76.9	W 441884	91.4	W 581504	123.4	W 707543	161.9	ESSENCES POUR MOTEURS
33411	MOTOR,AVIATION SPIRIT	W 324760	75.8	W 441262	90.4	W 580528	122.2	W 701343	159.8	ESSENCES MOTEURS D'AVIONS
3343	GAS OILS	W 18224	2.0	W 39558	7.0	W 43179	10.2	W 269578	59.5	GAS OILS
3345	LUBS,PETROLEUM OILS NES		30.3		35.1		40.2		48.3	HUILES LUBRIFIANTES
335	RESIDUAL PETRLM PROD NES	W 132823	26.1	W 236343	37.2	W 172607	33.0	W 147340	39.5	PRODUITS RESIDUELS NDA
4	ANIMAL,VEGETABLE OIL,FAT		43.8		53.0		64.9		59.8	HUILES,GRAISSES ANIM,VEG
42	FIXED VEGETABLE OIL,FAT		35.5		42.3		49.0		46.0	HUILES VEGETALES FIXES
5	CHEMCLS,RELATED PROD NES		1295.1		1498.6		1756.9		1783.6	PRODUITS CHIMIQUES
51	ORGANIC CHEMICALS		127.9		167.2		198.4		177.3	PROD CHIMIQ ORGANIQUES
513	CARBOXYLIC ACIDS ETC		31.8		34.1		48.6		40.5	ACIDES CARBOXYLIQUES
514	NITROGEN–FNCTN COMPOUNDS		32.2		43.5		49.8		46.9	COMPOSES FONCT AZOTEES
515	ORG–INORG COMPOUNDS ETC		25.2		43.1		39.8		46.0	COMPOSES ORGANO–MINERAUX
52	INORGANIC CHEMICALS		94.0		98.9		123.9		141.4	PROD CHIM INORGANIQUES
522	INORG ELEMNTS,OXIDES,ETC		33.4		37.5		47.9		57.9	ELEMENTS INORGANIQUES
523	OTHR INORG CHEMICALS ETC		59.4		60.2		75.0		82.5	AUT PRODUITS CHIMIQUES INORG
53	DYES,TANNING,COLOUR PROD		82.3		99.8		109.2		112.7	PROD TEINTURE,COLORANTS
533	PIGMENTS,PAINTS,ETC		47.5		62.7		74.2		79.5	PIGMENTS,PEINTURES,VERNIS
541	*MEDICINAL,PHARM PRODUCT		305.5		334.4		372.3		406.4	PROD MEDICINAUX PHARMACEUT
5417	MEDICAMENTS		248.5		266.3		298.5		331.5	MEDICAMENTS
54171	— CONTAINNG ANTIBIOTICS		37.2		40.0		40.3		44.6	MED CONTN ANTIBIOTIQUES
54172	— CONTAINING HORMONES		36.4		38.3		45.1		36.9	MED CONTENANT HORMONES
54179	— CONTNG OTH SUBSTANCES		159.4		172.1		195.8		223.8	MED CONT AUT SUBSTANCES
55	PERFUME,CLEANING ETC PRD		118.2		142.6		162.4		185.3	PROD POUR PARFUM,TOILETTE
553	PERFUMERY,COSMETICS,ETC		64.2		81.3		96.8		107.5	PRODUITS DE PARFUMERIE
554	SOAP,CLEANSING ETC PREPS		39.5		43.0		48.1		59.7	SAVONS,PRODUITS DETERSIFS
5542	WASHING PREPARATIONS ETC	W 2	30.0	W 6	32.6		36.8		45.6	PROD ORG TENSIO–ACT NDA
562	*FERTILIZERS,MANUFACTURE	W 614579	92.5	W 660962	111.9	W 786438	159.2		140.1	ENGRAIS MANUFACTURES
5623	CHEM POTASSIC FERTILIZER	W 239494	33.6	W 211011	30.6	W 259661	41.7	W 237020	35.7	ENGRAIS POTASSIQUES
56231	POTASSIUM CHLORIDE	W 234469	32.1	W 203561	28.6	W 246239	38.3	W 236234	35.4	CHLORURE DE POTASSIUM
5629	FERTILIZERS NES	W 212035	39.1	W 245457	53.6	W 296548	76.6		64.4	ENGRAIS NDA
56292	NITROG–PHOS FERTILZR NES	W 198741	32.7	W 237825	48.7	W 290581	71.9	W 211632	55.7	ENGRAIS NDA CONT N P
58	PLASTIC MATERIALS ETC		309.1		370.4		420.4		405.7	MAT PLAST ARTIFICIELLES
582	PROD OF CONDENSATION ETC		73.2		82.2		98.0		93.6	PROD CONDENS,POLYCOND
5823	ALKYDS,OTHER POLYESTERS	W 16831	41.1	W 19517	45.4		57.9		52.7	ALKYDES ET AUT POLYESTERS
58231	— IN PRIMARY FORMS	W 16579	30.2	W 19299	33.5	W 19046	43.0	W 20735	39.4	SOUS FORMES PRIMAIRES
583	POLYMERIZATION ETC PRODS		225.8		278.8		313.5		304.0	PROD POLYMERISATION
5831	POLYETHYLENE		74.4		95.5		106.6		109.0	POLYETHYLENE
58311	— IN PRIMARY FORMS	W 80886	64.0	W 103850	84.2	W 89882	94.1	W 101863	95.2	POLYETHYLENE PRIMAIRES
5834	POLYVINYL CHLORIDE	W 27521	34.5	W 33550	46.3		51.4		42.1	CHLORURE DE POLYVINYLE
5839	OTH POLYMRZTION ETC PROD	W 31	52.2	W 395	55.6		62.2		64.0	AUT PROD POLYMER COPOLYM
59	CHEMICAL MATERIALS NES		161.9		167.7		205.5		208.7	MAT PROD CHIMIQUES NDA
591	PESTICIDES,DISINFECTANTS		41.8		43.6		58.5		75.7	DESINF,INSECT,FONG,HERB
598	MISCEL CHEM PRODUCTS NES		99.8		100.3		118.3		105.4	PROD DIV INDUST CHIM NDA
5989	CHEM PRODUCTS,PREPS NES		71.5		75.8		87.0		80.6	PROD PREP CHIMIQUES NDA
59899	OTH CHEM PRODS,PREPS,NES		46.1		53.1		59.6		61.5	AUT PRODUITS CHIMIQUES NDA
6	BASIC MANUFACTURES		1575.2		1873.6		2251.2		2266.8	ART MANUFACTURES
62	RUBBER MANUFACTURES NES		116.1		127.9		156.2		162.1	CAOUTCHOUC MANUFACTURE
625	RUBBER TYRES, TUBES ETC	N 2146043	65.5	N 2215556	70.1	N 3177659	88.6	N 3118784	92.6	PNEUS CAOUTCHOUC VULCANISE
628	RUBBER ARTICLES NES		32.1		35.9		40.1		42.3	OUVRAGES CAOUTCHOUC NDA
63	WOOD,CORK MANUFACTRS NES		21.8		29.0		39.8		45.2	OUVRAGES LIEGE ET BOIS
64	PAPER,PAPERBOARD AND MFR		257.7		302.5		412.5		393.5	PAPIERS,CARTONS & OUVRAGES
641	PAPER AND PAPERBOARD		187.8		218.0		306.3		268.8	PAPIERS ET CARTONS
6412	PRINTG,WRITING PAPER NES	W 51324	70.6	W 62596	85.7		127.1		94.0	PAPIERS POUR L'IMPRESSION
64122	— COATED,IMPREGNATD ETC	W 51323	54.3	W 62594	64.4	W 70384	91.3	W 52362	62.1	PAPIERS IMPRESSION COUCHES
6415	PAPER,PAPERBRD,BULK,NES	W 51131	50.7	W 59132	57.4	W 69987	81.8	W 63495	71.0	PAPIERS,CARTONS ROULEAUX
64159	OTHER PAPER ETC,BULK,NES	W 50354	48.8	W 58464	55.5	W 69159	79.5	W 60838	67.2	AUT PAPIER ROULEAUX FEUILLES
6418	COATED ETC PAPER NES BLK	W 18757	47.8	W 18497	51.0	W 21353	61.0	W 21370	61.4	PAP,CARTONS COUCHES,ENDUITS
64189	COATED PAPER ETC NES	W 12994	35.2	W 13711	39.1	W 14963	45.8	W 14497	45.0	PAPIERS,CARTONS COUCHES
642	PAPER,ETC,PRECUT,ARTS OF		70.0		84.6		106.3		124.7	PAP,CARTONS DECOUPES
6428	PAPER ETC ARTICLES NES		24.7		31.6		42.1		52.8	OUVRAGES EN PATE A PAPIER
65	TEXTILE YARN,FABRICS,ETC		406.3		465.7		480.0		474.9	FILS,TISSUS,ARTICLES TEXTILE

4. General Imports C.I.F. by Commodities according to the S.I.T.C. (Rev. 2) in million U.S. Dollars
Importations Générales C.A.F. par Produits d'après la C.T.C.I. (Rév. 2) en millions de Dollars E.U.

SITC CTCI	COMMODITY	1993		1994		1995		1996		PRODUIT
		QUANTITY QUANTITE	VALUE VALEUR	QUANTITY QUANTITE	VALUE VALEUR	QUANTITY QUANTITE	VALUE VALEUR	QUANTITY QUANTITE	VALUE VALEUR	
651	TEXTILE YARN		65.3		76.1		69.7		64.5	FILS TEXTILES
652	COTTON FABRICS,WOVEN	A 34590	52.2	A 34911	56.3	A 30990	57.3	A 28330	56.0	TISSUS DE COTON
6522	WOVEN COTTON BLEACHD,ETC	A 29905	49.3	A 30500	53.3	A 26917	54.0	A 25387	53.7	TISSUS COTON BLANCHIS ETC
65224	BLCHED COTTON FABRIC NES	A 27017	42.6	A 26983	44.6	A 23721	44.4	A 21751	42.7	AUT TIS PLUS 85% COT BLANCHI
653	WOVN MAN–MADE FIB FABRIC	A 59780	90.9	A 63517	100.6	A 76439	102.3	A 69693	93.7	TISSUS FIBRES SYNTH,ARTIF
6534	DISC SYN BLEND FABRC NES	A 23718	32.2	A 22851	30.3	A 27898	30.9	A 20584	28.9	TISSUS FIBRES SYNTH DISCONT
657	SPECIAL TXTL FABRC,PRODS		67.5		75.1		73.6		74.8	TISSUS SPECIAUX
658	TEXTILE ARTICLES NES		48.8		60.1		70.1		77.4	ART FACONNES MAT TEXTILES
6584	LINENS ETC	MN 18688	32.4	MN 22455	39.6	MN 20359	43.2	MN 19513	47.3	LINGE DE MAISON
66	NONMETAL MINERAL MFS NES		151.4		186.9		235.7		239.9	ART MIN NON METALLIQUES
662	CLAY,REFRACTORY BLDG PRD		20.6		25.2		46.2		39.7	MAT CONST REFRACTAIRES
664	GLASS		43.5		56.1		62.6		67.2	VERRE
67	IRON AND STEEL		219.0		285.6		332.3		370.0	FER ET ACIER
673	IRON,STEEL SHAPES ETC	W 59543	41.7	W 70729	50.4	W 78750	61.7	W 109690	80.4	BARRES,PROFIL FER,ACIER
674	IRN,STL UNIV,PLATE,SHEET	W 121302	111.9	W 161821	146.4	W 149765	160.1	W 160512	162.3	LARGES PLATS,TOLES
6746	IRN,STL THIN PLATE,ROLLD	W 19514	30.9	W 20785	30.4	W 23518	47.2	W 21965	35.0	TOLES LAM MOINS 3MM
6747	TINNED PLATES,SHEETS	W 35054	28.1	W 42528	35.8	W 35518	31.6	W 40249	39.3	TOLES ETAMEES EN ACIER
6749	OTH IRN,STL PLATES,SHEET	W 39542	32.5	W 64776	56.4	W 49929	48.1	W 50802	49.8	AUTRES TOLES FER,ACIER
67491	— OF IRON OR SIMPLE STL	W 37795	28.6	W 62131	50.5	W 48256	44.2	W 49587	46.2	AUT TOLES AUTRES ACIER FIN
678	IRON,STL TUBES,PIPES,ETC	W 30211	32.5	W 39179	45.5	W 39892	51.4	W 46638	65.2	TUBES,TUYAUX EN FONTE,FER
68	NON–FERROUS METALS		157.2		185.0		236.8		204.8	METAUX NON FERREUX
682	COPPER EXC CEMENT COPPER		53.5		60.8		72.8		66.7	CUIVRE
6822	COPPER,ALLOYS WORKED		41.0		40.5		40.3		38.3	CUIVRE,ALLIAGES OUVRES
684	ALUMINIUM	W 29911	73.3	W 36392	91.7	W 41046	127.9	W 34910	103.3	ALUMINIUM
6842	ALUMINIUM,ALLOYS WORKED	W 25311	66.0	W 28272	76.6	W 29356	101.5	W 22462	80.6	ALUMINIUM,ALLIAGES OUVRE
68422	ALUMNM PLATE,SHEET,STRIP	W 17183	38.9	W 20568	48.8	W 20286	63.1	W 15208	48.5	TOLES, PLANCHES EN ALU
69	METAL MANUFACTURES NES		226.3		269.3		334.6		352.4	ART MANUFACT EN METAL NDA
695	TOOLS		50.4		58.7		69.7		68.1	OUTILS A MAIN
697	BASE MTL HOUSEHOLD EQUIP		26.8		33.1		41.5		46.9	ART MENAGE MET COMMUNS
699	BASE METAL MFRS NES		87.1		102.3		123.0		135.7	ART MANUFACTURES MET NDA
7	MACHINES,TRANSPORT EQUIP		3716.8		4963.8		5876.6		6153.6	MACHINES MATERIEL TRANSPORT
71	POWER GENERATING EQUIPMT		201.3		215.9		241.4		293.7	MACHINES GENERATRICES
713	INTRNL COMBUS PSTN ENGIN		69.4		86.2		105.9		103.6	MOTEURS EXPL COMB INT, PIECE
714	ENGINES AND MOTORS NES		90.0		77.7		66.1		58.5	MOTEURS NON ELECTRIQUES
7149	ENGINE & MOTOR PARTS NES		77.0		70.1		53.9		51.0	PIECES 714 ET 718.88
71491	PARTS NES OF 7144,71481		74.4		64.4		49.0		46.1	PIECES DES PROPULSEURS
716	ROTATING ELECTRIC PLANT		31.0		36.8		38.8		62.0	APP ELECTR ROTATIFS,PIECES
72	MACHS FOR SPCL INDUSTRYS		461.0		580.4		611.4		667.6	MAC SPECIALES POUR INDUST
721	AGRIC MACHY,EXC TRACTORS		46.2		59.0		75.1		79.2	MACHINES AGRICOLES
7212	HARVESTING ETC MACHINES		30.5		35.4		41.0		45.9	ENGINS POUR LA RECOLTE
722	TRACTORS NON–ROAD	N 6554	65.9	N 7541	80.4	N 4140	73.2	N 8256	81.7	TRACTEURS
7224	WHEELED TRACTORS NES	N 6553	65.8	N 7538	79.6	N 4129	72.1	N 8253	81.5	TRACTEURS A ROUES
723	CIVIL ENGNEERG EQUIP ETC		83.5		126.2		123.7		126.7	APPAREILS DE GENIE CIVIL
7234	CONST,MINING MACHNRY NES		72.9		105.6		107.3		112.5	MACH POUR LA CONST, MINES
72342	SLFPRP SHOVELS,EXCAVATRS		57.9	N 5	81.1		79.0		85.1	PELLES MECANIQUES
725	PAPER ETC MILL MACHINERY		38.6		23.2		33.3		78.9	MACHINES FABR PATE PAPIER
726	PRINTG,BKBINDG MACHY,PTS		52.1		106.0		91.5		70.8	MACHINES POUR IMPRIMERIE
7264	PRINTING PRESSES	W 1206	26.3	W 3090	69.5	W 1840	49.4	W 1401	38.1	MACHINES A IMPRIMER
72641	ROTARY PRINTING PRESSES	W 1206	26.3	W 3090	69.5	W 1840	49.4	W 1401	38.1	MACH IMPRIMER ROTATIVES
728	OTH MACHY FOR SPCL INDUS		124.4		132.4		150.1		179.8	AUT MACH IND PARTICULIERES
7281	MACH–TOOLS FR SPCL INDUS		36.5		35.8		31.3		49.5	MACH–OUTILS SPEC IND PART
72812	MACH–TOOLS TO WORK WOOD	W 2388	31.5	W 2710	29.4	W 2200	25.0	W 3076	39.4	MACH–OUT POUR TRAVAIL BOIS
7284	MACHY FOR SPCL INDUS NES		82.8		85.6		107.5		118.5	MACH SPEC IND PARTICUL.
72848	OTH MCHY WITH INDIV FNCT		30.2	N 22264	36.2	N 1366630	51.4	N 436186	57.8	AUTRES MACHINES NDA
73	METALWORKING MACHINERY		42.3		63.6		77.2		66.0	MACH TRAVAIL DES METAUX
736	METALWORKING MACH–TOOLS		27.6		46.3		47.8		44.5	MACH–OUTILS TRAVAIL METAUX
74	GENRL INDUSTRL MACHY NES		422.4		534.4		685.1		766.6	MACH APP INDUSTRIE
741	HEATING,COOLING EQUIPMNT		64.5		79.1		122.2		139.6	MACH CHAUFFAGE,PIECES
7416	HEATING,COOLING EQU NES		32.2		36.6		39.5		56.8	APP CHANGEMENT TEMP
742	PUMPS FOR LIQUIDS ETC		41.2		53.0		59.2		61.8	POMPES MOTO–POMPES
743	PUMPS NES,CENTRFUGES ETC		67.5		85.5		102.7		113.8	POMPES COMPRES,VENT ETC
744	MECHANICAL HANDLING EQU		68.4		94.3		146.3		178.3	EQUIP MANUTENTION PIECES
7441	FORK LIFT TRCKS,ETC,PTS		25.5		35.9		55.2		64.0	CHARIOTS POUR USINES ETC
74411	FORK LIFT TRUCKS ETC		25.3		35.8		55.2		64.0	CHARIOTS POUR LES GARES
7442	LIFTING,LOADING MACH NES		26.3		36.2		62.3		68.1	APP LEVAGE,MANUTENTION
74428	OTH HANDLING ETC MCH NES	W 161	21.0	W 16	29.1		46.0		55.6	AUT APP LEVAGE ETC
7449	PTS NES OF MACHY OF 7442		16.6		22.3		28.9		46.4	PIECES DU 744.2
745	NONELEC MACHY,TOOLS NES		70.9		87.7		109.0		114.6	AUT MACH NON ELEC,PIECES
7452	OTH NONELEC MCHS,PTS NES		54.8		69.7		88.0		93.1	AUT MACH NON ELEC,PIECES
749	NONELEC MACH PTS,ACC NES		110.2		135.1		145.9		158.6	PIECES MACH NON ELEC NDA
7492	COCKS,VALVES ETC NES		50.7		64.3		67.9	MN 15009	77.7	ART ROB,SIM POUR TUYAUX
75	OFFICE MACHNES,ADP EQUIP		479.3		635.2		776.9		767.5	MACH BUREAU TRAIT AUTOM
751	OFFICE MACHINES		56.1		61.8		69.8		69.1	MACH,APPAREILS DE BUREAU
7518	OFFICE MACHINES NES		40.3		50.3		58.8		52.4	MACH,APP DE BUREAU NDA
75182	PHOTO,THERMOCOPY APPARAT	N 11826	30.7	N 11751	33.3	N 14178	42.1	N 12855	39.6	APPAREILS DE PHOTOCOPIE
752	AUTOMTIC DATA PROC EQUIP		273.6		388.3		481.4		478.5	MACH TRAIT INFORMATION
7522	DIGITAL COMPUTERS		95.7		138.4		153.0		180.7	MACH DIGITALES COMPLETES
7523	DIGITL CENTRL PROCESSORS		25.1		49.5		88.0		50.4	UNITES CENTRALES
7524	DIGITL CENTRL STOR UNITS		17.1		45.9		64.5		62.2	UNITES MEMOIRE CENTRALES
7525	ADP PERIPHERAL UNITS		81.5		96.2		123.8		120.5	UNITES PERIPHERIQUES
7528	OFF–LINE DATA PROC EQUIP		51.9		56.9		51.0		54.7	MACH AUXIL TRAIT INFORM
759	OFFICE,ADP MCH PTS,ACCES		149.7		185.1		225.8		220.0	PIECES DU 751 ET 752
7599	ACCTG,ETC,ADP MCH PTS,AC		131.7		163.6		201.2		191.2	PIECES DU 751 ET 752
76	TELECOMM,SOUND EQUIPMENT		380.4		489.0		663.5		645.4	EQUIPMENT DE TELECOM
761	TELEVISION RECEIVERS	N 272354	74.0	N 358172	96.4	N 330645	97.0	N 230488	77.9	RECEPTEURS DE TELEVISION
7611	COLOUR TV RECEIVERS	N 267191	73.1	N 356007	95.9	N 328860	96.6	N 229514	77.7	RECEPTEURS COULEUR
762	RADIO BROADCAST RECEIVRS	N 648771	40.3	N 909177	62.5	N 1112447	78.9	N 813114	64.2	RECEPTEURS RADIODIFFUSION
7628	OTHER RADIO RECEIVERS	N 221514	23.5	N 322391	40.9	N 351398	55.3	N 287574	42.3	AUTRES RECEPT RADIO
763	SOUND RECORDRS,PHONOGRPH	N 330881	47.4	N 429092	53.6	N 386986	57.2	N 421162	63.9	PHONO,APP ENREGISTREMENT
7638	OTHR SOUND APPARATUS ETC	N 307997	46.0	N 416901	52.6	N 380620	56.3	N 415185	63.2	AUT APP D'ENREGIS,REPROD
76381	TV IMAGE,SND RECRDRS ETC	N 111463	29.9	N 128721	34.0	N 152677	38.9	N 160318	42.7	APP ENREG,REPRO IMAG,SON
764	TELECOM EQPT,PTS,ACC NES		218.8		276.5		430.6		439.6	EQUIP TELECOM,PIECES
7641	LINE TELEPHONE,ETC EQUIP	N 756	72.7	N 12802	82.7		117.4	N 1101409	138.9	APP TELEPHON PAR FIL
7643	TV,RADIO TRANSMITTRS ETC		54.6		85.7		133.2		105.4	APP EMET TELE RADIO
7648	TELECOMM EQUIPMENT NES		30.3		28.2		37.5		22.5	APP TELECOM NDA
7649	PTS NES OF EQUIPMT OF 76		49.0		64.1		122.5		150.6	PIECES DE LA DIV 76
76491	PTS NES OF APPAR OF 7641		30.2		37.9		90.4		108.3	PIECES POUR 764.1
77	ELECTRIC MACHNRY NES ETC		447.1		545.9		654.3		704.3	MACH APP ELECT NDA
771	ELECTRIC POWER MACHY NES		27.4		28.4		55.5		64.7	MACH PROD,TRANS ELECTR
772	SWITCHGEAR ETC,PARTS NES	MN 103552	91.5	MN 169353	120.1		137.1		141.8	APP COUPURE,SECT ETC
7721	SWITCHGEAR ETC	N 9077	84.3	N 33184	108.7		123.8		126.9	APP COUPURE,SECTIONMNT

4. General Imports C.I.F. by Commodities according to the S.I.T.C. (Rev. 2) in million U.S. Dollars
Importations Générales C.A.F. par Produits d'après la C.T.C.I. (Rév. 2) en millions de Dollars E.U.

SITC CTCI	COMMODITY	1993		1994		1995		1996		PRODUIT
		QUANTITY QUANTITE	VALUE VALEUR	QUANTITY QUANTITE	VALUE VALEUR	QUANTITY QUANTITE	VALUE VALEUR	QUANTITY QUANTITE	VALUE VALEUR	
773	ELECTR DISTRIBUTNG EQUIP		37.4		45.1		48.8		55.2	EQUIPMT DISTRIBUTION ELECT
7731	INSULATED WIRE,CABLE ETC	W 14	35.1	W 69	40.5	W 5661	44.1	W 6821	48.1	FILS,CABLES ISOLES ELECT
775	HOUSEHOLD TYPE EQUIP NES		103.3		125.0		138.2		148.1	MACH,APP USAGE DOMESTQUE
7758	ELECTRO–THERMIC APPL NES		46.6		58.3		65.9		67.5	APP ELECTROTHERMIQ NDA
776	TRANSISTORS,VALVES,ETC	MN 69804	39.1	MN 87683	53.5		74.7		74.3	LAMPES,TUBES,VALVES
7764	ELECTRONIC MICROCIRCUITS	MN 12610	22.9	MN 19022	33.7	MN 21048	49.5	MN 22485	51.7	MICROSTRUCTURES ELECTRON
778	ELECTRICAL MACHINERY NES		124.9		151.3		177.5		192.3	AUTRES MACH ELECT NDA
7788	OTH ELEC MACHY,EQUIP NES		48.4		59.2		71.1		86.5	AUT MACH APP ELEC NDA
78	ROAD VEHICLES		1035.8		1402.8		1679.7		1947.2	VEHICULES ROUTIERS
781	PASS MOTOR VEH EXC BUSES	N 108606	683.4	N 139874	961.3	N 158263	1140.8	N 197925	1418.6	AUTO TRANSPORT PERSONNES
782	LORRIES,SPCL MTR VEH NES	N 28871	206.2	N 32107	262.3	N 31907	321.7	N 60540	307.7	VEHICULES SPECIAUX,MARCH
7821	LORRIES,TRUCKS	N 28838	204.1	N 32034	257.4	N 31764	310.5	N 32385	298.8	VEHICULES TRANSP MARCHAND
784	MOTOR VEH PRTS,ACCES NES		81.0		98.2		117.8		120.2	PIECES 722,781,782,783
7849	OTHER MOTOR VEHCL PARTS		76.6		91.6		108.5		114.6	PIECES 722,781,782,783
785	CYCLES,ETC MOTRZD OR NOT		39.0		41.1		48.1		53.7	MOTOCYCLES SCOOTERS
79	OTHR TRANSPORT EQUIPMENT		247.6		497.2		487.5		295.9	AUTRE MATERIEL TRANSPORT
792	AIRCRAFT ETC		215.1		444.7		413.7		124.6	APP NAVIGATION AERIENNE
7923	AIRCRFT NES2000–15000KG	N 36	52.6	N 46	42.0	N 36	104.1	N 34	62.3	AERODYNES 2000 A 15000 KG
7924	AIRCRFT NES OVER 15000KG	N 3	100.6	N 8	326.4	N 3	239.9			AERODYNES PLUS 15000 KG
7929	AIRCRAFT PARTS NES		41.2		58.2		54.3		46.9	PIECES DU 792
793	SHIPS AND BOATS ETC		25.9		51.3		70.1	N 16582	165.6	NAVIRES BATEAUX,ETC
7932	SHIPS AND BOATS NES	N 1980	24.2	N 2402	49.5	N 7671	57.4	N 15545	163.7	NAVIRES ET BATEAUX
79322	TANKERS OF ALL KINDS							N 2	94.8	BATEAUX–CITERNES
8	MISC MANUFACTURED GOODS		1341.0		1618.3		1850.2		2021.6	ART MANUFACTURES DIVERS
812	*PLUMBG,HEATNG,LGHTNG EQ		27.2		36.9		46.7		50.2	APPAR SANITAIRES CHAUFFAGE
821	*FURNITURE,PARTS THEREOF		45.7		63.4		79.8		102.1	MEUBLES ET PIECES
8219	FURNITURE AND PARTS NES		18.6		27.6		37.1		50.8	AUTRES MEUBLES ET PIECES
84	CLOTHING AND ACCESSORIES		197.7		266.1		306.5		351.6	VETEMENTS
843	WOMENS OUTERWEAR NONKNIT	N 7893804	45.7	N 8974005	59.0	MN 9490	72.9	MN 10264	85.8	VET DESSUS FEMMES MAT TEX
845	OUTERWEAR KNIT NONELASTC	N 1078107	55.6	N 991775	78.2	MN 13253	80.5	MN 13080	92.5	VET DESSOUS,ACCES BONNET
8459	— OTHER,CLTHG ACCESRYS	N 566767	30.7	N 528825	47.7	MN 9965	48.8	MN 9513	55.2	AUT VET DESSUS DE BONNE
846	UNDER GARMENTS KNITTED	MN 16068	30.6	MN 21788	45.3		53.7		64.2	SOUS VETS DE BONNETERIE
8462	— OF COTTON NON ELASTIC	MN 13783	23.0	MN 19277	33.8	MN 19027	39.6	MN 19570	48.4	SOUS–VET BONNET COTON
851	*FOOTWEAR	P 7519863	65.5	MP 9497	79.8	MP 10373	89.8	MP 9606	100.1	CHAUSSURES
85102	FOOTWEAR LEATHER	P 4900693	50.5	P 6267519	63.2	P 6919089	71.0	P 6517879	79.9	CHAUS SEMELLES EN CUIR
87	PRECISION INSTRUMNTS NES		186.3		226.9		246.3		260.5	INSTRUM,APPAR SCIENT NDA
872	MEDICAL INSTRUMENTS NES		44.4		53.3		60.9		70.4	INSTR,APP MEDIC–CHIR NDA
87202	OTH MEDICAL INSTRUMENTS		39.5		47.1		52.9		62.0	INSTRUM,APP MEDECINE
874	MEASURNG,CONTROLNG INSTR		122.0		149.7		159.2		160.5	INSTRUMENTS DE MESURE
8748	ELEC MEAS,CONTRL EQU NES		30.1		42.5		43.4		46.9	APP ELEC ELECTRO MESURE
87483	OTH ELCTRNC MEAS ETC EQU		26.4		36.6		38.4		41.8	AUT APP ELECTRO DE MESURE
88	PHOTO EQU,OPTICL GDS ETC		135.3		156.7		170.2		192.4	APP,FOURN PHOTO,OP,MONTR
881	PHOTO APPARAT,EQUIPT NES		32.3		32.5		32.9		41.7	APP,EQUIP PHOTO NDA
882	PHOTO,CINEMA SUPPLIES		66.0		77.5		82.2		93.8	PRODUITS PHOTO,CINEMA
8822	PHOTO FILM EXC DEV CINMA		48.0		56.3		58.2		60.8	PLAQUES,PELLICULES,FILMS
89	MISC MANUFCTRD GOODS NES		659.8		757.3		876.8		929.2	ART MANUFACTURES DIVERS
892	PRINTED MATTER		179.6		208.5		219.0		230.9	IMPRIMES
8921	PRINTED BOOKS,GLOBES,ETC		90.1		101.1		105.7		111.2	LIVRES,BROCHURES,CARTES
89211	PRINTED BOOKS,PAMPHLETS		88.5		99.3		103.7		109.0	LIVRES,BROCHURES
8922	NEWSPAPERS,PERIODICALS		52.1		60.4		62.2		65.8	JOURNAUX ET PERIODIQUES
8928	PRINTED MATTER NES		33.6		42.3		45.5		47.3	IMPRIMES NDA
893	ARTICLES OF PLASTIC NES		142.6		173.8		208.5		219.7	OUVRAGES EN MAT DIVIS 58
8939	MISC PLASTIC ARTICLES		111.9		132.8		159.3		168.6	ART DIVERS EN MAT DIV 58
89399	OTHR PLASTC ARTICLES NES	W 7	91.0	W 1	110.5		134.0		146.0	AUT OUV MAT DIV 58
894	TOYS,SPORTING GOODS,ETC		110.4		120.9		158.2		173.7	VOITURES ENFANTS,JOUETS
8942	TOYS,INDOOR GAMES ETC		70.1		74.2		101.7		113.6	JOUETS,JEUX ETC
89423	TOYS NES		32.8		36.0		45.9		51.7	JOUETS,MODELES REDUITS
89424	INDOOR GAME EQUIPMENT		28.6		27.0		40.9		46.7	ART,JEUX DE SOCIETE
8947	OTH SPORT GDS,FAIR AMUSM		31.5		38.0		45.2		47.8	AUT ART DE SPORT
897	GOLD,SILVER WARE,JEWELRY		37.9		30.3		24.4		30.2	BIJOUTERIE,ORFEVRERIE
8973	PREC JEWLRY,GLD–SILVWARE		33.0		23.3		17.8		24.0	BIJOUX OR,ARGENT ORFEVRE
89731	PRECIOUS METAL JEWELLERY		31.3		21.2		15.0		21.7	ART BIJOUTERIE,JOAILLER
898	MUSICAL INSTRUMENTS,PTS		118.3		141.0		170.1		169.9	INSTRUMENTS DE MUSIQUE
8983	SOUND RECRDNG TAPE,DISCS		108.1		129.7		158.3		157.3	SUPPORTS SON POUR 763
89832	RECORDED DISCS,TAPES ETC		87.8		108.7		137.7		136.1	DISQUES,PHONO,BANDES
899	OTHER MANUFACTURED GOODS		43.2		48.3		56.8		64.4	AUT ART MANUF DIVERS NDA

5. General Exports F.O.B. by Commodities according to the S.I.T.C. (Rev. 2) in million U.S. Dollars
Exportations Générales F.O.B. par Produits d'après la C.T.C.I. (Rév. 2) en millions de Dollars E.U.

SITC CTCI	COMMODITY	1993 QUANTITY QUANTITE	1993 VALUE VALEUR	1994 QUANTITY QUANTITE	1994 VALUE VALEUR	1995 QUANTITY QUANTITE	1995 VALUE VALEUR	1996 QUANTITY QUANTITE	1996 VALUE VALEUR	PRODUIT
	ALL COMMODITIES		10558.2		12185.5		13745.5		14354.3	TOUS PRODUITS
0	FOOD AND LIVE ANIMALS		4692.1		5082.6		5645.8		6263.5	ALIMENTS,ANIMAUX VIVANTS
001	*LIVE ANIMALS FOR FOOD	N 1661907	98.6	N 1537871	100.3	N 977737	80.9	N 872282	91.1	ANIMAUX VIVANTS
0012	SHEEP AND GOATS,LIVE	N 1245144	47.9	N 831139	42.8	N 629581	24.2	N 551905	22.2	ESPECES OVINE ET CAPRINE
00121	SHEEP,LIVE	N 1244944	47.4	N 825486	30.9	N 627906	22.9	N 551155	21.9	ESPECE OVINE
0015	EQUINE SPECIES, LIVE	N 3165	46.6	N 3132	51.4	N 3149	53.6	N 3046	63.6	CHEVAUX,ANES,MULETS
01	MEAT AND PREPARATIONS		1653.2		1691.3		1785.9		1873.3	VIANDES ET PREPARATIONS
011	MEAT FRESH,CHILLD,FROZEN	W 696851	1632.4	W 722038	1660.8	W 776455	1749.6	W 776821	1836.5	VIANDES FRAICHES,REF,CONGE
0111	BOVINE MEAT FRESH,FROZEN	W 313829	773.0	W 319124	782.1	W 347058	767.6	W 343178	681.9	VIANDES BOVIN FRAI,REF
01111	BOVINE MEAT WITH BONE IN	W 22486	34.0	W 26697	50.0	W 28459	45.6	W 24921	41.8	VIANDES BOVIN NON DESOSS
01112	BOVINE MEAT BONELESS	W 291344	739.1	W 292427	732.2	W 318600	722.0	W 318257	640.1	VIANDES BOVIN DESOSSEES
0112	MUTTON ETC FRSH,CHLD,FRN	W 327894	729.4	W 344077	743.6	W 365013	809.9	W 371148	984.1	VIANDE DE MOUTON
0116	EDIBLE OFFAL FRESH,CH,FR	W 38719	53.8	W 43501	59.7	W 48704	69.1	W 49260	64.0	ABATS COMESTIBLES
0118	MEAT NES FRESH,CHLD,FRZN	W 14855	72.6	W 13953	71.6	W 14200	98.7	W 11568	102.4	AUTRES VIANDES,ABATS
01189	OTHER MEAT NES FRESH,ETC	W 14855	72.6	W 13953	71.6	W 14199	98.7	W 11568	102.4	VIANDE,ABATS COMESTIBLES
02	DAIRY PRODCTS,BIRDS'EGGS		1520.7		1661.2		1788.9		2309.5	PRODUITS LAITIERS,OEUFS
022	MILK AND CREAM	W 436209	794.1	W 516609	845.0	W 443412	882.5	W 564696	1175.2	LAIT ET CREME
0223	MILK AND CREAM FRESH	W 30453	39.7	W 48849	55.7	W 45700	61.9	W 66230	83.1	LAIT,CREME FRAIS
0224	MILK,CREAM PRESERVED ETC	W 405756	754.4	W 467760	789.3	W 397712	820.6	W 498465	1092.2	LAIT,CREME CONS,CONC
02242	MILK DRY,1.5% FAT OR LES	W 107268	194.9	W 149236	247.0	W 113315	239.3	W 169433	365.5	LAIT POUDRE INF 1.5%
02243	MILK DRY,OVER 1.5% FAT	W 293700	552.4	W 308117	530.1	W 276008	567.9	W 318997	706.2	LAIT POUDRE SUP 1.5%
023	BUTTER	W 248660	449.0	W 251671	469.5	W 233273	510.7	W 274250	624.4	BEURRE
024	CHEESE AND CURD	W 126499	276.3	W 159353	345.5	W 168793	394.2	W 204718	507.7	FROMAGE ET CAILLEBOTTE
03	FISH AND PREPARATIONS		641.0		686.8		802.3		796.7	POISSONS ET PREPARATIONS
034	FISH,FRESH,CHILLED,FROZN	W 210197	437.7	W 174931	419.0	W 175758	479.8	W 197169	484.5	POISSON FRAIS, REFRIG,CONG
0341	FISH FRSH,CHLLD,EX FILLT	W 8537	46.0	W 10401	54.1	W 9258	54.3	W 8844	51.5	POISSON FRAIS,REFRIGERE
0342	FISH FROZEN,EXCL FILLETS	W 136161	155.6	W 109079	148.4	W 107820	184.8	W 126610	206.0	POISSONS CONGELES
0344	FISH FILLETS,FROZEN	W 64451	230.8	W 54617	211.9	W 57878	236.1	W 60882	222.6	FILETS CONGELES
036	SHELL FISH FRESH,FROZEN	W 14114	149.4	W 4	0.1	W 104004	266.2	W 84275	257.5	CRUSTACES,MOLLUSQUES
037	FISH ETC PREPD,PRSVD NES	W 7267	48.9	W 7103	49.1	W 7356	48.9	W 7130	48.5	POIS,CRUST,MOL PREPARES
04	CEREALS AND PREPARATIONS		39.2		57.8		81.2		86.0	CEREALES ET PRODUITS
048	CEREAL ETC PREPARATIONS	W 21971	33.2	W 32407	53.9		74.1		79.8	PREPTNS A BASE CEREALES
05	VEGETABLES AND FRUIT		597.0		693.9		888.3		849.7	LEGUMES ET FRUITS
054	VEG ETC FRSH,SMPLY PRSVD	W 153	0.2	W 196	0.4		213.9		203.6	LEGUMES FRAIS,CONG,SECS
0545	OTHER FRESH VEGETABLES	W 170197	71.8	W 241435	105.8	W 214592	116.9	W 253639	107.7	AUTRES LEGUMES FRAIS,REF
05451	ALLIACEOUS VEGTBLS,FRESH	W 92761	29.0	W 136731	49.9	W 132168	62.6	W 160957	47.9	OIGNONS,ECHALOTES,AULX
05459	FRESH VEGETABLES NES	W 77436	42.8	W 104704	55.9	W 82423	54.3	W 92682	59.8	LEGUMES FRAIS,REFRI NDA
0546	VEGETABLES SIMPLY PRESVD	W 47347	36.5	W 68859	53.8	W 79043	65.7	W 76518	66.4	LEGUMES CONG,CONSER
05461	VEGETABLES FROZEN	W 47347	36.5	W 68859	53.8	W 78990	65.7	W 76518	66.4	LEGUMES CONGELES
057	FRUIT,NUTS,FRESH,DRIED	W 459096	411.7	W 422231	442.1	W 520162	602.6	W 544646	565.2	FRUITS FRAIS OU SECS
0574	APPLES FRESH	W 237414	194.3	W 209766	194.1	W 313057	314.7	W 310786	252.7	POMMES FRAICHES
0579	FRUIT FRESH OR DRIED NES	W 220877	215.9	W 211666	246.0	W 205843	284.9	W 232959	310.1	FRUITS FRAIS,SECS NDA
05798	OTHER FRESH FRUIT	W 210663	194.5	W 200103	220.5	W 193262	250.4	W 221617	280.3	AUTRES FRUITS FRAIS
058	FRUIT PRESERVED,PREPARED	W 18223	38.7	W 22904	48.9	W 198	0.4	W 45555	66.0	CONSERVES DE FRUITS
06	SUGAR AND PREPS,HONEY		28.9		35.9		41.3		64.4	SUCRES ET PRODUITS
061	SUGAR AND HONEY	W 29695	24.4	W 26909	30.0	W 46469	34.8	W 58166	58.0	SUCRES ET MIEL
081	*FEEDING STUFF FOR ANIML		25.1		31.6		35.8	W 6	0.1	NOURRITURE POUR ANIMAUX
09	MISC EDIBLE PRODUCTS		63.4		92.9		113.8		104.0	PREP ALIMENTAIRES DIVERSES
098	EDIBLE PRODCTS,PREPS NES		60.0		89.2		111.6		101.4	PREP ALIMENTAIRES NDA
09809	MISC FOOD PREPRTIONS NES	W 115	38.6	W 13	58.0		78.3		70.3	PREP ALIMENTAIRES NDA
1	BEVERAGES AND TOBACCO		48.7		60.6		68.2		81.9	BOISSONS ET TABACS
11	BEVERAGES		46.8		57.8		64.4		78.2	BOISSONS
112	ALCOHOLIC BEVERAGES	W 20894	44.8	W 20811	52.3	W 20022	57.7	W 15139	74.4	BOISSONS ALCOOLIQUES
1121	WINE OF FRESH GRAPES ETC	W 8580	24.9	W 8202	26.4	W 8627	32.1	W 12042	45.1	VINS DE RAISINS FRAIS
11212	WINE OF FRESH GRAPES	W 8579	24.9	W 8202	26.4	W 8601	32.0	W 12041	45.1	VINS DE MOUTS DE RAISINS
2	CRUDE MATERLS,EXCL FUELS		1902.8		2283.6		2537.3		2419.3	MAT BRUTES NON COMESTIBLES
21	HIDES,SKINS,FURS UNDRSSD		201.6		267.4		293.9		308.6	CUIRS,PEAUX BRUTS
211	HIDES,SKINS,EXC FURS,RAW		200.1		264.7		293.5	N 14723	0.3	CUIRS ET PEAUX
2111	BOVINE,EQUINE HIDES,RAW	N 833536	32.8	N 864816	39.9	N 905733	48.2	N 874011	40.6	PEAUX DE BOVINS
2117	SHEEP SKIN WITHOUT WOOL		149.7		202.3		217.7		238.6	PEAUX EPILEES D'OVINS
24	CORK AND WOOD		745.5		774.1		790.3		781.4	LIEGE ET BOIS
247	OTH WOOD ROUGH,SQUARED	W 3006395	441.0	W 3386338	427.6	W 3680484	427.7	W 3948048	461.7	BOIS BRUTS EQUARRIS
2471	SAW–,VENEER–LOGS CONIFER	W 3005754	440.8	W 3384469	427.2	W 3675808	427.1	W 3947890	461.6	CONIFERES POUR SCIAGE,PLACAG
24711	— IN THE ROUGH	W 3005754	440.8	W 3384469	427.2	W 3675808	427.1	W 3947890	461.6	ECORCES OU DEGROSSIS
248	WOOD SHAPED,SLEEPERS		282.7		323.5		321.5	W 131	0.2	BOIS SIMPLEMENT TRAVAILLES
2482	LUMBER SHAPED CONIFER		281.0		322.1		320.0	W 34	0.1	CONIFERES SCIES,RABOTES
24821	LUMBER SAWN ETC CONIFER	W 566022	255.6	W 601034	292.7	W 629025	287.4	W 575360	253.6	CONIFERES SCIES LONGITUD
251	*PULP AND WASTE PAPER	W 697590	189.9	W 721318	238.1	W 713834	352.0	W 774082	279.1	PATES A PAPIER,DECHETS
2512	MECHANICAL'WOOD PULP	W 309128	72.7	W 329627	95.2	W 341256	127.2	W 351124	99.5	PATES MECANIQUES DE BOIS
2517	SODA,SULPHATE WOOD PULP	W 342534	113.0	W 321421	135.2	W 299555	210.4	W 328756	168.1	PATES CHIMIQUES AU SULFATE
25171	— UNBLEACHED	W 142913	45.2	W 150932	58.4	W 117872	70.2	W 146226	78.2	PATES ECRUES
25172	— BLEACHED,NONDISSOLVNG	W 199621	67.9	W 170489	76.8	W 181683	140.2	W 182530	89.9	PATES BLANCHIES
26	TEXTILE FIBRES AND WASTE		507.8		712.9		785.9		714.0	FIBRES TEXTILES
268	WOOL(EXC TOPS),ANML HAIR	W 214720	506.7	W 246129	711.6	W 219828	784.4	W 203836	712.5	LAINES ET POILS
2681	WOOL GREASY,FLEECE–WSHED	W 52048	114.4	W 57827	168.6	W 64391	213.8	W 49567	162.1	LAINE EN SUINT
2682	WOOL DEGREASED,UNCOMBED	W 160610	385.0	W 185637	532.5	W 152816	559.8	W 151261	537.7	LAINE DEGRAISSEE
28	METALLIFEROUS ORES,SCRAP		32.9		37.0		40.6		34.7	MINERAIS METAL,DECHETS
29	CRUDE ANIMAL,VEG MAT NES		208.9		235.3		256.7		279.6	MATIERES BRUTES ANIM,VEGET
291	CRUDE ANIMAL MTRIALS NES		145.4		158.7		169.9		194.4	MATIERES BRUTES ANIMALES
2911	BONES,IVORY,HORNS,ETC		0.1		67.4	W 1	0.2		90.7	OS,CORNES,SABOTS
29111	BONE,HORN–CORE AND WASTE		32.9		31.2		38.6		50.5	OS
2919	OTH ANIMAL MATERIALS NES		84.1		91.4		99.8		103.7	MAT ORIGINE ANIMALE NDA
29193	GUT,BLADDERS,ETC NONFISH		70.2		75.5		86.0		86.9	BOYAUX,VESSIES
292	CRUDE VEG MATERIALS NES		63.6		76.6		86.8		85.2	MAT BRUTES VEGETALES NDA
2927	CUT FLOWERS AND FOLIAGE		30.9	N 7375	0.1		44.2	N 11595	0.1	FLEURS,FEUILLAGES COUPES
3	MINERAL FUELS ETC		267.4		244.0		218.0		323.1	COMBUSTIBLES MINERAUX LUB
32	COAL,COKE AND BRIQUETTES		42.6		49.9		63.4		75.8	HOUILLES,COKES,BRIQUETTES
322	COAL,LIGNITE AND PEAT	W 790980	42.6	W 1047235	49.9	W 1337589	63.4	W 1430008	75.8	HOUILLES,LIGNITES,TOURBE
3222	OTH COAL,NOT AGGLOMERATD	W 787644	42.1	W 1043606	49.3	W 1333751	62.8	W 1426258	75.0	AUTRES HOUILLES
33	PETROLEUM AND PRODUCTS		221.1		190.8		151.9		239.1	PETROLE ET DERIVES
333	CRUDE PETROLEUM	W 1072877	162.2	W 1137085	150.8	W 1011386	144.5	W 1312227	224.1	HUILES BRUTES DE PETROLE
334	PETROLEUM PRODUCTS,REFIN		58.0		39.7		5.0		13.8	PRODUITS RAFFINES
4	ANIMAL,VEGETABLE OIL,FAT		65.7		79.7		110.5		104.2	HUILES,GRAISSES ANIM,VEG
411	*ANIMAL OILS AND FATS		38.1		47.6		66.8	W 64	0.1	HUILES,GRAISSES ANIMALES
4113	ANIML OIL,FAT,GREASE NES	W 122175	37.3	W 139515	46.5		65.2	W 142025	58.4	HUILES,GRAISSES ANIMALES NDA
41132	FATS OF BOVINE,SHEEP,ETC	W 120855	36.4	W 137228	45.4	W 134768	63.6	W 138993	56.9	SUIFS BRUTS FONDUS
431	*PROCESD ANML VEG OIL,ET				31.5	W 36	0.1		42.8	HUILES,GRAISSES PREPAREES
5	CHEMCLS,RELATED PROD NES		606.1		920.7		1030.9		1032.3	PRODUITS CHIMIQUES
51	ORGANIC CHEMICALS		90.8		248.1		286.6		226.6	PROD CHIMIQ ORGANIQUES
512	ALCOHOLS,PHENOLS ETC		83.6		241.4		278.7		214.8	PHENOLS,PHENOLS–ALCOOLS
5121	ACYCLIC ALCOHOLS,DERIVS		83.5		241.3		278.7		214.7	ALCOOLS ACYCLIQUES

5. General Exports F.O.B. by Commodities according to the S.I.T.C. (Rev. 2) in million U.S. Dollars
Exportations Générales F.O.B. par Produits d'après la C.T.C.I. (Rév. 2) en millions de Dollars E.U.

SITC CTCI	COMMODITY	1993 QUANTITY QUANTITE	1993 VALUE VALEUR	1994 QUANTITY QUANTITE	1994 VALUE VALEUR	1995 QUANTITY QUANTITE	1995 VALUE VALEUR	1996 QUANTITY QUANTITE	1996 VALUE VALEUR	PRODUIT
51211	METHYL ALCOHOL(METHANOL)	V 972012	80.6	V 1186600	238.1	V 1599246	275.8	V 2315943	211.0	ALCOOLS METHYLIQUES
541	*MEDICINAL,PHARM PRODUCT		42.8		46.6		76.7		74.9	PROD MEDICINAUX PHARMACEUT
55	PERFUME,CLEANING ETC PRD		74.3		98.8		100.1		111.4	PROD POUR PARFUM,TOILETTE
553	PERFUMERY,COSMETICS,ETC		51.5		57.2		49.5		47.8	PRODUITS DE PARFUMERIE
554	SOAP,CLEANSING ETC PREPS		22.1		40.5		49.5		62.1	SAVONS,PRODUITS DETERSIFS
58	PLASTIC MATERIALS ETC		37.7		52.2		68.5		71.3	MAT PLAST ARTIFICIELLES
583	POLYMERIZATION ETC PRODS		26.5		36.7		49.8		55.3	PROD POLYMERISATION
59	CHEMICAL MATERIALS NES		332.1		441.5		457.4		496.9	MAT PROD CHIMIQUES NDA
591	PESTICIDES,DISINFECTANTS		8.4		32.7		43.7		43.7	DESINF,INSECT,FONG,HERB
592	STARCH,INULIN,GLUTEN,ETC		310.7		388.0		397.0		435.2	AMIDONS,INUL,GLUT FROM
5922	ALBUMINOID SUBSTAN,GLUES		310.2		387.7		396.6		434.7	MAT ALBUMIN,COLLES
59221	CASEIN AND DERIVATVS,ETC	W 65691	273.8	W 87559	341.7	W 73093	339.5	W 72482	379.6	CASEINES,CASEINATES
59222	ALBUMINS AND DERIVATIVES	W 6876	28.3	W 8829	35.8	W 11737	47.2	W 9820	45.0	ALBUMINES,ALBUMINATES
6	BASIC MANUFACTURES		1453.5		1684.4		2033.5		2039.2	ART MANUFACTURES
61	LEATHER,DRESSED FUR,ETC		145.6		166.3		199.9		233.9	CUIRS,PELLETERIES
611	LEATHER		119.0		138.2	A 8	0.2		181.3	CUIRS,PEAUX PREPARES
6114	LEATHR BOVINE NES,EQUINE	A 34	75.4	A 151	88.4	A 4	0.2	A 1	0.1	CUIRS DE BOVINS
6115	LEATHER FROM SHEEP,LAMBS		34.5		0.1	A 1	0.1		48.5	PEAUX D'OVINS PREPAREES
613	FUR SKINS TANNED,DRESSED	N 578812	21.5	N 369266	19.2	N 1684709	32.7	N 2016052	44.9	PELLETERIES
62	RUBBER MANUFACTURES NES		39.7		48.0		52.7		52.0	CAOUTCHOUC MANUFACTURE
63	WOOD,CORK MANUFACTRS NES		76.4		115.5		149.8		[illegible]	OUVRAGES LIEGE ET BOIS
634	VENEERS,PLYWOOD,ETC	V 22	0.1		90.5	V 87	0.1		132.5	PLACAGES,CONTRE–PLAQUES
6342	PLYWOOD OF WOOD SHEETS	V 6016	26.9	V 632	53.4	V 130581	69.1		77.4	BOIS CONTRE–PLAQUES
6343	IMPROVED,RECONSTIT WOOD	V 87963	23.7	V 109730	31.7	V 121416	42.0	V 116661	49.6	BOIS AMELIORES,RECONST
63432	RECONSTITUTED WOOD	V 87928	23.7	V 109678	31.7	V 121414	42.0	V 116661	49.6	BOIS RECONSTITUES
64	PAPER,PAPERBOARD AND MFR		329.6		374.8		428.4		443.9	PAPIERS,CARTONS & OUVRAGES
641	PAPER AND PAPERBOARD		295.5		332.2		378.9		401.8	PAPIERS ET CARTONS
6411	NEWSPRINT	W 254631	114.7	W 251604	128.6	W 228400	146.9	W 257328	187.0	PAPIER JOURNAL
6413	KRAFT PAPER,PAPERBOARD	W 82711	32.6	W 62700	29.0	W 50840	33.3	W 77588	35.1	PAPIER ET CARTON KRAFT
6416	FIBRE BUILDING BOARD	V 361007	103.9	V 366925	121.1	V 366724	135.4	V 353967	117.4	PLAQUES CONSTRUCT EN PATE
64162	INSULATING BOARD, ETC	V 358289	102.5	V 363175	119.2	V 363558	133.7	V 351289	116.0	PLAQUES CONST NON COMPR
642	PAPER,ETC,PRECUT,ARTS OF		34.1		42.7		49.6		42.1	PAP,CARTONS DECOUPES
65	TEXTILE YARN,FABRICS,ETC		129.4		146.8		160.8		164.1	FILS,TISSUS,ARTICLES TEXTILE
651	TEXTILE YARN		37.6		42.8		45.0		45.8	FILS TEXTILES
6512	WOOL,HAIR YARN,INCL TOPS	W 5768	36.0	W 5822	39.4	W 5635	41.4	W 5838	43.8	FILS DE LAINE,DE POILS
659	FLOOR COVERINGS,ETC		37.6		48.6		53.0		56.0	COUVRE–PARQUETS,TAPIS ETC
6594	WOOL CARPETS ETC NES		34.6		45.4		48.6	A 2590	51.3	TAPIS DE LAINE
66	NONMETAL MINERAL MFS NES		41.0		44.0		48.9		42.4	ART MIN NON METALLIQUES
67	IRON AND STEEL		173.5		171.6		205.9		190.5	FER ET ACIER
672	IRON,STEEL PRIMARY FORMS	W 232792	70.1	W 251487	75.7	W 220832	81.0	W 247904	73.8	LINGOTS FER,ACIER
6727	IRN,STL COIL FR REROLLNG	W 226508	68.9	W 251415	75.6	W 220717	80.9	W 239706	71.1	EBAUCHES POUR TOLES FER
67271	IRON,SIMPLE STEEL COILS	W 226435	68.9	W 251002	75.4	W 220589	80.7	W 239682	71.1	EBAUCHES NON EN ACIER
674	IRN,STL UNIV,PLATE,SHEET	W 120299	62.5	W 104970	53.3	W 146695	80.6	W 153773	87.0	LARGES PLATS,TOLES
6749	OTH IRN,STL PLATES,SHEET	W 78537	46.2	W 44470	29.9	W 56548	39.9	W 76635	55.1	AUTRES TOLES FER,ACIER
67491	— OF IRON OR SIMPLE STL	W 78481	46.0	W 44435	29.8	W 56490	39.8	W 76535	54.9	AUT TOLES AUTRES ACIER FIN
68	NON–FERROUS METALS		386.5		453.4		603.4		551.3	METAUX NON FERREUX
682	COPPER EXC CEMENT COPPER		42.4	W 15534	53.9	W 14294	59.7		57.0	CUIVRE
6822	COPPER,ALLOYS WORKED		41.3	W 15046	53.1	W 14204	59.5		56.9	CUIVRE,ALLIAGES OUVRES
684	ALUMINIUM	W 262944	341.4	W 254483	395.3	W 265367	536.0	W 279362	484.1	ALUMINIUM
6841	ALUMINIUM,ALLOYS,UNWRGHT	W 243257	287.0	W 232281	327.5	W 246230	470.6	W 258179	407.1	ALUMINIUM,ALLIAGES BRUTS
6842	ALUMINIUM,ALLOYS WORKED	W 19687	54.4	W 22202	67.9	W 19138	65.5	W 21183	77.1	ALUMINIUM,ALLIAGES OUVRE
68421	ALUMINIUM BARS,WIRE,ETC	W 10736	26.4	W 11759	33.3	W 9594	30.6	W 13308	44.4	BARRES,PROFILES FILS ALU
69	METAL MANUFACTURES NES		132.4		164.3		184.2		192.1	ART MANUFACT EN METAL NDA
699	BASE METAL MFRS NES		43.6		55.1		61.6		68.7	ART MANUFACTURES MET NDA
7	MACHINES,TRANSPORT EQUIP		785.5		1001.6		1175.7		1173.9	MACHINES MATERIEL TRANSPORT
71	POWER GENERATING EQUIPMT		22.8		38.7		28.1		46.0	MACHINES GENERATRICES
72	MACHS FOR SPCL INDUSTRYS		104.2		117.0		140.1		152.1	MAC SPECIALES POUR INDUST
721	AGRIC MACHY,EXC TRACTORS		40.4		45.1		56.8		55.4	MACHINES AGRICOLES
728	OTH MACHY FOR SPCL INDUS		23.1		34.5		39.5		48.9	AUT MACH IND PARTICULIERES
74	GENRL INDUSTRL MACHY NES		137.9		191.2		204.1		234.0	MACH APP INDUSTRIE
741	HEATING,COOLING EQUIPMNT		42.4		71.5		76.9		93.0	MACH CHAUFFAGE,PIECES
75	OFFICE MACHNES,ADP EQUIP		48.9		54.2		72.0		73.6	MACH BUREAU TRAIT AUTOM
759	OFFICE,ADP MCH PTS,ACCES		24.9		25.9		41.3		41.3	PIECES DU 751 ET 752
76	TELECOMM,SOUND EQUIPMENT		64.6		88.9		111.8		104.4	EQUIPMENT DE TELECOM
764	TELECOM EQPT,PTS,ACC NES		60.7		85.3		107.5		99.5	EQUIP TELECOM,PIECES
7643	TV,RADIO TRANSMITTRS ETC		24.2		41.7		54.3		53.9	APP EMET TELE RADIO
77	ELECTRIC MACHNRY NES ETC		206.6		291.3		324.4		357.4	MACH APP ELECT NDA
772	SWITCHGEAR ETC,PARTS NES	N 887074	34.2	N 3478574	54.0		62.0		77.8	APP COUPURE,SECT ETC
7721	SWITCHGEAR ETC	N 1186	31.2	N 49382	48.8		53.8		69.7	APP COUPURE,SECTIONMNT
773	ELECTR DISTRIBUTNG EQUIP		33.2		38.9		41.5		26.2	EQUIPMT DISTRIBUTION ELECT
775	HOUSEHOLD TYPE EQUIP NES		90.6		126.8		127.4		145.1	MACH,APP USAGE DOMESTQUE
7751	HOUSEHOLD LDRY EQUIP NES	N 88500	24.7	N 141989	43.0	N 147881	48.0	N 174567	59.0	MACH A LAVER ET SECHOIRS
77511	DOMESTIC WASHING MACHNES	N 55353	19.6	N 101657	36.6	N 104030	40.5	N 119993	49.1	MACH LAVER LINGE MOINS 6 KG
7752	DOM REFRIGERATRS,FREEZRS	N 109133	31.7	N 133504	41.5	N 118059	36.7	N 123207	38.1	REFRIG,CONGEL MENAGER
778	ELECTRICAL MACHINERY NES		36.3		44.2		54.6		59.5	AUTRES MACH ELECT NDA
78	ROAD VEHICLES		63.2		69.2		63.2		66.1	VEHICULES ROUTIERS
784	MOTOR VEH PRTS,ACCES NES	N 91	40.4	N 3448	2.1		41.9	N 1154331	40.9	PIECES 722,781,782,783
7849	OTHER MOTOR VEHCL PARTS	N 14	40.1	N 3424	1.8		41.6	N 1154266	40.4	PIECES 722,781,782,783
79	OTHR TRANSPORT EQUIPMENT		124.3		139.0		207.2		126.5	AUTRE MATERIEL TRANSPORT
792	AIRCRAFT ETC		97.2		50.5		146.5		82.8	APP NAVIGATION AERIENNE
7924	AIRCRFT NES OVER 15000KG	N 5	65.9	N 3	17.9	N 7	104.9	N 10	39.1	AERODYNES PLUS 15000 KG
793	SHIPS AND BOATS ETC		27.0		88.3		60.4		43.7	NAVIRES BATEAUX,ETC
7932	SHIPS AND BOATS NES	N 3638	23.4	N 3400	33.5	N 4479	48.0	N 5277	20.8	NAVIRES ET BATEAUX
7938	TUGS,SPECIAL VESSELS ETC	N 793	1.4	N 1639	51.0	N 1062	2.7	N 2202	4.6	REMORQUEURS,BATEAUX SPEC
79382	SPECL PURPOSE VESSLS ETC	N 5	0.7	N 2	46.9	N 1	0.7	N 4	0.1	BAT–PHARES,–POMPES,DRAGUES
8	MISC MANUFACTURED GOODS		459.8		539.0		563.0		538.9	ART MANUFACTURES DIVERS
821	*FURNITURE,PARTS THEREOF		42.4		52.8		47.5		45.3	MEUBLES ET PIECES
8219	FURNITURE AND PARTS NES		30.7		38.9		32.0		29.6	AUTRES MEUBLES ET PIECES
84	CLOTHING AND ACCESSORIES		107.6		124.2		141.1		124.3	VETEMENTS
848	HEADGEAR,NONTXTL CLOTHNG		29.5		42.3		37.2		27.6	VET ACCES MAT AUT QUE TEX
87	PRECISION INSTRUMNTS NES		83.3		110.0		105.6		83.7	INSTRUM,APPAR SCIENT NDA
874	MEASURNG,CONTROLNG INSTR		40.0		62.2		63.7		44.1	INSTRUMENTS DE MESURE
89	MISC MANUFCTRD GOODS NES		193.7		212.6		225.7		238.8	ART MANUFACTURES DIVERS
893	ARTICLES OF PLASTIC NES		89.8		101.3		111.5		112.4	OUVRAGES EN MAT DIVIS 58
8931	PLSTC PACKG CONTNRS,LIDS	N 42000	29.6	N 365200	37.3		35.6		37.1	ART TRANSP EMBALLAGE ETC
8939	MISC PLASTIC ARTICLES		52.0		52.9		65.8		65.8	ART DIVERS EN MAT DIV 58
89399	OTHR PLASTC ARTICLES NES	W 1	50.9		51.8		64.8		64.4	AUT OUV MAT DIV 58
897	GOLD,SILVER WARE,JEWELRY		39.0		32.1		21.7		25.7	BIJOUTERIE,ORFEVRERIE
8973	PREC JEWLRY,GLD–SILVWARE		37.0		29.8		19.4		23.7	BIJOUX OR,ARGENT ORFEVRE
89731	PRECIOUS METAL JEWELLERY		36.0		27.5		18.2		22.5	ART BIJOUTERIE,JOAILLER
9	GOODS NOT CLASSD BY KIND		276.9		289.9		363.0		378.5	ART TRANSACT NON CLASSES

5. General Exports F.O.B. by Commodities according to the S.I.T.C. (Rev. 2) in million U.S. Dollars
Exportations Générales F.O.B. par Produits d'après la C.T.C.I. (Rév. 2) en millions de Dollars E.U.

SITC CTCI	COMMODITY	1993 QUANTITY QUANTITE	1993 VALUE VALEUR	1994 QUANTITY QUANTITE	1994 VALUE VALEUR	1995 QUANTITY QUANTITE	1995 VALUE VALEUR	1996 QUANTITY QUANTITE	1996 VALUE VALEUR	PRODUIT
931	*SPECIAL TRANSACTIONS		146.9		141.7		168.0		197.5	TRANS.SPECIALES
971	*GOLD,NON MONETARY NES	K 26324	127.6	K 39671	144.9	K 11	0.1	K 8	0.1	OR NON MONETAIRE
97101	NONMON GLD UNWRT,SEMIMFD	K 26328	127.6	K 39682	145.0	K 40091	192.3	K 40897	177.2	OR,ALLIAGES D'OR BRUTS

1. HISTORICAL SERIES, 1962–1997 SPECIAL TRADE, IMPORTS C.I.F., EXPORTS F.O.B.
SERIES HISTORIQUES, 1962–1997 COMMERCE SPECIAL, IMPORTATIONS C.A.F., EXPORTATIONS F.O.B

YEAR ANNEE	VALUE IN MILLION U.S. DOLLARS VALEUR EN MILLION U.S. DOLLARS MERCHANDISE –MARCHANDISE IMPORTS	EXPORTS	GOLD –OR IMPORTS	EXPORTS	CONVERSION FACTORS FACTEURS DE CONVERSION CENTS E.U. PAR IMPORTS	EXPORTS	INDEX NUMBERS –INDICES QUANTUM IMPORTS	EXPORTS	UNIT VALUE VALEUR UNITAIRE IMPORTS	EXPORTS
1962	98.20	90.20	0.70	7.71						
1963	110.80	106.80		7.09						
1964	137.00	125.20	1.21	6.88						
1965	160.30	149.00		5.41						
1966	181.90	142.20		5.18						
1967	203.90	151.70	1.54	5.21						
1968	184.70	162.30	1.35	5.02						
1969	176.99	158.75	1.40	4.10						
1970	198.75	178.62	0.89	3.80						
1971	210.44	187.24		3.80						
1972	218.49	249.44	0.53	3.10						
1973	326.98	277.88	0.63	3.20						
1974	561.68	380.92								
1975	516.86	375.17								
1976	532.14	541.90								
1977	761.93	636.80								
1978	593.93	645.97								
1979	360.20	566.55								
1980	887.21	450.44								
1981	999.44	499.83								
1982	775.55	405.45								
1983	806.91	431.29								
1984	826.24	384.80								
1985	964.30	301.50								
1986	856.80	247.20								
1987	826.80	272.80								
1988	805.20	232.70								
1989	614.90	310.70								
1990	637.50	330.60								
1991	751.40	272.40								
1992	855.10	223.10								
1993	744.00	267.00								
1994	874.70	351.70								
1995	961.70	526.30								
1996	1160.20	670.60								
1997	1211.30	628.90								

2. IMPORTS BY BROAD ECONOMIC CATEGORY AND EXPORTS BY INDUSTRIAL ORIGIN. (PERCENTAGE OF TOTAL VALUE)
IMPORTATIONS PAR CATEGORIES ECONOMIQUES ET EXPORTATIONS PAR BRANCHE D'ACTIVITE.(EN POURCENTAGE DE LA VALEUR TOTALE)

IMPORTS – IMPORTATIONS

	1991	1992	1993	1994	1995	1996	1997
TOTAL IMPORTS–IMPORTATIONS TOTALES	100.	100.	100.	100.	100.	100.	100.
1 FOOD BEV–ALIMENTATION BOISSONS	20.8	20.8	19.3	17.1	16.6	16.1	12.7
11 PRIMARY–PRODUITS DE BASE	7.1	4.8	6.7	5.0	3.9	4.8	2.8
111 FOR INDUSTRY–POUR L'INDUSTRIE	3.4	1.7	3.9	3.2	2.2	3.2	1.4
112 FOR HOUSEHOLDS–POUR LES MENAGES	3.7	3.1	2.7	1.8	1.7	1.5	1.4
12 PROCESSED–PRODUITS ELABORES	13.7	16.0	12.7	12.1	12.7	11.4	9.9
121 FOR INDUSTRY–POUR L'INDUSTRIE	2.5	5.1	3.8	3.7	3.3	3.4	2.9
122 FOR HOUSEHOLDS–POUR LES MENAGES	11.1	10.9	8.9	8.5	9.4	8.0	7.1
2 IND SUPPLIES–APPROV INDUSTRIELS	27.4	22.1	24.3	27.9	27.0	30.3	32.5
21 PRIMARY–PRODUITS DE BASE	1.5	1.8	1.3	2.0	1.6	1.9	1.5
22 PROCESSED–PRODUITS ELABORES	25.9	20.3	23.1	25.9	25.4	28.4	31.0
3 FUELS–COMBUSTIBLES	4.5	14.9	13.9	12.7	17.9	9.0	12.1
31 PRIMARY–PRODUITS DE BASE	4.0	12.2	11.7	10.3	13.9	4.5	8.4
32 PROCESSED–PRODUITS ELABORES	0.5	2.7	2.2	2.5	4.0	4.5	3.7
321 MOTOR SPIRIT–ESSENCE	0.0	0.3	0.2	0.3	0.6	0.3	0.4
322 OTHER–AUTRES	0.5	2.4	2.0	2.1	3.4	4.2	3.3
4 MACHINERY–EQUIPEMENT	16.6	16.4	15.8	17.4	14.8	16.4	16.1
41 CAPITAL EQUIPMENT–MACHINES	15.2	15.2	14.4	16.1	13.2	14.6	14.5
42 PARTS–PIECES ACCESSOIRES	1.5	1.2	1.4	1.3	1.6	1.8	1.6
5 TRANSPORT–TRANSPORT	15.0	10.8	11.0	9.3	9.2	11.6	12.5
51 PASSENGER CARS–AUTOMOBILES	9.9	7.3	3.0	2.0	2.9	3.7	4.0
52 OTHER–AUTRES	1.3	0.8	5.4	4.5	3.2	4.5	4.8
521 INDUSTRIAL–INDUSTRIELS	0.5	0.2	4.9	4.1	3.0	4.3	4.6
522 NON INDUSTRIAL–NON INDUSTRIEL	0.8	0.6	0.4	0.4	0.2	0.2	0.3
53 PARTS–PIECES ACCESSOIRES	3.8	2.7	2.7	2.8	3.1	3.4	3.7
6 CONSUM GOODS–BIENS CONSOMMATION	15.7	14.7	15.4	15.3	14.3	16.4	13.6
61 DURABLE–DURABLES	2.6	1.8	1.8	1.7	2.0	2.2	2.0
62 SEMI DURABLE–SEMI DURABLES	4.7	4.4	4.9	5.0	4.5	4.6	3.6
63 NON DURABLE–NON DURABLES	8.4	8.5	8.7	8.6	7.7	9.5	8.0
7 GOODS NES–BIENS NDA	0.0	0.4	0.2	0.2	0.2	0.3	0.5

EXPORTS – EXPORTATIONS

	1991	1992	1993	1994	1995	1996	1997
TOTAL EXPORTS–EXPORTATIONS TOTALES	100.	100.	100.	100.	100.	100.	100.
1 AGRICULTURE	54.4	54.0	43.3	55.9	53.1	44.1	44.8
2 MINING QUARRY–INDUS EXTRACTIVES	0.3	0.3	0.1	0.0	0.1	0.0	0.0
3 MANUFACTURING–IND MANUFACTUR	45.3	45.7	56.6	44.1	46.8	55.8	55.2
31 FOOD BEV TOBACCO–ALIM BOISS TAB	33.2	35.8	37.8	27.6	22.5	17.9	25.6
32 TEXTILES–INDUSTRIES TEXTILES	1.3	1.2	1.7	1.7	1.5	1.3	1.6
33 WOOD & PRODUCTS–BOIS & PRODUITS	0.9	0.6	0.8	1.5	2.3	2.9	3.2
34 PAPER & PRODUCTS–PAPIER & PRODT	0.1	0.1	0.1	0.2	0.1	0.0	0.0
35 CHEMICALS–INDUSTRIES CHIMIQUES	4.3	4.0	3.0	2.5	2.0	1.7	2.5
36 NON METAL MIN–MIN NON METAL	0.3	0.6	1.5	0.9	0.9	0.7	0.6
37 BASIC METAL–IND METAL BASE	3.1	2.1	5.3	0.8	0.4	0.3	0.5
38 METAL MANUF–MANUF METAL	2.1	1.1	2.6	3.3	9.7	17.4	13.4
39 OTH MANUF IND–AUTRES MANUF	0.0	0.0	3.9	5.4	7.4	13.6	7.7

Nicaragua

3. TRADE BY PRINCIPAL COUNTRIES OF ORIGIN AND DESTINATION (VALUE IN MILLION U.S. DOLLARS)
ECHANGES SELON LES PRINCIPAUX PAYS D'ORIGINE ET DE DESTINATION (VALEUR EN MILLIONS DE DOLLARS EU)

COUNTRIES–PAYS	SPECIAL IMPORTS C.I.F. IMPORTATIONS SPECIALES C.A.F				
	1993	1994	1995	1996	1997
World	755.1	852.5	1009.2	1076.2	1469.7
Africa	1.4	0.9	1.1	2.4	0.7
Americas	576.9	599.9	794.2	828.6	1213.8
– Northern America	207.3	227.8	318.4	387.9	571.2
– LAIA	141.5	145.7	184.0	105.4	195.4
– CACM	197.4	190.2	228.3	260.0	331.5
– Caribbean	3.6	2.7	6.5	8.8	17.7
– Rest of America	27.2	33.5	57.0	66.5	98.0
Asia excl fmr USSR	92.2	105.0	91.1	120.2	110.2
– Middle East	0.0	0.0	0.1	0.1	0.3
Asia former USSR					
Europe excl fmr USSR	75.5	122.1	111.8	118.2	132.7
– European Union	65.1	100.4	101.6	111.1	124.5
– Eastern Europe	2.7	4.0	2.9	0.8	0.4
– Rest of Europe	7.7	17.7	7.3	6.3	7.8
Europe former USSR	5.2	21.2	7.0	2.8	6.2
Oceania	3.6	3.2	4.1	4.0	3.1
Other	0.2	0.3			3.1
USA/Etats–Unis d'Amer	200.7	214.7	304.4	365.3	549.2
Costa Rica	77.8	68.2	82.2	90.6	120.1
Guatemala	66.8	69.3	79.7	90.4	97.5
Venezuela	93.6	101.7	130.8	19.5	48.9
Japan/Japon	60.5	61.0	50.5	82.8	71.2
Panama	27.2	33.5	57.0	66.2	97.9
Mexico/Mexique	28.7	27.0	31.6	55.0	83.1
El Salvador	34.8	34.4	40.5	46.6	59.8
Honduras	18.0	18.3	25.9	32.4	54.0
Spain/Espagne	7.2	19.0	23.8	30.3	63.8
Germany/Allemagne	19.2	23.4	22.7	25.1	21.9
Other Asia n.e.s.	16.0	19.6	21.0	17.1	8.7
Canada	6.5	13.1	14.0	22.7	22.0
France, Monaco	7.8	11.7	10.7	14.3	10.8
Colombia/Colombie	5.5	8.8	6.4	12.8	17.9
Belgium–Luxembourg	6.5	16.6	5.7	9.5	7.4
Argentina/Argentine	6.8	1.5	1.6	3.8	29.1
Russian Federation	5.2	21.2	7.0	2.8	5.2
Italy/Italie	7.2	8.3	8.2	10.7	6.7
Korea, Republic of	3.0	4.7	9.7	8.5	10.9
Brazil/Brésil	6.0	4.9	5.4	8.7	5.8
Switzerland,Liechtenst.	3.7	6.4	5.4	4.5	7.7
Netherlands/Pays–Bas	4.1	5.4	6.7	6.3	4.1
Denmark/Danemark	1.3	5.5	11.5	2.8	3.2
United Kingdom	3.9	2.2	5.0	5.8	3.7
Viet Nam	4.0	14.5			0.1
Trinidad and Tobago	0.0	0.5	1.9	3.0	11.6
New Zealand	3.5	3.1	4.0	3.3	2.6
Korea Dem People's Rp	4.8	1.2	0.2	2.0	6.4
Sweden/Suède	2.3	3.0	2.7	3.9	1.7
Ecuador/Equateur	0.2	0.4	7.1	3.3	0.5
Other Europe n.e.s.		10.4	0.1	0.4	
Chile/Chili	0.5	0.9	0.7	1.4	6.9
Israel/Israël	0.7	0.8	1.5	2.2	3.9
China/Chine	0.1	0.9	1.6	2.4	4.1
Cuba	2.9	1.4	1.0	1.9	1.1
Finland/Finlande	4.6	0.6	2.7	0.2	0.1
Norway,Svalbard and JM	3.8	0.7	1.7	1.4	0.0
Netherlands Antilles	0.2	0.5	3.3	1.1	2.2
China, Hong Kong SAR	0.5	0.5	4.3	1.2	0.5

COUNTRIES–PAYS	SPECIAL EXPORTS F.O.B. EXPORTATIONS SPECIALES F.O.B.				
	1993	1994	1995	1996	1997
Monde	267.5	351.1	509.2	660.2	666.6
Afrique	0.0	0.2	0.1	0.2	5.6
Amériques	219.0	258.7	329.7	434.9	460.4
– Amérique du Nord	145.6	153.0	219.5	300.9	308.2
– ALAI	11.3	13.3	17.6	16.5	17.9
– MCAC	57.1	83.9	83.0	101.2	121.3
– Caraïbes	1.3	4.0	7.4	11.7	10.8
– Autre Amérique	3.6	4.6	2.1	4.6	2.3
Asie anc. URSS exclus	1.8	2.1	13.0	7.8	5.5
– Moyen–Orient	0.1		0.0	4.0	0.1
Asie ancienne URSS					
Europe anc. URSS exclus	45.6	88.5	166.0	216.9	186.7
– Union Européenne	44.3	85.2	161.9	211.2	181.7
– Europe de l'Est	0.6	0.2	0.0	3.9	0.6
– Autre de l'Europe	0.7	3.1	4.1	1.9	4.4
Europe ancienne URSS	1.0	1.6	0.3	0.2	5.2
Océanie	0.2	0.1	0.0	0.2	0.6
Autre			0.0		2.5
USA/Etats–Unis d'Amer	117.2	150.3	214.4	296.3	305.4
Germany/Allemagne	24.3	44.1	58.0	61.1	60.5
El Salvador	15.3	37.1	41.3	58.1	56.7
Spain/Espagne	2.4	13.6	39.5	73.3	60.0
Costa Rica	22.9	25.5	17.3	13.3	22.8
Honduras	11.5	12.6	14.0	19.6	28.5
Belgium–Luxembourg	4.7	9.7	17.5	16.8	15.1
United Kingdom	1.4	5.0	9.9	24.4	20.5
Mexico/Mexique	10.2	11.0	8.9	11.3	12.6
Guatemala	7.4	8.7	10.4	10.2	13.3
Netherlands/Pays–Bas	5.5	3.2	16.8	16.3	6.9
Canada	28.4	2.7	5.1	4.6	2.8
France, Monaco	1.4	4.4	10.0	9.1	8.4
Italy/Italie	3.6	3.7	8.0	4.5	5.0
Dominican Republic	0.7	1.8	3.1	5.8	6.3
Panama	3.5	4.5	2.1	4.5	2.2
Japan/Japon	1.3	1.3	7.0	0.9	4.7
Switzerland,Liechtenst.	0.5	1.7	3.2	1.5	4.3
Russian Federation	1.0	1.6	0.3	0.2	5.2
Colombia/Colombie	1.0	1.0	1.9	2.2	1.9
Cuba	0.4	0.9	2.9	2.6	0.8
Finland/Finlande	0.1	0.4	1.2	1.9	3.2
Venezuela		0.6	2.4	2.7	0.1
Haiti/Haïti		0.2	0.5	2.1	2.3
Morocco/Maroc			0.1		5.0
Chile/Chili	0.1	0.0	1.6	0.0	3.2
Denmark/Danemark	0.3	0.2	0.7	2.0	0.8
Jordan/Jordanie				3.9	
Bulgaria/Bulgarie				3.7	0.0
Other Asia n.e.s.	0.0	0.0	1.3	2.0	0.3
Jamaica/Jamaïque	0.1	0.8	0.8	1.0	0.4
Korea, Republic of			2.9	0.1	0.0
China, Hong Kong SAR	0.1	0.7	1.6	0.6	0.0
Norway,Svalbard and JM	0.2	1.4	0.9	0.1	0.1
Areas n.e.s.			0.0		2.5
Austria/Autriche	0.4	0.5	0.3	0.6	0.8
Sweden/Suède	0.1	0.3	0.0	1.0	0.4
Peru/Pérou	0.0	0.5	1.0	0.1	0.0
Ecuador/Equateur	0.0	0.0	1.3	0.0	0.1
Poland/Pologne	0.4	0.2			0.6

(VALUE AS PERCENTAGE OF WORLD TOTAL)(VALEURS EN POURCENTAGE DU TOTAL MONDIAL)

	1988	1989	1990	1991	1992	1993	1994	1995	1996	1997
Africa	0.0	0.0	0.6	0.0	0.0	0.2	0.1	0.1	0.2	0.0
Americas	29.2	35.3	53.5	67.5	76.4	76.4	70.4	78.7	77.0	82.6
– Northern America	6.5	6.3	14.9	28.9	26.6	27.5	26.7	31.5	36.0	38.9
– LAIA	9.4	13.9	21.3	8.7	19.9	18.7	17.1	18.2	9.8	13.3
– CACM	4.9	7.1	10.8	23.5	25.1	26.1	22.3	22.6	24.2	22.6
– Caribbean	3.8	1.4	1.2	0.8	0.4	0.5	0.3	0.6	0.8	1.2
– Rest of America	4.5	6.5	5.3	5.6	4.4	3.6	3.9	5.7	6.2	6.7
Asia excl fmr USSR	7.9	8.0	14.6	12.8	10.9	12.2	12.3	9.0	11.2	7.5
– Middle East	0.3	0.3		0.0	0.0	0.0	0.0	0.0	0.0	0.0
Asia former USSR										
Europe excl fmr USSR	33.1	31.1	21.1	16.2	10.9	10.0	14.3	11.1	11.0	9.0
– European Union	22.1	21.2	14.9	14.2	9.6	8.6	11.8	10.1	10.3	8.5
– Eastern Europe	7.4	6.7	5.0	0.6	0.4	0.4	0.5	0.3	0.1	0.0
– Rest of Europe	3.6	3.1	1.2	1.4	0.9	1.0	2.1	0.7	0.6	0.5
Europe former USSR	29.8	25.4	10.1	3.4	1.5	0.7	2.5	0.7	0.3	0.4
Oceania	0.0	0.0	0.0	0.0	0.3	0.5	0.4	0.4	0.4	0.2
Other		0.2	0.0		0.1	0.0	0.0			0.2
USA/Etats–Unis d'Amer	2.6	3.7	12.2	25.6	25.6	26.6	25.2	30.2	33.9	37.4
Costa Rica	1.7	3.0	4.0	9.8	9.9	10.3	8.0	8.1	8.4	8.2
Guatemala	2.2	2.7	4.6	8.6	7.6	8.9	8.1	7.9	8.4	6.6
Venezuela	0.1	0.2	9.8	1.8	13.7	12.4	11.9	13.0	1.8	3.3
Japan/Japon	3.4	5.1	7.1	6.6	6.0	8.0	7.2	5.0	7.7	4.8
Panama	4.5	6.4	5.3	5.6	4.4	3.6	3.9	5.6	6.2	6.7
Mexico/Mexique	1.8	2.1	2.6	2.1	3.1	3.8	3.2	3.1	5.1	5.7
El Salvador	0.9	0.9	1.7	3.8	5.5	4.6	4.0	4.0	4.3	4.1
Honduras	0.2	0.4	0.6	1.3	2.1	2.4	2.1	2.6	3.0	3.7
Spain/Espagne	4.0	2.4	1.2	0.5	0.7	0.9	2.2	2.4	2.8	4.3

	1988	1989	1990	1991	1992	1993	1994	1995	1996	1997
Afrique			0.0	0.0	0.0	0.0	0.0	0.0	0.0	0.8
Amériques	32.5	51.2	51.7	58.6	63.0	81.9	73.7	64.7	65.9	69.1
– Amérique du Nord	17.1	22.3	27.6	31.2	32.8	54.4	43.6	43.1	45.6	46.2
– ALAI	0.2	1.8	7.6	5.4	9.7	4.2	3.8	3.5	2.5	2.7
– MCAC	8.5	19.0	13.8	19.3	17.6	21.3	23.9	16.3	15.3	18.2
– Caraïbes	4.5	5.4	2.4	1.5	1.9	0.5	1.1	1.5	1.8	1.6
– Autre Amérique	2.1	2.7	0.3	1.2	1.0	1.3	1.3	0.4	0.7	0.3
Asie anc. URSS exclus	17.1	8.1	8.7	14.2	10.5	0.7	0.6	2.6	1.2	0.8
– Moyen–Orient					0.0	0.0		0.0	0.6	0.0
Asie ancienne URSS										
Europe anc. URSS exclus	49.1	36.8	34.8	27.1	26.2	17.0	25.2	32.6	32.9	28.0
– Union Européenne	42.5	33.5	33.3	26.2	25.7	16.6	24.3	31.8	32.0	27.3
– Europe de l'Est	6.6	3.2	0.4	0.2	0.1	0.2	0.1	0.0	0.6	0.1
– Autre de l'Europe		0.0	1.1	0.7	0.5	0.3	0.9	0.8	0.3	0.7
Europe ancienne URSS	1.3	4.0	3.5	0.0	0.1	0.4	0.5	0.1	0.0	0.8
Océanie				0.1	0.1	0.1	0.0	0.0	0.0	0.1
Autre			1.3	0.1	0.1			0.0		0.4
USA/Etats–Unis d'Amer	0.0	0.1	6.6	20.0	26.0	43.8	42.8	42.1	44.9	45.8
Germany/Allemagne				11.4	11.0	9.1	12.6	11.4	9.2	9.1
El Salvador	1.3	4.2	2.8	7.2	5.8	5.7	10.6	8.1	8.8	8.5
Spain/Espagne	4.9	3.1	3.6	1.0	2.1	0.9	3.9	7.8	11.1	9.0
Costa Rica	4.0	6.6	4.6	4.5	7.3	8.6	7.3	3.4	2.0	3.4
Honduras	0.8	3.9	2.6	3.3	2.3	4.3	3.6	2.8	3.0	4.3
Belgium–Luxembourg	10.6	10.4	11.2	11.3	9.0	1.8	2.8	3.4	2.5	2.3
United Kingdom	0.2	0.6	1.1	0.3	0.1	0.5	1.4	1.9	3.7	3.1
Mexico/Mexique	0.1	1.7	6.1	4.9	5.8	3.8	3.1	1.8	1.7	1.9
Guatemala	2.5	4.3	3.8	4.3	2.2	2.8	2.5	2.0	1.5	2.0

4. Special Imports C.I.F. by Commodities according to the S.I.T.C. (Rev. 2) in million U.S. Dollars
Importations Spéciales C.A.F. par Produits d'après la C.T.C.I. (Rév. 2) en millions de Dollars E.U.

SITC CTCI	COMMODITY	1994 QUANTITY QUANTITE	1994 VALUE VALEUR	1995 QUANTITY QUANTITE	1995 VALUE VALEUR	1996 QUANTITY QUANTITE	1996 VALUE VALEUR	1997 QUANTITY QUANTITE	1997 VALUE VALEUR	PRODUIT
	ALL COMMODITIES		852.5		1009.3		1076.2		1469.8	TOUS PRODUITS
0	FOOD AND LIVE ANIMALS		122.5		138.8		152.4		158.7	ALIMENTS,ANIMAUX VIVANTS
02	DAIRY PRODCTS,BIRDS'EGGS		15.4		18.9		11.5		16.7	PRODUITS LAITIERS,OEUFS
022	MILK AND CREAM	W 5715	11.3	W 6106	13.9	W 2602	5.9	W 3797	8.2	LAIT ET CREME
0224	MILK,CREAM PRESERVED ETC	W 5576	11.2	W 6053	13.8	W 2557	5.8	W 3694	8.2	LAIT,CREME CONS,CONC
02242	MILK DRY,1.5% FAT OR LES	W 2251	4.3	W 1351	3.3	W 867	2.2	W 1463	3.2	LAIT POUDRE INF 1.5%
02243	MILK DRY,OVER 1.5% FAT	W 3016	6.6	W 4413	10.3	W 1162	3.1	W 1581	4.4	LAIT POUDRE SUP 1.5%
025	EGGS,BIRDS,FRESH,PRSRVD	W 1114	3.2	W 1244	3.6	W 1137	3.5	W 1546	5.6	OEUFS
0251	— IN SHELL	W 1106	3.1	W 1242	3.6	W 1130	3.4	W 1538	5.6	OEUFS EN COQUILLE
04	CEREALS AND PREPARATIONS		58.4		61.0		84.9		74.0	CEREALES ET PRODUITS
041	WHEAT ETC UNMILLED	W 91900	14.9	W 89369	17.7	W 103338	26.4	W 65093	14.6	FROMENT,EPEAUTRE
0411	DURUM WHEAT UNMILLED	W 36385	5.9	W 89369	17.7	W 49828	13.3	W 61329	13.9	FROMENT DUR NON MOULU
0412	OTHER WHEAT ETC UNMILLED	W 55515	9.0			W 53510	13.1	W 3764	0.7	AUTRE FROMENT NON MOULU
042	RICE	W 46648	24.2	W 53299	21.9	W 70014	32.5	W 85201	34.4	RIZ
0421	RICE IN HUSK OR HUSKED	W 13047	8.3	W 4659	1.7	W 12129	3.8	W 11431	3.6	RIZ SANS AUTRE PREPARATION
04211	RICE IN THE HUSK	W 4571	2.0	W 1156	0.4	W 12066	3.8	W 11431	3.6	RIZ PADDY
04212	RICE HUSKED	W 8476	6.3	W 3503	1.3	W 63	0.1			RIZ CARGO
0422	RICE SEMI-MILLED,MILLED	W 33601	15.9	W 48639	20.2	W 57885	28.7	W 73770	30.9	RIZ POLI,GLACE INCL BRISURES
04221	RICE MILLED UNBROKEN	W 32713	15.7	W 44120	19.1	W 54391	28.1	W 66231	29.2	RIZ POLI,GLACE EXCL BRISURES
044	MAIZE UNMILLED	W 35411	5.0	W 32381	3.2	W 18865	4.0	W 16265	2.9	MAIS NON MOULU
047	OTHER CEREAL MEALS,FLOUR	W 3320	1.5	W 6836	2.8	W 11538	5.6	W 9914	5.0	AUTRES SEMOULES,FARINES
04701	CEREAL FLOUR(NON-WHEAT)	W 3294	1.5	W 6787	2.8	W 11478	5.5	W 9721	4.9	FARINES DE CEREALES
048	CEREAL ETC PREPARATIONS	W 12229	11.8	W 14879	14.7	W 13726	14.1	W 18161	16.5	PREPTNS A BASE CEREALES
0481	PREPD BREAKFAST FOOD ETC	W 2557	3.4	W 3567	3.9	W 2925	3.2	W 3033	3.4	CEREALES TRAVAILLEES
04812	CEREAL ROASTED, PUFFED	W 1867	3.0	W 2165	3.3	W 1420	2.4	W 1579	2.4	PRODTS BASE CEREALES
0488	OTH CEREAL PREPS,MALT EX	W 1528	3.9	W 1878	5.0	W 1580	4.3	W 3286	5.0	EXTRAITS DE MALT
05	VEGETABLES AND FRUIT		14.9		16.0		16.9		18.8	LEGUMES ET FRUITS
054	VEG ETC FRSH,SMPLY PRSVD	W 23863	8.8	W 28193	10.4	W 25366	10.2	W 31069	12.2	LEGUMES FRAIS,CONG,SECS
0541	POTATOES FRSH EXCL SWEET	W 12896	3.7	W 14673	4.4	W 12478	3.6	W 16982	5.1	POMMES DE TERRE
0545	OTHER FRESH VEGETABLES	W 7483	2.9	W 8828	4.0	W 7570	3.2	W 8979	3.8	AUTRES LEGUMES FRAIS,REF
06	SUGAR AND PREPS,HONEY		3.1		2.8		3.2		3.6	SUCRES ET PRODUITS
081	*FEEDING STUFF FOR ANIML	W 17746	5.4	W 12942	5.1	W 15007	5.6	W 21443	9.2	NOURRITURE POUR ANIMAUX
0813	OILCAKE AND OTH RESIDUES	W 17003	4.9	W 11730	3.3	W 13444	4.7	W 12839	4.8	TOURTEAUX
08131	— OF SOYA BEANS	W 17003	4.9	W 10956	3.1	W 13424	4.7	W 12534	4.7	TOURTEAUX DE SOJA
09	MISC EDIBLE PRODUCTS		19.4		28.8		23.4		28.1	PREP ALIMENTAIRES DIVERSES
091	MARGARINE AND SHORTENING	W 1288	1.3	W 16587	9.3	W 1547	1.5	W 1800	1.9	MARGARINE ET GRAISSES
0913	PIG,POULTRY FAT RENDERED			W 15242	7.9					SAINDOUX
098	EDIBLE PRODCTS,PREPS NES	W 7017	18.1	W 8476	19.6	W 8465	21.9	W 10450	26.3	PREP ALIMENTAIRES NDA
09804	SAUCES,MIXED SEASONINGS	W 3286	3.2	W 4599	4.9	W 3971	4.7	W 3798	4.4	SAUCES,ASSAISONNEMENTS
09805	SOUPS AND BROTHS	W 1229	2.8	W 1324	2.8	W 1449	3.1	W 1649	3.5	SOUPES,POTAGES,BOUILLONS
09809	MISC FOOD PREPRTIONS NES	W 1423	10.8	W 1390	10.6	W 1604	12.4	W 2147	16.5	PREP ALIMENTAIRES NDA
1	BEVERAGES AND TOBACCO		5.1		5.7		8.3		10.1	BOISSONS ET TABACS
11	BEVERAGES		1.9		3.2		3.2		7.1	BOISSONS
112	ALCOHOLIC BEVERAGES	W 955	1.4	W 1281	2.0	W 1287	1.9	W 3744	4.6	BOISSONS ALCOOLIQUES
12	TOBACCO AND MANUFACTURES		3.3		2.5		5.1		3.1	TABACS BRUTS FABRIQUES
121	TOBACCO UNMNFCTRD,REFUSE	W 1111	3.2	W 791	2.4	W 1844	4.9	W 659	2.5	TABACS BRUTS,DECHETS
1212	TOBACCO STRIPPED OR PART	W 843	2.6	W 624	2.1	W 1666	4.6	W 62	0.1	TABACS PART ECOTES
2	CRUDE MATERLS,EXCL FUELS		12.0		13.9		13.7		18.1	MAT BRUTES NON COMESTIBLES
26	TEXTILE FIBRES AND WASTE		5.1		6.3		7.7		7.6	FIBRES TEXTILES
269	WASTE OF TEXTILE FABRICS	W 3491	4.3	W 4326	4.7	W 4753	5.8	W 6711	5.6	FRIPERIE DRILLES,CHIFFONS
26901	BULK TEXT WSTE,OLD CLTHG	W 1822	2.8	W 2229	2.9	W 1859	2.7	W 3977	3.6	ART ET ACCESS D'HABILLEMENT
27	CRUDE FERTLZR,MINRLS NES		1.6		2.8		2.6		6.0	ENGRAIS MINERAUX BRUTS
3	MINERAL FUELS ETC		109.3		181.1		97.4		178.9	COMBUSTIBLES MINERAUX LUB
33	PETROLEUM AND PRODUCTS		106.9		176.8		92.4		172.2	PETROLE ET DERIVES
333	CRUDE PETROLEUM	W 604171	85.4	W 762808	136.1	W 277039	43.0	W 657197	117.3	HUILES BRUTES DE PETROLE
334	PETROLEUM PRODUCTS,REFIN	W 97353	21.0	W 211909	40.2	W 284790	48.6	W 196953	53.8	PRODUITS RAFFINES
3341	GASOLINE,OTH LIGHT OILS	W 8957	2.8	W 32272	6.4	W 9697	3.0	W 19712	5.6	ESSENCES POUR MOTEURS
33411	MOTOR,AVIATION SPIRIT	W 8957	2.8	W 32272	6.4	W 9695	3.0			ESSENCES MOTEURS D'AVIONS
33419	OTH LIGHT PETROLEUM OILS					W 2	0.1	W 19712	5.6	AUTRES HUILES LEGERES
3343	GAS OILS	W 78719	11.4	W 146936	22.5	W 169378	27.7			GAS OILS
3344	FUEL OILS,NES	W 405	0.3	W 21650	3.6	W 95008	10.7	W 162779	40.2	FUEL OILS
3345	LUBS,PETROLEUM OILS NES	W 9272	6.6	W 11046	7.8	W 10707	7.3	W 14462	8.1	HUILES LUBRIFIANTES
33451	LUBS(HIGH PETR CONT) ETC	W 9171	6.4	W 10853	7.5	W 10555	7.1	W 14307	7.9	HUILES LUBRIF,H LOURDES
341	*GAS,NATURAL AND MANUFCT	W 7591	2.3	W 13719	4.3	W 14297	5.0	W 18382	6.7	GAZ NATUREL,GAZ MANUFACT
3413	PETROLM GASES,LIQUEFIED	W 7591	2.3	W 13719	4.3	W 14297	5.0	W 18381	6.7	GAZ DE PETROLE LIQUEFIE
34131	LIQUEFIED PROPANE,BUTANE	W 7591	2.3	W 13718	4.3	W 6866	2.5	W 18379	6.7	PROPANE,BUTANE LIQUEFIES
4	ANIMAL,VEGETABLE OIL,FAT		37.1		34.4		39.3		42.2	HUILES,GRAISSES ANIM,VEG
411	*ANIMAL OILS AND FATS	W 13398	6.4	W 259	0.2	W 13550	7.2	W 8632	5.6	HUILES,GRAISSES ANIMALES
4113	ANIML OIL,FAT,GREASE NES	W 13397	6.4	W 253	0.2	W 13536	7.2	W 8616	5.6	HUILES,GRAISSES ANIMALES NDA
41132	FATS OF BOVINE,SHEEP,ETC	W 12997	6.2	W 91	0.1	W 13533	7.1	W 8581	5.6	SUIFS BRUTS FONDUS
42	FIXED VEGETABLE OIL,FAT		28.6		30.4		24.7		30.7	HUILES VEGETALES FIXES
423	FIXED VEG OILS,SOFT	W 28240	18.7	W 31814	24.9	W 18445	13.6	W 79165	17.6	HUILES VEGET DOUCES FIXES
4232	SOYA BEAN OIL	W 11182	6.7	W 8840	6.4	W 6165	4.8	W 73192	12.9	HUILE DE SOJA
4233	COTTON SEED OIL	W 10552	6.5	W 15157	11.5	W 9111	6.6	W 4792	3.6	HUILE DE COTON
4236	SUNFLOWER SEED OIL	W 5586	4.7	W 7312	6.8	W 499	0.6	W 416	0.3	HUILE DE TOURNESOL
424	FIXED VEG OIL NONSOFT	W 19440	9.9	W 8009	5.5	W 18752	11.2	W 20470	13.2	AUTRES HUILES VEG FIXES
4242	PALM OIL	W 14798	7.5	W 4752	3.4	W 15781	9.6	W 19170	12.1	HUILE DE PALME
431	*PROCESD ANML VEG OIL,ET	W 3207	2.2	W 6224	3.9	W 11120	7.5	W 9227	5.9	HUILES,GRAISSES PREPAREES
4313	FATTY ACIDS ETC,RESIDUES	W 576	0.2	W 4360	2.2	W 8479	5.2	W 7398	4.2	ACIDES GRAS INDUST,RESIDUS
43131	FATTY ACIDS,ACID OILS	W 476	0.2	W 4320	2.2	W 8479	5.2	W 7335	4.2	ACIDES GRAS INDUSTRIELS
5	CHEMCLS,RELATED PROD NES		137.1		172.2		197.3		275.6	PRODUITS CHIMIQUES
51	ORGANIC CHEMICALS		4.7		5.9		5.3		7.8	PROD CHIMIQ ORGANIQUES
52	INORGANIC CHEMICALS		5.8		7.3		6.7		7.7	PROD CHIM INORGANIQUES
522	INORG ELEMNTS,OXIDES,ETC	W 9367	3.1	W 8661	3.8	W 29828	3.0	W 9976	3.1	ELEMENTS INORGANIQUES
523	OTHR INORG CHEMICALS ETC	W 7369	2.8	W 8696	3.5	W 8793	3.7	W 10082	4.7	AUT PRODUITS CHIMIQUES INORG
53	DYES,TANNING,COLOUR PROD		4.4		7.1		10.7		35.1	PROD TEINTURE,COLORANTS
531	SYNT DYE,NAT INDGO,LAKES	W 164	0.4	W 302	1.0	W 296	2.2	W 2802	25.3	MAT COLOR ORGAN,LAQUES
5312	SYNTH LUMIN,INDIGO,LAKES	W 127	0.3	W 99	0.3	W 141	0.4	W 2109	24.9	LUMINOPHORES ORGAN SYNTH
53121	SYN ORG LUMIN ETC,INDIGO	W 94	0.2	W 18	0.1	W 30	0.1	W 2006	24.7	PROD ORGANIQ SYNTH LUMIN
533	PIGMENTS,PAINTS,ETC	W 2508	3.7	W 3046	5.6	W 3253	8.0	W 4002	9.3	PIGMENTS,PEINTURES,VERNIS
5334	VARNISHES,DISTEMPERS ETC	W 1962	2.8	W 2028	2.8	W 2175	3.3	W 2793	6.0	PEINTURES A L'EAU
541	*MEDICINAL,PHARM PRODUCT	K 3669680	51.1	K 4653702	53.3	K 6548036	75.0	K 6084000	75.3	PROD MEDICINAUX PHARMACEUT
5416	GLYCOSIDES,GLANDS,SERA	K 539174	2.9	K 1661632	3.1	K 2860904	4.0	K 2007007	3.9	HETEROSIDES
54164	ANTISERA,MICROB VACCINES	K 278803	2.0	K 1307131	2.3	K 2139264	3.5	K 1690187	3.3	SERUMS,VACCINS
5417	MEDICAMENTS	K 2547642	43.9	K 2348414	44.4	K 3084179	64.3	K 3429051	63.9	MEDICAMENTS
54171	— CONTAINNG ANTIBIOTICS	K 414497	5.8	K 314816	6.9	K 429920	6.4	K 433690	6.5	MED CONTN ANTIBIOTIQUES
54172	— CONTAINING HORMONES	K 149933	3.4	K 162169	4.2	K 111723	3.4	K 80422	3.5	MED CONTENANT HORMONES
54179	— CONTNG OTH SUBSTANCES	K 1890524	33.9	K 1859961	33.2	K 2533178	54.3	K 2911403	53.9	MED CONT AUT SUBSTANCES
5419	PHARMACEUTICAL GOODS NES	K 188007	2.3	K 221199	3.4	K 287311	4.5	K 357943	5.3	PREP,ART PHARMACEUTIQUES
54199	OTH PHARMACEUTICAL GOODS	K 72612	1.6	K 79544	2.7	K 99148	3.4	K 124471	3.2	AUT PREP PHARMACEUTIQUES
55	PERFUME,CLEANING ETC PRD		16.5		22.1		25.7		34.8	PROD POUR PARFUM,TOILETTE

4. Special Imports C.I.F. by Commodities according to the S.I.T.C. (Rev. 2) in million U.S. Dollars
Importations Spéciales C.A.F. par Produits d'après la C.T.C.I. (Rév. 2) en millions de Dollars E.U.

SITC CTCI	COMMODITY	1994 QUANTITY QUANTITE	1994 VALUE VALEUR	1995 QUANTITY QUANTITE	1995 VALUE VALEUR	1996 QUANTITY QUANTITE	1996 VALUE VALEUR	1997 QUANTITY QUANTITE	1997 VALUE VALEUR	PRODUIT
553	PERFUMERY,COSMETICS,ETC	W 3331	6.5	W 4324	8.9	W 4796	10.2	W 8210	14.5	PRODUITS DE PARFUMERIE
554	SOAP,CLEANSING ETC PREPS	W 9285	8.5	W 11127	11.5	W 14767	13.8	W 19352	18.4	SAVONS,PRODUITS DETERSIFS
5541	SOAPS	W 6672	4.9	W 7321	6.5	W 10523	8.1	W 14170	11.8	SAVONS,PROD TENSIO–ACTIFS
5542	WASHING PREPARATIONS ETC	W 2154	2.8	W 3342	4.3	W 3694	4.8	W 4612	5.6	PROD ORG TENSIO–ACT NDA
562	*FERTILIZERS,MANUFACTURE	W 65989	18.3	W 78953	19.0	W 68407	17.7	W 118625	30.6	ENGRAIS MANUFACTURES
5621	CHEM NITROGENOUS FERTLZR	W 43956	13.6	W 52834	12.6	W 51469	13.6	W 77796	21.0	ENGRAIS AZOTES
56216	UREA	W 43118	13.4	W 44801	11.3	W 39581	10.7	W 71077	17.9	UREE
5629	FERTILIZERS NES	W 17355	3.9	W 20456	5.4	W 13518	3.6	W 36523	8.7	ENGRAIS NDA
56292	NITROG–PHOS FERTILZR NES	W 16521	3.6	W 14596	3.6	W 7885	2.1	W 30824	7.0	ENGRAIS NDA CONT N P
58	PLASTIC MATERIALS ETC		14.2		31.2		31.1		54.4	MAT PLAST ARTIFICIELLES
582	PROD OF CONDENSATION ETC	W 3220	3.4	W 10601	14.4	W 2187	11.4	W 4266	31.9	PROD CONDENS,POLYCOND
5822	AMINOPLASTS	W 2057	1.8	W 8899	9.3	W 1035	7.9	W 546	21.4	AMINOPLASTES
58221	— IN PRIMARY FORMS	W 2057	1.8	W 8899	9.3	W 1035	7.9	W 546	21.4	AMINOPLASTES PRIMAIRES
5823	ALKYDS,OTHER POLYESTERS	W 905	1.1	W 1401	4.5	W 968	2.3	W 1241	4.5	ALKYDES ET AUT POLYESTERS
58231	— IN PRIMARY FORMS	W 905	1.1	W 1401	4.5	W 962	2.3	W 1238	4.5	SOUS FORMES PRIMAIRES
583	POLYMERIZATION ETC PRODS	W 9014	9.5	W 12661	15.6	W 14319	16.7	W 15457	20.8	PROD POLYMERISATION
5831	POLYETHYLENE	W 6337	5.7	W 7338	8.3	W 7661	7.9	W 7236	9.1	POLYETHYLENE
58311	— IN PRIMARY FORMS	W 5639	4.5	W 6661	6.7	W 6512	5.9	W 5929	6.2	POLYETHYLENE PRIMAIRES
5839	OTH POLYMRZTION ETC PROD	W 813	1.4	W 1002	1.9	W 1892	3.1	W 3462	4.7	AUT PROD POLYMER COPOLYM
59	CHEMICAL MATERIALS NES		21.7		25.9		24.5		28.7	MAT PROD CHIMIQUES NDA
591	PESTICIDES,DISINFECTANTS	W 3811	15.5	W 4446	19.9	W 4701	18.3	W 6221	21.7	DESINF,INSECT,FONG,HERB
5911	INSECTICIDES,FOR RETAIL	W 939	4.2	W 1358	6.1	W 1592	5.7	W 1627	6.4	INSECTICIDES VENTE DET
5912	FUNGICIDES,FOR RETAIL	W 424	3.1	W 572	4.7	W 791	4.4	W 619	5.0	FONGICIDES VENTE AU DET
5913	HERBICIDES,FOR RETAIL	W 1440	7.0	W 1541	8.0	W 1344	7.1	W 2604	9.2	HERBICIDES VENTE AU DET
598	MISCEL CHEM PRODUCTS NES	W 2768	4.4	W 3007	4.5	W 2646	4.5	W 2679	5.0	PROD DIV INDUST CHIM NDA
5989	CHEM PRODUCTS,PREPS NES	W 2246	3.1	W 2350	3.4	W 2118	3.6	W 1999	3.6	PROD PREP CHIMIQUES NDA
6	BASIC MANUFACTURES		136.7		150.4		179.2		234.9	ART MANUFACTURES
62	RUBBER MANUFACTURES NES		15.9		19.9		20.8		25.4	CAOUTCHOUC MANUFACTURE
625	RUBBER TYRES, TUBES ETC	W 6038	13.2	W 6865	16.8	W 6716	17.4	W 7537	20.7	PNEUS CAOUTCHOUC VULCANISE
6251	TYRES NEW FOR MOTOR CARS	W 1031	3.0	W 1094	3.5	W 1093	3.6	W 1250	4.2	PNEUS POUR VOITURES
6252	TYRES,NEW,BUS OR LORRY	W 2255	5.7	W 2238	7.7	W 2323	8.2	W 3268	11.6	PNEUS POUR AUTOBUS,CAMIONS
6259	OTH TYRES,TYRE CASES,ETC	W 2549	4.1	W 3344	5.3	W 3038	5.3	W 2813	4.6	AUTRES PNEUS RECHAPES FLAPS
62599	TYRES NES,TYRE CASES,ETC	W 2317	3.6	W 3102	4.6	W 2731	4.6	W 2553	4.0	PNEUS,FLAPS
63	WOOD,CORK MANUFACTRS NES		2.0		2.7		2.9		20.4	OUVRAGES LIEGE ET BOIS
635	WOOD MANUFACTURES NES	W 329	0.6	W 572	0.8	W 606	1.0	W 2125	17.4	ART MANUF EN BOIS NDA
6353	BUILDERS WOODWRK,PREFABS	W 142	0.3	W 148	0.3	W 111	0.5	W 849	16.3	OUVRAGES DE MENUISERIE
64	PAPER,PAPERBOARD AND MFR		19.3		25.6		31.9		37.7	PAPIERS,CARTONS & OUVRAGES
641	PAPER AND PAPERBOARD	W 13566	9.6	W 9338	11.2	W 14859	15.0	W 14412	13.1	PAPIERS ET CARTONS
6415	PAPER,PAPERBRD,BULK,NES	W 5806	3.3	W 2919	3.7	W 5569	4.9	W 4814	4.3	PAPIERS,CARTONS ROULEAUX
64159	OTHER PAPER ETC,BULK,NES	W 5759	3.2	W 2824	3.5	W 5529	4.8	W 4723	4.1	AUT PAPIER ROULEAUX FEUILLES
642	PAPER,ETC,PRECUT,ARTS OF	W 6269	9.8	W 9002	14.5	W 10494	16.9	W 18311	24.7	PAP,CARTONS DECOUPES
6421	PAPER ETC CONTAINERS	W 1688	2.6	W 3779	5.9	W 5250	7.2	W 10255	11.5	BOITES,SACS EMBALLAGES
6423	EXERCISE BOOKS ETC	W 1533	2.2	W 1941	2.8	W 2258	3.2	W 3034	4.9	REGISTRES,CAHIERS,CARNETS
6424	PAPER ETC CT TO SIZE NES	W 2140	2.8	W 2156	3.0	W 1945	3.6	W 3666	4.9	PAP,CARTONS DECOUPES
65	TEXTILE YARN,FABRICS,ETC		12.9		13.3		12.9		20.1	FILS,TISSUS,ARTICLES TEXTILE
653	WOVN MAN–MADE FIB FABRIC	W 3303	7.4	W 2679	7.6	W 3067	5.9	W 2842	7.0	TISSUS FIBRES SYNTH,ARTIF
6531	CONT SYNT WEAVES NONPILE	W 3215	6.9	W 2299	5.3	W 2605	3.5	W 2344	4.3	TISSUS FIBRES SYNTH CONTINUE
65315	CONT SYN TXTL FABRIC NES	W 3191	6.8	W 2257	5.1	W 2590	3.4	W 2258	4.1	TIS PLUS 85% TEXT SYNT CONT
656	LACE,RIBBONS,TULLE,ETC	W 114	0.5	W 119	0.5	W 95	1.2	W 174	6.1	TULLES,BRODERIE
65601	NARROW FABRICS NES	W 23	0.1	W 43	0.3	W 32	0.9	W 81	5.8	RUBANS SANS TRAME EN FILS
66	NONMETAL MINERAL MFS NES		15.4		17.3		23.9		30.7	ART MIN NON METALLIQUES
661	LIME,CEMENT,BLDG PRODS	W 30468	2.7	W 71943	4.9	W 46312	3.9	W 95563	10.3	CHAUX,CIMENTS MAT CONSTR
6612	CEMENT	W 27240	1.6	W 62751	3.3	W 39962	2.2	W 79445	6.8	CIMENTS HYDRAULIQUES
662	CLAY,REFRACTORY BLDG PRD	W 3040	1.9	W 5273	2.9	W 5841	3.2	W 9522	5.5	MAT CONST REFRACTAIRES
6624	BRICKS ETC NONREFRACTORY	W 2520	1.4	W 4019	1.9	W 4507	2.2	W 8721	4.7	BRIQUES ETC CERAM NON REFR
665	GLASSWARE	W 12495	7.7	W 8966	6.0	W 21181	12.5	W 12784	8.5	OUVRAGES EN VERRE
6651	BOTTLES ETC OF GLASS	W 11149	6.3	W 7955	4.6	W 19877	10.9	W 11791	6.8	RECIPIENTS EN VERRE
66511	GLASS BOTTLES ETC NONVAC	W 11149	6.3	W 7955	4.6	W 19874	10.9	W 11791	6.8	BONBONNES,BOUTEILLES,ETC
67	IRON AND STEEL		42.5		38.6		49.3		50.7	FER ET ACIER
672	IRON,STEEL PRIMARY FORMS	W 5422	1.7	W 2479	1.4	W 8168	3.6	W 9909	4.4	LINGOTS FER,ACIER
6727	IRN,STL COIL FR REROLLNG	W 2174	1.0	W 2371	1.4	W 7030	3.3	W 6027	3.1	EBAUCHES POUR TOLES FER
67271	IRON,SIMPLE STEEL COILS	W 780	0.4	W 1869	1.0	W 7011	3.3	W 5670	2.8	EBAUCHES NON EN ACIER
673	IRON,STEEL SHAPES ETC	W 24868	10.3	W 29067	13.1	W 28963	11.9	W 30910	14.2	BARRES,PROFIL FER,ACIER
6731	IRON,STEEL WIRE ROD	W 11928	4.2	W 11122	4.0	W 14908	5.2	W 13276	4.9	FIL MACHINE FER,ACIER
67315	OTHER ALLOY STL WIRE ROD	W 11181	3.9	W 9354	3.4	W 11923	4.1	W 11044	4.1	FIL MACH NON ACIERS ALL
6732	IRON,STEEL BARS ETC	W 10343	4.7	W 12926	5.8	W 11351	5.1	W 14336	6.7	BARRES FER,ACIER
67326	IRN,OTH STL BARS HOTROLD	W 8906	3.9	W 11675	5.1	W 10120	4.1	W 13684	6.1	BARRES PLEINES FER,ACIER
6733	IRON,STEEL PROFILES ETC	W 2597	1.5	W 5019	3.4	W 2704	1.7	W 3299	2.6	PROFILES,PALPLAN FER,ACIER
674	IRN,STL UNIV,PLATE,SHEET	W 22091	16.8	W 19645	14.5	W 22863	20.0	W 29121	19.6	LARGES PLATS,TOLES
6746	IRN,STL THIN PLATE,ROLLD	W 3863	2.6	W 5329	4.1	W 6400	4.8	W 7683	5.3	TOLES LAM MOINS 3MM
67461	— OF IRON OR SIMPLE STL	W 2771	2.0	W 3993	3.2	W 5921	4.3	W 7450	5.1	TOL NON AC FIN MOINS 3 MM
6749	OTH IRN,STL PLATES,SHEET	W 11724	11.2	W 9508	8.0	W 11530	12.4	W 12165	9.8	AUTRES TOLES FER,ACIER
67491	— OF IRON OR SIMPLE STL	W 11638	11.2	W 9084	7.7	W 11442	12.3	W 12052	9.7	AUT TOLES AUTRES ACIER FIN
678	IRON,STL TUBES,PIPES,ETC	W 11293	12.8	W 5882	8.0	W 8906	12.3	W 7325	8.9	TUBES,TUYAUX EN FONTE,FER
6783	IRON,STL TUBES,PIPES NES	W 9327	8.5	W 4933	5.5	W 6818	8.6	W 5711	5.4	AUT TUBES,TUYAUX FER,ACIER
68	NON–FERROUS METALS		3.2		3.7		4.9		6.6	METAUX NON FERREUX
684	ALUMINIUM	W 1020	1.9	W 678	2.3	W 1100	4.0	W 1749	5.3	ALUMINIUM
6842	ALUMINIUM,ALLOYS WORKED	W 391	1.4	W 643	2.3	W 1100	4.0	W 1749	5.2	ALUMINIUM,ALLIAGES OUVRE
69	METAL MANUFACTURES NES		25.3		29.2		32.4		42.7	ART MANUFACT EN METAL NDA
691	STRUCTURES AND PARTS NES	W 3520	7.0	W 1186	5.2	W 1069	2.6	W 1996	5.6	CONSTRUCT FER,ACIER,ALU
6911	STRUCTURES,PARTS IRN,STL	W 3410	6.8	W 1109	5.0	W 1005	2.3	W 1806	4.5	CONSTRUCT FER,ACIER,FONTE
693	WIRE PRODUCTS NON ELECTR	W 809	1.4	W 1475	2.8	W 1891	4.0	W 3465	4.6	OUVRAGES FILS METALLIQUES
694	STL,COPPR NAILS,NUTS,ETC	W 1349	1.9	W 1854	3.0	W 1445	2.6	W 3860	5.8	CLOUS,VIS,ECROUS
695	TOOLS	W 741	3.7	W 781	3.9	W 1031	4.8	W 1285	6.1	OUTILS A MAIN
697	BASE MTL HOUSEHOLD EQUIP	W 802	2.6	W 1087	3.3	W 1376	4.3	W 1176	4.1	ART MENAGE MET COMMUNS
699	BASE METAL MFRS NES	W 2683	6.2	W 2858	7.7	W 3249	9.9	W 4510	12.2	ART MANUFACTURES MET NDA
6996	BASE MTL MISC ARTICLES	W 1822	3.2	W 1664	3.1	W 1879	3.5	W 2653	5.1	ART DIVERS METAUX COMMUNS
7	MACHINES,TRANSPORT EQUIP		224.7		232.4		287.2		395.9	MACHINES MATERIEL TRANSPORT
71	POWER GENERATING EQUIPMT		19.4		19.5		16.0		30.5	MACHINES GENERATRICES
711	STEAM BOILERS & AUX PLNT	W 71	0.9	W 300	5.6	W 149	2.1	W 253	2.2	GENERATEURS VAPEUR EAU ETC
7119	PTS NES OF APP OF 711	W 36	0.7	W 231	5.1	W 50	1.5	W 155	1.8	PART,PIECES POUR 711
71191	PTS NES OF BOILERS	W 34	0.6	W 226	4.8	W 49	1.4	W 97	1.0	PART,PIECES POUR 711.1
712	STEAM ENGINES,TURBINES	W 271	6.5	W 2	0.1	W 1	0.1	W 36	1.1	MACHINES A VAPEUR D'EAU PIEC
7129	STM ENGINE ETC PARTS NES	W 269	6.4			W 1	0.1	W 11	0.5	PARTIES,PIECES DU 712.6
713	INTRNL COMBUS PSTN ENGIN	W 432	3.1	W 528	5.2	W 648	5.9	W 1448	16.5	MOTEURS EXPL COMB INT, PIECE
7139	PISTON ENGINE PARTS NES	W 158	2.1	W 259	3.9	W 320	3.9	W 583	10.1	PIECES POUR 713.2,3,8
716	ROTATING ELECTRIC PLANT	W 644	6.9	W 955	8.3	W 500	5.9	W 1049	10.3	APP ELECTR ROTATIFS,PIECES
7162	AC MTRS,GENRTRS,GEN SETS	W 519	5.4	W 613	4.4	W 390	4.5	W 571	6.8	MOTEURS ELECTRIQUES
71622	AC GENERATORS	W 319	4.0	W 233	1.9	W 157	2.2	W 289	4.1	GENER COURANT ALTERNATIF
72	MACHS FOR SPCL INDUSTRYS		36.6		21.9		35.5		49.2	MAC SPECIALES POUR INDUST
721	AGRIC MACHY,EXC TRACTORS	W 806	5.1	W 1067	5.2	W 1027	7.6	W 1489	9.4	MACHINES AGRICOLES

4. Special Imports C.I.F. by Commodities according to the S.I.T.C. (Rev. 2) in million U.S. Dollars
Importations Spéciales C.A.F. par Produits d'après la C.T.C.I. (Rév. 2) en millions de Dollars E.U.

SITC CTCI	COMMODITY	1994 QUANTITY QUANTITE	1994 VALUE VALEUR	1995 QUANTITY QUANTITE	1995 VALUE VALEUR	1996 QUANTITY QUANTITE	1996 VALUE VALEUR	1997 QUANTITY QUANTITE	1997 VALUE VALEUR	PRODUIT
7212	HARVESTING ETC MACHINES	W 383	3.6	W 351	2.4	W 525	5.0	W 1115	6.3	ENGINS POUR LA RECOLTE
722	TRACTORS NON-ROAD	W 1100	3.1	W 874	2.5	W 587	3.0	W 998	6.3	TRACTEURS
723	CIVIL ENGNEERG EQUIP ETC	W 3934	22.7	W 761	4.5	W 1398	8.4	W 2424	12.0	APPAREILS DE GENIE CIVIL
7234	CONST,MINING MACHNRY NES	W 3805	21.7	W 704	4.1	W 1064	6.9	W 1366	8.2	MACH POUR LA CONST, MINES
72342	SLFPRP SHOVELS,EXCAVATRS	W 391	2.9	W 294	1.5	W 252	2.0	W 640	3.7	PELLES MECANIQUES
72343	SLFPRP CONST ETC MCH NES	W 2972	15.5	W 128	1.0	W 195	1.5	W 112	0.5	AUT MACH EXTR,TERRASSEM
727	FOOD MACHRY NON-DOMESTIC	W 132	1.0	W 278	2.1	W 596	6.4	W 968	9.8	MACH INDUSTRIES ALIMENT
7272	OTH FOOD PROC MCHY,PARTS	W 100	0.8	W 183	1.5	W 517	5.4	W 898	9.1	AUT MACH IND ALIMENTAIRE
72722	INDUS FOOD PROC MACH NES	W 59	0.6	W 133	1.3	W 398	3.7	W 412	6.0	MACHINES BOULANGERIE
728	OTH MACHY FOR SPCL INDUS	W 348	2.8	W 438	5.5	W 1147	6.6	W 897	8.4	AUT MACH IND PARTICULIERES
7284	MACHY FOR SPCL INDUS NES	W 109	1.6	W 224	4.5	W 132	2.2	W 209	5.1	MACH SPEC IND PARTICUL.
74	GENRL INDUSTRL MACHY NES		25.4		38.8		42.8		47.0	MACH APP INDUSTRIE
741	HEATING,COOLING EQUIPMNT	W 762	5.6	W 1024	7.6	W 1481	9.5	W 1228	8.6	MACH CHAUFFAGE,PIECES
7414	NONDOM REFRIG EQUIPT,PTS	W 179	1.2	W 364	2.2	W 839	4.9	W 429	2.3	MAT PRODUCTION DU FROID
74141	REFRIG EQUIP NONDOMESTIC	W 124	0.7	W 248	1.7	W 774	4.5	W 299	1.5	REFIG INDUSTRIELS
742	PUMPS FOR LIQUIDS ETC	W 360	4.2	W 449	6.9	W 547	9.2	W 570	6.9	POMPES MOTO-POMPES
7428	OTHER PUMPS FOR LIQUIDS	W 245	3.1	W 378	5.6	W 443	7.7	W 461	4.9	AUTRES POMPES POUR LIQ
74288	PUMPS FR LIQUIDS NES ETC	W 209	2.5	W 354	5.1	W 402	6.9	W 387	3.9	POMPES POUR LIQUIDES NDA
743	PUMPS NES,CENTRFUGES ETC	W 500	3.5	W 711	5.4	W 658	5.2	W 950	6.9	POMPES COMPRES,VENT ETC
744	MECHANICAL HANDLING EQU	W 472	3.4	W 421	1.9	W 584	3.1	W 730	3.9	EQUIP MANUTENTION PIECES
745	NONELEC MACHY,TOOLS NES	W 244	2.9	W 456	6.9	W 310	5.4	W 600	7.1	AUT MACH NON ELEC,PIECES
7452	OTH NONELEC MCHS,PTS NES	W 210	2.3	W 405	5.6	W 270	4.2	W 550	6.0	AUT MACH NON ELEC,PIECES
749	NONELEC MACH PTS,ACC NES	W 751	6.1	W 1261	10.4	W 989	10.6	W 1140	13.8	PIECES MACH NON ELEC NDA
7492	COCKS,VALVES ETC NES	W 476	2.4	W 660	4.7	W 434	3.8	W 543	5.2	ART ROB,SIM POUR TUYAUX
75	OFFICE MACHNES,ADP EQUIP		14.1		16.5		21.4		27.0	MACH BUREAU TRAIT AUTOM
751	OFFICE MACHINES	W 164	1.9	W 240	2.9	W 294	3.8	W 283	3.3	MACH,APPAREILS DE BUREAU
752	AUTOMTIC DATA PROC EQUIP	W 292	9.0	W 352	10.6	W 405	13.8	W 515	17.6	MACH TRAIT INFORMATION
7521	ANALOG,HYBRID COMPUTERS	W 57	1.2	W 51	0.9	W 41	1.6	W 110	4.5	MACH POUR TRAIT INFORMAT
7522	DIGITAL COMPUTERS	W 151	5.6	W 159	6.3	W 168	7.4	W 169	5.3	MACH DIGITALES COMPLETES
7525	ADP PERIPHERAL UNITS	W 55	1.3	W 101	2.2	W 170	3.7	W 111	2.7	UNITES PERIPHERIQUES
759	OFFICE,ADP MCH PTS,ACCES	W 121	3.3	W 101	3.2	W 111	3.9	W 250	6.3	PIECES DU 751 ET 752
7599	ACCTG,ETC,ADP MCH PTS,AC	W 74	2.3	W 95	3.0	W 108	3.8	W 189	5.1	PIECES DU 751 ET 752
76	TELECOMM,SOUND EQUIPMENT		28.2		25.2		26.2		42.2	EQUIPMENT DE TELECOM
761	TELEVISION RECEIVERS	W 343	1.8	W 568	2.8	W 611	3.4	W 591	4.0	RECEPTEURS DE TELEVISION
762	RADIO BROADCAST RECEIVRS	W 360	1.5	W 594	2.7	W 556	3.9	W 513	3.6	RECEPTEURS RADIODIFFUSION
764	TELECOM EQPT,PTS,ACC NES	W 1032	24.5	W 675	19.1	W 628	18.4	W 817	33.8	EQUIP TELECOM,PIECES
7641	LINE TELEPHONE,ETC EQUIP	W 428	14.7	W 388	14.8	W 315	13.6	W 499	27.6	APP TELEPHON PAR FIL
7643	TV,RADIO TRANSMITTRS ETC	W 70	3.4	W 40	1.5	W 42	2.1	W 38	1.6	APP EMET TELE RADIO
7649	PTS NES OF EQUIPMT OF 76	W 468	5.8	W 117	2.0	W 121	1.7	W 155	3.2	PIECES DE LA DIV 76
76491	PTS NES OF APPAR OF 7641	W 358	3.3	W 59	1.0	W 18	0.6	W 62	2.3	PIECES POUR 764.1
77	ELECTRIC MACHNRY NES ETC		37.4		40.7		47.5		55.3	MACH APP ELECT NDA
771	ELECTRIC POWER MACHY NES	W 588	4.0	W 858	5.6	W 682	5.2	W 1097	6.0	MACH PROD,TRANS ELECTR
7711	TRANSFORMERS,ELECTRICAL	W 379	3.2	W 678	5.0	W 509	4.3	W 869	4.5	TRANSFO ELECTRIQUES
77111	LIQUID DIELEC TRANSFRMRS	W 127	1.7	W 278	3.3	W 226	3.0	W 401	2.8	TRANSFO DIELEC LIQUIDE
772	SWITCHGEAR ETC,PARTS NES	W 733	6.0	W 657	7.4	W 899	11.7	W 921	13.5	APP COUPURE,SECT ETC
7721	SWITCHGEAR ETC	W 672	5.7	W 652	7.3	W 896	11.6	W 918	13.3	APP COUPURE,SECTIONMNT
773	ELECTR DISTRIBUTNG EQUIP	W 1859	8.1	W 1920	8.6	W 2245	9.1	W 2037	7.2	EQUIPMT DISTRIBUTION ELECT
7731	INSULATED WIRE,CABLE ETC	W 1717	7.7	W 1792	8.0	W 1710	7.9	W 1735	6.5	FILS,CABLES ISOLES ELECT
774	ELECTRO-MEDCL,XRAY EQUIP	W 241	3.4	W 52	1.6	W 102	1.8	W 239	6.1	APPAREILS MEDICAUX
7741	ELECTRO-MEDICAL EQUIPMNT	W 236	3.2	W 46	1.5	W 80	1.3	W 222	5.8	APP ELECTRICITE MEDICALE
775	HOUSEHOLD TYPE EQUIP NES	W 1475	4.9	W 1928	6.7	W 2021	7.1	W 2062	7.3	MACH,APP USAGE DOMESTQUE
7752	DOM REFRIGERATRS,FREEZRS	W 740	2.9	W 941	3.9	W 1108	4.7	W 1149	4.8	REFRIG,CONGEL MENAGER
77521	DOMESTIC REFRIGERATORS	W 673	2.6	W 819	3.3	W 981	4.1	W 980	4.0	REFRIGERATEURS
778	ELECTRICAL MACHINERY NES	W 3235	10.7	W 3339	10.7	W 3239	12.1	W 4060	15.0	AUTRES MACH ELECT NDA
7781	BATTERIES,ACCUMULATORS	W 2558	6.0	W 2532	6.2	W 2438	6.2	W 3031	8.3	PILES ET ACCUMULATEURS
77811	PRIMARY BATTERIES,CELLS	W 1936	4.4	W 1798	4.4	W 1381	3.6	W 1789	4.5	PILES ELECTRIQUES,PIECES
78	ROAD VEHICLES		54.9		66.5		91.5		132.0	VEHICULES ROUTIERS
781	PASS MOTOR VEH EXC BUSES	W 3076	17.0	W 5258	29.3	W 6526	39.9	W 9529	58.3	AUTO TRANSPORT PERSONNES
782	LORRIES,SPCL MTR VEH NES	W 4013	21.3	W 5259	23.5	W 6869	35.0	W 10051	49.0	VEHICULES SPECIAUX,MARCH
7821	LORRIES,TRUCKS	W 3383	13.8	W 5011	22.9	W 6181	31.1	W 9845	47.1	VEHICULES TRANSP MARCHAND
7822	SPECIAL MOTOR VEHCLS NES	W 630	7.6	W 247	0.7	W 687	4.0	W 206	1.9	VEHICULES USAGES SPECIAUX
783	ROAD MOTOR VEHICLES NES	W 2143	7.6	W 2591	4.6	W 2949	6.0	W 4816	9.5	VEHICULES ROUTIERS NDA
7831	BUSES	W 1759	6.7	W 1990	3.3	W 2347	4.9	W 3330	5.9	VOITURES TRANSPORT COMMUN
784	MOTOR VEH PRTS,ACCES NES	W 375	3.7	W 538	4.5	W 649	5.7	W 1123	8.7	PIECES 722,781,782,783
7849	OTHER MOTOR VEHCL PARTS	W 369	3.7	W 530	4.5	W 621	5.6	W 1074	8.4	PIECES 722,781,782,783
785	CYCLES,ETC MOTRZD OR NOT	W 1196	4.6	W 1108	3.7	W 1180	4.0	W 3465	5.5	MOTOCYCLES SCOOTERS
79	OTHR TRANSPORT EQUIPMENT		8.1		1.4		4.8		11.1	AUTRE MATERIEL TRANSPORT
793	SHIPS AND BOATS ETC	W 2594	7.9	W 739	1.3	W 1820	4.6	W 1524	10.3	NAVIRES BATEAUX,ETC
7932	SHIPS AND BOATS NES	W 2292	5.1	W 725	1.2	W 1810	4.4	W 1392	7.5	NAVIRES ET BATEAUX
79324	FISHING VESSELS ETC	W 2169	4.8	W 642	0.5	W 1725	4.1	W 1324	7.2	BATEAUX DE PECHE
7938	TUGS,SPECIAL VESSELS ETC	W 302	2.8	W 14	0.1	W 5	0.2	W 9	0.2	REMORQUEURS,BATEAUX SPEC
79382	SPECL PURPOSE VESSLS ETC	W 300	2.8	W 10	0.1		0.1		0.1	BAT-PHARES,-POMPES,DRAGUES
8	MISC MANUFACTURED GOODS		68.2		80.5		101.3		152.2	ART MANUFACTURES DIVERS
821	*FURNITURE,PARTS THEREOF	W 1732	4.1	W 2192	6.2	W 2315	8.7	W 3654	12.3	MEUBLES ET PIECES
8212	MED FURN,STUFFD FURNSHGS	W 654	1.6	W 849	3.2	W 940	5.2	W 1166	4.7	MOB MEDICO-CHIRUR,PIECES
82121	MEDICAL FURNITURE,PARTS	W 123	0.6	W 211	2.0	W 217	3.6	W 168	2.8	MOBILIER MED,TABLE OPER ETC
8219	FURNITURE AND PARTS NES	W 741	1.8	W 877	2.2	W 864	2.6	W 1835	6.1	AUTRES MEUBLES ET PIECES
84	CLOTHING AND ACCESSORIES		12.1		11.4		9.3		9.7	VETEMENTS
851	*FOOTWEAR	W 1898	4.1	W 2196	4.8	W 1976	4.4	W 2216	5.4	CHAUSSURES
87	PRECISION INSTRUMNTS NES		8.8		14.5		18.4		27.3	INSTRUM,APPAR SCIENT NDA
872	MEDICAL INSTRUMENTS NES	W 317	3.1	W 449	9.3	W 598	8.0	W 876	18.2	INSTR,APP MEDIC-CHIR NDA
87202	OTH MEDICAL INSTRUMENTS	W 314	2.9	W 400	9.1	W 521	7.8	W 746	18.0	INSTRUM,APP MEDECINE
873	METERS AND COUNTERS NES	W 197	1.4	W 131	1.8	W 360	3.9	W 147	2.1	COMPTEURS,INST DE MESURE
8731	GAS SUPPLY METERS ETC	W 192	1.3	W 130	1.8	W 358	3.9	W 145	2.1	COMPTEURS GAZ,LIQ ELECT
874	MEASURNG,CONTROLNG INSTR	W 327	4.3	W 226	3.2	W 345	6.2	W 342	6.6	INSTRUMENTS DE MESURE
88	PHOTO EQU,OPTICL GDS ETC		4.2		5.0		4.9		6.3	APP,FOURN PHOTO,OP,MONTR
882	PHOTO,CINEMA SUPPLIES	W 258	2.8	W 275	3.1	W 284	2.9	W 310	3.2	PRODUITS PHOTO,CINEMA
89	MISC MANUFCTRD GOODS NES		32.6		36.1		52.4		87.5	ART MANUFACTURES DIVERS
892	PRINTED MATTER	W 1713	9.7	W 1441	9.3	W 1658	11.3	W 2808	13.9	IMPRIMES
8921	PRINTED BOOKS,GLOBES,ETC	W 1151	5.9	W 822	5.0	W 825	5.7	W 1905	9.5	LIVRES,BROCHURES,CARTES
89211	PRINTED BOOKS,PAMPHLETS	W 1140	5.8	W 687	4.6	W 789	5.6	W 1884	9.4	LIVRES,BROCHURES
8928	PRINTED MATTER NES	W 417	3.1	W 450	3.6	W 649	4.9	W 527	3.3	IMPRIMES NDA
893	ARTICLES OF PLASTIC NES		13.3		14.7		18.9		18.5	OUVRAGES EN MAT DIVIS 58
8931	PLSTC PACKG CONTNRS,LIDS	W 2250	6.0	W 2357	6.5	W 4176	9.2	W 2383	8.5	ART TRANSP EMBALLAGE ETC
8939	MISC PLASTIC ARTICLES	W 3404	7.2	W 3418	8.1	W 4337	9.7	W 4938	9.6	ART DIVERS EN MAT DIV 58
89399	OTHR PLASTC ARTICLES NES	W 3329	7.0	W 3344	7.8	W 4214	9.2	W 4708	8.9	AUT OUV MAT DIV 58
894	TOYS,SPORTING GOODS,ETC	W 1228	3.6	W 1275	3.9	W 1312	3.0	W 1537	3.8	VOITURES ENFANTS,JOUETS
8942	TOYS,INDOOR GAMES ETC	W 1117	2.7	W 1062	2.7	W 1142	2.3	W 1370	3.1	JOUETS,JEUX ETC
895	OFFICE SUPPLIES NES	W 513	2.4	W 525	3.6	W 753	13.8	W 1105	44.7	ART PAPET NDA
8959	OTHER OFFICE SUPPLIES	W 145	0.9	W 161	1.7	W 220	11.1	W 457	41.7	AUT ART DE PAPETERIE
89591	INK EXCL PRINTING INK	W 64	0.3	W 103	1.0	W 155	10.3	W 380	40.8	ENCRES A ECRIRE

Nicaragua

4. Special Imports C.I.F. by Commodities according to the S.I.T.C. (Rev. 2) in million U.S. Dollars
Importations Spéciales C.A.F. par Produits d'après la C.T.C.I. (Rév. 2) en millions de Dollars E.U.

SITC CTCI	COMMODITY	1994		1995		1996		1997		PRODUIT
		QUANTITY QUANTITE	VALUE VALEUR	QUANTITY QUANTITE	VALUE VALEUR	QUANTITY QUANTITE	VALUE VALEUR	QUANTITY QUANTITE	VALUE VALEUR	

Nicaragua

5. Special Exports F.O.B. by Commodities according to the S.I.T.C. (Rev. 2) in million U.S. Dollars
Exportations Spéciales F.O.B. par Produits d'après la C.T.C.I. (Rév. 2) en millions de Dollars E.U.

SITC CTCI	COMMODITY	1994		1995		1996		1997		PRODUIT
		QUANTITY QUANTITE	VALUE VALEUR	QUANTITY QUANTITE	VALUE VALEUR	QUANTITY QUANTITE	VALUE VALEUR	QUANTITY QUANTITE	VALUE VALEUR	
	ALL COMMODITIES		351.2		509.3		660.2		666.7	TOUS PRODUITS
0	FOOD AND LIVE ANIMALS		260.2		339.9		343.9		380.6	ALIMENTS,ANIMAUX VIVANTS
001	*LIVE ANIMALS FOR FOOD	W 13697	11.5	W 4684	3.3	W 3673	2.9	W 4672	3.9	ANIMAUX VIVANTS
0011	BOVINE SPECIES,LIVE	W 13648	11.4	W 3456	2.9	W 3289	2.8	W 4503	3.8	ESPECE BOVINE
00119	— OTHR THAN FR BREEDING	W 13642	11.4	W 2232	1.9	W 3248	2.7	W 4503	3.8	BOVINS NON REPRODUCTEURS
01	MEAT AND PREPARATIONS		65.1		55.9		42.1		42.5	VIANDES ET PREPARATIONS
011	MEAT FRESH,CHILLD,FROZEN	W 27392	64.8	W 26200	55.8	W 22696	41.9	W 24730	42.2	VIANDES FRAICHES,REF,CONGE
0111	BOVINE MEAT FRESH,FROZEN	W 26352	63.4	W 25360	54.8	W 21491	40.8	W 23135	40.8	VIANDES BOVIN FRAI,REF
01111	BOVINE MEAT WITH BONE IN	W 1445	2.8	W 3948	7.3	W 6229	11.0	W 2544	4.2	VIANDES BOVIN NON DESOSS
01112	BOVINE MEAT BONELESS	W 24907	60.7	W 21412	47.5	W 15263	29.8	W 20591	36.6	VIANDES BOVIN DESOSSEES
02	DAIRY PRODCTS,BIRDS'EGGS		1.9		7.7		11.0		13.9	PRODUITS LAITIERS,OEUFS
022	MILK AND CREAM	W 100	0.2	W 787	1.7	W 1290	3.0	W 648	1.5	LAIT ET CREME
0224	MILK,CREAM PRESERVED ETC	W 38	0.1	W 670	1.5	W 1119	2.7	W 388	1.1	LAIT,CREME CONS,CONC
02243	MILK DRY,OVER 1.5% FAT			W 644	1.5	W 1036	2.6	W 316	0.9	LAIT POUDRE SUP 1.5%
024	CHEESE AND CURD	W 830	1.3	W 2807	4.7	W 4783	8.1	W 40476	12.4	FROMAGE ET CAILLEBOTTE
03	FISH AND PREPARATIONS		53.1		98.0		78.4		81.9	POISSONS ET PREPARATIONS
034	FISH,FRESH,CHILLED,FROZN	W 3103	8.8	W 2414	9.5	W 2553	10.8	W 2700	10.7	POISSON FRAIS, REFRIG,CONG
0341	FISH FRSH,CHLLD,EX FILLT	W 2144	5.8	W 1404	4.6	W 1538	5.5	W 1778	6.9	POISSON FRAIS,REFRIGERE
0342	FISH FROZEN,EXCL FILLETS	W 671	1.9	W 518	2.2	W 619	3.1	W 548	2.5	POISSONS CONGELES
0344	FISH FILLETS,FROZEN	W 194	0.8	W 465	2.7	W 340	1.9	W 366	1.5	FILETS CONGELES
035	FISH SALTED,DRIED,SMOKED	W 91	1.2	W 717	1.6	W 135	3.6	W 163	7.4	POISSON SECHE,SALE,FUME
03503	FISH(EX COD)DRIED,SALTED	W 86	1.2	W 717	1.6	W 134	3.6	W 163	7.4	POISSONS SECHES,SALES
036	SHELL FISH FRESH,FROZEN	W 4839	43.2	W 7123	69.8	W 6972	64.0	W 9527	63.8	CRUSTACES,MOLLUSQUES
037	FISH ETC PREPD,PRSVD NES			W 50175	17.2	W 5	0.1	W 2	0.1	POIS,CRUST,MOL PREPARES
0371	FISH PREPARD,PRESRVD NES			W 50175	17.2	W 5	0.1	W 2	0.1	CONSERVES DE POISSONS
04	CEREALS AND PREPARATIONS		8.4		4.0		4.4		8.2	CEREALES ET PRODUITS
044	MAIZE UNMILLED	W 8957	1.5	W 4172	0.6	W 4544	0.8	W 14391	2.9	MAIS NON MOULU
045	CEREALS NES UNMILLED	W 21180	3.1	W 648	0.1	W 1992	0.3	W 6906	1.0	AUTRES CEREALES NON MOULUES
0459	OTHER CEREALS UNMILLED	W 21180	3.1	W 648	0.1	W 1992	0.3	W 6906	1.0	SARRASIN,MILLET,SORGHO
04592	SORGHUM UNMILLED	W 21180	3.1	W 648	0.1	W 1990	0.3	W 6888	1.0	SORGHO NON MOULU
048	CEREAL ETC PREPARATIONS	W 1441	3.1	W 1717	2.9	W 1278	2.3	W 1632	2.5	PREPTNS A BASE CEREALES
0484	BAKERY PRODUCTS	W 1370	3.0	W 1632	2.7	W 1186	2.1	W 1441	2.2	PRODUITS DE BOULANGERIE
04842	PASTRY, CAKES ETC	W 1357	3.0	W 1632	2.7	W 1185	2.1	W 732	1.2	PATISSERIE ETC.
05	VEGETABLES AND FRUIT		23.0		29.8		33.2		36.8	LEGUMES ET FRUITS
054	VEG ETC FRSH,SMPLY PRSVD	W 25701	13.3	W 28786	11.3	W 17417	7.5	W 20730	16.4	LEGUMES FRAIS,CONG,SECS
0542	LEGUMINOUS VEGETBLES DRY	W 19011	11.0	W 22256	8.8	W 11793	5.1	W 11337	9.9	LEGUMES A COSSE SECS
0546	VEGETABLES SIMPLY PRESVD	W 2547	0.9	W 848	0.7	W 1118	1.0	W 2296	3.0	LEGUMES CONG,CONSER
05461	VEGETABLES FROZEN			W 848	0.7	W 1098	0.9	W 2286	3.0	LEGUMES CONGELES
0548	EDIBLE VEG NES FRESH,DRY	W 2287	0.9	W 2217	1.2	W 2446	0.9	W 3418	2.5	RACINES,TUBERCULES
05481	ROOTS,TUBERS FRESH,DRY	W 2287	0.9	W 2217	1.2	W 2446	0.9	W 3418	2.5	RACINES DE MANIOC ETC
057	FRUIT,NUTS,FRESH,DRIED	W 42546	9.6	W 68399	18.2	W 95300	25.5	W 87378	20.4	FRUITS FRAIS OU SECS
0573	BANANA,PLANTAIN,FRSH,DRY	W 28544	6.2	W 54635	14.3	W 80900	22.3	W 72638	16.0	BANANES FRAICHES,SECHEES
0579	FRUIT FRESH OR DRIED NES	W 13562	3.3	W 13099	3.7	W 14109	3.2	W 13059	4.0	FRUITS FRAIS,SECS NDA
05797	OTH TROP FRUIT,FRESH,DRY	W 293	0.2	W 1314	0.8	W 1328	0.8	W 1439	2.1	AVOCATS,MANGUES,GOYAVES
05798	OTHER FRESH FRUIT	W 12631	2.8	W 10743	2.4	W 11751	2.0	W 10120	1.6	AUTRES FRUITS FRAIS
06	SUGAR AND PREPS,HONEY		17.9		16.2		37.1		56.8	SUCRES ET PRODUITS
061	SUGAR AND HONEY	W 101693	17.9	W 99563	16.2	W 171743	37.0	W 229337	56.7	SUCRES ET MIEL
0611	RAW BEET AND CANE SUGAR	W 55018	15.9	W 45126	12.5	W 121979	33.5	W 190731	53.2	SUCRES BRUTS
0615	MOLASSES	W 46590	2.0	W 54283	3.6	W 49537	3.3	W 34504	1.9	MELASSES
07	COFFEE,TEA,COCOA,SPICES		77.4		121.5		129.8		126.1	CAFE,THE,CACAO,EPICES
071	COFFEE AND SUBSTITUTES	W 38262	77.3	W 38043	121.1	W 53909	128.0	W 40314	123.6	CAFE ET SUCCEDANES
0711	COFFEE GREEN,ROASTED,SUB	W 37911	76.3	W 37850	119.9	W 53568	126.3	W 40302	123.6	CAFE TORREFIE OU DECAFEINE
07111	COFFEE GREEN,HUSKS,SKINS	W 37911	76.3	W 37781	119.4	W 53233	123.8	W 40301	123.6	CAFE NON TORREFIE
07113	COFFEE SUBST CONT COFFEE			W 67	0.6	W 335	2.5		0.1	SUCCEDANES DU CAFE
075	SPICES	W 110	0.1	W 654	0.4	W 2027	1.8	W 2791	2.4	EPICES
0752	SPICES,EX PEPPER,PIMENTO	W 70	0.1	W 654	0.4	W 2026	1.8	W 2771	2.4	AUTRES EPICES
07526	GINGER (EXCPT SWEETENED)	W 70	0.1	W 642	0.4	W 2021	1.8	W 2770	2.4	GINGEMBRE
081	*FEEDING STUFF FOR ANIML	W 21576	2.0	W 23704	3.0	W 23208	3.0	W 24626	7.7	NOURRITURE POUR ANIMAUX
0812	BRAN,POLLARD,SHARPS,ETC	W 18777	1.7	W 16073	1.5	W 17659	1.7	W 19236	1.9	SONS
08122	BRAN,ETC OF OTHR CEREALS	W 18460	1.6	W 16035	1.4	W 17210	1.7	W 17654	1.8	SONS D'AUTRES CEREALES
0814	MEAT OR FISH MEAL FODDER	W 886	0.2	W 1206	0.3	W 581	0.2	W 681	5.3	FARINES DE VIANDES,POISSONS
08142	FISH MEAL FODDER							W 189	5.1	FARINES DE POISSONS
09	MISC EDIBLE PRODUCTS		0.3		0.8		2.4		3.3	PREP ALIMENTAIRES DIVERSES
098	EDIBLE PRODCTS,PREPS NES	W 218	0.3	W 517	0.8	W 1574	2.4	W 2664	3.3	PREP ALIMENTAIRES NDA
1	BEVERAGES AND TOBACCO		4.0		5.6		17.1		45.1	BOISSONS ET TABACS
11	BEVERAGES		1.5		1.5		2.5		2.5	BOISSONS
112	ALCOHOLIC BEVERAGES	W 1789	1.5	W 1932	1.5	W 2722	1.9	W 3204	2.3	BOISSONS ALCOOLIQUES
1124	DISTILLED ALCOHOLIC BEVS	W 1788	1.5	W 1931	1.5	W 2645	1.9	W 3204	2.3	ALCOOLS,EAUX–DE–VIE
11249	OTH ALCOHOLC BEVS,CMPNDS	W 1788	1.5	W 1931	1.5	W 2645	1.9	W 3204	2.3	BOISSONS ALCOOLIQUES NDA
12	TOBACCO AND MANUFACTURES		2.5		4.1		14.6		42.6	TABACS BRUTS FABRIQUES
121	TOBACCO UNMNFCTRD,REFUSE	W 557	2.2	W 457	2.5	W 512	3.9	W 1310	11.0	TABACS BRUTS,DECHETS
1211	TOBACCO,NOT STRIPPED	W 273	1.1	W 205	1.2	W 170	2.0	W 623	6.5	TABACS NON ECOTES
1212	TOBACCO STRIPPED OR PART	W 264	1.1	W 246	1.3	W 323	1.9	W 503	4.1	TABACS PART ECOTES
122	TOBACCO,MANUFACTURED	W 45	0.4	W 175	1.7	W 566	10.7	W 1331	31.6	TABACS FABRIQUES
1221	CIGARS,CHEROOTS,ETC	W 30	0.3	W 126	1.6	W 480	10.5	W 1249	31.1	CIGARES
2	CRUDE MATERLS,EXCL FUELS		32.5		43.5		65.6		56.7	MAT BRUTES NON COMESTIBLES
21	HIDES,SKINS,FURS UNDRSSD		2.9		1.2		1.7		1.3	CUIRS,PEAUX BRUTS
211	HIDES,SKINS,EXC FURS,RAW	W 3624	2.9	W 1235	1.2	W 1680	1.7		1.3	CUIRS ET PEAUX
2111	BOVINE,EQUINE HIDES,RAW	W 3195	2.6	W 1074	1.0	W 1493	1.6	W 894	1.1	PEAUX DE BOVINS
22	OIL SEEDS,OLEAGINOUS FRT		17.6		24.6		29.8		28.1	GRAINES,FRUITS OLEAGINEUX
222	SEEDS FOR'SOFT'FIXED OIL	W 21725	17.2	W 35163	24.2	W 32789	28.2	W 36322	25.2	GRAINES HUILES FIXES
2221	GROUNDNUTS,GREEN	W 13913	9.8	W 20664	12.1	W 20159	13.4	W 23252	14.8	ARACHIDES NON GRILLEES
2225	SESAME SEEDS	W 7584	7.4	W 14048	12.0	W 12068	14.7	W 12600	10.3	GRAINES DE SESAME
223	SEEDS FOR OTH FIXED OILS	W 1321	0.4	W 1614	0.5	W 6599	1.7	W 6888	3.0	GRAINES AUTRES HUILES FIXES
24	CORK AND WOOD		5.0		11.4		18.0		19.5	LIEGE ET BOIS
248	WOOD SHAPED,SLEEPERS	W 14659	5.0	W 33127	11.3	W 55601	17.9	W 60250	19.5	BOIS SIMPLEMENT TRAVAILLES
2482	LUMBER SHAPED CONIFER	W 8126	1.2	W 18368	2.6	W 35372	5.3	W 44885	9.0	CONIFERES SCIES,RABOTES
24821	LUMBER SAWN ETC CONIFER	W 8126	1.2	W 18349	2.6	W 35330	5.3	W 44885	9.0	CONIFERES SCIES LONGITUD
2483	LUMBER SHAPED NON–CONIFR	W 6533	3.9	W 14758	8.8	W 20229	12.6	W 15289	10.4	NON CONIFERES SCIES,RABOTES
24831	LUMBER SAWN ETC NON–CON	W 6517	3.9	W 14714	8.8	W 20229	12.6	W 14778	9.8	SCIES LONGITUDINALEMENT
26	TEXTILE FIBRES AND WASTE		4.3		2.2		10.3		3.1	FIBRES TEXTILES
263	COTTON	W 1677	4.3	W 1540	2.2	W 6313	10.3	W 1941	3.1	COTON
2631	RAW COTTON,EXCL LINTERS	W 1677	4.3	W 1540	2.2	W 5844	10.1	W 1898	3.1	COTON EN MASSE
28	METALLIFEROUS ORES,SCRAP		2.4		3.8		5.3		4.0	MINERAIS METAL,DECHETS
288	NONFERR METAL SCRAP NES	W 1647	1.4	W 2783	2.9	W 2795	3.5	W 2546	3.1	DECHETS NON FERREUX
2882	OTHER BASE MTL SCRAP NES	W 1647	1.4	W 2783	2.9	W 2795	3.5	W 2537	3.0	AUTRES DECHETS
28821	COPPER WASTE AND SCRAP	W 782	1.1	W 1044	1.9	W 1606	3.0	W 1275	2.5	DECHETS DE CUIVRE
3	MINERAL FUELS ETC		3.6		3.2		4.6		6.6	COMBUSTIBLES MINERAUX LUB
33	PETROLEUM AND PRODUCTS		3.6		3.2		4.6		6.6	PETROLE ET DERIVES
334	PETROLEUM PRODUCTS,REFIN	W 13281	2.9	W 10894	2.5	W 20802	4.4	W 27124	6.4	PRODUITS RAFFINES
3341	GASOLINE,OTH LIGHT OILS	W 10739	2.5	W 10006	2.0	W 7986	1.2	W 6707	1.8	ESSENCES POUR MOTEURS

5. Special Exports F.O.B. by Commodities according to the S.I.T.C. (Rev. 2) in million U.S. Dollars
Exportations Spéciales F.O.B. par Produits d'après la C.T.C.I. (Rév. 2) en millions de Dollars E.U.

SITC CTCI	COMMODITY	1994 QUANTITY QUANTITE	1994 VALUE VALEUR	1995 QUANTITY QUANTITE	1995 VALUE VALEUR	1996 QUANTITY QUANTITE	1996 VALUE VALEUR	1997 QUANTITY QUANTITE	1997 VALUE VALEUR	PRODUIT
33419	OTH LIGHT PETROLEUM OILS	W 10739	2.5	W 10006	2.0	W 129	0.1	W 6707	1.8	AUTRES HUILES LEGERES
3344	FUEL OILS,NES	W 1033	0.2	W 342	0.1			W 14278	2.9	FUEL OILS
3345	LUBS,PETROLEUM OILS NES	W 8	0.1	W 160	0.2	W 12816	3.2	W 6139	1.7	HUILES LUBRIFIANTES
33451	LUBS(HIGH PETR CONT) ETC	W 8	0.1	W 160	0.2	W 12806	3.2	W 6139	1.7	HUILES LUBRIF,H LOURDES
4	ANIMAL,VEGETABLE OIL,FAT		0.1		3.4		0.8		3.1	HUILES,GRAISSES ANIM,VEG
42	FIXED VEGETABLE OIL,FAT		0.1		3.3		0.7		2.3	HUILES VEGETALES FIXES
423	FIXED VEG OILS,SOFT	W 40	0.1	W 3833	3.3	W 786	0.7	W 1606	2.2	HUILES VEGET DOUCES FIXES
4234	GROUNDNUT(PEANUT) OIL			W 3833	3.3	W 783	0.7	W 1598	2.2	HUILE D'ARACHIDE
5	CHEMCLS,RELATED PROD NES		4.8		6.0		6.2		9.7	PRODUITS CHIMIQUES
51	ORGANIC CHEMICALS		0.4		0.6		1.7		4.0	PROD CHIMIQ ORGANIQUES
512	ALCOHOLS,PHENOLS ETC	W 65	0.1	W 58	0.1	W 6343	1.2	W 13000	3.0	PHENOLS,PHENOLS–ALCOOLS
5121	ACYCLIC ALCOHOLS,DERIVS	W 65	0.1	W 58	0.1	W 6342	1.2	W 13000	3.0	ALCOOLS ACYCLIQUES
51216	ETHYL ALC,DENATRD SPIRIT			W 53	0.1	W 6341	1.2	W 12993	3.0	ALCOOL ETHYLIQUE NON DENAT
541	*MEDICINAL,PHARM PRODUCT	K 540163	1.3	K 170580	1.2	K 144351	1.1	K 87144	1.2	PROD MEDICINAUX PHARMACEUT
55	PERFUME,CLEANING ETC PRD		1.4		2.0		1.8		1.7	PROD POUR PARFUM,TOILETTE
554	SOAP,CLEANSING ETC PREPS	W 1451	1.4	W 2548	1.9	W 2190	1.7	W 2033	1.6	SAVONS,PRODUITS DETERSIFS
5542	WASHING PREPARATIONS ETC	W 1382	1.3	W 1246	1.2	W 485	0.5	W 223	0.3	PROD ORG TENSIO–ACT NDA
6	BASIC MANUFACTURES		12.1		11.7		12.6		13.8	ART MANUFACTURES
61	LEATHER,DRESSED FUR,ETC		1.3		4.0		4.3		4.7	CUIRS,PELLETERIES
611	LEATHER	W 671	1.2	W 2384	4.0	W 2701	4.3	W 2336	4.5	CUIRS,PEAUX PREPARES
6114	LEATHR BOVINE NES,EQUINE	W 466	0.6	W 1602	2.3	W 2272	3.3	W 2247	3.9	CUIRS DE BOVINS
65	TEXTILE YARN,FABRICS,ETC		3.6		2.7		3.0		3.1	FILS,TISSUS,ARTICLES TEXTILE
658	TEXTILE ARTICLES NES	W 615	1.1	W 811	1.4	W 1283	2.1	W 968	1.8	ART FACONNES MAT TEXTILES
66	NONMETAL MINERAL MFS NES		1.6		1.8		1.1		0.7	ART MIN NON METALLIQUES
67	IRON AND STEEL		2.4		1.5		1.8		0.2	FER ET ACIER
68	NON–FERROUS METALS		0.3		0.5		0.3		3.1	METAUX NON FERREUX
681	SILVER,PLATINUM,ETC				0.2		0.1		2.9	ARGENT ET PLATINE
6812	METALS OF PLATINUM GROUP								2.8	PLATINE
68122	ROLLED PLATINUM ETC								2.8	PLAQUE PLATINE BRUT MI–OU
69	METAL MANUFACTURES NES		2.0		0.8		0.8		0.6	ART MANUFACT EN METAL NDA
7	MACHINES,TRANSPORT EQUIP		6.1		31.1		63.1		50.3	MACHINES MATERIEL TRANSPORT
72	MACHS FOR SPCL INDUSTRYS		2.0		1.5		0.8		1.6	MAC SPECIALES POUR INDUST
75	OFFICE MACHNES,ADP EQUIP		0.5		22.7		41.0		23.8	MACH BUREAU TRAIT AUTOM
759	OFFICE,ADP MCH PTS,ACCES	W 5	0.5	W 138	22.7	W 147	41.0	W 59	23.8	PIECES DU 751 ET 752
7591	OFFICE MACHINE PARTS NES	W 5	0.5	W 138	22.7	W 147	41.0	W 59	23.7	PIECES DU 7511,7518
75919	COPY MACH PRTS,ACCES NES	W 5	0.5	W 138	22.7	W 147	41.0	W 57	23.7	PIECES DU 751.82
77	ELECTRIC MACHNRY NES ETC		1.4		1.4		17.6		22.8	MACH APP ELECT NDA
771	ELECTRIC POWER MACHY NES	W 4	0.1	W 1	0.1	W 64	16.6	W 51	21.6	MACH PROD,TRANS ELECTR
7712	OTH ELEC POWER MACHY NES	W 1	0.1	W 1	0.1	W 64	16.6	W 48	21.6	AUT APP PROD TRANSF ELEC
77121	STATIC CONVERTERS ETC					W 64	16.6	W 48	21.6	CONVERTISSEURS STATIQUES
775	HOUSEHOLD TYPE EQUIP NES	W 235	1.2	W 267	1.1	W 237	0.8	W 251	1.2	MACH,APP USAGE DOMESTQUE
7752	DOM REFRIGERATRS,FREEZRS	W 234	1.2	W 265	1.1	W 236	0.8	W 251	1.2	REFRIG,CONGEL MENAGER
77522	DOMESTIC DEEP–FREEZERS	W 234	1.2	W 265	1.1	W 236	0.8	W 251	1.2	MEUBLES CONGELATEURS
78	ROAD VEHICLES		1.0		2.6		1.4		0.8	VEHICULES ROUTIERS
784	MOTOR VEH PRTS,ACCES NES	W 437	0.4	W 1576	1.9	W 274	0.9	W 16	0.2	PIECES 722,781,782,783
7849	OTHER MOTOR VEHCL PARTS	W 126	0.2	W 1545	1.9	W 274	0.9	W 15	0.2	PIECES 722,781,782,783
8	MISC MANUFACTURED GOODS		23.5		55.0		138.5		90.8	ART MANUFACTURES DIVERS
812	*PLUMBG,HEATNG,LGHTNG EQ	W 1508	1.8	W 2006	2.6	W 2529	3.3	W 2822	3.5	APPAR SANITAIRES CHAUFFAGE
8122	CERAMIC PLUMBNG FIXTURES	W 1503	1.8	W 2005	2.6	W 2529	3.3	W 2820	3.5	EVIERS,LAVABOS,CUVETTES
851	*FOOTWEAR	W 105	0.7	W 91	0.7	W 140	1.2	W 422	2.4	CHAUSSURES
87	PRECISION INSTRUMNTS NES		0.2		0.2		0.1		16.6	INSTRUM,APPAR SCIENT NDA
872	MEDICAL INSTRUMENTS NES		0.1		0.1	W 1	0.1	W 51	16.5	INSTR,APP MEDIC–CHIR NDA
87202	OTH MEDICAL INSTRUMENTS		0.1		0.1	W 1	0.1	W 51	16.5	INSTRUM,APP MEDECINE
89	MISC MANUFCTRD GOODS NES		20.0		50.8		133.2		67.7	ART MANUFACTURES DIVERS
895	OFFICE SUPPLIES NES	W 123	9.0	W 234	28.0	W 192	52.0	W 86	27.9	ART PAPET NDA
8959	OTHER OFFICE SUPPLIES	W 44	8.9	W 177	27.9	W 174	52.0	W 72	27.8	AUT ART DE PAPETERIE
89594	TYPEWRTR RIBBON,INK PADS	W 43	8.9	W 177	27.9	W 174	52.0	W 72	27.8	RUBANS ENCREURS
897	GOLD,SILVER WARE,JEWELRY		9.9		9.2		36.8		22.5	BIJOUTERIE,ORFEVRERIE
8973	PREC JEWLRY,GLD–SILVWARE		9.9		9.2		36.8		16.0	BIJOUX OR,ARGENT ORFEVRE
89731	PRECIOUS METAL JEWELLERY		9.9		9.2		36.8		16.0	ART BIJOUTERIE,JOAILLER
8974	PREC MTL INDUS,LAB EQUIP								6.6	AUT OUV METAUX PRECIEUX
898	MUSICAL INSTRUMENTS,PTS	W 10	0.1	W 140	12.4	W 133	43.2	W 32	16.5	INSTRUMENTS DE MUSIQUE
8983	SOUND RECRDNG TAPE,DISCS			W 116	12.4	W 132	43.2	W 32	16.5	SUPPORTS SON POUR 763
89831	PREPD SND RECORDNG MEDIA			W 116	12.4	W 132	43.2	W 32	16.5	SUPPORTS PREPARES
9	GOODS NOT CLASSD BY KIND		4.7		10.3		8.4		10.4	ART TRANSACT NON CLASSES
971	*GOLD,NON MONETARY NES		3.6		9.3	K 4571	7.0	K 128693	9.1	OR NON MONETAIRE
97101	NONMON GLD UNWRT,SEMIMFD		3.6		9.3	K 4571	7.0	K 128693	9.1	OR,ALLIAGES D'OR BRUTS

1. HISTORICAL SERIES, 1956–1993 GENERAL TRADE, IMPORTS C.I.F., EXPORTS F.O.B.
SERIES HISTORIQUES, 1956–1993 COMMERCE GENERAL, IMPORTATIONS C.A.F., EXPORTATIONS F.O.B

YEAR ANNEE	VALUE IN MILLION N.Z. DOLLARS VALEUR EN MILLION N.Z. DOLLARS MERCHANDISE –MARCHANDISE		GOLD –OR		CONVERSION FACTORS U.S. CENTS PER N.Z. DOLLAR FACTEURS DE CONVERSION CENTS E.U. PAR N.Z. DOLLAR		INDEX NUMBERS –INDICES QUANTUM		UNIT VALUE VALEUR UNITAIRE	
	IMPORTS	EXPORTS	IMPORTS	EXPORTS	IMPORTS	EXPORTS	IMPORTS	EXPORTS	IMPORTS	EXPORTS
1956	0.33	0.13			140.0000	140.0000				
1957	0.31	0.12			140.0000	140.0000				
1958	0.30	0.11			140.0000	140.0000				
1959	0.34	0.05			140.0000	140.0000				
1960	0.46	0.04			140.0000	140.0000				
1961	0.48	0.07			140.0000	140.0000				
1962	0.37	0.06			139.0000	139.0000				
1963	0.33	0.10			139.0000	139.0000				
1964	0.46	0.16			139.0000	139.0000				
1965	0.50	0.13			139.0000	139.0000				
1966	0.52	0.11			139.0000	139.0000				
1967	0.60	0.13			137.0000	137.0000				
1968	0.69	0.06			112.0000	112.0000				
1969	0.77	0.07			112.0000	112.0000				
1970	0.75	0.18			112.0000	112.0000				
1971	0.81	0.18			113.6080	113.6080				
1972	0.92	0.14			119.5000	119.5000				
1973	0.72	0.14			136.1970	136.3000				
1974	1.15	0.17			140.1000	140.1000				
1975	2.09	0.20			121.4560	121.4560				
1976	1.75	0.15			99.6370	99.4150				
1977	2.11	0.26			97.0830	96.9150				
1978	2.32	0.24			103.7760	103.9250				
1979	2.09	0.37			102.3470	102.3470				
1980	3.38	0.31			97.3400	97.3400				
1981	3.84	0.59			87.0000	87.0000				
1982	3.43	0.64			75.1875	75.1875				
1983	3.16	0.63			66.8800	66.8800				
1984	4.21	0.25			57.8500	57.8500				
1985	3.75	0.18			49.8400	49.8400				
1986		0.17				52.7457				
1987		0.12				57.8485				
1988		0.09				66.3134				
1991	5.86	0.08			57.9200	57.9200				
1992	7.22	0.19			53.8100	53.8100				
1993	6.96	0.54			54.0700	54.0700				

2. IMPORTS BY BROAD ECONOMIC CATEGORY AND EXPORTS BY INDUSTRIAL ORIGIN. (PERCENTAGE OF TOTAL VALUE)
IMPORTATIONS PAR CATEGORIES ECONOMIQUES ET EXPORTATIONS PAR BRANCHE D'ACTIVITE.(EN POURCENTAGE DE LA VALEUR TOTALE)

IMPORTS – IMPORTATIONS

	1987	1988	1989	1990	1991	1992	1993
TOTAL IMPORTS–IMPORTATIONS TOTALES							
1 FOOD BEV–ALIMENTATION BOISSONS							
11 PRIMARY–PRODUITS DE BASE							
111 FOR INDUSTRY–POUR L'INDUSTRIE							
112 FOR HOUSEHOLDS–POUR LES MENAGES							
12 PROCESSED–PRODUITS ELABORES							
121 FOR INDUSTRY–POUR L'INDUSTRIE							
122 FOR HOUSEHOLDS–POUR LES MENAGES							
2 IND SUPPLIES–APPROV INDUSTRIELS							
21 PRIMARY–PRODUITS DE BASE							
22 PROCESSED–PRODUITS ELABORES							
3 FUELS–COMBUSTIBLES							
31 PRIMARY–PRODUITS DE BASE							
32 PROCESSED–PRODUITS ELABORES							
321 MOTOR SPIRIT–ESSENCE							
322 OTHER–AUTRES							
4 MACHINERY–EQUIPEMENT							
41 CAPITAL EQUIPMENT–MACHINES							
42 PARTS–PIECES ACCESSOIRES							
5 TRANSPORT–TRANSPORT							
51 PASSENGER CARS–AUTOMOBILES							
52 OTHER–AUTRES							
521 INDUSTRIAL–INDUSTRIELS							
522 NON INDUSTRIAL–NON INDUSTRIEL							
53 PARTS–PIECES ACCESSOIRES							
6 CONSUM GOODS–BIENS CONSOMMATION							
61 DURABLE–DURABLES							
62 SEMI DURABLE–SEMI DURABLES							
63 NON DURABLE–NON DURABLES							
7 GOODS NES–BIENS NDA							

EXPORTS – EXPORTATIONS

	1987	1988	1989	1990	1991	1992	1993
TOTAL EXPORTS–EXPORTATIONS TOTALES							
1 AGRICULTURE							
2 MINING QUARRY–INDUS EXTRACTIVES							
3 MANUFACTURING–IND MANUFACTUR							
31 FOOD BEV TOBACCO–ALIM BOISS TAB							
32 TEXTILES–INDUSTRIES TEXTILES							
33 WOOD & PRODUCTS–BOIS & PRODUITS							
34 PAPER & PRODUCTS–PAPIER & PRODT							
35 CHEMICALS–INDUSTRIES CHIMIQUES							
36 NON METAL MIN–MIN NON METAL							
37 BASIC METAL–IND METAL BASE							
38 METAL MANUF–MANUF METAL							
39 OTH MANUF IND–AUTRES MANUF							

3. TRADE BY PRINCIPAL COUNTRIES OF ORIGIN AND DESTINATION (VALUE IN MILLION U.S. DOLLARS)
ECHANGES SELON LES PRINCIPAUX PAYS D'ORIGINE ET DE DESTINATION (VALEUR EN MILLIONS DE DOLLARS EU)

COUNTRIES–PAYS	GENERAL IMPORTS C.I.F. IMPORTATIONS GENERALES C.A.F					COUNTRIES–PAYS	GENERAL EXPORTS F.O.B. EXPORTATIONS GENERALES F.O.B.				
	1989	1990	1991	1992	1993		1989	1990	1991	1992	1993
World				3.9	3.5	Monde					
Africa						Afrique					
Americas				0.0	0.1	Amériques					
– Northern America				0.0	0.1	– Amérique du Nord					
– LAIA						– ALAI					
– CACM						– MCAC					
– Caribbean						– Caraïbes					
– Rest of America						– Autre Amérique					
Asia excl fmr USSR				0.2	0.2	Asie anc. URSS exclus					
– Middle East						– Moyen–Orient					
Asia former USSR						Asie ancienne URSS					
Europe excl fmr USSR				0.0	0.0	Europe anc. URSS exclus					
– European Union				0.0	0.0	– Union Européenne					
– Eastern Europe						– Europe de l'Est					
– Rest of Europe						– Autre de l'Europe					
Europe former USSR						Europe ancienne URSS					
Oceania				3.6	3.2	Océanie					
Other						Autre					
New Zealand				3.2	3.0						
Australia/Australie				0.4	0.1						
Japan/Japon				0.2	0.2						
Fiji/Fidji				0.0	0.1						

(VALUE AS PERCENTAGE OF WORLD TOTAL)(VALEURS EN POURCENTAGE DU TOTAL MONDIAL)

	1984	1985	1986	1987	1988	1989	1990	1991	1992	1993		1984	1985	1986	1987	1988	1989	1990	1991	1992	1993
Africa											Afrique										
Americas	2.5								0.1	2.9	Amériques										
– Northern America	2.5								0.1	2.9	– Amérique du Nord										
– LAIA											– ALAI										
– CACM											– MCAC										
– Caribbean											– Caraïbes										
– Rest of America											– Autre Amérique										
Asia excl fmr USSR	5.7								5.9	6.1	Asie anc. URSS exclus										
– Middle East											– Moyen–Orient										
Asia former USSR											Asie ancienne URSS										
Europe excl fmr USSR	0.5								0.1	0.2	Europe anc. URSS exclus										
– European Union	0.5								0.1	0.2	– Union Européenne										
– Eastern Europe											– Europe de l'Est										
– Rest of Europe											– Autre de l'Europe										
Europe former USSR											Europe ancienne URSS										
Oceania	91.3								93.9	90.8	Océanie										
Other											Autre										
New Zealand	51.9								82.2	86.1											
Australia/Australie	1.4								10.7	1.5											
Japan/Japon	4.5								5.7	5.5											
Fiji/Fidji	34.5								0.3	2.0											

4. General Imports C.I.F. by Commodities according to the S.I.T.C. (Rev. 2) in million U.S. Dollars
Importations Générales C.A.F. par Produits d'après la C.T.C.I. (Rév. 2) en millions de Dollars E.U.

SITC CTCI	COMMODITY	1990		1991		1992		1993		PRODUIT
		QUANTITY QUANTITE	VALUE VALEUR	QUANTITY QUANTITE	VALUE VALEUR	QUANTITY QUANTITE	VALUE VALEUR	QUANTITY QUANTITE	VALUE VALEUR	
	ALL COMMODITIES						3.9		3.5	TOUS PRODUITS
0	FOOD AND LIVE ANIMALS						1.2		1.0	ALIMENTS,ANIMAUX VIVANTS
01	MEAT AND PREPARATIONS						0.2		0.3	VIANDES ET PREPARATIONS
011	MEAT FRESH,CHILLD,FROZEN						0.2		0.3	VIANDES FRAICHES,REF,CONGE
02	DAIRY PRODCTS,BIRDS'EGGS						0.1		0.1	PRODUITS LAITIERS,OEUFS
03	FISH AND PREPARATIONS						0.4		0.3	POISSONS ET PREPARATIONS
037	FISH ETC PREPD,PRSVD NES						0.4		0.2	POIS,CRUST,MOL PREPARES
04	CEREALS AND PREPARATIONS						0.2		0.2	CEREALES ET PRODUITS
048	CEREAL ETC PREPARATIONS						0.2		0.2	PREPTNS A BASE CEREALES
0484	BAKERY PRODUCTS						0.2		0.2	PRODUITS DE BOULANGERIE
05	VEGETABLES AND FRUIT						0.2		0.2	LEGUMES ET FRUITS
054	VEG ETC FRSH,SMPLY PRSVD						0.1		0.1	LEGUMES FRAIS,CONG,SECS
056	VEGTBLES ETC PRSVD,PREPD						0.1		0.1	CONSERVES DE LEGUMES
05651	VEGTBLS,FRUIT IN VINEGAR						0.1		0.1	LEGUM CONSERV AU VINAIGRE
057	FRUIT,NUTS,FRESH,DRIED						0.1		0.1	FRUITS FRAIS OU SECS
0572	LEMONS,GRAPEFRUIT ETC						0.1		0.1	AUTRES AGRUMES FRAIS,SECS
06	SUGAR AND PREPS,HONEY						0.1		0.1	SUCRES ET PRODUITS
061	SUGAR AND HONEY						0.1		0.1	SUCRES ET MIEL
07	COFFEE,TEA,COCOA,SPICES						0.1		0.1	CAFE,THE,CACAO,EPICES
081	*FEEDING STUFF FOR ANIML						0.1		0.1	NOURRITURE POUR ANIMAUX
09	MISC EDIBLE PRODUCTS						0.1		0.1	PREP ALIMENTAIRES DIVERSES
098	EDIBLE PRODCTS,PREPS NES						0.1		0.1	PREP ALIMENTAIRES NDA
09809	MISC FOOD PREPRTIONS NES						0.1		0.1	PREP ALIMENTAIRES NDA
1	BEVERAGES AND TOBACCO						0.4		0.2	BOISSONS ET TABACS
11	BEVERAGES						0.4		0.2	BOISSONS
112	ALCOHOLIC BEVERAGES						0.4		0.1	BOISSONS ALCOOLIQUES
1123	BEER,ALE,STOUT,PORTER						0.1	V 110	0.1	BIERES
12	TOBACCO AND MANUFACTURES						0.1		0.1	TABACS BRUTS FABRIQUES
122	TOBACCO,MANUFACTURED						0.1		0.1	TABACS FABRIQUES
1223	OTH MANUFACTURED TOBACCO						0.1		0.1	TABACS FUMER,CHIQUER,PRISER
2	CRUDE MATERLS,EXCL FUELS						0.1		0.1	MAT BRUTES NON COMESTIBLES
26	TEXTILE FIBRES AND WASTE						0.1		0.1	FIBRES TEXTILES
269	WASTE OF TEXTILE FABRICS						0.1		0.1	FRIPERIE DRILLES,CHIFFONS
26901	BULK TEXT WSTE,OLD CLTHG						0.1		0.1	ART ET ACCESS D'HABILLEMENT
27	CRUDE FERTLZR,MINRLS NES						0.1		0.1	ENGRAIS MINERAUX BRUTS
3	MINERAL FUELS ETC						0.5		0.2	COMBUSTIBLES MINERAUX LUB
33	PETROLEUM AND PRODUCTS						0.5		0.2	PETROLE ET DERIVES
334	PETROLEUM PRODUCTS,REFIN						0.2		0.1	PRODUITS RAFFINES
33411	MOTOR,AVIATION SPIRIT					W 266	0.1		0.1	ESSENCES MOTEURS D'AVIONS
33412	SPIRIT TYPE JET FUEL					W 269	0.1	W 81	0.1	CARBUREACTEURS
3344	FUEL OILS,NES					W 787	0.1	W 220	0.1	FUEL OILS
335	RESIDUAL PETRLM PROD NES						0.4		0.1	PRODUITS RESIDUELS NDA
4	ANIMAL,VEGETABLE OIL,FAT						0.1		0.1	HUILES,GRAISSES ANIM,VEG
431	*PROCESD ANML VEG OIL,ET						0.1		0.1	HUILES,GRAISSES PREPAREES
5	CHEMCLS,RELATED PROD NES						0.4		0.4	PRODUITS CHIMIQUES
53	DYES,TANNING,COLOUR PROD						0.1		0.1	PROD TEINTURE,COLORANTS
532	DYES NES,TANNING PROD						0.1		0.1	EXTRAITS TEINTURE,TANNAGE
541	*MEDICINAL,PHARM PRODUCT						0.1		0.1	PROD MEDICINAUX PHARMACEUT
55	PERFUME,CLEANING ETC PRD						0.2		0.1	PROD POUR PARFUM,TOILETTE
553	PERFUMERY,COSMETICS,ETC						0.1		0.1	PRODUITS DE PARFUMERIE
554	SOAP,CLEANSING ETC PREPS						0.1		0.1	SAVONS,PRODUITS DETERSIFS
58	PLASTIC MATERIALS ETC						0.1		0.1	MAT PLAST ARTIFICIELLES
59	CHEMICAL MATERIALS NES						0.1		0.1	MAT PROD CHIMIQUES NDA
592	STARCH,INULIN,GLUTEN,ETC						0.1		0.1	AMIDONS,INUL,GLUT FROM
5921	STARCH,INULIN,GLUTEN						0.1		0.1	AMID,INUL,GLUT FROMENT
6	BASIC MANUFACTURES						0.6		0.7	ART MANUFACTURES
62	RUBBER MANUFACTURES NES						0.1		0.1	CAOUTCHOUC MANUFACTURE
63	WOOD,CORK MANUFACTRS NES						0.2		0.2	OUVRAGES LIEGE ET BOIS
635	WOOD MANUFACTURES NES						0.1		0.1	ART MANUF EN BOIS NDA
6353	BUILDERS WOODWRK,PREFABS						0.1		0.1	OUVRAGES DE MENUISERIE
64	PAPER,PAPERBOARD AND MFR						0.2		0.1	PAPIERS,CARTONS & OUVRAGES
641	PAPER AND PAPERBOARD						0.2		0.1	PAPIERS ET CARTONS
65	TEXTILE YARN,FABRICS,ETC						0.1		0.1	FILS,TISSUS,ARTICLES TEXTILE
651	TEXTILE YARN						0.1		0.1	FILS TEXTILES
66	NONMETAL MINERAL MFS NES						0.1		0.1	ART MIN NON METALLIQUES
661	LIME,CEMENT,BLDG PRODS						0.1		0.1	CHAUX,CIMENTS MAT CONSTR
66181	ASPHALT ETC PRODUCTS						0.1		0.1	OUVRAGES EN ASPHALTE
665	GLASSWARE						0.1		0.1	OUVRAGES EN VERRE
67	IRON AND STEEL						0.1		0.1	FER ET ACIER
68	NON-FERROUS METALS						0.1		0.1	METAUX NON FERREUX
684	ALUMINIUM						0.1		0.1	ALUMINIUM
6841	ALUMINIUM,ALLOYS,UNWRGHT						0.1		0.1	ALUMINIUM,ALLIAGES BRUTS
69	METAL MANUFACTURES NES						0.2		0.2	ART MANUFACT EN METAL NDA
691	STRUCTURES AND PARTS NES						0.1		0.2	CONSTRUCT FER,ACIER,ALU
696	CUTLERY						0.1		0.1	COUTELLERIE
69606	BASE METAL TABLEWARE NES						0.1		0.1	CUILLERS,FOURCHETTES
699	BASE METAL MFRS NES						0.1		0.1	ART MANUFACTURES MET NDA
7	MACHINES,TRANSPORT EQUIP						0.7		1.0	MACHINES MATERIEL TRANSPORT
71	POWER GENERATING EQUIPMT						0.2		0.4	MACHINES GENERATRICES
716	ROTATING ELECTRIC PLANT								0.2	APP ELECTR ROTATIFS,PIECES
7163	ROTARY CONVERTERS								0.2	CONVERTISSEURS ROTATIFS
718	OTH POWER GENERATG MACHY						0.2		0.2	AUTRES MOTEURS PARTIES
7187	NUCLEAR REACTORS,PTS NES						0.2		0.2	REACTEURS NUCLEAIRES
72	MACHS FOR SPCL INDUSTRYS						0.1		0.1	MAC SPECIALES POUR INDUST
74	GENRL INDUSTRL MACHY NES						0.1		0.1	MACH APP INDUSTRIE
76	TELECOMM,SOUND EQUIPMENT						0.1		0.3	EQUIPMENT DE TELECOM
763	SOUND RECORDRS,PHONOGRPH						0.1		0.3	PHONO,APP ENREGISTREMENT
764	TELECOM EQPT,PTS,ACC NES						0.1		0.1	EQUIP TELECOM,PIECES
76481	RADIOTELEPHONE ETC RCVRS								0.1	RECEP RADIOTELEPHONIE
77	ELECTRIC MACHNRY NES ETC						0.1		0.1	MACH APP ELECT NDA
78	ROAD VEHICLES						0.4		0.3	VEHICULES ROUTIERS
781	PASS MOTOR VEH EXC BUSES					N 1683	0.1	N 13	0.1	AUTO TRANSPORT PERSONNES
782	LORRIES,SPCL MTR VEH NES					N 2307	0.1	N 59	0.1	VEHICULES SPECIAUX,MARCH
7821	LORRIES,TRUCKS					N 2307	0.1	N 59	0.1	VEHICULES TRANSP MARCHAND
783	ROAD MOTOR VEHICLES NES							N 2	0.1	VEHICULES ROUTIERS NDA
7831	BUSES							N 2	0.1	VOITURES TRANSPORT COMMUN
79	OTHR TRANSPORT EQUIPMENT						0.1		0.1	AUTRE MATERIEL TRANSPORT
793	SHIPS AND BOATS ETC						0.1		0.1	NAVIRES BATEAUX,ETC
8	MISC MANUFACTURED GOODS						0.3		0.3	ART MANUFACTURES DIVERS
821	*FURNITURE,PARTS THEREOF						0.1		0.1	MEUBLES ET PIECES
82122	MATTRESSES ETC						0.1		0.1	SOMMIERS,ARTICLES DE LITERIE

4. General Imports C.I.F. by Commodities according to the S.I.T.C. (Rev. 2) in million U.S. Dollars
Importations Générales C.A.F. par Produits d'après la C.T.C.I. (Rév. 2) en millions de Dollars E.U.

SITC CTCI	COMMODITY	1990 QUANTITY QUANTITE	1990 VALUE VALEUR	1991 QUANTITY QUANTITE	1991 VALUE VALEUR	1992 QUANTITY QUANTITE	1992 VALUE VALEUR	1993 QUANTITY QUANTITE	1993 VALUE VALEUR	PRODUIT
84	CLOTHING AND ACCESSORIES						0.1		0.1	VETEMENTS
847	TEXTILE CLTHNG ACCES NES						0.1		0.1	ACCES VET MAT TEXT NDA
84719	MADE-UP CLTHG ACCESS NES						0.1		0.1	AUT ACCES VET MAT TEXTIL
84722	KNIT SOCKS,ETC NONELASTC						0.1		0.1	CHAUSSETTES BON. NON ELAS
851	*FOOTWEAR						0.1		0.1	CHAUSSURES
85105	GAITERS,LEGGINGS,ETC						0.1		0.1	GUETRES,JAMBIERES ETC
87	PRECISION INSTRUMNTS NES						0.1		0.1	INSTRUM,APPAR SCIENT NDA
88	PHOTO EQU,OPTICL GDS ETC						0.1		0.1	APP,FOURN PHOTO,OP,MONTR
89	MISC MANUFCTRD GOODS NES						0.2		0.1	ART MANUFACTURES DIVERS
892	PRINTED MATTER						0.2		0.1	IMPRIMES
89282	PLANS,ETC NOT PRINTED						0.2		0.1	PLANS ARCHITECTES,INGEN
894	TOYS,SPORTING GOODS,ETC						0.1		0.1	VOITURES ENFANTS,JOUETS
89423	TOYS NES						0.1		0.1	JOUETS,MODELES REDUITS

5. General Exports F.O.B. by Commodities according to the S.I.T.C. (Rev. 2) in million U.S. Dollars
Exportations Générales F.O.B. par Produits d'après la C.T.C.I. (Rév. 2) en millions de Dollars E.U.

SITC CTCI	COMMODITY	1990		1991		1992		1993		PRODUIT
		QUANTITY QUANTITE	VALUE VALEUR	QUANTITY QUANTITE	VALUE VALEUR	QUANTITY QUANTITE	VALUE VALEUR	QUANTITY QUANTITE	VALUE VALEUR	
	ALL COMMODITIES						0.2		0.3	TOUS PRODUITS
0	FOOD AND LIVE ANIMALS						0.1		0.3	ALIMENTS,ANIMAUX VIVANTS
05	VEGETABLES AND FRUIT						0.1		0.3	LEGUMES ET FRUITS
054	VEG ETC FRSH,SMPLY PRSVD						0.1		0.3	LEGUMES FRAIS,CONG,SECS
0548	EDIBLE VEG NES FRESH,DRY						0.1		0.3	RACINES,TUBERCULES
05481	ROOTS,TUBERS FRESH,DRY						0.1		0.3	RACINES DE MANIOC ETC
056	VEGTBLES ETC PRSVD,PREPD						0.1			CONSERVES DE LEGUMES
0564	FLOUR ETC OF FRUIT,VEGET						0.1			FARINES,SEMOULES,FLOCONS
05645	TAPIOCA, SAGO, ETC						0.1			TAPIOCA
057	FRUIT,NUTS,FRESH,DRIED						0.1		0.1	FRUITS FRAIS OU SECS
0577	NUTS EDIBLE,FRESH,DRIED						0.1		0.1	FRUITS A COQUES
05771	COCONUTS FRESH OR DRIED						0.1		0.1	NOIX DE COCO
9	GOODS NOT CLASSD BY KIND						0.1			ART TRANSACT NON CLASSES

1. HISTORICAL SERIES, 1992–1994 GENERAL TRADE, IMPORTS F.O.B., EXPORTS F.O.B.
SERIES HISTORIQUES, 1992–1994 COMMERCE GENERAL, IMPORTATIONS F.O.B., EXPORTATIONS F.O.B

YEAR ANNEE	VALUE IN MILLION U.S. DOLLARS VALEUR EN MILLION U.S. DOLLARS MERCHANDISE –MARCHANDISE		GOLD –OR		CONVERSION FACTORS FACTEURS DE CONVERSION CENTS E.U. PAR		INDEX NUMBERS –INDICES QUANTUM		UNIT VALUE VALEUR UNITAIRE	
	IMPORTS	EXPORTS	IMPORTS	EXPORTS	IMPORTS	EXPORTS	IMPORTS	EXPORTS	IMPORTS	EXPORTS
1992	493.60									
1993	512.40									
1994	513.80									

2. IMPORTS BY BROAD ECONOMIC CATEGORY AND EXPORTS BY INDUSTRIAL ORIGIN. (PERCENTAGE OF TOTAL VALUE)
IMPORTATIONS PAR CATEGORIES ECONOMIQUES ET EXPORTATIONS PAR BRANCHE D'ACTIVITE.(EN POURCENTAGE DE LA VALEUR TOTALE)

IMPORTS – IMPORTATIONS

	1988	1989	1990	1991	1992	1993	1994
TOTAL IMPORTS–IMPORTATIONS TOTALES							
1 FOOD BEV–ALIMENTATION BOISSONS							
11 PRIMARY–PRODUITS DE BASE							
111 FOR INDUSTRY–POUR L'INDUSTRIE							
112 FOR HOUSEHOLDS–POUR LES MENAGES							
12 PROCESSED–PRODUITS ELABORES							
121 FOR INDUSTRY–POUR L'INDUSTRIE							
122 FOR HOUSEHOLDS–POUR LES MENAGES							
2 IND SUPPLIES–APPROV INDUSTRIELS							
21 PRIMARY–PRODUITS DE BASE							
22 PROCESSED–PRODUITS ELABORES							
3 FUELS–COMBUSTIBLES							
31 PRIMARY–PRODUITS DE BASE							
32 PROCESSED–PRODUITS ELABORES							
321 MOTOR SPIRIT–ESSENCE							
322 OTHER–AUTRES							
4 MACHINERY–EQUIPEMENT							
41 CAPITAL EQUIPMENT–MACHINES							
42 PARTS–PIECES ACCESSOIRES							
5 TRANSPORT–TRANSPORT							
51 PASSENGER CARS–AUTOMOBILES							
52 OTHER–AUTRES							
521 INDUSTRIAL–INDUSTRIELS							
522 NON INDUSTRIAL–NON INDUSTRIEL							
53 PARTS–PIECES ACCESSOIRES							
6 CONSUM GOODS–BIENS CONSOMMATION							
61 DURABLE–DURABLES							
62 SEMI DURABLE–SEMI DURABLES							
63 NON DURABLE–NON DURABLES							
7 GOODS NES–BIENS NDA							

EXPORTS – EXPORTATIONS

	1988	1989	1990	1991	1992	1993	1994
TOTAL EXPORTS–EXPORTATIONS TOTALES							
1 AGRICULTURE							
2 MINING QUARRY–INDUS EXTRACTIVES							
3 MANUFACTURING–IND MANUFACTUR							
31 FOOD BEV TOBACCO–ALIM BOISS TAB							
32 TEXTILES–INDUSTRIES TEXTILES							
33 WOOD & PRODUCTS–BOIS & PRODUITS							
34 PAPER & PRODUCTS–PAPIER & PRODT							
35 CHEMICALS–INDUSTRIES CHIMIQUES							
36 NON METAL MIN–MIN NON METAL							
37 BASIC METAL–IND METAL BASE							
38 METAL MANUF–MANUF METAL							
39 OTH MANUF IND–AUTRES MANUF							

3. TRADE BY PRINCIPAL COUNTRIES OF ORIGIN AND DESTINATION (VALUE IN MILLION U.S. DOLLARS)
ECHANGES SELON LES PRINCIPAUX PAYS D'ORIGINE ET DE DESTINATION (VALEUR EN MILLIONS DE DOLLARS EU)

COUNTRIES–PAYS	GENERAL IMPORTS F.O.B. IMPORTATIONS GENERALES F.O.B.					COUNTRIES–PAYS	GENERAL EXPORTS F.O.B. EXPORTATIONS GENERALES F.O.B.				
	1990	1991	1992	1993	1994		1990	1991	1992	1993	1994
World						Monde					
Africa						Afrique					
Americas						Amériques					
– Northern America						– Amérique du Nord					
– LAIA						– ALAI					
– CACM						– MCAC					
– Caribbean						– Caraïbes					
– Rest of America						– Autre Amérique					
Asia excl fmr USSR						Asie anc. URSS exclus					
– Middle East						– Moyen–Orient					
Asia former USSR						Asie ancienne URSS					
Europe excl fmr USSR						Europe anc. URSS exclus					
– European Union						– Union Européenne					
– Eastern Europe						– Europe de l'Est					
– Rest of Europe						– Autre de l'Europe					
Europe former USSR						Europe ancienne URSS					
Oceania						Océanie					
Other						Autre					

(VALUE AS PERCENTAGE OF WORLD TOTAL)(VALEURS EN POURCENTAGE DU TOTAL MONDIAL)

	1985	1986	1987	1988	1989	1990	1991	1992	1993	1994		1985	1986	1987	1988	1989	1990	1991	1992	1993	1994
Africa											Afrique										
Americas											Amériques										
– Northern America											– Amérique du Nord										
– LAIA											– ALAI										
– CACM											– MCAC										
– Caribbean											– Caraïbes										
– Rest of America											– Autre Amérique										
Asia excl fmr USSR											Asie anc. URSS exclus										
– Middle East											– Moyen–Orient										
Asia former USSR											Asie ancienne URSS										
Europe excl fmr USSR											Europe anc. URSS exclus										
– European Union											– Union Européenne										
– Eastern Europe											– Europe de l'Est										
– Rest of Europe											– Autre de l'Europe										
Europe former USSR											Europe ancienne URSS										
Oceania											Océanie										
Other											Autre										

4. General Imports F.O.B. by Commodities according to the S.I.T.C. (Rev. 2) in million U.S. Dollars
Importations Générales F.O.B. par Produits d'après la C.T.C.I. (Rév. 2) en millions de Dollars E.U.

SITC CTCI	COMMODITY	1991		1992		1993		1994		PRODUIT
		QUANTITY QUANTITE	VALUE VALEUR	QUANTITY QUANTITE	VALUE VALEUR	QUANTITY QUANTITE	VALUE VALEUR	QUANTITY QUANTITE	VALUE VALEUR	
	ALL COMMODITIES				493.6		512.4		513.8	TOUS PRODUITS
001	*LIVE ANIMALS FOR FOOD				2.8		0.1		1.4	ANIMAUX VIVANTS
01	MEAT AND PREPARATIONS				9.3		10.1		11.8	VIANDES ET PREPARATIONS
02	DAIRY PRODCTS,BIRDS'EGGS				3.4		3.2		3.5	PRODUITS LAITIERS,OEUFS
03	FISH AND PREPARATIONS				2.9		3.1		2.9	POISSONS ET PREPARATIONS
04	CEREALS AND PREPARATIONS				3.1		2.6		3.2	CEREALES ET PRODUITS
048	CEREAL ETC PREPARATIONS				0.7		0.9		2.2	PREPTNS A BASE CEREALES
05	VEGETABLES AND FRUIT						2.8		3.8	LEGUMES ET FRUITS
057	FRUIT,NUTS,FRESH,DRIED				1.6		1.1		1.9	FRUITS FRAIS OU SECS
06	SUGAR AND PREPS,HONEY				2.0		1.1		1.9	SUCRES ET PRODUITS
07	COFFEE,TEA,COCOA,SPICES						2.4			CAFE,THE,CACAO,EPICES
072	COCOA				3.1		1.4		2.0	CACAO
098	EDIBLE PRODCTS,PREPS NES				5.5		4.4		6.2	PREP ALIMENTAIRES NDA
11	BEVERAGES				15.9		15.2		16.0	BOISSONS
122	TOBACCO,MANUFACTURED				9.2		7.3		6.7	TABACS FABRIQUES
334	PETROLEUM PRODUCTS,REFIN				37.2		49.6		53.4	PRODUITS RAFFINES
53	DYES,TANNING,COLOUR PROD				2.2		1.2		0.9	PROD TEINTURE,COLORANTS
55	PERFUME,CLEANING ETC PRD				10.5		8.3		7.5	PROD POUR PARFUM,TOILETTE
553	PERFUMERY,COSMETICS,ETC				2.0		3.6		3.4	PRODUITS DE PARFUMERIE
598	MISCEL CHEM PRODUCTS NES				2.1		1.3		1.8	PROD DIV INDUST CHIM NDA
658	TEXTILE ARTICLES NES				10.8		7.6		5.7	ART FACONNES MAT TEXTILES
661	LIME,CEMENT,BLDG PRODS				1.6		1.5		1.0	CHAUX,CIMENTS MAT CONSTR
6639	CERAMIC ARTICLES NES				2.3		1.3		1.4	ARTICLES EN CERAMIQUE NDA
67	IRON AND STEEL				4.3		1.5		1.6	FER ET ACIER
69	METAL MANUFACTURES NES				3.9		4.8		8.3	ART MANUFACT EN METAL NDA
6996	BASE MTL MISC ARTICLES				1.7		1.6		1.6	ART DIVERS METAUX COMMUNS
78	ROAD VEHICLES				30.2		20.7		26.1	VEHICULES ROUTIERS
792	AIRCRAFT ETC				0.3		0.7		2.0	APP NAVIGATION AERIENNE
793	SHIPS AND BOATS ETC				1.2		2.7		1.6	NAVIRES BATEAUX,ETC
821	*FURNITURE,PARTS THEREOF				7.8		4.5		3.3	MEUBLES ET PIECES
84	CLOTHING AND ACCESSORIES				17.5		18.6		22.5	VETEMENTS
851	*FOOTWEAR				1.0		1.0		1.7	CHAUSSURES
88	PHOTO EQU,OPTICL GDS ETC						4.2			APP,FOURN PHOTO,OP,MONTR
885	WATCHES AND CLOCKS				4.8		3.6		6.2	HORLOGERIE
89	MISC MANUFCTRD GOODS NES				46.2		35.3		26.4	ART MANUFACTURES DIVERS
8942	TOYS,INDOOR GAMES ETC				2.2		2.4		2.6	JOUETS,JEUX ETC
931	*SPECIAL TRANSACTIONS				66.0		71.5		43.0	TRANS.SPECIALES

5. General Exports F.O.B. by Commodities according to the S.I.T.C. (Rev. 2) in million U.S. Dollars
Exportations Générales F.O.B. par Produits d'après la C.T.C.I. (Rév. 2) en millions de Dollars E.U.

SITC CTCI	COMMODITY	1991		1992		1993		1994		PRODUIT
		QUANTITY QUANTITE	VALUE VALEUR	QUANTITY QUANTITE	VALUE VALEUR	QUANTITY QUANTITE	VALUE VALEUR	QUANTITY QUANTITE	VALUE VALEUR	
	ALL COMMODITIES									TOUS PRODUITS

Norway, including Svalbard and Jan Mayen Islands

Norvège y compris iles Svalbard et Jan Mayen

1. HISTORICAL SERIES, 1962–1997 GENERAL TRADE, IMPORTS C.I.F., EXPORTS F.O.B.
SERIES HISTORIQUES, 1962–1997 COMMERCE GENERAL, IMPORTATIONS C.A.F., EXPORTATIONS F.O.B

YEAR ANNEE	VALUE IN MILLION NORWG. KRONER / VALEUR EN MILLION NORWG. KRONER — MERCHANDISE – MARCHANDISE		GOLD – OR		CONVERSION FACTORS U.S. CENTS PER NORWG. KRONE / FACTEURS DE CONVERSION CENTS E.U. PAR NORWG. KRONE		INDEX NUMBERS – INDICES — QUANTUM		UNIT VALUE / VALEUR UNITAIRE	
	IMPORTS	EXPORTS	IMPORTS	EXPORTS	IMPORTS	EXPORTS	IMPORTS	EXPORTS	IMPORTS	EXPORTS
1962	11885.00	6942.00	5.72	0.14	14.0000	14.0000				
1963	13013.00	7664.00	6.62	0.27	14.0000	14.0000				
1964	14169.00	9219.00	9.30	0.52	14.0000	14.0000				
1965	15787.00	10309.00	10.68	0.52	14.0000	14.0000				
1966	17169.00	11168.00	9.39	0.41	14.0000	14.0000				
1967	19627.00	12411.00	12.97	0.45	14.0000	14.0000				
1968	19331.00	13841.00	13.57	0.65	14.0000	14.0000				
1969	21011.00	15741.00	13.17	0.99	14.0000	14.0000				
1970	26443.00	17549.00	15.46	0.84	14.0000	14.0000				
1971	28715.00	18003.00	13.92	0.78	14.1800	14.1800				
1972	28808.00	21625.00	16.09	1.48	15.0400	15.0400				
1973	36040.00	27085.00	13.20	1.70	17.3130	17.3060				
1974	46556.00	34720.00	18.97	2.80	18.0730	18.0710				
1975	50545.00	37922.00			19.2020	19.0760				
1976	60533.00	43330.00			18.3710	18.3510				
1977	68579.00	47263.00			18.7860	18.7940				
1978	60169.00	57084.00			19.1090	19.0540				
1979	69339.00	68527.00			19.7690	19.7690				
1980	83602.00	91672.00			20.2490	20.2300	77	54	69	80
1981	89687.80	104265.40			17.4518	17.4745	76	54	72	93
1982	99747.30	113236.30			15.5182	15.5385	77	53	78	100
1983	98407.80	131397.00			13.4519	13.4160	74	60	80	103
1984	113102.10	154034.50			12.2799	12.2648	84	64	83	113
1985	132563.40	170732.80			11.7377	11.7087	94	67	88	118
1986	150052.00	133847.00			13.5330	13.5194	108	69	88	88
1987	152041.00	144543.00			14.8913	14.8698	106	78	91	85
1988	151101.00	146166.00			15.3690	15.3419	95	81	93	85
1989	163380.00	187146.00			14.4940	14.4869	90	93	99	96
1990	169998.00	211579.00			16.0113	16.0907	100	100	100	100
1991	165181.00	220316.00			15.4834	15.4848	102	107	98	96
1992	160821.00	218474.00			16.1148	16.1084	106	115	97	88
1993	170069.00	225714.00			14.0487	14.0788	107	121	97	89
1994	192073.00	243809.00			14.2147	14.2264	122	136	97	85
1995	208627.00	265883.00			15.8049	15.7947	134	145	98	88
1996	229720.00	315699.90			15.5041	15.5079	147	162	98	95
1997	250350.00	336720.10			14.1812	14.1790	160	170	97	97

2. IMPORTS BY BROAD ECONOMIC CATEGORY AND EXPORTS BY INDUSTRIAL ORIGIN. (PERCENTAGE OF TOTAL VALUE)
IMPORTATIONS PAR CATEGORIES ECONOMIQUES ET EXPORTATIONS PAR BRANCHE D'ACTIVITE.(EN POURCENTAGE DE LA VALEUR TOTALE)

IMPORTS – IMPORTATIONS

	1991	1992	1993	1994	1995	1996	1997
TOTAL IMPORTS–IMPORTATIONS TOTALES	100.	100.	100.	100.	100.	100.	100.
1 FOOD BEV–ALIMENTATION BOISSONS	5.5	5.9	5.9	6.1	6.0	6.2	5.8
11 PRIMARY–PRODUITS DE BASE	2.7	2.8	2.5	2.9	2.9	3.1	2.8
111 FOR INDUSTRY–POUR L'INDUSTRIE	0.7	0.7	0.5	1.0	0.8	0.9	0.8
112 FOR HOUSEHOLDS–POUR LES MENAGES	2.0	2.1	2.0	1.9	2.1	2.1	1.9
12 PROCESSED–PRODUITS ELABORES	2.9	3.1	3.4	3.2	3.1	3.1	3.0
121 FOR INDUSTRY–POUR L'INDUSTRIE	0.4	0.5	0.6	0.5	0.5	0.6	0.6
122 FOR HOUSEHOLDS–POUR LES MENAGES	2.4	2.6	2.8	2.7	2.6	2.6	2.4
2 IND SUPPLIES–APPROV INDUSTRIELS	31.0	30.5	30.0	32.1	32.6	30.1	29.2
21 PRIMARY–PRODUITS DE BASE	4.9	4.5	4.5	4.8	4.8	4.7	4.3
22 PROCESSED–PRODUITS ELABORES	26.1	26.0	25.5	27.3	27.8	25.4	24.8
3 FUELS–COMBUSTIBLES	3.9	3.1	3.0	2.7	2.5	4.1	3.0
31 PRIMARY–PRODUITS DE BASE	1.6	1.3	1.3	0.7	0.8	0.9	0.8
32 PROCESSED–PRODUITS ELABORES	2.3	1.8	1.7	2.0	1.7	3.2	2.1
321 MOTOR SPIRIT–ESSENCE	0.5	0.4	0.4	0.4	0.5	0.3	0.4
322 OTHER–AUTRES	1.8	1.5	1.3	1.7	1.3	2.9	1.8
4 MACHINERY–EQUIPEMENT	22.8	23.5	24.3	23.2	25.2	26.3	24.7
41 CAPITAL EQUIPMENT–MACHINES	18.5	18.9	19.4	18.5	20.3	21.8	20.2
42 PARTS–PIECES ACCESSOIRES	4.3	4.6	4.9	4.8	4.9	4.5	4.5
5 TRANSPORT–TRANSPORT	15.2	14.4	15.5	14.7	13.1	13.5	17.9
51 PASSENGER CARS–AUTOMOBILES	1.9	2.7	2.5	3.9	3.7	4.6	5.0
52 OTHER–AUTRES	9.9	8.3	9.6	7.1	5.7	5.1	9.3
521 INDUSTRIAL–INDUSTRIELS	9.7	8.0	9.3	6.8	5.4	4.9	9.0
522 NON INDUSTRIAL–NON INDUSTRIEL	0.2	0.2	0.2	0.3	0.2	0.3	0.3
53 PARTS–PIECES ACCESSOIRES	3.3	3.5	3.5	3.6	3.7	3.8	3.6
6 CONSUM GOODS–BIENS CONSOMMATION	19.4	20.6	20.2	19.5	19.0	18.5	18.0
61 DURABLE–DURABLES	4.5	4.6	4.5	4.4	4.3	4.3	4.4
62 SEMI DURABLE–SEMI DURABLES	10.8	11.6	11.4	10.8	10.3	9.9	9.6
63 NON DURABLE–NON DURABLES	4.2	4.3	4.4	4.3	4.4	4.2	4.0
7 GOODS NES–BIENS NDA	1.9	1.7	0.9	1.7	1.5	1.4	1.4

EXPORTS – EXPORTATIONS

	1991	1992	1993	1994	1995	1996	1997
TOTAL EXPORTS–EXPORTATIONS TOTALES	100.	100.	100.	100.	100.	100.	100.
1 AGRICULTURE	6.2	6.3	6.6	7.4	7.1	6.6	6.7
2 MINING QUARRY–INDUS EXTRACTIVES	45.6	46.1	47.6	46.0	44.1	51.1	49.8
3 MANUFACTURING–IND MANUFACTUR	48.2	47.6	45.8	46.7	48.7	42.3	43.5
31 FOOD BEV TOBACCO–ALIM BOISS TAB	1.8	2.1	1.9	1.8	1.6	1.5	1.5
32 TEXTILES–INDUSTRIES TEXTILES	0.8	0.8	0.8	0.9	0.8	0.7	0.7
33 WOOD & PRODUCTS–BOIS & PRODUITS	1.2	1.1	1.3	1.2	1.1	0.9	0.8
34 PAPER & PRODUCTS–PAPIER & PRODT	3.3	2.8	3.0	2.6	3.3	2.5	2.1
35 CHEMICALS–INDUSTRIES CHIMIQUES	10.8	11.0	11.0	7.6	7.1	7.2	7.7
36 NON METAL MIN–MIN NON METAL	0.6	0.6	0.5	0.4	0.4	0.4	0.3
37 BASIC METAL–IND METAL BASE	10.5	9.7	9.5	9.6	10.1	8.4	8.9
38 METAL MANUF–MANUF METAL	17.8	18.0	16.4	15.1	16.4	14.1	15.2
39 OTH MANUF IND–AUTRES MANUF	1.5	1.4	1.5	7.5	7.9	6.7	6.2

3. TRADE BY PRINCIPAL COUNTRIES OF ORIGIN AND DESTINATION (VALUE IN MILLION U.S. DOLLARS)
ECHANGES SELON LES PRINCIPAUX PAYS D'ORIGINE ET DE DESTINATION (VALEUR EN MILLIONS DE DOLLARS EU)

COUNTRIES–PAYS	GENERAL IMPORTS C.I.F. IMPORTATIONS GENERALES C.A.F				
	1993	1994	1995	1996	1997
World	24021.2	27294.9	32705.9	34309.2	35768.3
Africa	299.6	260.7	303.2	423.4	841.3
Americas	2921.8	3300.4	3734.1	3760.6	4097.2
– Northern America	2428.3	2546.2	2905.1	2983.2	3117.9
– LAIA	221.3	316.5	380.6	378.0	544.3
– CACM	26.5	23.0	30.6	36.0	47.5
– Caribbean	115.1	198.4	234.0	152.7	264.2
– Rest of America	130.6	216.3	183.8	210.5	123.4
Asia excl fmr USSR	3512.7	3363.5	3514.0	3925.1	4286.2
– Middle East	65.6	83.2	153.5	131.9	187.6
Asia former USSR	3.9	19.8	4.7	0.8	1.6
Europe excl fmr USSR	16778.6	19514.4	24281.7	25320.8	25457.5
– European Union	16132.2	18810.6	23365.6	24296.0	24326.5
– Eastern Europe	191.1	246.8	342.6	388.5	488.4
– Rest of Europe	455.3	457.0	573.4	636.3	642.5
Europe former USSR	410.1	736.7	778.0	730.8	880.5
Oceania	94.5	99.4	90.2	147.7	204.0
Other	0.0				
Sweden/Suède	3397.7	4094.4	5048.3	5855.3	5606.8
Germany/Allemagne	3254.7	3802.9	4558.0	4592.3	4842.9
United Kingdom	2197.4	2830.6	3203.7	3191.3	3369.7
Denmark/Danemark	1784.7	2015.6	2473.2	2654.6	2518.1
USA/Etats–Unis d'Amer	1938.2	2009.8	2189.4	2220.8	2383.9
Japan/Japon	1923.2	1629.7	1254.4	1332.9	1623.5
Netherlands/Pays–Bas	983.9	1158.4	1457.8	1528.4	1549.0
France, Monaco	1028.3	1105.7	1446.1	1444.1	1459.0
Italy/Italie	830.6	947.5	1155.1	1312.3	1383.6
Finland/Finlande	786.2	996.7	1290.6	1231.8	1156.3
Belgium–Luxembourg	584.4	696.1	947.1	878.6	742.8
Canada	485.3	534.0	703.3	741.3	620.4
China/Chine	425.1	515.8	621.9	693.9	800.3
Russian Federation	344.5	616.6	592.7	579.2	706.7
Spain/Espagne	484.4	282.9	614.8	486.4	580.7
Switzerland,Liechtenst.	370.9	368.0	457.5	485.3	416.9
Ireland/Irlande	269.3	320.4	497.2	464.7	424.5
Austria/Autriche	254.9	270.2	328.9	325.4	362.8
Korea, Republic of	137.9	219.0	388.9	203.9	490.7
Portugal	235.1	249.5	303.1	291.1	289.3
Other Asia n.e.s.	226.5	211.4	235.2	264.8	256.8
Singapore/Singapour	225.5	104.1	134.8	569.0	154.0
China, Hong Kong SAR	156.3	169.5	207.5	177.2	163.8
Poland/Pologne	112.9	134.7	172.9	194.5	245.2
So. African Customs Un	124.3	116.9	160.4	204.8	185.7
Liberia/Libéria	58.0	22.6	1.4	83.4	474.3
Brazil/Brésil	82.6	108.8	130.2	114.7	202.2
Jamaica/Jamaïque	105.6	105.4	147.1	124.7	115.4
Australia/Australie	87.8	90.7	76.4	135.9	190.8
Suriname/Surinam	81.1	111.3	146.5	129.5	102.2
India/Inde	76.0	98.8	108.7	110.7	121.5
Thailand/Thaïlande	63.1	76.3	97.5	103.4	102.6
Turkey/Turquie	45.8	61.4	93.1	94.5	128.4
Malaysia/Malaisie	52.4	71.8	91.1	95.1	97.2
Czech Republic	37.6	49.5	81.6	85.5	100.2
Iceland/Islande	52.7	41.9	61.5	79.2	108.1
Panama	49.3	104.8	37.1	79.9	20.9
Indonesia/Indonésie	41.0	43.8	51.2	64.2	76.1
Bahamas	8.7	90.6	49.6	9.0	112.5
Colombia/Colombie	29.3	56.1	49.7	47.1	50.2

COUNTRIES–PAYS	GENERAL EXPORTS F.O.B. EXPORTATIONS GENERALES F.O.B.				
	1993	1994	1995	1996	1997
Monde	31903.9	34743.5	41740.3	48955.0	48549.9
Afrique	499.3	380.9	282.7	287.2	351.5
Amériques	3490.0	4063.2	4911.0	6382.7	6222.3
– Amérique du Nord	2959.2	3612.6	4187.6	5656.5	5531.9
– ALAI	223.2	266.8	418.2	474.9	392.5
– MCAC	10.0	11.0	11.6	9.8	21.4
– Caraïbes	72.1	104.9	225.0	106.2	168.0
– Autre Amérique	225.5	67.9	68.6	135.4	108.5
Asie anc. URSS exclus	1838.6	2020.3	2816.8	2911.2	3198.9
– Moyen–Orient	279.5	241.8	375.2	303.1	380.3
Asie ancienne URSS	2.5	1.5	3.0	5.3	8.4
Europe anc. URSS exclus	25872.3	27978.0	33283.5	38767.3	38017.8
– Union Européenne	24969.7	27032.1	32232.5	37642.3	36874.6
– Europe de l'Est	389.2	417.9	484.4	464.0	528.2
– Autre de l'Europe	513.4	528.0	566.6	661.0	614.9
Europe ancienne URSS	119.6	191.9	309.0	459.4	583.5
Océanie	81.6	107.8	134.0	141.8	167.4
Autre	0.0		0.4		
United Kingdom	7842.9	7231.6	8362.0	9713.4	9357.8
Germany/Allemagne	4149.2	4322.3	4981.1	5456.8	5283.7
Netherlands/Pays–Bas	2706.1	3302.8	3977.4	5436.3	5539.7
Sweden/Suède	2777.8	3260.2	4119.1	4540.6	4268.7
France, Monaco	2524.4	2827.0	3246.6	4320.6	4119.7
USA/Etats–Unis d'Amer	1977.7	2345.1	2569.1	3626.8	3004.8
Denmark/Danemark	1399.9	1639.4	2099.0	2237.2	2449.6
Canada	740.0	1152.9	1576.6	1980.5	2307.2
Belgium–Luxembourg	731.7	978.7	1300.7	1553.9	1462.0
Italy/Italie	828.7	998.3	1145.1	1318.0	1286.5
Finland/Finlande	812.2	1034.5	1145.4	1076.1	1016.7
Japan/Japon	589.5	650.7	741.5	904.6	964.2
Spain/Espagne	363.3	482.0	702.6	938.2	801.2
Ireland/Irlande	319.6	422.4	386.2	435.4	578.4
Poland/Pologne	316.6	333.2	359.5	343.4	354.6
Portugal	285.7	305.5	372.6	346.8	347.4
Singapore/Singapour	146.6	192.9	506.0	196.3	267.1
Other Asia n.e.s.	89.5	97.4	153.5	319.3	434.3
China/Chine	202.5	170.7	185.1	202.4	307.1
Switzerland,Liechtenst.	184.6	210.4	226.9	217.3	223.6
Russian Federation	96.0	123.7	190.9	277.0	343.0
Brazil/Brésil	107.2	173.6	252.4	244.6	232.2
Iceland/Islande	163.1	198.9	166.4	249.8	218.5
Korea, Republic of	96.2	116.7	179.2	235.0	238.3
Austria/Autriche	116.2	139.5	181.8	172.2	162.3
Greece/Grèce	112.1	87.9	212.9	96.8	200.9
Liberia/Libéria	272.5	165.9	81.1	59.7	106.2
China, Hong Kong SAR	97.2	85.0	168.9	131.9	149.4
Thailand/Thaïlande	100.4	86.5	130.6	159.3	127.2
Panama	224.7	66.1	65.8	131.3	105.5
Bermuda/Bermudes	226.4	107.9	33.4	15.4	176.1
Israel/Israël	111.2	116.8	132.0	139.1	53.5
Turkey/Turquie	91.7	52.5	86.6	109.5	170.7
Australia/Australie	71.5	94.4	100.2	116.3	110.0
Czech Republic	38.5	48.2	66.8	65.2	121.2
India/Inde	27.2	77.4	99.0	61.8	71.4
Saudi Arabia	32.6	61.6	130.9	39.4	38.4
Malaysia/Malaisie	29.4	80.3	55.0	51.3	86.0
Cyprus/Chypre	75.4	56.7	68.3	24.0	38.2
Faeroe Islds/Is Féroé	37.4	43.2	44.6	61.2	65.9

(VALUE AS PERCENTAGE OF WORLD TOTAL)(VALEURS EN POURCENTAGE DU TOTAL MONDIAL)

	1988	1989	1990	1991	1992	1993	1994	1995	1996	1997
Africa	3.9	5.1	4.5	2.7	1.4	1.2	1.0	0.9	1.2	2.4
Americas	12.8	17.2	15.2	13.1	12.5	12.2	12.1	11.4	11.0	11.5
– Northern America	8.4	9.7	10.5	10.1	10.4	10.1	9.3	8.9	8.7	8.7
– LAIA	1.3	1.5	1.0	1.1	1.0	0.9	1.2	1.2	1.1	1.5
– CACM	0.1	0.1	0.1	0.1	0.1	0.1	0.1	0.1	0.1	0.1
– Caribbean	0.8	1.7	1.1	0.7	0.4	0.5	0.7	0.7	0.4	0.7
– Rest of America	2.2	4.1	2.5	1.2	0.7	0.5	0.8	0.6	0.6	0.3
Asia excl fmr USSR	10.0	10.6	9.2	11.8	12.3	14.6	12.3	10.7	11.4	12.0
– Middle East	0.6	1.9	0.6	1.3	0.3	0.3	0.3	0.5	0.4	0.5
Asia former USSR						0.0	0.1	0.0	0.0	0.0
Europe excl fmr USSR	72.2	65.6	69.5	70.7	71.8	69.8	71.5	74.2	73.8	71.2
– European Union	68.3	62.2	66.2	67.9	69.0	67.2	68.9	71.4	70.8	68.0
– Eastern Europe	1.5	1.3	1.1	0.7	0.8	0.8	0.9	1.0	1.1	1.4
– Rest of Europe	2.3	2.0	2.2	2.2	2.0	1.9	1.7	1.8	1.9	1.8
Europe former USSR	0.7	1.1	1.4	1.4	1.6	1.7	2.7	2.4	2.1	2.5
Oceania	0.5	0.5	0.3	0.2	0.4	0.4	0.4	0.3	0.4	0.6
Other	0.0	0.0	0.0	0.0	0.0	0.0				
Sweden/Suède	17.6	15.2	15.8	15.4	15.4	14.1	15.0	15.4	17.1	15.7
Germany/Allemagne				14.1	14.4	13.5	13.9	13.9	13.4	13.5
United Kingdom	7.8	7.4	9.0	8.7	9.3	9.1	10.4	9.8	9.3	9.4
Denmark/Danemark	7.6	6.7	6.7	7.3	7.5	7.4	7.4	7.6	7.7	7.0
USA/Etats–Unis d'Amer	6.6	7.4	8.1	7.8	8.5	8.1	7.4	6.7	6.5	6.7
Japan/Japon	4.6	3.7	4.4	4.9	6.3	8.0	6.0	3.8	3.9	4.5
Netherlands/Pays–Bas	3.9	3.3	4.0	5.3	3.9	4.1	4.2	4.5	4.5	4.3
France, Monaco	3.3	3.3	3.8	3.8	4.1	4.3	4.1	4.4	4.2	4.1
Italy/Italie	3.3	2.9	3.2	3.4	3.4	3.5	3.5	3.5	3.8	3.9
Finland/Finlande	3.5	3.0	3.1	3.1	3.5	3.3	3.7	3.9	3.6	3.2

	1988	1989	1990	1991	1992	1993	1994	1995	1996	1997
Afrique	1.6	1.4	1.1	2.3	2.0	1.6	1.1	0.7	0.6	0.7
Amériques	9.1	10.4	10.6	9.2	10.1	10.9	11.7	11.8	13.0	12.8
– Amérique du Nord	7.6	9.2	9.0	7.6	8.2	9.3	10.4	10.0	11.6	11.4
– ALAI	0.8	0.7	0.7	0.7	0.5	0.7	0.8	1.0	1.0	0.8
– MCAC	0.0	0.1	0.0	0.0	0.1	0.0	0.0	0.0	0.0	0.0
– Caraïbes	0.3	0.2	0.7	0.6	0.9	0.2	0.3	0.5	0.2	0.3
– Autre Amérique	0.3	0.2	0.1	0.4	0.5	0.7	0.2	0.2	0.3	0.2
Asie anc. URSS exclus	5.4	4.7	5.6	5.5	5.6	5.8	5.8	6.7	5.9	6.6
– Moyen–Orient	0.7	0.8	1.6	0.9	1.0	0.9	0.7	0.9	0.6	0.8
Asie ancienne URSS						0.0	0.0	0.0	0.0	0.0
Europe anc. URSS exclus	82.7	82.3	81.8	82.4	81.6	81.1	80.5	79.7	79.2	78.3
– Union Européenne	79.7	80.1	79.5	80.0	78.8	78.3	77.8	77.2	76.9	76.0
– Europe de l'Est	0.7	0.5	0.7	0.9	1.1	1.2	1.2	1.2	0.9	1.1
– Autre de l'Europe	2.3	1.7	1.7	1.5	1.8	1.6	1.5	1.4	1.4	1.3
Europe ancienne URSS	0.6	0.6	0.5	0.3	0.4	0.4	0.6	0.7	0.9	1.2
Océanie	0.6	0.5	0.4	0.3	0.3	0.3	0.3	0.3	0.3	0.3
Autre	0.0	0.0	0.0	0.0	0.0	0.0		0.0		
United Kingdom	26.0	26.7	26.0	26.5	24.2	24.6	20.8	20.0	19.8	19.3
Germany/Allemagne				11.1	13.2	13.0	12.4	11.9	11.1	10.9
Netherlands/Pays–Bas	6.9	6.6	8.0	7.9	7.1	8.5	9.5	9.5	11.1	11.4
Sweden/Suède	11.7	12.4	11.5	10.3	9.4	8.7	9.4	9.9	9.3	8.8
France, Monaco	7.3	9.0	7.8	7.5	7.7	7.9	8.1	7.8	8.8	8.5
USA/Etats–Unis d'Amer	6.1	6.8	6.5	4.8	5.3	6.2	6.7	6.2	7.4	6.2
Denmark/Danemark	5.3	4.7	4.8	5.6	5.4	4.4	4.7	5.0	4.6	5.0
Canada	1.2	2.2	2.5	2.7	2.6	2.3	3.3	3.8	4.0	4.8
Belgium–Luxembourg	2.4	2.5	2.2	2.4	2.9	2.3	2.8	3.1	3.2	3.0
Italy/Italie	2.8	2.4	2.6	2.3	2.6	2.6	2.9	2.7	2.7	2.6

4. General Imports C.I.F. by Commodities according to the S.I.T.C. (Rev. 2) in million U.S. Dollars
Importations Générales C.A.F. par Produits d'après la C.T.C.I. (Rév. 2) en millions de Dollars E.U.

SITC CTCI	COMMODITY	1994 QUANTITY QUANTITE	1994 VALUE VALEUR	1995 QUANTITY QUANTITE	1995 VALUE VALEUR	1996 QUANTITY QUANTITE	1996 VALUE VALEUR	1997 QUANTITY QUANTITE	1997 VALUE VALEUR	PRODUIT
	ALL COMMODITIES		27295.0		32705.9		34309.2		35768.4	TOUS PRODUITS
0	FOOD AND LIVE ANIMALS		1546.6		1817.2		1942.1		1858.2	ALIMENTS,ANIMAUX VIVANTS
03	FISH AND PREPARATIONS		242.3		342.4		381.8		366.1	POISSONS ET PREPARATIONS
034	FISH,FRESH,CHILLED,FROZN	W 171857	159.1	W 198173	218.2	W 243732	248.7	W 271018	249.4	POISSON FRAIS, REFRIG,CONG
0341	FISH FRSH,CHLLD,EX FILLT	W 134188	101.4	W 163090	158.6	W 192653	168.7	W 204693	145.6	POISSON FRAIS,REFRIGERE
04	CEREALS AND PREPARATIONS		205.5		209.0		287.8		230.3	CEREALES ET PRODUITS
048	CEREAL ETC PREPARATIONS	W 102463	118.9	W 93632	142.0	W 105230	156.6	W 109051	155.6	PREPTNS A BASE CEREALES
05	VEGETABLES AND FRUIT		419.0		469.2		498.0		462.5	LEGUMES ET FRUITS
054	VEG ETC FRSH,SMPLY PRSVD	W 110202	100.6	W 120984	123.6	W 132386	126.6	W 115023	113.8	LEGUMES FRAIS,CONG,SECS
057	FRUIT,NUTS,FRESH,DRIED	W 224277	205.6	W 216253	230.4	W 227563	250.4	W 224224	235.5	FRUITS FRAIS OU SECS
058	FRUIT PRESERVED,PREPARED	W 55381	83.7	W 48757	83.2	W 53577	90.4	W 55353	83.5	CONSERVES DE FRUITS
06	SUGAR AND PREPS,HONEY		129.6		149.9		155.7		148.3	SUCRES ET PRODUITS
07	COFFEE,TEA,COCOA,SPICES		255.5		270.3		256.6		283.7	CAFE,THE,CACAO,EPICES
071	COFFEE AND SUBSTITUTES	W 46752	142.3	W 38528	150.1	W 41594	126.1	W 39395	163.6	CAFE ET SUCCEDANES
0711	COFFEE GREEN,ROASTED,SUB	W 45729	128.1	W 37639	135.9	W 40447	109.6	W 38144	145.1	CAFE TORREFIE OU DECAFEINE
07111	COFFEE GREEN,HUSKS,SKINS	W 44786	123.6	W 37201	133.2	W 39790	106.3	W 37288	140.4	CAFE NON TORREFIE
081	*FEEDING STUFF FOR ANIML	W 278229	134.4	W 242507	173.8	W 271479	169.2	W 316318	186.2	NOURRITURE POUR ANIMAUX
09	MISC EDIBLE PRODUCTS		109.2		135.6		117.4		121.0	PREP ALIMENTAIRES DIVERSES
098	EDIBLE PRODCTS,PREPS NES	W 29720	106.1	W 33428	132.1	W 32393	114.5	W 35846	116.5	PREP ALIMENTAIRES NDA
09809	MISC FOOD PREPRTIONS NES	W 19452	80.1	W 22708	98.5	W 22209	83.9	W 24293	86.5	PREP ALIMENTAIRES NDA
1	BEVERAGES AND TOBACCO		192.2		219.2		218.9		228.7	BOISSONS ET TABACS
11	BEVERAGES		128.0		158.1		158.1		168.2	BOISSONS
112	ALCOHOLIC BEVERAGES	W 45678	112.8	W 49571	146.1	W 51153	149.6	W 59070	158.9	BOISSONS ALCOOLIQUES
2	CRUDE MATERLS,EXCL FUELS		2030.3		2471.0		2466.6		2401.5	MAT BRUTES NON COMESTIBLES
22	OIL SEEDS,OLEAGINOUS FRT		66.4		87.3		107.7		106.5	GRAINES,FRUITS OLEAGINEUX
222	SEEDS FOR'SOFT'FIXED OIL	W 230587	65.2	W 315243	86.0	W 334691	106.3	W 313300	105.1	GRAINES HUILES FIXES
24	CORK AND WOOD		421.2		583.3		492.8		508.6	LIEGE ET BOIS
247	OTH WOOD ROUGH,SQUARED	W 2033676	137.1	W 3008581	248.8	W 1917089	161.7	W 2211788	162.1	BOIS BRUTS EQUARRIS
2471	SAW-,VENEER-LOGS CONIFER	W 1416484	98.5	W 2216653	181.1	W 1435983	120.9	W 1725179	125.1	CONIFERES POUR SCIAGE,PLACAG
24711	— IN THE ROUGH	W 1416484	98.5	W 2216653	181.1	W 1435983	120.9	W 1725179	125.1	ECORCES OU DEGROSSIS
248	WOOD SHAPED,SLEEPERS	W 449520	256.6	W 433777	296.4	W 462400	290.2	W 523866	310.1	BOIS SIMPLEMENT TRAVAILLES
2482	LUMBER SHAPED CONIFER	W 408048	214.4	W 385380	240.2	W 414704	234.1	W 475809	254.2	CONIFERES SCIES,RABOTES
24821	LUMBER SAWN ETC CONIFER	W 393234	198.6	W 370248	221.8	W 397890	216.3	W 455746	235.3	CONIFERES SCIES LONGITUD
27	CRUDE FERTLZR,MINRLS NES		178.8		202.9		212.8		205.1	ENGRAIS MINERAUX BRUTS
278	OTHER CRUDE MINERALS	W 1896876	109.7	W 1973585	126.2	W 2011554	127.6	W 2002128	123.1	AUTRES MINERAUX BRUTS
28	METALLIFEROUS ORES,SCRAP		1146.0		1313.4		1412.6		1332.3	MINERAIS METAL,DECHETS
287	BASE METAL ORES,CONC NES	W 2821408	974.8	W 2658560	1120.8	W 2754033	1226.6	W 2983161	1113.8	MINERAIS METAUX COMMUNS
2872	NICKEL ORES,CONCENTRATES	W 146274	521.9	W 109318	594.8	W 141941	703.4	W 132146	574.5	MINERAIS DE NICKEL
28722	NICKEL MATTE,SINTERS,ETC	W 146274	521.9	W 109318	594.8	W 141941	703.4	W 132146	574.5	MATTES,SINTERS
2873	ALUMINIUM ORES,ALUMINA	W 1760049	322.6	W 1609533	395.4	W 1716114	401.4	W 1764736	384.4	MINERAIS D'ALUMINIUM
28732	ALUMINA(ALUMINIUM OXIDE)	W 1720504	321.0	W 1576786	393.8	W 1693565	400.3	W 1733334	383.0	ALUMINE (OXYDE ALUMINIUM)
288	NONFERR METAL SCRAP NES	W 265870	128.6	W 276764	142.9	W 290584	128.6	W 305011	148.8	DECHETS NON FERREUX
2882	OTHER BASE MTL SCRAP NES	W 77206	103.0	W 67712	119.9	W 71356	100.0	W 76318	112.2	AUTRES DECHETS
28823	ALUMINIUM WSTE AND SCRAP	W 68505	90.5	W 60576	108.1	W 63038	87.7	W 68723	100.1	DECHETS D'ALUMINIUM
29	CRUDE ANIMAL,VEG MAT NES		106.9		131.0		127.4		138.1	MATIERES BRUTES ANIM,VEGET
292	CRUDE VEG MATERIALS NES	W 23952	93.9	W 29826	117.0	W 29858	114.2	W 37609	117.7	MAT BRUTES VEGETALES NDA
3	MINERAL FUELS ETC		845.8		961.5		1550.5		1201.9	COMBUSTIBLES MINERAUX LUB
32	COAL,COKE AND BRIQUETTES		124.8		142.4		150.7		137.6	HOUILLES,COKES,BRIQUETTES
33	PETROLEUM AND PRODUCTS		608.1		769.3		870.0		866.8	PETROLE ET DERIVES
333	CRUDE PETROLEUM	W 981515	108.0	W 1398124	166.2	W 1332752	213.2	W 1559656	205.4	HUILES BRUTES DE PETROLE
334	PETROLEUM PRODUCTS,REFIN	W 2318361	384.3	W 2358882	452.1	W 2362430	486.8	W 2733574	507.0	PRODUITS RAFFINES
3341	GASOLINE,OTH LIGHT OILS	W 606267	109.7	W 810097	153.4	W 517702	114.4	W 664515	145.2	ESSENCES POUR MOTEURS
33411	MOTOR,AVIATION SPIRIT	W 551468	96.7	W 697005	130.2	W 484912	104.7	W 569482	122.3	ESSENCES MOTEURS D'AVIONS
3343	GAS OILS	W 441689	68.2	W 638567	104.7	W 520303	106.2	W 466711	85.6	GAS OILS
3344	FUEL OILS,NES	W 1022492	103.4	W 695546	81.9	W 1074128	140.8	W 1349925	159.4	FUEL OILS
335	RESIDUAL PETRLM PROD NES	W 792490	115.9	W 885750	151.2	W 855641	170.1	W 847057	154.5	PRODUITS RESIDUELS NDA
3354	PETROLM BITUMEN,COKE ETC	W 652592	77.3	W 742022	101.7	W 713356	120.0	W 704467	112.4	BITUME,COKE DE PETROLE
351	*ELECTRIC CURRENT	H 4519728	103.3	H 2200513	39.3	MH 13212	518.7	H 8692413	187.3	ENERGIE ELECTRIQUE
4	ANIMAL,VEGETABLE OIL,FAT		86.8		107.9		119.6		155.6	HUILES,GRAISSES ANIM,VEG
411	*ANIMAL OILS AND FATS	W 145099	49.4	W 182043	72.7	W 180016	79.7	W 209099	107.4	HUILES,GRAISSES ANIMALES
5	CHEMCLS,RELATED PROD NES		2415.5		3026.1		3002.0		2947.3	PRODUITS CHIMIQUES
51	ORGANIC CHEMICALS		294.5		372.3		372.7		342.6	PROD CHIMIQ ORGANIQUES
511	HYDROCARBONS NES,DERIVS	W 280596	77.8	W 350188	119.8	W 316727	89.9	W 307008	92.6	HYDROCARBURES NDA
52	INORGANIC CHEMICALS		189.0		238.6		240.7		246.4	PROD CHIM INORGANIQUES
522	INORG ELEMNTS,OXIDES,ETC	W 355619	102.4	W 455392	155.6	W 473754	150.8	W 580001	159.6	ELEMENTS INORGANIQUES
53	DYES,TANNING,COLOUR PROD		246.1		309.7		297.3		292.9	PROD TEINTURE,COLORANTS
531	SYNT DYE,NAT INDGO,LAKES	W 4256	85.8	W 4430	115.2	W 4395	96.5	W 4619	98.4	MAT COLOR ORGAN,LAQUES
5311	SYNTHIC ORGNIC DYESTUFFS	W 3371	81.7	W 3728	112.4	W 3443	93.3	W 3296	94.8	MAT COLOR ORGAN SYNTHET
533	PIGMENTS,PAINTS,ETC	W 71869	157.4	W 77551	191.6	W 82091	197.6	W 96757	191.5	PIGMENTS,PEINTURES,VERNIS
541	*MEDICINAL,PHARM PRODUCT	MK 9989	474.5	MK 9899	607.9		617.6	MK 11957	618.9	PROD MEDICINAUX PHARMACEUT
5417	MEDICAMENTS	K 5984999	381.5	K 5801256	498.4	K 6290821	504.8	K 6329402	506.9	MEDICAMENTS
54179	— CONTNG OTH SUBSTANCES	K 5541724	336.8	K 5272627	425.2	K 5976079	451.5	K 5847720	459.5	MED CONT AUT SUBSTANCES
55	PERFUME,CLEANING ETC PRD		354.0		409.0		437.9		428.5	PROD POUR PARFUM,TOILETTE
553	PERFUMERY,COSMETICS,ETC	W 20529	175.5	W 20375	201.9	W 21340	194.3	W 22968	195.7	PRODUITS DE PARFUMERIE
554	SOAP,CLEANSING ETC PREPS	W 69380	114.1	W 74019	134.2	W 84365	148.2	W 85202	134.8	SAVONS,PRODUITS DETERSIFS
5542	WASHING PREPARATIONS ETC	W 57362	85.3	W 61944	100.6	W 71372	110.6	W 73952	103.5	PROD ORG TENSIO-ACT NDA
562	*FERTILIZERS,MANUFACTURE	W 707473	98.7	W 716454	107.0	W 718424	107.8	W 682648	101.1	ENGRAIS MANUFACTURES
58	PLASTIC MATERIALS ETC		458.9		598.5		555.6		554.4	MAT PLAST ARTIFICIELLES
582	PROD OF CONDENSATION ETC	W 50663	112.2	W 53895	144.3	W 54752	137.3	W 49799	124.8	PROD CONDENS,POLYCOND
583	POLYMERIZATION ETC PRODS	W 210249	326.9	W 221470	434.0	W 225979	399.7	W 261673	415.0	PROD POLYMERISATION
5831	POLYETHYLENE	W 83079	91.9	W 85117	127.0	W 79862	105.4	W 85523	109.1	POLYETHYLENE
5839	OTH POLYMRZTION ETC PROD	W 31341	96.7	W 34058	124.3	W 38626	128.2	W 54371	139.4	AUT PROD POLYMER COPOLYM
59	CHEMICAL MATERIALS NES		280.4		358.0		343.3		335.2	MAT PROD CHIMIQUES NDA
598	MISCEL CHEM PRODUCTS NES	W 149021	207.5	W 164854	267.0	W 157903	244.2	W 167349	244.4	PROD DIV INDUST CHIM NDA
5989	CHEM PRODUCTS,PREPS NES	W 71099	159.4	W 84547	210.5	W 85249	191.7	W 93620	197.5	PROD PREP CHIMIQUES NDA
59899	OTH CHEM PRODS,PREPS,NES	W 50885	117.3	W 62496	158.9	W 71453	154.7	W 75861	151.7	AUT PRODUITS CHIMIQUES NDA
6	BASIC MANUFACTURES		5145.4		6163.1		5886.3		6058.8	ART MANUFACTURES
62	RUBBER MANUFACTURES NES		264.4		304.3		313.0		295.7	CAOUTCHOUC MANUFACTURE
625	RUBBER TYRES, TUBES ETC	W 41694	166.5	W 39969	183.4	W 40910	188.9	W 41608	178.2	PNEUS CAOUTCHOUC VULCANISE
6251	TYRES NEW FOR MOTOR CARS	W 21982	100.7	W 19704	106.0	W 21324	116.2	W 22255	113.4	PNEUS POUR VOITURES
63	WOOD,CORK MANUFACTRS NES		212.9		276.8		299.6		342.6	OUVRAGES LIEGE ET BOIS
635	WOOD MANUFACTURES NES	W 66222	130.3	W 75639	178.4	W 82345	196.1	W 113524	232.6	ART MANUF EN BOIS NDA
6353	BUILDERS WOODWRK,PREFABS	W 39856	87.8	W 46471	125.3	W 51115	142.6	W 73768	172.6	OUVRAGES DE MENUISERIE
64	PAPER,PAPERBOARD AND MFR		717.1		958.0		960.7		892.8	PAPIERS,CARTONS & OUVRAGES
641	PAPER AND PAPERBOARD	W 440302	396.8	W 468046	553.6	W 489072	544.1	W 545737	510.2	PAPIERS ET CARTONS
6412	PRINTG,WRITING PAPER NES	W 129970	121.8	W 116138	153.2	W 121500	144.7	W 139425	134.0	PAPIERS POUR L'IMPRESSION
64122	— COATED,IMPREGNATD ETC	W 104903	95.6	W 93592	118.7	W 97457	112.8	W 113653	104.4	PAPIERS IMPRESSION COUCHES
6415	PAPER,PAPERBRD,BULK,NES	W 114144	83.5	W 126236	125.8	W 138472	128.5	W 154998	123.2	PAPIERS,CARTONS ROULEAUX
64159	OTHER PAPER ETC,BULK,NES	W 85847	69.6	W 104734	110.5	W 112607	112.8	W 124354	107.2	AUT PAPIER ROULEAUX FEUILLES
6418	COATED ETC PAPER NES BLK	W 64108	98.4	W 60131	118.4	W 62791	119.3	W 68059	112.0	PAP,CARTONS COUCHES,ENDUITS
642	PAPER,ETC,PRECUT,ARTS OF	W 142857	320.4	W 148429	404.5	W 154330	416.7	W 158684	382.7	PAP,CARTONS DECOUPES

4. General Imports C.I.F. by Commodities according to the S.I.T.C. (Rev. 2) in million U.S. Dollars
Importations Générales C.A.F. par Produits d'après la C.T.C.I. (Rév. 2) en millions de Dollars E.U.

SITC CTCI	COMMODITY	1994 QUANTITY QUANTITE	1994 VALUE VALEUR	1995 QUANTITY QUANTITE	1995 VALUE VALEUR	1996 QUANTITY QUANTITE	1996 VALUE VALEUR	1997 QUANTITY QUANTITE	1997 VALUE VALEUR	PRODUIT
6421	PAPER ETC CONTAINERS	W 39592	76.5	W 45844	99.2	W 48616	99.5	W 51579	94.5	BOITES,SACS EMBALLAGES
6428	PAPER ETC ARTICLES NES	W 59670	149.3	W 58530	182.3	W 59795	188.8	W 60937	174.2	OUVRAGES EN PATE A PAPIER
65	TEXTILE YARN,FABRICS,ETC		535.6		620.5		641.3		618.4	FILS,TISSUS,ARTICLES TEXTILE
657	SPECIAL TXTL FABRC,PRODS	W 12054	95.7	W 13673	118.4	W 15133	127.2	W 15324	115.6	TISSUS SPECIAUX
658	TEXTILE ARTICLES NES	W 13862	112.4	W 15476	140.1	W 16625	149.3	W 18398	150.0	ART FACONNES MAT TEXTILES
66	NONMETAL MINERAL MFS NES		354.6		448.4		485.8		498.0	ART MIN NON METALLIQUES
663	MINERAL MANUFCTURES NES	W 173826	87.2	W 192934	109.6	W 197099	121.5	W 326532	136.7	ART MIN MANUF NDA
664	GLASS	W 83240	78.6	W 90981	102.4	W 99233	103.2	W 94624	102.5	VERRE
67	IRON AND STEEL		1212.1		1465.6		1383.9		1544.9	FER ET ACIER
672	IRON,STEEL PRIMARY FORMS	W 330580	101.9	W 402206	148.8	W 305484	110.3	W 377949	116.8	LINGOTS FER,ACIER
673	IRON,STEEL SHAPES ETC	W 252412	137.6	W 277546	186.1	W 278438	174.7	W 281628	160.7	BARRES,PROFIL FER,ACIER
674	IRN,STL UNIV,PLATE,SHEET	W 475477	301.8	W 513992	421.9	W 527623	401.7	W 534255	355.8	LARGES PLATS,TOLES
6744	IRN,STL HVY PLATE,ROLLED	W 214520	123.3	W 229331	172.3	W 215334	155.6	W 223450	129.8	TOLES LAMINEES PLUS 4.75 MM
67441	— OF IRON OR SIMPLE STL	W 203151	91.9	W 215589	124.6	W 202806	110.2	W 213911	101.7	TOLES NON ACIER FIN CARB
6749	OTH IRN,STL PLATES,SHEET	W 102738	77.2	W 117056	109.8	W 142951	127.6	W 143522	123.8	AUTRES TOLES FER,ACIER
67491	— OF IRON OR SIMPLE STL	W 97970	67.7	W 111351	94.0	W 137499	113.6	W 131392	98.0	AUT TOLES AUTRES ACIER FIN
678	IRON,STL TUBES,PIPES,ETC	W 443609	603.6	W 435743	621.0	W 388843	595.9	W 735147	812.2	TUBES,TUYAUX EN FONTE,FER
6782	IRON,STL SEAMLESS TUBES	W 90634	168.3	W 99409	179.3	W 122216	207.5	W 82896	174.4	TUBES,TUYAUX SANS SOUDURE
6783	IRON,STL TUBES,PIPES NES	W 331963	337.0	W 312944	319.0	W 241351	248.3	W 627797	486.2	AUT TUBES,TUYAUX FER,ACIER
6785	IRON,STEEL TUBE FITTINGS	W 12553	92.0	W 13882	114.7	W 15285	131.6	W 17297	145.9	ACCESSOIRES DE TUYAUTERIE
68	NON-FERROUS METALS		570.9		673.3		613.6		679.2	METAUX NON FERREUX
682	COPPER EXC CEMENT COPPER	W 26098	85.1	W 29128	118.7	W 28631	109.6	W 31767	110.9	CUIVRE
6822	COPPER,ALLOYS WORKED	W 23464	79.2	W 25864	109.3	W 25475	100.9	W 27346	101.1	CUIVRE,ALLIAGES OUVRES
684	ALUMINIUM	W 232755	408.0	W 190313	450.9	W 188960	394.0	W 236676	484.2	ALUMINIUM
6841	ALUMINIUM,ALLOYS,UNWRGHT	W 198663	292.8	W 152303	287.4	W 149540	234.8	W 196263	326.0	ALUMINIUM,ALLIAGES BRUTS
6842	ALUMINIUM,ALLOYS WORKED	W 34091	115.3	W 38010	163.5	W 39420	159.3	W 40412	158.3	ALUMINIUM,ALLIAGES OUVRE
69	METAL MANUFACTURES NES		1233.4		1369.3		1141.1		1138.8	ART MANUFACT EN METAL NDA
691	STRUCTURES AND PARTS NES	W 75122	472.4	W 88087	439.0	W 82455	230.9	W 112214	256.2	CONSTRUCT FER,ACIER,ALU
6911	STRUCTURES,PARTS IRN,STL	W 70658	446.0	W 82537	400.3	W 77217	190.6	W 106122	213.3	CONSTRUCT FER,ACIER,FONTE
694	STL,COPPR NAILS,NUTS,ETC	W 19669	76.1	W 22424	101.2	W 22479	100.8	W 23456	97.2	CLOUS,VIS,ECROUS
695	TOOLS	W 6839	129.9	W 7888	161.4	W 7736	169.6	W 8321	143.6	OUTILS A MAIN
699	BASE METAL MFRS NES	W 66302	343.4	W 67777	434.2	W 68223	388.2	W 80112	391.4	ART MANUFACTURES MET NDA
6991	LOCKSMITHS WARES,ETC	W 9025	71.7	W 10426	90.7	W 12100	108.1	W 13538	110.8	ARTICLES DE SERRURERIE
6996	BASE MTL MISC ARTICLES	W 16181	94.5	W 15456	126.5	W 9951	47.0	W 15518	55.7	ART DIVERS METAUX COMMUNS
6997	IRON,STEEL ARTICLES NES	W 21156	82.7	W 23008	104.3	W 24215	105.0	W 23762	94.5	OUV FONTE,FER,ACIER NDA
69979	IRN,STL MANUFACTURES NES	W 19859	80.3	W 21120	101.3	W 21350	98.6	W 21441	90.4	AUT OUVRAGES EN FER NDA
7	MACHINES,TRANSPORT EQUIP		10097.3		12307.1		13449.8		15146.6	MACHINES MATERIEL TRANSPORT
71	POWER GENERATING EQUIPMT		490.8		555.2		617.3		650.5	MACHINES GENERATRICES
713	INTRNL COMBUS PSTN ENGIN	W 12101	183.1	W 13138	220.7	W 12853	219.3	W 15434	237.5	MOTEURS EXPL COMB INT, PIECE
7133	MARINE PISTON ENGINES	W 4534	79.9	W 4676	90.6	W 5207	92.8	W 8463	125.6	MOTEURS EXPL POUR BATEAUX
714	ENGINES AND MOTORS NES	W 1574	157.6	W 1965	158.0	W 2572	189.3	W 2515	221.8	MOTEURS NON ELECTRIQUES
7149	ENGINE & MOTOR PARTS NES	W 1398	82.6	W 1556	90.6	W 2191	114.4	W 2174	123.8	PIECES 714 ET 718.88
716	ROTATING ELECTRIC PLANT	W 9760	116.9	W 10636	132.7	W 11546	132.6	W 12218	132.6	APP ELECTR ROTATIFS,PIECES
7162	AC MTRS,GENRTRS,GEN SETS	W 8002	87.7	W 8841	99.1	W 9763	105.0	W 10470	104.7	MOTEURS ELECTRIQUES
72	MACHS FOR SPCL INDUSTRYS		1038.7		1449.1		1624.1		1456.8	MAC SPECIALES POUR INDUST
721	AGRIC MACHY,EXC TRACTORS	W 15239	107.1	W 16576	132.5	W 17491	152.6	W 18305	135.5	MACHINES AGRICOLES
722	TRACTORS NON-ROAD	W 13638	93.5	W 17193	136.0	W 17492	142.1	W 14601	110.5	TRACTEURS
7224	WHEELED TRACTORS NES	W 13569	92.6	W 17072	135.0	W 17399	140.7	W 14530	109.5	TRACTEURS A ROUES
723	CIVIL ENGNEERG EQUIP ETC	W 31526	318.6	W 43789	476.6	W 51262	536.0	W 47515	392.7	APPAREILS DE GENIE CIVIL
7234	CONST,MINING MACHNRY NES	W 20424	128.0	W 30545	212.7	W 34399	229.3	W 34220	227.1	MACH POUR LA CONST, MINES
72342	SLFPRP SHOVELS,EXCAVATRS	W 17001	92.3	W 25501	160.0	W 26676	162.7	W 28695	168.0	PELLES MECANIQUES
7239	CONSTR ETC MACHY PTS NES	W 10914	189.2	W 12812	260.8	W 16491	303.3	W 12716	161.1	PIECES 723.41–723.46
725	PAPER ETC MILL MACHINERY	W 2564	48.1	W 6273	108.5	W 4244	92.7	W 3553	66.5	MACHINES FABR PATE PAPIER
726	PRINTG,BKBINDG MACHY,PTS	W 2391	91.0	W 2412	96.2	W 3754	123.8	W 4213	131.7	MACHINES POUR IMPRIMERIE
727	FOOD MACHRY NON-DOMESTIC	W 2559	66.1	W 2758	80.3	W 3438	107.9	W 3720	96.8	MACH INDUSTRIES ALIMENT
728	OTH MACHY FOR SPCL INDUS	W 19882	277.0	W 26606	375.9	W 27971	425.1	W 31929	477.6	AUT MACH IND PARTICULIERES
7284	MACHY FOR SPCL INDUS NES	W 10702	195.0	W 13574	243.1	W 14909	286.3	W 17530	330.0	MACH SPEC IND PARTICUL.
72848	OTH MCHY WITH INDIV FNCT	W 5595	98.1	W 7532	119.6	W 8077	144.5	W 8154	137.3	AUTRES MACHINES NDA
72849	PTS OF MACHS OF 7284 ETC	W 3735	66.4	W 4165	83.8	W 5217	103.6	W 7516	154.6	PIECES DU 728.4 ETC
73	METALWORKING MACHINERY		117.8		166.2		190.4		173.0	MACH TRAVAIL DES METAUX
736	METALWORKING MACH-TOOLS	W 5948	75.3	W 7640	117.6	W 8379	140.8	W 8618	129.4	MACH-OUTILS TRAVAIL METAUX
74	GENRL INDUSTRL MACHY NES		1399.9		1831.0		1930.5		1940.7	MACH APP INDUSTRIE
741	HEATING,COOLING EQUIPMNT	W 13840	186.1	W 21134	261.8	W 25700	311.1	W 23710	301.1	MACH CHAUFFAGE,PIECES
7416	HEATING,COOLING EQU NES	W 4174	75.1	W 9597	112.5	W 10184	128.0	W 6034	111.0	APP CHANGEMENT TEMP
742	PUMPS FOR LIQUIDS ETC	W 5943	127.1	W 7019	164.4	W 7252	165.6	W 6837	141.7	POMPES MOTO-POMPES
743	PUMPS NES,CENTRFUGES ETC	W 13839	217.9	W 16926	289.3	W 15861	292.2	W 18354	286.7	POMPES COMPRES,VENT ETC
744	MECHANICAL HANDLING EQU	W 37073	270.9	W 46449	405.1	W 50028	426.4	W 54729	414.6	EQUIP MANUTENTION PIECES
7442	LIFTING,LOADING MACH NES	W 14708	104.1	W 20350	155.9	W 21252	182.6	W 22285	167.4	APP LEVAGE,MANUTENTION
74428	OTH HANDLING ETC MCH NES	W 7734	56.2	W 10316	86.5	W 11760	110.3	W 13173	101.6	AUT APP LEVAGE ETC
7449	PTS NES OF MACHY OF 7442	W 13179	111.2	W 15384	176.7	W 14934	154.5	W 18157	153.3	PIECES DU 744.2
745	NONELEC MACHY,TOOLS NES	W 8711	171.3	W 11203	212.5	W 10898	214.9	W 10827	213.5	AUT MACH NON ELEC,PIECES
7452	OTH NONELEC MCHS,PTS NES	W 7626	144.4	W 10153	185.3	W 9848	186.7	W 9637	184.3	AUT MACH NON ELEC,PIECES
749	NONELEC MACH PTS,ACC NES	W 23976	426.9	W 25337	498.2	W 25775	520.5	W 30180	583.4	PIECES MACH NON ELEC NDA
7492	COCKS,VALVES ETC NES	W 11751	263.6	W 11493	292.1	W 10851	298.8	W 13391	362.1	ART ROB,SIM POUR TUYAUX
7493	SHAFT,CRANK,PULLEY ETC	W 6413	74.7	W 6969	96.1	W 7992	108.1	W 9229	106.8	ARBRES TRANS,VILEBREQUINS
75	OFFICE MACHNES,ADP EQUIP		1185.4		1585.6		1562.9		1722.1	MACH BUREAU TRAIT AUTOM
751	OFFICE MACHINES	W 3029	105.6		124.6	W 3443	116.2	W 3512	108.7	MACH,APPAREILS DE BUREAU
7518	OFFICE MACHINES NES	W 2587	82.5	W 2913	102.2	W 2992	95.5	W 3086	90.9	MACH,APP DE BUREAU NDA
752	AUTOMTIC DATA PROC EQUIP	W 8834	648.2	W 11786	908.9	W 12936	950.9	W 16531	1107.9	MACH TRAIT INFORMATION
7522	DIGITAL COMPUTERS	W 621	84.7	W 806	99.3	W 931	133.4	W 713	133.4	MACH DIGITALES COMPLETES
7523	DIGITL CENTRL PROCESSORS	W 2550	220.3	W 3798	368.8	W 4158	364.2	W 5501	453.1	UNITES CENTRALES
7524	DIGITL CENTRL STOR UNITS	W 372	44.0	W 502	67.2	W 489	80.0	W 887	134.2	UNITES MEMOIRE CENTRALES
7525	ADP PERIPHERAL UNITS	W 4462	229.8	W 5841	305.6	W 4774	220.8	W 6779	258.3	UNITES PERIPHERIQUES
7528	OFF-LINE DATA PROC EQUIP	W 793	64.3	W 805	62.3	W 2467	129.9	W 2531	102.6	MACH AUXIL TRAIT INFORM
759	OFFICE,ADP MCH PTS,ACCES	W 5226	431.7	W 5586	552.2	W 5718	495.9	W 6428	505.6	PIECES DU 751 ET 752
7599	ACCTG,ETC,ADP MCH PTS,AC	W 4212	386.3	W 4505	500.4	W 4578	449.7	W 5217	460.2	PIECES DU 751 ET 752
76	TELECOMM,SOUND EQUIPMENT		895.7		1168.9		1141.0		1170.5	EQUIPMENT DE TELECOM
761	TELEVISION RECEIVERS	W 7011	107.5	W 6878	117.3	W 7456	116.5	W 9289	126.4	RECEPTEURS DE TELEVISION
7611	COLOUR TV RECEIVERS	W 6982	105.9	W 6835	113.8	W. 7438	115.5	W 9255	124.4	RECEPTEURS COULEUR
764	TELECOM EQPT,PTS,ACC NES	W 7937	651.9	W 9202	894.0	W 9352	859.1	W 11001	888.4	EQUIP TELECOM,PIECES
7641	LINE TELEPHONE,ETC EQUIP	W 1194	107.6	W 1686	180.9	W 1896	211.5	W 2319	235.9	APP TELEPHON PAR FIL
7643	TV,RADIO TRANSMITTRS ETC	W 708	175.2	W 1189	293.9	W 925	240.1	W 1170	233.9	APP EMET TELE RADIO
7649	PTS NES OF EQUIPMT OF 76	W 3169	259.2	W 3187	315.6	W 3221	309.1	W 3641	325.3	PIECES DE LA DIV 76
76491	PTS NES OF APPAR OF 7641	W 980	138.8	W 1306	174.9	W 1513	192.8	W 1932	205.0	PIECES POUR 764.1
76493	TELECOMM EQUIPMT PTS NES	W 1934	112.1	W 1618	130.0	W 1446	105.4	W 1370	107.6	PIECES 761,762,764.3,8
77	ELECTRIC MACHNRY NES ETC		1419.4		1797.0		1875.4		1867.5	MACH APP ELECT NDA
771	ELECTRIC POWER MACHY NES	W 5203	92.2	W 6449	125.1	W 9695	147.3	W 8683	137.1	MACH PROD,TRANS ELECTR
772	SWITCHGEAR ETC,PARTS NES	W 9003	309.9	W 10715	432.6	W 11803	433.0	W 13148	430.2	APP COUPURE,SECT ETC
7721	SWITCHGEAR ETC	W 8704	272.3	W 10304	376.0	W 11402	383.3	W 12741	380.2	APP COUPURE,SECTIONMNT
773	ELECTR DISTRIBUTNG EQUIP	W 17201	111.9	W 19287	142.8	W 20330	153.7	W 22397	151.9	EQUIPMNT DISTRIBUTION ELECT
7731	INSULATED WIRE,CABLE ETC	W 15778	99.1	W 17949	126.3	W 19169	137.7	W 21236	139.0	FILS,CABLES ISOLES ELECT

4. General Imports C.I.F. by Commodities according to the S.I.T.C. (Rev. 2) in million U.S. Dollars
Importations Générales C.A.F. par Produits d'après la C.T.C.I. (Rév. 2) en millions de Dollars E.U.

SITC CTCI	COMMODITY	1994 QUANTITY QUANTITE	1994 VALUE VALEUR	1995 QUANTITY QUANTITE	1995 VALUE VALEUR	1996 QUANTITY QUANTITE	1996 VALUE VALEUR	1997 QUANTITY QUANTITE	1997 VALUE VALEUR	PRODUIT
775	HOUSEHOLD TYPE EQUIP NES	W 38913	274.7	W 41060	315.4	W 42697	327.8	W 49760	362.5	MACH,APP USAGE DOMESTQUE
7758	ELECTRO–THERMIC APPL NES	W 9994	84.9	W 10395	94.4	W 11451	102.4	W 13030	109.5	APP ELECTROTHERMIQ NDA
776	TRANSISTORS,VALVES,ETC	W 593	175.7	W 600	213.8	W 455	200.5	W 453	210.5	LAMPES,TUBES,VALVES
7764	ELECTRONIC MICROCIRCUITS	W 197	137.2	W 232	160.9	W 236	155.9	W 299	167.2	MICROSTRUCTURES ELECTRON
778	ELECTRICAL MACHINERY NES	W 170212	408.7	W 187023	514.8	W 184917	533.9	W 197523	509.8	AUTRES MACH ELECT NDA
7788	OTH ELEC MACHY,EQUIP NES	W 146722	193.9	W 162036	251.7	W 158037	258.8	W 170985	264.2	AUT MACH APP ELEC NDA
77887	ELECTRICAL CARBONS	W 144589	85.6	W 159397	103.1	W 154871	108.3	W 167713	106.3	PIECES CHARBON,GRAPHITE
78	ROAD VEHICLES		2113.6		2624.2		2982.5		3327.1	VEHICULES ROUTIERS
781	PASS MOTOR VEH EXC BUSES	W 127681	1063.4	W 126440	1221.4	W 157657	1564.7	W 185699	1779.0	AUTO TRANSPORT PERSONNES
782	LORRIES,SPCL MTR VEH NES	W 54730	463.0	W 65421	642.2	W 60097	616.1	W 81852	774.2	VEHICULES SPECIAUX,MARCH
7821	LORRIES,TRUCKS	W 52007	437.6	W 61907	605.1	W 55747	576.1	W 76823	702.3	VEHICULES TRANSP MARCHAND
783	ROAD MOTOR VEHICLES NES	W 5162	70.6	W 8140	114.5	W 5237	79.2	W 5072	67.4	VEHICULES ROUTIERS NDA
7831	BUSES	W 4376	62.2	W 7459	107.0	W 4849	76.5	W 4606	64.8	VOITURES TRANSPORT COMMUN
784	MOTOR VEH PRTS,ACCES NES	W 35278	309.0	W 40316	384.0	W 40111	428.1	W 39308	390.9	PIECES 722,781,782,783
7849	OTHER MOTOR VEHCL PARTS	W 33616	298.1	W 38430	370.5	W 37085	393.8	W 36999	367.6	PIECES 722,781,782,783
785	CYCLES,ETC MOTRZD OR NOT	W 7916	114.7	W 7141	128.4	W 9430	149.1	W 9616	158.3	MOTOCYCLES SCOOTERS
786	TRAILERS,NONMOTR VEH,NES	W 23529	93.3	W 28397	134.0	W 32897	145.6	W 40392	157.6	REMORQUES,CADRES,CONTAIN
7861	TRAILERS,TRANSP CONTAINR	W 17635	61.1	W 21750	92.9	W 25795	104.4	W 32196	111.8	REMORQUES TOUS VEHICULES
79	OTHR TRANSPORT EQUIPMENT		1436.4		1130.3		1526.0		2838.9	AUTRE MATERIEL TRANSPORT
791	RAILWAY VEHICLES	W 10333	64.2		61.4	W 8776	160.0	W 10774	148.5	VEHIC MAT CHEMINS DE FER
792	AIRCRAFT ETC	W 854	311.7	W 1768	262.9	W 1528	283.7	W 1377	319.8	APP NAVIGATION AERIENNE
7924	AIRCRFT NES OVER 15000KG	W 149	90.7	W 10	10.6	W 53	30.5	W 107	108.8	AERODYNES PLUS 15000 KG
7929	AIRCRAFT PARTS NES	W 565	132.4	W 1595	161.2	W 1300	167.5	W 1174	165.3	PIECES DU 792
793	SHIPS AND BOATS ETC	W 925124	1060.6	W 668759	806.2		1082.3	W 2822678	2370.7	NAVIRES BATEAUX,ETC
7932	SHIPS AND BOATS NES	W 891233	1019.6	W 654859	770.6	W 590459	616.6	W 2784953	1955.3	NAVIRES ET BATEAUX
79322	TANKERS OF ALL KINDS	W 295846	358.5	W 289990	357.1	W 28653	30.2	W 1399899	675.1	BATEAUX–CITERNES
79323	OTHER CARGO VESSELS	W 591281	627.5	W 354104	335.6	W 551969	513.4	W 1357573	1134.3	AUT BATEAUX TRANS MARCH
7938	TUGS,SPECIAL VESSELS ETC	W 26476	25.5	W 7463	10.7		449.0	W 5180	345.8	REMORQUEURS,BATEAUX SPEC
79382	SPECL PURPOSE VESSLS ETC	W 20589	11.8	W 5062	1.7	W 805	438.5	W 1833	301.4	BAT–PHARES,–POMPES,DRAGUES
8	MISC MANUFACTURED GOODS		4481.4		5150.5		5220.6		5328.0	ART MANUFACTURES DIVERS
812	*PLUMBG,HEATNG,LGHTNG EQ	W 15742	145.7	W 18572	184.2	W 20137	197.3	W 23823	214.2	APPAR SANITAIRES CHAUFFAGE
8124	LIGHTING EQUIPMENT NES	W 9663	115.4	W 12305	152.4	W 12887	158.0	W 15059	171.7	APPAREILS ECLAIRAGE ETC
81242	LAMPS,FITTINGS BASE METL	W 8089	91.0	W 9874	115.1	W 10438	122.2	W 11652	129.4	APPAREILS D'ECLAIRAGE
821	*FURNITURE,PARTS THEREOF	W 116175	506.2	W 120552	610.7	W 123041	651.0	W 146658	701.3	MEUBLES ET PIECES
8211	CHAIRS,SEATS AND PARTS	W 18398	118.6	W 21088	149.5	W 22384	160.4	W 24515	165.0	SIEGES ET PIECES
82111	CHAIRS AND OTHER SEATS	W 16677	107.8	W 19181	136.5	W 20493	147.7	W 22205	151.4	SIEGES
8219	FURNITURE AND PARTS NES	W 92152	330.8	W 93951	395.5	W 95564	425.0	W 115204	458.9	AUTRES MEUBLES ET PIECES
82192	WOOD FURNITURE NES	W 63797	229.7	W 66836	283.3	W 68141	305.6	W 81983	328.8	MEUBLES NDA EN BOIS
84	CLOTHING AND ACCESSORIES		1294.6		1420.9		1382.4		1396.8	VETEMENTS
842	MENS OUTERWEAR NOT KNIT	W 8393	229.7	W 9449	272.1	W 8328	242.2	W 8616	231.6	VET DESSUS POUR HOMMES
8423	— TROUSERS,BREECHES ETC	W 3827	87.5	W 4013	102.4	W 3876	100.4	W 3982	92.4	PANTALONS HOMMES MAT TEX
8429	— OTHER OUTER GARMENTS	W 3295	86.5	W 4129	105.9	W 3203	82.5	W 3155	76.0	AUT VET DES HOM MAT TEX
843	WOMENS OUTERWEAR NONKNIT	W 10660	367.8	W 10174	396.9	W 9305	364.5	W 9835	362.2	VET DESSUS FEMMES MAT TEX
8439	— OTHER OUTER GARMENTS	W 6006	163.6	W 5505	166.8	W 4980	155.3	W 5463	164.0	AUT VET DES FEM MAT TEXT
845	OUTERWEAR KNIT NONELASTC	W 13147	329.2	W 11976	327.1	W 12862	353.9	W 14938	387.0	VET DESSOUS,ACCES BONNET
8451	— JERSEYS,PULLOVERS ETC	W 7968	189.0	W 6693	176.9	W 7527	200.6	W 8293	208.9	CHANDAILS,PULL–OVERS ETC
8459	— OTHER,CLTHG ACCESRYS	W 4365	111.6	W 4454	118.5	W 4521	123.5	W 5786	147.0	AUT VET DESSUS DE BONNE
846	UNDER GARMENTS KNITTED	W 7068	145.6	W 7224	174.0	W 7392	176.6	W 8201	184.0	SOUS VETS DE BONNETERIE
8462	— OF COTTON NON ELASTIC	W 5953	102.8	W 5962	122.8	W 6131	125.3	W 6911	133.8	SOUS–VET BONNET COTON
84629	—— OTHER	W 5638	97.5	W 5709	117.3	W 5844	118.9	W 6599	126.8	AUT SOUS–VET BONNET COTON
848	HEADGEAR,NONTXTL CLOTHNG	W 5362	104.9	W 5824	112.6	W 5844	106.4	W 5790	100.7	VET ACCES MAT AUT QUE TEX
851	*FOOTWEAR	W 13398	259.3	W 13185	283.4	W 13031	285.1	W 13732	279.4	CHAUSSURES
85102	FOOTWEAR LEATHER	W 9288	215.9	W 9296	236.0	W 9275	236.2	W 9587	231.4	CHAUS SEMELLES EN CUIR
87	PRECISION INSTRUMNTS NES		533.7		580.1		569.8		548.0	INSTRUM,APPAR SCIENT NDA
872	MEDICAL INSTRUMENTS NES	W 2263	114.3	W 2794	153.2	W 2828	159.7	W 2779	155.4	INSTR,APP MEDIC–CHIR NDA
87202	OTH MEDICAL INSTRUMENTS	W 1851	93.7	W 2230	118.8	W 2311	135.2	W 2165	130.9	INSTRUM,APP MEDECINE
874	MEASURNG,CONTROLNG INSTR	W 4342	335.7	W 4041	355.9	W 4297	343.5	W 3747	326.0	INSTRUMENTS DE MESURE
88	PHOTO EQU,OPTICL GDS ETC		229.3		271.3		282.6		293.3	APP,FOURN PHOTO,OP,MONTR
882	PHOTO,CINEMA SUPPLIES	W 7232	93.7	W 7711	108.6	W 7220	99.8	W 7456	93.3	PRODUITS PHOTO,CINEMA
89	MISC MANUFCTRD GOODS NES		1446.3		1717.8		1770.4		1809.6	ART MANUFACTURES DIVERS
892	PRINTED MATTER	W 51593	278.1	W 54790	349.4	W 56171	359.5	W 61308	351.1	IMPRIMES
8921	PRINTED BOOKS,GLOBES,ETC	W 13362	89.0	W 14666	118.5	W 13570	114.7	W 16552	117.9	LIVRES,BROCHURES,CARTES
89211	PRINTED BOOKS,PAMPHLETS	W 12722	83.6	W 13891	111.6	W 13012	108.7	W 15690	110.7	LIVRES,BROCHURES
8928	PRINTED MATTER NES	W 29301	144.5	W 31599	178.8	W 34364	181.8	W 33772	172.8	IMPRIMES NDA
89286	TRADE ADV MATRL,CATALOGS	W 22038	80.5	W 23614	99.1	W 27283	109.1	W 25733	101.3	IMPRIMES PUBLICITAIRES
893	ARTICLES OF PLASTIC NES		454.9		525.4		562.4		566.5	OUVRAGES EN MAT DIVIS 58
8931	PLSTC PACKG CONTNRS,LIDS	W 41149	137.2	W 40785	166.1	W 45560	172.9	W 52993	175.7	ART TRANSP EMBALLAGE ETC
8939	MISC PLASTIC ARTICLES	W 61869	300.0	W 58259	338.1	W 64156	365.4	W 72055	365.3	ART DIVERS EN MAT DIV 58
89399	OTHR PLASTC ARTICLES NES	W 41756	237.1	W 39284	268.5	W 44221	289.4	W 50374	289.6	AUT OUV MAT DIV 58
894	TOYS,SPORTING GOODS,ETC	W 20910	219.7	W 23803	267.7	W 23221	274.1	W 26019	292.4	VOITURES ENFANTS,JOUETS
8942	TOYS,INDOOR GAMES ETC	W 13751	129.8	W 16131	164.5	W 15880	174.5	W 17799	190.2	JOUETS,JEUX ETC
898	MUSICAL INSTRUMENTS,PTS	W 6356	254.3	W 6859	298.9	W 6712	293.4	W 7167	293.9	INSTRUMENTS DE MUSIQUE
8983	SOUND RECRDNG TAPE,DISCS	W 5599	234.1	W 5991	274.9	W 5905	270.8	W 6326	271.1	SUPPORTS SON POUR 763
89832	RECORDED DISCS,TAPES ETC	W 3914	205.5	W 4409	246.3	W 4370	236.0	W 4797	238.8	DISQUES,PHONO,BANDES
899	OTHER MANUFACTURED GOODS		121.2		145.4		151.3		154.9	AUT ART MANUF DIVERS NDA
9	GOODS NOT CLASSD BY KIND		454.3		482.7		453.3		442.1	ART TRANSACT NON CLASSES
931	*SPECIAL TRANSACTIONS		256.3		286.6		270.6		277.5	TRANS.SPECIALES
951	*WAR FIREARMS,AMMUNITION	W 1274	178.4	W 2409	169.8	W 5225	159.5	W 1635	143.2	VEHIC BLINDES ARMES
95106	AMMUNITION NES	W 604	123.3	W 503	118.8	W 1865	97.2	W 752	118.4	PROJECTILES,MUNITIONS

5. General Exports F.O.B. by Commodities according to the S.I.T.C. (Rev. 2) in million U.S. Dollars
Exportations Générales F.O.B. par Produits d'après la C.T.C.I. (Rév. 2) en millions de Dollars E.U.

SITC CTCI	COMMODITY	1994 QUANTITY QUANTITE	1994 VALUE VALEUR	1995 QUANTITY QUANTITE	1995 VALUE VALEUR	1996 QUANTITY QUANTITE	1996 VALUE VALEUR	1997 QUANTITY QUANTITE	1997 VALUE VALEUR	PRODUIT
	ALL COMMODITIES		34743.6		41740.4		48955.0		48549.9	TOUS PRODUITS
0	FOOD AND LIVE ANIMALS		3002.5		3405.7		3730.0		3690.0	ALIMENTS,ANIMAUX VIVANTS
03	FISH AND PREPARATIONS		2678.8		3045.5		3321.7		3311.6	POISSONS ET PREPARATIONS
034	FISH,FRESH,CHILLED,FROZN	W 1023885	1751.7	W 1135785	2066.8	W 1291846	2360.3	W 1472649	2435.6	POISSON FRAIS, REFRIG,CONG
0341	FISH FRSH,CHLLD,EX FILLT	W 309157	849.0	W 344719	936.4	W 370704	949.2	W 428371	944.6	POISSON FRAIS,REFRIGERE
0342	FISH FROZEN,EXCL FILLETS	W 521024	425.9	W 582622	555.5	W 692756	788.5	W 806526	855.5	POISSONS CONGELES
0344	FISH FILLETS,FROZEN	W 177366	419.0	W 187290	500.7	W 195185	515.0	W 191655	515.0	FILETS CONGELES
035	FISH SALTED,DRIED,SMOKED	W 167811	659.6	W 167913	719.9	W 169245	696.3	W 159666	633.8	POISSON SECHE,SALE,FUME
03502	COD(NOT IN FILLETS)DRIED	W 36877	226.3	W 44309	293.4	W 46497	286.7	W 45189	256.6	MORUE SECHEE,SALEE
03503	FISH(EX COD)DRIED,SALTED	W 127053	393.3	W 119442	382.2	W 118672	365.2	W 110311	335.8	POISSONS SECHES,SALES
037	FISH ETC PREPD,PRSVD NES	W 50734	211.3	W 40769	204.2	W 43762	214.1	W 45325	198.3	POIS,CRUST,MOL PREPARES
0371	FISH PREPARD,PRESRVD NES	W 34307	105.8	W 29489	101.2	W 30092	104.9	W 28597	92.9	CONSERVES DE POISSONS
0372	SHELL FISH PREPRD,PRESVD	W 16426	105.5	W 11280	103.1	W 13670	109.2	W 16728	105.5	CRUSTACES,COQUIL PREPARES
081	*FEEDING STUFF FOR ANIML	W 217325	98.8	W 262516	117.7	W 289365	159.5	W 254155	155.8	NOURRITURE POUR ANIMAUX
2	CRUDE MATERLS,EXCL FUELS		799.5		1023.0		933.8		857.6	MAT BRUTES NON COMESTIBLES
24	CORK AND WOOD		202.0		223.1		204.2		193.1	LIEGE ET BOIS
248	WOOD SHAPED,SLEEPERS	W 385882	180.2	W 365313	191.9	W 385732	176.1	W 345180	163.6	BOIS SIMPLEMENT TRAVAILLES
2482	LUMBER SHAPED CONIFER	W 383814	177.4	W 364145	189.9	W 381385	172.9	W 342620	160.9	CONIFERES SCIES,RABOTES
24821	LUMBER SAWN ETC CONIFER	W 366600	163.9	W 352401	177.8	W 363317	157.5	W 332613	151.9	CONIFERES SCIES LONGITUD
251	*PULP AND WASTE PAPER	W 493795	163.7	W 555836	281.7	W 505932	209.2	W 513558	160.1	PATES A PAPIER,DECHETS
2516	CHEM WOOD PULP DISSOLVNG	W 104443	67.2	W 136488	126.2	W 148854	124.7	W 129860	94.6	PATES CHIMIQUES DE BOIS
27	CRUDE FERTLZR,MINRLS NES		199.0		229.1		233.0		242.6	ENGRAIS MINERAUX BRUTS
273	STONE,SAND AND GRAVEL	MW 9064	143.4	MW 10050	166.3	MW 9944	164.8	MW 12412	172.6	PIERRES,SABLES,GRAVIERS
28	METALLIFEROUS ORES,SCRAP		135.7		152.0		142.9		97.5	MINERAIS METAL,DECHETS
3	MINERAL FUELS ETC		17236.7		19736.9		26758.9		26115.6	COMBUSTIBLES MINERAUX LUB
33	PETROLEUM AND PRODUCTS		14618.8		16756.1		22886.9		21416.0	PETROLE ET DERIVES
333	CRUDE PETROLEUM	MW 111261	13168.6	MW 121730	15331.0	MW 136824	20987.9	MW 137548	19299.4	HUILES BRUTES DE PETROLE
334	PETROLEUM PRODUCTS,REFIN	MW 9706	1428.7	MW 9156	1390.6	MW 10259	1858.8	MW 12011	2082.9	PRODUITS RAFFINES
3341	GASOLINE,OTH LIGHT OILS	W 3781886	601.0	W 3933145	639.4	W 4785090	907.8	W 6367813	1175.6	ESSENCES POUR MOTEURS
33411	MOTOR,AVIATION SPIRIT	W 1848450	317.5	W 1360671	245.0	W 1949153	397.1	W 1819480	393.5	ESSENCES MOTEURS D'AVIONS
33419	OTH LIGHT PETROLEUM OILS	W 1931212	283.2	W 2561372	392.6	W 2817768	507.1	W 4526690	778.3	AUTRES HUILES LEGERES
3343	GAS OILS	W 3742631	569.9	W 2980056	464.8	W 3097136	595.4	W 3131656	563.8	GAS OILS
3344	FUEL OILS,NES	W 1754615	176.0	W 1902145	216.1	W 1906757	242.8	W 2185817	256.8	FUEL OILS
341	*GAS,NATURAL AND MANUFCT	MW 23973	2522.8	MW 25199	2791.0	MW 33664	3716.1	MW 37234	4611.7	GAZ NATUREL,GAZ MANUFACT
3413	PETROLM GASES,LIQUEFIED	W 2325798	325.1	W 2910821	506.7	W 3156414	638.0	W 3283206	702.6	GAZ DE PETROLE LIQUEFIE
34131	LIQUEFIED PROPANE,BUTANE	W 2212117	304.9	W 2770622	457.8	W 2986189	594.4	W 3073407	642.4	PROPANE,BUTANE LIQUEFIES
3414	PETROLEUM GASES, GASEOUS	MW 21647	2197.8	MW 22288	2284.4	MW 30507	3078.2	MW 33951	3909.2	GAZ DE PETROLE GAZEUX
351	*ELECTRIC CURRENT	H 4740918	93.4	H 8563380	188.8	H 4236276	153.2	H 4874224	87.0	ENERGIE ELECTRIQUE
5	CHEMCLS,RELATED PROD NES		990.6		1268.1		1369.8		1388.3	PRODUITS CHIMIQUES
51	ORGANIC CHEMICALS		202.9		247.7		276.3		305.4	PROD CHIMIQ ORGANIQUES
514	NITROGEN-FNCTN COMPOUNDS	W 2171	173.4	W 3891	220.0	W 23594	244.9	W 4365	267.0	COMPOSES FONCT AZOTEES
5147	AMIDE-FNCT CMPD,EXC UREA	W 1133	161.0	W 1584	197.5	W 19485	220.5	W 1899	241.4	COMPOSES CARBOXYAMIDE
52	INORGANIC CHEMICALS		158.6		201.5		235.0		235.7	PROD CHIM INORGANIQUES
522	INORG ELEMNTS,OXIDES,ETC	W 515946	142.8	W 839451	179.2	W 983824	207.7		213.1	ELEMENTS INORGANIQUES
5221	CHEMICAL ELEMENTS	W 97072	117.7	W 105855	146.9	W 111124	163.7		176.5	ELEMENTS CHIMIQUES
52212	NON-METALS NES	W 91798	117.0	W 97689	145.3	W 97136	161.9	W 109435	174.2	SELENIUM,PHOSPHORE
541	*MEDICINAL,PHARM PRODUCT	MK 14232	190.0		210.2		225.5		217.9	PROD MEDICINAUX PHARMACEUT
58	PLASTIC MATERIALS ETC		156.1		201.4		185.6		167.1	MAT PLAST ARTIFICIELLES
583	POLYMERIZATION ETC PRODS	W 84729	124.7	W 76673	160.2	W 74234	145.4	W 63844	128.2	PROD POLYMERISATION
59	CHEMICAL MATERIALS NES		184.1		270.4		294.4		323.3	MAT PROD CHIMIQUES NDA
598	MISCEL CHEM PRODUCTS NES	W 1161556	171.3	W 1626140	256.9	W 362436	280.1	W 2406202	310.5	PROD DIV INDUST CHIM NDA
5989	CHEM PRODUCTS,PREPS NES	W 1039452	128.1	W 1450716	187.8	W 212271	208.9	W 2255133	245.3	PROD PREP CHIMIQUES NDA
59899	OTH CHEM PRODS,PREPS,NES	W 1007738	112.3	W 1418625	164.0	W 178177	188.6	W 2220388	225.2	AUT PRODUITS CHIMIQUES NDA
6	BASIC MANUFACTURES		4908.4		6325.2		6155.4		6228.8	ART MANUFACTURES
63	WOOD,CORK MANUFACTRS NES		226.3		256.7		243.2		216.6	OUVRAGES LIEGE ET BOIS
635	WOOD MANUFACTURES NES	W 61853	185.7	W 59798	206.6	W 56132	189.2	W 50302	166.3	ART MANUF EN BOIS NDA
6353	BUILDERS WOODWRK,PREFABS	W 60187	179.8	W 57459	198.6	W 54010	181.9	W 48282	158.5	OUVRAGES DE MENUISERIE
64	PAPER,PAPERBOARD AND MFR		688.2		1053.2		938.7		819.2	PAPIERS,CARTONS & OUVRAGES
641	PAPER AND PAPERBOARD	W 990391	603.5	W 1111117	949.0	W 1008853	829.9	W 1079759	721.9	PAPIERS ET CARTONS
6413	KRAFT PAPER,PAPERBOARD	W 222324	129.0	W 214567	183.0	W 221367	147.6	W 231767	134.7	PAPIER ET CARTON KRAFT
64131	KRAFT LINER IN BULK	W 181947	92.5	W 180332	141.3	W 187961	113.4	W 199728	106.6	PAP KRAFT POUR COUVERTURES
6415	PAPER,PAPERBRD,BULK,NES	W 682855	407.7	W 810374	675.4	W 708389	599.6	W 753727	493.1	PAPIERS,CARTONS ROULEAUX
64159	OTHER PAPER ETC,BULK,NES	W 640779	350.8	W 769557	606.7	W 669107	533.3	W 710819	427.6	AUT PAPIER ROULEAUX FEUILLES
65	TEXTILE YARN,FABRICS,ETC		169.9		186.4		197.3		187.8	FILS,TISSUS,ARTICLES TEXTILE
66	NONMETAL MINERAL MFS NES		124.1		137.9		153.4		139.4	ART MIN NON METALLIQUES
67	IRON AND STEEL		759.8		942.7		1044.5		1193.4	FER ET ACIER
671	PIG IRON ETC	W 643306	413.2	W 790347	558.1	W 652076	582.2	W 654262	480.4	FONTE,SPIEGEL,POUDRES
6716	FERRO-ALLOYS	W 612529	407.4	W 621183	514.4	W 651376	581.7	W 653222	480.1	FERRO-ALLIAGES
67162	FERRO-SILICON	W 423410	283.7	W 415723	347.8	W 414036	372.0	W 412873	314.6	FERRO-SILICIUM
67169	OTHER FERRO-ALLOYS	W 189118	123.7	W 205460	166.6	W 237340	209.7	W 240349	165.5	AUTRES FERRO-ALLIAGES
673	IRON,STEEL SHAPES ETC	W 314973	116.4	W 249565	116.0	W 311937	129.2	W 345679	125.0	BARRES,PROFIL FER,ACIER
674	IRN,STL UNIV,PLATE,SHEET	W 168187	115.7	W 182032	143.9	W 170716	135.9	W 190502	134.9	LARGES PLATS,TOLES
678	IRON,STL TUBES,PIPES,ETC	W 33461	52.1	W 36605	57.9	W 96582	97.1	W 980207	363.1	TUBES,TUYAUX EN FONTE,FER
6783	IRON,STL TUBES,PIPES NES	W 16838	18.2	W 17481	21.0	W 79619	42.7	W 966396	321.2	AUT TUBES,TUYAUX FER,ACIER
68	NON-FERROUS METALS		2564.2		3260.2		3059.6		3115.2	METAUX NON FERREUX
682	COPPER EXC CEMENT COPPER	W 47442	114.3	W 40520	131.9	W 40187	104.9	W 42709	129.4	CUIVRE
683	NICKEL	W 67211	408.4	W 52660	448.5	W 61060	474.5	W 62305	442.0	NICKEL
6831	NICKEL,ALLOYS UNWROUGHT	W 67188	408.3	W 52644	448.3	W 61030	474.5	W 62304	441.9	NICKEL ET ALLIAGES BRUTS
684	ALUMINIUM	W 1041851	1718.7	W 978348	2298.7	W 1072138	2125.5	W 1129341	2148.5	ALUMINIUM
6841	ALUMINIUM,ALLOYS,UNWRGHT	W 866704	1333.6	W 810570	1782.0	W 875679	1600.4	W 915144	1610.2	ALUMINIUM,ALLIAGES BRUTS
6842	ALUMINIUM,ALLOYS WORKED	W 175148	385.1	W 167778	516.8	W 196459	525.2	W 214197	538.4	ALUMINIUM,ALLIAGES OUVRE
68421	ALUMINIUM BARS,WIRE,ETC	W 65394	140.2	W 62976	190.2	W 87317	212.8	W 95374	220.1	BARRES,PROFILES FILS ALU
68422	ALUMNM PLATE,SHEET,STRIP	W 105536	230.6	W 101632	306.8	W 105089	282.0	W 115421	286.5	TOLES, PLANCHES EN ALU
686	ZINC	W 125648	126.7	W 121262	130.4	W 122227	129.0	W 131742	173.0	ZINC
6861	ZINC,ALLOYS UNWROUGHT	W 124539	125.8	W 120148	129.5	W 121410	128.3	W 130838	172.1	ZINC ET ALLIAGES BRUTS
689	NON-FER BASE METALS NES	W 4042	138.2	W 3974	178.1	W 3562	174.4	W 3958	161.1	AUT METAUX NON FERREUX
6899	BASE METALS NES,CERMETS	W 4005	137.1	W 3969	178.1	W 3477	174.4	W 3855	161.0	METAUX COMMUNS NDA
68999	BASE MTL NES UNWRT,WASTE	W 3853	137.0	W 3969	178.1	W 3477	174.4	W 3855	161.0	AUT METAUX COM BRUTS NDA
69	METAL MANUFACTURES NES		298.4		408.0		439.1		482.0	ART MANUFACT EN METAL NDA
699	BASE METAL MFRS NES	W 20703	121.5	W 22212	150.7	W 26627	187.3	W 27733	190.7	ART MANUFACTURES MET NDA
7	MACHINES,TRANSPORT EQUIP		4196.8		5553.4		5418.0		5869.1	MACHINES MATERIEL TRANSPORT
71	POWER GENERATING EQUIPMT		261.0		311.8		338.3		314.3	MACHINES GENERATRICES
713	INTRNL COMBUS PSTN ENGIN	W 6901	130.3	W 6975	148.5	W 6624	146.7	W 5785	128.3	MOTEURS EXPL COMB INT, PIECE
72	MACHS FOR SPCL INDUSTRYS		390.6		522.5		650.6		623.7	MAC SPECIALES POUR INDUST
721	AGRIC MACHY,EXC TRACTORS	W 22278	113.4	W 23226	135.7	W 26242	148.5	W 27379	144.5	MACHINES AGRICOLES
723	CIVIL ENGINEERG EQUIP ETC	W 13666	84.3	W 14464	127.0	W 14835	163.8	W 15561	192.5	APPAREILS DE GENIE CIVIL
7239	CONSTR ETC MACHY PTS NES	W 3643	53.3	W 4644	84.9	W 3664	112.1	W 5816	156.5	PIECES 723.41-723.46
728	OTH MACHY FOR SPCL INDUS	W 9280	102.5	W 11867	139.5	W 12890	186.5	W 12794	170.9	AUT MACH IND PARTICULIERES
7284	MACHY FOR SPCL INDUS NES	W 5260	81.2	W 7618	115.4	W 9145	158.2	W 8485	148.5	MACH SPEC IND PARTICUL.
74	GENRL INDUSTRL MACHY NES		566.6		812.9		910.7		882.4	MACH APP INDUSTRIE
741	HEATING,COOLING EQUIPMNT	W 8357	94.5	W 9220	122.4	W 11479	158.2	W 11270	119.4	MACH CHAUFFAGE,PIECES

Norway, including Svalbard and Jan Mayen Islands

Norvège y compris iles Svalbard et Jan Mayen

5. General Exports F.O.B. by Commodities according to the S.I.T.C. (Rev. 2) in million U.S. Dollars
Exportations Générales F.O.B. par Produits d'après la C.T.C.I. (Rév. 2) en millions de Dollars E.U.

SITC CTCI	COMMODITY	1994		1995		1996		1997		PRODUIT
		QUANTITY QUANTITE	VALUE VALEUR	QUANTITY QUANTITE	VALUE VALEUR	QUANTITY QUANTITE	VALUE VALEUR	QUANTITY QUANTITE	VALUE VALEUR	
742	PUMPS FOR LIQUIDS ETC	W 3145	91.9	W 4048	134.0	W 4496	146.0	W 4320	168.6	POMPES MOTO–POMPES
744	MECHANICAL HANDLING EQU	W 19996	154.5	W 27849	245.8	W 26741	242.8	W 26077	262.3	EQUIP MANUTENTION PIECES
7442	LIFTING,LOADING MACH NES	W 10504	88.1	W 16382	155.2	W 14168	136.7	W 13419	155.8	APP LEVAGE,MANUTENTION
749	NONELEC MACH PTS,ACC NES	W 4664	78.3	W 7083	123.0	W 8638	162.1	W 8278	151.3	PIECES MACH NON ELEC NDA
75	OFFICE MACHNES,ADP EQUIP		326.9		353.3		409.6		431.2	MACH BUREAU TRAIT AUTOM
752	AUTOMTIC DATA PROC EQUIP	W 1386	201.4	W 1150	209.2	W 1262	222.5	W 1693	279.4	MACH TRAIT INFORMATION
759	OFFICE,ADP MCH PTS,ACCES	W 1340	98.5	W 964	105.8	W 1974	159.6	W 1809	136.1	PIECES DU 751 ET 752
7599	ACCTG,ETC,ADP MCH PTS,AC	W 1197	95.5	W 803	103.3	W 1751	154.4	W 1463	131.5	PIECES DU 751 ET 752
76	TELECOMM,SOUND EQUIPMENT		379.2		574.4		565.2		689.7	EQUIPMENT DE TELECOM
764	TELECOM EQPT,PTS,ACC NES	W 3166	359.3	W 4564	555.6	W 4492	547.1	W 4769	663.5	EQUIP TELECOM,PIECES
7641	LINE TELEPHONE,ETC EQUIP	W 487	89.7	W 917	167.2	W 486	143.2	W 589	155.1	APP TELEPHON PAR FIL
7643	TV,RADIO TRANSMITTRS ETC	W 246	85.7	W 326	129.2	W 475	163.7	W 680	200.1	APP EMET TELE RADIO
7649	PTS NES OF EQUIPMT OF 76	W 1489	129.7	W 2472	221.0	W 2450	200.6	W 2525	259.7	PIECES DE LA DIV 76
76493	TELECOMM EQUIPMT PTS NES	W 1045	55.6	W 1922	98.4	W 1980	115.6	W 1923	147.5	PIECES 761,762,764.3,8
77	ELECTRIC MACHNRY NES ETC		486.8		641.8		783.4		757.1	MACH APP ELECT NDA
772	SWITCHGEAR ETC,PARTS NES	W 4657	101.7	W 5764	141.7	W 6379	165.5	W 6866	175.0	APP COUPURE,SECT ETC
7721	SWITCHGEAR ETC	W 4640	98.4	W 5742	133.9	W 6363	160.7	W 6851	171.9	APP COUPURE,SECTIONMNT
773	ELECTR DISTRIBUTNG EQUIP	W 10427	67.8	W 11155	93.0	W 27978	199.5	W 20783	184.0	EQUIPMT DISTRIBUTION ELECT
7731	INSULATED WIRE,CABLE ETC	W 10266	66.2	W 10981	91.5	W 27755	197.4	W 20578	182.0	FILS,CABLES ISOLES ELECT
778	ELECTRICAL MACHINERY NES	W 5690	99.3	W 9464	142.7	W 26566	151.1	W 29718	129.7	AUTRES MACH ELECT NDA
78	ROAD VEHICLES		389.5		536.5		553.2		534.8	VEHICULES ROUTIERS
784	MOTOR VEH PRTS,ACCES NES	W 31489	250.8	W 36823	339.4	W 37706	353.3	W 41399	337.5	PIECES 722,781,782,783
7849	OTHER MOTOR VEHCL PARTS	W 31267	248.8	W 36529	337.1	W 37552	351.7	W 40996	332.7	PIECES 722,781,782,783
79	OTHR TRANSPORT EQUIPMENT		1365.0		1761.4		1167.4		1607.7	AUTRE MATERIEL TRANSPORT
793	SHIPS AND BOATS ETC	W 1428798	1323.0	W 1814488	1705.6	W 982206	1101.7		1504.0	NAVIRES BATEAUX,ETC
7931	WARSHIPS	W 6496	114.5	W 1344	108.2	W 2711	61.8	W 2105	34.3	NAVIRES DE GUERRE
7932	SHIPS AND BOATS NES	W 1246372	1050.1	W 1810510	1528.4	W 961130	947.3	W 1294392	1254.8	NAVIRES ET BATEAUX
79322	TANKERS OF ALL KINDS	W 281632	283.5	W 390546	264.1	W 145681	181.2	W 730917	288.4	BATEAUX–CITERNES
79323	OTHER CARGO VESSELS	W 948996	619.2	W 1400516	1081.6	W 789052	530.0	W 527282	689.5	AUT BATEAUX TRANS MARCH
79324	FISHING VESSELS ETC	W 13292	94.2	W 17461	139.3	W 24690	198.7	W 34690	241.5	BATEAUX DE PECHE
7938	TUGS,SPECIAL VESSELS ETC	W 1681	138.4	W 2634	69.0	W 1447	89.9		209.5	REMORQUEURS,BATEAUX SPEC
79382	SPECL PURPOSE VESSLS ETC	W 57	112.4	W 51	34.7	W 1370	86.3		134.2	BAT–PHARES,–POMPES,DRAGUES
8	MISC MANUFACTURED GOODS		1051.7		1252.2		1357.3		1397.9	ART MANUFACTURES DIVERS
821	*FURNITURE,PARTS THEREOF	W 25929	202.7	W 30045	265.8	W 35923	311.7	W 39918	321.7	MEUBLES ET PIECES
8211	CHAIRS,SEATS AND PARTS	W 7806	118.6	W 8564	153.7	W 10282	177.8	W 11230	187.1	SIEGES ET PIECES
82111	CHAIRS AND OTHER SEATS	W 7148	113.9	W 7820	147.1	W 9168	166.4	W 10183	176.9	SIEGES
87	PRECISION INSTRUMNTS NES		322.9		367.4		421.4		441.3	INSTRUM,APPAR SCIENT NDA
874	MEASURNG,CONTROLNG INSTR	W 2109	278.6	W 2134	313.0		352.6	W 2331	355.1	INSTRUMENTS DE MESURE
89	MISC MANUFCTRD GOODS NES		306.2		366.8		388.9		394.6	ART MANUFACTURES DIVERS
893	ARTICLES OF PLASTIC NES		131.5		177.7		173.0		189.2	OUVRAGES EN MAT DIVIS 58
9	GOODS NOT CLASSD BY KIND		2488.6		3104.3		3150.9		2909.7	ART TRANSACT NON CLASSES
931	*SPECIAL TRANSACTIONS		2411.0		3017.9		3028.5		2841.4	TRANS.SPECIALES

Oman

1. HISTORICAL SERIES, 1965–1997 GENERAL TRADE, IMPORTS C.I.F., EXPORTS F.O.B.
SERIES HISTORIQUES, 1965–1997 COMMERCE GENERAL, IMPORTATIONS C.A.F., EXPORTATIONS F.O.B

YEAR ANNEE	VALUE IN MILLION RIALS OMANI VALEUR EN MILLION RIALS OMANI MERCHANDISE –MARCHANDISE		GOLD –OR		CONVERSION FACTORS U.S. CENTS PER RIAL OMANI FACTEURS DE CONVERSION CENTS E.U. PAR RIAL OMANI		INDEX NUMBERS –INDICES QUANTUM		UNIT VALUE VALEUR UNITAIRE	
	IMPORTS	EXPORTS	IMPORTS	EXPORTS	IMPORTS	EXPORTS	IMPORTS	EXPORTS	IMPORTS	EXPORTS
1965	3.20	0.80			280.0340	280.0340				
1966	3.40	0.60			280.0340	280.0340				
1967	3.60	12.90			280.0340	280.0340				
1968	4.00	60.00			280.0340	280.0340				
1969	4.00	84.70			280.0340	280.0340				
1970	7.60	82.10			239.9820	239.9820				
1971	13.80	88.10			280.0340	280.0340				
1972	18.70	88.60			260.5520	260.5520				
1973	40.70	115.00			286.8610	286.8610				
1974	135.60	419.10			240.7320	240.7320				
1975	264.30	489.20			289.5190	289.5190				
1976	250.50	545.20			289.5190	289.5190				
1977	302.10	547.40			289.5190	289.5190				
1978	327.20	552.00			289.5190	289.5190				
1979	430.50	787.40			289.5190	289.5190				
1980	598.20	1294.50			289.5190	289.5190				
1981	790.30	1621.90			289.5194	289.5194				
1982	926.50	1526.90			289.5192	289.5192				
1983	860.90	1467.30			289.5192	289.5192				
1984	949.20	1527.50			289.5191	289.5193				
1985	1088.90	1778.10			289.5191	289.5190				
1986	916.70	1122.50			260.0776	262.7984				
1987	700.70	1484.90			260.0776	260.0776				
1988	846.50	1291.40			260.0778	260.0779				
1989	867.90	1564.00			260.0780	260.0780				
1990	1031.00	2118.00			260.0778	260.0780				
1991	1228.00	1872.00			260.0797	260.0780				
1992	1449.30	2086.00			260.0797	260.0796				
1993	1581.80	2037.00			260.0797	260.0796				
1994	1505.30	2132.00			260.0800	260.0800				
1995	1633.20	2196.00			260.0796	260.0796				
1996	1760.10	2824.50			260.0797	260.0796				
1997	1932.50	2933.80			260.0796	260.0797				

2. IMPORTS BY BROAD ECONOMIC CATEGORY AND EXPORTS BY INDUSTRIAL ORIGIN. (PERCENTAGE OF TOTAL VALUE)
IMPORTATIONS PAR CATEGORIES ECONOMIQUES ET EXPORTATIONS PAR BRANCHE D'ACTIVITE.(EN POURCENTAGE DE LA VALEUR TOTALE)

IMPORTS – IMPORTATIONS

	1990	1991	1992	1993	1994	1995	1996
TOTAL IMPORTS–IMPORTATIONS TOTALES	100.	100.	100.	100.	100.	100.	100.
1 FOOD BEV–ALIMENTATION BOISSONS	17.0	15.1	13.9	13.3	14.8	15.2	14.0
11 PRIMARY–PRODUITS DE BASE	8.9	7.9	7.2	6.5	7.4	8.0	7.0
111 FOR INDUSTRY–POUR L'INDUSTRIE	2.5	1.9	1.9	1.5	2.1	3.3	2.3
112 FOR HOUSEHOLDS–POUR LES MENAGES	6.4	6.0	5.2	5.0	5.3	4.7	4.7
12 PROCESSED–PRODUITS ELABORES	8.1	7.2	6.7	6.8	7.3	7.1	7.0
121 FOR INDUSTRY–POUR L'INDUSTRIE	0.4	0.5	0.4	0.5	0.6	0.8	0.7
122 FOR HOUSEHOLDS–POUR LES MENAGES	7.7	6.7	6.4	6.3	6.7	6.3	6.2
2 IND SUPPLIES–APPROV INDUSTRIELS	21.2	21.4	18.8	19.1	19.9	22.2	21.1
21 PRIMARY–PRODUITS DE BASE	1.1	0.9	0.8	1.6	2.2	2.3	2.0
22 PROCESSED–PRODUITS ELABORES	20.1	20.5	17.9	17.5	17.6	19.9	19.1
3 FUELS–COMBUSTIBLES	4.2	1.9	1.9	3.2	1.1	1.6	1.1
31 PRIMARY–PRODUITS DE BASE	0.1	0.0	0.1	0.1	0.1	0.1	0.1
32 PROCESSED–PRODUITS ELABORES	4.1	1.8	1.9	3.1	0.9	1.5	1.0
321 MOTOR SPIRIT–ESSENCE		1.7	1.7	2.9	0.9		
322 OTHER–AUTRES	4.1	0.1	0.1	0.2	0.1	1.5	1.0
4 MACHINERY–EQUIPEMENT	17.0	21.6	18.0	17.5	18.2	18.3	18.5
41 CAPITAL EQUIPMENT–MACHINES	15.4	19.7	16.5	16.0	16.7	16.7	16.9
42 PARTS–PIECES ACCESSOIRES	1.6	1.9	1.5	1.5	1.5	1.6	1.6
5 TRANSPORT–TRANSPORT	18.7	20.4	25.9	25.9	25.4	21.5	23.4
51 PASSENGER CARS–AUTOMOBILES	11.1	12.1	16.3	15.7	13.3	9.8	11.8
52 OTHER–AUTRES	2.0	2.2	3.0	4.1	6.0	4.8	3.4
521 INDUSTRIAL–INDUSTRIELS	2.0	2.1	2.9	4.1	5.9	4.8	3.4
522 NON INDUSTRIAL–NON INDUSTRIEL	0.1	0.1	0.1	0.1	0.1	0.0	0.0
53 PARTS–PIECES ACCESSOIRES	5.6	6.1	6.6	6.1	6.2	6.8	8.2
6 CONSUM GOODS–BIENS CONSOMMATION	15.0	16.3	18.1	16.4	17.1	16.6	16.7
61 DURABLE–DURABLES	6.4	6.0	6.1	5.0	5.1	5.0	5.9
62 SEMI DURABLE–SEMI DURABLES	4.4	4.2	3.7	3.4	3.6	3.6	3.7
63 NON DURABLE–NON DURABLES	4.2	6.1	8.4	8.0	8.5	8.0	7.1
7 GOODS NES–BIENS NDA	6.9	3.3	3.4	4.6	3.5	4.7	5.3

EXPORTS – EXPORTATIONS

	1990	1991	1992	1993	1994	1995	1996
TOTAL EXPORTS–EXPORTATIONS TOTALES	100.	100.	100.	100.	100.	100.	100.
1 AGRICULTURE	1.4	1.4	1.3	1.7	1.8	2.1	1.6
2 MINING QUARRY–INDUS EXTRACTIVES	89.1	84.1	83.3	78.3	75.9	78.1	80.1
3 MANUFACTURING–IND MANUFACTUR	9.5	14.5	15.4	20.0	22.3	19.7	18.3
31 FOOD BEV TOBACCO–ALIM BOISS TAB	0.3	1.2	2.0	3.0	3.1	2.9	2.3
32 TEXTILES–INDUSTRIES TEXTILES	0.6	0.8	1.0	1.2	1.4	1.7	1.5
33 WOOD & PRODUCTS–BOIS & PRODUITS	0.0	0.0	0.0	0.0	0.0	0.0	0.0
34 PAPER & PRODUCTS–PAPIER & PRODT	0.0	0.1	0.1	0.1	0.1	0.1	0.1
35 CHEMICALS–INDUSTRIES CHIMIQUES	3.2	4.1	1.2	1.5	1.5	1.7	1.7
36 NON METAL MIN–MIN NON METAL	0.1	0.1	0.1	0.2	0.2	0.2	0.2
37 BASIC METAL–IND METAL BASE	0.8	0.9	0.9	1.2	1.5	1.5	1.1
38 METAL MANUF–MANUF METAL	4.1	7.1	9.9	12.5	13.8	11.0	10.6
39 OTH MANUF IND–AUTRES MANUF	0.3	0.3	0.3	0.4	0.7	0.6	0.8

3. TRADE BY PRINCIPAL COUNTRIES OF ORIGIN AND DESTINATION (VALUE IN MILLION U.S. DOLLARS)
ECHANGES SELON LES PRINCIPAUX PAYS D'ORIGINE ET DE DESTINATION (VALEUR EN MILLIONS DE DOLLARS EU)

COUNTRIES–PAYS	GENERAL IMPORTS C.I.F. IMPORTATIONS GENERALES C.A.F				
	1992	1993	1994	1995	1996
World	3769.2	4114.0	3915.0	4248.6	4577.8
Africa	11.0	15.0	19.2	15.8	16.2
Americas	290.4	398.9	297.8	342.2	443.7
– Northern America	272.2	372.0	273.3	298.2	356.6
– LAIA	14.3	25.3	23.2	42.1	85.7
– CACM	4.0	1.5	1.2	1.8	1.4
– Caribbean	0.0	0.0	0.0	0.2	0.0
– Rest of America		0.0	0.0		0.0
Asia excl fmr USSR	2379.0	2586.0	2484.1	2489.8	2738.4
– Middle East	1192.8	1358.1	1305.1	1280.8	1344.8
Asia former USSR			0.0	0.2	0.1
Europe excl fmr USSR	979.8	945.6	993.6	1242.7	1231.9
– European Union	928.3	909.7	937.4	1185.1	1157.7
– Eastern Europe	3.4	2.8	17.0	9.4	6.4
– Rest of Europe	48.0	33.0	39.2	48.2	67.8
Europe former USSR	1.0	2.0	0.3	5.5	2.1
Oceania	86.4	143.1	99.3	125.5	118.1
Other	21.5	23.5	21.0	26.8	27.4
United Arab Emirates	1053.2	1154.0	1139.8	1012.8	1086.8
Japan/Japon	876.9	859.7	779.0	671.3	786.5
United Kingdom	319.8	343.2	346.2	444.7	403.8
USA/Etats–Unis d'Amer	257.0	331.8	263.8	276.1	345.4
Germany/Allemagne	200.6	181.5	192.1	215.6	236.0
India/Inde	95.6	105.9	122.1	141.4	181.9
France, Monaco	116.3	102.1	106.0	163.8	155.3
Saudi Arabia	75.1	87.7	97.2	161.7	140.5
Australia/Australie	74.9	132.2	87.3	114.4	106.2
Netherlands/Pays–Bas	118.3	87.7	101.1	105.9	90.3
Korea, Republic of	50.9	76.3	50.8	109.0	153.2
Italy/Italie	58.1	73.3	74.2	82.0	109.2
Malaysia/Malaisie	32.7	37.1	72.4	53.1	65.0
Switzerland,Liechtenst.	41.2	27.0	33.7	40.9	61.4
Belgium–Luxembourg	26.5	26.1	23.6	52.5	44.1
Pakistan	23.9	39.1	26.2	33.2	40.0
Bahrain/Bahreïn	28.0	70.6	13.8	19.1	30.2
Indonesia/Indonésie	8.9	15.9	36.1	66.2	30.8
Singapore/Singapour	26.0	31.1	30.2	36.2	33.2
Sweden/Suède	24.4	25.2	27.4	36.4	31.1
China/Chine	16.4	19.3	20.7	38.1	38.4
Denmark/Danemark	23.8	25.7	24.3	29.1	26.8
Special Categories	21.5	23.5	20.9	26.2	27.4
Thailand/Thaïlande	25.0	21.1	16.0	24.2	26.2
Canada	15.2	40.2	9.5	22.1	11.2
China, Hong Kong SAR	20.3	15.0	17.5	18.9	20.9
Turkey/Turquie	13.5	11.1	14.8	19.0	21.8
Spain/Espagne	12.6	11.8	14.1	18.4	22.7
Chile/Chili	3.8	10.7	9.1	12.1	41.4
Iran (Islamic Rep of)	1.4	2.5	9.5	30.7	29.0
Argentina/Argentine	3.8	10.9	7.7	17.3	26.6
New Zealand	11.5	10.9	11.9	11.1	12.0
Qatar	9.4	8.1	5.9	14.9	15.2
Austria/Autriche	10.3	12.2	9.5	12.1	8.3
Ireland/Irlande	5.9	8.8	7.6	12.2	16.5
Kuwait/ Koweït	4.5	8.4	8.4	9.6	9.8
Finland/Finlande	7.6	6.4	8.4	8.3	9.4
Brazil/Brésil	6.3	3.5	5.1	10.6	14.3
Philippines	2.1	2.1	2.3	11.1	10.2
So. African Customs Un	0.2	6.5	11.5	4.3	4.8

COUNTRIES–PAYS	GENERAL EXPORTS F.O.B. EXPORTATIONS GENERALES F.O.B.				
	1992	1993	1994	1995	1996
Monde	5451.2	5299.5	5418.3	5917.4	7221.9
Afrique	60.2	99.3	118.5	129.9	142.5
Amériques	53.8	211.1	55.0	164.4	75.2
– Amérique du Nord	53.7	210.9	54.6	164.2	75.1
– ALAI	0.0	0.0	0.4	0.3	0.0
– MCAC		0.0			0.0
– Caraïbes		0.0	0.0		0.0
– Autre Amérique	0.0	0.2			0.0
Asie anc. URSS exclus	5271.0	4873.0	5165.2	5305.7	1111.3
– Moyen–Orient	825.0	905.4	1012.7	996.0	883.1
Asie ancienne URSS			0.5	8.7	20.5
Europe anc. URSS exclus	51.3	58.6	50.8	53.3	57.6
– Union Européenne	51.0	58.0	50.0	52.6	55.2
– Europe de l'Est	0.0	0.2	0.1	0.1	0.1
– Autre de l'Europe	0.3	0.5	0.7	0.7	2.4
Europe ancienne URSS		0.9	0.9	6.2	31.0
Océanie	1.8	18.9	0.8	1.5	0.6
Autre	13.1	37.7	26.6	247.7	5783.3
Japan/Japon	1840.0	1418.7	1887.1	1688.5	31.4
Areas n.e.s.	12.9	34.0	21.7	238.6	5774.5
Korea, Republic of	1283.3	1069.7	769.4	936.3	17.6
United Arab Emirates	458.8	505.4	549.1	604.6	606.9
China/Chine	380.2	432.7	436.4	573.5	0.9
Thailand/Thaïlande	243.2	274.8	447.3	506.6	7.7
Other Asia n.e.s.	359.4	326.6	316.0	275.9	
Yemen/Yémen	190.1	189.4	250.8	167.4	17.5
Singapore/Singapour	227.1	276.8	29.2	161.2	14.1
China, Hong Kong SAR	94.2	143.4	222.1	129.0	113.3
Iran (Islamic Rep of)	109.9	131.4	119.7	124.8	135.4
USA/Etats–Unis d'Amer	53.4	210.5	53.5	163.9	74.3
Saudi Arabia	38.3	42.0	54.7	55.2	65.4
United Rep of Tanzania	27.8	44.9	47.9	58.7	64.2
United Kingdom	21.4	29.0	31.6	29.0	24.5
Kenya	14.4	20.5	18.4	28.5	32.7
India/Inde	15.7	19.9	24.5	27.3	26.7
Zambia/Zambie	13.1	20.9	19.6	29.2	26.5
Kuwait/ Koweït	9.6	9.6	13.7	18.0	15.3
France, Monaco	19.2	16.7	5.7	5.8	10.2
Qatar	5.9	7.2	6.9	8.5	15.4
Bahrain/Bahreïn	6.9	7.5	7.9	9.3	8.9
Russian Federation		0.9	0.9	5.6	29.1
Syrian Arab Republic	2.7	9.1	6.6	3.8	8.1
Special Categories	0.2	3.7	4.9	9.1	8.8
Australia/Australie	1.7	18.8	0.7	1.4	0.6
So. African Customs Un		0.0	21.7	0.1	0.9
Kazakhstan			0.2	5.6	15.4
Netherlands/Pays–Bas	2.9	2.4	3.4	4.9	7.1
Germany/Allemagne	1.9	3.5	2.7	4.7	4.8
Egypt/Egypte	0.8	2.7	3.0	4.8	5.2
Tunisia/Tunisie	1.2	5.0	4.0	2.2	3.3
Pakistan	1.2	1.6	2.1	2.3	6.8
Sri Lanka	0.7	1.6	8.4	2.0	1.4
Italy/Italie	2.0	2.4	3.3	3.5	2.6
Libyan Arab Jamahiriya	1.3	3.3	0.9	2.2	3.2
Jordan/Jordanie	0.9	1.6	1.6	2.1	4.2
Greece/Grèce	2.6	2.8	1.1	1.6	1.5
Malaysia/Malaisie	0.7	0.5	4.2	2.4	1.8
Philippines	0.1	1.1	3.1	1.1	3.2

(VALUE AS PERCENTAGE OF WORLD TOTAL)(VALEURS EN POURCENTAGE DU TOTAL MONDIAL)

	1987	1988	1989	1990	1991	1992	1993	1994	1995	1996
Africa	0.2	0.2	0.2	0.5	0.4	0.3	0.4	0.5	0.4	0.4
Americas	7.6	9.9	9.6	10.0	8.4	7.7	9.7	7.6	8.1	9.7
– Northern America	6.9	9.0	8.9	9.6	7.8	7.2	9.0	7.0	7.0	7.8
– LAIA	0.5	0.7	0.5	0.3	0.4	0.4	0.6	0.6	1.0	1.9
– CACM	0.1	0.2	0.2	0.0	0.1	0.1	0.0	0.0	0.0	0.0
– Caribbean	0.0	0.0	0.0	0.0	0.0	0.0	0.0	0.0	0.0	0.0
– Rest of America	0.0		0.0				0.0	0.0		0.0
Asia excl fmr USSR	48.8	51.4	53.2	53.8	59.1	63.1	62.9	63.4	58.6	59.8
– Middle East	24.1	23.9	28.4	27.6	29.3	31.6	33.0	33.3	30.1	29.4
Asia former USSR								0.0	0.0	0.0
Europe excl fmr USSR	39.6	34.9	32.5	32.1	29.0	26.0	23.0	25.4	29.3	26.9
– European Union	38.0	32.9	29.7	29.3	27.9	24.6	22.1	23.9	27.9	25.3
– Eastern Europe	0.1	0.1	0.1	0.2	0.1	0.1	0.1	0.4	0.2	0.1
– Rest of Europe	1.4	1.9	2.6	2.6	1.0	1.3	0.8	1.0	1.1	1.5
Europe former USSR	0.0	0.0	0.2	0.1	0.1	0.0	0.0	0.0	0.1	0.0
Oceania	3.2	2.9	3.6	2.7	2.3	2.3	3.5	2.5	3.0	2.6
Other	0.7	0.7	0.6	0.7	0.7	0.6	0.6	0.5	0.6	0.6
United Arab Emirates	21.0	21.0	24.2	23.2	25.3	27.9	28.1	29.1	23.8	23.7
Japan/Japon	15.2	16.8	15.7	17.0	20.5	23.3	20.9	19.9	15.8	17.2
United Kingdom	14.7	13.3	11.7	11.5	10.0	8.5	8.3	8.8	10.5	8.8
USA/Etats–Unis d'Amer	6.7	8.8	8.5	9.4	7.6	6.8	8.1	6.7	6.5	7.5
Germany/Allemagne					5.2	5.3	4.4	4.9	5.1	5.2
India/Inde	3.7	3.7	2.8	2.8	2.7	2.5	2.6	3.1	3.3	4.0
France, Monaco	3.6	3.5	3.3	4.3	3.3	3.1	2.5	2.7	3.9	3.4
Saudi Arabia	1.1	1.3	2.0	2.2	2.6	2.0	2.1	2.5	3.8	3.1
Australia/Australie	2.6	2.3	2.9	2.3	1.9	2.0	3.2	2.2	2.7	2.3
Netherlands/Pays–Bas	4.5	2.9	3.2	3.4	4.0	3.1	2.1	2.6	2.5	2.0

	1987	1988	1989	1990	1991	1992	1993	1994	1995	1996
Afrique	0.3	0.2	0.1	0.4	1.0	1.1	1.9	2.2	2.2	2.0
Amériques	5.6	1.6	2.8	0.3	0.5	1.0	4.0	1.0	2.8	1.0
– Amérique du Nord	5.6	1.6	2.8	0.3	0.5	1.0	4.0	1.0	2.8	1.0
– ALAI	0.0	0.0	0.0	0.0	0.0	0.0	0.0	0.0	0.0	0.0
– MCAC	0.0				0.0		0.0			0.0
– Caraïbes							0.0	0.0		0.0
– Autre Amérique						0.0	0.0			0.0
Asie anc. URSS exclus	82.3	85.7	86.4	6.4	10.3	96.7	92.0	95.3	89.7	15.4
– Moyen–Orient	4.9	7.1	7.8	5.4	8.8	15.1	17.1	18.7	16.8	12.2
Asie ancienne URSS								0.0	0.1	0.3
Europe anc. URSS exclus	6.6	3.0	2.0	1.0	1.0	0.9	1.1	0.9	0.9	0.8
– Union Européenne	6.6	3.0	2.0	0.9	1.0	0.9	1.1	0.9	0.9	0.8
– Europe de l'Est	0.0		0.0		0.0	0.0	0.0	0.0	0.0	0.0
– Autre de l'Europe	0.0	0.1	0.1	0.1	0.0	0.0	0.0	0.0	0.0	0.0
Europe ancienne URSS				0.0	0.0		0.0	0.0	0.1	0.4
Océanie	0.4	0.4	0.4	0.1	0.2	0.0	0.4	0.0	0.0	0.0
Autre	4.8	9.1	8.2	91.8	87.0	0.2	0.7	0.5	4.2	80.1
Japan/Japon	38.1	44.2	34.6	0.2	0.1	33.8	26.8	34.8	28.5	0.4
Areas n.e.s.	4.6	8.1	7.6	91.7	87.0	0.2	0.6	0.4	4.0	80.0
Korea, Republic of	14.8	20.6	28.8	0.3	0.4	23.5	20.2	14.2	15.8	0.2
United Arab Emirates	3.8	5.7	5.4	3.9	6.5	8.4	9.5	10.1	10.2	8.4
China/Chine	0.0	0.0	0.0	0.0	0.0	7.0	8.2	8.1	9.7	0.0
Thailand/Thaïlande	3.3	1.7	1.2	0.0	0.0	4.5	5.2	8.3	8.6	0.1
Other Asia n.e.s.	9.4	5.7	8.6			6.6	6.2	5.8	4.7	
Yemen/Yémen					0.0	3.5	3.6	4.6	2.8	0.2
Singapore/Singapour	6.6	2.4	5.2	0.2	0.3	4.2	5.2	0.5	2.7	0.2
China, Hong Kong SAR	0.0	0.0	0.0	0.1	0.5	1.7	2.7	4.1	2.2	1.6

4. General Imports C.I.F. by Commodities according to the S.I.T.C. (Rev. 2) in million U.S. Dollars
Importations Générales C.A.F. par Produits d'après la C.T.C.I. (Rév. 2) en millions de Dollars E.U.

SITC CTCI	COMMODITY	1993 QUANTITY QUANTITE	1993 VALUE VALEUR	1994 QUANTITY QUANTITE	1994 VALUE VALEUR	1995 QUANTITY QUANTITE	1995 VALUE VALEUR	1996 QUANTITY QUANTITE	1996 VALUE VALEUR	PRODUIT
	ALL COMMODITIES		4114.1		3915.1		4248.6		4577.9	TOUS PRODUITS
0	FOOD AND LIVE ANIMALS		482.1		499.1		568.2		577.4	ALIMENTS,ANIMAUX VIVANTS
001	*LIVE ANIMALS FOR FOOD	W 19550	20.7	W 25388	26.8	W 30537	45.7	W 34534	41.5	ANIMAUX VIVANTS
0012	SHEEP AND GOATS,LIVE	W 19437	19.6	W 25271	26.1	W 30453	45.2	W 34457	41.0	ESPECES OVINE ET CAPRINE
00121	SHEEP,LIVE	W 16897	16.5	W 23380	22.8	W 22673	25.0	W 26968	23.1	ESPECE OVINE
00122	GOATS,LIVE	W 2540	3.2	W 1891	3.3	W 7780	20.3	W 7489	17.9	ESPECE CAPRINE
01	MEAT AND PREPARATIONS		70.6		75.2		86.8		93.0	VIANDES ET PREPARATIONS
011	MEAT FRESH,CHILLD,FROZEN	W 52888	68.1	W 53824	71.4	W 58935	82.4	W 60437	87.6	VIANDES FRAICHES,REF,CONGE
0111	BOVINE MEAT FRESH,FROZEN	W 8593	11.0	W 8841	10.7	W 11557	15.9	W 11976	16.4	VIANDES BOVIN FRAI,REF
01112	BOVINE MEAT BONELESS	W 7925	10.3	W 8637	10.3	W 11361	15.6	W 11689	16.0	VIANDES BOVIN DESOSSEES
0112	MUTTON ETC FRSH,CHLD,FRN	W 8874	14.4	W 8043	14.8	W 6982	14.4	W 7187	13.9	VIANDE DE MOUTON
0114	POULTRY FRESH CHLLD,FRZN	W 34933	41.9	W 36590	45.0	W 40122	51.4	W 41031	56.7	VOLAILLES MORTES
02	DAIRY PRODCTS,BIRDS'EGGS		83.6		87.9		97.8		98.8	PRODUITS LAITIERS,OEUFS
022	MILK AND CREAM	W 31476	52.1	W 35917	57.5	W 35995	62.3	W 36665	65.2	LAIT ET CREME
0223	MILK AND CREAM FRESH	W 6494	9.4	W 7621	11.0	W 8142	11.1	W 10817	14.3	LAIT,CREME FRAIS
0224	MILK,CREAM PRESERVED ETC	W 24982	42.8	W 28297	46.6	W 27853	51.2	W 25848	51.0	LAIT,CREME CONS,CONC
02243	MILK DRY,OVER 1.5% FAT	W 10565	24.7	W 12854	28.0	W 11385	28.5	W 10426	29.5	LAIT POUDRE SUP 1.5%
02249	MILK(EX DRY) PRSVD,SWEET	W 13740	16.5	W 15285	18.3	W 15789	20.7	W 15177	20.5	LAIT CONS,CONC SUCRE
023	BUTTER	W 6090	12.8	W 5130	10.7	W 5381	12.4	W 4197	9.8	BEURRE
024	CHEESE AND CURD	W 4253	10.4	W 4156	10.6	W 4679	13.1	W 3815	12.5	FROMAGE ET CAILLEBOTTE
04	CEREALS AND PREPARATIONS		102.6		104.7		137.9		130.4	CEREALES ET PRODUITS
041	WHEAT ETC UNMILLED	W 156503	23.6	W 184561	32.6	W 195846	41.9	W 147768	30.7	FROMENT,EPEAUTRE
0411	DURUM WHEAT UNMILLED	W 155602	23.4	W 183458	32.3	W 194807	41.6	W 146624	30.3	FROMENT DUR NON MOULU
042	RICE	W 106833	50.4	W 75962	37.6	W 139876	42.1	W 90205	44.9	RIZ
0422	RICE SEMI–MILLED,MILLED	W 94815	46.0	W 73443	36.5	W 73979	37.3	W 82296	41.9	RIZ POLI,GLACE INCL BRISURES
04221	RICE MILLED UNBROKEN	W 94815	46.0	W 73441	36.5	W 73979	37.3	W 82296	41.9	RIZ POLI,GLACE EXCL BRISURES
043	BARLEY UNMILLED	W 47400	5.8	W 158076	12.9	W 71366	32.6	W 80955	19.3	ORGE NON MONDEE
048	CEREAL ETC PREPARATIONS	W 10010	15.0	W 10086	13.1	W 9021	16.6	W 11780	18.3	PREPTNS A BASE CEREALES
05	VEGETABLES AND FRUIT		126.2		118.2		102.4		106.0	LEGUMES ET FRUITS
054	VEG ETC FRSH,SMPLY PRSVD	W 63349	34.7	W 70377	34.2	W 68867	28.4	W 60630	30.4	LEGUMES FRAIS,CONG,SECS
0545	OTHER FRESH VEGETABLES	W 27613	15.2	W 32673	13.4	W 33235	10.6	W 30150	13.2	AUTRES LEGUMES FRAIS,REF
056	VEGTBLES ETC PRSVD,PREPD	W 14770	13.2	W 14122	13.8	W 15815	14.7	W 17621	16.8	CONSERVES DE LEGUMES
0565	VEGTBLES PRSVD,PREPD NES	W 13867	11.2	W 13024	11.7	W 14559	12.3	W 16415	14.1	LEGUMES PREPARES CONSERVE
057	FRUIT,NUTS,FRESH,DRIED	W 103530	68.0	W 76478	62.3	W 73025	52.3	W 80626	51.1	FRUITS FRAIS OU SECS
0571	ORANGES, MANDARINS ETC	W 35483	19.7	W 27922	18.9	W 40244	16.6	W 48862	18.1	ORANGES,MAND,CLEMENTINES
05711	ORANGES,FRESH OR DRIED	W 34130	18.4	W 27828	18.6	W 39957	15.7	W 48319	17.3	ORANGES FRAICHES,SECHEES
0579	FRUIT FRESH OR DRIED NES	W 40007	22.0	W 29431	18.3	W 17499	11.2	W 21421	11.2	FRUITS FRAIS,SECS NDA
05798	OTHER FRESH FRUIT	W 34046	15.2	W 25146	12.0	W 14579	7.6	W 17081	7.0	AUTRES FRUITS FRAIS
06	SUGAR AND PREPS,HONEY		15.6		17.4		17.8		28.6	SUCRES ET PRODUITS
061	SUGAR AND HONEY	W 35250	13.2	W 36185	15.4	W 34059	16.2	W 45599	27.3	SUCRES ET MIEL
0612	REFINED SUGAR ETC	W 33669	11.1	W 34595	13.5	W 32916	14.4	W 42212	21.6	SUCRES RAFFINES
07	COFFEE,TEA,COCOA,SPICES		28.1		33.3		39.2		37.8	CAFE,THE,CACAO,EPICES
073	CHOCOLATE AND PRODUCTS	W 4109	9.6	W 4367	12.0	W 4196	12.7	W 4939	14.9	CHOCOLAT
09	MISC EDIBLE PRODUCTS		25.6		23.7		27.6		27.3	PREP ALIMENTAIRES DIVERSES
098	EDIBLE PRODCTS,PREPS NES	W 10032	25.1	W 10422	23.3	W 11073	27.1	W 12322	26.7	PREP ALIMENTAIRES NDA
09809	MISC FOOD PREPRTIONS NES	W 8434	22.8	W 8464	20.0	W 8439	22.6	W 9725	22.5	PREP ALIMENTAIRES NDA
1	BEVERAGES AND TOBACCO		243.7		252.0		228.4		193.2	BOISSONS ET TABACS
11	BEVERAGES		47.9		49.8		35.4		38.3	BOISSONS
111	NON–ALCOHL BEVERAGES NES	W 94617	38.3	W 99986	41.3	W 72742	26.7	W 79251	28.1	BOISSONS NON ALCOOLIQUES
11102	FLAVORED WATERS NON–ALCO	W 63083	32.8	W 65152	35.7	W 41095	21.5	W 46903	22.3	LIMONADES,EAUX GAZEUSES
12	TOBACCO AND MANUFACTURES		195.9		202.2		193.1		155.0	TABACS BRUTS FABRIQUES
122	TOBACCO,MANUFACTURED	W 12589	195.5	W 18175	202.0	W 22502	192.9	W 17159	154.7	TABACS FABRIQUES
1222	CIGARETTES	W 12002	186.8	W 18093	201.7	W 22395	192.6	W 17077	154.5	CIGARETTES
2	CRUDE MATERLS,EXCL FUELS		84.7		96.7		116.0		102.0	MAT BRUTES NON COMESTIBLES
24	CORK AND WOOD		25.4		25.9		27.1		22.4	LIEGE ET BOIS
248	WOOD SHAPED,SLEEPERS	W 139601	24.0	W 74046	17.4	W 78245	20.6	W 52485	18.5	BOIS SIMPLEMENT TRAVAILLES
2483	LUMBER SHAPED NON–CONIFR	W 133701	22.6	W 72655	16.9	W 77880	20.4	W 49232	16.1	NON CONIFERES SCIES,RABOTES
24831	LUMBER SAWN ETC NON–CON	W 133701	22.6	W 72655	16.9	W 77879	20.4	W 49232	16.1	SCIES LONGITUDINALEMENT
27	CRUDE FERTLZR,MINRLS NES		13.9		11.2		14.4		15.0	ENGRAIS MINERAUX BRUTS
28	METALLIFEROUS ORES,SCRAP		37.4		51.6		65.7		55.7	MINERAIS METAL,DECHETS
287	BASE METAL ORES,CONC NES	W 66797	32.2	W 103681	51.6	W 104876	65.5	W 128566	54.9	MINERAIS METAUX COMMUNS
2871	CPR ORE ETC,CEMENT COPPR	W 57004	31.1	W 103673	51.5	W 94927	64.8	W 128454	54.8	MINERAIS DE CUIVRE,MATTES
28711	COPPER ORES,EXCL MATTE	W 57004	31.1	W 103673	51.5	W 94909	64.7	W 128454	54.8	MINERAIS DE CUIVRE
3	MINERAL FUELS ETC		131.5		42.2		64.7		47.5	COMBUSTIBLES MINERAUX LUB
33	PETROLEUM AND PRODUCTS		126.0		37.1		61.0		44.8	PETROLE ET DERIVES
334	PETROLEUM PRODUCTS,REFIN	W 462946	124.0	W 44534	35.3	W 180583	59.0	W 94749	43.6	PRODUITS RAFFINES
3341	GASOLINE,OTH LIGHT OILS	W 456585	115.6	W 42864	32.6					ESSENCES POUR MOTEURS
33419	OTH LIGHT PETROLEUM OILS	W 456585	115.6	W 42864	32.6					AUTRES HUILES LEGERES
4	ANIMAL,VEGETABLE OIL,FAT		21.3		30.2		39.6		27.5	HUILES,GRAISSES ANIM,VEG
42	FIXED VEGETABLE OIL,FAT		21.3		30.1		39.0		26.6	HUILES VEGETALES FIXES
424	FIXED VEG OIL NONSOFT	W 35953	18.0	W 39647	23.8	W 37635	29.7	W 34735	21.9	AUTRES HUILES VEG FIXES
4242	PALM OIL	W 23694	10.9	W 25342	14.6	W 30325	21.6	W 24801	13.1	HUILE DE PALME
5	CHEMCLS,RELATED PROD NES		231.8		228.6		279.1		293.5	PRODUITS CHIMIQUES
52	INORGANIC CHEMICALS		13.8		15.0		16.3		15.4	PROD CHIM INORGANIQUES
53	DYES,TANNING,COLOUR PROD		13.5		11.4		13.5		15.4	PROD TEINTURE,COLORANTS
533	PIGMENTS,PAINTS,ETC	W 8510	12.1	W 9728	10.8	W 10489	12.8	W 11198	14.7	PIGMENTS,PEINTURES,VERNIS
541	*MEDICINAL,PHARM PRODUCT	K 4596397	61.3	K 4559248	57.6	K 4811848	69.1	K 3888607	64.3	PROD MEDICINAUX PHARMACEUT
5413	ANTIBIOTICS IN BULK	K 5281	0.2	K 444655	7.1	K 1073204	17.4			ANTIBIOTIQUES NDA
54139	OTHER ANTIBIOTICS	K 5281	0.2	K 444655	7.1	K 1073204	17.4			AUTRES ANTIBIOTIQUES
5417	MEDICAMENTS	K 4407431	59.3	K 3609827	48.1	K 3558816	49.3	K 3516229	60.6	MEDICAMENTS
54171	— CONTAINNG ANTIBIOTICS	K 734759	15.2	K 336018	9.9	K 297965	4.3	K 187893	4.5	MED CONTN ANTIBIOTIQUES
54179	— CONTNG OTH SUBSTANCES	K 3654430	43.9	K 3270451	38.0	K 3249487	44.7	K 3319393	55.2	MED CONT AUT SUBSTANCES
55	PERFUME,CLEANING ETC PRD		55.3		57.7		72.1		82.5	PROD POUR PARFUM,TOILETTE
551	ESSENTL OILS,PERFUME,ETC	W 989	2.6	W 1197	4.6	W 2450	8.7	W 7257	14.4	HUILES ESSENTIELLES
5514	MIXED PERFUME SUBSTANCES	W 877	2.4	W 1115	4.4	W 2387	8.5	W 7152	14.3	MELANGES SUBSTAN ODORIFER
553	PERFUMERY,COSMETICS,ETC	W 5738	36.7	W 6423	39.8	W 6704	48.8	W 8266	52.9	PRODUITS DE PARFUMERIE
554	SOAP,CLEANSING ETC PREPS	W 10672	16.2	W 9493	13.4	W 9666	14.7	W 10692	15.3	SAVONS,PRODUITS DETERSIFS
58	PLASTIC MATERIALS ETC		26.8		25.2		32.4		36.1	MAT PLAST ARTIFICIELLES
583	POLYMERIZATION ETC PRODS	W 20159	22.1	W 20892	21.0	W 21900	28.9	W 34916	35.2	PROD POLYMERISATION
5831	POLYETHYLENE	W 10704	8.2	W 13501	12.3	W 13481	15.9	W 25885	22.6	POLYETHYLENE
58311	— IN PRIMARY FORMS	W 10704	8.2	W 13501	12.3	W 12880	14.4	W 25048	20.9	POLYETHYLENE PRIMAIRES
59	CHEMICAL MATERIALS NES		44.2		48.2		59.2		66.5	MAT PROD CHIMIQUES NDA
598	MISCEL CHEM PRODUCTS NES	W 21713	34.7	W 28737	39.4	W 27887	47.3	W 37343	53.2	PROD DIV INDUST CHIM NDA
5989	CHEM PRODUCTS,PREPS NES	W 20679	32.6	W 28007	38.3	W 25354	43.6	W 36017	51.2	PROD PREP CHIMIQUES NDA
59899	OTH CHEM PRODS,PREPS,NES	W 17957	26.6	W 26146	36.0	W 23639	41.4	W 34104	48.5	AUT PRODUITS CHIMIQUES NDA
6	BASIC MANUFACTURES		616.8		560.4		656.0		747.7	ART MANUFACTURES
62	RUBBER MANUFACTURES NES		48.0		38.3		52.2		73.3	CAOUTCHOUC MANUFACTURE
625	RUBBER TYRES, TUBES ETC	W 15353	46.4	W 12410	36.8	W 15466	51.2	W 21385	71.0	PNEUS CAOUTCHOUC VULCANISE
6251	TYRES NEW FOR MOTOR CARS	W 8763	28.2	W 7676	25.3	W 7270	24.3	W 8697	29.0	PNEUS POUR VOITURES
6252	TYRES,NEW,BUS OR LORRY	W 6459	17.9	W 4612	11.2	W 7983	26.3	W 12364	41.1	PNEUS POUR AUTOBUS,CAMIONS
63	WOOD,CORK MANUFACTRS NES		23.6		18.9		22.2		25.0	OUVRAGES LIEGE ET BOIS

4. General Imports C.I.F. by Commodities according to the S.I.T.C. (Rev. 2) in million U.S. Dollars
Importations Générales C.A.F. par Produits d'après la C.T.C.I. (Rév. 2) en millions de Dollars E.U.

SITC CTCI	COMMODITY	1993 QUANTITY QUANTITE	1993 VALUE VALEUR	1994 QUANTITY QUANTITE	1994 VALUE VALEUR	1995 QUANTITY QUANTITE	1995 VALUE VALEUR	1996 QUANTITY QUANTITE	1996 VALUE VALEUR	PRODUIT
634	VENEERS,PLYWOOD,ETC	W 33642	18.1	W 17930	15.3	W 24446	17.9	W 27652	21.7	PLACAGES,CONTRE–PLAQUES
6342	PLYWOOD OF WOOD SHEETS	W 28691	14.2	W 17677	14.5	W 23781	16.7	W 25399	20.1	BOIS CONTRE–PLAQUES
64	PAPER,PAPERBOARD AND MFR		45.3		47.4		63.2		60.2	PAPIERS,CARTONS & OUVRAGES
641	PAPER AND PAPERBOARD	W 13710	12.6	W 18349	15.1	W 19968	23.6	W 22732	19.0	PAPIERS ET CARTONS
6415	PAPER,PAPERBRD,BULK,NES	W 10365	8.9	W 11977	9.8	W 14562	17.3	W 19523	15.3	PAPIERS,CARTONS ROULEAUX
64159	OTHER PAPER ETC,BULK,NES	W 7503	7.1	W 11534	9.3	W 13010	15.9	W 18006	14.4	AUT PAPIER ROULEAUX FEUILLES
642	PAPER,ETC,PRECUT,ARTS OF	W 17968	32.8	W 22816	32.3	W 26001	39.7	W 25970	41.2	PAP,CARTONS DECOUPES
6421	PAPER ETC CONTAINERS	W 11290	13.7	W 13415	14.8	W 14314	16.3	W 14281	16.3	BOITES,SACS EMBALLAGES
6428	PAPER ETC ARTICLES NES	W 4680	14.7	W 7907	13.7	W 10545	20.1	W 10385	20.9	OUVRAGES EN PATE A PAPIER
65	TEXTILE YARN,FABRICS,ETC		131.3		129.5		162.7		172.6	FILS,TISSUS,ARTICLES TEXTILE
652	COTTON FABRICS,WOVEN	W 4967	25.9	W 6104	29.4	W 4887	29.8	W 4092	22.2	TISSUS DE COTON
6521	GREY WOVEN COTTON FABRIC	W 4944	25.6	W 6103	29.4	W 4878	29.6	W 4063	22.0	TISSUS COT ECRUS NON MERCER
65214	GREY WOVEN COTTON NES	W 4684	24.3	W 5356	28.9	W 4787	29.2	W 3993	21.6	AUT TISSUS 85% COTON ECRUS
653	WOVN MAN–MADE FIB FABRIC	W 6728	63.7	W 7345	59.8	W 11598	91.1	W 13755	107.3	TISSUS FIBRES SYNTH,ARTIF
6531	CONT SYNT WEAVES NONPILE	W 671	6.9	W 1286	10.5	W 2006	17.6	W 2197	18.9	TISSUS FIBRES SYNTH CONTINUE
65314	CONT SYN TYRE CORD FABRC	W 671	6.9	W 1286	10.5	W 2006	17.6	W 2197	18.9	TIS ARMATURE PNEUMATIQUES
6534	DISC SYN BLEND FABRC NES	W 5353	48.5	W 5530	44.2	W 8966	68.8	W 11320	86.0	TISSUS FIBRES SYNTH DISCONT
65341	DISC SYN FIB–COTTN FABRC	W 5348	48.4	W 5510	44.1	W 8966	68.8	W 11320	86.0	TISSUS FIB SYNT DIS MEL COTO
659	FLOOR COVERINGS,ETC	W 5069	15.7	W 4420	15.0	W 4889	13.9	W 5745	15.7	COUVRE–PARQUETS,TAPIS ETC
6596	OTH TXTL CARPETS ETC NES	W 4793	14.1	W 4220	13.9	W 4489	12.8	W 5500	14.9	TAPIS AUT MAT TEXT NDA
65961	— TUFTED	W 4574	12.8	W 4060	12.4	W 4317	11.7	W 5478	14.8	TAPIS AUT MAT TEXT TOUFF
66	NONMETAL MINERAL MFS NES		89.4		84.5		88.9		101.3	ART MIN NON METALLIQUES
661	LIME,CEMENT,BLDG PRODS	W 496660	40.5	W 449251	34.8	W 351397	25.2	W 569351	41.7	CHAUX,CIMENTS MAT CONSTR
6612	CEMENT	W 472371	33.1	W 437975	31.8	W 336228	22.2	W 554934	37.9	CIMENTS HYDRAULIQUES
662	CLAY,REFRACTORY BLDG PRD	W 25670	14.8	W 25944	14.5	W 22285	14.2	W 24076	14.9	MAT CONST REFRACTAIRES
665	GLASSWARE	W 30684	20.3	W 39023	23.4	W 39851	28.4	W 40858	24.9	OUVRAGES EN VERRE
6651	BOTTLES ETC OF GLASS	W 28966	13.3	W 36935	14.4	W 37862	19.6	W 38933	14.4	RECIPIENTS EN VERRE
66511	GLASS BOTTLES ETC NONVAC	W 28941	13.2	W 36932	14.3	W 37860	19.6	W 38931	14.4	BONBONNES,BOUTEILLES,ETC
67	IRON AND STEEL		153.8		131.8		134.7		190.7	FER ET ACIER
673	IRON,STEEL SHAPES ETC	W 184233	61.2	W 167433	52.5	W 155218	56.0	W 515398	70.5	BARRES,PROFIL FER,ACIER
6732	IRON,STEEL BARS ETC	W 151488	48.0	W 143450	43.8	W 132925	44.5	W 489602	56.9	BARRES FER,ACIER
67322	HIGH CARBON STL BARS ETC					W 129389	43.4	W 483680	55.1	BARRES ACIER FIN CARBONE
67326	IRN,OTH STL BARS HOTROLD	W 123214	39.1	W 119626	37.4					BARRES PLEINES FER,ACIER
674	IRN,STL UNIV,PLATE,SHEET	W 21063	10.9	W 10911	7.0	W 20987	14.2	W 26288	14.8	LARGES PLATS,TOLES
6747	TINNED PLATES,SHEETS					W 20672	13.9	W 25600	14.4	TOLES ETAMEES EN ACIER
678	IRON,STL TUBES,PIPES,ETC	W 97893	77.5	W 83021	69.0	W 51639	62.3	W 107988	102.2	TUBES,TUYAUX EN FONTE,FER
6782	IRON,STL SEAMLESS TUBES	W 55758	37.3	W 54122	42.3	W 30010	32.6	W 86131	74.1	TUBES,TUYAUX SANS SOUDURE
6783	IRON,STL TUBES,PIPES NES	W 38761	31.9	W 26475	19.3	W 17326	18.6	W 17197	16.3	AUT TUBES,TUYAUX FER,ACIER
68	NON–FERROUS METALS		15.4		15.8		21.3		27.1	METAUX NON FERREUX
69	METAL MANUFACTURES NES		108.9		93.3		110.0		96.4	ART MANUFACT EN METAL NDA
691	STRUCTURES AND PARTS NES	W 16328	29.2	W 15083	15.1	W 17301	27.9	W 7057	12.4	CONSTRUCT FER,ACIER,ALU
6911	STRUCTURES,PARTS IRN,STL	W 10506	21.3	W 10795	7.9	W 8077	12.4	W 3456	5.3	CONSTRUCT FER,ACIER,FONTE
6912	STRUCTURES,PARTS ALUMNM	W 5821	8.0	W 4288	7.3	W 9224	15.5	W 3601	7.1	CONSTRUCT ALUMINIUM
692	METAL TANKS,BOXES,ETC	W 15708	27.3	W 18839	25.7	W 12827	22.5	W 17806	28.6	RECIPIENTS METALLIQUES
6924	MTL TRANSPORT BOXES ETC	W 15186	26.2	W 17619	23.2	W 11953	20.4	W 14653	22.9	FUTS,TAMBOURS,BIDONS
697	BASE MTL HOUSEHOLD EQUIP	W 3893	14.3	W 3027	12.6	W 2608	14.0	W 2467	12.4	ART MENAGE MET COMMUNS
699	BASE METAL MFRS NES	W 9930	21.0	W 12616	23.9	W 9414	23.3	W 11335	26.9	ART MANUFACTURES MET NDA
6991	LOCKSMITHS WARES,ETC	W 7209	16.2	W 8694	18.7	W 7215	17.9	W 8823	21.2	ARTICLES DE SERRURERIE
69913	BASE MTL DOOR,ETC FITTNG	W 6955	14.2	W 8093	15.9	W 6879	15.4	W 8310	17.8	GARNITURES POUR MEUBLES
7	MACHINES,TRANSPORT EQUIP		1778.5		1670.1		1672.4		1900.4	MACHINES MATERIEL TRANSPORT
71	POWER GENERATING EQUIPMT		95.1		126.8		126.5		124.2	MACHINES GENERATRICES
713	INTRNL COMBUS PSTN ENGIN	W 2299	24.2	W 1287	14.3	W 1236	16.5	W 2499	27.4	MOTEURS EXPL COMB INT, PIECE
7139	PISTON ENGINE PARTS NES	W 1112	13.5	W 755	10.4	W 557	11.2	W 1098	18.6	PIECES POUR 713.2,3,8
714	ENGINES AND MOTORS NES	W 163	9.5	W 4947	60.6	W 2311	56.5	W 2962	60.3	MOTEURS NON ELECTRIQUES
7148	GAS TURBINES NES	W 112	8.2	W 2770	29.3	W 456	20.2	W 409	16.5	TURBINES A GAZ
71488	OTHER GAS TURBINES NES	W 112	8.2	W 2770	29.3	W 456	20.2	W 409	16.5	AUTRES TURBINES A GAZ
7149	ENGINE & MOTOR PARTS NES	W 48	1.3	W 2176	31.3	W 1851	36.4	W 2412	43.2	PIECES 714 ET 718.88
71499	PARTS NES,OF 71488,71888	W 48	1.3	W 2176	31.3	W 1851	36.4	W 2412	43.2	PIECES 714.88 ET 718.88
716	ROTATING ELECTRIC PLANT	W 2601	60.1	W 2432	48.4	W 2691	51.6	W 1754	26.6	APP ELECTR ROTATIFS,PIECES
7162	AC MTRS,GENRTRS,GEN SETS	W 831	9.1	W 885	8.4	W 1433	15.1	W 915	9.4	MOTEURS ELECTRIQUES
71623	GEN SETS WITH PISTN ENGN	W 480	6.3	W 798	7.7	W 1346	14.5	W 700	8.3	GROUPES MOTEUR EXPLOSION
7169	PTS NES OF ROT ELEC PLNT	W 1459	50.0	W 1489	39.9	W 1136	34.2	W 813	17.0	PIECES MAC APP ROTATIFS
72	MACHS FOR SPCL INDUSTRYS		244.6		216.8		210.5		242.6	MAC SPECIALES POUR INDUST
723	CIVIL ENGNEERG EQUIP ETC	W 23688	197.9	W 20449	173.4	W 14453	151.1	W 14653	138.5	APPAREILS DE GENIE CIVIL
7234	CONST,MINING MACHNRY NES	W 3654	13.2	W 2657	13.5	W 3903	17.5	W 3638	14.0	MACH POUR LA CONST, MINES
7239	CONSTR ETC MACHY PTS NES	W 19941	184.4	W 17707	159.6	W 10429	132.7	W 10747	122.5	PIECES 723.41–723.46
727	FOOD MACHRY NON–DOMESTIC	W 262	4.2	W 580	5.3	W 940	15.3	W 2700	10.5	MACH INDUSTRIES ALIMENT
728	OTH MACHY FOR SPCL INDUS	W 3426	25.2	W 2665	21.8	W 3328	28.0	W 7236	80.2	AUT MACH IND PARTICULIERES
7283	OTHR MINERAL WORKG MACHY	W 1448	4.5	W 625	3.7	W 525	3.4	W 1791	22.1	MACH TRIER,CRIBLER,BROYER
7284	MACHY FOR SPCL INDUS NES	W 1547	17.0	W 1690	16.4	W 2478	22.7	W 4983	54.4	MACH SPEC IND PARTICUL.
72848	OTH MCHY WITH INDIV FNCT	W 376	3.2	W 466	4.0	W 1041	6.3	W 1694	18.6	AUTRES MACHINES NDA
72849	PTS OF MACHS OF 7284 ETC	W 506	10.5	W 754	9.5	W 760	11.5	W 1256	20.8	PIECES DU 728.4 ETC
74	GENRL INDUSTRL MACHY NES		160.2		146.9		139.1		183.0	MACH APP INDUSTRIE
741	HEATING,COOLING EQUIPMNT	W 11383	50.4	W 11063	53.2	W 10042	54.7	W 9145	60.2	MACH CHAUFFAGE,PIECES
7415	AIR–CONDITIONING MACHNRY	W 10216	42.4	W 10199	46.3	W 8513	43.8	W 7751	48.1	GROUPES CONDITION AIR
742	PUMPS FOR LIQUIDS ETC	W 2338	17.9	W 2597	17.9	W 2994	20.3	W 2151	23.0	POMPES MOTO–POMPES
743	PUMPS NES,CENTRFUGES ETC	W 1173	21.8	W 2342	9.2	W 1404	9.8	W 4634	13.5	POMPES COMPRES,VENT ETC
7431	PUMPS FOR GASES ETC	W 717	17.4	W 473	3.3	W 306	2.4	W 365	4.7	POMPES AIR A VIDE,COMPRES
744	MECHANICAL HANDLING EQU	W 4943	45.1	W 3905	33.8	W 4765	29.4	W 9805	59.4	EQUIP MANUTENTION PIECES
7442	LIFTING,LOADING MACH NES	W 2298	17.1	W 1272	8.1	W 2274	7.7	W 1910	7.4	APP LEVAGE,MANUTENTION
7449	PTS NES OF MACHY OF 7442	W 2040	25.3	W 1190	20.5	W 1858	19.0	W 7065	48.1	PIECES DU 744.2
745	NONELEC MACHY,TOOLS NES	W 952	8.4	W 1301	15.4	W 1069	11.1	W 687	7.6	AUT MACH NON ELEC,PIECES
7452	OTH NONELEC MCHS,PTS NES	W 942	8.3	W 1282	15.3	W 1044	11.0	W 683	7.6	AUT MACH NON ELEC,PIECES
749	NONELEC MACH PTS,ACC NES	W 1322	16.9	W 1391	17.5	W 1129	14.0	W 2153	19.6	PIECES MACH NON ELEC NDA
7492	COCKS,VALVES ETC NES	W 1209	13.7	W 1224	15.2	W 1017	12.5	W 1872	17.4	ART ROB,SIM POUR TUYAUX
75	OFFICE MACHNES,ADP EQUIP		75.9		46.9		52.7		61.8	MACH BUREAU TRAIT AUTOM
752	AUTOMTIC DATA PROC EQUIP	W 1314	30.1	W 241	6.3	W 197	6.2	W 123	6.1	MACH TRAIT INFORMATION
7522	DIGITAL COMPUTERS	W 1125	25.5	W 127	3.2	W 92	2.8	W 85	4.6	MACH DIGITALES COMPLETES
759	OFFICE,ADP MCH PTS,ACCES	W 573	38.2	W 525	35.1	W 713	38.2	W 1235	50.8	PIECES DU 751 ET 752
7599	ACCTG,ETC,ADP MCH PTS,AC	W 473	35.9	W 461	32.9	W 625	35.6	W 1139	47.3	PIECES DU 751 ET 752
76	TELECOMM,SOUND EQUIPMENT		99.5		88.8		126.3		164.4	EQUIPMENT DE TELECOM
761	TELEVISION RECEIVERS	W 1567	17.8	W 1251	14.3	W 2399	26.0	W 3827	39.6	RECEPTEURS DE TELEVISION
7611	COLOUR TV RECEIVERS	W 1450	16.1	W 1219	14.0	W 2364	25.8	W 3814	39.4	RECEPTEURS COULEUR
762	RADIO BROADCAST RECEIVRS	W 604	10.2	W 353	6.5	W 662	10.6	W 866	14.1	RECEPTEURS RADIODIFFUSION
763	SOUND RECORDRS,PHONOGRPH	W 1521	22.2	W 869	16.2	W 509	10.7	W 904	22.8	PHONO,APP ENREGISTREMENT
7638	OTHR SOUND APPARATUS ETC	W 1504	21.9	W 845	15.8	W 504	10.7	W 831	21.9	AUT APP D'ENREGIS,REPROD
76381	TV IMAGE,SND RECRDRS ETC	W 1473	21.5	W 791	15.1	W 461	9.7	W 772	20.7	APP ENREG,REPRO IMAG,SON
764	TELECOM EQPT,PTS,ACC NES	W 1211	49.5	W 1602	51.9	W 2152	79.0	W 3307	88.0	EQUIP TELECOM,PIECES
7643	TV,RADIO TRANSMITTRS ETC	W 78	7.4	W 61	5.2	W 98	9.4	W 302	21.6	APP EMET TELE RADIO
7649	PTS NES OF EQUIPMT OF 76	W 896	33.5	W 1305	38.6	W 1596	56.5	W 2551	46.5	PIECES DE LA DIV 76
76491	PTS NES OF APPAR OF 7641	W 97	9.9	W 322	14.1	W 567	25.6	W 225	18.6	PIECES POUR 764.1

4. General Imports C.I.F. by Commodities according to the S.I.T.C. (Rev. 2) in million U.S. Dollars
Importations Générales C.A.F. par Produits d'après la C.T.C.I. (Rév. 2) en millions de Dollars E.U.

SITC CTCI	COMMODITY	1993 QUANTITY QUANTITE	1993 VALUE VALEUR	1994 QUANTITY QUANTITE	1994 VALUE VALEUR	1995 QUANTITY QUANTITE	1995 VALUE VALEUR	1996 QUANTITY QUANTITE	1996 VALUE VALEUR	PRODUIT
76493	TELECOMM EQUIPMT PTS NES	W 763	23.2	W 955	24.1	W 1020	30.7	W 2311	27.4	PIECES 761,762,764.3,8
77	ELECTRIC MACHNRY NES ETC		129.2		132.8		201.5		186.0	MACH APP ELECT NDA
771	ELECTRIC POWER MACHY NES	W 1603	5.0	W 1936	6.7	W 3570	29.8	W 2034	8.2	MACH PROD,TRANS ELECTR
7711	TRANSFORMERS,ELECTRICAL	W 1476	4.1	W 1868	6.0	W 3353	28.4	W 1703	6.1	TRANSFO ELECTRIQUES
77111	LIQUID DIELEC TRANSFRMRS	W 969	2.9	W 1679	5.6	W 3072	27.1	W 1446	5.1	TRANSFO DIELEC LIQUIDE
772	SWITCHGEAR ETC,PARTS NES	W 5069	38.4	W 5103	38.9	W 6782	58.3	W 8905	69.9	APP COUPURE,SECT ETC
7721	SWITCHGEAR ETC	W 5069	38.4	W 5100	38.9	W 6748	58.1	W 8895	69.8	APP COUPURE,SECTIONMNT
773	ELECTR DISTRIBUTNG EQUIP	W 12419	31.9	W 17102	32.9	W 18285	53.8	W 13663	33.2	EQUIPMT DISTRIBUTION ELECT
7731	INSULATED WIRE,CABLE ETC	W 11708	30.7	W 16272	31.6	W 16695	49.6	W 12116	27.9	FILS,CABLES ISOLES ELECT
775	HOUSEHOLD TYPE EQUIP NES	W 7381	37.5	W 6606	34.6	W 6347	36.2	W 8635	51.2	MACH,APP USAGE DOMESTQUE
7752	DOM REFRIGERATRS,FREEZRS	W 3447	13.6	W 2987	14.1	W 2990	14.2	W 3569	17.8	REFRIG,CONGEL MENAGER
77521	DOMESTIC REFRIGERATORS	W 2801	10.5	W 2536	12.0	W 2409	11.4	W 3128	15.3	REFRIGERATEURS
7757	DOMESTIC ELECTRC EQU NES	W 2044	13.2	W 1393	9.3	W 1431	9.3	W 2471	17.9	APP ELECTR DOMEST NDA
778	ELECTRICAL MACHINERY NES	W 4141	13.4	W 4588	13.3	W 8125	18.5	W 6040	20.4	AUTRES MACH ELECT NDA
78	ROAD VEHICLES		899.0		854.9		787.6		900.4	VEHICULES ROUTIERS
781	PASS MOTOR VEH EXC BUSES	W 69939	632.8	W 50978	500.9	W 37120	406.1	W 51918	524.4	AUTO TRANSPORT PERSONNES
782	LORRIES,SPCL MTR VEH NES	W 11254	67.6	W 14988	107.4	W 16123	127.3	W 14833	98.2	VEHICULES SPECIAUX,MARCH
7821	LORRIES,TRUCKS	W 10025	59.6	W 14265	104.3	W 15466	105.7	W 14279	91.1	VEHICULES TRANSP MARCHAND
7822	SPECIAL MOTOR VEHCLS NES	W 1229	8.0	W 723	3.1	W 657	21.7	W 554	7.1	VEHICULES USAGES SPECIAUX
783	ROAD MOTOR VEHICLES NES	W 4419	22.2	W 7164	59.7	W 5645	50.1	W 5511	31.5	VEHICULES ROUTIERS NDA
7831	BUSES	W 4410	22.1	W 7113	59.5	W 5645	50.1	W 5432	31.4	VOITURES TRANSPORT COMMUN
784	MOTOR VEH PRTS,ACCES NES	W 13759	159.3	W 12813	159.0	W 14144	182.8	W 17649	225.6	PIECES 722,781,782,783
7849	OTHER MOTOR VEHCL PARTS	W 12718	156.3	W 12006	157.3	W 13624	181.7	W 16472	224.2	PIECES 722,781,782,783
786	TRAILERS,NONMOTR VEH,NES	W 4800	13.9	W 4062	25.3	W 3598	19.6	W 5738	19.1	REMORQUES,CADRES,CONTAIN
7861	TRAILERS,TRANSP CONTAINR	W 3865	10.6	W 3507	20.3	W 3158	14.4	W 5168	17.4	REMORQUES TOUS VEHICULES
78612	OTHER TRAILERS	W 3685	10.3	W 3499	20.2	W 3031	13.6	W 4526	16.8	REMORQUES TRANSP MARCH
79	OTHR TRANSPORT EQUIPMENT		71.7		49.0		24.4		32.4	AUTRE MATERIEL TRANSPORT
792	AIRCRAFT ETC	W 664	68.1	W 513	45.8	W 182	22.6	W 175	28.8	APP NAVIGATION AERIENNE
7924	AIRCRFT NES OVER 15000KG	W 561	58.6	W 350	29.7					AERODYNES PLUS 15000 KG
7929	AIRCRAFT PARTS NES	W 103	9.5	W 163	16.1	W 181	22.5	W 175	28.8	PIECES DU 792
8	MISC MANUFACTURED GOODS		259.7		267.6		309.6		321.3	ART MANUFACTURES DIVERS
812	*PLUMBG,HEATNG,LGHTNG EQ	W 5267	21.7	W 5779	27.7	W 5060	27.3	W 5213	24.4	APPAR SANITAIRES CHAUFFAGE
8122	CERAMIC PLUMBNG FIXTURES	W 4025	11.7	W 3685	13.5	W 3375	11.2	W 3576	12.1	EVIERS,LAVABOS,CUVETTES
8124	LIGHTING EQUIPMENT NES	W 1139	9.7	W 1903	14.1	W 1656	16.1	W 1576	12.1	APPAREILS ECLAIRAGE ETC
821	*FURNITURE,PARTS THEREOF	W 12699	40.2	W 10263	36.4	W 11299	33.2	W 17272	40.6	MEUBLES ET PIECES
8219	FURNITURE AND PARTS NES	W 11729	35.0	W 9358	31.1	W 10455	29.4	W 16161	36.6	AUTRES MEUBLES ET PIECES
82192	WOOD FURNITURE NES	W 9879	29.4	W 8308	27.4	W 9055	25.9	W 14365	32.9	MEUBLES NDA EN BOIS
84	CLOTHING AND ACCESSORIES		30.4		27.9		30.6		37.1	VETEMENTS
845	OUTERWEAR KNIT NONELASTC	W 1377	17.9	W 1121	16.1	W 1267	18.7	W 2166	25.0	VET DESSOUS,ACCES BONNET
8459	— OTHER,CLTHG ACCESRYS	W 1358	17.7	W 1111	16.1	W 1253	18.4	W 2109	24.4	AUT VET DESSUS DE BONNE
851	*FOOTWEAR	W 2340	16.1	W 2091	14.6	W 1882	16.8	W 2945	20.2	CHAUSSURES
85102	FOOTWEAR LEATHER	W 1146	11.8	W 975	10.2	W 943	12.9	W 1297	14.9	CHAUS SEMELLES EN CUIR
87	PRECISION INSTRUMNTS NES		22.2		21.4		37.4		30.7	INSTRUM,APPAR SCIENT NDA
872	MEDICAL INSTRUMENTS NES	W 607	13.2	W 397	11.3	W 482	11.3	W 1172	22.1	INSTR,APP MEDIC–CHIR NDA
874	MEASURNG,CONTROLNG INSTR	W 250	7.3	W 302	8.2	W 376	24.9	W 166	5.5	INSTRUMENTS DE MESURE
88	PHOTO EQU,OPTICL GDS ETC		47.0		47.0		62.4		66.0	APP,FOURN PHOTO,OP,MONTR
882	PHOTO,CINEMA SUPPLIES	W 783	8.4	W 612	9.7	W 1132	14.9	W 1454	17.9	PRODUITS PHOTO,CINEMA
8822	PHOTO FILM EXC DEV CINMA	W 611	7.4	W 540	9.3	W 861	13.8	W 1073	17.1	PLAQUES,PELLICULES,FILMS
885	WATCHES AND CLOCKS		30.9		31.9		35.1		33.2	HORLOGERIE
8851	WATCHES,MOVEMENTS,CASES		29.2		31.3		34.8		32.7	MONTRES,MOUVEMENTS,BOITES
88511	WATCHES		29.0		30.3		33.5		31.4	MONTRES POCHE,BRACELET
89	MISC MANUFCTRD GOODS NES		78.4		88.1		98.0		96.3	ART MANUFACTURES DIVERS
893	ARTICLES OF PLASTIC NES	W 10385	23.9	W 13343	26.2	W 12924	33.7	W 19364	35.4	OUVRAGES EN MAT DIVIS 58
8939	MISC PLASTIC ARTICLES	W 7675	19.8	W 6999	20.4	W 7126	23.9	W 16245	27.7	ART DIVERS EN MAT DIV 58
89399	OTHR PLASTC ARTICLES NES	W 6858	17.2	W 6432	18.2	W 6109	20.7	W 15230	24.2	AUT OUV MAT DIV 58
897	GOLD,SILVER WARE,JEWELRY		18.6		29.0		26.8		24.8	BIJOUTERIE,ORFEVRERIE
8973	PREC JEWLRY,GLD–SILVWARE		16.7		28.2		24.9		23.7	BIJOUX OR,ARGENT ORFEVRE
89731	PRECIOUS METAL JEWELLERY		16.7		28.1		24.7		23.6	ART BIJOUTERIE,JOAILLER
9	GOODS NOT CLASSD BY KIND		264.4		268.7		315.1		367.9	ART TRANSACT NON CLASSES
931	*SPECIAL TRANSACTIONS	W 10884	179.6	W 10174	127.5	W 7891	187.9	W 9503	227.8	TRANS.SPECIALES
971	*GOLD,NON MONETARY NES	K 7132	80.4	K 11229	137.9	K 80269	123.2	K 14053	134.8	OR NON MONETAIRE
97101	NONMON GLD UNWRT,SEMIMFD	K 7018	80.4	K 11229	137.9	K 77167	123.2	K 13232	134.7	OR,ALLIAGES D'OR BRUTS

5. General Exports F.O.B. by Commodities according to the S.I.T.C. (Rev. 2) in million U.S. Dollars
Exportations Générales F.O.B. par Produits d'après la C.T.C.I. (Rév. 2) en millions de Dollars E.U.

SITC CTCI	COMMODITY	1993 QUANTITY QUANTITE	1993 VALUE VALEUR	1994 QUANTITY QUANTITE	1994 VALUE VALEUR	1995 QUANTITY QUANTITE	1995 VALUE VALEUR	1996 QUANTITY QUANTITE	1996 VALUE VALEUR	PRODUIT
	ALL COMMODITIES		5299.6		5418.3		5917.4		7222.0	TOUS PRODUITS
0	FOOD AND LIVE ANIMALS		98.4		112.1		149.7		148.9	ALIMENTS,ANIMAUX VIVANTS
001	*LIVE ANIMALS FOR FOOD	W 930	3.7	W 2795	9.1	W 9099	24.3	W 6201	16.8	ANIMAUX VIVANTS
0012	SHEEP AND GOATS,LIVE	W 906	3.6	W 2774	9.0	W 9062	24.0	W 6147	16.7	ESPECES OVINE ET CAPRINE
00122	GOATS,LIVE	W 906	3.6	W 2763	9.0	W 9054	24.0	W 6140	16.6	ESPECE CAPRINE
03	FISH AND PREPARATIONS		51.5		49.5		61.5		63.4	POISSONS ET PREPARATIONS
034	FISH,FRESH,CHILLED,FROZN	W 45022	45.8	W 43476	43.7	W 57675	55.6	W 54973	55.9	POISSON FRAIS, REFRIG,CONG
0342	FISH FROZEN,EXCL FILLETS	W 45022	45.8	W 43473	43.7	W 57670	55.6	W 54841	55.7	POISSONS CONGELES
04	CEREALS AND PREPARATIONS		12.8		17.8		23.2		24.7	CEREALES ET PRODUITS
1	BEVERAGES AND TOBACCO		124.6		120.0		113.0		109.9	BOISSONS ET TABACS
12	TOBACCO AND MANUFACTURES		121.5		117.2		107.6		103.4	TABACS BRUTS FABRIQUES
122	TOBACCO,MANUFACTURED	W 16615	120.5	W 16147	116.4	W 18198	106.9	W 18268	102.6	TABACS FABRIQUES
1222	CIGARETTES	W 16586	120.4	W 16147	116.4	W 18168	106.7	W 18265	102.6	CIGARETTES
2	CRUDE MATERLS,EXCL FUELS		13.5		17.2		26.7		30.1	MAT BRUTES NON COMESTIBLES
3	MINERAL FUELS ETC		4181.8		4144.3		4650.6		5808.1	COMBUSTIBLES MINERAUX LUB
33	PETROLEUM AND PRODUCTS		4181.8		4144.3		4650.6		5808.1	PETROLE ET DERIVES
333	CRUDE PETROLEUM	MW 36556	4148.0	MW 34192	4107.8	MW 35734	4606.9		5764.7	HUILES BRUTES DE PETROLE
334	PETROLEUM PRODUCTS,REFIN	W 30366	33.8	W 33639	36.6	W 36703	43.7	W 40587	43.4	PRODUITS RAFFINES
3341	GASOLINE,OTH LIGHT OILS	W 30255	33.5	W 33534	36.4					ESSENCES POUR MOTEURS
33419	OTH LIGHT PETROLEUM OILS	W 30255	33.5	W 33534	36.4					AUTRES HUILES LEGERES
4	ANIMAL,VEGETABLE OIL,FAT		11.9		17.1		22.0		11.7	HUILES,GRAISSES ANIM,VEG
42	FIXED VEGETABLE OIL,FAT		11.9		17.1		22.0		11.6	HUILES VEGETALES FIXES
424	FIXED VEG OIL NONSOFT	W 15205	11.9	W 20721	16.9	W 23370	22.0	W 12791	11.6	AUTRES HUILES VEG FIXES
4249	FIXED VEGETABLE OILS NES	W 15200	11.9	W 20639	16.8	W 23303	21.8	W 12769	11.6	HUILES VEGET FIXES NDA
5	CHEMCLS,RELATED PROD NES		22.1		17.7		21.1		30.7	PRODUITS CHIMIQUES
55	PERFUME,CLEANING ETC PRD		17.1		11.6		13.9		19.5	PROD POUR PARFUM,TOILETTE
6	BASIC MANUFACTURES		102.8		127.7		161.6		164.1	ART MANUFACTURES
62	RUBBER MANUFACTURES NES		15.2		14.8		22.4		30.3	CAOUTCHOUC MANUFACTURE
625	RUBBER TYRES, TUBES ETC	W 5208	15.2	W 5473	14.8	W 6703	22.3	W 8357	30.1	PNEUS CAOUTCHOUC VULCANISE
68	NON–FERROUS METALS		58.2		77.1		82.6		70.3	METAUX NON FERREUX
682	COPPER EXC CEMENT COPPER	W 20363	42.4	W 23073	54.5	W 22158	73.0	W 37783	60.3	CUIVRE
6821	COPPER NES,ALLOYS,UNWRT	W 20326	42.3	W 23064	54.5	W 22098	72.8	W 37757	60.2	CUIVRE BRUT
68212	COPPER REFINED,UNWROUGHT	W 20300	39.9	W 23017	49.4	W 22011	61.4	W 37679	55.8	CUIVRE AFFINE BRUT
684	ALUMINIUM	W 5672	15.8	W 8395	22.7	W 3322	9.7	W 3620	9.1	ALUMINIUM
6842	ALUMINIUM,ALLOYS WORKED	W 5672	15.8	W 8395	22.7	W 3322	9.7	W 3620	9.1	ALUMINIUM,ALLIAGES OUVRE
68421	ALUMINIUM BARS,WIRE,ETC	W 5672	15.8	W 8395	22.7	W 3198	9.3	W 3590	9.0	BARRES,PROFILES FILS ALU
69	METAL MANUFACTURES NES		8.4		12.3		24.1		21.5	ART MANUFACT EN METAL NDA
7	MACHINES,TRANSPORT EQUIP		619.8		696.0		569.9		677.7	MACHINES MATERIEL TRANSPORT
72	MACHS FOR SPCL INDUSTRYS		25.3		27.3		26.2		50.5	MAC SPECIALES POUR INDUST
723	CIVIL ENGNEERG EQUIP ETC	W 4770	23.4	W 5585	25.6	W 4546	24.8	W 8283	47.5	APPAREILS DE GENIE CIVIL
7239	CONSTR ETC MACHY PTS NES	W 2809	19.5	W 4660	23.1	W 4100	24.0	W 7589	45.8	PIECES 723.41–723.46
76	TELECOMM,SOUND EQUIPMENT		9.9		12.4		23.2		38.2	EQUIPMENT DE TELECOM
77	ELECTRIC MACHNRY NES ETC		14.7		16.9		23.7		35.9	MACH APP ELECT NDA
78	ROAD VEHICLES		514.6		578.7		461.0		518.2	VEHICULES ROUTIERS
781	PASS MOTOR VEH EXC BUSES	W 36710	401.4	W 35659	418.0	W 18492	246.5	W 24293	282.8	AUTO TRANSPORT PERSONNES
782	LORRIES,SPCL MTR VEH NES	W 3142	11.9	W 4864	19.2	W 6091	38.2	W 5667	32.5	VEHICULES SPECIAUX,MARCH
7821	LORRIES,TRUCKS	W 3095	11.7	W 4864	19.2	W 5962	37.9	W 5512	31.3	VEHICULES TRANSP MARCHAND
783	ROAD MOTOR VEHICLES NES	W 2840	17.4	W 4587	43.3	W 4635	53.2	W 5790	59.8	VEHICULES ROUTIERS NDA
7831	BUSES	W 2840	17.4	W 4587	43.3	W 4635	53.2	W 5790	59.8	VOITURES TRANSPORT COMMUN
784	MOTOR VEH PRTS,ACCES NES	W 6920	82.8	W 8332	94.6	W 9405	121.3	W 11054	137.6	PIECES 722,781,782,783
7849	OTHER MOTOR VEHCL PARTS	W 6920	82.8	W 8332	94.6	W 9405	121.3	W 11048	137.6	PIECES 722,781,782,783
79	OTHR TRANSPORT EQUIPMENT		45.5		44.0		16.8		15.5	AUTRE MATERIEL TRANSPORT
792	AIRCRAFT ETC	W 47	45.2	W 49	43.5	W 49	16.7	W 61	14.8	APP NAVIGATION AERIENNE
7929	AIRCRAFT PARTS NES	W 47	45.2	W 49	43.5	W 49	16.7	W 61	14.8	PIECES DU 792
8	MISC MANUFACTURED GOODS		94.7		115.4		150.4		169.3	ART MANUFACTURES DIVERS
84	CLOTHING AND ACCESSORIES		59.3		73.4		89.1		91.2	VETEMENTS
843	WOMENS OUTERWEAR NONKNIT	W 818	8.0	W 898	9.6	W 1853	18.6	W 1184	12.5	VET DESSUS FEMMES MAT TEX
844	UNDER GARMENTS NOT KNIT	W 4047	34.5	W 5114	47.0	W 2929	31.3	W 2412	25.3	VETEMENT DESSOUS MAT TEX
8441	— MENS SHIRTS	W 4047	34.5	W 5114	47.0	W 2929	31.3	W 2412	25.3	CHEMISES HOMMES MAT TEXT
84412	—— OF SYNTHETIC FIBRES	W 4047	34.5	W 5114	47.0	W 2929	31.3	W 2412	25.3	CHEMISES HOMMES FIB SYNT
845	OUTERWEAR KNIT NONELASTC	W 1948	16.3	W 1870	15.8	W 3900	35.0	W 4032	38.9	VET DESSOUS,ACCES BONNET
8459	— OTHER,CLTHG ACCESRYS	W 1936	16.2	W 1650	14.5	W 3558	31.6	W 3581	33.6	AUT VET DESSUS DE BONNE
88	PHOTO EQU,OPTICL GDS ETC		16.4		15.0		24.4		35.4	APP,FOURN PHOTO,OP,MONTR
9	GOODS NOT CLASSD BY KIND		30.5		51.3		52.7		71.9	ART TRANSACT NON CLASSES
931	*SPECIAL TRANSACTIONS	W 4931	17.5	W 7604	34.8	W 9008	30.7	W 11121	51.5	TRANS.SPECIALES

1. HISTORICAL SERIES, 1962–1997 GENERAL TRADE, IMPORTS C.I.F., EXPORTS F.O.B.
SERIES HISTORIQUES, 1962–1997 COMMERCE GENERAL, IMPORTATIONS C.A.F., EXPORTATIONS F.O.B

YEAR ANNEE	VALUE IN MILLION PAK. RUPEES VALEUR EN MILLION PAK. RUPEES MERCHANDISE –MARCHANDISE		GOLD –OR		CONVERSION FACTORS U.S. CENTS PER PAK. RUPEE FACTEURS DE CONVERSION CENTS E.U. PAR PAK. RUPEE		INDEX NUMBERS –INDICES QUANTUM		UNIT VALUE VALEUR UNITAIRE	
	IMPORTS	EXPORTS	IMPORTS	EXPORTS	IMPORTS	EXPORTS	IMPORTS	EXPORTS	IMPORTS	EXPORTS
1962	3514.90	1891.70			21.0000	21.0000				
1963	4231.70	1983.40			21.0000	21.0000				
1964	4749.30	2351.90			21.0000	21.0000				
1965	4967.00	2515.20			21.0000	21.0000				
1966	4284.40	2860.80			21.0000	21.0000				
1967	5243.40	3071.80			21.0000	21.0000				
1968	4742.20	3429.50			21.0000	21.0000				
1969	4929.50	3245.00			21.0000	21.0000				
1970	5575.70	3444.10			21.0000	21.0000				
1971	4409.20	3171.50			21.0000	21.0000				
1972	5936.90	5818.40			11.2172	11.6734				
1973	9698.30	9523.80			9.9872	9.9839				
1974	17201.30	10857.40			10.1010	10.1010				
1975	21361.30	10242.10			10.1010	10.1010				
1976	21587.60	11550.80			10.1010	10.1010				
1977	24297.80	11626.10			10.1010	10.1010				
1978	32521.00	14603.90			10.1010	10.1010				
1979	40158.30	20354.40			10.1010	10.1010				
1980	52966.00	25620.90			10.1010	10.1010	67	51	42	51
1981	54936.50	28516.00			10.1010	10.1010	72	61	49	48
1982	63803.00	28246.20			8.4399	8.4781	66	49	56	56
1983	70048.20	40308.60			7.6251	7.6266	66	56	60	56
1984	82058.50	36636.40			7.1576	7.1343	74	44	70	61
1985	93811.00	43646.00			6.2792	6.2774	77	56	73	62
1986	89355.41	56245.31			6.0174	6.0068	75	75	65	65
1987	101440.50	72685.89			5.7467	5.7476	77	82	76	79
1988	119212.60	81442.10			5.5530	5.5588	100	90	78	84
1989	146444.30	98412.40			4.8615	4.8561	105	94	92	91
1990	160134.00	121345.00			4.6060	4.6056	100	100	100	100
1991	201409.00	155398.00			4.1900	4.2009	105	113	107	104
1992	235296.00	183599.00			3.9861	3.9854	122	124	110	106
1993	265142.00	187786.00			3.5833	3.5615	124	112	118	116
1994	271744.00	225200.00			3.2711	3.2706	120	139	138	136
1995	362685.90	252714.00			3.1600	3.1623	129	110	156	171
1996	437768.90	335312.90			2.7712	2.7798	127	130	172	189
1997	476346.10	359045.80			2.4342	2.4278	130	123	199	217

2. IMPORTS BY BROAD ECONOMIC CATEGORY AND EXPORTS BY INDUSTRIAL ORIGIN. (PERCENTAGE OF TOTAL VALUE)
IMPORTATIONS PAR CATEGORIES ECONOMIQUES ET EXPORTATIONS PAR BRANCHE D'ACTIVITE.(EN POURCENTAGE DE LA VALEUR TOTALE)

IMPORTS – IMPORTATIONS

	1991	1992	1993	1994	1995	1996	1997
TOTAL IMPORTS–IMPORTATIONS TOTALES	100.	100.	100.	100.	100.	100.	100.
1 FOOD BEV–ALIMENTATION BOISSONS	11.5	14.5	13.6	15.6	17.3	14.5	18.6
11 PRIMARY–PRODUITS DE BASE	5.1	8.2	7.2	6.4	7.2	6.7	10.0
111 FOR INDUSTRY–POUR L'INDUSTRIE	1.9	4.9	3.7	3.3	4.0	4.1	7.5
112 FOR HOUSEHOLDS–POUR LES MENAGES	3.2	3.3	3.5	3.1	3.2	2.5	2.5
12 PROCESSED–PRODUITS ELABORES	6.4	6.3	6.4	9.1	10.1	7.9	8.6
121 FOR INDUSTRY–POUR L'INDUSTRIE	5.0	5.1	5.8	8.5	9.3	6.0	6.9
122 FOR HOUSEHOLDS–POUR LES MENAGES	1.4	1.2	0.6	0.6	0.8	1.9	1.7
2 IND SUPPLIES–APPROV INDUSTRIELS	32.5	31.9	30.5	33.4	33.5	33.0	30.4
21 PRIMARY–PRODUITS DE BASE	4.4	4.6	4.0	6.0	5.5	3.5	3.9
22 PROCESSED–PRODUITS ELABORES	28.1	27.3	26.5	27.4	28.0	29.5	26.5
3 FUELS–COMBUSTIBLES	17.9	16.3	17.1	18.3	16.4	20.7	19.8
31 PRIMARY–PRODUITS DE BASE	6.6	6.6	5.9	7.7	5.6	6.1	6.4
32 PROCESSED–PRODUITS ELABORES	11.3	9.7	11.1	10.6	10.8	14.5	13.5
321 MOTOR SPIRIT–ESSENCE	0.4	0.2	1.4	0.4	0.3	0.6	0.5
322 OTHER–AUTRES	10.8	9.6	9.8	10.2	10.5	14.0	12.9
4 MACHINERY–EQUIPEMENT	23.8	25.6	21.4	21.9	23.6	20.6	21.8
41 CAPITAL EQUIPMENT–MACHINES	21.9	23.5	19.6	19.2	21.9	18.7	20.5
42 PARTS–PIECES ACCESSOIRES	1.9	2.0	1.8	2.7	1.7	1.9	1.3
5 TRANSPORT–TRANSPORT	10.7	8.6	14.1	7.1	5.5	7.1	5.7
51 PASSENGER CARS–AUTOMOBILES	1.9	2.2	4.2	2.0	1.9	2.1	1.4
52 OTHER–AUTRES	5.5	3.7	6.6	2.6	1.6	2.1	1.5
521 INDUSTRIAL–INDUSTRIELS	5.2	3.2	6.2	2.3	1.2	1.6	1.1
522 NON INDUSTRIAL–NON INDUSTRIEL	0.4	0.4	0.4	0.4	0.4	0.5	0.4
53 PARTS–PIECES ACCESSOIRES	3.3	2.8	3.3	2.5	2.1	3.0	2.9
6 CONSUM GOODS–BIENS CONSOMMATION	3.4	2.9	3.2	3.2	3.4	3.6	3.1
61 DURABLE–DURABLES	0.6	0.7	0.6	0.5	0.6	0.4	0.4
62 SEMI DURABLE–SEMI DURABLES	0.9	0.6	0.8	0.8	0.9	1.2	1.0
63 NON DURABLE–NON DURABLES	1.8	1.6	1.8	2.0	1.9	2.0	1.7
7 GOODS NES–BIENS NDA	0.2	0.1	0.2	0.5	0.2	0.5	0.5

EXPORTS – EXPORTATIONS

	1991	1992	1993	1994	1995	1996	1997
TOTAL EXPORTS–EXPORTATIONS TOTALES	100.	100.	100.	100.	100.	100.	100.
1 AGRICULTURE	10.0	11.2	7.2	4.0	5.2	7.5	4.8
2 MINING QUARRY–INDUS EXTRACTIVES	1.1	1.1	1.0	0.6	0.7	0.8	0.8
3 MANUFACTURING–IND MANUFACTUR	88.9	87.6	91.8	95.3	94.1	91.8	94.4
31 FOOD BEV TOBACCO–ALIM BOISS TAB	7.7	7.2	5.7	6.8	9.4	6.7	7.2
32 TEXTILES–INDUSTRIES TEXTILES	73.7	74.0	79.0	81.3	77.6	77.9	78.6
33 WOOD & PRODUCTS–BOIS & PRODUITS	0.0	0.0	0.1	0.0	0.0	0.0	0.0
34 PAPER & PRODUCTS–PAPIER & PRODT	0.1	0.1	0.1	0.1	0.1	0.1	0.1
35 CHEMICALS–INDUSTRIES CHIMIQUES	1.1	0.9	0.7	1.0	1.1	1.1	0.9
36 NON METAL MIN–MIN NON METAL	0.3	0.2	0.2	0.2	0.2	0.2	0.2
37 BASIC METAL–IND METAL BASE	0.0	0.0	0.0	0.0	0.0	0.0	0.0
38 METAL MANUF–MANUF METAL	3.0	2.7	2.9	2.3	2.4	2.5	3.3
39 OTH MANUF IND–AUTRES MANUF	3.0	2.5	3.0	3.6	3.2	3.2	4.0

3. TRADE BY PRINCIPAL COUNTRIES OF CONSIGNMENT AND DESTINATION (VALUE IN MILLION U.S. DOLLARS)
ECHANGES SELON LES PRINCIPAUX PAYS DE CONSIGNATION ET DE DESTINATION (VALEUR EN MILLIONS DE DOLLARS EU)

COUNTRIES–PAYS	GENERAL IMPORTS C.I.F. IMPORTATIONS GENERALES C.A.F					COUNTRIES–PAYS	EXPORTS EXPORTATIONS ES F.O.B.				
	1993	1994	1995	1996	1997		1993	1994	1995	1996	1997
World	9739.7	8881.5	11703.6	12140.6	11595.2	Monde	6877.5	7356.9	8157.9	9322.2	8717.0
Africa	211.3	206.0	316.1	338.8	260.3	Afrique	249.9	334.0	359.4	428.8	483.5
Americas	1119.9	1017.2	1421.1	1599.4	1645.1	Amériques	1262.6	1409.4	1508.1	1858.0	1969.2
– Northern America	971.8	937.9	1225.4	1391.3	1477.5	– Amérique du Nord	1179.9	1323.3	1375.8	1700.2	1802.8
– LAIA	147.2	77.5	191.0	204.5	164.9	– ALAI	67.0	64.8	108.3	126.5	136.6
– CACM	0.6	0.5	2.4	1.3	2.0	– MCAC	4.1	10.2	11.8	17.5	17.8
– Caribbean	0.1	0.4	0.5	1.5	0.3	– Caraïbes	2.2	2.6	5.8	3.7	2.8
– Rest of America	0.1	0.9	1.7	0.8	0.4	– Autre Amérique	9.4	8.6	6.4	10.1	9.1
Asia excl fmr USSR	5417.6	4750.0	6351.0	6597.4	6349.8	Asie anc. URSS exclus	2885.1	2940.2	3515.7	3826.9	3139.8
– Middle East	1789.7	1895.0	2350.4	2837.2	2947.2	– Moyen–Orient	1015.3	840.0	1067.0	1051.5	925.9
Asia former USSR	0.4	1.4	7.2	4.9	6.4	Asie ancienne URSS	27.1	36.6	56.8	94.5	92.8
Europe excl fmr USSR	2701.3	2554.4	3266.2	3209.0	2762.5	Europe anc. URSS exclus	2281.6	2475.7	2580.3	2916.6	2824.7
– European Union	2372.1	2289.2	2754.1	2528.8	2418.5	– Union Européenne	2193.8	2388.7	2486.9	2809.5	2722.8
– Eastern Europe	77.6	57.1	125.6	92.7	70.7	– Europe de l'Est	14.5	13.5	30.0	30.8	26.0
– Rest of Europe	251.6	208.1	386.4	587.5	273.3	– Autre de l'Europe	73.4	73.5	63.5	76.3	75.9
Europe former USSR	33.5	153.3	163.1	137.0	74.0	Europe ancienne URSS	38.1	19.7	19.4	26.5	42.6
Oceania	255.8	199.2	178.9	254.1	497.2	Océanie	133.0	141.2	118.1	170.9	164.4
Other		0.0	0.0			Autre	0.0				
Japan/Japon	1515.3	831.3	1254.0	1241.8	872.7	USA/Etats–Unis d'Amer	1006.2	1159.2	1230.8	1556.6	1636.7
USA/Etats–Unis d'Amer	906.8	867.7	1093.2	1308.7	1370.9	China, Hong Kong SAR	375.6	566.6	617.5	875.1	732.6
Germany/Allemagne	694.8	699.2	734.6	601.4	722.3	Germany/Allemagne	569.4	541.3	561.6	664.0	581.3
Malaysia/Malaisie	492.8	658.1	988.2	642.8	641.0	United Kingdom	508.2	563.7	529.1	629.0	615.8
Kuwait/ Koweït	361.9	565.9	668.3	905.4	699.5	Japan/Japon	502.1	537.2	552.4	606.0	449.8
Saudi Arabia	518.7	487.7	584.0	706.1	782.5	United Arab Emirates	414.7	402.4	374.0	448.4	448.5
United Arab Emirates	335.0	295.5	562.1	621.0	1028.5	France, Monaco	300.1	271.5	274.6	270.0	255.5
United Kingdom	465.6	474.0	553.9	565.8	491.4	Netherlands/Pays–Bas	197.6	228.6	271.9	276.2	294.9
China/Chine	436.6	420.8	515.3	574.3	584.8	Saudi Arabia	293.6	207.0	229.6	246.6	207.6
Italy/Italie	290.7	276.1	585.1	351.9	373.9	Korea, Republic of	175.4	219.7	277.4	273.2	207.8
Korea, Republic of	456.2	286.7	350.3	324.1	308.8	Italy/Italie	166.5	213.6	235.9	256.8	247.4
Switzerland,Liechtenst.	223.6	193.8	366.3	549.8	258.4	Belgium–Luxembourg	136.4	188.7	206.1	232.8	230.3
France, Monaco	356.9	360.8	257.8	204.9	217.9	Other Asia n.e.s.	177.0	184.4	216.5	210.9	137.9
Australia/Australie	241.1	181.3	164.8	238.8	485.2	Canada	173.0	125.7	144.4	143.1	165.9
Iran (Islamic Rep of)	152.7	129.4	191.1	272.0	207.2	Spain/Espagne	92.2	125.7	129.9	130.0	162.1
Singapore/Singapour	167.2	163.3	225.0	197.1	189.7	Bangladesh	119.0	118.6	154.7	107.0	91.7
Netherlands/Pays–Bas	170.0	136.6	153.0	249.5	154.0	Australia/Australie	104.5	112.7	92.4	136.9	128.6
Indonesia/Indonésie	124.2	116.3	119.1	139.3	196.2	Other Africa n.e.s.	84.7	139.5	117.3	138.5	79.3
Other Asia n.e.s.	129.1	105.8	159.0	143.8	125.4	China/Chine	60.0	54.1	121.2	118.9	158.2
Bahrain/Bahreïn	157.8	138.3	68.9	135.9	96.0	Singapore/Singapour	131.1	94.9	95.1	90.4	67.7
Belgium–Luxembourg	121.4	114.1	116.8	107.0	129.7	Indonesia/Indonésie	51.1	39.8	108.4	139.1	93.5
India/Inde	68.3	72.2	82.4	187.8	142.2	Turkey/Turquie	103.9	35.7	136.5	76.1	59.3
Kenya	112.3	96.7	123.9	109.4	105.2	Portugal	49.3	64.7	74.1	101.5	102.8
Thailand/Thaïlande	61.1	71.0	110.3	126.4	150.0	Sweden/Suède	72.3	76.5	71.6	81.8	86.5
Russian Federation	32.7	147.7	107.5	122.7	50.0	Sri Lanka	58.7	70.0	56.5	82.6	96.6
Canada	59.8	69.0	130.0	81.9	106.1	Thailand/Thaïlande	64.4	39.8	62.0	96.6	28.1
Sweden/Suède	110.8	72.7	81.2	84.0	96.5	Iran (Islamic Rep of)	18.3	26.4	124.7	67.3	18.8
Brazil/Brésil	76.3	46.6	108.6	119.8	61.3	Denmark/Danemark	37.9	40.0	49.9	52.9	46.7
Qatar	155.1	99.4	71.4	32.0	11.6	Malaysia/Malaisie	50.3	48.7	47.1	39.0	34.3
Turkey/Turquie	59.5	56.1	86.9	75.0	64.3	India/Inde	49.0	46.5	39.8	42.2	33.3
Spain/Espagne	44.4	44.7	64.0	79.6	95.0	Brazil/Brésil	21.2	16.5	58.4	59.2	41.3
Argentina/Argentine	64.2	23.5	65.4	55.3	90.5	Greece/Grèce	17.0	20.6	31.4	59.4	52.5
Finland/Finlande	16.7	27.5	47.3	115.3	59.8	So. African Customs Un	17.8	14.3	9.8	43.5	94.1
Denmark/Danemark	29.4	35.5	76.3	98.3	27.1	Kenya	14.6	30.1	19.9	36.0	75.8
Sri Lanka	42.3	42.1	50.7	44.4	40.0	Switzerland,Liechtenst.	38.8	34.5	27.8	34.8	37.5
China, Hong Kong SAR	48.5	31.3	49.8	46.4	40.7	Oman	28.5	22.8	32.5	43.0	42.9
Oman	24.0	64.0	53.6	40.6	31.7	Egypt/Egypte	10.1	21.4	46.4	50.6	40.6
Bangladesh	39.2	23.9	35.7	36.3	43.9	Philippines	27.7	24.2	30.8	50.9	29.1
Ireland/Irlande	21.6	22.9	44.5	37.5	28.6	Norway,Svalbard and JM	27.5	32.1	29.6	33.5	32.2
Morocco/Maroc	30.5	5.8	24.3	54.6	29.4	Uzbekistan/Ouzbékistan	14.6	17.9	36.1	44.8	39.3

(VALUE AS PERCENTAGE OF WORLD TOTAL)(VALEURS EN POURCENTAGE DU TOTAL MONDIAL)

	1988	1989	1990	1991	1992	1993	1994	1995	1996	1997
Africa	1.1	1.8	2.6	2.2	2.1	2.2	2.3	2.7	2.8	2.2
Americas	15.8	17.6	15.1	14.0	13.1	11.5	11.5	12.1	13.2	14.2
– Northern America	14.5	16.2	14.1	12.0	11.6	10.0	10.6	10.5	11.5	12.7
– LAIA	1.2	1.3	0.9	1.9	1.5	1.5	0.9	1.6	1.7	1.4
– CACM	0.0	0.1	0.0	0.0	0.0	0.0	0.0	0.0	0.0	0.0
– Caribbean	0.0	0.0	0.0	0.1	0.0	0.0	0.0	0.0	0.0	0.0
– Rest of America	0.0	0.0	0.0	0.0	0.0	0.0	0.0	0.0	0.0	0.0
Asia excl fmr USSR	48.7	50.2	50.7	49.2	50.0	55.6	53.5	54.3	54.3	54.8
– Middle East	16.6	19.3	19.6	15.9	16.0	18.4	21.3	20.1	23.4	25.4
Asia former USSR					0.0	0.0	0.0	0.1	0.0	0.1
Europe excl fmr USSR	31.8	27.2	28.5	31.2	31.4	27.7	28.8	27.9	26.4	23.8
– European Union	27.4	22.8	24.1	27.0	27.2	24.4	25.8	23.5	20.8	20.9
– Eastern Europe	1.4	1.4	1.3	1.2	1.2	0.8	0.6	1.1	0.8	0.6
– Rest of Europe	3.0	3.0	3.1	3.0	3.0	2.6	2.3	3.3	4.8	2.4
Europe former USSR	0.4	0.5	0.9	1.0	1.0	0.3	1.7	1.4	1.1	0.6
Oceania	2.2	2.8	2.4	1.9	2.4	2.6	2.2	1.5	2.1	4.3
Other				0.5			0.0	0.0		
Japan/Japon	14.7	13.0	11.9	14.7	14.2	15.6	9.4	10.7	10.2	7.5
USA/Etats–Unis d'Amer	13.0	15.3	12.8	11.1	10.5	9.3	9.8	9.3	10.8	11.8
Germany/Allemagne				7.9	7.8	7.1	7.9	6.3	5.0	6.2
Malaysia/Malaisie	3.9	3.4	3.3	4.5	4.5	5.1	7.4	8.4	5.3	5.5
Kuwait/ Koweït	7.3	10.2	6.0	0.4	1.9	3.7	6.4	5.7	7.5	6.0
Saudi Arabia	4.4	4.6	6.3	5.1	5.3	5.3	5.5	5.0	5.8	6.7
United Arab Emirates	1.5	1.6	2.1	3.7	3.1	3.4	3.3	4.8	5.1	8.9
United Kingdom	6.3	5.5	4.9	5.1	5.9	4.8	5.3	4.7	4.7	4.2
China/Chine	3.8	4.5	4.6	4.2	4.5	4.5	4.7	4.4	4.7	5.0
Italy/Italie	3.1	2.1	3.1	3.2	4.1	3.0	3.1	5.0	2.9	3.2

	1988	1989	1990	1991	1992	1993	1994	1995	1996	1997
Afrique	4.2	4.4	4.2	4.3	4.0	3.6	4.5	4.4	4.6	5.5
Amériques	12.9	14.1	14.4	13.9	15.4	18.4	19.2	18.5	19.9	22.6
– Amérique du Nord	12.8	13.8	14.1	13.2	14.7	17.2	18.0	16.9	18.2	20.7
– ALAI	0.1	0.1	0.2	0.5	0.4	1.0	0.9	1.3	1.4	1.6
– MCAC	0.0	0.1	0.0	0.0	0.0	0.1	0.1	0.1	0.2	0.2
– Caraïbes	0.0	0.0	0.0	0.1	0.0	0.0	0.0	0.1	0.0	0.0
– Autre Amérique	0.0	0.0	0.1	0.1	0.1	0.1	0.1	0.1	0.1	0.1
Asie anc. URSS exclus	44.1	45.6	39.4	44.0	46.8	41.9	40.0	43.1	41.1	36.0
– Moyen–Orient	11.4	10.9	10.3	13.4	14.3	14.8	11.4	13.1	11.3	10.6
Asie ancienne URSS					0.0	0.4	0.5	0.7	1.0	1.1
Europe anc. URSS exclus	34.9	32.7	39.3	35.3	31.4	33.2	33.7	31.6	31.3	32.4
– Union Européenne	32.1	30.4	36.0	32.3	30.0	31.9	32.5	30.5	30.1	31.2
– Europe de l'Est	1.2	1.0	1.9	1.7	0.4	0.2	0.2	0.4	0.3	0.3
– Autre de l'Europe	1.5	1.4	1.5	1.2	1.0	1.1	1.0	0.8	0.8	0.9
Europe ancienne URSS	2.0	1.4	1.3	0.9	0.6	0.6	0.3	0.2	0.3	0.5
Océanie	1.9	1.8	1.4	1.4	1.7	1.9	1.9	1.4	1.8	1.9
Autre				0.1		0.0				
USA/Etats–Unis d'Amer	11.2	12.2	12.4	11.5	12.8	14.6	15.8	15.1	16.7	18.8
China, Hong Kong SAR	4.5	5.2	5.0	5.9	7.8	5.5	7.7	7.6	9.4	8.4
Germany/Allemagne				8.3	7.0	8.3	7.4	6.9	7.1	6.7
United Kingdom	6.8	6.3	7.4	6.9	7.0	7.4	7.7	6.5	6.7	7.1
Japan/Japon	11.5	10.5	8.2	8.0	7.7	7.3	7.3	6.8	6.5	5.2
United Arab Emirates	4.2	3.7	3.3	3.7	5.2	6.0	5.5	4.6	4.8	5.1
France, Monaco	3.1	3.2	4.0	3.9	4.0	4.4	3.7	3.4	2.9	2.9
Netherlands/Pays–Bas	2.1	1.7	2.0	2.0	2.4	2.9	3.1	3.3	3.0	3.4
Saudi Arabia	3.8	2.3	2.9	3.9	4.3	4.3	2.8	2.8	2.6	2.4
Korea, Republic of	3.0	3.2	3.0	4.1	2.3	2.5	3.0	3.4	2.9	2.4

4. General Imports C.I.F. by Commodities according to the S.I.T.C. (Rev. 2) in million U.S. Dollars
Importations Générales C.A.F. par Produits d'après la C.T.C.I. (Rév. 2) en millions de Dollars E.U.

SITC CTCI	COMMODITY	1994 QUANTITY QUANTITE	1994 VALUE VALEUR	1995 QUANTITY QUANTITE	1995 VALUE VALEUR	1996 QUANTITY QUANTITE	1996 VALUE VALEUR	1997 QUANTITY QUANTITE	1997 VALUE VALEUR	PRODUIT
	ALL COMMODITIES		8881.6		11703.6		12140.7		11595.3	TOUS PRODUITS
0	FOOD AND LIVE ANIMALS		626.7		898.9		1030.1		1346.4	ALIMENTS,ANIMAUX VIVANTS
04	CEREALS AND PREPARATIONS		300.4		463.6		486.9		824.8	CEREALES ET PRODUITS
041	WHEAT ETC UNMILLED	W 2228361	282.5	W 2285520	444.4	W 2112697	466.0	W 4458265	809.9	FROMENT,EPEAUTRE
0411	DURUM WHEAT UNMILLED	W 2228361	282.5	W 2285520	444.4	W 2112661	466.0	W 4458247	809.8	FROMENT DUR NON MOULU
05	VEGETABLES AND FRUIT		100.5		162.5		136.6		109.5	LEGUMES ET FRUITS
054	VEG ETC FRSH,SMPLY PRSVD	W 206973	58.7	W 385314	116.6	W 239631	84.1	W 192744	56.0	LEGUMES FRAIS,CONG,SECS
0542	LEGUMINOUS VEGETBLES DRY	W 169796	50.0	W 298982	102.6	W 162514	65.7	W 121215	38.7	LEGUMES A COSSE SECS
057	FRUIT,NUTS,FRESH,DRIED	W 97635	39.5	W 89395	42.1	W 133165	49.7	W 122811	50.5	FRUITS FRAIS OU SECS
0577	NUTS EDIBLE,FRESH,DRIED	W 36357	28.2	W 39099	31.7	W 38732	33.1	W 42667	36.1	FRUITS A COQUES
06	SUGAR AND PREPS,HONEY		6.9		7.7		194.3		177.1	SUCRES ET PRODUITS
061	SUGAR AND HONEY	W 13161	6.3	W 9035	6.4	W 493336	193.3	W 490272	176.3	SUCRES ET MIEL
0611	RAW BEET AND CANE SUGAR	W 130	0.1	W 224	0.2	W 85199	25.4	W 98492	35.6	SUCRES BRUTS
0612	REFINED SUGAR ETC	W 7859	2.7	W 3724	1.8	W 403284	163.4	W 388264	137.5	SUCRES RAFFINES
07	COFFEE,TEA,COCOA,SPICES		188.3		217.0		179.7		188.8	CAFE,THE,CACAO,EPICES
074	TEA AND MATE	W 106549	174.4	W 115719	182.0	W 110773	163.5	W 86883	171.5	THE ET MATE
0741	TEA	W 106549	174.4	W 115719	182.0	W 110773	163.5	W 86871	171.5	THE
2	CRUDE MATERLS,EXCL FUELS		719.4		817.6		628.2		618.0	MAT BRUTES NON COMESTIBLES
21	HIDES,SKINS,FURS UNDRSSD		41.3		27.3		29.0		24.6	CUIRS,PEAUX BRUTS
211	HIDES,SKINS,EXC FURS,RAW	W 18414	41.2	W 10456	27.3	W 13464	28.2	W 15302	24.6	CUIRS ET PEAUX
22	OIL SEEDS,OLEAGINOUS FRT		27.2		35.6		34.8		27.8	GRAINES,FRUITS OLEAGINEUX
223	SEEDS FOR OTH FIXED OILS	W 119639	26.7	W 111657	27.4	W 100056	26.7	W 28891	12.9	GRAINES AUTRES HUILES FIXES
23	RUBBER, CRUDE		41.4		64.0		63.8		52.9	CAOUTCHOUC BRUT
232	NATURAL RUBBER,GUMS	W 28309	26.3	W 29558	42.4	W 29613	39.4	W 31780	33.0	LATEX CAOUTCHOUC NATUREL
251	*PULP AND WASTE PAPER	W 77501	23.3	W 70344	37.9	W 71006	26.0	W 91277	30.7	PATES A PAPIER,DECHETS
26	TEXTILE FIBRES AND WASTE		405.8		458.9		263.2		290.2	FIBRES TEXTILES
263	COTTON	W 138784	218.5	W 134020	223.1	W 42062	54.5	W 67716	104.5	COTON
2631	RAW COTTON,EXCL LINTERS	W 121507	218.4	W 107708	222.9	W 27359	54.2	W 54653	104.2	COTON EN MASSE
266	SYNTHETIC FIBRES TO SPIN	W 62644	96.5	W 53474	113.4	W 48391	81.9	W 39003	63.5	FIBRES SYNTHETIQUES
2665	DISCN SYNTH FIBRE UNCMBD	W 52811	78.5	W 43968	92.7	W 39962	64.8	W 27903	43.4	DISCONTINUES EN MASSE
26652	— POLYESTER	W 29860	41.9	W 23548	49.4	W 21105	31.7	W 11378	14.7	FIBRES EN POLYESTERS
26653	— ACRYLIC	W 22251	35.5	W 19597	41.5	W 18261	32.1	W 15525	26.9	FIBRES ACRYLIQUES
267	OTHER MAN-MADE FIBRES	W 21758	40.4	W 22125	50.7	W 26416	53.9	W 26448	47.8	AUTR FIBR TEXT ARTIF SYNTH
2671	REGENERATD FIBRE TO SPIN	W 21707	40.3	W 22010	50.5	W 26408	53.9	W 26447	47.8	FIBRES TEXT ARTIFIC
26711	DISCN REGEN FIBRE UNCMBD	W 20226	35.3	W 20326	44.1	W 24367	46.0	W 23958	38.4	FIBRES TEX ARTIF DISCONT
269	WASTE OF TEXTILE FABRICS	W 87699	20.7	W 83099	31.8	W 99050	37.2	W 95635	35.7	FRIPERIE DRILLES,CHIFFONS
26901	BULK TEXT WSTE,OLD CLTHG	W 86939	20.4	W 82586	31.6	W 98797	37.1	W 94926	35.6	ART ET ACCESS D'HABILLEMENT
27	CRUDE FERTLZR,MINRLS NES		28.0		34.0		31.1		25.5	ENGRAIS MINERAUX BRUTS
28	METALLIFEROUS ORES,SCRAP		110.0		109.3		124.6		111.3	MINERAIS METAL,DECHETS
281	IRON ORE,CONCENTRATES	W 1888647	49.4	W 1697986	55.0	W 1591355	51.7	W 1650020	49.6	MINERAIS DE FER
2816	IRON ORE AGGLOMERATES	W 1888617	49.3	W 1697978	55.0	W 1591353	51.7	W 1649949	49.6	MINERAIS AGGLOMERES
282	IRON AND STEEL SCRAP	W 184425	28.6	W 120606	22.2	W 257965	41.4	W 222022	32.6	FERRAILLES
288	NONFERR METAL SCRAP NES	W 89019	30.0	W 64781	30.1	W 59826	28.8	W 67817	27.1	DECHETS NON FERREUX
2882	OTHER BASE MTL SCRAP NES	W 88380	29.7	W 64588	30.0	W 59616	28.8	W 67777	27.1	AUTRES DECHETS
28823	ALUMINIUM WSTE AND SCRAP	W 82991	28.2	W 58891	28.3	W 53440	25.7	W 66014	26.4	DECHETS D'ALUMINIUM
29	CRUDE ANIMAL,VEG MAT NES		32.2		39.0		39.5		31.7	MATIERES BRUTES ANIM,VEGET
292	CRUDE VEG MATERIALS NES	W 43776	31.8	W 51114	38.3	W 54358	38.8	W 45766	31.5	MAT BRUTES VEGETALES NDA
3	MINERAL FUELS ETC		1631.8		1901.8		2446.7		2226.9	COMBUSTIBLES MINERAUX LUB
32	COAL,COKE AND BRIQUETTES		56.6		54.0		63.6		58.0	HOUILLES,COKES,BRIQUETTES
322	COAL,LIGNITE AND PEAT	W 1050200	56.6	W 884495	54.0	W 982141	63.1	W 902615	55.6	HOUILLES,LIGNITES,TOURBE
3222	OTH COAL,NOT AGGLOMERATD	W 1049284	56.2	W 884069	53.9	W 981989	63.0	W 901613	55.2	AUTRES HOUILLES
33	PETROLEUM AND PRODUCTS		1401.7		1780.2		2290.1		2082.2	PETROLE ET DERIVES
333	CRUDE PETROLEUM	W 3907964	454.1	W 4174043	529.5	W 3858984	567.8	W 4077477	569.2	HUILES BRUTES DE PETROLE
334	PETROLEUM PRODUCTS,REFIN	W 7393565	942.0	MW 9185	1244.2	MW 10340	1715.7	MW 10399	1505.3	PRODUITS RAFFINES
3341	GASOLINE,OTH LIGHT OILS	W 209986	39.5	W 133876	29.0	W 314405	65.5	W 319406	61.0	ESSENCES POUR MOTEURS
33411	MOTOR,AVIATION SPIRIT	W 200148	37.9	W 129639	28.2	W 314101	65.4	W 318777	60.7	ESSENCES MOTEURS D'AVIONS
3342	KEROSENE,OTH MEDIUM OILS	W 161185	28.4	W 68748	13.4	W 148431	32.0	W 67109	14.7	PETR LAMPANTS,AUT HUIL
33421	KEROSENE INCL JET FUEL	W 161185	28.4	W 68738	13.4	W 148360	31.9	W 65566	14.0	PETROLES LAMPANTS
3343	GAS OILS	W 3530662	541.3	W 4401427	716.1	W 5044838	1022.2	W 4399380	786.7	GAS OILS
3344	FUEL OILS,NES	W 3453840	308.3	W 4548146	458.2	W 4759162	554.3	W 5574601	614.1	FUEL OILS
3345	LUBS,PETROLEUM OILS NES	W 37892	24.7	W 32503	27.6	W 72821	41.9	W 38042	29.0	HUILES LUBRIFIANTES
341	*GAS,NATURAL AND MANUFCT		173.6		67.6		93.1		86.8	GAZ NATUREL,GAZ MANUFACT
3413	PETROLM GASES,LIQUEFIED	W 460370	173.5	W 324031	67.6	W 340941	93.1	W 2370140	86.8	GAZ DE PETROLE LIQUEFIE
34139	OTH HYDROCARBON GAS LQFD	W 458930	173.5	W 324031	67.6	W 340941	93.1	W 2369920	86.8	HYDROCARBURES GAZEUX NDA
4	ANIMAL,VEGETABLE OIL,FAT		789.5		1103.0		724.9		773.9	HUILES,GRAISSES ANIM,VEG
411	*ANIMAL OILS AND FATS	W 73855	32.6	W 22940	14.6	W 72608	41.9	W 45416	24.4	HUILES,GRAISSES ANIMALES
4113	ANIML OIL,FAT,GREASE NES	W 73749	32.5	W 22853	14.5	W 72521	41.9	W 45230	24.2	HUILES,GRAISSES ANIMALES NDA
41132	FATS OF BOVINE,SHEEP,ETC	W 70389	29.8	W 20633	12.5	W 72383	41.7	W 45104	24.0	SUIFS BRUTS FONDUS
42	FIXED VEGETABLE OIL,FAT		723.8		1062.6		651.1		722.4	HUILES VEGETALES FIXES
423	FIXED VEG OILS,SOFT	W 201309	125.3	W 228074	181.2	W 150281	93.2	W 218440	136.5	HUILES VEGET DOUCES FIXES
4232	SOYA BEAN OIL	W 198072	122.7	W 196549	157.3	W 140357	86.3	W 209487	130.6	HUILE DE SOJA
424	FIXED VEG OIL NONSOFT	W 1106337	598.6	W 1057237	881.4	W 905838	557.9	W 949087	585.9	AUTRES HUILES VEG FIXES
4242	PALM OIL	W 1099783	594.0	W 1049173	874.2	W 899455	552.3	W 941337	579.2	HUILE DE PALME
431	*PROCESD ANML VEG OIL,ET	W 106569	33.2	W 62047	25.9	W 85984	32.0	W 70279	27.3	HUILES,GRAISSES PREPAREES
4313	FATTY ACIDS ETC,RESIDUES	W 103770	30.3	W 59759	22.8	W 84096	29.2	W 66677	23.2	ACIDES GRAS INDUST,RESIDUS
43131	FATTY ACIDS,ACID OILS	W 96603	29.2	W 52730	21.9	W 62897	25.7	W 53739	20.3	ACIDES GRAS INDUSTRIELS
5	CHEMCLS,RELATED PROD NES		1443.8		1965.9		2141.9		1827.7	PRODUITS CHIMIQUES
51	ORGANIC CHEMICALS		373.6		498.6		529.9		538.4	PROD CHIMIQ ORGANIQUES
512	ALCOHOLS,PHENOLS ETC		41.6		50.7	W 161687	91.6		106.4	PHENOLS,PHENOLS-ALCOOLS
5121	ACYCLIC ALCOHOLS,DERIVS		37.9		46.4	W 158310	87.2		102.3	ALCOOLS ACYCLIQUES
51215	ETHYLENE GLYCOL	V 40680	17.1	V 34378	23.5	W 103751	58.9	V 118133	76.8	ETHYLENE-GLYCOL
513	CARBOXYLIC ACIDS ETC	W 176154	135.6	W 216089	225.5	W 206167	203.5	W 380799	245.0	ACIDES CARBOXYLIQUES
5138	POLYACIDS AND DERIVATIVS	W 148535	104.3	W 187129	184.0	W 175047	156.4	W 348195	207.0	ACIDES POLYCARBOXYLIQUES
51389	OTH POLYACIDS ETC,DERIVS	W 131291	91.7	W 180237	173.5	W 161118	144.4	W 342847	203.6	ACIDES POLYCARBOXYLIQUES
514	NITROGEN-FNCTN COMPOUNDS	W 11869	81.4	W 14962	113.4	W 20187	118.6	W 17659	96.9	COMPOSES FONCT AZOTEES
5148	OTH NITROGN-FNCTN CMPNDS	W 6265	46.9	W 8291	70.6	W 12510	78.3	W 10046	57.9	AUTRES COMPOSES AZOTES
51482	IMIDE-,IMIDE-FNCT CMPNDS	W 1491	35.5	W 2416	47.7	W 6636	54.0	W 2389	40.6	COMPOSES A FONCTION IMIDE
515	ORG-INORG COMPOUNDS ETC	W 14205	55.5	W 9816	62.0	W 8032	61.1	W 5274	48.6	COMPOSES ORGANO-MINERAUX
5156	HETEROCYCLIC CMPDS ETC	W 2046	31.9	W 2924	37.1	W 2766	33.6	W 2131	32.8	COMPOSES HETEROCYCLIQUES
51569	OTH HETEROCYC CMPDS,ETC	W 1922	31.4	W 2606	36.4	W 2322	32.0	W 1841	31.3	AUT COMP HETEROCYCLIQUES
516	OTHER ORGANIC CHEMICALS	W 70545	39.7	W 15122	30.3	W 14839	25.0	W 15145	15.4	AUTRES PROD ORGANIQUES
5161	ETHERS,EPOXIDES,ACETALS	W 64416	28.5	W 8977	7.9	W 6388	6.8	W 9428	4.9	ETHERS-OXYDES,ALCOOLS
51611	ETHERS,ETHER-ALCOHOL,ETC	W 64385	28.3	W 8926	7.6	W 5657	5.8	W 9390	4.8	ETHERS-OXYDES
52	INORGANIC CHEMICALS		52.2		63.9		66.8		64.5	PROD CHIM INORGANIQUES
523	OTHR INORG CHEMICALS ETC	W 78714	32.5	W 94268	40.6	W 93215	44.1	W 86820	41.4	AUT PRODUITS CHIMIQUES INORG
53	DYES,TANNING,COLOUR PROD		132.7		147.9		139.6		134.5	PROD TEINTURE,COLORANTS
531	SYNT DYE,NAT INDGO,LAKES	W 16735	80.2	W 15845	85.3	W 14056	80.8	W 15965	78.6	MAT COLOR ORGAN,LAQUES
5311	SYNTHIC ORGNIC DYESTUFFS	W 15747	77.0	W 14972	81.6	W 13242	77.2	W 15218	75.5	MAT COLOR ORGAN SYNTHET
533	PIGMENTS,PAINTS,ETC	W 21383	32.5	W 20375	40.2	W 21139	38.7	W 18413	36.3	PIGMENTS,PEINTURES,VERNIS
541	*MEDICINAL,PHARM PRODUCT	MK 10732	242.7	MK 11707	297.6	MK 11612	315.6	MK 9217	265.4	PROD MEDICINAUX PHARMACEUT
5413	ANTIBIOTICS IN BULK	K 830283	54.1	K 953784	66.5	K 862462	65.6	K 871613	62.9	ANTIBIOTIQUES NDA

4. General Imports C.I.F. by Commodities according to the S.I.T.C. (Rev. 2) in million U.S. Dollars
Importations Générales C.A.F. par Produits d'après la C.T.C.I. (Rév. 2) en millions de Dollars E.U.

SITC CTCI	COMMODITY	1994 QUANTITY QUANTITE	1994 VALUE VALEUR	1995 QUANTITY QUANTITE	1995 VALUE VALEUR	1996 QUANTITY QUANTITE	1996 VALUE VALEUR	1997 QUANTITY QUANTITE	1997 VALUE VALEUR	PRODUIT
54139	OTHER ANTIBIOTICS	K 386805	44.5	K 504193	57.4	K 428784	54.3	K 496697	51.0	AUTRES ANTIBIOTIQUES
5417	MEDICAMENTS	K 8045936	136.2	K 8679710	167.7	K 8919084	180.4	K 6543719	140.9	MEDICAMENTS
54179	— CONTNG OTH SUBSTANCES	K 5370160	102.2	K 5464484	113.9	K 5594671	124.9	K 3883507	93.8	MED CONT AUT SUBSTANCES
55	PERFUME,CLEANING ETC PRD		21.5		43.6		36.7		34.7	PROD POUR PARFUM,TOILETTE
562	*FERTILIZERS,MANUFACTURE	W 913792	170.6	W 1159038	276.0	W 1844473	433.2	W 1037117	235.5	ENGRAIS MANUFACTURES
5621	CHEM NITROGENOUS FERTLZR	W 79052	11.4	W 190542	53.3	W 673168	154.6	W 405666	80.9	ENGRAIS AZOTES
56216	UREA	W 77531	11.0	W 189226	52.9	W 641460	147.3	W 403009	80.1	UREE
5629	FERTILIZERS NES	W 787158	152.8	W 847874	198.9	W 1078984	260.1	W 630066	154.2	ENGRAIS NDA
56292	NITROG–PHOS FERTILZR NES	W 725928	139.4	W 700320	161.4	W 970988	233.3	W 630048	154.2	ENGRAIS NDA CONT N P
58	PLASTIC MATERIALS ETC		274.8		367.3		353.7		312.0	MAT PLAST ARTIFICIELLES
582	PROD OF CONDENSATION ETC	W 110937	64.7	W 52078	92.5	W 61113	84.9	W 38230	48.3	PROD CONDENS,POLYCOND
5823	ALKYDS,OTHER POLYESTERS	W 92671	39.7	W 36596	66.1	W 46635	57.0	W 22619	23.0	ALKYDES ET AUT POLYESTERS
58231	— IN PRIMARY FORMS	W 91550	37.2	W 34846	60.4	W 46051	55.2	W 22104	21.4	SOUS FORMES PRIMAIRES
583	POLYMERIZATION ETC PRODS	W 240426	201.2	W 226055	264.3	W 277285	257.2	W 284228	252.4	PROD POLYMERISATION
5831	POLYETHYLENE	W 86303	53.7	W 76647	68.4	W 95531	74.2	W 91342	74.7	POLYETHYLENE
58311	— IN PRIMARY FORMS	W 75372	51.1	W 61144	63.3	W 82074	69.9	W 82895	71.5	POLYETHYLENE PRIMAIRES
5832	POLYPROPYLENE	W 69315	49.5	W 54590	67.2	W 62486	58.0	W 77373	66.1	POLYPROPYLENE
58321	— IN PRIMARY FORMS	W 67713	45.0	W 52669	60.5	W 60388	52.3	W 74047	59.4	POLYPROPYLENE PRIMAIRES
5834	POLYVINYL CHLORIDE	W 44541	42.3	W 50276	58.2	W 70018	54.3	W 66010	53.0	CHLORURE DE POLYVINYLE
58341	— IN PRIMARY FORMS	W 39435	33.4	W 41059	44.6	W 53787	41.3	W 48571	40.1	SOUS FORMES PRIMAIRES
5839	OTH POLYMRZTION ETC PROD	W 14826	21.5	W 22677	33.5	W 26281	38.1	W 25937	30.9	AUT PROD POLYMER COPOLYM
59	CHEMICAL MATERIALS NES		175.3		269.2		265.5		242.0	MAT PROD CHIMIQUES NDA
591	PESTICIDES,DISINFECTANTS	W 14695	64.2	W 29127	148.0	W 29211	139.5	W 32056	126.0	DESINF,INSECT,FONG,HERB
5911	INSECTICIDES,FOR RETAIL	W 10276	48.6	W 23019	121.9	W 23525	115.0	W 23704	89.1	INSECTICIDES VENTE DET
598	MISCEL CHEM PRODUCTS NES	W 56126	105.9	W 58152	115.7	W 69711	120.9	W 63039	112.5	PROD DIV INDUST CHIM NDA
5982	ANTI–KNOCK PREPARTNS ETC	W 14561	32.5	W 13447	27.8	W 16797	34.8	W 12537	25.6	PREPARAT ANTIDETONANTES
5989	CHEM PRODUCTS,PREPS NES	W 34179	67.1	W 36445	79.4	W 45052	77.8	W 43167	77.4	PROD PREP CHIMIQUES NDA
59899	OTH CHEM PRODS,PREPS,NES	W 24811	51.7	W 25333	60.8	W 32877	58.4	W 31344	57.6	AUT PRODUITS CHIMIQUES NDA
6	BASIC MANUFACTURES		881.9		1166.9		1231.8		1021.4	ART MANUFACTURES
62	RUBBER MANUFACTURES NES		58.1		74.4		90.1		91.0	CAOUTCHOUC MANUFACTURE
625	RUBBER TYRES, TUBES ETC	N 2772194	48.6	N 3412461	59.0	N 2811407	69.7	N 3493959	70.7	PNEUS CAOUTCHOUC VULCANISE
6259	OTH TYRES,TYRE CASES,ETC	N 2210491	38.3	N 2386721	35.0	N 1999708	47.5	N 2618632	44.6	AUTRES PNEUS RECHAPES FLAPS
62599	TYRES NES,TYRE CASES,ETC	N 1216123	37.3	N 1049381	33.2	N 1254808	45.1	N 1407411	42.5	PNEUS,FLAPS
64	PAPER,PAPERBOARD AND MFR		122.7		153.9		140.8		131.8	PAPIERS,CARTONS & OUVRAGES
641	PAPER AND PAPERBOARD	W 193610	115.7	W 154052	143.1	W 154840	130.0	W 176725	120.3	PAPIERS ET CARTONS
6411	NEWSPRINT	W 78343	36.6	W 67000	56.4	W 61470	45.1	W 76241	40.4	PAPIER JOURNAL
65	TEXTILE YARN,FABRICS,ETC		76.8		121.5		110.5		85.4	FILS,TISSUS,ARTICLES TEXTILE
651	TEXTILE YARN	W 19120	53.6	W 16013	55.1	W 17224	62.2	W 15102	46.1	FILS TEXTILES
66	NONMETAL MINERAL MFS NES		75.4		66.9		61.5		52.8	ART MIN NON METALLIQUES
661	LIME,CEMENT,BLDG PRODS	W 564663	28.0	W 232030	12.8	W 22485	2.5	W 40545	1.8	CHAUX,CIMENTS MAT CONSTR
6612	CEMENT	W 495821	27.3	W 207475	12.2	W 16968	2.0	W 7034	1.2	CIMENTS HYDRAULIQUES
67	IRON AND STEEL		332.9		447.6		490.9		403.2	FER ET ACIER
672	IRON,STEEL PRIMARY FORMS	W 41233	14.6	W 101422	39.2	W 114066	41.9	W 54333	19.0	LINGOTS FER,ACIER
674	IRN,STL UNIV,PLATE,SHEET	W 378046	181.8	W 501749	239.0	W 573420	245.6	W 466977	187.2	LARGES PLATS,TOLES
6747	TINNED PLATES,SHEETS	W 89653	42.0	W 158538	59.6	W 119541	47.4	W 93711	42.5	TOLES ETAMEES EN ACIER
6749	OTH IRN,STL PLATES,SHEET	W 228505	100.3	W 229592	116.6	W 293637	120.5	W 285895	110.5	AUTRES TOLES FER,ACIER
67491	— OF IRON OR SIMPLE STL	W 215468	81.0	W 210575	94.5	W 280584	102.1	W 272306	92.3	AUT TOLES AUTRES ACIER FIN
678	IRON,STL TUBES,PIPES,ETC	W 98302	92.7	W 105605	112.8	W 191734	134.1	W 169427	143.0	TUBES,TUYAUX EN FONTE,FER
6782	IRON,STL SEAMLESS TUBES	W 23626	33.2	W 25435	22.6	W 51598	51.7	W 51064	54.9	TUBES,TUYAUX SANS SOUDURE
6783	IRON,STL TUBES,PIPES NES	W 51840	39.6	W 62828	63.3	W 122003	57.3	W 96157	55.1	AUT TUBES,TUYAUX FER,ACIER
68	NON–FERROUS METALS		102.8		161.9		164.0		113.1	METAUX NON FERREUX
682	COPPER EXC CEMENT COPPER	W 12578	33.2	W 18465	63.9	W 19934	58.4	W 13688	37.1	CUIVRE
6821	COPPER NES,ALLOYS,UNWRT	W 5456	12.2	W 10657	35.5	W 11697	27.5	W 10799	26.0	CUIVRE BRUT
68212	COPPER REFINED,UNWROUGHT	W 5452	12.2	W 10646	35.5	W 11689	27.5	W 10788	26.0	CUIVRE AFFINE BRUT
684	ALUMINIUM	W 22535	45.6	W 29863	61.8	W 26033	66.9	W 14770	39.0	ALUMINIUM
69	METAL MANUFACTURES NES		97.9		125.6		157.6		128.7	ART MANUFACT EN METAL NDA
691	STRUCTURES AND PARTS NES	W 31848	41.6	W 42632	50.8	W 46069	63.4	W 37527	49.9	CONSTRUCT FER,ACIER,ALU
6911	STRUCTURES,PARTS IRN,STL	W 31830	41.5	W 42541	50.3	W 45972	62.8	W 37160	48.2	CONSTRUCT FER,ACIER,FONTE
699	BASE METAL MFRS NES	W 15617	30.8	W 14528	42.3	W 18633	40.4	W 15783	38.5	ART MANUFACTURES MET NDA
7	MACHINES,TRANSPORT EQUIP		2524.8		3381.1		3226.6		3037.9	MACHINES MATERIEL TRANSPORT
71	POWER GENERATING EQUIPMT		331.3		797.1		736.7		902.5	MACHINES GENERATRICES
711	STEAM BOILERS & AUX PLNT		45.7		157.3		110.1		39.4	GENERATEURS VAPEUR EAU ETC
7112	AUXILIARY BOILER PLANT	N 581	23.8	N 217	37.5	N 303	11.0	N 197	20.2	APPAREILS AUXIL DU 711.1
7119	PTS NES OF APP OF 711	W 3293	13.9	W 17043	107.6	W 5423	96.3	W 3074	14.2	PART,PIECES POUR 711
71191	PTS NES OF BOILERS	W 3193	13.5	W 16269	105.3	W 4038	82.4	W 2357	9.0	PART,PIECES POUR 711.1
712	STEAM ENGINES,TURBINES		71.0		314.0		234.5		108.5	MACHINES A VAPEUR D'EAU PIEC
7126	STEAM POWR UNITS,ENGINES	N 99	35.0	N 39	4.9	N 581	81.2	N 143	22.0	MACHINES A VAPEUR D EAU
7129	STM ENGINE ETC PARTS NES	W 2152	36.1	W 95934	309.1	W 15807	153.3	W 9218	86.6	PARTIES,PIECES DU 712.6
713	INTRNL COMBUS PSTN ENGIN		30.0		43.5		103.0		92.5	MOTEURS EXPL COMB INT, PIECE
7138	PISTON ENGINES NES	N 130413	9.7	N 3509	20.3	N 49312	57.9	N 20256	41.7	MOTEURS A PISTONS NDA
7139	PISTON ENGINE PARTS NES	W 11109	13.9	W 11134	16.9	W 11867	33.3	W 11324	36.1	PIECES POUR 713.2,3,8
714	ENGINES AND MOTORS NES		35.2		41.8		21.9		239.3	MOTEURS NON ELECTRIQUES
7148	GAS TURBINES NES	N 7	21.7	N 4	11.0	N 23	8.4	N 39	179.1	TURBINES A GAZ
71488	OTHER GAS TURBINES NES	N 7	21.7	N 4	11.0	N 2	8.4	N 39	179.1	AUTRES TURBINES A GAZ
7149	ENGINE & MOTOR PARTS NES	W 4020	13.5	W 3427	30.8	W 318	13.5	W 2537	60.2	PIECES 714 ET 718.88
71499	PARTS NES,OF 71488,71888	W 4013	13.4	W 3427	30.8	W 318	13.5	W 2533	59.9	PIECES 714.88 ET 718.88
716	ROTATING ELECTRIC PLANT		133.5		201.2		220.3		282.8	APP ELECTR ROTATIFS,PIECES
7162	AC MTRS,GENRTRS,GEN SETS	N 103675	106.0	N 74574	170.7	N 150391	133.8	N 224673	225.3	MOTEURS ELECTRIQUES
71623	GEN SETS WITH PISTN ENGN	N 12928	101.2	N 4990	155.6	N 4714	123.2	N 5406	214.7	GROUPES MOTEUR EXPLOSION
7169	PTS NES OF ROT ELEC PLNT	W 2049	18.2	W 1486	22.5	W 5159	81.6	W 3868	53.0	PIECES MAC APP ROTATIFS
718	OTH POWER GENERATG MACHY		16.0		39.7		47.2		140.3	AUTRES MOTEURS PARTIES
7188	WIND,WATER,ETC ENGINES		16.0		39.7		47.2		140.3	MOT MACHINES MOTRICES NDA
71889	PARTS NES OF 71881,71882	W 526	4.6	W 1631	36.8	W 3041	41.2	W 19402	138.7	PARTIES DES POS 718.81,82
72	MACHS FOR SPCL INDUSTRYS		664.5		799.1		632.0		531.6	MAC SPECIALES POUR INDUST
722	TRACTORS NON–ROAD		37.2	N 241	141.4		50.3	N 14357	54.6	TRACTEURS
7224	WHEELED TRACTORS NES		37.2	N 240	141.4		50.3	N 14337	54.3	TRACTEURS A ROUES
723	CIVIL ENGNEERG EQUIP ETC		83.9		71.0		100.2		44.6	APPAREILS DE GENIE CIVIL
7234	CONST,MINING MACHNRY NES	N 19675	72.3	N 44044	64.3	N 8070	96.4	N 69741	35.2	MACH POUR LA CONST, MINES
724	TEXTILE,LEATHER MACHNRY		304.5		291.3		165.2		174.9	MACH POUR INDUSTRIE TEXTILE
7244	SPINNING,EXTRDNG,ETC MCH		135.5		177.0		90.9		64.4	MACH POUR LE FILAGE
72441	TEXTILE EXTRUDING MACHS	N 290	17.4	N 4164	114.6	N 512	34.8	N 50	1.2	MACH FILAGE TEXT SYNTH
72442	FIBRE PROCESSNG MACH NES	N 5931	48.6	N 714	16.9	N 701	14.2	N 768	20.3	MACH PREP MAT TEXTILES
72443	SPINNING,REELING,ETC MCH	N 26067	53.5	N 6870	28.9	N 3088	15.5	N 3428	25.4	MACH POUR LA FILATURE
7245	WEAVING,FELT MFG,ETC MCH	N 17758	80.0	N 8046	36.0	N 12631	23.9	N 24893	60.0	METIERS A TISSER,PIECES
72451	WEAVING MACHINES (LOOMS)	N 9732	50.5	N 791	16.1	N 8193	15.1	N 22538	40.1	METIERS A TISSER
7247	TEXTILE MACHINERY NES		52.0		48.3		32.8		24.1	MACH LAVAGE,TEINTURE TEX
72474	OTH TEXTILE MACHNERY NES	N 15677	46.3	N 22440	45.4	N 13620	29.2	N 4772	22.0	MACH LAVAGE ETC MAT TEXT
728	OTH MACHY FOR SPCL INDUS		174.7		240.9		257.6		213.3	AUT MACH IND PARTICULIERES
7283	OTHR MINERAL WORKG MACHY		49.3		37.3		28.2		7.6	MACH TRIER,CRIBLER,BROYER
72834	MINRL MOULDING ETC MACHY	N 5727	30.3	N 4798	25.6	N 450	2.6	N 931	1.3	MACH AGGLO CIMENT ETC
7284	MACHY FOR SPCL INDUS NES		123.3		199.5		224.6		204.3	MACH SPEC IND PARTICUL.

4. General Imports C.I.F. by Commodities according to the S.I.T.C. (Rev. 2) in million U.S. Dollars
Importations Générales C.A.F. par Produits d'après la C.T.C.I. (Rév. 2) en millions de Dollars E.U.

SITC CTCI	COMMODITY	1994		1995		1996		1997		PRODUIT
		QUANTITY QUANTITE	VALUE VALEUR	QUANTITY QUANTITE	VALUE VALEUR	QUANTITY QUANTITE	VALUE VALEUR	QUANTITY QUANTITE	VALUE VALEUR	
72848	OTH MCHY WITH INDIV FNCT	N 71756	78.8	N 72430	128.4	N 39694	82.0	N 29533	79.8	AUTRES MACHINES NDA
72849	PTS OF MACHS OF 7284 ETC	W 2844	31.3	W 4116	50.2	W 21966	133.3	W 12956	116.6	PIECES DU 728.4 ETC
74	GENRL INDUSTRL MACHY NES		413.3		487.5		529.9		510.4	MACH APP INDUSTRIE
741	HEATING,COOLING EQUIPMNT		120.3		99.1		144.3		140.3	MACH CHAUFFAGE,PIECES
7416	HEATING,COOLING EQU NES		65.8		46.1	N 16961	98.9		103.0	APP CHANGEMENT TEMP
742	PUMPS FOR LIQUIDS ETC		21.4		25.4		33.9		36.6	POMPES MOTO–POMPES
743	PUMPS NES,CENTRFUGES ETC		55.1		122.4		97.1		83.3	POMPES COMPRES,VENT ETC
7431	PUMPS FOR GASES ETC	N 362425	28.8	N 625626	53.2	N 401687	36.8	N 381772	32.9	POMPES AIR A VIDE,COMPRES
7436	GAS,LIQUID FILTERS ETC	N 1359784	13.0	N 1108653	37.3	N 920309	33.5	N 735187	18.6	APP POUR FILT DES LIQUIDES
744	MECHANICAL HANDLING EQU		139.0		128.0		119.0		165.7	EQUIP MANUTENTION PIECES
7449	PTS NES OF MACHY OF 7442	W 18037	110.9	W 9118	98.3	W 12739	90.4	W 23625	144.4	PIECES DU 744.2
749	NONELEC MACH PTS,ACC NES		58.7		91.3		108.4		72.5	PIECES MACH NON ELEC NDA
7492	COCKS,VALVES ETC NES		22.5		30.9	MN 11775	54.9	N 3250485	26.0	ART ROB,SIM POUR TUYAUX
75	OFFICE MACHNES,ADP EQUIP		62.8		85.7		55.0		62.0	MACH BUREAU TRAIT AUTOM
752	AUTOMTIC DATA PROC EQUIP	N 158027	46.9	N 243525	60.7	N 196487	34.8	N 336993	43.6	MACH TRAIT INFORMATION
76	TELECOMM,SOUND EQUIPMENT		163.9		202.8		140.4		94.7	EQUIPMENT DE TELECOM
764	TELECOM EQPT,PTS,ACC NES		156.8		174.8		128.5		87.9	EQUIP TELECOM,PIECES
7649	PTS NES OF EQUIPMT OF 76	W 7191	134.5	W 5812	152.6	W 5514	97.5	W 3706	61.5	PIECES DE LA DIV 76
76491	PTS NES OF APPAR OF 7641	W 2087	98.8	W 1220	92.7	W 1108	51.9	W 608	35.0	PIECES POUR 764.1
76493	TELECOMM EQUIPMT PTS NES	W 3236	24.7	W 3276	44.4	W 2659	36.7	W 1999	22.2	PIECES 761,762,764.3,8
77	ELECTRIC MACHNRY NES ETC		298.4		365.0		439.0		434.5	MACH APP ELECT NDA
771	ELECTRIC POWER MACHY NES		34.6		95.1		86.2		136.9	MACH PROD,TRANS ELECTR
7711	TRANSFORMERS,ELECTRICAL	N 9075	23.4	N 17322	71.2	N 7339	72.2	N 9495	93.6	TRANSFO ELECTRIQUES
77118	OTHER ELEC TRANSFORMERS	N 6075	22.6	N 17032	71.2	N 4850	72.1	N 7658	93.5	AUTRES TRANSFO ELECTRIQ
7712	OTH ELEC POWER MACHY NES		11.2		23.9		14.1		43.3	AUT APP PROD TRANSF ELEC
77129	PTS NES OF MACHY OF 771	W 212	2.7	W 892	22.2	W 893	10.1	W 3796	39.5	PIECES MACH DU 771
772	SWITCHGEAR ETC,PARTS NES		41.4		82.9	MN 102454	106.2		109.0	APP COUPURE,SECT ETC
7721	SWITCHGEAR ETC		37.9		78.1	MN 67507	103.5	MN 42935	106.5	APP COUPURE,SECTIONMNT
773	ELECTR DISTRIBUTNG EQUIP	W 15019	40.4	W 17921	57.6	W 47413	118.0	W 46325	111.6	EQUIPMT DISTRIBUTION ELECT
7731	INSULATED WIRE,CABLE ETC	W 9809	30.8	W 11274	43.9	W 33331	92.6	W 33359	88.8	FILS,CABLES ISOLES ELECT
778	ELECTRICAL MACHINERY NES		135.0		63.5		78.8		44.9	AUTRES MACH ELECT NDA
7788	OTH ELEC MACHY,EQUIP NES		121.5		42.9		58.0		25.2	AUT MACH APP ELEC NDA
77889	ELEC PARTS OF MACHY NES	W 19077	113.8	W 1053	15.9	W 5149	40.5	W 690	9.0	PIECES ELEC DE MACH NDA
78	ROAD VEHICLES		386.8		453.8		551.3		369.1	VEHICULES ROUTIERS
781	PASS MOTOR VEH EXC BUSES	N 29786	174.0	N 35123	217.3	N 186468	244.9	N 32904	153.1	AUTO TRANSPORT PERSONNES
782	LORRIES,SPCL MTR VEH NES		114.4	N 15523	109.5	N 14111	162.1	N 11876	109.2	VEHICULES SPECIAUX,MARCH
7821	LORRIES,TRUCKS	N 9111	100.4	N 15355	93.4	N 13780	132.9	N 11621	80.7	VEHICULES TRANSP MARCHAND
784	MOTOR VEH PRTS,ACCES NES		35.8		42.6		47.0		39.0	PIECES 722,781,782,783
7849	OTHER MOTOR VEHCL PARTS		34.4		41.6		45.9	W 12299	38.3	PIECES 722,781,782,783
785	CYCLES,ETC MOTRZD OR NOT		47.5		66.8		69.8		52.7	MOTOCYCLES SCOOTERS
7851	MOTORCYCLES ETC	N 76863	31.9	N 96071	45.6	N 122414	54.1	N 121637	39.7	MOTO VELO MOTEUR AUXIL
79	OTHR TRANSPORT EQUIPMENT		180.7		158.3		118.6		108.9	AUTRE MATERIEL TRANSPORT
792	AIRCRAFT ETC		136.8		45.5		85.3		87.9	APP NAVIGATION AERIENNE
7924	AIRCRFT NES OVER 15000KG	N 217	64.6	N 23	0.1	N 1742	0.1	N 758	0.1	AERODYNES PLUS 15000 KG
7929	AIRCRAFT PARTS NES	W 1233	69.6	W 698	43.1	W 1080	84.2	W 1496	87.6	PIECES DU 792
793	SHIPS AND BOATS ETC		26.8		90.0		6.7		6.2	NAVIRES BATEAUX,ETC
7933	VESSELS FOR BREAKING UP	N 5	12.5	N 30	67.3			N 1	3.3	BATEAUX A DEPECER
8	MISC MANUFACTURED GOODS		217.9		270.5		317.7		274.7	ART MANUFACTURES DIVERS
87	PRECISION INSTRUMNTS NES		90.4		97.4		116.0		98.8	INSTRUM,APPAR SCIENT NDA
874	MEASURNG,CONTROLNG INSTR		58.9		65.2		70.8		67.4	INSTRUMENTS DE MESURE
88	PHOTO EQU,OPTICL GDS ETC		32.3		43.7		40.5		37.1	APP,FOURN PHOTO,OP,MONTR
882	PHOTO,CINEMA SUPPLIES		27.3		33.0		29.2		26.2	PRODUITS PHOTO,CINEMA
89	MISC MANUFCTRD GOODS NES		87.0		118.5		148.2		125.9	ART MANUFACTURES DIVERS
899	OTHER MANUFACTURED GOODS		35.2		56.2		78.7		65.8	AUT ART MANUF DIVERS NDA
8991	CARVED,MOULDED GOODS		27.3		47.6		68.4		54.6	MAT A TAILLER,A MOULER
89911	GOODS OF ANML CARVNG MTL		24.6		45.1		66.1		53.7	ECAILLE,NACRE,IVOIRE ETC
9	GOODS NOT CLASSD BY KIND		41.4		189.4		384.9		463.5	ART TRANSACT NON CLASSES
931	*SPECIAL TRANSACTIONS		37.4		19.3		55.1		49.6	TRANS.SPECIALES
971	*GOLD,NON MONETARY NES	K 188	2.3	K 12843	168.3	K 28916	328.8	K 39058	413.5	OR NON MONETAIRE
97101	NONMON GLD UNWRT,SEMIMFD	K 188	2.3	K 12843	168.3	K 28450	325.9	K 39058	413.5	OR,ALLIAGES D'OR BRUTS

5. General Exports F.O.B. by Commodities according to the S.I.T.C. (Rev. 2) in million U.S. Dollars
Exportations Générales F.O.B. par Produits d'après la C.T.C.I. (Rév. 2) en millions de Dollars E.U.

SITC CTCI	COMMODITY	1994 QUANTITY QUANTITE	1994 VALUE VALEUR	1995 QUANTITY QUANTITE	1995 VALUE VALEUR	1996 QUANTITY QUANTITE	1996 VALUE VALEUR	1997 QUANTITY QUANTITE	1997 VALUE VALEUR	PRODUIT
	ALL COMMODITIES		7357.0		8157.9		9322.2		8717.0	TOUS PRODUITS
0	FOOD AND LIVE ANIMALS		700.5		930.9		818.1		859.0	ALIMENTS,ANIMAUX VIVANTS
03	FISH AND PREPARATIONS		143.2		150.5		147.1		177.0	POISSONS ET PREPARATIONS
034	FISH,FRESH,CHILLED,FROZN	W 20007	31.7	W 21076	31.6	W 26465	34.0	W 29823	37.7	POISSON FRAIS, REFRIG,CONG
036	SHELL FISH FRESH,FROZEN	W 23891	97.2	W 21943	97.2	W 25160	95.3	W 28820	120.5	CRUSTACES,MOLLUSQUES
04	CEREALS AND PREPARATIONS		319.2		482.4		506.6		491.6	CEREALES ET PRODUITS
042	RICE	W 1398506	316.5	W 1579244	478.8	W 1677545	500.7	W 1873896	485.7	RIZ
0422	RICE SEMI-MILLED,MILLED	W 1398506	316.5	W 1579244	478.8	W 1677545	500.7	W 1873896	485.7	RIZ POLI,GLACE INCL BRISURES
04221	RICE MILLED UNBROKEN	W 1398506	316.5	W 1579244	478.8	W 1677545	500.7	W 1873896	485.7	RIZ POLI,GLACE EXCL BRISURES
05	VEGETABLES AND FRUIT		55.8		53.2		84.7		91.0	LEGUMES ET FRUITS
057	FRUIT,NUTS,FRESH,DRIED	W 133377	42.9	W 119255	37.3	W 179033	60.6	W 234324	71.3	FRUITS FRAIS OU SECS
0579	FRUIT FRESH OR DRIED NES	W 100624	34.8	W 78085	29.6	W 126328	50.1	W 138442	54.6	FRUITS FRAIS,SECS NDA
06	SUGAR AND PREPS,HONEY		143.3		230.0		57.5		76.8	SUCRES ET PRODUITS
061	SUGAR AND HONEY	W 1858368	135.4	W 1953681	222.1	W 751695	51.9	W 1360457	69.3	SUCRES ET MIEL
0612	REFINED SUGAR ETC	W 148862	49.1	W 317623	123.4	W 100	0.1	W 300	0.2	SUCRES RAFFINES
0615	MOLASSES	W 1707164	83.8	W 1630505	95.5	W 746787	47.8	W 1353359	64.7	MELASSES
07	COFFEE,TEA,COCOA,SPICES		30.8		10.4		13.7		12.3	CAFE,THE,CACAO,EPICES
2	CRUDE MATERLS,EXCL FUELS		188.0		348.0		599.0		260.0	MAT BRUTES NON COMESTIBLES
26	TEXTILE FIBRES AND WASTE		103.8		246.5		481.5		178.2	FIBRES TEXTILES
263	COTTON	W 127133	85.0	W 172582	224.6	W 468171	458.7	W 164544	156.1	COTON
2631	RAW COTTON,EXCL LINTERS	W 17129	19.4	W 84197	161.1	W 260365	403.7	W 72380	107.7	COTON EN MASSE
2633	COTTON WASTE,UNCOMBED	W 109802	65.6	W 83465	61.5	W 95534	52.8	W 86065	46.7	DECHETS DE COTON
29	CRUDE ANIMAL,VEG MAT NES		55.3		66.1		83.3		56.9	MATIERES BRUTES ANIM,VEGET
291	CRUDE ANIMAL MTRIALS NES	W 24870	13.9	W 34027	19.6	W 38701	28.7	W 29445	21.1	MATIERES BRUTES ANIMALES
292	CRUDE VEG MATERIALS NES	W 62989	41.5	W 62335	46.6	W 59094	54.7	W 29312	35.9	MAT BRUTES VEGETALES NDA
2922	NAT GUMS,RESINS,LACS,ETC	W 41270	30.4	W 42700	33.5	W 36384	38.5	W 20900	27.3	GOMME LAQUE
3	MINERAL FUELS ETC		57.3		79.8		70.6		75.3	COMBUSTIBLES MINERAUX LUB
33	PETROLEUM AND PRODUCTS		57.3		78.9		69.4		75.3	PETROLE ET DERIVES
333	CRUDE PETROLEUM	W 235159	36.5	W 308217	44.3	W 347075	50.8	W 351470	56.5	HUILES BRUTES DE PETROLE
334	PETROLEUM PRODUCTS,REFIN	W 113300	14.3	W 179023	27.5	W 112021	16.9	W 98625	18.4	PRODUITS RAFFINES
3344	FUEL OILS,NES	W 113300	14.3	W 172709	25.5	W 112010	16.9	W 98625	18.4	FUEL OILS
5	CHEMCLS,RELATED PROD NES		45.3		54.8		72.6		47.7	PRODUITS CHIMIQUES
541	*MEDICINAL,PHARM PRODUCT	K 3597978	32.0	K 3636271	32.4	K 5590706	43.6	K 4870043	32.3	PROD MEDICINAUX PHARMACEUT
5417	MEDICAMENTS	K 2760781	24.4	K 2750759	25.7	K 3529443	28.9	K 2817184	26.5	MEDICAMENTS
54179	— CONTNG OTH SUBSTANCES	K 2760781	24.4	K 2747574	25.6	K 3529257	28.9	K 2803170	26.5	MED CONT AUT SUBSTANCES
6	BASIC MANUFACTURES		4295.9		4584.1		5248.3		4904.8	ART MANUFACTURES
61	LEATHER,DRESSED FUR,ETC		268.6		279.6		275.4		237.3	CUIRS,PELLETERIES
611	LEATHER	A 17244	248.1	A 16794	266.4	A 16379	263.2	A 13441	224.4	CUIRS,PEAUX PREPARES
6113	CALF LEATHER	A 2823	46.6	A 2384	47.5	A 2496	50.9	A 2616	50.2	CUIRS,PEAUX DE VEAUX
6114	LEATHR BOVINE NES,EQUINE	A 5029	75.2	A 4588	71.4	A 4632	70.9	A 2645	44.3	CUIRS DE BOVINS
6115	LEATHER FROM SHEEP,LAMBS	A 1870	29.0	A 1676	27.5	A 1663	29.5	A 1006	18.1	PEAUX D'OVINS PREPAREES
6116	LEATHER OF OTH HIDE,SKIN	A 7519	97.5	A 8141	120.0	A 7589	112.0	A 7165	111.9	PEAUX PREP D'AUTRES ANIMAUX
61161	LEATHER FROM GOAT,KID	A 7485	97.0	A 8078	118.7	A 7468	110.2	A 7145	111.6	PEAUX DE CAPRINS PREPAREES
65	TEXTILE YARN,FABRICS,ETC		3977.7		4256.0		4919.1		4607.8	FILS,TISSUS,ARTICLES TEXTILE
651	TEXTILE YARN	W 562229	1421.6	W 526644	1648.2	W 594825	1672.6	W 542986	1459.1	FILS TEXTILES
6513	COTTON YARN	W 533329	1345.3	W 507338	1587.5	W 570045	1601.6	W 503180	1359.5	FILS DE COTON
6514	SYN FIB YRN,BULK,MONOFIL	W 27973	73.4	W 14626	46.1	W 20544	59.1	W 28641	72.3	FILS CONT 85% FIB TEXT SYNTH
65144	— TEXTRD,CONT POLYESTER	W 27217	71.3	W 13476	42.5	W 19583	55.3	W 27885	70.4	FILS TEX FI CONT POLYESTERS
6516	DISCON SYN FIB BLEND YRN	W 559	1.6	W 4483	14.0	W 4117	11.4	W 10919	26.5	FILS FIBR TEX SYNT DIS MOINS
65166	DISCON SYN FIB–COTTN YRN	W 536	1.5	W 4462	13.8	W 4114	11.4	W 10881	26.4	FILS TEXT SYNT MELANGE COTON
652	COTTON FABRICS,WOVEN	A 1123817	962.5	A 1062294	1072.6	A 1448568	1403.1	A 1284128	1294.4	TISSUS DE COTON
6521	GREY WOVEN COTTON FABRIC	A 525235	461.6	A 502205	516.0	A 603827	583.9	A 513748	519.4	TISSUS COT ECRUS NON MERCER
65214	GREY WOVEN COTTON NES	A 493878	437.5	A 444244	468.6	A 476621	492.5	A 445864	463.8	AUT TISSUS 85% COTON ECRUS
65215	GREY WOVN COTN BLEND NES	A 27909	20.8	A 54874	44.3	A 121946	86.4	A 62283	49.3	AUT TIS MOINS 85% COT ECRUS
6522	WOVEN COTTON BLEACHD,ETC	A 598582	501.0	A 560089	556.6	A 844741	819.2	A 770379	775.1	TISSUS COTON BLANCHIS ETC
65221	COTTON GAUZE BLEACHD,ETC	A 14742	18.1	A 27803	32.4	A 23422	26.0	A 23010	27.9	TISSUS COTON POINT DE GAZE
65224	BLCHED COTTON FABRIC NES	A 482641	385.9	A 407499	378.7	A 478384	432.4	A 388476	395.8	AUT TIS PLUS 85% COT BLANCHI
65225	BLCHD COTN BLEND FAB NES	A 96615	93.4	A 123186	143.9	A 341957	359.8	A 358664	351.2	AUT TIS MOINS 85% COT BLANCH
653	WOVN MAN–MADE FIB FABRIC		651.7		503.1	A 53	0.1	A 120	0.2	TISSUS FIBRES SYNTH,ARTIF
6531	CONT SYNT WEAVES NONPILE	A 853452	650.3	A 533268	502.3	A 594849	517.9	A 649941	566.3	TISSUS FIBRES SYNTH CONTINUE
65314	CONT SYN TYRE CORD FABRC	A 299876	224.5	A 132912	129.6	A 148529	139.4	A 198293	183.1	TIS ARMATURE PNEUMATIQUES
65315	CONT SYN TXTL FABRIC NES	A 553576	425.9	A 400357	372.8	A 446320	378.5	A 451648	383.2	TIS PLUS 85% TEXT SYNT CONT
655	KNITTED,ETC FABRICS		92.0		94.2	W 19353	93.5	W 16309	83.1	ETOF BONNETERIE PIECES ETC
6552	OTHER KNIT ETC FAB NONEL		92.0		94.2	W 19353	93.5	W 16309	83.1	ETOF BON NON ELAS NON SYNT
657	SPECIAL TXTL FABRC,PRODS	W 10723	34.8	W 9917	40.6	W 10300	41.6	W 9546	36.8	TISSUS SPECIAUX
6577	TEXTILES FOR MACHINERY	W 8293	31.1	W 7947	36.8	W 8402	37.7	W 8036	33.7	OUATES,MECHES ART TEXT
65771	TEXTILE WADDING NES ETC	W 8146	30.1	W 7759	36.3	W 8260	37.2	W 7932	33.2	OUATES,ARTICLES EN OUATE
658	TEXTILE ARTICLES NES	N 48000	0.1		726.1	W 5	0.1		956.4	ART FACONNES MAT TEXTILES
6581	BAGS,SACKS OF TEXTILES	W 5722	18.5	W 4685	20.9	W 6970	29.7	W 5666	27.2	SACS EMBALLAGE TEXTILES
6582	MADE-UP CANVAS GOODS	W 15100	33.8	W 14653	38.6	W 14601	36.1	W 15572	46.9	BACHES,TENTES ETC
6584	LINENS ETC		448.8		536.5		0.1		716.9	LINGE DE MAISON
65841	BED LINEN OF COTTON	W 37096	234.2	W 41536	288.6	W 51958	337.0	W 52688	335.3	LINGE DE LIT DE COTON
65842	BED LINEN OF OTHR FIBRES	W 8220	53.1	W 9761	68.8	W 17756	120.6	W 21962	140.3	LINGE DE LIT AUT FIBRES
65845	OTHER LINEN OF COTTON	W 30280	137.2	W 30641	154.6	W 42249	205.4	W 41435	195.1	LINGE DE TOILETTE COTON
65849	OTH FURN ART OF OTH FIBR	N 6172308	16.2	N 4473024	15.7	N 8951760	28.3	MN 9283	35.5	AUT ART AMEUBLEMENT AUT FIBR
6589	OTH TEXTILE ARTICLES NES	N 48000	0.1		125.1		154.8	MN 543426	160.4	AUT ART EN TEXTILES NDA
65898	KNITTED ETC ARTICLES NES		90.5		105.2	MN 532303718	119.5	MN 513432	114.2	ART BONNET NON ELASTIQUE
65899	TXTL ARTCLES NONKNIT NES	MN 17491	18.6	MN 17143	20.0	MN 28382	35.3	MN 29994	46.3	ART TIS AUT QUE BONNETERIE
659	FLOOR COVERINGS,ETC	A 3430	191.2	A 2602	151.8	A 4450	238.5	A 3428	197.3	COUVRE-PARQUETS,TAPIS ETC
6592	CARPETS ETC KNOTTED	A 3011	187.6	A 2317	149.0	A 3789	230.9	A 2875	192.2	TAPIS POINTS NOUES,ENROULES
65921	— OF WOOL OR FINE HAIR	A 3011	187.5	A 2317	149.0	A 3789	230.9	A 2871	192.2	TAP NOUES,ENROULES LAINE
69	METAL MANUFACTURES NES		28.6		30.1		29.7		28.9	ART MANUFACT EN METAL NDA
7	MACHINES,TRANSPORT EQUIP		34.3		43.9		55.2		110.0	MACHINES MATERIEL TRANSPORT
72	MACHS FOR SPCL INDUSTRYS		13.6		14.3		19.6		36.9	MAC SPECIALES POUR INDUST
8	MISC MANUFACTURED GOODS		2011.2		2090.6		2441.1		2444.4	ART MANUFACTURES DIVERS
84	CLOTHING AND ACCESSORIES		1615.1		1665.1		1941.0		1888.5	VETEMENTS
842	MENS OUTERWEAR NOT KNIT	MN 100924	242.6	MN 82900	222.6	MN 290891	280.0	MN 107514	333.8	VET DESSUS POUR HOMMES
8422	— SUITS	MN 12942	28.7	MN 14902	27.6	MN 15036	30.0	N 782364	2.3	COMPLETS HOMMES MAT TEXT
84223	—— OF MAN-MADE FIBRES	MN 12932	28.7	MN 14898	27.6	MN 15036	30.0	N 773004	2.3	COMPLETS HOMMES FIB SYNT
8423	— TROUSERS,BREECHES ETC	MN 48503	112.1	MN 44614	123.4	MN 50492	159.2	MN 60700	199.7	PANTALONS HOMMES MAT TEX
8424	— JACKETS,BLAZERS ETC	MN 10869	34.1	N 5595624	23.3	MN 156661	31.7	MN 9136	37.5	VESTES HOMMES MAT TEXTIL
8429	— OTHER OUTER GARMENTS	MN 28554	67.7	MN 17786	48.5	MN 68683	59.2	MN 36895	94.3	AUT VET DES HOM MAT TEX
843	WOMENS OUTERWEAR NONKNIT	MN 73255	184.7	MN 61332	163.7	MN 72752	221.0	MN 51216	155.2	VET DESSUS FEMMES MAT TEX
8432	— SUITS AND COSTUMES	N 7889052	19.5	MN 10856	27.5	MN 24083	58.4	N 5022672	15.5	COSTUMES-TAIL MAT TEXIL
8433	— DRESSES	MN 16751	38.9	MN 12432	36.9	MN 9962	32.2	MN 11375	37.7	ROBES EN MAT-TEXTILES
8435	— BLOUSES	MN 13423	34.9	N 7723668	21.2	MN 9123	27.0	N 6383916	19.1	BLOUSES FEM MAT TEXTILES
8439	— OTHER OUTER GARMENTS	MN 30907	80.4	MN 27253	68.8	MN 25425	90.4	MN 26420	75.7	AUT VET DES FEM MAT TEXT
844	UNDER GARMENTS NOT KNIT	MN 61919	155.8	MN 54767	167.9	MN 62650	204.6	MN 63972	232.0	VETEMENT DESSOUS MAT TEX
8441	— MENS SHIRTS	MN 43131	109.6	MN 40443	122.2	MN 49142	165.7	MN 50071	187.6	CHEMISES HOMMES MAT TEXT
84411	—— OF COTTON	MN 39786	102.4	MN 38201	116.5	MN 46669	158.6	MN 47382	180.1	CHEMISES HOMMES DE COTON
8442	— MENS,OTHR THAN SHIRTS	MN 18182	45.3	MN 14065	45.0	MN 13362	38.6	MN 13590	43.7	SOUS-VET HOMMES MAT TEXT

5. General Exports F.O.B. by Commodities according to the S.I.T.C. (Rev. 2) in million U.S. Dollars
Exportations Générales F.O.B. par Produits d'après la C.T.C.I. (Rév. 2) en millions de Dollars E.U.

SITC CTCI	COMMODITY	1994		1995		1996		1997		PRODUIT
		QUANTITY QUANTITE	VALUE VALEUR	QUANTITY QUANTITE	VALUE VALEUR	QUANTITY QUANTITE	VALUE VALEUR	QUANTITY QUANTITE	VALUE VALEUR	
845	OUTERWEAR KNIT NONELASTC	MN 65212	183.3	MN 63858	195.1	MN 783382	238.4	MN 69629	214.5	VET DESSOUS,ACCES BONNET
8459	— OTHER,CLTHG ACCESRYS	MN 53926	157.8	MN 55471	171.8	MN 396737	209.1	MN 60866	190.6	AUT VET DESSUS DE BONNE
846	UNDER GARMENTS KNITTED	MN 132654	319.9	MN 125016	365.7	MN 1186200	398.1	MN 99000	373.1	SOUS VETS DE BONNETERIE
8462	— OF COTTON NON ELASTIC	MN 54070	118.5	MN 42200	110.3	MN 399582	118.0	MN 29383	85.8	SOUS–VET BONNET COTON
84629	—— OTHER	MN 54070	118.5	MN 42200	110.3	MN 399582	118.0	MN 29383	85.8	AUT SOUS–VET BONNET COTON
8463	— OF SYNTH FBR NONELAST	MN 77733	200.4	MN 81921	254.2	MN 784875	279.0	MN 69015	286.7	SOUS–VET BONNET FIB SYNT
84632	—— MENS SHIRTS	MN 77362	200.0	MN 81637	253.9	MN 211395	278.9	MN 68918	286.6	CHEMISES DE BON FIB SYNMT
847	TEXTILE CLTHNG ACCES NES	MN 257976	139.0	MN 254893	167.4	MN *********	161.0	MN 289145	145.6	ACCES VET MAT TEXT NDA
8471	— NOT KNITTED	MN 106023	51.6	MN 79455	46.7	MN 107815507	48.7	MN 117861	50.8	ACCES VET MAT TEX NON BON
84712	SHAWLS,VEILS ETC,NOT KNT	MN 26467	28.8	MN 20944	28.1	MN 15033	20.5	MN 18392	23.4	ECHARPES ETC MAT TEXT
8472	CLTHNG ACCESRYS ETC KNIT	MN 151953	87.5	MN 175438	120.7	MN *********	112.4	MN 171283	94.8	ACCES VET BONNE NDA
84721	KNIT GLOVES,ETC NONELAST	MN 95403	27.9	MN 107009	38.5	MN *********	35.2	MN 108111	32.1	GANTERIE BONNET NON ELAS
84722	KNIT SOCKS,ETC NONELASTC	MN 56551	59.7	MN 68429	82.2	MN 320743321	77.3	MN 63172	62.8	CHAUSSETTES BON. NON ELAS
848	HEADGEAR,NONTXTL CLOTHNG	MN 56733	389.9	MN 64048	382.9	MN 55904	438.3	MN 58401	434.6	VET ACCES MAT AUT QUE TEX
8481	LEATHER CLOTHES,ACCESSOR	MN 56286	389.5	MN 63864	382.6	MN 55261	437.8	MN 58224	434.3	VET ACCES MAT CUIR ARTIF
851	*FOOTWEAR	P 8440551	31.7	MP 10078	48.0	P 8085522	48.0	P 7857454	45.4	CHAUSSURES
85102	FOOTWEAR LEATHER	P 8332896	31.0	MP 9923	47.2	P 7729997	45.3	P 7546092	42.9	CHAUS SEMELLES EN CUIR
87	PRECISION INSTRUMNTS NES		94.7		110.8		138.2		136.3	INSTRUM,APPAR SCIENT NDA
872	MEDICAL INSTRUMENTS NES	MN 65698	93.9	MN 76250	108.2	MN 96893	135.6	MN 96133	131.7	INSTR,APP MEDIC–CHIR NDA
87202	OTH MEDICAL INSTRUMENTS	MN 65698	93.9	MN 76250	108.2	MN 96891	135.6	MN 96132	131.6	INSTRUM,APP MEDECINE
89	MISC MANUFCTRD GOODS NES		257.5		257.9		305.8		364.6	ART MANUFACTURES DIVERS
894	TOYS,SPORTING GOODS,ETC		194.6	MN 57130	189.1		223.4	N 21804	0.1	VOITURES ENFANTS,JOUETS
8947	OTH SPORT GDS,FAIR AMUSM	MN 68722	194.0	MN 55622	188.2	MN 4665086	222.5	MN 73918	275.9	AUT ART DE SPORT
89472	OTH OUTDOOR SPORT GOODS	MN 66871	193.7	MN 55217	188.1	MN 61407	222.3	MN 73477	275.7	ART POUR JEUX PLEIN AIR
899	OTHER MANUFACTURED GOODS		43.5		47.5		59.0		65.3	AUT ART MANUF DIVERS NDA
8991	CARVED,MOULDED GOODS		41.7		44.9		53.9		55.1	MAT A TAILLER,A MOULER
89911	GOODS OF ANML CARVNG MTL		41.7		44.8		53.9		55.0	ECAILLE,NACRE,IVOIRE ETC

1. HISTORICAL SERIES, 1962–1997 SPECIAL TRADE, IMPORTS C.I.F., EXPORTS F.O.B. # 1
SERIES HISTORIQUES, 1962–1997 COMMERCE SPECIAL, IMPORTATIONS C.A.F., EXPORTATIONS F.O.B

YEAR ANNEE	VALUE IN MILLION BALBOAS VALEUR EN MILLION BALBOAS MERCHANDISE –MARCHANDISE		GOLD –OR		CONVERSION FACTORS U.S. CENTS PER BALBOA FACTEURS DE CONVERSION CENTS E.U. PAR BALBOA		INDEX NUMBERS –INDICES QUANTUM		UNIT VALUE VALEUR UNITAIRE	
	IMPORTS	EXPORTS	IMPORTS	EXPORTS	IMPORTS	EXPORTS	IMPORTS	EXPORTS	IMPORTS	EXPORTS
1962	145.20	48.00	0.39		100.0000	100.0000				
1963	162.80	60.00	0.31		100.0000	100.0000				
1964	181.40	69.70	0.53		100.0000	100.0000				
1965	208.40	79.30	0.43		100.0000	100.0000				
1966	234.80	89.50	0.34		100.0000	100.0000				
1967	250.70	93.90	0.66		100.0000	100.0000				
1968	266.30	99.80	0.71		100.0000	100.0000				
1969	305.40	112.70	2.30		100.0000	100.0000				
1970	357.00	106.30	0.86		100.0000	100.0000				
1971	395.80	114.90	0.95		100.0000	100.0000				
1972	440.50	121.10	0.57		100.0000	100.0000				
1973	508.00	135.30	0.66		100.0000	100.0000				
1974	829.20	204.30			100.0000	100.0000				
1975	952.50	304.90			100.0000	100.0000				
1976	912.20	256.50			100.0000	100.0000				
1977	938.10	270.80			100.0000	100.0000				
1978	845.00	247.00			100.0000	100.0000				
1979	1063.00	295.00			100.0000	100.0000				
1980	1288.90	353.40			100.0000	100.0000		117		110
1981	1562.10	319.40			100.0000	100.0000		103		110
1982	1568.30	309.30			100.0000	100.0000		116		99
1983	1413.00	303.50			100.0000	100.0000		102		110
1984	1429.60	256.30			100.0000	100.0000		81		111
1985	1391.80	306.50			100.0000	100.0000		97		106
1986	1283.75	327.05			100.0000	100.0000		95		93
1987	1306.36	336.16			100.0000	100.0000		94		103
1988	815.07	292.45			100.0000	100.0000		79		94
1989	964.76	297.21			100.0000	100.0000		93		95
1990	1538.60	340.10			100.0000	100.0000		100		100
1991	1695.00	358.40			100.0000	100.0000		95		101
1992	2023.60	501.50			100.0000	100.0000		97		
1993	2187.80	553.20			100.0000	100.0000		116		
1994	2404.10	583.30			100.0000	100.0000				
1995	2510.70	625.20			100.0000	100.0000				
1996	2779.90	622.62			100.0000	100.0000				
1997		684.00				100.0000				

2. IMPORTS BY BROAD ECONOMIC CATEGORY AND EXPORTS BY INDUSTRIAL ORIGIN. (PERCENTAGE OF TOTAL VALUE)
IMPORTATIONS PAR CATEGORIES ECONOMIQUES ET EXPORTATIONS PAR BRANCHE D'ACTIVITE.(EN POURCENTAGE DE LA VALEUR TOTALE)

IMPORTS – IMPORTATIONS

	1990	1991	1992	1993	1994	1995	1996
TOTAL IMPORTS–IMPORTATIONS TOTALES	100.	100.	100.	100.	100.	100.	100.
1 FOOD BEV–ALIMENTATION BOISSONS	10.7	9.3	8.7	8.2	8.4	8.3	8.3
11 PRIMARY–PRODUITS DE BASE	2.9	2.4	2.1	2.0	2.1	2.3	2.3
111 FOR INDUSTRY–POUR L'INDUSTRIE	1.3	1.1	1.0	0.9	1.1	1.1	1.1
112 FOR HOUSEHOLDS–POUR LES MENAGES	1.6	1.3	1.1	1.0	1.0	1.2	1.2
12 PROCESSED–PRODUITS ELABORES	7.8	6.9	6.6	6.3	6.3	6.0	6.0
121 FOR INDUSTRY–POUR L'INDUSTRIE	2.2	1.8	1.3	1.4	1.5	1.5	1.2
122 FOR HOUSEHOLDS–POUR LES MENAGES	5.6	5.1	5.3	4.8	4.8	4.5	4.8
2 IND SUPPLIES–APPROV INDUSTRIELS	29.6	28.1	28.7	28.2	29.0	29.7	27.0
21 PRIMARY–PRODUITS DE BASE	1.3	1.0	1.8	2.0	2.0	2.1	2.2
22 PROCESSED–PRODUITS ELABORES	28.3	27.0	26.9	26.2	27.1	27.6	24.9
3 FUELS–COMBUSTIBLES	16.4	14.9	15.0	12.6	12.8	13.5	15.8
31 PRIMARY–PRODUITS DE BASE	14.1	10.0	12.3	9.6	6.1	6.8	11.8
32 PROCESSED–PRODUITS ELABORES	2.3	4.9	2.7	3.0	6.7	6.7	4.0
321 MOTOR SPIRIT–ESSENCE	0.9	1.5	0.9	1.2	1.5	0.6	1.0
322 OTHER–AUTRES	1.4	3.4	1.8	1.8	5.2	6.2	3.0
4 MACHINERY–EQUIPEMENT	9.1	12.2	13.2	16.0	15.6	15.7	15.4
41 CAPITAL EQUIPMENT–MACHINES	7.9	10.8	11.6	14.1	13.5	13.7	13.2
42 PARTS–PIECES ACCESSOIRES	1.2	1.3	1.6	1.8	2.0	2.0	2.2
5 TRANSPORT–TRANSPORT	9.4	13.1	13.9	14.7	14.3	13.2	14.3
51 PASSENGER CARS–AUTOMOBILES	3.5	5.2	5.3	5.8	5.5	6.8	8.5
52 OTHER–AUTRES	2.5	3.9	4.4	4.9	4.9	2.6	2.3
521 INDUSTRIAL–INDUSTRIELS	2.3	3.8	4.2	4.7	4.7	2.4	2.1
522 NON INDUSTRIAL–NON INDUSTRIEL	0.1	0.2	0.2	0.2	0.2	0.1	0.1
53 PARTS–PIECES ACCESSOIRES	3.5	3.9	4.2	4.0	3.9	3.9	3.5
6 CONSUM GOODS–BIENS CONSOMMATION	24.7	22.4	20.3	20.3	19.8	19.5	19.1
61 DURABLE–DURABLES	4.8	4.9	4.5	4.4	4.4	4.2	4.3
62 SEMI DURABLE–SEMI DURABLES	12.5	10.7	9.7	9.7	9.0	8.9	8.7
63 NON DURABLE–NON DURABLES	7.4	6.9	6.1	6.2	6.4	6.4	6.1
7 GOODS NES–BIENS NDA	0.1	0.1	0.1	0.1	0.1	0.0	0.0

EXPORTS – EXPORTATIONS

	1990	1991	1992	1993	1994	1995	1996
TOTAL EXPORTS–EXPORTATIONS TOTALES	100.	100.	100.	100.	100.	100.	100.
1 AGRICULTURE	53.9	67.3	68.4	65.0	65.0	63.9	60.6
2 MINING QUARRY–INDUS EXTRACTIVES	0.0	0.0	0.0	0.0	0.0	0.0	0.1
3 MANUFACTURING–IND MANUFACTUR	46.1	32.7	31.6	35.0	35.0	36.0	39.3
31 FOOD BEV TOBACCO–ALIM BOISS TAB	23.4	15.8	13.4	16.4	13.2	11.3	12.3
32 TEXTILES–INDUSTRIES TEXTILES	8.1	7.1	7.6	6.8	6.2	6.0	6.0
33 WOOD & PRODUCTS–BOIS & PRODUITS	0.2	0.1	0.2	0.3	0.4	0.4	0.4
34 PAPER & PRODUCTS–PAPIER & PRODT	1.9	1.4	1.3	1.2	2.0	2.9	2.3
35 CHEMICALS–INDUSTRIES CHIMIQUES	5.5	5.4	6.0	6.8	7.8	8.7	10.5
36 NON METAL MIN–MIN NON METAL	0.5	0.5	0.6	0.6	0.6	0.5	0.4
37 BASIC METAL–IND METAL BASE	0.8	0.6	0.5	0.4	0.6	0.2	0.5
38 METAL MANUF–MANUF METAL	4.5	1.4	1.5	1.4	1.8	2.6	4.2
39 OTH MANUF IND–AUTRES MANUF	1.2	0.5	0.5	1.1	2.6	3.4	2.6

3. TRADE BY PRINCIPAL COUNTRIES OF ORIGIN AND DESTINATION (VALUE IN MILLION U.S. DOLLARS)
ECHANGES SELON LES PRINCIPAUX PAYS D'ORIGINE ET DE DESTINATION (VALEUR EN MILLIONS DE DOLLARS EU)

COUNTRIES–PAYS	SPECIAL IMPORTS C.I.F. IMPORTATIONS SPECIALES C.A.F				
	1992	1993	1994	1995	1996
World	2018.4	2199.8	2402.1	2510.7	2779.7
Africa	5.6	4.8	8.5	5.2	2.7
Americas	1250.0	1336.0	1475.2	1632.2	1844.2
– Northern America	762.2	837.1	969.5	1042.1	1079.2
– LAIA	307.1	303.1	329.9	422.4	589.5
– CACM	95.7	107.8	125.3	138.0	148.4
– Caribbean	85.1	88.0	50.4	29.7	26.8
– Rest of America	0.0	0.0	0.0	0.0	0.3
Asia excl fmr USSR	261.9	271.2	287.8	252.0	295.6
– Middle East	0.2	1.1	0.6	1.7	3.8
Asia former USSR					
Europe excl fmr USSR	157.6	197.5	231.3	222.2	231.1
– European Union	144.2	170.8	204.7	202.8	216.7
– Eastern Europe	2.1	10.8	15.6	4.2	1.4
– Rest of Europe	11.3	15.8	11.0	15.2	13.0
Europe former USSR	0.0	4.2	3.1	2.6	0.2
Oceania	9.2	9.1	9.3	12.1	11.8
Other	334.0	377.0	386.8	384.4	394.1
USA/Etats–Unis d'Amer	746.6	819.0	943.7	1009.2	1052.0
Free zones/Zone franches	327.8	370.1	379.1	375.4	384.4
Japan/Japon	165.3	170.9	173.0	126.8	168.0
Ecuador/Equateur	126.8	84.3	104.9	134.0	107.4
Venezuela	41.9	38.2	53.4	78.0	198.8
Mexico/Mexique	40.6	60.9	47.3	85.8	106.9
Costa Rica	54.7	61.0	68.2	75.0	75.5
Colombia/Colombie	35.3	52.4	47.6	48.9	98.3
Korea, Republic of	40.9	38.8	56.2	54.7	55.8
Germany/Allemagne	34.5	41.5	43.6	46.9	46.7
Brazil/Brésil	31.1	32.9	40.7	37.2	30.9
Guatemala	25.5	29.3	32.7	37.4	42.1
Aruba	64.5	66.4	15.6	9.3	5.0
Other Asia n.e.s.	27.5	28.5	25.0	28.1	24.2
Spain/Espagne	15.4	22.5	24.6	31.2	27.5
Netherlands/Pays–Bas	9.5	8.8	42.1	33.9	25.4
Canada	15.5	18.0	25.8	32.5	25.8
China, Hong Kong SAR	20.2	22.3	21.6	21.7	26.9
Italy/Italie	16.0	18.6	33.3	23.0	21.0
United Kingdom	17.1	14.9	14.0	16.0	17.9
Chile/Chili	12.1	14.0	15.2	17.5	19.2
France, Monaco	16.9	18.1	14.3	14.1	14.3
El Salvador	11.2	12.3	13.4	14.8	20.8
Argentina/Argentine	10.7	14.2	14.1	12.2	19.1
Trinidad and Tobago	9.1	17.0	15.9	9.9	8.1
Belgium–Luxembourg	8.0	7.7	9.1	12.4	16.5
Denmark/Danemark	8.3	8.4	7.4	8.9	19.9
Sweden/Suède	9.4	9.7	7.1	5.8	19.2
New Zealand	8.3	8.8	8.8	11.8	11.4
Switzerland,Liechtenst.	9.0	7.9	8.8	9.7	10.4
Peru/Pérou	8.5	6.2	6.6	8.5	8.2
Bunkers, ship stores	6.2	6.9	7.8	7.6	8.4
Netherlands Antilles	4.9	1.5	14.4	6.3	8.5
Honduras	3.8	5.0	9.4	9.0	7.0
Ireland/Irlande	6.1	5.9	5.5	5.2	5.1
So. African Customs Un	5.1	4.8	8.5	5.2	2.7
China/Chine	1.4	1.6	2.5	6.5	6.1
Norway,Svalbard and JM	2.2	7.9	2.0	3.2	1.0
Thailand/Thaïlande	1.7	1.8	2.8	3.4	4.3
Bulgaria/Bulgarie	0.0	4.6	6.8	1.9	

COUNTRIES–PAYS	SPECIAL EXPORTS F.O.B. EXPORTATIONS SPECIALES F.O.B.				
	1992	1993	1994	1995	1996
Monde	480.9	506.8	539.8	577.2	569.2
Afrique		0.0	0.2	0.1	0.0
Amériques	238.3	297.0	334.8	384.4	418.0
– Amérique du Nord	153.6	190.9	225.3	264.8	299.0
– ALAI	18.7	28.8	22.4	21.9	25.7
– MCAC	56.4	64.0	72.4	83.4	76.4
– Caraïbes	9.4	12.5	14.2	14.2	16.4
– Autre Amérique	0.3	0.8	0.5	0.2	0.5
Asie anc. URSS exclus	2.9	2.7	4.2	7.2	7.9
– Moyen–Orient	0.7	0.0	0.0	0.0	0.2
Asie ancienne URSS					
Europe anc. URSS exclus	219.7	193.3	182.8	177.2	130.3
– Union Européenne	218.9	193.3	182.3	176.8	130.2
– Europe de l'Est			0.4	0.2	0.0
– Autre de l'Europe	0.8	0.0	0.2	0.2	0.1
Europe ancienne URSS		0.0	2.6	1.4	0.7
Océanie	4.6	8.0	8.2	0.5	1.1
Autre	15.4	5.8	7.0	6.2	11.3
USA/Etats–Unis d'Amer	151.3	187.2	220.7	257.4	286.3
Germany/Allemagne	134.9	72.4	69.0	71.7	25.2
Sweden/Suède	22.0	49.1	48.5	28.0	57.8
Costa Rica	30.9	32.4	36.5	41.8	37.7
Belgium–Luxembourg	10.0	27.9	37.9	27.5	23.7
Italy/Italie	39.9	27.8	9.5	6.2	5.8
Guatemala	7.6	9.1	11.6	14.8	15.0
Spain/Espagne	8.8	7.4	10.7	12.6	14.4
El Salvador	9.7	8.1	10.9	9.9	9.4
Honduras	5.1	11.4	9.0	12.4	9.9
Free zones/Zone franches	15.4	5.8	7.0	6.2	11.1
Mexico/Mexique	6.3	18.1	7.6	0.5	2.1
Portugal		3.9	0.9	26.3	
Colombia/Colombie	2.8	3.8	5.7	9.0	9.2
Canada	2.2	3.5	4.6	7.2	11.4
New Zealand	4.6	8.0	7.4		
Ecuador/Equateur	1.8	2.0	3.5	7.0	5.4
Nicaragua	3.1	3.1	4.6	4.5	4.4
Netherlands Antilles	3.7	3.5	4.4	3.0	4.0
Cuba	1.0	2.0	1.8	3.4	4.5
Venezuela	3.9	2.1	1.9	0.9	2.8
China, Hong Kong SAR	1.1	1.9	2.2	3.2	2.7
Japan/Japon	1.0	0.4	1.9	3.5	4.4
Netherlands/Pays–Bas	2.0	2.0	3.8	2.1	0.3
Dominican Republic	1.2	1.2	1.5	2.0	3.5
Aruba	1.6	1.4	1.5	2.0	1.7
Peru/Pérou	1.0	0.9	1.1	2.1	2.3
United Kingdom	0.1	0.9	0.7	2.0	2.0
Haiti/Haïti	0.0	2.2	2.0	1.1	0.1
Russian Federation		0.0	2.6	1.4	0.7
Jamaica/Jamaïque	0.3	0.9	1.0	1.0	1.5
France, Monaco	1.0	1.8	0.9	0.3	0.6
Bolivia/Bolivie	0.4	0.3	0.9	0.7	1.9
Chile/Chili	0.2	0.5	0.4	1.0	1.4
Argentina/Argentine	1.8	0.6	0.2	0.2	0.2
Australia/Australie	0.0	0.0	0.8	0.5	1.1
Barbados/Barbade	0.5	0.4	1.0	0.0	0.1
Bahamas	0.2	0.3	0.3	0.9	0.3
Trinidad and Tobago	0.1	0.2	0.5	0.5	0.7
Brazil/Brésil	0.2	0.1	0.9	0.3	0.4

(VALUE AS PERCENTAGE OF WORLD TOTAL)(VALEURS EN POURCENTAGE DU TOTAL MONDIAL)

	1987	1988	1989	1990	1991	1992	1993	1994	1995	1996
Africa	0.0	0.0	0.2	0.1	0.3	0.3	0.2	0.4	0.2	0.1
Americas	61.3	66.2	65.0	62.2	60.6	61.9	60.7	61.4	65.0	66.3
– Northern America	35.4	38.6	39.1	35.7	37.3	37.8	38.1	40.4	41.5	38.8
– LAIA	20.2	21.0	17.4	20.2	15.8	15.2	13.8	13.7	16.8	21.2
– CACM	5.0	6.2	6.1	5.0	4.8	4.7	4.9	5.2	5.5	5.3
– Caribbean	0.7	0.3	2.5	1.3	2.7	4.2	4.0	2.1	1.2	1.0
– Rest of America	0.0	0.0	0.0	0.0	0.0	0.0	0.0	0.0	0.0	0.0
Asia excl fmr USSR	14.7	8.9	9.6	9.5	12.2	13.0	12.3	12.0	10.0	10.6
– Middle East	1.5	0.0	0.6	0.0	0.0	0.0	0.0	0.0	0.1	0.1
Asia former USSR										
Europe excl fmr USSR	11.0	12.3	10.8	8.7	8.6	7.8	9.0	9.6	8.9	8.3
– European Union	10.2	11.3	9.7	7.7	7.7	7.1	7.8	8.5	8.1	7.8
– Eastern Europe	0.2	0.2	0.2	0.2	0.2	0.1	0.5	0.7	0.2	0.1
– Rest of Europe	0.7	0.8	0.8	0.7	0.7	0.6	0.7	0.5	0.6	0.5
Europe former USSR	0.0	0.0	0.0	0.0	0.0	0.0	0.2	0.1	0.1	0.0
Oceania	0.4	0.6	0.7	0.4	0.4	0.5	0.4	0.4	0.5	0.4
Other	12.6	12.1	13.7	19.1	17.9	16.5	17.1	16.1	15.3	14.2
USA/Etats–Unis d'Amer	34.4	37.7	38.4	34.9	35.8	37.0	37.2	39.3	40.2	37.8
Free zones/Zone franches	12.6	12.1	13.7	19.1	17.9	16.2	16.8	15.8	15.0	13.8
Japan/Japon	7.4	4.6	4.3	5.0	6.8	8.2	7.8	7.2	5.1	6.0
Ecuador/Equateur	2.0	4.1	6.2	11.1	6.2	6.3	3.8	4.4	5.3	3.9
Venezuela	4.0	4.2	3.2	2.4	2.7	2.1	1.7	2.2	3.1	7.2
Mexico/Mexique	8.5	7.6	2.9	1.7	1.8	2.0	2.8	2.0	3.4	3.8
Costa Rica	3.0	3.3	3.4	2.9	2.7	2.7	2.8	2.8	3.0	2.7
Colombia/Colombie	1.7	1.3	1.2	1.8	2.0	1.8	2.4	2.0	1.9	3.5
Korea, Republic of	2.0	1.4	1.3	1.7	2.3	2.0	1.8	2.3	2.2	2.0
Germany/Allemagne					2.3	1.7	1.9	1.8	1.9	1.7

	1987	1988	1989	1990	1991	1992	1993	1994	1995	1996
Afrique	0.0	0.2	0.1	0.0			0.0	0.0	0.0	0.0
Amériques	80.9	69.1	69.0	66.5	49.8	49.6	58.6	62.0	66.6	73.4
– Amérique du Nord	68.9	50.7	47.4	46.2	32.3	31.9	37.7	41.7	45.9	52.5
– ALAI	2.1	4.3	4.1	5.4	5.5	3.9	5.7	4.1	3.8	4.5
– MCAC	8.6	11.5	12.2	13.2	10.2	11.7	12.6	13.4	14.4	13.4
– Caraïbes	1.3	2.4	4.5	1.7	1.7	2.0	2.5	2.6	2.5	2.9
– Autre Amérique	0.1	0.1	0.8	0.1	0.1	0.1	0.2	0.1	0.0	0.1
Asie anc. URSS exclus	1.8	1.5	1.1	1.0	1.7	0.6	0.5	0.8	1.3	1.4
– Moyen–Orient	1.2	0.4	0.5	0.0	0.0	0.1	0.0	0.0	0.0	0.0
Asie ancienne URSS										
Europe anc. URSS exclus	16.5	27.8	28.0	30.1	44.5	45.7	38.1	33.9	30.7	22.9
– Union Européenne	16.2	25.7	27.3	29.9	44.4	45.5	38.1	33.8	30.6	22.9
– Europe de l'Est	0.0	2.1	0.7	0.2	0.0			0.1	0.0	0.0
– Autre de l'Europe	0.3	0.0	0.0	0.1	0.1	0.2	0.0	0.0	0.0	0.0
Europe ancienne URSS				0.0			0.0	0.5	0.3	0.1
Océanie		0.0		0.0	0.4	1.0	1.6	1.5	0.1	0.2
Autre	0.7	1.4	1.8	2.3	3.6	3.2	1.2	1.3	1.1	2.0
USA/Etats–Unis d'Amer	67.5	49.0	46.1	45.1	31.6	31.5	36.9	40.9	44.6	50.3
Germany/Allemagne					25.6	28.0	14.3	12.8	12.4	4.4
Sweden/Suède	1.6	2.1	1.6	1.9	3.6	4.6	9.7	9.0	4.9	10.2
Costa Rica	5.8	7.0	8.2	9.0	5.9	6.4	6.4	6.8	7.2	6.6
Belgium–Luxembourg	4.1	4.3	6.0	5.4	4.7	2.1	5.5	7.0	4.8	4.2
Italy/Italie	2.5	4.7	3.7	4.5	8.6	8.3	5.5	1.8	1.1	1.0
Guatemala	0.8	1.3	1.6	1.1	1.4	1.6	1.8	2.1	2.6	2.6
Spain/Espagne	0.9	1.1	1.6	2.1	1.6	1.8	1.5	2.0	2.2	2.5
El Salvador	0.8	1.0	0.9	1.1	1.4	2.0	1.6	2.0	1.7	1.7
Honduras	0.6	0.7	0.9	1.1	0.8	1.1	2.2	1.7	2.1	1.7

4. Special Imports C.I.F. by Commodities according to the S.I.T.C. (Rev. 2) in million U.S. Dollars
Importations Spéciales C.A.F. par Produits d'après la C.T.C.I. (Rév. 2) en millions de Dollars E.U.

SITC CTCI	COMMODITY	1993		1994		1995		1996		PRODUIT
		QUANTITY QUANTITE	VALUE VALEUR	QUANTITY QUANTITE	VALUE VALEUR	QUANTITY QUANTITE	VALUE VALEUR	QUANTITY QUANTITE	VALUE VALEUR	
	ALL COMMODITIES		2199.8		2402.1		2510.8		2779.8	TOUS PRODUITS
0	FOOD AND LIVE ANIMALS		199.0		215.8		233.2		268.7	ALIMENTS,ANIMAUX VIVANTS
01	MEAT AND PREPARATIONS		11.0		11.8		8.9		10.3	VIANDES ET PREPARATIONS
014	MEAT PREPD,PRSVD,NES ETC	W 3073	6.8	W 3672	7.3	W 2854	6.1	W 3616	7.4	CONSERVES DE VIANDES
02	DAIRY PRODCTS,BIRDS'EGGS		11.4		13.0		15.7		16.6	PRODUITS LAITIERS,OEUFS
022	MILK AND CREAM	W 2142	4.3	W 3010	5.6	W 5163	11.3	W 4814	11.7	LAIT ET CREME
03	FISH AND PREPARATIONS		12.0		11.2		11.3		14.3	POISSONS ET PREPARATIONS
037	FISH ETC PREPD,PRSVD NES	W 4606	10.1	W 4599	9.2	W 4782	8.9	W 5808	11.4	POIS,CRUST,MOL PREPARES
0371	FISH PREPARD,PRESRVD NES	W 4575	9.9	W 4569	9.0	W 4753	8.8	W 5754	11.1	CONSERVES DE POISSONS
04	CEREALS AND PREPARATIONS		64.3		70.0		79.9		91.6	CEREALES ET PRODUITS
041	WHEAT ETC UNMILLED	W 82818	17.1	W 116722	22.5	W 94304	19.9	W 102045	24.7	FROMENT,EPEAUTRE
0411	DURUM WHEAT UNMILLED	W 82818	17.1	W 116722	22.5	W 94304	19.9	W 95754	23.3	FROMENT DUR NON MOULU
044	MAIZE UNMILLED	W 166754	23.6	W 148519	22.1	W 165307	26.1	W 183034	34.0	MAIS NON MOULU
048	CEREAL ETC PREPARATIONS	W 18996	21.1	W 22376	22.4	W 24252	28.0	W 24425	31.4	PREPTNS A BASE CEREALES
0481	PREPD BREAKFAST FOOD ETC	W 1941	8.8	W 1970	8.0	W 3309	10.4	W 3988	12.8	CEREALES TRAVAILLEES
04812	CEREAL ROASTED, PUFFED	W 1941	8.8	W 1970	8.0	W 2548	9.6	W 3094	11.7	PRODTS BASE CEREALES
0482	MALT INCLUDING FLOUR	W 14400	5.3	W 15925	5.2	W 16610	6.5	W 15756	8.5	MALT MEME TORREFIE
05	VEGETABLES AND FRUIT		40.4		43.0		44.0		47.5	LEGUMES ET FRUITS
054	VEG ETC FRSH,SMPLY PRSVD	W 8711	6.5	W 6655	5.5	W 12919	10.0	W 16223	10.2	LEGUMES FRAIS,CONG,SECS
056	VEGTBLES ETC PRSVD,PREPD	W 5212	7.7	W 4754	7.7	W 4072	7.0	W 4462	7.0	CONSERVES DE LEGUMES
057	FRUIT,NUTS,FRESH,DRIED	W 11276	12.6	W 13801	14.8	W 12227	13.1	W 12678	14.1	FRUITS FRAIS OU SECS
058	FRUIT PRESERVED,PREPARED	W 6728	13.7	W 7339	15.1	W 6623	14.1	W 8076	16.4	CONSERVES DE FRUITS
0585	FRUIT OR VEGETABLE JUICE	W 4737	10.5	W 4861	11.3	W 4323	10.0	W 4868	10.9	JUS DE FRUITS
06	SUGAR AND PREPS,HONEY		6.0		7.1		10.8		7.6	SUCRES ET PRODUITS
07	COFFEE,TEA,COCOA,SPICES		9.0		10.0		10.8		11.1	CAFE,THE,CACAO,EPICES
081	*FEEDING STUFF FOR ANIML	W 66342	21.5	W 76138	24.5	W 91944	28.7	W 94154	36.0	NOURRITURE POUR ANIMAUX
0813	OILCAKE AND OTH RESIDUES	W 54838	14.3	W 66189	16.9	W 73072	17.4	W 76924	23.8	TOURTEAUX
08131	— OF SOYA BEANS					W 73070	17.4	W 76921	23.8	TOURTEAUX DE SOJA
0819	FOOD WASTE AND FEED NES	W 11330	7.2	W 9742	7.6	W 18622	11.2	W 16980	12.2	DECHETS,ALIMENTS NDA
08199	FODDER NES,INCL SWEETNED	W 11330	7.2	W 9742	7.6	W 12088	9.1	W 11959	10.1	PREPARATIONS FOURRAGERES
09	MISC EDIBLE PRODUCTS		22.1		23.7		21.5		31.6	PREP ALIMENTAIRES DIVERSES
098	EDIBLE PRODCTS,PREPS NES	W 6149	21.9	W 6877	23.6	W 7164	21.5	W 10744	31.4	PREP ALIMENTAIRES NDA
09809	MISC FOOD PREPRTIONS NES	W 3398	14.2	W 3670	15.5	W 3986	14.4	W 6245	21.8	PREP ALIMENTAIRES NDA
1	BEVERAGES AND TOBACCO		10.5		13.8		12.8		15.8	BOISSONS ET TABACS
11	BEVERAGES		8.4		10.4		10.6		13.2	BOISSONS
112	ALCOHOLIC BEVERAGES	W 2322	7.8	W 2866	8.9	W 3138	9.0	W 3700	11.5	BOISSONS ALCOOLIQUES
2	CRUDE MATERLS,EXCL FUELS		23.0		31.0		27.3		27.6	MAT BRUTES NON COMESTIBLES
251	*PULP AND WASTE PAPER	W 8419	3.1	W 12014	4.9	W 17218	7.9	W 10115	4.5	PATES A PAPIER,DECHETS
3	MINERAL FUELS ETC		279.0		310.3		343.3		443.7	COMBUSTIBLES MINERAUX LUB
33	PETROLEUM AND PRODUCTS		259.5		289.7		317.7		417.6	PETROLE ET DERIVES
333	CRUDE PETROLEUM	W 1720857	192.0	W 1188791	125.5	W 1223452	144.7	W 2040499	301.7	HUILES BRUTES DE PETROLE
334	PETROLEUM PRODUCTS,REFIN	W 352155	65.3	W 1040743	161.1	W 1056746	168.2	W 557843	111.2	PRODUITS RAFFINES
3341	GASOLINE,OTH LIGHT OILS	W 102685	25.9	W 150313	37.3	W 118654	28.0	W 106158	27.5	ESSENCES POUR MOTEURS
33411	MOTOR,AVIATION SPIRIT	W 14301	7.0	W 8585	7.5	W 56311	13.0	W 105014	27.1	ESSENCES MOTEURS D'AVIONS
33412	SPIRIT TYPE JET FUEL	W 148	0.2	W 93	0.1	W 60450	14.2			CARBUREACTEURS
33419	OTH LIGHT PETROLEUM OILS	W 88237	18.9	W 141635	29.8	W 1893	0.9	W 1144	0.4	AUTRES HUILES LEGERES
3342	KEROSENE,OTH MEDIUM OILS	W 237070	36.1	W 521846	87.0	W 65453	16.0	W 92857	24.4	PETR LAMPANTS,AUT HUIL
33421	KEROSENE INCL JET FUEL	W 15341	3.8	W 78486	18.2	W 65416	15.9	W 92857	24.4	PETROLES LAMPANTS
33429	OTH MEDIUM PETROLEUM OIL	W 221729	32.4	W 443360	68.8	W 36	0.1			AUTRES HUILES MOYENNES
3343	GAS OILS	W 10555	0.8	W 351366	31.1	W 858065	113.7	W 220060	33.1	GAS OILS
3344	FUEL OILS,NES	W 1264	1.7	W 16457	4.5	W 11257	6.6	W 133896	21.1	FUEL OILS
341	*GAS,NATURAL AND MANUFCT	W 66103	17.4	W 71488	18.2	W 76990	22.9	W 63052	22.8	GAZ NATUREL,GAZ MANUFACT
3413	PETROLM GASES,LIQUEFIED	W 66102	17.4	W 71488	18.1	W 76989	22.9	W 63051	22.7	GAZ DE PETROLE LIQUEFIE
34131	LIQUEFIED PROPANE,BUTANE					W 76975	22.9	W 63038	22.7	PROPANE,BUTANE LIQUEFIES
4	ANIMAL,VEGETABLE OIL,FAT		14.5		20.2		22.0		23.6	HUILES,GRAISSES ANIM,VEG
42	FIXED VEGETABLE OIL,FAT		13.6		18.7		20.0		21.3	HUILES VEGETALES FIXES
423	FIXED VEG OILS,SOFT	W 24771	13.6	W 28108	18.7	W 23815	18.3	W 28189	17.9	HUILES VEGET DOUCES FIXES
4232	SOYA BEAN OIL					W 23327	17.1	W 27732	16.6	HUILE DE SOJA
5	CHEMCLS,RELATED PROD NES		284.2		310.1		331.7		355.1	PRODUITS CHIMIQUES
51	ORGANIC CHEMICALS		18.5		19.3		21.0		21.8	PROD CHIMIQ ORGANIQUES
514	NITROGEN–FNCTN COMPOUNDS	W 1291	5.0	W 1822	6.3	W 1330	6.4	W 1563	8.7	COMPOSES FONCT AZOTEES
52	INORGANIC CHEMICALS		17.4		17.9		18.3		16.7	PROD CHIM INORGANIQUES
523	OTHR INORG CHEMICALS ETC	W 24688	12.2	W 23762	11.5	W 25618	11.7	W 22531	10.9	AUT PRODUITS CHIMIQUES INORG
5232	OTH MTL CMPD OF INRG ACD	W 17849	9.1	W 16231	8.0	W 15641	7.5	W 16683	7.7	SELS METALLIQUES
53	DYES,TANNING,COLOUR PROD		13.7		14.4		17.1		19.1	PROD TEINTURE,COLORANTS
533	PIGMENTS,PAINTS,ETC	W 5724	10.6	W 7036	11.1	W 9187	13.0	W 8767	14.9	PIGMENTS,PEINTURES,VERNIS
541	*MEDICINAL,PHARM PRODUCT	K 3985664	77.6	K 3935997	80.3	K 4868530	95.1	K 6121248	103.2	PROD MEDICINAUX PHARMACEUT
5417	MEDICAMENTS	K 2088971	65.3	K 2627681	70.3	K 3523894	82.2	K 4668600	91.5	MEDICAMENTS
54171	— CONTAINNG ANTIBIOTICS					K 900925	27.9	K 873226	28.3	MED CONTN ANTIBIOTIQUES
54172	— CONTAINING HORMONES					K 379784	15.1	K 482310	25.1	MED CONTENANT HORMONES
54179	— CONTNG OTH SUBSTANCES					K 2238837	39.2	K 3302538	38.1	MED CONT AUT SUBSTANCES
55	PERFUME,CLEANING ETC PRD		38.0		40.9		40.3		46.2	PROD POUR PARFUM,TOILETTE
553	PERFUMERY,COSMETICS,ETC	W 3618	24.1	W 5193	26.9	W 4394	26.6	W 4646	28.8	PRODUITS DE PARFUMERIE
554	SOAP,CLEANSING ETC PREPS	W 4929	7.8	W 6098	8.7	W 5732	7.7	W 7941	9.8	SAVONS,PRODUITS DETERSIFS
562	*FERTILIZERS,MANUFACTURE	W 95092	16.0	W 100896	19.9	W 105199	23.4	W 124212	28.8	ENGRAIS MANUFACTURES
5621	CHEM NITROGENOUS FERTLZR	W 62918	10.0	W 59695	11.5	W 52021	11.5	W 54068	12.5	ENGRAIS AZOTES
5629	FERTILIZERS NES	W 4954	1.3	W 4940	1.6	W 21735	6.1	W 32239	9.0	ENGRAIS NDA
58	PLASTIC MATERIALS ETC		48.5		56.0		56.2		50.8	MAT PLAST ARTIFICIELLES
582	PROD OF CONDENSATION ETC	W 4171	8.6	W 4527	9.6	W 6465	10.1	W 6487	9.0	PROD CONDENS,POLYCOND
583	POLYMERIZATION ETC PRODS	W 33769	34.9	W 38287	41.1	W 32527	43.2	W 32243	39.6	PROD POLYMERISATION
5831	POLYETHYLENE					W 17056	17.7	W 16785	17.0	POLYETHYLENE
58311	— IN PRIMARY FORMS					W 16902	17.4	W 16425	16.4	POLYETHYLENE PRIMAIRES
5839	OTH POLYMRZTION ETC PROD					W 3768	8.4	W 2931	6.6	AUT PROD POLYMER COPOLYM
59	CHEMICAL MATERIALS NES		53.8		60.4		58.7		66.6	MAT PROD CHIMIQUES NDA
591	PESTICIDES,DISINFECTANTS	W 9312	28.7	W 9196	32.1	W 8386	34.6	W 11695	38.2	DESINF,INSECT,FONG,HERB
5912	FUNGICIDES,FOR RETAIL					W 1456	12.5	W 4828	14.6	FONGICIDES VENTE AU DET
5913	HERBICIDES,FOR RETAIL					W 2981	12.1	W 3822	15.3	HERBICIDES VENTE AU DET
5914	DISINFECTANTS,ETC,FR RET	W 9312	28.7	W 9196	32.1	W 2468	3.2	W 1961	2.8	DESINFECTANTS VENTE DET
592	STARCH,INULIN,GLUTEN,ETC	W 16097	10.4	W 16415	10.9	W 5567	7.1	W 7140	9.5	AMIDONS,INUL,GLUT FROM
5922	ALBUMINOID SUBSTAN,GLUES	W 4012	5.7	W 4780	6.5	W 4653	6.7	W 4987	8.6	MAT ALBUMIN,COLLES
598	MISCEL CHEM PRODUCTS NES	W 6891	14.8	W 8151	17.5	W 7212	17.0	W 7468	19.0	PROD DIV INDUST CHIM NDA
5989	CHEM PRODUCTS,PREPS NES	W 4502	9.3	W 5332	11.2	W 4820	11.4	W 4637	12.5	PROD PREP CHIMIQUES NDA
59898	COMPOUND CATALYSTS	W 2754	7.3	W 3443	8.7	W 47	0.3	W 27	0.2	CATALYSEURS COMPOSITES
59899	OTH CHEM PRODS,PREPS,NES					W 2956	8.8	W 3196	10.2	AUT PRODUITS CHIMIQUES NDA
6	BASIC MANUFACTURES		419.2		457.9		484.1		454.3	ART MANUFACTURES
61	LEATHER,DRESSED FUR,ETC		9.6		6.6		8.1		6.9	CUIRS,PELLETERIES
612	LEATHER ETC MANUFACTURES	W 1028	8.6	W 947	5.9	W 1087	7.1	W 968	6.4	OUVRAGES EN CUIRS NDA
6123	PREPRD PARTS OF FOOTWEAR	W 1016	8.4	W 938	5.8	W 1073	7.0	W 955	6.3	PARTIES DE CHAUSSURES
62	RUBBER MANUFACTURES NES		31.8		31.5		37.2		37.9	CAOUTCHOUC MANUFACTURE
625	RUBBER TYRES, TUBES ETC	W 8952	25.1	W 8920	24.4	W 14001	29.8	W 10596	30.2	PNEUS CAOUTCHOUC VULCANISE
6251	TYRES NEW FOR MOTOR CARS	W 8826	24.8	W 8803	24.1	W 7280	13.2	W 3871	13.0	PNEUS POUR VOITURES

4. Special Imports C.I.F. by Commodities according to the S.I.T.C. (Rev. 2) in million U.S. Dollars
Importations Spéciales C.A.F. par Produits d'après la C.T.C.I. (Rév. 2) en millions de Dollars E.U.

SITC CTCI	COMMODITY	1993 QUANTITY QUANTITE	1993 VALUE VALEUR	1994 QUANTITY QUANTITE	1994 VALUE VALEUR	1995 QUANTITY QUANTITE	1995 VALUE VALEUR	1996 QUANTITY QUANTITE	1996 VALUE VALEUR	PRODUIT
6252	TYRES,NEW,BUS OR LORRY					W 3257	9.5	W 2839	8.9	PNEUS POUR AUTOBUS,CAMIONS
63	WOOD,CORK MANUFACTRS NES		6.5		10.8		9.8		9.0	OUVRAGES LIEGE ET BOIS
64	PAPER,PAPERBOARD AND MFR		96.6		110.6		121.3		103.6	PAPIERS,CARTONS & OUVRAGES
641	PAPER AND PAPERBOARD	W 106189	66.2	W 135829	82.7	W 112885	94.2	W 98615	74.1	PAPIERS ET CARTONS
6411	NEWSPRINT	W 96828	55.4	W 124758	70.7	W 12495	8.2	W 12150	9.7	PAPIER JOURNAL
6413	KRAFT PAPER,PAPERBOARD					W 57739	41.2	W 46241	25.9	PAPIER ET CARTON KRAFT
64132	SACK KRAFT PAPER IN BULK					W 30399	21.8	W 24439	11.7	PAPIER KRAFT POUR SACS
64139	KRAFT PAPER PAPERBD,NES					W 19835	15.2	W 18729	12.2	PAPIER,CARTON KRAFT NDA
6415	PAPER,PAPERBRD,BULK,NES	W 114	0.3	W 67	0.3	W 16729	20.0	W 16986	17.5	PAPIERS,CARTONS ROULEAUX
64159	OTHER PAPER ETC,BULK,NES					W 15122	18.9	W 16710	17.1	AUT PAPIER ROULEAUX FEUILLES
6418	COATED ETC PAPER NES BLK	W 1855	4.0	W 1721	3.9	W 20016	17.6	W 16609	13.6	PAP,CARTONS COUCHES,ENDUITS
64181	PLASTIC COATED PAPER ETC					W 14544	11.8	W 14132	8.8	PAP,CARTONS ENDUITS,RESINES
642	PAPER,ETC,PRECUT,ARTS OF	W 15489	30.4	W 12517	27.9	W 10873	27.1	W 12207	29.6	PAP,CARTONS DECOUPES
6421	PAPER ETC CONTAINERS	W 11255	17.1	W 7882	12.7	W 6445	12.6	W 6606	12.9	BOITES,SACS EMBALLAGES
6428	PAPER ETC ARTICLES NES	W 2006	7.2	W 2251	8.4	W 2714	8.9	W 3758	11.2	OUVRAGES EN PATE A PAPIER
65	TEXTILE YARN,FABRICS,ETC		81.6		73.8		74.7		76.3	FILS,TISSUS,ARTICLES TEXTILE
652	COTTON FABRICS,WOVEN	W 1531	12.0	W 1772	10.6	W 1197	9.1	W 1456	10.3	TISSUS DE COTON
6521	GREY WOVEN COTTON FABRIC	W 1452	11.7	W 1711	10.3	W 247	1.6	W 204	1.9	TISSUS COT ECRUS NON MERCER
65214	GREY WOVEN COTTON NES	W 1440	11.6	W 1702	10.3	W 166	1.0	W 154	1.5	AUT TISSUS 85% COTON ECRUS
653	WOVN MAN–MADE FIB FABRIC	W 5004	32.2	W 4760	27.0	W 3969	25.7	W 4712	29.9	TISSUS FIBRES SYNTH,ARTIF
6531	CONT SYNT WEAVES NONPILE	W 4504	28.3	W 4207	23.4	W 2480	14.6	W 3547	22.3	TISSUS FIBRES SYNTH CONTINUE
65315	CONT SYN TXTL FABRIC NES					W 2317	13.3	W 3115	18.5	TIS PLUS 85% TEXT SYNT CONT
657	SPECIAL TXTL FABRC,PRODS	W 2380	8.2	W 2109	8.3	W 1923	8.0	W 1569	6.4	TISSUS SPECIAUX
658	TEXTILE ARTICLES NES	W 1211	8.7	W 876	6.7	W 1278	9.2	W 1485	10.4	ART FACONNES MAT TEXTILES
6584	LINENS ETC	W 998	7.4	W 733	5.5	W 1124	7.9	W 1280	8.8	LINGE DE MAISON
66	NONMETAL MINERAL MFS NES		30.3		38.4		40.1		47.0	ART MIN NON METALLIQUES
661	LIME,CEMENT,BLDG PRODS	W 65766	3.9	W 166342	9.7	W 31025	7.9	W 23425	8.3	CHAUX,CIMENTS MAT CONSTR
6612	CEMENT	W 62682	2.6	W 161685	7.7	W 24775	4.8	W 15848	3.7	CIMENTS HYDRAULIQUES
662	CLAY,REFRACTORY BLDG PRD	W 18653	9.5	W 23698	11.1	W 20575	10.4	W 26521	12.5	MAT CONST REFRACTAIRES
6624	BRICKS ETC NONREFRACTORY	W 18023	8.8	W 22397	10.3	W 19227	9.3	W 24022	9.9	BRIQUES ETC CERAM NON REFR
66245	GLAZED CERAMIC SETTS ETC	W 17997	8.8	W 22363	10.2	W 18721	9.2	W 23090	9.6	AUT CARREAUX CERAMIQUE
664	GLASS	W 5779	5.0	W 6710	5.7	W 7239	8.8	W 9101	12.1	VERRE
67	IRON AND STEEL		78.7		94.3		90.5		79.6	FER ET ACIER
672	IRON,STEEL PRIMARY FORMS	W 35357	9.9	W 36713	10.1	W 35128	10.8	W 27202	7.3	LINGOTS FER,ACIER
6725	IRN,STL BLOOMS,SLABS,ETC	W 35356	9.9	W 36712	10.1	W 34594	10.2	W 27008	7.1	BLOOMS,BILLETTES FER ACIER
67251	IRN,SMPLE STL BLOOMS,ETC	W 35356	9.9	W 36712	10.1	W 34584	10.2	W 27008	7.1	BLOOMS ETC NON ACIER FIN
673	IRON,STEEL SHAPES ETC	W 41980	17.8	W 42333	17.5	W 29192	13.0	W 29691	13.3	BARRES,PROFIL FER,ACIER
6732	IRON,STEEL BARS ETC	W 18583	7.7	W 24752	9.3	W 11870	4.8	W 14707	5.9	BARRES FER,ACIER
67326	IRN,OTH STL BARS HOTROLD	W 18583	7.7	W 24752	9.3	W 7358	2.7	W 8400	3.0	BARRES PLEINES FER,ACIER
6733	IRON,STEEL PROFILES ETC	W 18247	8.0	W 13068	6.3	W 13977	6.8	W 13512	6.9	PROFILES,PALPLAN FER,ACIER
674	IRN,STL UNIV,PLATE,SHEET	W 53366	34.8	W 69803	44.8	W 64084	49.7	W 60107	41.4	LARGES PLATS,TOLES
6745	IRN,STL MED PLATE,ROLLED	W 30683	18.9	W 47526	29.5	W 1920	1.1	W 5953	2.7	TOLES 3 A 4.75 MM
67451	— OF IRON OR SIMPLE STL	W 30683	18.9	W 47526	29.5	W 1672	0.9	W 5803	2.6	TOLES AUT NON ACIER FIN
6747	TINNED PLATES,SHEETS	W 11052	10.3	W 8652	8.1	W 11963	11.5	W 7370	7.6	TOLES ETAMEES EN ACIER
6749	OTH IRN,STL PLATES,SHEET	W 2368	1.6	W 3645	2.5	W 43249	33.0	W 40257	27.4	AUTRES TOLES FER,ACIER
67491	— OF IRON OR SIMPLE STL	W 2368	1.6	W 3645	2.5	W 42638	32.5	W 39901	27.2	AUT TOLES AUTRES ACIER FIN
678	IRON,STL TUBES,PIPES,ETC	W 10999	9.0	W 17469	13.0	W 13243	11.3	W 11716	11.5	TUBES,TUYAUX EN FONTE,FER
6783	IRON,STL TUBES,PIPES NES	W 7065	4.8	W 6118	4.6	W 11032	8.1	W 8189	7.3	AUT TUBES,TUYAUX FER,ACIER
68	NON–FERROUS METALS		15.5		20.1		28.4		27.2	METAUX NON FERREUX
682	COPPER EXC CEMENT COPPER	W 1877	5.2	W 2217	6.5	W 2214	8.4	W 2565	7.7	CUIVRE
6822	COPPER,ALLOYS WORKED	W 1875	5.2	W 2215	6.5	W 2210	8.3	W 2563	7.7	CUIVRE,ALLIAGES OUVRES
684	ALUMINIUM	W 3370	9.7	W 4949	13.1	W 5988	19.6	W 7029	19.3	ALUMINIUM
6842	ALUMINIUM,ALLOYS WORKED	W 3370	9.7	W 4949	13.1	W 4361	15.9	W 5339	16.0	ALUMINIUM,ALLIAGES OUVRE
68422	ALUMNM PLATE,SHEET,STRIP	W 2070	5.2	W 3094	7.2	W 2555	8.1	W 3205	8.6	TOLES, PLANCHES EN ALU
69	METAL MANUFACTURES NES		69.0		72.2		74.5		67.2	ART MANUFACT EN METAL NDA
692	METAL TANKS,BOXES,ETC	W 2018	8.2	W 1789	6.6	W 4118	12.5	W 1736	6.3	RECIPIENTS METALLIQUES
6924	MTL TRANSPORT BOXES ETC	W 1699	5.6	W 1322	5.3	W 3729	10.8	W 1460	5.5	FUTS,TAMBOURS,BIDONS
69242	ALUMNM TRNSPRT BOXES ETC	W 1114	4.3	W 647	3.6	W 2354	7.8	W 875	3.9	FUTS,TAMBOURS,BIDONS ALU
695	TOOLS	W 1176	8.1	W 1412	8.9	W 1402	9.0	W 1131	8.3	OUTILS A MAIN
697	BASE MTL HOUSEHOLD EQUIP	W 3366	15.4	W 4040	14.7	W 2709	10.3	W 3045	10.8	ART MENAGE MET COMMUNS
6973	DMSTC HEATG,COOKG APPARA	W 2542	11.2	W 3074	10.1	W 1932	6.0	W 2040	6.2	APPS CHAUF NON ELECTRIQ
699	BASE METAL MFRS NES	W 5828	21.6	W 7276	24.3	W 6117	24.5	W 6141	25.1	ART MANUFACTURES MET NDA
6991	LOCKSMITHS WARES,ETC	W 1675	8.8	W 1895	10.0	W 1645	9.1	W 1599	9.4	ARTICLES DE SERRURERIE
6996	BASE MTL MISC ARTICLES	W 1933	6.3	W 2125	6.2	W 2355	8.1	W 2351	7.2	ART DIVERS METAUX COMMUNS
7	MACHINES,TRANSPORT EQUIP		686.8		741.2		727.8		848.1	MACHINES MATERIEL TRANSPORT
71	POWER GENERATING EQUIPMT		43.0		33.6		25.4		28.3	MACHINES GENERATRICES
713	INTRNL COMBUS PSTN ENGIN	W 909	12.1	W 970	11.7	W 781	14.5	W 857	12.0	MOTEURS EXPL COMB INT, PIECE
7139	PISTON ENGINE PARTS NES	W 304	6.2	W 453	7.8	W 330	7.1	W 329	7.2	PIECES POUR 713.2,3,8
716	ROTATING ELECTRIC PLANT	W 2774	23.3	W 2407	14.3	W 945	9.6	W 1040	12.5	APP ELECTR ROTATIFS,PIECES
7161	DC MOTORS AND GENERATORS	W 1077	13.2	W 516	4.5	W 381	3.6	W 341	4.2	MOTEURS COURANT CONTINU
7163	ROTARY CONVERTERS	W 1450	7.4	W 1591	7.1	W 4	0.1	W 11	0.2	CONVERTISSEURS ROTATIFS
72	MACHS FOR SPCL INDUSTRYS		83.6		77.1		78.4		69.9	MAC SPECIALES POUR INDUST
722	TRACTORS NON–ROAD	W 4317	8.6	W 5512	11.7	W 2013	11.5	W 1372	7.7	TRACTEURS
7223	TRACK–LAYING TRACTORS	W 4317	8.6	W 5512	11.7	W 221	0.7	W 403	2.3	TRACTEURS A CHENILLES
7224	WHEELED TRACTORS NES					W 1791	10.8	W 969	5.4	TRACTEURS A ROUES
723	CIVIL ENGNEERG EQUIP ETC	W 5522	24.2	W 4044	17.2	W 3471	19.7	W 2418	13.1	APPAREILS DE GENIE CIVIL
7234	CONST,MINING MACHNRY NES	W 5486	24.1	W 4021	17.1	W 3190	18.2	W 2268	11.8	MACH POUR LA CONST, MINES
72342	SLFPRP SHOVELS,EXCAVATRS					W 1785	9.4	W 1382	7.5	PELLES MECANIQUES
724	TEXTILE,LEATHER MACHNRY	W 2392	9.9	W 2173	9.0	W 690	6.1	W 551	3.0	MACH POUR INDUSTRIE TEXTILE
7247	TEXTILE MACHINERY NES	W 2015	7.3	W 1816	6.4	W 302	1.7	W 151	0.9	MACH LAVAGE,TEINTURE TEX
725	PAPER ETC MILL MACHINERY	W 297	9.0	W 102	2.2	W 281	3.9	W 116	3.1	MACHINES FABR PATE PAPIER
726	PRINTG,BKBINDG MACHY,PTS	W 477	7.9	W 719	12.6	W 307	6.0	W 379	7.3	MACHINES POUR IMPRIMERIE
7264	PRINTING PRESSES	W 263	3.6	W 414	8.0	W 75	1.2	W 46	0.9	MACHINES A IMPRIMER
727	FOOD MACHRY NON–DOMESTIC	W 567	5.1	W 803	6.0	W 1204	9.7	W 642	5.2	MACH INDUSTRIES ALIMENT
7272	OTH FOOD PROC MCHY,PARTS	W 295	3.7	W 667	5.1	W 1034	8.7	W 558	4.4	AUT MACH IND ALIMENTAIRE
72722	INDUS FOOD PROC MACH NES					W 1034	8.6	W 556	4.4	MACHINES BOULANGERIE
728	OTH MACHY FOR SPCL INDUS	W 1307	13.0	W 1760	12.9	W 1294	14.3	W 2506	22.4	AUT MACH IND PARTICULIERES
7283	OTHR MINERAL WORKG MACHY	W 938	6.8	W 1219	6.3	W 642	4.0	W 1783	13.2	MACH TRIER,CRIBLER,BROYER
73	METALWORKING MACHINERY		9.5		10.1		8.3		8.0	MACH TRAVAIL DES METAUX
736	METALWORKING MACH–TOOLS	W 505	6.4	W 758	8.9	W 609	5.5	W 380	5.2	MACH–OUTILS TRAVAIL METAUX
74	GENRL INDUSTRL MACHY NES		76.6		82.3		102.1		107.4	MACH APP INDUSTRIE
741	HEATING,COOLING EQUIPMNT	W 2266	16.4	W 2561	20.1	W 4166	28.2	W 3740	30.8	MACH CHAUFFAGE,PIECES
7415	AIR–CONDITIONING MACHNRY	W 1316	9.8	W 1652	12.4	W 2418	14.1	W 2247	18.1	GROUPES CONDITION AIR
742	PUMPS FOR LIQUIDS ETC	W 574	7.2	W 586	7.6	W 724	7.9	W 661	7.7	POMPES MOTO–POMPES
743	PUMPS NES,CENTRFUGES ETC	W 1215	12.7	W 1310	13.0	W 1383	12.1	W 1420	14.1	POMPES COMPRES,VENT ETC
744	MECHANICAL HANDLING EQU	W 4031	14.6	W 3589	14.1	W 3839	20.0	W 3441	20.2	EQUIP MANUTENTION PIECES
7442	LIFTING,LOADING MACH NES	W 1808	6.5	W 1475	5.7	W 2797	12.7	W 2556	14.7	APP LEVAGE,MANUTENTION
74424	LIFTS AND SKIP HOISTS					W 1862	7.8	W 1672	8.5	ASCENSEURS,MONTE–CHARGE
745	NONELEC MACHY,TOOLS NES	W 553	8.1	W 719	9.0	W 994	17.4	W 922	16.4	AUT MACH NON ELEC,PIECES
7452	OTH NONELEC MCHS,PTS NES	W 491	7.0	W 631	7.5	W 922	16.5	W 795	13.8	AUT MACH NON ELEC,PIECES
74522	PACKAGNG,BOTTLNG,ETC MCH	W 1	0.1	W 12	0.3	W 323	8.1	W 294	7.3	MACH NETT BOUTEILLES,ETC

4. Special Imports C.I.F. by Commodities according to the S.I.T.C. (Rev. 2) in million U.S. Dollars
Importations Spéciales C.A.F. par Produits d'après la C.T.C.I. (Rév. 2) en millions de Dollars E.U.

SITC CTCI	COMMODITY	1993		1994		1995		1996		PRODUIT
		QUANTITY QUANTITE	VALUE VALEUR	QUANTITY QUANTITE	VALUE VALEUR	QUANTITY QUANTITE	VALUE VALEUR	QUANTITY QUANTITE	VALUE VALEUR	
749	NONELEC MACH PTS,ACC NES	W 2245	17.8	W 1937	18.7	W 1625	16.7	W 1915	18.5	PIECES MACH NON ELEC NDA
7492	COCKS,VALVES ETC NES	W 714	6.9	W 818	8.5	W 988	7.2	W 890	8.1	ART ROB,SIM POUR TUYAUX
75	OFFICE MACHNES,ADP EQUIP		42.0		51.8		61.4		74.1	MACH BUREAU TRAIT AUTOM
751	OFFICE MACHINES	W 401	9.1	W 349	8.2	W 392	9.0	W 389	8.4	MACH,APPAREILS DE BUREAU
752	AUTOMTIC DATA PROC EQUIP	W 353	17.4	W 359	22.9	W 411	26.2	W 431	31.6	MACH TRAIT INFORMATION
7521	ANALOG,HYBRID COMPUTERS					W 205	11.9	W 198	13.1	MACH POUR TRAIT INFORMAT
7522	DIGITAL COMPUTERS					W 106	8.0	W 145	12.4	MACH DIGITALES COMPLETES
759	OFFICE,ADP MCH PTS,ACCES	W 404	15.6	W 460	20.8	W 621	26.4	W 777	34.1	PIECES DU 751 ET 752
7591	OFFICE MACHINE PARTS NES	W 404	15.6	W 460	20.8	W 46	1.7	W 43	1.5	PIECES DU 7511,7518
75911	TYPEWRTR PARTS,ACCES NES	W 390	15.2	W 450	20.4	W 2	0.2	W 1	0.1	PIECES DU 7511
7599	ACCTG,ETC,ADP MCH PTS,AC					W 575	24.7	W 734	32.7	PIECES DU 751 ET 752
76	TELECOMM,SOUND EQUIPMENT		68.6		81.9		79.6		98.9	EQUIPMENT DE TELECOM
761	TELEVISION RECEIVERS	W 5	0.3	W 7	0.4	W 1150	12.4	W 1397	15.4	RECEPTEURS DE TELEVISION
7611	COLOUR TV RECEIVERS	W 4	0.3	W 7	0.3	W 1080	11.9	W 1301	14.6	RECEPTEURS COULEUR
762	RADIO BROADCAST RECEIVRS	W 2098	25.9	W 2223	28.3	W 442	9.7	W 464	11.8	RECEPTEURS RADIODIFFUSION
7621	MTR VEHC RADIO RECEIVERS	W 828	11.9	W 824	11.4	W 238	5.5	W 150	4.3	RECEPTEURS RADIO AUTO
7628	OTHER RADIO RECEIVERS	W 1237	12.9	W 1378	14.8	W 85	1.9	W 157	3.0	AUTRES RECEPT RADIO
763	SOUND RECORDRS,PHONOGRPH	W 278	9.5	W 373	10.5	W 660	12.2	W 712	13.8	PHONO,APP ENREGISTREMENT
7638	OTHR SOUND APPARATUS ETC	W 203	7.3	W 267	7.6	W 464	9.8	W 508	10.8	AUT APP D'ENREGIS,REPROD
76388	DICTATING MACHINES ETC	W 144	6.8	W 152	6.0	W 331	4.8	W 332	5.2	MACHINES A DICTER
764	TELECOM EQPT,PTS,ACC NES	W 944	33.0	W 1067	42.8	W 1064	45.6	W 1535	58.0	EQUIP TELECOM,PIECES
7641	LINE TELEPHONE,ETC EQUIP	W 351	17.5	W 405	19.9	W 305	20.6	W 616	38.7	APP TELEPHON PAR FIL
7643	TV,RADIO TRANSMITTRS ETC	W 70	7.9	W 114	12.1	W 103	9.8	W 43	4.9	APP EMET TELE RADIO
77	ELECTRIC MACHNRY NES ETC		84.9		105.1		93.9		116.6	MACH APP ELECT NDA
771	ELECTRIC POWER MACHY NES	W 79	3.5	W 136	3.9	W 2018	9.5	W 2635	13.0	MACH PROD,TRANS ELECTR
7711	TRANSFORMERS,ELECTRICAL	W 32	0.8	W 53	1.4	W 1593	5.7	W 2116	9.0	TRANSFO ELECTRIQUES
772	SWITCHGEAR ETC,PARTS NES	W 1788	17.0	W 1919	19.8	W 1376	13.0	W 1758	21.5	APP COUPURE,SECT ETC
7721	SWITCHGEAR ETC	W 1180	10.1	W 1344	13.4	W 1372	12.7	W 1755	21.2	APP COUPURE,SECTIONMNT
773	ELECTR DISTRIBUTNG EQUIP	W 1425	7.0	W 2778	11.4	W 2638	11.9	W 2848	14.2	EQUIPMT DISTRIBUTION ELECT
7731	INSULATED WIRE,CABLE ETC	W 1269	6.5	W 2554	10.3	W 2469	11.1	W 2579	12.1	FILS,CABLES ISOLES ELECT
774	ELECTRO–MEDCL,XRAY EQUIP	W 69	5.2	W 87	9.2	W 87	5.9	W 76	5.9	APPAREILS MEDICAUX
775	HOUSEHOLD TYPE EQUIP NES	W 5256	29.3	W 5827	36.3	W 6980	28.7	W 6760	33.0	MACH,APP USAGE DOMESTQUE
7752	DOM REFRIGERATRS,FREEZRS	W 3131	14.1	W 3365	15.6	W 3755	13.6	W 3274	16.1	REFRIG,CONGEL MENAGER
77521	DOMESTIC REFRIGERATORS					W 2606	10.7	W 2440	11.2	REFRIGERATEURS
7753	DOMSTC DISHWASHING MACHS	W 202	5.9	W 630	11.5	W 7	0.1	W 3	0.1	MACH A LAVER VAISSELLE
778	ELECTRICAL MACHINERY NES	W 4580	22.2	W 5028	23.6	W 4967	23.4	W 5425	26.5	AUTRES MACH ELECT NDA
7781	BATTERIES,ACCUMULATORS	W 3020	7.9	W 3318	9.1	W 3515	9.4	W 3757	10.7	PILES ET ACCUMULATEURS
78	ROAD VEHICLES		273.5		292.4		273.4		330.6	VEHICULES ROUTIERS
781	PASS MOTOR VEH EXC BUSES	W 19609	127.5	W 21037	130.8	W 22723	170.3	W 27963	235.1	AUTO TRANSPORT PERSONNES
782	LORRIES,SPCL MTR VEH NES	W 750	3.0	W 1243	5.4	W 6359	28.8	W 4286	18.2	VEHICULES SPECIAUX,MARCH
7821	LORRIES,TRUCKS	W 41	0.5	W 81	0.7	W 4167	16.0	W 3238	12.3	VEHICULES TRANSP MARCHAND
7822	SPECIAL MOTOR VEHCLS NES	W 708	2.6	W 1162	4.8	W 2192	12.8	W 1048	5.9	VEHICULES USAGES SPECIAUX
783	ROAD MOTOR VEHICLES NES	W 18661	93.1	W 18895	101.4	W 6556	24.4	W 6447	25.7	VEHICULES ROUTIERS NDA
7831	BUSES	W 18135	90.8	W 18721	100.7	W 4412	18.7	W 4742	18.9	VOITURES TRANSPORT COMMUN
784	MOTOR VEH PRTS,ACCES NES	W 4475	41.0	W 4785	45.4	W 4591	41.7	W 4487	44.1	PIECES 722,781,782,783
7849	OTHER MOTOR VEHCL PARTS	W 4367	40.9	W 4717	45.3	W 4472	41.3	W 4355	43.7	PIECES 722,781,782,783
79	OTHR TRANSPORT EQUIPMENT		5.5		7.4		5.7		14.9	AUTRE MATERIEL TRANSPORT
792	AIRCRAFT ETC	W 22	3.1	W 38	4.1	W 42	3.3	W 78	12.1	APP NAVIGATION AERIENNE
7923	AIRCRFT NES2000–15000KG							W 54	10.9	AERODYNES 2000 A 15000 KG
8	MISC MANUFACTURED GOODS		282.0		298.1		320.1		340.8	ART MANUFACTURES DIVERS
812	*PLUMBG,HEATNG,LGHTNG EQ	W 1493	5.4	W 1699	6.6	W 2969	8.2	W 2805	9.6	APPAR SANITAIRES CHAUFFAGE
821	*FURNITURE,PARTS THEREOF	W 1117	6.2	W 2569	9.9	W 4437	15.8	W 5089	18.2	MEUBLES ET PIECES
8219	FURNITURE AND PARTS NES	W 681	3.2	W 1801	6.1	W 3464	9.8	W 4048	11.9	AUTRES MEUBLES ET PIECES
831	*TRAVEL GOODS,HANDBAGS	W 613	6.7	W 616	6.3	W 783	7.0	W 809	7.7	ARTICLES DE VOYAGE ETC
84	CLOTHING AND ACCESSORIES		78.9		75.4		74.8		81.3	VETEMENTS
842	MENS OUTERWEAR NOT KNIT	W 1514	18.4	W 1445	17.6	W 1046	13.4	W 1242	15.5	VET DESSUS POUR HOMMES
8423	— TROUSERS,BREECHES ETC					W 732	9.7	W 906	11.0	PANTALONS HOMMES MAT TEX
843	WOMENS OUTERWEAR NONKNIT	W 1403	21.1	W 1363	23.0	W 1545	26.6	W 1825	29.4	VET DESSUS FEMMES MAT TEX
8439	— OTHER OUTER GARMENTS					W 1117	18.0	W 1378	20.1	AUT VET DES FEM MAT TEXT
844	UNDER GARMENTS NOT KNIT	W 437	6.3	W 456	7.0	W 513	8.0	W 582	8.7	VETEMENT DESSOUS MAT TEX
845	OUTERWEAR KNIT NONELASTC	W 1783	14.1	W 1373	9.9	W 1212	15.2	W 1120	14.2	VET DESSOUS,ACCES BONNET
8451	— JERSEYS,PULLOVERS ETC	W 1050	9.9	W 731	6.8	W 634	8.8	W 707	9.9	CHANDAILS,PULL–OVERS ETC
846	UNDER GARMENTS KNITTED	W 1286	13.3	W 1168	12.6	W 401	6.0	W 480	6.5	SOUS VETS DE BONNETERIE
851	*FOOTWEAR	W 2977	33.8	W 3100	36.7	W 2855	36.3	W 2867	38.7	CHAUSSURES
85101	FOOTWEAR RUBBER,PLASTIC	W 115	0.5	W 192	1.6	W 1574	20.1	W 1805	21.6	CHAUS SEMELLES CAOUTCH
85102	FOOTWEAR LEATHER	W 2849	33.2	W 2899	35.0	W 1267	16.0	W 1058	17.1	CHAUS SEMELLES EN CUIR
87	PRECISION INSTRUMNTS NES		24.8		24.7		30.7		31.3	INSTRUM,APPAR SCIENT NDA
872	MEDICAL INSTRUMENTS NES	W 540	12.5	W 390	11.3	W 564	13.0	W 512	12.1	INSTR,APP MEDIC–CHIR NDA
87201	DENTAL INSTRUMENTS	W 507	10.2	W 359	9.5	W 17	0.4		0.1	INSTRUM,APPAR DENTAIRE
87202	OTH MEDICAL INSTRUMENTS					W 507	11.4	W 476	10.9	INSTRUM,APP MEDECINE
874	MEASURNG,CONTROLNG INSTR	W 343	9.2	W 492	11.3	W 527	14.1	W 727	15.6	INSTRUMENTS DE MESURE
88	PHOTO EQU,OPTICL GDS ETC		24.4		23.8		24.5		24.9	APP,FOURN PHOTO,OP,MONTR
882	PHOTO,CINEMA SUPPLIES	W 894	8.4	W 873	8.3	W 873	8.6	W 817	9.5	PRODUITS PHOTO,CINEMA
8822	PHOTO FILM EXC DEV CINMA	W 647	6.7	W 666	7.2	W 696	7.7	W 626	8.6	PLAQUES,PELLICULES,FILMS
885	WATCHES AND CLOCKS		7.4		7.5		7.3		7.0	HORLOGERIE
89	MISC MANUFCTRD GOODS NES		102.2		115.0		123.2		129.3	ART MANUFACTURES DIVERS
892	PRINTED MATTER	W 2495	19.4	W 2860	23.3	W 3136	24.2	W 2737	23.9	IMPRIMES
8921	PRINTED BOOKS,GLOBES,ETC	W 1195	9.8	W 1465	12.0	W 1801	13.5	W 1399	12.5	LIVRES,BROCHURES,CARTES
89211	PRINTED BOOKS,PAMPHLETS	W 1167	9.6	W 1394	11.5	W 1749	12.9	W 1292	11.9	LIVRES,BROCHURES
893	ARTICLES OF PLASTIC NES	W 7805	30.6	W 8496	33.6		36.3		36.6	OUVRAGES EN MAT DIVIS 58
8931	PLSTC PACKG CONTNRS,LIDS	W 6126	24.1	W 6863	27.0	W 3095	13.4	W 2662	11.4	ART TRANSP EMBALLAGE ETC
8939	MISC PLASTIC ARTICLES	W 1679	6.5	W 1633	6.6	W 5966	22.3	W 7036	24.7	ART DIVERS EN MAT DIV 58
89399	OTHR PLASTC ARTICLES NES	W 1679	6.5	W 1633	6.6	W 4976	20.8	W 5511	22.9	AUT OUV MAT DIV 58
894	TOYS,SPORTING GOODS,ETC	W 3632	20.9	W 4054	23.7	W 3909	24.7	W 4140	26.8	VOITURES ENFANTS,JOUETS
8942	TOYS,INDOOR GAMES ETC	W 3009	17.2	W 3365	19.8	W 3346	20.7	W 3387	20.9	JOUETS,JEUX ETC
89423	TOYS NES	W 1851	10.5	W 2109	12.5	W 1656	10.6	W 1701	10.1	JOUETS,MODELES REDUITS
895	OFFICE SUPPLIES NES	W 597	5.1	W 583	7.0	W 646	8.7	W 964	11.2	ART PAPET NDA
897	GOLD,SILVER WARE,JEWELRY		10.4		8.9		8.9		8.6	BIJOUTERIE,ORFEVRERIE
898	MUSICAL INSTRUMENTS,PTS	W 485	9.0	W 515	10.9	W 508	11.9	W 609	12.6	INSTRUMENTS DE MUSIQUE
8983	SOUND RECRDNG TAPE,DISCS	W 398	7.8	W 433	9.7	W 416	10.6	W 508	11.3	SUPPORTS SON POUR 763
89832	RECORDED DISCS,TAPES ETC					W 180	8.3	W 187	8.0	DISQUES,PHONO,BANDES
899	OTHER MANUFACTURED GOODS		6.9		7.5		8.3		9.3	AUT ART MANUF DIVERS NDA
9	GOODS NOT CLASSD BY KIND		2.1		4.1		8.9		2.4	ART TRANSACT NON CLASSES
971	*GOLD,NON MONETARY NES	K 500	0.5	K 1228	2.8	K 1113	8.6	K 668	2.2	OR NON MONETAIRE
97101	NONMON GLD UNWRT,SEMIMFD	K 428	0.4	K 254	2.8	K 836	8.6	K 251	2.2	OR,ALLIAGES D'OR BRUTS

5. Special Exports F.O.B. by Commodities according to the S.I.T.C. (Rev. 2) in million U.S. Dollars
Exportations Spéciales F.O.B. par Produits d'après la C.T.C.I. (Rév. 2) en millions de Dollars E.U.

SITC CTCI	COMMODITY	1993 QUANTITY QUANTITE	1993 VALUE VALEUR	1994 QUANTITY QUANTITE	1994 VALUE VALEUR	1995 QUANTITY QUANTITE	1995 VALUE VALEUR	1996 QUANTITY QUANTITE	1996 VALUE VALEUR	PRODUIT
	ALL COMMODITIES		506.9		539.9		577.3		569.3	TOUS PRODUITS
0	FOOD AND LIVE ANIMALS		390.0		399.5		413.9		392.5	ALIMENTS,ANIMAUX VIVANTS
001	*LIVE ANIMALS FOR FOOD	W 93	0.2	W 221	0.7	W 78	0.3	W 672	2.8	ANIMAUX VIVANTS
0011	BOVINE SPECIES,LIVE	W 72	0.2	W 204	0.7	W 61	0.3	W 603	2.7	ESPECE BOVINE
00111	— PURE BRED FR BREEDING	W 72	0.2	W 204	0.7	W 61	0.3	W 603	2.7	BOVINS REPRODUCTEURS
01	MEAT AND PREPARATIONS		16.7		5.5		4.2		6.4	VIANDES ET PREPARATIONS
011	MEAT FRESH,CHILLD,FROZEN	W 4619	16.7	W 1592	5.5	W 1460	4.2	W 2697	5.8	VIANDES FRAICHES,REF,CONGE
0111	BOVINE MEAT FRESH,FROZEN	W 4547	16.4	W 1565	5.4	W 1284	3.8	W 2340	5.1	VIANDES BOVIN FRAI,REF
01112	BOVINE MEAT BONELESS					W 1275	3.7	W 2340	5.1	VIANDES BOVIN DESOSSEES
02	DAIRY PRODCTS,BIRDS'EGGS		8.2		9.2		9.7		12.0	PRODUITS LAITIERS,OEUFS
022	MILK AND CREAM	W 3604	5.3	W 4060	5.7	W 4571	6.4	W 5853	8.1	LAIT ET CREME
0224	MILK,CREAM PRESERVED ETC	W 3581	5.3	W 4013	5.6	W 4523	6.3	W 5850	8.1	LAIT,CREME CONS,CONC
02249	MILK(EX DRY) PRSVD,SWEET					W 4523	6.3	W 5847	8.0	LAIT CONS,CONC SUCRE
024	CHEESE AND CURD	W 708	2.8	W 703	2.8	W 610	2.5	W 500	2.1	FROMAGE ET CAILLEBOTTE
025	EGGS,BIRDS,FRESH,PRSRVD	W 124	0.2	W 554	0.9	W 558	0.9	W 1003	1.9	OEUFS
0251	— IN SHELL	W 124	0.2	W 554	0.9	W 558	0.9	W 1003	1.9	OEUFS EN COQUILLE
03	FISH AND PREPARATIONS		87.0		102.6		118.4		112.7	POISSONS ET PREPARATIONS
034	FISH,FRESH,CHILLED,FROZN	W 6366	18.7	W 6188	18.5	W 6512	19.4	W 7223	22.1	POISSON FRAIS, REFRIG,CONG
0341	FISH FRSH,CHLLD,EX FILLT	W 111	0.1	W 26	0.1	W 4767	12.8	W 5135	14.2	POISSON FRAIS,REFRIGERE
0343	FISH FILLETS,FRESH,CHLLD					W 1720	6.6	W 2035	7.8	FILETS FRAIS,REFRIGERES
0344	FISH FILLETS,FROZEN	W 6254	18.6	W 6162	18.5			W 5	0.1	FILETS CONGELES
035	FISH SALTED,DRIED,SMOKED	W 75	2.5	W 84	2.8	W 109	3.8	W 194	4.6	POISSON SECHE,SALE,FUME
03503	FISH(EX COD)DRIED,SALTED					W 86	3.4	W 153	4.1	POISSONS SECHES,SALES
036	SHELL FISH FRESH,FROZEN	W 9282	65.9	W 10321	81.4	W 13254	95.3	W 13131	86.0	CRUSTACES,MOLLUSQUES
05	VEGETABLES AND FRUIT		225.4		231.3		208.1		199.9	LEGUMES ET FRUITS
054	VEG ETC FRSH,SMPLY PRSVD	W 6147	2.4	W 12196	5.2	W 12043	3.7	W 20578	5.9	LEGUMES FRAIS,CONG,SECS
0545	OTHER FRESH VEGETABLES	W 3465	0.9	W 6227	1.5	W 9179	2.0	W 17564	4.1	AUTRES LEGUMES FRAIS,REF
05459	FRESH VEGETABLES NES	W 3465	0.9	W 6227	1.5	W 9113	2.0	W 17564	4.1	LEGUMES FRAIS,REFRI NDA
0548	EDIBLE VEG NES FRESH,DRY	W 2574	1.5	W 3855	2.6	W 1280	0.9	W 2885	1.7	RACINES,TUBERCULES
05481	ROOTS,TUBERS FRESH,DRY	W 2574	1.5	W 3855	2.6	W 1280	0.9	W 2885	1.7	RACINES DE MANIOC ETC
057	FRUIT,NUTS,FRESH,DRIED	W 729081	216.7	W 782518	220.1	W 718205	203.8	W 656797	192.8	FRUITS FRAIS OU SECS
0573	BANANA,PLANTAIN,FRSH,DRY	W 694167	201.9	W 747016	206.9	W 690028	190.4	W 632264	184.2	BANANES FRAICHES,SECHEES
0579	FRUIT FRESH OR DRIED NES	W 34885	14.8	W 35502	13.3	W 28161	13.4	W 24533	8.6	FRUITS FRAIS,SECS NDA
05798	OTHER FRESH FRUIT	W 34885	14.8	W 35502	13.3	W 27980	13.4	W 23339	8.2	AUTRES FRUITS FRAIS
058	FRUIT PRESERVED,PREPARED	W 10523	5.8	W 19376	5.6	W 431	0.7	W 726	1.3	CONSERVES DE FRUITS
0582	FRUIT PRESERVED BY SUGAR	W 10022	5.0	W 19214	5.4					FRUITS CONFITS AU SUCRE
06	SUGAR AND PREPS,HONEY		22.3		17.8		20.0		22.9	SUCRES ET PRODUITS
061	SUGAR AND HONEY	W 65221	22.0	W 54777	17.1	W 45775	19.0	W 46645	22.6	SUCRES ET MIEL
0611	RAW BEET AND CANE SUGAR	W 63110	21.9	W 54777	17.1	W 44215	18.0	W 46645	22.6	SUCRES BRUTS
07	COFFEE,TEA,COCOA,SPICES		13.3		15.8		36.1		21.0	CAFE,THE,CACAO,EPICES
071	COFFEE AND SUBSTITUTES	W 8079	11.9	W 5266	14.0	W 10945	33.5	W 8400	18.9	CAFE ET SUCCEDANES
0711	COFFEE GREEN,ROASTED,SUB	W 8079	11.9	W 5266	14.0	W 10945	33.5	W 8400	18.9	CAFE TORREFIE OU DECAFEINE
07111	COFFEE GREEN,HUSKS,SKINS					W 10945	33.5	W 8345	18.8	CAFE NON TORREFIE
081	*FEEDING STUFF FOR ANIML	W 16290	4.9	W 20365	5.7	W 21226	5.5	W 8013	2.7	NOURRITURE POUR ANIMAUX
0814	MEAT OR FISH MEAL FODDER	W 15734	4.5	W 19082	5.1	W 20468	5.0	W 7095	2.2	FARINES DE VIANDES,POISSONS
08142	FISH MEAL FODDER					W 20468	5.0	W 7095	2.2	FARINES DE POISSONS
09	MISC EDIBLE PRODUCTS		12.0		10.9		11.7		11.0	PREP ALIMENTAIRES DIVERSES
098	EDIBLE PRODCTS,PREPS NES	W 5910	12.0	W 5610	10.8	W 6136	11.6	W 5639	11.0	PREP ALIMENTAIRES NDA
09804	SAUCES,MIXED SEASONINGS	W 3165	5.5	W 5005	9.7	W 5504	10.4	W 4956	9.9	SAUCES,ASSAISONNEMENTS
09809	MISC FOOD PREPRTIONS NES	W 2581	6.2	W 356	0.7	W 484	1.0	W 412	0.7	PREP ALIMENTAIRES NDA
1	BEVERAGES AND TOBACCO		14.6		14.2		10.3		10.6	BOISSONS ET TABACS
11	BEVERAGES		6.3		7.5		5.5		4.8	BOISSONS
112	ALCOHOLIC BEVERAGES	W 5052	5.7	W 5607	7.0	W 2623	4.6	W 2273	4.5	BOISSONS ALCOOLIQUES
1124	DISTILLED ALCOHOLIC BEVS	W 4189	5.1	W 3589	5.7	W 2485	4.5	W 2069	4.4	ALCOOLS,EAUX–DE–VIE
11249	OTH ALCOHOLC BEVS,CMPNDS					W 2478	4.5	W 2060	4.3	BOISSONS ALCOOLIQUES NDA
12	TOBACCO AND MANUFACTURES		8.3		6.7		4.8		5.9	TABACS BRUTS FABRIQUES
121	TOBACCO UNMNFCTRD,REFUSE	W 1290	5.7	W 559	1.7	W 248	0.5	W 170	0.7	TABACS BRUTS,DECHETS
1211	TOBACCO,NOT STRIPPED	W 1290	5.7	W 559	1.7	W 248	0.5	W 163	0.7	TABACS NON ECOTES
122	TOBACCO,MANUFACTURED	W 400	2.7	W 746	5.0	W 710	4.3	W 822	5.2	TABACS FABRIQUES
1222	CIGARETTES	W 400	2.7	W 745	4.9	W 709	4.2	W 822	5.2	CIGARETTES
2	CRUDE MATERLS,EXCL FUELS		5.7		5.0		10.9		9.8	MAT BRUTES NON COMESTIBLES
22	OIL SEEDS,OLEAGINOUS FRT						2.9		0.5	GRAINES,FRUITS OLEAGINEUX
223	SEEDS FOR OTH FIXED OILS					W 37874	2.9	W 8300	0.5	GRAINES AUTRES HUILES FIXES
2232	PALM NUTS AND KERNELS					W 37874	2.9	W 8300	0.5	NOIX,AMANDES DE PALMISTE
28	METALLIFEROUS ORES,SCRAP		1.5		1.9		5.3		6.7	MINERAIS METAL,DECHETS
288	NONFERR METAL SCRAP NES	W 1148	0.9	W 1118	0.9	W 5332	4.4	W 6861	5.9	DECHETS NON FERREUX
2882	OTHER BASE MTL SCRAP NES	W 1148	0.9	W 1118	0.9	W 5332	4.4	W 6861	5.9	AUTRES DECHETS
28823	ALUMINIUM WSTE AND SCRAP	W 313	0.3	W 80	0.1	W 4387	3.3	W 5973	5.0	DECHETS D'ALUMINIUM
29	CRUDE ANIMAL,VEG MAT NES		2.9		2.5		2.3		2.0	MATIERES BRUTES ANIM,VEGET
292	CRUDE VEG MATERIALS NES	W 786	1.9	W 685	1.6	W 572	1.3	W 546	1.4	MAT BRUTES VEGETALES NDA
3	MINERAL FUELS ETC		10.2		13.0		18.2		28.1	COMBUSTIBLES MINERAUX LUB
33	PETROLEUM AND PRODUCTS		10.2		13.0		18.2		27.8	PETROLE ET DERIVES
334	PETROLEUM PRODUCTS,REFIN	W 81601	10.2	W 96712	13.0	W 143313	18.2	W 193312	27.8	PRODUITS RAFFINES
3341	GASOLINE,OTH LIGHT OILS	W 3430	1.2	W 5465	1.6	W 2259	0.8	W 36329	7.2	ESSENCES POUR MOTEURS
33411	MOTOR,AVIATION SPIRIT					W 2259	0.8	W 36329	7.2	ESSENCES MOTEURS D'AVIONS
3342	KEROSENE,OTH MEDIUM OILS			W 11610	2.0					PETR LAMPANTS,AUT HUIL
3343	GAS OILS	W 75884	6.5	W 77325	7.3	W 139014	15.6	W 24406	4.0	GAS OILS
3344	FUEL OILS,NES	W 2287	2.5	W 2312	2.4			W 130242	14.3	FUEL OILS
3345	LUBS,PETROLEUM OILS NES					W 2041	1.9	W 2335	2.4	HUILES LUBRIFIANTES
33451	LUBS(HIGH PETR CONT) ETC					W 2041	1.9	W 2335	2.4	HUILES LUBRIF,H LOURDES
4	ANIMAL,VEGETABLE OIL,FAT		2.1		2.5		1.9		1.7	HUILES,GRAISSES ANIM,VEG
411	*ANIMAL OILS AND FATS	W 8645	2.1	W 12623	2.5	W 7357	1.9	W 2323	0.7	HUILES,GRAISSES ANIMALES
4111	OILS OF FISH,WHALES ETC	W 8645	2.1	W 12623	2.5	W 7357	1.9	W 2323	0.7	GRAISSES,HUILES DE POISSONS
41112	OTHER FISH OILS AND FATS					W 7357	1.9	W 2323	0.7	AUTRES HUILES ET GRAISSES
5	CHEMCLS,RELATED PROD NES		22.2		26.7		28.8		28.5	PRODUITS CHIMIQUES
51	ORGANIC CHEMICALS		2.0		3.2		1.4		3.2	PROD CHIMIQ ORGANIQUES
512	ALCOHOLS,PHENOLS ETC	W 6043	2.0	W 8751	3.1	W 3360	1.4	W 5540	2.9	PHENOLS,PHENOLS–ALCOOLS
5121	ACYCLIC ALCOHOLS,DERIVS	W 6043	2.0	W 8751	3.1	W 3360	1.4	W 5540	2.9	ALCOOLS ACYCLIQUES
51216	ETHYL ALC,DENATRD SPIRIT	W 6043	2.0	W 8751	3.1	W 3360	1.4	W 5540	2.9	ALCOOL ETHYLIQUE NON DENAT
53	DYES,TANNING,COLOUR PROD		3.9		3.9		5.7		6.9	PROD TEINTURE,COLORANTS
531	SYNT DYE,NAT INDGO,LAKES	W 1110	3.1	W 844	2.3	W 796	2.6	W 848	2.9	MAT COLOR ORGAN,LAQUES
5311	SYNTHIC ORGNIC DYESTUFFS	W 1110	3.1	W 844	2.3	W 791	2.6	W 845	2.8	MAT COLOR ORGAN SYNTHET
533	PIGMENTS,PAINTS,ETC	W 269	0.9	W 480	1.6	W 1138	3.1	W 1608	4.0	PIGMENTS,PEINTURES,VERNIS
5334	VARNISHES,DISTEMPERS ETC	W 206	0.5	W 294	0.9	W 1006	2.7	W 1530	3.7	PEINTURES A L'EAU
53342	OTH PAINTS,VARNISHES ETC					W 672	1.9	W 1355	3.3	AUTRES PEINTURES,VERNIS
541	*MEDICINAL,PHARM PRODUCT	K 559515	10.0	K 712344	12.2	K 984812	15.9	K 866164	13.1	PROD MEDICINAUX PHARMACEUT
5417	MEDICAMENTS	K 559515	10.0	K 711997	12.1	K 983807	15.8	K 865691	13.1	MEDICAMENTS
54179	— CONTNG OTH SUBSTANCES					K 978508	15.2	K 863861	13.0	MED CONT AUT SUBSTANCES
55	PERFUME,CLEANING ETC PRD		5.2		5.9		4.5		3.6	PROD POUR PARFUM,TOILETTE
553	PERFUMERY,COSMETICS,ETC	W 726	4.6	W 948	5.6	W 610	4.1	W 618	3.3	PRODUITS DE PARFUMERIE
6	BASIC MANUFACTURES		24.7		33.7		39.2		44.3	ART MANUFACTURES

5. Special Exports F.O.B. by Commodities according to the S.I.T.C. (Rev. 2) in million U.S. Dollars
Exportations Spéciales F.O.B. par Produits d'après la C.T.C.I. (Rév. 2) en millions de Dollars E.U.

SITC CTCI	COMMODITY	1993		1994		1995		1996		PRODUIT
		QUANTITY QUANTITE	VALUE VALEUR	QUANTITY QUANTITE	VALUE VALEUR	QUANTITY QUANTITE	VALUE VALEUR	QUANTITY QUANTITE	VALUE VALEUR	
61	LEATHER,DRESSED FUR,ETC		8.0		9.1		8.7		9.1	CUIRS,PELLETERIES
611	LEATHER	W 4519	8.0	W 4957	9.1	W 4373	8.7	W 4945	9.0	CUIRS,PEAUX PREPARES
6114	LEATHR BOVINE NES,EQUINE	W 4519	8.0	W 4956	9.1	W 4373	8.7	W 4945	9.0	CUIRS DE BOVINS
63	WOOD,CORK MANUFACTRS NES		1.0		1.7		1.9		2.3	OUVRAGES LIEGE ET BOIS
635	WOOD MANUFACTURES NES	W 525	0.8	W 775	1.2	W 1175	1.8	W 1396	2.2	ART MANUF EN BOIS NDA
6359	OTHER WOOD MANUFACTURES	W 525	0.8	W 748	1.1	W 1144	1.8	W 1284	2.0	OUVRAGES EN BOIS NDA
63591	TOOLS,HANDLES ETC WOOD	W 522	0.8	W 744	1.1	W 1135	1.8	W 1260	2.0	OUTILS MANCHES D'OUTILS
64	PAPER,PAPERBOARD AND MFR		5.4		10.3		16.1		12.8	PAPIERS,CARTONS & OUVRAGES
641	PAPER AND PAPERBOARD	W 1224	0.7	W 4969	2.1	W 8817	5.4	W 7889	3.6	PAPIERS ET CARTONS
6411	NEWSPRINT	W 1218	0.7	W 4953	2.1	W 8377	4.8	W 7498	3.0	PAPIER JOURNAL
642	PAPER,ETC,PRECUT,ARTS OF	W 4647	4.7	W 7277	8.2	W 9447	10.7	W 5279	9.3	PAP,CARTONS DECOUPES
6421	PAPER ETC CONTAINERS	W 3522	2.3	W 5096	3.4	W 6907	5.3	W 1939	2.7	BOITES,SACS EMBALLAGES
6428	PAPER ETC ARTICLES NES	W 1086	2.3	W 2085	4.6	W 2420	5.1	W 3267	6.5	OUVRAGES EN PATE A PAPIER
64283	PAPER DISHES,CUPS,ETC					W 1066	2.6	W 1196	2.8	ASSIETTES ETC EN PAPIER
64284	PAPER TISSUES,TOWELS ETC		0.1	W 496	1.9	W 6	0.1			MOUCHOIRS SERVIETTES EN PAP
64285	PAPER ETC DIAPERS ETC	W 1025	2.3	W 1036	2.4	W 410	1.8	W 693	2.9	SERVIETTES HYGIENIQUES
66	NONMETAL MINERAL MFS NES		2.9		3.2		3.0		2.1	ART MIN NON METALLIQUES
68	NON–FERROUS METALS		1.6		2.3		1.2		2.5	METAUX NON FERREUX
684	ALUMINIUM	W 2192	1.6	W 3072	2.3	W 135	0.5	W 297	1.2	ALUMINIUM
6841	ALUMINIUM,ALLOYS,UNWRGHT	W 2168	1.5	W 3051	2.2					ALUMINIUM,ALLIAGES BRUTS
69	METAL MANUFACTURES NES		4.6		6.7		8.0		14.8	ART MANUFACT EN METAL NDA
692	METAL TANKS,BOXES,ETC	W 1184	3.2	W 1118	5.3	W 1476	6.2	W 3577	12.4	RECIPIENTS METALLIQUES
6924	MTL TRANSPORT BOXES ETC	W 1181	3.2	W 1118	5.3	W 1476	6.2	W 3571	12.4	FUTS,TAMBOURS,BIDONS
69242	ALUMNM TRNSPRT BOXES ETC	W 1172	3.2	W 1118	5.3	W 1476	6.2	W 3531	12.3	FUTS,TAMBOURS,BIDONS ALU
8	MISC MANUFACTURED GOODS		32.9		40.3		48.7		41.6	ART MANUFACTURES DIVERS
84	CLOTHING AND ACCESSORIES		24.1		23.3		25.8		24.2	VETEMENTS
842	MENS OUTERWEAR NOT KNIT	W 74	2.5	W 63	2.3	W 56	2.0	W 55	1.6	VET DESSUS POUR HOMMES
843	WOMENS OUTERWEAR NONKNIT	W 105	4.6	W 114	4.3	W 137	5.2	W 132	5.0	VET DESSUS FEMMES MAT TEX
8439	— OTHER OUTER GARMENTS					W 92	3.2	W 82	2.8	AUT VET DES FEM MAT TEXT
844	UNDER GARMENTS NOT KNIT	W 354	11.6	W 311	11.5	W 419	15.2	W 375	13.5	VETEMENT DESSOUS MAT TEX
8441	— MENS SHIRTS	W 288	10.1	W 278	10.4	W 328	12.8	W 285	10.9	CHEMISES HOMMES MAT TEXT
84412	—— OF SYNTHETIC FIBRES					W 328	12.8	W 285	10.9	CHEMISES HOMMES FIB SYNT
8442	— MENS,OTHR THAN SHIRTS		0.1		0.1	W 75	1.9	W 70	1.9	SOUS–VET HOMMES MAT TEXT
8443	— WOMENS	W 65	1.6	W 33	1.1	W 16	0.6	W 20	0.8	VET DESSOUS FEM MAT TEXT
847	TEXTILE CLTHNG ACCES NES	W 97	2.5	W 83	2.2			W 3	0.1	ACCES VET MAT TEXT NDA
8471	— NOT KNITTED	W 92	2.4	W 77	2.0				0.1	ACCES VET MAT TEX NON BON
84714	GLOVES,SOCKS ETC,NOT KNT	W 92	2.4	W 77	2.0					BAS,CHAUSSETTES MAT TEXT
848	HEADGEAR,NONTXTL CLOTHNG	W 854	2.7	W 882	2.8	W 1072	3.6	W 1086	4.0	VET ACCES MAT AUT QUE TEX
8482	PLASTC,RUBBR CLTHG,ACCES	W 853	2.6	W 880	2.7	W 1072	3.6	W 1085	4.0	VET ACCES MAT PLAS ARTIF
84822	RUBBER CLOTHING,ACCESRYS	W 853	2.6	W 880	2.7	W 1072	3.6	W 1085	4.0	VET ACCES CAOUT VULCAN
89	MISC MANUFCTRD GOODS NES		7.7		16.4		22.4		16.7	ART MANUFACTURES DIVERS
893	ARTICLES OF PLASTIC NES	W 889	1.8	W 969	1.8		2.1	W 770	1.7	OUVRAGES EN MAT DIVIS 58
8931	PLSTC PACKG CONTNRS,LIDS	W 883	1.8	W 925	1.7	W 428	1.2	W 257	0.8	ART TRANSP EMBALLAGE ETC
897	GOLD,SILVER WARE,JEWELRY		1.1		6.8		7.9		1.8	BIJOUTERIE,ORFEVRERIE
8973	PREC JEWLRY,GLD–SILVWARE		1.1		6.8		7.9		1.8	BIJOUX OR,ARGENT ORFEVRE
89731	PRECIOUS METAL JEWELLERY		1.1		6.1		7.9		1.8	ART BIJOUTERIE,JOAILLER
899	OTHER MANUFACTURED GOODS	W 1899	4.8	W 3058	7.6	W 4722	10.6	W 4690	11.6	AUT ART MANUF DIVERS NDA
8997	BASKETWORK,BROOMS ETC	W 1768	4.1	W 2823	6.6	W 4439	9.7	W 4581	11.2	OUVRAGES VANNERIE NDA
89972	BRUSHES,BROOMS,MOPS ETC	W 1767	4.1	W 2822	6.6	W 4439	9.7	W 4581	11.2	BALAIS ET BALAYETTES
9	GOODS NOT CLASSD BY KIND		3.3		4.0		4.5		10.9	ART TRANSACT NON CLASSES
971	*GOLD,NON MONETARY NES	K 850	3.2	K 585	3.8	K 1234	4.5	K 2442	10.9	OR NON MONETAIRE
97101	NONMON GLD UNWRT,SEMIMFD	K 468	3.1	K 577	3.8	K 1075	4.4	K 2427	10.9	OR,ALLIAGES D'OR BRUTS

FOOT NOTES – NOTES

TABLE 1 –
1 Prior to 1964, imports f.o.b.
TABLEAU 1 –
1 Avant 1964, les importations sont f.a.b.

1. HISTORICAL SERIES, 1962–1997 GENERAL TRADE, IMPORTS F.O.B., EXPORTS F.O.B. #1
SERIES HISTORIQUES, 1962–1997 COMMERCE GENERAL, IMPORTATIONS F.O.B., EXPORTATIONS F.O.B

YEAR ANNEE	VALUE IN MILLION KINA / VALEUR EN MILLION KINA — MERCHANDISE –MARCHANDISE		GOLD –OR		CONVERSION FACTORS U.S. CENTS PER KINA / FACTEURS DE CONVERSION CENTS E.U. PAR KINA		INDEX NUMBERS –INDICES — QUANTUM		UNIT VALUE / VALEUR UNITAIRE	
	IMPORTS	EXPORTS	IMPORTS	EXPORTS	IMPORTS	EXPORTS	IMPORTS	EXPORTS	IMPORTS	EXPORTS
1962	51.90	30.40		1.44	112.0000	112.0000				
1963	57.10	35.00		1.34	112.0000	112.0000				
1964	70.70	39.60		1.32	112.0000	112.0000				
1965	86.90	48.10		1.08	112.0000	112.0000				
1966	110.40	48.90		0.95	112.0000	112.0000				
1967	127.40	52.30		0.91	112.0000	112.0000				
1968	145.30	69.40		0.82	112.0000	112.0000				
1969	150.50	74.40		0.81	112.0000	112.0000				
1970	239.50	91.70		0.80	112.0000	112.0000				
1971	275.40	106.30		0.70	113.8760	113.7580				
1972	247.40	182.00		0.81	119.0990	119.0990				
1973	214.40	362.70		0.95	142.1660	143.0970				
1974	298.90	477.80		1.62	143.2280	145.1130				
1975	362.80	335.90			131.0860	131.1220				
1976	351.50	435.50			122.2990	122.4960				
1977	448.30	539.80			126.5470	126.5680				
1978	478.30	504.00			141.2820	141.6820				
1979	561.60	629.10			140.4000	140.3790				
1980	684.20	694.20			149.4710	148.7350				89
1981	738.10	581.80			148.5438	148.3945		100		70
1982	751.70	570.90			135.3008	135.1002		108		69
1983	821.70	682.20			119.5202	119.1071		116		80
1984	851.10	783.50			111.7249	111.5829		126		89
1985	866.90	917.00			99.8319	99.7706		134		91
1986	1037.38	1000.80			102.9352	102.9934		141		90
1987	1144.94	1123.20			110.2289	110.5110		147		98
1988	1378.85	1256.30			115.5184	115.5419				114
1989	1324.80	1111.60			116.7165	116.9369				96
1990	1138.61	1122.40			104.6084	104.8583				100
1991	1535.94	1390.50			105.0583	104.9507				99
1992	1431.17	1862.60			103.7504	103.4645				101
1993	1270.50	2527.30			102.2448	102.2374				113
1994	1534.10	2662.00			99.1461	98.8071				132
1995	1862.90	3400.00			77.9239	78.0476				185
1996	2296.00	3314.00			75.8440	75.9001				182
1997	2428.90	3043.50			69.8142	70.2029				204

2. IMPORTS BY BROAD ECONOMIC CATEGORY AND EXPORTS BY INDUSTRIAL ORIGIN. (PERCENTAGE OF TOTAL VALUE)
IMPORTATIONS PAR CATEGORIES ECONOMIQUES ET EXPORTATIONS PAR BRANCHE D'ACTIVITE.(EN POURCENTAGE DE LA VALEUR TOTALE)

IMPORTS – IMPORTATIONS

	1987	1988	1989	1990	1991	1992	1993
TOTAL IMPORTS–IMPORTATIONS TOTALES	100.	100.	100.	100.			
1 FOOD BEV–ALIMENTATION BOISSONS	16.2	15.8	14.4	16.9			
11 PRIMARY–PRODUITS DE BASE	4.1	4.1	4.0	4.7			
111 FOR INDUSTRY–POUR L'INDUSTRIE	0.6	0.8	1.0	1.2			
112 FOR HOUSEHOLDS–POUR LES MENAGES	3.5	3.4	3.0	3.5			
12 PROCESSED–PRODUITS ELABORES	12.1	11.6	10.3	12.2			
121 FOR INDUSTRY–POUR L'INDUSTRIE	0.6	0.6	0.5	0.5			
122 FOR HOUSEHOLDS–POUR LES MENAGES	11.4	11.1	9.8	11.7			
2 IND SUPPLIES–APPROV INDUSTRIELS	22.8	22.7	21.8	24.0			
21 PRIMARY–PRODUITS DE BASE	1.2	1.2	0.9	1.1			
22 PROCESSED–PRODUITS ELABORES	21.6	21.4	20.9	23.0			
3 FUELS–COMBUSTIBLES	10.6	8.4	4.7	6.8			
31 PRIMARY–PRODUITS DE BASE	0.0	0.0	0.0	0.1			
32 PROCESSED–PRODUITS ELABORES	10.6	8.3	4.7	6.7			
321 MOTOR SPIRIT–ESSENCE	2.4	1.8	0.8	1.2			
322 OTHER–AUTRES	8.2	6.6	3.8	5.5			
4 MACHINERY–EQUIPEMENT	23.5	25.9	25.2	23.7			
41 CAPITAL EQUIPMENT–MACHINES	20.3	22.9	22.2	20.8			
42 PARTS–PIECES ACCESSOIRES	3.2	3.0	3.0	2.9			
5 TRANSPORT–TRANSPORT	15.1	16.3	22.6	16.7			
51 PASSENGER CARS–AUTOMOBILES	3.9	1.9	2.4	2.8			
52 OTHER–AUTRES	6.0	8.5	13.1	7.6			
521 INDUSTRIAL–INDUSTRIELS	5.9	8.3	13.0	7.5			
522 NON INDUSTRIAL–NON INDUSTRIEL	0.1	0.1	0.1	0.1			
53 PARTS–PIECES ACCESSOIRES	5.2	5.9	7.1	6.3			
6 CONSUM GOODS–BIENS CONSOMMATION	11.2	10.5	10.0	10.3			
61 DURABLE–DURABLES	2.2	1.7	1.8	1.6			
62 SEMI DURABLE–SEMI DURABLES	5.7	5.7	5.3	5.2			
63 NON DURABLE–NON DURABLES	3.3	3.2	2.9	3.5			
7 GOODS NES–BIENS NDA	0.7	0.5	1.4	1.6			

EXPORTS – EXPORTATIONS

	1987	1988	1989	1990	1991	1992	1993
TOTAL EXPORTS–EXPORTATIONS TOTALES	100.	100.	100.	100.	100.	100.	100.
1 AGRICULTURE	35.7	25.7	26.8	24.9	21.8	27.2	28.1
2 MINING QUARRY–INDUS EXTRACTIVES	57.3	64.7	60.5	56.6	53.8	50.3	62.3
3 MANUFACTURING–IND MANUFACTUR	7.0	9.6	12.7	18.4	24.4	22.5	9.6
31 FOOD BEV TOBACCO–ALIM BOISS TAB	4.8	5.0	5.5	5.4	6.2	9.1	4.9
32 TEXTILES–INDUSTRIES TEXTILES	0.0	0.0	0.0	0.0	0.2	0.1	0.1
33 WOOD & PRODUCTS–BOIS & PRODUITS	0.9	0.7	0.6	0.9	0.7	0.7	0.5
34 PAPER & PRODUCTS–PAPIER & PRODT	0.0	0.0	0.0	0.0	0.0	0.0	0.0
35 CHEMICALS–INDUSTRIES CHIMIQUES	0.4	0.5	0.3	0.5	0.4	0.2	0.1
36 NON METAL MIN–MIN NON METAL	0.1	0.1	0.1	0.1	0.0	0.0	0.0
37 BASIC METAL–IND METAL BASE	0.2	0.0	0.6	1.5	1.3	1.0	0.4
38 METAL MANUF–MANUF METAL	0.6	3.4	4.0	8.6	15.0	10.8	3.4
39 OTH MANUF IND–AUTRES MANUF	0.0	0.0	1.6	1.5	0.5	0.5	0.2

3. TRADE BY PRINCIPAL COUNTRIES OF ORIGIN AND DESTINATION (VALUE IN MILLION U.S. DOLLARS)
ECHANGES SELON LES PRINCIPAUX PAYS D'ORIGINE ET DE DESTINATION (VALEUR EN MILLIONS DE DOLLARS EU)

COUNTRIES–PAYS	GENERAL IMPORTS F.O.B. IMPORTATIONS GENERALES F.O.B.				
	1989	1990	1991	1992	1993
World	1576.5	1233.1			
Africa	2.5	3.2			
Americas	245.3	149.2			
– Northern America	239.7	143.3			
– LAIA	5.6	5.9			
– CACM	0.0				
– Caribbean	0.0	0.0			
– Rest of America	0.0	0.0			
Asia excl fmr USSR	477.4	366.1			
– Middle East	6.3	0.2			
Asia former USSR					
Europe excl fmr USSR	170.8	87.6			
– European Union	164.1	84.2			
– Eastern Europe	0.8	0.4			
– Rest of Europe	5.9	3.0			
Europe former USSR	0.1	13.6			
Oceania	678.3	609.9			
Other	2.1	3.4			
Australia/Australie	625.4	567.9			
Japan/Japon	236.7	160.5			
USA/Etats–Unis d'Amer	205.7	119.6			
Singapore/Singapour	106.2	105.7			
New Zealand	49.5	40.8			
United Kingdom	45.1	29.0			
France, Monaco	56.1	14.0			
Canada	34.0	23.7			
China/Chine	31.3	25.0			
China, Hong Kong SAR	33.8	19.7			
Former Fed Rep Germany	23.0	16.3			
Korea, Republic of	16.2	11.3			
Netherlands/Pays–Bas	21.2	4.9			
Other Asia n.e.s.	13.9	8.7			
Malaysia/Malaisie	11.7	9.2			
Indonesia/Indonésie	7.5	11.6			
Thailand/Thaïlande	8.8	8.0			
Former USSR/Anc. URSS	0.1	13.6			
Italy/Italie	3.9	8.9			
Denmark/Danemark	4.9	3.7			
Chile/Chili	4.0	4.7			
Belgium–Luxembourg	4.6	2.2			
Saudi Arabia	6.0	0.0			
Sweden/Suède	2.6	2.8			
Philippines	1.8	3.2			
Areas n.e.s.	1.3	3.2			
Norway,Svalbard and JM	3.4	0.9			
Sudan/Soudan	1.4	2.2			
India/Inde	1.4	1.2			
Switzerland,Liechtenst.	1.5	1.0			
Fiji/Fidji	1.7	0.7			
Brazil/Brésil	1.3	1.0			
Former SFR Yugoslavia	1.0	1.1			
Malawi	1.0	1.0			
Bangladesh	1.0	0.8			
Vanuatu	1.5	0.2			
Ireland/Irlande	0.9	0.5			
Spain/Espagne	0.9	0.5			
Finland/Finlande	0.4	0.9			
Special Categories	0.8	0.2			

COUNTRIES–PAYS	GENERAL EXPORTS F.O.B. EXPORTATIONS GENERALES F.O.B.				
	1989	1990	1991	1992	1993
Monde	1453.8	1261.7	1641.8	1698.9	2624.6
Afrique	0.1	2.1	1.7	0.1	0.1
Amériques	28.5	34.3	37.2	40.0	110.9
– Amérique du Nord	28.4	34.3	36.4	39.9	110.9
– ALAI	0.2	0.0	0.8	0.0	0.0
– MCAC					
– Caraïbes	0.0	0.0		0.0	0.0
– Autre Amérique					
Asie anc. URSS exclus	740.4	568.8	645.7	642.0	1234.5
– Moyen–Orient	5.6	0.3	1.9	6.9	2.1
Asie ancienne URSS					
Europe anc. URSS exclus	509.3	312.1	300.9	309.7	318.4
– Union Européenne	461.4	304.8	262.2	309.1	318.4
– Europe de l'Est	46.1		38.1	0.0	
– Autre de l'Europe	1.7	7.3	0.6	0.6	0.0
Europe ancienne URSS			15.0	4.2	
Océanie	174.4	344.0	639.8	700.8	960.2
Autre	1.0	0.5	1.5	2.2	0.4
Australia/Australie	165.5	328.5	608.0	691.8	933.7
Japan/Japon	544.0	351.4	361.7	360.0	563.2
Korea, Republic of	126.8	124.9	147.8	133.8	262.3
Former Fed Rep Germany	341.6	201.2			
Germany/Allemagne			147.3	163.9	167.0
United Kingdom	66.0	54.2	65.7	72.9	81.3
Philippines	31.6	53.7	69.5	47.2	70.3
USA/Etats–Unis d'Amer	28.1	30.1	36.1	36.0	109.7
Singapore/Singapour	9.9	18.5	34.3	62.4	82.8
China/Chine	1.1	2.5	4.2	4.6	173.2
Finland/Finlande	5.6	35.8	33.0	40.9	26.8
Netherlands/Pays–Bas	21.5	8.1	8.4	25.6	27.0
New Zealand	5.7	11.6	27.4	5.3	19.5
Other Asia n.e.s.	2.1	3.4	1.1	1.5	32.6
China, Hong Kong SAR	7.1	2.7	9.5	10.4	8.3
Bulgaria/Bulgarie			37.8	0.0	
Former Czechoslovakia	30.8				
Indonesia/Indonésie	3.4	4.0	0.5	6.6	12.5
Belgium–Luxembourg	6.6	2.2	4.9	3.5	3.2
Thailand/Thaïlande	0.5	0.8	1.3	1.9	15.5
Malaysia/Malaisie	1.9	1.0	2.4	2.6	10.6
Spain/Espagne	14.3	0.1	0.8	0.1	0.0
Jordan/Jordanie	5.0	0.2	1.0	6.9	2.0
Former USSR/Anc. URSS			15.0		
India/Inde	3.3	5.0	1.8	3.7	0.3
Poland/Pologne	11.7		0.3		
Solomon Islands	2.2	2.7	3.0	2.7	1.3
Denmark/Danemark	0.0		0.0		11.3
France, Monaco	5.4	2.6	1.3	0.9	0.4
Switzerland,Liechtenst.	1.7	7.3	0.6	0.6	0.0
Canada	0.3	4.1	0.3	3.9	1.2
Myanmar			9.5		
Fiji/Fidji	0.5	0.5	0.3	0.2	4.8
Russian Federation				4.2	
Bunkers, ship stores	0.0	0.2	1.3	0.7	0.4
Korea Dem People's Rp	2.5				
Areas n.e.s.	0.5	0.2	0.0	1.4	0.0
Italy/Italie	0.2	0.3	0.4	0.5	0.6
Hungary/Hongrie	2.0				
So. African Customs Un	0.1	1.8	0.0	0.0	

(VALUE AS PERCENTAGE OF WORLD TOTAL)(VALEURS EN POURCENTAGE DU TOTAL MONDIAL)

	1984	1985	1986	1987	1988	1989	1990	1991	1992	1993
Africa	0.1	0.1	0.1	0.1	0.1	0.2	0.3			
Americas	12.0	12.3	12.9	14.0	11.9	15.6	12.1			
– Northern America	11.7	12.0	12.3	13.3	11.5	15.2	11.6			
– LAIA	0.2	0.3	0.6	0.4	0.5	0.4	0.5			
– CACM	0.0	0.0	0.0	0.1		0.0				
– Caribbean	0.0	0.0	0.0	0.0	0.0	0.0	0.0			
– Rest of America	0.0	0.0	0.0	0.2	0.0	0.0	0.0			
Asia excl fmr USSR	35.1	33.8	31.3	32.4	31.9	30.3	29.7			
– Middle East	0.0	0.0	0.0	0.0	0.1	0.4	0.0			
Asia former USSR										
Europe excl fmr USSR	7.6	8.1	10.8	9.1	8.5	10.8	7.1			
– European Union	7.2	7.7	10.4	8.7	8.3	10.4	6.8			
– Eastern Europe	0.1	0.0	0.0	0.0	0.0	0.1	0.0			
– Rest of Europe	0.3	0.4	0.4	0.4	0.2	0.4	0.2			
Europe former USSR	0.0	0.0	0.0	0.0	0.0	0.0	1.1			
Oceania	44.9	45.2	44.4	44.2	47.4	43.0	49.5			
Other	0.4	0.5	0.4	0.2	0.1	0.1	0.3			
Australia/Australie	39.5	39.6	39.9	40.6	43.6	39.7	46.1			
Japan/Japon	15.8	17.0	17.7	17.6	17.8	15.0	13.0			
USA/Etats–Unis d'Amer	11.1	11.6	10.2	10.9	10.4	13.0	9.7			
Singapore/Singapour	11.9	10.0	6.2	6.5	5.9	6.7	8.6			
New Zealand	5.2	5.4	4.4	3.5	3.7	3.1	3.3			
United Kingdom	3.5	2.9	3.4	2.9	3.1	2.9	2.4			
France, Monaco	0.8	0.9	0.8	0.7	0.7	3.6	1.1			
Canada	0.6	0.4	2.2	2.4	1.1	2.2	1.9			
China/Chine	2.0	1.7	1.9	1.9	2.2	2.0	2.0			
China, Hong Kong SAR	2.3	2.3	1.8	2.0	2.0	2.1	1.6			

	1984	1985	1986	1987	1988	1989	1990	1991	1992	1993
Afrique	0.0	0.0	0.0		0.0	0.0	0.2	0.1	0.0	0.0
Amériques	3.7	7.9	3.2	2.0	3.2	2.0	2.7	2.3	2.4	4.2
– Amérique du Nord	3.7	7.9	3.2	2.0	3.2	2.0	2.7	2.2	2.4	4.2
– ALAI			0.0	0.0	0.0	0.0	0.0	0.0	0.0	0.0
– MCAC										
– Caraïbes			0.0			0.0	0.0		0.0	0.0
– Autre Amérique										
Asie anc. URSS exclus	41.0	32.0	37.0	51.3	56.8	50.9	45.1	39.3	37.8	47.0
– Moyen–Orient	0.1	0.1	0.1	0.1	0.2	0.4	0.0	0.1	0.4	0.1
Asie ancienne URSS										
Europe anc. URSS exclus	44.8	47.6	44.4	38.1	33.0	35.0	24.7	18.3	18.2	12.1
– Union Européenne	43.1	47.5	44.4	38.1	32.1	31.7	24.2	16.0	18.2	12.1
– Europe de l'Est	1.0	0.1			1.0	3.2		2.3	0.0	
– Autre de l'Europe	0.8	0.0	0.0	0.0	0.0	0.1	0.6	0.0	0.0	0.0
Europe ancienne URSS	0.0		0.3					0.9	0.2	
Océanie	10.4	12.2	15.0	8.5	6.9	12.0	27.3	39.0	41.3	36.6
Autre	0.0	0.2	0.1	0.1	0.0	0.1	0.0	0.1	0.1	0.0
Australia/Australie	9.0	10.6	13.7	7.7	6.4	11.4	26.0	37.0	40.7	35.6
Japan/Japon	28.7	22.3	26.4	28.2	41.2	37.4	27.9	22.0	21.2	21.5
Korea, Republic of	5.7	6.1	6.3	16.4	6.6	8.7	9.9	9.0	7.9	10.0
Former Fed Rep Germany	20.9	29.5	34.8	27.7	21.6	23.5	15.9			
Germany/Allemagne								9.0	9.6	6.4
United Kingdom	11.2	7.8	4.5	4.6	5.0	4.5	4.3	4.0	4.3	3.1
Philippines	0.1	0.3	0.0	2.5	5.8	2.2	4.3	4.2	2.8	2.7
USA/Etats–Unis d'Amer	3.4	3.9	3.2	2.0	3.0	1.9	2.4	2.2	2.1	4.2
Singapore/Singapour	1.2	0.6	1.7	0.5	0.5	0.7	1.5	2.1	3.7	3.2
China/Chine	3.1	1.9	1.9	2.1	0.1	0.1	0.2	0.3	0.3	6.6

4. General Imports F.O.B. by Commodities according to the S.I.T.C. (Rev. 2) in million U.S. Dollars
Importations Générales F.O.B. par Produits d'après la C.T.C.I. (Rév. 2) en millions de Dollars E.U.

SITC CTCI	COMMODITY	1990 QUANTITY QUANTITE	1990 VALUE VALEUR	1991 QUANTITY QUANTITE	1991 VALUE VALEUR	1992 QUANTITY QUANTITE	1992 VALUE VALEUR	1993 QUANTITY QUANTITE	1993 VALUE VALEUR	PRODUIT
	ALL COMMODITIES		1233.1							TOUS PRODUITS
0	FOOD AND LIVE ANIMALS		206.1							ALIMENTS,ANIMAUX VIVANTS
01	MEAT AND PREPARATIONS		43.9							VIANDES ET PREPARATIONS
011	MEAT FRESH,CHILLD,FROZEN	W 43009	36.5							VIANDES FRAICHES,REF,CONGE
0111	BOVINE MEAT FRESH,FROZEN	W 10156	15.1							VIANDES BOVIN FRAI,REF
01112	BOVINE MEAT BONELESS	W 9784	14.3							VIANDES BOVIN DESOSSEES
0112	MUTTON ETC FRSH,CHLD,FRN	W 30095	18.1							VIANDE DE MOUTON
012	MEAT DRIED,SALTED,SMOKED	W 2387	4.6							VIANDE,ABATS SALES,SECHES
02	DAIRY PRODCTS,BIRDS'EGGS		14.2							PRODUITS LAITIERS,OEUFS
022	MILK AND CREAM	W 9814	10.9							LAIT ET CREME
0224	MILK,CREAM PRESERVED ETC	W 9199	10.5							LAIT,CREME CONS,CONC
02243	MILK DRY,OVER 1.5% FAT	W 1614	5.4							LAIT POUDRE SUP 1.5%
02249	MILK(EX DRY) PRSVD,SWEET	W 7473	4.9							LAIT CONS,CONC SUCRE
03	FISH AND PREPARATIONS		36.2							POISSONS ET PREPARATIONS
037	FISH ETC PREPD,PRSVD NES	W 31721	35.0							POIS,CRUST,MOL PREPARES
0371	FISH PREPARD,PRESRVD NES	W 31705	34.9							CONSERVES DE POISSONS
04	CEREALS AND PREPARATIONS		65.0							CEREALES ET PRODUITS
041	WHEAT ETC UNMILLED	W 52851	11.7							FROMENT,EPEAUTRE
0412	OTHER WHEAT ETC UNMILLED	W 36882	9.2							AUTRE FROMENT NON MOULU
042	RICE	W 154182	41.1							RIZ
0422	RICE SEMI-MILLED,MILLED	W 148896	40.1							RIZ POLI,GLACE INCL BRISURES
04221	RICE MILLED UNBROKEN	W 148896	40.1							RIZ POLI,GLACE EXCL BRISURES
048	CEREAL ETC PREPARATIONS	W 17155	9.7							PREPTNS A BASE CEREALES
05	VEGETABLES AND FRUIT		11.5							LEGUMES ET FRUITS
058	FRUIT PRESERVED,PREPARED	W 4471	4.5							CONSERVES DE FRUITS
07	COFFEE,TEA,COCOA,SPICES		4.5							CAFE,THE,CACAO,EPICES
081	*FEEDING STUFF FOR ANIML		9.0							NOURRITURE POUR ANIMAUX
0819	FOOD WASTE AND FEED NES	W 19645	6.6							DECHETS,ALIMENTS NDA
08199	FODDER NES,INCL SWEETNED	W 19628	6.6							PREPARATIONS FOURRAGERES
09	MISC EDIBLE PRODUCTS		18.8							PREP ALIMENTAIRES DIVERSES
091	MARGARINE AND SHORTENING	W 5864	6.8							MARGARINE ET GRAISSES
0914	MARGARINE,EDIBLE FAT NES	W 5827	6.7							MARGARINES,SIMILI SAINDOUX
09149	OTH PREPARED EDIBLE FATS	W 4021	3.9							SIMILI-SAINDOUX
098	EDIBLE PRODCTS,PREPS NES	W 12366	12.1							PREP ALIMENTAIRES NDA
09809	MISC FOOD PREPRTIONS NES	W 10226	7.0							PREP ALIMENTAIRES NDA
1	BEVERAGES AND TOBACCO		15.5							BOISSONS ET TABACS
11	BEVERAGES		10.3							BOISSONS
111	NON-ALCOHL BEVERAGES NES	W 10570	6.0							BOISSONS NON ALCOOLIQUES
11102	FLAVORED WATERS NON-ALCO	W 10517	6.0							LIMONADES,EAUX GAZEUSES
112	ALCOHOLIC BEVERAGES	W 751	4.4							BOISSONS ALCOOLIQUES
12	TOBACCO AND MANUFACTURES		5.2							TABACS BRUTS FABRIQUES
2	CRUDE MATERLS,EXCL FUELS		9.5							MAT BRUTES NON COMESTIBLES
26	TEXTILE FIBRES AND WASTE		4.2							FIBRES TEXTILES
27	CRUDE FERTLZR,MINRLS NES		3.9							ENGRAIS MINERAUX BRUTS
3	MINERAL FUELS ETC		83.9							COMBUSTIBLES MINERAUX LUB
33	PETROLEUM AND PRODUCTS		83.1							PETROLE ET DERIVES
334	PETROLEUM PRODUCTS,REFIN	W 377292	82.8							PRODUITS RAFFINES
3341	GASOLINE,OTH LIGHT OILS	W 56448	14.9							ESSENCES POUR MOTEURS
33411	MOTOR,AVIATION SPIRIT	W 56029	14.5							ESSENCES MOTEURS D'AVIONS
3342	KEROSENE,OTH MEDIUM OILS	W 58905	11.7							PETR LAMPANTS,AUT HUIL
33421	KEROSENE INCL JET FUEL	W 58507	11.5							PETROLES LAMPANTS
3343	GAS OILS	W 240202	45.9							GAS OILS
3345	LUBS,PETROLEUM OILS NES	W 10396	8.7							HUILES LUBRIFIANTES
33451	LUBS(HIGH PETR CONT) ETC	W 10375	8.6							HUILES LUBRIF,H LOURDES
4	ANIMAL,VEGETABLE OIL,FAT		5.1							HUILES,GRAISSES ANIM,VEG
5	CHEMCLS,RELATED PROD NES		86.2							PRODUITS CHIMIQUES
51	ORGANIC CHEMICALS		3.8							PROD CHIMIQ ORGANIQUES
52	INORGANIC CHEMICALS		16.9							PROD CHIM INORGANIQUES
522	INORG ELEMNTS,OXIDES,ETC	W 13028	5.7							ELEMENTS INORGANIQUES
523	OTHR INORG CHEMICALS ETC		11.2							AUT PRODUITS CHIMIQUES INORG
5232	OTH MTL CMPD OF INRG ACD	W 10656	9.1							SELS METALLIQUES
52325	CYANIDES,COMPLEX CYANIDE	W 4074	6.4							CYANURES SIMPLES,COMPLEXES
541	*MEDICINAL,PHARM PRODUCT		12.6							PROD MEDICINAUX PHARMACEUT
5417	MEDICAMENTS	K 8694262	7.9							MEDICAMENTS
54179	— CONTNG OTH SUBSTANCES	K 412654	4.2							MED CONT AUT SUBSTANCES
5419	PHARMACEUTICAL GOODS NES		4.2							PREP,ART PHARMACEUTIQUES
55	PERFUME,CLEANING ETC PRD		12.8							PROD POUR PARFUM,TOILETTE
554	SOAP,CLEANSING ETC PREPS		9.6							SAVONS,PRODUITS DETERSIFS
5542	WASHING PREPARATIONS ETC	W 5742	6.6							PROD ORG TENSIO-ACT NDA
562	*FERTILIZERS,MANUFACTURE	W 34840	6.6							ENGRAIS MANUFACTURES
5621	CHEM NITROGENOUS FERTLZR	W 26342	4.1							ENGRAIS AZOTES
58	PLASTIC MATERIALS ETC		9.9							MAT PLAST ARTIFICIELLES
583	POLYMERIZATION ETC PRODS	W 2864	5.7							PROD POLYMERISATION
59	CHEMICAL MATERIALS NES		17.9							MAT PROD CHIMIQUES NDA
591	PESTICIDES,DISINFECTANTS	W 2263	5.1							DESINF,INSECT,FONG,HERB
598	MISCEL CHEM PRODUCTS NES	W 3303	11.5							PROD DIV INDUST CHIM NDA
5989	CHEM PRODUCTS,PREPS NES	W 3020	10.6							PROD PREP CHIMIQUES NDA
59899	OTH CHEM PRODS,PREPS,NES	W 2470	9.3							AUT PRODUITS CHIMIQUES NDA
6	BASIC MANUFACTURES		237.4							ART MANUFACTURES
62	RUBBER MANUFACTURES NES		28.0							CAOUTCHOUC MANUFACTURE
625	RUBBER TYRES, TUBES ETC	N 385632	18.5							PNEUS CAOUTCHOUC VULCANISE
6252	TYRES,NEW,BUS OR LORRY	N 124408	6.2							PNEUS POUR AUTOBUS,CAMIONS
6259	OTH TYRES,TYRE CASES,ETC	N 186212	9.9							AUTRES PNEUS RECHAPES FLAPS
62599	TYRES NES,TYRE CASES,ETC	N 32148	7.6							PNEUS,FLAPS
628	RUBBER ARTICLES NES		6.0							OUVRAGES CAOUTCHOUC NDA
6289	OTH RUBBER ARTICLES NES		4.3							AUT OUVR CAOUTCHOUC NDA
62898	UNHARD RUBBER PRODS NES		4.1							OUV CAOUT VULC NON DURCI
64	PAPER,PAPERBOARD AND MFR		25.3							PAPIERS,CARTONS & OUVRAGES
641	PAPER AND PAPERBOARD		12.4							PAPIERS ET CARTONS
642	PAPER,ETC,PRECUT,ARTS OF		13.0							PAP,CARTONS DECOUPES
6421	PAPER ETC CONTAINERS		3.8							BOITES,SACS EMBALLAGES
65	TEXTILE YARN,FABRICS,ETC		24.2							FILS,TISSUS,ARTICLES TEXTILE
652	COTTON FABRICS,WOVEN	A 6050	6.6							TISSUS DE COTON
6522	WOVEN COTTON BLEACHD,ETC	A 4340	4.3							TISSUS COTON BLANCHIS ETC
658	TEXTILE ARTICLES NES		8.3							ART FACONNES MAT TEXTILES
66	NONMETAL MINERAL MFS NES		23.3							ART MIN NON METALLIQUES
661	LIME,CEMENT,BLDG PRODS		12.4							CHAUX,CIMENTS MAT CONSTR
6612	CEMENT	W 1026641	7.6							CIMENTS HYDRAULIQUES
664	GLASS		4.0							VERRE
67	IRON AND STEEL		52.7							FER ET ACIER
672	IRON,STEEL PRIMARY FORMS		6.3							LINGOTS FER,ACIER

4. General Imports F.O.B. by Commodities according to the S.I.T.C. (Rev. 2) in million U.S. Dollars
Importations Générales F.O.B. par Produits d'après la C.T.C.I. (Rév. 2) en millions de Dollars E.U.

SITC CTCI	COMMODITY	1990 QUANTITY QUANTITE	1990 VALUE VALEUR	1991 QUANTITY QUANTITE	1991 VALUE VALEUR	1992 QUANTITY QUANTITE	1992 VALUE VALEUR	1993 QUANTITY QUANTITE	1993 VALUE VALEUR	PRODUIT
6727	IRN,STL COIL FR REROLLNG		4.7							EBAUCHES POUR TOLES FER
673	IRON,STEEL SHAPES ETC	W 233461	9.9							BARRES,PROFIL FER,ACIER
6732	IRON,STEEL BARS ETC	W 92217	5.6							BARRES FER,ACIER
674	IRN,STL UNIV,PLATE,SHEET		7.7							LARGES PLATS,TOLES
678	IRON,STL TUBES,PIPES,ETC	W 14131	22.1							TUBES,TUYAUX EN FONTE,FER
6782	IRON,STL SEAMLESS TUBES	W 2713	5.2							TUBES,TUYAUX SANS SOUDURE
6783	IRON,STL TUBES,PIPES NES	W 8181	9.6							AUT TUBES,TUYAUX FER,ACIER
6785	IRON,STEEL TUBE FITTINGS	W 904	5.3							ACCESSOIRES DE TUYAUTERIE
679	IRN,STL CASTINGS UNWORKD	W 6797	4.4							OUVRAGES EN FONTE,FER,ACIER
68	NON-FERROUS METALS		4.3							METAUX NON FERREUX
69	METAL MANUFACTURES NES		77.4							ART MANUFACT EN METAL NDA
691	STRUCTURES AND PARTS NES		20.5							CONSTRUCT FER,ACIER,ALU
6911	STRUCTURES,PARTS IRN,STL		19.3							CONSTRUCT FER,ACIER,FONTE
692	METAL TANKS,BOXES,ETC	MN 69440	10.7							RECIPIENTS METALLIQUES
6924	MTL TRANSPORT BOXES ETC	MN 69438	7.6							FUTS,TAMBOURS,BIDONS
69241	STL TRANSPORT BOXES ETC	MN 69368	6.9							FUTS,TAMBOURS,BIDONS FER
693	WIRE PRODUCTS NON ELECTR	W 3519	4.9							OUVRAGES FILS METALLIQUES
694	STL,COPPR NAILS,NUTS,ETC	W 3445	6.3							CLOUS,VIS,ECROUS
69402	IRN,STL NUTS,BOLTS,ETC	W 2472	5.5							BOULONS,VIS,ECROUS FER,AC
695	TOOLS		12.7							OUTILS A MAIN
6953	OTHER HAND TOOLS	MN 73069	5.2							AUTRES OUTILS A MAIN
6954	BLADES,TIPS,ETC FR TOOLS		6.2							OUTILS POUR MACHINE–OUTIL
69541	PARTS TO INSERT IN TOOLS	N 195525	5.6							OUTILS DE FORAGE
697	BASE MTL HOUSEHOLD EQUIP		6.0							ART MENAGE MET COMMUNS
699	BASE METAL MFRS NES		15.2							ART MANUFACTURES MET NDA
6991	LOCKSMITHS WARES,ETC		4.8							ARTICLES DE SERRURERIE
6997	IRON,STEEL ARTICLES NES		4.0							OUV FONTE,FER,ACIER NDA
69979	IRN,STL MANUFACTURES NES		3.9							AUT OUVRAGES EN FER NDA
7	MACHINES,TRANSPORT EQUIP		472.2							MACHINES MATERIEL TRANSPORT
71	POWER GENERATING EQUIPMT		38.0							MACHINES GENERATRICES
713	INTRNL COMBUS PSTN ENGIN		20.2							MOTEURS EXPL COMB INT, PIECE
7131	AIRCRAFT PSTN ENGINS,PTS		10.4							MOTEURS EXPL P.AVIATION, PIE
71311	AIRCRAFT PISTON ENGINES	N 79	7.9							MOTEURS EXPL P.AVIATION
7139	PISTON ENGINE PARTS NES		4.2							PIECES POUR 713.2,3,8
716	ROTATING ELECTRIC PLANT		13.4							APP ELECTR ROTATIFS,PIECES
7162	AC MTRS,GENRTRS,GEN SETS	N 5609	10.2							MOTEURS ELECTRIQUES
71623	GEN SETS WITH PSTN ENGN	N 1099	6.7							GROUPES MOTEUR EXPLOSION
72	MACHS FOR SPCL INDUSTRYS		101.6							MAC SPECIALES POUR INDUST
722	TRACTORS NON-ROAD	N 146	3.9							TRACTEURS
723	CIVIL ENGNEERG EQUIP ETC		74.2							APPAREILS DE GENIE CIVIL
7234	CONST,MINING MACHNRY NES		37.9							MACH POUR LA CONST, MINES
72341	SELF-PROPELLD DOZERS,ETC	N 259	12.5							BULLDOZERS
72342	SLFPRP SHOVELS,EXCAVATRS	N 65	5.6							PELLES MECANIQUES
72343	SLFPRP CONST ETC MCH NES	N 275	12.2							AUT MACH EXTR,TERRASSEM
72346	OTH CONST,MINING MCH NES	N 1471	6.1							AUT MACH EXTRACTION,EXCAV ET
7239	CONSTR ETC MACHY PTS NES		36.2							PIECES 723.41–723.46
728	OTH MACHY FOR SPCL INDUS		14.3							AUT MACH IND PARTICULIERES
7283	OTHR MINERAL WORKG MACHY		9.8							MACH TRIER,CRIBLER,BROYER
73	METALWORKING MACHINERY		4.7							MACH TRAVAIL DES METAUX
74	GENRL INDUSTRL MACHY NES		64.7							MACH APP INDUSTRIE
741	HEATING,COOLING EQUIPMNT		12.3							MACH CHAUFFAGE,PIECES
7416	HEATING,COOLING EQU NES		5.2							APP CHANGEMENT TEMP
742	PUMPS FOR LIQUIDS ETC		8.8							POMPES MOTO–POMPES
7428	OTHER PUMPS FOR LIQUIDS	N 46898	6.6							AUTRES POMPES POUR LIQ
74288	PUMPS FR LIQUIDS NES ETC	N 44778	6.0							POMPES POUR LIQUIDES NDA
743	PUMPS NES,CENTRFUGES ETC		9.4							POMPES COMPRES,VENT ETC
7436	GAS,LIQUID FILTERS ETC	N 283478	4.1							APP POUR FILT DES LIQUIDES
744	MECHANICAL HANDLING EQU		12.8							EQUIP MANUTENTION PIECES
7441	FORK LIFT TRCKS,ETC,PTS		4.1							CHARIOTS POUR USINES ETC
7442	LIFTING,LOADING MACH NES	N 7055	6.2							APP LEVAGE,MANUTENTION
745	NONELEC MACHY,TOOLS NES		4.3							AUT MACH NON ELEC,PIECES
749	NONELEC MACH PTS,ACC NES		17.4							PIECES MACH NON ELEC NDA
7491	BALL,ROLLER,ETC BEARINGS	N 160557	3.9							ROULEMENTS BILLES ETC
7492	COCKS,VALVES ETC NES	N 342757	7.6							ART ROB,SIM POUR TUYAUX
7493	SHAFT,CRANK,PULLEY ETC		4.2							ARBRES TRANS,VILEBREQUINS
75	OFFICE MACHNES,ADP EQUIP		22.2							MACH BUREAU TRAIT AUTOM
751	OFFICE MACHINES	N 172877	4.2							MACH,APPAREILS DE BUREAU
752	AUTOMTIC DATA PROC EQUIP		11.8							MACH TRAIT INFORMATION
7528	OFF-LINE DATA PROC EQUIP	N 12429	7.9							MACH AUXIL TRAIT INFORM
759	OFFICE,ADP MCH PTS,ACCES		6.3							PIECES DU 751 ET 752
7599	ACCTG,ETC,ADP MCH PTS,AC		5.3							PIECES DU 751 ET 752
76	TELECOMM,SOUND EQUIPMENT		20.0							EQUIPMENT DE TELECOM
764	TELECOM EQPT,PTS,ACC NES		16.3							EQUIP TELECOM,PIECES
7643	TV,RADIO TRANSMITTRS ETC	N 14682	5.0							APP EMET TELE RADIO
7648	TELECOMM EQUIPMENT NES		5.5							APP TELECOM NDA
76483	RADAR APPARATUS ETC		5.2							APP DE RADIOGUIDAGE ETC
77	ELECTRIC MACHNRY NES ETC		58.4							MACH APP ELECT NDA
771	ELECTRIC POWER MACHY NES		5.6							MACH PROD,TRANS ELECTR
7711	TRANSFORMERS,ELECTRICAL	N 3903	4.0							TRANSFO ELECTRIQUES
77118	OTHER ELEC TRANSFORMERS	N 3892	3.9							AUTRES TRANSFO ELECTRIQ
772	SWITCHGEAR ETC,PARTS NES		14.4							APP COUPURE,SECT ETC
7721	SWITCHGEAR ETC		14.1							APP COUPURE,SECTIONMNT
773	ELECTR DISTRIBUTNG EQUIP		15.4							EQUIPMT DISTRIBUTION ELECT
7731	INSULATED WIRE,CABLE ETC		14.1							FILS,CABLES ISOLES ELECT
775	HOUSEHOLD TYPE EQUIP NES		5.5							MACH,APP USAGE DOMESTQUE
778	ELECTRICAL MACHINERY NES		15.6							AUTRES MACH ELECT NDA
7781	BATTERIES,ACCUMULATORS		7.1							PILES ET ACCUMULATEURS
77811	PRIMARY BATTERIES,CELLS		5.3							PILES ELECTRIQUES,PIECES
78	ROAD VEHICLES		98.5							VEHICULES ROUTIERS
781	PASS MOTOR VEH EXC BUSES	N 3029	34.9							AUTO TRANSPORT PERSONNES
782	LORRIES,SPCL MTR VEH NES	N 4628	43.3							VEHICULES SPECIAUX,MARCH
7821	LORRIES,TRUCKS	N 4581	35.4							VEHICULES TRANSP MARCHAND
7822	SPECIAL MOTOR VEHCLS NES	N 47	8.0							VEHICULES USAGES SPECIAUX
783	ROAD MOTOR VEHICLES NES	N 708	6.2							VEHICULES ROUTIERS NDA
7831	BUSES	N 706	6.0							VOITURES TRANSPORT COMMUN
784	MOTOR VEH PRTS,ACCES NES		10.1							PIECES 722,781,782,783
7849	OTHER MOTOR VEHCL PARTS		9.3							PIECES 722,781,782,783
79	OTHR TRANSPORT EQUIPMENT		64.5							AUTRE MATERIEL TRANSPORT
792	AIRCRAFT ETC		51.1							APP NAVIGATION AERIENNE
7921	HELICOPTERS	N 15	18.7							HELICOPTERES
7924	AIRCRFT NES OVER 15000KG	N 2	6.8							AERODYNES PLUS 15000 KG

4. General Imports F.O.B. by Commodities according to the S.I.T.C. (Rev. 2) in million U.S. Dollars
Importations Générales F.O.B. par Produits d'après la C.T.C.I. (Rév. 2) en millions de Dollars E.U.

SITC CTCI	COMMODITY	1990 QUANTITY QUANTITE	1990 VALUE VALEUR	1991 QUANTITY QUANTITE	1991 VALUE VALEUR	1992 QUANTITY QUANTITE	1992 VALUE VALEUR	1993 QUANTITY QUANTITE	1993 VALUE VALEUR	PRODUIT
7929	AIRCRAFT PARTS NES		23.9							PIECES DU 792
793	SHIPS AND BOATS ETC	N 837	13.3							NAVIRES BATEAUX,ETC
7932	SHIPS AND BOATS NES	N 499	12.2							NAVIRES ET BATEAUX
79323	OTHER CARGO VESSELS	N 26	9.2							AUT BATEAUX TRANS MARCH
8	MISC MANUFACTURED GOODS		105.5							ART MANUFACTURES DIVERS
821	*FURNITURE,PARTS THEREOF		4.7							MEUBLES ET PIECES
84	CLOTHING AND ACCESSORIES		20.4							VETEMENTS
842	MENS OUTERWEAR NOT KNIT	N 3793582	8.2							VET DESSUS POUR HOMMES
8423	— TROUSERS,BREECHES ETC	N 3254922	6.4							PANTALONS HOMMES MAT TEX
84232	—— OF COTTON	N 2965113	5.3							PANTALONS HOMMES COTON
844	UNDER GARMENTS NOT KNIT	N 4699231	4.4							VETEMENT DESSOUS MAT TEX
851	*FOOTWEAR		7.3							CHAUSSURES
85102	FOOTWEAR LEATHER		4.4							CHAUS SEMELLES EN CUIR
87	PRECISION INSTRUMNTS NES		20.1							INSTRUM,APPAR SCIENT NDA
874	MEASURNG,CONTROLNG INSTR		18.0							INSTRUMENTS DE MESURE
8748	ELEC MEAS,CONTRL EQU NES	N 24712	8.9							APP ELEC ELECTRO MESURE
87483	OTH ELCTRNC MEAS ETC EQU	N 13786	7.2							AUT APP ELECTRO DE MESURE
88	PHOTO EQU,OPTICL GDS ETC		6.4							APP,FOURN PHOTO,OP,MONTR
89	MISC MANUFCTRD GOODS NES		40.5							ART MANUFACTURES DIVERS
892	PRINTED MATTER		14.9							IMPRIMES
8921	PRINTED BOOKS,GLOBES,ETC	N 2192305	5.3							LIVRES,BROCHURES,CARTES
89211	PRINTED BOOKS,PAMPHLETS	N 2169259	5.2							LIVRES,BROCHURES
8928	PRINTED MATTER NES		9.3							IMPRIMES NDA
89283	UNISSUED BANKNOTES ETC		7.1							TIMBRES–POSTE FISCAUX
893	ARTICLES OF PLASTIC NES		12.8							OUVRAGES EN MAT DIVIS 58
8939	MISC PLASTIC ARTICLES		10.2							ART DIVERS EN MAT DIV 58
89399	OTHR PLASTC ARTICLES NES		9.0							AUT OUV MAT DIV 58
894	TOYS,SPORTING GOODS,ETC		4.5							VOITURES ENFANTS,JOUETS
9	GOODS NOT CLASSD BY KIND		12.2							ART TRANSACT NON CLASSES
931	*SPECIAL TRANSACTIONS		8.6							TRANS.SPECIALES

5. General Exports F.O.B. by Commodities according to the S.I.T.C. (Rev. 2) in million U.S. Dollars
Exportations Générales F.O.B. par Produits d'après la C.T.C.I. (Rév. 2) en millions de Dollars E.U.

SITC CTCI	COMMODITY	1990		1991		1992		1993		PRODUIT
		QUANTITY QUANTITE	VALUE VALEUR	QUANTITY QUANTITE	VALUE VALEUR	QUANTITY QUANTITE	VALUE VALEUR	QUANTITY QUANTITE	VALUE VALEUR	
	ALL COMMODITIES		1261.8		1641.8		1698.9		2624.6	TOUS PRODUITS
0	FOOD AND LIVE ANIMALS		168.2		140.9		134.0		151.0	ALIMENTS,ANIMAUX VIVANTS
03	FISH AND PREPARATIONS		10.8		14.0		13.0		9.2	POISSONS ET PREPARATIONS
036	SHELL FISH FRESH,FROZEN	W 1294	9.9	W 1490	13.1	W 1527	12.3	W 1110	9.0	CRUSTACES,MOLLUSQUES
06	SUGAR AND PREPS,HONEY		4.9		3.1		3.2			SUCRES ET PRODUITS
061	SUGAR AND HONEY	W 9712	4.9	W 7664	3.1	W 6923	3.2			SUCRES ET MIEL
0611	RAW BEET AND CANE SUGAR	W 9700	4.9	W 7664	3.1	W 6909	3.1			SUCRES BRUTS
07	COFFEE,TEA,COCOA,SPICES		150.3		121.6		113.4		137.2	CAFE,THE,CACAO,EPICES
071	COFFEE AND SUBSTITUTES	W 63426	108.6	W 44911	80.1	W 55125	70.6	W 63576	94.6	CAFE ET SUCCEDANES
0711	COFFEE GREEN,ROASTED,SUB	W 63426	108.6	W 44911	80.1	W 55125	70.6	W 63576	94.6	CAFE TORREFIE OU DECAFEINE
07111	COFFEE GREEN,HUSKS,SKINS	W 63416	108.5	W 44892	80.0	W 55093	70.4	W 63545	94.4	CAFE NON TORREFIE
072	COCOA	W 36433	34.2	W 37618	36.8	W 39327	35.7	W 38325	34.9	CACAO
0721	COCOA BEANS,RAW,ROASTED	W 36433	34.2	W 37615	36.8	W 39327	35.7	W 38325	34.9	CACAO EN FEVES
074	TEA AND MATE	W 5408	7.1	W 3747	4.5	W 5638	6.8	W 6441	7.4	THE ET MATE
0741	TEA	W 5408	7.1	W 3747	4.5	W 5638	6.8	W 6441	7.4	THE
2	CRUDE MATERLS,EXCL FUELS		692.0		711.3		716.6		966.0	MAT BRUTES NON COMESTIBLES
22	OIL SEEDS,OLEAGINOUS FRT		10.4		7.5		14.6		16.7	GRAINES,FRUITS OLEAGINEUX
223	SEEDS FOR OTH FIXED OILS	W 71919	10.4	W 59286	7.5	W 59131	14.6	W 75645	16.7	GRAINES AUTRES HUILES FIXES
2231	COPRA	W 60699	9.4	W 45341	5.7	W 45640	12.3	W 58461	14.2	COPRAH
24	CORK AND WOOD		90.1		101.6		154.6		432.4	LIEGE ET BOIS
246	PULPWOOD,CHIPS,WOODWASTE	W 156957	7.5	W 105543	5.8	W 57024	6.3	W 96170	7.1	BOIS DE TRITURATION
24602	PULPWOOD CHIPS,PARTICLES	W 156957	7.5	W 105543	5.8	W 55580	5.3	W 96132	7.1	EN FORME DE PLAQUETTES
247	OTH WOOD ROUGH,SQUARED	W 970895	80.9	W 1047927	93.9	W 1463167	146.6	W 2130544	423.8	BOIS BRUTS EQUARRIS
2471	SAW–,VENEER–LOGS CONIFER	W 35043	4.9	W 44384	7.6	W 83330	15.9	W 89051	27.7	CONIFERES POUR SCIAGE,PLACAG
24711	— IN THE ROUGH	W 35043	4.9	W 44196	7.6	W 83330	15.9	W 89051	27.7	ECORCES OU DEGROSSIS
2472	SAW–,VENEER–LOGS NON–CON	W 429989	44.4	W 419553	47.8	W 536110	66.7	W 852511	212.9	NON CONIFERES SCIAGE,PLAC
24721	— IN THE ROUGH	W 429132	44.2	W 419484	47.8	W 535539	66.7	W 852511	212.9	BRUTS ECORCES DEGROSSIS
2479	PTPROPS,POLES,PILING,ETC	W 505863	31.7	W 583990	38.6	W 843726	64.1	W 1188982	183.3	POTEAUX DE MINES
28	METALLIFEROUS ORES,SCRAP		583.6		595.9		541.9		510.7	MINERAIS METAL,DECHETS
287	BASE METAL ORES,CONC NES	W 471939	582.7	W 576039	595.1	W 550099	541.2	W 556231	510.4	MINERAIS METAUX COMMUNS
2871	CPR ORE ETC,CEMENT COPPR	W 471939	582.7	W 576039	595.1	W 550099	541.2	W 556231	510.4	MINERAIS DE CUIVRE,MATTES
28711	COPPER ORES,EXCL MATTE	W 471934	582.7	W 576039	595.1	W 550099	541.2	W 556188	510.3	MINERAIS DE CUIVRE
29	CRUDE ANIMAL,VEG MAT NES		4.4		3.1		2.3		1.8	MATIERES BRUTES ANIM,VEGET
3	MINERAL FUELS ETC		1.7		3.7		1.8		803.5	COMBUSTIBLES MINERAUX LUB
33	PETROLEUM AND PRODUCTS		1.7		3.7		1.8		803.5	PETROLE ET DERIVES
333	CRUDE PETROLEUM		0.1		0.1			W 6187316	802.1	HUILES BRUTES DE PETROLE
4	ANIMAL,VEGETABLE OIL,FAT		43.8		61.3		88.7		96.6	HUILES,GRAISSES ANIM,VEG
42	FIXED VEGETABLE OIL,FAT		43.8		61.2		87.8		95.9	HUILES VEGETALES FIXES
424	FIXED VEG OIL NONSOFT	W 160924	43.8	W 199596	61.2	W 227411	87.8	W 268934	95.9	AUTRES HUILES VEG FIXES
4242	PALM OIL	W 115623	28.5	W 166295	47.3	W 178410	58.7	W 213217	72.4	HUILE DE PALME
4243	COCONUT (COPRA) OIL	W 37865	12.8	W 25771	11.7	W 40913	25.1	W 36502	16.2	HJUILE DE COPRAH
6	BASIC MANUFACTURES		22.4		20.1		18.6		13.7	ART MANUFACTURES
68	NON–FERROUS METALS		14.8		14.1		10.6		8.5	METAUX NON FERREUX
681	SILVER,PLATINUM,ETC		14.7		14.0		10.6		8.5	ARGENT ET PLATINE
6811	SILVER UNWKD,PARTLY WRKD		14.7		14.0		10.6		8.5	ARGENT BRUT MI–OUVRE
68113	SILVER UNWROUGHT		14.7		14.0		10.6		8.5	ARGENT ET ALLIAGES BRUTS
69	METAL MANUFACTURES NES		4.6		4.1		6.4		1.6	ART MANUFACT EN METAL NDA
7	MACHINES,TRANSPORT EQUIP		72.3		135.6		102.9		66.4	MACHINES MATERIEL TRANSPORT
71	POWER GENERATING EQUIPMT		8.3		1.7		2.5		2.9	MACHINES GENERATRICES
713	INTRNL COMBUS PSTN ENGIN		7.9		0.9		0.1		0.5	MOTEURS EXPL COMB INT, PIECE
7131	AIRCRAFT PSTN ENGINS,PTS		7.1		0.6				0.2	MOTEURS EXPL P.AVIATION, PIE
71311	AIRCRAFT PISTON ENGINES	N 19	6.5	N 6	0.5			N 10	0.2	MOTEURS EXPL P.AVIATION
72	MACHS FOR SPCL INDUSTRYS		20.2		16.9		43.0		17.2	MAC SPECIALES POUR INDUST
723	CIVIL ENGNEERG EQUIP ETC		18.4		14.6		36.3		16.3	APPAREILS DE GENIE CIVIL
7234	CONST,MINING MACHNRY NES	N 212	12.3	N 261	10.1	N 230	32.2	N 401	8.9	MACH POUR LA CONST, MINES
72341	SELF–PROPELLD DOZERS,ETC	N 36	1.9	N 35	2.1	N 67	10.9	N 37	2.5	BULLDOZERS
72342	SLFPRP SHOVELS,EXCAVATRS	N 10	5.7	N 17	1.7	N 7	0.2	N 5	0.3	PELLES MECANIQUES
72343	SLFPRP CONST ETC MCH NES	N 22	1.1	N 42	1.5	N 107	18.7	N 88	3.0	AUT MACH EXTR,TERRASSEM
7239	CONSTR ETC MACHY PTS NES		6.1		4.5		4.0		7.4	PIECES 723.41–723.46
74	GENRL INDUSTRL MACHY NES		6.2		4.1		7.9		3.0	MACH APP INDUSTRIE
78	ROAD VEHICLES		10.9		11.6		3.9		3.1	VEHICULES ROUTIERS
782	LORRIES,SPCL MTR VEH NES	N 151	9.7	N 197	8.0	N 51	2.8	N 59	2.1	VEHICULES SPECIAUX,MARCH
7822	SPECIAL MOTOR VEHCLS NES	N 142	6.7	N 163	7.3	N 12	0.5	N 28	1.1	VEHICULES USAGES SPECIAUX
79	OTHR TRANSPORT EQUIPMENT		23.5		99.4		41.9		38.1	AUTRE MATERIEL TRANSPORT
792	AIRCRAFT ETC		21.3		96.4		38.9		22.3	APP NAVIGATION AERIENNE
7921	HELICOPTERS	N 4	3.0	N 17	26.3	N 13	12.9	N 9	2.8	HELICOPTERES
7922	AIRCRFT NES 2000KG OR LS	N 1	0.2	N 2	18.7			N 3	1.2	AERODYNES MOINS 2000 KG
7924	AIRCRFT NES OVER 15000KG	N 1	3.9	N 1	36.9	N 2	18.4	N 5	4.6	AERODYNES PLUS 15000 KG
7929	AIRCRAFT PARTS NES		14.2		14.7		6.8		13.5	PIECES DU 792
793	SHIPS AND BOATS ETC	N 100	2.3	N 29	3.1	N 63	3.0	N 30	15.9	NAVIRES BATEAUX,ETC
7932	SHIPS AND BOATS NES	N 86	2.1	N 26	3.0	N 26	1.9	N 14	14.4	NAVIRES ET BATEAUX
79323	OTHER CARGO VESSELS	N 3	0.4	N 6	2.1	N 10	1.5	N 5	14.2	AUT BATEAUX TRANS MARCH
8	MISC MANUFACTURED GOODS		11.1		27.6		7.9		4.9	ART MANUFACTURES DIVERS
87	PRECISION INSTRUMNTS NES		10.0		25.0		5.7		3.0	INSTRUM,APPAR SCIENT NDA
874	MEASURNG,CONTROLNG INSTR		10.0		25.0		5.3		2.8	INSTRUMENTS DE MESURE
8741	SURVEYING INSTRUMENTS		7.0		23.7		2.6		2.2	INST GEODESIE,TOPO ETC
87412	SURVEY INSTR ETC NONELEC		5.9		23.7		1.6		2.2	INSTR GEODESIE,TOPO ETC
9	GOODS NOT CLASSD BY KIND		248.9		540.5		628.2		522.0	ART TRANSACT NON CLASSES
931	*SPECIAL TRANSACTIONS		15.7		5.4		5.1		4.3	TRANS.SPECIALES
971	*GOLD,NON MONETARY NES	K 18742	233.2	K 45383	535.1	K 58489	623.1	K 44773	517.7	OR NON MONETAIRE
97101	NONMON GLD UNWRT,SEMIMFD	K 18742	233.2	K 45383	535.1	K 58435	622.7	K 44773	517.7	OR,ALLIAGES D'OR BRUTS

FOOT NOTES – NOTES

TABLE 1 –
1 Prior to 1981, special trade.
TABLEAU 1 –
1 Avant 1981, commerce spéciale.

1. HISTORICAL SERIES, 1961–1996 SPECIAL TRADE, IMPORTS C.I.F., EXPORTS F.O.B.
SERIES HISTORIQUES, 1961–1996 COMMERCE SPECIAL, IMPORTATIONS C.A.F., EXPORTATIONS F.O.B

YEAR ANNEE	VALUE IN MILLION U.S. DOLLARS VALEUR EN MILLION U.S. DOLLARS MERCHANDISE –MARCHANDISE		GOLD –OR		CONVERSION FACTORS FACTEURS DE CONVERSION CENTS E.U. PAR		INDEX NUMBERS –INDICES QUANTUM		UNIT VALUE VALEUR UNITAIRE	
	IMPORTS	EXPORTS	IMPORTS	EXPORTS	IMPORTS	EXPORTS	IMPORTS	EXPORTS	IMPORTS	EXPORTS
1961	34.70	30.70								
1962	34.70	33.50								
1963	32.60	40.20								
1964	33.80	49.80								
1965	47.40	57.30								
1966	50.20	49.40								
1967	60.70	48.30								
1968	61.50	47.60								
1969	70.40	51.00								
1970	63.80	64.10								
1971	70.30	65.21								
1972	69.85	86.19								
1973	104.79	126.93								
1974	171.39	169.81								
1975	178.67	176.71								
1976	180.14	181.25								
1977	255.38	278.91								
1978	317.74	256.96								
1979	437.72	305.08								
1980	614.70	310.20								9
1981	599.60	295.60								10
1982	672.00	329.80								11
1983	545.90	269.20								9
1984	586.00	334.50								16
1985	501.50	303.90								16
1986	578.10	232.50								12
1987	595.30	353.40								29
1988	573.90	509.80								39
1989	759.70	1009.40								
1990	1352.00	958.70								
1991	1460.30	737.10								
1992	1421.60	656.60								
1993	1688.80	725.20								
1994	2370.20	816.80								
1995	3143.80	919.30								
1996	3107.35	1043.50								

2. IMPORTS BY BROAD ECONOMIC CATEGORY AND EXPORTS BY INDUSTRIAL ORIGIN. (PERCENTAGE OF TOTAL VALUE)
IMPORTATIONS PAR CATEGORIES ECONOMIQUES ET EXPORTATIONS PAR BRANCHE D'ACTIVITE.(EN POURCENTAGE DE LA VALEUR TOTALE)

IMPORTS – IMPORTATIONS

	1990	1991	1992	1993	1994	1995	1996
TOTAL IMPORTS–IMPORTATIONS TOTALES	100.	100.	100.	100.	100.	100.	100.
1 FOOD BEV–ALIMENTATION BOISSONS	6.1	7.5	9.5	8.3	10.6	12.0	11.0
11 PRIMARY–PRODUITS DE BASE	0.3	0.5	1.4	1.3	2.2	2.5	2.2
111 FOR INDUSTRY–POUR L'INDUSTRIE	0.2	0.4	1.3	1.1	1.9	2.2	2.0
112 FOR HOUSEHOLDS–POUR LES MENAGES	0.1	0.1	0.1	0.2	0.3	0.3	0.3
12 PROCESSED–PRODUITS ELABORES	5.8	7.0	8.0	7.0	8.4	9.5	8.7
121 FOR INDUSTRY–POUR L'INDUSTRIE	0.5	0.4	0.5	0.5	0.4	0.5	0.5
122 FOR HOUSEHOLDS–POUR LES MENAGES	5.3	6.6	7.5	6.5	8.0	9.1	8.2
2 IND SUPPLIES–APPROV INDUSTRIELS	16.7	17.7	18.0	18.6	18.5	16.3	20.2
21 PRIMARY–PRODUITS DE BASE	0.5	1.0	0.9	0.8	0.9	0.7	3.4
22 PROCESSED–PRODUITS ELABORES	16.2	16.6	17.1	17.8	17.6	15.6	16.7
3 FUELS–COMBUSTIBLES	14.2	11.8	13.5	11.9	8.1	6.5	8.0
31 PRIMARY–PRODUITS DE BASE	6.4	5.4	4.9	3.5	2.2	1.5	1.3
32 PROCESSED–PRODUITS ELABORES	7.8	6.3	8.6	8.4	5.8	5.0	6.7
321 MOTOR SPIRIT–ESSENCE	1.7	1.5	1.6	1.7	1.2	3.5	4.9
322 OTHER–AUTRES	6.1	4.8	7.1	6.7	4.6	1.6	1.8
4 MACHINERY–EQUIPEMENT	15.9	15.3	17.9	19.1	18.9	17.2	18.9
41 CAPITAL EQUIPMENT–MACHINES	14.3	13.6	16.2	16.8	16.8	15.7	17.2
42 PARTS–PIECES ACCESSOIRES	1.6	1.7	1.7	2.2	2.2	1.5	1.7
5 TRANSPORT–TRANSPORT	10.4	13.9	15.7	15.4	14.0	13.8	12.6
51 PASSENGER CARS–AUTOMOBILES	2.3	3.9	6.0	5.4	4.1	4.3	4.5
52 OTHER–AUTRES	4.4	5.1	6.1	6.2	6.0	5.9	4.8
521 INDUSTRIAL–INDUSTRIELS	4.2	4.8	5.5	5.3	5.2	5.1	4.4
522 NON INDUSTRIAL–NON INDUSTRIEL	0.2	0.4	0.6	0.9	0.8	0.8	0.4
53 PARTS–PIECES ACCESSOIRES	3.6	4.8	3.7	3.8	4.0	3.6	3.2
6 CONSUM GOODS–BIENS CONSOMMATION	36.5	33.8	25.4	26.4	29.4	33.9	29.1
61 DURABLE–DURABLES	23.6	18.3	11.1	11.6	12.5	14.4	7.6
62 SEMI DURABLE–SEMI DURABLES	8.7	9.0	7.0	7.9	8.3	9.3	8.2
63 NON DURABLE–NON DURABLES	4.2	6.5	7.2	6.9	8.5	10.1	13.3
7 GOODS NES–BIENS NDA	0.3	0.0	0.0	0.2	0.5	0.3	0.2

EXPORTS – EXPORTATIONS

	1990	1991	1992	1993	1994	1995	1996
TOTAL EXPORTS–EXPORTATIONS TOTALES	100.	100.	100.	100.	100.	100.	100.
1 AGRICULTURE	68.1	67.0	53.7	55.2	52.5	54.0	54.0
2 MINING QUARRY–INDUS EXTRACTIVES	0.0	0.0	0.1	0.1	0.1	0.1	0.1
3 MANUFACTURING–IND MANUFACTUR	31.9	33.0	46.2	44.6	47.4	45.9	45.9
31 FOOD BEV TOBACCO–ALIM BOISS TAB	18.7	16.5	24.1	21.5	19.4	19.4	22.0
32 TEXTILES–INDUSTRIES TEXTILES	5.6	5.7	8.4	9.4	11.2	10.6	8.4
33 WOOD & PRODUCTS–BOIS & PRODUITS	3.9	6.0	8.0	8.7	9.6	9.6	8.8
34 PAPER & PRODUCTS–PAPIER & PRODT	0.1	0.1	0.3	0.3	0.4	0.5	0.4
35 CHEMICALS–INDUSTRIES CHIMIQUES	3.2	3.5	3.6	2.2	2.8	3.2	4.1
36 NON METAL MIN–MIN NON METAL	0.0	0.0	0.1	0.1	0.2	0.2	0.1
37 BASIC METAL–IND METAL BASE	0.2	0.8	1.3	1.7	2.5	1.0	0.8
38 METAL MANUF–MANUF METAL	0.2	0.3	0.3	0.8	1.3	1.3	1.1
39 OTH MANUF IND–AUTRES MANUF	0.0	0.0	0.0	0.0	0.0	0.0	0.1

3. TRADE BY PRINCIPAL COUNTRIES OF CONSIGNMENT AND DESTINATION (VALUE IN MILLION U.S. DOLLARS)
ECHANGES SELON LES PRINCIPAUX PAYS DE CONSIGNATION ET DE DESTINATION (VALEUR EN MILLIONS DE DOLLARS EU)

COUNTRIES–PAYS	SPECIAL IMPORTS C.I.F. IMPORTATIONS SPECIALES C.A.F				
	1992	1993	1994	1995	1996
World	1420.4	1688.0	2424.6	3135.9	3107.4
Africa	44.3	65.0	51.1	28.2	13.2
Americas	817.8	980.2	1422.4	1774.4	2106.6
– Northern America	201.1	245.4	309.2	410.9	354.5
– LAIA	596.8	706.7	1093.9	1353.1	1741.7
– CACM	0.4	0.1	0.2	0.4	0.2
– Caribbean	0.6	0.1	0.0	0.6	3.7
– Rest of America	18.8	27.8	19.0	9.3	6.5
Asia excl fmr USSR	338.0	426.9	628.2	961.2	645.7
– Middle East	0.2	0.3	0.5	0.6	1.3
Asia former USSR					
Europe excl fmr USSR	216.9	212.9	314.8	363.7	340.8
– European Union	202.8	199.4	275.7	346.2	317.9
– Eastern Europe	3.9	2.4	23.1	2.2	4.4
– Rest of Europe	10.1	11.1	16.1	15.3	18.4
Europe former USSR	3.1	2.8	7.2	0.0	0.3
Oceania	0.3	0.3	0.9	1.3	0.8
Other				7.0	0.0
Brazil/Brésil	283.1	369.5	598.7	681.3	982.0
Argentina/Argentine	231.0	242.4	349.4	518.6	587.4
USA/Etats–Unis d'Amer	199.0	237.7	284.5	392.4	348.3
Japan/Japon	174.2	204.2	226.6	272.5	204.4
Other Asia n.e.s.	71.3	112.9	152.6	237.4	217.2
Korea, Republic of	55.5	67.0	119.2	207.2	109.5
Germany/Allemagne	55.7	57.8	82.0	83.3	103.4
China, Hong Kong SAR	21.2	23.3	90.6	169.7	71.6
United Kingdom	59.6	55.1	61.6	96.1	86.8
Chile/Chili	39.6	47.7	84.5	85.2	71.7
Italy/Italie	28.2	21.2	49.5	66.2	33.5
Uruguay	12.0	20.7	31.7	36.9	63.2
France, Monaco	24.4	23.7	33.7	37.8	28.3
Algeria/Algérie	37.4	60.6	29.2	15.8	3.2
Spain/Espagne	10.8	9.6	15.9	21.8	27.9
Mexico/Mexique	12.3	15.3	14.2	20.1	20.2
Singapore/Singapour	7.9	6.9	19.4	36.3	11.1
Panama	18.8	27.8	19.0	9.3	6.5
Netherlands/Pays–Bas	10.7	20.8	10.2	13.8	14.7
Switzerland,Liechtenst.	9.9	10.8	15.8	15.0	17.9
Canada	2.1	7.7	24.6	18.5	6.2
So. African Customs Un	6.9	4.4	21.8	12.3	9.9
Venezuela	14.9	4.7	9.1	1.5	8.9
Malaysia/Malaisie	1.4	3.6	4.7	15.6	8.8
Sweden/Suède	4.3	4.8	4.9	11.2	8.8
India/Inde	2.8	5.1	7.5	10.0	8.4
Belgium–Luxembourg	4.6	3.0	8.2	7.2	3.9
Romania/Roumanie	0.4	0.1	20.3	0.9	0.5
Russian Federation	3.1	2.8	7.2	0.0	0.2
Colombia/Colombie	1.2	1.0	2.1	4.7	3.6
Thailand/Thaïlande	1.1	1.4	1.6	4.2	4.2
Indonesia/Indonésie	0.4	0.8	2.6	4.5	4.0
Denmark/Danemark	1.2	1.7	2.8	3.1	3.1
Austria/Autriche	1.5	0.9	3.5	2.7	2.9
Israel/Israël	1.4	1.2	2.2	1.9	2.8
Bolivia/Bolivie	1.3	2.4	1.9	2.1	1.2
Areas n.e.s.				7.0	0.0
Peru/Pérou	0.8	2.1	1.0	1.3	1.7
Czech Republic		1.7	1.8	0.0	2.9
Ecuador/Equateur	0.5	0.9	1.1	1.4	1.7

COUNTRIES–PAYS	SPECIAL EXPORTS F.O.B. EXPORTATIONS SPECIALES F.O.B.				
	1992	1993	1994	1995	1996
Monde	656.6	725.2	816.8	919.3	1043.0
Afrique	3.6	2.1	4.7	5.7	2.3
Amériques	384.5	435.0	553.5	656.9	775.4
– Amérique du Nord	49.5	68.5	76.7	55.9	39.5
– ALAI	312.4	342.8	468.6	596.3	723.3
– MCAC	3.2	0.3	0.7	0.6	0.2
– Caraïbes	14.3	17.1	7.5	3.7	5.5
– Autre Amérique	5.1	6.3	0.1	0.5	6.9
Asie anc. URSS exclus	32.1	12.0	19.9	73.4	28.3
– Moyen–Orient	1.3	0.8	1.0	0.9	0.7
Asie ancienne URSS					
Europe anc. URSS exclus	236.2	275.2	237.8	182.4	236.9
– Union Européenne	225.1	248.4	226.7	178.1	226.7
– Europe de l'Est	0.2	0.0	0.1	0.0	0.0
– Autre de l'Europe	10.8	26.8	11.0	4.3	10.2
Europe ancienne URSS	0.2	0.8	0.7	0.4	0.0
Océanie	0.0	0.0	0.1	0.3	
Autre	0.0		0.1	0.2	
Brazil/Brésil	171.4	215.1	323.7	410.8	520.7
Netherlands/Pays–Bas	138.9	189.3	160.0	89.7	172.7
Argentina/Argentine	64.1	64.9	90.7	83.3	95.4
USA/Etats–Unis d'Amer	35.0	53.2	57.1	43.9	37.5
Chile/Chili	47.4	42.2	32.8	31.1	24.8
Italy/Italie	22.5	17.1	24.2	29.1	20.1
Uruguay	10.8	7.2	10.4	33.9	43.5
Other Asia n.e.s.	12.3	4.2	9.0	48.9	19.0
France, Monaco	14.1	11.6	12.2	19.7	11.6
Switzerland,Liechtenst.	8.8	26.0	10.9	4.3	10.1
Germany/Allemagne	20.3	6.7	13.2	10.5	7.4
Bermuda/Bermudes	13.7	12.6	18.7	11.5	1.7
Venezuela	8.3	0.4	2.2	21.6	14.7
Spain/Espagne	7.5	5.2	5.6	9.5	7.2
United Kingdom	5.3	14.0	4.7	7.0	3.8
Peru/Pérou	4.8	5.2	0.5	3.2	11.4
Belgium–Luxembourg	8.3	2.1	1.3	9.0	1.9
Cayman Is/Is Caïmans	4.3	7.1	2.8	1.6	4.4
Israel/Israël	5.9	3.3	5.2	2.7	1.9
Panama	5.1	6.3	0.1	0.5	6.9
Portugal	7.8	1.9	4.3	3.3	1.4
Mexico/Mexique	1.6	3.4	3.9	0.9	8.2
Bahamas	8.8	6.3		0.6	0.0
China, Hong Kong SAR	1.1	1.4	2.7	7.5	2.4
Bolivia/Bolivie	1.5	2.9	3.1	3.6	3.4
So. African Customs Un	2.6	1.2	1.6	3.7	1.5
Colombia/Colombie	1.3	1.0	0.8	6.9	0.4
British Virgin Islds	1.1	3.4	3.0	1.2	1.0
Thailand/Thaïlande	2.1	0.2	0.0	1.9	2.3
Indonesia/Indonésie	2.2	0.1	0.1	3.8	0.2
Korea, Republic of	2.6	0.3	0.3	2.2	0.8
Japan/Japon	2.4	0.8	1.0	0.7	0.7
Canada	0.8	2.8	1.0	0.5	0.3
Tunisia/Tunisie	0.6	0.5	1.7	0.9	
Ecuador/Equateur	1.1	0.5	0.5	1.0	0.7
Iceland/Islande	2.1	0.8	0.1	0.0	0.2
Guatemala	1.5	0.0	0.5	0.4	0.1
Philippines			0.0	2.0	0.2
Singapore/Singapour	1.5	0.1	0.1	0.3	
Russian Federation	0.2	0.8	0.7	0.2	

(VALUE AS PERCENTAGE OF WORLD TOTAL)(VALEURS EN POURCENTAGE DU TOTAL MONDIAL)

	1987	1988	1989	1990	1991	1992	1993	1994	1995	1996
Africa	10.8	11.0	10.0	6.0	4.3	3.1	3.9	2.1	0.9	0.4
Americas	56.0	54.9	55.3	47.7	51.8	57.6	58.1	58.7	56.6	67.8
– Northern America	10.5	10.3	14.2	12.9	15.3	14.2	14.5	12.8	13.1	11.4
– LAIA	44.5	44.2	39.7	32.9	33.9	42.0	41.9	45.1	43.1	56.0
– CACM	0.0	0.0	0.0	0.0	0.0	0.0	0.0	0.0	0.0	0.0
– Caribbean	0.0		0.0	0.0	1.0	0.0	0.0	0.0	0.0	0.1
– Rest of America	1.0	0.4	1.3	1.8	1.7	1.3	1.6	0.8	0.3	0.2
Asia excl fmr USSR	11.0	13.0	20.5	30.4	28.5	23.8	25.3	25.9	30.7	20.8
– Middle East	0.0	0.0	0.0	0.0	0.0	0.0	0.0	0.0	0.0	0.0
Asia former USSR										
Europe excl fmr USSR	22.2	21.1	14.2	15.9	15.1	15.3	12.6	13.0	11.6	11.0
– European Union	21.0	19.6	13.1	15.0	14.2	14.3	11.8	11.4	11.0	10.2
– Eastern Europe	0.2	0.3	0.2	0.1	0.2	0.3	0.1	1.0	0.1	0.1
– Rest of Europe	1.1	1.2	0.9	0.7	0.7	0.7	0.7	0.7	0.5	0.6
Europe former USSR			0.0	0.0	0.3	0.2	0.2	0.3	0.0	0.0
Oceania	0.0		0.0	0.0	0.0	0.0	0.0	0.0	0.0	0.0
Other	0.0								0.2	0.0
Brazil/Brésil	31.2	29.0	25.5	16.5	17.2	19.9	21.9	24.7	21.7	31.6
Argentina/Argentine	8.9	12.0	10.7	12.8	12.0	16.3	14.4	14.4	16.5	18.9
USA/Etats–Unis d'Amer	10.4	10.0	14.1	12.7	15.0	14.0	14.1	11.7	12.5	11.2
Japan/Japon	6.0	7.6	12.2	15.5	13.1	12.3	12.1	9.3	8.7	6.6
Other Asia n.e.s.	3.1	3.1	3.6	6.3	6.5	5.0	6.7	6.3	7.6	7.0
Korea, Republic of	0.5	0.8	2.0	4.4	4.8	3.9	4.0	4.9	6.6	3.5
Germany/Allemagne					4.0	3.9	3.4	3.4	2.7	3.3
China, Hong Kong SAR	1.2	1.1	2.4	4.0	3.5	1.5	1.4	3.7	5.4	2.3
United Kingdom	6.3	6.5	3.8	3.6	4.1	4.2	3.3	2.5	3.1	2.8
Chile/Chili	1.2	1.7	2.1	2.1	2.7	2.8	2.8	3.5	2.7	2.3

	1987	1988	1989	1990	1991	1992	1993	1994	1995	1996
Afrique	0.7	1.8	0.4	0.3	0.4	0.5	0.3	0.6	0.6	0.2
Amériques	53.0	50.2	56.7	58.0	54.4	58.6	60.0	67.8	71.5	74.3
– Amérique du Nord	4.2	8.1	6.3	5.6	7.7	7.5	9.5	9.4	6.1	3.8
– ALAI	44.6	38.5	41.8	44.4	44.3	47.6	47.3	57.4	64.9	69.3
– MCAC	0.0	0.0	0.0	0.1	0.1	0.5	0.0	0.1	0.1	0.0
– Caraïbes	0.1	0.0	2.9	4.2	2.0	2.2	2.4	0.9	0.4	0.5
– Autre Amérique	4.1	3.6	5.6	3.7	0.3	0.8	0.9	0.0	0.0	0.7
Asie anc. URSS exclus	3.4	8.0	3.3	4.6	8.3	4.9	1.7	2.4	8.0	2.7
– Moyen–Orient	0.1	0.8	0.2	0.2	0.1	0.2	0.1	0.1	0.1	0.1
Asie ancienne URSS										
Europe anc. URSS exclus	42.8	40.0	39.6	37.0	36.8	36.0	37.9	29.1	19.8	22.7
– Union Européenne	36.0	32.2	32.2	31.7	32.0	34.3	34.3	27.8	19.4	21.7
– Europe de l'Est		0.0	0.1	0.0	0.0	0.0	0.0	0.0	0.0	0.0
– Autre de l'Europe	6.8	7.7	7.4	5.3	4.8	1.7	3.7	1.3	0.5	1.0
Europe ancienne URSS					0.0	0.0	0.1	0.1	0.0	0.0
Océanie				0.0	0.0	0.0	0.0	0.0	0.0	
Autre		0.0				0.0		0.0	0.0	
Brazil/Brésil	17.6	23.0	32.5	32.6	27.5	26.1	29.7	39.6	44.7	49.9
Netherlands/Pays–Bas	18.0	13.3	18.5	15.3	14.9	21.2	26.1	19.6	9.8	16.6
Argentina/Argentine	15.2	6.6	4.9	5.8	6.1	9.8	9.0	11.1	9.1	9.1
USA/Etats–Unis d'Amer	4.2	3.8	4.2	4.3	4.7	5.3	7.3	7.0	4.8	3.6
Chile/Chili	6.0	5.2	2.8	3.1	6.5	7.2	5.8	4.0	3.4	2.4
Italy/Italie	3.4	2.5	2.4	2.7	5.3	3.4	2.4	3.0	3.2	1.9
Uruguay	3.2	0.9	1.0	1.2	1.5	1.6	1.0	1.3	3.7	4.2
Other Asia n.e.s.	0.9	2.7	1.3	1.9	4.6	1.9	0.6	1.1	5.3	1.8
France, Monaco	1.8	1.3	0.8	1.1	1.5	2.1	1.6	1.5	2.1	1.1
Switzerland,Liechtenst.	6.8	7.6	7.3	5.2	4.8	1.3	3.6	1.3	0.5	1.0

4. Special Imports C.I.F. by Commodities according to the S.I.T.C. (Rev. 2) in million U.S. Dollars
Importations Spéciales C.A.F. par Produits d'après la C.T.C.I. (Rév. 2) en millions de Dollars E.U.

SITC CTCI	COMMODITY	1993 QUANTITY QUANTITE	1993 VALUE VALEUR	1994 QUANTITY QUANTITE	1994 VALUE VALEUR	1995 QUANTITY QUANTITE	1995 VALUE VALEUR	1996 QUANTITY QUANTITE	1996 VALUE VALEUR	PRODUIT
	ALL COMMODITIES		1688.1		2424.7		3135.9		3107.4	TOUS PRODUITS
0	FOOD AND LIVE ANIMALS		71.7		150.7		217.5		199.6	ALIMENTS,ANIMAUX VIVANTS
001	*LIVE ANIMALS FOR FOOD	W 2913	3.1	W 60096	43.1	W 82954	57.0	W 40288	27.5	ANIMAUX VIVANTS
0011	BOVINE SPECIES,LIVE	W 2814	2.4	W 59658	41.2	W 82417	54.2	W 39951	25.6	ESPECE BOVINE
00111	— PURE BRED FR BREEDING	W 119	0.2	W 719	1.2	W 28849	19.3	W 6330	3.3	BOVINS REPRODUCTEURS
00119	— OTHR THAN FR BREEDING	W 2695	2.3	W 58938	40.1	W 53568	34.9	W 33621	22.4	BOVINS NON REPRODUCTEURS
02	DAIRY PRODCTS,BIRDS'EGGS		6.1		19.0		22.1		22.9	PRODUITS LAITIERS,OEUFS
022	MILK AND CREAM	W 2889	5.8	W 7645	17.5	W 7241	19.0	W 7127	19.2	LAIT ET CREME
0224	MILK,CREAM PRESERVED ETC	W 2850	5.8	W 7510	17.4	W 7129	18.8	W 6935	19.0	LAIT,CREME CONS,CONC
02243	MILK DRY,OVER 1.5% FAT	W 1954	4.5	W 4521	11.9	W 6534	18.0	W 5942	16.8	LAIT POUDRE SUP 1.5%
04	CEREALS AND PREPARATIONS		27.7		24.5		54.0		62.9	CEREALES ET PRODUITS
041	WHEAT ETC UNMILLED	W 81914	11.2	W 7000	0.9	W 38059	6.0	W 79073	18.8	FROMENT,EPEAUTRE
0411	DURUM WHEAT UNMILLED	W 79814	10.9	W 7000	0.9	W 133	0.1	W 2204	0.6	FROMENT DUR NON MOULU
0412	OTHER WHEAT ETC UNMILLED	W 2100	0.4			W 37927	6.0	W 76869	18.2	AUTRE FROMENT NON MOULU
048	CEREAL ETC PREPARATIONS	W 26309	15.6	W 33211	21.3	W 37074	42.8	W 34728	37.8	PREPTNS A BASE CEREALES
0482	MALT INCLUDING FLOUR	W 19153	6.9	W 21957	6.7	W 18873	11.0	W 18607	12.5	MALT MEME TORREFIE
0484	BAKERY PRODUCTS	W 5375	6.0	W 8325	10.2	W 12554	22.5	W 11291	17.0	PRODUITS DE BOULANGERIE
04842	PASTRY, CAKES ETC	W 5255	5.8	W 7938	9.5	W 10445	20.4	W 8770	13.0	PATISSERIE ETC.
05	VEGETABLES AND FRUIT		5.9		10.4		16.0		15.8	LEGUMES ET FRUITS
06	SUGAR AND PREPS,HONEY		5.3		12.5		19.4		15.5	SUCRES ET PRODUITS
062	SUGAR CANDY NON-CHOCLATE	W 2641	4.5	W 5082	8.7	W 7663	14.4	W 7050	15.2	SUCRERIES
07	COFFEE,TEA,COCOA,SPICES		4.3		7.1		11.6		13.6	CAFE,THE,CACAO,EPICES
09	MISC EDIBLE PRODUCTS		16.0		24.1		26.3		30.1	PREP ALIMENTAIRES DIVERSES
098	EDIBLE PRODCTS,PREPS NES	W 5338	15.9	W 8948	23.8	W 9221	25.8	W 9759	29.6	PREP ALIMENTAIRES NDA
09809	MISC FOOD PREPRTIONS NES	W 2387	11.9	W 4020	17.3	W 4140	17.0	W 5348	22.5	PREP ALIMENTAIRES NDA
1	BEVERAGES AND TOBACCO		116.8		197.7		355.9		429.8	BOISSONS ET TABACS
11	BEVERAGES		65.4		108.0		158.0		136.4	BOISSONS
111	NON-ALCOHL BEVERAGES NES	W 5475	3.1	W 12214	6.6	W 18396	11.2	W 16875	10.6	BOISSONS NON ALCOOLIQUES
11102	FLAVORED WATERS NON-ALCO	W 5403	3.1	W 12161	6.6	W 18220	10.9	W 16815	10.6	LIMONADES,EAUX GAZEUSES
112	ALCOHOLIC BEVERAGES	W 37455	62.4	W 85433	101.5	W 97860	146.8	W 98866	125.8	BOISSONS ALCOOLIQUES
1121	WINE OF FRESH GRAPES ETC	W 6633	8.3	W 11396	10.8	W 10957	15.9	W 10200	11.2	VINS DE RAISINS FRAIS
11212	WINE OF FRESH GRAPES	W 6281	7.6	W 10864	10.3	W 10434	15.4	W 9182	10.2	VINS DE MOUTS DE RAISINS
1123	BEER,ALE,STOUT,PORTER	W 16220	9.6	W 54010	30.4	W 56481	33.7	W 61113	39.6	BIERES
1124	DISTILLED ALCOHOLIC BEVS	W 13949	44.3	W 17317	59.2	W 27333	94.7	W 20246	71.4	ALCOOLS,EAUX-DE-VIE
11241	WHISKY	W 12697	41.5	W 15065	53.9	W 24202	87.3	W 16818	64.4	WHISKY
12	TOBACCO AND MANUFACTURES		51.4		89.7		197.9		293.5	TABACS BRUTS FABRIQUES
121	TOBACCO UNMNFCTRD,REFUSE	W 2387	4.6	W 3101	5.5	W 3675	7.4	W 4960	10.6	TABACS BRUTS,DECHETS
1212	TOBACCO STRIPPED OR PART	W 224	0.7	W 2257	5.1	W 2631	6.6	W 3599	9.4	TABACS PART ECOTES
122	TOBACCO,MANUFACTURED	W 3692	46.8	W 9039	84.3	W 22971	190.6	W 35366	283.0	TABACS FABRIQUES
1222	CIGARETTES	W 3668	46.6	W 9024	84.2	W 22811	190.1	W 33762	276.4	CIGARETTES
2	CRUDE MATERLS,EXCL FUELS		13.2		17.6		15.9		105.6	MAT BRUTES NON COMESTIBLES
22	OIL SEEDS,OLEAGINOUS FRT		4.0		1.0		4.0		12.3	GRAINES,FRUITS OLEAGINEUX
222	SEEDS FOR'SOFT'FIXED OIL	W 2809	4.0	W 303	1.0	W 4666	4.0	W 14856	12.3	GRAINES HUILES FIXES
27	CRUDE FERTLZR,MINRLS NES		3.2		10.4		4.5		83.6	ENGRAIS MINERAUX BRUTS
278	OTHER CRUDE MINERALS	W 12466	1.4	W 28848	2.1	W 33459	3.2	MW 9922	81.2	AUTRES MINERAUX BRUTS
2782	REFRACTORY MINERALS NES	W 4336	0.2	W 779	0.2	W 10494	0.3	MW 9905	79.2	ARGILE MINERAUX REFRACTAIRES
27823	DOLOMITE	W 3706	0.1	W 400	0.1	W 9855	0.1	MW 9904	79.1	DOLOMIE BRUTE
3	MINERAL FUELS ETC		206.6		201.8		206.5		252.6	COMBUSTIBLES MINERAUX LUB
33	PETROLEUM AND PRODUCTS		192.0		189.7		192.5		236.9	PETROLE ET DERIVES
333	CRUDE PETROLEUM	W 219913	44.5	W 234222	43.3	W 228423	31.5	W 148261	25.6	HUILES BRUTES DE PETROLE
334	PETROLEUM PRODUCTS,REFIN	W 567973	142.4	W 664735	140.1	W 716850	157.8	W 793013	208.6	PRODUITS RAFFINES
3341	GASOLINE,OTH LIGHT OILS	W 116376	29.3	W 143140	29.2	W 543327	108.6	W 615429	153.2	ESSENCES POUR MOTEURS
33411	MOTOR,AVIATION SPIRIT	W 115381	28.9	W 142269	28.9	W 530537	104.8	W 585732	143.1	ESSENCES MOTEURS D'AVIONS
33419	OTH LIGHT PETROLEUM OILS	W 996	0.4	W 871	0.4	W 12789	3.8	W 29697	10.1	AUTRES HUILES LEGERES
3343	GAS OILS	W 415033	94.7	W 478145	89.0	W 15051	11.1	W 18094	14.7	GAS OILS
3345	LUBS,PETROLEUM OILS NES	W 17895	14.0	W 20274	17.1	W 158424	38.2	W 159449	40.8	HUILES LUBRIFIANTES
33451	LUBS(HIGH PETR CONT) ETC	W 16862	11.6	W 19100	14.6	W 157519	36.8	W 158547	39.7	HUILES LUBRIF,H LOURDES
335	RESIDUAL PETRLM PROD NES	W 28552	5.1	W 44692	6.4	W 21688	3.2	W 20058	2.8	PRODUITS RESIDUELS NDA
341	*GAS,NATURAL AND MANUFCT	W 55587	14.7	W 70328	11.2	W 70367	14.1	W 60138	15.7	GAZ NATUREL,GAZ MANUFACT
3413	PETROLM GASES,LIQUEFIED	W 55587	14.7	W 70328	11.2	W 70352	14.0	W 58243	15.3	GAZ DE PETROLE LIQUEFIE
34139	OTH HYDROCARBON GAS LQFD	W 55587	14.7	W 70328	11.2	W 69501	13.8	W 58191	15.3	HYDROCARBURES GAZEUX NDA
5	CHEMCLS,RELATED PROD NES		180.0		270.0		278.6		322.8	PRODUITS CHIMIQUES
51	ORGANIC CHEMICALS		18.1		15.2		17.7		20.2	PROD CHIMIQ ORGANIQUES
52	INORGANIC CHEMICALS		7.9		8.5		8.9		7.2	PROD CHIM INORGANIQUES
53	DYES,TANNING,COLOUR PROD		12.8		23.2		16.5		15.7	PROD TEINTURE,COLORANTS
531	SYNT DYE,NAT INDGO,LAKES	W 423	2.9	W 1540	11.0	W 538	3.5	W 353	2.5	MAT COLOR ORGAN,LAQUES
5312	SYNTH LUMIN,INDIGO,LAKES	W 102	0.5	W 1211	8.5	W 152	0.6	W 155	0.4	LUMINOPHORES ORGAN SYNTH
53121	SYN ORG LUMIN ETC,INDIGO	W 56	0.3	W 1152	8.3	W 126	0.5	W 75	0.4	PROD ORGANIQ SYNTH LUMIN
533	PIGMENTS,PAINTS,ETC	W 4924	8.5	W 6376	10.6	W 6944	12.1	W 8483	12.3	PIGMENTS,PEINTURES,VERNIS
5334	VARNISHES,DISTEMPERS ETC	W 3353	5.2	W 3918	5.8	W 3760	6.2	W 4808	7.0	PEINTURES A L'EAU
541	*MEDICINAL,PHARM PRODUCT	K 2496304	36.2	K 7191099	62.1	K 6128531	51.1	K 6263119	58.2	PROD MEDICINAUX PHARMACEUT
5417	MEDICAMENTS	K 2192642	27.4	K 6759462	51.1	K 5569281	37.4	K 5593692	42.6	MEDICAMENTS
54179	— CONTNG OTH SUBSTANCES	K 2051396	20.6	K 5935772	41.2	K 5185152	29.1	K 4714649	32.6	MED CONT AUT SUBSTANCES
55	PERFUME,CLEANING ETC PRD		27.5		45.1		55.4		56.4	PROD POUR PARFUM,TOILETTE
553	PERFUMERY,COSMETICS,ETC	W 5425	19.6	W 10747	32.7	W 11269	39.0	W 8216	33.4	PRODUITS DE PARFUMERIE
554	SOAP,CLEANSING ETC PREPS	W 2970	3.2	W 9515	9.3	W 14571	14.4	W 18361	20.7	SAVONS,PRODUITS DETERSIFS
5542	WASHING PREPARATIONS ETC	W 2211	2.2	W 7645	7.5	W 11479	11.6	W 15615	17.1	PROD ORG TENSIO-ACT NDA
562	*FERTILIZERS,MANUFACTURE	W 74892	12.0	W 107407	18.1	W 81268	22.7	W 148065	40.7	ENGRAIS MANUFACTURES
5629	FERTILIZERS NES	W 66887	10.7	W 87379	15.0	W 64899	18.3	W 130277	34.5	ENGRAIS NDA
56291	NIT-PHOS-POT FERTLZR NES	W 37146	5.4	W 56619	9.3	W 41945	13.1	W 87546	22.6	ENGRAIS CONT N P K
58	PLASTIC MATERIALS ETC		25.4		38.2		44.4		43.7	MAT PLAST ARTIFICIELLES
582	PROD OF CONDENSATION ETC	W 4402	4.5	W 8219	7.9	W 7433	8.9	W 8297	10.6	PROD CONDENS,POLYCOND
583	POLYMERIZATION ETC PRODS	W 22188	20.6	W 31688	29.7	W 32994	34.7	W 29649	32.1	PROD POLYMERISATION
5831	POLYETHYLENE	W 11991	8.3	W 16996	11.9	W 13320	17.7	W 14783	14.0	POLYETHYLENE
58311	— IN PRIMARY FORMS	W 11725	7.8	W 16717	11.4	W 12996	16.6	W 14545	13.5	POLYETHYLENE PRIMAIRES
59	CHEMICAL MATERIALS NES		39.1		59.2		61.3		80.0	MAT PROD CHIMIQUES NDA
591	PESTICIDES,DISINFECTANTS	W 3733	26.1	W 8111	46.5	W 8549	47.0	W 14618	65.5	DESINF,INSECT,FONG,HERB
5911	INSECTICIDES,FOR RETAIL	W 1176	9.0	W 2083	12.0	W 1593	9.5	W 2267	17.3	INSECTICIDES VENTE DET
5913	HERBICIDES,FOR RETAIL	W 1937	12.7	W 3300	27.9	W 3987	30.9	W 4891	37.4	HERBICIDES VENTE AU DET
598	MISCEL CHEM PRODUCTS NES	W 4395	10.7	W 5704	9.4	W 5381	10.1	W 6062	10.2	PROD DIV INDUST CHIM NDA
5982	ANTI-KNOCK PREPARTNS ETC	W 1459	6.0	W 1001	2.3	W 988	2.9	W 645	1.4	PREPARAT ANTIDETONANTES
6	BASIC MANUFACTURES		210.0		314.8		372.2		346.6	ART MANUFACTURES
62	RUBBER MANUFACTURES NES		36.1		56.7		64.0		61.5	CAOUTCHOUC MANUFACTURE
625	RUBBER TYRES, TUBES ETC	W 10212	30.7	W 16119	50.2	W 18511	54.5	W 16031	52.4	PNEUS CAOUTCHOUC VULCANISE
6251	TYRES NEW FOR MOTOR CARS	W 2384	6.7	W 3940	12.5	W 4518	13.3	W 4080	14.5	PNEUS POUR VOITURES
6252	TYRES,NEW,BUS OR LORRY	W 5511	18.8	W 7837	29.0	W 9207	30.0	W 6428	27.5	PNEUS POUR AUTOBUS,CAMIONS
6259	OTH TYRES,TYRE CASES,ETC	W 2013	4.5	W 3816	7.5	W 4083	9.5	W 3562	8.9	AUTRES PNEUS RECHAPES FLAPS
64	PAPER,PAPERBOARD AND MFR		36.6		51.4		71.4		68.5	PAPIERS,CARTONS & OUVRAGES
641	PAPER AND PAPERBOARD	W 35248	24.6	W 50385	33.6	W 46790	44.2	W 43070	37.4	PAPIERS ET CARTONS
6411	NEWSPRINT	W 14440	9.4	W 19959	12.2	W 17500	14.3	W 7341	6.0	PAPIER JOURNAL
6415	PAPER,PAPERBRD,BULK,NES	W 9840	7.1	W 12193	9.0	W 11136	13.5	W 15456	13.6	PAPIERS,CARTONS ROULEAUX

4. Special Imports C.I.F. by Commodities according to the S.I.T.C. (Rev. 2) in million U.S. Dollars
Importations Spéciales C.A.F. par Produits d'après la C.T.C.I. (Rév. 2) en millions de Dollars E.U.

SITC CTCI	COMMODITY	1993 QUANTITY QUANTITE	1993 VALUE VALEUR	1994 QUANTITY QUANTITE	1994 VALUE VALEUR	1995 QUANTITY QUANTITE	1995 VALUE VALEUR	1996 QUANTITY QUANTITE	1996 VALUE VALEUR	PRODUIT
64159	OTHER PAPER ETC,BULK,NES	W 9705	6.8	W 11943	8.6	W 9989	12.6	W 14837	13.3	AUT PAPIER ROULEAUX FEUILLES
642	PAPER,ETC,PRECUT,ARTS OF	W 5107	12.1	W 8811	17.9	W 10920	27.3	W 11525	31.1	PAP,CARTONS DECOUPES
6428	PAPER ETC ARTICLES NES	W 3598	9.3	W 5575	13.4	W 7223	20.9	W 7435	22.4	OUVRAGES EN PATE A PAPIER
64285	PAPER ETC DIAPERS ETC	W 3085	8.6	W 4634	12.1	W 5955	18.8	W 6023	19.8	SERVIETTES HYGIENIQUES
65	TEXTILE YARN,FABRICS,ETC		37.6		57.6		64.6		49.0	FILS,TISSUS,ARTICLES TEXTILE
652	COTTON FABRICS,WOVEN	W 1968	6.2	W 3893	13.5	W 3634	10.3	W 2489	9.6	TISSUS DE COTON
6522	WOVEN COTTON BLEACHD,ETC	W 1955	6.1	W 3857	13.5	W 3626	10.3	W 2488	9.5	TISSUS COTON BLANCHIS ETC
65224	BLCHED COTTON FABRIC NES	W 1762	5.6	W 3691	12.8	W 2770	9.8	W 2378	9.0	AUT TIS PLUS 85% COT BLANCHI
653	WOVN MAN–MADE FIB FABRIC	W 4416	17.1	W 6896	22.6	W 7741	30.0	W 4158	15.3	TISSUS FIBRES SYNTH,ARTIF
6531	CONT SYNT WEAVES NONPILE	W 2773	10.5	W 4282	12.6	W 4310	15.6	W 1554	6.0	TISSUS FIBRES SYNTH CONTINUE
65315	CONT SYN TXTL FABRIC NES	W 2609	9.8	W 4082	11.8	W 4144	14.7	W 1459	5.5	TIS PLUS 85% TEXT SYNT CONT
66	NONMETAL MINERAL MFS NES		19.2		27.0		34.3		39.4	ART MIN NON METALLIQUES
664	GLASS	W 6697	4.7	W 7877	6.2	W 8824	7.9	W 8270	12.5	VERRE
665	GLASSWARE	W 7315	6.4	W 8388	7.6	W 7114	8.8	W 6466	8.5	OUVRAGES EN VERRE
67	IRON AND STEEL		24.3		39.2		41.4		42.7	FER ET ACIER
674	IRN,STL UNIV,PLATE,SHEET	W 27118	14.5	W 35270	22.3	W 40793	25.9	W 44865	25.3	LARGES PLATS,TOLES
6749	OTH IRN,STL PLATES,SHEET	W 7583	5.3	W 17346	14.2	W 18477	12.4	W 14183	11.0	AUTRES TOLES FER,ACIER
67491	— OF IRON OR SIMPLE STL	W 5328	3.4	W 15453	9.8	W 18108	11.9	W 14138	10.9	AUT TOLES AUTRES ACIER FIN
68	NON–FERROUS METALS		10.2		11.7		16.5		14.6	METAUX NON FERREUX
684	ALUMINIUM	W 1932	6.6	W 2225	7.8	W 2432	10.4	W 3396	10.3	ALUMINIUM
6842	ALUMINIUM,ALLOYS WORKED	W 1864	6.5	W 2185	7.7	W 2382	10.3	W 3358	10.2	ALUMINIUM,ALLIAGES OUVRE
69	METAL MANUFACTURES NES		45.4		70.3		76.8		69.2	ART MANUFACT EN METAL NDA
692	METAL TANKS,BOXES,ETC	W 2220	6.1	W 4082	14.0	W 3148	8.2	W 2404	5.9	RECIPIENTS METALLIQUES
695	TOOLS	W 2194	7.3	W 4813	11.5	W 7385	12.7	W 4693	10.0	OUTILS A MAIN
6953	OTHER HAND TOOLS	W 1740	5.1	W 3976	7.6	W 6636	9.6	W 4159	7.6	AUTRES OUTILS A MAIN
696	CUTLERY	W 1074	4.6	W 2167	7.5	W 4057	8.4	W 1704	8.2	COUTELLERIE
697	BASE MTL HOUSEHOLD EQUIP	W 3798	7.8	W 8375	13.1	W 18498	17.0	W 7996	15.7	ART MENAGE MET COMMUNS
6974	BASE MTL DMSTC ARTIC NES	W 1712	3.0	W 4975	5.3	W 9301	9.9	W 4258	5.8	ARTICLES NDA FONTE,FER,ETC
699	BASE METAL MFRS NES	W 3533	11.0	W 5288	12.3	W 5995	14.5	W 15615	13.3	ART MANUFACTURES MET NDA
7	MACHINES,TRANSPORT EQUIP		704.4		999.4		1323.6		1124.3	MACHINES MATERIEL TRANSPORT
71	POWER GENERATING EQUIPMT		30.5		41.1		37.5		48.1	MACHINES GENERATRICES
713	INTRNL COMBUS PSTN ENGIN	W 1705	9.5	W 2239	11.1	W 3134	13.9	W 1591	10.6	MOTEURS EXPL COMB INT, PIECE
7139	PISTON ENGINE PARTS NES	W 495	6.3	W 1081	8.2	W 2349	8.7	W 922	7.3	PIECES POUR 713.2,3,8
716	ROTATING ELECTRIC PLANT	W 625	2.9	W 696	2.8	W 1911	9.4	W 4179	28.7	APP ELECTR ROTATIFS,PIECES
7169	PTS NES OF ROT ELEC PLNT	W 28	0.1	W 90	0.1	W 1019	4.4	W 2458	20.9	PIECES MAC APP ROTATIFS
718	OTH POWER GENERATG MACHY	W 2174	17.0	W 2481	26.2	W 1038	13.5	W 893	7.8	AUTRES MOTEURS PARTIES
7188	WIND,WATER,ETC ENGINES	W 2174	17.0	W 2462	26.2	W 1038	13.5	W 893	7.7	MOT MACHINES MOTRICES NDA
71889	PARTS NES OF 71881,71882	W 2159	16.9	W 2451	26.1	W 1027	13.5	W 867	7.5	PARTIES DES POS 718.81,82
72	MACHS FOR SPCL INDUSTRYS		70.6		103.2		100.5		113.2	MAC SPECIALES POUR INDUST
721	AGRIC MACHY,EXC TRACTORS	W 3466	9.1	W 5609	15.6	W 4601	15.3	W 7237	30.4	MACHINES AGRICOLES
7211	CULTIVATING MACHINERY	W 1621	2.3	W 2632	3.8	W 2369	4.1	W 3371	9.5	MACH PREPARATION DU SOL
7212	HARVESTING ETC MACHINES	W 1591	4.3	W 2750	10.5	W 1926	9.3	W 3551	17.5	ENGINS POUR LA RECOLTE
72122	COMBINE HARVESTR–THRESHR	W 1063	2.7	W 1975	7.9	W 1290	6.4	W 2588	13.4	MOISSONNEUSES–BATTEUSES
722	TRACTORS NON–ROAD	W 2861	11.5	W 3219	13.9	W 2610	13.4	W 3849	20.0	TRACTEURS
7224	WHEELED TRACTORS NES	W 2761	11.1	W 3042	12.9	W 2503	12.9	W 3801	19.7	TRACTEURS A ROUES
723	CIVIL ENGNEERG EQUIP ETC	W 3970	17.0	W 3419	17.3	W 4525	25.6	W 3863	20.2	APPAREILS DE GENIE CIVIL
7234	CONST,MINING MACHNRY NES	W 3736	16.3	W 2968	15.5	W 4117	24.2	W 3247	17.7	MACH POUR LA CONST, MINES
72341	SELF–PROPELLD DOZERS,ETC	W 2259	10.8	W 842	3.9	W 1702	12.7	W 1110	8.1	BULLDOZERS
72342	SLFPRP SHOVELS,EXCAVATRS	W 1084	4.6	W 1334	6.1	W 1965	9.6	W 1427	6.5	PELLES MECANIQUES
724	TEXTILE,LEATHER MACHNRY	W 1288	9.4	W 2495	19.5	W 1712	13.6	W 869	6.9	MACH POUR INDUSTRIE TEXTILE
7244	SPINNING,EXTRDNG,ETC MCH	W 437	2.9	W 1440	11.6	W 636	4.9	W 214	2.5	MACH POUR LE FILAGE
726	PRINTG,BKBINDG MACHY,PTS	W 646	7.2	W 1038	10.8	W 1175	8.6	W 1442	7.3	MACHINES POUR IMPRIMERIE
728	OTH MACHY FOR SPCL INDUS	W 1740	10.6	W 2081	18.8	W 2069	13.5	W 2062	16.9	AUT MACH IND PARTICULIERES
7284	MACHY FOR SPCL INDUS NES	W 902	6.8	W 993	13.0	W 981	9.4	W 1033	11.3	MACH SPEC IND PARTICUL.
72842	RUBBER,PLASTICS WRKG MCH	W 409	4.5	W 710	8.2	W 329	4.6	W 302	3.7	MACH IND CAOUT MAT PLAST
74	GENRL INDUSTRL MACHY NES		64.3		109.3		99.0		114.3	MACH APP INDUSTRIE
741	HEATING,COOLING EQUIPMNT	W 3634	17.6	W 4756	31.7	W 4693	31.3	W 5858	36.8	MACH CHAUFFAGE,PIECES
7414	NONDOM REFRIG EQUIPT,PTS	W 519	3.1	W 784	4.4	W 1025	7.3	W 1570	12.2	MAT PRODUCTION DU FROID
74141	REFRIG EQUIP NONDOMESTIC	W 450	2.7	W 675	4.0	W 871	6.3	W 1334	10.6	REFIG INDUSTRIELS
7415	AIR–CONDITIONING MACHNRY	W 1493	8.9	W 2137	15.3	W 2682	18.6	W 2728	17.1	GROUPES CONDITION AIR
7416	HEATING,COOLING EQU NES	W 1454	4.6	W 1151	9.8	W 771	4.4	W 1090	4.9	APP CHANGEMENT TEMP
742	PUMPS FOR LIQUIDS ETC	W 463	4.7	W 981	8.2	W 1388	7.6	W 783	7.4	POMPES MOTO–POMPES
743	PUMPS NES,CENTRFUGES ETC	W 1577	8.1	W 2515	14.3	W 3254	15.0	W 5080	15.2	POMPES COMPRES,VENT ETC
744	MECHANICAL HANDLING EQU	W 2078	9.9	W 2335	9.8	W 2123	9.7	W 3000	13.6	EQUIP MANUTENTION PIECES
7442	LIFTING,LOADING MACH NES	W 1624	7.2	W 1623	5.6	W 1512	6.5	W 1948	8.0	APP LEVAGE,MANUTENTION
745	NONELEC MACHY,TOOLS NES	W 1233	11.4	W 3191	25.1	W 1207	13.8	W 1605	19.0	AUT MACH NON ELEC,PIECES
7452	OTH NONELEC MCHS,PTS NES	W 1160	9.9	W 3076	22.5	W 1052	10.8	W 1520	16.9	AUT MACH NON ELEC,PIECES
74522	PACKAGNG,BOTTLNG,ETC MCH	W 376	5.5	W 720	13.1	W 171	4.9	W 257	7.2	MACH NETT BOUTEILLES,ETC
749	NONELEC MACH PTS,ACC NES	W 1348	12.9	W 2280	20.5	W 2531	21.8	W 4197	22.6	PIECES MACH NON ELEC NDA
75	OFFICE MACHNES,ADP EQUIP		56.8		77.1		152.1		131.9	MACH BUREAU TRAIT AUTOM
751	OFFICE MACHINES	W 1882	7.3	W 2387	11.2	W 1845	15.1	W 2016	10.3	MACH,APPAREILS DE BUREAU
752	AUTOMTIC DATA PROC EQUIP	W 2880	36.5	W 3097	48.1	W 11234	119.4	W 10313	98.3	MACH TRAIT INFORMATION
7522	DIGITAL COMPUTERS	W 177	5.0	W 100	5.7	W 268	4.1	W 3174	31.9	MACH DIGITALES COMPLETES
7523	DIGITL CENTRL PROCESSORS	W 44	0.3	W 32	0.6	W 493	5.1	W 1120	14.4	UNITES CENTRALES
7524	DIGITL CENTRL STOR UNITS	W 2	0.1	W 1	0.1	W 485	14.0	W 312	5.2	UNITES MEMOIRE CENTRALES
7525	ADP PERIPHERAL UNITS	W 1492	18.3	W 2603	37.2	W 9612	88.0	W 5239	39.1	UNITES PERIPHERIQUES
7528	OFF–LINE DATA PROC EQUIP	W 1139	12.5	W 330	4.3	W 370	7.9	W 191	2.5	MACH AUXIL TRAIT INFORM
759	OFFICE,ADP MCH PTS,ACCES	W 2962	13.1	W 4669	17.8	W 3242	17.8	W 4025	23.4	PIECES DU 751 ET 752
7599	ACCTG,ETC,ADP MCH PTS,AC	W 2941	12.5	W 4611	16.9	W 3107	16.3	W 3924	21.9	PIECES DU 751 ET 752
76	TELECOMM,SOUND EQUIPMENT		181.2		269.9		428.8		239.9	EQUIPMENT DE TELECOM
761	TELEVISION RECEIVERS	W 14111	64.2	W 18039	101.7	W 17328	118.5	W 5338	35.8	RECEPTEURS DE TELEVISION
7611	COLOUR TV RECEIVERS	W 7903	47.3	W 11096	81.7	W 11064	96.9	W 3042	21.3	RECEPTEURS COULEUR
7612	MONOCHROME TV RECEIVERS	W 6208	16.9	W 6943	20.1	W 6265	21.7	W 2296	14.5	RECEPTEURS NOIR ET BLANC
762	RADIO BROADCAST RECEIVRS	W 11974	43.0	W 17152	73.0	W 27078	143.9	W 20603	77.4	RECEPTEURS RADIODIFFUSION
7621	MTR VEHC RADIO RECEIVERS	W 1419	11.1	W 2340	19.4	W 2572	30.6	W 2318	13.7	RECEPTEURS RADIO AUTO
7622	PORTABLE RADIO RECEIVERS	W 4114	11.4	W 5475	17.1	W 8552	36.9	W 5038	15.6	RECEPT PORTATIFS RADIO
7628	OTHER RADIO RECEIVERS	W 6441	20.6	W 9338	36.6	W 15953	76.6	W 13248	48.2	AUTRES RECEPT RADIO
763	SOUND RECORDRS,PHONOGRPH	W 1821	30.2	W 2079	39.9	W 2921	78.6	W 1050	23.3	PHONO,APP ENREGISTREMENT
7638	OTHR SOUND APPARATUS ETC	W 1716	28.8	W 1845	36.4	W 2835	77.7	W 987	22.9	AUT APP D'ENREGIS,REPROD
76381	TV IMAGE,SND RECRDRS ETC	W 1389	25.8	W 1428	32.7	W 2241	66.6	W 601	17.2	APP ENREG,REPRO IMAG,SON
76388	DICTATING MACHINES ETC	W 327	3.0	W 417	3.8	W 594	11.2	W 385	5.8	MACHINES A DICTER
764	TELECOM EQPT,PTS,ACC NES	W 2901	44.0	W 4844	55.5	W 6620	88.0	W 8715	103.5	EQUIP TELECOM,PIECES
7641	LINE TELEPHONE,ETC EQUIP	W 1810	22.5	W 2427	31.0	W 2894	39.2	W 2987	36.4	APP TELEPHON PAR FIL
7642	MICROPH,LOUDSPKR,AMPLIFR	W 480	2.7	W 1529	6.8	W 2394	9.9	W 3908	10.4	MICRO,HAUT–PARLEUR,AMPLI
7643	TV,RADIO TRANSMITTRS ETC	W 116	3.7	W 144	3.7	W 343	12.3	W 266	14.9	APP EMET TELE RADIO
7648	TELECOMM EQUIPMENT NES	W 147	8.0	W 286	10.0	W 502	18.6	W 440	17.8	APP TELECOM NDA
76482	TELEVISION CAMERAS	W 101	2.8	W 128	8.7	W 294	16.9	W 128	6.1	APP PRISE DE VUES TELE
76483	RADAR APPARATUS ETC	W 15	4.8	W 20	0.2	W 17	0.3	W 270	10.0	APP DE RADIOGUIDAGE ETC
7649	PTS NES OF EQUIPMT OF 76	W 348	7.3	W 458	4.2	W 487	8.2	W 1114	24.3	PIECES DE LA DIV 76
76491	PTS NES OF APPAR OF 7641	W 131	5.7	W 65	1.0	W 67	5.3	W 216	16.2	PIECES POUR 764.1
77	ELECTRIC MACHNRY NES ETC		83.6		129.2		150.1		159.2	MACH APP ELECT NDA

4. Special Imports C.I.F. by Commodities according to the S.I.T.C. (Rev. 2) in million U.S. Dollars
Importations Spéciales C.A.F. par Produits d'après la C.T.C.I. (Rév. 2) en millions de Dollars E.U.

SITC CTCI	COMMODITY	1993 QUANTITY QUANTITE	1993 VALUE VALEUR	1994 QUANTITY QUANTITE	1994 VALUE VALEUR	1995 QUANTITY QUANTITE	1995 VALUE VALEUR	1996 QUANTITY QUANTITE	1996 VALUE VALEUR	PRODUIT
771	ELECTRIC POWER MACHY NES	W 1592	7.3	W 4719	10.8	W 4043	12.8	W 3261	14.1	MACH PROD,TRANS ELECTR
7711	TRANSFORMERS,ELECTRICAL	W 1280	5.4	W 2943	8.1	W 2416	8.9	W 2165	10.0	TRANSFO ELECTRIQUES
77118	OTHER ELEC TRANSFORMERS	W 1188	5.1	W 1429	2.5	W 2133	7.2	W 927	4.5	AUTRES TRANSFO ELECTRIQ
772	SWITCHGEAR ETC,PARTS NES	W 832	12.9	W 1792	13.4	W 1542	15.2	W 2334	12.7	APP COUPURE,SECT ETC
7721	SWITCHGEAR ETC	W 823	12.7	W 1741	13.2	W 1539	15.1	W 2325	12.6	APP COUPURE,SECTIONMNT
773	ELECTR DISTRIBUTNG EQUIP	W 1095	3.6	W 2164	8.1	W 2290	9.7	W 3996	16.2	EQUIPMT DISTRIBUTION ELECT
7731	INSULATED WIRE,CABLE ETC	W 857	3.3	W 1505	6.7	W 1967	8.6	W 3476	15.4	FILS,CABLES ISOLES ELECT
775	HOUSEHOLD TYPE EQUIP NES	W 13083	33.8	W 20316	55.6	W 27347	70.7	W 22313	62.4	MACH,APP USAGE DOMESTQUE
7751	HOUSEHOLD LDRY EQUIP NES	W 1479	5.4	W 2140	9.5	W 1858	7.5	W 2366	8.9	MACH A LAVER ET SECHOIRS
77511	DOMESTIC WASHING MACHNES	W 1413	5.1	W 2069	9.1	W 1794	7.2	W 2296	8.6	MACH LAVER LINGE MOINS 6 KG
7752	DOM REFRIGERATRS,FREEZRS	W 5685	11.7	W 4550	12.4	W 3117	9.6	W 3426	11.5	REFRIG,CONGEL MENAGER
77521	DOMESTIC REFRIGERATORS	W 3917	7.7	W 2817	7.9	W 2187	6.6	W 2462	8.1	REFRIGERATEURS
7757	DOMESTIC ELECTRC EQU NES	W 3800	9.9	W 10403	22.8	W 16079	33.8	W 9681	19.7	APP ELECTR DOMEST NDA
77572	DOM ELEC ROOM FANS ETC	W 3391	7.0	W 9671	18.0	W 15135	28.2	W 8013	13.0	HOTTES ASPIRANTES,VENTIL
7758	ELECTRO–THERMIC APPL NES	W 1903	6.2	W 2893	10.0	W 5546	17.9	W 5836	19.8	APP ELECTROTHERMIQ NDA
77586	ELECTROTHERM DOM APP NES	W 1004	4.1	W 1998	7.0	W 3691	13.0	W 4198	15.3	APP ELECTRO THERMIQUES
776	TRANSISTORS,VALVES,ETC	W 629	8.1	W 941	9.5	W 339	4.5	W 166	2.9	LAMPES,TUBES,VALVES
7764	ELECTRONIC MICROCIRCUITS	W 601	7.8	W 914	9.1	W 316	4.1	W 88	2.3	MICROSTRUCTURES ELECTRON
778	ELECTRICAL MACHINERY NES	W 4926	16.5	W 11762	27.4	W 13973	34.1	W 13174	44.1	AUTRES MACH ELECT NDA
7781	BATTERIES,ACCUMULATORS	W 3037	5.3	W 6914	9.2	W 8729	13.7	W 9310	16.6	PILES ET ACCUMULATEURS
77811	PRIMARY BATTERIES,CELLS	W 1348	2.4	W 3779	4.6	W 5351	8.2	W 5678	10.0	PILES ELECTRIQUES,PIECES
78	ROAD VEHICLES		211.3		259.0		336.3		307.1	VEHICULES ROUTIERS
781	PASS MOTOR VEH EXC BUSES	W 12134	91.1	W 13671	99.0	W 20109	135.3	W 19616	139.5	AUTO TRANSPORT PERSONNES
782	LORRIES,SPCL MTR VEH NES	W 10972	65.8	W 13935	76.4	W 18230	99.4	W 18050	86.9	VEHICULES SPECIAUX,MARCH
7821	LORRIES,TRUCKS	W 10559	63.5	W 12981	70.7	W 17182	92.8	W 17180	84.4	VEHICULES TRANSP MARCHAND
783	ROAD MOTOR VEHICLES NES	W 4194	20.6	W 6673	39.5	W 8526	41.4	W 7917	39.0	VEHICULES ROUTIERS NDA
7831	BUSES	W 2852	15.5	W 3789	27.0	W 3907	23.3	W 4246	26.1	VOITURES TRANSPORT COMMUN
7832	TRACTORS FOR TR–TRAILERS	W 1342	5.1	W 2884	12.6	W 4620	18.1	W 3671	12.9	TRACTEURS ROUTIERS
784	MOTOR VEH PRTS,ACCES NES	W 2113	14.1	W 3690	19.9	W 5356	25.6	W 4195	22.6	PIECES 722,781,782,783
7849	OTHER MOTOR VEHCL PARTS	W 1905	13.0	W 3324	17.9	W 4826	21.7	W 3821	20.0	PIECES 722,781,782,783
785	CYCLES,ETC MOTRZD OR NOT	W 4482	18.6	W 6533	22.7	W 6773	30.4	W 3505	15.2	MOTOCYCLES SCOOTERS
7851	MOTORCYCLES ETC	W 1151	7.5	W 1276	7.7	W 2014	16.3	W 1043	8.5	MOTO VELO MOTEUR AUXIL
7852	CYCLES, ETC NON–MOTOR	W 2787	7.7	W 4374	11.3	W 3405	8.4	W 1745	4.6	VELOCIPEDES SANS MOTEUR
79	OTHR TRANSPORT EQUIPMENT		3.8		8.9		16.3		7.6	AUTRE MATERIEL TRANSPORT
793	SHIPS AND BOATS ETC	W 1477	2.1		6.4	W 5495	13.0	W 2534	4.9	NAVIRES BATEAUX,ETC
8	MISC MANUFACTURED GOODS		184.0		259.0		354.2		318.3	ART MANUFACTURES DIVERS
831	*TRAVEL GOODS,HANDBAGS	W 1190	2.9	W 4071	5.8	W 5794	10.0	W 3242	7.2	ARTICLES DE VOYAGE ETC
84	CLOTHING AND ACCESSORIES		13.6		26.6		28.5		24.9	VETEMENTS
846	UNDER GARMENTS KNITTED	W 1373	5.6	W 2564	9.9	W 2090	9.4	W 2097	8.8	SOUS VETS DE BONNETERIE
851	*FOOTWEAR	W 3841	13.2	W 8301	24.9	W 10512	41.8	W 7412	36.5	CHAUSSURES
85102	FOOTWEAR LEATHER	W 3566	12.4	W 6630	20.1	W 8960	36.7	W 5770	29.1	CHAUS SEMELLES EN CUIR
87	PRECISION INSTRUMNTS NES		17.9		18.8		18.6		20.9	INSTRUM,APPAR SCIENT NDA
874	MEASURNG,CONTROLNG INSTR	W 794	11.1	W 1239	9.3	W 2354	8.6	W 1886	8.7	INSTRUMENTS DE MESURE
88	PHOTO EQU,OPTICL GDS ETC		24.9		28.5		38.1		35.4	APP,FOURN PHOTO,OP,MONTR
882	PHOTO,CINEMA SUPPLIES	W 792	9.2	W 815	10.8	W 1636	13.3	W 1130	14.2	PRODUITS PHOTO,CINEMA
8822	PHOTO FILM EXC DEV CINMA	W 533	7.2	W 520	9.0	W 576	10.9	W 855	12.2	PLAQUES,PELLICULES,FILMS
885	WATCHES AND CLOCKS		9.3		10.3		15.1		12.2	HORLOGERIE
8851	WATCHES,MOVEMENTS,CASES		6.2		4.8		6.4		7.9	MONTRES,MOUVEMENTS,BOITES
88511	WATCHES		5.6		4.0		5.9		7.8	MONTRES POCHE,BRACELET
89	MISC MANUFCTRD GOODS NES		105.6		145.0		204.0		179.5	ART MANUFACTURES DIVERS
892	PRINTED MATTER	W 869	6.1	W 1191	6.5	W 1831	9.7	W 1980	10.9	IMPRIMES
893	ARTICLES OF PLASTIC NES		19.0		23.9		30.5		32.7	OUVRAGES EN MAT DIVIS 58
8931	PLSTC PACKG CONTNRS,LIDS	W 1694	6.7	W 2204	6.9	W 3544	9.9	W 2885	10.9	ART TRANSP EMBALLAGE ETC
8939	MISC PLASTIC ARTICLES	W 4119	12.2	W 10312	15.6	W 15200	20.1	W 9245	21.2	ART DIVERS EN MAT DIV 58
89399	OTHR PLASTC ARTICLES NES	W 4017	12.0	W 9910	15.0	W 14817	19.3	W 8918	20.5	AUT OUV MAT DIV 58
894	TOYS,SPORTING GOODS,ETC	W 20298	36.7	W 34198	57.0	W 46676	97.2	W 39772	81.4	VOITURES ENFANTS,JOUETS
8942	TOYS,INDOOR GAMES ETC	W 18691	30.5	W 30903	44.2	W 41193	79.5	W 34832	65.8	JOUETS,JEUX ETC
89423	TOYS NES	W 12756	15.5	W 21031	23.8	W 28472	47.3	W 23669	38.7	JOUETS,MODELES REDUITS
89424	INDOOR GAME EQUIPMENT	W 1758	9.3	W 2776	11.7	W 3224	16.3	W 2725	11.4	ART,JEUX DE SOCIETE
8947	OTH SPORT GDS,FAIR AMUSM	W 1150	3.6	W 1566	5.4	W 4526	11.1	W 3591	8.1	AUT ART DE SPORT
895	OFFICE SUPPLIES NES	W 2018	6.3	W 4578	7.9	W 4584	10.9	W 2699	7.9	ART PAPET NDA
898	MUSICAL INSTRUMENTS,PTS	W 5175	23.5	W 7148	32.4	W 8479	32.1	W 7127	28.2	INSTRUMENTS DE MUSIQUE
8983	SOUND RECRDNG TAPE,DISCS	W 3709	18.9	W 5408	26.5	W 6390	26.1	W 5723	25.0	SUPPORTS SON POUR 763
89831	PREPD SND RECORDNG MEDIA	W 3546	17.1	W 5140	22.2	W 6195	20.7	W 5504	18.1	SUPPORTS PREPARES
899	OTHER MANUFACTURED GOODS		13.4		16.5		22.1		17.7	AUT ART MANUF DIVERS NDA
9	GOODS NOT CLASSD BY KIND		1.1		11.8		8.1		6.8	ART TRANSACT NON CLASSES
951	*WAR FIREARMS,AMMUNITION	W 205	1.1	W 1463	11.8	W 1068	7.8	W 531	6.8	VEHIC BLINDES ARMES

5. Special Exports F.O.B. by Commodities according to the S.I.T.C. (Rev. 2) in million U.S. Dollars
Exportations Spéciales F.O.B. par Produits d'après la C.T.C.I. (Rév. 2) en millions de Dollars E.U.

SITC CTCI	COMMODITY	1993 QUANTITY QUANTITE	1993 VALUE VALEUR	1994 QUANTITY QUANTITE	1994 VALUE VALEUR	1995 QUANTITY QUANTITE	1995 VALUE VALEUR	1996 QUANTITY QUANTITE	1996 VALUE VALEUR	PRODUIT
	ALL COMMODITIES		725.3		816.9		919.4		1043.0	TOUS PRODUITS
0	FOOD AND LIVE ANIMALS		123.8		137.0		152.2		189.0	ALIMENTS,ANIMAUX VIVANTS
001	*LIVE ANIMALS FOR FOOD	W 8838	6.2	W 19841	14.6	W 12400	12.2	W 11731	10.7	ANIMAUX VIVANTS
0011	BOVINE SPECIES,LIVE	W 8808	6.1	W 19831	14.5	W 12366	12.1	W 11725	10.7	ESPECE BOVINE
00119	— OTHR THAN FR BREEDING	W 8500	5.9	W 19741	14.4	W 11897	11.7	W 10494	9.5	BOVINS NON REPRODUCTEURS
01	MEAT AND PREPARATIONS		47.1		55.5		54.9		46.9	VIANDES ET PREPARATIONS
011	MEAT FRESH,CHILLD,FROZEN	W 29383	46.3	W 32098	52.8	W 29065	51.1	W 25469	45.9	VIANDES FRAICHES,REF,CONGE
0111	BOVINE MEAT FRESH,FROZEN	W 25967	43.8	W 27004	47.0	W 25531	48.1	W 23463	44.3	VIANDES BOVIN FRAI,REF
01111	BOVINE MEAT WITH BONE IN	W 7953	9.8	W 8478	10.9	W 9647	14.0	W 10261	15.9	VIANDES BOVIN NON DESOSS
01112	BOVINE MEAT BONELESS	W 18014	34.0	W 18526	36.2	W 15884	34.1	W 13202	28.4	VIANDES BOVIN DESOSSEES
0116	EDIBLE OFFAL FRESH,CH,FR	W 3416	2.6	W 4895	5.6	W 3386	3.0	W 2006	1.7	ABATS COMESTIBLES
014	MEAT PREPD,PRSVD,NES ETC	W 647	0.9	W 1526	2.7	W 1576	3.9	W 481	1.0	CONSERVES DE VIANDES
0149	OTH PREPARD,PRESRVD MEAT	W 647	0.9	W 1526	2.7	W 1503	3.6	W 481	1.0	AUTRES PREP DE VIANDES
04	CEREALS AND PREPARATIONS		0.8		24.6		26.9		26.6	CEREALES ET PRODUITS
041	WHEAT ETC UNMILLED			W 78440	15.2	W 37000	5.0	W 55700	7.2	FROMENT,EPEAUTRE
0411	DURUM WHEAT UNMILLED			W 78440	15.2	W 37000	5.0	W 55700	7.2	FROMENT DUR NON MOULU
044	MAIZE UNMILLED	W 1676	0.2	W 74288	9.1	W 187917	21.7	W 125139	17.2	MAIS NON MOULU
05	VEGETABLES AND FRUIT		4.0		6.0		5.8		8.0	LEGUMES ET FRUITS
058	FRUIT PRESERVED,PREPARED	W 698	2.1	W 556	3.3	W 1806	3.9	W 2511	5.5	CONSERVES DE FRUITS
0589	FRUIT PREPRD,PRESRVD,NES	W 602	2.0	W 527	3.3	W 686	2.6	W 986	3.9	FRUITS PREPARES CONSERV
05899	FRUIT,NUTS NES,PRESERVED	W 602	2.0	W 527	3.3	W 686	2.6	W 986	3.9	FRUITS PREP CONSERV NDA
06	SUGAR AND PREPS,HONEY		2.4		1.2		6.1		3.8	SUCRES ET PRODUITS
061	SUGAR AND HONEY	W 5940	2.3	W 1408	0.6	W 11144	6.0	W 6273	3.8	SUCRES ET MIEL
0611	RAW BEET AND CANE SUGAR	W 5940	2.3	W 1408	0.6	W 11144	6.0	W 6273	3.8	SUCRES BRUTS
07	COFFEE,TEA,COCOA,SPICES		4.6		5.6		3.0		2.1	CAFE,THE,CACAO,EPICES
071	COFFEE AND SUBSTITUTES	W 2150	4.5	W 1625	5.4	W 635	2.7	W 547	1.9	CAFE ET SUCCEDANES
0712	COFFEE EXTRACTS,ESSENCES	W 770	2.6	W 798	3.6	W 376	1.9	W 252	1.1	EXTRAITS DE CAFE
081	*FEEDING STUFF FOR ANIML	W 413540	58.7	W 184172	29.0	W 308048	43.4	W 539200	91.2	NOURRITURE POUR ANIMAUX
0813	OILCAKE AND OTH RESIDUES	W 412560	57.6	W 180889	27.5	W 306235	40.9	W 536558	87.8	TOURTEAUX
08131	— OF SOYA BEANS	W 344094	51.2	W 155100	25.6	W 272662	38.0	W 472636	81.0	TOURTEAUX DE SOJA
08133	— OF COTTON SEEDS	W 43965	3.3	W 21181	1.6	W 32925	2.9	W 43172	5.0	TOURTEAUX DE COTON
08139	— OF OTHER OILSEEDS ETC	W 17000	2.8					W 50	0.1	TOURTEAUX D'AUTRES OLEAGINEU
0819	FOOD WASTE AND FEED NES	W 455	1.0	W 868	1.2	W 1763	2.5	W 2517	3.5	DECHETS,ALIMENTS NDA
08199	FODDER NES,INCL SWEETNED	W 455	1.0	W 868	1.2	W 1763	2.5	W 2517	3.5	PREPARATIONS FOURRAGERES
1	BEVERAGES AND TOBACCO		7.3		7.8		9.4		12.0	BOISSONS ET TABACS
11	BEVERAGES		0.2		0.9		2.6		3.2	BOISSONS
12	TOBACCO AND MANUFACTURES		7.2		7.0		6.9		8.9	TABACS BRUTS FABRIQUES
121	TOBACCO UNMNFCTRD,REFUSE	W 6524	7.1	W 6531	7.0	W 5903	6.9	W 6173	8.9	TABACS BRUTS,DECHETS
1211	TOBACCO,NOT STRIPPED	W 1514	1.9	W 1514	1.3	W 5153	5.8	W 4616	6.9	TABACS NON ECOTES
1212	TOBACCO STRIPPED OR PART	W 4926	5.2	W 4961	5.7	W 727	1.1	W 1557	2.0	TABACS PART ECOTES
2	CRUDE MATERLS,EXCL FUELS		430.9		432.2		514.5		583.7	MAT BRUTES NON COMESTIBLES
21	HIDES,SKINS,FURS UNDRSSD		2.6		1.3		1.4		0.4	CUIRS,PEAUX BRUTS
211	HIDES,SKINS,EXC FURS,RAW	W 4739	2.6	W 3348	1.3	W 3130	1.4	W 330	0.4	CUIRS ET PEAUX
22	OIL SEEDS,OLEAGINOUS FRT		226.7		224.8		177.8		325.7	GRAINES,FRUITS OLEAGINEUX
222	SEEDS FOR'SOFT'FIXED OIL	W 1364085	225.7	W 1190075	224.0	W 1076731	177.6	W 1458420	325.3	GRAINES HUILES FIXES
2222	SOYA BEANS	W 1360434	223.7	W 1186520	222.3	W 1074110	176.0	W 1456689	324.2	FEVES DE SOJA
24	CORK AND WOOD		41.8		48.2		57.7		62.2	LIEGE ET BOIS
248	WOOD SHAPED,SLEEPERS	W 224186	41.4	W 216615	47.9	W 271083	57.1	W 340481	61.2	BOIS SIMPLEMENT TRAVAILLES
2483	LUMBER SHAPED NON–CONIFR	W 223786	41.4	W 215465	47.8	W 268834	56.8	W 337955	60.9	NON CONIFERES SCIES,RABOTES
24831	LUMBER SAWN ETC NON–CON	W 194339	22.8	W 180581	25.2	W 231585	29.3	W 298530	32.8	SCIES LONGITUDINALEMENT
24832	LUMBER PLANED ETC NONCON	W 29446	18.7	W 34884	22.7	W 37249	27.5	W 39424	28.1	RABOTES,RAINES,LANGUETES
26	TEXTILE FIBRES AND WASTE		157.5		155.3		274.0		190.7	FIBRES TEXTILES
263	COTTON	W 136127	156.8	W 108014	154.0	W 143975	271.1	W 121675	189.8	COTON
2631	RAW COTTON,EXCL LINTERS	W 132179	155.6	W 96264	151.5	W 135858	268.1	W 116639	188.2	COTON EN MASSE
3	MINERAL FUELS ETC		1.6		2.1		1.9		6.5	COMBUSTIBLES MINERAUX LUB
33	PETROLEUM AND PRODUCTS		1.6		2.1		1.9		6.5	PETROLE ET DERIVES
334	PETROLEUM PRODUCTS,REFIN	W 13653	1.6	W 23756	2.1	W 19899	1.9	W 22604	6.5	PRODUITS RAFFINES
3345	LUBS,PETROLEUM OILS NES		0.1	W 4	0.1	W 2	0.1	W 1197	4.9	HUILES LUBRIFIANTES
33451	LUBS(HIGH PETR CONT) ETC		0.1	W 3	0.1	W 2	0.1	W 1197	4.9	HUILES LUBRIF,H LOURDES
4	ANIMAL,VEGETABLE OIL,FAT		40.8		63.8		64.4		74.4	HUILES,GRAISSES ANIM,VEG
42	FIXED VEGETABLE OIL,FAT		40.5		63.2		64.0		73.6	HUILES VEGETALES FIXES
423	FIXED VEG OILS,SOFT	W 75864	33.9	W 123426	55.5	W 206886	59.5	W 130586	67.8	HUILES VEGET DOUCES FIXES
4232	SOYA BEAN OIL	W 72350	32.0	W 115314	51.6	W 204099	57.8	W 112750	58.2	HUILE DE SOJA
4233	COTTON SEED OIL	W 2000	1.3	W 1200	0.8	W 1786	1.0	W 10875	5.9	HUILE DE COTON
4236	SUNFLOWER SEED OIL	W 3	0.1	W 6650	3.1	W 922	0.6	W 6349	3.4	HUILE DE TOURNESOL
424	FIXED VEG OIL NONSOFT	W 7826	6.6	W 9099	7.7	W 5183	4.6	W 6024	5.8	AUTRES HUILES VEG FIXES
4244	PALM KERNEL OIL	W 3224	2.3	W 3908	2.7	W 486	0.5	W 2437	2.0	HUILE DE PALMISTE
4249	FIXED VEGETABLE OILS NES	W 4302	4.1	W 4606	4.7	W 4593	4.1	W 3156	3.4	HUILES VEGET FIXES NDA
5	CHEMCLS,RELATED PROD NES		14.2		20.6		23.6		22.3	PRODUITS CHIMIQUES
51	ORGANIC CHEMICALS		1.7		1.8		3.0		3.0	PROD CHIMIQ ORGANIQUES
512	ALCOHOLS,PHENOLS ETC	W 129	1.6	W 331	1.8	W 184	2.9	W 233	2.8	PHENOLS,PHENOLS–ALCOOLS
5122	CYCLIC ALCOHOLS,DERIVATS	W 129	1.6	W 131	1.8	W 184	2.9	W 233	2.8	ALCOOLS CYCLIQUES
53	DYES,TANNING,COLOUR PROD		3.5		5.7		3.6		0.2	PROD TEINTURE,COLORANTS
532	DYES NES,TANNING PROD	W 3896	3.5	W 7266	5.7	W 4336	3.5	W 18	0.1	EXTRAITS TEINTURE,TANNAGE
5322	DYE,TANN EXTRCTS,TANNINS	W 3896	3.5	W 7264	5.7	W 4333	3.5	W 10	0.1	EXT TAN ORIG VEG,TANNINS
53221	VEG TANN EXTRCTS,TANNINS	W 3896	3.5	W 7264	5.7	W 4333	3.5	W 10	0.1	EXTR TANNANTS ORIG VEGET
541	*MEDICINAL,PHARM PRODUCT		2.1	K 956329	3.8	K 2876135	5.9	K 140534	4.3	PROD MEDICINAUX PHARMACEUT
5417	MEDICAMENTS	K 763544	2.0	K 769297	3.7	K 2310379	3.7	K 120183	3.9	MEDICAMENTS
54179	— CONTNG OTH SUBSTANCES	K 693870	1.4	K 541499	2.6	K 2240061	3.6	K 92002	3.6	MED CONT AUT SUBSTANCES
55	PERFUME,CLEANING ETC PRD		6.9		8.8		8.4		11.7	PROD POUR PARFUM,TOILETTE
551	ESSENTL OILS,PERFUME,ETC	W 726	6.6	W 678	8.5	W 595	8.0	W 630	10.7	HUILES ESSENTIELLES
5513	ESSENTL OIL,RESINOID,ETC	W 726	6.6	W 678	8.5	W 595	8.0	W 630	10.7	HUILES ESSENTIELLES,RESIN
6	BASIC MANUFACTURES		95.2		137.9		134.7		130.4	ART MANUFACTURES
61	LEATHER,DRESSED FUR,ETC		51.9		63.7		55.7		40.8	CUIRS,PELLETERIES
611	LEATHER	W 8440	50.5	W 7598	60.6	W 6866	54.8	W 7645	38.2	CUIRS,PEAUX PREPARES
6113	CALF LEATHER	W 416	0.9	W 838	2.3	W 2966	9.4	W 5308	15.4	CUIRS,PEAUX DE VEAUX
6114	LEATHR BOVINE NES,EQUINE	W 6606	37.9	W 5697	42.4	W 3201	35.5	W 2287	20.2	CUIRS DE BOVINS
6116	LEATHER OF OTH HIDE,SKIN	W 55	0.9	W 16	4.4	W 8	1.8	W 14	2.5	PEAUX PREP D'AUTRES ANIMAUX
61169	LEATHER NES	W 55	0.9	W 16	4.4	W 8	1.8	W 14	2.5	PEAUX PREPAREES NDA
6118	LEATHER SPECIALLY FINSHD	W 938	10.4	W 972	11.5	W 691	8.3	W 35	0.2	CUIRS,PEAUX TANNES
61183	LEATHER PATENT,METALIZED	W 938	10.4	W 972	11.5	W 691	8.3	W 35	0.2	CUIRS,PEAUX VERNIS
612	LEATHER ETC MANUFACTURES	W 275	1.5	W 143	3.2	W 202	1.0	W 102	2.7	OUVRAGES EN CUIRS NDA
6129	LEATHER MANUFACTURES NES	W 196	1.0	W 77	2.5	W 27	0.9	W 86	2.3	AUT OUV CUIR NAT,ARTIF
62	RUBBER MANUFACTURES NES		0.1		0.1		3.2		12.4	CAOUTCHOUC MANUFACTURE
625	RUBBER TYRES, TUBES ETC	W 1	0.1			W 450	3.2	W 1376	11.4	PNEUS CAOUTCHOUC VULCANISE
6259	OTH TYRES,TYRE CASES,ETC	W 1	0.1			W 450	3.2	W 1376	11.4	AUTRES PNEUS RECHAPES FLAPS
62599	TYRES NES,TYRE CASES,ETC	W 1	0.1			W 450	3.2	W 1376	11.4	PNEUS,FLAPS
63	WOOD,CORK MANUFACTRS NES		21.7		30.5		31.3		31.2	OUVRAGES LIEGE ET BOIS
634	VENEERS,PLYWOOD,ETC	W 57732	19.9	W 71252	28.1	W 66453	25.9	W 65384	28.0	PLACAGES,CONTRE–PLAQUES
6341	VENEER SHEETS ETC	W 35296	11.0	W 29169	9.2	W 27435	8.7	W 26800	7.9	BOIS SIMPLEMENT SCIES

Paraguay

5. Special Exports F.O.B. by Commodities according to the S.I.T.C. (Rev. 2) in million U.S. Dollars
Exportations Spéciales F.O.B. par Produits d'après la C.T.C.I. (Rév. 2) en millions de Dollars E.U.

SITC CTCI	COMMODITY	1993		1994		1995		1996		PRODUIT
		QUANTITY QUANTITE	VALUE VALEUR	QUANTITY QUANTITE	VALUE VALEUR	QUANTITY QUANTITE	VALUE VALEUR	QUANTITY QUANTITE	VALUE VALEUR	
6342	PLYWOOD OF WOOD SHEETS	W 22264	8.8	W 42010	18.9	W 34742	15.3	W 38447	20.1	BOIS CONTRE–PLAQUES
635	WOOD MANUFACTURES NES	W 3710	1.8	W 3903	2.4	W 9600	5.5	W 6605	3.3	ART MANUF EN BOIS NDA
6353	BUILDERS WOODWRK,PREFABS	W 1199	0.8	W 2175	1.6	W 6727	4.3	W 5208	2.6	OUVRAGES DE MENUISERIE
65	TEXTILE YARN,FABRICS,ETC		8.5		18.5		28.2		30.9	FILS,TISSUS,ARTICLES TEXTILE
651	TEXTILE YARN	W 1497	3.5	W 5747	10.4	W 4014	13.5	W 5448	17.5	FILS TEXTILES
6513	COTTON YARN	W 1497	3.5	W 5747	10.4	W 4014	13.5	W 5448	17.5	FILS DE COTON
652	COTTON FABRICS,WOVEN	W 1110	4.7	W 1310	6.7	W 2070	12.9	W 1664	10.6	TISSUS DE COTON
6521	GREY WOVEN COTTON FABRIC	W 690	2.4	W 628	2.8	W 484	2.7	W 634	3.8	TISSUS COT ECRUS NON MERCER
65214	GREY WOVEN COTTON NES	W 690	2.4	W 628	2.8	W 484	2.7	W 634	3.8	AUT TISSUS 85% COTON ECRUS
6522	WOVEN COTTON BLEACHD,ETC	W 420	2.3	W 682	3.9	W 1586	10.2	W 1030	6.9	TISSUS COTON BLANCHIS ETC
65224	BLCHED COTTON FABRIC NES	W 420	2.3	W 663	3.9	W 1405	9.1	W 826	5.7	AUT TIS PLUS 85% COT BLANCHI
67	IRON AND STEEL		12.0		20.8		9.5		8.4	FER ET ACIER
672	IRON,STEEL PRIMARY FORMS	W 12327	3.0	W 1211	0.3	W 26108	5.7	W 12148	2.7	LINGOTS FER,ACIER
6725	IRN,STL BLOOMS,SLABS,ETC	W 12327	3.0	W 1211	0.3	W 26108	5.7	W 12148	2.7	BLOOMS,BILLETTES FER ACIER
67251	IRN,SMPLE STL BLOOMS,ETC	W 12327	3.0	W 1211	0.3	W 26108	5.7	W 12148	2.7	BLOOMS ETC NON ACIER FIN
673	IRON,STEEL SHAPES ETC	W 30465	8.9	W 96839	20.4	W 10124	3.4	W 15757	5.4	BARRES,PROFIL FER,ACIER
6732	IRON,STEEL BARS ETC	W 24554	7.2	W 94519	19.7	W 5943	2.0	W 9033	3.2	BARRES FER,ACIER
67326	IRN,OTH STL BARS HOTROLD	W 21353	6.2	W 93646	19.6	W 1686	0.6	W 1894	0.7	BARRES PLEINES FER,ACIER
69	METAL MANUFACTURES NES		0.4		1.8		2.5		3.7	ART MANUFACT EN METAL NDA
7	MACHINES,TRANSPORT EQUIP		4.6		7.7		7.2		4.7	MACHINES MATERIEL TRANSPORT
72	MACHS FOR SPCL INDUSTRYS		0.4		0.4		3.9		0.7	MAC SPECIALES POUR INDUST
78	ROAD VEHICLES		2.3		6.6		1.2		0.8	VEHICULES ROUTIERS
783	ROAD MOTOR VEHICLES NES	W 198	1.6	W 543	4.7	W 10	0.2	W 5	0.1	VEHICULES ROUTIERS NDA
7831	BUSES	W 198	1.6	W 543	4.7	W 10	0.2	W 5	0.1	VOITURES TRANSPORT COMMUN
8	MISC MANUFACTURED GOODS		7.2		8.2		11.9		20.3	ART MANUFACTURES DIVERS
84	CLOTHING AND ACCESSORIES		3.3		3.4		6.4		12.5	VETEMENTS
842	MENS OUTERWEAR NOT KNIT	W 25	0.3	W 74	0.4	W 693	1.6	W 633	6.7	VET DESSUS POUR HOMMES
8423	— TROUSERS,BREECHES ETC	W 24	0.2	W 73	0.4	W 690	1.5	W 612	6.5	PANTALONS HOMMES MAT TEX
843	WOMENS OUTERWEAR NONKNIT	W 117	1.7	W 104	1.6	W 247	3.6	W 340	4.3	VET DESSUS FEMMES MAT TEX
8439	— OTHER OUTER GARMENTS	W 86	0.9	W 96	1.4	W 236	3.3	W 306	4.0	AUT VET DES FEM MAT TEXT
89	MISC MANUFCTRD GOODS NES		1.5		1.8		2.3		4.7	ART MANUFACTURES DIVERS

1. HISTORICAL SERIES, 1962–1997 SPECIAL TRADE, IMPORTS C.I.F., EXPORTS F.O.B.
SERIES HISTORIQUES, 1962–1997 COMMERCE SPECIAL, IMPORTATIONS C.A.F., EXPORTATIONS F.O.B

YEAR ANNEE	VALUE IN MILLION U.S. DOLLARS VALEUR EN MILLION U.S. DOLLARS MERCHANDISE –MARCHANDISE		GOLD –OR		CONVERSION FACTORS FACTEURS DE CONVERSION CENTS E.U. PAR		INDEX NUMBERS –INDICES QUANTUM		UNIT VALUE VALEUR UNITAIRE	
	IMPORTS	EXPORTS	IMPORTS	EXPORTS	IMPORTS	EXPORTS	IMPORTS	EXPORTS	IMPORTS	EXPORTS
1962	539.00	542.90								
1963	552.80	539.70								
1964	570.90	666.20								
1965	718.70	666.20								
1966	816.50	762.80								
1967	819.80	755.20								
1968	629.70	866.10								
1969	600.00	865.50								
1970	621.70	1044.40								
1971	749.60	892.90								
1972	796.30	944.40								
1973	1024.20	1049.50								
1974	1595.30	1517.40								
1975	2379.60	1314.60								
1976	1798.00	1296.10								
1977	1598.30	1647.40								
1978	1356.30	1805.30								
1979	1475.50	3379.60								
1980	2573.30	3265.50						120		137
1981	3803.00	3249.00						121		113
1982	3079.80	3227.00						133		98
1983	2147.20	3027.10						115		104
1984	1869.50	3130.50						115		93
1985	1806.00	2978.00						118		85
1986	2908.80	2530.60						106		69
1987	3562.30	2660.80						96		86
1988	3348.00	2701.00						85		95
1989	2749.20	3488.00						100		104
1990	3469.80	3230.90						100		100
1991	4194.70	3329.10						104		93
1992	4861.30	3484.40						111		94
1993	4859.20	3514.50						121		75
1994	6690.70	4554.60						132		86
1995	9224.00	5575.10						133		106
1996	9472.60	5897.10						142		107
1997	10282.00	6753.60						155		109

2. IMPORTS BY BROAD ECONOMIC CATEGORY AND EXPORTS BY INDUSTRIAL ORIGIN. (PERCENTAGE OF TOTAL VALUE)
IMPORTATIONS PAR CATEGORIES ECONOMIQUES ET EXPORTATIONS PAR BRANCHE D'ACTIVITE.(EN POURCENTAGE DE LA VALEUR TOTALE)

IMPORTS – IMPORTATIONS

	1991	1992	1993	1994	1995	1996	1997
TOTAL IMPORTS–IMPORTATIONS TOTALES	100.	100.	100.	100.	100.	100.	100.
1 FOOD BEV–ALIMENTATION BOISSONS	16.3	17.4	16.3	14.5	10.6	13.7	11.5
11 PRIMARY–PRODUITS DE BASE	5.2	6.5	6.0	5.0	3.7	4.9	4.1
111 FOR INDUSTRY–POUR L'INDUSTRIE	3.3	4.6	4.8	3.6	2.8	3.9	3.1
112 FOR HOUSEHOLDS–POUR LES MENAGES	1.9	1.9	1.2	1.3	0.9	1.0	1.0
12 PROCESSED–PRODUITS ELABORES	11.1	10.9	10.3	9.5	6.9	8.8	7.4
121 FOR INDUSTRY–POUR L'INDUSTRIE	2.7	3.6	2.5	2.6	1.4	1.6	1.9
122 FOR HOUSEHOLDS–POUR LES MENAGES	8.4	7.3	7.9	6.9	5.5	7.2	5.5
2 IND SUPPLIES–APPROV INDUSTRIELS	30.1	29.1	31.0	30.2	31.2	28.7	28.3
21 PRIMARY–PRODUITS DE BASE	3.7	4.3	3.6	3.6	3.5	3.0	2.9
22 PROCESSED–PRODUITS ELABORES	26.3	24.8	27.4	26.6	27.6	25.7	25.5
3 FUELS–COMBUSTIBLES	10.8	9.9	7.9	6.4	8.6	10.0	10.3
31 PRIMARY–PRODUITS DE BASE	6.8	5.5	3.7	2.7	4.7	6.0	6.6
32 PROCESSED–PRODUITS ELABORES	4.0	4.4	4.2	3.7	4.0	4.0	3.7
321 MOTOR SPIRIT–ESSENCE	0.3	0.1	0.1	0.1	0.2	0.2	0.1
322 OTHER–AUTRES	3.7	4.3	4.1	3.6	3.8	3.8	3.6
4 MACHINERY–EQUIPEMENT	19.7	18.1	22.6	21.8	22.7	25.5	27.6
41 CAPITAL EQUIPMENT–MACHINES	16.9	15.5	19.5	18.9	19.9	22.8	24.7
42 PARTS–PIECES ACCESSOIRES	2.8	2.6	3.1	2.9	2.8	2.7	2.9
5 TRANSPORT–TRANSPORT	15.7	18.3	13.4	15.6	14.8	10.7	10.7
51 PASSENGER CARS–AUTOMOBILES	6.1	5.4	3.9	4.5	4.6	3.7	3.8
52 OTHER–AUTRES	4.6	8.5	5.1	6.8	6.4	3.9	3.7
521 INDUSTRIAL–INDUSTRIELS	4.4	8.2	4.8	6.4	5.8	3.4	3.4
522 NON INDUSTRIAL–NON INDUSTRIEL	0.2	0.3	0.2	0.4	0.6	0.4	0.3
53 PARTS–PIECES ACCESSOIRES	5.0	4.4	4.4	4.3	3.7	3.2	3.2
6 CONSUM GOODS–BIENS CONSOMMATION	7.3	7.0	8.7	11.5	12.1	11.4	11.6
61 DURABLE–DURABLES	2.1	2.3	2.7	4.5	4.2	3.7	3.2
62 SEMI DURABLE–SEMI DURABLES	2.4	2.3	2.9	3.8	4.5	4.5	4.8
63 NON DURABLE–NON DURABLES	2.8	2.4	3.1	3.3	3.4	3.2	3.6
7 GOODS NES–BIENS NDA	0.2	0.2	0.1	0.0	0.1	0.1	0.1

EXPORTS – EXPORTATIONS

	1991	1992	1993	1994	1995	1996	1997
TOTAL EXPORTS–EXPORTATIONS TOTALES	100.	100.	100.	100.	100.	100.	100.
1 AGRICULTURE	8.8	7.0	7.0	10.3	11.5	10.0	12.2
2 MINING QUARRY–INDUS EXTRACTIVES	15.8	17.5	15.0	16.6	20.3	20.4	19.0
3 MANUFACTURING–IND MANUFACTUR	75.5	75.5	78.0	73.1	68.2	69.6	68.8
31 FOOD BEV TOBACCO–ALIM BOISS TAB	20.1	19.3	24.4	25.5	21.2	23.3	24.0
32 TEXTILES–INDUSTRIES TEXTILES	11.8	10.1	9.8	9.3	8.2	8.5	9.0
33 WOOD & PRODUCTS–BOIS & PRODUITS	0.2	0.2	0.4	0.5	0.3	0.5	0.7
34 PAPER & PRODUCTS–PAPIER & PRODT	0.1	0.4	0.1	0.1	0.3	0.1	0.2
35 CHEMICALS–INDUSTRIES CHIMIQUES	9.7	9.8	9.6	7.7	5.9	6.4	6.4
36 NON METAL MIN–MIN NON METAL	0.5	0.5	0.6	0.5	0.5	0.5	0.5
37 BASIC METAL–IND METAL BASE	28.9	31.2	28.8	26.5	28.2	26.6	24.6
38 METAL MANUF–MANUF METAL	2.3	2.0	2.0	1.5	1.4	1.2	1.1
39 OTH MANUF IND–AUTRES MANUF	1.9	2.0	2.2	1.6	2.3	2.5	2.2

3. TRADE BY PRINCIPAL COUNTRIES OF ORIGIN AND DESTINATION (VALUE IN MILLION U.S. DOLLARS)
ECHANGES SELON LES PRINCIPAUX PAYS D'ORIGINE ET DE DESTINATION (VALEUR EN MILLIONS DE DOLLARS EU)

COUNTRIES–PAYS	SPECIAL IMPORTS C.I.F. IMPORTATIONS SPECIALES C.A.F				
	1993	1994	1995	1996	1997
World	4230.8	5626.3	7584.1	7947.2	8558.3
Africa	10.5	18.0	15.2	15.3	19.2
Americas	2758.3	3507.0	4692.8	5078.7	5658.0
– Northern America	1317.4	1669.3	2064.0	2299.4	2561.2
– LAIA	1376.0	1735.8	2530.2	2693.7	3033.1
– CACM	23.8	36.0	42.2	50.3	39.6
– Caribbean	15.5	24.7	25.6	19.9	6.9
– Rest of America	25.6	41.1	30.8	15.3	17.2
Asia excl fmr USSR	665.7	991.0	1273.6	1193.7	1264.2
– Middle East	3.2	15.0	20.4	5.0	6.8
Asia former USSR	0.1	0.0	0.0		0.0
Europe excl fmr USSR	674.7	1018.9	1462.4	1513.1	1483.2
– European Union	608.1	925.5	1353.9	1423.3	1361.8
– Eastern Europe	18.5	25.5	35.7	24.5	32.2
– Rest of Europe	48.1	67.9	72.8	65.3	89.3
Europe former USSR	19.4	19.4	14.3	38.0	33.8
Oceania	63.6	68.1	72.3	106.7	99.0
Other	38.6	3.9	53.4	1.7	0.9
USA/Etats–Unis d'Amer	1251.5	1583.1	1911.4	2089.3	2271.3
Colombia/Colombie	230.7	254.9	611.7	677.2	613.3
Japan/Japon	330.8	490.4	532.6	439.7	479.4
Venezuela	118.2	154.3	384.7	591.0	566.8
Brazil/Brésil	256.3	372.8	426.8	363.5	375.3
Argentina/Argentine	275.0	299.2	347.2	278.8	360.7
Germany/Allemagne	173.7	262.3	260.4	305.8	302.8
Chile/Chili	155.2	216.5	284.5	284.6	311.3
Mexico/Mexique	111.4	162.6	241.7	272.4	350.1
Spain/Espagne	47.5	75.0	325.4	338.4	257.2
Korea, Republic of	100.2	171.9	229.7	241.2	253.9
China/Chine	90.6	109.8	242.0	190.0	216.5
Italy/Italie	83.8	165.5	180.6	185.4	213.4
Canada	65.9	85.8	152.5	210.1	289.9
Ecuador/Equateur	127.1	159.9	70.5	44.5	240.3
France, Monaco	63.2	91.9	130.8	142.1	156.6
Bolivia/Bolivie	46.2	74.9	123.4	124.3	151.3
United Kingdom	52.4	73.7	98.4	109.7	119.8
Other Asia n.e.s.	59.9	82.3	90.6	92.0	120.9
Sweden/Suède	49.5	90.7	130.3	79.6	79.5
Belgium–Luxembourg	48.3	58.9	66.4	60.9	68.8
Switzerland,Liechtenst.	42.8	60.6	62.1	52.6	75.2
New Zealand	46.2	54.1	55.0	74.9	61.9
Netherlands/Pays–Bas	43.9	51.7	60.2	60.0	70.3
Uruguay	36.1	24.7	23.8	39.3	39.2
Denmark/Danemark	23.1	22.1	28.0	44.2	29.4
Guatemala	19.1	28.7	34.9	35.1	18.1
Panama	25.1	40.6	30.7	15.0	16.9
Australia/Australie	17.4	13.9	17.2	31.8	37.1
China, Hong Kong SAR	12.4	22.8	37.0	22.7	19.5
Thailand/Thaïlande	21.7	8.6	24.3	37.9	21.0
India/Inde	9.9	12.1	22.8	40.5	24.0
Russian Federation	15.3	16.5	13.7	34.0	26.3
Finland/Finlande	6.7	8.4	26.1	42.8	17.5
Austria/Autriche	9.3	12.4	25.5	29.1	24.8
Areas n.e.s.	38.6	3.9	53.4	1.7	0.9
Paraguay	19.9	16.0	15.8	18.2	25.0
Viet Nam	6.6	28.8	0.8	30.4	24.3
Singapore/Singapour	10.5	14.5	21.3	18.2	16.6
Malaysia/Malaisie	5.3	12.8	19.9	18.1	23.6

COUNTRIES–PAYS	SPECIAL EXPORTS F.O.B. EXPORTATIONS SPECIALES F.O.B.				
	1993	1994	1995	1996	1997
Monde	3343.4	4388.9	5439.7	5835.0	6759.4
Afrique	18.8	30.0	38.1	65.7	74.9
Amériques	1420.9	1674.0	2031.3	2312.1	2905.8
– Amérique du Nord	800.4	851.6	1078.2	1318.0	1718.1
– ALAI	581.9	782.1	888.7	919.9	1073.0
– MCAC	20.1	25.2	21.9	28.9	41.7
– Caraïbes	10.4	5.6	22.6	19.5	35.8
– Autre Amérique	8.2	9.6	19.9	25.8	37.2
Asie anc. URSS exclus	771.6	1098.3	1396.7	1447.3	1562.7
– Moyen–Orient	39.9	20.3	45.4	73.9	48.0
Asie ancienne URSS	0.6	0.0	0.1	0.0	0.0
Europe anc. URSS exclus	1065.6	1510.8	1905.5	1934.5	2149.7
– Union Européenne	998.3	1404.1	1660.6	1558.5	1630.7
– Europe de l'Est	6.1	19.8	21.9	40.1	53.9
– Autre de l'Europe	61.3	86.9	223.0	336.0	465.0
Europe ancienne URSS	9.9	21.3	11.6	20.4	10.5
Océanie	17.5	26.3	12.8	20.1	23.0
Autre	38.4	28.2	43.7	34.8	32.9
USA/Etats–Unis d'Amer	717.4	727.0	937.6	1159.6	1597.6
Japan/Japon	298.8	384.6	455.5	388.0	473.6
United Kingdom	283.8	405.3	409.5	424.2	299.6
China/Chine	140.5	284.8	349.0	419.4	490.6
Germany/Allemagne	204.0	279.4	331.9	300.7	386.9
Netherlands/Pays–Bas	116.1	233.6	277.6	208.4	219.3
Italy/Italie	162.0	197.5	246.5	198.7	229.4
Brazil/Brésil	124.3	180.9	199.9	239.3	256.1
Switzerland,Liechtenst.	43.9	53.7	179.8	291.2	412.6
Other Asia n.e.s.	118.6	152.4	200.2	155.4	159.1
Belgium–Luxembourg	85.2	118.1	155.3	154.2	183.3
Canada	82.7	123.5	139.9	157.8	119.7
Venezuela	75.9	84.0	163.2	125.7	138.6
Colombia/Colombie	87.1	99.5	118.2	120.3	154.6
Chile/Chili	72.6	86.2	152.1	123.2	132.3
Mexico/Mexique	91.2	165.5	96.3	95.6	114.2
Spain/Espagne	57.4	76.6	121.7	139.9	157.8
Korea, Republic of	59.4	61.5	111.2	145.1	91.5
Bolivia/Bolivie	62.8	78.0	76.9	101.2	111.3
France, Monaco	66.2	63.6	71.2	80.1	91.3
Ecuador/Equateur	43.3	60.6	46.8	70.3	111.2
Malaysia/Malaisie	26.6	57.5	70.3	73.8	59.8
China, Hong Kong SAR	28.6	33.8	49.5	54.6	68.8
Areas n.e.s.	38.4	28.2	43.7	34.8	32.9
Philippines	24.0	31.8	41.7	32.0	48.0
Argentina/Argentine	19.1	22.7	30.8	37.7	48.3
Iran (Islamic Rep of)	24.5	9.7	32.7	52.3	22.9
Indonesia/Indonésie	12.3	32.6	25.5	30.0	36.3
Norway,Svalbard and JM	9.5	22.2	27.4	24.3	40.6
Thailand/Thaïlande	1.8	11.8	22.9	34.9	36.2
So. African Customs Un	1.1	7.1	19.7	41.7	37.1
Panama	8.1	9.5	19.7	25.6	37.1
Australia/Australie	15.0	23.5	11.5	18.5	16.4
Russian Federation	9.9	21.0	9.9	20.1	9.5
Algeria/Algérie	10.8	9.8	13.6	12.8	21.9
Denmark/Danemark	11.3	13.1	14.7	14.7	14.8
Bulgaria/Bulgarie	3.2	8.6	7.9	12.4	35.9
Israel/Israël	10.0	19.6	15.1	3.8	11.6
Turkey/Turquie	9.3	6.0	7.3	15.5	14.5
Poland/Pologne	2.0	10.8	12.7	17.1	9.3

(VALUE AS PERCENTAGE OF WORLD TOTAL)(VALEURS EN POURCENTAGE DU TOTAL MONDIAL)

	1988	1989	1990	1991	1992	1993	1994	1995	1996	1997
Africa	1.0	0.9	0.6	0.4	0.3	0.2	0.3	0.2	0.2	0.2
Americas	48.0	65.1	66.2	66.3	66.0	65.2	62.3	61.9	63.9	66.1
– Northern America	23.9	32.7	29.9	28.0	30.9	31.1	29.7	27.2	28.9	29.9
– LAIA	23.4	30.9	35.5	36.8	33.5	32.5	30.9	33.4	33.9	35.4
– CACM	0.1	0.0	0.0	0.0	0.1	0.6	0.6	0.6	0.6	0.5
– Caribbean	0.1	0.8	0.2	0.3	0.5	0.4	0.4	0.3	0.3	0.1
– Rest of America	0.5	0.7	0.5	1.1	1.0	0.6	0.7	0.4	0.2	0.2
Asia excl fmr USSR	6.1	8.2	7.3	10.9	14.0	15.7	17.6	16.8	15.0	14.8
– Middle East	0.1	0.0	0.1	0.0	0.0	0.1	0.3	0.3	0.1	0.1
Asia former USSR						0.0	0.0	0.0		0.0
Europe excl fmr USSR	23.1	24.1	22.6	20.8	16.9	15.9	18.1	19.3	19.0	17.3
– European Union	20.8	20.9	19.8	19.0	15.4	14.4	16.4	17.9	17.9	15.9
– Eastern Europe	0.5	1.1	0.5	0.3	0.3	0.4	0.5	0.5	0.3	0.4
– Rest of Europe	1.8	2.1	2.3	1.5	1.2	1.1	1.2	1.0	0.8	1.0
Europe former USSR	0.1	0.2	0.3	0.3	0.2	0.5	0.3	0.2	0.5	0.4
Oceania	2.1	1.3	2.5	1.1	1.1	1.5	1.2	1.0	1.3	1.2
Other	19.6	0.0	0.6	0.1	1.4	0.9	0.1	0.7	0.0	0.0
USA/Etats–Unis d'Amer	22.2	30.9	28.2	25.7	28.9	29.6	28.1	25.2	26.3	26.5
Colombia/Colombie	2.4	3.6	3.8	7.5	7.9	5.5	4.5	8.1	8.5	7.2
Japan/Japon	3.9	4.3	3.4	6.2	8.0	7.8	8.7	7.0	5.5	5.6
Venezuela	1.9	1.8	2.1	3.5	3.4	2.8	2.7	5.1	7.4	6.6
Brazil/Brésil	6.5	6.2	6.4	5.9	5.4	6.1	6.6	5.6	4.6	4.4
Argentina/Argentine	6.8	8.2	8.8	7.3	6.5	6.5	5.3	4.6	3.5	4.2
Germany/Allemagne				5.9	4.8	4.1	4.7	3.4	3.8	3.5
Chile/Chili	2.3	2.2	3.4	3.0	3.1	3.7	3.8	3.8	3.6	3.6
Mexico/Mexique	1.8	2.4	3.8	3.0	2.3	2.6	2.9	3.2	3.4	4.1
Spain/Espagne	1.8	1.2	1.2	1.0	1.0	1.1	1.3	4.3	4.3	3.0

	1988	1989	1990	1991	1992	1993	1994	1995	1996	1997
Afrique	0.9	0.8	0.7	0.6	0.5	0.6	0.7	0.7	1.1	1.1
Amériques	37.5	43.0	38.7	39.2	44.0	42.5	38.1	37.3	39.6	43.0
– Amérique du Nord	24.8	27.5	23.8	20.7	24.3	23.9	19.4	19.8	22.6	25.4
– ALAI	11.4	14.0	13.0	17.5	18.9	17.4	17.8	16.3	15.8	15.9
– MCAC	0.5	0.6	0.7	0.6	0.4	0.6	0.6	0.4	0.5	0.6
– Caraïbes	0.6	0.7	0.8	0.1	0.2	0.3	0.1	0.4	0.3	0.5
– Autre Amérique	0.2	0.3	0.5	0.2	0.2	0.2	0.2	0.4	0.4	0.6
Asie anc. URSS exclus	22.2	20.3	20.4	26.8	23.9	23.1	25.0	25.7	24.8	23.1
– Moyen–Orient	0.5	0.9	0.6	0.8	1.4	1.2	0.5	0.8	1.3	0.7
Asie ancienne URSS						0.0	0.0	0.0	0.0	0.0
Europe anc. URSS exclus	37.8	31.2	35.7	31.4	29.8	31.9	34.4	35.0	33.2	31.8
– Union Européenne	34.6	27.6	32.6	29.4	27.9	29.9	32.0	30.5	26.7	24.1
– Europe de l'Est	1.8	1.9	1.5	0.9	0.4	0.2	0.5	0.4	0.7	0.8
– Autre de l'Europe	1.4	1.7	1.7	1.1	1.5	1.8	2.0	4.1	5.8	6.9
Europe ancienne URSS	1.0	4.4	1.9	0.8	0.2	0.3	0.5	0.2	0.4	0.2
Océanie	0.2	0.1	0.1	0.2	0.5	0.5	0.6	0.2	0.3	0.3
Autre	0.3	0.2	2.5	0.9	1.1	1.1	0.6	0.8	0.6	0.5
USA/Etats–Unis d'Amer	23.9	26.5	23.1	19.1	21.0	21.5	16.6	17.2	19.9	23.6
Japan/Japon	10.8	10.9	12.7	10.1	8.7	8.9	8.8	8.4	6.6	7.0
United Kingdom	9.8	4.6	4.5	3.7	6.5	8.5	9.2	7.5	7.3	4.4
China/Chine	4.4	2.6	1.7	7.2	7.5	4.2	6.5	6.4	7.2	7.3
Germany/Allemagne				6.1	4.4	6.1	6.4	6.1	5.2	5.7
Netherlands/Pays–Bas	3.6	3.2	3.3	4.0	3.6	3.5	5.3	5.1	3.6	3.2
Italy/Italie	4.7	4.2	8.3	7.8	5.8	4.8	4.5	4.5	3.4	3.4
Brazil/Brésil	2.5	3.7	3.2	3.5	4.7	3.7	4.1	3.7	4.1	3.8
Switzerland,Liechtenst.	0.4	0.3	0.2	0.2	0.9	1.3	1.2	3.3	5.0	6.1
Other Asia n.e.s.	4.2	3.2	1.5	2.8	1.9	3.5	3.5	3.7	2.7	2.4

4. Special Imports C.I.F. by Commodities according to the S.I.T.C. (Rev. 2) in million U.S. Dollars
Importations Spéciales C.A.F. par Produits d'après la C.T.C.I. (Rév. 2) en millions de Dollars E.U.

SITC CTCI	COMMODITY	1994 QUANTITY QUANTITE	1994 VALUE VALEUR	1995 QUANTITY QUANTITE	1995 VALUE VALEUR	1996 QUANTITY QUANTITE	1996 VALUE VALEUR	1997 QUANTITY QUANTITE	1997 VALUE VALEUR	PRODUIT
	ALL COMMODITIES		5626.3		7584.1		7947.2		8558.4	TOUS PRODUITS
0	FOOD AND LIVE ANIMALS		856.3		909.7		1195.9		1044.9	ALIMENTS,ANIMAUX VIVANTS
01	MEAT AND PREPARATIONS		23.0		24.3		31.9		33.2	VIANDES ET PREPARATIONS
011	MEAT FRESH,CHILLD,FROZEN	W 16025	21.2	W 16827	22.2	W 23540	29.3	W 26281	30.9	VIANDES FRAICHES,REF,CONGE
02	DAIRY PRODCTS,BIRDS'EGGS		102.8		112.2		134.7		125.7	PRODUITS LAITIERS,OEUFS
022	MILK AND CREAM	W 51279	88.7	W 52055	97.5	W 59314	117.8	W 62222	108.6	LAIT ET CREME
0224	MILK,CREAM PRESERVED ETC	W 50030	87.3	W 50284	94.6	W 57171	115.9	W 58455	105.9	LAIT,CREME CONS,CONC
02242	MILK DRY,1.5% FAT OR LES	W 10499	18.4	W 8956	18.1	W 9254	21.3	W 11826	24.1	LAIT POUDRE INF 1.5%
02243	MILK DRY,OVER 1.5% FAT	W 30243	59.8	W 29727	65.3	W 33015	80.2	W 30385	67.1	LAIT POUDRE SUP 1.5%
04	CEREALS AND PREPARATIONS		434.3		475.7		681.6		555.8	CEREALES ET PRODUITS
041	WHEAT ETC UNMILLED	W 1079559	175.4	W 1008872	188.2	W 1125638	264.3	W 1156817	217.2	FROMENT,EPEAUTRE
0411	DURUM WHEAT UNMILLED	W 1031467	166.7	W 987367	184.3	W 1065202	250.3	W 1114792	208.5	FROMENT DUR NON MOULU
042	RICE	W 245811	76.2	W 174613	59.6	W 411900	159.4	W 233861	90.9	RIZ
0422	RICE SEMI–MILLED,MILLED	W 219675	69.4	W 159001	56.0	W 372507	147.1	W 191423	75.0	RIZ POLI,GLACE INCL BRISURES
04221	RICE MILLED UNBROKEN	W 216462	68.3	W 159001	56.0	W 371844	146.7	W 191314	75.0	RIZ POLI,GLACE EXCL BRISURES
044	MAIZE UNMILLED	W 855105	118.3	W 1066392	154.4	W 776962	146.1	W 937143	134.3	MAIS NON MOULU
048	CEREAL ETC PREPARATIONS	W 76903	37.3	W 97320	55.3	W 104193	64.5	W 115261	74.5	PREPTNS A BASE CEREALES
0483	MACARONI,SPAGHETTI ETC	W 3647	2.7	W 7715	5.1	W 20274	13.3	W 57054	34.8	PATES ALIMENTAIRES
05	VEGETABLES AND FRUIT		59.7		49.6		58.3		65.2	LEGUMES ET FRUITS
054	VEG ETC FRSH,SMPLY PRSVD	W 55125	27.4	W 29441	15.9	W 48942	25.9	W 55013	30.6	LEGUMES FRAIS,CONG,SECS
0542	LEGUMINOUS VEGETBLES DRY	W 44715	21.0	W 27120	13.1	W 45404	23.0	W 48845	25.0	LEGUMES A COSSE SECS
057	FRUIT,NUTS,FRESH,DRIED	W 35729	20.7	W 36968	21.0	W 34859	17.9	W 35102	19.0	FRUITS FRAIS OU SECS
06	SUGAR AND PREPS,HONEY		128.6		118.6		143.8		109.7	SUCRES ET PRODUITS
061	SUGAR AND HONEY	W 333742	107.9	W 239716	91.8	W 316136	118.0	W 257680	87.6	SUCRES ET MIEL
0612	REFINED SUGAR ETC	W 301608	97.2	W 237222	90.1	W 313118	116.3	W 255828	86.3	SUCRES RAFFINES
062	SUGAR CANDY NON–CHOCLATE	W 10162	20.8	W 12935	26.9	W 12373	25.8	W 10155	22.2	SUCRERIES
07	COFFEE,TEA,COCOA,SPICES		20.3		18.4		17.2		14.7	CAFE,THE,CACAO,EPICES
081	*FEEDING STUFF FOR ANIML	W 186134	49.3	W 246689	61.9	W 237060	75.2	W 265802	87.8	NOURRITURE POUR ANIMAUX
0813	OILCAKE AND OTH RESIDUES	W 174887	40.4	W 233057	52.7	W 228576	64.2	W 260541	78.5	TOURTEAUX
08131	— OF SOYA BEANS	W 174065	40.3	W 228390	51.9	W 220512	62.6	W 253680	77.1	TOURTEAUX DE SOJA
09	MISC EDIBLE PRODUCTS		29.4		38.8		42.2		40.6	PREP ALIMENTAIRES DIVERSES
098	EDIBLE PRODCTS,PREPS NES	W 5401	28.5	W 7291	36.1	W 8933	39.0	W 10201	32.9	PREP ALIMENTAIRES NDA
09809	MISC FOOD PREPRTIONS NES	W 3009	23.7	W 4278	30.2	W 5042	32.0	W 5548	25.0	PREP ALIMENTAIRES NDA
1	BEVERAGES AND TOBACCO		31.5		36.4		36.1		42.1	BOISSONS ET TABACS
11	BEVERAGES		27.2		31.8		30.1		34.9	BOISSONS
112	ALCOHOLIC BEVERAGES	W 10662	25.1	W 12696	29.2	W 11473	28.3	W 13151	30.7	BOISSONS ALCOOLIQUES
2	CRUDE MATERLS,EXCL FUELS		129.2		175.7		139.9		159.4	MAT BRUTES NON COMESTIBLES
23	RUBBER, CRUDE		14.9		23.3		19.9		17.7	CAOUTCHOUC BRUT
251	*PULP AND WASTE PAPER	W 28461	14.0		23.3	W 24830	13.3	W 25876	12.7	PATES A PAPIER,DECHETS
26	TEXTILE FIBRES AND WASTE		52.0		67.1		42.2		64.4	FIBRES TEXTILES
263	COTTON	W 19634	30.0	W 21521	44.1	W 12921	23.3		47.6	COTON
2631	RAW COTTON,EXCL LINTERS	W 19110	29.5	W 21503	44.0	W 12902	23.2	W 25583	47.6	COTON EN MASSE
3	MINERAL FUELS ETC		367.5		666.6		806.9		888.2	COMBUSTIBLES MINERAUX LUB
32	COAL,COKE AND BRIQUETTES		33.5		34.9		41.3		44.6	HOUILLES,COKES,BRIQUETTES
322	COAL,LIGNITE AND PEAT	W 354703	17.9	W 287030	15.7	W 360483	19.0	W 489673	27.2	HOUILLES,LIGNITES,TOURBE
3222	OTH COAL,NOT AGGLOMERATD	W 354702	17.9	W 287007	15.7	W 360236	18.9	W 486441	26.6	AUTRES HOUILLES
33	PETROLEUM AND PRODUCTS		311.1		598.5		733.4		816.5	PETROLE ET DERIVES
333	CRUDE PETROLEUM	W 965667	112.3	W 2463147	304.9	W 2909915	426.8	W 3977618	507.5	HUILES BRUTES DE PETROLE
334	PETROLEUM PRODUCTS,REFIN	W 1166056	191.2	W 1507926	282.9	W 1303913	296.7	W 1416954	299.1	PRODUITS RAFFINES
3342	KEROSENE,OTH MEDIUM OILS	W 23657	4.3	W 48404	9.2	W 35472	7.9	W 127046	28.0	PETR LAMPANTS,AUT HUIL
33429	OTH MEDIUM PETROLEUM OIL	W 23657	4.3	W 35634	6.7	W 12731	3.4	W 127046	28.0	AUTRES HUILES MOYENNES
3343	GAS OILS	W 1050573	148.5	W 1311551	217.0	W 1130700	233.8	W 1136139	217.4	GAS OILS
3345	LUBS,PETROLEUM OILS NES	W 70717	32.2	W 75482	39.7	W 68672	36.6	W 82213	39.6	HUILES LUBRIFIANTES
33451	LUBS(HIGH PETR CONT) ETC	W 70014	30.1	W 74376	36.9	W 67718	34.0	W 81123	36.8	HUILES LUBRIF,H LOURDES
341	*GAS,NATURAL AND MANUFCT	W 92698	23.0	W 114041	33.3	W 112238	32.3	W 108280	27.2	GAZ NATUREL,GAZ MANUFACT
3413	PETROLM GASES,LIQUEFIED	W 92687	22.9	W 114041	33.3	W 112238	32.3	W 108280	27.2	GAZ DE PETROLE LIQUEFIE
34139	OTH HYDROCARBON GAS LQFD	W 92687	22.9	W 114035	33.3	W 112236	32.3	W 39546	10.1	HYDROCARBURES GAZEUX NDA
4	ANIMAL,VEGETABLE OIL,FAT		97.2		71.3		73.3		114.8	HUILES,GRAISSES ANIM,VEG
42	FIXED VEGETABLE OIL,FAT		92.8		66.2		66.7		109.1	HUILES VEGETALES FIXES
423	FIXED VEG OILS,SOFT	W 136572	89.8	W 87721	64.9	W 97223	65.7	W 165572	106.7	HUILES VEGET DOUCES FIXES
4232	SOYA BEAN OIL	W 122399	79.7	W 82384	60.0	W 86013	57.2	W 154518	97.5	HUILE DE SOJA
5	CHEMCLS,RELATED PROD NES		747.6		971.7		963.2		1085.5	PRODUITS CHIMIQUES
51	ORGANIC CHEMICALS		121.8		152.0		135.4		134.1	PROD CHIMIQ ORGANIQUES
513	CARBOXYLIC ACIDS ETC	W 22125	25.7	W 18592	33.6	W 20665	28.2	W 24786	30.0	ACIDES CARBOXYLIQUES
514	NITROGEN–FNCTN COMPOUNDS	W 20691	36.0	W 12422	40.6	W 23189	41.8	W 20841	39.1	COMPOSES FONCT AZOTEES
5148	OTH NITROGN–FNCTN CMPNDS	W 18388	26.3	W 9923	27.0	W 19883	30.0	W 16753	25.6	AUTRES COMPOSES AZOTES
515	ORG–INORG COMPOUNDS ETC	W 2682	21.5	W 3541	27.9	W 2986	21.0	W 3710	21.1	COMPOSES ORGANO–MINERAUX
52	INORGANIC CHEMICALS		47.3		53.2		58.8		67.6	PROD CHIM INORGANIQUES
523	OTHR INORG CHEMICALS ETC	W 60563	31.7	W 64488	35.7	W 80002	42.9	W 96418	47.8	AUT PRODUITS CHIMIQUES INORG
5232	OTH MTL CMPD OF INRG ACD	W 47633	22.6	W 48928	24.3	W 57976	28.6	W 72545	33.7	SELS METALLIQUES
53	DYES,TANNING,COLOUR PROD		54.3		61.3		62.5		75.8	PROD TEINTURE,COLORANTS
531	SYNT DYE,NAT INDGO,LAKES	W 2516	29.1	W 3218	29.9	W 2434	28.3	W 3634	35.9	MAT COLOR ORGAN,LAQUES
5311	SYNTHIC ORGNIC DYESTUFFS	W 2172	25.5	W 2711	25.8	W 2131	25.2	W 3188	32.3	MAT COLOR ORGAN SYNTHET
533	PIGMENTS,PAINTS,ETC	W 7977	21.7	W 8485	27.5	W 9579	31.0	W 12016	36.2	PIGMENTS,PEINTURES,VERNIS
541	*MEDICINAL,PHARM PRODUCT	K 5407638	100.4		160.6	K 5589175	151.8	K 7111342	179.6	PROD MEDICINAUX PHARMACEUT
5417	MEDICAMENTS	K 4428273	62.9	K 3946475	105.5	K 4200250	103.3	K 5595107	124.9	MEDICAMENTS
54171	— CONTAINNG ANTIBIOTICS	K 2472862	16.9	K 479553	25.4	K 495214	23.8	K 724106	32.8	MED CONTN ANTIBIOTIQUES
54179	— CONTNG OTH SUBSTANCES	K 1806877	36.0	K 3048390	62.1	K 3334779	60.5	K 4546879	71.0	MED CONT AUT SUBSTANCES
55	PERFUME,CLEANING ETC PRD		62.7		74.3		79.2		97.6	PROD POUR PARFUM,TOILETTE
553	PERFUMERY,COSMETICS,ETC	W 8463	32.6	W 8377	38.4	W 8884	39.7	W 11852	50.0	PRODUITS DE PARFUMERIE
554	SOAP,CLEANSING ETC PREPS	W 8762	16.4	W 9734	19.3	W 10512	22.4	W 13047	26.1	SAVONS,PRODUITS DETERSIFS
562	*FERTILIZERS,MANUFACTURE	W 400994	63.6	W 345145	79.7	W 412604	95.5	W 472389	94.6	ENGRAIS MANUFACTURES
5621	CHEM NITROGENOUS FERTLZR	W 249191	38.7	W 268068	61.8	W 299742	69.3	W 315229	59.9	ENGRAIS AZOTES
56216	UREA	W 220509	32.8	W 235773	54.4	W 223180	53.0	W 223186	40.2	UREE
58	PLASTIC MATERIALS ETC		187.0		254.1		247.0		279.9	MAT PLAST ARTIFICIELLES
582	PROD OF CONDENSATION ETC	W 18403	32.0	W 22128	48.3	W 24581	47.7	W 35950	55.2	PROD CONDENS,POLYCOND
5823	ALKYDS,OTHER POLYESTERS	W 8304	12.6	W 12723	27.0	W 14796	24.6	W 25102	30.8	ALKYDES ET AUT POLYESTERS
58231	— IN PRIMARY FORMS	W 7968	11.2	W 12175	24.1	W 14541	23.1	W 24683	28.7	SOUS FORMES PRIMAIRES
583	POLYMERIZATION ETC PRODS	W 148706	146.7	W 143071	196.7	W 170701	191.5	W 187086	216.1	PROD POLYMERISATION
5831	POLYETHYLENE	W 64255	49.7	W 55403	63.6	W 68363	67.0	W 74305	80.2	POLYETHYLENE
58311	— IN PRIMARY FORMS	W 62704	47.3	W 54628	61.6	W 67474	64.0	W 70344	71.6	POLYETHYLENE PRIMAIRES
5832	POLYPROPYLENE	W 23594	22.9	W 21719	34.6	W 24740	32.2	W 32064	37.8	POLYPROPYLENE
58321	— IN PRIMARY FORMS	W 21070	17.3	W 18011	23.3	W 20437	20.5	W 26891	25.0	POLYPROPYLENE PRIMAIRES
5834	POLYVINYL CHLORIDE	W 40958	42.0	W 46768	55.9	W 55497	50.2	W 56097	55.1	CHLORURE DE POLYVINYLE
58341	— IN PRIMARY FORMS	W 40121	39.7	W 45492	52.4	W 54223	46.3	W 54106	49.5	SOUS FORMES PRIMAIRES
59	CHEMICAL MATERIALS NES		108.4		134.5		130.3		151.0	MAT PROD CHIMIQUES NDA
591	PESTICIDES,DISINFECTANTS	W 5316	34.8	W 5597	33.9	W 5998	36.8	W 6788	44.6	DESINF,INSECT,FONG,HERB
5911	INSECTICIDES,FOR RETAIL	W 2120	17.9	W 2428	18.2	W 2397	18.6	W 3053	24.2	INSECTICIDES VENTE DET
598	MISCEL CHEM PRODUCTS NES	W 31774	62.7	W 36799	84.1	W 38218	76.5	W 42324	88.4	PROD DIV INDUST CHIM NDA
5982	ANTI–KNOCK PREPARTNS ETC	W 7559	19.5	W 10672	33.0	W 8073	20.0	W 10801	27.4	PREPARAT ANTIDETONANTES
5989	CHEM PRODUCTS,PREPS NES	W 22388	40.0	W 23768	46.5	W 27901	51.8	W 28779	55.9	PROD PREP CHIMIQUES NDA

4. Special Imports C.I.F. by Commodities according to the S.I.T.C. (Rev. 2) in million U.S. Dollars
Importations Spéciales C.A.F. par Produits d'après la C.T.C.I. (Rév. 2) en millions de Dollars E.U.

SITC CTCI	COMMODITY	1994 QUANTITY QUANTITE	1994 VALUE VALEUR	1995 QUANTITY QUANTITE	1995 VALUE VALEUR	1996 QUANTITY QUANTITE	1996 VALUE VALEUR	1997 QUANTITY QUANTITE	1997 VALUE VALEUR	PRODUIT
59899	OTH CHEM PRODS,PREPS,NES	W 18980	31.0	W 20377	36.8	W 23054	40.1	W 22835	42.9	AUT PRODUITS CHIMIQUES NDA
6	BASIC MANUFACTURES		822.6		1201.0		1156.9		1248.5	ART MANUFACTURES
62	RUBBER MANUFACTURES NES		77.7		93.2		94.4		109.7	CAOUTCHOUC MANUFACTURE
625	RUBBER TYRES, TUBES ETC	W 22167	49.4	W 18897	58.4	W 19605	61.6	W 23996	73.9	PNEUS CAOUTCHOUC VULCANISE
6252	TYRES,NEW,BUS OR LORRY	W 11698	18.7	W 6893	21.8	W 6478	21.9	W 8333	27.1	PNEUS POUR AUTOBUS,CAMIONS
6259	OTH TYRES,TYRE CASES,ETC	W 6041	17.7	W 6781	21.0	W 8162	23.9	W 9362	27.3	AUTRES PNEUS RECHAPES FLAPS
628	RUBBER ARTICLES NES	W 1817	17.1	W 2356	21.6	W 2146	19.8	W 2245	22.4	OUVRAGES CAOUTCHOUC NDA
64	PAPER,PAPERBOARD AND MFR		142.3		230.8		244.5		229.5	PAPIERS,CARTONS & OUVRAGES
641	PAPER AND PAPERBOARD	W 166885	116.1	W 175571	179.8	W 190255	181.1	W 215530	169.3	PAPIERS ET CARTONS
6411	NEWSPRINT	W 54551	28.4	W 55540	41.4	W 54784	42.8	W 60721	33.1	PAPIER JOURNAL
6412	PRINTG,WRITING PAPER NES	W 18675	16.9	W 27595	35.1	W 27283	31.4	W 35253	35.6	PAPIERS POUR L'IMPRESSION
64122	— COATED,IMPREGNATD ETC	W 13929	12.7	W 21654	26.9	W 19102	22.2	W 24186	24.7	PAPIERS IMPRESSION COUCHES
6415	PAPER,PAPERBRD,BULK,NES	W 60285	45.3	W 48240	58.3	W 60208	63.0	W 54261	47.3	PAPIERS,CARTONS ROULEAUX
64159	OTHER PAPER ETC,BULK,NES	W 58704	42.6	W 46852	55.5	W 58938	61.1	W 52934	45.2	AUT PAPIER ROULEAUX FEUILLES
6418	COATED ETC PAPER NES BLK	W 13907	13.6	W 18303	23.4	W 18586	21.1	W 24705	26.0	PAP,CARTONS COUCHES,ENDUITS
642	PAPER,ETC,PRECUT,ARTS OF	W 14736	26.3	W 24223	51.1	W 27657	63.4		60.2	PAP,CARTONS DECOUPES
6428	PAPER ETC ARTICLES NES	W 3163	10.4	W 5676	20.5	W 8303	28.1		28.8	OUVRAGES EN PATE A PAPIER
65	TEXTILE YARN,FABRICS,ETC		131.8		153.2		154.0		159.4	FILS,TISSUS,ARTICLES TEXTILE
651	TEXTILE YARN		32.8		42.1	W 12315	45.2	W 13483	50.2	FILS TEXTILES
6514	SYN FIB YRN,BULK,MONOFIL	W 6733	25.3	W 8840	32.4	W 9274	34.4	W 9285	34.4	FILS CONT 85% FIB TEXT SYNTH
65142	— NONTXT ETC CONT PAMID	W 4022	13.9	W 5705	20.5	W 6495	24.0	W 6969	25.3	FILS NON TEX FI CON POLYAMID
653	WOVN MAN-MADE FIB FABRIC	W 7824	43.1	W 7705	42.3	W 6350	35.3	W 6117	37.3	TISSUS FIBRES SYNTH,ARTIF
657	SPECIAL TXTL FABRC,PRODS	W 4798	24.5	W 6236	31.6	W 5365	29.4	W 6404	30.6	TISSUS SPECIAUX
66	NONMETAL MINERAL MFS NES		84.8		147.8		126.4		146.8	ART MIN NON METALLIQUES
661	LIME,CEMENT,BLDG PRODS	W 62385	5.8	W 779039	41.5	W 380314	24.5	W 683985	38.6	CHAUX,CIMENTS MAT CONSTR
6612	CEMENT	W 61608	4.8	W 777382	40.0	W 377478	21.9	W 678914	34.4	CIMENTS HYDRAULIQUES
662	CLAY,REFRACTORY BLDG PRD	W 17800	14.8	W 19790	15.5	W 32415	21.1	W 37781	25.8	MAT CONST REFRACTAIRES
664	GLASS	W 48532	30.9	W 60502	53.0	W 56870	39.9	W 70063	44.2	VERRE
665	GLASSWARE	W 13233	17.5	W 23116	17.5	W 13137	18.0	W 12703	19.1	OUVRAGES EN VERRE
67	IRON AND STEEL		202.4		321.5		280.3		308.7	FER ET ACIER
671	PIG IRON ETC	W 78942	17.1	W 83884	18.4	W 72038	17.0	W 21652	10.5	FONTE,SPIEGEL,POUDRES
672	IRON,STEEL PRIMARY FORMS	W 41733	13.4	W 72573	23.5	W 98198	30.2		30.1	LINGOTS FER,ACIER
673	IRON,STEEL SHAPES ETC	W 125740	48.2	W 223193	81.4	W 98940	41.4	W 205721	74.4	BARRES,PROFIL FER,ACIER
6731	IRON,STEEL WIRE ROD	W 61281	21.3	W 71682	25.6	W 56885	19.7	W 90376	30.4	FIL MACHINE FER,ACIER
67311	IRON,SIMPLE STL WIRE ROD	W 52820	18.1	W 44416	16.0	W 44355	15.5	W 74267	25.2	FIL MACH AUT ACIER FIN
6732	IRON,STEEL BARS ETC	W 59041	23.2	W 139212	49.8	W 27628	14.2	W 93560	34.4	BARRES FER,ACIER
67326	IRN,OTH STL BARS HOTROLD	W 42353	13.6	W 121013	37.9	W 18573	6.3	W 84544	26.6	BARRES PLEINES FER,ACIER
674	IRN,STL UNIV,PLATE,SHEET	W 96232	70.3	W 168561	124.0	W 146407	107.6	W 138562	100.4	LARGES PLATS,TOLES
6746	IRN,STL THIN PLATE,ROLLD	W 32049	20.7	W 55541	37.2	W 47449	30.5	W 43295	26.3	TOLES LAM MOINS 3MM
67461	— OF IRON OR SIMPLE STL	W 26190	12.6	W 50252	26.7	W 43024	22.2	W 38279	17.5	TOL NON AC FIN MOINS 3 MM
6747	TINNED PLATES,SHEETS	W 28446	23.4	W 31543	28.0	W 32209	31.4	W 36421	31.1	TOLES ETAMEES EN ACIER
6749	OTH IRN,STL PLATES,SHEET	W 21517	16.6	W 40408	34.6	W 22481	21.6	W 31835	27.9	AUTRES TOLES FER,ACIER
67491	— OF IRON OR SIMPLE STL	W 20353	15.3	W 38195	31.7	W 21838	19.6	W 31143	26.4	AUT TOLES AUTRES ACIER FIN
678	IRON,STL TUBES,PIPES,ETC	W 35180	39.4	W 47828	61.7	W 51385	67.1	W 69137	81.8	TUBES,TUYAUX EN FONTE,FER
6782	IRON,STL SEAMLESS TUBES	W 21652	21.1	W 33180	32.1	W 33860	37.5	W 37800	43.5	TUBES,TUYAUX SANS SOUDURE
68	NON-FERROUS METALS		22.7		35.3		31.3		30.8	METAUX NON FERREUX
69	METAL MANUFACTURES NES		143.7		199.5		199.5		237.7	ART MANUFACT EN METAL NDA
691	STRUCTURES AND PARTS NES	W 6143	14.1	W 11619	16.8	W 10156	21.6	W 18212	32.9	CONSTRUCT FER,ACIER,ALU
6911	STRUCTURES,PARTS IRN,STL	W 6068	13.6	W 11545	16.2	W 9965	20.2	W 17869	29.1	CONSTRUCT FER,ACIER,FONTE
693	WIRE PRODUCTS NON ELECTR	W 5618	11.1	W 5570	13.2	W 8470	19.9	W 12204	27.6	OUVRAGES FILS METALLIQUES
695	TOOLS	W 5535	31.9	W 8719	50.0	W 5105	41.3	W 6306	54.4	OUTILS A MAIN
6954	BLADES,TIPS,ETC FR TOOLS	W 1363	13.9	W 1822	22.3	W 1174	22.1	W 1302	29.5	OUTILS POUR MACHINE-OUTIL
69541	PARTS TO INSERT IN TOOLS	W 1114	11.5	W 1494	18.6	W 1022	19.1	W 1137	26.2	OUTILS DE FORAGE
697	BASE MTL HOUSEHOLD EQUIP	W 7338	19.2	W 7449	25.5	W 6606	25.7	W 5924	22.0	ART MENAGE MET COMMUNS
699	BASE METAL MFRS NES	W 8853	38.0	W 9309	50.6	W 14572	53.9	W 15466	58.1	ART MANUFACTURES MET NDA
7	MACHINES,TRANSPORT EQUIP		2189.1		2952.7		2955.9		3274.3	MACHINES MATERIEL TRANSPORT
71	POWER GENERATING EQUIPMT		152.2		174.5		232.6		283.0	MACHINES GENERATRICES
713	INTRNL COMBUS PSTN ENGIN	W 10477	81.8	W 13589	94.3	W 10276	89.3	W 11873	92.3	MOTEURS EXPL COMB INT, PIECE
7132	MOTOR VEHCL PISTN ENGINS	W 5287	19.1	W 5788	18.3	W 5142	11.2	W 6652	11.6	MOTEURS EXPL POUR VEHICULES
7139	PISTON ENGINE PARTS NES	W 2247	41.0	W 2239	47.2	W 2178	41.7	W 2139	41.3	PIECES POUR 713.2,3,8
714	ENGINES AND MOTORS NES	W 42	7.0	W 59	6.8	W 60	4.6	W 1571	38.0	MOTEURS NON ELECTRIQUES
7148	GAS TURBINES NES	W 1	0.1	W 2	0.2	W 4	0.2	W 1434	34.0	TURBINES A GAZ
71488	OTHER GAS TURBINES NES	W 1	0.1	W 1	0.2	W 2	0.2	W 1433	34.0	AUTRES TURBINES A GAZ
716	ROTATING ELECTRIC PLANT	W 5527	46.8	W 6411	53.1	W 10269	122.5	W 7751	130.8	APP ELECTR ROTATIFS,PIECES
7161	DC MOTORS AND GENERATORS	W 1174	6.9	W 793	6.6	W 515	6.1	W 1830	45.0	MOTEURS COURANT CONTINU
7162	AC MTRS,GENRTRS,GEN SETS	W 4000	35.7	W 5250	43.9	W 9578	111.8	W 5692	81.0	MOTEURS ELECTRIQUES
71622	AC GENERATORS	W 471	6.6	W 281	2.3	W 4296	52.2	W 1618	44.2	GENER COURANT ALTERNATIF
71623	GEN SETS WITH PISTN ENGN	W 1596	16.8	W 2232	26.3	W 3271	43.8	W 1784	20.2	GROUPES MOTEUR EXPLOSION
72	MACHS FOR SPCL INDUSTRYS		312.3		371.1		444.4		532.0	MAC SPECIALES POUR INDUST
722	TRACTORS NON-ROAD	W 3693	24.2	W 5085	18.2	W 2061	12.5	W 2784	16.2	TRACTEURS
7224	WHEELED TRACTORS NES	W 2742	18.4	W 4388	14.0	W 1908	11.4	W 2108	12.6	TRACTEURS A ROUES
723	CIVIL ENGNEERG EQUIP ETC	W 17196	102.3	W 19744	126.9	W 21106	145.9	W 27705	197.4	APPAREILS DE GENIE CIVIL
7234	CONST,MINING MACHNRY NES	W 16919	100.8	W 16694	103.1	W 20269	142.0	W 26478	189.6	MACH POUR LA CONST, MINES
72341	SELF-PROPELLD DOZERS,ETC	W 4288	26.9	W 3502	22.1	W 5057	32.7	W 8239	61.1	BULLDOZERS
72342	SLFPRP SHOVELS,EXCAVATRS	W 10421	59.6	W 10510	63.1	W 11968	79.6	W 16083	103.2	PELLES MECANIQUES
724	TEXTILE,LEATHER MACHNRY	W 6522	65.3	W 6283	71.9	W 4975	71.2	W 8029	100.1	MACH POUR INDUSTRIE TEXTILE
7245	WEAVING,FELT MFG,ETC MCH	W 1677	18.5	W 1629	21.1	W 1311	19.5	W 2252	28.8	METIERS A TISSER,PIECES
726	PRINTG,BKBINDG MACHY,PTS	W 1460	18.8	W 1756	23.2	W 2603	43.7	W 1668	32.2	MACHINES POUR IMPRIMERIE
7264	PRINTING PRESSES	W 791	8.8	W 1155	13.4	W 1956	31.1	W 1231	19.7	MACHINES A IMPRIMER
72641	ROTARY PRINTING PRESSES	W 791	8.8	W 1155	13.4	W 1956	31.1	W 1231	19.7	MACH IMPRIMER ROTATIVES
727	FOOD MACHRY NON-DOMESTIC	W 3143	26.3	W 4108	21.8	W 2088	24.2	W 2687	42.7	MACH INDUSTRIES ALIMENT
7272	OTH FOOD PROC MCHY,PARTS	W 2412	20.7	W 1472	13.0	W 1344	18.5	W 1965	34.8	AUT MACH IND ALIMENTAIRE
72722	INDUS FOOD PROC MACH NES	W 2252	17.6	W 1224	11.6	W 1214	17.1	W 1883	34.2	MACHINES BOULANGERIE
728	OTH MACHY FOR SPCL INDUS	W 7337	65.9	W 9502	86.2	W 11927	118.2	W 10789	111.9	AUT MACH IND PARTICULIERES
7283	OTHR MINERAL WORKG MACHY	W 3461	19.7	W 4729	27.4	W 6434	44.1	W 4206	31.2	MACH TRIER,CRIBLER,BROYER
72839	PTS NES OF MACHY OF 7283	W 1073	7.0	W 1116	8.0	W 3612	26.1	W 1930	14.0	PIECES MACH DU 728.3
7284	MACHY FOR SPCL INDUS NES	W 3131	43.0	W 3356	51.9	W 4480	67.8	W 6032	76.8	MACH SPEC IND PARTICUL.
72842	RUBBER,PLASTICS WRKG MCH	W 1382	16.9	W 1463	22.8	W 1696	26.7	W 1725	31.5	MACH IND CAOUT MAT PLAST
72848	OTH MCHY WITH INDIV FNCT	W 1138	12.7	W 1399	17.5	W 2199	30.9	W 2650	27.7	AUTRES MACHINES NDA
73	METALWORKING MACHINERY		24.4		38.1		38.9		54.3	MACH TRAVAIL DES METAUX
736	METALWORKING MACH-TOOLS	W 2593	15.3	W 5226	24.4	W 6699	28.4	W 7720	40.3	MACH-OUTILS TRAVAIL METAUX
74	GENRL INDUSTRL MACHY NES		334.5		406.9		471.0		515.0	MACH APP INDUSTRIE
741	HEATING,COOLING EQUIPMNT	W 6017	49.9	W 7044	64.5	W 12497	98.8	W 8698	98.9	MACH CHAUFFAGE,PIECES
7416	HEATING,COOLING EQU NES	W 2359	25.6	W 2268	23.0	W 4250	43.0	W 2310	45.9	APP CHANGEMENT TEMP
742	PUMPS FOR LIQUIDS ETC	W 2872	39.3	W 9086	60.2	W 3932	60.0	W 5374	60.2	POMPES MOTO-POMPES
7428	OTHER PUMPS FOR LIQUIDS	W 1439	18.6	W 4692	32.0	W 1553	27.2	W 3330	26.6	AUTRES POMPES POUR LIQ
74288	PUMPS FR LIQUIDS NES ETC	W 1122	13.4	W 4241	23.9	W 1050	18.7	W 2986	21.2	POMPES POUR LIQUIDES NDA
743	PUMPS NES,CENTRFUGES ETC	W 6027	58.4	W 7256	74.7	W 5987	74.7	W 7255	87.6	POMPES COMPRES,VENT ETC
7431	PUMPS FOR GASES ETC	W 3531	19.9	W 4526	29.6	W 3158	23.7	W 3849	33.9	POMPES AIR A VIDE,COMPRES
744	MECHANICAL HANDLING EQU	W 7051	51.4	W 6045	37.0	W 10641	74.8	W 11831	87.5	EQUIP MANUTENTION PIECES
7442	LIFTING,LOADING MACH NES	W 2800	20.1	W 3123	21.7	W 4166	28.3	W 4465	32.2	APP LEVAGE,MANUTENTION

4. Special Imports C.I.F. by Commodities according to the S.I.T.C. (Rev. 2) in million U.S. Dollars
Importations Spéciales C.A.F. par Produits d'après la C.T.C.I. (Rév. 2) en millions de Dollars E.U.

SITC CTCI	COMMODITY	1994			1995			1996			1997			PRODUIT
		QUANTITY QUANTITE		VALUE VALEUR	QUANTITY QUANTITE		VALUE VALEUR	QUANTITY QUANTITE		VALUE VALEUR	QUANTITY QUANTITE		VALUE VALEUR	
7449	PTS NES OF MACHY OF 7442	W	2447	24.5	W	538	4.4	W	4051	35.8	W	4429	41.3	PIECES DU 744.2
745	NONELEC MACHY,TOOLS NES	W	2980	42.1	W	3472	55.7	W	2679	53.2	W	3234	59.5	AUT MACH NON ELEC,PIECES
7452	OTH NONELEC MCHS,PTS NES	W	2702	33.8	W	3090	46.2	W	2364	44.8	W	2910	49.2	AUT MACH NON ELEC,PIECES
74522	PACKAGNG,BOTTLNG,ETC MCH	W	1112	18.0	W	1113	20.0	W	938	22.0	W	1043	25.6	MACH NETT BOUTEILLES,ETC
749	NONELEC MACH PTS,ACC NES	W	5695	93.7	W	7692	115.1	W	6514	109.9	W	7465	121.5	PIECES MACH NON ELEC NDA
7491	BALL,ROLLER,ETC BEARINGS	W	1167	19.3	W	1171	22.0	W	1030	20.0	W	1081	21.2	ROULEMENTS BILLES ETC
7492	COCKS,VALVES ETC NES	W	2160	28.2	W	2944	36.9	W	2915	37.5	W	3703	44.3	ART ROB,SIM POUR TUYAUX
7493	SHAFT,CRANK,PULLEY ETC	W	1542	29.6	W	2620	34.3	W	1757	34.9	W	1712	34.8	ARBRES TRANS,VILEBREQUINS
75	OFFICE MACHNES,ADP EQUIP			135.4			207.8			259.7			299.9	MACH BUREAU TRAIT AUTOM
751	OFFICE MACHINES	W	1070	22.2	W	1517	32.2	W	1485	33.8	W	1466	26.9	MACH,APPAREILS DE BUREAU
7518	OFFICE MACHINES NES	W	613	14.4	W	862	21.0	W	1020	24.8	W	1066	20.8	MACH,APP DE BUREAU NDA
752	AUTOMTIC DATA PROC EQUIP	W	2671	91.6	W	3202	144.2	W	4012	182.1	W	4574	216.4	MACH TRAIT INFORMATION
7522	DIGITAL COMPUTERS	W	691	36.0	W	961	61.5	W	1265	80.0	W	1244	86.1	MACH DIGITALES COMPLETES
7524	DIGITL CENTRL STOR UNITS	W	100	5.1	W	177	12.9	W	246	19.9	W	365	29.9	UNITES MEMOIRE CENTRALES
7525	ADP PERIPHERAL UNITS	W	1730	38.7	W	1893	55.0	W	2305	66.2	W	2572	69.6	UNITES PERIPHERIQUES
759	OFFICE,ADP MCH PTS,ACCES	W	765	21.6	W	4794	31.5	W	1020	43.9	W	1149	56.7	PIECES DU 751 ET 752
7599	ACCTG,ETC,ADP MCH PTS,AC	W	688	18.4	W	4697	27.3	W	906	38.8	W	1012	51.4	PIECES DU 751 ET 752
76	TELECOMM,SOUND EQUIPMENT			269.3			461.0			490.4			525.2	EQUIPMENT DE TELECOM
761	TELEVISION RECEIVERS	W	6173	72.2	W	6933	76.9	W	5987	69.5	W	6060	62.8	RECEPTEURS DE TELEVISION
7611	COLOUR TV RECEIVERS	W	5132	67.2	W	5433	70.9	W	5416	66.6	W	5184	58.4	RECEPTEURS COULEUR
762	RADIO BROADCAST RECEIVRS	W	4696	42.6	W	4547	54.0	W	3332	44.2	W	3709	43.5	RECEPTEURS RADIODIFFUSION
7628	OTHER RADIO RECEIVERS	W	4000	36.9	W	4000	47.6	W	2945	38.8	W	3087	35.2	AUTRES RECEPT RADIO
763	SOUND RECORDRS,PHONOGRPH	W	808	20.8	W	813	25.3	W	593	20.3	W	407	12.3	PHONO,APP ENREGISTREMENT
7638	OTHR SOUND APPARATUS ETC	W	763	20.0	W	780	24.5	W	585	20.2	W	401	12.2	AUT APP D'ENREGIS,REPROD
76381	TV IMAGE,SND RECRDRS ETC	W	650	17.5	W	672	21.4	W	504	17.7	W	335	9.9	APP ENREG,REPRO IMAG,SON
764	TELECOM EQPT,PTS,ACC NES	W	3866	133.9	W	6993	305.0	W	7022	356.5	W	5271	406.7	EQUIP TELECOM,PIECES
7641	LINE TELEPHONE,ETC EQUIP	W	1367	60.2	W	3506	179.7	W	2823	132.6	W	528	51.4	APP TELEPHON PAR FIL
7643	TV,RADIO TRANSMITTRS ETC	W	255	33.3	W	780	66.2	W	689	85.8	W	1262	198.6	APP EMET TELE RADIO
7649	PTS NES OF EQUIPMT OF 76	W	1550	26.3	W	1405	40.7	W	2392	117.2	W	2326	135.2	PIECES DE LA DIV 76
76491	PTS NES OF APPAR OF 7641	W	248	11.9	W	943	28.8	W	1727	97.7	W	1439	87.8	PIECES POUR 764.1
76493	TELECOMM EQUIPMT PTS NES	W	1071	11.5	W	321	10.1	W	504	17.3	W	777	46.0	PIECES 761,762,764.3,8
77	ELECTRIC MACHNRY NES ETC			231.8			351.4			347.2			344.9	MACH APP ELECT NDA
771	ELECTRIC POWER MACHY NES	W	2353	16.9	W	4338	25.3	W	4369	31.9	W	4460	39.2	MACH PROD,TRANS ELECTR
772	SWITCHGEAR ETC,PARTS NES	W	2680	45.4	W	2783	58.7	W	3436	64.8	W	4232	87.1	APP COUPURE,SECT ETC
7721	SWITCHGEAR ETC	W	2586	39.6	W	2689	55.3	W	3365	62.3	W	4177	85.1	APP COUPURE,SECTIONMNT
773	ELECTR DISTRIBUTNG EQUIP	W	6233	26.9	W	15145	80.0	W	11257	74.2	W	7855	47.9	EQUIPMT DISTRIBUTION ELECT
7731	INSULATED WIRE,CABLE ETC	W	4149	21.6	W	12972	66.2	W	8830	51.7	W	6095	37.5	FILS,CABLES ISOLES ELECT
775	HOUSEHOLD TYPE EQUIP NES	W	9490	53.4	W	14516	75.6	W	10477	66.3	W	9670	58.3	MACH,APP USAGE DOMESTQUE
778	ELECTRICAL MACHINERY NES	W	11350	71.2	W	15942	80.7	W	12531	85.0	W	13264	85.3	AUTRES MACH ELECT NDA
7788	OTH ELEC MACHY,EQUIP NES	W	2425	24.1	W	2457	17.0	W	2607	25.9	W	2819	25.6	AUT MACH APP ELEC NDA
78	ROAD VEHICLES			699.3			895.5			652.4			698.5	VEHICULES ROUTIERS
781	PASS MOTOR VEH EXC BUSES	W	46679	252.5	W	91264	352.1	W	51980	291.3	W	56361	328.6	AUTO TRANSPORT PERSONNES
782	LORRIES,SPCL MTR VEH NES	W	45085	194.4	W	70505	234.6	W	34489	190.6	W	41001	218.5	VEHICULES SPECIAUX,MARCH
7821	LORRIES,TRUCKS	W	42007	183.4	W	68555	226.3	W	32219	173.1	W	37333	194.1	VEHICULES TRANSP MARCHAND
783	ROAD MOTOR VEHICLES NES	W	48813	131.1	W	59092	156.0	W	17920	60.4	W	13666	47.0	VEHICULES ROUTIERS NDA
7831	BUSES	W	38783	111.9	W	42816	122.8	W	13554	48.0	W	7545	29.1	VOITURES TRANSPORT COMMUN
7832	TRACTORS FOR TR–TRAILERS	W	10030	19.2	W	16276	33.3	W	4366	12.4	W	6121	18.0	TRACTEURS ROUTIERS
784	MOTOR VEH PRTS,ACCES NES	W	10247	76.5	W	13587	88.1	W	9305	64.6	W	9746	62.7	PIECES 722,781,782,783
7849	OTHER MOTOR VEHCL PARTS	W	8747	65.1	W	12479	80.6	W	8685	61.1	W	8970	59.7	PIECES 722,781,782,783
785	CYCLES,ETC MOTRZD OR NOT	W	6775	36.1	W	10609	56.9	W	6641	39.9	W	6485	35.0	MOTOCYCLES SCOOTERS
7851	MOTORCYCLES ETC	W	1706	17.2	W	4538	35.2	W	2259	25.1	W	1719	20.0	MOTO VELO MOTEUR AUXIL
79	OTHR TRANSPORT EQUIPMENT			30.4			46.8			19.6			21.8	AUTRE MATERIEL TRANSPORT
791	RAILWAY VEHICLES	W	2106	19.1	W	1123	24.1	W	553	5.5	W	1174	7.2	VEHIC MAT CHEMINS DE FER
8	MISC MANUFACTURED GOODS			384.9			598.4			618.6			699.0	ART MANUFACTURES DIVERS
821	*FURNITURE,PARTS THEREOF	W	3364	14.1	W	4603	23.9	W	6500	36.2	W	7500	40.1	MEUBLES ET PIECES
84	CLOTHING AND ACCESSORIES			25.1			36.4			42.7			65.4	VETEMENTS
851	*FOOTWEAR	W	6610	24.8	W	6061	31.2	W	2825	27.3	W	2595	31.9	CHAUSSURES
85102	FOOTWEAR LEATHER	W	5528	18.6	W	4330	18.6	W	1454	16.3	W	1250	20.8	CHAUS SEMELLES EN CUIR
87	PRECISION INSTRUMNTS NES			80.3			133.9			114.7			126.5	INSTRUM,APPAR SCIENT NDA
872	MEDICAL INSTRUMENTS NES	W	649	17.7	W	1303	31.6	W	1134	29.4	W	1313	30.1	INSTR,APP MEDIC–CHIR NDA
87202	OTH MEDICAL INSTRUMENTS	W	590	16.2	W	1150	26.6	W	987	25.5	W	1201	26.9	INSTRUM,APP MEDECINE
874	MEASURNG,CONTROLNG INSTR	W	1648	45.6	W	2398	77.7	W	1654	66.2	W	2198	74.8	INSTRUMENTS DE MESURE
88	PHOTO EQU,OPTICL GDS ETC			51.3			66.4			68.3			75.6	APP,FOURN PHOTO,OP,MONTR
882	PHOTO,CINEMA SUPPLIES	W	3334	30.6	W	3278	40.5	W	3124	42.2	W	3494	46.5	PRODUITS PHOTO,CINEMA
8822	PHOTO FILM EXC DEV CINMA	W	2425	24.8	W	2089	31.1	W	2317	32.1	W	2227	33.5	PLAQUES,PELLICULES,FILMS
89	MISC MANUFCTRD GOODS NES			176.5			285.2			305.5			334.0	ART MANUFACTURES DIVERS
892	PRINTED MATTER	W	4359	30.3	W	5156	42.4	W	6928	50.7	W	7939	55.5	IMPRIMES
8921	PRINTED BOOKS,GLOBES,ETC	W	2264	16.4	W	2881	22.7	W	4572	30.5	W	5585	34.8	LIVRES,BROCHURES,CARTES
89211	PRINTED BOOKS,PAMPHLETS	W	2207	16.0	W	2777	22.0	W	4488	29.9	W	5484	34.1	LIVRES,BROCHURES
893	ARTICLES OF PLASTIC NES			49.3			89.4			83.3			90.9	OUVRAGES EN MAT DIVIS 58
8931	PLSTC PACKG CONTNRS,LIDS	W	5821	21.1	W	9185	34.3	W	7715	26.4	W	9536	29.9	ART TRANSP EMBALLAGE ETC
8939	MISC PLASTIC ARTICLES	W	6789	27.6	W	13454	54.2	W	15215	55.8	W	15750	60.0	ART DIVERS EN MAT DIV 58
89399	OTHR PLASTC ARTICLES NES	W	6019	25.7	W	11781	50.6	W	12447	50.1	W	14056	57.3	AUT OUV MAT DIV 58
894	TOYS,SPORTING GOODS,ETC	W	8311	33.8	W	11113	67.4	W	10375	80.4	W	12312	82.5	VOITURES ENFANTS,JOUETS
8942	TOYS,INDOOR GAMES ETC	W	7719	30.3	W	9880	60.2	W	8774	71.3	W	9865	72.1	JOUETS,JEUX ETC
89423	TOYS NES	W	4072	13.6	W	5396	26.5	W	4557	24.3	W	5583	33.8	JOUETS,MODELES REDUITS
89424	INDOOR GAME EQUIPMENT	W	1254	7.6	W	1695	19.7	W	1980	35.9	W	1555	24.7	ART,JEUX DE SOCIETE
898	MUSICAL INSTRUMENTS,PTS	W	2461	26.0	W	3284	35.7	W	3150	39.7	W	3422	52.5	INSTRUMENTS DE MUSIQUE
8983	SOUND RECRDNG TAPE,DISCS	W	2273	23.8	W	3028	32.3	W	2930	36.7	W	3195	49.2	SUPPORTS SON POUR 763
89832	RECORDED DISCS,TAPES ETC	W	213	11.4	W	240	17.2	W	426	22.8	W	742	36.1	DISQUES,PHONO,BANDES
899	OTHER MANUFACTURED GOODS			17.1			23.4			23.9			24.5	AUT ART MANUF DIVERS NDA

5. Special Exports F.O.B. by Commodities according to the S.I.T.C. (Rev. 2) in million U.S. Dollars
Exportations Spéciales F.O.B. par Produits d'après la C.T.C.I. (Rév. 2) en millions de Dollars E.U.

SITC CTCI	COMMODITY	1994		1995		1996		1997		PRODUIT
		QUANTITY QUANTITE	VALUE VALEUR	QUANTITY QUANTITE	VALUE VALEUR	QUANTITY QUANTITE	VALUE VALEUR	QUANTITY QUANTITE	VALUE VALEUR	
	ALL COMMODITIES		4389.0		5439.8		5835.1		6759.4	TOUS PRODUITS
0	FOOD AND LIVE ANIMALS		1349.4		1481.2		1573.2		2029.4	ALIMENTS,ANIMAUX VIVANTS
03	FISH AND PREPARATIONS		168.8		208.0		209.2		276.7	POISSONS ET PREPARATIONS
034	FISH,FRESH,CHILLED,FROZN	W 48074	51.9	W 56533	69.6	W 79331	87.3	W 64333	76.4	POISSON FRAIS, REFRIG,CONG
0342	FISH FROZEN,EXCL FILLETS	W 15367	12.6	W 10375	10.2	W 18261	17.1	W 22414	20.9	POISSONS CONGELES
0344	FISH FILLETS,FROZEN	W 30628	35.8	W 45436	57.1	W 59790	66.0	W 40906	50.7	FILETS CONGELES
036	SHELL FISH FRESH,FROZEN	W 24690	83.7	W 26322	103.3	W 17410	76.3	W 25044	124.6	CRUSTACES,MOLLUSQUES
037	FISH ETC PREPD,PRSVD NES	W 20424	31.2	W 22890	31.5	W 25057	38.7	W 46980	65.4	POIS,CRUST,MOL PREPARES
0371	FISH PREPARD,PRESRVD NES	W 19715	24.9	W 22552	29.3	W 24434	35.4	W 46043	58.2	CONSERVES DE POISSONS
04	CEREALS AND PREPARATIONS		13.7		9.6		5.8		11.3	CEREALES ET PRODUITS
05	VEGETABLES AND FRUIT		139.7		171.4		207.5		215.7	LEGUMES ET FRUITS
054	VEG ETC FRSH,SMPLY PRSVD	W 41342	48.7	W 50394	59.1	W 67853	68.8	W 61087	76.0	LEGUMES FRAIS,CONG,SECS
0545	OTHER FRESH VEGETABLES	W 12485	19.4	W 21101	26.6	W 40617	35.6	W 28020	37.3	AUTRES LEGUMES FRAIS,REF
05459	FRESH VEGETABLES NES	W 11314	18.7	W 14555	24.2	W 14615	27.9	W 16667	33.6	LEGUMES FRAIS,REFRI NDA
0546	VEGETABLES SIMPLY PRESVD	W 14389	17.9	W 11894	19.0	W 14005	23.3	W 19473	29.0	LEGUMES CONG,CONSER
05461	VEGETABLES FROZEN	W 13477	16.1	W 10503	16.2	W 11087	18.3	W 14904	22.6	LEGUMES CONGELES
056	VEGTBLES ETC PRSVD,PREPD	W 48248	70.8	W 45956	88.3	W 47204	103.8	W 48742	102.1	CONSERVES DE LEGUMES
0565	VEGTBLES PRSVD,PREPD NES	W 47786	64.0	W 44581	81.1	W 45450	94.6	W 47246	95.4	LEGUMES PREPARES CONSERVE
05659	OTH VEG PRESVD,PREPD NES	W 47656	63.9	W 44347	80.7	W 45341	94.5	W 47190	95.2	LEGUM PREPAP,CONSERV NDA
057	FRUIT,NUTS,FRESH,DRIED	W 12241	12.1	W 14994	13.2	W 33676	22.5		23.4	FRUITS FRAIS OU SECS
06	SUGAR AND PREPS,HONEY		31.7		30.6		39.2		38.1	SUCRES ET PRODUITS
061	SUGAR AND HONEY	W 69795	31.1		30.5	W 98881	38.5	W 126447	36.8	SUCRES ET MIEL
0611	RAW BEET AND CANE SUGAR	W 56014	24.9	W 64633	30.3	W 82515	37.2	W 76921	33.4	SUCRES BRUTS
07	COFFEE,TEA,COCOA,SPICES		223.2		310.4		247.5		421.1	CAFE,THE,CACAO,EPICES
071	COFFEE AND SUBSTITUTES	W 68861	206.8	W 105262	286.2	W 100337	223.5	W 98040	397.3	CAFE ET SUCCEDANES
0711	COFFEE GREEN,ROASTED,SUB	W 68861	206.8	W 105204	285.7	W 100296	223.1	W 98005	396.9	CAFE TORREFIE OU DECAFEINE
07111	COFFEE GREEN,HUSKS,SKINS	W 66022	199.5	W 104733	284.0	W 100098	222.7	W 98004	396.9	CAFE NON TORREFIE
072	COCOA	W 4639	14.1	W 6631	21.6	W 7485	20.1	W 5776	18.0	CACAO
0723	COCOA BUTTER AND PASTE	W 4266	13.9	W 6432	21.5	W 6825	19.7	W 5195	17.6	BEURRE ET PATE DE CACAO
07232	COCOA BUTTER	W 4194	13.9	W 5428	20.6	W 4957	18.9	W 4269	16.8	BEURRE DE CACAO
081	*FEEDING STUFF FOR ANIML	W 2323311	766.3	W 1859432	739.1	W 1627559	856.3		1058.7	NOURRITURE POUR ANIMAUX
0811	HAY, FODDER, GREEN, DRY	W 11170	19.4	W 8789	14.0	W 7732	15.0		20.3	FOIN ET FOURRAGE
08119	FODDER OF VEG ORIGIN NES	W 11170	19.4	W 8749	13.9	W 7716	15.0	W 10556	20.3	AUTRES FOURRAGES
0814	MEAT OR FISH MEAL FODDER	W 2306016	743.5	W 1845589	722.1	W 1611805	836.2	W 1926205	1031.5	FARINES DE VIANDES,POISSONS
08142	FISH MEAL FODDER	W 2305369	743.3	W 1845242	722.0	W 1611805	836.2	W 1926205	1031.5	FARINES DE POISSONS
2	CRUDE MATERLS,EXCL FUELS		773.0		1014.1		973.9		1095.8	MAT BRUTES NON COMESTIBLES
24	CORK AND WOOD		12.5		9.0		15.5		30.0	LIEGE ET BOIS
248	WOOD SHAPED,SLEEPERS	W 19344	12.3	W 11529	9.0	W 17773	15.5	W 32874	30.0	BOIS SIMPLEMENT TRAVAILLES
2483	LUMBER SHAPED NON–CONIFR	W 19123	12.1	W 11527	9.0	W 13719	12.9	W 32840	29.9	NON CONIFERES SCIES,RABOTES
24831	LUMBER SAWN ETC NON–CON	W 18790	11.8	W 10601	8.4	W 12818	12.4	W 32204	29.6	SCIES LONGITUDINALEMENT
26	TEXTILE FIBRES AND WASTE		66.5		92.9		73.4		85.4	FIBRES TEXTILES
263	COTTON	W 2248	5.1	W 8127	24.4	W 11576	30.3	W 13652	32.3	COTON
2631	RAW COTTON,EXCL LINTERS	W 2133	4.9	W 8006	24.2	W 11509	30.2	W 13395	31.9	COTON EN MASSE
266	SYNTHETIC FIBRES TO SPIN		36.8	W 21889	44.4	W 14484	27.0	W 22249	38.3	FIBRES SYNTHETIQUES
2666	CONTIN FILAMNT TOW SYNTH	W 10944	19.5	W 11757	23.8	W 8890	16.1	W 14360	24.3	CABLES POUR DISCONTINUS
26663	— OF ACRYLIC FIBRES	W 10944	19.5	W 11757	23.8	W 8890	16.1	W 14360	24.3	DE FIBRES ACRYLIQUES
268	WOOL(EXC TOPS),ANML HAIR	W 4411	24.6	W 4283	24.1	W 3443	16.2	W 4159	15.0	LAINES ET POILS
2687	WOOL OR HAIR COMBED ETC	W 2712	21.2	W 2628	21.2	W 1419	13.2	W 1664	12.6	LAINE CARDEE PEIGNEE
28	METALLIFEROUS ORES,SCRAP		666.4		872.4		823.3		909.7	MINERAIS METAL,DECHETS
281	IRON ORE,CONCENTRATES	W 6547332	108.9	W 6007510	100.4	W 4030664	84.1	W 3712385	78.0	MINERAIS DE FER
2815	IRON ORE,CONC,NOT AGGLOM	W 3471635	43.5	W 3023187	35.0	W 1584219	20.6	W 1899218	26.1	MINERAIS NON AGGLOMERES
2816	IRON ORE AGGLOMERATES	W 3074773	65.1	W 2983255	65.1	W 2445812	63.3	W 1813142	52.0	MINERAIS AGGLOMERES
287	BASE METAL ORES,CONC NES	W 1369206	540.3	W 1451488	736.5	W 1565511	711.1	W 1763787	806.3	MINERAIS METAUX COMMUNS
2871	CPR ORE ETC,CEMENT COPPR	W 150734	89.8	W 217386	176.1	W 242419	137.4	W 293108	153.1	MINERAIS DE CUIVRE,MATTES
28711	COPPER ORES,EXCL MATTE	W 150734	89.8	W 217386	176.1	W 242419	137.4	W 293108	153.1	MINERAIS DE CUIVRE
2874	LEAD ORES,CONCENTRATES	W 222366	141.6	W 231524	177.7	W 234993	183.4	W 234285	159.2	MINERAIS DE PLOMB
2875	ZINC ORES,CONCENTRATES	W 944942	208.9	W 956836	236.4	W 1041170	273.4	W 1195970	397.4	MINERAIS DE ZINC
2876	TIN ORES,CONCENTRATES	W 44863	81.6	W 37099	81.5	W 38271	87.8	W 31627	63.3	MINERAIS D'ETAIN
2879	OTH NONFER ORE,CONCNTRTE	W 5622	17.9	W 8596	65.0	W 8658	29.3	W 8798	33.5	MINERAIS D'AUTRES METAUX
28793	MOLYBD, NIOBIUM ETC ORES	W 4844	16.1	W 7326	60.5	W 7683	26.8	W 8368	32.3	MINERAIS DE MOLYBDENE,TITANE
289	PREC MTAL ORES,WASTE NES	K 7630759	13.3	MK 12107	27.6	MK 10675	23.0	MK 10050	17.6	MINERAIS,DECHETS MET PREC
28901	PRECIOUS METAL ORES,CONC	K 7630759	13.3	MK 12107	27.6	MK 10675	23.0	MK 10050	17.6	MINERAIS METAUX PRECIEUX
29	CRUDE ANIMAL,VEG MAT NES		16.8		31.4		49.7		46.8	MATIERES BRUTES ANIM,VEGET
291	CRUDE ANIMAL MTRIALS NES	W 500	3.2	W 1065	13.7	W 921	33.1	W 1002	27.1	MATIERES BRUTES ANIMALES
2919	OTH ANIMAL MATERIALS NES	W 257	3.1	W 414	13.6	W 746	33.0	W 742	27.0	MAT ORIGINE ANIMALE NDA
29199	ANIMAL PRODUCTS,NES	W 168	2.8	W 246	13.0	W 602	32.4	W 528	26.4	PROD ORIGINE ANIMALE NDA
292	CRUDE VEG MATERIALS NES	W 10778	13.7	W 11219	17.7	W 10780	16.6	W 14492	19.7	MAT BRUTES VEGETALES NDA
3	MINERAL FUELS ETC		177.1		268.3		384.9		401.9	COMBUSTIBLES MINERAUX LUB
33	PETROLEUM AND PRODUCTS		177.1		268.3		384.9		401.9	PETROLE ET DERIVES
333	CRUDE PETROLEUM			W 1522089	140.5	W 2019579	236.6	W 2468984	239.6	HUILES BRUTES DE PETROLE
334	PETROLEUM PRODUCTS,REFIN	W 471965	177.1	W 1209976	127.9	W 1228442	147.0	W 1360387	159.9	PRODUITS RAFFINES
3341	GASOLINE,OTH LIGHT OILS	W 145295	22.4	W 75562	13.0	W 115956	22.4	W 171156	34.6	ESSENCES POUR MOTEURS
33411	MOTOR,AVIATION SPIRIT	W 145295	22.4	W 75562	13.0	W 115956	22.4	W 170734	34.5	ESSENCES MOTEURS D'AVIONS
3343	GAS OILS	W 316247	150.0	W 60984	15.7	W 66274	16.2	W 64520	15.3	GAS OILS
3344	FUEL OILS,NES			W 1069020	96.6	W 1042601	106.3	W 1117169	107.4	FUEL OILS
4	ANIMAL,VEGETABLE OIL,FAT		72.8		83.0		78.4		96.0	HUILES,GRAISSES ANIM,VEG
411	*ANIMAL OILS AND FATS	W 285597	67.5	W 270145	77.7	W 225145	75.3		95.2	HUILES,GRAISSES ANIMALES
4111	OILS OF FISH,WHALES ETC	W 285597	67.5	W 270145	77.7	W 225145	75.3		95.2	GRAISSES,HUILES DE POISSONS
41112	OTHER FISH OILS AND FATS	W 285562	67.5	W 268467	76.9	W 225145	75.3	W 242588	95.2	AUTRES HUILES ET GRAISSES
5	CHEMCLS,RELATED PROD NES		96.9		118.9		153.6		180.8	PRODUITS CHIMIQUES
52	INORGANIC CHEMICALS		26.1		32.2		39.2		45.9	PROD CHIM INORGANIQUES
522	INORG ELEMNTS,OXIDES,ETC	W 103204	19.1	W 152387	23.1	W 219519	24.7	W 238355	24.1	ELEMENTS INORGANIQUES
523	OTHR INORG CHEMICALS ETC	W 20220	7.1	W 23359	9.1		14.5	W 40540	21.8	AUT PRODUITS CHIMIQUES INORG
53	DYES,TANNING,COLOUR PROD		17.6		28.9		41.5		38.9	PROD TEINTURE,COLORANTS
531	SYNT DYE,NAT INDGO,LAKES	W 166	0.5	W 12	1.6	W 70	19.8	W 71	18.2	MAT COLOR ORGAN,LAQUES
5312	SYNTH LUMIN,INDIGO,LAKES	W 3	0.3	W 7	1.4	W 66	19.7	W 61	18.0	LUMINOPHORES ORGAN SYNTH
53122	COLOUR LAKES	W 2	0.3	W 6	1.4	W 65	19.7	W 61	18.0	LAQUES COLORANTES
532	DYES NES,TANNING PROD	W 1248	16.7	W 1944	26.7	W 2435	21.0	W 2321	19.7	EXTRAITS TEINTURE,TANNAGE
5322	DYE,TANN EXTRCTS,TANNINS	W 423	15.9	W 568	25.6	W 1050	20.0	W 1539	19.1	EXT TAN ORIG VEG,TANNINS
53222	DYEING EXTRCTS VEG,ANMAL	W 258	15.5	W 346	25.2	W 618	19.2	W 1212	18.3	MATI COLOR VEGET ANIMALE
541	*MEDICINAL,PHARM PRODUCT	K 301243	12.9	K 399674	16.1		21.8	K 581293	22.6	PROD MEDICINAUX PHARMACEUT
55	PERFUME,CLEANING ETC PRD		21.1		20.3		24.9		28.3	PROD POUR PARFUM,TOILETTE
554	SOAP,CLEANSING ETC PREPS	W 9682	13.3	W 7744	10.9	W 9773	11.9	W 10930	13.3	SAVONS,PRODUITS DETERSIFS
59	CHEMICAL MATERIALS NES		4.6		6.2		8.3		24.6	MAT PROD CHIMIQUES NDA
6	BASIC MANUFACTURES		1279.9		1642.7		1605.6		1770.7	ART MANUFACTURES
65	TEXTILE YARN,FABRICS,ETC		149.9		171.6		159.4		196.1	FILS,TISSUS,ARTICLES TEXTILE
651	TEXTILE YARN	W 16279	89.0	W 13942	102.6	W 13664	84.7	W 15491	93.9	FILS TEXTILES
6512	WOOL,HAIR YARN,INCL TOPS	W 3032	29.6	W 3266	35.1	W 2186	22.9	W 2612	25.0	FILS DE LAINE,DE POILS
6513	COTTON YARN	W 12018	55.3	W 10001	63.8	W 10810	58.1	W 11714	63.2	FILS DE COTON
652	COTTON FABRICS,WOVEN	W 15342	26.9	W 3409	28.0	W 5473	35.4	W 8406	53.8	TISSUS DE COTON
6522	WOVEN COTTON BLEACHD,ETC	W 1556	16.2	W 2708	24.6	W 4386	30.7	W 6926	47.5	TISSUS COTON BLANCHIS ETC

5. Special Exports F.O.B. by Commodities according to the S.I.T.C. (Rev. 2) in million U.S. Dollars
Exportations Spéciales F.O.B. par Produits d'après la C.T.C.I. (Rév. 2) en millions de Dollars E.U.

SITC CTCI	COMMODITY	1994		1995		1996		1997		PRODUIT
		QUANTITY QUANTITE	VALUE VALEUR	QUANTITY QUANTITE	VALUE VALEUR	QUANTITY QUANTITE	VALUE VALEUR	QUANTITY QUANTITE	VALUE VALEUR	
65224	BLCHED COTTON FABRIC NES	W 1549	16.1	W 2600	23.4	W 4077	27.8	W 6398	41.5	AUT TIS PLUS 85% COT BLANCHI
654	OTH WOVEN TEXTILE FABRIC	W 794	20.6	W 804	22.4	W 1027	22.0		27.2	TISSUS AUT COTON SYNT,ARTIF
6542	WOVEN WOOL,HAIR NONPILE	W 760	19.5	W 762	21.1	W 567	15.6	W 497	12.4	TIS PLUS 85% LAINE,POILS
65422	WOVN COMB WOOL,FINE HAIR	W 568	15.8	W 621	17.3	W 508	14.1	W 474	11.8	TISSUS 85% LAINE,PLS PEIG
66	NONMETAL MINERAL MFS NES		20.2		23.0		28.1		31.9	ART MIN NON METALLIQUES
67	IRON AND STEEL		9.2		10.4		15.4		24.7	FER ET ACIER
68	NON–FERROUS METALS		1062.5		1389.9		1376.1		1477.5	METAUX NON FERREUX
681	SILVER,PLATINUM,ETC		100.2		111.2		125.3		121.7	ARGENT ET PLATINE
6811	SILVER UNWKD,PARTLY WRKD		100.2		111.0		125.3		121.7	ARGENT BRUT MI–OUVRE
68113	SILVER UNWROUGHT		100.0		109.7		124.9		111.0	ARGENT ET ALLIAGES BRUTS
682	COPPER EXC CEMENT COPPER	W 360747	771.7	W 375457	1077.6	W 425968	959.8	W 445596	1001.3	CUIVRE
6821	COPPER NES,ALLOYS,UNWRT	W 342717	729.8	W 356465	1017.5	W 407724	911.4	W 420809	938.6	CUIVRE BRUT
68211	COPPER UNREF,EXC CEMENT	W 105518	216.9	W 91046	246.4	W 82722	175.4	W 57100	122.8	CUIVRE POUR AFFINAGE
68212	COPPER REFINED,UNWROUGHT	W 237199	512.9	W 265419	771.2	W 325002	736.0	W 363709	815.9	CUIVRE AFFINE BRUT
6822	COPPER,ALLOYS WORKED	W 18030	42.0	W 18993	60.1	W 18244	48.5	W 24786	62.7	CUIVRE,ALLIAGES OUVRES
68221	COPPER BARS,WIRE,ETC	W 17469	40.4	W 18485	58.2	W 15059	39.8	W 23302	59.0	BARRES,PROFILES ET FILS
685	LEAD	W 76401	40.5	W 80224	53.3	W 87898	70.1	W 99354	67.5	PLOMB
6851	LEAD,ALLOYS UNWROUGHT	W 76173	40.4	W 80222	53.3	W 87898	70.1	W 98856	67.3	PLOMB,ALLIAGES BRUTS
68512	REF LEAD(EXC ALLOY)UNWRT	W 75529	40.1	W 79762	53.0	W 85932	68.5	W 91286	60.6	PLOMB AFFINE BRUT
686	ZINC	W 140547	141.3	W 120023	140.2	W 171366	193.1	W 156531	219.3	ZINC
6861	ZINC,ALLOYS UNWROUGHT	W 136337	133.4	W 112350	127.6	W 151304	162.6	W 133735	179.2	ZINC ET ALLIAGES BRUTS
6863	ZINC,ALLOYS WKD,INC DUST	W 4210	7.9	W 7673	12.6	W 20062	30.6	W 22796	40.2	ZINC ET ALLIAGES OUVRES
68632	ZINC SHEETS,STRIP,FOIL	W 4140	7.8	W 5546	10.2	W 19806	30.5	W 22751	40.1	PLANCHES,FEUILLES EN ZINC
687	TIN	W 40	0.3	W 78	0.5	W 4523	21.0	W 10966	57.3	ETAIN
6871	TIN,ALLOYS UNWROUGHT	W 34	0.3	W 65	0.5	W 4510	21.0	W 10957	57.3	ETAIN ET ALLIAGES BRUTS
69	METAL MANUFACTURES NES		21.3		24.9		7.4		7.4	ART MANUFACT EN METAL NDA
699	BASE METAL MFRS NES	W 15957	19.0	W 15707	22.5	W 1920	4.1	W 1143	2.8	ART MANUFACTURES MET NDA
6998	MFRS NES OF CPR,NIKL,ETC	W 14746	17.9	W 14657	20.4	W 840	1.5	W 150	0.5	OUVRAGES EN CU,NI,AL,PB,ZN
69985	ZINC MANUFACTURES NES	W 13392	16.5	W 14267	19.8	W 707	1.0	W 77	0.2	OUVRAGES EN ZINC
7	MACHINES,TRANSPORT EQUIP		31.5		31.9		35.2		43.8	MACHINES MATERIEL TRANSPORT
8	MISC MANUFACTURED GOODS		265.6		334.1		416.7		492.2	ART MANUFACTURES DIVERS
84	CLOTHING AND ACCESSORIES		189.6		202.1		256.8		325.8	VETEMENTS
845	OUTERWEAR KNIT NONELASTC	W 4316	79.2	W 3090	71.6	W 3522	90.8	W 3852	99.1	VET DESSOUS,ACCES BONNET
8451	— JERSEYS,PULLOVERS ETC	W 808	37.3	W 1360	34.6	W 1644	44.8	W 2215	56.7	CHANDAILS,PULL–OVERS ETC
8459	— OTHER,CLTHG ACCESRYS	W 3479	41.1	W 1654	34.5	W 1754	42.3	W 1492	37.7	AUT VET DESSUS DE BONNE
846	UNDER GARMENTS KNITTED	W 3317	95.0	W 5460	114.5	W 6481	143.2	W 7875	193.2	SOUS VETS DE BONNETERIE
8462	— OF COTTON NON ELASTIC	W 2105	56.7	W 4172	84.3	W 3550	69.3	W 3580	81.5	SOUS–VET BONNET COTON
84629	—— OTHER	W 2105	56.7	W 4172	84.3	W 3550	69.3	W 3580	81.5	AUT SOUS–VET BONNET COTON
8463	— OF SYNTH FBR NONELAST	W 1211	38.3	W 1287	30.1	W 2930	73.9	W 4293	111.7	SOUS–VET BONNET FIB SYNT
84632	—— MENS SHIRTS	W 1211	38.3	W 1286	30.1	W 2930	73.9	W 4289	111.7	CHEMISES DE BON FIB SYNMT
89	MISC MANUFCTRD GOODS NES		69.8		126.5		145.1		154.5	ART MANUFACTURES DIVERS
897	GOLD,SILVER WARE,JEWELRY		59.5		111.4		126.6		129.5	BIJOUTERIE,ORFEVRERIE
8973	PREC JEWLRY,GLD–SILVWARE		54.8		106.7		101.9		82.9	BIJOUX OR,ARGENT ORFEVRE
89731	PRECIOUS METAL JEWELLERY		52.5		104.6		99.2		55.0	ART BIJOUTERIE,JOAILLER
89732	GOLD,SILVER,ETC WARE		2.2		2.1		2.6		27.9	ORFEVRERIE MET PRECIEUX
8974	PREC MTL INDUS,LAB EQUIP		0.1		0.1		19.3		38.0	AUT OUV METAUX PRECIEUX
9	GOODS NOT CLASSD BY KIND		341.7		464.3		611.5		645.8	ART TRANSACT NON CLASSES
971	*GOLD,NON MONETARY NES	K 33919	340.6	K 49051	463.0	K 67105	609.2	K 111158	644.9	OR NON MONETAIRE
97101	NONMON GLD UNWRT,SEMIMFD	K 33919	340.6	K 49029	463.0	K 66383	601.3	K 105752	598.3	OR,ALLIAGES D'OR BRUTS
97102	ROLLED GLD UNWKD,SEMIMFD			K 22	0.1	K 722	7.9	K 5406	46.7	MET COMMUNS PLAQUES OR

1. HISTORICAL SERIES, 1962–1997 GENERAL TRADE, IMPORTS C.I.F., EXPORTS F.O.B.
SERIES HISTORIQUES, 1962–1997 COMMERCE GENERAL, IMPORTATIONS C.A.F., EXPORTATIONS F.O.B

YEAR ANNEE	VALUE IN MILLION U.S. DOLLARS VALEUR EN MILLION U.S. DOLLARS MERCHANDISE –MARCHANDISE IMPORTS	EXPORTS	GOLD –OR IMPORTS	EXPORTS	CONVERSION FACTORS FACTEURS DE CONVERSION CENTS E.U. PAR IMPORTS	EXPORTS	INDEX NUMBERS –INDICES QUANTUM IMPORTS	EXPORTS	UNIT VALUE VALEUR UNITAIRE IMPORTS	EXPORTS
1962	655.20	580.30	5.83	20.79						
1963	716.40	770.60		8.86						
1964	890.30	779.40		8.62						
1965	928.00	795.70		1.56						
1966	1177.70	877.40		16.10						
1967	1178.70	891.50		16.75						
1968	1331.40	962.10		16.15						
1969	1327.20	983.20		18.44						
1970	1286.20	1142.20		22.87						
1971	1404.80	1189.30		11.45						
1972	1485.00	1168.40		8.96						
1973	1789.50	1837.20		39.15						
1974	3467.60	2725.00		48.06						
1975	3776.20	2294.50		53.50						
1976	3953.30	2573.70		65.35						
1977	4269.80	3150.90		71.27						
1978	5143.40	3424.90		75.74						
1979	6612.90	4601.20		103.28						
1980	8295.20	5787.80		238.38			63	62	32	36
1981	7945.70	5722.20		210.70			58	63	38	37
1982	8255.30	5020.60					66	66	35	34
1983	7979.50	5005.30					63	63	46	46
1984	6051.20	5321.60					45	62	78	76
1985	5445.00	4629.00					41	60	81	75
1986	5134.29	4841.78					49	70	73	73
1987	6811.48	5720.24					64	75	74	80
1988	8731.40	7034.80					78	83	76	91
1989	10732.07	7746.74					93	93	83	92
1990	13041.00	8067.90					100	100	100	100
1991	12785.70	8767.10					102	103	108	115
1992	15449.20	9751.50								
1993	18754.40	11088.70								
1994	22545.50	13304.00								
1995	28336.70	17501.81								
1996	34121.90	20416.80								
1997		25088.00								

2. IMPORTS BY BROAD ECONOMIC CATEGORY AND EXPORTS BY INDUSTRIAL ORIGIN. (PERCENTAGE OF TOTAL VALUE)
IMPORTATIONS PAR CATEGORIES ECONOMIQUES ET EXPORTATIONS PAR BRANCHE D'ACTIVITE.(EN POURCENTAGE DE LA VALEUR TOTALE)

IMPORTS – IMPORTATIONS

	1990	1991	1992	1993	1994	1995	1996
TOTAL IMPORTS–IMPORTATIONS TOTALES	100.	100.	100.	100.	100.	100.	100.
1 FOOD BEV–ALIMENTATION BOISSONS	7.8	6.3	6.3	5.7	6.2	6.6	6.9
11 PRIMARY–PRODUITS DE BASE	3.3	3.2	3.2	2.9	3.2	3.0	2.8
111 FOR INDUSTRY–POUR L'INDUSTRIE	2.4	2.1	2.2	2.0	2.2	2.0	1.8
112 FOR HOUSEHOLDS–POUR LES MENAGES	0.9	1.1	1.0	0.8	1.0	0.9	0.9
12 PROCESSED–PRODUITS ELABORES	4.5	3.1	3.1	2.8	3.1	3.7	4.1
121 FOR INDUSTRY–POUR L'INDUSTRIE	0.8	0.7	0.7	0.5	0.5	0.7	1.0
122 FOR HOUSEHOLDS–POUR LES MENAGES	3.7	2.4	2.4	2.4	2.5	2.9	3.1
2 IND SUPPLIES–APPROV INDUSTRIELS	33.1	39.9	32.0	30.5	28.9	28.7	28.2
21 PRIMARY–PRODUITS DE BASE	4.3	5.3	3.8	3.3	3.3	3.5	3.4
22 PROCESSED–PRODUITS ELABORES	28.8	34.6	28.2	27.2	25.6	25.2	24.8
3 FUELS–COMBUSTIBLES	14.8	15.0	13.8	11.3	9.4	9.1	9.2
31 PRIMARY–PRODUITS DE BASE	13.5	12.8	11.8	8.4	6.9	8.1	8.3
32 PROCESSED–PRODUITS ELABORES	1.4	2.2	1.9	3.0	2.5	1.0	0.8
321 MOTOR SPIRIT–ESSENCE	0.0	0.0	0.0	0.2	0.3	0.2	0.2
322 OTHER–AUTRES	1.3	2.2	1.9	2.8	2.2	0.8	0.6
4 MACHINERY–EQUIPEMENT	18.0	27.7	20.6	22.6	25.5	23.3	41.4
41 CAPITAL EQUIPMENT–MACHINES	13.3	14.0	14.9	17.1	19.5	17.2	20.0
42 PARTS–PIECES ACCESSOIRES	4.7	13.7	5.7	5.5	6.0	6.1	21.4
5 TRANSPORT–TRANSPORT	7.7	6.8	7.4	10.0	7.5	8.7	9.7
51 PASSENGER CARS–AUTOMOBILES	1.4	1.8	1.9	2.1	2.4	2.4	2.3
52 OTHER–AUTRES	3.0	2.9	3.2	4.4	1.8	2.9	4.6
521 INDUSTRIAL–INDUSTRIELS	2.7	2.7	2.9	4.0	1.4	2.6	4.1
522 NON INDUSTRIAL–NON INDUSTRIEL	0.3	0.2	0.3	0.4	0.4	0.4	0.4
53 PARTS–PIECES ACCESSOIRES	3.3	2.1	2.4	3.4	3.4	3.4	2.9
6 CONSUM GOODS–BIENS CONSOMMATION	2.8	4.0	3.5	3.8	4.3	4.3	4.6
61 DURABLE–DURABLES	0.5	0.7	0.7	0.7	0.9	1.1	1.2
62 SEMI DURABLE–SEMI DURABLES	1.0	1.9	1.3	1.5	1.5	1.7	1.9
63 NON DURABLE–NON DURABLES	1.3	1.4	1.4	1.6	1.8	1.5	1.4
7 GOODS NES–BIENS NDA	15.8	0.4	16.4	16.1	18.2	19.3	0.1

EXPORTS – EXPORTATIONS

	1990	1991	1992	1993	1994	1995	1996
TOTAL EXPORTS–EXPORTATIONS TOTALES	100.	100.	100.	100.	100.	100.	100.
1 AGRICULTURE	8.8	9.5	7.6	7.7	6.8	5.7	4.6
2 MINING QUARRY–INDUS EXTRACTIVES	4.9	5.0	4.4	2.9	2.5	2.1	1.7
3 MANUFACTURING–IND MANUFACTUR	86.3	85.6	87.9	89.4	90.7	92.2	93.7
31 FOOD BEV TOBACCO–ALIM BOISS TAB	11.3	10.4	10.6	8.8	8.2	8.2	6.3
32 TEXTILES–INDUSTRIES TEXTILES	10.8	24.8	11.6	10.5	10.2	9.1	15.1
33 WOOD & PRODUCTS–BOIS & PRODUITS	2.6	2.8	1.7	1.4	1.2	1.0	1.0
34 PAPER & PRODUCTS–PAPIER & PRODT	0.5	0.6	0.6	0.6	0.5	0.5	0.5
35 CHEMICALS–INDUSTRIES CHIMIQUES	5.5	6.4	4.6	3.9	3.6	3.4	3.8
36 NON METAL MIN–MIN NON METAL	0.7	0.9	0.8	0.8	0.7	0.6	0.5
37 BASIC METAL–IND METAL BASE	4.6	3.4	2.7	3.0	2.7	3.0	2.3
38 METAL MANUF–MANUF METAL	15.5	32.3	19.7	22.0	24.8	25.1	61.6
39 OTH MANUF IND–AUTRES MANUF	34.9	4.1	35.4	38.3	38.7	41.2	2.5

3. TRADE BY PRINCIPAL COUNTRIES OF ORIGIN AND DESTINATION (VALUE IN MILLION U.S. DOLLARS)
ECHANGES SELON LES PRINCIPAUX PAYS D'ORIGINE ET DE DESTINATION (VALEUR EN MILLIONS DE DOLLARS EU)

COUNTRIES–PAYS	GENERAL IMPORTS C.I.F. IMPORTATIONS GENERALES C.A.F					COUNTRIES–PAYS	GENERAL EXPORTS F.O.B. EXPORTATIONS GENERALES F.O.B.				
	1992	1993	1994	1995	1996		1992	1993	1994	1995	1996
World	15465.3	18772.7	22738.0	28487.3	34701.2	Monde	9824.3	11374.8	13482.9	17447.2	20542.5
Africa	121.0	173.0	122.8	174.7	161.1	Afrique	29.3	40.5	51.4	44.0	63.0
Americas	3341.6	4269.3	4769.2	6151.5	7712.1	Amériques	4134.3	4703.6	5525.2	6638.8	7406.0
– Northern America	3043.1	3929.4	4342.5	5658.7	7058.4	– Amérique du Nord	4003.4	4579.3	5390.1	6447.3	7244.0
– LAIA	297.4	318.0	418.7	471.5	645.1	– ALAI	53.0	72.4	77.6	114.7	116.4
– CACM	0.5	0.5	0.7	16.2	2.5	– MCAC	0.5	0.8	0.7	0.6	1.3
– Caribbean	0.2	21.1	6.7	3.6	3.7	– Caraïbes	29.3	15.7	17.1	26.8	12.5
– Rest of America	0.4	0.3	0.7	1.6	2.5	– Autre Amérique	48.1	35.4	39.7	49.3	31.9
Asia excl fmr USSR	9217.8	11162.6	13992.3	17302.9	20810.6	Asie anc. URSS exclus	3553.9	4401.2	5286.8	7426.9	9170.8
– Middle East	1575.4	1396.2	1466.5	2229.4	2723.0	– Moyen–Orient	193.9	247.4	217.2	209.9	225.1
Asia former USSR		0.9	4.3	0.2	0.4	Asie ancienne URSS					0.0
Europe excl fmr USSR	2053.6	2288.3	2712.1	3263.1	4261.6	Europe anc. URSS exclus	1944.9	2061.7	2407.9	3128.6	3669.8
– European Union	1859.9	2051.5	2506.5	3035.1	3868.6	– Union Européenne	1906.0	2016.9	2358.6	3073.4	3602.9
– Eastern Europe	100.0	120.2	72.8	38.4	94.2	– Europe de l'Est	4.8	8.6	10.5	13.3	17.9
– Rest of Europe	93.7	116.6	132.8	189.6	298.8	– Autre de l'Europe	34.0	36.1	38.8	41.9	49.0
Europe former USSR	100.5	112.8	267.6	500.2	562.5	Europe ancienne URSS	7.8	11.7	20.2	11.8	16.3
Oceania	630.7	765.8	869.7	1092.1	1192.6	Océanie	153.7	156.1	187.8	197.1	216.6
Other	0.1		0.0	2.6	0.4	Autre	0.5		3.5	0.0	
Japan/Japon	3277.4	4283.0	5561.4	6304.7	7578.2	USA/Etats–Unis d'Amer	3843.3	4384.8	5194.2	6245.1	7037.8
USA/Etats–Unis d'Amer	2823.8	3763.4	4187.9	5386.4	6770.8	Japan/Japon	1745.0	1827.0	2034.7	2747.5	3671.2
Other Asia n.e.s.	996.8	1071.6	1280.9	1543.3	1708.0	Singapore/Singapour	252.3	379.5	708.5	995.7	1223.5
Singapore/Singapour	575.0	1016.1	1494.3	1636.0	1826.5	United Kingdom	466.8	540.5	638.6	923.2	936.4
Saudi Arabia	921.4	796.5	994.3	1718.7	1751.2	China, Hong Kong SAR	463.7	548.2	651.4	824.0	868.3
Korea, Republic of	740.0	943.7	1172.4	1429.3	1785.9	Germany/Allemagne	521.7	586.0	665.3	699.1	847.0
China, Hong Kong SAR	745.4	913.8	1164.8	1385.0	1459.0	Netherlands/Pays–Bas	406.3	361.8	516.1	805.1	1114.6
Germany/Allemagne	702.3	647.2	797.6	977.1	1283.1	Other Asia n.e.s.	286.8	346.1	452.8	568.5	661.2
Australia/Australie	458.2	534.5	639.0	828.5	887.4	Thailand/Thaïlande	98.4	168.7	363.8	798.9	780.1
Malaysia/Malaisie	409.8	378.2	458.1	623.7	857.6	Malaysia/Malaisie	127.8	161.1	222.1	315.4	687.1
Indonesia/Indonésie	196.5	368.1	399.4	620.7	707.9	Korea, Republic of	175.8	221.0	292.1	443.7	370.7
United Kingdom	313.8	393.4	406.3	573.4	506.3	France, Monaco	178.9	208.9	185.0	203.2	227.7
China/Chine	200.2	201.9	332.9	660.8	763.4	China/Chine	113.9	173.9	164.5	214.0	327.9
Thailand/Thaïlande	146.0	189.5	212.2	427.9	660.4	Canada	159.8	194.1	195.8	202.1	205.8
Netherlands/Pays–Bas	192.0	249.0	294.9	343.5	358.3	Australia/Australie	112.6	114.4	139.8	143.3	160.8
France, Monaco	223.2	215.4	258.0	323.3	417.1	United Arab Emirates	110.5	149.7	130.2	105.1	124.0
Russian Federation	98.7	106.8	216.2	406.8	530.6	Belgium–Luxembourg	76.8	94.1	97.2	105.4	107.7
Brazil/Brésil	211.3	235.4	282.2	290.9	338.6	Italy/Italie	99.5	85.5	90.5	111.2	93.9
United Arab Emirates	276.4	272.2	230.2	184.0	318.2	Indonesia/Indonésie	40.3	48.3	71.1	129.1	142.5
Canada	219.3	166.0	154.6	272.2	287.6	Viet Nam	29.7	37.4	62.5	123.6	130.0
Italy/Italie	125.7	143.2	178.9	244.4	325.0	Spain/Espagne	69.7	50.3	55.1	79.5	88.8
Belgium–Luxembourg	99.7	118.1	245.9	192.1	236.8	India/Inde	8.6	225.6	13.0	20.2	36.6
Israel/Israël	101.2	170.2	203.7	162.5	183.9	Saudi Arabia	57.0	68.1	58.7	64.9	54.6
India/Inde	95.4	123.2	148.2	176.1	242.0	Panama	47.4	35.3	39.6	49.1	31.7
Iran (Islamic Rep of)	173.7	72.5	71.2	114.9	298.3	Mexico/Mexique	21.3	35.0	39.9	38.7	36.0
Switzerland,Liechtenst.	86.9	112.6	125.2	177.4	208.4	Ireland/Irlande	9.4	13.1	20.9	53.9	67.8
New Zealand	101.4	133.2	136.7	147.0	171.3	Switzerland,Liechtenst.	21.6	27.1	28.1	27.5	34.2
Sweden/Suède	29.2	68.2	76.7	104.9	224.2	Chile/Chili	17.5	17.5	16.9	33.9	39.4
Kuwait/ Koweït	86.8	202.3	86.8	35.6	20.4	Denmark/Danemark	20.3	23.5	24.0	26.9	28.3
Ireland/Irlande	30.4	34.8	36.8	78.8	246.2	So. African Customs Un	8.5	19.0	29.2	24.3	30.3
Papua New Guinea	59.5	82.1	77.7	88.4	102.0	Sweden/Suède	23.6	17.0	17.9	20.2	24.5
Finland/Finlande	22.2	85.5	82.8	64.0	96.9	New Zealand	12.5	13.8	18.2	22.3	20.5
Spain/Espagne	65.9	43.7	61.7	64.5	86.6	US Misc Pacific Islands	16.3	13.4	15.9	17.2	16.8
So. African Customs Un	24.5	76.2	54.9	65.1	75.6	Finland/Finlande	7.4	9.7	19.7	14.4	27.2
Oman	0.0	0.3	25.1	88.8	178.5	Austria/Autriche	11.2	14.4	15.5	13.7	19.8
Chile/Chili	49.3	38.6	47.7	44.2	111.0	Netherlands Antilles	23.8	11.9	13.4	18.4	6.0
Viet Nam	15.8	13.7	16.9	42.9	196.9	Egypt/Egypte	9.7	11.7	11.8	10.6	21.7
Poland/Pologne	61.3	71.4	35.7	14.5	60.7	Russian Federation	7.8	10.4	20.2	11.4	15.4
Brunei Darussalam	94.0	52.0	36.3	7.9	0.4	Brazil/Brésil	4.3	5.3	9.3	20.9	13.4
Qatar	77.1	28.8	23.8	15.5	44.7	Kuwait/ Koweït	6.9	10.2	8.6	9.8	17.7

(VALUE AS PERCENTAGE OF WORLD TOTAL)(VALEURS EN POURCENTAGE DU TOTAL MONDIAL)

	1987	1988	1989	1990	1991	1992	1993	1994	1995	1996		1987	1988	1989	1990	1991	1992	1993	1994	1995	1996
Africa	1.3	1.1	1.0	0.7	0.5	0.8	0.9	0.5	0.6	0.5	Afrique	0.3	0.3	0.3	0.3	0.3	0.3	0.4	0.4	0.3	0.3
Americas	24.7	24.2	23.9	23.7	23.9	21.6	22.7	21.0	21.6	22.2	Amériques	38.5	37.9	40.7	40.3	38.4	42.1	41.4	41.0	38.1	36.1
– Northern America	23.3	22.2	20.7	21.0	21.6	19.7	20.9	19.1	19.9	20.3	– Amérique du Nord	37.6	37.2	39.4	39.4	37.3	40.7	40.3	40.0	37.0	35.3
– LAIA	1.5	2.0	3.2	2.7	2.3	1.9	1.7	1.8	1.7	1.9	– ALAI	0.1	0.1	0.4	0.2	0.4	0.5	0.6	0.6	0.7	0.6
– CACM	0.0	0.0	0.0	0.0	0.0	0.0	0.0	0.0	0.1	0.0	– MCAC	0.0	0.0	0.0	0.0	0.0	0.0	0.0	0.0	0.0	0.0
– Caribbean	0.0	0.0	0.0	0.0	0.0	0.0	0.1	0.0	0.0	0.0	– Caraïbes	0.1	0.1	0.2	0.3	0.2	0.3	0.1	0.1	0.2	0.1
– Rest of America	0.0	0.0	0.0	0.0	0.0	0.0	0.0	0.0	0.0	0.0	– Autre Amérique	0.6	0.5	0.7	0.5	0.5	0.5	0.3	0.3	0.3	0.2
Asia excl fmr USSR	56.0	54.6	57.1	58.2	58.6	59.6	59.5	61.5	60.7	60.0	Asie anc. URSS exclus	38.9	40.7	38.9	38.9	40.0	36.2	38.7	39.2	42.6	44.6
– Middle East	12.2	9.0	9.4	11.5	10.0	10.2	7.4	6.4	7.8	7.8	– Moyen–Orient	1.7	1.3	1.5	1.6	1.6	2.0	2.2	1.6	1.2	1.1
Asia former USSR							0.0	0.0	0.0	0.0	Asie ancienne URSS										0.0
Europe excl fmr USSR	13.8	14.6	13.0	12.9	12.2	13.3	12.2	11.9	11.5	12.3	Europe anc. URSS exclus	19.9	18.4	17.7	18.6	19.5	19.8	18.1	17.9	17.9	17.9
– European Union	12.2	13.2	11.9	11.7	10.8	12.0	10.9	11.0	10.7	11.1	– Union Européenne	19.4	18.1	17.4	18.2	19.1	19.4	17.7	17.5	17.6	17.5
– Eastern Europe	0.5	0.4	0.5	0.5	0.6	0.6	0.6	0.3	0.1	0.3	– Europe de l'Est	0.1	0.0	0.0	0.0	0.1	0.0	0.1	0.1	0.1	0.1
– Rest of Europe	1.2	1.0	0.6	0.7	0.8	0.6	0.6	0.6	0.7	0.9	– Autre de l'Europe	0.3	0.3	0.3	0.3	0.3	0.3	0.3	0.3	0.2	0.2
Europe former USSR	0.2	0.4	0.2	0.2	0.3	0.6	0.6	1.2	1.8	1.6	Europe ancienne URSS	0.5	0.3	0.3	0.2	0.2	0.1	0.1	0.1	0.1	0.1
Oceania	3.9	5.1	4.8	4.3	4.5	4.1	4.1	3.8	3.8	3.4	Océanie	2.1	2.4	2.1	1.6	1.6	1.6	1.4	1.4	1.1	1.1
Other	0.0			0.0		0.0		0.0	0.0	0.0	Autre	0.0			0.0		0.0		0.0	0.0	
Japan/Japon	16.9	17.4	19.5	18.4	19.6	21.2	22.8	24.5	22.1	21.8	USA/Etats–Unis d'Amer	36.2	35.7	37.8	37.9	35.7	39.1	38.5	38.5	35.8	34.3
USA/Etats–Unis d'Amer	22.0	21.2	19.1	19.5	20.3	18.3	20.0	18.4	18.9	19.5	Japan/Japon	17.2	20.1	20.3	19.8	20.0	17.8	16.1	15.1	15.7	17.9
Other Asia n.e.s.	5.5	6.1	6.5	6.4	6.6	6.4	5.7	5.6	5.4	4.9	Singapore/Singapour	3.4	3.2	2.8	2.9	2.6	2.6	3.3	5.3	5.7	6.0
Singapore/Singapour	3.4	4.0	4.7	3.9	3.7	3.7	5.4	6.6	5.7	5.3	United Kingdom	4.3	4.6	4.2	4.3	4.2	4.8	4.8	4.7	5.3	4.6
Saudi Arabia	3.2	1.4	2.4	4.4	5.4	6.0	4.2	4.4	6.0	5.0	China, Hong Kong SAR	4.9	4.9	3.9	4.0	4.4	4.7	4.8	4.8	4.7	4.2
Korea, Republic of	2.9	4.0	4.0	3.8	5.0	4.8	5.0	5.2	5.0	5.1	Germany/Allemagne					5.7	5.3	5.2	4.9	4.0	4.1
China, Hong Kong SAR	4.6	4.4	4.5	4.4	4.8	4.8	4.9	5.1	4.9	4.2	Netherlands/Pays–Bas	5.4	4.5	4.2	4.4	3.8	4.1	3.2	3.8	4.6	5.4
Germany/Allemagne					3.8	4.5	3.4	3.5	3.4	3.7	Other Asia n.e.s.	2.5	2.8	2.7	2.6	2.4	2.9	3.0	3.4	3.3	3.2
Australia/Australie	3.0	3.6	3.5	3.1	3.3	3.0	2.8	2.8	2.9	2.6	Thailand/Thaïlande	2.2	1.7	2.0	1.9	2.5	1.0	1.5	2.7	4.6	3.8
Malaysia/Malaisie	4.0	3.0	2.5	2.2	2.5	2.6	2.0	2.0	2.2	2.5	Malaysia/Malaisie	2.1	1.7	1.3	1.5	1.4	1.3	1.4	1.6	1.8	3.3

4. General Imports C.I.F. by Commodities according to the S.I.T.C. (Rev. 2) in million U.S. Dollars
Importations Générales C.A.F. par Produits d'après la C.T.C.I. (Rév. 2) en millions de Dollars E.U.

SITC CTCI	COMMODITY	1993 QUANTITY QUANTITE	1993 VALUE VALEUR	1994 QUANTITY QUANTITE	1994 VALUE VALEUR	1995 QUANTITY QUANTITE	1995 VALUE VALEUR	1996 QUANTITY QUANTITE	1996 VALUE VALEUR	PRODUIT
	ALL COMMODITIES		18772.7		22738.0		28487.4		34701.3	TOUS PRODUITS
0	FOOD AND LIVE ANIMALS		1267.6		1505.9		2107.3		2548.9	ALIMENTS,ANIMAUX VIVANTS
001	*LIVE ANIMALS FOR FOOD	W 26571	43.7	N 1119330	53.6	N 2254861	88.1	W 53129	84.9	ANIMAUX VIVANTS
01	MEAT AND PREPARATIONS		32.9		66.1		79.6		109.5	VIANDES ET PREPARATIONS
02	DAIRY PRODCTS,BIRDS'EGGS		272.7		332.1		438.9		404.2	PRODUITS LAITIERS,OEUFS
022	MILK AND CREAM	W 148031	230.4	W 182944	278.9	W 201838	379.1	W 191069	342.2	LAIT ET CREME
0224	MILK,CREAM PRESERVED ETC	W 127385	202.2	W 154707	243.3	W 166333	330.8	W 151480	293.8	LAIT,CREME CONS,CONC
02242	MILK DRY,1.5% FAT OR LES	W 77031	130.9	W 88424	146.9	W 103592	229.9	W 83237	177.9	LAIT POUDRE INF 1.5%
02243	MILK DRY,OVER 1.5% FAT	W 29123	57.2	W 35379	74.0	W 34239	80.3	W 36982	90.2	LAIT POUDRE SUP 1.5%
04	CEREALS AND PREPARATIONS		425.9		516.8		688.6		1051.5	CEREALES ET PRODUITS
041	WHEAT ETC UNMILLED	W 1802564	297.8	W 2146889	368.9	W 2101745	409.6	W 1887093	427.0	FROMENT,EPEAUTRE
0412	OTHER WHEAT ETC UNMILLED	W 1802564	297.8	W 2146889	368.9	W 2101745	409.6	W 1887093	427.0	AUTRE FROMENT NON MOULU
042	RICE	W 203943	37.2	W 1638	0.7	W 263251	82.8	W 866949	309.0	RIZ
0422	RICE SEMI-MILLED,MILLED	W 203943	37.2	W 1638	0.7	W 263248	82.8	W 866949	309.0	RIZ POLI,GLACE INCL BRISURES
04221	RICE MILLED UNBROKEN	W 203943	37.2	W 1638	0.7	W 263248	82.8	W 866905	309.0	RIZ POLI,GLACE EXCL BRISURES
048	CEREAL ETC PREPARATIONS	W 166529	82.8	W 222654	132.1	W 192809	145.3	W 189449	166.4	PREPTNS A BASE CEREALES
05	VEGETABLES AND FRUIT		74.1		118.0		122.5		151.3	LEGUMES ET FRUITS
06	SUGAR AND PREPS,HONEY		25.6		43.8		190.8		287.3	SUCRES ET PRODUITS
061	SUGAR AND HONEY	W 45738	23.5	W 71529	36.0	W 464846	176.8	W 904423	280.0	SUCRES ET MIEL
0611	RAW BEET AND CANE SUGAR					W 235754	87.5	W 439371	135.7	SUCRES BRUTS
081	*FEEDING STUFF FOR ANIML	W 973498	276.3	W 812597	227.4	W 1094516	313.5	W 595511	230.5	NOURRITURE POUR ANIMAUX
0813	OILCAKE AND OTH RESIDUES	W 828591	206.6	W 657120	151.2	W 901335	204.4	W 446194	117.0	TOURTEAUX
08131	— OF SOYA BEANS	W 825710	206.2	W 655066	150.9	W 898392	204.0	W 431147	112.9	TOURTEAUX DE SOJA
1	BEVERAGES AND TOBACCO		136.2		237.4		169.5		123.1	BOISSONS ET TABACS
12	TOBACCO AND MANUFACTURES		98.6		183.0		123.1		82.1	TABACS BRUTS FABRIQUES
121	TOBACCO UNMNFCTRD,REFUSE	W 14410	57.3	W 26642	93.6	W 25233	91.2	W 15318	72.1	TABACS BRUTS,DECHETS
1212	TOBACCO STRIPPED OR PART	W 14409	57.2	W 26642	93.6	W 25190	91.1	W 15305	71.9	TABACS PART ECOTES
122	TOBACCO,MANUFACTURED	W 4951	41.4	W 9833	89.5	W 4418	31.9	W 1168	10.1	TABACS FABRIQUES
1222	CIGARETTES	W 4949	41.4	W 9789	89.0	W 4413	31.8	W 1154	9.8	CIGARETTES
2	CRUDE MATERLS,EXCL FUELS		775.1		977.4		1236.3		1474.8	MAT BRUTES NON COMESTIBLES
24	CORK AND WOOD		127.8		123.0		164.5		289.2	LIEGE ET BOIS
247	OTH WOOD ROUGH,SQUARED	W 480975	82.5	W 300896	56.3	W 513120	82.1	W 728411	126.5	BOIS BRUTS EQUARRIS
2472	SAW-,VENEER-LOGS NON-CON	W 396039	57.2	W 270751	47.5	W 399784	62.7	W 630957	105.2	NON CONIFERES SCIAGE,PLAC
24721	— IN THE ROUGH	W 396039	57.2	W 270751	47.5	W 399784	62.7	W 630957	105.2	BRUTS ECORCES DEGROSSIS
248	WOOD SHAPED,SLEEPERS	W 201476	45.3	W 207948	66.7	W 259623	82.3	W 461988	162.4	BOIS SIMPLEMENT TRAVAILLES
2483	LUMBER SHAPED NON-CONIFR	W 198709	44.0	W 201322	63.3	W 227468	67.3	W 394861	118.4	NON CONIFERES SCIES,RABOTES
24831	LUMBER SAWN ETC NON-CON	W 198705	44.0	W 201235	63.2	W 227465	67.3	W 394825	118.3	SCIES LONGITUDINALEMENT
251	*PULP AND WASTE PAPER	W 323450	81.0	W 322009	79.4	W 360088	139.1	W 351006	114.0	PATES A PAPIER,DECHETS
26	TEXTILE FIBRES AND WASTE		156.4		241.0		248.3		272.5	FIBRES TEXTILES
263	COTTON	W 59194	72.3	W 76673	114.0	W 61605	116.7	W 77824	143.6	COTON
2631	RAW COTTON,EXCL LINTERS	W 55299	69.9	W 74102	111.6	W 59295	113.4	W 75228	140.8	COTON EN MASSE
266	SYNTHETIC FIBRES TO SPIN	W 34474	47.8	W 45052	73.2	W 37997	74.0	W 52886	71.3	FIBRES SYNTHETIQUES
2665	DISCN SYNTH FIBRE UNCMBD	W 32433	42.7	W 43255	68.8	W 36416	69.6	W 50558	66.3	DISCONTINUES EN MASSE
27	CRUDE FERTLZR,MINRLS NES		74.3		101.2		149.2		144.8	ENGRAIS MINERAUX BRUTS
28	METALLIFEROUS ORES,SCRAP		244.1		318.4		412.9		505.2	MINERAIS METAL,DECHETS
287	BASE METAL ORES,CONC NES	W 383977	234.0	W 429687	312.3	W 532280	402.4	W 533170	382.4	MINERAIS METAUX COMMUNS
2871	CPR ORE ETC,CEMENT COPPR	W 371318	229.7	W 420065	307.8	W 499033	394.3	W 509068	373.6	MINERAIS DE CUIVRE,MATTES
28711	COPPER ORES,EXCL MATTE	W 371318	229.7	W 420065	307.8	W 499033	394.3	W 509068	373.6	MINERAIS DE CUIVRE
3	MINERAL FUELS ETC		2167.0		2166.0		2629.5		3200.2	COMBUSTIBLES MINERAUX LUB
32	COAL,COKE AND BRIQUETTES		57.7		44.7		80.5		126.1	HOUILLES,COKES,BRIQUETTES
322	COAL,LIGNITE AND PEAT	W 925979	51.7	W 1061580	38.2	W 1629454	66.6	W 3356925	112.2	HOUILLES,LIGNITES,TOURBE
33	PETROLEUM AND PRODUCTS		1952.2		1942.2		2324.9		2849.5	PETROLE ET DERIVES
333	CRUDE PETROLEUM	MW 11251	1366.4	MW 11764	1350.7	MW 15975	2010.4	MW 17065	2555.2	HUILES BRUTES DE PETROLE
334	PETROLEUM PRODUCTS,REFIN	W 2897321	549.2	W 3657277	567.1	W 1374175	282.1	W 1263858	267.4	PRODUITS RAFFINES
3341	GASOLINE,OTH LIGHT OILS	W 142614	32.6	W 332210	72.9	W 230696	67.1	W 242454	56.6	ESSENCES POUR MOTEURS
3343	GAS OILS	W 2310519	426.5	W 2002085	324.9	W 585391	100.0	W 535458	117.6	GAS OILS
3344	FUEL OILS,NES	W 357469	30.4	W 1176243	115.9	W 463698	56.4	W 427632	55.4	FUEL OILS
341	*GAS,NATURAL AND MANUFCT	W 882953	157.2	W 1100668	179.1	W 1066188	224.2	W 960734	224.7	GAZ NATUREL,GAZ MANUFACT
3413	PETROLM GASES,LIQUEFIED	W 882953	157.2	W 1100659	179.1	W 1066186	224.2	W 960711	224.6	GAZ DE PETROLE LIQUEFIE
34131	LIQUEFIED PROPANE,BUTANE	W 744666	120.8	W 962210	151.8	W 957623	196.3	W 835992	192.9	PROPANE,BUTANE LIQUEFIES
5	CHEMCLS,RELATED PROD NES		1784.3		2151.0		2566.4		2833.9	PRODUITS CHIMIQUES
51	ORGANIC CHEMICALS		343.5		384.7		488.1		463.2	PROD CHIMIQ ORGANIQUES
511	HYDROCARBONS NES,DERIVS	W 97330	56.6	W 95513	64.2	W 103714	90.3	W 122763	74.5	HYDROCARBURES NDA
513	CARBOXYLIC ACIDS ETC	W 94021	86.8	W 96309	94.7	W 93319	124.1	W 83405	107.4	ACIDES CARBOXYLIQUES
514	NITROGEN-FNCTN COMPOUNDS	W 24128	66.7	W 23390	80.3	W 27948	103.3	W 32950	112.5	COMPOSES FONCT AZOTEES
52	INORGANIC CHEMICALS		172.0		190.7		244.8		261.0	PROD CHIM INORGANIQUES
522	INORG ELEMNTS,OXIDES,ETC	W 438716	82.9	W 513690	86.9	W 406979	111.1	W 525429	118.1	ELEMENTS INORGANIQUES
523	OTHR INORG CHEMICALS ETC	W 284638	88.9	W 346321	103.3	W 419523	133.1	W 379091	142.3	AUT PRODUITS CHIMIQUES INORG
53	DYES,TANNING,COLOUR PROD		140.1		148.5		175.1		179.9	PROD TEINTURE,COLORANTS
531	SYNT DYE,NAT INDGO,LAKES	W 8641	60.0	W 8266	54.8	W 8612	58.0	W 8091	55.8	MAT COLOR ORGAN,LAQUES
533	PIGMENTS,PAINTS,ETC	W 37986	77.2	W 42849	90.7	W 46840	113.1	W 49820	120.8	PIGMENTS,PEINTURES,VERNIS
541	*MEDICINAL,PHARM PRODUCT	MK 11661	206.6	MK 12095	269.5	MK 11415	303.8	MK 15686	341.8	PROD MEDICINAUX PHARMACEUT
5417	MEDICAMENTS	K 7044269	112.6	K 8467024	165.8	K 6633596	184.5	K 8940545	223.4	MEDICAMENTS
54179	— CONTNG OTH SUBSTANCES	K 6349455	88.4	K 7718466	129.4	K 5539328	138.3	K 8043036	167.4	MED CONT AUT SUBSTANCES
55	PERFUME,CLEANING ETC PRD		108.8		126.4		155.2		160.6	PROD POUR PARFUM,TOILETTE
551	ESSENTL OILS,PERFUME,ETC	W 7095	62.1	W 7192	69.7	W 6596	81.5	W 7628	83.8	HUILES ESSENTIELLES
562	*FERTILIZERS,MANUFACTURE	W 1212873	147.5	W 1379070	199.8	W 1267879	227.9	W 1342922	243.3	ENGRAIS MANUFACTURES
5621	CHEM NITROGENOUS FERTLZR	W 796526	101.2	W 999814	137.5	W 906291	158.7	W 961674	170.5	ENGRAIS AZOTES
56216	UREA	W 596775	79.0	W 689279	102.3	W 630865	125.3	W 650415	124.9	UREE
58	PLASTIC MATERIALS ETC		458.8		590.6		710.6		848.0	MAT PLAST ARTIFICIELLES
582	PROD OF CONDENSATION ETC	W 30959	69.3	W 43142	92.1	W 42410	113.1	W 51603	143.7	PROD CONDENS,POLYCOND
583	POLYMERIZATION ETC PRODS	W 468600	373.7	W 567894	482.3	W 463617	578.7	W 637510	685.5	PROD POLYMERISATION
5831	POLYETHYLENE	W 172701	121.2	W 224150	165.4	W 161145	167.4	W 241144	221.4	POLYETHYLENE
58311	— IN PRIMARY FORMS	W 159818	108.0	W 218665	150.6	W 154632	150.1	W 231560	200.4	POLYETHYLENE PRIMAIRES
5832	POLYPROPYLENE	W 187063	122.7	W 184074	139.3	W 159865	183.2	W 202367	196.2	POLYPROPYLENE
58321	— IN PRIMARY FORMS	W 182974	115.3	W 177982	126.7	W 151953	161.6	W 189913	168.4	POLYPROPYLENE PRIMAIRES
5834	POLYVINYL CHLORIDE	W 59903	47.4	W 104291	79.8	W 75204	85.9	W 101885	89.6	CHLORURE DE POLYVINYLE
5839	OTH POLYMRZTION ETC PROD	W 27392	50.1	W 29480	58.0	W 38559	92.1	W 55956	121.3	AUT PROD POLYMER COPOLYM
59	CHEMICAL MATERIALS NES		204.2		237.8		257.3		332.6	MAT PROD CHIMIQUES NDA
598	MISCEL CHEM PRODUCTS NES	W 78878	139.3	W 79405	163.0	W 95196	169.4	W 125862	208.8	PROD DIV INDUST CHIM NDA
5989	CHEM PRODUCTS,PREPS NES	W 53101	100.0	W 56401	126.8	W 66819	121.5	W 94196	157.0	PROD PREP CHIMIQUES NDA
59899	OTH CHEM PRODS,PREPS,NES	W 32585	67.7	W 37938	87.1	W 40804	85.3	W 67283	113.5	AUT PRODUITS CHIMIQUES NDA
6	BASIC MANUFACTURES		2846.5		3178.0		4002.6		4919.5	ART MANUFACTURES
61	LEATHER,DRESSED FUR,ETC		99.4		95.0		93.7		126.0	CUIRS,PELLETERIES
611	LEATHER	W 5953	71.8	W 7114	68.1	W 6358	69.7	W 7607	94.6	CUIRS,PEAUX PREPARES
6114	LEATHR BOVINE NES,EQUINE	W 4755	61.8	W 4822	56.4	W 4437	60.1	W 5202	73.4	CUIRS DE BOVINS
62	RUBBER MANUFACTURES NES		116.9		130.9		165.1		222.2	CAOUTCHOUC MANUFACTURE
625	RUBBER TYRES, TUBES ETC	W 32600	72.5	N 5015734	81.9	N 6530425	111.0	W 65279	158.5	PNEUS CAOUTCHOUC VULCANISE
64	PAPER,PAPERBOARD AND MFR		223.2		306.6		363.3		403.8	PAPIERS,CARTONS & OUVRAGES
641	PAPER AND PAPERBOARD	W 310447	178.2	W 430161	245.0	W 392861	299.4	W 475544	310.7	PAPIERS ET CARTONS
6413	KRAFT PAPER,PAPERBOARD	W 108644	50.1	W 152527	70.8	W 137591	84.9	W 175456	90.8	PAPIER ET CARTON KRAFT

4. General Imports C.I.F. by Commodities according to the S.I.T.C. (Rev. 2) in million U.S. Dollars
Importations Générales C.A.F. par Produits d'après la C.T.C.I. (Rév. 2) en millions de Dollars E.U.

SITC CTCI	COMMODITY	1993 QUANTITY QUANTITE	1993 VALUE VALEUR	1994 QUANTITY QUANTITE	1994 VALUE VALEUR	1995 QUANTITY QUANTITE	1995 VALUE VALEUR	1996 QUANTITY QUANTITE	1996 VALUE VALEUR	PRODUIT
65	TEXTILE YARN,FABRICS,ETC		740.4		821.9		943.5		1256.3	FILS,TISSUS,ARTICLES TEXTILE
651	TEXTILE YARN	W 41693	110.3	W 39072	122.3	W 45008	160.5	W 50813	176.7	FILS TEXTILES
652	COTTON FABRICS,WOVEN	W 30297	151.6		166.1		205.3	W 39729	252.3	TISSUS DE COTON
6522	WOVEN COTTON BLEACHD,ETC	W 29421	149.0		162.3		200.1	W 38453	246.1	TISSUS COTON BLANCHIS ETC
65224	BLCHED COTTON FABRIC NES	W 27055	132.4		146.3		179.6	W 34578	215.2	AUT TIS PLUS 85% COT BLANCHI
653	WOVN MAN-MADE FIB FABRIC	W 22457	140.7		158.0		186.3	W 40405	274.2	TISSUS FIBRES SYNTH,ARTIF
6531	CONT SYNT WEAVES NONPILE	W 11059	74.2		72.7		91.0	W 23615	137.6	TISSUS FIBRES SYNTH CONTINUE
65315	CONT SYN TXTL FABRIC NES	W 10907	73.1		72.1		89.6	W 23328	135.8	TIS PLUS 85% TEXT SYNT CONT
655	KNITTED,ETC FABRICS		176.0	W 29408	197.2	W 30126	213.2	W 38055	261.6	ETOF BONNETERIE PIECES ETC
6552	OTHER KNIT ETC FAB NONEL		176.0	W 29408	197.2	W 30126	213.2	W 38055	261.6	ETOF BON NON ELAS NON SYNT
657	SPECIAL TXTL FABRC,PRODS	W 24064	98.8		111.8		105.7	W 29929	138.4	TISSUS SPECIAUX
6573	COATED ETC TEXTILES NES	W 19807	75.6	W 21038	82.1	W 17823	73.8	W 22717	97.3	TISSUS,ART MATIERE TEXT NDA
66	NONMETAL MINERAL MFS NES		121.9		138.9		247.6		388.1	ART MIN NON METALLIQUES
661	LIME,CEMENT,BLDG PRODS	W 753531	43.0	W 705229	37.4	W 1467974	87.7	W 2598312	160.8	CHAUX,CIMENTS MAT CONSTR
6612	CEMENT	W 745694	38.4	W 696467	32.0	W 1452740	78.9	W 2572057	145.6	CIMENTS HYDRAULIQUES
67	IRON AND STEEL		925.0		973.5		1475.8		1620.3	FER ET ACIER
672	IRON,STEEL PRIMARY FORMS	W 1706461	447.0	W 1800409	439.7	W 2443828	697.9	W 2284057	632.0	LINGOTS FER,ACIER
6725	IRN,STL BLOOMS,SLABS,ETC	W 1273004	301.5	W 1627115	375.6	W 2223571	614.5	W 1950977	506.0	BLOOMS,BILLETTES FER ACIER
67251	IRN,SMPLE STL BLOOMS,ETC	W 1273004	301.5	W 1627083	375.6	W 2223469	614.0	W 1950974	506.0	BLOOMS ETC NON ACIER FIN
6727	IRN,STL COIL FR REROLLNG	W 433454	145.6	W 173290	64.1	W 219684	83.3	W 333028	126.0	EBAUCHES POUR TOLES FER
67271	IRON,SIMPLE STEEL COILS	W 427898	134.3	W 169078	57.3	W 214861	73.8	W 323469	118.0	EBAUCHES NON EN ACIER
673	IRON,STEEL SHAPES ETC	W 154447	71.9	W 249081	111.6	W 387052	159.0	W 750324	317.7	BARRES,PROFIL FER,ACIER
6731	IRON,STEEL WIRE ROD	W 69313	25.4	W 127254	45.2	W 224400	72.2	W 288360	120.6	FIL MACHINE FER,ACIER
67311	IRON,SIMPLE STL WIRE ROD	W 62454	21.4	W 114632	37.7	W 217845	68.5	W 270928	110.5	FIL MACH AUT ACIER FIN
6732	IRON,STEEL BARS ETC	W 36499	25.8	W 27282	26.4	W 64150	37.8	W 273374	108.8	BARRES FER,ACIER
674	IRN,STL UNIV,PLATE,SHEET	W 477362	272.3	W 469640	290.4	W 835118	511.3	W 844343	489.1	LARGES PLATS,TOLES
6744	IRN,STL HVY PLATE,ROLLED	W 123502	49.4	W 91708	38.2	W 235270	95.0	W 260999	103.0	TOLES LAMINEES PLUS 4.75 MM
67441	— OF IRON OR SIMPLE STL	W 121911	46.8	W 90080	35.5	W 233230	90.9	W 258249	96.0	TOLES NON ACIER FIN CARB
6746	IRN,STL THIN PLATE,ROLLD	W 207015	124.5	W 192145	131.1	W 301968	213.9	W 304257	191.2	TOLES LAM MOINS 3MM
67461	— OF IRON OR SIMPLE STL	W 191831	97.2	W 169050	90.7	W 282066	169.4	W 277705	143.1	TOL NON AC FIN MOINS 3 MM
6749	OTH IRN,STL PLATES,SHEET	W 65936	46.3	W 84023	61.1	W 131983	103.0	W 132517	104.2	AUTRES TOLES FER,ACIER
67491	— OF IRON OR SIMPLE STL	W 61274	39.8	W 82087	57.9	W 127624	97.7	W 128802	100.5	AUT TOLES AUTRES ACIER FIN
678	IRON,STL TUBES,PIPES,ETC	W 49638	72.5	W 59366	92.0	W 51984	64.1	W 82590	122.4	TUBES,TUYAUX EN FONTE,FER
68	NON-FERROUS METALS		219.7		270.0		359.2		365.8	METAUX NON FERREUX
682	COPPER EXC CEMENT COPPER	W 30402	73.2	W 38219	99.4	W 32239	115.6	W 48953	116.0	CUIVRE
684	ALUMINIUM	W 49853	88.1	W 86653	106.8	W 55652	155.7	W 66649	162.9	ALUMINIUM
6842	ALUMINIUM,ALLOYS WORKED	W 26815	57.0	W 18616	59.7	W 22387	86.9	W 28985	97.1	ALUMINIUM,ALLIAGES OUVRE
69	METAL MANUFACTURES NES		388.8		424.3		325.1		474.1	ART MANUFACT EN METAL NDA
691	STRUCTURES AND PARTS NES	W 57212	215.6	W 60745	205.1	W 40632	75.7	W 64237	125.6	CONSTRUCT FER,ACIER,ALU
6911	STRUCTURES,PARTS IRN,STL	W 57072	215.1	W 60452	203.8	W 39860	71.2	W 62589	119.3	CONSTRUCT FER,ACIER,FONTE
699	BASE METAL MFRS NES	W 75460	81.3		95.6		98.3	W 57985	149.9	ART MANUFACTURES MET NDA
7	MACHINES,TRANSPORT EQUIP		6139.3		7576.1		9238.1		17955.7	MACHINES MATERIEL TRANSPORT
71	POWER GENERATING EQUIPMT		815.5		886.5		561.9		596.0	MACHINES GENERATRICES
711	STEAM BOILERS & AUX PLNT	W 4407	59.3		21.6		10.7	W 6532	28.6	GENERATEURS VAPEUR EAU ETC
712	STEAM ENGINES,TURBINES	W 5043	92.3		367.2		73.8	W 4764	43.5	MACHINES A VAPEUR D'EAU PIEC
7129	STM ENGINE ETC PARTS NES	W 4912	91.4	W 20347	359.1	W 7993	72.1	W 4703	41.1	PARTIES,PIECES DU 712.6
713	INTRNL COMBUS PSTN ENGIN	W 74179	195.8		293.3		293.9	W 84222	306.7	MOTEURS EXPL COMB INT, PIECE
7132	MOTOR VEHCL PSTN ENGINS	W 55852	59.5	N 438603	99.6	N 247051	174.1	W 65315	174.1	MOTEURS EXPL POUR VEHICULES
7138	PISTON ENGINES NES	W 6999	34.3	N 208500	97.4	N 169944	53.3	W 12905	67.2	MOTEURS A PISTONS NDA
7139	PISTON ENGINE PARTS NES	W 10411	94.1	W 9239	88.9	W 5559	59.4	W 4902	56.3	PIECES POUR 713.2,3,8
714	ENGINES AND MOTORS NES	W 5690	126.9		40.8		28.9	W 2086	19.9	MOTEURS NON ELECTRIQUES
7149	ENGINE & MOTOR PARTS NES	W 5047	111.1	W 3261	40.0	W 1001	28.5	W 2085	19.9	PIECES 714 ET 718.88
71499	PARTS NES,OF 71488,71888	W 5045	110.7	W 3260	39.9	W 1000	28.4	W 2085	19.9	PIECES 714.88 ET 718.88
716	ROTATING ELECTRIC PLANT	W 43275	339.6		162.7		151.8	W 25111	192.7	APP ELECTR ROTATIFS,PIECES
7162	AC MTRS,GENRTRS,GEN SETS	W 38411	304.1	N 1710991	128.8	N 1978786	116.9	W 21133	158.4	MOTEURS ELECTRIQUES
71623	GEN SETS WITH PISTN ENGN	W 29826	279.2	N 6339	93.6	N 3625	85.4	W 10761	107.9	GROUPES MOTEUR EXPLOSION
72	MACHS FOR SPCL INDUSTRYS		635.4		893.4		1365.1		1833.4	MAC SPECIALES POUR INDUST
723	CIVIL ENGNEERG EQUIP ETC	W 39972	55.7		66.2		130.0	W 112999	265.3	APPAREILS DE GENIE CIVIL
7234	CONST,MINING MACHNRY NES	W 36079	45.1	N 7162	47.7	N 28638	110.5	W 101562	227.7	MACH POUR LA CONST, MINES
72342	SLFPRP SHOVELS,EXCAVATRS	W 21171	23.2	N 1942	28.4	N 3064	63.1	W 60964	107.9	PELLES MECANIQUES
724	TEXTILE,LEATHER MACHNRY	W 13374	110.6		162.7		159.2	W 13130	117.2	MACH POUR INDUSTRIE TEXTILE
727	FOOD MACHRY NON-DOMESTIC	W 4023	35.2		68.5		90.9	W 9952	106.9	MACH INDUSTRIES ALIMENT
728	OTH MACHY FOR SPCL INDUS	W 30241	374.3		472.5		840.2	W 67079	1183.3	AUT MACH IND PARTICULIERES
7283	OTHR MINERAL WORKG MACHY	W 5036	24.9		21.4		65.5	W 24448	164.9	MACH TRIER,CRIBLER,BROYER
7284	MACHY FOR SPCL INDUS NES	W 22792	337.4		440.7		748.6	W 38721	994.4	MACH SPEC IND PARTICUL.
72848	OTH MCHY WITH INDIV FNCT	W 6228	108.5	N 5	163.6	N 40	272.8	W 12213	400.9	AUTRES MACHINES NDA
72849	PTS OF MACHS OF 7284 ETC	W 5464	168.6	W 5194	169.5	W 10003	313.0	W 11015	421.7	PIECES DU 728.4 ETC
73	METALWORKING MACHINERY		104.4		92.0		210.6		281.7	MACH TRAVAIL DES METAUX
736	METALWORKING MACH-TOOLS	W 15985	77.0		68.5		165.4	W 28449	223.5	MACH-OUTILS TRAVAIL METAUX
74	GENRL INDUSTRL MACHY NES		621.1		754.2		914.7		1265.8	MACH APP INDUSTRIE
741	HEATING,COOLING EQUIPMNT	W 18186	124.2		164.6		199.5	W 29845	287.9	MACH CHAUFFAGE,PIECES
7416	HEATING,COOLING EQU NES	W 7750	51.4		64.6		63.7	W 9531	110.3	APP CHANGEMENT TEMP
742	PUMPS FOR LIQUIDS ETC	W 6609	60.5		66.9		74.6	W 11739	97.4	POMPES MOTO-POMPES
743	PUMPS NES,CENTRFUGES ETC	W 17680	99.4		127.4		175.0	W 35616	205.7	POMPES COMPRES,VENT ETC
744	MECHANICAL HANDLING EQU	W 31316	129.3		165.7		187.5	W 68505	302.4	EQUIP MANUTENTION PIECES
7442	LIFTING,LOADING MACH NES	W 15551	76.5	N 254667	86.8	N 213193	92.4	W 34080	159.1	APP LEVAGE,MANUTENTION
745	NONELEC MACHY,TOOLS NES	W 7119	68.3		86.2		102.9	W 10792	140.6	AUT MACH NON ELEC,PIECES
7452	OTH NONELEC MCHS,PTS NES	W 6701	64.4		81.3		97.4	W 9605	125.6	AUT MACH NON ELEC,PIECES
749	NONELEC MACH PTS,ACC NES	W 16804	139.7	W 17916	143.6	W 20209	175.4	W 26007	232.2	PIECES MACH NON ELEC NDA
75	OFFICE MACHNES,ADP EQUIP		280.7		342.0		541.5		1942.8	MACH BUREAU TRAIT AUTOM
752	AUTOMTIC DATA PROC EQUIP	W 2993	97.0	N 463050	115.1	N 768285	172.7	W 7614	244.1	MACH TRAIT INFORMATION
7525	ADP PERIPHERAL UNITS	W 2424	62.7	N 401769	72.5	N 688011	95.3	W 5612	140.8	UNITES PERIPHERIQUES
759	OFFICE,ADP MCH PTS,ACCES	W 4126	149.4	W 5268	186.4	W 6392	310.3	W 15767	1636.7	PIECES DU 751 ET 752
7599	ACCTG,ETC,ADP MCH PTS,AC	W 3833	142.7	W 4824	176.7	W 5925	298.2	W 15074	1618.0	PIECES DU 751 ET 752
76	TELECOMM,SOUND EQUIPMENT		613.2		895.4		1321.7		2007.5	EQUIPMENT DE TELECOM
764	TELECOM EQPT,PTS,ACC NES	W 21338	572.9		824.7		1206.0	W 53410	1917.4	EQUIP TELECOM,PIECES
7641	LINE TELEPHONE,ETC EQUIP	W 1587	111.8		246.8		282.8	W 7777	355.4	APP TELEPHON PAR FIL
7643	TV,RADIO TRANSMITTRS ETC	W 740	78.3		108.5		294.5	W 10210	323.8	APP EMET TELE RADIO
7649	PTS NES OF EQUIPMT OF 76	W 17627	371.2		449.7		602.5	W 32794	1208.7	PIECES DE LA DIV 76
76491	PTS NES OF APPAR OF 7641	W 2913	99.8	W 5226	135.6	W 3466	186.8	W 9968	471.4	PIECES POUR 764.1
76493	TELECOMM EQUIPMT PTS NES	W 8968	213.6		237.8		329.8	W 14709	574.3	PIECES 761,762,764.3,8
76499	PARTS ETC OF SOUND EQUIP	W 2754	42.7	W 2890	42.1	W 2715	49.5	W 3631	125.7	PIECES NDA POUR 763
77	ELECTRIC MACHNRY NES ETC		1419.2		1802.7		2183.2		7129.1	MACH APP ELECT NDA
771	ELECTRIC POWER MACHY NES	W 12557	100.6		100.5		113.6	W 31722	243.7	MACH PROD,TRANS ELECTR
7711	TRANSFORMERS,ELECTRICAL	W 6719	54.5	N 4781588	42.9	N 7415206	48.5	W 21047	109.8	TRANSFO ELECTRIQUES
7712	OTH ELEC POWER MACHY NES	W 5837	46.1	W 6378	57.6	W 6443	65.2	W 10675	134.0	AUT APP PROD TRANSF ELEC
772	SWITCHGEAR ETC,PARTS NES	W 19720	278.0		303.5		322.6	W 32412	601.3	APP COUPURE,SECT ETC
7721	SWITCHGEAR ETC	W 18693	242.0		251.5		233.9	W 22131	390.0	APP COUPURE,SECTIONMNT
7722	PRINTED CIRCUITS,PTS NES	W 565	19.3	W 1010	23.5	W 1418	53.0	W 9456	161.4	CIRCUITS ET PIECES
773	ELECTR DISTRIBUTNG EQUIP	W 40369	179.1	W 38808	243.1	W 48644	298.6	W 72235	457.6	EQUIPMT DISTRIBUTION ELECT
7731	INSULATED WIRE,CABLE ETC	W 25389	100.8	W 25464	141.5	W 30683	174.5	W 49744	335.2	FILS,CABLES ISOLES ELECT

4. General Imports C.I.F. by Commodities according to the S.I.T.C. (Rev. 2) in million U.S. Dollars
Importations Générales C.A.F. par Produits d'après la C.T.C.I. (Rév. 2) en millions de Dollars E.U.

SITC CTCI	COMMODITY	1993 QUANTITY QUANTITE	1993 VALUE VALEUR	1994 QUANTITY QUANTITE	1994 VALUE VALEUR	1995 QUANTITY QUANTITE	1995 VALUE VALEUR	1996 QUANTITY QUANTITE	1996 VALUE VALEUR	PRODUIT
7732	ELECTRC INSULATING EQUIP	W 14980	78.3	W 13344	101.7	W 17961	124.1	W 22491	122.5	EQUIP ISOL ELECTRIQUE
77327	OTH ELEC INSUL FITTG NES	W 4017	48.6	W 5251	80.8	W 5921	96.4	W 6861	96.3	PIECES ISOL EN AUT MATIERES
776	TRANSISTORS,VALVES,ETC	W 7677	671.0		929.2		1125.6	W 24253	5345.9	LAMPES,TUBES,VALVES
7763	DIODES,TRANSISTORS,ETC	W 675	38.5	W 570	52.4	W 898	92.7	W 1151	182.6	DIODES,TRANSISTORS
7764	ELECTRONIC MICROCIRCUITS	W 556	107.4	W 786	131.6	W 781	189.2	W 2202	857.6	MICROSTRUCTURES ELECTRON
7768	ELCTRNC COMP PTS,CRYSTLS	W 2268	497.7		707.8	W 3925	787.1	W 9815	4238.4	CRIST PIEZO–ELEC,PCS 776
77689	ELECTRNIC COMPON PTS NES	W 2209	484.3	W 2572	686.5	W 3846	735.2	W 9725	4200.2	PIECES DU GROUPE 776
778	ELECTRICAL MACHINERY NES	W 50273	159.9		187.2		262.7	W 52951	404.2	AUTRES MACH ELECT NDA
7788	OTH ELEC MACHY,EQUIP NES	W 9752	93.6		113.0		162.3	W 16282	256.9	AUT MACH APP ELEC NDA
77884	ELECTRICAL CONDENSERS	W 1386	42.5	W 1722	69.5	W 2036	101.8	W 2387	159.5	CONDENSATEURS ELECTRIQUES
78	ROAD VEHICLES		911.4		1097.0		1517.0		1870.0	VEHICULES ROUTIERS
781	PASS MOTOR VEH EXC BUSES	W 72688	402.4	N 106959	540.6	N 129586	694.7	W 112022	785.9	AUTO TRANSPORT PERSONNES
782	LORRIES,SPCL MTR VEH NES	W 62358	191.6	N 29447	194.3	N 60173	251.4	W 100525	284.3	VEHICULES SPECIAUX,MARCH
7821	LORRIES,TRUCKS	W 50365	163.2	N 28787	176.7	N 58996	217.3	W 78650	228.6	VEHICULES TRANSP MARCHAND
783	ROAD MOTOR VEHICLES NES	W 18202	32.0	N 2532	37.7	N 16904	140.0	W 60405	294.3	VEHICULES ROUTIERS NDA
7831	BUSES	W 10637	20.9	N 1630	21.6	N 14951	105.0	W 43906	258.9	VOITURES TRANSPORT COMMUN
784	MOTOR VEH PRTS,ACCES NES	W 92946	187.4		203.0		277.0	W 163130	300.2	PIECES 722,781,782,783
7849	OTHER MOTOR VEHCL PARTS	W 87833	182.3	W 243623	187.9	W 106183	246.8	W 129361	275.2	PIECES 722,781,782,783
785	CYCLES,ETC MOTRZD OR NOT	W 18229	89.7		112.6		138.3	W 30658	183.0	MOTOCYCLES SCOOTERS
7851	MOTORCYCLES ETC	W 8539	75.7	N 106628	86.1	N 113899	106.0	W 14085	146.2	MOTO VELO MOTEUR AUXIL
79	OTHR TRANSPORT EQUIPMENT		738.7		813.4		622.7		1029.8	AUTRE MATERIEL TRANSPORT
792	AIRCRAFT ETC	W 1227	622.1		140.7		469.0	W 2855	918.3	APP NAVIGATION AERIENNE
7924	AIRCRFT NES OVER 15000KG	W 724	489.2	N 2	8.2	N 8	271.6	W 1950	747.4	AERODYNES PLUS 15000 KG
7929	AIRCRAFT PARTS NES	W 470	130.3	W 644	118.8	W 853	185.9	W 778	138.0	PIECES DU 792
793	SHIPS AND BOATS ETC	W 48657	110.7	N 4091	668.1	N 40043	147.8	W 63205	100.8	NAVIRES BATEAUX,ETC
7938	TUGS,SPECIAL VESSELS ETC	W 6182	81.2	N 3751	607.1	N 3553	107.2	W 3132	47.9	REMORQUEURS,BATEAUX SPEC
79382	SPECL PURPOSE VESSLS ETC	W 6051	80.5	N 13	606.2	N 36	105.2	W 2557	45.2	BAT–PHARES,–POMPES,DRAGUES
8	MISC MANUFACTURED GOODS		618.4		779.2		1014.5		1527.6	ART MANUFACTURES DIVERS
87	PRECISION INSTRUMNTS NES		157.6		172.5		219.6		294.7	INSTRUM,APPAR SCIENT NDA
874	MEASURNG,CONTROLNG INSTR	W 3915	114.5		119.3		158.5	W 5666	209.7	INSTRUMENTS DE MESURE
88	PHOTO EQU,OPTICL GDS ETC		105.9		145.4		158.3		363.9	APP,FOURN PHOTO,OP,MONTR
881	PHOTO APPARAT,EQUIPT NES	W 923	32.3		60.1		67.2	W 1982	185.2	APP,EQUIP PHOTO NDA
8811	CAMERAS STILL,FLASH APP	W 270	19.5		36.6		37.7	W 1233	151.9	APPAREILS PHOTO,PIECES
88119	PTS NES OF APPAR OF 8811	W 152	16.8	W 202	32.8	W 238	31.8	W 1004	144.8	PIECES POUR 881.1
882	PHOTO,CINEMA SUPPLIES	W 6160	56.9		66.7		68.6	W 8497	76.1	PRODUITS PHOTO,CINEMA
89	MISC MANUFCTRD GOODS NES		269.2		355.6		478.8		627.1	ART MANUFACTURES DIVERS
892	PRINTED MATTER	W 9629	50.1		68.3		92.3	W 14398	104.5	IMPRIMES
893	ARTICLES OF PLASTIC NES		90.7		118.5		171.8		265.0	OUVRAGES EN MAT DIVIS 58
8939	MISC PLASTIC ARTICLES	W 20218	70.1		91.7		130.2	W 44597	192.4	ART DIVERS EN MAT DIV 58
89399	OTHR PLASTC ARTICLES NES	W 16794	66.3	W 10890	83.5	W 13854	120.0	W 36735	181.5	AUT OUV MAT DIV 58
9	GOODS NOT CLASSD BY KIND		3013.0		4126.9		5481.9		55.0	ART TRANSACT NON CLASSES
931	*SPECIAL TRANSACTIONS	W 4724649	3009.9	W 1972407	4121.0	W 123095	5473.8			TRANS.SPECIALES

5. General Exports F.O.B. by Commodities according to the S.I.T.C. (Rev. 2) in million U.S. Dollars
Exportations Générales F.O.B. par Produits d'après la C.T.C.I. (Rév. 2) en millions de Dollars E.U.

SITC CTCI	COMMODITY	1993 QUANTITY QUANTITE	1993 VALUE VALEUR	1994 QUANTITY QUANTITE	1994 VALUE VALEUR	1995 QUANTITY QUANTITE	1995 VALUE VALEUR	1996 QUANTITY QUANTITE	1996 VALUE VALEUR	PRODUIT
	ALL COMMODITIES		11374.9		13482.9		17447.2		20542.5	TOUS PRODUITS
0	FOOD AND LIVE ANIMALS		1327.6		1329.9		1337.2		1397.6	ALIMENTS,ANIMAUX VIVANTS
03	FISH AND PREPARATIONS		476.6		532.5		502.0		437.0	POISSONS ET PREPARATIONS
034	FISH,FRESH,CHILLED,FROZN	W 38058	58.4	W 39128	66.8	W 41496	84.6	W 34899	72.9	POISSON FRAIS, REFRIG,CONG
0341	FISH FRSH,CHLLD,EX FILLT	W 23380	36.6	W 19156	31.4	W 24749	51.3	W 20289	40.3	POISSON FRAIS,REFRIGERE
036	SHELL FISH FRESH,FROZEN	W 55370	282.2	W 38688	310.4	W 34498	291.0	W 39755	219.5	CRUSTACES, MOLLUSQUES
037	FISH ETC PREPD,PRSVD NES	W 73685	133.9	W 63224	153.3	W 50306	124.4	W 73497	142.1	POIS,CRUST,MOL PREPARES
0371	FISH PREPARD,PRESRVD NES	W 71801	127.5	W 61219	144.5	W 48559	115.3	W 71103	134.3	CONSERVES DE POISSONS
05	VEGETABLES AND FRUIT		600.4		571.8		581.6		632.4	LEGUMES ET FRUITS
057	FRUIT,NUTS,FRESH,DRIED	W 1450180	370.2		348.2	W 19	0.1	W 1522050	393.9	FRUITS FRAIS OU SECS
0573	BANANA,PLANTAIN,FRSH,DRY	W 1153468	226.1	W 1155182	215.3	W 1213411	223.8	W 1253175	236.5	BANANES FRAICHES,SECHEES
0577	NUTS EDIBLE,FRESH,DRIED	W 105826	87.6		73.0		70.6	W 78218	86.9	FRUITS A COQUES
05771	COCONUTS FRESH OR DRIED	W 101771	85.4		72.1		69.7	W 77914	86.7	NOIX DE COCO
0579	FRUIT FRESH OR DRIED NES	W 190885	56.5	W 197016	60.0	W 213968	74.6	W 190653	70.6	FRUITS FRAIS,SECS NDA
058	FRUIT PRESERVED,PREPARED	W 405217	200.2	W 367333	192.6	W 349863	179.0	W 441931	203.0	CONSERVES DE FRUITS
0585	FRUIT OR VEGETABLE JUICE	W 96728	38.5	W 91997	39.1	W 101845	43.3	W 120544	47.3	JUS DE FRUITS
0589	FRUIT PREPRD,PRESRVD,NES	W 295202	147.8	W 265466	143.0	W 238590	125.5	W 311729	144.3	FRUITS PREPARES CONSERV
05899	FRUIT,NUTS NES,PRESERVED	W 294072	145.9	W 264394	140.5	W 237521	122.8	W 309823	140.6	FRUITS PREP CONSERV NDA
06	SUGAR AND PREPS,HONEY		137.8		85.2		88.8		157.9	SUCRES ET PRODUITS
061	SUGAR AND HONEY	W 824663	128.1	W 438329	75.8	W 246810	74.7	W 352837	140.2	SUCRES ET MIEL
0611	RAW BEET AND CANE SUGAR	W 324739	102.3	W 183013	61.5	W 153837	66.5	W 319657	136.7	SUCRES BRUTS
081	*FEEDING STUFF FOR ANIML	W 509947	55.4	W 596210	63.1	W 776928	80.4	W 512609	72.0	NOURRITURE POUR ANIMAUX
0813	OILCAKE AND OTH RESIDUES	W 490791	45.5	W 575370	53.2	W 757002	67.0	W 474568	56.3	TOURTEAUX
08137	— OF COCONUT(COPRA)	W 489369	45.4	W 574223	53.1	W 756343	66.9	W 471423	56.0	TOURTEAUX DE COPRAH
1	BEVERAGES AND TOBACCO		44.4		44.7		41.9		58.7	BOISSONS ET TABACS
12	TOBACCO AND MANUFACTURES		34.9		32.7		28.0		45.1	TABACS BRUTS FABRIQUES
2	CRUDE MATERLS,EXCL FUELS		387.8		411.1		531.1		522.0	MAT BRUTES NON COMESTIBLES
24	CORK AND WOOD		39.0		20.7		27.1		36.7	LIEGE ET BOIS
28	METALLIFEROUS ORES,SCRAP		200.4		226.7		283.6		261.6	MINERAIS METAL,DECHETS
281	IRON ORE,CONCENTRATES	W 17506	0.6	W 10385	0.5			W 4481872	70.2	MINERAIS DE FER
2816	IRON ORE AGGLOMERATES							W 4481872	70.2	MINERAIS AGGLOMERES
287	BASE METAL ORES,CONC NES	W 1031786	132.1	W 846589	135.7	W 1008978	171.0	W 1501464	93.0	MINERAIS METAUX COMMUNS
2871	CPR ORE ETC,CEMENT COPPR	W 370805	109.6	W 309107	113.6	W 282284	134.3	W 178678	52.2	MINERAIS DE CUIVRE,MATTES
28711	COPPER ORES,EXCL MATTE	W 370789	109.5	W 309007	113.5	W 282266	134.3	W 178678	52.2	MINERAIS DE CUIVRE
289	PREC MTAL ORES,WASTE NES	K 32880	53.5	K 22104	67.4	K 22485	64.8	K 31613	59.0	MINERAIS,DECHETS MET PREC
28901	PRECIOUS METAL ORES,CONC	K 23544	52.7	K 22104	67.4	K 22485	64.8	K 30716	57.1	MINERAIS METAUX PRECIEUX
29	CRUDE ANIMAL,VEG MAT NES		54.3		64.4		93.8		104.7	MATIERES BRUTES ANIM,VEGET
292	CRUDE VEG MATERIALS NES	W 35139	50.7	W 37164	59.6	W 43449	89.1	W 42616	100.6	MAT BRUTES VEGETALES NDA
2929	OTH CRUDE VEG MATERIALS	W 32146	46.6	W 34560	56.1	W 40455	84.3	W 39207	94.9	MATIERES VEGETALES NDA
3	MINERAL FUELS ETC		228.9		215.6		262.9		382.3	COMBUSTIBLES MINERAUX LUB
33	PETROLEUM AND PRODUCTS		136.5		119.8		154.9		274.0	PETROLE ET DERIVES
334	PETROLEUM PRODUCTS,REFIN	W 675932	103.4	W 730993	101.0	W 960754	143.1	W 1517084	272.7	PRODUITS RAFFINES
3341	GASOLINE,OTH LIGHT OILS	W 455038	75.8	W 579800	77.3	W 609510	90.7	W 663715	124.9	ESSENCES POUR MOTEURS
33419	OTH LIGHT PETROLEUM OILS	W 417357	68.2	W 569253	75.6	W 562348	82.7	W 663715	124.9	AUTRES HUILES LEGERES
3343	GAS OILS	W 24613	3.9	W 7288	1.1	W 107857	22.2	W 488717	89.7	GAS OILS
341	*GAS,NATURAL AND MANUFCT	W 528636	92.4	W 553534	95.9	W 491217	108.0	W 475775	108.3	GAZ NATUREL,GAZ MANUFACT
3413	PETROLM GASES,LIQUEFIED	W 528636	92.4	W 553534	95.9	W 491217	108.0	W 475774	108.3	GAZ DE PETROLE LIQUEFIE
34139	OTH HYDROCARBON GAS LQFD	W 500382	86.9	W 542825	94.1	W 487438	107.3	W 474774	108.1	HYDROCARBURES GAZEUX NDA
4	ANIMAL,VEGETABLE OIL,FAT		370.3		490.7		844.5		588.9	HUILES,GRAISSES ANIM,VEG
42	FIXED VEGETABLE OIL,FAT		358.9		475.9		826.5		570.8	HUILES VEGETALES FIXES
424	FIXED VEG OIL NONSOFT	W 860880	358.9	W 849465	475.9	W 1340768	826.5	W 792732	570.8	AUTRES HUILES VEG FIXES
4243	COCONUT (COPRA) OIL	W 859208	357.7	W 848756	475.2	W 1340410	826.1	W 792652	570.7	HJUILE DE COPRAH
5	CHEMCLS,RELATED PROD NES		257.5		298.3		329.6		342.6	PRODUITS CHIMIQUES
51	ORGANIC CHEMICALS		41.4		43.4		48.7		45.9	PROD CHIMIQ ORGANIQUES
512	ALCOHOLS,PHENOLS ETC	W 34797	35.6	W 31475	38.5	W 30639	43.4	W 31333	40.3	PHENOLS,PHENOLS–ALCOOLS
5121	ACYCLIC ALCOHOLS,DERIVS	W 34797	35.6	W 31475	38.5	W 30639	43.4	W 31314	40.2	ALCOOLS ACYCLIQUES
562	*FERTILIZERS,MANUFACTURE	W 555327	85.5	W 584602	101.3	W 670444	120.0	W 583967	104.7	ENGRAIS MANUFACTURES
5629	FERTILIZERS NES	W 520805	78.0	W 552189	92.3	W 641539	110.8	W 531133	90.8	ENGRAIS NDA
56292	NITROG–PHOS FERTILZR NES	W 239681	33.6	W 230305	41.9	W 169915	31.3	W 98249	20.2	ENGRAIS NDA CONT N P
56299	OTHER FERTILIZERS NES	W 150127	21.0	W 287984	42.3	W 471624	79.6	W 432885	70.6	AUTRES ENGRAIS NDA
6	BASIC MANUFACTURES		806.8		880.0		1124.0		1298.1	ART MANUFACTURES
63	WOOD,CORK MANUFACTRS NES		125.6		145.9		154.4		178.2	OUVRAGES LIEGE ET BOIS
635	WOOD MANUFACTURES NES	W 65759	100.8		127.0		131.6	W 79066	159.6	ART MANUF EN BOIS NDA
6353	BUILDERS WOODWRK,PREFABS	W 52234	54.1		74.3		68.1	W 55929	93.7	OUVRAGES DE MENUISERIE
6354	WOOD MFRS DOMESTIC ETC	W 12258	43.7		47.9		56.6	W 12941	58.2	ART MANUF USAGE DOMESTIQUE
64	PAPER,PAPERBOARD AND MFR		32.7		33.3		54.7		55.6	PAPIERS,CARTONS & OUVRAGES
65	TEXTILE YARN,FABRICS,ETC		123.2		177.7		213.1		318.7	FILS,TISSUS,ARTICLES TEXTILE
651	TEXTILE YARN	W 11568	26.5	W 16639	42.7	W 17767	49.3	W 25674	60.2	FILS TEXTILES
655	KNITTED,ETC FABRICS	W 6068	18.8	W 12092	43.8	W 12171	49.8	W 16467	67.1	ETOF BONNETERIE PIECES ETC
6552	OTHER KNIT ETC FAB NONEL	W 6068	18.8	W 12092	43.8	W 12171	49.8	W 16467	67.1	ETOF BON NON ELAS NON SYNT
658	TEXTILE ARTICLES NES	W 2877	28.7		30.9		43.4	W 10931	81.1	ART FACONNES MAT TEXTILES
66	NONMETAL MINERAL MFS NES		86.9		96.2		108.1		103.6	ART MIN NON METALLIQUES
666	POTTERY	W 17775	47.6	MN 31734	51.5	MN 36360	56.4	W 21691	57.6	POTERIE
67	IRON AND STEEL		54.1		57.0		61.0		87.5	FER ET ACIER
68	NON–FERROUS METALS		284.8		297.8		446.0		369.2	METAUX NON FERREUX
682	COPPER EXC CEMENT COPPER	W 141567	273.3	W 145414	286.3	W 148057	430.7	W 145878	348.8	CUIVRE
6821	COPPER NES,ALLOYS,UNWRT	W 136920	264.7	W 137465	269.9	W 139637	406.4	W 143329	343.1	CUIVRE BRUT
68212	COPPER REFINED,UNWROUGHT	W 136920	264.7	W 137465	269.9	W 139637	406.4	W 143329	343.1	CUIVRE AFFINE BRUT
69	METAL MANUFACTURES NES		81.9		54.7		61.5		142.5	ART MANUFACT EN METAL NDA
691	STRUCTURES AND PARTS NES	W 82716	48.6	W 9377	6.8	W 6646	7.9	W 44152	46.3	CONSTRUCT FER,ACIER,ALU
6911	STRUCTURES,PARTS IRN,STL	W 82609	48.0	W 6924	5.1	W 6589	7.4	W 44026	45.6	CONSTRUCT FER,ACIER,FONTE
7	MACHINES,TRANSPORT EQUIP		2119.4		2906.7		3869.6		11624.1	MACHINES MATERIEL TRANSPORT
72	MACHS FOR SPCL INDUSTRYS		11.6		13.2		17.1		89.6	MAC SPECIALES POUR INDUST
74	GENRL INDUSTRL MACHY NES		22.4		29.5		37.0		119.6	MACH APP INDUSTRIE
75	OFFICE MACHNES,ADP EQUIP		215.1		233.0		442.7		2772.3	MACH BUREAU TRAIT AUTOM
752	AUTOMTIC DATA PROC EQUIP	W 4609	188.0	MN 12874	179.3	MN 10073	268.9	W 15173	1081.8	MACH TRAIT INFORMATION
7525	ADP PERIPHERAL UNITS	W 4593	187.4	MN 12863	177.9	MN 9787	195.4	W 14678	1014.7	UNITES PERIPHERIQUES
7528	OFF–LINE DATA PROC EQUIP	W 2	0.2	N 9	0.1	N 286482	73.5	W 317	63.4	MACH AUXIL TRAIT INFORM
759	OFFICE,ADP MCH PTS,ACCES	W 253	27.1	W 774	53.7	W 3553	172.0	W 15257	1677.3	PIECES DU 751 ET 752
7599	ACCTG,ETC,ADP MCH PTS,AC	W 253	27.1	W 774	53.7	W 3552	172.0	W 14935	1672.2	PIECES DU 751 ET 752
76	TELECOMM,SOUND EQUIPMENT		506.1		681.2		805.6		1156.8	EQUIPMENT DE TELECOM
761	TELEVISION RECEIVERS	W 1314	17.7	N 257341	35.7	N 493512	71.0	W 10901	121.2	RECEPTEURS DE TELEVISION
7611	COLOUR TV RECEIVERS	W 856	12.3	N 160920	24.7	N 438622	63.3	W 10738	115.3	RECEPTEURS COULEUR
762	RADIO BROADCAST RECEIVRS	W 3561	69.4	N 2448368	121.0	N 2575805	119.5	W 3717	86.6	RECEPTEURS RADIODIFFUSION
7621	MTR VEHC RADIO RECEIVERS	W 546	29.6	N 1027979	62.9	N 1346291	77.0	W 1294	55.3	RECEPTEURS RADIO AUTO
7628	OTHER RADIO RECEIVERS	W 2976	39.1	N 1413191	58.1	N 1229514	42.6	W 2339	30.4	AUTRES RECEPT RADIO
764	TELECOM EQPT,PTS,ACC NES	W 13773	393.6		499.9		596.2	W 31444	931.3	EQUIP TELECOM,PIECES
7641	LINE TELEPHONE,ETC EQUIP	W 3055	65.4		105.3	N 38080	0.2	W 16636	430.5	APP TELEPHON PAR FIL
7643	TV,RADIO TRANSMITTRS ETC	W 5234	173.3	N 4752989	193.5	N 4231453	191.0	W 3575	141.9	APP EMET TELE RADIO
7648	TELECOMM EQUIPMENT NES	W 794	57.7	N 1228093	61.1	N 845575	37.3	W 815	38.6	APP TELECOM NDA
76483	RADAR APPARATUS ETC	W 625	45.8	N 1129744	50.3	N 735361	25.9	W 622	24.7	APP DE RADIOGUIDAGE ETC

5. General Exports F.O.B. by Commodities according to the S.I.T.C. (Rev. 2) in million U.S. Dollars
Exportations Générales F.O.B. par Produits d'après la C.T.C.I. (Rév. 2) en millions de Dollars E.U.

SITC CTCI	COMMODITY	1993 QUANTITY QUANTITE	1993 VALUE VALEUR	1994 QUANTITY QUANTITE	1994 VALUE VALEUR	1995 QUANTITY QUANTITE	1995 VALUE VALEUR	1996 QUANTITY QUANTITE	1996 VALUE VALEUR	PRODUIT
7649	PTS NES OF EQUIPMT OF 76	W 3101	85.2		118.2		196.3	W 7724	296.1	PIECES DE LA DIV 76
76491	PTS NES OF APPAR OF 7641	W 262	13.8	W 258	14.0	W 673	49.6	W 1390	106.4	PIECES POUR 764.1
76493	TELECOMM EQUIPMT PTS NES	W 2476	58.5		89.8		132.3	W 5689	154.5	PIECES 761,762,764.3,8
77	ELECTRIC MACHNRY NES ETC		1249.3		1756.7		2313.1		7055.9	MACH APP ELECT NDA
772	SWITCHGEAR ETC,PARTS NES	W 1354	56.8		0.1	W 2526	118.7	W 5442	252.7	APP COUPURE,SECT ETC
7721	SWITCHGEAR ETC	W 434	5.2		0.1	W 774	12.4	W 3370	97.7	APP COUPURE,SECTIONMNT
7722	PRINTED CIRCUITS,PTS NES	W 351	20.6	W 358	20.8	W 568	36.2	W 1145	98.0	CIRCUITS ET PIECES
7723	FIXED,VARIABLE RESISTORS	W 569	31.1	W 1029	67.5	W 1184	70.2	W 926	57.1	POTENTIOMETRES PIECES
773	ELECTR DISTRIBUTNG EQUIP	W 29131	310.1	W 38051	450.9	W 39213	477.5	W 47014	521.6	EQUIPMT DISTRIBUTION ELECT
7731	INSULATED WIRE,CABLE ETC	W 25598	303.1	W 33407	442.7	W 33624	467.7	W 41703	513.6	FILS,CABLES ISOLES ELECT
776	TRANSISTORS,VALVES,ETC	W 5859	805.7	W 154	27.5	W 118	59.8	W 17350	6127.0	LAMPES,TUBES,VALVES
7763	DIODES,TRANSISTORS,ETC	W 2705	197.8	W 3369	263.8	W 3646	383.6	W 5067	682.6	DIODES,TRANSISTORS
7764	ELECTRONIC MICROCIRCUITS	W 2854	575.1	W 3193	798.8	W 4191	1140.4	W 11629	5302.8	MICROSTRUCTURES ELECTRON
7768	ELCTRNC COMP PTS,CRYSTLS	W 288	32.9	W 338	37.3	W 322	62.9	W 635	141.5	CRIST PIEZO–ELEC,PCS 776
77689	ELECTRNIC COMPON PTS NES	W 196	20.7	W 244	23.6	W 257	49.2	W 585	131.0	PIECES DU GROUPE 776
778	ELECTRICAL MACHINERY NES	W 10858	30.8		47.4		65.5	W 13113	67.4	AUTRES MACH ELECT NDA
78	ROAD VEHICLES		109.1		180.2		238.4		333.6	VEHICULES ROUTIERS
784	MOTOR VEH PRTS,ACCES NES	W 9082	96.3		165.7		208.6	W 25309	281.7	PIECES 722,781,782,783
7849	OTHER MOTOR VEHCL PARTS	W 8829	95.6	W 14488	164.9	W 20495	208.1	W 25170	281.1	PIECES 722,781,782,783
8	MISC MANUFACTURED GOODS		1769.3		1983.6		2248.9		4111.1	ART MANUFACTURES DIVERS
821	*FURNITURE,PARTS THEREOF	W 57460	203.3		240.2		276.3	W 74363	294.2	MEUBLES ET PIECES
8211	CHAIRS,SEATS AND PARTS	W 10592	42.2		47.1		56.2	W 12637	54.9	SIEGES ET PIECES
82111	CHAIRS AND OTHER SEATS	W 10188	41.3	N 1132216	46.0	N 1236088	55.2	W 12298	53.9	SIEGES
8219	FURNITURE AND PARTS NES	W 46602	159.0		191.3		217.4	W 61302	235.3	AUTRES MEUBLES ET PIECES
82192	WOOD FURNITURE NES	W 8431	37.7	N 746306	50.9	N 1090926	76.5	W 20157	86.1	MEUBLES NDA EN BOIS
82199	OTHR FURN,FURN PARTS NES	W 35453	111.2		120.5		112.2	W 33761	119.3	MEUBLES NDA AUTRES MATIERES
831	*TRAVEL GOODS,HANDBAGS	W 9710	53.8	MN 19264	76.1	MN 27221	110.3	W 32226	180.6	ARTICLES DE VOYAGE ETC
83102	TRAVEL GDS,TOILET–CASES	W 6315	30.5	N 8715312	53.5	MN 9469	68.4	W 21004	104.8	ARTICLES DE VOYAGE
83109	OTHER TRAVEL BAGS,CASES	W 2515	17.6	N 8193615	13.6	MN 11470	24.0	W 8971	63.0	AUT CONTENANTS SIMILAIRES
84	CLOTHING AND ACCESSORIES		868.4		924.8		1092.0		2411.9	VETEMENTS
842	MENS OUTERWEAR NOT KNIT	W 7949	110.4	MN 18929	129.2	MN 22198	147.9	W 24839	378.7	VET DESSUS POUR HOMMES
8423	— TROUSERS,BREECHES ETC	W 4833	57.7	MN 12311	66.2	MN 14730	81.8	W 14312	196.0	PANTALONS HOMMES MAT TEX
8424	— JACKETS,BLAZERS ETC	W 2057	35.0	N 3456380	43.6	N 3650329	43.4	W 6055	102.7	VESTES HOMMES MAT TEXTIL
843	WOMENS OUTERWEAR NONKNIT		163.4	MN 40950	193.4	MN 61863	264.2	W 45129	721.6	VET DESSUS FEMMES MAT TEX
8431	— COATS AND JACKETS	W 1585	28.6	N 2218090	27.0	N 1437010	19.6	W 3965	76.4	MANT,VEST FEM MAT TEXTIL
8433	— DRESSES	W 1509	23.9	N 7016434	41.9	MN 10873	65.2	W 9976	160.7	ROBES EN MAT–TEXTILES
8439	— OTHER OUTER GARMENTS		85.2	MN 26183	102.0	MN 41275	142.1	W 23747	357.7	AUT VET DES FEM MAT TEXT
844	UNDER GARMENTS NOT KNIT	W 2396	41.2	N 6420812	38.6	MN 9404	56.1	W 11135	179.2	VETEMENT DESSOUS MAT TEX
8441	— MENS SHIRTS	W 1647	30.0	N 4287033	25.2	N 6676386	41.1	W 7327	123.4	CHEMISES HOMMES MAT TEXT
84411	—— OF COTTON	W 1499	27.5	N 3080261	20.0	N 3474613	24.5	W 4667	86.9	CHEMISES HOMMES DE COTON
845	OUTERWEAR KNIT NONELASTC	W 26573	304.7	MN 90745	314.6	MN 98691	343.7	W 41054	514.8	VET DESSOUS,ACCES BONNET
8451	— JERSEYS,PULLOVERS ETC	W 5011	69.2	MN 15322	82.1	MN 14350	82.2	W 7804	106.6	CHANDAILS,PULL–OVERS ETC
8459	— OTHER,CLTHG ACCESRYS	W 20024	218.4	MN 71690	218.3	MN 79203	241.3	W 30240	367.9	AUT VET DESSUS DE BONNE
846	UNDER GARMENTS KNITTED	W 18945	181.8	MN 68829	173.9	MN 71568	199.0	W 29432	423.6	SOUS VETS DE BONNETERIE
8462	— OF COTTON NON ELASTIC	W 12762	112.4	MN 42365	87.5	MN 31572	70.7	W 16641	220.6	SOUS–VET BONNET COTON
84621	—— MENS SHIRTS							W 11536	162.5	CHEMISES DE COTON
84629	—— OTHER	W 12762	112.4	MN 42365	87.5	MN 31572	70.7	W 5105	58.1	AUT SOUS–VET BONNET COTON
8463	— OF SYNTH FBR NONELAST	W 6124	67.9	MN 24560	83.8	MN 38277	126.7	W 9358	100.4	SOUS–VET BONNET FIB SYNT
84632	—— MENS SHIRTS	W 6119	67.8	MN 23028	82.4	MN 35093	124.5	W 9237	98.9	CHEMISES DE BON FIB SYNMT
8465	CORSETS,GARTERS,ETC	W 59	1.7	N 1904164	2.7	N 1718849	1.7	W 3433	102.6	CORSETS,GAINES ART SIM
84651	BRASSIERES	W 55	1.5	N 1696301	2.1	N 631781	1.2	W 2925	88.0	SOUTIENS–GORGE,BUSTIERS
848	HEADGEAR,NONTXTL CLOTHNG	W 3093	51.8		49.0	N 740	0.1	W 8113	134.2	VET ACCES MAT AUT QUE TEX
8481	LEATHER CLOTHES,ACCESSOR	W 1656	40.2		35.8		32.2	W 2426	70.7	VET ACCES MAT CUIR ARTIF
851	*FOOTWEAR	W 15814	142.2	MP 26516	175.9	MP 21430	153.9	W 15977	167.9	CHAUSSURES
85102	FOOTWEAR LEATHER	W 9510	85.2	MP 12020	72.9	MP 9082	63.1	W 13557	148.5	CHAUS SEMELLES EN CUIR
85103	SHOES WOOD–,CORK–SOLED	W 3387	39.4	MP 9241	91.7	P 7396028	80.5	W 74	0.5	CHAUS SEMELLES BOIS,LIEGE
87	PRECISION INSTRUMNTS NES		23.0		21.2		26.9		78.9	INSTRUM,APPAR SCIENT NDA
88	PHOTO EQU,OPTICL GDS ETC		11.6		35.3		34.6		338.1	APP,FOURN PHOTO,OP,MONTR
881	PHOTO APPARAT,EQUIPT NES	W 45	2.9		24.7			W 774	175.1	APP,EQUIP PHOTO NDA
8811	CAMERAS STILL,FLASH APP	W 35	2.3		22.7			W 694	169.2	APPAREILS PHOTO,PIECES
88111	STILL CAMERAS	W 28	1.5	N 342219	22.6	N 326016	21.8	W 526	142.3	APPAREILS PHOTOGRAPHIQ
885	WATCHES AND CLOCKS		0.8		0.8		1.2		151.4	HORLOGERIE
8851	WATCHES,MOVEMENTS,CASES		0.7		0.3		1.1		119.7	MONTRES,MOUVEMENTS,BOITES
88511	WATCHES		0.6		0.1		0.1		107.9	MONTRES POCHE,BRACELET
89	MISC MANUFCTRD GOODS NES		452.1		492.4		537.3		619.1	ART MANUFACTURES DIVERS
893	ARTICLES OF PLASTIC NES		42.3		0.1	W 34	0.4		109.6	OUVRAGES EN MAT DIVIS 58
8939	MISC PLASTIC ARTICLES	W 10868	24.2		0.1	W 13	0.3	W 29101	72.5	ART DIVERS EN MAT DIV 58
89399	OTHR PLASTC ARTICLES NES	W 8362	21.7	W 11656	27.5	W 16228	42.3	W 26075	69.3	AUT OUV MAT DIV 58
894	TOYS,SPORTING GOODS,ETC	W 18735	137.1		165.8	W 2	0.1	W 28914	246.8	VOITURES ENFANTS,JOUETS
8942	TOYS,INDOOR GAMES ETC	W 16470	119.4		141.5		169.4	W 24551	202.2	JOUETS,JEUX ETC
89425	XMAS DECORATIONS ETC	W 10421	77.5		96.7		123.6	W 17310	133.7	ART DIVERTIS,FETES
897	GOLD,SILVER WARE,JEWELRY		54.8		50.6		29.6		23.0	BIJOUTERIE,ORFEVRERIE
8972	IMITATION JEWELLERY		51.5		46.7		25.1		17.8	BIJOUTERIE DE FANTAISIE
899	OTHER MANUFACTURED GOODS		207.5		0.1		0.1		195.1	AUT ART MANUF DIVERS NDA
8997	BASKETWORK,BROOMS ETC	W 35881	132.2		134.4		125.0	W 27307	102.2	OUVRAGES VANNERIE NDA
89971	BASKETWORK,WICKERWRK,ETC	W 35750	132.0	MN 95329	134.2	MN 89429	124.7	W 27188	101.7	OUVRAGES DE VANNERIE
9	GOODS NOT CLASSD BY KIND		4063.4		4922.9		6858.1		217.6	ART TRANSACT NON CLASSES
931	*SPECIAL TRANSACTIONS	W 4262093	3898.3	W 5127154	4707.5		6659.5	W 1	0.1	TRANS.SPECIALES
971	*GOLD,NON MONETARY NES	K 49846	162.8	K 61902	212.1	K 50237	195.7	K 60238	215.0	OR NON MONETAIRE
97101	NONMON GLD UNWRT,SEMIMFD	K 49308	160.7	K 61239	209.5	K 50131	195.5	K 60199	214.7	OR,ALLIAGES D'OR BRUTS

1. HISTORICAL SERIES, 1962–1997 SPECIAL TRADE, IMPORTS C.I.F., EXPORTS F.O.B.
SERIES HISTORIQUES, 1962–1997 COMMERCE SPECIAL, IMPORTATIONS C.A.F., EXPORTATIONS F.O.B

YEAR ANNEE	VALUE IN MILLION U.S. DOLLARS / VALEUR EN MILLION U.S. DOLLARS — MERCHANDISE –MARCHANDISE IMPORTS	MERCHANDISE –MARCHANDISE EXPORTS	GOLD –OR IMPORTS	GOLD –OR EXPORTS	CONVERSION FACTORS FACTEURS DE CONVERSION CENTS E.U. PAR IMPORTS	CONVERSION FACTORS EXPORTS	INDEX NUMBERS –INDICES — QUANTUM IMPORTS	QUANTUM EXPORTS	UNIT VALUE VALEUR UNITAIRE IMPORTS	UNIT VALUE VALEUR UNITAIRE EXPORTS
1962	1885.50	1646.30								
1963	1979.00	1770.00								
1964	2072.30	2096.50								
1965	2340.30	2227.80								
1966	2494.00	2272.00								
1967	2644.80	2526.50								
1968	2853.00	2857.80								
1969	3209.80	3141.50								
1970	3607.50	3547.80								
1971	4037.80	3872.30								
1972	5335.30	4932.00								
1973	7813.20	6373.60								
1974	10481.70	8315.10								
1975	12537.00	10282.50								
1976	13867.40	11016.60								
1977	14616.00	12265.10								
1978	16088.90	13667.10								
1979	17583.90	16249.00								
1980	19089.10	16996.90					127	72	1	1
1981	12043.00	14508.00					106	58	1	1
1982	10244.00	11172.00					91	63	1	1
1983	10590.00	11572.00					96	70	1	1
1984	10638.00	11750.00					104	76	2	1
1985	10799.00	11488.00					113	77	2	2
1986	11208.00	12074.00					118	81	2	2
1987	10844.00	12205.00					124	85	3	3
1988	12240.00	13956.00					136	92	5	5
1989	10085.00	13155.00					138	92	14	16
1990	8413.00	13627.00					100	100	100	100
1991	15757.00	14903.00					156	103	130	118
1992	15701.00	13324.00							152	
1993	18834.00	14143.00					210	96	177	191
1994	21383.01	17042.00					238	114	225	246
1995	29050.00	22895.01							268	
1996	37137.01	24440.00								
1997	42308.00	25751.01								

2. IMPORTS BY BROAD ECONOMIC CATEGORY AND EXPORTS BY INDUSTRIAL ORIGIN. (PERCENTAGE OF TOTAL VALUE)
IMPORTATIONS PAR CATEGORIES ECONOMIQUES ET EXPORTATIONS PAR BRANCHE D'ACTIVITE.(EN POURCENTAGE DE LA VALEUR TOTALE)

IMPORTS – IMPORTATIONS

	1990	1991	1992	1993	1994	1995	1996
TOTAL IMPORTS–IMPORTATIONS TOTALES	100.	100.	100.	100.	100.	100.	100.
1 FOOD BEV–ALIMENTATION BOISSONS	5.1	8.9	9.4	8.9	8.5	7.7	8.1
11 PRIMARY–PRODUITS DE BASE	2.1	4.9	5.2	5.5	5.2	4.4	5.1
111 FOR INDUSTRY–POUR L'INDUSTRIE	0.8	1.4	2.0	2.4	2.0	2.1	2.9
112 FOR HOUSEHOLDS–POUR LES MENAGES	1.3	3.6	3.2	3.1	3.1	2.3	2.3
12 PROCESSED–PRODUITS ELABORES	2.9	4.0	4.3	3.4	3.3	3.3	3.0
121 FOR INDUSTRY–POUR L'INDUSTRIE	0.2	0.2	0.8	0.8	0.8	0.8	0.8
122 FOR HOUSEHOLDS–POUR LES MENAGES	2.7	3.8	3.5	2.6	2.5	2.4	2.1
2 IND SUPPLIES–APPROV INDUSTRIELS	23.5	16.9	27.5	33.9	37.7	39.5	36.2
21 PRIMARY–PRODUITS DE BASE	5.9	3.8	4.7	4.5	4.4	4.5	3.9
22 PROCESSED–PRODUITS ELABORES	17.6	13.1	22.9	29.3	33.3	35.0	32.2
3 FUELS–COMBUSTIBLES	21.9	18.8	16.7	12.3	10.4	9.2	9.2
31 PRIMARY–PRODUITS DE BASE	16.5	14.9	13.3	10.3	8.6	7.3	7.2
32 PROCESSED–PRODUITS ELABORES	5.4	3.9	3.4	2.0	1.9	1.8	2.0
321 MOTOR SPIRIT–ESSENCE			2.0	0.0	0.9		
322 OTHER–AUTRES	5.4	3.9	1.4	2.0	1.0	1.8	2.0
4 MACHINERY–EQUIPEMENT	25.0	21.1	23.8	22.6	22.7	22.9	23.8
41 CAPITAL EQUIPMENT–MACHINES	24.1	20.6	21.1	19.4	19.4	19.4	20.3
42 PARTS–PIECES ACCESSOIRES	0.9	0.5	2.7	3.3	3.3	3.5	3.5
5 TRANSPORT–TRANSPORT	5.9	8.5	6.1	7.2	6.9	7.4	9.4
51 PASSENGER CARS–AUTOMOBILES			2.0	2.3	1.8	1.6	2.5
52 OTHER–AUTRES	1.3	1.1	1.6	1.7	1.4	1.1	1.3
521 INDUSTRIAL–INDUSTRIELS	1.3	1.1	1.5	1.6	1.2	1.0	1.2
522 NON INDUSTRIAL–NON INDUSTRIEL			0.0	0.1	0.1	0.1	0.1
53 PARTS–PIECES ACCESSOIRES	4.7	7.4	2.5	3.1	3.8	4.7	5.5
6 CONSUM GOODS–BIENS CONSOMMATION	9.9	15.2	14.2	13.5	13.7	12.8	13.0
61 DURABLE–DURABLES	3.0	3.9	3.2	2.7	2.7	2.6	2.9
62 SEMI DURABLE–SEMI DURABLES	3.9	6.5	5.3	5.3	5.7	5.4	5.5
63 NON DURABLE–NON DURABLES	3.0	4.8	5.6	5.4	5.3	4.8	4.6
7 GOODS NES–BIENS NDA	8.7	10.6	2.3	1.6	0.1	0.5	0.1

EXPORTS – EXPORTATIONS

	1990	1991	1992	1993	1994	1995	1996
TOTAL EXPORTS–EXPORTATIONS TOTALES	100.	100.	100.	100.	100.	100.	100.
1 AGRICULTURE	5.9	8.4	7.1	4.2	3.6	3.5	2.8
2 MINING QUARRY–INDUS EXTRACTIVES	10.6	10.8	11.2	9.5	8.8	7.9	6.4
3 MANUFACTURING–IND MANUFACTUR	83.5	80.8	81.7	86.3	87.6	88.7	90.8
31 FOOD BEV TOBACCO–ALIM BOISS TAB	6.6	6.0	8.5	8.2	9.0	7.8	8.8
32 TEXTILES–INDUSTRIES TEXTILES	6.1	6.2	8.4	15.3	14.7	14.0	13.7
33 WOOD & PRODUCTS–BOIS & PRODUITS	1.3	3.1	3.4	3.4	3.8	3.6	3.3
34 PAPER & PRODUCTS–PAPIER & PRODT	0.8	0.9	1.5	1.4	1.7	2.8	2.7
35 CHEMICALS–INDUSTRIES CHIMIQUES	10.6	10.4	11.1	9.3	9.8	11.2	11.4
36 NON METAL MIN–MIN NON METAL	1.5	3.0	2.6	2.8	3.0	2.8	2.9
37 BASIC METAL–IND METAL BASE	13.6	13.5	15.0	13.9	13.8	12.3	10.3
38 METAL MANUF–MANUF METAL	32.3	25.2	28.3	29.6	30.4	32.9	36.2
39 OTH MANUF IND–AUTRES MANUF	10.5	12.6	3.0	2.4	1.4	1.4	1.5

3. TRADE BY PRINCIPAL COUNTRIES OF ORIGIN AND DESTINATION (VALUE IN MILLION U.S. DOLLARS)
ECHANGES SELON LES PRINCIPAUX PAYS D'ORIGINE ET DE DESTINATION (VALEUR EN MILLIONS DE DOLLARS EU)

COUNTRIES–PAYS	SPECIAL IMPORTS C.I.F. IMPORTATIONS SPECIALES C.A.F				
	1992	1993	1994	1995	1996
World	15894.1	18845.3	21433.5	29019.5	37094.9
Africa	188.0	256.5	305.5	472.1	474.4
Americas	787.2	1268.7	1145.3	1673.2	2520.9
– Northern America	595.4	1073.1	816.8	1252.3	1829.1
– LAIA	168.2	168.8	311.2	376.8	627.7
– CACM	18.3	22.4	11.8	36.1	55.3
– Caribbean	3.2	2.1	3.6	4.6	5.6
– Rest of America	2.1	2.4	1.9	3.3	3.2
Asia excl fmr USSR	1678.7	1741.5	1769.7	2513.9	3517.2
– Middle East	550.4	389.3	276.9	249.4	137.8
Asia former USSR	128.9	105.7	183.7	210.5	160.4
Europe excl fmr USSR	11336.1	13740.2	15466.1	21519.8	27012.4
– European Union	9850.3	12206.1	13707.5	18781.6	23739.2
– Eastern Europe	703.9	719.6	902.3	1677.2	2112.3
– Rest of Europe	781.9	814.5	856.2	1061.0	1161.0
Europe former USSR	1755.7	1703.5	1878.8	2588.0	3352.1
Oceania	19.4	29.3	26.2	42.0	57.6
Other	0.0		658.2	0.0	0.0
Germany/Allemagne	3798.0	5289.4	5843.9	7736.6	9166.3
Italy/Italie	1097.9	1469.2	1778.5	2482.6	3688.2
Russian Federation	1351.0	1271.2	1440.0	1959.8	2525.8
United Kingdom	1055.6	1085.0	1102.9	1502.7	2186.9
France, Monaco	705.7	803.7	937.8	1421.2	2027.9
Netherlands/Pays–Bas	757.0	877.0	956.9	1318.0	1413.0
USA/Etats–Unis d'Amer	538.2	1000.3	754.2	1140.4	1645.9
Austria/Autriche	720.9	613.5	525.5	737.8	815.4
Sweden/Suède	303.6	421.6	578.8	909.5	996.9
Belgium–Luxembourg	400.6	434.1	513.8	766.9	950.8
Czech Republic		350.3	474.5	891.7	1150.5
Denmark/Danemark	335.4	456.0	492.6	635.0	811.8
Finland/Finlande	378.8	383.3	505.8	540.5	610.8
Japan/Japon	334.7	329.6	335.0	478.7	604.8
Switzerland,Liechtenst.	306.1	328.0	354.2	504.2	557.4
Spain/Espagne	190.5	253.5	326.7	473.4	757.1
China/Chine	157.9	224.9	296.1	465.1	734.8
Norway,Svalbard and JM	354.9	355.8	367.9	393.2	373.9
Korea, Republic of	112.3	165.2	200.1	263.0	665.4
Hungary/Hongrie	143.9	165.5	210.4	352.2	426.0
Ukraine	161.9	199.0	194.6	290.8	418.5
Slovakia/Slovaquie		161.5	185.3	380.8	432.5
Iran (Islamic Rep of)	400.0	297.0	180.9	158.1	28.7
Other Asia n.e.s.	99.9	149.6	155.1	246.5	353.8
Belarus/Bélarus	161.2	113.9	157.4	238.4	257.4
Brazil/Brésil	52.4	58.4	125.4	154.6	331.1
Areas n.e.s.	0.0		646.2	0.0	0.0
Ireland/Irlande	46.2	66.6	83.0	151.4	189.7
Singapore/Singapour	81.8	86.5	73.9	129.2	164.6
Former Czechoslovakia	503.5				
Canada	57.0	72.7	62.6	111.9	182.8
Indonesia/Indonésie	35.4	66.3	88.2	119.7	166.9
India/Inde	64.3	75.5	82.4	108.1	139.9
Slovenia/Slovénie	4.8	82.1	86.4	103.6	151.5
China, Hong Kong SAR	87.8	77.6	63.1	87.2	92.1
Turkey/Turquie	80.5	65.0	84.6	76.1	93.2
Lithuania/Lituanie	57.0	90.4	71.8	66.7	109.7
Uzbekistan/Ouzbékistan	47.0	41.0	78.6	120.5	108.5
Thailand/Thaïlande	60.7	34.5	41.8	87.0	101.6
Greece/Grèce	55.1	47.6	54.3	79.3	77.2

COUNTRIES–PAYS	SPECIAL EXPORTS F.O.B. EXPORTATIONS SPECIALES F.O.B.				
	1992	1993	1994	1995	1996
Monde	13164.6	14044.1	17194.4	22862.1	24393.1
Afrique	359.1	380.9	288.1	303.1	330.4
Amériques	661.1	666.7	1024.8	999.9	914.5
– Amérique du Nord	343.2	455.0	730.0	688.9	678.1
– ALAI	234.4	186.4	210.2	211.1	184.0
– MCAC	7.9	10.8	3.5	9.7	9.1
– Caraïbes	51.3	7.2	77.2	80.6	15.1
– Autre Amérique	24.3	7.3	3.9	9.6	28.2
Asie anc. URSS exclus	966.5	995.2	1012.4	1075.4	1217.9
– Moyen–Orient	344.8	218.3	308.1	321.8	336.4
Asie ancienne URSS	115.1	96.1	61.4	68.5	98.3
Europe anc. URSS exclus	9905.7	10865.5	12933.4	17855.2	18497.4
– Union Européenne	8642.2	9761.8	11752.4	16038.7	16250.2
– Europe de l'Est	779.4	757.8	838.6	1349.7	1561.6
– Autre de l'Europe	484.1	345.8	342.4	466.9	685.6
Europe ancienne URSS	1131.8	1009.0	1422.6	2535.6	3306.1
Océanie	25.3	30.4	22.1	24.6	28.5
Autre	0.0	0.3	429.6	0.0	0.0
Germany/Allemagne	4132.7	5117.3	6114.6	8777.5	8417.3
Russian Federation	723.3	644.5	902.9	1274.2	1653.8
Netherlands/Pays–Bas	790.6	825.7	996.9	1288.6	1169.6
Italy/Italie	727.6	740.6	842.2	1124.3	1356.9
United Kingdom	567.0	609.4	769.7	916.9	960.8
France, Monaco	478.5	593.8	672.4	819.2	1077.4
Denmark/Danemark	330.5	418.9	534.2	688.2	743.0
USA/Etats–Unis d'Amer	304.2	407.4	582.9	622.7	563.7
Ukraine	188.2	184.9	257.4	742.6	977.7
Czech Republic		342.5	429.4	698.2	847.2
Belgium–Luxembourg	355.9	369.5	414.2	564.1	607.9
Sweden/Suède	328.9	307.1	426.4	581.0	582.6
Austria/Autriche	421.5	339.8	366.7	489.0	484.1
Finland/Finlande	259.2	195.9	293.1	352.8	315.4
Hungary/Hongrie	171.0	174.2	172.5	267.4	310.2
Switzerland,Liechtenst.	188.1	186.8	159.8	208.0	225.9
Slovakia/Slovaquie		166.7	169.2	279.4	280.0
Spain/Espagne	117.9	101.5	171.3	249.8	249.7
Belarus/Bélarus	158.8	103.2	115.0	240.6	272.4
Other Asia n.e.s.	125.3	226.0	160.8	141.2	148.6
Norway,Svalbard and JM	159.3	76.9	107.7	147.1	299.2
Lithuania/Lituanie	36.4	45.6	96.0	189.4	230.3
Brazil/Brésil	105.5	106.4	128.8	121.7	100.0
Thailand/Thaïlande	91.3	70.7	101.5	94.2	145.2
Former Czechoslovakia	498.0				
Greece/Grèce	47.5	64.6	61.6	95.3	182.6
Areas n.e.s.	0.0	0.3	414.5	0.0	0.0
Cyprus/Chypre	42.0	14.5	165.6	98.0	66.1
Morocco/Maroc	74.8	56.9	60.0	101.1	55.1
China/Chine	49.2	164.9	61.4	35.4	33.7
Ireland/Irlande	72.9	63.3	63.0	54.4	64.9
Turkey/Turquie	87.5	62.2	31.9	74.4	58.6
Egypt/Egypte	86.7	43.2	49.7	60.6	70.2
Canada	39.0	45.1	58.7	66.2	84.8
Korea, Republic of	24.0	40.6	39.6	55.3	121.6
India/Inde	52.4	42.1	40.5	80.2	51.4
Romania/Roumanie	66.5	36.4	27.2	57.6	73.8
Singapore/Singapour	36.5	48.5	54.5	57.0	58.4
Japan/Japon	67.7	48.7	36.5	42.9	52.1
Iran (Islamic Rep of)	110.9	33.7	23.5	31.8	24.1

(VALUE AS PERCENTAGE OF WORLD TOTAL)(VALEURS EN POURCENTAGE DU TOTAL MONDIAL)

	1987	1988	1989	1990	1991	1992	1993	1994	1995	1996
Africa	0.6	0.5	0.5	0.5	0.4	1.2	1.4	1.4	1.6	1.3
Americas	4.3	4.8	3.8	2.7	3.2	5.0	6.7	5.3	5.8	6.8
– Northern America	1.4	2.1	1.6	1.8	2.5	3.7	5.7	3.8	4.3	4.9
– LAIA	2.5	2.5	2.0	0.8	0.6	1.1	0.9	1.5	1.3	1.7
– CACM	0.0	0.0	0.0	0.0	0.0	0.1	0.1	0.1	0.1	0.1
– Caribbean	0.3	0.2	0.2	0.0	0.0	0.0	0.0	0.0	0.0	0.0
– Rest of America	0.1	0.0	0.0	0.0	0.0	0.0	0.0	0.0	0.0	0.0
Asia excl fmr USSR	7.3	7.8	9.0	9.2	11.3	10.6	9.2	8.3	8.7	9.5
– Middle East	0.8	1.5	2.4	3.6	4.5	3.5	2.1	1.3	0.9	0.4
Asia former USSR						0.8	0.6	0.9	0.7	0.4
Europe excl fmr USSR	52.2	61.3	67.1	66.8	70.7	71.3	72.9	72.2	74.2	72.8
– European Union	28.2	35.6	42.6	51.4	59.0	62.0	64.8	64.0	64.7	64.0
– Eastern Europe	16.0	17.2	14.1	5.4	4.9	4.4	3.8	4.2	5.8	5.7
– Rest of Europe	7.9	8.6	10.4	9.9	6.8	4.9	4.3	4.0	3.7	3.1
Europe former USSR	24.7	23.3	18.1	19.8	14.1	11.0	9.0	8.8	8.9	9.0
Oceania	1.3	1.4	1.1	0.4	0.2	0.1	0.2	0.1	0.1	0.2
Other	9.6	0.8	0.4	0.6	0.1	0.0		3.1	0.0	0.0
Germany/Allemagne					26.5	23.9	28.1	27.3	26.7	24.7
Italy/Italie	2.5	3.3	4.1	7.5	4.5	6.9	7.8	8.3	8.6	9.9
Russian Federation						8.5	6.7	6.7	6.8	6.8
United Kingdom	3.2	4.2	4.5	5.7	4.0	6.6	5.8	5.1	5.2	5.9
France, Monaco	2.3	2.5	3.1	3.0	3.6	4.4	4.3	4.4	4.9	5.5
Netherlands/Pays–Bas	1.7	2.7	3.0	2.6	4.9	4.8	4.7	4.5	4.5	3.8
USA/Etats–Unis d'Amer	1.3	2.0	1.4	1.6	2.3	3.4	5.3	3.5	3.9	4.4
Austria/Autriche	3.6	4.4	6.0	5.7	6.3	4.5	3.3	2.5	2.5	2.2
Sweden/Suède	1.2	1.6	1.7	2.0	1.8	1.9	2.2	2.7	3.1	2.7
Belgium–Luxembourg	1.3	1.4	1.5	1.4	2.8	2.5	2.3	2.4	2.6	2.6

	1987	1988	1989	1990	1991	1992	1993	1994	1995	1996
Afrique	2.2	2.7	2.5	2.3	2.0	2.7	2.7	1.7	1.3	1.4
Amériques	4.8	4.6	4.7	4.7	4.2	5.0	4.7	6.0	4.4	3.7
– Amérique du Nord	3.1	3.1	3.3	3.2	2.9	2.6	3.2	4.2	3.0	2.8
– ALAI	1.3	1.3	0.9	1.4	1.2	1.8	1.3	1.2	0.9	0.8
– MCAC	0.0	0.0	0.0	0.0	0.0	0.1	0.1	0.0	0.0	0.0
– Caraïbes	0.3	0.2	0.2	0.1	0.0	0.4	0.1	0.4	0.4	0.1
– Autre Amérique	0.0	0.0	0.3	0.0	0.1	0.2	0.1	0.0	0.0	0.1
Asie anc. URSS exclus	7.6	7.6	8.8	7.5	5.1	7.3	7.1	5.9	4.7	5.0
– Moyen–Orient	2.1	2.4	2.9	3.0	2.4	2.6	1.6	1.8	1.4	1.4
Asie ancienne URSS						0.9	0.7	0.4	0.3	0.4
Europe anc. URSS exclus	51.6	57.8	60.7	68.9	76.8	75.2	77.4	75.2	78.1	75.8
– Union Européenne	32.5	35.4	40.3	54.8	64.1	65.6	69.5	68.4	70.2	66.6
– Europe de l'Est	13.7	16.2	14.0	6.8	5.8	5.9	5.4	4.9	5.9	6.4
– Autre de l'Europe	5.4	6.1	6.4	7.3	6.9	3.7	2.5	2.0	2.0	2.8
Europe ancienne URSS	21.3	24.5	20.8	15.3	11.0	8.6	7.2	8.3	11.1	13.6
Océanie	0.2	0.2	0.2	0.2	0.1	0.2	0.2	0.1	0.1	0.1
Autre	12.4	2.6	2.3	1.2	0.7	0.0	0.0	2.5	0.0	0.0
Germany/Allemagne					29.3	31.4	36.4	35.6	38.4	34.5
Russian Federation						5.5	4.6	5.3	5.6	6.8
Netherlands/Pays–Bas	1.8	2.2	2.6	3.1	5.2	6.0	5.9	5.8	5.6	4.8
Italy/Italie	2.9	2.3	2.3	2.9	4.1	5.5	5.3	4.9	4.9	5.6
United Kingdom	4.3	5.0	6.5	7.1	7.1	4.3	4.3	4.5	4.0	3.9
France, Monaco	2.3	2.3	2.4	3.2	3.8	3.6	4.2	3.9	3.6	4.4
Denmark/Danemark	1.2	1.3	1.4	1.8	2.3	2.5	3.0	3.1	3.0	3.0
USA/Etats–Unis d'Amer	2.6	2.6	2.8	2.8	2.5	2.3	2.9	3.4	2.7	2.3
Ukraine						1.4	1.3	1.5	3.2	4.0
Czech Republic							2.4	2.5	3.1	3.5

4. Special Imports C.I.F. by Commodities according to the S.I.T.C. (Rev. 2) in million U.S. Dollars
Importations Spéciales C.A.F. par Produits d'après la C.T.C.I. (Rév. 2) en millions de Dollars E.U.

SITC CTCI	COMMODITY	1993 QUANTITY QUANTITE	1993 VALUE VALEUR	1994 QUANTITY QUANTITE	1994 VALUE VALEUR	1995 QUANTITY QUANTITE	1995 VALUE VALEUR	1996 QUANTITY QUANTITE	1996 VALUE VALEUR	PRODUIT
	ALL COMMODITIES		18845.4		21433.5		29019.5		37095.0	TOUS PRODUITS
0	FOOD AND LIVE ANIMALS		1819.1		1868.4		2327.1		3137.1	ALIMENTS,ANIMAUX VIVANTS
01	MEAT AND PREPARATIONS		167.5		206.7		140.9		189.4	VIANDES ET PREPARATIONS
011	MEAT FRESH,CHILLD,FROZEN	W 157738	162.8	W 190994	203.1	W 96907	133.3	W 118784	177.8	VIANDES FRAICHES,REF,CONGE
0113	PIG MEAT FRESH,CHLD,FRZN	W 47365	69.3	W 97803	114.7	W 46178	76.1	W 36523	79.2	VIANDE DE PORC
0114	POULTRY FRESH CHLLD,FRZN	W 72595	60.5	W 58314	59.5	W 31095	35.3	W 44017	51.1	VOLAILLES MORTES
02	DAIRY PRODCTS,BIRDS'EGGS		90.0		49.6		40.2		44.6	PRODUITS LAITIERS,OEUFS
03	FISH AND PREPARATIONS		126.0		169.1		181.1		241.4	POISSONS ET PREPARATIONS
034	FISH,FRESH,CHILLED,FROZN	W 146304	92.1	W 182450	136.4	W 170010	141.0	W 198491	203.9	POISSON FRAIS, REFRIG,CONG
0342	FISH FROZEN,EXCL FILLETS	W 108225	56.4	W 135477	81.7	W 133813	93.0	W 151763	135.7	POISSONS CONGELES
04	CEREALS AND PREPARATIONS		423.2		125.0		323.9		856.7	CEREALES ET PRODUITS
041	WHEAT ETC UNMILLED	W 818054	104.1	W 207540	35.7	W 976617	125.2	W 2187478	453.0	FROMENT,EPEAUTRE
0412	OTHER WHEAT ETC UNMILLED	W 546277	67.1	W 82469	7.8	W 859474	103.7	W 2142031	441.4	AUTRE FROMENT NON MOULU
043	BARLEY UNMILLED	W 675480	76.7	W 100953	7.4	W 679963	56.2	W 595766	101.0	ORGE NON MONDEE
044	MAIZE UNMILLED	W 926688	118.7	W 93027	13.7	W 198930	29.7	W 609352	118.8	MAIS NON MOULU
05	VEGETABLES AND FRUIT		278.5		308.5		388.3		485.5	LEGUMES ET FRUITS
054	VEG ETC FRSH,SMPLY PRSVD	W 256725	66.0	W 169016	65.0	W 198494	76.7	W 164770	73.1	LEGUMES FRAIS,CONG,SECS
057	FRUIT,NUTS,FRESH,DRIED	W 533556	168.7	W 587054	189.8	W 699823	233.2	W 796172	305.2	FRUITS FRAIS OU SECS
0573	BANANA,PLANTAIN,FRSH,DRY	W 144598	52.6	W 177889	73.6	W 245426	99.4	W 255862	126.0	BANANES FRAICHES,SECHEES
06	SUGAR AND PREPS,HONEY		46.1		48.0		135.6		99.1	SUCRES ET PRODUITS
061	SUGAR AND HONEY	W 25636	8.8	W 14792	6.6	W 201284	90.8	W 96310	49.5	SUCRES ET MIEL
07	COFFEE,TEA,COCOA,SPICES		296.2		447.8		565.7		531.9	CAFE,THE,CACAO,EPICES
071	COFFEE AND SUBSTITUTES	W 91902	134.9	W 101895	256.0	W 99206	338.8	W 106452	267.2	CAFE ET SUCCEDANES
0711	COFFEE GREEN,ROASTED,SUB	W 89057	116.0	W 97397	224.4	W 94605	301.9	W 100632	227.4	CAFE TORREFIE OU DECAFEINE
07111	COFFEE GREEN,HUSKS,SKINS	W 68333	73.8	W 85259	186.0	W 90647	282.5	W 97056	213.1	CAFE NON TORREFIE
072	COCOA	W 43883	63.8	W 51176	83.5	W 53538	93.8	W 62986	108.6	CACAO
074	TEA AND MATE	W 32832	60.6	W 32348	60.1	W 32552	65.8	W 33145	69.8	THE ET MATE
0741	TEA	W 32824	60.5	W 32348	60.1	W 32552	65.8	W 33145	69.8	THE
081	*FEEDING STUFF FOR ANIML	W 716613	196.1	W 937294	269.7	W 1181306	316.8	W 1451223	451.8	NOURRITURE POUR ANIMAUX
0813	OILCAKE AND OTH RESIDUES	W 428540	102.5	W 599544	134.0	W 707631	159.4	W 906955	255.6	TOURTEAUX
08131	— OF SOYA BEANS	W 415298	100.5	W 596407	133.5	W 703545	158.5	W 882139	251.8	TOURTEAUX DE SOJA
0814	MEAT OR FISH MEAL FODDER	W 138985	40.5	W 225198	73.8	W 243531	82.0	W 268841	100.8	FARINES DE VIANDES,POISSONS
08141	MEAT MEAL FODDER	W 132287	38.1	W 221405	72.1	W 241739	81.0	W 267213	99.8	FARINES DE VIANDES
09	MISC EDIBLE PRODUCTS		165.3		187.2		201.8		196.9	PREP ALIMENTAIRES DIVERSES
098	EDIBLE PRODCTS,PREPS NES	W 71985	144.0	W 96996	177.3	W 95252	191.9	W 93217	187.3	PREP ALIMENTAIRES NDA
09809	MISC FOOD PREPRTIONS NES	W 45615	96.4	W 71346	132.3	W 64650	135.3	W 57580	123.9	PREP ALIMENTAIRES NDA
1	BEVERAGES AND TOBACCO		144.6		184.8		216.1		249.4	BOISSONS ET TABACS
12	TOBACCO AND MANUFACTURES		107.5		141.2		163.2		165.1	TABACS BRUTS FABRIQUES
121	TOBACCO UNMNFCTRD,REFUSE	W 28040	98.4	W 41208	125.7	W 44534	142.0	W 42049	154.6	TABACS BRUTS,DECHETS
1212	TOBACCO STRIPPED OR PART	W 15698	68.0	W 28500	98.1	W 31602	113.7	W 29672	129.5	TABACS PART ECOTES
2	CRUDE MATERLS,EXCL FUELS		836.9		1085.1		1524.8		1695.8	MAT BRUTES NON COMESTIBLES
22	OIL SEEDS,OLEAGINOUS FRT		34.3		56.9		39.4		151.9	GRAINES,FRUITS OLEAGINEUX
222	SEEDS FOR'SOFT'FIXED OIL	W 80022	29.5	W 120497	49.9	W 55287	35.5	W 383264	144.9	GRAINES HUILES FIXES
23	RUBBER, CRUDE		48.4		81.7		121.5		127.5	CAOUTCHOUC BRUT
251	*PULP AND WASTE PAPER	W 110900	37.5	W 143335	58.4	W 223356	138.3	W 198703	103.7	PATES A PAPIER,DECHETS
26	TEXTILE FIBRES AND WASTE		186.8		269.7		344.4		321.4	FIBRES TEXTILES
263	COTTON	W 69402	70.7	W 88111	125.4	W 90665	178.5	W 85142	149.9	COTON
2631	RAW COTTON,EXCL LINTERS	W 58565	65.4	W 81688	121.1	W 86472	174.2	W 80573	144.5	COTON EN MASSE
27	CRUDE FERTLZR,MINRLS NES		123.1		147.3		187.9		212.6	ENGRAIS MINERAUX BRUTS
278	OTHER CRUDE MINERALS		54.9	W 426228	66.1	W 463762	84.3	W 492699	84.9	AUTRES MINERAUX BRUTS
28	METALLIFEROUS ORES,SCRAP		261.5		278.5		390.6		389.6	MINERAIS METAL,DECHETS
281	IRON ORE,CONCENTRATES	W 8775959	191.6	W 8447731	192.6	MW 10875	278.4	MW 9804	274.6	MINERAIS DE FER
2815	IRON ORE,CONC,NOT AGGLOM	W 6926919	135.3	W 6162680	124.4	W 7544496	169.8	W 6774335	167.5	MINERAIS NON AGGLOMERES
2816	IRON ORE AGGLOMERATES	W 1849040	56.3	W 2250918	67.1	W 2984589	97.2	W 2699187	95.1	MINERAIS AGGLOMERES
287	BASE METAL ORES,CONC NES	W 509272	68.6	W 604346	84.2	W 585840	108.9	W 570741	110.6	MINERAIS METAUX COMMUNS
29	CRUDE ANIMAL,VEG MAT NES		104.8		122.4		171.4		212.1	MATIERES BRUTES ANIM,VEGET
292	CRUDE VEG MATERIALS NES		55.4	W 28790	64.2	W 47055	88.6	W 38849	101.2	MAT BRUTES VEGETALES NDA
3	MINERAL FUELS ETC		2353.4		2271.3		2676.7		3421.8	COMBUSTIBLES MINERAUX LUB
33	PETROLEUM AND PRODUCTS		2033.3		1875.1		2111.7		2694.7	PETROLE ET DERIVES
333	CRUDE PETROLEUM	MW 13674	1625.2	MW 12720	1442.4	MW 13037	1576.4	MW 13351	1976.4	HUILES BRUTES DE PETROLE
334	PETROLEUM PRODUCTS,REFIN	W 1763346	378.2	W 2045991	396.6	W 2432036	491.7	W 2958144	674.4	PRODUITS RAFFINES
3341	GASOLINE,OTH LIGHT OILS	W 1105534	213.6	W 1065952	184.7					ESSENCES POUR MOTEURS
33411	MOTOR,AVIATION SPIRIT	W 8678	3.3	W 982119	172.4					ESSENCES MOTEURS D'AVIONS
33412	SPIRIT TYPE JET FUEL	W 1075074	206.1							CARBUREACTEURS
3343	GAS OILS	W 435339	75.5	W 548502	83.4					GAS OILS
3345	LUBS,PETROLEUM OILS NES	W 92912	66.5	W 88170	70.6					HUILES LUBRIFIANTES
341	*GAS,NATURAL AND MANUFCT		313.5		351.1	W 5473648	480.7	W 5510161	608.3	GAZ NATUREL,GAZ MANUFACT
3413	PETROLM GASES,LIQUEFIED	W 121949	18.5	W 218491	36.6	W 426639	75.9	W 629202	113.0	GAZ DE PETROLE LIQUEFIE
3414	PETROLEUM GASES, GASEOUS		295.1		314.5	W 5047009	404.9	W 4880959	495.4	GAZ DE PETROLE GAZEUX
4	ANIMAL,VEGETABLE OIL,FAT		113.6		158.1		187.9		214.6	HUILES,GRAISSES ANIM,VEG
42	FIXED VEGETABLE OIL,FAT		88.7		119.8		125.1		140.1	HUILES VEGETALES FIXES
423	FIXED VEG OILS,SOFT	W 142133	64.9	W 151118	85.0	W 125873	83.5	W 157508	99.7	HUILES VEGET DOUCES FIXES
5	CHEMCLS,RELATED PROD NES		2363.6		3023.7		4134.2		4878.2	PRODUITS CHIMIQUES
51	ORGANIC CHEMICALS		332.5		510.3		694.7		634.3	PROD CHIMIQ ORGANIQUES
511	HYDROCARBONS NES,DERIVS	W 287604	95.4	W 483543	170.3	W 488946	262.2	W 435124	162.1	HYDROCARBURES NDA
5111	ACYCLIC HYDROCARBONS	W 102662	31.0	W 140573	45.2	W 166390	87.6	W 142093	61.5	HYDROCARBURES ACYCLIQUES
5112	CYCLIC HYDROCARBONS	W 159434	49.6	W 279139	98.4	W 235496	118.4	W 217130	71.9	HYDROCARBURES CYCLIQUES
512	ALCOHOLS,PHENOLS ETC	W 137018	51.9	W 179918	87.1	W 139116	91.9	W 173366	93.2	PHENOLS,PHENOLS–ALCOOLS
514	NITROGEN–FNCTN COMPOUNDS	W 23061	62.6	W 32056	85.0	W 39319	121.4	W 41333	139.4	COMPOSES FONCT AZOTEES
52	INORGANIC CHEMICALS		93.2		112.2		142.9		179.2	PROD CHIM INORGANIQUES
53	DYES,TANNING,COLOUR PROD		213.8		275.3		362.3		431.9	PROD TEINTURE,COLORANTS
533	PIGMENTS,PAINTS,ETC	W 70443	170.5	W 77564	221.1	W 95934	297.6	W 120738	358.0	PIGMENTS,PEINTURES,VERNIS
5334	VARNISHES,DISTEMPERS ETC	W 25689	83.4	W 31807	105.4	W 39368	151.0	W 45837	182.3	PEINTURES A L'EAU
53342	OTH PAINTS,VARNISHES ETC	W 18097	61.0	W 22923	77.5	W 27991	112.0	W 29224	127.0	AUTRES PEINTURES,VERNIS
541	*MEDICINAL,PHARM PRODUCT	MK 24104	654.1		738.0	MK 25420	911.8	MK 27709	1068.2	PROD MEDICINAUX PHARMACEUT
5417	MEDICAMENTS	MK 15676	489.8	MK 16677	561.3	MK 16876	697.8	MK 18332	846.5	MEDICAMENTS
54171	— CONTAINNG ANTIBIOTICS	K 1955114	121.4	K 1460000	84.9	K 1591596	122.9	K 2013417	151.5	MED CONTN ANTIBIOTIQUES
54179	— CONTNG OTH SUBSTANCES	MK 12650	319.2	MK 14567	414.1	MK 14676	484.2	MK 15700	586.3	MED CONT AUT SUBSTANCES
55	PERFUME,CLEANING ETC PRD		295.3		316.7		407.6		566.7	PROD POUR PARFUM,TOILETTE
553	PERFUMERY,COSMETICS,ETC	W 35084	127.7	W 37951	135.8	W 41138	152.4	W 56136	225.6	PRODUITS DE PARFUMERIE
554	SOAP,CLEANSING ETC PREPS	W 121326	125.7	W 471042	127.1	W 163921	175.3	W 230460	234.8	SAVONS,PRODUITS DETERSIFS
5542	WASHING PREPARATIONS ETC	W 99805	95.3	W 448619	94.7	W 138375	134.1	W 198394	184.9	PROD ORG TENSIO–ACT NDA
562	*FERTILIZERS,MANUFACTURE	W 685778	51.7	W 912084	65.3	W 907709	76.6	W 1089532	103.2	ENGRAIS MANUFACTURES
58	PLASTIC MATERIALS ETC		412.2		595.3		1001.2		1200.4	MAT PLAST ARTIFICIELLES
582	PROD OF CONDENSATION ETC	W 43101	92.4	W 65514	122.7	W 86695	194.8	W 115595	228.8	PROD CONDENS,POLYCOND
583	POLYMERIZATION ETC PRODS	W 197472	305.2	W 292113	448.2	W 435662	769.2	W 576861	927.3	PROD POLYMERISATION
5831	POLYETHYLENE	W 49544	39.6	W 88366	95.1	W 137574	179.0	W 178924	201.2	POLYETHYLENE
58311	— IN PRIMARY FORMS	W 46387	35.1	W 69469	59.7	W 112845	129.3	W 149496	141.5	POLYETHYLENE PRIMAIRES
5832	POLYPROPYLENE	W 36355	54.8	W 41857	58.3	W 55260	103.5	W 72848	118.7	POLYPROPYLENE
5833	POLYSTYRENE,ITS COPOLYMR	W 35736	46.3	W 53768	72.0	W 59019	105.7	W 96359	131.4	POLYPROPYLENE COPOLYMERES
5834	POLYVINYL CHLORIDE	W 30801	42.2	W 42293	60.7	W 84759	129.0	W 112016	166.5	CHLORURE DE POLYVINYLE

4. Special Imports C.I.F. by Commodities according to the S.I.T.C. (Rev. 2) in million U.S. Dollars
Importations Spéciales C.A.F. par Produits d'après la C.T.C.I. (Rév. 2) en millions de Dollars E.U.

SITC CTCI	COMMODITY	1993 QUANTITY QUANTITE	1993 VALUE VALEUR	1994 QUANTITY QUANTITE	1994 VALUE VALEUR	1995 QUANTITY QUANTITE	1995 VALUE VALEUR	1996 QUANTITY QUANTITE	1996 VALUE VALEUR	PRODUIT
5839	OTH POLYMRZTION ETC PROD	W 30190	90.9	W 42828	112.0	W 64797	167.6	W 70365	199.5	AUT PROD POLYMER COPOLYM
59	CHEMICAL MATERIALS NES		309.2		407.8		531.9		689.6	MAT PROD CHIMIQUES NDA
591	PESTICIDES,DISINFECTANTS	W 12559	89.8	W 14965	121.3	W 18730	139.4	W 23898	174.2	DESINF,INSECT,FONG,HERB
592	STARCH,INULIN,GLUTEN,ETC	W 62042	58.6	W 43776	78.8	W 94975	120.2	W 93710	147.9	AMIDONS,INUL,GLUT FROM
5922	ALBUMINOID SUBSTAN,GLUES	W 28189	50.5	W 38247	76.3	W 48358	99.3	W 51295	128.9	MAT ALBUMIN,COLLES
598	MISCEL CHEM PRODUCTS NES	W 223082	160.9	W 257879	207.7	W 275114	272.3	W 353187	367.6	PROD DIV INDUST CHIM NDA
5989	CHEM PRODUCTS,PREPS NES	W 64967	118.3	W 83355	150.6	W 93534	198.5	W 152743	278.0	PROD PREP CHIMIQUES NDA
59899	OTH CHEM PRODS,PREPS,NES	W 49140	81.0	W 67926	108.1	W 78480	147.7	W 109800	206.0	AUT PRODUITS CHIMIQUES NDA
6	BASIC MANUFACTURES		3478.6		4415.6		6355.4		7576.7	ART MANUFACTURES
61	LEATHER,DRESSED FUR,ETC		101.8		130.8		188.3		243.0	CUIRS,PELLETERIES
611	LEATHER	W 6713	78.2	W 9596	98.6	W 10578	142.2	W 14275	177.0	CUIRS,PEAUX PREPARES
6114	LEATHR BOVINE NES,EQUINE	W 4265	52.7	W 5731	67.1	W 6648	106.3	W 8947	136.3	CUIRS DE BOVINS
62	RUBBER MANUFACTURES NES		137.8		164.5		223.0		296.3	CAOUTCHOUC MANUFACTURE
628	RUBBER ARTICLES NES	W 7666	53.9	W 10297	67.5	W 12052	90.1	W 15207	115.8	OUVRAGES CAOUTCHOUC NDA
63	WOOD,CORK MANUFACTRS NES		51.4		72.4		122.4		164.0	OUVRAGES LIEGE ET BOIS
64	PAPER,PAPERBOARD AND MFR		456.9		599.5		938.5		1134.8	PAPIERS,CARTONS & OUVRAGES
641	PAPER AND PAPERBOARD	W 282642	288.0	W 362839	399.9	W 479787	647.2	W 673538	807.9	PAPIERS ET CARTONS
6412	PRINTG,WRITING PAPER NES	W 57698	58.3	W 99923	102.5	W 137626	175.0	W 169486	180.6	PAPIERS POUR L'IMPRESSION
64122	— COATED,IMPREGNATD ETC	W 53179	53.9	W 92392	94.3	W 126684	159.1	W 152652	161.2	PAPIERS IMPRESSION COUCHES
6415	PAPER,PAPERBRD,BULK,NES	W 87165	64.0	W 126179	79.8	W 159300	148.6	W 217613	175.5	PAPIERS,CARTONS ROULEAUX
64159	OTHER PAPER ETC,BULK,NES	W 83278	62.1	W 123511	76.8	W 154686	141.9	W 210993	167.8	AUT PAPIER ROULEAUX FEUILLES
6418	COATED ETC PAPER NES BLK	W 57284	113.9	W 69268	158.8	W 88849	217.7	W 118440	271.4	PAP,CARTONS COUCHES,ENDUITS
64181	PLASTIC COATED PAPER ETC	W 13138	44.5	W 17033	78.4	W 21143	96.8	W 29067	124.6	PAP,CARTONS ENDUITS,RESINES
64189	COATED PAPER ETC NES	W 42744	68.1	W 51709	79.9	W 67375	120.4	W 88696	145.9	PAPIERS,CARTONS COUCHES
642	PAPER,ETC,PRECUT,ARTS OF	W 87854	169.0	W 94718	199.7	W 118884	291.4	W 148473	327.0	PAP,CARTONS DECOUPES
6421	PAPER ETC CONTAINERS	W 52565	80.7	W 57251	103.2	W 71981	146.9	W 86040	166.9	BOITES,SACS EMBALLAGES
6428	PAPER ETC ARTICLES NES	W 22201	58.0	W 22037	56.4	W 27022	76.2	W 33000	82.4	OUVRAGES EN PATE A PAPIER
65	TEXTILE YARN,FABRICS,ETC		1381.3		1728.0		2194.1		2389.2	FILS,TISSUS,ARTICLES TEXTILE
651	TEXTILE YARN		124.9	W 33096	162.0	W 37398	210.0	W 62401	286.0	FILS TEXTILES
6514	SYN FIB YRN,BULK,MONOFIL		55.6	W 14289	77.8	W 16891	102.3	W 33107	141.7	FILS CONT 85% FIB TEXT SYNTH
652	COTTON FABRICS,WOVEN	W 33345	258.7	W 37390	322.8	W 39737	402.4	W 43430	419.6	TISSUS DE COTON
6522	WOVEN COTTON BLEACHD,ETC	W 26032	224.0	W 29936	293.7	W 34409	383.3	W 37818	397.5	TISSUS COTON BLANCHIS ETC
65224	BLCHED COTTON FABRIC NES	W 19965	179.3	W 25035	239.7	W 29941	318.5	W 33012	333.3	AUT TIS PLUS 85% COT BLANCHI
653	WOVN MAN-MADE FIB FABRIC	W 37714	486.9	W 52428	553.1	W 64781	701.4	W 97607	681.3	TISSUS FIBRES SYNTH,ARTIF
6531	CONT SYNT WEAVES NONPILE	W 10292	107.8	W 16701	125.0	W 21028	145.3	W 24742	147.6	TISSUS FIBRES SYNTH CONTINUE
65315	CONT SYN TXTL FABRIC NES	W 9264	95.7	W 15126	109.3	W 19057	126.8	W 22197	124.9	TIS PLUS 85% TEXT SYNT CONT
6534	DISC SYN BLEND FABRC NES	W 9650	122.6	W 13663	140.0	W 15239	167.8	W 42115	180.5	TISSUS FIBRES SYNTH DISCONT
6535	CONT REGN WEAVES NONPILE	W 3838	74.4	W 5232	92.1	W 5375	136.6	W 4796	109.5	TISSUS FIB TEXT ART CONTINU
65355	CONT REGN TXTL FABRC NES	W 2671	49.4	W 3853	63.8	W 3747	94.3	W 3431	75.3	TISSUS 85% TEXT ART CONT
6538	DISC REG BLEND FABRC NES	W 4366	80.8	W 3759	79.8	W 4625	104.1	W 4789	97.7	TIS MOINS 85% TEXT ART DISC
654	OTH WOVEN TEXTILE FABRIC	W 7434	155.4	W 9144	187.9	W 9435	216.0	W 11256	229.0	TISSUS AUT COTON SYNT,ARTIF
6542	WOVEN WOOL,HAIR NONPILE	W 2769	72.0	W 3194	85.1	W 3345	93.4	W 3287	97.6	TIS PLUS 85% LAINE,POILS
6543	WOVEN WOOL ETC FABRC NES	W 2948	60.3	W 3316	63.8	W 3473	79.1	W 4606	91.7	TISSUS LAINE,POILS FINS NDA
655	KNITTED,ETC FABRICS	W 10758	104.0	W 14592	135.2	W 15415	157.8	W 18597	187.6	ETOF BONNETERIE PIECES ETC
6552	OTHER KNIT ETC FAB NONEL	W 10758	104.0	W 14592	135.2	W 15415	157.8	W 18597	187.6	ETOF BON NON ELAS NON SYNT
657	SPECIAL TXTL FABRC,PRODS	W 75999	158.1	W 594070	231.7	W 43857	317.3	W 52075	362.9	TISSUS SPECIAUX
6572	BONDED FIBRE TEXTLS NES	W 60579	44.6	W 568459	64.9	W 12309	91.2	W 14720	90.2	TISSUS NON TISSES
6573	COATED ETC TEXTILES NES	W 10109	76.1	W 16267	116.1	W 21305	157.2	W 24419	184.4	TISSUS,ART MATIERE TEXT PLAST
658	TEXTILE ARTICLES NES	W 3859	28.2	W 6855	58.0	W 8271	88.4	W 11603	104.0	ART FACONNES MAT TEXTILES
66	NONMETAL MINERAL MFS NES		304.1		394.2		611.9		798.7	ART MIN NON METALLIQUES
662	CLAY,REFRACTORY BLDG PRD	W 248927	99.2	W 335151	130.4	W 457132	200.8	W 634895	284.0	MAT CONST REFRACTAIRES
6624	BRICKS ETC NONREFRACTORY	W 231846	80.3	W 321216	112.5	W 429506	164.1	W 604127	237.0	BRIQUES ETC CERAM NON REFR
66245	GLAZED CERAMIC SETTS ETC	W 129498	58.9	W 172672	79.4	W 215564	107.4	W 305023	156.3	AUT CARREAUX CERAMIQUE
663	MINERAL MANUFCTURES NES	W 61025	50.0	W 90880	65.8	W 184303	111.0	W 319250	140.6	ART MIN MANUF NDA
664	GLASS	W 76432	83.9	W 114727	114.1	W 148421	171.4	W 168883	204.9	VERRE
67	IRON AND STEEL		430.5		566.3		934.8		1075.1	FER ET ACIER
673	IRON,STEEL SHAPES ETC	W 69672	40.2	W 142947	73.4	W 200927	134.3	W 199540	134.2	BARRES,PROFIL FER,ACIER
674	IRN,STL UNIV,PLATE,SHEET	W 353922	195.9	W 440460	258.9	W 505115	391.1	W 501868	398.8	LARGES PLATS,TOLES
6744	IRN,STL HVY PLATE,ROLLED	W 114134	45.3	W 121781	58.7	W 155643	101.9	W 105878	73.5	TOLES LAMINEES PLUS 4.75 MM
6746	IRN,STL THIN PLATE,ROLLD	W 56920	38.6	W 101536	62.6	W 112054	103.2	W 120372	110.4	TOLES LAM MOINS 3MM
6749	OTH IRN,STL PLATES,SHEET	W 113772	72.6	W 138267	97.9	W 136660	122.9	W 138853	133.4	AUTRES TOLES FER,ACIER
67491	— OF IRON OR SIMPLE STL	W 109340	67.8	W 135059	92.7	W 132972	114.0	W 134234	120.8	AUT TOLES AUTRES ACIER FIN
678	IRON,STL TUBES,PIPES,ETC	W 71467	101.0	W 76604	103.4	W 157914	236.0	W 244861	347.9	TUBES,TUYAUX EN FONTE,FER
6783	IRON,STL TUBES,PIPES NES	W 31229	35.7	W 35308	37.9	W 97214	125.9	W 173422	208.0	AUT TUBES,TUYAUX FER,ACIER
68	NON-FERROUS METALS		196.2		220.6		367.5		429.6	METAUX NON FERREUX
684	ALUMINIUM	W 67480	137.9	W 65795	165.1	W 88133	268.4	W 114210	320.0	ALUMINIUM
6841	ALUMINIUM,ALLOYS,UNWRGHT	W 42317	49.6	W 38258	58.3	W 45141	88.0	W 49529	81.7	ALUMINIUM,ALLIAGES BRUTS
6842	ALUMINIUM,ALLOYS WORKED	W 25163	88.3	W 27537	106.9	W 42992	180.4	W 64681	238.4	ALUMINIUM,ALLIAGES OUVRE
69	METAL MANUFACTURES NES		419.0		539.7		775.2		1046.4	ART MANUFACT EN METAL NDA
691	STRUCTURES AND PARTS NES	W 37278	61.8	W 39446	84.6	W 48334	118.4	W 62162	162.2	CONSTRUCT FER,ACIER,ALU
695	TOOLS	W 5477	44.5	W 6620	60.0	W 9236	89.8	W 13641	124.3	OUTILS A MAIN
697	BASE MTL HOUSEHOLD EQUIP	W 13935	68.5	W 13762	71.7	W 16603	93.0	W 23191	134.2	ART MENAGE MET COMMUNS
699	BASE METAL MFRS NES	W 31062	136.3	W 41509	189.1	W 57276	287.9	W 77702	388.7	ART MANUFACTURES MET NDA
6991	LOCKSMITHS WARES,ETC	W 8003	60.1	W 11386	81.4	W 15508	124.0	W 22546	168.6	ARTICLES DE SERRURERIE
69913	BASE MTL DOOR,ETC FITTNG	W 6092	44.8	W 9320	64.4	W 12862	96.0	W 18982	131.5	GARNITURES POUR MEUBLES
7	MACHINES,TRANSPORT EQUIP		5496.5		6208.0		8667.3		12237.5	MACHINES MATERIEL TRANSPORT
71	POWER GENERATING EQUIPMT		283.7		393.0		562.5		700.2	MACHINES GENERATRICES
713	INTRNL COMBUS PSTN ENGIN	W 21253	166.1	W 27004	243.3	W 32409	336.3	W 47499	447.1	MOTEURS EXPL COMB INT, PIECE
7132	MOTOR VEHCL PISTN ENGINS	W 13663	104.2	W 19091	171.9	W 25266	236.1	W 34942	306.7	MOTEURS EXPL POUR VEHICULES
72	MACHS FOR SPCL INDUSTRYS		867.5		1025.6		1294.7		1764.1	MAC SPECIALES POUR INDUST
721	AGRIC MACHY,EXC TRACTORS	W 22663	48.3	W 39333	78.0	W 32612	135.3	W 61243	237.3	MACHINES AGRICOLES
7212	HARVESTING ETC MACHINES	W 14161	20.4	W 24613	33.3	W 16493	54.8	W 37182	130.5	ENGINS POUR LA RECOLTE
723	CIVIL ENGNEERG EQUIP ETC	W 15144	111.6	W 14265	50.1	W 21759	82.7	W 41530	113.2	APPAREILS DE GENIE CIVIL
7234	CONST,MINING MACHNRY NES	W 14262	104.6	W 12762	45.3	W 19136	68.3	W 38768	99.5	MACH POUR LA CONST, MINES
72344	BORING,SINKING MACHINERY	W 7778	71.9	W 1181	8.6	W 808	11.8	W 1908	13.7	MACHINES DE FORAGE
724	TEXTILE,LEATHER MACHNRY	W 10691	134.3	W 14722	171.9	W 14689	183.8	W 19917	223.6	MACH POUR INDUSTRIE TEXTILE
725	PAPER ETC MILL MACHINERY	W 3732	55.4	W 3994	63.0	W 6363	96.2	W 7769	113.8	MACHINES FABR PATE PAPIER
726	PRINTG,BKBINDG MACHY,PTS	W 6232	70.4	W 7462	115.8	W 8618	108.6	W 12486	178.2	MACHINES POUR IMPRIMERIE
727	FOOD MACHRY NON-DOMESTIC	W 11179	155.7	W 11100	156.0	W 17701	236.8	W 14851	216.3	MACH INDUSTRIES ALIMENT
7272	OTH FOOD PROC MCHY,PARTS	W 10216	154.4	W 10371	152.1	W 16957	232.8	W 13732	210.4	AUT MACH IND ALIMENTAIRE
72722	INDUS FOOD PROC MACH NES	W 10010	149.4	W 10203	146.7	W 16643	225.0	W 13196	195.2	MACHINES BOULANGERIE
728	OTH MACHY FOR SPCL INDUS	W 28268	283.7	W 39460	381.8	W 38876	438.3	W 50975	633.7	AUT MACH IND PARTICULIERES
7284	MACHY FOR SPCL INDUS NES	W 15214	212.9	W 25234	299.9	W 22332	327.8	W 30816	492.9	MACH SPEC IND PARTICUL.
72842	RUBBER,PLASTICS WRKG MCH	W 5476	41.6	W 7957	56.2	W 9607	93.5	W 11091	108.0	MACH IND CAOUT MAT PLAST
72844	WOOD TREATING MACHNS NES	W 1938	14.3	W 6722	71.3	W 2973	32.1	W 3808	44.6	MACH TRAITEMENT DU BOIS
72848	OTH MCHY WITH INDIV FNCT	W 4492	75.9	W 7382	110.4	W 5712	110.1	W 10379	185.1	AUTRES MACHINES NDA
73	METALWORKING MACHINERY		122.4		186.7		248.4		310.5	MACH TRAVAIL DES METAUX
736	METALWORKING MACH-TOOLS	W 8330	84.4	W 12220	112.1	W 13649	121.1	W 24054	189.6	MACH-OUTILS TRAVAIL METAUX
737	METALWORKING MACHNRY NES	W 3313	38.1	W 7727	74.7	W 23563	127.4	W 17314	121.0	MACH TRAV METAUX PIECES
74	GENRL INDUSTRL MACHY NES		1056.9		1268.7		1767.6		2316.4	MACH APP INDUSTRIE
741	HEATING,COOLING EQUIPMNT	W 21515	218.7	W 28162	260.3	W 32609	382.0	W 60779	598.7	MACH CHAUFFAGE,PIECES

4. Special Imports C.I.F. by Commodities according to the S.I.T.C. (Rev. 2) in million U.S. Dollars
Importations Spéciales C.A.F. par Produits d'après la C.T.C.I. (Rév. 2) en millions de Dollars E.U.

SITC CTCI	COMMODITY	1993 QUANTITY QUANTITE	1993 VALUE VALEUR	1994 QUANTITY QUANTITE	1994 VALUE VALEUR	1995 QUANTITY QUANTITE	1995 VALUE VALEUR	1996 QUANTITY QUANTITE	1996 VALUE VALEUR	PRODUIT
7413	INDUS FURNACES ETC,PARTS	W 6319	41.8	W 11269	67.0	W 8081	77.4	W 18844	121.1	FOURS IND,LABOR,PIECES
7416	HEATING,COOLING EQU NES	W 5955	72.2	W 7204	88.5	W 12216	156.1	W 24008	267.8	APP CHANGEMENT TEMP
742	PUMPS FOR LIQUIDS ETC	W 3787	70.2	W 3922	77.5	W 6234	113.9	W 6535	129.5	POMPES MOTO-POMPES
743	PUMPS NES,CENTRFUGES ETC	W 99625	217.4	W 19710	264.2	W 25801	365.3	W 35266	467.0	POMPES COMPRES,VENT ETC
7436	GAS,LIQUID FILTERS ETC	W 92379	132.4	W 10833	155.5	W 14401	226.0	W 18742	274.4	APP POUR FILT DES LIQUIDES
744	MECHANICAL HANDLING EQU	W 18964	127.8	W 24770	160.3	W 58161	201.1	W 42640	234.0	EQUIP MANUTENTION PIECES
7442	LIFTING,LOADING MACH NES	W 9165	76.0	W 11931	96.6	W 13705	125.2	W 18450	133.5	APP LEVAGE,MANUTENTION
74428	OTH HANDLING ETC MCH NES	W 7231	57.6	W 8317	68.0	W 10623	99.1	W 13012	94.4	AUT APP LEVAGE ETC
745	NONELEC MACHY,TOOLS NES	W 12371	190.8	W 11899	208.9	W 14113	286.1	W 16230	364.2	AUT MACH NON ELEC,PIECES
7452	OTH NONELEC MCHS,PTS NES	W 11751	171.0	W 11017	179.7	W 12935	245.0	W 14707	311.3	AUT MACH NON ELEC,PIECES
74522	PACKAGNG,BOTTLNG,ETC MCH	W 5088	108.8	W 4621	103.7	W 5115	144.8	W 5515	173.0	MACH NETT BOUTEILLES,ETC
749	NONELEC MACH PTS,ACC NES	W 18086	232.3	W 871409	297.7	W 30199	419.6	W 39042	523.1	PIECES MACH NON ELEC NDA
7492	COCKS,VALVES ETC NES	W 8946	143.5	W 11027	169.6	W 14156	231.5	W 18451	289.9	ART ROB,SIM POUR TUYAUX
75	OFFICE MACHNES,ADP EQUIP		577.7		593.8		841.4		1120.7	MACH BUREAU TRAIT AUTOM
751	OFFICE MACHINES	W 2654	60.1	W 3119	65.6	W 3186	82.1	W 4408	114.6	MACH,APPAREILS DE BUREAU
752	AUTOMTIC DATA PROC EQUIP		407.6	W 7639	416.3	W 10199	591.1	W 15189	790.5	MACH TRAIT INFORMATION
7522	DIGITAL COMPUTERS	W 1849	122.3	W 1199	133.3	W 1401	197.1	W 1266	175.8	MACH DIGITALES COMPLETES
7524	DIGITL CENTRL STOR UNITS		77.0	W 486	76.9	W 621	104.5	W 1088	148.5	UNITES MEMOIRE CENTRALES
7525	ADP PERIPHERAL UNITS	W 5245	157.1	W 5585	158.1	W 7799	225.9	W 11766	310.3	UNITES PERIPHERIQUES
759	OFFICE,ADP MCH PTS,ACCES	W 4619	110.1	W 3017	112.0	W 4462	168.3	W 6771	215.7	PIECES DU 751 ET 752
7599	ACCTG,ETC,ADP MCH PTS,AC	W 4247	98.3	W 2662	98.2	W 4040	149.8	W 6277	192.4	PIECES DU 751 ET 752
76	TELECOMM,SOUND EQUIPMENT		583.9		546.8		729.8		1048.3	EQUIPMENT DE TELECOM
762	RADIO BROADCAST RECEIVRS	W 9226	57.9	W 8118	42.0	W 8512	76.4	W 9722	126.4	RECEPTEURS RADIODIFFUSION
764	TELECOM EQPT,PTS,ACC NES	W 11884	451.6	W 11804	425.4	W 14200	569.0	W 17347	804.4	EQUIP TELECOM,PIECES
7641	LINE TELEPHONE,ETC EQUIP	W 4205	271.7	W 2865	196.6	W 2185	154.0	W 2913	220.3	APP TELEPHON PAR FIL
7643	TV,RADIO TRANSMITTRS ETC	W 419	57.3	W 468	76.9	W 514	94.7	W 980	187.0	APP EMET TELE RADIO
7649	PTS NES OF EQUIPMT OF 76	W 5969	97.1	W 6827	123.1	W 9010	269.0	W 9968	339.1	PIECES DE LA DIV 76
76491	PTS NES OF APPAR OF 7641	W 429	17.3	W 702	40.2	W 1090	103.2	W 1257	159.2	PIECES POUR 764.1
76493	TELECOMM EQUIPMT PTS NES	W 4944	66.9	W 5784	75.0	W 7320	124.9	W 8050	146.4	PIECES 761,762,764.3,8
77	ELECTRIC MACHNRY NES ETC		940.2		1096.9		1595.7		2207.6	MACH APP ELECT NDA
771	ELECTRIC POWER MACHY NES	W 5334	44.9	W 7841	75.3	W 9697	104.7	W 12274	151.6	MACH PROD,TRANS ELECTR
7712	OTH ELEC POWER MACHY NES	W 4975	39.0	W 7320	65.5	W 8918	92.2	W 10537	122.6	AUT APP PROD TRANSF ELEC
772	SWITCHGEAR ETC,PARTS NES	W 6340	179.1	W 9222	240.0	W 12006	361.1	W 17957	501.0	APP COUPURE,SECT ETC
7721	SWITCHGEAR ETC	W 6053	167.9	W 8877	226.2	W 11647	345.2	W 17125	471.3	APP COUPURE,SECTIONMNT
773	ELECTR DISTRIBUTNG EQUIP	W 11857	76.2	W 13531	86.0	W 17276	128.3	W 24248	180.3	EQUIPMT DISTRIBUTION ELECT
7731	INSULATED WIRE,CABLE ETC	W 10867	64.5	W 12411	72.3	W 16141	112.5	W 22594	156.8	FILS,CABLES ISOLES ELECT
774	ELECTRO-MEDCL,XRAY EQUIP	W 999	92.0	W 699	64.8	W 871	112.8	W 1157	128.9	APPAREILS MEDICAUX
775	HOUSEHOLD TYPE EQUIP NES	W 28749	134.3	W 32924	170.7	W 45942	254.5	W 66105	385.3	MACH,APP USAGE DOMESTQUE
7758	ELECTRO-THERMIC APPL NES	W 5157	46.2	W 6367	63.7	W 8661	91.5	W 14679	137.5	APP ELECTROTHERMIQ NDA
776	TRANSISTORS,VALVES,ETC	W 11310	167.5	W 10756	174.8	W 14043	243.5	W 16901	367.0	LAMPES,TUBES,VALVES
7761	TV PICTURE TUBES	W 9331	57.9	W 9573	53.2	W 12909	76.9	W 15261	107.1	TUBES CATHODIQUES
7764	ELECTRONIC MICROCIRCUITS	W 287	70.6	W 278	83.0	W 375	117.4	W 720	194.0	MICROSTRUCTURES ELECTRON
778	ELECTRICAL MACHINERY NES	W 33545	246.4	W 33329	285.7	W 40677	391.0	W 48523	493.7	AUTRES MACH ELECT NDA
7788	OTH ELEC MACHY,EQUIP NES	W 13995	100.8	W 13502	114.3	W 14784	161.2	W 15634	200.4	AUT MACH APP ELEC NDA
78	ROAD VEHICLES		1023.3		1033.2		1556.3		2622.3	VEHICULES ROUTIERS
781	PASS MOTOR VEH EXC BUSES	W 65758	441.3	W 57246	376.1	W 64308	466.3	W 123474	919.9	AUTO TRANSPORT PERSONNES
782	LORRIES,SPCL MTR VEH NES	W 49684	188.5	W 35820	129.5	W 23735	113.2	W 33609	166.0	VEHICULES SPECIAUX,MARCH
7821	LORRIES,TRUCKS	W 39249	140.5	W 28699	101.4	W 21864	96.2	W 31293	141.9	VEHICULES TRANSP MARCHAND
783	ROAD MOTOR VEHICLES NES	W 27639	68.6	W 32393	66.9	W 16492	64.4	W 15580	47.0	VEHICULES ROUTIERS NDA
784	MOTOR VEH PRTS,ACCES NES	W 42273	263.3	W 82008	360.8	W 109114	752.6	W 198619	1262.6	PIECES 722,781,782,783
7841	MOTOR VEHICLE CHASSIS	W 1292	13.0	W 3395	35.3	W 13634	143.7	W 11462	107.4	CHASSIS 722,781,782,783
7842	MOTOR VEHICLE BODIES	W 5129	39.2	W 32984	79.4	W 27658	187.1	W 68217	440.5	CARROS 722,781,782,783
7849	OTHER MOTOR VEHCL PARTS	W 35851	211.3	W 45629	246.2	W 67822	421.9	W 118941	714.8	PIECES 722,781,782,783
785	CYCLES,ETC MOTRZD OR NOT	W 4673	22.0	W 9436	52.3	W 13966	81.3	W 19565	112.6	MOTOCYCLES SCOOTERS
786	TRAILERS,NONMOTR VEH,NES	W 37877	39.9	W 47497	47.8	W 48533	78.8	W 66603	114.5	REMORQUES,CADRES,CONTAIN
79	OTHR TRANSPORT EQUIPMENT		41.3		63.5		71.3		147.8	AUTRE MATERIEL TRANSPORT
8	MISC MANUFACTURED GOODS		1939.0		2208.2		2794.2		3558.3	ART MANUFACTURES DIVERS
812	*PLUMBG,HEATNG,LGHTNG EQ	W 42215	89.4	W 31016	115.0	W 34999	157.1	W 54702	215.1	APPAR SANITAIRES CHAUFFAGE
8121	CENTRAL HEATING EQUIPMNT	W 33794	44.2	W 18673	57.3	W 21615	80.0	W 37429	114.2	CHAUDIERES,RADIATEURS
821	*FURNITURE,PARTS THEREOF	W 35830	117.1	W 40321	122.0	W 47135	167.0	W 60337	212.6	MEUBLES ET PIECES
8219	FURNITURE AND PARTS NES	W 23892	65.0	W 26829	67.5	W 30585	90.4	W 38179	114.9	AUTRES MEUBLES ET PIECES
84	CLOTHING AND ACCESSORIES		255.8		268.9		316.5		452.2	VETEMENTS
851	*FOOTWEAR	W 23186	82.1	W 27798	99.6	W 38318	122.3	W 50636	171.1	CHAUSSURES
85102	FOOTWEAR LEATHER	W 15856	57.0	W 20509	74.4	W 27856	87.4	W 33084	115.0	CHAUS SEMELLES EN CUIR
87	PRECISION INSTRUMNTS NES		356.3		386.8		503.2		602.9	INSTRUM,APPAR SCIENT NDA
872	MEDICAL INSTRUMENTS NES	W 2831	111.0	W 3584	101.8	W 3613	127.3	W 4843	157.4	INSTR,APP MEDIC-CHIR NDA
87202	OTH MEDICAL INSTRUMENTS	W 2234	88.4	W 2909	84.3	W 2771	104.2	W 3612	125.2	INSTRUM,APP MEDECINE
874	MEASURNG,CONTROLNG INSTR		223.6	W 3879	256.8	W 5330	333.3	W 5888	391.8	INSTRUMENTS DE MESURE
8748	ELEC MEAS,CONTRL EQU NES	W 1320	84.5	W 645	96.0	W 809	113.7	W 890	131.8	APP ELEC ELECTRO MESURE
87483	OTH ELCTRNC MEAS ETC EQU	W 1179	72.4	W 442	82.3	W 577	93.6	W 618	110.6	AUT APP ELECTRO DE MESURE
88	PHOTO EQU,OPTICL GDS ETC		113.8		111.8		134.2		171.3	APP,FOURN PHOTO,OP,MONTR
882	PHOTO,CINEMA SUPPLIES	W 4380	64.0	W 5070	61.8	W 5382	67.9	W 5995	74.6	PRODUITS PHOTO,CINEMA
89	MISC MANUFCTRD GOODS NES		910.5		1084.8		1367.8		1699.7	ART MANUFACTURES DIVERS
892	PRINTED MATTER	W 72426	239.1	W 79002	232.9	W 82042	277.5	W 83253	339.4	IMPRIMES
8921	PRINTED BOOKS,GLOBES,ETC	W 24283	102.5	W 25984	90.4	W 30806	109.4	W 31077	121.4	LIVRES,BROCHURES,CARTES
89211	PRINTED BOOKS,PAMPHLETS	W 23538	99.6	W 24825	85.3	W 29845	104.7	W 30284	116.6	LIVRES,BROCHURES
8922	NEWSPAPERS,PERIODICALS	W 36196	74.7	W 42567	80.6	W 38886	87.3	W 35246	76.6	JOURNAUX ET PERIODIQUES
8928	PRINTED MATTER NES	W 11210	54.5	W 9682	52.6	W 11578	70.2	W 15998	128.8	IMPRIMES NDA
893	ARTICLES OF PLASTIC NES	W 110302	353.3	W 146317	481.0	W 147185	621.5	W 174483	756.1	OUVRAGES EN MAT DIVIS 58
8931	PLSTC PACKG CONTNRS,LIDS	W 47017	115.5	W 70868	170.2	W 55271	179.3	W 57843	190.9	ART TRANSP EMBALLAGE ETC
8939	MISC PLASTIC ARTICLES	W 61871	228.3	W 73664	297.8	W 89061	419.7	W 112804	534.7	ART DIVERS EN MAT DIV 58
89399	OTHR PLASTC ARTICLES NES	W 47071	194.1	W 55623	250.2	W 67401	356.0	W 86496	453.4	AUT OUV MAT DIV 58
894	TOYS,SPORTING GOODS,ETC	W 17155	111.1	W 21383	121.8	W 24332	152.0	W 32411	210.3	VOITURES ENFANTS,JOUETS
8942	TOYS,INDOOR GAMES ETC	W 15085	88.1	W 17310	96.2	W 19741	112.7	W 25295	144.2	JOUETS,JEUX ETC
89423	TOYS NES	W 10536	70.3	W 12323	76.7	W 12250	83.0	W 14917	99.9	JOUETS,MODELES REDUITS
899	OTHER MANUFACTURED GOODS		105.3		129.1		161.5		200.0	AUT ART MANUF DIVERS NDA
8998	SMALLWARES,TOILETRYS ETC	W 2872	55.7	W 3529	67.4	W 3831	78.4	W 4556	82.8	ART MERCERIE,TOILETTE
9	GOODS NOT CLASSD BY KIND		12.1		10.7		136.4		21.2	ART TRANSACT NON CLASSES
931	*SPECIAL TRANSACTIONS						115.0			TRANS.SPECIALES

5. Special Exports F.O.B. by Commodities according to the S.I.T.C. (Rev. 2) in million U.S. Dollars
Exportations Spéciales F.O.B. par Produits d'après la C.T.C.I. (Rév. 2) en millions de Dollars E.U.

SITC CTCI	COMMODITY	1993 QUANTITY QUANTITE	1993 VALUE VALEUR	1994 QUANTITY QUANTITE	1994 VALUE VALEUR	1995 QUANTITY QUANTITE	1995 VALUE VALEUR	1996 QUANTITY QUANTITE	1996 VALUE VALEUR	PRODUIT
	ALL COMMODITIES		14044.2		17194.4		22862.2		24393.2	TOUS PRODUITS
0	FOOD AND LIVE ANIMALS		1389.4		1726.1		2089.5		2455.0	ALIMENTS,ANIMAUX VIVANTS
001	*LIVE ANIMALS FOR FOOD	W 118339	166.1	W 109900	175.4	W 97771	174.7	W 92802	171.6	ANIMAUX VIVANTS
0011	BOVINE SPECIES,LIVE	W 33772	47.6	W 49874	77.3	W 50915	88.8	W 37326	72.9	ESPECE BOVINE
00119	— OTHR THAN FR BREEDING	W 33617	47.3	W 48715	75.2	W 50476	87.8	W 37326	72.9	BOVINS NON REPRODUCTEURS
0015	EQUINE SPECIES, LIVE	W 61561	92.6	W 49764	81.7	W 37513	68.1	W 44258	79.3	CHEVAUX,ANES,MULETS
01	MEAT AND PREPARATIONS		178.0		215.3		320.2		437.4	VIANDES ET PREPARATIONS
011	MEAT FRESH,CHILLD,FROZEN	W 31351	114.4	W 30639	123.7	W 59471	177.2	W 81750	205.8	VIANDES FRAICHES,REF,CONGE
0114	POULTRY FRESH CHLLD,FRZN	W 14680	51.6	W 13832	54.5	W 16043	66.2	W 21105	81.8	VOLAILLES MORTES
014	MEAT PREPD,PRSVD,NES ETC	W 22536	63.6	W 39842	89.2	W 71271	141.8	W 132079	227.6	CONSERVES DE VIANDES
0142	SAUSAGES INCLDING TINNED	W 3051	8.4	W 18117	32.9	W 44460	76.1	W 86996	137.4	SAUCISSES,SAUCISSONS
0149	OTH PREPARD,PRESRVD MEAT	W 19485	55.3	W 21725	56.4	W 26811	65.7	W 45083	90.2	AUTRES PREP DE VIANDES
02	DAIRY PRODCTS,BIRDS'EGGS		218.1		207.7		252.7		221.4	PRODUITS LAITIERS,OEUFS
022	MILK AND CREAM	W 129102	181.8	W 119598	158.8	W 104046	195.9	W 86929	145.5	LAIT ET CREME
0224	MILK,CREAM PRESERVED ETC	W 129015	181.8	W 119112	158.5	W 102144	193.9	W 81859	140.2	LAIT,CREME CONS,CONC
02242	MILK DRY,1.5% FAT OR LES	W 125610	176.9	W 112024	150.2	W 97654	185.0	W 76777	132.6	LAIT POUDRE INF 1.5%
03	FISH AND PREPARATIONS		69.0		116.7		148.3		168.3	POISSONS ET PREPARATIONS
037	FISH ETC PREPD,PRSVD NES	W 23540	39.8	W 29585	61.1	W 29822	66.3	W 34108	71.4	POIS,CRUST,MOL PREPARES
04	CEREALS AND PREPARATIONS		20.0		45.8		100.4		126.8	CEREALES ET PRODUITS
048	CEREAL ETC PREPARATIONS	W 13896	18.7	W 28672	42.4	W 47354	75.2	W 70149	104.0	PREPTNS A BASE CEREALES
0484	BAKERY PRODUCTS	W 5951	14.2	W 12245	27.0	W 25040	53.8	W 40051	76.1	PRODUITS DE BOULANGERIE
05	VEGETABLES AND FRUIT		532.5		646.2		708.2		703.7	LEGUMES ET FRUITS
054	VEG ETC FRSH,SMPLY PRSVD	W 663081	144.8	W 554493	164.8	W 410949	175.7	W 395224	172.6	LEGUMES FRAIS,CONG,SECS
0545	OTHER FRESH VEGETABLES	W 219181	55.9	W 247362	67.9	W 146865	59.7	W 172117	74.8	AUTRES LEGUMES FRAIS,REF
0546	VEGETABLES SIMPLY PRSVD	W 78756	38.4	W 113023	58.5	W 108633	78.3	W 116719	74.7	LEGUMES CONG,CONSER
056	VEGTBLES ETC PRSVD,PREPD	W 39580	34.1	W 80996	63.4	W 59978	67.2	W 71796	92.1	CONSERVES DE LEGUMES
057	FRUIT,NUTS,FRESH,DRIED	W 253895	91.9	W 181464	101.3	W 243962	136.4	W 204890	95.9	FRUITS FRAIS OU SECS
0579	FRUIT FRESH OR DRIED NES	W 69051	46.7	W 51509	59.6	W 81425	66.3	W 80392	48.1	FRUITS FRAIS,SECS NDA
05794	BERRIES FRESH	W 46245	39.6	W 42747	54.6	W 54776	50.8	W 63914	37.0	BAIES FRAICHES
058	FRUIT PRESERVED,PREPARED	W 310304	261.9	W 312001	316.8	W 280532	329.0	W 350300	343.2	CONSERVES DE FRUITS
0585	FRUIT OR VEGETABLE JUICE	W 119713	91.0	W 128130	97.6	W 107124	148.3	W 120900	131.3	JUS DE FRUITS
05857	JUICE OF OTHER FRUIT,VEG	W 116437	88.7	W 120602	93.2	W 99021	143.0	W 112926	124.5	JUS AUTRES FRUITS,LEGUMES
0586	FRUIT TEMPORARILY PRESVD	W 173240	154.7	W 171019	204.8	W 162852	166.0	W 214792	191.8	FRUITS CONSERV TEMPORAIRE
05861	FRUIT,FRZN WITHOUT SUGAR	W 164087	148.9	W 165919	199.4	W 158886	163.0	W 208000	188.3	FRUITS CONG SANS SUCRE
06	SUGAR AND PREPS,HONEY		108.4		145.6		112.1		220.3	SUCRES ET PRODUITS
061	SUGAR AND HONEY	W 597267	86.2	W 602981	98.2	W 366216	37.6	W 636182	99.8	SUCRES ET MIEL
062	SUGAR CANDY NON–CHOCLATE	W 12725	22.3	W 25899	47.4	W 36119	74.6	W 56002	120.5	SUCRERIES
07	COFFEE,TEA,COCOA,SPICES		38.2		61.6		129.5		209.1	CAFE,THE,CACAO,EPICES
073	CHOCOLATE AND PRODUCTS	W 5925	17.9	W 12519	36.2	W 29297	83.0	W 48410	140.1	CHOCOLAT
09	MISC EDIBLE PRODUCTS		32.1		72.7		98.2		129.2	PREP ALIMENTAIRES DIVERSES
098	EDIBLE PRODCTS,PREPS NES	W 18593	28.3	W 37394	68.3	W 43367	80.3	W 61339	117.2	PREP ALIMENTAIRES NDA
09809	MISC FOOD PREPRTIONS NES	W 15333	22.6	W 25288	46.7	W 28316	57.0	W 40510	87.5	PREP ALIMENTAIRES NDA
1	BEVERAGES AND TOBACCO		133.9		239.5		163.3		130.3	BOISSONS ET TABACS
11	BEVERAGES		87.8		186.0		136.4		86.7	BOISSONS
111	NON–ALCOHL BEVERAGES NES	W 192029	51.9	W 514379	120.2	W 203380	50.8	W 104326	23.7	BOISSONS NON ALCOOLIQUES
11102	FLAVORED WATERS NON–ALCO	W 189614	51.1	W 501742	117.3	W 180498	45.7	W 78619	18.9	LIMONADES,EAUX GAZEUSES
112	ALCOHOLIC BEVERAGES	W 39977	36.0	W 87225	65.8	W 115355	85.6	W 73089	63.1	BOISSONS ALCOOLIQUES
12	TOBACCO AND MANUFACTURES		46.1		53.5		27.0		43.6	TABACS BRUTS FABRIQUES
2	CRUDE MATERLS,EXCL FUELS		775.5		803.6		1019.1		820.3	MAT BRUTES NON COMESTIBLES
22	OIL SEEDS,OLEAGINOUS FRT		8.4		2.7		99.3		15.5	GRAINES,FRUITS OLEAGINEUX
222	SEEDS FOR'SOFT'FIXED OIL	W 34331	7.5	W 5567	1.6	W 369149	98.4	W 48630	13.7	GRAINES HUILES FIXES
2226	RAPE AND COLZA SEEDS	W 34283	7.4	W 4978	1.3	W 368858	98.0	W 48533	13.5	GRAINES DE NAVETTE,COLZA
23	RUBBER, CRUDE		25.3		34.5		70.9		60.7	CAOUTCHOUC BRUT
233	RUBBER,SYNTHTIC,RECLAIMD	W 39578	25.0	W 49190	34.5	W 57532	70.2	W 58646	60.3	LATEX CAOUTCH SYNTH REGEN
2331	SYNTHETIC RUBBER ETC	W 34332	24.5	W 43738	33.7	W 52107	69.3	W 53881	59.2	LATEX CAOUTCH SYNTHETIQUE
23315	POLYBUTADIENE–STYRN(SBR)	W 34158	24.4	W 43704	33.7	W 51918	69.0	W 52963	57.8	POLYBUTADIENE–STYRENE
24	CORK AND WOOD		280.2		334.7		326.4		266.4	LIEGE ET BOIS
247	OTH WOOD ROUGH,SQUARED	W 767018	70.3	W 540408	65.2	W 282307	44.7	W 200391	30.2	BOIS BRUTS EQUARRIS
2471	SAW–,VENEER–LOGS CONIFER	W 554585	51.6	W 366889	46.2	W 182813	34.0	W 151577	22.8	CONIFERES POUR SCIAGE,PLACAG
24711	— IN THE ROUGH	W 554585	51.6	W 366889	46.2	W 182813	34.0	W 151577	22.8	ECORCES OU DEGROSSIS
248	WOOD SHAPED,SLEEPERS	W 805147	194.6	W 985897	252.4	W 732701	264.3	W 555571	217.2	BOIS SIMPLEMENT TRAVAILLES
2482	LUMBER SHAPED CONIFER	W 622131	134.8	W 735751	172.2	W 507385	167.9	W 351771	122.2	CONIFERES SCIES,RABOTES
24821	LUMBER SAWN ETC CONIFER	W 601446	126.8	W 713840	164.4	W 486488	156.2	W 325769	109.5	CONIFERES SCIES LONGITUD
2483	LUMBER SHAPED NON–CONIFR	W 171713	58.0	W 232507	77.1	W 210876	94.1	W 189858	92.5	NON CONIFERES SCIES,RABOTES
24831	LUMBER SAWN ETC NON–CON	W 136781	40.8	W 205591	60.2	W 181163	70.3	W 166691	70.9	SCIES LONGITUDINALEMENT
26	TEXTILE FIBRES AND WASTE		37.3		57.8		66.0		41.3	FIBRES TEXTILES
27	CRUDE FERTLZR,MINRLS NES		152.3		158.4		195.4		162.4	ENGRAIS MINERAUX BRUTS
273	STONE,SAND AND GRAVEL		49.8	W 7274052	54.9	W 6872998	60.6	W 6625735	61.3	PIERRES,SABLES,GRAVIERS
274	SULPHUR,UNRSTD IRN PYRTE	W 2259662	77.2	W 1813369	73.5	W 1643505	96.1	W 1302430	58.5	SOUFRE ET PYRITES
2741	SULPHUR,EX SULP IN 52215	W 2259662	77.2	W 1813369	73.5	W 1643505	96.1	W 1302430	58.5	SOUFRE
28	METALLIFEROUS ORES,SCRAP		157.1		90.4		92.9		98.0	MINERAIS METAL,DECHETS
282	IRON AND STEEL SCRAP	W 988862	83.8	W 432882	48.6	W 422504	57.5	W 414033	52.8	FERRAILLES
28209	— OF OTHR IRON OR STEEL	W 849828	65.9	W 405587	37.5	W 402256	44.7	W 399514	42.1	FERRAILLES DE FER
29	CRUDE ANIMAL,VEG MAT NES		66.2		75.3		94.9		105.2	MATIERES BRUTES ANIM,VEGET
3	MINERAL FUELS ETC		1260.6		1565.6		1869.9		1677.5	COMBUSTIBLES MINERAUX LUB
32	COAL,COKE AND BRIQUETTES		1126.5		1324.2		1577.0		1355.6	HOUILLES,COKES,BRIQUETTES
322	COAL,LIGNITE AND PEAT	MW 23615	978.9	MW 28381	1057.3	MW 32281	1245.0	MW 29015	1140.2	HOUILLES,LIGNITES,TOURBE
3222	OTH COAL,NOT AGGLOMERATD	MW 22539	951.1	MW 27474	1035.0	MW 31794	1231.6	MW 28885	1135.3	AUTRES HOUILLES
323	BRIQUETS,COKE,SEMI–COKE	W 1987911	147.7	W 3185368	267.0	W 3429921	332.1	W 2289065	215.4	BRIQUETTES
3232	COKE,SEMI–COKE,RTRT CRBN	W 1873354	141.9	W 3104690	261.8	W 3331368	326.4	W 2205006	210.6	COKES ET SEMI–COKES
33	PETROLEUM AND PRODUCTS		132.4		153.5		188.2		196.1	PETROLE ET DERIVES
334	PETROLEUM PRODUCTS,REFIN	W 1159489	97.3	W 1104459	108.2	W 1121442	131.0	W 1212475	150.3	PRODUITS RAFFINES
3344	FUEL OILS,NES	W 964937	56.1	W 893681	60.9					FUEL OILS
351	*ELECTRIC CURRENT		0.1		84.9		101.8		122.1	ENERGIE ELECTRIQUE
5	CHEMCLS,RELATED PROD NES		925.0		1140.1		1739.5		1845.3	PRODUITS CHIMIQUES
51	ORGANIC CHEMICALS		199.9		268.1		471.4		393.3	PROD CHIMIQ ORGANIQUES
512	ALCOHOLS,PHENOLS ETC	W 146874	61.7	W 159661	87.4	W 175747	173.3	W 181380	111.7	PHENOLS,PHENOLS–ALCOOLS
5121	ACYCLIC ALCOHOLS,DERIVS	W 134519	57.1	W 125187	72.6	W 139115	145.6	W 140029	88.4	ALCOOLS ACYCLIQUES
51214	OCTYL ALCOHOLS(OCTANOLS)	W 83207	38.7	W 73101	44.2	W 74453	97.3	W 76849	52.7	ALCOOLS OCTYLIQUES
515	ORG–INORG COMPOUNDS ETC	W 73175	75.6	W 65966	77.4	W 79743	134.9	W 82948	128.6	COMPOSES ORGANO–MINERAUX
5156	HETEROCYCLIC CMPDS ETC	W 72694	70.0	W 64910	66.1	W 78859	124.1	W 82305	119.5	COMPOSES HETEROCYCLIQUES
51561	LACTAMS	W 72571	68.5	W 64816	64.4	W 78828	123.1	W 82204	113.7	LACTAMES .
52	INORGANIC CHEMICALS		163.8		213.5		242.5		226.8	PROD CHIM INORGANIQUES
522	INORG ELEMNTS,OXIDES,ETC		63.5	W 746170	101.1	W 747883	112.4	W 615080	101.4	ELEMENTS INORGANIQUES
5225	INORGANIC BASES ETC NES	W 145421	21.1	W 398819	57.0	W 330399	58.6	W 273120	48.5	AUTRES BASES OXYDES METAL
523	OTHR INORG CHEMICALS ETC	W 570575	99.2	W 721238	111.4	W 699563	129.0	W 635536	124.0	AUT PRODUITS CHIMIQUES INORG
5232	OTH MTL CMPD OF INRG ACD	W 467913	73.0	W 606830	85.3	W 582855	93.3	W 528266	88.3	SELS METALLIQUES
52323	NEUTRAL SODIUM CARBONATE	W 260646	32.5	W 490644	58.8	W 482827	63.7	W 384811	55.5	CARBONATE NEUTRE SODIUM
541	*MEDICINAL,PHARM PRODUCT		206.7	K 8956000	200.2	MK 9395	223.9	MK 12067	256.1	PROD MEDICINAUX PHARMACEUT
5417	MEDICAMENTS	K 6423814	171.1	K 5848000	153.8	K 6219185	169.5	K 7128606	190.1	MEDICAMENTS
54179	— CONTNG OTH SUBSTANCES	K 4436241	122.9	K 4202000	110.4	K 4706068	138.8	K 5792728	158.2	MED CONT AUT SUBSTANCES

5. Special Exports F.O.B. by Commodities according to the S.I.T.C. (Rev. 2) in million U.S. Dollars
Exportations Spéciales F.O.B. par Produits d'après la C.T.C.I. (Rév. 2) en millions de Dollars E.U.

SITC CTCI	COMMODITY	1993		1994		1995		1996		PRODUIT
		QUANTITY QUANTITE	VALUE VALEUR	QUANTITY QUANTITE	VALUE VALEUR	QUANTITY QUANTITE	VALUE VALEUR	QUANTITY QUANTITE	VALUE VALEUR	
55	PERFUME,CLEANING ETC PRD		28.9		63.8		161.8		303.6	PROD POUR PARFUM,TOILETTE
553	PERFUMERY,COSMETICS,ETC	W 7669	17.7	W 12819	30.9	W 26464	76.0	W 44668	160.0	PRODUITS DE PARFUMERIE
554	SOAP,CLEANSING ETC PREPS	W 12364	9.9	W 56595	31.5	W 79684	82.2	W 143531	138.7	SAVONS,PRODUITS DETERSIFS
5542	WASHING PREPARATIONS ETC	W 10258	8.3	W 53652	28.1	W 75285	76.2	W 130331	123.5	PROD ORG TENSIO–ACT NDA
562	*FERTILIZERS,MANUFACTURE	W 1434417	108.7	W 1795803	173.7	W 2342344	297.2	W 2317286	303.8	ENGRAIS MANUFACTURES
5621	CHEM NITROGENOUS FERTLZR	W 1325271	94.3	W 1431670	121.1	W 1799200	209.7	W 1675613	193.8	ENGRAIS AZOTES
56219	CHEM NITROG FERTILZR NES	W 741184	57.1	W 392412	34.5	W 858462	101.2	W 842479	99.7	ENGRAIS AZOTES NDA
5629	FERTILIZERS NES	W 96961	13.3	W 284965	43.5	W 473113	79.4	W 568101	99.8	ENGRAIS NDA
58	PLASTIC MATERIALS ETC		108.3		106.8		191.4		187.5	MAT PLAST ARTIFICIELLES
583	POLYMERIZATION ETC PRODS	W 135258	82.3	W 99518	72.1	W 123861	129.5	W 154646	132.9	PROD POLYMERISATION
59	CHEMICAL MATERIALS NES		72.8		61.9		82.2		103.6	MAT PROD CHIMIQUES NDA
592	STARCH,INULIN,GLUTEN,ETC	W 16710	45.2	W 13093	30.9	W 17617	40.0	W 34704	54.9	AMIDONS,INUL,GLUT FROM
5922	ALBUMINOID SUBSTAN,GLUES	W 16710	45.2	W 13093	30.9	W 17590	39.9	W 33973	54.3	MAT ALBUMIN,COLLES
6	BASIC MANUFACTURES		3792.0		4832.0		6423.9		6450.9	ART MANUFACTURES
61	LEATHER,DRESSED FUR,ETC		132.8		147.5		202.0		216.8	CUIRS,PELLETERIES
611	LEATHER	W 11439	50.3	W 9217	57.3	W 8510	71.0	W 5152	58.0	CUIRS,PEAUX PREPARES
612	LEATHER ETC MANUFACTURES	W 4342	72.5	W 5413	73.1	W 6494	99.2	W 9117	120.1	OUVRAGES EN CUIRS NDA
6123	PREPRD PARTS OF FOOTWEAR	W 3868	67.3	W 5083	66.4	W 5704	77.9	W 7809	89.6	PARTIES DE CHAUSSURES
62	RUBBER MANUFACTURES NES		92.3		140.5		210.2		237.7	CAOUTCHOUC MANUFACTURE
625	RUBBER TYRES, TUBES ETC	W 30414	66.2	W 46344	104.7	W 59767	159.3	W 58490	168.8	PNEUS CAOUTCHOUC VULCANISE
6251	TYRES NEW FOR MOTOR CARS	W 12363	34.1	W 19276	49.6	W 26941	78.7	W 28406	88.7	PNEUS POUR VOITURES
63	WOOD,CORK MANUFACTRS NES		275.9		405.9		561.7		596.6	OUVRAGES LIEGE ET BOIS
634	VENEERS,PLYWOOD,ETC	W 133866	55.5	W 217440	94.4	W 227812	117.0	W 189868	110.9	PLACAGES,CONTRE–PLAQUES
635	WOOD MANUFACTURES NES	W 635200	220.4	W 894295	311.3	W 892188	444.7	W 871100	485.5	ART MANUF EN BOIS NDA
6351	BOXES,CASES,CRATES,ETC	W 482264	95.4	W 648861	124.5	W 606746	147.2	W 525418	128.1	CAISSES EMBALLAGES BOIS
6353	BUILDERS WOODWRK,PREFABS	W 64512	59.6	W 105286	89.9	W 114939	146.6	W 121313	164.3	OUVRAGES DE MENUISERIE
6359	OTHER WOOD MANUFACTURES	W 79157	48.5	W 128945	74.9	W 159255	123.7	W 211267	158.5	OUVRAGES EN BOIS NDA
63599	OTHER WOOD ARTICLES NES	W 77577	47.3	W 127363	73.1	W 157451	121.3	W 209148	156.0	AUTRES OUVRAGES EN BOIS NDA
64	PAPER,PAPERBOARD AND MFR		166.7		240.8		525.0		541.4	PAPIERS,CARTONS & OUVRAGES
641	PAPER AND PAPERBOARD	W 393567	123.6	W 472367	174.4	W 632700	417.9	W 717309	397.3	PAPIERS ET CARTONS
6412	PRINTG,WRITING PAPER NES	W 1818	1.3	W 21439	16.4	W 102439	96.3	W 115774	83.2	PAPIERS POUR L'IMPRESSION
64121	— UNCOATED	W 395	0.5	W 20094	15.2	W 101095	94.5	W 113968	79.5	PAPIERS IMPRES NON COUCHES
6413	KRAFT PAPER,PAPERBOARD	W 123249	45.6	W 144480	59.9	W 127733	84.1	W 148987	79.1	PAPIER ET CARTON KRAFT
6415	PAPER,PAPERBRD,BULK,NES	W 115555	37.6	W 129558	44.8	W 148607	103.2	W 182480	105.6	PAPIERS,CARTONS ROULEAUX
64159	OTHER PAPER ETC,BULK,NES	W 43003	19.1	W 35498	17.8	W 62198	58.6	W 103686	78.6	AUT PAPIER ROULEAUX FEUILLES
6416	FIBRE BUILDING BOARD	W 128602	29.0	W 157108	39.2	W 195793	76.7	W 185980	66.8	PLAQUES CONSTRUCT EN PATE
642	PAPER,ETC,PRECUT,ARTS OF	W 67623	43.1	W 82685	66.4	W 79240	107.2	W 87031	144.2	PAP,CARTONS DECOUPES
65	TEXTILE YARN,FABRICS,ETC		309.8		398.7		515.6		563.3	FILS,TISSUS,ARTICLES TEXTILE
651	TEXTILE YARN	W 12189	41.4	W 18223	62.0	W 21727	96.2	W 18240	87.6	FILS TEXTILES
654	OTH WOVEN TEXTILE FABRIC	W 5119	48.7	W 7183	62.8	W 5943	55.6	W 5005	40.6	TISSUS AUT COTON SYNT,ARTIF
658	TEXTILE ARTICLES NES	W 19489	107.2	W 24668	155.7	W 27311	213.2	W 29341	235.6	ART FACONNES MAT TEXTILES
6584	LINENS ETC	W 7330	57.3	W 9952	83.8	W 11559	113.5	W 12011	121.1	LINGE DE MAISON
66	NONMETAL MINERAL MFS NES		389.0		500.4		618.0		671.1	ART MIN NON METALLIQUES
661	LIME,CEMENT,BLDG PRODS	W 3661230	151.3	W 4773549	196.4	W 4334188	215.2	W 3798152	184.0	CHAUX,CIMENTS MAT CONSTR
6612	CEMENT	W 3241313	130.9	W 4401312	171.6	W 4035343	186.5	W 3480128	152.6	CIMENTS HYDRAULIQUES
663	MINERAL MANUFCTURES NES	W 209575	28.8	W 294354	42.1	W 311076	58.8	W 339687	100.5	ART MIN MANUF NDA
664	GLASS		46.4	W 125314	50.4	W 134248	58.2	W 141198	64.9	VERRE
665	GLASSWARE	W 110236	99.6	W 149384	131.3	W 166593	173.5	W 169629	189.3	OUVRAGES EN VERRE
6652	HOUSEHLD,HOTEL ETC GLASS	W 22772	74.8	W 32207	97.0	W 39494	127.2	W 45098	140.5	OBJETS VERRE TABLE,CUISINE
666	POTTERY	W 28410	54.1	W 33073	64.6	W 35940	82.1	W 38663	93.5	POTERIE
67	IRON AND STEEL		1006.5		1223.5		1426.4		1346.2	FER ET ACIER
672	IRON,STEEL PRIMARY FORMS	W 1116170	238.3	W 1537117	304.7	W 721323	175.1	W 1088728	246.6	LINGOTS FER,ACIER
6725	IRN,STL BLOOMS,SLABS,ETC	W 1075989	226.7	W 1446809	288.4	W 682072	165.4	W 1073443	241.1	BLOOMS,BILLETTES FER ACIER
67251	IRN,SMPLE STL BLOOMS,ETC	W 1069385	219.4	W 1428558	278.1	W 679097	158.5	W 1064555	231.6	BLOOMS ETC NON ACIER FIN
673	IRON,STEEL SHAPES ETC	W 1504252	462.3	W 1584028	436.5	W 1668862	548.4	W 1660938	493.6	BARRES,PROFIL FER,ACIER
6732	IRON,STEEL BARS ETC	W 253116	78.3	W 366572	101.6	W 262898	113.1	W 221583	91.0	BARRES FER,ACIER
67326	IRN,OTH STL BARS HOTROLD	W 212779	55.7	W 320260	77.0	W 206553	66.2	W 142601	41.3	BARRES PLEINES FER,ACIER
6733	IRON,STEEL PROFILES ETC	W 1115158	347.5	W 1044829	288.4	W 1200797	372.9	W 1187108	338.7	PROFILES,PALPLAN FER,ACIER
67331	SMALL U,I,H SECTIONS ETC	W 86786	60.1	W 51047	13.8	W 22607	8.0	W 11780	3.9	PROFILES MOINS 80MM
67332	LARGE U,I,H SECTIONS ETC	W 899714	250.7	W 789256	218.3	W 939593	285.9	W 1005883	280.2	PROFILES PLUS 80MM
674	IRN,STL UNIV,PLATE,SHEET	W 299503	89.8	W 561239	177.8	W 639505	251.8	W 487190	194.3	LARGES PLATS,TOLES
6744	IRN,STL HVY PLATE,ROLLED	W 226981	59.3	W 345303	96.9	W 304499	114.6	W 263865	103.3	TOLES LAMINEES PLUS 4.75 MM
67441	— OF IRON OR SIMPLE STL	W 219002	57.2	W 345002	96.6	W 304144	114.1	W 263598	103.0	TOLES NON ACIER FIN CARB
676	RAILWY RAILS ETC IRN,STL	W 121281	30.9	W 206201	62.7	W 229414	76.0	W 154654	59.2	RAILS,ELEMENTS VOIES FERREE
67601	RAILWAY RAILS IRN,STL	W 114346	26.1	W 191180	55.3	W 218974	68.4	W 145200	52.1	RAILS,ELEMENTS FER,ACIER
678	IRON,STL TUBES,PIPES,ETC	W 82343	58.0	W 128502	85.3	W 156696	127.7	W 121555	119.2	TUBES,TUYAUX EN FONTE,FER
679	IRN,STL CASTINGS UNWORKD	W 83605	65.9	W 109599	94.7	W 137397	143.3	W 132956	144.9	OUVRAGES EN FONTE,FER,ACIER
6794	IRON,STL CASTINGS ROUGH	W 80159	61.4	W 104269	87.5	W 131186	124.9	W 126441	124.8	OUVRAGES COULES,MOULES
67941	IRON CASTINGS ROUGH	W 80159	61.4	W 104269	87.5	W 131186	124.9	W 126441	124.8	OUVRAGES A L'ETAT BRUT
68	NON–FERROUS METALS		943.5		1130.9		1370.1		1162.6	METAUX NON FERREUX
681	SILVER,PLATINUM,ETC		96.1		166.3		152.8		151.5	ARGENT ET PLATINE
6811	SILVER UNWKD,PARTLY WRKD		94.7		165.8		151.9		150.7	ARGENT BRUT MI–OUVRE
68113	SILVER UNWROUGHT		94.3		165.2		151.3		150.2	ARGENT ET ALLIAGES BRUTS
682	COPPER EXC CEMENT COPPER	W 332597	663.4	W 350522	794.2	W 336661	1005.9	W 335120	811.4	CUIVRE
6821	COPPER NES,ALLOYS,UNWRT	W 266212	521.0	W 264516	590.5	W 201683	596.1	W 207969	474.5	CUIVRE BRUT
68212	COPPER REFINED,UNWROUGHT	W 266212	521.0	W 264058	589.7	W 201344	595.4	W 207903	474.4	CUIVRE AFFINE BRUT
6822	COPPER,ALLOYS WORKED	W 66386	142.5	W 86006	203.7	W 134979	409.8	W 127152	336.9	CUIVRE,ALLIAGES OUVRES
68221	COPPER BARS,WIRE,ETC	W 50217	101.0	W 62518	140.5	W 111499	329.1	W 104935	264.6	BARRES,PROFILES ET FILS
68222	COPPER PLATE,SHEET,STRIP	W 14424	35.6	W 21309	55.1	W 20173	66.3	W 18901	58.9	TOLES DE PLUS 0.15 MM
684	ALUMINIUM	W 43608	62.0	W 41828	72.1	W 52747	112.8	W 52375	100.0	ALUMINIUM
686	ZINC		114.0	W 89866	85.0	W 78821	83.8	W 75888	80.6	ZINC
6861	ZINC,ALLOYS UNWROUGHT	W 71429	92.0	W 81808	72.6	W 69381	67.5	W 65814	64.4	ZINC ET ALLIAGES BRUTS
69	METAL MANUFACTURES NES		476.0		644.3		995.5		1115.6	ART MANUFACT EN METAL NDA
691	STRUCTURES AND PARTS NES	W 152966	164.5	W 195853	226.6	W 256241	355.6	W 273907	386.5	CONSTRUCT FER,ACIER,ALU
6911	STRUCTURES,PARTS IRN,STL	W 152259	160.3	W 194516	216.6	W 253369	333.8	W 270183	360.2	CONSTRUCT FER,ACIER,FONTE
692	METAL TANKS,BOXES,ETC	W 51943	58.9	W 43980	54.0	W 53580	84.6	W 65969	124.2	RECIPIENTS METALLIQUES
6924	MTL TRANSPORT BOXES ETC	W 13713	17.3	W 14836	20.1	W 21948	44.3	W 30117	78.0	FUTS,TAMBOURS,BIDONS
694	STL,COPPR NAILS,NUTS,ETC	W 56514	41.8	W 65014	53.3	W 69573	74.5	W 54946	61.7	CLOUS,VIS,ECROUS
699	BASE METAL MFRS NES	W 81335	112.3	W 133513	199.2	W 208229	336.0	W 226085	388.7	ART MANUFACTURES MET NDA
6997	IRON,STEEL ARTICLES NES	W 59021	64.1	W 97158	111.7	W 156987	191.6	W 171126	223.1	OUV FONTE,FER,ACIER NDA
69979	IRN,STL MANUFACTURES NES	W 59013	64.1	W 96931	111.3	W 156579	191.0	W 170814	222.5	AUT OUVRAGES EN FER NDA
6998	MFRS NES OF CPR,NIKL,ETC	W 4378	16.5	W 10746	38.9	W 16424	68.0	W 19715	75.3	OUVRAGES EN CU,NI,AL,PB,ZN
7	MACHINES,TRANSPORT EQUIP		2879.9		3397.0		4808.6		5703.2	MACHINES MATERIEL TRANSPORT
71	POWER GENERATING EQUIPMT		207.8		211.2		364.7		421.3	MACHINES GENERATRICES
713	INTRNL COMBUS PSTN ENGIN	W 16071	81.5	W 17249	88.1	W 18870	109.4	W 24971	152.0	MOTEURS EXPL COMB INT, PIECE
7139	PISTON ENGINE PARTS NES	W 11262	44.7	W 13883	58.1	W 14780	75.5	W 17870	97.6	PIECES POUR 713.2,3,8
716	ROTATING ELECTRIC PLANT	W 16128	53.8	W 17133	59.4	W 21983	87.1	W 24759	105.0	APP ELECTR ROTATIFS,PIECES
7162	AC MTRS,GENRTRS,GEN SETS	W 14456	44.8	W 14284	41.0	W 16424	57.3	W 15611	57.4	MOTEURS ELECTRIQUES
72	MACHS FOR SPCL INDUSTRYS		246.2		327.1		425.2		460.5	MAC SPECIALES POUR INDUST
722	TRACTORS NON–ROAD	W 10397	26.3	W 18429	56.0	W 17497	66.3	W 14284	68.0	TRACTEURS
7224	WHEELED TRACTORS NES	W 10352	26.2	W 18429	56.0	W 17417	66.2	W 14284	68.0	TRACTEURS A ROUES

5. Special Exports F.O.B. by Commodities according to the S.I.T.C. (Rev. 2) in million U.S. Dollars
Exportations Spéciales F.O.B. par Produits d'après la C.T.C.I. (Rév. 2) en millions de Dollars E.U.

SITC CTCI	COMMODITY	1993 QUANTITY QUANTITE	1993 VALUE VALEUR	1994 QUANTITY QUANTITE	1994 VALUE VALEUR	1995 QUANTITY QUANTITE	1995 VALUE VALEUR	1996 QUANTITY QUANTITE	1996 VALUE VALEUR	PRODUIT
723	CIVIL ENGNEERG EQUIP ETC	W 18234	64.1	W 24220	88.3	W 23439	97.8	W 22059	102.6	APPAREILS DE GENIE CIVIL
7234	CONST,MINING MACHNRY NES	W 15208	58.0	W 20683	79.3	W 19445	87.7	W 18390	93.5	MACH POUR LA CONST, MINES
728	OTH MACHY FOR SPCL INDUS	W 21023	70.8	W 23258	78.0	W 36087	118.5	W 34969	133.8	AUT MACH IND PARTICULIERES
7284	MACHY FOR SPCL INDUS NES	W 11266	38.9	W 12764	45.4	W 24773	78.0	W 25458	97.9	MACH SPEC IND PARTICUL.
73	METALWORKING MACHINERY		54.9		57.7		83.1		97.9	MACH TRAVAIL DES METAUX
736	METALWORKING MACH-TOOLS	W 11166	46.7	W 11493	45.6	W 15468	68.2	W 16823	77.2	MACH-OUTILS TRAVAIL METAUX
74	GENRL INDUSTRL MACHY NES		268.7		340.5		519.6		622.8	MACH APP INDUSTRIE
741	HEATING,COOLING EQUIPMNT	W 9193	25.8	W 10263	39.1	W 13859	60.8	W 19699	86.5	MACH CHAUFFAGE,PIECES
744	MECHANICAL HANDLING EQU	W 34192	87.5	W 44909	96.7	W 55478	145.4	W 58307	159.5	EQUIP MANUTENTION PIECES
7449	PTS NES OF MACHY OF 7442	W 20823	49.6	W 29532	61.3	W 37682	94.4	W 37625	94.9	PIECES DU 744.2
749	NONELEC MACH PTS,ACC NES	W 31471	104.2	W 33678	130.2	W 49323	207.4	W 58893	243.2	PIECES MACH NON ELEC NDA
7491	BALL,ROLLER,ETC BEARINGS	W 7520	41.6	W 9789	57.2	W 16004	93.5	W 13779	92.0	ROULEMENTS BILLES ETC
76	TELECOMM,SOUND EQUIPMENT		35.2		81.1		168.5		287.0	EQUIPMENT DE TELECOM
761	TELEVISION RECEIVERS	W 61	0.9	W 1736	22.9	W 3877	47.3	W 11098	133.6	RECEPTEURS DE TELEVISION
7611	COLOUR TV RECEIVERS	W 60	0.9	W 1736	22.9	W 3877	47.3	W 10602	127.2	RECEPTEURS COULEUR
764	TELECOM EQPT,PTS,ACC NES	W 3775	30.8	W 4965	54.3	W 6306	95.6	W 9599	145.3	EQUIP TELECOM,PIECES
7649	PTS NES OF EQUIPMT OF 76	W 1304	16.3	W 2139	34.9	W 3336	69.9	W 6497	116.2	PIECES DE LA DIV 76
76493	TELECOMM EQUIPMT PTS NES	W 915	10.6	W 1644	27.6	W 2239	46.0	W 4607	75.6	PIECES 761,762,764.3,8
77	ELECTRIC MACHNRY NES ETC		594.8		702.1		1023.3		1223.9	MACH APP ELECT NDA
771	ELECTRIC POWER MACHY NES	W 2842	14.2	W 5669	32.9	W 6614	50.5	W 9396	91.9	MACH PROD,TRANS ELECTR
772	SWITCHGEAR ETC,PARTS NES	W 8439	88.5	W 9325	108.0	W 8694	137.8	W 9212	169.2	APP COUPURE,SECT ETC
7721	SWITCHGEAR ETC	W 8382	85.0	W 9253	103.0	W 8626	133.1	W 9048	159.6	APP COUPURE,SECTIONMNT
773	ELECTR DISTRIBUTNG EQUIP	W 56031	144.3	W 50958	156.5	W 73710	278.7	W 86581	338.6	EQUIPMT DISTRIBUTION ELECT
7731	INSULATED WIRE,CABLE ETC	W 53557	138.0	W 47915	149.3	W 68880	268.8	W 81835	326.2	FILS,CABLES ISOLES ELECT
775	HOUSEHOLD TYPE EQUIP NES	W 19135	82.5	W 19340	87.8	W 18529	99.0	W 20325	112.9	MACH,APP USAGE DOMESTQUE
776	TRANSISTORS,VALVES,ETC	W 15912	86.4	W 18944	112.3	W 27510	205.5	W 28640	201.3	LAMPES,TUBES,VALVES
7761	TV PICTURE TUBES	W 15530	76.7	W 18086	92.4	W 26825	165.0	W 27753	171.4	TUBES CATHODIQUES
778	ELECTRICAL MACHINERY NES	W 57897	173.9	W 56480	200.0	W 64866	248.7	W 74926	306.8	AUTRES MACH ELECT NDA
7782	ELECTRIC LAMPS,BULBS	W 10691	86.3	W 13514	103.5	W 16580	132.9	W 18978	147.3	LAMPES, TUBES ELECTRIQUES
77822	ELEC DISCHARGE LAMPS NES	W 4256	50.2	W 5873	56.7	W 7339	70.1	W 8574	85.8	LAMPES NON ULTRA-VIOLETS
7788	OTH ELEC MACHY,EQUIP NES	W 40672	61.9	W 37604	74.0	W 41204	84.5	W 38926	94.8	AUT MACH APP ELEC NDA
77887	ELECTRICAL CARBONS	W 39203	51.5	W 36060	55.8	W 39034	65.8	W 36969	69.6	PIECES CHARBON,GRAPHITE
78	ROAD VEHICLES		730.6		794.0		1127.8		1324.3	VEHICULES ROUTIERS
781	PASS MOTOR VEH EXC BUSES	W 107745	553.2	W 104822	523.8	W 124212	658.9	W 135182	783.4	AUTO TRANSPORT PERSONNES
782	LORRIES,SPCL MTR VEH NES	W 8057	33.5	W 10690	68.5	W 19092	182.2	W 17205	160.9	VEHICULES SPECIAUX,MARCH
7821	LORRIES,TRUCKS	W 5098	21.8	W 8698	62.7	W 18465	180.0	W 16408	158.7	VEHICULES TRANSP MARCHAND
784	MOTOR VEH PRTS,ACCES NES	W 14378	48.0	W 21155	62.8	W 35513	123.5	W 51471	206.8	PIECES 722,781,782,783
7849	OTHER MOTOR VEHCL PARTS	W 13547	44.8	W 20851	61.6	W 34497	116.6	W 49698	187.1	PIECES 722,781,782,783
786	TRAILERS,NONMOTR VEH,NES	W 58720	77.1	W 75630	101.7	W 78810	116.6	W 80651	119.2	REMORQUES,CADRES,CONTAIN
7861	TRAILERS,TRANSP CONTAINR	W 44869	53.8	W 59741	66.7	W 59751	72.9	W 58940	74.4	REMORQUES TOUS VEHICULES
79	OTHR TRANSPORT EQUIPMENT		728.2		854.2		1065.4		1202.6	AUTRE MATERIEL TRANSPORT
791	RAILWAY VEHICLES	W 84029	51.9	W 53664	38.1	W 37284	51.9	W 20304	31.0	VEHIC MAT CHEMINS DE FER
792	AIRCRAFT ETC	W 479	30.4	W 624	29.5	W 765	37.6	W 628	84.9	APP NAVIGATION AERIENNE
793	SHIPS AND BOATS ETC		646.0	W 2486822	786.6	W 1670934	976.0	W 962359	1086.8	NAVIRES BATEAUX,ETC
7932	SHIPS AND BOATS NES	W 1691186	618.9	W 2458414	770.5	W 1646067	950.4	W 927994	1012.2	NAVIRES ET BATEAUX
79322	TANKERS OF ALL KINDS	W 37656	62.1			W 778	0.4	W 3906	0.4	BATEAUX-CITERNES
79323	OTHER CARGO VESSELS	W 1638528	528.7	W 2448802	751.3	W 1632468	930.2	W 912643	978.7	AUT BATEAUX TRANS MARCH
8	MISC MANUFACTURED GOODS		2607.1		3415.9		4624.5		5239.4	ART MANUFACTURES DIVERS
812	*PLUMBG,HEATNG,LGHTNG EQ	W 10419	34.3	W 14148	52.1	W 18496	78.5	W 24409	104.5	APPAR SANITAIRES CHAUFFAGE
8124	LIGHTING EQUIPMENT NES	W 8242	31.2	W 10997	47.5	W 14857	70.4	W 16952	88.3	APPAREILS ECLAIRAGE ETC
821	*FURNITURE,PARTS THEREOF	W 1256794	581.0	W 470367	894.8	W 599374	1337.9	W 722993	1617.4	MEUBLES ET PIECES
8211	CHAIRS,SEATS AND PARTS	W 1029513	230.8	W 145667	380.0	W 199821	583.8	W 236522	700.3	SIEGES ET PIECES
82111	CHAIRS AND OTHER SEATS	W 1024684	210.0	W 137575	348.2	W 191247	547.7	W 225140	651.6	SIEGES
8212	MED FURN,STUFFD FURNSHGS	W 7348	29.5	W 12369	40.4	W 11931	63.1	W 14655	74.8	MOB MEDICO-CHIRUR,PIECES
8219	FURNITURE AND PARTS NES	W 219933	320.8	W 312331	474.6	W 387621	691.0	W 471816	842.4	AUTRES MEUBLES ET PIECES
82192	WOOD FURNITURE NES	W 198578	288.4	W 280691	422.2	W 343936	605.7	W 415311	726.7	MEUBLES NDA EN BOIS
82199	OTHR FURN,FURN PARTS NES	W 12630	18.5	W 19816	32.4	W 30401	56.2	W 42873	81.8	MEUBLES NDA AUTRES MATIERES
84	CLOTHING AND ACCESSORIES		1577.8		1842.7		2298.7		2369.3	VETEMENTS
842	MENS OUTERWEAR NOT KNIT	W 15536	396.4	W 18078	466.8	W 20016	550.9	W 22560	616.2	VET DESSUS POUR HOMMES
8421	— OVERCOATS,OTHER COATS	W 2012	56.7	W 2254	70.5	W 1615	60.7	W 2058	69.3	MANTEAUX HOMMES MAT TEXT
8422	— SUITS	W 1264	48.8	W 1428	54.2	W 1396	59.8	W 1405	62.7	COMPLETS HOMMES MAT TEXT
8423	— TROUSERS,BREECHES ETC	W 4877	99.9	W 6246	123.2	W 8090	170.7	W 9585	203.3	PANTALONS HOMMES MAT TEX
8424	— JACKETS,BLAZERS ETC	W 2983	104.5	W 3127	106.8	W 3584	129.0	W 3731	141.6	VESTES HOMMES MAT TEXTIL
8429	— OTHER OUTER GARMENTS	W 4400	86.8	W 5023	112.4	W 5331	130.8	W 5781	139.5	AUT VET DES HOM MAT TEX
843	WOMENS OUTERWEAR NONKNIT	W 22557	738.9	W 26791	867.7	W 30049	1115.1	W 31482	1128.2	VET DESSUS FEMMES MAT TEX
8431	— COATS AND JACKETS	W 5863	223.0	W 6441	248.0	W 6551	289.3	W 6532	278.3	MANT,VEST FEM MAT TEXTIL
8433	— DRESSES	W 860	34.1	W 1139	38.5	W 1900	71.9	W 2088	77.6	ROBES EN MAT-TEXTILES
8434	— SKIRTS	W 2308	69.1	W 2824	82.7	W 3689	124.2	W 3593	119.6	JUPES EN MAT TEXTILES
8435	— BLOUSES	W 4879	174.2	W 5848	207.3	W 6572	270.0	W 6410	250.2	BLOUSES FEM MAT TEXTILES
8439	— OTHER OUTER GARMENTS	W 7617	203.2	W 9517	259.4	W 10303	318.1	W 11695	353.8	AUT VET DES FEM MAT TEXT
844	UNDER GARMENTS NOT KNIT	W 3239	127.2	W 3706	142.6	W 4613	186.0	W 4498	162.9	VETEMENT DESSOUS MAT TEX
8441	— MENS SHIRTS	W 2924	119.9	W 3382	137.3	W 4214	179.4	W 3932	154.3	CHEMISES HOMMES MAT TEXT
84411	—— OF COTTON	W 1208	50.9	W 1503	60.8	W 2005	87.0	W 2111	90.0	CHEMISES HOMMES DE COTON
84412	—— OF SYNTHETIC FIBRES	W 1716	69.1	W 1879	76.5	W 2209	92.4	W 1821	64.3	CHEMISES HOMMES FIB SYNT
845	OUTERWEAR KNIT NONELASTC	W 11527	210.1	W 12387	229.2	W 13813	278.7	W 15745	284.9	VET DESSOUS,ACCES BONNET
8451	— JERSEYS,PULLOVERS ETC	W 4160	71.7	W 4528	78.7	W 5438	98.9	W 6989	129.1	CHANDAILS,PULL-OVERS ETC
8459	— OTHER,CLTHG ACCESRYS	W 6196	110.5	W 6530	121.1	W 6787	139.7	W 6710	119.6	AUT VET DESSUS DE BONNE
846	UNDER GARMENTS KNITTED	W 4332	66.5	W 5467	91.1	W 5664	114.6	W 6376	123.8	SOUS VETS DE BONNETERIE
8462	— OF COTTON NON ELASTIC	W 3324	46.7	W 4316	64.5	W 4422	82.7	W 4906	87.4	SOUS-VET BONNET COTON
84629	—— OTHER	W 3324	46.7	W 4316	64.5	W 4422	82.7	W 4906	87.4	AUT SOUS-VET BONNET COTON
851	*FOOTWEAR	W 10281	109.4	W 11203	121.9	W 13383	175.2	W 15675	221.7	CHAUSSURES
85102	FOOTWEAR LEATHER	W 4667	53.4	W 5459	67.2	W 7139	107.7	W 7970	122.2	CHAUS SEMELLES EN CUIR
85103	SHOES WOOD-,CORK-SOLED	W 3454	43.2	W 3470	40.2	W 2986	34.2	W 1888	27.2	CHAUS SEMELLES BOIS,LIEGE
87	PRECISION INSTRUMNTS NES		46.8		94.5		105.0		117.8	INSTRUM,APPAR SCIENT NDA
874	MEASURNG,CONTROLNG INSTR	W 1259	27.7	W 1525	41.1	W 1841	58.0	W 2261	74.1	INSTRUMENTS DE MESURE
89	MISC MANUFCTRD GOODS NES		234.0		380.7		593.3		766.7	ART MANUFACTURES DIVERS
892	PRINTED MATTER	W 4813	19.4	W 8058	35.5	W 12799	53.9	W 18496	78.2	IMPRIMES
893	ARTICLES OF PLASTIC NES		87.5		149.6		261.5		333.7	OUVRAGES EN MAT DIVIS 58
8931	PLSTC PACKG CONTNRS,LIDS	W 10768	16.2	W 13101	25.4	W 20042	58.2	W 33379	74.9	ART TRANSP EMBALLAGE ETC
8939	MISC PLASTIC ARTICLES	W 20844	66.8	W 39568	116.7	W 57742	191.7	W 71864	244.3	ART DIVERS EN MAT DIV 58
89399	OTHR PLASTC ARTICLES NES	W 19289	63.9	W 35144	108.0	W 48466	172.2	W 63274	224.5	AUT OUV MAT DIV 58
894	TOYS,SPORTING GOODS,ETC		51.1	W 14150	67.9	W 13651	86.5	W 15659	101.9	VOITURES ENFANTS,JOUETS
8942	TOYS,INDOOR GAMES ETC		32.4	W 9928	49.5	W 9618	64.8	W 11007	78.0	JOUETS,JEUX ETC
898	MUSICAL INSTRUMENTS,PTS		9.6	W 1220	44.4	W 1544	82.3	W 1577	78.4	INSTRUMENTS DE MUSIQUE
8983	SOUND RECRDNG TAPE,DISCS		5.9	W 543	40.4	W 644	75.3	W 670	71.3	SUPPORTS SON POUR 763
89832	RECORDED DISCS,TAPES ETC		5.0	W 287	38.4	W 338	72.6	W 292	69.1	DISQUES,PHONO,BANDES
899	OTHER MANUFACTURED GOODS		45.4		54.1		71.7		76.7	AUT ART MANUF DIVERS NDA
9	GOODS NOT CLASSD BY KIND		27.9		57.6		94.8		34.9	ART TRANSACT NON CLASSES

1. HISTORICAL SERIES, 1962–1997 SPECIAL TRADE, IMPORTS C.I.F., EXPORTS F.O.B.
SERIES HISTORIQUES, 1962–1997 COMMERCE SPECIAL, IMPORTATIONS C.A.F., EXPORTATIONS F.O.B

YEAR ANNEE	VALUE IN MILLION PORT. ESCUDOS / VALEUR EN MILLION PORT. ESCUDOS — MERCHANDISE –MARCHANDISE		GOLD # 1 –OR		CONVERSION FACTORS U.S. CENTS PER PORT. ESCUDO / FACTEURS DE CONVERSION CENTS E.U. PAR PORT. ESCUDO		INDEX NUMBERS –INDICES — QUANTUM		UNIT VALUE / VALEUR UNITAIRE	
	IMPORTS	EXPORTS	IMPORTS	EXPORTS	IMPORTS	EXPORTS	IMPORTS	EXPORTS	IMPORTS	EXPORTS
1962	16829.00	10632.00	386.20	0.30	3.4780	3.4780				
1963	18865.00	12023.00	426.20	0.80	3.4780	3.4780				
1964	22376.00	14830.00	405.60	0.80	3.4780	3.4780				
1965	26551.00	16572.00	238.90	1.00	3.4780	3.4780				
1966	29406.00	17811.00	353.60	0.80	3.4780	3.4780				
1967	30451.00	20164.00	303.80	0.80	3.4780	3.4780				
1968	33856.00	21909.00	301.60	0.80	3.4780	3.4780				
1969	37261.00	24526.00	104.10	0.40	3.4780	3.4780				
1970	45493.00	27296.00	777.00	0.20	3.4780	3.4780				
1971	52416.00	30248.00	793.90	0.70	3.4780	3.4780				
1972	60684.00	35255.00	515.40	0.60	3.6700	3.6700				
1973	74776.00	45410.00	512.70	0.10	4.1100	4.1010				
1974	118095.00	58014.00	736.40	1.90	3.9680	3.9620				
1975	97692.00	49310.00			3.9350	3.9310				
1976	130859.00	55089.00			3.3000	3.3110				
1977	190685.00	77685.00			2.6020	2.6040				
1978	230128.00	106451.00			2.2720	2.2650				
1979	331927.00	176051.00			2.0400	2.0400				
1980	473018.40	231623.20			1.9970	1.9980	38	35	34	28
1981	608965.40	256912.70			1.6342	1.6269			39	
1982	753980.90	331742.70			1.2731	1.2573			46	
1983	899340.30	508568.60			0.9163	0.9043	43	44	60	49
1984	1160633.00	760580.00			0.6874	0.6847	41	51	81	64
1985	1326529.00	971747.10			0.5874	0.5877	43	56	86	74
1986	1442000.00	1082000.00			0.6691	0.6693	52	61	79	77
1987	1964999.00	1311000.00			0.7107	0.7110	66	68	84	83
1988	2580999.00	1582000.00			0.6951	0.6947	81	74	90	92
1989	3024000.00	2016000.00			0.6351	0.6350	88	89	97	97
1990	3603000.00	2336000.00			0.7038	0.7028	100	100	100	100
1991	3808000.00	2352000.00			0.6934	0.6938	106	101	100	100
1992	4086000.00	2474000.00			0.7415	0.7425	119	107	95	98
1993	3888999.00	2468999.00			0.6254	0.6231				
1994	4453998.00	2976000.00			0.6048	0.6051				
1995	4883001.00	3052000.00			0.6625	0.6628				
1996	5262000.00	3675000.00			0.6482	0.6482				
1997	5742252.00	3983933.00			0.5716	0.5719				

2. IMPORTS BY BROAD ECONOMIC CATEGORY AND EXPORTS BY INDUSTRIAL ORIGIN. (PERCENTAGE OF TOTAL VALUE)
IMPORTATIONS PAR CATEGORIES ECONOMIQUES ET EXPORTATIONS PAR BRANCHE D'ACTIVITE.(EN POURCENTAGE DE LA VALEUR TOTALE)

IMPORTS – IMPORTATIONS

	1991	1992	1993	1994	1995	1996	1997
TOTAL IMPORTS–IMPORTATIONS TOTALES	100.	100.	100.	100.	100.	100.	100.
1 FOOD BEV–ALIMENTATION BOISSONS	10.9	10.1	11.4	12.3	12.1	11.6	10.8
11 PRIMARY–PRODUITS DE BASE	7.9	7.2	7.9	8.4	7.9	7.4	6.9
111 FOR INDUSTRY–POUR L'INDUSTRIE	3.0	2.7	2.8	2.8	2.8	2.7	2.4
112 FOR HOUSEHOLDS–POUR LES MENAGES	4.9	4.5	5.1	5.6	5.1	4.7	4.4
12 PROCESSED–PRODUITS ELABORES	3.0	2.9	3.5	3.9	4.2	4.2	3.9
121 FOR INDUSTRY–POUR L'INDUSTRIE	0.9	0.7	0.6	0.6'	0.7	0.8	0.7
122 FOR HOUSEHOLDS–POUR LES MENAGES	2.2	2.2	2.9	3.3	3.5	3.4	3.2
2 IND SUPPLIES–APPROV INDUSTRIELS	32.3	31.1	30.5	32.5	33.7	31.5	32.0
21 PRIMARY–PRODUITS DE BASE	4.5	4.2	4.3	4.5	4.1	3.7	3.7
22 PROCESSED–PRODUITS ELABORES	27.8	26.9	26.3	28.1	29.5	27.8	28.4
3 FUELS–COMBUSTIBLES	9.0	8.0	8.9	8.5	8.2	7.8	8.1
31 PRIMARY–PRODUITS DE BASE	6.7	6.1	6.8	7.0	6.3	6.1	6.6
32 PROCESSED–PRODUITS ELABORES	2.3	1.9	2.1	1.5	1.9	1.7	1.6
321 MOTOR SPIRIT–ESSENCE	0.9	0.7		0.7			
322 OTHER–AUTRES	1.3	1.2	2.1	0.8	1.9	1.7	1.6
4 MACHINERY–EQUIPEMENT	19.8	18.9	17.4	16.1	16.9	17.3	17.9
41 CAPITAL EQUIPMENT–MACHINES	17.0	16.4	14.9	13.5	13.4	14.1	14.8
42 PARTS–PIECES ACCESSOIRES	2.8	2.5	2.5	2.6	3.6	3.3	3.0
5 TRANSPORT–TRANSPORT	15.3	18.1	16.9	17.4	15.7	18.1	17.2
51 PASSENGER CARS–AUTOMOBILES	6.2	7.9	7.8	7.1	6.2	6.8	6.2
52 OTHER–AUTRES	3.1	4.0	3.0	4.5	3.4	2.9	3.5
521 INDUSTRIAL–INDUSTRIELS	2.8	3.6	2.5	4.2	3.1	2.7	3.2
522 NON INDUSTRIAL–NON INDUSTRIEL	0.4	0.5	0.5	0.3	0.3	0.3	0.3
53 PARTS–PIECES ACCESSOIRES	6.0	6.1	6.0	5.8	6.2	8.4	7.5
6 CONSUM GOODS–BIENS CONSOMMATION	12.7	13.7	14.8	13.1	13.2	13.5	13.9
61 DURABLE–DURABLES	4.4	4.4	4.4	3.7	3.5	3.6	3.6
62 SEMI DURABLE–SEMI DURABLES	6.0	6.6	7.1	6.3	6.3	6.4	6.7
63 NON DURABLE–NON DURABLES	2.3	2.7	3.3	3.2	3.4	3.6	3.6
7 GOODS NES–BIENS NDA	0.1	0.1	0.1	0.1	0.2	0.1	0.1

EXPORTS – EXPORTATIONS

	1991	1992	1993	1994	1995	1996	1997
TOTAL EXPORTS–EXPORTATIONS TOTALES	100.	100.	100.	100.	100.	100.	100.
1 AGRICULTURE	2.4	2.1	1.8	1.8	2.0	1.8	2.0
2 MINING QUARRY–INDUS EXTRACTIVES	2.5	2.1	2.1	2.0	1.9	1.5	1.6
3 MANUFACTURING–IND MANUFACTUR	95.0	95.8	96.1	96.2	96.2	96.7	96.5
31 FOOD BEV TOBACCO–ALIM BOISS TAB	6.1	6.1	6.0	6.0	6.0	6.1	5.8
32 TEXTILES–INDUSTRIES TEXTILES	38.6	38.4	38.0	35.6	31.3	30.6	29.7
33 WOOD & PRODUCTS–BOIS & PRODUITS	5.2	4.7	4.7	4.5	4.1	4.1	4.2
34 PAPER & PRODUCTS–PAPIER & PRODT	5.7	5.4	5.4	6.0	6.6	5.3	5.2
35 CHEMICALS–INDUSTRIES CHIMIQUES	8.7	8.6	9.3	10.6	9.6	8.8	8.8
36 NON METAL MIN–MIN NON METAL	4.5	4.5	4.6	4.8	4.4	4.0	3.9
37 BASIC METAL–IND METAL BASE	1.2	1.2	1.2	1.2	1.1	1.2	1.1
38 METAL MANUF–MANUF METAL	24.2	26.3	26.2	27.1	32.5	36.0	37.2
39 OTH MANUF IND–AUTRES MANUF	0.8	0.7	0.6	0.6	0.6	0.6	0.5

3. TRADE BY PRINCIPAL COUNTRIES OF CONSIGNMENT AND DESTINATION (VALUE IN MILLION U.S. DOLLARS)
ECHANGES SELON LES PRINCIPAUX PAYS DE CONSIGNATION ET DE DESTINATION (VALEUR EN MILLIONS DE DOLLARS EU)

COUNTRIES–PAYS	SPECIAL IMPORTS C.I.F. IMPORTATIONS SPECIALES C.A.F				
	1993	1994	1995	1996	1997
World	24244.3	27065.1	33565.2	34121.9	32964.6
Africa	1367.2	1506.9	1728.7	1847.3	1557.4
Americas	1638.6	1887.9	2299.7	2181.9	2268.9
– Northern America	866.7	1051.0	1199.0	1197.8	1183.9
– LAIA	650.2	705.5	955.3	853.9	949.4
– CACM	30.7	30.6	38.7	38.9	57.8
– Caribbean	81.6	87.7	69.1	73.0	57.8
– Rest of America	9.5	13.1	37.6	18.2	19.9
Asia excl fmr USSR	1971.9	2468.3	2948.0	2839.4	2988.2
– Middle East	358.1	761.0	813.8	702.6	853.6
Asia former USSR	15.4	20.2	27.0	25.4	28.9
Europe excl fmr USSR	18968.1	20880.3	26172.5	26772.6	25693.7
– European Union	18066.9	19891.3	25020.9	25820.0	24812.3
– Eastern Europe	53.7	74.9	128.7	110.9	126.1
– Rest of Europe	847.5	914.1	1022.9	841.7	755.4
Europe former USSR	205.0	242.9	311.0	372.0	336.6
Oceania	44.3	48.7	62.0	72.5	71.0
Other	33.8	9.9	16.3	10.9	19.8
Spain/Espagne	4330.8	5384.7	7118.3	7666.3	7568.3
Germany/Allemagne	3642.9	3761.0	4952.1	5285.4	4952.0
France, Monaco	3084.0	3468.3	3964.8	3782.2	3550.3
Italy/Italie	2103.6	2318.4	2809.1	2825.0	2657.4
United Kingdom	1795.3	1775.1	2216.2	2295.1	2317.5
Netherlands/Pays–Bas	1193.6	1168.1	1513.8	1511.8	1483.0
Belgium–Luxembourg	917.6	919.7	1114.5	1128.4	1028.2
USA/Etats–Unis d'Amer	768.2	978.8	1099.6	1082.1	1080.0
Japan/Japon	782.7	770.6	742.0	759.8	823.8
Switzerland,Liechtenst.	472.2	447.1	506.6	483.9	438.8
Brazil/Brésil	337.1	412.6	514.4	471.5	579.5
Nigeria/Nigéria	344.5	384.5	464.1	584.1	487.8
Sweden/Suède	291.2	306.8	404.5	401.2	378.8
Norway,Svalbard and JM	333.9	429.8	409.6	275.8	251.4
Saudi Arabia	207.6	304.2	356.9	356.1	380.2
Korea, Republic of	79.0	174.7	446.8	328.0	275.0
Russian Federation	186.6	192.5	258.9	306.2	286.8
Iran (Islamic Rep of)	70.2	362.3	342.6	198.3	243.8
Denmark/Danemark	185.1	232.2	282.2	277.8	219.6
China/Chine	185.8	172.0	198.9	231.7	244.6
Austria/Autriche	201.4	211.1	202.2	213.0	196.8
Algeria/Algérie	324.0	252.7	158.1	127.8	65.6
Ireland/Irlande	136.1	183.1	191.3	189.2	217.7
Finland/Finlande	157.9	131.1	198.6	185.3	204.4
Libyan Arab Jamahiriya	161.4	97.3	180.0	123.7	122.8
Egypt/Egypte	92.4	150.4	116.3	194.8	120.0
So. African Customs Un	106.8	119.2	153.7	153.2	132.4
Thailand/Thaïlande	113.3	105.1	115.8	114.9	123.2
India/Inde	71.4	80.9	117.0	138.6	141.8
Other Asia n.e.s.	100.7	83.2	100.4	121.8	121.6
Canada	98.3	71.9	99.3	115.2	103.9
Mexico/Mexique	81.6	68.4	108.0	76.7	97.5
Argentina/Argentine	91.0	74.3	110.1	90.7	63.2
Pakistan	55.4	62.3	88.7	111.3	95.9
Malaysia/Malaisie	51.0	71.9	94.9	94.6	82.7
Turkey/Turquie	48.0	75.3	76.2	73.4	110.2
Colombia/Colombie	49.5	47.7	72.9	84.4	85.2
Morocco/Maroc	34.2	48.6	62.1	63.7	58.7
Singapore/Singapour	51.8	46.1	48.4	52.3	48.9
Cameroon/Cameroun	37.4	40.3	58.8	42.2	56.6

COUNTRIES–PAYS	SPECIAL EXPORTS F.O.B. EXPORTATIONS SPECIALES F.O.B.				
	1993	1994	1995	1996	1997
Monde	15417.4	17980.8	23370.0	23185.6	22745.7
Afrique	771.5	786.4	888.7	1019.1	996.3
Amériques	940.5	1299.9	1578.8	1599.3	1683.5
– Amérique du Nord	801.9	1052.6	1183.7	1202.9	1249.0
– ALAI	111.3	219.2	318.2	360.2	395.5
– MCAC	4.3	5.1	8.5	7.0	12.3
– Caraïbes	20.6	19.2	46.9	14.4	13.5
– Autre Amérique	2.4	4.0	21.6	14.7	13.3
Asie anc. URSS exclus	549.1	614.4	880.4	917.2	819.6
– Moyen–Orient	148.9	156.4	208.3	229.0	227.7
Asie ancienne URSS	1.0	2.7	0.8	1.4	2.0
Europe anc. URSS exclus	12905.9	15002.3	19690.8	19256.0	18913.5
– Union Européenne	12349.6	14399.7	18883.0	18438.0	18225.4
– Europe de l'Est	28.1	48.9	80.4	152.1	160.0
– Autre de l'Europe	528.2	553.7	727.4	665.8	528.1
Europe ancienne URSS	74.6	73.4	91.6	136.8	93.6
Océanie	50.6	64.5	82.7	103.3	101.1
Autre	124.1	137.2	156.2	152.3	136.0
Germany/Allemagne	3012.2	3400.9	5033.2	4413.6	4546.4
Spain/Espagne	2248.3	2639.7	3559.8	3425.9	3207.6
France, Monaco	2331.3	2645.9	3294.6	3376.6	3199.0
United Kingdom	1749.5	2085.6	2596.8	2567.7	2755.1
Netherlands/Pays–Bas	801.6	966.8	1232.0	1164.5	1086.0
USA/Etats–Unis d'Amer	678.9	929.2	1056.1	1087.0	1099.8
Belgium–Luxembourg	541.8	654.9	717.5	997.3	1015.3
Italy/Italie	461.4	603.4	796.8	885.8	882.1
Sweden/Suède	396.2	436.9	507.0	488.6	483.5
Denmark/Danemark	329.8	413.8	512.8	423.0	414.0
Angola	346.6	293.6	347.2	397.3	442.5
Switzerland,Liechtenst.	320.1	333.3	453.6	402.4	300.0
Austria/Autriche	181.4	196.1	237.2	287.5	263.0
Norway,Svalbard and JM	159.4	179.8	231.1	233.5	198.6
Finland/Finlande	152.8	186.8	205.9	185.3	180.5
Brazil/Brésil	60.2	88.1	191.6	248.8	228.9
Japan/Japon	121.2	136.0	177.9	179.3	148.6
Canada	122.4	122.1	126.6	115.3	148.5
Bunkers, ship stores	100.8	100.5	118.2	124.0	111.8
Cape Verde/Cap–Vert	58.9	84.1	119.7	125.4	122.9
Israel/Israël	69.5	85.3	115.2	112.4	102.2
Greece/Grèce	80.9	79.8	95.0	115.9	94.3
Ireland/Irlande	62.4	89.2	94.5	106.5	98.7
Morocco/Maroc	49.8	70.5	80.1	95.8	84.1
Russian Federation	47.6	58.2	68.9	116.3	76.0
Singapore/Singapour	22.4	27.0	82.6	124.9	87.1
Australia/Australie	40.9	51.8	67.7	87.6	85.8
Turkey/Turquie	47.8	35.9	60.5	68.6	98.1
So. African Customs Un	38.5	46.8	63.3	80.9	74.0
China, Hong Kong SAR	30.1	41.0	56.5	58.1	54.4
Mozambique	37.4	43.4	49.1	49.9	48.8
Saudi Arabia	34.5	41.2	37.8	44.8	45.1
Argentina/Argentine	13.6	64.4	50.8	30.4	37.5
Tunisia/Tunisie	10.5	54.6	59.7	25.0	30.5
Hungary/Hongrie	10.6	19.9	29.4	55.4	64.9
Algeria/Algérie	48.0	46.8	32.2	23.3	24.3
China/Chine	30.1	17.8	33.7	32.4	46.7
Chile/Chili	9.8	23.2	33.5	39.2	51.8
Other Asia n.e.s.	24.0	30.3	35.9	26.7	29.8
Liberia/Libéria	79.4	0.0	0.4	42.6	18.3

(VALUE AS PERCENTAGE OF WORLD TOTAL)(VALEURS EN POURCENTAGE DU TOTAL MONDIAL)

	1988	1989	1990	1991	1992	1993	1994	1995	1996	1997
Africa	5.8	6.5	7.3	5.8	5.5	5.6	5.6	5.2	5.4	4.7
Americas	9.5	8.9	8.3	7.5	6.7	6.8	7.0	6.9	6.4	6.9
– Northern America	5.3	5.3	4.7	4.0	3.6	3.6	3.9	3.6	3.5	3.6
– LAIA	3.8	3.2	3.3	3.2	2.7	2.7	2.6	2.8	2.5	2.9
– CACM	0.1	0.1	0.1	0.1	0.1	0.1	0.1	0.1	0.1	0.2
– Caribbean	0.2	0.3	0.1	0.1	0.2	0.3	0.3	0.2	0.2	0.2
– Rest of America	0.1	0.1	0.1	0.1	0.1	0.0	0.0	0.1	0.1	0.1
Asia excl fmr USSR	9.2	9.0	8.1	7.8	7.1	8.1	9.1	8.8	8.3	9.1
– Middle East	2.5	3.4	2.8	2.2	1.3	1.5	2.8	2.4	2.1	2.6
Asia former USSR					0.0	0.1	0.1	0.1	0.1	0.1
Europe excl fmr USSR	74.8	74.8	75.8	78.3	80.1	78.2	77.1	78.0	78.5	77.9
– European Union	70.4	71.0	72.1	74.8	76.6	74.5	73.5	74.5	75.7	75.3
– Eastern Europe	0.4	0.3	0.3	0.2	0.2	0.2	0.3	0.4	0.3	0.4
– Rest of Europe	4.1	3.5	3.4	3.3	3.4	3.5	3.4	3.0	2.5	2.3
Europe former USSR	0.3	0.3	0.2	0.2	0.4	0.8	0.9	0.9	1.1	1.0
Oceania	0.4	0.4	0.3	0.2	0.2	0.2	0.2	0.2	0.2	0.2
Other	0.1	0.0	0.1	0.1	0.0	0.1	0.0	0.0	0.0	0.1
Spain/Espagne	13.1	14.5	14.4	15.8	16.6	17.9	19.9	21.2	22.5	23.0
Germany/Allemagne				15.0	15.1	15.0	13.9	14.8	15.5	15.0
France, Monaco	11.5	11.7	11.5	11.9	12.9	12.7	12.8	11.8	11.1	10.8
Italy/Italie	9.2	9.1	10.0	10.2	10.2	8.7	8.6	8.4	8.3	8.1
United Kingdom	8.3	7.5	7.6	7.5	7.1	7.4	6.6	6.6	6.7	7.0
Netherlands/Pays–Bas	4.8	5.5	5.7	6.1	6.9	4.9	4.3	4.5	4.4	4.5
Belgium–Luxembourg	4.1	3.9	4.1	4.0	3.8	3.8	3.4	3.3	3.3	3.1
USA/Etats–Unis d'Amer	4.3	4.4	3.9	3.4	3.0	3.2	3.6	3.3	3.2	3.3
Japan/Japon	3.6	3.1	2.7	2.9	3.1	3.2	2.8	2.2	2.2	2.5
Switzerland,Liechtenst.	2.4	2.1	2.1	1.8	1.7	1.9	1.7	1.5	1.4	1.3

	1988	1989	1990	1991	1992	1993	1994	1995	1996	1997
Afrique	4.2	4.6	4.6	5.3	6.6	5.0	4.4	3.8	4.4	4.4
Amériques	7.4	7.6	6.3	5.1	4.8	6.1	7.2	6.8	6.9	7.4
– Amérique du Nord	6.7	6.9	5.6	4.6	4.3	5.2	5.9	5.1	5.2	5.5
– ALAI	0.5	0.5	0.4	0.5	0.4	0.7	1.2	1.4	1.6	1.7
– MCAC	0.0	0.0	0.0	0.0	0.0	0.0	0.0	0.0	0.0	0.1
– Caraïbes	0.1	0.1	0.1	0.1	0.1	0.1	0.1	0.2	0.1	0.1
– Autre Amérique	0.0	0.1	0.1	0.0	0.0	0.0	0.0	0.1	0.1	0.1
Asie anc. URSS exclus	3.2	3.1	3.0	2.9	2.8	3.6	3.4	3.8	4.0	3.6
– Moyen–Orient	0.8	0.7	0.5	0.6	0.7	1.0	0.9	0.9	1.0	1.0
Asie ancienne URSS					0.0	0.0	0.0	0.0	0.0	0.0
Europe anc. URSS exclus	82.9	82.2	84.2	85.1	84.1	83.7	83.4	84.3	83.1	83.2
– Union Européenne	78.5	78.0	80.5	81.6	80.8	80.1	80.1	80.8	79.5	80.1
– Europe de l'Est	0.3	0.2	0.2	0.1	0.2	0.2	0.3	0.3	0.7	0.7
– Autre de l'Europe	4.1	3.9	3.5	3.4	3.2	3.4	3.1	3.1	2.9	2.3
Europe ancienne URSS	0.6	0.9	0.4	0.1	0.3	0.5	0.4	0.4	0.6	0.4
Océanie	0.4	0.5	0.3	0.3	0.3	0.3	0.4	0.4	0.4	0.4
Autre	1.3	1.2	1.2	1.2	1.0	0.8	0.8	0.7	0.7	0.6
Germany/Allemagne				19.1	19.1	19.5	18.9	21.5	19.0	20.0
Spain/Espagne	11.5	12.7	13.5	15.1	15.0	14.6	14.7	15.2	14.8	14.1
France, Monaco	15.2	15.0	15.5	14.3	14.2	15.1	14.7	14.1	14.6	14.1
United Kingdom	14.3	12.2	12.1	10.8	11.1	11.3	11.6	11.1	11.1	12.1
Netherlands/Pays–Bas	5.9	5.8	5.7	5.7	5.4	5.2	5.4	5.3	5.0	4.8
USA/Etats–Unis d'Amer	5.9	5.9	4.8	3.8	3.5	4.4	5.2	4.5	4.7	4.8
Belgium–Luxembourg	3.2	3.1	3.1	3.2	3.3	3.5	3.6	3.1	4.3	4.5
Italy/Italie	4.2	4.2	4.1	4.0	3.8	3.0	3.4	3.4	3.8	3.9
Sweden/Suède	4.0	4.0	4.1	3.7	3.4	2.6	2.4	2.2	2.1	2.1
Denmark/Danemark	2.3	2.0	2.2	2.1	2.2	2.1	2.3	2.2	1.8	1.8

4. Special Imports C.I.F. by Commodities according to the S.I.T.C. (Rev. 2) in million U.S. Dollars
Importations Spéciales C.A.F. par Produits d'après la C.T.C.I. (Rév. 2) en millions de Dollars E.U.

SITC CTCI	COMMODITY	1994 QUANTITY QUANTITE	1994 VALUE VALEUR	1995 QUANTITY QUANTITE	1995 VALUE VALEUR	1996 QUANTITY QUANTITE	1996 VALUE VALEUR	1997 QUANTITY QUANTITE	1997 VALUE VALEUR	PRODUIT
	ALL COMMODITIES		27065.1		33565.2		34122.0		32964.7	TOUS PRODUITS
0	FOOD AND LIVE ANIMALS		3148.0		3676.6		3698.4		3364.9	ALIMENTS,ANIMAUX VIVANTS
01	MEAT AND PREPARATIONS		453.6		490.8		397.3		381.5	VIANDES ET PREPARATIONS
011	MEAT FRESH,CHILLD,FROZEN	W 138348	423.3	W 138549	449.2	W 117147	350.9	W 125352	335.9	VIANDES FRAICHES,REF,CONGE
0111	BOVINE MEAT FRESH,FROZEN	W 72106	282.4	W 63734	269.8	W 32688	133.0	W 40169	144.8	VIANDES BOVIN FRAI,REF
01111	BOVINE MEAT WITH BONE IN	W 65006	245.8	W 55304	221.9	W 25513	95.5	W 30426	101.2	VIANDES BOVIN NON DESOSS
0113	PIG MEAT FRESH,CHLD,FRZN	W 43377	86.0	W 51710	118.3	W 57194	144.5	W 59224	131.4	VIANDE DE PORC
02	DAIRY PRODCTS,BIRDS'EGGS		99.7		138.9		140.0		138.8	PRODUITS LAITIERS,OEUFS
03	FISH AND PREPARATIONS		705.3		806.6		776.6		727.9	POISSONS ET PREPARATIONS
034	FISH,FRESH,CHILLED,FROZN	W 159898	247.3	W 161014	282.9	W 155956	285.8	W 155600	269.8	POISSON FRAIS, REFRIG,CONG
0342	FISH FROZEN,EXCL FILLETS	W 112743	180.2	W 115917	205.8	W 120535	207.9	W 106387	180.6	POISSONS CONGELES
035	FISH SALTED,DRIED,SMOKED	W 75207	285.6	W 79829	331.4	W 84649	315.3	W 80026	280.4	POISSON SECHE,SALE,FUME
03502	COD(NOT IN FILLETS)DRIED	W 19458	92.8	W 19957	111.0	W 17710	90.5	W 18703	83.8	MORUE SECHEE,SALEE
03503	FISH(EX COD)DRIED,SALTED	W 55696	192.1	W 59814	219.7	W 66876	223.9	W 61242	195.6	POISSONS SECHES,SALES
036	SHELL FISH FRESH,FROZEN	W 35216	141.4	W 38089	156.5	W 35450	147.5	W 39613	149.4	CRUSTACES,MOLLUSQUES
04	CEREALS AND PREPARATIONS		632.6		722.9		765.8		650.1	CEREALES ET PRODUITS
041	WHEAT ETC UNMILLED	W 999696	200.5	W 1092992	239.6	W 1140383	238.4	W 1238799	215.5	FROMENT,EPEAUTRE
0412	OTHER WHEAT ETC UNMILLED	W 917050	181.6	W 946079	203.2	W 1054678	220.1	W 1088276	185.0	AUTRE FROMENT NON MOULU
042	RICE	W 136671	82.9	W 126226	83.7	W 116679	81.8	W 102384	51.4	RIZ
044	MAIZE UNMILLED	W 1045914	197.1	W 939454	181.7	W 905776	198.1	W 1086737	180.7	MAIS NON MOULU
048	CEREAL ETC PREPARATIONS	W 65714	113.1	W 94083	161.1	W 107396	169.6	W 105677	152.4	PREPTNS A BASE CEREALES
05	VEGETABLES AND FRUIT		523.4		591.6		607.7		533.9	LEGUMES ET FRUITS
054	VEG ETC FRSH,SMPLY PRSVD	W 773731	202.9	W 598558	217.3	W 579270	208.5	W 738194	172.8	LEGUMES FRAIS,CONG,SECS
057	FRUIT,NUTS,FRESH,DRIED	W 336184	253.2	W 336109	277.7	W 361621	290.2	W 336098	251.5	FRUITS FRAIS OU SECS
0573	BANANA,PLANTAIN,FRSH,DRY	W 142245	96.4	W 154619	110.1	W 161338	101.2	W 139858	92.2	BANANES FRAICHES,SECHEES
06	SUGAR AND PREPS,HONEY		132.4		199.3		238.5		199.1	SUCRES ET PRODUITS
061	SUGAR AND HONEY	W 433186	110.9	W 465722	166.7	W 440526	205.1	W 420421	165.9	SUCRES ET MIEL
0611	RAW BEET AND CANE SUGAR	W 292630	92.7	W 310944	142.6	W 310075	181.9	W 295398	144.4	SUCRES BRUTS
07	COFFEE,TEA,COCOA,SPICES		180.7		254.5		232.5		231.6	CAFE,THE,CACAO,EPICES
071	COFFEE AND SUBSTITUTES	W 38921	102.9	W 36955	152.2	W 43090	132.8	W 41928	132.3	CAFE ET SUCCEDANES
0711	COFFEE GREEN,ROASTED,SUB	W 38093	96.2	W 35713	138.9	W 42007	123.3	W 40817	123.2	CAFE TORREFIE OU DECAFEINE
07111	COFFEE GREEN,HUSKS,SKINS	W 35537	82.9	W 33052	121.0	W 39503	107.8	W 38190	107.8	CAFE NON TORREFIE
081	*FEEDING STUFF FOR ANIML		270.6	W 1270101	257.2	W 1340982	311.9	W 1415420	304.8	NOURRITURE POUR ANIMAUX
0813	OILCAKE AND OTH RESIDUES	W 455633	83.6	W 265561	40.9	W 390755	84.1	W 423637	97.2	TOURTEAUX
0819	FOOD WASTE AND FEED NES		148.8	W 825251	186.1	W 720447	187.9	W 747000	171.0	DECHETS,ALIMENTS NDA
08193	BEET–PULP,BAGASSE,ETC	W 678674	93.1	W 752110	106.8	W 286800	48.8	W 111687	16.5	PULPES,AUTRES DECHETS
08199	FODDER NES,INCL SWEETNED		55.2	W 73021	79.1	W 433598	139.0	W 634748	154.5	PREPARATIONS FOURRAGERES
09	MISC EDIBLE PRODUCTS		86.5		116.0		131.5		116.0	PREP ALIMENTAIRES DIVERSES
098	EDIBLE PRODCTS,PREPS NES		83.8	W 36323	107.5	W 41396	119.2	W 44014	107.4	PREP ALIMENTAIRES NDA
1	BEVERAGES AND TOBACCO		314.2		330.1		327.3		289.5	BOISSONS ET TABACS
11	BEVERAGES		243.7		261.9		241.8		224.2	BOISSONS
112	ALCOHOLIC BEVERAGES	W 193159	193.1	W 144793	207.5	W 99696	189.7	W 105924	191.0	BOISSONS ALCOOLIQUES
1124	DISTILLED ALCOHOLIC BEVS	W 41478	114.2	W 32083	121.1	W 24356	122.6	W 31709	132.1	ALCOOLS,EAUX–DE–VIE
2	CRUDE MATERLS,EXCL FUELS		1224.1		1609.7		1465.2		1424.6	MAT BRUTES NON COMESTIBLES
22	OIL SEEDS,OLEAGINOUS FRT		245.7		319.9		315.0		275.5	GRAINES,FRUITS OLEAGINEUX
222	SEEDS FOR'SOFT'FIXED OIL	W 827721	244.7	W 1158264	318.7	W 976945	313.5	W 896070	274.4	GRAINES HUILES FIXES
2222	SOYA BEANS	W 584041	158.5	W 895290	233.1	W 709333	226.0	W 624054	199.2	FEVES DE SOJA
24	CORK AND WOOD		264.0		382.3		312.3		348.9	LIEGE ET BOIS
247	OTH WOOD ROUGH,SQUARED	W 837743	155.6	W 1329984	235.3	W 823803	163.1	W 1321140	182.9	BOIS BRUTS EQUARRIS
2472	SAW–,VENEER–LOGS NON–CON	W 756481	150.0	W 1186931	226.2	W 784996	159.7	W 1224578	178.1	NON CONIFERES SCIAGE,PLAC
24721	— IN THE ROUGH	W 756481	150.0	W 1186931	226.2	W 784996	159.7	W 1224578	178.1	BRUTS ECORCES DEGROSSIS
248	WOOD SHAPED,SLEEPERS	W 107101	64.7	W 130719	93.3	W 136803	98.8	W 155905	103.4	BOIS SIMPLEMENT TRAVAILLES
26	TEXTILE FIBRES AND WASTE		355.3		441.9		418.5		384.2	FIBRES TEXTILES
263	COTTON	W 169225	263.6	W 173355	343.3	W 172428	336.8	W 168183	298.5	COTON
2631	RAW COTTON,EXCL LINTERS	W 167814	262.1	W 171393	340.4	W 169427	331.7	W 166418	294.7	COTON EN MASSE
29	CRUDE ANIMAL,VEG MAT NES		82.3		106.9		107.1		103.8	MATIERES BRUTES ANIM,VEGET
3	MINERAL FUELS ETC		2333.1		2754.2		2671.5		2681.5	COMBUSTIBLES MINERAUX LUB
32	COAL,COKE AND BRIQUETTES		206.2		260.1		237.3		239.0	HOUILLES,COKES,BRIQUETTES
322	COAL,LIGNITE AND PEAT	W 5094903	203.9	W 5735006	257.6	W 5110885	235.1	W 5619830	236.8	HOUILLES,LIGNITES,TOURBE
3222	OTH COAL,NOT AGGLOMERATD	W 4416946	182.4	W 5348886	240.8	W 4776331	219.9	W 5160295	216.8	AUTRES HOUILLES
33	PETROLEUM AND PRODUCTS		2001.4		2316.5		2215.3		2165.7	PETROLE ET DERIVES
333	CRUDE PETROLEUM	MW 13437	1581.6	MW 13237	1695.3	MW 11132	1653.9	MW 12701	1712.2	HUILES BRUTES DE PETROLE
334	PETROLEUM PRODUCTS,REFIN	W 2750626	387.6	W 3647141	559.0	W 2567678	514.4	W 2000919	395.8	PRODUITS RAFFINES
3341	GASOLINE,OTH LIGHT OILS	W 1152622	179.8							ESSENCES POUR MOTEURS
33419	OTH LIGHT PETROLEUM OILS	W 1132812	176.1							AUTRES HUILES LEGERES
3344	FUEL OILS,NES	W 1420552	137.5							FUEL OILS
341	*GAS,NATURAL AND MANUFCT	W 611630	111.4	W 919096	162.8	W 721585	189.8	W 881389	220.1	GAZ NATUREL,GAZ MANUFACT
3413	PETROLM GASES,LIQUEFIED	W 611628	111.4	W 640140	150.4	W 663557	187.2	W 711615	188.9	GAZ DE PETROLE LIQUEFIE
34131	LIQUEFIED PROPANE,BUTANE	W 605342	109.9	W 630353	148.6	W 651700	184.9	W 701327	186.8	PROPANE,BUTANE LIQUEFIES
4	ANIMAL,VEGETABLE OIL,FAT		146.6		232.6		208.8		174.8	HUILES,GRAISSES ANIM,VEG
42	FIXED VEGETABLE OIL,FAT		134.2		215.7		190.3		157.5	HUILES VEGETALES FIXES
423	FIXED VEG OILS,SOFT	W 54690	111.2	W 82280	189.8	W 62010	165.1	W 88602	140.3	HUILES VEGET DOUCES FIXES
4235	OLIVE OIL	W 36892	98.4	W 44666	161.4	W 29985	143.6	W 43901	112.4	HUILE D'OLIVE
5	CHEMCLS,RELATED PROD NES		2640.4		3373.2		3349.2		3178.3	PRODUITS CHIMIQUES
51	ORGANIC CHEMICALS		510.1		651.6		601.5		552.2	PROD CHIMIQ ORGANIQUES
511	HYDROCARBONS NES,DERIVS		85.7	W 151344	111.6		88.6		99.0	HYDROCARBURES NDA
514	NITROGEN–FNCTN COMPOUNDS		160.6	W 49294	193.7	W 77050	198.5	W 71223	161.3	COMPOSES FONCT AZOTEES
5148	OTH NITROGN–FNCTN CMPNDS		102.9	W 39624	138.5	W 64478	132.7	W 59814	103.7	AUTRES COMPOSES AZOTES
515	ORG–INORG COMPOUNDS ETC		106.1	W 5136	121.5	W 6328	115.7	W 5266	99.0	COMPOSES ORGANO–MINERAUX
52	INORGANIC CHEMICALS		143.6		172.8		176.7		159.9	PROD CHIM INORGANIQUES
53	DYES,TANNING,COLOUR PROD		284.0		351.1		358.1		345.0	PROD TEINTURE,COLORANTS
531	SYNT DYE,NAT INDGO,LAKES		107.5	W 12159	116.2	W 15359	109.9	W 17645	104.7	MAT COLOR ORGAN,LAQUES
5311	SYNTHIC ORGNIC DYESTUFFS		98.7	W 8448	106.4	W 9332	96.3	W 9612	90.7	MAT COLOR ORGAN SYNTHET
533	PIGMENTS,PAINTS,ETC		161.2	W 86186	222.2	W 90440	235.4	W 99786	227.5	PIGMENTS,PEINTURES,VERNIS
5334	VARNISHES,DISTEMPERS ETC	W 24619	65.2	W 27513	95.3	W 28431	106.8	W 29732	100.5	PEINTURES A L'EAU
541	*MEDICINAL,PHARM PRODUCT		492.8		630.1	MK 18059	701.4	MK 17462	700.6	PROD MEDICINAUX PHARMACEUT
5417	MEDICAMENTS		337.6	MK 18828	437.5	MK 12964	503.8	MK 12703	523.1	MEDICAMENTS
54179	— CONTNG OTH SUBSTANCES	K 8329505	256.5	MK 17776	344.4	MK 11895	398.3	MK 11655	424.5	MED CONT AUT SUBSTANCES
55	PERFUME,CLEANING ETC PRD		306.4		388.2		392.8		339.4	PROD POUR PARFUM,TOILETTE
553	PERFUMERY,COSMETICS,ETC	W 26006	158.4	W 29001	211.6	W 33730	215.4	W 33355	207.7	PRODUITS DE PARFUMERIE
554	SOAP,CLEANSING ETC PREPS		116.5	W 111674	142.8	W 113595	140.0	W 85234	99.9	SAVONS,PRODUITS DETERSIFS
5542	WASHING PREPARATIONS ETC		95.0	W 98422	115.5	W 94811	111.5	W 70911	76.2	PROD ORG TENSIO–ACT NDA
58	PLASTIC MATERIALS ETC		525.7		726.4		667.3		653.3	MAT PLAST ARTIFICIELLES
582	PROD OF CONDENSATION ETC		116.8	W 69449	162.8	W 66886	159.7	W 88184	162.3	PROD CONDENS,POLYCOND
583	POLYMERIZATION ETC PRODS		392.4	W 334834	544.5	W 361008	490.1	W 381536	472.9	PROD POLYMERISATION
5831	POLYETHYLENE	W 84772	74.3	W 86403	110.8	W 99774	105.1	W 101512	105.4	POLYETHYLENE
5832	POLYPROPYLENE	W 71051	67.0	W 76286	103.8	W 74096	84.2	W 79797	84.6	POLYPROPYLENE
5834	POLYVINYL CHLORIDE		75.7	W 66717	102.9	W 66626	82.1	W 72507	81.0	CHLORURE DE POLYVINYLE
5839	OTH POLYMRZTION ETC PROD	W 41207	86.9	W 45387	124.1	W 49614	113.7	W 49219	104.7	AUT PROD POLYMER COPOLYM
59	CHEMICAL MATERIALS NES		301.9		373.1		370.1		350.9	MAT PROD CHIMIQUES NDA
598	MISCEL CHEM PRODUCTS NES		192.4	W 144961	233.4	W 112226	218.4	W 131127	218.9	PROD DIV INDUST CHIM NDA

4. Special Imports C.I.F. by Commodities according to the S.I.T.C. (Rev. 2) in million U.S. Dollars
Importations Spéciales C.A.F. par Produits d'après la C.T.C.I. (Rév. 2) en millions de Dollars E.U.

SITC CTCI	COMMODITY	1994 QUANTITY QUANTITE	1994 VALUE VALEUR	1995 QUANTITY QUANTITE	1995 VALUE VALEUR	1996 QUANTITY QUANTITE	1996 VALUE VALEUR	1997 QUANTITY QUANTITE	1997 VALUE VALEUR	PRODUIT
5989	CHEM PRODUCTS,PREPS NES		148.9	W 83659	181.8	W 83510	181.8	W 92893	180.2	PROD PREP CHIMIQUES NDA
59899	OTH CHEM PRODS,PREPS,NES	W 52568	99.5	W 59687	124.8	W 57807	122.3	W 66707	124.9	AUT PRODUITS CHIMIQUES NDA
6	BASIC MANUFACTURES		5209.8		6800.2		6485.3		6536.8	ART MANUFACTURES
61	LEATHER,DRESSED FUR,ETC		548.1		602.0		573.4		550.3	CUIRS,PELLETERIES
611	LEATHER		423.2	W 50329	458.0	W 51285	430.9	W 48807	407.3	CUIRS,PEAUX PREPARES
6114	LEATHR BOVINE NES,EQUINE		318.8	W 42638	347.1	W 44208	336.1	W 41587	317.3	CUIRS DE BOVINS
612	LEATHER ETC MANUFACTURES		122.9	W 9401	138.5	W 10426	137.2	W 11398	137.8	OUVRAGES EN CUIRS NDA
6123	PREPRD PARTS OF FOOTWEAR		119.6	W 9162	134.1	W 10092	131.4	W 11005	132.8	PARTIES DE CHAUSSURES
62	RUBBER MANUFACTURES NES		248.0		351.2		402.6		400.7	CAOUTCHOUC MANUFACTURE
625	RUBBER TYRES, TUBES ETC	W 41804	153.5	W 50260	206.8	W 54897	227.6	W 62126	223.1	PNEUS CAOUTCHOUC VULCANISE
6251	TYRES NEW FOR MOTOR CARS	W 15165	72.2	W 18617	98.2	W 22319	115.6	W 24581	110.2	PNEUS POUR VOITURES
63	WOOD,CORK MANUFACTRS NES		97.9		115.9		131.0		151.4	OUVRAGES LIEGE ET BOIS
64	PAPER,PAPERBOARD AND MFR		505.9		710.3		701.8		616.4	PAPIERS,CARTONS & OUVRAGES
641	PAPER AND PAPERBOARD		352.1	W 438803	509.9	W 465657	494.2	W 539528	427.3	PAPIERS ET CARTONS
6412	PRINTG,WRITING PAPER NES	W 81094	77.2	W 81311	109.5	W 94005	105.2	W 132845	113.2	PAPIERS POUR L'IMPRESSION
64122	— COATED,IMPREGNATD ETC	W 74292	68.7	W 74380	97.6	W 87227	95.5	W 121715	100.1	PAPIERS IMPRESSION COUCHES
6418	COATED ETC PAPER NES BLK	W 72844	132.9	W 71857	165.3	W 79444	170.8	W 68434	115.9	PAP,CARTONS COUCHES,ENDUITS
64189	COATED PAPER ETC NES	W 66214	120.1	W 52223	108.2	W 43257	74.8	W 47852	65.1	PAPIERS,CARTONS COUCHES
642	PAPER,ETC,PRECUT,ARTS OF		153.8	W 75990	200.4	W 86437	207.6	W 96800	189.2	PAP,CARTONS DECOUPES
6428	PAPER ETC ARTICLES NES		99.4	W 39304	118.4	W 45244	122.3	W 46325	104.2	OUVRAGES EN PATE A PAPIER
65	TEXTILE YARN,FABRICS,ETC		1650.6		2012.3		1964.3		1919.0	FILS,TISSUS,ARTICLES TEXTILE
651	TEXTILE YARN		500.1	W 123901	628.6	W 131914	616.5	W 164760	660.1	FILS TEXTILES
6513	COTTON YARN	W 40733	146.1	W 43561	186.1	W 46581	187.0	W 58113	209.1	FILS DE COTON
6514	SYN FIB YRN,BULK,MONOFIL		136.2	W 31115	163.0	W 29570	149.1	W 42155	175.6	FILS CONT 85% FIB TEXT SYNTH
6516	DISCON SYN FIB BLEND YRN	W 24731	83.8	W 27019	108.8	W 33033	117.8	W 40017	122.9	FILS FIBR TEX SYNT DIS MOINS
65166	DISCON SYN FIB–COTTN YRN	W 22379	73.2	W 23690	92.9	W 28130	97.7	W 32730	99.2	FILS TEXT SYNT MELANGE COTON
652	COTTON FABRICS,WOVEN	W 24639	242.1	W 24938	279.9	W 26504	291.5	W 26550	258.2	TISSUS DE COTON
6522	WOVEN COTTON BLEACHD,ETC	W 18979	211.2	W 17726	239.2	W 19662	254.3	W 18087	215.9	TISSUS COTON BLANCHIS ETC
65224	BLCHED COTTON FABRIC NES	W 15589	157.6	W 14143	177.5	W 14858	189.2	W 13314	156.2	AUT TIS PLUS 85% COT BLANCHI
653	WOVN MAN–MADE FIB FABRIC		349.0	W 24257	414.4	W 22806	378.8	W 23623	346.5	TISSUS FIBRES SYNTH,ARTIF
6531	CONT SYNT WEAVES NONPILE	W 6861	105.9	W 7857	132.5	W 7007	118.3	W 7373	108.8	TISSUS FIBRES SYNTH CONTINUE
65315	CONT SYN TXTL FABRIC NES	W 5777	92.0	W 6535	112.8	W 5943	100.7	W 6298	94.3	TIS PLUS 85% TEXT SYNT CONT
6534	DISC SYN BLEND FABRC NES	W 8933	110.0	W 9952	133.6	W 9345	131.6	W 10000	124.9	TISSUS FIBRES SYNTH DISCONT
654	OTH WOVEN TEXTILE FABRIC	W 6045	156.8	W 5896	170.9	W 5112	153.7	W 5019	132.0	TISSUS AUT COTON SYNT,ARTIF
655	KNITTED,ETC FABRICS	W 6724	102.1	W 7084	124.7	W 7631	131.9	W 9397	144.2	ETOF BONNETERIE PIECES ETC
6552	OTHER KNIT ETC FAB NONEL	W 6724	102.1	W 7084	124.7	W 7631	131.9	W 9397	144.2	ETOF BON NON ELAS NON SYNT
657	SPECIAL TXTL FABRC,PRODS		175.9	W 22793	236.0	W 22074	226.9	W 25736	220.5	TISSUS SPECIAUX
6573	COATED ETC TEXTILES NES	W 7794	106.7	W 10275	149.5	W 10503	143.2	W 12545	142.3	TISSUS,ART MATIERE TEXT NDA
65732	PLASTIC COATED TEXTILES	W 6727	93.6	W 7837	124.6	W 8816	125.1	W 10144	121.6	TISSUS IMPREGNES
66	NONMETAL MINERAL MFS NES		390.4		454.5		476.7		531.4	ART MIN NON METALLIQUES
662	CLAY,REFRACTORY BLDG PRD	W 161991	75.3	W 196906	109.8	W 195645	101.3	W 221552	95.7	MAT CONST REFRACTAIRES
664	GLASS		63.9	W 87795	86.9	W 107873	102.9	W 123279	97.1	VERRE
667	PEARL,PREC–,SEMI–P STONE		86.6		57.6		63.5		89.8	PERLES, PIERRES GEMMES
6672	DIAMONDS NONINDUST,UNSET		84.1		54.3		60.5		87.0	DIAMANTS BRUTS
67	IRON AND STEEL		852.3		1274.2		1045.8		1100.3	FER ET ACIER
672	IRON,STEEL PRIMARY FORMS	W 520614	159.0	W 538588	256.8	W 200167	82.3	W 441721	151.2	LINGOTS FER,ACIER
6727	IRN,STL COIL FR REROLLNG	W 493506	148.8	W 527055	249.1	W 196975	78.1	W 427595	135.4	EBAUCHES POUR TOLES FER
67271	IRON,SIMPLE STEEL COILS	W 492121	147.8	W 525247	246.8	W 196299	76.9	W 426810	134.2	EBAUCHES NON EN ACIER
673	IRON,STEEL SHAPES ETC		194.4	W 709392	322.5	W 589773	244.2	W 729436	263.2	BARRES,PROFIL FER,ACIER
6732	IRON,STEEL BARS ETC	W 341499	132.0	W 444847	203.7	W 268285	115.4	W 343598	129.4	BARRES FER,ACIER
67326	IRN,OTH STL BARS HOTROLD	W 305179	100.8	W 392310	150.5	W 230125	77.3	W 304442	95.6	BARRES PLEINES FER,ACIER
674	IRN,STL UNIV,PLATE,SHEET	W 364680	252.9	W 497282	427.4	W 735132	484.2	W 697595	418.2	LARGES PLATS,TOLES
6745	IRN,STL MED PLATE,ROLLED	W 51189	34.8	W 61889	50.8	W 227914	102.7	W 112110	49.1	TOLES 3 A 4.75 MM
6746	IRN,STL THIN PLATE,ROLLD	W 86650	78.8	W 145729	146.7	W 151123	131.1	W 191545	135.4	TOLES LAM MOINS 3MM
6749	OTH IRN,STL PLATES,SHEET	W 130680	82.2	W 166348	137.6	W 183940	137.4	W 239610	153.6	AUTRES TOLES FER,ACIER
67491	— OF IRON OR SIMPLE STL	W 128252	77.6	W 164035	130.4	W 181461	131.3	W 233364	145.8	AUT TOLES AUTRES ACIER FIN
678	IRON,STL TUBES,PIPES,ETC		174.4	W 152297	167.1	W 128864	141.7	W 195999	171.3	TUBES,TUYAUX EN FONTE,FER
6783	IRON,STL TUBES,PIPES NES	W 137555	127.4	W 111915	100.1	W 77100	61.5	W 83320	58.6	AUT TUBES,TUYAUX FER,ACIER
68	NON–FERROUS METALS		400.7		583.1		496.6		541.7	METAUX NON FERREUX
682	COPPER EXC CEMENT COPPER		148.8	W 65136	223.7	W 62471	198.3	W 77476	212.6	CUIVRE
6822	COPPER,ALLOYS WORKED		132.7	W 63554	219.1	W 58367	188.7	W 73520	204.2	CUIVRE,ALLIAGES OUVRES
68221	COPPER BARS,WIRE,ETC	W 34054	77.2	W 46765	141.5	W 42324	115.6	W 52792	132.3	BARRES,PROFILES ET FILS
684	ALUMINIUM		192.3	W 100364	280.4	W 95966	216.8	W 120267	254.5	ALUMINIUM
6841	ALUMINIUM,ALLOYS,UNWRGHT	W 68257	107.7	W 73352	164.3	W 67676	114.5	W 79769	143.5	ALUMINIUM,ALLIAGES BRUTS
6842	ALUMINIUM,ALLOYS WORKED		84.7	W 27012	116.1	W 28290	102.4	W 40498	111.0	ALUMINIUM,ALLIAGES OUVRE
69	METAL MANUFACTURES NES		516.3		697.4		693.7		725.9	ART MANUFACT EN METAL NDA
695	TOOLS		76.8	W 11485	99.2	W 11756	104.5	W 13198	106.4	OUTILS A MAIN
699	BASE METAL MFRS NES		160.5	W 39237	227.0	W 43395	232.1	W 55326	247.2	ART MANUFACTURES MET NDA
7	MACHINES,TRANSPORT EQUIP		9310.8		11327.5		12378.9		11806.4	MACHINES MATERIEL TRANSPORT
71	POWER GENERATING EQUIPMT		441.2		638.4		815.8		730.6	MACHINES GENERATRICES
713	INTRNL COMBUS PSTN ENGIN	W 42801	348.8	W 50345	525.9	W 45818	669.9	W 38939	576.7	MOTEURS EXPL COMB INT, PIECE
7132	MOTOR VEHCL PISTN ENGINS	W 13509	143.3	W 16042	223.5	W 24183	385.9	W 31473	465.1	MOTEURS EXPL POUR VEHICULES
7139	PISTON ENGINE PARTS NES	W 27698	174.6	W 32660	266.8	W 19821	249.1	W 5396	78.0	PIECES POUR 713.2,3,8
72	MACHS FOR SPCL INDUSTRYS		815.3		1034.2		1088.0		1115.6	MAC SPECIALES POUR INDUST
722	TRACTORS NON–ROAD	W 9948	69.7	W 12955	101.6	W 16844	129.1	W 17988	122.9	TRACTEURS
7224	WHEELED TRACTORS NES	W 9904	69.4	W 12773	100.3	W 16543	127.3	W 17418	119.5	TRACTEURS A ROUES
723	CIVIL ENGNEERG EQUIP ETC	W 20759	119.9	W 23456	135.1	W 29977	176.1	W 44772	228.9	APPAREILS DE GENIE CIVIL
7234	CONST,MINING MACHNRY NES	W 18086	103.5	W 18541	105.1	W 24461	143.1	W 38578	194.6	MACH POUR LA CONST, MINES
72342	SLFPRP SHOVELS,EXCAVATRS	W 12728	60.8	W 14422	72.5	W 19743	103.6	W 32345	146.4	PELLES MECANIQUES
724	TEXTILE,LEATHER MACHNRY		219.5	W 11604	263.7	W 10771	263.0	W 12071	264.5	MACH POUR INDUSTRIE TEXTILE
728	OTH MACHY FOR SPCL INDUS		253.7	W 22017	312.3	W 20515	302.7	W 21834	300.1	AUT MACH IND PARTICULIERES
7284	MACHY FOR SPCL INDUS NES		185.8	W 11756	209.3	W 10958	204.5	W 10702	201.9	MACH SPEC IND PARTICUL.
73	METALWORKING MACHINERY		134.8		140.6		148.4		173.9	MACH TRAVAIL DES METAUX
736	METALWORKING MACH–TOOLS		106.5	W 8216	100.4	W 9943	110.9	W 9796	139.0	MACH–OUTILS TRAVAIL METAUX
74	GENRL INDUSTRL MACHY NES		835.2		1092.4		1185.8		1132.6	MACH APP INDUSTRIE
741	HEATING,COOLING EQUIPMNT		211.9	W 23372	277.9	W 22197	303.7	W 22679	249.9	MACH CHAUFFAGE,PIECES
7415	AIR–CONDITIONING MACHNRY	W 5000	70.2	W 6239	105.7	W 8346	138.1	W 7016	94.4	GROUPES CONDITION AIR
743	PUMPS NES,CENTRFUGES ETC		131.6	W 18025	167.5	W 20191	205.5	W 22423	193.6	POMPES COMPRES,VENT ETC
744	MECHANICAL HANDLING EQU		139.2	W 31427	179.5	W 36231	195.7	W 43265	221.3	EQUIP MANUTENTION PIECES
745	NONELEC MACHY,TOOLS NES		136.2	W 10413	156.5	W 11329	155.2	W 12042	150.4	AUT MACH NON ELEC,PIECES
7452	OTH NONELEC MCHS,PTS NES		116.6	W 9574	131.5	W 10258	128.9	W 11101	126.5	AUT MACH NON ELEC,PIECES
749	NONELEC MACH PTS,ACC NES		159.7	W 15860	233.3	W 14688	228.9	W 17669	232.0	PIECES MACH NON ELEC NDA
7492	COCKS,VALVES ETC NES		78.4	W 7728	95.9	W 8633	108.1	W 10783	112.9	ART ROB,SIM POUR TUYAUX
75	OFFICE MACHNES,ADP EQUIP		609.9		802.9		871.2		818.6	MACH BUREAU TRAIT AUTOM
751	OFFICE MACHINES	W 2935	88.9	W 2807	95.9	W 3295	81.6	W 3328	78.4	MACH,APPAREILS DE BUREAU
752	AUTOMTIC DATA PROC EQUIP		365.3	W 7063	493.7	W 8694	535.4	W 25547	517.4	MACH TRAIT INFORMATION
7523	DIGITL CENTRL PROCESSORS	W 1365	112.9	W 1251	126.9	W 1732	158.7	W 14042	160.1	UNITES CENTRALES
7525	ADP PERIPHERAL UNITS	W 2924	111.2	W 3920	158.8	W 5066	165.9	W 9927	163.1	UNITES PERIPHERIQUES
759	OFFICE,ADP MCH PTS,ACCES		155.8	W 3359	213.4	W 4361	254.3	W 4562	222.9	PIECES DU 751 ET 752
7599	ACCTG,ETC,ADP MCH PTS,AC	W 1754	130.5	W 2524	177.2	W 3509	223.9	W 3599	187.0	PIECES DU 751 ET 752
76	TELECOMM,SOUND EQUIPMENT		758.3		931.9		896.3		966.9	EQUIPMENT DE TELECOM

4. Special Imports C.I.F. by Commodities according to the S.I.T.C. (Rev. 2) in million U.S. Dollars
Importations Spéciales C.A.F. par Produits d'après la C.T.C.I. (Rév. 2) en millions de Dollars E.U.

SITC CTCI	COMMODITY	1994 QUANTITY QUANTITE	1994 VALUE VALEUR	1995 QUANTITY QUANTITE	1995 VALUE VALEUR	1996 QUANTITY QUANTITE	1996 VALUE VALEUR	1997 QUANTITY QUANTITE	1997 VALUE VALEUR	PRODUIT
761	TELEVISION RECEIVERS	W 11404	156.3	W 11405	171.0	W 10762	153.2	W 13303	143.8	RECEPTEURS DE TELEVISION
7611	COLOUR TV RECEIVERS	W 11315	154.5	W 11253	168.7	W 10694	151.3	W 13229	142.0	RECEPTEURS COULEUR
762	RADIO BROADCAST RECEIVRS		89.7	W 4050	96.1	W 3557	83.2	W 3707	74.5	RECEPTEURS RADIODIFFUSION
764	TELECOM EQPT,PTS,ACC NES		437.7	W 10090	582.2	W 10433	565.2	W 11576	665.1	EQUIP TELECOM,PIECES
7641	LINE TELEPHONE,ETC EQUIP	W 1104	73.0	W 1188	86.0	W 1344	95.1	W 1731	110.2	APP TELEPHON PAR FIL
7643	TV,RADIO TRANSMITTRS ETC	W 273	60.2	W 297	91.2	W 423	123.4	W 710	201.1	APP EMET TELE RADIO
7649	PTS NES OF EQUIPMT OF 76		220.2	W 5680	319.0	W 5749	290.8	W 5665	298.2	PIECES DE LA DIV 76
76491	PTS NES OF APPAR OF 7641		92.5	W 667	121.2	W 742	119.6	W 966	142.0	PIECES POUR 764.1
76493	TELECOMM EQUIPMT PTS NES	W 2986	89.2	W 2935	102.5	W 2405	82.3	W 2418	80.1	PIECES 761,762,764.3,8
77	ELECTRIC MACHNRY NES ETC		1635.4		2317.7		2323.7		2244.8	MACH APP ELECT NDA
771	ELECTRIC POWER MACHY NES		97.4	W 8665	104.1	W 9795	111.8	W 14510	128.1	MACH PROD,TRANS ELECTR
7712	OTH ELEC POWER MACHY NES		81.2	W 6703	84.7	W 7725	91.7	W 12114	107.2	AUT APP PROD TRANSF ELEC
772	SWITCHGEAR ETC,PARTS NES		378.7	W 16468	497.4	W 17798	521.3	W 24540	523.7	APP COUPURE,SECT ETC
7721	SWITCHGEAR ETC		318.2	W 15226	417.3	W 16411	450.5	W 23130	461.1	APP COUPURE,SECTIONMNT
773	ELECTR DISTRIBUTNG EQUIP		254.5	W 42014	374.5	W 44684	370.1	W 46063	367.9	EQUIPMT DISTRIBUTION ELECT
7731	INSULATED WIRE,CABLE ETC		161.0	W 34917	242.5	W 36611	234.6	W 38565	220.9	FILS,CABLES ISOLES ELECT
7732	ELECTRC INSULATING EQUIP	W 6646	93.5	W 7097	132.1	W 8073	135.5	W 7499	147.0	EQUIP ISOL ELECTRIQUE
77327	OTH ELEC INSUL FITTG NES	W 4712	65.5	W 5104	103.8	W 5616	102.7	W 5564	110.2	PIECES ISOL EN AUT MATIERES
775	HOUSEHOLD TYPE EQUIP NES		281.1	W 54031	332.2	W 56231	358.7	W 63721	349.9	MACH,APP USAGE DOMESTQUE
7758	ELECTRO–THERMIC APPL NES		98.5	W 13136	116.9	W 14529	129.5	W 15566	120.3	APP ELECTROTHERMIQ NDA
776	TRANSISTORS,VALVES,ETC		268.9	W 1866	594.0	W 1747	488.2	W 1389	398.2	LAMPES,TUBES,VALVES
7764	ELECTRONIC MICROCIRCUITS		218.9	W 1116	526.2	W 1031	408.7	W 574	331.0	MICROSTRUCTURES ELECTRON
778	ELECTRICAL MACHINERY NES		318.3	W 30543	376.4	W 34512	425.5	W 38409	430.3	AUTRES MACH ELECT NDA
7783	AUTOMOTIVE ELECTR EQUIP		68.9	W 5997	98.3	W 6784	131.1	W 7705	136.6	EQUIP ELECT MOTEURS EXPL
7788	OTH ELEC MACHY,EQUIP NES		141.8	W 5492	154.0	W 5281	157.8	W 5778	147.0	AUT MACH APP ELEC NDA
78	ROAD VEHICLES		3551.1		3869.0		4899.3		4326.2	VEHICULES ROUTIERS
781	PASS MOTOR VEH EXC BUSES	W 206048	1910.9	W 197336	2064.3	W 226953	2300.9	W 227438	2032.9	AUTO TRANSPORT PERSONNES
782	LORRIES,SPCL MTR VEH NES	W 81387	625.7	W 62558	519.9	W 85548	697.9	W 109803	755.8	VEHICULES SPECIAUX,MARCH
7821	LORRIES,TRUCKS	W 79642	615.9	W 60265	505.1	W 83242	685.5	W 106819	738.5	VEHICULES TRANSP MARCHAND
784	MOTOR VEH PRTS,ACCES NES		830.1	W 119186	1026.3	W 166018	1638.2	W 168033	1278.8	PIECES 722,781,782,783
7849	OTHER MOTOR VEHCL PARTS		810.1	W 116142	997.1	W 162580	1608.3	W 161970	1245.0	PIECES 722,781,782,783
785	CYCLES,ETC MOTRZD OR NOT	W 8600	120.9	W 9284	135.9	W 9017	127.7	W 11128	128.1	MOTOCYCLES SCOOTERS
7851	MOTORCYCLES ETC	W 4413	86.8	W 4276	94.0	W 4156	86.5	W 4776	85.1	MOTO VELO MOTEUR AUXIL
79	OTHR TRANSPORT EQUIPMENT		529.9		500.7		150.8		297.6	AUTRE MATERIEL TRANSPORT
792	AIRCRAFT ETC		368.4	W 583	348.5	W 564	93.9	W 662	204.4	APP NAVIGATION AERIENNE
7924	AIRCRFT NES OVER 15000KG	W 406	343.0	W 422	303.6	W 173	15.0	W 224	63.3	AERODYNES PLUS 15000 KG
793	SHIPS AND BOATS ETC	W 58588	87.4	W 28974	72.7	W 17823	41.9		35.4	NAVIRES BATEAUX,ETC
7932	SHIPS AND BOATS NES	W 54571	83.9	W 6162	57.8	W 7646	32.8		27.2	NAVIRES ET BATEAUX
8	MISC MANUFACTURED GOODS		2581.4		3251.1		3358.2		3394.3	ART MANUFACTURES DIVERS
812	*PLUMBG,HEATNG,LGHTNG EQ		72.3	W 13948	94.7	W 17117	108.1	W 19694	122.9	APPAR SANITAIRES CHAUFFAGE
821	*FURNITURE,PARTS THEREOF		169.7	W 41224	213.7	W 45668	230.9	W 56714	244.4	MEUBLES ET PIECES
8219	FURNITURE AND PARTS NES	W 22708	89.1	W 26003	112.3	W 29964	119.4	W 34312	122.8	AUTRES MEUBLES ET PIECES
84	CLOTHING AND ACCESSORIES		715.7		852.4		870.1		849.6	VETEMENTS
842	MENS OUTERWEAR NOT KNIT		114.1	W 3756	130.7	W 3521	131.3	W 3540	124.3	VET DESSUS POUR HOMMES
843	WOMENS OUTERWEAR NONKNIT		144.9	W 3573	185.6	W 3817	189.4	W 3679	182.7	VET DESSUS FEMMES MAT TEX
845	OUTERWEAR KNIT NONELASTC		197.5	W 5302	211.8	W 5067	212.2	W 6097	221.5	VET DESSOUS,ACCES BONNET
8451	— JERSEYS,PULLOVERS ETC		103.3	W 2656	105.8	W 2250	98.8	W 2795	108.6	CHANDAILS,PULL–OVERS ETC
8459	— OTHER,CLTHG ACCESRYS		82.4	W 2300	89.9	W 2461	96.6	W 2881	97.8	AUT VET DESSUS DE BONNE
846	UNDER GARMENTS KNITTED		121.4	W 5613	157.2	W 5351	163.8	W 5215	145.6	SOUS VETS DE BONNETERIE
8462	— OF COTTON NON ELASTIC		74.1	W 3990	97.5	W 3917	102.6	W 3889	91.8	SOUS–VET BONNET COTON
851	*FOOTWEAR		117.7	W 10947	158.2	W 11183	158.3	W 11127	166.6	CHAUSSURES
85102	FOOTWEAR LEATHER		100.1	W 8498	132.1	W 8293	128.8	W 7943	132.1	CHAUS SEMELLES EN CUIR
87	PRECISION INSTRUMNTS NES		332.8		397.5		420.8		423.2	INSTRUM,APPAR SCIENT NDA
872	MEDICAL INSTRUMENTS NES		95.8	W 3555	117.3	W 3684	130.1	W 3394	117.4	INSTR,APP MEDIC–CHIR NDA
87202	OTH MEDICAL INSTRUMENTS	W 2222	84.2	W 3239	105.7	W 3313	117.9	W 2937	102.3	INSTRUM,APP MEDECINE
874	MEASURNG,CONTROLNG INSTR		199.7	W 3559	234.0	W 3524	247.0	W 4538	264.3	INSTRUMENTS DE MESURE
88	PHOTO EQU,OPTICL GDS ETC		219.3		274.0		274.6		271.5	APP,FOURN PHOTO,OP,MONTR
89	MISC MANUFCTRD GOODS NES		919.2		1214.6		1245.8		1265.1	ART MANUFACTURES DIVERS
892	PRINTED MATTER		164.3	W 27074	232.5	W 27400	220.4	W 27896	215.9	IMPRIMES
893	ARTICLES OF PLASTIC NES		261.8		371.9		377.5		387.8	OUVRAGES EN MAT DIVIS 58
8939	MISC PLASTIC ARTICLES		199.9	W 45708	293.6	W 48706	298.6	W 63177	305.1	ART DIVERS EN MAT DIV 58
89399	OTHR PLASTC ARTICLES NES		184.2	W 40283	274.0	W 42093	274.6	W 55505	284.3	AUT OUV MAT DIV 58
894	TOYS,SPORTING GOODS,ETC		155.9	W 20561	188.3	W 23190	226.5	W 25263	221.1	VOITURES ENFANTS,JOUETS
8942	TOYS,INDOOR GAMES ETC		119.9	W 15081	140.5	W 17164	176.4	W 18213	170.4	JOUETS,JEUX ETC
898	MUSICAL INSTRUMENTS,PTS		115.2		153.4	W 11550	138.8	W 10077	150.4	INSTRUMENTS DE MUSIQUE
8983	SOUND RECRDNG TAPE,DISCS		102.2	W 8285	137.1	W 10827	122.7	W 9315	135.1	SUPPORTS SON POUR 763
899	OTHER MANUFACTURED GOODS		114.6		133.7		138.2		143.6	AUT ART MANUF DIVERS NDA
9	GOODS NOT CLASSD BY KIND		157.1		210.4		179.6		114.1	ART TRANSACT NON CLASSES
971	*GOLD,NON MONETARY NES		129.4	K 14091	171.5	K 13380	143.0	K 9519	94.0	OR NON MONETAIRE
97101	NONMON GLD UNWRT,SEMIMFD		129.4	K 14088	171.5	K 12375	143.0	K 9505	94.0	OR,ALLIAGES D'OR BRUTS

5. Special Exports F.O.B. by Commodities according to the S.I.T.C. (Rev. 2) in million U.S. Dollars
Exportations Spéciales F.O.B. par Produits d'après la C.T.C.I. (Rév. 2) en millions de Dollars E.U.

SITC CTCI	COMMODITY	1994 QUANTITY QUANTITE	1994 VALUE VALEUR	1995 QUANTITY QUANTITE	1995 VALUE VALEUR	1996 QUANTITY QUANTITE	1996 VALUE VALEUR	1997 QUANTITY QUANTITE	1997 VALUE VALEUR	PRODUIT
	ALL COMMODITIES		17980.8		23370.1		23185.6		22745.7	TOUS PRODUITS
0	FOOD AND LIVE ANIMALS		687.8		941.0		897.8		891.3	ALIMENTS,ANIMAUX VIVANTS
02	DAIRY PRODCTS,BIRDS'EGGS		78.9		124.6		132.1		139.7	PRODUITS LAITIERS,OEUFS
022	MILK AND CREAM	W 54316	46.7	W 84757	70.8	W 93366	79.8	W 130647	93.2	LAIT ET CREME
03	FISH AND PREPARATIONS		234.9		301.3		268.6		249.6	POISSONS ET PREPARATIONS
034	FISH,FRESH,CHILLED,FROZN	W 48718	90.5	W 51795	106.5	W 42123	88.4	W 42152	94.2	POISSON FRAIS, REFRIG,CONG
037	FISH ETC PREPD,PRSVD NES	W 34591	112.7	W 37348	136.8	W 26696	107.7	W 25817	87.0	POIS,CRUST,MOL PREPARES
0371	FISH PREPARD,PRESRVD NES	W 34497	112.3	W 37232	136.2	W 26602	107.2	W 25654	86.6	CONSERVES DE POISSONS
04	CEREALS AND PREPARATIONS		47.1		81.7		90.9		82.6	CEREALES ET PRODUITS
048	CEREAL ETC PREPARATIONS	W 17267	35.7	W 30716	61.3	W 37135	70.8	W 35404	51.9	PREPTNS A BASE CEREALES
05	VEGETABLES AND FRUIT		204.2		272.9		242.8		250.9	LEGUMES ET FRUITS
054	VEG ETC FRSH,SMPLY PRSVD	W 173111	135.7	W 200003	183.9	W 165395	139.4	W 173916	128.7	LEGUMES FRAIS,CONG,SECS
0546	VEGETABLES SIMPLY PRESVD	W 122308	106.2	W 146162	141.4	W 120482	108.4	W 128939	100.4	LEGUMES CONG,CONSER
05461	VEGETABLES FROZEN	W 121968	105.9	W 145278	140.9	W 120352	108.1	W 128883	100.3	LEGUMES CONGELES
057	FRUIT,NUTS,FRESH,DRIED	W 48745	41.7	W 59307	55.0	W 62093	56.1	W 100698	78.9	FRUITS FRAIS OU SECS
1	BEVERAGES AND TOBACCO		514.8		585.5		632.2		595.0	BOISSONS ET TABACS
11	BEVERAGES		507.6		575.2		615.5		584.2	BOISSONS
112	ALCOHOLIC BEVERAGES	W 256603	496.4	W 247490	560.9	W 268984	599.0	W 305206	567.3	BOISSONS ALCOOLIQUES
1121	WINE OF FRESH GRAPES ETC	W 190631	447.0	W 169618	496.1	W 196398	539.4	W 246259	516.1	VINS DE RAISINS FRAIS
11212	WINE OF FRESH GRAPES	W 190318	446.3	W 169311	495.3	W 196005	538.3	W 245934	515.0	VINS DE MOUTS DE RAISINS
2	CRUDE MATERLS,EXCL FUELS		1092.4		1466.5		1045.1		1066.7	MAT BRUTES NON COMESTIBLES
24	CORK AND WOOD		152.9		203.4		158.7		154.6	LIEGE ET BOIS
248	WOOD SHAPED,SLEEPERS	W 456666	84.0	W 444022	95.2	W 393780	75.4	W 345948	71.1	BOIS SIMPLEMENT TRAVAILLES
2482	LUMBER SHAPED CONIFER	W 444523	78.8	W 433151	90.8	W 386534	72.3	W 341000	67.4	CONIFERES SCIES,RABOTES
24821	LUMBER SAWN ETC CONIFER	W 443008	78.5	W 416886	87.4	W 348145	66.5	W 332231	57.6	CONIFERES SCIES LONGITUD
251	*PULP AND WASTE PAPER	W 1102760	509.4	W 1015846	739.2	W 1034748	462.2	W 1136945	486.4	PATES A PAPIER,DECHETS
2517	SODA,SULPHATE WOOD PULP	W 967385	456.7	W 904733	671.3	W 929169	429.9	W 1029503	457.9	PATES CHIMIQUES AU SULFATE
25171	— UNBLEACHED	W 116644	49.3	W 100940	73.2	W 89900	38.0	W 94000	37.8	PATES ECRUES
25172	— BLEACHED,NONDISSOLVNG	W 850740	407.5	W 803793	598.2	W 839270	392.0	W 935503	420.2	PATES BLANCHIES
26	TEXTILE FIBRES AND WASTE		60.8		66.9		65.8		79.1	FIBRES TEXTILES
28	METALLIFEROUS ORES,SCRAP		264.1		324.3		232.1		223.3	MINERAIS METAL,DECHETS
287	BASE METAL ORES,CONC NES	W 564665	218.4	W 527288	275.2	W 503450	197.1	W 474721	176.9	MINERAIS METAUX COMMUNS
2871	CPR ORE ETC,CEMENT COPPR	W 554815	195.9	W 516154	244.5	W 492279	167.7	W 465392	155.4	MINERAIS DE CUIVRE,MATTES
28711	COPPER ORES,EXCL MATTE	W 554815	195.9	W 516154	244.5	W 492279	167.7	W 465368	155.3	MINERAIS DE CUIVRE
3	MINERAL FUELS ETC		736.0		747.3		560.4		533.5	COMBUSTIBLES MINERAUX LUB
33	PETROLEUM AND PRODUCTS		725.8		708.9		536.4		501.2	PETROLE ET DERIVES
334	PETROLEUM PRODUCTS,REFIN	W 5001879	670.2	W 4117745	652.1	W 2711559	487.3	W 2562350	449.5	PRODUITS RAFFINES
3341	GASOLINE,OTH LIGHT OILS	W 782819	127.0							ESSENCES POUR MOTEURS
33411	MOTOR,AVIATION SPIRIT	W 550609	92.2							ESSENCES MOTEURS D'AVIONS
3342	KEROSENE,OTH MEDIUM OILS	W 810166	136.6							PETR LAMPANTS,AUT HUIL
33421	KEROSENE INCL JET FUEL	W 810160	136.6							PETROLES LAMPANTS
3343	GAS OILS	W 1461199	213.0							GAS OILS
3344	FUEL OILS,NES	W 1845179	158.2							FUEL OILS
335	RESIDUAL PETRLM PROD NES	W 339462	55.6	W 325317	56.8	W 266258	49.2	W 286570	51.7	PRODUITS RESIDUELS NDA
4	ANIMAL,VEGETABLE OIL,FAT		70.2		151.2		166.0		145.8	HUILES,GRAISSES ANIM,VEG
42	FIXED VEGETABLE OIL,FAT		63.3		141.8		156.8		136.4	HUILES VEGETALES FIXES
423	FIXED VEG OILS,SOFT	W 53528	61.9	W 102967	130.6	W 112890	155.0	W 121188	130.3	HUILES VEGET DOUCES FIXES
4235	OLIVE OIL	W 16931	37.4	W 21782	69.4	W 20297	90.1	W 26901	71.1	HUILE D'OLIVE
5	CHEMCLS,RELATED PROD NES		842.7		1083.5		1028.1		1009.6	PRODUITS CHIMIQUES
51	ORGANIC CHEMICALS		234.1		315.9		204.2		192.2	PROD CHIMIQ ORGANIQUES
511	HYDROCARBONS NES,DERIVS	W 497105	169.0	W 483806	252.5	W 408703	156.0	W 406738	152.3	HYDROCARBURES NDA
5111	ACYCLIC HYDROCARBONS	W 238355	68.0	W 204818	90.0	W 174529	57.3	W 193600	77.8	HYDROCARBURES ACYCLIQUES
5112	CYCLIC HYDROCARBONS	W 246120	93.6	W 261788	153.6	W 218619	90.0	W 194739	67.2	HYDROCARBURES CYCLIQUES
51124	XYLENES,CHEMICALLY PURE	W 129525	64.8	W 145469	126.6	W 115876	66.2	W 94970	40.4	XYLENES PURS
541	*MEDICINAL,PHARM PRODUCT		94.8	K 6259685	143.6	K 6079838	169.3	K 8168446	169.5	PROD MEDICINAUX PHARMACEUT
5417	MEDICAMENTS		55.1	K 4268648	89.3	K 4153669	121.8	K 6271684	118.4	MEDICAMENTS
54179	— CONTNG OTH SUBSTANCES	K 2007174	47.7	K 3589649	69.2	K 2227344	73.7	K 4027972	74.4	MED CONT AUT SUBSTANCES
55	PERFUME,CLEANING ETC PRD		50.9		76.2		91.9		85.9	PROD POUR PARFUM,TOILETTE
58	PLASTIC MATERIALS ETC		244.1		253.5		221.7		241.8	MAT PLAST ARTIFICIELLES
583	POLYMERIZATION ETC PRODS		227.3	W 180639	218.2	W 160002	182.8	W 180025	198.9	PROD POLYMERISATION
5831	POLYETHYLENE	W 178473	125.0	W 108586	106.0	W 76108	67.6	W 97031	87.0	POLYETHYLENE
58311	— IN PRIMARY FORMS	W 174216	121.4	W 102429	99.9	W 72203	61.8	W 93630	80.5	POLYETHYLENE PRIMAIRES
5834	POLYVINYL CHLORIDE	W 77064	66.5	W 52633	67.9	W 63688	66.9	W 59671	62.2	CHLORURE DE POLYVINYLE
58341	— IN PRIMARY FORMS	W 73648	58.1	W 48075	54.8	W 57417	45.8	W 53513	43.2	SOUS FORMES PRIMAIRES
59	CHEMICAL MATERIALS NES		134.3		178.4		208.1		190.5	MAT PROD CHIMIQUES NDA
598	MISCEL CHEM PRODUCTS NES		118.9	W 114669	159.7	W 115802	194.3	W 114896	176.5	PROD DIV INDUST CHIM NDA
5989	CHEM PRODUCTS,PREPS NES		81.2	W 68704	113.2	W 77089	150.6	W 77375	131.3	PROD PREP CHIMIQUES NDA
59899	OTH CHEM PRODS,PREPS,NES		79.6	W 68032	111.4	W 76297	148.6	W 76326	129.1	AUT PRODUITS CHIMIQUES NDA
6	BASIC MANUFACTURES		4457.3		5511.7		5361.3		5267.2	ART MANUFACTURES
61	LEATHER,DRESSED FUR,ETC		204.5		218.6		213.3		200.8	CUIRS,PELLETERIES
612	LEATHER ETC MANUFACTURES	W 7171	148.5	W 6585	158.6	W 6988	151.8	W 8113	141.5	OUVRAGES EN CUIRS NDA
6123	PREPRD PARTS OF FOOTWEAR	W 7123	147.5	W 6530	157.2	W 6899	150.2	W 7965	139.6	PARTIES DE CHAUSSURES
62	RUBBER MANUFACTURES NES		103.6		147.6		167.1		179.7	CAOUTCHOUC MANUFACTURE
625	RUBBER TYRES, TUBES ETC	W 27322	93.4	W 35658	126.5	W 38925	146.3	W 48770	157.3	PNEUS CAOUTCHOUC VULCANISE
6251	TYRES NEW FOR MOTOR CARS	W 24653	86.3	W 32555	116.4	W 35517	135.5	W 44276	146.1	PNEUS POUR VOITURES
63	WOOD,CORK MANUFACTRS NES		718.3		846.5		860.9		869.8	OUVRAGES LIEGE ET BOIS
633	CORK MANUFACTURES	W 94545	549.6	W 92011	641.0	W 95698	662.3	W 98131	665.5	OUVRAGES EN LIEGE
63301	NATURAL CORK ARTICLES	W 21774	320.1	W 22487	386.6	W 26834	407.9	W 25795	429.2	OUVRAGES EN LIEGE NATUREL
63302	AGGLOMERATD CORK,ARTS OF	W 72771	229.5	W 69523	254.5	W 68864	254.5	W 72336	236.4	LIEGE AGGLOM ET OUVRAGES
634	VENEERS,PLYWOOD,ETC	W 374068	100.4	W 320466	109.4	W 284002	94.5	W 363456	100.9	PLACAGES,CONTRE–PLAQUES
6343	IMPROVED,RECONSTIT WOOD	W 307967	75.1	W 255543	79.7	W 239828	70.6	W 313653	79.6	BOIS AMELIORES,RECONST
63432	RECONSTITUTED WOOD	W 307945	75.1	W 255492	79.7	W 239761	70.5	W 313575	79.5	BOIS RECONSTITUES
635	WOOD MANUFACTURES NES	W 79503	68.4	W 101138	96.2	W 80809	104.2	W 82578	103.5	ART MANUF EN BOIS NDA
64	PAPER,PAPERBOARD AND MFR		546.0		764.0		738.4		657.9	PAPIERS,CARTONS & OUVRAGES
641	PAPER AND PAPERBOARD		502.0	W 763697	702.0	W 916657	667.5	W 978439	598.7	PAPIERS ET CARTONS
6413	KRAFT PAPER,PAPERBOARD	W 220289	107.4	W 223424	162.9	W 209099	122.7	W 218957	109.8	PAPIER ET CARTON KRAFT
64131	KRAFT LINER IN BULK	W 180299	82.4	W 180835	123.1	W 165825	84.6	W 164778	72.2	PAP KRAFT POUR COUVERTURES
6415	PAPER,PAPERBRD,BULK,NES	W 307627	252.9	W 295574	354.7	W 351528	316.4	W 354757	295.0	PAPIERS,CARTONS ROULEAUX
64159	OTHER PAPER ETC,BULK,NES	W 307589	252.8	W 295526	354.5	W 351109	316.2	W 354644	294.8	AUT PAPIER ROULEAUX FEUILLES
6416	FIBRE BUILDING BOARD	W 203748	79.9	W 186156	83.9	W 256173	86.3	W 300731	94.9	PLAQUES CONSTRUCT EN PATE
64162	INSULATING BOARD, ETC	W 161305	63.4	W 147518	67.3	W 200202	67.6	W 239843	75.3	PLAQUES CONST NON COMPR
642	PAPER,ETC,PRECUT,ARTS OF		44.0	W 30998	62.0	W 46095	71.0	W 38156	59.3	PAP,CARTONS DECOUPES
65	TEXTILE YARN,FABRICS,ETC		1348.5		1632.8		1615.8		1633.5	FILS,TISSUS,ARTICLES TEXTILE
651	TEXTILE YARN	W 27450	125.3	W 25012	141.4	W 28604	151.0	W 30980	154.5	FILS TEXTILES
652	COTTON FABRICS,WOVEN		157.6	W 13107	187.5	W 12462	196.7	W 14403	198.9	TISSUS DE COTON
6522	WOVEN COTTON BLEACHD,ETC		145.6	W 11351	175.9	W 11612	190.9	W 12801	189.6	TISSUS COTON BLANCHIS ETC
65224	BLCHED COTTON FABRIC NES		123.7	W 10137	155.1	W 10572	171.4	W 11249	166.0	AUT TIS PLUS 85% COT BLANCHI
653	WOVN MAN–MADE FIB FABRIC		175.1	W 13441	194.4	W 13113	199.0	W 14207	198.4	TISSUS FIBRES SYNTH,ARTIF
6534	DISC SYN BLEND FABRC NES	W 6806	104.0	W 7002	118.0	W 7194	122.8	W 8070	130.3	TISSUS FIBRES SYNTH DISCONT
65342	DISC SYN FIB–WOOL FABRIC	W 2576	53.8	W 2678	63.6	W 2742	65.7	W 3465	69.6	TISSUS FIB SYNT MEL LAINE
657	SPECIAL TXTL FABRC,PRODS		154.7	W 78774	206.9	W 79090	195.9	W 83918	203.1	TISSUS SPECIAUX

5. Special Exports F.O.B. by Commodities according to the S.I.T.C. (Rev. 2) in million U.S. Dollars
Exportations Spéciales F.O.B. par Produits d'après la C.T.C.I. (Rév. 2) en millions de Dollars E.U.

SITC CTCI	COMMODITY	1994 QUANTITY QUANTITE	1994 VALUE VALEUR	1995 QUANTITY QUANTITE	1995 VALUE VALEUR	1996 QUANTITY QUANTITE	1996 VALUE VALEUR	1997 QUANTITY QUANTITE	1997 VALUE VALEUR	PRODUIT
6575	CORDAGE AND MANUFACTURES	W 66513	105.5	W 66344	131.2	W 67009	122.6	W 65322	112.9	FICELLES,CORDES,CORDAGES
65751	CORDAGE,CABLE,ROPE,TWINE	W 62140	86.5	W 62770	110.3	W 63630	103.0	W 61817	95.1	CORDAGES TRESSES OU NON
658	TEXTILE ARTICLES NES		624.0	W 70789	757.8	W 70206	743.8	W 76416	732.9	ART FACONNES MAT TEXTILES
6584	LINENS ETC		544.5	W 58785	651.5	W 58705	649.2	W 62185	633.5	LINGE DE MAISON
65841	BED LINEN OF COTTON	W 20221	190.8	W 21825	233.8	W 22709	252.9	W 24225	260.6	LINGE DE LIT DE COTON
65845	OTHER LINEN OF COTTON		255.1	W 27793	304.3	W 27456	292.2	W 27469	260.0	LINGE DE TOILETTE COTON
6589	OTH TEXTILE ARTICLES NES		54.1	W 6175	77.5	W 5916	69.1	W 8352	73.2	AUT ART EN TEXTILES NDA
66	NONMETAL MINERAL MFS NES		884.0		1010.4		908.4		884.9	ART MIN NON METALLIQUES
661	LIME,CEMENT,BLDG PRODS	W 1230574	176.7	W 887091	186.7	W 807920	183.7	W 710801	158.0	CHAUX,CIMENTS MAT CONSTR
6613	BUILDING STONE ETC WORKD	W 738334	159.7	W 719737	173.7	W 634771	167.2	W 596612	146.5	PIERRES A BATIR
66132	BUILDING STONE WORKED	W 235570	117.3	W 222586	126.8	W 214751	126.6	W 228136	113.8	OUVR EN PIERRES DE TAILLE
662	CLAY,REFRACTORY BLDG PRD	W 263875	116.9	W 275675	129.9	W 264521	119.2	W 285388	115.0	MAT CONST REFRACTAIRES
6624	BRICKS ETC NONREFRACTORY	W 260452	116.1	W 270602	128.0	W 257758	116.9	W 281858	113.6	BRIQUES ETC CERAM NON REFR
66245	GLAZED CERAMIC SETTS ETC	W 183976	91.5	W 194459	100.8	W 193369	95.5	W 218871	91.9	AUT CARREAUX CERAMIQUE
665	GLASSWARE		168.6	W 351921	215.6	W 266440	170.4	W 293310	162.8	OUVRAGES EN VERRE
6651	BOTTLES ETC OF GLASS	W 303571	114.9	W 333204	145.1	W 249947	112.4	W 270925	102.4	RECIPIENTS EN VERRE
66511	GLASS BOTTLES ETC NONVAC	W 303571	114.9	W 333203	145.1	W 249947	112.4	W 270925	102.4	BONBONNES,BOUTEILLES,ETC
666	POTTERY	W 107278	288.2	W 113770	343.0	W 108459	317.1	W 125404	302.9	POTERIE
6665	COARSE CERAMIC HOUSEWARE	W 38776	91.2	W 40296	103.7	W 40354	102.5	W 47883	115.0	VAISSELLE,ART MEN CERAM
6666	CERAMIC ORNAMENTS ETC	W 57623	154.6	W 62849	193.9	W 55953	161.0	W 64967	142.7	OBJETS PORCELAINE,CERAM
667	PEARL,PREC–,SEMI–P STONE		81.9		65.1		54.5		84.0	PERLES, PIERRES GEMMES
6672	DIAMONDS NONINDUST,UNSET		81.9		64.9		54.3		83.9	DIAMANTS BRUTS
66729	— CUT ETC NOT SET		76.6		61.2		53.6		56.9	DIAMANTS TAILLES
67	IRON AND STEEL		178.2		223.7		238.2		208.3	FER ET ACIER
673	IRON,STEEL SHAPES ETC	W 187713	60.3	W 178035	73.6	W 80105	34.4	W 78932	29.2	BARRES,PROFIL FER,ACIER
674	IRN,STL UNIV,PLATE,SHEET	W 109143	66.3	W 95294	72.9	W 164793	97.0	W 171263	97.0	LARGES PLATS,TOLES
69	METAL MANUFACTURES NES		444.9		628.1		582.8		588.5	ART MANUFACT EN METAL NDA
692	METAL TANKS,BOXES,ETC		56.4	W 33369	66.7	W 34412	76.1	W 37841	68.4	RECIPIENTS METALLIQUES
6924	MTL TRANSPORT BOXES ETC		54.3	W 32027	60.8	W 32778	66.0	W 35968	61.7	FUTS,TAMBOURS,BIDONS
697	BASE MTL HOUSEHOLD EQUIP	W 19770	76.6	W 24162	102.7	W 25933	117.3	W 32671	124.1	ART MENAGE MET COMMUNS
699	BASE METAL MFRS NES		184.4		238.2		214.9		224.4	ART MANUFACTURES MET NDA
6991	LOCKSMITHS WARES,ETC		80.3	W 10675	106.6	W 9613	86.4	W 16313	90.1	ARTICLES DE SERRURERIE
69913	BASE MTL DOOR,ETC FITTNG	W 7055	58.8	W 7693	75.5	W 6439	61.3	W 7971	62.4	GARNITURES POUR MEUBLES
7	MACHINES,TRANSPORT EQUIP		3888.6		6252.7		7080.8		7186.2	MACHINES MATERIEL TRANSPORT
71	POWER GENERATING EQUIPMT		260.2		399.1		253.9		150.6	MACHINES GENERATRICES
713	INTRNL COMBUS PSTN ENGIN		221.6	W 47629	332.1	W 34338	224.2	W 16407	79.7	MOTEURS EXPL COMB INT, PIECE
7132	MOTOR VEHCL PISTN ENGINS	W 20282	153.0	W 31125	257.7	W 17027	141.4	W 222	3.8	MOTEURS EXPL POUR VEHICULES
7139	PISTON ENGINE PARTS NES		65.4	W 16333	68.0	W 17166	73.9	W 15985	68.4	PIECES POUR 713.2,3,8
72	MACHS FOR SPCL INDUSTRYS		143.8		184.1		198.6		195.9	MAC SPECIALES POUR INDUST
74	GENRL INDUSTRL MACHY NES		371.3		478.0		546.6		508.6	MACH APP INDUSTRIE
741	HEATING,COOLING EQUIPMNT		103.5	W 16096	126.3	W 19154	153.1	W 18859	119.3	MACH CHAUFFAGE,PIECES
7416	HEATING,COOLING EQU NES	W 6836	64.6	W 8530	78.5	W 9109	90.2	W 6504	57.9	APP CHANGEMENT TEMP
749	NONELEC MACH PTS,ACC NES		209.8	W 12420	276.9	W 12862	313.6	W 15158	313.9	PIECES MACH NON ELEC NDA
7499	OTH NONELEC MCHY PTS NES		160.7	W 6617	204.6	W 7339	241.3	W 8695	244.4	PIECES NON ELECT NDA
74991	FOUNDRY MOULDS ETC NES	W 5927	159.1	W 6438	201.7	W 7072	237.9	W 8199	238.9	MOULES POUR METAUX
75	OFFICE MACHNES,ADP EQUIP		44.2		47.0		60.8		84.4	MACH BUREAU TRAIT AUTOM
76	TELECOMM,SOUND EQUIPMENT		553.8		726.8		777.9		708.7	EQUIPMENT DE TELECOM
762	RADIO BROADCAST RECEIVRS	W 5118	420.7	W 6564	531.7	W 7662	565.3	W 7819	474.4	RECEPTEURS RADIODIFFUSION
7621	MTR VEHC RADIO RECEIVERS	W 4310	392.9	W 5377	499.8	W 6220	538.1	W 7076	461.6	RECEPTEURS RADIO AUTO
764	TELECOM EQPT,PTS,ACC NES		99.3	W 7367	142.0	W 8731	160.6	W 11502	188.7	EQUIP TELECOM,PIECES
7649	PTS NES OF EQUIPMT OF 76	W 2871	59.7	W 5608	92.4	W 6165	109.9	W 9338	143.6	PIECES DE LA DIV 76
76499	PARTS ETC OF SOUND EQUIP	W 200	7.2	W 305	14.3	W 603	42.4	W 1145	74.7	PIECES NDA POUR 763
77	ELECTRIC MACHNRY NES ETC		1425.1		2126.6		2074.4		1891.4	MACH APP ELECT NDA
771	ELECTRIC POWER MACHY NES		122.1	W 14040	171.3	W 20600	198.7	W 21260	187.4	MACH PROD,TRANS ELECTR
7711	TRANSFORMERS,ELECTRICAL		94.3	W 12956	135.3	W 19104	174.6	W 14976	141.1	TRANSFO ELECTRIQUES
77111	LIQUID DIELEC TRANSFRMRS	W 6535	24.8	W 9537	44.7	W 15554	84.6	W 10979	59.7	TRANSFO DIELEC LIQUIDE
77118	OTHER ELEC TRANSFORMERS		69.6	W 3418	90.6	W 3551	90.1	W 3998	81.5	AUTRES TRANSFO ELECTRIQ
772	SWITCHGEAR ETC,PARTS NES		149.3	W 7956	186.2	W 8023	180.3	W 13488	272.1	APP COUPURE,SECT ETC
7721	SWITCHGEAR ETC		127.6	W 7599	163.2	W 7746	161.5	W 13190	254.0	APP COUPURE,SECTIONMNT
773	ELECTR DISTRIBUTNG EQUIP		718.0	W 60210	958.5	W 63311	1016.7	W 69276	889.1	EQUIPMT DISTRIBUTION ELECT
7731	INSULATED WIRE,CABLE ETC		711.1	W 58523	948.1	W 61271	1008.2	W 67417	878.6	FILS,CABLES ISOLES ELECT
775	HOUSEHOLD TYPE EQUIP NES		145.4	W 36046	179.4	W 29216	158.4	W 35191	150.2	MACH,APP USAGE DOMESTQUE
7752	DOM REFRIGERATRS,FREEZRS	W 17655	68.7	W 16538	70.3	W 9285	42.7	W 10849	41.9	REFRIG,CONGEL MENAGER
7758	ELECTRO–THERMIC APPL NES		54.5	W 15901	89.8	W 17650	95.1	W 22355	93.5	APP ELECTROTHERMIQ NDA
77586	ELECTROTHERM DOM APP NES	W 5279	37.9	W 7757	62.7	W 9305	71.3	W 10081	62.9	APP ELECTRO THERMIQUES
776	TRANSISTORS,VALVES,ETC		145.8	W 306	429.5	W 248	296.5	W 629	200.8	LAMPES,TUBES,VALVES
7764	ELECTRONIC MICROCIRCUITS		142.3	W 205	424.2	W 162	291.3	W 228	193.4	MICROSTRUCTURES ELECTRON
778	ELECTRICAL MACHINERY NES		141.2	W 28392	196.0	W 27868	218.6	W 23632	187.8	AUTRES MACH ELECT NDA
7788	OTH ELEC MACHY,EQUIP NES		88.1	W 3412	123.1	W 2956	103.0	W 3265	87.9	AUT MACH APP ELEC NDA
78	ROAD VEHICLES		928.4		2084.1		2932.3		3375.2	VEHICULES ROUTIERS
781	PASS MOTOR VEH EXC BUSES	W 24640	228.6	W 84450	1134.2	W 221139	2005.0	W 257457	2539.6	AUTO TRANSPORT PERSONNES
782	LORRIES,SPCL MTR VEH NES	W 51164	371.0	W 62969	488.6	W 51495	417.7	W 52749	371.7	VEHICULES SPECIAUX,MARCH
7821	LORRIES,TRUCKS	W 50970	370.1	W 62828	487.8	W 51359	416.7	W 52491	370.0	VEHICULES TRANSP MARCHAND
784	MOTOR VEH PRTS,ACCES NES	W 53143	242.1	W 61915	353.5	W 63597	390.5	W 76786	345.3	PIECES 722,781,782,783
7849	OTHER MOTOR VEHCL PARTS	W 53109	241.3	W 61817	352.3	W 63474	389.4	W 76667	344.5	PIECES 722,781,782,783
785	CYCLES,ETC MOTRZD OR NOT		56.5	W 11397	71.0	W 12070	77.5	W 13320	75.0	MOTOCYCLES SCOOTERS
79	OTHR TRANSPORT EQUIPMENT		134.5		176.6		207.6		238.6	AUTRE MATERIEL TRANSPORT
792	AIRCRAFT ETC		83.8	W 471	85.9	W 364	59.0	W 856	57.7	APP NAVIGATION AERIENNE
7924	AIRCRFT NES OVER 15000KG	W 66	63.8	W 312	60.1	W 191	30.2	W 414	20.5	AERODYNES PLUS 15000 KG
793	SHIPS AND BOATS ETC	W 22146	43.5	W 38665	82.5	W 41707	120.0	W 63008	153.1	NAVIRES BATEAUX,ETC
7932	SHIPS AND BOATS NES	W 21602	43.3	W 38599	82.2	W 41699	119.9	W 62767	150.8	NAVIRES ET BATEAUX
79323	OTHER CARGO VESSELS	W 19574	36.4	W 36719	77.9	W 34418	103.7	W 62225	146.0	AUT BATEAUX TRANS MARCH
8	MISC MANUFACTURED GOODS		5652.4		6576.5		6355.7		6001.6	ART MANUFACTURES DIVERS
812	*PLUMBG,HEATNG,LGHTNG EQ	W 36083	68.9	W 43326	88.1	W 50989	98.6	W 60469	104.0	APPAR SANITAIRES CHAUFFAGE
8122	CERAMIC PLUMBNG FIXTURES	W 32178	46.2	W 39331	61.9	W 45414	67.6	W 53540	69.8	EVIERS,LAVABOS,CUVETTES
821	*FURNITURE,PARTS THEREOF	W 49011	218.7	W 54946	285.3	W 66784	308.6	W 63525	310.2	MEUBLES ET PIECES
8211	CHAIRS,SEATS AND PARTS	W 7636	105.6	W 11388	142.2	W 18110	162.8	W 13201	163.6	SIEGES ET PIECES
82119	PTS NES OF CHAIRS ETC	W 5753	94.7	W 8564	125.6	W 15540	145.3	W 9408	137.3	PIECES DU 821.11
8219	FURNITURE AND PARTS NES	W 37666	100.4	W 39992	127.4	W 45197	130.9	W 46458	130.2	AUTRES MEUBLES ET PIECES
82192	WOOD FURNITURE NES	W 31049	81.0	W 33846	104.5	W 38493	106.7	W 38089	103.3	MEUBLES NDA EN BOIS
84	CLOTHING AND ACCESSORIES		3286.8		3805.1		3590.8		3303.5	VETEMENTS
842	MENS OUTERWEAR NOT KNIT		741.6	W 21967	859.1	W 20806	807.1	W 20111	721.0	VET DESSUS POUR HOMMES
8422	— SUITS	W 1510	70.8	W 1823	100.9	W 1896	107.0	W 2353	122.3	COMPLETS HOMMES MAT TEXT
84221	—— OF WOOL,FINE HAIR	W 719	39.4	W 973	62.4	W 1103	69.4	W 1327	76.1	COMPLETS HOMMES LAINE
8423	— TROUSERS,BREECHES ETC	W 10806	307.8	W 11781	369.9	W 11018	347.9	W 9954	288.5	PANTALONS HOMMES MAT TEX
8424	— JACKETS,BLAZERS ETC	W 4199	193.5	W 4021	212.5	W 3889	195.9	W 3933	180.0	VESTES HOMMES MAT TEXTIL
8429	— OTHER OUTER GARMENTS		147.2	W 3801	152.0	W 3406	128.0	W 3379	109.5	AUT VET DES HOM MAT TEX
843	WOMENS OUTERWEAR NONKNIT		419.4	W 10709	486.4	W 10577	463.3	W 10230	419.1	VET DESSUS FEMMES MAT TEX
8431	— COATS AND JACKETS		76.8	W 1929	101.1	W 1900	104.3	W 2068	98.3	MANT,VEST FEM MAT TEXTIL
8435	— BLOUSES	W 1516	81.8	W 1711	99.2	W 1729	94.1	W 1818	83.6	BLOUSES FEM MAT TEXTILES
8439	— OTHER OUTER GARMENTS		189.4	W 5266	193.7	W 5216	181.2	W 4799	166.7	AUT VET DES FEM MAT TEXT

Portugal

5. Special Exports F.O.B. by Commodities according to the S.I.T.C. (Rev. 2) in million U.S. Dollars
Exportations Spéciales F.O.B. par Produits d'après la C.T.C.I. (Rév. 2) en millions de Dollars E.U.

SITC CTCI	COMMODITY	1994 QUANTITY QUANTITE	1994 VALUE VALEUR	1995 QUANTITY QUANTITE	1995 VALUE VALEUR	1996 QUANTITY QUANTITE	1996 VALUE VALEUR	1997 QUANTITY QUANTITE	1997 VALUE VALEUR	PRODUIT
844	UNDER GARMENTS NOT KNIT		291.0	W 9404	335.8	W 8372	286.7	W 7707	236.2	VETEMENT DESSOUS MAT TEX
8441	— MENS SHIRTS		267.0	W 7822	308.8	W 6420	256.7	W 5899	208.8	CHEMISES HOMMES MAT TEXT
84411	—— OF COTTON	W 7156	234.2	W 6827	265.5	W 5580	224.6	W 4944	177.9	CHEMISES HOMMES DE COTON
845	OUTERWEAR KNIT NONELASTC		1023.0	W 42018	1181.0	W 41557	1131.6	W 43347	1059.7	VET DESSOUS,ACCES BONNET
8451	— JERSEYS,PULLOVERS ETC	W 20942	489.6	W 22298	583.4	W 22630	581.8	W 23834	553.3	CHANDAILS,PULL–OVERS ETC
8452	— WOMENS DRESSES ETC		61.4	W 2221	77.8	W 1844	62.8	W 1885	55.0	ROBES,JUPES BONNETERIE
8459	— OTHER,CLTHG ACCESRYS		472.1	W 17499	519.9	W 17083	487.2	W 17627	451.6	AUT VET DESSUS DE BONNE
846	UNDER GARMENTS KNITTED		649.5	W 24942	748.3	W 24594	721.2	W 26432	694.8	SOUS VETS DE BONNETERIE
8462	— OF COTTON NON ELASTIC		575.9	W 22734	665.9	W 22217	636.0	W 24049	616.6	SOUS–VET BONNET COTON
84621	—— MENS SHIRTS	W 3034	83.8	W 2886	87.7	W 2804	86.6	W 3451	96.0	CHEMISES DE COTON
84629	—— OTHER		492.1	W 19847	578.2	W 19414	549.4	W 20598	520.6	AUT SOUS–VET BONNET COTON
847	TEXTILE CLTHNG ACCES NES		144.9	W 16179	170.7	W 15254	155.3	W 17232	151.8	ACCES VET MAT TEXT NDA
8472	CLTHNG ACCESRYS ETC KNIT		136.3	W 15798	160.6	W 14899	146.5	W 16930	145.0	ACCES VET BONNE NDA
84722	KNIT SOCKS,ETC NONELASTC		127.7	W 14710	146.8	W 13999	135.0	W 16156	136.9	CHAUSSETTES BON. NON ELAS
851	*FOOTWEAR	W 73034	1555.5	W 70239	1689.7	W 75475	1709.7	W 80071	1635.3	CHAUSSURES
85102	FOOTWEAR LEATHER	W 70737	1530.0	W 67309	1648.9	W 70270	1637.4	W 73327	1561.0	CHAUS SEMELLES EN CUIR
87	PRECISION INSTRUMNTS NES		130.1		204.9		172.9		190.8	INSTRUM,APPAR SCIENT NDA
874	MEASURNG,CONTROLNG INSTR		76.6	W 939	127.8	W 1045	115.8	W 1445	141.1	INSTRUMENTS DE MESURE
8743	GAS,LIQUID CONTROL INSTR		57.7	W 346	82.5	W 323	65.8	W 274	50.3	APP,INSTR MESURE FLUIDES
89	MISC MANUFCTRD GOODS NES		330.7		427.5		402.8		392.5	ART MANUFACTURES DIVERS
893	ARTICLES OF PLASTIC NES		157.0		199.1		176.0		184.0	OUVRAGES EN MAT DIVIS 58
8939	MISC PLASTIC ARTICLES		119.0	W 43749	159.3	W 44175	136.0	W 45701	142.1	ART DIVERS EN MAT DIV 58
89399	OTHR PLASTC ARTICLES NES		116.7	W 43031	156.7	W 43546	134.1	W 45067	140.6	AUT OUV MAT DIV 58
894	TOYS,SPORTING GOODS,ETC		55.9	W 5453	76.9	W 5163	72.4	W 4644	53.2	VOITURES ENFANTS,JOUETS

FOOT NOTES – NOTES

TABLE 1 –

1 The gold trade is comprised of gold bullion and specie, including government gold transactions, and partly–worked gold, jewellers' sweepings, dust, concentrates, etc.

TABLEAU 1 –

1 Le commerce de l'or comprend l'or en lingots ou en pièces de monnaie, y compris les transactions en or du gouvernement, ainsi que l'or partiellement travaillé, les balayures des bijoutiers, les poussières, les concentrés etc.

1. HISTORICAL SERIES, 1969–1995 GENERAL TRADE, IMPORTS C.I.F., EXPORTS F.O.B.
SERIES HISTORIQUES, 1969–1995 COMMERCE GENERAL, IMPORTATIONS C.A.F., EXPORTATIONS F.O.B

YEAR ANNEE	VALUE IN MILLION QATAR RIYALS / VALEUR EN MILLION QATAR RIYALS — MERCHANDISE –MARCHANDISE IMPORTS	MERCHANDISE –MARCHANDISE EXPORTS	GOLD –OR IMPORTS	GOLD –OR EXPORTS	CONVERSION FACTORS U.S. CENTS PER QATAR RIYAL / FACTEURS DE CONVERSION CENTS E.U. PAR QATAR RIYAL — IMPORTS	EXPORTS	INDEX NUMBERS –INDICES — QUANTUM IMPORTS	QUANTUM EXPORTS	UNIT VALUE / VALEUR UNITAIRE IMPORTS	UNIT VALUE / VALEUR UNITAIRE EXPORTS
1969	252.20	1088.60			21.0000	21.0000				
1970	305.50	1124.30			21.0000	21.0000				
1971	561.90	1689.00			21.0000	21.0000				
1972	607.30	2092.60			22.8000	22.8000				
1973	778.50	2841.70			24.9850	24.9838				
1974	1068.90	7958.20			25.3330	25.3330				
1975	1609.80	7107.00			25.4592	25.4559				
1976	3300.30	8754.10			25.2428	25.2389				
1977	4850.10	7964.00			25.2603	25.2588				
1978	4589.70	8993.00			25.8112	25.7997				
1979	5377.70	14655.00			26.4920	26.5819				
1980	5267.90	20787.00			27.4725	27.4725				
1981	5524.90	21272.00			27.4725	27.4725				
1982	7087.50	16405.00			27.4725	27.4725				
1983	5298.00	12002.00			27.4725	27.4725				
1984	4229.60	16427.00			27.4725	27.4725				
1985	4146.50	12894.00			27.4725	27.4725				
1986	3999.70	7676.47			27.4725	27.4725				
1987	4127.90	7219.58			27.4725	27.4725				
1988	4613.10				27.4730					
1989	4826.70	9779.91			27.4725	27.4725				
1990	6169.40	12846.87			27.4725	27.4725				
1991	6261.20	11307.96			27.4725	27.4725				
1992	7336.00	13600.08			27.4725	27.4725				
1993	6882.10	11578.23			27.4725	27.4725				
1994	7015.60	11695.12			27.4725	27.4725				
1995	7713.17	13744.65			27.4725	27.4725				

2. IMPORTS BY BROAD ECONOMIC CATEGORY AND EXPORTS BY INDUSTRIAL ORIGIN. (PERCENTAGE OF TOTAL VALUE)
IMPORTATIONS PAR CATEGORIES ECONOMIQUES ET EXPORTATIONS PAR BRANCHE D'ACTIVITE.(EN POURCENTAGE DE LA VALEUR TOTALE)

IMPORTS – IMPORTATIONS

	1989	1990	1991	1992	1993	1994	1995
TOTAL IMPORTS–IMPORTATIONS TOTALES	100.	100.	100.	100.	100.	100.	
1 FOOD BEV–ALIMENTATION BOISSONS	15.0	15.6	15.1	12.6	12.8	13.4	
11 PRIMARY–PRODUITS DE BASE	9.2	10.1	9.3	7.6	7.2	7.5	
111 FOR INDUSTRY–POUR L'INDUSTRIE	3.9	4.9	4.1	2.7	2.3	2.4	
112 FOR HOUSEHOLDS–POUR LES MENAGES	5.3	5.2	5.2	4.9	4.9	5.1	
12 PROCESSED–PRODUITS ELABORES	5.7	5.4	5.7	5.0	5.6	5.9	
121 FOR INDUSTRY–POUR L'INDUSTRIE	0.4	0.4	0.3	0.3	0.4	0.4	
122 FOR HOUSEHOLDS–POUR LES MENAGES	5.3	5.1	5.4	4.7	5.2	5.5	
2 IND SUPPLIES–APPROV INDUSTRIELS	31.0	24.7	26.2	25.2	26.0	30.2	
21 PRIMARY–PRODUITS DE BASE	3.6	3.1	3.2	2.9	2.3	3.3	
22 PROCESSED–PRODUITS ELABORES	27.4	21.6	23.0	22.2	23.7	26.9	
3 FUELS–COMBUSTIBLES	0.8	0.6	0.7	0.7	0.6	0.6	
31 PRIMARY–PRODUITS DE BASE	0.0	0.0	0.0	0.0	0.0	0.0	
32 PROCESSED–PRODUITS ELABORES	0.7	0.6	0.7	0.7	0.6	0.6	
321 MOTOR SPIRIT–ESSENCE							
322 OTHER–AUTRES	0.7	0.6	0.7	0.7	0.6	0.6	
4 MACHINERY–EQUIPEMENT	18.6	29.0	25.5	23.6	20.8	21.3	
41 CAPITAL EQUIPMENT–MACHINES	17.8	28.4	22.6	21.6	19.4	19.8	
42 PARTS–PIECES ACCESSOIRES	0.8	0.6	2.8	2.1	1.4	1.5	
5 TRANSPORT–TRANSPORT	16.5	14.2	15.1	19.8	20.5	16.5	
51 PASSENGER CARS–AUTOMOBILES	9.7	8.0	8.3	10.5	11.8	8.8	
52 OTHER–AUTRES	2.5	2.6	2.7	4.5	3.8	3.4	
521 INDUSTRIAL–INDUSTRIELS	2.5	2.5	2.6	4.5	3.7	3.3	
522 NON INDUSTRIAL–NON INDUSTRIEL	0.0	0.1	0.1	0.1	0.1	0.1	
53 PARTS–PIECES ACCESSOIRES	4.2	3.6	4.1	4.8	5.0	4.3	
6 CONSUM GOODS–BIENS CONSOMMATION	18.1	15.8	17.4	17.9	19.0	17.8	
61 DURABLE–DURABLES	7.2	5.9	7.1	7.6	8.2	7.4	
62 SEMI DURABLE–SEMI DURABLES	7.3	6.3	6.6	6.7	6.7	6.5	
63 NON DURABLE–NON DURABLES	3.7	3.6	3.7	3.6	4.0	3.9	
7 GOODS NES–BIENS NDA	0.1	0.1	0.1	0.1	0.2	0.1	

EXPORTS – EXPORTATIONS

	1989	1990	1991	1992	1993	1994	1995
TOTAL EXPORTS–EXPORTATIONS TOTALES	100.	100.	100.	100.	100.	100.	
1 AGRICULTURE	0.1	0.1	0.1	0.1	0.1	0.2	
2 MINING QUARRY–INDUS EXTRACTIVES	72.1	79.3	73.7	75.2	75.1	67.0	
3 MANUFACTURING–IND MANUFACTUR	27.9	20.6	26.2	24.7	24.9	32.8	
31 FOOD BEV TOBACCO–ALIM BOISS TAB	0.1	0.1	0.4	0.2	0.3	0.3	
32 TEXTILES–INDUSTRIES TEXTILES	0.1	0.2	0.5	0.9	1.2	2.0	
33 WOOD & PRODUCTS–BOIS & PRODUITS	0.0	0.0	0.0	0.0	0.0	0.0	
34 PAPER & PRODUCTS–PAPIER & PRODT	0.0	0.0	0.0	0.0	0.0	0.0	
35 CHEMICALS–INDUSTRIES CHIMIQUES	21.0	12.6	18.0	16.6	15.4	23.1	
36 NON METAL MIN–MIN NON METAL	0.0	0.0	0.1	0.0	0.0	0.0	
37 BASIC METAL–IND METAL BASE	5.1	4.9	4.4	4.7	6.3	5.8	
38 METAL MANUF–MANUF METAL	1.5	2.5	2.7	2.3	1.6	1.6	
39 OTH MANUF IND–AUTRES MANUF	0.1	0.2	0.0	0.0	0.1	0.0	

3. TRADE BY PRINCIPAL COUNTRIES OF ORIGIN AND SALE (VALUE IN MILLION U.S. DOLLARS)
ECHANGES SELON LES PRINCIPAUX PAYS D'ORIGINE ET DE VENTE (VALEUR EN MILLIONS DE DOLLARS EU)

COUNTRIES–PAYS	GENERAL IMPORTS C.I.F. IMPORTATIONS GENERALES C.A.F				
	1991	1992	1993	1994	1995
World	1720.1	2015.4	1890.7	1927.4	2119.0
Africa	13.6	24.2	19.2	16.1	
Americas	249.6	292.5	254.4	256.0	
– Northern America	206.4	246.1	224.4	214.8	
– LAIA	42.1	45.3	29.2	38.9	
– CACM	1.2	1.0	0.8	2.2	
– Caribbean	0.0	0.1	0.0	0.1	
– Rest of America		0.0	0.0	0.0	
Asia excl fmr USSR	681.4	838.2	898.1	890.6	
– Middle East	241.3	286.6	339.6	344.5	
Asia former USSR					
Europe excl fmr USSR	710.0	806.5	665.4	702.3	
– European Union	677.7	763.3	628.6	653.0	
– Eastern Europe	2.9	4.4	5.0	5.7	
– Rest of Europe	29.4	38.8	31.9	43.6	
Europe former USSR	1.4	4.8	11.7	21.0	
Oceania	63.4	48.4	41.2	41.1	
Other	0.5	0.8	0.7	0.2	
Japan/Japon	234.1	314.5	310.3	257.7	
USA/Etats–Unis d'Amer	199.6	230.4	220.2	204.2	
United Kingdom	203.4	225.2	194.5	197.9	
Germany/Allemagne	147.0	146.2	150.9	128.1	
United Arab Emirates	73.5	101.7	136.1	133.7	120.0
Saudi Arabia	70.0	72.5	100.5	95.4	118.0
Italy/Italie	97.1	132.3	85.5	83.6	
France, Monaco	89.2	111.2	64.8	75.9	
Netherlands/Pays–Bas	35.9	55.8	45.9	57.7	
India/Inde	30.4	39.2	53.9	63.2	
Australia/Australie	59.7	44.5	38.1	38.0	
Korea, Republic of	27.8	36.8	36.1	38.4	
Belgium–Luxembourg	43.9	30.1	25.2	25.9	
Bahrain/Bahreïn	23.2	27.4	18.1	30.8	20.0
Brazil/Brésil	28.8	34.0	22.4	30.2	
Switzerland,Liechtenst.	20.8	23.4	27.1	39.7	
Other Asia n.e.s.	26.7	29.1	28.8	26.1	
China/Chine	22.0	24.7	27.1	28.3	
Singapore/Singapour	25.1	28.5	19.3	15.4	
Jordan/Jordanie	19.4	20.3	18.6	13.1	16.0
Iran (Islamic Rep of)	14.2	17.3	15.6	21.9	14.0
Indonesia/Indonésie	10.2	18.1	18.7	21.8	14.0
Pakistan	15.1	13.8	12.9	17.5	19.0
Malaysia/Malaisie	10.0	12.7	17.1	25.3	12.0
Spain/Espagne	18.2	13.9	16.5	23.3	
Thailand/Thaïlande	18.9	19.4	16.9	16.6	
Sweden/Suède	14.0	18.2	9.1	24.2	
Syrian Arab Republic	11.1	11.0	9.8	9.1	16.0
Egypt/Egypte	8.2	17.7	13.1	8.9	8.0
Denmark/Danemark	14.2	12.7	13.5	14.4	
Lebanon/Liban	10.9	12.0	10.4	9.8	11.0
Turkey/Turquie	7.5	8.3	9.9	9.5	18.0
China, Hong Kong SAR	12.1	6.2	8.4	26.3	
Russian Federation		4.8	11.7	21.0	
Canada	6.7	15.8	4.2	10.6	
Oman	5.2	6.1	7.4	8.5	7.0
Austria/Autriche	6.2	8.0	8.5	8.8	
Kuwait/ Koweït	1.1	6.7	10.0	9.3	
Ireland/Irlande	3.7	5.4	6.7	7.2	
Argentina/Argentine	8.8	7.1	1.9	2.2	

COUNTRIES–PAYS	GENERAL EXPORTS F.O.B. EXPORTATIONS GENERALES F.O.B.				
	1991	1992	1993	1994	1995
Monde	3209.8	3840.7	3245.4	3212.9	3776.0
Afrique	19.4	7.7	4.1	32.9	
Amériques	18.8	35.4	46.9	73.3	
– Amérique du Nord	18.8	35.4	46.9	65.1	
– ALAI	0.0	0.0	0.0	4.8	
– MCAC			0.0		
– Caraïbes					
– Autre Amérique				3.5	
Asie anc. URSS exclus	856.7	1222.5	998.8	1026.4	
– Moyen–Orient	344.8	409.6	406.1	352.4	
Asie ancienne URSS					
Europe anc. URSS exclus	33.5	30.2	15.5	15.4	
– Union Européenne	31.4	28.7	13.4	14.5	
– Europe de l'Est		0.0	0.0	0.0	
– Autre de l'Europe	2.1	1.5	2.0	0.9	
Europe ancienne URSS	0.0	0.0	0.0	0.2	
Océanie	46.4	57.9	63.6	54.0	
Autre	2235.1	2486.9	2116.5	2010.7	
Areas n.e.s.	2235.1	2486.9	2116.5	2010.7	
Japan/Japon	187.8	307.7	180.1	183.4	
United Arab Emirates	142.8	162.3	162.7	190.0	123.0
Korea, Republic of	19.0	149.8	170.3	143.3	
Saudi Arabia	77.2	110.3	101.8	91.6	60.0
India/Inde	35.5	56.7	82.3	141.0	
China/Chine	82.8	59.1	47.5	52.2	
Iran (Islamic Rep of)	50.2	80.5	83.5	18.5	4.0
Pakistan	54.1	75.5	8.8	21.4	63.0
Australia/Australie	46.1	57.4	63.3	53.8	
USA/Etats–Unis d'Amer	17.8	34.2	46.6	64.1	
Singapore/Singapour	55.2	35.2	13.8	23.7	
Kuwait/ Koweït	27.5	22.1	24.5	16.6	
Philippines	17.2	27.2	15.1	24.7	
Other Asia n.e.s.	19.6	27.1	16.8	16.2	
Indonesia/Indonésie	10.4	25.4	19.6	13.4	10.0
Maldives					69.0
Bahrain/Bahreïn	11.2	10.7	14.4	16.6	8.0
Oman	14.3	10.2	9.0	6.7	6.0
Malaysia/Malaisie	4.8	7.7	11.9	12.4	9.0
Thailand/Thaïlande	13.4	13.3	6.5	8.0	
Jordan/Jordanie	5.8	9.9	7.2	6.6	7.0
Sri Lanka	2.1	4.6	7.1	20.1	
France, Monaco	8.4	11.7	5.6	3.1	
China, Hong Kong SAR	4.0	10.6	6.2	5.9	
Viet Nam	4.5	7.9	4.9	6.3	
Netherlands/Pays–Bas	12.2	5.8	0.4	3.4	
United Rep of Tanzania	0.0	1.2		17.4	
Yemen/Yémen	13.3	0.3	0.1	4.4	
United Kingdom	2.7	5.1	4.3	5.2	
Sudan/Soudan	3.1	2.2	0.3	10.6	
Egypt/Egypte	2.9	2.7	2.6	1.1	
Bangladesh	0.4	4.8	1.7	1.5	1.0
Other Africa n.e.s.	8.7		0.3	0.0	
Italy/Italie	4.6	2.5	0.2	0.3	
Germany/Allemagne	1.7	1.2	0.7	2.3	
Switzerland,Liechtenst.	1.9	0.8	1.9	0.7	
Brazil/Brésil	0.0	0.0		4.7	
Syrian Arab Republic	0.5	1.0	1.3	0.7	1.0
Lebanon/Liban	1.3	1.3	1.1	0.7	

(VALUE AS PERCENTAGE OF WORLD TOTAL)(VALEURS EN POURCENTAGE DU TOTAL MONDIAL)

	1986	1987	1988	1989	1990	1991	1992	1993	1994	1995
Africa	0.1	0.5	0.6	0.7	0.7	0.8	1.2	1.0	0.8	
Americas	8.5	14.6	13.0	12.2	11.9	14.5	14.5	13.5	13.3	
– Northern America	6.3	12.2	9.7	9.1	9.7	12.0	12.2	11.9	11.1	
– LAIA	2.2	2.4	3.2	3.0	2.1	2.4	2.2	1.5	2.0	
– CACM		0.0	0.0	0.0	0.0	0.1	0.0	0.0	0.1	
– Caribbean			0.0	0.0	0.0	0.0	0.0	0.0	0.0	
– Rest of America		0.0	0.0	0.0	0.0		0.0	0.0	0.0	
Asia excl fmr USSR	36.3	36.8	39.9	42.4	38.8	39.6	41.6	47.5	46.2	
– Middle East	9.6	10.5	11.4	12.0	12.6	14.0	14.2	18.0	17.9	
Asia former USSR										
Europe excl fmr USSR	48.8	43.2	40.7	41.5	45.7	41.3	40.0	35.2	36.4	
– European Union	45.6	41.0	38.3	39.8	43.4	39.4	37.9	33.2	33.9	
– Eastern Europe	0.3	0.4	0.4	0.3	0.3	0.2	0.2	0.3	0.3	
– Rest of Europe	3.0	1.8	2.0	1.4	2.1	1.7	1.9	1.7	2.3	
Europe former USSR		0.0	0.1	0.1	0.1	0.1	0.2	0.6	1.1	
Oceania	3.4	2.7	3.3	3.0	2.6	3.7	2.4	2.2	2.1	
Other	2.9	2.2	2.6	0.1	0.2	0.0	0.0	0.0	0.0	
Japan/Japon	17.0	16.3	17.6	18.8	14.7	13.6	15.6	16.4	13.4	
USA/Etats–Unis d'Amer	5.9	11.9	9.3	8.8	9.5	11.6	11.4	11.6	10.6	
United Kingdom	16.5	16.0	13.8	11.7	14.5	11.8	11.2	10.3	10.3	
Germany/Allemagne						8.5	7.3	8.0	6.6	
United Arab Emirates	3.1	3.0	3.1	4.4	3.0	4.3	5.0	7.2	6.9	5.7
Saudi Arabia	2.1	2.7	3.0	2.9	4.1	4.1	3.6	5.3	5.0	5.6
Italy/Italie	5.3	4.9	4.3	7.8	9.4	5.6	6.6	4.5	4.3	
France, Monaco	5.1	4.3	4.0	4.7	4.7	5.2	5.5	3.4	3.9	
Netherlands/Pays–Bas	2.6	2.5	2.5	2.6	2.0	2.1	2.8	2.4	3.0	
India/Inde	1.8	1.5	1.5	1.7	1.8	1.8	1.9	2.9	3.3	

	1986	1987	1988	1989	1990	1991	1992	1993	1994	1995
Afrique				0.4	0.6	0.6	0.2	0.1	1.0	
Amériques				1.0	0.4	0.6	0.9	1.4	2.3	
– Amérique du Nord				0.6	0.3	0.6	0.9	1.4	2.0	
– ALAI				0.4	0.1	0.0	0.0	0.0	0.1	
– MCAC								0.0		
– Caraïbes										
– Autre Amérique									0.1	
Asie anc. URSS exclus				26.4	21.5	26.7	31.8	30.8	31.9	
– Moyen–Orient				9.9	8.9	10.7	10.7	12.5	11.0	
Asie ancienne URSS										
Europe anc. URSS exclus				0.5	0.7	1.0	0.8	0.5	0.5	
– Union Européenne				0.5	0.6	1.0	0.7	0.4	0.5	
– Europe de l'Est				0.0			0.0	0.0	0.0	
– Autre de l'Europe				0.0	0.1	0.1	0.0	0.1	0.0	
Europe ancienne URSS					0.0	0.0	0.0	0.0	0.0	
Océanie				2.1	0.4	1.4	1.5	2.0	1.7	
Autre				69.6	76.4	69.6	64.8	65.2	62.6	
Areas n.e.s.				69.6	76.4	69.6	64.8	65.2	62.6	
Japan/Japon				6.9	4.7	5.8	8.0	5.6	5.7	
United Arab Emirates				4.7	4.5	4.4	4.2	5.0	5.9	3.3
Korea, Republic of				0.7	0.9	0.6	3.9	5.2	4.5	
Saudi Arabia				3.0	1.8	2.4	2.9	3.1	2.9	1.6
India/Inde				1.4	0.6	1.1	1.5	2.5	4.4	
China/Chine				2.3	1.4	2.6	1.5	1.5	1.6	
Iran (Islamic Rep of)				0.2	0.4	1.6	2.1	2.6	0.6	0.1
Pakistan				0.5	0.4	1.7	2.0	0.3	0.7	1.7
Australia/Australie				2.0	0.4	1.4	1.5	2.0	1.7	

4. General Imports C.I.F. by Commodities according to the S.I.T.C. (Rev. 2) in million U.S. Dollars
Importations Générales C.A.F. par Produits d'après la C.T.C.I. (Rév. 2) en millions de Dollars E.U.

SITC CTCI	COMMODITY	1992		1993		1994		1995		PRODUIT
		QUANTITY QUANTITE	VALUE VALEUR	QUANTITY QUANTITE	VALUE VALEUR	QUANTITY QUANTITE	VALUE VALEUR	QUANTITY QUANTITE	VALUE VALEUR	
	ALL COMMODITIES		2015.4		1890.7		1927.4			TOUS PRODUITS
0	FOOD AND LIVE ANIMALS		253.9		241.8		253.6			ALIMENTS,ANIMAUX VIVANTS
001	*LIVE ANIMALS FOR FOOD	W 19986	40.3		31.0	W 20218	34.3			ANIMAUX VIVANTS
0012	SHEEP AND GOATS,LIVE	W 19473	39.5	W 16375	29.7	W 19465	33.1			ESPECES OVINE ET CAPRINE
01	MEAT AND PREPARATIONS		32.6		30.9		33.8			VIANDES ET PREPARATIONS
011	MEAT FRESH,CHILLD,FROZEN	W 19193	30.6	W 18580	28.5	W 21085	31.2			VIANDES FRAICHES,REF,CONGE
0114	POULTRY FRESH CHLLD,FRZN	W 14020	20.1	W 13702	17.7	W 16714	21.6			VOLAILLES MORTES
02	DAIRY PRODCTS,BIRDS'EGGS		36.3		36.4		37.8			PRODUITS LAITIERS,OEUFS
022	MILK AND CREAM	W 13779	26.0	W 13274	25.3	W 14666	26.5			LAIT ET CREME
0223	MILK AND CREAM FRESH	W 3850	5.1	W 3743	4.9	W 5390	6.9			LAIT,CREME FRAIS
0224	MILK,CREAM PRESERVED ETC	W 9929	20.9	W 9531	20.4	W 9276	19.6			LAIT,CREME CONS,CONC
02243	MILK DRY,OVER 1.5% FAT	W 3257	10.8	W 3776	10.5	W 3889	10.8			LAIT POUDRE SUP 1.5%
02249	MILK(EX DRY) PRSVD,SWEET	W 6339	8.8	W 5386	8.0	W 4984	7.3			LAIT CONS,CONC SUCRE
024	CHEESE AND CURD	W 1818	5.3	W 2267	6.2	W 2522	6.3			FROMAGE ET CAILLEBOTTE
04	CEREALS AND PREPARATIONS		36.8		38.0		34.6			CEREALES ET PRODUITS
041	WHEAT ETC UNMILLED	W 40747	7.6	W 44623	8.2	W 28848	5.7			FROMENT,EPEAUTRE
0411	DURUM WHEAT UNMILLED	W 40747	7.6	W 44623	8.2	W 28848	5.7			FROMENT DUR NON MOULU
042	RICE	W 26992	12.9	W 29600	13.2	W 29218	13.1			RIZ
048	CEREAL ETC PREPARATIONS	W 4018	7.8	W 4523	8.9	W 4340	9.0			PREPTNS A BASE CEREALES
05	VEGETABLES AND FRUIT		61.2		59.0		60.3			LEGUMES ET FRUITS
054	VEG ETC FRSH,SMPLY PRSVD	W 58673	23.0	W 60906	22.0	W 60807	23.9			LEGUMES FRAIS,CONG,SECS
0545	OTHER FRESH VEGETABLES	W 34913	13.9	W 34990	13.5	W 36094	14.1			AUTRES LEGUMES FRAIS,REF
05459	FRESH VEGETABLES NES	W 21587	11.2	W 21763	10.8	W 23066	11.0			LEGUMES FRAIS,REFRI NDA
056	VEGTBLES ETC PRSVD,PREPD	W 3793	4.8	W 4115	5.7	W 4530	5.2			CONSERVES DE LEGUMES
057	FRUIT,NUTS,FRESH,DRIED	W 49114	28.5	W 53680	26.3	W 53226	26.1			FRUITS FRAIS OU SECS
0571	ORANGES, MANDARINS ETC	W 12297	5.7	W 14970	6.6	W 13201	5.4			ORANGES,MAND,CLEMENTINES
0579	FRUIT FRESH OR DRIED NES	W 18100	9.5	W 18841	8.3	W 20408	9.7			FRUITS FRAIS,SECS NDA
06	SUGAR AND PREPS,HONEY		8.5		7.9		10.7			SUCRES ET PRODUITS
061	SUGAR AND HONEY	W 11230	4.7	W 10014	4.5	W 17038	7.7			SUCRES ET MIEL
0612	REFINED SUGAR ETC	W 10968	4.0	W 9727	3.8	W 16708	7.1			SUCRES RAFFINES
07	COFFEE,TEA,COCOA,SPICES		16.3		15.0		18.4			CAFE,THE,CACAO,EPICES
073	CHOCOLATE AND PRODUCTS	W 1021	5.8	W 929	5.8	W 1112	6.8			CHOCOLAT
074	TEA AND MATE	W 1135	6.4	W 1022	5.9	W 1170	6.6			THE ET MATE
0741	TEA	W 1135	6.4	W 1022	5.9	W 1170	6.6			THE
081	*FEEDING STUFF FOR ANIML	W 45732	9.0	W 40616	8.1	W 55485	9.5			NOURRITURE POUR ANIMAUX
09	MISC EDIBLE PRODUCTS		10.9		12.9		10.9			PREP ALIMENTAIRES DIVERSES
098	EDIBLE PRODCTS,PREPS NES	W 5480	10.5	W 6288	12.3	W 4274	10.4			PREP ALIMENTAIRES NDA
09809	MISC FOOD PREPRTIONS NES	W 3937	8.0	W 4355	9.3	W 2162	7.2			PREP ALIMENTAIRES NDA
1	BEVERAGES AND TOBACCO		24.2		24.2		25.6			BOISSONS ET TABACS
11	BEVERAGES		9.1		9.5		12.1			BOISSONS
111	NON–ALCOHL BEVERAGES NES	W 13642	6.8	W 16501	7.5	W 21490	9.8			BOISSONS NON ALCOOLIQUES
11102	FLAVORED WATERS NON–ALCO	W 7511	5.1	W 8450	5.9	W 12509	8.0			LIMONADES,EAUX GAZEUSES
12	TOBACCO AND MANUFACTURES		15.2		14.7		13.6			TABACS BRUTS FABRIQUES
122	TOBACCO,MANUFACTURED	W 1079	15.1	W 1138	14.7	W 924	13.5			TABACS FABRIQUES
1222	CIGARETTES	W 1077	15.1	W 1137	14.6	W 773	13.0			CIGARETTES
2	CRUDE MATERLS,EXCL FUELS		63.2		48.0		66.1			MAT BRUTES NON COMESTIBLES
24	CORK AND WOOD		12.2		11.2		9.8			LIEGE ET BOIS
248	WOOD SHAPED,SLEEPERS	W 22430	10.6	W 26913	10.6	W 19378	8.4			BOIS SIMPLEMENT TRAVAILLES
27	CRUDE FERTLZR,MINRLS NES		12.6		21.1		12.7			ENGRAIS MINERAUX BRUTS
273	STONE,SAND AND GRAVEL	W 511637	8.3		17.8	W 821489	9.6			PIERRES,SABLES,GRAVIERS
2731	BLDG,DIMENSION STONE	W 416647	6.6	W 1512036	16.4	W 786558	8.2			PIERRES DE TAILLE
27313	GRANITE,SANDSTONE,ETC	W 407384	5.0	W 1507263	15.7	W 782120	7.3			GYPSE,BASALTE,GRES
28	METALLIFEROUS ORES,SCRAP		33.0		11.1		38.7			MINERAIS METAL,DECHETS
281	IRON ORE,CONCENTRATES	W 787205	32.4	W 222630	9.2	W 895266	38.6			MINERAIS DE FER
3	MINERAL FUELS ETC		14.8		13.2		13.6			COMBUSTIBLES MINERAUX LUB
33	PETROLEUM AND PRODUCTS		14.7		13.2		13.6			PETROLE ET DERIVES
334	PETROLEUM PRODUCTS,REFIN	W 13343	12.7	W 12186	11.8	W 12373	11.2			PRODUITS RAFFINES
3345	LUBS,PETROLEUM OILS NES	W 13035	12.7	W 12186	11.8	W 12373	11.2			HUILES LUBRIFIANTES
33451	LUBS(HIGH PETR CONT) ETC	W 12494	11.8	W 11728	10.4	W 11817	10.1			HUILES LUBRIF,H LOURDES
4	ANIMAL,VEGETABLE OIL,FAT		10.7		9.5		10.3			HUILES,GRAISSES ANIM,VEG
42	FIXED VEGETABLE OIL,FAT		10.6		9.4		10.3			HUILES VEGETALES FIXES
424	FIXED VEG OIL NONSOFT	W 9530	9.4	W 8300	8.2	W 9181	9.3			AUTRES HUILES VEG FIXES
4249	FIXED VEGETABLE OILS NES	W 8761	8.8	W 7544	7.4	W 8576	8.7			HUILES VEGET FIXES NDA
5	CHEMCLS,RELATED PROD NES		119.5		140.6		126.9			PRODUITS CHIMIQUES
52	INORGANIC CHEMICALS		9.9		7.9		8.7			PROD CHIM INORGANIQUES
53	DYES,TANNING,COLOUR PROD		9.6		9.0		10.4			PROD TEINTURE,COLORANTS
533	PIGMENTS,PAINTS,ETC	W 5566	8.5	W 5588	8.5	W 5754	10.0			PIGMENTS,PEINTURES,VERNIS
5334	VARNISHES,DISTEMPERS ETC	W 4214	6.4	W 4882	7.3	W 4976	8.1			PEINTURES A L'EAU
541	*MEDICINAL,PHARM PRODUCT	K 1225333	23.9		32.2	K 1604987	26.7			PROD MEDICINAUX PHARMACEUT
5417	MEDICAMENTS	K 992529	21.0		27.8	K 1138398	23.0			MEDICAMENTS
54179	— CONTNG OTH SUBSTANCES	K 992529	21.0		27.8	K 1138398	23.0			MED CONT AUT SUBSTANCES
55	PERFUME,CLEANING ETC PRD		33.8		33.5		38.0			PROD POUR PARFUM,TOILETTE
551	ESSENTL OILS,PERFUME,ETC	W 425	5.6	W 617	7.5	W 474	9.0			HUILES ESSENTIELLES
553	PERFUMERY,COSMETICS,ETC	W 2460	18.5	W 2333	17.6	W 2739	19.2			PRODUITS DE PARFUMERIE
554	SOAP,CLEANSING ETC PREPS	W 6017	9.8	W 5519	8.5	W 6720	9.9			SAVONS,PRODUITS DETERSIFS
5542	WASHING PREPARATIONS ETC	W 3987	5.8	W 4264	5.7	W 4623	6.0			PROD ORG TENSIO–ACT NDA
58	PLASTIC MATERIALS ETC		7.1		9.7		10.2			MAT PLAST ARTIFICIELLES
583	POLYMERIZATION ETC PRODS	W 5174	5.6	W 7008	8.0	W 7419	8.3			PROD POLYMERISATION
59	CHEMICAL MATERIALS NES		28.0		44.0		27.2			MAT PROD CHIMIQUES NDA
598	MISCEL CHEM PRODUCTS NES	W 14662	23.9	W 81439	39.3	W 16236	22.7			PROD DIV INDUST CHIM NDA
5983	ORGANIC CHEM PRODCTS NES	W 1216	4.3	W 69378	22.9	W 1838	4.7			PROD ORGAN NDA IND CHIMIQ
59832	ARTIFICIAL,ETC GRAPHITE	W 1213	4.3	W 69378	22.9	W 1835	4.7			GRAPHITE ARTIFICIEL COLLOIDA
5989	CHEM PRODUCTS,PREPS NES	W 12539	15.7	W 11579	13.7	W 13941	16.7			PROD PREP CHIMIQUES NDA
59899	OTH CHEM PRODS,PREPS,NES	W 10538	11.3	W 9469	9.7	W 11232	11.8			AUT PRODUITS CHIMIQUES NDA
6	BASIC MANUFACTURES		376.1		364.2		424.2			ART MANUFACTURES
62	RUBBER MANUFACTURES NES		23.6		24.1		21.9			CAOUTCHOUC MANUFACTURE
625	RUBBER TYRES, TUBES ETC	W 7209	22.0	W 6988	22.4	W 5956	19.5			PNEUS CAOUTCHOUC VULCANISE
6251	TYRES NEW FOR MOTOR CARS	W 4669	13.8	W 4295	14.2	W 3609	12.1			PNEUS POUR VOITURES
6252	TYRES,NEW,BUS OR LORRY	W 2440	7.9	W 2503	7.5	W 2028	5.9			PNEUS POUR AUTOBUS,CAMIONS
63	WOOD,CORK MANUFACTRS NES		24.1		19.1		26.3			OUVRAGES LIEGE ET BOIS
634	VENEERS,PLYWOOD,ETC	W 18452	13.4	W 21182	17.2	W 25237	20.7			PLACAGES,CONTRE–PLAQUES
6342	PLYWOOD OF WOOD SHEETS	W 13311	9.7	W 13630	11.1	W 14942	12.9			BOIS CONTRE–PLAQUES
6349	WOOD SIMPLY SHAPED NES	W 4682	3.5	W 7012	5.7	W 9923	7.6			BOIS SIMPL TRAVAILLES NDA
635	WOOD MANUFACTURES NES	W 1947	10.8	W 1078	1.9	W 2800	5.6			ART MANUF EN BOIS NDA
6353	BUILDERS WOODWRK,PREFABS	W 1561	9.8	W 644	0.9	W 2176	4.2			OUVRAGES DE MENUISERIE
64	PAPER,PAPERBOARD AND MFR		24.4		24.3		22.4			PAPIERS,CARTONS & OUVRAGES
641	PAPER AND PAPERBOARD	W 4941	5.2	W 7323	6.4	W 4582	4.4			PAPIERS ET CARTONS
642	PAPER,ETC,PRECUT,ARTS OF	W 9622	19.2	W 23447	18.0	W 9498	18.1			PAP,CARTONS DECOUPES
6428	PAPER ETC ARTICLES NES	W 3513	10.6	W 4112	11.6	W 4415	11.3			OUVRAGES EN PATE A PAPIER
64285	PAPER ETC DIAPERS ETC	W 1600	5.5	W 1696	6.7	W 2065	6.6			SERVIETTES HYGIENIQUES
65	TEXTILE YARN,FABRICS,ETC		82.0		83.1		98.1			FILS,TISSUS,ARTICLES TEXTILE

4. General Imports C.I.F. by Commodities according to the S.I.T.C. (Rev. 2) in million U.S. Dollars
Importations Générales C.A.F. par Produits d'après la C.T.C.I. (Rév. 2) en millions de Dollars E.U.

SITC CTCI	COMMODITY	1992 QUANTITY QUANTITE	1992 VALUE VALEUR	1993 QUANTITY QUANTITE	1993 VALUE VALEUR	1994 QUANTITY QUANTITE	1994 VALUE VALEUR	1995 QUANTITY QUANTITE	1995 VALUE VALEUR	PRODUIT
652	COTTON FABRICS,WOVEN	W 437	5.1	W 1524	6.8	W 3902	24.6			TISSUS DE COTON
653	WOVN MAN–MADE FIB FABRIC	W 1784	25.1	W 3349	31.3	W 3013	30.8			TISSUS FIBRES SYNTH,ARTIF
654	OTH WOVEN TEXTILE FABRIC	W 657	13.0	W 237	6.9	W 222	7.3			TISSUS AUT COTON SYNT,ARTIF
658	TEXTILE ARTICLES NES	W 4070	18.1	W 3663	18.0	W 3235	14.9			ART FACONNES MAT TEXTILES
6584	LINENS ETC	W 1287	11.5	W 1227	11.2	W 471	5.4			LINGE DE MAISON
659	FLOOR COVERINGS,ETC	W 7147	18.4		18.3	W 4319	16.3			COUVRE–PARQUETS,TAPIS ETC
6592	CARPETS ETC KNOTTED	W 4695	15.5	W 4476	15.3	W 3990	13.5			TAPIS POINTS NOUES,ENROULES
66	NONMETAL MINERAL MFS NES		53.3		75.0		87.8			ART MIN NON METALLIQUES
661	LIME,CEMENT,BLDG PRODS	W 304061	19.0	W 543571	36.7	W 537773	38.6			CHAUX,CIMENTS MAT CONSTR
6612	CEMENT	W 291728	12.2	W 526306	25.5	W 516911	26.9			CIMENTS HYDRAULIQUES
6613	BUILDING STONE ETC WORKD	W 7273	4.7	W 10544	7.1	W 12678	7.9			PIERRES A BATIR
66132	BUILDING STONE WORKED	W 6621	4.5	W 9466	6.8	W 12161	7.8			OUVR EN PIERRES DE TAILLE
662	CLAY,REFRACTORY BLDG PRD	W 27784	15.7	W 41501	20.1	W 41396	18.3			MAT CONST REFRACTAIRES
6623	REFRACTORY BUILDING PROD	W 8754	6.8	W 16917	9.1	W 10669	5.6			BRIQUES REFRACTAIRES
66232	REFRACTRY BRICKS ETC NES	W 5367	4.0	W 10800	7.0	W 5200	4.0			BRIQUES ETC REFRACTAIRES
6624	BRICKS ETC NONREFRACTORY	W 19030	9.0	W 24584	11.0	W 30727	12.8			BRIQUES ETC CERAM NON REFR
66245	GLAZED CERAMIC SETTS ETC	W 7846	5.6	W 11054	7.0	W 13948	7.7			AUT CARREAUX CERAMIQUE
663	MINERAL MANUFCTURES NES	W 5890	3.2	W 7669	3.0	W 22632	10.4			ART MIN MANUF NDA
6633	MINRL MFS NES NONCERAMIC	W 3678	1.1	W 5986	1.4	W 19994	7.5			OUVR MAT MINERALE NDA
66332	CEMENT,ARTFCL STONE PROD	W 2226	0.6	W 4695	0.9	W 18435	7.2			OUVRAGES EN CIMENT
664	GLASS	W 5652	6.9	W 5311	6.5	W 6672	10.6			VERRE
6649	GLASS NES	W 2093	4.1	W 1606	3.4	W 1853	6.8			VERRE NDA
665	GLASSWARE	W 5021	5.6	W 7817	6.3	W 7804	6.9			OUVRAGES EN VERRE
67	IRON AND STEEL		88.4		63.3		75.3			FER ET ACIER
671	PIG IRON ETC	W 108992	12.0	W 4329	2.7	W 1144	1.3			FONTE,SPIEGEL,POUDRES
6716	FERRO–ALLOYS	W 16071	8.2	W 3969	2.5	W 828	1.0			FERRO–ALLIAGES
672	IRON,STEEL PRIMARY FORMS	W 30647	8.9	W 6671	3.8	W 6281	4.6			LINGOTS FER,ACIER
673	IRON,STEEL SHAPES ETC	W 21708	10.5	W 24240	10.4	W 23251	12.4			BARRES,PROFIL FER,ACIER
6733	IRON,STEEL PROFILES ETC	W 11411	6.4	W 11929	5.9	W 14002	8.8			PROFILES,PALPLAN FER,ACIER
678	IRON,STL TUBES,PIPES,ETC	W 40171	51.9	W 38224	40.3	W 48359	50.7			TUBES,TUYAUX EN FONTE,FER
6783	IRON,STL TUBES,PIPES NES	W 37854	42.8	W 36987	35.1	W 46112	46.3			AUT TUBES,TUYAUX FER,ACIER
6785	IRON,STEEL TUBE FITTINGS	W 2317	9.2	W 1237	5.2	W 2247	4.5			ACCESSOIRES DE TUYAUTERIE
68	NON–FERROUS METALS		18.1		14.0		21.8			METAUX NON FERREUX
682	COPPER EXC CEMENT COPPER	W 1583	7.6	W 1022	3.9	W 1565	4.8			CUIVRE
6822	COPPER,ALLOYS WORKED	W 1583	7.6	W 1022	3.9	W 1565	4.8			CUIVRE,ALLIAGES OUVRES
68225	COPPER TUBES,PIPES,ETC	W 1583	7.6	W 1022	3.9	W 1565	4.8			TUBES,TUYAUX EN CUIVRE
684	ALUMINIUM	W 3806	10.4	W 3784	10.1	W 4022	11.9			ALUMINIUM
6842	ALUMINIUM,ALLOYS WORKED	W 3800	10.4	W 3776	10.1	W 4018	11.8			ALUMINIUM,ALLIAGES OUVRE
68421	ALUMINIUM BARS,WIRE,ETC	W 2127	5.6	W 2175	6.8	W 2346	7.5			BARRES,PROFILES FILS ALU
69	METAL MANUFACTURES NES		61.7		60.7		70.3			ART MANUFACT EN METAL NDA
691	STRUCTURES AND PARTS NES	W 8871	12.7	W 6543	13.6	W 10132	19.5			CONSTRUCT FER,ACIER,ALU
6911	STRUCTURES,PARTS IRN,STL	W 8297	10.3	W 6077	11.1	W 9475	15.4			CONSTRUCT FER,ACIER,FONTE
692	METAL TANKS,BOXES,ETC	W 3213	7.8	W 2773	8.9	W 2552	7.5			RECIPIENTS METALLIQUES
697	BASE MTL HOUSEHOLD EQUIP	W 4034	14.0	W 2442	11.8	W 3365	12.7			ART MENAGE MET COMMUNS
699	BASE METAL MFRS NES	W 4878	13.6	W 5115	12.0	W 8733	16.9			ART MANUFACTURES MET NDA
6991	LOCKSMITHS WARES,ETC	W 1173	6.1	W 1384	5.6	W 2055	7.2			ARTICLES DE SERRURERIE
7	MACHINES,TRANSPORT EQUIP		888.1		800.8		764.1			MACHINES MATERIEL TRANSPORT
71	POWER GENERATING EQUIPMT		42.5		70.7		59.0			MACHINES GENERATRICES
711	STEAM BOILERS & AUX PLNT	W 635	4.8		27.7	W 676	5.3			GENERATEURS VAPEUR EAU ETC
7111	STEAM BOILERS ETC	W 631	4.7	W 2970	25.7	W 646	5.1			GENERATEURS VAPEUR EAU
713	INTRNL COMBUS PSTN ENGIN	W 802	13.2	W 1171	14.9	W 540	9.6			MOTEURS EXPL COMB INT, PIECE
7139	PISTON ENGINE PARTS NES	W 411	7.3	W 889	11.7	W 348	7.5			PIECES POUR 713.2,3,8
714	ENGINES AND MOTORS NES	W 139	12.5	W 101	15.6	W 464	31.7			MOTEURS NON ELECTRIQUES
7148	GAS TURBINES NES	W 87	4.3	W 31	0.8	W 197	11.2			TURBINES A GAZ
71488	OTHER GAS TURBINES NES	W 87	4.3	W 31	0.8	W 197	11.2			AUTRES TURBINES A GAZ
7149	ENGINE & MOTOR PARTS NES	W 52	8.2	W 70	14.9	W 267	20.5			PIECES 714 ET 718.88
71499	PARTS NES,OF 71488,71888	W 52	8.2	W 70	14.9	W 267	20.5			PIECES 714.88 ET 718.88
716	ROTATING ELECTRIC PLANT	W 1590	12.2		12.6	W 1044	12.5			APP ELECTR ROTATIFS,PIECES
7162	AC MTRS,GENRTRS,GEN SETS	W 461	6.2	W 504	6.6	W 716	7.8			MOTEURS ELECTRIQUES
72	MACHS FOR SPCL INDUSTRYS		166.0		91.4		107.2			MAC SPECIALES POUR INDUST
723	CIVIL ENGNEERG EQUIP ETC	W 17124	139.4	W 10587	66.0	W 7336	62.9			APPAREILS DE GENIE CIVIL
7234	CONST,MINING MACHNRY NES	W 7993	46.3	W 4994	15.9	W 3577	14.5			MACH POUR LA CONST, MINES
72342	SLFPRP SHOVELS,EXCAVATRS	W 2763	10.0	W 3763	11.2	W 2506	7.1			PELLES MECANIQUES
72343	SLFPRP CONST ETC MCH NES	W 3561	23.2	W 197	0.5	W 23	0.1			AUT MACH EXTR,TERRASSEM
72346	OTH CONST,MINING MCH NES	W 804	7.3			W 321	2.9			AUT MACH EXTRACTION,EXCAV ET
7239	CONSTR ETC MACHY PTS NES	W 9042	92.5	W 5407	49.8	W 3599	47.8			PIECES 723.41–723.46
726	PRINTG,BKBINDG MACHY,PTS	W 113	2.2	W 480	6.6	W 124	1.9			MACHINES POUR IMPRIMERIE
727	FOOD MACHRY NON–DOMESTIC	W 93	2.8		1.9	W 859	20.3			MACH INDUSTRIES ALIMENT
7272	OTH FOOD PROC MCHY,PARTS	W 72	2.2	W 86	0.8	W 755	16.3			AUT MACH IND ALIMENTAIRE
72722	INDUS FOOD PROC MACH NES	W 72	2.2	W 86	0.8	W 739	16.0			MACHINES BOULANGERIE
728	OTH MACHY FOR SPCL INDUS	W 1652	15.4	W 1167	12.1	W 1748	18.7			AUT MACH IND PARTICULIERES
7283	OTHR MINERAL WORKG MACHY	W 1466	13.6	W 756	9.0	W 1367	16.2			MACH TRIER,CRIBLER,BROYER
72839	PTS NES OF MACHY OF 7283	W 628	8.9	W 401	7.2	W 759	12.2			PIECES MACH DU 728.3
74	GENRL INDUSTRL MACHY NES		121.6		117.2		140.8			MACH APP INDUSTRIE
741	HEATING,COOLING EQUIPMNT	W 6124	52.0	W 6384	58.9	W 12891	85.1			MACH CHAUFFAGE,PIECES
7413	INDUS FURNACES ETC,PARTS	W 1298	4.7	W 1278	11.8	W 1391	8.6			FOURS IND,LABOR,PIECES
74132	INDUST FURNACES NONELECT	W 1298	4.7	W 1278	11.8	W 1391	8.6			FOURS NON ELECTRIQUES
7415	AIR–CONDITIONING MACHNRY	W 3602	24.9	W 4075	29.9	W 4391	29.7			GROUPES CONDITION AIR
7416	HEATING,COOLING EQU NES	W 725	18.8	W 520	13.5	W 6361	42.7			APP CHANGEMENT TEMP
742	PUMPS FOR LIQUIDS ETC	W 1009	16.3		18.7	W 1037	17.0			POMPES MOTO–POMPES
7428	OTHER PUMPS FOR LIQUIDS	W 581	4.8	W 570	6.5	W 681	6.6			AUTRES POMPES POUR LIQ
74288	PUMPS FR LIQUIDS NES ETC	W 558	4.5	W 564	6.3	W 640	6.1			POMPES POUR LIQUIDES NDA
7429	PTS NES OF PUMPS OF 742	W 177	7.1	W 231	10.5	W 224	8.8			PIECES POUR GROUPE 742
743	PUMPS NES,CENTRFUGES ETC	W 1329	13.8	W 806	8.3	W 951	7.1			POMPES COMPRES,VENT ETC
7436	GAS,LIQUID FILTERS ETC	W 572	6.4	W 399	3.6	W 346	2.2			APP POUR FILT DES LIQUIDES
744	MECHANICAL HANDLING EQU	W 3251	16.6	W 3713	16.2	W 3376	16.0			EQUIP MANUTENTION PIECES
7442	LIFTING,LOADING MACH NES	W 2237	11.7	W 1946	6.2	W 2032	8.7			APP LEVAGE,MANUTENTION
7449	PTS NES OF MACHY OF 7442	W 318	2.1	W 1023	6.6	W 741	4.4			PIECES DU 744.2
745	NONELEC MACHY,TOOLS NES	W 542	6.2	W 551	4.7	W 759	5.8			AUT MACH NON ELEC,PIECES
749	NONELEC MACH PTS,ACC NES	W 1098	17.0		10.6	W 877	10.1			PIECES MACH NON ELEC NDA
7492	COCKS,VALVES ETC NES	W 839	15.1	W 1134	9.0	W 795	8.7			ART ROB,SIM POUR TUYAUX
75	OFFICE MACHNES,ADP EQUIP		26.0		23.1		26.3			MACH BUREAU TRAIT AUTOM
752	AUTOMTIC DATA PROC EQUIP	W 143	8.7	W 143	9.6	W 139	10.4			MACH TRAIT INFORMATION
759	OFFICE,ADP MCH PTS,ACCES	W 242	13.2	W 212	9.7	W 267	12.1			PIECES DU 751 ET 752
76	TELECOMM,SOUND EQUIPMENT		53.4		54.9		44.7			EQUIPMENT DE TELECOM
761	TELEVISION RECEIVERS	W 748	8.7	W 522	7.7	W 576	8.0			RECEPTEURS DE TELEVISION
7611	COLOUR TV RECEIVERS	W 744	8.7	W 522	7.7	W 574	8.0			RECEPTEURS COULEUR
762	RADIO BROADCAST RECEIVRS	W 305	5.3	W 364	5.8	W 414	5.2			RECEPTEURS RADIODIFFUSION
764	TELECOM EQPT,PTS,ACC NES	W 685	34.5	W 808	36.1	W 558	25.9			EQUIP TELECOM,PIECES
7641	LINE TELEPHONE,ETC EQU!P	W 378	22.3	W 314	11.2	W 228	14.2			APP TELEPHON PAR FIL
7643	TV,RADIO TRANSMITTRS ETC	W 16	2.0	W 100	7.7	W 7	2.2			APP EMET TELE RADIO

4. General Imports C.I.F. by Commodities according to the S.I.T.C. (Rev. 2) in million U.S. Dollars
Importations Générales C.A.F. par Produits d'après la C.T.C.I. (Rév. 2) en millions de Dollars E.U.

SITC CTCI	COMMODITY	1992		1993		1994		1995		PRODUIT
		QUANTITY QUANTITE	VALUE VALEUR	QUANTITY QUANTITE	VALUE VALEUR	QUANTITY QUANTITE	VALUE VALEUR	QUANTITY QUANTITE	VALUE VALEUR	
7649	PTS NES OF EQUIPMT OF 76	W 256	8.1	W 347	14.0	W 289	7.3			PIECES DE LA DIV 76
77	ELECTRIC MACHNRY NES ETC		112.4		92.1		95.5			MACH APP ELECT NDA
771	ELECTRIC POWER MACHY NES	W 2065	7.0	W 587	5.4	W 964	4.6			MACH PROD,TRANS ELECTR
7711	TRANSFORMERS,ELECTRICAL	W 2052	6.9	W 566	5.3	W 932	4.4			TRANSFO ELECTRIQUES
772	SWITCHGEAR ETC,PARTS NES	W 2732	29.1	W 2669	22.8	W 1931	15.5			APP COUPURE,SECT ETC
7721	SWITCHGEAR ETC	W 2729	29.1	W 2644	22.7	W 1917	15.4			APP COUPURE,SECTIONMNT
773	ELECTR DISTRIBUTNG EQUIP	W 9958	33.7	W 26478	28.4	W 17519	39.5			EQUIPMT DISTRIBUTION ELECT
7731	INSULATED WIRE,CABLE ETC	W 9810	33.1	W 26089	27.3	W 17027	38.0			FILS,CABLES ISOLES ELECT
775	HOUSEHOLD TYPE EQUIP NES	W 3941	25.3		20.4	W 3150	19.5			MACH,APP USAGE DOMESTQUE
7752	DOM REFRIGERATRS,FREEZRS	W 1035	6.1	W 844	4.6	W 933	5.0			REFRIG,CONGEL MENAGER
7757	DOMESTIC ELECTRC EQU NES	W 651	5.9		6.4	W 643	5.7			APP ELECTR DOMEST NDA
7758	ELECTRO-THERMIC APPL NES	W 1677	9.9	W 1195	6.9	W 1197	6.4			APP ELECTROTHERMIQ NDA
778	ELECTRICAL MACHINERY NES	W 2278	16.9		14.3	W 2553	15.2			AUTRES MACH ELECT NDA
7788	OTH ELEC MACHY,EQUIP NES	W 205	6.4		2.9	W 102	3.8			AUT MACH APP ELEC NDA
78	ROAD VEHICLES		345.7		338.0		271.8			VEHICULES ROUTIERS
781	PASS MOTOR VEH EXC BUSES	W 17502	212.0	W 18389	222.3	W 12790	170.4			AUTO TRANSPORT PERSONNES
782	LORRIES,SPCL MTR VEH NES	W 16729	69.3	W 10633	55.2	W 7707	45.1			VEHICULES SPECIAUX,MARCH
7821	LORRIES,TRUCKS	W 11643	58.3	W 9884	52.2	W 6667	40.7			VEHICULES TRANSP MARCHAND
7822	SPECIAL MOTOR VEHCLS NES	W 5086	11.1	W 749	3.0	W 1040	4.5			VEHICULES USAGES SPECIAUX
783	ROAD MOTOR VEHICLES NES	W 2101	9.4	W 2167	9.8	W 2671	10.7			VEHICULES ROUTIERS NDA
7831	BUSES	W 903	5.8	W 1234	7.4	W 1963	9.0			VOITURES TRANSPORT COMMUN
784	MOTOR VEH PRTS,ACCES NES	W 4689	49.7	W 4818	47.2	W 3713	40.7			PIECES 722,781,782,783
7849	OTHER MOTOR VEHCL PARTS	W 4273	49.0	W 4233	45.8	W 3367	39.5			PIECES 722,781,782,783
79	OTHR TRANSPORT EQUIPMENT		15.3		9.7		14.9			AUTRE MATERIEL TRANSPORT
792	AIRCRAFT ETC	W 34	8.5	W 23	5.9	W 62	11.4			APP NAVIGATION AERIENNE
7929	AIRCRAFT PARTS NES	W 31	7.0	W 23	5.9	W 59	9.5			PIECES DU 792
793	SHIPS AND BOATS ETC	W 827	6.8	W 366	3.8	W 1058	3.5			NAVIRES BATEAUX,ETC
8	MISC MANUFACTURED GOODS		263.6		246.3		241.8			ART MANUFACTURES DIVERS
812	*PLUMBG,HEATNG,LGHTNG EQ	W 4082	17.2	W 3678	16.6	W 4286	18.9			APPAR SANITAIRES CHAUFFAGE
8122	CERAMIC PLUMBNG FIXTURES	W 3136	9.3	W 2876	9.8	W 3361	10.7			EVIERS,LAVABOS,CUVETTES
8124	LIGHTING EQUIPMENT NES	W 854	7.5	W 736	6.5	W 845	7.9			APPAREILS ECLAIRAGE ETC
81242	LAMPS,FITTINGS BASE METL	W 799	7.1	W 663	6.1	W 709	6.8			APPAREILS D'ECLAIRAGE
821	*FURNITURE,PARTS THEREOF	W 11577	37.7	W 9484	30.3	W 9768	31.3			MEUBLES ET PIECES
8211	CHAIRS,SEATS AND PARTS	W 2865	9.0	W 2641	7.7	W 3026	8.8			SIEGES ET PIECES
8219	FURNITURE AND PARTS NES	W 8079	27.0	W 6136	20.7	W 6049	20.7			AUTRES MEUBLES ET PIECES
82192	WOOD FURNITURE NES	W 6822	22.9	W 5156	17.5	W 4842	16.5			MEUBLES NDA EN BOIS
84	CLOTHING AND ACCESSORIES		39.1		39.3		38.4			VETEMENTS
842	MENS OUTERWEAR NOT KNIT	W 733	8.6	W 754	9.0	W 668	9.3			VET DESSUS POUR HOMMES
8422	— SUITS	W 415	5.6	W 542	6.8	W 530	7.6			COMPLETS HOMMES MAT TEXT
843	WOMENS OUTERWEAR NONKNIT	W 1093	14.6	W 1315	15.6	W 858	15.9			VET DESSUS FEMMES MAT TEX
8432	— SUITS AND COSTUMES	W 460	6.5	W 756	8.0	W 372	7.0			COSTUMES-TAIL MAT TEXIL
8439	— OTHER OUTER GARMENTS	W 389	5.3	W 318	4.8	W 303	5.9			AUT VET DES FEM MAT TEXT
844	UNDER GARMENTS NOT KNIT	W 852	8.5	W 644	7.6	W 629	7.2			VETEMENT DESSOUS MAT TEX
851	*FOOTWEAR	W 1236	14.9	W 1118	13.3	W 1040	13.1			CHAUSSURES
85101	FOOTWEAR RUBBER,PLASTIC	W 1236	14.9	W 1118	13.3	W 942	11.9			CHAUS SEMELLES CAOUTCH
87	PRECISION INSTRUMNTS NES		38.5		20.5		18.9			INSTRUM,APPAR SCIENT NDA
872	MEDICAL INSTRUMENTS NES	W 213	6.3	W 252	10.0	W 234	7.5			INSTR,APP MEDIC-CHIR NDA
87202	OTH MEDICAL INSTRUMENTS	W 120	4.3	W 198	7.6	W 203	6.4			INSTRUM,APP MEDECINE
874	MEASURNG,CONTROLNG INSTR	W 451	31.9	W 210	10.0	W 340	10.6			INSTRUMENTS DE MESURE
8743	GAS,LIQUID CONTROL INSTR	W 163	6.4	W 89	4.7	W 176	5.8			APP,INSTR MESURE FLUIDES
8745	MEAS,CONTRL,SCI INST NES	W 132	18.3	W 56	1.5	W 59	1.1			APP SCIENT MESURE NDA
87452	INSTRMNTS ETC FR DEMONST	W 127	18.2	W 50	1.3	W 58	1.1			INSTR POUR DEMONSTRATION
88	PHOTO EQU,OPTICL GDS ETC		28.8		28.4		27.9			APP,FOURN PHOTO,OP,MONTR
885	WATCHES AND CLOCKS		18.6		19.8		18.5			HORLOGERIE
8851	WATCHES,MOVEMENTS,CASES		17.7		19.1		17.5			MONTRES,MOUVEMENTS,BOITES
88511	WATCHES		17.7		19.1		17.5			MONTRES POCHE,BRACELET
89	MISC MANUFCTRD GOODS NES		82.7		94.1		89.0			ART MANUFACTURES DIVERS
893	ARTICLES OF PLASTIC NES	W 9520	18.6	W 7516	15.0	W 7428	15.4			OUVRAGES EN MAT DIVIS 58
8939	MISC PLASTIC ARTICLES	W 6563	13.7	W 6193	12.2	W 6480	13.6			ART DIVERS EN MAT DIV 58
89399	OTHR PLASTC ARTICLES NES	W 6299	13.1	W 5959	11.7	W 6221	13.0			AUT OUV MAT DIV 58
894	TOYS,SPORTING GOODS,ETC	W 2236	10.9	W 1993	10.1	W 2531	9.9			VOITURES ENFANTS,JOUETS
8942	TOYS,INDOOR GAMES ETC	W 1053	5.0	W 1091	6.0	W 1332	6.2			JOUETS,JEUX ETC
895	OFFICE SUPPLIES NES	W 2116	9.4	W 1626	8.7	W 1830	9.0			ART PAPET NDA
8959	OTHER OFFICE SUPPLIES	W 1769	7.2	W 1377	6.7	W 1275	6.0			AUT ART DE PAPETERIE
897	GOLD,SILVER WARE,JEWELRY		30.2		46.9		34.7			BIJOUTERIE,ORFEVRERIE
8973	PREC JEWLRY,GLD-SILVWARE		28.9		45.2		33.3			BIJOUX OR,ARGENT ORFEVRE
89732	GOLD,SILVER,ETC WARE		28.4		45.1		33.1			ORFEVRERIE MET PRECIEUX
899	OTHER MANUFACTURED GOODS		5.3		6.4		11.7			AUT ART MANUF DIVERS NDA
8998	SMALLWARES,TOILETRYS ETC	W 177	1.5	W 237	2.7	W 1534	7.6			ART MERCERIE,TOILETTE

5. General Exports F.O.B. by Commodities according to the S.I.T.C. (Rev. 2) in million U.S. Dollars
Exportations Générales F.O.B. par Produits d'après la C.T.C.I. (Rév. 2) en millions de Dollars E.U.

SITC CTCI	COMMODITY	1992 QUANTITY QUANTITE	1992 VALUE VALEUR	1993 QUANTITY QUANTITE	1993 VALUE VALEUR	1994 QUANTITY QUANTITE	1994 VALUE VALEUR	1995 QUANTITY QUANTITE	1995 VALUE VALEUR	PRODUIT
	ALL COMMODITIES		3840.7		3245.5		3213.0			TOUS PRODUITS
0	FOOD AND LIVE ANIMALS		9.3		10.8		16.0			ALIMENTS,ANIMAUX VIVANTS
3	MINERAL FUELS ETC		3200.7		2641.8		2372.8			COMBUSTIBLES MINERAUX LUB
33	PETROLEUM AND PRODUCTS		2803.8		2328.1		2238.8			PETROLE ET DERIVES
333	CRUDE PETROLEUM	MW 17000	2487.0	MW 17341	2116.6	W 16666	2010.7			HUILES BRUTES DE PETROLE
334	PETROLEUM PRODUCTS,REFIN	W 2220910	316.8	W 1683183	211.5	W 1895074	228.0			PRODUITS RAFFINES
3341	GASOLINE,OTH LIGHT OILS	W 236452	46.2	W 114987	21.0	W 216776	32.6			ESSENCES POUR MOTEURS
33411	MOTOR,AVIATION SPIRIT	W 100815	20.6	W 83844	15.8	W 216776	32.6			ESSENCES MOTEURS D'AVIONS
33419	OTH LIGHT PETROLEUM OILS	W 135637	25.7	W 31143	5.3					AUTRES HUILES LEGERES
3342	KEROSENE,OTH MEDIUM OILS	W 311726	63.7	W 260668	51.1	W 301625	50.4			PETR LAMPANTS,AUT HUIL
33421	KEROSENE INCL JET FUEL	W 311726	63.7	W 260668	51.1	W 301625	50.4			PETROLES LAMPANTS
3343	GAS OILS	W 631368	116.7	W 423928	73.2	W 472301	69.6			GAS OILS
3344	FUEL OILS,NES	W 1041326	90.1	W 883458	66.3	W 904360	75.6			FUEL OILS
341	*GAS,NATURAL AND MANUFCT	W 2468668	397.0	W 2308711	313.8	W 1087057	134.1			GAZ NATUREL,GAZ MANUFACT
3413	PETROLM GASES,LIQUEFIED	W 2468668	397.0	W 2308711	313.8	W 1087057	134.1			GAZ DE PETROLE LIQUEFIE
34131	LIQUEFIED PROPANE,BUTANE	W 1081471	154.4	W 1102086	135.0	W 1087057	134.1			PROPANE,BUTANE LIQUEFIES
34139	OTH HYDROCARBON GAS LQFD	W 1387197	242.7	W 1206625	178.8					HYDROCARBURES GAZEUX NDA
5	CHEMCLS,RELATED PROD NES		316.2		285.5		510.0			PRODUITS CHIMIQUES
51	ORGANIC CHEMICALS		33.4		40.4		56.7			PROD CHIMIQ ORGANIQUES
511	HYDROCARBONS NES,DERIVS	W 144786	33.3	W 168205	40.4	W 175785	56.6			HYDROCARBURES NDA
5111	ACYCLIC HYDROCARBONS	W 144726	33.3	W 168205	40.4	W 175785	56.6			HYDROCARBURES ACYCLIQUES
51111	ETHYLENE	W 144678	33.2	W 168205	40.4	W 175785	56.6			ETHYLENE
52	INORGANIC CHEMICALS		23.7		27.8		47.9			PROD CHIM INORGANIQUES
522	INORG ELEMNTS,OXIDES,ETC	W 260026	23.6	W 281659	27.7	W 297767	47.8			ELEMENTS INORGANIQUES
5225	INORGANIC BASES ETC NES	W 241934	23.0	W 281637	27.7	W 297756	47.8			AUTRES BASES OXYDES METAL
52251	AMMONIA,ANHYDROUS ETC	W 241934	23.0	W 281637	27.7	W 297756	47.8			AMMONIAC LIQUEFIE
562	*FERTILIZERS,MANUFACTURE	W 769097	104.0	W 872930	92.5	W 885869	115.5			ENGRAIS MANUFACTURES
5621	CHEM NITROGENOUS FERTLZR	W 769065	104.0	W 872930	92.5	W 885869	115.5			ENGRAIS AZOTES
56216	UREA	W 769065	104.0	W 872930	92.5	W 885869	115.5			UREE
58	PLASTIC MATERIALS ETC		146.8		119.6		284.0			MAT PLAST ARTIFICIELLES
582	PROD OF CONDENSATION ETC	W 21	0.1			W 1298984	181.6			PROD CONDENS,POLYCOND
5829	OTH CONDNSATION,ETC PROD					W 1298984	181.6			AUT PROD CONDENSATION
583	POLYMERIZATION ETC PRODS	W 180660	146.8	W 173105	119.6	W 156767	102.5			PROD POLYMERISATION
5831	POLYETHYLENE	W 180497	146.6	W 172928	119.4	W 156599	102.4			POLYETHYLENE
58311	— IN PRIMARY FORMS	W 180484	146.6	W 172928	119.4	W 156517	102.3			POLYETHYLENE PRIMAIRES
6	BASIC MANUFACTURES		187.8		212.4		194.3			ART MANUFACTURES
67	IRON AND STEEL		180.2		204.8		186.2			FER ET ACIER
673	IRON,STEEL SHAPES ETC	W 519121	176.4	W 551319	203.2	W 529128	185.1			BARRES,PROFIL FER,ACIER
6732	IRON,STEEL BARS ETC	W 519000	176.3	W 551205	203.1	W 528965	185.0			BARRES FER,ACIER
67326	IRN,OTH STL BARS HOTROLD	W 519000	176.3	W 551205	203.1					BARRES PLEINES FER,ACIER
7	MACHINES,TRANSPORT EQUIP		79.6		42.0		45.8			MACHINES MATERIEL TRANSPORT
72	MACHS FOR SPCL INDUSTRYS		11.6		9.2		12.1			MAC SPECIALES POUR INDUST
723	CIVIL ENGNEERG EQUIP ETC	W 2705	11.4		8.7	W 2273	11.6			APPAREILS DE GENIE CIVIL
7239	CONSTR ETC MACHY PTS NES	W 904	8.5	W 1612	6.7	W 1766	10.4			PIECES 723.41–723.46
78	ROAD VEHICLES		49.4		21.8		16.9			VEHICULES ROUTIERS
781	PASS MOTOR VEH EXC BUSES	W 2739	24.4	W 1492	13.5	W 1190	8.3			AUTO TRANSPORT PERSONNES
782	LORRIES,SPCL MTR VEH NES	W 3880	21.0		5.6	W 1087	5.1			VEHICULES SPECIAUX,MARCH
7821	LORRIES,TRUCKS	W 3829	20.8	W 1180	5.5	W 980	4.9			VEHICULES TRANSP MARCHAND
8	MISC MANUFACTURED GOODS		39.0		44.7		64.8			ART MANUFACTURES DIVERS
84	CLOTHING AND ACCESSORIES		31.0		36.2		58.3			VETEMENTS
842	MENS OUTERWEAR NOT KNIT	W 2399	18.8	W 2943	25.5	W 1976	28.6			VET DESSUS POUR HOMMES
8422	— SUITS	W 2356	18.4	W 2932	25.4	W 1967	28.5			COMPLETS HOMMES MAT TEXT
843	WOMENS OUTERWEAR NONKNIT	W 1373	10.4	W 968	9.5	W 1809	28.2			VET DESSUS FEMMES MAT TEX
8432	— SUITS AND COSTUMES	W 1200	8.8	W 929	9.2	W 1786	27.9			COSTUMES–TAIL MAT TEXIL

1. HISTORICAL SERIES, 1992–1997 GENERAL TRADE, IMPORTS C.I.F., EXPORTS F.O.B.
SERIES HISTORIQUES, 1992–1997 COMMERCE GENERAL, IMPORTATIONS C.A.F., EXPORTATIONS F.O.B

YEAR ANNEE	VALUE IN MILLION U.S. DOLLARS VALEUR EN MILLION U.S. DOLLARS MERCHANDISE –MARCHANDISE		GOLD –OR		CONVERSION FACTORS U.S. CENTS PER MOLDOVAN LEU FACTEURS DE CONVERSION CENTS E.U. PAR MOLDOVAN LEU		INDEX NUMBERS –INDICES QUANTUM		UNIT VALUE VALEUR UNITAIRE	
	IMPORTS	EXPORTS	IMPORTS	EXPORTS	IMPORTS	EXPORTS	IMPORTS	EXPORTS	IMPORTS	EXPORTS
1992	170.00	157.00								
1993	184.00	178.00								
1994	659.30	565.40								
1995	840.70	745.50								
1996	1079.20	801.60								
1997	1147.61	842.87								

2. IMPORTS BY BROAD ECONOMIC CATEGORY AND EXPORTS BY INDUSTRIAL ORIGIN. (PERCENTAGE OF TOTAL VALUE)
IMPORTATIONS PAR CATEGORIES ECONOMIQUES ET EXPORTATIONS PAR BRANCHE D'ACTIVITE.(EN POURCENTAGE DE LA VALEUR TOTALE)

IMPORTS – IMPORTATIONS

	1991	1992	1993	1994	1995	1996	1997
TOTAL IMPORTS–IMPORTATIONS TOTALES				100.	100.		
1 FOOD BEV–ALIMENTATION BOISSONS				4.0	6.7		
11 PRIMARY–PRODUITS DE BASE				2.3	3.3		
111 FOR INDUSTRY–POUR L'INDUSTRIE				1.5	1.7		
112 FOR HOUSEHOLDS–POUR LES MENAGES				0.8	1.5		
12 PROCESSED–PRODUITS ELABORES				1.7	3.4		
121 FOR INDUSTRY–POUR L'INDUSTRIE				0.3	0.8		
122 FOR HOUSEHOLDS–POUR LES MENAGES				1.3	2.6		
2 IND SUPPLIES–APPROV INDUSTRIELS				20.5	26.1		
21 PRIMARY–PRODUITS DE BASE				3.6	3.5		
22 PROCESSED–PRODUITS ELABORES				16.9	22.7		
3 FUELS–COMBUSTIBLES				54.6	45.8		
31 PRIMARY–PRODUITS DE BASE				33.6	18.5		
32 PROCESSED–PRODUITS ELABORES				21.0	27.3		
321 MOTOR SPIRIT–ESSENCE				5.5	21.4		
322 OTHER–AUTRES				15.5	5.9		
4 MACHINERY–EQUIPEMENT				9.0	11.5		
41 CAPITAL EQUIPMENT–MACHINES				7.4	10.4		
42 PARTS–PIECES ACCESSOIRES				1.7	1.1		
5 TRANSPORT–TRANSPORT				3.9	3.9		
51 PASSENGER CARS–AUTOMOBILES				0.7	0.7		
52 OTHER–AUTRES				1.0	0.8		
521 INDUSTRIAL–INDUSTRIELS				0.9	0.8		
522 NON INDUSTRIAL–NON INDUSTRIEL				0.1	0.0		
53 PARTS–PIECES ACCESSOIRES				2.2	2.4		
6 CONSUM GOODS–BIENS CONSOMMATION				7.8	5.9		
61 DURABLE–DURABLES				1.3	0.9		
62 SEMI DURABLE–SEMI DURABLES				2.7	2.2		
63 NON DURABLE–NON DURABLES				3.7	2.8		
7 GOODS NES–BIENS NDA				0.1	0.0		

EXPORTS – EXPORTATIONS

	1991	1992	1993	1994	1995	1996	1997
TOTAL EXPORTS–EXPORTATIONS TOTALES				100.	100.		
1 AGRICULTURE				20.3	13.2		
2 MINING QUARRY–INDUS EXTRACTIVES				0.1	0.2		
3 MANUFACTURING–IND MANUFACTUR				79.6	86.6		
31 FOOD BEV TOBACCO–ALIM BOISS TAB				47.8	60.2		
32 TEXTILES–INDUSTRIES TEXTILES				6.2	5.6		
33 WOOD & PRODUCTS–BOIS & PRODUITS				0.4	0.2		
34 PAPER & PRODUCTS–PAPIER & PRODT				1.4	1.1		
35 CHEMICALS–INDUSTRIES CHIMIQUES				2.8	1.9		
36 NON METAL MIN–MIN NON METAL				1.0	2.1		
37 BASIC METAL–IND METAL BASE				1.6	1.3		
38 METAL MANUF–MANUF METAL				15.7	12.8		
39 OTH MANUF IND–AUTRES MANUF				2.8	1.3		

3. TRADE BY PRINCIPAL COUNTRIES OF PURCHASE AND SALE (VALUE IN MILLION U.S. DOLLARS)
ECHANGES SELON LES PRINCIPAUX PAYS D'ACHAT ET DE VENTE (VALEUR EN MILLIONS DE DOLLARS EU)

COUNTRIES–PAYS	GENERAL IMPORTS C.I.F. IMPORTATIONS GENERALES C.A.F				
	1993	1994	1995	1996	1997
World	628.0	659.3	840.7	1079.2	1171.7
Africa		0.6	0.2	0.4	2.4
Americas	19.8	20.0	11.9	29.5	51.7
– Northern America	16.4	19.8	11.3	13.5	42.3
– LAIA	1.7	0.1	0.3	0.4	6.8
– CACM			0.1		0.1
– Caribbean	1.7	0.2	0.0	15.6	1.3
– Rest of America	0.0		0.2		1.2
Asia excl fmr USSR	4.5	17.8	16.7	29.2	44.5
– Middle East	1.2	5.3	7.2	12.9	14.8
Asia former USSR	60.1	23.8	11.7	10.4	11.5
Europe excl fmr USSR	154.2	137.2	230.6	341.1	459.4
– European Union	67.2	67.5	115.2	162.6	234.0
– Eastern Europe	82.8	65.4	105.0	161.2	204.5
– Rest of Europe	4.2	4.4	10.4	17.3	20.8
Europe former USSR	389.4	459.7	569.2	666.2	601.9
Oceania		0.1	0.4		0.0
Other			0.1		
Russian Federation	221.7	309.3	278.0	295.3	333.3
Ukraine	129.7	122.7	228.5	297.1	211.3
Romania/Roumanie	68.4	42.6	56.0	72.1	101.3
Germany/Allemagne	23.6	35.6	45.6	65.9	94.7
Belarus/Bélarus	32.5	20.1	50.7	61.1	48.6
Bulgaria/Bulgarie	4.9	10.1	31.9	58.4	61.7
Italy/Italie	8.7	8.7	19.3	33.9	48.6
USA/Etats–Unis d'Amer	14.2	19.2	10.7	12.1	40.8
Azerbaijan/Azerbaïdjan	39.0	12.0	5.5	4.6	3.5
Hungary/Hongrie	7.0	7.0	8.5	14.2	15.8
Netherlands/Pays–Bas	10.4	3.2	6.5	10.5	12.0
Switzerland,Liechtenst.	3.3	2.4	8.6	10.8	12.8
Turkey/Turquie	0.5	3.4	6.8	11.9	13.5
France, Monaco	5.6	2.0	6.5	6.9	13.3
Poland/Pologne	1.8	4.4	4.2	9.8	13.4
Austria/Autriche	2.9	2.1	7.8	9.0	11.2
Israel/Israël	1.4	1.7	5.8	12.3	9.5
Belgium–Luxembourg	2.8	4.0	9.4	5.5	7.7
Lithuania/Lituanie	2.0	4.1	7.3	8.2	6.1
Spain/Espagne	4.7	0.3	1.3	9.1	11.1
United Kingdom	5.1	2.1	5.5	3.3	8.5
Kazakhstan	9.4	3.1	2.5	2.5	4.9
Greece/Grèce	0.2	3.8	5.0	3.6	8.9
Denmark/Danemark	0.4	1.9	4.1	4.9	7.2
Cuba				15.6	1.2
Czech Republic	0.5	1.4	2.6	2.8	9.0
Turkmenistan/Turkménistn	5.9	5.0	0.8		1.3
Latvia/Lettonie	1.7	2.3	3.1	3.3	1.8
India/Inde	0.0	4.3	1.1	2.0	3.6
Uzbekistan/Ouzbékistan	1.8	1.8	2.1	2.5	1.2
Slovakia/Slovaquie	0.1		1.9	3.9	3.4
Sweden/Suède	1.2	2.3	1.2	2.3	2.1
Finland/Finlande	1.6	0.4	1.9	2.9	2.2
Portugal		0.1	0.2	3.5	4.9
Korea, Republic of		0.5	0.6	0.6	6.7
China/Chine	0.7	5.6	0.2		1.6
Slovenia/Slovénie	0.2	1.2	0.8	2.8	2.3
Japan/Japon	0.2	0.1	1.3	1.1	4.5
Estonia/Estonie	1.8	1.1	1.7	1.2	0.9
Canada	2.2	0.6	0.6	1.4	1.5

COUNTRIES–PAYS	GENERAL EXPORTS F.O.B. EXPORTATIONS GENERALES F.O.B.				
	1993	1994	1995	1996	1997
Monde	483.4	566.0	745.5	801.6	874.4
Afrique	0.0	0.1	0.6	1.6	1.5
Amériques	1.0	3.6	11.9	21.6	64.8
– Amérique du Nord	1.0	3.6	9.6	18.3	64.0
– ALAI		0.0		3.3	0.3
– MCAC			2.3		
– Caraïbes		0.0			0.2
– Autre Amérique		0.0	0.1		0.3
Asie anc. URSS exclus	6.0	5.0	19.3	18.1	11.2
– Moyen–Orient	4.2	3.4	13.1	11.5	7.7
Asie ancienne URSS	52.7	24.2	21.4	34.1	12.5
Europe anc. URSS exclus	163.8	143.0	230.0	177.1	166.9
– Union Européenne	36.8	39.1	86.2	77.9	90.0
– Europe de l'Est	125.8	100.7	138.0	97.4	74.4
– Autre de l'Europe	1.2	3.1	5.7	1.8	2.5
Europe ancienne URSS	259.8	390.1	462.2	546.5	614.7
Océanie	0.0	0.0	0.1	1.4	
Autre			0.0		
Russian Federation	172.1	289.7	360.1	430.1	508.9
Romania/Roumanie	104.0	83.4	103.7	74.9	58.9
Ukraine	62.9	68.6	58.9	47.5	49.4
Germany/Allemagne	15.3	19.7	45.4	29.9	32.4
Belarus/Bélarus	17.3	23.7	26.5	34.4	35.4
USA/Etats–Unis d'Amer	0.9	1.8	7.9	11.0	58.2
Italy/Italie	6.2	7.8	15.6	21.1	23.9
Bulgaria/Bulgarie	16.5	10.4	21.4	12.8	10.0
Azerbaijan/Azerbaïdjan	31.3	13.0	5.4	6.5	1.5
Lithuania/Lituanie	3.7	4.1	9.8	14.3	11.0
Latvia/Lettonie	1.8	2.9	4.6	14.6	8.0
Kazakhstan	6.7	7.2	8.6	7.6	0.4
Turkey/Turquie	1.7	1.4	11.5	9.5	5.5
Austria/Autriche	0.7	1.1	9.9	3.7	7.5
Netherlands/Pays–Bas	0.6	1.4	2.3	8.7	5.6
Greece/Grèce	0.9	5.1	2.7	4.3	4.8
United Kingdom	1.0	3.5	6.2	5.3	1.3
Canada	0.2	1.8	1.6	7.3	5.8
Uzbekistan/Ouzbékistan	2.4	1.4	2.8	3.3	6.3
Hungary/Hongrie	3.0	2.6	5.7	2.7	1.7
Turkmenistan/Turkménistn	9.7	1.1	1.5	2.9	0.1
Estonia/Estonie	2.0	1.1	2.3	5.6	1.9
Ireland/Irlande	5.5	0.2	0.5		5.4
Switzerland,Liechtenst.	1.0	2.4	4.1	1.4	1.8
Poland/Pologne	0.7	2.5	3.0	1.7	1.6
France, Monaco	0.1	0.1	1.4	2.1	5.7
Kyrgyzstan/Kirghizistan	1.1	0.4	0.3	6.2	0.1
Armenia/Arménie	0.2	0.2	2.6	4.7	0.2
Georgia/Géorgie	0.5	0.6	0.1	2.7	3.9
Spain/Espagne		0.1	1.6	2.5	2.7
Slovakia/Slovaquie	0.2		3.0	2.8	0.6
Israel/Israël	0.2	0.9	3.4	1.9	
Sweden/Suède	5.9		0.1		0.2
Czech Republic	1.1	1.6	0.7	1.9	0.8
Cyprus/Chypre	1.8	0.7	0.9	0.6	1.1
Peru/Pérou				3.0	0.2
India/Inde	0.0	0.1	0.3	2.3	0.2
Albania/Albanie	0.2	0.3	0.7	0.6	0.8
Viet Nam	0.3	0.0	1.3	0.7	0.2
El Salvador			2.3		

(VALUE AS PERCENTAGE OF WORLD TOTAL)(VALEURS EN POURCENTAGE DU TOTAL MONDIAL)

	1988	1989	1990	1991	1992	1993	1994	1995	1996	1997
Africa							0.1	0.0	0.0	0.2
Americas						3.2	3.0	1.4	2.7	4.4
– Northern America						2.6	3.0	1.3	1.3	3.6
– LAIA						0.3	0.0	0.0	0.0	0.6
– CACM								0.0		0.0
– Caribbean						0.3	0.0	0.0	1.4	0.1
– Rest of America						0.0		0.0		0.1
Asia excl fmr USSR						0.7	2.7	2.0	2.7	3.8
– Middle East						0.2	0.8	0.9	1.2	1.3
Asia former USSR						9.6	3.6	1.4	1.0	1.0
Europe excl fmr USSR						24.6	20.8	27.4	31.6	39.2
– European Union						10.7	10.2	13.7	15.1	20.0
– Eastern Europe						13.2	9.9	12.5	14.9	17.5
– Rest of Europe						0.7	0.7	1.2	1.6	1.8
Europe former USSR						62.0	69.7	67.7	61.7	51.4
Oceania							0.0	0.0		0.0
Other								0.0		
Russian Federation						35.3	46.9	33.1	27.4	28.4
Ukraine						20.7	18.6	27.2	27.5	18.0
Romania/Roumanie						10.9	6.5	6.7	6.7	8.6
Germany/Allemagne						3.8	5.4	5.4	6.1	8.1
Belarus/Bélarus						5.2	3.0	6.0	5.7	4.1
Bulgaria/Bulgarie						0.8	1.5	3.8	5.4	5.3
Italy/Italie						1.4	1.3	2.3	3.1	4.1
USA/Etats–Unis d'Amer						2.3	2.9	1.3	1.1	3.5
Azerbaijan/Azerbaïdjan						6.2	1.8	0.7	0.4	0.3
Hungary/Hongrie						1.1	1.1	1.0	1.3	1.3

	1988	1989	1990	1991	1992	1993	1994	1995	1996	1997
Afrique						0.0	0.0	0.1	0.2	0.2
Amériques						0.2	0.6	1.6	2.7	7.4
– Amérique du Nord						0.2	0.6	1.3	2.3	7.3
– ALAI							0.0		0.4	0.0
– MCAC								0.3		
– Caraïbes							0.0			0.0
– Autre Amérique							0.0	0.0		0.0
Asie anc. URSS exclus						1.2	0.9	2.6	2.3	1.3
– Moyen–Orient						0.9	0.6	1.8	1.4	0.9
Asie ancienne URSS						10.9	4.3	2.9	4.3	1.4
Europe anc. URSS exclus						33.9	25.3	30.8	22.1	19.1
– Union Européenne						7.6	6.9	11.6	9.7	10.3
– Europe de l'Est						26.0	17.8	18.5	12.2	8.5
– Autre de l'Europe						0.2	0.6	0.8	0.2	0.3
Europe ancienne URSS						53.7	68.9	62.0	68.2	70.3
Océanie						0.0	0.0	0.0	0.2	
Autre								0.0		
Russian Federation						35.6	51.2	48.3	53.7	58.2
Romania/Roumanie						21.5	14.7	13.9	9.3	6.7
Ukraine						13.0	12.1	7.9	5.9	5.7
Germany/Allemagne						3.2	3.5	6.1	3.7	3.7
Belarus/Bélarus						3.6	4.2	3.6	4.3	4.1
USA/Etats–Unis d'Amer						0.2	0.3	1.1	1.4	6.7
Italy/Italie						1.3	1.4	2.1	2.6	2.7
Bulgaria/Bulgarie						3.4	1.8	2.9	1.6	1.1
Azerbaijan/Azerbaïdjan						6.5	2.3	0.7	0.8	0.2
Lithuania/Lituanie						0.8	0.7	1.3	1.8	1.3

4. General Imports C.I.F. by Commodities according to the S.I.T.C. (Rev. 2) in million U.S. Dollars
Importations Générales C.A.F. par Produits d'après la C.T.C.I. (Rév. 2) en millions de Dollars E.U.

SITC CTCI	COMMODITY	1994 QUANTITY QUANTITE	1994 VALUE VALEUR	1995 QUANTITY QUANTITE	1995 VALUE VALEUR	1996 QUANTITY QUANTITE	1996 VALUE VALEUR	1997 QUANTITY QUANTITE	1997 VALUE VALEUR	PRODUIT
	ALL COMMODITIES		659.3		840.8		1079.2			TOUS PRODUITS
0	FOOD AND LIVE ANIMALS		34.6		49.5					ALIMENTS,ANIMAUX VIVANTS
03	FISH AND PREPARATIONS		2.4		5.5					POISSONS ET PREPARATIONS
034	FISH,FRESH,CHILLED,FROZN	W 1495	0.9	W 4888	3.4					POISSON FRAIS, REFRIG,CONG
0342	FISH FROZEN,EXCL FILLETS	W 1450	0.9	W 4543	3.3					POISSONS CONGELES
04	CEREALS AND PREPARATIONS		19.3		20.5		15.1			CEREALES ET PRODUITS
041	WHEAT ETC UNMILLED	W 38574	6.2	W 62753	5.1					FROMENT,EPEAUTRE
0411	DURUM WHEAT UNMILLED	W 7198	1.3	W 42194	3.2					FROMENT DUR NON MOULU
0412	OTHER WHEAT ETC UNMILLED	W 31376	5.0	W 20559	1.9					AUTRE FROMENT NON MOULU
044	MAIZE UNMILLED	W 39266	9.8	W 39224	6.4					MAIS NON MOULU
045	CEREALS NES UNMILLED	W 16838	1.1	W 64264	4.8					AUTRES CEREALES NON MOULUES
0451	RYE UNMILLED	W 16470	1.1	W 63559	4.4					SEIGLE NON MOULU
05	VEGETABLES AND FRUIT		4.5		7.3					LEGUMES ET FRUITS
054	VEG ETC FRSH,SMPLY PRSVD	W 15911	2.5	W 21937	4.5		13.1			LEGUMES FRAIS,CONG,SECS
0541	POTATOES FRSH EXCL SWEET	W 13877	1.8	W 18120	3.3					POMMES DE TERRE
06	SUGAR AND PREPS,HONEY		2.1		4.9		25.1			SUCRES ET PRODUITS
061	SUGAR AND HONEY	W 15051	1.9	W 19927	4.6					SUCRES ET MIEL
0611	RAW BEET AND CANE SUGAR	W 3165	1.0	W 7306	2.8					SUCRES BRUTS
07	COFFEE,TEA,COCOA,SPICES		2.2		2.1					CAFE,THE,CACAO,EPICES
081	*FEEDING STUFF FOR ANIML	W 7729	2.3	W 19179	3.5					NOURRITURE POUR ANIMAUX
1	BEVERAGES AND TOBACCO		7.0		15.7					BOISSONS ET TABACS
11	BEVERAGES		3.0		14.0		34.1			BOISSONS
111	NON-ALCOHL BEVERAGES NES	W 915	0.4	W 5020	2.7					BOISSONS NON ALCOOLIQUES
112	ALCOHOLIC BEVERAGES	W 2801	2.7	W 12924	11.4					BOISSONS ALCOOLIQUES
1121	WINE OF FRESH GRAPES ETC	W 1737	1.4	W 10501	7.8					VINS DE RAISINS FRAIS
11212	WINE OF FRESH GRAPES	W 1725	1.4	W 9991	7.7					VINS DE MOUTS DE RAISINS
1124	DISTILLED ALCOHOLIC BEVS	W 309	1.0	W 1075	3.2					ALCOOLS,EAUX-DE-VIE
11249	OTH ALCOHOLC BEVS,CMPNDS	W 279	0.8	W 1069	3.2					BOISSONS ALCOOLIQUES NDA
12	TOBACCO AND MANUFACTURES		4.0		1.7		5.1			TABACS BRUTS FABRIQUES
121	TOBACCO UNMNFCTRD,REFUSE	W 1921	2.4	W 1307	1.3					TABACS BRUTS,DECHETS
2	CRUDE MATERLS,EXCL FUELS		19.2		31.6					MAT BRUTES NON COMESTIBLES
21	HIDES,SKINS,FURS UNDRSSD		2.1		1.7					CUIRS,PEAUX BRUTS
22	OIL SEEDS,OLEAGINOUS FRT		0.5		1.9		9.1			GRAINES,FRUITS OLEAGINEUX
24	CORK AND WOOD		3.9		6.3		15.1			LIEGE ET BOIS
248	WOOD SHAPED,SLEEPERS		2.8		4.8					BOIS SIMPLEMENT TRAVAILLES
2482	LUMBER SHAPED CONIFER		2.4		3.6					CONIFERES SCIES,RABOTES
24821	LUMBER SAWN ETC CONIFER	W 24668	1.9	W 33029	3.2					CONIFERES SCIES LONGITUD
26	TEXTILE FIBRES AND WASTE		6.6		6.7					FIBRES TEXTILES
263	COTTON	W 376	0.4	W 656	1.1		6.1			COTON
266	SYNTHETIC FIBRES TO SPIN	W 1390	3.2	W 1217	2.3					FIBRES SYNTHETIQUES
268	WOOL(EXC TOPS),ANML HAIR	W 1439	2.3	W 778	1.9		10.1			LAINES ET POILS
27	CRUDE FERTLZR,MINRLS NES		1.8		3.7					ENGRAIS MINERAUX BRUTS
28	METALLIFEROUS ORES,SCRAP		0.7		4.4					MINERAIS METAL,DECHETS
288	NONFERR METAL SCRAP NES	W 837	0.7	W 4194	4.2					DECHETS NON FERREUX
2882	OTHER BASE MTL SCRAP NES	W 837	0.7	W 4148	4.2					AUTRES DECHETS
28821	COPPER WASTE AND SCRAP	W 767	0.7	W 2843	3.0					DECHETS DE CUIVRE
29	CRUDE ANIMAL,VEG MAT NES		3.3		5.7					MATIERES BRUTES ANIM,VEGET
292	CRUDE VEG MATERIALS NES		3.3		5.5					MAT BRUTES VEGETALES NDA
2925	SEEDS,ETC FOR PLANTING	W 454	2.7	W 846	4.8					SEMENCES NDA
3	MINERAL FUELS ETC		364.3		386.9		392.0			COMBUSTIBLES MINERAUX LUB
32	COAL,COKE AND BRIQUETTES		55.7		50.3					HOUILLES,COKES,BRIQUETTES
322	COAL,LIGNITE AND PEAT	W 2443968	55.4	W 1315092	49.0					HOUILLES,LIGNITES,TOURBE
3221	ANTHRACITE,NOT AGGLOMRTD	W 2357931	53.3	W 1106026	41.5					ANTHRACITE
3222	OTH COAL,NOT AGGLOMERATD	W 85693	2.1	W 208702	7.5					AUTRES HOUILLES
33	PETROLEUM AND PRODUCTS		133.3		183.2					PETROLE ET DERIVES
334	PETROLEUM PRODUCTS,REFIN	W 998635	128.1	W 1165896	180.5					PRODUITS RAFFINES
3341	GASOLINE,OTH LIGHT OILS	W 208587	37.4	W 1165357	179.8					ESSENCES POUR MOTEURS
33411	MOTOR,AVIATION SPIRIT	W 183965	32.4	W 1165357	179.8					ESSENCES MOTEURS D'AVIONS
33419	OTH LIGHT PETROLEUM OILS	W 20087	4.2							AUTRES HUILES LEGERES
3342	KEROSENE,OTH MEDIUM OILS	W 14225	2.4							PETR LAMPANTS,AUT HUIL
3343	GAS OILS	W 263608	37.0							GAS OILS
3344	FUEL OILS,NES	W 492633	42.9							FUEL OILS
3345	LUBS,PETROLEUM OILS NES	W 19582	8.6	W 539	0.7					HUILES LUBRIFIANTES
33451	LUBS(HIGH PETR CONT) ETC	W 18548	7.7							HUILES LUBRIF,H LOURDES
335	RESIDUAL PETRLM PROD NES	W 27682	4.5	W 19017	2.7					PRODUITS RESIDUELS NDA
3352	MINERAL TARS AND PRODCTS	W 8141	2.7	W 3237	0.8					GOUDRONS MINERAUX
341	*GAS,NATURAL AND MANUFCT		165.4	W 30710	105.9					GAZ NATUREL,GAZ MANUFACT
3413	PETROLM GASES,LIQUEFIED	W 45259	12.6	W 30615	3.7					GAZ DE PETROLE LIQUEFIE
34139	OTH HYDROCARBON GAS LQFD	W 44453	12.5	W 13966	1.4					HYDROCARBURES GAZEUX NDA
3414	PETROLEUM GASES, GASEOUS	W 393	152.8	W 95	102.3					GAZ DE PETROLE GAZEUX
351	*ELECTRIC CURRENT	H 615400	10.0	H 1996709	47.6					ENERGIE ELECTRIQUE
5	CHEMCLS,RELATED PROD NES		43.0		76.2					PRODUITS CHIMIQUES
51	ORGANIC CHEMICALS		5.6		8.0		4.1			PROD CHIMIQ ORGANIQUES
512	ALCOHOLS,PHENOLS ETC		4.4		5.4					PHENOLS,PHENOLS-ALCOOLS
5121	ACYCLIC ALCOHOLS,DERIVS		4.4		5.3					ALCOOLS ACYCLIQUES
51216	ETHYL ALC,DENATRD SPIRIT	V 7139	4.3	V 8275	5.2					ALCOOL ETHYLIQUE NON DENAT
52	INORGANIC CHEMICALS		3.5		8.8		9.1			PROD CHIM INORGANIQUES
523	OTHR INORG CHEMICALS ETC		2.5		7.1					AUT PRODUITS CHIMIQUES INORG
5232	OTH MTL CMPD OF INRG ACD	W 12291	1.7	W 39268	5.2					SELS METALLIQUES
52323	NEUTRAL SODIUM CARBONATE	W 9483	0.9	W 37471	4.2					CARBONATE NEUTRE SODIUM
53	DYES,TANNING,COLOUR PROD		2.1		4.2		7.1			PROD TEINTURE,COLORANTS
533	PIGMENTS,PAINTS,ETC	W 1677	1.8	W 2236	3.7					PIGMENTS,PEINTURES,VERNIS
5334	VARNISHES,DISTEMPERS ETC	W 1330	1.4	W 1938	2.9					PEINTURES A L'EAU
53342	OTH PAINTS,VARNISHES ETC	W 1127	1.3	W 1680	2.7					AUTRES PEINTURES,VERNIS
541	*MEDICINAL,PHARM PRODUCT		17.6	K 1636130	18.2		23.1			PROD MEDICINAUX PHARMACEUT
5417	MEDICAMENTS	K 849400	15.1	K 1234130	16.3					MEDICAMENTS
54171	— CONTAINNG ANTIBIOTICS	K 243100	3.6	K 185400	3.0					MED CONTN ANTIBIOTIQUES
54179	— CONTNG OTH SUBSTANCES	K 565200	10.7	K 1021430	12.7					MED CONT AUT SUBSTANCES
55	PERFUME,CLEANING ETC PRD		5.3		6.9		4.1			PROD POUR PARFUM,TOILETTE
553	PERFUMERY,COSMETICS,ETC	W 699	2.5	W 22	1.7					PRODUITS DE PARFUMERIE
554	SOAP,CLEANSING ETC PREPS	W 3638	2.5	W 4070	4.0					SAVONS,PRODUITS DETERSIFS
5542	WASHING PREPARATIONS ETC	W 2470	1.8	W 3106	3.0					PROD ORG TENSIO-ACT NDA
572	*EXPLOSIVES,PYROTECH PRO	W 3	0.1	W 109	0.3		22.1			EXPLOSIFS
58	PLASTIC MATERIALS ETC		5.0		7.7					MAT PLAST ARTIFICIELLES
583	POLYMERIZATION ETC PRODS	W 4493	3.4	W 5335	6.4					PROD POLYMERISATION
59	CHEMICAL MATERIALS NES		3.5		21.3					MAT PROD CHIMIQUES NDA
591	PESTICIDES,DISINFECTANTS	W 453	2.0	W 2046	17.8					DESINF,INSECT,FONG,HERB
5911	INSECTICIDES,FOR RETAIL	W 16	0.1	W 206	2.6					INSECTICIDES VENTE DET
5912	FUNGICIDES,FOR RETAIL	W 68	0.1	W 286	4.4					FONGICIDES VENTE AU DET
5913	HERBICIDES,FOR RETAIL	W 229	1.8	W 1108	10.1					HERBICIDES VENTE AU DET
6	BASIC MANUFACTURES		75.4		121.1					ART MANUFACTURES

4. General Imports C.I.F. by Commodities according to the S.I.T.C. (Rev. 2) in million U.S. Dollars
Importations Générales C.A.F. par Produits d'après la C.T.C.I. (Rév. 2) en millions de Dollars E.U.

SITC CTCI	COMMODITY	1994 QUANTITY QUANTITE	1994 VALUE VALEUR	1995 QUANTITY QUANTITE	1995 VALUE VALEUR	1996 QUANTITY QUANTITE	1996 VALUE VALEUR	1997 QUANTITY QUANTITE	1997 VALUE VALEUR	PRODUIT
62	RUBBER MANUFACTURES NES		2.8		5.7		15.1			CAOUTCHOUC MANUFACTURE
625	RUBBER TYRES, TUBES ETC		2.3		4.6					PNEUS CAOUTCHOUC VULCANISE
63	WOOD,CORK MANUFACTRS NES		3.8		5.3					OUVRAGES LIEGE ET BOIS
64	PAPER,PAPERBOARD AND MFR		11.1		27.3		47.1			PAPIERS,CARTONS & OUVRAGES
641	PAPER AND PAPERBOARD		7.5		18.4					PAPIERS ET CARTONS
6411	NEWSPRINT	W 792	0.3	W 4203	2.8					PAPIER JOURNAL
6415	PAPER,PAPERBRD,BULK,NES	W 12894	3.8	W 6042	8.5					PAPIERS,CARTONS ROULEAUX
64159	OTHER PAPER ETC,BULK,NES	W 12148	3.5	W 2569	5.8					AUT PAPIER ROULEAUX FEUILLES
642	PAPER,ETC,PRECUT,ARTS OF		3.6	W 6930	8.9					PAP,CARTONS DECOUPES
6421	PAPER ETC CONTAINERS	W 4832	2.5	W 5531	6.0					BOITES,SACS EMBALLAGES
65	TEXTILE YARN,FABRICS,ETC		23.4		28.2		13.1			FILS,TISSUS,ARTICLES TEXTILE
651	TEXTILE YARN	W 2244	4.3		5.4					FILS TEXTILES
652	COTTON FABRICS,WOVEN		3.6		3.2					TISSUS DE COTON
6522	WOVEN COTTON BLEACHD,ETC		3.2		2.2					TISSUS COTON BLANCHIS ETC
65224	BLCHED COTTON FABRIC NES		2.5		1.2					AUT TIS PLUS 85% COT BLANCHI
653	WOVN MAN-MADE FIB FABRIC		2.9		5.3					TISSUS FIBRES SYNTH,ARTIF
654	OTH WOVEN TEXTILE FABRIC		7.2		6.2					TISSUS AUT COTON SYNT,ARTIF
6543	WOVEN WOOL ETC FABRC NES	A 2003	5.0	A 892	2.3					TISSUS LAINE,POILS FINS NDA
65432	WOOL-DISC SYN FIBR FABRC	A 1941	4.8	A 876	2.2					TISSUS LAINE MEL SYNT DISC
655	KNITTED,ETC FABRICS	A 279	0.9	A 3444	2.8					ETOF BONNETERIE PIECES ETC
6552	OTHER KNIT ETC FAB NONEL	A 279	0.9	A 3444	2.8					ETOF BON NON ELAS NON SYNT
657	SPECIAL TXTL FABRC,PRODS		1.6		3.9					TISSUS SPECIAUX
658	TEXTILE ARTICLES NES		2.5		1.0					ART FACONNES MAT TEXTILES
66	NONMETAL MINERAL MFS NES		14.0		23.7		41.1			ART MIN NON METALLIQUES
661	LIME,CEMENT,BLDG PRODS		3.5		3.6					CHAUX,CIMENTS MAT CONSTR
6618	MNRL BLDG PRD UNFIRD NES		2.1		1.8					MAT CONST AMIANTE-CIMENT
662	CLAY,REFRACTORY BLDG PRD		4.1		1.8					MAT CONST REFRACTAIRES
6623	REFRACTORY BUILDING PROD	W 4086	3.4	W 4297	0.6					BRIQUES REFRACTAIRES
66233	REFRACTORY CEMENT,MORTAR	W 1726	3.2	W 173	0.3					CIMENTS REFRACTAIRES
665	GLASSWARE		5.2		14.9					OUVRAGES EN VERRE
6651	BOTTLES ETC OF GLASS	MN 51106	4.8		14.6					RECIPIENTS EN VERRE
66511	GLASS BOTTLES ETC NONVAC	MN 51106	4.8		14.6					BONBONNES,BOUTEILLES,ETC
67	IRON AND STEEL		12.1		16.4		15.1			FER ET ACIER
673	IRON,STEEL SHAPES ETC	W 16066	2.3	W 3269	1.1					BARRES,PROFIL FER,ACIER
674	IRN,STL UNIV,PLATE,SHEET	W 21359	5.4	W 16800	6.8					LARGES PLATS,TOLES
6745	IRN,STL MED PLATE,ROLLED	W 2975	0.7	W 9608	3.1					TOLES 3 A 4.75 MM
678	IRON,STL TUBES,PIPES,ETC	W 11145	2.8	W 13000	6.7					TUBES,TUYAUX EN FONTE,FER
6782	IRON,STL SEAMLESS TUBES	W 7245	1.9	W 5538	3.2					TUBES,TUYAUX SANS SOUDURE
6783	IRON,STL TUBES,PIPES NES	W 3368	0.8	W 6856	3.1					AUT TUBES,TUYAUX FER,ACIER
68	NON-FERROUS METALS		2.4		4.9					METAUX NON FERREUX
684	ALUMINIUM	W 986	1.8	W 1284	3.7		6.1			ALUMINIUM
6842	ALUMINIUM,ALLOYS WORKED	W 895	1.8	W 843	3.5					ALUMINIUM,ALLIAGES OUVRE
69	METAL MANUFACTURES NES		5.5		7.9		23.1			ART MANUFACT EN METAL NDA
699	BASE METAL MFRS NES		2.5		3.5					ART MANUFACTURES MET NDA
7	MACHINES,TRANSPORT EQUIP		84.4		127.9		188.0			MACHINES MATERIEL TRANSPORT
71	POWER GENERATING EQUIPMT		3.7		6.6					MACHINES GENERATRICES
713	INTRNL COMBUS PSTN ENGIN		2.1		4.1					MOTEURS EXPL COMB INT, PIECE
72	MACHS FOR SPCL INDUSTRYS		16.6		33.9					MAC SPECIALES POUR INDUST
721	AGRIC MACHY,EXC TRACTORS		5.9		9.7					MACHINES AGRICOLES
7212	HARVESTING ETC MACHINES		1.0		3.0					ENGINS POUR LA RECOLTE
7219	AGRICULTURE MACHINES NES		2.9		4.6					ENGINS AGRICOLES NDA
72191	WINE-MAKING ETC MACHINERY	N 36	2.5	N 235	3.0					APPAREILS DE VINIFICATION
727	FOOD MACHRY NON-DOMESTIC		6.5		15.6					MACH INDUSTRIES ALIMENT
7272	OTH FOOD PROC MCHY,PARTS		5.8		14.2					AUT MACH IND ALIMENTAIRE
72722	INDUS FOOD PROC MACH NES	N 2053	5.2	N 419	10.8					MACHINES BOULANGERIE
72729	PTS NES OF MCHY OF 72722	W 54	0.4		3.1					PIECES MACH DU 727.22
728	OTH MACHY FOR SPCL INDUS		1.6		4.7					AUT MACH IND PARTICULIERES
7284	MACHY FOR SPCL INDUS NES		1.2		4.4					MACH SPEC IND PARTICUL.
72841	GLASS-WORKING MACHY NES			W 163	3.5					MACH TRAVAIL VERRE ETC
74	GENRL INDUSTRL MACHY NES		12.5		18.9					MACH APP INDUSTRIE
741	HEATING,COOLING EQUIPMNT		2.3		4.1					MACH CHAUFFAGE,PIECES
743	PUMPS NES,CENTRFUGES ETC		2.9		1.7					POMPES COMPRES,VENT ETC
745	NONELEC MACHY,TOOLS NES		3.8		8.7					AUT MACH NON ELEC,PIECES
7452	OTH NONELEC MCHS,PTS NES		3.8		8.6					AUT MACH NON ELEC,PIECES
74522	PACKAGNG,BOTTLNG,ETC MCH	W 115	2.9	W 211	6.1					MACH NETT BOUTEILLES,ETC
75	OFFICE MACHNES,ADP EQUIP		5.5		5.5					MACH BUREAU TRAIT AUTOM
752	AUTOMTIC DATA PROC EQUIP		3.3		2.9					MACH TRAIT INFORMATION
76	TELECOMM,SOUND EQUIPMENT		8.4		19.4					EQUIPMENT DE TELECOM
764	TELECOM EQPT,PTS,ACC NES		7.0		18.5					EQUIP TELECOM,PIECES
7641	LINE TELEPHONE,ETC EQUIP		3.1	N 480	5.4					APP TELEPHON PAR FIL
7643	TV,RADIO TRANSMITTRS ETC	N 430	0.3	N 657	2.7					APP EMET TELE RADIO
7649	PTS NES OF EQUIPMT OF 76	W 81	3.4		10.0					PIECES DE LA DIV 76
76491	PTS NES OF APPAR OF 7641	W 6	0.2	W 55	4.5					PIECES POUR 764.1
76493	TELECOMM EQUIPMT PTS NES	W 57	3.2		5.0					PIECES 761,762,764.3,8
77	ELECTRIC MACHNRY NES ETC		18.6		21.6					MACH APP ELECT NDA
773	ELECTR DISTRIBUTNG EQUIP	W 841	2.1	W 601	3.5					EQUIPMT DISTRIBUTION ELECT
7731	INSULATED WIRE,CABLE ETC	W 765	2.1	W 438	3.2					FILS,CABLES ISOLES ELECT
776	TRANSISTORS,VALVES,ETC		3.7		5.0					LAMPES,TUBES,VALVES
7761	TV PICTURE TUBES	N 113676	2.9	N 111484	3.9					TUBES CATHODIQUES
778	ELECTRICAL MACHINERY NES		9.3		6.6					AUTRES MACH ELECT NDA
7781	BATTERIES,ACCUMULATORS		2.4		2.9					PILES ET ACCUMULATEURS
77812	ELECTRIC ACCUMULATORS	N 46524	2.3	N 1896	2.4					ACCUMULATEURS ELECTRIQ
7788	OTH ELEC MACHY,EQUIP NES	W 1680	6.0	W 135	2.0					AUT MACH APP ELEC NDA
77887	ELECTRICAL CARBONS	W 1469	4.4	W 11	0.2					PIECES CHARBON,GRAPHITE
78	ROAD VEHICLES		18.4		19.4		31.1			VEHICULES ROUTIERS
781	PASS MOTOR VEH EXC BUSES	N 947	4.7	N 574	6.2					AUTO TRANSPORT PERSONNES
782	LORRIES,SPCL MTR VEH NES	N 1129	4.1	N 549	3.3					VEHICULES SPECIAUX,MARCH
7821	LORRIES,TRUCKS	N 1043	3.5	N 469	2.6					VEHICULES TRANSP MARCHAND
784	MOTOR VEH PRTS,ACCES NES		7.2		6.6					PIECES 722,781,782,783
7849	OTHER MOTOR VEHCL PARTS	W 10721	7.1	W 11	6.2					PIECES 722,781,782,783
8	MISC MANUFACTURED GOODS		30.5		29.9					ART MANUFACTURES DIVERS
821	*FURNITURE,PARTS THEREOF		4.4		2.5		4.1			MEUBLES ET PIECES
8219	FURNITURE AND PARTS NES	W 2336	3.9	W 1407	2.1					AUTRES MEUBLES ET PIECES
82192	WOOD FURNITURE NES	W 2103	3.6	W 1178	1.8					MEUBLES NDA EN BOIS
84	CLOTHING AND ACCESSORIES		9.8		7.3		8.1			VETEMENTS
843	WOMENS OUTERWEAR NONKNIT		3.7	N 14176	0.6					VET DESSUS FEMMES MAT TEX
8439	— OTHER OUTER GARMENTS		3.1	N 717	0.2					AUT VET DES FEM MAT TEXT
844	UNDER GARMENTS NOT KNIT		1.6		3.5					VETEMENT DESSOUS MAT TEX
8441	— MENS SHIRTS		1.6		3.4					CHEMISES HOMMES MAT TEXT
84412	—— OF SYNTHETIC FIBRES		1.4		3.3					CHEMISES HOMMES FIB SYNT
845	OUTERWEAR KNIT NONELASTC		2.4	N 32194	0.3					VET DESSOUS,ACCES BONNET

4. General Imports C.I.F. by Commodities according to the S.I.T.C. (Rev. 2) in million U.S. Dollars
Importations Générales C.A.F. par Produits d'après la C.T.C.I. (Rév. 2) en millions de Dollars E.U.

SITC CTCI	COMMODITY	1994 QUANTITY QUANTITE	1994 VALUE VALEUR	1995 QUANTITY QUANTITE	1995 VALUE VALEUR	1996 QUANTITY QUANTITE	1996 VALUE VALEUR	1997 QUANTITY QUANTITE	1997 VALUE VALEUR	PRODUIT
851	*FOOTWEAR	P 582996	2.9	P 299902	1.8		3.1			CHAUSSURES
87	PRECISION INSTRUMNTS NES		3.5		3.9					INSTRUM,APPAR SCIENT NDA
89	MISC MANUFCTRD GOODS NES		8.8		12.0					ART MANUFACTURES DIVERS
892	PRINTED MATTER	W 1410	3.8		2.1		1.1			IMPRIMES
8921	PRINTED BOOKS,GLOBES,ETC	W 1181	3.0	W 197	0.4					LIVRES,BROCHURES,CARTES
89211	PRINTED BOOKS,PAMPHLETS	W 1179	3.0	W 196	0.4					LIVRES,BROCHURES
893	ARTICLES OF PLASTIC NES		2.7		6.8					OUVRAGES EN MAT DIVIS 58
8931	PLSTC PACKG CONTNRS,LIDS	W 712	1.3	W 1704	4.5					ART TRANSP EMBALLAGE ETC

5. General Exports F.O.B. by Commodities according to the S.I.T.C. (Rev. 2) in million U.S. Dollars
Exportations Générales F.O.B. par Produits d'après la C.T.C.I. (Rév. 2) en millions de Dollars E.U.

SITC CTCI	COMMODITY	1994 QUANTITY QUANTITE	1994 VALUE VALEUR	1995 QUANTITY QUANTITE	1995 VALUE VALEUR	1996 QUANTITY QUANTITE	1996 VALUE VALEUR	1997 QUANTITY QUANTITE	1997 VALUE VALEUR	PRODUIT
	ALL COMMODITIES		566.1		745.6		801.6			TOUS PRODUITS
0	FOOD AND LIVE ANIMALS		230.6		296.0					ALIMENTS,ANIMAUX VIVANTS
001	*LIVE ANIMALS FOR FOOD	N 17328	0.8		7.3					ANIMAUX VIVANTS
0011	BOVINE SPECIES,LIVE	N 7243	0.5	N 14622	3.5					ESPECE BOVINE
00119	— OTHR THAN FR BREEDING	N 7098	0.4	N 14622	3.5					BOVINS NON REPRODUCTEURS
0013	SWINE,LIVE	N 1243	0.2	N 29760	3.3					ESPECE PORCINE
01	MEAT AND PREPARATIONS		34.4		49.1		44.1			VIANDES ET PREPARATIONS
011	MEAT FRESH,CHILLD,FROZEN	W 30066	32.5	W 37128	44.8					VIANDES FRAICHES,REF,CONGE
0111	BOVINE MEAT FRESH,FROZEN	W 23235	24.1	W 29578	35.0					VIANDES BOVIN FRAI,REF
01111	BOVINE MEAT WITH BONE IN	W 23161	24.1	W 28867	34.2					VIANDES BOVIN NON DESOSS
0113	PIG MEAT FRESH,CHLD,FRZN	W 5682	7.8	W 4948	7.5					VIANDE DE PORC
014	MEAT PREPD,PRSVD,NES ETC	W 1112	2.0	W 1840	4.4					CONSERVES DE VIANDES
0149	OTH PREPARD,PRESRVD MEAT	W 850	1.5	W 1614	3.7					AUTRES PREP DE VIANDES
02	DAIRY PRODCTS,BIRDS'EGGS		11.5		15.3		13.1			PRODUITS LAITIERS,OEUFS
022	MILK AND CREAM	W 6160	3.9	W 8637	8.8					LAIT ET CREME
0224	MILK,CREAM PRESERVED ETC	W 3886	3.5	W 5950	8.2					LAIT,CREME CONS,CONC
02242	MILK DRY,1.5% FAT OR LES	W 2836	2.7	W 4772	6.4					LAIT POUDRE INF 1.5%
023	BUTTER	W 3496	6.6	W 1739	5.2					BEURRE
04	CEREALS AND PREPARATIONS		31.9		30.8		24.1			CEREALES ET PRODUITS
041	WHEAT ETC UNMILLED	W 665	0.1	W 110529	12.8					FROMENT,EPEAUTRE
0411	DURUM WHEAT UNMILLED	W 665	0.1	W 83949	9.5					FROMENT DUR NON MOULU
0412	OTHER WHEAT ETC UNMILLED			W 26581	3.3					AUTRE FROMENT NON MOULU
044	MAIZE UNMILLED	W 48628	31.0	W 27573	12.4					MAIS NON MOULU
046	WHEAT ETC MEAL OR FLOUR	W 78	0.1	W 13024	3.8					SEMOULE FARINE,FROMENT
04601	FLOUR OF WHEAT OR MESLIN	W 78	0.1	W 12698	3.7					FARINE DE FROMENT
05	VEGETABLES AND FRUIT		107.5		118.9					LEGUMES ET FRUITS
054	VEG ETC FRSH,SMPLY PRSVD	W 48799	15.4	W 39250	17.0		4.1			LEGUMES FRAIS,CONG,SECS
0544	TOMATOES FRESH	W 12849	2.6	W 6989	1.9					TOMATES FRAICHES
0545	OTHER FRESH VEGETABLES	W 17480	3.6	W 14538	3.6					AUTRES LEGUMES FRAIS,REF
05459	FRESH VEGETABLES NES	W 14452	2.8	W 11975	2.7					LEGUMES FRAIS,REFRI NDA
0546	VEGETABLES SIMPLY PRESVD	W 17759	8.9	W 15232	11.1					LEGUMES CONG,CONSER
05461	VEGETABLES FROZEN	W 17676	8.9	W 15140	11.1					LEGUMES CONGELES
056	VEGTBLES ETC PRSVD,PREPD	W 19499	8.5	W 20825	12.6					CONSERVES DE LEGUMES
0565	VEGTBLES PRSVD,PREPD NES	W 19464	8.5	W 20825	12.6					LEGUMES PREPARES CONSERVE
05651	VEGTBLS,FRUIT IN VINEGAR	W 12678	4.5	W 12855	6.5					LEGUM CONSERV AU VINAIGRE
05659	OTH VEG PRESVD,PREPD NES	W 6786	4.1	W 7970	6.1					LEGUM PREPAP,CONSERV NDA
057	FRUIT,NUTS,FRESH,DRIED	W 254933	55.4	W 100859	31.7		29.1			FRUITS FRAIS OU SECS
0574	APPLES FRESH	W 96393	23.3	W 67189	19.0					POMMES FRAICHES
0575	GRAPES FRESH OR DRIED	W 137014	24.0	W 13703	3.7					RAISINS FRAIS OU SECS
05751	GRAPES FRESH	W 136999	24.0	W 13658	3.7					RAISINS FRAIS
0577	NUTS EDIBLE,FRESH,DRIED	W 1694	3.2	W 3459	4.4					FRUITS A COQUES
05779	NUTS EDIBLE,FRSH,DRY,NES	W 1449	2.8	W 3432	4.4					FRUITS A COQUES NDA
0579	FRUIT FRESH OR DRIED NES	W 19805	5.0	W 16487	4.7					FRUITS FRAIS,SECS NDA
05793	STONE FRUIT FRESH NES	W 14632	3.6	W 13439	3.1					FRUITS A NOYAU NDA FRAIS
058	FRUIT PRESERVED,PREPARED	W 71271	28.4	W 78815	57.8					CONSERVES DE FRUITS
0583	FRUIT JAMS,JELLIES ETC	W 5628	3.0	W 7476	5.0					PATES DE FRUITS CONFITURES
0585	FRUIT OR VEGETABLE JUICE	W 53468	21.4	W 61162	48.2					JUS DE FRUITS
05855	TOMATO JUICE	W 3047	1.0	W 6508	3.0					JUS DE TOMATE
05857	JUICE OF OTHER FRUIT,VEG	W 47495	19.8	W 53350	44.8					JUS AUTRES FRUITS,LEGUMES
0589	FRUIT PREPRD,PRESRVD,NES	W 9916	3.5	W 8668	4.4					FRUITS PREPARES CONSERV
05899	FRUIT,NUTS NES,PRESERVED	W 9737	3.5	W 8668	4.4					FRUITS PREP CONSERV NDA
06	SUGAR AND PREPS,HONEY		37.8		65.8		59.1			SUCRES ET PRODUITS
061	SUGAR AND HONEY	W 138592	34.0	W 179458	63.1					SUCRES ET MIEL
0611	RAW BEET AND CANE SUGAR	W 84456	25.6	W 117478	51.5					SUCRES BRUTS
0612	REFINED SUGAR ETC	W 16085	5.5	W 17498	7.5					SUCRES RAFFINES
0615	MOLASSES	W 36893	2.5	W 44270	3.9					MELASSES
062	SUGAR CANDY NON–CHOCLATE	W 3338	3.9	W 2198	2.8					SUCRERIES
07	COFFEE,TEA,COCOA,SPICES		1.1		3.2					CAFE,THE,CACAO,EPICES
09	MISC EDIBLE PRODUCTS		5.4		4.5					PREP ALIMENTAIRES DIVERSES
098	EDIBLE PRODCTS,PREPS NES		5.4		4.4					PREP ALIMENTAIRES NDA
09804	SAUCES,MIXED SEASONINGS	W 6430	4.3	W 4723	4.0					SAUCES,ASSAISONNEMENTS
1	BEVERAGES AND TOBACCO		132.2		220.9					BOISSONS ET TABACS
11	BEVERAGES		96.7		174.4		225.0			BOISSONS
112	ALCOHOLIC BEVERAGES	W 163091	96.4	W 273253	173.1					BOISSONS ALCOOLIQUES
1121	WINE OF FRESH GRAPES ETC	W 154662	62.8	W 259751	113.1					VINS DE RAISINS FRAIS
11211	GRAPE MUST	W 16538	3.7	W 93462	20.9					MOUTS DE RAISIN
11212	WINE OF FRESH GRAPES	W 137303	58.7	W 165551	91.3					VINS DE MOUTS DE RAISINS
1124	DISTILLED ALCOHOLIC BEVS	W 8210	33.5	W 13459	59.9					ALCOOLS,EAUX–DE–VIE
11242	DISTILLD WINE,GRAPE MARC	W 2210	17.0	W 3000	30.0					EAUX–DE–VIE NATURELLES
11249	OTH ALCOHOLC BEVS,CMPNDS	W 5999	16.5	W 10436	29.8					BOISSONS ALCOOLIQUES NDA
12	TOBACCO AND MANUFACTURES		35.6		46.6		77.1			TABACS BRUTS FABRIQUES
121	TOBACCO UNMNFCTRD,REFUSE	W 17429	14.1	W 17804	15.6					TABACS BRUTS,DECHETS
1211	TOBACCO,NOT STRIPPED	W 13491	11.3	W 7794	6.0					TABACS NON ECOTES
1212	TOBACCO STRIPPED OR PART	W 3810	2.8	W 9949	9.6					TABACS PART ECOTES
122	TOBACCO,MANUFACTURED		21.5		31.0					TABACS FABRIQUES
1222	CIGARETTES		9.8	W 3002	24.4					CIGARETTES
1223	OTH MANUFACTURED TOBACCO	W 13323	11.7	W 7756	6.5					TABACS FUMER,CHIQUER,PRISER
2	CRUDE MATERLS,EXCL FUELS		18.7		40.1					MAT BRUTES NON COMESTIBLES
21	HIDES,SKINS,FURS UNDRSSD		5.3		8.9					CUIRS,PEAUX BRUTS
211	HIDES,SKINS,EXC FURS,RAW		5.3		8.8					CUIRS ET PEAUX
2111	BOVINE,EQUINE HIDES,RAW	W 2294	2.1	W 1984	2.5					PEAUX DE BOVINS
2112	CALF AND KIP SKINS,RAW	W 2599	2.4	W 3804	4.4					PEAUX DE VEAUX
22	OIL SEEDS,OLEAGINOUS FRT		4.3		6.6		11.1			GRAINES,FRUITS OLEAGINEUX
222	SEEDS FOR'SOFT'FIXED OIL	W 21119	4.3	W 25083	6.6					GRAINES HUILES FIXES
2224	SUNFLOWER SEEDS	W 20622	4.2	W 24988	6.6					GRAINES DE TOURNESOL
26	TEXTILE FIBRES AND WASTE		0.9		2.3					FIBRES TEXTILES
28	METALLIFEROUS ORES,SCRAP		6.0		18.7					MINERAIS METAL,DECHETS
288	NONFERR METAL SCRAP NES	W 8462	5.7	W 19357	17.4					DECHETS NON FERREUX
2882	OTHER BASE MTL SCRAP NES	W 8462	5.7	W 19356	17.3					AUTRES DECHETS
28821	COPPER WASTE AND SCRAP	W 6281	4.7	W 11515	11.6					DECHETS DE CUIVRE
28823	ALUMINIUM WSTE AND SCRAP	W 2081	1.0	W 7748	5.6					DECHETS D'ALUMINIUM
29	CRUDE ANIMAL,VEG MAT NES		1.8		1.6					MATIERES BRUTES ANIM,VEGET
3	MINERAL FUELS ETC		14.4		6.6					COMBUSTIBLES MINERAUX LUB
351	*ELECTRIC CURRENT	H 264800	13.5	H 126860	6.5					ENERGIE ELECTRIQUE
4	ANIMAL,VEGETABLE OIL,FAT		11.2		11.2		3.1			HUILES,GRAISSES ANIM,VEG
411	*ANIMAL OILS AND FATS	W 1543	2.7	W 772	0.5					HUILES,GRAISSES ANIMALES
4113	ANIML OIL,FAT,GREASE NES	W 1543	2.7	W 772	0.5					HUILES,GRAISSES ANIMALES NDA
41139	ANIMAL OILS,FATS NES	W 1062	2.3							GRAISSES,HUILES ANIM NDA
42	FIXED VEGETABLE OIL,FAT		8.5		10.6					HUILES VEGETALES FIXES
423	FIXED VEG OILS,SOFT	W 16031	8.5	W 13612	10.6					HUILES VEGET DOUCES FIXES
4236	SUNFLOWER SEED OIL	W 16029	8.5	W 13606	10.6					HUILE DE TOURNESOL

5. General Exports F.O.B. by Commodities according to the S.I.T.C. (Rev. 2) in million U.S. Dollars
Exportations Générales F.O.B. par Produits d'après la C.T.C.I. (Rév. 2) en millions de Dollars E.U.

SITC CTCI	COMMODITY	1994 QUANTITY QUANTITE	1994 VALUE VALEUR	1995 QUANTITY QUANTITE	1995 VALUE VALEUR	1996 QUANTITY QUANTITE	1996 VALUE VALEUR	1997 QUANTITY QUANTITE	1997 VALUE VALEUR	PRODUIT
5	CHEMCLS,RELATED PROD NES		12.1		10.1					PRODUITS CHIMIQUES
51	ORGANIC CHEMICALS		4.0		3.6		2.1			PROD CHIMIQ ORGANIQUES
512	ALCOHOLS,PHENOLS ETC		3.0	V 2018	1.6					PHENOLS,PHENOLS–ALCOOLS
5121	ACYCLIC ALCOHOLS,DERIVS		3.0	V 2018	1.6					ALCOOLS ACYCLIQUES
51216	ETHYL ALC,DENATRD SPIRIT	V 4157	3.0	V 2018	1.6					ALCOOL ETHYLIQUE NON DENAT
55	PERFUME,CLEANING ETC PRD		4.8		3.6		3.1			PROD POUR PARFUM,TOILETTE
553	PERFUMERY,COSMETICS,ETC	W 1743	2.9	W 883	2.1					PRODUITS DE PARFUMERIE
572	*EXPLOSIVES,PYROTECH PRO						5.1			EXPLOSIFS
6	BASIC MANUFACTURES		44.9		54.0					ART MANUFACTURES
61	LEATHER,DRESSED FUR,ETC		2.5		4.4					CUIRS,PELLETERIES
611	LEATHER		2.0		4.2		10.1			CUIRS,PEAUX PREPARES
6114	LEATHR BOVINE NES,EQUINE	A 220	1.2	A 242	2.5					CUIRS DE BOVINS
63	WOOD,CORK MANUFACTRS NES		2.5		1.7					OUVRAGES LIEGE ET BOIS
635	WOOD MANUFACTURES NES		2.3		1.4					ART MANUF EN BOIS NDA
6353	BUILDERS WOODWRK,PREFABS		2.3	W 4482	1.3					OUVRAGES DE MENUISERIE
64	PAPER,PAPERBOARD AND MFR		5.5		6.9		7.1			PAPIERS,CARTONS & OUVRAGES
641	PAPER AND PAPERBOARD		3.5		3.6					PAPIERS ET CARTONS
6415	PAPER,PAPERBRD,BULK,NES	W 5108	2.0	W 3653	2.0					PAPIERS,CARTONS ROULEAUX
64159	OTHER PAPER ETC,BULK,NES	W 4877	1.9	W 3129	1.7					AUT PAPIER ROULEAUX FEUILLES
642	PAPER,ETC,PRECUT,ARTS OF	W 3464	2.1		3.3					PAP,CARTONS DECOUPES
6421	PAPER ETC CONTAINERS	W 2808	1.7	W 3205	2.6					BOITES,SACS EMBALLAGES
65	TEXTILE YARN,FABRICS,ETC		15.4		10.8		10.1			FILS,TISSUS,ARTICLES TEXTILE
659	FLOOR COVERINGS,ETC		12.1		9.3		10.1			COUVRE–PARQUETS,TAPIS ETC
6594	WOOL CARPETS ETC NES	A 393	4.5	A 304	5.0					TAPIS DE LAINE
65942	— WOVEN	A 384	4.4	A 302	4.9					TAPIS DE LAINE TISSES
6596	OTH TXTL CARPETS ETC NES	A 803	7.5	A 399	4.1					TAPIS AUT MAT TEXT NDA
65962	— OTHR THAN KNOTTED ETC	A 802	7.4	A 396	4.1					TAPIS AUT QUE NOUES TOUF
66	NONMETAL MINERAL MFS NES		5.7		15.4		28.1			ART MIN NON METALLIQUES
661	LIME,CEMENT,BLDG PRODS		2.4		1.5					CHAUX,CIMENTS MAT CONSTR
6618	MNRL BLDG PRD UNFIRD NES		2.2		1.0					MAT CONST AMIANTE–CIMENT
66183	ASBESTOS–,FIBRE–CMNT PRD		2.2		1.0					OUVRAGES AMIANTE–CIMENT
665	GLASSWARE		2.0		12.2					OUVRAGES EN VERRE
6651	BOTTLES ETC OF GLASS	MN 22577	1.9		12.2					RECIPIENTS EN VERRE
66511	GLASS BOTTLES ETC NONVAC	MN 22577	1.9		12.2					BONBONNES,BOUTEILLES,ETC
67	IRON AND STEEL		8.0		8.1		5.1			FER ET ACIER
673	IRON,STEEL SHAPES ETC	W 16624	3.5	W 13001	3.2					BARRES,PROFIL FER,ACIER
674	IRN,STL UNIV,PLATE,SHEET		2.8	W 7324	2.0					LARGES PLATS,TOLES
682	COPPER EXC CEMENT COPPER	W 70	0.2	W 325	0.6		4.1			CUIVRE
69	METAL MANUFACTURES NES		4.1		3.9		2.1			ART MANUFACT EN METAL NDA
699	BASE METAL MFRS NES		2.5		2.0					ART MANUFACTURES MET NDA
7	MACHINES,TRANSPORT EQUIP		65.2		58.8		54.1			MACHINES MATERIEL TRANSPORT
72	MACHS FOR SPCL INDUSTRYS		10.4		12.8					MAC SPECIALES POUR INDUST
722	TRACTORS NON–ROAD	N 1311	6.6	N 995	6.5					TRACTEURS
7223	TRACK–LAYING TRACTORS	N 1236	6.5	N 892	6.3					TRACTEURS A CHENILLES
74	GENRL INDUSTRL MACHY NES		16.1		16.9					MACH APP INDUSTRIE
742	PUMPS FOR LIQUIDS ETC	N 92752	13.0	N 95479	13.6					POMPES MOTO–POMPES
7422	CENTRIFUGAL PUMPS NES	N 33327	7.8	N 20222	10.5					POMPES CENTRIF NON 742.81
7428	OTHER PUMPS FOR LIQUIDS	N 25372	4.8	N 17964	2.6					AUTRES POMPES POUR LIQ
74288	PUMPS FR LIQUIDS NES ETC	N 25044	4.7	N 17250	2.4					POMPES POUR LIQUIDES NDA
76	TELECOMM,SOUND EQUIPMENT		14.8		6.2					EQUIPMENT DE TELECOM
761	TELEVISION RECEIVERS	N 93572	13.5	N 28505	4.2					RECEPTEURS DE TELEVISION
7611	COLOUR TV RECEIVERS	N 60924	11.1	N 13983	3.1					RECEPTEURS COULEUR
7612	MONOCHROME TV RECEIVERS	N 32648	2.5	N 14522	1.2					RECEPTEURS NOIR ET BLANC
77	ELECTRIC MACHNRY NES ETC		17.8		16.1					MACH APP ELECT NDA
775	HOUSEHOLD TYPE EQUIP NES		13.0		7.9					MACH,APP USAGE DOMESTQUE
7751	HOUSEHOLD LDRY EQUIP NES	N 71124	6.4	N 36234	3.2					MACH A LAVER ET SECHOIRS
77511	DOMESTIC WASHING MACHNES	N 70680	6.2	N 32374	3.0					MACH LAVER LINGE MOINS 6 KG
7752	DOM REFRIGERATRS,FREEZRS	N 46704	5.4	N 20545	2.7					REFRIG,CONGEL MENAGER
77522	DOMESTIC DEEP–FREEZERS	N 45862	5.4	N 20295	2.6					MEUBLES CONGELATEURS
776	TRANSISTORS,VALVES,ETC		1.2		2.7					LAMPES,TUBES,VALVES
778	ELECTRICAL MACHINERY NES		1.6		2.5					AUTRES MACH ELECT NDA
78	ROAD VEHICLES		4.2		4.0		11.1			VEHICULES ROUTIERS
784	MOTOR VEH PRTS,ACCES NES		2.3		1.6					PIECES 722,781,782,783
7849	OTHER MOTOR VEHCL PARTS	W 1590	2.3	W 2	1.6					PIECES 722,781,782,783
8	MISC MANUFACTURED GOODS		37.1		48.3					ART MANUFACTURES DIVERS
812	*PLUMBG,HEATNG,LGHTNG EQ		2.4		3.4					APPAR SANITAIRES CHAUFFAGE
8124	LIGHTING EQUIPMENT NES		1.9		3.0					APPAREILS ECLAIRAGE ETC
81242	LAMPS,FITTINGS BASE METL	W 1487	1.9	W 1309	2.9					APPAREILS D'ECLAIRAGE
821	*FURNITURE,PARTS THEREOF		10.4		9.7		10.1			MEUBLES ET PIECES
8211	CHAIRS,SEATS AND PARTS		2.1		1.1					SIEGES ET PIECES
82111	CHAIRS AND OTHER SEATS	N 1011300	2.1		1.1					SIEGES
8219	FURNITURE AND PARTS NES	W 10196	8.2	W 6469	8.6					AUTRES MEUBLES ET PIECES
82192	WOOD FURNITURE NES	W 10011	8.0	W 6360	8.5					MEUBLES NDA EN BOIS
84	CLOTHING AND ACCESSORIES		14.3		23.4		34.1			VETEMENTS
842	MENS OUTERWEAR NOT KNIT	N 494091	5.4	N 568920	7.8					VET DESSUS POUR HOMMES
8421	— OVERCOATS,OTHER COATS	N 97079	1.0	N 120211	2.7					MANTEAUX HOMMES MAT TEXT
84219	—— OF OTHER FIBRES	N 93585	0.9	N 99811	2.5					MANTEAUX HOMMES AUT FIBR
8423	— TROUSERS,BREECHES ETC	N 254208	2.1	N 264719	1.8					PANTALONS HOMMES MAT TEX
843	WOMENS OUTERWEAR NONKNIT		3.6		8.0					VET DESSUS FEMMES MAT TEX
8431	— COATS AND JACKETS	N 305425	2.0	N 362225	5.1					MANT,VEST FEM MAT TEXTIL
845	OUTERWEAR KNIT NONELASTC		1.6		2.4					VET DESSOUS,ACCES BONNET
846	UNDER GARMENTS KNITTED	N 2616320	1.9	N 1972124	2.7					SOUS VETS DE BONNETERIE
8462	— OF COTTON NON ELASTIC	N 1726994	1.6	N 1753283	2.6					SOUS–VET BONNET COTON
851	*FOOTWEAR	P 1210420	2.4	P 858700	2.7		4.1			CHAUSSURES
89	MISC MANUFCTRD GOODS NES		5.9		7.1					ART MANUFACTURES DIVERS
892	PRINTED MATTER		2.1		1.5		1.1			IMPRIMES
893	ARTICLES OF PLASTIC NES		1.4		2.7					OUVRAGES EN MAT DIVIS 58
8931	PLSTC PACKG CONTNRS,LIDS	W 450	1.0	W 1167	2.3					ART TRANSP EMBALLAGE ETC

1. HISTORICAL SERIES, 1962–1997 SPECIAL TRADE, IMPORTS C.I.F., EXPORTS F.O.B.
SERIES HISTORIQUES, 1962–1997 COMMERCE SPECIAL, IMPORTATIONS C.A.F., EXPORTATIONS F.O.B

YEAR ANNEE	VALUE IN MILLION U.S. DOLLARS VALEUR EN MILLION U.S. DOLLARS MERCHANDISE –MARCHANDISE IMPORTS	EXPORTS	GOLD –OR IMPORTS	EXPORTS	CONVERSION FACTORS FACTEURS DE CONVERSION CENTS E.U. PAR IMPORTS	EXPORTS	INDEX NUMBERS –INDICES QUANTUM IMPORTS	EXPORTS	UNIT VALUE VALEUR UNITAIRE IMPORTS	EXPORTS
1962	941.02	818.02								
1963	1022.02	915.02								
1964	1168.19	1000.02								
1965	1077.19	1101.52								
1966	1213.19	1186.19								
1967	1546.20	1395.36								
1968	1609.03	1468.53								
1969	1740.53	1633.20								
1970	1960.20	1850.87								
1971	2102.71	2101.04								
1972	2615.73	2599.10								
1973	3467.90	3698.52								
1974	5143.53	4874.40								
1975	5341.74	5341.42								
1976	6095.34	6137.72								
1977	7017.98	6978.66								
1978	8909.59	8076.60								
1979	10915.45	9724.17								
1980	13843.40	11209.00								
1981	13453.60	12610.00								
1982	10524.60	11559.00								
1983	10414.40	11512.00								
1984	11160.70	12646.00								
1985	11266.60	12167.00								
1986	11437.20	9763.10								
1987	8977.70	10491.80								
1988	8254.00	11392.40								
1989	9122.40	10487.30								
1990	9843.40	5775.40								
1991	5793.40	4265.70								
1992	6259.60	4363.40								
1993	6521.70	4892.20								
1994	7109.00	6151.30								
1995	10277.90	7910.00								
1996	11435.30	8084.50								
1997	11275.40	8428.30								

2. IMPORTS BY BROAD ECONOMIC CATEGORY AND EXPORTS BY INDUSTRIAL ORIGIN. (PERCENTAGE OF TOTAL VALUE)
IMPORTATIONS PAR CATEGORIES ECONOMIQUES ET EXPORTATIONS PAR BRANCHE D'ACTIVITE.(EN POURCENTAGE DE LA VALEUR TOTALE)

IMPORTS – IMPORTATIONS

	1991	1992	1993	1994	1995	1996	1997
TOTAL IMPORTS–IMPORTATIONS TOTALES	100.	100.	100.	100.	100.	100.	100.
1 FOOD BEV–ALIMENTATION BOISSONS	10.7	12.8	11.1	7.3	6.8	5.4	4.5
11 PRIMARY–PRODUITS DE BASE	5.9	6.2	6.8	2.7	2.1	1.6	1.5
111 FOR INDUSTRY–POUR L'INDUSTRIE	4.9	4.0	5.5	1.2	0.4	0.7	0.5
112 FOR HOUSEHOLDS–POUR LES MENAGES	1.0	2.2	1.2	1.6	1.6	0.9	0.9
12 PROCESSED–PRODUITS ELABORES	4.8	6.6	4.4	4.6	4.7	3.8	3.0
121 FOR INDUSTRY–POUR L'INDUSTRIE	1.5	1.9	0.9	1.2	1.3	1.7	1.1
122 FOR HOUSEHOLDS–POUR LES MENAGES	3.3	4.7	3.5	3.4	3.4	2.1	2.0
2 IND SUPPLIES–APPROV INDUSTRIELS	24.4	28.2	31.7	34.4	36.0	36.5	37.9
21 PRIMARY–PRODUITS DE BASE	8.7	6.0	5.8	4.8	4.4	4.2	4.0
22 PROCESSED–PRODUITS ELABORES	15.7	22.2	25.8	29.6	31.5	32.3	33.9
3 FUELS–COMBUSTIBLES	39.7	29.7	25.9	23.7	21.4	20.9	18.9
31 PRIMARY–PRODUITS DE BASE	31.4	24.3	22.0	21.1	17.6	17.1	14.5
32 PROCESSED–PRODUITS ELABORES	8.3	5.4	3.9	2.7	3.8	3.8	4.5
321 MOTOR SPIRIT–ESSENCE							
322 OTHER–AUTRES	8.3	5.4	3.9	2.7	3.8	3.8	4.5
4 MACHINERY–EQUIPEMENT	13.2	12.4	17.1	19.8	20.7	20.9	22.3
41 CAPITAL EQUIPMENT–MACHINES	11.7	10.7	14.7	17.3	17.9	18.1	19.9
42 PARTS–PIECES ACCESSOIRES	1.5	1.7	2.3	2.5	2.8	2.7	2.4
5 TRANSPORT–TRANSPORT	3.2	6.0	5.5	5.5	4.7	4.8	4.5
51 PASSENGER CARS–AUTOMOBILES		0.2	0.1	0.2	1.7	0.7	0.6
52 OTHER–AUTRES	1.4	3.9	3.6	3.6	1.3	1.2	1.5
521 INDUSTRIAL–INDUSTRIELS	1.4	3.8	3.6	3.6	1.3	1.2	1.5
522 NON INDUSTRIAL–NON INDUSTRIEL	0.0	0.1	0.0	0.0	0.0	0.0	0.0
53 PARTS–PIECES ACCESSOIRES	1.8	1.9	1.7	1.6	1.7	2.9	2.5
6 CONSUM GOODS–BIENS CONSOMMATION	8.1	8.3	8.3	8.2	9.3	9.9	9.9
61 DURABLE–DURABLES	2.8	2.7	1.6	1.5	1.8	2.2	2.1
62 SEMI DURABLE–SEMI DURABLES	2.8	3.3	3.8	4.2	4.4	4.3	4.7
63 NON DURABLE–NON DURABLES	2.5	2.3	3.0	2.5	3.2	3.4	3.1
7 GOODS NES–BIENS NDA	0.7	2.7	0.5	1.1	1.3	1.5	2.0

EXPORTS – EXPORTATIONS

	1991	1992	1993	1994	1995	1996	1997
TOTAL EXPORTS–EXPORTATIONS TOTALES	100.	100.	100.	100.	100.	100.	100.
1 AGRICULTURE	3.2	3.1	2.4	2.6	3.9	5.4	3.1
2 MINING QUARRY–INDUS EXTRACTIVES	0.5	0.5	0.4	0.5	0.5	0.5	0.4
3 MANUFACTURING–IND MANUFACTUR	96.3	96.4	97.1	96.9	95.7	94.1	96.5
31 FOOD BEV TOBACCO–ALIM BOISS TAB	3.0	3.7	4.6	4.2	3.0	3.4	4.2
32 TEXTILES–INDUSTRIES TEXTILES	11.4	11.8	19.3	23.8	25.2	27.8	29.7
33 WOOD & PRODUCTS–BOIS & PRODUITS	2.2	3.0	3.3	3.4	3.1	3.6	4.1
34 PAPER & PRODUCTS–PAPIER & PRODT	0.6	0.6	0.6	0.7	1.2	0.8	0.8
35 CHEMICALS–INDUSTRIES CHIMIQUES	21.1	23.4	19.1	21.0	20.1	18.6	15.3
36 NON METAL MIN–MIN NON METAL	3.3	3.6	3.4	2.8	2.8	2.8	2.9
37 BASIC METAL–IND METAL BASE	13.2	15.1	18.0	16.3	16.6	13.9	16.6
38 METAL MANUF–MANUF METAL	39.2	32.6	27.4	23.3	22.9	22.7	22.1
39 OTH MANUF IND–AUTRES MANUF	2.2	2.6	1.6	1.3	0.7	0.5	0.9

3. TRADE BY PRINCIPAL COUNTRIES OF ORIGIN AND DESTINATION (VALUE IN MILLION U.S. DOLLARS)
ECHANGES SELON LES PRINCIPAUX PAYS D'ORIGINE ET DE DESTINATION (VALEUR EN MILLIONS DE DOLLARS EU)

COUNTRIES–PAYS	SPECIAL IMPORTS C.I.F. IMPORTATIONS SPECIALES C.A.F				
	1993	1994	1995	1996	1997
World	6521.7	7109.0	10277.9	11435.3	11279.7
Africa	183.4	169.9	482.5	308.3	189.1
Americas	565.9	666.2	670.5	825.8	852.9
– Northern America	436.1	508.5	450.0	472.2	550.0
– LAIA	117.7	137.4	174.5	270.4	258.5
– CACM	3.3	2.0	5.0	3.3	0.7
– Caribbean	8.5	17.4	37.0	77.9	42.6
– Rest of America	0.3	1.0	4.0	1.9	1.1
Asia excl fmr USSR	1194.2	948.3	1349.1	1504.0	1529.1
– Middle East	827.7	636.7	594.8	594.4	416.4
Asia former USSR	27.3	26.5	63.9	33.7	40.3
Europe excl fmr USSR	3493.7	3925.0	5957.2	6764.4	6872.5
– European Union	2955.8	3391.7	5125.3	5889.7	5924.3
– Eastern Europe	328.1	336.7	558.6	600.8	669.5
– Rest of Europe	209.8	196.6	273.3	274.0	278.7
Europe former USSR	998.4	1245.7	1561.6	1726.6	1640.5
Oceania	28.2	55.5	73.5	121.4	124.0
Other	30.7	72.0	119.6	151.1	31.3
Germany/Allemagne	1031.2	1258.6	1766.2	1949.4	1850.7
Italy/Italie	614.6	841.5	1363.7	1747.3	1786.1
Russian Federation	764.1	980.2	1228.7	1432.1	1356.2
France, Monaco	506.7	359.1	532.0	555.3	648.5
USA/Etats–Unis d'Amer	372.9	459.8	407.4	418.9	461.5
Iran (Islamic Rep of)	604.1	443.0	255.8	314.9	105.4
Korea, Republic of	46.8	48.6	319.8	418.6	578.1
United Kingdom	170.5	220.8	299.7	324.2	387.8
Austria/Autriche	165.5	192.2	308.8	339.9	304.0
Hungary/Hongrie	167.7	166.0	314.5	288.0	346.6
Netherlands/Pays–Bas	157.0	175.3	270.1	259.3	228.8
Turkey/Turquie	147.2	150.2	250.4	218.1	212.7
Egypt/Egypte	86.5	122.9	400.6	239.7	116.5
Ukraine	133.3	150.1	193.6	181.7	186.5
Switzerland,Liechtenst.	150.9	149.0	203.3	189.8	150.6
Belgium–Luxembourg	87.0	83.5	158.0	190.6	194.2
Greece/Grèce	69.5	89.3	158.1	185.3	191.9
China/Chine	93.5	60.1	89.8	115.0	119.9
Israel/Israël	55.4	58.1	105.3	100.4	136.7
Japan/Japon	57.7	57.5	76.2	104.2	131.5
Republic of Moldova	85.2	92.5	104.5	79.8	62.4
Brazil/Brésil	51.9	77.6	85.9	109.6	91.6
Australia/Australie	28.1	53.8	71.1	120.8	123.0
Areas n.e.s.	2.0	72.0	119.6	150.8	31.3
Sweden/Suède	33.5	39.1	75.7	75.7	142.6
Spain/Espagne	40.9	46.4	88.1	101.3	82.3
Czech Republic	36.0	50.0	61.7	82.1	104.6
Bulgaria/Bulgarie	67.9	59.0	76.7	73.2	55.6
Canada	63.2	48.7	42.6	53.3	88.5
Poland/Pologne	33.1	29.8	57.0	85.5	90.4
Denmark/Danemark	48.2	45.5	54.0	86.7	50.2
Slovakia/Slovaquie	23.2	31.8	48.6	59.1	72.2
Argentina/Argentine	45.7	31.2	31.6	50.1	39.2
Venezuela	4.1	10.7	19.3	59.1	72.8
India/Inde	19.3	18.1	42.2	36.0	27.9
Cuba	7.7	17.0	36.5	62.9	17.5
Yugoslavia/Yougoslavie	0.2	20.3	19.9	30.9	54.1
Finland/Finlande	13.5	27.5	23.8	33.6	26.6
So. African Customs Un	39.8	14.6	18.8	15.1	34.8
China, Hong Kong SAR	16.0	16.7	35.9	30.3	23.9

COUNTRIES–PAYS	SPECIAL EXPORTS F.O.B. EXPORTATIONS SPECIALES F.O.B.				
	1993	1994	1995	1996	1997
Monde	4892.2	6151.2	7910.0	8084.5	8431.0
Afrique	219.4	395.6	569.4	536.7	457.2
Amériques	201.4	352.1	407.4	408.4	485.2
– Amérique du Nord	95.3	237.4	231.9	216.7	355.1
– ALAI	76.6	88.7	124.1	150.4	104.0
– MCAC	2.2	4.9	13.4	5.3	3.1
– Caraïbes	27.0	16.5	36.7	34.8	22.6
– Autre Amérique	0.3	4.6	1.3	1.2	0.5
Asie anc. URSS exclus	1475.7	1446.1	1606.7	1462.8	1411.5
– Moyen–Orient	697.6	696.7	762.3	806.2	804.0
Asie ancienne URSS	22.7	36.5	66.9	96.7	53.7
Europe anc. URSS exclus	2480.2	3484.3	4833.2	5214.5	5531.2
– Union Européenne	2024.4	2964.2	4281.9	4574.0	4775.7
– Europe de l'Est	257.9	364.6	328.4	365.6	386.8
– Autre de l'Europe	197.9	155.5	222.9	274.8	368.6
Europe ancienne URSS	423.4	359.8	384.3	333.7	476.8
Océanie	6.5	8.5	7.0	7.0	12.9
Autre	62.9	68.3	35.2	24.6	2.6
Germany/Allemagne	699.4	985.9	1434.2	1486.0	1419.2
Italy/Italie	409.4	798.0	1246.6	1392.9	1651.1
France, Monaco	219.3	315.8	456.5	459.8	465.3
Turkey/Turquie	277.4	250.7	347.0	389.7	353.9
Netherlands/Pays–Bas	212.1	216.1	238.8	343.0	264.1
United Kingdom	183.4	200.2	235.9	247.3	299.3
China/Chine	419.0	275.6	179.3	92.9	43.9
Russian Federation	220.4	207.3	157.9	164.3	249.8
USA/Etats–Unis d'Amer	69.0	194.1	201.2	192.6	319.8
Egypt/Egypte	101.0	157.8	199.1	232.6	236.5
Hungary/Hongrie	117.0	160.9	174.3	171.4	182.6
Greece/Grèce	84.3	141.1	205.0	177.3	175.0
Syrian Arab Republic	132.7	145.9	164.0	157.9	106.9
Austria/Autriche	75.8	96.4	154.8	169.2	177.6
Belgium–Luxembourg	76.2	103.2	134.1	125.3	147.7
Ukraine	104.7	94.8	137.4	64.8	91.8
Israel/Israël	53.9	95.1	107.0	89.6	123.0
Republic of Moldova	94.2	47.9	81.3	97.0	128.6
Bulgaria/Bulgarie	102.3	102.2	70.9	70.6	57.5
Yugoslavia/Yougoslavie	7.9	47.0	68.8	136.8	139.8
India/Inde	24.6	45.8	73.9	177.1	64.1
Spain/Espagne	28.2	56.0	101.6	94.5	83.0
Singapore/Singapour	34.3	107.8	117.7	43.3	38.4
Switzerland,Liechtenst.	119.9	45.5	65.4	41.9	46.4
Lebanon/Liban	46.6	47.1	66.2	61.5	67.4
Algeria/Algérie	4.7	24.2	95.7	48.4	58.1
Poland/Pologne	20.1	14.0	39.1	52.9	101.7
Iran (Islamic Rep of)	81.8	28.7	23.0	27.3	64.0
Japan/Japon	52.8	53.0	35.5	39.0	37.4
Saudi Arabia	31.2	41.9	35.6	33.7	67.1
Morocco/Maroc	25.5	38.8	46.2	47.3	36.8
Sweden/Suède	21.4	34.1	38.8	43.9	51.2
Nigeria/Nigéria	32.4	86.5	27.1	23.9	13.9
United Arab Emirates	28.3	48.0	26.8	28.4	50.0
Korea, Republic of	3.1	34.9	52.6	42.5	43.6
Thailand/Thaïlande	29.9	21.8	38.3	41.0	38.4
Jordan/Jordanie	42.8	35.7	27.1	37.4	25.6
Cyprus/Chypre	20.4	48.6	35.7	36.0	24.7
Canada	26.2	38.6	30.6	24.1	35.3
Brazil/Brésil	3.7	11.0	63.3	55.8	17.5

(VALUE AS PERCENTAGE OF WORLD TOTAL)(VALEURS EN POURCENTAGE DU TOTAL MONDIAL)

	1988	1989	1990	1991	1992	1993	1994	1995	1996	1997
Africa	3.1	2.7	7.0	8.8	4.6	2.8	2.4	4.7	2.7	1.7
Americas	5.4	4.7	6.8	6.3	6.0	8.7	9.4	6.5	7.2	7.6
– Northern America	3.4	2.6	4.7	3.6	4.2	6.7	7.2	4.4	4.1	4.9
– LAIA	0.7	0.7	1.5	2.6	1.6	1.8	1.9	1.7	2.4	2.3
– CACM			0.0	0.0	0.0	0.1	0.0	0.0	0.0	0.0
– Caribbean	1.3	1.4	0.6	0.1	0.1	0.1	0.2	0.4	0.7	0.4
– Rest of America			0.0	0.1	0.0	0.0	0.0	0.0	0.0	0.0
Asia excl fmr USSR	24.8	28.5	23.1	23.8	18.6	18.3	13.3	13.1	13.2	13.6
– Middle East	18.3	23.1	18.3	17.3	13.4	12.7	9.0	5.8	5.2	3.7
Asia former USSR					0.3	0.4	0.4	0.6	0.3	0.4
Europe excl fmr USSR	33.3	30.8	38.2	41.7	52.0	53.6	55.2	58.0	59.2	60.9
– European Union	14.6	13.8	21.5	28.7	41.3	45.3	47.7	49.9	51.5	52.5
– Eastern Europe	16.1	14.7	12.3	7.6	6.0	5.0	4.7	5.4	5.3	5.9
– Rest of Europe	2.6	2.3	4.4	5.4	4.7	3.2	2.8	2.7	2.4	2.5
Europe former USSR	31.6	31.2	23.4	17.7	15.3	15.3	17.5	15.2	15.1	14.5
Oceania	1.2	1.2	1.2	1.1	0.5	0.4	0.8	0.7	1.1	1.1
Other		0.8	0.4	0.7	2.6	0.5	1.0	1.2	1.3	0.3
Germany/Allemagne				10.2	13.2	15.8	17.7	17.2	17.0	16.4
Italy/Italie	0.7	0.6	1.2	3.6	7.8	9.4	11.8	13.3	15.3	15.8
Russian Federation					11.0	11.7	13.8	12.0	12.5	12.0
France, Monaco	0.9	0.6	1.9	3.8	7.6	7.8	5.1	5.2	4.9	5.7
USA/Etats–Unis d'Amer	2.7	2.0	4.6	3.2	3.6	5.7	6.5	4.0	3.7	4.1
Iran (Islamic Rep of)	12.2	12.0	5.9	7.9	7.5	9.3	6.2	2.5	2.8	0.9
Korea, Republic of			0.1	0.3	0.4	0.7	0.7	3.1	3.7	5.1
United Kingdom	0.8	0.8	1.8	2.6	3.0	2.6	3.1	2.9	2.8	3.4
Austria/Autriche	0.7	0.6	1.6	3.2	3.0	2.5	2.7	3.0	3.0	2.7
Hungary/Hongrie	3.8	3.2	2.4	2.1	2.8	2.6	2.3	3.1	2.5	3.1

	1988	1989	1990	1991	1992	1993	1994	1995	1996	1997
Afrique	4.6	3.7	3.6	3.5	3.6	4.5	6.4	7.2	6.6	5.4
Amériques	8.2	8.9	8.1	4.2	4.0	4.1	5.7	5.2	5.1	5.8
– Amérique du Nord	5.8	6.1	6.3	3.3	2.3	1.9	3.9	2.9	2.7	4.2
– ALAI	0.6	1.2	0.6	0.7	1.0	1.6	1.4	1.6	1.9	1.2
– MCAC		0.1	0.1	0.2	0.1	0.0	0.1	0.2	0.1	0.0
– Caraïbes	1.5	1.3	1.1	0.0	0.2	0.6	0.3	0.5	0.4	0.3
– Autre Amérique	0.2	0.2	0.0	0.0	0.4	0.0	0.1	0.0	0.0	0.0
Asie anc. URSS exclus	19.0	17.6	14.9	18.1	27.1	30.2	23.5	20.3	18.1	16.7
– Moyen–Orient	10.8	9.5	7.8	9.3	16.2	14.3	11.3	9.6	10.0	9.5
Asie ancienne URSS					0.3	0.5	0.6	0.8	1.2	0.6
Europe anc. URSS exclus	44.7	46.2	46.5	49.5	49.3	50.7	56.6	61.1	64.5	65.6
– Union Européenne	30.7	32.8	33.3	36.7	35.1	41.4	48.2	54.1	56.6	56.6
– Europe de l'Est	11.7	10.7	9.2	7.1	6.4	5.3	5.9	4.2	4.5	4.6
– Autre de l'Europe	2.3	2.6	4.0	5.7	7.9	4.0	2.5	2.8	3.4	4.4
Europe ancienne URSS	21.7	21.9	24.2	22.7	13.6	8.7	5.8	4.9	4.1	5.7
Océanie	0.4	0.2	0.1	0.1	0.2	0.1	0.1	0.1	0.1	0.2
Autre		1.6	2.5	1.8	1.8	1.3	1.1	0.4	0.3	0.0
Germany/Allemagne				10.9	11.0	14.3	16.0	18.1	18.4	16.8
Italy/Italie	7.4	9.5	8.8	6.1	6.1	8.4	13.0	15.8	17.2	19.6
France, Monaco	2.8	2.4	3.4	4.1	3.9	4.5	5.1	5.8	5.7	5.5
Turkey/Turquie	2.2	3.0	2.8	3.6	5.0	5.7	4.1	4.4	4.8	4.2
Netherlands/Pays–Bas	3.6	1.4	2.7	5.3	2.5	4.3	3.5	3.0	4.2	3.1
United Kingdom	2.4	2.4	2.2	3.6	3.6	3.7	3.3	3.0	3.1	3.5
China/Chine	4.3	3.3	2.6	3.3	4.6	8.6	4.5	2.3	1.1	0.5
Russian Federation					9.5	4.5	3.4	2.0	2.0	3.0
USA/Etats–Unis d'Amer	4.9	5.4	5.8	2.9	1.9	1.4	3.2	2.5	2.4	3.8
Egypt/Egypte	2.8	1.8	1.4	1.6	1.8	2.1	2.6	2.5	2.9	2.8

4. Special Imports C.I.F. by Commodities according to the S.I.T.C. (Rev. 2) in million U.S. Dollars
Importations Spéciales C.A.F. par Produits d'après la C.T.C.I. (Rév. 2) en millions de Dollars E.U.

SITC CTCI	COMMODITY	1994 QUANTITY QUANTITE	1994 VALUE VALEUR	1995 QUANTITY QUANTITE	1995 VALUE VALEUR	1996 QUANTITY QUANTITE	1996 VALUE VALEUR	1997 QUANTITY QUANTITE	1997 VALUE VALEUR	PRODUIT
	ALL COMMODITIES		7109.1		10277.9		11435.3		11279.8	TOUS PRODUITS
0	FOOD AND LIVE ANIMALS		532.6		745.8		657.8		530.8	ALIMENTS,ANIMAUX VIVANTS
01	MEAT AND PREPARATIONS		63.9		94.1		20.0		36.4	VIANDES ET PREPARATIONS
011	MEAT FRESH,CHILLD,FROZEN	W 54349	57.3		69.3	W 14271	15.3		21.4	VIANDES FRAICHES,REF,CONGE
0114	POULTRY FRESH CHLLD,FRZN	W 38579	41.5	W 23325	35.5	W 2944	1.2	W 14441	13.6	VOLAILLES MORTES
02	DAIRY PRODCTS,BIRDS'EGGS		22.7		22.8		25.9		19.2	PRODUITS LAITIERS,OEUFS
04	CEREALS AND PREPARATIONS		86.9		82.8		57.5		80.9	CEREALES ET PRODUITS
043	BARLEY UNMILLED	W 395741	35.8	W 4061	0.5	W 47288	9.1	W 84636	15.8	ORGE NON MONDEE
046	WHEAT ETC MEAL OR FLOUR	W 52873	10.9	W 144241	31.2	W 19809	7.6	W 61967	16.9	SEMOULE FARINE,FROMENT
04601	FLOUR OF WHEAT OR MESLIN	W 52659	10.8	W 143106	31.0	W 18985	7.3	W 61263	16.7	FARINE DE FROMENT
048	CEREAL ETC PREPARATIONS	W 42658	25.5	W 54131	39.4	W 48981	31.3	W 25481	19.9	PREPTNS A BASE CEREALES
05	VEGETABLES AND FRUIT		57.1		107.3		87.7		91.1	LEGUMES ET FRUITS
057	FRUIT,NUTS,FRESH,DRIED		31.6		56.2		46.5		47.1	FRUITS FRAIS OU SECS
06	SUGAR AND PREPS,HONEY		86.5		127.3		171.4		85.8	SUCRES ET PRODUITS
061	SUGAR AND HONEY	W 288305	72.8		111.4		164.9	W 257021	80.5	SUCRES ET MIEL
0611	RAW BEET AND CANE SUGAR	W 141846	43.1	W 156419	62.3	W 336488	121.4	W 136324	47.9	SUCRES BRUTS
0612	REFINED SUGAR ETC	W 70180	23.7	W 105619	42.9	W 99127	37.8	W 79095	27.4	SUCRES RAFFINES
07	COFFEE,TEA,COCOA,SPICES		62.1		71.3		62.1		55.6	CAFE,THE,CACAO,EPICES
071	COFFEE AND SUBSTITUTES	W 14119	23.7		27.2	W 34515	33.3	W 32383	30.9	CAFE ET SUCCEDANES
073	CHOCOLATE AND PRODUCTS	W 20414	27.3	W 22049	29.9	W 11437	11.9	W 8383	10.9	CHOCOLAT
081	*FEEDING STUFF FOR ANIML		68.6	W 302261	96.0		99.1	W 156786	64.1	NOURRITURE POUR ANIMAUX
0813	OILCAKE AND OTH RESIDUES		48.0	W 236950	56.0		57.8	W 118961	40.1	TOURTEAUX
08131	— OF SOYA BEANS	W 205001	47.9	W 236015	55.8	W 191529	57.7	W 118959	40.1	TOURTEAUX DE SOJA
09	MISC EDIBLE PRODUCTS		68.5		107.7		102.6		75.3	PREP ALIMENTAIRES DIVERSES
098	EDIBLE PRODCTS,PREPS NES	W 31420	57.4		96.2		99.3		72.2	PREP ALIMENTAIRES NDA
09809	MISC FOOD PREPRTIONS NES	W 6662	41.1	W 12097	66.3	W 11893	69.3	W 9906	42.2	PREP ALIMENTAIRES NDA
1	BEVERAGES AND TOBACCO		68.8		96.7		115.9		98.7	BOISSONS ET TABACS
11	BEVERAGES		22.1		27.6		8.7		6.5	BOISSONS
12	TOBACCO AND MANUFACTURES		46.8		69.1		107.3		92.3	TABACS BRUTS FABRIQUES
121	TOBACCO UNMNFCTRD,REFUSE	W 10504	10.3	W 8496	5.6	W 18854	22.4	W 18097	36.0	TABACS BRUTS,DECHETS
122	TOBACCO,MANUFACTURED		36.5	W 23202	63.5	W 11535	84.9	W 6897	56.4	TABACS FABRIQUES
1222	CIGARETTES	W 13240	35.8	W 22335	60.5	W 8706	73.3	W 5460	50.0	CIGARETTES
2	CRUDE MATERLS,EXCL FUELS		406.0		533.0		603.2		518.8	MAT BRUTES NON COMESTIBLES
22	OIL SEEDS,OLEAGINOUS FRT		21.2		9.5		39.3		13.4	GRAINES,FRUITS OLEAGINEUX
222	SEEDS FOR'SOFT'FIXED OIL	W 76598	21.1	W 7447	9.4	W 105799	39.0	W 29215	13.1	GRAINES HUILES FIXES
23	RUBBER, CRUDE		35.9		62.3		71.1		50.1	CAOUTCHOUC BRUT
233	RUBBER,SYNTHTIC,RECLAIMD	W 23551	22.5		32.9	W 25453	38.1		26.1	LATEX CAOUTCH SYNTH REGEN
2331	SYNTHETIC RUBBER ETC	W 23067	22.0	W 22613	32.5	W 25077	37.4	W 19538	25.8	LATEX CAOUTCH SYNTHETIQUE
26	TEXTILE FIBRES AND WASTE		79.0		120.6		120.2		110.5	FIBRES TEXTILES
263	COTTON	W 30609	45.9	W 43819	86.5	W 40081	78.9	W 34050	62.6	COTON
2631	RAW COTTON,EXCL LINTERS	W 30293	45.5	W 43734	86.4	W 39352	77.7	W 33591	62.0	COTON EN MASSE
27	CRUDE FERTLZR,MINRLS NES		63.0		66.2		75.7		55.4	ENGRAIS MINERAUX BRUTS
271	FERTILIZERS,CRUDE	W 830766	34.7		31.9		33.7	W 480604	25.6	ENGRAIS BRUTS
2713	NAT CALCM PHOSPHATES ETC	W 830765	34.7	W 733321	31.9	W 683211	32.7	W 480313	25.5	PHOSPHATES DE CALCIUM
27131	— UNGROUND	W 772130	31.8	W 715854	31.0	W 667895	31.8	W 405749	20.8	PHOSPHATES NON MOULUS
278	OTHER CRUDE MINERALS	W 131269	22.2		25.9		33.8		22.4	AUTRES MINERAUX BRUTS
28	METALLIFEROUS ORES,SCRAP		167.3		225.2		245.3		251.5	MINERAIS METAL,DECHETS
281	IRON ORE,CONCENTRATES	W 5452091	128.6	W 6278469	157.1	W 5843451	158.2	W 6625324	180.1	MINERAIS DE FER
2815	IRON ORE,CONC,NOT AGGLOM	W 1493241	38.8	W 2786480	70.3	W 3252767	87.9	W 3044316	85.7	MINERAIS NON AGGLOMERES
2816	IRON ORE AGGLOMERATES	W 3958850	89.9	W 3491989	86.8	W 2590684	70.3	W 3581008	94.4	MINERAIS AGGLOMERES
287	BASE METAL ORES,CONC NES	W 716549	38.6		67.8		87.0	W 956345	71.4	MINERAIS METAUX COMMUNS
2873	ALUMINIUM ORES,ALUMINA	W 562179	20.7	W 674412	28.7	W 643201	42.9	W 811851	52.5	MINERAIS D'ALUMINIUM
3	MINERAL FUELS ETC		1681.7		2197.6		2394.5		2135.2	COMBUSTIBLES MINERAUX LUB
32	COAL,COKE AND BRIQUETTES		241.6		290.7		315.8		362.8	HOUILLES,COKES,BRIQUETTES
322	COAL,LIGNITE AND PEAT	W 4090005	229.9	W 4737827	280.0	W 4730346	303.3	W 5249071	342.1	HOUILLES,LIGNITES,TOURBE
3221	ANTHRACITE,NOT AGGLOMRTD	W 333902	22.0	W 6011	0.5	W 9089	0.8	W 6901	0.6	ANTHRACITE
3222	OTH COAL,NOT AGGLOMERATD	W 3745593	207.8	W 4726767	279.2	W 4719027	302.4	W 5241746	341.3	AUTRES HOUILLES
33	PETROLEUM AND PRODUCTS		1053.6		1424.6		1447.7		1305.7	PETROLE ET DERIVES
333	CRUDE PETROLEUM	W 8122294	895.8	W 8657249	1053.6	W 7155735	1037.0	W 6244782	838.4	HUILES BRUTES DE PETROLE
334	PETROLEUM PRODUCTS,REFIN	W 1631463	154.6	W 2858488	365.0	W 3220823	404.9	W 3916286	461.2	PRODUITS RAFFINES
341	*GAS,NATURAL AND MANUFCT		367.3		478.3		614.4		449.3	GAZ NATUREL,GAZ MANUFACT
3414	PETROLEUM GASES, GASEOUS		367.3		478.2		611.9		448.1	GAZ DE PETROLE GAZEUX
5	CHEMCLS,RELATED PROD NES		624.9		1043.2		1092.7		1040.0	PRODUITS CHIMIQUES
51	ORGANIC CHEMICALS		128.6		213.9		179.5		159.7	PROD CHIMIQ ORGANIQUES
511	HYDROCARBONS NES,DERIVS	W 90054	34.2		80.9		41.0		38.0	HYDROCARBURES NDA
5111	ACYCLIC HYDROCARBONS	W 37415	10.8	W 104080	41.6	W 64905	20.2	W 48251	12.9	HYDROCARBURES ACYCLIQUES
512	ALCOHOLS,PHENOLS ETC	W 37320	31.5	W 46714	42.4		40.9		28.4	PHENOLS,PHENOLS–ALCOOLS
513	CARBOXYLIC ACIDS ETC	W 23261	21.4	W 21977	32.0	W 34828	32.6	W 43818	37.3	ACIDES CARBOXYLIQUES
52	INORGANIC CHEMICALS		48.8		60.6		70.5		73.4	PROD CHIM INORGANIQUES
522	INORG ELEMNTS,OXIDES,ETC	W 132312	24.6		30.8		30.8		35.1	ELEMENTS INORGANIQUES
523	OTHR INORG CHEMICALS ETC		23.6		29.3		39.0		38.0	AUT PRODUITS CHIMIQUES INORG
53	DYES,TANNING,COLOUR PROD		68.9		109.8		123.2		113.6	PROD TEINTURE,COLORANTS
533	PIGMENTS,PAINTS,ETC	W 22135	49.4	W 33399	83.6	W 40009	95.4	W 47961	89.8	PIGMENTS,PEINTURES,VERNIS
5334	VARNISHES,DISTEMPERS ETC	W 15352	36.2	W 20110	58.0	W 22057	63.3	W 26294	57.8	PEINTURES A L'EAU
53342	OTH PAINTS,VARNISHES ETC	W 12830	29.4	W 14992	44.5	W 15130	50.5	W 15640	42.4	AUTRES PEINTURES,VERNIS
541	*MEDICINAL,PHARM PRODUCT	MK 18806	105.3		172.8		195.4		181.2	PROD MEDICINAUX PHARMACEUT
5417	MEDICAMENTS	K 2239000	68.3	K 3339326	115.9	K 3773884	139.1		138.5	MEDICAMENTS
54171	— CONTAINNG ANTIBIOTICS	K 696000	21.7	K 975796	36.2	K 835991	34.6	K 636973	30.4	MED CONTN ANTIBIOTIQUES
54179	— CONTNG OTH SUBSTANCES	K 1184000	33.0	K 2049396	61.4	K 2425563	82.1	K 2904394	88.8	MED CONT AUT SUBSTANCES
55	PERFUME,CLEANING ETC PRD		75.0		133.2		143.9		125.3	PROD POUR PARFUM,TOILETTE
553	PERFUMERY,COSMETICS,ETC	W 8531	27.1	W 10928	54.8	W 12934	63.6	W 11451	49.3	PRODUITS DE PARFUMERIE
554	SOAP,CLEANSING ETC PREPS	W 35040	39.2	W 61647	66.6	W 59786	65.5	W 44063	47.1	SAVONS,PRODUITS DETERSIFS
5542	WASHING PREPARATIONS ETC	W 26730	31.0	W 51355	55.5	W 47680	53.5	W 34033	35.4	PROD ORG TENSIO–ACT NDA
58	PLASTIC MATERIALS ETC		70.2		134.7		141.9		157.6	MAT PLAST ARTIFICIELLES
582	PROD OF CONDENSATION ETC	W 15735	22.4	W 18331	47.7	W 21970	44.4	W 34989	52.4	PROD CONDENS,POLYCOND
583	POLYMERIZATION ETC PRODS	W 21899	44.4		82.3	W 35015	91.6	W 47647	97.3	PROD POLYMERISATION
59	CHEMICAL MATERIALS NES		116.6		206.7		227.8		217.8	MAT PROD CHIMIQUES NDA
591	PESTICIDES,DISINFECTANTS	W 5412	47.9	W 9065	87.7	W 12016	107.3	W 12091	106.9	DESINF,INSECT,FONG,HERB
5912	FUNGICIDES,FOR RETAIL	W 1695	22.2	W 2694	31.2	W 2675	30.4	W 3095	32.8	FONGICIDES VENTE AU DET
5913	HERBICIDES,FOR RETAIL	W 1184	11.0	W 2884	34.1	W 5244	54.4	W 4688	47.5	HERBICIDES VENTE AU DET
598	MISCEL CHEM PRODUCTS NES		55.7		96.9		94.4		87.8	PROD DIV INDUST CHIM NDA
5989	CHEM PRODUCTS,PREPS NES		38.6		76.1		73.5		65.9	PROD PREP CHIMIQUES NDA
59899	OTH CHEM PRODS,PREPS,NES	W 9914	21.4	W 18154	42.4	W 18476	38.0	W 22025	40.1	AUT PRODUITS CHIMIQUES NDA
6	BASIC MANUFACTURES		1383.3		2140.1		2564.0		2760.9	ART MANUFACTURES
61	LEATHER,DRESSED FUR,ETC		168.7		265.7		337.7		378.4	CUIRS,PELLETERIES
611	LEATHER	W 7812	122.0	W 9540	185.9	W 11390	230.3	W 13602	250.5	CUIRS,PEAUX PREPARES
6113	CALF LEATHER	W 2519	28.3	W 1521	27.4	W 1951	33.6	W 1781	34.5	CUIRS,PEAUX DE VEAUX
6114	LEATHR BOVINE NES,EQUINE	W 4093	77.8	W 7010	140.7	W 8401	177.3	W 10595	193.9	CUIRS DE BOVINS
612	LEATHER ETC MANUFACTURES	W 7245	45.8		78.4		103.8		125.8	OUVRAGES EN CUIRS NDA
6123	PREPRD PARTS OF FOOTWEAR	W 7210	45.5	W 11800	77.8	W 15128	103.0	W 19777	125.1	PARTIES DE CHAUSSURES
62	RUBBER MANUFACTURES NES		45.1		53.0		69.0		67.5	CAOUTCHOUC MANUFACTURE

4. Special Imports C.I.F. by Commodities according to the S.I.T.C. (Rev. 2) in million U.S. Dollars
Importations Spéciales C.A.F. par Produits d'après la C.T.C.I. (Rév. 2) en millions de Dollars E.U.

SITC CTCI	COMMODITY	1994		1995		1996		1997		PRODUIT
		QUANTITY QUANTITE	VALUE VALEUR	QUANTITY QUANTITE	VALUE VALEUR	QUANTITY QUANTITE	VALUE VALEUR	QUANTITY QUANTITE	VALUE VALEUR	
625	RUBBER TYRES, TUBES ETC	W 7423	13.9	W 13880	26.0	W 16728	31.3	W 22040	38.9	PNEUS CAOUTCHOUC VULCANISE
628	RUBBER ARTICLES NES	W 6532	24.7	W 2796	18.5	W 2753	24.4	W 1594	17.1	OUVRAGES CAOUTCHOUC NDA
63	WOOD,CORK MANUFACTRS NES		21.8		59.5		50.2		57.2	OUVRAGES LIEGE ET BOIS
634	VENEERS,PLYWOOD,ETC	W 23049	13.8	W 28358	38.6	W 41210	34.4	W 41124	35.7	PLACAGES,CONTRE–PLAQUES
64	PAPER,PAPERBOARD AND MFR		89.2		160.9		190.9		179.0	PAPIERS,CARTONS & OUVRAGES
641	PAPER AND PAPERBOARD	W 68079	56.3	W 79727	99.2	W 102614	114.2	W 99327	96.8	PAPIERS ET CARTONS
642	PAPER,ETC,PRECUT,ARTS OF	W 22805	32.9	W 31244	61.7		76.7	W 46006	82.3	PAP,CARTONS DECOUPES
6421	PAPER ETC CONTAINERS	W 15317	18.8	W 18819	30.5	W 25926	44.0	W 33988	48.4	BOITES,SACS EMBALLAGES
65	TEXTILE YARN,FABRICS,ETC		624.6		938.9		1054.9		1258.0	FILS,TISSUS,ARTICLES TEXTILE
651	TEXTILE YARN		46.8		66.2		73.1		90.3	FILS TEXTILES
6514	SYN FIB YRN,BULK,MONOFIL	W 1542	19.6	W 2238	30.0	W 2276	34.0	W 2653	36.7	FILS CONT 85% FIB TEXT SYNTH
652	COTTON FABRICS,WOVEN	W 9758	103.0		146.9		170.2		199.1	TISSUS DE COTON
6522	WOVEN COTTON BLEACHD,ETC	W 8020	92.2		129.1		147.0		174.0	TISSUS COTON BLANCHIS ETC
65224	BLCHED COTTON FABRIC NES	W 5655	59.6	W 6804	91.4	W 7416	108.9	W 9378	138.7	AUT TIS PLUS 85% COT BLANCHI
65225	BLCHD COTN BLEND FAB NES	W 1663	24.9	W 1581	26.3	W 1613	23.7	W 1539	24.2	AUT TIS MOINS 85% COT BLANCH
653	WOVN MAN–MADE FIB FABRIC	W 16957	268.3	W 21608	392.3	W 25543	419.7	W 35026	491.7	TISSUS FIBRES SYNTH,ARTIF
6531	CONT SYNT WEAVES NONPILE	W 6134	96.9	W 7450	133.4	W 8446	126.3	W 10563	148.4	TISSUS FIBRES SYNTH CONTINUE
65314	CONT SYN TYRE CORD FABRC	W 875	19.7	W 1422	31.4	W 1324	25.0	W 1246	20.0	TIS ARMATURE PNEUMATIQUES
65315	CONT SYN TXTL FABRIC NES	W 5259	77.2	W 6029	102.0	W 7122	101.3	W 9317	128.5	TIS PLUS 85% TEXT SYNT CONT
6532	DISC SYN TXTL FABRIC NES	W 651	9.0	W 1186	16.4	W 1858	24.7	W 3028	34.5	TIS DISC MOINS 85% FIBR TEXT
6534	DISC SYN BLEND FABRC NES	W 4622	67.7	W 5908	100.2	W 6800	115.1	W 10204	149.5	TISSUS FIBRES SYNTH DISCONT
6535	CONT REGN WEAVES NONPILE	W 1535	27.9	W 2058	42.5	W 2660	48.9	W 3008	50.5	TISSUS FIB TEXT ART CONTINU
6536	DISC REGN TXTL FABRC NES	W 1838	27.3	W 2254	39.8	W 2159	38.5	W 1940	37.0	TISSUS 85% TEXT ART DISC
6538	DISC REG BLEND FABRC NES	W 1739	34.6	W 2146	52.3	W 2581	56.9	W 3132	59.6	TIS MOINS 85% TEXT ART DISC
65383	DISC REG–CONT MAN–MD FAB	W 884	18.7	W 1018	24.8	W 1251	28.2	W 1895	37.1	TISSUS TEX ART CONT MEL SYNT
654	OTH WOVEN TEXTILE FABRIC	W 5068	100.4		152.2		163.0		196.1	TISSUS AUT COTON SYNT,ARTIF
6542	WOVEN WOOL,HAIR NONPILE	W 2052	50.5	W 2489	75.2	W 2937	90.2	W 4143	110.0	TIS PLUS 85% LAINE,POILS
65422	WOVN COMB WOOL,FINE HAIR	W 1457	37.9	W 1706	56.7	W 2189	71.2	W 2985	82.9	TISSUS 85% LAINE,PLS PEIG
6543	WOVEN WOOL ETC FABRC NES	W 1934	32.5		51.3	W 2611	52.0	W 3502	64.6	TISSUS LAINE,POILS FINS NDA
65432	WOOL–DISC SYN FIBR FABRC	W 1699	28.4	W 2193	47.2	W 2382	47.4	W 3392	61.7	TISSUS LAINE MEL SYNT DISC
655	KNITTED,ETC FABRICS	W 1621	18.5	W 2755	36.3	W 4163	47.4	W 5686	53.5	ETOF BONNETERIE PIECES ETC
6552	OTHER KNIT ETC FAB NONEL	W 1621	18.5	W 2755	36.3	W 4163	47.4	W 5686	53.5	ETOF BON NON ELAS NON SYNT
656	LACE,RIBBONS,TULLE,ETC	W 1064	19.9	W 1439	29.4	W 1818	33.4	W 1954	39.0	TULLES,BRODERIE
657	SPECIAL TXTL FABRC,PRODS		55.4		94.9		122.4		147.4	TISSUS SPECIAUX
6572	BONDED FIBRE TEXTLS NES	W 2265	27.2	W 3509	41.7	W 4474	47.7	W 12727	61.5	TISSUS NON TISSES
6573	COATED ETC TEXTILES NES	W 2153	17.4	W 3295	34.3	W 3689	42.9	W 137285	56.0	TISSUS,ART MATIERE TEXT NDA
65732	PLASTIC COATED TEXTILES	W 1437	13.1	W 2152	25.6	W 2553	33.0	W 135859	42.3	TISSUS IMPREGNES
66	NONMETAL MINERAL MFS NES		83.2		121.4		156.3		160.1	ART MIN NON METALLIQUES
662	CLAY,REFRACTORY BLDG PRD	W 41185	29.2		43.2	W 109065	52.8		52.2	MAT CONST REFRACTAIRES
6623	REFRACTORY BUILDING PROD	W 24046	21.9	W 29998	31.7	W 32923	32.5		31.9	BRIQUES REFRACTAIRES
663	MINERAL MANUFCTURES NES	W 8108	15.4		30.5		34.9		33.3	ART MIN MANUF NDA
664	GLASS	W 9486	23.6		22.5	W 14496	35.2		37.6	VERRE
67	IRON AND STEEL		208.4		292.6		370.7		336.3	FER ET ACIER
671	PIG IRON ETC	W 59380	31.8	W 71904	46.2	W 56818	38.4	W 103665	53.3	FONTE,SPIEGEL,POUDRES
6716	FERRO–ALLOYS	W 54727	30.3	W 61531	43.0	W 47740	36.0	W 80568	52.2	FERRO–ALLIAGES
672	IRON,STEEL PRIMARY FORMS	W 287121	75.2	W 361822	141.1	W 416708	175.6	W 415124	151.2	LINGOTS FER,ACIER
6725	IRN,STL BLOOMS,SLABS,ETC	W 234659	53.0	W 304445	88.5	W 328255	116.7	W 339264	107.0	BLOOMS,BILLETTES FER ACIER
67251	IRN,SMPLE STL BLOOMS,ETC	W 220227	42.9	W 234767	53.7	W 248688	70.9	W 271585	75.6	BLOOMS ETC NON ACIER FIN
67255	OTH ALLOY STL BLOOMS ETC	W 13362	8.3	W 68529	32.3	W 78462	43.5	W 67126	30.2	BLOOMS ETC AUT AC ALLIES
6727	IRN,STL COIL FR REROLLNG	W 47913	21.4	W 38626	45.4	W 70736	50.5	W 73433	42.3	EBAUCHES POUR TOLES FER
674	IRN,STL UNIV,PLATE,SHEET	W 48112	38.4	W 53519	44.8	W 84142	64.4	W 71455	48.7	LARGES PLATS,TOLES
678	IRON,STL TUBES,PIPES,ETC	W 33550	38.9	W 19552	32.3	W 27641	51.9	W 14862	35.6	TUBES,TUYAUX EN FONTE,FER
6782	IRON,STL SEAMLESS TUBES	W 18026	26.3	W 11678	18.5	W 19780	34.0	W 7444	16.9	TUBES,TUYAUX SANS SOUDURE
68	NON–FERROUS METALS		36.5		75.1		102.4		77.3	METAUX NON FERREUX
684	ALUMINIUM	W 2491	12.9		29.4	W 6530	47.3		41.3	ALUMINIUM
6842	ALUMINIUM,ALLOYS WORKED	W 2454	12.8		29.4	W 6432	47.2		41.1	ALUMINIUM,ALLIAGES OUVRE
69	METAL MANUFACTURES NES		106.2		173.4		232.3		247.5	ART MANUFACT EN METAL NDA
691	STRUCTURES AND PARTS NES	W 5052	11.7	W 8217	24.6	W 10952	30.5	W 20283	52.8	CONSTRUCT FER,ACIER,ALU
6911	STRUCTURES,PARTS IRN,STL	W 4123	7.6	W 7186	15.8	W 9994	22.1	W 19232	44.3	CONSTRUCT FER,ACIER,FONTE
692	METAL TANKS,BOXES,ETC	W 4686	9.8	W 7267	22.7		39.2		35.5	RECIPIENTS METALLIQUES
699	BASE METAL MFRS NES		50.1		66.9		87.2		92.9	ART MANUFACTURES MET NDA
7	MACHINES,TRANSPORT EQUIP		1784.7		2538.4		2916.7		2980.1	MACHINES MATERIEL TRANSPORT
71	POWER GENERATING EQUIPMT		55.7		85.2		129.3		95.4	MACHINES GENERATRICES
713	INTRNL COMBUS PSTN ENGIN		24.4		30.8		70.6		52.8	MOTEURS EXPL COMB INT, PIECE
7132	MOTOR VEHCL PSTN ENGINS	W 939	5.9	W 1531	10.3	W 6698	49.2	W 4503	31.5	MOTEURS EXPL POUR VEHICULES
72	MACHS FOR SPCL INDUSTRYS		466.8		603.0		697.6		473.5	MAC SPECIALES POUR INDUST
721	AGRIC MACHY,EXC TRACTORS	W 12849	88.1	W 15829	103.4		79.8		36.1	MACHINES AGRICOLES
7212	HARVESTING ETC MACHINES	W 11475	79.3	W 12839	75.4	W 4885	33.1	W 3748	20.0	ENGINS POUR LA RECOLTE
723	CIVIL ENGNEERG EQUIP ETC	W 3513	30.0	W 5798	46.8	W 6914	49.3	W 5087	25.8	APPAREILS DE GENIE CIVIL
7234	CONST,MINING MACHNRY NES	W 2909	17.0	W 4216	32.0	W 5796	40.1	W 3846	17.9	MACH POUR LA CONST, MINES
724	TEXTILE,LEATHER MACHNRY	W 6115	100.6	W 7081	136.6		154.7		124.6	MACH POUR INDUSTRIE TEXTILE
7243	SEWING MACHS,NEEDLES ETC	W 1451	31.6	W 1587	43.1	W 1534	44.1	W 1980	41.6	MACHINES A COUDRE,PIECES
72431	SEWING MACHINES	W 1263	26.8	W 1340	36.6	W 1314	35.3	W 1664	33.6	MACHINES A COUDRE
7245	WEAVING,FELT MFG,ETC MCH	W 904	18.3	W 1098	23.8	W 1324	47.0	W 1198	24.3	METIERS A TISSER,PIECES
7247	TEXTILE MACHINERY NES	W 872	18.5	W 2394	37.9	W 2674	35.3	W 1860	23.6	MACH LAVAGE,TEINTURE TEX
726	PRINTG,BKBINDG MACHY,PTS	W 1754	16.3		32.9		40.2		32.4	MACHINES POUR IMPRIMERIE
727	FOOD MACHRY NON–DOMESTIC	W 5036	55.5	W 6512	73.3	W 8321	121.8	W 4960	55.8	MACH INDUSTRIES ALIMENT
7272	OTH FOOD PROC MCHY,PARTS	W 3802	41.7	W 5080	65.0	W 7127	112.1	W 3843	49.0	AUT MACH IND ALIMENTAIRE
72722	INDUS FOOD PROC MACH NES	W 3741	40.9	W 4977	62.7	W 6030	95.0	W 3455	42.8	MACHINES BOULANGERIE
728	OTH MACHY FOR SPCL INDUS	W 11936	152.8	W 16093	180.5	W 20354	226.6		173.3	AUT MACH IND PARTICULIERES
7281	MACH–TOOLS FR SPCL INDUS	W 4467	42.5	W 6706	58.0	W 7421	58.6	W 6219	32.8	MACH–OUTILS SPEC IND PART
72812	MACH–TOOLS TO WORK WOOD	W 3715	31.6	W 4784	33.4	W 6477	47.5	W 5388	25.6	MACH–OUT POUR TRAVAIL BOIS
7283	OTHR MINERAL WORKG MACHY	W 2790	24.5	W 3387	25.9	W 4794	28.2	W 3682	20.9	MACH TRIER,CRIBLER,BROYER
7284	MACHY FOR SPCL INDUS NES	W 4679	86.0	W 6000	96.7	W 8139	139.9		119.7	MACH SPEC IND PARTICUL.
72842	RUBBER,PLASTICS WRKG MCH	W 1882	38.1	W 2069	34.0	W 2617	37.5	W 1710	30.4	MACH IND CAOUT MAT PLAST
72848	OTH MCHY WITH INDIV FNCT	W 1622	29.1	W 1288	27.1	W 1028	27.5	W 1167	34.7	AUTRES MACHINES NDA
72849	PTS OF MACHS OF 7284 ETC	W 526	13.6	W 1951	30.9	W 2084	34.9	W 1228	33.9	PIECES DU 728.4 ETC
73	METALWORKING MACHINERY		37.7		81.5		84.2		383.3	MACH TRAVAIL DES METAUX
736	METALWORKING MACH–TOOLS	W 1743	22.9		40.0	W 3317	57.7		321.8	MACH–OUTILS TRAVAIL METAUX
7361	METAL CUTTING MACH–TOOLS	W 761	10.8	W 974	15.9	W 1473	27.9	W 5427	234.9	MACH–OUT ENLEVEMENT METAL
7367	OTH METALWRKG MACH–TOOLS	W 103	2.0	W 174	3.6	W 475	7.0	W 1082	56.3	AUT MACH–OUT POUR METAUX
737	METALWORKING MACHNRY NES	W 1318	14.9		41.5		26.5	W 3198	61.5	MACH TRAV METAUX PIECES
74	GENRL INDUSTRL MACHY NES		282.8		517.8		619.7		588.2	MACH APP INDUSTRIE
741	HEATING,COOLING EQUIPMNT	W 10525	95.5	W 15324	171.6	W 20546	245.3	W 21084	218.9	MACH CHAUFFAGE,PIECES
7413	INDUS FURNACES ETC,PARTS	W 4440	30.9	W 3635	44.6	W 6477	67.3	W 8129	89.2	FOURS IND,LABOR,PIECES
74131	INDUS FURNACES ETC ELCTR	W 2691	16.5	W 1257	15.6	W 1006	13.6	W 2123	42.0	FOURS ELECTRIQUES
74132	INDUST FURNACES NONELECT	W 1749	14.5	W 2378	29.1	W 5471	53.8	W 6006	47.2	FOURS NON ELECTRIQUES
7414	NONDOM REFRIG EQUIPT,PTS	W 3097	20.4	W 7392	50.6	W 5697	44.4	W 5206	33.9	MAT PRODUCTION DU FROID
74141	REFRIG EQUIP NONDOMESTIC	W 2484	16.7	W 5026	37.4	W 3894	34.3	W 3861	26.6	REFIG INDUSTRIELS
7415	AIR–CONDITIONING MACHNRY	W 1129	15.6	W 1652	33.7	W 1680	26.6	W 2044	30.7	GROUPES CONDITION AIR
7416	HEATING,COOLING EQU NES	W 1314	14.3	W 2015	29.0	W 4594	76.3	W 5110	50.3	APP CHANGEMENT TEMP

4. Special Imports C.I.F. by Commodities according to the S.I.T.C. (Rev. 2) in million U.S. Dollars
Importations Spéciales C.A.F. par Produits d'après la C.T.C.I. (Rév. 2) en millions de Dollars E.U.

SITC CTCI	COMMODITY	1994 QUANTITY QUANTITE	1994 VALUE VALEUR	1995 QUANTITY QUANTITE	1995 VALUE VALEUR	1996 QUANTITY QUANTITE	1996 VALUE VALEUR	1997 QUANTITY QUANTITE	1997 VALUE VALEUR	PRODUIT
742	PUMPS FOR LIQUIDS ETC	W 1567	22.8	W 2528	34.1	W 2083	45.9	W 1748	40.0	POMPES MOTO–POMPES
743	PUMPS NES,CENTRFUGES ETC	W 3231	37.5	W 5340	62.5	W 6660	91.7	W 6890	85.4	POMPES COMPRES,VENT ETC
7439	PTS NES OF APP OF 7435,6	W 295	8.6	W 763	16.2	W 1172	37.3	W 1470	21.0	PIECES 743.5 ET 743.6
744	MECHANICAL HANDLING EQU	W 3774	24.3	W 8548	72.4	W 6539	40.2	W 7706	63.6	EQUIP MANUTENTION PIECES
7442	LIFTING,LOADING MACH NES	W 1139	8.3	W 3856	33.6	W 2222	16.3	W 3761	42.0	APP LEVAGE,MANUTENTION
74428	OTH HANDLING ETC MCH NES	W 700	4.8	W 3107	26.2	W 1693	10.9	W 2871	34.1	AUT APP LEVAGE ETC
745	NONELEC MACHY,TOOLS NES	W 3521	61.4		110.3		111.9		88.7	AUT MACH NON ELEC,PIECES
7452	OTH NONELEC MCHS,PTS NES	W 3431	57.7		97.0		102.2		79.6	AUT MACH NON ELEC,PIECES
74522	PACKAGNG,BOTTLNG,ETC MCH	W 1797	39.2	W 2829	59.5	W 2540	61.3	W 1736	44.3	MACH NETT BOUTEILLES,ETC
749	NONELEC MACH PTS,ACC NES	W 2022	41.6		67.3		84.9		91.8	PIECES MACH NON ELEC NDA
7492	COCKS,VALVES ETC NES	W 610	15.7	W 1758	29.3	W 1986	41.9	W 2635	42.1	ART ROB,SIM POUR TUYAUX
75	OFFICE MACHNES,ADP EQUIP		128.8		188.3		205.9		200.3	MACH BUREAU TRAIT AUTOM
752	AUTOMTIC DATA PROC EQUIP	W 969	63.5	W 1846	99.4	W 2300	118.3	W 2418	132.0	MACH TRAIT INFORMATION
759	OFFICE,ADP MCH PTS,ACCES	W 751	46.8	W 1114	63.6	W 1323	63.9	W 1105	48.4	PIECES DU 751 ET 752
7599	ACCTG,ETC,ADP MCH PTS,AC	W 681	42.0	W 1052	56.9	W 1254	57.3	W 1044	42.5	PIECES DU 751 ET 752
76	TELECOMM,SOUND EQUIPMENT		202.5		249.4		274.1		368.0	EQUIPMENT DE TELECOM
764	TELECOM EQPT,PTS,ACC NES		186.7		222.9		241.0		338.0	EQUIP TELECOM,PIECES
7643	TV,RADIO TRANSMITTRS ETC	W 98	18.0	W 193	31.9	W 124	22.9	W 612	96.9	APP EMET TELE RADIO
7649	PTS NES OF EQUIPMT OF 76		139.5		151.6	W 5911	169.1		189.3	PIECES DE LA DIV 76
76491	PTS NES OF APPAR OF 7641	W 859	63.6	W 636	49.9	W 772	70.5	W 1123	98.4	PIECES POUR 764.1
76493	TELECOMM EQUIPMT PTS NES	W 3461	72.2	W 5081	100.3	W 5044	96.4	W 3022	89.8	PIECES 761,762,764.3,8
77	ELECTRIC MACHNRY NES ETC		285.6		428.1		504.2		502.2	MACH APP ELECT NDA
772	SWITCHGEAR ETC,PARTS NES	W 1389	51.8		49.9		68.1		81.6	APP COUPURE,SECT ETC
7721	SWITCHGEAR ETC	W 1303	49.7	W 1507	47.7	W 1885	63.9	W 2261	76.3	APP COUPURE,SECTIONMNT
773	ELECTR DISTRIBUTNG EQUIP	W 13902	92.4	W 12767	100.9	W 14977	114.8	W 17101	124.2	EQUIPMT DISTRIBUTION ELECT
7731	INSULATED WIRE,CABLE ETC	W 13781	89.2	W 12653	97.7	W 14826	111.4	W 16876	120.3	FILS,CABLES ISOLES ELECT
774	ELECTRO–MEDCL,XRAY EQUIP	W 66	20.6	W 264	44.2	W 197	20.1	W 291	30.1	APPAREILS MEDICAUX
7742	X–RAY APPARATUS ETC	W 34	9.1	W 205	33.1	W 143	9.6	W 179	15.6	APPAREILS A RAYONS X
775	HOUSEHOLD TYPE EQUIP NES		21.0		45.1		89.4		69.8	MACH,APP USAGE DOMESTQUE
776	TRANSISTORS,VALVES,ETC	W 4905	41.7		85.8		90.3		61.4	LAMPES,TUBES,VALVES
7761	TV PICTURE TUBES	W 4694	33.4	W 7783	64.0	W 7235	60.0	W 3280	28.2	TUBES CATHODIQUES
778	ELECTRICAL MACHINERY NES		51.8		92.0		105.5		103.4	AUTRES MACH ELECT NDA
7788	OTH ELEC MACHY,EQUIP NES		23.5		36.3		41.9		43.5	AUT MACH APP ELEC NDA
78	ROAD VEHICLES		120.8		310.4		346.6		284.3	VEHICULES ROUTIERS
781	PASS MOTOR VEH EXC BUSES	W 3029	16.6	W 23013	175.4	W 10908	79.1	W 8522	65.9	AUTO TRANSPORT PERSONNES
782	LORRIES,SPCL MTR VEH NES	W 13590	49.1	W 14210	51.7	W 14764	53.5	W 12055	48.4	VEHICULES SPECIAUX,MARCH
7821	LORRIES,TRUCKS	W 10881	23.2	W 10984	34.2	W 12276	42.8	W 10196	36.3	VEHICULES TRANSP MARCHAND
7822	SPECIAL MOTOR VEHCLS NES	W 2709	25.9	W 3226	17.5	W 2488	10.8	W 1859	12.1	VEHICULES USAGES SPECIAUX
783	ROAD MOTOR VEHICLES NES	W 7743	29.9	W 10567	41.8	W 8912	49.0	W 8695	39.1	VEHICULES ROUTIERS NDA
784	MOTOR VEH PRTS,ACCES NES	W 4141	15.5	W 5148	26.0	W 20959	145.1	W 14435	106.6	PIECES 722,781,782,783
7849	OTHER MOTOR VEHCL PARTS	W 3749	14.5	W 4342	23.8	W 20039	142.9	W 13188	94.9	PIECES 722,781,782,783
79	OTHR TRANSPORT EQUIPMENT		204.4		75.3		55.6		85.2	AUTRE MATERIEL TRANSPORT
791	RAILWAY VEHICLES	W 8043	21.1		45.0	W 8163	14.2		31.0	VEHIC MAT CHEMINS DE FER
792	AIRCRAFT ETC		181.9		28.3		38.2		52.3	APP NAVIGATION AERIENNE
7923	AIRCRFT NES2000–15000KG	W 74	26.1	W 25	0.2		6.7	W 37	6.6	AERODYNES 2000 A 15000 KG
7924	AIRCRFT NES OVER 15000KG	W 199	126.4	W 195	1.5	W 92	1.5	W 24	21.1	AERODYNES PLUS 15000 KG
7929	AIRCRAFT PARTS NES	W 115	27.6		21.6	W 57	25.3	W 32	12.2	PIECES DU 792
8	MISC MANUFACTURED GOODS		521.8		842.9		907.5		960.6	ART MANUFACTURES DIVERS
812	*PLUMBG,HEATNG,LGHTNG EQ	W 6578	15.0	W 10683	34.9	W 11028	44.7	W 12234	46.7	APPAR SANITAIRES CHAUFFAGE
821	*FURNITURE,PARTS THEREOF	W 7563	23.6	W 15100	45.2	W 19416	60.3		56.7	MEUBLES ET PIECES
8219	FURNITURE AND PARTS NES	W 6477	17.7	W 12988	35.4	W 16715	43.6	W 14924	39.6	AUTRES MEUBLES ET PIECES
84	CLOTHING AND ACCESSORIES		122.6		170.2		189.1		218.9	VETEMENTS
844	UNDER GARMENTS NOT KNIT	W 3949	27.1	W 6863	46.3	W 5266	83.3		110.8	VETEMENT DESSOUS MAT TEX
8441	— MENS SHIRTS	W 3676	26.6	W 6117	45.3	W 4894	82.0	W 6085	109.7	CHEMISES HOMMES MAT TEXT
84412	—— OF SYNTHETIC FIBRES	W 2713	24.5	W 4838	43.7	W 4795	80.4	W 5997	108.3	CHEMISES HOMMES FIB SYNT
846	UNDER GARMENTS KNITTED	W 3106	27.1	W 3179	34.6		31.6	W 2573	22.3	SOUS VETS DE BONNETERIE
847	TEXTILE CLTHNG ACCES NES	W 1555	29.0		47.5		30.4		28.1	ACCES VET MAT TEXT NDA
8471	— NOT KNITTED	W 1309	26.6		45.1		28.5		26.3	ACCES VET MAT TEX NON BON
84719	MADE–UP CLTHG ACCESS NES	W 1148	25.8	W 1644	44.2	W 1458	28.0	W 1521	25.4	AUT ACCES VET MAT TEXTIL
87	PRECISION INSTRUMNTS NES		112.0		197.0		171.1		187.7	INSTRUM,APPAR SCIENT NDA
872	MEDICAL INSTRUMENTS NES	W 974	16.0		55.8		44.4		37.5	INSTR,APP MEDIC–CHIR NDA
87202	OTH MEDICAL INSTRUMENTS	W 938	14.7	W 1855	53.0	W 2046	39.0	W 1660	33.7	INSTRUM,APP MEDECINE
874	MEASURNG,CONTROLNG INSTR	W 998	83.9		127.6		111.5		135.6	INSTRUMENTS DE MESURE
8742	MEASUR,DRAW ETC INST,PTS	W 333	31.4		50.2		12.0	W 338	26.8	INST DESSIN,TRACAGE,PCS
87421	MEASURNG,DRAWNG ETC INST	W 267	30.6	W 476	47.7	W 330	10.3	W 266	20.9	INSTRUM DESSIN,TRACAGE
8748	ELEC MEAS,CONTRL EQU NES	W 120	24.1		31.8		39.1		32.3	APP ELEC ELECTRO MESURE
87483	OTH ELCTRNC MEAS ETC EQU	W 106	21.7		29.0		32.7		27.7	AUT APP ELECTRO DE MESURE
88	PHOTO EQU,OPTICL GDS ETC		19.9		34.9		40.8		36.2	APP,FOURN PHOTO,OP,MONTR
89	MISC MANUFCTRD GOODS NES		208.1		335.4		379.6		382.1	ART MANUFACTURES DIVERS
892	PRINTED MATTER		37.6		59.7		68.7		67.9	IMPRIMES
8928	PRINTED MATTER NES		20.6		29.2		36.0		33.1	IMPRIMES NDA
893	ARTICLES OF PLASTIC NES	W 65598	70.1	W 40620	130.6	W 41961	157.7		159.4	OUVRAGES EN MAT DIVIS 58
8931	PLSTC PACKG CONTNRS,LIDS	W 54951	29.1	W 23858	48.6	W 19068	42.7	W 21660	44.4	ART TRANSP EMBALLAGE ETC
8939	MISC PLASTIC ARTICLES	W 10266	40.4	W 16451	80.5	W 22483	113.0	W 86918	112.3	ART DIVERS EN MAT DIV 58
89399	OTHR PLASTC ARTICLES NES	W 8425	36.3	W 13548	71.5	W 19816	104.0	W 84041	104.3	AUT OUV MAT DIV 58
894	TOYS,SPORTING GOODS,ETC	W 8018	39.3		55.2		50.4		49.2	VOITURES ENFANTS,JOUETS
8942	TOYS,INDOOR GAMES ETC	W 7496	34.0	W 9898	42.6	W 8893	39.1	W 11792	42.6	JOUETS,JEUX ETC
899	OTHER MANUFACTURED GOODS		44.3		62.9		75.0		77.4	AUT ART MANUF DIVERS NDA
8998	SMALLWARES,TOILETRYS ETC		35.1		48.1		58.4		63.1	ART MERCERIE,TOILETTE
89983	BUTTONS,STUDS,ETC	W 96791	23.0	W 825	30.5	W 899	33.3	W 1152	36.0	BOUTONS,BOUTONS–PRESSION
9	GOODS NOT CLASSD BY KIND		86.1		123.0		164.6		223.9	ART TRANSACT NON CLASSES
931	*SPECIAL TRANSACTIONS		67.4		103.5		140.7		213.7	TRANS.SPECIALES

5. Special Exports F.O.B. by Commodities according to the S.I.T.C. (Rev. 2) in million U.S. Dollars
Exportations Spéciales F.O.B. par Produits d'après la C.T.C.I. (Rév. 2) en millions de Dollars E.U.

SITC CTCI	COMMODITY	1994 QUANTITY QUANTITE	1994 VALUE VALEUR	1995 QUANTITY QUANTITE	1995 VALUE VALEUR	1996 QUANTITY QUANTITE	1996 VALUE VALEUR	1997 QUANTITY QUANTITE	1997 VALUE VALEUR	PRODUIT
	ALL COMMODITIES		6151.3		7910.1		8084.5		8431.1	TOUS PRODUITS
0	FOOD AND LIVE ANIMALS		310.0		398.8		557.5		383.6	ALIMENTS,ANIMAUX VIVANTS
001	*LIVE ANIMALS FOR FOOD	W 83137	85.1	W 81754	85.6	W 73018	71.8	W 77425	77.8	ANIMAUX VIVANTS
0011	BOVINE SPECIES,LIVE	W 24439	26.4	W 24426	28.7	W 13667	16.1	W 22769	22.7	ESPECE BOVINE
0012	SHEEP AND GOATS,LIVE	W 48318	50.6	W 44049	44.8	W 41027	39.9	W 38720	41.8	ESPECES OVINE ET CAPRINE
01	MEAT AND PREPARATIONS		132.0		76.0		64.8		97.6	VIANDES ET PREPARATIONS
011	MEAT FRESH,CHILLD,FROZEN	W 97869	118.3	W 42061	65.5	W 37492	59.8	W 60231	94.6	VIANDES FRAICHES,REF,CONGE
0113	PIG MEAT FRESH,CHLD,FRZN	W 86282	94.0	W 37667	50.2	W 34456	48.6	W 57236	84.2	VIANDE DE PORC
04	CEREALS AND PREPARATIONS		7.8		143.7		305.5		91.3	CEREALES ET PRODUITS
041	WHEAT ETC UNMILLED	W 100	0.1	W 649684	109.4	W 1281017	232.8	W 451193	49.7	FROMENT,EPEAUTRE
0412	OTHER WHEAT ETC UNMILLED	W 100	0.1	W 649384	109.3	W 1281017	232.8	W 428948	47.0	AUTRE FROMENT NON MOULU
043	BARLEY UNMILLED	W 175	0.1	W 8535	0.9	W 166669	24.8	W 259048	28.9	ORGE NON MONDEE
044	MAIZE UNMILLED	W 6985	7.4	W 220546	29.9	W 187578	27.2	W 83360	10.5	MAIS NON MOULU
05	VEGETABLES AND FRUIT		62.1		67.3		73.9		66.4	LEGUMES ET FRUITS
054	VEG ETC FRSH,SMPLY PRSVD	W 53848	24.8		24.8	W 25460	24.9	W 39685	20.4	LEGUMES FRAIS,CONG,SECS
057	FRUIT,NUTS,FRESH,DRIED	W 47060	18.4		23.5	W 133697	25.8	W 129788	26.9	FRUITS FRAIS OU SECS
1	BEVERAGES AND TOBACCO		23.6		31.2		55.0		57.4	BOISSONS ET TABACS
11	BEVERAGES		23.5		30.4		54.9		57.3	BOISSONS
112	ALCOHOLIC BEVERAGES	W 39014	20.2		26.3		36.2	W 93143	46.8	BOISSONS ALCOOLIQUES
1121	WINE OF FRESH GRAPES ETC	W 37809	19.2		25.4	W 49184	34.7	W 91974	46.1	VINS DE RAISINS FRAIS
11212	WINE OF FRESH GRAPES	W 36622	18.7	W 33292	24.6	W 45454	33.0	W 80657	42.5	VINS DE MOUTS DE RAISINS
2	CRUDE MATERLS,EXCL FUELS		277.8		295.3		309.3		394.2	MAT BRUTES NON COMESTIBLES
24	CORK AND WOOD		156.4		174.9		218.0		248.2	LIEGE ET BOIS
248	WOOD SHAPED,SLEEPERS	W 423937	154.3	W 455285	171.4	W 544004	214.5	W 706996	245.3	BOIS SIMPLEMENT TRAVAILLES
2482	LUMBER SHAPED CONIFER	W 221223	72.4	W 265395	88.8	W 290361	96.4	W 474804	140.2	CONIFERES SCIES,RABOTES
24821	LUMBER SAWN ETC CONIFER	W 220068	71.8	W 260941	86.4	W 285525	94.4	W 463364	136.2	CONIFERES SCIES LONGITUD
2483	LUMBER SHAPED NON–CONIFR	W 202714	82.0	W 189890	82.7	W 253643	118.2	W 232164	105.1	NON CONIFERES SCIES,RABOTES
24831	LUMBER SAWN ETC NON–CON	W 190362	77.4	W 170799	74.9	W 238461	109.0	W 215659	94.7	SCIES LONGITUDINALEMENT
26	TEXTILE FIBRES AND WASTE		46.2		61.1		34.3		35.1	FIBRES TEXTILES
266	SYNTHETIC FIBRES TO SPIN	W 18505	26.4	W 18604	37.2	W 11438	16.9	W 14081	20.7	FIBRES SYNTHETIQUES
2665	DISCN SYNTH FIBRE UNCMBD	W 15183	21.2	W 15625	31.0	W 9968	13.8	W 9573	13.9	DISCONTINUES EN MASSE
27	CRUDE FERTLZR,MINRLS NES		15.5		14.9		20.9		28.3	ENGRAIS MINERAUX BRUTS
28	METALLIFEROUS ORES,SCRAP		28.6		11.7		5.8		47.3	MINERAIS METAL,DECHETS
3	MINERAL FUELS ETC		613.6		628.3		596.2		517.9	COMBUSTIBLES MINERAUX LUB
33	PETROLEUM AND PRODUCTS		608.2		605.2		579.2		492.6	PETROLE ET DERIVES
334	PETROLEUM PRODUCTS,REFIN	W 4068913	598.5	W 3847430	589.4	W 2944234	563.6	W 2658592	480.1	PRODUITS RAFFINES
4	ANIMAL,VEGETABLE OIL,FAT		47.9		82.0		71.3		128.5	HUILES,GRAISSES ANIM,VEG
42	FIXED VEGETABLE OIL,FAT		45.2		78.5		65.7		123.2	HUILES VEGETALES FIXES
423	FIXED VEG OILS,SOFT		45.1	W 127742	78.4	W 123767	65.6	W 240084	123.0	HUILES VEGET DOUCES FIXES
4236	SUNFLOWER SEED OIL	W 56790	33.5	W 106589	66.3	W 111645	59.1	W 221811	113.9	HUILE DE TOURNESOL
5	CHEMCLS,RELATED PROD NES		589.7		849.4		794.8		656.1	PRODUITS CHIMIQUES
51	ORGANIC CHEMICALS		151.4		204.6		137.5		176.0	PROD CHIMIQ ORGANIQUES
512	ALCOHOLS,PHENOLS ETC	W 241587	68.7	W 159448	59.3	W 135239	37.5	W 265041	55.2	PHENOLS,PHENOLS–ALCOOLS
5121	ACYCLIC ALCOHOLS,DERIVS	W 236535	66.7	W 152073	55.1	W 133570	35.6	W 255584	48.0	ALCOOLS ACYCLIQUES
513	CARBOXYLIC ACIDS ETC	W 33163	28.5	W 25765	32.6	W 17239	23.1	W 17798	22.4	ACIDES CARBOXYLIQUES
5138	POLYACIDS AND DERIVATIVS	W 29143	23.1	W 18298	21.0	W 12665	14.6	W 12246	13.3	ACIDES POLYCARBOXYLIQUES
514	NITROGEN–FNCTN COMPOUNDS		38.3		75.5		57.9		64.1	COMPOSES FONCT AZOTEES
5148	OTH NITROGN–FNCTN CMPNDS	W 56488	34.9		68.0	W 65768	52.0	W 71846	60.1	AUTRES COMPOSES AZOTES
51483	ACRYLONITRILE	W 43915	24.9	W 53049	54.6	W 53221	35.9	W 56914	40.7	ACRYLONITRILE
52	INORGANIC CHEMICALS		73.6		114.7		122.8		110.0	PROD CHIM INORGANIQUES
522	INORG ELEMNTS,OXIDES,ETC	W 193272	24.7		41.2		32.6	W 220345	29.1	ELEMENTS INORGANIQUES
5225	INORGANIC BASES ETC NES	W 183495	22.1	W 163705	36.7	W 174553	28.9	W 181753	22.9	AUTRES BASES OXYDES METAL
523	OTHR INORG CHEMICALS ETC		48.9		73.5		90.1		80.8	AUT PRODUITS CHIMIQUES INORG
5232	OTH MTL CMPD OF INRG ACD	W 285681	33.8	W 344532	46.1	W 394278	54.3	W 399054	52.8	SELS METALLIQUES
52323	NEUTRAL SODIUM CARBONATE	W 263877	28.7	W 309325	37.2	W 362329	46.7	W 372307	47.0	CARBONATE NEUTRE SODIUM
541	*MEDICINAL,PHARM PRODUCT		33.1		43.8		39.5		30.9	PROD MEDICINAUX PHARMACEUT
562	*FERTILIZERS,MANUFACTURE	W 2082531	208.2		334.8	W 2489514	353.8	W 1370423	180.1	ENGRAIS MANUFACTURES
5621	CHEM NITROGENOUS FERTLZR	W 1527492	143.4	W 2133998	285.0	W 2204099	306.9	W 1084260	136.4	ENGRAIS AZOTES
56211	AMMONIUM NITRATE	W 245327	20.5	W 233082	24.6	W 288783	36.0	W 125489	13.9	NITRATE D'AMMONIUM
56216	UREA	W 974341	98.2	W 1293827	204.1	W 1340837	210.0	W 600582	88.7	UREE
56219	CHEM NITROG FERTILZR NES	W 252608	22.3	W 499541	49.3	W 496293	55.8	W 278521	28.7	ENGRAIS AZOTES NDA
5629	FERTILIZERS NES	W 407409	54.0		47.8	W 242632	42.4	W 243336	39.6	ENGRAIS NDA
56291	NIT–PHOS–POT FERTLZR NES	W 359841	46.8	W 259019	41.3	W 211924	36.9	W 225524	36.7	ENGRAIS CONT N P K
58	PLASTIC MATERIALS ETC		102.9		129.6		109.1		114.7	MAT PLAST ARTIFICIELLES
583	POLYMERIZATION ETC PRODS	W 137645	99.6		116.7		95.4		99.7	PROD POLYMERISATION
5834	POLYVINYL CHLORIDE	W 111502	83.8	W 101146	92.7		63.7	W 105678	70.5	CHLORURE DE POLYVINYLE
58341	— IN PRIMARY FORMS	W 111471	83.8	W 101072	92.6	W 108955	63.5	W 105332	70.0	SOUS FORMES PRIMAIRES
6	BASIC MANUFACTURES		1627.2		2231.0		2074.1		2396.1	ART MANUFACTURES
61	LEATHER,DRESSED FUR,ETC		138.3		185.1		232.2		233.8	CUIRS,PELLETERIES
612	LEATHER ETC MANUFACTURES		125.4		171.9	W 9028	217.6		217.1	OUVRAGES EN CUIRS NDA
6123	PREPRD PARTS OF FOOTWEAR	W 6686	124.1	W 7696	170.2	W 8956	216.0	W 10328	215.1	PARTIES DE CHAUSSURES
62	RUBBER MANUFACTURES NES		31.1		51.6		59.1		48.6	CAOUTCHOUC MANUFACTURE
625	RUBBER TYRES, TUBES ETC		23.7	W 22887	40.4	W 21905	41.4	W 19645	36.2	PNEUS CAOUTCHOUC VULCANISE
6259	OTH TYRES,TYRE CASES,ETC	W 11999	17.7	W 18580	31.7	W 16727	30.3	W 16452	29.6	AUTRES PNEUS RECHAPES FLAPS
62599	TYRES NES,TYRE CASES,ETC	W 11689	17.4	W 17931	30.6	W 16358	29.5	W 16237	29.2	PNEUS,FLAPS
63	WOOD,CORK MANUFACTRS NES		54.9		72.2		76.8		97.9	OUVRAGES LIEGE ET BOIS
634	VENEERS,PLYWOOD,ETC	W 76656	28.5		31.9		28.1	W 53621	29.9	PLACAGES,CONTRE–PLAQUES
6342	PLYWOOD OF WOOD SHEETS	W 36013	18.6	W 41724	23.9	W 35732	21.2	W 39462	22.7	BOIS CONTRE–PLAQUES
635	WOOD MANUFACTURES NES	W 47572	26.5	W 63110	40.4	W 82915	48.7	W 141663	67.6	ART MANUF EN BOIS NDA
6353	BUILDERS WOODWRK,PREFABS	W 15386	11.5	W 33681	23.7	W 50804	30.0	W 97567	43.5	OUVRAGES DE MENUISERIE
64	PAPER,PAPERBOARD AND MFR		37.9		91.8		60.3		67.1	PAPIERS,CARTONS & OUVRAGES
641	PAPER AND PAPERBOARD	W 119253	36.6		89.2	W 122378	56.2		57.8	PAPIERS ET CARTONS
6413	KRAFT PAPER,PAPERBOARD	W 20343	9.8	W 53336	39.9	W 42614	25.5	W 41839	22.2	PAPIER ET CARTON KRAFT
6415	PAPER,PAPERBRD,BULK,NES	W 33111	11.9	W 63004	30.1	W 35105	19.1	W 56857	21.4	PAPIERS,CARTONS ROULEAUX
65	TEXTILE YARN,FABRICS,ETC		138.5		180.9		170.0		190.8	FILS,TISSUS,ARTICLES TEXTILE
651	TEXTILE YARN		62.1		88.0		81.7		90.4	FILS TEXTILES
6514	SYN FIB YRN,BULK,MONOFIL	W 10334	26.0	W 11366	37.0	W 11560	34.4	W 13444	37.0	FILS CONT 85% FIB TEXT SYNTH
6516	DISCON SYN FIB BLEND YRN	W 6504	19.9	W 7621	26.9	W 8802	29.2	W 10352	34.0	FILS FIBR TEX SYNT DIS MOINS
65168	OTH DISC SYN BLEND YARN	W 6173	19.2	W 7014	24.8	W 8270	27.0	W 10056	32.7	FILS TEXT SYNT MELANGE AUT F
658	TEXTILE ARTICLES NES	W 4416	24.9		32.7		33.8		43.0	ART FACONNES MAT TEXTILES
6584	LINENS ETC	W 3156	18.5	W 3270	24.1	W 3314	24.0	W 4849	30.6	LINGE DE MAISON
66	NONMETAL MINERAL MFS NES		162.9		214.2		211.4		226.1	ART MIN NON METALLIQUES
661	LIME,CEMENT,BLDG PRODS	W 2400672	64.1	W 2966859	81.7	W 2663864	79.3	W 3060294	94.5	CHAUX,CIMENTS MAT CONSTR
6612	CEMENT	W 2378777	60.8	W 2951903	79.0	W 2638309	75.7	W 3036495	90.4	CIMENTS HYDRAULIQUES
664	GLASS	W 114916	22.9		32.4	W 114783	29.7		21.1	VERRE
665	GLASSWARE	W 23331	47.0		62.0		61.5		68.0	OUVRAGES EN VERRE
6652	HOUSEHLD,HOTEL ETC GLASS	W 11386	44.6	W 12163	55.1	W 13443	54.3	W 17983	59.8	OBJETS VERRE TABLE,CUISINE
666	POTTERY	W 14939	22.5	W 20506	33.8	W 23017	37.3	W 25174	36.8	POTERIE
67	IRON AND STEEL		804.0		1059.4		886.2		1089.1	FER ET ACIER
671	PIG IRON ETC	W 45914	15.7	W 113138	42.1	W 156402	61.8	W 135959	42.1	FONTE,SPIEGEL,POUDRES
6716	FERRO–ALLOYS	W 25410	12.6	W 60584	34.1	W 86951	49.3	W 56162	27.2	FERRO–ALLIAGES

5. Special Exports F.O.B. by Commodities according to the S.I.T.C. (Rev. 2) in million U.S. Dollars
Exportations Spéciales F.O.B. par Produits d'après la C.T.C.I. (Rév. 2) en millions de Dollars E.U.

SITC CTCI	COMMODITY	1994		1995		1996		1997		PRODUIT
		QUANTITY QUANTITE	VALUE VALEUR	QUANTITY QUANTITE	VALUE VALEUR	QUANTITY QUANTITE	VALUE VALEUR	QUANTITY QUANTITE	VALUE VALEUR	
67169	OTHER FERRO–ALLOYS	W 7639	2.8	W 46022	24.7	W 70216	37.1	W 51497	23.8	AUTRES FERRO–ALLIAGES
672	IRON,STEEL PRIMARY FORMS	W 389953	104.1	W 398156	124.0	W 198173	58.5	W 446568	125.3	LINGOTS FER,ACIER
6727	IRN,STL COIL FR REROLLNG	W 388048	103.4	W 397725	123.4	W 196909	57.4	W 371869	109.1	EBAUCHES POUR TOLES FER
673	IRON,STEEL SHAPES ETC		268.6	W 967622	283.2	W 630360	181.3	W 905146	244.1	BARRES,PROFIL FER,ACIER
6731	IRON,STEEL WIRE ROD		157.3	W 472452	131.0	W 333688	88.0	W 514782	131.7	FIL MACHINE FER,ACIER
67311	IRON,SIMPLE STL WIRE ROD	W 598371	157.3	W 469030	129.9	W 332501	87.1	W 513898	131.2	FIL MACH AUT ACIER FIN
6732	IRON,STEEL BARS ETC	W 199667	48.0	W 183238	60.2	W 79136	31.2	W 138740	42.2	BARRES FER,ACIER
67326	IRN,OTH STL BARS HOTROLD	W 164382	38.7	W 147815	43.3	W 55734	17.6	W 118393	32.5	BARRES PLEINES FER,ACIER
6733	IRON,STEEL PROFILES ETC	W 227738	63.4	W 311932	92.2	W 217536	62.2	W 251624	70.3	PROFILES,PALPLAN FER,ACIER
67332	LARGE U,I,H SECTIONS ETC	W 142036	39.2	W 241924	71.4	W 145946	41.6	W 172507	47.3	PROFILES PLUS 80MM
674	IRN,STL UNIV,PLATE,SHEET	W 1106631	307.5	W 1158144	400.8	W 1069750	375.5		440.2	LARGES PLATS,TOLES
6744	IRN,STL HVY PLATE,ROLLED	W 972525	260.1	W 1057425	328.3	W 1021268	328.3	W 1256948	393.2	TOLES LAMINEES PLUS 4.75 MM
67441	— OF IRON OR SIMPLE STL	W 972357	260.0	W 1055695	327.3	W 1021214	328.0	W 1255960	392.6	TOLES NON ACIER FIN CARB
6745	IRN,STL MED PLATE,ROLLED	W 85258	21.0	W 11791	5.2	W 9352	4.9	W 19227	6.3	TOLES 3 A 4.75 MM
67451	— OF IRON OR SIMPLE STL	W 84925	20.9	W 9464	3.5	W 5300	2.0	W 17955	5.4	TOLES AUT NON ACIER FIN
6746	IRN,STL THIN PLATE,ROLLD	W 37652	22.7	W 73486	60.2	W 33589	39.5	W 34909	34.3	TOLES LAM MOINS 3MM
67463	— OF STAINLESS ETC STL	W 11769	14.0	W 16697	36.9	W 15923	30.9	W 17361	27.7	TOL ACIER INOX MOINS 3 MM
677	IRN,STL WIRE(EXCL W ROD)	W 82708	25.1	W 206119	61.3	W 102112	32.8	W 134704	40.8	FILS EN FER,ACIER
678	IRON,STL TUBES,PIPES,ETC	W 130701	72.8	W 216930	127.8	W 244343	152.9	W 287846	180.7	TUBES,TUYAUX EN FONTE,FER
6782	IRON,STL SEAMLESS TUBES	W 67346	32.8	W 120535	65.5	W 149597	89.6	W 188187	112.2	TUBES,TUYAUX SANS SOUDURE
6783	IRON,STL TUBES,PIPES NES	W 41064	18.8	W 71444	33.2	W 46171	21.7	W 68421	27.3	AUT TUBES,TUYAUX FER,ACIER
6785	IRON,STEEL TUBE FITTINGS	W 21924	21.0	W 24793	29.1	W 48443	41.6	W 31017	40.9	ACCESSOIRES DE TUYAUTERIE
68	NON–FERROUS METALS		180.1		247.5		234.2		300.2	METAUX NON FERREUX
682	COPPER EXC CEMENT COPPER	W 14182	21.1		18.7		30.2	W 20121	32.6	CUIVRE
684	ALUMINIUM	W 110469	154.3	W 128502	221.1	W 128375	191.9		246.3	ALUMINIUM
6841	ALUMINIUM,ALLOYS,UNWRGHT	W 99568	134.0	W 106243	169.6	W 105345	149.2	W 107483	167.8	ALUMINIUM,ALLIAGES BRUTS
6842	ALUMINIUM,ALLOYS WORKED	W 10901	20.3	W 22259	51.5	W 23030	42.7		78.6	ALUMINIUM,ALLIAGES OUVRE
68421	ALUMINIUM BARS,WIRE,ETC	W 3032	5.4	W 12041	25.3	W 17459	30.4	W 30703	55.6	BARRES,PROFILES FILS ALU
69	METAL MANUFACTURES NES		79.9		128.7		144.2		142.9	ART MANUFACT EN METAL NDA
691	STRUCTURES AND PARTS NES	W 13475	12.5	W 13099	13.5	W 97784	31.9		27.3	CONSTRUCT FER,ACIER,ALU
6911	STRUCTURES,PARTS IRN,STL	W 13375	12.3	W 13028	13.4	W 97693	31.5	W 29176	26.9	CONSTRUCT FER,ACIER,FONTE
694	STL,COPPR NAILS,NUTS,ETC	W 33149	11.6	W 27575	24.8	W 24372	23.2	W 25486	18.5	CLOUS,VIS,ECROUS
699	BASE METAL MFRS NES		16.5		26.9		22.4		27.3	ART MANUFACTURES MET NDA
7	MACHINES,TRANSPORT EQUIP		879.2		1037.0		1100.4		1179.3	MACHINES MATERIEL TRANSPORT
71	POWER GENERATING EQUIPMT		82.5		101.2		103.2		122.1	MACHINES GENERATRICES
711	STEAM BOILERS & AUX PLNT	W 6555	27.8		20.8	W 3504	14.0	W 3999	18.5	GENERATEURS VAPEUR EAU ETC
713	INTRNL COMBUS PSTN ENGIN	W 1473	6.9	W 1099	7.5		8.1		25.9	MOTEURS EXPL COMB INT, PIECE
716	ROTATING ELECTRIC PLANT	W 13439	32.5		57.8		65.1		62.8	APP ELECTR ROTATIFS,PIECES
7162	AC MTRS,GENRTRS,GEN SETS	W 12141	29.2	W 18177	51.1		58.4		52.6	MOTEURS ELECTRIQUES
71621	AC MTRS,INC UNIVRSL MTRS	W 12036	28.6	W 17995	50.2	W 18526	56.8	W 19027	52.1	MOT ELEC NON COUR CONTINU
72	MACHS FOR SPCL INDUSTRYS		89.6		109.9		103.7		145.0	MAC SPECIALES POUR INDUST
722	TRACTORS NON–ROAD	W 99079	26.1	W 14623	33.1	W 12321	28.6	W 17219	39.7	TRACTEURS
7224	WHEELED TRACTORS NES	W 98782	25.6	W 14153	32.1	W 12048	28.0	W 17162	39.6	TRACTEURS A ROUES
723	CIVIL ENGNEERG EQUIP ETC	W 6063	28.8	W 6933	33.2	W 11098	30.3	W 8027	36.6	APPAREILS DE GENIE CIVIL
728	OTH MACHY FOR SPCL INDUS		16.7	W 12021	30.3		28.8		49.5	AUT MACH IND PARTICULIERES
7283	OTHR MINERAL WORKG MACHY	W 3352	11.3	W 9916	24.8	W 6898	19.8	W 12419	40.2	MACH TRIER,CRIBLER,BROYER
72839	PTS NES OF MACHY OF 7283	W 1856	6.9	W 9359	23.6	W 6697	19.1	W 12100	39.1	PIECES MACH DU 728.3
73	METALWORKING MACHINERY		41.1		53.2		61.8		69.9	MACH TRAVAIL DES METAUX
736	METALWORKING MACH–TOOLS	W 10650	25.1	W 12418	38.7	W 16988	46.4	W 21099	51.0	MACH–OUTILS TRAVAIL METAUX
74	GENRL INDUSTRL MACHY NES		160.7		214.8		235.0		246.0	MACH APP INDUSTRIE
741	HEATING,COOLING EQUIPMNT		14.8	W 7023	36.5		21.6		32.3	MACH CHAUFFAGE,PIECES
744	MECHANICAL HANDLING EQU	W 6360	10.2		15.4	W 15047	25.6		25.7	EQUIP MANUTENTION PIECES
749	NONELEC MACH PTS,ACC NES	W 32318	119.9		142.5	W 37267	165.2		165.1	PIECES MACH NON ELEC NDA
7491	BALL,ROLLER,ETC BEARINGS	W 17038	77.9	W 16743	99.5	W 17462	107.9	W 18337	98.4	ROULEMENTS BILLES ETC
7492	COCKS,VALVES ETC NES	W 12497	29.9	W 10814	24.7	W 12708	31.2	W 15596	39.0	ART ROB,SIM POUR TUYAUX
77	ELECTRIC MACHNRY NES ETC		131.2		184.8		179.0		183.3	MACH APP ELECT NDA
772	SWITCHGEAR ETC,PARTS NES	W 3666	25.4		37.9		24.6		20.3	APP COUPURE,SECT ETC
7721	SWITCHGEAR ETC	W 3619	24.7	W 4401	37.5	W 3607	24.0	W 4071	19.3	APP COUPURE,SECTIONMNT
773	ELECTR DISTRIBUTNG EQUIP	W 6951	54.9	W 9314	83.3	W 8213	77.4	W 8039	76.3	EQUIPMT DISTRIBUTION ELECT
7731	INSULATED WIRE,CABLE ETC	W 6258	53.5	W 8595	81.5	W 7544	76.0	W 7313	74.7	FILS,CABLES ISOLES ELECT
778	ELECTRICAL MACHINERY NES		20.3		32.1		35.4		44.5	AUTRES MACH ELECT NDA
7788	OTH ELEC MACHY,EQUIP NES		5.1		12.5		16.8		26.1	AUT MACH APP ELEC NDA
78	ROAD VEHICLES		163.7		173.0		165.9		195.0	VEHICULES ROUTIERS
781	PASS MOTOR VEH EXC BUSES	W 31101	104.2	W 15026	75.0	W 9310	59.5	W 10535	69.4	AUTO TRANSPORT PERSONNES
782	LORRIES,SPCL MTR VEH NES	W 6848	24.2	W 5831	21.9	W 4367	14.6	W 1390	5.2	VEHICULES SPECIAUX,MARCH
7821	LORRIES,TRUCKS	W 5594	18.9	W 5109	17.7	W 4020	13.4	W 1228	4.6	VEHiCULES TRANSP MARCHAND
784	MOTOR VEH PRTS,ACCES NES	W 5378	20.0	W 12913	52.6	W 17147	72.2	W 20808	101.4	PIECES 722,781,782,783
7842	MOTOR VEHICLE BODIES	W 48	0.2	W 142	0.5	W 258	0.7	W 5271	34.4	CARROS 722,781,782,783
7849	OTHER MOTOR VEHCL PARTS	W 4472	18.1	W 7184	40.8	W 11975	59.1	W 12788	59.1	PIECES 722,781,782,783
79	OTHR TRANSPORT EQUIPMENT		193.6		182.4		236.3		210.9	AUTRE MATERIEL TRANSPORT
791	RAILWAY VEHICLES	W 39325	40.0	W 36108	25.4	W 62423	64.1	W 52723	80.1	VEHIC MAT CHEMINS DE FER
7911	ELEC LOCOS NON–SELF–GEN	W 25	0.1			W 1561	12.2	W 3612	27.9	LOCOMOTIVES ELECTRIQUES
7915	FRT,MAINT CARS NOT POWRD	W 26170	18.8	W 19939	9.0	W 31695	21.5	W 11568	13.4	WAGONS DE SERVICE
7919	RY TRACK FIXT,ETC,PARTS	W 12894	19.6	W 15992	15.6	W 29143	30.4	W 37490	38.8	MATER FIXE VOIES FERREES
79199	PARTS NES OF 7911–7915	W 12651	19.4	W 15449	15.2	W 28846	30.1	W 36991	38.2	PIECES 791.1 ET 5
792	AIRCRAFT ETC		26.9		8.4		9.7		19.2	APP NAVIGATION AERIENNE
793	SHIPS AND BOATS ETC		126.8	W 621325	148.7	W 120579	162.6	W 162603	111.7	NAVIRES BATEAUX,ETC
7932	SHIPS AND BOATS NES	W 151924	113.8	W 618856	146.5	W 105541	147.9	W 149837	107.6	NAVIRES ET BATEAUX
79323	OTHER CARGO VESSELS	W 124022	104.3	W 614331	142.5	W 92433	131.3	W 56075	76.2	AUT BATEAUX TRANS MARCH
8	MISC MANUFACTURED GOODS		1687.1		2258.2		2469.8		2668.3	ART MANUFACTURES DIVERS
812	*PLUMBG,HEATNG,LGHTNG EQ	W 17292	36.0		20.2		16.6		19.0	APPAR SANITAIRES CHAUFFAGE
8121	CENTRAL HEATING EQUIPMNT	W 4946	23.5	W 2039	6.8	W 445	1.4	W 505	2.0	CHAUDIERES,RADIATEURS
821	*FURNITURE,PARTS THEREOF	W 334165	397.5		514.2		485.6		446.3	MEUBLES ET PIECES
8211	CHAIRS,SEATS AND PARTS	W 18053	40.2	W 18046	46.3	W 18047	46.6	W 21001	44.9	SIEGES ET PIECES
82111	CHAIRS AND OTHER SEATS	W 17681	39.5	W 17127	45.3	W 15997	44.4	W 16359	40.7	SIEGES
8219	FURNITURE AND PARTS NES	W 315352	355.4	W 233115	465.3	W 233653	437.0	W 252501	399.7	AUTRES MEUBLES ET PIECES
82192	WOOD FURNITURE NES	W 299286	337.4	W 213565	441.1	W 214208	411.3	W 227221	370.6	MEUBLES NDA EN BOIS
84	CLOTHING AND ACCESSORIES		995.3		1360.4		1559.1		1752.8	VETEMENTS
842	MENS OUTERWEAR NOT KNIT	W 14553	331.5	W 15457	422.9	W 17026	503.6	W 19584	537.6	VET DESSUS POUR HOMMES
8421	— OVERCOATS,OTHER COATS	W 1760	46.4	W 1852	55.5	W 1616	53.1	W 2250	62.7	MANTEAUX HOMMES MAT TEXT
84219	—— OF OTHER FIBRES	W 1466	36.8	W 1678	50.5	W 1404	46.6	W 2001	55.5	MANTEAUX HOMMES AUT FIBR
8422	— SUITS	W 1512	31.5	W 1177	39.6	W 1778	63.3	W 1867	61.9	COMPLETS HOMMES MAT TEXT
8423	— TROUSERS,BREECHES ETC	W 5629	115.8	W 5974	153.8	W 6750	189.0	W 7904	205.7	PANTALONS HOMMES MAT TEX
8424	— JACKETS,BLAZERS ETC	W 2667	81.7	W 2869	100.9	W 2939	97.6	W 3342	100.4	VESTES HOMMES MAT TEXTIL
8429	— OTHER OUTER GARMENTS	W 2985	56.2	W 3585	73.3	W 3943	100.8	W 4222	107.2	AUT VET DES HOM MAT TEX
843	WOMENS OUTERWEAR NONKNIT	W 17709	398.6	W 22111	577.2	W 24416	651.5	W 30841	729.0	VET DESSUS FEMMES MAT TEX
8431	— COATS AND JACKETS	W 6725	169.8	W 6902	211.9	W 7097	221.1	W 10242	259.0	MANT,VEST FEM MAT TEXTIL
8432	— SUITS AND COSTUMES	W 726	17.3	W 899	25.2	W 1080	33.4	W 1138	33.7	COSTUMES–TAIL MAT TEXIL
8433	— DRESSES	W 1161	24.5	W 1877	51.5	W 2118	54.0	W 2031	51.0	ROBES EN MAT–TEXTILES
8434	— SKIRTS	W 1633	28.0	W 2287	50.8	W 2527	54.4	W 2660	52.5	JUPES EN MAT TEXTILES
8435	— BLOUSES	W 2498	57.4	W 2936	77.3	W 2924	78.1	W 4022	95.7	BLOUSES FEM MAT TEXTILES

5. Special Exports F.O.B. by Commodities according to the S.I.T.C. (Rev. 2) in million U.S. Dollars
Exportations Spéciales F.O.B. par Produits d'après la C.T.C.I. (Rév. 2) en millions de Dollars E.U.

SITC CTCI	COMMODITY	1994		1995		1996		1997		PRODUIT
		QUANTITY QUANTITE	VALUE VALEUR	QUANTITY QUANTITE	VALUE VALEUR	QUANTITY QUANTITE	VALUE VALEUR	QUANTITY QUANTITE	VALUE VALEUR	
8439	— OTHER OUTER GARMENTS	W 4966	101.8	W 7209	160.6	W 8671	210.8	W 10747	237.4	AUT VET DES FEM MAT TEXT
844	UNDER GARMENTS NOT KNIT	W 4926	60.4	W 5680	95.1	W 5556	105.9	W 5988	117.7	VETEMENT DESSOUS MAT TEX
8441	— MENS SHIRTS	W 4378	56.1	W 4865	85.0	W 4730	93.3	W 5292	108.8	CHEMISES HOMMES MAT TEXT
84411	—— OF COTTON	W 2771	32.7	W 3008	50.3	W 2998	64.4	W 3335	77.0	CHEMISES HOMMES DE COTON
84412	—— OF SYNTHETIC FIBRES	W 1607	23.4	W 1857	34.8	W 1732	29.0	W 1956	31.8	CHEMISES HOMMES FIB SYNT
845	OUTERWEAR KNIT NONELASTC	W 8080	97.2	W 8305	124.5	W 10035	151.4	W 13031	183.0	VET DESSOUS,ACCES BONNET
8451	— JERSEYS,PULLOVERS ETC	W 5274	61.3	W 5279	75.3	W 6754	95.6	W 8888	117.1	CHANDAILS,PULL–OVERS ETC
8459	— OTHER,CLTHG ACCESRYS	W 2538	31.6	W 2752	43.6	W 2969	49.9	W 3734	57.3	AUT VET DESSUS DE BONNE
846	UNDER GARMENTS KNITTED	W 4467	82.8		107.9	W 6283	112.4	W 8477	141.8	SOUS VETS DE BONNETERIE
8462	— OF COTTON NON ELASTIC	W 2319	35.1	W 3608	48.9	W 4217	62.9	W 5791	79.0	SOUS–VET BONNET COTON
84629	—— OTHER	W 2319	35.1	W 3608	48.9	W 4217	62.9	W 5791	79.0	AUT SOUS–VET BONNET COTON
8463	— OF SYNTH FBR NONELAST	W 1794	33.3	W 2078	39.7	W 1529	27.6	W 1846	33.0	SOUS–VET BONNET FIB SYNT
84631	—— PANTY HOSE (TIGHTS)	W 1121	25.7	W 1292	29.5	W 867	19.4	W 1039	22.6	COLLANTS BON FIBR SYNT
8465	CORSETS,GARTERS,ETC	W 354	14.6		19.4	W 537	22.0	W 840	29.9	CORSETS,GAINES ART SIM
84651	BRASSIERES	W 351	14.6	W 516	19.2	W 508	20.9	W 821	29.2	SOUTIENS–GORGE,BUSTIERS
848	HEADGEAR,NONTXTL CLOTHNG		15.4		20.3		22.0		28.0	VET ACCES MAT AUT QUE TEX
851	*FOOTWEAR	W 17983	182.6	W 21492	252.9	W 23791	284.3	W 29714	324.7	CHAUSSURES
85102	FOOTWEAR LEATHER	W 15030	154.7	W 18551	225.5	W 20470	257.9	W 24812	285.4	CHAUS SEMELLES EN CUIR
89	MISC MANUFCTRD GOODS NES		53.1		79.7		90.1		91.1	ART MANUFACTURES DIVERS
894	TOYS,SPORTING GOODS,ETC	W 5315	26.7		44.4		47.3		47.0	VOITURES ENFANTS,JOUETS
8942	TOYS,INDOOR GAMES ETC	W 4633	24.9	W 6616	34.8	W 6786	37.6	W 10391	41.7	JOUETS,JEUX ETC
9	GOODS NOT CLASSD BY KIND		95.7		99.1		56.7		50.1	ART TRANSACT NON CLASSES
931	*SPECIAL TRANSACTIONS		67.5		31.0		22.5		36.4	TRANS.SPECIALES
951	*WAR FIREARMS,AMMUNITION	W 1174	8.0		66.7		32.7	W 68	1.6	VEHIC BLINDES ARMES
95101	ARMORED FIGHTNG VEHICLES	W 1174	8.0	W 4730	38.5	W 4484	7.8	W 68	1.6	CHARS DE COMBAT
971	*GOLD,NON MONETARY NES		18.9					K 1264	10.6	OR NON MONETAIRE
97101	NONMON GLD UNWRT,SEMIMFD		18.9					K 1264	10.6	OR,ALLIAGES D'OR BRUTS

1. HISTORICAL SERIES, 1992–1997 GENERAL TRADE, IMPORTS C.I.F., EXPORTS F.O.B. # 1
SERIES HISTORIQUES, 1992–1997 COMMERCE GENERAL, IMPORTATIONS C.A.F., EXPORTATIONS F.O.B

YEAR ANNEE	VALUE IN MILLION U.S. DOLLARS VALEUR EN MILLION U.S. DOLLARS MERCHANDISE –MARCHANDISE		GOLD –OR		CONVERSION FACTORS FACTEURS DE CONVERSION CENTS E.U. PAR		INDEX NUMBERS –INDICES QUANTUM		UNIT VALUE VALEUR UNITAIRE	
	IMPORTS	EXPORTS	IMPORTS	EXPORTS	IMPORTS	EXPORTS	IMPORTS	EXPORTS	IMPORTS	EXPORTS
1992	36984.00	42376.30								
1993	32806.00	44297.01								
1994	50518.00	67642.00								
1995	60916.00	81137.01								
1996	62278.00	89110.00								
1997	67619.01	87368.00								

2. IMPORTS BY BROAD ECONOMIC CATEGORY AND EXPORTS BY INDUSTRIAL ORIGIN. (PERCENTAGE OF TOTAL VALUE)
IMPORTATIONS PAR CATEGORIES ECONOMIQUES ET EXPORTATIONS PAR BRANCHE D'ACTIVITE.(EN POURCENTAGE DE LA VALEUR TOTALE)

IMPORTS – IMPORTATIONS

	1991	1992	1993	1994	1995	1996	1997
TOTAL IMPORTS–IMPORTATIONS TOTALES						100.	100.
1 FOOD BEV–ALIMENTATION BOISSONS						16.4	16.5
11 PRIMARY–PRODUITS DE BASE						6.8	7.3
111 FOR INDUSTRY–POUR L'INDUSTRIE						1.2	0.9
112 FOR HOUSEHOLDS–POUR LES MENAGES						5.6	6.4
12 PROCESSED–PRODUITS ELABORES						9.6	9.2
121 FOR INDUSTRY–POUR L'INDUSTRIE						2.2	2.2
122 FOR HOUSEHOLDS–POUR LES MENAGES						7.5	6.9
2 IND SUPPLIES–APPROV INDUSTRIELS						18.5	17.2
21 PRIMARY–PRODUITS DE BASE						2.2	2.4
22 PROCESSED–PRODUITS ELABORES						16.4	14.7
3 FUELS–COMBUSTIBLES						2.5	2.8
31 PRIMARY–PRODUITS DE BASE						1.7	1.3
32 PROCESSED–PRODUITS ELABORES						0.8	1.5
321 MOTOR SPIRIT–ESSENCE						0.3	
322 OTHER–AUTRES						0.5	1.5
4 MACHINERY–EQUIPEMENT						16.1	17.4
41 CAPITAL EQUIPMENT–MACHINES						14.8	16.2
42 PARTS–PIECES ACCESSOIRES						1.3	1.2
5 TRANSPORT–TRANSPORT						4.5	5.8
51 PASSENGER CARS–AUTOMOBILES						0.5	1.5
52 OTHER–AUTRES						2.2	2.7
521 INDUSTRIAL–INDUSTRIELS						2.2	2.7
522 NON INDUSTRIAL–NON INDUSTRIEL						0.0	0.0
53 PARTS–PIECES ACCESSOIRES						1.8	1.6
6 CONSUM GOODS–BIENS CONSOMMATION						10.3	10.3
61 DURABLE–DURABLES						2.5	1.9
62 SEMI DURABLE–SEMI DURABLES						3.3	3.0
63 NON DURABLE–NON DURABLES						4.5	5.5
7 GOODS NES–BIENS NDA						31.7	30.0

EXPORTS – EXPORTATIONS

	1991	1992	1993	1994	1995	1996	1997
TOTAL EXPORTS–EXPORTATIONS TOTALES						100.	100.
1 AGRICULTURE						2.1	2.2
2 MINING QUARRY–INDUS EXTRACTIVES						35.0	35.7
3 MANUFACTURING–IND MANUFACTUR						62.9	62.1
31 FOOD BEV TOBACCO–ALIM BOISS TAB						1.1	1.0
32 TEXTILES–INDUSTRIES TEXTILES						1.0	0.9
33 WOOD & PRODUCTS–BOIS & PRODUITS						1.0	1.1
34 PAPER & PRODUCTS–PAPIER & PRODT						1.9	1.7
35 CHEMICALS–INDUSTRIES CHIMIQUES						15.5	14.4
36 NON METAL MIN–MIN NON METAL						0.4	0.3
37 BASIC METAL–IND METAL BASE						17.1	17.3
38 METAL MANUF–MANUF METAL						8.7	7.7
39 OTH MANUF IND–AUTRES MANUF						16.3	17.7

3. TRADE BY PRINCIPAL COUNTRIES OF ORIGIN AND DESTINATION (VALUE IN MILLION U.S. DOLLARS)
ECHANGES SELON LES PRINCIPAUX PAYS D'ORIGINE ET DE DESTINATION (VALEUR EN MILLIONS DE DOLLARS EU)

COUNTRIES–PAYS	GENERAL IMPORTS C.I.F. # 1 IMPORTATIONS GENERALES C.A.F					COUNTRIES–PAYS	GENERAL EXPORTS F.O.B. # 1 EXPORTATIONS GENERALES F.O.B.				
	1993	1994	1995	1996	1997		1993	1994	1995	1996	1997
World	26806.7	38661.4	46710.2	61147.0	67619.0	Monde	44297.4	66861.8	79869.1	88703.0	87368.0
Africa	380.3			332.4	369.6	Afrique	521.6	304.9	393.6	774.9	795.7
Americas	3286.0	2788.2	3484.5	4373.3	5897.3	Amériques	2890.2	3991.6	6309.2	8323.0	6699.1
– Northern America	2597.3	2256.7	2870.3	3264.2	4394.4	– Amérique du Nord	2245.8	3561.5	4575.9	5399.4	4712.9
– LAIA	232.9	231.0	418.0	543.9	1008.3	– ALAI	202.3			226.8	399.4
– CACM	4.9			47.1	31.3	– MCAC	17.6			30.9	43.1
– Caribbean	437.5	300.5	196.2	468.5	429.0	– Caraïbes	347.1	304.4	1489.1	2337.4	1303.2
– Rest of America	13.4			49.7	34.3	– Autre Amérique	77.4	125.7	244.2	328.5	240.5
Asia excl fmr USSR	8148.2	3920.3	3877.5	5386.3	6086.2	Asie anc. URSS exclus	10852.0	10036.2	13876.9	16269.5	14469.9
– Middle East	1129.4	400.5	541.5	735.5	994.1	– Moyen–Orient	3081.3	1473.2	2483.5	3110.6	3565.4
Asia former USSR		3147.4	3951.7	4408.5	4630.7	Asie ancienne URSS		2688.3	3278.9	4449.5	4331.1
Europe excl fmr USSR	14704.8	19211.7	22735.1	20125.4	24863.0	Europe anc. URSS exclus	29431.8	34497.8	39298.0	43747.3	43215.6
– European Union	11197.6	15321.6	17902.8	15963.1	19596.7	– Union Européenne	19922.3	23774.1	26110.1	28190.8	28207.9
– Eastern Europe	2191.0	2837.3	3499.1	2768.1	3609.8	– Europe de l'Est	7137.1	6595.1	9088.6	10247.1	9586.5
– Rest of Europe	1316.2	1052.8	1333.2	1394.2	1656.5	– Autre de l'Europe	2372.4	4128.6	4099.3	5309.4	5421.2
Europe former USSR	172.0	7643.8	10379.3	10677.7	10477.4	Europe ancienne URSS	589.4	12070.4	12614.4	13966.3	15377.1
Oceania	115.4	299.3	246.2	254.0	327.6	Océanie	12.4			14.5	32.8
Other				15589.2	14967.3	Autre				1158.1	2446.8
Germany/Allemagne	5142.1	5675.2	6483.1	5213.5	6643.3	Germany/Allemagne	5074.4	6375.5	6049.1	7080.3	6531.1
Ukraine		4404.1	6616.6	6294.5	3982.1	Ukraine		6885.3	6980.5	7555.1	7239.7
Special Categories				15584.0		USA/Etats–Unis d'Amer	1998.1	3561.1	4537.4	5068.5	4486.1
Areas n.e.s.				5.2	14967.3	China/Chine	3067.8	2888.9	3431.8	4750.4	3981.4
USA/Etats–Unis d'Amer	2303.7	2069.6	2647.9	2921.7	4060.0	United Kingdom	3353.4	4258.7	3187.1	3543.9	3054.6
Belarus/Bélarus		2094.1	2088.9	2907.6	4626.2	Switzerland,Liechtenst.	1726.3	3809.1	3746.5	4009.5	3752.1
Kazakhstan		1996.2	2675.1	3041.9	2743.5	Italy/Italie	2629.2	2983.8	3397.0	2823.3	3564.3
Italy/Italie	1105.8	1595.9	1850.6	2342.3	2640.2	Japan/Japon	2005.1	2823.4	3622.2	3367.3	2935.1
Finland/Finlande	723.6	1628.1	2040.7	1676.1	1873.7	Netherlands/Pays–Bas	979.1	2470.9	3201.1	3328.3	4553.1
China/Chine	2334.6	952.0	865.4	1003.9	1261.4	Belarus/Bélarus		2998.1	2940.0	3356.9	4631.3
Netherlands/Pays–Bas	431.1	1611.2	1646.0	1020.1	1205.8	Finland/Finlande	1364.1	1890.8	2364.9	2637.8	2774.0
France, Monaco	899.2	1009.5	1083.9	1277.6	1594.7	Poland/Pologne	1311.1	1414.2	2002.9	2477.9	2514.6
United Kingdom	652.7	895.8	1099.6	1146.3	1505.4	Ireland/Irlande	604.9	926.2	2511.1	2907.0	2499.4
Japan/Japon	1366.9	1113.7	762.6	999.5	985.2	Kazakhstan		1938.0	2458.1	2552.2	2472.0
Poland/Pologne	528.8	945.8	1321.4	928.4	1354.4	Hungary/Hongrie	2098.2	1407.8	1804.4	1978.1	1853.7
Austria/Autriche	855.2	979.4	981.5	667.2	708.3	Czech Republic	1378.5	1278.9	1904.9	1939.1	1822.2
Hungary/Hongrie	622.3	761.2	842.1	657.9	920.6	France, Monaco	1839.6	1330.2	1543.2	1602.5	1626.1
Belgium–Luxembourg	472.9	614.4	866.5	669.5	815.1	Slovakia/Slovaquie	932.4	1234.6	1754.6	1879.4	1741.2
Uzbekistan/Ouzbékistan		851.8	888.7	655.5	1015.3	Turkey/Turquie	1078.4	1014.3	1660.7	1686.0	1983.3
India/Inde	632.6	586.9	614.1	602.8	801.2	Belgium–Luxembourg	1079.0	1379.9	1462.3	1427.4	860.4
Turkey/Turquie	661.2	400.5	541.5	588.5	794.5	Austria/Autriche	1404.9	884.2	855.2	823.1	734.8
Switzerland,Liechtenst.	679.6	539.3	667.9	502.7	535.2	Bulgaria/Bulgarie	941.5	784.9	885.6	1077.2	914.1
Korea, Republic of	305.6	429.1	502.1	835.9	837.1	Lithuania/Lituanie	299.0	691.9	1080.6	1131.7	1337.3
Republic of Moldova		475.8	636.0	829.2	841.2	Sweden/Suède	783.0	855.2	750.8	1100.0	984.5
Sweden/Suède	313.6	310.5	546.6	569.6	874.5	Korea, Republic of	391.2	567.6	918.8	1340.4	835.4
Czech Republic	460.7	429.9	438.2	534.7	585.8	British Virgin Islds	36.7	217.4	1277.8	1616.6	789.3
Denmark/Danemark	189.8	322.7	483.3	456.7	584.8	Latvia/Lettonie	207.6	627.6	784.4	1042.1	1228.5
Cuba	436.3	300.5	196.2	405.8	351.5	India/Inde	474.0	379.0	997.8	793.6	917.7
Bulgaria/Bulgarie	309.5	345.3	471.4	246.1	260.6	Uzbekistan/Ouzbékistan		750.3	820.8	1089.9	874.6
Spain/Espagne	174.7	244.7	241.0	364.0	528.1	Romania/Roumanie	475.0	474.7	736.2	894.2	739.6
Lithuania/Lituanie	53.4	274.7	386.9	255.3	460.0	Areas n.e.s.					2446.8
Slovenia/Slovénie	232.2	229.6	340.7	279.5	330.4	Iran (Islamic Rep of)	1004.5	146.6	249.3	377.1	461.4
Ireland/Irlande	83.3	249.8	322.8	322.5	408.9	Israel/Israël	168.5	424.2	624.4	564.6	426.8
Canada	293.6	187.1	222.4	342.2	333.9	Cyprus/Chypre	539.6	270.5	272.9	490.7	630.9
Brazil/Brésil	113.9	192.8	359.4	204.5	466.6	Singapore/Singapour	241.6	417.4	499.3	601.6	208.5
Slovakia/Slovaquie	167.9	208.8	294.2	265.9	284.8	Spain/Espagne	384.8	200.9	307.7	425.8	630.2
Singapore/Singapour	290.3	211.0	267.7	240.8	202.0	Estonia/Estonie	82.8	337.3	415.7	490.9	559.4
Latvia/Lettonie	77.4	197.4	376.1	235.5	308.2	Other Asia n.e.s.	284.6	194.2	463.8	495.2	289.1
Norway,Svalbard and JM	87.6	110.6	175.2	283.5	374.9	Republic of Moldova		530.2	413.2	389.7	380.9
Israel/Israël	139.1	154.7	242.7	274.8	183.8	Egypt/Egypte	169.9	304.9	393.6	387.8	438.8

(VALUE AS PERCENTAGE OF WORLD TOTAL)(VALEURS EN POURCENTAGE DU TOTAL MONDIAL)

	1988	1989	1990	1991	1992	1993	1994	1995	1996	1997		1988	1989	1990	1991	1992	1993	1994	1995	1996	1997
Africa						1.4			0.5	0.5	Afrique						1.2	0.5	0.5	0.9	0.9
Americas						12.3	7.2	7.5	7.2	8.7	Amériques						6.5	6.0	7.9	9.4	7.7
– Northern America						9.7	5.8	6.1	5.3	6.5	– Amérique du Nord						5.1	5.3	5.7	6.1	5.4
– LAIA						0.9	0.6	0.9	0.9	1.5	– ALAI						0.5			0.3	0.5
– CACM						0.0			0.1	0.0	– MCAC						0.0			0.0	0.0
– Caribbean						1.6	0.8	0.4	0.8	0.6	– Caraïbes						0.8	0.5	1.9	2.6	1.5
– Rest of America						0.0			0.1	0.1	– Autre Amérique						0.2	0.2	0.3	0.4	0.3
Asia excl fmr USSR						30.4	10.1	8.3	8.8	9.0	Asie anc. URSS exclus						24.5	15.0	17.4	18.3	16.6
– Middle East						4.2	1.0	1.2	1.2	1.5	– Moyen–Orient						7.0	2.2	3.1	3.5	4.1
Asia former USSR							8.1	8.5	7.2	6.8	Asie ancienne URSS							4.0	4.1	5.0	5.0
Europe excl fmr USSR						54.9	49.7	48.7	32.9	36.8	Europe anc. URSS exclus						66.4	51.6	49.2	49.3	49.5
– European Union						41.8	39.6	38.3	26.1	29.0	– Union Européenne						45.0	35.6	32.7	31.8	32.3
– Eastern Europe						8.2	7.3	7.5	4.5	5.3	– Europe de l'Est						16.1	9.9	11.4	11.6	11.0
– Rest of Europe						4.9	2.7	2.9	2.3	2.4	– Autre de l'Europe						5.4	6.2	5.1	6.0	6.2
Europe former USSR						0.6	19.8	22.2	17.5	15.5	Europe ancienne URSS						1.3	18.1	15.8	15.7	17.6
Oceania						0.4	0.8	0.5	0.4	0.5	Océanie						0.0			0.0	0.0
Other									25.5	22.1	Autre									1.3	2.8
Germany/Allemagne						19.2	14.7	13.9	8.5	9.8	Germany/Allemagne						11.5	9.5	7.6	8.0	7.5
Ukraine							11.4	14.2	10.3	5.9	Ukraine							10.3	8.7	8.5	8.3
Special Categories									25.5		USA/Etats–Unis d'Amer						4.5	5.3	5.7	5.7	5.1
Areas n.e.s.									0.0	22.1	China/Chine						6.9	4.3	4.3	5.4	4.6
USA/Etats–Unis d'Amer						8.6	5.4	5.7	4.8	6.0	United Kingdom						7.6	6.4	4.0	4.0	3.5
Belarus/Bélarus							5.4	4.5	4.8	6.8	Switzerland,Liechtenst.						3.9	5.7	4.7	4.5	4.3
Kazakhstan							5.2	5.7	5.0	4.1	Italy/Italie						5.9	4.5	4.3	3.2	4.1
Italy/Italie						4.1	4.1	4.0	3.8	3.9	Japan/Japon						4.5	4.2	4.5	3.8	3.4
Finland/Finlande						2.7	4.2	4.4	2.7	2.8	Netherlands/Pays–Bas						2.2	3.7	4.0	3.8	5.2
China/Chine						8.7	2.5	1.9	1.6	1.9	Belarus/Bélarus							4.5	3.7	3.8	5.3

4. General Imports C.I.F. by Commodities according to the S.I.T.C. (Rev. 2) in million U.S. Dollars
Importations Générales C.A.F. par Produits d'après la C.T.C.I. (Rév. 2) en millions de Dollars E.U.

SITC CTCI	COMMODITY	1994 QUANTITY QUANTITE	1994 VALUE VALEUR	1995 QUANTITY QUANTITE	1995 VALUE VALEUR	1996 QUANTITY QUANTITE	1996 VALUE VALEUR	1997 QUANTITY QUANTITE	1997 VALUE VALEUR	PRODUIT
	ALL COMMODITIES				46710.2		61147.0		67619.0	TOUS PRODUITS
0	FOOD AND LIVE ANIMALS						8962.7		9927.9	ALIMENTS,ANIMAUX VIVANTS
01	MEAT AND PREPARATIONS				1848.0		2068.5		2766.2	VIANDES ET PREPARATIONS
011	MEAT FRESH,CHILLD,FROZEN					W 1615151	1658.7	W 2314902	2318.3	VIANDES FRAICHES,REF,CONGE
0111	BOVINE MEAT FRESH,FROZEN					W 448934	636.8	W 618072	850.7	VIANDES BOVIN FRAI,REF
01111	BOVINE MEAT WITH BONE IN					W 297191	414.2	W 352475	462.1	VIANDES BOVIN NON DESOSS
01112	BOVINE MEAT BONELESS					W 151743	222.6	W 265596	388.6	VIANDES BOVIN DESOSSEES
0113	PIG MEAT FRESH,CHLD,FRZN					W 303914	442.5	W 308946	518.8	VIANDE DE PORC
0114	POULTRY FRESH CHLLD,FRZN					W 747727	504.7	W 1146555	815.3	VOLAILLES MORTES
014	MEAT PREPD,PRSVD,NES ETC					W 251266	380.9	W 267446	352.4	CONSERVES DE VIANDES
0149	OTH PREPARD,PRESRVD MEAT					W 129814	219.7	W 133275	187.5	AUTRES PREP DE VIANDES
02	DAIRY PRODCTS,BIRDS'EGGS				867.0		530.7		652.8	PRODUITS LAITIERS,OEUFS
023	BUTTER					W 112848	208.2	W 169698	269.2	BEURRE
03	FISH AND PREPARATIONS						379.8		394.6	POISSONS ET PREPARATIONS
034	FISH,FRESH,CHILLED,FROZN					W 328740	232.4	W 496526	271.0	POISSON FRAIS, REFRIG,CONG
0342	FISH FROZEN,EXCL FILLETS					W 294450	195.0	W 447065	222.8	POISSONS CONGELES
04	CEREALS AND PREPARATIONS						1475.9		1248.0	CEREALES ET PRODUITS
041	WHEAT ETC UNMILLED					W 2057161	388.0	W 2142978	343.3	FROMENT,EPEAUTRE
0412	OTHER WHEAT ETC UNMILLED					W 1772995	328.2	W 2001807	317.6	AUTRE FROMENT NON MOULU
046	WHEAT ETC MEAL OR FLOUR					W 731938	230.8	W 392710	113.9	SEMOULE FARINE,FROMENT
04601	FLOUR OF WHEAT OR MESLIN					W 720327	226.6	W 386895	111.7	FARINE DE FROMENT
048	CEREAL ETC PREPARATIONS					W 750233	497.2	W 971653	512.3	PREPTNS A BASE CEREALES
0484	BAKERY PRODUCTS					W 223489	205.5	W 360301	213.9	PRODUITS DE BOULANGERIE
05	VEGETABLES AND FRUIT						1715.8		1842.5	LEGUMES ET FRUITS
054	VEG ETC FRSH,SMPLY PRSVD				278.0	W 822829	382.2	W 1272410	438.0	LEGUMES FRAIS,CONG,SECS
0545	OTHER FRESH VEGETABLES					W 484868	172.6	W 734110	206.1	AUTRES LEGUMES FRAIS,REF
057	FRUIT,NUTS,FRESH,DRIED				1065.0	W 1603131	900.5	W 2318435	963.8	FRUITS FRAIS OU SECS
0574	APPLES FRESH					W 419586	256.7	W 451098	217.8	POMMES FRAICHES
0579	FRUIT FRESH OR DRIED NES					W 310504	206.5	W 495050	274.0	FRUITS FRAIS,SECS NDA
058	FRUIT PRESERVED,PREPARED					W 478114	284.5	W 383048	238.4	CONSERVES DE FRUITS
06	SUGAR AND PREPS,HONEY				1523.0		1448.6		1320.9	SUCRES ET PRODUITS
061	SUGAR AND HONEY					W 3209208	1313.9	W 3525046	1181.8	SUCRES ET MIEL
0611	RAW BEET AND CANE SUGAR					W 1696132	600.1	W 2528820	809.3	SUCRES BRUTS
0612	REFINED SUGAR ETC					W 1453358	675.8	W 956442	338.8	SUCRES RAFFINES
07	COFFEE,TEA,COCOA,SPICES						672.5		883.4	CAFE,THE,CACAO,EPICES
071	COFFEE AND SUBSTITUTES					W 41068	119.8	W 88954	259.2	CAFE ET SUCCEDANES
0712	COFFEE EXTRACTS,ESSENCES					W 15990	86.7	W 61129	234.7	EXTRAITS DE CAFE
073	CHOCOLATE AND PRODUCTS					W 102052	190.5	W 79924	152.6	CHOCOLAT
074	TEA AND MATE					W 118578	203.0	W 158205	281.3	THE ET MATE
0741	TEA					W 118520	203.0	W 158162	281.2	THE
09	MISC EDIBLE PRODUCTS						511.7		609.2	PREP ALIMENTAIRES DIVERSES
098	EDIBLE PRODCTS,PREPS NES					W 307395	419.6	W 459417	437.9	PREP ALIMENTAIRES NDA
09809	MISC FOOD PREPRTIONS NES					W 125528	260.0	W 170047	265.7	PREP ALIMENTAIRES NDA
1	BEVERAGES AND TOBACCO						1517.6		2048.6	BOISSONS ET TABACS
11	BEVERAGES				1963.0		908.6		952.5	BOISSONS
112	ALCOHOLIC BEVERAGES					W 843857	772.7	W 722505	844.8	BOISSONS ALCOOLIQUES
1121	WINE OF FRESH GRAPES ETC					W 486167	437.3	W 543394	575.2	VINS DE RAISINS FRAIS
11212	WINE OF FRESH GRAPES					W 351691	346.0	W 432036	474.4	VINS DE MOUTS DE RAISINS
1124	DISTILLED ALCOHOLIC BEVS					W 127730	209.7	W 55665	192.7	ALCOOLS,EAUX-DE-VIE
12	TOBACCO AND MANUFACTURES						609.0		1096.1	TABACS BRUTS FABRIQUES
121	TOBACCO UNMNFCTRD,REFUSE					W 125296	177.1	W 173734	308.5	TABACS BRUTS,DECHETS
122	TOBACCO,MANUFACTURED					W 59052	432.0	W 110596	787.6	TABACS FABRIQUES
1222	CIGARETTES					W 49373	390.7	W 93400	716.7	CIGARETTES
2	CRUDE MATERLS,EXCL FUELS						2283.3		2382.3	MAT BRUTES NON COMESTIBLES
24	CORK AND WOOD				198.0		27.1		33.1	LIEGE ET BOIS
26	TEXTILE FIBRES AND WASTE						286.5		410.2	FIBRES TEXTILES
263	COTTON				578.0	W 168160	249.2	W 228400	360.6	COTON
2631	RAW COTTON,EXCL LINTERS					W 143856	238.1	W 211994	350.5	COTON EN MASSE
27	CRUDE FERTLZR,MINRLS NES						217.3		225.7	ENGRAIS MINERAUX BRUTS
28	METALLIFEROUS ORES,SCRAP						1498.4		1430.7	MINERAIS METAL,DECHETS
287	BASE METAL ORES,CONC NES					W 5297824	1341.4	W 7115288	1194.7	MINERAIS METAUX COMMUNS
2873	ALUMINIUM ORES,ALUMINA					W 3669652	1098.4	W 5202959	932.8	MINERAIS D'ALUMINIUM
28732	ALUMINA(ALUMINIUM OXIDE)					W 3434909	1042.1	W 4181960	898.9	ALUMINE (OXYDE ALUMINIUM)
3	MINERAL FUELS ETC				1934.0		1696.5		1901.7	COMBUSTIBLES MINERAUX LUB
32	COAL,COKE AND BRIQUETTES						328.9		260.6	HOUILLES,COKES,BRIQUETTES
322	COAL,LIGNITE AND PEAT					MW 20155	311.2	MW 15181	253.3	HOUILLES,LIGNITES,TOURBE
3222	OTH COAL,NOT AGGLOMERATD					MW 17545	279.5	MW 9722	198.0	AUTRES HOUILLES
33	PETROLEUM AND PRODUCTS						1202.8		1493.2	PETROLE ET DERIVES
333	CRUDE PETROLEUM					W 8983372	591.5	W 7905006	535.3	HUILES BRUTES DE PETROLE
334	PETROLEUM PRODUCTS,REFIN					W 2473916	465.2	W 4012775	747.2	PRODUITS RAFFINES
3341	GASOLINE,OTH LIGHT OILS					W 1298360	202.5			ESSENCES POUR MOTEURS
33411	MOTOR,AVIATION SPIRIT					W 1255486	195.3			ESSENCES MOTEURS D'AVIONS
335	RESIDUAL PETRLM PROD NES					W 810706	146.2	W 1101094	210.8	PRODUITS RESIDUELS NDA
4	ANIMAL,VEGETABLE OIL,FAT						367.8		525.9	HUILES,GRAISSES ANIM,VEG
42	FIXED VEGETABLE OIL,FAT						319.7		456.1	HUILES VEGETALES FIXES
423	FIXED VEG OILS,SOFT					W 264044	201.5	W 554153	288.5	HUILES VEGET DOUCES FIXES
4236	SUNFLOWER SEED OIL					W 167279	139.8	W 321897	204.3	HUILE DE TOURNESOL
5	CHEMCLS,RELATED PROD NES						4173.0		4952.1	PRODUITS CHIMIQUES
51	ORGANIC CHEMICALS				416.0		428.5		351.6	PROD CHIMIQ ORGANIQUES
52	INORGANIC CHEMICALS				848.0		282.3		274.5	PROD CHIM INORGANIQUES
53	DYES,TANNING,COLOUR PROD				317.0		364.4		438.0	PROD TEINTURE,COLORANTS
533	PIGMENTS,PAINTS,ETC					W 193508	340.3	W 311319	402.1	PIGMENTS,PEINTURES,VERNIS
5334	VARNISHES,DISTEMPERS ETC					W 94824	216.6	W 115477	231.9	PEINTURES A L'EAU
541	*MEDICINAL,PHARM PRODUCT				1055.0		1247.6	MK 66702	1768.5	PROD MEDICINAUX PHARMACEUT
5417	MEDICAMENTS					MK 48815	1120.3	MK 59703	1577.1	MEDICAMENTS
54179	— CONTNG OTH SUBSTANCES					MK 45496	945.6	MK 52091	1211.6	MED CONT AUT SUBSTANCES
55	PERFUME,CLEANING ETC PRD				328.0		708.2		796.9	PROD POUR PARFUM,TOILETTE
553	PERFUMERY,COSMETICS,ETC					W 200570	492.9	W 240975	542.7	PRODUITS DE PARFUMERIE
572	*EXPLOSIVES,PYROTECH PRO				831.0	W 986	1.8	W 1306	2.2	EXPLOSIFS
58	PLASTIC MATERIALS ETC						477.6		560.1	MAT PLAST ARTIFICIELLES
583	POLYMERIZATION ETC PRODS					W 185030	371.4	W 244209	418.3	PROD POLYMERISATION
59	CHEMICAL MATERIALS NES						626.3		749.3	MAT PROD CHIMIQUES NDA
591	PESTICIDES,DISINFECTANTS					W 36228	203.7	W 86522	205.5	DESINF,INSECT,FONG,HERB
598	MISCEL CHEM PRODUCTS NES					W 247334	326.6	W 295872	413.1	PROD DIV INDUST CHIM NDA
5989	CHEM PRODUCTS,PREPS NES					W 113281	217.5	W 119413	269.0	PROD PREP CHIMIQUES NDA
6	BASIC MANUFACTURES						6595.8		6385.2	ART MANUFACTURES
62	RUBBER MANUFACTURES NES				456.0		403.6		317.8	CAOUTCHOUC MANUFACTURE
625	RUBBER TYRES, TUBES ETC					W 104694	299.5	W 81932	206.8	PNEUS CAOUTCHOUC VULCANISE
63	WOOD,CORK MANUFACTRS NES						229.5		285.0	OUVRAGES LIEGE ET BOIS
635	WOOD MANUFACTURES NES					W 82523	187.6	W 117397	206.6	ART MANUF EN BOIS NDA
64	PAPER,PAPERBOARD AND MFR				624.0		772.5		944.0	PAPIERS,CARTONS & OUVRAGES

4. General Imports C.I.F. by Commodities according to the S.I.T.C. (Rev. 2) in million U.S. Dollars
Importations Générales C.A.F. par Produits d'après la C.T.C.I. (Rév. 2) en millions de Dollars E.U.

SITC CTCI	COMMODITY	1994		1995		1996		1997		PRODUIT
		QUANTITY QUANTITE	VALUE VALEUR	QUANTITY QUANTITE	VALUE VALEUR	QUANTITY QUANTITE	VALUE VALEUR	QUANTITY QUANTITE	VALUE VALEUR	
641	PAPER AND PAPERBOARD					W 262500	351.2	W 412567	401.1	PAPIERS ET CARTONS
642	PAPER,ETC,PRECUT,ARTS OF					W 192685	421.3	W 278725	543.0	PAP,CARTONS DECOUPES
6421	PAPER ETC CONTAINERS					W 80966	147.7	W 121841	215.0	BOITES,SACS EMBALLAGES
6428	PAPER ETC ARTICLES NES					W 71211	210.1	W 95246	238.0	OUVRAGES EN PATE A PAPIER
65	TEXTILE YARN,FABRICS,ETC				322.0		794.4		810.8	FILS,TISSUS,ARTICLES TEXTILE
657	SPECIAL TXTL FABRC,PRODS					W 79458	188.6	W 120623	203.9	TISSUS SPECIAUX
66	NONMETAL MINERAL MFS NES				833.0		649.1		718.7	ART MIN NON METALLIQUES
67	IRON AND STEEL				1404.0		2432.5		1840.6	FER ET ACIER
671	PIG IRON ETC					W 4490465	484.0	W 992388	252.1	FONTE,SPIEGEL,POUDRES
6716	FERRO–ALLOYS					W 417037	282.9	W 349583	212.1	FERRO–ALLIAGES
673	IRON,STEEL SHAPES ETC					W 1119178	381.8	W 736762	263.2	BARRES,PROFIL FER,ACIER
674	IRN,STL UNIV,PLATE,SHEET					W 634170	369.4	W 557876	300.9	LARGES PLATS,TOLES
678	IRON,STL TUBES,PIPES,ETC					W 1231048	948.0	W 1097391	887.2	TUBES,TUYAUX EN FONTE,FER
6782	IRON,STL SEAMLESS TUBES					W 708394	534.5	W 537672	433.1	TUBES,TUYAUX SANS SOUDURE
6783	IRON,STL TUBES,PIPES NES					W 509663	380.4	W 545019	430.2	AUT TUBES,TUYAUX FER,ACIER
68	NON–FERROUS METALS						346.4		379.3	METAUX NON FERREUX
682	COPPER EXC CEMENT COPPER				165.0	W 31234	94.5	W 46051	125.3	CUIVRE
684	ALUMINIUM				280.0	W 45152	128.5	W 64088	143.2	ALUMINIUM
69	METAL MANUFACTURES NES				1421.0		901.7		1016.5	ART MANUFACT EN METAL NDA
691	STRUCTURES AND PARTS NES					W 81320	193.1	W 90310	229.8	CONSTRUCT FER,ACIER,ALU
699	BASE METAL MFRS NES					W 77798	208.6	W 97353	262.3	ART MANUFACTURES MET NDA
7	MACHINES,TRANSPORT EQUIP				13261.0		12007.1		14776.7	MACHINES MATERIEL TRANSPORT
71	POWER GENERATING EQUIPMT						816.7		914.0	MACHINES GENERATRICES
714	ENGINES AND MOTORS NES					W 5481	251.3	W 10294	393.0	MOTEURS NON ELECTRIQUES
716	ROTATING ELECTRIC PLANT					W 29967	184.1	W 29913	177.2	APP ELECTR ROTATIFS,PIECES
72	MACHS FOR SPCL INDUSTRYS						2409.8		2498.9	MAC SPECIALES POUR INDUST
721	AGRIC MACHY,EXC TRACTORS					W 43415	217.2	W 30556	201.6	MACHINES AGRICOLES
723	CIVIL ENGNEERG EQUIP ETC					W 57473	468.9	W 66397	572.1	APPAREILS DE GENIE CIVIL
7234	CONST,MINING MACHNRY NES					W 49122	400.6	W 56958	470.5	MACH POUR LA CONST, MINES
727	FOOD MACHRY NON–DOMESTIC					W 26999	403.6	W 30694	377.4	MACH INDUSTRIES ALIMENT
7272	OTH FOOD PROC MCHY,PARTS					W 20648	366.3	W 19373	330.5	AUT MACH IND ALIMENTAIRE
72722	INDUS FOOD PROC MACH NES					W 20110	357.5	W 17165	295.3	MACHINES BOULANGERIE
728	OTH MACHY FOR SPCL INDUS					W 83911	967.5	W 88357	956.3	AUT MACH IND PARTICULIERES
7284	MACHY FOR SPCL INDUS NES					W 49798	724.5	W 57187	736.7	MACH SPEC IND PARTICUL.
72842	RUBBER,PLASTICS WRKG MCH					W 8734	216.1	W 8159	188.5	MACH IND CAOUT MAT PLAST
72845	MTL ETC TREATNG MACH NES					W 4429	210.6	W 1497	24.3	MACH TRAITEMENT METAUX
72848	OTH MCHY WITH INDIV FNCT					W 25281	136.1	W 37351	295.2	AUTRES MACHINES NDA
73	METALWORKING MACHINERY						375.4		355.0	MACH TRAVAIL DES METAUX
736	METALWORKING MACH–TOOLS					W 19422	226.2	W 16000	242.0	MACH–OUTILS TRAVAIL METAUX
74	GENRL INDUSTRL MACHY NES						2446.6		3469.0	MACH APP INDUSTRIE
741	HEATING,COOLING EQUIPMNT					W 60840	514.7	W 103849	1095.3	MACH CHAUFFAGE,PIECES
7416	HEATING,COOLING EQU NES					W 17202	184.7	W 41574	652.2	APP CHANGEMENT TEMP
742	PUMPS FOR LIQUIDS ETC					W 31231	292.4	W 32072	309.5	POMPES MOTO–POMPES
743	PUMPS NES,CENTRFUGES ETC					W 49174	521.7	W 73669	773.9	POMPES COMPRES,VENT ETC
7431	PUMPS FOR GASES ETC					W 24571	260.2	W 31632	444.6	POMPES AIR A VIDE,COMPRES
744	MECHANICAL HANDLING EQU					W 80680	464.6	W 86046	505.8	EQUIP MANUTENTION PIECES
7442	LIFTING,LOADING MACH NES					W 31922	215.5	W 34888	246.8	APP LEVAGE,MANUTENTION
745	NONELEC MACHY,TOOLS NES					W 20034	344.6	W 27380	450.3	AUT MACH NON ELEC,PIECES
7452	OTH NONELEC MCHS,PTS NES					W 19615	331.3	W 26711	436.6	AUT MACH NON ELEC,PIECES
74522	PACKAGNG,BOTTLNG,ETC MCH					W 8726	218.0	W 13427	293.0	MACH NETT BOUTEILLES,ETC
749	NONELEC MACH PTS,ACC NES					W 126092	308.9	W 46624	334.6	PIECES MACH NON ELEC NDA
75	OFFICE MACHNES,ADP EQUIP						473.8		493.0	MACH BUREAU TRAIT AUTOM
752	AUTOMTIC DATA PROC EQUIP					W 6458	247.2	W 6042	280.0	MACH TRAIT INFORMATION
76	TELECOMM,SOUND EQUIPMENT						1589.7		1821.0	EQUIPMENT DE TELECOM
761	TELEVISION RECEIVERS					W 40986	386.3	W 17700	170.2	RECEPTEURS DE TELEVISION
7611	COLOUR TV RECEIVERS					W 39705	380.1	W 15093	163.7	RECEPTEURS COULEUR
764	TELECOM EQPT,PTS,ACC NES					W 54331	1028.4	W 97354	1573.2	EQUIP TELECOM,PIECES
7641	LINE TELEPHONE,ETC EQUIP					W 10192	551.2	W 29584	752.3	APP TELEPHON PAR FIL
7643	TV,RADIO TRANSMITTRS ETC					W 1940	285.5	W 2717	426.6	APP EMET TELE RADIO
7649	PTS NES OF EQUIPMT OF 76					W 38850	149.2	W 60972	339.5	PIECES DE LA DIV 76
77	ELECTRIC MACHNRY NES ETC						1831.0		1896.5	MACH APP ELECT NDA
772	SWITCHGEAR ETC,PARTS NES					W 16838	229.4	W 39384	286.7	APP COUPURE,SECT ETC
7721	SWITCHGEAR ETC					W 16517	223.9	W 39223	282.6	APP COUPURE,SECTIONMNT
774	ELECTRO–MEDCL,XRAY EQUIP					W 9659	460.3	W 3131	449.3	APPAREILS MEDICAUX
7742	X–RAY APPARATUS ETC					W 8629	327.4	W 2320	275.3	APPAREILS A RAYONS X
775	HOUSEHOLD TYPE EQUIP NES					W 92782	347.1	W 139713	303.7	MACH,APP USAGE DOMESTQUE
778	ELECTRICAL MACHINERY NES					W 174304	441.0	W 216176	502.4	AUTRES MACH ELECT NDA
7788	OTH ELEC MACHY,EQUIP NES					W 87911	209.4	W 96125	256.7	AUT MACH APP ELEC NDA
78	ROAD VEHICLES				1824.0		1232.9		2262.0	VEHICULES ROUTIERS
781	PASS MOTOR VEH EXC BUSES					W 63006	308.1	W 226533	987.9	AUTO TRANSPORT PERSONNES
782	LORRIES,SPCL MTR VEH NES					W 68209	331.4	W 79029	335.7	VEHICULES SPECIAUX,MARCH
7821	LORRIES,TRUCKS					W 52958	203.0	W 67149	209.6	VEHICULES TRANSP MARCHAND
783	ROAD MOTOR VEHICLES NES					W 51901	268.6	W 86588	466.8	VEHICULES ROUTIERS NDA
7831	BUSES					W 46698	247.0	W 67375	403.2	VOITURES TRANSPORT COMMUN
784	MOTOR VEH PRTS,ACCES NES					W 48352	256.6	W 74477	380.2	PIECES 722,781,782,783
7849	OTHER MOTOR VEHCL PARTS					W 42228	230.2	W 54019	286.6	PIECES 722,781,782,783
79	OTHR TRANSPORT EQUIPMENT						831.7		1067.7	AUTRE MATERIEL TRANSPORT
791	RAILWAY VEHICLES					W 279224	428.0	W 132798	220.7	VEHIC MAT CHEMINS DE FER
792	AIRCRAFT ETC				190.0	W 2258	60.6			APP NAVIGATION AERIENNE
793	SHIPS AND BOATS ETC				188.0		343.2		847.0	NAVIRES BATEAUX,ETC
7932	SHIPS AND BOATS NES						321.6	W 1248254	736.5	NAVIRES ET BATEAUX
79323	OTHER CARGO VESSELS					MV 811232	173.8	W 867813	370.3	AUT BATEAUX TRANS MARCH
79324	FISHING VESSELS ETC					MV 274503	134.7	W 227330	287.1	BATEAUX DE PECHE
8	MISC MANUFACTURED GOODS						4212.4		4416.8	ART MANUFACTURES DIVERS
812	*PLUMBG,HEATNG,LGHTNG EQ					W 69656	191.6	W 93847	234.0	APPAR SANITAIRES CHAUFFAGE
821	*FURNITURE,PARTS THEREOF				1055.0	W 865450	520.2	W 188837	576.5	MEUBLES ET PIECES
8219	FURNITURE AND PARTS NES					W 828806	342.5	W 144579	381.7	AUTRES MEUBLES ET PIECES
82192	WOOD FURNITURE NES					W 779502	224.6	W 117675	283.9	MEUBLES NDA EN BOIS
84	CLOTHING AND ACCESSORIES				598.0		427.2		456.2	VETEMENTS
851	*FOOTWEAR				491.0	W 96627	480.8	W 45877	303.3	CHAUSSURES
85102	FOOTWEAR LEATHER					W 58873	352.9	W 26090	226.7	CHAUS SEMELLES EN CUIR
87	PRECISION INSTRUMNTS NES						971.6		1024.2	INSTRUM,APPAR SCIENT NDA
872	MEDICAL INSTRUMENTS NES					W 15195	407.3	W 15327	372.3	INSTR,APP MEDIC–CHIR NDA
87202	OTH MEDICAL INSTRUMENTS					W 7129	254.6	W 8124	256.2	INSTRUM,APP MEDECINE
874	MEASURNG,CONTROLNG INSTR					W 19385	492.5	W 13566	576.9	INSTRUMENTS DE MESURE
88	PHOTO EQU,OPTICL GDS ETC						296.1		270.9	APP,FOURN PHOTO,OP,MONTR
89	MISC MANUFCTRD GOODS NES						1278.0		1510.9	ART MANUFACTURES DIVERS
892	PRINTED MATTER				255.0	W 117814	476.9	W 179300	545.8	IMPRIMES
8922	NEWSPAPERS,PERIODICALS					W 60914	211.9	W 73712	220.4	JOURNAUX ET PERIODIQUES
893	ARTICLES OF PLASTIC NES						418.2		513.4	OUVRAGES EN MAT DIVIS 58
8939	MISC PLASTIC ARTICLES					W 112216	282.6	W 135403	324.6	ART DIVERS EN MAT DIV 58

4. General Imports C.I.F. by Commodities according to the S.I.T.C. (Rev. 2) in million U.S. Dollars
Importations Générales C.A.F. par Produits d'après la C.T.C.I. (Rév. 2) en millions de Dollars E.U.

SITC CTCI	COMMODITY	1994 QUANTITY QUANTITE	1994 VALUE VALEUR	1995 QUANTITY QUANTITE	1995 VALUE VALEUR	1996 QUANTITY QUANTITE	1996 VALUE VALEUR	1997 QUANTITY QUANTITE	1997 VALUE VALEUR	PRODUIT
89399	OTHR PLASTC ARTICLES NES					W 102268	264.5	W 116486	300.6	AUT OUV MAT DIV 58
9	GOODS NOT CLASSD BY KIND						18797.2		20302.4	ART TRANSACT NON CLASSES
931	*SPECIAL TRANSACTIONS						18795.3		20299.6	TRANS.SPECIALES

5. General Exports F.O.B. by Commodities according to the S.I.T.C. (Rev. 2) in million U.S. Dollars
Exportations Générales F.O.B. par Produits d'après la C.T.C.I. (Rév. 2) en millions de Dollars E.U.

SITC CTCI	COMMODITY	1994 QUANTITY QUANTITE	1994 VALUE VALEUR	1995 QUANTITY QUANTITE	1995 VALUE VALEUR	1996 QUANTITY QUANTITE	1996 VALUE VALEUR	1997 QUANTITY QUANTITE	1997 VALUE VALEUR	PRODUIT
	ALL COMMODITIES				79869.1		88703.0		87368.0	TOUS PRODUITS
0	FOOD AND LIVE ANIMALS						895.6		939.6	ALIMENTS,ANIMAUX VIVANTS
03	FISH AND PREPARATIONS						251.9		316.0	POISSONS ET PREPARATIONS
2	CRUDE MATERLS,EXCL FUELS						4830.2		5321.5	MAT BRUTES NON COMESTIBLES
21	HIDES,SKINS,FURS UNDRSSD						313.3		345.8	CUIRS,PEAUX BRUTS
211	HIDES,SKINS,EXC FURS,RAW					W 238026	245.3	W 243163	307.5	CUIRS ET PEAUX
22	OIL SEEDS,OLEAGINOUS FRT						440.9		251.4	GRAINES,FRUITS OLEAGINEUX
222	SEEDS FOR'SOFT'FIXED OIL					W 1911313	430.6	W 1187307	244.2	GRAINES HUILES FIXES
2224	SUNFLOWER SEEDS					W 1779045	399.2	W 1049168	209.5	GRAINES DE TOURNESOL
23	RUBBER, CRUDE						478.8		380.6	CAOUTCHOUC BRUT
233	RUBBER,SYNTHTIC,RECLAIMD					W 352510	477.6	W 303633	369.3	LATEX CAOUTCH SYNTH REGEN
2331	SYNTHETIC RUBBER ETC					W 348729	475.9	W 299743	367.9	LATEX CAOUTCH SYNTHETIQUE
24	CORK AND WOOD				2115.0		1597.4		1728.1	LIEGE ET BOIS
247	OTH WOOD ROUGH,SQUARED					MW 12874	945.3	MW 14637	1025.6	BOIS BRUTS EQUARRIS
2471	SAW–,VENEER–LOGS CONIFER					W 7713083	663.7	MW 9543	758.9	CONIFERES POUR SCIAGE,PLACAG
24711	— IN THE ROUGH					W 7713083	663.7	MW 9543	758.9	ECORCES OU DEGROSSIS
2472	SAW–,VENEER–LOGS NON–CON					W 5160648	281.7	W 5093680	266.7	NON CONIFERES SCIAGE,PLAC
24721	— IN THE ROUGH					W 5160648	281.7	W 5093680	266.7	BRUTS ECORCES DEGROSSIS
248	WOOD SHAPED,SLEEPERS					W 2850691	630.6	W 2960997	682.5	BOIS SIMPLEMENT TRAVAILLES
2482	LUMBER SHAPED CONIFER					W 2584882	581.3	W 2708676	637.6	CONIFERES SCIES,RABOTES
24821	LUMBER SAWN ETC CONIFER					W 2575064	578.3	W 2697830	635.0	CONIFERES SCIES LONGITUD
251	*PULP AND WASTE PAPER					W 1112750	449.5	W 1014686	373.6	PATES A PAPIER,DECHETS
2517	SODA,SULPHATE WOOD PULP					W 932294	364.8	W 876606	317.8	PATES CHIMIQUES AU SULFATE
25172	— BLEACHED,NONDISSOLVNG					W 771160	311.0	W 680582	256.6	PATES BLANCHIES
27	CRUDE FERTLZR,MINRLS NES						283.0		339.6	ENGRAIS MINERAUX BRUTS
28	METALLIFEROUS ORES,SCRAP						1188.6		1811.6	MINERAIS METAL,DECHETS
281	IRON ORE,CONCENTRATES					MW 11322	283.6	MW 11773	269.2	MINERAIS DE FER
282	IRON AND STEEL SCRAP					W 2724761	358.9	W 5232775	573.3	FERRAILLES
28209	— OF OTHR IRON OR STEEL					W 2153702	162.7	W 4585310	347.2	FERRAILLES DE FER
288	NONFERR METAL SCRAP NES					W 383168	386.8	W 679567	791.1	DECHETS NON FERREUX
2882	OTHER BASE MTL SCRAP NES					W 303925	366.4	W 612424	752.1	AUTRES DECHETS
28821	COPPER WASTE AND SCRAP					W 214141	308.6	W 355359	528.2	DECHETS DE CUIVRE
3	MINERAL FUELS ETC				32565.0		38257.8		38053.7	COMBUSTIBLES MINERAUX LUB
32	COAL,COKE AND BRIQUETTES						1143.3		924.8	HOUILLES,COKES,BRIQUETTES
322	COAL,LIGNITE AND PEAT					MW 27387	1050.6	MW 23695	839.0	HOUILLES,LIGNITES,TOURBE
3222	OTH COAL,NOT AGGLOMERATD					MW 21744	886.4	MW 20695	746.7	AUTRES HOUILLES
33	PETROLEUM AND PRODUCTS						22514.0		20873.4	PETROLE ET DERIVES
333	CRUDE PETROLEUM					MW 115830	15012.3	MW 116847	13688.5	HUILES BRUTES DE PETROLE
334	PETROLEUM PRODUCTS,REFIN					MW 56613	7443.5	MW 60605	7132.9	PRODUITS RAFFINES
3341	GASOLINE,OTH LIGHT OILS					W 5679168	917.4			ESSENCES POUR MOTEURS
33411	MOTOR,AVIATION SPIRIT					W 3701024	614.1			ESSENCES MOTEURS D'AVIONS
33419	OTH LIGHT PETROLEUM OILS					W 1895504	291.2			AUTRES HUILES LEGERES
3344	FUEL OILS,NES					MW 24261	3990.3			FUEL OILS
3345	LUBS,PETROLEUM OILS NES					MW 24262	2150.8			HUILES LUBRIFIANTES
33451	LUBS(HIGH PETR CONT) ETC					MW 24255	2143.7			HUILES LUBRIF,H LOURDES
341	*GAS,NATURAL AND MANUFCT					MW 161985	14167.1	MW 162466	15844.0	GAZ NATUREL,GAZ MANUFACT
3414	PETROLEUM GASES, GASEOUS					MW 160675	13992.2	MW 160983	15644.2	GAZ DE PETROLE GAZEUX
351	*ELECTRIC CURRENT						433.6	MH 16884	411.6	ENERGIE ELECTRIQUE
5	CHEMCLS,RELATED PROD NES						5242.7		4517.7	PRODUITS CHIMIQUES
51	ORGANIC CHEMICALS				2015.0		1046.2		1039.3	PROD CHIMIQ ORGANIQUES
511	HYDROCARBONS NES,DERIVS					W 979198	343.5	W 957597	273.6	HYDROCARBURES NDA
512	ALCOHOLS,PHENOLS ETC					W 1034125	357.6	W 1298901	347.1	PHENOLS,PHENOLS–ALCOOLS
5121	ACYCLIC ALCOHOLS,DERIVS					W 972879	304.0	W 1240700	296.0	ALCOOLS ACYCLIQUES
515	ORG–INORG COMPOUNDS ETC					W 126330	196.3	W 174514	269.4	COMPOSES ORGANO–MINERAUX
52	INORGANIC CHEMICALS				1900.0		1220.2		867.8	PROD CHIM INORGANIQUES
522	INORG ELEMNTS,OXIDES,ETC					W 3740394	736.1		685.8	ELEMENTS INORGANIQUES
5225	INORGANIC BASES ETC NES					W 3413335	527.2	W 3276747	481.3	AUTRES BASES OXYDES METAL
52251	AMMONIA,ANHYDROUS ETC					W 3199192	403.6	W 3058471	346.0	AMMONIAC LIQUEFIE
524	RADIOACTIVE ETC MATERIAL						301.6		20.9	MATIERES RADIOACTIVES
5241	RADIOACTIVE ELEMENTS ETC						283.7			RADIOELEMENTS,ISOTOPES
562	*FERTILIZERS,MANUFACTURE				1881.0	MW 15523	1937.5	MW 15168	1598.6	ENGRAIS MANUFACTURES
5621	CHEM NITROGENOUS FERTLZR					W 8322319	1060.5	W 6159681	561.0	ENGRAIS AZOTES
56211	AMMONIUM NITRATE					W 3218087	369.0	W 2402296	209.7	NITRATE D'AMMONIUM
56216	UREA					W 3758067	602.2	W 2743162	303.8	UREE
5623	CHEM POTASSIC FERTILIZER					W 3606585	279.0	W 4928892	393.7	ENGRAIS POTASSIQUES
56231	POTASSIUM CHLORIDE					W 3590036	276.4	W 4909164	389.9	CHLORURE DE POTASSIUM
5629	FERTILIZERS NES					W 3590646	598.0	W 4077467	643.8	ENGRAIS NDA
56292	NITROG–PHOS FERTILZR NES					W 2014063	374.1	W 2265909	395.4	ENGRAIS NDA CONT N P
572	*EXPLOSIVES,PYROTECH PRO				630.0	W 76131	86.0	W 88715	98.9	EXPLOSIFS
58	PLASTIC MATERIALS ETC						452.7		446.1	MAT PLAST ARTIFICIELLES
583	POLYMERIZATION ETC PRODS					W 556088	421.4	W 535022	424.1	PROD POLYMERISATION
6	BASIC MANUFACTURES						17714.1		17419.8	ART MANUFACTURES
62	RUBBER MANUFACTURES NES				897.0		368.8		315.1	CAOUTCHOUC MANUFACTURE
63	WOOD,CORK MANUFACTRS NES						264.7		299.7	OUVRAGES LIEGE ET BOIS
64	PAPER,PAPERBOARD AND MFR				1266.0		790.1		677.3	PAPIERS,CARTONS & OUVRAGES
641	PAPER AND PAPERBOARD					W 1472533	736.4	W 1601297	649.1	PAPIERS ET CARTONS
6411	NEWSPRINT					W 867958	423.3	W 822386	324.2	PAPIER JOURNAL
65	TEXTILE YARN,FABRICS,ETC				322.0		478.9		410.0	FILS,TISSUS,ARTICLES TEXTILE
66	NONMETAL MINERAL MFS NES						317.5		300.3	ART MIN NON METALLIQUES
67	IRON AND STEEL				7267.0		7651.3		7299.8	FER ET ACIER
671	PIG IRON ETC					W 2688231	643.0	W 3161682	635.4	FONTE,SPIEGEL,POUDRES
6712	PIG IRN,SPIEGELEISEN ETC					W 2078031	288.6	W 2419872	302.8	FONTES BRUTES
6716	FERRO–ALLOYS					W 283872	316.4	W 342459	284.4	FERRO–ALLIAGES
672	IRON,STEEL PRIMARY FORMS					MW 15762	3401.3	MW 16710	3455.7	LINGOTS FER,ACIER
6725	IRN,STL BLOOMS,SLABS,ETC					MW 10968	2257.6	MW 11203	2210.3	BLOOMS,BILLETTES FER ACIER
67251	IRN,SMPLE STL BLOOMS,ETC					MW 10806	2220.7	MW 10580	2072.9	BLOOMS ETC NON ACIER FIN
6727	IRN,STL COIL FR REROLLNG					W 4692846	1109.8	W 5283114	1205.9	EBAUCHES POUR TOLES FER
67271	IRON,SIMPLE STEEL COILS					W 4661857	1098.8	W 5283011	1205.3	EBAUCHES NON EN ACIER
673	IRON,STEEL SHAPES ETC					W 5385420	1419.8	W 4796350	1212.8	BARRES,PROFIL FER,ACIER
6731	IRON,STEEL WIRE ROD					W 2096294	499.9	W 1895931	446.1	FIL MACHINE FER,ACIER
67311	IRON,SIMPLE STL WIRE ROD					W 2061662	488.9	W 1888161	443.0	FIL MACH AUT ACIER FIN
6732	IRON,STEEL BARS ETC					W 2598939	710.2	W 2199083	571.7	BARRES FER,ACIER
67325	OTH ALLOY STEEL BARS ETC					W 997401	296.8	W 587941	179.5	BARRES NON ACIERS ALLIES
67326	IRN,OTH STL BARS HOTROLD					W 1519307	369.7	W 1549260	356.2	BARRES PLEINES FER,ACIER
674	IRN,STL UNIV,PLATE,SHEET					W 4860788	1685.0	W 4845716	1609.1	LARGES PLATS,TOLES
6744	IRN,STL HVY PLATE,ROLLED					W 1651122	410.6	W 1312591	311.6	TOLES LAMINEES PLUS 4.75 MM
67441	— OF IRON OR SIMPLE STL					W 1648195	403.2	W 1307995	302.9	TOLES NON ACIER FIN CARB
6745	IRN,STL MED PLATE,ROLLED					W 874270	367.3	W 828964	306.8	TOLES 3 A 4.75 MM
6746	IRN,STL THIN PLATE,ROLLD					W 1894683	663.8	W 2152044	709.4	TOLES LAM MOINS 3MM
67461	— OF IRON OR SIMPLE STL					W 1880881	650.8	W 2138676	696.2	TOL NON AC FIN MOINS 3 MM
678	IRON,STL TUBES,PIPES,ETC					W 458073	302.9	W 293867	185.4	TUBES,TUYAUX EN FONTE,FER

5. General Exports F.O.B. by Commodities according to the S.I.T.C. (Rev. 2) in million U.S. Dollars
Exportations Générales F.O.B. par Produits d'après la C.T.C.I. (Rév. 2) en millions de Dollars E.U.

SITC CTCI	COMMODITY	1994 QUANTITY QUANTITE	1994 VALUE VALEUR	1995 QUANTITY QUANTITE	1995 VALUE VALEUR	1996 QUANTITY QUANTITE	1996 VALUE VALEUR	1997 QUANTITY QUANTITE	1997 VALUE VALEUR	PRODUIT
68	NON–FERROUS METALS						7325.2		7584.7	METAUX NON FERREUX
682	COPPER EXC CEMENT COPPER				1437.0	W 601811	1293.3	W 589555	1253.3	CUIVRE
6821	COPPER NES,ALLOYS,UNWRT					W 562843	1202.8	W 571661	1201.7	CUIVRE BRUT
68212	COPPER REFINED,UNWROUGHT					W 529364	1134.6	W 536203	1126.1	CUIVRE AFFINE BRUT
683	NICKEL					W 171490	1258.4	W 223798	1515.9	NICKEL
6831	NICKEL,ALLOYS UNWROUGHT					W 167202	1217.0	W 221857	1496.3	NICKEL ET ALLIAGES BRUTS
684	ALUMINIUM				4159.0	W 2821559	4254.9	W 2940531	4175.6	ALUMINIUM
6841	ALUMINIUM,ALLOYS,UNWRGHT					W 2618442	3928.9	W 2708823	3797.6	ALUMINIUM,ALLIAGES BRUTS
6842	ALUMINIUM,ALLOYS WORKED					W 203117	326.0	W 231708	378.1	ALUMINIUM,ALLIAGES OUVRE
689	NON–FER BASE METALS NES						337.7	W 77508	464.6	AUT METAUX NON FERREUX
6899	BASE METALS NES,CERMETS						250.6	W 41479	370.4	METAUX COMMUNS NDA
68999	BASE MTL NES UNWRT,WASTE					W 25997	250.6	W 41479	370.4	AUT METAUX COM BRUTS NDA
69	METAL MANUFACTURES NES				702.0		471.2		497.3	ART MANUFACT EN METAL NDA
699	BASE METAL MFRS NES						246.1	W 62557	285.6	ART MANUFACTURES MET NDA
7	MACHINES,TRANSPORT EQUIP				7464.0		6217.0		4572.6	MACHINES MATERIEL TRANSPORT
71	POWER GENERATING EQUIPMT						1115.4		1164.3	MACHINES GENERATRICES
714	ENGINES AND MOTORS NES					W 3791	314.4	W 3539	270.6	MOTEURS NON ELECTRIQUES
718	OTH POWER GENERATG MACHY					W 3472	330.3	W 3302	388.1	AUTRES MOTEURS PARTIES
7187	NUCLEAR REACTORS,PTS NES					W 1223	310.8	W 845	367.8	REACTEURS NUCLEAIRES
72	MACHS FOR SPCL INDUSTRYS						360.7		288.3	MAC SPECIALES POUR INDUST
74	GENRL INDUSTRL MACHY NES						676.4		664.1	MACH APP INDUSTRIE
749	NONELEC MACH PTS,ACC NES					W 71462	283.1	W 45768	235.0	PIECES MACH NON ELEC NDA
76	TELECOMM,SOUND EQUIPMENT						408.2		592.6	EQUIPMENT DE TELECOM
764	TELECOM EQPT,PTS,ACC NES					W 4582	304.0	W 5097	347.7	EQUIP TELECOM,PIECES
77	ELECTRIC MACHNRY NES ETC						609.1		611.5	MACH APP ELECT NDA
78	ROAD VEHICLES				1710.0		1175.4		791.8	VEHICULES ROUTIERS
781	PASS MOTOR VEH EXC BUSES					W 158381	633.2	W 106020	406.8	AUTO TRANSPORT PERSONNES
79	OTHR TRANSPORT EQUIPMENT						1646.9		262.2	AUTRE MATERIEL TRANSPORT
791	RAILWAY VEHICLES					W 915152	238.4	W 364705	262.2	VEHIC MAT CHEMINS DE FER
792	AIRCRAFT ETC					W 7882	290.0			APP NAVIGATION AERIENNE
793	SHIPS AND BOATS ETC				..		1118.6			NAVIRES BATEAUX,ETC
7932	SHIPS AND BOATS NES						1034.8			NAVIRES ET BATEAUX
79323	OTHER CARGO VESSELS					MV 2676119	496.6			AUT BATEAUX TRANS MARCH
79324	FISHING VESSELS ETC					MV 1312807	450.6			BATEAUX DE PECHE
8	MISC MANUFACTURED GOODS						1295.2		1399.4	ART MANUFACTURES DIVERS
84	CLOTHING AND ACCESSORIES				282.0		293.7		264.5	VETEMENTS
87	PRECISION INSTRUMNTS NES						234.2		267.4	INSTRUM,APPAR SCIENT NDA
89	MISC MANUFCTRD GOODS NES						562.8		662.2	ART MANUFACTURES DIVERS
892	PRINTED MATTER				87.1	W 11284	407.6	W 10897	450.5	IMPRIMES
8921	PRINTED BOOKS,GLOBES,ETC					W 8638	263.3	W 7177	305.0	LIVRES,BROCHURES,CARTES
89211	PRINTED BOOKS,PAMPHLETS					W 8492	261.9	W 7127	303.8	LIVRES,BROCHURES
9	GOODS NOT CLASSD BY KIND						14020.1		14996.2	ART TRANSACT NON CLASSES
931	*SPECIAL TRANSACTIONS						14017.9		14995.7	TRANS.SPECIALES

FOOT NOTES – NOTES

TABLE 1 –
1 Excludes trade with the Commonwealth of Independent State s prior to 1994.
TABLE 3 –
1 Excludes trade with the Commonwealth of Independent State s prior to 1994.
TABLEAU 1 –
1 Y exclu le commerce avec la confédération des états indépendants avant 1994.
TABLEAU 3 –
1 Y exclu le commerce avec la confédération des états indépendants avant 1994.

1. HISTORICAL SERIES, 1961–1997 SPECIAL TRADE, IMPORTS C.I.F., EXPORTS F.O.B.
SERIES HISTORIQUES, 1961–1997 COMMERCE SPECIAL, IMPORTATIONS C.A.F., EXPORTATIONS F.O.B

YEAR ANNEE	VALUE IN MILLION E.C. DOLLARS VALEUR EN MILLION E.C. DOLLARS MERCHANDISE –MARCHANDISE IMPORTS	EXPORTS	GOLD –OR IMPORTS	EXPORTS	CONVERSION FACTORS U.S. CENTS PER E.C. DOLLAR FACTEURS DE CONVERSION CENTS E.U. PAR E.C. DOLLAR IMPORTS	EXPORTS	INDEX NUMBERS –INDICES QUANTUM IMPORTS	EXPORTS	UNIT VALUE VALEUR UNITAIRE IMPORTS	EXPORTS
1961	13.43	9.82			58.3300	58.3300				
1963	12.28	8.29			58.3300	58.3300				
1964	13.45	9.77			58.3300	58.3300				
1965	14.63	8.81			58.3300	58.3300				
1966	15.82	8.61			58.3300	58.3300				
1967	16.24	9.05			57.6500	57.6500				
1968	17.07	6.95			50.0000	50.0000				
1969	19.30	8.62			50.0000	50.0000				
1970	23.43	8.29			50.0000	50.0000				
1971	30.50	8.06			50.7170	50.7170				
1972	30.56	12.12			52.1220	52.1220				
1973	35.59	16.58			51.0810	51.0810				
1974	39.37	24.13			48.7300	48.7300				
1975	51.36	46.84			46.2880	46.2880				
1976	57.77	46.40			38.3480	38.3480				
1977	59.18	40.54			37.0370	37.0370				
1978	65.41	45.21			37.0370	37.0370				
1979	86.71	45.47			37.0370	37.0370				
1980	121.07	65.13			37.0370	37.0370				
1981	128.83	65.51			37.0370	37.0370				
1982	118.15	50.86			37.0370	37.0370				
1983	132.00	64.00			37.0370	37.0370				
1984	132.00	64.00			37.0370	37.0370				
1985	144.72	58.86			37.0370	37.0370				
1986	169.82	67.90			37.0370	37.0370				
1987	214.63	75.58			37.0370	37.0370				
1988	251.52	74.10			37.0370	37.0370				
1989	276.71	77.25			37.0370	37.0370				
1990	298.97	74.66			37.0370	37.0370				
1991	297.76	74.20			37.0370	37.0370				
1992	258.19	70.62			37.0370	37.0370				
1993	318.89	72.87			37.0370	37.0370				
1994	343.28	60.14			37.0370	37.0370				
1995	357.11	50.72			37.0370	37.0370				
1996	393.81	58.10			37.0370	37.0370				
1997	397.36	110.90			37.0370	37.0370				

2. IMPORTS BY BROAD ECONOMIC CATEGORY AND EXPORTS BY INDUSTRIAL ORIGIN. (PERCENTAGE OF TOTAL VALUE)
IMPORTATIONS PAR CATEGORIES ECONOMIQUES ET EXPORTATIONS PAR BRANCHE D'ACTIVITE.(EN POURCENTAGE DE LA VALEUR TOTALE)

IMPORTS – IMPORTATIONS

	1991	1992	1993	1994	1995	1996	1997
TOTAL IMPORTS–IMPORTATIONS TOTALES			100.	100.	100.	100.	100.
1 FOOD BEV–ALIMENTATION BOISSONS			20.7	20.0	20.1	19.5	18.4
11 PRIMARY–PRODUITS DE BASE			6.5	6.2	6.2	6.3	6.4
111 FOR INDUSTRY–POUR L'INDUSTRIE			0.5	0.5	0.4	0.5	0.4
112 FOR HOUSEHOLDS–POUR LES MENAGES			5.9	5.7	5.8	5.8	5.9
12 PROCESSED–PRODUITS ELABORES			14.2	13.8	13.9	13.2	12.0
121 FOR INDUSTRY–POUR L'INDUSTRIE			2.8	2.2	2.5	2.4	2.0
122 FOR HOUSEHOLDS–POUR LES MENAGES			11.5	11.6	11.3	10.8	10.1
2 IND SUPPLIES–APPROV INDUSTRIELS			29.7	28.6	30.4	28.8	27.1
21 PRIMARY–PRODUITS DE BASE			0.6	0.6	0.8	0.7	0.9
22 PROCESSED–PRODUITS ELABORES			29.1	28.0	29.6	28.1	26.2
3 FUELS–COMBUSTIBLES			3.5	3.0	4.3	5.7	7.4
31 PRIMARY–PRODUITS DE BASE			0.8	0.5	0.5	1.0	0.9
32 PROCESSED–PRODUITS ELABORES			2.7	2.5	3.8	4.7	6.5
321 MOTOR SPIRIT–ESSENCE			1.6	1.6	2.3	2.1	4.7
322 OTHER–AUTRES			1.1	0.9	1.6	2.7	1.8
4 MACHINERY–EQUIPEMENT			17.2	21.3	16.9	16.1	18.8
41 CAPITAL EQUIPMENT–MACHINES			15.1	18.9	14.4	13.2	15.8
42 PARTS–PIECES ACCESSOIRES			2.1	2.5	2.5	2.9	3.0
5 TRANSPORT–TRANSPORT			8.0	8.6	9.5	9.9	7.6
51 PASSENGER CARS–AUTOMOBILES			4.0	4.4	4.8	5.3	3.9
52 OTHER–AUTRES			1.9	2.2	2.5	2.2	1.6
521 INDUSTRIAL–INDUSTRIELS			1.8	2.1	2.5	2.1	1.5
522 NON INDUSTRIAL–NON INDUSTRIEL			0.1	0.1	0.0	0.1	0.1
53 PARTS–PIECES ACCESSOIRES			2.2	2.0	2.1	2.5	2.2
6 CONSUM GOODS–BIENS CONSOMMATION			18.4	18.0	16.8	18.3	19.9
61 DURABLE–DURABLES			3.9	4.8	4.1	5.2	6.3
62 SEMI DURABLE–SEMI DURABLES			9.0	8.3	8.0	8.2	8.7
63 NON DURABLE–NON DURABLES			5.5	4.8	4.7	4.9	4.8
7 GOODS NES–BIENS NDA			2.6	0.5	2.0	1.7	0.8

EXPORTS – EXPORTATIONS

	1991	1992	1993	1994	1995	1996	1997
TOTAL EXPORTS–EXPORTATIONS TOTALES			100.	100.	100.	100.	100.
1 AGRICULTURE			2.2	1.1	1.5	0.8	0.4
2 MINING QUARRY–INDUS EXTRACTIVES			0.0	0.0	0.0		
3 MANUFACTURING–IND MANUFACTUR			97.8	98.9	98.4	99.2	99.6
31 FOOD BEV TOBACCO–ALIM BOISS TAB			54.4	59.1	52.9	61.3	57.5
32 TEXTILES–INDUSTRIES TEXTILES			5.6	2.0	2.5	2.8	1.0
33 WOOD & PRODUCTS–BOIS & PRODUITS			0.0	0.0	0.1	0.1	0.2
34 PAPER & PRODUCTS–PAPIER & PRODT			1.3	1.4	0.4	0.6	0.9
35 CHEMICALS–INDUSTRIES CHIMIQUES			0.3	0.7	1.0	0.8	0.3
36 NON METAL MIN–MIN NON METAL			1.0	1.4	1.1	0.5	0.2
37 BASIC METAL–IND METAL BASE			0.1	0.3	0.1	0.3	0.1
38 METAL MANUF–MANUF METAL			34.2	32.2	38.8	32.5	38.7
39 OTH MANUF IND–AUTRES MANUF			0.9	1.8	1.5	0.4	0.8

3. TRADE BY PRINCIPAL COUNTRIES OF ORIGIN AND DESTINATION (VALUE IN MILLION U.S. DOLLARS)
ECHANGES SELON LES PRINCIPAUX PAYS D'ORIGINE ET DE DESTINATION (VALEUR EN MILLIONS DE DOLLARS EU)

COUNTRIES–PAYS	SPECIAL IMPORTS C.I.F. IMPORTATIONS SPECIALES C.A.F				
	1993	1994	1995	1996	1997
World	117.9	127.1	132.3	145.9	147.2
Africa	0.0	0.0	0.0	0.0	0.2
Americas	93.0	103.2	104.4	116.8	119.2
– Northern America	66.1	76.5	76.0	84.3	85.8
– LAIA	1.0	1.1	0.7	1.5	1.2
– CACM	0.9	0.5	0.1	0.1	0.1
– Caribbean	24.3	24.5	26.4	29.8	31.0
– Rest of America	0.7	0.6	1.1	1.2	1.0
Asia excl fmr USSR	7.0	8.7	9.3	10.5	9.0
– Middle East	0.1	0.1	0.1	0.0	0.1
Asia former USSR					
Europe excl fmr USSR	17.7	15.0	18.2	18.1	18.5
– European Union	17.3	14.4	17.5	17.5	17.9
– Eastern Europe	0.1	0.0	0.0	0.1	0.1
– Rest of Europe	0.3	0.6	0.7	0.6	0.5
Europe former USSR	0.0	0.0	0.0	0.0	0.0
Oceania	0.2	0.2	0.3	0.4	0.4
Other			0.0		
USA/Etats–Unis d'Amer	63.4	73.5	73.0	80.5	82.5
United Kingdom	14.4	12.0	14.2	13.8	13.9
Trinidad and Tobago	10.4	10.7	13.1	15.0	18.0
Japan/Japon	5.7	6.3	7.0	8.0	6.2
Barbados/Barbade	3.3	3.3	3.4	3.7	3.2
Canada	2.7	3.0	3.1	3.7	3.4
Netherlands Antilles	2.8	2.7	2.8	3.5	2.8
St Vincent & Grenadines	1.6	1.8	1.8	2.1	1.9
Jamaica/Jamaïque	1.8	2.2	1.8	1.9	1.5
Other Asia n.e.s.	0.6	1.1	1.2	1.4	1.8
Antigua and Barbuda	0.9	0.8	0.8	0.9	1.4
France, Monaco	0.5	0.4	0.7	1.2	1.6
Netherlands/Pays–Bas	0.6	0.5	1.0	0.9	0.8
Denmark/Danemark	0.8	0.8	0.6	0.7	0.6
Dominica/Dominique	0.6	0.7	0.5	0.7	0.7
Dominican Republic	0.5	0.5	0.6	0.8	0.7
Saint Lucia/Ste–Lucie	0.7	0.6	0.5	0.4	0.5
Guyana	0.6	0.2	0.7	0.9	0.4
Norway,Svalbard and JM	0.2	0.5	0.6	0.5	0.4
Germany/Allemagne	0.4	0.4	0.4	0.2	0.4
Panama	0.1	0.3	0.5	0.3	0.6
Brazil/Brésil	0.2	0.4	0.3	0.4	0.4
Grenada/Grenade	0.5	0.4	0.2	0.1	0.1
Italy/Italie	0.4	0.2	0.3	0.2	0.2
British Virgin Islds	0.5	0.3	0.3	0.2	0.1
China/Chine	0.2	0.4	0.2	0.3	0.2
Mexico/Mexique	0.1	0.1	0.1	0.4	0.5
Venezuela	0.4	0.2	0.1	0.2	0.1
Argentina/Argentine	0.2	0.3	0.1	0.2	0.1
New Zealand	0.1	0.2	0.2	0.2	0.2
Korea, Republic of	0.0	0.3	0.3	0.1	0.2
Guatemala	0.8	0.0	0.0	0.0	0.0
Guadeloupe	0.3	0.2	0.3		
Korea Dem People's Rp	0.1	0.1	0.2	0.2	0.0
Colombia/Colombie	0.1	0.2	0.1	0.2	0.1
Montserrat	0.1	0.1	0.1	0.3	0.0
Honduras	0.1	0.4	0.0	0.0	0.0
Australia/Australie	0.1	0.0	0.1	0.2	0.2
Belgium–Luxembourg	0.0	0.0	0.1	0.1	0.2
Anguilla	0.0	0.2	0.2	0.0	0.0

COUNTRIES–PAYS	EXPORTS EXPORTATIONS ES F.O.B.				
	1993	1994	1995	1996	1997
Monde	26.9	22.3	18.8	21.5	41.1
Afrique			0.0	0.0	
Amériques	14.3	10.8	10.7	13.5	25.4
– Amérique du Nord	10.0	6.9	7.6	3.9	23.6
– ALAI		0.0		0.0	0.0
– MCAC		0.0		0.0	0.0
– Caraïbes	4.3	3.7	3.0	9.4	1.7
– Autre Amérique	0.0	0.2	0.1	0.2	0.1
Asie anc. URSS exclus	0.0	0.1	0.0	0.1	1.9
– Moyen–Orient					0.0
Asie ancienne URSS					
Europe anc. URSS exclus	12.6	11.5	8.0	7.9	13.8
– Union Européenne	12.6	11.5	8.0	7.9	13.8
– Europe de l'Est					
– Autre de l'Europe		0.0	0.0	0.0	
Europe ancienne URSS					
Océanie		0.0		0.0	
Autre					
United Kingdom	12.5	11.2	7.9	7.9	13.5
USA/Etats–Unis d'Amer	10.0	6.9	7.6	3.9	23.6
Anguilla	0.4	0.2	0.2	8.5	0.1
Dominica/Dominique	0.4	0.6	0.6	0.1	0.5
Japan/Japon	0.0	0.1	0.0	0.1	1.9
Trinidad and Tobago	1.0	0.7	0.1	0.2	0.0
Netherlands Antilles	0.3	0.4	0.5	0.1	0.2
Antigua and Barbuda	0.7	0.3	0.2	0.1	0.2
Saint Lucia/Ste–Lucie	0.4	0.2	0.3	0.1	0.2
Montserrat	0.2	0.3	0.2	0.0	0.2
Barbados/Barbade	0.2	0.2	0.3	0.1	0.1
Grenada/Grenade	0.3	0.2	0.2	0.1	0.0
St Vincent & Grenadines	0.2	0.2	0.2	0.0	0.1
Guyana	0.0	0.2	0.1	0.2	0.1
Guadeloupe	0.2	0.2	0.1		
British Virgin Islds	0.1	0.1	0.1	0.0	0.1
Netherlands/Pays–Bas	0.1	0.1	0.1	0.0	0.0
France, Monaco	0.0	0.0	0.0	0.1	0.1
Italy/Italie		0.0	0.1		0.1
Germany/Allemagne	0.0	0.0	0.0		0.1
Jamaica/Jamaïque	0.0	0.0	0.0	0.0	0.0
Canada	0.0	0.0	0.0	0.0	0.0
Cayman Is/Is Caïmans		0.1			
Dominican Republic	0.0	0.0	0.0		0.0
Denmark/Danemark		0.0			0.0
Argentina/Argentine				0.0	0.0
Other Asia n.e.s.		0.0		0.0	0.0
Australia/Australie		0.0		0.0	
Panama		0.0			0.0
China/Chine	0.0				0.0
Brazil/Brésil					0.0
India/Inde		0.0		0.0	
Mexico/Mexique		0.0			
Indonesia/Indonésie				0.0	0.0
Belgium–Luxembourg				0.0	0.0
Guatemala		0.0		0.0	0.0
Korea, Republic of	0.0				
Switzerland,Liechtenst.		0.0	0.0	0.0	
Venezuela				0.0	

(VALUE AS PERCENTAGE OF WORLD TOTAL)(VALEURS EN POURCENTAGE DU TOTAL MONDIAL)

	1988	1989	1990	1991	1992	1993	1994	1995	1996	1997
Africa	0.1					0.0	0.0	0.0	0.0	0.1
Americas	72.1					78.9	81.2	78.9	80.1	81.0
– Northern America	52.7					56.1	60.2	57.5	57.8	58.3
– LAIA	1.6					0.9	0.9	0.6	1.0	0.8
– CACM	0.6					0.8	0.4	0.1	0.1	0.1
– Caribbean	16.9					20.6	19.3	20.0	20.4	21.1
– Rest of America	0.4					0.6	0.5	0.9	0.8	0.7
Asia excl fmr USSR	5.8					6.0	6.9	7.0	7.2	6.1
– Middle East	0.1					0.1	0.1	0.0	0.0	0.0
Asia former USSR										
Europe excl fmr USSR	21.9					15.0	11.8	13.8	12.4	12.5
– European Union	21.1					14.7	11.3	13.2	12.0	12.2
– Eastern Europe	0.1					0.1	0.0	0.0	0.0	0.1
– Rest of Europe	0.7					0.3	0.4	0.5	0.4	0.3
Europe former USSR	0.0					0.0	0.0	0.0	0.0	0.0
Oceania	0.1					0.1	0.2	0.3	0.3	0.3
Other	0.0							0.0		
USA/Etats–Unis d'Amer	48.5					53.8	57.8	55.2	55.2	56.0
United Kingdom	18.0					12.2	9.4	10.7	9.5	9.5
Trinidad and Tobago	6.5					8.8	8.4	9.9	10.3	12.2
Japan/Japon	3.8					4.8	4.9	5.3	5.5	4.2
Barbados/Barbade	2.7					2.8	2.6	2.5	2.6	2.1
Canada	4.2					2.3	2.3	2.3	2.6	2.3
Netherlands Antilles	2.0					2.4	2.1	2.1	2.4	1.9
St Vincent & Grenadines	2.1					1.4	1.5	1.4	1.5	1.3
Jamaica/Jamaïque	1.3					1.6	1.7	1.4	1.3	1.0
Other Asia n.e.s.	0.3					0.5	0.9	0.9	0.9	1.2

	1988	1989	1990	1991	1992	1993	1994	1995	1996	1997
Afrique	0.0							0.0	0.0	
Amériques	71.2					53.0	48.3	57.1	62.9	61.8
– Amérique du Nord	58.0					37.2	31.2	40.7	18.2	57.5
– ALAI	0.1						0.0		0.1	0.0
– MCAC	0.0						0.0		0.0	0.0
– Caraïbes	13.0					15.8	16.4	16.1	43.7	4.1
– Autre Amérique	0.1					0.0	0.7	0.4	0.9	0.2
Asie anc. URSS exclus	0.1					0.1	0.3	0.1	0.3	4.6
– Moyen–Orient										0.0
Asie ancienne URSS										
Europe anc. URSS exclus	22.4					46.9	51.4	42.7	36.8	33.7
– Union Européenne	22.4					46.9	51.4	42.7	36.8	33.7
– Europe de l'Est										
– Autre de l'Europe	0.0						0.0	0.0	0.0	
Europe ancienne URSS										
Océanie							0.0		0.0	
Autre	6.3									
United Kingdom	21.8					46.5	50.4	41.8	36.5	32.8
USA/Etats–Unis d'Amer	57.8					37.1	31.1	40.5	18.2	57.4
Anguilla	1.1					1.4	1.0	1.1	39.6	0.2
Dominica/Dominique	0.5					1.3	2.7	3.4	0.5	1.2
Japan/Japon						0.1	0.2	0.1	0.2	4.6
Trinidad and Tobago	4.3					3.7	3.0	0.4	0.7	0.1
Netherlands Antilles	1.4					1.2	1.6	2.5	0.7	0.4
Antigua and Barbuda	2.3					2.4	1.5	0.9	0.3	0.4
Saint Lucia/Ste–Lucie	0.1					1.3	1.1	1.8	0.4	0.5
Montserrat	0.9					0.9	1.3	1.3	0.1	0.5

4. Special Imports C.I.F. by Commodities according to the S.I.T.C. (Rev. 2) in million U.S. Dollars
Importations Spéciales C.A.F. par Produits d'après la C.T.C.I. (Rév. 2) en millions de Dollars E.U.

SITC CTCI	COMMODITY	1994 QUANTITY QUANTITE	1994 VALUE VALEUR	1995 QUANTITY QUANTITE	1995 VALUE VALEUR	1996 QUANTITY QUANTITE	1996 VALUE VALEUR	1997 QUANTITY QUANTITE	1997 VALUE VALEUR	PRODUIT
	ALL COMMODITIES		127.2		132.3		145.9		147.2	TOUS PRODUITS
0	FOOD AND LIVE ANIMALS		22.0		22.8		24.8		23.4	ALIMENTS,ANIMAUX VIVANTS
01	MEAT AND PREPARATIONS		5.3		5.3		5.9		5.3	VIANDES ET PREPARATIONS
011	MEAT FRESH,CHILLD,FROZEN	W 2491	3.7	W 2937	4.0	W 7963	4.3	W 2943	4.1	VIANDES FRAICHES,REF,CONGE
0111	BOVINE MEAT FRESH,FROZEN	W 168	0.6	W 130	0.5	W 141	0.5	W 79	0.3	VIANDES BOVIN FRAI,REF
0114	POULTRY FRESH CHLLD,FRZN	W 1976	2.5	W 2430	2.8	W 7422	3.0	W 2460	2.8	VOLAILLES MORTES
014	MEAT PREPD,PRSVD,NES ETC	W 574	1.4	W 411	1.2	W 638	1.4	W 401	1.1	CONSERVES DE VIANDES
0142	SAUSAGES INCLDING TINNED	W 258	0.6	W 160	0.5	W 225	0.7	W 187	0.5	SAUCISSES,SAUCISSONS
0149	OTH PREPARD,PRESRVD MEAT	W 317	0.9	W 250	0.7	W 413	0.7	W 214	0.6	AUTRES PREP DE VIANDES
02	DAIRY PRODCTS,BIRDS'EGGS		2.4		2.3		2.2		2.4	PRODUITS LAITIERS,OEUFS
022	MILK AND CREAM	W 1187	1.4	W 1110	1.3	W 844	1.1	W 1023	1.4	LAIT ET CREME
0223	MILK AND CREAM FRESH	W 357	0.4	W 198	0.3	W 286	0.4	W 564	0.8	LAIT,CREME FRAIS
0224	MILK,CREAM PRESERVED ETC	W 831	1.0	W 912	1.0	W 558	0.8	W 459	0.7	LAIT,CREME CONS,CONC
02249	MILK(EX DRY) PRSVD,SWEET	W 795	0.9	W 879	0.9	W 526	0.7	W 426	0.6	LAIT CONS,CONC SUCRE
024	CHEESE AND CURD	W 231	0.9	W 271	0.9	W 233	1.0	W 237	0.9	FROMAGE ET CAILLEBOTTE
03	FISH AND PREPARATIONS		1.6		1.8		1.9		2.0	POISSONS ET PREPARATIONS
034	FISH,FRESH,CHILLED,FROZN	W 67	0.4	W 71	0.5	W 93	0.5	W 138	0.7	POISSON FRAIS, REFRIG,CONG
035	FISH SALTED,DRIED,SMOKED	W 155	0.6	W 302	0.8	W 324	0.8	W 188	0.8	POISSON SECHE,SALE,FUME
03503	FISH(EX COD)DRIED,SALTED	W 107	0.4	W 268	0.7	W 313	0.8	W 175	0.7	POISSONS SECHES,SALES
037	FISH ETC PREPD,PRSVD NES	W 111	0.4	W 95	0.5	W 104	0.5	W 133	0.5	POIS,CRUST,MOL PREPARES
0371	FISH PREPARD,PRESRVD NES	W 109	0.4	W 94	0.5	W 102	0.4	W 131	0.5	CONSERVES DE POISSONS
04	CEREALS AND PREPARATIONS		3.8		4.2		4.7		4.4	CEREALES ET PRODUITS
042	RICE	W 1174	0.7	W 867	0.7	W 921	0.8	W 1140	0.8	RIZ
0421	RICE IN HUSK OR HUSKED	W 917	0.5	W 637	0.5	W 736	0.6	W 951	0.6	RIZ SANS AUTRE PREPARATION
04212	RICE HUSKED	W 917	0.5	W 637	0.5	W 717	0.6	W 951	0.6	RIZ CARGO
046	WHEAT ETC MEAL OR FLOUR	W 3142	1.1	W 2349	1.3	W 2093	1.4	W 2187	1.3	SEMOULE FARINE,FROMENT
04601	FLOUR OF WHEAT OR MESLIN	W 3123	1.1	W 2337	1.2	W 2077	1.3	W 2174	1.2	FARINE DE FROMENT
048	CEREAL ETC PREPARATIONS	W 734	1.7	W 794	2.0	W 1021	2.4	W 743	2.2	PREPTNS A BASE CEREALES
0481	PREPD BREAKFAST FOOD ETC	W 118	0.5	W 114	0.6	W 127	0.7	W 87	0.5	CEREALES TRAVAILLEES
04812	CEREAL ROASTED, PUFFED	W 110	0.5	W 107	0.6	W 104	0.6	W 77	0.5	PRODTS BASE CEREALES
0484	BAKERY PRODUCTS	W 184	0.6	W 216	0.6	W 276	0.8	W 206	0.8	PRODUITS DE BOULANGERIE
0488	OTH CEREAL PREPS,MALT EX	W 127	0.4	W 111	0.5	W 216	0.6	W 118	0.5	EXTRAITS DE MALT
05	VEGETABLES AND FRUIT		4.1		4.1		4.4		4.1	LEGUMES ET FRUITS
054	VEG ETC FRSH,SMPLY PRSVD	W 1696	1.8	W 1758	1.9	W 1844	1.9	W 2474	1.9	LEGUMES FRAIS,CONG,SECS
0545	OTHER FRESH VEGETABLES	W 751	0.8	W 775	0.9	W 732	0.9	W 1579	1.0	AUTRES LEGUMES FRAIS,REF
05459	FRESH VEGETABLES NES	W 508	0.6	W 533	0.7	W 491	0.7	W 514	0.8	LEGUMES FRAIS,REFRI NDA
0546	VEGETABLES SIMPLY PRESVD	W 283	0.4	W 342	0.5	W 355	0.5	W 227	0.4	LEGUMES CONG,CONSER
05461	VEGETABLES FROZEN	W 281	0.4	W 342	0.5	W 355	0.5	W 227	0.4	LEGUMES CONGELES
057	FRUIT,NUTS,FRESH,DRIED	W 442	0.7	W 441	0.8	W 557	1.0	W 716	0.9	FRUITS FRAIS OU SECS
058	FRUIT PRESERVED,PREPARED	W 778	1.4	W 821	1.3	W 958	1.5	W 845	1.2	CONSERVES DE FRUITS
0585	FRUIT OR VEGETABLE JUICE	W 667	1.1	W 719	1.0	W 847	1.1	W 735	0.9	JUS DE FRUITS
06	SUGAR AND PREPS,HONEY		0.9		1.4		1.6		1.2	SUCRES ET PRODUITS
061	SUGAR AND HONEY	W 1202	0.5	W 1896	1.1	W 1889	1.3	W 1619	0.9	SUCRES ET MIEL
0611	RAW BEET AND CANE SUGAR	W 3	0.1	W 816	0.5	W 710	0.7	W 300	0.3	SUCRES BRUTS
0612	REFINED SUGAR ETC	W 1191	0.5	W 1021	0.6	W 1136	0.6	W 1298	0.6	SUCRES RAFFINES
07	COFFEE,TEA,COCOA,SPICES		0.6		0.5		0.6		0.7	CAFE,THE,CACAO,EPICES
081	*FEEDING STUFF FOR ANIML	W 3753	1.1	W 1963	0.8	W 2027	0.8	W 1113	0.6	NOURRITURE POUR ANIMAUX
0819	FOOD WASTE AND FEED NES	W 3721	1.1	W 1953	0.8	W 2011	0.8	W 1102	0.6	DECHETS,ALIMENTS NDA
08199	FODDER NES,INCL SWEETNED	W 3712	1.1	W 1946	0.8	W 2008	0.8	W 1100	0.6	PREPARATIONS FOURRAGERES
09	MISC EDIBLE PRODUCTS		2.6		2.8		2.9		3.0	PREP ALIMENTAIRES DIVERSES
098	EDIBLE PRODCTS,PREPS NES	W 1891	2.4	W 1091	2.6	W 1368	2.7	W 1212	2.8	PREP ALIMENTAIRES NDA
09804	SAUCES,MIXED SEASONINGS	W 355	0.8	W 310	0.8	W 278	0.8	W 336	0.9	SAUCES,ASSAISONNEMENTS
09809	MISC FOOD PREPRTIONS NES	W 1431	1.4	W 684	1.6	W 958	1.7	W 693	1.7	PREP ALIMENTAIRES NDA
1	BEVERAGES AND TOBACCO		3.9		4.1		3.9		3.9	BOISSONS ET TABACS
11	BEVERAGES		3.6		3.7		3.6		3.6	BOISSONS
111	NON-ALCOHL BEVERAGES NES	W 2494	1.6	W 1728	1.7	W 2703	2.0	W 2186	2.0	BOISSONS NON ALCOOLIQUES
11102	FLAVORED WATERS NON-ALCO	W 2332	1.5	W 1491	1.6	W 2438	1.8	W 2020	1.9	LIMONADES,EAUX GAZEUSES
112	ALCOHOLIC BEVERAGES	W 830	2.0	W 720	2.0	W 589	1.7	W 657	1.6	BOISSONS ALCOOLIQUES
1121	WINE OF FRESH GRAPES ETC	W 144	0.5	W 176	0.5	W 127	0.5	W 148	0.5	VINS DE RAISINS FRAIS
11212	WINE OF FRESH GRAPES	W 137	0.5	W 163	0.5	W 123	0.5	W 138	0.5	VINS DE MOUTS DE RAISINS
1123	BEER,ALE,STOUT,PORTER	W 351	0.5	W 232	0.4	W 160	0.3	W 249	0.4	BIERES
1124	DISTILLED ALCOHOLIC BEVS	W 310	1.1	W 288	1.0	W 259	0.8	W 227	0.8	ALCOOLS,EAUX-DE-VIE
11249	OTH ALCOHOLC BEVS,CMPNDS	W 253	0.8	W 220	0.7	W 217	0.7	W 181	0.6	BOISSONS ALCOOLIQUES NDA
2	CRUDE MATERLS,EXCL FUELS		3.3		3.9		3.4		3.8	MAT BRUTES NON COMESTIBLES
24	CORK AND WOOD		2.6		2.7		2.3		2.4	LIEGE ET BOIS
248	WOOD SHAPED,SLEEPERS	W 7270	2.4	W 4047	2.6	W 2658	2.3	W 4385	2.3	BOIS SIMPLEMENT TRAVAILLES
2482	LUMBER SHAPED CONIFER	W 6954	2.0	W 3442	2.2	W 2032	1.9	W 4064	2.1	CONIFERES SCIES,RABOTES
24821	LUMBER SAWN ETC CONIFER	W 4427	1.4	W 2097	1.4	W 1032	1.1	W 2526	1.1	CONIFERES SCIES LONGITUD
24822	LUMBER PLANED ETC CONIFR	W 2528	0.7	W 1345	0.8	W 1001	0.9	W 1538	1.0	CONIFER RABOTES,RAINES
2483	LUMBER SHAPED NON-CONIFR	W 316	0.5	W 605	0.5	W 626	0.4	W 321	0.3	NON CONIFERES SCIES,RABOTES
24831	LUMBER SAWN ETC NON-CON	W 260	0.3	W 450	0.5	W 582	0.3	W 296	0.2	SCIES LONGITUDINALEMENT
27	CRUDE FERTLZR,MINRLS NES		0.2		0.5		0.6		0.7	ENGRAIS MINERAUX BRUTS
278	OTHER CRUDE MINERALS	W 249	0.2	W 515	0.5	W 383	0.2	W 1378	0.2	AUTRES MINERAUX BRUTS
29	CRUDE ANIMAL,VEG MAT NES		0.4		0.5		0.5		0.7	MATIERES BRUTES ANIM,VEGET
292	CRUDE VEG MATERIALS NES	W 124	0.4	W 94	0.5	W 104	0.5	W 267	0.7	MAT BRUTES VEGETALES NDA
3	MINERAL FUELS ETC		4.0		5.8		8.4		11.0	COMBUSTIBLES MINERAUX LUB
33	PETROLEUM AND PRODUCTS		3.3		5.2		7.0		9.6	PETROLE ET DERIVES
334	PETROLEUM PRODUCTS,REFIN	W 12600	3.3	W 12976	5.1	W 21659	7.0	W 22586	9.5	PRODUITS RAFFINES
3341	GASOLINE,OTH LIGHT OILS	W 9311	2.1	W 8601	3.1	W 10428	3.1	W 12093	6.9	ESSENCES POUR MOTEURS
33411	MOTOR,AVIATION SPIRIT	W 9307	2.1	W 8599	3.1	W 10407	3.1	W 12092	6.9	ESSENCES MOTEURS D'AVIONS
3342	KEROSENE,OTH MEDIUM OILS	W 181	0.1	W 292	0.1	W 1099	0.5	W 426	0.1	PETR LAMPANTS,AUT HUIL
33421	KEROSENE INCL JET FUEL	W 27	0.1	W 122	0.1	W 826	0.5	W 165	0.1	PETROLES LAMPANTS
3343	GAS OILS	W 2596	0.5	W 3360	1.3	W 9477	2.7	W 9619	2.0	GAS OILS
3345	LUBS,PETROLEUM OILS NES	W 513	0.7	W 722	0.8	W 655	0.8	W 447	0.7	HUILES LUBRIFIANTES
33451	LUBS(HIGH PETR CONT) ETC	W 510	0.7	W 714	0.8	W 648	0.8	W 446	0.7	HUILES LUBRIF,H LOURDES
341	*GAS,NATURAL AND MANUFCT	W 1936	0.7	W 1493	0.7	W 2253	1.4	W 3613	1.4	GAZ NATUREL,GAZ MANUFACT
3413	PETROLM GASES,LIQUEFIED	W 1936	0.7	W 1493	0.7	W 2253	1.4	W 3613	1.4	GAZ DE PETROLE LIQUEFIE
34131	LIQUEFIED PROPANE,BUTANE	W 1844	0.7	W 1493	0.7	W 2209	1.4	W 3612	1.4	PROPANE,BUTANE LIQUEFIES
4	ANIMAL,VEGETABLE OIL,FAT		1.1		1.1		1.0		0.9	HUILES,GRAISSES ANIM,VEG
411	*ANIMAL OILS AND FATS	W 474	0.4	W 423	0.5	W 914	0.5	W 344	0.4	HUILES,GRAISSES ANIMALES
4111	OILS OF FISH,WHALES ETC	W 469	0.4	W 419	0.5	W 908	0.5	W 339	0.4	GRAISSES,HUILES DE POISSONS
41111	FISH LIVER OIL	W 469	0.4	W 419	0.5	W 908	0.5	W 339	0.4	HUILES DE FOIES
42	FIXED VEGETABLE OIL,FAT		0.7		0.6		0.5		0.4	HUILES VEGETALES FIXES
423	FIXED VEG OILS,SOFT	W 416	0.5	W 367	0.5	W 360	0.3	W 205	0.3	HUILES VEGET DOUCES FIXES
4232	SOYA BEAN OIL	W 406	0.5	W 361	0.5	W 343	0.3	W 200	0.3	HUILE DE SOJA
5	CHEMCLS,RELATED PROD NES		9.4		9.7		11.2		10.4	PRODUITS CHIMIQUES
53	DYES,TANNING,COLOUR PROD		1.9		1.7		2.1		2.0	PROD TEINTURE,COLORANTS
533	PIGMENTS,PAINTS,ETC	W 872	1.8	W 597	1.7	W 726	2.1	W 743	2.0	PIGMENTS,PEINTURES,VERNIS
5334	VARNISHES,DISTEMPERS ETC	W 488	1.4	W 301	1.3	W 397	1.7	W 420	1.6	PEINTURES A L'EAU
53341	WATER-THINNED PAINTS	W 128	0.5	W 96	0.4	W 102	0.5	W 72	0.3	PEINTURES DILUEES
53342	OTH PAINTS,VARNISHES ETC	W 356	0.9	W 201	0.9	W 291	1.2	W 346	1.2	AUTRES PEINTURES,VERNIS

4. Special Imports C.I.F. by Commodities according to the S.I.T.C. (Rev. 2) in million U.S. Dollars
Importations Spéciales C.A.F. par Produits d'après la C.T.C.I. (Rév. 2) en millions de Dollars E.U.

SITC CTCI	COMMODITY	1994 QUANTITY QUANTITE	1994 VALUE VALEUR	1995 QUANTITY QUANTITE	1995 VALUE VALEUR	1996 QUANTITY QUANTITE	1996 VALUE VALEUR	1997 QUANTITY QUANTITE	1997 VALUE VALEUR	PRODUIT
5335	GLAZES,DRIERS,PUTTY ETC	W 382	0.4	W 292	0.4	W 327	0.4	W 319	0.4	PREPTNS COLOR UTILISES CERAM
53354	PUTTY,OTHER FILLINGS ETC	W 381	0.4	W 291	0.4	W 326	0.4	W 317	0.4	MASTICS ENDUITS
541	*MEDICINAL,PHARM PRODUCT	K 174021	1.5	K 91434	1.4	K 137370	1.6	K 87602	1.7	PROD MEDICINAUX PHARMACEUT
5417	MEDICAMENTS	K 165080	1.3	K 72335	1.2	K 128039	1.5	K 80488	1.5	MEDICAMENTS
54179	— CONTNG OTH SUBSTANCES	K 157935	1.1	K 67345	1.0	K 122550	1.3	K 73505	1.3	MED CONT AUT SUBSTANCES
55	PERFUME,CLEANING ETC PRD		3.0		3.1		3.4		3.1	PROD POUR PARFUM,TOILETTE
553	PERFUMERY,COSMETICS,ETC	W 197	1.6	W 188	1.6	W 313	1.6	W 187	1.5	PRODUITS DE PARFUMERIE
554	SOAP,CLEANSING ETC PREPS	W 1275	1.5	W 949	1.5	W 1240	1.8	W 1014	1.7	SAVONS,PRODUITS DETERSIFS
5542	WASHING PREPARATIONS ETC	W 1142	1.1	W 820	1.2	W 963	1.4	W 888	1.3	PROD ORG TENSIO-ACT NDA
562	*FERTILIZERS,MANUFACTURE	W 1904	0.6	W 2054	0.6	W 2402	0.8	W 1633	0.5	ENGRAIS MANUFACTURES
5629	FERTILIZERS NES	W 1853	0.6	W 1661	0.5	W 2383	0.8	W 1619	0.5	ENGRAIS NDA
56291	NIT-PHOS-POT FERTLZR NES	W 1843	0.5	W 1647	0.5	W 2340	0.8	W 1604	0.5	ENGRAIS CONT N P K
58	PLASTIC MATERIALS ETC		0.3		0.4		0.6		0.9	MAT PLAST ARTIFICIELLES
583	POLYMERIZATION ETC PRODS	W 64	0.3	W 81	0.4	W 114	0.6	W 104	0.7	PROD POLYMERISATION
5839	OTH POLYMRZTION ETC PROD	W 63	0.3	W 81	0.4	W 114	0.5	W 104	0.7	AUT PROD POLYMER COPOLYM
59	CHEMICAL MATERIALS NES		2.0		2.4		2.4		2.0	MAT PROD CHIMIQUES NDA
591	PESTICIDES,DISINFECTANTS	W 273	1.3	W 304	1.5	W 318	1.5	W 252	1.1	DESINF,INSECT,FONG,HERB
5911	INSECTICIDES,FOR RETAIL	W 111	0.6	W 125	0.7	W 103	0.7	W 64	0.4	INSECTICIDES VENTE DET
5913	HERBICIDES,FOR RETAIL	W 70	0.4	W 85	0.6	W 95	0.6	W 74	0.5	HERBICIDES VENTE AU DET
598	MISCEL CHEM PRODUCTS NES	W 184	0.6	W 197	0.6	W 225	0.7	W 232	0.6	PROD DIV INDUST CHIM NDA
5989	CHEM PRODUCTS,PREPS NES	W 170	0.5	W 190	0.6	W 213	0.6	W 220	0.6	PROD PREP CHIMIQUES NDA
6	BASIC MANUFACTURES		26.0		30.1		32.1		30.2	ART MANUFACTURES
62	RUBBER MANUFACTURES NES		1.3		1.3		1.8		1.7	CAOUTCHOUC MANUFACTURE
625	RUBBER TYRES, TUBES ETC	W 236	0.9	W 286	1.0	W 338	1.4	W 336	1.2	PNEUS CAOUTCHOUC VULCANISE
6252	TYRES,NEW,BUS OR LORRY	W 77	0.3	W 94	0.4	W 121	0.6	W 131	0.5	PNEUS POUR AUTOBUS,CAMIONS
6259	OTH TYRES,TYRE CASES,ETC	W 82	0.3	W 107	0.3	W 123	0.5	W 105	0.4	AUTRES PNEUS RECHAPES FLAPS
63	WOOD,CORK MANUFACTRS NES		2.9		3.2		2.8		3.3	OUVRAGES LIEGE ET BOIS
634	VENEERS,PLYWOOD,ETC	W 1869	1.7	W 2215	2.0	W 1822	1.6	W 2475	1.8	PLACAGES,CONTRE-PLAQUES
6342	PLYWOOD OF WOOD SHEETS	W 1710	1.6	W 2110	1.9	W 1812	1.6	W 2359	1.7	BOIS CONTRE-PLAQUES
635	WOOD MANUFACTURES NES	W 473	1.3	W 406	1.2	W 353	1.3	W 1378	1.6	ART MANUF EN BOIS NDA
6353	BUILDERS WOODWRK,PREFABS	W 393	1.1	W 346	1.1	W 274	1.0	W 1260	1.4	OUVRAGES DE MENUISERIE
64	PAPER,PAPERBOARD AND MFR		3.8		3.3		4.1		3.6	PAPIERS,CARTONS & OUVRAGES
641	PAPER AND PAPERBOARD	W 288	0.6	W 227	0.6	W 301	1.1	W 593	0.7	PAPIERS ET CARTONS
6415	PAPER,PAPERBRD,BULK,NES	W 63	0.2	W 53	0.2	W 108	0.6	W 287	0.3	PAPIERS,CARTONS ROULEAUX
64159	OTHER PAPER ETC,BULK,NES	W 49	0.2	W 47	0.2	W 101	0.5	W 281	0.3	AUT PAPIER ROULEAUX FEUILLES
642	PAPER,ETC,PRECUT,ARTS OF	W 776	3.3	W 744	2.7	W 1131	3.1	W 782	2.9	PAP,CARTONS DECOUPES
6421	PAPER ETC CONTAINERS	W 343	1.0	W 353	0.9	W 607	0.9	W 330	0.9	BOITES,SACS EMBALLAGES
6424	PAPER ETC CT TO SIZE NES	W 151	0.4	W 102	0.4	W 174	0.5	W 141	0.5	PAP,CARTONS DECOUPES
6428	PAPER ETC ARTICLES NES	W 201	1.6	W 215	1.0	W 254	1.2	W 228	1.1	OUVRAGES EN PATE A PAPIER
64281	SPOOLS ETC OF PAPER ETC	W 6	0.4	W 1	0.1	W 1	0.1			TAMBOURS,BOBINES EN PAPIER
64284	PAPER TISSUES,TOWELS ETC	W 67	0.5	W 65	0.3	W 87	0.4	W 81	0.4	MOUCHOIRS SERVIETTES EN PAP
64285	PAPER ETC DIAPERS ETC	W 104	0.6	W 129	0.6	W 149	0.7	W 134	0.7	SERVIETTES HYGIENIQUES
65	TEXTILE YARN,FABRICS,ETC		2.1		2.1		2.4		1.8	FILS,TISSUS,ARTICLES TEXTILE
652	COTTON FABRICS,WOVEN	W 71	0.6	W 92	0.5	W 71	0.7	W 32	0.3	TISSUS DE COTON
6522	WOVEN COTTON BLEACHD,ETC	W 60	0.5	W 74	0.5	W 69	0.7	W 26	0.3	TISSUS COTON BLANCHIS ETC
65224	BLCHED COTTON FABRIC NES	W 52	0.5	W 66	0.5	W 65	0.6	W 22	0.2	AUT TIS PLUS 85% COT BLANCHI
653	WOVN MAN-MADE FIB FABRIC	W 51	0.4	W 53	0.4	W 34	0.4	W 30	0.4	TISSUS FIBRES SYNTH,ARTIF
658	TEXTILE ARTICLES NES	W 49	0.5	W 43	0.5	W 40	0.6	W 36	0.4	ART FACONNES MAT TEXTILES
66	NONMETAL MINERAL MFS NES		4.3		4.3		5.4		5.2	ART MIN NON METALLIQUES
661	LIME,CEMENT,BLDG PRODS	W 27360	2.2	W 16530	2.1	W 27207	2.4	W 19391	2.6	CHAUX,CIMENTS MAT CONSTR
6612	CEMENT	W 26839	1.9	W 15820	1.6	W 26584	2.1	W 18827	2.3	CIMENTS HYDRAULIQUES
6618	MNRL BLDG PRD UNFIRD NES	W 481	0.3	W 689	0.5	W 593	0.3	W 439	0.3	MAT CONST AMIANTE-CIMENT
662	CLAY,REFRACTORY BLDG PRD	W 1165	1.0	W 687	0.6	W 1313	1.2	W 1068	1.0	MAT CONST REFRACTAIRES
6624	BRICKS ETC NONREFRACTORY	W 1132	0.9	W 672	0.6	W 1303	1.2	W 1053	1.0	BRIQUES ETC CERAM NON REFR
66245	GLAZED CERAMIC SETTS ETC	W 953	0.8	W 527	0.5	W 998	0.9	W 824	0.8	AUT CARREAUX CERAMIQUE
664	GLASS	W 75	0.3	W 100	0.4	W 148	0.4	W 113	0.7	VERRE
665	GLASSWARE	W 502	0.6	W 789	1.0	W 1152	1.1	W 406	0.7	OUVRAGES EN VERRE
6651	BOTTLES ETC OF GLASS	W 475	0.4	W 748	0.7	W 1109	0.8	W 370	0.4	RECIPIENTS EN VERRE
66511	GLASS BOTTLES ETC NONVAC	W 475	0.4	W 747	0.7	W 1109	0.8	W 370	0.4	BONBONNES,BOUTEILLES,ETC
67	IRON AND STEEL		2.8		6.5		5.1		3.7	FER ET ACIER
673	IRON,STEEL SHAPES ETC	W 2217	1.2	W 7844	4.6	W 5693	2.2	W 2375	1.6	BARRES,PROFIL FER,ACIER
6732	IRON,STEEL BARS ETC	W 1792	0.9	W 1306	0.7	W 2475	0.9	W 1847	1.0	BARRES FER,ACIER
67322	HIGH CARBON STL BARS ETC	W 1766	0.9	W 1197	0.6	W 2463	0.9	W 1835	0.9	BARRES ACIER FIN CARBONE
6733	IRON,STEEL PROFILES ETC	W 274	0.3	W 5845	3.8	W 365	1.2	W 334	0.6	PROFILES,PALPLAN FER,ACIER
67336	IRN,SMPL STL SHEET PILNG	W 262	0.3	W 5831	3.8	W 351	1.1	W 303	0.6	PALPLANCHES EN FER,ACIER
674	IRN,STL UNIV,PLATE,SHEET	W 343	0.5	W 469	0.5	W 524	0.7	W 516	0.5	LARGES PLATS,TOLES
6749	OTH IRN,STL PLATES,SHEET	W 242	0.5	W 441	0.5	W 464	0.7	W 493	0.5	AUTRES TOLES FER,ACIER
67491	— OF IRON OR SIMPLE STL	W 242	0.4	W 441	0.5	W 459	0.7	W 492	0.5	AUT TOLES AUTRES ACIER FIN
678	IRON,STL TUBES,PIPES,ETC	W 339	1.0	W 709	1.3	W 943	1.8	W 438	1.3	TUBES,TUYAUX EN FONTE,FER
6782	IRON,STL SEAMLESS TUBES	W 112	0.2	W 44	0.1	W 754	0.7	W 249	0.3	TUBES,TUYAUX SANS SOUDURE
6783	IRON,STL TUBES,PIPES NES	W 74	0.2	W 580	0.6	W 82	0.3	W 22	0.1	AUT TUBES,TUYAUX FER,ACIER
6785	IRON,STEEL TUBE FITTINGS	W 97	0.7	W 75	0.7	W 84	0.8	W 149	0.9	ACCESSOIRES DE TUYAUTERIE
68	NON-FERROUS METALS		0.6		0.7		0.7		0.5	METAUX NON FERREUX
682	COPPER EXC CEMENT COPPER	W 120	0.4	W 89	0.5	W 68	0.4	W 43	0.4	CUIVRE
6822	COPPER,ALLOYS WORKED	W 120	0.3	W 89	0.5	W 68	0.4	W 43	0.3	CUIVRE,ALLIAGES OUVRES
69	METAL MANUFACTURES NES		8.5		9.1		10.0		10.6	ART MANUFACT EN METAL NDA
691	STRUCTURES AND PARTS NES	W 694	2.2	W 483	1.6	W 617	2.3	W 645	2.2	CONSTRUCT FER,ACIER,ALU
6911	STRUCTURES,PARTS IRN,STL	W 326	0.9	W 247	0.6	W 380	1.1	W 357	0.9	CONSTRUCT FER,ACIER,FONTE
6912	STRUCTURES,PARTS ALUMNM	W 368	1.3	W 236	1.1	W 237	1.3	W 289	1.4	CONSTRUCT ALUMINIUM
692	METAL TANKS,BOXES,ETC	W 106	0.3	W 147	0.4	W 105	0.3	W 353	0.8	RECIPIENTS METALLIQUES
6924	MTL TRANSPORT BOXES ETC	W 92	0.3	W 89	0.3	W 91	0.2	W 217	0.5	FUTS,TAMBOURS,BIDONS
693	WIRE PRODUCTS NON ELECTR	W 428	1.0	W 424	0.9	W 512	0.8	W 606	1.0	OUVRAGES FILS METALLIQUES
6931	WIRE CABLES, ROPES ETC	W 46	0.5	W 67	0.4	W 46	0.3	W 98	0.6	CORDAGES EN FILS DE FER
6935	METAL FENCING,GAUZE,ETC	W 337	0.5	W 332	0.5	W 319	0.5	W 351	0.5	TOILES EN FER,ACIER,CUIVRE
69351	IRN,STL FENCNG,GAUZE ETC	W 337	0.5	W 332	0.5	W 319	0.5	W 351	0.5	TOILES EN FER,ACIER
694	STL,COPPR NAILS,NUTS,ETC	W 234	1.0	W 212	1.3	W 263	1.6	W 245	1.9	CLOUS,VIS,ECROUS
69402	IRN,STL NUTS,BOLTS,ETC	W 94	0.8	W 121	1.1	W 164	1.3	W 156	1.7	BOULONS,VIS,ECROUS FER,AC
695	TOOLS	W 67	0.5	W 56	0.5	W 125	0.6	W 68	0.6	OUTILS A MAIN
697	BASE MTL HOUSEHOLD EQUIP	W 286	0.8	W 138	0.8	W 143	0.9	W 182	1.0	ART MENAGE MET COMMUNS
6973	DMSTC HEATG,COOKG APPARA	W 203	0.4	W 81	0.5	W 81	0.5	W 112	0.6	APPS CHAUF NON ELECTRIQ
69731	IRN,STL DOM COOKG APPARA	W 201	0.4	W 76	0.4	W 78	0.5	W 109	0.6	APPS CUISSON FER,ACIER
699	BASE METAL MFRS NES	W 382	3.0	W 481	3.8	W 974	3.8	W 398	3.3	ART MANUFACTURES MET NDA
6991	LOCKSMITHS WARES,ETC	W 77	0.4	W 53	0.4	W 49	0.5	W 54	0.5	ARTICLES DE SERRURERIE
6993	PINS,HOOKS,EYES,ETC	W 58	0.6	W 35	0.3	W 26	0.2	W 26	0.3	EPINGLES,AIGUILLES FER,AC
69933	BASE METL HOOKS,EYES ETC	W 57	0.6	W 30	0.3	W 25	0.2	W 26	0.3	FERMOIRS,BOUCLES,AGRAFES
6996	BASE MTL MISC ARTICLES	W 90	0.3	W 92	0.5	W 118	0.5	W 98	0.4	ART DIVERS METAUX COMMUNS
6997	IRON,STEEL ARTICLES NES	W 97	1.3	W 139	1.8	W 704	1.9	W 134	1.4	OUV FONTE,FER,ACIER NDA
69979	IRN,STL MANUFACTURES NES	W 95	1.3	W 123	1.8	W 703	1.9	W 127	1.4	AUT OUVRAGES EN FER NDA
6998	MFRS NES OF CPR,NIKL,ETC	W 48	0.4	W 109	0.8	W 52	0.6	W 64	0.7	OUVRAGES EN CU,NI,AL,PB,ZN
69981	COPPER MANUFACTURES NES	W 24	0.3	W 47	0.5	W 34	0.5	W 36	0.6	OUVRAGES EN CUIVRE
7	MACHINES,TRANSPORT EQUIP		40.8		36.7		39.8		42.5	MACHINES MATERIEL TRANSPORT

4. Special Imports C.I.F. by Commodities according to the S.I.T.C. (Rev. 2) in million U.S. Dollars
Importations Spéciales C.A.F. par Produits d'après la C.T.C.I. (Rév. 2) en millions de Dollars E.U.

SITC CTCI	COMMODITY	1994 QUANTITY QUANTITE	1994 VALUE VALEUR	1995 QUANTITY QUANTITE	1995 VALUE VALEUR	1996 QUANTITY QUANTITE	1996 VALUE VALEUR	1997 QUANTITY QUANTITE	1997 VALUE VALEUR	PRODUIT
71	POWER GENERATING EQUIPMT		7.8		1.6		1.7		1.5	MACHINES GENERATRICES
713	INTRNL COMBUS PSTN ENGIN	W 44	0.8	W 62	0.8	W 35	0.8	W 25	0.6	MOTEURS EXPL COMB INT, PIECE
7139	PISTON ENGINE PARTS NES	W 24	0.5	W 15	0.5	W 10	0.5	W 12	0.5	PIECES POUR 713.2,3,8
716	ROTATING ELECTRIC PLANT	W 157	7.0	W 58	0.8	W 93	0.9	W 65	0.9	APP ELECTR ROTATIFS,PIECES
7162	AC MTRS,GENRTRS,GEN SETS	W 151	6.9	W 43	0.5	W 69	0.5	W 56	0.5	MOTEURS ELECTRIQUES
71621	AC MTRS,INC UNIVRSL MTRS	W 135	6.8	W 19	0.2	W 50	0.3	W 10	0.2	MOT ELEC NON COUR CONTINU
72	MACHS FOR SPCL INDUSTRYS		1.6		1.9		2.2		3.3	MAC SPECIALES POUR INDUST
723	CIVIL ENGNEERG EQUIP ETC	W 465	0.7	W 261	0.7	W 142	0.7	W 207	1.0	APPAREILS DE GENIE CIVIL
7234	CONST,MINING MACHNRY NES	W 411	0.6	W 193	0.5	W 135	0.7	W 180	0.9	MACH POUR LA CONST, MINES
72342	SLFPRP SHOVELS,EXCAVATRS	W 132	0.5	W 91	0.3	W 119	0.6	W 55	0.4	PELLES MECANIQUES
728	OTH MACHY FOR SPCL INDUS	W 47	0.5	W 36	0.5	W 71	0.6	W 268	1.5	AUT MACH IND PARTICULIERES
7283	OTHR MINERAL WORKG MACHY	W 34	0.3	W 28	0.3	W 50	0.3	W 230	1.3	MACH TRIER,CRIBLER,BROYER
72833	MNRL MIXING,KNEADING MCH	W 26	0.2	W 16	0.2	W 21	0.2	W 120	0.9	MACH MELANGER MAT MINER
74	GENRL INDUSTRL MACHY NES		3.6		3.0		4.3		4.6	MACH APP INDUSTRIE
741	HEATING,COOLING EQUIPMNT	W 170	1.3	W 71	0.9	W 120	1.1	W 105	1.2	MACH CHAUFFAGE,PIECES
7415	AIR–CONDITIONING MACHNRY	W 102	0.8	W 46	0.5	W 78	0.7	W 64	0.7	GROUPES CONDITION AIR
743	PUMPS NES,CENTRFUGES ETC	W 85	0.7	W 25	0.3	W 47	0.5	W 43	0.6	POMPES COMPRES,VENT ETC
744	MECHANICAL HANDLING EQU	W 74	0.4	W 134	0.5	W 86	0.6	W 78	0.7	EQUIP MANUTENTION PIECES
745	NONELEC MACHY,TOOLS NES	W 32	0.2	W 52	0.3	W 27	0.3	W 47	0.6	AUT MACH NON ELEC,PIECES
749	NONELEC MACH PTS,ACC NES	W 80	0.9	W 64	0.9	W 108	1.5	W 92	1.2	PIECES MACH NON ELEC NDA
7492	COCKS,VALVES ETC NES	W 53	0.3	W 37	0.4	W 44	0.5	W 41	0.5	ART ROB,SIM POUR TUYAUX
7493	SHAFT,CRANK,PULLEY ETC	W 11	0.2	W 7	0.2	W 18	0.5	W 36	0.3	ARBRES TRANS,VILEBREQUINS
75	OFFICE MACHNES,ADP EQUIP		2.6		2.3		2.9		4.0	MACH BUREAU TRAIT AUTOM
751	OFFICE MACHINES	W 19	0.6	W 17	0.4	W 13	0.4	W 15	0.5	MACH,APPAREILS DE BUREAU
7518	OFFICE MACHINES NES	W 12	0.5	W 12	0.3	W 9	0.3	W 9	0.4	MACH,APP DE BUREAU NDA
752	AUTOMTIC DATA PROC EQUIP	W 22	1.6	W 23	1.4	W 29	2.0	W 45	2.5	MACH TRAIT INFORMATION
7522	DIGITAL COMPUTERS	W 12	1.2	W 14	0.9	W 10	1.4	W 28	1.8	MACH DIGITALES COMPLETES
7525	ADP PERIPHERAL UNITS	W 7	0.4	W 7	0.4	W 12	0.4	W 10	0.4	UNITES PERIPHERIQUES
759	OFFICE,ADP MCH PTS,ACCES	W 7	0.4	W 7	0.6	W 9	0.6	W 15	1.1	PIECES DU 751 ET 752
7599	ACCTG,ETC,ADP MCH PTS,AC	W 4	0.4	W 5	0.5	W 7	0.5	W 13	1.0	PIECES DU 751 ET 752
76	TELECOMM,SOUND EQUIPMENT		1.6		2.9		3.0		5.8	EQUIPMENT DE TELECOM
761	TELEVISION RECEIVERS	W 37	0.4	W 51	0.4	W 48	0.5	W 91	0.8	RECEPTEURS DE TELEVISION
7611	COLOUR TV RECEIVERS	W 37	0.3	W 50	0.4	W 47	0.5	W 91	0.8	RECEPTEURS COULEUR
762	RADIO BROADCAST RECEIVRS	W 19	0.2	W 30	0.3	W 17	0.2	W 78	0.7	RECEPTEURS RADIODIFFUSION
7628	OTHER RADIO RECEIVERS	W 10	0.1	W 13	0.2	W 8	0.1	W 60	0.6	AUTRES RECEPT RADIO
763	SOUND RECORDRS,PHONOGRPH	W 15	0.2	W 9	0.2	W 29	0.3	W 45	0.5	PHONO,APP ENREGISTREMENT
7638	OTHR SOUND APPARATUS ETC	W 15	0.2	W 9	0.2	W 29	0.3	W 44	0.5	AUT APP D'ENREGIS,REPROD
764	TELECOM EQPT,PTS,ACC NES	W 34	1.0	W 42	2.2	W 76	2.1	W 74	3.8	EQUIP TELECOM,PIECES
7641	LINE TELEPHONE,ETC EQUIP	W 18	0.7	W 22	1.3	W 12	0.8	W 37	2.8	APP TELEPHON PAR FIL
7649	PTS NES OF EQUIPMT OF 76	W 4	0.2	W 7	0.6	W 14	0.8	W 9	0.5	PIECES DE LA DIV 76
76491	PTS NES OF APPAR OF 7641	W 2	0.2	W 3	0.5	W 4	0.7	W 3	0.3	PIECES POUR 764.1
77	ELECTRIC MACHNRY NES ETC		14.7		14.6		14.0		14.4	MACH APP ELECT NDA
771	ELECTRIC POWER MACHY NES	W 114	0.7	W 124	1.0	W 94	0.7	W 94	0.8	MACH PROD,TRANS ELECTR
7711	TRANSFORMERS,ELECTRICAL	W 101	0.5	W 113	0.7	W 85	0.4	W 88	0.6	TRANSFO ELECTRIQUES
772	SWITCHGEAR ETC,PARTS NES	W 309	6.2	W 316	5.7	W 202	4.9	W 306	4.9	APP COUPURE,SECT ETC
7721	SWITCHGEAR ETC	W 244	3.7	W 249	3.4	W 130	2.6	W 166	2.5	APP COUPURE,SECTIONMNT
7722	PRINTED CIRCUITS,PTS NES	W 10	0.7	W 11	0.6	W 6	0.5	W 3	0.3	CIRCUITS ET PIECES
7723	FIXED,VARIABLE RESISTORS	W 55	2.0	W 57	1.8	W 65	1.9	W 137	2.1	POTENTIOMETRES PIECES
773	ELECTR DISTRIBUTNG EQUIP	W 323	2.5	W 260	1.9	W 263	1.7	W 275	1.7	EQUIPMT DISTRIBUTION ELECT
7731	INSULATED WIRE,CABLE ETC	W 285	2.2	W 237	1.7	W 253	1.6	W 269	1.6	FILS,CABLES ISOLES ELECT
774	ELECTRO–MEDCL,XRAY EQUIP	W 1	0.1	W 3	0.6	W 6	0.2	W 1	0.1	APPAREILS MEDICAUX
7742	X–RAY APPARATUS ETC		0.1	W 3	0.6	W 4	0.1	W 1	0.1	APPAREILS A RAYONS X
775	HOUSEHOLD TYPE EQUIP NES	W 334	1.5	W 343	1.3	W 321	1.8	W 425	2.4	MACH,APP USAGE DOMESTQUE
7751	HOUSEHOLD LDRY EQUIP NES	W 49	0.2	W 96	0.2	W 64	0.3	W 104	0.5	MACH A LAVER ET SECHOIRS
77511	DOMESTIC WASHING MACHNES	W 48	0.2	W 95	0.2	W 62	0.3	W 103	0.5	MACH LAVER LINGE MOINS 6 KG
7752	DOM REFRIGERATRS,FREEZRS	W 226	1.0	W 195	0.7	W 190	1.0	W 243	1.4	REFRIG,CONGEL MENAGER
77521	DOMESTIC REFRIGERATORS	W 192	0.8	W 166	0.6	W 155	0.8	W 201	1.2	REFRIGERATEURS
776	TRANSISTORS,VALVES,ETC	W 48	1.7	W 37	1.7	W 35	2.0	W 65	1.9	LAMPES,TUBES,VALVES
7763	DIODES,TRANSISTORS,ETC	W 46	1.6	W 36	1.7	W 34	1.9	W 65	1.9	DIODES,TRANSISTORS
778	ELECTRICAL MACHINERY NES	W 262	2.3	W 241	2.7	W 224	3.0	W 213	2.9	AUTRES MACH ELECT NDA
7781	BATTERIES,ACCUMULATORS	W 114	0.5	W 114	0.5	W 96	0.6	W 80	0.6	PILES ET ACCUMULATEURS
7782	ELECTRIC LAMPS,BULBS	W 64	0.4	W 38	0.5	W 37	0.7	W 33	0.4	LAMPES, TUBES ELECTRIQUES
77822	ELEC DISCHARGE LAMPS NES	W 37	0.2	W 31	0.4	W 32	0.6	W 24	0.3	LAMPES NON ULTRA–VIOLETS
7788	OTH ELEC MACHY,EQUIP NES	W 55	1.2	W 61	1.6	W 53	1.3	W 69	1.6	AUT MACH APP ELEC NDA
77881	ELECTRO–MAGNETS ETC		0.1		0.1	W 1	0.1	W 19	0.5	ELECTRO–AIMANTS
77884	ELECTRICAL CONDENSERS	W 51	1.1	W 38	1.1	W 49	1.2	W 48	1.0	CONDENSATEURS ELECTRIQUES
78	ROAD VEHICLES		8.6		10.2		11.6		8.6	VEHICULES ROUTIERS
781	PASS MOTOR VEH EXC BUSES	W 1924	5.6	W 818	6.4	W 1048	7.7	W 1166	5.8	AUTO TRANSPORT PERSONNES
782	LORRIES,SPCL MTR VEH NES	W 276	1.3	W 422	2.2	W 346	2.0	W 271	1.2	VEHICULES SPECIAUX,MARCH
7821	LORRIES,TRUCKS	W 197	1.1	W 341	1.6	W 287	1.8	W 218	1.1	VEHICULES TRANSP MARCHAND
7822	SPECIAL MOTOR VEHCLS NES	W 79	0.3	W 81	0.6	W 59	0.2	W 53	0.2	VEHICULES USAGES SPECIAUX
783	ROAD MOTOR VEHICLES NES	W 125	1.0	W 105	1.0	W 105	0.9	W 98	0.7	VEHICULES ROUTIERS NDA
7831	BUSES	W 108	0.9	W 96	0.9	W 88	0.9	W 98	0.7	VOITURES TRANSPORT COMMUN
784	MOTOR VEH PRTS,ACCES NES	W 45	0.6	W 70	0.6	W 126	0.9	W 73	0.8	PIECES 722,781,782,783
7849	OTHER MOTOR VEHCL PARTS	W 43	0.6	W 66	0.6	W 119	0.9	W 69	0.8	PIECES 722,781,782,783
79	OTHR TRANSPORT EQUIPMENT		0.4		0.2		0.4		0.6	AUTRE MATERIEL TRANSPORT
8	MISC MANUFACTURED GOODS		17.0		18.5		21.6		21.2	ART MANUFACTURES DIVERS
812	*PLUMBG,HEATNG,LGHTNG EQ	W 215	0.8	W 121	0.7	W 133	1.0	W 164	1.0	APPAR SANITAIRES CHAUFFAGE
8124	LIGHTING EQUIPMENT NES	W 51	0.4	W 54	0.4	W 54	0.6	W 61	0.7	APPAREILS ECLAIRAGE ETC
81242	LAMPS,FITTINGS BASE METL	W 43	0.3	W 47	0.4	W 40	0.5	W 56	0.6	APPAREILS D'ECLAIRAGE
821	*FURNITURE,PARTS THEREOF	W 719	3.1	W 601	2.3	W 836	3.9	W 958	3.7	MEUBLES ET PIECES
8211	CHAIRS,SEATS AND PARTS	W 132	0.7	W 110	0.6	W 121	0.9	W 152	0.9	SIEGES ET PIECES
82111	CHAIRS AND OTHER SEATS	W 131	0.6	W 109	0.6	W 120	0.9	W 151	0.9	SIEGES
8212	MED FURN,STUFFD FURNSHGS	W 104	0.4	W 90	0.3	W 113	0.6	W 251	0.7	MOB MEDICO–CHIRUR,PIECES
82122	MATTRESSES ETC	W 103	0.4	W 88	0.3	W 103	0.5	W 249	0.6	SOMMIERS,ARTICLES DE LITERIE
8219	FURNITURE AND PARTS NES	W 484	2.1	W 402	1.5	W 602	2.5	W 555	2.2	AUTRES MEUBLES ET PIECES
82192	WOOD FURNITURE NES	W 370	1.7	W 302	1.0	W 429	1.9	W 438	1.7	MEUBLES NDA EN BOIS
84	CLOTHING AND ACCESSORIES		3.1		2.5		2.7		2.7	VETEMENTS
842	MENS OUTERWEAR NOT KNIT	W 23	0.4	W 17	0.4	W 15	0.4	W 10	0.4	VET DESSUS POUR HOMMES
843	WOMENS OUTERWEAR NONKNIT	W 70	1.1	W 52	0.7	W 51	0.7	W 77	1.1	VET DESSUS FEMMES MAT TEX
8439	— OTHER OUTER GARMENTS	W 54	0.9	W 43	0.5	W 24	0.3	W 39	0.8	AUT VET DES FEM MAT TEXT
844	UNDER GARMENTS NOT KNIT	W 27	0.4	W 23	0.3	W 22	0.4	W 13	0.4	VETEMENT DESSOUS MAT TEX
846	UNDER GARMENTS KNITTED	W 56	0.7	W 64	0.7	W 44	0.7	W 39	0.6	SOUS VETS DE BONNETERIE
8462	— OF COTTON NON ELASTIC	W 48	0.6	W 56	0.6	W 39	0.6	W 33	0.5	SOUS–VET BONNET COTON
84629	—— OTHER	W 48	0.6	W 56	0.6	W 39	0.6	W 33	0.5	AUT SOUS–VET BONNET COTON
851	*FOOTWEAR	W 74	0.6	W 68	0.6	W 59	0.7	W 56	0.6	CHAUSSURES
85102	FOOTWEAR LEATHER	W 61	0.5	W 52	0.6	W 47	0.6	W 42	0.5	CHAUS SEMELLES EN CUIR
87	PRECISION INSTRUMNTS NES		0.9		1.1		1.4		1.0	INSTRUM,APPAR SCIENT NDA
872	MEDICAL INSTRUMENTS NES	W 7	0.1	W 11	0.3	W 37	0.7	W 15	0.2	INSTR,APP MEDIC–CHIR NDA
87202	OTH MEDICAL INSTRUMENTS	W 5	0.1	W 9	0.2	W 26	0.7	W 13	0.2	INSTRUM,APP MEDECINE
874	MEASURNG,CONTROLNG INSTR	W 29	0.7	W 15	0.7	W 23	0.6	W 17	0.6	INSTRUMENTS DE MESURE

4. Special Imports C.I.F. by Commodities according to the S.I.T.C. (Rev. 2) in million U.S. Dollars
Importations Spéciales C.A.F. par Produits d'après la C.T.C.I. (Rév. 2) en millions de Dollars E.U.

SITC CTCI	COMMODITY	1994 QUANTITY QUANTITE	1994 VALUE VALEUR	1995 QUANTITY QUANTITE	1995 VALUE VALEUR	1996 QUANTITY QUANTITE	1996 VALUE VALEUR	1997 QUANTITY QUANTITE	1997 VALUE VALEUR	PRODUIT
88	PHOTO EQU,OPTICL GDS ETC		0.7		0.7		1.0		0.9	APP,FOURN PHOTO,OP,MONTR
89	MISC MANUFCTRD GOODS NES		7.8		10.7		11.1		11.5	ART MANUFACTURES DIVERS
892	PRINTED MATTER	W 228	2.1	W 247	4.1	W 246	4.0	W 224	2.9	IMPRIMES
8921	PRINTED BOOKS,GLOBES,ETC	W 141	1.1	W 90	0.9	W 84	0.9	W 114	1.2	LIVRES,BROCHURES,CARTES
89211	PRINTED BOOKS,PAMPHLETS	W 140	1.1	W 89	0.9	W 80	0.9	W 112	1.2	LIVRES,BROCHURES
8928	PRINTED MATTER NES	W 67	0.9	W 115	2.9	W 130	2.8	W 62	1.4	IMPRIMES NDA
89283	UNISSUED BANKNOTES ETC	W 11	0.6	W 61	2.7	W 88	2.5	W 20	0.9	TIMBRES–POSTE FISCAUX
893	ARTICLES OF PLASTIC NES		4.2		4.8		5.0		6.0	OUVRAGES EN MAT DIVIS 58
8931	PLSTC PACKG CONTNRS,LIDS	W 277	1.4	W 737	1.8	W 340	1.8	W 344	1.7	ART TRANSP EMBALLAGE ETC
8939	MISC PLASTIC ARTICLES	W 697	2.9	W 666	3.0	W 652	3.2	W 955	4.4	ART DIVERS EN MAT DIV 58
89399	OTHR PLASTC ARTICLES NES	W 591	2.7	W 517	2.8	W 596	3.1	W 784	4.1	AUT OUV MAT DIV 58
894	TOYS,SPORTING GOODS,ETC	W 61	0.5	W 55	0.5	W 80	0.7	W 83	0.7	VOITURES ENFANTS,JOUETS
8942	TOYS,INDOOR GAMES ETC	W 46	0.3	W 48	0.4	W 69	0.5	W 71	0.6	JOUETS,JEUX ETC
898	MUSICAL INSTRUMENTS,PTS	W 11	0.2	W 17	0.4	W 17	0.4	W 45	0.7	INSTRUMENTS DE MUSIQUE
899	OTHER MANUFACTURED GOODS		0.4		0.4		0.6		0.5	AUT ART MANUF DIVERS NDA

5. Special Exports F.O.B. by Commodities according to the S.I.T.C. (Rev. 2) in million U.S. Dollars
Exportations Spéciales F.O.B. par Produits d'après la C.T.C.I. (Rév. 2) en millions de Dollars E.U.

SITC CTCI	COMMODITY	1994		1995		1996		1997		PRODUIT
		QUANTITY QUANTITE	VALUE VALEUR	QUANTITY QUANTITE	VALUE VALEUR	QUANTITY QUANTITE	VALUE VALEUR	QUANTITY QUANTITE	VALUE VALEUR	
	ALL COMMODITIES		22.3		18.8		21.6		41.1	TOUS PRODUITS
0	FOOD AND LIVE ANIMALS		12.7		9.4		12.8		23.0	ALIMENTS,ANIMAUX VIVANTS
03	FISH AND PREPARATIONS		0.2		0.2		0.2		0.1	POISSONS ET PREPARATIONS
036	SHELL FISH FRESH,FROZEN	W 27	0.2	W 28	0.2	W 35	0.2	W 21	0.1	CRUSTACES,MOLLUSQUES
04	CEREALS AND PREPARATIONS		0.3		0.3		0.3		0.3	CEREALES ET PRODUITS
048	CEREAL ETC PREPARATIONS	W 139	0.3	W 149	0.3	W 95	0.3	W 101	0.3	PREPTNS A BASE CEREALES
0481	PREPD BREAKFAST FOOD ETC	W 32	0.1	W 39	0.2	W 22	0.1	W 19	0.1	CEREALES TRAVAILLEES
04811	CEREAL FLAKED,ROLLED,ETC	W 32	0.1	W 39	0.2	W 22	0.1	W 19	0.1	GRAINS GERMES DE CEREALES
0483	MACARONI,SPAGHETTI ETC	W 107	0.2	W 110	0.2	W 71	0.2	W 77	0.2	PATES ALMENTAIRES
06	SUGAR AND PREPS,HONEY		11.4		7.9		11.9		22.0	SUCRES ET PRODUITS
061	SUGAR AND HONEY	W 24413	11.4	W 12878	7.9	W 20031	11.9	W 45942	22.0	SUCRES ET MIEL
0611	RAW BEET AND CANE SUGAR	W 14850	10.9	W 12849	7.9	W 20029	11.9	W 40201	21.8	SUCRES BRUTS
0615	MOLASSES	W 9500	0.5	W 24	0.1			W 5740	0.2	MELASSES
09	MISC EDIBLE PRODUCTS		0.8		1.0		0.5		0.6	PREP ALIMENTAIRES DIVERSES
091	MARGARINE AND SHORTENING	W 579	0.8	W 584	1.0	W 266	0.5	W 286	0.6	MARGARINE ET GRAISSES
0914	MARGARINE,EDIBLE FAT NES	W 579	0.8	W 584	1.0	W 266	0.5	W 286	0.6	MARGARINES,SIMILI SAINDOUX
09141	MARGARINE	W 374	0.6	W 332	0.6	W 162	0.3	W 183	0.4	MARGARINE
09149	OTH PREPARED EDIBLE FATS	W 205	0.3	W 252	0.4	W 105	0.2	W 103	0.2	SIMILI–SAINDOUX
1	BEVERAGES AND TOBACCO		0.8		0.8		0.7		0.8	BOISSONS ET TABACS
11	BEVERAGES		0.8		0.8		0.7		0.8	BOISSONS
111	NON–ALCOHL BEVERAGES NES	W 1128	0.7	W 1086	0.8	W 897	0.7	W 1022	0.7	BOISSONS NON ALCOOLIQUES
11102	FLAVORED WATERS NON–ALCO	W 1128	0.7	W 1086	0.8	W 876	0.6	W 1021	0.7	LIMONADES,EAUX GAZEUSES
2	CRUDE MATERLS,EXCL FUELS		0.1		0.1		0.1		0.1	MAT BRUTES NON COMESTIBLES
26	TEXTILE FIBRES AND WASTE		0.1		0.1		0.1		0.1	FIBRES TEXTILES
269	WASTE OF TEXTILE FABRICS	W 10	0.1	W 3	0.1	W 10	0.1		0.1	FRIPERIE DRILLES,CHIFFONS
26901	BULK TEXT WSTE,OLD CLTHG	W 10	0.1	W 3	0.1	W 10	0.1		0.1	ART ET ACCESS D'HABILLEMENT
5	CHEMCLS,RELATED PROD NES		0.2		0.2		0.2		0.1	PRODUITS CHIMIQUES
51	ORGANIC CHEMICALS		0.1		0.1		0.1		0.1	PROD CHIMIQ ORGANIQUES
512	ALCOHOLS,PHENOLS ETC	W 92	0.1	W 135	0.1	W 31	0.1		0.1	PHENOLS,PHENOLS–ALCOOLS
5121	ACYCLIC ALCOHOLS,DERIVS	W 92	0.1	W 135	0.1	W 31	0.1		0.1	ALCOOLS ACYCLIQUES
51216	ETHYL ALC,DENATRD SPIRIT	W 92	0.1	W 135	0.1	W 31	0.1		0.1	ALCOOL ETHYLIQUE NON DENAT
6	BASIC MANUFACTURES		0.7		0.4		0.4		0.6	ART MANUFACTURES
65	TEXTILE YARN,FABRICS,ETC		0.2		0.1		0.1		0.1	FILS,TISSUS,ARTICLES TEXTILE
66	NONMETAL MINERAL MFS NES		0.4		0.3		0.2		0.1	ART MIN NON METALLIQUES
663	MINERAL MANUFCTURES NES	W 4500	0.3	W 2139	0.2	W 1141	0.1	W 1126	0.1	ART MIN MANUF NDA
6633	MINRL MFS NES NONCERAMIC	W 4500	0.3	W 2137	0.2	W 1140	0.1	W 1126	0.1	OUVR MAT MINERALE NDA
66332	CEMENT,ARTFCL STONE PROD	W 4500	0.3	W 2137	0.2	W 1140	0.1	W 1126	0.1	OUVRAGES EN CIMENT
69	METAL MANUFACTURES NES		0.1		0.1		0.2		0.4	ART MANUFACT EN METAL NDA
692	METAL TANKS,BOXES,ETC	W 13	0.1	W 35	0.1	W 39	0.1	W 94	0.1	RECIPIENTS METALLIQUES
6924	MTL TRANSPORT BOXES ETC	W 3	0.1	W 24	0.1	W 39	0.1	W 93	0.1	FUTS,TAMBOURS,BIDONS
69243	IRN,STL COMP GAS CYLINDR	W 2	0.1	W 24	0.1	W 35	0.1	W 92	0.1	RECIP FER,ACIER GAZ COMP
695	TOOLS	W 20	0.1	W 1	0.1	W 1	0.1	W 5	0.2	OUTILS A MAIN
6953	OTHER HAND TOOLS	W 20	0.1		0.1		0.1	W 5	0.2	AUTRES OUTILS A MAIN
7	MACHINES,TRANSPORT EQUIP		6.5		6.9		6.8		15.4	MACHINES MATERIEL TRANSPORT
71	POWER GENERATING EQUIPMT		1.9		2.7		2.1		3.6	MACHINES GENERATRICES
716	ROTATING ELECTRIC PLANT	W 49	1.9	W 134	2.7	W 117	2.1	W 213	3.6	APP ELECTR ROTATIFS,PIECES
7161	DC MOTORS AND GENERATORS		0.1	W 40	0.9		0.1	W 3	0.1	MOTEURS COURANT CONTINU
7162	AC MTRS,GENRTRS,GEN SETS	W 25	1.2	W 93	1.7	W 1	0.1	W 10	0.1	MOTEURS ELECTRIQUES
71621	AC MTRS,INC UNIVRSL MTRS	W 23	1.2	W 93	1.7	W 1	0.1			MOT ELEC NON COUR CONTINU
7169	PTS NES OF ROT ELEC PLNT	W 23	0.7	W 1	0.1	W 116	2.1	W 200	3.5	PIECES MAC APP ROTATIFS
72	MACHS FOR SPCL INDUSTRYS		0.8		0.1		0.4		0.1	MAC SPECIALES POUR INDUST
723	CIVIL ENGNEERG EQUIP ETC	W 149	0.5	W 22	0.1	W 88	0.3	W 6	0.1	APPAREILS DE GENIE CIVIL
7234	CONST,MINING MACHNRY NES	W 130	0.5	W 22	0.1	W 78	0.2	W 6	0.1	MACH POUR LA CONST, MINES
72341	SELF–PROPELLD DOZERS,ETC	W 94	0.3		0.1	W 23	0.1			BULLDOZERS
72342	SLFPRP SHOVELS,EXCAVATRS	W 36	0.2	W 20	0.1	W 39	0.2			PELLES MECANIQUES
724	TEXTILE,LEATHER MACHNRY	W 16	0.2		0.1		0.1	W 2	0.1	MACH POUR INDUSTRIE TEXTILE
7243	SEWING MACHS,NEEDLES ETC	W 16	0.2		0.1		0.1			MACHINES A COUDRE,PIECES
72431	SEWING MACHINES	W 12	0.2		0.1		0.1			MACHINES A COUDRE
74	GENRL INDUSTRL MACHY NES		0.3		0.1		0.2		0.1	MACH APP INDUSTRIE
744	MECHANICAL HANDLING EQU	W 88	0.2	W 1	0.1	W 5	0.1	W 1	0.1	EQUIP MANUTENTION PIECES
7442	LIFTING,LOADING MACH NES	W 85	0.2		0.1				0.1	APP LEVAGE,MANUTENTION
74422	SHIP DERRICKS,CRANES ETC	W 80	0.1							GRUES,PONTS ROULANTS
749	NONELEC MACH PTS,ACC NES	W 1	0.1		0.1	W 14	0.1	W 2	0.1	PIECES MACH NON ELEC NDA
7493	SHAFT,CRANK,PULLEY ETC	W 1	0.1		0.1	W 13	0.1	W 2	0.1	ARBRES TRANS,VILEBREQUINS
75	OFFICE MACHNES,ADP EQUIP		0.1		0.1		0.1		0.1	MACH BUREAU TRAIT AUTOM
76	TELECOMM,SOUND EQUIPMENT		0.2		0.7		0.4		1.1	EQUIPMENT DE TELECOM
764	TELECOM EQPT,PTS,ACC NES	W 12	0.2	W 220	0.7	W 61	0.4	W 72	1.0	EQUIP TELECOM,PIECES
7642	MICROPH,LOUDSPKR,AMPLIFR		0.1	W 29	0.2	W 36	0.1	W 4	0.1	MICRO,HAUT–PARLEUR,AMPLI
7643	TV,RADIO TRANSMITTRS ETC	W 12	0.2	W 3	0.1					APP EMET TELE RADIO
7649	PTS NES OF EQUIPMT OF 76			W 188	0.4	W 25	0.4	W 66	1.0	PIECES DE LA DIV 76
76493	TELECOMM EQUIPMT PTS NES			W 188	0.4	W 25	0.4	W 66	0.9	PIECES 761,762,764.3,8
77	ELECTRIC MACHNRY NES ETC		3.2		3.2		3.4		8.6	MACH APP ELECT NDA
771	ELECTRIC POWER MACHY NES	W 26	0.3	W 27	0.2	W 7	0.1		0.1	MACH PROD,TRANS ELECTR
7712	OTH ELEC POWER MACHY NES	W 21	0.2	W 9	0.1	W 2	0.1		0.1	AUT APP PROD TRANSF ELEC
77122	INDUCTORS	W 19	0.2	W 9	0.1	W 2	0.1		0.1	BOBINES REACTANCE,SELFS
772	SWITCHGEAR ETC,PARTS NES	W 527	2.9	W 384	2.9	W 521	3.3	W 626	7.5	APP COUPURE,SECT ETC
7721	SWITCHGEAR ETC	W 523	2.7	W 383	2.9	W 518	3.3	W 626	7.5	APP COUPURE,SECTIONMNT
7722	PRINTED CIRCUITS,PTS NES	W 4	0.2		0.1					CIRCUITS ET PIECES
778	ELECTRICAL MACHINERY NES		0.1	W 23	0.2	W 6	0.1	W 23	1.0	AUTRES MACH ELECT NDA
7788	OTH ELEC MACHY,EQUIP NES		0.1	W 22	0.2	W 5	0.1	W 17	1.0	AUT MACH APP ELEC NDA
77881	ELECTRO–MAGNETS ETC						0.1	W 15	0.9	ELECTRO–AIMANTS
77884	ELECTRICAL CONDENSERS		0.1	W 21	0.1		0.1		0.1	CONDENSATEURS ELECTRIQUES
78	ROAD VEHICLES		0.3		0.2		0.5		2.0	VEHICULES ROUTIERS
781	PASS MOTOR VEH EXC BUSES	W 16	0.2	W 16	0.1	W 14	0.3	W 129	2.0	AUTO TRANSPORT PERSONNES
782	LORRIES,SPCL MTR VEH NES	W 28	0.1	W 8	0.1	W 11	0.1		0.1	VEHICULES SPECIAUX,MARCH
7821	LORRIES,TRUCKS	W 15	0.1	W 7	0.1	W 11	0.1		0.1	VEHICULES TRANSP MARCHAND
784	MOTOR VEH PRTS,ACCES NES	W 2	0.1	W 3	0.1	W 6	0.2	W 1	0.1	PIECES 722,781,782,783
7849	OTHER MOTOR VEHCL PARTS	W 2	0.1	W 2	0.1	W 6	0.2	W 1	0.1	PIECES 722,781,782,783
786	TRAILERS,NONMOTR VEH,NES	W 7	0.1	W 2	0.1		0.1	W 1	0.1	REMORQUES,CADRES,CONTAIN
7861	TRAILERS,TRANSP CONTAINR	W 6	0.1	W 2	0.1				0.1	REMORQUES TOUS VEHICULES
78612	OTHER TRAILERS	W 6	0.1	W 2	0.1					REMORQUES TRANSP MARCH
79	OTHR TRANSPORT EQUIPMENT		0.1		0.1		0.1		0.1	AUTRE MATERIEL TRANSPORT
793	SHIPS AND BOATS ETC	W 1	0.1	W 11	0.1		0.1		0.1	NAVIRES BATEAUX,ETC
7932	SHIPS AND BOATS NES	W 1	0.1	W 11	0.1		0.1		0.1	NAVIRES ET BATEAUX
79323	OTHER CARGO VESSELS			W 11	0.1					AUT BATEAUX TRANS MARCH
8	MISC MANUFACTURED GOODS		1.6		1.2		0.9		1.3	ART MANUFACTURES DIVERS
821	*FURNITURE,PARTS THEREOF	W 11	0.1	W 6	0.1	W 18	0.1	W 14	0.1	MEUBLES ET PIECES
84	CLOTHING AND ACCESSORIES		0.3		0.5		0.6		0.4	VETEMENTS
842	MENS OUTERWEAR NOT KNIT	W 6	0.1	W 4	0.1	W 2	0.1	W 2	0.1	VET DESSUS POUR HOMMES
8423	— TROUSERS,BREECHES ETC	W 6	0.1	W 3	0.1	W 2	0.1	W 2	0.1	PANTALONS HOMMES MAT TEX
843	WOMENS OUTERWEAR NONKNIT	W 15	0.2	W 80	0.3	W 17	0.5	W 49	0.4	VET DESSUS FEMMES MAT TEX

5. Special Exports F.O.B. by Commodities according to the S.I.T.C. (Rev. 2) in million U.S. Dollars
Exportations Spéciales F.O.B. par Produits d'après la C.T.C.I. (Rév. 2) en millions de Dollars E.U.

SITC CTCI	COMMODITY	1994		1995		1996		1997		PRODUIT
		QUANTITY QUANTITE	VALUE VALEUR	QUANTITY QUANTITE	VALUE VALEUR	QUANTITY QUANTITE	VALUE VALEUR	QUANTITY QUANTITE	VALUE VALEUR	
8439	— OTHER OUTER GARMENTS	W 9	0.2	W 80	0.3	W 16	0.5	W 42	0.3	AUT VET DES FEM MAT TEXT
844	UNDER GARMENTS NOT KNIT	W 4	0.1	W 10	0.2	W 2	0.1	W 2	0.1	VETEMENT DESSOUS MAT TEX
8441	— MENS SHIRTS	W 4	0.1	W 8	0.1	W 2	0.1	W 2	0.1	CHEMISES HOMMES MAT TEXT
88	PHOTO EQU,OPTICL GDS ETC		0.6		0.2		0.1		0.1	APP,FOURN PHOTO,OP,MONTR
884	OPTICAL GOODS NES	W 36	0.6	W 15	0.2					ELEMENTS OPTIQ,ART LUNET
8841	OPTICAL ELEMENTS	W 36	0.6	W 15	0.2					LENTILLES,PRISMES,MIROIR
88412	OPTICAL ELEMENTS MOUNTED	W 36	0.6	W 15	0.2					LENT,MIROIRS MONTES
89	MISC MANUFCTRD GOODS NES		0.7		0.4		0.3		0.8	ART MANUFACTURES DIVERS
892	PRINTED MATTER	W 9	0.4	W 7	0.1	W 10	0.2	W 14	0.4	IMPRIMES
8928	PRINTED MATTER NES	W 4	0.3	W 2	0.1	W 3	0.1	W 5	0.4	IMPRIMES NDA
89283	UNISSUED BANKNOTES ETC	W 3	0.3		0.1	W 1	0.1	W 5	0.4	TIMBRES–POSTE FISCAUX
898	MUSICAL INSTRUMENTS,PTS	W 5	0.2	W 2	0.1	W 9	0.1	W 40	0.2	INSTRUMENTS DE MUSIQUE
8982	MUSICAL INSTRUMENTS NES	W 4	0.2	W 1	0.1	W 9	0.1	W 39	0.2	AUT INSTRUM DE MUSIQUE
89825	ELECTRICAL MUSICAL INSTR	W 3	0.2	W 1	0.1			W 23	0.1	INSTRUM ELECTROMAGNETIQ
899	OTHER MANUFACTURED GOODS	W 20	0.2	W 24	0.3	W 5	0.1	W 20	0.2	AUT ART MANUF DIVERS NDA
8997	BASKETWORK,BROOMS ETC	W 20	0.2	W 24	0.3	W 5	0.1	W 20	0.2	OUVRAGES VANNERIE NDA
89972	BRUSHES,BROOMS,MOPS ETC	W 20	0.2	W 24	0.3	W 5	0.1	W 20	0.2	BALAIS ET BALAYETTES

1. HISTORICAL SERIES, 1961–1996 GENERAL TRADE, IMPORTS C.I.F., EXPORTS F.O.B. #1
SERIES HISTORIQUES, 1961–1996 COMMERCE GENERAL, IMPORTATIONS C.A.F., EXPORTATIONS F.O.B

YEAR ANNEE	VALUE IN MILLION E.C. DOLLARS VALEUR EN MILLION E.C. DOLLARS MERCHANDISE –MARCHANDISE IMPORTS	EXPORTS	GOLD –OR IMPORTS	EXPORTS	CONVERSION FACTORS U.S. CENTS PER E.C. DOLLAR FACTEURS DE CONVERSION CENTS E.U. PAR E.C. DOLLAR IMPORTS	EXPORTS	INDEX NUMBERS –INDICES QUANTUM IMPORTS	EXPORTS	UNIT VALUE VALEUR UNITAIRE IMPORTS	EXPORTS
1961	13.30	7.70			58.3300	58.3300				
1962	16.70	7.60			58.3300	58.3300				
1963	16.70	8.00			58.3300	58.3300				
1964	20.40	9.80			58.3300	58.3300				
1965	22.00	11.20			58.3300	58.3300				
1966	28.40	12.10			58.3300	58.3300				
1967	29.50	11.70			57.6500	57.6500				
1968	29.50	12.60			50.0000	50.0000				
1969	41.50	16.30			50.0000	50.0000				
1970	54.60	8.70			50.0000	50.0000				
1971	69.00	12.20			50.7166	50.7166				
1972	68.70	15.10			52.1216	52.1216				
1973	74.20	19.20			51.0808	51.0808				
1974	91.10	32.90			48.7301	48.7301				
1975	100.40	34.50			46.2878	46.2878				
1976	125.70	49.90			38.0480	38.0480				
1977	160.20	61.00			37.0370	37.0370				
1978	219.90	72.40			37.0370	37.0370				
1979	273.20	86.00			37.0370	37.0370				
1980	334.20	124.20			37.0370	37.0370				
1981	348.90	111.30			37.0370	37.0370				
1982	318.70	112.30			37.0370	37.0370				
1983	288.40	128.30			37.0370	37.0370				
1984	320.00	129.10			37.0370	37.0370				
1985	337.50	140.50			37.0370	37.0370				
1986	417.90	234.59			37.0370	37.0370				
1987	483.90	214.80			37.0370	37.0370				
1988	595.00	312.00			37.0370	37.0370				
1989	739.10	294.70			37.0370	37.0370				
1990	731.60	343.70			37.0370	37.0370				
1991	797.00	297.80			37.0370	37.0370				
1992	845.00	331.50			37.0370	37.0370				
1993	807.84	322.94			37.0370	37.0370				
1994	814.78	256.10			37.0370	37.0370				
1995	826.27	294.21			37.0370	37.0370				
1996	846.48	214.67			37.0370	37.0370				

2. IMPORTS BY BROAD ECONOMIC CATEGORY AND EXPORTS BY INDUSTRIAL ORIGIN. (PERCENTAGE OF TOTAL VALUE)
IMPORTATIONS PAR CATEGORIES ECONOMIQUES ET EXPORTATIONS PAR BRANCHE D'ACTIVITE.(EN POURCENTAGE DE LA VALEUR TOTALE)

IMPORTS – IMPORTATIONS

	1990	1991	1992	1993	1994	1995	1996
TOTAL IMPORTS–IMPORTATIONS TOTALES	100.	100.	100.	100.	100.	100.	100.
1 FOOD BEV–ALIMENTATION BOISSONS	22.3	22.8	22.8	23.4	24.2	25.7	24.8
11 PRIMARY–PRODUITS DE BASE	6.7	6.9	6.8	7.4	8.1	8.5	8.3
111 FOR INDUSTRY–POUR L'INDUSTRIE	0.1	0.2	0.1	0.2	0.3	0.4	0.3
112 FOR HOUSEHOLDS–POUR LES MENAGES	6.6	6.7	6.7	7.2	7.8	8.1	8.0
12 PROCESSED–PRODUITS ELABORES	15.6	16.0	16.0	16.0	16.1	17.2	16.5
121 FOR INDUSTRY–POUR L'INDUSTRIE	2.8	2.8	2.3	2.4	2.5	2.9	2.3
122 FOR HOUSEHOLDS–POUR LES MENAGES	12.7	13.2	13.7	13.6	13.5	14.3	14.2
2 IND SUPPLIES–APPROV INDUSTRIELS	32.4	31.7	32.2	27.9	29.1	29.9	27.4
21 PRIMARY–PRODUITS DE BASE	1.2	1.6	1.6	1.0	1.4	1.3	1.1
22 PROCESSED–PRODUITS ELABORES	31.2	30.0	30.6	26.9	27.7	28.6	26.3
3 FUELS–COMBUSTIBLES	7.2	6.5	4.8	7.4	6.5	7.6	8.3
31 PRIMARY–PRODUITS DE BASE	0.8	0.7	0.7	0.7	0.7	0.8	0.8
32 PROCESSED–PRODUITS ELABORES	6.4	5.9	4.1	6.7	5.9	6.8	7.4
321 MOTOR SPIRIT–ESSENCE	2.7	2.3	2.4	2.4	2.5	2.5	3.0
322 OTHER–AUTRES	3.7	3.6	1.7	4.3	3.4	4.3	4.4
4 MACHINERY–EQUIPEMENT	11.5	11.9	12.0	11.9	12.2	10.1	11.1
41 CAPITAL EQUIPMENT–MACHINES	10.6	10.7	11.0	10.8	11.0	8.4	9.8
42 PARTS–PIECES ACCESSOIRES	0.9	1.2	1.0	1.2	1.2	1.7	1.2
5 TRANSPORT–TRANSPORT	8.5	8.2	8.1	9.2	8.4	7.8	9.4
51 PASSENGER CARS–AUTOMOBILES	2.8	3.8	4.0	3.0	1.9	2.3	2.9
52 OTHER–AUTRES	3.4	2.1	1.8	3.6	2.6	2.9	2.8
521 INDUSTRIAL–INDUSTRIELS	3.3	2.0	1.7	3.5	2.5	2.9	2.7
522 NON INDUSTRIAL–NON INDUSTRIEL	0.1	0.1	0.1	0.1	0.1	0.1	0.1
53 PARTS–PIECES ACCESSOIRES	2.3	2.4	2.3	2.6	3.9	2.5	3.8
6 CONSUM GOODS–BIENS CONSOMMATION	18.0	18.8	19.9	20.0	19.6	18.8	18.9
61 DURABLE–DURABLES	3.7	4.1	4.2	4.9	4.3	3.9	4.1
62 SEMI DURABLE–SEMI DURABLES	9.9	10.3	10.8	10.1	10.3	9.6	9.6
63 NON DURABLE–NON DURABLES	4.4	4.4	4.9	5.0	5.0	5.4	5.2
7 GOODS NES–BIENS NDA	0.1	0.1	0.1	0.1	0.1	0.1	0.2

EXPORTS – EXPORTATIONS

	1990	1991	1992	1993	1994	1995	1996
TOTAL EXPORTS–EXPORTATIONS TOTALES	100.	100.	100.	100.	100.	100.	100.
1 AGRICULTURE	59.3	56.1	58.9	49.9	51.7	52.8	67.6
2 MINING QUARRY–INDUS EXTRACTIVES	0.0	0.0	0.1	0.0	0.0	0.0	
3 MANUFACTURING–IND MANUFACTUR	40.7	43.9	41.0	50.1	48.3	47.1	32.4
31 FOOD BEV TOBACCO–ALIM BOISS TAB	8.6	8.9	6.3	6.3	6.6	5.9	5.0
32 TEXTILES–INDUSTRIES TEXTILES	16.1	17.6	18.1	22.8	20.5	16.8	10.2
33 WOOD & PRODUCTS–BOIS & PRODUITS	0.0	0.1	0.0	0.1	0.1	0.0	0.0
34 PAPER & PRODUCTS–PAPIER & PRODT	5.7	4.8	2.8	7.5	6.2	7.3	7.6
35 CHEMICALS–INDUSTRIES CHIMIQUES	1.3	1.9	2.9	3.2	3.5	3.0	2.7
36 NON METAL MIN–MIN NON METAL	0.0	0.0	0.1	0.1	0.1	0.1	0.1
37 BASIC METAL–IND METAL BASE	0.0	0.2	0.2	0.2	0.3	0.1	0.0
38 METAL MANUF–MANUF METAL	8.6	9.8	10.1	9.7	10.0	12.7	6.2
39 OTH MANUF IND–AUTRES MANUF	0.3	0.4	0.4	0.3	1.0	1.2	0.5

3. TRADE BY PRINCIPAL COUNTRIES OF ORIGIN AND DESTINATION (VALUE IN MILLION U.S. DOLLARS)
ECHANGES SELON LES PRINCIPAUX PAYS D'ORIGINE ET DE DESTINATION (VALEUR EN MILLIONS DE DOLLARS EU)

COUNTRIES–PAYS	GENERAL IMPORTS C.I.F. IMPORTATIONS GENERALES C.A.F				
	1992	1993	1994	1995	1996
World	303.3	299.2	301.8	306.0	313.5
Africa	0.0	0.0	0.0	0.1	0.1
Americas	198.9	205.6	212.6	217.5	218.8
– Northern America	124.4	131.0	130.9	128.3	133.8
– LAIA	9.0	9.1	7.8	8.0	8.2
– CACM	2.5	1.9	3.2	3.0	2.3
– Caribbean	61.6	60.9	67.4	74.5	71.3
– Rest of America	1.4	2.6	3.4	3.6	3.0
Asia excl fmr USSR	32.5	32.9	27.0	28.2	30.7
– Middle East	0.1	0.3	0.6	0.4	0.2
Asia former USSR					
Europe excl fmr USSR	69.7	59.1	60.1	57.5	61.2
– European Union	67.4	57.5	58.7	56.4	58.1
– Eastern Europe	0.3	0.3	0.4	0.4	0.4
– Rest of Europe	1.9	1.3	1.0	0.7	2.8
Europe former USSR	0.1	0.1	0.0	0.1	0.1
Oceania	1.9	1.5	1.9	2.7	2.7
Other	0.0			0.0	0.0
USA/Etats–Unis d'Amer	113.7	120.9	119.1	116.5	125.0
United Kingdom	43.8	37.7	40.4	34.1	32.6
Trinidad and Tobago	29.3	30.2	34.4	37.8	40.1
Japan/Japon	18.2	16.6	12.7	14.1	15.2
Canada	10.7	10.1	11.8	11.8	8.8
Barbados/Barbade	8.2	9.3	8.7	10.4	11.3
France, Monaco	9.7	6.6	6.1	6.2	8.0
St Vincent & Grenadines	7.9	7.0	7.2	7.4	6.0
Germany/Allemagne	3.8	3.5	3.2	4.5	6.9
Jamaica/Jamaïque	4.2	4.8	4.8	4.1	3.8
Netherlands/Pays–Bas	3.6	2.7	2.7	4.7	4.5
China/Chine	2.4	3.7	4.1	4.3	3.6
Other Asia n.e.s.	4.4	4.1	3.0	2.2	1.4
Netherlands Antilles	1.8	2.0	2.6	4.9	2.0
Korea, Republic of	2.1	2.5	1.5	1.7	4.9
Brazil/Brésil	2.5	2.6	2.8	2.8	2.1
Colombia/Colombie	3.1	2.5	2.3	2.2	1.9
Dominica/Dominique	1.6	2.1	2.9	2.8	2.5
Italy/Italie	2.7	2.2	1.7	2.2	2.3
Guyana	0.8	2.0	2.8	2.7	1.9
Honduras	1.8	1.6	2.8	2.3	1.5
Venezuela	1.6	1.8	1.3	1.7	2.8
Grenada/Grenade	1.9	1.7	1.7	2.0	1.8
Martinique	2.1	1.6	2.7	2.6	
New Zealand	1.2	1.1	1.5	2.1	2.1
Thailand/Thaïlande	1.3	1.0	1.3	1.4	2.0
Switzerland,Liechtenst.	1.7	1.0	0.8	0.5	2.5
Dominican Republic	0.7	0.7	1.0	1.5	2.6
Antigua and Barbuda	2.9	1.2	1.0	0.6	0.7
Belgium–Luxembourg	0.9	2.3	0.6	1.4	1.1
China, Hong Kong SAR	1.8	1.5	0.8	1.0	0.7
Mexico/Mexique	1.3	1.4	1.0	0.6	0.7
Denmark/Danemark	0.9	0.8	0.8	0.8	1.2
Ireland/Irlande	0.8	0.6	1.1	0.9	0.4
Panama	0.5	0.6	0.5	0.8	1.1
Malaysia/Malaisie	0.6	0.6	1.0	0.6	0.4
Indonesia/Indonésie	0.3	0.6	0.5	0.7	0.9
Australia/Australie	0.7	0.4	0.5	0.6	0.6
India/Inde	0.4	0.5	0.6	0.5	0.5
Argentina/Argentine	0.5	0.7	0.3	0.4	0.6

COUNTRIES–PAYS	EXPORTS EXPORTATIONS ES F.O.B.				
	1992	1993	1994	1995	1996
Monde	123.9	119.6	94.9	109.0	79.5
Afrique	2.1	0.0		0.0	
Amériques	44.6	55.7	42.6	47.9	23.1
– Amérique du Nord	27.5	33.0	26.9	29.3	12.0
– ALAI	0.2	0.4	0.2	0.2	0.1
– MCAC	0.0	0.1	0.0		0.0
– Caraïbes	16.3	21.4	15.0	17.7	10.3
– Autre Amérique	0.6	0.9	0.5	0.6	0.7
Asie anc. URSS exclus	0.4	0.2	0.4	0.5	0.6
– Moyen–Orient			0.0		
Asie ancienne URSS					
Europe anc. URSS exclus	76.8	63.8	51.9	59.8	55.8
– Union Européenne	76.7	63.8	51.9	59.7	55.8
– Europe de l'Est			0.0		
– Autre de l'Europe	0.2	0.0	0.0	0.1	0.0
Europe ancienne URSS					
Océanie	0.0		0.0	0.0	
Autre				0.7	
United Kingdom	66.1	59.4	49.9	57.8	53.8
USA/Etats–Unis d'Amer	27.2	32.6	26.7	28.4	11.9
Dominica/Dominique	3.3	9.2	4.8	5.8	3.0
Barbados/Barbade	4.0	2.3	2.1	2.8	1.9
Trinidad and Tobago	1.8	2.3	2.1	3.2	2.3
Italy/Italie	7.4	0.9	0.0	0.0	0.0
Germany/Allemagne	1.3	2.9	1.2	1.4	1.1
Antigua and Barbuda	1.7	1.4	1.4	1.7	0.9
Grenada/Grenade	1.4	1.0	1.0	1.3	0.7
St Vincent & Grenadines	1.5	1.2	0.6	0.8	0.4
Jamaica/Jamaïque	0.4	1.5	1.2	0.3	0.0
Martinique	0.5	1.1	0.6	0.8	
Saint Kitts and Nevis	0.7	0.7	0.6	0.4	0.5
France, Monaco	1.5	0.2	0.4	0.1	0.6
Guyana	0.4	0.6	0.3	0.4	0.4
Madagascar	2.1				
Canada	0.3	0.4	0.3	1.0	0.1
Montserrat	0.4	0.3	0.4	0.4	0.3
Japan/Japon	0.4	0.1	0.2	0.3	0.2
Guadeloupe	0.6	0.2	0.2	0.1	
Venezuela	0.2	0.4	0.2	0.2	0.1
Belize/Bélize	0.2	0.2	0.2	0.2	0.1
Free zones/Zone franches				0.7	
Belgium–Luxembourg	0.0	0.1	0.1	0.2	0.2
Netherlands/Pays–Bas	0.2	0.2	0.1	0.1	0.0
Austria/Autriche	0.1	0.0	0.1	0.2	0.1
Netherlands Antilles	0.1	0.1	0.1	0.0	0.1
Korea Dem People's Rp			0.0	0.0	0.3
Switzerland,Liechtenst.	0.2	0.0	0.0	0.1	0.0
China, Hong Kong SAR	0.0	0.0	0.1	0.1	0.0
Suriname/Surinam	0.0	0.0		0.0	0.1
Bahamas	0.0	0.1	0.0		0.0
Korea, Republic of	0.0	0.0	0.0		0.1
Guatemala		0.1			
India/Inde		0.0	0.0	0.0	0.0
Other Asia n.e.s.	0.0	0.0	0.0	0.0	0.0
Brazil/Brésil	0.0	0.0		0.0	
Dominican Republic	0.0	0.0		0.0	0.0
Mexico/Mexique			0.0	0.0	
Sweden/Suède	0.0	0.0	0.0	0.0	

(VALUE AS PERCENTAGE OF WORLD TOTAL)(VALEURS EN POURCENTAGE DU TOTAL MONDIAL)

	1987	1988	1989	1990	1991	1992	1993	1994	1995	1996
Africa	0.1	0.0	0.0	0.0	0.1	0.0	0.0	0.0	0.0	0.0
Americas	60.7	61.4	61.2	65.1	65.1	65.6	68.7	70.5	71.1	69.8
– Northern America	38.4	38.7	38.1	40.1	40.7	41.0	43.8	43.4	41.9	42.7
– LAIA	3.2	3.1	3.2	3.8	4.4	3.0	3.0	2.6	2.6	2.6
– CACM	1.6	1.7	1.7	1.3	0.9	0.8	0.6	1.1	1.0	0.7
– Caribbean	17.0	17.0	17.5	19.0	18.4	20.3	20.4	22.3	24.4	22.8
– Rest of America	0.5	0.9	0.7	1.0	0.7	0.5	0.9	1.1	1.2	1.0
Asia excl fmr USSR	12.5	14.0	12.5	9.1	10.8	10.7	11.0	9.0	9.2	9.8
– Middle East	0.1	0.1	0.0	0.0	0.0	0.0	0.1	0.2	0.1	0.1
Asia former USSR										
Europe excl fmr USSR	26.5	24.1	25.8	22.9	23.5	23.0	19.8	19.9	18.8	19.5
– European Union	25.8	23.4	25.2	22.2	22.8	22.2	19.2	19.5	18.4	18.5
– Eastern Europe	0.2	0.2	0.2	0.1	0.1	0.1	0.1	0.1	0.1	0.1
– Rest of Europe	0.5	0.5	0.4	0.6	0.6	0.6	0.4	0.3	0.2	0.9
Europe former USSR	0.0	0.0	0.0	0.1	0.0	0.0	0.0	0.0	0.0	0.0
Oceania	0.2	0.5	0.3	0.9	0.4	0.6	0.5	0.6	0.9	0.9
Other	0.0	0.0	0.0	1.8	0.0	0.0			0.0	0.0
USA/Etats–Unis d'Amer	34.6	34.7	34.8	37.1	37.2	37.5	40.4	39.5	38.1	39.9
United Kingdom	15.5	15.4	14.6	14.2	13.3	14.5	12.6	13.4	11.1	10.4
Trinidad and Tobago	8.3	8.5	8.5	9.4	9.0	9.7	10.1	11.4	12.4	12.8
Japan/Japon	6.5	8.3	7.2	6.2	6.1	6.0	5.5	4.2	4.6	4.9
Canada	3.8	4.0	3.3	3.0	3.5	3.5	3.4	3.9	3.9	2.8
Barbados/Barbade	2.1	2.5	2.2	2.8	2.6	2.7	3.1	2.9	3.4	3.6
France, Monaco	2.4	1.7	2.1	2.0	4.0	3.2	2.2	2.0	2.0	2.5
St Vincent & Grenadines	2.0	1.9	2.0	2.2	2.2	2.6	2.3	2.4	2.4	1.9
Germany/Allemagne					1.3	1.2	1.2	1.1	1.5	2.2
Jamaica/Jamaïque	1.3	1.1	1.2	1.2	1.2	1.4	1.6	1.6	1.3	1.2

	1987	1988	1989	1990	1991	1992	1993	1994	1995	1996
Afrique	0.0	0.0	0.0	0.0	0.0	1.7	0.0		0.0	
Amériques	41.3	40.2	42.3	39.8	42.1	36.0	46.6	44.9	44.0	29.0
– Amérique du Nord	19.3	20.3	19.7	22.0	22.1	22.2	27.6	28.4	26.9	15.1
– ALAI	0.4	0.7	0.5	0.3	1.0	0.2	0.3	0.2	0.2	0.2
– MCAC			0.2	0.0		0.0	0.1	0.0		0.0
– Caraïbes	21.3	18.9	21.6	17.3	18.6	13.2	17.9	15.8	16.3	13.0
– Autre Amérique	0.3	0.3	0.4	0.1	0.4	0.5	0.8	0.5	0.6	0.8
Asie anc. URSS exclus	0.2	0.0	0.1	0.1	0.2	0.3	0.1	0.4	0.4	0.8
– Moyen–Orient	0.0	0.0		0.0				0.0		
Asie ancienne URSS										
Europe anc. URSS exclus	58.5	59.7	57.6	60.1	57.7	62.0	53.3	54.7	54.9	70.2
– Union Européenne	58.5	59.7	57.6	60.1	57.7	61.9	53.3	54.7	54.8	70.1
– Europe de l'Est			0.0					0.0		
– Autre de l'Europe	0.0	0.0	0.0	0.0	0.0	0.1	0.0	0.0	0.1	0.0
Europe ancienne URSS										
Océanie	0.0	0.0	0.0	0.0	0.0	0.0		0.0	0.0	
Autre	0.0	0.0	0.0	0.0	0.0				0.7	
United Kingdom	53.2	52.6	50.1	53.1	50.0	53.3	49.7	52.6	53.1	67.7
USA/Etats–Unis d'Amer	18.9	20.0	19.2	21.5	21.7	22.0	27.3	28.1	26.0	14.9
Dominica/Dominique	7.8	5.8	3.5	4.1	4.0	2.6	7.7	5.1	5.4	3.8
Barbados/Barbade	4.5	4.2	5.3	3.0	3.9	3.3	1.9	2.2	2.6	2.3
Trinidad and Tobago	1.2	2.1	3.2	1.7	2.2	1.4	1.9	2.2	3.0	2.9
Italy/Italie	4.4	6.8	6.8	6.2	6.4	6.0	0.7	0.0	0.0	0.0
Germany/Allemagne					0.7	1.1	2.4	1.3	1.3	1.4
Antigua and Barbuda	1.2	1.1	1.5	1.4	1.3	1.4	1.2	1.5	1.6	1.2
Grenada/Grenade	1.7	1.9	1.8	1.5	1.5	1.1	0.9	1.0	1.2	0.8
St Vincent & Grenadines	1.1	1.2	2.0	1.6	1.2	1.2	1.0	0.6	0.7	0.5

4. General Imports C.I.F. by Commodities according to the S.I.T.C. (Rev. 2) in million U.S. Dollars
Importations Générales C.A.F. par Produits d'après la C.T.C.I. (Rév. 2) en millions de Dollars E.U.

SITC CTCI	COMMODITY	1993		1994		1995		1996		PRODUIT
		QUANTITY QUANTITE	VALUE VALEUR	QUANTITY QUANTITE	VALUE VALEUR	QUANTITY QUANTITE	VALUE VALEUR	QUANTITY QUANTITE	VALUE VALEUR	
	ALL COMMODITIES		299.2		301.8		306.1		313.6	TOUS PRODUITS
0	FOOD AND LIVE ANIMALS		61.1		64.2		69.9		69.1	ALIMENTS,ANIMAUX VIVANTS
01	MEAT AND PREPARATIONS		17.7		19.0		19.4		20.3	VIANDES ET PREPARATIONS
011	MEAT FRESH,CHILLD,FROZEN	W 9534	14.6	W 10382	16.0	W 10400	16.4	W 10551	17.3	VIANDES FRAICHES,REF,CONGE
0111	BOVINE MEAT FRESH,FROZEN	W 887	2.8	W 1231	3.0	W 702	2.9	W 640	2.4	VIANDES BOVIN FRAI,REF
01112	BOVINE MEAT BONELESS	W 835	2.6	W 1197	2.8	W 685	2.8	W 600	2.3	VIANDES BOVIN DESOSSEES
0112	MUTTON ETC FRSH,CHLD,FRN	W 512	1.2	W 554	1.4	W 583	1.4	W 1275	1.5	VIANDE DE MOUTON
0114	POULTRY FRESH CHLLD,FRZN	W 6953	9.3	W 7745	10.4	W 7696	10.8	W 7838	12.1	VOLAILLES MORTES
014	MEAT PREPD,PRSVD,NES ETC	W 758	2.5	W 847	2.4	W 772	2.5	W 792	2.4	CONSERVES DE VIANDES
0142	SAUSAGES INCLDING TINNED	W 254	0.8	W 329	0.9	W 354	1.0	W 335	0.9	SAUCISSES,SAUCISSONS
0149	OTH PREPARD,PRESRVD MEAT	W 504	1.8	W 518	1.6	W 418	1.6	W 457	1.5	AUTRES PREP DE VIANDES
02	DAIRY PRODCTS,BIRDS'EGGS		7.1		7.9		8.5		9.0	PRODUITS LAITIERS,OEUFS
022	MILK AND CREAM	W 2766	4.6	W 2999	5.0	W 3164	5.7	W 3051	5.9	LAIT ET CREME
0224	MILK,CREAM PRESERVED ETC	W 2571	4.3	W 2558	4.4	W 2643	4.9	W 2580	5.2	LAIT,CREME CONS,CONC
02243	MILK DRY,OVER 1.5% FAT	W 462	1.7	W 477	1.7	W 451	1.8	W 529	2.1	LAIT POUDRE SUP 1.5%
02249	MILK(EX DRY) PRSVD,SWEET	W 1993	2.5	W 1947	2.4	W 2056	2.7	W 1934	2.8	LAIT CONS,CONC SUCRE
024	CHEESE AND CURD	W 528	1.8	W 607	2.2	W 604	2.1	W 649	2.4	FROMAGE ET CAILLEBOTTE
03	FISH AND PREPARATIONS		3.3		4.0		4.4		5.0	POISSONS ET PREPARATIONS
035	FISH SALTED,DRIED,SMOKED	W 371	1.3	W 329	1.4	W 285	1.4	W 337	1.6	POISSON SECHE,SALE,FUME
03503	FISH(EX COD)DRIED,SALTED	W 219	0.9	W 290	1.2	W 255	1.3	W 268	1.2	POISSONS SECHES,SALES
036	SHELL FISH FRESH,FROZEN	W 60	0.7	W 73	0.9	W 93	1.0	W 71	0.8	CRUSTACES,MOLLUSQUES
037	FISH ETC PREPD,PRSVD NES	W 435	1.3	W 517	1.6	W 521	1.7	W 758	2.4	POIS,CRUST,MOL PREPARES
0371	FISH PREPARD,PRESRVD NES	W 432	1.2	W 513	1.6	W 515	1.6	W 754	2.3	CONSERVES DE POISSONS
04	CEREALS AND PREPARATIONS		13.1		13.3		14.8		13.9	CEREALES ET PRODUITS
042	RICE	W 2036	1.6	W 2740	1.9	W 3089	2.1	W 2759	2.0	RIZ
0422	RICE SEMI–MILLED,MILLED	W 1575	1.4	W 1605	1.4	W 1481	1.4	W 1800	1.4	RIZ POLI,GLACE INCL BRISURES
04221	RICE MILLED UNBROKEN	W 1209	0.9	W 1568	1.4	W 1439	1.3	W 1756	1.4	RIZ POLI,GLACE EXCL BRISURES
046	WHEAT ETC MEAL OR FLOUR	W 9537	4.5	W 10077	4.6	W 10828	4.9	W 7502	4.1	SEMOULE FARINE,FROMENT
04601	FLOUR OF WHEAT OR MESLIN	W 9530	4.5	W 10052	4.6	W 10826	4.9	W 7138	3.9	FARINE DE FROMENT
048	CEREAL ETC PREPARATIONS	W 4127	6.9	W 3304	6.7	W 3824	7.6	W 3797	7.7	PREPTNS A BASE CEREALES
0481	PREPD BREAKFAST FOOD ETC	W 325	1.3	W 303	1.2	W 377	1.4	W 347	1.4	CEREALES TRAVAILLEES
04812	CEREAL ROASTED, PUFFED	W 242	1.0	W 259	1.1	W 302	1.2	W 309	1.3	PRODTS BASE CEREALES
0484	BAKERY PRODUCTS	W 1224	3.1	W 1250	3.1	W 1498	3.8	W 1496	3.8	PRODUITS DE BOULANGERIE
04841	BREAD,BISCUIT,COM WAFERS	W 621	1.6	W 559	1.6	W 684	1.9	W 673	1.9	PAINS,BISCUITS DE MER
04842	PASTRY, CAKES ETC	W 603	1.5	W 692	1.6	W 814	2.0	W 823	1.9	PATISSERIE ETC.
0488	OTH CEREAL PREPS,MALT EX	W 329	1.2	W 374	1.4	W 290	1.2	W 426	1.4	EXTRAITS DE MALT
05	VEGETABLES AND FRUIT		9.2		9.5		9.8		9.4	LEGUMES ET FRUITS
054	VEG ETC FRSH,SMPLY PRSVD	W 4438	4.2	W 4602	4.2	W 5216	4.4	W 4538	4.0	LEGUMES FRAIS,CONG,SECS
0541	POTATOES FRSH EXCL SWEET	W 1348	0.7	W 1396	0.8	W 1924	1.1	W 1329	0.8	POMMES DE TERRE
0545	OTHER FRESH VEGETABLES	W 1598	1.4	W 1686	1.7	W 1698	1.8	W 1716	1.7	AUTRES LEGUMES FRAIS,REF
057	FRUIT,NUTS,FRESH,DRIED	W 588	0.9	W 586	0.9	W 568	1.0	W 654	1.1	FRUITS FRAIS OU SECS
058	FRUIT PRESERVED,PREPARED	W 2530	3.7	W 2666	3.9	W 2901	3.8	W 2313	3.7	CONSERVES DE FRUITS
0585	FRUIT OR VEGETABLE JUICE	W 2236	2.9	W 2354	2.9	W 2619	3.1	W 2036	2.9	JUS DE FRUITS
05851	ORANGE JUICE	W 1346	1.7	W 1284	1.8	W 1407	1.7	W 1162	1.7	JUS D'ORANGE
06	SUGAR AND PREPS,HONEY		3.1		3.2		4.4		2.7	SUCRES ET PRODUITS
061	SUGAR AND HONEY	W 8421	2.3	W 16523	2.5	W 11763	3.7	W 7130	2.1	SUCRES ET MIEL
0611	RAW BEET AND CANE SUGAR	W 3174	1.1	W 12132	1.1	W 3906	1.5	W 2211	0.8	SUCRES BRUTS
0612	REFINED SUGAR ETC	W 3235	1.1	W 2385	1.1	W 3360	1.8	W 2386	1.0	SUCRES RAFFINES
07	COFFEE,TEA,COCOA,SPICES		1.7		1.8		2.0		1.7	CAFE,THE,CACAO,EPICES
081	*FEEDING STUFF FOR ANIML	W 4432	1.4	W 4780	1.3	W 4663	1.6	W 4994	1.6	NOURRITURE POUR ANIMAUX
0819	FOOD WASTE AND FEED NES	W 4154	1.3	W 4606	1.3	W 4408	1.6	W 4570	1.5	DECHETS,ALIMENTS NDA
08199	FODDER NES,INCL SWEETNED	W 4154	1.3	W 4606	1.3	W 4408	1.6	W 4570	1.5	PREPARATIONS FOURRAGERES
09	MISC EDIBLE PRODUCTS		4.8		4.5		5.4		5.9	PREP ALIMENTAIRES DIVERSES
091	MARGARINE AND SHORTENING	W 198	0.4	W 235	0.5	W 388	0.8	W 641	1.3	MARGARINE ET GRAISSES
0914	MARGARINE,EDIBLE FAT NES	W 198	0.4	W 235	0.5	W 388	0.8	W 623	1.3	MARGARINES,SIMILI SAINDOUX
098	EDIBLE PRODCTS,PREPS NES	W 1759	4.4	W 1522	4.1	W 1597	4.6	W 1639	4.6	PREP ALIMENTAIRES NDA
09804	SAUCES,MIXED SEASONINGS	W 686	1.0	W 589	1.0	W 565	1.1	W 623	1.2	SAUCES,ASSAISONNEMENTS
09809	MISC FOOD PREPRTIONS NES	W 787	2.8	W 722	2.5	W 766	2.8	W 774	2.8	PREP ALIMENTAIRES NDA
1	BEVERAGES AND TOBACCO		11.0		10.4		11.0		10.8	BOISSONS ET TABACS
11	BEVERAGES		9.9		9.3		9.5		9.5	BOISSONS
111	NON–ALCOHL BEVERAGES NES	W 2719	2.7	W 2754	2.7	W 3019	2.7	W 2951	3.3	BOISSONS NON ALCOOLIQUES
11102	FLAVORED WATERS NON–ALCO	W 2370	2.5	W 1823	2.3	W 2193	2.4	W 2419	3.0	LIMONADES,EAUX GAZEUSES
112	ALCOHOLIC BEVERAGES	W 2401	7.2	W 5669	6.6	W 2490	6.9	W 2087	6.3	BOISSONS ALCOOLIQUES
1121	WINE OF FRESH GRAPES ETC	W 602	1.9	W 482	1.4	W 587	1.7	W 600	1.7	VINS DE RAISINS FRAIS
11212	WINE OF FRESH GRAPES	W 539	1.8	W 431	1.3	W 528	1.6	W 550	1.6	VINS DE MOUTS DE RAISINS
1123	BEER,ALE,STOUT,PORTER	W 550	0.7	W 601	0.8	W 766	1.2	W 348	0.5	BIERES
1124	DISTILLED ALCOHOLIC BEVS	W 1000	4.4	W 1117	4.2	W 850	3.7	W 747	3.6	ALCOOLS,EAUX–DE–VIE
11241	WHISKY	W 250	1.5	W 207	1.5	W 155	1.1	W 145	1.3	WHISKY
11249	OTH ALCOHOLC BEVS,CMPNDS	W 628	2.5	W 693	2.5	W 597	2.3	W 540	2.0	BOISSONS ALCOOLIQUES NDA
12	TOBACCO AND MANUFACTURES		1.2		1.1		1.5		1.3	TABACS BRUTS FABRIQUES
122	TOBACCO,MANUFACTURED	W 31	0.8	W 35	1.0		1.3	W 50	1.2	TABACS FABRIQUES
1222	CIGARETTES	W 30	0.8	W 34	1.0	W 45	1.3	W 49	1.2	CIGARETTES
2	CRUDE MATERLS,EXCL FUELS		8.2		10.2		9.9		8.5	MAT BRUTES NON COMESTIBLES
24	CORK AND WOOD		6.1		6.8		6.5		5.3	LIEGE ET BOIS
248	WOOD SHAPED,SLEEPERS	W 12169	5.4	W 12355	6.0	W 12662	5.9	W 10823	5.0	BOIS SIMPLEMENT TRAVAILLES
2482	LUMBER SHAPED CONIFER	W 10652	4.6	W 11857	5.7	W 12148	5.7	W 10376	4.8	CONIFERES SCIES,RABOTES
24821	LUMBER SAWN ETC CONIFER	W 4049	1.7	W 7322	3.4	W 11093	5.0	W 9108	4.3	CONIFERES SCIES LONGITUD
24822	LUMBER PLANED ETC CONIFR	W 6603	3.0	W 4535	2.3	W 1055	0.7	W 1268	0.6	CONIFER RABOTES,RAINES
27	CRUDE FERTLZR,MINRLS NES		1.5		2.6		2.3		2.5	ENGRAIS MINERAUX BRUTS
273	STONE,SAND AND GRAVEL		0.5	W 85716	1.2	W 91264	1.0	W 167957	1.5	PIERRES,SABLES,GRAVIERS
278	OTHER CRUDE MINERALS	W 3595	1.0	W 6793	1.4	W 4630	1.3	W 3419	1.0	AUTRES MINERAUX BRUTS
2789	MINERALS CRUDE NES	W 2968	0.8	W 5393	1.1	W 3576	1.1	W 2642	0.8	MINERAUX BRUTS NDA
27896	NATURAL ASPHALT,BITUMEN	W 2933	0.8	W 5340	1.0	W 3536	1.0	W 2618	0.7	BITUMES,ASPHALTES NATURELS
3	MINERAL FUELS ETC		22.9		19.8		23.4		26.0	COMBUSTIBLES MINERAUX LUB
33	PETROLEUM AND PRODUCTS		20.8		17.8		21.0		23.5	PETROLE ET DERIVES
334	PETROLEUM PRODUCTS,REFIN	W 75126	20.0	W 79287	17.7	W 80201	20.8	W 94190	23.4	PRODUITS RAFFINES
3341	GASOLINE,OTH LIGHT OILS	W 29966	7.3	W 38677	8.0	W 32754	8.0	W 38427	9.7	ESSENCES POUR MOTEURS
33411	MOTOR,AVIATION SPIRIT	W 29881	7.3	W 34455	7.6	W 31987	7.8	W 37638	9.5	ESSENCES MOTEURS D'AVIONS
3343	GAS OILS	W 41598	11.0	W 36137	7.7	W 43402	10.5	W 51530	11.3	GAS OILS
3345	LUBS,PETROLEUM OILS NES	W 1401	1.5	W 1415	1.7	W 1433	1.8	W 1482	1.9	HUILES LUBRIFIANTES
33451	LUBS(HIGH PETR CONT) ETC	W 1390	1.5	W 1406	1.7	W 1427	1.8	W 1470	1.8	HUILES LUBRIF,H LOURDES
341	*GAS,NATURAL AND MANUFCT	W 6572	2.2	W 6212	2.1	W 5184	2.5	W 7208	2.6	GAZ NATUREL,GAZ MANUFACT
3413	PETROLM GASES,LIQUEFIED	W 6410	2.1	W 6203	2.1	W 5184	2.5	W 7207	2.6	GAZ DE PETROLE LIQUEFIE
34131	LIQUEFIED PROPANE,BUTANE	W 5127	1.6	W 3251	1.0	W 1786	1.0	W 4761	1.8	PROPANE,BUTANE LIQUEFIES
34139	OTH HYDROCARBON GAS LQFD	W 1282	0.6	W 2953	1.1	W 3398	1.5	W 2446	0.8	HYDROCARBURES GAZEUX NDA
5	CHEMCLS,RELATED PROD NES		26.2		26.8		26.8		30.3	PRODUITS CHIMIQUES
53	DYES,TANNING,COLOUR PROD		3.9		4.1		3.4		3.5	PROD TEINTURE,COLORANTS
533	PIGMENTS,PAINTS,ETC	W 1602	3.9	W 1717	4.0	W 1422	3.3	W 1527	3.5	PIGMENTS,PEINTURES,VERNIS
5334	VARNISHES,DISTEMPERS ETC	W 984	3.1	W 944	3.0	W 776	2.4	W 816	2.5	PEINTURES A L'EAU
53342	OTH PAINTS,VARNISHES ETC	W 839	2.6	W 721	2.3	W 591	1.8	W 634	1.9	AUTRES PEINTURES,VERNIS
541	*MEDICINAL,PHARM PRODUCT	K 195015	3.0	K 216830	3.0		3.3	K 227325	3.9	PROD MEDICINAUX PHARMACEUT

4. General Imports C.I.F. by Commodities according to the S.I.T.C. (Rev. 2) in million U.S. Dollars
Importations Générales C.A.F. par Produits d'après la C.T.C.I. (Rév. 2) en millions de Dollars E.U.

SITC CTCI	COMMODITY	1993			1994			1995			1996			PRODUIT
		QUANTITY QUANTITE		VALUE VALEUR	QUANTITY QUANTITE		VALUE VALEUR	QUANTITY QUANTITE		VALUE VALEUR	QUANTITY QUANTITE		VALUE VALEUR	
5417	MEDICAMENTS	K	182256	2.7	K	196373	2.6	K	195982	2.8	K	203684	3.5	MEDICAMENTS
54179	— CONTNG OTH SUBSTANCES	K	126613	1.8	K	184496	2.3	K	186774	2.5	K	193689	3.1	MED CONT AUT SUBSTANCES
55	PERFUME,CLEANING ETC PRD			6.9			6.8			7.4			7.0	PROD POUR PARFUM,TOILETTE
553	PERFUMERY,COSMETICS,ETC	W	534	3.2	W	543	3.2	W	596	3.6	W	558	3.6	PRODUITS DE PARFUMERIE
554	SOAP,CLEANSING ETC PREPS	W	2137	3.7	W	2078	3.7	W	2158	3.8	W	2030	3.4	SAVONS,PRODUITS DETERSIFS
5541	SOAPS	W	805	1.3	W	724	1.2	W	744	1.3	W	614	1.1	SAVONS,PROD TENSIO–ACTIFS
5542	WASHING PREPARATIONS ETC	W	1295	2.3	W	1297	2.4	W	1377	2.4	W	1384	2.2	PROD ORG TENSIO–ACT NDA
562	*FERTILIZERS,MANUFACTURE	W	7285	1.7	W	5537	2.5	W	7115	2.5	W	9044	3.3	ENGRAIS MANUFACTURES
5621	CHEM NITROGENOUS FERTLZR	W	7247	1.7	W	2389	1.6	W	831	0.4	W	1072	0.7	ENGRAIS AZOTES
56212	AMMONIUM SULPHONITRATE	W	1734	0.4	W	2011	1.5	W	445	0.2	W	1050	0.6	SULFONITRATE D'AMMONIUM
5629	FERTILIZERS NES	W	15	0.1	W	2841	0.8	W	6196	2.1	W	7965	2.7	ENGRAIS NDA
56299	OTHER FERTILIZERS NES	W	11	0.1	W	2705	0.7	W	6195	2.1	W	7952	2.6	AUTRES ENGRAIS NDA
58	PLASTIC MATERIALS ETC			2.9			2.6			2.6			2.5	MAT PLAST ARTIFICIELLES
583	POLYMERIZATION ETC PRODS	W	1543	2.5	W	884	1.8	W	697	1.8	W	849	1.9	PROD POLYMERISATION
5839	OTH POLYMRZTION ETC PROD	W	1259	1.9	W	879	1.8	W	697	1.8	W	847	1.9	AUT PROD POLYMER COPOLYM
59	CHEMICAL MATERIALS NES			6.7			6.5			6.4			8.8	MAT PROD CHIMIQUES NDA
591	PESTICIDES,DISINFECTANTS	W	1893	4.9	W	1083	4.3	W	1037	4.1	W	1525	6.3	DESINF,INSECT,FONG,HERB
5911	INSECTICIDES,FOR RETAIL	W	1383	2.4	W	475	1.8	W	495	1.9	W	960	4.0	INSECTICIDES VENTE DET
5912	FUNGICIDES,FOR RETAIL	W	78	1.6	W	265	1.0	W	43	0.8	W	130	0.5	FONGICIDES VENTE AU DET
5913	HERBICIDES,FOR RETAIL	W	287	0.6	W	208	1.1	W	352	1.2	W	276	1.5	HERBICIDES VENTE AU DET
592	STARCH,INULIN,GLUTEN,ETC	W	744	1.0	W	1134	1.3	W	1160	1.2	W	1055	1.2	AMIDONS,INUL,GLUT FROM
598	MISCEL CHEM PRODUCTS NES	W	253	1.0	W	499	1.0			1.2			1.4	PROD DIV INDUST CHIM NDA
5989	CHEM PRODUCTS,PREPS NES	W	236	0.9	W	446	0.9	W	321	1.1	W	341	1.3	PROD PREP CHIMIQUES NDA
6	BASIC MANUFACTURES			58.4			63.0			66.2			58.1	ART MANUFACTURES
62	RUBBER MANUFACTURES NES			4.2			4.4			4.0			3.9	CAOUTCHOUC MANUFACTURE
625	RUBBER TYRES, TUBES ETC	W	744	2.7	W	1501	2.8	W	696	2.3	W	842	2.4	PNEUS CAOUTCHOUC VULCANISE
6252	TYRES,NEW,BUS OR LORRY	W	218	1.1	W	749	1.3	W	310	1.2	W	299	1.1	PNEUS POUR AUTOBUS,CAMIONS
6259	OTH TYRES,TYRE CASES,ETC	W	377	1.1	W	565	1.0	W	245	0.7	W	311	0.7	AUTRES PNEUS RECHAPES FLAPS
62599	TYRES NES,TYRE CASES,ETC	W	339	1.0	W	541	0.9	W	229	0.6	W	294	0.6	PNEUS,FLAPS
63	WOOD,CORK MANUFACTRS NES			5.1			4.8			5.5			5.3	OUVRAGES LIEGE ET BOIS
634	VENEERS,PLYWOOD,ETC	W	6387	3.1	W	7577	3.3	W	6088	3.6	W	5786	3.2	PLACAGES,CONTRE–PLAQUES
6342	PLYWOOD OF WOOD SHEETS	W	6324	3.1	W	7405	3.3	W	5983	3.5	W	5709	3.1	BOIS CONTRE–PLAQUES
635	WOOD MANUFACTURES NES	W	552	2.0	W	544	1.5	W	682	2.0	W	751	2.2	ART MANUF EN BOIS NDA
6353	BUILDERS WOODWRK,PREFABS	W	295	1.4	W	276	1.0	W	455	1.5	W	509	1.7	OUVRAGES DE MENUISERIE
64	PAPER,PAPERBOARD AND MFR			12.2			14.3			19.0			14.3	PAPIERS,CARTONS & OUVRAGES
641	PAPER AND PAPERBOARD	W	9678	7.6	W	18936	10.0	W	19682	14.0	W	13612	10.0	PAPIERS ET CARTONS
6413	KRAFT PAPER,PAPERBOARD	W	7645	4.5	W	15436	7.1	W	18131	11.2	W	11742	6.6	PAPIER ET CARTON KRAFT
64139	KRAFT PAPER PAPERBD,NES	W	7645	4.5	W	15436	7.1	W	18131	11.2	W	11742	6.6	PAPIER,CARTON KRAFT NDA
6415	PAPER,PAPERBRD,BULK,NES	W	355	0.8	W	2210	1.3	W	176	0.5	W	233	0.6	PAPIERS,CARTONS ROULEAUX
6417	CORRUGATED PAPER ETC,BLK	W	1005	1.5	W	605	0.7	W	928	1.3	W	1117	1.8	PAPIERS,CARTONS ONDULES
64172	CREPED HSHOLD PAPER ETC	W	666	1.1	W	404	0.6	W	727	1.1	W	319	1.0	PAPIER NON KRAFT CREPE
642	PAPER,ETC,PRECUT,ARTS OF	W	1407	4.6	W	1417	4.3	W	1618	5.0	W	1153	4.4	PAP,CARTONS DECOUPES
6421	PAPER ETC CONTAINERS	W	653	1.6	W	639	1.1	W	856	1.4	W	260	0.6	BOITES,SACS EMBALLAGES
6428	PAPER ETC ARTICLES NES	W	419	1.7	W	487	1.9	W	477	2.0	W	590	2.3	OUVRAGES EN PATE A PAPIER
64285	PAPER ETC DIAPERS ETC	W	242	1.1	W	332	1.3	W	332	1.5	W	343	1.6	SERVIETTES HYGIENIQUES
65	TEXTILE YARN,FABRICS,ETC			7.7			7.3			7.0			6.7	FILS,TISSUS,ARTICLES TEXTILE
653	WOVN MAN–MADE FIB FABRIC	W	316	1.5	W	226	1.4	W	264	1.3	W	228	1.3	TISSUS FIBRES SYNTH,ARTIF
656	LACE,RIBBONS,TULLE,ETC	W	67	0.9	W	64	1.5	W	57	0.9	W	52	0.8	TULLES,BRODERIE
65601	NARROW FABRICS NES	W	41	0.6	W	42	1.2	W	34	0.7	W	29	0.5	RUBANS SANS TRAME EN FILS
657	SPECIAL TXTL FABRC,PRODS	W	282	1.6	W	224	1.5	W	274	1.4	W	222	1.3	TISSUS SPECIAUX
6575	CORDAGE AND MANUFACTURES	W	147	0.9	W	120	1.1	W	176	1.1	W	158	1.0	FICELLES,CORDES,CORDAGES
65751	CORDAGE,CABLE,ROPE,TWINE	W	138	0.8	W	115	1.0	W	167	1.1	W	146	0.9	CORDAGES TRESSES OU NON
658	TEXTILE ARTICLES NES	W	193	1.8	W	149	1.5	W	149	1.4	W	144	1.3	ART FACONNES MAT TEXTILES
6584	LINENS ETC	W	147	1.4	W	117	1.2	W	110	1.0	W	98	0.9	LINGE DE MAISON
66	NONMETAL MINERAL MFS NES			11.9			13.2			13.3			10.1	ART MIN NON METALLIQUES
661	LIME,CEMENT,BLDG PRODS	W	53571	4.4	W	70720	5.1	W	61060	4.6	W	56500	4.4	CHAUX,CIMENTS MAT CONSTR
6612	CEMENT	W	52862	3.8	W	70144	4.6	W	59701	4.2	W	54094	3.9	CIMENTS HYDRAULIQUES
662	CLAY,REFRACTORY BLDG PRD	W	2887	2.4	W	2128	1.5	W	3017	1.9	W	1795	1.3	MAT CONST REFRACTAIRES
6624	BRICKS ETC NONREFRACTORY	W	2226	2.2	W	2128	1.5	W	3016	1.9	W	1792	1.3	BRIQUES ETC CERAM NON REFR
66245	GLAZED CERAMIC SETTS ETC	W	1899	1.8	W	1885	1.4	W	2443	1.6	W	1408	1.1	AUT CARREAUX CERAMIQUE
664	GLASS	W	481	1.1	W	437	0.8			1.3			0.9	VERRE
665	GLASSWARE	W	6598	3.1	W	3719	2.6	W	6024	4.2	W	3509	2.5	OUVRAGES EN VERRE
6651	BOTTLES ETC OF GLASS	W	6146	2.4	W	3549	2.0	W	5838	3.6	W	3283	2.0	RECIPIENTS EN VERRE
66511	GLASS BOTTLES ETC NONVAC	W	6146	2.4	W	3549	2.0	W	5838	3.6	W	3282	2.0	BONBONNES,BOUTEILLES,ETC
666	POTTERY	W	111	0.6	W	383	2.7	W	152	0.7	W	103	0.4	POTERIE
6665	COARSE CERAMIC HOUSEWARE	W	66	0.3	W	327	2.4	W	56	0.3	W	85	0.3	VAISSELLE,ART MEN CERAM
67	IRON AND STEEL			4.7			5.6			4.6			5.3	FER ET ACIER
673	IRON,STEEL SHAPES ETC	W	3129	1.7	W	4200	2.5	W	4256	2.2	W	5338	2.6	BARRES,PROFIL FER,ACIER
6732	IRON,STEEL BARS ETC	W	2455	1.1	W	3731	2.0	W	3846	1.7	W	3449	1.6	BARRES FER,ACIER
67322	HIGH CARBON STL BARS ETC	W	1349	0.6	W	3329	1.8	W	3645	1.6	W	3217	1.4	BARRES ACIER FIN CARBONE
674	IRN,STL UNIV,PLATE,SHEET	W	1904	1.8	W	1998	2.1	W	1365	1.6	W	1720	2.0	LARGES PLATS,TOLES
6749	OTH IRN,STL PLATES,SHEET	W	1279	1.3	W	1688	1.8	W	1304	1.6	W	1402	1.7	AUTRES TOLES FER,ACIER
67491	— OF IRON OR SIMPLE STL	W	1276	1.3	W	1680	1.8	W	1296	1.6	W	1400	1.7	AUT TOLES AUTRES ACIER FIN
678	IRON,STL TUBES,PIPES,ETC	W	279	0.7	W	272	1.0	W	283	0.8	W	263	0.7	TUBES,TUYAUX EN FONTE,FER
68	NON–FERROUS METALS			0.9			1.3			0.8			1.0	METAUX NON FERREUX
69	METAL MANUFACTURES NES			12.1			12.4			12.3			11.8	ART MANUFACT EN METAL NDA
691	STRUCTURES AND PARTS NES	W	607	1.8	W	1246	2.5	W	598	2.2	W	949	3.1	CONSTRUCT FER,ACIER,ALU
6911	STRUCTURES,PARTS IRN,STL	W	355	1.0	W	1025	1.3	W	414	0.9	W	681	1.4	CONSTRUCT FER,ACIER,FONTE
6912	STRUCTURES,PARTS ALUMNM	W	251	0.9	W	222	1.2	W	184	1.3	W	268	1.8	CONSTRUCT ALUMINIUM
693	WIRE PRODUCTS NON ELECTR	W	946	1.3	W	854	1.1	W	925	1.2	W	743	0.9	OUVRAGES FILS METALLIQUES
6935	METAL FENCING,GAUZE,ETC	W	843	1.0	W	797	0.9	W	873	1.0	W	699	0.7	TOILES EN FER,ACIER,CUIVRE
69351	IRN,STL FENCNG,GAUZE ETC	W	843	1.0	W	797	0.9	W	873	1.0	W	699	0.7	TOILES EN FER,ACIER
694	STL,COPPR NAILS,NUTS,ETC	W	362	1.1	W	388	1.2	W	318	1.0	W	324	0.9	CLOUS,VIS,ECROUS
695	TOOLS	W	119	1.1	W	125	0.9	W	117	1.1			1.0	OUTILS A MAIN
697	BASE MTL HOUSEHOLD EQUIP	W	397	2.3	W	446	1.7	W	370	2.0	W	326	1.9	ART MENAGE MET COMMUNS
6973	DMSTC HEATG,COOKG APPARA	W	199	1.2	W	291	0.8	W	199	1.1	W	195	1.1	APPS CHAUF NON ELECTRIQ
69731	IRN,STL DOM COOKG APPARA	W	191	1.1	W	281	0.7	W	193	1.1	W	191	1.0	APPS CUISSON FER,ACIER
699	BASE METAL MFRS NES			3.8	W	1024	4.0			3.7			3.1	ART MANUFACTURES MET NDA
6991	LOCKSMITHS WARES,ETC	W	162	1.2	W	208	1.3	W	144	1.1	W	124	1.2	ARTICLES DE SERRURERIE
6997	IRON,STEEL ARTICLES NES	W	336	1.2	W	458	1.4	W	312	1.2	W	152	0.9	OUV FONTE,FER,ACIER NDA
69979	IRN,STL MANUFACTURES NES	W	311	1.1	W	455	1.4	W	309	1.2	W	152	0.9	AUT OUVRAGES EN FER NDA
7	MACHINES,TRANSPORT EQUIP			68.4			65.5			58.1			68.2	MACHINES MATERIEL TRANSPORT
71	POWER GENERATING EQUIPMT			4.8			7.1			2.9			7.2	MACHINES GENERATRICES
713	INTRNL COMBUS PSTN ENGIN	W	101	1.8	W	326	5.4	W	114	2.1	W	201	5.8	MOTEURS EXPL COMB INT, PIECE
7138	PISTON ENGINES NES	W	6	0.1	W	161	2.9			0.1	W	59	2.8	MOTEURS A PISTONS NDA
7139	PISTON ENGINE PARTS NES	W	45	1.1	W	108	2.0	W	61	1.5	W	58	2.4	PIECES POUR 713.2,3,8
716	ROTATING ELECTRIC PLANT	W	301	2.9	W	98	1.5	W	77	0.8	W	158	1.0	APP ELECTR ROTATIFS,PIECES
7161	DC MOTORS AND GENERATORS	W	193	1.5	W	14	0.2	W	31	0.4	W	113	0.5	MOTEURS COURANT CONTINU
7162	AC MTRS,GENRTRS,GEN SETS	W	104	1.2	W	82	1.0	W	44	0.4	W	43	0.5	MOTEURS ELECTRIQUES
72	MACHS FOR SPCL INDUSTRYS			7.0			4.2			3.7			7.2	MAC SPECIALES POUR INDUST
721	AGRIC MACHY,EXC TRACTORS	W	52	0.3	W	16	0.2	W	21	0.2	W	29	3.2	MACHINES AGRICOLES

4. General Imports C.I.F. by Commodities according to the S.I.T.C. (Rev. 2) in million U.S. Dollars
Importations Générales C.A.F. par Produits d'après la C.T.C.I. (Rév. 2) en millions de Dollars E.U.

SITC CTCI	COMMODITY	1993 QUANTITY QUANTITE	1993 VALUE VALEUR	1994 QUANTITY QUANTITE	1994 VALUE VALEUR	1995 QUANTITY QUANTITE	1995 VALUE VALEUR	1996 QUANTITY QUANTITE	1996 VALUE VALEUR	PRODUIT
7211	CULTIVATING MACHINERY	W 1	0.1	W 2	0.1	W 9	0.1	W 10	3.0	MACH PREPARATION DU SOL
72111	PLOUGHS			W 1	0.1	W 2	0.1	W 9	2.9	CHARRUES
723	CIVIL ENGINEERG EQUIP ETC	W 636	2.7	W 147	0.9		1.3	W 413	2.2	APPAREILS DE GENIE CIVIL
7234	CONST,MINING MACHNRY NES	W 533	2.2	W 122	0.8		1.3	W 360	2.1	MACH POUR LA CONST, MINES
72342	SLFPRP SHOVELS,EXCAVATRS	W 117	0.6	W 103	0.7	W 257	1.1	W 201	1.2	PELLES MECANIQUES
727	FOOD MACHRY NON–DOMESTIC	W 61	1.2	W 17	0.3	W 19	0.5	W 9	0.3	MACH INDUSTRIES ALIMENT
7272	OTH FOOD PROC MCHY,PARTS	W 59	1.2	W 17	0.3	W 19	0.5	W 9	0.3	AUT MACH IND ALIMENTAIRE
728	OTH MACHY FOR SPCL INDUS		1.9	W 135	2.1	W 120	0.9	W 78	0.9	AUT MACH IND PARTICULIERES
7283	OTHR MINERAL WORKG MACHY	W 252	1.2	W 36	0.3	W 79	0.4	W 38	0.2	MACH TRIER,CRIBLER,BROYER
7284	MACHY FOR SPCL INDUS NES		0.6	W 84	1.6	W 36	0.4	W 21	0.5	MACH SPEC IND PARTICUL.
72842	RUBBER,PLASTICS WRKG MCH	W 9	0.2	W 27	1.0	W 14	0.2	W 7	0.4	MACH IND CAOUT MAT PLAST
74	GENRL INDUSTRL MACHY NES		10.2		10.9		10.8		8.5	MACH APP INDUSTRIE
741	HEATING,COOLING EQUIPMNT	W 231	2.6	W 241	2.2	W 255	2.7	W 208	2.3	MACH CHAUFFAGE,PIECES
7414	NONDOM REFRIG EQUIPT,PTS	W 63	0.7	W 90	0.9	W 130	1.2	W 72	0.8	MAT PRODUCTION DU FROID
7415	AIR–CONDITIONING MACHNRY	W 78	1.0	W 69	0.6	W 83	0.9	W 78	0.8	GROUPES CONDITION AIR
742	PUMPS FOR LIQUIDS ETC	W 64	0.9	W 79	1.1	W 53	1.0	W 50	1.1	POMPES MOTO–POMPES
7428	OTHER PUMPS FOR LIQUIDS	W 55	0.7	W 69	0.9	W 49	0.9	W 46	1.0	AUTRES POMPES POUR LIQ
743	PUMPS NES,CENTRFUGES ETC	W 146	1.3	W 174	1.2	W 86	1.0	W 937	1.2	POMPES COMPRES,VENT ETC
744	MECHANICAL HANDLING EQU	W 429	2.3	W 641	3.2	W 211	1.3	W 96	0.7	EQUIP MANUTENTION PIECES
7441	FORK LIFT TRCKS,ETC,PTS	W 130	0.5	W 242	1.9	W 40	0.2	W 28	0.2	CHARIOTS POUR USINES ETC
74411	FORK LIFT TRUCKS ETC	W 129	0.5	W 242	1.8	W 39	0.2	W 28	0.2	CHARIOTS POUR LES GARES
7442	LIFTING,LOADING MACH NES	W 263	1.5	W 315	0.7	W 132	0.8	W 27	0.2	APP LEVAGE,MANUTENTION
745	NONELEC MACHY,TOOLS NES	W 95	1.0	W 126	1.1	W 72	1.3	W 122	1.2	AUT MACH NON ELEC,PIECES
7452	OTH NONELEC MCHS,PTS NES	W 81	0.8	W 110	0.9	W 58	1.1	W 77	0.9	AUT MACH NON ELEC,PIECES
749	NONELEC MACH PTS,ACC NES	W 119	2.2	W 161	2.3	W 84970	3.7	W 117	2.1	PIECES MACH NON ELEC NDA
7492	COCKS,VALVES ETC NES	W 65	1.0	W 78	1.2	W 84915	1.4	W 78	1.1	ART ROB,SIM POUR TUYAUX
7493	SHAFT,CRANK,PULLEY ETC	W 25	0.7	W 30	0.6	W 37	1.7	W 18	0.5	ARBRES TRANS,VILEBREQUINS
75	OFFICE MACHNES,ADP EQUIP		4.4		5.2		4.8		6.4	MACH BUREAU TRAIT AUTOM
751	OFFICE MACHINES	W 31	1.0	W 28	1.0	W 38	0.8	W 28	0.7	MACH,APPAREILS DE BUREAU
752	AUTOMTIC DATA PROC EQUIP	W 49	2.7	W 56	3.2	W 63	3.1	W 82	4.5	MACH TRAIT INFORMATION
7522	DIGITAL COMPUTERS	W 20	1.1	W 10	0.7	W 9	0.6	W 7	0.5	MACH DIGITALES COMPLETES
7523	DIGITL CENTRL PROCESSORS	W 12	0.8	W 16	1.1	W 23	1.3	W 41	2.6	UNITES CENTRALES
7525	ADP PERIPHERAL UNITS	W 14	0.7	W 24	1.2	W 29	1.1	W 32	1.2	UNITES PERIPHERIQUES
759	OFFICE,ADP MCH PTS,ACCES	W 36	0.8	W 22	1.0	W 16	1.0	W 21	1.3	PIECES DU 751 ET 752
7599	ACCTG,ETC,ADP MCH PTS,AC	W 8	0.6	W 15	0.8	W 12	0.8	W 16	1.1	PIECES DU 751 ET 752
76	TELECOMM,SOUND EQUIPMENT		6.9		8.5		6.6		7.1	EQUIPMENT DE TELECOM
761	TELEVISION RECEIVERS	W 122	1.5	W 133	1.5	W 107	1.4	W 105	1.4	RECEPTEURS DE TELEVISION
7611	COLOUR TV RECEIVERS	W 119	1.4	W 128	1.4	W 103	1.4	W 102	1.4	RECEPTEURS COULEUR
762	RADIO BROADCAST RECEIVRS	W 75	0.9	W 72	0.9	W 63	0.8	W 48	1.1	RECEPTEURS RADIODIFFUSION
764	TELECOM EQPT,PTS,ACC NES	W 150	4.0	W 183	5.7	W 124	3.9	W 95	4.1	EQUIP TELECOM,PIECES
7641	LINE TELEPHONE,ETC EQUIP	W 76	1.9	W 116	3.7	W 59	1.9	W 34	1.7	APP TELEPHON PAR FIL
7649	PTS NES OF EQUIPMT OF 76	W 23	0.9	W 20	1.0	W 18	1.0	W 14	1.1	PIECES DE LA DIV 76
77	ELECTRIC MACHNRY NES ETC		13.1		13.1		10.8		11.3	MACH APP ELECT NDA
771	ELECTRIC POWER MACHY NES	W 163	1.0	W 175	1.2	W 97	0.9	W 90	0.9	MACH PROD,TRANS ELECTR
7711	TRANSFORMERS,ELECTRICAL	W 158	0.8	W 168	1.0	W 88	0.6	W 78	0.6	TRANSFO ELECTRIQUES
772	SWITCHGEAR ETC,PARTS NES	W 113	1.8	W 133	3.0	W 80	1.8	W 99	1.8	APP COUPURE,SECT ETC
7721	SWITCHGEAR ETC	W 106	1.7	W 133	3.0	W 79	1.7	W 99	1.8	APP COUPURE,SECTIONMNT
773	ELECTR DISTRIBUTNG EQUIP	W 726	3.4	W 751	3.0	W 438	2.2	W 461	2.2	EQUIPMT DISTRIBUTION ELECT
7731	INSULATED WIRE,CABLE ETC	W 690	3.1	W 739	2.8	W 421	2.1	W 429	2.1	FILS,CABLES ISOLES ELECT
775	HOUSEHOLD TYPE EQUIP NES	W 663	4.0	W 515	3.2	W 591	3.6	W 686	3.7	MACH,APP USAGE DOMESTQUE
7752	DOM REFRIGERATRS,FREEZRS	W 417	2.6	W 309	1.8	W 332	1.8	W 401	1.8	REFRIG,CONGEL MENAGER
77521	DOMESTIC REFRIGERATORS	W 356	2.1	W 267	1.6	W 266	1.5	W 340	1.6	REFRIGERATEURS
778	ELECTRICAL MACHINERY NES	W 374	2.7	W 455	2.5	W 358	2.5	W 423	2.6	AUTRES MACH ELECT NDA
7781	BATTERIES,ACCUMULATORS	W 210	0.9	W 268	0.9	W 250	1.0	W 228	0.8	PILES ET ACCUMULATEURS
78	ROAD VEHICLES		17.9		14.7		17.1		18.8	VEHICULES ROUTIERS
781	PASS MOTOR VEH EXC BUSES	W 1094	9.0	W 778	5.7	W 1085	7.1	W 1876	9.1	AUTO TRANSPORT PERSONNES
782	LORRIES,SPCL MTR VEH NES	W 856	3.8	W 664	4.2	W 1020	5.4	W 1310	4.6	VEHICULES SPECIAUX,MARCH
7821	LORRIES,TRUCKS	W 732	3.1	W 565	3.5	W 850	4.4	W 1097	4.1	VEHICULES TRANSP MARCHAND
7822	SPECIAL MOTOR VEHCLS NES	W 124	0.8	W 99	0.7	W 170	1.0	W 213	0.5	VEHICULES USAGES SPECIAUX
783	ROAD MOTOR VEHICLES NES	W 343	2.2	W 287	1.9	W 356	2.0	W 406	2.3	VEHICULES ROUTIERS NDA
7831	BUSES	W 287	2.0	W 259	1.7	W 279	1.9	W 374	2.2	VOITURES TRANSPORT COMMUN
784	MOTOR VEH PRTS,ACCES NES	W 242	2.3	W 269	2.2	W 185	2.2	W 282	2.5	PIECES 722,781,782,783
7849	OTHER MOTOR VEHCL PARTS	W 223	2.2	W 263	2.1	W 171	2.1	W 264	2.4	PIECES 722,781,782,783
79	OTHR TRANSPORT EQUIPMENT		4.4		1.5		1.4		1.9	AUTRE MATERIEL TRANSPORT
792	AIRCRAFT ETC	W 27	2.9	W 15	0.6		0.6	W 6	0.4	APP NAVIGATION AERIENNE
7921	HELICOPTERS	W 10	1.5	W 3	0.1		0.4			HELICOPTERES
7923	AIRCRFT NES2000–15000KG	W 13	1.2	W 5	0.3					AERODYNES 2000 A 15000 KG
793	SHIPS AND BOATS ETC	W 99	1.5	W 161	1.0	W 165	0.8	W 231	1.5	NAVIRES BATEAUX,ETC
7932	SHIPS AND BOATS NES	W 87	1.4	W 130	0.8	W 163	0.8	W 132	1.4	NAVIRES ET BATEAUX
8	MISC MANUFACTURED GOODS		42.8		41.3		40.1		41.7	ART MANUFACTURES DIVERS
812	*PLUMBG,HEATNG,LGHTNG EQ	W 377	1.9	W 266	1.8	W 261	1.5	W 252	1.5	APPAR SANITAIRES CHAUFFAGE
8124	LIGHTING EQUIPMENT NES	W 158	1.3	W 105	1.3	W 87	0.9	W 98	1.1	APPAREILS ECLAIRAGE ETC
81242	LAMPS,FITTINGS BASE METL	W 134	1.0	W 91	1.1	W 77	0.8	W 78	1.0	APPAREILS D'ECLAIRAGE
821	*FURNITURE,PARTS THEREOF	W 932	5.8	W 761	5.0	W 708	3.6	W 770	4.0	MEUBLES ET PIECES
8211	CHAIRS,SEATS AND PARTS	W 272	1.6	W 199	1.4	W 168	1.0	W 187	1.3	SIEGES ET PIECES
82111	CHAIRS AND OTHER SEATS	W 271	1.6	W 199	1.4	W 167	0.9	W 186	1.3	SIEGES
8219	FURNITURE AND PARTS NES	W 600	3.8	W 511	3.3	W 423	2.2	W 491	2.3	AUTRES MEUBLES ET PIECES
82191	METAL FURNITURE NES	W 196	1.1	W 189	1.2	W 186	0.9	W 172	1.0	MEUBLES NDA EN METAL
82192	WOOD FURNITURE NES	W 272	1.9	W 234	1.7	W 179	1.0	W 243	0.9	MEUBLES NDA EN BOIS
84	CLOTHING AND ACCESSORIES		9.5		9.9		8.5		9.6	VETEMENTS
842	MENS OUTERWEAR NOT KNIT	W 116	1.4	W 93	1.2	W 100	1.2	W 128	1.4	VET DESSUS POUR HOMMES
8423	— TROUSERS,BREECHES ETC	W 93	1.1	W 74	0.9	W 88	1.0	W 115	1.1	PANTALONS HOMMES MAT TEX
843	WOMENS OUTERWEAR NONKNIT	W 131	2.3	W 131	2.3	W 125	2.2	W 109	2.5	VET DESSUS FEMMES MAT TEX
8439	— OTHER OUTER GARMENTS	W 60	1.0	W 72	1.1	W 66	1.0	W 52	1.2	AUT VET DES FEM MAT TEXT
845	OUTERWEAR KNIT NONELASTC	W 317	2.6	W 53	1.0	W 58	1.0	W 68	1.1	VET DESSOUS,ACCES BONNET
8459	— OTHER,CLTHG ACCESRYS	W 130	2.1	W 15	0.6	W 15	0.5	W 17	0.5	AUT VET DESSUS DE BONNE
846	UNDER GARMENTS KNITTED	W 482	1.9	W 189	3.9	W 122	2.9	W 100	2.8	SOUS VETS DE BONNETERIE
8462	— OF COTTON NON ELASTIC	W 96	1.0	W 129	1.6	W 92	1.3	W 83	1.2	SOUS–VET BONNET COTON
84629	—— OTHER	W 95	1.0	W 127	1.6	W 91	1.3	W 82	1.2	AUT SOUS–VET BONNET COTON
8465	CORSETS,GARTERS,ETC	W 386	0.9	W 58	2.3	W 29	1.6	W 17	1.6	CORSETS,GAINES ART SIM
84651	BRASSIERES	W 386	0.9	W 58	1.9	W 24	1.5	W 16	1.6	SOUTIENS–GORGE,BUSTIERS
851	*FOOTWEAR	W 348	4.4	W 302	3.7	W 305	3.4	W 325	3.5	CHAUSSURES
85101	FOOTWEAR RUBBER,PLASTIC	W 188	1.8	W 126	1.3	W 161	1.4	W 196	1.5	CHAUS SEMELLES CAOUTCH
85102	FOOTWEAR LEATHER	W 120	2.1	W 160	2.2	W 135	1.9	W 127	2.0	CHAUS SEMELLES EN CUIR
87	PRECISION INSTRUMNTS NES		1.9		2.2		2.1		2.0	INSTRUM,APPAR SCIENT NDA
874	MEASURNG,CONTROLNG INSTR	W 32	1.1	W 55	1.5	W 32	1.3	W 27	1.2	INSTRUMENTS DE MESURE
88	PHOTO EQU,OPTICL GDS ETC		1.7		1.4		1.4		1.5	APP,FOURN PHOTO,OP,MONTR
89	MISC MANUFCTRD GOODS NES		17.2		17.1		19.2		19.3	ART MANUFACTURES DIVERS
892	PRINTED MATTER	W 559	4.5	W 405	4.7	W 419	5.1	W 386	4.9	IMPRIMES
8921	PRINTED BOOKS,GLOBES,ETC	W 396	2.4	W 220	3.0	W 185	2.8	W 160	2.3	LIVRES,BROCHURES,CARTES
89211	PRINTED BOOKS,PAMPHLETS	W 387	2.3	W 212	2.9	W 178	2.7	W 149	2.2	LIVRES,BROCHURES

4. General Imports C.I.F. by Commodities according to the S.I.T.C. (Rev. 2) in million U.S. Dollars
Importations Générales C.A.F. par Produits d'après la C.T.C.I. (Rév. 2) en millions de Dollars E.U.

SITC CTCI	COMMODITY	1993		1994		1995		1996		PRODUIT
		QUANTITY QUANTITE	VALUE VALEUR	QUANTITY QUANTITE	VALUE VALEUR	QUANTITY QUANTITE	VALUE VALEUR	QUANTITY QUANTITE	VALUE VALEUR	
8928	PRINTED MATTER NES	W 121	1.5	W 107	1.2	W 173	1.6	W 156	1.8	IMPRIMES NDA
89281	LABELS PAPER,PAPERBOARD	W 62	0.9	W 51	0.7	W 82	1.0	W 76	1.2	ETIQUETTES TOUS GENRES
893	ARTICLES OF PLASTIC NES		7.5		7.2	W 3027	9.0		9.2	OUVRAGES EN MAT DIVIS 58
8931	PLSTC PACKG CONTNRS,LIDS	W 748	2.3	W 757	2.1	W 834	3.5	W 1041	4.1	ART TRANSP EMBALLAGE ETC
8939	MISC PLASTIC ARTICLES	W 1326	5.1	W 1568	5.1	W 2172	5.5	W 1384	5.1	ART DIVERS EN MAT DIV 58
89399	OTHR PLASTC ARTICLES NES	W 1006	4.5	W 1101	4.7	W 1843	5.0	W 1114	4.8	AUT OUV MAT DIV 58
894	TOYS,SPORTING GOODS,ETC	W 161	1.7	W 177	1.6	W 169	1.5	W 195	1.6	VOITURES ENFANTS,JOUETS
8942	TOYS,INDOOR GAMES ETC	W 105	1.2	W 116	1.0	W 128	1.0	W 148	1.1	JOUETS,JEUX ETC
898	MUSICAL INSTRUMENTS,PTS	W 120	1.1	W 39	1.2	W 694	1.2	W 42	1.3	INSTRUMENTS DE MUSIQUE
8983	SOUND RECRDNG TAPE,DISCS	W 115	0.9	W 30	1.0	W 688	1.0	W 37	1.1	SUPPORTS SON POUR 763
899	OTHER MANUFACTURED GOODS		1.6		1.5		1.6		1.6	AUT ART MANUF DIVERS NDA

5. General Exports F.O.B. by Commodities according to the S.I.T.C. (Rev. 2) in million U.S. Dollars
Exportations Générales F.O.B. par Produits d'après la C.T.C.I. (Rév. 2) en millions de Dollars E.U.

SITC CTCI	COMMODITY	1993 QUANTITY QUANTITE	1993 VALUE VALEUR	1994 QUANTITY QUANTITE	1994 VALUE VALEUR	1995 QUANTITY QUANTITE	1995 VALUE VALEUR	1996 QUANTITY QUANTITE	1996 VALUE VALEUR	PRODUIT
	ALL COMMODITIES		119.7		94.9		109.0		79.6	TOUS PRODUITS
0	FOOD AND LIVE ANIMALS		60.1		49.4		57.9		54.1	ALIMENTS,ANIMAUX VIVANTS
05	VEGETABLES AND FRUIT		59.0		48.2		56.9		53.5	LEGUMES ET FRUITS
057	FRUIT,NUTS,FRESH,DRIED	W 134745	59.0	W 93500	48.2	W 114294	56.9	W 103486	53.5	FRUITS FRAIS OU SECS
0573	BANANA,PLANTAIN,FRSH,DRY	W 132978	58.2	W 91729	47.1	W 112920	56.1	W 102320	52.9	BANANES FRAICHES,SECHEES
0579	FRUIT FRESH OR DRIED NES	W 1731	0.8	W 1736	1.1	W 1318	0.8	W 1157	0.7	FRUITS FRAIS,SECS NDA
05797	OTH TROP FRUIT,FRESH,DRY	W 566	0.3	W 744	0.5	W 428	0.3	W 391	0.3	AVOCATS,MANGUES,GOYAVES
05798	OTHER FRESH FRUIT	W 978	0.4	W 833	0.5	W 833	0.4	W 734	0.4	AUTRES FRUITS FRAIS
07	COFFEE,TEA,COCOA,SPICES		0.4		0.8		0.6		0.3	CAFE,THE,CACAO,EPICES
075	SPICES	W 120	0.3	W 184	0.6	W 240	0.5	W 144	0.3	EPICES
0751	PEPPER AND PIMENTO	W 95	0.2	W 167	0.6	W 234	0.4	W 141	0.3	POIVRE,PIMENTS
09	MISC EDIBLE PRODUCTS		0.6		0.5		0.4		0.3	PREP ALIMENTAIRES DIVERSES
098	EDIBLE PRODCTS,PREPS NES	W 213	0.4	W 146	0.4	W 134	0.3	W 158	0.3	PREP ALIMENTAIRES NDA
1	BEVERAGES AND TOBACCO		5.2		5.0		5.7		3.8	BOISSONS ET TABACS
11	BEVERAGES		5.2		5.0		5.7		3.8	BOISSONS
111	NON–ALCOHL BEVERAGES NES	W 550	0.7	W 575	0.5	W 536	0.6	W 256	0.4	BOISSONS NON ALCOOLIQUES
11102	FLAVORED WATERS NON–ALCO	W 412	0.6	W 316	0.5	W 276	0.4	W 195	0.3	LIMONADES,EAUX GAZEUSES
112	ALCOHOLIC BEVERAGES	W 3380	4.6	W 3262	4.6	W 4188	5.2	W 2255	3.4	BOISSONS ALCOOLIQUES
1123	BEER,ALE,STOUT,PORTER	W 2776	4.3	W 2863	4.0	W 3863	4.8	W 2219	3.3	BIERES
1124	DISTILLED ALCOHOLIC BEVS	W 604	0.4	W 344	0.5	W 220	0.3	W 2	0.1	ALCOOLS,EAUX–DE–VIE
11249	OTH ALCOHOLC BEVS,CMPNDS	W 598	0.4	W 340	0.5	W 216	0.3	W 2	0.1	BOISSONS ALCOOLIQUES NDA
2	CRUDE MATERLS,EXCL FUELS		0.6		0.6		0.5		0.2	MAT BRUTES NON COMESTIBLES
4	ANIMAL,VEGETABLE OIL,FAT		1.7		0.8		0.3			HUILES,GRAISSES ANIM,VEG
42	FIXED VEGETABLE OIL,FAT		1.7		0.8		0.3			HUILES VEGETALES FIXES
424	FIXED VEG OIL NONSOFT	W 2522	1.6	W 1019	0.8	W 326	0.3			AUTRES HUILES VEG FIXES
4243	COCONUT (COPRA) OIL	W 2507	1.6	W 1019	0.8	W 326	0.3			HJUILE DE COPRAH
5	CHEMCLS,RELATED PROD NES		1.5		0.8		1.0		0.8	PRODUITS CHIMIQUES
55	PERFUME,CLEANING ETC PRD		0.4		0.2		0.2		0.2	PROD POUR PARFUM,TOILETTE
59	CHEMICAL MATERIALS NES		0.9		0.5		0.7		0.7	MAT PROD CHIMIQUES NDA
591	PESTICIDES,DISINFECTANTS	W 354	0.5	W 7	0.2	W 15	0.3	W 304	0.3	DESINF,INSECT,FONG,HERB
592	STARCH,INULIN,GLUTEN,ETC	W 91	0.4	W 73	0.3	W 86	0.4	W 108	0.5	AMIDONS,INUL,GLUT FROM
5922	ALBUMINOID SUBSTAN,GLUES	W 82	0.4	W 73	0.3	W 86	0.4	W 108	0.5	MAT ALBUMIN,COLLES
59229	PREPARED GLUES NES,ETC	W 81	0.4	W 71	0.3	W 81	0.4	W 98	0.4	COLLES PREPAREES NDA
6	BASIC MANUFACTURES		10.8		7.1		10.0		7.3	ART MANUFACTURES
64	PAPER,PAPERBOARD AND MFR		8.7		5.7		7.8		6.0	PAPIERS,CARTONS & OUVRAGES
641	PAPER AND PAPERBOARD	W 1723	6.1	W 27	0.1	W 6	0.1	W 408	0.4	PAPIERS ET CARTONS
6417	CORRUGATED PAPER ETC,BLK	W 1182	5.9	W 17	0.1	W 6	0.1	W 408	0.4	PAPIERS,CARTONS ONDULES
64173	OTHER CREPED ETC PAPER	W 1168	5.8	W 8	0.1					AUT PAPIER CREPE,PLISSE
64174	PAPER ETC CORRUGATED ETC			W 8	0.1			W 408	0.4	PAP,CARTONS SIMPL ONDULES
642	PAPER,ETC,PRECUT,ARTS OF	W 2143	2.7	W 5363	5.7	W 8442	7.8	W 4926	5.7	PAP,CARTONS DECOUPES
6421	PAPER ETC CONTAINERS	W 1775	1.7	W 5080	4.9	W 8257	7.3	W 4757	5.2	BOITES,SACS EMBALLAGES
6424	PAPER ETC CT TO SIZE NES	W 248	0.6	W 199	0.6	W 129	0.4	W 154	0.5	PAP,CARTONS DECOUPES
64243	TOILET PAPER CUT TO SIZE	W 248	0.6	W 199	0.6	W 129	0.4	W 154	0.5	PAPIER HYGIENIQUE
6428	PAPER ETC ARTICLES NES	W 103	0.4	W 81	0.3	W 55	0.2	W 14	0.1	OUVRAGES EN PATE A PAPIER
65	TEXTILE YARN,FABRICS,ETC		1.0		0.4		0.6		1.1	FILS,TISSUS,ARTICLES TEXTILE
652	COTTON FABRICS,WOVEN	W 115	0.4	W 19	0.2	W 5	0.1		0.1	TISSUS DE COTON
6522	WOVEN COTTON BLEACHD,ETC	W 115	0.4	W 19	0.2				0.1	TISSUS COTON BLANCHIS ETC
65224	BLCHED COTTON FABRIC NES	W 113	0.4	W 19	0.2				0.1	AUT TIS PLUS 85% COT BLANCHI
658	TEXTILE ARTICLES NES		0.1		0.1	W 6	0.2	W 60	1.1	ART FACONNES MAT TEXTILES
6584	LINENS ETC				0.1	W 4	0.1	W 59	1.1	LINGE DE MAISON
65845	OTHER LINEN OF COTTON				0.1	W 4	0.1	W 48	1.1	LINGE DE TOILETTE COTON
69	METAL MANUFACTURES NES		0.4		0.4		1.0		0.1	ART MANUFACT EN METAL NDA
697	BASE MTL HOUSEHOLD EQUIP	W 44	0.2	W 18	0.1	W 36	0.5	W 1	0.1	ART MENAGE MET COMMUNS
6978	BASE MTL HOUSE EQUIP NES			W 2	0.1	W 31	0.4			ART MENAGE MET COMMUNS
69782	BASE MTL DECOR ARTICLES			W 2	0.1	W 31	0.4			AUT OBJETS ORNEM INTERIEUR
7	MACHINES,TRANSPORT EQUIP		10.3		8.5		12.2		4.8	MACHINES MATERIEL TRANSPORT
71	POWER GENERATING EQUIPMT		1.4		0.3		0.5		0.2	MACHINES GENERATRICES
713	INTRNL COMBUS PSTN ENGIN	W 50	0.6	W 13	0.3	W 18	0.3	W 2	0.1	MOTEURS EXPL COMB INT, PIECE
7139	PISTON ENGINE PARTS NES	W 36	0.5	W 9	0.2	W 9	0.2		0.1	PIECES POUR 713.2,3,8
716	ROTATING ELECTRIC PLANT	W 73	0.8	W 5	0.1	W 8	0.2	W 11	0.2	APP ELECTR ROTATIFS,PIECES
7162	AC MTRS,GENRTRS,GEN SETS	W 70	0.7	W 5	0.1	W 5	0.2	W 5	0.1	MOTEURS ELECTRIQUES
71622	AC GENERATORS	W 56	0.7		0.1		0.1			GENER COURANT ALTERNATIF
72	MACHS FOR SPCL INDUSTRYS		1.3		0.8		2.3		0.5	MAC SPECIALES POUR INDUST
723	CIVIL ENGNEERG EQUIP ETC	W 180	1.1	W 160	0.7	W 119	1.3	W 54	0.4	APPAREILS DE GENIE CIVIL
7234	CONST,MINING MACHNRY NES	W 167	1.1	W 139	0.6	W 119	1.3	W 54	0.4	MACH POUR LA CONST, MINES
72341	SELF–PROPELLD DOZERS,ETC	W 44	0.2	W 132	0.5	W 34	0.8	W 31	0.3	BULLDOZERS
72342	SLFPRP SHOVELS,EXCAVATRS	W 81	0.7	W 7	0.1	W 29	0.1	W 23	0.2	PELLES MECANIQUES
72345	PILE DRIVERS,ETC					W 51	0.5			CHASSE–NEIGE
728	OTH MACHY FOR SPCL INDUS	W 26	0.1	W 16	0.1	W 72	0.9	W 9	0.1	AUT MACH IND PARTICULIERES
7284	MACHY FOR SPCL INDUS NES	W 5	0.1	W 4	0.1	W 64	0.8		0.1	MACH SPEC IND PARTICUL.
72842	RUBBER,PLASTICS WRKG MCH					W 51	0.5			MACH IND CAOUT MAT PLAST
74	GENRL INDUSTRL MACHY NES		0.4		0.3		2.0		0.1	MACH APP INDUSTRIE
742	PUMPS FOR LIQUIDS ETC	W 1	0.1	W 2	0.1	W 37	0.5		0.1	POMPES MOTO–POMPES
7428	OTHER PUMPS FOR LIQUIDS	W 1	0.1	W 2	0.1	W 37	0.5		0.1	AUTRES POMPES POUR LIQ
74288	PUMPS FR LIQUIDS NES ETC	W 1	0.1	W 1	0.1	W 27	0.4		0.1	POMPES POUR LIQUIDES NDA
744	MECHANICAL HANDLING EQU	W 149	0.2	W 11	0.1	W 44	0.9	W 20	0.1	EQUIP MANUTENTION PIECES
7442	LIFTING,LOADING MACH NES	W 111	0.1	W 1	0.1	W 17	0.7	W 16	0.1	APP LEVAGE,MANUTENTION
76	TELECOMM,SOUND EQUIPMENT		0.5		2.6		1.9		0.1	EQUIPMENT DE TELECOM
763	SOUND RECORDRS,PHONOGRPH		0.1	W 3	0.8	W 1	0.1		0.1	PHONO,APP ENREGISTREMENT
7638	OTHR SOUND APPARATUS ETC		0.1	W 3	0.8	W 1	0.1		0.1	AUT APP D'ENREGIS,REPROD
76381	TV IMAGE,SND RECRDRS ETC		0.1	W 3	0.8		0.1			APP ENREG,REPRO IMAG,SON
764	TELECOM EQPT,PTS,ACC NES	W 8	0.5	W 17	1.9	W 33	1.9		0.1	EQUIP TELECOM,PIECES
7643	TV,RADIO TRANSMITTRS ETC	W 3	0.2	W 12	1.5	W 30	1.8		0.1	APP EMET TELE RADIO
7649	PTS NES OF EQUIPMT OF 76	W 1	0.1	W 1	0.4	W 1	0.1			PIECES DE LA DIV 76
76491	PTS NES OF APPAR OF 7641	W 1	0.1		0.4		0.1			PIECES POUR 764.1
77	ELECTRIC MACHNRY NES ETC		6.0		3.4		4.0		3.3	MACH APP ELECT NDA
771	ELECTRIC POWER MACHY NES	W 44	0.3	W 4	0.2	W 13	0.4	W 8	0.3	MACH PROD,TRANS ELECTR
7711	TRANSFORMERS,ELECTRICAL	W 43	0.2	W 3	0.1	W 12	0.4	W 6	0.2	TRANSFO ELECTRIQUES
77118	OTHER ELEC TRANSFORMERS	W 43	0.2	W 3	0.1	W 12	0.4	W 6	0.2	AUTRES TRANSFO ELECTRIQ
772	SWITCHGEAR ETC,PARTS NES	W 30	2.9	W 27	2.0	W 41	2.5	W 18	1.7	APP COUPURE,SECT ETC
7721	SWITCHGEAR ETC	W 19	1.6	W 11	0.2	W 24	0.4		0.1	APP COUPURE,SECTIONMNT
7723	FIXED,VARIABLE RESISTORS	W 9	1.2	W 13	1.6	W 15	1.8	W 17	1.6	POTENTIOMETRES PIECES
775	HOUSEHOLD TYPE EQUIP NES	W 163	1.6	W 27	0.3	W 4	0.1		0.1	MACH,APP USAGE DOMESTQUE
7752	DOM REFRIGERATRS,FREEZRS	W 162	1.6	W 27	0.3		0.1			REFRIG,CONGEL MENAGER
77521	DOMESTIC REFRIGERATORS	W 157	1.5	W 27	0.3					REFRIGERATEURS
776	TRANSISTORS,VALVES,ETC	W 1	0.9	W 2	1.0	W 1	1.1	W 1	1.3	LAMPES,TUBES,VALVES
7763	DIODES,TRANSISTORS,ETC	W 1	0.4	W 2	1.0	W 1	1.1	W 1	1.3	DIODES,TRANSISTORS
78	ROAD VEHICLES		0.8		1.1		0.6		0.6	VEHICULES ROUTIERS
781	PASS MOTOR VEH EXC BUSES	W 16	0.2	W 29	0.3	W 31	0.4	W 60	0.5	AUTO TRANSPORT PERSONNES
782	LORRIES,SPCL MTR VEH NES	W 96	0.5	W 117	0.4	W 70	0.2	W 9	0.1	VEHICULES SPECIAUX,MARCH
786	TRAILERS,NONMOTR VEH,NES	W 3	0.1	W 20	0.3	W 5	0.1		0.1	REMORQUES,CADRES,CONTAIN

5. General Exports F.O.B. by Commodities according to the S.I.T.C. (Rev. 2) in million U.S. Dollars
Exportations Générales F.O.B. par Produits d'après la C.T.C.I. (Rév. 2) en millions de Dollars E.U.

SITC CTCI	COMMODITY	1993		1994		1995		1996		PRODUIT
		QUANTITY QUANTITE	VALUE VALEUR	QUANTITY QUANTITE	VALUE VALEUR	QUANTITY QUANTITE	VALUE VALEUR	QUANTITY QUANTITE	VALUE VALEUR	
79	OTHR TRANSPORT EQUIPMENT		0.1		0.3		0.9		0.3	AUTRE MATERIEL TRANSPORT
792	AIRCRAFT ETC	W 2	0.1	W 3	0.2	W 4	0.5		0.1	APP NAVIGATION AERIENNE
7929	AIRCRAFT PARTS NES	W 2	0.1	W 3	0.2	W 4	0.5		0.1	PIECES DU 792
793	SHIPS AND BOATS ETC	W 3	0.1		0.1	W 25	0.5	W 53	0.3	NAVIRES BATEAUX,ETC
7932	SHIPS AND BOATS NES	W 1	0.1		0.1	W 25	0.5	W 53	0.3	NAVIRES ET BATEAUX
8	MISC MANUFACTURED GOODS		29.7		22.6		21.5		9.0	ART MANUFACTURES DIVERS
84	CLOTHING AND ACCESSORIES		26.2		18.9		17.5		7.0	VETEMENTS
842	MENS OUTERWEAR NOT KNIT	W 340	3.1	W 16	0.3	W 124	0.8		0.1	VET DESSUS POUR HOMMES
8422	— SUITS	W 70	0.7				0.1			COMPLETS HOMMES MAT TEXT
84223	—— OF MAN–MADE FIBRES	W 70	0.7				0.1			COMPLETS HOMMES FIB SYNT
8423	— TROUSERS,BREECHES ETC	W 218	2.0	W 15	0.3	W 123	0.8		0.1	PANTALONS HOMMES MAT TEX
8429	— OTHER OUTER GARMENTS	W 51	0.5		0.1					AUT VET DES HOM MAT TEX
843	WOMENS OUTERWEAR NONKNIT	W 731	6.5	W 196	1.9	W 78	0.4	W 3	0.1	VET DESSUS FEMMES MAT TEX
8432	— SUITS AND COSTUMES	W 302	3.1		0.1					COSTUMES–TAIL MAT TEXIL
8433	— DRESSES	W 52	0.5	W 1	0.1	W 15	0.1		0.1	ROBES EN MAT–TEXTILES
8435	— BLOUSES	W 168	1.0	W 4	0.1	W 1	0.1		0.1	BLOUSES FEM MAT TEXTILES
8439	— OTHER OUTER GARMENTS	W 200	1.9	W 187	1.8	W 60	0.3	W 2	0.1	AUT VET DES FEM MAT TEXT
844	UNDER GARMENTS NOT KNIT	W 142	1.5	W 136	1.3	W 71	0.8	W 9	0.2	VETEMENT DESSOUS MAT TEX
8441	— MENS SHIRTS	W 142	1.5	W 136	1.3	W 70	0.8	W 9	0.2	CHEMISES HOMMES MAT TEXT
84411	—— OF COTTON	W 120	1.4	W 82	1.0	W 68	0.8	W 9	0.2	CHEMISES HOMMES DE COTON
84412	—— OF SYNTHETIC FIBRES	W 22	0.1	W 53	0.4	W 2	0.1			CHEMISES HOMMES FIB SYNT
845	OUTERWEAR KNIT NONELASTC	W 1063	11.3	W 1210	12.9	W 1325	12.0	W 691	6.6	VET DESSOUS,ACCES BONNET
8451	— JERSEYS,PULLOVERS ETC	W 482	6.1	W 568	4.2	W 640	4.0	W 258	1.4	CHANDAILS,PULL–OVERS ETC
8459	— OTHER,CLTHG ACCESRYS	W 580	5.2	W 640	8.8	W 685	8.0	W 424	5.2	AUT VET DESSUS DE BONNE
846	UNDER GARMENTS KNITTED	W 104	3.6	W 72	2.5	W 56	0.6	W 21	0.2	SOUS VETS DE BONNETERIE
8462	— OF COTTON NON ELASTIC	W 27	0.6	W 26	0.3	W 56	0.6	W 21	0.2	SOUS–VET BONNET COTON
84629	—— OTHER	W 26	0.6	W 26	0.3	W 56	0.6	W 21	0.2	AUT SOUS–VET BONNET COTON
8465	CORSETS,GARTERS,ETC	W 76	3.0	W 46	2.2	W 74	3.1			CORSETS,GAINES ART SIM
84651	BRASSIERES	W 76	3.0	W 46	2.2	W 73	3.0			SOUTIENS–GORGE,BUSTIERS
848	HEADGEAR,NONTXTL CLOTHNG	W 46	0.5		0.1		0.1			VET ACCES MAT AUT QUE TEX
8482	PLASTC,RUBBR CLTHG,ACCES	W 43	0.4		0.1		0.1			VET ACCES MAT PLAS ARTIF
851	*FOOTWEAR	W 2	0.1	W 8	0.4	W 5	0.1		0.1	CHAUSSURES
85101	FOOTWEAR RUBBER,PLASTIC	W 1	0.1	W 8	0.4	W 2	0.1			CHAUS SEMELLES CAOUTCH
87	PRECISION INSTRUMNTS NES		0.2		0.2		0.4		0.1	INSTRUM,APPAR SCIENT NDA
88	PHOTO EQU,OPTICL GDS ETC		0.7		0.3		0.2		0.1	APP,FOURN PHOTO,OP,MONTR
881	PHOTO APPARAT,EQUIPT NES	W 5	0.6	W 2	0.3	W 1	0.1		0.1	APP,EQUIP PHOTO NDA
8812	CINEMA CAMERAS,PROJ,ETC	W 5	0.6	W 1	0.2	W 1	0.1		0.1	APPAREILS CINEMA,PIECES
88121	— FOR FILM UNDER 16MM	W 5	0.6	W 1	0.2		0.1		0.1	APP CINEMA MOINS 16 MM
89	MISC MANUFCTRD GOODS NES		2.4		2.7		3.1		1.9	ART MANUFACTURES DIVERS
893	ARTICLES OF PLASTIC NES	W 159	2.0	W 7	0.1	W 91	2.0	W 64	1.5	OUVRAGES EN MAT DIVIS 58
8939	MISC PLASTIC ARTICLES	W 134	1.9	W 117	2.0	W 90	2.0	W 64	1.4	ART DIVERS EN MAT DIV 58
89399	OTHR PLASTC ARTICLES NES	W 111	1.9	W 117	2.0	W 90	2.0	W 64	1.4	AUT OUV MAT DIV 58
899	OTHER MANUFACTURED GOODS	W 23	0.1	W 19	0.3	W 16	0.4	W 17	0.4	AUT ART MANUF DIVERS NDA
8998	SMALLWARES,TOILETRYS ETC	W 22	0.1	W 13	0.3	W 11	0.4	W 13	0.4	ART MERCERIE,TOILETTE
89985	COMBS,HAIR–SLIDES,ETC		0.1	W 12	0.3	W 11	0.4	W 13	0.4	PEIGNES,BARRETTES ETC
9	GOODS NOT CLASSD BY KIND		0.1		0.5		0.3		0.1	ART TRANSACT NON CLASSES
931	*SPECIAL TRANSACTIONS	W 1	0.1	W 573	0.5	W 339	0.3	W 1	0.1	TRANS.SPECIALES

FOOT NOTES – NOTES

TABLE 1 –
1 Prior to 1981, special trade.
TABLEAU 1 –
1 Avant 1981, commerce spécial.

1. HISTORICAL SERIES, 1959–1994 SPECIAL TRADE, IMPORTS C.I.F., EXPORTS F.O.B. # 1
SERIES HISTORIQUES, 1959–1994 COMMERCE SPECIAL, IMPORTATIONS C.A.F., EXPORTATIONS F.O.B

YEAR ANNEE	VALUE IN MILLION FRANCS / VALEUR EN MILLION FRANCS: MERCHANDISE – MARCHANDISE		GOLD – OR		CONVERSION FACTORS U.S. CENTS PER FRANC / FACTEURS DE CONVERSION CENTS E.U. PAR FRANC		INDEX NUMBERS – INDICES: QUANTUM		UNIT VALUE / VALEUR UNITAIRE	
	IMPORTS	EXPORTS	IMPORTS	EXPORTS	IMPORTS	EXPORTS	IMPORTS	EXPORTS	IMPORTS	EXPORTS
1959	20.10	8.90			20.2550	20.2550				
1960	21.80	8.90			20.2550	20.2550				
1961	22.60	12.20			20.2550	20.2550				
1962	21.20	8.30			20.2550	20.2550				
1963	25.40	6.20			20.2550	20.2550				
1964	25.10	7.10			20.2550	20.2550				
1965	27.30	6.60			20.2550	20.2550				
1966	32.30	7.60			20.2550	20.2550				
1967	38.40	6.70			20.2550	20.2550				
1968	39.10	5.10			20.2550	20.2550				
1969	49.70	5.90			19.3650	19.3650				
1970	65.20	15.00			18.0050	18.0050				
1971	62.30	14.30			18.0050	18.0050				
1972	73.70	21.30			19.8269	19.8315				
1973	77.90	23.60			22.5579	22.5660				
1974	125.60	25.20			20.8098	20.8216				
1975	102.30	26.70			23.3459	23.3824				
1976	129.40	39.00			20.9027	20.9217				
1977	126.00	16.90			20.3537	20.3616				
1978	134.40	17.10			22.1937	22.2006				
1979	148.60	19.00			23.5355	23.5297				
1980	177.20	24.20			23.6663	23.6566				
1981	220.40	38.60			18.4753	18.4478				
1982	276.30	41.20			15.2158	15.2158				
1983	281.00	44.40			13.1780	13.1600				
1984	359.50	64.20			12.2121	12.2121				
1985	280.00	44.00			12.0000	12.0000				
1986	348.30	113.30			14.4991	14.4686				
1987	343.48	134.45			16.6585	16.6382				
1988	366.72	74.89			16.7873	16.7873				
1989	533.13	127.49			15.6737	15.6737				
1990	470.99	139.94			18.3645	18.3645				
1991	458.72	170.78			17.7239	17.7239				
1992	404.19	134.08			18.8900	18.8900				
1993	344.05	4.42			20.2042	20.2042				
1994	413.65	68.67			17.0590	17.0590				

2. IMPORTS BY BROAD ECONOMIC CATEGORY AND EXPORTS BY INDUSTRIAL ORIGIN. (PERCENTAGE OF TOTAL VALUE)
IMPORTATIONS PAR CATEGORIES ECONOMIQUES ET EXPORTATIONS PAR BRANCHE D'ACTIVITE. (EN POURCENTAGE DE LA VALEUR TOTALE)

IMPORTS – IMPORTATIONS

	1988	1989	1990	1991	1992	1993	1994
TOTAL IMPORTS–IMPORTATIONS TOTALES	100.	100.					
1 FOOD BEV–ALIMENTATION BOISSONS	18.1	17.4					
11 PRIMARY–PRODUITS DE BASE	7.0	8.9					
111 FOR INDUSTRY–POUR L'INDUSTRIE	0.7	0.5					
112 FOR HOUSEHOLDS–POUR LES MENAGES	6.3	8.4					
12 PROCESSED–PRODUITS ELABORES	11.1	8.6					
121 FOR INDUSTRY–POUR L'INDUSTRIE	0.6	0.4					
122 FOR HOUSEHOLDS–POUR LES MENAGES	10.5	8.2					
2 IND SUPPLIES–APPROV INDUSTRIELS	19.8	10.7					
21 PRIMARY–PRODUITS DE BASE	1.1	0.6					
22 PROCESSED–PRODUITS ELABORES	18.7	10.1					
3 FUELS–COMBUSTIBLES	19.7	18.5					
31 PRIMARY–PRODUITS DE BASE	0.2	0.1					
32 PROCESSED–PRODUITS ELABORES	19.6	18.4					
321 MOTOR SPIRIT–ESSENCE							
322 OTHER–AUTRES	19.6	18.4					
4 MACHINERY–EQUIPEMENT	12.1	7.6					
41 CAPITAL EQUIPMENT–MACHINES	10.3	6.4					
42 PARTS–PIECES ACCESSOIRES	1.8	1.2					
5 TRANSPORT–TRANSPORT	13.2	29.4					
51 PASSENGER CARS–AUTOMOBILES	1.8	1.5					
52 OTHER–AUTRES	7.4	25.2					
521 INDUSTRIAL–INDUSTRIELS	7.2	25.1					
522 NON INDUSTRIAL–NON INDUSTRIEL	0.1	0.2					
53 PARTS–PIECES ACCESSOIRES	4.1	2.6					
6 CONSUM GOODS–BIENS CONSOMMATION	16.2	11.3					
61 DURABLE–DURABLES	4.7	3.4					
62 SEMI DURABLE–SEMI DURABLES	7.4	4.9					
63 NON DURABLE–NON DURABLES	4.1	3.1					
7 GOODS NES–BIENS NDA	0.8	5.1					

EXPORTS – EXPORTATIONS

	1988	1989	1990	1991	1992	1993	1994
TOTAL EXPORTS–EXPORTATIONS TOTALES	100.	100.					
1 AGRICULTURE	99.6	93.2					
2 MINING QUARRY–INDUS EXTRACTIVES							
3 MANUFACTURING–IND MANUFACTUR	0.4	6.8					
31 FOOD BEV TOBACCO–ALIM BOISS TAB							
32 TEXTILES–INDUSTRIES TEXTILES							
33 WOOD & PRODUCTS–BOIS & PRODUITS							
34 PAPER & PRODUCTS–PAPIER & PRODT							
35 CHEMICALS–INDUSTRIES CHIMIQUES							
36 NON METAL MIN–MIN NON METAL							
37 BASIC METAL–IND METAL BASE							
38 METAL MANUF–MANUF METAL	0.4	6.8					
39 OTH MANUF IND–AUTRES MANUF							

3. TRADE BY PRINCIPAL COUNTRIES OF ORIGIN AND DESTINATION (VALUE IN MILLION U.S. DOLLARS)
ECHANGES SELON LES PRINCIPAUX PAYS D'ORIGINE ET DE DESTINATION (VALEUR EN MILLIONS DE DOLLARS EU)

COUNTRIES–PAYS	SPECIAL IMPORTS C.I.F. IMPORTATIONS SPECIALES C.A.F				
	1990	1991	1992	1993	1994
World	86.5	81.3	76.4	69.5	70.6
Africa					
Americas	46.2	46.0	41.2	40.6	32.4
– Northern America	46.2	46.0	41.2	40.6	32.4
– LAIA					
– CACM					
– Caribbean					
– Rest of America					
Asia excl fmr USSR					
– Middle East					
Asia former USSR					
Europe excl fmr USSR	36.6	31.4	30.7	24.4	33.2
– European Union	31.2	27.6	27.8	24.4	33.2
– Eastern Europe					
– Rest of Europe	5.5	3.8	2.9		
Europe former USSR					
Oceania					
Other	3.7	3.8	4.5	4.5	5.0
Canada	46.2	46.0	41.2	38.2	30.2
France, Monaco	31.2	27.6	27.8	24.4	33.2
Areas n.e.s.	3.7	3.8	4.5	4.5	5.0
Other Europe n.e.s.	5.5	3.8	2.9		
USA/Etats–Unis d'Amer				2.5	2.2

COUNTRIES–PAYS	SPECIAL EXPORTS F.O.B. # 1 EXPORTATIONS SPECIALES F.O.B.				
	1990	1991	1992	1993	1994
Monde	41.6	44.0	37.7	5.8	14.1
Afrique					
Amériques	0.1	0.1	0.1	0.1	0.0
– Amérique du Nord	0.1	0.1	0.1	0.1	0.0
– ALAI					
– MCAC					
– Caraïbes					
– Autre Amérique					
Asie anc. URSS exclus					
– Moyen–Orient					
Asie ancienne URSS					
Europe anc. URSS exclus	20.7	24.2	23.5	0.3	11.7
– Union Européenne	16.0	17.3	13.0	0.0	11.3
– Europe de l'Est					
– Autre de l'Europe	4.7	6.9	10.5	0.3	0.3
Europe ancienne URSS					
Océanie					
Autre	20.8	19.6	14.1	5.4	2.4
France, Monaco	16.0	17.3	13.0	0.0	11.3
Bunkers, ship stores	15.9	13.7	12.4	4.9	2.4
Other Europe n.e.s.	4.7	6.9	10.5	0.3	0.3
Areas n.e.s.	4.9	5.9	1.7	0.5	
Canada	0.1	0.1	0.1	0.1	0.0

(VALUE AS PERCENTAGE OF WORLD TOTAL)(VALEURS EN POURCENTAGE DU TOTAL MONDIAL)

	1985	1986	1987	1988	1989	1990	1991	1992	1993	1994
Africa		0.1		0.2	0.1					
Americas		50.0		51.3	43.1	53.4	56.6	53.9	58.5	45.9
– Northern America		49.9		51.3	43.1	53.4	56.6	53.9	58.5	45.9
– LAIA		0.0		0.0	0.0					
– CACM										
– Caribbean		0.0		0.0	0.0					
– Rest of America		0.0		0.0	0.0					
Asia excl fmr USSR		1.6		2.3	6.0					
– Middle East		0.0		0.0	0.0					
Asia former USSR										
Europe excl fmr USSR		48.2		46.2	50.7	42.4	38.7	40.2	35.0	47.1
– European Union		48.0		46.0	50.4	36.0	33.9	36.4	35.0	47.1
– Eastern Europe		0.1		0.0	0.0					
– Rest of Europe		0.1		0.2	0.3	6.3	4.7	3.8		
Europe former USSR		0.1			0.0					
Oceania		0.0		0.1	0.0					
Other		0.1		0.0	0.0	4.3	4.7	5.8	6.5	7.0
Canada		48.4		49.5	42.3	53.4	56.6	53.9	54.9	42.8
France, Monaco		35.0		38.0	47.6	36.0	33.9	36.4	35.0	47.1
Areas n.e.s.		0.1		0.0	0.0	4.3	4.7	5.8	6.5	7.0
Other Europe n.e.s.						6.3	4.7	3.8		
USA/Etats–Unis d'Amer		1.5		1.7	0.9				3.6	3.1

	1985	1986	1987	1988	1989	1990	1991	1992	1993	1994
Afrique										
Amériques		46.3		26.7	35.1	0.3	0.3	0.3	0.9	0.3
– Amérique du Nord		46.3		26.7	35.1	0.3	0.3	0.3	0.9	0.3
– ALAI										
– MCAC										
– Caraïbes										
– Autre Amérique										
Asie anc. URSS exclus					24.0					
– Moyen–Orient										
Asie ancienne URSS										
Europe anc. URSS exclus		53.7		73.3	40.9	49.7	55.1	62.2	5.8	82.7
– Union Européenne		53.7		73.3	40.9	38.5	39.3	34.4	0.4	80.3
– Europe de l'Est										
– Autre de l'Europe						11.2	15.8	27.8	5.4	2.4
Europe ancienne URSS										
Océanie										
Autre		0.0		0.0	0.0	49.9	44.6	37.5	93.4	17.0
France, Monaco		35.7		57.2	25.2	38.5	39.3	34.4	0.4	80.3
Bunkers, ship stores						38.2	31.2	32.9	84.7	17.0
Other Europe n.e.s.						11.2	15.8	27.8	5.4	2.4
Areas n.e.s.		0.0		0.0	0.0	11.7	13.4	4.6	8.7	
Canada		3.9		2.4	12.0	0.3	0.3	0.3	0.9	0.3

4. Special Imports C.I.F. by Commodities according to the S.I.T.C. (Rev. 2) in million U.S. Dollars
Importations Spéciales C.A.F. par Produits d'après la C.T.C.I. (Rév. 2) en millions de Dollars E.U.

SITC CTCI	COMMODITY	1991 QUANTITY QUANTITE	1991 VALUE VALEUR	1992 QUANTITY QUANTITE	1992 VALUE VALEUR	1993 QUANTITY QUANTITE	1993 VALUE VALEUR	1994 QUANTITY QUANTITE	1994 VALUE VALEUR	PRODUIT
	ALL COMMODITIES		81.4		76.4		69.6		70.6	TOUS PRODUITS
0	FOOD AND LIVE ANIMALS						15.4		13.2	ALIMENTS,ANIMAUX VIVANTS
334	PETROLEUM PRODUCTS,REFIN		18.2		15.1	W 41104	8.9	W 37646	6.7	PRODUITS RAFFINES
931	*SPECIAL TRANSACTIONS					W 16647	45.4	W 17327	50.9	TRANS.SPECIALES

5. Special Exports F.O.B. by Commodities according to the S.I.T.C. (Rev. 2) in million U.S. Dollars
Exportations Spéciales F.O.B. par Produits d'après la C.T.C.I. (Rév. 2) en millions de Dollars E.U.

SITC CTCI	COMMODITY	1991		1992		1993		1994		PRODUIT
		QUANTITY QUANTITE	VALUE VALEUR	QUANTITY QUANTITE	VALUE VALEUR	QUANTITY QUANTITE	VALUE VALEUR	QUANTITY QUANTITE	VALUE VALEUR	
	ALL COMMODITIES # 1		44.0		37.8		5.9		14.2	TOUS PRODUITS
034	FISH,FRESH,CHILLED,FROZN		24.9		19.7			W 20	0.1	POISSON FRAIS, REFRIG,CONG
035	FISH SALTED,DRIED,SMOKED		5.2		5.5	W 34	0.4	W 43	0.4	POISSON SECHE,SALE,FUME
081	*FEEDING STUFF FOR ANIML		0.3		0.3					NOURRITURE POUR ANIMAUX
931	*SPECIAL TRANSACTIONS		13.8		12.4	W 20834	5.5	W 14654	13.7	TRANS.SPECIALES

FOOT NOTES – NOTES

TABLE 1 –
1 Export data for 1993 reflect the moratorium on the shipmen t of fish products.
TABLE 3 –
1 Export data for 1993 reflect the moratorium on the shipmen t of fish products.
TABLE 5 –
1 Data for 1993 reflect the moratorium on the shipment of fish products.
TABLEAU 1 –
1 En 1993 les données des exportations réfléchissen t l'application du moratoire sur les produits de la pêche
TABLEAU 3 –
1 En 1993 les données des exportations réfléchissen t l'application du moratoire sur les produits de la pêche
TABLEAU 5 –
1 En 1993 les données réfléchissent l'application d u moratoire sur les produits de la pêche.

1. HISTORICAL SERIES, 1962–1997 SPECIAL TRADE, IMPORTS C.I.F., EXPORTS F.O.B.
SERIES HISTORIQUES, 1962–1997 COMMERCE SPECIAL, IMPORTATIONS C.A.F., EXPORTATIONS F.O.B

YEAR ANNEE	VALUE IN MILLION E.C. DOLLARS VALEUR EN MILLION E.C. DOLLARS MERCHANDISE –MARCHANDISE		GOLD –OR		CONVERSION FACTORS U.S. CENTS PER E.C. DOLLAR FACTEURS DE CONVERSION CENTS E.U. PAR E.C. DOLLAR		INDEX NUMBERS –INDICES QUANTUM		UNIT VALUE VALEUR UNITAIRE	
	IMPORTS	EXPORTS	IMPORTS	EXPORTS	IMPORTS	EXPORTS	IMPORTS	EXPORTS	IMPORTS	EXPORTS
1962	12.50	6.10			58.3300	58.3300				
1963	12.80	6.30			58.3300	58.3300				
1964	16.10	6.50			58.3300	58.3300				
1965	14.80	6.40			58.3300	58.3300				
1966	16.10	6.70			58.3300	58.3300				
1967	15.80	6.30			57.6500	57.6500				
1968	20.00	7.50			50.0000	50.0000				
1969	24.40	7.60			50.0000	50.0000				
1970	30.50	7.10			50.0000	50.0000				
1971	36.00	5.90			50.7166	50.7166				
1972	35.20	6.60			52.1216	52.1216				
1973	38.10	10.10			51.0808	51.0808				
1974	52.30	14.60			48.7301	48.7301				
1975	53.90	16.50			46.2878	46.2878				
1976	62.00	24.70			38.0480	38.0480				
1977	81.90	27.00			37.0370	37.0370				
1978	97.70	44.30			37.0370	37.0370				
1979	125.10	39.90			37.0370	37.0370				
1980	154.20	42.50			37.0370	37.0370				
1981	157.10	65.90			37.0370	37.0370				
1982	175.80	87.10			37.0370	37.0370				
1983	190.00	110.80			37.0370	37.0370				
1984	206.80	144.60			37.0370	37.0370				
1985	213.80	170.90			37.0370	37.0370				
1986	235.70	172.30			37.0370	37.0370				
1987	266.40	141.30			37.0370	37.0370				
1988	330.10	230.20			37.0370	37.0370				
1989	344.20	201.40			37.0370	37.0370				
1990	367.40	223.40			37.0370	37.0370				
1991	377.10	181.20			37.0370	37.0370				
1992	356.60	210.90			37.0370	37.0370				
1993	362.70	156.10			37.0370	37.0370				
1994	351.00	136.10			37.0370	37.0370				
1995	366.70	115.20			37.0370	37.0370				
1996	356.00	125.20			37.0370	37.0370				
1997		124.50				37.0370				

2. IMPORTS BY BROAD ECONOMIC CATEGORY AND EXPORTS BY INDUSTRIAL ORIGIN. (PERCENTAGE OF TOTAL VALUE)
IMPORTATIONS PAR CATEGORIES ECONOMIQUES ET EXPORTATIONS PAR BRANCHE D'ACTIVITE.(EN POURCENTAGE DE LA VALEUR TOTALE)

IMPORTS – IMPORTATIONS

	1991	1992	1993	1994	1995	1996	1997
TOTAL IMPORTS–IMPORTATIONS TOTALES			100.	100.	100.		
1 FOOD BEV–ALIMENTATION BOISSONS			24.4	22.1	22.1		
11 PRIMARY–PRODUITS DE BASE			11.5	9.4	8.2		
111 FOR INDUSTRY–POUR L'INDUSTRIE			6.6	4.1	2.6		
112 FOR HOUSEHOLDS–POUR LES MENAGES			4.9	5.3	5.6		
12 PROCESSED–PRODUITS ELABORES			12.9	12.7	13.9		
121 FOR INDUSTRY–POUR L'INDUSTRIE			1.3	1.9	1.5		
122 FOR HOUSEHOLDS–POUR LES MENAGES			11.5	10.8	12.4		
2 IND SUPPLIES–APPROV INDUSTRIELS			37.4	35.7	34.9		
21 PRIMARY–PRODUITS DE BASE			1.1	1.0	0.6		
22 PROCESSED–PRODUITS ELABORES			36.3	34.7	34.2		
3 FUELS–COMBUSTIBLES			5.5	6.1	5.9		
31 PRIMARY–PRODUITS DE BASE			1.0	0.9	0.9		
32 PROCESSED–PRODUITS ELABORES			4.5	5.2	5.0		
321 MOTOR SPIRIT–ESSENCE			2.0	2.0	1.9		
322 OTHER–AUTRES			2.5	3.2	3.1		
4 MACHINERY–EQUIPEMENT			10.1	13.3	13.1		
41 CAPITAL EQUIPMENT–MACHINES			8.7	11.9	11.9		
42 PARTS–PIECES ACCESSOIRES			1.4	1.4	1.2		
5 TRANSPORT–TRANSPORT			7.0	6.1	6.1		
51 PASSENGER CARS–AUTOMOBILES			1.7	1.6	1.6		
52 OTHER–AUTRES			2.2	2.1	2.3		
521 INDUSTRIAL–INDUSTRIELS			2.2	2.0	2.2		
522 NON INDUSTRIAL–NON INDUSTRIEL			0.1	0.1	0.1		
53 PARTS–PIECES ACCESSOIRES			3.0	2.4	2.2		
6 CONSUM GOODS–BIENS CONSOMMATION			15.5	16.5	17.6		
61 DURABLE–DURABLES			2.9	3.4	4.2		
62 SEMI DURABLE–SEMI DURABLES			7.3	7.8	8.2		
63 NON DURABLE–NON DURABLES			5.3	5.3	5.2		
7 GOODS NES–BIENS NDA			0.0	0.1	0.3		

EXPORTS – EXPORTATIONS

	1991	1992	1993	1994	1995	1996	1997
TOTAL EXPORTS–EXPORTATIONS TOTALES			100.	100.	100.	100.	100.
1 AGRICULTURE			56.1	41.5	53.8	54.9	42.4
2 MINING QUARRY–INDUS EXTRACTIVES				0.2			
3 MANUFACTURING–IND MANUFACTUR			43.9	58.3	46.2	45.1	57.6
31 FOOD BEV TOBACCO–ALIM BOISS TAB			28.6	33.8	27.7	25.7	39.3
32 TEXTILES–INDUSTRIES TEXTILES			3.7	4.3	4.6	1.6	1.3
33 WOOD & PRODUCTS–BOIS & PRODUITS			0.0	0.0	0.0	0.0	0.1
34 PAPER & PRODUCTS–PAPIER & PRODT			1.3	1.3	1.5	1.8	2.0
35 CHEMICALS–INDUSTRIES CHIMIQUES			1.8	1.1	1.6	1.7	1.6
36 NON METAL MIN–MIN NON METAL			0.0	0.0	0.0	0.2	0.3
37 BASIC METAL–IND METAL BASE			1.2	2.2	2.7	3.6	2.5
38 METAL MANUF–MANUF METAL			6.1	14.0	6.5	7.4	9.6
39 OTH MANUF IND–AUTRES MANUF			1.1	1.4	1.5	2.9	0.8

3. TRADE BY PRINCIPAL COUNTRIES OF ORIGIN AND DESTINATION (VALUE IN MILLION U.S. DOLLARS) ECHANGES SELON LES PRINCIPAUX PAYS D'ORIGINE ET DE DESTINATION (VALEUR EN MILLIONS DE DOLLARS EU)

COUNTRIES–PAYS	SPECIAL IMPORTS C.I.F. IMPORTATIONS SPECIALES C.A.F				
	1993	1994	1995	1996	1997
World	133.7	130.0	134.4		
Africa	0.0	0.1	0.1		
Americas	92.3	88.6	96.8		
– Northern America	54.4	49.5	55.0		
– LAIA	4.2	2.8	2.9		
– CACM	0.9	0.8	0.5		
– Caribbean	31.6	33.2	36.0		
– Rest of America	1.3	2.3	2.4		
Asia excl fmr USSR	8.1	8.0	7.8		
– Middle East	0.0	0.1	0.0		
Asia former USSR					
Europe excl fmr USSR	33.0	33.1	29.5		
– European Union	32.1	32.2	28.9		
– Eastern Europe	0.2	0.4	0.1		
– Rest of Europe	0.7	0.5	0.4		
Europe former USSR	0.1	0.0	0.0		
Oceania	0.2	0.2	0.2		
Other					
USA/Etats–Unis d'Amer	49.6	46.6	50.7		
Trinidad and Tobago	20.2	21.9	23.0		
United Kingdom	15.8	16.4	17.4		
Italy/Italie	9.2	8.0	3.0		
Barbados/Barbade	5.2	5.1	6.0		
Canada	4.7	2.9	4.3		
Japan/Japon	3.4	3.6	3.1		
Germany/Allemagne	2.5	1.9	2.3		
Jamaica/Jamaïque	2.4	2.2	2.1		
Netherlands/Pays–Bas	1.5	2.1	2.5		
Brazil/Brésil	2.7	1.3	1.2		
Guyana	1.1	1.8	1.9		
Other Asia n.e.s.	1.6	1.5	1.5		
China/Chine	1.1	1.1	1.4		
France, Monaco	0.8	1.5	1.2		
Dominica/Dominique	0.9	1.1	1.0		
Saint Lucia/Ste–Lucie	0.7	0.6	1.6		
Venezuela	0.7	0.9	0.9		
Spain/Espagne	0.9	0.5	0.8		
Netherlands Antilles	1.0	0.7	0.5		
Denmark/Danemark	0.7	0.7	0.5		
Honduras	0.7	0.6	0.3		
Korea, Republic of	0.2	0.5	0.7		
Grenada/Grenade	0.4	0.5	0.4		
Belgium–Luxembourg	0.4	0.5	0.4		
Ireland/Irlande	0.2	0.5	0.4		
Switzerland,Liechtenst.	0.6	0.3	0.2		
Martinique	0.1	0.0	0.9		
Antigua and Barbuda	0.3	0.5	0.2		
Colombia/Colombie	0.3	0.3	0.3		
Panama	0.1	0.3	0.5		
China, Hong Kong SAR	0.3	0.3	0.2		
Indonesia/Indonésie	0.2	0.3	0.3		
Saint Kitts and Nevis	0.2	0.2	0.2		
Argentina/Argentine	0.3	0.1	0.2		
Thailand/Thaïlande	0.5	0.1	0.1		
Guatemala	0.2	0.2	0.2		
Singapore/Singapour	0.2	0.2	0.2		
Sweden/Suède	0.1	0.1	0.3		
Norway,Svalbard and JM	0.1	0.2	0.2		

COUNTRIES–PAYS	SPECIAL EXPORTS F.O.B. EXPORTATIONS SPECIALES F.O.B.				
	1993	1994	1995	1996	1997
Monde	57.8	50.4	59.4	50.4	46.1
Afrique				0.0	0.0
Amériques	32.1	33.7	35.0	29.3	30.7
– Amérique du Nord	4.4	4.7	5.7	3.7	3.4
– ALAI	0.0	0.0	0.0	0.1	0.1
– MCAC	0.0	0.0			
– Caraïbes	27.4	28.1	28.8	25.0	26.5
– Autre Amérique	0.2	0.8	0.5	0.5	0.7
Asie anc. URSS exclus	0.0	0.0	0.0	0.0	0.1
– Moyen–Orient					0.0
Asie ancienne URSS					
Europe anc. URSS exclus	25.7	16.6	24.4	21.1	15.3
– Union Européenne	25.7	16.6	24.4	21.1	15.3
– Europe de l'Est				0.0	
– Autre de l'Europe	0.0		0.0		0.0
Europe ancienne URSS					
Océanie	0.0				0.0
Autre		0.0			
United Kingdom	23.5	15.8	24.2	19.9	14.4
Saint Lucia/Ste–Lucie	6.8	6.5	6.8	5.5	6.3
Trinidad and Tobago	6.0	5.3	5.2	5.2	4.6
USA/Etats–Unis d'Amer	4.3	4.7	5.6	3.6	3.3
Antigua and Barbuda	3.7	3.8	3.8	3.7	4.2
Barbados/Barbade	2.1	3.4	3.7	3.5	2.9
Dominica/Dominique	3.1	2.8	2.7	2.2	2.1
Saint Kitts and Nevis	1.7	2.6	2.0	1.6	2.3
Grenada/Grenade	1.8	1.3	1.9	1.3	1.7
Jamaica/Jamaïque	0.9	0.9	0.7	1.0	1.6
Guyana	0.2	0.8	0.5	0.5	0.7
Italy/Italie	1.9	0.4	0.0	0.0	0.1
Martinique	0.4	0.6	1.0		
Montserrat	0.4	0.5	0.4	0.3	0.3
France, Monaco	0.0	0.0	0.1	0.5	0.7
Netherlands Antilles	0.2	0.2	0.2	0.3	0.3
Netherlands/Pays–Bas	0.2	0.2	0.0	0.6	0.0
Haiti/Haïti	0.2	0.1	0.0	0.2	0.1
Canada	0.1	0.1	0.1	0.1	0.1
Venezuela	0.0	0.0	0.0	0.1	0.1
Portugal		0.2			
Germany/Allemagne	0.0	0.0	0.1	0.0	0.0
Japan/Japon	0.0	0.0	0.0	0.0	0.1
Turks and Caicos Isls			0.0		0.1
Guadeloupe	0.0	0.0	0.1		
Cuba			0.1		
Belize/Bélize	0.0				0.0
Colombia/Colombie					0.0
Belgium–Luxembourg	0.0	0.0		0.0	
Guatemala	0.0				
Ireland/Irlande				0.0	0.0
Other Asia n.e.s.		0.0	0.0		0.0
Poland/Pologne				0.0	
China, Hong Kong SAR			0.0		
Korea, Republic of	0.0				
Switzerland,Liechtenst.	0.0		0.0		0.0
Singapore/Singapour			0.0		
Indonesia/Indonésie					0.0
China/Chine		0.0	0.0	0.0	0.0
Areas n.e.s.		0.0			

(VALUE AS PERCENTAGE OF WORLD TOTAL)(VALEURS EN POURCENTAGE DU TOTAL MONDIAL)

	1988	1989	1990	1991	1992	1993	1994	1995	1996	1997
Africa			0.0	0.1	0.0	0.0	0.1	0.1		
Americas	15.9	63.7	65.7	67.9	69.9	69.0	68.2	72.0		
– Northern America		44.8	40.3	38.5	39.8	40.7	38.1	40.9		
– LAIA			3.0	2.5	3.1	3.1	2.1	2.2		
– CACM			0.5	1.5	1.4	0.7	0.6	0.3		
– Caribbean	15.5	18.6	21.2	24.9	24.7	23.6	25.6	26.8		
– Rest of America	0.4	0.4	0.5	0.5	0.9	1.0	1.7	1.8		
Asia excl fmr USSR			7.2	5.9	6.5	6.0	6.1	5.8		
– Middle East			0.0	0.0	0.0	0.0	0.1	0.0		
Asia former USSR										
Europe excl fmr USSR		21.3	27.0	25.8	23.6	24.7	25.5	21.9		
– European Union		21.3	26.3	25.2	23.0	24.0	24.8	21.5		
– Eastern Europe			0.3	0.2	0.1	0.1	0.3	0.1		
– Rest of Europe			0.4	0.4	0.4	0.5	0.4	0.3		
Europe former USSR			0.0	0.0	0.0	0.1	0.0	0.0		
Oceania			0.1	0.2	0.0	0.1	0.1	0.2		
Other	84.1	15.0	0.1	0.1	0.0					
USA/Etats–Unis d'Amer		41.8	36.4	35.1	36.7	37.1	35.8	37.7		
Trinidad and Tobago	9.2	10.8	12.5	16.0	16.7	15.1	16.8	17.1		
United Kingdom		14.5	17.7	12.5	17.1	11.8	12.6	12.9		
Italy/Italie		0.9	0.9	0.7	0.5	6.9	6.2	2.2		
Barbados/Barbade	3.2	3.9	4.1	3.9	3.4	3.9	4.0	4.4		
Canada		3.0	3.9	3.4	3.1	3.5	2.3	3.2		
Japan/Japon			3.3	2.4	2.8	2.6	2.8	2.3		
Germany/Allemagne				2.0	2.0	1.9	1.5	1.7		
Jamaica/Jamaïque	1.2	1.3	1.3	1.4	1.5	1.8	1.7	1.5		
Netherlands/Pays–Bas		1.9	3.0	5.9	1.7	1.1	1.6	1.9		

	1988	1989	1990	1991	1992	1993	1994	1995	1996	1997
Afrique									0.0	0.0
Amériques	41.7	52.2	45.4	43.5	46.4	55.5	66.9	58.9	58.1	66.6
– Amérique du Nord		14.8	10.7	5.6	4.8	7.6	9.4	9.5	7.3	7.4
– ALAI			0.0	0.0	0.0	0.0	0.1	0.1	0.1	0.2
– MCAC				0.0	0.0	0.0	0.0			
– Caraïbes	41.6	37.2	33.5	37.8	41.5	47.5	55.7	48.5	49.7	57.4
– Autre Amérique	0.1	0.1	1.2	0.1	0.1	0.3	1.7	0.8	1.1	1.5
Asie anc. URSS exclus			0.0	0.1	0.0	0.0	0.1	0.1	0.0	0.2
– Moyen–Orient										0.0
Asie ancienne URSS										
Europe anc. URSS exclus		46.9	54.6	56.4	53.6	44.4	33.0	41.0	41.8	33.3
– Union Européenne		46.9	54.6	56.4	53.6	44.4	33.0	41.0	41.8	33.2
– Europe de l'Est			0.0						0.0	
– Autre de l'Europe				0.0	0.0	0.0		0.0		0.0
Europe ancienne URSS										
Océanie						0.0				0.0
Autre	58.3	1.0	0.0	0.0			0.0			
United Kingdom		43.2	54.0	54.7	41.6	40.7	31.4	40.7	39.5	31.1
Saint Lucia/Ste–Lucie	5.4	7.0	6.8	9.1	10.2	11.8	12.9	11.5	11.0	13.7
Trinidad and Tobago	25.9	14.0	12.4	12.4	12.3	10.3	10.4	8.7	10.4	10.0
USA/Etats–Unis d'Amer		14.6	10.5	5.3	4.5	7.4	9.3	9.4	7.1	7.1
Antigua and Barbuda	2.5	3.9	3.5	3.3	4.0	6.5	7.5	6.3	7.3	9.0
Barbados/Barbade	2.0	3.7	3.4	2.8	3.2	3.6	6.8	6.2	7.0	6.3
Dominica/Dominique	1.8	2.7	2.7	3.9	3.7	5.3	5.6	4.6	4.4	4.6
Saint Kitts and Nevis	1.3	2.2	2.3	2.3	2.2	3.0	5.2	3.3	3.1	4.9
Grenada/Grenade	0.6	1.1	0.8	1.4	2.5	3.1	2.6	3.2	2.6	3.6
Jamaica/Jamaïque	1.7	2.0	0.8	1.6	2.0	1.5	1.8	1.3	2.0	3.4

4. Special Imports C.I.F. by Commodities according to the S.I.T.C. (Rev. 2) in million U.S. Dollars
Importations Spéciales C.A.F. par Produits d'après la C.T.C.I. (Rév. 2) en millions de Dollars E.U.

SITC CTCI	COMMODITY	1994 QUANTITY QUANTITE	1994 VALUE VALEUR	1995 QUANTITY QUANTITE	1995 VALUE VALEUR	1996 QUANTITY QUANTITE	1996 VALUE VALEUR	1997 QUANTITY QUANTITE	1997 VALUE VALEUR	PRODUIT
	ALL COMMODITIES		130.1		134.5					TOUS PRODUITS
0	FOOD AND LIVE ANIMALS		27.1		27.3					ALIMENTS,ANIMAUX VIVANTS
01	MEAT AND PREPARATIONS		7.0		8.0					VIANDES ET PREPARATIONS
011	MEAT FRESH,CHILLD,FROZEN	W 5199	5.5	W 5822	6.0					VIANDES FRAICHES,REF,CONGE
0111	BOVINE MEAT FRESH,FROZEN	W 131	0.5	W 169	0.6					VIANDES BOVIN FRAI,REF
01112	BOVINE MEAT BONELESS	W 127	0.5	W 151	0.6					VIANDES BOVIN DESOSSEES
0114	POULTRY FRESH CHLLD,FRZN	W 4858	4.7	W 5392	5.1					VOLAILLES MORTES
012	MEAT DRIED,SALTED,SMOKED	W 179	0.4	W 215	0.5					VIANDE,ABATS SALES,SECHES
014	MEAT PREPD,PRSVD,NES ETC	W 464	1.2	W 2123	1.6					CONSERVES DE VIANDES
0142	SAUSAGES INCLDING TINNED	W 206	0.5	W 413	0.7					SAUCISSES,SAUCISSONS
0149	OTH PREPARD,PRESRVD MEAT	W 257	0.7	W 1709	1.0					AUTRES PREP DE VIANDES
02	DAIRY PRODCTS,BIRDS'EGGS		2.6		3.0					PRODUITS LAITIERS,OEUFS
022	MILK AND CREAM	W 1246	1.8	W 1203	2.2					LAIT ET CREME
0224	MILK,CREAM PRESERVED ETC	W 1183	1.7	W 1154	2.1					LAIT,CREME CONS,CONC
02242	MILK DRY,1.5% FAT OR LES	W 254	0.5	W 277	0.8					LAIT POUDRE INF 1.5%
02243	MILK DRY,OVER 1.5% FAT	W 334	0.7	W 270	0.8					LAIT POUDRE SUP 1.5%
02249	MILK(EX DRY) PRSVD,SWEET	W 595	0.6	W 606	0.6					LAIT CONS,CONC SUCRE
024	CHEESE AND CURD	W 200	0.7	W 178	0.8					FROMAGE ET CAILLEBOTTE
03	FISH AND PREPARATIONS		0.9		1.0					POISSONS ET PREPARATIONS
035	FISH SALTED,DRIED,SMOKED	W 165	0.6	W 160	0.6					POISSON SECHE,SALE,FUME
04	CEREALS AND PREPARATIONS		8.4		6.6					CEREALES ET PRODUITS
041	WHEAT ETC UNMILLED	W 10105	2.2							FROMENT,EPEAUTRE
0411	DURUM WHEAT UNMILLED	W 10105	2.2							FROMENT DUR NON MOULU
042	RICE	W 6750	3.0	W 6913	3.3					RIZ
0421	RICE IN HUSK OR HUSKED	W 6750	3.0	W 6913	3.3					RIZ SANS AUTRE PREPARATION
04212	RICE HUSKED	W 6750	3.0	W 6413	3.1					RIZ CARGO
048	CEREAL ETC PREPARATIONS	W 1885	2.8	W 1779	3.2					PREPTNS A BASE CEREALES
0481	PREPD BREAKFAST FOOD ETC	W 374	0.7	W 208	0.7					CEREALES TRAVAILLEES
04812	CEREAL ROASTED, PUFFED	W 363	0.6	W 189	0.7					PRODTS BASE CEREALES
0484	BAKERY PRODUCTS	W 739	1.5	W 746	1.6					PRODUITS DE BOULANGERIE
04841	BREAD,BISCUIT,COM WAFERS	W 272	0.7	W 292	0.8					PAINS,BISCUITS DE MER
04842	PASTRY, CAKES ETC	W 467	0.9	W 453	0.9					PATISSERIE ETC.
05	VEGETABLES AND FRUIT		1.8		2.0					LEGUMES ET FRUITS
054	VEG ETC FRSH,SMPLY PRSVD	W 1002	0.7	W 1586	0.9					LEGUMES FRAIS,CONG,SECS
058	FRUIT PRESERVED,PREPARED	W 497	1.0	W 571	1.0					CONSERVES DE FRUITS
0585	FRUIT OR VEGETABLE JUICE	W 396	0.6	W 469	0.7					JUS DE FRUITS
06	SUGAR AND PREPS,HONEY		2.6		2.7					SUCRES ET PRODUITS
061	SUGAR AND HONEY	W 8179	2.4	W 5774	2.4					SUCRES ET MIEL
0611	RAW BEET AND CANE SUGAR	W 4471	1.5	W 3039	1.2					SUCRES BRUTS
0612	REFINED SUGAR ETC	W 3656	0.9	W 2696	1.2					SUCRES RAFFINES
07	COFFEE,TEA,COCOA,SPICES		0.7		0.8					CAFE,THE,CACAO,EPICES
09	MISC EDIBLE PRODUCTS		3.2		3.4					PREP ALIMENTAIRES DIVERSES
091	MARGARINE AND SHORTENING	W 690	1.2	W 749	1.3					MARGARINE ET GRAISSES
0914	MARGARINE,EDIBLE FAT NES	W 690	1.2	W 749	1.3					MARGARINES,SIMILI SAINDOUX
09141	MARGARINE	W 518	0.9	W 562	1.0					MARGARINE
098	EDIBLE PRODCTS,PREPS NES	W 977	2.1	W 1059	2.2					PREP ALIMENTAIRES NDA
09804	SAUCES,MIXED SEASONINGS	W 300	0.6	W 362	0.7					SAUCES,ASSAISONNEMENTS
09809	MISC FOOD PREPRTIONS NES	W 513	1.3	W 529	1.3					PREP ALIMENTAIRES NDA
1	BEVERAGES AND TOBACCO		2.1		2.7					BOISSONS ET TABACS
11	BEVERAGES		1.8		2.4					BOISSONS
111	NON–ALCOHL BEVERAGES NES	W 412	0.5	W 437	0.5					BOISSONS NON ALCOOLIQUES
11102	FLAVORED WATERS NON–ALCO	W 381	0.4	W 428	0.5					LIMONADES,EAUX GAZEUSES
112	ALCOHOLIC BEVERAGES	W 459	1.4	W 594	1.9					BOISSONS ALCOOLIQUES
1121	WINE OF FRESH GRAPES ETC	W 78	0.3	W 119	0.6					VINS DE RAISINS FRAIS
11212	WINE OF FRESH GRAPES	W 76	0.3	W 118	0.6					VINS DE MOUTS DE RAISINS
1124	DISTILLED ALCOHOLIC BEVS	W 179	0.8	W 194	1.0					ALCOOLS,EAUX–DE–VIE
11249	OTH ALCOHOLC BEVS,CMPNDS	W 146	0.6	W 151	0.7					BOISSONS ALCOOLIQUES NDA
2	CRUDE MATERLS,EXCL FUELS		4.7		3.9					MAT BRUTES NON COMESTIBLES
24	CORK AND WOOD		3.8		3.3					LIEGE ET BOIS
248	WOOD SHAPED,SLEEPERS	W 5908	3.5	W 5293	3.1					BOIS SIMPLEMENT TRAVAILLES
2482	LUMBER SHAPED CONIFER	W 4598	2.5	W 4561	2.5					CONIFERES SCIES,RABOTES
24821	LUMBER SAWN ETC CONIFER	W 1701	0.8	W 1686	0.9					CONIFERES SCIES LONGITUD
24822	LUMBER PLANED ETC CONIFR	W 2897	1.7	W 2875	1.6					CONIFER RABOTES,RAINES
2483	LUMBER SHAPED NON–CONIFR	W 1310	1.1	W 732	0.6					NON CONIFERES SCIES,RABOTES
24831	LUMBER SAWN ETC NON–CON	W 976	0.6	W 553	0.5					SCIES LONGITUDINALEMENT
24832	LUMBER PLANED ETC NONCON	W 335	0.5	W 179	0.2					RABOTES,RAINES,LANGUETES
27	CRUDE FERTLZR,MINRLS NES		0.6		0.3					ENGRAIS MINERAUX BRUTS
3	MINERAL FUELS ETC		8.2		8.2					COMBUSTIBLES MINERAUX LUB
33	PETROLEUM AND PRODUCTS		7.0		7.0					PETROLE ET DERIVES
334	PETROLEUM PRODUCTS,REFIN	W 36524	6.8	W 36175	6.8					PRODUITS RAFFINES
3341	GASOLINE,OTH LIGHT OILS	W 14765	2.6	W 14456	2.7					ESSENCES POUR MOTEURS
33411	MOTOR,AVIATION SPIRIT	W 14764	2.6	W 14456	2.7					ESSENCES MOTEURS D'AVIONS
3343	GAS OILS	W 19812	3.3	W 20692	3.4					GAS OILS
3345	LUBS,PETROLEUM OILS NES	W 1037	0.8	W 576	0.7					HUILES LUBRIFIANTES
33451	LUBS(HIGH PETR CONT) ETC	W 1035	0.8	W 571	0.7					HUILES LUBRIF,H LOURDES
341	*GAS,NATURAL AND MANUFCT	W 3184	1.2	W 3675	1.3					GAZ NATUREL,GAZ MANUFACT
3413	PETROLM GASES,LIQUEFIED	W 3184	1.2	W 3675	1.3					GAZ DE PETROLE LIQUEFIE
34131	LIQUEFIED PROPANE,BUTANE	W 3184	1.2	W 3675	1.3					PROPANE,BUTANE LIQUEFIES
5	CHEMCLS,RELATED PROD NES		13.7		16.5					PRODUITS CHIMIQUES
52	INORGANIC CHEMICALS		0.4		0.5					PROD CHIM INORGANIQUES
53	DYES,TANNING,COLOUR PROD		2.0		1.9					PROD TEINTURE,COLORANTS
533	PIGMENTS,PAINTS,ETC	W 674	2.0	W 579	1.9					PIGMENTS,PEINTURES,VERNIS
5334	VARNISHES,DISTEMPERS ETC	W 506	1.7	W 402	1.5					PEINTURES A L'EAU
53341	WATER–THINNED PAINTS	W 153	0.4	W 101	0.4					PEINTURES DILUEES
53342	OTH PAINTS,VARNISHES ETC	W 343	1.2	W 289	1.1					AUTRES PEINTURES,VERNIS
541	*MEDICINAL,PHARM PRODUCT	K 431614	1.9	K 161408	1.8					PROD MEDICINAUX PHARMACEUT
5417	MEDICAMENTS	K 167082	1.7	K 154036	1.6					MEDICAMENTS
54179	— CONTNG OTH SUBSTANCES	K 160799	1.6	K 147914	1.5					MED CONT AUT SUBSTANCES
55	PERFUME,CLEANING ETC PRD		3.1		3.6					PROD POUR PARFUM,TOILETTE
553	PERFUMERY,COSMETICS,ETC	W 256	1.3	W 289	1.6					PRODUITS DE PARFUMERIE
554	SOAP,CLEANSING ETC PREPS	W 1346	1.8	W 2051	2.0					SAVONS,PRODUITS DETERSIFS
5541	SOAPS	W 584	0.8	W 1121	0.9					SAVONS,PROD TENSIO–ACTIFS
5542	WASHING PREPARATIONS ETC	W 738	1.0	W 906	1.1					PROD ORG TENSIO–ACT NDA
562	*FERTILIZERS,MANUFACTURE	W 5261	1.7	W 3838	2.1					ENGRAIS MANUFACTURES
5629	FERTILIZERS NES	W 5257	1.7	W 3033	2.0					ENGRAIS NDA
56291	NIT–PHOS–POT FERTLZR NES	W 4441	1.4	W 3027	2.0					ENGRAIS CONT N P K
58	PLASTIC MATERIALS ETC		1.3		2.2					MAT PLAST ARTIFICIELLES
583	POLYMERIZATION ETC PRODS	W 689	1.2	W 868	1.9					PROD POLYMERISATION
5839	OTH POLYMRZTION ETC PROD	W 688	1.2	W 867	1.9					AUT PROD POLYMER COPOLYM
59	CHEMICAL MATERIALS NES		3.4		4.5					MAT PROD CHIMIQUES NDA
591	PESTICIDES,DISINFECTANTS	W 963	2.6	W 874	3.5					DESINF,INSECT,FONG,HERB

4. Special Imports C.I.F. by Commodities according to the S.I.T.C. (Rev. 2) in million U.S. Dollars
Importations Spéciales C.A.F. par Produits d'après la C.T.C.I. (Rév. 2) en millions de Dollars E.U.

SITC CTCI	COMMODITY	1994		1995		1996		1997		PRODUIT
		QUANTITY QUANTITE	VALUE VALEUR	QUANTITY QUANTITE	VALUE VALEUR	QUANTITY QUANTITE	VALUE VALEUR	QUANTITY QUANTITE	VALUE VALEUR	
5911	INSECTICIDES,FOR RETAIL	W 178	1.1	W 250	1.1					INSECTICIDES VENTE DET
5912	FUNGICIDES,FOR RETAIL	W 617	1.0	W 477	2.0					FONGICIDES VENTE AU DET
592	STARCH,INULIN,GLUTEN,ETC	W 241	0.5	W 263	0.6					AMIDONS,INUL,GLUT FROM
598	MISCEL CHEM PRODUCTS NES	W 137	0.4	W 279	0.5					PROD DIV INDUST CHIM NDA
6	BASIC MANUFACTURES		33.1		32.3					ART MANUFACTURES
62	RUBBER MANUFACTURES NES		1.4		1.2					CAOUTCHOUC MANUFACTURE
625	RUBBER TYRES, TUBES ETC	W 339	0.9	W 430	0.9					PNEUS CAOUTCHOUC VULCANISE
6259	OTH TYRES,TYRE CASES,ETC	W 258	0.6	W 359	0.6					AUTRES PNEUS RECHAPES FLAPS
62599	TYRES NES,TYRE CASES,ETC	W 251	0.6	W 345	0.6					PNEUS,FLAPS
628	RUBBER ARTICLES NES	W 33	0.5	W 25	0.3					OUVRAGES CAOUTCHOUC NDA
63	WOOD,CORK MANUFACTRS NES		2.5		2.6					OUVRAGES LIEGE ET BOIS
634	VENEERS,PLYWOOD,ETC	W 1810	1.3	W 2010	1.6					PLACAGES,CONTRE–PLAQUES
6342	PLYWOOD OF WOOD SHEETS	W 1764	1.2	W 1939	1.5					BOIS CONTRE–PLAQUES
635	WOOD MANUFACTURES NES	W 336	1.3	W 500	1.1					ART MANUF EN BOIS NDA
6353	BUILDERS WOODWRK,PREFABS	W 201	1.0	W 415	0.9					OUVRAGES DE MENUISERIE
64	PAPER,PAPERBOARD AND MFR		4.8		8.4					PAPIERS,CARTONS & OUVRAGES
641	PAPER AND PAPERBOARD	W 3030	2.9	W 5563	6.1					PAPIERS ET CARTONS
6413	KRAFT PAPER,PAPERBOARD	W 979	1.0	W 3784	3.5					PAPIER ET CARTON KRAFT
64139	KRAFT PAPER PAPERBD,NES	W 979	1.0	W 3784	3.5					PAPIER,CARTON KRAFT NDA
6415	PAPER,PAPERBRD,BULK,NES	W 1056	0.9	W 1607	2.0					PAPIERS,CARTONS ROULEAUX
64151	SEMI–CHEM FLUTING PAPER	W 977	0.7	W 1508	1.8					PAPIER FLUTING
6417	CORRUGATED PAPER ETC,BLK	W 852	0.8	W 1	0.2					PAPIERS,CARTONS ONDULES
64171	KRAFT PAPER CREPED ETC	W 616	0.5							PAPIER KRAFT CREPE ROULEAU
642	PAPER,ETC,PRECUT,ARTS OF	W 643	2.0	W 650	2.4					PAP,CARTONS DECOUPES
6421	PAPER ETC CONTAINERS	W 316	0.6	W 218	0.7					BOITES,SACS EMBALLAGES
6423	EXERCISE BOOKS ETC	W 78	0.5	W 74	0.5					REGISTRES,CAHIERS,CARNETS
6428	PAPER ETC ARTICLES NES	W 206	0.8	W 277	1.1					OUVRAGES EN PATE A PAPIER
64285	PAPER ETC DIAPERS ETC	W 123	0.5	W 130	0.6					SERVIETTES HYGIENIQUES
65	TEXTILE YARN,FABRICS,ETC		3.0		2.7					FILS,TISSUS,ARTICLES TEXTILE
653	WOVN MAN–MADE FIB FABRIC	W 127	0.9	W 171	1.1					TISSUS FIBRES SYNTH,ARTIF
6534	DISC SYN BLEND FABRC NES	W 92	0.6	W 130	0.9					TISSUS FIBRES SYNTH DISCONT
65341	DISC SYN FIB–COTTN FABRC	W 86	0.6	W 122	0.8					TISSUS FIB SYNT DIS MEL COTO
657	SPECIAL TXTL FABRC,PRODS	W 51	0.9	W 48	0.3					TISSUS SPECIAUX
6575	CORDAGE AND MANUFACTURES	W 42	0.9	W 39	0.2					FICELLES,CORDES,CORDAGES
65751	CORDAGE,CABLE,ROPE,TWINE	W 37	0.8	W 28	0.2					CORDAGES TRESSES OU NON
658	TEXTILE ARTICLES NES	W 55	0.5	W 83	0.7					ART FACONNES MAT TEXTILES
66	NONMETAL MINERAL MFS NES		8.5		6.9					ART MIN NON METALLIQUES
661	LIME,CEMENT,BLDG PRODS	W 63483	4.0	W 47085	3.6					CHAUX,CIMENTS MAT CONSTR
6612	CEMENT	W 63190	3.9	W 46992	3.4					CIMENTS HYDRAULIQUES
662	CLAY,REFRACTORY BLDG PRD	W 833	0.9	W 899	0.7					MAT CONST REFRACTAIRES
6624	BRICKS ETC NONREFRACTORY	W 831	0.9	W 896	0.7					BRIQUES ETC CERAM NON REFR
66245	GLAZED CERAMIC SETTS ETC	W 549	0.7	W 527	0.5					AUT CARREAUX CERAMIQUE
663	MINERAL MANUFCTURES NES	W 1552	2.3	W 393	1.1					ART MIN MANUF NDA
6633	MINRL MFS NES NONCERAMIC	W 1536	2.2	W 379	1.0					OUVR MAT MINERALE NDA
66332	CEMENT,ARTFCL STONE PROD	W 1519	2.1	W 328	1.0					OUVRAGES EN CIMENT
664	GLASS	W 136	0.4	W 152	0.5					VERRE
665	GLASSWARE	W 1946	1.0	W 1519	1.1					OUVRAGES EN VERRE
6651	BOTTLES ETC OF GLASS	W 1914	0.9	W 1446	0.9					RECIPIENTS EN VERRE
66511	GLASS BOTTLES ETC NONVAC	W 1914	0.9	W 1446	0.9					BONBONNES,BOUTEILLES,ETC
67	IRON AND STEEL		2.9		3.7					FER ET ACIER
673	IRON,STEEL SHAPES ETC	W 2930	1.3	W 2596	1.7					BARRES,PROFIL FER,ACIER
6731	IRON,STEEL WIRE ROD	W 1177	0.4	W 1009	0.4					FIL MACHINE FER,ACIER
67311	IRON,SIMPLE STL WIRE ROD	W 1162	0.4	W 1009	0.4					FIL MACH AUT ACIER FIN
6732	IRON,STEEL BARS ETC	W 1643	0.8	W 1138	0.8					BARRES FER,ACIER
67322	HIGH CARBON STL BARS ETC	W 1449	0.7	W 906	0.5					BARRES ACIER FIN CARBONE
6733	IRON,STEEL PROFILES ETC	W 110	0.1	W 450	0.6					PROFILES,PALPLAN FER,ACIER
67336	IRN,SMPL STL SHEET PILNG	W 88	0.1	W 421	0.5					PALPLANCHES EN FER,ACIER
674	IRN,STL UNIV,PLATE,SHEET	W 929	1.0	W 1496	1.4					LARGES PLATS,TOLES
6746	IRN,STL THIN PLATE,ROLLD	W 625	0.4	W 1268	1.1					TOLES LAM MOINS 3MM
67461	— OF IRON OR SIMPLE STL	W 625	0.4	W 1268	1.1					TOL NON AC FIN MOINS 3 MM
6749	OTH IRN,STL PLATES,SHEET	W 284	0.6	W 197	0.4					AUTRES TOLES FER,ACIER
67491	— OF IRON OR SIMPLE STL	W 283	0.6	W 196	0.4					AUT TOLES AUTRES ACIER FIN
678	IRON,STL TUBES,PIPES,ETC	W 299	0.6	W 289	0.6					TUBES,TUYAUX EN FONTE,FER
68	NON–FERROUS METALS		0.4		0.4					METAUX NON FERREUX
69	METAL MANUFACTURES NES		9.8		6.7					ART MANUFACT EN METAL NDA
691	STRUCTURES AND PARTS NES	W 804	5.2	W 618	2.1					CONSTRUCT FER,ACIER,ALU
6911	STRUCTURES,PARTS IRN,STL	W 423	4.2	W 337	0.9					CONSTRUCT FER,ACIER,FONTE
6912	STRUCTURES,PARTS ALUMNM	W 381	1.1	W 281	1.2					CONSTRUCT ALUMINIUM
694	STL,COPPR NAILS,NUTS,ETC	W 153	0.7	W 197	0.7					CLOUS,VIS,ECROUS
69402	IRN,STL NUTS,BOLTS,ETC	W 66	0.5	W 63	0.4					BOULONS,VIS,ECROUS FER,AC
695	TOOLS	W 70	0.7	W 73	0.7					OUTILS A MAIN
6953	OTHER HAND TOOLS	W 45	0.5	W 46	0.4					AUTRES OUTILS A MAIN
697	BASE MTL HOUSEHOLD EQUIP	W 261	1.2	W 233	1.2					ART MENAGE MET COMMUNS
6973	DMSTC HEATG,COOKG APPARA	W 194	0.8	W 175	0.8					APPS CHAUF NON ELECTRIQ
69731	IRN,STL DOM COOKG APPARA	W 135	0.6	W 173	0.8					APPS CUISSON FER,ACIER
699	BASE METAL MFRS NES	W 233	1.4	W 453	1.6					ART MANUFACTURES MET NDA
6991	LOCKSMITHS WARES,ETC	W 70	0.6	W 63	0.5					ARTICLES DE SERRURERIE
6997	IRON,STEEL ARTICLES NES	W 63	0.4	W 207	0.6					OUV FONTE,FER,ACIER NDA
69979	IRN,STL MANUFACTURES NES	W 62	0.4	W 194	0.6					AUT OUVRAGES EN FER NDA
7	MACHINES,TRANSPORT EQUIP		26.7		23.8					MACHINES MATERIEL TRANSPORT
71	POWER GENERATING EQUIPMT		1.5		3.2					MACHINES GENERATRICES
713	INTRNL COMBUS PSTN ENGIN	W 90	1.0	W 80	1.0					MOTEURS EXPL COMB INT, PIECE
7133	MARINE PISTON ENGINES	W 32	0.7	W 38	0.7					MOTEURS EXPL POUR BATEAUX
71331	—— OUTBOARD	W 23	0.5	W 26	0.6					MOTEURS BATEAUX HORSBORD
716	ROTATING ELECTRIC PLANT	W 27	0.5	W 117	2.2					APP ELECTR ROTATIFS,PIECES
7162	AC MTRS,GENRTRS,GEN SETS	W 17	0.2	W 100	2.1					MOTEURS ELECTRIQUES
71623	GEN SETS WITH PISTN ENGN	W 9	0.1	W 96	2.0					GROUPES MOTEUR EXPLOSION
72	MACHS FOR SPCL INDUSTRYS		3.2		2.0					MAC SPECIALES POUR INDUST
723	CIVIL ENGNEERG EQUIP ETC	W 163	1.0	W 218	0.8					APPAREILS DE GENIE CIVIL
7234	CONST,MINING MACHNRY NES	W 139	1.0	W 181	0.7					MACH POUR LA CONST, MINES
72342	SLFPRP SHOVELS,EXCAVATRS	W 112	0.8	W 106	0.5					PELLES MECANIQUES
724	TEXTILE,LEATHER MACHNRY	W 24	0.5	W 12	0.2					MACH POUR INDUSTRIE TEXTILE
728	OTH MACHY FOR SPCL INDUS	W 71	1.2	W 32	0.4					AUT MACH IND PARTICULIERES
7284	MACHY FOR SPCL INDUS NES	W 25	0.8	W 7	0.2					MACH SPEC IND PARTICUL.
72842	RUBBER,PLASTICS WRKG MCH	W 6	0.5	W 1	0.1					MACH IND CAOUT MAT PLAST
74	GENRL INDUSTRL MACHY NES		5.1		3.8					MACH APP INDUSTRIE
741	HEATING,COOLING EQUIPMNT	W 109	1.7	W 120	1.1					MACH CHAUFFAGE,PIECES
7414	NONDOM REFRIG EQUIPT,PTS	W 41	0.9	W 48	0.4					MAT PRODUCTION DU FROID
74141	REFRIG EQUIP NONDOMESTIC	W 27	0.5	W 39	0.3					REFIG INDUSTRIELS
74149	PTS NES OF REFRIG EQUIPT	W 15	0.5	W 9	0.1					PIECES POUR MACH FROID
7415	AIR–CONDITIONING MACHNRY	W 34	0.5	W 56	0.6					GROUPES CONDITION AIR

4. Special Imports C.I.F. by Commodities according to the S.I.T.C. (Rev. 2) in million U.S. Dollars
Importations Spéciales C.A.F. par Produits d'après la C.T.C.I. (Rév. 2) en millions de Dollars E.U.

SITC CTCI	COMMODITY	1994 QUANTITY QUANTITE	1994 VALUE VALEUR	1995 QUANTITY QUANTITE	1995 VALUE VALEUR	1996 QUANTITY QUANTITE	1996 VALUE VALEUR	1997 QUANTITY QUANTITE	1997 VALUE VALEUR	PRODUIT
743	PUMPS NES,CENTRFUGES ETC	W 49	0.7	W 38	0.5					POMPES COMPRES,VENT ETC
744	MECHANICAL HANDLING EQU	W 125	1.1	W 167	0.6					EQUIP MANUTENTION PIECES
7442	LIFTING,LOADING MACH NES	W 64	0.6	W 85	0.4					APP LEVAGE,MANUTENTION
745	NONELEC MACHY,TOOLS NES	W 44	0.5	W 65	0.5					AUT MACH NON ELEC,PIECES
749	NONELEC MACH PTS,ACC NES	W 62	1.1	W 112	1.0					PIECES MACH NON ELEC NDA
7492	COCKS,VALVES ETC NES	W 43	0.7	W 94	0.7					ART ROB,SIM POUR TUYAUX
75	OFFICE MACHNES,ADP EQUIP		1.7		1.7					MACH BUREAU TRAIT AUTOM
752	AUTOMTIC DATA PROC EQUIP	W 22	1.1	W 41	1.2					MACH TRAIT INFORMATION
7522	DIGITAL COMPUTERS	W 17	0.9	W 20	0.9					MACH DIGITALES COMPLETES
759	OFFICE,ADP MCH PTS,ACCES	W 7	0.5	W 6	0.3					PIECES DU 751 ET 752
7599	ACCTG,ETC,ADP MCH PTS,AC	W 5	0.4	W 3	0.2					PIECES DU 751 ET 752
76	TELECOMM,SOUND EQUIPMENT		3.7		1.6					EQUIPMENT DE TELECOM
764	TELECOM EQPT,PTS,ACC NES	W 44	3.3	W 39	1.0					EQUIP TELECOM,PIECES
7641	LINE TELEPHONE,ETC EQUIP	W 15	1.2	W 9	0.5					APP TELEPHON PAR FIL
7643	TV,RADIO TRANSMITTRS ETC	W 8	1.6	W 3	0.1					APP EMET TELE RADIO
7649	PTS NES OF EQUIPMT OF 76	W 15	0.5	W 17	0.3					PIECES DE LA DIV 76
77	ELECTRIC MACHNRY NES ETC		5.9		5.3					MACH APP ELECT NDA
771	ELECTRIC POWER MACHY NES	W 63	0.7	W 71	0.5					MACH PROD,TRANS ELECTR
7711	TRANSFORMERS,ELECTRICAL	W 49	0.5	W 65	0.4					TRANSFO ELECTRIQUES
77118	OTHER ELEC TRANSFORMERS	W 45	0.5	W 61	0.4					AUTRES TRANSFO ELECTRIQ
772	SWITCHGEAR ETC,PARTS NES	W 65	1.3	W 100	1.3					APP COUPURE,SECT ETC
7721	SWITCHGEAR ETC	W 65	1.3	W 100	1.3					APP COUPURE,SECTIONMNT
773	ELECTR DISTRIBUTNG EQUIP	W 199	1.4	W 250	1.1					EQUIPMT DISTRIBUTION ELECT
7731	INSULATED WIRE,CABLE ETC	W 188	1.3	W 239	1.0					FILS,CABLES ISOLES ELECT
775	HOUSEHOLD TYPE EQUIP NES	W 215	1.3	W 252	1.4					MACH,APP USAGE DOMESTQUE
7752	DOM REFRIGERATRS,FREEZRS	W 147	0.8	W 161	0.9					REFRIG,CONGEL MENAGER
77521	DOMESTIC REFRIGERATORS	W 113	0.7	W 136	0.8					REFRIGERATEURS
778	ELECTRICAL MACHINERY NES	W 202	1.4	W 195	1.1					AUTRES MACH ELECT NDA
7781	BATTERIES,ACCUMULATORS	W 132	0.6	W 143	0.6					PILES ET ACCUMULATEURS
78	ROAD VEHICLES		5.4		5.8					VEHICULES ROUTIERS
781	PASS MOTOR VEH EXC BUSES	W 386	2.2	W 398	2.2					AUTO TRANSPORT PERSONNES
782	LORRIES,SPCL MTR VEH NES	W 260	1.4	W 399	1.9					VEHICULES SPECIAUX,MARCH
7821	LORRIES,TRUCKS	W 244	1.3	W 352	1.8					VEHICULES TRANSP MARCHAND
783	ROAD MOTOR VEHICLES NES	W 139	0.9	W 137	0.9					VEHICULES ROUTIERS NDA
7831	BUSES	W 97	0.8	W 114	0.8					VOITURES TRANSPORT COMMUN
784	MOTOR VEH PRTS,ACCES NES	W 91	0.8	W 102	0.7					PIECES 722,781,782,783
7849	OTHER MOTOR VEHCL PARTS	W 89	0.8	W 97	0.7					PIECES 722,781,782,783
79	OTHR TRANSPORT EQUIPMENT		0.5		0.6					AUTRE MATERIEL TRANSPORT
793	SHIPS AND BOATS ETC	W 29	0.4	W 24	0.5					NAVIRES BATEAUX,ETC
8	MISC MANUFACTURED GOODS		14.7		19.9					ART MANUFACTURES DIVERS
812	*PLUMBG,HEATNG,LGHTNG EQ	W 153	0.9	W 142	0.7					APPAR SANITAIRES CHAUFFAGE
8124	LIGHTING EQUIPMENT NES	W 44	0.6	W 53	0.5					APPAREILS ECLAIRAGE ETC
81242	LAMPS,FITTINGS BASE METL	W 39	0.5	W 45	0.4					APPAREILS D'ECLAIRAGE
821	*FURNITURE,PARTS THEREOF	W 362	1.9	W 533	2.4					MEUBLES ET PIECES
8211	CHAIRS,SEATS AND PARTS	W 76	0.5	W 143	0.6					SIEGES ET PIECES
82111	CHAIRS AND OTHER SEATS	W 76	0.5	W 142	0.6					SIEGES
8219	FURNITURE AND PARTS NES	W 222	1.1	W 325	1.4					AUTRES MEUBLES ET PIECES
82191	METAL FURNITURE NES	W 42	0.3	W 89	0.5					MEUBLES NDA EN METAL
82192	WOOD FURNITURE NES	W 145	0.7	W 184	0.7					MEUBLES NDA EN BOIS
84	CLOTHING AND ACCESSORIES		3.6		3.7					VETEMENTS
842	MENS OUTERWEAR NOT KNIT	W 24	0.4	W 33	0.5					VET DESSUS POUR HOMMES
843	WOMENS OUTERWEAR NONKNIT	W 243	0.8	W 159	1.0					VET DESSUS FEMMES MAT TEX
8439	— OTHER OUTER GARMENTS	W 224	0.6	W 136	0.6					AUT VET DES FEM MAT TEXT
844	UNDER GARMENTS NOT KNIT	W 47	1.2	W 45	1.1					VETEMENT DESSOUS MAT TEX
8441	— MENS SHIRTS	W 43	1.2	W 40	1.1					CHEMISES HOMMES MAT TEXT
84412	—— OF SYNTHETIC FIBRES	W 41	1.1	W 36	1.0					CHEMISES HOMMES FIB SYNT
846	UNDER GARMENTS KNITTED	W 69	0.8	W 63	0.7					SOUS VETS DE BONNETERIE
8462	— OF COTTON NON ELASTIC	W 59	0.7	W 55	0.6					SOUS–VET BONNET COTON
84629	—— OTHER	W 58	0.7	W 55	0.6					AUT SOUS–VET BONNET COTON
851	*FOOTWEAR	W 185	1.1	W 188	1.3					CHAUSSURES
85102	FOOTWEAR LEATHER	W 114	0.9	W 148	1.1					CHAUS SEMELLES EN CUIR
87	PRECISION INSTRUMNTS NES		0.7		4.5					INSTRUM,APPAR SCIENT NDA
872	MEDICAL INSTRUMENTS NES	W 4	0.2	W 11	1.2					INSTR,APP MEDIC–CHIR NDA
87202	OTH MEDICAL INSTRUMENTS	W 3	0.2	W 9	1.2					INSTRUM,APP MEDECINE
874	MEASURNG,CONTROLNG INSTR	W 16	0.4	W 27	3.1					INSTRUMENTS DE MESURE
8748	ELEC MEAS,CONTRL EQU NES	W 1	0.1	W 7	2.8					APP ELEC ELECTRO MESURE
87483	OTH ELCTRNC MEAS ETC EQU	W 1	0.1	W 7	2.8					AUT APP ELECTRO DE MESURE
88	PHOTO EQU,OPTICL GDS ETC		0.5		0.5					APP,FOURN PHOTO,OP,MONTR
89	MISC MANUFCTRD GOODS NES		6.0		6.9					ART MANUFACTURES DIVERS
892	PRINTED MATTER	W 196	1.7	W 166	1.6					IMPRIMES
8921	PRINTED BOOKS,GLOBES,ETC	W 107	0.9	W 66	0.9					LIVRES,BROCHURES,CARTES
89211	PRINTED BOOKS,PAMPHLETS	W 104	0.9	W 64	0.8					LIVRES,BROCHURES
8928	PRINTED MATTER NES	W 31	0.5	W 33	0.5					IMPRIMES NDA
893	ARTICLES OF PLASTIC NES	W 941	3.0		3.2					OUVRAGES EN MAT DIVIS 58
8931	PLSTC PACKG CONTNRS,LIDS	W 239	0.9	W 301	1.0					ART TRANSP EMBALLAGE ETC
8939	MISC PLASTIC ARTICLES	W 688	2.0	W 555	2.2					ART DIVERS EN MAT DIV 58
89399	OTHR PLASTC ARTICLES NES	W 517	1.8	W 444	1.9					AUT OUV MAT DIV 58
894	TOYS,SPORTING GOODS,ETC	W 64	0.4	W 84	0.7					VOITURES ENFANTS,JOUETS
897	GOLD,SILVER WARE,JEWELRY		0.2		0.6					BIJOUTERIE,ORFEVRERIE
8973	PREC JEWLRY,GLD–SILVWARE		0.1		0.6					BIJOUX OR,ARGENT ORFEVRE
89731	PRECIOUS METAL JEWELLERY		0.1		0.6					ART BIJOUTERIE,JOAILLER
899	OTHER MANUFACTURED GOODS		0.7		0.7					AUT ART MANUF DIVERS NDA

5. Special Exports F.O.B. by Commodities according to the S.I.T.C. (Rev. 2) in million U.S. Dollars
Exportations Spéciales F.O.B. par Produits d'après la C.T.C.I. (Rév. 2) en millions de Dollars E.U.

SITC CTCI	COMMODITY	1994		1995		1996		1997		PRODUIT
		QUANTITY QUANTITE	VALUE VALEUR	QUANTITY QUANTITE	VALUE VALEUR	QUANTITY QUANTITE	VALUE VALEUR	QUANTITY QUANTITE	VALUE VALEUR	
	ALL COMMODITIES		50.4		59.4		50.4		46.2	TOUS PRODUITS
0	FOOD AND LIVE ANIMALS		36.5		47.2		39.2		36.0	ALIMENTS,ANIMAUX VIVANTS
03	FISH AND PREPARATIONS		0.3		1.1		0.3		0.8	POISSONS ET PREPARATIONS
034	FISH,FRESH,CHILLED,FROZN	W 494	0.2	W 213	0.8	W 101	0.3	W 218	0.6	POISSON FRAIS, REFRIG,CONG
0341	FISH FRSH,CHLLD,EX FILLT	W 26	0.1	W 114	0.4	W 54	0.1	W 116	0.4	POISSON FRAIS,REFRIGERE
0342	FISH FROZEN,EXCL FILLETS	W 466	0.2	W 99	0.5	W 45	0.2	W 102	0.3	POISSONS CONGELES
036	SHELL FISH FRESH,FROZEN	W 4	0.1	W 33	0.3	W 4	0.1	W 18	0.2	CRUSTACES,MOLLUSQUES
04	CEREALS AND PREPARATIONS		14.8		15.2		12.1		14.8	CEREALES ET PRODUITS
042	RICE	W 13255	6.1	W 11142	6.4	W 8005	5.4	W 8783	6.0	RIZ
0421	RICE IN HUSK OR HUSKED	W 2043	1.3	W 3869	2.2	W 2955	1.9	W 686	0.5	RIZ SANS AUTRE PREPARATION
04212	RICE HUSKED	W 2041	1.3	W 3869	2.2	W 2955	1.9	W 686	0.5	RIZ CARGO
0422	RICE SEMI–MILLED,MILLED	W 11212	4.9	W 7273	4.3	W 5050	3.6	W 8096	5.5	RIZ POLI,GLACE INCL BRISURES
04221	RICE MILLED UNBROKEN	W 11065	4.8	W 7269	4.3	W 5050	3.6	W 8096	5.5	RIZ POLI,GLACE EXCL BRISURES
046	WHEAT ETC MEAL OR FLOUR	W 19055	8.5	W 17919	8.7	W 12584	6.4	W 17236	8.7	SEMOULE FARINE,FROMENT
04601	FLOUR OF WHEAT OR MESLIN	W 19046	8.5	W 17918	8.7	W 12552	6.4	W 17212	8.7	FARINE DE FROMENT
048	CEREAL ETC PREPARATIONS	W 129	0.2	W 111	0.2	W 88	0.2	W 79	0.2	PREPTNS A BASE CEREALES
0483	MACARONI,SPAGHETTI ETC	W 111	0.2	W 96	0.2	W 86	0.2	W 79	0.2	PATES ALMENTAIRES
05	VEGETABLES AND FRUIT		19.4		28.8		25.1		18.1	LEGUMES ET FRUITS
054	VEG ETC FRSH,SMPLY PRSVD	W 2820	1.6	W 4163	2.5	W 4842	2.8	W 4369	2.6	LEGUMES FRAIS,CONG,SECS
0548	EDIBLE VEG NES FRESH,DRY	W 2730	1.6	W 4095	2.5	W 4789	2.8	W 4313	2.6	RACINES,TUBERCULES
05481	ROOTS,TUBERS FRESH,DRY	W 2730	1.6	W 4095	2.5	W 4789	2.8	W 4313	2.6	RACINES DE MANIOC ETC
057	FRUIT,NUTS,FRESH,DRIED	W 36607	17.6	W 58252	26.0	W 52747	22.3	W 35175	15.5	FRUITS FRAIS OU SECS
0573	BANANA,PLANTAIN,FRSH,DRY	W 35191	17.0	W 55924	25.0	W 50153	21.1	W 33469	14.7	BANANES FRAICHES,SECHEES
0577	NUTS EDIBLE,FRESH,DRIED	W 375	0.2	W 700	0.3	W 937	0.4	W 612	0.3	FRUITS A COQUES
05771	COCONUTS FRESH OR DRIED	W 375	0.2	W 699	0.3	W 937	0.4	W 612	0.3	NOIX DE COCO
0579	FRUIT FRESH OR DRIED NES	W 930	0.5	W 1424	0.8	W 1593	0.9	W 1066	0.6	FRUITS FRAIS,SECS NDA
05797	OTH TROP FRUIT,FRESH,DRY	W 517	0.3	W 874	0.6	W 1050	0.7	W 565	0.4	AVOCATS,MANGUES,GOYAVES
05798	OTHER FRESH FRUIT	W 400	0.2	W 546	0.3	W 522	0.2	W 434	0.2	AUTRES FRUITS FRAIS
058	FRUIT PRESERVED,PREPARED	W 167	0.2	W 102	0.3	W 75	0.1	W 32	0.1	CONSERVES DE FRUITS
0585	FRUIT OR VEGETABLE JUICE	W 166	0.2	W 100	0.3	W 75	0.1	W 32	0.1	JUS DE FRUITS
07	COFFEE,TEA,COCOA,SPICES		0.2		0.3		0.4		0.4	CAFE,THE,CACAO,EPICES
075	SPICES	W 249	0.2	W 400	0.3	W 613	0.4	W 700	0.4	EPICES
0752	SPICES,EX PEPPER,PIMENTO	W 233	0.2	W 373	0.2	W 589	0.4	W 656	0.4	AUTRES EPICES
07526	GINGER (EXCPT SWEETENED)	W 192	0.1	W 321	0.2	W 569	0.3	W 603	0.4	GINGEMBRE
081	*FEEDING STUFF FOR ANIML	W 13648	2.0	W 12268	1.9	W 9396	1.3	W 9972	1.8	NOURRITURE POUR ANIMAUX
0812	BRAN,POLLARD,SHARPS,ETC	W 7847	0.5	W 7201	0.5	W 6630	0.5	W 5628	0.5	SONS
08122	BRAN,ETC OF OTHR CEREALS	W 7144	0.5	W 5771	0.4	W 5473	0.4	W 4764	0.4	SONS D'AUTRES CEREALES
0819	FOOD WASTE AND FEED NES	W 5350	1.5	W 5067	1.5	W 2756	0.9	W 4331	1.4	DECHETS,ALIMENTS NDA
08199	FODDER NES,INCL SWEETNED	W 5350	1.5	W 5067	1.5	W 2756	0.9	W 4331	1.4	PREPARATIONS FOURRAGERES
09	MISC EDIBLE PRODUCTS		0.1		0.1		0.1		0.2	PREP ALIMENTAIRES DIVERSES
098	EDIBLE PRODCTS,PREPS NES	W 15	0.1	W 9	0.1	W 7	0.1	W 20	0.2	PREP ALIMENTAIRES NDA
09809	MISC FOOD PREPRTIONS NES	W 10	0.1	W 5	0.1	W 5	0.1	W 17	0.2	PREP ALIMENTAIRES NDA
1	BEVERAGES AND TOBACCO		1.2		1.0		1.0		1.3	BOISSONS ET TABACS
11	BEVERAGES		1.2		1.0		1.0		1.3	BOISSONS
111	NON–ALCOHL BEVERAGES NES	W 525	0.7	W 609	0.6	W 684	0.8	W 693	1.1	BOISSONS NON ALCOOLIQUES
11102	FLAVORED WATERS NON–ALCO	W 455	0.6	W 462	0.6	W 593	0.8	W 619	1.0	LIMONADES,EAUX GAZEUSES
112	ALCOHOLIC BEVERAGES	W 541	0.6	W 470	0.4	W 173	0.2	W 188	0.3	BOISSONS ALCOOLIQUES
1123	BEER,ALE,STOUT,PORTER	W 540	0.6	W 469	0.4	W 173	0.2	W 187	0.3	BIERES
2	CRUDE MATERLS,EXCL FUELS		0.3		0.2		0.2		0.2	MAT BRUTES NON COMESTIBLES
4	ANIMAL,VEGETABLE OIL,FAT		0.1		0.1		0.1		0.2	HUILES,GRAISSES ANIM,VEG
42	FIXED VEGETABLE OIL,FAT		0.1				0.1		0.2	HUILES VEGETALES FIXES
424	FIXED VEG OIL NONSOFT	W 26	0.1			W 134	0.1	W 181	0.2	AUTRES HUILES VEG FIXES
4243	COCONUT (COPRA) OIL	W 26	0.1			W 134	0.1	W 181	0.2	HJUILE DE COPRAH
5	CHEMCLS,RELATED PROD NES		0.2		0.4		0.5		0.5	PRODUITS CHIMIQUES
59	CHEMICAL MATERIALS NES		0.2		0.3		0.4		0.4	MAT PROD CHIMIQUES NDA
592	STARCH,INULIN,GLUTEN,ETC	W 98	0.2	W 95	0.3	W 152	0.4	W 154	0.4	AMIDONS,INUL,GLUT FROM
5921	STARCH,INULIN,GLUTEN	W 98	0.2	W 95	0.3	W 152	0.4	W 154	0.4	AMID,INUL,GLUT FROMENT
59211	STARCHES,INULIN	W 98	0.2	W 95	0.3	W 152	0.4	W 154	0.4	AMIDONS FECULES INULINE
6	BASIC MANUFACTURES		2.6		3.4		3.6		3.0	ART MANUFACTURES
64	PAPER,PAPERBOARD AND MFR		0.7		0.9		0.9		0.9	PAPIERS,CARTONS & OUVRAGES
642	PAPER,ETC,PRECUT,ARTS OF	W 1805	0.7	W 636	0.9	W 631	0.9	W 731	0.9	PAP,CARTONS DECOUPES
6421	PAPER ETC CONTAINERS	W 1663	0.5	W 562	0.8	W 592	0.8	W 658	0.8	BOITES,SACS EMBALLAGES
6424	PAPER ETC CT TO SIZE NES	W 139	0.2	W 74	0.2	W 38	0.1	W 72	0.1	PAP,CARTONS DECOUPES
64243	TOILET PAPER CUT TO SIZE	W 139	0.2	W 74	0.2	W 38	0.1	W 72	0.1	PAPIER HYGIENIQUE
66	NONMETAL MINERAL MFS NES		0.1		0.1		0.2		0.2	ART MIN NON METALLIQUES
663	MINERAL MANUFCTURES NES					W 24	0.1	W 6	0.2	ART MIN MANUF NDA
67	IRON AND STEEL		1.1		1.6		1.9		1.2	FER ET ACIER
673	IRON,STEEL SHAPES ETC	W 561	0.3	W 546	0.3	W 831	0.4	W 534	0.3	BARRES,PROFIL FER,ACIER
6732	IRON,STEEL BARS ETC	W 418	0.2	W 535	0.3	W 830	0.4	W 534	0.3	BARRES FER,ACIER
67322	HIGH CARBON STL BARS ETC	W 418	0.2	W 533	0.3	W 830	0.4	W 534	0.3	BARRES ACIER FIN CARBONE
674	IRN,STL UNIV,PLATE,SHEET	W 947	0.9	W 1107	1.3	W 1052	1.5	W 832	1.0	LARGES PLATS,TOLES
6749	OTH IRN,STL PLATES,SHEET	W 780	0.8	W 1054	1.3	W 1052	1.5	W 819	0.9	AUTRES TOLES FER,ACIER
67491	— OF IRON OR SIMPLE STL	W 779	0.8	W 1054	1.3	W 1052	1.5	W 819	0.9	AUT TOLES AUTRES ACIER FIN
69	METAL MANUFACTURES NES		0.9		0.9		0.8		0.8	ART MANUFACT EN METAL NDA
691	STRUCTURES AND PARTS NES	W 39	0.1	W 27	0.1	W 52	0.3	W 119	0.4	CONSTRUCT FER,ACIER,ALU
6912	STRUCTURES,PARTS ALUMNM			W 27	0.1	W 52	0.3	W 52	0.4	CONSTRUCT ALUMINIUM
697	BASE MTL HOUSEHOLD EQUIP	W 148	0.6	W 141	0.5	W 55	0.3	W 34	0.2	ART MENAGE MET COMMUNS
6973	DMSTC HEATG,COOKG APPARA	W 147	0.6	W 86	0.4	W 55	0.3	W 34	0.2	APPS CHAUF NON ELECTRIQ
69731	IRN,STL DOM COOKG APPARA	W 147	0.6	W 86	0.4	W 55	0.3	W 34	0.2	APPS CUISSON FER,ACIER
7	MACHINES,TRANSPORT EQUIP		6.2		2.4		2.7		3.4	MACHINES MATERIEL TRANSPORT
71	POWER GENERATING EQUIPMT		0.2		0.3		0.2		0.7	MACHINES GENERATRICES
713	INTRNL COMBUS PSTN ENGIN	W 5	0.1	W 7	0.2	W 16	0.2	W 18	0.7	MOTEURS EXPL COMB INT, PIECE
7131	AIRCRAFT PSTN ENGINS,PTS	W 1	0.1	W 2	0.2	W 2	0.1	W 5	0.5	MOTEURS EXPL P.AVIATION, PIE
71311	AIRCRAFT PISTON ENGINES		0.1	W 1	0.1	W 2	0.1	W 5	0.5	MOTEURS EXPL P.AVIATION
72	MACHS FOR SPCL INDUSTRYS		1.6		0.5		0.5		0.6	MAC SPECIALES POUR INDUST
723	CIVIL ENGNEERG EQUIP ETC	W 285	1.0	W 33	0.5	W 127	0.4	W 84	0.5	APPAREILS DE GENIE CIVIL
7234	CONST,MINING MACHNRY NES	W 218	0.9	W 23	0.4	W 108	0.4	W 75	0.4	MACH POUR LA CONST, MINES
72341	SELF–PROPELLD DOZERS,ETC	W 123	0.4	W 20	0.1	W 95	0.3	W 15	0.1	BULLDOZERS
72342	SLFPRP SHOVELS,EXCAVATRS	W 88	0.5			W 13	0.1	W 48	0.2	PELLES MECANIQUES
72348	PUBLIC WORKS MACHNRY NES	W 1	0.1	W 3	0.4					MACHINES TRAVAUX PUBLICS
728	OTH MACHY FOR SPCL INDUS	W 57	0.6	W 6	0.1	W 20	0.1	W 27	0.1	AUT MACH IND PARTICULIERES
7283	OTHR MINERAL WORKG MACHY	W 49	0.6			W 19	0.1	W 27	0.1	MACH TRIER,CRIBLER,BROYER
72833	MNRL MIXING,KNEADING MCH	W 33	0.5			W 19	0.1	W 27	0.1	MACH MELANGER MAT MINER
74	GENRL INDUSTRL MACHY NES		0.6		0.2		0.3		0.2	MACH APP INDUSTRIE
744	MECHANICAL HANDLING EQU	W 54	0.4	W 23	0.2	W 16	0.3	W 28	0.1	EQUIP MANUTENTION PIECES
7441	FORK LIFT TRCKS,ETC,PTS	W 42	0.4	W 22	0.2		0.1	W 24	0.1	CHARIOTS POUR USINES ETC
74411	FORK LIFT TRUCKS ETC	W 42	0.4	W 22	0.2			W 24	0.1	CHARIOTS POUR LES GARES
7442	LIFTING,LOADING MACH NES					W 11	0.2	W 2	0.1	APP LEVAGE,MANUTENTION
74422	SHIP DERRICKS,CRANES ETC					W 11	0.2			GRUES,PONTS ROULANTS
76	TELECOMM,SOUND EQUIPMENT		1.6		0.3		0.3		0.2	EQUIPMENT DE TELECOM
764	TELECOM EQPT,PTS,ACC NES	W 4	1.6	W 6	0.3	W 36	0.3	W 20	0.2	EQUIP TELECOM,PIECES

5. Special Exports F.O.B. by Commodities according to the S.I.T.C. (Rev. 2) in million U.S. Dollars
Exportations Spéciales F.O.B. par Produits d'après la C.T.C.I. (Rév. 2) en millions de Dollars E.U.

SITC CTCI	COMMODITY	1994		1995		1996		1997		PRODUIT
		QUANTITY QUANTITE	VALUE VALEUR	QUANTITY QUANTITE	VALUE VALEUR	QUANTITY QUANTITE	VALUE VALEUR	QUANTITY QUANTITE	VALUE VALEUR	
7642	MICROPH,LOUDSPKR,AMPLIFR		0.1	W 3	0.1	W 33	0.2	W 18	0.1	MICRO,HAUT–PARLEUR,AMPLI
7643	TV,RADIO TRANSMITTRS ETC	W 3	1.5		0.1		0.1		0.1	APP EMET TELE RADIO
77	ELECTRIC MACHNRY NES ETC		0.9		0.5		0.4		0.4	MACH APP ELECT NDA
771	ELECTRIC POWER MACHY NES	W 16	0.1	W 44	0.3	W 41	0.3	W 30	0.3	MACH PROD,TRANS ELECTR
7711	TRANSFORMERS,ELECTRICAL	W 15	0.1			W 27	0.3	W 30	0.3	TRANSFO ELECTRIQUES
77111	LIQUID DIELEC TRANSFRMRS					W 27	0.3	W 30	0.3	TRANSFO DIELEC LIQUIDE
7712	OTH ELEC POWER MACHY NES	W 1	0.1	W 44	0.3	W 14	0.1		0.1	AUT APP PROD TRANSF ELEC
77122	INDUCTORS	W 1	0.1	W 43	0.3	W 14	0.1		0.1	BOBINES REACTANCE,SELFS
772	SWITCHGEAR ETC,PARTS NES	W 3	0.1	W 7	0.1	W 3	0.1	W 19	0.2	APP COUPURE,SECT ETC
778	ELECTRICAL MACHINERY NES	W 153	0.8	W 15	0.2	W 3	0.1	W 2	0.1	AUTRES MACH ELECT NDA
7782	ELECTRIC LAMPS,BULBS	W 143	0.3	W 14	0.2				0.1	LAMPES, TUBES ELECTRIQUES
77829	PTS NES OF LAMPS OF 7782	W 143	0.3	W 14	0.2					PIECES DU 778.2
7788	OTH ELEC MACHY,EQUIP NES	W 5	0.5			W 2	0.1		0.1	AUT MACH APP ELEC NDA
77886	OTH ELEC MACHINERY NES	W 5	0.5							AUT MACH APP ELECTRIQUES
78	ROAD VEHICLES		0.8		0.4		0.6		0.3	VEHICULES ROUTIERS
781	PASS MOTOR VEH EXC BUSES	W 10	0.1	W 16	0.1	W 16	0.2	W 16	0.2	AUTO TRANSPORT PERSONNES
782	LORRIES,SPCL MTR VEH NES	W 141	0.6	W 32	0.2	W 53	0.4	W 12	0.1	VEHICULES SPECIAUX,MARCH
7821	LORRIES,TRUCKS	W 103	0.5	W 16	0.1	W 52	0.4	W 11	0.1	VEHICULES TRANSP MARCHAND
79	OTHR TRANSPORT EQUIPMENT		0.8		0.4		0.7		1.2	AUTRE MATERIEL TRANSPORT
792	AIRCRAFT ETC	W 5	0.2	W 16	0.2	W 2	0.2	W 3	0.1	APP NAVIGATION AERIENNE
7929	AIRCRAFT PARTS NES	W 5	0.2	W 16	0.2	W 2	0.2	W 3	0.1	PIECES DU 792
793	SHIPS AND BOATS ETC	W 37	0.6	W 38	0.2	W 37	0.5	W 214	1.2	NAVIRES BATEAUX,ETC
7932	SHIPS AND BOATS NES	W 37	0.6	W 38	0.2	W 36	0.5	W 26	0.5	NAVIRES ET BATEAUX
79321	YACHTS,SPORTS VESSLS ETC	W 19	0.2	W 27	0.2	W 2	0.1	W 15	0.3	BATEAUX DE PLAISANCE
79323	OTHER CARGO VESSELS	W 18	0.4	W 11	0.1	W 34	0.5	W 10	0.3	AUT BATEAUX TRANS MARCH
7938	TUGS,SPECIAL VESSELS ETC		0.1				0.1	W 188	0.7	REMORQUEURS,BATEAUX SPEC
79382	SPECL PURPOSE VESSLS ETC							W 188	0.7	BAT–PHARES,–POMPES,DRAGUES
8	MISC MANUFACTURED GOODS		3.5		5.2		3.3		2.0	ART MANUFACTURES DIVERS
821	*FURNITURE,PARTS THEREOF	W 5	0.1	W 17	0.1	W 15	0.2	W 20	0.1	MEUBLES ET PIECES
8219	FURNITURE AND PARTS NES	W 4	0.1	W 16	0.1	W 14	0.2	W 19	0.1	AUTRES MEUBLES ET PIECES
84	CLOTHING AND ACCESSORIES		2.2		2.7		0.9		0.7	VETEMENTS
843	WOMENS OUTERWEAR NONKNIT	W 62	1.6	W 89	2.1	W 82	0.2	W 118	0.2	VET DESSUS FEMMES MAT TEX
8433	— DRESSES	W 36	1.5	W 45	2.0		0.1		0.1	ROBES EN MAT–TEXTILES
8439	— OTHER OUTER GARMENTS	W 27	0.1	W 44	0.1	W 81	0.2	W 118	0.2	AUT VET DES FEM MAT TEXT
845	OUTERWEAR KNIT NONELASTC		0.1	W 5	0.1	W 7	0.1	W 11	0.2	VET DESSOUS,ACCES BONNET
846	UNDER GARMENTS KNITTED	W 70	0.6	W 59	0.6	W 44	0.5	W 10	0.1	SOUS VETS DE BONNETERIE
8463	— OF SYNTH FBR NONELAST	W 70	0.6	W 54	0.6	W 41	0.4	W 6	0.1	SOUS–VET BONNET FIB SYNT
84632	—— MENS SHIRTS	W 70	0.6	W 54	0.6	W 41	0.4	W 6	0.1	CHEMISES DE BON FIB SYNMT
87	PRECISION INSTRUMNTS NES		0.1		0.3		0.1		0.3	INSTRUM,APPAR SCIENT NDA
874	MEASURNG,CONTROLNG INSTR	W 3	0.1	W 2	0.3	W 2	0.1		0.3	INSTRUMENTS DE MESURE
89	MISC MANUFCTRD GOODS NES		1.2		2.0		2.3		1.1	ART MANUFACTURES DIVERS
893	ARTICLES OF PLASTIC NES	W 232	0.5	W 455	0.9	W 494	0.8	W 30	0.1	OUVRAGES EN MAT DIVIS 58
8931	PLSTC PACKG CONTNRS,LIDS	W 121	0.3	W 282	0.6	W 359	0.5	W 229	0.4	ART TRANSP EMBALLAGE ETC
8939	MISC PLASTIC ARTICLES	W 111	0.3	W 173	0.3	W 132	0.3	W 201	0.4	ART DIVERS EN MAT DIV 58
89399	OTHR PLASTC ARTICLES NES	W 110	0.3	W 173	0.3	W 131	0.3	W 201	0.4	AUT OUV MAT DIV 58
894	TOYS,SPORTING GOODS,ETC	W 3	0.1	W 92	0.3		0.1	W 6	0.1	VOITURES ENFANTS,JOUETS
8947	OTH SPORT GDS,FAIR AMUSM	W 2	0.1	W 91	0.3		0.1	W 1	0.1	AUT ART DE SPORT
89473	AMUSEMENTS ETC FOR FAIRS			W 91	0.3					MANEGES,BALANCOIRES
897	GOLD,SILVER WARE,JEWELRY		0.7		0.9		1.5		0.4	BIJOUTERIE,ORFEVRERIE
8973	PREC JEWLRY,GLD–SILVWARE		0.7		0.9		1.5		0.4	BIJOUX OR,ARGENT ORFEVRE
89731	PRECIOUS METAL JEWELLERY		0.7		0.9		1.5		0.4	ART BIJOUTERIE,JOAILLER

1. HISTORICAL SERIES, 1957–1995 SPECIAL TRADE, IMPORTS C.I.F., EXPORTS F.O.B.
SERIES HISTORIQUES, 1957–1995 COMMERCE SPECIAL, IMPORTATIONS C.A.F., EXPORTATIONS F.O.B

YEAR ANNEE	VALUE IN MILLION U.S. DOLLARS VALEUR EN MILLION U.S. DOLLARS MERCHANDISE –MARCHANDISE IMPORTS	EXPORTS	GOLD –OR IMPORTS	EXPORTS	CONVERSION FACTORS FACTEURS DE CONVERSION CENTS E.U. PAR IMPORTS	EXPORTS	INDEX NUMBERS –INDICES QUANTUM IMPORTS	EXPORTS	UNIT VALUE VALEUR UNITAIRE IMPORTS	EXPORTS
1957	4.53	7.29								
1958	4.46	8.05								
1959	5.53	6.49								
1960	4.71	7.37								
1961	4.92	5.58								
1962	4.52	5.29								
1963	4.74	5.52								
1964	5.01	5.64								
1965	5.05	5.08								
1966	5.51	6.14								
1967	5.43	7.89								
1968	6.35	8.66								
1969	7.82	8.64								
1970	9.04	8.26								
1971	7.81	6.64								
1972	7.96	7.35								
1973	10.06	13.13								
1974	9.86	17.35								
1975	11.31	7.08								
1976	9.15	8.25								
1977	14.23	22.95								
1980	47.78	63.88								
1981	28.55	42.89								
1984		12.44								
1990	26.60	4.38								
1991	30.00	6.00								
1992	28.10	5.40								
1993	32.00	6.59								
1994	30.40	6.47								
1995	22.50	5.10								

2. IMPORTS BY BROAD ECONOMIC CATEGORY AND EXPORTS BY INDUSTRIAL ORIGIN. (PERCENTAGE OF TOTAL VALUE)
IMPORTATIONS PAR CATEGORIES ECONOMIQUES ET EXPORTATIONS PAR BRANCHE D'ACTIVITE.(EN POURCENTAGE DE LA VALEUR TOTALE)

IMPORTS – IMPORTATIONS

	1989	1990	1991	1992	1993	1994	1995
TOTAL IMPORTS–IMPORTATIONS TOTALES							
1 FOOD BEV–ALIMENTATION BOISSONS							
11 PRIMARY–PRODUITS DE BASE							
111 FOR INDUSTRY–POUR L'INDUSTRIE							
112 FOR HOUSEHOLDS–POUR LES MENAGES							
12 PROCESSED–PRODUITS ELABORES							
121 FOR INDUSTRY–POUR L'INDUSTRIE							
122 FOR HOUSEHOLDS–POUR LES MENAGES							
2 IND SUPPLIES–APPROV INDUSTRIELS							
21 PRIMARY–PRODUITS DE BASE							
22 PROCESSED–PRODUITS ELABORES							
3 FUELS–COMBUSTIBLES							
31 PRIMARY–PRODUITS DE BASE							
32 PROCESSED–PRODUITS ELABORES							
321 MOTOR SPIRIT–ESSENCE							
322 OTHER–AUTRES							
4 MACHINERY–EQUIPEMENT							
41 CAPITAL EQUIPMENT–MACHINES							
42 PARTS–PIECES ACCESSOIRES							
5 TRANSPORT–TRANSPORT							
51 PASSENGER CARS–AUTOMOBILES							
52 OTHER–AUTRES							
521 INDUSTRIAL–INDUSTRIELS							
522 NON INDUSTRIAL–NON INDUSTRIEL							
53 PARTS–PIECES ACCESSOIRES							
6 CONSUM GOODS–BIENS CONSOMMATION							
61 DURABLE–DURABLES							
62 SEMI DURABLE–SEMI DURABLES							
63 NON DURABLE–NON DURABLES							
7 GOODS NES–BIENS NDA							

EXPORTS – EXPORTATIONS

	1989	1990	1991	1992	1993	1994	1995
TOTAL EXPORTS–EXPORTATIONS TOTALES							
1 AGRICULTURE							
2 MINING QUARRY–INDUS EXTRACTIVES							
3 MANUFACTURING–IND MANUFACTUR							
31 FOOD BEV TOBACCO–ALIM BOISS TAB							
32 TEXTILES–INDUSTRIES TEXTILES							
33 WOOD & PRODUCTS–BOIS & PRODUITS							
34 PAPER & PRODUCTS–PAPIER & PRODT							
35 CHEMICALS–INDUSTRIES CHIMIQUES							
36 NON METAL MIN–MIN NON METAL							
37 BASIC METAL–IND METAL BASE							
38 METAL MANUF–MANUF METAL							
39 OTH MANUF IND–AUTRES MANUF							

3. TRADE BY PRINCIPAL COUNTRIES OF (VALUE IN MILLION U.S. DOLLARS)
ECHANGES SELON LES PRINCIPAUX PAYS (VALEUR EN MILLIONS DE DOLLARS EU)

COUNTRIES–PAYS	SPECIAL IMPORTS C.I.F. IMPORTATIONS SPECIALES C.A.F					COUNTRIES–PAYS	SPECIAL EXPORTS F.O.B. EXPORTATIONS SPECIALES F.O.B.				
	1991	1992	1993	1994	1995		1991	1992	1993	1994	1995
World						Monde					
Africa						Afrique					
Americas						Amériques					
– Northern America						– Amérique du Nord					
– LAIA						– ALAI					
– CACM						– MCAC					
– Caribbean						– Caraïbes					
– Rest of America						– Autre Amérique					
Asia excl fmr USSR						Asie anc. URSS exclus					
– Middle East						– Moyen–Orient					
Asia former USSR						Asie ancienne URSS					
Europe excl fmr USSR						Europe anc. URSS exclus					
– European Union						– Union Européenne					
– Eastern Europe						– Europe de l'Est					
– Rest of Europe						– Autre de l'Europe					
Europe former USSR						Europe ancienne URSS					
Oceania						Océanie					
Other						Autre					

(VALUE AS PERCENTAGE OF WORLD TOTAL)(VALEURS EN POURCENTAGE DU TOTAL MONDIAL)

	1986	1987	1988	1989	1990	1991	1992	1993	1994	1995		1986	1987	1988	1989	1990	1991	1992	1993	1994	1995
Africa											Afrique										
Americas											Amériques										
– Northern America											– Amérique du Nord										
– LAIA											– ALAI										
– CACM											– MCAC										
– Caribbean											– Caraïbes										
– Rest of America											– Autre Amérique										
Asia excl fmr USSR											Asie anc. URSS exclus										
– Middle East											– Moyen–Orient										
Asia former USSR											Asie ancienne URSS										
Europe excl fmr USSR											Europe anc. URSS exclus										
– European Union											– Union Européenne										
– Eastern Europe											– Europe de l'Est										
– Rest of Europe											– Autre de l'Europe										
Europe former USSR											Europe ancienne URSS										
Oceania											Océanie										
Other											Autre										

4. Special Imports C.I.F. by Commodities according to the S.I.T.C. (Rev. 2) in million U.S. Dollars
Importations Spéciales C.A.F. par Produits d'après la C.T.C.I. (Rév. 2) en millions de Dollars E.U.

SITC CTCI	COMMODITY	1992		1993		1994		1995		PRODUIT
		QUANTITY QUANTITE	VALUE VALEUR	QUANTITY QUANTITE	VALUE VALEUR	QUANTITY QUANTITE	VALUE VALEUR	QUANTITY QUANTITE	VALUE VALEUR	
	ALL COMMODITIES									TOUS PRODUITS

5. Special Exports F.O.B. by Commodities according to the S.I.T.C. (Rev. 2) in million U.S. Dollars
Exportations Spéciales F.O.B. par Produits d'après la C.T.C.I. (Rév. 2) en millions de Dollars E.U.

SITC CTCI	COMMODITY	1992 QUANTITY QUANTITE		1992 VALUE VALEUR	1993 QUANTITY QUANTITE		1993 VALUE VALEUR	1994 QUANTITY QUANTITE		1994 VALUE VALEUR	1995 QUANTITY QUANTITE		1995 VALUE VALEUR	PRODUIT
	ALL COMMODITIES			5.5			6.6			6.5			5.2	TOUS PRODUITS
071	COFFEE AND SUBSTITUTES	W	22	0.1	W	24	0.1	W	24	0.1				CAFE ET SUCCEDANES
0711	COFFEE GREEN,ROASTED,SUB	W	22	0.1	W	24	0.1	W	24	0.1				CAFE TORREFIE OU DECAFEINE
072	COCOA	W	4383	4.3	W	4305	4.2	W	3352	4.9	W	4577	4.8	CACAO
0721	COCOA BEANS,RAW,ROASTED	W	4383	4.3	W	4305	4.2	W	3352	4.9	W	4577	4.8	CACAO EN FEVES
2231	COPRA	W	1360	0.4										COPRAH

1. HISTORICAL SERIES, 1961–1996 GENERAL TRADE, IMPORTS C.I.F., EXPORTS F.O.B.
SERIES HISTORIQUES, 1961–1996 COMMERCE GENERAL, IMPORTATIONS C.A.F., EXPORTATIONS F.O.B

YEAR ANNEE	VALUE IN MILLION S. ARABIAN RIYAL / VALEUR EN MILLION S. ARABIAN RIYAL — MERCHANDISE –MARCHANDISE		GOLD –OR		CONVERSION FACTORS U.S. CENTS PER S. ARABIAN RIYAL / FACTEURS DE CONVERSION CENTS E.U. PAR S. ARABIAN RIYAL		INDEX NUMBERS –INDICES — QUANTUM		UNIT VALUE / VALEUR UNITAIRE	
	IMPORTS	EXPORTS	IMPORTS	EXPORTS	IMPORTS	EXPORTS	IMPORTS	EXPORTS	IMPORTS	EXPORTS
1961	1053.00	4095.00			22.2222	22.2222				
1962	1155.10	4392.00			22.2222	22.2222				
1963	1266.00	4797.00			22.2222	22.2222				
1964	1270.70	5400.00	72.90	28.00	22.2222	22.2222				
1965	1574.90	6268.50	103.40	2.00	22.2222	22.2222				
1966	2327.70	7850.00	70.30		22.2222	22.2222				
1967	2280.90	8093.30	66.10		22.2222	22.2222				
1968	2534.80	9117.20	52.50		22.2222	22.2222				
1969	3361.50	9003.10	71.90		22.2222	22.2222				
1970	3114.40	10906.50	82.40		22.2222	22.2222				
1971	3625.10	17304.00	42.40		22.2222	22.2222				
1972	4664.50	22757.80	43.80	3.00	24.1270	24.1270				
1973	7310.00	33309.00	46.10	13.00	27.1993	27.2929				
1974	10148.90	126223.00	0.30		28.1690	28.1690				
1975	14822.50	104412.00	0.60	1.00	28.4298	28.4220				
1976	30691.00	135153.00	0.20		28.3286	28.3286				
1977	51638.90	153209.00	23.10		28.3716	28.3699				
1978	69179.70	138242.00			29.5224	29.4530				
1979	82223.00	213183.00			29.7510	29.7525				
1980	100350.00	362886.00			30.1059	30.0677				
1981	119298.00	405481.00			29.5425	29.6537				
1982	139335.10	271090.20			29.1769	29.1872				
1983	135417.00	158443.90			28.9521	28.9283				
1984	118737.00	129794.40			28.3785	28.3785				
1985	85563.60	99535.80			27.6083	27.6083				
1986	70779.01	74750.00			26.9974	27.0054				
1987	75312.00	86880.00			26.7023	26.7023				
1988	81582.00	91290.00			26.7023	26.7023				
1989	79220.00	106290.00			26.7023	26.7023				
1990	90140.00	166340.00			26.7023	26.7023				
1991	108900.00	179000.00			26.7023	26.7023				
1992	124600.00	188300.00			26.7023	26.7023				
1993	105600.00	158770.00			26.7023	26.7023				
1994	87400.00	159590.00			26.7023	26.7023				
1995	105200.00	187400.00			26.7023	26.7023				
1996	103980.00	211628.00			26.7023	26.7023				

2. IMPORTS BY BROAD ECONOMIC CATEGORY AND EXPORTS BY INDUSTRIAL ORIGIN. (PERCENTAGE OF TOTAL VALUE)
IMPORTATIONS PAR CATEGORIES ECONOMIQUES ET EXPORTATIONS PAR BRANCHE D'ACTIVITE.(EN POURCENTAGE DE LA VALEUR TOTALE)

IMPORTS – IMPORTATIONS

	1990	1991	1992	1993	1994	1995	1996
TOTAL IMPORTS–IMPORTATIONS TOTALES	100.	100.	100.	100.	100.	100.	100.
1 FOOD BEV–ALIMENTATION BOISSONS	13.0	11.8	10.0	9.7	10.4	14.4	15.8
11 PRIMARY–PRODUITS DE BASE	6.9	6.4	6.6	6.3	6.8	8.1	8.9
111 FOR INDUSTRY–POUR L'INDUSTRIE	2.8	2.3	3.7	2.9	3.4	3.5	4.3
112 FOR HOUSEHOLDS–POUR LES MENAGES	4.1	4.1	2.9	3.3	3.4	4.6	4.6
12 PROCESSED–PRODUITS ELABORES	6.1	5.5	3.4	3.4	3.6	6.3	6.9
121 FOR INDUSTRY–POUR L'INDUSTRIE	0.3	0.4	0.3	0.3	0.5	0.7	0.7
122 FOR HOUSEHOLDS–POUR LES MENAGES	5.7	5.1	3.0	3.1	3.1	5.6	6.2
2 IND SUPPLIES–APPROV INDUSTRIELS	25.4	25.2	24.0	27.7	28.1	29.0	27.8
21 PRIMARY–PRODUITS DE BASE	1.3	1.0	1.0	2.1	1.7	1.6	1.7
22 PROCESSED–PRODUITS ELABORES	24.2	24.1	23.0	25.6	26.4	27.4	26.1
3 FUELS–COMBUSTIBLES	0.3	0.2	0.1	0.2	0.2	0.2	0.2
31 PRIMARY–PRODUITS DE BASE	0.0	0.0	0.0	0.0	0.0	0.0	0.0
32 PROCESSED–PRODUITS ELABORES	0.2	0.2	0.1	0.2	0.2	0.2	0.2
321 MOTOR SPIRIT–ESSENCE	0.0	0.0	0.0	0.0	0.0	0.0	0.0
322 OTHER–AUTRES	0.2	0.2	0.1	0.1	0.2	0.2	0.2
4 MACHINERY–EQUIPEMENT	15.0	17.3	19.0	19.0	19.5	21.2	20.1
41 CAPITAL EQUIPMENT–MACHINES	10.5	13.7	14.7	15.3	15.7	17.4	16.1
42 PARTS–PIECES ACCESSOIRES	4.6	3.6	4.2	3.7	3.9	3.8	4.0
5 TRANSPORT–TRANSPORT	24.2	24.7	27.7	23.7	22.4	15.8	17.4
51 PASSENGER CARS–AUTOMOBILES	6.4	7.1	6.9	6.2	7.4	4.7	4.4
52 OTHER–AUTRES	3.6	4.6	3.5	2.7	3.3	1.8	1.6
521 INDUSTRIAL–INDUSTRIELS	3.5	4.5	3.4	2.6	3.3	1.7	1.6
522 NON INDUSTRIAL–NON INDUSTRIEL	0.1	0.1	0.1	0.1	0.1	0.1	0.0
53 PARTS–PIECES ACCESSOIRES	14.2	13.1	17.3	14.8	11.6	9.4	11.3
6 CONSUM GOODS–BIENS CONSOMMATION	21.7	20.2	18.4	18.6	17.3	17.3	17.0
61 DURABLE–DURABLES	6.6	6.3	5.9	6.1	5.5	4.3	3.9
62 SEMI DURABLE–SEMI DURABLES	9.1	8.8	7.9	8.1	7.6	7.7	7.8
63 NON DURABLE–NON DURABLES	6.1	5.1	4.5	4.4	4.2	5.2	5.3
7 GOODS NES–BIENS NDA	0.4	0.5	0.8	1.2	2.1	2.0	1.7

EXPORTS – EXPORTATIONS

	1990	1991	1992	1993	1994	1995	1996
TOTAL EXPORTS–EXPORTATIONS TOTALES	100.	100.	100.	100.	100.	100.	100.
1 AGRICULTURE	0.6	0.3	0.8	0.7	0.4	0.4	0.2
2 MINING QUARRY–INDUS EXTRACTIVES	78.7	82.5	78.3	80.4	74.8	74.4	73.9
3 MANUFACTURING–IND MANUFACTUR	20.7	17.2	20.9	19.0	24.8	25.2	25.9
31 FOOD BEV TOBACCO–ALIM BOISS TAB	0.3	0.4	0.4	0.5	0.4	0.5	0.5
32 TEXTILES–INDUSTRIES TEXTILES	0.2	0.2	0.1	0.1	0.2	0.3	0.3
33 WOOD & PRODUCTS–BOIS & PRODUITS	0.0	0.1	0.1	0.0	0.0	0.0	0.1
34 PAPER & PRODUCTS–PAPIER & PRODT	0.2	0.2	0.2	0.2	0.2	0.3	0.3
35 CHEMICALS–INDUSTRIES CHIMIQUES	17.6	14.4	17.4	16.3	22.2	21.1	21.8
36 NON METAL MIN–MIN NON METAL	0.2	0.2	0.3	0.2	0.2	0.3	0.4
37 BASIC METAL–IND METAL BASE	0.5	0.3	0.4	0.2	0.3	0.8	0.6
38 METAL MANUF–MANUF METAL	1.6	1.4	1.9	1.4	1.3	1.8	1.9
39 OTH MANUF IND–AUTRES MANUF	0.2	0.0	0.0	0.0	0.0	0.1	0.1

3. TRADE BY PRINCIPAL COUNTRIES OF ORIGIN AND DESTINATION (VALUE IN MILLION U.S. DOLLARS)
ECHANGES SELON LES PRINCIPAUX PAYS D'ORIGINE ET DE DESTINATION (VALEUR EN MILLIONS DE DOLLARS EU)

COUNTRIES–PAYS	GENERAL IMPORTS C.I.F. IMPORTATIONS GENERALES C.A.F					COUNTRIES–PAYS	EXPORTS EXPORTATIONS ES F.O.B.				
	1992	1993	1994	1995	1996		1992	1993	1994	1995	1996
World	33272.7	28201.4	23042.7	28085.1	27764.9	Monde	53486.4	42395.8	42874.2	49029.6	56509.5
Africa	604.1	656.4	563.5	740.0	922.8	Afrique	912.0	607.5	241.9	516.0	764.2
Americas	8315.5	6792.6	5740.3	7011.8	7160.9	Amériques	12757.0	9081.9	7586.2	8381.2	9737.5
– Northern America	7782.5	6119.8	5362.2	6358.3	6478.1	– Amérique du Nord	11307.1	7753.0	7578.1	8367.6	9727.1
– LAIA	493.1	649.3	362.3	610.0	645.4	– ALAI	1449.7	1328.4	7.9	13.1	9.5
– CACM	31.8	21.5	14.9	40.6	35.4	– MCAC	0.0	0.1	0.0	0.2	0.0
– Caribbean	5.3	1.9	0.8	2.8	2.0	– Caraïbes	0.1	0.1	0.2	0.3	0.8
– Rest of America	2.9	0.2	0.1	0.2	0.0	– Autre Amérique	0.0	0.2	0.0	0.0	0.1
Asia excl fmr USSR	10186.9	9097.4	7246.3	8231.7	7819.9	Asie anc. URSS exclus	24445.4	19974.0	8089.1	10364.6	10979.3
– Middle East	1314.9	1663.5	1453.0	1609.2	1703.9	– Moyen–Orient	4763.7	3596.2	1438.6	2048.2	2146.0
Asia former USSR	1.4	1.2	2.0	5.7	22.1	Asie ancienne URSS	0.0	0.1	1.4	1.6	2.4
Europe excl fmr USSR	13727.1	11257.1	9151.2	11485.0	11085.3	Europe anc. URSS exclus	11694.5	9755.2	7603.4	8123.8	8833.1
– European Union	11978.2	10041.2	8025.6	9870.8	9579.1	– Union Européenne	11528.3	9734.3	7581.4	8088.7	8809.5
– Eastern Europe	144.7	131.0	114.2	174.2	146.9	– Europe de l'Est	147.9	3.3	0.4	0.6	3.4
– Rest of Europe	1604.3	1085.0	1011.4	1439.9	1359.3	– Autre de l'Europe	18.4	17.5	21.5	34.4	20.2
Europe former USSR	14.1	4.9	21.5	235.1	218.1	Europe ancienne URSS		0.0	0.4	0.4	0.6
Oceania	328.2	296.1	224.1	296.3	438.7	Océanie	717.3	504.7	82.1	173.3	188.2
Other	95.4	95.8	93.7	79.7	97.2	Autre	2960.2	2472.5	19269.6	21468.6	26004.3
USA/Etats–Unis d'Amer	7497.0	5801.5	4969.3	6043.6	6081.0	Special Categories	0.0		19261.7	21404.0	25977.2
Japan/Japon	4724.8	3573.8	2744.2	2486.5	1953.0	USA/Etats–Unis d'Amer	11303.3	7749.7	7322.5	7980.1	9433.1
United Kingdom	3583.0	3111.5	1974.8	2377.5	2492.5	Other Asia n.e.s.	16997.9	15010.5			301.4
Germany/Allemagne	2473.1	1977.4	1930.3	2209.1	2082.2	European Union n.e.s.	10608.3	9345.9			
Italy/Italie	1650.4	1429.6	1097.5	1233.8	1308.6	Japan/Japon	405.9	233.4	5215.6	6039.3	6934.8
France, Monaco	1602.8	1161.4	979.9	1340.2	1151.6	France, Monaco	121.4	60.3	2465.2	2401.0	2592.0
Switzerland,Liechtenst.	1520.6	1043.3	970.5	1388.1	1296.7	Netherlands/Pays–Bas	379.7	134.7	1625.5	1799.1	2012.7
China/Chine	1267.0	1119.5	873.9	1175.6	854.8	Areas n.e.s.	2960.2	2472.5	8.0	64.6	27.1
Viet Nam	919.6	805.4	712.5	1011.6	10.2	Middle East n.e.s.	2512.4	2237.2			
Belgium–Luxembourg	622.3	539.5	453.9	517.8	567.7	Italy/Italie	132.2	56.2	1288.2	1396.4	1482.1
India/Inde	410.8	520.9	419.7	509.7	598.3	Spain/Espagne	48.5	30.2	897.2	1079.1	1274.1
Netherlands/Pays–Bas	527.5	486.6	392.6	529.5	472.6	United Arab Emirates	598.3	429.2	492.7	672.2	733.4
Turkey/Turquie	359.1	610.2	404.5	420.2	299.9	LAIA n.e.s.	1430.5	1311.9			
Brazil/Brésil	349.2	491.9	252.0	443.2	475.4	Germany/Allemagne	9.6	7.7	744.5	742.4	872.3
Sweden/Suède	416.1	391.1	339.6	399.0	343.9	Kuwait/ Koweït	626.7	366.5	344.5	464.9	454.4
Spain/Espagne	386.9	328.5	352.8	414.1	377.5	India/Inde	544.7	224.9	272.2	353.5	297.1
Indonesia/Indonésie	363.3	357.9	267.8	385.3	411.9	Australia/Australie	713.2	502.3	77.1	165.3	184.0
Canada	285.4	318.2	392.8	314.7	396.9	United Kingdom	102.8	54.6	514.1	511.0	431.6
United Arab Emirates	261.0	283.7	292.3	362.8	403.2	China/Chine	383.5	180.5	269.2	452.6	99.9
Thailand/Thaïlande	326.6	276.9	202.8	285.9	325.5	Singapore/Singapour	232.7	91.7	157.7	301.1	222.3
Egypt/Egypte	246.7	284.0	214.5	236.8	258.3	Bahrain/Bahreïn	270.4	157.3	165.7	185.5	180.3
Malaysia/Malaisie	220.3	191.8	193.3	274.7	240.9	Canada	3.8	3.4	255.5	387.5	294.0
Australia/Australie	203.3	166.2	183.7	214.6	337.3	China, Hong Kong SAR	173.7	66.2	126.8	311.9	214.3
Bahrain/Bahreïn	131.1	158.2	167.9	200.6	260.8	Other Africa n.e.s.	518.4	350.6			
Denmark/Danemark	139.3	121.1	113.7	295.1	233.6	Viet Nam	242.2	111.6	153.9	278.7	20.7
Pakistan	183.5	187.5	106.0	153.7	242.1	Egypt/Egypte	75.9	38.9	51.7	212.8	352.6
Austria/Autriche	229.7	176.7	132.2	144.6	147.8	Qatar	158.3	83.3	95.2	157.9	205.6
Korea, Republic of					785.0	Indonesia/Indonésie	172.6	160.4	120.9	151.4	77.8
Singapore/Singapour	227.3	161.9	111.7	132.3	102.6	Thailand/Thaïlande	158.4	92.1	126.4	120.7	133.1
Syrian Arab Republic	136.7	119.8	114.1	149.7	160.7	Pakistan	164.9	84.1	80.6	145.8	140.3
Ireland/Irlande	138.9	99.6	77.3	184.3	158.8	Morocco/Maroc	148.7	96.0	110.2	94.3	119.1
Zambia/Zambie	72.2	85.6	116.8	160.8	120.9	Oman	85.8	62.0	77.6	124.0	115.2
Finland/Finlande	86.7	94.1	90.4	122.3	142.1	Yemen/Yémen	120.0	46.9	38.9	81.8	130.9
China, Hong Kong SAR	156.5	147.4	81.7	83.8	57.0	Jordan/Jordanie	76.2	52.9	82.0	92.5	104.3
Lebanon/Liban	109.6	108.9	103.7	93.6	110.1	Belgium–Luxembourg	69.2	22.1	34.2	134.7	107.9
Jordan/Jordanie	97.2	107.5	74.2	86.7	129.5	Syrian Arab Republic	92.4	48.0	50.7	74.1	77.8
New Zealand	124.8	129.9	40.1	80.8	101.1	Turkey/Turquie	88.7	46.8	36.0	94.4	60.4
Other Asia n.e.s.					413.2	Malaysia/Malaisie	79.9	61.0	45.9	58.6	80.4
Greece/Grèce	90.4	96.4	64.7	79.1	72.0	Philippines	61.3	41.4	59.7	70.1	71.5
Russian Federation	3.4		15.6	223.8	159.3	Lebanon/Liban	44.7	35.4	39.0	65.0	64.7

(VALUE AS PERCENTAGE OF WORLD TOTAL)(VALEURS EN POURCENTAGE DU TOTAL MONDIAL)

	1987	1988	1989	1990	1991	1992	1993	1994	1995	1996
Africa	1.4	1.7	1.3	2.0	1.7	1.8	2.3	2.4	2.6	3.3
Americas	17.6	18.8	20.8	19.0	23.1	25.0	24.1	24.9	25.0	25.8
– Northern America	16.1	16.9	19.2	17.4	21.1	23.4	21.7	23.3	22.6	23.3
– LAIA	1.2	1.7	1.5	1.4	1.8	1.5	2.3	1.6	2.2	2.3
– CACM	0.3	0.2	0.1	0.1	0.1	0.1	0.1	0.1	0.1	0.1
– Caribbean	0.0	0.0	0.0	0.0	0.0	0.0	0.0	0.0	0.0	0.0
– Rest of America	0.0	0.0	0.0	0.0	0.0	0.0	0.0	0.0	0.0	0.0
Asia excl fmr USSR	38.7	37.8	35.2	33.0	30.3	30.6	32.3	31.4	29.3	28.2
– Middle East	5.0	5.5	6.1	4.7	4.0	4.0	5.9	6.3	5.7	6.1
Asia former USSR						0.0	0.0	0.0	0.0	0.1
Europe excl fmr USSR	40.2	39.6	41.0	43.4	42.1	41.3	39.9	39.7	40.9	39.9
– European Union	36.9	35.9	34.7	35.9	36.4	36.0	35.6	34.8	35.1	34.5
– Eastern Europe	0.5	0.8	1.0	0.7	0.7	0.4	0.5	0.5	0.6	0.5
– Rest of Europe	2.8	2.8	5.4	6.8	5.1	4.8	3.8	4.4	5.1	4.9
Europe former USSR	0.1	0.1	0.1	0.2	0.2	0.0	0.0	0.1	0.8	0.8
Oceania	1.6	1.4	1.2	1.5	1.3	1.0	1.1	1.0	1.1	1.6
Other	0.4	0.5	0.4	0.9	1.2	0.3	0.3	0.4	0.3	0.3
USA/Etats–Unis d'Amer	15.3	16.2	18.2	16.7	20.2	22.5	20.6	21.6	21.5	21.9
Japan/Japon	17.3	16.0	14.2	15.3	13.7	14.2	12.7	11.9	8.9	7.0
United Kingdom	7.8	7.3	10.2	11.3	11.2	10.8	11.0	8.6	8.5	9.0
Germany/Allemagne					7.8	7.4	7.0	8.4	7.9	7.5
Italy/Italie	6.8	6.5	5.7	4.6	4.6	5.0	5.1	4.8	4.4	4.7
France, Monaco	5.3	5.2	4.3	3.9	4.0	4.8	4.1	4.3	4.8	4.1
Switzerland,Liechtenst.	2.5	2.3	5.0	6.6	4.8	4.6	3.7	4.2	4.9	4.7
China/Chine	1.6	1.8	1.9	1.8	2.1	3.8	4.0	3.8	4.2	3.1
Viet Nam			0.0	0.0	0.0	2.8	2.9	3.1	3.6	0.0
Belgium–Luxembourg	1.7	1.9	1.5	1.7	1.9	1.9	1.9	2.0	1.8	2.0

	1987	1988	1989	1990	1991	1992	1993	1994	1995	1996
Afrique				1.0	1.5	1.7	1.4	0.6	1.1	1.4
Amériques				28.3	26.6	23.9	21.4	17.7	17.1	17.2
– Amérique du Nord				24.9	23.8	21.1	18.3	17.7	17.1	17.2
– ALAI				3.3	2.8	2.7	3.1	0.0	0.0	0.0
– MCAC					0.0	0.0	0.0	0.0	0.0	0.0
– Caraïbes					0.0	0.0	0.0	0.0	0.0	0.0
– Autre Amérique					0.0	0.0	0.0	0.0	0.0	0.0
Asie anc. URSS exclus				46.9	43.3	45.7	47.1	18.9	21.1	19.4
– Moyen–Orient				10.6	9.0	8.9	8.5	3.4	4.2	3.8
Asie ancienne URSS						0.0	0.0	0.0	0.0	0.0
Europe anc. URSS exclus				19.1	22.0	21.9	23.0	17.7	16.6	15.6
– Union Européenne				18.4	21.3	21.6	23.0	17.7	16.5	15.6
– Europe de l'Est				0.7	0.7	0.3	0.0	0.0	0.0	0.0
– Autre de l'Europe					0.0	0.0	0.0	0.1	0.1	0.0
Europe ancienne URSS					0.0		0.0	0.0	0.0	0.0
Océanie				1.0	1.3	1.3	1.2	0.2	0.4	0.3
Autre				3.7	5.3	5.5	5.8	44.9	43.8	46.0
Special Categories						0.0		44.9	43.7	46.0
USA/Etats–Unis d'Amer				24.9	23.8	21.1	18.3	17.1	16.3	16.7
Other Asia n.e.s.				36.4	31.4	31.8	35.4			0.5
European Union n.e.s.				18.4	19.9	19.8	22.0			
Japan/Japon					0.5	0.8	0.6	12.2	12.3	12.3
France, Monaco					0.1	0.2	0.1	5.7	4.9	4.6
Netherlands/Pays–Bas					0.5	0.7	0.3	3.8	3.7	3.6
Areas n.e.s.				3.7	5.3	5.5	5.8	0.0	0.1	0.0
Middle East n.e.s.				10.6	6.1	4.7	5.3			
Italy/Italie					0.2	0.2	0.1	3.0	2.8	2.6

4. General Imports C.I.F. by Commodities according to the S.I.T.C. (Rev. 2) in million U.S. Dollars
Importations Générales C.A.F. par Produits d'après la C.T.C.I. (Rév. 2) en millions de Dollars E.U.

SITC CTCI	COMMODITY	1993 QUANTITY QUANTITE	1993 VALUE VALEUR	1994 QUANTITY QUANTITE	1994 VALUE VALEUR	1995 QUANTITY QUANTITE	1995 VALUE VALEUR	1996 QUANTITY QUANTITE	1996 VALUE VALEUR	PRODUIT
	ALL COMMODITIES		28201.5		23042.7		28085.2		27765.0	TOUS PRODUITS
0	FOOD AND LIVE ANIMALS		2746.4		2406.7		4013.3		4301.9	ALIMENTS,ANIMAUX VIVANTS
001	*LIVE ANIMALS FOR FOOD	W 250230	457.7	W 131680	226.3	W 210943	335.9	W 206521	330.9	ANIMAUX VIVANTS
0012	SHEEP AND GOATS,LIVE	W 234796	423.2	W 121279	204.7	W 202253	310.6	W 201352	313.4	ESPECES OVINE ET CAPRINE
00121	SHEEP,LIVE	W 209247	379.7	W 104875	182.9	W 165165	266.4	W 168187	273.5	ESPECE OVINE
01	MEAT AND PREPARATIONS		319.6		206.3		581.5		550.9	VIANDES ET PREPARATIONS
011	MEAT FRESH,CHILLD,FROZEN	W 222093	307.7	W 138690	197.1	W 376961	567.0	W 344542	536.1	VIANDES FRAICHES,REF,CONGE
0111	BOVINE MEAT FRESH,FROZEN	W 18575	33.5	W 13684	25.7	W 55413	113.1	W 41833	93.2	VIANDES BOVIN FRAI,REF
01112	BOVINE MEAT BONELESS	W 11035	14.7	W 7621	12.6	W 42486	84.9	W 32353	70.1	VIANDES BOVIN DESOSSEES
0112	MUTTON ETC FRSH,CHLD,FRN	W 32922	66.4	W 23759	49.8	W 48903	98.4	W 49163	103.8	VIANDE DE MOUTON
0114	POULTRY FRESH CHLLD,FRZN	W 168548	205.1	W 99811	119.6	W 263187	341.4	W 239990	322.5	VOLAILLES MORTES
02	DAIRY PRODCTS,BIRDS'EGGS		181.1		118.4		410.5		400.8	PRODUITS LAITIERS,OEUFS
022	MILK AND CREAM	W 51066	98.8	W 36072	63.6	W 88508	205.9	W 83513	202.8	LAIT ET CREME
0224	MILK,CREAM PRESERVED ETC	W 45805	92.7	W 30799	56.8	W 83201	196.4	W 76442	189.2	LAIT,CREME CONS,CONC
02243	MILK DRY,OVER 1.5% FAT	W 13423	39.2	W 9639	26.7	W 38440	116.8	W 32286	101.9	LAIT POUDRE SUP 1.5%
024	CHEESE AND CURD	W 18500	58.5	W 13803	38.9	W 54084	153.9	W 49992	149.0	FROMAGE ET CAILLEBOTTE
03	FISH AND PREPARATIONS		46.8		35.2		86.8		82.6	POISSONS ET PREPARATIONS
04	CEREALS AND PREPARATIONS		794.8		888.8		1115.0		1397.1	CEREALES ET PRODUITS
042	RICE	W 576561	310.3	W 433565	228.6	W 522942	277.9	W 721276	363.6	RIZ
0422	RICE SEMI-MILLED,MILLED	W 576561	310.3	W 433565	228.6	W 522821	277.9	W 721276	363.6	RIZ POLI,GLACE INCL BRISURES
04221	RICE MILLED UNBROKEN	W 576502	310.2	W 433563	228.6	W 522817	277.9	W 721237	363.6	RIZ POLI,GLACE EXCL BRISURES
043	BARLEY UNMILLED	W 1908381	233.3	W 5140263	496.7	W 3937123	523.6	W 4105660	739.4	ORGE NON MONDEE
044	MAIZE UNMILLED	W 1195406	168.3	W 580550	84.0	W 1134817	161.4	W 1031468	152.5	MAIS NON MOULU
048	CEREAL ETC PREPARATIONS	W 82543	68.9	W 93136	72.0	W 116257	144.3	W 114072	132.1	PREPTNS A BASE CEREALES
05	VEGETABLES AND FRUIT		562.0		546.5		650.7		656.6	LEGUMES ET FRUITS
054	VEG ETC FRSH,SMPLY PRSVD	W 635473	168.0	W 569966	155.8	W 522020	176.2	W 545773	199.1	LEGUMES FRAIS,CONG,SECS
057	FRUIT,NUTS,FRESH,DRIED	W 792264	315.2	W 823828	315.6	W 797167	341.3	W 730317	321.4	FRUITS FRAIS OU SECS
0571	ORANGES, MANDARINS ETC	W 285241	95.0	W 297456	94.8	W 298104	101.0	W 253514	90.1	ORANGES,MAND,CLEMENTINES
05711	ORANGES,FRESH OR DRIED	W 239638	80.3	W 250430	80.5	W 253705	86.3	W 209232	73.7	ORANGES FRAICHES,SECHEES
058	FRUIT PRESERVED,PREPARED	W 49509	54.7	W 50280	52.0	W 76303	91.8	W 80446	96.7	CONSERVES DE FRUITS
06	SUGAR AND PREPS,HONEY		77.2		81.8		256.0		343.7	SUCRES ET PRODUITS
061	SUGAR AND HONEY	W 182173	65.1	W 156789	67.5	W 495177	227.4	W 707945	316.3	SUCRES ET MIEL
0612	REFINED SUGAR ETC	W 177482	55.8	W 150143	57.4	W 474453	206.5	W 672480	288.0	SUCRES RAFFINES
07	COFFEE,TEA,COCOA,SPICES		135.8		112.4		239.6		232.1	CAFE,THE,CACAO,EPICES
081	*FEEDING STUFF FOR ANIML	W 213137	74.7	W 353032	103.9	W 527409	149.9	W 392083	128.8	NOURRITURE POUR ANIMAUX
0813	OILCAKE AND OTH RESIDUES	W 160603	41.4	W 281796	71.9	W 470135	110.5	W 330212	88.8	TOURTEAUX
08131	— OF SOYA BEANS	W 157650	40.7	W 279717	71.5	W 467314	109.9	W 326455	88.3	TOURTEAUX DE SOJA
09	MISC EDIBLE PRODUCTS		97.1		87.6		187.8		178.8	PREP ALIMENTAIRES DIVERSES
098	EDIBLE PRODCTS,PREPS NES	W 36683	94.8	W 40937	85.5	W 64851	180.9	W 62812	171.6	PREP ALIMENTAIRES NDA
09809	MISC FOOD PREPRTIONS NES	W 11982	68.8	W 18448	58.3	W 24672	133.6	W 20155	120.5	PREP ALIMENTAIRES NDA
1	BEVERAGES AND TOBACCO		64.5		118.0		243.4		187.9	BOISSONS ET TABACS
12	TOBACCO AND MANUFACTURES		57.2		107.1		225.3		169.2	TABACS BRUTS FABRIQUES
122	TOBACCO,MANUFACTURED	W 11167	56.1	W 8569	106.4	W 20955	224.7	W 18744	168.2	TABACS FABRIQUES
1222	CIGARETTES	W 3002	47.8	W 4933	102.1	W 11774	214.7	W 8697	157.3	CIGARETTES
2	CRUDE MATERLS,EXCL FUELS		764.8		528.1		555.7		567.4	MAT BRUTES NON COMESTIBLES
22	OIL SEEDS,OLEAGINOUS FRT		85.0		11.7		32.3		28.7	GRAINES,FRUITS OLEAGINEUX
24	CORK AND WOOD		192.5		151.7		148.0		125.6	LIEGE ET BOIS
248	WOOD SHAPED,SLEEPERS	W 345395	149.9	W 315419	124.0	W 289369	122.7	W 258251	101.9	BOIS SIMPLEMENT TRAVAILLES
2483	LUMBER SHAPED NON-CONIFR	W 149572	66.4	W 195409	74.1	W 146379	59.2	W 132952	52.9	NON CONIFERES SCIES,RABOTES
24831	LUMBER SAWN ETC NON-CON	W 146847	62.9	W 191392	70.2	W 144418	55.9	W 132206	51.1	SCIES LONGITUDINALEMENT
26	TEXTILE FIBRES AND WASTE		86.7		79.0		114.8		109.0	FIBRES TEXTILES
266	SYNTHETIC FIBRES TO SPIN	W 16088	65.5	W 16290	58.5	W 25945	96.2	W 23735	92.2	FIBRES SYNTHETIQUES
28	METALLIFEROUS ORES,SCRAP		295.2		173.2		158.7		197.2	MINERAIS METAL,DECHETS
281	IRON ORE,CONCENTRATES	W 2760458	255.4	W 3277315	121.2	W 2865826	117.7	W 2552775	124.3	MINERAIS DE FER
2815	IRON ORE,CONC,NOT AGGLOM	W 2760377	255.2	W 2902534	107.7	W 2753944	110.2	W 2551638	122.6	MINERAIS NON AGGLOMERES
4	ANIMAL,VEGETABLE OIL,FAT		103.9		120.3		232.7		204.9	HUILES,GRAISSES ANIM,VEG
42	FIXED VEGETABLE OIL,FAT		96.8		111.3		220.1		187.9	HUILES VEGETALES FIXES
424	FIXED VEG OIL NONSOFT	W 142102	83.9	W 130199	102.1	W 253996	197.1	W 238851	169.6	AUTRES HUILES VEG FIXES
4242	PALM OIL	W 72079	39.8	W 75724	60.1	W 163840	122.9	W 160251	103.3	HUILE DE PALME
5	CHEMCLS,RELATED PROD NES		2288.8		1935.4		2604.7		2533.6	PRODUITS CHIMIQUES
51	ORGANIC CHEMICALS		188.1		205.8		319.0		343.5	PROD CHIMIQ ORGANIQUES
516	OTHER ORGANIC CHEMICALS	W 11517	26.8	W 13174	30.1	W 20494	74.3	W 21381	87.5	AUTRES PROD ORGANIQUES
52	INORGANIC CHEMICALS		182.5		207.7		228.5		231.2	PROD CHIM INORGANIQUES
522	INORG ELEMNTS,OXIDES,ETC	W 310208	83.2	W 342605	95.0	W 234273	80.7	W 200087	84.1	ELEMENTS INORGANIQUES
523	OTHR INORG CHEMICALS ETC	W 214032	93.4	W 224732	95.9	W 289974	134.4	W 355030	142.9	AUT PRODUITS CHIMIQUES INORG
53	DYES,TANNING,COLOUR PROD		99.5		88.2		112.2		100.1	PROD TEINTURE,COLORANTS
533	PIGMENTS,PAINTS,ETC	W 47661	84.9	W 38391	73.5	W 45858	92.5	W 43488	81.1	PIGMENTS,PEINTURES,VERNIS
541	*MEDICINAL,PHARM PRODUCT	MK 32700	733.6	MK 16564	529.8	MK 24498	761.1	MK 23317	775.6	PROD MEDICINAUX PHARMACEUT
5417	MEDICAMENTS	MK 16824	629.3	MK 12180	453.7	MK 18479	673.3	MK 19792	705.4	MEDICAMENTS
54171	— CONTAINNG ANTIBIOTICS	K 5360634	308.5	K 3435326	216.4	K 8166902	385.0	K 8282006	407.4	MED CONTN ANTIBIOTIQUES
54172	— CONTAINING HORMONES	K 5925407	172.1	K 3361512	115.0	K 3203471	99.1	K 3078941	109.9	MED CONTENANT HORMONES
54179	— CONTNG OTH SUBSTANCES	K 5533667	147.5	K 5257177	121.1	K 7025984	187.0	K 8389978	187.8	MED CONT AUT SUBSTANCES
55	PERFUME,CLEANING ETC PRD		306.6		250.2		350.3		338.5	PROD POUR PARFUM,TOILETTE
553	PERFUMERY,COSMETICS,ETC	W 35768	207.8	W 23889	155.4	W 34691	243.6	W 35517	231.2	PRODUITS DE PARFUMERIE
554	SOAP,CLEANSING ETC PREPS	W 55820	74.5	W 62328	71.2	W 62365	74.4	W 63196	73.1	SAVONS,PRODUITS DETERSIFS
58	PLASTIC MATERIALS ETC		331.8		330.8		446.1		360.4	MAT PLAST ARTIFICIELLES
583	POLYMERIZATION ETC PRODS	W 211816	278.4	W 221292	279.4	W 209275	363.9	W 170133	277.3	PROD POLYMERISATION
5831	POLYETHYLENE	W 65935	71.5	W 66544	74.3	W 56004	81.4	W 49583	69.5	POLYETHYLENE
5839	OTH POLYMRZTION ETC PROD	W 63607	97.4	W 56632	95.2	W 80498	148.8	W 64046	106.5	AUT PROD POLYMER COPOLYM
59	CHEMICAL MATERIALS NES		384.8		303.6		362.3		357.3	MAT PROD CHIMIQUES NDA
598	MISCEL CHEM PRODUCTS NES	W 112606	277.7	W 100072	231.9	W 118983	274.4	W 120802	271.2	PROD DIV INDUST CHIM NDA
5989	CHEM PRODUCTS,PREPS NES	W 79355	191.5	W 68596	158.8	W 78003	184.5	W 87296	205.4	PROD PREP CHIMIQUES NDA
59899	OTH CHEM PRODS,PREPS,NES	W 54913	136.0	W 48168	114.0	W 50358	118.4	W 52691	138.6	AUT PRODUITS CHIMIQUES NDA
6	BASIC MANUFACTURES		6110.7		4847.8		5947.1		5606.8	ART MANUFACTURES
62	RUBBER MANUFACTURES NES		452.2		352.7		360.1		402.9	CAOUTCHOUC MANUFACTURE
625	RUBBER TYRES, TUBES ETC	W 136942	383.9	W 105765	297.4	W 103906	286.8	W 110769	333.5	PNEUS CAOUTCHOUC VULCANISE
6251	TYRES NEW FOR MOTOR CARS	W 48014	139.7	W 35690	107.7	W 29125	96.5	W 30761	104.7	PNEUS POUR VOITURES
6252	TYRES,NEW,BUS OR LORRY	W 67246	194.1	W 54212	149.1	W 54057	135.8	W 58465	168.6	PNEUS POUR AUTOBUS,CAMIONS
63	WOOD,CORK MANUFACTRS NES		316.5		241.8		243.2		243.4	OUVRAGES LIEGE ET BOIS
634	VENEERS,PLYWOOD,ETC	W 410246	247.3	W 368829	197.1	W 359300	208.2	W 320681	203.6	PLACAGES,CONTRE-PLAQUES
6341	VENEER SHEETS ETC	W 148160	75.5	W 173982	86.1	W 166822	81.3	W 111148	60.2	BOIS SIMPLEMENT SCIES
6342	PLYWOOD OF WOOD SHEETS	W 216793	143.9	W 116673	74.8	W 125043	86.1	W 164045	112.3	BOIS CONTRE-PLAQUES
64	PAPER,PAPERBOARD AND MFR		519.8		518.7		725.7		534.6	PAPIERS,CARTONS & OUVRAGES
641	PAPER AND PAPERBOARD	W 537222	397.1	W 564604	402.7	W 634153	600.6	W 469001	411.3	PAPIERS ET CARTONS
6413	KRAFT PAPER,PAPERBOARD	W 154744	75.6	W 166352	89.2	W 180878	138.2	W 184038	106.7	PAPIER ET CARTON KRAFT
6415	PAPER,PAPERBRD,BULK,NES	W 88461	82.5	W 67525	63.2	W 104891	121.0	W 64046	72.3	PAPIERS,CARTONS ROULEAUX
64159	OTHER PAPER ETC,BULK,NES	W 73404	69.1	W 49337	51.2	W 83210	101.3	W 51119	60.4	AUT PAPIER ROULEAUX FEUILLES
6417	CORRUGATED PAPER ETC,BLK	W 93757	85.5	W 99073	86.0	W 104797	119.7	W 62675	77.7	PAPIERS,CARTONS ONDULES
642	PAPER,ETC,PRECUT,ARTS OF	W 75692	122.7	W 79733	116.1	W 76204	125.1	W 66197	123.3	PAP,CARTONS DECOUPES
65	TEXTILE YARN,FABRICS,ETC		1353.6		1052.0		1229.7		1165.6	FILS,TISSUS,ARTICLES TEXTILE
651	TEXTILE YARN	W 30036	100.2	W 31157	100.7	W 47305	151.8	W 41625	126.4	FILS TEXTILES

4. General Imports C.I.F. by Commodities according to the S.I.T.C. (Rev. 2) in million U.S. Dollars
Importations Générales C.A.F. par Produits d'après la C.T.C.I. (Rév. 2) en millions de Dollars E.U.

SITC CTCI	COMMODITY	1993		1994		1995		1996		PRODUIT
		QUANTITY QUANTITE	VALUE VALEUR	QUANTITY QUANTITE	VALUE VALEUR	QUANTITY QUANTITE	VALUE VALEUR	QUANTITY QUANTITE	VALUE VALEUR	
653	WOVN MAN–MADE FIB FABRIC	W 45926	509.2	W 38767	418.3	W 50377	518.0	W 58672	511.2	TISSUS FIBRES SYNTH,ARTIF
6531	CONT SYNT WEAVES NONPILE	W 17174	183.9	W 11307	127.6	W 19784	207.0	W 22283	196.6	TISSUS FIBRES SYNTH CONTINUE
65315	CONT SYN TXTL FABRIC NES	W 16474	178.3	W 10539	120.6	W 17906	191.2	W 20223	180.1	TIS PLUS 85% TEXT SYNT CONT
6532	DISC SYN TXTL FABRIC NES	W 22908	255.3	W 20571	221.5	W 22794	249.0	W 24162	246.5	TIS DISC MOINS 85% FIBR TEXT
655	KNITTED,ETC FABRICS	W 13231	99.5	W 12273	95.2	W 12005	85.4	W 12424	90.7	ETOF BONNETERIE PIECES ETC
6552	OTHER KNIT ETC FAB NONEL	W 13231	99.5	W 12273	95.2	W 12005	85.4	W 12424	90.7	ETOF BON NON ELAS NON SYNT
658	TEXTILE ARTICLES NES	W 58280	211.2	W 32622	115.2	W 42505	151.6	W 50521	167.0	ART FACONNES MAT TEXTILES
6583	BLANKETS ETC NON ELECTRC	W 20405	93.3	W 14118	53.7	W 17507	66.9	W 17473	69.3	COUVERTURES
659	FLOOR COVERINGS,ETC	W 64880	222.4	W 41346	143.7	W 35509	130.1	W 32394	116.5	COUVRE–PARQUETS,TAPIS ETC
6595	MAN–MADE TXTL CARPTS NES	W 50448	159.1	W 29203	93.9	W 24223	79.9	W 21246	71.1	TAPIS MAT TEXT SYNT ARTIF
65952	— WOVEN	W 40056	124.3	W 24275	74.5	W 18383	58.3	W 13094	45.7	TAPIS MAT TEXT SYNT TISSES
66	NONMETAL MINERAL MFS NES		632.2		519.9		489.8		478.5	ART MIN NON METALLIQUES
661	LIME,CEMENT,BLDG PRODS	W 2658210	263.3	W 2358855	204.8	W 1537126	148.9	W 757152	142.2	CHAUX,CIMENTS MAT CONSTR
6612	CEMENT	W 2220238	106.6	W 2002725	100.2	W 1233162	65.9	W 411386	31.3	CIMENTS HYDRAULIQUES
6613	BUILDING STONE ETC WORKD	W 420569	144.8	W 336207	95.7	W 290361	69.8	W 332497	104.5	PIERRES A BATIR
66132	BUILDING STONE WORKED	W 162551	84.8	W 122598	56.2	W 155228	49.4	W 185691	69.0	OUVR EN PIERRES DE TAILLE
662	CLAY,REFRACTORY BLDG PRD	W 251110	100.0	W 254360	91.7	W 259146	94.2	W 194609	110.2	MAT CONST REFRACTAIRES
664	GLASS	W 95361	105.9	W 90986	88.0	W 96251	100.5	W 88466	99.0	VERRE
67	IRON AND STEEL		1406.5		920.6		1363.4		1379.4	FER ET ACIER
672	IRON,STEEL PRIMARY FORMS	W 1495628	503.8	W 605732	241.7	W 808175	375.7	W 760096	319.7	LINGOTS FER,ACIER
6724	IRN,STL INGOTS,LUMPS,ETC	W 834594	208.6	W 171443	49.4	W 165367	45.8	W 155049	41.4	FER,ACIER LINGOTS,MASSES
67243	STNLESS STEEL ETC INGOTS	W 832022	206.6	W 139097	39.1	W 132132	36.9	W 128963	33.5	LINGOTS ACIER INOXYDABLE
6727	IRN,STL COIL FR REROLLNG	W 650402	286.9	W 426822	187.8	W 518204	292.3	W 562381	263.0	EBAUCHES POUR TOLES FER
67271	IRON,SIMPLE STEEL COILS	W 561310	245.2	W 393200	172.0	W 462609	258.6	W 496894	227.3	EBAUCHES NON EN ACIER
673	IRON,STEEL SHAPES ETC	W 705475	255.3	W 498799	194.9	W 499563	212.2	W 588189	242.3	BARRES,PROFIL FER,ACIER
6732	IRON,STEEL BARS ETC	W 397233	133.0	W 205982	75.5	W 150709	56.2	W 241570	95.3	BARRES FER,ACIER
6733	IRON,STEEL PROFILES ETC	W 289430	114.5	W 249582	103.5	W 303252	137.2	W 300809	128.2	PROFILES,PALPLAN FER,ACIER
67332	LARGE U,I,H SECTIONS ETC	W 168829	63.7	W 131839	55.0	W 194268	88.0	W 186742	75.7	PROFILES PLUS 80MM
674	IRN,STL UNIV,PLATE,SHEET	W 437228	242.1	W 350566	209.7	W 617055	406.5	W 537917	333.0	LARGES PLATS,TOLES
6744	IRN,STL HVY PLATE,ROLLED	W 95658	46.2	W 83431	46.7	W 202107	107.6	W 144975	77.6	TOLES LAMINEES PLUS 4.75 MM
67441	— OF IRON OR SIMPLE STL	W 88150	41.9	W 81492	45.4	W 200114	106.0	W 143870	76.0	TOLES NON ACIER FIN CARB
6749	OTH IRN,STL PLATES,SHEET	W 200897	115.4	W 168704	100.9	W 242215	187.4	W 223687	152.6	AUTRES TOLES FER,ACIER
67491	— OF IRON OR SIMPLE STL	W 177179	100.1	W 142687	85.9	W 227413	176.0	W 200588	135.8	AUT TOLES AUTRES ACIER FIN
678	IRON,STL TUBES,PIPES,ETC	W 303728	311.8	W 176041	211.0	W 177887	302.0	W 291045	435.0	TUBES,TUYAUX EN FONTE,FER
6783	IRON,STL TUBES,PIPES NES	W 110183	103.7	W 79077	69.1	W 97391	118.6	W 215197	232.7	AUT TUBES,TUYAUX FER,ACIER
6785	IRON,STEEL TUBE FITTINGS	W 68525	118.7	W 22060	81.4	W 28384	118.5	W 32693	142.0	ACCESSOIRES DE TUYAUTERIE
68	NON–FERROUS METALS		591.8		605.3		774.7		700.4	METAUX NON FERREUX
682	COPPER EXC CEMENT COPPER	W 98586	235.9	W 124844	291.8	W 114465	360.2	W 133933	348.0	CUIVRE
6821	COPPER NES,ALLOYS,UNWRT	W 58464	117.6	W 104351	230.7	W 94805	283.6	W 105224	258.5	CUIVRE BRUT
68212	COPPER REFINED,UNWROUGHT	W 58023	116.1	W 104344	230.7	W 94733	283.3	W 105012	258.1	CUIVRE AFFINE BRUT
6822	COPPER,ALLOYS WORKED	W 40122	118.4	W 20494	61.1	W 19660	76.7	W 28709	89.6	CUIVRE,ALLIAGES OUVRES
684	ALUMINIUM	W 249571	326.0	W 190353	279.7	W 145717	379.5	W 136971	320.0	ALUMINIUM
6842	ALUMINIUM,ALLOYS WORKED	W 243535	316.5	W 139948	273.8	W 144497	376.2	W 131947	310.2	ALUMINIUM,ALLIAGES OUVRE
68421	ALUMINIUM BARS,WIRE,ETC	W 65539	109.8	W 77843	134.0	W 62952	146.8	W 81205	164.5	BARRES,PROFILES FILS ALU
68422	ALUMNM PLATE,SHEET,STRIP	W 159146	175.1	W 48749	104.3	W 61457	173.6	W 41402	115.1	TOLES, PLANCHES EN ALU
69	METAL MANUFACTURES NES		824.4		626.4		750.7		690.1	ART MANUFACT EN METAL NDA
691	STRUCTURES AND PARTS NES	W 82311	137.3	W 59246	85.4	W 74847	124.3	W 77998	103.0	CONSTRUCT FER,ACIER,ALU
6911	STRUCTURES,PARTS IRN,STL	W 79260	123.0	W 57419	75.4	W 73219	114.5	W 76434	91.6	CONSTRUCT FER,ACIER,FONTE
697	BASE MTL HOUSEHOLD EQUIP	W 44911	175.5	W 30398	129.5	W 37654	148.6	W 37307	148.6	ART MENAGE MET COMMUNS
699	BASE METAL MFRS NES	W 84148	240.3	W 64948	198.1	W 67460	222.2	W 60288	210.9	ART MANUFACTURES MET NDA
6991	LOCKSMITHS WARES,ETC	W 24117	101.1	W 20901	87.0	W 22703	101.4	W 19669	87.6	ARTICLES DE SERRURERIE
7	MACHINES,TRANSPORT EQUIP		11802.6		9357.9		9986.5		9843.3	MACHINES MATERIEL TRANSPORT
71	POWER GENERATING EQUIPMT		738.7		624.7		987.3		813.7	MACHINES GENERATRICES
711	STEAM BOILERS & AUX PLNT	W 4400	46.0	W 6551	99.0	W 21788	225.3	W 11077	78.7	GENERATEURS VAPEUR EAU ETC
7112	AUXILIARY BOILER PLANT	W 758	4.9	W 4951	82.9	W 7859	133.5	W 3127	19.4	APPAREILS AUXIL DU 711.1
713	INTRNL COMBUS PSTN ENGIN	W 23353	301.7	W 16515	159.4	W 14349	131.8	W 15122	216.2	MOTEURS EXPL COMB INT, PIECE
7131	AIRCRAFT PSTN ENGINS,PTS	W 471	111.2	W 261	45.9	W 145	31.8	W 152	106.7	MOTEURS EXPL P.AVIATION, PIE
71311	AIRCRAFT PISTON ENGINES	W 326	109.8	W 167	44.3	W 113	30.0	W 138	105.9	MOTEURS EXPL P.AVIATION
714	ENGINES AND MOTORS NES	W 2131	129.9	W 629	43.9	W 3665	156.4	W 5185	234.2	MOTEURS NON ELECTRIQUES
7149	ENGINE & MOTOR PARTS NES	W 1326	77.7	W 545	43.1	W 1283	73.9	W 3710	143.5	PIECES 714 ET 718.88
71499	PARTS NES,OF 71488,71888	W 1141	63.6	W 405	32.2	W 695	54.5	W 3497	134.5	PIECES 714.88 ET 718.88
716	ROTATING ELECTRIC PLANT	W 18447	191.3	W 16122	144.3	W 24876	307.1	W 19160	205.5	APP ELECTR ROTATIFS,PIECES
7161	DC MOTORS AND GENERATORS	W 4546	33.9	W 5514	45.8	W 10384	118.3	W 5557	53.9	MOTEURS COURANT CONTINU
7162	AC MTRS,GENRTRS,GEN SETS	W 11920	115.8	W 9368	69.5	W 13011	143.6	W 11516	108.7	MOTEURS ELECTRIQUES
718	OTH POWER GENERATG MACHY	W 2087	63.6	W 2855	171.5	W 2448	129.2	W 2587	73.2	AUTRES MOTEURS PARTIES
7188	WIND,WATER,ETC ENGINES	W 1563	60.7	W 2806	171.2	W 2433	129.1	W 2538	72.6	MOT MACHINES MOTRICES NDA
71882	OTH HYDRAULIC ENGNS,MTRS	W 419	9.8	W 1775	96.8	W 714	14.9	W 736	31.2	MACH MOTRICES HYDRAULQUES
71889	PARTS NES OF 71881,71882	W 671	45.5	W 675	69.7	W 1434	112.0	W 662	31.6	PARTIES DES POS 718.81,82
72	MACHS FOR SPCL INDUSTRYS		680.0		576.4		582.1		542.7	MAC SPECIALES POUR INDUST
721	AGRIC MACHY,EXC TRACTORS	W 12350	86.7	W 6769	52.5	W 5115	66.2	W 5909	42.0	MACHINES AGRICOLES
723	CIVIL ENGNEERG EQUIP ETC	W 53628	216.3	W 28489	137.4	W 14606	95.6	W 19433	141.8	APPAREILS DE GENIE CIVIL
7234	CONST,MINING MACHNRY NES	W 46716	146.5	W 24456	102.9	W 10792	60.7	W 14516	92.4	MACH POUR LA CONST, MINES
724	TEXTILE,LEATHER MACHNRY	W 5693	50.8	W 6853	84.2	W 7021	80.3	W 5289	74.4	MACH POUR INDUSTRIE TEXTILE
728	OTH MACHY FOR SPCL INDUS	W 20145	190.8	W 18144	164.4	W 23754	220.5	W 20458	175.5	AUT MACH IND PARTICULIERES
7284	MACHY FOR SPCL INDUS NES	W 8059	98.8	W 5642	83.5	W 8351	117.0	W 8088	91.7	MACH SPEC IND PARTICUL.
73	METALWORKING MACHINERY		145.8		123.6		137.5		98.7	MACH TRAVAIL DES METAUX
736	METALWORKING MACH–TOOLS	W 13370	111.4	W 13656	102.9	W 10191	104.3	W 7257	72.3	MACH–OUTILS TRAVAIL METAUX
74	GENRL INDUSTRL MACHY NES		1959.6		1528.1		2049.6		1865.1	MACH APP INDUSTRIE
741	HEATING,COOLING EQUIPMNT	W 57372	464.8	W 44434	333.6	W 60259	470.5	W 50602	389.7	MACH CHAUFFAGE,PIECES
7414	NONDOM REFRIG EQUIPT,PTS	W 10377	77.8	W 11086	76.6	W 14013	97.1	W 11228	78.6	MAT PRODUCTION DU FROID
7415	AIR–CONDITIONING MACHNRY	W 32369	219.3	W 26408	190.4	W 23159	175.3	W 18947	139.7	GROUPES CONDITION AIR
7416	HEATING,COOLING EQU NES	W 7389	83.5	W 3206	36.7	W 7746	72.1	W 11175	101.0	APP CHANGEMENT TEMP
742	PUMPS FOR LIQUIDS ETC	W 23329	209.8	W 14302	149.7	W 15026	182.7	W 15414	192.6	POMPES MOTO–POMPES
7428	OTHER PUMPS FOR LIQUIDS	W 14811	130.2	W 9662	92.6	W 11177	119.5	W 11869	129.6	AUTRES POMPES POUR LIQ
74288	PUMPS FR LIQUIDS NES ETC	W 14048	121.6	W 9239	87.0	W 10439	111.4	W 11044	120.9	POMPES POUR LIQUIDES NDA
743	PUMPS NES,CENTRFUGES ETC	W 39034	301.7	W 46553	260.0	W 62016	437.4	W 44607	331.8	POMPES COMPRES,VENT ETC
7431	PUMPS FOR GASES ETC	W 26524	145.6	W 34591	149.3	W 32552	167.7	W 29299	182.9	POMPES AIR A VIDE,COMPRES
7436	GAS,LIQUID FILTERS ETC	W 5222	58.8	W 4109	48.0	W 18028	179.5	W 5714	66.8	APP POUR FILT DES LIQUIDES
744	MECHANICAL HANDLING EQU	W 31373	187.2	W 26988	153.6	W 30319	188.1	W 30743	220.3	EQUIP MANUTENTION PIECES
7442	LIFTING,LOADING MACH NES	W 18226	101.7	W 15389	79.5	W 17947	120.7	W 18619	120.5	APP LEVAGE,MANUTENTION
745	NONELEC MACHY,TOOLS NES	W 20699	117.8	W 7455	107.3	W 8263	116.5	W 6354	94.2	AUT MACH NON ELEC,PIECES
7452	OTH NONELEC MCHS,PTS NES	W 18867	97.4	W 5738	88.9	W 6488	99.6	W 4780	79.7	AUT MACH NON ELEC,PIECES
749	NONELEC MACH PTS,ACC NES	W 49950	678.5	W 33083	524.2	W 44786	654.6	W 35616	636.7	PIECES MACH NON ELEC NDA
7492	COCKS,VALVES ETC NES	W 17824	204.8	W 11698	151.3	W 13842	181.9	W 17489	239.0	ART ROB,SIM POUR TUYAUX
7499	OTH NONELEC MCHY PTS NES	W 22639	380.1	W 15633	309.5	W 25070	397.2	W 11665	319.6	PIECES NON ELECT NDA
74999	MACH PARTS NONELEC NES	W 19483	328.9	W 13165	272.1	W 22434	348.7	W 9364	264.6	PIECES MACHINES NDA
75	OFFICE MACHNES,ADP EQUIP		400.5		342.7		366.7		386.8	MACH BUREAU TRAIT AUTOM
752	AUTOMTIC DATA PROC EQUIP	W 1733	115.2	W 863	54.1	W 1046	81.6	W 1307	109.4	MACH TRAIT INFORMATION
759	OFFICE,ADP MCH PTS,ACCES	W 5437	226.8	W 4265	235.5	W 5566	247.0	W 5766	238.7	PIECES DU 751 ET 752
7599	ACCTG,ETC,ADP MCH PTS,AC	W 3353	177.2	W 3163	209.3	W 4248	213.4	W 4843	214.0	PIECES DU 751 ET 752
76	TELECOMM,SOUND EQUIPMENT		704.1		593.1		809.3		684.7	EQUIPMENT DE TELECOM

4. General Imports C.I.F. by Commodities according to the S.I.T.C. (Rev. 2) in million U.S. Dollars
Importations Générales C.A.F. par Produits d'après la C.T.C.I. (Rév. 2) en millions de Dollars E.U.

SITC CTCI	COMMODITY	1993 QUANTITY QUANTITE	1993 VALUE VALEUR	1994 QUANTITY QUANTITE	1994 VALUE VALEUR	1995 QUANTITY QUANTITE	1995 VALUE VALEUR	1996 QUANTITY QUANTITE	1996 VALUE VALEUR	PRODUIT
761	TELEVISION RECEIVERS	W 9735	146.1	W 9467	141.6	W 6482	83.2	W 7307	86.9	RECEPTEURS DE TELEVISION
7611	COLOUR TV RECEIVERS	W 9421	141.4	W 8730	129.9	W 5811	74.6	W 7171	85.0	RECEPTEURS COULEUR
763	SOUND RECORDRS,PHONOGRPH	W 7199	148.2	W 4407	91.5	W 5610	93.1	W 5068	73.6	PHONO,APP ENREGISTREMENT
7638	OTHR SOUND APPARATUS ETC	W 6964	143.9	W 4155	89.3	W 5168	89.1	W 4747	70.6	AUT APP D'ENREGIS,REPROD
76388	DICTATING MACHINES ETC	W 5227	86.0	W 2601	45.4	W 3690	45.3	W 3642	43.3	MACHINES A DICTER
764	TELECOM EQPT,PTS,ACC NES	W 8337	358.9	W 6468	308.5	W 9291	583.1	W 8423	485.5	EQUIP TELECOM,PIECES
7641	LINE TELEPHONE,ETC EQUIP	W 2893	112.1	W 2327	71.7	W 2961	96.6	W 3419	149.8	APP TELEPHON PAR FIL
7643	TV,RADIO TRANSMITTRS ETC	W 1158	63.6	W 957	82.0	W 1611	114.2	W 1120	124.9	APP EMET TELE RADIO
7648	TELECOMM EQUIPMENT NES	W 377	55.2	W 243	39.8	W 306	190.2	W 303	67.3	APP TELECOM NDA
76483	RADAR APPARATUS ETC	W 203	49.2	W 113	29.5	W 172	178.5	W 190	57.0	APP DE RADIOGUIDAGE ETC
7649	PTS NES OF EQUIPMT OF 76	W 3228	116.3	W 2491	107.5	W 3765	173.2	W 2974	135.7	PIECES DE LA DIV 76
76491	PTS NES OF APPAR OF 7641	W 940	65.2	W 718	51.0	W 1857	123.6	W 1000	89.4	PIECES POUR 764.1
77	ELECTRIC MACHNRY NES ETC		1427.5		1110.4		1253.4		1449.4	MACH APP ELECT NDA
771	ELECTRIC POWER MACHY NES	W 15448	128.6	W 15173	126.2	W 15979	122.6	W 18845	146.2	MACH PROD,TRANS ELECTR
7711	TRANSFORMERS,ELECTRICAL	W 9676	90.1	W 8632	88.3	W 9109	85.9	W 9784	89.2	TRANSFO ELECTRIQUES
772	SWITCHGEAR ETC,PARTS NES	W 30353	384.8	W 26019	339.0	W 22736	398.0	W 26661	511.8	APP COUPURE,SECT ETC
7721	SWITCHGEAR ETC	W 30011	370.3	W 25634	330.7	W 22342	386.5	W 26276	501.7	APP COUPURE,SECTIONMNT
773	ELECTR DISTRIBUTNG EQUIP	W 48038	176.7	W 36023	103.3	W 23052	117.2	W 37885	161.9	EQUIPMT DISTRIBUTION ELECT
7731	INSULATED WIRE,CABLE ETC	W 43571	155.1	W 31916	85.8	W 19993	98.8	W 33559	131.7	FILS,CABLES ISOLES ELECT
775	HOUSEHOLD TYPE EQUIP NES	W 55237	321.6	W 40651	229.2	W 44509	239.1	W 34881	196.4	MACH,APP USAGE DOMESTQUE
7752	DOM REFRIGERATRS,FREEZRS	W 16732	90.7	W 13363	71.5	W 11316	61.8	W 9784	51.0	REFRIG,CONGEL MENAGER
7757	DOMESTIC ELECTRC EQU NES	W 14888	94.6	W 11102	63.6	W 14225	72.5	W 9436	50.4	APP ELECTR DOMEST NDA
7758	ELECTRO-THERMIC APPL NES	W 15405	89.1	W 10495	57.9	W 13114	67.9	W 10640	63.3	APP ELECTROTHERMIQ NDA
778	ELECTRICAL MACHINERY NES	W 53157	307.7	W 41132	230.5	W 51412	281.7	W 47806	333.5	AUTRES MACH ELECT NDA
7788	OTH ELEC MACHY,EQUIP NES	W 6545	94.4	W 9405	93.7	W 8556	108.9	W 8050	154.1	AUT MACH APP ELEC NDA
78	ROAD VEHICLES		3016.3		2834.2		2131.3		1855.2	VEHICULES ROUTIERS
781	PASS MOTOR VEH EXC BUSES	W 183657	1707.9	W 171633	1651.7	W 120684	1260.2	W 114367	1171.9	AUTO TRANSPORT PERSONNES
782	LORRIES,SPCL MTR VEH NES	W 77479	532.7	W 74812	521.6	W 36299	352.2	W 32756	234.2	VEHICULES SPECIAUX,MARCH
7821	LORRIES,TRUCKS	W 72414	496.0	W 70502	491.1	W 34057	263.8	W 30748	216.7	VEHICULES TRANSP MARCHAND
7822	SPECIAL MOTOR VEHCLS NES	W 5065	36.8	W 4310	30.6	W 2242	88.4	W 2008	17.6	VEHICULES USAGES SPECIAUX
783	ROAD MOTOR VEHICLES NES	W 17178	103.1	W 25428	164.9	W 10880	73.3	W 4904	33.2	VEHICULES ROUTIERS NDA
7831	BUSES	W 9442	64.7	W 18206	124.8	W 7510	56.3	W 2665	18.8	VOITURES TRANSPORT COMMUN
784	MOTOR VEH PRTS,ACCES NES	W 78880	621.3	W 60705	452.9	W 54039	410.9	W 58649	384.4	PIECES 722,781,782,783
7849	OTHER MOTOR VEHCL PARTS	W 76078	605.4	W 59222	447.6	W 53260	407.0	W 55158	366.9	PIECES 722,781,782,783
79	OTHR TRANSPORT EQUIPMENT		2730.3		1625.1		1669.7		2147.4	AUTRE MATERIEL TRANSPORT
792	AIRCRAFT ETC	W 6440	2693.6	W 3687	1602.3	W 4288	1623.5	W 4391	2070.4	APP NAVIGATION AERIENNE
7928	AIRCRAFT NES,ASSOC EQUIP	W 28	0.4	W 13	0.4	W 15	0.9	W 10	95.4	APP NAVIG AERIENNE NDA
79282	BALLOONS AND AIRSHIPS	W 7	0.2	W 8	0.3	W 3	0.1	W 8	95.0	AEROSTATS
7929	AIRCRAFT PARTS NES	W 6364	2654.3	W 3653	1592.6	W 3960	1600.5	W 4364	1965.3	PIECES DU 792
8	MISC MANUFACTURED GOODS		3243.6		2482.4		2901.3		2931.5	ART MANUFACTURES DIVERS
812	*PLUMBG,HEATNG,LGHTNG EQ	W 32850	146.7	W 34248	133.0	W 36323	124.5	W 30973	116.9	APPAR SANITAIRES CHAUFFAGE
8124	LIGHTING EQUIPMENT NES	W 12492	93.0	W 10983	86.8	W 12930	81.6	W 10421	70.8	APPAREILS ECLAIRAGE ETC
81242	LAMPS,FITTINGS BASE METL	W 8767	68.5	W 9035	74.6	W 10054	62.8	W 7173	49.7	APPAREILS D'ECLAIRAGE
821	*FURNITURE,PARTS THEREOF	W 114699	345.5	W 100807	266.7	W 107690	268.6	W 105743	254.8	MEUBLES ET PIECES
8219	FURNITURE AND PARTS NES	W 97329	262.6	W 84694	200.0	W 93606	202.7	W 87013	188.7	AUTRES MEUBLES ET PIECES
82192	WOOD FURNITURE NES	W 81154	209.9	W 71474	162.8	W 77795	158.5	W 68409	144.1	MEUBLES NDA EN BOIS
831	*TRAVEL GOODS,HANDBAGS	W 23434	90.7	W 22726	74.7	W 24799	85.2	W 21951	79.9	ARTICLES DE VOYAGE ETC
84	CLOTHING AND ACCESSORIES		856.6		651.0		880.1		846.0	VETEMENTS
842	MENS OUTERWEAR NOT KNIT	W 26260	206.7	W 22303	156.7	W 32905	251.7	W 33741	250.4	VET DESSUS POUR HOMMES
8422	— SUITS	W 14786	100.3	W 12748	72.1	W 18015	129.6	W 18306	128.5	COMPLETS HOMMES MAT TEXT
84223	—— OF MAN-MADE FIBRES	W 14544	94.1	W 12597	68.0	W 17863	127.7	W 18186	126.6	COMPLETS HOMMES FIB SYNT
8429	— OTHER OUTER GARMENTS	W 6694	63.1	W 6384	58.1	W 12085	101.8	W 11293	92.7	AUT VET DES HOM MAT TEX
843	WOMENS OUTERWEAR NONKNIT	W 25589	263.5	W 21051	248.1	W 30202	313.6	W 29664	306.1	VET DESSUS FEMMES MAT TEX
8439	— OTHER OUTER GARMENTS	W 11844	127.2	W 11471	133.6	W 18735	178.9	W 17264	173.5	AUT VET DES FEM MAT TEXT
844	UNDER GARMENTS NOT KNIT	W 16800	123.8	W 10365	79.6	W 12945	93.2	W 11973	87.4	VETEMENT DESSOUS MAT TEX
845	OUTERWEAR KNIT NONELASTC	W 16377	114.5	W 7527	58.7	W 8764	68.0	W 8149	68.4	VET DESSOUS,ACCES BONNET
848	HEADGEAR,NONTXTL CLOTHNG	W 7331	72.8	W 5473	56.6	W 7425	94.0	W 7777	79.5	VET ACCES MAT AUT QUE TEX
851	*FOOTWEAR	W 33972	205.0	W 24445	169.4	W 30783	206.3	W 35610	223.7	CHAUSSURES
85102	FOOTWEAR LEATHER	W 16631	135.0	W 11847	109.2	W 16837	137.9	W 19273	149.0	CHAUS SEMELLES EN CUIR
87	PRECISION INSTRUMNTS NES		382.0		274.4		320.0		358.0	INSTRUM,APPAR SCIENT NDA
872	MEDICAL INSTRUMENTS NES	W 3094	104.2	W 2574	85.7	W 2620	77.0	W 2724	73.3	INSTR,APP MEDIC-CHIR NDA
87202	OTH MEDICAL INSTRUMENTS	W 2636	91.2	W 2053	74.5	W 2158	64.7	W 2099	59.6	INSTRUM,APP MEDECINE
874	MEASURNG,CONTROLNG INSTR	W 6085	241.0	W 4831	159.6	W 5814	211.6	W 6310	264.1	INSTRUMENTS DE MESURE
8748	ELEC MEAS,CONTRL EQU NES	W 1038	67.8	W 931	51.1	W 1264	74.2	W 1314	91.8	APP ELEC ELECTRO MESURE
88	PHOTO EQU,OPTICL GDS ETC		369.0		303.5		324.7		325.8	APP,FOURN PHOTO,OP,MONTR
885	WATCHES AND CLOCKS		227.9		199.2		193.8		204.3	HORLOGERIE
8851	WATCHES,MOVEMENTS,CASES		208.9		184.5		174.3		185.7	MONTRES,MOUVEMENTS,BOITES
88511	WATCHES		203.4		180.7		171.2		181.4	MONTRES POCHE,BRACELET
89	MISC MANUFCTRD GOODS NES		848.4		609.9		692.3		726.8	ART MANUFACTURES DIVERS
892	PRINTED MATTER	W 10633	77.2	W 10185	49.3	W 9108	56.2	W 8133	88.3	IMPRIMES
893	ARTICLES OF PLASTIC NES		257.9		221.1		254.1		230.9	OUVRAGES EN MAT DIVIS 58
8939	MISC PLASTIC ARTICLES	W 63000	196.6	W 51414	165.4	W 59657	194.8	W 56186	170.9	ART DIVERS EN MAT DIV 58
89399	OTHR PLASTC ARTICLES NES	W 57067	180.1	W 45922	150.4	W 53393	175.9	W 50598	155.1	AUT OUV MAT DIV 58
894	TOYS,SPORTING GOODS,ETC	W 42766	100.7	W 25729	86.2	W 25706	95.6	W 28157	133.5	VOITURES ENFANTS,JOUETS
897	GOLD,SILVER WARE,JEWELRY		158.7		50.8		63.6		56.1	BIJOUTERIE,ORFEVRERIE
8973	PREC JEWLRY,GLD-SILVWARE		124.5		23.8		30.7		25.4	BIJOUX OR,ARGENT ORFEVRE
89731	PRECIOUS METAL JEWELLERY		119.9		17.9		25.2		20.0	ART BIJOUTERIE,JOAILLER
899	OTHER MANUFACTURED GOODS		106.1		88.4		99.8		93.6	AUT ART MANUF DIVERS NDA
9	GOODS NOT CLASSD BY KIND		1023.5		1192.0		1533.2		1527.9	ART TRANSACT NON CLASSES
931	*SPECIAL TRANSACTIONS		79.3		80.4		67.8		88.3	TRANS.SPECIALES
951	*WAR FIREARMS,AMMUNITION	W 8944	230.6	W 9444	368.8	W 4947	389.2	W 4255	307.1	VEHIC BLINDES ARMES
95101	ARMORED FIGHTNG VEHICLES	W 5398	98.2	W 8040	349.0	W 4152	236.9	W 3604	234.4	CHARS DE COMBAT
971	*GOLD,NON MONETARY NES	K 63104	706.2	K 59470	734.4		996.7	K 88739	1114.2	OR NON MONETAIRE
97101	NONMON GLD UNWRT,SEMIMFD	K 62984	706.1	K 59451	734.4	K 151911	996.6	K 88738	1114.2	OR,ALLIAGES D'OR BRUTS

5. General Exports F.O.B. by Commodities according to the S.I.T.C. (Rev. 2) in million U.S. Dollars
Exportations Générales F.O.B. par Produits d'après la C.T.C.I. (Rév. 2) en millions de Dollars E.U.

SITC CTCI	COMMODITY	1993 QUANTITY QUANTITE	1993 VALUE VALEUR	1994 QUANTITY QUANTITE	1994 VALUE VALEUR	1995 QUANTITY QUANTITE	1995 VALUE VALEUR	1996 QUANTITY QUANTITE	1996 VALUE VALEUR	PRODUIT
	ALL COMMODITIES		42395.8		42874.2		49029.6		56509.6	TOUS PRODUITS
0	FOOD AND LIVE ANIMALS		433.4		299.2		395.2		357.5	ALIMENTS,ANIMAUX VIVANTS
04	CEREALS AND PREPARATIONS		204.7		116.0		117.8		36.3	CEREALES ET PRODUITS
041	WHEAT ETC UNMILLED	W 1568970	180.1	W 815584	95.6	W 595937	89.1			FROMENT,EPEAUTRE
0412	OTHER WHEAT ETC UNMILLED	W 1568970	180.1	W 798584	93.4	W 595937	89.1			AUTRE FROMENT NON MOULU
2	CRUDE MATERLS,EXCL FUELS		164.2		142.6		208.7		177.1	MAT BRUTES NON COMESTIBLES
3	MINERAL FUELS ETC		38613.4		38617.1		42539.8		50051.1	COMBUSTIBLES MINERAUX LUB
33	PETROLEUM AND PRODUCTS		36675.8		38598.7		42509.0		50050.9	PETROLE ET DERIVES
333	CRUDE PETROLEUM	MW 297454	32017.8	MW 310705	31967.5	MW 313556	36336.5	MW 304510	41699.1	HUILES BRUTES DE PETROLE
334	PETROLEUM PRODUCTS,REFIN	MW 44286	4586.5	W 310	0.2	W 101	0.2	W 69	0.1	PRODUITS RAFFINES
3341	GASOLINE,OTH LIGHT OILS	MW 11862	1702.5				1839.0		2504.1	ESSENCES POUR MOTEURS
33411	MOTOR,AVIATION SPIRIT	MW 11861	1702.1							ESSENCES MOTEURS D'AVIONS
33419	OTH LIGHT PETROLEUM OILS	W 988	0.5				1839.0		2504.1	AUTRES HUILES LEGERES
3342	KEROSENE,OTH MEDIUM OILS	W 4530319	777.1		615.1		897.0		1168.6	PETR LAMPANTS,AUT HUIL
33421	KEROSENE INCL JET FUEL	W 4530319	777.1	W 43	0.1					PETROLES LAMPANTS
33429	OTH MEDIUM PETROLEUM OIL				615.0		897.0		1168.6	AUTRES HUILES MOYENNES
3343	GAS OILS	MW 22800	1982.1		1430.0		2230.4		3088.4	GAS OILS
3344	FUEL OILS,NES	W 5076843	113.3		2429.0				1586.0	FUEL OILS
341	*GAS,NATURAL AND MANUFCT	MW 15574	1937.5	W 42368	18.4	W 50002	30.8	W 43	0.1	GAZ NATUREL,GAZ MANUFACT
3413	PETROLM GASES,LIQUEFIED	MW 15574	1937.5	W 42356	18.4	W 49844	30.8	W 3	0.1	GAZ DE PETROLE LIQUEFIE
34131	LIQUEFIED PROPANE,BUTANE	MW 14846	1802.2	W 37929	15.5	W 31723	19.1			PROPANE,BUTANE LIQUEFIES
34139	OTH HYDROCARBON GAS LQFD	W 727750	135.4	W 4427	2.9	W 18120	11.7	W 3	0.1	HYDROCARBURES GAZEUX NDA
5	CHEMCLS,RELATED PROD NES		2203.6		2851.8		4117.5		3894.6	PRODUITS CHIMIQUES
51	ORGANIC CHEMICALS		969.7		1347.4		1865.7		1792.0	PROD CHIMIQ ORGANIQUES
511	HYDROCARBONS NES,DERIVS	W 1145526	319.0	W 1032511	331.0	W 947249	488.3	W 1281291	483.4	HYDROCARBURES NDA
5111	ACYCLIC HYDROCARBONS	W 309954	96.5	W 432721	122.0	W 312208	129.5	W 634472	241.2	HYDROCARBURES ACYCLIQUES
5112	CYCLIC HYDROCARBONS	W 250932	105.0	W 215715	105.3	W 350566	265.1	W 337662	154.0	HYDROCARBURES CYCLIQUES
51125	STYRENE	W 250613	104.7	W 173810	94.3	W 342072	261.2	W 335967	152.9	STYRENE
512	ALCOHOLS,PHENOLS ETC	W 2947312	569.2	W 2909887	800.9	W 2594069	919.9	W 2974543	834.4	PHENOLS,PHENOLS–ALCOOLS
5121	ACYCLIC ALCOHOLS,DERIVS	W 2780366	530.1	W 2663340	751.0	W 2589724	917.8	W 2974215	834.2	ALCOOLS ACYCLIQUES
51211	METHYL ALCOHOL(METHANOL)	W 1647452	152.1	W 1335572	378.2	W 1292981	308.0	W 1741346	218.0	ALCOOLS METHYLIQUES
51215	ETHYLENE GLYCOL	W 748388	271.3	W 1036081	292.3	W 1120086	548.2	W 1190152	602.1	ETHYLENE–GLYCOL
516	OTHER ORGANIC CHEMICALS	W 295771	66.1	W 928123	209.8	W 1642614	444.6	W 2048269	470.0	AUTRES PROD ORGANIQUES
5161	ETHERS,EPOXIDES,ACETALS	W 292825	64.6	W 798746	186.7	W 1637611	440.1	W 2017678	457.1	ETHERS–OXYDES,ALCOOLS
51611	ETHERS,ETHER–ALCOHOL,ETC	W 292661	64.5	W 798746	186.7	W 1637092	439.9	W 2017620	457.0	ETHERS–OXYDES
52	INORGANIC CHEMICALS		276.7		215.8		345.6		355.0	PROD CHIM INORGANIQUES
522	INORG ELEMNTS,OXIDES,ETC	W 1821404	274.1	W 2010408	204.3	W 2098211	340.9	W 2166122	346.4	ELEMENTS INORGANIQUES
5221	CHEMICAL ELEMENTS	W 1056824	112.4	W 1270127	132.6	W 940322	107.1	W 1415125	156.0	ELEMENTS CHIMIQUES
52215	SULPHUR,PURIFIED	W 1048700	109.4	W 1267673	131.5	W 901533	101.8	W 1397763	153.2	SOUFRE SUBLIME,PRECIPITE
5225	INORGANIC BASES ETC NES	W 739543	132.8	W 722237	57.5	W 1110475	167.4	W 717095	148.1	AUTRES BASES OXYDES METAL
52253	SODIUM HYDROXIDE, OTHER	W 738296	132.3	W 715829	56.0	W 1102368	164.8	W 700511	143.4	HYDROXYDE SODIUM AQUEUX
562	*FERTILIZERS,MANUFACTURE	W 1166112	148.9	W 1871355	249.6	W 1683467	307.8	W 1938422	410.9	ENGRAIS MANUFACTURES
5621	CHEM NITROGENOUS FERTLZR	W 1162972	148.0	W 1777196	236.3	W 1671960	306.7	W 1881097	398.0	ENGRAIS AZOTES
56219	CHEM NITROG FERTILZR NES	W 822435	103.7	W 1494073	197.8	W 1173573	210.0	W 1334980	275.6	ENGRAIS AZOTES NDA
58	PLASTIC MATERIALS ETC		648.5		868.8		1403.3		1101.9	MAT PLAST ARTIFICIELLES
583	POLYMERIZATION ETC PRODS	W 1294267	641.7	W 1613814	861.1	W 1850891	1386.3	W 1617882	1056.1	PROD POLYMERISATION
5831	POLYETHYLENE	W 1089415	533.4	W 1324188	683.4	W 1347611	1020.3	W 1340864	888.1	POLYETHYLENE
58311	— IN PRIMARY FORMS	W 1088704	532.8	W 1323575	682.9	W 1346544	1019.7	W 1340006	887.2	POLYETHYLENE PRIMAIRES
5834	POLYVINYL CHLORIDE	W 106305	53.7	W 98692	63.5	W 230601	181.0	W 62082	49.3	CHLORURE DE POLYVINYLE
58341	— IN PRIMARY FORMS	W 106194	53.6	W 98619	63.4	W 230492	180.9	W 61667	48.9	SOUS FORMES PRIMAIRES
6	BASIC MANUFACTURES		460.6		485.8		1097.7		1178.3	ART MANUFACTURES
66	NONMETAL MINERAL MFS NES		66.6		80.4		137.5		208.0	ART MIN NON METALLIQUES
67	IRON AND STEEL		63.2		66.0		251.5		287.5	FER ET ACIER
673	IRON,STEEL SHAPES ETC	W 24920	11.1	W 32179	16.2	W 465911	156.9	W 644928	203.9	BARRES,PROFIL FER,ACIER
6732	IRON,STEEL BARS ETC	W 14615	6.0	W 18700	7.1	W 388051	124.0	W 622754	187.1	BARRES FER,ACIER
69	METAL MANUFACTURES NES		133.4		138.2		309.9		276.0	ART MANUFACT EN METAL NDA
7	MACHINES,TRANSPORT EQUIP		404.8		363.5		502.4		708.6	MACHINES MATERIEL TRANSPORT
78	ROAD VEHICLES		93.7		75.9		153.5		250.3	VEHICULES ROUTIERS

1. HISTORICAL SERIES, 1962–1997 SPECIAL TRADE, IMPORTS C.I.F., EXPORTS F.O.B.
SERIES HISTORIQUES, 1962–1997 COMMERCE SPECIAL, IMPORTATIONS C.A.F., EXPORTATIONS F.O.B

YEAR ANNEE	VALUE IN MILLION C.F.A. FRANCS / VALEUR EN MILLION C.F.A. FRANCS — MERCHANDISE – MARCHANDISE		GOLD – OR		CONVERSION FACTORS U.S. CENTS PER C.F.A. FRANC / FACTEURS DE CONVERSION CENTS E.U. PAR C.F.A. FRANC		INDEX NUMBERS – INDICES — QUANTUM		UNIT VALUE / VALEUR UNITAIRE	
	IMPORTS	EXPORTS	IMPORTS	EXPORTS	IMPORTS	EXPORTS	IMPORTS	EXPORTS	IMPORTS	EXPORTS
1962	38204.00	30671.00	2.00		0.4051	0.4051				
1963	38508.00	27279.00	18.00		0.4051	0.4051				
1964	42371.00	30243.00	16.00		0.4051	0.4051				
1965	39568.00	31712.00	16.00		0.4051	0.4051				
1966	38283.00	36764.00	30.00		0.4051	0.4051				
1967	38898.00	33890.00	6.00		0.4051	0.4051				
1968	44527.00	37369.00	2.00		0.4051	0.4051				
1969	51294.00	31907.00	5.00		0.3905	0.3962				
1970	53557.00	42182.00	6.00		0.3601	0.3601				
1971	60561.00	34707.00	49.00	5.00	0.3601	0.3601				
1972	70289.00	54412.00	26.00		0.3966	0.3969				
1973	79767.00	43237.00			0.4506	0.4512				
1974	119382.00	93983.00			0.4167	0.4158				
1975	124616.00	99101.00			0.4678	0.4643				
1976	139164.00	117094.00			0.4160	0.4105				
1977	187547.00	152920.00			0.4074	0.4080				
1978	170314.00	84909.00			0.4440	0.4418				
1979	197979.00	113858.00			0.4704	0.4704				
1980	222256.00	100767.00			0.4733	0.4733				
1981	292341.00	135900.00			0.3679	0.3677				
1982	325935.10	180037.00			0.3043	0.3043				
1983	396079.10	206976.00			0.2624	0.2624				
1984	437100.00	233974.00			0.2310	0.2284				
1985	370970.90	252492.00			0.2189	0.2196				
1986	332930.00	216580.00			0.2888	0.2888				
1987	307600.10	182250.00			0.3327	0.3327				
1988	321570.00	176080.00			0.3357	0.3357				
1989	389540.10	221100.00			0.3135	0.3135				
1990	332120.00	207380.00			0.3673	0.3673				
1991	330939.90	197710.00			0.3555	0.3554				
1992	273720.00	178080.00			0.3785	0.3787				
1993	332300.00	180500.00			0.3541	0.3541				
1994	611200.00	395500.00			0.1800	0.1800				
1995	650000.10	430200.00			0.2002	0.2002				
1996	648400.10	504499.90			0.1954	0.1954				
1997	694299.90	539600.10			0.1713	0.1713				

2. IMPORTS BY BROAD ECONOMIC CATEGORY AND EXPORTS BY INDUSTRIAL ORIGIN. (PERCENTAGE OF TOTAL VALUE)
IMPORTATIONS PAR CATEGORIES ECONOMIQUES ET EXPORTATIONS PAR BRANCHE D'ACTIVITE.(EN POURCENTAGE DE LA VALEUR TOTALE)

IMPORTS – IMPORTATIONS

	1991	1992	1993	1994	1995	1996	1997
TOTAL IMPORTS–IMPORTATIONS TOTALES	100.	100.	100.	100.	100.		
1 FOOD BEV–ALIMENTATION BOISSONS	27.5	27.9	31.2	23.7	30.4		
11 PRIMARY–PRODUITS DE BASE	8.5	7.5	7.5	7.1	6.7		
111 FOR INDUSTRY–POUR L'INDUSTRIE	3.4	3.0	3.4	3.8	4.5		
112 FOR HOUSEHOLDS–POUR LES MENAGES	5.1	4.5	4.2	3.3	2.2		
12 PROCESSED–PRODUITS ELABORES	19.0	20.4	23.7	16.6	23.6		
121 FOR INDUSTRY–POUR L'INDUSTRIE	4.7	4.3	6.1	4.1	5.9		
122 FOR HOUSEHOLDS–POUR LES MENAGES	14.3	16.1	17.6	12.4	17.7		
2 IND SUPPLIES–APPROV INDUSTRIELS	29.1	29.1	27.2	28.5	32.0		
21 PRIMARY–PRODUITS DE BASE	2.8	3.4	3.9	3.6	3.5		
22 PROCESSED–PRODUITS ELABORES	26.3	25.7	23.3	25.0	28.5		
3 FUELS–COMBUSTIBLES	10.7	8.7	8.9	19.0	9.8		
31 PRIMARY–PRODUITS DE BASE	8.3	6.8	7.4	5.3	7.2		
32 PROCESSED–PRODUITS ELABORES	2.4	1.9	1.5	13.6	2.5		
321 MOTOR SPIRIT–ESSENCE	0.4	0.0	0.0	1.3	0.2		
322 OTHER–AUTRES	2.0	1.8	1.5	12.3	2.3		
4 MACHINERY–EQUIPEMENT	14.9	14.4	12.9	11.9	10.9		
41 CAPITAL EQUIPMENT–MACHINES	13.4	12.6	11.4	10.5	9.8		
42 PARTS–PIECES ACCESSOIRES	1.5	1.8	1.5	1.4	1.1		
5 TRANSPORT–TRANSPORT	8.2	9.3	9.2	7.8	7.7		
51 PASSENGER CARS–AUTOMOBILES	2.4	3.2	3.3	2.1	2.0		
52 OTHER–AUTRES	3.1	2.9	2.9	2.3	2.8		
521 INDUSTRIAL–INDUSTRIELS	3.0	2.7	2.8	2.1	2.7		
522 NON INDUSTRIAL–NON INDUSTRIEL	0.1	0.1	0.1	0.2	0.1		
53 PARTS–PIECES ACCESSOIRES	2.7	3.3	3.0	3.4	2.9		
6 CONSUM GOODS–BIENS CONSOMMATION	9.6	10.6	10.5	8.9	8.8		
61 DURABLE–DURABLES	1.2	1.6	1.5	1.3	1.3		
62 SEMI DURABLE–SEMI DURABLES	2.6	3.2	3.3	2.9	3.3		
63 NON DURABLE–NON DURABLES	5.8	5.9	5.8	4.8	4.2		
7 GOODS NES–BIENS NDA	0.0	0.0	0.0	0.2	0.5		

EXPORTS – EXPORTATIONS

	1991	1992	1993	1994	1995	1996	1997
TOTAL EXPORTS–EXPORTATIONS TOTALES	100.	100.	100.	100.	100.		
1 AGRICULTURE	17.6	17.6	20.1	14.5	10.7		
2 MINING QUARRY–INDUS EXTRACTIVES	8.6	12.2	10.8	6.8	9.9		
3 MANUFACTURING–IND MANUFACTUR	73.7	70.2	69.1	78.7	79.4		
31 FOOD BEV TOBACCO–ALIM BOISS TAB	35.9	28.4	21.2	23.6	13.4		
32 TEXTILES–INDUSTRIES TEXTILES	1.0	1.2	1.0	1.1	0.7		
33 WOOD & PRODUCTS–BOIS & PRODUITS	0.1	0.1	0.1	0.1	0.1		
34 PAPER & PRODUCTS–PAPIER & PRODT	1.0	2.0	2.6	1.8	2.7		
35 CHEMICALS–INDUSTRIES CHIMIQUES	31.4	31.9	32.7	42.1	56.5		
36 NON METAL MIN–MIN NON METAL	0.1	0.1	0.2	0.5	0.4		
37 BASIC METAL–IND METAL BASE	0.3	0.6	1.1	0.7	0.6		
38 METAL MANUF–MANUF METAL	3.8	5.7	9.7	8.6	4.9		
39 OTH MANUF IND–AUTRES MANUF	0.1	0.2	0.3	0.3	0.3		

3. TRADE BY PRINCIPAL COUNTRIES OF ORIGIN AND DESTINATION (VALUE IN MILLION U.S. DOLLARS)
ECHANGES SELON LES PRINCIPAUX PAYS D'ORIGINE ET DE DESTINATION (VALEUR EN MILLIONS DE DOLLARS EU)

COUNTRIES–PAYS	SPECIAL IMPORTS C.I.F. IMPORTATIONS SPECIALES C.A.F				
	1993	1994	1995	1996	1997
World	1139.2	876.8	1224.4	1307.6	1205.9
Africa	170.5	92.2	144.3	150.3	165.2
Americas	98.9	72.8	160.5	137.6	113.9
– Northern America	69.7	51.4	84.2	78.2	74.2
– LAIA	27.2	18.0	69.9	56.0	36.3
– CACM	0.0	0.0	0.0	0.0	0.1
– Caribbean	1.4	3.4	6.3	3.4	0.2
– Rest of America	0.6	0.0		0.0	3.1
Asia excl fmr USSR	181.8	126.8	231.2	285.1	241.9
– Middle East	9.2	6.2	5.7	8.9	8.1
Asia former USSR					
Europe excl fmr USSR	665.7	569.6	668.3	726.8	660.3
– European Union	650.4	556.9	654.4	708.0	643.8
– Eastern Europe	7.5	4.8	5.9	8.6	9.4
– Rest of Europe	7.9	7.8	8.0	10.2	7.1
Europe former USSR	9.8	9.2	16.4	7.1	23.5
Oceania	11.8	5.8	3.7	0.5	0.8
Other	0.6	0.3	0.1		
France, Monaco	403.1	300.9	386.9	378.7	370.3
Nigeria/Nigéria	71.0	39.3	77.9	76.6	87.6
USA/Etats–Unis d'Amer	59.2	43.8	70.0	67.5	58.3
Germany/Allemagne	42.4	28.4	59.9	89.7	44.8
Spain/Espagne	40.1	46.9	41.8	56.4	53.6
Italy/Italie	48.1	55.6	43.4	45.5	40.3
Thailand/Thaïlande	46.7	32.8	60.5	43.6	35.5
Japan/Japon	40.7	35.4	45.8	39.6	36.3
Cote d'Ivoire	57.8	34.1	32.2	34.2	31.2
India/Inde	3.1	2.6	43.6	90.2	47.0
Belgium–Luxembourg	30.4	32.7	38.0	37.2	45.5
Netherlands/Pays–Bas	38.7	34.4	33.6	41.9	32.8
Brazil/Brésil	20.4	14.8	44.5	30.1	19.9
China/Chine	23.4	21.9	29.3	28.4	25.2
United Kingdom	17.0	19.8	22.1	24.2	21.9
Viet Nam	16.1	4.9	1.5	14.9	31.2
Russian Federation	9.8	9.2	16.4	7.1	23.5
Canada	10.5	7.6	14.3	10.7	15.9
Korea, Republic of	9.8	8.1	11.1	13.4	11.8
Gabon	19.9	2.1	13.7	15.3	1.2
Portugal	2.1	23.5	5.8	6.2	8.6
Israel/Israël	0.0	2.3	0.3	16.0	23.0
China, Hong Kong SAR	9.4	6.0	10.0	7.8	4.9
Ireland/Irlande	5.1	2.0	5.4	10.5	12.0
Uruguay		1.0	12.5	12.7	8.4
Morocco/Maroc	10.4	2.5	4.9	8.6	6.0
Cameroon/Cameroun	4.0	2.3	8.5	6.8	8.7
Switzerland,Liechtenst.	5.8	6.0	5.7	8.3	3.9
Pakistan	7.0	0.5	12.4	5.2	3.4
Argentina/Argentine	2.0	0.3	11.1	10.7	3.5
Sweden/Suède	5.9	3.7	6.2	5.7	5.1
Algeria/Algérie	0.1	0.7	0.2	0.2	21.8
Indonesia/Indonésie	4.5	1.5	2.1	6.9	5.2
Finland/Finlande	5.7	3.5	5.5	2.5	2.7
Other Asia n.e.s.	3.2	2.5	3.7	7.1	3.3
Denmark/Danemark	5.7	3.4	2.9	4.6	2.4
New Zealand	11.1	4.1	3.2	0.5	0.1
Turkey/Turquie	3.0	1.7	3.0	5.7	5.2
Austria/Autriche	5.7	1.7	1.5	3.5	2.5
Malaysia/Malaisie	1.4	1.0	4.1	2.4	6.0

COUNTRIES–PAYS	SPECIAL EXPORTS F.O.B. EXPORTATIONS SPECIALES F.O.B.				
	1993	1994	1995	1996	1997
Monde	605.1	444.4	530.8	530.9	393.5
Afrique	141.1	110.5	142.0	166.1	
Amériques	23.6	6.1	5.8	14.5	
– Amérique du Nord	18.0	5.1	3.2	2.2	
– ALAI	3.8	0.9	2.5	12.2	
– MCAC	1.7				
– Caraïbes	0.1	0.0	0.1	0.1	
– Autre Amérique			0.0		
Asie anc. URSS exclus	132.4	102.8	186.3	135.6	
– Moyen–Orient	13.7	9.5	12.2	12.9	
Asie ancienne URSS					
Europe anc. URSS exclus	244.8	164.0	127.6	144.3	
– Union Européenne	244.1	163.2	126.5	143.4	
– Europe de l'Est	0.1	0.0		0.0	
– Autre de l'Europe	0.6	0.8	1.1	0.9	
Europe ancienne URSS	0.0	0.4		0.5	
Océanie	0.0	0.0	0.0	0.0	
Autre	63.2	60.6	69.1		
India/Inde	76.9	67.0	136.4	110.6	101.3
France, Monaco	157.3	80.0	58.9	76.0	32.8
Mali	31.3	40.7	45.0	47.8	37.0
Bunkers, ship stores	61.7	60.0	51.0		
Italy/Italie	41.4	22.4	38.1	28.1	8.0
Cote d'Ivoire	13.4	7.8	8.1	15.1	17.5
Mauritania/Mauritanie	12.4	7.1	11.6	15.4	14.2
Other Asia n.e.s.	17.8	9.4	21.9	3.2	3.7
Netherlands/Pays–Bas	7.1	22.4	8.1	11.9	5.8
Gambia/Gambie	12.6	7.0	8.8	12.6	12.2
Guinea/Guinée	11.8	7.0	6.7	10.2	9.2
Benin/Bénin	10.2	2.9	13.4	16.7	1.6
Iran (Islamic Rep of)	13.5	7.9	9.9	9.1	3.4
Germany/Allemagne	9.6	9.7	4.2	5.6	6.2
Cameroon/Cameroun	7.3	4.5	8.6	9.9	4.7
United Kingdom	4.0	9.8	5.0	11.8	2.7
Nigeria/Nigéria	3.8	7.5	11.8	7.7	2.3
Spain/Espagne	9.4	11.9	2.1	6.4	2.4
Guinea–Bissau	3.1	3.5	4.1	7.1	8.0
USA/Etats–Unis d'Amer	12.2	5.1	3.1	1.2	1.1
Areas n.e.s.	1.4	0.7	18.1		
Togo	1.6	3.8	5.3	5.6	3.8
Philippines	3.3	3.6	10.0	2.2	
Burkina Faso	3.8	1.4	4.7	3.9	4.7
Japan/Japon	10.3	3.5	1.9	0.3	1.2
Portugal	2.1	2.3	6.2	1.2	4.1
Congo	5.9	3.1	1.9	2.4	1.6
Brazil/Brésil	0.0	0.4	2.1	10.0	2.2
Belgium–Luxembourg	7.1	2.7	2.0	2.0	0.9
Gabon	4.1	1.9	0.9	1.4	2.3
Greece/Grèce	5.4	1.3	1.9	0.0	0.2
Chad/Tchad	1.5	0.7	1.3	2.2	2.6
Sierra Leone	2.1	1.6	1.4	2.6	0.3
Thailand/Thaïlande	2.3	3.1	1.1	0.5	0.4
Canada	5.8	0.1	0.2	1.0	0.2
Morocco/Maroc	4.5	0.1	0.7	0.6	1.3
Indonesia/Indonésie	0.1	0.4	1.0	5.3	
Ethiopia/Ethiopie	6.1			0.0	
United Arab Emirates		0.3	2.0	3.6	
China, Hong Kong SAR	2.8	1.1	0.7	0.0	0.6

(VALUE AS PERCENTAGE OF WORLD TOTAL)(VALEURS EN POURCENTAGE DU TOTAL MONDIAL)

	1988	1989	1990	1991	1992	1993	1994	1995	1996	1997
Africa	15.1	23.4	16.1	16.2	15.1	15.0	10.5	11.8	11.5	13.7
Americas	9.6	9.2	9.5	10.4	10.1	8.7	8.3	13.1	10.5	9.4
– Northern America	7.5	7.2	6.4	8.5	8.1	6.1	5.9	6.9	6.0	6.2
– LAIA	2.0	1.7	1.8	1.7	1.8	2.4	2.1	5.7	4.3	3.0
– CACM	0.0	0.0	0.0	0.0	0.0	0.0	0.0	0.0	0.0	0.0
– Caribbean	0.0	0.4	1.3	0.1	0.2	0.1	0.4	0.5	0.3	0.0
– Rest of America	0.0	0.0	0.0	0.1	0.0	0.1	0.0		0.0	0.3
Asia excl fmr USSR	16.1	14.0	14.0	13.0	15.2	16.0	14.5	18.9	21.8	20.1
– Middle East	0.8	0.7	1.0	0.6	0.5	0.8	0.7	0.5	0.7	0.7
Asia former USSR										
Europe excl fmr USSR	55.3	52.0	59.0	58.7	58.1	58.4	65.0	54.6	55.6	54.8
– European Union	53.6	50.1	57.3	56.9	56.4	57.1	63.5	53.4	54.1	53.4
– Eastern Europe	1.0	1.1	1.1	1.0	0.8	0.7	0.6	0.5	0.7	0.8
– Rest of Europe	0.7	0.8	0.6	0.8	0.9	0.7	0.9	0.7	0.8	0.6
Europe former USSR	0.2	0.2	0.4	0.5	0.5	0.9	1.1	1.3	0.5	1.9
Oceania	0.1	0.1	0.0	0.3	0.8	1.0	0.7	0.3	0.0	0.1
Other	3.7	1.2	0.9	0.8	0.2	0.1	0.0	0.0		
France, Monaco	31.5	28.6	32.9	34.3	33.2	35.4	34.3	31.6	29.0	30.7
Nigeria/Nigéria	4.3	8.1	7.5	7.3	6.1	6.2	4.5	6.4	5.9	7.3
USA/Etats–Unis d'Amer	6.4	5.9	5.3	7.2	6.1	5.2	5.0	5.7	5.2	4.8
Germany/Allemagne				3.5	3.6	3.7	3.2	4.9	6.9	3.7
Spain/Espagne	4.7	4.5	4.2	3.3	3.6	3.5	5.4	3.4	4.3	4.4
Italy/Italie	3.9	5.0	6.5	5.2	6.0	4.2	6.3	3.5	3.5	3.3
Thailand/Thaïlande	2.3	2.5	2.9	5.2	3.0	4.1	3.7	4.9	3.3	2.9
Japan/Japon	4.2	3.7	3.6	3.0	3.8	3.6	4.0	3.7	3.0	3.0
Cote d'Ivoire	5.7	4.4	4.5	5.6	6.0	5.1	3.9	2.6	2.6	2.6
India/Inde	0.8	0.1	0.1	0.2	0.5	0.3	0.3	3.6	6.9	3.9

	1988	1989	1990	1991	1992	1993	1994	1995	1996	1997
Afrique	18.7	22.6	20.1	14.4	19.8	23.3	24.9	26.8	31.3	
Amériques	0.9	0.6	0.3	2.4	1.1	3.9	1.4	1.1	2.7	
– Amérique du Nord	0.8	0.2	0.2	1.8	0.5	3.0	1.2	0.6	0.4	
– ALAI	0.0	0.2	0.0	0.3	0.2	0.6	0.2	0.5	2.3	
– MCAC	0.0			0.3	0.3	0.3				
– Caraïbes	0.1	0.2	0.0	0.1	0.2	0.0	0.0	0.0	0.0	
– Autre Amérique			0.0	0.0				0.0		
Asie anc. URSS exclus	16.3	16.8	17.0	19.8	25.7	21.9	23.1	35.1	25.5	
– Moyen–Orient	0.2	0.7	1.9	1.9	3.2	2.3	2.1	2.3	2.4	
Asie ancienne URSS										
Europe anc. URSS exclus	57.1	50.8	53.4	51.2	43.8	40.5	36.9	24.0	27.2	
– Union Européenne	56.2	50.6	53.4	51.2	43.5	40.3	36.7	23.8	27.0	
– Europe de l'Est	0.2	0.0	0.0		0.0	0.0	0.0		0.0	
– Autre de l'Europe	0.8	0.3	0.0	0.0	0.3	0.1	0.2	0.2	0.2	
Europe ancienne URSS	0.0	0.0	0.0	0.0	0.0	0.0	0.1		0.1	
Océanie	0.2	0.0		0.0	0.0	0.0	0.0	0.0	0.0	
Autre	6.8	9.2	9.3	12.2	9.6	10.4	13.6	13.0		
India/Inde	9.7	9.3	10.6	11.8	15.4	12.7	15.1	25.7	20.8	25.7
France, Monaco	37.6	33.4	34.9	31.6	27.2	26.0	18.0	11.1	14.3	8.3
Mali	4.1	6.5	7.1	3.7	5.4	5.2	9.1	8.5	9.0	9.4
Bunkers, ship stores		7.7	8.8	12.1	9.3	10.2	13.5	9.6		
Italy/Italie	4.1	6.2	7.0	10.1	5.8	6.8	5.0	7.2	5.3	2.0
Cote d'Ivoire	3.2	2.8	2.8	2.7	2.9	2.2	1.7	1.5	2.8	4.5
Mauritania/Mauritanie	3.1	1.5	0.0	0.0	0.7	2.0	1.6	2.2	2.9	3.6
Other Asia n.e.s.	0.8	0.5	0.3	2.0	1.6	2.9	2.1	4.1	0.6	0.9
Netherlands/Pays–Bas	4.1	3.0	5.3	1.6	3.7	1.2	5.0	1.5	2.2	1.5
Gambia/Gambie	0.7	1.2	0.9	1.5	1.7	2.1	1.6	1.7	2.4	3.1

4. Special Imports C.I.F. by Commodities according to the S.I.T.C. (Rev. 2) in million U.S. Dollars
Importations Spéciales C.A.F. par Produits d'après la C.T.C.I. (Rév. 2) en millions de Dollars E.U.

SITC CTCI	COMMODITY	1994 QUANTITY QUANTITE	1994 VALUE VALEUR	1995 QUANTITY QUANTITE	1995 VALUE VALEUR	1996 QUANTITY QUANTITE	1996 VALUE VALEUR	1997 QUANTITY QUANTITE	1997 VALUE VALEUR	PRODUIT
	ALL COMMODITIES		876.8		1224.5					TOUS PRODUITS
0	FOOD AND LIVE ANIMALS		174.5		317.2					ALIMENTS,ANIMAUX VIVANTS
02	DAIRY PRODCTS,BIRDS'EGGS		39.7		34.5					PRODUITS LAITIERS,OEUFS
022	MILK AND CREAM	W 21058	35.4	W 15587	30.5					LAIT ET CREME
0224	MILK,CREAM PRESERVED ETC	W 19097	34.4	W 13849	29.3					LAIT,CREME CONS,CONC
02242	MILK DRY,1.5% FAT OR LES	W 18775	34.0	W 12635	28.3					LAIT POUDRE INF 1.5%
023	BUTTER	W 1727	3.1	W 1203	2.7					BEURRE
03	FISH AND PREPARATIONS		7.9		0.9					POISSONS ET PREPARATIONS
034	FISH,FRESH,CHILLED,FROZN	W 7299	6.8	W 26	0.1					POISSON FRAIS, REFRIG,CONG
0341	FISH FRSH,CHLLD,EX FILLT	W 7299	6.8	W 26	0.1					POISSON FRAIS,REFRIGERE
04	CEREALS AND PREPARATIONS		76.7		195.9					CEREALES ET PRODUITS
041	WHEAT ETC UNMILLED	W 185102	31.6	W 223899	54.0					FROMENT,EPEAUTRE
0412	OTHER WHEAT ETC UNMILLED	W 185097	31.6	W 219513	53.1					AUTRE FROMENT NON MOULU
042	RICE	W 335146	41.0	W 441295	132.5					RIZ
0422	RICE SEMI–MILLED,MILLED	W 335143	41.0	W 441295	132.5					RIZ POLI,GLACE INCL BRISURES
04222	RICE BROKEN	W 335082	41.0	W 441033	132.5					BRISURES DE RIZ
044	MAIZE UNMILLED	W 9355	1.1	W 25549	4.2					MAIS NON MOULU
05	VEGETABLES AND FRUIT		11.9		19.5					LEGUMES ET FRUITS
054	VEG ETC FRSH,SMPLY PRSVD	W 19481	8.3	W 22126	11.0					LEGUMES FRAIS,CONG,SECS
0541	POTATOES FRSH EXCL SWEET	W 7438	3.0	W 7248	3.5					POMMES DE TERRE
0545	OTHER FRESH VEGETABLES	W 11550	4.8	W 13389	6.3					AUTRES LEGUMES FRAIS,REF
05451	ALLIACEOUS VEGTBLS,FRESH	W 11391	4.7	W 12921	6.0					OIGNONS,ECHALOTES,AULX
056	VEGTBLES ETC PRSVD,PREPD	W 989	0.9	W 4538	5.1					CONSERVES DE LEGUMES
0565	VEGTBLES PRSVD,PREPD NES	W 937	0.8	W 4482	5.0					LEGUMES PREPARES CONSERVE
05659	OTH VEG PRESVD,PREPD NES	W 924	0.8	W 4445	4.9					LEGUM PREPAP,CONSERV NDA
06	SUGAR AND PREPS,HONEY		10.4		27.5					SUCRES ET PRODUITS
061	SUGAR AND HONEY	W 20125	9.7	W 58204	26.2					SUCRES ET MIEL
0611	RAW BEET AND CANE SUGAR			W 30501	10.9					SUCRES BRUTS
0612	REFINED SUGAR ETC	W 18668	9.1	W 26557	14.7					SUCRES RAFFINES
07	COFFEE,TEA,COCOA,SPICES		12.2		17.1					CAFE,THE,CACAO,EPICES
071	COFFEE AND SUBSTITUTES	W 265	1.7	W 486	5.0					CAFE ET SUCCEDANES
0712	COFFEE EXTRACTS,ESSENCES	W 222	1.6	W 449	4.9					EXTRAITS DE CAFE
074	TEA AND MATE	W 3350	8.9	W 3657	9.7					THE ET MATE
0741	TEA	W 3350	8.9	W 3657	9.7					THE
09	MISC EDIBLE PRODUCTS		13.7		19.9					PREP ALIMENTAIRES DIVERSES
098	EDIBLE PRODCTS,PREPS NES	W 5958	12.5	W 7060	19.0					PREP ALIMENTAIRES NDA
09806	YEASTS,BAKING POWDERS	W 1797	2.8	W 1998	3.6					LEVURES
09809	MISC FOOD PREPRTIONS NES	W 2964	8.7	W 3708	13.4					PREP ALIMENTAIRES NDA
1	BEVERAGES AND TOBACCO		10.5		13.3					BOISSONS ET TABACS
12	TOBACCO AND MANUFACTURES		8.3		10.0					TABACS BRUTS FABRIQUES
121	TOBACCO UNMNFCTRD,REFUSE	W 1231	8.0	W 999	9.4					TABACS BRUTS,DECHETS
1212	TOBACCO STRIPPED OR PART	W 1207	8.0	W 967	9.3					TABACS PART ECOTES
2	CRUDE MATERLS,EXCL FUELS		34.0		40.8					MAT BRUTES NON COMESTIBLES
24	CORK AND WOOD		10.6		15.1					LIEGE ET BOIS
247	OTH WOOD ROUGH,SQUARED	W 15764	2.9	W 21606	6.5					BOIS BRUTS EQUARRIS
2472	SAW–,VENEER–LOGS NON–CON	W 15354	2.7	W 21342	6.3					NON CONIFERES SCIAGE,PLAC
24721	— IN THE ROUGH	W 15277	2.7	W 21342	6.3					BRUTS ECORCES DEGROSSIS
248	WOOD SHAPED,SLEEPERS	W 18181	7.7	W 16577	8.6					BOIS SIMPLEMENT TRAVAILLES
2483	LUMBER SHAPED NON–CONIFR	W 18144	7.7	W 16551	8.6					NON CONIFERES SCIES,RABOTES
24831	LUMBER SAWN ETC NON–CON	W 18143	7.7	W 16551	8.6					SCIES LONGITUDINALEMENT
26	TEXTILE FIBRES AND WASTE		6.4		9.0					FIBRES TEXTILES
269	WASTE OF TEXTILE FABRICS	W 4169	3.9	W 6516	6.9					FRIPERIE DRILLES,CHIFFONS
26901	BULK TEXT WSTE,OLD CLTHG	W 3942	3.7	W 6051	6.6					ART ET ACCESS D'HABILLEMENT
27	CRUDE FERTLZR,MINRLS NES		13.6		13.8					ENGRAIS MINERAUX BRUTS
274	SULPHUR,UNRSTD IRN PYRTE	W 390594	11.8	W 121044	10.9					SOUFRE ET PYRITES
2741	SULPHUR,EX SULP IN 52215	W 390594	11.8	W 121044	10.9					SOUFRE
3	MINERAL FUELS ETC		168.8		122.4					COMBUSTIBLES MINERAUX LUB
33	PETROLEUM AND PRODUCTS		157.8		122.1					PETROLE ET DERIVES
333	CRUDE PETROLEUM	W 302782	35.9	W 650686	88.7					HUILES BRUTES DE PETROLE
334	PETROLEUM PRODUCTS,REFIN	W 848601	119.5	W 127631	30.6					PRODUITS RAFFINES
3341	GASOLINE,OTH LIGHT OILS	W 214636	38.2	W 9510	2.2					ESSENCES POUR MOTEURS
33411	MOTOR,AVIATION SPIRIT	W 61562	11.9	W 9085	2.2					ESSENCES MOTEURS D'AVIONS
33412	SPIRIT TYPE JET FUEL	W 153048	26.4	W 405	0.1					CARBUREACTEURS
3343	GAS OILS	W 281444	41.4	W 72390	12.1					GAS OILS
3344	FUEL OILS,NES	W 331544	30.0	W 21774	3.3					FUEL OILS
3345	LUBS,PETROLEUM OILS NES	W 20790	10.0	W 23742	13.0					HUILES LUBRIFIANTES
33451	LUBS(HIGH PETR CONT) ETC	W 20704	9.7	W 23657	12.8					HUILES LUBRIF,H LOURDES
341	*GAS,NATURAL AND MANUFCT	W 49597	10.9	W 44	0.1					GAZ NATUREL,GAZ MANUFACT
3413	PETROLM GASES,LIQUEFIED	W 49597	10.9	W 44	0.1					GAZ DE PETROLE LIQUEFIE
34131	LIQUEFIED PROPANE,BUTANE	W 49597	10.9	W 44	0.1					PROPANE,BUTANE LIQUEFIES
4	ANIMAL,VEGETABLE OIL,FAT		34.5		67.4					HUILES,GRAISSES ANIM,VEG
411	*ANIMAL OILS AND FATS	W 4063	1.9	W 15681	8.6					HUILES,GRAISSES ANIMALES
4113	ANIML OIL,FAT,GREASE NES	W 3959	1.9	W 15681	8.6					HUILES,GRAISSES ANIMALES NDA
41132	FATS OF BOVINE,SHEEP,ETC	W 3922	1.8	W 15372	8.4					SUIFS BRUTS FONDUS
42	FIXED VEGETABLE OIL,FAT		32.1		56.0					HUILES VEGETALES FIXES
423	FIXED VEG OILS,SOFT	W 44404	24.2	W 71363	50.6					HUILES VEGET DOUCES FIXES
4232	SOYA BEAN OIL	W 4671	3.1	W 28182	19.5					HUILE DE SOJA
4239	OTH FIXED VEG OILS,SOFT	W 39613	20.9	W 42781	30.1					AUTRES HUILES FIXES
42391	RAPE,COLZA,MUSTARD OILS	W 39613	20.9	W 42781	30.1					H NAVETTE COLZA MOUTARDE
424	FIXED VEG OIL NONSOFT	W 20922	8.0	W 8476	5.4					AUTRES HUILES VEG FIXES
4242	PALM OIL	W 17998	6.0	W 6212	3.8					HUILE DE PALME
5	CHEMCLS,RELATED PROD NES		114.7		170.3					PRODUITS CHIMIQUES
51	ORGANIC CHEMICALS		9.7		12.9					PROD CHIMIQ ORGANIQUES
515	ORG–INORG COMPOUNDS ETC	W 330	2.0	W 486	3.7					COMPOSES ORGANO–MINERAUX
52	INORGANIC CHEMICALS		10.8		29.0					PROD CHIM INORGANIQUES
522	INORG ELEMNTS,OXIDES,ETC	W 40699	7.5	W 209418	25.5					ELEMENTS INORGANIQUES
5221	CHEMICAL ELEMENTS	W 368	0.9	W 167436	13.8					ELEMENTS CHIMIQUES
52215	SULPHUR,PURIFIED			W 166987	12.4					SOUFRE SUBLIME,PRECIPITE
5225	INORGANIC BASES ETC NES	W 38522	5.9	W 39789	10.4					AUTRES BASES OXYDES METAL
52251	AMMONIA,ANHYDROUS ETC	W 25564	4.0	W 26412	6.8					AMMONIAC LIQUEFIE
523	OTHR INORG CHEMICALS ETC	W 7533	3.3	W 6281	3.5					AUT PRODUITS CHIMIQUES INORG
53	DYES,TANNING,COLOUR PROD		4.2		7.8					PROD TEINTURE,COLORANTS
531	SYNT DYE,NAT INDGO,LAKES	W 294	1.8	W 453	3.9					MAT COLOR ORGAN,LAQUES
533	PIGMENTS,PAINTS,ETC	W 912	2.4	W 1399	3.8					PIGMENTS,PEINTURES,VERNIS
541	*MEDICINAL,PHARM PRODUCT	K 2296159	32.8	K 2558881	36.1					PROD MEDICINAUX PHARMACEUT
5417	MEDICAMENTS	K 2047397	28.4	K 2229923	31.9					MEDICAMENTS
55	PERFUME,CLEANING ETC PRD		6.4		10.3					PROD POUR PARFUM,TOILETTE
553	PERFUMERY,COSMETICS,ETC	W 1215	2.6	W 1816	4.4					PRODUITS DE PARFUMERIE
562	*FERTILIZERS,MANUFACTURE	W 94593	9.1	W 83921	13.6					ENGRAIS MANUFACTURES
5621	CHEM NITROGENOUS FERTLZR	W 45190	4.3	W 38895	7.6					ENGRAIS AZOTES
56216	UREA	W 19577	2.6	W 25884	6.4					UREE

4. Special Imports C.I.F. by Commodities according to the S.I.T.C. (Rev. 2) in million U.S. Dollars
Importations Spéciales C.A.F. par Produits d'après la C.T.C.I. (Rév. 2) en millions de Dollars E.U.

SITC CTCI	COMMODITY	1994		1995		1996		1997		PRODUIT
		QUANTITY QUANTITE	VALUE VALEUR	QUANTITY QUANTITE	VALUE VALEUR	QUANTITY QUANTITE	VALUE VALEUR	QUANTITY QUANTITE	VALUE VALEUR	
5623	CHEM POTASSIC FERTILIZER	W 33389	3.3	W 44290	5.6					ENGRAIS POTASSIQUES
56231	POTASSIUM CHLORIDE	W 33201	3.2	W 44101	5.5					CHLORURE DE POTASSIUM
58	PLASTIC MATERIALS ETC		23.6		36.2					MAT PLAST ARTIFICIELLES
582	PROD OF CONDENSATION ETC	W 2444	2.9	W 2388	4.0					PROD CONDENS,POLYCOND
583	POLYMERIZATION ETC PRODS	W 27304	19.7	W 25755	30.7					PROD POLYMERISATION
5831	POLYETHYLENE	W 9040	6.1	W 9937	11.7					POLYETHYLENE
58311	— IN PRIMARY FORMS	W 8930	5.7	W 9776	11.0					POLYETHYLENE PRIMAIRES
5832	POLYPROPYLENE	W 5062	4.2	W 4949	6.7					POLYPROPYLENE
58321	— IN PRIMARY FORMS	W 4856	3.5	W 4768	6.2					POLYPROPYLENE PRIMAIRES
5834	POLYVINYL CHLORIDE	W 12083	7.7	W 9057	9.0					CHLORURE DE POLYVINYLE
58341	— IN PRIMARY FORMS	W 9862	5.9	W 7397	7.3					SOUS FORMES PRIMAIRES
59	CHEMICAL MATERIALS NES		18.4		24.0					MAT PROD CHIMIQUES NDA
591	PESTICIDES,DISINFECTANTS	W 1381	7.4	W 1164	8.1					DESINF,INSECT,FONG,HERB
5914	DISINFECTANTS,ETC,FR RET	W 1085	6.6	W 940	7.4					DESINFECTANTS VENTE DET
59149	RAT POISONS ETC FR RTAIL	W 1014	6.5	W 843	7.1					ANTIPARASITES VENTE DET
598	MISCEL CHEM PRODUCTS NES	W 7419	9.6	W 10391	14.3					PROD DIV INDUST CHIM NDA
5982	ANTI-KNOCK PREPARTNS ETC	W 1875	4.4	W 2311	7.0					PREPARAT ANTIDETONANTES
5989	CHEM PRODUCTS,PREPS NES	W 2370	4.0	W 2701	4.8					PROD PREP CHIMIQUES NDA
6	BASIC MANUFACTURES		132.7		212.6					ART MANUFACTURES
62	RUBBER MANUFACTURES NES		10.6		17.2					CAOUTCHOUC MANUFACTURE
625	RUBBER TYRES, TUBES ETC	W 3490	7.0	W 4679	11.7					PNEUS CAOUTCHOUC VULCANISE
6252	TYRES,NEW,BUS OR LORRY	W 850	3.2	W 1392	6.0					PNEUS POUR AUTOBUS,CAMIONS
6259	OTH TYRES,TYRE CASES,ETC	W 2374	2.8	W 2893	3.9					AUTRES PNEUS RECHAPES FLAPS
628	RUBBER ARTICLES NES	W 338	2.2	W 424	3.8					OUVRAGES CAOUTCHOUC NDA
63	WOOD,CORK MANUFACTRS NES		3.8		4.8					OUVRAGES LIEGE ET BOIS
634	VENEERS,PLYWOOD,ETC	W 4542	3.3	W 4460	4.0					PLACAGES,CONTRE-PLAQUES
6342	PLYWOOD OF WOOD SHEETS	W 4288	3.0	W 3972	3.6					BOIS CONTRE-PLAQUES
64	PAPER,PAPERBOARD AND MFR		22.5		36.1					PAPIERS,CARTONS & OUVRAGES
641	PAPER AND PAPERBOARD	W 18821	14.6	W 23129	26.0					PAPIERS ET CARTONS
6412	PRINTG,WRITING PAPER NES	W 2818	2.6	W 3493	4.9					PAPIERS POUR L'IMPRESSION
64121	— UNCOATED	W 2509	2.2	W 2870	3.9					PAPIERS IMPRES NON COUCHES
6413	KRAFT PAPER,PAPERBOARD	W 7073	4.3	W 9893	9.3					PAPIER ET CARTON KRAFT
64131	KRAFT LINER IN BULK	W 7073	4.3	W 9893	9.3					PAP KRAFT POUR COUVERTURES
6415	PAPER,PAPERBRD,BULK,NES	W 4144	2.6	W 4429	4.4					PAPIERS,CARTONS ROULEAUX
6418	COATED ETC PAPER NES BLK	W 4210	4.8	W 3762	5.8					PAP,CARTONS COUCHES,ENDUITS
64189	COATED PAPER ETC NES	W 4114	4.7	W 3680	5.7					PAPIERS,CARTONS COUCHES
642	PAPER,ETC,PRECUT,ARTS OF	W 4137	7.9	W 4166	10.1					PAP,CARTONS DECOUPES
6424	PAPER ETC CT TO SIZE NES	W 2858	5.1	W 2138	4.6					PAP,CARTONS DECOUPES
64249	OTH PAPER CT TO SIZE NES	W 2586	4.2	W 1779	3.4					AUT PAP CARTON DECOUP NDA
65	TEXTILE YARN,FABRICS,ETC		16.3		35.6					FILS,TISSUS,ARTICLES TEXTILE
651	TEXTILE YARN	W 395	2.2	W 760	4.0					FILS TEXTILES
652	COTTON FABRICS,WOVEN	W 329	1.2	W 2374	11.1					TISSUS DE COTON
6521	GREY WOVEN COTTON FABRIC	W 160	0.6	W 1887	9.4					TISSUS COT ECRUS NON MERCER
65214	GREY WOVEN COTTON NES	W 160	0.6	W 1886	9.4					AUT TISSUS 85% COTON ECRUS
653	WOVN MAN-MADE FIB FABRIC	W 1261	4.2	W 1496	5.6					TISSUS FIBRES SYNTH,ARTIF
657	SPECIAL TXTL FABRC,PRODS	W 1066	3.3	W 1651	5.6					TISSUS SPECIAUX
658	TEXTILE ARTICLES NES	W 1620	4.1	W 3713	6.4					ART FACONNES MAT TEXTILES
66	NONMETAL MINERAL MFS NES		14.6		21.6					ART MIN NON METALLIQUES
662	CLAY,REFRACTORY BLDG PRD	W 14290	5.8	W 16072	7.9					MAT CONST REFRACTAIRES
6624	BRICKS ETC NONREFRACTORY	W 13888	5.3	W 14927	6.6					BRIQUES ETC CERAM NON REFR
66245	GLAZED CERAMIC SETTS ETC	W 11076	4.0	W 12536	5.2					AUT CARREAUX CERAMIQUE
665	GLASSWARE	W 4166	4.4	W 6230	7.4					OUVRAGES EN VERRE
6651	BOTTLES ETC OF GLASS	W 3501	2.9	W 4643	5.3					RECIPIENTS EN VERRE
66511	GLASS BOTTLES ETC NONVAC	W 3501	2.9	W 4643	5.3					BONBONNES,BOUTEILLES,ETC
67	IRON AND STEEL		42.8		58.7					FER ET ACIER
673	IRON,STEEL SHAPES ETC	W 68747	20.3	W 62056	25.0					BARRES,PROFIL FER,ACIER
6731	IRON,STEEL WIRE ROD	W 60390	17.0	W 51661	19.7					FIL MACHINE FER,ACIER
67311	IRON,SIMPLE STL WIRE ROD	W 60390	17.0	W 51661	19.7					FIL MACH AUT ACIER FIN
674	IRN,STL UNIV,PLATE,SHEET	W 31292	17.5	W 26451	21.4					LARGES PLATS,TOLES
6744	IRN,STL HVY PLATE,ROLLED	W 1026	0.8	W 7013	4.5					TOLES LAMINEES PLUS 4.75 MM
6746	IRN,STL THIN PLATE,ROLLD	W 15948	5.7	W 6882	3.8					TOLES LAM MOINS 3MM
6747	TINNED PLATES,SHEETS	W 12909	10.2	W 10088	10.6					TOLES ETAMEES EN ACIER
678	IRON,STL TUBES,PIPES,ETC	W 2992	3.8	W 4140	7.5					TUBES,TUYAUX EN FONTE,FER
6782	IRON,STL SEAMLESS TUBES	W 511	0.5	W 1952	3.9					TUBES,TUYAUX SANS SOUDURE
68	NON-FERROUS METALS		3.6		6.4					METAUX NON FERREUX
684	ALUMINIUM	W 582	2.4	W 989	4.5					ALUMINIUM
6842	ALUMINIUM,ALLOYS WORKED	W 582	2.4	W 989	4.5					ALUMINIUM,ALLIAGES OUVRE
69	METAL MANUFACTURES NES		18.6		32.2					ART MANUFACT EN METAL NDA
691	STRUCTURES AND PARTS NES	W 547	1.4	W 1494	6.6					CONSTRUCT FER,ACIER,ALU
6911	STRUCTURES,PARTS IRN,STL	W 433	0.9	W 1342	6.3					CONSTRUCT FER,ACIER,FONTE
692	METAL TANKS,BOXES,ETC	W 1219	2.5	W 1800	5.6					RECIPIENTS METALLIQUES
6924	MTL TRANSPORT BOXES ETC	W 1203	2.4	W 1543	4.3					FUTS,TAMBOURS,BIDONS
697	BASE MTL HOUSEHOLD EQUIP	W 1152	2.6	W 1340	3.7					ART MENAGE MET COMMUNS
699	BASE METAL MFRS NES	W 2846	7.4	W 3624	10.3					ART MANUFACTURES MET NDA
7	MACHINES,TRANSPORT EQUIP		161.9		221.4					MACHINES MATERIEL TRANSPORT
71	POWER GENERATING EQUIPMT		20.3		17.2					MACHINES GENERATRICES
713	INTRNL COMBUS PSTN ENGIN	W 2184	10.8	W 3109	8.7					MOTEURS EXPL COMB INT, PIECE
7138	PISTON ENGINES NES	W 2032	4.2	W 2866	3.9					MOTEURS A PISTONS NDA
7139	PISTON ENGINE PARTS NES	W 74	4.3	W 83	2.4					PIECES POUR 713.2,3,8
714	ENGINES AND MOTORS NES	W 56	4.3	W 5	0.1					MOTEURS NON ELECTRIQUES
7148	GAS TURBINES NES	W 26	3.4							TURBINES A GAZ
71488	OTHER GAS TURBINES NES	W 26	3.4							AUTRES TURBINES A GAZ
716	ROTATING ELECTRIC PLANT	W 465	4.2	W 405	4.8					APP ELECTR ROTATIFS,PIECES
7161	DC MOTORS AND GENERATORS	W 346	3.1	W 339	4.1					MOTEURS COURANT CONTINU
72	MACHS FOR SPCL INDUSTRYS		25.0		36.0					MAC SPECIALES POUR INDUST
723	CIVIL ENGNEERG EQUIP ETC	W 3835	8.9	W 3508	12.7					APPAREILS DE GENIE CIVIL
7234	CONST,MINING MACHNRY NES	W 3542	6.4	W 2843	8.5					MACH POUR LA CONST, MINES
724	TEXTILE,LEATHER MACHNRY	W 819	3.9	W 893	3.7					MACH POUR INDUSTRIE TEXTILE
727	FOOD MACHRY NON-DOMESTIC	W 366	3.9	W 631	3.6					MACH INDUSTRIES ALIMENT
7272	OTH FOOD PROC MCHY,PARTS	W 308	3.4	W 546	3.0					AUT MACH IND ALIMENTAIRE
728	OTH MACHY FOR SPCL INDUS	W 744	5.7	W 1157	11.6					AUT MACH IND PARTICULIERES
7284	MACHY FOR SPCL INDUS NES	W 452	4.6	W 534	8.7					MACH SPEC IND PARTICUL.
73	METALWORKING MACHINERY		4.1		2.8					MACH TRAVAIL DES METAUX
736	METALWORKING MACH-TOOLS	W 212	3.8	W 360	1.9					MACH-OUTILS TRAVAIL METAUX
74	GENRL INDUSTRL MACHY NES		30.3		41.3					MACH APP INDUSTRIE
741	HEATING,COOLING EQUIPMNT	W 409	4.3	W 522	6.2					MACH CHAUFFAGE,PIECES
742	PUMPS FOR LIQUIDS ETC	W 356	6.1	W 360	6.4					POMPES MOTO-POMPES
743	PUMPS NES,CENTRFUGES ETC	W 468	4.2	W 607	7.2					POMPES COMPRES,VENT ETC
7436	GAS,LIQUID FILTERS ETC	W 125	1.3	W 246	4.1					APP POUR FILT DES LIQUIDES
744	MECHANICAL HANDLING EQU	W 976	4.5	W 1394	7.0					EQUIP MANUTENTION PIECES
7442	LIFTING,LOADING MACH NES	W 623	3.0	W 970	4.6					APP LEVAGE,MANUTENTION

4. Special Imports C.I.F. by Commodities according to the S.I.T.C. (Rev. 2) in million U.S. Dollars
Importations Spéciales C.A.F. par Produits d'après la C.T.C.I. (Rév. 2) en millions de Dollars E.U.

SITC CTCI	COMMODITY	1994		1995		1996		1997		PRODUIT
		QUANTITY QUANTITE	VALUE VALEUR	QUANTITY QUANTITE	VALUE VALEUR	QUANTITY QUANTITE	VALUE VALEUR	QUANTITY QUANTITE	VALUE VALEUR	
745	NONELEC MACHY,TOOLS NES	W 193	2.5	W 252	4.8					AUT MACH NON ELEC,PIECES
7452	OTH NONELEC MCHS,PTS NES	W 179	2.4	W 244	4.5					AUT MACH NON ELEC,PIECES
749	NONELEC MACH PTS,ACC NES	W 683	9.1	W 666	10.0					PIECES MACH NON ELEC NDA
7492	COCKS,VALVES ETC NES	W 371	3.0	W 354	4.0					ART ROB,SIM POUR TUYAUX
7493	SHAFT,CRANK,PULLEY ETC	W 149	3.5	W 110	3.2					ARBRES TRANS,VILEBREQUINS
75	OFFICE MACHNES,ADP EQUIP		3.5		4.7					MACH BUREAU TRAIT AUTOM
76	TELECOMM,SOUND EQUIPMENT		11.4		16.4					EQUIPMENT DE TELECOM
764	TELECOM EQPT,PTS,ACC NES	W 352	9.1	W 482	13.0					EQUIP TELECOM,PIECES
7649	PTS NES OF EQUIPMT OF 76	W 73	5.1	W 80	6.8					PIECES DE LA DIV 76
76491	PTS NES OF APPAR OF 7641	W 52	4.2	W 73	6.5					PIECES POUR 764.1
77	ELECTRIC MACHNRY NES ETC		19.8		32.5					MACH APP ELECT NDA
772	SWITCHGEAR ETC,PARTS NES	W 294	5.1	W 360	6.6					APP COUPURE,SECT ETC
7721	SWITCHGEAR ETC	W 281	4.9	W 348	6.5					APP COUPURE,SECTIONMNT
773	ELECTR DISTRIBUTNG EQUIP	W 1036	3.2	W 1910	8.0					EQUIPMT DISTRIBUTION ELECT
7731	INSULATED WIRE,CABLE ETC	W 1018	3.0	W 1833	7.5					FILS,CABLES ISOLES ELECT
775	HOUSEHOLD TYPE EQUIP NES	W 1112	4.6	W 1249	6.2					MACH,APP USAGE DOMESTQUE
7752	DOM REFRIGERATRS,FREEZRS	W 913	3.8	W 1041	4.8					REFRIG,CONGEL MENAGER
778	ELECTRICAL MACHINERY NES	W 1354	4.7	W 1601	7.5					AUTRES MACH ELECT NDA
78	ROAD VEHICLES		42.7		67.0					VEHICULES ROUTIERS
781	PASS MOTOR VEH EXC BUSES	W 2621	18.1	W 3946	24.2					AUTO TRANSPORT PERSONNES
782	LORRIES,SPCL MTR VEH NES	W 3227	11.7	W 5769	20.6					VEHICULES SPECIAUX,MARCH
7821	LORRIES,TRUCKS	W 2816	10.0	W 5063	18.5					VEHICULES TRANSP MARCHAND
783	ROAD MOTOR VEHICLES NES	W 723	3.0	W 1774	8.0					VEHICULES ROUTIERS NDA
7832	TRACTORS FOR TR-TRAILERS	W 509	1.8	W 1147	4.7					TRACTEURS ROUTIERS
784	MOTOR VEH PRTS,ACCES NES	W 1520	6.9	W 2128	9.4					PIECES 722,781,782,783
7849	OTHER MOTOR VEHCL PARTS	W 1508	6.9	W 2098	9.3					PIECES 722,781,782,783
79	OTHR TRANSPORT EQUIPMENT		5.1		3.9					AUTRE MATERIEL TRANSPORT
793	SHIPS AND BOATS ETC	W 217	2.8	W 310	1.1					NAVIRES BATEAUX,ETC
8	MISC MANUFACTURED GOODS		44.2		54.1					ART MANUFACTURES DIVERS
812	*PLUMBG,HEATNG,LGHTNG EQ	W 1100	2.6	W 1374	4.9					APPAR SANITAIRES CHAUFFAGE
821	*FURNITURE,PARTS THEREOF	W 1288	3.7	W 1160	4.1					MEUBLES ET PIECES
84	CLOTHING AND ACCESSORIES		5.1		7.5					VETEMENTS
851	*FOOTWEAR	W 580	1.9	W 1134	3.8					CHAUSSURES
87	PRECISION INSTRUMNTS NES		10.6		5.3					INSTRUM,APPAR SCIENT NDA
872	MEDICAL INSTRUMENTS NES	W 273	4.4	W 144	1.4					INSTR,APP MEDIC-CHIR NDA
87202	OTH MEDICAL INSTRUMENTS	W 270	4.2	W 130	1.3					INSTRUM,APP MEDECINE
874	MEASURNG,CONTROLNG INSTR	W 495	4.2	W 127	2.5					INSTRUMENTS DE MESURE
89	MISC MANUFCTRD GOODS NES		18.0		24.3					ART MANUFACTURES DIVERS
892	PRINTED MATTER	W 1020	5.7	W 922	6.9					IMPRIMES
8921	PRINTED BOOKS,GLOBES,ETC	W 607	3.3	W 550	4.6					LIVRES,BROCHURES,CARTES
89211	PRINTED BOOKS,PAMPHLETS	W 592	3.3	W 537	4.5					LIVRES,BROCHURES
893	ARTICLES OF PLASTIC NES	W 2088	8.0	W 2286	9.9					OUVRAGES EN MAT DIVIS 58
8931	PLSTC PACKG CONTNRS,LIDS	W 1093	4.1	W 1147	5.3					ART TRANSP EMBALLAGE ETC
8939	MISC PLASTIC ARTICLES	W 912	3.5	W 937	4.0					ART DIVERS EN MAT DIV 58
89399	OTHR PLASTC ARTICLES NES	W 911	3.5	W 935	4.0					AUT OUV MAT DIV 58
9	GOODS NOT CLASSD BY KIND		1.3		5.2					ART TRANSACT NON CLASSES
951	*WAR FIREARMS,AMMUNITION	W 20	1.3	W 79	5.2					VEHIC BLINDES ARMES

5. Special Exports F.O.B. by Commodities according to the S.I.T.C. (Rev. 2) in million U.S. Dollars
Exportations Spéciales F.O.B. par Produits d'après la C.T.C.I. (Rév. 2) en millions de Dollars E.U.

SITC CTCI	COMMODITY	1994 QUANTITY QUANTITE	1994 VALUE VALEUR	1995 QUANTITY QUANTITE	1995 VALUE VALEUR	1996 QUANTITY QUANTITE	1996 VALUE VALEUR	1997 QUANTITY QUANTITE	1997 VALUE VALEUR	PRODUIT
	ALL COMMODITIES		444.5		530.8					TOUS PRODUITS
0	FOOD AND LIVE ANIMALS		63.6		21.3					ALIMENTS,ANIMAUX VIVANTS
03	FISH AND PREPARATIONS		42.9		9.9					POISSONS ET PREPARATIONS
034	FISH,FRESH,CHILLED,FROZN	W 22467	21.5	W 1607	8.6					POISSON FRAIS, REFRIG,CONG
0341	FISH FRSH,CHLLD,EX FILLT	W 22467	21.5	W 1607	8.6					POISSON FRAIS,REFRIGERE
035	FISH SALTED,DRIED,SMOKED	W 2830	2.4	W 1744	1.0					POISSON SECHE,SALE,FUME
03503	FISH(EX COD)DRIED,SALTED	W 2445	2.3	W 1607	1.0					POISSONS SECHES,SALES
036	SHELL FISH FRESH,FROZEN	W 2569	10.6	W 4	0.1					CRUSTACES,MOLLUSQUES
037	FISH ETC PREPD,PRSVD NES	W 3432	8.5	W 212	0.3					POIS,CRUST,MOL PREPARES
0371	FISH PREPARD,PRESRVD NES	W 771	2.2	W 175	0.2					CONSERVES DE POISSONS
0372	SHELL FISH PREPRD,PRESVD	W 2661	6.3	W 38	0.1					CRUSTACES,COQUIL PREPARES
05	VEGETABLES AND FRUIT		2.9		2.4					LEGUMES ET FRUITS
054	VEG ETC FRSH,SMPLY PRSVD	W 2712	1.7	W 1738	0.9					LEGUMES FRAIS,CONG,SECS
0545	OTHER FRESH VEGETABLES	W 2069	1.5	W 187	0.2					AUTRES LEGUMES FRAIS,REF
05459	FRESH VEGETABLES NES	W 2036	1.5	W 186	0.2					LEGUMES FRAIS,REFRI NDA
06	SUGAR AND PREPS,HONEY		2.3		0.9					SUCRES ET PRODUITS
061	SUGAR AND HONEY	W 35644	2.2	W 7388	0.6					SUCRES ET MIEL
0615	MOLASSES	W 35636	2.2	W 7200	0.5					MELASSES
081	*FEEDING STUFF FOR ANIML	W 90662	13.6	W 43823	6.4					NOURRITURE POUR ANIMAUX
0813	OILCAKE AND OTH RESIDUES	W 84851	12.6	W 38163	5.1					TOURTEAUX
08132	— OF GROUNDNUTS	W 83768	12.4	W 37163	5.1					TOURTEAUX D'ARACHIDES
2	CRUDE MATERLS,EXCL FUELS		63.0		104.6					MAT BRUTES NON COMESTIBLES
21	HIDES,SKINS,FURS UNDRSSD		3.8		5.1					CUIRS,PEAUX BRUTS
211	HIDES,SKINS,EXC FURS,RAW	W 1637	3.8	W 1659	5.1					CUIRS ET PEAUX
2111	BOVINE,EQUINE HIDES,RAW	W 1168	1.8	W 468	1.2					PEAUX DE BOVINS
22	OIL SEEDS,OLEAGINOUS FRT		4.6		3.7					GRAINES,FRUITS OLEAGINEUX
222	SEEDS FOR'SOFT'FIXED OIL	W 13230	4.6	W 6617	3.7					GRAINES HUILES FIXES
2221	GROUNDNUTS,GREEN	W 6549	3.9	W 6617	3.7					ARACHIDES NON GRILLEES
26	TEXTILE FIBRES AND WASTE		19.1		33.6					FIBRES TEXTILES
263	COTTON	W 15242	19.1	W 9079	33.6					COTON
2631	RAW COTTON,EXCL LINTERS	W 15242	19.1	W 9079	33.6					COTON EN MASSE
27	CRUDE FERTLZR,MINRLS NES		29.8		51.7					ENGRAIS MINERAUX BRUTS
271	FERTILIZERS,CRUDE	W 529991	16.8	W 846468	43.3					ENGRAIS BRUTS
2713	NAT CALCM PHOSPHATES ETC	W 529990	16.8	W 846468	43.3					PHOSPHATES DE CALCIUM
27131	— UNGROUND	W 529989	16.8	W 846466	43.3					PHOSPHATES NON MOULUS
278	OTHER CRUDE MINERALS	W 288842	13.0	W 158856	8.3					AUTRES MINERAUX BRUTS
2782	REFRACTORY MINERALS NES	W 121120	5.6	W 58960	2.9					ARGILE MINERAUX REFRACTAIRES
27821	CLAY ETC	W 121120	5.5	W 58960	2.9					ARGILES
2783	COMMON SALT,ETC	W 167427	7.4	W 99558	5.3					SEL
28	METALLIFEROUS ORES,SCRAP		1.9		4.1					MINERAIS METAL,DECHETS
282	IRON AND STEEL SCRAP	W 19912	1.4	W 20867	2.3					FERRAILLES
288	NONFERR METAL SCRAP NES	W 655	0.5	W 1340	1.9					DECHETS NON FERREUX
2882	OTHER BASE MTL SCRAP NES	W 655	0.5	W 1340	1.9					AUTRES DECHETS
28821	COPPER WASTE AND SCRAP	W 477	0.5	W 1276	1.8					DECHETS DE CUIVRE
29	CRUDE ANIMAL,VEG MAT NES		4.0		6.5					MATIERES BRUTES ANIM,VEGET
292	CRUDE VEG MATERIALS NES	W 1739	4.0	W 2102	6.5					MAT BRUTES VEGETALES NDA
2922	NAT GUMS,RESINS,LACS,ETC	W 1656	3.8	W 2038	6.4					GOMME LAQUE
3	MINERAL FUELS ETC		73.1		80.0					COMBUSTIBLES MINERAUX LUB
33	PETROLEUM AND PRODUCTS		72.7		79.4					PETROLE ET DERIVES
334	PETROLEUM PRODUCTS,REFIN	W 438507	72.5	W 396186	78.9					PRODUITS RAFFINES
3341	GASOLINE,OTH LIGHT OILS	W 199799	31.9	W 173968	35.2					ESSENCES POUR MOTEURS
33411	MOTOR,AVIATION SPIRIT	W 25163	4.5	W 19551	4.4					ESSENCES MOTEURS D'AVIONS
33412	SPIRIT TYPE JET FUEL	W 174636	27.4	W 154417	30.9					CARBUREACTEURS
3343	GAS OILS	W 149555	23.1	W 138793	22.4					GAS OILS
3344	FUEL OILS,NES	W 68247	4.9	W 64650	8.2					FUEL OILS
3345	LUBS,PETROLEUM OILS NES	W 15176	11.8	W 14709	12.4					HUILES LUBRIFIANTES
33451	LUBS(HIGH PETR CONT) ETC	W 15168	11.8	W 14704	12.3					HUILES LUBRIF,H LOURDES
4	ANIMAL,VEGETABLE OIL,FAT		74.2		55.8					HUILES,GRAISSES ANIM,VEG
42	FIXED VEGETABLE OIL,FAT		74.0		54.4					HUILES VEGETALES FIXES
423	FIXED VEG OILS,SOFT	W 73704	74.0	W 54653	54.3					HUILES VEGET DOUCES FIXES
4234	GROUNDNUT(PEANUT) OIL	W 73471	73.8	W 54518	53.9					HUILE D'ARACHIDE
5	CHEMCLS,RELATED PROD NES		109.4		209.8					PRODUITS CHIMIQUES
51	ORGANIC CHEMICALS		3.5		4.3					PROD CHIMIQ ORGANIQUES
512	ALCOHOLS,PHENOLS ETC	W 2875	1.7	W 1540	1.8					PHENOLS,PHENOLS–ALCOOLS
5121	ACYCLIC ALCOHOLS,DERIVS	W 2870	1.7	W 1535	1.8					ALCOOLS ACYCLIQUES
52	INORGANIC CHEMICALS		71.4		119.7					PROD CHIM INORGANIQUES
522	INORG ELEMNTS,OXIDES,ETC	W 275333	71.3	W 263168	119.5					ELEMENTS INORGANIQUES
5221	CHEMICAL ELEMENTS	W 498	1.4	W 45	0.3					ELEMENTS CHIMIQUES
52211	GASES,EXCL HALOGENS	W 496	1.4	W 42	0.3					OXYGENE,AZOTE,HYDROGENE
5222	INORGANIC ACIDS ETC	W 273215	69.4	W 262558	119.0					ACIDES INORGANIQUES
52224	PHOSPHORIC ACIDS ETC	W 273177	69.4	W 262488	119.0					ACIDES PHOSPHORIQUES
55	PERFUME,CLEANING ETC PRD		4.3		8.5					PROD POUR PARFUM,TOILETTE
553	PERFUMERY,COSMETICS,ETC	W 1240	3.8	W 1774	7.0					PRODUITS DE PARFUMERIE
562	*FERTILIZERS,MANUFACTURE	W 143816	21.3	W 170846	63.6					ENGRAIS MANUFACTURES
5623	CHEM POTASSIC FERTILIZER			W 5755	15.2					ENGRAIS POTASSIQUES
56239	CHEM POTASS FERTILZR NES			W 5755	15.2					ENGRAIS POTASSIQUES NDA
5629	FERTILIZERS NES	W 112127	19.7	W 134281	47.1					ENGRAIS NDA
58	PLASTIC MATERIALS ETC		2.5		5.1					MAT PLAST ARTIFICIELLES
583	POLYMERIZATION ETC PRODS	W 3762	2.4	W 3959	4.8					PROD POLYMERISATION
5831	POLYETHYLENE	W 760	0.5	W 1513	1.8					POLYETHYLENE
58311	— IN PRIMARY FORMS	W 732	0.4	W 1497	1.8					POLYETHYLENE PRIMAIRES
59	CHEMICAL MATERIALS NES		5.0		6.9					MAT PROD CHIMIQUES NDA
591	PESTICIDES,DISINFECTANTS	W 1092	3.4	W 949	4.7					DESINF,INSECT,FONG,HERB
5914	DISINFECTANTS,ETC,FR RET	W 837	2.9	W 907	4.5					DESINFECTANTS VENTE DET
59149	RAT POISONS ETC FR RTAIL	W 837	2.9	W 907	4.5					ANTIPARASITES VENTE DET
598	MISCEL CHEM PRODUCTS NES	W 671	1.2	W 755	1.8					PROD DIV INDUST CHIM NDA
6	BASIC MANUFACTURES		23.5		27.9					ART MANUFACTURES
64	PAPER,PAPERBOARD AND MFR		7.7		13.8					PAPIERS,CARTONS & OUVRAGES
641	PAPER AND PAPERBOARD	W 4579	2.0	W 3774	3.2					PAPIERS ET CARTONS
642	PAPER,ETC,PRECUT,ARTS OF	W 3178	5.8	W 4402	10.6					PAP,CARTONS DECOUPES
6421	PAPER ETC CONTAINERS	W 2060	2.9	W 3299	6.9					BOITES,SACS EMBALLAGES
6423	EXERCISE BOOKS ETC	W 792	1.4	W 747	1.9					REGISTRES,CAHIERS,CARNETS
6424	PAPER ETC CT TO SIZE NES	W 297	1.4	W 307	1.8					PAP,CARTONS DECOUPES
64249	OTH PAPER CT TO SIZE NES	W 288	1.4	W 261	1.7					AUT PAP CARTON DECOUP NDA
65	TEXTILE YARN,FABRICS,ETC		3.9		3.2					FILS,TISSUS,ARTICLES TEXTILE
66	NONMETAL MINERAL MFS NES		2.1		2.3					ART MIN NON METALLIQUES
661	LIME,CEMENT,BLDG PRODS	W 7451	1.5	W 7040	1.0					CHAUX,CIMENTS MAT CONSTR
67	IRON AND STEEL		2.8		2.7					FER ET ACIER
674	IRN,STL UNIV,PLATE,SHEET	W 4429	2.3	W 1480	1.2					LARGES PLATS,TOLES
6747	TINNED PLATES,SHEETS	W 3759	2.0	W 654	0.8					TOLES ETAMEES EN ACIER
69	METAL MANUFACTURES NES		6.2		5.1					ART MANUFACT EN METAL NDA

5. Special Exports F.O.B. by Commodities according to the S.I.T.C. (Rev. 2) in million U.S. Dollars
Exportations Spéciales F.O.B. par Produits d'après la C.T.C.I. (Rév. 2) en millions de Dollars E.U.

SITC CTCI	COMMODITY	1994 QUANTITY QUANTITE	1994 VALUE VALEUR	1995 QUANTITY QUANTITE	1995 VALUE VALEUR	1996 QUANTITY QUANTITE	1996 VALUE VALEUR	1997 QUANTITY QUANTITE	1997 VALUE VALEUR	PRODUIT
692	METAL TANKS,BOXES,ETC	W 4136	4.9	W 1936	4.3					RECIPIENTS METALLIQUES
6924	MTL TRANSPORT BOXES ETC	W 4087	4.8	W 1935	4.3					FUTS,TAMBOURS,BIDONS
69241	STL TRANSPORT BOXES ETC	W 3588	4.3	W 1473	3.7					FUTS,TAMBOURS,BIDONS FER
7	MACHINES,TRANSPORT EQUIP		25.6		13.5					MACHINES MATERIEL TRANSPORT
71	POWER GENERATING EQUIPMT		7.8		1.8					MACHINES GENERATRICES
714	ENGINES AND MOTORS NES	W 18	6.9	W 11	0.5					MOTEURS NON ELECTRIQUES
7144	REACTION ENGINES	W 6	6.3		0.1					PROPULSEURS A REACTION
72	MACHS FOR SPCL INDUSTRYS		3.7		3.2					MAC SPECIALES POUR INDUST
723	CIVIL ENGNEERG EQUIP ETC	W 1510	2.2	W 590	1.6					APPAREILS DE GENIE CIVIL
7234	CONST,MINING MACHNRY NES	W 1496	2.1	W 527	1.4					MACH POUR LA CONST, MINES
74	GENRL INDUSTRL MACHY NES		1.8		1.4					MACH APP INDUSTRIE
78	ROAD VEHICLES		2.7		4.9					VEHICULES ROUTIERS
781	PASS MOTOR VEH EXC BUSES	W 268	1.7	W 242	3.6					AUTO TRANSPORT PERSONNES
79	OTHR TRANSPORT EQUIPMENT		8.3		0.4					AUTRE MATERIEL TRANSPORT
792	AIRCRAFT ETC	W 89	8.1	W 2	0.3					APP NAVIGATION AERIENNE
7929	AIRCRAFT PARTS NES	W 89	8.1	W 1	0.2					PIECES DU 792
8	MISC MANUFACTURED GOODS		11.5		11.8					ART MANUFACTURES DIVERS
87	PRECISION INSTRUMNTS NES		2.3		1.3					INSTRUM,APPAR SCIENT NDA
874	MEASURNG,CONTROLNG INSTR	W 23	2.2	W 12	1.3					INSTRUMENTS DE MESURE
88	PHOTO EQU,OPTICL GDS ETC		2.1		0.1					APP,FOURN PHOTO,OP,MONTR
881	PHOTO APPARAT,EQUIPT NES	W 59	2.1							APP,EQUIP PHOTO NDA
8813	OTH PHOTO,CINE EQUIP NES	W 59	2.1							APP,MAT PHOTO,CINEMA
88139	PHOTO,CINE LAB EQUIP NES	W 59	2.1							APP TYPES UTIL LABOR
89	MISC MANUFCTRD GOODS NES		5.5		9.6					ART MANUFACTURES DIVERS
893	ARTICLES OF PLASTIC NES	W 2059	3.6	W 3147	7.6					OUVRAGES EN MAT DIVIS 58
8931	PLSTC PACKG CONTNRS,LIDS	W 1004	2.0	W 2040	5.4					ART TRANSP EMBALLAGE ETC
8939	MISC PLASTIC ARTICLES	W 1053	1.7	W 861	1.7					ART DIVERS EN MAT DIV 58
89399	OTHR PLASTC ARTICLES NES	W 1053	1.7	W 861	1.7					AUT OUV MAT DIV 58
9	GOODS NOT CLASSD BY KIND		0.3		5.3					ART TRANSACT NON CLASSES
951	*WAR FIREARMS,AMMUNITION	W 8	0.3	W 35	1.7					VEHIC BLINDES ARMES
971	*GOLD,NON MONETARY NES			K 397	3.7					OR NON MONETAIRE
97101	NONMON GLD UNWRT,SEMIMFD			K 397	3.7					OR,ALLIAGES D'OR BRUTS

1. HISTORICAL SERIES, 1961–1996 GENERAL TRADE, IMPORTS C.I.F., EXPORTS F.O.B.
SERIES HISTORIQUES, 1961–1996 COMMERCE GENERAL, IMPORTATIONS C.A.F., EXPORTATIONS F.O.B

YEAR ANNEE	VALUE IN MILLION SEYCH. RUPEES / VALEUR EN MILLION SEYCH. RUPEES MERCHANDISE –MARCHANDISE		GOLD –OR		CONVERSION FACTORS U.S. CENTS PER SEYCH. RUPEE FACTEURS DE CONVERSION CENTS E.U. PAR SEYCH. RUPEE		INDEX NUMBERS –INDICES QUANTUM		UNIT VALUE VALEUR UNITAIRE	
	IMPORTS	EXPORTS	IMPORTS	EXPORTS	IMPORTS	EXPORTS	IMPORTS	EXPORTS	IMPORTS	EXPORTS
1961	12.03	6.71			21.0000	21.0000				
1962	12.80	7.40			21.0000	21.0000				
1963	14.60	6.87			21.0000	21.0000				
1964	15.72	8.69			21.0000	21.0000				
1965	18.67	9.77			21.0000	21.0000				
1966	19.96	8.60			21.0000	21.0000				
1967	24.60	10.04			21.0000	21.0000				
1968	33.88	17.39			18.0000	18.0000				
1969	40.00	13.91			18.0000	18.0000				
1970	55.92	11.90			18.0000	18.0000				
1971	84.00	9.83			18.0801	18.0801				
1972	111.67	12.77			18.7567	18.7567				
1973	135.12	18.86			18.3824	18.3824				
1974	160.46	39.13			17.5448	17.5448				
1975	191.35	35.00			16.6616	16.6616				
1976	290.62	57.63			14.9652	14.9652				
1977	349.74	84.76			13.1142	13.0839				
1978	402.05	96.00			14.3544	14.3544				
1979	534.78	138.63			15.9782	15.9835				
1980	631.44	135.21			15.6446	15.6446				
1981	589.01	108.34			15.8638	15.7884				
1982	641.32	100.09			15.2835	15.1691				
1983	594.14	136.86			14.8031	14.8110				
1984	619.00	181.48			14.1596	14.1344				
1985	704.72	199.69			14.0930	13.9654	60	18	118	169
1986	651.96	113.66			16.0901	15.9725	64	17	103	110
1987	633.90	124.07			17.9297	17.8579	63	44	102	112
1988	856.63	171.33			18.5649	18.5778	87	93	100	112
1989	930.15	193.52			17.7039	17.6545	97	102	96	94
1990	993.78	301.50			18.8052	18.9142	100	100	100	100
1991	910.42	258.27			18.9528	18.9750	95	136	97	88
1992	980.87	245.66			19.4576	19.4468	107	126	93	101
1993	1234.86	265.02			19.3068	19.2845	147	106	85	102
1994	1042.38	262.15			19.8173	19.8258				
1995	1109.20	252.00			20.9893	20.9588				
1996	1362.81	256.40			20.1196	20.1135				

2. IMPORTS BY BROAD ECONOMIC CATEGORY AND EXPORTS BY INDUSTRIAL ORIGIN. (PERCENTAGE OF TOTAL VALUE)
IMPORTATIONS PAR CATEGORIES ECONOMIQUES ET EXPORTATIONS PAR BRANCHE D'ACTIVITE.(EN POURCENTAGE DE LA VALEUR TOTALE)

IMPORTS – IMPORTATIONS

	1990	1991	1992	1993	1994	1995	1996
TOTAL IMPORTS–IMPORTATIONS TOTALES	100.	100.	100.	100.	100.	100.	100.
1 FOOD BEV–ALIMENTATION BOISSONS	16.5	17.7	20.7	17.8	19.5	20.2	18.9
11 PRIMARY–PRODUITS DE BASE	6.1	7.2	6.7	7.0	7.8	7.3	8.5
111 FOR INDUSTRY–POUR L'INDUSTRIE	0.3	0.7	0.3	0.4	0.3	0.4	0.3
112 FOR HOUSEHOLDS–POUR LES MENAGES	5.9	6.5	6.4	6.5	7.5	6.8	8.2
12 PROCESSED–PRODUITS ELABORES	10.4	10.5	14.0	10.8	11.7	12.9	10.4
121 FOR INDUSTRY–POUR L'INDUSTRIE	1.7	1.9	3.3	1.6	2.1	2.3	1.8
122 FOR HOUSEHOLDS–POUR LES MENAGES	8.7	8.6	10.7	9.3	9.6	10.6	8.5
2 IND SUPPLIES–APPROV INDUSTRIELS	23.4	24.5	24.3	21.9	24.6	19.4	17.1
21 PRIMARY–PRODUITS DE BASE	2.2	1.7	0.9	1.1	1.7	0.8	0.9
22 PROCESSED–PRODUITS ELABORES	21.2	22.8	23.4	20.9	22.9	18.6	16.2
3 FUELS–COMBUSTIBLES	19.2	21.7	17.1	14.1	15.5	17.3	3.2
31 PRIMARY–PRODUITS DE BASE	0.3	0.2	0.2	0.2	0.2	0.2	0.2
32 PROCESSED–PRODUITS ELABORES	18.9	21.5	16.9	13.9	15.3	17.1	3.0
321 MOTOR SPIRIT–ESSENCE	1.2	1.2	0.8	0.7	15.3	17.1	0.6
322 OTHER–AUTRES	17.7	20.3	16.1	13.2	0.0	0.0	2.4
4 MACHINERY–EQUIPEMENT	18.2	17.5	14.2	21.5	18.0	17.7	15.6
41 CAPITAL EQUIPMENT–MACHINES	17.4	16.9	13.5	20.6	16.2	15.4	14.1
42 PARTS–PIECES ACCESSOIRES	0.8	0.6	0.7	0.9	1.7	2.3	1.5
5 TRANSPORT–TRANSPORT	8.2	5.4	6.3	9.5	6.2	10.2	33.7
51 PASSENGER CARS–AUTOMOBILES	1.9	0.8	0.5	2.5	1.0	1.8	1.6
52 OTHER–AUTRES	2.4	0.7	1.2	2.6	1.9	4.1	28.3
521 INDUSTRIAL–INDUSTRIELS	2.4	0.6	1.1	2.5	1.8	4.0	28.2
522 NON INDUSTRIAL–NON INDUSTRIEL	0.1	0.1	0.1	0.1	0.1	0.1	0.1
53 PARTS–PIECES ACCESSOIRES	3.9	3.9	4.6	4.5	3.3	4.3	3.7
6 CONSUM GOODS–BIENS CONSOMMATION	14.3	13.2	17.2	14.9	16.1	14.9	11.1
61 DURABLE–DURABLES	3.0	2.2	4.2	3.7	3.6	3.6	2.7
62 SEMI DURABLE–SEMI DURABLES	7.4	6.9	8.7	7.3	7.9	7.2	5.5
63 NON DURABLE–NON DURABLES	3.9	4.0	4.3	3.9	4.6	4.0	2.8
7 GOODS NES–BIENS NDA	0.2	0.1	0.2	0.2	0.2	0.3	0.5

EXPORTS – EXPORTATIONS

	1990	1991	1992	1993	1994	1995	1996
TOTAL EXPORTS–EXPORTATIONS TOTALES	100.	100.	100.	100.	100.	100.	100.
1 AGRICULTURE	5.5	8.4	9.6	7.3	10.4	9.8	4.8
2 MINING QUARRY–INDUS EXTRACTIVES			0.0	0.1	0.0	0.0	0.1
3 MANUFACTURING–IND MANUFACTUR	94.5	91.6	90.3	92.7	89.5	90.2	95.1
31 FOOD BEV TOBACCO–ALIM BOISS TAB	19.1	25.7	29.5	23.1	36.3	36.1	25.1
32 TEXTILES–INDUSTRIES TEXTILES		0.0	0.1	0.0	0.1	0.1	0.0
33 WOOD & PRODUCTS–BOIS & PRODUITS					0.0	0.0	0.0
34 PAPER & PRODUCTS–PAPIER & PRODT	0.0	0.0	0.1	0.0	0.0	0.0	0.0
35 CHEMICALS–INDUSTRIES CHIMIQUES	49.6	60.7	58.0	55.4	46.1	47.2	22.1
36 NON METAL MIN–MIN NON METAL		0.0		0.1	0.0	0.5	0.0
37 BASIC METAL–IND METAL BASE		0.0		0.0		0.0	
38 METAL MANUF–MANUF METAL	25.8	5.1	2.6	13.9	6.6	5.9	47.6
39 OTH MANUF IND–AUTRES MANUF	0.0	0.0	0.1	0.2	0.4	0.3	0.2

3. TRADE BY PRINCIPAL COUNTRIES OF ORIGIN AND DESTINATION (VALUE IN MILLION U.S. DOLLARS)
ECHANGES SELON LES PRINCIPAUX PAYS D'ORIGINE ET DE DESTINATION (VALEUR EN MILLIONS DE DOLLARS EU)

COUNTRIES–PAYS	GENERAL IMPORTS C.I.F. IMPORTATIONS GENERALES C.A.F				
	1992	1993	1994	1995	1996
World	191.4	241.6	206.5	254.7	346.7
Africa	34.2	41.7	37.8	41.9	47.8
Americas	5.8	19.5	8.6	10.2	100.8
– Northern America	4.9	18.7	8.1	9.6	100.5
– LAIA	0.8	0.7	0.4	0.4	0.3
– CACM				0.0	0.0
– Caribbean	0.0	0.0	0.0	0.1	0.0
– Rest of America	0.1	0.0	0.0	0.1	0.0
Asia excl fmr USSR	89.9	99.1	82.7	115.8	81.7
– Middle East	31.5	32.9	30.4	42.4	12.0
Asia former USSR					
Europe excl fmr USSR	57.4	74.9	73.3	83.2	110.5
– European Union	56.8	73.7	72.4	82.0	109.0
– Eastern Europe	0.0	0.0	0.0	0.1	0.1
– Rest of Europe	0.6	1.2	0.9	1.2	1.4
Europe former USSR	0.1	0.0		0.0	0.0
Oceania	3.9	4.3	4.0	3.4	5.3
Other	0.0	2.1	0.0	0.1	0.5
United Kingdom	24.7	32.2	36.4	35.4	42.5
Singapore/Singapour	31.0	31.6	30.2	37.4	35.2
So. African Customs Un	27.5	31.1	27.6	31.4	39.4
USA/Etats–Unis d'Amer	4.8	18.7	7.9	9.4	100.4
Yemen/Yémen		31.7	29.2	40.6	9.3
France, Monaco	8.7	15.0	11.9	18.1	26.9
Japan/Japon	9.2	13.9	6.8	14.5	8.2
Italy/Italie	6.8	6.3	6.5	8.8	13.9
Bahrain/Bahreïn	30.9	0.0	0.0	0.1	0.1
Germany/Allemagne	4.2	7.8	2.8	3.8	7.8
India/Inde	2.3	5.1	3.1	5.0	9.1
Netherlands/Pays–Bas	4.6	4.3	4.7	5.7	5.0
Thailand/Thaïlande	2.4	5.2	3.7	5.1	6.7
Spain/Espagne	1.9	2.3	3.4	5.1	6.7
Kenya	2.4	3.5	4.6	4.4	3.5
Australia/Australie	3.2	3.6	3.3	3.1	4.9
Mauritius/Maurice	3.0	3.6	3.5	3.6	4.0
Malaysia/Malaisie	3.4	3.0	2.4	2.9	3.5
Belgium–Luxembourg	3.4	1.3	2.3	2.4	2.6
China/Chine	3.3	2.6	2.1	2.0	1.5
China, Hong Kong SAR	1.8	1.7	1.5	1.6	1.5
Ireland/Irlande	0.5	1.2	2.7	1.1	1.6
Pakistan	2.4	1.3	0.9	2.0	0.1
Sweden/Suède	0.9	2.3	0.9	0.9	1.2
United Arab Emirates	0.6	0.4	1.0	1.5	2.1
Switzerland,Liechtenst.	0.6	1.1	0.8	1.2	1.3
Other Asia n.e.s.	0.8	0.8	0.7	1.2	1.4
Reunion/Réunion	0.9	1.8	1.1	0.9	
Korea, Republic of	0.8	0.4	0.3	0.9	1.1
Denmark/Danemark	1.1	0.7	0.5	0.6	0.7
Madagascar	0.0	1.4	0.9	0.8	0.1
New Zealand	0.7	0.7	0.7	0.3	0.5
Areas n.e.s.	0.0	2.0	0.0	0.1	0.5
Indonesia/Indonésie	0.7	0.4	0.4	0.6	0.5
Brazil/Brésil	0.4	0.7	0.4	0.4	0.3
Zimbabwe	0.3	0.4	0.0	0.8	0.7
Israel/Israël	0.0	0.0	0.0	0.1	0.7
Sri Lanka	0.1	0.2	0.1	0.1	0.3
Turkey/Turquie	0.0	0.3	0.0	0.1	0.4
Canada	0.1	0.0	0.3	0.2	0.2

COUNTRIES–PAYS	EXPORTS EXPORTATIONS ES F.O.B.				
	1992	1993	1994	1995	1996
Monde	48.0	51.6	51.8	53.1	139.4
Afrique	3.9	3.6	3.2	2.6	2.2
Amériques	1.0	3.6	2.1	2.1	52.1
– Amérique du Nord	1.0	3.6	2.1	2.1	52.1
– ALAI	0.0	0.0	0.0	0.0	0.0
– MCAC					
– Caraïbes	0.0	0.0	0.0	0.0	0.0
– Autre Amérique	0.0	0.0	0.0	0.0	0.0
Asie anc. URSS exclus	29.0	29.5	24.4	26.7	44.2
– Moyen–Orient	27.5	28.0	23.3	24.3	29.4
Asie ancienne URSS					
Europe anc. URSS exclus	14.0	14.9	22.0	21.5	40.1
– Union Européenne	14.0	14.8	22.0	21.3	39.9
– Europe de l'Est	0.0	0.0	0.0		0.0
– Autre de l'Europe	0.0	0.1	0.0	0.2	0.2
Europe ancienne URSS				0.0	0.0
Océanie	0.0	0.0	0.1	0.0	0.1
Autre	0.0	0.0	0.0	0.0	0.7
Yemen/Yémen		28.0	23.2	24.3	29.4
USA/Etats–Unis d'Amer	1.0	3.5	2.1	2.0	52.0
United Kingdom	4.3	10.5	13.3	12.7	12.8
Bahrain/Bahreïn	27.3		0.0	0.0	0.0
France, Monaco	8.2	2.5	1.2	1.1	10.8
Germany/Allemagne	0.4	0.6	3.4	4.9	7.9
Singapore/Singapour	0.7	0.8	0.5	0.8	12.8
Italy/Italie	0.0	0.0	2.3	0.1	6.6
Reunion/Réunion	2.0	1.5	1.9	1.7	
Mauritius/Maurice	1.5	1.8	0.3	0.3	0.5
Japan/Japon	0.0	0.1	0.3	1.4	1.9
Belgium–Luxembourg	0.8	0.7	0.6	0.3	0.4
So. African Customs Un	0.4	0.3	0.5	0.4	1.1
Netherlands/Pays–Bas	0.3	0.3	0.2	0.2	0.4
Spain/Espagne	0.0	0.1	0.2	0.8	0.3
Denmark/Danemark	0.0	0.0	0.7	0.6	0.0
Kenya	0.0	0.0	0.0	0.2	0.6
China, Hong Kong SAR	0.2	0.2	0.1	0.1	0.1
Sweden/Suède	0.0	0.0	0.0	0.0	0.6
Areas n.e.s.			0.0		0.6
Thailand/Thaïlande	0.1	0.2	0.2	0.1	0.0
Switzerland,Liechtenst.	0.0	0.1	0.0	0.2	0.2
Madagascar		0.0	0.4	0.0	0.1
Greece/Grèce		0.0	0.0	0.3	0.0
United Arab Emirates	0.2	0.0	0.1	0.0	0.0
Other Asia n.e.s.	0.3	0.1			
Portugal	0.0	0.0	0.1	0.2	0.0
Australia/Australie	0.0	0.0	0.1	0.0	0.1
Canada	0.0	0.0	0.0	0.1	0.0
Pakistan	0.1	0.1			
Sri Lanka	0.1	0.0			
India/Inde	0.0		0.0	0.1	0.0
Bunkers, ship stores	0.0	0.0	0.0	0.0	0.0
Malaysia/Malaisie		0.0	0.0	0.0	
United Rep of Tanzania		0.0	0.0	0.0	0.0
Ireland/Irlande	0.0	0.0	0.0	0.0	0.0
Brazil/Brésil	0.0				
China/Chine	0.0				
Czech Republic					0.0
New Zealand			0.0	0.0	

(VALUE AS PERCENTAGE OF WORLD TOTAL)(VALEURS EN POURCENTAGE DU TOTAL MONDIAL)

	1987	1988	1989	1990	1991	1992	1993	1994	1995	1996
Africa	16.7	12.9	16.2	18.7	17.0	17.9	17.3	18.3	16.5	13.8
Americas	3.1	10.7	2.7	2.1	2.5	3.0	8.1	4.2	4.0	29.1
– Northern America	3.0	10.6	2.2	1.9	2.5	2.5	7.7	3.9	3.8	29.0
– LAIA	0.1	0.1	0.4	0.2	0.0	0.4	0.3	0.2	0.2	0.1
– CACM									0.0	0.0
– Caribbean	0.0	0.0	0.0	0.0	0.0	0.0	0.0	0.0	0.0	0.0
– Rest of America	0.0	0.0	0.0	0.0	0.0	0.0	0.0	0.0	0.0	0.0
Asia excl fmr USSR	34.5	36.1	42.6	40.2	45.6	47.0	41.0	40.1	45.5	23.6
– Middle East	14.2	11.8	17.0	17.0	17.6	16.4	13.6	14.7	16.6	3.5
Asia former USSR										
Europe excl fmr USSR	44.6	38.3	37.2	37.3	33.5	30.0	31.0	35.5	32.7	31.9
– European Union	44.0	37.6	36.9	37.0	33.2	29.7	30.5	35.1	32.2	31.4
– Eastern Europe	0.0	0.1	0.0	0.0	0.0	0.0	0.0	0.0	0.0	0.0
– Rest of Europe	0.5	0.6	0.3	0.3	0.3	0.3	0.5	0.4	0.5	0.4
Europe former USSR	0.0	0.9	0.1	0.1	0.1	0.1	0.0		0.0	0.0
Oceania	1.2	1.1	1.1	1.6	1.2	2.0	1.8	1.9	1.3	1.5
Other	0.0	0.0	0.1	0.0	0.0	0.0	0.9	0.0	0.0	0.1
United Kingdom	19.9	14.9	14.3	14.4	11.5	12.9	13.3	17.6	13.9	12.2
Singapore/Singapour	7.5	10.3	10.0	10.2	11.6	16.2	13.1	14.6	14.7	10.2
So. African Customs Un	13.2	10.3	13.1	13.6	13.0	14.4	12.9	13.4	12.3	11.4
USA/Etats–Unis d'Amer	3.0	10.6	2.2	1.9	2.5	2.5	7.7	3.8	3.7	28.9
Yemen/Yémen							13.1	14.1	16.0	2.7
France, Monaco	14.3	10.4	9.6	11.3	8.8	4.5	6.2	5.8	7.1	7.8
Japan/Japon	5.5	6.5	7.0	6.1	5.2	4.8	5.8	3.3	5.7	2.4
Italy/Italie	1.3	2.2	5.4	2.2	2.5	3.5	2.6	3.1	3.5	4.0
Bahrain/Bahreïn	0.0	0.0	0.0	8.1	16.2	16.1	0.0	0.0	0.0	0.0
Germany/Allemagne					3.2	2.2	3.2	1.3	1.5	2.3

	1987	1988	1989	1990	1991	1992	1993	1994	1995	1996
Afrique	3.5	5.1	7.9	6.2	6.0	8.1	6.9	6.1	5.0	1.6
Amériques	2.5	2.6	3.0	1.2	1.2	2.2	6.9	4.0	4.0	37.4
– Amérique du Nord	2.4	2.3	2.5	1.1	1.2	2.1	6.9	4.0	4.0	37.4
– ALAI	0.1	0.3	0.5	0.1	0.0	0.0	0.0	0.0	0.0	0.0
– MCAC										
– Caraïbes		0.0	0.0	0.0		0.0	0.0	0.0	0.0	0.0
– Autre Amérique			0.0			0.0	0.0	0.0	0.0	0.0
Asie anc. URSS exclus	5.1	39.9	30.3	25.4	2.7	60.5	57.2	47.2	50.3	31.7
– Moyen–Orient	0.0	36.4	26.3	23.5	0.0	57.2	54.2	45.0	45.7	21.1
Asie ancienne URSS										
Europe anc. URSS exclus	25.9	45.3	32.0	17.2	28.9	29.1	28.9	42.5	40.6	28.8
– Union Européenne	24.8	45.2	31.9	17.2	28.9	29.1	28.7	42.5	40.1	28.6
– Europe de l'Est	0.0	0.0	0.0	0.0		0.0	0.0	0.0		0.0
– Autre de l'Europe	1.1	0.1	0.1	0.0	0.0	0.1	0.2	0.1	0.4	0.2
Europe ancienne URSS	0.0	1.9							0.0	0.0
Océanie	0.3	0.1	0.0	0.0	0.1	0.1	0.1	0.2	0.1	0.0
Autre	62.6	5.0	26.8	50.0	61.1	0.0	0.0	0.0	0.1	0.5
Yemen/Yémen							54.2	44.7	45.7	21.1
USA/Etats–Unis d'Amer	2.4	2.3	2.5	1.1	1.2	2.1	6.8	4.0	3.7	37.3
United Kingdom	5.9	12.2	3.7	4.0	18.9	8.9	20.4	25.7	23.9	9.2
Bahrain/Bahreïn		0.0				56.8		0.0	0.0	0.0
France, Monaco	18.3	26.3	24.9	11.2	9.0	17.0	4.8	2.3	2.1	7.8
Germany/Allemagne					0.7	0.7	1.2	6.6	9.3	5.6
Singapore/Singapour	0.4	0.6	0.7	0.5	0.6	1.4	1.6	1.0	1.5	9.2
Italy/Italie	0.3	0.5	0.3	1.3	0.1	0.1	0.0	4.5	0.3	4.8
Reunion/Réunion	3.0	4.4	7.3	5.8	4.7	4.3	2.8	3.6	3.2	
Mauritius/Maurice	0.2	0.2	0.1	0.2	1.0	3.0	3.5	0.7	0.5	0.3

4. General Imports C.I.F. by Commodities according to the S.I.T.C. (Rev. 2) in million U.S. Dollars
Importations Générales C.A.F. par Produits d'après la C.T.C.I. (Rév. 2) en millions de Dollars E.U.

SITC CTCI	COMMODITY	1993		1994		1995		1996		PRODUIT
		QUANTITY QUANTITE	VALUE VALEUR	QUANTITY QUANTITE	VALUE VALEUR	QUANTITY QUANTITE	VALUE VALEUR	QUANTITY QUANTITE	VALUE VALEUR	
	ALL COMMODITIES		241.6		206.5		254.7		346.8	TOUS PRODUITS
0	FOOD AND LIVE ANIMALS		37.9		37.8		42.6		58.2	ALIMENTS,ANIMAUX VIVANTS
01	MEAT AND PREPARATIONS		3.5		2.2		3.3		3.4	VIANDES ET PREPARATIONS
011	MEAT FRESH,CHILLD,FROZEN	W 928	2.8	W 535	1.7	W 851	2.6	W 879	2.8	VIANDES FRAICHES,REF,CONGE
0111	BOVINE MEAT FRESH,FROZEN	W 375	1.1	W 380	1.1	W 342	1.3	W 367	1.2	VIANDES BOVIN FRAI,REF
01112	BOVINE MEAT BONELESS	W 372	1.0	W 378	1.1	W 340	1.2	W 366	1.2	VIANDES BOVIN DESOSSEES
0113	PIG MEAT FRESH,CHLD,FRZN	W 320	0.9	W 49	0.2	W 95	0.4	W 191	0.7	VIANDE DE PORC
02	DAIRY PRODCTS,BIRDS'EGGS		4.9		6.0		6.1		7.4	PRODUITS LAITIERS,OEUFS
022	MILK AND CREAM	W 1482	3.3	W 2069	4.2	W 1410	4.0	W 1624	5.0	LAIT ET CREME
0224	MILK,CREAM PRESERVED ETC	W 1276	2.9	W 1788	3.8	W 1310	3.7	W 1462	4.7	LAIT,CREME CONS,CONC
02242	MILK DRY,1.5% FAT OR LES	W 39	0.1	W 860	2.1	W 385	1.5	W 766	3.1	LAIT POUDRE INF 1.5%
02243	MILK DRY,OVER 1.5% FAT	W 489	1.6	W 468	1.0	W 302	1.1	W 181	0.5	LAIT POUDRE SUP 1.5%
02249	MILK(EX DRY) PRSVD,SWEET	W 748	1.3	W 459	0.8	W 623	1.3	W 515	1.2	LAIT CONS,CONC SUCRE
024	CHEESE AND CURD	W 214	0.9	W 250	1.0	W 243	1.0	W 237	1.1	FROMAGE ET CAILLEBOTTE
03	FISH AND PREPARATIONS		7.1		8.0		8.9		18.9	POISSONS ET PREPARATIONS
034	FISH,FRESH,CHILLED,FROZN	W 9702	6.7	W 8210	7.5	W 11955	8.6	W 19391	17.5	POISSON FRAIS, REFRIG,CONG
0342	FISH FROZEN,EXCL FILLETS	W 9700	6.7	W 8192	7.3	W 11953	8.6	W 19390	17.5	POISSONS CONGELES
036	SHELL FISH FRESH,FROZEN	W 39	0.4	W 59	0.6	W 19	0.3	W 146	1.4	CRUSTACES,MOLLUSQUES
04	CEREALS AND PREPARATIONS		8.2		7.1		10.3		12.3	CEREALES ET PRODUITS
042	RICE	W 3263	1.8	W 1191	1.0	W 5958	3.6	W 5639	4.9	RIZ
0422	RICE SEMI-MILLED,MILLED	W 1732	1.3	W 1191	1.0	W 5957	3.6	W 5638	4.9	RIZ POLI,GLACE INCL BRISURES
04221	RICE MILLED UNBROKEN	W 1732	1.3	W 581	0.6	W 3058	2.2	W 5136	4.6	RIZ POLI,GLACE EXCL BRISURES
04222	RICE BROKEN			W 610	0.5	W 2899	1.4	W 502	0.3	BRISURES DE RIZ
044	MAIZE UNMILLED	W 6072	1.7	W 6112	1.6	W 2769	0.8	W 3730	1.1	MAIS NON MOULU
046	WHEAT ETC MEAL OR FLOUR	W 2801	1.4	W 2325	1.3	W 2561	1.6	W 3813	2.1	SEMOULE FARINE,FROMENT
04601	FLOUR OF WHEAT OR MESLIN	W 2795	1.4	W 2267	1.1	W 2477	1.4	W 2838	1.8	FARINE DE FROMENT
048	CEREAL ETC PREPARATIONS	W 2094	3.3	W 1922	2.9	W 2057	3.6	W 1921	3.6	PREPTNS A BASE CEREALES
0484	BAKERY PRODUCTS	W 534	1.9	W 415	1.5	W 475	1.8	W 463	1.7	PRODUITS DE BOULANGERIE
04841	BREAD,BISCUIT,COM WAFERS	W 168	0.8		0.2	W 123	0.5	W 14	0.1	PAINS,BISCUITS DE MER
04842	PASTRY, CAKES ETC	W 366	1.2	W 415	1.4	W 353	1.4	W 449	1.6	PATISSERIE ETC.
05	VEGETABLES AND FRUIT		7.2		8.8		8.0		9.5	LEGUMES ET FRUITS
054	VEG ETC FRSH,SMPLY PRSVD	W 4087	3.7	W 4254	4.1	W 4000	4.1	W 4479	4.3	LEGUMES FRAIS,CONG,SECS
0541	POTATOES FRSH EXCL SWEET	W 1338	0.8	W 1581	1.0	W 1347	1.0	W 1779	1.1	POMMES DE TERRE
0545	OTHER FRESH VEGETABLES	W 1763	1.6	W 1997	2.1	W 1606	1.6	W 1799	1.8	AUTRES LEGUMES FRAIS,REF
05451	ALLIACEOUS VEGTBLS,FRESH	W 1169	0.9	W 1064	0.9	W 846	0.7	W 1041	0.7	OIGNONS,ECHALOTES,AULX
05459	FRESH VEGETABLES NES	W 594	0.8	W 934	1.2	W 759	1.0	W 758	1.2	LEGUMES FRAIS,REFRI NDA
057	FRUIT,NUTS,FRESH,DRIED	W 908	1.8	W 740	1.4	W 821	1.5	W 1078	1.9	FRUITS FRAIS OU SECS
058	FRUIT PRESERVED,PREPARED	W 1345	1.4	W 2025	2.9	W 920	2.0	W 1481	2.9	CONSERVES DE FRUITS
0585	FRUIT OR VEGETABLE JUICE	W 1112	1.0	W 1758	2.3	W 603	1.3	W 1331	2.5	JUS DE FRUITS
05857	JUICE OF OTHER FRUIT,VEG	W 743	0.4	W 1081	1.3	W 328	0.8	W 509	1.1	JUS AUTRES FRUITS,LEGUMES
06	SUGAR AND PREPS,HONEY		2.2		1.5		2.3		2.4	SUCRES ET PRODUITS
061	SUGAR AND HONEY	W 4493	1.7	W 3077	1.2	W 3141	1.8	W 3360	2.0	SUCRES ET MIEL
0612	REFINED SUGAR ETC	W 4215	1.4	W 3050	1.1	W 2922	1.6	W 3348	2.0	SUCRES RAFFINES
07	COFFEE,TEA,COCOA,SPICES		1.8		1.4		1.4		1.7	CAFE,THE,CACAO,EPICES
073	CHOCOLATE AND PRODUCTS	W 200	0.8	W 200	0.7	W 181	0.7	W 165	0.7	CHOCOLAT
081	*FEEDING STUFF FOR ANIML	W 2829	1.4	W 2903	1.6	W 855	0.9	W 1865	1.0	NOURRITURE POUR ANIMAUX
0819	FOOD WASTE AND FEED NES	W 355	0.6	W 647	1.0	W 493	0.7	W 217	0.2	DECHETS,ALIMENTS NDA
08199	FODDER NES,INCL SWEETNED	W 355	0.6	W 647	1.0	W 493	0.7	W 217	0.2	PREPARATIONS FOURRAGERES
09	MISC EDIBLE PRODUCTS		1.9		1.5		1.8		1.9	PREP ALIMENTAIRES DIVERSES
098	EDIBLE PRODCTS,PREPS NES	W 494	1.3	W 381	1.1	W 448	1.2	W 461	1.2	PREP ALIMENTAIRES NDA
1	BEVERAGES AND TOBACCO		8.4		3.9		7.0		4.3	BOISSONS ET TABACS
11	BEVERAGES		7.5		3.3		6.2		3.7	BOISSONS
112	ALCOHOLIC BEVERAGES	W 3810	6.8	W 991	3.0	W 1615	5.9	W 885	3.5	BOISSONS ALCOOLIQUES
1121	WINE OF FRESH GRAPES ETC	W 764	1.9	W 407	1.3	W 744	2.3	W 431	1.4	VINS DE RAISINS FRAIS
11211	GRAPE MUST	W 503	1.0		0.1	W 52	0.2	W 28	0.1	MOUTS DE RAISIN
11212	WINE OF FRESH GRAPES	W 112	0.6	W 347	1.2	W 606	1.9	W 346	1.3	VINS DE MOUTS DE RAISINS
1123	BEER,ALE,STOUT,PORTER	W 2255	2.0	W 394	0.5	W 339	0.5	W 209	0.4	BIERES
1124	DISTILLED ALCOHOLIC BEVS	W 783	3.0	W 188	1.3	W 529	3.1	W 240	1.8	ALCOOLS,EAUX-DE-VIE
11241	WHISKY	W 147	0.9	W 84	0.7	W 284	1.8	W 129	1.0	WHISKY
11242	DISTILLD WINE,GRAPE MARC	W 449	1.3	W 41	0.3	W 102	0.6	W 41	0.4	EAUX-DE-VIE NATURELLES
11249	OTH ALCOHOLC BEVS,CMPNDS	W 187	0.9	W 64	0.5	W 144	0.8	W 70	0.5	BOISSONS ALCOOLIQUES NDA
12	TOBACCO AND MANUFACTURES		1.0		0.6		0.9		0.7	TABACS BRUTS FABRIQUES
2	CRUDE MATERLS,EXCL FUELS		3.4		3.7		4.2		5.1	MAT BRUTES NON COMESTIBLES
24	CORK AND WOOD		3.0		2.6		3.3		3.6	LIEGE ET BOIS
248	WOOD SHAPED,SLEEPERS	W 5971	2.8		2.0	W 4701	3.2	W 10687	3.4	BOIS SIMPLEMENT TRAVAILLES
2482	LUMBER SHAPED CONIFER	W 5877	2.8	W 3434	1.7	W 4480	2.9	W 10637	3.3	CONIFERES SCIES,RABOTES
24821	LUMBER SAWN ETC CONIFER	W 5863	2.7	W 3433	1.6	W 4445	2.8	W 10128	3.0	CONIFERES SCIES LONGITUD
27	CRUDE FERTLZR,MINRLS NES		0.2		0.7		0.3		0.5	ENGRAIS MINERAUX BRUTS
3	MINERAL FUELS ETC		34.4		32.2		44.4		11.4	COMBUSTIBLES MINERAUX LUB
33	PETROLEUM AND PRODUCTS		33.9		31.8		43.9		10.8	PETROLE ET DERIVES
334	PETROLEUM PRODUCTS,REFIN	W 203891	33.7	W 212666	31.6	W 230498	43.6	W 42844	10.4	PRODUITS RAFFINES
3341	GASOLINE,OTH LIGHT OILS	W 11287	1.9	W 212665	31.6	W 230488	43.5	W 10715	2.2	ESSENCES POUR MOTEURS
33411	MOTOR,AVIATION SPIRIT	W 11138	1.8					W 10715	2.2	ESSENCES MOTEURS D'AVIONS
3342	KEROSENE,OTH MEDIUM OILS	W 55382	8.9					W 16941	4.0	PETR LAMPANTS,AUT HUIL
33421	KEROSENE INCL JET FUEL	W 55382	8.9					W 16941	4.0	PETROLES LAMPANTS
3343	GAS OILS	W 133179	20.9					W 13745	3.1	GAS OILS
3345	LUBS,PETROLEUM OILS NES	W 1756	2.0	W 2	0.1	W 10	0.1	W 860	1.2	HUILES LUBRIFIANTES
33451	LUBS(HIGH PETR CONT) ETC	W 1754	2.0					W 856	1.2	HUILES LUBRIF,H LOURDES
4	ANIMAL,VEGETABLE OIL,FAT		1.9		2.3		4.4		5.8	HUILES,GRAISSES ANIM,VEG
42	FIXED VEGETABLE OIL,FAT		1.9		2.3		4.3		5.7	HUILES VEGETALES FIXES
423	FIXED VEG OILS,SOFT	W 721	0.7	W 1135	1.1	W 1846	2.5	W 1806	3.6	HUILES VEGET DOUCES FIXES
4232	SOYA BEAN OIL	W 511	0.4	W 877	0.8	W 1217	1.2	W 1118	1.1	HUILE DE SOJA
4235	OLIVE OIL	W 5	0.1	W 12	0.1	W 232	0.8	W 345	2.0	HUILE D'OLIVE
424	FIXED VEG OIL NONSOFT	W 973	1.2	W 919	1.3	W 1137	1.9	W 871	2.1	AUTRES HUILES VEG FIXES
4242	PALM OIL		0.1	W 917	1.3	W 1018	1.7	W 869	2.1	HUILE DE PALME
4249	FIXED VEGETABLE OILS NES	W 972	1.2	W 2	0.1	W 115	0.2	W 1	0.1	HUILES VEGET FIXES NDA
5	CHEMCLS,RELATED PROD NES		14.4		12.8		15.8		16.2	PRODUITS CHIMIQUES
53	DYES,TANNING,COLOUR PROD		1.4		1.2		1.8		1.8	PROD TEINTURE,COLORANTS
533	PIGMENTS,PAINTS,ETC	W 408	1.4	W 241	1.2	W 484	1.7	W 536	1.8	PIGMENTS,PEINTURES,VERNIS
5334	VARNISHES,DISTEMPERS ETC	W 330	1.1	W 179	0.8	W 368	1.4	W 407	1.5	PEINTURES A L'EAU
541	*MEDICINAL,PHARM PRODUCT	K 142765	3.4	K 210303	2.7	K 497879	3.8	K 272334	2.9	PROD MEDICINAUX PHARMACEUT
5413	ANTIBIOTICS IN BULK	K 6826	0.2	K 24223	0.8	K 19414	0.9	K 24490	0.6	ANTIBIOTIQUES NDA
54139	OTHER ANTIBIOTICS	K 6673	0.2	K 21010	0.8	K 16725	0.9	K 21201	0.6	AUTRES ANTIBIOTIQUES
5417	MEDICAMENTS	K 40896	1.2	K 123832	1.4	K 142468	1.9	K 141791	1.5	MEDICAMENTS
54179	— CONTNG OTH SUBSTANCES	K 35479	0.9	K 85470	0.9	K 108752	1.3	K 113784	1.2	MED CONT AUT SUBSTANCES
5419	PHARMACEUTICAL GOODS NES	K 77615	1.9	K 48806	0.4	K 24271	0.3	K 26216	0.4	PREP,ART PHARMACEUTIQUES
54199	OTH PHARMACEUTICAL GOODS	K 63136	1.7	K 4840	0.1	K 4250	0.1	K 3657	0.1	AUT PREP PHARMACEUTIQUES
55	PERFUME,CLEANING ETC PRD		5.1		4.8		5.7		5.9	PROD POUR PARFUM,TOILETTE
553	PERFUMERY,COSMETICS,ETC	W 340	2.3	W 456	2.3	W 346	2.7	W 409	2.8	PRODUITS DE PARFUMERIE
554	SOAP,CLEANSING ETC PREPS	W 821	2.1	W 845	2.3	W 798	2.5	W 1652	2.7	SAVONS,PRODUITS DETERSIFS
5541	SOAPS	W 447	1.1	W 345	0.9	W 354	1.0	W 453	1.0	SAVONS,PROD TENSIO-ACTIFS

4. General Imports C.I.F. by Commodities according to the S.I.T.C. (Rev. 2) in million U.S. Dollars
Importations Générales C.A.F. par Produits d'après la C.T.C.I. (Rév. 2) en millions de Dollars E.U.

SITC CTCI	COMMODITY	1993 QUANTITY QUANTITE	1993 VALUE VALEUR	1994 QUANTITY QUANTITE	1994 VALUE VALEUR	1995 QUANTITY QUANTITE	1995 VALUE VALEUR	1996 QUANTITY QUANTITE	1996 VALUE VALEUR	PRODUIT
5542	WASHING PREPARATIONS ETC	W 299	0.7	W 381	0.9	W 372	1.2	W 1096	1.3	PROD ORG TENSIO-ACT NDA
58	PLASTIC MATERIALS ETC		1.4		1.3		1.2		1.5	MAT PLAST ARTIFICIELLES
583	POLYMERIZATION ETC PRODS	W 377	1.2	W 309	1.1	W 256	0.9	W 341	1.3	PROD POLYMERISATION
59	CHEMICAL MATERIALS NES		2.3		2.0		2.0		2.4	MAT PROD CHIMIQUES NDA
591	PESTICIDES,DISINFECTANTS	W 163	0.8	W 262	0.7	W 126	0.7	W 509	0.9	DESINF,INSECT,FONG,HERB
598	MISCEL CHEM PRODUCTS NES	W 552	1.2	W 538	1.0	W 213	1.0	W 357	1.2	PROD DIV INDUST CHIM NDA
5989	CHEM PRODUCTS,PREPS NES	W 525	1.2	W 505	1.0	W 163	0.8	W 191	0.8	PROD PREP CHIMIQUES NDA
59899	OTH CHEM PRODS,PREPS,NES	W 495	1.0	W 476	0.8	W 134	0.6	W 144	0.5	AUT PRODUITS CHIMIQUES NDA
6	BASIC MANUFACTURES		44.8		41.3		40.5		50.7	ART MANUFACTURES
62	RUBBER MANUFACTURES NES		2.2		1.7		2.4		2.7	CAOUTCHOUC MANUFACTURE
625	RUBBER TYRES, TUBES ETC		1.2		1.1	W 313	1.7	W 408	1.8	PNEUS CAOUTCHOUC VULCANISE
63	WOOD,CORK MANUFACTRS NES		4.0		4.0		3.5		6.2	OUVRAGES LIEGE ET BOIS
634	VENEERS,PLYWOOD,ETC	W 3817	2.5	W 7416	1.7	W 2178	1.8	W 1521	2.1	PLACAGES,CONTRE-PLAQUES
6342	PLYWOOD OF WOOD SHEETS	W 3228	2.0	W 6867	1.2	W 1831	1.4	W 1014	1.6	BOIS CONTRE-PLAQUES
635	WOOD MANUFACTURES NES		1.5	W 274	2.3	W 586	1.6	W 1063	4.1	ART MANUF EN BOIS NDA
6351	BOXES,CASES,CRATES,ETC	W 57	0.9	W 5	0.1	W 3	0.1	W 22	0.1	CAISSES EMBALLAGES BOIS
6353	BUILDERS WOODWRK,PREFABS		0.6	W 248	2.2	W 555	1.4	W 985	3.8	OUVRAGES DE MENUISERIE
64	PAPER,PAPERBOARD AND MFR		5.1		5.8		6.3		6.2	PAPIERS,CARTONS & OUVRAGES
641	PAPER AND PAPERBOARD	W 691	2.0	W 642	1.6	W 968	2.2	W 947	1.8	PAPIERS ET CARTONS
6412	PRINTG,WRITING PAPER NES	W 221	0.9	W 271	0.6	W 51	0.2	W 20	0.1	PAPIERS POUR L'IMPRESSION
64122	— COATED,IMPREGNATD ETC	W 191	0.8	W 179	0.3	W 34	0.1	W 15	0.1	PAPIERS IMPRESSION COUCHES
6415	PAPER,PAPERBRD,BULK,NES	W 120	0.4	W 77	0.4	W 323	1.2	W 331	1.0	PAPIERS,CARTONS ROULEAUX
64159	OTHER PAPER ETC,BULK,NES	W 115	0.4	W 73	0.4	W 321	1.2	W 326	1.0	AUT PAPIER ROULEAUX FEUILLES
642	PAPER,ETC,PRECUT,ARTS OF	W 934	3.1	W 1385	4.2	W 890	4.1	W 1332	4.4	PAP,CARTONS DECOUPES
6421	PAPER ETC CONTAINERS	W 438	0.9	W 726	1.6	W 432	1.4	W 689	1.7	BOITES,SACS EMBALLAGES
6428	PAPER ETC ARTICLES NES	W 199	1.3	W 355	1.5	W 232	1.6	W 314	1.6	OUVRAGES EN PATE A PAPIER
64285	PAPER ETC DIAPERS ETC	W 104	0.8	W 138	0.9	W 144	1.2	W 216	1.1	SERVIETTES HYGIENIQUES
65	TEXTILE YARN,FABRICS,ETC		4.2		4.1		5.1		5.2	FILS,TISSUS,ARTICLES TEXTILE
652	COTTON FABRICS,WOVEN		1.6		1.0	W 130	1.1	W 131	1.3	TISSUS DE COTON
6522	WOVEN COTTON BLEACHD,ETC		0.9		0.7	W 97	0.8	W 103	1.0	TISSUS COTON BLANCHIS ETC
653	WOVN MAN-MADE FIB FABRIC		0.4		0.5	W 68	0.8	W 46	0.4	TISSUS FIBRES SYNTH,ARTIF
657	SPECIAL TXTL FABRC,PRODS		0.3		0.7	W 152	1.2	W 187	1.4	TISSUS SPECIAUX
658	TEXTILE ARTICLES NES		1.4		1.2	W 122	1.2	W 162	1.5	ART FACONNES MAT TEXTILES
6584	LINENS ETC		1.1	N 93338	0.8	W 84	0.7	W 104	0.9	LINGE DE MAISON
66	NONMETAL MINERAL MFS NES		7.6		7.7		6.5		8.3	ART MIN NON METALLIQUES
661	LIME,CEMENT,BLDG PRODS	W 27300	2.9	W 26780	2.8	W 25989	2.6	W 29110	3.4	CHAUX,CIMENTS MAT CONSTR
6612	CEMENT	W 27188	2.7	W 26741	2.7	W 25915	2.4	W 28859	2.9	CIMENTS HYDRAULIQUES
662	CLAY,REFRACTORY BLDG PRD	W 4909	2.2	W 2224	1.9	W 1338	1.4	W 1911	1.7	MAT CONST REFRACTAIRES
6623	REFRACTORY BUILDING PROD	W 3623	0.9	W 116	0.2	W 25	0.1	W 54	0.2	BRIQUES REFRACTAIRES
6624	BRICKS ETC NONREFRACTORY	W 1285	1.3	W 2108	1.8	W 1313	1.3	W 1857	1.6	BRIQUES ETC CERAM NON REFR
66245	GLAZED CERAMIC SETTS ETC	W 1175	1.2	W 1910	1.4	W 1034	0.9	W 1371	1.2	AUT CARREAUX CERAMIQUE
664	GLASS		0.6		0.8	W 251	0.8	W 260	1.0	VERRE
665	GLASSWARE		1.5		1.6	W 477	1.2	W 414	1.0	OUVRAGES EN VERRE
6651	BOTTLES ETC OF GLASS		0.9		1.1	W 306	0.6	W 241	0.4	RECIPIENTS EN VERRE
66511	GLASS BOTTLES ETC NONVAC	W 1296	0.9	W 1358	1.1	W 306	0.6	W 241	0.4	BONBONNES,BOUTEILLES,ETC
67	IRON AND STEEL		4.4		5.2		3.9		4.7	FER ET ACIER
673	IRON,STEEL SHAPES ETC	W 1321	1.2	W 1805	1.7	W 654	0.9	W 1519	1.2	BARRES,PROFIL FER,ACIER
6733	IRON,STEEL PROFILES ETC	W 454	0.4	W 731	0.9	W 278	0.5	W 372	0.6	PROFILES,PALPLAN FER,ACIER
67336	IRN,SMPL STL SHEET PILNG	W 297	0.2	W 624	0.7	W 105	0.3	W 67	0.3	PALPLANCHES EN FER,ACIER
674	IRN,STL UNIV,PLATE,SHEET	W 1407	1.7	W 1119	1.6	W 1094	1.6	W 1059	2.2	LARGES PLATS,TOLES
6749	OTH IRN,STL PLATES,SHEET	W 1242	1.5	W 942	1.3	W 945	1.4	W 850	2.0	AUTRES TOLES FER,ACIER
67491	— OF IRON OR SIMPLE STL	W 1241	1.5	W 915	1.3	W 938	1.4	W 719	1.8	AUT TOLES AUTRES ACIER FIN
678	IRON,STL TUBES,PIPES,ETC	W 673	1.2	W 1150	1.8	W 270	1.1	W 532	1.2	TUBES,TUYAUX EN FONTE,FER
6783	IRON,STL TUBES,PIPES NES	W 289	0.5	W 991	1.2	W 30	0.1	W 46	0.1	AUT TUBES,TUYAUX FER,ACIER
68	NON-FERROUS METALS		1.4		1.4		1.5		1.3	METAUX NON FERREUX
684	ALUMINIUM	W 200	1.1	W 141	1.0	W 144	1.1	W 143	0.9	ALUMINIUM
6842	ALUMINIUM,ALLOYS WORKED	W 199	1.1	W 141	1.0	W 144	1.1	W 117	0.8	ALUMINIUM,ALLIAGES OUVRE
69	METAL MANUFACTURES NES		16.1		11.7		11.6		16.6	ART MANUFACT EN METAL NDA
691	STRUCTURES AND PARTS NES	W 437	3.7	W 732	2.8	W 504	1.7	W 1214	2.3	CONSTRUCT FER,ACIER,ALU
6911	STRUCTURES,PARTS IRN,STL	W 235	0.9	W 696	2.6	W 424	1.2	W 1009	1.5	CONSTRUCT FER,ACIER,FONTE
6912	STRUCTURES,PARTS ALUMNM	W 203	2.8	W 36	0.3	W 80	0.6	W 205	0.8	CONSTRUCT ALUMINIUM
692	METAL TANKS,BOXES,ETC		6.9		2.9	W 2166	4.2	W 3702	7.4	RECIPIENTS METALLIQUES
6921	METAL STORAGE TANKS ETC	W 439	3.3	W 8	0.1	W 12	0.2	W 21	0.1	CUVES EN FONTE,FER,ALU
69211	STEEL STORAGE TANKS ETC	W 381	3.0	W 8	0.1	W 11	0.2	W 10	0.1	CUVES EN FONTE FER OU ACIER
6924	MTL TRANSPORT BOXES ETC		3.7		2.9	W 2153	4.0	W 3681	7.3	FUTS,TAMBOURS,BIDONS
69241	STL TRANSPORT BOXES ETC		3.6	W 35	2.7	W 2126	3.9	W 3539	7.0	FUTS,TAMBOURS,BIDONS FER
695	TOOLS	W 186	1.0	W 143	1.0	W 126	1.1	W 99	0.9	OUTILS A MAIN
6953	OTHER HAND TOOLS	W 149	0.7	W 102	0.8	W 78	0.7	W 56	0.6	AUTRES OUTILS A MAIN
697	BASE MTL HOUSEHOLD EQUIP		1.8		1.6	W 247	1.5	W 233	1.5	ART MENAGE MET COMMUNS
6973	DMSTC HEATG,COOKG APPARA		0.7	N 2316	0.7	W 120	0.7	W 92	0.6	APPS CHAUF NON ELECTRIQ
699	BASE METAL MFRS NES		1.8	W 415	2.3	W 396	2.0	W 472	2.9	ART MANUFACTURES MET NDA
6991	LOCKSMITHS WARES,ETC	W 148	0.8	W 105	0.9	W 111	0.9	W 235	1.4	ARTICLES DE SERRURERIE
6996	BASE MTL MISC ARTICLES	W 153	0.5	W 250	0.8	W 190	0.6	W 123	0.7	ART DIVERS METAUX COMMUNS
7	MACHINES,TRANSPORT EQUIP		60.5		47.9		68.8		166.2	MACHINES MATERIEL TRANSPORT
71	POWER GENERATING EQUIPMT		4.8		2.7		7.7		10.3	MACHINES GENERATRICES
713	INTRNL COMBUS PSTN ENGIN		1.1		1.3	W 121	3.9	W 156	3.9	MOTEURS EXPL COMB INT, PIECE
7131	AIRCRAFT PSTN ENGINS,PTS		0.1		0.1	W 8	1.5	W 12	2.2	MOTEURS EXPL P.AVIATION, PIE
71319	PTS NES OF ENGN OF 71311		0.1		0.1	W 7	1.5	W 9	1.7	PIECES POUR 713.11
7133	MARINE PISTON ENGINES	N 1083	0.7	N 78	0.5	W 70	1.6	W 63	0.8	MOTEURS EXPL POUR BATEAUX
71331	—— OUTBOARD	N 1067	0.6	N 73	0.4	W 41	0.9	W 27	0.6	MOTEURS BATEAUX HORSBORD
716	ROTATING ELECTRIC PLANT		3.2		1.3	W 260	3.5	W 610	6.2	APP ELECTR ROTATIFS,PIECES
7161	DC MOTORS AND GENERATORS		1.8	N 2	0.3	W 74	2.2	W 554	5.4	MOTEURS COURANT CONTINU
7162	AC MTRS,GENRTRS,GEN SETS		0.3		0.5	W 179	1.0	W 34	0.5	MOTEURS ELECTRIQUES
7169	PTS NES OF ROT ELEC PLNT		1.2		0.5	W 7	0.4	W 22	0.4	PIECES MAC APP ROTATIFS
72	MACHS FOR SPCL INDUSTRYS		6.1		5.8		5.3		4.7	MAC SPECIALES POUR INDUST
721	AGRIC MACHY,EXC TRACTORS		0.5		1.7	W 43	0.6	W 60	0.6	MACHINES AGRICOLES
7219	AGRICULTURE MACHINES NES		0.2		1.4	W 20	0.2	W 12	0.2	ENGINS AGRICOLES NDA
72197	OTH AGRIC ETC MACHINERY		0.1		1.3	W 18	0.2	W 7	0.1	AUT APP POUR AGRICULTURE
723	CIVIL ENGNEERG EQUIP ETC		0.8		1.3	W 89	0.8	W 100	0.7	APPAREILS DE GENIE CIVIL
7234	CONST,MINING MACHNRY NES		0.7		1.2	W 83	0.8	W 44	0.3	MACH POUR LA CONST, MINES
72342	SLFPRP SHOVELS,EXCAVATRS	N 14	0.4	N 1	1.1	W 66	0.7	W 38	0.3	PELLES MECANIQUES
727	FOOD MACHRY NON-DOMESTIC		1.0		1.0	W 63	2.6	W 108	2.1	MACH INDUSTRIES ALIMENT
7272	OTH FOOD PROC MCHY,PARTS		1.0		1.0	W 63	2.6	W 104	2.1	AUT MACH IND ALIMENTAIRE
72722	INDUS FOOD PROC MACH NES		0.6	N 16430	0.4	W 54	2.4	W 57	0.8	MACHINES BOULANGERIE
72729	PTS NES OF MCHY OF 72722		0.5		0.7	W 9	0.3	W 47	1.3	PIECES MACH DU 727.22
728	OTH MACHY FOR SPCL INDUS		3.4		1.0	W 165	1.1	W 111	1.0	AUT MACH IND PARTICULIERES
7283	OTHR MINERAL WORKG MACHY		2.0		0.3	W 134	0.7	W 46	0.4	MACH TRIER,CRIBLER,BROYER
72832	MINRL CRUSHING ETC MACHY		1.2			W 109	0.5	W 1	0.1	MACH CONCASSER MAT MINER
7284	MACHY FOR SPCL INDUS NES		0.9		0.6	W 9	0.2	W 32	0.4	MACH SPEC IND PARTICUL.
73	METALWORKING MACHINERY		0.4		0.9		0.5		0.5	MACH TRAVAIL DES METAUX
736	METALWORKING MACH-TOOLS		0.3		0.7	W 52	0.4	W 22	0.3	MACH-OUTILS TRAVAIL METAUX

4. General Imports C.I.F. by Commodities according to the S.I.T.C. (Rev. 2) in million U.S. Dollars
Importations Générales C.A.F. par Produits d'après la C.T.C.I. (Rév. 2) en millions de Dollars E.U.

SITC CTCI	COMMODITY	1993 QUANTITY QUANTITE	1993 VALUE VALEUR	1994 QUANTITY QUANTITE	1994 VALUE VALEUR	1995 QUANTITY QUANTITE	1995 VALUE VALEUR	1996 QUANTITY QUANTITE	1996 VALUE VALEUR	PRODUIT
74	GENRL INDUSTRL MACHY NES		6.1		11.6		10.1		11.4	MACH APP INDUSTRIE
741	HEATING,COOLING EQUIPMNT		2.4		3.3	W 290	2.6	W 361	3.4	MACH CHAUFFAGE,PIECES
7414	NONDOM REFRIG EQUIPT,PTS		0.5		1.7	W 88	1.0	W 96	0.6	MAT PRODUCTION DU FROID
74141	REFRIG EQUIP NONDOMESTIC	N 210	0.4	N 115	1.5	W 60	0.5	W 51	0.4	REFIG INDUSTRIELS
7415	AIR–CONDITIONING MACHNRY		1.3	N 33	1.2	W 141	1.2	W 154	1.3	GROUPES CONDITION AIR
7416	HEATING,COOLING EQU NES		0.4		0.4	W 43	0.3	W 97	1.5	APP CHANGEMENT TEMP
742	PUMPS FOR LIQUIDS ETC		0.7		0.9	W 38	0.7	W 63	0.8	POMPES MOTO–POMPES
7428	OTHER PUMPS FOR LIQUIDS		0.2		0.8	W 30	0.5	W 39	0.6	AUTRES POMPES POUR LIQ
74288	PUMPS FR LIQUIDS NES ETC		0.2		0.7	W 30	0.5	W 39	0.6	POMPES POUR LIQUIDES NDA
743	PUMPS NES,CENTRFUGES ETC		0.6		0.9	W 61	1.0	W 101	1.1	POMPES COMPRES,VENT ETC
744	MECHANICAL HANDLING EQU		1.8		4.4	W 147	1.4	W 178	1.8	EQUIP MANUTENTION PIECES
7441	FORK LIFT TRCKS,ETC,PTS		0.7		3.7	W 69	0.5	W 35	0.4	CHARIOTS POUR USINES ETC
74419	PTS NES OF VEHC OF 74411		0.6		3.4	W 8	0.2	W 7	0.2	PIECES POUR 744.11
7449	PTS NES OF MACHY OF 7442		0.7		0.7	W 33	0.6	W 49	0.7	PIECES DU 744.2
745	NONELEC MACHY,TOOLS NES		0.5		0.7	W 132	1.7	W 292	3.1	AUT MACH NON ELEC,PIECES
7452	OTH NONELEC MCHS,PTS NES		0.3		0.5	W 126	1.6	W 273	2.8	AUT MACH NON ELEC,PIECES
74522	PACKAGNG,BOTTLNG,ETC MCH		0.1		0.1	W 40	0.5	W 165	1.4	MACH NETT BOUTEILLES,ETC
749	NONELEC MACH PTS,ACC NES		0.3		1.7	W 204	2.9	W 168	1.5	PIECES MACH NON ELEC NDA
7492	COCKS,VALVES ETC NES		0.3		1.3	W 64	0.6	W 53	0.6	ART ROB,SIM POUR TUYAUX
7499	OTH NONELEC MCHY PTS NES		0.1		0.1	W 112	1.8	W 20	0.3	PIECES NON ELECT NDA
74992	METAL–PLASTIC GASKETS		0.1	N 3	0.1	W 99	1.6	W 12	0.2	JOINTS METALLOPLASTIQUES
75	OFFICE MACHNES,ADP EQUIP		3.0		3.3		5.4		4.5	MACH BUREAU TRAIT AUTOM
751	OFFICE MACHINES		0.6		0.5	W 24	0.9	W 25	0.6	MACH,APPAREILS DE BUREAU
752	AUTOMTIC DATA PROC EQUIP		1.9		2.2	W 47	3.2	W 45	2.0	MACH TRAIT INFORMATION
7522	DIGITAL COMPUTERS	N 329	0.5	N 143	0.7	W 11	0.8	W 8	0.5	MACH DIGITALES COMPLETES
7525	ADP PERIPHERAL UNITS	N 361	0.4	N 139	0.5	W 17	1.2	W 26	1.2	UNITES PERIPHERIQUES
7528	OFF–LINE DATA PROC EQUIP		1.0	N 6635	0.6	W 12	0.6	W 7	0.3	MACH AUXIL TRAIT INFORM
759	OFFICE,ADP MCH PTS,ACCES		0.6		0.8	W 33	1.5	W 57	1.9	PIECES DU 751 ET 752
7599	ACCTG,ETC,ADP MCH PTS,AC		0.4		0.5	W 20	1.0	W 44	1.6	PIECES DU 751 ET 752
76	TELECOMM,SOUND EQUIPMENT		10.0		5.5		10.9		14.1	EQUIPMENT DE TELECOM
761	TELEVISION RECEIVERS	N 2917	1.9	N 1224	0.7	W 94	1.3	W 43	0.6	RECEPTEURS DE TELEVISION
7611	COLOUR TV RECEIVERS	N 2817	0.8	N 974	0.6	W 94	1.3	W 41	0.6	RECEPTEURS COULEUR
7612	MONOCHROME TV RECEIVERS	N 100	1.2	N 250	0.1		0.1	W 2	0.1	RECEPTEURS NOIR ET BLANC
763	SOUND RECORDRS,PHONOGRPH	N 4260	0.7	N 677	0.8	W 25	0.6	W 47	0.8	PHONO,APP ENREGISTREMENT
7638	OTHR SOUND APPARATUS ETC	N 4127	0.6	N 606	0.7	W 24	0.6	W 45	0.8	AUT APP D'ENREGIS,REPROD
764	TELECOM EQPT,PTS,ACC NES		7.1		3.8	W 161	8.6	W 219	12.4	EQUIP TELECOM,PIECES
7641	LINE TELEPHONE,ETC EQUIP	N 6236	5.0	N 336	1.8	W 70	4.7	W 46	2.3	APP TELEPHON PAR FIL
7648	TELECOMM EQUIPMENT NES		0.2	N 28	0.3	W 1	0.1	W 96	7.3	APP TELECOM NDA
76483	RADAR APPARATUS ETC		0.1	N 2	0.1		0.1	W 94	7.1	APP DE RADIOGUIDAGE ETC
7649	PTS NES OF EQUIPMT OF 76		1.6		1.2	W 77	3.3	W 52	1.8	PIECES DE LA DIV 76
76491	PTS NES OF APPAR OF 7641		0.9		0.7	W 67	2.9	W 33	1.5	PIECES POUR 764.1
77	ELECTRIC MACHNRY NES ETC		9.2		8.4		9.0		10.8	MACH APP ELECT NDA
771	ELECTRIC POWER MACHY NES		1.5		0.4	W 30	0.4	W 38	0.3	MACH PROD,TRANS ELECTR
7712	OTH ELEC POWER MACHY NES		1.3		0.2	W 3	0.1	W 5	0.1	AUT APP PROD TRANSF ELEC
77129	PTS NES OF MACHY OF 771		1.3		0.2	W 1	0.1	W 1	0.1	PIECES MACH DU 771
772	SWITCHGEAR ETC,PARTS NES		1.6		1.5	W 87	1.4	W 157	1.8	APP COUPURE,SECT ETC
7721	SWITCHGEAR ETC		1.2		1.3	W 76	1.1	W 151	1.6	APP COUPURE,SECTIONMNT
773	ELECTR DISTRIBUTNG EQUIP		1.3		1.0	W 251	1.2	W 350	2.2	EQUIPMT DISTRIBUTION ELECT
7731	INSULATED WIRE,CABLE ETC		1.1		0.9	W 234	1.1	W 334	2.1	FILS,CABLES ISOLES ELECT
774	ELECTRO–MEDCL,XRAY EQUIP		1.0		0.1	W 1	0.1	W 4	0.1	APPAREILS MEDICAUX
7742	X–RAY APPARATUS ETC		1.0		0.1		0.1	W 1	0.1	APPAREILS A RAYONS X
775	HOUSEHOLD TYPE EQUIP NES		2.4		2.6	W 491	3.0	W 1020	2.7	MACH,APP USAGE DOMESTQUE
7752	DOM REFRIGERATRS,FREEZRS	N 3090	1.1	N 3115	1.1	W 273	1.5	W 374	1.2	REFRIG,CONGEL MENAGER
77521	DOMESTIC REFRIGERATORS	N 2012	0.7	N 2034	0.8	W 195	1.1	W 324	0.8	REFRIGERATEURS
7758	ELECTRO–THERMIC APPL NES		0.8		0.7	W 95	0.8	W 89	0.8	APP ELECTROTHERMIQ NDA
776	TRANSISTORS,VALVES,ETC		0.1		1.0	W 16	1.0	W 24	1.6	LAMPES,TUBES,VALVES
7764	ELECTRONIC MICROCIRCUITS		0.1		0.6	W 11	0.9	W 2	0.1	MICROSTRUCTURES ELECTRON
7768	ELCTRNC COMP PTS,CRYSTLS		0.1		0.1	W 1	0.1	W 18	1.4	CRIST PIEZO–ELEC,PCS 776
77689	ELECTRNIC COMPON PTS NES		0.1		0.1	W 1	0.1	W 18	1.4	PIECES DU GROUPE 776
778	ELECTRICAL MACHINERY NES		1.6		2.1	W 224	2.2	W 252	2.4	AUTRES MACH ELECT NDA
78	ROAD VEHICLES		16.6		6.2		12.9		13.5	VEHICULES ROUTIERS
781	PASS MOTOR VEH EXC BUSES	N 1210	6.0	N 48	2.1	W 492	4.8	W 800	5.7	AUTO TRANSPORT PERSONNES
782	LORRIES,SPCL MTR VEH NES	N 335	3.7	N 56	2.6	W 336	3.3	W 209	2.3	VEHICULES SPECIAUX,MARCH
7821	LORRIES,TRUCKS	N 306	2.7	N 55	1.4	W 193	1.4	W 167	1.7	VEHICULES TRANSP MARCHAND
7822	SPECIAL MOTOR VEHCLS NES	N 29	1.0	N 1	1.3	W 144	2.0	W 42	0.7	VEHICULES USAGES SPECIAUX
783	ROAD MOTOR VEHICLES NES	N 74	1.9		0.2	W 271	0.7	W 171	1.1	VEHICULES ROUTIERS NDA
7831	BUSES	N 71	1.9	N 3	0.1	W 271	0.7	W 155	1.0	VOITURES TRANSPORT COMMUN
784	MOTOR VEH PRTS,ACCES NES		4.7		1.0	W 295	3.8	W 456	4.0	PIECES 722,781,782,783
7849	OTHER MOTOR VEHCL PARTS		4.6	W 2	1.0	W 272	3.7	W 430	3.9	PIECES 722,781,782,783
79	OTHR TRANSPORT EQUIPMENT		4.8		3.9		7.4		96.7	AUTRE MATERIEL TRANSPORT
792	AIRCRAFT ETC		3.6		3.0	W 10	1.2	W 28	93.4	APP NAVIGATION AERIENNE
7924	AIRCRFT NES OVER 15000KG							W 15	91.1	AERODYNES PLUS 15000 KG
7929	AIRCRAFT PARTS NES		3.6		3.0	W 8	1.0	W 12	2.3	PIECES DU 792
793	SHIPS AND BOATS ETC		1.1		0.9	W 742	6.1	W 620	3.3	NAVIRES BATEAUX,ETC
7932	SHIPS AND BOATS NES	N 143	0.4		0.8	W 731	6.0	W 607	3.2	NAVIRES ET BATEAUX
79321	YACHTS,SPORTS VESSLS ETC	N 43	0.2	N 4	0.2	W 12	0.2	W 588	2.8	BATEAUX DE PLAISANCE
79323	OTHER CARGO VESSELS	N 100	0.2		0.1	W 598	2.4	W 3	0.1	AUT BATEAUX TRANS MARCH
79324	FISHING VESSELS ETC				0.7	W 122	3.5	W 16	0.4	BATEAUX DE PECHE
8	MISC MANUFACTURED GOODS		36.0		24.9		27.1		27.5	ART MANUFACTURES DIVERS
812	*PLUMBG,HEATNG,LGHTNG EQ		2.0		1.3	W 204	1.5	W 395	2.7	APPAR SANITAIRES CHAUFFAGE
8122	CERAMIC PLUMBNG FIXTURES		0.8	W 112	0.6	W 126	0.7	W 250	1.1	EVIERS,LAVABOS,CUVETTES
8124	LIGHTING EQUIPMENT NES		1.3		0.7	W 74	0.8	W 117	1.2	APPAREILS ECLAIRAGE ETC
81242	LAMPS,FITTINGS BASE METL		1.2		0.6	W 54	0.5	W 99	1.1	APPAREILS D'ECLAIRAGE
821	*FURNITURE,PARTS THEREOF		2.6		2.5	W 803	3.1	W 1280	4.0	MEUBLES ET PIECES
8212	MED FURN,STUFFD FURNSHGS		0.9		0.7	W 213	0.8	W 382	0.8	MOB MEDICO–CHIRUR,PIECES
82122	MATTRESSES ETC		0.8	N 2398	0.6	W 210	0.7	W 376	0.8	SOMMIERS,ARTICLES DE LITERIE
8219	FURNITURE AND PARTS NES		1.6		1.7	W 521	2.0	W 829	2.9	AUTRES MEUBLES ET PIECES
82192	WOOD FURNITURE NES		0.8		1.1	W 351	1.1	W 559	1.6	MEUBLES NDA EN BOIS
84	CLOTHING AND ACCESSORIES		2.9		2.7		3.6		3.3	VETEMENTS
846	UNDER GARMENTS KNITTED	N 750855	1.1	N 473470	0.9	W 158	1.5	W 109	1.2	SOUS VETS DE BONNETERIE
8462	— OF COTTON NON ELASTIC	N 674419	1.0	N 426195	0.7	W 138	1.3	W 96	1.0	SOUS–VET BONNET COTON
84629	—— OTHER	N 672708	1.0	N 419895	0.7	W 135	1.3	W 85	1.0	AUT SOUS–VET BONNET COTON
851	*FOOTWEAR	P 323729	1.6	P 382658	2.1	W 230	2.3	W 181	2.2	CHAUSSURES
85102	FOOTWEAR LEATHER	P 146300	0.8	P 199543	1.3	W 159	1.7	W 142	1.8	CHAUS SEMELLES EN CUIR
87	PRECISION INSTRUMNTS NES		13.7		3.3		3.3		2.3	INSTRUM,APPAR SCIENT NDA
872	MEDICAL INSTRUMENTS NES		1.1		1.1	W 21	1.0	W 36	0.6	INSTR,APP MEDIC–CHIR NDA
87202	OTH MEDICAL INSTRUMENTS		1.0		1.1	W 20	0.9	W 34	0.6	INSTRUM,APP MEDECINE
874	MEASURNG,CONTROLNG INSTR		12.5		2.1	W 74	2.3		1.6	INSTRUMENTS DE MESURE
8748	ELEC MEAS,CONTRL EQU NES		10.7		1.4	W 10	1.1		0.5	APP ELEC ELECTRO MESURE
87483	OTH ELCTRNC MEAS ETC EQU		10.3	N 70	1.2	W 10	1.0	W 12	0.3	AUT APP ELECTRO DE MESURE
8749	INSTR PTS NES,ACCESSORYS		1.2		0.1	W 8	0.4	W 4	0.1	PIECES 873,874.3,54,874.8

4. General Imports C.I.F. by Commodities according to the S.I.T.C. (Rev. 2) in million U.S. Dollars
Importations Générales C.A.F. par Produits d'après la C.T.C.I. (Rév. 2) en millions de Dollars E.U.

SITC CTCI	COMMODITY	1993		1994		1995		1996		PRODUIT
		QUANTITY QUANTITE	VALUE VALEUR	QUANTITY QUANTITE	VALUE VALEUR	QUANTITY QUANTITE	VALUE VALEUR	QUANTITY QUANTITE	VALUE VALEUR	
88	PHOTO EQU,OPTICL GDS ETC		1.4		1.1		1.2		1.3	APP,FOURN PHOTO,OP,MONTR
89	MISC MANUFCTRD GOODS NES		11.6		11.8		11.8		11.6	ART MANUFACTURES DIVERS
892	PRINTED MATTER		2.5		2.9	W 302	3.0	W 282	2.4	IMPRIMES
8921	PRINTED BOOKS,GLOBES,ETC		1.1		1.2	W 105	1.0	W 99	0.8	LIVRES,BROCHURES,CARTES
89211	PRINTED BOOKS,PAMPHLETS		1.0		1.2	W 100	1.0	W 90	0.8	LIVRES,BROCHURES
8928	PRINTED MATTER NES		1.2		1.3	W 132	1.3	W 138	1.1	IMPRIMES NDA
893	ARTICLES OF PLASTIC NES		4.5		4.1		4.6		5.2	OUVRAGES EN MAT DIVIS 58
8931	PLSTC PACKG CONTNRS,LIDS		1.1	W 27	1.0	W 399	1.8	W 460	2.6	ART TRANSP EMBALLAGE ETC
8939	MISC PLASTIC ARTICLES		3.3		2.8	W 431	2.7	W 586	2.5	ART DIVERS EN MAT DIV 58
89399	OTHR PLASTC ARTICLES NES		3.1	W 6	2.5	W 399	2.4	W 438	2.2	AUT OUV MAT DIV 58
894	TOYS,SPORTING GOODS,ETC		2.1		2.2	W 837	1.9	W 182	1.8	VOITURES ENFANTS,JOUETS
8942	TOYS,INDOOR GAMES ETC		1.7		1.7	W 570	1.1	W 136	1.2	JOUETS,JEUX ETC
89423	TOYS NES		0.7		0.7	W 533	0.5	W 74	0.7	JOUETS,MODELES REDUITS
89424	INDOOR GAME EQUIPMENT		0.8		0.8	W 16	0.5	W 30	0.3	ART,JEUX DE SOCIETE
898	MUSICAL INSTRUMENTS,PTS		1.1		0.7	W 45	0.9	W 43	0.7	INSTRUMENTS DE MUSIQUE
8983	SOUND RECRDNG TAPE,DISCS	N 300560	1.0	N 86576	0.6	W 42	0.8	W 40	0.7	SUPPORTS SON POUR 763
899	OTHER MANUFACTURED GOODS		0.8		1.4		0.9		0.9	AUT ART MANUF DIVERS NDA
9	GOODS NOT CLASSD BY KIND		0.3		0.2		0.5		1.8	ART TRANSACT NON CLASSES
931	*SPECIAL TRANSACTIONS	W 1	0.1		0.1		0.4		1.6	TRANS.SPECIALES

5. General Exports F.O.B. by Commodities according to the S.I.T.C. (Rev. 2) in million U.S. Dollars
Exportations Générales F.O.B. par Produits d'après la C.T.C.I. (Rév. 2) en millions de Dollars E.U.

SITC CTCI	COMMODITY	1993		1994		1995		1996		PRODUIT
		QUANTITY QUANTITE	VALUE VALEUR	QUANTITY QUANTITE	VALUE VALEUR	QUANTITY QUANTITE	VALUE VALEUR	QUANTITY QUANTITE	VALUE VALEUR	
	ALL COMMODITIES		51.7		51.8		53.2		139.4	TOUS PRODUITS
0	FOOD AND LIVE ANIMALS		15.2		23.6		23.5		40.8	ALIMENTS,ANIMAUX VIVANTS
02	DAIRY PRODCTS,BIRDS'EGGS		0.2		0.1		0.1		0.1	PRODUITS LAITIERS,OEUFS
022	MILK AND CREAM	W 51	0.2	W 5	0.1		0.1	W 1	0.1	LAIT ET CREME
0224	MILK,CREAM PRESERVED ETC	W 51	0.2	W 3	0.1					LAIT,CREME CONS,CONC
03	FISH AND PREPARATIONS		14.4		22.5		22.7		39.8	POISSONS ET PREPARATIONS
034	FISH,FRESH,CHILLED,FROZN	W 445	1.8	W 438	1.9	W 406	2.2	W 496	2.6	POISSON FRAIS, REFRIG,CONG
0341	FISH FRSH,CHLLD,EX FILLT	W 193	1.2	W 246	1.4	W 262	1.8	W 297	2.1	POISSON FRAIS,REFRIGERE
0342	FISH FROZEN,EXCL FILLETS	W 252	0.7	W 192	0.5	W 145	0.4	W 198	0.6	POISSONS CONGELES
035	FISH SALTED,DRIED,SMOKED	W 15	0.6	W 619	2.6	W 17	0.7	W 918	0.9	POISSON SECHE,SALE,FUME
03503	FISH(EX COD)DRIED,SALTED	W 15	0.6	W 9	0.4	W 11	0.7	W 10	0.5	POISSONS SECHES,SALES
03504	FISH SMOKED			W 610	2.3	W 6	0.1	W 16	0.2	POISSONS FUMES
036	SHELL FISH FRESH,FROZEN	W 68	0.7	W 39	0.4	W 131	1.5	W 191	2.2	CRUSTACES,MOLLUSQUES
037	FISH ETC PREPD,PRSVD NES	W 4466	11.4	W 7362	17.7	W 6291	18.5	W 13019	34.2	POIS,CRUST,MOL PREPARES
0371	FISH PREPARD,PRESRVD NES	W 4466	11.4	W 7362	17.7	W 6291	18.5	W 13016	34.2	CONSERVES DE POISSONS
07	COFFEE,TEA,COCOA,SPICES		0.5		0.6		0.8		1.0	CAFE,THE,CACAO,EPICES
075	SPICES	W 446	0.5	W 435	0.5	W 637	0.8	W 746	1.0	EPICES
0752	SPICES,EX PEPPER,PIMENTO	W 446	0.5	W 435	0.5	W 637	0.8	W 746	1.0	AUTRES EPICES
07522	CINNAMON,ETC	W 446	0.5	W 435	0.5	W 637	0.8	W 743	1.0	CANNELLE
081	*FEEDING STUFF FOR ANIML	W 196	0.1	W 1440	0.5					NOURRITURE POUR ANIMAUX
0814	MEAT OR FISH MEAL FODDER	W 196	0.1	W 1440	0.5					FARINES DE VIANDES,POISSONS
08142	FISH MEAL FODDER	W 196	0.1	W 1440	0.5					FARINES DE POISSONS
1	BEVERAGES AND TOBACCO		0.4		0.6		0.8		0.7	BOISSONS ET TABACS
11	BEVERAGES		0.3		0.4		0.5		0.6	BOISSONS
112	ALCOHOLIC BEVERAGES	W 93	0.3	W 107	0.4	W 102	0.5	W 92	0.4	BOISSONS ALCOOLIQUES
1124	DISTILLED ALCOHOLIC BEVS	W 30	0.2	W 73	0.3	W 42	0.4	W 43	0.3	ALCOOLS,EAUX-DE-VIE
11241	WHISKY	W 14	0.1	W 9	0.1	W 17	0.3	W 28	0.3	WHISKY
12	TOBACCO AND MANUFACTURES		0.1		0.2		0.3		0.2	TABACS BRUTS FABRIQUES
122	TOBACCO,MANUFACTURED	W 9	0.1	W 18	0.2	W 421	0.3	W 10	0.2	TABACS FABRIQUES
1222	CIGARETTES	W 8	0.1	W 17	0.2	W 415	0.2	W 9	0.2	CIGARETTES
2	CRUDE MATERLS,EXCL FUELS		0.3		0.2		0.3		0.2	MAT BRUTES NON COMESTIBLES
22	OIL SEEDS,OLEAGINOUS FRT		0.2		0.1		0.2		0.1	GRAINES,FRUITS OLEAGINEUX
223	SEEDS FOR OTH FIXED OILS	W 226	0.2	W 101	0.1	W 157	0.1		0.1	GRAINES AUTRES HUILES FIXES
2231	COPRA	W 226	0.2	W 101	0.1	W 157	0.1			COPRAH
3	MINERAL FUELS ETC		28.5		23.8		24.9		30.5	COMBUSTIBLES MINERAUX LUB
33	PETROLEUM AND PRODUCTS		28.5		23.8		24.9		30.5	PETROLE ET DERIVES
334	PETROLEUM PRODUCTS,REFIN	W 133816	28.5	W 116151	23.8	W 103916	24.8	W 110050	30.5	PRODUITS RAFFINES
3341	GASOLINE,OTH LIGHT OILS			W 116151	23.8	W 103916	24.8			ESSENCES POUR MOTEURS
3342	KEROSENE,OTH MEDIUM OILS	W 37923	9.0					W 32580	10.4	PETR LAMPANTS,AUT HUIL
33421	KEROSENE INCL JET FUEL	W 37923	9.0					W 32580	10.4	PETROLES LAMPANTS
3343	GAS OILS	W 92191	18.7					W 72552	18.5	GAS OILS
3344	FUEL OILS,NES	W 3062	0.5					W 3786	0.7	FUEL OILS
3345	LUBS,PETROLEUM OILS NES	W 640	0.5					W 1131	1.1	HUILES LUBRIFIANTES
33451	LUBS(HIGH PETR CONT) ETC	W 640	0.5					W 1131	1.1	HUILES LUBRIF,H LOURDES
5	CHEMCLS,RELATED PROD NES		0.2		0.1		0.3		0.3	PRODUITS CHIMIQUES
55	PERFUME,CLEANING ETC PRD		0.2		0.1		0.3		0.3	PROD POUR PARFUM,TOILETTE
553	PERFUMERY,COSMETICS,ETC	W 5	0.2	W 5	0.1	W 14	0.3	W 11	0.1	PRODUITS DE PARFUMERIE
6	BASIC MANUFACTURES		0.1		0.1		0.4		0.2	ART MANUFACTURES
66	NONMETAL MINERAL MFS NES		0.1		0.1		0.3		0.1	ART MIN NON METALLIQUES
661	LIME,CEMENT,BLDG PRODS	W 402	0.1	W 7	0.1	W 2023	0.3	W 29	0.1	CHAUX,CIMENTS MAT CONSTR
6612	CEMENT					W 2000	0.2			CIMENTS HYDRAULIQUES
7	MACHINES,TRANSPORT EQUIP		4.1		1.4		1.6		64.4	MACHINES MATERIEL TRANSPORT
71	POWER GENERATING EQUIPMT		0.1		0.3		0.1		0.3	MACHINES GENERATRICES
74	GENRL INDUSTRL MACHY NES		0.5		0.2		0.8		0.1	MACH APP INDUSTRIE
741	HEATING,COOLING EQUIPMNT					W 8	0.7		0.1	MACH CHAUFFAGE,PIECES
7413	INDUS FURNACES ETC,PARTS					W 7	0.7			FOURS IND,LABOR,PIECES
74132	INDUST FURNACES NONELECT					W 7	0.7			FOURS NON ELECTRIQUES
744	MECHANICAL HANDLING EQU		0.4		0.2				0.1	EQUIP MANUTENTION PIECES
7441	FORK LIFT TRCKS,ETC,PTS			W 5	0.2				0.1	CHARIOTS POUR USINES ETC
74419	PTS NES OF VEHC OF 74411			W 5	0.2				0.1	PIECES POUR 744.11
7449	PTS NES OF MACHY OF 7442		0.4		0.1					PIECES DU 744.2
76	TELECOMM,SOUND EQUIPMENT		2.2		0.1		0.2		0.4	EQUIPMENT DE TELECOM
764	TELECOM EQPT,PTS,ACC NES		2.2		0.1	W 1	0.2	W 3	0.2	EQUIP TELECOM,PIECES
7649	PTS NES OF EQUIPMT OF 76		2.1		0.1	W 1	0.2	W 1	0.2	PIECES DE LA DIV 76
76499	PARTS ETC OF SOUND EQUIP		2.1							PIECES NDA POUR 763
77	ELECTRIC MACHNRY NES ETC		0.1		0.1		0.1		11.0	MACH APP ELECT NDA
778	ELECTRICAL MACHINERY NES		0.1		0.1		0.1	W 42	10.9	AUTRES MACH ELECT NDA
7788	OTH ELEC MACHY,EQUIP NES		0.1				0.1	W 40	10.9	AUT MACH APP ELEC NDA
77882	ELEC TRAFFIC CONTROL EQU							W 36	9.6	APP ELECT SIGNAL,SECURITE ET
77886	OTH ELEC MACHINERY NES							W 4	1.4	AUT MACH APP ELECTRIQUES
78	ROAD VEHICLES		0.1		0.1		0.1		1.8	VEHICULES ROUTIERS
782	LORRIES,SPCL MTR VEH NES							W 34	1.8	VEHICULES SPECIAUX,MARCH
7822	SPECIAL MOTOR VEHCLS NES							W 34	1.8	VEHICULES USAGES SPECIAUX
79	OTHR TRANSPORT EQUIPMENT		1.4		0.8		0.4		51.0	AUTRE MATERIEL TRANSPORT
792	AIRCRAFT ETC		1.4		0.8	W 16	0.4	W 36	50.9	APP NAVIGATION AERIENNE
7924	AIRCRFT NES OVER 15000KG					W 15	0.1	W 25	49.3	AERODYNES PLUS 15000 KG
7929	AIRCRAFT PARTS NES		1.4		0.8	W 1	0.4	W 11	1.7	PIECES DU 792
8	MISC MANUFACTURED GOODS		3.3		2.3		1.7		2.4	ART MANUFACTURES DIVERS
87	PRECISION INSTRUMNTS NES		3.0		1.8		1.2		1.8	INSTRUM,APPAR SCIENT NDA
874	MEASURNG,CONTROLNG INSTR		3.0		1.8	W 4	1.2	W 8	1.8	INSTRUMENTS DE MESURE
8741	SURVEYING INSTRUMENTS						0.1	W 4	0.7	INST GEODESIE,TOPO ETC
87412	SURVEY INSTR ETC NONELEC						0.1	W 4	0.7	INSTR GEODESIE,TOPO ETC
8748	ELEC MEAS,CONTRL EQU NES		0.4		1.6	W 3	1.1	W 4	1.1	APP ELEC ELECTRO MESURE
87483	OTH ELCTRNC MEAS ETC EQU		0.4		1.6	W 3	1.1	W 3	1.1	AUT APP ELECTRO DE MESURE
8749	INSTR PTS NES,ACCESSORYS		2.6		0.2				0.1	PIECES 873,874.3,54,874.8
88	PHOTO EQU,OPTICL GDS ETC		0.1		0.2		0.2		0.2	APP,FOURN PHOTO,OP,MONTR
89	MISC MANUFCTRD GOODS NES		0.2		0.3		0.3		0.4	ART MANUFACTURES DIVERS
899	OTHER MANUFACTURED GOODS		0.1		0.3	W 4	0.2	W 3	0.1	AUT ART MANUF DIVERS NDA
8998	SMALLWARES,TOILETRYS ETC		0.1		0.3	W 3	0.2	W 3	0.1	ART MERCERIE,TOILETTE
89983	BUTTONS,STUDS,ETC		0.1		0.3	W 3	0.2	W 3	0.1	BOUTONS,BOUTONS-PRESSION

TABLEAU 1 –

1 En 1969 les valeurs des importations sont estimées.

1. HISTORICAL SERIES, 1961–1996 GENERAL TRADE, IMPORTS C.I.F., EXPORTS F.O.B.
SERIES HISTORIQUES, 1961–1996 COMMERCE GENERAL, IMPORTATIONS C.A.F., EXPORTATIONS F.O.B

YEAR ANNEE	VALUE IN MILLION LEONES / VALEUR EN MILLION LEONES: MERCHANDISE – MARCHANDISE IMPORTS	MERCHANDISE – MARCHANDISE EXPORTS	GOLD – OR IMPORTS	GOLD – OR EXPORTS	CONVERSION FACTORS U.S. CENTS PER LEONE / FACTEURS DE CONVERSION CENTS E.U. PAR LEONE IMPORTS	CONVERSION FACTORS EXPORTS	INDEX NUMBERS – INDICES: QUANTUM IMPORTS	QUANTUM EXPORTS	UNIT VALUE / VALEUR UNITAIRE IMPORTS	UNIT VALUE / VALEUR UNITAIRE EXPORTS
1961	65.08	58.74			140.0000	140.0000				
1962	60.87	41.04			140.0000	140.0000				
1963	59.70	57.88			140.0000	140.0000				
1964	70.92	67.91			140.0000	140.0000				
1965	76.97	63.22			140.0000	140.0000				
1966	71.70	59.06			140.0000	140.0000				
1967	65.27	50.54			138.4400	139.0500				
1968	75.46	79.71			120.0000	120.0000				
1969	93.02	90.08			120.0000	120.0000				
1970	96.89	84.55			120.0000	120.0000				
1971	94.27	83.38			120.0000	120.0000				
1972	95.37	91.61			126.8930	128.2470				
1973	127.20	106.00			123.9510	123.9740				
1974	188.40	123.11			118.5230	118.7840				
1975	167.88	108.00			110.3250	111.8070				
1976	171.26	112.50			89.3210	90.0510				
1977	260.53	140.30			87.6030	85.9500				
1978	272.88	170.47			95.4620	94.6860				
1979	314.13	217.90			94.5650	94.5050				
1980	433.74	214.51			95.3450	95.2800				
1981	360.44	176.25			86.4340	87.0900				
1982	297.00	109.10			80.8650	81.3590				
1983	278.10	151.69			59.5800	60.3440				
1984	417.65	370.95			39.8400	39.8400				
1985	781.56	668.00			19.7022	19.3443				
1986	2022.00	1952.00			6.5241	7.2910				
1987	4424.00	4656.00			3.0859	2.7668				
1988	5215.00	3329.00			2.9901	3.1986				
1989	10902.00	8270.00			1.6716	1.6683				
1990	23607.01	21093.01			0.6554	0.6524				
1991	45488.00	43946.00			0.3580	0.3297				
1992	72776.00	74918.00			0.2005	0.1991				
1993	83461.01	66908.00			0.1762	0.1763				
1994	88438.00	67696.00			0.1702	0.1700				
1995	103751.00	18008.00			0.1304	0.1403				
1996	193936.00	43006.00			0.1092	0.1092				

2. IMPORTS BY BROAD ECONOMIC CATEGORY AND EXPORTS BY INDUSTRIAL ORIGIN. (PERCENTAGE OF TOTAL VALUE)
IMPORTATIONS PAR CATEGORIES ECONOMIQUES ET EXPORTATIONS PAR BRANCHE D'ACTIVITE. (EN POURCENTAGE DE LA VALEUR TOTALE)

IMPORTS – IMPORTATIONS

	1989	1990	1991	1992	1993	1994	1995
TOTAL IMPORTS–IMPORTATIONS TOTALES							
1 FOOD BEV–ALIMENTATION BOISSONS							
11 PRIMARY–PRODUITS DE BASE							
111 FOR INDUSTRY–POUR L'INDUSTRIE							
112 FOR HOUSEHOLDS–POUR LES MENAGES							
12 PROCESSED–PRODUITS ELABORES							
121 FOR INDUSTRY–POUR L'INDUSTRIE							
122 FOR HOUSEHOLDS–POUR LES MENAGES							
2 IND SUPPLIES–APPROV INDUSTRIELS							
21 PRIMARY–PRODUITS DE BASE							
22 PROCESSED–PRODUITS ELABORES							
3 FUELS–COMBUSTIBLES							
31 PRIMARY–PRODUITS DE BASE							
32 PROCESSED–PRODUITS ELABORES							
321 MOTOR SPIRIT–ESSENCE							
322 OTHER–AUTRES							
4 MACHINERY–EQUIPEMENT							
41 CAPITAL EQUIPMENT–MACHINES							
42 PARTS–PIECES ACCESSOIRES							
5 TRANSPORT–TRANSPORT							
51 PASSENGER CARS–AUTOMOBILES							
52 OTHER–AUTRES							
521 INDUSTRIAL–INDUSTRIELS							
522 NON INDUSTRIAL–NON INDUSTRIEL							
53 PARTS–PIECES ACCESSOIRES							
6 CONSUM GOODS–BIENS CONSOMMATION							
61 DURABLE–DURABLES							
62 SEMI DURABLE–SEMI DURABLES							
63 NON DURABLE–NON DURABLES							
7 GOODS NES–BIENS NDA							

EXPORTS – EXPORTATIONS

	1989	1990	1991	1992	1993	1994	1995
TOTAL EXPORTS–EXPORTATIONS TOTALES							
1 AGRICULTURE							
2 MINING QUARRY–INDUS EXTRACTIVES							
3 MANUFACTURING–IND MANUFACTUR							
31 FOOD BEV TOBACCO–ALIM BOISS TAB							
32 TEXTILES–INDUSTRIES TEXTILES							
33 WOOD & PRODUCTS–BOIS & PRODUITS							
34 PAPER & PRODUCTS–PAPIER & PRODT							
35 CHEMICALS–INDUSTRIES CHIMIQUES							
36 NON METAL MIN–MIN NON METAL							
37 BASIC METAL–IND METAL BASE							
38 METAL MANUF–MANUF METAL							
39 OTH MANUF IND–AUTRES MANUF							

3. TRADE BY PRINCIPAL COUNTRIES OF ORIGIN AND DESTINATION (VALUE IN MILLION U.S. DOLLARS)
ECHANGES SELON LES PRINCIPAUX PAYS D'ORIGINE ET DE DESTINATION (VALEUR EN MILLIONS DE DOLLARS EU)

COUNTRIES–PAYS	GENERAL IMPORTS C.I.F. IMPORTATIONS GENERALES C.A.F				
	1991	1992	1993	1994	1995
World				151.3	
Africa					
Americas					
– Northern America					
– LAIA					
– CACM					
– Caribbean					
– Rest of America					
Asia excl fmr USSR					
– Middle East					
Asia former USSR					
Europe excl fmr USSR					
– European Union					
– Eastern Europe					
– Rest of Europe					
Europe former USSR					
Oceania					
Other					
Nigeria/Nigéria				8.0	
Malaysia/Malaisie				3.0	
Senegal/Sénégal				2.0	
Indonesia/Indonésie				1.0	
Morocco/Maroc				1.0	
Turkey/Turquie				1.0	

COUNTRIES–PAYS	GENERAL EXPORTS F.O.B. EXPORTATIONS GENERALES F.O.B.				
	1991	1992	1993	1994	1995
Monde				117.3	
Afrique					
Amériques					
– Amérique du Nord					
– ALAI					
– MCAC					
– Caraïbes					
– Autre Amérique					
Asie anc. URSS exclus					
– Moyen–Orient					
Asie ancienne URSS					
Europe anc. URSS exclus					
– Union Européenne					
– Europe de l'Est					
– Autre de l'Europe					
Europe ancienne URSS					
Océanie					
Autre					
Malaysia/Malaisie				1.0	

(VALUE AS PERCENTAGE OF WORLD TOTAL)(VALEURS EN POURCENTAGE DU TOTAL MONDIAL)

	1986	1987	1988	1989	1990	1991	1992	1993	1994	1995
Africa	10.6									
Americas	10.7									
– Northern America	10.0									
– LAIA	0.7									
– CACM										
– Caribbean										
– Rest of America										
Asia excl fmr USSR	21.8									
– Middle East										
Asia former USSR										
Europe excl fmr USSR	52.3									
– European Union	45.8									
– Eastern Europe	0.8									
– Rest of Europe	5.7									
Europe former USSR	0.4									
Oceania	2.9									
Other	1.1									
Areas n.e.s.	1.1									
Nigeria/Nigéria	9.0								5.3	
Malaysia/Malaisie									2.0	
Senegal/Sénégal									1.3	
Indonesia/Indonésie									0.7	
Morocco/Maroc									0.7	
Turkey/Turquie									0.7	

	1986	1987	1988	1989	1990	1991	1992	1993	1994	1995
Afrique	4.4									
Amériques	15.4									
– Amérique du Nord	15.1									
– ALAI	0.2									
– MCAC										
– Caraïbes										
– Autre Amérique										
Asie anc. URSS exclus	0.0									
– Moyen–Orient										
Asie ancienne URSS										
Europe anc. URSS exclus	25.9									
– Union Européenne	24.5									
– Europe de l'Est										
– Autre de l'Europe	1.3									
Europe ancienne URSS	0.0									
Océanie										
Autre	54.3									
Areas n.e.s.	54.3									
Malaysia/Malaisie									0.9	

4. General Imports C.I.F. by Commodities according to the S.I.T.C. (Rev. 2) in million U.S. Dollars
Importations Générales C.A.F. par Produits d'après la C.T.C.I. (Rév. 2) en millions de Dollars E.U.

SITC CTCI	COMMODITY	1992		1993		1994		1995		PRODUIT
		QUANTITY QUANTITE	VALUE VALEUR	QUANTITY QUANTITE	VALUE VALEUR	QUANTITY QUANTITE	VALUE VALEUR	QUANTITY QUANTITE	VALUE VALEUR	
	ALL COMMODITIES		154.5		146.6		151.3		136.3	TOUS PRODUITS
0	FOOD AND LIVE ANIMALS		51.7		59.5		54.1		54.0	ALIMENTS,ANIMAUX VIVANTS
1	BEVERAGES AND TOBACCO		1.5		2.8		4.2		4.4	BOISSONS ET TABACS
2	CRUDE MATERLS,EXCL FUELS		1.9		3.4		3.3		3.1	MAT BRUTES NON COMESTIBLES
3	MINERAL FUELS ETC		29.1		25.0		24.7		23.7	COMBUSTIBLES MINERAUX LUB
4	ANIMAL,VEGETABLE OIL,FAT		3.4		4.3		4.2		3.8	HUILES,GRAISSES ANIM,VEG
5	CHEMCLS,RELATED PROD NES		16.1		9.7		12.0		10.6	PRODUITS CHIMIQUES
6	BASIC MANUFACTURES		16.8		13.4		18.2		11.3	ART MANUFACTURES
7	MACHINES,TRANSPORT EQUIP		28.8		21.1		24.9		20.0	MACHINES MATERIEL TRANSPORT
8	MISC MANUFACTURED GOODS		5.5		7.8		6.1		5.8	ART MANUFACTURES DIVERS

5. General Exports F.O.B. by Commodities according to the S.I.T.C. (Rev. 2) in million U.S. Dollars
Exportations Générales F.O.B. par Produits d'après la C.T.C.I. (Rév. 2) en millions de Dollars E.U.

SITC CTCI	COMMODITY	1992		1993		1994		1995		PRODUIT
		QUANTITY QUANTITE	VALUE VALEUR	QUANTITY QUANTITE	VALUE VALEUR	QUANTITY QUANTITE	VALUE VALEUR	QUANTITY QUANTITE	VALUE VALEUR	
	ALL COMMODITIES		145.6		139.5		117.3		76.1	TOUS PRODUITS
03	FISH AND PREPARATIONS		0.6		0.5		0.8		1.4	POISSONS ET PREPARATIONS
071	COFFEE AND SUBSTITUTES		2.5		3.0		2.9		4.4	CAFE ET SUCCEDANES
0711	COFFEE GREEN,ROASTED,SUB		2.5		3.0		2.9		4.4	CAFE TORREFIE OU DECAFEINE
072	COCOA		2.3		2.0		3.7		2.6	CACAO
0721	COCOA BEANS,RAW,ROASTED		2.3		2.0		3.7		2.6	CACAO EN FEVES
121	TOBACCO UNMNFCTRD,REFUSE		1.9		1.0		1.1		1.7	TABACS BRUTS,DECHETS
2873	ALUMINIUM ORES,ALUMINA		26.1		34.3		20.0		11.2	MINERAIS D'ALUMINIUM
28731	ALUMINIUM ORE,CONCNTRATE		26.1		34.3		20.0		11.2	MINERAIS D'ALUMINIUM
2879	OTH NONFER ORE,CONCNTRTE		73.4		70.7		61.5		27.7	MINERAIS D'AUTRES METAUX
28793	MOLYBD, NIOBIUM ETC ORES		73.4		70.7		61.5		27.7	MINERAIS DE MOLYBDENE,TITANE
667	PEARL,PREC–,SEMI–P STONE		35.2		23.0		21.2		19.7	PERLES, PIERRES GEMMES
6672	DIAMONDS NONINDUST,UNSET		35.2		23.0		21.2		19.7	DIAMANTS BRUTS
931	*SPECIAL TRANSACTIONS		3.4		4.2		5.1		7.6	TRANS.SPECIALES
971	*GOLD,NON MONETARY NES		0.5		1.1		1.4		0.1	OR NON MONETAIRE

1. HISTORICAL SERIES, 1962–1997 GENERAL TRADE, IMPORTS C.I.F., EXPORTS F.O.B.
SERIES HISTORIQUES, 1962–1997 COMMERCE GENERAL, IMPORTATIONS C.A.F., EXPORTATIONS F.O.B

YEAR ANNEE	VALUE IN MILLION SINGAPOR.DOLLARS VALEUR EN MILLION SINGAPOR.DOLLARS MERCHANDISE – MARCHANDISE		GOLD – OR		CONVERSION FACTORS U.S. CENTS PER SINGAPORE DOLLAR FACTEURS DE CONVERSION CENTS E.U. PAR SINGAPORE DOLLAR		INDEX NUMBERS – INDICES QUANTUM		UNIT VALUE VALEUR UNITAIRE	
	IMPORTS	EXPORTS	IMPORTS	EXPORTS	IMPORTS	EXPORTS	IMPORTS	EXPORTS	IMPORTS	EXPORTS
1962	4036.00	3417.00	0.25	0.20	32.6667	32.6667				
1963	4279.00	3475.00	5.07		32.6667	32.6667				
1964	3479.00	2772.00	6.46		32.6667	32.6667				
1965	3807.00	3004.00	4.09		32.6667	32.6667				
1966	4066.00	3374.00	3.57	0.20	32.6667	32.6667				
1967	4407.00	3491.00	14.57		32.6667	32.6667				
1968	5084.00	3891.00	15.67		32.6667	32.6667				
1969	6244.00	4741.00	16.51		32.6667	32.6667				
1970	7534.00	4756.00	5.55		32.6667	32.6667				
1971	8664.00	5371.00			32.6667	32.6667				
1972	9538.00	6149.00			35.6248	35.6325				
1973	12513.00	8907.00			41.1362	41.1643				
1974	20405.00	14155.00			41.0666	41.0425				
1975	19270.00	12758.00			42.2079	42.1395				
1976	22404.00	16266.00			40.4830	40.4859				
1977	25522.00	20090.00			41.0261	41.0185				
1978	29601.00	22986.00			44.0811	44.0888				
1979	38352.00	30940.00			46.0041	46.0026				
1980	50481.00	41453.00			46.7290	46.7414	40	34	115	127
1981	58325.30	44290.80			47.3338	47.3398	45	35	128	146
1982	60244.50	44472.70			46.7552	46.7431	49	37	122	141
1983	59504.20	46154.90			47.3210	47.3027	49	40	119	134
1984	61133.60	51340.40			46.9654	46.9572	51	46	119	129
1985	57817.40	50178.70			45.4624	45.4633	50	46	105	114
1986	55543.01	48986.00			45.9306	45.9218	54	53	93	98
1987	68416.00	60266.00			47.5993	47.6089	62	62	101	101
1988	88228.00	79051.01			49.7149	49.7205	79	83	101	100
1989	96864.00	87117.01			51.2643	51.2659	87	92	101	100
1990	109806.00	95206.00			55.3467	55.3853	100	100	100	100
1991	114195.00	101880.00			57.8777	57.8760	107	113	97	95
1992	117530.00	103351.00			61.3735	61.3784	114	123	94	88
1993	137602.00	119475.00			61.9390	61.9441	137	145	92	86
1994	156397.00	147327.00			65.6471	65.7214	157	187	91	83
1995	176317.00	167515.00			70.6125	70.5984	177	216	91	82
1996	185183.00	176271.00			70.9243	70.9225	188	230	90	81
1997	196610.00	185664.00			67.3643	67.3382	203	245		80

2. IMPORTS BY BROAD ECONOMIC CATEGORY AND EXPORTS BY INDUSTRIAL ORIGIN. (PERCENTAGE OF TOTAL VALUE)
IMPORTATIONS PAR CATEGORIES ECONOMIQUES ET EXPORTATIONS PAR BRANCHE D'ACTIVITE.(EN POURCENTAGE DE LA VALEUR TOTALE)

IMPORTS – IMPORTATIONS

	1991	1992	1993	1994	1995	1996	1997
TOTAL IMPORTS–IMPORTATIONS TOTALES	100.	100.	100.	100.	100.	100.	100.
1 FOOD BEV–ALIMENTATION BOISSONS	5.1	4.9	4.4	4.1	3.6	3.6	3.3
11 PRIMARY–PRODUITS DE BASE	2.5	2.5	2.2	2.0	1.7	1.6	1.5
111 FOR INDUSTRY–POUR L'INDUSTRIE	0.7	0.7	0.6	0.6	0.5	0.4	0.3
112 FOR HOUSEHOLDS–POUR LES MENAGES	1.8	1.8	1.6	1.4	1.2	1.2	1.2
12 PROCESSED–PRODUITS ELABORES	2.6	2.5	2.1	2.0	1.9	2.0	1.8
121 FOR INDUSTRY–POUR L'INDUSTRIE	0.6	0.5	0.4	0.3	0.3	0.3	0.3
122 FOR HOUSEHOLDS–POUR LES MENAGES	2.0	2.0	1.8	1.7	1.6	1.7	1.5
2 IND SUPPLIES–APPROV INDUSTRIELS	23.2	22.9	21.2	19.6	19.9	17.5	17.3
21 PRIMARY–PRODUITS DE BASE	1.8	1.5	1.3	1.2	1.3	1.2	1.1
22 PROCESSED–PRODUITS ELABORES	21.5	21.4	19.9	18.5	18.6	16.3	16.1
3 FUELS–COMBUSTIBLES	14.1	12.7	10.9	8.8	8.1	9.4	9.5
31 PRIMARY–PRODUITS DE BASE	10.1	8.8	7.6	5.7	5.2	6.1	6.1
32 PROCESSED–PRODUITS ELABORES	4.0	3.9	3.3	3.1	2.9	3.3	3.4
321 MOTOR SPIRIT–ESSENCE	3.4	0.8	2.4	0.6		0.4	
322 OTHER–AUTRES	0.6	3.1	1.0	2.5	2.9	2.9	3.4
4 MACHINERY–EQUIPEMENT	35.3	36.2	39.9	45.7	48.9	48.8	49.8
41 CAPITAL EQUIPMENT–MACHINES	21.1	21.0	22.7	24.9	23.6	24.5	25.2
42 PARTS–PIECES ACCESSOIRES	14.2	15.2	17.2	20.7	25.3	24.2	24.6
5 TRANSPORT–TRANSPORT	7.4	8.3	7.9	6.4	6.2	7.4	7.0
51 PASSENGER CARS–AUTOMOBILES		0.7		0.7	0.7	0.6	0.5
52 OTHER–AUTRES	4.0	3.8	4.5	2.8	2.7	3.8	3.5
521 INDUSTRIAL–INDUSTRIELS	3.8	3.6	4.3	2.7	2.7	3.7	3.4
522 NON INDUSTRIAL–NON INDUSTRIEL	0.2	0.2	0.2	0.1	0.1	0.1	0.1
53 PARTS–PIECES ACCESSOIRES	3.4	3.8	3.5	3.0	2.8	3.1	3.0
6 CONSUM GOODS–BIENS CONSOMMATION	13.8	13.8	14.6	13.9	12.3	12.4	12.0
61 DURABLE–DURABLES	6.1	5.6	6.5	6.4	5.2	5.0	4.6
62 SEMI DURABLE–SEMI DURABLES	5.4	5.7	5.4	5.1	4.9	5.3	5.1
63 NON DURABLE–NON DURABLES	2.3	2.5	2.7	2.4	2.1	2.1	2.3
7 GOODS NES–BIENS NDA	1.2	1.2	1.1	1.4	1.0	0.9	1.0

EXPORTS – EXPORTATIONS

	1991	1992	1993	1994	1995	1996	1997
TOTAL EXPORTS–EXPORTATIONS TOTALES	100.	100.	100.	100.	100.	100.	100.
1 AGRICULTURE	3.2	2.9	2.3	2.2	2.0	1.6	1.5
2 MINING QUARRY–INDUS EXTRACTIVES	0.5	0.4	0.4	0.3	0.3	0.4	0.4
3 MANUFACTURING–IND MANUFACTUR	96.3	96.7	97.3	97.4	97.6	98.0	98.1
31 FOOD BEV TOBACCO–ALIM BOISS TAB	3.9	4.0	3.6	3.1	2.7	2.7	2.6
32 TEXTILES–INDUSTRIES TEXTILES	5.0	4.8	4.0	3.2	2.7	2.4	2.4
33 WOOD & PRODUCTS–BOIS & PRODUITS	0.9	0.8	0.7	0.5	0.3	0.3	0.3
34 PAPER & PRODUCTS–PAPIER & PRODT	1.2	1.2	1.0	1.0	1.1	0.9	0.9
35 CHEMICALS–INDUSTRIES CHIMIQUES	24.9	20.9	19.9	16.4	14.0	14.6	14.2
36 NON METAL MIN–MIN NON METAL	0.5	0.5	0.5	0.5	0.5	0.4	0.4
37 BASIC METAL–IND METAL BASE	2.0	2.1	1.9	1.9	2.4	2.1	2.2
38 METAL MANUF–MANUF METAL	55.4	59.9	63.0	68.5	70.3	70.7	71.3
39 OTH MANUF IND–AUTRES MANUF	2.4	2.5	2.5	2.4	3.6	3.9	4.0

3. TRADE BY PRINCIPAL COUNTRIES OF ORIGIN AND DESTINATION (VALUE IN MILLION U.S. DOLLARS)
ECHANGES SELON LES PRINCIPAUX PAYS D'ORIGINE ET DE DESTINATION (VALEUR EN MILLIONS DE DOLLARS EU)

COUNTRIES–PAYS	GENERAL IMPORTS C.I.F. IMPORTATIONS GENERALES C.A.F				
	1993	1994	1995	1996	1997
World	85231.1	102669.3	124503.5	131340.0	132441.7
Africa	705.7	637.6	687.1	707.0	661.3
Americas	14969.6	17017.7	20375.6	23553.5	24451.5
– Northern America	14189.9	16117.6	19264.4	22144.0	23069.0
– LAIA	497.3	668.0	877.6	1094.4	1099.3
– CACM	13.4	8.5	13.9	12.6	14.9
– Caribbean	114.3	49.8	81.9	98.7	55.4
– Rest of America	154.8	173.8	137.8	203.8	212.9
Asia excl fmr USSR	55785.0	67913.8	82057.0	83294.5	84105.6
– Middle East	6212.9	6625.2	8005.1	10394.5	10268.0
Asia former USSR	0.7		0.3	10.6	6.9
Europe excl fmr USSR	11910.6	15110.8	18947.0	21315.9	20781.8
– European Union	10613.5	13451.4	16591.1	18982.2	18515.0
– Eastern Europe	163.8	218.0	313.1	216.1	305.4
– Rest of Europe	1133.3	1441.4	2042.8	2117.6	1961.4
Europe former USSR	162.0	188.3	381.7	167.1	339.0
Oceania	1697.4	1801.2	2054.6	2291.4	2095.7
Other			0.0		
Japan/Japon	18650.4	22597.1	26330.3	23842.4	23283.5
USA/Etats–Unis d'Amer	13852.7	15701.7	18740.3	21551.8	22376.7
Malaysia/Malaisie	14041.3	16805.6	19267.9	19722.6	19905.0
Thailand/Thaïlande	3515.8	4904.4	6423.4	7175.5	6790.6
Other Asia n.e.s.	3381.4	3951.2	5120.4	5263.4	5690.6
Saudi Arabia	3319.4	3680.9	3798.8	4994.2	5371.7
Korea, Republic of	2743.0	3929.3	5405.5	4512.2	4079.8
Germany/Allemagne	2603.3	3459.3	4326.5	4794.3	4529.0
China/Chine	2401.5	2896.3	4045.8	4439.0	5690.0
China, Hong Kong SAR	2687.4	3469.7	4111.1	4199.8	3893.8
United Kingdom	2225.4	2839.7	3309.4	3593.4	3713.9
France, Monaco	1939.2	2178.1	2798.8	3723.3	3658.6
Australia/Australie	1476.9	1570.9	1804.6	1983.9	1797.5
Italy/Italie	1135.9	1450.0	1772.4	2261.3	1955.9
United Arab Emirates	900.5	876.6	1436.8	2055.2	1636.9
Switzerland,Liechtenst.	921.4	1111.8	1530.7	1664.6	1543.7
Philippines	503.6	783.2	1100.4	1389.8	1989.6
Netherlands/Pays–Bas	789.8	1075.5	1129.8	1267.6	1141.9
Kuwait/ Koweït	684.8	768.6	1167.8	1355.5	1191.5
India/Inde	668.7	792.7	922.2	1012.0	1043.0
Belgium–Luxembourg	516.4	612.0	741.7	710.6	903.0
Sweden/Suède	415.1	518.5	665.9	772.8	906.1
Iran (Islamic Rep of)	649.6	591.7	476.5	362.4	588.4
Canada	337.2	415.9	524.1	588.9	692.3
Spain/Espagne	259.3	353.3	554.3	578.1	557.3
Viet Nam	352.4	451.4	449.2	436.1	543.8
Qatar	121.1	112.6	293.3	603.9	729.2
Finland/Finlande	298.9	351.1	381.4	418.8	350.3
Brazil/Brésil	301.5	353.1	360.0	338.0	259.2
Ireland/Irlande	132.1	194.6	262.1	286.2	311.8
Turkey/Turquie	141.1	208.5	188.6	247.3	391.4
Israel/Israël	126.3	155.9	232.4	271.4	341.2
Austria/Autriche	121.2	168.0	356.6	259.5	204.6
Norway,Svalbard and JM	138.5	176.1	337.1	198.9	228.5
New Zealand	179.7	191.4	206.9	236.3	225.8
Brunei Darussalam	216.5	209.1	223.6	205.7	182.3
Chile/Chili	88.4	136.9	236.1	292.2	277.1
Mexico/Mexique	39.5	61.1	160.2	304.9	463.6
Denmark/Danemark	132.2	181.8	218.7	228.7	185.3
Oman	237.5	99.0	224.2	225.0	142.1

COUNTRIES–PAYS	GENERAL EXPORTS F.O.B. EXPORTATIONS GENERALES F.O.B.				
	1993	1994	1995	1996	1997
Monde	74006.8	96824.6	118263.2	125008.9	124988.1
Afrique	1317.1	1420.2	1548.1	1516.3	1492.6
Amériques	16867.2	20234.8	23774.0	25451.5	25539.3
– Amérique du Nord	15548.3	18783.6	22168.2	23471.1	23421.0
– ALAI	747.4	828.5	975.2	1209.3	1265.3
– MCAC	51.3	28.7	33.1	34.2	35.0
– Caraïbes	101.0	102.5	116.8	147.2	128.0
– Autre Amérique	419.2	491.5	480.8	589.7	690.1
Asie anc. URSS exclus	41106.7	57182.2	71564.9	76004.8	74945.7
– Moyen–Orient	1686.3	1629.3	1843.4	1962.6	2042.1
Asie ancienne URSS	11.5		11.1	5.1	2.8
Europe anc. URSS exclus	11767.6	14045.3	16830.0	17297.1	18339.8
– Union Européenne	10800.8	13034.0	15836.2	16298.0	17493.4
– Europe de l'Est	145.3	176.9	190.9	205.0	153.8
– Autre de l'Europe	821.5	834.4	802.9	794.1	692.6
Europe ancienne URSS	540.9	830.6	966.1	921.1	784.7
Océanie	2395.7	3111.5	3568.9	3813.0	3883.2
Autre			0.0		
USA/Etats–Unis d'Amer	15062.5	18177.2	21590.0	23063.4	23025.0
Malaysia/Malaisie	10494.7	19118.0	22679.7	22512.8	21820.8
China, Hong Kong SAR	6419.8	8421.7	10132.5	11125.9	12018.8
Japan/Japon	5526.2	6797.3	9224.6	10251.6	8837.8
Thailand/Thaïlande	4215.3	5380.1	6828.2	7096.6	5745.6
Other Asia n.e.s.	2880.5	3912.1	4818.8	4874.6	5636.5
Germany/Allemagne	2940.3	3437.1	4000.3	3839.0	3621.4
United Kingdom	2214.7	2619.0	3072.3	3534.6	4168.3
Korea, Republic of	2060.1	2544.0	3245.1	3796.4	3692.1
China/Chine	1900.1	2107.5	2760.9	3392.9	4065.6
Netherlands/Pays–Bas	1920.3	2583.4	3149.5	2888.8	3069.2
Australia/Australie	1673.7	2293.9	2593.8	2846.9	2914.6
Philippines	1371.6	1584.8	1929.2	2296.1	2950.6
France, Monaco	1089.5	1313.5	2013.5	2476.5	2474.9
India/Inde	949.8	1267.2	1878.6	2075.9	2220.5
Viet Nam	980.2	1334.3	1791.2	1716.1	1665.6
Brunei Darussalam	634.7	819.2	1466.7	1710.3	1391.6
Ireland/Irlande	500.5	705.4	1205.3	1430.9	1996.0
United Arab Emirates	681.3	799.6	849.6	901.0	938.4
Russian Federation	489.0	830.6	911.6	876.3	738.1
Italy/Italie	652.5	690.3	770.4	507.8	519.5
Myanmar	335.0	393.0	637.9	721.9	705.1
Bangladesh	347.1	432.6	589.2	669.8	555.7
Panama	385.0	453.0	465.9	577.1	666.2
Canada	480.2	601.1	571.9	401.0	382.3
Cambodia/Cambodge	369.1	384.8	500.5	517.1	429.7
Belgium–Luxembourg	413.2	477.5	445.4	414.0	416.1
Switzerland,Liechtenst.	436.6	516.1	400.5	400.3	251.0
Brazil/Brésil	294.0	242.2	436.1	487.7	419.7
Sri Lanka	311.4	339.1	376.8	387.3	398.0
Saudi Arabia	386.0	330.7	325.8	379.7	374.0
New Zealand	226.8	316.4	384.4	384.2	376.7
Spain/Espagne	297.8	371.9	339.6	317.9	346.7
Liberia/Libéria	222.7	411.0	315.5	315.4	299.7
Pakistan	261.7	309.4	308.3	269.5	274.1
Mexico/Mexique	130.7	204.9	187.3	388.4	487.0
So. African Customs Un	0.3	0.2	459.4	436.7	338.0
Other Africa n.e.s.	413.3	427.2	28.4	76.1	56.1
US Misc Pacific Islands	158.0	182.3	209.3	196.5	160.5
Israel/Israël	113.3	161.5	234.6	229.8	167.2

(VALUE AS PERCENTAGE OF WORLD TOTAL)(VALEURS EN POURCENTAGE DU TOTAL MONDIAL)

	1988	1989	1990	1991	1992	1993	1994	1995	1996	1997
Africa	0.7	0.9	0.7	0.6	0.8	0.8	0.6	0.6	0.5	0.5
Americas	17.2	18.9	17.8	17.6	18.0	17.6	16.6	16.4	17.9	18.5
– Northern America	16.2	17.7	16.6	16.5	16.9	16.6	15.7	15.5	16.9	17.4
– LAIA	1.0	1.0	1.0	1.0	0.9	0.6	0.7	0.7	0.8	0.8
– CACM	0.0	0.0	0.0	0.0	0.0	0.0	0.0	0.0	0.0	0.0
– Caribbean	0.0	0.1	0.0	0.1	0.1	0.1	0.0	0.1	0.1	0.0
– Rest of America	0.1	0.1	0.2	0.1	0.1	0.2	0.2	0.1	0.2	0.2
Asia excl fmr USSR	64.9	62.9	63.4	64.7	63.8	65.5	66.1	65.9	63.4	63.5
– Middle East	9.2	9.8	10.8	9.2	8.3	7.3	6.5	6.4	7.9	7.8
Asia former USSR						0.0		0.0	0.0	0.0
Europe excl fmr USSR	14.6	15.1	15.7	14.5	15.2	14.0	14.7	15.2	16.2	15.7
– European Union	12.9	13.5	13.8	13.1	13.6	12.5	13.1	13.3	14.5	14.0
– Eastern Europe	0.3	0.3	0.3	0.2	0.2	0.2	0.2	0.3	0.2	0.2
– Rest of Europe	1.3	1.3	1.7	1.3	1.4	1.3	1.4	1.6	1.6	1.5
Europe former USSR	0.2	0.3	0.2	0.3	0.2	0.2	0.2	0.3	0.1	0.3
Oceania	2.3	1.9	2.2	2.2	2.0	2.0	1.8	1.7	1.7	1.6
Other			0.0	0.0				0.0		
Japan/Japon	21.9	21.3	20.2	21.3	21.1	21.9	22.0	21.1	18.2	17.6
USA/Etats–Unis d'Amer	15.6	17.1	16.0	15.8	16.5	16.3	15.3	15.1	16.4	16.9
Malaysia/Malaisie	14.7	13.2	13.6	15.2	14.7	16.5	16.4	15.5	15.0	15.0
Thailand/Thaïlande	2.7	2.5	2.7	3.2	3.7	4.1	4.8	5.2	5.5	5.1
Other Asia n.e.s.	4.9	4.9	4.8	4.7	4.3	4.0	3.8	4.1	4.0	4.3
Saudi Arabia	4.4	4.8	5.3	5.1	5.1	3.9	3.6	3.1	3.8	4.1
Korea, Republic of	2.9	3.0	2.9	2.8	3.3	3.2	3.8	4.3	3.4	3.1
Germany/Allemagne				3.2	3.3	3.1	3.4	3.5	3.7	3.4
China/Chine	3.8	3.4	3.4	3.4	3.1	2.8	2.8	3.2	3.4	4.3
China, Hong Kong SAR	2.8	2.8	3.1	3.0	3.1	3.2	3.4	3.3	3.2	2.9

	1988	1989	1990	1991	1992	1993	1994	1995	1996	1997
Afrique	2.3	1.9	2.1	2.2	2.1	1.8	1.5	1.3	1.2	1.2
Amériques	26.3	25.5	23.5	22.2	23.5	22.8	20.9	20.1	20.4	20.4
– Amérique du Nord	24.8	24.3	22.2	20.5	21.8	21.0	19.4	18.7	18.8	18.7
– ALAI	0.7	0.6	0.5	0.7	0.8	1.0	0.9	0.8	1.0	1.0
– MCAC	0.0	0.0	0.0	0.0	0.0	0.1	0.0	0.0	0.0	0.0
– Caraïbes	0.1	0.1	0.1	0.2	0.1	0.1	0.1	0.1	0.1	0.1
– Autre Amérique	0.7	0.6	0.7	0.7	0.7	0.6	0.5	0.4	0.5	0.6
Asie anc. URSS exclus	52.3	52.5	53.3	55.2	53.2	55.5	59.1	60.5	60.8	60.0
– Moyen–Orient	2.7	2.6	2.6	3.1	2.9	2.3	1.7	1.6	1.6	1.6
Asie ancienne URSS						0.0		0.0	0.0	0.0
Europe anc. URSS exclus	15.0	15.3	16.5	16.2	17.0	15.9	14.5	14.2	13.8	14.7
– Union Européenne	13.5	13.9	15.0	14.5	15.8	14.6	13.5	13.4	13.0	14.0
– Europe de l'Est	0.3	0.3	0.4	0.4	0.3	0.2	0.2	0.2	0.2	0.1
– Autre de l'Europe	1.2	1.1	1.1	1.2	1.0	1.1	0.9	0.7	0.6	0.6
Europe ancienne URSS	0.3	0.4	0.6	0.5	0.5	0.7	0.9	0.8	0.7	0.6
Océanie	3.8	4.2	3.9	3.7	3.7	3.2	3.2	3.0	3.1	3.1
Autre		0.0	0.0	0.0				0.0		
USA/Etats–Unis d'Amer	23.8	23.3	21.3	19.8	21.1	20.4	18.8	18.3	18.4	18.4
Malaysia/Malaisie	13.6	13.7	13.1	15.0	12.5	14.2	19.7	19.2	18.0	17.5
China, Hong Kong SAR	6.3	6.3	6.5	7.2	7.8	8.7	8.7	8.6	8.9	9.6
Japan/Japon	8.6	8.5	8.7	8.7	7.6	7.5	7.0	7.8	8.2	7.1
Thailand/Thaïlande	5.5	5.5	6.6	6.3	6.2	5.7	5.6	5.8	5.7	4.6
Other Asia n.e.s.	3.8	4.2	4.9	4.9	4.9	3.9	4.0	4.1	3.9	4.5
Germany/Allemagne				4.2	4.2	4.0	3.5	3.4	3.1	2.9
United Kingdom	2.9	3.4	3.2	3.0	2.9	3.0	2.7	2.6	2.8	3.3
Korea, Republic of	2.0	1.9	2.2	2.4	2.3	2.8	2.6	2.7	3.0	3.0
China/Chine	3.0	2.7	1.5	1.5	1.8	2.6	2.2	2.3	2.7	3.3

4. General Imports C.I.F. by Commodities according to the S.I.T.C. (Rev. 2) in million U.S. Dollars
Importations Générales C.A.F. par Produits d'après la C.T.C.I. (Rév. 2) en millions de Dollars E.U.

SITC CTCI	COMMODITY	1994 QUANTITY QUANTITE	1994 VALUE VALEUR	1995 QUANTITY QUANTITE	1995 VALUE VALEUR	1996 QUANTITY QUANTITE	1996 VALUE VALEUR	1997 QUANTITY QUANTITE	1997 VALUE VALEUR	PRODUIT
	ALL COMMODITIES		102669.4		124503.5		131340.1		132441.8	TOUS PRODUITS
0	FOOD AND LIVE ANIMALS		3420.9		3635.8		3657.0		3515.5	ALIMENTS,ANIMAUX VIVANTS
03	FISH AND PREPARATIONS		613.1		656.2		639.0		623.5	POISSONS ET PREPARATIONS
04	CEREALS AND PREPARATIONS		367.3		398.9		435.2		424.2	CEREALES ET PRODUITS
05	VEGETABLES AND FRUIT		813.6		872.3		872.1		787.7	LEGUMES ET FRUITS
057	FRUIT,NUTS,FRESH,DRIED		358.8		375.0		385.1		356.7	FRUITS FRAIS OU SECS
07	COFFEE,TEA,COCOA,SPICES		460.5		423.4		347.3		410.1	CAFE,THE,CACAO,EPICES
1	BEVERAGES AND TOBACCO		1405.8		1429.3		1697.5		1779.2	BOISSONS ET TABACS
11	BEVERAGES		508.2		605.5		737.6		601.2	BOISSONS
112	ALCOHOLIC BEVERAGES	W 55006	458.9	W 61540	534.8	W 67193	664.4	W 74548	530.7	BOISSONS ALCOOLIQUES
1124	DISTILLED ALCOHOLIC BEVS	W 17550	372.8	W 19475	427.0	W 20480	381.0	W 19560	367.9	ALCOOLS,EAUX-DE-VIE
12	TOBACCO AND MANUFACTURES		897.6		823.9		960.0		1178.0	TABACS BRUTS FABRIQUES
122	TOBACCO,MANUFACTURED	W 48869	833.3	W 41925	756.0	W 48547	883.6	W 59238	1091.4	TABACS FABRIQUES
1222	CIGARETTES	W 44556	801.9	W 38396	738.7	W 46848	871.1	W 57690	1077.0	CIGARETTES
2	CRUDE MATERLS,EXCL FUELS		1272.5		1473.3		1339.7		1203.8	MAT BRUTES NON COMESTIBLES
23	RUBBER, CRUDE		349.8		482.9		392.0		306.5	CAOUTCHOUC BRUT
232	NATURAL RUBBER,GUMS	W 308478	303.9	W 298741	435.9	W 260881	344.6	W 279579	261.3	LATEX CAOUTCHOUC NATUREL
3	MINERAL FUELS ETC		9081.2		10063.4		12314.4		12588.3	COMBUSTIBLES MINERAUX LUB
33	PETROLEUM AND PRODUCTS		9075.0		10057.8		12307.8		12582.0	PETROLE ET DERIVES
333	CRUDE PETROLEUM	MW 50947	5861.7	MW 51159	6489.2	MW 55192	7983.1	MW 55342	8033.3	HUILES BRUTES DE PETROLE
334	PETROLEUM PRODUCTS,REFIN	MW 25768	3186.7	MW 26824	3536.8	MW 30545	4298.7	MW 32987	4520.1	PRODUITS RAFFINES
3341	GASOLINE,OTH LIGHT OILS	W 4286954	721.0			W 3524416	695.6			ESSENCES POUR MOTEURS
33411	MOTOR,AVIATION SPIRIT	W 2352562	408.0			W 1583531	298.4			ESSENCES MOTEURS D'AVIONS
3343	GAS OILS	W 5164586	814.4			W 4158661	813.0			GAS OILS
3344	FUEL OILS,NES	MW 15574	1384.4			MW 21583	2381.4			FUEL OILS
4	ANIMAL,VEGETABLE OIL,FAT		438.0		550.0		366.6		346.4	HUILES,GRAISSES ANIM,VEG
5	CHEMCLS,RELATED PROD NES		6457.9		7842.5		7558.6		7384.8	PRODUITS CHIMIQUES
51	ORGANIC CHEMICALS		1188.7		1655.6		1547.1		1672.9	PROD CHIMIQ ORGANIQUES
52	INORGANIC CHEMICALS		305.4		405.1		402.9		434.0	PROD CHIM INORGANIQUES
53	DYES,TANNING,COLOUR PROD		465.0		496.4		494.4		504.7	PROD TEINTURE,COLORANTS
541	*MEDICINAL,PHARM PRODUCT		524.5		661.8		683.8		722.3	PROD MEDICINAUX PHARMACEUT
55	PERFUME,CLEANING ETC PRD		644.4		780.1		815.1		790.5	PROD POUR PARFUM,TOILETTE
553	PERFUMERY,COSMETICS,ETC		464.7		560.2		586.5		557.0	PRODUITS DE PARFUMERIE
58	PLASTIC MATERIALS ETC		1480.5		1759.3		1600.8		1701.4	MAT PLAST ARTIFICIELLES
582	PROD OF CONDENSATION ETC	W 262137	541.6	W 308842	727.1	W 279883	685.2	W 320623	757.8	PROD CONDENS,POLYCOND
583	POLYMERIZATION ETC PRODS	W 617394	902.5		990.7	W 659425	878.0	W 545512	892.5	PROD POLYMERISATION
59	CHEMICAL MATERIALS NES		1811.1		2045.7		1962.7		1526.4	MAT PROD CHIMIQUES NDA
598	MISCEL CHEM PRODUCTS NES		1684.5		1897.6		1804.0		1356.7	PROD DIV INDUST CHIM NDA
5989	CHEM PRODUCTS,PREPS NES		1399.5		1539.5		1502.3		1047.9	PROD PREP CHIMIQUES NDA
59899	OTH CHEM PRODS,PREPS,NES	W 68012	1307.3	W 70008	1428.8	W 75423	1388.5	W 75011	911.1	AUT PRODUITS CHIMIQUES NDA
6	BASIC MANUFACTURES		10899.8		13599.2		13017.0		13314.9	ART MANUFACTURES
62	RUBBER MANUFACTURES NES		450.6		573.0		594.0		556.1	CAOUTCHOUC MANUFACTURE
64	PAPER,PAPERBOARD AND MFR		942.1		1198.5		1038.1		942.1	PAPIERS,CARTONS & OUVRAGES
641	PAPER AND PAPERBOARD		650.4		873.1		708.1		618.0	PAPIERS ET CARTONS
65	TEXTILE YARN,FABRICS,ETC		2017.4		2109.2		1916.3		1722.2	FILS,TISSUS,ARTICLES TEXTILE
653	WOVN MAN–MADE FIB FABRIC	A 609075	662.0	A 569588	643.5	A 537720	568.8	A 470852	464.2	TISSUS FIBRES SYNTH,ARTIF
6532	DISC SYN TXTL FABRIC NES	A 287176	360.9	A 252348	322.8	A 252900	285.2	A 185952	222.6	TIS DISC MOINS 85% FIBR TEXT
66	NONMETAL MINERAL MFS NES		1510.3		1904.4		2209.6		2087.9	ART MIN NON METALLIQUES
661	LIME,CEMENT,BLDG PRODS	W 4332731	297.2	W 4794007	367.8	W 5689002	454.0	W 6412076	454.5	CHAUX,CIMENTS MAT CONSTR
664	GLASS		293.0		337.1		397.1		389.4	VERRE
667	PEARL,PREC–,SEMI–P STONE		261.4		479.8		606.8		586.3	PERLES, PIERRES GEMMES
6672	DIAMONDS NONINDUST,UNSET		240.5		426.4		533.2		491.5	DIAMANTS BRUTS
66729	— CUT ETC NOT SET		239.8		403.0		523.2		489.8	DIAMANTS TAILLES
67	IRON AND STEEL		2167.6		2815.3		2726.6		2930.4	FER ET ACIER
673	IRON,STEEL SHAPES ETC	W 1426665	557.6	W 1953427	822.9	W 2068224	805.6	W 2422433	884.4	BARRES,PROFIL FER,ACIER
6732	IRON,STEEL BARS ETC	W 740008	293.8	W 882163	377.9	W 1079628	417.6	W 1149123	428.0	BARRES FER,ACIER
674	IRN,STL UNIV,PLATE,SHEET	W 1298182	777.1	W 1524442	1063.1	W 1315275	891.9	W 1407588	906.9	LARGES PLATS,TOLES
678	IRON,STL TUBES,PIPES,ETC	W 489236	525.7	W 512713	590.8	W 570464	706.6	W 628159	778.8	TUBES,TUYAUX EN FONTE,FER
68	NON–FERROUS METALS		1675.2		2548.9		1940.7		2357.2	METAUX NON FERREUX
682	COPPER EXC CEMENT COPPER	W 227089	794.5	W 410809	1456.6	W 335754	1065.5	W 371894	1064.9	CUIVRE
6821	COPPER NES,ALLOYS,UNWRT	W 93805	293.2	W 263138	778.8	W 196245	482.7	W 213121	505.5	CUIVRE BRUT
68212	COPPER REFINED,UNWROUGHT	W 93497	291.9	W 261523	773.5	W 190834	468.2	W 211967	501.2	CUIVRE AFFINE BRUT
6822	COPPER,ALLOYS WORKED	W 133284	501.4	W 147672	677.9	W 139509	582.8	W 158774	559.5	CUIVRE,ALLIAGES OUVRES
684	ALUMINIUM	W 203804	457.6	W 297596	742.8	W 189926	496.0	W 211660	553.1	ALUMINIUM
6842	ALUMINIUM,ALLOYS WORKED	W 83351	282.1	W 98904	379.4	W 90593	335.7	W 109075	381.3	ALUMINIUM,ALLIAGES OUVRE
69	METAL MANUFACTURES NES		1719.8		2069.3		2188.3		2328.1	ART MANUFACT EN METAL NDA
695	TOOLS		347.4		420.9		448.3		440.7	OUTILS A MAIN
699	BASE METAL MFRS NES		654.6		761.1		819.4		907.1	ART MANUFACTURES MET NDA
7	MACHINES,TRANSPORT EQUIP		57890.1		71991.9		75942.3		76128.1	MACHINES MATERIEL TRANSPORT
71	POWER GENERATING EQUIPMT		2935.5		2988.3		2805.0		2782.3	MACHINES GENERATRICES
713	INTRNL COMBUS PSTN ENGIN		821.5		852.5		775.3		779.1	MOTEURS EXPL COMB INT, PIECE
7139	PISTON ENGINE PARTS NES		377.9		394.7		385.9		409.5	PIECES POUR 713.2,3,8
714	ENGINES AND MOTORS NES		652.5		306.8		320.7		248.5	MOTEURS NON ELECTRIQUES
7149	ENGINE & MOTOR PARTS NES		445.3		245.6		224.0		197.0	PIECES 714 ET 718.88
71491	PARTS NES OF 7144,71481		318.0		148.4		112.9		82.0	PIECES DES PROPULSEURS
716	ROTATING ELECTRIC PLANT		1292.7		1607.9		1550.8		1597.5	APP ELECTR ROTATIFS,PIECES
7162	AC MTRS,GENRTRS,GEN SETS	MN 351906	988.6	MN 485102	1229.3	MN 442806	1260.2	MN 483688	1341.8	MOTEURS ELECTRIQUES
71621	AC MTRS,INC UNIVRSL MTRS	MN 351852	755.0	MN 485057	1008.6	MN 442765	1048.6	MN 483649	1087.9	MOT ELEC NON COUR CONTINU
72	MACHS FOR SPCL INDUSTRYS		2997.2		3801.4		4640.8		4497.0	MAC SPECIALES POUR INDUST
723	CIVIL ENGNEERG EQUIP ETC		700.1		898.6		1065.9		1214.7	APPAREILS DE GENIE CIVIL
7234	CONST,MINING MACHNRY NES	N 11888	301.9	N 12474	438.5	N 10377	490.5	N 9959	487.4	MACH POUR LA CONST, MINES
7239	CONSTR ETC MACHY PTS NES		388.2		445.1		556.6		710.0	PIECES 723.41–723.46
728	OTH MACHY FOR SPCL INDUS		1761.2		2176.8		2639.7		2598.3	AUT MACH IND PARTICULIERES
7284	MACHY FOR SPCL INDUS NES		1525.7		1951.3		2389.4		2367.3	MACH SPEC IND PARTICUL.
72848	OTH MCHY WITH INDIV FNCT	N 96410	869.8	N 93985	1122.8	N 358828	1505.0	N 57917	1434.3	AUTRES MACHINES NDA
72849	PTS OF MACHS OF 7284 ETC		368.7		535.5		669.6		722.6	PIECES DU 728.4 ETC
73	METALWORKING MACHINERY		613.8		759.3		728.5		772.2	MACH TRAVAIL DES METAUX
736	METALWORKING MACH–TOOLS		481.5		596.2		591.1		620.9	MACH–OUTILS TRAVAIL METAUX
74	GENRL INDUSTRL MACHY NES		4917.7		5407.5		6143.7		5849.8	MACH APP INDUSTRIE
741	HEATING,COOLING EQUIPMNT		1068.1		1134.1		1232.9		1146.0	MACH CHAUFFAGE,PIECES
7415	AIR–CONDITIONING MACHNRY	N 1607888	598.7	N 1500397	598.2	N 1563311	631.7	N 1590467	599.4	GROUPES CONDITION AIR
742	PUMPS FOR LIQUIDS ETC		364.8		385.9		425.1		439.1	POMPES MOTO–POMPES
743	PUMPS NES,CENTRFUGES ETC		672.7		683.3		772.8		702.3	POMPES COMPRES,VENT ETC
744	MECHANICAL HANDLING EQU		1039.7		1195.2		1497.1		1564.2	EQUIP MANUTENTION PIECES
7442	LIFTING,LOADING MACH NES	N 337573	528.3	N 423404	453.1	N 205631	441.9	N 177518	418.3	APP LEVAGE,MANUTENTION
7449	PTS NES OF MACHY OF 7442		297.5		478.4		740.1		755.7	PIECES DU 744.2
749	NONELEC MACH PTS,ACC NES		1514.5		1721.7		1893.1		1726.4	PIECES MACH NON ELEC NDA
7491	BALL,ROLLER,ETC BEARINGS		505.1		683.9		795.2		658.5	ROULEMENTS BILLES ETC
7492	COCKS,VALVES ETC NES	MN 53551	434.4	MN 66035	412.5	MN 43804	491.0	MN 42955	446.3	ART ROB,SIM POUR TUYAUX
7499	OTH NONELEC MCHY PTS NES		313.1		370.4		345.2		346.8	PIECES NON ELECT NDA
75	OFFICE MACHNES,ADP EQUIP		9933.5		13180.6		15303.8		16662.0	MACH BUREAU TRAIT AUTOM

4. General Imports C.I.F. by Commodities according to the S.I.T.C. (Rev. 2) in million U.S. Dollars
Importations Générales C.A.F. par Produits d'après la C.T.C.I. (Rév. 2) en millions de Dollars E.U.

SITC CTCI	COMMODITY	1994		1995		1996		1997		PRODUIT
		QUANTITY QUANTITE	VALUE VALEUR	QUANTITY QUANTITE	VALUE VALEUR	QUANTITY QUANTITE	VALUE VALEUR	QUANTITY QUANTITE	VALUE VALEUR	
751	OFFICE MACHINES	MN 32169	460.1	MN 36689	488.8	MN 44048	550.9	MN 36393	555.1	MACH,APPAREILS DE BUREAU
752	AUTOMTIC DATA PROC EQUIP	MN 61971	5087.4	MN 70709	5253.1	MN 73838	6798.4	MN 78794	7182.7	MACH TRAIT INFORMATION
7522	DIGITAL COMPUTERS	N 1317189	593.6	N 1730910	617.6	N 155580	234.3	N 281337	388.2	MACH DIGITALES COMPLETES
7523	DIGITL CENTRL PROCESSORS	N 186509	175.4	N 251543	228.2	N 417771	632.5	N 336854	542.0	UNITES CENTRALES
7524	DIGITL CENTRL STOR UNITS	MN 38509	3109.8	MN 36125	2654.7	MN 48554	4302.1	MN 48627	4673.4	UNITES MEMOIRE CENTRALES
7525	ADP PERIPHERAL UNITS	MN 16376	914.9	MN 27411	1303.5	MN 23623	1365.2	MN 28694	1322.7	UNITES PERIPHERIQUES
7528	OFF–LINE DATA PROC EQUIP	N 5581358	292.8	N 5190660	448.6	N 1087744	264.4	N 854420	256.6	MACH AUXIL TRAIT INFORM
759	OFFICE,ADP MCH PTS,ACCES		4386.2		7438.7		7954.7		8924.3	PIECES DU 751 ET 752
7599	ACCTG,ETC,ADP MCH PTS,AC		4239.6		7238.6		7770.2		8720.2	PIECES DU 751 ET 752
76	TELECOMM,SOUND EQUIPMENT		9115.3		9203.7		8120.3		7858.2	EQUIPMENT DE TELECOM
761	TELEVISION RECEIVERS	N 4042706	1003.4	N 3238531	854.4	N 3547069	892.1	N 2865222	640.1	RECEPTEURS DE TELEVISION
7611	COLOUR TV RECEIVERS	N 3927143	997.0	N 3160728	849.8	N 3446735	882.4	N 2821022	636.9	RECEPTEURS COULEUR
762	RADIO BROADCAST RECEIVRS	MN 32743	1447.5	MN 22953	1229.1	MN 15468	916.8	MN 14287	843.4	RECEPTEURS RADIODIFFUSION
7622	PORTABLE RADIO RECEIVERS	MN 21974	685.1	MN 13867	520.9	N 7647674	251.9	N 6831942	197.3	RECEPT PORTATIFS RADIO
7628	OTHER RADIO RECEIVERS	N 6327944	556.8	N 4637768	447.9	N 4598312	430.5	N 5223205	471.3	AUTRES RECEPT RADIO
763	SOUND RECORDRS,PHONOGRPH	MN 24494	1687.2	MN 12771	1135.6	N 8698841	978.4	N 7813072	907.7	PHONO,APP ENREGISTREMENT
7638	OTHR SOUND APPARATUS ETC	MN 24205	1678.1	MN 12522	1125.9	N 8687186	977.4	N 7792378	906.4	AUT APP D'ENREGIS,REPROD
76381	TV IMAGE,SND RECRDRS ETC	N 5883494	867.8	N 4323352	731.9	N 3840546	658.7	N 3377357	631.3	APP ENREG,REPRO IMAG,SON
76388	DICTATING MACHINES ETC	MN 18322	810.4	N 8198607	394.1	N 4846640	318.8	N 4415021	275.1	MACHINES A DICTER
764	TELECOM EQPT,PTS,ACC NES		4977.4		5984.8		5333.1		5467.2	EQUIP TELECOM,PIECES
7641	LINE TELEPHONE,ETC EQUIP	MN 32225	621.9	MN 33237	663.0	MN 24444	621.2	MN 20051	645.3	APP TELEPHON PAR FIL
7642	MICROPH,LOUDSPKR,AMPLIFR	MN 495588	441.7	MN 121794	434.0	MN 98030	398.1	MN 118035	387.1	MICRO,HAUT–PARLEUR,AMPLI
7643	TV,RADIO TRANSMITTRS ETC	N 1623481	250.3	N 2317987	574.3	N 5067079	653.5	N 3095059	909.2	APP EMET TELE RADIO
7648	TELECOMM EQUIPMENT NES	MN 15377	377.0	MN 17120	573.6	MN 15891	348.7	MN 14346	337.0	APP TELECOM NDA
7649	PTS NES OF EQUIPMT OF 76		3286.7		3740.2		3311.9		3188.8	PIECES DE LA DIV 76
76491	PTS NES OF APPAR OF 7641		252.5		380.4		396.4		419.8	PIECES POUR 764.1
76493	TELECOMM EQUIPMT PTS NES		1318.1		1229.7		1281.3		1348.9	PIECES 761,762,764.3,8
76499	PARTS ETC OF SOUND EQUIP		1646.9		2059.8		1555.5		1330.9	PIECES NDA POUR 763
77	ELECTRIC MACHNRY NES ETC		22348.5		30494.7		30025.4		29857.4	MACH APP ELECT NDA
771	ELECTRIC POWER MACHY NES		1135.5		1418.6		1401.5		1418.5	MACH PROD,TRANS ELECTR
7711	TRANSFORMERS,ELECTRICAL	MN 544742	428.8	MN 564752	428.4	MN 430252	341.1	MN 375514	349.2	TRANSFO ELECTRIQUES
77118	OTHER ELEC TRANSFORMERS	MN 533999	401.5	MN 559707	408.5	MN 420730	329.5	MN 368135	319.6	AUTRES TRANSFO ELECTRIQ
7712	OTH ELEC POWER MACHY NES		706.7		990.2		1060.5		1069.4	AUT APP PROD TRANSF ELEC
77121	STATIC CONVERTERS ETC	MN 311573	273.4	MN 219925	413.4	MN 161501	532.4	MN 127696	548.4	CONVERTISSEURS STATIQUES
772	SWITCHGEAR ETC,PARTS NES		2914.3		3470.6		3465.2		3367.6	APP COUPURE,SECT ETC
7721	SWITCHGEAR ETC		1713.3		2074.2		2134.0		2008.1	APP COUPURE,SECTIONMNT
7722	PRINTED CIRCUITS,PTS NES		736.9		930.9		942.6		1011.1	CIRCUITS ET PIECES
7723	FIXED,VARIABLE RESISTORS		464.2		465.6		388.7		348.5	POTENTIOMETRES PIECES
773	ELECTR DISTRIBUTNG EQUIP		697.7		743.4		814.3		751.2	EQUIPMT DISTRIBUTION ELECT
7731	INSULATED WIRE,CABLE ETC	W 127603	615.2	W 119931	660.1	W 109432	722.1	W 115682	662.3	FILS,CABLES ISOLES ELECT
775	HOUSEHOLD TYPE EQUIP NES		375.4		393.6		422.0		408.3	MACH,APP USAGE DOMESTQUE
776	TRANSISTORS,VALVES,ETC		14649.0		21384.6		21020.1		20925.9	LAMPES,TUBES,VALVES
7761	TV PICTURE TUBES	N 5083337	376.8	N 6124968	527.0	N 5844515	567.3	N 2915918	316.3	TUBES CATHODIQUES
7762	OTH ELECTRONIC TUBES ETC		349.0		412.6		669.3		541.4	AUT LAMPES ELECTRONIQUES
7763	DIODES,TRANSISTORS,ETC		1570.4		2170.5		2284.4		2167.9	DIODES,TRANSISTORS
7764	ELECTRONIC MICROCIRCUITS		10716.6		15573.5		14739.2		15498.2	MICROSTRUCTURES ELECTRON
7768	ELCTRNC COMP PTS,CRYSTLS		1636.4		2701.2		2760.1		2402.4	CRIST PIEZO–ELEC,PCS 776
77681	PIEZO–ELEC CRYSTALS,MNTD		341.4		423.7		361.7		294.4	CRISTAUX PIEZO–ELECTRIQ
77689	ELECTRNIC COMPON PTS NES		1295.1		2277.5		2398.4		2108.0	PIECES DU GROUPE 776
778	ELECTRICAL MACHINERY NES		2514.4		3016.4		2812.3		2891.8	AUTRES MACH ELECT NDA
7788	OTH ELEC MACHY,EQUIP NES		1865.1		2296.7		2081.6		2165.9	AUT MACH APP ELEC NDA
77884	ELECTRICAL CONDENSERS		1154.3		1381.9		1234.0		1209.5	CONDENSATEURS ELECTRIQUES
77886	OTH ELEC MACHINERY NES	MN 34181	252.6		406.0		455.3		516.8	AUT MACH APP ELECTRIQUES
78	ROAD VEHICLES		2125.6		2686.6		2566.4		2394.3	VEHICULES ROUTIERS
781	PASS MOTOR VEH EXC BUSES	N 42588	695.2	N 38229	853.6	N 39323	767.3	N 38831	670.8	AUTO TRANSPORT PERSONNES
782	LORRIES,SPCL MTR VEH NES	N 13422	284.9	N 22056	451.6	N 19008	454.0	N 19334	503.5	VEHICULES SPECIAUX,MARCH
784	MOTOR VEH PRTS,ACCES NES		759.9		972.1		917.4		820.0	PIECES 722,781,782,783
7849	OTHER MOTOR VEHCL PARTS		703.3		872.9		860.0		762.6	PIECES 722,781,782,783
79	OTHR TRANSPORT EQUIPMENT		2903.4		3470.2		5608.9		5455.3	AUTRE MATERIEL TRANSPORT
792	AIRCRAFT ETC		1627.1		1677.9		3011.2		3225.6	APP NAVIGATION AERIENNE
7924	AIRCRFT NES OVER 15000KG	N 9	1244.3	N 8	922.2	N 11	1591.2	N 12	1649.4	AERODYNES PLUS 15000 KG
7929	AIRCRAFT PARTS NES		341.2		674.0		1343.5		1501.4	PIECES DU 792
793	SHIPS AND BOATS ETC	N 14144	1228.9	N 15277	1659.3	N 21407	2569.2	N 21262	2218.9	NAVIRES BATEAUX,ETC
7932	SHIPS AND BOATS NES	N 3354	983.6	N 1977	1554.7	N 7663	2418.5	N 6504	2129.2	NAVIRES ET BATEAUX
79322	TANKERS OF ALL KINDS	N 21	211.9	N 35	184.0	N 56	1098.1	N 57	481.9	BATEAUX–CITERNES
79323	OTHER CARGO VESSELS	N 195	750.3	N 229	1338.4	N 229	1286.0	N 226	1613.7	AUT BATEAUX TRANS MARCH
8	MISC MANUFACTURED GOODS		10234.0		12400.4		13859.8		14064.8	ART MANUFACTURES DIVERS
821	*FURNITURE,PARTS THEREOF		383.5		447.0		511.5		515.8	MEUBLES ET PIECES
84	CLOTHING AND ACCESSORIES		1574.6		1645.2		1732.3		1806.9	VETEMENTS
843	WOMENS OUTERWEAR NONKNIT	MN 51916	331.6	MN 49277	336.3	MN 48152	350.6	MN 54795	361.2	VET DESSUS FEMMES MAT TEX
845	OUTERWEAR KNIT NONELASTC	MN 118286	428.1	MN 83192	422.5	MN 81936	448.2	MN 88398	514.4	VET DESSOUS,ACCES BONNET
846	UNDER GARMENTS KNITTED	MN 136773	314.6	MN 126968	390.7	MN 124674	410.4	MN 133384	430.3	SOUS VETS DE BONNETERIE
87	PRECISION INSTRUMNTS NES		2068.1		2508.2		2625.8		3099.3	INSTRUM,APPAR SCIENT NDA
871	OPTICAL INSTRUMENTS		649.1		699.9		539.3		794.5	APPAR,INSTRUM D'OPTIQUE
87109	OPTICAL INSTRUMENTS NES	MN 109797	611.2	MN 137751	665.8	MN 103414	493.3	MN 120845	747.4	APP,INSTRUM OPTIQUE NDA
874	MEASURNG,CONTROLNG INSTR		1165.0		1550.2		1812.3		1973.7	INSTRUMENTS DE MESURE
8742	MEASUR,DRAW ETC INST,PTS		270.8		385.4		481.2		532.4	INST DESSIN,TRACAGE,PCS
87421	MEASURNG,DRAWNG ETC INST	MN 19525	225.9	MN 21048	306.5	MN 18942	379.3	MN 15900	422.2	INSTRUM DESSIN,TRACAGE
88	PHOTO EQU,OPTICL GDS ETC		2012.2		2270.8		2376.7		2334.5	APP,FOURN PHOTO,OP,MONTR
881	PHOTO APPARAT,EQUIPT NES		324.9		388.7		451.5		403.4	APP,EQUIP PHOTO NDA
882	PHOTO,CINEMA SUPPLIES		604.4		680.7		637.0		619.3	PRODUITS PHOTO,CINEMA
8822	PHOTO FILM EXC DEV CINMA		403.0		415.4		360.5		318.6	PLAQUES,PELLICULES,FILMS
885	WATCHES AND CLOCKS		921.5		1019.8		1093.2		1110.1	HORLOGERIE
8851	WATCHES,MOVEMENTS,CASES		716.1		845.4		910.8		925.3	MONTRES,MOUVEMENTS,BOITES
88511	WATCHES		667.7		806.5		870.2		871.6	MONTRES POCHE,BRACELET
89	MISC MANUFCTRD GOODS NES		3473.3		4730.2		5722.0		5462.3	ART MANUFACTURES DIVERS
893	ARTICLES OF PLASTIC NES		722.8		757.1		773.9		841.8	OUVRAGES EN MAT DIVIS 58
8939	MISC PLASTIC ARTICLES		524.8		549.3		566.6		607.9	ART DIVERS EN MAT DIV 58
89399	OTHR PLASTC ARTICLES NES		493.2		509.9		526.7		566.2	AUT OUV MAT DIV 58
894	TOYS,SPORTING GOODS,ETC		420.0		471.5		493.7		438.3	VOITURES ENFANTS,JOUETS
897	GOLD,SILVER WARE,JEWELRY		419.9		871.0		1212.7		1169.9	BIJOUTERIE,ORFEVRERIE
8973	PREC JEWLRY,GLD–SILVWARE		376.5		836.7		1179.8		1141.8	BIJOUX OR,ARGENT ORFEVRE
89731	PRECIOUS METAL JEWELLERY		339.4		789.2		1118.6		1102.3	ART BIJOUTERIE,JOAILLER
898	MUSICAL INSTRUMENTS,PTS		1195.1		1829.6		2357.9		2113.8	INSTRUMENTS DE MUSIQUE
8983	SOUND RECRDNG TAPE,DISCS	MN 393443	1133.5	MN 532499	1758.7	MN 936635	2279.4	MN 621441	2029.7	SUPPORTS SON POUR 763
89831	PREPD SND RECORDNG MEDIA	MN 343211	863.2	MN 490605	1347.3	MN 802111	1984.0	MN 563450	1792.9	SUPPORTS PREPARES
89832	RECORDED DISCS,TAPES ETC	MN 50232	270.4	MN 41894	411.5	MN 134524	295.4	MN 57991	236.9	DISQUES,PHONO,BANDES
9	GOODS NOT CLASSD BY KIND		1569.6		1518.3		1587.5		2116.4	ART TRANSACT NON CLASSES
931	*SPECIAL TRANSACTIONS		1282.8		1193.5		1184.0		1318.2	TRANS.SPECIALES
971	*GOLD,NON MONETARY NES	K 25714	277.0	K 26813	318.4	K 39766	397.0	K 74521	790.3	OR NON MONETAIRE
97101	NONMON GLD UNWRT,SEMIMFD	K 23199	271.6	K 26392	314.7	K 31380	389.7	K 71859	767.3	OR,ALLIAGES D'OR BRUTS

4. General Imports C.I.F. by Commodities according to the S.I.T.C. (Rev. 2) in million U.S. Dollars
Importations Générales C.A.F. par Produits d'après la C.T.C.I. (Rév. 2) en millions de Dollars E.U.

SITC CTCI	COMMODITY	1994		1995		1996		1997		PRODUIT
		QUANTITY QUANTITE	VALUE VALEUR	QUANTITY QUANTITE	VALUE VALEUR	QUANTITY QUANTITE	VALUE VALEUR	QUANTITY QUANTITE	VALUE VALEUR	

5. General Exports F.O.B. by Commodities according to the S.I.T.C. (Rev. 2) in million U.S. Dollars
Exportations Générales F.O.B. par Produits d'après la C.T.C.I. (Rév. 2) en millions de Dollars E.U.

SITC CTCI	COMMODITY	1994 QUANTITY QUANTITE	1994 VALUE VALEUR	1995 QUANTITY QUANTITE	1995 VALUE VALEUR	1996 QUANTITY QUANTITE	1996 VALUE VALEUR	1997 QUANTITY QUANTITE	1997 VALUE VALEUR	PRODUIT
	ALL COMMODITIES		96824.6		118263.2		125009.0		124988.2	TOUS PRODUITS
0	FOOD AND LIVE ANIMALS		2324.8		2506.6		2261.2		2165.5	ALIMENTS,ANIMAUX VIVANTS
03	FISH AND PREPARATIONS		562.1		582.1		539.6		492.2	POISSONS ET PREPARATIONS
05	VEGETABLES AND FRUIT		366.0		399.8		394.7		329.8	LEGUMES ET FRUITS
07	COFFEE,TEA,COCOA,SPICES		708.2		753.6		574.0		674.3	CAFE,THE,CACAO,EPICES
071	COFFEE AND SUBSTITUTES	W 157922	318.0	W 95997	282.7	W 62663	137.9	W 74782	149.7	CAFE ET SUCCEDANES
0711	COFFEE GREEN,ROASTED,SUB	W 152160	302.2	W 86133	247.6	W 49703	94.4	W 56530	95.0	CAFE TORREFIE OU DECAFEINE
07111	COFFEE GREEN,HUSKS,SKINS	W 151773	300.0	W 85511	244.1	W 46798	84.8	W 52088	80.9	CAFE NON TORREFIE
1	BEVERAGES AND TOBACCO		1608.6		1605.6		1866.3		1862.5	BOISSONS ET TABACS
11	BEVERAGES		566.8		599.6		584.7		514.7	BOISSONS
112	ALCOHOLIC BEVERAGES	W 57025	465.6		513.4	W 69526	505.2	W 56004	456.5	BOISSONS ALCOOLIQUES
1124	DISTILLED ALCOHOLIC BEVS	W 13100	397.4		421.3	W 14733	406.0	W 14288	362.1	ALCOOLS,EAUX–DE–VIE
11242	DISTILLD WINE,GRAPE MARC	W 5702	354.9	W 6574	366.1	W 6640	345.7	W 6793	309.5	EAUX–DE–VIE NATURELLES
12	TOBACCO AND MANUFACTURES		1041.8		1006.1		1281.6		1347.9	TABACS BRUTS FABRIQUES
122	TOBACCO,MANUFACTURED	W 55527	1034.1	W 50715	998.7	W 59333	1272.9	W 65283	1337.5	TABACS FABRIQUES
1222	CIGARETTES	W 54425	1025.8	W 49044	986.6	W 56153	1251.6	W 60844	1310.2	CIGARETTES
2	CRUDE MATERLS,EXCL FUELS		1441.0		1697.7		1408.6		1210.1	MAT BRUTES NON COMESTIBLES
23	RUBBER, CRUDE		538.4		692.9		551.3		382.2	CAOUTCHOUC BRUT
232	NATURAL RUBBER,GUMS	W 498389	516.0	W 432330	669.8	W 375798	527.9	W 346919	357.8	LATEX CAOUTCHOUC NATUREL
23202	OTHER NATURAL RUBBER	W 435778	453.6	W 379904	590.9	W 332913	470.2	W 286360	300.8	CAOUTCHOUC NATUREL
3	MINERAL FUELS ETC		9183.1		8121.1		9851.5		8810.3	COMBUSTIBLES MINERAUX LUB
33	PETROLEUM AND PRODUCTS		9040.7		7968.6		9656.3		8593.8	PETROLE ET DERIVES
334	PETROLEUM PRODUCTS,REFIN	MW 60543	8834.9	MW 45074	7756.9	MW 48530	9464.3	MW 44393	8319.4	PRODUITS RAFFINES
3341	GASOLINE,OTH LIGHT OILS	MW 16704	2975.1			MW 17661	3769.6			ESSENCES POUR MOTEURS
33411	MOTOR,AVIATION SPIRIT	W 5938455	1144.9			W 6773522	1399.2			ESSENCES MOTEURS D'AVIONS
33412	SPIRIT TYPE JET FUEL	W 6265447	1123.4			W 6685347	1564.9			CARBUREACTEURS
33419	OTH LIGHT PETROLEUM OILS	W 4500450	707.0			W 4202568	805.6			AUTRES HUILES LEGERES
3343	GAS OILS	MW 30706	4116.9			MW 16318	3318.9			GAS OILS
3344	FUEL OILS,NES	MW 11625	1191.0			MW 12323	1548.9			FUEL OILS
3345	LUBS,PETROLEUM OILS NES	W 978511	450.9			W 1123074	566.1	W 9410	28.5	HUILES LUBRIFIANTES
33451	LUBS(HIGH PETR CONT) ETC	W 972430	433.9			W 1111663	537.5			HUILES LUBRIF,H LOURDES
4	ANIMAL,VEGETABLE OIL,FAT		378.1		511.7		368.5		342.4	HUILES,GRAISSES ANIM,VEG
5	CHEMCLS,RELATED PROD NES		5412.9		6902.4		6861.7		7357.3	PRODUITS CHIMIQUES
51	ORGANIC CHEMICALS		1715.1		2331.4		2269.2		2594.9	PROD CHIMIQ ORGANIQUES
511	HYDROCARBONS NES,DERIVS		300.4		484.5		361.6		484.7	HYDROCARBURES NDA
5112	CYCLIC HYDROCARBONS	V 587643	223.1	V 796809	406.9	V 778842	285.1	V 1178599	405.5	HYDROCARBURES CYCLIQUES
514	NITROGEN–FNCTN COMPOUNDS	W 85731	230.8	W 125938	413.5	W 136539	692.7	W 150133	824.7	COMPOSES FONCT AZOTEES
5148	OTH NITROGN–FNCTN CMPNDS	W 42439	107.8	W 67527	258.4	W 80153	501.4	W 87925	538.0	AUTRES COMPOSES AZOTES
51482	IMIDE–,IMIDE–FNCT CMPNDS	W 4444	41.3	W 14402	149.1	W 6194	368.1	W 5781	413.8	COMPOSES A FONCTION IMIDE
515	ORG–INORG COMPOUNDS ETC	W 17946	715.3	W 15651	766.2	W 27328	627.6	W 29299	578.5	COMPOSES ORGANO–MINERAUX
5156	HETEROCYCLIC CMPDS ETC	W 6765	667.5	W 4955	709.6	W 6966	407.4	W 7664	216.8	COMPOSES HETEROCYCLIQUES
51569	OTH HETEROCYC CMPDS,ETC	W 5025	662.3	W 3053	704.2	W 5429	403.4	W 5043	210.7	AUT COMP HETEROCYCLIQUES
53	DYES,TANNING,COLOUR PROD		466.7		537.6		494.7		479.3	PROD TEINTURE,COLORANTS
533	PIGMENTS,PAINTS,ETC		327.9		387.5		367.1		357.7	PIGMENTS,PEINTURES,VERNIS
541	*MEDICINAL,PHARM PRODUCT		494.8		601.2		616.2		616.6	PROD MEDICINAUX PHARMACEUT
55	PERFUME,CLEANING ETC PRD		485.2		627.2		714.8		708.2	PROD POUR PARFUM,TOILETTE
553	PERFUMERY,COSMETICS,ETC		302.8		388.1		433.5		420.7	PRODUITS DE PARFUMERIE
58	PLASTIC MATERIALS ETC		1288.3		1617.9		1604.4		1773.6	MAT PLAST ARTIFICIELLES
582	PROD OF CONDENSATION ETC	W 250773	393.7	W 268681	589.9	W 291801	655.8	W 332777	650.6	PROD CONDENS,POLYCOND
583	POLYMERIZATION ETC PRODS	W 881126	873.8	W 827729	1005.6	W 815903	929.1	W 1055295	1104.0	PROD POLYMERISATION
5831	POLYETHYLENE	W 370199	286.3	W 319871	326.7	W 331583	296.3	W 458038	395.7	POLYETHYLENE
59	CHEMICAL MATERIALS NES		750.4		968.5		939.2		990.4	MAT PROD CHIMIQUES NDA
598	MISCEL CHEM PRODUCTS NES		640.9		832.8		792.4		843.5	PROD DIV INDUST CHIM NDA
5989	CHEM PRODUCTS,PREPS NES		367.9		515.9		463.4		486.8	PROD PREP CHIMIQUES NDA
59899	OTH CHEM PRODS,PREPS,NES	W 68712	291.1	W 69953	400.8	W 74037	356.8	W 81109	371.0	AUT PRODUITS CHIMIQUES NDA
6	BASIC MANUFACTURES		5846.8		7525.4		7178.4		7053.6	ART MANUFACTURES
62	RUBBER MANUFACTURES NES		266.3		344.4		382.3		348.9	CAOUTCHOUC MANUFACTURE
64	PAPER,PAPERBOARD AND MFR		469.1		581.1		519.9		463.3	PAPIERS,CARTONS & OUVRAGES
641	PAPER AND PAPERBOARD		296.5		366.7		317.6		266.1	PAPIERS ET CARTONS
65	TEXTILE YARN,FABRICS,ETC		1415.9		1496.1		1346.8		1241.8	FILS,TISSUS,ARTICLES TEXTILE
653	WOVN MAN–MADE FIB FABRIC		540.2		527.4		470.2		422.0	TISSUS FIBRES SYNTH,ARTIF
6532	DISC SYN TXTL FABRIC NES	A 251360	323.8	A 236776	324.4	A 231472	283.4	A 213362	253.7	TIS DISC MOINS 85% FIBR TEXT
66	NONMETAL MINERAL MFS NES		518.8		692.5		805.1		764.3	ART MIN NON METALLIQUES
67	IRON AND STEEL		738.1		894.5		856.4		864.6	FER ET ACIER
68	NON–FERROUS METALS		1035.8		1953.4		1702.6		1795.0	METAUX NON FERREUX
682	COPPER EXC CEMENT COPPER	W 153203	436.5	W 251272	828.4	W 256108	702.1	W 251299	687.5	CUIVRE
6821	COPPER NES,ALLOYS,UNWRT	W 97835	216.9	W 199118	587.0	W 197161	496.2	W 201849	468.3	CUIVRE BRUT
68212	COPPER REFINED,UNWROUGHT	W 97733	216.4	W 197122	581.2	W 191887	481.3	W 201672	467.5	CUIVRE AFFINE BRUT
69	METAL MANUFACTURES NES		1035.9		1247.8		1287.9		1299.6	ART MANUFACT EN METAL NDA
699	BASE METAL MFRS NES		444.2		520.6		506.7		478.4	ART MANUFACTURES MET NDA
7	MACHINES,TRANSPORT EQUIP		61828.1		77568.0		82365.9		82425.4	MACHINES MATERIEL TRANSPORT
71	POWER GENERATING EQUIPMT		1613.8		1717.1		1652.0		1603.5	MACHINES GENERATRICES
713	INTRNL COMBUS PSTN ENGIN		436.4		410.1		398.6		376.2	MOTEURS EXPL COMB INT, PIECE
716	ROTATING ELECTRIC PLANT		900.8		1123.6		1133.1		1096.0	APP ELECTR ROTATIFS,PIECES
7162	AC MTRS,GENRTRS,GEN SETS	MN 392708	682.9	MN 512563	855.7	MN 424158	857.3	MN 421834	849.8	MOTEURS ELECTRIQUES
71621	AC MTRS,INC UNIVRSL MTRS	MN 392686	539.5	MN 512539	730.1	MN 424134	665.6	MN 421791	673.5	MOT ELEC NON COUR CONTINU
72	MACHS FOR SPCL INDUSTRYS		1699.6		2108.7		2187.6		2248.2	MAC SPECIALES POUR INDUST
723	CIVIL ENGNEERG EQUIP ETC		519.2		718.1		729.7		836.1	APPAREILS DE GENIE CIVIL
7239	CONSTR ETC MACHY PTS NES		396.9		501.2		486.6		629.8	PIECES 723.41–723.46
728	OTH MACHY FOR SPCL INDUS		851.5		1015.3		999.9		1028.9	AUT MACH IND PARTICULIERES
7284	MACHY FOR SPCL INDUS NES		696.7		851.3		859.4		893.1	MACH SPEC IND PARTICUL.
72848	OTH MCHY WITH INDIV FNCT	N 42653	390.5	N 44160	488.1	N 42757	440.9	N 43873	418.3	AUTRES MACHINES NDA
73	METALWORKING MACHINERY		374.1		471.3		440.0		431.3	MACH TRAVAIL DES METAUX
736	METALWORKING MACH–TOOLS		301.5		370.3		351.8		337.5	MACH–OUTILS TRAVAIL METAUX
74	GENRL INDUSTRL MACHY NES		3267.4		3602.7		3841.0		3642.3	MACH APP INDUSTRIE
741	HEATING,COOLING EQUIPMNT		666.6		666.1		690.0		645.5	MACH CHAUFFAGE,PIECES
7415	AIR–CONDITIONING MACHNRY	N 1018203	384.2	N 1031921	416.9	N 1061138	437.9	N 1055037	397.3	GROUPES CONDITION AIR
743	PUMPS NES,CENTRFUGES ETC		681.3		677.2		643.3		631.6	POMPES COMPRES,VENT ETC
7431	PUMPS FOR GASES ETC	MN 10513	486.0	MN 9637	474.7	MN 9045	439.8	N 7283792	413.6	POMPES AIR A VIDE,COMPRES
744	MECHANICAL HANDLING EQU		542.6		622.5		766.0		726.1	EQUIP MANUTENTION PIECES
7449	PTS NES OF MACHY OF 7442		244.8		299.6		387.8		377.7	PIECES DU 744.2
749	NONELEC MACH PTS,ACC NES		1062.7		1279.8		1343.1		1265.8	PIECES MACH NON ELEC NDA
7491	BALL,ROLLER,ETC BEARINGS		473.9		652.6		707.8		636.6	ROULEMENTS BILLES ETC
75	OFFICE MACHNES,ADP EQUIP		22567.8		28962.6		33071.4		34122.0	MACH BUREAU TRAIT AUTOM
751	OFFICE MACHINES	MN 27471	522.7	MN 30014	523.3	MN 29633	535.0	MN 31903	590.4	MACH,APPAREILS DE BUREAU
7512	CALCULATNG,ACCTG,ETC MCH	MN 24802	302.4	MN 27377	338.4	MN 27507	405.8	MN 29971	436.3	MACHINE A CALCULER ETC
752	AUTOMTIC DATA PROC EQUIP	MN 104128	14668.4	MN 107981	19538.3	MN 118360	23079.4	MN 131207	23224.0	MACH TRAIT INFORMATION
7522	DIGITAL COMPUTERS	N 3751669	2790.4	N 3699420	3496.4	N 1312255	1911.4	N 1040897	1454.3	MACH DIGITALES COMPLETES
7523	DIGITL CENTRL PROCESSORS	N 438570	461.1	N 774173	691.8	N 2336075	2199.9	N 2673261	2361.3	UNITES CENTRALES
7524	DIGITL CENTRL STOR UNITS	MN 59447	8924.6	MN 68559	11460.1	MN 79367	14236.6	MN 82776	14629.1	UNITES MEMOIRE CENTRALES
7525	ADP PERIPHERAL UNITS	MN 35887	1967.7	MN 29726	2951.2	MN 30343	3859.5	MN 39763	3930.2	UNITES PERIPHERIQUES

5. General Exports F.O.B. by Commodities according to the S.I.T.C. (Rev. 2) in million U.S. Dollars
Exportations Générales F.O.B. par Produits d'après la C.T.C.I. (Rév. 2) en millions de Dollars E.U.

SITC CTCI	COMMODITY	1994 QUANTITY QUANTITE	1994 VALUE VALEUR	1995 QUANTITY QUANTITE	1995 VALUE VALEUR	1996 QUANTITY QUANTITE	1996 VALUE VALEUR	1997 QUANTITY QUANTITE	1997 VALUE VALEUR	PRODUIT
7528	OFF–LINE DATA PROC EQUIP	N 4603959	524.7	N 5222283	939.0	N 5002273	872.1	N 4954043	849.4	MACH AUXIL TRAIT INFORM
759	OFFICE,ADP MCH PTS,ACCES		7376.8		8901.1		9457.1		10307.7	PIECES DU 751 ET 752
7599	ACCTG,ETC,ADP MCH PTS,AC		7226.8		8714.3		9183.5		10069.3	PIECES DU 751 ET 752
76	TELECOMM,SOUND EQUIPMENT		12394.3		12966.6		11652.6		9974.8	EQUIPMENT DE TELECOM
761	TELEVISION RECEIVERS	N 7407270	1654.8	N 7461391	1731.3	N 7632702	1795.2	N 5019760	1125.3	RECEPTEURS DE TELEVISION
7611	COLOUR TV RECEIVERS	N 7318860	1650.0	N 7415159	1728.6	N 7586523	1792.1	N 4988141	1123.4	RECEPTEURS COULEUR
762	RADIO BROADCAST RECEIVRS	MN 29014	2303.9	MN 23286	2098.9	MN 20460	1910.6	MN 16863	1517.1	RECEPTEURS RADIODIFFUSION
7621	MTR VEHC RADIO RECEIVERS	N 4646453	389.6	N 4905489	426.2	N 4908351	452.4	N 3860508	335.0	RECEPTEURS RADIO AUTO
7622	PORTABLE RADIO RECEIVERS	MN 16116	749.1	MN 11818	601.4	N 8821054	396.2	N 6919157	266.5	RECEPT PORTATIFS RADIO
7628	OTHER RADIO RECEIVERS	N 8251482	1165.4	N 6562639	1071.3	N 6730150	1062.0	N 6083177	915.7	AUTRES RECEPT RADIO
763	SOUND RECORDRS,PHONOGRPH	MN 26632	2349.2	MN 22143	2262.0	MN 16227	1787.5	MN 13542	1336.1	PHONO,APP ENREGISTREMENT
7638	OTHR SOUND APPARATUS ETC	MN 26424	2341.3	MN 21892	2254.5	MN 16200	1786.0	MN 13530	1335.4	AUT APP D'ENREGIS,REPROD
76381	TV IMAGE,SND RECRDRS ETC	N 8953588	1480.6	N 8986843	1516.0	N 7763120	1306.1	N 5801702	935.6	APP ENREG,REPRO IMAG,SON
76388	DICTATING MACHINES ETC	MN 17471	860.7	MN 12905	738.6	N 8437166	480.0	N 7728728	399.9	MACHINES A DICTER
764	TELECOM EQPT,PTS,ACC NES		6086.5		6874.6		6159.4		5996.5	EQUIP TELECOM,PIECES
7641	LINE TELEPHONE,ETC EQUIP	MN 25890	695.4	MN 29551	794.4	MN 22986	611.1	MN 17959	533.7	APP TELEPHON PAR FIL
7642	MICROPH,LOUDSPKR,AMPLIFR	MN 156386	375.0	MN 148269	406.6	MN 138472	380.4	MN 147994	351.7	MICRO,HAUT–PARLEUR,AMPLI
7643	TV,RADIO TRANSMITTRS ETC	MN 10421	127.0	N 5625410	288.0	N 4730452	542.8	N 6463523	817.1	APP EMET TELE RADIO
7648	TELECOMM EQUIPMENT NES	MN 22744	848.9	MN 28625	1253.5	MN 24821	874.2	MN 26238	810.5	APP TELECOM NDA
76481	RADIOTELEPHONE ETC RCVRS	N 5737630	632.0	N 8257415	921.8	N 6436139	720.0	N 7672638	675.7	RECEP RADIOTELEPHONIE
7649	PTS NES OF EQUIPMT OF 76		4040.5		4132.3		3751.1		3483.7	PIECES DE LA DIV 76
76493	TELECOMM EQUIPMT PTS NES		2001.3		2079.8		1829.9		1701.4	PIECES 761,762,764.3,8
76499	PARTS ETC OF SOUND EQUIP		1688.3		1722.4		1545.1		1425.5	PIECES NDA POUR 763
77	ELECTRIC MACHNRY NES ETC		17838.6		25511.2		27019.8		27794.9	MACH APP ELECT NDA
771	ELECTRIC POWER MACHY NES		819.4		1046.4		1072.1		1014.9	MACH PROD,TRANS ELECTR
7712	OTH ELEC POWER MACHY NES		587.5		787.9		835.6		816.4	AUT APP PROD TRANSF ELEC
772	SWITCHGEAR ETC,PARTS NES		2081.3		2451.5		2470.6		2507.4	APP COUPURE,SECT ETC
7721	SWITCHGEAR ETC		1180.8		1422.4		1413.8		1501.8	APP COUPURE,SECTIONMNT
7722	PRINTED CIRCUITS,PTS NES		492.3		590.8		617.8		585.3	CIRCUITS ET PIECES
7723	FIXED,VARIABLE RESISTORS		408.2		438.4		439.1		420.4	POTENTIOMETRES PIECES
773	ELECTR DISTRIBUTNG EQUIP		419.2		504.5		486.5		482.5	EQUIPMT DISTRIBUTION ELECT
7731	INSULATED WIRE,CABLE ETC	W 61357	372.9	W 54243	462.5	W 47288	438.1	W 48160	432.6	FILS,CABLES ISOLES ELECT
775	HOUSEHOLD TYPE EQUIP NES		492.5		531.7		557.6		536.8	MACH,APP USAGE DOMESTQUE
7758	ELECTRO–THERMIC APPL NES		312.2		315.4		321.4		321.4	APP ELECTROTHERMIQ NDA
776	TRANSISTORS,VALVES,ETC		12054.0		18392.6		19751.3		20519.4	LAMPES,TUBES,VALVES
7761	TV PICTURE TUBES	MN 9409	720.7	MN 9351	775.9	MN 9265	923.9	N 8772322	822.7	TUBES CATHODIQUES
7762	OTH ELECTRONIC TUBES ETC		218.6		482.9		594.3		610.7	AUT LAMPES ELECTRONIQUES
7763	DIODES,TRANSISTORS,ETC		1152.5		2024.8		2140.4		1998.0	DIODES,TRANSISTORS
7764	ELECTRONIC MICROCIRCUITS		9206.2		14242.2		14598.2		15687.5	MICROSTRUCTURES ELECTRON
7768	ELCTRNC COMP PTS,CRYSTLS		756.1		866.9		1494.6		1400.7	CRIST PIEZO–ELEC,PCS 776
77689	ELECTRNIC COMPON PTS NES		627.7		673.9		1307.1		1224.9	PIECES DU GROUPE 776
778	ELECTRICAL MACHINERY NES		1929.5		2525.3		2608.3		2667.8	AUTRES MACH ELECT NDA
7781	BATTERIES,ACCUMULATORS		279.7		372.2		447.2		458.4	PILES ET ACCUMULATEURS
7788	OTH ELEC MACHY,EQUIP NES		1385.1		1850.3		1852.0		1892.6	AUT MACH APP ELEC NDA
77884	ELECTRICAL CONDENSERS		933.5		1310.5		1317.9		1268.3	CONDENSATEURS ELECTRIQUES
78	ROAD VEHICLES		967.2		1193.2		1289.4		1300.6	VEHICULES ROUTIERS
784	MOTOR VEH PRTS,ACCES NES		287.8		392.6		488.0		503.0	PIECES 722,781,782,783
7849	OTHER MOTOR VEHCL PARTS		283.6		387.9		483.8		500.1	PIECES 722,781,782,783
785	CYCLES,ETC MOTRZD OR NOT		399.6		394.0		370.7		371.1	MOTOCYCLES SCOOTERS
7853	INVAL CARR, PTS OF 785		354.9		348.8		294.7		287.4	FAUTEUILS INVALIDES,PIECES
78539	PARTS,ACCES NES OF 785		354.7		348.5		294.6		287.2	PIECES DU 785
79	OTHR TRANSPORT EQUIPMENT		1105.5		1035.0		1212.4		1308.2	AUTRE MATERIEL TRANSPORT
792	AIRCRAFT ETC		233.3		380.4		539.1		672.1	APP NAVIGATION AERIENNE
7929	AIRCRAFT PARTS NES		196.6		268.5		384.0		527.4	PIECES DU 792
793	SHIPS AND BOATS ETC	N 5424	868.6		650.7	N 3992	670.4	N 13196	632.4	NAVIRES BATEAUX,ETC
7932	SHIPS AND BOATS NES	N 1356	841.6	N 1147	463.7	N 1182	585.0	N 1825	577.9	NAVIRES ET BATEAUX
79323	OTHER CARGO VESSELS	N 198	652.8	N 156	318.2	N 180	407.9	N 124	457.8	AUT BATEAUX TRANS MARCH
8	MISC MANUFACTURED GOODS		7438.5		8971.1		9390.1		9689.4	ART MANUFACTURES DIVERS
84	CLOTHING AND ACCESSORIES		1526.3		1464.9		1398.9		1491.5	VETEMENTS
845	OUTERWEAR KNIT NONELASTC	MN 116007	553.1	MN 105922	519.0	MN 104391	541.3	MN 110538	622.7	VET DESSOUS,ACCES BONNET
8459	— OTHER,CLTHG ACCESRYS	MN 78664	343.4	MN 73512	333.3	MN 66909	317.5	MN 71706	370.9	AUT VET DESSUS DE BONNE
846	UNDER GARMENTS KNITTED	MN 85753	338.0	MN 93063	372.3	MN 87302	353.1	MN 92937	378.8	SOUS VETS DE BONNETERIE
87	PRECISION INSTRUMNTS NES		1343.9		1648.1		1591.3		1733.6	INSTRUM,APPAR SCIENT NDA
872	MEDICAL INSTRUMENTS NES		412.0		507.0		484.4		536.4	INSTR,APP MEDIC–CHIR NDA
87202	OTH MEDICAL INSTRUMENTS		403.7		500.0		474.7		523.1	INSTRUM,APP MEDECINE
874	MEASURNG,CONTROLNG INSTR		730.1		866.7		865.9		897.9	INSTRUMENTS DE MESURE
88	PHOTO EQU,OPTICL GDS ETC		1368.5		1768.4		2038.0		2073.9	APP,FOURN PHOTO,OP,MONTR
882	PHOTO,CINEMA SUPPLIES		493.3		554.1		572.4		530.5	PRODUITS PHOTO,CINEMA
8822	PHOTO FILM EXC DEV CINMA		315.3		325.7		276.9		220.0	PLAQUES,PELLICULES,FILMS
885	WATCHES AND CLOCKS		563.9		815.3		977.3		1013.8	HORLOGERIE
8851	WATCHES,MOVEMENTS,CASES		400.8		619.2		752.1		771.4	MONTRES,MOUVEMENTS,BOITES
88511	WATCHES		329.3		558.7		729.1		728.9	MONTRES POCHE,BRACELET
89	MISC MANUFCTRD GOODS NES		2732.0		3574.5		3806.5		3853.1	ART MANUFACTURES DIVERS
892	PRINTED MATTER		483.8		609.1		594.9		568.5	IMPRIMES
8921	PRINTED BOOKS,GLOBES,ETC		355.1		458.8		438.3		395.8	LIVRES,BROCHURES,CARTES
89211	PRINTED BOOKS,PAMPHLETS		310.6		419.3		402.2		367.7	LIVRES,BROCHURES
893	ARTICLES OF PLASTIC NES		593.2		665.5		653.4		651.2	OUVRAGES EN MAT DIVIS 58
8939	MISC PLASTIC ARTICLES		415.2		448.3		466.5		461.2	ART DIVERS EN MAT DIV 58
89399	OTHR PLASTC ARTICLES NES		403.7		432.3		443.8		434.9	AUT OUV MAT DIV 58
894	TOYS,SPORTING GOODS,ETC		328.2		463.9		458.9		245.1	VOITURES ENFANTS,JOUETS
897	GOLD,SILVER WARE,JEWELRY		316.8		658.2		788.3		693.4	BIJOUTERIE,ORFEVRERIE
8973	PREC JEWLRY,GLD–SILVWARE		295.9		646.7		777.7		681.6	BIJOUX OR,ARGENT ORFEVRE
89731	PRECIOUS METAL JEWELLERY		280.5		614.8		745.7		655.9	ART BIJOUTERIE,JOAILLER
898	MUSICAL INSTRUMENTS,PTS		703.9		841.5		932.3		1298.9	INSTRUMENTS DE MUSIQUE
8983	SOUND RECRDNG TAPE,DISCS	MN 282778	663.4	MN 365446	800.9	MN 406723	885.0	MN 448495	1243.8	SUPPORTS SON POUR 763
89831	PREPD SND RECORDNG MEDIA	MN 251610	262.9	MN 338259	347.1	MN 384806	592.6	MN 413772	826.3	SUPPORTS PREPARES
89832	RECORDED DISCS,TAPES ETC	MN 31168	400.6	MN 27187	453.9	MN 21917	292.4	MN 34723	417.5	DISQUES,PHONO,BANDES
9	GOODS NOT CLASSD BY KIND		1363.3		2854.2		3457.3		4072.1	ART TRANSACT NON CLASSES
931	*SPECIAL TRANSACTIONS		1189.7		2640.0		3096.1		3512.1	TRANS.SPECIALES
971	*GOLD,NON MONETARY NES	K 13120	163.1		210.5	K 28055	358.6	K 52510	557.3	OR NON MONETAIRE
97101	NONMON GLD UNWRT,SEMIMFD	K 12191	161.6	K 14295	195.0	K 23700	313.8	K 42243	470.1	OR,ALLIAGES D'OR BRUTS

1. HISTORICAL SERIES, 1993–1997 GENERAL TRADE, IMPORTS F.O.B., EXPORTS F.O.B.
SERIES HISTORIQUES, 1993–1997 COMMERCE GENERAL, IMPORTATIONS F.O.B., EXPORTATIONS F.O.B

YEAR ANNEE	VALUE IN MILLION CS KORUNY (CSK) VALEUR EN MILLION CS KORUNY (CSK) MERCHANDISE –MARCHANDISE IMPORTS	EXPORTS	GOLD –OR IMPORTS	EXPORTS	CONVERSION FACTORS U.S. CENTS PER CS KORUNA (CSK) FACTEURS DE CONVERSION CENTS E.U. PAR CS KORUNA (CSK) IMPORTS	EXPORTS	INDEX NUMBERS –INDICES QUANTUM IMPORTS	EXPORTS	UNIT VALUE VALEUR UNITAIRE IMPORTS	EXPORTS
1993	195034.00	167724.00			3.2610	3.2610				
1994	208227.00	211085.00			3.1230	3.1230				
1995	260791.00	255096.00			3.3693	3.3695				
1996	340902.90	270642.90			3.2583	3.2583				
1997	345049.00	295574.00			2.9768	2.9742				

2. IMPORTS BY BROAD ECONOMIC CATEGORY AND EXPORTS BY INDUSTRIAL ORIGIN. (PERCENTAGE OF TOTAL VALUE)
IMPORTATIONS PAR CATEGORIES ECONOMIQUES ET EXPORTATIONS PAR BRANCHE D'ACTIVITE.(EN POURCENTAGE DE LA VALEUR TOTALE)

IMPORTS – IMPORTATIONS

	1991	1992	1993	1994	1995	1996	1997
TOTAL IMPORTS–IMPORTATIONS TOTALES				100.	100.	100.	100.
1 FOOD BEV–ALIMENTATION BOISSONS				7.0	6.7	5.7	6.0
11 PRIMARY–PRODUITS DE BASE				3.3	3.0	2.4	2.5
111 FOR INDUSTRY–POUR L'INDUSTRIE				1.4	1.1	0.9	1.0
112 FOR HOUSEHOLDS–POUR LES MENAGES				1.9	1.9	1.5	1.5
12 PROCESSED–PRODUITS ELABORES				3.7	3.8	3.3	3.5
121 FOR INDUSTRY–POUR L'INDUSTRIE				0.3	0.3	0.2	0.3
122 FOR HOUSEHOLDS–POUR LES MENAGES				3.3	3.5	3.0	3.3
2 IND SUPPLIES–APPROV INDUSTRIELS				32.8	33.7	26.2	27.0
21 PRIMARY–PRODUITS DE BASE				4.3	4.3	3.3	2.0
22 PROCESSED–PRODUITS ELABORES				28.5	29.5	22.9	25.0
3 FUELS–COMBUSTIBLES				19.2	11.9	11.7	11.8
31 PRIMARY–PRODUITS DE BASE				18.0	10.5	9.8	9.4
32 PROCESSED–PRODUITS ELABORES				1.2	1.5	1.9	2.4
321 MOTOR SPIRIT–ESSENCE				0.6			
322 OTHER–AUTRES				0.6	1.5	1.9	2.4
4 MACHINERY–EQUIPEMENT				22.9	22.3	19.2	24.0
41 CAPITAL EQUIPMENT–MACHINES				19.9	18.9	16.4	20.5
42 PARTS–PIECES ACCESSOIRES				3.0	3.4	2.8	3.5
5 TRANSPORT–TRANSPORT				6.2	7.0	11.4	9.2
51 PASSENGER CARS–AUTOMOBILES				1.9	2.3	6.6	4.1
52 OTHER–AUTRES				1.7	2.0	2.0	2.6
521 INDUSTRIAL–INDUSTRIELS				1.6	1.9	2.0	2.5
522 NON INDUSTRIAL–NON INDUSTRIEL				0.1	0.1	0.1	0.1
53 PARTS–PIECES ACCESSOIRES				2.6	2.7	2.8	2.6
6 CONSUM GOODS–BIENS CONSOMMATION				11.3	11.3	10.8	13.1
61 DURABLE–DURABLES				2.2	2.3	2.3	2.8
62 SEMI DURABLE–SEMI DURABLES				4.6	4.3	4.0	5.0
63 NON DURABLE–NON DURABLES				4.5	4.7	4.5	5.3
7 GOODS NES–BIENS NDA				0.7	7.1	15.1	8.9

EXPORTS – EXPORTATIONS

	1991	1992	1993	1994	1995	1996	1997
TOTAL EXPORTS–EXPORTATIONS TOTALES				100.	100.	100.	100.
1 AGRICULTURE				2.9	3.0	1.7	2.0
2 MINING QUARRY–INDUS EXTRACTIVES				1.1	0.9	0.9	0.7
3 MANUFACTURING–IND MANUFACTUR				96.0	96.1	97.3	97.2
31 FOOD BEV TOBACCO–ALIM BOISS TAB				4.0	3.9	3.5	3.6
32 TEXTILES–INDUSTRIES TEXTILES				10.5	9.0	8.3	9.2
33 WOOD & PRODUCTS–BOIS & PRODUITS				3.1	3.1	2.6	2.7
34 PAPER & PRODUCTS–PAPIER & PRODT				5.1	5.7	5.8	5.6
35 CHEMICALS–INDUSTRIES CHIMIQUES				21.3	20.4	18.7	17.5
36 NON METAL MIN–MIN NON METAL				4.0	4.3	3.7	3.6
37 BASIC METAL–IND METAL BASE				19.5	19.6	8.6	16.7
38 METAL MANUF–MANUF METAL				28.1	27.2	30.7	34.6
39 OTH MANUF IND–AUTRES MANUF				0.5	2.9	15.5	3.7

3. TRADE BY PRINCIPAL COUNTRIES OF ORIGIN AND DESTINATION (VALUE IN MILLION U.S. DOLLARS)
ECHANGES SELON LES PRINCIPAUX PAYS D'ORIGINE ET DE DESTINATION (VALEUR EN MILLIONS DE DOLLARS EU)

COUNTRIES–PAYS	GENERAL IMPORTS F.O.B. IMPORTATIONS GENERALES F.O.B.				
	1993	1994	1995	1996	1997
World	6453.7	6611.0	8770.4	10936.3	10264.4
Africa		34.2	59.6	57.4	43.4
Americas	9.0	271.7	328.1	415.4	462.3
– Northern America		201.7	235.6	322.5	378.0
– LAIA	9.0	49.0	61.0	59.9	65.4
– CACM		16.7	25.0	23.8	14.2
– Caribbean		0.7	1.5	2.4	1.6
– Rest of America		3.5	5.1	6.7	3.1
Asia excl fmr USSR	41.0	275.9	466.5	730.4	597.3
– Middle East		18.1	35.6	39.5	31.1
Asia former USSR		40.0	46.3	37.3	19.9
Europe excl fmr USSR	4115.0	4610.5	6181.0	7489.8	7210.7
– European Union	1524.0	2212.7	3048.7	4030.5	4054.7
– Eastern Europe	2546.0	2244.8	2892.2	3193.3	2895.2
– Rest of Europe	45.0	153.0	240.2	266.0	260.9
Europe former USSR	1459.0	1338.0	1625.5	2142.7	1882.0
Oceania		12.0	17.1	14.7	15.3
Other		28.7	46.2	48.7	33.6
Czech Republic	2321.0	1957.9	2433.6	2682.0	2360.1
Russian Federation	1302.0	1194.7	1456.0	1933.1	1596.7
Germany/Allemagne	746.0	888.1	1251.5	1591.2	1552.4
Austria/Autriche	399.0	381.5	447.7	509.4	498.6
Italy/Italie	197.0	289.7	405.8	650.6	572.3
France, Monaco	99.0	147.7	214.8	348.0	382.7
Poland/Pologne	127.0	157.5	243.3	269.5	286.0
USA/Etats–Unis d'Amer		187.7	215.3	293.7	336.9
Hungary/Hongrie	86.0	110.8	193.2	217.0	225.5
Ukraine	157.0	118.6	122.7	173.3	259.5
United Kingdom	83.0	105.7	148.2	203.2	256.1
Netherlands/Pays–Bas		110.1	150.6	199.2	219.8
Japan/Japon		81.6	130.7	189.4	179.1
Switzerland,Liechtenst.		95.1	148.1	161.3	152.4
Belgium–Luxembourg		85.1	109.1	151.7	156.5
Sweden/Suède		43.3	101.1	87.6	109.3
China/Chine	31.0	37.6	57.8	81.0	105.1
Finland/Finlande		55.2	73.6	88.5	86.1
Spain/Espagne		40.0	61.6	95.6	103.7
Korea, Republic of		16.8	37.6	191.4	36.5
Other Asia n.e.s.		40.0	53.0	72.7	77.7
Denmark/Danemark		40.5	50.9	62.7	64.8
Slovenia/Slovénie		29.6	48.0	56.4	52.8
Areas n.e.s.		5.9	46.2	48.7	6.5
Belarus/Bélarus		19.0	39.0	28.0	20.3
India/Inde	10.0	17.8	31.2	26.2	20.7
Canada		11.6	20.2	28.8	41.2
Malaysia/Malaisie		8.4	26.6	36.1	30.5
China, Hong Kong SAR		17.3	32.1	23.2	25.4
Ireland/Irlande		13.9	18.2	27.5	31.1
Turkey/Turquie		11.8	26.8	29.3	21.0
So. African Customs Un		16.6	31.2	22.3	17.4
Brazil/Brésil	9.0	15.6	15.8	18.5	20.2
Croatia/Croatie		17.3	20.3	21.3	20.2
Israel/Israël		7.6	11.3	18.0	28.8
Yugoslavia/Yougoslavie	45.0	0.4	0.2	5.3	12.9
Indonesia/Indonésie		8.6	16.4	17.5	18.5
Norway,Svalbard and JM		6.8	17.6	17.2	18.7
Uzbekistan/Ouzbékistan		10.8	21.0	15.7	10.2
Kazakhstan		22.5	14.6	11.5	6.0

COUNTRIES–PAYS	GENERAL EXPORTS F.O.B. EXPORTATIONS GENERALES F.O.B.				
	1993	1994	1995	1996	1997
Monde	5392.5	6690.2	8577.5	8824.1	8790.0
Afrique		54.1	77.7	49.3	37.5
Amériques	2.0	211.2	189.9	183.1	220.1
– Amérique du Nord		145.7	127.6	130.2	165.3
– ALAI	2.0	56.4	47.9	38.1	38.3
– MCAC		5.1	7.4	5.8	4.6
– Caraïbes		3.0	4.7	7.3	8.9
– Autre Amérique		0.9	2.3	1.7	2.9
Asie anc. URSS exclus	127.0	331.4	342.2	312.8	192.1
– Moyen–Orient	47.0	93.5	128.3	98.4	77.6
Asie ancienne URSS		29.8	23.8	28.9	19.5
Europe anc. URSS exclus	4212.0	5620.0	7343.7	7629.7	7639.9
– Union Européenne	1389.0	2343.0	3208.2	3644.9	3955.0
– Europe de l'Est	2733.0	3095.6	3854.6	3645.8	3325.5
– Autre de l'Europe	90.0	181.4	280.9	339.0	359.4
Europe ancienne URSS	396.0	437.3	588.3	612.2	665.3
Océanie		4.0	4.8	6.6	9.2
Autre		2.4	7.2	1.5	6.4
Czech Republic	2310.0	2501.7	3024.0	2737.8	2343.5
Germany/Allemagne	828.0	1143.9	1612.5	1871.1	1958.3
Austria/Autriche	271.0	351.4	425.9	533.9	629.0
Hungary/Hongrie	247.0	365.7	390.9	403.3	412.2
Italy/Italie	148.0	288.3	413.4	431.4	497.8
Poland/Pologne	159.0	189.3	378.0	426.9	484.3
Russian Federation	256.0	277.6	330.8	307.8	328.4
Ukraine	140.0	116.7	190.8	235.9	255.6
France, Monaco	87.0	113.3	171.4	186.8	204.4
Netherlands/Pays–Bas		119.0	150.8	166.7	167.1
United Kingdom	55.0	85.6	112.4	135.3	144.6
USA/Etats–Unis d'Amer		108.4	107.6	119.0	142.0
Belgium–Luxembourg		88.4	93.7	112.2	138.1
Slovenia/Slovénie		45.2	94.8	87.5	96.2
Switzerland,Liechtenst.		46.2	70.4	95.9	98.8
Croatia/Croatie		60.6	72.3	73.4	78.1
India/Inde	15.0	61.2	67.1	64.7	37.5
Spain/Espagne		39.8	61.8	54.3	66.9
Yugoslavia/Yougoslavie	90.0	2.6	4.0	49.1	57.5
Romania/Roumanie		26.7	42.6	57.2	61.8
Sweden/Suède		39.7	58.6	39.8	42.3
China/Chine	65.0	23.1	17.0	38.6	10.8
Finland/Finlande		21.7	38.2	32.9	31.5
Turkey/Turquie		29.3	40.8	19.0	21.7
Syrian Arab Republic	47.0	24.6	17.3	14.8	7.0
Greece/Grèce		20.1	26.2	32.6	30.7
Denmark/Danemark		19.6	28.5	31.7	26.0
Belarus/Bélarus		18.2	33.6	24.8	27.9
Thailand/Thaïlande		53.0	19.0	21.0	4.3
Bulgaria/Bulgarie	17.0	11.6	18.1	19.7	23.5
Canada		37.3	20.1	10.9	21.6
Lithuania/Lituanie		18.2	22.6	25.3	22.5
Egypt/Egypte		18.8	21.3	16.8	9.3
Malaysia/Malaisie		20.4	20.0	13.1	4.5
Japan/Japon		6.2	17.7	19.0	12.0
Indonesia/Indonésie		12.4	10.9	22.0	8.9
Lebanon/Liban		11.5	14.7	11.9	12.3
Argentina/Argentine		10.7	11.6	13.3	13.7
TFYR Macedonia		16.3	18.4	6.7	5.5
Saudi Arabia		5.7	20.3	16.3	4.4

(VALUE AS PERCENTAGE OF WORLD TOTAL)(VALEURS EN POURCENTAGE DU TOTAL MONDIAL)

	1988	1989	1990	1991	1992	1993	1994	1995	1996	1997
Africa							0.5	0.7	0.5	0.4
Americas						0.1	4.1	3.7	3.8	4.5
– Northern America							3.1	2.7	2.9	3.7
– LAIA						0.1	0.7	0.7	0.5	0.6
– CACM							0.3	0.3	0.2	0.1
– Caribbean							0.0	0.0	0.0	0.0
– Rest of America							0.1	0.1	0.1	0.0
Asia excl fmr USSR						0.6	4.2	5.3	6.7	5.8
– Middle East							0.3	0.4	0.4	0.3
Asia former USSR							0.6	0.5	0.3	0.2
Europe excl fmr USSR						63.8	69.7	70.5	68.5	70.2
– European Union						23.6	33.5	34.8	36.9	39.5
– Eastern Europe						39.5	34.0	33.0	29.2	28.2
– Rest of Europe						0.7	2.3	2.7	2.4	2.5
Europe former USSR						22.6	20.2	18.5	19.6	18.3
Oceania							0.2	0.2	0.1	0.1
Other							0.4	0.5	0.4	0.3
Czech Republic						36.0	29.6	27.7	24.5	23.0
Russian Federation						20.2	18.1	16.6	17.7	15.6
Germany/Allemagne						11.6	13.4	14.3	14.5	15.1
Austria/Autriche						6.2	5.8	5.1	4.7	4.9
Italy/Italie						3.1	4.4	4.6	5.9	5.6
France, Monaco						1.5	2.2	2.4	3.2	3.7
Poland/Pologne						2.0	2.4	2.8	2.5	2.8
USA/Etats–Unis d'Amer							2.8	2.5	2.7	3.3
Hungary/Hongrie						1.3	1.7	2.2	2.0	2.2
Ukraine						2.4	1.8	1.4	1.6	2.5

	1988	1989	1990	1991	1992	1993	1994	1995	1996	1997
Afrique							0.8	0.9	0.6	0.4
Amériques						0.0	3.2	2.2	2.1	2.5
– Amérique du Nord							2.2	1.5	1.5	1.9
– ALAI						0.0	0.8	0.6	0.4	0.4
– MCAC							0.1	0.1	0.1	0.1
– Caraïbes							0.0	0.1	0.1	0.1
– Autre Amérique							0.0	0.0	0.0	0.0
Asie anc. URSS exclus						2.4	5.0	4.0	3.5	2.2
– Moyen–Orient						0.9	1.4	1.5	1.1	0.9
Asie ancienne URSS							0.4	0.3	0.3	0.2
Europe anc. URSS exclus						78.1	84.0	85.6	86.5	86.9
– Union Européenne						25.8	35.0	37.4	41.3	45.0
– Europe de l'Est						50.7	46.3	44.9	41.3	37.8
– Autre de l'Europe						1.7	2.7	3.3	3.8	4.1
Europe ancienne URSS						7.3	6.5	6.9	6.9	7.6
Océanie							0.1	0.1	0.1	0.1
Autre							0.0	0.1	0.0	0.1
Czech Republic						42.8	37.4	35.3	31.0	26.7
Germany/Allemagne						15.4	17.1	18.8	21.2	22.3
Austria/Autriche						5.0	5.3	5.0	6.1	7.2
Hungary/Hongrie						4.6	5.5	4.6	4.6	4.7
Italy/Italie						2.7	4.3	4.8	4.9	5.7
Poland/Pologne						2.9	2.8	4.4	4.8	5.5
Russian Federation						4.7	4.1	3.9	3.5	3.7
Ukraine						2.6	1.7	2.2	2.7	2.9
France, Monaco						1.6	1.7	2.0	2.1	2.3
Netherlands/Pays–Bas							1.8	1.8	1.9	1.9

4. General Imports F.O.B. by Commodities according to the S.I.T.C. (Rev. 2) in million U.S. Dollars
Importations Générales F.O.B. par Produits d'après la C.T.C.I. (Rév. 2) en millions de Dollars E.U.

SITC CTCI	COMMODITY	1994 QUANTITY QUANTITE	1994 VALUE VALEUR	1995 QUANTITY QUANTITE	1995 VALUE VALEUR	1996 QUANTITY QUANTITE	1996 VALUE VALEUR	1997 QUANTITY QUANTITE	1997 VALUE VALEUR	PRODUIT
	ALL COMMODITIES		6611.0		8770.5		10936.4		10264.5	TOUS PRODUITS
0	FOOD AND LIVE ANIMALS		458.1		594.3		628.9		632.5	ALIMENTS,ANIMAUX VIVANTS
02	DAIRY PRODCTS,BIRDS'EGGS		25.3		25.7		25.4		23.0	PRODUITS LAITIERS,OEUFS
03	FISH AND PREPARATIONS		27.8		30.9		34.3		35.7	POISSONS ET PREPARATIONS
04	CEREALS AND PREPARATIONS		54.9		55.9		87.5		105.9	CEREALES ET PRODUITS
048	CEREAL ETC PREPARATIONS	W 20009	24.8	W 26935	37.8	W 45270	46.2	W 39467	50.4	PREPTNS A BASE CEREALES
0484	BAKERY PRODUCTS	W 9061	15.4	W 14309	26.3	W 17366	31.0	W 17969	31.0	PRODUITS DE BOULANGERIE
05	VEGETABLES AND FRUIT		109.1		159.0		170.7		158.0	LEGUMES ET FRUITS
054	VEG ETC FRSH,SMPLY PRSVD	W 140823	21.6	W 122535	41.3	W 89181	28.5	W 61375	24.9	LEGUMES FRAIS,CONG,SECS
057	FRUIT,NUTS,FRESH,DRIED	W 151723	63.6	W 184994	81.3	W 239124	93.5	W 177975	86.4	FRUITS FRAIS OU SECS
0573	BANANA,PLANTAIN,FRSH,DRY	W 56876	24.1	W 74790	30.0	W 78120	36.0	W 66401	30.9	BANANES FRAICHES,SECHEES
058	FRUIT PRESERVED,PREPARED	W 23458	19.8	W 36128	30.3	W 57938	40.7	W 51218	36.4	CONSERVES DE FRUITS
06	SUGAR AND PREPS,HONEY		25.2		45.1		25.3		16.7	SUCRES ET PRODUITS
061	SUGAR AND HONEY	W 37973	14.6	W 57334	29.8	W 21021	10.9	W 9389	3.7	SUCRES ET MIEL
07	COFFEE,TEA,COCOA,SPICES		87.5		114.1		102.4		104.2	CAFE,THE,CACAO,EPICES
071	COFFEE AND SUBSTITUTES		37.2	W 13909	57.0	W 13415	37.7	W 13637	48.1	CAFE ET SUCCEDANES
0711	COFFEE GREEN,ROASTED,SUB		33.9	W 13324	51.0	W 13297	37.1	W 12584	38.7	CAFE TORREFIE OU DECAFEINE
07111	COFFEE GREEN,HUSKS,SKINS	W 11823	26.8	W 11523	42.9	W 11356	29.4	W 9359	26.6	CAFE NON TORREFIE
073	CHOCOLATE AND PRODUCTS	W 10765	28.4	W 10813	36.3	W 12979	35.2	W 13746	34.0	CHOCOLAT
081	*FEEDING STUFF FOR ANIML	W 157124	55.1	W 211626	73.5	W 197458	84.4	W 202763	81.8	NOURRITURE POUR ANIMAUX
0813	OILCAKE AND OTH RESIDUES	W 110362	27.4	W 134505	32.6	W 134157	38.1	W 145989	42.4	TOURTEAUX
08131	— OF SOYA BEANS	W 105282	26.2	W 134505	32.6	W 134157	38.1	W 145989	42.4	TOURTEAUX DE SOJA
0819	FOOD WASTE AND FEED NES	W 29140	20.6	W 61941	33.5	W 47814	37.5	W 43923	31.7	DECHETS,ALIMENTS NDA
08199	FODDER NES,INCL SWEETNED	W 27824	20.1	W 61599	33.4	W 47451	37.4	W 42104	31.1	PREPARATIONS FOURRAGERES
09	MISC EDIBLE PRODUCTS		42.3		52.7		67.9		70.7	PREP ALIMENTAIRES DIVERSES
098	EDIBLE PRODCTS,PREPS NES	W 19555	31.0	W 21952	37.2	W 30711	49.8	W 32344	55.5	PREP ALIMENTAIRES NDA
09809	MISC FOOD PREPRTIONS NES	W 7185	14.9	W 9464	19.6	W 14650	29.6	W 18634	36.3	PREP ALIMENTAIRES NDA
1	BEVERAGES AND TOBACCO		85.4		95.7		111.9		118.9	BOISSONS ET TABACS
11	BEVERAGES		37.5		46.7		55.9		54.0	BOISSONS
112	ALCOHOLIC BEVERAGES		23.9	W 79396	31.5	W 94453	33.7	W 77463	34.0	BOISSONS ALCOOLIQUES
12	TOBACCO AND MANUFACTURES		47.9		49.0		56.1		64.9	TABACS BRUTS FABRIQUES
122	TOBACCO,MANUFACTURED		36.3	W 4688	38.8	W 5495	46.0	W 6083	55.6	TABACS FABRIQUES
1222	CIGARETTES		34.2	W 4607	38.2	W 5455	45.7	W 5124	49.0	CIGARETTES
2	CRUDE MATERLS,EXCL FUELS		348.7		509.6		517.6		334.0	MAT BRUTES NON COMESTIBLES
23	RUBBER, CRUDE		45.0		95.8		84.1		49.4	CAOUTCHOUC BRUT
232	NATURAL RUBBER,GUMS	W 13445	14.4	W 19679	33.4	W 20751	36.6	W 16654	23.3	LATEX CAOUTCHOUC NATUREL
23202	OTHER NATURAL RUBBER	W 12536	13.0	W 19140	32.3	W 19863	35.2	W 14896	20.9	CAOUTCHOUC NATUREL
233	RUBBER,SYNTHTIC,RECLAIMD	W 30837	30.6	W 44793	62.4	W 33666	47.6	W 20832	26.1	LATEX CAOUTCH SYNTH REGEN
2331	SYNTHETIC RUBBER ETC	W 29549	30.1	W 43366	61.7	W 32389	46.9	W 19888	25.6	LATEX CAOUTCH SYNTHETIQUE
251	*PULP AND WASTE PAPER	W 63259	19.4	W 49088	32.0	W 143421	49.1	W 169409	36.2	PATES A PAPIER,DECHETS
26	TEXTILE FIBRES AND WASTE		36.5		39.2		43.0		38.9	FIBRES TEXTILES
27	CRUDE FERTLZR,MINRLS NES		37.7		42.6		45.2		45.0	ENGRAIS MINERAUX BRUTS
278	OTHER CRUDE MINERALS	W 451262	23.7	W 389967	25.8	W 500723	30.6	W 464677	29.8	AUTRES MINERAUX BRUTS
28	METALLIFEROUS ORES,SCRAP		149.3		220.5		227.2		98.3	MINERAIS METAL,DECHETS
281	IRON ORE,CONCENTRATES	W 4233539	90.4	W 4888071	128.8	W 4180036	113.8	W 5178	0.3	MINERAIS DE FER
2816	IRON ORE AGGLOMERATES	W 3408231	76.6	W 4523565	111.7	W 4129280	111.5			MINERAIS AGGLOMERES
287	BASE METAL ORES,CONC NES	W 546745	44.9	W 434239	63.3	W 556615	93.8	W 454485	75.9	MINERAIS METAUX COMMUNS
2873	ALUMINIUM ORES,ALUMINA	W 198299	6.6	W 242095	25.5	W 354143	57.5	W 300882	55.9	MINERAIS D'ALUMINIUM
28732	ALUMINA(ALUMINIUM OXIDE)	W 7186	1.6	W 103624	21.5	W 222508	54.1	W 215852	53.2	ALUMINE (OXYDE ALUMINIUM)
2877	MANGANESE ORE,CONCENTRTE	W 195929	20.3	W 80197	8.2	W 120870	16.1	W 113852	13.6	MINERAIS DE MANGANESE
29	CRUDE ANIMAL,VEG MAT NES		22.9		32.2		33.6		38.4	MATIERES BRUTES ANIM,VEGET
292	CRUDE VEG MATERIALS NES	W 13568	19.8	W 8502	28.1	W 7685	27.3	W 10231	32.1	MAT BRUTES VEGETALES NDA
3	MINERAL FUELS ETC		1280.2		1045.7		1278.0		1211.1	COMBUSTIBLES MINERAUX LUB
32	COAL,COKE AND BRIQUETTES		274.2		310.1		328.2		295.2	HOUILLES,COKES,BRIQUETTES
322	COAL,LIGNITE AND PEAT	W 8604941	247.3	W 8625242	289.3	W 8524314	304.1	W 7018137	278.2	HOUILLES,LIGNITES,TOURBE
3222	OTH COAL,NOT AGGLOMERATD	W 4956290	186.8	W 4842520	221.5	W 4994457	237.8	W 4689823	236.6	AUTRES HOUILLES
3223	LIGNITE,NOT AGGLOMERATED	W 3460896	54.1	W 3695506	64.7	W 3355351	59.3	W 2175449	34.9	LIGNITES
323	BRIQUETS,COKE,SEMI–COKE	W 519101	26.9	W 256607	20.9	W 274202	24.1	W 201468	17.0	BRIQUETTES
3232	COKE,SEMI–COKE,RTRT CRBN	W 265528	22.3	W 200281	19.4	W 237402	23.1	W 180238	16.4	COKES ET SEMI–COKES
33	PETROLEUM AND PRODUCTS		554.6		703.2		850.1		802.1	PETROLE ET DERIVES
333	CRUDE PETROLEUM	W 4825407	498.6	W 5301328	622.7	W 5443068	762.5	W 5335407	681.6	HUILES BRUTES DE PETROLE
334	PETROLEUM PRODUCTS,REFIN	W 262286	44.0	W 368254	63.6	W 354734	69.2	W 476346	96.0	PRODUITS RAFFINES
3341	GASOLINE,OTH LIGHT OILS	W 259937	37.2							ESSENCES POUR MOTEURS
341	*GAS,NATURAL AND MANUFCT		441.6	W 9013	2.4	W 20318	3.5	W 15821	3.2	GAZ NATUREL,GAZ MANUFACT
3414	PETROLEUM GASES, GASEOUS	W 3688848	439.7	W 1201	0.2		0.1		0.1	GAZ DE PETROLE GAZEUX
351	*ELECTRIC CURRENT		9.9		30.1		96.4		110.8	ENERGIE ELECTRIQUE
5	CHEMCLS,RELATED PROD NES		844.3		1142.3		1172.3		1194.0	PRODUITS CHIMIQUES
51	ORGANIC CHEMICALS		190.8		261.5		200.4		192.6	PROD CHIMIQ ORGANIQUES
511	HYDROCARBONS NES,DERIVS	W 101473	33.0	W 122198	55.0	W 104133	40.9	W 97507	44.7	HYDROCARBURES NDA
5111	ACYCLIC HYDROCARBONS	W 42668	12.7	W 55217	29.6	W 53748	24.6	W 49892	26.8	HYDROCARBURES ACYCLIQUES
512	ALCOHOLS,PHENOLS ETC	W 147775	46.0	W 57081	39.4	W 35459	21.3	W 37047	17.6	PHENOLS,PHENOLS–ALCOOLS
5121	ACYCLIC ALCOHOLS,DERIVS	W 145158	41.4	W 54027	33.1	W 33328	17.9	W 34808	14.4	ALCOOLS ACYCLIQUES
513	CARBOXYLIC ACIDS ETC		38.9	W 48016	61.6	W 39571	39.4	W 42333	33.9	ACIDES CARBOXYLIQUES
5138	POLYACIDS AND DERIVATIVS		19.1	W 26926	37.2	W 21402	18.7	W 26301	17.0	ACIDES POLYCARBOXYLIQUES
514	NITROGEN–FNCTN COMPOUNDS		23.6	W 26872	36.8	W 37502	44.2	W 34180	38.0	COMPOSES FONCT AZOTEES
515	ORG–INORG COMPOUNDS ETC	W 29412	40.7	W 29516	54.0	W 18596	37.6	W 25017	41.9	COMPOSES ORGANO–MINERAUX
5156	HETEROCYCLIC CMPDS ETC	W 28853	38.0	W 28484	49.3	W 17211	32.0	W 23647	36.5	COMPOSES HETEROCYCLIQUES
51561	LACTAMS	W 27967	33.6	W 27701	43.1	W 16231	23.7	W 22843	30.4	LACTAMES .
52	INORGANIC CHEMICALS		76.8		95.0		99.0		80.4	PROD CHIM INORGANIQUES
522	INORG ELEMNTS,OXIDES,ETC	W 214361	45.4	W 235884	60.8	W 239170	60.1	W 236936	48.8	ELEMENTS INORGANIQUES
523	OTHR INORG CHEMICALS ETC	W 111757	30.7	W 105314	33.1	W 126564	37.6	W 117650	29.9	AUT PRODUITS CHIMIQUES INORG
53	DYES,TANNING,COLOUR PROD		74.5		90.0		99.3		98.5	PROD TEINTURE,COLORANTS
533	PIGMENTS,PAINTS,ETC	W 68336	60.2	W 36105	75.9	W 41217	82.6	W 45010	84.3	PIGMENTS,PEINTURES,VERNIS
5334	VARNISHES,DISTEMPERS ETC	W 48379	27.4	W 15342	35.1	W 15338	40.9	W 15575	40.0	PEINTURES A L'EAU
541	*MEDICINAL,PHARM PRODUCT	K 8284936	162.1	MK 10396	266.5	MK 10612	314.4	MK 10534	341.0	PROD MEDICINAUX PHARMACEUT
5417	MEDICAMENTS	K 6050657	124.9	K 7575683	210.0	K 8318448	253.5	K 8444350	282.7	MEDICAMENTS
54171	— CONTAINNG ANTIBIOTICS	K 385169	11.9	K 576052	27.6	K 609124	39.3	K 533188	39.2	MED CONTN ANTIBIOTIQUES
54172	— CONTAINING HORMONES	K 756212	17.7	K 1245486	42.3	K 1583689	58.8	K 1333281	60.7	MED CONTENANT HORMONES
54179	— CONTNG OTH SUBSTANCES	K 4847488	94.4	K 5702988	138.8	K 6031773	150.8	K 6467653	178.2	MED CONT AUT SUBSTANCES
55	PERFUME,CLEANING ETC PRD		84.5		95.7		105.0		119.4	PROD POUR PARFUM,TOILETTE
553	PERFUMERY,COSMETICS,ETC	W 10955	39.1	W 10759	44.8	W 14459	56.0	W 18396	65.3	PRODUITS DE PARFUMERIE
554	SOAP,CLEANSING ETC PREPS		39.5	W 46775	44.3	W 45558	41.4	W 51020	45.6	SAVONS,PRODUITS DETERSIFS
5542	WASHING PREPARATIONS ETC	W 30104	31.6	W 39341	34.2	W 38096	31.6	W 41893	34.4	PROD ORG TENSIO–ACT NDA
562	*FERTILIZERS,MANUFACTURE	W 256445	24.1	W 221849	24.4	W 247791	35.1	W 189346	27.5	ENGRAIS MANUFACTURES
58	PLASTIC MATERIALS ETC		133.5		193.8		202.4		194.1	MAT PLAST ARTIFICIELLES
582	PROD OF CONDENSATION ETC	W 21723	29.4	W 19151	42.1	W 20864	43.6	W 20775	37.6	PROD CONDENS,POLYCOND
583	POLYMERIZATION ETC PRODS	W 70210	99.4	W 79089	146.1	W 91204	153.4	W 98138	150.5	PROD POLYMERISATION
5834	POLYVINYL CHLORIDE	W 21969	25.4	W 25759	40.3	W 26672	37.6	W 23235	34.3	CHLORURE DE POLYVINYLE
5839	OTH POLYMRZTION ETC PROD	W 13147	32.8	W 11984	41.4	W 16785	48.1	W 16703	41.6	AUT PROD POLYMER COPOLYM
59	CHEMICAL MATERIALS NES		96.7		112.5		114.1		138.1	MAT PROD CHIMIQUES NDA
591	PESTICIDES,DISINFECTANTS	W 6279	31.1	W 7283	39.0	W 8639	49.6	W 10040	54.3	DESINF,INSECT,FONG,HERB

4. General Imports F.O.B. by Commodities according to the S.I.T.C. (Rev. 2) in million U.S. Dollars
Importations Générales F.O.B. par Produits d'après la C.T.C.I. (Rév. 2) en millions de Dollars E.U.

SITC CTCI	COMMODITY	1994 QUANTITY QUANTITE	1994 VALUE VALEUR	1995 QUANTITY QUANTITE	1995 VALUE VALEUR	1996 QUANTITY QUANTITE	1996 VALUE VALEUR	1997 QUANTITY QUANTITE	1997 VALUE VALEUR	PRODUIT
5913	HERBICIDES,FOR RETAIL	W 1795	16.4	W 2100	21.1	W 2835	28.5	W 3202	32.5	HERBICIDES VENTE AU DET
598	MISCEL CHEM PRODUCTS NES		57.9	W 51192	63.7	W 34879	53.2	W 67310	72.4	PROD DIV INDUST CHIM NDA
5989	CHEM PRODUCTS,PREPS NES		46.1	W 38456	51.9	W 20339	38.9	W 51169	58.6	PROD PREP CHIMIQUES NDA
59899	OTH CHEM PRODS,PREPS,NES		27.0	W 27170	33.8	W 6668	16.0	W 35030	36.6	AUT PRODUITS CHIMIQUES NDA
6	BASIC MANUFACTURES		1133.5		1573.6		1504.7		1567.9	ART MANUFACTURES
61	LEATHER,DRESSED FUR,ETC		25.8		30.8		48.1		31.7	CUIRS,PELLETERIES
62	RUBBER MANUFACTURES NES		44.6		59.6		71.9		76.5	CAOUTCHOUC MANUFACTURE
625	RUBBER TYRES, TUBES ETC	W 7929	18.8	W 9121	27.4	W 10794	33.6	W 12210	36.2	PNEUS CAOUTCHOUC VULCANISE
63	WOOD,CORK MANUFACTRS NES		32.0		39.9		35.2		54.6	OUVRAGES LIEGE ET BOIS
64	PAPER,PAPERBOARD AND MFR		133.0		196.5		215.1		208.1	PAPIERS,CARTONS & OUVRAGES
641	PAPER AND PAPERBOARD		89.0	W 140199	134.6	W 172497	148.7	W 183517	134.7	PAPIERS ET CARTONS
6412	PRINTG,WRITING PAPER NES	W 24147	22.8	W 26503	33.3	W 36147	37.5	W 34072	32.6	PAPIERS POUR L'IMPRESSION
64122	— COATED,IMPREGNATD ETC	W 23440	21.7	W 24931	30.2	W 34267	34.6	W 32576	30.4	PAPIERS IMPRESSION COUCHES
6415	PAPER,PAPERBRD,BULK,NES	W 36712	21.3	W 42815	34.9	W 61906	44.0	W 60104	35.3	PAPIERS,CARTONS ROULEAUX
64159	OTHER PAPER ETC,BULK,NES	W 32601	19.0	W 40409	32.3	W 51847	38.0	W 53498	31.5	AUT PAPIER ROULEAUX FEUILLES
6418	COATED ETC PAPER NES BLK	W 17053	20.0	W 20254	31.3	W 28035	36.6	W 34857	36.5	PAP,CARTONS COUCHES,ENDUITS
64189	COATED PAPER ETC NES	W 13394	14.9	W 18875	27.4	W 25564	31.6	W 29913	30.7	PAPIERS,CARTONS COUCHES
642	PAPER,ETC,PRECUT,ARTS OF	W 31596	44.0	W 36060	62.0	W 39348	66.5	W 47343	73.5	PAP,CARTONS DECOUPES
65	TEXTILE YARN,FABRICS,ETC		185.6		215.3		205.4		188.8	FILS,TISSUS,ARTICLES TEXTILE
651	TEXTILE YARN	W 7861	30.3	W 10997	39.3	W 8635	32.3	W 6769	28.3	FILS TEXTILES
652	COTTON FABRICS,WOVEN		21.3	W 3738	23.7	W 3386	23.1	W 3284	20.6	TISSUS DE COTON
653	WOVN MAN–MADE FIB FABRIC		31.7	W 3092	34.4	W 3343	39.3	W 3574	38.8	TISSUS FIBRES SYNTH,ARTIF
657	SPECIAL TXTL FABRC,PRODS		54.1	W 11334	67.2	W 9044	55.8	W 7202	41.2	TISSUS SPECIAUX
6573	COATED ETC TEXTILES NES	W 7478	35.0	W 7512	43.7	W 6083	35.4	W 2581	15.4	TISSUS,ART MATIERE TEXT NDA
65733	RUBBERIZED TEXT NOT KNIT	W 5094	22.1	W 4426	26.3	W 2558	15.9	W 459	2.3	TISSUS CAOUTCHOUTES
66	NONMETAL MINERAL MFS NES		105.9		143.5		169.8		178.3	ART MIN NON METALLIQUES
662	CLAY,REFRACTORY BLDG PRD	W 78797	26.1	W 67512	33.2	W 98059	39.7	W 168159	38.4	MAT CONST REFRACTAIRES
663	MINERAL MANUFCTURES NES	W 87437	29.6	W 106605	41.0	W 134140	49.0	W 143438	48.0	ART MIN MANUF NDA
664	GLASS		22.9	W 53997	33.7	W 56558	39.6	W 52146	46.1	VERRE
67	IRON AND STEEL		300.8		436.3		308.7		386.3	FER ET ACIER
671	PIG IRON ETC	W 59257	21.8	W 43597	17.2	W 41633	17.9	W 36306	16.6	FONTE,SPIEGEL,POUDRES
673	IRON,STEEL SHAPES ETC	W 247717	78.5	W 371413	137.8	W 196583	78.0	W 397224	126.8	BARRES,PROFIL FER,ACIER
6731	IRON,STEEL WIRE ROD	W 80150	23.2	W 158599	51.2	W 2309	0.9	W 137204	37.3	FIL MACHINE FER,ACIER
67311	IRON,SIMPLE STL WIRE ROD	W 79729	22.9	W 137981	41.8	W 1850	0.6	W 136881	37.1	FIL MACH AUT ACIER FIN
6732	IRON,STEEL BARS ETC	W 97833	33.6	W 125732	55.9	W 107358	46.5	W 145777	53.1	BARRES FER,ACIER
67326	IRN,OTH STL BARS HOTROLD	W 68781	18.5	W 86015	28.6	W 72617	20.6	W 111304	31.3	BARRES PLEINES FER,ACIER
6733	IRON,STEEL PROFILES ETC	W 69734	21.9	W 87082	30.7	W 86917	30.7	W 114243	36.5	PROFILES,PALPLAN FER,ACIER
674	IRN,STL UNIV,PLATE,SHEET	W 103907	51.1	W 152971	86.0	W 38371	35.2	W 142432	71.6	LARGES PLATS,TOLES
6744	IRN,STL HVY PLATE,ROLLED	W 59605	25.9	W 99099	48.0	W 12533	10.0	W 89229	37.3	TOLES LAMINEES PLUS 4.75 MM
67441	— OF IRON OR SIMPLE STL	W 58549	24.2	W 97862	45.4	W 10777	6.1	W 87389	34.1	TOLES NON ACIER FIN CARB
678	IRON,STL TUBES,PIPES,ETC		88.9	W 146558	121.0	W 144512	112.5	W 132490	104.8	TUBES,TUYAUX EN FONTE,FER
6782	IRON,STL SEAMLESS TUBES		23.3	W 42282	31.3	W 43722	34.0	W 41625	33.2	TUBES,TUYAUX SANS SOUDURE
6783	IRON,STL TUBES,PIPES NES	W 79408	53.3	W 95443	73.2	W 87998	55.8	W 81805	51.9	AUT TUBES,TUYAUX FER,ACIER
679	IRN,STL CASTINGS UNWORKD	W 18612	20.0	W 23920	28.4	W 29540	36.0	W 29602	34.2	OUVRAGES EN FONTE,FER,ACIER
68	NON–FERROUS METALS		127.8		216.1		168.2		167.8	METAUX NON FERREUX
682	COPPER EXC CEMENT COPPER		35.6	W 23647	74.8	W 15922	45.8	W 14584	41.2	CUIVRE
6821	COPPER NES,ALLOYS,UNWRT	W 5351	10.9	W 10523	28.1	W 5820	13.5	W 5692	13.1	CUIVRE BRUT
68212	COPPER REFINED,UNWROUGHT	W 5330	10.9	W 10059	27.6	W 5784	13.3	W 5658	13.0	CUIVRE AFFINE BRUT
6822	COPPER,ALLOYS WORKED		24.7	W 13124	46.8	W 10102	32.4	W 8891	28.1	CUIVRE,ALLIAGES OUVRES
68221	COPPER BARS,WIRE,ETC	W 6939	17.4	W 10842	35.0	W 7639	20.9	W 5773	14.7	BARRES,PROFILES ET FILS
684	ALUMINIUM		58.4	W 37138	92.6	W 31642	82.2	W 40477	86.4	ALUMINIUM
6841	ALUMINIUM,ALLOYS,UNWRGHT	W 11983	16.1	W 19658	33.0	W 14876	22.2	W 23442	30.7	ALUMINIUM,ALLIAGES BRUTS
6842	ALUMINIUM,ALLOYS WORKED		42.3	W 17480	59.7	W 16766	60.0	W 17034	55.7	ALUMINIUM,ALLIAGES OUVRE
686	ZINC	W 24947	23.1	W 26371	29.5	W 25545	28.3	W 23554	33.0	ZINC
6861	ZINC,ALLOYS UNWROUGHT	W 24531	22.5	W 26062	29.0	W 25305	27.8	W 23294	32.4	ZINC ET ALLIAGES BRUTS
69	METAL MANUFACTURES NES		178.4		235.9		282.7		276.2	ART MANUFACT EN METAL NDA
691	STRUCTURES AND PARTS NES	W 22422	23.1	W 26433	27.7	W 32693	39.8	W 40727	48.6	CONSTRUCT FER,ACIER,ALU
6911	STRUCTURES,PARTS IRN,STL	W 21915	19.4	W 25897	22.7	W 31621	32.0	W 39472	41.2	CONSTRUCT FER,ACIER,FONTE
692	METAL TANKS,BOXES,ETC	W 14769	20.6	W 13108	24.5	W 14455	31.6	W 9721	21.6	RECIPIENTS METALLIQUES
695	TOOLS	W 2173	19.2	W 2743	30.0	W 3683	40.4	W 3704	45.2	OUTILS A MAIN
697	BASE MTL HOUSEHOLD EQUIP	W 5279	20.3	W 5733	25.9	W 7349	32.9	W 6773	28.4	ART MENAGE MET COMMUNS
699	BASE METAL MFRS NES	W 28964	72.6	W 30956	90.8	W 30990	91.5	W 31120	95.2	ART MANUFACTURES MET NDA
6991	LOCKSMITHS WARES,ETC	W 4189	24.2	W 4503	30.0	W 5082	35.2	W 5406	35.7	ARTICLES DE SERRURERIE
7	MACHINES,TRANSPORT EQUIP		1831.9		2460.4		3203.4		3333.9	MACHINES MATERIEL TRANSPORT
71	POWER GENERATING EQUIPMT		128.4		100.8		113.1		140.4	MACHINES GENERATRICES
713	INTRNL COMBUS PSTN ENGIN	W 2859	20.5	W 3401	28.1	W 4043	35.5	W 4918	24.2	MOTEURS EXPL COMB INT, PIECE
714	ENGINES AND MOTORS NES	W 670	16.8	W 694	12.4	W 379	9.1	W 1738	35.6	MOTEURS NON ELECTRIQUES
7149	ENGINE & MOTOR PARTS NES	W 464	5.7	W 606	7.5	W 330	5.8	W 1713	33.7	PIECES 714 ET 718.88
71499	PARTS NES,OF 71488,71888	W 460	4.4	W 603	5.7	W 326	4.5	W 1700	32.9	PIECES 714.88 ET 718.88
716	ROTATING ELECTRIC PLANT	W 11624	37.7	W 3076	20.0	W 2870	25.1	W 3351	30.1	APP ELECTR ROTATIFS,PIECES
7169	PTS NES OF ROT ELEC PLNT	W 8434	22.5	W 643	3.9	W 319	4.1	W 1079	10.4	PIECES MAC APP ROTATIFS
718	OTH POWER GENERATG MACHY	W 2075	34.2	W 1506	16.5	W 1465	24.6	W 1259	18.5	AUTRES MOTEURS PARTIES
7187	NUCLEAR REACTORS,PTS NES	W 48	24.6	W 157	7.6	W 315	5.9			REACTEURS NUCLEAIRES
72	MACHS FOR SPCL INDUSTRYS		274.4		410.1		510.0		439.9	MAC SPECIALES POUR INDUST
721	AGRIC MACHY,EXC TRACTORS	W 9532	41.0	W 13167	76.2	W 12796	89.7	W 11885	78.1	MACHINES AGRICOLES
7212	HARVESTING ETC MACHINES	W 4723	17.8	W 7381	43.8	W 6829	47.2	W 6153	46.1	ENGINS POUR LA RECOLTE
723	CIVIL ENGNEERG EQUIP ETC		17.7	W 5850	30.4	W 7069	43.1	W 7784	43.6	APPAREILS DE GENIE CIVIL
7234	CONST,MINING MACHNRY NES		13.3	W 5178	24.9	W 5839	35.3	W 6492	36.9	MACH POUR LA CONST, MINES
724	TEXTILE,LEATHER MACHNRY		46.1	W 3219	52.6	W 3916	53.6	W 3514	50.8	MACH POUR INDUSTRIE TEXTILE
725	PAPER ETC MILL MACHINERY		16.5	W 2762	29.5	W 1987	38.3	W 2117	32.9	MACHINES FABR PATE PAPIER
726	PRINTG,BKBINDG MACHY,PTS	W 1286	24.7	W 2382	53.7	W 2208	47.0	W 1988	37.0	MACHINES POUR IMPRIMERIE
7264	PRINTING PRESSES	W 559	11.2	W 1513	34.9	W 1024	26.2	W 1012	17.9	MACHINES A IMPRIMER
72641	ROTARY PRINTING PRESSES	W 559	11.2	W 1513	34.9	W 1024	26.2	W 1012	17.9	MACH IMPRIMER ROTATIVES
727	FOOD MACHRY NON–DOMESTIC	W 2337	29.2	W 2503	48.2	W 3544	56.4	W 2147	31.1	MACH INDUSTRIES ALIMENT
7272	OTH FOOD PROC MCHY,PARTS	W 1738	26.1	W 2296	46.4	W 3322	54.5	W 1905	29.9	AUT MACH IND ALIMENTAIRE
72722	INDUS FOOD PROC MACH NES	W 1634	23.3	W 2139	45.0	W 3281	53.9	W 1898	29.7	MACHINES BOULANGERIE
728	OTH MACHY FOR SPCL INDUS	W 9495	93.1	W 11561	109.9	W 14322	162.6	W 16217	147.7	AUT MACH IND PARTICULIERES
7281	MACH–TOOLS FR SPCL INDUS	W 3560	25.0	W 4316	35.8	W 4345	40.0	W 3775	21.0	MACH–OUTILS SPEC IND PART
72812	MACH–TOOLS TO WORK WOOD	W 3070	20.7	W 3853	31.7	W 3319	30.1	W 2996	14.3	MACH–OUT POUR TRAVAIL BOIS
7284	MACHY FOR SPCL INDUS NES	W 3720	52.9	W 3697	52.8	W 6567	95.7	W 9270	104.6	MACH SPEC IND PARTICUL.
72842	RUBBER,PLASTICS WRKG MCH	W 1102	14.9	W 1197	13.7	W 2514	37.0	W 1951	20.3	MACH IND CAOUT MAT PLAST
72849	PTS OF MACHS OF 7284 ETC	W 1078	16.9	W 1056	14.3	W 1962	29.9	W 4978	49.7	PIECES DU 728.4 ETC
73	METALWORKING MACHINERY		89.4		113.4		143.2		131.3	MACH TRAVAIL DES METAUX
736	METALWORKING MACH–TOOLS	W 7771	67.6	W 9713	68.7	W 12309	92.9	W 12022	96.9	MACH–OUTILS TRAVAIL METAUX
7361	METAL CUTTING MACH–TOOLS	W 2681	41.1	W 2229	22.4	W 4750	36.2	W 4076	32.0	MACH–OUT ENLEVEMENT METAL
73619	OTH MTL CUTTNG MCH–TOOLS	W 815	22.2	W 520	5.0	W 1032	7.3	W 933	8.1	MACH A AFFUTER ETC METAL
737	METALWORKING MACHNRY NES	W 5020	21.8	W 9138	44.7	W 7008	50.4	W 5602	34.5	MACH TRAV METAUX PIECES
74	GENRL INDUSTRL MACHY NES		332.2		430.0		547.2		547.1	MACH APP INDUSTRIE
741	HEATING,COOLING EQUIPMNT		62.4	W 8488	81.6	W 11108	118.5	W 14856	115.7	MACH CHAUFFAGE,PIECES
7416	HEATING,COOLING EQU NES	W 1273	13.6	W 1575	20.9	W 2763	31.6	W 6557	48.2	APP CHANGEMENT TEMP
742	PUMPS FOR LIQUIDS ETC	W 3197	30.4	W 3034	39.2	W 3779	47.8	W 3272	42.6	POMPES MOTO–POMPES

4. General Imports F.O.B. by Commodities according to the S.I.T.C. (Rev. 2) in million U.S. Dollars
Importations Générales F.O.B. par Produits d'après la C.T.C.I. (Rév. 2) en millions de Dollars E.U.

SITC CTCI	COMMODITY	1994		1995		1996		1997		PRODUIT
		QUANTITY QUANTITE	VALUE VALEUR	QUANTITY QUANTITE	VALUE VALEUR	QUANTITY QUANTITE	VALUE VALEUR	QUANTITY QUANTITE	VALUE VALEUR	
743	PUMPS NES,CENTRFUGES ETC	W 8108	70.2	W 7457	79.0	W 8917	87.1	W 9881	97.4	POMPES COMPRES,VENT ETC
7431	PUMPS FOR GASES ETC	W 3493	25.4	W 2832	24.3	W 2825	24.2	W 2989	33.5	POMPES AIR A VIDE,COMPRES
7436	GAS,LIQUID FILTERS ETC	W 2098	24.0	W 2427	33.4	W 3118	34.6	W 3555	31.2	APP POUR FILT DES LIQUIDES
744	MECHANICAL HANDLING EQU		50.2	W 11148	58.9	W 15649	68.4	W 14484	69.2	EQUIP MANUTENTION PIECES
7442	LIFTING,LOADING MACH NES	W 4559	23.1	W 4048	21.8	W 6144	28.1	W 5659	27.2	APP LEVAGE,MANUTENTION
745	NONELEC MACHY,TOOLS NES	W 2832	37.7	W 3693	59.6	W 5412	84.1	W 7339	90.6	AUT MACH NON ELEC,PIECES
7452	OTH NONELEC MCHS,PTS NES	W 2646	32.8	W 3482	52.1	W 5035	75.0	W 7039	82.2	AUT MACH NON ELEC,PIECES
74522	PACKAGNG,BOTTLNG,ETC MCH	W 675	14.9	W 620	19.7	W 1299	33.3	W 1866	39.0	MACH NETT BOUTEILLES,ETC
749	NONELEC MACH PTS,ACC NES	W 10510	81.5	W 95723	111.9	W 13971	141.6	W 98009	131.9	PIECES MACH NON ELEC NDA
7492	COCKS,VALVES ETC NES	W 5443	42.6	W 5360	62.8	W 7252	84.2	W 6828	84.2	ART ROB,SIM POUR TUYAUX
75	OFFICE MACHNES,ADP EQUIP		203.6		298.3		106.4		335.3	MACH BUREAU TRAIT AUTOM
751	OFFICE MACHINES	W 840	26.7	W 1796	61.0	W 1156	32.0	W 880	22.5	MACH,APPAREILS DE BUREAU
7512	CALCULATNG,ACCTG,ETC MCH	W 197	8.0	W 1149	42.6	W 451	14.8	W 162	5.5	MACHINE A CALCULER ETC
75123	CASH REGISTERS	W 121	4.9	W 989	34.9	W 154	5.8	W 68	2.6	CAISSES ENREGISTREUSES
752	AUTOMTIC DATA PROC EQUIP	W 2250	146.5	W 3206	199.0	W 221	19.6	W 4088	254.8	MACH TRAIT INFORMATION
7522	DIGITAL COMPUTERS	W 490	48.8	W 598	73.4	W 19	2.0	W 474	48.1	MACH DIGITALES COMPLETES
7523	DIGITL CENTRL PROCESSORS	W 172	19.4	W 188	14.3	W 8	0.4	W 176	31.7	UNITES CENTRALES
7524	DIGITL CENTRL STOR UNITS	W 115	15.7	W 108	16.1	W 3	0.4	W 195	36.8	UNITES MEMOIRE CENTRALES
7525	ADP PERIPHERAL UNITS	W 1142	45.2	W 1928	75.1	W 46	2.7	W 2645	75.3	UNITES PERIPHERIQUES
7528	OFF–LINE DATA PROC EQUIP	W 317	15.2	W 360	16.6	W 25	1.2	W 518	53.2	MACH AUXIL TRAIT INFORM
759	OFFICE,ADP MCH PTS,ACCES	W 848	30.5	W 1551	38.3	W 1434	55.0	W 1325	58.1	PIECES DU 751 ET 752
7599	ACCTG,ETC,ADP MCH PTS,AC	W 644	23.2	W 750	28.9	W 1185	43.8	W 1048	47.4	PIECES DU 751 ET 752
76	TELECOMM,SOUND EQUIPMENT		135.2		181.9		208.8		348.1	EQUIPMENT DE TELECOM
764	TELECOM EQPT,PTS,ACC NES		117.8	W 2730	152.1	W 2772	177.5	W 3797	291.2	EQUIP TELECOM,PIECES
7641	LINE TELEPHONE,ETC EQUIP	W 85450	24.8	W 427	30.9	W 158	12.5	W 456	45.4	APP TELEPHON PAR FIL
7643	TV,RADIO TRANSMITTRS ETC	W 158	22.6	W 122	23.5	W 175	31.6	W 863	99.9	APP EMET TELE RADIO
7649	PTS NES OF EQUIPMT OF 76	W 1254	63.8	W 1849	89.1	W 1938	122.9	W 1795	125.2	PIECES DE LA DIV 76
76491	PTS NES OF APPAR OF 7641	W 781	52.1	W 659	73.7	W 841	99.6	W 834	99.4	PIECES POUR 764.1
77	ELECTRIC MACHNRY NES ETC		324.1		410.1		431.1		538.5	MACH APP ELECT NDA
771	ELECTRIC POWER MACHY NES		19.9	W 3083	29.6	W 4012	36.2	W 4792	39.2	MACH PROD,TRANS ELECTR
772	SWITCHGEAR ETC,PARTS NES		45.6	W 3572	62.6	W 4212	95.8	W 5386	117.9	APP COUPURE,SECT ETC
7721	SWITCHGEAR ETC		43.1	W 3442	58.6	W 4108	92.2	W 5297	114.3	APP COUPURE,SECTIONMNT
773	ELECTR DISTRIBUTNG EQUIP		42.7	W 14545	52.5	W 17838	62.7	W 19947	82.5	EQUIPMT DISTRIBUTION ELECT
7731	INSULATED WIRE,CABLE ETC	W 13705	39.0	W 13321	47.9	W 16370	57.2	W 18041	62.7	FILS,CABLES ISOLES ELECT
774	ELECTRO–MEDCL,XRAY EQUIP	W 381	63.3	W 227	32.4	W 242	32.9	W 233	32.0	APPAREILS MEDICAUX
7742	X-RAY APPARATUS ETC	W 307	50.1	W 128	18.0	W 140	14.0	W 122	13.3	APPAREILS A RAYONS X
775	HOUSEHOLD TYPE EQUIP NES	W 7220	39.0	W 9234	55.9	W 12465	75.6	W 15602	85.3	MACH,APP USAGE DOMESTQUE
7758	ELECTRO–THERMIC APPL NES	W 2124	14.4	W 2556	20.5	W 3771	28.2	W 5865	37.3	APP ELECTROTHERMIQ NDA
776	TRANSISTORS,VALVES,ETC		44.1	W 2861	79.5	W 2260	31.7	W 2560	79.7	LAMPES,TUBES,VALVES
7764	ELECTRONIC MICROCIRCUITS		29.2	W 279	55.3	W 30	9.8	W 436	60.9	MICROSTRUCTURES ELECTRON
778	ELECTRICAL MACHINERY NES		69.8	W 17199	97.9	W 96733	96.5	W 99884	102.1	AUTRES MACH ELECT NDA
7788	OTH ELEC MACHY,EQUIP NES		28.4	W 6822	40.9	W 3121	37.9	W 2873	41.8	AUT MACH APP ELEC NDA
78	ROAD VEHICLES		280.9		459.4		1077.8		790.6	VEHICULES ROUTIERS
781	PASS MOTOR VEH EXC BUSES	W 21996	125.8	W 28544	204.3	W 94788	724.2	W 57962	417.4	AUTO TRANSPORT PERSONNES
782	LORRIES,SPCL MTR VEH NES	W 12481	41.9	W 17084	68.5	W 23299	108.2	W 27415	132.3	VEHICULES SPECIAUX,MARCH
7821	LORRIES,TRUCKS	W 8509	34.2	W 12511	53.9	W 18393	93.8	W 22290	110.6	VEHICULES TRANSP MARCHAND
783	ROAD MOTOR VEHICLES NES	W 4685	25.2	W 7418	56.2	W 8543	70.1	W 8732	75.6	VEHICULES ROUTIERS NDA
7832	TRACTORS FOR TR–TRAILERS	W 2202	13.0	W 3050	30.5	W 5686	53.5	W 6596	60.1	TRACTEURS ROUTIERS
784	MOTOR VEH PRTS,ACCES NES	W 13599	62.8	W 17734	95.8	W 22887	132.4	W 22007	117.8	PIECES 722,781,782,783
7849	OTHER MOTOR VEHCL PARTS	W 12300	58.2	W 16500	89.4	W 20874	119.3	W 21014	112,3	PIECES 722,781,782,783
79	OTHR TRANSPORT EQUIPMENT		64.0		56.8		66.2		63.1	AUTRE MATERIEL TRANSPORT
791	RAILWAY VEHICLES	W 27351	34.7	W 18213	33.9	W 17008	44.5	W 22361	51.6	VEHIC MAT CHEMINS DE FER
7919	RY TRACK FIXT,ETC,PARTS	W 17631	30.9	W 14274	26.6	W 13486	32.1	W 17510	38.4	MATER FIXE VOIES FERREES
79199	PARTS NES OF 7911–7915	W 17027	30.4	W 13645	25.9	W 13062	31.5	W 17237	37.8	PIECES 791.1 ET 5
792	AIRCRAFT ETC	W 207	28.7	W 158	22.6	W 221	20.7	W 124	10.5	APP NAVIGATION AERIENNE
7923	AIRCRFT NES2000–15000KG	W 33	23.6	W 59	18.3	W 33	0.5	W 21	1.4	AERODYNES 2000 A 15000 KG
8	MISC MANUFACTURED GOODS		567.1		708.4		847.4		943.6	ART MANUFACTURES DIVERS
812	*PLUMBG,HEATNG,LGHTNG EQ	W 110026	35.1	W 15254	43.1	W 17996	55.5	W 18984	61.4	APPAR SANITAIRES CHAUFFAGE
8124	LIGHTING EQUIPMENT NES	W 96748	18.1	W 3099	22.7	W 3255	25.4	W 3858	31.4	APPAREILS ECLAIRAGE ETC
821	*FURNITURE,PARTS THEREOF	W 11890	36.6	W 14952	45.3	W 19870	68.4	W 20581	68.7	MEUBLES ET PIECES
8219	FURNITURE AND PARTS NES	W 8236	19.9	W 10226	25.0	W 14118	35.6	W 14872	37.9	AUTRES MEUBLES ET PIECES
84	CLOTHING AND ACCESSORIES		76.0		86.5		102.4		110.3	VETEMENTS
851	*FOOTWEAR	W 4067	29.9	W 5085	38.7	W 6474	48.9	W 6687	57.4	CHAUSSURES
85102	FOOTWEAR LEATHER	W 2272	16.7	W 3101	21.8	W 4292	33.3	W 4279	42.1	CHAUS SEMELLES EN CUIR
87	PRECISION INSTRUMNTS NES		124.3		157.3		185.6		187.1	INSTRUM,APPAR SCIENT NDA
872	MEDICAL INSTRUMENTS NES		26.4	W 914	36.9	W 1191	44.1	W 1351	39.2	INSTR,APP MEDIC–CHIR NDA
87202	OTH MEDICAL INSTRUMENTS		23.5	W 689	29.8	W 917	36.9	W 1109	32.3	INSTRUM,APP MEDECINE
874	MEASURNG,CONTROLNG INSTR		85.0	W 3293	108.3	W 3321	127.5	W 3711	135.3	INSTRUMENTS DE MESURE
8743	GAS,LIQUID CONTROL INSTR	W 2680	27.6	W 909	32.1	W 898	34.8	W 1130	43.7	APP,INSTR MESURE FLUIDES
8748	ELEC MEAS,CONTRL EQU NES		22.6	W 290	27.2	W 352	30.6	W 285	31.2	APP ELEC ELECTRO MESURE
88	PHOTO EQU,OPTICL GDS ETC		34.6		42.7		47.4		48.6	APP,FOURN PHOTO,OP,MONTR
89	MISC MANUFCTRD GOODS NES		224.2		285.7		327.2		397.9	ART MANUFACTURES DIVERS
892	PRINTED MATTER		43.1	W 8346	50.9	W 9200	67.9	W 11638	83.5	IMPRIMES
8928	PRINTED MATTER NES		15.1	W 2070	18.1	W 3039	22.1	W 3490	35.4	IMPRIMES NDA
893	ARTICLES OF PLASTIC NES		79.6		104.1		133.3		148.9	OUVRAGES EN MAT DIVIS 58
8931	PLSTC PACKG CONTNRS,LIDS	W 9585	23.1	W 11392	32.7	W 16164	44.7	W 16295	42.6	ART TRANSP EMBALLAGE ETC
8939	MISC PLASTIC ARTICLES	W 17043	54.5	W 15652	67.7	W 19425	83.7	W 24835	100.2	ART DIVERS EN MAT DIV 58
89399	OTHR PLASTC ARTICLES NES	W 14229	49.6	W 12776	61.2	W 16070	75.6	W 20558	91.2	AUT OUV MAT DIV 58
894	TOYS,SPORTING GOODS,ETC		30.7	W 4748	34.1	W 101273	41.5	W 6508	45.6	VOITURES ENFANTS,JOUETS
8942	TOYS,INDOOR GAMES ETC	W 3363	21.7	W 3231	22.5	W 99064	25.1	W 4106	27.2	JOUETS,JEUX ETC
898	MUSICAL INSTRUMENTS,PTS		23.7	W 1098	35.5	W 923	12.5	W 1519	49.6	INSTRUMENTS DE MUSIQUE
8983	SOUND RECRDNG TAPE,DISCS		21.9	W 1008	33.6	W 808	10.0	W 1394	47.0	SUPPORTS SON POUR 763
89832	RECORDED DISCS,TAPES ETC		15.6	W 343	26.0	W 10	0.8	W 524	38.3	DISQUES,PHONO,BANDES
899	OTHER MANUFACTURED GOODS		26.5		36.0		43.5		40.3	AUT ART MANUF DIVERS NDA
9	GOODS NOT CLASSD BY KIND		43.8		624.3		1656.8		909.1	ART TRANSACT NON CLASSES
931	*SPECIAL TRANSACTIONS				608.6		1526.3		895.9	TRANS.SPECIALES
951	*WAR FIREARMS,AMMUNITION	W 765	40.5	W 2198	7.3	W 2382	118.3	W 960	8.2	VEHIC BLINDES ARMES
95106	AMMUNITION NES	W 514	33.7	W 124	0.8	W 1064	108.9	W 205	4.0	PROJECTILES,MUNITIONS

5. General Exports F.O.B. by Commodities according to the S.I.T.C. (Rev. 2) in million U.S. Dollars
Exportations Générales F.O.B. par Produits d'après la C.T.C.I. (Rév. 2) en millions de Dollars E.U.

SITC CTCI	COMMODITY	1994		1995		1996		1997		PRODUIT
		QUANTITY QUANTITE	VALUE VALEUR	QUANTITY QUANTITE	VALUE VALEUR	QUANTITY QUANTITE	VALUE VALEUR	QUANTITY QUANTITE	VALUE VALEUR	
	ALL COMMODITIES		6690.3		8577.5		8824.1		8790.0	TOUS PRODUITS
0	FOOD AND LIVE ANIMALS		301.4		421.5		304.6		313.2	ALIMENTS,ANIMAUX VIVANTS
001	*LIVE ANIMALS FOR FOOD	W 19812	27.9	W 10404	19.6	W 7689	13.4	W 11516	18.4	ANIMAUX VIVANTS
0011	BOVINE SPECIES,LIVE	W 17515	21.8	W 8511	14.5	W 6190	9.3	W 9613	12.9	ESPECE BOVINE
00119	— OTHR THAN FR BREEDING	W 16427	20.3	W 6399	10.8	W 5584	8.3	W 9008	11.9	BOVINS NON REPRODUCTEURS
02	DAIRY PRODCTS,BIRDS'EGGS		35.9		45.2		46.0		43.6	PRODUITS LAITIERS,OEUFS
024	CHEESE AND CURD	W 9355	20.6	W 9562	22.6	W 10953	26.3	W 10255	25.0	FROMAGE ET CAILLEBOTTE
04	CEREALS AND PREPARATIONS		62.0		177.6		71.9		65.0	CEREALES ET PRODUITS
041	WHEAT ETC UNMILLED	W 27792	3.1	W 621868	77.9	W 11205	1.9	W 26312	3.0	FROMENT,EPEAUTRE
0412	OTHER WHEAT ETC UNMILLED	W 19918	2.1	W 539383	67.9	W 10233	1.8	W 26312	3.0	AUTRE FROMENT NON MOULU
048	CEREAL ETC PREPARATIONS	W 76082	35.5	W 171339	60.7	W 113357	54.8	W 89750	44.1	PREPTNS A BASE CEREALES
0482	MALT INCLUDING FLOUR	W 55610	12.1	W 149757	37.5	W 80389	25.5	W 65935	19.3	MALT MEME TORREFIE
05	VEGETABLES AND FRUIT		76.9		65.1		59.4		52.6	LEGUMES ET FRUITS
054	VEG ETC FRSH,SMPLY PRSVD	W 163056	50.6	W 134714	43.8	W 100512	37.8	W 74825	30.4	LEGUMES FRAIS,CONG,SECS
0545	OTHER FRESH VEGETABLES	W 63303	25.3	W 53768	19.2	W 40461	17.4	W 33164	14.0	AUTRES LEGUMES FRAIS,REF
05459	FRESH VEGETABLES NES	W 59757	23.7	W 48204	17.3	W 37734	16.1	W 31122	13.4	LEGUMES FRAIS,REFRI NDA
07	COFFEE,TEA,COCOA,SPICES		35.1		43.7		33.9		34.8	CAFE,THE,CACAO,EPICES
073	CHOCOLATE AND PRODUCTS	W 10756	27.8	W 10089	35.0	W 11576	28.7	W 14034	28.2	CHOCOLAT
081	*FEEDING STUFF FOR ANIML	W 93496	10.8	W 134946	14.2	W 94483	21.7	W 103680	33.2	NOURRITURE POUR ANIMAUX
09	MISC EDIBLE PRODUCTS		12.4		19.3		32.6		36.0	PREP ALIMENTAIRES DIVERSES
1	BEVERAGES AND TOBACCO		62.8		74.1		58.8		60.9	BOISSONS ET TABACS
11	BEVERAGES		35.9		40.3		35.6		32.5	BOISSONS
112	ALCOHOLIC BEVERAGES	W 63031	32.9	W 66888	36.5	W 75745	32.0	W 54700	28.5	BOISSONS ALCOOLIQUES
12	TOBACCO AND MANUFACTURES		27.0		33.9		23.3		28.5	TABACS BRUTS FABRIQUES
122	TOBACCO,MANUFACTURED		26.8	W 4680	33.9	W 3520	23.3	W 3456	25.4	TABACS FABRIQUES
1222	CIGARETTES		25.2	W 4144	31.3	W 2823	20.9	W 3456	25.4	CIGARETTES
2	CRUDE MATERLS,EXCL FUELS		341.6		409.3		363.4		384.3	MAT BRUTES NON COMESTIBLES
24	CORK AND WOOD		153.5		190.4		175.2		194.7	LIEGE ET BOIS
247	OTH WOOD ROUGH,SQUARED	W 2468826	35.4	W 456669	33.0	W 528887	34.9	W 910751	50.6	BOIS BRUTS EQUARRIS
2471	SAW-,VENEER-LOGS CONIFER	W 1233886	20.1	W 218894	18.1	W 301244	22.9	W 578873	36.6	CONIFERES POUR SCIAGE,PLACAG
24711	— IN THE ROUGH	W 1233886	20.1	W 218894	18.1	W 301244	22.9	W 578873	36.6	ECORCES OU DEGROSSIS
248	WOOD SHAPED,SLEEPERS	W 522622	115.4	W 586095	153.5	W 620247	135.5	W 625247	139.6	BOIS SIMPLEMENT TRAVAILLES
2482	LUMBER SHAPED CONIFER	W 364589	80.8	W 382950	98.2	W 445504	84.0	W 452739	92.6	CONIFERES SCIES,RABOTES
24821	LUMBER SAWN ETC CONIFER	W 361534	78.8	W 380457	96.1	W 441200	81.2	W 447963	90.8	CONIFERES SCIES LONGITUD
2483	LUMBER SHAPED NON-CONIFR	W 151132	33.3	W 192805	52.4	W 170650	50.4	W 169445	46.3	NON CONIFERES SCIES,RABOTES
24831	LUMBER SAWN ETC NON-CON	W 131827	26.3	W 165083	40.8	W 139421	36.2	W 144624	34.2	SCIES LONGITUDINALEMENT
251	*PULP AND WASTE PAPER	W 94181	40.1	W 88322	66.0	W 86821	37.9	W 81620	33.4	PATES A PAPIER,DECHETS
2517	SODA,SULPHATE WOOD PULP	W 74316	31.3	W 68378	52.4	W 66373	26.9	W 63293	24.2	PATES CHIMIQUES AU SULFATE
25172	— BLEACHED,NONDISSOLVNG	W 69915	30.4	W 68016	52.3	W 66075	26.8	W 63293	24.2	PATES BLANCHIES
27	CRUDE FERTLZR,MINRLS NES		47.4		57.7		60.9		54.7	ENGRAIS MINERAUX BRUTS
278	OTHER CRUDE MINERALS	W 759352	39.2	W 819037	49.1	W 932393	53.0	W 1228778	49.4	AUTRES MINERAUX BRUTS
2782	REFRACTORY MINERALS NES	W 588221	30.7	W 682689	40.0	W 797529	43.1	W 1125966	41.6	ARGILE MINERAUX REFRACTAIRES
27824	MAGNESITE, ETC	W 162533	25.2	W 259712	35.0	W 249117	37.3	W 261920	34.9	CARBONATE DE MAGNESIUM
28	METALLIFEROUS ORES,SCRAP		44.9		37.9		28.9		35.1	MINERAIS METAL,DECHETS
282	IRON AND STEEL SCRAP	W 2578321	22.2	W 197836	20.7	W 212688	18.8	W 213340	19.2	FERRAILLES
3	MINERAL FUELS ETC		314.4		358.9		416.8		431.1	COMBUSTIBLES MINERAUX LUB
33	PETROLEUM AND PRODUCTS		302.9		345.4		397.9		418.0	PETROLE ET DERIVES
334	PETROLEUM PRODUCTS,REFIN	W 1845089	283.0	W 1952382	329.9	W 1983063	383.3	W 2312287	406.4	PRODUITS RAFFINES
3341	GASOLINE,OTH LIGHT OILS	W 1841148	279.1							ESSENCES POUR MOTEURS
5	CHEMCLS,RELATED PROD NES		828.1		1018.7		935.2		818.7	PRODUITS CHIMIQUES
51	ORGANIC CHEMICALS		168.1		164.3		142.9		141.5	PROD CHIMIQ ORGANIQUES
511	HYDROCARBONS NES,DERIVS	W 247681	60.3	W 134108	38.8	W 98327	26.7	W 49927	19.5	HYDROCARBURES NDA
5112	CYCLIC HYDROCARBONS	W 156982	37.0	W 57778	17.1	W 54928	13.0	W 38181	11.8	HYDROCARBURES CYCLIQUES
512	ALCOHOLS,PHENOLS ETC	W 179055	40.3	W 63010	43.0	W 61488	33.3	W 52814	32.3	PHENOLS,PHENOLS-ALCOOLS
5121	ACYCLIC ALCOHOLS,DERIVS	W 121004	25.2	W 31245	21.8	W 26496	14.3	W 23302	13.6	ALCOOLS ACYCLIQUES
514	NITROGEN-FNCTN COMPOUNDS	W 3555	6.6	W 275	0.7	W 223	0.4	W 18609	45.4	COMPOSES FONCT AZOTEES
5145	AMINE-FUNCTION COMPOUNDS	W 1704	1.7	W 22	0.4		0.1	W 17012	42.8	COMPOSES FONCTION AMINE
515	ORG-INORG COMPOUNDS ETC	W 9707	8.8	W 2612	4.0	W 4058	17.1	W 8329	29.6	COMPOSES ORGANO-MINERAUX
516	OTHER ORGANIC CHEMICALS	W 86233	44.7	W 94110	70.9	W 101054	60.6	W 18114	9.3	AUTRES PROD ORGANIQUES
5162	ALDEHYDE ETC FNCT CMPNDS	W 81766	41.9	W 93953	69.3	W 100872	58.4	W 17992	7.4	COMP FONCTION ALDEHYDE
51629	OTHER KETONES ETC,DERIVS	W 53809	33.1	W 64982	54.1	W 67664	48.5			AUTRES CETONES
52	INORGANIC CHEMICALS		65.2		55.8		65.1		61.3	PROD CHIM INORGANIQUES
522	INORG ELEMNTS,OXIDES,ETC	W 205950	45.2	W 179532	38.0	W 170206	39.5	W 229445	40.4	ELEMENTS INORGANIQUES
5221	CHEMICAL ELEMENTS	W 63725	21.3	W 36615	7.6	W 50034	12.9	W 71614	17.2	ELEMENTS CHIMIQUES
53	DYES,TANNING,COLOUR PROD		24.0		29.8		25.7		22.5	PROD TEINTURE,COLORANTS
533	PIGMENTS,PAINTS,ETC	W 18521	22.5	W 19612	28.2	W 16097	24.0	W 23840	20.9	PIGMENTS,PEINTURES,VERNIS
5334	VARNISHES,DISTEMPERS ETC	W 16658	20.9	W 17254	26.1	W 14087	21.9	W 12323	18.3	PEINTURES A L'EAU
541	*MEDICINAL,PHARM PRODUCT		120.3	K 6670109	138.1	K 7280343	131.5	K 3669185	105.3	PROD MEDICINAUX PHARMACEUT
5413	ANTIBIOTICS IN BULK	K 1971292	21.3	K 604214	17.9	K 541145	16.2			ANTIBIOTIQUES NDA
5417	MEDICAMENTS		80.8	K 5590985	107.1	K 6287885	104.0	K 3325208	95.2	MEDICAMENTS
54179	— CONTNG OTH SUBSTANCES	K 4228188	57.3	K 4554133	72.9	K 5174316	70.4	K 2728342	64.3	MED CONT AUT SUBSTANCES
55	PERFUME,CLEANING ETC PRD		39.2		44.4		51.1		48.6	PROD POUR PARFUM,TOILETTE
554	SOAP,CLEANSING ETC PREPS	W 28788	25.0	W 32078	32.0	W 78632	39.9	W 49917	37.9	SAVONS,PRODUITS DETERSIFS
5542	WASHING PREPARATIONS ETC	W 25794	21.7	W 27264	27.7	W 38327	34.4	W 45718	34.2	PROD ORG TENSIO-ACT NDA
562	*FERTILIZERS,MANUFACTURE	W 811189	77.3	W 852177	103.1	W 938783	112.2	W 590525	62.9	ENGRAIS MANUFACTURES
5621	CHEM NITROGENOUS FERTLZR	W 658956	55.0	W 665364	73.0	W 756543	83.9	W 474506	45.5	ENGRAIS AZOTES
56219	CHEM NITROG FERTILZR NES	W 495804	41.8	W 511682	58.8	W 573472	65.7	W 300418	29.9	ENGRAIS AZOTES NDA
5629	FERTILIZERS NES	W 146241	21.7	W 186813	30.1	W 182240	28.4	W 116019	17.5	ENGRAIS NDA
58	PLASTIC MATERIALS ETC		255.0		363.7		331.5		327.9	MAT PLAST ARTIFICIELLES
582	PROD OF CONDENSATION ETC	W 44797	26.0	W 63300	39.9	W 99487	37.0	W 107295	36.5	PROD CONDENS,POLYCOND
583	POLYMERIZATION ETC PRODS		211.6	W 314320	305.1	W 277346	272.7	W 273117	271.9	PROD POLYMERISATION
5831	POLYETHYLENE	W 194514	103.8	W 189058	142.1	W 154430	131.4	W 149783	135.2	POLYETHYLENE
58311	— IN PRIMARY FORMS	W 179340	87.5	W 172457	118.6	W 134923	104.6	W 128359	106.4	POLYETHYLENE PRIMAIRES
58313	— PLATES,FILM,STRIP,ETC	W 14028	15.9	W 15399	22.9	W 18071	26.3	W 20770	28.6	POLYETHYLENE PLAQUES
5832	POLYPROPYLENE	W 44923	42.9	W 50387	66.4	W 54577	71.7	W 50971	65.6	POLYPROPYLENE
58321	— IN PRIMARY FORMS	W 37496	22.9	W 42552	35.2	W 45470	31.2	W 40693	27.6	POLYPROPYLENE PRIMAIRES
58322	— PLATES,FILM,STRIP,ETC	W 7427	20.1	W 7835	31.2	W 9108	40.5	W 10278	38.1	POLYPROPYLENE PLAQUES
5834	POLYVINYL CHLORIDE	W 45531	36.2	W 54632	53.9	W 55487	41.0	W 54458	40.8	CHLORURE DE POLYVINYLE
58341	— IN PRIMARY FORMS	W 42813	31.6	W 51282	48.1	W 53661	37.1	W 52680	37.5	SOUS FORMES PRIMAIRES
59	CHEMICAL MATERIALS NES		75.3		114.8		71.4		46.0	MAT PROD CHIMIQUES NDA
598	MISCEL CHEM PRODUCTS NES	W 39155	53.4	W 50962	89.1	W 33075	51.8	W 62591	28.9	PROD DIV INDUST CHIM NDA
5989	CHEM PRODUCTS,PREPS NES	W 31782	41.6	W 44556	70.6	W 17842	31.5	W 37653	18.6	PROD PREP CHIMIQUES NDA
59899	OTH CHEM PRODS,PREPS,NES	W 26323	35.5	W 38081	63.3	W 12235	25.1	W 33173	13.6	AUT PRODUITS CHIMIQUES NDA
6	BASIC MANUFACTURES		2668.6		3461.9		2364.9		3063.0	ART MANUFACTURES
61	LEATHER,DRESSED FUR,ETC		37.3		37.9		38.8		48.2	CUIRS,PELLETERIES
62	RUBBER MANUFACTURES NES		186.5		264.1		207.5		191.7	CAOUTCHOUC MANUFACTURE
621	MATERIALS OF RUBBER	W 14012	22.5	W 14080	30.3	W 111797	31.7	W 18198	32.5	PRODUITS EN CAOUTCHOUC
62104	UNHARD VULC RUBBER,BASIC	W 11772	17.9	W 11732	24.5	W 110147	27.1	W 16589	27.9	PLAQUES,FEUILLES CAOUT
625	RUBBER TYRES, TUBES ETC	W 91656	119.4	W 65189	170.2	W 102310	165.3	W 54912	122.7	PNEUS CAOUTCHOUC VULCANISE
6251	TYRES NEW FOR MOTOR CARS	W 63005	56.1	W 20591	56.7	W 21873	62.9	W 20464	51.6	PNEUS POUR VOITURES
6252	TYRES,NEW,BUS OR LORRY	W 22572	54.5	W 39554	102.5	W 36063	92.3	W 31647	65.4	PNEUS POUR AUTOBUS,CAMIONS

5. General Exports F.O.B. by Commodities according to the S.I.T.C. (Rev. 2) in million U.S. Dollars
Exportations Générales F.O.B. par Produits d'après la C.T.C.I. (Rév. 2) en millions de Dollars E.U.

SITC CTCI	COMMODITY	1994 QUANTITY QUANTITE	1994 VALUE VALEUR	1995 QUANTITY QUANTITE	1995 VALUE VALEUR	1996 QUANTITY QUANTITE	1996 VALUE VALEUR	1997 QUANTITY QUANTITE	1997 VALUE VALEUR	PRODUIT
628	RUBBER ARTICLES NES		44.6	W 22389	63.7	W 4792	10.6	W 15133	36.7	OUVRAGES CAOUTCHOUC NDA
6282	VULCANIZD RUBBER BELTING	W 13264	35.7	W 16083	52.9			W 11099	26.6	COURROIES EN CAOUTCHOUC
63	WOOD,CORK MANUFACTRS NES		88.7		109.5		89.4		93.7	OUVRAGES LIEGE ET BOIS
634	VENEERS,PLYWOOD,ETC		35.7	W 64288	39.7	W 17337	17.9	W 48226	29.7	PLACAGES,CONTRE–PLAQUES
6342	PLYWOOD OF WOOD SHEETS		22.9	W 21855	25.2	W 13549	15.3	W 20126	18.6	BOIS CONTRE–PLAQUES
635	WOOD MANUFACTURES NES	W 257209	52.8	W 84957	69.8	W 91278	71.5	W 91110	64.1	ART MANUF EN BOIS NDA
6353	BUILDERS WOODWRK,PREFABS	W 223053	38.0	W 40642	52.6	W 40674	53.6	W 37298	43.9	OUVRAGES DE MENUISERIE
64	PAPER,PAPERBOARD AND MFR		233.1		339.2		371.2		364.3	PAPIERS,CARTONS & OUVRAGES
641	PAPER AND PAPERBOARD		170.1	W 279357	244.6	W 334598	247.4	W 378387	244.8	PAPIERS ET CARTONS
6412	PRINTG,WRITING PAPER NES	W 1574	1.8	W 2475	3.1	W 40887	31.9	W 54931	40.1	PAPIERS POUR L'IMPRESSION
64121	— UNCOATED	W 217	0.5	W 304	0.6	W 38691	29.6	W 48616	35.1	PAPIERS IMPRES NON COUCHES
6415	PAPER,PAPERBRD,BULK,NES	W 162455	90.2	W 189051	153.2	W 198435	112.5	W 213159	103.3	PAPIERS,CARTONS ROULEAUX
64151	SEMI–CHEM FLUTING PAPER	W 29362	9.4	W 56148	27.6	W 68334	29.6	W 76023	23.3	PAPIER FLUTING
64159	OTHER PAPER ETC,BULK,NES	W 131650	79.5	W 131103	123.0	W 128759	80.7	W 136193	79.1	AUT PAPIER ROULEAUX FEUILLES
6417	CORRUGATED PAPER ETC,BLK	W 23635	17.0	W 27985	30.5	W 41977	39.7	W 40541	33.9	PAPIERS,CARTONS ONDULES
64172	CREPED HSHOLD PAPER ETC	W 22892	16.5	W 25659	29.0	W 37561	37.0	W 35527	31.6	PAPIER NON KRAFT CREPE
6418	COATED ETC PAPER NES BLK	W 106075	46.5	W 22139	35.4	W 20859	42.3	W 22819	43.2	PAP,CARTONS COUCHES,ENDUITS
64181	PLASTIC COATED PAPER ETC	W 7003	19.7	W 9223	29.5	W 11867	38.1	W 14575	39.6	PAP,CARTONS ENDUITS,RESINES
64182	TARRED ETC PAPER,PAPERBD	W 97793	26.1	W 11986	4.2	W 7808	2.8	W 6514	2.5	PAPIERS,CARTONS GOUDRONNES
642	PAPER,ETC,PRECUT,ARTS OF		63.0	W 70224	94.6	W 86504	123.9	W 143132	119.6	PAP,CARTONS DECOUPES
6421	PAPER ETC CONTAINERS	W 24334	22.1	W 30576	34.4	W 29112	32.4	W 80343	26.9	BOITES,SACS EMBALLAGES
6424	PAPER ETC CT TO SIZE NES	W 28339	19.9	W 25447	26.1	W 36182	38.4	W 33903	28.5	PAP,CARTONS DECOUPES
64243	TOILET PAPER CUT TO SIZE	W 28081	19.6	W 25181	25.6	W 36030	38.0	W 33826	28.3	PAPIER HYGIENIQUE
6428	PAPER ETC ARTICLES NES	W 10516	16.8	W 11212	27.2	W 17835	46.9	W 26242	60.2	OUVRAGES EN PATE A PAPIER
64285	PAPER ETC DIAPERS ETC	W 3924	8.2	W 3630	14.8	W 7032	29.4	W 13079	40.4	SERVIETTES HYGIENIQUES
65	TEXTILE YARN,FABRICS,ETC		327.7		370.8		294.9		315.3	FILS,TISSUS,ARTICLES TEXTILE
651	TEXTILE YARN		217.2	W 86757	264.7	W 62818	209.2	W 86593	222.2	FILS TEXTILES
6514	SYN FIB YRN,BULK,MONOFIL		161.6	W 56824	186.1	W 54879	174.3	W 57178	160.6	FILS CONT 85% FIB TEXT SYNTH
65141	— TEXTRD,CONT POLYAMIDE	W 8889	27.8	W 4960	20.6	W 5552	22.5	W 4720	17.1	FILS TEXT FIB CONT POLYAMID
65142	— NONTXT ETC CONT PAMID	W 31366	83.6	W 33742	112.8	W 33871	107.2	W 37142	105.3	FILS NON TEX FI CON POLYAMID
65144	— TEXTRD,CONT POLYESTER	W 14727	34.4	W 11266	34.2	W 9236	26.4	W 8611	21.4	FILS TEX FI CONT POLYESTERS
6517	REGEN FIBRE YARN,MONOFIL	W 6422	25.6	W 7011	34.4	W 5682	27.4	W 6017	24.0	FILS TEXT ART NON VENTE DT
65171	CONT VISCOSE RAYON YARN	W 5697	23.9	W 6364	32.9	W 5045	26.5	W 5262	22.7	FILS RAY,VIS NON VENTE DET
6519	TEXTILE FIBRE YARN NES	W 16053	21.3	W 21307	36.3	W 112	0.4	W 22424	32.0	FILS TEXT NDA FILE FIB VER
65195	YARN ETC OF GLASS FIBRE	W 15575	19.3	W 21120	35.6			W 22197	31.6	FILS DE FIBRES DE VERRE
652	COTTON FABRICS,WOVEN		21.4	W 4519	18.3	W 2976	17.3	W 3254	16.2	TISSUS DE COTON
653	WOVN MAN–MADE FIB FABRIC		18.4	W 2552	25.8	W 2588	29.1	W 3853	32.3	TISSUS FIBRES SYNTH,ARTIF
654	OTH WOVEN TEXTILE FABRIC	W 5538	26.7	W 5291	26.0	W 1394	9.0	W 4516	15.5	TISSUS AUT COTON SYNT,ARTIF
658	TEXTILE ARTICLES NES	W 4125	23.3	W 3894	19.6	W 3244	20.7	W 3268	20.1	ART FACONNES MAT TEXTILES
66	NONMETAL MINERAL MFS NES		272.1		362.5		314.4		303.6	ART MIN NON METALLIQUES
661	LIME,CEMENT,BLDG PRODS	W 1722116	84.5	W 1975128	131.7	W 1784344	107.5	W 1799038	101.0	CHAUX,CIMENTS MAT CONSTR
6612	CEMENT	W 1603145	76.3	W 1760692	97.5	W 1450918	76.5	W 1535633	71.0	CIMENTS HYDRAULIQUES
6618	MNRL BLDG PRD UNFIRD NES	W 17722	3.5	W 110942	29.2	W 202257	25.3	W 105640	23.8	MAT CONST AMIANTE–CIMENT
662	CLAY,REFRACTORY BLDG PRD	W 215344	64.1	W 249124	82.9	W 288369	77.6	W 202962	66.8	MAT CONST REFRACTAIRES
6623	REFRACTORY BUILDING PROD	W 132065	43.4	W 150519	58.1	W 144059	54.4	W 139159	49.4	BRIQUES REFRACTAIRES
66232	REFRACTRY BRICKS ETC NES	W 126341	42.1	W 141300	55.7	W 130519	52.1	W 124421	47.4	BRIQUES ETC REFRACTAIRES
6624	BRICKS ETC NONREFRACTORY	W 83279	20.8	W 98605	24.8	W 144310	23.2	W 63803	17.4	BRIQUES ETC CERAM NON REFR
663	MINERAL MANUFCTURES NES		33.6	W 368889	40.2	W 296284	40.5	W 249464	30.5	ART MIN MANUF NDA
6633	MINRL MFS NES NONCERAMIC	W 315320	25.4	W 341916	27.3	W 268000	27.0	W 225251	19.2	OUVR MAT MINERALE NDA
66332	CEMENT,ARTFCL STONE PROD	W 314450	24.1	W 337631	24.4	W 263260	23.4	W 208794	16.1	OUVRAGES EN CIMENT
664	GLASS	W 18426	25.4	W 20072	33.8	W 19141	36.2	W 17996	31.9	VERRE
6649	GLASS NES	W 12536	20.0	W 11969	23.0	W 13151	26.7	W 13278	22.9	VERRE NDA
665	GLASSWARE	W 75543	56.4	W 163317	72.5	W 12757	51.0	W 92488	71.6	OUVRAGES EN VERRE
6651	BOTTLES ETC OF GLASS	W 64631	19.4	W 82720	29.7	W 1381	2.9	W 82440	25.3	RECIPIENTS EN VERRE
66511	GLASS BOTTLES ETC NONVAC	W 64110	17.4	W 81805	26.0	W 567	0.2	W 81622	23.1	BONBONNES,BOUTEILLES,ETC
6652	HOUSEHLD,HOTEL ETC GLASS	W 10134	35.0	W 79702	39.3	W 10712	44.4	W 9521	42.6	OBJETS VERRE TABLE,CUISINE
67	IRON AND STEEL		1156.5		1474.4		454.3		1162.9	FER ET ACIER
671	PIG IRON ETC	W 1695789	93.5	W 139185	99.0	W 113176	86.2	W 170514	100.5	FONTE,SPIEGEL,POUDRES
6716	FERRO–ALLOYS	W 1689402	93.1	W 139061	98.9	W 113171	86.1	W 152904	98.4	FERRO–ALLIAGES
67162	FERRO–SILICON	W 486533	27.1	W 35679	23.7	W 66475	49.8	W 64601	43.5	FERRO–SILICIUM
67169	OTHER FERRO–ALLOYS	W 881435	50.7	W 79570	61.9	W 23164	23.8	W 67552	44.9	AUTRES FERRO–ALLIAGES
672	IRON,STEEL PRIMARY FORMS	MW 11496	292.0	W 1079000	326.8	W 130862	31.2	W 793197	212.9	LINGOTS FER,ACIER
6725	IRN,STL BLOOMS,SLABS,ETC	W 2581607	55.0	W 339666	86.8	W 127427	30.1	W 120843	25.5	BLOOMS,BILLETTES FER ACIER
67251	IRN,SMPLE STL BLOOMS,ETC	W 2580826	54.9	W 339536	86.7	W 127333	29.9	W 120265	25.3	BLOOMS ETC NON ACIER FIN
6727	IRN,STL COIL FR REROLLNG	W 8862611	236.6	W 739334	240.1	W 3435	1.2	W 672355	187.4	EBAUCHES POUR TOLES FER
67271	IRON,SIMPLE STEEL COILS	W 8811368	235.0	W 736428	239.0	W 3423	1.1	W 672355	187.4	EBAUCHES NON EN ACIER
674	IRN,STL UNIV,PLATE,SHEET	MW 18404	648.1	W 2131471	875.5	W 397537	212.4	W 1794690	700.5	LARGES PLATS,TOLES
6744	IRN,STL HVY PLATE,ROLLED	W 4041653	111.0	W 332573	115.2	W 17643	5.7	W 212220	64.1	TOLES LAMINEES PLUS 4.75 MM
67441	— OF IRON OR SIMPLE STL	W 4020727	110.4	W 332467	115.1	W 17614	5.6	W 212007	64.0	TOLES NON ACIER FIN CARB
6745	IRN,STL MED PLATE,ROLLED	W 4824331	147.6	W 610302	209.4	W 94651	30.1	W 580590	180.4	TOLES 3 A 4.75 MM
67451	— OF IRON OR SIMPLE STL	W 4792256	146.3	W 590313	198.1	W 94647	30.1	W 523131	151.0	TOLES AUT NON ACIER FIN
67454	— OF OTHER ALLOY STEEL	W 22964	1.1	W 19983	11.3			W 57451	29.4	TOLES NON ACIERS ALLIES
6746	IRN,STL THIN PLATE,ROLLD	W 5952688	225.2	W 807445	337.5	W 1890	0.9	W 687842	276.8	TOLES LAM MOINS 3MM
67461	— OF IRON OR SIMPLE STL	W 5925059	224.1	W 806012	336.7	W 1707	0.8	W 687680	276.7	TOL NON AC FIN MOINS 3 MM
6747	TINNED PLATES,SHEETS	W 905090	55.2	W 96530	71.4	W 80000	61.0	W 79125	52.5	TOLES ETAMEES EN ACIER
6749	OTH IRN,STL PLATES,SHEET	W 2680231	109.4	W 284622	142.2	W 203354	114.9	W 234913	126.9	AUTRES TOLES FER,ACIER
67491	— OF IRON OR SIMPLE STL	W 2678754	109.3	W 283964	141.8	W 203353	114.9	W 234910	126.9	AUT TOLES AUTRES ACIER FIN
678	IRON,STL TUBES,PIPES,ETC	W 1322084	71.0	W 154165	100.1	W 129174	89.9	W 137481	86.4	TUBES,TUYAUX EN FONTE,FER
6782	IRON,STL SEAMLESS TUBES	W 786815	40.2	W 96552	61.6	W 106438	67.3	W 113613	64.5	TUBES,TUYAUX SANS SOUDURE
679	IRN,STL CASTINGS UNWORKD	W 248726	17.2	W 31946	27.4	W 30297	29.1	W 23808	22.7	OUVRAGES EN FONTE,FER,ACIER
68	NON–FERROUS METALS		143.3		207.7		302.8		302.0	METAUX NON FERREUX
682	COPPER EXC CEMENT COPPER		77.2	W 104156	82.8	W 29458	64.8	W 28875	57.1	CUIVRE
6821	COPPER NES,ALLOYS,UNWRT	W 91962	21.0	W 6043	16.9	W 2182	4.8	W 1648	2.7	CUIVRE BRUT
68212	COPPER REFINED,UNWROUGHT	W 90650	20.8	W 5909	16.5	W 2182	4.8	W 1648	2.7	CUIVRE AFFINE BRUT
6822	COPPER,ALLOYS WORKED		56.3	W 98113	65.9	W 27276	60.1	W 27227	54.5	CUIVRE,ALLIAGES OUVRES
68221	COPPER BARS,WIRE,ETC		48.5	W 96266	57.6	W 25598	53.3	W 25877	49.0	BARRES,PROFILES ET FILS
684	ALUMINIUM		62.0	W 56645	114.4	W 136443	234.0	W 132586	239.3	ALUMINIUM
6841	ALUMINIUM,ALLOYS,UNWRGHT	W 228531	32.4	W 40613	76.6	W 128598	214.6	W 123826	216.5	ALUMINIUM,ALLIAGES BRUTS
6842	ALUMINIUM,ALLOYS WORKED		29.7	W 16032	37.8	W 7845	19.4	W 8761	22.8	ALUMINIUM,ALLIAGES OUVRE
68421	ALUMINIUM BARS,WIRE,ETC	W 151686	27.0	W 13941	34.2	W 6394	15.9	W 7596	19.1	BARRES,PROFILES FILS ALU
69	METAL MANUFACTURES NES		223.7		296.2		292.0		281.7	ART MANUFACT EN METAL NDA
691	STRUCTURES AND PARTS NES	W 504055	54.9	W 60857	69.9	W 58631	71.1	W 57174	59.4	CONSTRUCT FER,ACIER,ALU
6911	STRUCTURES,PARTS IRN,STL	W 486565	47.0	W 59755	63.8	W 57508	63.9	W 56254	54.1	CONSTRUCT FER,ACIER,FONTE
692	METAL TANKS,BOXES,ETC	W 303519	35.1	W 34866	43.8	W 30527	39.6	W 29527	36.7	RECIPIENTS METALLIQUES
6921	METAL STORAGE TANKS ETC	W 209615	21.4	W 23191	25.8	W 18481	20.7	W 15070	16.3	CUVES EN FONTE,FER,ALU
69211	STEEL STORAGE TANKS ETC	W 209362	21.2	W 23182	25.8	W 18474	20.7	W 14919	16.0	CUVES EN FONTE FER OU ACIER
693	WIRE PRODUCTS NON ELECTR	W 683257	34.8	W 46855	44.3	W 38686	39.8	W 34407	32.1	OUVRAGES FILS METALLIQUES
697	BASE MTL HOUSEHOLD EQUIP	W 83556	13.8	W 9645	18.6	W 13011	24.7	W 14920	33.4	ART MENAGE MET COMMUNS
699	BASE METAL MFRS NES		60.3	W 50724	89.2	W 55422	85.9	W 54397	93.8	ART MANUFACTURES MET NDA
6997	IRON,STEEL ARTICLES NES		33.6	W 40133	50.4	W 45276	58.2	W 41541	50.3	OUV FONTE,FER,ACIER NDA
69979	IRN,STL MANUFACTURES NES		33.4	W 39949	50.1	W 45248	58.1	W 41352	50.1	AUT OUVRAGES EN FER NDA

5. General Exports F.O.B. by Commodities according to the S.I.T.C. (Rev. 2) in million U.S. Dollars
Exportations Générales F.O.B. par Produits d'après la C.T.C.I. (Rév. 2) en millions de Dollars E.U.

SITC CTCI	COMMODITY	1994 QUANTITY QUANTITE	1994 VALUE VALEUR	1995 QUANTITY QUANTITE	1995 VALUE VALEUR	1996 QUANTITY QUANTITE	1996 VALUE VALEUR	1997 QUANTITY QUANTITE	1997 VALUE VALEUR	PRODUIT
7	MACHINES,TRANSPORT EQUIP		1274.2		1587.2		1992.5		2382.7	MACHINES MATERIEL TRANSPORT
71	POWER GENERATING EQUIPMT		121.9		147.5		168.8		142.7	MACHINES GENERATRICES
713	INTRNL COMBUS PSTN ENGIN	W 34539	24.2	W 3933	34.5	W 4391	38.4	W 4187	32.4	MOTEURS EXPL COMB INT, PIECE
714	ENGINES AND MOTORS NES	W 8074	24.1	W 1038	7.9	W 986	7.4	W 1418	9.9	MOTEURS NON ELECTRIQUES
716	ROTATING ELECTRIC PLANT	W 165967	53.0	W 19412	81.7	W 19584	85.1	W 21815	69.6	APP ELECTR ROTATIFS,PIECES
7162	AC MTRS,GENRTRS,GEN SETS	W 147458	45.8	W 17080	73.2	W 15907	75.3	W 16586	56.8	MOTEURS ELECTRIQUES
71621	AC MTRS,INC UNIVRSL MTRS	W 146197	45.2	W 16997	72.9	W 15800	74.8	W 16393	55.9	MOT ELEC NON COUR CONTINU
72	MACHS FOR SPCL INDUSTRYS		111.6		131.3		148.9		175.1	MAC SPECIALES POUR INDUST
721	AGRIC MACHY,EXC TRACTORS	W 61908	10.8	W 5833	17.2	W 8239	23.4	W 22172	38.3	MACHINES AGRICOLES
7212	HARVESTING ETC MACHINES	W 29680	4.5	W 3263	11.6	W 5628	16.1	W 19250	30.7	ENGINS POUR LA RECOLTE
722	TRACTORS NON-ROAD	W 59188	19.9	W 5532	21.8	W 6790	32.2	W 6452	28.0	TRACTEURS
7224	WHEELED TRACTORS NES	W 59065	19.9	W 5457	21.7	W 6757	32.1	W 6357	27.9	TRACTEURS A ROUES
723	CIVIL ENGNEERG EQUIP ETC	W 133869	39.6	W 9995	35.1	W 10289	38.0	W 8487	31.4	APPAREILS DE GENIE CIVIL
7234	CONST,MINING MACHNRY NES	W 117465	36.4	W 8352	31.9	W 7906	32.5	W 6782	27.0	MACH POUR LA CONST, MINES
72342	SLFPRP SHOVELS,EXCAVATRS	W 92095	27.6	W 6785	25.8	W 6209	26.4	W 4489	19.2	PELLES MECANIQUES
728	OTH MACHY FOR SPCL INDUS		18.8	W 6307	32.7	W 6589	29.4	W 97124	41.6	AUT MACH IND PARTICULIERES
7284	MACHY FOR SPCL INDUS NES	W 21256	8.6	W 2248	19.5	W 2004	15.3	W 2928	27.6	MACH SPEC IND PARTICUL.
73	METALWORKING MACHINERY		55.3		92.3		91.2		93.3	MACH TRAVAIL DES METAUX
736	METALWORKING MACH-TOOLS	W 158853	46.2	W 20223	73.2	W 19275	74.7	W 17087	68.3	MACH-OUTILS TRAVAIL METAUX
7361	METAL CUTTING MACH-TOOLS	W 60065	20.4	W 7026	27.6	W 7482	30.6	W 6785	29.0	MACH-OUT ENLEVEMENT METAL
74	GENRL INDUSTRL MACHY NES		217.3		283.7		296.1		289.2	MACH APP INDUSTRIE
744	MECHANICAL HANDLING EQU	W 218495	47.4	W 29099	67.0	W 30694	69.5	W 33501	69.4	EQUIP MANUTENTION PIECES
7449	PTS NES OF MACHY OF 7442	W 143146	28.2	W 20225	43.3	W 21098	45.3	W 24998	47.0	PIECES DU 744.2
749	NONELEC MACH PTS,ACC NES	W 1056072	120.3	W 24317	159.6	W 22884	167.6	W 23041	158.2	PIECES MACH NON ELEC NDA
7491	BALL,ROLLER,ETC BEARINGS	W 111691	69.2	W 13500	102.5	W 13693	109.1	W 13643	100.1	ROULEMENTS BILLES ETC
7492	COCKS,VALVES ETC NES	W 40215	33.1	W 2727	25.8	W 2575	24.3	W 2119	19.1	ART ROB,SIM POUR TUYAUX
7493	SHAFT,CRANK,PULLEY ETC	W 885052	13.1	W 5569	22.4	W 5031	24.8	W 5591	29.0	ARBRES TRANS,VILEBREQUINS
75	OFFICE MACHNES,ADP EQUIP		24.0		17.5		11.5		32.4	MACH BUREAU TRAIT AUTOM
76	TELECOMM,SOUND EQUIPMENT		67.9		83.4		78.2		138.1	EQUIPMENT DE TELECOM
761	TELEVISION RECEIVERS	W 18435	25.7	W 1639	25.6	W 1	0.1	W 1789	19.4	RECEPTEURS DE TELEVISION
7611	COLOUR TV RECEIVERS	W 18255	25.5	W 1638	25.5	W 1	0.1	W 1789	19.4	RECEPTEURS COULEUR
764	TELECOM EQPT,PTS,ACC NES	W 19055	39.6	W 1910	56.4	W 2131	76.9	W 3219	115.4	EQUIP TELECOM,PIECES
7641	LINE TELEPHONE,ETC EQUIP	W 4159	18.2	W 493	35.6	W 486	42.8	W 659	46.6	APP TELEPHON PAR FIL
7649	PTS NES OF EQUIPMT OF 76	W 13517	18.8	W 1331	18.3	W 1537	30.5	W 2417	62.2	PIECES DE LA DIV 76
76493	TELECOMM EQUIPMT PTS NES	W 7957	10.2	W 829	6.7	W 1105	19.3	W 1968	49.0	PIECES 761,762,764.3,8
77	ELECTRIC MACHNRY NES ETC		235.0		307.7		348.0		409.2	MACH APP ELECT NDA
772	SWITCHGEAR ETC,PARTS NES	W 42120	30.1	W 5139	35.7	W 5201	37.6	W 4757	50.4	APP COUPURE,SECT ETC
7721	SWITCHGEAR ETC	W 41419	27.8	W 4926	31.3	W 4974	30.4	W 4467	40.0	APP COUPURE,SECTIONMNT
773	ELECTR DISTRIBUTNG EQUIP	W 211856	52.8	W 31764	111.6	W 40199	157.9	W 51579	185.2	EQUIPMT DISTRIBUTION ELECT
7731	INSULATED WIRE,CABLE ETC	W 177059	42.8	W 28233	97.7	W 36982	145.9	W 48340	174.6	FILS,CABLES ISOLES ELECT
775	HOUSEHOLD TYPE EQUIP NES	W 289981	89.6	W 30015	105.7	W 32150	111.4	W 36451	97.1	MACH,APP USAGE DOMESTQUE
7751	HOUSEHOLD LDRY EQUIP NES	W 51858	19.4	W 11947	45.1	W 13335	49.5	W 19096	42.9	MACH A LAVER ET SECHOIRS
77511	DOMESTIC WASHING MACHNES	W 51805	19.4	W 11944	45.1	W 13330	49.4	W 19095	42.9	MACH LAVER LINGE MOINS 6 KG
7752	DOM REFRIGERATRS,FREEZRS	W 156670	53.1	W 11953	45.7	W 13003	47.2	W 11006	34.9	REFRIG,CONGEL MENAGER
77521	DOMESTIC REFRIGERATORS	W 123562	40.1	W 9815	35.8	W 11223	39.4	W 9063	28.3	REFRIGERATEURS
778	ELECTRICAL MACHINERY NES		27.5	W 9234	29.2	W 4051	21.5	W 6875	31.9	AUTRES MACH ELECT NDA
78	ROAD VEHICLES		293.7		369.1		677.4		917.7	VEHICULES ROUTIERS
781	PASS MOTOR VEH EXC BUSES	W 99454	69.4	W 29394	67.0	W 32115	274.2	W 42801	437.6	AUTO TRANSPORT PERSONNES
782	LORRIES,SPCL MTR VEH NES	W 279284	43.6	W 14908	38.3	W 10501	29.4	W 13935	55.4	VEHICULES SPECIAUX,MARCH
7821	LORRIES,TRUCKS	W 182781	27.0	W 8288	23.3	W 6115	18.2	W 4026	6.7	VEHICULES TRANSP MARCHAND
7822	SPECIAL MOTOR VEHCLS NES	W 96503	16.6	W 6619	15.1	W 4386	11.2	W 9910	48.8	VEHICULES USAGES SPECIAUX
784	MOTOR VEH PRTS,ACCES NES	W 383403	134.9	W 179221	194.4	W 65666	300.9	W 76378	365.4	PIECES 722,781,782,783
7849	OTHER MOTOR VEHCL PARTS	W 343811	128.2	W 174822	184.6	W 59026	283.1	W 69357	349.9	PIECES 722,781,782,783
786	TRAILERS,NONMOTR VEH,NES	W 286265	31.9	W 38038	53.3	W 35349	54.7	W 33137	42.5	REMORQUES,CADRES,CONTAIN
7861	TRAILERS,TRANSP CONTAINR	W 222902	23.4	W 26897	35.3	W 25313	37.5	W 21513	26.8	REMORQUES TOUS VEHICULES
78613	CONTAINERS INC ROAD-RAIL	W 153573	15.3	W 22927	28.4	W 21971	30.4	W 17405	18.4	CADRES ET CONTAINERS
79	OTHR TRANSPORT EQUIPMENT		147.8		155.1		172.9		185.5	AUTRE MATERIEL TRANSPORT
791	RAILWAY VEHICLES	W 513019	79.4	W 62034	82.5	W 52269	86.3	W 44873	88.2	VEHIC MAT CHEMINS DE FER
7915	FRT,MAINT CARS NOT POWRD	W 286268	38.3	W 34997	32.7	W 26591	34.4	W 20877	31.3	WAGONS DE SERVICE
79152	RAILWAY FREIGHT CARS NES	W 280776	36.7	W 32769	28.9	W 25705	26.0	W 20311	28.7	WAGONS MARCHANDISES
7919	RY TRACK FIXT,ETC,PARTS	W 197937	38.7	W 16213	34.5	W 13523	25.1	W 17740	36.6	MATER FIXE VOIES FERREES
79199	PARTS NES OF 7911-7915	W 197406	38.6	W 16110	34.3	W 13513	25.0	W 17690	36.5	PIECES 791.1 ET 5
793	SHIPS AND BOATS ETC	W 239204	60.6	W 19038	68.8	W 24511	83.2	W 25028	87.3	NAVIRES BATEAUX,ETC
7932	SHIPS AND BOATS NES	W 219912	60.2	W 19038	68.8	W 24511	83.2	W 23480	85.8	NAVIRES ET BATEAUX
79323	OTHER CARGO VESSELS	W 215462	59.8	W 18993	68.5	W 24454	82.9	W 23369	85.5	AUT BATEAUX TRANS MARCH
8	MISC MANUFACTURED GOODS		832.3		970.7		982.7		1010.6	ART MANUFACTURES DIVERS
812	*PLUMBG,HEATNG,LGHTNG EQ		46.4	W 19435	55.7	W 22219	59.5	W 24438	59.4	APPAR SANITAIRES CHAUFFAGE
8121	CENTRAL HEATING EQUIPMNT	W 156619	21.8	W 12992	26.0	W 15794	30.9	W 17494	34.1	CHAUDIERES,RADIATEURS
8124	LIGHTING EQUIPMENT NES		23.9	W 5894	28.7	W 4427	26.5	W 4418	22.6	APPAREILS ECLAIRAGE ETC
821	*FURNITURE,PARTS THEREOF	W 1789622	144.2	W 97794	192.5	W 189748	192.7	W 110539	173.9	MEUBLES ET PIECES
8211	CHAIRS,SEATS AND PARTS	W 160724	35.9	W 21427	49.8	W 21024	49.4	W 47613	55.1	SIEGES ET PIECES
82111	CHAIRS AND OTHER SEATS	W 138751	33.5	W 16179	43.3	W 15883	42.1	W 39119	36.3	SIEGES
8219	FURNITURE AND PARTS NES	W 1618999	100.1	W 74763	130.5	W 73001	132.4	W 61676	109.5	AUTRES MEUBLES ET PIECES
82191	METAL FURNITURE NES	W 186576	25.1	W 20226	31.5	W 23409	30.8	W 17047	23.7	MEUBLES NDA EN METAL
82192	WOOD FURNITURE NES	W 382757	62.6	W 42667	84.7	W 38211	86.4	W 34759	73.6	MEUBLES NDA EN BOIS
84	CLOTHING AND ACCESSORIES		237.5		256.7		269.4		336.4	VETEMENTS
842	MENS OUTERWEAR NOT KNIT	W 8603	105.7	W 8700	113.6	W 8525	114.2	W 8174	150.8	VET DESSUS POUR HOMMES
8422	— SUITS	W 931	21.3	W 955	23.0	W 1007	24.7	W 1110	37.4	COMPLETS HOMMES MAT TEXT
8423	— TROUSERS,BREECHES ETC	W 3250	32.8	W 3509	33.8	W 3720	34.5	W 3307	47.2	PANTALONS HOMMES MAT TEX
8424	— JACKETS,BLAZERS ETC	W 2233	31.4	W 2192	36.7	W 1965	37.0	W 1846	41.7	VESTES HOMMES MAT TEXTIL
843	WOMENS OUTERWEAR NONKNIT		53.2	W 4630	62.1	W 4609	63.9	W 4597	83.0	VET DESSUS FEMMES MAT TEX
8431	— COATS AND JACKETS	W 2526	27.4	W 2042	29.0	W 1975	28.3	W 1631	36.1	MANT,VEST FEM MAT TEXTIL
845	OUTERWEAR KNIT NONELASTC	W 3127	37.2	W 3071	39.3	W 3613	44.5	W 3300	49.9	VET DESSOUS,ACCES BONNET
8451	— JERSEYS,PULLOVERS ETC	W 1583	20.1	W 1773	22.7	W 2162	29.1	W 2121	34.3	CHANDAILS,PULL-OVERS ETC
846	UNDER GARMENTS KNITTED		21.7	W 1944	21.0	W 2537	24.0	W 2231	22.2	SOUS VETS DE BONNETERIE
8462	— OF COTTON NON ELASTIC	W 2015	20.8	W 1879	19.9	W 2423	22.1	W 2058	19.0	SOUS-VET BONNET COTON
84629	—— OTHER	W 2015	20.8	W 1879	19.9	W 2423	22.1	W 2058	19.0	AUT SOUS-VET BONNET COTON
851	*FOOTWEAR	W 11438	102.0	W 10503	111.1	W 10340	123.0	W 10366	107.8	CHAUSSURES
85102	FOOTWEAR LEATHER	W 7558	65.7	W 8043	91.9	W 8257	108.4	W 8337	93.3	CHAUS SEMELLES EN CUIR
85103	SHOES WOOD-,CORK-SOLED	W 1669	24.3	W 385	6.7	W 436	3.8	W 565	7.2	CHAUS SEMELLES BOIS,LIEGE
87	PRECISION INSTRUMNTS NES		88.5		101.5		90.5		86.8	INSTRUM,APPAR SCIENT NDA
872	MEDICAL INSTRUMENTS NES	W 31273	44.7	W 3179	46.3	W 2792	37.5	W 2195	27.7	INSTR,APP MEDIC-CHIR NDA
87201	DENTAL INSTRUMENTS	W 10058	26.1	W 826	24.5	W 526	17.6	W 348	10.9	INSTRUM,APPAR DENTAIRE
873	METERS AND COUNTERS NES	W 21806	23.3	W 2909	32.4	W 2870	32.6	W 3096	36.2	COMPTEURS,INST DE MESURE
8731	GAS SUPPLY METERS ETC	W 21777	23.3	W 2881	32.0	W 2867	32.1	W 3095	36.1	COMPTEURS GAZ,LIQ ELECT
874	MEASURNG,CONTROLNG INSTR		20.2	W 1276	22.7	W 1206	20.3	W 1389	22.7	INSTRUMENTS DE MESURE
89	MISC MANUFCTRD GOODS NES		199.4		238.4		231.2		231.6	ART MANUFACTURES DIVERS
892	PRINTED MATTER		70.4	W 29518	86.8	W 105974	101.4	W 34338	99.0	IMPRIMES
8921	PRINTED BOOKS,GLOBES,ETC		45.2	W 18237	54.0	W 18126	58.9	W 15977	51.6	LIVRES,BROCHURES,CARTES
89211	PRINTED BOOKS,PAMPHLETS		41.9	W 17596	50.4	W 17535	55.3	W 15280	48.4	LIVRES,BROCHURES
8922	NEWSPAPERS,PERIODICALS	W 9724	15.4	W 9755	19.8	W 85975	28.6	W 16560	34.3	JOURNAUX ET PERIODIQUES

5. General Exports F.O.B. by Commodities according to the S.I.T.C. (Rev. 2) in million U.S. Dollars
Exportations Générales F.O.B. par Produits d'après la C.T.C.I. (Rév. 2) en millions de Dollars E.U.

SITC CTCI	COMMODITY	1994 QUANTITY QUANTITE	1994 VALUE VALEUR	1995 QUANTITY QUANTITE	1995 VALUE VALEUR	1996 QUANTITY QUANTITE	1996 VALUE VALEUR	1997 QUANTITY QUANTITE	1997 VALUE VALEUR	PRODUIT
893	ARTICLES OF PLASTIC NES		81.7		96.1		89.5		84.0	OUVRAGES EN MAT DIVIS 58
8939	MISC PLASTIC ARTICLES		55.9	W 91527	63.6	W 25899	57.8	W 23722	51.0	ART DIVERS EN MAT DIV 58
89399	OTHR PLASTC ARTICLES NES		52.8	W 86704	59.4	W 23090	54.9	W 22263	49.4	AUT OUV MAT DIV 58
9	GOODS NOT CLASSD BY KIND		61.2		268.0		1395.6		312.6	ART TRANSACT NON CLASSES
931	*SPECIAL TRANSACTIONS				203.3		1333.2		281.9	TRANS.SPECIALES
951	*WAR FIREARMS,AMMUNITION	W 60049	58.2	W 4859	61.5	W 4839	59.0	W 1786	27.7	VEHIC BLINDES ARMES
95101	ARMORED FIGHTNG VEHICLES	W 55979	52.4	W 3514	55.1	W 3097	55.2	W 1359	25.0	CHARS DE COMBAT

1. HISTORICAL SERIES, 1992–1997 SPECIAL TRADE, IMPORTS C.I.F., EXPORTS F.O.B.
SERIES HISTORIQUES, 1992–1997 COMMERCE SPECIAL, IMPORTATIONS C.A.F., EXPORTATIONS F.O.B

YEAR ANNEE	VALUE IN MILLION U.S. DOLLARS VALEUR EN MILLION U.S. DOLLARS MERCHANDISE –MARCHANDISE		GOLD –OR		CONVERSION FACTORS FACTEURS DE CONVERSION CENTS E.U. PAR		INDEX NUMBERS –INDICES QUANTUM		UNIT VALUE VALEUR UNITAIRE	
	IMPORTS	EXPORTS	IMPORTS	EXPORTS	IMPORTS	EXPORTS	IMPORTS	EXPORTS	IMPORTS	EXPORTS
1992	6142.00	6681.00								
1993	6529.00	6083.00								
1994	7304.00	6828.00								
1995	9490.00	8315.00								
1996	9423.00	8312.00								
1997	9357.00	8372.00								

2. IMPORTS BY BROAD ECONOMIC CATEGORY AND EXPORTS BY INDUSTRIAL ORIGIN. (PERCENTAGE OF TOTAL VALUE)
IMPORTATIONS PAR CATEGORIES ECONOMIQUES ET EXPORTATIONS PAR BRANCHE D'ACTIVITE.(EN POURCENTAGE DE LA VALEUR TOTALE)

IMPORTS – IMPORTATIONS

	1991	1992	1993	1994	1995	1996	1997
TOTAL IMPORTS–IMPORTATIONS TOTALES		100.	100.	100.	100.	100.	100.
1 FOOD BEV–ALIMENTATION BOISSONS		7.2	6.9	7.2	6.7	6.5	6.2
11 PRIMARY–PRODUITS DE BASE		3.2	3.3	3.5	2.9	2.8	2.9
111 FOR INDUSTRY–POUR L'INDUSTRIE		1.0	1.1	1.1	0.9	0.8	0.9
112 FOR HOUSEHOLDS–POUR LES MENAGES		2.2	2.2	2.4	2.0	2.0	2.0
12 PROCESSED–PRODUITS ELABORES		4.0	3.6	3.7	3.8	3.6	3.3
121 FOR INDUSTRY–POUR L'INDUSTRIE		0.5	0.6	0.5	0.6	0.6	0.5
122 FOR HOUSEHOLDS–POUR LES MENAGES		3.5	3.1	3.2	3.2	3.0	2.8
2 IND SUPPLIES–APPROV INDUSTRIELS		39.7	34.6	38.0	37.4	35.7	36.5
21 PRIMARY–PRODUITS DE BASE		4.4	3.3	4.0	3.9	3.3	3.2
22 PROCESSED–PRODUITS ELABORES		35.3	31.3	34.0	33.5	32.3	33.3
3 FUELS–COMBUSTIBLES		10.2	10.2	6.8	6.3	7.7	8.0
31 PRIMARY–PRODUITS DE BASE		5.8	5.8	2.1	2.3	2.3	2.6
32 PROCESSED–PRODUITS ELABORES		4.3	4.4	4.7	3.9	5.4	5.4
321 MOTOR SPIRIT–ESSENCE		1.7	1.6	2.1	1.6	2.1	2.2
322 OTHER–AUTRES		2.6	2.8	2.6	2.3	3.3	3.3
4 MACHINERY–EQUIPEMENT		16.2	16.8	18.5	18.6	18.5	19.0
41 CAPITAL EQUIPMENT–MACHINES		13.4	13.9	15.4	15.6	15.3	15.8
42 PARTS–PIECES ACCESSOIRES		2.8	2.9	3.1	3.0	3.2	3.2
5 TRANSPORT–TRANSPORT		10.2	13.7	13.5	15.6	16.1	14.9
51 PASSENGER CARS–AUTOMOBILES		3.1	7.1	5.9	6.4	6.7	6.0
52 OTHER–AUTRES		1.1	1.7	1.9	2.7	2.4	1.9
521 INDUSTRIAL–INDUSTRIELS		1.0	1.5	1.8	2.6	2.3	1.7
522 NON INDUSTRIAL–NON INDUSTRIEL		0.1	0.1	0.1	0.1	0.1	0.2
53 PARTS–PIECES ACCESSOIRES		6.0	4.9	5.7	6.5	7.0	7.0
6 CONSUM GOODS–BIENS CONSOMMATION		12.1	13.9	12.6	12.5	15.2	15.0
61 DURABLE–DURABLES		2.5	2.8	2.9	2.9	2.9	2.8
62 SEMI DURABLE–SEMI DURABLES		7.2	8.3	6.7	6.6	9.1	8.9
63 NON DURABLE–NON DURABLES		2.5	2.7	2.9	3.0	3.3	3.3
7 GOODS NES–BIENS NDA		4.5	4.0	3.3	2.9	0.3	0.3

EXPORTS – EXPORTATIONS

	1991	1992	1993	1994	1995	1996	1997
TOTAL EXPORTS–EXPORTATIONS TOTALES		100.	100.	100.	100.	100.	100.
1 AGRICULTURE		1.5	1.0	1.0	0.7	0.7	0.6
2 MINING QUARRY–INDUS EXTRACTIVES		1.9	3.9	0.2	0.1	0.1	0.1
3 MANUFACTURING–IND MANUFACTUR		96.6	95.1	98.7	99.2	99.2	99.3
31 FOOD BEV TOBACCO–ALIM BOISS TAB		5.7	4.3	4.3	3.6	3.9	3.8
32 TEXTILES–INDUSTRIES TEXTILES		17.7	18.2	16.3	14.5	13.5	12.5
33 WOOD & PRODUCTS–BOIS & PRODUITS		4.4	4.5	4.8	4.7	4.5	4.2
34 PAPER & PRODUCTS–PAPIER & PRODT		5.4	5.0	5.4	6.0	5.2	5.1
35 CHEMICALS–INDUSTRIES CHIMIQUES		13.2	13.1	13.9	14.3	14.6	15.5
36 NON METAL MIN–MIN NON METAL		2.7	2.7	2.7	2.6	2.8	2.7
37 BASIC METAL–IND METAL BASE		5.7	5.3	6.0	6.9	6.4	6.7
38 METAL MANUF–MANUF METAL		40.8	40.0	43.2	44.4	46.7	46.9
39 OTH MANUF IND–AUTRES MANUF		1.1	2.0	2.0	2.2	1.7	1.8

3. TRADE BY PRINCIPAL COUNTRIES OF ORIGIN AND DESTINATION (VALUE IN MILLION U.S. DOLLARS)
ECHANGES SELON LES PRINCIPAUX PAYS D'ORIGINE ET DE DESTINATION (VALEUR EN MILLIONS DE DOLLARS EU)

COUNTRIES–PAYS	SPECIAL IMPORTS C.I.F. IMPORTATIONS SPECIALES C.A.F				
	1993	1994	1995	1996	1997
World	6500.9	7303.9	9491.7	9420.7	9365.7
Africa	86.9	88.9	113.7	125.7	159.1
Americas	282.0	321.1	429.1	478.4	434.5
– Northern America	207.3	232.1	337.9	365.7	320.5
– LAIA	64.8	80.8	86.4	107.9	108.7
– CACM	1.0	0.8	1.1	0.9	1.9
– Caribbean	7.9	6.4	1.5	1.8	0.9
– Rest of America	1.2	0.9	2.2	2.1	2.5
Asia excl fmr USSR	437.8	373.2	505.2	552.6	624.2
– Middle East	133.2	30.2	35.8	43.6	63.4
Asia former USSR	6.3	9.6	14.7	12.6	13.8
Europe excl fmr USSR	5467.7	6336.6	8146.5	7975.4	7818.6
– European Union	4265.9	5052.3	6531.5	6358.7	6310.8
– Eastern Europe	370.5	501.1	693.9	647.1	719.0
– Rest of Europe	831.4	783.2	921.1	969.6	788.9
Europe former USSR	210.6	159.8	260.1	223.8	270.4
Oceania	9.7	14.7	22.3	21.7	19.1
Other	0.0	0.0	0.0	30.6	26.0
Germany/Allemagne	1626.0	1734.2	2206.0	2043.9	1935.5
Italy/Italie	1051.2	1258.2	1611.2	1591.8	1557.7
Austria/Autriche	553.2	755.5	918.9	834.7	788.4
France, Monaco	521.8	612.7	798.1	924.5	980.1
Croatia/Croatie	595.4	498.2	575.6	590.4	466.4
USA/Etats–Unis d'Amer	188.1	197.2	291.4	325.4	287.7
Hungary/Hongrie	165.0	192.6	266.8	238.6	292.8
Russian Federation	202.5	147.4	241.4	208.5	250.2
Czech Republic	152.2	177.8	246.9	236.4	233.7
Netherlands/Pays–Bas	122.0	167.5	206.6	194.3	200.1
United Kingdom	103.0	129.6	189.9	208.3	240.5
Switzerland,Liechtenst.	129.7	157.2	202.5	180.1	162.9
Spain/Espagne	70.8	115.4	224.6	170.0	199.2
Japan/Japon	125.1	126.2	156.7	162.5	161.1
Belgium–Luxembourg	67.2	88.8	153.8	153.3	159.8
Sweden/Suède	65.4	83.5	100.7	110.5	109.8
TFYR Macedonia	89.3	80.4	85.7	70.8	56.1
Korea, Republic of	47.0	47.1	78.4	91.7	84.8
Slovakia/Slovaquie		58.1	82.3	91.5	102.5
Algeria/Algérie	42.0	44.0	62.0	65.2	99.8
China/Chine	29.4	37.2	52.9	49.6	82.1
Brazil/Brésil	30.1	43.8	51.2	54.9	53.6
Other Asia n.e.s.	32.4	38.4	48.0	46.2	42.6
Denmark/Danemark	24.7	32.4	46.2	41.8	46.5
Finland/Finlande	25.0	45.5	39.5	39.1	41.2
Poland/Pologne	14.0	22.5	37.7	48.4	58.4
Canada	19.1	34.8	46.3	40.1	32.8
Norway,Svalbard and JM	4.7	30.6	34.4	67.7	30.2
Turkey/Turquie	26.9	21.7	31.8	32.9	40.3
Israel/Israël	5.7	20.7	20.8	25.8	53.9
Ireland/Irlande	20.4	18.0	19.9	28.6	26.1
Romania/Roumanie	15.7	20.6	33.4	24.7	16.5
Indonesia/Indonésie	13.1	12.0	21.8	29.8	32.0
Iran (Islamic Rep of)	87.1	1.1	1.2	4.0	1.5
Bulgaria/Bulgarie	22.6	28.6	23.1	4.1	12.8
Argentina/Argentine	16.9	7.4	9.3	23.7	25.8
Australia/Australie	8.8	13.6	21.3	20.5	17.3
China, Hong Kong SAR	10.7	13.4	18.5	18.5	18.1
Malaysia/Malaisie	6.2	8.1	18.4	25.3	20.8
Thailand/Thaïlande	11.7	13.3	17.2	18.1	17.5

COUNTRIES–PAYS	SPECIAL EXPORTS F.O.B. EXPORTATIONS SPECIALES F.O.B.				
	1993	1994	1995	1996	1997
Monde	6082.9	6827.8	8315.8	8309.8	8368.9
Afrique	39.8	39.3	58.2	48.5	62.5
Amériques	267.9	325.7	344.0	316.5	319.2
– Amérique du Nord	247.3	292.3	298.7	278.7	270.7
– ALAI	15.8	23.0	31.1	35.1	44.8
– MCAC	0.6	1.4	1.3	1.3	0.7
– Caraïbes	2.9	8.1	10.9	0.9	2.4
– Autre Amérique	1.4	0.9	2.0	0.5	0.6
Asie anc. URSS exclus	252.4	189.2	204.2	202.9	216.1
– Moyen–Orient	166.9	92.0	92.2	100.2	120.6
Asie ancienne URSS	8.5	3.9	11.0	7.0	9.9
Europe anc. URSS exclus	5208.0	5937.0	7315.6	7328.7	7317.6
– Union Européenne	3847.1	4480.2	5574.5	5366.7	5319.7
– Europe de l'Est	329.2	339.6	442.7	489.9	523.1
– Autre de l'Europe	1031.7	1117.1	1298.4	1472.1	1474.7
Europe ancienne URSS	289.0	312.3	364.0	383.2	422.2
Océanie	17.2	20.3	18.7	17.0	16.9
Autre	0.0	0.0	0.0	6.0	4.6
Germany/Allemagne	1797.6	2067.7	2507.8	2545.4	2459.5
Italy/Italie	756.0	923.6	1211.8	1103.3	1248.3
Croatia/Croatie	738.5	737.7	891.1	855.0	837.2
France, Monaco	527.8	586.3	681.5	598.0	463.2
Austria/Autriche	303.0	373.3	534.6	550.6	565.4
Russian Federation	249.1	264.9	305.2	298.3	326.5
USA/Etats–Unis d'Amer	216.0	250.3	261.9	246.2	243.1
TFYR Macedonia	198.2	218.0	189.3	170.5	149.2
United Kingdom	148.1	208.2	229.1	161.5	149.9
Bosnia and Herzegovina	20.1	68.6	118.9	263.6	287.9
Czech Republic	86.1	82.5	132.0	146.6	147.4
Poland/Pologne	87.4	96.3	104.9	141.5	155.5
Netherlands/Pays–Bas	89.8	99.5	117.2	124.9	123.1
Hungary/Hongrie	87.7	98.7	114.6	105.4	120.5
Belgium–Luxembourg	53.8	60.3	73.7	78.0	86.0
Switzerland,Liechtenst.	53.3	59.9	74.0	70.4	72.0
Sweden/Suède	45.4	50.4	58.5	54.2	55.9
Yugoslavia/Yougoslavie	7.6	15.7	9.5	95.7	112.4
Spain/Espagne	48.0	36.2	42.4	43.9	52.7
Denmark/Danemark	23.3	32.3	42.2	47.2	54.3
Slovakia/Slovaquie		30.3	51.7	57.2	56.4
Canada	31.3	42.0	36.8	32.5	27.6
Iran (Islamic Rep of)	59.8	31.7	20.8	25.4	32.4
Ukraine	19.0	24.7	29.2	33.4	45.9
Turkey/Turquie	34.1	7.7	20.5	24.4	33.0
Egypt/Egypte	18.4	20.1	24.5	25.7	30.5
Greece/Grèce	18.2	16.9	31.9	22.9	24.0
Belarus/Bélarus	15.7	13.3	16.5	33.1	28.7
Romania/Roumanie	19.0	12.4	21.0	22.3	24.4
Japan/Japon	25.5	18.2	21.0	19.1	15.4
Bulgaria/Bulgarie	45.3	14.3	12.6	9.3	12.6
United Arab Emirates	22.1	16.9	14.4	14.4	14.8
Australia/Australie	15.9	17.9	16.9	15.4	14.7
Finland/Finlande	9.9	12.6	18.0	19.6	18.2
Saudi Arabia	17.1	15.3	15.8	13.6	15.9
Norway,Svalbard and JM	11.5	14.3	12.4	11.8	14.0
Ireland/Irlande	18.3	6.2	17.0	4.3	5.3
Brazil/Brésil	2.0	4.3	10.7	18.0	15.8
Portugal	7.9	6.6	8.8	13.0	14.1
Korea, Republic of	7.6	11.1	13.1	9.3	9.4

(VALUE AS PERCENTAGE OF WORLD TOTAL)(VALEURS EN POURCENTAGE DU TOTAL MONDIAL)

	1988	1989	1990	1991	1992	1993	1994	1995	1996	1997
Africa					1.2	1.3	1.2	1.2	1.3	1.7
Americas					3.8	4.3	4.4	4.5	5.1	4.6
– Northern America					3.0	3.2	3.2	3.6	3.9	3.4
– LAIA					0.7	1.0	1.1	0.9	1.1	1.2
– CACM					0.0	0.0	0.0	0.0	0.0	0.0
– Caribbean					0.1	0.1	0.1	0.0	0.0	0.0
– Rest of America					0.0	0.0	0.0	0.0	0.0	0.0
Asia excl fmr USSR					4.1	6.7	5.1	5.3	5.9	6.7
– Middle East					0.7	2.0	0.4	0.4	0.5	0.7
Asia former USSR					0.0	0.1	0.1	0.2	0.1	0.1
Europe excl fmr USSR					86.5	84.1	86.8	85.8	84.7	83.5
– European Union					59.6	65.6	69.2	68.8	67.5	67.4
– Eastern Europe					5.3	5.7	6.9	7.3	6.9	7.7
– Rest of Europe					21.6	12.8	10.7	9.7	10.3	8.4
Europe former USSR					4.1	3.2	2.2	2.7	2.4	2.9
Oceania					0.3	0.1	0.2	0.2	0.2	0.2
Other					0.0	0.0	0.0	0.0	0.3	0.3
Germany/Allemagne					22.7	25.0	23.7	23.2	21.7	20.7
Italy/Italie					13.7	16.2	17.2	17.0	16.9	16.6
Austria/Autriche					8.1	8.5	10.3	9.7	8.9	8.4
France, Monaco					8.0	8.0	8.4	8.4	9.8	10.5
Croatia/Croatie					13.9	9.2	6.8	6.1	6.3	5.0
USA/Etats–Unis d'Amer					2.7	2.9	2.7	3.1	3.5	3.1
Hungary/Hongrie					2.5	2.5	2.6	2.8	2.5	3.1
Russian Federation					4.0	3.1	2.0	2.5	2.2	2.7
Czech Republic						2.3	2.4	2.6	2.5	2.5
Netherlands/Pays–Bas					1.7	1.9	2.3	2.2	2.1	2.1

	1988	1989	1990	1991	1992	1993	1994	1995	1996	1997
Afrique					0.9	0.7	0.6	0.7	0.6	0.7
Amériques					3.7	4.4	4.8	4.1	3.8	3.8
– Amérique du Nord					3.4	4.1	4.3	3.6	3.4	3.2
– ALAI					0.3	0.3	0.3	0.4	0.4	0.5
– MCAC					0.0	0.0	0.0	0.0	0.0	0.0
– Caraïbes					0.0	0.0	0.1	0.1	0.0	0.0
– Autre Amérique					0.0	0.0	0.0	0.0	0.0	0.0
Asie anc. URSS exclus					3.5	4.1	2.8	2.5	2.4	2.6
– Moyen–Orient					2.6	2.7	1.3	1.1	1.2	1.4
Asie ancienne URSS					0.0	0.1	0.1	0.1	0.1	0.1
Europe anc. URSS exclus					88.3	85.6	87.0	88.0	88.2	87.4
– Union Européenne					60.9	63.2	65.6	67.0	64.6	63.6
– Europe de l'Est					3.9	5.4	5.0	5.3	5.9	6.3
– Autre de l'Europe					23.6	17.0	16.4	15.6	17.7	17.6
Europe ancienne URSS					3.3	4.8	4.6	4.4	4.6	5.0
Océanie					0.2	0.3	0.3	0.2	0.2	0.2
Autre					0.0	0.0	0.0	0.0	0.1	0.1
Germany/Allemagne					27.0	29.6	30.3	30.2	30.6	29.4
Italy/Italie					13.2	12.4	13.5	14.6	13.3	14.9
Croatia/Croatie					14.2	12.1	10.8	10.7	10.3	10.0
France, Monaco					9.2	8.7	8.6	8.2	7.2	5.5
Austria/Autriche					5.1	5.0	5.5	6.4	6.6	6.8
Russian Federation					3.0	4.1	3.9	3.7	3.6	3.9
USA/Etats–Unis d'Amer					2.9	3.6	3.7	3.1	3.0	2.9
TFYR Macedonia						3.3	3.2	2.3	2.1	1.8
United Kingdom					2.1	2.4	3.0	2.8	1.9	1.8
Bosnia and Herzegovina					0.3	0.3	1.0	1.4	3.2	3.4

4. Special Imports C.I.F. by Commodities according to the S.I.T.C. (Rev. 2) in million U.S. Dollars
Importations Spéciales C.A.F. par Produits d'après la C.T.C.I. (Rév. 2) en millions de Dollars E.U.

SITC CTCI	COMMODITY	1994 QUANTITY QUANTITE	1994 VALUE VALEUR	1995 QUANTITY QUANTITE	1995 VALUE VALEUR	1996 QUANTITY QUANTITE	1996 VALUE VALEUR	1997 QUANTITY QUANTITE	1997 VALUE VALEUR	PRODUIT
	ALL COMMODITIES		7304.0		9491.7		9420.7		9365.7	TOUS PRODUITS
0	FOOD AND LIVE ANIMALS		555.3		637.5		637.5		595.6	ALIMENTS,ANIMAUX VIVANTS
01	MEAT AND PREPARATIONS		81.2		76.0		66.5		72.4	VIANDES ET PREPARATIONS
011	MEAT FRESH,CHILLD,FROZEN	W 37438	73.3	W 26933	64.4	W 24403	57.2	W 27328	64.6	VIANDES FRAICHES,REF,CONGE
0113	PIG MEAT FRESH,CHLD,FRZN	W 24119	46.6	W 19327	45.1	W 18564	43.8	W 22651	52.6	VIANDE DE PORC
04	CEREALS AND PREPARATIONS		106.0		108.5		140.6		118.9	CEREALES ET PRODUITS
041	WHEAT ETC UNMILLED	W 125140	16.6	W 82377	13.7	W 64747	12.9	W 167873	30.0	FROMENT,EPEAUTRE
0412	OTHER WHEAT ETC UNMILLED	W 115568	15.6	W 82189	13.6	W 64708	12.9	W 167848	30.0	AUTRE FROMENT NON MOULU
044	MAIZE UNMILLED	W 210344	28.8	W 188841	24.6	W 215317	43.5	W 198287	26.5	MAIS NON MOULU
048	CEREAL ETC PREPARATIONS	W 35119	37.2	W 38826	47.9	W 42763	49.7	W 39004	42.9	PREPTNS A BASE CEREALES
0484	BAKERY PRODUCTS	W 10849	23.2	W 10791	28.3	W 9391	26.5	W 8881	22.6	PRODUITS DE BOULANGERIE
05	VEGETABLES AND FRUIT		122.2		158.9		157.9		141.7	LEGUMES ET FRUITS
054	VEG ETC FRSH,SMPLY PRSVD	W 72795	45.4	W 100961	61.5	W 110803	61.8	W 73626	47.7	LEGUMES FRAIS,CONG,SECS
0545	OTHER FRESH VEGETABLES	W 40696	22.4	W 43496	27.5	W 41073	29.8	W 38424	24.5	AUTRES LEGUMES FRAIS,REF
057	FRUIT,NUTS,FRESH,DRIED	W 86681	46.1	W 89580	57.2	W 89729	61.9	W 94315	62.0	FRUITS FRAIS OU SECS
058	FRUIT PRESERVED,PREPARED	W 24991	22.3	W 28201	29.4	W 18632	23.6	W 21306	22.2	CONSERVES DE FRUITS
06	SUGAR AND PREPS,HONEY		35.9		42.2		33.3		27.7	SUCRES ET PRODUITS
061	SUGAR AND HONEY	W 59668	23.2	W 70041	30.0	W 55261	22.5	W 49689	17.9	SUCRES ET MIEL
07	COFFEE,TEA,COCOA,SPICES		66.1		76.4		72.4		69.8	CAFE,THE,CACAO,EPICES
071	COFFEE AND SUBSTITUTES	W 9714	29.6	W 9030	34.0	W 10265	32.6	W 9996	32.1	CAFE ET SUCCEDANES
0711	COFFEE GREEN,ROASTED,SUB	W 9244	28.0	W 8542	32.0	W 9659	29.4	W 9426	29.1	CAFE TORREFIE OU DECAFEINE
07111	COFFEE GREEN,HUSKS,SKINS	W 8597	24.8	W 7852	27.3	W 9154	26.2	W 8861	25.9	CAFE NON TORREFIE
073	CHOCOLATE AND PRODUCTS	W 7141	31.3	W 7331	37.2	W 7167	34.4	W 7670	32.0	CHOCOLAT
081	*FEEDING STUFF FOR ANIML	W 143078	46.2	W 163149	52.1	W 154912	56.1	W 150509	57.4	NOURRITURE POUR ANIMAUX
0813	OILCAKE AND OTH RESIDUES	W 104178	25.3	W 116500	26.5	W 110555	32.2	W 112710	34.7	TOURTEAUX
08131	— OF SOYA BEANS	W 96158	24.1	W 103168	24.6	W 93752	29.4	W 93185	31.2	TOURTEAUX DE SOJA
09	MISC EDIBLE PRODUCTS		49.6		65.0		61.0		60.2	PREP ALIMENTAIRES DIVERSES
098	EDIBLE PRODCTS,PREPS NES	W 11217	41.0	W 13216	54.8	W 13696	51.2	W 16962	51.2	PREP ALIMENTAIRES NDA
09809	MISC FOOD PREPRTIONS NES	W 7159	30.1	W 8214	40.7	W 8743	36.2	W 11876	39.0	PREP ALIMENTAIRES NDA
1	BEVERAGES AND TOBACCO		47.0		61.1		60.1		58.3	BOISSONS ET TABACS
11	BEVERAGES		20.9		36.3		38.1		29.8	BOISSONS
12	TOBACCO AND MANUFACTURES		26.1		24.8		22.0		28.5	TABACS BRUTS FABRIQUES
2	CRUDE MATERLS,EXCL FUELS		462.7		610.3		471.1		478.2	MAT BRUTES NON COMESTIBLES
21	HIDES,SKINS,FURS UNDRSSD		23.7		31.6		27.4		34.5	CUIRS,PEAUX BRUTS
211	HIDES,SKINS,EXC FURS,RAW	W 25436	23.2	W 25699	31.0	W 21654	27.1	W 24303	34.2	CUIRS ET PEAUX
23	RUBBER, CRUDE		41.2		63.7		53.8		48.1	CAOUTCHOUC BRUT
233	RUBBER,SYNTHTIC,RECLAIMD	W 24635	26.7	W 27939	40.0	W 25778	31.3	W 28390	29.6	LATEX CAOUTCH SYNTH REGEN
2331	SYNTHETIC RUBBER ETC	W 24367	26.5	W 27624	39.7	W 25254	30.9	W 27826	29.0	LATEX CAOUTCH SYNTHETIQUE
24	CORK AND WOOD		61.4		72.1		58.1		59.1	LIEGE ET BOIS
248	WOOD SHAPED,SLEEPERS	W 88943	42.5	W 75171	47.6	W 73955	47.3	W 87024	43.7	BOIS SIMPLEMENT TRAVAILLES
2483	LUMBER SHAPED NON–CONIFR	W 70162	31.7	W 55949	34.0	W 55712	34.8	W 62633	32.2	NON CONIFERES SCIES,RABOTES
24831	LUMBER SAWN ETC NON–CON	W 65311	25.3	W 51992	27.5	W 51636	27.5	W 58904	25.8	SCIES LONGITUDINALEMENT
251	*PULP AND WASTE PAPER	W 257436	95.6	W 263979	159.0	W 232721	84.3	W 276247	90.1	PATES A PAPIER,DECHETS
2511	WASTE PAPER,PPRBOARD ETC	W 115083	18.6	W 125256	41.0	W 103474	17.7	W 114789	14.3	DECHETS DE PAPIER
2517	SODA,SULPHATE WOOD PULP	W 83877	48.4	W 90772	82.8	W 88154	47.8	W 103109	52.1	PATES CHIMIQUES AU SULFATE
25172	— BLEACHED,NONDISSOLVNG	W 81726	47.4	W 88919	81.3	W 86444	46.8	W 101914	51.6	PATES BLANCHIES
2518	SULPHITE WOOD PULP	W 44494	23.5	W 34156	27.8	W 28233	14.0	W 39820	17.6	PATES AU BISULFITE
25182	— BLEACHED,NONDISSOLVNG	W 42761	22.6	W 30994	25.4	W 27878	13.8	W 39815	17.6	PATES BLANCHES
26	TEXTILE FIBRES AND WASTE		54.4		56.6		45.3		45.2	FIBRES TEXTILES
263	COTTON	W 13998	23.4	W 11609	25.9	W 10135	19.8	W 12112	22.6	COTON
27	CRUDE FERTLZR,MINRLS NES		50.0		65.2		60.3		66.2	ENGRAIS MINERAUX BRUTS
278	OTHER CRUDE MINERALS	W 315481	31.9	W 387201	44.5	W 344789	33.3	W 371495	41.6	AUTRES MINERAUX BRUTS
28	METALLIFEROUS ORES,SCRAP		101.0		116.6		94.7		90.5	MINERAIS METAL,DECHETS
282	IRON AND STEEL SCRAP	W 278290	46.7	W 259960	63.2	W 142581	34.6	W 203099	38.9	FERRAILLES
28209	— OF OTHR IRON OR STEEL	W 239773	32.5	W 239103	38.1	W 119951	17.0	W 174571	22.8	FERRAILLES DE FER
287	BASE METAL ORES,CONC NES	W 237759	39.6	W 246356	43.7	W 225541	42.3	W 241283	44.4	MINERAIS METAUX COMMUNS
2873	ALUMINIUM ORES,ALUMINA	W 169427	33.4	W 160394	32.6	W 155465	32.5	W 205434	39.6	MINERAIS D'ALUMINIUM
28732	ALUMINA(ALUMINIUM OXIDE)	W 140833	30.2	W 145071	31.0	W 140532	30.8	W 159547	34.6	ALUMINE (OXYDE ALUMINIUM)
29	CRUDE ANIMAL,VEG MAT NES		34.3		43.6		44.8		42.0	MATIERES BRUTES ANIM,VEGET
292	CRUDE VEG MATERIALS NES		30.0	W 13070	38.4	W 10595	39.8	W 13810	37.6	MAT BRUTES VEGETALES NDA
3	MINERAL FUELS ETC		528.2		632.3		764.0		792.4	COMBUSTIBLES MINERAUX LUB
32	COAL,COKE AND BRIQUETTES		18.2		27.7		29.1		24.0	HOUILLES,COKES,BRIQUETTES
33	PETROLEUM AND PRODUCTS		410.7		458.9		595.6		607.5	PETROLE ET DERIVES
333	CRUDE PETROLEUM	W 410871	53.0	W 515575	73.3	W 460493	77.8	W 507859	86.0	HUILES BRUTES DE PETROLE
334	PETROLEUM PRODUCTS,REFIN	W 1778199	325.5	W 1800396	347.0	W 2215621	482.9	W 2210989	483.0	PRODUITS RAFFINES
3341	GASOLINE,OTH LIGHT OILS	W 754560	152.0	W 770880	158.1	W 917165	199.2	W 903885	203.1	ESSENCES POUR MOTEURS
33411	MOTOR,AVIATION SPIRIT	W 734530	147.6	W 762598	154.0	W 898434	195.0	W 894825	200.1	ESSENCES MOTEURS D'AVIONS
3343	GAS OILS	W 982104	142.7	W 985632	154.7	W 847067	166.0	W 470382	92.3	GAS OILS
3344	FUEL OILS,NES	W 2889	0.4	W 840	0.2	W 357374	69.4	W 720129	136.8	FUEL OILS
3345	LUBS,PETROLEUM OILS NES	W 15557	25.8	W 16501	28.3	W 27420	33.2	W 29008	32.9	HUILES LUBRIFIANTES
335	RESIDUAL PETRLM PROD NES	W 272395	32.3	W 238375	38.7	W 233804	35.0	W 263379	38.6	PRODUITS RESIDUELS NDA
341	*GAS,NATURAL AND MANUFCT	W 621910	92.2	W 744701	126.8	W 646267	117.7	W 703902	143.7	GAZ NATUREL,GAZ MANUFACT
3414	PETROLEUM GASES, GASEOUS	W 568344	85.1	W 683447	115.8	W 575675	101.1	W 628361	124.2	GAZ DE PETROLE GAZEUX
4	ANIMAL,VEGETABLE OIL,FAT		29.1		38.1		38.2		41.4	HUILES,GRAISSES ANIM,VEG
42	FIXED VEGETABLE OIL,FAT		21.1		29.8		29.1		33.4	HUILES VEGETALES FIXES
423	FIXED VEG OILS,SOFT	W 29747	19.7	W 39324	28.0		27.2	W 50432	31.7	HUILES VEGET DOUCES FIXES
5	CHEMCLS,RELATED PROD NES		862.5		1109.8		1083.9		1092.2	PRODUITS CHIMIQUES
51	ORGANIC CHEMICALS		161.8		214.0		194.1		211.0	PROD CHIMIQ ORGANIQUES
511	HYDROCARBONS NES,DERIVS	W 34583	27.3	W 33392	31.1	W 34927	18.9	W 40435	24.5	HYDROCARBURES NDA
512	ALCOHOLS,PHENOLS ETC	W 25930	20.8	W 25034	32.6	W 27145	25.9	W 27340	23.9	PHENOLS,PHENOLS–ALCOOLS
513	CARBOXYLIC ACIDS ETC	W 25372	30.3	W 22461	38.0	W 24727	36.4	W 24650	33.3	ACIDES CARBOXYLIQUES
514	NITROGEN–FNCTN COMPOUNDS	W 9683	38.8	W 11171	47.6	W 12022	51.6	W 13969	52.4	COMPOSES FONCT AZOTEES
5148	OTH NITROGN–FNCTN CMPNDS	W 6581	26.1	W 8460	35.5	W 9018	37.0	W 11198	38.8	AUTRES COMPOSES AZOTES
515	ORG–INORG COMPOUNDS ETC	W 3688	34.1	W 10160	51.3	W 13021	48.9	W 21313	65.8	COMPOSES ORGANO–MINERAUX
5156	HETEROCYCLIC CMPDS ETC	W 2356	26.0	W 8650	39.3	W 11411	37.5	W 19985	56.7	COMPOSES HETEROCYCLIQUES
51561	LACTAMS	W 1505	2.4	W 7742	13.2	W 10773	16.6	W 19239	28.7	LACTAMES .
51569	OTH HETEROCYC CMPDS,ETC	W 850	23.7	W 909	26.2	W 638	20.9	W 746	28.0	AUT COMP HETEROCYCLIQUES
52	INORGANIC CHEMICALS		64.3		85.3		88.4		79.9	PROD CHIM INORGANIQUES
522	INORG ELEMNTS,OXIDES,ETC	W 94498	35.5	W 129856	52.6	W 134550	55.4		50.7	ELEMENTS INORGANIQUES
523	OTHR INORG CHEMICALS ETC	W 78238	26.0	W 73316	30.5	W 71604	31.4	W 68429	27.8	AUT PRODUITS CHIMIQUES INORG
53	DYES,TANNING,COLOUR PROD		80.7		96.3		92.1		90.9	PROD TEINTURE,COLORANTS
531	SYNT DYE,NAT INDGO,LAKES	W 1754	23.4	W 1960	23.6	W 1827	21.1	W 2118	20.5	MAT COLOR ORGAN,LAQUES
533	PIGMENTS,PAINTS,ETC	W 19230	55.1	W 32371	69.9	W 38726	68.2	W 47179	67.7	PIGMENTS,PEINTURES,VERNIS
5334	VARNISHES,DISTEMPERS ETC	W 7547	31.1	W 8152	37.4	W 8043	36.5	W 9457	35.8	PEINTURES A L'EAU
53342	OTH PAINTS,VARNISHES ETC	W 5623	23.2	W 5658	27.1	W 4991	25.2	W 5428	23.8	AUTRES PEINTURES,VERNIS
541	*MEDICINAL,PHARM PRODUCT		137.2	K 4050886	165.8		183.7		187.6	PROD MEDICINAUX PHARMACEUT
5417	MEDICAMENTS	K 3224312	90.8	K 3255823	118.3	K 2932892	131.5	K 3397473	137.2	MEDICAMENTS
54179	— CONTNG OTH SUBSTANCES	K 2495579	57.5	K 2540351	75.4	K 2446502	84.8	K 3009162	91.5	MED CONT AUT SUBSTANCES
55	PERFUME,CLEANING ETC PRD		63.9		83.4		87.8		92.1	PROD POUR PARFUM,TOILETTE
553	PERFUMERY,COSMETICS,ETC	W 3366	22.4	W 4399	33.0	W 4344	32.8	W 5463	37.1	PRODUITS DE PARFUMERIE
554	SOAP,CLEANSING ETC PREPS	W 21346	33.6	W 24302	42.1	W 29189	46.9	W 32234	46.0	SAVONS,PRODUITS DETERSIFS

4. Special Imports C.I.F. by Commodities according to the S.I.T.C. (Rev. 2) in million U.S. Dollars
Importations Spéciales C.A.F. par Produits d'après la C.T.C.I. (Rév. 2) en millions de Dollars E.U.

SITC CTCI	COMMODITY	1994		1995		1996		1997		PRODUIT
		QUANTITY QUANTITE	VALUE VALEUR	QUANTITY QUANTITE	VALUE VALEUR	QUANTITY QUANTITE	VALUE VALEUR	QUANTITY QUANTITE	VALUE VALEUR	
5542	WASHING PREPARATIONS ETC	W 19023	28.1	W 21492	34.9	W 26323	39.1	W 29488	38.9	PROD ORG TENSIO–ACT NDA
562	*FERTILIZERS,MANUFACTURE	W 196953	29.7	W 219888	40.3	W 222785	40.6	W 252052	38.6	ENGRAIS MANUFACTURES
58	PLASTIC MATERIALS ETC		225.7		301.4		279.0		282.6	MAT PLAST ARTIFICIELLES
582	PROD OF CONDENSATION ETC	W 56705	80.1	W 55070	105.2	W 44365	93.6	W 48044	92.2	PROD CONDENS,POLYCOND
583	POLYMERIZATION ETC PRODS	W 92979	137.3	W 96521	186.9	W 106144	177.0	W 120135	183.1	PROD POLYMERISATION
5831	POLYETHYLENE	W 31802	29.8	W 33372	43.6	W 37807	40.2	W 40498	42.3	POLYETHYLENE
58311	— IN PRIMARY FORMS	W 27360	20.3	W 28320	30.9	W 32561	29.1	W 34299	31.6	POLYETHYLENE PRIMAIRES
5833	POLYSTYRENE,ITS COPOLYMR	W 18211	23.4	W 19339	33.0	W 18741	26.7	W 23379	27.4	POLYPROPYLENE COPOLYMERES
58331	— IN PRIMARY FORMS	W 16179	20.2	W 17884	29.6	W 17694	24.2	W 22073	25.2	SOUS FORMES PRIMAIRES
5834	POLYVINYL CHLORIDE	W 17835	22.8	W 18422	31.9	W 20386	30.8	W 21672	31.4	CHLORURE DE POLYVINYLE
5839	OTH POLYMRZTION ETC PROD	W 8993	32.8	W 9145	40.3	W 10152	43.3	W 13565	45.9	AUT PROD POLYMER COPOLYM
59	CHEMICAL MATERIALS NES		97.7		121.6		117.1		108.3	MAT PROD CHIMIQUES NDA
598	MISCEL CHEM PRODUCTS NES	W 44633	70.8	W 43946	84.5	W 41350	81.3	W 49321	76.8	PROD DIV INDUST CHIM NDA
5989	CHEM PRODUCTS,PREPS NES	W 38390	61.9	W 35871	73.6	W 34470	71.4	W 42385	68.0	PROD PREP CHIMIQUES NDA
59899	OTH CHEM PRODS,PREPS,NES	W 24664	42.1	W 23045	49.3	W 18410	42.8	W 24318	40.6	AUT PRODUITS CHIMIQUES NDA
6	BASIC MANUFACTURES		1467.9		1923.9		1894.8		1971.8	ART MANUFACTURES
61	LEATHER,DRESSED FUR,ETC		79.8		73.5		71.4		88.6	CUIRS,PELLETERIES
611	LEATHER	W 3781	46.1	W 2965	40.4	W 2572	41.4	W 2730	41.2	CUIRS,PEAUX PREPARES
6114	LEATHR BOVINE NES,EQUINE	W 1788	30.8	W 1442	29.1	W 1603	32.5	W 1804	33.4	CUIRS DE BOVINS
612	LEATHER ETC MANUFACTURES	W 2207	32.0	W 2188	32.3	W 2191	28.2	W 3205	45.7	OUVRAGES EN CUIRS NDA
6123	PREPRD PARTS OF FOOTWEAR	W 2125	30.9	W 2028	28.8	W 1903	23.0	W 2206	29.5	PARTIES DE CHAUSSURES
62	RUBBER MANUFACTURES NES		57.1		85.5		87.1		82.5	CAOUTCHOUC MANUFACTURE
625	RUBBER TYRES, TUBES ETC	W 5289	19.4	W 7131	34.3	W 8578	33.7	W 10320	34.3	PNEUS CAOUTCHOUC VULCANISE
628	RUBBER ARTICLES NES	W 2447	21.5	W 2980	28.4	W 3547	29.6	W 3196	28.6	OUVRAGES CAOUTCHOUC NDA
63	WOOD,CORK MANUFACTRS NES		51.3		68.0		68.2		66.7	OUVRAGES LIEGE ET BOIS
634	VENEERS,PLYWOOD,ETC	W 43546	38.8	W 42843	49.3	W 41072	46.7	W 45860	44.2	PLACAGES,CONTRE–PLAQUES
64	PAPER,PAPERBOARD AND MFR		147.8		210.9		203.2		202.7	PAPIERS,CARTONS & OUVRAGES
641	PAPER AND PAPERBOARD	W 128486	98.9	W 129199	143.2	W 136384	133.3	W 163856	134.1	PAPIERS ET CARTONS
6415	PAPER,PAPERBRD,BULK,NES	W 58729	38.1	W 54210	48.3	W 60247	36.7	W 75091	37.9	PAPIERS,CARTONS ROULEAUX
64159	OTHER PAPER ETC,BULK,NES	W 41212	29.5	W 37539	36.6	W 52163	31.6	W 61687	32.2	AUT PAPIER ROULEAUX FEUILLES
6418	COATED ETC PAPER NES BLK	W 10295	18.5	W 12536	35.8	W 13331	39.9	W 15456	38.8	PAP,CARTONS COUCHES,ENDUITS
642	PAPER,ETC,PRECUT,ARTS OF	W 24779	49.0	W 27011	67.7	W 28390	69.9	W 30133	68.7	PAP,CARTONS DECOUPES
6421	PAPER ETC CONTAINERS	W 15041	24.1	W 14154	29.3	W 13516	27.9	W 13514	26.6	BOITES,SACS EMBALLAGES
6428	PAPER ETC ARTICLES NES	W 6445	17.0	W 8699	26.2	W 8711	27.4	W 10499	28.7	OUVRAGES EN PATE A PAPIER
65	TEXTILE YARN,FABRICS,ETC		267.8		345.2		327.4		335.2	FILS,TISSUS,ARTICLES TEXTILE
651	TEXTILE YARN	W 26933	92.2	W 21991	103.3	W 17162	84.2	W 19310	85.8	FILS TEXTILES
6514	SYN FIB YRN,BULK,MONOFIL	W 13745	37.6	W 8647	37.2	W 6214	32.5	W 7521	34.6	FILS CONT 85% FIB TEXT SYNTH
653	WOVN MAN–MADE FIB FABRIC	W 2566	32.9	W 2268	38.1	W 2017	34.2	W 2572	36.4	TISSUS FIBRES SYNTH,ARTIF
655	KNITTED,ETC FABRICS	W 982	12.5	W 1416	22.8	W 2032	36.2	W 1773	26.9	ETOF BONNETERIE PIECES ETC
6552	OTHER KNIT ETC FAB NONEL	W 982	12.5	W 1416	22.8	W 2032	36.2	W 1773	26.9	ETOF BON NON ELAS NON SYNT
657	SPECIAL TXTL FABRC,PRODS	W 5616	59.0	W 8006	87.2	W 8104	87.7	W 9261	97.7	TISSUS SPECIAUX
6573	COATED ETC TEXTILES NES	W 3878	44.0	W 5685	67.6	W 5688	66.9	W 6784	77.3	TISSUS,ART MATIERE TEXT NDA
65732	PLASTIC COATED TEXTILES	W 2285	32.1	W 3544	50.1	W 3748	51.7	W 4951	64.6	TISSUS IMPREGNES
66	NONMETAL MINERAL MFS NES		142.2		187.8		187.9		196.1	ART MIN NON METALLIQUES
662	CLAY,REFRACTORY BLDG PRD	W 79214	29.3	W 108507	41.2	W 90445	37.1	W 122202	38.7	MAT CONST REFRACTAIRES
663	MINERAL MANUFCTURES NES	W 43950	30.8	W 51669	39.8	W 59618	38.4	W 67730	39.7	ART MIN MANUF NDA
664	GLASS	W 32581	38.2	W 34912	46.9	W 37706	51.9	W 44315	58.6	VERRE
665	GLASSWARE	W 30105	22.9	W 37675	31.4	W 35518	30.8	W 35396	28.5	OUVRAGES EN VERRE
67	IRON AND STEEL		312.0		415.5		394.5		398.1	FER ET ACIER
671	PIG IRON ETC	W 21129	15.6	W 26030	25.5	W 28935	23.6	W 32908	29.6	FONTE,SPIEGEL,POUDRES
672	IRON,STEEL PRIMARY FORMS	W 95092	31.0	W 71774	30.2	W 65918	25.6	W 67555	24.1	LINGOTS FER,ACIER
6727	IRN,STL COIL FR REROLLNG	W 85244	27.6	W 68898	28.0	W 63724	22.4	W 65022	19.2	EBAUCHES POUR TOLES FER
67271	IRON,SIMPLE STEEL COILS	W 83776	23.4	W 67993	24.9	W 62509	20.5	W 64639	18.3	EBAUCHES NON EN ACIER
673	IRON,STEEL SHAPES ETC	W 136809	56.2	W 201058	85.4	W 191886	82.4	W 189829	74.6	BARRES,PROFIL FER,ACIER
6731	IRON,STEEL WIRE ROD	W 69527	22.9	W 90860	36.6	W 85636	30.9	W 81243	26.2	FIL MACHINE FER,ACIER
6732	IRON,STEEL BARS ETC	W 42903	20.3	W 84560	33.0	W 80335	36.0	W 76106	31.1	BARRES FER,ACIER
674	IRN,STL UNIV,PLATE,SHEET		140.3	W 214849	179.9	W 232080	176.2	W 282175	187.2	LARGES PLATS,TOLES
6744	IRN,STL HVY PLATE,ROLLED	W 39541	24.8	W 40245	32.9	W 31345	20.8	W 38114	21.8	TOLES LAMINEES PLUS 4.75 MM
6746	IRN,STL THIN PLATE,ROLLD		65.5	W 87143	81.3	W 84141	75.4	W 106790	82.8	TOLES LAM MOINS 3MM
67461	— OF IRON OR SIMPLE STL		38.3	W 68347	43.8	W 61115	37.1	W 78889	39.8	TOL NON AC FIN MOINS 3 MM
67463	— OF STAINLESS ETC STL	W 8450	20.8	W 7698	26.3	W 9985	26.8	W 14141	31.7	TOL ACIER INOX MOINS 3 MM
6749	OTH IRN,STL PLATES,SHEET	W 44397	32.1	W 44915	39.1	W 54100	43.4	W 66092	49.2	AUTRES TOLES FER,ACIER
67491	— OF IRON OR SIMPLE STL	W 42996	30.3	W 44581	38.3	W 53098	41.4	W 65688	47.5	AUT TOLES AUTRES ACIER FIN
678	IRON,STL TUBES,PIPES,ETC	W 40744	39.7	W 47642	58.4	W 50252	59.8	W 53474	55.9	TUBES,TUYAUX EN FONTE,FER
68	NON–FERROUS METALS		184.0		227.4		225.9		274.4	METAUX NON FERREUX
682	COPPER EXC CEMENT COPPER	W 14063	43.6	W 14568	59.1	W 14003	51.0	W 16511	54.8	CUIVRE
6822	COPPER,ALLOYS WORKED	W 9074	34.3	W 10984	49.8	W 10303	42.6	W 12434	46.4	CUIVRE,ALLIAGES OUVRES
683	NICKEL	W 3503	20.5	W 3327	26.8	W 3515	30.2	W 4850	40.1	NICKEL
6831	NICKEL,ALLOYS UNWROUGHT	W 1053	6.9	W 1648	14.8	W 1942	16.3	W 4375	34.8	NICKEL ET ALLIAGES BRUTS
684	ALUMINIUM	W 39655	90.7	W 36876	105.0	W 44051	105.2	W 58271	133.3	ALUMINIUM
6841	ALUMINIUM,ALLOYS,UNWRGHT	W 27204	42.9	W 25173	50.9	W 29570	49.1	W 41750	74.7	ALUMINIUM,ALLIAGES BRUTS
6842	ALUMINIUM,ALLOYS WORKED	W 12451	47.9	W 11703	54.2	W 14481	56.2	W 16522	58.6	ALUMINIUM,ALLIAGES OUVRE
686	ZINC	W 14081	15.8	W 16523	20.5	W 17557	21.1	W 20044	28.2	ZINC
69	METAL MANUFACTURES NES		226.2		310.4		329.8		327.9	ART MANUFACT EN METAL NDA
691	STRUCTURES AND PARTS NES	W 8607	18.5	W 12734	28.4	W 15554	32.7	W 16597	34.8	CONSTRUCT FER,ACIER,ALU
692	METAL TANKS,BOXES,ETC	W 7702	25.0	W 11072	39.7	W 11550	40.5	W 12697	39.1	RECIPIENTS METALLIQUES
6924	MTL TRANSPORT BOXES ETC	W 7137	21.3	W 10130	34.0	W 11054	37.2	W 12084	34.7	FUTS,TAMBOURS,BIDONS
69241	STL TRANSPORT BOXES ETC	W 5743	16.2	W 8644	27.9	W 9898	31.6	W 10162	26.6	FUTS,TAMBOURS,BIDONS FER
693	WIRE PRODUCTS NON ELECTR	W 9290	19.8	W 11283	27.3	W 13067	29.0	W 14320	23.6	OUVRAGES FILS METALLIQUES
694	STL,COPPR NAILS,NUTS,ETC	W 4731	19.3	W 6030	27.5	W 7548	35.6	W 8795	35.5	CLOUS,VIS,ECROUS
69402	IRN,STL NUTS,BOLTS,ETC	W 3787	17.8	W 4949	25.9	W 5896	33.7	W 7118	33.5	BOULONS,VIS,ECROUS FER,AC
695	TOOLS	W 2120	31.7	W 2134	41.3	W 2606	47.0	W 3139	49.6	OUTILS A MAIN
6954	BLADES,TIPS,ETC FR TOOLS	W 660	20.5	W 760	26.5	W 1081	31.6	W 1557	34.2	OUTILS POUR MACHINE–OUTIL
699	BASE METAL MFRS NES		87.5		117.1	W 25419	114.7	W 32894	115.7	ART MANUFACTURES MET NDA
6991	LOCKSMITHS WARES,ETC	W 8630	34.9	W 10272	45.3	W 11310	48.7	W 14528	51.2	ARTICLES DE SERRURERIE
69913	BASE MTL DOOR,ETC FITTNG	W 8079	29.2	W 9595	37.9	W 10783	40.6	W 13829	42.5	GARNITURES POUR MEUBLES
6997	IRON,STEEL ARTICLES NES	W 5736	22.0	W 7528	32.6	W 6912	25.9	W 10167	25.4	OUV FONTE,FER,ACIER NDA
69979	IRN,STL MANUFACTURES NES	W 5707	21.9	W 7449	32.5	W 6686	25.5	W 9858	25.0	AUT OUVRAGES EN FER NDA
7	MACHINES,TRANSPORT EQUIP		2319.9		3200.8		3170.4		3089.2	MACHINES MATERIEL TRANSPORT
71	POWER GENERATING EQUIPMT		150.9		227.2		254.6		236.4	MACHINES GENERATRICES
713	INTRNL COMBUS PSTN ENGIN	W 13421	112.7	W 15925	160.8	W 11479	163.6	W 11795	151.2	MOTEURS EXPL COMB INT, PIECE
7132	MOTOR VEHCL PSTN ENGINS	W 12656	101.3	W 14909	145.5	W 10707	151.0	W 10949	137.1	MOTEURS EXPL POUR VEHICULES
716	ROTATING ELECTRIC PLANT	W 5712	30.8	W 4419	35.5	W 7004	56.6	W 9872	58.7	APP ELECTR ROTATIFS,PIECES
7162	AC MTRS,GENRTRS,GEN SETS	W 2820	18.8	W 2640	21.4	W 3938	31.9	W 4861	34.4	MOTEURS ELECTRIQUES
72	MACHS FOR SPCL INDUSTRYS		272.7		376.6		290.7		301.7	MAC SPECIALES POUR INDUST
721	AGRIC MACHY,EXC TRACTORS	W 3353	17.1	W 5327	28.7	W 4540	26.0	W 4329	23.1	MACHINES AGRICOLES
722	TRACTORS NON–ROAD	W 5690	22.5	W 6316	32.9	W 5430	31.1	W 3801	21.8	TRACTEURS
7224	WHEELED TRACTORS NES	W 5653	22.0	W 6261	32.1	W 5349	30.6	W 3779	21.7	TRACTEURS A ROUES
723	CIVIL ENGNEERG EQUIP ETC	W 6557	27.8	W 10211	49.9	W 7672	37.9	W 7583	37.0	APPAREILS DE GENIE CIVIL
7234	CONST,MINING MACHNRY NES	W 5175	21.9	W 8861	44.1	W 6729	32.4	W 6728	33.3	MACH POUR LA CONST, MINES
72342	SLFPRP SHOVELS,EXCAVATRS	W 4469	15.9	W 7470	33.0	W 5311	21.8	W 5453	21.1	PELLES MECANIQUES

4. Special Imports C.I.F. by Commodities according to the S.I.T.C. (Rev. 2) in million U.S. Dollars
Importations Spéciales C.A.F. par Produits d'après la C.T.C.I. (Rév. 2) en millions de Dollars E.U.

SITC CTCI	COMMODITY	1994		1995		1996		1997		PRODUIT
		QUANTITY QUANTITE	VALUE VALEUR	QUANTITY QUANTITE	VALUE VALEUR	QUANTITY QUANTITE	VALUE VALEUR	QUANTITY QUANTITE	VALUE VALEUR	
724	TEXTILE,LEATHER MACHNRY	W 6510	48.4	W 6865	60.5	W 3561	42.1	W 3368	39.7	MACH POUR INDUSTRIE TEXTILE
726	PRINTG,BKBINDG MACHY,PTS	W 1493	25.3	W 1405	27.8	W 1298	20.0	W 1147	21.1	MACHINES POUR IMPRIMERIE
728	OTH MACHY FOR SPCL INDUS	W 8104	98.7	W 11717	137.5	W 9456	106.7	W 12059	133.4	AUT MACH IND PARTICULIERES
7281	MACH–TOOLS FR SPCL INDUS	W 3127	23.6	W 3568	34.3	W 3236	29.4	W 3201	27.4	MACH–OUTILS SPEC IND PART
7284	MACHY FOR SPCL INDUS NES	W 4173	70.5	W 5843	88.7	W 4747	68.4	W 5862	87.5	MACH SPEC IND PARTICUL.
72848	OTH MCHY WITH INDIV FNCT	W 1838	39.2	W 2440	46.9	W 1855	32.8	W 2892	55.6	AUTRES MACHINES NDA
73	METALWORKING MACHINERY		44.5		66.8		62.3		76.7	MACH TRAVAIL DES METAUX
736	METALWORKING MACH–TOOLS	W 5076	36.7	W 7754	52.1	W 5117	42.8	W 6623	53.5	MACH–OUTILS TRAVAIL METAUX
74	GENRL INDUSTRL MACHY NES		373.6		422.7		410.4		422.8	MACH APP INDUSTRIE
741	HEATING,COOLING EQUIPMNT	W 5640	72.5	W 6366	77.6	W 6923	81.7	W 7066	70.4	MACH CHAUFFAGE,PIECES
7416	HEATING,COOLING EQU NES	W 1207	28.5	W 1213	20.1	W 1321	20.1	W 1640	19.9	APP CHANGEMENT TEMP
742	PUMPS FOR LIQUIDS ETC	W 1545	22.1	W 1852	29.8	W 1289	27.6	W 1395	24.0	POMPES MOTO–POMPES
743	PUMPS NES,CENTRFUGES ETC	W 18888	129.7	W 16357	96.5	W 15303	79.7	W 21160	87.7	POMPES COMPRES,VENT ETC
7431	PUMPS FOR GASES ETC	W 6933	34.0	W 7379	43.8	W 6412	37.2	W 8157	38.4	POMPES AIR A VIDE,COMPRES
7436	GAS,LIQUID FILTERS ETC	W 6355	79.5	W 2169	30.5	W 1311	19.9	W 1868	25.8	APP POUR FILT DES LIQUIDES
744	MECHANICAL HANDLING EQU	W 4922	25.9	W 6433	41.1	W 8142	53.0	W 10049	58.5	EQUIP MANUTENTION PIECES
7442	LIFTING,LOADING MACH NES	W 1947	12.5	W 2839	20.7	W 3789	29.3	W 4050	32.0	APP LEVAGE,MANUTENTION
745	NONELEC MACHY,TOOLS NES	W 1875	40.0	W 2760	67.4	W 2608	54.4	W 2982	62.1	AUT MACH NON ELEC,PIECES
7452	OTH NONELEC MCHS,PTS NES	W 1629	33.7	W 2348	57.4	W 2243	45.1	W 2609	53.0	AUT MACH NON ELEC,PIECES
74522	PACKAGNG,BOTTLNG,ETC MCH	W 634	19.3	W 1042	36.2	W 724	22.2	W 789	27.6	MACH NETT BOUTEILLES,ETC
749	NONELEC MACH PTS,ACC NES	W 6532	83.7	W 8461	110.5	W 8588	114.2	W 10639	120.4	PIECES MACH NON ELEC NDA
7492	COCKS,VALVES ETC NES	W 2194	32.1	W 2374	43.2	W 3259	50.0	W 3618	52.0	ART ROB,SIM POUR TUYAUX
75	OFFICE MACHNES,ADP EQUIP		160.5		223.7		211.7		206.2	MACH BUREAU TRAIT AUTOM
752	AUTOMTIC DATA PROC EQUIP	W 1525	101.3	W 1948	143.8	W 2321	150.5	W 2586	148.3	MACH TRAIT INFORMATION
7523	DIGITL CENTRL PROCESSORS	W 182	28.0	W 266	36.4	W 391	36.5	W 474	41.4	UNITES CENTRALES
7524	DIGITL CENTRL STOR UNITS	W 159	23.0	W 175	32.1	W 205	29.2	W 198	27.8	UNITES MEMOIRE CENTRALES
7525	ADP PERIPHERAL UNITS	W 1073	36.6	W 1408	53.5	W 1454	49.3	W 1566	43.7	UNITES PERIPHERIQUES
759	OFFICE,ADP MCH PTS,ACCES	W 778	44.1	W 1013	58.9	W 781	44.0	W 758	40.0	PIECES DU 751 ET 752
7599	ACCTG,ETC,ADP MCH PTS,AC	W 709	41.0	W 915	54.3	W 688	39.8	W 638	36.4	PIECES DU 751 ET 752
76	TELECOMM,SOUND EQUIPMENT		105.2		173.2		159.3		189.0	EQUIPMENT DE TELECOM
764	TELECOM EQPT,PTS,ACC NES	W 1772	70.4	W 1900	123.7	W 2002	118.0	W 2364	148.3	EQUIP TELECOM,PIECES
7643	TV,RADIO TRANSMITTRS ETC	W 69	21.3	W 52	23.1	W 77	28.4	W 202	50.4	APP EMET TELE RADIO
7648	TELECOMM EQUIPMENT NES	W 53	3.0	W 153	34.2	W 52	7.0	W 61	16.5	APP TELECOM NDA
76483	RADAR APPARATUS ETC	W 23	1.4	W 77	28.8	W 11	4.0	W 19	5.6	APP DE RADIOGUIDAGE ETC
7649	PTS NES OF EQUIPMT OF 76	W 1215	26.2	W 1008	39.4	W 1227	55.3	W 1225	47.9	PIECES DE LA DIV 76
77	ELECTRIC MACHNRY NES ETC		390.9		467.3		516.3		501.9	MACH APP ELECT NDA
771	ELECTRIC POWER MACHY NES	W 992	15.5	W 1466	24.5	W 2082	29.9	W 2750	27.1	MACH PROD,TRANS ELECTR
772	SWITCHGEAR ETC,PARTS NES	W 3272	76.2	W 3852	91.5	W 3859	108.3	W 4267	109.2	APP COUPURE,SECT ETC
7721	SWITCHGEAR ETC	W 3185	71.4	W 3703	82.7	W 3633	98.6	W 4059	100.3	APP COUPURE,SECTIONMNT
773	ELECTR DISTRIBUTNG EQUIP	W 22215	95.0	W 19431	106.7	W 22039	112.7	W 25518	111.7	EQUIPMT DISTRIBUTION ELECT
7731	INSULATED WIRE,CABLE ETC	W 21584	90.7	W 18835	101.3	W 21213	105.7	W 24751	105.8	FILS,CABLES ISOLES ELECT
775	HOUSEHOLD TYPE EQUIP NES	W 6310	55.4	W 7145	64.8	W 6565	62.3	W 7077	59.1	MACH,APP USAGE DOMESTQUE
7758	ELECTRO–THERMIC APPL NES	W 2784	26.6	W 2921	30.0	W 2772	29.3	W 2929	27.1	APP ELECTROTHERMIQ NDA
776	TRANSISTORS,VALVES,ETC	W 2420	46.3	W 1858	52.0	W 3274	69.8	W 3935	65.5	LAMPES,TUBES,VALVES
7764	ELECTRONIC MICROCIRCUITS	W 76	24.2	W 66	29.5	W 142	37.9	W 128	34.3	MICROSTRUCTURES ELECTRON
778	ELECTRICAL MACHINERY NES	W 10124	82.9	W 12125	112.4	W 31112	113.6	W 32523	117.5	AUTRES MACH ELECT NDA
7783	AUTOMOTIVE ELECTR EQUIP	W 2234	23.9	W 3051	34.0	W 2956	33.7	W 3229	35.2	EQUIP ELECT MOTEURS EXPL
7788	OTH ELEC MACHY,EQUIP NES	W 4109	29.5	W 3998	38.9	W 3754	39.8	W 4529	40.6	AUT MACH APP ELEC NDA
78	ROAD VEHICLES		799.2		1194.4		1197.4		1141.7	VEHICULES ROUTIERS
781	PASS MOTOR VEH EXC BUSES	W 53337	431.7	W 64204	611.2	W 64277	628.5	W 64445	561.1	AUTO TRANSPORT PERSONNES
782	LORRIES,SPCL MTR VEH NES	W 10273	66.4	W 13902	110.4	W 13074	108.2	W 13349	96.3	VEHICULES SPECIAUX,MARCH
7821	LORRIES,TRUCKS	W 9860	61.3	W 13251	101.7	W 12145	97.6	W 12712	91.6	VEHICULES TRANSP MARCHAND
783	ROAD MOTOR VEHICLES NES	W 4158	34.2	W 5925	68.8	W 2994	31.6	W 3946	36.7	VEHICULES ROUTIERS NDA
7832	TRACTORS FOR TR–TRAILERS	W 3436	26.6	W 4345	43.8	W 2148	19.5	W 2648	21.5	TRACTEURS ROUTIERS
784	MOTOR VEH PRTS,ACCES NES	W 31567	235.0	W 40718	356.2	W 58813	383.5	W 74447	400.4	PIECES 722,781,782,783
7849	OTHER MOTOR VEHCL PARTS	W 30809	233.2	W 40213	354.4	W 57934	377.9	W 72701	390.6	PIECES 722,781,782,783
786	TRAILERS,NONMOTR VEH,NES	W 6697	19.4	W 7801	29.3	W 6432	25.3	W 6932	25.9	REMORQUES,CADRES,CONTAIN
79	OTHR TRANSPORT EQUIPMENT		22.8		49.3		68.3		13.1	AUTRE MATERIEL TRANSPORT
792	AIRCRAFT ETC	W 65	17.1	W 286	33.3	W 114	54.1	W 42	7.1	APP NAVIGATION AERIENNE
7924	AIRCRFT NES OVER 15000KG					W 60	35.0			AERODYNES PLUS 15000 KG
8	MISC MANUFACTURED GOODS		785.2		1000.1		1261.8		1208.7	ART MANUFACTURES DIVERS
812	*PLUMBG,HEATNG,LGHTNG EQ	W 11206	37.1	W 12965	49.1	W 14186	57.1	W 15522	56.7	APPAR SANITAIRES CHAUFFAGE
821	*FURNITURE,PARTS THEREOF	W 16932	82.8	W 22063	114.2	W 23521	125.1	W 30387	124.4	MEUBLES ET PIECES
8211	CHAIRS,SEATS AND PARTS	W 8774	53.5	W 9524	69.2	W 11230	78.4	W 13196	69.0	SIEGES ET PIECES
82111	CHAIRS AND OTHER SEATS	W 4247	20.3	W 6197	34.4	W 6075	39.6	W 7723	41.2	SIEGES
82119	PTS NES OF CHAIRS ETC	W 4527	33.3	W 3327	34.8	W 5156	38.9	W 5472	27.9	PIECES DU 821.11
8219	FURNITURE AND PARTS NES	W 7175	22.1	W 11034	34.7	W 10674	36.1	W 15259	43.5	AUTRES MEUBLES ET PIECES
84	CLOTHING AND ACCESSORIES		219.6		262.0		481.0		446.7	VETEMENTS
842	MENS OUTERWEAR NOT KNIT	W 1652	40.0	W 1594	42.3	W 3714	104.3	W 3956	104.1	VET DESSUS POUR HOMMES
8423	— TROUSERS,BREECHES ETC	W 667	14.8	W 800	19.0	W 1534	37.6	W 1640	39.3	PANTALONS HOMMES MAT TEX
843	WOMENS OUTERWEAR NONKNIT	W 2271	62.7	W 2376	77.1	W 4913	172.9	W 4954	160.2	VET DESSUS FEMMES MAT TEX
8431	— COATS AND JACKETS	W 549	17.9	W 520	19.2	W 1368	55.7	W 1359	49.7	MANT,VEST FEM MAT TEXTIL
8439	— OTHER OUTER GARMENTS	W 1319	30.1	W 1416	38.7	W 2485	73.0	W 2582	71.2	AUT VET DES FEM MAT TEXT
845	OUTERWEAR KNIT NONELASTC	W 1845	40.0	W 1940	53.1	W 2706	74.0	W 2583	63.9	VET DESSOUS,ACCES BONNET
8451	— JERSEYS,PULLOVERS ETC	W 879	19.7	W 926	25.1	W 1436	36.0	W 1350	31.2	CHANDAILS,PULL–OVERS ETC
8459	— OTHER,CLTHG ACCESRYS	W 916	19.1	W 967	26.5	W 1158	33.7	W 1128	29.4	AUT VET DESSUS DE BONNE
846	UNDER GARMENTS KNITTED	W 2492	41.5	W 2788	50.4	W 4328	81.3	W 4178	72.9	SOUS VETS DE BONNETERIE
8462	— OF COTTON NON ELASTIC	W 1410	25.4	W 1571	31.9	W 1603	40.0	W 1691	36.2	SOUS–VET BONNET COTON
84629	—— OTHER	W 1410	25.4	W 1571	31.9	W 1603	40.0	W 1691	36.2	AUT SOUS–VET BONNET COTON
851	*FOOTWEAR	W 3755	49.1	W 4042	61.6	W 3758	60.3	W 4084	64.6	CHAUSSURES
85102	FOOTWEAR LEATHER	W 2749	40.5	W 2963	50.3	W 2723	49.2	W 2967	53.1	CHAUS SEMELLES EN CUIR
87	PRECISION INSTRUMNTS NES		117.8		143.3		145.8		139.6	INSTRUM,APPAR SCIENT NDA
872	MEDICAL INSTRUMENTS NES	W 1358	39.3	W 1562	42.3	W 1692	40.6	W 2154	41.9	INSTR,APP MEDIC–CHIR NDA
87202	OTH MEDICAL INSTRUMENTS	W 1216	32.1	W 1367	34.5	W 1471	31.9	W 1930	34.5	INSTRUM,APP MEDECINE
874	MEASURNG,CONTROLNG INSTR	W 1090	64.8	W 1457	83.8	W 1531	81.8	W 1825	78.4	INSTRUMENTS DE MESURE
88	PHOTO EQU,OPTICL GDS ETC		47.2		65.0		65.0		64.7	APP,FOURN PHOTO,OP,MONTR
89	MISC MANUFCTRD GOODS NES		219.8		289.2		313.7		298.9	ART MANUFACTURES DIVERS
892	PRINTED MATTER	W 6610	28.7	W 7188	41.4	W 8983	55.6	W 7156	42.3	IMPRIMES
893	ARTICLES OF PLASTIC NES		87.2		115.8		123.1		122.1	OUVRAGES EN MAT DIVIS 58
8931	PLSTC PACKG CONTNRS,LIDS	W 8352	22.8	W 10039	33.9	W 11489	30.8	W 13374	30.5	ART TRANSP EMBALLAGE ETC
8939	MISC PLASTIC ARTICLES	W 11577	59.8	W 13457	76.6	W 14167	85.7	W 15362	85.0	ART DIVERS EN MAT DIV 58
89399	OTHR PLASTC ARTICLES NES	W 8447	52.7	W 10685	67.5	W 11176	76.4	W 12557	76.7	AUT OUV MAT DIV 58
894	TOYS,SPORTING GOODS,ETC	W 2910	31.0	W 3425	39.6	W 3420	38.9	W 4051	41.3	VOITURES ENFANTS,JOUETS
898	MUSICAL INSTRUMENTS,PTS	W 822	25.5	W 1036	37.4	W 1096	40.4	W 1104	34.9	INSTRUMENTS DE MUSIQUE
8983	SOUND RECRDNG TAPE,DISCS	W 527	20.9	W 684	30.4	W 790	34.2	W 837	29.3	SUPPORTS SON POUR 763
89832	RECORDED DISCS,TAPES ETC	W 235	16.3	W 368	25.2	W 424	28.6	W 430	23.4	DISQUES,PHONO,BANDES
899	OTHER MANUFACTURED GOODS		28.0		33.0		33.4		35.1	AUT ART MANUF DIVERS NDA
9	GOODS NOT CLASSD BY KIND		246.5		278.3		39.3		38.4	ART TRANSACT NON CLASSES
931	*SPECIAL TRANSACTIONS	W 20531	239.7	W 60012	272.1	W 3908	29.6	W 1190	26.6	TRANS.SPECIALES

5. Special Exports F.O.B. by Commodities according to the S.I.T.C. (Rev. 2) in million U.S. Dollars
Exportations Spéciales F.O.B. par Produits d'après la C.T.C.I. (Rév. 2) en millions de Dollars E.U.

SITC CTCI	COMMODITY	1994			1995			1996			1997			PRODUIT
		QUANTITY QUANTITE		VALUE VALEUR	QUANTITY QUANTITE		VALUE VALEUR	QUANTITY QUANTITE		VALUE VALEUR	QUANTITY QUANTITE		VALUE VALEUR	
	ALL COMMODITIES			6827.9			8315.9			8309.9			8368.9	TOUS PRODUITS
0	FOOD AND LIVE ANIMALS			274.6			263.2			263.9			240.4	ALIMENTS,ANIMAUX VIVANTS
01	MEAT AND PREPARATIONS			87.4			80.5			83.3			75.6	VIANDES ET PREPARATIONS
011	MEAT FRESH,CHILLD,FROZEN	W	17379	36.8	W	14119	31.0	W	13581	28.6	W	15672	31.0	VIANDES FRAICHES,REF,CONGE
014	MEAT PREPD,PRSVD,NES ETC	W	16374	42.7	W	14445	43.5	W	15335	49.2	W	14165	40.1	CONSERVES DE VIANDES
0142	SAUSAGES INCLDING TINNED	W	7805	22.8	W	6147	21.4	W	10771	32.8	W	9576	25.1	SAUCISSES,SAUCISSONS
02	DAIRY PRODCTS,BIRDS'EGGS			29.2			37.0			36.5			33.7	PRODUITS LAITIERS,OEUFS
022	MILK AND CREAM	W	73566	22.2	W	83979	29.6	W	68538	28.5	W	56436	24.4	LAIT ET CREME
0223	MILK AND CREAM FRESH	W	62266	18.6	W	77696	26.3	W	65814	26.6	W	55779	23.2	LAIT,CREME FRAIS
04	CEREALS AND PREPARATIONS			16.9			14.3			27.9			28.4	CEREALES ET PRODUITS
05	VEGETABLES AND FRUIT			64.3			57.5			44.1			38.6	LEGUMES ET FRUITS
054	VEG ETC FRSH,SMPLY PRSVD	W	21564	32.6	W	14237	23.7	W	8057	16.8	W	12914	15.2	LEGUMES FRAIS,CONG,SECS
09	MISC EDIBLE PRODUCTS			26.8			28.4			24.1			21.8	PREP ALIMENTAIRES DIVERSES
098	EDIBLE PRODCTS,PREPS NES	W	9788	26.4	W	10934	28.0	W	12019	23.7	W	11565	21.5	PREP ALIMENTAIRES NDA
1	BEVERAGES AND TOBACCO			49.6			51.1			72.4			70.8	BOISSONS ET TABACS
11	BEVERAGES			38.1			41.6			60.7			53.1	BOISSONS
111	NON–ALCOHL BEVERAGES NES	W	1964145	17.1	W	1979467	18.9	W	2111227	33.0	W	2068484	31.8	BOISSONS NON ALCOOLIQUES
11102	FLAVORED WATERS NON–ALCO	W	33684	11.5	W	26051	14.1	W	36934	26.9	W	34529	24.7	LIMONADES,EAUX GAZEUSES
112	ALCOHOLIC BEVERAGES	W	45686	21.1	W	43486	22.7	W	47829	27.8	W	45833	21.3	BOISSONS ALCOOLIQUES
2	CRUDE MATERLS,EXCL FUELS			131.0			170.6			138.9			166.0	MAT BRUTES NON COMESTIBLES
24	CORK AND WOOD			75.0			84.4			74.2			80.9	LIEGE ET BOIS
248	WOOD SHAPED,SLEEPERS	W	232952	60.7	W	221389	71.6	W	199060	62.4	W	228840	65.8	BOIS SIMPLEMENT TRAVAILLES
2482	LUMBER SHAPED CONIFER	W	152081	37.3	W	136406	42.3	W	127593	36.3	W	154621	35.7	CONIFERES SCIES,RABOTES
24821	LUMBER SAWN ETC CONIFER	W	148161	34.2	W	132764	39.1	W	122927	33.2	W	149630	32.5	CONIFERES SCIES LONGITUD
2483	LUMBER SHAPED NON–CONIFR	W	80870	23.5	W	84875	29.4	W	71391	26.1	W	74210	30.1	NON CONIFERES SCIES,RABOTES
24831	LUMBER SAWN ETC NON–CON	W	79729	22.0	W	84100	28.1	W	70124	24.4	W	72976	27.9	SCIES LONGITUDINALEMENT
251	*PULP AND WASTE PAPER	W	46328	19.6	W	57105	38.2	W	39129	15.6	W	65539	23.2	PATES A PAPIER,DECHETS
2518	SULPHITE WOOD PULP	W	33139	18.3	W	46505	36.3	W	36209	15.4	W	59014	22.8	PATES AU BISULFITE
25182	— BLEACHED,NONDISSOLVNG	W	32952	18.2	W	46505	36.3	W	36197	15.4	W	58993	22.8	PATES BLANCHES
28	METALLIFEROUS ORES,SCRAP			10.9			14.9			17.2			28.6	MINERAIS METAL,DECHETS
3	MINERAL FUELS ETC			77.4			99.8			78.0			101.8	COMBUSTIBLES MINERAUX LUB
33	PETROLEUM AND PRODUCTS			22.6			14.3			26.2			33.5	PETROLE ET DERIVES
334	PETROLEUM PRODUCTS,REFIN	W	39855	11.3	W	55973	13.8	W	128051	25.3	W	164133	32.8	PRODUITS RAFFINES
351	*ELECTRIC CURRENT			53.1			85.0			51.2			68.0	ENERGIE ELECTRIQUE
5	CHEMCLS,RELATED PROD NES			692.9			852.7			864.8			924.7	PRODUITS CHIMIQUES
51	ORGANIC CHEMICALS			84.9			114.7			77.1			64.7	PROD CHIMIQ ORGANIQUES
513	CARBOXYLIC ACIDS ETC	W	27810	21.5	W	27586	38.4	W	34794	26.5	W	33175	24.2	ACIDES CARBOXYLIQUES
5138	POLYACIDS AND DERIVATIVS	W	27329	20.6	W	27122	37.5	W	34361	25.7	W	32328	22.9	ACIDES POLYCARBOXYLIQUES
515	ORG–INORG COMPOUNDS ETC	W	1428	49.5	W	1466	56.2	W	1261	39.9	W	1488	21.3	COMPOSES ORGANO–MINERAUX
5156	HETEROCYCLIC CMPDS ETC	W	1380	49.2	W	1448	56.1	W	1245	39.8	W	1476	21.2	COMPOSES HETEROCYCLIQUES
51569	OTH HETEROCYC CMPDS,ETC	W	1380	49.2	W	1448	56.1	W	1245	39.8	W	1474	21.2	AUT COMP HETEROCYCLIQUES
52	INORGANIC CHEMICALS			52.8			64.0			76.5			84.1	PROD CHIM INORGANIQUES
522	INORG ELEMNTS,OXIDES,ETC	W	58633	15.1	W	48550	20.2	W	59109	19.4	W	73926	26.7	ELEMENTS INORGANIQUES
523	OTHR INORG CHEMICALS ETC	W	154482	37.7	W	100517	43.9	W	123533	57.1	W	145761	57.5	AUT PRODUITS CHIMIQUES INORG
5232	OTH MTL CMPD OF INRG ACD	W	63599	19.7	W	45235	25.3	W	72939	37.8	W	88876	37.7	SELS METALLIQUES
53	DYES,TANNING,COLOUR PROD			83.5			118.5			124.5			139.2	PROD TEINTURE,COLORANTS
533	PIGMENTS,PAINTS,ETC	W	52488	79.0	W	63094	113.4	W	72996	119.2	W	90892	132.8	PIGMENTS,PEINTURES,VERNIS
5331	COLOURING MATERIAL NES	W	25580	38.4	W	25003	50.3	W	21758	39.6	W	32760	50.1	AUT MATIERES COLORANTES
5334	VARNISHES,DISTEMPERS ETC	W	17960	31.5	W	24699	48.8	W	25937	53.7	W	15350	44.3	PEINTURES A L'EAU
53342	OTH PAINTS,VARNISHES ETC	W	7206	22.4	W	10123	35.4	W	11561	41.9	W	11706	40.1	AUTRES PEINTURES,VERNIS
5335	GLAZES,DRIERS,PUTTY ETC	W	8774	7.6	W	13258	13.1	W	25165	24.9	W	42609	37.4	PREPTNS COLOR UTILISES CERAM
53354	PUTTY,OTHER FILLINGS ETC	W	7184	5.1	W	11286	10.1	W	22712	20.8	W	39544	32.7	MASTICS ENDUITS
541	*MEDICINAL,PHARM PRODUCT			283.1			318.8			357.8			402.1	PROD MEDICINAUX PHARMACEUT
5417	MEDICAMENTS	K	6918050	254.0	K	7870657	293.9	K	8503636	338.2	MK	9254	380.0	MEDICAMENTS
54171	— CONTAINNG ANTIBIOTICS	K	1209309	39.3	K	1487709	52.4	K	1439649	68.3	K	1519078	76.0	MED CONTN ANTIBIOTIQUES
54179	— CONTNG OTH SUBSTANCES	K	5404577	204.7	K	6148317	231.0	K	6746341	251.7	K	7367668	282.9	MED CONT AUT SUBSTANCES
55	PERFUME,CLEANING ETC PRD			78.6			85.5			92.7			89.0	PROD POUR PARFUM,TOILETTE
553	PERFUMERY,COSMETICS,ETC	W	14624	44.6	W	8909	48.8	W	11445	55.3	W	11662	57.6	PRODUITS DE PARFUMERIE
554	SOAP,CLEANSING ETC PREPS	W	26612	23.7	W	26661	25.1	W	27091	24.9	W	17205	16.6	SAVONS,PRODUITS DETERSIFS
58	PLASTIC MATERIALS ETC			67.9			110.1			99.4			113.2	MAT PLAST ARTIFICIELLES
582	PROD OF CONDENSATION ETC	W	40632	28.2	W	121600	54.2	W	93410	48.3	W	112857	58.8	PROD CONDENS,POLYCOND
583	POLYMERIZATION ETC PRODS	W	28507	39.6	W	30590	55.8	W	32084	50.8	W	27733	54.1	PROD POLYMERISATION
5839	OTH POLYMRZTION ETC PROD	W	10943	20.7	W	11450	29.3	W	12929	26.9	W	11957	33.1	AUT PROD POLYMER COPOLYM
59	CHEMICAL MATERIALS NES			37.6			37.1			32.7			28.5	MAT PROD CHIMIQUES NDA
6	BASIC MANUFACTURES			1952.6			2468.6			2376.7			2349.9	ART MANUFACTURES
61	LEATHER,DRESSED FUR,ETC			100.3			99.9			94.0			92.8	CUIRS,PELLETERIES
611	LEATHER	W	6311	68.6	W	4952	61.5	W	3048	55.2	W	3400	57.6	CUIRS,PEAUX PREPARES
6116	LEATHER OF OTH HIDE,SKIN	W	2979	55.9	W	2555	54.3	W	2397	51.4	W	2761	53.0	PEAUX PREP D'AUTRES ANIMAUX
61169	LEATHER NES	W	2976	55.9	W	2554	54.3	W	2394	51.4	W	2760	53.0	PEAUX PREPAREES NDA
612	LEATHER ETC MANUFACTURES	W	3163	28.4	W	3396	34.5	W	2875	32.5	W	3037	30.1	OUVRAGES EN CUIRS NDA
6123	PREPRD PARTS OF FOOTWEAR	W	3009	25.8	W	3134	29.5	W	2531	26.7	W	2500	23.1	PARTIES DE CHAUSSURES
62	RUBBER MANUFACTURES NES			155.2			199.8			199.6			204.2	CAOUTCHOUC MANUFACTURE
621	MATERIALS OF RUBBER	W	6028	18.4	W	7122	24.0	W	7157	23.9	W	8070	25.4	PRODUITS EN CAOUTCHOUC
625	RUBBER TYRES, TUBES ETC	W	58555	125.3	W	46651	158.1	W	42169	154.4	W	49278	155.9	PNEUS CAOUTCHOUC VULCANISE
6251	TYRES NEW FOR MOTOR CARS	W	16426	50.8	W	18086	65.3	W	16908	66.1	W	21037	72.0	PNEUS POUR VOITURES
6252	TYRES,NEW,BUS OR LORRY	W	21593	49.7	W	20314	65.8	W	18414	64.2	W	20198	59.4	PNEUS POUR AUTOBUS,CAMIONS
63	WOOD,CORK MANUFACTRS NES			267.5			316.0			313.3			283.4	OUVRAGES LIEGE ET BOIS
634	VENEERS,PLYWOOD,ETC	W	66568	36.1	W	71218	48.1	W	68758	43.2	W	77143	39.9	PLACAGES,CONTRE–PLAQUES
635	WOOD MANUFACTURES NES	W	121052	231.3	W	113961	267.9	W	117560	270.2	W	124380	243.5	ART MANUF EN BOIS NDA
6353	BUILDERS WOODWRK,PREFABS	W	105152	204.2	W	97456	235.6	W	99801	235.4	W	107604	212.9	OUVRAGES DE MENUISERIE
64	PAPER,PAPERBOARD AND MFR			302.5			408.1			350.4			349.0	PAPIERS,CARTONS & OUVRAGES
641	PAPER AND PAPERBOARD	W	289542	214.4	W	302604	301.8	W	298251	247.4	W	349342	253.7	PAPIERS ET CARTONS
6411	NEWSPRINT	W	18761	8.8	W	32733	25.8	W	29755	21.9	W	40790	19.1	PAPIER JOURNAL
6412	PRINTG,WRITING PAPER NES	W	66919	65.4	W	59331	78.9	W	63347	68.1	W	66017	63.7	PAPIERS POUR L'IMPRESSION
64122	— COATED,IMPREGNATD ETC	W	64961	63.3	W	55955	74.4	W	61083	66.0	W	62185	60.6	PAPIERS IMPRESSION COUCHES
6415	PAPER,PAPERBRD,BULK,NES	W	71239	55.1	W	74129	81.5	W	67145	57.5	W	84663	63.1	PAPIERS,CARTONS ROULEAUX
64159	OTHER PAPER ETC,BULK,NES	W	70272	54.4	W	73393	80.7	W	66609	57.0	W	84276	62.7	AUT PAPIER ROULEAUX FEUILLES
6418	COATED ETC PAPER NES BLK	W	90173	67.5	W	97704	94.7	W	101443	82.0	W	131874	94.8	PAP,CARTONS COUCHES,ENDUITS
64189	COATED PAPER ETC NES	W	90109	67.4	W	97567	94.5	W	101279	81.5	W	131662	94.3	PAPIERS,CARTONS COUCHES
642	PAPER,ETC,PRECUT,ARTS OF	W	74750	88.2	W	70679	106.4	W	67902	103.1	W	71155	95.4	PAP,CARTONS DECOUPES
6421	PAPER ETC CONTAINERS	W	18154	20.1	W	17990	25.0	W	15474	22.6	W	16386	21.3	BOITES,SACS EMBALLAGES
6424	PAPER ETC CT TO SIZE NES	W	26759	29.0	W	26211	36.9	W	23054	29.9	W	24771	29.0	PAP,CARTONS DECOUPES
64243	TOILET PAPER CUT TO SIZE	W	24917	24.6	W	22011	26.7	W	19681	21.9	W	20074	19.9	PAPIER HYGIENIQUE
6428	PAPER ETC ARTICLES NES	W	27013	34.4	W	23604	37.1	W	25875	42.1	W	25992	37.0	OUVRAGES EN PATE A PAPIER
64284	PAPER TISSUES,TOWELS ETC	W	21846	27.3	W	19165	29.6	W	20862	33.2	W	21101	29.0	MOUCHOIRS SERVIETTES EN PAP
65	TEXTILE YARN,FABRICS,ETC			268.9			322.0			325.2			305.1	FILS,TISSUS,ARTICLES TEXTILE
651	TEXTILE YARN			80.1	W	21240	95.3			99.9			104.1	FILS TEXTILES
6514	SYN FIB YRN,BULK,MONOFIL	W	10948	39.2	W	13363	56.2	W	16555	67.2	W	18158	71.4	FILS CONT 85% FIB TEXT SYNTH
65141	— TEXTRD,CONT POLYAMIDE	W	6854	26.0	W	6795	30.2	W	11046	43.9	W	14387	56.4	FILS TEXT FIB CONT POLYAMID
652	COTTON FABRICS,WOVEN	W	4336	30.2	W	5406	42.6	W	5542	47.4			39.5	TISSUS DE COTON
6522	WOVEN COTTON BLEACHD,ETC	W	3004	23.8	W	2868	29.6	W	2814	32.7			24.0	TISSUS COTON BLANCHIS ETC

5. Special Exports F.O.B. by Commodities according to the S.I.T.C. (Rev. 2) in million U.S. Dollars
Exportations Spéciales F.O.B. par Produits d'après la C.T.C.I. (Rév. 2) en millions de Dollars E.U.

SITC CTCI	COMMODITY	1994 QUANTITY QUANTITE	1994 VALUE VALEUR	1995 QUANTITY QUANTITE	1995 VALUE VALEUR	1996 QUANTITY QUANTITE	1996 VALUE VALEUR	1997 QUANTITY QUANTITE	1997 VALUE VALEUR	PRODUIT
65224	BLCHED COTTON FABRIC NES	W 2522	19.0	W 2348	23.4	W 2321	27.3	W 1707	19.6	AUT TIS PLUS 85% COT BLANCHI
653	WOVN MAN-MADE FIB FABRIC	W 5329	47.8	W 66132	54.5	W 4887	52.0	W 5055	51.1	TISSUS FIBRES SYNTH,ARTIF
657	SPECIAL TXTL FABRC,PRODS	W 11269	36.6	W 11167	42.6		44.8	W 11205	39.6	TISSUS SPECIAUX
658	TEXTILE ARTICLES NES	W 7215	49.3	W 6242	57.7	W 5342	52.3	W 5118	41.3	ART FACONNES MAT TEXTILES
6584	LINENS ETC	W 2599	26.8	W 2535	30.8	W 2085	26.3	W 1940	20.0	LINGE DE MAISON
66	NONMETAL MINERAL MFS NES		165.5		198.5		213.5		208.7	ART MIN NON METALLIQUES
663	MINERAL MANUFCTURES NES	W 139119	63.2	W 266000	75.6	W 155605	82.7	W 174160	84.9	ART MIN MANUF NDA
6631	GRINDING STONES ETC	W 6527	20.2	W 7338	25.6	W 8029	27.0	W 10659	31.6	PIERRES A AIGUISER,MEULES
6635	MINRL INSULATNG PROD NES	W 55322	26.5	W 165963	29.8	W 58080	32.1	W 61154	29.6	LAINES DE LAITIER
664	GLASS	W 22963	20.1	W 22365	21.4	W 22707	26.8	W 23478	26.9	VERRE
665	GLASSWARE	W 22142	49.0	W 27084	64.9	W 32235	68.1	W 28787	62.3	OUVRAGES EN VERRE
6652	HOUSEHLD,HOTEL ETC GLASS	W 12435	42.3	W 17224	55.5	W 16925	56.1	W 20118	55.9	OBJETS VERRE TABLE,CUISINE
67	IRON AND STEEL		203.6		311.6		274.5		262.1	FER ET ACIER
671	PIG IRON ETC	W 29195	20.0	W 37387	31.6	W 39213	32.5	W 31406	22.7	FONTE,SPIEGEL,POUDRES
6716	FERRO-ALLOYS	W 17210	14.6	W 23683	24.6	W 26011	25.8	W 16703	16.1	FERRO-ALLIAGES
672	IRON,STEEL PRIMARY FORMS	W 16403	9.7	W 21262	26.4	W 11302	10.0	W 14627	11.8	LINGOTS FER,ACIER
673	IRON,STEEL SHAPES ETC	W 100657	65.6	W 97720	90.1	W 82145	88.6	W 92395	77.7	BARRES,PROFIL FER,ACIER
6732	IRON,STEEL BARS ETC	W 77332	49.5	W 80911	71.2	W 72699	83.0	W 79385	71.9	BARRES FER,ACIER
67325	OTH ALLOY STEEL BARS ETC	W 50884	30.0	W 54991	46.1	W 50968	59.4	W 52481	50.7	BARRES NON ACIERS ALLIES
674	IRN,STL UNIV,PLATE,SHEET	W 89682	65.3	W 87122	100.0	W 69906	83.9	W 86552	91.9	LARGES PLATS,TOLES
6744	IRN,STL HVY PLATE,ROLLED	W 26922	13.7	W 24890	27.6	W 16661	28.2	W 25495	39.3	TOLES LAMINEES PLUS 4.75 MM
67443	— OF STAINLESS ETC STL	W 1193	1.9	W 6589	15.6	W 11127	25.0	W 17148	35.3	TOLES ACIER INOXYDABLE
6745	IRN,STL MED PLATE,ROLLED	W 40828	22.7	W 42091	30.5	W 25418	19.6	W 31334	19.3	TOLES 3 A 4.75 MM
67454	— OF OTHER ALLOY STEEL	W 34672	19.7	W 35766	25.4	W 23108	17.4	W 28269	16.4	TOLES NON ACIERS ALLIES
6746	IRN,STL THIN PLATE,ROLLD	W 18653	26.1	W 18189	39.1	W 22066	30.9	W 24504	29.2	TOLES LAM MOINS 3MM
67463	— OF STAINLESS ETC STL	W 13521	22.0	W 13631	33.5	W 11286	23.8	W 12695	22.8	TOL ACIER INOX MOINS 3 MM
678	IRON,STL TUBES,PIPES,ETC	W 87202	26.4	W 52840	39.9	W 51411	35.9	W 68073	40.1	TUBES,TUYAUX EN FONTE,FER
6783	IRON,STL TUBES,PIPES NES	W 82826	17.0	W 47895	26.3	W 45961	21.5	W 60656	23.1	AUT TUBES,TUYAUX FER,ACIER
68	NON-FERROUS METALS		207.9		263.2		255.7		300.8	METAUX NON FERREUX
684	ALUMINIUM	W 85199	158.0	W 80088	208.2	W 89609	199.7	W 105992	232.2	ALUMINIUM
6841	ALUMINIUM,ALLOYS,UNWRGHT	W 47317	71.3	W 42101	86.7	W 47750	83.1	W 55970	99.7	ALUMINIUM,ALLIAGES BRUTS
6842	ALUMINIUM,ALLOYS WORKED	W 37881	86.8	W 37986	121.5	W 41859	116.6	W 50022	132.5	ALUMINIUM,ALLIAGES OUVRE
68421	ALUMINIUM BARS,WIRE,ETC	W 16517	39.5	W 15415	56.0	W 15262	46.6	W 18242	53.3	BARRES,PROFILES FILS ALU
68422	ALUMNM PLATE,SHEET,STRIP	W 14272	30.1	W 14955	40.5	W 19692	47.8	W 22472	52.8	TOLES, PLANCHES EN ALU
69	METAL MANUFACTURES NES		281.5		349.8		350.9		344.3	ART MANUFACT EN METAL NDA
691	STRUCTURES AND PARTS NES	W 16251	41.0	W 19075	57.0	W 19291	56.7	W 19987	49.3	CONSTRUCT FER,ACIER,ALU
6911	STRUCTURES,PARTS IRN,STL	W 14783	29.3	W 17046	40.7	W 17713	41.6	W 18050	36.8	CONSTRUCT FER,ACIER,FONTE
695	TOOLS	W 7358	46.1	W 7550	59.5	W 6321	57.4	W 7781	57.2	OUTILS A MAIN
6953	OTHER HAND TOOLS	W 3842	26.3	W 3690	32.8	W 3191	30.8	W 3306	29.2	AUTRES OUTILS A MAIN
69539	HAND TOOLS ETC NES	W 3421	23.8	W 3180	29.1	W 2290	22.3	W 1733	14.6	OUTILLAGE A MAIN NDA
697	BASE MTL HOUSEHOLD EQUIP	W 8974	35.1	W 7177	35.8	W 7352	36.7	W 7247	32.6	ART MENAGE MET COMMUNS
699	BASE METAL MFRS NES	W 46229	122.5	W 45394	149.6	W 47152	151.9		158.9	ART MANUFACTURES MET NDA
6991	LOCKSMITHS WARES,ETC	W 16721	60.7	W 17178	69.4	W 17781	69.6	W 22061	75.0	ARTICLES DE SERRURERIE
69913	BASE MTL DOOR,ETC FITTNG	W 14753	51.7	W 15730	59.5	W 16069	57.0	W 20217	62.7	GARNITURES POUR MEUBLES
6998	MFRS NES OF CPR,NIKL,ETC	W 5412	16.9	W 5368	22.3	W 4704	22.2	W 6828	27.4	OUVRAGES EN CU,NI,AL,PB,ZN
7	MACHINES,TRANSPORT EQUIP		2066.0		2612.7		2771.3		2811.7	MACHINES MATERIEL TRANSPORT
71	POWER GENERATING EQUIPMT		164.7		213.5		220.5		202.7	MACHINES GENERATRICES
713	INTRNL COMBUS PSTN ENGIN	W 7609	28.4	W 7474	41.8	W 5638	28.6	W 6069	25.1	MOTEURS EXPL COMB INT, PIECE
716	ROTATING ELECTRIC PLANT	W 21510	126.5	W 21725	158.9	W 23458	175.8	W 28685	164.1	APP ELECTR ROTATIFS,PIECES
7162	AC MTRS,GENRTRS,GEN SETS	W 6140	43.8	W 5797	48.0	W 6821	59.6	W 5408	45.7	MOTEURS ELECTRIQUES
71621	AC MTRS,INC UNIVRSL MTRS	W 6131	43.7	W 5781	47.9	W 6788	59.3	W 5348	44.9	MOT ELEC NON COUR CONTINU
7169	PTS NES OF ROT ELEC PLNT	W 13848	71.0	W 13913	91.7	W 14691	94.2	W 21195	98.9	PIECES MAC APP ROTATIFS
72	MACHS FOR SPCL INDUSTRYS		89.6		116.4		127.5		126.4	MAC SPECIALES POUR INDUST
728	OTH MACHY FOR SPCL INDUS	W 10002	45.0	W 10086	56.2	W 10643	57.0	W 11472	55.7	AUT MACH IND PARTICULIERES
7284	MACHY FOR SPCL INDUS NES	W 3248	22.0	W 3971	25.7	W 5219	29.4	W 5030	28.5	MACH SPEC IND PARTICUL.
73	METALWORKING MACHINERY		42.7		54.2		64.2		84.6	MACH TRAVAIL DES METAUX
736	METALWORKING MACH-TOOLS	W 4552	22.1	W 6406	31.3	W 5380	34.8	W 7133	40.6	MACH-OUTILS TRAVAIL METAUX
737	METALWORKING MACHNRY NES	W 5242	20.6	W 5634	22.9	W 6837	29.4	W 9449	44.1	MACH TRAV METAUX PIECES
7372	ROLLING MILLS AND ROLLS	W 3607	13.1	W 3872	13.4	W 5211	18.2	W 6990	27.5	LAMINOIRS CYLINDRES PIEC
74	GENRL INDUSTRL MACHY NES		263.1		348.6		360.8		396.3	MACH APP INDUSTRIE
741	HEATING,COOLING EQUIPMNT	W 5612	35.4	W 6170	45.9	W 7427	42.1	W 9540	47.8	MACH CHAUFFAGE,PIECES
743	PUMPS NES,CENTRFUGES ETC	W 15250	58.2	W 14246	68.6	W 16330	74.2	W 22016	86.6	POMPES COMPRES,VENT ETC
7431	PUMPS FOR GASES ETC	W 7725	29.1	W 9349	42.7	W 11141	48.0	W 16465	59.4	POMPES AIR A VIDE,COMPRES
7436	GAS,LIQUID FILTERS ETC	W 6039	23.3	W 3395	18.2	W 3746	18.7	W 2896	17.5	APP POUR FILT DES LIQUIDES
744	MECHANICAL HANDLING EQU	W 20600	58.7	W 24666	88.4	W 23925	94.7	W 29967	111.9	EQUIP MANUTENTION PIECES
7442	LIFTING,LOADING MACH NES	W 3813	15.3	W 4740	23.7	W 6380	31.4	W 7711	40.6	APP LEVAGE,MANUTENTION
7449	PTS NES OF MACHY OF 7442	W 15578	37.8	W 17815	58.2	W 15933	56.0	W 20503	64.6	PIECES DU 744.2
745	NONELEC MACHY,TOOLS NES	W 2139	20.7	W 2110	24.7	W 3145	31.8	W 2737	28.1	AUT MACH NON ELEC,PIECES
7452	OTH NONELEC MCHS,PTS NES	W 1998	16.8	W 1878	19.2	W 2972	27.0	W 2504	22.7	AUT MACH NON ELEC,PIECES
749	NONELEC MACH PTS,ACC NES	W 14870	74.1	W 18249	97.2	W 12451	94.8	W 16308	103.6	PIECES MACH NON ELEC NDA
7492	COCKS,VALVES ETC NES	W 4752	35.9	W 4463	45.2	W 5143	56.6	W 5826	57.1	ART ROB,SIM POUR TUYAUX
7493	SHAFT,CRANK,PULLEY ETC	W 8752	24.5	W 12322	32.1	W 4754	16.5	W 9002	25.1	ARBRES TRANS,VILEBREQUINS
76	TELECOMM,SOUND EQUIPMENT		84.0		116.4		161.9		139.9	EQUIPMENT DE TELECOM
761	TELEVISION RECEIVERS	W 2870	34.2	W 2630	37.1	W 4130	49.2	W 4796	48.0	RECEPTEURS DE TELEVISION
7611	COLOUR TV RECEIVERS	W 2870	34.2	W 2629	37.0	W 4128	49.1	W 4795	48.0	RECEPTEURS COULEUR
764	TELECOM EQPT,PTS,ACC NES	W 1461	49.6	W 1376	79.2	W 1648	112.1	W 1516	91.5	EQUIP TELECOM,PIECES
7641	LINE TELEPHONE,ETC EQUIP	W 267	13.2	W 212	12.5	W 331	28.5	W 769	72.5	APP TELEPHON PAR FIL
7649	PTS NES OF EQUIPMT OF 76	W 1167	34.5	W 1132	63.2	W 1280	78.9	W 690	14.0	PIECES DE LA DIV 76
76491	PTS NES OF APPAR OF 7641	W 280	22.6	W 527	54.5	W 788	73.4	W 109	8.2	PIECES POUR 764.1
77	ELECTRIC MACHNRY NES ETC		636.9		759.6		781.2		833.1	MACH APP ELECT NDA
771	ELECTRIC POWER MACHY NES	W 3540	23.6	W 2878	29.5	W 3860	36.7	W 5003	37.3	MACH PROD,TRANS ELECTR
772	SWITCHGEAR ETC,PARTS NES	W 5241	76.2	W 5440	89.4	W 5187	95.7	W 6017	98.6	APP COUPURE,SECT ETC
7721	SWITCHGEAR ETC	W 4840	62.9	W 4626	74.8	W 4736	80.8	W 5495	83.0	APP COUPURE,SECTIONMNT
773	ELECTR DISTRIBUTNG EQUIP	W 31807	21.7	W 3589	29.5	W 3947	28.4	W 4833	35.2	EQUIPMT DISTRIBUTION ELECT
7731	INSULATED WIRE,CABLE ETC	W 29900	17.0	W 2230	24.1	W 2363	21.9	W 3210	29.6	FILS,CABLES ISOLES ELECT
775	HOUSEHOLD TYPE EQUIP NES	W 84960	342.4	W 87146	402.2	W 91656	427.6	W 109412	456.1	MACH,APP USAGE DOMESTQUE
7751	HOUSEHOLD LDRY EQUIP NES	W 15362	41.1	W 14904	46.6	W 20666	67.3	W 27077	82.3	MACH A LAVER ET SECHOIRS
77511	DOMESTIC WASHING MACHNES	W 14869	39.3	W 14320	44.0	W 19976	64.3	W 26692	80.7	MACH LAVER LINGE MOINS 6 KG
7752	DOM REFRIGERATRS,FREEZRS	W 34829	124.0	W 35568	146.3	W 32106	135.7	W 38117	142.0	REFRIG,CONGEL MENAGER
77521	DOMESTIC REFRIGERATORS	W 24893	89.6	W 26263	109.2	W 24621	104.6	W 29241	108.7	REFRIGERATEURS
77522	DOMESTIC DEEP-FREEZERS	W 9936	34.5	W 9305	37.1	W 7484	31.2	W 8876	33.3	MEUBLES CONGELATEURS
7757	DOMESTIC ELECTRC EQU NES	W 6051	55.8	W 6791	70.5	W 7809	84.3	W 9980	89.3	APP ELECTR DOMEST NDA
77578	OTH DOMSTC ELEC APPL ETC	W 3030	31.1	W 3201	37.2	W 3321	42.5	W 3197	39.4	AUT APP ELECT USAGE DOM
7758	ELECTRO-THERMIC APPL NES	W 28653	121.0	W 29853	138.8	W 31063	140.3	W 34200	142.6	APP ELECTROTHERMIQ NDA
77586	ELECTROTHERM DOM APP NES	W 16325	67.1	W 15427	74.2	W 15460	79.5	W 17160	79.3	APP ELECTRO THERMIQUES
77589	ELECTRTHRMC APPL PTS NES	W 10089	39.7	W 12092	47.7	W 13203	42.7	W 14171	43.6	PIECES APP ELECTR THERM
778	ELECTRICAL MACHINERY NES	W 22597	161.7		198.8	W 26554	183.9		199.2	AUTRES MACH ELECT NDA
7781	BATTERIES,ACCUMULATORS	W 13011	23.1	W 16510	30.2	W 16976	32.6	W 20879	37.0	PILES ET ACCUMULATEURS
77812	ELECTRIC ACCUMULATORS	W 10281	17.3	W 12626	22.4	W 14042	25.1	W 16940	28.5	ACCUMULATEURS ELECTRIQ
7783	AUTOMOTIVE ELECTR EQUIP	W 5807	62.0	W 6660	77.2	W 6206	75.1	W 7446	82.2	EQUIP ELECT MOTEURS EXPL
77831	IGNITION,STARTING EQUIP	W 3950	41.0	W 5077	57.0	W 4547	53.2	W 5602	60.0	APP ELEC ALLUM,DEMARRAGE

5. Special Exports F.O.B. by Commodities according to the S.I.T.C. (Rev. 2) in million U.S. Dollars
Exportations Spéciales F.O.B. par Produits d'après la C.T.C.I. (Rév. 2) en millions de Dollars E.U.

SITC CTCI	COMMODITY	1994 QUANTITY QUANTITE	1994 VALUE VALEUR	1995 QUANTITY QUANTITE	1995 VALUE VALEUR	1996 QUANTITY QUANTITE	1996 VALUE VALEUR	1997 QUANTITY QUANTITE	1997 VALUE VALEUR	PRODUIT
77832	ELECT VEHICLE LGHTNG EQU	W 1857	21.0	W 1583	20.3	W 1659	21.9	W 1844	22.3	APP ELEC ECLAIR,SIGNAL AUTO
7784	ELECTRO–MECH HAND TOOLS	W 1968	27.5	W 2076	32.3	W 1484	23.5	W 2088	26.5	OUTILS ELECTROMEC,PIECES
7788	OTH ELEC MACHY,EQUIP NES	W 1569	44.7		53.3	W 1578	46.0	W 1923	49.1	AUT MACH APP ELEC NDA
77884	ELECTRICAL CONDENSERS	W 1055	31.8	W 2143	36.7	W 1124	31.3	W 1391	33.6	CONDENSATEURS ELECTRIQUES
78	ROAD VEHICLES		729.6		952.3		1014.5		997.7	VEHICULES ROUTIERS
781	PASS MOTOR VEH EXC BUSES	W 47351	513.6	W 54260	698.6	W 60391	783.0	W 67844	771.9	AUTO TRANSPORT PERSONNES
784	MOTOR VEH PRTS,ACCES NES	W 24987	117.7	W 27643	145.2	W 27752	141.7	W 34188	140.4	PIECES 722,781,782,783
7849	OTHER MOTOR VEHCL PARTS	W 24726	116.0	W 27407	144.3	W 27495	139.6	W 33910	138.7	PIECES 722,781,782,783
785	CYCLES,ETC MOTRZD OR NOT	W 4530	24.7	W 4047	27.0	W 3131	24.7	W 1918	14.9	MOTOCYCLES SCOOTERS
786	TRAILERS,NONMOTR VEH,NES	W 14509	41.6	W 54512	49.6	W 11656	46.9	W 15129	51.6	REMORQUES,CADRES,CONTAIN
7861	TRAILERS,TRANSP CONTAINR	W 7545	28.4	W 8664	34.4	W 6502	33.3	W 8567	36.4	REMORQUES TOUS VEHICULES
78611	HOUSING,CAMPING TRAILERS	W 2989	18.7	W 2920	20.9	W 2919	23.2	W 3458	25.5	REMORQUES POUR CAMPING
79	OTHR TRANSPORT EQUIPMENT		42.1		39.7		27.1		17.7	AUTRE MATERIEL TRANSPORT
792	AIRCRAFT ETC	W 138	32.3	W 116	26.1	W 78	12.4	W 30	3.2	APP NAVIGATION AERIENNE
7924	AIRCRFT NES OVER 15000KG	W 105	29.4	W 70	19.8	W 50	5.3			AERODYNES PLUS 15000 KG
8	MISC MANUFACTURED GOODS		1563.2		1771.3		1733.5		1686.3	ART MANUFACTURES DIVERS
812	*PLUMBG,HEATNG,LGHTNG EQ	W 12640	40.7	W 106539	51.4	W 11905	51.3	W 13901	55.1	APPAR SANITAIRES CHAUFFAGE
8124	LIGHTING EQUIPMENT NES	W 9773	32.5	W 104402	44.6	W 9820	45.5	W 11235	48.4	APPAREILS ECLAIRAGE ETC
81242	LAMPS,FITTINGS BASE METL	W 3413	15.9	W 3823	25.5	W 4061	26.4	W 4765	29.4	APPAREILS D'ECLAIRAGE
821	*FURNITURE,PARTS THEREOF	W 234945	374.1	W 486374	454.1	W 122336	473.7	W 127272	472.4	MEUBLES ET PIECES
8211	CHAIRS,SEATS AND PARTS	W 137911	178.2	W 32806	226.1	W 32189	252.4	W 33579	268.7	SIEGES ET PIECES
82111	CHAIRS AND OTHER SEATS	W 113165	85.0	W 16219	81.8	W 16164	83.5	W 16912	84.3	SIEGES
82119	PTS NES OF CHAIRS ETC	W 24746	93.3	W 16586	144.4	W 16024	168.9	W 16666	184.5	PIECES DU 821.11
8219	FURNITURE AND PARTS NES	W 95118	186.7	W 451573	216.3	W 87945	208.3	W 91053	191.6	AUTRES MEUBLES ET PIECES
82192	WOOD FURNITURE NES	W 61673	124.1	W 403349	145.3	W 56553	135.4	W 59544	126.9	MEUBLES NDA EN BOIS
82199	OTHR FURN,FURN PARTS NES	W 27080	48.5	W 42420	55.3	W 25705	56.9	W 25196	50.0	MEUBLES NDA AUTRES MATIERES
84	CLOTHING AND ACCESSORIES		615.8		659.1		593.6		550.5	VETEMENTS
842	MENS OUTERWEAR NOT KNIT	W 2524	127.8	W 30223	132.0	W 2241	122.7	W 2341	122.3	VET DESSUS POUR HOMMES
8422	— SUITS	W 673	37.5	W 28610	39.0	W 537	38.5	W 643	40.6	COMPLETS HOMMES MAT TEXT
84221	—— OF WOOL,FINE HAIR	W 558	33.6	W 499	35.7	W 507	37.1	W 596	38.7	COMPLETS HOMMES LAINE
8423	— TROUSERS,BREECHES ETC	W 786	34.5	W 737	36.4	W 834	33.1	W 811	36.5	PANTALONS HOMMES MAT TEX
8424	— JACKETS,BLAZERS ETC	W 614	32.7	W 518	35.2	W 500	31.0	W 526	29.2	VESTES HOMMES MAT TEXTIL
843	WOMENS OUTERWEAR NONKNIT	W 32259	237.7	W 37822	271.8	W 4242	237.4	W 4101	227.3	VET DESSUS FEMMES MAT TEX
8431	— COATS AND JACKETS	W 29172	75.0	W 34897	89.2	W 1306	71.5	W 1299	81.4	MANT,VEST FEM MAT TEXTIL
8432	— SUITS AND COSTUMES	W 283	22.2	W 363	32.9	W 374	32.8	W 363	27.7	COSTUMES–TAIL MAT TEXIL
8435	— BLOUSES	W 271	22.7	W 232	21.5	W 248	19.7	W 223	15.4	BLOUSES FEM MAT TEXTILES
8439	— OTHER OUTER GARMENTS	W 2095	90.3	W 1886	96.0	W 1901	87.3	W 1938	87.1	AUT VET DES FEM MAT TEXT
844	UNDER GARMENTS NOT KNIT	W 694	28.4	W 500	24.6	W 420	21.0	W 392	16.8	VETEMENT DESSOUS MAT TEX
845	OUTERWEAR KNIT NONELASTC	W 14108	74.1	W 1656	83.0	W 1702	77.9	W 1661	68.7	VET DESSOUS,ACCES BONNET
8451	— JERSEYS,PULLOVERS ETC	W 13170	35.5	W 835	35.9	W 967	34.3	W 891	32.4	CHANDAILS,PULL–OVERS ETC
8459	— OTHER,CLTHG ACCESRYS	W 865	35.4	W 739	42.6	W 670	40.2	W 704	32.5	AUT VET DESSUS DE BONNE
846	UNDER GARMENTS KNITTED	W 3421	104.4	W 3305	103.2	W 2922	94.8	W 2702	76.2	SOUS VETS DE BONNETERIE
8462	— OF COTTON NON ELASTIC	W 891	28.7	W 838	32.1	W 735	32.0	W 683	24.9	SOUS–VET BONNET COTON
84629	—— OTHER	W 891	28.7	W 838	32.1	W 735	32.0	W 683	24.9	AUT SOUS–VET BONNET COTON
8463	— OF SYNTH FBR NONELAST	W 2243	46.6	W 2164	39.2	W 1908	34.9	W 1685	24.5	SOUS–VET BONNET FIB SYNT
84631	—— PANTY HOSE (TIGHTS)	W 2222	45.5	W 2143	38.1	W 1859	32.5	W 1655	23.1	COLLANTS BON FIBR SYNT
8465	CORSETS,GARTERS,ETC	W 288	29.2	W 303	32.0	W 279	28.1	W 334	26.9	CORSETS,GAINES ART SIM
84651	BRASSIERES	W 198	21.9	W 206	23.1	W 191	20.6	W 247	20.3	SOUTIENS–GORGE,BUSTIERS
848	HEADGEAR,NONTXTL CLOTHNG		27.2	W 464	26.6	W 431	23.5	W 409	20.7	VET ACCES MAT AUT QUE TEX
8481	LEATHER CLOTHES,ACCESSOR	W 321	21.8	W 286	21.0	W 284	18.3	W 273	15.7	VET ACCES MAT CUIR ARTIF
851	*FOOTWEAR	W 6344	137.3	W 5459	130.0	W 4552	104.7	W 4407	93.1	CHAUSSURES
85102	FOOTWEAR LEATHER	W 5128	119.9	W 4397	113.6	W 3934	93.8	W 3657	81.9	CHAUS SEMELLES EN CUIR
87	PRECISION INSTRUMNTS NES		136.6		158.6		170.4		167.5	INSTRUM,APPAR SCIENT NDA
873	METERS AND COUNTERS NES	W 3672	71.2	W 4175	94.3	W 4127	87.9	W 4241	78.1	COMPTEURS,INST DE MESURE
8731	GAS SUPPLY METERS ETC	W 3633	69.6	W 4134	92.1	W 4107	86.6	W 4225	77.3	COMPTEURS GAZ,LIQ ELECT
874	MEASURNG,CONTROLNG INSTR	W 2446	42.9	W 2145	52.5	W 2345	61.8	W 2482	65.2	INSTRUMENTS DE MESURE
8743	GAS,LIQUID CONTROL INSTR	W 769	21.6	W 791	26.8	W 874	31.1	W 1188	37.1	APP,INSTR MESURE FLUIDES
88	PHOTO EQU,OPTICL GDS ETC		45.5		57.5		52.7		55.3	APP,FOURN PHOTO,OP,MONTR
884	OPTICAL GOODS NES	W 245	21.2	W 205	23.6	W 158	16.0	W 194	17.1	ELEMENTS OPTIQ,ART LUNET
89	MISC MANUFCTRD GOODS NES		204.9		249.6		276.8		284.1	ART MANUFACTURES DIVERS
892	PRINTED MATTER	W 16194	51.5	W 46270	58.0	W 15252	68.0	W 17971	65.2	IMPRIMES
8921	PRINTED BOOKS,GLOBES,ETC	W 13390	38.5	W 11549	43.6	W 10727	39.2	W 13244	39.3	LIVRES,BROCHURES,CARTES
89211	PRINTED BOOKS,PAMPHLETS	W 13088	37.8	W 11466	43.3	W 10648	38.8	W 12606	38.1	LIVRES,BROCHURES
893	ARTICLES OF PLASTIC NES	W 20698	67.7	W 25270	93.7		103.1		114.4	OUVRAGES EN MAT DIVIS 58
8939	MISC PLASTIC ARTICLES	W 13712	43.3	W 16395	60.4	W 17861	66.0	W 21559	73.5	ART DIVERS EN MAT DIV 58
89399	OTHR PLASTC ARTICLES NES	W 10745	35.5	W 12417	48.6	W 12118	50.4	W 13899	53.8	AUT OUV MAT DIV 58
894	TOYS,SPORTING GOODS,ETC	W 4464	44.5	W 4963	52.1	W 4211	53.5	W 4927	54.7	VOITURES ENFANTS,JOUETS
8942	TOYS,INDOOR GAMES ETC	W 3588	21.7	W 3834	27.6	W 2651	21.7	W 3009	21.7	JOUETS,JEUX ETC
8947	OTH SPORT GDS,FAIR AMUSM	W 862	22.7	W 1120	24.4	W 1547	31.7	W 1899	32.8	AUT ART DE SPORT
89472	OTH OUTDOOR SPORT GOODS	W 860	22.7	W 1087	24.3	W 1508	31.5	W 1880	32.7	ART POUR JEUX PLEIN AIR
895	OFFICE SUPPLIES NES	W 5755	20.9	W 8672	24.3	W 5611	26.8	W 6196	24.4	ART PAPET NDA

1. HISTORICAL SERIES, 1961–1996 SPECIAL TRADE, IMPORTS C.I.F., EXPORTS F.O.B. # 1
SERIES HISTORIQUES, 1961–1996 COMMERCE SPECIAL, IMPORTATIONS C.A.F., EXPORTATIONS F.O.B

YEAR ANNEE	VALUE IN MILLION S.I. DOLLARS / VALEUR EN MILLION S.I. DOLLARS: MERCHANDISE –MARCHANDISE IMPORTS	MERCHANDISE –MARCHANDISE EXPORTS	GOLD –OR IMPORTS	GOLD –OR EXPORTS	CONVERSION FACTORS U.S. CENTS PER S.I. DOLLAR / FACTEURS DE CONVERSION CENTS E.U. PAR S.I. DOLLAR: IMPORTS	CONVERSION FACTORS EXPORTS	INDEX NUMBERS –INDICES: QUANTUM IMPORTS	QUANTUM EXPORTS	UNIT VALUE / VALEUR UNITAIRE IMPORTS	UNIT VALUE / VALEUR UNITAIRE EXPORTS
1961	4.15	3.56			112.0000	112.0000				
1962	4.47	3.25			112.0000	112.0000				
1963	4.62	3.71			112.0000	112.0000				
1964	5.47	4.76			112.0000	112.0000				
1965	6.58	4.83		8.00	112.0000	112.0000				
1966	8.52	3.75		9.00	112.0000	112.0000				
1967	8.20	5.09		17.00	112.0000	112.0000				
1968	9.20	5.54		18.00	112.0000	112.0000				
1969	8.54	6.46		12.00	112.0000	112.0000				
1970	10.02	7.11		7.00	112.0000	112.0000				
1971	11.52	9.08		13.00	113.5720	112.8080				
1972	12.05	9.14		20.00	119.1000	119.1000				
1973	11.26	9.55		61.00	142.6120	144.1660				
1974	16.37	18.25		72.00	142.7390	144.8740				
1975	21.77	11.82		45.00	130.9450	131.1830				
1976	21.09	19.95		47.00	121.8460	121.3170				
1977	25.75	29.61		56.00	110.9850	110.8880				
1978	30.88	30.59		89.00	114.5150	114.5680				
1979	50.57	59.26			111.6850	111.6030				
1980	61.54	60.80			120.3530	120.4370		76		95
1981	65.78	57.55			114.9151	114.5287		83		76
1982	57.43	56.56			103.1025	102.5989		79		77
1983	70.63	71.22			86.7251	86.1231		96		79
1984	83.84	118.56			78.1544	78.4026		106		118
1985	102.67	103.86			67.1944	67.1541		96		112
1986	125.19	114.90			57.5333	56.9522		119		79
1987	162.08	128.30			50.2190	50.1490		87		85
1988	203.30	170.57			48.0443	47.7344		93		94
1989	262.50	171.45			43.5642	43.3447		94		93
1990	238.96	178.11			39.5887	39.5546		100		100
1991	299.60	228.71			36.7934	36.7658		122		106
1992	285.90	301.18			33.9819	34.0332		136		103
1993	321.10	411.44			31.4288	31.7276				
1994	468.11	467.87			30.3552	30.3772				
1995	525.28	573.15			29.3449	29.3764				
1996	580.27				28.0765					

2. IMPORTS BY BROAD ECONOMIC CATEGORY AND EXPORTS BY INDUSTRIAL ORIGIN. (PERCENTAGE OF TOTAL VALUE)
IMPORTATIONS PAR CATEGORIES ECONOMIQUES ET EXPORTATIONS PAR BRANCHE D'ACTIVITE.(EN POURCENTAGE DE LA VALEUR TOTALE)

IMPORTS – IMPORTATIONS

	1990	1991	1992	1993	1994	1995	1996
TOTAL IMPORTS–IMPORTATIONS TOTALES							100.
1 FOOD BEV–ALIMENTATION BOISSONS							13.7
11 PRIMARY–PRODUITS DE BASE							7.3
111 FOR INDUSTRY–POUR L'INDUSTRIE							6.2
112 FOR HOUSEHOLDS–POUR LES MENAGES							1.1
12 PROCESSED–PRODUITS ELABORES							6.5
121 FOR INDUSTRY–POUR L'INDUSTRIE							1.6
122 FOR HOUSEHOLDS–POUR LES MENAGES							4.8
2 IND SUPPLIES–APPROV INDUSTRIELS							20.1
21 PRIMARY–PRODUITS DE BASE							1.1
22 PROCESSED–PRODUITS ELABORES							19.0
3 FUELS–COMBUSTIBLES							24.7
31 PRIMARY–PRODUITS DE BASE							1.2
32 PROCESSED–PRODUITS ELABORES							23.4
321 MOTOR SPIRIT–ESSENCE							23.4
322 OTHER–AUTRES							
4 MACHINERY–EQUIPEMENT							13.2
41 CAPITAL EQUIPMENT–MACHINES							12.2
42 PARTS–PIECES ACCESSOIRES							1.0
5 TRANSPORT–TRANSPORT							12.8
51 PASSENGER CARS–AUTOMOBILES							
52 OTHER–AUTRES							9.2
521 INDUSTRIAL–INDUSTRIELS							9.0
522 NON INDUSTRIAL–NON INDUSTRIEL							0.1
53 PARTS–PIECES ACCESSOIRES							3.6
6 CONSUM GOODS–BIENS CONSOMMATION							13.4
61 DURABLE–DURABLES							2.3
62 SEMI DURABLE–SEMI DURABLES							7.7
63 NON DURABLE–NON DURABLES							3.4
7 GOODS NES–BIENS NDA							2.1

EXPORTS – EXPORTATIONS

	1990	1991	1992	1993	1994	1995	1996
TOTAL EXPORTS–EXPORTATIONS TOTALES							
1 AGRICULTURE							
2 MINING QUARRY–INDUS EXTRACTIVES							
3 MANUFACTURING–IND MANUFACTUR							
31 FOOD BEV TOBACCO–ALIM BOISS TAB							
32 TEXTILES–INDUSTRIES TEXTILES							
33 WOOD & PRODUCTS–BOIS & PRODUITS							
34 PAPER & PRODUCTS–PAPIER & PRODT							
35 CHEMICALS–INDUSTRIES CHIMIQUES							
36 NON METAL MIN–MIN NON METAL							
37 BASIC METAL–IND METAL BASE							
38 METAL MANUF–MANUF METAL							
39 OTH MANUF IND–AUTRES MANUF							

3. TRADE BY PRINCIPAL COUNTRIES OF ORIGIN AND DESTINATION (VALUE IN MILLION U.S. DOLLARS)
ECHANGES SELON LES PRINCIPAUX PAYS D'ORIGINE ET DE DESTINATION (VALEUR EN MILLIONS DE DOLLARS EU)

COUNTRIES–PAYS	SPECIAL IMPORTS C.I.F. IMPORTATIONS SPECIALES C.A.F				
	1992	1993	1994	1995	1996
World	111.0	137.1	142.1		162.9
Africa	0.5				0.8
Americas	7.2	7.8	4.0		3.0
– Northern America	6.9	7.8	4.0		2.9
– LAIA	0.3				0.1
– CACM					
– Caribbean					0.0
– Rest of America					
Asia excl fmr USSR	42.2	56.2	62.7		43.9
– Middle East					0.0
Asia former USSR					0.0
Europe excl fmr USSR	6.6	3.8	3.6		3.5
– European Union	6.5	3.8	3.6		3.5
– Eastern Europe	0.0				
– Rest of Europe	0.1	0.0	0.0		0.0
Europe former USSR					
Oceania	54.4	64.2	70.0		110.0
Other	0.0				1.8
Australia/Australie	41.7	48.1	52.9		84.3
Japan/Japon	16.3	20.1	24.3		16.4
New Zealand	9.5	13.2	13.7		21.4
Singapore/Singapour	13.2	16.4	12.0		9.8
Other Asia n.e.s.	4.8	6.7	14.8		0.9
USA/Etats–Unis d'Amer	6.9	7.8	4.0		2.8
China/Chine	3.2	3.8	3.8		4.6
Thailand/Thaïlande	0.9	4.3	3.9		2.7
China, Hong Kong SAR	3.0	3.4	2.4		1.4
United Kingdom	1.9	2.0	1.9		2.3
Papua New Guinea	1.8	1.4	1.5		3.3
Germany/Allemagne	3.7	1.5	1.1		0.7
Korea, Republic of	0.9	1.6	1.6		0.7
Fiji/Fidji	1.3	1.0	1.1		
Indonesia/Indonésie					3.1
Malaysia/Malaisie					2.6
Areas n.e.s.	0.0				1.8
Vanuatu		0.2	0.6		0.9
Korea Dem People's Rp					1.3
Belgium–Luxembourg	0.4	0.2	0.2		0.1
So. African Customs Un					0.7
Oceania n.e.s.	0.2	0.2	0.3		
Malawi	0.5				0.1
Netherlands/Pays–Bas	0.1	0.0	0.2		0.1
Sweden/Suède	0.1	0.1	0.1		0.1
European Union n.e.s.	0.3				
LAIA n.e.s.	0.3				
India/Inde					0.1
Canada					0.1
Philippines					0.1
Italy/Italie					0.1
France, Monaco					0.0
Norway,Svalbard and JM	0.0	0.0	0.0		
New Caledonia					0.0
US Misc Pacific Islands					0.0
Eastern Europe n.e.s.	0.0				

COUNTRIES–PAYS	SPECIAL EXPORTS F.O.B. EXPORTATIONS SPECIALES F.O.B.				
	1992	1993	1994	1995	1996
Monde	102.3	130.5	142.1		
Afrique					
Amériques	1.5	0.9	0.7		
– Amérique du Nord	1.5	0.9	0.7		
– ALAI	0.0				
– MCAC					
– Caraïbes					
– Autre Amérique					
Asie anc. URSS exclus	64.6	90.2	100.8		
– Moyen–Orient					
Asie ancienne URSS					
Europe anc. URSS exclus	29.6	32.5	34.6		
– Union Européenne	29.6	32.5	34.6		
– Europe de l'Est					
– Autre de l'Europe					
Europe ancienne URSS					
Océanie	6.6	6.8	6.0		
Autre					
Japan/Japon	35.6	54.5	58.4		
United Kingdom	24.1	18.7	18.6		
Korea, Republic of	12.5	21.5	20.0		
Other Asia n.e.s.	5.9	5.9	9.9		
Netherlands/Pays–Bas		8.5	12.1		
Singapore/Singapour	3.9	4.1	4.9		
Thailand/Thaïlande	2.5	2.0	6.4		
Australia/Australie	2.5	2.8	2.2		
Belgium–Luxembourg	2.3	3.1	1.8		
Germany/Allemagne	2.8	2.2	2.1		
China, Hong Kong SAR	3.8	2.1	0.9		
Oceania n.e.s.	1.4	1.3	2.0		
Fiji/Fidji	1.6	1.5	0.9		
USA/Etats–Unis d'Amer	1.5	0.9	0.7		
New Zealand	0.7	0.4	0.3		
Papua New Guinea	0.2	0.7	0.4		
India/Inde	0.5		0.4		
Vanuatu	0.2	0.1	0.2		
European Union n.e.s.	0.3				
LAIA n.e.s.	0.0				

(VALUE AS PERCENTAGE OF WORLD TOTAL)(VALEURS EN POURCENTAGE DU TOTAL MONDIAL)

	1987	1988	1989	1990	1991	1992	1993	1994	1995	1996
Africa	0.5	0.2	0.3	0.3	0.3	0.5				0.5
Americas	3.0	3.1	3.0	5.4	5.5	6.5	5.7	2.8		1.8
– Northern America	3.0	3.0	2.8	5.2	5.5	6.2	5.7	2.8		1.8
– LAIA	0.1	0.1				0.2				0.0
– CACM										
– Caribbean	0.0	0.0								0.0
– Rest of America			0.2	0.2						
Asia excl fmr USSR	37.2	31.4	43.6	42.0	39.9	38.0	41.0	44.1		27.0
– Middle East		0.0								0.0
Asia former USSR										0.0
Europe excl fmr USSR	6.8	8.0	4.9	3.2	5.0	6.0	2.8	2.5		2.2
– European Union	6.8	7.9	4.4	2.6	4.8	5.9	2.7	2.5		2.1
– Eastern Europe	0.0	0.0	0.1	0.1	0.0	0.0				
– Rest of Europe	0.0	0.1	0.4	0.5	0.2	0.1	0.0	0.0		0.0
Europe former USSR	0.0	0.0								
Oceania	52.1	56.9	48.2	49.1	47.9	49.0	46.8	49.3		67.5
Other	0.4	0.4				0.0				1.1
Australia/Australie	41.4	45.5	37.1	34.7	36.0	37.6	35.1	37.2		51.8
Japan/Japon	19.1	16.2	23.3	15.4	19.8	14.7	14.6	17.1		10.1
New Zealand	7.9	8.3	7.7	9.3	8.2	8.5	9.6	9.6		13.1
Singapore/Singapour	9.2	5.4	8.1	15.2	11.4	11.9	11.9	8.4		6.0
Other Asia n.e.s.	0.7	1.4	4.2	2.3	2.9	4.3	4.9	10.4		0.6
USA/Etats–Unis d'Amer	2.9	2.9	2.8	5.2	5.5	6.2	5.7	2.8		1.7
China/Chine	3.5	3.3	3.9	3.5	2.3	2.9	2.8	2.7		2.8
Thailand/Thaïlande	0.1	0.1	0.4	0.3	0.4	0.8	3.1	2.7		1.7
China, Hong Kong SAR	2.5	2.7	2.6	2.2	2.3	2.7	2.5	1.7		0.9
United Kingdom	4.4	5.3	3.0	1.5	2.8	1.7	1.4	1.4		1.4

	1987	1988	1989	1990	1991	1992	1993	1994	1995	1996
Afrique										
Amériques	7.2	4.2	0.1	0.1	0.1	1.5	0.7	0.5		
– Amérique du Nord	7.2	4.2	0.1	0.1	0.1	1.5	0.7	0.5		
– ALAI	0.0					0.0				
– MCAC										
– Caraïbes										
– Autre Amérique				0.0	0.0					
Asie anc. URSS exclus	57.2	56.6	53.3	53.4	58.0	63.1	69.1	70.9		
– Moyen–Orient										
Asie ancienne URSS										
Europe anc. URSS exclus	23.2	22.3	29.3	32.1	29.6	28.9	24.9	24.3		
– Union Européenne	23.2	22.3	29.3	31.9	29.0	28.9	24.9	24.3		
– Europe de l'Est										
– Autre de l'Europe		0.0	0.1	0.2	0.6					
Europe ancienne URSS										
Océanie	12.3	16.9	17.2	14.4	11.3	6.5	5.2	4.2		
Autre										
Japan/Japon	35.6	34.5	33.2	39.2	28.2	34.8	41.7	41.1		
United Kingdom	13.8	14.5	17.0	23.4	15.3	23.6	14.3	13.1		
Korea, Republic of	6.0	3.2	2.9	7.9	6.9	12.2	16.5	14.1		
Other Asia n.e.s.	1.6	0.7	0.5	0.3	3.3	5.8	4.5	6.9		
Netherlands/Pays–Bas	2.0	1.7	6.7	1.4	7.6		6.5	8.5		
Singapore/Singapour	0.9	1.1	2.8	2.1	2.0	3.8	3.2	3.4		
Thailand/Thaïlande	12.2	14.6	13.1	0.4	13.8	2.4	1.6	4.5		
Australia/Australie	3.7	4.7	7.2	4.6	2.8	2.5	2.1	1.5		
Belgium–Luxembourg	2.2	1.2	2.1	3.1	2.7	2.3	2.4	1.3		
Germany/Allemagne					3.4	2.8	1.7	1.5		

4. Special Imports C.I.F. by Commodities according to the S.I.T.C. (Rev. 2) in million U.S. Dollars
Importations Spéciales C.A.F. par Produits d'après la C.T.C.I. (Rév. 2) en millions de Dollars E.U.

SITC CTCI	COMMODITY	1993 QUANTITY QUANTITE	1993 VALUE VALEUR	1994 QUANTITY QUANTITE	1994 VALUE VALEUR	1995 QUANTITY QUANTITE	1995 VALUE VALEUR	1996 QUANTITY QUANTITE	1996 VALUE VALEUR	PRODUIT
	ALL COMMODITIES		137.2		142.1				163.0	TOUS PRODUITS
0	FOOD AND LIVE ANIMALS		16.7		18.6				20.8	ALIMENTS,ANIMAUX VIVANTS
01	MEAT AND PREPARATIONS								2.3	VIANDES ET PREPARATIONS
011	MEAT FRESH,CHILLD,FROZEN								0.8	VIANDES FRAICHES,REF,CONGE
0111	BOVINE MEAT FRESH,FROZEN								0.7	VIANDES BOVIN FRAI,REF
014	MEAT PREPD,PRSVD,NES ETC	W 393	0.9	W 435	1.1				1.5	CONSERVES DE VIANDES
02	DAIRY PRODCTS,BIRDS'EGGS								1.2	PRODUITS LAITIERS,OEUFS
022	MILK AND CREAM								0.9	LAIT ET CREME
0224	MILK,CREAM PRESERVED ETC								0.7	LAIT,CREME CONS,CONC
04	CEREALS AND PREPARATIONS								11.7	CEREALES ET PRODUITS
041	WHEAT ETC UNMILLED								1.6	FROMENT,EPEAUTRE
0411	DURUM WHEAT UNMILLED								1.6	FROMENT DUR NON MOULU
042	RICE	W 17749	6.4	W 60543	7.9				8.2	RIZ
0421	RICE IN HUSK OR HUSKED								8.2	RIZ SANS AUTRE PREPARATION
04211	RICE IN THE HUSK								8.2	RIZ PADDY
048	CEREAL ETC PREPARATIONS								1.8	PREPTNS A BASE CEREALES
0483	MACARONI,SPAGHETTI ETC								0.9	PATES ALMENTAIRES
0488	OTH CEREAL PREPS,MALT EX								0.7	EXTRAITS DE MALT
05	VEGETABLES AND FRUIT								0.8	LEGUMES ET FRUITS
06	SUGAR AND PREPS,HONEY								2.0	SUCRES ET PRODUITS
061	SUGAR AND HONEY								1.7	SUCRES ET MIEL
0611	RAW BEET AND CANE SUGAR	W 54	0.1	W 60	0.1				1.7	SUCRES BRUTS
0612	REFINED SUGAR ETC	W 2613	1.1	W 2909	1.0					SUCRES RAFFINES
07	COFFEE,TEA,COCOA,SPICES								0.7	CAFE,THE,CACAO,EPICES
081	*FEEDING STUFF FOR ANIML								1.2	NOURRITURE POUR ANIMAUX
0819	FOOD WASTE AND FEED NES								1.1	DECHETS,ALIMENTS NDA
08199	FODDER NES,INCL SWEETNED								1.1	PREPARATIONS FOURRAGERES
09	MISC EDIBLE PRODUCTS								0.9	PREP ALIMENTAIRES DIVERSES
098	EDIBLE PRODCTS,PREPS NES								0.8	PREP ALIMENTAIRES NDA
1	BEVERAGES AND TOBACCO		1.8		2.1				3.8	BOISSONS ET TABACS
11	BEVERAGES								2.1	BOISSONS
111	NON-ALCOHL BEVERAGES NES								0.9	BOISSONS NON ALCOOLIQUES
11102	FLAVORED WATERS NON-ALCO								0.8	LIMONADES,EAUX GAZEUSES
112	ALCOHOLIC BEVERAGES								1.2	BOISSONS ALCOOLIQUES
1123	BEER,ALE,STOUT,PORTER	W 917	0.8	W 919	0.8				0.7	BIERES
12	TOBACCO AND MANUFACTURES								1.7	TABACS BRUTS FABRIQUES
121	TOBACCO UNMNFCTRD,REFUSE								0.8	TABACS BRUTS,DECHETS
122	TOBACCO,MANUFACTURED	W 42	0.2	W 7	0.1				1.0	TABACS FABRIQUES
2	CRUDE MATERLS,EXCL FUELS		0.9		1.4				1.1	MAT BRUTES NON COMESTIBLES
3	MINERAL FUELS ETC		12.9		11.7				40.3	COMBUSTIBLES MINERAUX LUB
33	PETROLEUM AND PRODUCTS								38.3	PETROLE ET DERIVES
334	PETROLEUM PRODUCTS,REFIN								38.2	PRODUITS RAFFINES
3341	GASOLINE,OTH LIGHT OILS	W 11974	1.8	W 14814	2.1					ESSENCES POUR MOTEURS
3343	GAS OILS	W 47647	8.2	W 46612	6.5					GAS OILS
341	*GAS,NATURAL AND MANUFCT								2.0	GAZ NATUREL,GAZ MANUFACT
3413	PETROLM GASES,LIQUEFIED								2.0	GAZ DE PETROLE LIQUEFIE
34139	OTH HYDROCARBON GAS LQFD								2.0	HYDROCARBURES GAZEUX NDA
4	ANIMAL,VEGETABLE OIL,FAT		0.5		1.1				2.1	HUILES,GRAISSES ANIM,VEG
42	FIXED VEGETABLE OIL,FAT								2.1	HUILES VEGETALES FIXES
424	FIXED VEG OIL NONSOFT								1.6	AUTRES HUILES VEG FIXES
4241	LINSEED OIL								1.4	HUILE DE LIN
5	CHEMCLS,RELATED PROD NES		6.6		7.4				6.3	PRODUITS CHIMIQUES
52	INORGANIC CHEMICALS								0.7	PROD CHIM INORGANIQUES
53	DYES,TANNING,COLOUR PROD								0.7	PROD TEINTURE,COLORANTS
533	PIGMENTS,PAINTS,ETC								0.7	PIGMENTS,PEINTURES,VERNIS
541	*MEDICINAL,PHARM PRODUCT								1.3	PROD MEDICINAUX PHARMACEUT
5419	PHARMACEUTICAL GOODS NES								0.9	PREP,ART PHARMACEUTIQUES
55	PERFUME,CLEANING ETC PRD								1.0	PROD POUR PARFUM,TOILETTE
554	SOAP,CLEANSING ETC PREPS								0.6	SAVONS,PRODUITS DETERSIFS
562	*FERTILIZERS,MANUFACTURE	W 1147	0.2	W 2288	0.6				0.9	ENGRAIS MANUFACTURES
58	PLASTIC MATERIALS ETC								0.8	MAT PLAST ARTIFICIELLES
583	POLYMERIZATION ETC PRODS								0.7	PROD POLYMERISATION
59	CHEMICAL MATERIALS NES								1.0	MAT PROD CHIMIQUES NDA
6	BASIC MANUFACTURES		28.9		28.4				30.5	ART MANUFACTURES
62	RUBBER MANUFACTURES NES								1.6	CAOUTCHOUC MANUFACTURE
625	RUBBER TYRES, TUBES ETC								1.3	PNEUS CAOUTCHOUC VULCANISE
6251	TYRES NEW FOR MOTOR CARS								1.1	PNEUS POUR VOITURES
63	WOOD,CORK MANUFACTRS NES								2.2	OUVRAGES LIEGE ET BOIS
634	VENEERS,PLYWOOD,ETC								0.9	PLACAGES,CONTRE-PLAQUES
6342	PLYWOOD OF WOOD SHEETS								0.7	BOIS CONTRE-PLAQUES
635	WOOD MANUFACTURES NES								1.3	ART MANUF EN BOIS NDA
6353	BUILDERS WOODWRK,PREFABS								1.3	OUVRAGES DE MENUISERIE
64	PAPER,PAPERBOARD AND MFR								3.0	PAPIERS,CARTONS & OUVRAGES
641	PAPER AND PAPERBOARD								1.6	PAPIERS ET CARTONS
642	PAPER,ETC,PRECUT,ARTS OF								1.4	PAP,CARTONS DECOUPES
6421	PAPER ETC CONTAINERS								0.6	BOITES,SACS EMBALLAGES
65	TEXTILE YARN,FABRICS,ETC								3.7	FILS,TISSUS,ARTICLES TEXTILE
652	COTTON FABRICS,WOVEN								0.7	TISSUS DE COTON
6521	GREY WOVEN COTTON FABRIC								0.7	TISSUS COT ECRUS NON MERCER
65215	GREY WOVN COTN BLEND NES								0.6	AUT TIS MOINS 85% COT ECRUS
657	SPECIAL TXTL FABRC,PRODS								0.9	TISSUS SPECIAUX
6575	CORDAGE AND MANUFACTURES								0.8	FICELLES,CORDES,CORDAGES
658	TEXTILE ARTICLES NES								1.7	ART FACONNES MAT TEXTILES
6589	OTH TEXTILE ARTICLES NES								1.2	AUT ART EN TEXTILES NDA
66	NONMETAL MINERAL MFS NES								3.4	ART MIN NON METALLIQUES
661	LIME,CEMENT,BLDG PRODS								1.7	CHAUX,CIMENTS MAT CONSTR
6612	CEMENT	W 7484	1.0	W 8207	1.1				1.5	CIMENTS HYDRAULIQUES
665	GLASSWARE								0.8	OUVRAGES EN VERRE
6658	GLASS ARTICLES NES								0.7	ARTICLES FAB EN VERRE NDA
66581	LABORATORY ETC GLASS								0.7	VERRERIE LABOR,HYG,PHAR ETC
67	IRON AND STEEL								3.6	FER ET ACIER
673	IRON,STEEL SHAPES ETC								1.7	BARRES,PROFIL FER,ACIER
6732	IRON,STEEL BARS ETC								0.7	BARRES FER,ACIER
6733	IRON,STEEL PROFILES ETC								0.8	PROFILES,PALPLAN FER,ACIER
674	IRN,STL UNIV,PLATE,SHEET								0.9	LARGES PLATS,TOLES
6744	IRN,STL HVY PLATE,ROLLED								0.7	TOLES LAMINEES PLUS 4.75 MM
67441	— OF IRON OR SIMPLE STL								0.7	TOLES NON ACIER FIN CARB
678	IRON,STL TUBES,PIPES,ETC								0.8	TUBES,TUYAUX EN FONTE,FER
68	NON-FERROUS METALS								3.5	METAUX NON FERREUX
687	TIN								2.9	ETAIN
6872	TIN,ALLOYS WORKED								2.9	ETAIN ET ALLIAGES OUVRES

4. Special Imports C.I.F. by Commodities according to the S.I.T.C. (Rev. 2) in million U.S. Dollars
Importations Spéciales C.A.F. par Produits d'après la C.T.C.I. (Rév. 2) en millions de Dollars E.U.

SITC CTCI	COMMODITY	1993		1994		1995		1996		PRODUIT
		QUANTITY QUANTITE	VALUE VALEUR	QUANTITY QUANTITE	VALUE VALEUR	QUANTITY QUANTITE	VALUE VALEUR	QUANTITY QUANTITE	VALUE VALEUR	
68721	TIN BARS,RODS,WIRE ETC								2.9	BARRES,PROFILES FILS SN
69	METAL MANUFACTURES NES								9.9	ART MANUFACT EN METAL NDA
691	STRUCTURES AND PARTS NES								1.4	CONSTRUCT FER,ACIER,ALU
6911	STRUCTURES,PARTS IRN,STL								1.2	CONSTRUCT FER,ACIER,FONTE
693	WIRE PRODUCTS NON ELECTR								1.1	OUVRAGES FILS METALLIQUES
6931	WIRE CABLES, ROPES ETC								0.6	CORDAGES EN FILS DE FER
694	STL,COPPR NAILS,NUTS,ETC								0.9	CLOUS,VIS,ECROUS
695	TOOLS								0.7	OUTILS A MAIN
697	BASE MTL HOUSEHOLD EQUIP								0.9	ART MENAGE MET COMMUNS
699	BASE METAL MFRS NES								4.4	ART MANUFACTURES MET NDA
6998	MFRS NES OF CPR,NIKL,ETC								3.4	OUVRAGES EN CU,NI,AL,PB,ZN
69986	TIN MANUFACTURES NES								3.3	OUVRAGES EN ETAIN
7	MACHINES,TRANSPORT EQUIP		54.1		54.0				41.6	MACHINES MATERIEL TRANSPORT
71	POWER GENERATING EQUIPMT								3.8	MACHINES GENERATRICES
713	INTRNL COMBUS PSTN ENGIN								2.4	MOTEURS EXPL COMB INT, PIECE
7131	AIRCRAFT PSTN ENGINS,PTS								2.0	MOTEURS EXPL P.AVIATION, PIE
71311	AIRCRAFT PISTON ENGINES								1.0	MOTEURS EXPL P.AVIATION
71319	PTS NES OF ENGN OF 71311								1.0	PIECES POUR 713.11
71331	—— OUTBOARD	N 1501	1.0	N 998	1.2					MOTEURS BATEAUX HORSBORD
716	ROTATING ELECTRIC PLANT								1.3	APP ELECTR ROTATIFS,PIECES
7162	AC MTRS,GENRTRS,GEN SETS								0.8	MOTEURS ELECTRIQUES
71621	AC MTRS,INC UNIVRSL MTRS								0.6	MOT ELEC NON COUR CONTINU
7169	PTS NES OF ROT ELEC PLNT								0.6	PIECES MAC APP ROTATIFS
72	MACHS FOR SPCL INDUSTRYS								3.4	MAC SPECIALES POUR INDUST
723	CIVIL ENGNEERG EQUIP ETC								2.2	APPAREILS DE GENIE CIVIL
7234	CONST,MINING MACHNRY NES								2.2	MACH POUR LA CONST, MINES
72341	SELF–PROPELLD DOZERS,ETC								1.8	BULLDOZERS
73	METALWORKING MACHINERY								0.6	MACH TRAVAIL DES METAUX
74	GENRL INDUSTRL MACHY NES								9.9	MACH APP INDUSTRIE
741	HEATING,COOLING EQUIPMNT								1.4	MACH CHAUFFAGE,PIECES
7416	HEATING,COOLING EQU NES								1.2	APP CHANGEMENT TEMP
742	PUMPS FOR LIQUIDS ETC								1.4	POMPES MOTO–POMPES
7428	OTHER PUMPS FOR LIQUIDS								1.4	AUTRES POMPES POUR LIQ
744	MECHANICAL HANDLING EQU								4.7	EQUIP MANUTENTION PIECES
7442	LIFTING,LOADING MACH NES								0.6	APP LEVAGE,MANUTENTION
7449	PTS NES OF MACHY OF 7442								4.0	PIECES DU 744.2
745	NONELEC MACHY,TOOLS NES								1.0	AUT MACH NON ELEC,PIECES
7451	POWER TOOLS NONELEC, PTS								0.9	OUT MACH PNEUM A MOTEUR
749	NONELEC MACH PTS,ACC NES								1.2	PIECES MACH NON ELEC NDA
75	OFFICE MACHNES,ADP EQUIP								1.4	MACH BUREAU TRAIT AUTOM
752	AUTOMTIC DATA PROC EQUIP								0.8	MACH TRAIT INFORMATION
7521	ANALOG,HYBRID COMPUTERS								0.8	MACH POUR TRAIT INFORMAT
76	TELECOMM,SOUND EQUIPMENT								1.7	EQUIPMENT DE TELECOM
764	TELECOM EQPT,PTS,ACC NES								1.3	EQUIP TELECOM,PIECES
7643	TV,RADIO TRANSMITTRS ETC								0.7	APP EMET TELE RADIO
77	ELECTRIC MACHNRY NES ETC								4.6	MACH APP ELECT NDA
771	ELECTRIC POWER MACHY NES								0.6	MACH PROD,TRANS ELECTR
7712	OTH ELEC POWER MACHY NES								0.6	AUT APP PROD TRANSF ELEC
772	SWITCHGEAR ETC,PARTS NES								0.8	APP COUPURE,SECT ETC
7721	SWITCHGEAR ETC								0.8	APP COUPURE,SECTIONMNT
775	HOUSEHOLD TYPE EQUIP NES								1.1	MACH,APP USAGE DOMESTQUE
7752	DOM REFRIGERATRS,FREEZRS								0.9	REFRIG,CONGEL MENAGER
77521	DOMESTIC REFRIGERATORS								0.9	REFRIGERATEURS
778	ELECTRICAL MACHINERY NES								1.4	AUTRES MACH ELECT NDA
7781	BATTERIES,ACCUMULATORS								0.6	PILES ET ACCUMULATORS
78	ROAD VEHICLES								8.5	VEHICULES ROUTIERS
781	PASS MOTOR VEH EXC BUSES	N 142	1.0	N 169	1.2					AUTO TRANSPORT PERSONNES
782	LORRIES,SPCL MTR VEH NES								6.4	VEHICULES SPECIAUX,MARCH
7821	LORRIES,TRUCKS								6.3	VEHICULES TRANSP MARCHAND
783	ROAD MOTOR VEHICLES NES								0.6	VEHICULES ROUTIERS NDA
7831	BUSES								0.6	VOITURES TRANSPORT COMMUN
784	MOTOR VEH PRTS,ACCES NES								1.1	PIECES 722,781,782,783
7849	OTHER MOTOR VEHCL PARTS								1.1	PIECES 722,781,782,783
79	OTHR TRANSPORT EQUIPMENT								8.1	AUTRE MATERIEL TRANSPORT
792	AIRCRAFT ETC								7.8	APP NAVIGATION AERIENNE
7921	HELICOPTERS								7.4	HELICOPTERES
8	MISC MANUFACTURED GOODS		13.4		13.3				14.9	ART MANUFACTURES DIVERS
821	*FURNITURE,PARTS THEREOF								0.8	MEUBLES ET PIECES
84	CLOTHING AND ACCESSORIES								2.5	VETEMENTS
846	UNDER GARMENTS KNITTED								0.6	SOUS VETS DE BONNETERIE
848	HEADGEAR,NONTXTL CLOTHNG								0.9	VET ACCES MAT AUT QUE TEX
8484	HEADGEAR								0.8	COIFFURES ET PARTIES NDA
84848	HEAD–BANDS,LININGS,ETC								0.8	BANDES POUR GARNIT INTER
851	*FOOTWEAR								1.0	CHAUSSURES
87	PRECISION INSTRUMNTS NES								0.8	INSTRUM,APPAR SCIENT NDA
874	MEASURNG,CONTROLNG INSTR								0.7	INSTRUMENTS DE MESURE
89	MISC MANUFCTRD GOODS NES								9.1	ART MANUFACTURES DIVERS
892	PRINTED MATTER								3.4	IMPRIMES
8921	PRINTED BOOKS,GLOBES,ETC								1.0	LIVRES,BROCHURES,CARTES
8922	NEWSPAPERS,PERIODICALS								0.7	JOURNAUX ET PERIODIQUES
8928	PRINTED MATTER NES								1.7	IMPRIMES NDA
89283	UNISSUED BANKNOTES ETC								1.4	TIMBRES–POSTE FISCAUX
893	ARTICLES OF PLASTIC NES								2.9	OUVRAGES EN MAT DIVIS 58
8931	PLSTC PACKG CONTNRS,LIDS								1.5	ART TRANSP EMBALLAGE ETC
8939	MISC PLASTIC ARTICLES								1.4	ART DIVERS EN MAT DIV 58
89399	OTHR PLASTC ARTICLES NES								1.3	AUT OUV MAT DIV 58
894	TOYS,SPORTING GOODS,ETC								1.5	VOITURES ENFANTS,JOUETS
8947	OTH SPORT GDS,FAIR AMUSM								1.2	AUT ART DE SPORT
899	OTHER MANUFACTURED GOODS								0.8	AUT ART MANUF DIVERS NDA
9	GOODS NOT CLASSD BY KIND		1.8						2.1	ART TRANSACT NON CLASSES
931	*SPECIAL TRANSACTIONS								2.0	TRANS.SPECIALES

5. Special Exports F.O.B. by Commodities according to the S.I.T.C. (Rev. 2) in million U.S. Dollars
Exportations Spéciales F.O.B. par Produits d'après la C.T.C.I. (Rév. 2) en millions de Dollars E.U.

SITC CTCI	COMMODITY	1993		1994		1995		1996		PRODUIT
		QUANTITY QUANTITE	VALUE VALEUR	QUANTITY QUANTITE	VALUE VALEUR	QUANTITY QUANTITE	VALUE VALEUR	QUANTITY QUANTITE	VALUE VALEUR	
	ALL COMMODITIES		130.6		142.2					TOUS PRODUITS
0	FOOD AND LIVE ANIMALS		33.0		35.0					ALIMENTS,ANIMAUX VIVANTS
011	MEAT FRESH,CHILLD,FROZEN	W 316	1.1	W 284	0.8					VIANDES FRAICHES,REF,CONGE
0118	MEAT NES FRESH,CHLD,FRZN	W 316	1.1	W 284	0.8					AUTRES VIANDES,ABATS
01189	OTHER MEAT NES FRESH,ETC	W 316	1.1	W 284	0.8					VIANDE,ABATS COMESTIBLES
03	FISH AND PREPARATIONS		26.5		30.2					POISSONS ET PREPARATIONS
034	FISH,FRESH,CHILLED,FROZN	W 15507	9.2	W 23173	10.1					POISSON FRAIS, REFRIG,CONG
035	FISH SALTED,DRIED,SMOKED	W 699	2.2	W 842	1.8					POISSON SECHE,SALE,FUME
03504	FISH SMOKED	W 624	2.0	W 840	1.8					POISSONS FUMES
037	FISH ETC PREPD,PRSVD NES	W 5661	15.3	W 7712	18.4					POIS,CRUST,MOL PREPARES
0371	FISH PREPARD,PRESRVD NES	W 5661	15.3	W 7712	18.4					CONSERVES DE POISSONS
072	COCOA	W 3936	5.4	W 3683	3.9					CACAO
0721	COCOA BEANS,RAW,ROASTED	W 3936	5.4	W 3683	3.9					CACAO EN FEVES
2	CRUDE MATERLS,EXCL FUELS		81.6		93.0					MAT BRUTES NON COMESTIBLES
223	SEEDS FOR OTH FIXED OILS	W 33406	6.7	W 25093	7.4					GRAINES AUTRES HUILES FIXES
2231	COPRA	W 26669	5.9	W 19108	6.1					COPRAH
2232	PALM NUTS AND KERNELS	W 6737	0.8	W 5985	1.4					NOIX,AMANDES DE PALMISTE
247	OTH WOOD ROUGH,SQUARED	W 451	73.6	W 502	84.2					BOIS BRUTS EQUARRIS
2472	SAW–,VENEER–LOGS NON–CON	W 451	73.6	W 502	84.2					NON CONIFERES SCIAGE,PLAC
291	CRUDE ANIMAL MTRIALS NES	W 58	1.5		1.6					MATIERES BRUTES ANIMALES
2911	BONES,IVORY,HORNS,ETC	W 58	1.5		1.6					OS,CORNES,SABOTS
29115	CORAL, SHELLS, AND WASTE	W 58	1.5		1.6					CORAIL & SIMILAIRES
424	FIXED VEG OIL NONSOFT	W 34432	12.8	W 29217	12.8					AUTRES HUILES VEG FIXES
4242	PALM OIL	W 30987	11.4	W 28041	12.2					HUILE DE PALME
4243	COCONUT (COPRA) OIL	W 3445	1.4	W 1176	0.7					HJUILE DE COPRAH
9	GOODS NOT CLASSD BY KIND		3.2		1.4					ART TRANSACT NON CLASSES
931	*SPECIAL TRANSACTIONS		2.1		1.0					TRANS.SPECIALES

FOOT NOTES – NOTES

TABLE 1 –
1 Prior to 1978, imports f.o.b.
TABLEAU 1 –
1 Avant 1978, les importations sont f.a.b.

1. HISTORICAL SERIES, 1962–1997 GENERAL TRADE, IMPORTS C.I.F., EXPORTS F.O.B.
SERIES HISTORIQUES, 1962–1997 COMMERCE GENERAL, IMPORTATIONS C.A.F., EXPORTATIONS F.O.B

YEAR ANNEE	VALUE IN MILLION RAND VALEUR EN MILLION RAND: MERCHANDISE – MARCHANDISE IMPORTS	MERCHANDISE – MARCHANDISE EXPORTS	GOLD – OR IMPORTS	GOLD – OR EXPORTS	CONVERSION FACTORS U.S. CENTS PER RAND FACTEURS DE CONVERSION CENTS E.U. PAR RAND: IMPORTS	EXPORTS	INDEX NUMBERS – INDICES: QUANTUM IMPORTS	QUANTUM EXPORTS	UNIT VALUE VALEUR UNITAIRE IMPORTS	UNIT VALUE VALEUR UNITAIRE EXPORTS
1962	1013.10	949.50	0.10	636.60	140.0000	140.0000				
1963	1212.60	999.90	0.20	685.70	140.0000	140.0000				
1964	1539.90	1041.50	0.10	730.50	140.0000	140.0000				
1965	1756.40	1059.10	0.10	766.50	140.0000	140.0000				
1966	1645.50	1206.30	0.10	776.20	140.0000	140.0000				
1967	1919.30	1364.10	0.10	763.00	140.0000	140.0000				
1968	1880.10	1506.30	0.20	771.20	140.0000	140.0000				
1969	2134.60	1534.00	0.20	779.20	140.0000	140.0000				
1970	2811.90	1536.50	0.20	837.00	140.0000	140.0000				
1971	3184.40	1554.10	0.20	759.30	140.0000	140.0000				
1972	2840.50	1955.30	0.20	1161.00	129.3730	129.2230				
1973	3564.20	2375.80		1769.00	144.1460	144.0120				
1974	5344.30	3016.90		2565.00	147.0020	146.9250				
1975	5545.50	3408.10		2540.00	136.3360	136.0310				
1976	5859.40	4331.90		2346.00	115.0000	115.0000				
1977	5188.30	5863.20		2795.00	115.0000	115.0000				
1978	6253.40	7333.30		3906.00	115.0000	115.0000				
1979	9904.30	8808.70		6002.00	118.7930	118.9110				
1980	14381.30	9774.80		10041.00	129.0110	128.3670	109	85	30	30
1981	18511.20	9675.50		8338.60	113.8625	114.4715	123	77	34	33
1982	18391.20	10440.90		8626.80	92.2800	92.2800	104	77	41	36
1983	16228.80	10779.00		9929.00	89.5183	89.7286	86	69	44	40
1984	21687.00	13671.00			68.9623	68.2741	103	76	48	46
1985	22707.70	20622.90			45.4447	45.2196	88	90	62	58
1986	29688.00	42011.30		16719.00	43.7375	43.7736	85	94	72	66
1987	31105.01	43202.00		17808.00	49.1760	49.1327	89	91	75	69
1988	42566.00	49723.90		19622.00	43.8696	43.8769	109	98	83	79
1989	48515.01	58198.80		19122.00	38.1184	38.0553	109	106	93	95
1990	47605.01	60928.50		18069.00	38.6506	38.6830	100	100	100	100
1991	52006.00	64354.90		19351.00	36.2071	36.1759	100	100	110	106
1992	56358.00	66773.90		18195.00	35.0245	35.1056	103	88	117	112
1993	65411.01	79279.01		22229.00	30.6410	30.6410	107	107	127	122
1994	83042.00	89907.01			28.1348	28.1502	123	116	141	131
1995	110826.00	101052.00			27.5624	27.5661	136	119	157	161
1996	129522.00	126101.00			23.3067	23.1775	155	169	166	177
1997	151779.00	142938.00			21.7444	21.7076				

2. IMPORTS BY BROAD ECONOMIC CATEGORY AND EXPORTS BY INDUSTRIAL ORIGIN. (PERCENTAGE OF TOTAL VALUE)
IMPORTATIONS PAR CATEGORIES ECONOMIQUES ET EXPORTATIONS PAR BRANCHE D'ACTIVITE. (EN POURCENTAGE DE LA VALEUR TOTALE)

IMPORTS – IMPORTATIONS

	1990	1991	1992	1993	1994	1995	1996
TOTAL IMPORTS–IMPORTATIONS TOTALES	100.	100.	100.	100.	100.	100.	100.
1 FOOD BEV–ALIMENTATION BOISSONS	3.9	3.8	4.8	4.8	5.2	5.2	5.0
11 PRIMARY–PRODUITS DE BASE	1.6	1.8	2.3	2.3	2.1	2.2	2.0
111 FOR INDUSTRY–POUR L'INDUSTRIE	0.9	1.0	1.2	1.5	1.0	1.1	1.1
112 FOR HOUSEHOLDS–POUR LES MENAGES	0.7	0.7	1.1	0.8	1.1	1.1	0.9
12 PROCESSED–PRODUITS ELABORES	2.3	2.1	2.5	2.5	3.2	3.0	2.9
121 FOR INDUSTRY–POUR L'INDUSTRIE	0.8	0.7	0.8	0.8	0.8	0.8	0.8
122 FOR HOUSEHOLDS–POUR LES MENAGES	1.5	1.3	1.7	1.7	2.4	2.3	2.1
2 IND SUPPLIES–APPROV INDUSTRIELS	29.3	29.1	29.6	29.4	28.8	28.5	27.1
21 PRIMARY–PRODUITS DE BASE	3.2	3.1	4.8	4.6	3.9	3.5	3.2
22 PROCESSED–PRODUITS ELABORES	26.1	26.0	24.7	24.9	24.9	25.0	23.9
3 FUELS–COMBUSTIBLES	0.6	0.6	0.3	0.2	0.2	8.2	9.2
31 PRIMARY–PRODUITS DE BASE	0.2	0.2	0.2	0.1	0.1	8.1	8.2
32 PROCESSED–PRODUITS ELABORES	0.4	0.3	0.1	0.1	0.1	0.1	1.0
321 MOTOR SPIRIT–ESSENCE							0.4
322 OTHER–AUTRES	0.4	0.3	0.1	0.1	0.1	0.1	0.6
4 MACHINERY–EQUIPEMENT	29.3	27.8	28.0	28.9	33.0	30.8	31.7
41 CAPITAL EQUIPMENT–MACHINES	23.7	22.1	22.3	23.0	26.7	24.7	25.9
42 PARTS–PIECES ACCESSOIRES	5.6	5.7	5.7	5.9	6.2	6.1	5.8
5 TRANSPORT–TRANSPORT	15.3	16.9	15.0	17.4	17.0	15.5	7.8
51 PASSENGER CARS–AUTOMOBILES	5.0	4.2	3.4	5.1	4.4	4.0	1.8
52 OTHER–AUTRES	4.4	6.1	4.8	5.2	4.8	5.0	1.7
521 INDUSTRIAL–INDUSTRIELS	4.4	6.0	4.7	5.1	4.7	4.9	1.5
522 NON INDUSTRIAL–NON INDUSTRIEL	0.1	0.1	0.1	0.1	0.1	0.1	0.2
53 PARTS–PIECES ACCESSOIRES	5.8	6.6	6.8	7.0	7.8	6.5	4.3
6 CONSUM GOODS–BIENS CONSOMMATION	8.3	9.5	9.9	10.3	9.8	9.3	11.0
61 DURABLE–DURABLES	2.1	2.3	2.6	2.6	2.4	2.3	2.7
62 SEMI DURABLE–SEMI DURABLES	3.8	4.6	4.2	4.5	4.2	4.1	5.2
63 NON DURABLE–NON DURABLES	2.4	2.6	3.1	3.2	3.2	2.9	3.1
7 GOODS NES–BIENS NDA	13.3	12.2	12.4	9.0	6.0	2.5	8.3

EXPORTS – EXPORTATIONS

	1990	1991	1992	1993	1994	1995	1996
TOTAL EXPORTS–EXPORTATIONS TOTALES	100.	100.	100.	100.	100.	100.	100.
1 AGRICULTURE	5.4	4.9	4.4	4.1	5.8	4.4	6.1
2 MINING QUARRY–INDUS EXTRACTIVES	15.0	14.2	18.6	22.0	18.7	18.5	24.0
3 MANUFACTURING–IND MANUFACTUR	79.6	80.9	77.0	73.9	75.5	77.0	69.9
31 FOOD BEV TOBACCO–ALIM BOISS TAB	4.3	4.9	3.9	3.3	3.6	4.5	6.2
32 TEXTILES–INDUSTRIES TEXTILES	2.4	2.9	2.6	2.5	2.3	2.6	3.2
33 WOOD & PRODUCTS–BOIS & PRODUITS	0.5	0.6	0.5	0.7	0.7	0.8	0.8
34 PAPER & PRODUCTS–PAPIER & PRODT	3.0	3.0	2.8	2.5	3.0	4.0	3.7
35 CHEMICALS–INDUSTRIES CHIMIQUES	4.4	5.2	6.1	5.5	7.2	10.8	14.2
36 NON METAL MIN–MIN NON METAL	0.5	0.6	0.9	0.8	0.7	0.8	0.9
37 BASIC METAL–IND METAL BASE	9.6	10.1	14.1	11.9	11.1	13.1	16.3
38 METAL MANUF–MANUF METAL	6.7	8.0	8.3	8.7	9.7	12.5	16.2
39 OTH MANUF IND–AUTRES MANUF	48.0	45.6	37.8	38.1	37.1	28.1	8.2

3. TRADE BY PRINCIPAL COUNTRIES OF ORIGIN AND DESTINATION (VALUE IN MILLION U.S. DOLLARS)
ECHANGES SELON LES PRINCIPAUX PAYS D'ORIGINE ET DE DESTINATION (VALEUR EN MILLIONS DE DOLLARS EU)

COUNTRIES–PAYS	GENERAL IMPORTS C.I.F. IMPORTATIONS GENERALES C.A.F				
	1992	1993	1994	1995	1996
World	18373.4	18026.5	21109.6	26744.6	26872.4
Africa	420.4	456.8	585.7	736.0	782.4
Americas	3097.3	2835.3	3191.7	4111.6	4384.0
– Northern America	2658.6	2545.1	2690.6	3436.7	3706.0
– LAIA	422.8	272.5	475.5	653.1	626.3
– CACM	2.4	3.7	3.0	7.1	4.8
– Caribbean	12.0	11.4	20.3	12.3	11.7
– Rest of America	1.6	2.5	2.4	2.4	35.1
Asia excl fmr USSR	4148.4	4777.0	5179.9	8075.5	7960.6
– Middle East	59.6	75.2	85.9	1784.8	2076.3
Asia former USSR				3.7	2.4
Europe excl fmr USSR	8112.9	8000.5	10376.3	12832.0	12670.7
– European Union	7606.5	7511.1	9766.6	12055.1	11873.1
– Eastern Europe	60.6	60.3	61.1	89.3	70.1
– Rest of Europe	445.8	429.1	548.6	687.6	727.5
Europe former USSR	27.9	35.3	111.3	41.2	37.3
Oceania	244.8	235.6	327.0	486.3	715.9
Other	2321.7	1686.1	1337.7	458.3	319.2
Germany/Allemagne	3005.9	2838.0	3626.8	4411.5	4041.8
USA/Etats–Unis d'Amer	2512.3	2393.0	2390.4	3158.0	3479.0
United Kingdom	1875.3	1977.5	2455.3	2934.7	3094.6
Japan/Japon	1948.3	2279.1	2217.8	2719.0	2098.4
Special Categories	2285.3	1647.1	40.8	377.6	260.6
Italy/Italie	645.2	637.1	837.7	1094.8	1184.2
France, Monaco	717.3	641.3	779.0	1044.4	918.0
Other Asia n.e.s.	618.6	623.8	726.9	890.3	842.6
Netherlands/Pays–Bas	436.8	424.1	530.4	628.0	681.6
Switzerland,Liechtenst.	428.0	401.4	520.2	648.4	685.6
Belgium–Luxembourg	413.4	406.0	508.2	609.1	544.8
Iran (Islamic Rep of)	5.8	5.2	13.8	1206.9	1229.4
China/Chine	228.5	307.0	360.5	509.1	577.2
China, Hong Kong SAR	309.6	339.9	401.6	447.9	435.0
Australia/Australie	220.7	210.9	297.3	450.1	668.3
Korea, Republic of	247.3	269.6	303.4	411.3	542.2
Areas n.e.s.	36.5	38.9	1296.9	80.7	58.6
Singapore/Singapour	225.9	241.6	275.9	322.8	327.7
Zimbabwe	267.1	202.9	281.6	268.8	277.8
Sweden/Suède	44.6	72.6	232.2	408.9	448.6
Canada	145.3	150.3	299.8	278.3	226.5
Brazil/Brésil	162.5	169.7	205.8	240.5	264.4
Malaysia/Malaisie	125.0	178.0	210.4	245.7	251.9
Argentina/Argentine	182.7	63.1	160.4	249.3	232.5
Spain/Espagne	126.2	115.9	145.3	210.1	258.6
Thailand/Thaïlande	135.6	132.8	156.7	191.2	167.8
Israel/Israël	105.7	152.8	171.4	169.7	177.3
Austria/Autriche	124.0	112.7	174.7	173.7	163.8
India/Inde	38.4	50.4	114.2	195.5	259.4
Ireland/Irlande	71.6	96.3	128.6	167.8	188.5
Finland/Finlande	55.4	64.1	175.8	167.4	156.6
Kuwait/Koweït	0.3	0.4	0.2	165.0	383.3
Denmark/Danemark	46.0	67.4	103.3	129.3	107.8
Saudi Arabia	5.9	11.3	10.0	207.9	217.4
Dem Rep of the Congo	4.0	80.3	99.5	101.1	111.9
Indonesia/Indonésie	46.5	57.0	74.3	99.1	113.4
Chile/Chili	61.9	26.5	84.7	94.3	54.8
Malawi	46.9	48.9	52.0	56.5	69.0
Portugal	38.0	52.2	56.1	58.2	67.2
Turkey/Turquie	43.5	47.5	37.1	53.1	51.2

COUNTRIES–PAYS	GENERAL EXPORTS F.O.B. EXPORTATIONS GENERALES F.O.B.				
	1992	1993	1994	1995	1996
Monde	23883.7	24265.7	25621.5	28226.3	23468.8
Afrique	2082.0	2305.8	2390.9	3833.0	4036.1
Amériques	1967.7	2172.2	1963.1	2930.0	3127.2
– Amérique du Nord	1649.3	1799.5	1374.1	2318.2	2440.5
– ALAI	284.1	335.6	494.9	562.4	609.4
– MCAC	8.3	8.4	9.8	9.0	8.7
– Caraïbes	19.9	24.9	77.2	35.7	32.0
– Autre Amérique	5.9	3.7	7.1	4.8	36.5
Asie anc. URSS exclus	3780.6	4432.7	4063.9	5884.7	6400.4
– Moyen–Orient	383.3	393.0	327.7	377.9	458.7
Asie ancienne URSS		0.2	0.2	0.3	4.3
Europe anc. URSS exclus	5683.3	7778.3	7314.9	8961.7	9285.2
– Union Européenne	5195.6	5076.7	5395.9	7548.7	8242.0
– Europe de l'Est	80.7	80.5	66.5	99.4	68.6
– Autre de l'Europe	406.9	2621.0	1852.5	1313.6	974.7
Europe ancienne URSS	216.8	162.5	49.4	69.5	66.7
Océanie	129.9	182.0	220.3	333.6	431.7
Autre	10023.5	7232.1	9618.8	6213.5	117.3
Special Categories	9787.4	6900.3	9600.1	5704.6	0.0
United Kingdom	1553.9	1448.9	1654.0	2347.8	3107.0
USA/Etats–Unis d'Amer	1572.7	1678.7	1238.1	2145.0	2256.7
Japan/Japon	1116.1	1323.3	1169.5	1799.7	2022.4
Switzerland,Liechtenst.	194.8	2418.0	1703.8	1153.4	805.7
Germany/Allemagne	1032.7	940.2	987.7	1402.1	1307.5
Zimbabwe	542.4	757.0	678.0	1254.3	1248.0
Belgium–Luxembourg	454.6	710.1	727.3	899.7	840.0
Netherlands/Pays–Bas	609.5	652.8	591.3	855.6	785.5
Other Asia n.e.s.	681.9	662.5	521.3	700.1	737.0
Italy/Italie	549.8	443.0	494.4	669.4	625.4
China, Hong Kong SAR	448.2	533.0	418.5	566.7	611.0
Korea, Republic of	294.1	389.4	489.2	577.9	667.2
Mozambique	238.1	295.5	388.4	617.6	565.2
Spain/Espagne	314.2	284.7	339.6	466.6	634.9
Zambia/Zambie	389.8	399.9	317.8	377.5	417.2
Israel/Israël	282.2	513.9	303.4	387.1	394.1
France, Monaco	322.5	253.3	281.8	358.7	428.2
Bunkers, ship stores	235.2	323.7		508.7	112.5
Australia/Australie	115.8	159.0	186.5	289.0	384.5
Singapore/Singapour	100.9	131.0	128.9	315.4	391.6
Malawi	243.7	181.1	171.3	192.0	222.8
China/Chine	174.0	183.7	163.0	289.5	187.8
Brazil/Brésil	61.3	120.7	226.4	289.4	276.9
Mauritius/Maurice	137.3	144.3	150.2	191.1	214.0
Kenya	52.3	62.6	185.7	260.0	220.6
Angola	127.6	80.7	87.1	123.1	353.2
Norway,Svalbard and JM	187.1	174.3	129.8	116.0	149.3
Dem Rep of the Congo	101.2	95.9	104.2	194.7	222.6
Canada	76.6	120.7	135.4	173.2	183.5
Thailand/Thaïlande	118.4	122.0	95.6	164.2	141.9
India/Inde	7.0	28.4	136.8	189.7	245.9
Russian Federation	216.8	162.4	46.7	65.0	52.2
Turkey/Turquie	118.6	130.9	65.5	97.9	101.8
Indonesia/Indonésie	44.7	36.0	79.3	156.5	175.0
Ireland/Irlande	100.2	98.9	52.2	126.8	93.1
Malaysia/Malaisie	3.1	8.4	96.2	185.4	165.6
Portugal	105.8	85.7	73.6	106.6	82.3
Argentina/Argentine	75.8	85.3	77.2	113.0	89.7
Denmark/Danemark	14.4	71.5	74.8	114.7	151.0

(VALUE AS PERCENTAGE OF WORLD TOTAL)(VALEURS EN POURCENTAGE DU TOTAL MONDIAL)

	1987	1988	1989	1990	1991	1992	1993	1994	1995	1996
Africa						2.3	2.5	2.8	2.8	2.9
Americas						16.9	15.7	15.1	15.4	16.3
– Northern America						14.5	14.1	12.7	12.8	13.8
– LAIA						2.3	1.5	2.3	2.4	2.3
– CACM						0.0	0.0	0.0	0.0	0.0
– Caribbean						0.1	0.1	0.1	0.0	0.0
– Rest of America						0.0	0.0	0.0	0.0	0.1
Asia excl fmr USSR						22.6	26.5	24.5	30.2	29.6
– Middle East						0.3	0.4	0.4	6.7	7.7
Asia former USSR									0.0	0.0
Europe excl fmr USSR						44.2	44.4	49.2	48.0	47.2
– European Union						41.4	41.7	46.3	45.1	44.2
– Eastern Europe						0.3	0.3	0.3	0.3	0.3
– Rest of Europe						2.4	2.4	2.6	2.6	2.7
Europe former USSR						0.2	0.2	0.5	0.2	0.1
Oceania						1.3	1.3	1.5	1.8	2.7
Other						12.6	9.4	6.3	1.7	1.2
Germany/Allemagne						16.4	15.7	17.2	16.5	15.0
USA/Etats–Unis d'Amer						13.7	13.3	11.3	11.8	12.9
United Kingdom						10.2	11.0	11.6	11.0	11.5
Japan/Japon						10.6	12.6	10.5	10.2	7.8
Special Categories						12.4	9.1	0.2	1.4	1.0
Italy/Italie						3.5	3.5	4.0	4.1	4.4
France, Monaco						3.9	3.6	3.7	3.9	3.4
Other Asia n.e.s.						3.4	3.5	3.4	3.3	3.1
Netherlands/Pays–Bas						2.4	2.4	2.5	2.3	2.5
Switzerland,Liechtenst.						2.3	2.2	2.5	2.4	2.6

	1987	1988	1989	1990	1991	1992	1993	1994	1995	1996
Afrique						8.7	9.5	9.3	13.6	17.2
Amériques						8.2	9.0	7.7	10.4	13.3
– Amérique du Nord						6.9	7.4	5.4	8.2	10.4
– ALAI						1.2	1.4	1.9	2.0	2.6
– MCAC						0.0	0.0	0.0	0.0	0.0
– Caraïbes						0.1	0.1	0.3	0.1	0.1
– Autre Amérique						0.0	0.0	0.0	0.0	0.2
Asie anc. URSS exclus						15.8	18.3	15.9	20.8	27.3
– Moyen–Orient						1.6	1.6	1.3	1.3	2.0
Asie ancienne URSS							0.0	0.0	0.0	0.0
Europe anc. URSS exclus						23.8	32.1	28.5	31.7	39.6
– Union Européenne						21.8	20.9	21.1	26.7	35.1
– Europe de l'Est						0.3	0.3	0.3	0.4	0.3
– Autre de l'Europe						1.7	10.8	7.2	4.7	4.2
Europe ancienne URSS						0.9	0.7	0.2	0.2	0.3
Océanie						0.5	0.8	0.9	1.2	1.8
Autre						42.0	29.8	37.5	22.0	0.5
Special Categories						41.0	28.4	37.5	20.2	0.0
United Kingdom						6.5	6.0	6.5	8.3	13.2
USA/Etats–Unis d'Amer						6.6	6.9	4.8	7.6	9.6
Japan/Japon						4.7	5.5	4.6	6.4	8.6
Switzerland,Liechtenst.						0.8	10.0	6.6	4.1	3.4
Germany/Allemagne						4.3	3.9	3.9	5.0	5.6
Zimbabwe						2.3	3.1	2.6	4.4	5.3
Belgium–Luxembourg						1.9	2.9	2.8	3.2	3.6
Netherlands/Pays–Bas						2.6	2.7	2.3	3.0	3.3
Other Asia n.e.s.						2.9	2.7	2.0	2.5	3.1

4. General Imports C.I.F. by Commodities according to the S.I.T.C. (Rev. 2) in million U.S. Dollars
Importations Générales C.A.F. par Produits d'après la C.T.C.I. (Rév. 2) en millions de Dollars E.U.

SITC CTCI	COMMODITY	1993 QUANTITY QUANTITE	1993 VALUE VALEUR	1994 QUANTITY QUANTITE	1994 VALUE VALEUR	1995 QUANTITY QUANTITE	1995 VALUE VALEUR	1996 QUANTITY QUANTITE	1996 VALUE VALEUR	PRODUIT
	ALL COMMODITIES		18026.6		21109.6		26744.6		26872.5	TOUS PRODUITS
0	FOOD AND LIVE ANIMALS		758.4		868.9		1232.6		1245.6	ALIMENTS,ANIMAUX VIVANTS
01	MEAT AND PREPARATIONS		44.7		171.2		192.1		136.7	VIANDES ET PREPARATIONS
011	MEAT FRESH,CHILLD,FROZEN		43.7	W 122491	121.1	W 133113	146.8	W 161949	133.3	VIANDES FRAICHES,REF,CONGE
03	FISH AND PREPARATIONS		57.1		57.0		66.1		64.8	POISSONS ET PREPARATIONS
04	CEREALS AND PREPARATIONS		394.8		258.9		471.2		498.4	CEREALES ET PRODUITS
041	WHEAT ETC UNMILLED	W 1172377	145.4	W 728182	72.8	W 983913	155.5	W 1143901	191.3	FROMENT,EPEAUTRE
0412	OTHER WHEAT ETC UNMILLED	W 1142900	141.3	W 702697	68.0	W 957675	149.9	W 1114842	184.5	AUTRE FROMENT NON MOULU
042	RICE	W 385466	99.5	W 430640	127.0	W 466235	137.1	W 482689	163.2	RIZ
0422	RICE SEMI–MILLED,MILLED	W 276061	70.2	W 320349	87.6	W 424134	125.4	W 427835	142.3	RIZ POLI,GLACE INCL BRISURES
04221	RICE MILLED UNBROKEN	W 274496	69.8	W 317442	86.9	W 397950	118.1	W 418172	139.4	RIZ POLI,GLACE EXCL BRISURES
044	MAIZE UNMILLED	W 830244	103.3	W 29760	11.6	W 750253	114.3	W 506761	66.2	MAIS NON MOULU
05	VEGETABLES AND FRUIT		62.1		68.8		113.1		99.7	LEGUMES ET FRUITS
07	COFFEE,TEA,COCOA,SPICES		70.2		103.4		116.8		113.6	CAFE,THE,CACAO,EPICES
081	*FEEDING STUFF FOR ANIML		58.6	W 447717	116.8		142.8		190.2	NOURRITURE POUR ANIMAUX
0813	OILCAKE AND OTH RESIDUES	W 116068	18.0	W 182829	29.8	W 300308	38.2	W 426109	90.4	TOURTEAUX
0814	MEAT OR FISH MEAL FODDER	W 73196	27.6	W 194784	70.6	W 223738	79.9	W 123816	61.4	FARINES DE VIANDES,POISSONS
08142	FISH MEAL FODDER	W 73195	27.6	W 191867	70.0	W 214673	77.5	W 97835	52.7	FARINES DE POISSONS
1	BEVERAGES AND TOBACCO		131.0		156.3		170.1		188.7	BOISSONS ET TABACS
11	BEVERAGES		78.9		97.8		106.6		121.1	BOISSONS
112	ALCOHOLIC BEVERAGES		78.1	W 13772	95.8	W 30520	104.7	W 48386	114.9	BOISSONS ALCOOLIQUES
1124	DISTILLED ALCOHOLIC BEVS		73.1	W 9785	88.9	W 21123	95.2	W 21826	93.7	ALCOOLS,EAUX–DE–VIE
11241	WHISKY		63.7	W 8179	76.0	W 17918	80.7	W 17073	74.6	WHISKY
2	CRUDE MATERLS,EXCL FUELS		653.3		695.7		996.3		950.7	MAT BRUTES NON COMESTIBLES
22	OIL SEEDS,OLEAGINOUS FRT		62.2		44.4		70.1		25.5	GRAINES,FRUITS OLEAGINEUX
222	SEEDS FOR'SOFT'FIXED OIL		59.8	W 168970	41.3	W 268235	66.8	W 78984	25.1	GRAINES HUILES FIXES
23	RUBBER, CRUDE		70.7		85.5		129.2		107.8	CAOUTCHOUC BRUT
232	NATURAL RUBBER,GUMS	W 50020	45.5	W 58042	56.4	W 56983	87.6	W 56237	75.5	LATEX CAOUTCHOUC NATUREL
24	CORK AND WOOD		115.2		116.2		132.3		112.3	LIEGE ET BOIS
248	WOOD SHAPED,SLEEPERS		109.8	W 6956259	111.0	W 1651134	121.9	W 485821	101.3	BOIS SIMPLEMENT TRAVAILLES
2483	LUMBER SHAPED NON–CONIFR	W 776094	104.5	W 2692071	101.9	W 1579482	108.9	W 388114	88.4	NON CONIFERES SCIES,RABOTES
24831	LUMBER SAWN ETC NON–CON	W 771936	104.1	W 2632134	100.7	W 1577632	105.7	W 383154	81.4	SCIES LONGITUDINALEMENT
26	TEXTILE FIBRES AND WASTE		145.7		153.8		204.3		167.8	FIBRES TEXTILES
263	COTTON	W 44581	52.4	W 46749	65.7	W 46932	85.5	W 40938	74.6	COTON
2631	RAW COTTON,EXCL LINTERS	W 41105	50.5	W 44414	62.7	W 44114	80.8	W 38449	70.7	COTON EN MASSE
27	CRUDE FERTLZR,MINRLS NES		91.6		97.9		123.2		103.0	ENGRAIS MINERAUX BRUTS
28	METALLIFEROUS ORES,SCRAP		88.9		93.0		186.2		280.8	MINERAIS METAL,DECHETS
287	BASE METAL ORES,CONC NES	W 356431	71.9		77.7		166.0	W 1144827	252.6	MINERAIS METAUX COMMUNS
2873	ALUMINIUM ORES,ALUMINA	W 339701	64.7	W 329971	62.7	W 617271	129.6	W 1112759	219.5	MINERAIS D'ALUMINIUM
28732	ALUMINA(ALUMINIUM OXIDE)	W 330890	63.9	W 314278	61.7	W 606335	128.5	W 1099356	218.1	ALUMINE (OXYDE ALUMINIUM)
29	CRUDE ANIMAL,VEG MAT NES		57.8		62.1		81.4		83.8	MATIERES BRUTES ANIM,VEGET
3	MINERAL FUELS ETC		83.3		79.0		2238.3		2572.8	COMBUSTIBLES MINERAUX LUB
32	COAL,COKE AND BRIQUETTES		25.3		30.0		43.8		87.7	HOUILLES,COKES,BRIQUETTES
33	PETROLEUM AND PRODUCTS		57.9		48.6		2194.2		2484.6	PETROLE ET DERIVES
333	CRUDE PETROLEUM						2118.6		2137.3	HUILES BRUTES DE PETROLE
334	PETROLEUM PRODUCTS,REFIN	W 2711	9.2	W 3225	10.9	W 4188	13.8	W 984731	242.8	PRODUITS RAFFINES
3341	GASOLINE,OTH LIGHT OILS							W 469472	106.8	ESSENCES POUR MOTEURS
33411	MOTOR,AVIATION SPIRIT							W 469472	106.8	ESSENCES MOTEURS D'AVIONS
335	RESIDUAL PETRLM PROD NES	W 182998	48.7	W 132687	37.7	W 228290	62.0	W 395417	104.6	PRODUITS RESIDUELS NDA
4	ANIMAL,VEGETABLE OIL,FAT		158.9		267.6		312.6		256.9	HUILES,GRAISSES ANIM,VEG
42	FIXED VEGETABLE OIL,FAT		111.3		193.2		223.5		178.7	HUILES VEGETALES FIXES
423	FIXED VEG OILS,SOFT		52.2	W 211141	128.0	W 236231	150.2	W 170400	95.9	HUILES VEGET DOUCES FIXES
4236	SUNFLOWER SEED OIL	W 61402	29.2	W 195835	117.0	W 185749	113.9	W 139203	75.5	HUILE DE TOURNESOL
424	FIXED VEG OIL NONSOFT	W 146208	59.1	W 137857	65.2	W 130247	73.4	W 147220	82.8	AUTRES HUILES VEG FIXES
5	CHEMCLS,RELATED PROD NES		2280.0		2632.7		3250.1		3178.0	PRODUITS CHIMIQUES
51	ORGANIC CHEMICALS		561.3		700.2		892.1		783.7	PROD CHIMIQ ORGANIQUES
511	HYDROCARBONS NES,DERIVS		56.6		68.3	W 114944	91.2		66.9	HYDROCARBURES NDA
512	ALCOHOLS,PHENOLS ETC		53.2		84.6	W 145788	130.3	W 113129	92.5	PHENOLS,PHENOLS–ALCOOLS
5121	ACYCLIC ALCOHOLS,DERIVS		40.5		68.7	W 138135	110.6	W 105677	74.3	ALCOOLS ACYCLIQUES
513	CARBOXYLIC ACIDS ETC	W 144791	118.0	W 153280	139.6	W 175154	215.6	W 152899	170.7	ACIDES CARBOXYLIQUES
5137	MONOACIDS AND DERIVATIVS	W 49149	54.6	W 52903	59.4	W 66413	93.5	W 61623	83.9	ACIDES MONOCARBOXYLIQUES
5138	POLYACIDS AND DERIVATIVS	W 88237	47.5	W 90686	61.3	W 95579	96.7	W 78892	61.1	ACIDES POLYCARBOXYLIQUES
51389	OTH POLYACIDS ETC,DERIVS	W 87082	46.8	W 90013	60.9	W 94037	94.7	W 76755	59.5	ACIDES POLYCARBOXYLIQUES
514	NITROGEN–FNCTN COMPOUNDS		192.0	W 99199	239.2	W 95328	256.3	W 80798	255.5	COMPOSES FONCT AZOTEES
5148	OTH NITROGN–FNCTN CMPNDS	W 41397	113.2	W 59799	147.0	W 63787	168.9	W 50230	157.5	AUTRES COMPOSES AZOTES
51482	IMIDE–,IMIDE–FNCT CMPNDS	W 13295	61.9	W 15964	81.3	W 15012	76.5	W 13964	77.7	COMPOSES A FONCTION IMIDE
515	ORG–INORG COMPOUNDS ETC	W 11721	96.5	W 15982	112.7	W 17415	121.5	W 18723	128.6	COMPOSES ORGANO–MINERAUX
52	INORGANIC CHEMICALS		181.9		189.0		228.5		248.9	PROD CHIM INORGANIQUES
522	INORG ELEMNTS,OXIDES,ETC	W 129144	67.8	W 194658	75.6		82.3		84.4	ELEMENTS INORGANIQUES
523	OTHR INORG CHEMICALS ETC	W 329810	105.9	W 332101	104.4	W 378496	135.8	W 403820	152.9	AUT PRODUITS CHIMIQUES INORG
5232	OTH MTL CMPD OF INRG ACD	W 239537	58.6	W 189115	56.4	W 271888	73.2	W 293791	71.0	SELS METALLIQUES
53	DYES,TANNING,COLOUR PROD		160.7		183.4		209.7		199.7	PROD TEINTURE,COLORANTS
531	SYNT DYE,NAT INDGO,LAKES	W 7512	93.5	W 7988	100.4	W 8620	109.4	W 8974	100.3	MAT COLOR ORGAN,LAQUES
5311	SYNTHIC ORGNIC DYESTUFFS	W 6016	81.9	W 6481	88.8	W 6760	96.2	W 7194	88.0	MAT COLOR ORGAN SYNTHET
533	PIGMENTS,PAINTS,ETC	W 23416	63.5	W 25653	77.9	W 24729	94.7	W 25778	94.4	PIGMENTS,PEINTURES,VERNIS
541	*MEDICINAL,PHARM PRODUCT		359.1		441.2		538.5		590.8	PROD MEDICINAUX PHARMACEUT
5417	MEDICAMENTS		230.3		289.4	K 3755110	352.2	K 4533108	400.6	MEDICAMENTS
54171	— CONTAINNG ANTIBIOTICS		47.6		61.7	K 1174237	74.6	K 914380	91.9	MED CONTN ANTIBIOTIQUES
54179	— CONTNG OTH SUBSTANCES		155.4		187.7	K 2189225	226.9	K 3193471	257.6	MED CONT AUT SUBSTANCES
55	PERFUME,CLEANING ETC PRD		110.4		129.6		148.4		166.9	PROD POUR PARFUM,TOILETTE
551	ESSENTL OILS,PERFUME,ETC		55.1	W 4296	65.7	W 4054	72.6	W 4405	84.8	HUILES ESSENTIELLES
58	PLASTIC MATERIALS ETC		444.6		489.0		670.6		581.5	MAT PLAST ARTIFICIELLES
582	PROD OF CONDENSATION ETC		167.0	W 82041	175.1	W 97689	230.0	W 97448	213.2	PROD CONDENS,POLYCOND
5824	POLYAMIDES	W 32137	67.9	W 28134	58.2	W 32200	65.3	W 33849	64.6	POLYAMIDES
58241	— IN PRIMARY FORMS	W 32137	67.9	W 28134	58.2	W 32200	65.3	W 33849	64.6	POLYAMIDES PRIMAIRES
583	POLYMERIZATION ETC PRODS		250.9	W 187274	287.0	W 239467	409.2	W 208237	336.3	PROD POLYMERISATION
5831	POLYETHYLENE	W 43457	40.4	W 50691	46.8	W 110150	116.7	W 53766	50.1	POLYETHYLENE
58311	— IN PRIMARY FORMS	W 42464	36.6	W 49314	41.2	W 108688	110.4	W 51752	43.1	POLYETHYLENE PRIMAIRES
5839	OTH POLYMRZTION ETC PROD		89.4	W 30635	95.8	W 32207	115.7	W 35043	115.7	AUT PROD POLYMER COPOLYM
59	CHEMICAL MATERIALS NES		408.9		446.1		500.4		521.6	MAT PROD CHIMIQUES NDA
591	PESTICIDES,DISINFECTANTS	W 12340	77.6	W 13067	85.0	W 13502	94.9	W 15734	115.1	DESINF,INSECT,FONG,HERB
598	MISCEL CHEM PRODUCTS NES		286.3		308.4	W 159914	349.7	W 159306	348.0	PROD DIV INDUST CHIM NDA
5982	ANTI–KNOCK PREPARTNS ETC	W 45015	108.1	W 46962	119.8	W 48394	125.8	W 49766	126.3	PREPARAT ANTIDETONANTES
5989	CHEM PRODUCTS,PREPS NES		158.6	W 96495	169.8	W 97936	202.9	W 95838	199.5	PROD PREP CHIMIQUES NDA
59899	OTH CHEM PRODS,PREPS,NES		99.1	W 64666	105.6	W 68068	126.4	W 66630	124.1	AUT PRODUITS CHIMIQUES NDA
6	BASIC MANUFACTURES		2609.7		3078.8		3696.9		3493.2	ART MANUFACTURES
61	LEATHER,DRESSED FUR,ETC		67.4		108.0		111.8		102.6	CUIRS,PELLETERIES
611	LEATHER		50.9		91.3	W 12110	95.0	W 10175	87.9	CUIRS,PEAUX PREPARES
62	RUBBER MANUFACTURES NES		172.8		203.9		261.7		259.2	CAOUTCHOUC MANUFACTURE
625	RUBBER TYRES, TUBES ETC	W 27906	82.7	MN 36771	97.3	MN 9801	131.8	N 6361975	126.6	PNEUS CAOUTCHOUC VULCANISE
628	RUBBER ARTICLES NES		63.4		75.9		96.6		92.0	OUVRAGES CAOUTCHOUC NDA

4. General Imports C.I.F. by Commodities according to the S.I.T.C. (Rev. 2) in million U.S. Dollars
Importations Générales C.A.F. par Produits d'après la C.T.C.I. (Rév. 2) en millions de Dollars E.U.

SITC CTCI	COMMODITY	1993 QUANTITY QUANTITE	1993 VALUE VALEUR	1994 QUANTITY QUANTITE	1994 VALUE VALEUR	1995 QUANTITY QUANTITE	1995 VALUE VALEUR	1996 QUANTITY QUANTITE	1996 VALUE VALEUR	PRODUIT
63	WOOD,CORK MANUFACTRS NES		43.2		56.9		70.5		83.9	OUVRAGES LIEGE ET BOIS
64	PAPER,PAPERBOARD AND MFR		347.1		412.3		537.2		446.9	PAPIERS,CARTONS & OUVRAGES
641	PAPER AND PAPERBOARD		305.4	W 331095	364.1	W 336792	461.5	W 322848	376.2	PAPIERS ET CARTONS
6412	PRINTG,WRITING PAPER NES	W 96963	92.0	W 127792	116.8	W 136836	153.5	W 103819	107.2	PAPIERS POUR L'IMPRESSION
64122	— COATED,IMPREGNATD ETC	W 93501	88.5	W 126910	114.9	W 134501	150.0	W 96189	103.0	PAPIERS IMPRESSION COUCHES
6415	PAPER,PAPERBRD,BULK,NES	W 58621	68.5	W 62048	71.3	W 60360	91.8	W 54239	73.4	PAPIERS,CARTONS ROULEAUX
6418	COATED ETC PAPER NES BLK	W 59848	101.9	W 68073	115.6	W 75387	150.9	W 78933	131.6	PAP,CARTONS COUCHES,ENDUITS
65	TEXTILE YARN,FABRICS,ETC		550.1		651.9		736.7		675.5	FILS,TISSUS,ARTICLES TEXTILE
651	TEXTILE YARN	W 24568	87.4		108.7		114.9	W 29531	109.4	FILS TEXTILES
652	COTTON FABRICS,WOVEN	A 41304	47.6	W 63128	64.1	W 30142	86.0	W 11817	85.8	TISSUS DE COTON
6522	WOVEN COTTON BLEACHD,ETC	A 38530	45.7	W 52747	61.0	W 22339	81.9	W 10697	82.5	TISSUS COTON BLANCHIS ETC
653	WOVN MAN-MADE FIB FABRIC		202.6	W 192885	204.5		212.6		163.3	TISSUS FIBRES SYNTH,ARTIF
6531	CONT SYNT WEAVES NONPILE		98.4	W 89498	101.2	W 16967	89.5	W 15143	70.5	TISSUS FIBRES SYNTH CONTINUE
65315	CONT SYN TXTL FABRIC NES		94.0	W 82582	94.7	W 15906	82.9	W 14391	63.9	TIS PLUS 85% TEXT SYNT CONT
654	OTH WOVEN TEXTILE FABRIC		30.3	W 51442	68.4		69.6		54.4	TISSUS AUT COTON SYNT,ARTIF
657	SPECIAL TXTL FABRC,PRODS		91.2		93.8	W 15110	113.8	W 13675	116.0	TISSUS SPECIAUX
66	NONMETAL MINERAL MFS NES		630.7		705.3		652.3		691.2	ART MIN NON METALLIQUES
662	CLAY,REFRACTORY BLDG PRD		77.5		88.1		126.9		118.5	MAT CONST REFRACTAIRES
663	MINERAL MANUFCTURES NES		54.3	W 12764	55.0	W 18305	73.6	W 21257	96.1	ART MIN MANUF NDA
667	PEARL,PREC-,SEMI-P STONE		374.7		423.0		287.6		302.7	PERLES, PIERRES GEMMES
6672	DIAMONDS NONINDUST,UNSET		372.6		421.2		285.9		301.1	DIAMANTS BRUTS
66721	— ROUGH,UNSORTED		72.1		96.5		40.5		24.2	DIAMANTS BRUTS NON TRIES
66722	— SRTD,ROUGH,SIMPLY WKD		299.5		308.2		244.7		276.7	DIAMANTS TRIES BRUTS
67	IRON AND STEEL		260.0		326.0		419.0		432.6	FER ET ACIER
674	IRN,STL UNIV,PLATE,SHEET	W 126255	105.9	W 176140	139.7	W 164164	161.6	W 192925	170.0	LARGES PLATS,TOLES
678	IRON,STL TUBES,PIPES,ETC	W 53263	77.2	W 49389	81.4	W 59575	116.8	W 51934	107.7	TUBES,TUYAUX EN FONTE,FER
68	NON-FERROUS METALS		122.2		146.9		326.9		226.6	METAUX NON FERREUX
683	NICKEL	W 428	5.1	W 531	6.2	W 16730	107.3	W 4315	35.4	NICKEL
6831	NICKEL,ALLOYS UNWROUGHT	W 155	1.0	W 201	1.5	W 16354	100.6	W 3966	29.1	NICKEL ET ALLIAGES BRUTS
684	ALUMINIUM	W 26352	64.8	W 28944	70.0	W 40924	111.2	W 38321	108.4	ALUMINIUM
6842	ALUMINIUM,ALLOYS WORKED	W 26152	64.4	W 27799	67.6	W 40201	108.8	W 36626	104.6	ALUMINIUM,ALLIAGES OUVRE
69	METAL MANUFACTURES NES		416.7		468.1		581.4		575.0	ART MANUFACT EN METAL NDA
695	TOOLS		98.4		119.8	W 20156	144.1	W 12835	146.0	OUTILS A MAIN
6954	BLADES,TIPS,ETC FR TOOLS		50.5		61.6	W 7735	72.0	W 3760	82.5	OUTILS POUR MACHINE-OUTIL
699	BASE METAL MFRS NES		141.3		161.2		205.6		184.5	ART MANUFACTURES MET NDA
7	MACHINES,TRANSPORT EQUIP		8011.0		10202.5		11989.6		10209.9	MACHINES MATERIEL TRANSPORT
71	POWER GENERATING EQUIPMT		446.7		485.8		592.0		562.8	MACHINES GENERATRICES
713	INTRNL COMBUS PSTN ENGIN		231.4		260.9		307.6		267.5	MOTEURS EXPL COMB INT, PIECE
7139	PISTON ENGINE PARTS NES		117.0		139.9	W 8465	160.3	W 15873	128.7	PIECES POUR 713.2,3,8
714	ENGINES AND MOTORS NES		100.9		94.7		95.9		129.2	MOTEURS NON ELECTRIQUES
7149	ENGINE & MOTOR PARTS NES		75.6		55.8	W 100347	71.7	W 678	76.8	PIECES 714 ET 718.88
71491	PARTS NES OF 7144,71481		68.8		46.9	W 100099	60.1	W 436	68.6	PIECES DES PROPULSEURS
716	ROTATING ELECTRIC PLANT		80.0		94.8		114.5		106.8	APP ELECTR ROTATIFS,PIECES
72	MACHS FOR SPCL INDUSTRYS		973.3		1401.2		1746.0		1945.2	MAC SPECIALES POUR INDUST
721	AGRIC MACHY,EXC TRACTORS		51.1		73.8		102.2		108.6	MACHINES AGRICOLES
722	TRACTORS NON-ROAD	N 13728	71.0	N 21628	130.1	N 18856	147.2	N 32449	183.5	TRACTEURS
7224	WHEELED TRACTORS NES	N 13698	65.2	N 21586	119.8	N 18792	132.3	N 32404	173.7	TRACTEURS A ROUES
723	CIVIL ENGNEERG EQUIP ETC		114.9		163.3		248.2		382.4	APPAREILS DE GENIE CIVIL
7234	CONST,MINING MACHNRY NES	N 10091	103.5	N 22877	145.4	N 31563	225.8	N 23462	339.9	MACH POUR LA CONST, MINES
72342	SLFPRP SHOVELS,EXCAVATRS	N 794	51.1	N 1682	93.1	N 2055	165.6	N 2620	228.6	PELLES MECANIQUES
724	TEXTILE,LEATHER MACHNRY		178.9		228.1		308.9		239.7	MACH POUR INDUSTRIE TEXTILE
725	PAPER ETC MILL MACHINERY		48.9		117.3		121.5		150.7	MACHINES FABR PATE PAPIER
7251	PAPER,PULP MAKING MACHRY	N 59	3.1	N 4284	74.9	N 394	29.4	N 5397	73.8	MACHINES FABR PATE CARTON
72511	CELLULOSE PULP MFG MACHY	N 39	1.3	N 4239	70.5	N 302	13.2	N 1272	8.6	MACH FABR PATE CELLULOSE
726	PRINTG,BKBINDG MACHY,PTS		211.6		246.1		312.3		302.5	MACHINES POUR IMPRIMERIE
7267	OTH PRINTG & ANCILL MACH	N 230195	111.6	N 273123	121.6	N 324863	165.4	N 319029	137.6	AUT MACH IMPRIMERIE,PIEC
72671	PRINTING MACHINERY NES	N 229547	96.5	N 272727	118.5	N 322873	152.5	N 307298	125.3	AUT MACH IMPRIMERIE
727	FOOD MACHRY NON-DOMESTIC		47.2		53.7		57.6		91.0	MACH INDUSTRIES ALIMENT
728	OTH MACHY FOR SPCL INDUS		250.1		389.2		448.5		487.1	AUT MACH IND PARTICULIERES
7281	MACH-TOOLS FR SPCL INDUS		49.8		54.6		82.3		61.0	MACH-OUTILS SPEC IND PART
7283	OTHR MINERAL WORKG MACHY		17.1		89.0		55.4		43.0	MACH TRIER,CRIBLER,BROYER
7284	MACHY FOR SPCL INDUS NES		183.3		245.7		310.9		383.2	MACH SPEC IND PARTICUL.
72842	RUBBER,PLASTICS WRKG MCH	N 2419	57.4	N 65293	94.1	N 9176	98.5	N 38749	110.2	MACH IND CAOUT MAT PLAST
72848	OTH MCHY WITH INDIV FNCT		82.0	N 2168952	102.2	N 2334539	121.0	N 2546478	195.0	AUTRES MACHINES NDA
73	METALWORKING MACHINERY		180.4		402.8		286.2		328.2	MACH TRAVAIL DES METAUX
736	METALWORKING MACH-TOOLS		102.8		120.1		170.7		217.7	MACH-OUTILS TRAVAIL METAUX
7361	METAL CUTTING MACH-TOOLS	N 45848	40.9	N 50449	48.2	N 55474	72.0	N 87807	98.4	MACH-OUT ENLEVEMENT METAL
737	METALWORKING MACHNRY NES		77.6		282.8		115.6		110.5	MACH TRAV METAUX PIECES
7372	ROLLING MILLS AND ROLLS		30.3	N 6933558	236.6		63.1		41.3	LAMINOIRS CYLINDRES PIEC
73721	ROLLING MILLS	N 2638	15.8	N 6929323	226.2	N 81368	37.5	N 602	18.9	LAMINOIRS ET TRAINS
74	GENRL INDUSTRL MACHY NES		1260.0		1439.1		1861.3		1896.7	MACH APP INDUSTRIE
741	HEATING,COOLING EQUIPMNT		236.8		236.2		307.9		315.7	MACH CHAUFFAGE,PIECES
7414	NONDOM REFRIG EQUIPT,PTS		49.8		62.1		84.2		68.9	MAT PRODUCTION DU FROID
7416	HEATING,COOLING EQU NES		125.6	N 230335	95.0	N 364525	115.7	N 264873	122.9	APP CHANGEMENT TEMP
742	PUMPS FOR LIQUIDS ETC		108.4		123.7		151.5		138.1	POMPES MOTO-POMPES
743	PUMPS NES,CENTRFUGES ETC		185.3		216.6		285.8		289.7	POMPES COMPRES,VENT ETC
7431	PUMPS FOR GASES ETC	N 2013937	85.7	N 2319541	98.9	N 4534369	128.6	N 5815873	122.4	POMPES AIR A VIDE,COMPRES
7436	GAS,LIQUID FILTERS ETC	N 6159541	41.3	N 7162724	57.2	MN 9135	72.2	N 8613560	83.3	APP POUR FILT DES LIQUIDES
744	MECHANICAL HANDLING EQU		139.4		165.8		239.9		286.6	EQUIP MANUTENTION PIECES
7442	LIFTING,LOADING MACH NES	N 269438	46.4	N 308333	53.4	N 401312	73.7	N 397964	99.8	APP LEVAGE,MANUTENTION
7449	PTS NES OF MACHY OF 7442		65.5		85.8	W 14836	115.5	W 15202	109.6	PIECES DU 744.2
745	NONELEC MACHY,TOOLS NES		157.5		187.2		249.8		277.9	AUT MACH NON ELEC,PIECES
7452	OTH NONELEC MCHS,PTS NES		137.0		162.4		222.8		249.0	AUT MACH NON ELEC,PIECES
74522	PACKAGNG,BOTTLNG,ETC MCH	N 85768	64.6	N 246146	81.9	N 106295	109.4	N 98856	120.9	MACH NETT BOUTEILLES,ETC
749	NONELEC MACH PTS,ACC NES		432.7		509.8		626.8		588.9	PIECES MACH NON ELEC NDA
7491	BALL,ROLLER,ETC BEARINGS	MN 21575	94.3	MN 121772	125.5	MN 30115	147.7	MN 49584	137.4	ROULEMENTS BILLES ETC
7492	COCKS,VALVES ETC NES		126.8		138.5	W 12133	181.3	W 9298	171.4	ART ROB,SIM POUR TUYAUX
7493	SHAFT,CRANK,PULLEY ETC		137.0	MN 71878	159.3	MN 20419	206.7	MN 267618	192.3	ARBRES TRANS,VILEBREQUINS
7499	OTH NONELEC MCHY PTS NES		74.6		86.6	W 3622	91.2	W 5189	87.9	PIECES NON ELECT NDA
75	OFFICE MACHNES,ADP EQUIP		928.2		1162.4		1332.3		1333.0	MACH BUREAU TRAIT AUTOM
751	OFFICE MACHINES	N 3151634	91.7	N 3426368	117.4	N 4239476	130.2	N 4737797	132.4	MACH,APPAREILS DE BUREAU
7518	OFFICE MACHINES NES	N 864613	62.7	N 1016576	92.6	N 1313688	100.7	N 1429608	106.5	MACH,APP DE BUREAU NDA
75182	PHOTO,THERMOCOPY APPARAT	N 29240	51.5	N 37494	76.2	N 44276	85.7	N 49545	83.2	APPAREILS DE PHOTOCOPIE
752	AUTOMTIC DATA PROC EQUIP		521.2	N 1916484	627.5	N 2259491	688.6	N 3041178	741.8	MACH TRAIT INFORMATION
7522	DIGITAL COMPUTERS	N 1446821	164.0	N 313457	242.6	N 282812	233.0	N 133044	131.3	MACH DIGITALES COMPLETES
7523	DIGITL CENTRL PROCESSORS	N 471249	79.7	N 72216	83.2	N 114104	114.3	N 187739	195.4	UNITES CENTRALES
7524	DIGITL CENTRL STOR UNITS	N 385627	76.9	N 279500	67.7	N 240469	53.0	N 132666	34.8	UNITES MEMOIRE CENTRALES
7525	ADP PERIPHERAL UNITS	N 960699	172.0	N 1142563	202.1	N 1445542	230.1	N 2108441	230.1	UNITES PERIPHERIQUES
7528	OFF-LINE DATA PROC EQUIP		27.3	N 108271	31.5	N 175604	57.8	N 470917	142.9	MACH AUXIL TRAIT INFORM
759	OFFICE,ADP MCH PTS,ACCES		315.4		417.6		513.5		458.9	PIECES DU 751 ET 752
7599	ACCTG,ETC,ADP MCH PTS,AC		285.4		374.5		466.6		391.9	PIECES DU 751 ET 752

4. General Imports C.I.F. by Commodities according to the S.I.T.C. (Rev. 2) in million U.S. Dollars
Importations Générales C.A.F. par Produits d'après la C.T.C.I. (Rév. 2) en millions de Dollars E.U.

SITC CTCI	COMMODITY	1993 QUANTITY QUANTITE	1993 VALUE VALEUR	1994 QUANTITY QUANTITE	1994 VALUE VALEUR	1995 QUANTITY QUANTITE	1995 VALUE VALEUR	1996 QUANTITY QUANTITE	1996 VALUE VALEUR	PRODUIT
76	TELECOMM,SOUND EQUIPMENT		507.4		863.9		1037.9		1158.8	EQUIPMENT DE TELECOM
764	TELECOM EQPT,PTS,ACC NES		390.8		745.6		894.3		954.8	EQUIP TELECOM,PIECES
7641	LINE TELEPHONE,ETC EQUIP	N 1076038	158.8	N 1552984	231.3	N 1892521	276.8	N 2984364	207.1	APP TELEPHON PAR FIL
7643	TV,RADIO TRANSMITTRS ETC	N 181710	54.5	N 555885	267.2	N 716753	325.8	N 888454	385.6	APP EMET TELE RADIO
7649	PTS NES OF EQUIPMT OF 76		104.7		171.0		174.2		215.2	PIECES DE LA DIV 76
76491	PTS NES OF APPAR OF 7641		49.2		94.8	W 450	86.7	W 643	120.8	PIECES POUR 764.1
76493	TELECOMM EQUIPMT PTS NES		44.4		64.5		74.2		84.3	PIECES 761,762,764.3,8
77	ELECTRIC MACHNRY NES ETC		1060.6		1396.7		1617.2		1491.7	MACH APP ELECT NDA
771	ELECTRIC POWER MACHY NES		64.4		89.7		87.5		89.2	MACH PROD,TRANS ELECTR
7712	OTH ELEC POWER MACHY NES		48.8		67.4		68.8		70.9	AUT APP PROD TRANSF ELEC
772	SWITCHGEAR ETC,PARTS NES		295.0		346.5		386.4		363.2	APP COUPURE,SECT ETC
7721	SWITCHGEAR ETC		255.9		307.5		349.7		332.6	APP COUPURE,SECTIONMNT
773	ELECTR DISTRIBUTNG EQUIP		66.8		78.8	W 20358	99.5	W 14387	95.9	EQUIPMT DISTRIBUTION ELECT
774	ELECTRO–MEDCL,XRAY EQUIP	N 5962755	68.0	MN 11069	68.4	N 1990843	79.2	N 2065876	77.0	APPAREILS MEDICAUX
775	HOUSEHOLD TYPE EQUIP NES		139.6		151.8		174.4		197.6	MACH,APP USAGE DOMESTQUE
7758	ELECTRO–THERMIC APPL NES		57.8		63.9		76.4		94.4	APP ELECTROTHERMIQ NDA
776	TRANSISTORS,VALVES,ETC		184.0		256.3		323.3		330.1	LAMPES,TUBES,VALVES
7764	ELECTRONIC MICROCIRCUITS	MN 82254	112.7	MN 141563	161.7	MN 126788	218.1	MN 97998	243.8	MICROSTRUCTURES ELECTRON
778	ELECTRICAL MACHINERY NES		243.2		405.4		467.3		338.9	AUTRES MACH ELECT NDA
7783	AUTOMOTIVE ELECTR EQUIP		69.3		81.0		88.6		79.2	EQUIP ELECT MOTEURS EXPL
7788	OTH ELEC MACHY,EQUIP NES		77.4		204.4		243.1		114.1	AUT MACH APP ELEC NDA
77886	OTH ELEC MACHINERY NES	N 2367954	32.6	N 6606956	153.6	MN 11007	184.4	N 3676900	62.5	AUT MACH APP ELECTRIQUES
78	ROAD VEHICLES		2180.5		2658.6		2992.5		1196.1	VEHICULES ROUTIERS
781	PASS MOTOR VEH EXC BUSES		927.3	N 756733	927.0	N 694779	1064.0	N 39594	482.6	AUTO TRANSPORT PERSONNES
782	LORRIES,SPCL MTR VEH NES	N 335488	450.6	N 511367	564.0	N 522114	677.8	N 4802	111.4	VEHICULES SPECIAUX,MARCH
7821	LORRIES,TRUCKS	N 335309	436.0	N 511111	550.6	N 493305	659.3	N 4478	71.0	VEHICULES TRANSP MARCHAND
783	ROAD MOTOR VEHICLES NES	N 241514	74.7	N 569580	105.2	N 574921	188.3	N 32397	81.9	VEHICULES ROUTIERS NDA
7832	TRACTORS FOR TR–TRAILERS	N 221198	. 35.9	N 525417	73.4	N 555009	142.4	N 1206	62.6	TRACTEURS ROUTIERS
784	MOTOR VEH PRTS,ACCES NES		674.5		1002.7		985.7		428.5	PIECES 722,781,782,783
7842	MOTOR VEHICLE BODIES	N 3972	16.1	N 12285	51.5	N 11037	111.7	N 5095	21.0	CARROS 722,781,782,783
7849	OTHER MOTOR VEHCL PARTS	W 1143311	644.2	W 105197	941.7	W 86905	856.1	W 42572	393.0	PIECES 722,781,782,783
79	OTHR TRANSPORT EQUIPMENT		474.3		392.4		524.6		297.8	AUTRE MATERIEL TRANSPORT
792	AIRCRAFT ETC		437.2		369.6		492.9		246.4	APP NAVIGATION AERIENNE
7923	AIRCRFT NES2000–15000KG	N 52	142.8	N 72	98.7	N 112	244.9	N 81	97.8	AERODYNES 2000 A 15000 KG
7924	AIRCRFT NES OVER 15000KG	N 62	173.2	N 54	156.9	N 17	95.3	N 5	43.8	AERODYNES PLUS 15000 KG
7929	AIRCRAFT PARTS NES		80.8		77.2	W 318	80.8	W 426	74.6	PIECES DU 792
8	MISC MANUFACTURED GOODS		1718.1		1867.1		2187.8		2559.6	ART MANUFACTURES DIVERS
821	*FURNITURE,PARTS THEREOF		48.6		61.2		76.7		98.5	MEUBLES ET PIECES
84	CLOTHING AND ACCESSORIES		143.9		156.7		141.6		194.1	VETEMENTS
851	*FOOTWEAR		111.6	MP 29817	116.6	MP 63531	166.1	MP 48767	183.2	CHAUSSURES
85102	FOOTWEAR LEATHER	MP 22238	89.1	MP 21466	94.9	MP 40069	135.2	MP 29423	142.4	CHAUS SEMELLES EN CUIR
87	PRECISION INSTRUMNTS NES		527.2		558.0		633.0		669.8	INSTRUM,APPAR SCIENT NDA
872	MEDICAL INSTRUMENTS NES		114.9		132.3		147.4		162.6	INSTR,APP MEDIC–CHIR NDA
87202	OTH MEDICAL INSTRUMENTS		101.5		116.3	MN 236889	125.0	MN 193378	140.1	INSTRUM,APP MEDECINE
874	MEASURNG,CONTROLNG INSTR		373.8		384.1		436.0		461.6	INSTRUMENTS DE MESURE
8742	MEASUR,DRAW ETC INST,PTS		78.5		80.7		94.6		86.1	INST DESSIN,TRACAGE,PCS
87421	MEASURNG,DRAWNG ETC INST		70.3	N 7027595	71.6	N 8440352	84.4	MN 10871	76.1	INSTRUM DESSIN,TRACAGE
8743	GAS,LIQUID CONTROL INSTR		92.5	N 8728267	119.9	MN 9214	139.3	MN 9085	141.5	APP,INSTR MESURE FLUIDES
8745	MEAS,CONTRL,SCI INST NES		55.0		22.2		17.8		33.0	APP SCIENT MESURE NDA
8748	ELEC MEAS,CONTRL EQU NES		76.9	N 1570290	79.2	N 1572792	100.4	N 3113952	116.2	APP ELEC ELECTRO MESURE
87483	OTH ELCTRNC MEAS ETC EQU		70.6	N 1095201	71.9	N 927034	92.4	N 853407	104.7	AUT APP ELECTRO DE MESURE
88	PHOTO EQU,OPTICL GDS ETC		209.9		228.7		254.5		265.8	APP,FOURN PHOTO,OP,MONTR
882	PHOTO,CINEMA SUPPLIES		100.3		109.1		121.8		119.1	PRODUITS PHOTO,CINEMA
8822	PHOTO FILM EXC DEV CINMA		76.2		78.9		85.2		83.1	PLAQUES,PELLICULES,FILMS
89	MISC MANUFCTRD GOODS NES		623.6		681.5		830.9		1064.4	ART MANUFACTURES DIVERS
892	PRINTED MATTER		165.6		164.6	W 32091	180.4	W 22182	186.9	IMPRIMES
8921	PRINTED BOOKS,GLOBES,ETC		131.7		124.5	W 26466	139.4	W 14718	136.9	LIVRES,BROCHURES,CARTES
89211	PRINTED BOOKS,PAMPHLETS		128.7		122.4	W 25657	136.3	W 13878	133.7	LIVRES,BROCHURES
893	ARTICLES OF PLASTIC NES		116.0		132.4		163.5		161.0	OUVRAGES EN MAT DIVIS 58
8939	MISC PLASTIC ARTICLES		97.4		108.2	W 34484	134.6	W 32356	128.2	ART DIVERS EN MAT DIV 58
89399	OTHR PLASTC ARTICLES NES		85.2		94.8	W 20744	120.5	W 18118	114.1	AUT OUV MAT DIV 58
894	TOYS,SPORTING GOODS,ETC		91.4		95.2		115.3		140.7	VOITURES ENFANTS,JOUETS
8942	TOYS,INDOOR GAMES ETC		63.7		58.2		64.3		89.5	JOUETS,JEUX ETC
898	MUSICAL INSTRUMENTS,PTS		106.6		137.1		191.6		372.7	INSTRUMENTS DE MUSIQUE
8983	SOUND RECRDNG TAPE,DISCS		97.4	MN 51526	126.0	MN 88301	181.2	MN 92281	362.5	SUPPORTS SON POUR 763
89832	RECORDED DISCS,TAPES ETC	N 7174695	66.6	N 6654338	94.5	MN 13971	147.2	MN 15111	323.8	DISQUES,PHONO,BANDES
899	OTHER MANUFACTURED GOODS		73.9		84.6		95.9		101.5	AUT ART MANUF DIVERS NDA
9	GOODS NOT CLASSD BY KIND		1623.4		1261.5		670.8		2217.7	ART TRANSACT NON CLASSES
931	*SPECIAL TRANSACTIONS		1619.6		1254.0		665.3		2207.4	TRANS.SPECIALES

5. General Exports F.O.B. by Commodities according to the S.I.T.C. (Rev. 2) in million U.S. Dollars
Exportations Générales F.O.B. par Produits d'après la C.T.C.I. (Rév. 2) en millions de Dollars E.U.

SITC CTCI	COMMODITY	1993 QUANTITY QUANTITE	1993 VALUE VALEUR	1994 QUANTITY QUANTITE	1994 VALUE VALEUR	1995 QUANTITY QUANTITE	1995 VALUE VALEUR	1996 QUANTITY QUANTITE	1996 VALUE VALEUR	PRODUIT
	ALL COMMODITIES		24265.8		25621.6		28226.3		23468.9	TOUS PRODUITS
0	FOOD AND LIVE ANIMALS		1371.4		1909.0		1795.6		2137.9	ALIMENTS,ANIMAUX VIVANTS
01	MEAT AND PREPARATIONS		75.0		43.6		56.1		76.0	VIANDES ET PREPARATIONS
011	MEAT FRESH,CHILLD,FROZEN		68.9	W 457699	39.0		50.1		71.9	VIANDES FRAICHES,REF,CONGE
03	FISH AND PREPARATIONS		196.4		250.8		239.3		197.9	POISSONS ET PREPARATIONS
034	FISH,FRESH,CHILLED,FROZN		114.0	W 143368	159.2		141.6		103.3	POISSON FRAIS, REFRIG,CONG
0342	FISH FROZEN,EXCL FILLETS		90.7	W 124461	117.3		71.3		45.5	POISSONS CONGELES
04	CEREALS AND PREPARATIONS		103.9		531.7		265.9		502.4	CEREALES ET PRODUITS
044	MAIZE UNMILLED		41.1	W 3810176	463.7		167.3		368.0	MAIS NON MOULU
05	VEGETABLES AND FRUIT		808.3		800.3		899.8		868.1	LEGUMES ET FRUITS
054	VEG ETC FRSH,SMPLY PRSVD		25.8	W 46374	29.6		36.9		115.2	LEGUMES FRAIS,CONG,SECS
0545	OTHER FRESH VEGETABLES		8.5	W 9139	8.7		11.7		89.4	AUTRES LEGUMES FRAIS,REF
05451	ALLIACEOUS VEGTBLS,FRESH		1.3	W 5198	1.6		3.5		81.7	OIGNONS,ECHALOTES,AULX
057	FRUIT,NUTS,FRESH,DRIED		556.1	W 1080596	545.4		581.6		483.6	FRUITS FRAIS OU SECS
0571	ORANGES, MANDARINS ETC		125.8	W 322313	120.4		169.1		128.6	ORANGES,MAND,CLEMENTINES
05711	ORANGES,FRESH OR DRIED		120.8	W 319932	118.8		162.2		123.2	ORANGES FRAICHES,SECHEES
0572	LEMONS,GRAPEFRUIT ETC		39.8	W 221314	94.7		55.3		33.0	AUTRES AGRUMES FRAIS,SECS
05722	GRAPEFRUITS,FRESH,DRIED		28.8	W 189479	82.2		39.9		23.8	PAMPLEMOUSSES,POMELOS
0574	APPLES FRESH		125.3	W 245375	74.0		115.7		91.8	POMMES FRAICHES
0575	GRAPES FRESH OR DRIED		125.9	W 120380	144.6		139.6		117.0	RAISINS FRAIS OU SECS
05751	GRAPES FRESH		93.5	W 99899	122.7		116.0		90.3	RAISINS FRAIS
0579	FRUIT FRESH OR DRIED NES		136.1	W 168829	106.9		96.7		105.4	FRUITS FRAIS,SECS NDA
058	FRUIT PRESERVED,PREPARED		217.4	W 307810	216.1		270.7		256.0	CONSERVES DE FRUITS
0585	FRUIT OR VEGETABLE JUICE		62.9	W 113411	65.5		87.1		78.0	JUS DE FRUITS
0589	FRUIT PREPRD,PRESRVD,NES		145.7	W 185497	142.2		165.0		158.3	FRUITS PREPARES CONSERV
05899	FRUIT,NUTS NES,PRESERVED		142.9	W 181980	138.0		157.9		154.4	FRUITS PREP CONSERV NDA
06	SUGAR AND PREPS,HONEY		69.7		151.3		180.8		341.7	SUCRES ET PRODUITS
061	SUGAR AND HONEY		56.7	W 922773	134.3		167.1		321.0	SUCRES ET MIEL
0611	RAW BEET AND CANE SUGAR		33.7	W 419766	91.2		120.4		227.2	SUCRES BRUTS
0612	REFINED SUGAR ETC		16.1	W 340064	31.0		41.4		78.8	SUCRES RAFFINES
1	BEVERAGES AND TOBACCO		141.0		197.0		360.6		346.1	BOISSONS ET TABACS
11	BEVERAGES		113.0		160.7		301.5		286.5	BOISSONS
112	ALCOHOLIC BEVERAGES		84.0	W 712	3.6		274.8		252.1	BOISSONS ALCOOLIQUES
1121	WINE OF FRESH GRAPES ETC		45.6	W 52728	69.4		186.5		185.1	VINS DE RAISINS FRAIS
11212	WINE OF FRESH GRAPES		45.6	W 52714	69.4		186.3		185.0	VINS DE MOUTS DE RAISINS
2	CRUDE MATERLS,EXCL FUELS		1967.6		1995.4		2803.8		2524.1	MAT BRUTES NON COMESTIBLES
21	HIDES,SKINS,FURS UNDRSSD		79.8		76.6		96.7		112.4	CUIRS,PEAUX BRUTS
211	HIDES,SKINS,EXC FURS,RAW		79.7	W 30312	76.6		96.7		112.2	CUIRS ET PEAUX
24	CORK AND WOOD		66.1		116.6		155.2		146.5	LIEGE ET BOIS
246	PULPWOOD,CHIPS,WOODWASTE		20.0	W 1180524	74.7		109.7		102.4	BOIS DE TRITURATION
24602	PULPWOOD CHIPS,PARTICLES		20.0	W 1179619	74.5		109.6		102.3	EN FORME DE PLAQUETTES
251	*PULP AND WASTE PAPER		295.0	W 815820	371.0		613.6		346.9	PATES A PAPIER,DECHETS
2516	CHEM WOOD PULP DISSOLVNG		191.6	W 455545	220.2		388.3		229.1	PATES CHIMIQUES DE BOIS
2517	SODA,SULPHATE WOOD PULP		38.1	W 235927	116.8		187.3		105.9	PATES CHIMIQUES AU SULFATE
25172	— BLEACHED,NONDISSOLVNG		20.2	W 197040	103.5		171.4		89.7	PATES BLANCHIES
26	TEXTILE FIBRES AND WASTE		135.3		190.1		195.7		184.4	FIBRES TEXTILES
268	WOOL(EXC TOPS),ANML HAIR		127.1	W 46417	160.5		153.5		146.6	LAINES ET POILS
27	CRUDE FERTLZR,MINRLS NES		363.0		222.2		255.9		207.8	ENGRAIS MINERAUX BRUTS
278	OTHER CRUDE MINERALS		234.7	W 883168	123.5		144.2		124.9	AUTRES MINERAUX BRUTS
2786	SLAG,SCALINGS,DROSS,ETC		107.8	W 56652	12.7		20.1		13.5	SCORIES,LAITIERS
27861	SLAG ETC FRM IRN,STL MFR		107.7	W 56111	12.6		18.9		13.4	SCORIES,LAITIER,BATTIT
28	METALLIFEROUS ORES,SCRAP		961.9		927.4		1382.2		1407.4	MINERAIS METAL,DECHETS
281	IRON ORE,CONCENTRATES		283.8	MW 15998	257.5		362.6		286.9	MINERAIS DE FER
2816	IRON ORE AGGLOMERATES		283.8	MW 15998	257.4		362.5		286.8	MINERAIS AGGLOMERES
287	BASE METAL ORES,CONC NES		526.6	W 3694792	557.1		810.7		832.7	MINERAIS METAUX COMMUNS
2871	CPR ORE ETC,CEMENT COPPR		123.1	W 86646	119.9		90.4		58.7	MINERAIS DE CUIVRE,MATTES
28712	COPPER MATTE,CEMENT COPR		76.7	W 54665	93.6		65.8		25.8	MATTES DE CUIVRE
2872	NICKEL ORES,CONCENTRATES		151.7	W 54286	118.8		158.1		246.9	MINERAIS DE NICKEL
28722	NICKEL MATTE,SINTERS,ETC		151.7	W 54283	118.7		158.1		246.9	MATTES,SINTERS
2877	MANGANESE ORE,CONCENTRTE		113.7	W 1673004	108.4		126.8		128.1	MINERAIS DE MANGANESE
2879	OTH NONFER ORE,CONCNTRTE		107.0	W 1742897	162.0		380.6		365.8	MINERAIS D'AUTRES METAUX
28791	CHROMIUM ORE,CONCENTRATE		70.0	W 1061314	62.3		125.6		129.3	MINERAIS DE CHROME
28793	MOLYBD, NIOBIUM ETC ORES		36.8	W 658194	78.8		144.0		181.2	MINERAIS DE MOLYBDENE,TITANE
28799	OTH BASE MTL ORE,CON NES		0.3	W 23389	20.9	W 110816	111.1		55.3	AUTRES MINERAIS
289	PREC MTAL ORES,WASTE NES		56.6	MK 103951	54.3		73.4		151.4	MINERAIS,DECHETS MET PREC
28902	PREC METAL SCRAP, WASTE		56.6	MK 103951	54.3		73.4		90.0	CENDRES D'ORFEVRERIE
3	MINERAL FUELS ETC		1659.9		1368.0		2508.5		2549.8	COMBUSTIBLES MINERAUX LUB
32	COAL,COKE AND BRIQUETTES		1608.9		1296.1		1610.7		1525.8	HOUILLES,COKES,BRIQUETTES
322	COAL,LIGNITE AND PEAT		1601.9	MW 52402	1289.9		1606.6		1525.6	HOUILLES,LIGNITES,TOURBE
3222	OTH COAL,NOT AGGLOMERATD		1544.0	MW 51465	1242.8		1563.8		1467.4	AUTRES HOUILLES
33	PETROLEUM AND PRODUCTS		48.7		64.9		890.4		1016.0	PETROLE ET DERIVES
333	CRUDE PETROLEUM						101.6		108.2	HUILES BRUTES DE PETROLE
334	PETROLEUM PRODUCTS,REFIN		6.3	W 44090	3.8		713.0		821.4	PRODUITS RAFFINES
3341	GASOLINE,OTH LIGHT OILS					W 935084	148.0		133.6	ESSENCES POUR MOTEURS
33411	MOTOR,AVIATION SPIRIT					W 935084	148.0		133.6	ESSENCES MOTEURS D'AVIONS
3343	GAS OILS					W 2495967	396.5		338.7	GAS OILS
3344	FUEL OILS,NES					W 499568	42.5		204.7	FUEL OILS
3345	LUBS,PETROLEUM OILS NES		6.3	W 1756	2.2		75.9		76.5	HUILES LUBRIFIANTES
33451	LUBS(HIGH PETR CONT) ETC					W 271344	73.7		74.4	HUILES LUBRIF,H LOURDES
335	RESIDUAL PETRLM PROD NES		42.5	W 185366	61.2		75.8		86.5	PRODUITS RESIDUELS NDA
5	CHEMCLS,RELATED PROD NES		1161.2		1623.6		1963.9		2123.8	PRODUITS CHIMIQUES
51	ORGANIC CHEMICALS		154.2		270.7		325.6		386.8	PROD CHIMIQ ORGANIQUES
512	ALCOHOLS,PHENOLS ETC		62.0		159.7		143.3		168.0	PHENOLS,PHENOLS–ALCOOLS
5121	ACYCLIC ALCOHOLS,DERIVS		44.2		141.3		117.8		146.2	ALCOOLS ACYCLIQUES
51216	ETHYL ALC,DENATRD SPIRIT		31.1	V 255215	120.4		82.4		119.6	ALCOOL ETHYLIQUE NON DENAT
516	OTHER ORGANIC CHEMICALS		36.6		48.7		68.4		89.2	AUTRES PROD ORGANIQUES
52	INORGANIC CHEMICALS		527.8		706.0		826.6		838.8	PROD CHIM INORGANIQUES
522	INORG ELEMNTS,OXIDES,ETC		228.1	W 1203656	379.2		591.3		581.3	ELEMENTS INORGANIQUES
5222	INORGANIC ACIDS ETC		53.2	W 449417	69.2		108.4		86.7	ACIDES INORGANIQUES
52224	PHOSPHORIC ACIDS ETC		46.5	W 417247	65.4	W 571660	104.7		79.7	ACIDES PHOSPHORIQUES
5224	ZINC,IRON,LEAD ETC OXIDE		79.2	W 551215	206.2		351.8		361.8	OXYDES METALLIQUES
52246	TITANIUM OXIDES		64.1	W 526276	182.2		317.0		331.4	OXYDES DE TITANE
5225	INORGANIC BASES ETC NES		37.7	W 151391	52.4		85.9		83.8	AUTRES BASES OXYDES METAL
523	OTHR INORG CHEMICALS ETC		244.5	W 1502624	284.2		185.3		198.5	AUT PRODUITS CHIMIQUES INORG
5231	METAL CMPD OF INORG ACID		110.8	W 289306	144.4		26.0		35.1	SELS METALLIQUES
52312	CHLORIDES, BROMIDES ETC		85.3	W 250940	118.2		0.7		5.1	CHLORURES,OXYCHLORURES
5232	OTH MTL CMPD OF INRG ACD		111.4	W 1199815	120.7		122.9		129.6	SELS METALLIQUES
53	DYES,TANNING,COLOUR PROD		61.3		72.7		78.3		76.5	PROD TEINTURE,COLORANTS
55	PERFUME,CLEANING ETC PRD		44.1		151.9		88.2		127.0	PROD POUR PARFUM,TOILETTE
554	SOAP,CLEANSING ETC PREPS		20.5		125.8		39.6		60.3	SAVONS,PRODUITS DETERSIFS
5541	SOAPS		11.4		114.0		16.1		26.2	SAVONS,PROD TENSIO–ACTIFS

5. General Exports F.O.B. by Commodities according to the S.I.T.C. (Rev. 2) in million U.S. Dollars
Exportations Générales F.O.B. par Produits d'après la C.T.C.I. (Rév. 2) en millions de Dollars E.U.

SITC CTCI	COMMODITY	1993 QUANTITY QUANTITE	1993 VALUE VALEUR	1994 QUANTITY QUANTITE	1994 VALUE VALEUR	1995 QUANTITY QUANTITE	1995 VALUE VALEUR	1996 QUANTITY QUANTITE	1996 VALUE VALEUR	PRODUIT
562	*FERTILIZERS,MANUFACTURE		79.7	W 444937	84.1		159.6		202.4	ENGRAIS MANUFACTURES
5621	CHEM NITROGENOUS FERTLZR		28.0	W 189069	38.0		54.5		75.3	ENGRAIS AZOTES
5629	FERTILIZERS NES		48.5	W 217102	41.4		85.6		103.2	ENGRAIS NDA
58	PLASTIC MATERIALS ETC		114.2		131.1		175.6		148.7	MAT PLAST ARTIFICIELLES
583	POLYMERIZATION ETC PRODS		101.0	W 164860	110.9		134.3		119.4	PROD POLYMERISATION
59	CHEMICAL MATERIALS NES		127.5		150.6		228.8		260.1	MAT PROD CHIMIQUES NDA
591	PESTICIDES,DISINFECTANTS		74.2	W 30782	82.6		126.1		167.3	DESINF,INSECT,FONG,HERB
5913	HERBICIDES,FOR RETAIL		36.1	W 16133	39.7		63.6		89.8	HERBICIDES VENTE AU DET
598	MISCEL CHEM PRODUCTS NES		46.4		61.5		95.2		81.4	PROD DIV INDUST CHIM NDA
6	BASIC MANUFACTURES		6576.0		6586.7		7403.9		8093.8	ART MANUFACTURES
61	LEATHER,DRESSED FUR,ETC		83.3		126.7		145.1		144.7	CUIRS,PELLETERIES
611	LEATHER		77.5		120.2		139.1		136.9	CUIRS,PEAUX PREPARES
6116	LEATHER OF OTH HIDE,SKIN		45.9	A 1423	71.0		86.7		85.0	PEAUX PREP D'AUTRES ANIMAUX
61169	LEATHER NES		45.5	A 1358	70.3		85.9		84.5	PEAUX PREPAREES NDA
62	RUBBER MANUFACTURES NES		57.3		62.8		101.1		111.8	CAOUTCHOUC MANUFACTURE
625	RUBBER TYRES, TUBES ETC		44.3	MN 17806	49.9		82.5		90.1	PNEUS CAOUTCHOUC VULCANISE
63	WOOD,CORK MANUFACTRS NES		127.8		101.4		87.6		65.2	OUVRAGES LIEGE ET BOIS
634	VENEERS,PLYWOOD,ETC		73.0		19.5		21.8		15.3	PLACAGES,CONTRE-PLAQUES
635	WOOD MANUFACTURES NES		54.2		81.6		64.6		49.5	ART MANUF EN BOIS NDA
64	PAPER,PAPERBOARD AND MFR		290.5		348.3		450.8		458.0	PAPIERS,CARTONS & OUVRAGES
641	PAPER AND PAPERBOARD		259.3	W 622857	258.1		371.4		338.0	PAPIERS ET CARTONS
6411	NEWSPRINT		72.5	W 228393	91.1		138.6		98.9	PAPIER JOURNAL
6413	KRAFT PAPER,PAPERBOARD		110.1	W 276810	96.6		137.4		79.9	PAPIER ET CARTON KRAFT
64131	KRAFT LINER IN BULK		109.4	W 274368	94.9		135.1		77.8	PAP KRAFT POUR COUVERTURES
6415	PAPER,PAPERBRD,BULK,NES		45.9	W 75134	34.4		41.3		80.7	PAPIERS,CARTONS ROULEAUX
64159	OTHER PAPER ETC,BULK,NES		36.5	W 61910	31.6		39.0		72.2	AUT PAPIER ROULEAUX FEUILLES
642	PAPER,ETC,PRECUT,ARTS OF		31.2	W 90371	90.3		79.4		120.0	PAP,CARTONS DECOUPES
65	TEXTILE YARN,FABRICS,ETC		220.2		240.5		324.1		332.5	FILS,TISSUS,ARTICLES TEXTILE
651	TEXTILE YARN		125.6	W 41658	123.8		190.2		173.3	FILS TEXTILES
6512	WOOL,HAIR YARN,INCL TOPS		65.6	W 14623	79.9		92.2		81.7	FILS DE LAINE,DE POILS
65121	WOOL TOPS		62.5	W 13831	76.2		86.3		77.8	RUBANS LAINE PEIGN,TOPS
6514	SYN FIB YRN,BULK,MONOFIL		47.8	W 24214	38.2		90.2		81.0	FILS CONT 85% FIB TEXT SYNTH
66	NONMETAL MINERAL MFS NES		3029.1		2844.7		2500.1		3044.5	ART MIN NON METALLIQUES
661	LIME,CEMENT,BLDG PRODS		53.9	W 959460	66.6		89.4		80.8	CHAUX,CIMENTS MAT CONSTR
667	PEARL,PREC-,SEMI-P STONE		2885.9		2692.9		2326.7		2862.2	PERLES, PIERRES GEMMES
6672	DIAMONDS NONINDUST,UNSET		2876.9		2687.4		2319.9		2854.1	DIAMANTS BRUTS
66721	— ROUGH,UNSORTED		510.0		145.3		221.8		455.9	DIAMANTS BRUTS NON TRIES
66722	— SRTD,ROUGH,SIMPLY WKD		2088.5		2206.2		1794.4		2039.4	DIAMANTS TRIES BRUTS
66729	— CUT ETC NOT SET		278.5		336.0		303.8		358.9	DIAMANTS TAILLES
67	IRON AND STEEL		2014.7		2133.0		2791.8		2429.9	FER ET ACIER
671	PIG IRON ETC		625.7	W 2115616	806.5		1232.8		1056.4	FONTE,SPIEGEL,POUDRES
6712	PIG IRN,SPIEGELEISEN ETC		62.0	W 321592	53.3		86.3		85.4	FONTES BRUTES
6716	FERRO-ALLOYS		561.4	W 1786196	750.2	W 2165360	1141.2		963.2	FERRO-ALLIAGES
67161	FERRO-MANGANESE		132.3	W 419453	166.5	W 484015	202.2		187.4	FERRO-MANGANESE
67169	OTHER FERRO-ALLOYS		398.1	W 1311183	555.1	W 1623652	903.1		748.9	AUTRES FERRO-ALLIAGES
672	IRON,STEEL PRIMARY FORMS		388.6	W 1778259	502.1		499.4		517.6	LINGOTS FER,ACIER
6725	IRN,STL BLOOMS,SLABS,ETC		106.1	W 683010	167.0		224.5		196.1	BLOOMS,BILLETTES FER ACIER
67251	IRN,SMPLE STL BLOOMS,ETC		51.8	W 541272	117.8		101.0		134.3	BLOOMS ETC NON ACIER FIN
6727	IRN,STL COIL FR REROLLNG		280.1	W 1094955	334.9		272.2		314.9	EBAUCHES POUR TOLES FER
67271	IRON,SIMPLE STEEL COILS		227.4	W 1016707	270.7		219.5		159.4	EBAUCHES NON EN ACIER
67274	STNLESS STEEL ETC COILS		46.8	W 38948	52.2		47.9		155.3	EBAUCHES ACIER INOXYDBLE
673	IRON,STEEL SHAPES ETC		419.1	W 796488	228.4		317.2		292.0	BARRES,PROFIL FER,ACIER
6731	IRON,STEEL WIRE ROD		76.1	W 86671	26.9		51.2		84.0	FIL MACHINE FER,ACIER
67311	IRON,SIMPLE STL WIRE ROD		71.3	W 77654	24.0		48.4		81.6	FIL MACH AUT ACIER FIN
6732	IRON,STEEL BARS ETC		144.9	W 316646	85.7		73.0		40.3	BARRES FER,ACIER
6733	IRON,STEEL PROFILES ETC		198.2	W 393170	115.9		193.1		167.9	PROFILES,PALPLAN FER,ACIER
67333	OTH PRFILES HOTROLLD ETC		120.1	W 232579	64.2		115.7		90.2	AUT PROFILES LAMINES,FILES
674	IRN,STL UNIV,PLATE,SHEET		447.5	W 1117618	463.3		574.1		419.6	LARGES PLATS,TOLES
6744	IRN,STL HVY PLATE,ROLLED		149.7	W 318035	129.3		81.9		109.8	TOLES LAMINEES PLUS 4.75 MM
67441	— OF IRON OR SIMPLE STL		107.3	W 288811	87.8		51.9		77.3	TOLES NON ACIER FIN CARB
6746	IRN,STL THIN PLATE,ROLLD		97.6	W 307855	125.5		102.5		104.2	TOLES LAM MOINS 3MM
67461	— OF IRON OR SIMPLE STL		85.1	W 299155	114.3		95.7		89.3	TOL NON AC FIN MOINS 3 MM
6747	TINNED PLATES,SHEETS		24.7	W 71469	29.8		180.1		23.4	TOLES ETAMEES EN ACIER
6749	OTH IRN,STL PLATES,SHEET		120.8	W 300312	134.7		167.6		149.7	AUTRES TOLES FER,ACIER
67491	— OF IRON OR SIMPLE STL		119.7	W 299682	133.9		165.6		147.6	AUT TOLES AUTRES ACIER FIN
678	IRON,STL TUBES,PIPES,ETC		91.4	W 173324	86.8		108.3		88.7	TUBES,TUYAUX EN FONTE,FER
6783	IRON,STL TUBES,PIPES NES		80.5	W 139509	65.9		74.8		48.9	AUT TUBES,TUYAUX FER,ACIER
68	NON-FERROUS METALS		540.0		470.4		620.0		1053.8	METAUX NON FERREUX
682	COPPER EXC CEMENT COPPER		250.8	W 108033	195.8		263.0		191.0	CUIVRE
6821	COPPER NES,ALLOYS,UNWRT		215.6	W 86511	152.0		180.2		123.2	CUIVRE BRUT
68211	COPPER UNREF,EXC CEMENT		102.7	W 37989	75.4		30.7		3.7	CUIVRE POUR AFFINAGE
68212	COPPER REFINED,UNWROUGHT		113.0	W 48514	76.6		149.4		119.6	CUIVRE AFFINE BRUT
684	ALUMINIUM		157.4	W 95595	134.2		220.6		729.9	ALUMINIUM
6841	ALUMINIUM,ALLOYS,UNWRGHT		120.0	W 75871	95.2	W 96079	172.4		670.9	ALUMINIUM,ALLIAGES BRUTS
69	METAL MANUFACTURES NES		213.4		259.3		383.8		453.9	ART MANUFACT EN METAL NDA
691	STRUCTURES AND PARTS NES		46.9	W 50346	48.7		96.0		108.0	CONSTRUCT FER,ACIER,ALU
6911	STRUCTURES,PARTS IRN,STL		35.8	W 45490	35.9		83.7		98.8	CONSTRUCT FER,ACIER,FONTE
692	METAL TANKS,BOXES,ETC		24.4	W 46878	50.7		67.0		107.8	RECIPIENTS METALLIQUES
6921	METAL STORAGE TANKS ETC		14.5	W 28729	38.7		49.2		90.8	CUVES EN FONTE,FER,ALU
69211	STEEL STORAGE TANKS ETC		14.4	W 28707	38.6		49.0		90.6	CUVES EN FONTE FER OU ACIER
699	BASE METAL MFRS NES		40.4		40.9		54.8		70.8	ART MANUFACTURES MET NDA
7	MACHINES,TRANSPORT EQUIP		1680.8		1865.4		2476.5		2633.1	MACHINES MATERIEL TRANSPORT
71	POWER GENERATING EQUIPMT		90.1		111.6		112.0		123.1	MACHINES GENERATRICES
713	INTRNL COMBUS PSTN ENGIN		43.0		62.8		56.5		77.5	MOTEURS EXPL COMB INT, PIECE
72	MACHS FOR SPCL INDUSTRYS		172.0		209.0		292.8		411.4	MAC SPECIALES POUR INDUST
723	CIVIL ENGNEERG EQUIP ETC		35.8		49.4		42.9		165.3	APPAREILS DE GENIE CIVIL
7234	CONST,MINING MACHNRY NES		24.4	N 6499	22.1		29.7		150.5	MACH POUR LA CONST, MINES
72346	OTH CONST,MINING MCH NES		1.0	N 1775	1.1		1.6		118.3	AUT MACH EXTRACTION,EXCAV ET
728	OTH MACHY FOR SPCL INDUS		91.2		104.1		177.6		163.8	AUT MACH IND PARTICULIERES
7283	OTHR MINERAL WORKG MACHY		58.5		52.3		96.6		87.5	MACH TRIER,CRIBLER,BROYER
74	GENRL INDUSTRL MACHY NES		301.0		317.8		474.6		534.0	MACH APP INDUSTRIE
743	PUMPS NES,CENTRFUGES ETC		102.3		101.9		147.5		171.1	POMPES COMPRES,VENT ETC
7436	GAS,LIQUID FILTERS ETC		72.2	N 7331800	84.6		126.1		137.2	APP POUR FILT DES LIQUIDES
744	MECHANICAL HANDLING EQU		62.3		56.7		103.9		102.2	EQUIP MANUTENTION PIECES
749	NONELEC MACH PTS,ACC NES		58.0		60.7		88.5		114.0	PIECES MACH NON ELEC NDA
75	OFFICE MACHNES,ADP EQUIP		58.6		91.6		88.4		117.4	MACH BUREAU TRAIT AUTOM
759	OFFICE,ADP MCH PTS,ACCES		33.0		45.9		52.0		77.0	PIECES DU 751 ET 752
76	TELECOMM,SOUND EQUIPMENT		72.3		66.1		97.6		117.5	EQUIPMENT DE TELECOM
764	TELECOM EQPT,PTS,ACC NES		64.2		59.2		79.1		93.7	EQUIP TELECOM,PIECES
77	ELECTRIC MACHNRY NES ETC		153.1		184.3		295.0		293.7	MACH APP ELECT NDA
772	SWITCHGEAR ETC,PARTS NES		42.5		45.1		96.0		55.0	APP COUPURE,SECT ETC

5. General Exports F.O.B. by Commodities according to the S.I.T.C. (Rev. 2) in million U.S. Dollars
Exportations Générales F.O.B. par Produits d'après la C.T.C.I. (Rév. 2) en millions de Dollars E.U.

SITC CTCI	COMMODITY	1993		1994		1995		1996		PRODUIT
		QUANTITY QUANTITE	VALUE VALEUR	QUANTITY QUANTITE	VALUE VALEUR	QUANTITY QUANTITE	VALUE VALEUR	QUANTITY QUANTITE	VALUE VALEUR	
7721	SWITCHGEAR ETC		41.1		43.1		93.9		52.8	APP COUPURE,SECTIONMNT
778	ELECTRICAL MACHINERY NES		40.2		56.3		81.3		103.6	AUTRES MACH ELECT NDA
78	ROAD VEHICLES		671.7		634.8		921.2		826.3	VEHICULES ROUTIERS
781	PASS MOTOR VEH EXC BUSES		144.1	N 1068	4.2		233.7		122.2	AUTO TRANSPORT PERSONNES
782	LORRIES,SPCL MTR VEH NES		57.8	N 117143	89.5		171.2		209.5	VEHICULES SPECIAUX,MARCH
7821	LORRIES,TRUCKS		55.9	N 105716	87.2		165.3		196.8	VEHICULES TRANSP MARCHAND
784	MOTOR VEH PRTS,ACCES NES		288.8		236.5		291.8		275.8	PIECES 722,781,782,783
7849	OTHER MOTOR VEHCL PARTS		283.2	W 39437	232.6		288.8		270.6	PIECES 722,781,782,783
786	TRAILERS,NONMOTR VEH,NES		163.7		154.2		194.0		191.6	REMORQUES,CADRES,CONTAIN
7861	TRAILERS,TRANSP CONTAINR		151.8	N 70445	145.4		176.8		176.2	REMORQUES TOUS VEHICULES
78613	CONTAINERS INC ROAD–RAIL		146.7	N 48377	142.8		174.5		173.6	CADRES ET CONTAINERS
79	OTHR TRANSPORT EQUIPMENT		149.6		232.8		161.9		162.6	AUTRE MATERIEL TRANSPORT
791	RAILWAY VEHICLES		25.1		20.2		20.1		73.4	VEHIC MAT CHEMINS DE FER
792	AIRCRAFT ETC		45.3		197.4		114.1		74.5	APP NAVIGATION AERIENNE
793	SHIPS AND BOATS ETC		79.3	N 13122	15.4		27.8		14.9	NAVIRES BATEAUX,ETC
7932	SHIPS AND BOATS NES		78.4	N 9960	14.0		26.5		11.7	NAVIRES ET BATEAUX
8	MISC MANUFACTURED GOODS		553.7		684.9		945.3		1017.3	ART MANUFACTURES DIVERS
821	*FURNITURE,PARTS THEREOF		82.6		211.6		397.0		416.1	MEUBLES ET PIECES
8211	CHAIRS,SEATS AND PARTS		6.1		132.7		287.5		299.2	SIEGES ET PIECES
82119	PTS NES OF CHAIRS ETC		0.4	W 3341	126.5		277.9		286.3	PIECES DU 821.11
8219	FURNITURE AND PARTS NES		67.9		69.7		101.3		97.7	AUTRES MEUBLES ET PIECES
82192	WOOD FURNITURE NES		53.5	N 3658819	51.7		76.2		76.2	MEUBLES NDA EN BOIS
84	CLOTHING AND ACCESSORIES		206.7		125.0		157.5		164.2	VETEMENTS
842	MENS OUTERWEAR NOT KNIT		73.7	N 1213409	2.2		59.3		43.8	VET DESSUS POUR HOMMES
87	PRECISION INSTRUMNTS NES		50.3		70.7		84.6		98.4	INSTRUM,APPAR SCIENT NDA
89	MISC MANUFCTRD GOODS NES		167.6		220.6		236.6		260.3	ART MANUFACTURES DIVERS
893	ARTICLES OF PLASTIC NES		49.3		53.4		91.4		88.7	OUVRAGES EN MAT DIVIS 58
9	GOODS NOT CLASSD BY KIND		9114.0		9354.8		7915.7		1982.9	ART TRANSACT NON CLASSES
931	*SPECIAL TRANSACTIONS		9087.7		9337.6		7717.3		1736.9	TRANS.SPECIALES
971	*GOLD,NON MONETARY NES		23.1	K 38935	13.8		187.2		242.4	OR NON MONETAIRE
97101	NONMON GLD UNWRT,SEMIMFD		21.2	K 2021	13.6		126.2		241.3	OR,ALLIAGES D'OR BRUTS

1. HISTORICAL SERIES, 1962–1997 SPECIAL TRADE, IMPORTS C.I.F., EXPORTS F.O.B.
SERIES HISTORIQUES, 1962–1997 COMMERCE SPECIAL, IMPORTATIONS C.A.F., EXPORTATIONS F.O.B

YEAR ANNEE	VALUE IN MILLION PESETAS # 1 VALEUR EN MILLION PESETAS # 1 MERCHANDISE –MARCHANDISE		GOLD –OR		CONVERSION FACTORS U.S. CENTS PER PESETA FACTEURS DE CONVERSION CENTS E.U. PAR PESETA		INDEX NUMBERS –INDICES QUANTUM		UNIT VALUE VALEUR UNITAIRE	
	IMPORTS	EXPORTS	IMPORTS	EXPORTS	IMPORTS	EXPORTS	IMPORTS	EXPORTS	IMPORTS	EXPORTS
1962	94.17	44.16	0.0		1.6670	1.6670				
1963	117.30	44.13	0.01		1.6670	1.6670				
1964	134.64	57.27	0.89		1.6670	1.6670				
1965	180.21	57.99	0.92		1.6670	1.6670				
1966	214.34	75.21	1.10		1.6670	1.6670				
1967	211.01	84.66	0.81		1.6360	1.6240				
1968	245.15	111.24	1.40		1.4290	1.4290				
1969	294.11	133.01	2.19	0.03	1.4290	1.4290				
1970	330.04	167.09	2.25		1.4290	1.4290				
1971	347.41	205.64	1.87		1.4290	1.4290				
1972	437.57	245.21	2.04		1.5545	1.5534				
1973	561.54	302.67	3.38		1.7218	1.7187				
1974	883.66	407.89	5.03	0.08	1.7353	1.7355				
1975	931.99	441.09			1.7419	1.7387				
1976	1169.41	583.22			1.4933	1.4964				
1977	1350.35	775.15			1.3215	1.3196				
1978	1431.03	1001.38			1.3073	1.3097				
1979	1704.01	1221.44			1.4925	1.4903				
1980	2450.75	1493.19			1.3907	1.3877	58	110	64	54
1981	2975.97	1889.72			1.0826	1.0769	42	53	83	62
1982	3474.81	2233.93			0.9080	0.9080	42	57	93	68
1983	4177.03	2846.75			0.6991	0.6953	42	62	113	80
1984	4628.99	3778.07			0.6236	0.6243	41	74	127	90
1985	5073.24	4104.14			0.6109	0.6119	44	76	129	96
1986	4891.00	3802.00			0.7174	0.7162	53	74	107	92
1987	6030.00	4196.00			0.8146	0.8150	66	80	103	94
1988	7040.00	4686.00			0.8598	0.8609	78	85	102	98
1989	8396.00	5135.00			0.8451	0.8464	91	89	104	103
1990	8915.00	5643.00			0.9840	0.9861	100	100	100	100
1991	9637.00	6065.00			0.9650	0.9669	112	112	97	99
1992	10205.00	6658.00			0.9776	0.9740	122	117	96	100
1993	10131.00	7755.00			0.7872	0.7877	118	135	101	104
1994	12306.00	9747.00			0.7491	0.7482	131	160	107	109
1995	14107.00	11340.00			0.8033	0.8029			112	116
1996	15436.00	12931.00			0.7890	0.7888			114	119
1997	17966.00	15267.00			0.6831	0.6836			119	122

2. IMPORTS BY BROAD ECONOMIC CATEGORY AND EXPORTS BY INDUSTRIAL ORIGIN. (PERCENTAGE OF TOTAL VALUE)
IMPORTATIONS PAR CATEGORIES ECONOMIQUES ET EXPORTATIONS PAR BRANCHE D'ACTIVITE.(EN POURCENTAGE DE LA VALEUR TOTALE)

IMPORTS – IMPORTATIONS

	1990	1991	1992	1993	1994	1995	1996
TOTAL IMPORTS–IMPORTATIONS TOTALES	100.	100.	100.	100.	100.	100.	100.
1 FOOD BEV–ALIMENTATION BOISSONS	9.1	10.1	10.4	11.4	11.5	11.6	10.6
11 PRIMARY–PRODUITS DE BASE	6.2	6.8	6.6	7.2	7.3	7.4	6.6
111 FOR INDUSTRY–POUR L'INDUSTRIE	2.1	2.2	2.1	2.4	2.5	2.9	2.4
112 FOR HOUSEHOLDS–POUR LES MENAGES	4.2	4.5	4.6	4.8	4.7	4.5	4.1
12 PROCESSED–PRODUITS ELABORES	2.9	3.3	3.8	4.2	4.2	4.2	4.0
121 FOR INDUSTRY–POUR L'INDUSTRIE	0.2	0.3	0.3	0.4	0.3	0.3	0.3
122 FOR HOUSEHOLDS–POUR LES MENAGES	2.7	3.1	3.5	3.8	3.8	3.9	3.7
2 IND SUPPLIES–APPROV INDUSTRIELS	29.3	28.3	27.3	27.2	29.5	31.5	29.2
21 PRIMARY–PRODUITS DE BASE	4.7	4.1	3.8	4.1	4.6	4.6	4.1
22 PROCESSED–PRODUITS ELABORES	24.6	24.2	23.5	23.1	24.9	26.9	25.1
3 FUELS–COMBUSTIBLES	11.6	10.7	10.0	10.8	9.3	8.2	9.2
31 PRIMARY–PRODUITS DE BASE	9.8	9.0	8.7	8.7	7.9	7.0	7.9
32 PROCESSED–PRODUITS ELABORES	1.8	1.7	1.3	2.0	1.4	1.2	1.3
321 MOTOR SPIRIT–ESSENCE	0.7	1.7	0.3	0.6	0.4	1.0	0.3
322 OTHER–AUTRES	1.1	0.0	1.0	1.4	0.9	0.2	1.0
4 MACHINERY–EQUIPEMENT	22.3	21.3	19.8	17.6	17.3	17.8	18.8
41 CAPITAL EQUIPMENT–MACHINES	18.6	17.7	16.2	14.0	13.7	14.4	15.3
42 PARTS–PIECES ACCESSOIRES	3.7	3.6	3.6	3.6	3.6	3.5	3.5
5 TRANSPORT–TRANSPORT	16.4	16.3	17.6	18.4	18.4	18.1	19.2
51 PASSENGER CARS–AUTOMOBILES	5.1	4.9	6.7	6.7	5.8	5.4	5.9
52 OTHER–AUTRES	4.4	4.5	3.4	2.4	2.5	2.4	2.9
521 INDUSTRIAL–INDUSTRIELS	4.0	4.1	2.9	2.0	2.2	2.2	2.7
522 NON INDUSTRIAL–NON INDUSTRIEL	0.4	0.4	0.5	0.4	0.2	0.2	0.2
53 PARTS–PIECES ACCESSOIRES	6.8	6.9	7.5	9.4	10.1	10.3	10.4
6 CONSUM GOODS–BIENS CONSOMMATION	11.2	13.1	14.9	14.5	14.0	12.7	12.9
61 DURABLE–DURABLES	4.2	4.5	4.5	4.5	4.1	3.5	3.5
62 SEMI DURABLE–SEMI DURABLES	5.1	6.5	7.7	6.9	6.5	5.9	6.3
63 NON DURABLE–NON DURABLES	1.8	2.2	2.6	3.1	3.3	3.4	3.1
7 GOODS NES–BIENS NDA	0.1	0.2	0.1	0.2	0.2	0.1	0.2

EXPORTS – EXPORTATIONS

	1990	1991	1992	1993	1994	1995	1996
TOTAL EXPORTS–EXPORTATIONS TOTALES	100.	100.	100.	100.	100.	100.	100.
1 AGRICULTURE	8.4	8.9	9.0	9.3	9.0	8.7	8.5
2 MINING QUARRY–INDUS EXTRACTIVES	0.7	0.6	0.6	0.6	0.5	0.5	0.5
3 MANUFACTURING–IND MANUFACTUR	90.8	90.5	90.4	90.1	90.5	90.8	91.0
31 FOOD BEV TOBACCO–ALIM BOISS TAB	7.1	7.3	6.9	7.2	7.5	7.5	7.7
32 TEXTILES–INDUSTRIES TEXTILES	7.6	6.7	6.5	6.7	7.1	7.1	7.1
33 WOOD & PRODUCTS–BOIS & PRODUITS	0.6	0.6	0.7	0.6	0.6	0.6	0.6
34 PAPER & PRODUCTS–PAPIER & PRODT	3.0	2.8	2.9	2.8	2.9	3.2	2.7
35 CHEMICALS–INDUSTRIES CHIMIQUES	16.6	14.6	13.2	13.3	13.2	13.1	13.4
36 NON METAL MIN–MIN NON METAL	3.3	3.2	3.5	3.6	3.7	3.7	3.6
37 BASIC METAL–IND METAL BASE	6.8	6.7	5.9	6.5	6.2	6.0	5.5
38 METAL MANUF–MANUF METAL	44.2	46.1	48.5	47.1	47.4	47.8	48.5
39 OTH MANUF IND–AUTRES MANUF	1.6	2.5	2.2	2.4	1.9	1.7	1.9

3. TRADE BY PRINCIPAL COUNTRIES OF ORIGIN AND DESTINATION (VALUE IN MILLION U.S. DOLLARS)
ECHANGES SELON LES PRINCIPAUX PAYS D'ORIGINE ET DE DESTINATION (VALEUR EN MILLIONS DE DOLLARS EU)

COUNTRIES–PAYS	SPECIAL IMPORTS C.I.F. IMPORTATIONS SPECIALES C.A.F				
	1992	1993	1994	1995	1996
World	99746.8	79739.4	92502.4	113398.6	123182.9
Africa	6533.5	4766.8	5880.7	6489.2	7419.1
Americas	12298.1	9790.9	11219.6	13114.2	13263.6
– Northern America	7955.6	6217.8	7183.0	8195.7	8262.1
– LAIA	4006.5	3317.8	3546.3	4232.8	4300.1
– CACM	83.5	79.4	175.4	227.1	202.8
– Caribbean	185.4	132.6	219.1	327.6	388.3
– Rest of America	67.0	43.4	95.7	131.0	110.3
Asia excl fmr USSR	13156.0	10755.2	11540.5	13973.4	14850.7
– Middle East	2168.6	2264.2	2280.0	2766.1	3239.5
Asia former USSR	17.8	43.4	71.5	70.8	83.4
Europe excl fmr USSR	66221.3	52303.9	62044.8	77624.9	85594.5
– European Union	63395.8	49649.6	59293.4	73895.7	81812.5
– Eastern Europe	587.2	412.7	720.5	1205.7	1164.6
– Rest of Europe	2238.3	2241.6	2030.9	2523.5	2617.3
Europe former USSR	886.4	1123.6	1167.2	1659.8	1585.8
Oceania	351.2	309.6	401.4	429.3	376.5
Other	282.5	646.0	176.7	37.1	9.3
France, Monaco	15828.1	13381.3	16148.2	19523.9	21959.9
Germany/Allemagne	16359.7	11923.4	13511.5	17286.2	18228.5
Italy/Italie	9805.4	6740.6	8274.2	10321.4	11850.1
United Kingdom	7281.6	5931.0	7259.7	8812.3	10195.4
USA/Etats–Unis d'Amer	7380.1	5818.6	6750.2	7526.6	7609.0
Netherlands/Pays–Bas	3460.1	2738.3	3606.3	4889.8	4904.7
Japan/Japon	4649.2	3420.0	3295.9	3793.9	3440.6
Belgium–Luxembourg	3175.8	2766.3	3090.9	3866.4	4372.9
Portugal	2696.1	2114.7	2570.9	3309.0	3621.7
China/Chine	1618.5	1407.7	1800.5	2241.1	2417.4
Switzerland,Liechtenst.	1538.9	1687.3	1363.4	1686.1	1547.0
Sweden/Suède	1328.9	980.4	1213.2	1413.3	1832.6
Nigeria/Nigéria	1303.7	758.6	1072.7	1054.8	1769.5
Saudi Arabia	1081.1	1050.6	1115.5	1210.2	1343.9
Russian Federation	826.2	995.4	1020.0	1437.9	1362.8
Libyan Arab Jamahiriya	1242.8	901.7	1012.8	1168.0	1142.4
Mexico/Mexique	1353.0	1007.3	960.2	1018.4	1049.0
Brazil/Brésil	972.2	862.2	926.8	1117.0	1163.7
Austria/Autriche	747.8	839.4	975.2	1012.4	1255.8
Algeria/Algérie	1023.3	791.9	837.1	987.5	1172.0
Ireland/Irlande	887.6	692.4	850.3	1190.0	1161.4
Finland/Finlande	740.6	710.7	814.7	992.0	964.5
Denmark/Danemark	836.1	666.8	744.1	911.9	1043.3
Other Asia n.e.s.	1152.3	729.8	691.3	729.6	766.3
Korea, Republic of	793.3	632.1	691.6	968.1	957.6
Argentina/Argentine	632.3	608.1	688.7	816.1	865.9
Iran (Islamic Rep of)	357.4	573.0	643.3	789.2	976.1
Indonesia/Indonésie	393.0	395.5	584.9	695.2	990.1
So. African Customs Un	525.3	468.5	508.7	730.3	663.4
Norway,Svalbard and JM	475.5	386.0	468.0	642.8	890.1
Morocco/Maroc	472.6	428.3	511.2	585.4	637.4
Canada	569.0	394.1	407.6	637.3	558.6
Thailand/Thaïlande	490.7	378.2	442.9	522.7	603.4
India/Inde	313.0	299.1	334.4	470.0	555.9
Malaysia/Malaisie	294.1	262.5	321.5	505.4	488.3
Chile/Chili	459.7	307.8	309.8	417.4	338.0
Turkey/Turquie	416.9	252.5	272.2	399.3	448.7
Cameroon/Cameroun	329.7	318.8	314.4	316.3	405.0
Singapore/Singapour	322.4	264.5	320.3	322.8	320.7
Greece/Grèce	248.1	164.3	234.2	367.0	421.9

COUNTRIES–PAYS	SPECIAL EXPORTS F.O.B. EXPORTATIONS SPECIALES F.O.B.				
	1992	1993	1994	1995	1996
Monde	64310.9	60968.5	73187.9	89616.1	101592.4
Afrique	3141.9	3126.9	2987.0	3445.8	3481.3
Amériques	6478.4	7068.5	8569.5	9362.7	10760.4
– Amérique du Nord	3421.4	3293.0	4053.8	4257.6	4749.2
– ALAI	2412.3	3009.8	3770.7	4016.1	4619.5
– MCAC	101.1	122.4	185.8	194.7	179.2
– Caraïbes	482.3	577.2	492.3	796.1	1126.3
– Autre Amérique	61.3	66.1	66.9	98.2	86.4
Asie anc. URSS exclus	4131.8	5289.8	6353.6	7425.1	8466.3
– Moyen–Orient	1547.4	1836.5	1643.9	1966.2	2465.0
Asie ancienne URSS	0.7	5.5	15.2	10.2	20.5
Europe anc. URSS exclus	49612.3	44639.3	54530.5	68427.5	76490.4
– Union Européenne	47185.5	42077.0	51717.0	64773.8	72372.8
– Europe de l'Est	402.8	599.2	872.9	1029.0	1489.0
– Autre de l'Europe	2024.0	1963.1	1940.6	2624.7	2628.6
Europe ancienne URSS	427.4	336.5	347.4	472.2	746.0
Océanie	197.2	200.6	327.3	414.3	403.6
Autre	321.1	301.3	57.4	58.4	1223.9
France, Monaco	13002.0	11539.7	14746.5	18401.5	20602.5
Germany/Allemagne	10087.5	8912.0	10397.4	13809.8	14920.1
Italy/Italie	7006.3	5540.0	6741.4	8152.6	8853.2
United Kingdom	4925.3	5021.0	6016.5	7160.9	8425.9
Portugal	4835.5	4422.7	5694.4	7485.7	8922.1
USA/Etats–Unis d'Amer	3081.7	2934.4	3606.6	3799.7	4239.5
Netherlands/Pays–Bas	2766.4	2238.7	3046.3	3296.0	3473.0
Belgium–Luxembourg	2084.9	1868.5	2190.6	2774.7	3016.9
Switzerland,Liechtenst.	863.2	790.7	885.3	998.5	1156.0
Japan/Japon	593.0	562.6	981.9	1232.9	1223.1
Mexico/Mexique	879.4	1180.6	1372.8	600.2	534.7
Argentina/Argentine	446.7	617.2	904.0	956.8	1314.4
Algeria/Algérie	713.6	786.9	853.2	1010.5	701.9
Morocco/Maroc	699.9	759.3	686.3	743.0	809.4
Sweden/Suède	640.1	691.3	558.7	797.4	927.2
Greece/Grèce	485.6	499.0	679.5	895.9	987.7
Austria/Autriche	572.1	548.9	610.5	719.9	853.4
China/Chine	270.0	649.9	800.1	850.5	596.5
Turkey/Turquie	325.3	468.8	382.4	616.4	925.4
Brazil/Brésil	164.8	241.2	359.3	836.9	956.8
Denmark/Danemark	395.8	373.7	465.7	616.5	632.9
Saudi Arabia	459.6	462.9	517.9	481.0	488.4
Israel/Israël	248.1	304.4	459.3	610.1	720.1
China, Hong Kong SAR	276.9	374.6	497.4	485.5	598.7
Korea, Republic of	205.3	341.2	556.0	456.7	634.5
Andorra/Andorre	429.8	381.5	418.6	494.6	439.6
Norway,Svalbard and JM	463.8	448.8	248.3	558.7	376.9
Canada	338.0	356.8	420.8	433.9	434.5
Russian Federation	414.0	297.2	292.9	379.3	589.7
Singapore/Singapour	214.4	283.9	342.4	460.8	535.5
Chile/Chili	217.5	262.2	363.6	465.0	521.5
Poland/Pologne	158.5	250.5	345.0	436.9	624.8
Ireland/Irlande	186.4	252.6	317.9	327.8	464.6
Cuba	200.0	189.8	289.5	395.9	464.0
Other Asia n.e.s.	168.2	236.2	301.3	335.7	281.5
Special Categories	23.2	2.1		42.6	1201.1
Colombia/Colombie	231.2	188.7	237.9	288.4	317.0
Australia/Australie	140.2	146.4	276.0	356.0	333.6
Finland/Finlande	197.7	168.9	251.7	335.2	293.3
Tunisia/Tunisie	184.9	203.7	216.8	335.3	289.5

(VALUE AS PERCENTAGE OF WORLD TOTAL)(VALEURS EN POURCENTAGE DU TOTAL MONDIAL)

	1987	1988	1989	1990	1991	1992	1993	1994	1995	1996
Africa	7.4	6.3	6.4	6.8	6.9	6.6	6.0	6.4	5.7	6.0
Americas	14.9	14.7	14.4	13.5	13.0	12.3	12.3	12.1	11.6	10.8
– Northern America	8.7	9.3	9.5	8.8	8.4	8.0	7.8	7.8	7.2	6.7
– LAIA	5.6	4.8	4.5	4.4	4.2	4.0	4.2	3.8	3.7	3.5
– CACM	0.2	0.1	0.1	0.1	0.1	0.1	0.1	0.2	0.2	0.2
– Caribbean	0.3	0.3	0.2	0.2	0.2	0.2	0.2	0.2	0.3	0.3
– Rest of America	0.1	0.1	0.1	0.1	0.1	0.1	0.1	0.1	0.1	0.1
Asia excl fmr USSR	13.5	13.0	12.9	12.0	13.0	13.2	13.5	12.5	12.3	12.1
– Middle East	4.9	3.1	3.5	2.9	2.6	2.2	2.8	2.5	2.4	2.6
Asia former USSR						0.0	0.1	0.1	0.1	0.1
Europe excl fmr USSR	60.8	63.2	63.6	65.6	65.7	66.4	65.6	67.1	68.5	69.5
– European Union	57.7	60.2	60.5	62.8	63.0	63.6	62.3	64.1	65.2	66.4
– Eastern Europe	0.8	0.7	0.7	0.6	0.5	0.6	0.5	0.8	1.1	0.9
– Rest of Europe	2.3	2.2	2.3	2.2	2.2	2.2	2.8	2.2	2.2	2.1
Europe former USSR	1.8	1.8	1.8	1.5	0.8	0.9	1.4	1.3	1.5	1.3
Oceania	0.8	0.7	0.6	0.3	0.3	0.4	0.4	0.4	0.4	0.3
Other	0.7	0.3	0.3	0.3	0.3	0.3	0.8	0.2	0.0	0.0
France, Monaco	12.8	13.5	13.7	14.7	15.2	15.9	16.8	17.5	17.2	17.8
Germany/Allemagne					16.2	16.4	15.0	14.6	15.2	14.8
Italy/Italie	8.8	9.6	10.4	10.1	10.0	9.8	8.5	8.9	9.1	9.6
United Kingdom	7.0	7.1	6.5	7.2	7.5	7.3	7.4	7.8	7.8	8.3
USA/Etats–Unis d'Amer	8.3	8.9	9.0	8.3	8.0	7.4	7.3	7.3	6.6	6.2
Netherlands/Pays–Bas	3.2	3.5	3.3	3.7	3.5	3.5	3.4	3.9	4.3	4.0
Japan/Japon	4.5	5.1	4.8	4.4	4.7	4.7	4.3	3.6	3.3	2.8
Belgium–Luxembourg	3.2	3.3	3.2	3.1	3.0	3.2	3.5	3.3	3.4	3.5
Portugal	1.7	2.1	2.3	2.5	2.7	2.7	2.7	2.8	2.9	2.9
China/Chine	0.5	0.6	0.7	0.8	1.2	1.6	1.8	1.9	2.0	2.0

	1987	1988	1989	1990	1991	1992	1993	1994	1995	1996
Afrique	5.9	5.4	4.6	4.7	4.5	4.9	5.1	4.1	3.8	3.4
Amériques	13.5	13.0	12.3	10.4	9.3	10.1	11.6	11.7	10.4	10.6
– Amérique du Nord	9.2	9.1	8.2	6.5	5.5	5.3	5.4	5.5	4.8	4.7
– ALAI	3.1	2.8	2.7	2.7	2.8	3.8	4.9	5.2	4.5	4.5
– MCAC	0.2	0.2	0.2	0.2	0.1	0.2	0.2	0.3	0.2	0.2
– Caraïbes	0.8	0.8	0.7	0.7	0.7	0.7	0.9	0.7	0.9	1.1
– Autre Amérique	0.2	0.2	0.4	0.4	0.2	0.1	0.1	0.1	0.1	0.1
Asie anc. URSS exclus	7.5	7.8	7.6	6.5	6.6	6.4	8.7	8.7	8.3	8.3
– Moyen–Orient	3.2	3.5	3.1	2.5	2.4	2.4	3.0	2.2	2.2	2.4
Asie ancienne URSS						0.0	0.0	0.0	0.0	0.0
Europe anc. URSS exclus	70.0	71.4	72.4	75.3	76.6	77.1	73.2	74.5	76.4	75.3
– Union Européenne	66.0	67.7	68.7	71.4	73.1	73.4	69.0	70.7	72.3	71.2
– Europe de l'Est	0.7	0.6	0.6	0.5	0.5	0.6	1.0	1.2	1.1	1.5
– Autre de l'Europe	3.3	3.1	3.1	3.4	3.1	3.1	3.2	2.7	2.9	2.6
Europe ancienne URSS	0.9	0.7	0.9	0.7	0.9	0.7	0.6	0.5	0.5	0.7
Océanie	0.4	0.5	0.5	0.3	0.3	0.3	0.3	0.4	0.5	0.4
Autre	1.8	1.3	1.8	2.1	1.9	0.5	0.5	0.1	0.1	1.2
France, Monaco	18.8	18.5	19.5	20.8	20.0	20.2	18.9	20.1	20.5	20.3
Germany/Allemagne					15.9	15.7	14.6	14.2	15.4	14.7
Italy/Italie	8.9	9.7	9.7	10.7	11.4	10.9	9.1	9.2	9.1	8.7
United Kingdom	9.5	9.8	10.0	9.0	7.7	7.7	8.2	8.2	8.0	8.3
Portugal	4.5	5.6	6.2	6.1	6.6	7.5	7.3	7.8	8.4	8.8
USA/Etats–Unis d'Amer	8.1	7.9	7.4	5.8	4.9	4.8	4.8	4.9	4.2	4.2
Netherlands/Pays–Bas	5.4	4.9	4.5	4.7	4.3	4.3	3.7	4.2	3.7	3.4
Belgium–Luxembourg	3.0	3.4	3.2	3.0	3.1	3.2	3.1	3.0	3.1	3.0
Switzerland,Liechtenst.	1.8	1.7	1.5	1.6	1.6	1.3	1.3	1.2	1.1	1.1
Japan/Japon	1.1	1.2	1.4	1.1	1.0	0.9	0.9	1.3	1.4	1.2

4. Special Imports C.I.F. by Commodities according to the S.I.T.C. (Rev. 2) in million U.S. Dollars
Importations Spéciales C.A.F. par Produits d'après la C.T.C.I. (Rév. 2) en millions de Dollars E.U.

SITC CTCI	COMMODITY	1993 QUANTITY QUANTITE	1993 VALUE VALEUR	1994 QUANTITY QUANTITE	1994 VALUE VALEUR	1995 QUANTITY QUANTITE	1995 VALUE VALEUR	1996 QUANTITY QUANTITE	1996 VALUE VALEUR	PRODUIT
	ALL COMMODITIES		79739.4		92502.5		113398.7		123183.0	TOUS PRODUITS
0	FOOD AND LIVE ANIMALS		8613.7		9876.8		11739.3		11870.2	ALIMENTS,ANIMAUX VIVANTS
001	*LIVE ANIMALS FOR FOOD	W 119073	335.2	W 153922	450.6		499.2	W 171901	524.2	ANIMAUX VIVANTS
0011	BOVINE SPECIES,LIVE	W 61098	209.5	W 89596	307.0	W 85983	328.9	W 99949	319.8	ESPECE BOVINE
01	MEAT AND PREPARATIONS		729.1		802.2		811.3		812.9	VIANDES ET PREPARATIONS
011	MEAT FRESH,CHILLD,FROZEN	W 232513	623.3	W 258240	694.0	W 224768	692.9	W 243252	688.7	VIANDES FRAICHES,REF,CONGE
0111	BOVINE MEAT FRESH,FROZEN	W 67859	299.5	W 86864	348.6	W 64231	341.6	W 57759	300.3	VIANDES BOVIN FRAI,REF
02	DAIRY PRODCTS,BIRDS'EGGS		696.9		816.8		874.4		900.8	PRODUITS LAITIERS,OEUFS
022	MILK AND CREAM	W 446672	374.7	W 598243	461.5	W 503780	462.3	W 491286	465.8	LAIT ET CREME
024	CHEESE AND CURD	W 57358	259.1	W 103179	305.3	W 80699	369.9	W 80692	382.9	FROMAGE ET CAILLEBOTTE
03	FISH AND PREPARATIONS		2368.3		2601.9		3065.8		3121.4	POISSONS ET PREPARATIONS
034	FISH,FRESH,CHILLED,FROZN	W 441370	1078.5	W 497269	1175.6	W 505752	1321.4	W 552373	1408.0	POISSON FRAIS, REFRIG,CONG
0341	FISH FRSH,CHLLD,EX FILLT	W 179864	598.2	W 190369	609.6	W 179183	663.1	W 194204	697.2	POISSON FRAIS,REFRIGERE
0342	FISH FROZEN,EXCL FILLETS	W 204087	343.5	W 240274	407.2	W 255999	461.9	W 267962	457.7	POISSONS CONGELES
036	SHELL FISH FRESH,FROZEN	W 267127	969.5	W 316354	1090.0	W 322418	1353.8	W 325533	1300.2	CRUSTACES,MOLLUSQUES
04	CEREALS AND PREPARATIONS		1198.2		1321.1		1852.0		1705.2	CEREALES ET PRODUITS
041	WHEAT ETC UNMILLED	W 1752923	382.7	W 2049334	406.3	W 2757498	581.7	W 2136521	436.7	FROMENT,EPEAUTRE
0412	OTHER WHEAT ETC UNMILLED	W 1624694	352.6	W 1720619	341.9	W 2358393	490.3	W 1917044	391.7	AUTRE FROMENT NON MOULU
044	MAIZE UNMILLED	W 2425172	397.8	W 2339155	406.9	W 2912371	461.6	W 2139434	440.1	MAIS NON MOULU
048	CEREAL ETC PREPARATIONS	W 123508	253.1	W 137780	297.2	W 154751	345.8	W 256066	396.7	PREPTNS A BASE CEREALES
05	VEGETABLES AND FRUIT		1146.8		1464.6		1786.6		1810.9	LEGUMES ET FRUITS
054	VEG ETC FRSH,SMPLY PRSVD	W 2595333	601.7	W 2845326	715.7	W 2195798	799.0	W 2026986	687.4	LEGUMES FRAIS,CONG,SECS
057	FRUIT,NUTS,FRESH,DRIED	W 406295	367.7	W 557531	515.6	W 670625	674.1	W 698364	767.4	FRUITS FRAIS OU SECS
06	SUGAR AND PREPS,HONEY		347.3		265.0		387.0		475.3	SUCRES ET PRODUITS
061	SUGAR AND HONEY	W 588029	287.7	W 488362	192.4	W 620612	314.8	W 799615	405.6	SUCRES ET MIEL
07	COFFEE,TEA,COCOA,SPICES		516.3		754.0		1003.7		860.8	CAFE,THE,CACAO,EPICES
071	COFFEE AND SUBSTITUTES	W 188006	252.2	W 183490	444.0	W 185720	652.8	W 207043	511.1	CAFE ET SUCCEDANES
0711	COFFEE GREEN,ROASTED,SUB	W 183459	228.9	W 180299	416.1	W 181925	614.8	W 202898	477.0	CAFE TORREFIE OU DECAFEINE
07111	COFFEE GREEN,HUSKS,SKINS	W 180733	218.8	W 176643	400.7	W 176898	587.8	W 196248	439.2	CAFE NON TORREFIE
081	*FEEDING STUFF FOR ANIML	W 3837291	809.8	W 3751752	840.1	W 3893173	852.8	W 3775517	988.8	NOURRITURE POUR ANIMAUX
0813	OILCAKE AND OTH RESIDUES	W 2291932	443.8	W 2364847	462.6	W 2208230	399.6	W 2088938	488.9	TOURTEAUX
08131	— OF SOYA BEANS	W 1836906	386.5	W 1978783	412.2	W 1703720	334.0	W 1719459	435.2	TOURTEAUX DE SOJA
0819	FOOD WASTE AND FEED NES	W 1208904	298.4	W 1041557	297.3	W 1291536	363.7	W 1169978	378.5	DECHETS,ALIMENTS NDA
09	MISC EDIBLE PRODUCTS		466.3		561.1		606.9		670.4	PREP ALIMENTAIRES DIVERSES
098	EDIBLE PRODCTS,PREPS NES	W 105182	433.2	W 128113	535.6	W 126882	579.3	W 148559	635.4	PREP ALIMENTAIRES NDA
09809	MISC FOOD PREPRTIONS NES	W 58577	373.6	W 77432	469.8	W 75562	504.5	W 91449	548.9	PREP ALIMENTAIRES NDA
1	BEVERAGES AND TOBACCO		1233.6		1494.4		1870.9		1600.8	BOISSONS ET TABACS
11	BEVERAGES		860.9		924.3		1124.5		1098.4	BOISSONS
112	ALCOHOLIC BEVERAGES	W 312443	815.1	W 371572	870.4	W 593541	1068.5	W 461434	1036.0	BOISSONS ALCOOLIQUES
1124	DISTILLED ALCOHOLIC BEVS	W 121760	641.2	W 109276	661.4	W 137843	755.6	W 150993	798.0	ALCOOLS,EAUX–DE–VIE
11241	WHISKY	W 70948	446.6	W 58281	448.9	W 76626	486.6	W 84871	511.0	WHISKY
12	TOBACCO AND MANUFACTURES		372.8		570.1		746.4		502.5	TABACS BRUTS FABRIQUES
121	TOBACCO UNMNFCTRD,REFUSE	W 44767	224.1	W 53510	282.9	W 48413	262.9	W 52780	296.8	TABACS BRUTS,DECHETS
122	TOBACCO,MANUFACTURED	W 8605	148.7	W 11143	287.3	W 14198	483.5	W 11508	205.7	TABACS FABRIQUES
1222	CIGARETTES	W 2538	87.2	W 5200	209.4	W 7146	380.7	W 7673	138.5	CIGARETTES
2	CRUDE MATERLS,EXCL FUELS		4025.8		5265.9		6837.3		6568.0	MAT BRUTES NON COMESTIBLES
22	OIL SEEDS,OLEAGINOUS FRT		644.7		687.8		998.8		975.3	GRAINES,FRUITS OLEAGINEUX
222	SEEDS FOR'SOFT'FIXED OIL	W 2393443	635.2	W 2430917	676.8	W 3640399	987.0	W 3026635	961.9	GRAINES HUILES FIXES
2222	SOYA BEANS	W 2114528	517.1	W 2019350	514.5	W 2854706	714.7	W 2322303	701.1	FEVES DE SOJA
23	RUBBER, CRUDE		256.6		326.3		487.9		482.7	CAOUTCHOUC BRUT
24	CORK AND WOOD		544.5		693.3		912.9		852.4	LIEGE ET BOIS
248	WOOD SHAPED,SLEEPERS	W 891989	400.6	W 998745	513.0	W 1119726	642.9	W 1201043	618.7	BOIS SIMPLEMENT TRAVAILLES
2483	LUMBER SHAPED NON–CONIFR	W 387261	220.2	W 423196	266.7	W 508514	349.7	W 552335	357.9	NON CONIFERES SCIES,RABOTES
251	*PULP AND WASTE PAPER	W 1019719	269.2	W 1211166	373.5	W 1145541	560.9	W 1257280	372.0	PATES A PAPIER,DECHETS
2517	SODA,SULPHATE WOOD PULP	W 508382	203.7	W 529964	265.5	W 433557	356.3	W 454733	238.8	PATES CHIMIQUES AU SULFATE
25172	— BLEACHED,NONDISSOLVNG	W 498519	199.0	W 519566	260.3	W 425068	349.8	W 446459	234.6	PATES BLANCHIES
26	TEXTILE FIBRES AND WASTE		371.0		538.0		642.4		622.0	FIBRES TEXTILES
27	CRUDE FERTLZR,MINRLS NES		313.1		377.8		426.4		460.2	ENGRAIS MINERAUX BRUTS
28	METALLIFEROUS ORES,SCRAP		1213.9		1718.5		2066.3		2007.3	MINERAIS METAL,DECHETS
282	IRON AND STEEL SCRAP	W 4033327	537.7	W 4622645	753.8	W 4878557	963.8	W 4537643	802.8	FERRAILLES
28209	— OF OTHR IRON OR STEEL	W 3899020	473.3	W 4329866	561.6	W 4534198	675.6	W 4086412	503.6	FERRAILLES DE FER
287	BASE METAL ORES,CONC NES	W 2859833	418.8	W 3272841	635.7	W 3573624	714.9	W 4449902	750.0	MINERAIS METAUX COMMUNS
2871	CPR ORE ETC,CEMENT COPPR	W 476062	217.7	W 518428	367.7	W 465617	383.3	W 736656	389.9	MINERAIS DE CUIVRE,MATTES
28711	COPPER ORES,EXCL MATTE	W 476001	217.6	W 518428	367.7	W 465547	383.0	W 736576	389.6	MINERAIS DE CUIVRE
29	CRUDE ANIMAL,VEG MAT NES		290.9		327.9		508.8		534.6	MATIERES BRUTES ANIM,VEGET
292	CRUDE VEG MATERIALS NES	W 85019	229.0	W 82909	256.8	W 106282	425.3		442.7	MAT BRUTES VEGETALES NDA
3	MINERAL FUELS ETC		8719.8		8733.2		9480.7		11546.7	COMBUSTIBLES MINERAUX LUB
32	COAL,COKE AND BRIQUETTES		593.2		565.3		758.2		670.4	HOUILLES,COKES,BRIQUETTES
322	COAL,LIGNITE AND PEAT	MW 12731	582.5	MW 11876	540.0	MW 14062	676.3	MW 12779	618.8	HOUILLES,LIGNITES,TOURBE
3222	OTH COAL,NOT AGGLOMERATD	MW 12454	553.0	MW 11482	502.6	MW 13761	638.2	MW 12370	575.2	AUTRES HOUILLES
33	PETROLEUM AND PRODUCTS		7292.7		7260.9		7540.2		9474.2	PETROLE ET DERIVES
333	CRUDE PETROLEUM	MW 50565	5564.2	MW 53567	5904.3	MW 50032	6205.5	MW 53375	7870.7	HUILES BRUTES DE PETROLE
334	PETROLEUM PRODUCTS,REFIN	MW 11497	1576.2	W 7525873	1184.3	W 6647769	1113.9	W 6692436	1357.5	PRODUITS RAFFINES
3341	GASOLINE,OTH LIGHT OILS	W 3729303	479.8	W 2285130	412.9			W 2013625	407.4	ESSENCES POUR MOTEURS
33411	MOTOR,AVIATION SPIRIT	W 2738185	312.8	W 750055	135.9			W 583206	129.5	ESSENCES MOTEURS D'AVIONS
3343	GAS OILS	W 4640934	714.1	W 2966547	442.0			W 2896650	604.4	GAS OILS
341	*GAS,NATURAL AND MANUFCT		799.1		858.0	W 7466047	1023.9	W 8080352	1190.9	GAZ NATUREL,GAZ MANUFACT
3413	PETROLM GASES,LIQUEFIED	W 5663707	784.0	W 6163510	784.5	W 6685493	918.7	W 7000031	1042.9	GAZ DE PETROLE LIQUEFIE
34139	OTH HYDROCARBON GAS LQFD	W 4447164	572.2	W 5050021	600.1	W 5644513	690.1	W 5817964	778.1	HYDROCARBURES GAZEUX NDA
4	ANIMAL,VEGETABLE OIL,FAT		287.9		493.8		807.6		695.7	HUILES,GRAISSES ANIM,VEG
42	FIXED VEGETABLE OIL,FAT		157.5		338.7		577.8		515.0	HUILES VEGETALES FIXES
423	FIXED VEG OILS,SOFT	W 89856	89.4	W 213551	232.7	W 225039	438.0	W 182482	380.9	HUILES VEGET DOUCES FIXES
4235	OLIVE OIL	W 40861	60.2	W 125579	172.6	W 137581	375.2	W 98153	322.9	HUILE D'OLIVE
5	CHEMCLS,RELATED PROD NES		8606.2		10558.2		13445.9		13909.1	PRODUITS CHIMIQUES
51	ORGANIC CHEMICALS		2314.1		2851.0		3626.5		3488.3	PROD CHIMIQ ORGANIQUES
511	HYDROCARBONS NES,DERIVS	W 530920	261.9	W 592810	349.5	W 693484	492.9	W 612866	393.8	HYDROCARBURES NDA
512	ALCOHOLS,PHENOLS ETC	W 603774	220.8	W 682382	332.7	W 749613	421.3	W 756809	372.7	PHENOLS,PHENOLS–ALCOOLS
5121	ACYCLIC ALCOHOLS,DERIVS	W 574282	177.7	W 649693	285.2	W 717599	360.8	W 713654	308.8	ALCOOLS ACYCLIQUES
513	CARBOXYLIC ACIDS ETC	W 304907	331.9	W 381929	440.9	W 387608	586.2	W 352365	550.3	ACIDES CARBOXYLIQUES
514	NITROGEN–FNCTN COMPOUNDS	W 210859	495.2	W 278505	584.0	W 338656	1015.2	W 338584	1016.5	COMPOSES FONCT AZOTEES
5148	OTH NITROGN–FNCTN CMPNDS	W 96285	131.5	W 132060	170.7	W 164486	540.4	W 153618	491.8	AUTRES COMPOSES AZOTES
515	ORG–INORG COMPOUNDS ETC	W 88475	762.2	W 106265	872.0	W 74522	758.0	W 73873	805.3	COMPOSES ORGANO–MINERAUX
5156	HETEROCYCLIC CMPDS ETC	W 47370	595.4	W 58588	676.1	W 24944	558.7	W 22620	580.7	COMPOSES HETEROCYCLIQUES
51569	OTH HETEROCYC CMPDS,ETC	W 40099	576.6	W 46558	650.3	W 18384	531.0	W 18560	557.9	AUT COMP HETEROCYCLIQUES
516	OTHER ORGANIC CHEMICALS	W 266577	242.3	W 258207	272.2	W 221057	353.1	W 220041	350.0	AUTRES PROD ORGANIQUES
52	INORGANIC CHEMICALS		698.7		775.8		946.2		965.6	PROD CHIM INORGANIQUES
522	INORG ELEMNTS,OXIDES,ETC	W 888298	251.1	W 1226265	325.3	W 1401751	452.5	W 1337857	461.6	ELEMENTS INORGANIQUES
53	DYES,TANNING,COLOUR PROD		533.3		660.4		791.8		827.0	PROD TEINTURE,COLORANTS
533	PIGMENTS,PAINTS,ETC	W 119787	334.7	W 153319	420.2	W 163931	527.1	W 172172	550.4	PIGMENTS,PEINTURES,VERNIS
541	*MEDICINAL,PHARM PRODUCT		1532.8		1855.3	MK 34234	2242.3	MK 48070	2474.1	PROD MEDICINAUX PHARMACEUT
5417	MEDICAMENTS	MK 11517	883.4	MK 16301	1172.3	MK 19465	1407.3	MK 29604	1615.0	MEDICAMENTS

4. Special Imports C.I.F. by Commodities according to the S.I.T.C. (Rev. 2) in million U.S. Dollars
Importations Spéciales C.A.F. par Produits d'après la C.T.C.I. (Rév. 2) en millions de Dollars E.U.

SITC CTCI	COMMODITY	1993			1994			1995			1996			PRODUIT
		QUANTITY QUANTITE		VALUE VALEUR	QUANTITY QUANTITE		VALUE VALEUR	QUANTITY QUANTITE		VALUE VALEUR	QUANTITY QUANTITE		VALUE VALEUR	
54179	— CONTNG OTH SUBSTANCES	MK	9636	576.0	MK	13993	809.5	MK	16253	1026.8	MK	25288	1137.5	MED CONT AUT SUBSTANCES
55	PERFUME,CLEANING ETC PRD			686.1			858.3			999.2			1055.3	PROD POUR PARFUM,TOILETTE
553	PERFUMERY,COSMETICS,ETC	W	51974	373.2	W	61663	476.2	W	71827	568.8	W	85797	625.6	PRODUITS DE PARFUMERIE
562	*FERTILIZERS,MANUFACTURE	W	1676482	217.1	W	2329528	324.5	W	2347306	401.9	W	2886101	503.4	ENGRAIS MANUFACTURES
58	PLASTIC MATERIALS ETC			1547.1			1973.4			2867.0			2918.9	MAT PLAST ARTIFICIELLES
582	PROD OF CONDENSATION ETC	W	171478	405.3	W	241295	539.5	W	302017	806.1	W	320270	819.4	PROD CONDENS,POLYCOND
5823	ALKYDS,OTHER POLYESTERS	W	61308	158.5	W	90811	211.0	W	127092	349.1	W	146516	349.2	ALKYDES ET AUT POLYESTERS
583	POLYMERIZATION ETC PRODS	W	915687	1075.4	W	1302334	1355.0	W	1182832	1967.4	W	1388455	1994.1	PROD POLYMERISATION
5831	POLYETHYLENE	W	338442	255.2	W	419978	321.1	W	400262	469.4	W	472729	494.7	POLYETHYLENE
58311	— IN PRIMARY FORMS	W	295955	196.2	W	367955	247.4	W	343836	370.1	W	406076	385.4	POLYETHYLENE PRIMAIRES
5839	OTH POLYMRZTION ETC PROD	W	126858	295.9	W	359444	359.5	W	187984	496.3	W	246061	567.3	AUT PROD POLYMER COPOLYM
59	CHEMICAL MATERIALS NES			1069.9			1251.3			1552.8			1659.8	MAT PROD CHIMIQUES NDA
598	MISCEL CHEM PRODUCTS NES	W	344481	725.0	W	355797	832.6	W	418352	1009.6	W	444991	1060.0	PROD DIV INDUST CHIM NDA
5989	CHEM PRODUCTS,PREPS NES	W	213234	557.8	W	216101	638.0	W	243486	757.8	W	254365	806.6	PROD PREP CHIMIQUES NDA
59899	OTH CHEM PRODS,PREPS,NES	W	167779	443.9	W	164620	509.2	W	186982	604.3	W	187510	634.2	AUT PRODUITS CHIMIQUES NDA
6	BASIC MANUFACTURES			10191.3			13042.2			17648.9			17891.2	ART MANUFACTURES
61	LEATHER,DRESSED FUR,ETC			344.7			541.4			591.5			599.2	CUIRS,PELLETERIES
611	LEATHER	W	51684	300.1	W	84827	489.5	W	77027	538.1	W	79097	538.3	CUIRS,PEAUX PREPARES
62	RUBBER MANUFACTURES NES			848.6			1068.6			1432.2			1511.2	CAOUTCHOUC MANUFACTURE
625	RUBBER TYRES, TUBES ETC	W	119950	493.9	W	154417	608.1	W	194170	828.0	W	227122	896.8	PNEUS CAOUTCHOUC VULCANISE
6251	TYRES NEW FOR MOTOR CARS	W	59609	282.9	W	71193	339.2	W	91170	466.8	W	118061	505.3	PNEUS POUR VOITURES
63	WOOD,CORK MANUFACTRS NES			284.7			337.8			433.1			444.8	OUVRAGES LIEGE ET BOIS
64	PAPER,PAPERBOARD AND MFR			1744.1			2146.4			2969.3			2850.0	PAPIERS,CARTONS & OUVRAGES
641	PAPER AND PAPERBOARD	W	2146753	1428.5	W	2521681	1818.5	W	2574132	2549.6	W	2636812	2398.3	PAPIERS ET CARTONS
6412	PRINTG,WRITING PAPER NES	W	564747	440.7	W	679558	562.8	W	663248	782.6	W	635353	632.8	PAPIERS POUR L'IMPRESSION
64122	— COATED,IMPREGNATD ETC	W	498391	389.4	W	598467	489.9	W	582751	676.3	W	555053	548.3	PAPIERS IMPRESSION COUCHES
6413	KRAFT PAPER,PAPERBOARD	W	469578	242.2	W	547539	317.3	W	546655	439.3	W	574455	392.8	PAPIER ET CARTON KRAFT
6415	PAPER,PAPERBRD,BULK,NES	W	475258	282.7	W	573064	377.2	W	578520	532.4	W	572236	475.5	PAPIERS,CARTONS ROULEAUX
64159	OTHER PAPER ETC,BULK,NES	W	329333	218.1	W	391579	290.4	W	400799	411.2	W	418850	387.1	AUT PAPIER ROULEAUX FEUILLES
6418	COATED ETC PAPER NES BLK	W	138128	202.5	W	196929	283.6	W	212838	384.6	W	230345	423.5	PAP,CARTONS COUCHES,ENDUITS
642	PAPER,ETC,PRECUT,ARTS OF	W	145222	315.6	W	170792	327.9	W	186661	419.7	W	189605	451.8	PAP,CARTONS DECOUPES
65	TEXTILE YARN,FABRICS,ETC			1710.3			2252.2			2758.4			2967.6	FILS,TISSUS,ARTICLES TEXTILE
651	TEXTILE YARN	W	116875	453.2	W	197521	674.8			860.6	W	207258	896.2	FILS TEXTILES
6514	SYN FIB YRN,BULK,MONOFIL	W	54232	230.4	W	86318	341.4	W	97156	451.4	W	110921	476.0	FILS CONT 85% FIB TEXT SYNTH
653	WOVN MAN–MADE FIB FABRIC	W	38005	346.1	W	52388	471.1	W	60874	581.6	W	59833	570.1	TISSUS FIBRES SYNTH,ARTIF
657	SPECIAL TXTL FABRC,PRODS	W	43584	278.9	W	65264	343.5	W	65718	415.0	W	71390	477.3	TISSUS SPECIAUX
66	NONMETAL MINERAL MFS NES			924.9			1033.6			1360.1			1466.8	ART MIN NON METALLIQUES
664	GLASS	W	191175	199.0	W	197024	248.7	W	298082	343.3	W	343037	337.8	VERRE
67	IRON AND STEEL			1776.2			2387.0			3766.5			3735.0	FER ET ACIER
671	PIG IRON ETC	W	516367	189.6	W	774996	292.2	W	829469	397.0	W	880645	373.1	FONTE,SPIEGEL,POUDRES
672	IRON,STEEL PRIMARY FORMS	W	1036643	304.0	W	1131970	384.1			766.9	W	2199200	752.1	LINGOTS FER,ACIER
6727	IRN,STL COIL FR REROLLNG	W	985176	284.1	W	1066058	356.5	W	1647043	664.4	W	1728147	621.0	EBAUCHES POUR TOLES FER
67271	IRON,SIMPLE STEEL COILS	W	976071	278.4	W	1051095	348.3	W	1628306	646.0	W	1711384	604.5	EBAUCHES NON EN ACIER
673	IRON,STEEL SHAPES ETC	W	489377	223.0	W	652056	328.8	W	970503	478.1	W	824850	448.1	BARRES,PROFIL FER,ACIER
674	IRN,STL UNIV,PLATE,SHEET	W	1257104	761.4	W	1543607	945.9	W	2032856	1482.4	W	2099045	1442.6	LARGES PLATS,TOLES
6746	IRN,STL THIN PLATE,ROLLD	W	385909	233.8	W	423309	255.6	W	584324	429.6	W	516879	359.2	TOLES LAM MOINS 3MM
6749	OTH IRN,STL PLATES,SHEET	W	471152	290.5	W	583392	376.7	W	709984	545.6	W	869157	634.5	AUTRES TOLES FER,ACIER
67491	— OF IRON OR SIMPLE STL	W	468747	284.8	W	579389	368.8	W	704276	530.9	W	861410	619.6	AUT TOLES AUTRES ACIER FIN
678	IRON,STL TUBES,PIPES,ETC	W	175850	222.9	W	326976	335.3	W	415999	506.9	W	556002	574.6	TUBES,TUYAUX EN FONTE,FER
68	NON–FERROUS METALS			970.9			1308.3			1947.5			1721.7	METAUX NON FERREUX
682	COPPER EXC CEMENT COPPER	W	167066	409.3	W	178749	513.2	W	233030	827.3	W	196488	681.0	CUIVRE
6822	COPPER,ALLOYS WORKED	W	97273	284.0	W	130074	411.4	W	170312	653.9	W	154567	582.7	CUIVRE,ALLIAGES OUVRES
684	ALUMINIUM	W	170741	372.6	W	209427	465.4	W	233332	685.9	W	258126	700.2	ALUMINIUM
6842	ALUMINIUM,ALLOYS WORKED	W	82371	265.2	W	92885	294.7	W	103518	422.1	W	127914	487.8	ALUMINIUM,ALLIAGES OUVRE
69	METAL MANUFACTURES NES			1587.4			1967.2			2390.8			2595.4	ART MANUFACT EN METAL NDA
695	TOOLS	W	32308	252.5	W	37255	336.8	W	125409	350.3	W	38094	343.1	OUTILS A MAIN
699	BASE METAL MFRS NES	W	118475	593.4	W	155772	756.4	W	180797	969.2	W	244145	1074.4	ART MANUFACTURES MET NDA
6991	LOCKSMITHS WARES,ETC	W	28461	228.8	W	40268	316.3	W	43995	402.9	W	86239	426.2	ARTICLES DE SERRURERIE
7	MACHINES,TRANSPORT EQUIP			28460.9			32658.7			40284.1			46279.0	MACHINES MATERIEL TRANSPORT
71	POWER GENERATING EQUIPMT			2868.1			3443.7			4145.7			4667.4	MACHINES GENERATRICES
713	INTRNL COMBUS PSTN ENGIN	W	216703	2161.7	W	228395	2625.1	W	255392	3174.5	W	305387	3562.0	MOTEURS EXPL COMB INT, PIECE
7132	MOTOR VEHCL PISTN ENGINS	W	155813	1659.6	W	179940	2051.2	W	192025	2456.9	W	220705	2658.7	MOTEURS EXPL POUR VEHICULES
7139	PISTON ENGINE PARTS NES	W	54361	422.1	W	39637	430.5	W	52832	509.7	W	72112	697.6	PIECES POUR 713.2,3,8
714	ENGINES AND MOTORS NES	W	4817	273.1	W	3808	312.7	W	35509	276.5	W	5121	382.8	MOTEURS NON ELECTRIQUES
716	ROTATING ELECTRIC PLANT	W	32935	278.1	W	40956	339.1	W	53111	484.1	W	55842	515.6	APP ELECTR ROTATIFS,PIECES
7162	AC MTRS,GENRTRS,GEN SETS	W	21494	188.0	W	28062	248.1	W	35231	337.4	W	38404	375.7	MOTEURS ELECTRIQUES
72	MACHS FOR SPCL INDUSTRYS			1693.0			2032.6			2673.5			3137.1	MAC SPECIALES POUR INDUST
722	TRACTORS NON–ROAD	W	24301	134.7	W	45938	255.8	W	51404	323.1	W	75296	497.9	TRACTEURS
7224	WHEELED TRACTORS NES	W	23558	131.4	W	44368	249.0	W	49671	314.8	W	72250	483.2	TRACTEURS A ROUES
723	CIVIL ENGNEERG EQUIP ETC	W	22347	155.5	W	35920	230.2	W	55399	377.6	W	62418	398.5	APPAREILS DE GENIE CIVIL
724	TEXTILE,LEATHER MACHNRY	W	13968	221.1	W	19314	308.9	W	20709	369.6	W	19420	373.3	MACH POUR INDUSTRIE TEXTILE
728	OTH MACHY FOR SPCL INDUS	W	41110	637.0	W	46252	668.3	W	59953	897.8	W	64332	1010.3	AUT MACH IND PARTICULIERES
7284	MACHY FOR SPCL INDUS NES	W	24779	488.5	W	25657	486.1	W	33525	632.3	W	36961	718.0	MACH SPEC IND PARTICUL.
73	METALWORKING MACHINERY			430.8			476.7			623.3			694.8	MACH TRAVAIL DES METAUX
736	METALWORKING MACH–TOOLS	W	17057	251.2	W	18243	297.5	W	20049	346.8	W	28373	505.5	MACH–OUTILS TRAVAIL METAUX
74	GENRL INDUSTRL MACHY NES			3070.2			3356.8			4729.8			5214.5	MACH APP INDUSTRIE
741	HEATING,COOLING EQUIPMNT	W	61519	652.1	W	74928	680.4	W	95475	1022.1	W	106521	1224.1	MACH CHAUFFAGE,PIECES
7415	AIR–CONDITIONING MACHNRY	W	19937	253.0	W	17624	240.4	W	27183	428.8	W	38185	538.5	GROUPES CONDITION AIR
742	PUMPS FOR LIQUIDS ETC	W	22710	340.6	W	21765	391.3	W	27390	558.2	W	34297	612.6	POMPES MOTO–POMPES
743	PUMPS NES,CENTRFUGES ETC	W	50808	513.7	W	60468	591.0	W	73707	849.3	W	78713	921.9	POMPES COMPRES,VENT ETC
744	MECHANICAL HANDLING EQU	W	54765	398.4	W	65809	422.0	W	90048	678.9	W	92743	681.9	EQUIP MANUTENTION PIECES
745	NONELEC MACHY,TOOLS NES	W	22749	420.1	W	25088	408.7	W	29042	508.3	W	63513	562.3	AUT MACH NON ELEC,PIECES
7452	OTH NONELEC MCHS,PTS NES	W	21156	377.9	W	22774	353.5	W	26509	439.3	W	60840	489.0	AUT MACH NON ELEC,PIECES
749	NONELEC MACH PTS,ACC NES	W	73879	745.6	W	83306	863.7	W	96327	1113.2	W	113426	1211.9	PIECES MACH NON ELEC NDA
7492	COCKS,VALVES ETC NES	W	17850	262.8	W	20582	300.5	W	27228	407.7	W	31791	453.0	ART ROB,SIM POUR TUYAUX
75	OFFICE MACHNES,ADP EQUIP			2903.2			3132.9			3561.0			3939.8	MACH BUREAU TRAIT AUTOM
751	OFFICE MACHINES	W	10697	307.4	W	10907	298.7	W	11410	331.5	W	12119	367.7	MACH,APPAREILS DE BUREAU
752	AUTOMTIC DATA PROC EQUIP	W	47704	1434.8	W	114161	1618.9	W	33090	1938.6	W	35658	2220.3	MACH TRAIT INFORMATION
7523	DIGITL CENTRL PROCESSORS	W	4014	424.6	W	4866	502.4	W	4788	571.5	W	5117	626.5	UNITES CENTRALES
7524	DIGITL CENTRL STOR UNITS	W	3931	244.4	W	88221	272.0	W	5285	342.1	W	2562	305.6	UNITES MEMOIRE CENTRALES
7525	ADP PERIPHERAL UNITS	W	23847	373.8	W	14658	479.1	W	15480	572.0	W	19393	649.8	UNITES PERIPHERIQUES
7528	OFF–LINE DATA PROC EQUIP	W	14617	277.8	W	5195	256.6	W	5315	280.6	W	7488	431.0	MACH AUXIL TRAIT INFORM
759	OFFICE,ADP MCH PTS,ACCES	W	17464	1161.1	W	21994	1215.4	W	24230	1291.0	W	26381	1351.9	PIECES DU 751 ET 752
7599	ACCTG,ETC,ADP MCH PTS,AC	W	14124	1055.8	W	18646	1106.8	W	21093	1174.0	W	21635	1207.0	PIECES DU 751 ET 752
76	TELECOMM,SOUND EQUIPMENT			2199.3			2575.4			3233.5			4319.9	EQUIPMENT DE TELECOM
761	TELEVISION RECEIVERS	W	26557	372.6	W	31470	436.7	W	1415704	506.1	W	63999	540.5	RECEPTEURS DE TELEVISION
7611	COLOUR TV RECEIVERS	W	25684	365.3	W	30595	426.3	W	1414985	497.1	W	63598	534.2	RECEPTEURS COULEUR
762	RADIO BROADCAST RECEIVRS	W	17498	342.9	W	20044	419.8	W	23165	482.4	W	22083	467.0	RECEPTEURS RADIODIFFUSION
763	SOUND RECORDRS,PHONOGRPH	W	8128	283.9	W	8335	302.8	W	9485	330.9	W	9908	399.6	PHONO,APP ENREGISTREMENT
7638	OTHR SOUND APPARATUS ETC	W	7472	272.1	W	7690	289.7	W	8980	320.2	W	9552	394.1	AUT APP D'ENREGIS,REPROD
764	TELECOM EQPT,PTS,ACC NES	W	44024	1200.1	W	41181	1416.2	W	47593	1914.2	W	43629	2912.9	EQUIP TELECOM,PIECES

4. Special Imports C.I.F. by Commodities according to the S.I.T.C. (Rev. 2) in million U.S. Dollars
Importations Spéciales C.A.F. par Produits d'après la C.T.C.I. (Rév. 2) en millions de Dollars E.U.

SITC CTCI	COMMODITY	1993 QUANTITY QUANTITE	1993 VALUE VALEUR	1994 QUANTITY QUANTITE	1994 VALUE VALEUR	1995 QUANTITY QUANTITE	1995 VALUE VALEUR	1996 QUANTITY QUANTITE	1996 VALUE VALEUR	PRODUIT
7641	LINE TELEPHONE,ETC EQUIP	W 8807	237.4	W 5576	343.5	W 5826	521.8	W 5810	630.9	APP TELEPHON PAR FIL
7643	TV,RADIO TRANSMITTRS ETC	W 2035	102.7	W 784	107.9	W 1272	209.5	W 3014	674.9	APP EMET TELE RADIO
7649	PTS NES OF EQUIPMT OF 76	W 22511	587.4	W 23515	678.7	W 23296	854.2	W 22202	1398.9	PIECES DE LA DIV 76
76491	PTS NES OF APPAR OF 7641	W 2539	189.7	W 3154	226.3	W 3963	392.6	W 6333	897.3	PIECES POUR 764.1
76493	TELECOMM EQUIPMT PTS NES	W 8856	285.6	W 9666	305.7	W 11897	313.7	W 10328	361.2	PIECES 761,762,764.3,8
77	ELECTRIC MACHNRY NES ETC		3909.5		4653.4		5834.5		6200.6	MACH APP ELECT NDA
772	SWITCHGEAR ETC,PARTS NES	W 35668	759.3	W 44119	1006.5	W 46946	1252.6	W 55035	1295.7	APP COUPURE,SECT ETC
7721	SWITCHGEAR ETC	W 28172	688.8	W 38132	902.0	W 42020	1149.9	W 50998	1204.2	APP COUPURE,SECTIONMNT
773	ELECTR DISTRIBUTNG EQUIP	W 38680	330.2	W 44526	436.1	W 76461	600.5	W 64599	590.3	EQUIPMT DISTRIBUTION ELECT
7731	INSULATED WIRE,CABLE ETC	W 32152	252.6	W 34984	335.4	W 60194	459.6	W 52033	439.0	FILS,CABLES ISOLES ELECT
775	HOUSEHOLD TYPE EQUIP NES	W 133239	784.2	W 139330	830.5	W 151807	954.9	W 161186	1026.9	MACH,APP USAGE DOMESTQUE
7758	ELECTRO–THERMIC APPL NES	W 44872	318.4	W 44057	334.7	W 49271	369.7	W 46317	372.4	APP ELECTROTHERMIQ NDA
776	TRANSISTORS,VALVES,ETC	W 31839	563.3	W 38146	666.5	W 41118	854.3	W 57736	1020.2	LAMPES,TUBES,VALVES
7764	ELECTRONIC MICROCIRCUITS	W 6212	303.9	W 3381	353.9	W 1783	421.1	W 1797	536.1	MICROSTRUCTURES ELECTRON
778	ELECTRICAL MACHINERY NES	W 128395	1125.2	W 146359	1338.0	W 216284	1747.9	W 172471	1740.2	AUTRES MACH ELECT NDA
7783	AUTOMOTIVE ELECTR EQUIP	W 33723	386.2	W 40038	487.6	W 89197	641.1	W 40873	616.7	EQUIP ELECT MOTEURS EXPL
77831	IGNITION,STARTING EQUIP	W 21793	238.7	W 25774	300.8	W 28271	392.4	W 24834	363.5	APP ELEC ALLUM,DEMARRAGE
7788	OTH ELEC MACHY,EQUIP NES	W 20516	340.6	W 22065	387.2	W 27864	508.2	W 24178	504.1	AUT MACH APP ELEC NDA
78	ROAD VEHICLES		10098.0		11436.2		13934.0		15998.8	VEHICULES ROUTIERS
781	PASS MOTOR VEH EXC BUSES	W 536145	5314.9	W 584180	5378.9	W 563617	6106.2	W 664400	7282.1	AUTO TRANSPORT PERSONNES
782	LORRIES,SPCL MTR VEH NES	W 57673	385.0	W 74707	538.6	W 108478	908.6	W 136329	1147.2	VEHICULES SPECIAUX,MARCH
7821	LORRIES,TRUCKS	W 46174	347.8	W 68941	498.1	W 102941	866.2	W 127718	1077.4	VEHICULES TRANSP MARCHAND
784	MOTOR VEH PRTS,ACCES NES	W 577092	3739.1	W 801618	4860.4	W 762594	6063.0	W 918162	6587.2	PIECES 722,781,782,783
7849	OTHER MOTOR VEHCL PARTS	W 571105	3677.3	W 788384	4743.9	W 742399	5860.7	W 901735	6398.0	PIECES 722,781,782,783
785	CYCLES,ETC MOTRZD OR NOT	W 48361	455.3	W 31910	382.6	W 29716	400.0	W 31126	453.8	MOTOCYCLES SCOOTERS
79	OTHR TRANSPORT EQUIPMENT		1289.2		1551.5		1549.1		2106.4	AUTRE MATERIEL TRANSPORT
792	AIRCRAFT ETC	W 3881	1042.5	W 2166	1274.9		1128.5		1634.0	APP NAVIGATION AERIENNE
7924	AIRCRFT NES OVER 15000KG	W 2854	761.2	W 1285	954.6	W 1156	736.5	W 1896	1113.3	AERODYNES PLUS 15000 KG
793	SHIPS AND BOATS ETC	W 45742	173.6	W 65042	193.2	W 129181	334.9		387.5	NAVIRES BATEAUX,ETC
8	MISC MANUFACTURED GOODS		9381.2		10059.2		10803.9		12289.0	ART MANUFACTURES DIVERS
812	*PLUMBG,HEATNG,LGHTNG EQ	W 60155	311.9	W 59284	323.1	W 69938	385.0	W 80540	419.9	APPAR SANITAIRES CHAUFFAGE
821	*FURNITURE,PARTS THEREOF	W 94051	436.1	W 103951	509.3	W 105650	555.2	W 133064	634.1	MEUBLES ET PIECES
84	CLOTHING AND ACCESSORIES		2201.3		2404.7		2610.2		2930.4	VETEMENTS
842	MENS OUTERWEAR NOT KNIT	W 21692	427.1	W 24732	488.6	W 22998	504.2	W 24006	560.4	VET DESSUS POUR HOMMES
843	WOMENS OUTERWEAR NONKNIT	W 27268	490.3	W 82320	520.7	W 17896	561.4	W 20045	594.5	VET DESSUS FEMMES MAT TEX
845	OUTERWEAR KNIT NONELASTC	W 36819	406.7	W 20433	453.3	W 18827	502.4	W 25355	613.4	VET DESSOUS,ACCES BONNET
846	UNDER GARMENTS KNITTED	W 21545	350.2	W 25004	395.2	W 25269	472.9	W 47535	543.8	SOUS VETS DE BONNETERIE
8462	— OF COTTON NON ELASTIC	W 18274	250.6	W 21107	278.1	W 17306	278.5	W 21091	314.9	SOUS–VET BONNET COTON
851	*FOOTWEAR	W 22787	300.8	W 24886	341.9	W 30630	389.4	W 32128	484.3	CHAUSSURES
85102	FOOTWEAR LEATHER	W 16877	241.5	W 17731	272.9	W 22733	303.5	W 22070	358.8	CHAUS SEMELLES EN CUIR
87	PRECISION INSTRUMNTS NES		1520.8		1696.3		1944.7		2053.8	INSTRUM,APPAR SCIENT NDA
872	MEDICAL INSTRUMENTS NES	W 12414	430.1	W 13763	450.3	W 13874	516.6	W 12160	582.1	INSTR,APP MEDIC–CHIR NDA
87202	OTH MEDICAL INSTRUMENTS	W 10923	384.3	W 12314	406.8	W 12334	466.7	W 10521	518.7	INSTRUM,APP MEDECINE
874	MEASURNG,CONTROLNG INSTR	W 19069	972.4	W 18692	1096.4	W 19939	1249.0	W 20064	1288.7	INSTRUMENTS DE MESURE
8742	MEASUR,DRAW ETC INST,PTS	W 5282	250.6	W 5490	300.6	W 5762	320.4	W 5794	330.7	INST DESSIN,TRACAGE,PCS
8748	ELEC MEAS,CONTRL EQU NES	W 3088	293.4	W 2724	301.7	W 2153	309.2	W 2347	318.1	APP ELEC ELECTRO MESURE
87483	OTH ELCTRNC MEAS ETC EQU	W 2448	266.3	W 2233	268.3	W 1671	266.6	W 1816	276.0	AUT APP ELECTRO DE MESURE
88	PHOTO EQU,OPTICL GDS ETC		962.8		1037.6		1216.8		1310.7	APP,FOURN PHOTO,OP,MONTR
882	PHOTO,CINEMA SUPPLIES	W 29815	337.9	W 34195	350.7	W 37584	422.5	W 36364	432.8	PRODUITS PHOTO,CINEMA
8822	PHOTO FILM EXC DEV CINMA	W 19376	254.4	W 22594	263.4	W 24372	315.7	W 22069	324.0	PLAQUES,PELLICULES,FILMS
885	WATCHES AND CLOCKS		330.2		374.5		435.3		444.0	HORLOGERIE
8851	WATCHES,MOVEMENTS,CASES		272.6		305.8		354.7		355.3	MONTRES,MOUVEMENTS,BOITES
88511	WATCHES		261.0		295.0		341.5		343.3	MONTRES POCHE,BRACELET
89	MISC MANUFCTRD GOODS NES		3505.1		3596.6		3511.2		4221.8	ART MANUFACTURES DIVERS
892	PRINTED MATTER	W 51167	382.1	W 68537	374.7	W 53932	445.6	W 55356	472.3	IMPRIMES
893	ARTICLES OF PLASTIC NES		660.3		801.9		1064.8		1189.8	OUVRAGES EN MAT DIVIS 58
8939	MISC PLASTIC ARTICLES	W 131915	508.6	W 153050	588.2	W 175318	787.3	W 185987	882.7	ART DIVERS EN MAT DIV 58
89399	OTHR PLASTC ARTICLES NES	W 92950	478.0	W 116383	551.0	W 161930	738.4	W 166271	823.2	AUT OUV MAT DIV 58
894	TOYS,SPORTING GOODS,ETC	W 72499	691.6	W 83731	701.8	W 70666	558.9	W 87648	838.7	VOITURES ENFANTS,JOUETS
8942	TOYS,INDOOR GAMES ETC	W 55992	530.0	W 62313	510.8	W 48634	382.5	W 64353	598.7	JOUETS,JEUX ETC
896	WORKS OF ART ETC		568.7		464.2		100.5		104.5	OBJETS D'ART
89601	HAND PAINTINGS ETC NES		512.8		405.8		77.5		47.9	TABLEAUX,PEINTURES
898	MUSICAL INSTRUMENTS,PTS	W 27156	487.1	W 24038	490.2	W 23230	559.8		638.8	INSTRUMENTS DE MUSIQUE
8983	SOUND RECRDNG TAPE,DISCS	W 23554	433.1	W 20771	431.5	W 19286	495.1	W 20907	571.5	SUPPORTS SON POUR 763
89832	RECORDED DISCS,TAPES ETC	W 8460	235.0	W 8560	279.7	W 6168	333.8	W 8436	426.1	DISQUES,PHONO,BANDES
899	OTHER MANUFACTURED GOODS		382.9		416.2		424.8		523.0	AUT ART MANUF DIVERS NDA
9	GOODS NOT CLASSD BY KIND		219.4		320.4		480.6		533.8	ART TRANSACT NON CLASSES

5. Special Exports F.O.B. by Commodities according to the S.I.T.C. (Rev. 2) in million U.S. Dollars
Exportations Spéciales F.O.B. par Produits d'après la C.T.C.I. (Rév. 2) en millions de Dollars E.U.

SITC CTCI	COMMODITY	1993		1994		1995		1996		PRODUIT
		QUANTITY QUANTITE	VALUE VALEUR	QUANTITY QUANTITE	VALUE VALEUR	QUANTITY QUANTITE	VALUE VALEUR	QUANTITY QUANTITE	VALUE VALEUR	
	ALL COMMODITIES		60968.6		73188.0		89616.2		101592.4	TOUS PRODUITS
0	FOOD AND LIVE ANIMALS		7951.8		9471.9		11486.3		12802.5	ALIMENTS,ANIMAUX VIVANTS
01	MEAT AND PREPARATIONS		359.5		500.7		728.8		1027.4	VIANDES ET PREPARATIONS
011	MEAT FRESH,CHILLD,FROZEN		287.2		390.7	W 221550	576.8	W 319531	822.5	VIANDES FRAICHES,REF,CONGE
0113	PIG MEAT FRESH,CHLD,FRZN	W 45865	90.2	W 83067	164.5	W 101126	251.9	W 161021	437.2	VIANDE DE PORC
02	DAIRY PRODCTS,BIRDS'EGGS		159.9		219.1		316.6		357.6	PRODUITS LAITIERS,OEUFS
03	FISH AND PREPARATIONS		752.1		1004.1		1178.5		1430.1	POISSONS ET PREPARATIONS
034	FISH,FRESH,CHILLED,FROZN	W 179461	323.2	W 251100	450.7	W 271120	552.1	W 311340	667.3	POISSON FRAIS, REFRIG,CONG
0342	FISH FROZEN,EXCL FILLETS	W 131958	203.0	W 193885	292.0	W 203737	357.7	W 214922	383.2	POISSONS CONGELES
036	SHELL FISH FRESH,FROZEN	W 104649	238.2	W 106195	324.5	W 114045	317.8	W 139323	433.9	CRUSTACES,MOLLUSQUES
04	CEREALS AND PREPARATIONS		573.7		682.3		721.7		830.5	CEREALES ET PRODUITS
048	CEREAL ETC PREPARATIONS	W 107259	144.3	W 172934	203.6	W 213152	280.1	W 247074	342.0	PREPTNS A BASE CEREALES
05	VEGETABLES AND FRUIT		5335.7		5922.3		7044.7		7442.4	LEGUMES ET FRUITS
054	VEG ETC FRSH,SMPLY PRSVD	W 2137527	1737.2	W 2576603	1951.5		2475.1		2596.9	LEGUMES FRAIS,CONG,SECS
0544	TOMATOES FRESH	W 545496	420.7	W 686249	536.0	W 720753	636.4	W 751221	661.7	TOMATES FRAICHES
0545	OTHER FRESH VEGETABLES	W 1250356	1101.6	W 1470674	1130.0	W 1638248	1428.6	W 1866034	1606.8	AUTRES LEGUMES FRAIS,REF
05459	FRESH VEGETABLES NES	W 1034815	1005.0	W 1208489	1017.5	W 1352843	1299.1	W 1572563	1481.7	LEGUMES FRAIS,REFRI NDA
056	VEGTBLES ETC PRSVD,PREPD	W 225870	417.5	W 265456	490.4	W 241441	511.6	W 672547	527.7	CONSERVES DE LEGUMES
0565	VEGTBLES PRSVD,PREPD NES	W 214815	394.0	W 250839	463.7	W 226116	482.6	W 663166	502.9	LEGUMES PREPARES CONSERVE
05659	OTH VEG PRESVD,PREPD NES	W 210734	382.7	W 243180	447.5	W 218965	466.7	W 627862	479.8	LEGUM PREPAP,CONSERV NDA
057	FRUIT,NUTS,FRESH,DRIED	W 4096002	2754.3	W 4205121	3033.3	W 4193686	3518.7		3763.8	FRUITS FRAIS OU SECS
0571	ORANGES, MANDARINS ETC	W 2556906	1445.3	W 2592324	1537.6	W 2469240	1786.0	W 2301077	1876.2	ORANGES,MAND,CLEMENTINES
05711	ORANGES,FRESH OR DRIED	W 1415957	598.9	W 1358746	621.9	W 1361261	792.3	W 1215713	800.7	ORANGES FRAICHES,SECHEES
05712	MANDARINS ETC FRESH, DRY	W 1140950	846.4	W 1233578	915.8	W 1107979	993.8	W 1085363	1075.5	MANDARINES,CLEMENTINES
0572	LEMONS,GRAPEFRUIT ETC	W 472722	220.3	W 374855	222.6	W 347428	235.4	W 376956	287.6	AUTRES AGRUMES FRAIS,SECS
05721	LEMONS,LIMES,FRESH,DRIED	W 457253	213.6	W 356087	214.0	W 324253	223.3	W 358764	278.2	CITRONS ET LIMES
0577	NUTS EDIBLE,FRESH,DRIED	W 47941	207.2	W 44510	195.9	W 34593	175.0		249.7	FRUITS A COQUES
0579	FRUIT FRESH OR DRIED NES	W 857319	755.6	W 982809	898.7	W 1066487	1063.9	W 1176585	1095.9	FRUITS FRAIS,SECS NDA
05793	STONE FRUIT FRESH NES	W 208147	223.1	W 234393	260.3	W 196237	280.5	W 232074	303.3	FRUITS A NOYAU NDA FRAIS
05794	BERRIES FRESH	W 123687	223.7	W 159917	262.1	W 173387	327.1	W 159550	304.7	BAIES FRAICHES
05798	OTHER FRESH FRUIT	W 447331	238.9	W 479792	280.2	W 590755	356.0	W 663300	376.9	AUTRES FRUITS FRAIS
058	FRUIT PRESERVED,PREPARED	W 487643	426.8	W 540063	447.3	W 525456	539.5	W 587653	554.1	CONSERVES DE FRUITS
0589	FRUIT PREPRD,PRESRVD,NES	W 225760	215.9	W 256381	227.1	W 253073	284.8	W 311281	296.2	FRUITS PREPARES CONSERV
05899	FRUIT,NUTS NES,PRESERVED	W 222483	204.2	W 252836	214.3	W 248133	266.0	W 304717	273.9	FRUITS PREP CONSERV NDA
06	SUGAR AND PREPS,HONEY		227.9		367.1		480.1		475.9	SUCRES ET PRODUITS
062	SUGAR CANDY NON–CHOCLATE	W 38794	139.1	W 69099	219.5	W 79467	292.3	W 73768	294.1	SUCRERIES
07	COFFEE,TEA,COCOA,SPICES		182.6		280.7		374.3		396.7	CAFE,THE,CACAO,EPICES
09	MISC EDIBLE PRODUCTS		177.8		199.8		271.5		351.9	PREP ALIMENTAIRES DIVERSES
098	EDIBLE PRODCTS,PREPS NES	W 83932	170.4	W 97779	194.8	W 117535	260.5	W 153638	342.2	PREP ALIMENTAIRES NDA
1	BEVERAGES AND TOBACCO		1006.3		1162.6		1353.5		1593.6	BOISSONS ET TABACS
11	BEVERAGES		964.1		1101.1		1250.2		1475.7	BOISSONS
112	ALCOHOLIC BEVERAGES	W 1073221	928.2	W 926141	1026.3	W 746804	1144.3	W 826349	1381.1	BOISSONS ALCOOLIQUES
1121	WINE OF FRESH GRAPES ETC	W 999306	796.2	W 835716	849.9	W 669296	992.5	W 740339	1164.2	VINS DE RAISINS FRAIS
11212	WINE OF FRESH GRAPES	W 952573	769.4	W 775146	805.8	W 626179	952.1	W 678789	1103.6	VINS DE MOUTS DE RAISINS
2	CRUDE MATERLS,EXCL FUELS		1190.1		1522.5		2078.7		2003.1	MAT BRUTES NON COMESTIBLES
251	*PULP AND WASTE PAPER	W 616421	206.9	W 749961	319.3	W 699525	539.1	W 717295	325.7	PATES A PAPIER,DECHETS
2517	SODA,SULPHATE WOOD PULP	W 563293	186.6	W 688785	286.3	W 617524	481.6	W 627905	277.3	PATES CHIMIQUES AU SULFATE
25172	— BLEACHED,NONDISSOLVNG	W 563269	186.6	W 688693	286.2	W 617344	481.4	W 627905	277.3	PATES BLANCHIES
27	CRUDE FERTLZR,MINRLS NES		246.9		294.5		353.7		412.8	ENGRAIS MINERAUX BRUTS
28	METALLIFEROUS ORES,SCRAP		194.2		202.5		259.2		306.7	MINERAIS METAL,DECHETS
29	CRUDE ANIMAL,VEG MAT NES		218.4		274.3		370.1		348.8	MATIERES BRUTES ANIM,VEGET
292	CRUDE VEG MATERIALS NES	W 51047	189.6	W 71759	241.0	W 80537	327.2	W 101839	295.1	MAT BRUTES VEGETALES NDA
3	MINERAL FUELS ETC		1765.4		1613.9		1596.0		2557.1	COMBUSTIBLES MINERAUX LUB
33	PETROLEUM AND PRODUCTS		1704.0		1566.2		1488.1		2427.9	PETROLE ET DERIVES
334	PETROLEUM PRODUCTS,REFIN	MW 11502	1470.4	MW 10036	1308.9	W 8241197	1245.6	MW 12040	2196.6	PRODUITS RAFFINES
3341	GASOLINE,OTH LIGHT OILS	W 2824659	487.5	W 2828129	459.3			W 1852123	372.4	ESSENCES POUR MOTEURS
33411	MOTOR,AVIATION SPIRIT	W 1497115	269.8	W 1777560	298.5			W 1379479	276.5	ESSENCES MOTEURS D'AVIONS
33419	OTH LIGHT PETROLEUM OILS	W 1327544	217.8	W 1050569	160.9			W 461920	93.1	AUTRES HUILES LEGERES
3343	GAS OILS	W 1541595	251.3	W 1471657	209.3			W 1621684	321.8	GAS OILS
3344	FUEL OILS,NES	W 6049537	482.4	W 4816707	415.9			W 5056282	594.6	FUEL OILS
3345	LUBS,PETROLEUM OILS NES	W 390906	116.0	W 278142	116.3			W 2730248	761.6	HUILES LUBRIFIANTES
33451	LUBS(HIGH PETR CONT) ETC	W 377162	96.6	W 257685	89.5			W 2700064	716.7	HUILES LUBRIF,H LOURDES
335	RESIDUAL PETRLM PROD NES	W 1915764	233.6	W 1756681	244.3	W 1412358	240.4	W 1298500	231.3	PRODUITS RESIDUELS NDA
4	ANIMAL,VEGETABLE OIL,FAT		721.5		932.9		966.9		1308.8	HUILES,GRAISSES ANIM,VEG
42	FIXED VEGETABLE OIL,FAT		696.4		899.6		924.3		1244.4	HUILES VEGETALES FIXES
423	FIXED VEG OILS,SOFT		688.8		865.5	W 537669	887.1	W 424548	1203.6	HUILES VEGET DOUCES FIXES
4235	OLIVE OIL	W 219468	575.6	W 266441	749.9	W 175907	638.9	W 213804	1073.1	HUILE D'OLIVE
5	CHEMCLS,RELATED PROD NES		4619.6		5894.5		7424.8		7875.7	PRODUITS CHIMIQUES
51	ORGANIC CHEMICALS		943.9		1186.8		1374.4		1424.3	PROD CHIMIQ ORGANIQUES
514	NITROGEN–FNCTN COMPOUNDS	W 25016	149.6	W 38575	236.9	W 45499	299.6	W 51970	347.4	COMPOSES FONCT AZOTEES
515	ORG–INORG COMPOUNDS ETC	W 88174	318.5	W 84661	337.3	W 65610	285.5	W 82676	360.3	COMPOSES ORGANO–MINERAUX
5156	HETEROCYCLIC CMPDS ETC	W 67343	250.2	W 61017	259.2	W 40130	195.1	W 54296	256.2	COMPOSES HETEROCYCLIQUES
51569	OTH HETEROCYC CMPDS,ETC	W 15974	195.2	W 19093	214.6	W 9361	144.4	W 7062	189.3	AUT COMP HETEROCYCLIQUES
52	INORGANIC CHEMICALS		308.0		350.8		491.9		482.4	PROD CHIM INORGANIQUES
523	OTHR INORG CHEMICALS ETC	W 956538	201.0	W 1046322	213.5	W 1145349	263.9	W 1215402	297.7	AUT PRODUITS CHIMIQUES INORG
53	DYES,TANNING,COLOUR PROD		518.0		607.9		740.9		837.0	PROD TEINTURE,COLORANTS
533	PIGMENTS,PAINTS,ETC	W 292737	348.2	W 419414	432.1	W 506438	553.3	W 1321571	619.7	PIGMENTS,PEINTURES,VERNIS
5335	GLAZES,DRIERS,PUTTY ETC	W 213387	197.5	W 326712	251.3	W 423436	340.9	W 1201450	366.5	PREPTNS COLOR UTILISES CERAM
53351	PREPRD PIGMENT,GLAZE ETC	W 201521	165.5	W 309741	211.8	W 367916	282.6	W 1154979	306.8	PIGMENTS OPACIFIANTS
541	*MEDICINAL,PHARM PRODUCT		837.1	MK 36094	1061.2	MK 42608	1164.9	MK 54918	1414.1	PROD MEDICINAUX PHARMACEUT
5413	ANTIBIOTICS IN BULK	K 3338040	332.8	K 3645875	365.3	K 4125162	407.4	K 5461947	455.3	ANTIBIOTIQUES NDA
54131	PENICILLINS AND DERIVTVS	K 2847230	193.4	K 3086077	210.0	K 3677091	262.3	K 3816079	260.4	PENICILLINES ET DERIVES
5417	MEDICAMENTS	MK 14856	378.5	MK 26100	536.3	MK 30963	567.8	MK 39795	708.3	MEDICAMENTS
54179	— CONTNG OTH SUBSTANCES	MK 12300	295.4	MK 21956	423.8	MK 25991	419.7	MK 35652	529.3	MED CONT AUT SUBSTANCES
55	PERFUME,CLEANING ETC PRD		467.3		625.7		825.7		935.1	PROD POUR PARFUM,TOILETTE
553	PERFUMERY,COSMETICS,ETC	W 35455	229.6	W 50001	292.3	W 58201	394.8	W 61267	445.8	PRODUITS DE PARFUMERIE
554	SOAP,CLEANSING ETC PREPS	W 161816	172.0	W 259712	255.1	W 300024	335.6	W 358381	381.3	SAVONS,PRODUITS DETERSIFS
58	PLASTIC MATERIALS ETC		1086.9		1429.6		2036.9		1912.9	MAT PLAST ARTIFICIELLES
582	PROD OF CONDENSATION ETC	W 218775	238.6	W 299550	311.9	W 330324	491.6	W 385104	564.2	PROD CONDENS,POLYCOND
583	POLYMERIZATION ETC PRODS	W 887228	805.6	W 1103927	1068.4		1489.0	W 1047759	1291.1	PROD POLYMERISATION
5831	POLYETHYLENE	W 352921	245.4	W 364815	275.4		387.4	W 328766	313.3	POLYETHYLENE
58311	— IN PRIMARY FORMS	W 337524	222.9	W 335951	241.0	W 334929	336.0	W 299113	261.0	POLYETHYLENE PRIMAIRES
5839	OTH POLYMRZTION ETC PROD	W 146167	224.6	W 220966	303.4	W 247744	419.2	W 209939	367.6	AUT PROD POLYMER COPOLYM
59	CHEMICAL MATERIALS NES		330.9		480.4		541.7		634.5	MAT PROD CHIMIQUES NDA
598	MISCEL CHEM PRODUCTS NES	W 219383	235.1	W 409806	365.3		372.3	W 326283	429.2	PROD DIV INDUST CHIM NDA
5989	CHEM PRODUCTS,PREPS NES	W 179495	198.0	W 212277	227.2	W 244959	313.2	W 255464	354.7	PROD PREP CHIMIQUES NDA
6	BASIC MANUFACTURES		12073.4		14295.6		17762.5		19394.4	ART MANUFACTURES
61	LEATHER,DRESSED FUR,ETC		510.7		627.3		686.3		836.0	CUIRS,PELLETERIES
611	LEATHER	W 16029	256.1	W 16104	310.1	W 16938	344.3	W 20692	427.3	CUIRS,PEAUX PREPARES
613	FUR SKINS TANNED,DRESSED	W 4534	191.7	W 4278	234.4	W 4117	242.3	W 4979	316.5	PELLETERIES
62	RUBBER MANUFACTURES NES		1134.2		1367.0		1676.1		1899.4	CAOUTCHOUC MANUFACTURE

5. Special Exports F.O.B. by Commodities according to the S.I.T.C. (Rev. 2) in million U.S. Dollars
Exportations Spéciales F.O.B. par Produits d'après la C.T.C.I. (Rév. 2) en millions de Dollars E.U.

SITC CTCI	COMMODITY	1993 QUANTITY QUANTITE	1993 VALUE VALEUR	1994 QUANTITY QUANTITE	1994 VALUE VALEUR	1995 QUANTITY QUANTITE	1995 VALUE VALEUR	1996 QUANTITY QUANTITE	1996 VALUE VALEUR	PRODUIT
625	RUBBER TYRES, TUBES ETC	W 276911	894.2	W 320077	1060.3	W 340439	1234.3	W 351098	1383.5	PNEUS CAOUTCHOUC VULCANISE
6251	TYRES NEW FOR MOTOR CARS	W 90487	393.7	W 103156	443.1	W 104847	497.1	W 127538	586.0	PNEUS POUR VOITURES
6252	TYRES,NEW,BUS OR LORRY	W 74143	250.6	W 89962	309.3	W 99698	363.5	W 105036	384.0	PNEUS POUR AUTOBUS,CAMIONS
6259	OTH TYRES,TYRE CASES,ETC	W 107171	220.0	W 122656	272.9	W 131002	331.0	W 113197	367.1	AUTRES PNEUS RECHAPES FLAPS
62599	TYRES NES,TYRE CASES,ETC	W 106144	215.8	W 121525	269.0	W 130068	327.2	W 112492	364.1	PNEUS,FLAPS
63	WOOD,CORK MANUFACTRS NES		315.1		373.3		466.1		556.9	OUVRAGES LIEGE ET BOIS
64	PAPER,PAPERBOARD AND MFR		883.2		1091.2		1530.9		1483.2	PAPIERS,CARTONS & OUVRAGES
641	PAPER AND PAPERBOARD	W 942027	637.2	W 1054458	776.8	W 1095197	1120.2	W 1225561	1026.7	PAPIERS ET CARTONS
6418	COATED ETC PAPER NES BLK	W 186929	181.9	W 234006	215.2	W 226075	326.3	W 152259	260.1	PAP,CARTONS COUCHES,ENDUITS
642	PAPER,ETC,PRECUT,ARTS OF	W 144924	246.0	W 182653	314.4	W 198050	410.7	W 234588	456.6	PAP,CARTONS DECOUPES
65	TEXTILE YARN,FABRICS,ETC		1587.3		1962.3		2616.7		2934.4	FILS,TISSUS,ARTICLES TEXTILE
651	TEXTILE YARN	W 137204	482.2	W 167013	623.7		786.8	W 169973	798.5	FILS TEXTILES
652	COTTON FABRICS,WOVEN	W 34263	221.9	W 37658	264.4	W 42364	337.6	W 46273	389.2	TISSUS DE COTON
6522	WOVEN COTTON BLEACHD,ETC	W 29982	202.7	W 31035	238.3	W 36933	307.5	W 43720	370.6	TISSUS COTON BLANCHIS ETC
653	WOVN MAN-MADE FIB FABRIC	W 22641	266.3	W 29239	340.4	W 36683	501.9	W 39359	579.2	TISSUS FIBRES SYNTH,ARTIF
657	SPECIAL TXTL FABRC,PRODS	W 33780	182.2		226.1		325.7		387.4	TISSUS SPECIAUX
66	NONMETAL MINERAL MFS NES		2103.4		2601.7		3161.3		3449.1	ART MIN NON METALLIQUES
661	LIME,CEMENT,BLDG PRODS	W 4243576	463.0	W 5719876	589.2	W 5772719	735.4	W 7227430	849.4	CHAUX,CIMENTS MAT CONSTR
6613	BUILDING STONE ETC WORKD	W 628453	327.9	W 746707	404.4	W 811877	525.2	W 846251	576.9	PIERRES A BATIR
662	CLAY,REFRACTORY BLDG PRD	W 2146326	936.0	W 2951531	1192.9	W 3092252	1426.5	W 3357981	1504.8	MAT CONST REFRACTAIRES
6624	BRICKS ETC NONREFRACTORY	W 2056558	881.2	W 2822366	1129.1	W 2938827	1349.2	W 3235602	1433.8	BRIQUES ETC CERAM NON REFR
66245	GLAZED CERAMIC SETTS ETC	W 1905537	843.5	W 2638670	1076.5	W 2773399	1295.9	W 3053850	1377.5	AUT CARREAUX CERAMIQUE
663	MINERAL MANUFCTURES NES	W 241405	213.7	W 343379	200.0	W 410918	271.2	W 414821	300.7	ART MIN MANUF NDA
664	GLASS	W 145889	211.4	W 248966	274.8	W 244275	339.1	W 299708	384.9	VERRE
665	GLASSWARE	W 208856	169.3	W 273931	222.1	W 194981	254.1	W 213217	267.7	OUVRAGES EN VERRE
67	IRON AND STEEL		2836.1		3258.4		3853.3		3838.3	FER ET ACIER
672	IRON,STEEL PRIMARY FORMS	W 755361	275.9	W 595774	322.0	W 391326	413.1	W 611556	438.2	LINGOTS FER,ACIER
6727	IRN,STL COIL FR REROLLNG	W 528925	223.1	W 486508	268.8	W 294669	269.7	W 258348	237.6	EBAUCHES POUR TOLES FER
673	IRON,STEEL SHAPES ETC	W 2909543	983.8	W 3006249	1077.4	W 2652753	1267.0	W 4362699	1167.6	BARRES,PROFIL FER,ACIER
6731	IRON,STEEL WIRE ROD	W 594379	191.2	W 535836	176.7	W 464840	196.3	W 695889	202.4	FIL MACHINE FER,ACIER
6732	IRON,STEEL BARS ETC	W 1389697	493.3	W 1587000	594.8	W 1278500	699.6	W 2390233	620.2	BARRES FER,ACIER
67326	IRN,OTH STL BARS HOTROLD	W 1180577	325.8	W 1321283	382.8	W 946636	325.2	W 1028501	310.7	BARRES PLEINES FER,ACIER
6733	IRON,STEEL PROFILES ETC	W 925466	299.5	W 883413	306.0	W 909413	371.2	W 1276578	345.2	PROFILES,PALPLAN FER,ACIER
67332	LARGE U,I,H SECTIONS ETC	W 742691	226.7	W 678457	226.5	W 738727	285.7	W 742349	258.9	PROFILES PLUS 80MM
674	IRN,STL UNIV,PLATE,SHEET	W 1539335	994.6	W 1713135	1164.3	W 1427295	1328.6	W 1623782	1333.6	LARGES PLATS,TOLES
6746	IRN,STL THIN PLATE,ROLLD	W 535962	408.9	W 647475	508.8	W 483061	592.4	W 491323	522.7	TOLES LAM MOINS 3MM
67463	— OF STAINLESS ETC STL	W 171292	251.6	W 200698	313.6	W 175295	421.0	W 201578	369.7	TOL ACIER INOX MOINS 3 MM
6749	OTH IRN,STL PLATES,SHEET	W 354527	207.2	W 490486	294.8	W 396999	295.2	W 460687	310.2	AUTRES TOLES FER,ACIER
67491	— OF IRON OR SIMPLE STL	W 339914	183.9	W 475458	271.8	W 386640	271.2	W 444483	280.4	AUT TOLES AUTRES ACIER FIN
678	IRON,STL TUBES,PIPES,ETC	W 351884	409.3	W 471091	433.4	W 425908	543.7	W 443121	590.7	TUBES,TUYAUX EN FONTE,FER
6782	IRON,STL SEAMLESS TUBES	W 163659	202.3	W 156481	165.5	W 167264	255.5	W 182000	314.1	TUBES,TUYAUX SANS SOUDURE
68	NON-FERROUS METALS		1067.1		1221.2		1502.7		1655.6	METAUX NON FERREUX
682	COPPER EXC CEMENT COPPER	W 142118	329.0	W 152307	380.5	W 137250	452.9	W 221606	591.8	CUIVRE
6822	COPPER,ALLOYS WORKED	W 58428	184.5	W 79599	234.1	W 90230	344.5	W 104494	340.2	CUIVRE,ALLIAGES OUVRES
684	ALUMINIUM	W 333094	446.9	W 472777	594.2	W 283038	789.6	W 317380	801.9	ALUMINIUM
6841	ALUMINIUM,ALLOYS,UNWRGHT	W 167767	215.4	W 146090	225.5	W 119714	250.5	W 136320	238.6	ALUMINIUM,ALLIAGES BRUTS
6842	ALUMINIUM,ALLOYS WORKED	W 165327	231.5	W 326687	368.7	W 163323	539.2	W 181060	563.3	ALUMINIUM,ALLIAGES OUVRE
69	METAL MANUFACTURES NES		1636.8		1793.7		2269.5		2742.0	ART MANUFACT EN METAL NDA
691	STRUCTURES AND PARTS NES	W 84622	257.2	W 101990	141.0	W 105362	188.0	W 142476	256.5	CONSTRUCT FER,ACIER,ALU
6911	STRUCTURES,PARTS IRN,STL	W 82305	240.1	W 98784	123.6	W 100114	166.1	W 138430	229.3	CONSTRUCT FER,ACIER,FONTE
695	TOOLS	W 18538	234.1	W 20557	302.7	W 25372	328.8	W 32010	413.2	OUTILS A MAIN
697	BASE MTL HOUSEHOLD EQUIP	W 42127	199.1	W 49798	216.9	W 55738	274.9	W 64165	321.0	ART MENAGE MET COMMUNS
699	BASE METAL MFRS NES	W 123816	546.1	W 170703	671.3	W 185853	873.8	W 221044	1030.9	ART MANUFACTURES MET NDA
6991	LOCKSMITHS WARES,ETC	W 23490	179.0	W 29976	222.6	W 35269	301.6	W 49341	369.9	ARTICLES DE SERRURERIE
7	MACHINES,TRANSPORT EQUIP		25356.9		30806.6		37969.6		43438.9	MACHINES MATERIEL TRANSPORT
71	POWER GENERATING EQUIPMT		1164.0		1435.4		1778.8		2477.8	MACHINES GENERATRICES
713	INTRNL COMBUS PSTN ENGIN	W 124862	749.1	W 115422	931.7	W 128877	1232.2	W 188939	1797.6	MOTEURS EXPL COMB INT, PIECE
7132	MOTOR VEHCL PSTN ENGINS	W 50742	446.0	W 60981	631.0	W 72271	881.7	W 97186	1332.0	MOTEURS EXPL POUR VEHICULES
7139	PISTON ENGINE PARTS NES	W 68479	229.0	W 51598	269.5	W 53542	308.6	W 86467	411.2	PIECES POUR 713.2,3,8
716	ROTATING ELECTRIC PLANT	W 21765	186.1	W 35980	260.6	W 30548	300.2	W 30089	316.4	APP ELECTR ROTATIFS,PIECES
72	MACHS FOR SPCL INDUSTRYS		975.1		1085.5		1334.1		1575.7	MAC SPECIALES POUR INDUST
724	TEXTILE,LEATHER MACHNRY	W 19750	207.9	W 21618	225.0	W 22945	275.4		275.8	MACH POUR INDUSTRIE TEXTILE
728	OTH MACHY FOR SPCL INDUS	W 37445	360.6	W 42986	393.3	W 58952	491.8	W 58798	578.8	AUT MACH IND PARTICULIERES
7284	MACHY FOR SPCL INDUS NES	W 15841	202.1	W 16069	209.5	W 20064	264.8	W 22556	329.4	MACH SPEC IND PARTICUL.
73	METALWORKING MACHINERY		418.3		504.3		655.6		804.7	MACH TRAVAIL DES METAUX
736	METALWORKING MACH-TOOLS	W 29039	286.2	W 37226	314.0	W 46590	455.3	W 56613	619.3	MACH-OUTILS TRAVAIL METAUX
74	GENRL INDUSTRL MACHY NES		2242.3		2445.6		3054.5		3620.0	MACH APP INDUSTRIE
741	HEATING,COOLING EQUIPMNT	W 47592	380.4	W 51193	428.0	W 60996	510.3	W 75377	628.4	MACH CHAUFFAGE,PIECES
742	PUMPS FOR LIQUIDS ETC	W 15524	168.4	W 20258	223.5	W 23910	272.3	W 22133	361.5	POMPES MOTO-POMPES
743	PUMPS NES,CENTRFUGES ETC	W 43195	305.2	W 55704	389.8	W 62371	479.5	W 65212	548.9	POMPES COMPRES,VENT ETC
744	MECHANICAL HANDLING EQU	W 63755	362.6	W 77212	388.5	W 92079	522.0	W 100064	591.2	EQUIP MANUTENTION PIECES
7442	LIFTING,LOADING MACH NES	W 30158	187.0	W 40021	206.2	W 45169	264.2	W 48626	295.7	APP LEVAGE,MANUTENTION
745	NONELEC MACHY,TOOLS NES	W 16539	232.4	W 18303	265.3	W 20044	342.8	W 23971	391.4	AUT MACH NON ELEC,PIECES
7452	OTH NONELEC MCHS,PTS NES	W 16286	227.4	W 17879	260.1	W 19687	337.0	W 23581	384.9	AUT MACH NON ELEC,PIECES
749	NONELEC MACH PTS,ACC NES	W 65605	793.5	W 70408	750.7	W 84812	927.8	W 100818	1098.9	PIECES MACH NON ELEC NDA
7492	COCKS,VALVES ETC NES	W 32262	477.6	W 26857	324.3	W 35676	427.8	W 41012	495.1	ART ROB,SIM POUR TUYAUX
75	OFFICE MACHNES,ADP EQUIP		1026.0		1215.2		1472.3		1617.0	MACH BUREAU TRAIT AUTOM
752	AUTOMTIC DATA PROC EQUIP	W 11508	661.5	W 13719	838.2	W 20072	1163.2	W 22038	1247.4	MACH TRAIT INFORMATION
7523	DIGITL CENTRL PROCESSORS	W 857	222.0	W 478	88.8	W 361	37.5	W 794	83.4	UNITES CENTRALES
7525	ADP PERIPHERAL UNITS	W 3861	217.1	W 11045	539.8	W 15574	775.5	W 18507	864.8	UNITES PERIPHERIQUES
759	OFFICE,ADP MCH PTS,ACCES	W 2752	323.4	W 2503	299.5	W 3111	226.8	W 4049	292.8	PIECES DU 751 ET 752
7599	ACCTG,ETC,ADP MCH PTS,AC	W 2206	308.2	W 2153	285.1	W 2588	208.6	W 3161	272.6	PIECES DU 751 ET 752
76	TELECOMM,SOUND EQUIPMENT		1260.4		1518.6		1996.4		2099.9	EQUIPMENT DE TELECOM
761	TELEVISION RECEIVERS	W 27961	414.6	W 37008	473.7	W 53501	708.7	W 67585	850.4	RECEPTEURS DE TELEVISION
7611	COLOUR TV RECEIVERS	W 27916	413.7	W 36882	471.0	W 53248	702.9	W 67299	844.6	RECEPTEURS COULEUR
764	TELECOM EQPT,PTS,ACC NES	W 19500	736.1	W 24194	920.9	W 29265	1133.5	W 31912	1078.4	EQUIP TELECOM,PIECES
7641	LINE TELEPHONE,ETC EQUIP	W 2822	276.5	W 4627	363.9	W 6943	569.0	W 4718	316.3	APP TELEPHON PAR FIL
7649	PTS NES OF EQUIPMT OF 76	W 8021	332.8	W 8966	421.4	W 9417	438.3	W 12060	562.1	PIECES DE LA DIV 76
76491	PTS NES OF APPAR OF 7641	W 3291	214.4	W 4313	299.9	W 3683	280.3	W 5435	426.4	PIECES POUR 764.1
77	ELECTRIC MACHNRY NES ETC		2651.6		3343.0		4097.4		4762.9	MACH APP ELECT NDA
772	SWITCHGEAR ETC,PARTS NES	W 19845	451.5	W 29075	569.0	W 36586	719.8	W 41980	822.8	APP COUPURE,SECT ETC
7721	SWITCHGEAR ETC	W 18308	373.4	W 27386	478.5	W 34849	602.8	W 39971	669.7	APP COUPURE,SECTIONMNT
773	ELECTR DISTRIBUTNG EQUIP	W 76883	482.4	W 85608	616.9	W 100374	766.3	W 101622	760.7	EQUIPMT DISTRIBUTION ELECT
7731	INSULATED WIRE,CABLE ETC	W 71868	434.6	W 79186	560.7	W 94062	694.9	W 93593	687.8	FILS,CABLES ISOLES ELECT
775	HOUSEHOLD TYPE EQUIP NES	W 112026	606.9	W 132320	738.5	W 145674	915.0	W 192989	1101.6	MACH,APP USAGE DOMESTQUE
7758	ELECTRO-THERMIC APPL NES	W 24702	168.4	W 26860	206.1	W 28437	249.2	W 38950	316.8	APP ELECTROTHERMIQ NDA
776	TRANSISTORS,VALVES,ETC	W 3073	180.8	W 7595	263.6	W 9712	298.0	W 11202	329.3	LAMPES,TUBES,VALVES
778	ELECTRICAL MACHINERY NES	W 121601	738.6	W 151706	897.7	W 186052	1138.7	W 216932	1359.9	AUTRES MACH ELECT NDA
7783	AUTOMOTIVE ELECTR EQUIP	W 26123	329.6	W 37350	425.9	W 42141	551.6	W 45580	661.3	EQUIP ELECT MOTEURS EXPL
77831	IGNITION,STARTING EQUIP	W 13249	179.3	W 18341	211.6	W 18330	277.9	W 16807	325.4	APP ELEC ALLUM,DEMARRAGE
77832	ELECT VEHICLE LGHTNG EQU	W 12874	150.4	W 19008	214.3	W 23811	273.7	W 28773	336.0	APP ELEC ECLAIR,SIGNAL AUTO

5. Special Exports F.O.B. by Commodities according to the S.I.T.C. (Rev. 2) in million U.S. Dollars
Exportations Spéciales F.O.B. par Produits d'après la C.T.C.I. (Rév. 2) en millions de Dollars E.U.

SITC CTCI	COMMODITY	1993		1994		1995		1996		PRODUIT
		QUANTITY QUANTITE	VALUE VALEUR	QUANTITY QUANTITE	VALUE VALEUR	QUANTITY QUANTITE	VALUE VALEUR	QUANTITY QUANTITE	VALUE VALEUR	
7788	OTH ELEC MACHY,EQUIP NES	W 32334	204.2	W 31445	222.1	W 49994	275.5	W 53516	341.0	AUT MACH APP ELEC NDA
78	ROAD VEHICLES		13330.3		17075.7		21534.8		23894.1	VEHICULES ROUTIERS
781	PASS MOTOR VEH EXC BUSES	W 1153019	9883.1	W 1394973	12296.6	W 1551532	15097.6	W 1693372	16023.9	AUTO TRANSPORT PERSONNES
782	LORRIES,SPCL MTR VEH NES	W 112575	723.4	W 165619	1150.0	W 191907	1365.2	W 270620	2162.4	VEHICULES SPECIAUX,MARCH
7821	LORRIES,TRUCKS	W 108079	696.8	W 160891	1114.3	W 188990	1337.0	W 266787	2107.5	VEHICULES TRANSP MARCHAND
783	ROAD MOTOR VEHICLES NES	W 19528	199.8	W 37886	345.5	W 128937	533.6	W 51111	457.0	VEHICULES ROUTIERS NDA
7832	TRACTORS FOR TR–TRAILERS	W 13872	137.3	W 30977	270.6	W 120127	448.3	W 40816	343.2	TRACTEURS ROUTIERS
784	MOTOR VEH PRTS,ACCES NES	W 549598	2284.6	W 720552	3011.8	W 843210	4186.1	W 911638	4818.3	PIECES 722,781,782,783
7849	OTHER MOTOR VEHCL PARTS	W 522393	2254.3	W 707717	2973.0	W 836365	4131.8	W 902434	4767.9	PIECES 722,781,782,783
785	CYCLES,ETC MOTRZD OR NOT	W 13493	203.3	W 14634	219.8	W 17919	264.0	W 19912	323.2	MOTOCYCLES SCOOTERS
79	OTHR TRANSPORT EQUIPMENT		2289.3		2183.8		2046.0		2587.3	AUTRE MATERIEL TRANSPORT
791	RAILWAY VEHICLES	W 28440	63.7	W 48571	246.3	W 16021	143.1	W 24651	223.2	VEHIC MAT CHEMINS DE FER
792	AIRCRAFT ETC	W 2674	1104.5	W 3169	1354.9		1037.8	W 2976	1306.7	APP NAVIGATION AERIENNE
7923	AIRCRFT NES2000–15000KG	W 137	153.3	W 397	349.9	W 187	202.5	W 242	181.7	AERODYNES 2000 A 15000 KG
7924	AIRCRFT NES OVER 15000KG	W 995	442.5	W 1291	507.7	W 527	318.9	W 1181	556.9	AERODYNES PLUS 15000 KG
7929	AIRCRAFT PARTS NES	W 1484	507.0	W 1447	490.5	W 1448	507.5	W 1503	556.2	PIECES DU 792
793	SHIPS AND BOATS ETC	W 645309	1121.1	W 381519	582.8	W 375450	865.1	W 307918	1057.5	NAVIRES BATEAUX,ETC
7932	SHIPS AND BOATS NES	W 569292	823.0	W 373060	556.8	W 299535	802.3	W 261613	699.8	NAVIRES ET BATEAUX
79322	TANKERS OF ALL KINDS	W 284508	393.5	W 24399	25.6	W 102802	259.7	W 138221	164.0	BATEAUX–CITERNES
79323	OTHER CARGO VESSELS	W 223282	215.0	W 305661	344.9	W 166260	216.0	W 96731	234.6	AUT BATEAUX TRANS MARCH
79324	FISHING VESSELS ETC	W 44591	197.3	W 28924	131.7	W 22761	78.3	W 19681	83.9	BATEAUX DE PECHE
7938	TUGS,SPECIAL VESSELS ETC	W 75894	293.2	W 6484	10.5	W 26244	52.9	W 43817	339.4	REMORQUEURS,BATEAUX SPEC
79382	SPECL PURPOSE VESSLS ETC	W 75435	282.5	W 6105	9.3	W 24224	38.2	W 41462	314.5	BAT–PHARES,–POMPES,DRAGUES
8	MISC MANUFACTURED GOODS		5405.8		6681.1		8125.9		9712.6	ART MANUFACTURES DIVERS
812	*PLUMBG,HEATNG,LGHTNG EQ	W 53573	262.5	W 73108	331.8	W 81373	447.3	W 89300	502.2	APPAR SANITAIRES CHAUFFAGE
8124	LIGHTING EQUIPMENT NES	W 16425	188.6	W 23946	235.1	W 30432	327.2	W 32987	362.8	APPAREILS ECLAIRAGE ETC
821	*FURNITURE,PARTS THEREOF	W 127838	552.6	W 184671	728.6	W 200001	1037.9	W 262726	1283.7	MEUBLES ET PIECES
8211	CHAIRS,SEATS AND PARTS	W 39488	165.6	W 45947	217.5	W 42622	327.5	W 52598	380.0	SIEGES ET PIECES
8219	FURNITURE AND PARTS NES	W 84568	351.8	W 132994	464.5	W 152273	652.0	W 203229	836.5	AUTRES MEUBLES ET PIECES
82192	WOOD FURNITURE NES	W 43552	218.1	W 78290	300.4	W 89755	431.9	W 123616	569.0	MEUBLES NDA EN BOIS
84	CLOTHING AND ACCESSORIES		697.4		835.1		1115.3		1377.8	VETEMENTS
842	MENS OUTERWEAR NOT KNIT	W 3704	140.8	W 3699	163.5	W 5530	231.2	W 7595	307.2	VET DESSUS POUR HOMMES
845	OUTERWEAR KNIT NONELASTC	W 5893	160.6	W 6242	188.7	W 6583	240.0	W 8812	306.7	VET DESSOUS,ACCES BONNET
851	*FOOTWEAR	W 59417	1214.7	W 87192	1649.2	W 81539	1871.1	W 90176	1985.7	CHAUSSURES
85102	FOOTWEAR LEATHER	W 55242	1146.0	W 80377	1548.9	W 73619	1741.5	W 80869	1849.2	CHAUS SEMELLES EN CUIR
87	PRECISION INSTRUMNTS NES		539.1		626.1		671.0		819.1	INSTRUM,APPAR SCIENT NDA
874	MEASURNG,CONTROLNG INSTR		412.2	W 10593	480.9	W 7825	496.1	W 9076	598.4	INSTRUMENTS DE MESURE
8743	GAS,LIQUID CONTROL INSTR	W 3101	221.9	W 3855	263.2	W 3699	255.9	W 3931	301.8	APP,INSTR MESURE FLUIDES
88	PHOTO EQU,OPTICL GDS ETC		205.0		238.0		262.9		305.8	APP,FOURN PHOTO,OP,MONTR
89	MISC MANUFCTRD GOODS NES		1859.0		2161.9		2574.0		3268.9	ART MANUFACTURES DIVERS
892	PRINTED MATTER	W 126786	613.4	W 165643	693.6	W 181469	825.0	W 219665	905.8	IMPRIMES
8921	PRINTED BOOKS,GLOBES,ETC	W 71866	377.1	W 100597	466.9	W 102907	525.6	W 126832	580.7	LIVRES,BROCHURES,CARTES
89211	PRINTED BOOKS,PAMPHLETS	W 71384	374.5	W 99397	462.0	W 101839	513.8	W 125786	572.7	LIVRES,BROCHURES
893	ARTICLES OF PLASTIC NES		403.7		506.8		727.3		950.3	OUVRAGES EN MAT DIVIS 58
8939	MISC PLASTIC ARTICLES	W 56034	276.4	W 71868	334.3	W 98307	467.2	W 126234	634.4	ART DIVERS EN MAT DIV 58
89399	OTHR PLASTC ARTICLES NES	W 53805	268.4	W 69253	325.1	W 94995	452.3	W 122906	617.2	AUT OUV MAT DIV 58
894	TOYS,SPORTING GOODS,ETC	W 43851	405.6	W 51063	412.0	W 47186	416.3	W 67934	600.3	VOITURES ENFANTS,JOUETS
8942	TOYS,INDOOR GAMES ETC	W 32196	289.4	W 37477	302.1	W 31096	303.0	W 47131	449.0	JOUETS,JEUX ETC
9	GOODS NOT CLASSD BY KIND		878.1		806.8		852.4		906.2	ART TRANSACT NON CLASSES
931	*SPECIAL TRANSACTIONS	W 1122343	750.8	W 1151863	588.9	W 1071192	624.6	W 2276906	694.9	TRANS.SPECIALES

FOOT NOTES – NOTES

TABLE 1 –
1 Values are in thousand million pesetas.
TABLEAU 1 –
1 Les valeurs sont exprimées en milliards de pesetas.

1. HISTORICAL SERIES, 1962–1997 GENERAL TRADE, IMPORTS C.I.F., EXPORTS F.O.B.
SERIES HISTORIQUES, 1962–1997 COMMERCE GENERAL, IMPORTATIONS C.A.F., EXPORTATIONS F.O.B

YEAR ANNEE	VALUE IN MILLION SRI LANKA RUPEES VALEUR EN MILLION SRI LANKA RUPEES MERCHANDISE –MARCHANDISE		GOLD –OR		CONVERSION FACTORS U.S. CENTS PER SRI LANKA RUPEE FACTEURS DE CONVERSION CENTS E.U. PAR SRI LANKA RUPEE		INDEX NUMBERS –INDICES QUANTUM		UNIT VALUE VALEUR UNITAIRE	
	IMPORTS	EXPORTS	IMPORTS	EXPORTS	IMPORTS	EXPORTS	IMPORTS	EXPORTS	IMPORTS	EXPORTS
1962	1660.00	1808.00	1.90		21.0000	21.0000				
1963	1490.00	1731.00	1.90		21.0000	21.0000				
1964	1975.00	1876.00	2.30		21.0000	21.0000				
1965	1474.00	1949.00	1.90		21.0000	21.0000				
1966	2028.00	1700.00	2.20		21.0000	21.0000				
1967	1738.00	1690.00			20.7030	20.6040				
1968	2173.00	2035.00			16.8010	16.8010				
1969	2543.00	1916.00			16.8010	16.8010				
1970	2313.00	2033.00			16.8010	16.8010				
1971	1986.00	1947.00			16.8024	16.8024				
1972	2064.00	2009.00			17.0176	16.8119				
1973	2715.00	2617.00			15.5567	15.6169				
1974	4554.00	3472.00			15.1098	15.0752				
1975	5251.00	3933.00			14.3028	14.2154				
1976	4689.00	4815.00			11.7836	11.7702				
1977	6007.00	6638.00			11.7093	11.4932				
1978	14663.00	13206.00			6.4034	6.4056				
1979	22560.00	15273.00			6.4205	6.4202				
1980	33637.00	17273.00			6.0511	6.0311	107	66	33	35
1981	35530.20	20199.10			5.2052	5.1702	97	69	39	38
1982	36875.40	21124.20			4.8040	4.8029	97	73	40	38
1983	42020.10	25182.70			4.2518	4.2330	106	69	42	48
1984	46913.30	37005.70			3.9335	3.9282	110	81	44	62
1985	49068.00	35035.00			3.6331	3.6398	105	83	48	55
1986	51281.50	34092.30			3.5666	3.5656	120	89	44	48
1987	59749.70	39860.59			3.3930	3.3826	106	87	53	60
1988	70320.40	47092.00			3.1436	3.1445	101	84	66	70
1989	75352.75	55511.17			2.7710	2.7545	95	86	79	83
1990	107729.00	76624.00			2.4961	2.4961	100	100	100	100
1991	126643.00	82225.01			2.4178	2.4178	114	104	104	102
1992	153555.00	107855.00			2.2826	2.2826	132	108	109	128
1993	193550.00	138175.00			2.0631	2.0631	154	124	115	140
1994	235576.00	158554.00			2.0237	2.0237	173	136	121	147
1995	272200.90	195117.00			1.9495	1.9464	178	145	140	169
1996	299424.00	226801.00			1.8074	1.8056	182	151	153	189
1997	344531.90	275741.90			1.6947	1.6922				

2. IMPORTS BY BROAD ECONOMIC CATEGORY AND EXPORTS BY INDUSTRIAL ORIGIN. (PERCENTAGE OF TOTAL VALUE)
IMPORTATIONS PAR CATEGORIES ECONOMIQUES ET EXPORTATIONS PAR BRANCHE D'ACTIVITE.(EN POURCENTAGE DE LA VALEUR TOTALE)

IMPORTS – IMPORTATIONS

	1988	1989	1990	1991	1992	1993	1994
TOTAL IMPORTS–IMPORTATIONS TOTALES	100.	100.	100.	100.	100.	100.	100.
1 FOOD BEV–ALIMENTATION BOISSONS	18.9	19.5	18.0	16.0	14.7	12.2	14.1
11 PRIMARY–PRODUITS DE BASE	9.4	7.9	6.3	6.6	5.4	3.1	5.9
111 FOR INDUSTRY–POUR L'INDUSTRIE	6.5	5.8	3.4	2.7	2.0	0.2	2.9
112 FOR HOUSEHOLDS–POUR LES MENAGES	3.0	2.2	2.9	3.8	3.4	2.8	2.9
12 PROCESSED–PRODUITS ELABORES	9.5	11.5	11.7	9.4	9.3	9.2	8.2
121 FOR INDUSTRY–POUR L'INDUSTRIE	3.9	3.0	6.2	4.7	4.1	4.8	4.8
122 FOR HOUSEHOLDS–POUR LES MENAGES	5.5	8.5	5.5	4.7	5.2	4.3	3.4
2 IND SUPPLIES–APPROV INDUSTRIELS	43.4	44.9	44.7	47.6	48.1	50.5	50.0
21 PRIMARY–PRODUITS DE BASE	4.2	6.2	5.1	4.7	4.8	5.9	5.3
22 PROCESSED–PRODUITS ELABORES	39.2	38.8	39.6	43.0	43.3	44.6	44.7
3 FUELS–COMBUSTIBLES	10.7	10.6	12.6	10.9	8.8	7.7	6.2
31 PRIMARY–PRODUITS DE BASE	9.6	7.5	10.9	8.6	4.9	5.8	5.0
32 PROCESSED–PRODUITS ELABORES	1.1	3.1	1.7	2.3	3.9	1.9	1.2
321 MOTOR SPIRIT–ESSENCE	0.0	0.0					
322 OTHER–AUTRES	1.1	3.1	1.7	2.3	3.9	1.9	1.2
4 MACHINERY–EQUIPEMENT	11.8	10.3	10.7	10.0	12.6	12.4	12.6
41 CAPITAL EQUIPMENT–MACHINES	10.2	8.8	9.2	8.5	10.9	10.9	10.9
42 PARTS–PIECES ACCESSOIRES	1.6	1.5	1.5	1.5	1.7	1.6	1.6
5 TRANSPORT–TRANSPORT	8.0	8.3	8.3	9.3	8.3	9.7	9.9
51 PASSENGER CARS–AUTOMOBILES	1.8	1.7	1.3	0.7	1.0	1.0	1.9
52 OTHER–AUTRES	3.1	3.7	4.4	5.6	4.7	4.6	4.1
521 INDUSTRIAL–INDUSTRIELS	2.7	2.5	3.0	4.6	4.1	4.0	3.4
522 NON INDUSTRIAL–NON INDUSTRIEL	0.4	1.2	1.4	1.0	0.6	0.6	0.6
53 PARTS–PIECES ACCESSOIRES	3.1	2.9	2.7	3.0	2.6	4.0	3.9
6 CONSUM GOODS–BIENS CONSOMMATION	6.9	6.2	5.5	6.0	7.3	7.2	7.0
61 DURABLE–DURABLES	2.7	2.3	1.4	1.8	2.5	2.4	2.0
62 SEMI DURABLE–SEMI DURABLES	2.0	2.1	1.7	2.2	2.3	2.6	2.6
63 NON DURABLE–NON DURABLES	2.3	1.8	2.3	2.0	2.5	2.1	2.5
7 GOODS NES–BIENS NDA	0.3	0.3	0.3	0.2	0.2	0.3	0.2

EXPORTS – EXPORTATIONS

	1988	1989	1990	1991	1992	1993	1994
TOTAL EXPORTS–EXPORTATIONS TOTALES	100.	100.	100.	100.	100.	100.	100.
1 AGRICULTURE	43.9	39.9	38.5	33.1	25.5	24.1	23.1
2 MINING QUARRY–INDUS EXTRACTIVES	9.0	10.8	9.4	6.6	7.0	7.8	7.3
3 MANUFACTURING–IND MANUFACTUR	47.0	49.4	52.1	60.3	67.5	68.2	69.6
31 FOOD BEV TOBACCO–ALIM BOISS TAB	1.2	2.8	1.2	1.1	1.0	1.2	1.6
32 TEXTILES–INDUSTRIES TEXTILES	31.9	33.2	35.5	43.7	52.6	52.6	52.6
33 WOOD & PRODUCTS–BOIS & PRODUITS	0.4	0.5	0.6	1.0	0.6	0.6	0.7
34 PAPER & PRODUCTS–PAPIER & PRODT	0.1	0.1	0.1	0.3	0.3	0.5	0.5
35 CHEMICALS–INDUSTRIES CHIMIQUES	4.5	4.4	4.4	4.1	3.5	3.9	4.0
36 NON METAL MIN–MIN NON METAL	0.8	0.8	0.8	1.2	1.2	1.2	1.3
37 BASIC METAL–IND METAL BASE	0.0	0.1	0.1	0.1	0.1	0.1	0.1
38 METAL MANUF–MANUF METAL	3.0	3.1	4.6	4.6	3.1	3.2	3.6
39 OTH MANUF IND–AUTRES MANUF	5.1	4.4	4.9	4.3	5.0	4.9	5.2

3. TRADE BY PRINCIPAL COUNTRIES OF ORIGIN AND DESTINATION (VALUE IN MILLION U.S. DOLLARS)
ECHANGES SELON LES PRINCIPAUX PAYS D'ORIGINE ET DE DESTINATION (VALEUR EN MILLIONS DE DOLLARS EU)

COUNTRIES–PAYS	GENERAL IMPORTS C.I.F. IMPORTATIONS GENERALES C.A.F				
	1990	1991	1992	1993	1994
World	2634.1	3089.7	3419.2	3742.9	4483.4
Africa	116.8	116.7	78.0	75.1	84.4
Americas	251.4	215.5	219.7	168.6	391.1
– Northern America	226.7	190.5	180.7	145.7	298.5
– LAIA	8.4	24.8	38.1	17.7	73.9
– CACM	11.8	0.0	0.0	0.0	17.1
– Caribbean	4.5	0.1	0.9	0.7	1.5
– Rest of America	0.0	0.1	0.0	4.5	0.2
Asia excl fmr USSR	1720.5	2140.9	2394.7	2635.2	2960.5
– Middle East	316.7	275.1	203.9	203.5	248.1
Asia former USSR				0.4	0.0
Europe excl fmr USSR	468.0	542.9	618.9	750.8	898.4
– European Union	410.9	483.1	537.8	656.1	804.0
– Eastern Europe	24.2	29.4	43.6	53.7	24.8
– Rest of Europe	32.9	30.4	37.5	41.1	69.6
Europe former USSR	3.5	3.7	19.8	10.0	8.0
Oceania	73.2	69.2	87.2	102.0	140.2
Other	0.7	0.9	1.0	0.9	0.8
Japan/Japon	325.4	357.9	415.8	451.2	526.5
India/Inde	118.1	220.1	302.0	341.8	404.4
China, Hong Kong SAR	120.3	212.7	241.1	311.5	316.5
Korea, Republic of	127.9	219.1	209.6	260.8	326.2
Other Asia n.e.s.	155.8	207.4	214.1	225.0	250.2
USA/Etats–Unis d'Amer	207.7	174.5	159.4	130.9	284.7
United Kingdom	146.0	167.3	174.2	186.0	249.6
Singapore/Singapour	102.5	135.0	237.7	207.3	234.0
Malaysia/Malaisie	114.4	139.9	127.8	171.1	181.2
Iran (Islamic Rep of)	222.3	144.8	117.1	95.8	90.9
China/Chine	121.2	101.5	121.0	149.5	156.4
Germany/Allemagne		101.9	127.4	137.9	169.8
Thailand/Thaïlande	85.1	99.1	96.9	108.9	122.6
Belgium–Luxembourg	56.7	54.0	77.8	116.5	127.1
So. African Customs Un	83.4	87.7	71.4	48.6	52.1
Indonesia/Indonésie	39.4	41.1	65.2	85.8	84.5
Pakistan	50.8	73.7	66.0	55.1	60.7
Australia/Australie	43.4	36.6	50.9	59.6	91.8
Netherlands/Pays–Bas	19.8	48.1	42.7	55.1	70.8
France, Monaco	42.4	34.8	43.3	50.4	55.2
United Arab Emirates	15.0	41.4	25.4	50.5	72.7
New Zealand	29.5	32.3	36.0	42.0	48.2
Switzerland,Liechtenst.	18.2	25.9	32.4	36.5	60.3
Italy/Italie	18.9	19.3	26.1	43.5	47.8
Romania/Roumanie	11.5	18.3	31.6	43.6	8.0
Sweden/Suède	15.9	19.7	20.7	24.3	24.3
Turkey/Turquie	19.0	23.9	9.2	18.4	31.1
Viet Nam	11.9	28.1	35.0	16.7	2.6
Saudi Arabia	32.8	9.4	16.1	11.3	23.4
Canada	19.0	16.0	21.2	14.8	13.7
Former Fed Rep Germany	83.9				
Brazil/Brésil	2.6	7.1	14.4	8.0	43.6
Denmark/Danemark	8.0	7.7	8.4	20.6	19.4
Egypt/Egypte	1.4	20.2	1.9	16.7	16.9
Maldives	6.2	10.1	9.2	10.9	14.9
Bahrain/Bahreïn	10.9	4.1	14.7	5.8	7.4
Bangladesh	8.9	3.9	14.9	6.9	8.3
Nepal/Népal	0.0	5.3	23.4	12.2	0.9
Chile/Chili	4.1	7.0	10.6	5.6	12.5
Russian Federation			19.8	9.3	7.5

COUNTRIES–PAYS	EXPORTS EXPORTATIONS ES F.O.B.				
	1990	1991	1992	1993	1994
Monde	1912.6	1987.2	2454.0	2846.9	3209.7
Afrique	104.6	83.8	68.9	65.4	88.3
Amériques	560.4	629.2	921.0	1084.8	1208.0
– Amérique du Nord	521.6	591.0	876.8	1040.0	1165.7
– ALAI	30.6	35.9	39.6	38.1	38.1
– MCAC	0.9	1.0	1.6	2.1	1.8
– Caraïbes	6.9	0.6	0.4	1.2	0.5
– Autre Amérique	0.4	0.6	2.7	3.5	2.0
Asie anc. URSS exclus	549.1	582.9	508.7	601.5	712.0
– Moyen–Orient	251.0	260.5	196.0	224.5	228.3
Asie ancienne URSS				0.4	0.2
Europe anc. URSS exclus	552.4	595.0	865.5	951.4	1069.6
– Union Européenne	505.9	564.2	825.8	906.8	1023.2
– Europe de l'Est	22.9	9.6	18.3	17.5	20.0
– Autre de l'Europe	23.5	21.2	21.4	27.2	26.4
Europe ancienne URSS	40.5	11.5	8.8	49.9	37.2
Océanie	30.7	29.1	30.5	33.8	34.5
Autre	74.9	55.8	50.6	59.7	59.9
USA/Etats–Unis d'Amer	492.6	559.0	838.0	1003.8	1115.0
United Kingdom	115.1	126.2	170.3	202.9	285.3
Germany/Allemagne		148.9	211.9	226.9	222.4
Belgium–Luxembourg	96.9	78.9	135.0	176.3	189.1
Japan/Japon	102.4	101.6	128.1	147.5	165.2
Netherlands/Pays–Bas	48.6	59.0	97.8	107.3	112.1
France, Monaco	43.7	63.5	90.1	85.9	85.7
Singapore/Singapour	49.5	67.5	33.3	48.5	76.4
Iran (Islamic Rep of)	64.7	78.0	48.3	20.2	16.8
Areas n.e.s.	0.0	55.8	50.6	59.7	59.9
United Arab Emirates	27.8	36.7	27.6	66.2	62.4
Italy/Italie	36.6	37.1	47.4	42.4	56.1
Egypt/Egypte	59.1	36.4	35.0	25.6	32.1
Canada	29.0	32.0	38.8	36.2	50.7
Saudi Arabia	42.3	38.4	36.6	29.3	39.6
Jordan/Jordanie	16.4	56.3	31.1	41.4	39.8
Pakistan	32.5	32.0	28.6	35.3	43.4
Syrian Arab Republic	31.2	16.7	22.0	31.4	37.1
Australia/Australie	24.2	24.5	24.1	27.2	28.1
Former Fed Rep Germany	126.7				
China, Hong Kong SAR	17.1	14.9	24.3	32.0	35.6
Korea, Republic of	5.1	11.3	27.7	26.7	38.9
Thailand/Thaïlande	21.7	14.0	17.3	21.5	31.1
Russian Federation			8.8	48.2	35.8
Mexico/Mexique	18.1	20.3	19.8	18.3	15.0
Libyan Arab Jamahiriya	22.8	28.1	11.2	15.4	12.8
India/Inde	20.6	12.6	11.5	19.7	23.7
Sweden/Suède	10.0	13.7	19.4	16.3	19.2
Switzerland,Liechtenst.	13.9	12.1	12.7	17.2	20.2
Special Categories	74.9				
Spain/Espagne	10.0	12.4	16.4	15.8	15.8
So. African Customs Un	12.3	9.8	12.1	11.1	13.7
Poland/Pologne	8.2	5.5	14.8	13.4	15.8
Former USSR/Anc. URSS	40.5	11.5			
Maldives	7.4	11.2	8.6	8.8	10.1
Denmark/Danemark	6.6	10.2	10.6	8.3	9.7
Israel/Israël	6.0	6.7	7.7	6.3	16.4
Malaysia/Malaisie	2.7	26.6	4.5	3.3	5.8
Iraq	38.8	1.3	0.0	0.1	0.0
Other Asia n.e.s.	8.5	7.9	6.1	6.1	10.6

(VALUE AS PERCENTAGE OF WORLD TOTAL)(VALEURS EN POURCENTAGE DU TOTAL MONDIAL)

	1985	1986	1987	1988	1989	1990	1991	1992	1993	1994
Africa	2.0	5.5	5.4	5.8	6.0	4.4	3.8	2.3	2.0	1.9
Americas	10.6	10.2	7.8	10.1	8.3	9.5	7.0	6.4	4.5	8.7
– Northern America	9.0	8.4	6.7	8.8	7.3	8.6	6.2	5.3	3.9	6.7
– LAIA	1.0	1.0	0.7	1.0	1.0	0.3	0.8	1.1	0.5	1.6
– CACM	0.4	0.6	0.2	0.2	0.0	0.4	0.0	0.0	0.0	0.4
– Caribbean	0.1	0.0	0.1	0.2	0.0	0.2	0.0	0.0	0.0	0.0
– Rest of America	0.0	0.1	0.1	0.0	0.0	0.0	0.0	0.0	0.1	0.0
Asia excl fmr USSR	64.1	61.7	63.4	61.2	62.1	65.3	69.3	70.0	70.4	66.0
– Middle East	21.2	9.4	11.6	9.6	9.5	12.0	8.9	6.0	5.4	5.5
Asia former USSR									0.0	0.0
Europe excl fmr USSR	18.7	18.9	20.9	20.6	20.5	17.8	17.6	18.1	20.1	20.0
– European Union	17.2	16.9	19.4	19.0	17.8	15.6	15.6	15.7	17.5	17.9
– Eastern Europe	0.5	0.3	0.3	0.6	1.6	0.9	1.0	1.3	1.4	0.6
– Rest of Europe	1.1	1.8	1.2	1.0	1.2	1.3	1.0	1.1	1.1	1.6
Europe former USSR	0.4	1.1	0.6	0.1	0.1	0.1	0.1	0.6	0.3	0.2
Oceania	4.2	2.6	1.9	2.2	2.9	2.8	2.2	2.6	2.7	3.1
Other	0.0	0.0	0.0	0.0	0.0	0.0	0.0	0.0	0.0	0.0
Japan/Japon	15.6	17.1	15.0	13.8	12.4	12.4	11.6	12.2	12.1	11.7
India/Inde	4.1	4.2	4.1	4.1	3.1	4.5	7.1	8.8	9.1	9.0
China, Hong Kong SAR	3.2	4.6	6.4	5.3	5.3	4.6	6.9	7.1	8.3	7.1
Korea, Republic of	2.5	3.8	3.9	4.0	4.5	4.9	7.1	6.1	7.0	7.3
Other Asia n.e.s.	3.2	5.1	5.2	4.8	5.6	5.9	6.7	6.3	6.0	5.6
USA/Etats–Unis d'Amer	7.1	7.3	5.8	6.9	6.6	7.9	5.6	4.7	3.5	6.3
United Kingdom	5.5	5.5	6.9	5.7	6.0	5.5	5.4	5.1	5.0	5.6
Singapore/Singapour	4.1	3.8	4.9	4.2	4.5	3.9	4.4	7.0	5.5	5.2
Malaysia/Malaisie	1.6	2.2	2.9	2.8	2.9	4.3	4.5	3.7	4.6	4.0
Iran (Islamic Rep of)	9.2	2.0	5.1	4.6	4.6	8.4	4.7	3.4	2.6	2.0

	1985	1986	1987	1988	1989	1990	1991	1992	1993	1994
Afrique	8.2	7.4	8.3	6.4	6.2	5.5	4.2	2.8	2.3	2.8
Amériques	25.2	29.2	29.5	28.0	29.9	29.3	31.7	37.5	38.1	37.6
– Amérique du Nord	23.9	28.0	28.0	26.3	27.6	27.3	29.7	35.7	36.5	36.3
– ALAI	1.2	1.1	1.1	1.5	1.8	1.6	1.8	1.6	1.3	1.2
– MCAC	0.0	0.1	0.0	0.1	0.1	0.0	0.1	0.1	0.1	0.1
– Caraïbes	0.1	0.0	0.0	0.0	0.4	0.4	0.0	0.0	0.0	0.0
– Autre Amérique	0.0	0.0	0.3	0.1	0.1	0.0	0.0	0.1	0.1	0.1
Asie anc. URSS exclus	32.4	28.2	29.0	33.0	28.7	28.7	29.3	20.7	21.1	22.2
– Moyen–Orient	16.2	11.5	13.1	12.7	11.2	13.1	13.1	8.0	7.9	7.1
Asie ancienne URSS									0.0	0.0
Europe anc. URSS exclus	23.3	27.0	25.8	26.4	28.8	28.9	29.9	35.3	33.4	33.3
– Union Européenne	20.7	24.0	22.5	24.1	26.3	26.5	28.4	33.7	31.9	31.9
– Europe de l'Est	1.9	1.6	1.9	1.3	1.4	1.2	0.5	0.7	0.6	0.6
– Autre de l'Europe	0.8	1.4	1.4	0.9	1.1	1.2	1.1	0.9	1.0	0.8
Europe ancienne URSS	2.4	1.3	1.3	0.8	1.7	2.1	0.6	0.4	1.8	1.2
Océanie	1.8	1.8	1.6	1.7	1.5	1.6	1.5	1.2	1.2	1.1
Autre	6.7	5.2	4.6	3.7	3.2	3.9	2.8	2.1	2.1	1.9
USA/Etats–Unis d'Amer	22.0	26.1	26.2	24.8	26.0	25.8	28.1	34.1	35.3	34.7
United Kingdom	6.4	5.7	5.6	5.5	5.7	6.0	6.4	6.9	7.1	8.9
Germany/Allemagne							7.5	8.6	8.0	6.9
Belgium–Luxembourg	1.5	3.0	2.0	3.5	5.4	5.1	4.0	5.5	6.2	5.9
Japan/Japon	5.1	5.5	5.0	5.7	5.8	5.4	5.1	5.2	5.2	5.1
Netherlands/Pays–Bas	3.4	3.8	2.6	3.2	2.9	2.5	3.0	4.0	3.8	3.5
France, Monaco	1.3	1.4	1.9	1.9	2.5	2.3	3.2	3.7	3.0	2.7
Singapore/Singapour	3.4	2.6	2.4	3.0	2.4	2.6	3.4	1.4	1.7	2.4
Iran (Islamic Rep of)	1.3	1.3	2.1	2.1	2.2	3.4	3.9	2.0	0.7	0.5
Areas n.e.s.	6.7	5.2		0.0	0.0	0.0	2.8	2.1	2.1	1.9

4. General Imports C.I.F. by Commodities according to the S.I.T.C. (Rev. 2) in million U.S. Dollars
Importations Générales C.A.F. par Produits d'après la C.T.C.I. (Rév. 2) en millions de Dollars E.U.

SITC CTCI	COMMODITY	1991 QUANTITY QUANTITE	1991 VALUE VALEUR	1992 QUANTITY QUANTITE	1992 VALUE VALEUR	1993 QUANTITY QUANTITE	1993 VALUE VALEUR	1994 QUANTITY QUANTITE	1994 VALUE VALEUR	PRODUIT
	ALL COMMODITIES		3089.7		3419.3		3743.0		4483.4	TOUS PRODUITS
0	FOOD AND LIVE ANIMALS		497.5		496.9		434.1		627.6	ALIMENTS,ANIMAUX VIVANTS
02	DAIRY PRODCTS,BIRDS'EGGS		66.4		65.9		74.3		85.1	PRODUITS LAITIERS,OEUFS
022	MILK AND CREAM		63.1	W 30474	63.0	W 53417	71.5	W 46002	81.5	LAIT ET CREME
0224	MILK,CREAM PRESERVED ETC		62.9	W 30400	62.7	W 53364	71.3	W 45812	81.0	LAIT,CREME CONS,CONC
02242	MILK DRY,1.5% FAT OR LES		8.1	W 3401	5.9	W 3743	6.3	W 8791	13.8	LAIT POUDRE INF 1.5%
02243	MILK DRY,OVER 1.5% FAT		54.6	W 25847	55.8	W 32113	64.4	W 36118	66.6	LAIT POUDRE SUP 1.5%
03	FISH AND PREPARATIONS		50.5		55.9		50.7		59.8	POISSONS ET PREPARATIONS
035	FISH SALTED,DRIED,SMOKED		40.8		41.2		39.9	W 47620	42.4	POISSON SECHE,SALE,FUME
03503	FISH(EX COD)DRIED,SALTED		40.7	W 44290	41.1	W 64771	39.7	W 47569	42.2	POISSONS SECHES,SALES
037	FISH ETC PREPD,PRSVD NES		9.5	W 11952	14.1		10.1	W 13168	16.5	POIS,CRUST,MOL PREPARES
0371	FISH PREPARD,PRESRVD NES		9.5	W 11949	14.1	W 7458	10.1	W 13145	16.5	CONSERVES DE POISSONS
04	CEREALS AND PREPARATIONS		136.7		145.1		83.7		154.7	CEREALES ET PRODUITS
041	WHEAT ETC UNMILLED		81.3	W 462307	65.1	W 7322	1.1	W 881814	120.7	FROMENT,EPEAUTRE
0411	DURUM WHEAT UNMILLED		34.4	W 14	0.1			W 681656	98.9	FROMENT DUR NON MOULU
0412	OTHER WHEAT ETC UNMILLED		46.9	W 462294	65.1	W 7322	1.1	W 200158	21.9	AUTRE FROMENT NON MOULU
042	RICE		38.5	W 237224	65.1	W 208811	49.3	W 58434	13.3	RIZ
0422	RICE SEMI–MILLED,MILLED		38.4	W 234119	64.0	W 202707	48.0	W 45675	10.5	RIZ POLI,GLACE INCL BRISURES
04221	RICE MILLED UNBROKEN		12.0	W 67662	19.9	W 72582	18.2	W 9877	2.6	RIZ POLI,GLACE EXCL BRISURES
04222	RICE BROKEN		26.5	W 166458	44.1	W 130125	29.8	W 35798	8.0	BRISURES DE RIZ
044	MAIZE UNMILLED	W 53332	11.8	W 34843	7.7	W 80873	11.1	W 84824	11.9	MAIS NON MOULU
046	WHEAT ETC MEAL OR FLOUR		0.1		0.1	W 34420	11.4	W 2545	0.4	SEMOULE FARINE,FROMENT
04601	FLOUR OF WHEAT OR MESLIN		0.1	W 93	0.1	W 34420	11.4	W 2545	0.4	FARINE DE FROMENT
05	VEGETABLES AND FRUIT		62.9		59.0		55.6		80.2	LEGUMES ET FRUITS
054	VEG ETC FRSH,SMPLY PRSVD		53.9		48.6		44.0	W 119432	66.6	LEGUMES FRAIS,CONG,SECS
0542	LEGUMINOUS VEGETBLES DRY		37.1	W 76800	38.7	W 78317	32.2	W 106027	43.0	LEGUMES A COSSE SECS
0545	OTHER FRESH VEGETABLES		15.5	W 34093	8.7	W 35327	8.6	W 1468	12.5	AUTRES LEGUMES FRAIS,REF
05451	ALLIACEOUS VEGTBLS,FRESH		15.5	W 33928	8.5	W 35150	8.4	W 431	12.0	OIGNONS,ECHALOTES,AULX
06	SUGAR AND PREPS,HONEY		127.0		116.6		118.9		183.2	SUCRES ET PRODUITS
061	SUGAR AND HONEY		126.7		116.0		118.5	W 498520	182.6	SUCRES ET MIEL
0611	RAW BEET AND CANE SUGAR		121.9	W 358597	109.6	W 394753	116.4	W 491546	179.5	SUCRES BRUTS
07	COFFEE,TEA,COCOA,SPICES		20.8		23.4		17.9		18.0	CAFE,THE,CACAO,EPICES
075	SPICES		18.6	W 38985	18.9		10.3	W 22990	13.7	EPICES
0751	PEPPER AND PIMENTO		11.8	W 6850	11.1	W 944	1.2	W 8314	6.2	POIVRE,PIMENTS
081	*FEEDING STUFF FOR ANIML		14.4		13.3		17.1	W 220291	25.1	NOURRITURE POUR ANIMAUX
09	MISC EDIBLE PRODUCTS		16.3		14.9		13.7		19.4	PREP ALIMENTAIRES DIVERSES
098	EDIBLE PRODCTS,PREPS NES		15.2		13.5		12.1		17.3	PREP ALIMENTAIRES NDA
09809	MISC FOOD PREPRTIONS NES		9.4		7.5		5.2	W 57263	8.9	PREP ALIMENTAIRES NDA
1	BEVERAGES AND TOBACCO		23.0		34.7		36.5		47.2	BOISSONS ET TABACS
12	TOBACCO AND MANUFACTURES		16.1		27.8		28.6		37.2	TABACS BRUTS FABRIQUES
121	TOBACCO UNMNFCTRD,REFUSE		14.2	W 2703	26.8	W 1929	26.7	W 2394	24.9	TABACS BRUTS,DECHETS
1211	TOBACCO,NOT STRIPPED		14.2	W 2687	26.5	W 1929	26.7	W 2389	24.9	TABACS NON ECOTES
2	CRUDE MATERLS,EXCL FUELS		78.9		84.5		96.1		111.4	MAT BRUTES NON COMESTIBLES
26	TEXTILE FIBRES AND WASTE		41.4		42.4		47.2		59.2	FIBRES TEXTILES
263	COTTON		21.8		22.2		24.7	W 18616	33.8	COTON
2631	RAW COTTON,EXCL LINTERS		20.3	W 13381	19.6	W 15999	22.5	W 17819	30.0	COTON EN MASSE
266	SYNTHETIC FIBRES TO SPIN		7.8		10.8		14.0	W 9571	15.8	FIBRES SYNTHETIQUES
267	OTHER MAN–MADE FIBRES		11.4		8.4		7.6	W 4282	8.6	AUTR FIBR TEXT ARTIF SYNTH
2671	REGENERATD FIBRE TO SPIN		11.4		8.2	W 3245	7.6	W 4278	8.5	FIBRES TEXT ARTIFIC
26711	DISCN REGEN FIBRE UNCMBD		11.4	W 4041	8.0	W 2880	6.0	W 3711	6.3	FIBRES TEX ARTIF DISCONT
27	CRUDE FERTLZR,MINRLS NES		10.2		15.0		15.3		15.0	ENGRAIS MINERAUX BRUTS
29	CRUDE ANIMAL,VEG MAT NES		11.6		12.2		11.4		12.5	MATIERES BRUTES ANIM,VEGET
292	CRUDE VEG MATERIALS NES		10.3		9.9		9.6	W 5002	10.2	MAT BRUTES VEGETALES NDA
3	MINERAL FUELS ETC		339.8		304.6		289.2		279.5	COMBUSTIBLES MINERAUX LUB
33	PETROLEUM AND PRODUCTS		334.6		294.3		278.8		266.3	PETROLE ET DERIVES
333	CRUDE PETROLEUM		260.0	W 1176367	159.0	W 1614821	207.1	W 1806309	211.8	HUILES BRUTES DE PETROLE
334	PETROLEUM PRODUCTS,REFIN		71.5	W 30484	132.1		68.0		50.5	PRODUITS RAFFINES
4	ANIMAL,VEGETABLE OIL,FAT		17.1		23.0		46.2		27.9	HUILES,GRAISSES ANIM,VEG
42	FIXED VEGETABLE OIL,FAT		13.2		18.1		40.6		22.1	HUILES VEGETALES FIXES
424	FIXED VEG OIL NONSOFT		12.9	W 42214	17.7	W 83410	39.5	W 44832	21.2	AUTRES HUILES VEG FIXES
4242	PALM OIL		10.8	W 38592	15.4	W 44965	19.4	W 41820	19.3	HUILE DE PALME
4243	COCONUT (COPRA) OIL			W 300	0.2	W 29381	14.9	W 1051	0.7	HJUILE DE COPRAH
5	CHEMCLS,RELATED PROD NES		282.4		305.1		329.0		382.2	PRODUITS CHIMIQUES
51	ORGANIC CHEMICALS		39.8		34.3		37.8		37.7	PROD CHIMIQ ORGANIQUES
515	ORG–INORG COMPOUNDS ETC		15.0	W 3586	10.4		9.4		8.0	COMPOSES ORGANO–MINERAUX
5154	ORGANO–SULPHUR CMPNDS		10.3	W 1657	5.2	W 1391	4.1	W 580	3.4	THIOCOMPOSES ORGANIQUES
52	INORGANIC CHEMICALS		24.9		25.9		25.7		29.4	PROD CHIM INORGANIQUES
522	INORG ELEMNTS,OXIDES,ETC		16.6		16.4		16.4		17.1	ELEMENTS INORGANIQUES
53	DYES,TANNING,COLOUR PROD		22.0		35.5		29.5		32.2	PROD TEINTURE,COLORANTS
531	SYNT DYE,NAT INDGO,LAKES		9.8	W 11450	11.7	W 11110	12.8	W 2675	12.8	MAT COLOR ORGAN,LAQUES
533	PIGMENTS,PAINTS,ETC		11.6	W 5492	23.2		16.1	W 19372	18.7	PIGMENTS,PEINTURES,VERNIS
5334	VARNISHES,DISTEMPERS ETC		3.6	W 665	12.5		4.6	W 2240	5.5	PEINTURES A L'EAU
541	*MEDICINAL,PHARM PRODUCT		38.9		54.9		49.4		62.6	PROD MEDICINAUX PHARMACEUT
5417	MEDICAMENTS		30.8		46.4		41.7		53.3	MEDICAMENTS
54179	— CONTNG OTH SUBSTANCES		24.4	K 4857028	39.1	K 4664337	34.4		43.0	MED CONT AUT SUBSTANCES
55	PERFUME,CLEANING ETC PRD		9.0		12.7		14.5		19.0	PROD POUR PARFUM,TOILETTE
562	*FERTILIZERS,MANUFACTURE		59.5	W 293547	48.5	W 440317	63.8	W 413257	64.9	ENGRAIS MANUFACTURES
5621	CHEM NITROGENOUS FERTLZR		39.9	W 193358	29.6	W 283090	38.9	W 262371	40.0	ENGRAIS AZOTES
56213	AMMONIUM SULPHATE		8.6	W 69871	7.4	W 102349	12.4	W 76248	9.5	SULFATE D'AMMONIUM
56216	UREA		30.7	W 117945	21.0	W 164366	24.3	W 185370	30.3	UREE
5623	CHEM POTASSIC FERTILIZER		6.1	W 49405	9.5	W 83127	13.0	W 106419	16.6	ENGRAIS POTASSIQUES
58	PLASTIC MATERIALS ETC		62.3		62.4		68.8		89.3	MAT PLAST ARTIFICIELLES
583	POLYMERIZATION ETC PRODS		53.1		49.7		56.1		73.7	PROD POLYMERISATION
5831	POLYETHYLENE		16.8		14.6		14.3		18.9	POLYETHYLENE
58311	— IN PRIMARY FORMS		16.2	W 17494	14.0	W 19165	13.7	W 24915	18.0	POLYETHYLENE PRIMAIRES
5834	POLYVINYL CHLORIDE		10.6		8.9		14.7		17.3	CHLORURE DE POLYVINYLE
58341	— IN PRIMARY FORMS		9.2	W 30006	7.6	W 14538	11.3	W 18218	14.9	SOUS FORMES PRIMAIRES
5839	OTH POLYMRZTION ETC PROD		13.3		13.9		15.2		21.2	AUT PROD POLYMER COPOLYM
59	CHEMICAL MATERIALS NES		25.0		30.3		39.4		46.6	MAT PROD CHIMIQUES NDA
591	PESTICIDES,DISINFECTANTS		11.5	W 4672	14.1	W 5757	18.3	W 6671	20.2	DESINF,INSECT,FONG,HERB
598	MISCEL CHEM PRODUCTS NES		10.6		12.7		16.7	W 5885	20.6	PROD DIV INDUST CHIM NDA
5989	CHEM PRODUCTS,PREPS NES		6.3		8.2		10.6	W 1653	13.8	PROD PREP CHIMIQUES NDA
6	BASIC MANUFACTURES		1049.5		1228.2		1415.3		1672.8	ART MANUFACTURES
61	LEATHER,DRESSED FUR,ETC		6.9		7.2		11.6		19.0	CUIRS,PELLETERIES
611	LEATHER		6.1		5.9		9.7		15.1	CUIRS,PEAUX PREPARES
62	RUBBER MANUFACTURES NES		19.7		24.7		32.3		26.3	CAOUTCHOUC MANUFACTURE
625	RUBBER TYRES, TUBES ETC		10.0	N 1223402	11.9	N 2004505	20.5	N 1737007	13.9	PNEUS CAOUTCHOUC VULCANISE
6252	TYRES,NEW,BUS OR LORRY		4.6	N 151557	5.9	N 269778	11.3	N 128388	5.8	PNEUS POUR AUTOBUS,CAMIONS
63	WOOD,CORK MANUFACTRS NES		12.2		13.0		16.8		15.5	OUVRAGES LIEGE ET BOIS
634	VENEERS,PLYWOOD,ETC		11.5		11.1		11.5	W 19654	12.6	PLACAGES,CONTRE–PLAQUES
6342	PLYWOOD OF WOOD SHEETS		10.5	W 5351	10.2		10.4	W 17000	11.0	BOIS CONTRE–PLAQUES

4. General Imports C.I.F. by Commodities according to the S.I.T.C. (Rev. 2) in million U.S. Dollars
Importations Générales C.A.F. par Produits d'après la C.T.C.I. (Rév. 2) en millions de Dollars E.U.

SITC CTCI	COMMODITY	1991 QUANTITY QUANTITE	1991 VALUE VALEUR	1992 QUANTITY QUANTITE	1992 VALUE VALEUR	1993 QUANTITY QUANTITE	1993 VALUE VALEUR	1994 QUANTITY QUANTITE	1994 VALUE VALEUR	PRODUIT
64	PAPER,PAPERBOARD AND MFR		84.2		85.8		92.3		107.9	PAPIERS,CARTONS & OUVRAGES
641	PAPER AND PAPERBOARD		66.9		67.5		69.1		82.1	PAPIERS ET CARTONS
6411	NEWSPRINT		16.1	W 19098	9.9	W 25666	12.8	W 25546	12.2	PAPIER JOURNAL
6412	PRINTG,WRITING PAPER NES		14.0	W 43560	17.8	W 45562	18.7	W 26620	20.3	PAPIERS POUR L'IMPRESSION
64122	— COATED,IMPREGNATD ETC		13.6	W 43023	16.9	W 44381	17.3	W 25953	18.8	PAPIERS IMPRESSION COUCHES
6413	KRAFT PAPER,PAPERBOARD		12.9	W 24620	14.1	W 24558	12.4	W 59435	18.2	PAPIER ET CARTON KRAFT
6415	PAPER,PAPERBRD,BULK,NES		18.7	W 93999	21.4	W 75970	19.9		22.7	PAPIERS,CARTONS ROULEAUX
64159	OTHER PAPER ETC,BULK,NES		15.4	W 84997	17.6	W 66840	16.2	W 12369	17.8	AUT PAPIER ROULEAUX FEUILLES
642	PAPER,ETC,PRECUT,ARTS OF		17.4		18.4		23.2		25.8	PAP,CARTONS DECOUPES
6428	PAPER ETC ARTICLES NES		8.3		8.9		12.5		14.9	OUVRAGES EN PATE A PAPIER
65	TEXTILE YARN,FABRICS,ETC		610.9		737.6		851.7		1024.2	FILS,TISSUS,ARTICLES TEXTILE
651	TEXTILE YARN		73.8		79.0		84.1		95.1	FILS TEXTILES
6513	COTTON YARN		22.0		23.4		27.4	W 704	35.4	FILS DE COTON
6514	SYN FIB YRN,BULK,MONOFIL		32.1	W 9685	29.8	W 5790	23.0		24.4	FILS CONT 85% FIB TEXT SYNTH
65142	— NONTXT ETC CONT PAMID		16.1	W 918	4.2	W 749	3.6	W 1386	4.8	FILS NON TEX FI CON POLYAMID
6516	DISCON SYN FIB BLEND YRN		10.9		16.4		20.1	W 4761	22.5	FILS FIBR TEX SYNT DIS MOINS
65166	DISCON SYN FIB–COTTN YRN		2.9	W 1416	6.2		11.6	W 2392	9.4	FILS TEXT SYNT MELANGE COTON
652	COTTON FABRICS,WOVEN		141.8		203.9		240.2	A 112492	256.8	TISSUS DE COTON
6521	GREY WOVEN COTTON FABRIC		34.3		42.7		56.3	A 12318	53.2	TISSUS COT ECRUS NON MERCER
65214	GREY WOVEN COTTON NES		26.7		32.9		45.7	A 94	41.1	AUT TISSUS 85% COTON ECRUS
6522	WOVEN COTTON BLEACHD,ETC		107.6		161.3		184.0	A 100174	203.6	TISSUS COTON BLANCHIS ETC
65224	BLCHED COTTON FABRIC NES		92.9		137.1		163.2	A 97867	182.6	AUT TIS PLUS 85% COT BLANCHI
65225	BLCHD COTN BLEND FAB NES		11.0	A 12521	19.0		15.7	A 410	15.6	AUT TIS MOINS 85% COT BLANCH
653	WOVN MAN–MADE FIB FABRIC		205.8		236.9		255.3	A 15764	320.6	TISSUS FIBRES SYNTH,ARTIF
6531	CONT SYNT WEAVES NONPILE		41.5		42.2		50.6	A 659	60.1	TISSUS FIBRES SYNTH CONTINUE
65315	CONT SYN TXTL FABRIC NES		40.5		40.7		49.0	A 398	57.8	TIS PLUS 85% TEXT SYNT CONT
6532	DISC SYN TXTL FABRIC NES		57.3		52.2		69.2	A 208	82.0	TIS DISC MOINS 85% FIBR TEXT
6534	DISC SYN BLEND FABRC NES		66.2		86.0		79.2	A 9991	95.7	TISSUS FIBRES SYNTH DISCONT
65341	DISC SYN FIB–COTTN FABRC		58.3		71.5		65.5	A 147	78.2	TISSUS FIB SYNT DIS MEL COTO
65349	OTH DISC SYN BLEND FABRC		6.1		11.2		9.7	A 7755	12.4	TISSUS FIB SYNT MEL MAT AUT
6536	DISC REGN TXTL FABRC NES		29.6		41.6	A 24119	44.7	A 42	68.6	TISSUS 85% TEXT ART DISC
654	OTH WOVEN TEXTILE FABRIC		7.9		8.6		15.0		21.4	TISSUS AUT COTON SYNT,ARTIF
655	KNITTED,ETC FABRICS		111.6	A 68622	128.5	A 142632	163.6	A 81	195.9	ETOF BONNETERIE PIECES ETC
6552	OTHER KNIT ETC FAB NONEL		111.6	A 68622	128.5	A 142632	163.6	A 81	195.9	ETOF BON NON ELAS NON SYNT
656	LACE,RIBBONS,TULLE,ETC		18.7		26.2		37.1		51.7	TULLES,BRODERIE
65601	NARROW FABRICS NES		7.7		10.0		12.3		19.9	RUBANS SANS TRAME EN FILS
657	SPECIAL TXTL FABRC,PRODS		41.2		47.7		53.0		75.1	TISSUS SPECIAUX
6573	COATED ETC TEXTILES NES		24.5		25.2	A 12171	27.4	A 1905	42.6	TISSUS,ART MATIERE TEXT NDA
65732	PLASTIC COATED TEXTILES		14.1	A 8885	16.3	A 9110	19.2	A 196	31.5	TISSUS IMPREGNES
66	NONMETAL MINERAL MFS NES		136.4		164.4		215.2		234.5	ART MIN NON METALLIQUES
661	LIME,CEMENT,BLDG PRODS		41.4		52.4		58.5		69.0	CHAUX,CIMENTS MAT CONSTR
6612	CEMENT		41.1	W 830362	50.5	W 933196	56.3	W 1091954	65.6	CIMENTS HYDRAULIQUES
664	GLASS		10.7		13.6		11.0		11.9	VERRE
665	GLASSWARE		7.4		10.8		13.2		9.9	OUVRAGES EN VERRE
667	PEARL,PREC–,SEMI–P STONE		70.7		77.8		124.9		133.5	PERLES, PIERRES GEMMES
6672	DIAMONDS NONINDUST,UNSET		65.4		75.3		122.4		127.9	DIAMANTS BRUTS
66722	— SRTD,ROUGH,SIMPLY WKD		58.7		60.1		112.4		121.6	DIAMANTS TRIES BRUTS
66729	— CUT ETC NOT SET		6.8		15.1		10.0		6.3	DIAMANTS TAILLES
67	IRON AND STEEL		91.2		101.7		102.6		127.9	FER ET ACIER
672	IRON,STEEL PRIMARY FORMS		15.3		13.8		15.4	W 91639	25.7	LINGOTS FER,ACIER
6725	IRN,STL BLOOMS,SLABS,ETC		14.2		12.2		14.0	W 87102	23.2	BLOOMS,BILLETTES FER ACIER
67251	IRN,SMPLE STL BLOOMS,ETC		14.2	W 48404	12.2	W 244767	14.0	W 87043	23.1	BLOOMS ETC NON ACIER FIN
673	IRON,STEEL SHAPES ETC		22.6		29.5		31.1	W 161100	34.7	BARRES,PROFIL FER,ACIER
6732	IRON,STEEL BARS ETC		10.5		11.7	W 141121	14.3	W 106757	12.2	BARRES FER,ACIER
674	IRN,STL UNIV,PLATE,SHEET		28.9		27.8		26.7	W 53678	34.5	LARGES PLATS,TOLES
678	IRON,STL TUBES,PIPES,ETC		14.4		20.2		15.7	W 17696	18.8	TUBES,TUYAUX EN FONTE,FER
68	NON–FERROUS METALS		32.9		25.7		28.9		29.8	METAUX NON FERREUX
684	ALUMINIUM		22.0		13.2		14.6	W 7326	16.1	ALUMINIUM
6842	ALUMINIUM,ALLOYS WORKED		19.9		11.4		12.1	W 5635	13.4	ALUMINIUM,ALLIAGES OUVRE
69	METAL MANUFACTURES NES		55.5		68.5		64.5		88.1	ART MANUFACT EN METAL NDA
691	STRUCTURES AND PARTS NES		5.8	W 2796	12.3		8.8		20.2	CONSTRUCT FER,ACIER,ALU
6911	STRUCTURES,PARTS IRN,STL		5.2	W 2367	11.0	W 2603	6.9		14.4	CONSTRUCT FER,ACIER,FONTE
695	TOOLS		12.0	MN 85125	14.0	MN 15686	12.0	MN 12024	11.1	OUTILS A MAIN
699	BASE METAL MFRS NES		17.9		20.2		23.9		29.8	ART MANUFACTURES MET NDA
7	MACHINES,TRANSPORT EQUIP		607.7		725.9		859.9		1046.7	MACHINES MATERIEL TRANSPORT
71	POWER GENERATING EQUIPMT		46.9		47.9		63.8		99.9	MACHINES GENERATRICES
713	INTRNL COMBUS PSTN ENGIN		17.1		16.7	N 656350	13.3	N 725503	12.2	MOTEURS EXPL COMB INT, PIECE
714	ENGINES AND MOTORS NES		15.9	N 5113	11.8		30.8	N 24485	62.8	MOTEURS NON ELECTRIQUES
7149	ENGINE & MOTOR PARTS NES		13.7	N 5106	11.7		30.7	N 24438	62.5	PIECES 714 ET 718.88
71491	PARTS NES OF 7144,71481		13.5	N 3605	11.2	N 6116	29.6	N 22580	61.4	PIECES DES PROPULSEURS
716	ROTATING ELECTRIC PLANT		11.2	N 468861	17.8	N 557836	15.8	N 537843	21.5	APP ELECTR ROTATIFS,PIECES
72	MACHS FOR SPCL INDUSTRYS		102.8		147.3		178.1		154.9	MAC SPECIALES POUR INDUST
722	TRACTORS NON–ROAD		9.7	N 5537	9.8	N 5734	11.4	N 6613	18.5	TRACTEURS
7224	WHEELED TRACTORS NES		9.6	N 5395	9.3	N 5700	11.3	N 6589	18.4	TRACTEURS A ROUES
723	CIVIL ENGNEERG EQUIP ETC		3.0	N 9461	4.9	N 15096	24.2	N 42677	11.8	APPAREILS DE GENIE CIVIL
7234	CONST,MINING MACHNRY NES		2.3	N 2070	4.2	N 13369	23.1	N 39614	10.9	MACH POUR LA CONST, MINES
72341	SELF–PROPELLD DOZERS,ETC	N 10	0.4	N 38	0.8	N 169	11.7	N 197	2.4	BULLDOZERS
724	TEXTILE,LEATHER MACHNRY		46.7	MN 37010	76.2		75.8	MN 104408	58.8	MACH POUR INDUSTRIE TEXTILE
7243	SEWING MACHS,NEEDLES ETC		21.5	MN 21043	37.0		33.1	MN 87585	23.7	MACHINES A COUDRE,PIECES
72431	SEWING MACHINES		18.9	N 6278562	32.5		27.6	N 2351597	17.9	MACHINES A COUDRE
7244	SPINNING,EXTRDNG,ETC MCH		5.5	N 717872	12.1	N 2691004	7.1	N 6451423	5.8	MACH POUR LE FILAGE
7245	WEAVING,FELT MFG,ETC MCH		7.4	N 116490	12.4		17.1	N 269703	9.0	METIERS A TISSER,PIECES
7247	TEXTILE MACHINERY NES		9.1	N 275257	7.9		12.1	N 218960	13.9	MACH LAVAGE,TEINTURE TEX
726	PRINTG,BKBINDG MACHY,PTS		11.2	N 78666	13.9		12.9	N 928386	10.5	MACHINES POUR IMPRIMERIE
727	FOOD MACHRY NON–DOMESTIC		6.2	N 282282	8.3		13.5	N 405484	10.9	MACH INDUSTRIES ALIMENT
7272	OTH FOOD PROC MCHY,PARTS		4.9	N 23236	7.4		12.3	N 41081	9.4	AUT MACH IND ALIMENTAIRE
728	OTH MACHY FOR SPCL INDUS		22.2	N 1764062	28.3		34.0	MN 45751	38.3	AUT MACH IND PARTICULIERES
7283	OTHR MINERAL WORKG MACHY		2.5	N 87672	5.9		11.5	N 6539690	9.4	MACH TRIER,CRIBLER,BROYER
7284	MACHY FOR SPCL INDUS NES		15.6	N 641076	17.7		18.6	N 5243499	24.4	MACH SPEC IND PARTICUL.
73	METALWORKING MACHINERY		9.7		7.6		9.9		12.0	MACH TRAVAIL DES METAUX
74	GENRL INDUSTRL MACHY NES		71.3		97.8		96.0		114.1	MACH APP INDUSTRIE
741	HEATING,COOLING EQUIPMNT		10.5		21.2		24.1		25.9	MACH CHAUFFAGE,PIECES
743	PUMPS NES,CENTRFUGES ETC		11.4		10.7		14.6	N 1188342	15.4	POMPES COMPRES,VENT ETC
744	MECHANICAL HANDLING EQU		13.2	N 132777	16.5		12.6	N 67211	21.4	EQUIP MANUTENTION PIECES
7442	LIFTING,LOADING MACH NES		9.0	N 26139	12.3		8.2	N 31768	14.1	APP LEVAGE,MANUTENTION
745	NONELEC MACHY,TOOLS NES		7.3		12.4		10.2	N 5465240	10.0	AUT MACH NON ELEC,PIECES
7452	OTH NONELEC MCHS,PTS NES		6.9		11.9		9.4	N 5461988	9.4	AUT MACH NON ELEC,PIECES
749	NONELEC MACH PTS,ACC NES		22.8	MN 40584	27.4	MN 92065	27.2	MN 143615	32.4	PIECES MACH NON ELEC NDA
75	OFFICE MACHNES,ADP EQUIP		25.2		37.0		37.6		47.8	MACH BUREAU TRAIT AUTOM
752	AUTOMTIC DATA PROC EQUIP		10.8	N 25698	13.2	N 59589	15.0	N 34121	19.6	MACH TRAIT INFORMATION
759	OFFICE,ADP MCH PTS,ACCES		8.2	MN 51906	15.2	MN 47871	15.7	MN 42894	21.0	PIECES DU 751 ET 752

4. General Imports C.I.F. by Commodities according to the S.I.T.C. (Rev. 2) in million U.S. Dollars
Importations Générales C.A.F. par Produits d'après la C.T.C.I. (Rév. 2) en millions de Dollars E.U.

SITC CTCI	COMMODITY	1991 QUANTITY QUANTITE	1991 VALUE VALEUR	1992 QUANTITY QUANTITE	1992 VALUE VALEUR	1993 QUANTITY QUANTITE	1993 VALUE VALEUR	1994 QUANTITY QUANTITE	1994 VALUE VALEUR	PRODUIT
7599	ACCTG,ETC,ADP MCH PTS,AC		7.2	MN 50864	14.0	MN 47788	14.3	MN 42739	19.8	PIECES DU 751 ET 752
76	TELECOMM,SOUND EQUIPMENT		32.8		65.1		73.5		111.4	EQUIPMENT DE TELECOM
761	TELEVISION RECEIVERS		10.8	N 110531	13.0	N 103689	13.9	N 152570	18.0	RECEPTEURS DE TELEVISION
7611	COLOUR TV RECEIVERS		5.3	N 36234	8.0	N 48304	10.7	N 69593	13.7	RECEPTEURS COULEUR
764	TELECOM EQPT,PTS,ACC NES		15.9	MN 620011	44.8	MN 667398	48.7	MN 539329	83.1	EQUIP TELECOM,PIECES
7641	LINE TELEPHONE,ETC EQUIP		4.0	N 604052	22.6	N 182131	22.3	N 518135	23.4	APP TELEPHON PAR FIL
7643	TV,RADIO TRANSMITTRS ETC		2.5	N 4019	10.6	N 24158	8.5	N 27334	32.5	APP EMET TELE RADIO
7649	PTS NES OF EQUIPMT OF 76		5.7	MN 619194	9.6	MN 666729	13.3	MN 536928	21.0	PIECES DE LA DIV 76
77	ELECTRIC MACHNRY NES ETC		77.0		87.9		109.7		164.5	MACH APP ELECT NDA
771	ELECTRIC POWER MACHY NES		6.6	MN 15925	5.5	MN 29316	14.9	MN 39588	20.3	MACH PROD,TRANS ELECTR
772	SWITCHGEAR ETC,PARTS NES		27.4	MN 119246	27.0	MN 131795	31.9	MN 263936	44.8	APP COUPURE,SECT ETC
7721	SWITCHGEAR ETC		22.0	MN 48502	19.8	MN 60181	24.4	MN 97729	36.8	APP COUPURE,SECTIONMNT
773	ELECTR DISTRIBUTNG EQUIP		7.7		10.9		13.3		33.2	EQUIPMT DISTRIBUTION ELECT
7731	INSULATED WIRE,CABLE ETC		6.9	W 40465	6.1	W 4627	10.5		29.1	FILS,CABLES ISOLES ELECT
775	HOUSEHOLD TYPE EQUIP NES		8.3	N 696839	13.4		16.3	MN 85113	19.1	MACH,APP USAGE DOMESTQUE
778	ELECTRICAL MACHINERY NES		20.0	MN 277298	23.7		26.8	MN 947921	33.9	AUTRES MACH ELECT NDA
78	ROAD VEHICLES		199.5		205.7		240.6		338.2	VEHICULES ROUTIERS
781	PASS MOTOR VEH EXC BUSES		21.2	N 7815	35.5	N 14352	39.1	N 16261	85.3	AUTO TRANSPORT PERSONNES
782	LORRIES,SPCL MTR VEH NES		60.7	N 12909	76.4	N 12706	89.3	N 4413	113.6	VEHICULES SPECIAUX,MARCH
7821	LORRIES,TRUCKS		59.2	N 12596	74.3	N 12185	84.9	N 4314	109.7	VEHICULES TRANSP MARCHAND
783	ROAD MOTOR VEHICLES NES		52.7	N 3694	37.4	N 2390	16.1	N 10011	36.5	VEHICULES ROUTIERS NDA
7831	BUSES		51.2	N 2618	33.1	N 1125	11.3	N 9662	33.3	VOITURES TRANSPORT COMMUN
784	MOTOR VEH PRTS,ACCES NES		22.0	N 2491986	24.4	N 1957409	60.6	N 2677184	60.0	PIECES 722,781,782,783
7841	MOTOR VEHICLE CHASSIS	N 419	4.7	N 545	2.9	N 2208	28.9	N 981	12.2	CHASSIS 722,781,782,783
7842	MOTOR VEHICLE BODIES		3.4	N 1475	8.1	N 1221	17.1	N 7558	24.9	CARROS 722,781,782,783
7849	OTHER MOTOR VEHCL PARTS		14.0	N 2489966	13.5	N 1953980	14.8	N 2668645	23.1	PIECES 722,781,782,783
785	CYCLES,ETC MOTRZD OR NOT		42.1	MN 34779	30.7	MN 42132	33.8	MN 59588	40.9	MOTOCYCLES SCOOTERS
7851	MOTORCYCLES ETC		31.1	N 64655	21.7	N 58504	22.1	N 6605	27.4	MOTO VELO MOTEUR AUXIL
7853	INVAL CARR, PTS OF 785		10.5	MN 34698	8.6	MN 42030	10.4	MN 59560	13.0	FAUTEUILS INVALIDES,PIECES
78539	PARTS,ACCES NES OF 785		10.4	MN 34638	8.6	MN 42029	10.4	MN 59559	12.9	PIECES DU 785
79	OTHR TRANSPORT EQUIPMENT		42.9		30.0		51.0		4.3	AUTRE MATERIEL TRANSPORT
791	RAILWAY VEHICLES		28.9		25.4	N 610307	42.4		1.6	VEHIC MAT CHEMINS DE FER
7912	OTH RAIL LOCOMOTIVES ETC	N 20	15.0	N 4	1.0					AUTRES LOCOMOTIVES
7913	MECHAN–PROPELLED RY CARS	N 12	0.1		14.1	N 25	5.5			AUTOMOTRICES,DRAISINES
7914	RY COACHES NES NOT POWRD	N 50	11.3	N 42	9.3	N 188	34.9			VOITURES A VOYAGEURS
8	MISC MANUFACTURED GOODS		183.8		210.9		212.8		257.1	ART MANUFACTURES DIVERS
84	CLOTHING AND ACCESSORIES		21.8		25.5		33.4		43.3	VETEMENTS
847	TEXTILE CLTHNG ACCES NES		5.3	MN 22787	9.3	MN 42898	11.8	MN 34404	12.1	ACCES VET MAT TEXT NDA
848	HEADGEAR,NONTXTL CLOTHNG		9.5		10.3		13.8		16.2	VET ACCES MAT AUT QUE TEX
87	PRECISION INSTRUMNTS NES		30.7		54.8		31.1		41.6	INSTRUM,APPAR SCIENT NDA
872	MEDICAL INSTRUMENTS NES		7.4		27.0	MN 18672	5.0	MN 16189	10.9	INSTR,APP MEDIC–CHIR NDA
87202	OTH MEDICAL INSTRUMENTS		6.8	MN 1008337	26.6	MN 18580	4.7	MN 16154	8.0	INSTRUM,APP MEDECINE
874	MEASURNG,CONTROLNG INSTR		19.0	N 2754367	20.4		21.3	N 2950998	25.3	INSTRUMENTS DE MESURE
88	PHOTO EQU,OPTICL GDS ETC		15.3		17.7		18.4		17.5	APP,FOURN PHOTO,OP,MONTR
882	PHOTO,CINEMA SUPPLIES		10.2		11.1		11.0		11.7	PRODUITS PHOTO,CINEMA
89	MISC MANUFCTRD GOODS NES		105.4		102.3		115.9		137.9	ART MANUFACTURES DIVERS
892	PRINTED MATTER		13.7	MN 746735	21.0	MN 874510	22.9	MN 1235183	27.8	IMPRIMES
8928	PRINTED MATTER NES		8.0	MN 729329	13.3	MN 859950	16.0	MN 1204842	17.8	IMPRIMES NDA
893	ARTICLES OF PLASTIC NES		15.6		21.7		28.6		34.2	OUVRAGES EN MAT DIVIS 58
8939	MISC PLASTIC ARTICLES		10.6		15.4		17.8		24.1	ART DIVERS EN MAT DIV 58
89399	OTHR PLASTC ARTICLES NES		9.9		14.3		16.9	N 65901	22.6	AUT OUV MAT DIV 58
899	OTHER MANUFACTURED GOODS		63.3		41.8		43.6		54.0	AUT ART MANUF DIVERS NDA
8998	SMALLWARES,TOILETRYS ETC		58.1	MN 1139340	36.5	MN 3510801	39.1	MN 1629029	47.6	ART MERCERIE,TOILETTE
89983	BUTTONS,STUDS,ETC		34.5	MN 1022534	23.0	MN 1359276	20.8	MN 1430854	24.1	BOUTONS,BOUTONS–PRESSION
89984	SLIDE FASTENERS,PARTS		23.4	MN 103663	13.2	MN 2123780	18.0	MN 159345	23.1	FERMETURES A GLISSIERE
9	GOODS NOT CLASSD BY KIND		10.4		5.9		24.2		31.5	ART TRANSACT NON CLASSES
971	*GOLD,NON MONETARY NES		4.7	MK 9711	3.0		21.3		28.6	OR NON MONETAIRE
97101	NONMON GLD UNWRT,SEMIMFD		4.7	MK 9491	2.9		21.3	K 9	27.8	OR,ALLIAGES D'OR BRUTS

5. General Exports F.O.B. by Commodities according to the S.I.T.C. (Rev. 2) in million U.S. Dollars
Exportations Générales F.O.B. par Produits d'après la C.T.C.I. (Rév. 2) en millions de Dollars E.U.

SITC CTCI	COMMODITY	1991 QUANTITY QUANTITE	1991 VALUE VALEUR	1992 QUANTITY QUANTITE	1992 VALUE VALEUR	1993 QUANTITY QUANTITE	1993 VALUE VALEUR	1994 QUANTITY QUANTITE	1994 VALUE VALEUR	PRODUIT
	ALL COMMODITIES		1987.3		2454.0		2847.0		3209.7	TOUS PRODUITS
0	FOOD AND LIVE ANIMALS		568.0		500.3		576.3		635.8	ALIMENTS,ANIMAUX VIVANTS
03	FISH AND PREPARATIONS		21.4		30.4		43.9		63.6	POISSONS ET PREPARATIONS
034	FISH,FRESH,CHILLED,FROZN		3.4		6.8		16.6	W 2536	15.7	POISSON FRAIS, REFRIG,CONG
0342	FISH FROZEN,EXCL FILLETS		1.1		2.9	W 2442	10.7	W 2158	9.2	POISSONS CONGELES
036	SHELL FISH FRESH,FROZEN		16.3	W 2121	19.8	W 2107	24.1	W 1100	44.9	CRUSTACES,MOLLUSQUES
04	CEREALS AND PREPARATIONS		1.2		1.4		2.1		15.3	CEREALES ET PRODUITS
042	RICE		0.4	W 474	0.4	W 756	0.7	W 60299	13.7	RIZ
0422	RICE SEMI–MILLED,MILLED		0.3	W 318	0.3	W 531	0.5	W 60157	13.6	RIZ POLI,GLACE INCL BRISURES
05	VEGETABLES AND FRUIT		66.3		81.7		67.0		75.6	LEGUMES ET FRUITS
054	VEG ETC FRSH,SMPLY PRSVD		9.8	W 12491	7.1		10.2	W 13601	14.7	LEGUMES FRAIS,CONG,SECS
0546	VEGETABLES SIMPLY PRESVD		4.7	W 6294	4.0	W 9949	6.5	W 12140	10.7	LEGUMES CONG,CONSER
05462	VEG PRSVD UNFRZN UNTINND		4.6	W 6209	3.9	W 9923	6.5	W 12115	10.6	LEGUMES CONSER PROVISOIR
057	FRUIT,NUTS,FRESH,DRIED	W 50	0.1		67.1		46.7	N 9500	0.1	FRUITS FRAIS OU SECS
0577	NUTS EDIBLE,FRESH,DRIED		50.4		65.3		44.5	N 9500	0.1	FRUITS A COQUES
05771	COCONUTS FRESH OR DRIED		41.1		59.1		37.2	N 9500	0.1	NOIX DE COCO
05773	CASHEW NUTS,FRESH,DRIED		7.1	W 1062	5.4	W 1384	7.1	W 390	2.3	NOIX DE CAJOU
07	COFFEE,TEA,COCOA,SPICES		472.3		379.1		451.1		467.1	CAFE,THE,CACAO,EPICES
074	TEA AND MATE	W 12	0.1	W 181263	336.7	W 217700	404.4	W 228986	416.8	THE ET MATE
0741	TEA	W 12	0.1	W 181263	336.7	W 217700	404.4	W 228986	416.8	THE
075	SPICES		41.0		41.0		45.7	W 14252	42.5	EPICES
0752	SPICES,EX PEPPER,PIMENTO		37.6		38.1		37.4	W 10780	36.1	AUTRES EPICES
07522	CINNAMON,ETC		34.8	W 8238	34.8	W 8756	34.0	W 9054	33.0	CANNELLE
09	MISC EDIBLE PRODUCTS		4.7		5.5		9.3		8.9	PREP ALIMENTAIRES DIVERSES
098	EDIBLE PRODCTS,PREPS NES		4.7		5.5		9.3	W 1	0.1	PREP ALIMENTAIRES NDA
1	BEVERAGES AND TOBACCO		13.5		42.8		40.7		39.5	BOISSONS ET TABACS
12	TOBACCO AND MANUFACTURES		13.1		42.4		40.2		38.9	TABACS BRUTS FABRIQUES
121	TOBACCO UNMNFCTRD,REFUSE		5.9	W 4279	39.2	W 4353	36.5		32.7	TABACS BRUTS,DECHETS
1212	TOBACCO STRIPPED OR PART		3.6	W 3536	32.6	W 3465	29.6		26.6	TABACS PART ECOTES
122	TOBACCO,MANUFACTURED		7.2	W 856	3.3	W 828	3.8	W 1057	6.3	TABACS FABRIQUES
1222	CIGARETTES		7.2	W 842	2.9	W 826	3.6	W 1016	4.1	CIGARETTES
2	CRUDE MATERLS,EXCL FUELS		115.3		126.6		121.8		135.8	MAT BRUTES NON COMESTIBLES
23	RUBBER, CRUDE		64.7		68.8		63.8		73.1	CAOUTCHOUC BRUT
232	NATURAL RUBBER,GUMS		63.9	W 78612	67.6	W 69620	63.7	W 69141	72.5	LATEX CAOUTCHOUC NATUREL
23202	OTHER NATURAL RUBBER		31.7	W 39594	32.0	W 36485	31.1	W 34540	35.0	CAOUTCHOUC NATUREL
23203	BALATA,GUTTA–PERCHA, ETC		32.0	W 35041	33.2	W 31457	31.3	W 31947	35.3	BALATA,GUTTA–PERCHA
26	TEXTILE FIBRES AND WASTE		16.4		17.2		16.0		21.4	FIBRES TEXTILES
265	VEG FIBRE,EXCL COTN,JUTE		14.0	W 74165	16.1		14.9	W 94286	19.5	FIBRES VEGETALES
2659	VEG TEXT FIBRE,WASTE,NES		13.9	W 74165	16.1		14.9	W 94247	19.5	FIBRES TEXTILES VEGET NDA
26591	COIR FIBRE AND WASTE		13.9	W 74161	16.1	W 101109	14.9	W 94160	19.5	FIBRES DE COCO
27	CRUDE FERTLZR,MINRLS NES		8.1		11.2		9.4		6.2	ENGRAIS MINERAUX BRUTS
28	METALLIFEROUS ORES,SCRAP		5.3		7.1		11.8		13.1	MINERAIS METAL,DECHETS
29	CRUDE ANIMAL,VEG MAT NES		12.1		13.4		15.5		15.3	MATIERES BRUTES ANIM,VEGET
292	CRUDE VEG MATERIALS NES	W 10	0.1	W 16537	12.5	W 18008	14.2	W 14251	13.7	MAT BRUTES VEGETALES NDA
3	MINERAL FUELS ETC		27.5		13.2		17.9		22.4	COMBUSTIBLES MINERAUX LUB
33	PETROLEUM AND PRODUCTS		27.5		13.2		17.9		22.4	PETROLE ET DERIVES
334	PETROLEUM PRODUCTS,REFIN		8.3	W 6	0.1		1.2		7.2	PRODUITS RAFFINES
335	RESIDUAL PETRLM PROD NES		19.2		13.1		16.7		15.3	PRODUITS RESIDUELS NDA
3352	MINERAL TARS AND PRODCTS	W 96417	19.2	W 64154	13.1	W 88219	16.7		15.3	GOUDRONS MINERAUX
33525	MINERAL TAR OILS ETC NES	W 96416	19.2	W 64148	13.1	W 88218	16.7	W 117600	15.3	AUTRES PRODUITS NDA
5	CHEMCLS,RELATED PROD NES		20.2		24.2		31.7		27.8	PRODUITS CHIMIQUES
59	CHEMICAL MATERIALS NES		14.0		16.5		16.3		15.4	MAT PROD CHIMIQUES NDA
598	MISCEL CHEM PRODUCTS NES		13.4		15.8	W 3	0.1	W 13829	14.6	PROD DIV INDUST CHIM NDA
5989	CHEM PRODUCTS,PREPS NES		13.4		15.8	W 13745	15.7	W 13412	14.4	PROD PREP CHIMIQUES NDA
59892	ACTIVTED NAT MINRL PROD		13.3	W 14363	15.7	W 13681	15.6	W 13322	14.3	CHARBONS ACTIVES
6	BASIC MANUFACTURES		273.8		346.0		424.7		497.1	ART MANUFACTURES
61	LEATHER,DRESSED FUR,ETC		23.6		1.1		1.6		1.9	CUIRS,PELLETERIES
611	LEATHER	W 1	0.1		1.0		1.1		1.0	CUIRS,PEAUX PREPARES
6114	LEATHR BOVINE NES,EQUINE	W 412	23.4	W 685	0.7	W 472	0.6	W 265	0.7	CUIRS DE BOVINS
62	RUBBER MANUFACTURES NES		19.6		32.1		40.2		54.0	CAOUTCHOUC MANUFACTURE
625	RUBBER TYRES, TUBES ETC		10.9		20.4	N 5768438	25.3	N 7375624	37.6	PNEUS CAOUTCHOUC VULCANISE
6259	OTH TYRES,TYRE CASES,ETC		10.9		20.3	N 5684265	25.0	N 7251032	37.3	AUTRES PNEUS RECHAPES FLAPS
62599	TYRES NES,TYRE CASES,ETC		10.9	N 3044004	20.2	N 5301860	24.9	N 7000001	37.0	PNEUS,FLAPS
628	RUBBER ARTICLES NES		7.6		11.0	W 2	0.1			OUVRAGES CAOUTCHOUC NDA
6289	OTH RUBBER ARTICLES NES		7.5		10.8	W 20506	13.9	W 78	14.0	AUT OUVR CAOUTCHOUC NDA
62898	UNHARD RUBBER PRODS NES		7.5		10.8	W 20496	13.8	W 76	14.0	OUV CAOUT VULC NON DURCI
63	WOOD,CORK MANUFACTRS NES		19.4		13.8		17.7		21.9	OUVRAGES LIEGE ET BOIS
635	WOOD MANUFACTURES NES		19.3		13.8		17.5		21.6	ART MANUF EN BOIS NDA
6354	WOOD MFRS DOMESTIC ETC		15.4		10.6		13.9		17.9	ART MANUF USAGE DOMESTIQUE
63549	WOOD MFRS,DOMESTIC NES		15.4	MN 14517	10.6	MN 22187	13.9	MN 23257	17.9	OUVRAGES DE TABLETTERIE
65	TEXTILE YARN,FABRICS,ETC		41.4		81.2		103.3		133.0	FILS,TISSUS,ARTICLES TEXTILE
651	TEXTILE YARN		8.1		24.2		32.0		35.0	FILS TEXTILES
6516	DISCON SYN FIB BLEND YRN		3.9		19.7		25.2	W 340	26.5	FILS FIBR TEX SYNT DIS MOINS
65166	DISCON SYN FIB–COTTN YRN		3.6		19.6	W 10701	25.0	W 183	26.0	FILS TEXT SYNT MELANGE COTON
652	COTTON FABRICS,WOVEN		2.3		6.8		9.5		18.2	TISSUS DE COTON
6521	GREY WOVEN COTTON FABRIC		0.8		3.7		6.1	A 8724	13.5	TISSUS COT ECRUS NON MERCER
65214	GREY WOVEN COTTON NES		0.8		1.3		3.3	A 2062	10.6	AUT TISSUS 85% COTON ECRUS
653	WOVN MAN–MADE FIB FABRIC		4.6		9.3		18.8		23.4	TISSUS FIBRES SYNTH,ARTIF
6536	DISC REGN TXTL FABRC NES		1.8	A 1882	5.5	A 7729	9.9	A 3960	5.8	TISSUS 85% TEXT ART DISC
658	TEXTILE ARTICLES NES		20.8		33.8		30.9		44.4	ART FACONNES MAT TEXTILES
6582	MADE–UP CANVAS GOODS		5.3	N 187869	9.8	N 730228	13.9	N 661063	25.4	BACHES,TENTES ETC
6584	LINENS ETC		13.0		21.5	MN 2293666	13.2	MN 24780	12.8	LINGE DE MAISON
65841	BED LINEN OF COTTON		2.5	N 2360156	7.5	N 1573620	3.2	N 854598	1.6	LINGE DE LIT DE COTON
65845	OTHER LINEN OF COTTON		8.7	MN 36897	13.0	MN 2291287	8.4	MN 22845	8.0	LINGE DE TOILETTE COTON
66	NONMETAL MINERAL MFS NES		144.9		189.1		244.8		265.3	ART MIN NON METALLIQUES
666	POTTERY		17.1	MN 26699	23.8	MN 26674	27.1	MN 30437	29.7	POTERIE
6664	PORCELN,CHINA HOUSE WARE		7.1	MN 10702	9.5	MN 13038	12.0	MN 14828	14.3	VAISSELLE,ARTS MEN PORC
6666	CERAMIC ORNAMENTS ETC		9.8	MN 15580	13.7	MN 13243	14.3	MN 15447	15.1	OBJETS PORCELAINE,CERAM
667	PEARL,PREC–,SEMI–P STONE		121.8		158.9		209.8		226.0	PERLES, PIERRES GEMMES
6672	DIAMONDS NONINDUST,UNSET		65.1		101.8		137.2		145.0	DIAMANTS BRUTS
66722	— SRTD,ROUGH,SIMPLY WKD		20.3		17.7		23.9		39.9	DIAMANTS TRIES BRUTS
66729	— CUT ETC NOT SET		44.8		84.2		112.6		105.2	DIAMANTS TAILLES
6673	PREC–,SEMI–PR STONES NES		56.7		56.8		71.3		79.4	AUTRES PIERRES NON SERTIES
69	METAL MANUFACTURES NES		18.8		21.9		8.2		9.4	ART MANUFACT EN METAL NDA
694	STL,COPPR NAILS,NUTS,ETC		8.1		10.7		2.0	W 301	0.3	CLOUS,VIS,ECROUS
69402	IRN,STL NUTS,BOLTS,ETC		8.1		10.7		2.0	W 219	0.2	BOULONS,VIS,ECROUS FER,AC
695	TOOLS		6.3	N 102	0.1		0.5	N 20203	0.2	OUTILS A MAIN
6953	OTHER HAND TOOLS		6.1		5.6		0.5	N 19414	0.2	AUTRES OUTILS A MAIN
69532	WRENCHES AND SPANNERS		6.0	N 2087529	5.6		0.4	N 3908	0.1	CLES DE SERRAGE
7	MACHINES,TRANSPORT EQUIP		64.0		44.9		68.9		82.3	MACHINES MATERIEL TRANSPORT
72	MACHS FOR SPCL INDUSTRYS		3.0		2.1		16.0		6.1	MAC SPECIALES POUR INDUST

5. General Exports F.O.B. by Commodities according to the S.I.T.C. (Rev. 2) in million U.S. Dollars
Exportations Générales F.O.B. par Produits d'après la C.T.C.I. (Rév. 2) en millions de Dollars E.U.

SITC CTCI	COMMODITY	1991		1992		1993		1994		PRODUIT
		QUANTITY QUANTITE	VALUE VALEUR	QUANTITY QUANTITE	VALUE VALEUR	QUANTITY QUANTITE	VALUE VALEUR	QUANTITY QUANTITE	VALUE VALEUR	
728	OTH MACHY FOR SPCL INDUS		1.8	N 6	0.1		14.6	N 4776	2.7	AUT MACH IND PARTICULIERES
7284	MACHY FOR SPCL INDUS NES		1.5	N 495	0.6		14.5	N 192	2.5	MACH SPEC IND PARTICUL.
72848	OTH MCHY WITH INDIV FNCT		1.4	N 1	0.3		14.0	N 36	2.1	AUTRES MACHINES NDA
74	GENRL INDUSTRL MACHY NES		12.1		2.4		2.7		4.5	MACH APP INDUSTRIE
744	MECHANICAL HANDLING EQU		10.7		0.9		0.4	N 90	1.4	EQUIP MANUTENTION PIECES
7442	LIFTING,LOADING MACH NES		10.6		0.4		0.2	N 90	1.4	APP LEVAGE,MANUTENTION
74428	OTH HANDLING ETC MCH NES		9.6	N 1	0.2	N 2	0.1			AUT APP LEVAGE ETC
75	OFFICE MACHNES,ADP EQUIP		5.4		15.4		19.1		18.9	MACH BUREAU TRAIT AUTOM
759	OFFICE,ADP MCH PTS,ACCES		5.3		15.2		18.8	MN 152731	18.7	PIECES DU 751 ET 752
7599	ACCTG,ETC,ADP MCH PTS,AC		5.2	MN 92837	15.1	MN 2214164	18.7	MN 152215	18.7	PIECES DU 751 ET 752
77	ELECTRIC MACHNRY NES ETC		17.3		20.2		26.5		40.8	MACH APP ELECT NDA
772	SWITCHGEAR ETC,PARTS NES		8.4	MN 39849	9.4	MN 39414	7.8	MN 26904	16.6	APP COUPURE,SECT ETC
7721	SWITCHGEAR ETC		6.6	MN 15553	6.9	MN 16103	5.1	MN 11337	11.6	APP COUPURE,SECTIONMNT
778	ELECTRICAL MACHINERY NES		7.5	N 1301	0.1			MN 24351	11.5	AUTRES MACH ELECT NDA
7782	ELECTRIC LAMPS,BULBS		4.6	N 1451331	7.9	N 2718204	12.5	N 4030660	9.0	LAMPES, TUBES ELECTRIQUES
77822	ELEC DISCHARGE LAMPS NES		4.6	N 1444422	7.9	N 2231034	12.5	N 2101930	8.7	LAMPES NON ULTRA–VIOLETS
79	OTHR TRANSPORT EQUIPMENT		21.8		1.7		1.8		1.5	AUTRE MATERIEL TRANSPORT
792	AIRCRAFT ETC		20.9		0.8		1.0		0.5	APP NAVIGATION AERIENNE
7929	AIRCRAFT PARTS NES		20.7		0.3		0.5	N 1	0.1	PIECES DU 792
8	MISC MANUFACTURED GOODS		848.4		1302.8		1502.7		1705.0	ART MANUFACTURES DIVERS
821	*FURNITURE,PARTS THEREOF		2.1	N 803050	2.5	N 1	0.1	N 681011	10.8	MEUBLES ET PIECES
831	*TRAVEL GOODS,HANDBAGS		1.8		9.5	N 3831681	16.2	N 7109747	34.8	ARTICLES DE VOYAGE ETC
83102	TRAVEL GDS,TOILET–CASES	N 391641	1.7	N 2963658	9.2	N 3635655	14.5	N 5396148	21.1	ARTICLES DE VOYAGE
83109	OTHER TRAVEL BAGS,CASES		0.1		0.1	N 164233	1.6	N 1438374	12.7	AUT CONTENANTS SIMILAIRES
84	CLOTHING AND ACCESSORIES		790.6		1183.4		1356.0		1484.1	VETEMENTS
842	MENS OUTERWEAR NOT KNIT	N 4427	0.1	MN 28814	191.5	MN 31546	216.2	MN 36724	241.0	VET DESSUS POUR HOMMES
8421	— OVERCOATS,OTHER COATS		10.6	N 1183377	19.0	N 1542278	25.3	N 1759363	26.2	MANTEAUX HOMMES MAT TEXT
84219	—— OF OTHER FIBRES		10.5	N 1181205	18.9	N 1485517	24.6	N 1660859	24.5	MANTEAUX HOMMES AUT FIBR
8423	— TROUSERS,BREECHES ETC		60.2	MN 14641	75.4	MN 15817	80.7	MN 19589	86.2	PANTALONS HOMMES MAT TEX
8424	— JACKETS,BLAZERS ETC		47.0	N 7470912	72.1	N 8166927	79.3	N 8735613	94.0	VESTES HOMMES MAT TEXTIL
8429	— OTHER OUTER GARMENTS	N 4427	0.1	N 5156825	21.9	N 5204664	25.7	N 5578749	28.7	AUT VET DES HOM MAT TEX
843	WOMENS OUTERWEAR NONKNIT	N 9490	0.1	MN 3349806	462.6	MN 89296	506.3	MN 95632	557.1	VET DESSUS FEMMES MAT TEX
8431	— COATS AND JACKETS	N 3600	0.1	N 8445410	82.7	MN 9047	89.5	MN 10098	90.8	MANT,VEST FEM MAT TEXTIL
8432	— SUITS AND COSTUMES	N 840	0.1	N 1244047	8.7	N 1790189	11.7	N 2436419	14.3	COSTUMES–TAIL MAT TEXIL
8433	— DRESSES	N 600	0.1	MN 3279591	48.2	N 7171508	49.7	MN 10742	70.6	ROBES EN MAT–TEXTILES
8434	— SKIRTS		22.7	N 6234444	43.7	N 8134072	36.8	N 7136978	34.9	JUPES EN MAT TEXTILES
8435	— BLOUSES	N 4000	0.1	MN 31920	164.9	MN 34334	181.9	MN 34309	185.6	BLOUSES FEM MAT TEXTILES
8439	— OTHER OUTER GARMENTS	N 450	0.1	MN 22372	114.8	MN 28825	137.0	MN 30909	161.1	AUT VET DES FEM MAT TEXT
844	UNDER GARMENTS NOT KNIT		84.4	MN 27779	136.7	MN 35042	166.2	MN 33867	165.4	VETEMENT DESSOUS MAT TEX
8441	— MENS SHIRTS		67.3	MN 23485	110.5	MN 27107	123.0	MN 23848	109.3	CHEMISES HOMMES MAT TEXT
84411	—— OF COTTON		47.7	MN 15419	78.5	MN 16307	82.1	MN 12744	69.1	CHEMISES HOMMES DE COTON
84412	—— OF SYNTHETIC FIBRES		19.7	N 8066166	32.0	MN 10801	40.9	MN 11104	40.2	CHEMISES HOMMES FIB SYNT
8442	— MENS,OTHR THAN SHIRTS		3.3	N 898307	4.0	N 2402681	10.1	N 2386533	11.9	SOUS–VET HOMMES MAT TEXT
8443	— WOMENS		14.0	N 3395650	22.4	N 5531934	33.2	N 7632939	44.3	VET DESSOUS FEM MAT TEXT
845	OUTERWEAR KNIT NONELASTC		115.3	MN 28172	142.6	MN 39968	179.4	MN 42927	180.5	VET DESSOUS,ACCES BONNET
8451	— JERSEYS,PULLOVERS ETC	N 3685	0.1	N 5783432	35.3	N 6909613	39.1	MN 10298	49.8	CHANDAILS,PULL–OVERS ETC
8452	— WOMENS DRESSES ETC		17.9	N 3522150	23.9	N 4926950	26.0	N 4822049	27.4	ROBES,JUPES BONNETERIE
8459	— OTHER,CLTHG ACCESRYS		71.3	MN 18867	83.4	MN 28131	114.4	MN 27807	103.4	AUT VET DESSUS DE BONNE
846	UNDER GARMENTS KNITTED	N 7436	0.1	MN 79132	146.6	MN 84574	171.3	MN 90100	192.4	SOUS VETS DE BONNETERIE
8462	— OF COTTON NON ELASTIC		38.3	MN 22372	51.7	MN 23729	60.4	MN 29735	65.0	SOUS–VET BONNET COTON
84629	—— OTHER		38.3	MN 22372	51.7	MN 23729	60.4	MN 29735	65.0	AUT SOUS–VET BONNET COTON
8463	— OF SYNTH FBR NONELAST	N 7436	0.1	MN 49267	82.8	MN 52314	96.8	MN 51137	108.3	SOUS–VET BONNET FIB SYNT
84631	—— PANTY HOSE (TIGHTS)	N 6500	0.1	MN 37259	30.4	MN 37075	29.7	MN 32841	25.8	COLLANTS BON FIBR SYNT
84632	—— MENS SHIRTS	N 936	0.1	MN 12008	52.4	MN 15239	67.1	MN 18296	82.6	CHEMISES DE BON FIB SYNMT
8465	CORSETS,GARTERS,ETC		8.3	N 7492781	12.1	N 8531645	14.3	MN 9228	19.1	CORSETS,GAINES ART SIM
84651	BRASSIERES		6.7	N 5987301	9.6	N 7240565	12.3	N 8625983	17.6	SOUTIENS–GORGE,BUSTIERS
847	TEXTILE CLTHNG ACCES NES	N 5340	0.1	MN 74018	42.8	MN 82495	47.3	MN 112675	58.9	ACCES VET MAT TEXT NDA
8471	— NOT KNITTED	N 5340	0.1	N 2771943	9.7	N 3786626	9.4	MN 15788	13.7	ACCES VET MAT TEX NON BON
8472	CLTHNG ACCESRYS ETC KNIT		22.2	MN 71246	33.2	MN 78708	37.9	MN 96887	45.2	ACCES VET BONNE NDA
84721	KNIT GLOVES,ETC NONELAST		17.5	MN 65819	29.6	MN 69401	33.3	MN 86970	39.1	GANTERIE BONNET NON ELAS
848	HEADGEAR,NONTXTL CLOTHNG			MN 623665	60.8	N 15170	0.1	N 40307	0.1	VET ACCES MAT AUT QUE TEX
8481	LEATHER CLOTHES,ACCESSOR			N 2651900	12.5	N 3128121	15.8	N 3699411	15.5	VET ACCES MAT CUIR ARTIF
8482	PLASTC,RUBBR CLTHG,ACCES		11.2	MN 597947	28.8	MN 546822.	33.7	MN 714099	49.5	VET ACCES MAT PLAS ARTIF
84822	RUBBER CLOTHING,ACCESRYS		11.1	MN 597350	28.3	MN 545263	32.1	MN 711842	47.4	VET ACCES CAOUT VULCAN
8484	HEADGEAR		5.8	MN 23067	19.7			MN 30404	24.3	COIFFURES ET PARTIES NDA
84843	HEADGEAR TEXTILE NONFELT		5.6	MN 16846	19.4			MN 24251	22.9	CHAPEAUX EN BONNETERIE
851	*FOOTWEAR		10.3	N 4470661	17.2	N 5244029	25.3	N 5216890	38.2	CHAUSSURES
85102	FOOTWEAR LEATHER		8.5	N 3179486	14.3	N 3869432	21.5	N 3851437	34.5	CHAUS SEMELLES EN CUIR
89	MISC MANUFCTRD GOODS NES		41.8		87.9		99.1		132.8	ART MANUFACTURES DIVERS
893	ARTICLES OF PLASTIC NES				11.6		14.0		15.6	OUVRAGES EN MAT DIVIS 58
8931	PLSTC PACKG CONTNRS,LIDS		8.3	W 14612	7.4	W 7583	8.4	W 2	0.1	ART TRANSP EMBALLAGE ETC
894	TOYS,SPORTING GOODS,ETC		5.4		32.3	MN 60220	40.9	MN 49217	48.0	VOITURES ENFANTS,JOUETS
8942	TOYS,INDOOR GAMES ETC		4.7	MN 32298	31.2	MN 52443	38.8	MN 37054	44.8	JOUETS,JEUX ETC
89423	TOYS NES		3.6	MN 25406	28.0	MN 26339	34.2	MN 26968	40.1	JOUETS,MODELES REDUITS
897	GOLD,SILVER WARE,JEWELRY		8.0		10.7		12.6		24.8	BIJOUTERIE,ORFEVRERIE
8973	PREC JEWLRY,GLD–SILVWARE		7.2		7.2		7.3		17.9	BIJOUX OR,ARGENT ORFEVRE
89731	PRECIOUS METAL JEWELLERY		7.2		6.9		7.2		16.8	ART BIJOUTERIE,JOAILLER
899	OTHER MANUFACTURED GOODS		16.3		29.4		24.6	N 1200197	0.1	AUT ART MANUF DIVERS NDA
8997	BASKETWORK,BROOMS ETC		10.0		21.2		14.7		17.7	OUVRAGES VANNERIE NDA
89972	BRUSHES,BROOMS,MOPS ETC		9.8	MN 72356	21.0	MN 72654	14.5	MN 76159	17.6	BALAIS ET BALAYETTES
9	GOODS NOT CLASSD BY KIND		55.8		50.9		59.8		60.2	ART TRANSACT NON CLASSES
931	*SPECIAL TRANSACTIONS		55.8	W 333960	50.6	W 434259	59.7	W 453119	60.0	TRANS.SPECIALES

1. HISTORICAL SERIES, 1962–1997 GENERAL TRADE, IMPORTS C.I.F., EXPORTS F.O.B.
SERIES HISTORIQUES, 1962–1997 COMMERCE GENERAL, IMPORTATIONS C.A.F., EXPORTATIONS F.O.B

YEAR ANNEE	VALUE IN MILLION U.S. DOLLARS VALEUR EN MILLION U.S. DOLLARS MERCHANDISE –MARCHANDISE		GOLD –OR		CONVERSION FACTORS FACTEURS DE CONVERSION CENTS E.U. PAR		INDEX NUMBERS –INDICES QUANTUM		UNIT VALUE VALEUR UNITAIRE	
	IMPORTS	EXPORTS	IMPORTS	EXPORTS	IMPORTS	EXPORTS	IMPORTS	EXPORTS	IMPORTS	EXPORTS
1962	260.82	228.15	0.05	0.05						
1963	284.97	226.25	0.05	0.05						
1964	274.20	197.07								
1965	207.58	195.15								
1966	222.43	203.11								
1967	213.44	214.24								
1968	257.61	233.03								
1969	265.56	247.52								
1970	287.50	298.40								
1971	331.49	328.43								
1972	338.57	357.08								
1973	436.02	436.97								
1974	710.72	350.36								
1975	1033.40	437.92								
1976	980.33	554.21								
1977	1081.10	661.04								
1978	1197.83	532.92								
1979	1109.98	534.92								
1980	1576.40	542.70								
1981	1552.90	656.80								
1982	1282.40	498.10								
1983	1354.40	623.50								
1984	1146.70	628.70								
1985	770.70	373.90								
1986	960.90	333.30								
1987	871.00	503.90								
1988	1060.50	509.10								
1989		671.80								
1990	618.50	374.10								
1991	890.30	305.00								
1992	820.90	319.30								
1993	944.90	417.30								
1994	1161.50	523.90								
1995	1218.80	555.60								
1996	1547.30	620.30								
1997	1597.70	594.20								

2. IMPORTS BY BROAD ECONOMIC CATEGORY AND EXPORTS BY INDUSTRIAL ORIGIN. (PERCENTAGE OF TOTAL VALUE)
IMPORTATIONS PAR CATEGORIES ECONOMIQUES ET EXPORTATIONS PAR BRANCHE D'ACTIVITE.(EN POURCENTAGE DE LA VALEUR TOTALE)

IMPORTS – IMPORTATIONS

	1990	1991	1992	1993	1994	1995	1996
TOTAL IMPORTS–IMPORTATIONS TOTALES			100.	100.	100.	100.	100.
1 FOOD BEV–ALIMENTATION BOISSONS			9.3	13.3	15.9	19.0	13.9
11 PRIMARY–PRODUITS DE BASE			6.0	7.0	4.5	7.2	8.6
111 FOR INDUSTRY–POUR L'INDUSTRIE			2.6	3.3	1.9	5.4	6.1
112 FOR HOUSEHOLDS–POUR LES MENAGES			3.4	3.7	2.6	1.8	2.4
12 PROCESSED–PRODUITS ELABORES			3.3	6.2	11.4	11.8	5.3
121 FOR INDUSTRY–POUR L'INDUSTRIE			1.5	3.6	8.9	10.8	3.9
122 FOR HOUSEHOLDS–POUR LES MENAGES			1.8	2.6	2.5	1.1	1.4
2 IND SUPPLIES–APPROV INDUSTRIELS			28.0	33.0	27.5	31.3	32.1
21 PRIMARY–PRODUITS DE BASE			0.4	0.9	2.0	2.9	2.5
22 PROCESSED–PRODUITS ELABORES			27.6	32.1	25.4	28.4	29.6
3 FUELS–COMBUSTIBLES			19.1	15.1	22.4	13.8	19.1
31 PRIMARY–PRODUITS DE BASE			8.4	4.6	8.3	2.9	0.2
32 PROCESSED–PRODUITS ELABORES			10.7	10.5	14.1	10.9	18.8
321 MOTOR SPIRIT–ESSENCE			2.2	1.8	2.6	4.0	1.1
322 OTHER–AUTRES			8.4	8.7	11.4	7.0	17.8
4 MACHINERY–EQUIPEMENT			14.7	16.7	14.8	14.8	15.9
41 CAPITAL EQUIPMENT–MACHINES			13.5	15.6	13.8	13.4	14.9
42 PARTS–PIECES ACCESSOIRES			1.2	1.1	1.0	1.3	1.0
5 TRANSPORT–TRANSPORT			23.0	14.4	11.3	13.6	10.3
51 PASSENGER CARS–AUTOMOBILES			2.9	2.0	2.3	4.6	1.5
52 OTHER–AUTRES			14.3	6.6	4.4	6.0	5.1
521 INDUSTRIAL–INDUSTRIELS			14.1	6.5	4.2	5.9	4.9
522 NON INDUSTRIAL–NON INDUSTRIEL			0.2	0.1	0.2	0.1	0.2
53 PARTS–PIECES ACCESSOIRES			5.7	5.7	4.6	3.0	3.7
6 CONSUM GOODS–BIENS CONSOMMATION			5.6	7.5	7.9	7.3	7.3
61 DURABLE–DURABLES			1.1	1.4	1.7	0.9	0.9
62 SEMI DURABLE–SEMI DURABLES			1.7	2.6	2.3	2.6	3.2
63 NON DURABLE–NON DURABLES			2.8	3.5	3.9	3.8	3.2
7 GOODS NES–BIENS NDA			0.3	0.1	0.2	0.2	1.4

EXPORTS – EXPORTATIONS

	1990	1991	1992	1993	1994	1995	1996
TOTAL EXPORTS–EXPORTATIONS TOTALES			100.	100.	100.	100.	100.
1 AGRICULTURE			78.0	80.4	78.4	63.9	70.5
2 MINING QUARRY–INDUS EXTRACTIVES			0.0	0.1	0.1	0.3	0.1
3 MANUFACTURING–IND MANUFACTUR			21.9	19.5	21.5	35.7	29.4
31 FOOD BEV TOBACCO–ALIM BOISS TAB			19.7	16.6	17.8	20.7	20.9
32 TEXTILES–INDUSTRIES TEXTILES			1.2	1.9	1.6	14.7	7.5
33 WOOD & PRODUCTS–BOIS & PRODUITS				0.0			
34 PAPER & PRODUCTS–PAPIER & PRODT			0.0	0.0	0.0	0.0	0.0
35 CHEMICALS–INDUSTRIES CHIMIQUES			0.1	0.1	0.1	0.3	0.0
36 NON METAL MIN–MIN NON METAL					0.0		
37 BASIC METAL–IND METAL BASE				0.0			0.2
38 METAL MANUF–MANUF METAL			0.9	0.8	1.9	0.1	0.7
39 OTH MANUF IND–AUTRES MANUF			0.1	0.0	0.0	0.0	0.0

3. TRADE BY PRINCIPAL COUNTRIES OF CONSIGNMENT AND DESTINATION (VALUE IN MILLION U.S. DOLLARS)
ECHANGES SELON LES PRINCIPAUX PAYS DE CONSIGNATION ET DE DESTINATION (VALEUR EN MILLIONS DE DOLLARS EU)

GENERAL IMPORTS C.I.F. IMPORTATIONS GENERALES C.A.F

COUNTRIES–PAYS	1992	1993	1994	1995	1996
World	1225.1	1261.5	1486.0	1184.9	1072.8
Africa	132.5	173.5	189.5	158.6	100.7
Americas	72.9	65.9	83.8	132.4	121.6
– Northern America	64.7	58.0	74.9	125.5	104.6
– LAIA	8.0	7.8	7.3	4.8	12.6
– CACM				0.2	0.4
– Caribbean	0.1	0.0	1.4	1.6	3.4
– Rest of America	0.1		0.1	0.3	0.5
Asia excl fmr USSR	592.8	541.2	654.6	406.8	481.3
– Middle East	277.0	277.2	402.1	161.3	255.2
Asia former USSR					
Europe excl fmr USSR	415.1	473.9	549.9	480.8	341.4
– European Union	326.7	379.4	439.5	393.3	275.1
– Eastern Europe	73.5	79.7	78.2	55.4	51.5
– Rest of Europe	14.9	14.8	32.2	32.1	14.9
Europe former USSR	3.0	3.2	5.8	4.5	17.5
Oceania	5.5	3.8	2.5	1.9	10.3
Other	3.3	0.0		0.0	0.0
Saudi Arabia	141.5	128.3	242.3	65.7	103.0
Japan/Japon	174.3	63.1	77.7	114.3	59.7
United Kingdom	97.1	94.8	129.1	74.3	71.8
USA/Etats–Unis d'Amer	62.3	56.8	70.1	122.6	91.6
France, Monaco	26.5	63.2	73.0	86.7	57.5
Egypt/Egypte	56.4	86.5	68.8	63.6	30.3
Germany/Allemagne	60.5	45.4	50.0	72.3	48.6
Netherlands/Pays–Bas	48.0	46.5	51.4	41.5	24.5
Romania/Roumanie	41.9	58.7	45.1	15.3	30.9
Belgium–Luxembourg	23.1	41.0	55.2	52.0	11.6
Iran (Islamic Rep of)	51.3	29.1	37.1	8.4	55.9
China/Chine	29.6	31.0	30.0	31.1	46.9
United Arab Emirates	10.3	19.0	54.5	40.8	40.9
Italy/Italie	37.5	50.6	21.2	20.6	25.5
Libyan Arab Jamahiriya	31.5	29.1	48.5	25.4	6.7
Yemen/Yémen	48.1	69.2	5.8	0.4	12.8
Malaysia/Malaisie	26.1	45.1	17.9	30.4	16.2
India/Inde	19.8	26.1	31.2	17.9	34.2
Kenya	26.5	35.0	18.5	9.8	18.2
Korea, Republic of	11.9	24.8	22.8	16.9	20.7
Turkey/Turquie	6.7	6.8	33.0	23.5	18.9
Bangladesh	18.4	11.3	25.5	11.1	13.5
Switzerland,Liechtenst.	6.5	9.9	14.0	30.0	11.7
Indonesia/Indonésie	10.8	22.5	17.9	8.0	12.5
Singapore/Singapour	18.2	28.8	7.3	6.9	8.3
Bulgaria/Bulgarie	20.9	17.1	9.0	8.6	5.7
Jordan/Jordanie	12.2	16.7	11.8	6.8	13.0
Sweden/Suède	11.7	13.1	16.8	8.8	9.1
Greece/Grèce	8.4	7.5	6.7	12.5	8.7
Austria/Autriche	6.0	7.8	17.6	9.7	2.3
Poland/Pologne	7.5	2.2	21.5	5.7	4.9
Djibouti	2.9	11.4	23.0	0.0	0.0
Hungary/Hongrie	0.4	0.1	0.2	24.7	8.9
Zimbabwe				15.3	15.9
Denmark/Danemark	3.2	2.4	9.3	6.9	8.4
Canada	2.4	1.2	4.9	2.8	13.0
Australia/Australie	5.5	3.8	2.5	1.8	9.4
Syrian Arab Republic	1.2	5.5	11.0	1.6	3.4
Spain/Espagne	2.4	5.4	5.9	3.4	3.8
So. African Customs Un			0.2	7.8	12.9

EXPORTS EXPORTATIONS ES F.O.B.

COUNTRIES–PAYS	1992	1993	1994	1995	1996
Monde	281.6	294.2	394.9	685.2	273.1
Afrique	49.7	50.3	40.3	27.2	26.2
Amériques	3.0	6.6	17.2	57.9	5.8
– Amérique du Nord	3.0	4.4	17.0	56.2	5.4
– ALAI		2.2	0.3	0.4	0.3
– MCAC					0.0
– Caraïbes				1.2	0.0
– Autre Amérique				0.0	0.1
Asie anc. URSS exclus	142.6	137.2	255.6	329.6	154.8
– Moyen–Orient	93.7	112.7	106.4	177.4	96.8
Asie ancienne URSS					
Europe anc. URSS exclus	84.0	88.4	80.1	270.6	86.3
– Union Européenne	80.4	87.0	77.8	235.7	85.6
– Europe de l'Est	0.0	0.9	0.5	10.3	0.2
– Autre de l'Europe	3.5	0.5	1.8	24.5	0.4
Europe ancienne URSS	0.1	0.0	1.7	0.0	0.1
Océanie					0.0
Autre	2.2	11.6			0.0
Saudi Arabia	58.4	60.8	81.0	95.1	54.8
United Kingdom	11.3	18.6	25.4	38.6	41.0
China/Chine	0.8	0.4	45.7	50.2	22.2
Italy/Italie	26.8	19.4	0.0	50.9	15.8
Thailand/Thaïlande	21.6	12.9	20.3	40.9	12.8
France, Monaco	8.8	11.9	20.4	50.8	4.5
Japan/Japon	13.4	6.5	14.7	39.0	12.2
USA/Etats–Unis d'Amer	3.0	4.3	16.9	56.2	5.2
Germany/Allemagne	19.9	14.7	10.4	27.5	6.7
Libyan Arab Jamahiriya	22.6	32.6	16.2	0.3	2.5
Belgium–Luxembourg	2.4	12.7	8.6	47.4	1.7
Egypt/Egypte	19.7	6.4	9.1	20.3	14.4
Jordan/Jordanie	13.5	6.1	7.2	16.0	12.4
Turkey/Turquie	3.5	30.2	2.9	12.1	3.6
United Arab Emirates	0.4	2.6	1.9	27.3	12.4
Other Asia n.e.s.			35.3	0.6	0.1
India/Inde	5.6	0.6	10.4	11.8	0.9
Lebanon/Liban	4.2	0.0	0.0	16.0	5.3
Greece/Grèce	7.5	3.8	3.9	2.7	5.6
Netherlands/Pays–Bas	1.5	2.8	5.5	6.6	6.1
Switzerland,Liechtenst.	3.5	0.4	1.7	16.0	0.3
Yemen/Yémen	1.3	3.2	4.1	7.4	3.9
Syrian Arab Republic	5.1	4.3	4.7	1.9	2.9
Somalia/Somalie		2.7	7.5		3.9
Areas n.e.s.	2.2	11.6			0.0
Korea Dem People's Rp	0.0	0.2	11.6	1.2	0.0
Korea, Republic of	0.7	1.3	5.3	1.4	4.0
Iraq	6.6	4.7		1.3	0.0
Bangladesh	3.1	0.6	4.2	3.7	0.9
Tunisia/Tunisie	2.0	1.1	4.0	2.6	1.7
Sweden/Suède	0.7	0.6	1.3	6.3	1.4
Norway,Svalbard and JM		0.0	0.0	8.5	
Romania/Roumanie				8.5	0.0
Djibouti		2.5	0.6	1.5	3.1
China, Hong Kong SAR	2.7	0.3	0.8	0.2	3.3
Spain/Espagne	0.4	0.2	0.7	2.9	1.7
Kenya	1.3	1.8	1.0	0.4	0.6
Kuwait/ Koweït	0.3	0.0	4.0		0.0
Ethiopia, incl Eritrea	4.1				
Ethiopia/Ethiopie		1.6	1.8	0.3	0.0

(VALUE AS PERCENTAGE OF WORLD TOTAL)(VALEURS EN POURCENTAGE DU TOTAL MONDIAL)

	1987	1988	1989	1990	1991	1992	1993	1994	1995	1996
Africa	8.2	13.5				10.8	13.8	12.8	13.4	9.4
Americas	12.8	10.4				6.0	5.2	5.6	11.2	11.3
– Northern America	11.2	9.8				5.3	4.6	5.0	10.6	9.8
– LAIA	1.5	0.6				0.7	0.6	0.5	0.4	1.2
– CACM									0.0	0.0
– Caribbean		0.0				0.0	0.0	0.1	0.1	0.3
– Rest of America						0.0		0.0	0.0	0.0
Asia excl fmr USSR	38.6	38.0				48.4	42.9	44.1	34.3	44.9
– Middle East	24.2	20.8				22.6	22.0	27.1	13.6	23.8
Asia former USSR										
Europe excl fmr USSR	39.5	37.7				33.9	37.6	37.0	40.6	31.8
– European Union	36.0	33.2				26.7	30.1	29.6	33.2	25.6
– Eastern Europe	1.8	2.1				6.0	6.3	5.3	4.7	4.8
– Rest of Europe	1.7	2.4				1.2	1.2	2.2	2.7	1.4
Europe former USSR	0.1	0.3				0.2	0.3	0.4	0.4	1.6
Oceania	0.2	0.0				0.5	0.3	0.2	0.2	1.0
Other	0.6					0.3	0.0		0.0	0.0
Saudi Arabia	20.9	16.3				11.5	10.2	16.3	5.5	9.6
Japan/Japon	7.4	3.7				14.2	5.0	5.2	9.6	5.6
United Kingdom	10.5	7.5				7.9	7.5	8.7	6.3	6.7
USA/Etats–Unis d'Amer	10.4	8.7				5.1	4.5	4.7	10.3	8.5
France, Monaco	3.5	3.0				2.2	5.0	4.9	7.3	5.4
Egypt/Egypte	6.5	3.4				4.6	6.9	4.6	5.4	2.8
Germany/Allemagne						4.9	3.6	3.4	6.1	4.5
Netherlands/Pays–Bas	4.5	4.9				3.9	3.7	3.5	3.5	2.3
Romania/Roumanie	0.8	0.9				3.4	4.7	3.0	1.3	2.9
Belgium–Luxembourg	4.8	5.0				1.9	3.3	3.7	4.4	1.1

	1987	1988	1989	1990	1991	1992	1993	1994	1995	1996
Afrique	4.1	5.3				17.6	17.1	10.2	4.0	9.6
Amériques	4.8	3.2				1.1	2.2	4.4	8.4	2.1
– Amérique du Nord	4.7	3.2				1.1	1.5	4.3	8.2	2.0
– ALAI	0.1						0.8	0.1	0.1	0.1
– MCAC										0.0
– Caraïbes									0.2	0.0
– Autre Amérique									0.0	0.0
Asie anc. URSS exclus	34.5	49.1				50.6	46.7	64.7	48.1	56.7
– Moyen–Orient	14.3	17.0				33.3	38.3	26.9	25.9	35.4
Asie ancienne URSS										
Europe anc. URSS exclus	56.3	41.6				29.8	30.1	20.3	39.5	31.6
– Union Européenne	49.9	32.5				28.6	29.6	19.7	34.4	31.4
– Europe de l'Est	1.7	1.8				0.0	0.3	0.1	1.5	0.1
– Autre de l'Europe	4.8	7.2				1.3	0.2	0.5	3.6	0.2
Europe ancienne URSS	0.2	0.8				0.0	0.0	0.4	0.0	0.0
Océanie	0.0									0.0
Autre						0.8	3.9			0.0
Saudi Arabia	9.5	11.7				20.7	20.7	20.5	13.9	20.1
United Kingdom	8.2	6.8				4.0	6.3	6.4	5.6	15.0
China/Chine	0.0	2.2				0.3	0.1	11.6	7.3	8.1
Italy/Italie	10.8	7.7				9.5	6.6	0.0	7.4	5.8
Thailand/Thaïlande	5.3	9.0				7.7	4.4	5.1	6.0	4.7
France, Monaco	4.0	2.7				3.1	4.0	5.2	7.4	1.7
Japan/Japon	6.3	11.1				4.8	2.2	3.7	5.7	4.5
USA/Etats–Unis d'Amer	4.7	3.2				1.1	1.5	4.3	8.2	1.9
Germany/Allemagne						7.1	5.0	2.6	4.0	2.5
Libyan Arab Jamahiriya	0.1	0.1				8.0	11.1	4.1	0.0	0.9

4. General Imports C.I.F. by Commodities according to the S.I.T.C. (Rev. 2) in million U.S. Dollars
Importations Générales C.A.F. par Produits d'après la C.T.C.I. (Rév. 2) en millions de Dollars E.U.

SITC CTCI	COMMODITY	1993		1994		1995		1996		PRODUIT
		QUANTITY QUANTITE	VALUE VALEUR	QUANTITY QUANTITE	VALUE VALEUR	QUANTITY QUANTITE	VALUE VALEUR	QUANTITY QUANTITE	VALUE VALEUR	
	ALL COMMODITIES		1261.6		1486.1		1185.0		1072.9	TOUS PRODUITS
0	FOOD AND LIVE ANIMALS		167.2		235.9		216.2		141.7	ALIMENTS,ANIMAUX VIVANTS
02	DAIRY PRODCTS,BIRDS'EGGS		10.3		9.5		4.4		4.7	PRODUITS LAITIERS,OEUFS
022	MILK AND CREAM	W 4905	9.6	W 3972	9.1	W 1009	4.1	W 2058	4.4	LAIT ET CREME
0224	MILK,CREAM PRESERVED ETC	W 4905	9.6	W 3972	9.1	W 1007	4.1	W 2058	4.4	LAIT,CREME CONS,CONC
02242	MILK DRY,1.5% FAT OR LES	W 4905	9.6	W 3972	9.1	W 698	3.2	W 1473	2.7	LAIT POUDRE INF 1.5%
04	CEREALS AND PREPARATIONS		85.1		153.8		172.2		84.1	CEREALES ET PRODUITS
041	WHEAT ETC UNMILLED	W 164912	30.5	W 111098	14.9	W 57620	48.3	W 224811	47.0	FROMENT,EPEAUTRE
0411	DURUM WHEAT UNMILLED					W 57620	48.3	W 224811	47.0	FROMENT DUR NON MOULU
042	RICE	W 37760	12.5	W 20367	9.7	W 28636	9.1	W 25403	8.2	RIZ
0421	RICE IN HUSK OR HUSKED					W 28630	9.1	W 25323	8.2	RIZ SANS AUTRE PREPARATION
04211	RICE IN THE HUSK					W 17227	6.0	W 14051	4.2	RIZ PADDY
04212	RICE HUSKED					W 11403	3.1	W 11272	4.0	RIZ CARGO
0422	RICE SEMI–MILLED,MILLED	W 37760	12.5	W 20367	9.7	W 6	0.1	W 80	0.1	RIZ POLI,GLACE INCL BRISURES
046	WHEAT ETC MEAL OR FLOUR	W 158910	36.8	W 417844	113.5	W 681645	111.5	W 127192	27.9	SEMOULE FARINE,FROMENT
04601	FLOUR OF WHEAT OR MESLIN	W 158910	36.8	W 417844	113.5	W 681645	111.5	W 127192	27.9	FARINE DE FROMENT
047	OTHER CEREAL MEALS,FLOUR	W 13235	4.0	W 48744	13.4	W 64	0.1	W 86	0.1	AUTRES SEMOULES,FARINES
04701	CEREAL FLOUR(NON–WHEAT)	W 7180	1.6	W 21154	5.3			W 86	0.1	FARINES DE CEREALES
04702	MEAL OR GROATS NON–WHEAT	W 6055	2.4	W 27591	8.2	W 64	0.1			GRUAUX,SEMOULES DE CEREALES
05	VEGETABLES AND FRUIT		19.6		24.2		10.6		8.0	LEGUMES ET FRUITS
054	VEG ETC FRSH,SMPLY PRSVD	W 31659	16.9	W 37750	18.4	W 20450	9.9	W 17377	6.7	LEGUMES FRAIS,CONG,SECS
0542	LEGUMINOUS VEGETBLES DRY	W 31659	16.9	W 37738	18.4	W 19790	9.2	W 13682	4.3	LEGUMES A COSSE SECS
07	COFFEE,TEA,COCOA,SPICES		38.5		31.4		16.9		30.4	CAFE,THE,CACAO,EPICES
071	COFFEE AND SUBSTITUTES	W 5200	8.7	W 7608	11.1	W 3380	5.6	W 6087	9.4	CAFE ET SUCCEDANES
0711	COFFEE GREEN,ROASTED,SUB	W 5200	8.7	W 7608	11.1	W 3380	5.6	W 6087	9.4	CAFE TORREFIE OU DECAFEINE
07111	COFFEE GREEN,HUSKS,SKINS					W 3360	5.6	W 6049	9.3	CAFE NON TORREFIE
074	TEA AND MATE	W 17452	28.4	W 11239	18.1	W 10533	10.2	W 21236	19.0	THE ET MATE
0741	TEA	W 17452	28.4	W 11239	18.1	W 10533	10.2	W 21236	19.0	THE
09	MISC EDIBLE PRODUCTS		10.5		13.7		7.5		10.7	PREP ALIMENTAIRES DIVERSES
098	EDIBLE PRODCTS,PREPS NES	W 2699	10.4	W 3781	13.5	W 2377	7.1	W 3321	10.3	PREP ALIMENTAIRES NDA
09806	YEASTS,BAKING POWDERS	W 1385	3.6	W 1353	4.0	W 432	2.0	W 2135	4.9	LEVURES
09809	MISC FOOD PREPRTIONS NES	W 1021	6.2	W 1883	8.5	W 968	2.8	W 610	2.3	PREP ALIMENTAIRES NDA
1	BEVERAGES AND TOBACCO		6.1		22.6		18.1		18.1	BOISSONS ET TABACS
12	TOBACCO AND MANUFACTURES		6.0		22.5		17.9		17.8	TABACS BRUTS FABRIQUES
121	TOBACCO UNMNFCTRD,REFUSE	W 1053	5.6	W 2625	21.5	W 3624	17.4	W 3666	17.1	TABACS BRUTS,DECHETS
1211	TOBACCO,NOT STRIPPED					W 3624	17.4	W 3625	16.9	TABACS NON ECOTES
2	CRUDE MATERLS,EXCL FUELS		27.4		25.3		23.5		19.2	MAT BRUTES NON COMESTIBLES
23	RUBBER, CRUDE		2.7		2.8		2.7		4.6	CAOUTCHOUC BRUT
232	NATURAL RUBBER,GUMS	W 1276	2.0	W 129	0.2	W 1349	2.0	W 2696	3.8	LATEX CAOUTCHOUC NATUREL
23203	BALATA,GUTTA–PERCHA, ETC					W 1339	2.0	W 2644	3.7	BALATA,GUTTA–PERCHA
24	CORK AND WOOD		20.7		12.8		12.3		10.4	LIEGE ET BOIS
247	OTH WOOD ROUGH,SQUARED	W 65	0.1			W 11989	4.9	W 5761	1.9	BOIS BRUTS EQUARRIS
2472	SAW–,VENEER–LOGS NON–CON	W 20	0.1			W 11950	4.9	W 5761	1.9	NON CONIFERES SCIAGE,PLAC
24721	— IN THE ROUGH					W 11950	4.9	W 5761	1.9	BRUTS ECORCES DEGROSSIS
248	WOOD SHAPED,SLEEPERS		20.7		12.8	W 16087	7.5	W 23013	8.5	BOIS SIMPLEMENT TRAVAILLES
2481	RAILWAY SLEEPERS,TIES		5.1		1.3	W 8436	3.3	W 8485	3.7	TRAVERSES VOIES FERREES
2482	LUMBER SHAPED CONIFER	W 37190	15.7	W 24464	11.5	W 1322	0.7	W 359	0.2	CONIFERES SCIES,RABOTES
2483	LUMBER SHAPED NON–CONIFR	W 37	0.1	W 12	0.1	W 6328	3.5	W 14169	4.7	NON CONIFERES SCIES,RABOTES
24831	LUMBER SAWN ETC NON–CON					W 6328	3.5	W 14155	4.7	SCIES LONGITUDINALEMENT
26	TEXTILE FIBRES AND WASTE		0.2		3.7		5.9		0.8	FIBRES TEXTILES
269	WASTE OF TEXTILE FABRICS	W 48	0.1	W 659	3.4	W 224632	5.9	W 1797	0.7	FRIPERIE DRILLES,CHIFFONS
26901	BULK TEXT WSTE,OLD CLTHG					W 224632	5.9	W 1789	0.7	ART ET ACCESS D'HABILLEMENT
3	MINERAL FUELS ETC		195.9		336.5		164.6		207.8	COMBUSTIBLES MINERAUX LUB
32	COAL,COKE AND BRIQUETTES								6.1	HOUILLES,COKES,BRIQUETTES
323	BRIQUETS,COKE,SEMI–COKE							W 56977	6.1	BRIQUETTES
3231	BRIQUETTES,OVOIDS ETC							W 56962	6.1	BRIQUETTES ET BOULETS
32311	BRIQUETTES OF COAL							W 56962	6.1	BRIQUETTES DE HOUILLE
33	PETROLEUM AND PRODUCTS		182.5		331.7		162.3		199.2	PETROLE ET DERIVES
333	CRUDE PETROLEUM	W 334190	44.5	W 677447	119.1	W 108527	31.5			HUILES BRUTES DE PETROLE
334	PETROLEUM PRODUCTS,REFIN	W 745774	132.3	W 891495	209.1	W 406714	129.7	W 1417085	196.2	PRODUITS RAFFINES
3341	GASOLINE,OTH LIGHT OILS	W 158232	23.0	W 152701	40.9	W 109219	47.3	W 67661	11.8	ESSENCES POUR MOTEURS
33411	MOTOR,AVIATION SPIRIT	W 158171	23.0	W 147633	39.1	W 109207	47.3	W 67661	11.8	ESSENCES MOTEURS D'AVIONS
3342	KEROSENE,OTH MEDIUM OILS					W 6236	3.5	W 36440	4.6	PETR LAMPANTS,AUT HUIL
33421	KEROSENE INCL JET FUEL					W 6236	3.5	W 36440	4.6	PETROLES LAMPANTS
3343	GAS OILS	W 504124	86.5	W 581029	136.4	W 31386	23.7	W 463781	57.1	GAS OILS
3344	FUEL OILS,NES	W 59847	4.6	W 144270	19.9	W 243902	41.2	W 690823	86.6	FUEL OILS
3345	LUBS,PETROLEUM OILS NES	W 23571	18.3	W 13496	12.0	W 15971	14.3	W 158381	36.3	HUILES LUBRIFIANTES
33451	LUBS(HIGH PETR CONT) ETC	W 23571	18.3	W 13496	12.0	W 15970	14.3	W 158292	36.2	HUILES LUBRIF,H LOURDES
335	RESIDUAL PETRLM PROD NES	W 38101	5.8	W 8085	3.7	W 737	1.1	W 13796	3.0	PRODUITS RESIDUELS NDA
3353	MIN TAR PITCH,PITCH COKE	W 31794	3.9	W 6082	1.2	W 112	0.5	W 12545	2.0	BRAI,COKE DE BRAI
33531	PITCH FROM MINERAL TARS	W 31794	3.9	W 6082	1.2	W 112	0.5	W 12545	2.0	BRAI DE GOUDRON
341	*GAS,NATURAL AND MANUFCT	W 5712	13.5	W 11622	4.9	W 3316	2.4	W 13735	2.6	GAZ NATUREL,GAZ MANUFACT
4	ANIMAL,VEGETABLE OIL,FAT		63.4		29.2		54.7		26.1	HUILES,GRAISSES ANIM,VEG
411	*ANIMAL OILS AND FATS	W 126651	32.5	W 33156	14.8	W 77389	40.7	W 51211	17.5	HUILES,GRAISSES ANIMALES
4113	ANIML OIL,FAT,GREASE NES	W 126651	32.5	W 33156	14.8	W 77389	40.7	W 51211	17.5	HUILES,GRAISSES ANIMALES NDA
41133	LARD STEARIN AND OIL,ETC					W 73889	38.7	W 51195	17.5	STEARINE SOLAIRE
42	FIXED VEGETABLE OIL,FAT		30.2		13.6		12.2		7.9	HUILES VEGETALES FIXES
424	FIXED VEG OIL NONSOFT	W 44508	30.2	W 17864	13.6	W 24651	11.4	W 20189	7.9	AUTRES HUILES VEG FIXES
4242	PALM OIL					W 21285	9.3	W 16010	5.8	HUILE DE PALME
4249	FIXED VEGETABLE OILS NES	W 44508	30.2	W 17864	13.6	W 2053	1.3	W 2133	1.2	HUILES VEGET FIXES NDA
5	CHEMCLS,RELATED PROD NES		139.6		130.0		123.1		160.6	PRODUITS CHIMIQUES
51	ORGANIC CHEMICALS		5.8		6.7		4.5		32.7	PROD CHIMIQ ORGANIQUES
511	HYDROCARBONS NES,DERIVS	W 752	4.9	W 420	3.7	W 318	2.2	W 6028	28.8	HYDROCARBURES NDA
5113	HALOG DERIV OF HYDROCARB					W 209	1.7	W 5646	28.1	DERIVES HALOGENES HYDROCAR
51139	OTH HALOG HYDRCARB DERIV					W 209	1.7	W 5633	28.1	AUTRE DERIVES HALOGENES
52	INORGANIC CHEMICALS		15.8		14.5		12.4		15.2	PROD CHIM INORGANIQUES
522	INORG ELEMNTS,OXIDES,ETC	W 24551	12.6	W 13797	11.4	W 11297	7.8	W 17814	7.4	ELEMENTS INORGANIQUES
5225	INORGANIC BASES ETC NES	W 20199	8.4	W 9580	7.0	W 9225	4.8	W 11015	3.7	AUTRES BASES OXYDES METAL
52252	SODIUM HYDROXIDE, SOLID	W 20042	8.1	W 9485	6.7	W 8995	3.9	W 10718	3.4	HYDROXYDE DE SODIUM
523	OTHR INORG CHEMICALS ETC	W 9207	3.3	W 4604	3.1	W 9481	4.6	W 15104	7.7	AUT PRODUITS CHIMIQUES INORG
5232	OTH MTL CMPD OF INRG ACD	W 1736	0.7	W 2260	1.2	W 3168	1.8	W 6353	3.7	SELS METALLIQUES
53	DYES,TANNING,COLOUR PROD		2.5		4.4		3.8		6.4	PROD TEINTURE,COLORANTS
533	PIGMENTS,PAINTS,ETC	W 1418	1.8	W 3318	3.4	W 904	2.7	W 6945	5.1	PIGMENTS,PEINTURES,VERNIS
5334	VARNISHES,DISTEMPERS ETC	W 828	1.1	W 2385	2.2	W 561	1.7	W 4946	3.5	PEINTURES A L'EAU
541	*MEDICINAL,PHARM PRODUCT	K 5727479	40.8	K 6213891	44.2	K 7863371	37.1	K 3821641	25.4	PROD MEDICINAUX PHARMACEUT
5416	GLYCOSIDES,GLANDS,SERA	K 2499851	5.8	K 357512	1.2	K 324214	4.3	K 1541565	2.9	HETEROSIDES
54164	ANTISERA,MICROB VACCINES					K 322512	4.2	K 57676	1.2	SERUMS,VACCINS
5417	MEDICAMENTS	K 2958663	31.1	K 5502868	40.1	K 7016228	27.8	K 1907990	19.2	MEDICAMENTS
54171	— CONTAINNG ANTIBIOTICS					K 2629609	18.4	K 818197	11.4	MED CONTN ANTIBIOTIQUES
54179	— CONTNG OTH SUBSTANCES					K 4377739	9.2	K 1020130	7.3	MED CONT AUT SUBSTANCES
55	PERFUME,CLEANING ETC PRD		3.2		5.6		5.6		7.5	PROD POUR PARFUM,TOILETTE

4. General Imports C.I.F. by Commodities according to the S.I.T.C. (Rev. 2) in million U.S. Dollars
Importations Générales C.A.F. par Produits d'après la C.T.C.I. (Rév. 2) en millions de Dollars E.U.

SITC CTCI	COMMODITY	1993 QUANTITY QUANTITE	1993 VALUE VALEUR	1994 QUANTITY QUANTITE	1994 VALUE VALEUR	1995 QUANTITY QUANTITE	1995 VALUE VALEUR	1996 QUANTITY QUANTITE	1996 VALUE VALEUR	PRODUIT
554	SOAP,CLEANSING ETC PREPS	W 619	1.2	W 789	1.9	W 573	1.5	W 4222	4.0	SAVONS,PRODUITS DETERSIFS
5541	SOAPS	W 374	0.9	W 642	1.6	W 500	1.3	W 3867	3.7	SAVONS,PROD TENSIO–ACTIFS
562	*FERTILIZERS,MANUFACTURE	W 234245	44.4	W 101660	19.7	W 84067	28.8	W 189445	38.9	ENGRAIS MANUFACTURES
5621	CHEM NITROGENOUS FERTLZR	W 199234	37.7	W 73242	14.5	W 84051	25.6	W 183551	37.4	ENGRAIS AZOTES
56216	UREA					W 83977	25.5	W 182633	37.2	UREE
5622	CHEM PHOSPHATIC FERTILZR	W 35006	6.8	W 28400	5.3	W 12	3.3	W 3630	1.2	ENGRAIS PHOSPHATES
56229	CHEM PHOSPH FERTILZR NES	W 35006	6.8	W 28400	5.3					ENGRAIS PHOSPHATES NDA
58	PLASTIC MATERIALS ETC		9.2		12.2		10.0		18.1	MAT PLAST ARTIFICIELLES
583	POLYMERIZATION ETC PRODS	W 5736	6.1	W 8979	9.3	W 3483	6.0	W 8951	11.0	PROD POLYMERISATION
5832	POLYPROPYLENE					W 1121	2.5	W 4061	5.8	POLYPROPYLENE
58322	— PLATES,FILM,STRIP,ETC					W 1086	2.4	W 3969	5.7	POLYPROPYLENE PLAQUES
5839	OTH POLYMRZTION ETC PROD					W 1048	1.6	W 3040	3.3	AUT PROD POLYMER COPOLYM
584	CELLULOSE DERIVATIVS ETC	W 1907	3.2	W 1817	2.0	W 444	1.9	W 6994	5.8	CEL REGEN NIT ACETATE
5841	REGENERATED CELLULOSE					W 400	1.6	W 6864	5.6	CELLULOSE REGENEREE
59	CHEMICAL MATERIALS NES		17.3		22.6		20.8		15.0	MAT PROD CHIMIQUES NDA
591	PESTICIDES,DISINFECTANTS	W 2940	11.4	W 1983	17.3	W 1581	16.4	W 1334	9.8	DESINF,INSECT,FONG,HERB
5911	INSECTICIDES,FOR RETAIL					W 1197	12.3	W 614	4.7	INSECTICIDES VENTE DET
5913	HERBICIDES,FOR RETAIL					W 370	4.0	W 508	4.1	HERBICIDES VENTE AU DET
598	MISCEL CHEM PRODUCTS NES	W 1927	3.9	W 3986	4.1	W 906	2.5	W 1755	3.9	PROD DIV INDUST CHIM NDA
5989	CHEM PRODUCTS,PREPS NES	W 1860	3.8	W 3977	4.0	W 726	2.1	W 1613	3.5	PROD PREP CHIMIQUES NDA
6	BASIC MANUFACTURES		241.2		280.9		209.8		170.9	ART MANUFACTURES
62	RUBBER MANUFACTURES NES		14.3		23.2		12.1		12.4	CAOUTCHOUC MANUFACTURE
625	RUBBER TYRES, TUBES ETC	N 795488	12.3	N 549991	20.4	W 5625	9.2	W 5900	10.0	PNEUS CAOUTCHOUC VULCANISE
6252	TYRES,NEW,BUS OR LORRY					W 1545	5.1	W 3547	5.7	PNEUS POUR AUTOBUS,CAMIONS
63	WOOD,CORK MANUFACTRS NES		1.3		1.1		4.8		1.4	OUVRAGES LIEGE ET BOIS
64	PAPER,PAPERBOARD AND MFR		20.1		21.5		24.3		25.7	PAPIERS,CARTONS & OUVRAGES
641	PAPER AND PAPERBOARD	W 25862	9.5	W 17682	11.2	W 24098	15.4	W 26743	12.2	PAPIERS ET CARTONS
6412	PRINTG,WRITING PAPER NES	W 9214	4.8	W 7207	5.1	W 736	0.8	W 1563	1.6	PAPIERS POUR L'IMPRESSION
6415	PAPER,PAPERBRD,BULK,NES	W 21	0.1	W 598	0.4	W 10962	9.3	W 7170	4.7	PAPIERS,CARTONS ROULEAUX
64159	OTHER PAPER ETC,BULK,NES					W 10929	8.8	W 6219	4.2	AUT PAPIER ROULEAUX FEUILLES
642	PAPER,ETC,PRECUT,ARTS OF		10.7		10.4	W 5443	8.9	W 9149	13.6	PAP,CARTONS DECOUPES
6421	PAPER ETC CONTAINERS	W 10667	5.8	W 2746	4.0	W 3563	5.2	W 6286	9.3	BOITES,SACS EMBALLAGES
65	TEXTILE YARN,FABRICS,ETC		31.0		55.1		37.7		32.0	FILS,TISSUS,ARTICLES TEXTILE
653	WOVN MAN–MADE FIB FABRIC	L 1334	1.6	L 4391	5.7	W 838	5.3	W 973	3.7	TISSUS FIBRES SYNTH,ARTIF
6531	CONT SYNT WEAVES NONPILE	L 1297	1.5	L 4391	5.7	W 13	0.1	W 19	0.1	TISSUS FIBRES SYNTH CONTINUE
656	LACE,RIBBONS,TULLE,ETC	W 23	0.1	W 468	0.9	W 36876	17.4	W 17	0.2	TULLES,BRODERIE
65606	EMBROIDERY	W 1	0.1	W 467	0.9	W 36867	17.4	W 4	0.1	BRODERIES PIECES,BANDES
657	SPECIAL TXTL FABRC,PRODS	W 2554	5.3	W 3339	7.1	W 1110	4.0	W 4839	8.6	TISSUS SPECIAUX
6573	COATED ETC TEXTILES NES	W 331	0.5	W 326	0.8	W 259	1.8	W 1972	3.9	TISSUS,ART MATIERE TEXT NDA
65733	RUBBERIZED TEXT NOT KNIT	W 42	0.1	W 146	0.3	W 128	1.5	W 1594	3.4	TISSUS CAOUTCHOUTES
658	TEXTILE ARTICLES NES		21.1		38.7	W 28409	10.2	W 35630	17.5	ART FACONNES MAT TEXTILES
6581	BAGS,SACKS OF TEXTILES	MN 57712	19.1	MN 77873	37.8	W 28274	9.7	W 35499	16.5	SACS EMBALLAGE TEXTILES
66	NONMETAL MINERAL MFS NES		58.5		58.7		20.1		23.5	ART MIN NON METALLIQUES
661	LIME,CEMENT,BLDG PRODS	W 721254	42.6	W 429803	41.2	W 99065	8.6	W 122387	8.5	CHAUX,CIMENTS MAT CONSTR
6612	CEMENT	W 713282	40.6	W 425422	40.2	W 97402	5.9	W 116981	7.5	CIMENTS HYDRAULIQUES
662	CLAY,REFRACTORY BLDG PRD	W 5418	2.1	W 7415	3.1	W 4005	1.9	W 11527	3.4	MAT CONST REFRACTAIRES
665	GLASSWARE	W 18601	10.1	W 7772	11.0	W 6862	5.4	W 14219	7.8	OUVRAGES EN VERRE
6651	BOTTLES ETC OF GLASS	W 12635	4.8	W 4377	6.1	W 2346	2.4	W 6512	3.5	RECIPIENTS EN VERRE
66511	GLASS BOTTLES ETC NONVAC					W 2346	2.4	W 6512	3.5	BONBONNES,BOUTEILLES,ETC
6652	HOUSEHLD,HOTEL ETC GLASS	W 5929	5.2	W 3330	4.7	W 4005	2.7	W 7507	3.9	OBJETS VERRE TABLE,CUISINE
67	IRON AND STEEL		79.3		85.1		72.9		43.3	FER ET ACIER
673	IRON,STEEL SHAPES ETC		60.4	W 148213	58.7	W 175313	46.7	W 81469	24.5	BARRES,PROFIL FER,ACIER
6732	IRON,STEEL BARS ETC	W 152138	51.1	W 143509	57.2	W 154912	36.1	W 50033	14.3	BARRES FER,ACIER
67324	STNLESS STL ETC BARS ETC					W 154894	35.8	W 39558	10.3	BARRES ACIER INOXYDABLE
67327	IRN, OTH STL BARS FORGED					W 10	0.1	W 10414	3.9	BARRES FORGEES CREUSES
6733	IRON,STEEL PROFILES ETC	W 30203	9.4	W 4654	1.5	W 20291	10.7	W 26723	8.6	PROFILES,PALPLAN FER,ACIER
67332	LARGE U,I,H SECTIONS ETC					W 655	3.6	W 13587	4.5	PROFILES PLUS 80MM
67338	STNLESS STL ETC PROFILES					W 17089	5.9	W 9746	2.9	PROFILES ACIER INOXYDABLE
674	IRN,STL UNIV,PLATE,SHEET	W 22449	9.4	W 22895	13.0	W 22499	16.3	W 22138	9.3	LARGES PLATS,TOLES
6744	IRN,STL HVY PLATE,ROLLED					W 17173	11.7	W 10719	4.0	TOLES LAMINEES PLUS 4.75 MM
67444	— OF OTHER ALLOY STEEL					W 16270	10.0	W 9276	3.4	TOLES NON ACIER ALLIES
6746	IRN,STL THIN PLATE,ROLLD	W 17973	6.7	W 16783	8.4	W 194	0.2	W 1543	0.7	TOLES LAM MOINS 3MM
6749	OTH IRN,STL PLATES,SHEET	W 4300	2.5	W 5609	4.0	W 4948	4.3	W 8602	4.2	AUTRES TOLES FER,ACIER
67491	— OF IRON OR SIMPLE STL					W 4817	4.0	W 8108	3.9	AUT TOLES AUTRES ACIER FIN
678	IRON,STL TUBES,PIPES,ETC	W 18919	8.7	W 20637	12.4	W 16674	9.1	W 11111	6.3	TUBES,TUYAUX EN FONTE,FER
6781	CAST IRON TUBES,PIPES					W 15534	7.3	W 8482	3.1	TUBES,TUYAUX EN FONTE
6782	IRON,STL SEAMLESS TUBES	W 18366	8.1	W 19704	11.6	W 110	0.2	W 1792	1.6	TUBES,TUYAUX SANS SOUDURE
68	NON–FERROUS METALS		3.8		4.3		4.1		2.8	METAUX NON FERREUX
69	METAL MANUFACTURES NES		32.4		31.4		33.4		28.3	ART MANUFACT EN METAL NDA
691	STRUCTURES AND PARTS NES	W 21575	5.2	W 3269	3.3	W 2365	3.6	W 1706	3.4	CONSTRUCT FER,ACIER,ALU
692	METAL TANKS,BOXES,ETC	W 2494	7.2	W 2412	4.8	W 1653	2.6	W 2088	3.6	RECIPIENTS METALLIQUES
6924	MTL TRANSPORT BOXES ETC	W 2452	7.1	W 1991	3.9	W 657	2.2	W 1929	3.3	FUTS,TAMBOURS,BIDONS
69243	IRN,STL COMP GAS CYLINDR	W 2417	7.1	W 1959	3.6	W 323	1.1	W 1844	2.7	RECIP FER,ACIER GAZ COMP
694	STL,COPPR NAILS,NUTS,ETC	W 2161	2.2	W 3333	3.8	W 8963	10.3	W 2921	5.8	CLOUS,VIS,ECROUS
69402	IRN,STL NUTS,BOLTS,ETC	W 1323	1.7	W 2198	3.1	W 8158	9.5	W 2212	5.4	BOULONS,VIS,ECROUS FER,AC
699	BASE METAL MFRS NES	W 4537	10.1	W 5534	12.3	W 4116	8.1	W 6454	7.7	ART MANUFACTURES MET NDA
6991	LOCKSMITHS WARES,ETC	W 1331	5.9	W 1398	5.7	W 796	1.8	W 917	1.8	ARTICLES DE SERRURERIE
69912	BASE METAL SAFES ETC	W 507	3.9	W 279	2.6	W 43	0.3	W 37	0.2	COFFRE–FORTS
7	MACHINES,TRANSPORT EQUIP		370.5		372.4		329.7		275.4	MACHINES MATERIEL TRANSPORT
71	POWER GENERATING EQUIPMT		20.9		25.3		20.2		25.3	MACHINES GENERATRICES
713	INTRNL COMBUS PSTN ENGIN	W 13739	8.7	W 2408	6.9	W 23973	8.4	W 62564	7.9	MOTEURS EXPL COMB INT, PIECE
7139	PISTON ENGINE PARTS NES					W 23030	5.9	W 2370	5.0	PIECES POUR 713.2,3,8
716	ROTATING ELECTRIC PLANT		10.1		12.9	W 707	7.7	W 1959	14.9	APP ELECTR ROTATIFS,PIECES
7162	AC MTRS,GENRTRS,GEN SETS					W 437	4.6	W 984	5.9	MOTEURS ELECTRIQUES
7169	PTS NES OF ROT ELEC PLNT					W 36	0.6	W 863	8.2	PIECES MAC APP ROTATIFS
72	MACHS FOR SPCL INDUSTRYS		77.9		59.6		55.8		66.6	MAC SPECIALES POUR INDUST
721	AGRIC MACHY,EXC TRACTORS	W 1736	7.5	W 1538	6.3	W 1234	5.4	W 2931	14.2	MACHINES AGRICOLES
7211	CULTIVATING MACHINERY	W 791	2.6	W 493	2.7	W 52	0.3	W 943	6.4	MACH PREPARATION DU SOL
72119	PTS NES OF MACHY OF 7211					W 23	0.2	W 153	3.9	PIECES DU S–GROUPE 721.1
7212	HARVESTING ETC MACHINES	W 829	4.5	W 825	3.4	W 1114	4.9	W 1722	7.2	ENGINS POUR LA RECOLTE
72124	AGRIC CLEAN,GRADING MACH					W 303	0.2	W 991	4.7	MACH NETTOYAGE DES GRAINS
722	TRACTORS NON–ROAD	N 1603	20.6	N 262	3.4	W 539	4.0	W 574	2.6	TRACTEURS
7224	WHEELED TRACTORS NES					W 520	3.8	W 574	2.6	TRACTEURS A ROUES
723	CIVIL ENGNEERG EQUIP ETC	W 3180	19.3	W 2960	19.3	W 8614	27.7	W 2518	18.2	APPAREILS DE GENIE CIVIL
7234	CONST,MINING MACHNRY NES	W 3086	18.8	W 2886	18.9	W 8554	23.7	W 2151	13.4	MACH POUR LA CONST, MINES
72341	SELF–PROPELLD DOZERS,ETC					W 1017	8.3	W 1110	5.9	BULLDOZERS
72343	SLFPRP CONST ETC MCH NES					W 7276	13.9	W 522	3.3	AUT MACH EXTR,TERRASSEM
7239	CONSTR ETC MACHY PTS NES					W 59	4.0	W 291	4.4	PIECES 723.41–723.46
724	TEXTILE,LEATHER MACHNRY		4.0		15.0	W 793	6.5	W 2218	8.8	MACH POUR INDUSTRIE TEXTILE
7244	SPINNING,EXTRDNG,ETC MCH	W 452	1.9	W 1823	13.0	W 535	4.9	W 1516	4.6	MACH POUR LE FILAGE
72449	PTS NES OF MACHS OF 7244	W 434	1.8	W 1783	12.3	W 288	2.9	W 858	1.5	PIECES DES MACH DU 724.4

4. General Imports C.I.F. by Commodities according to the S.I.T.C. (Rev. 2) in million U.S. Dollars
Importations Générales C.A.F. par Produits d'après la C.T.C.I. (Rév. 2) en millions de Dollars E.U.

SITC CTCI	COMMODITY	1993		1994		1995		1996		PRODUIT
		QUANTITY QUANTITE	VALUE VALEUR	QUANTITY QUANTITE	VALUE VALEUR	QUANTITY QUANTITE	VALUE VALEUR	QUANTITY QUANTITE	VALUE VALEUR	
726	PRINTG,BKBINDG MACHY,PTS	W 620	7.0	W 137	1.2	W 69	0.5	W 188	1.2	MACHINES POUR IMPRIMERIE
7264	PRINTING PRESSES	W 587	6.7	W 86	0.9	W 14	0.1	W 83	0.7	MACHINES A IMPRIMER
727	FOOD MACHRY NON-DOMESTIC	W 1597	8.3	W 1887	6.7	W 1378	6.8	W 2603	15.0	MACH INDUSTRIES ALIMENT
7271	GRAIN WORKING MCHY,PARTS	W 629	1.8	W 599	1.2	W 250	2.2	W 870	3.4	MACH POUR MINOTERIE,PIEC
7272	OTH FOOD PROC MCHY,PARTS	W 967	6.6	W 1288	5.6	W 1127	4.6	W 1733	11.7	AUT MACH IND ALIMENTAIRE
72722	INDUS FOOD PROC MACH NES	W 967	6.6	W 1288	5.6	W 124	0.8	W 572	6.3	MACHINES BOULANGERIE
72729	PTS NES OF MCHY OF 72722					W 462	2.8	W 1097	5.3	PIECES MACH DU 727.22
728	OTH MACHY FOR SPCL INDUS	W 1705	11.1	W 2204	7.1	W 6412	5.2	W 3457	6.6	AUT MACH IND PARTICULIERES
7284	MACHY FOR SPCL INDUS NES	W 1350	8.6	W 977	4.8	W 4418	3.4	W 3073	4.2	MACH SPEC IND PARTICUL.
74	GENRL INDUSTRL MACHY NES		57.2		50.9		31.8		38.2	MACH APP INDUSTRIE
741	HEATING,COOLING EQUIPMNT		10.0		8.2	W 603	5.0	W 1413	6.4	MACH CHAUFFAGE,PIECES
7415	AIR-CONDITIONING MACHNRY	N 12698	5.9	N 22156	5.3	W 375	2.8	W 562	3.5	GROUPES CONDITION AIR
742	PUMPS FOR LIQUIDS ETC	W 1936	16.0	W 1565	20.8	W 520	4.2	W 2127	9.3	POMPES MOTO-POMPES
7428	OTHER PUMPS FOR LIQUIDS					W 310	3.0	W 970	6.3	AUTRES POMPES POUR LIQ
74288	PUMPS FR LIQUIDS NES ETC					W 293	2.6	W 888	5.1	POMPES POUR LIQUIDES NDA
743	PUMPS NES,CENTRFUGES ETC	W 1477	15.6	W 745	3.2	W 360	2.9	W 892	4.1	POMPES COMPRES,VENT ETC
7439	PTS NES OF APP OF 7435,6	W 980	12.7	W 526	1.7	W 12	0.7	W 98	0.8	PIECES 743.5 ET 743.6
744	MECHANICAL HANDLING EQU	W 1111	5.6	W 1071	8.9	W 1063	7.5	W 1455	8.9	EQUIP MANUTENTION PIECES
7442	LIFTING,LOADING MACH NES	W 820	4.2	W 943	6.8	W 589	4.0	W 518	2.0	APP LEVAGE,MANUTENTION
7449	PTS NES OF MACHY OF 7442					W 301	3.0	W 775	6.1	PIECES DU 744.2
745	NONELEC MACHY,TOOLS NES	W 1061	4.1	W 461	2.7	W 95	2.3	W 447	2.6	AUT MACH NON ELEC,PIECES
749	NONELEC MACH PTS,ACC NES	W 999	6.1	W 1080	7.3	W 4236	10.2	W 2296	7.2	PIECES MACH NON ELEC NDA
7499	OTH NONELEC MCHY PTS NES	W 830	4.3	W 838	5.5	W 104	3.5	W 149	2.2	PIECES NON ELECT NDA
74999	MACH PARTS NONELEC NES	W 830	4.3	W 838	5.5	W 33	2.7	W 59	1.7	PIECES MACHINES NDA
75	OFFICE MACHNES,ADP EQUIP		8.0		9.9		29.2		8.1	MACH BUREAU TRAIT AUTOM
752	AUTOMTIC DATA PROC EQUIP	N 1201	2.7	N 2633	5.5	W 142	24.9	W 152	4.7	MACH TRAIT INFORMATION
7522	DIGITAL COMPUTERS					W 40	19.0	W 39	1.5	MACH DIGITALES COMPLETES
759	OFFICE,ADP MCH PTS,ACCES		3.9		1.6	W 12741	1.9	W 20	0.7	PIECES DU 751 ET 752
7591	OFFICE MACHINE PARTS NES		3.9		1.6	W 26	0.3	W 8	0.3	PIECES DU 7511,7518
75911	TYPEWRTR PARTS,ACCES NES		3.9		1.6	W 18	0.2	W 2	0.1	PIECES DU 7511
76	TELECOMM,SOUND EQUIPMENT		16.5		57.6		25.9		22.0	EQUIPMENT DE TELECOM
764	TELECOM EQPT,PTS,ACC NES		13.9		50.7	W 862	22.1	W 727	20.0	EQUIP TELECOM,PIECES
7641	LINE TELEPHONE,ETC EQUIP	W 154	0.4	W 885	1.8	W 193	8.2	W 533	10.4	APP TELEPHON PAR FIL
7643	TV,RADIO TRANSMITTRS ETC	W 501	13.1	W 20978	48.7	W 71	3.4	W 32	1.5	APP EMET TELE RADIO
7649	PTS NES OF EQUIPMT OF 76	W 15	0.4	W 15	0.2	W 516	8.5	W 113	4.9	PIECES DE LA DIV 76
76493	TELECOMM EQUIPMT PTS NES					W 509	5.8	W 87	3.9	PIECES 761,762,764.3,8
77	ELECTRIC MACHNRY NES ETC		39.3		33.2		22.6		25.0	MACH APP ELECT NDA
772	SWITCHGEAR ETC,PARTS NES	W 822	10.6	W 724	4.4	W 4144	2.8	W 1152	3.8	APP COUPURE,SECT ETC
7721	SWITCHGEAR ETC					W 4143	2.8	W 1150	3.8	APP COUPURE,SECTIONMNT
773	ELECTR DISTRIBUTNG EQUIP	W 1776	7.3	W 1126	4.1	W 2730	3.8	W 1906	4.8	EQUIPMT DISTRIBUTION ELECT
7731	INSULATED WIRE,CABLE ETC	W 1702	6.9	W 978	3.6	W 2385	3.1	W 1838	4.6	FILS,CABLES ISOLES ELECT
775	HOUSEHOLD TYPE EQUIP NES		7.7		11.4	W 1732	3.1	W 1559	3.6	MACH,APP USAGE DOMESTQUE
7752	DOM REFRIGERATRS,FREEZRS	N 5324	2.2	N 20469	4.6	W 298	1.4	W 400	1.2	REFRIG,CONGEL MENAGER
778	ELECTRICAL MACHINERY NES		13.8		12.4	W 3441	10.3	W 10706	11.0	AUTRES MACH ELECT NDA
7781	BATTERIES,ACCUMULATORS	W 4395	10.3	W 2759	8.0	W 3096	7.7	W 8213	6.0	PILES ET ACCUMULATEURS
77811	PRIMARY BATTERIES,CELLS					W 2220	4.5	W 1354	2.0	PILES ELECTRIQUES,PIECES
77812	ELECTRIC ACCUMULATORS					W 877	3.2	W 6847	4.0	ACCUMULATEURS ELECTRIQ
78	ROAD VEHICLES		140.4		109.7		124.3		78.7	VEHICULES ROUTIERS
781	PASS MOTOR VEH EXC BUSES	N 2007	24.9	N 4538	34.4	W 2701	54.8	W 1597	16.1	AUTO TRANSPORT PERSONNES
782	LORRIES,SPCL MTR VEH NES	N 4050	65.0	N 3068	42.8	W 12606	48.0	W 10949	36.0	VEHICULES SPECIAUX,MARCH
7821	LORRIES,TRUCKS	N 4030	64.2	N 3048	42.0	W 12466	46.4	W 10383	31.7	VEHICULES TRANSP MARCHAND
7822	SPECIAL MOTOR VEHCLS NES	N 20	0.9	N 20	0.8	W 140	1.6	W 567	4.4	VEHICULES USAGES SPECIAUX
783	ROAD MOTOR VEHICLES NES	N 745	16.1	N 310	5.8	W 688	8.7	W 843	4.9	VEHICULES ROUTIERS NDA
7831	BUSES	N 745	16.1	N 310	5.8	W 663	8.2	W 754	4.1	VOITURES TRANSPORT COMMUN
784	MOTOR VEH PRTS,ACCES NES	W 3452	31.1	W 4750	20.6	W 756	7.4	W 3730	12.4	PIECES 722,781,782,783
7849	OTHER MOTOR VEHCL PARTS	W 3442	31.0	W 4737	20.6	W 755	7.4	W 3664	12.3	PIECES 722,781,782,783
785	CYCLES,ETC MOTRZD OR NOT		2.6		4.6	W 447	1.7	W 1464	2.8	MOTOCYCLES SCOOTERS
786	TRAILERS,NONMOTR VEH,NES		1.0		1.8	W 2644	4.0	W 2429	6.7	REMORQUES,CADRES,CONTAIN
7861	TRAILERS,TRANSP CONTAINR		1.0		1.8	W 2569	3.5	W 2066	4.2	REMORQUES TOUS VEHICULES
79	OTHR TRANSPORT EQUIPMENT		8.8		22.9		17.8		9.3	AUTRE MATERIEL TRANSPORT
791	RAILWAY VEHICLES	W 513	2.9		7.3	W 2002	6.3	W 2462	5.8	VEHIC MAT CHEMINS DE FER
7915	FRT,MAINT CARS NOT POWRD			N 70	5.9	W 878	2.2	W 1470	3.8	WAGONS DE SERVICE
79152	RAILWAY FREIGHT CARS NES			N 70	5.9	W 878	2.2	W 1470	3.8	WAGONS MARCHANDISES
792	AIRCRAFT ETC	W 100	5.7		15.1	W 366	5.9	W 346	2.9	APP NAVIGATION AERIENNE
7921	HELICOPTERS			N 8	6.1	W 7	0.1	W 7	0.1	HELICOPTERES
7929	AIRCRAFT PARTS NES	W 95	5.7	W 112	8.9	W 314	5.2	W 40	2.1	PIECES DU 792
793	SHIPS AND BOATS ETC	N 57	0.2		0.7	W 6517	5.7	W 62	0.7	NAVIRES BATEAUX,ETC
7938	TUGS,SPECIAL VESSELS ETC	N 4	0.1		0.1	W 6500	5.4	W 57	0.7	REMORQUEURS,BATEAUX SPEC
8	MISC MANUFACTURED GOODS		50.5		53.6		45.7		38.8	ART MANUFACTURES DIVERS
84	CLOTHING AND ACCESSORIES		4.2		3.1		4.0		3.4	VETEMENTS
851	*FOOTWEAR	P 2617504	3.2	P 2888578	3.9	W 837	2.8	W 2531	4.2	CHAUSSURES
87	PRECISION INSTRUMNTS NES		14.3		10.1		7.8		4.4	INSTRUM,APPAR SCIENT NDA
872	MEDICAL INSTRUMENTS NES		7.6		5.1	W 529	4.4	W 271	2.2	INSTR,APP MEDIC-CHIR NDA
87201	DENTAL INSTRUMENTS	W 415	7.5	W 822	5.0	W 3	0.1	W 2	0.1	INSTRUM,APPAR DENTAIRE
87202	OTH MEDICAL INSTRUMENTS					W 524	4.2	W 263	2.1	INSTRUM,APP MEDECINE
88	PHOTO EQU,OPTICL GDS ETC		4.6		3.7		2.4		1.0	APP,FOURN PHOTO,OP,MONTR
89	MISC MANUFCTRD GOODS NES		21.2		28.3		26.5		22.3	ART MANUFACTURES DIVERS
892	PRINTED MATTER		4.0		8.5	W 1301389	4.7	W 1080	2.1	IMPRIMES
893	ARTICLES OF PLASTIC NES		11.3	W 4106	11.1		12.9	W 35524	13.3	OUVRAGES EN MAT DIVIS 58
8931	PLSTC PACKG CONTNRS,LIDS					W 3393	3.4	W 2475	4.0	ART TRANSP EMBALLAGE ETC
8939	MISC PLASTIC ARTICLES					W 13730	9.5	W 32997	9.4	ART DIVERS EN MAT DIV 58
89399	OTHR PLASTC ARTICLES NES					W 13235	8.2	W 27585	8.3	AUT OUV MAT DIV 58
899	OTHER MANUFACTURED GOODS		3.6		2.5		4.7		3.6	AUT ART MANUF DIVERS NDA
9	GOODS NOT CLASSD BY KIND		0.2		0.1		0.1		14.8	ART TRANSACT NON CLASSES
931	*SPECIAL TRANSACTIONS							W 10399	14.8	TRANS.SPECIALES

5. General Exports F.O.B. by Commodities according to the S.I.T.C. (Rev. 2) in million U.S. Dollars
Exportations Générales F.O.B. par Produits d'après la C.T.C.I. (Rév. 2) en millions de Dollars E.U.

SITC CTCI	COMMODITY	1993 QUANTITY QUANTITE	1993 VALUE VALEUR	1994 QUANTITY QUANTITE	1994 VALUE VALEUR	1995 QUANTITY QUANTITE	1995 VALUE VALEUR	1996 QUANTITY QUANTITE	1996 VALUE VALEUR	PRODUIT
	ALL COMMODITIES		294.2		395.0		685.2		273.2	TOUS PRODUITS
0	FOOD AND LIVE ANIMALS		154.4		137.4		114.9		75.9	ALIMENTS,ANIMAUX VIVANTS
001	*LIVE ANIMALS FOR FOOD	N 709257	55.5	N 903359	67.1	W 25235	48.0	W 36023	31.7	ANIMAUX VIVANTS
0011	BOVINE SPECIES,LIVE					W 950	0.7	W 1918	0.9	ESPECE BOVINE
0012	SHEEP AND GOATS,LIVE	N 690578	46.3	N 889201	58.5	W 24284	47.4	W 34104	30.8	ESPECES OVINE ET CAPRINE
00121	SHEEP,LIVE					W 24196	47.2	W 33598	30.4	ESPECE OVINE
0015	EQUINE SPECIES, LIVE	N 11679	9.2	N 14149	8.7			W 1	0.1	CHEVAUX,ANES,MULETS
01	MEAT AND PREPARATIONS		10.6		9.0		7.7		20.1	VIANDES ET PREPARATIONS
011	MEAT FRESH,CHILLD,FROZEN	W 3434	10.6	W 3482	9.0	W 4102	7.7	W 10950	20.1	VIANDES FRAICHES,REF,CONGE
0111	BOVINE MEAT FRESH,FROZEN	W 1676	4.7	W 1023	2.5	W 728	1.4	W 2368	2.6	VIANDES BOVIN FRAI,REF
01111	BOVINE MEAT WITH BONE IN					W 728	1.4	W 2366	2.6	VIANDES BOVIN NON DESOSS
0112	MUTTON ETC FRSH,CHLD,FRN	W 1730	6.0	W 2397	6.5	W 3211	6.2	W 8537	17.5	VIANDE DE MOUTON
04	CEREALS AND PREPARATIONS		43.7		7.6		32.4		0.6	CEREALES ET PRODUITS
045	CEREALS NES UNMILLED	W 616639	43.3	W 95822	7.6	W 408094	32.4	W 7764	0.6	AUTRES CEREALES NON MOULUES
0459	OTHER CEREALS UNMILLED	W 616639	43.3	W 95822	7.6	W 408094	32.4	W 7764	0.6	SARRASIN,MILLET,SORGHO
04592	SORGHUM UNMILLED					W 406911	32.3	W 7750	0.6	SORGHO NON MOULU
05	VEGETABLES AND FRUIT		3.7		1.8		1.4		2.0	LEGUMES ET FRUITS
054	VEG ETC FRSH,SMPLY PRSVD	W 8163	1.5	W 236	0.2	W 110	0.1	W 258	0.1	LEGUMES FRAIS,CONG,SECS
0542	LEGUMINOUS VEGETBLES DRY	W 7035	1.4	W 148	0.1	W 33	0.1	W 135	0.1	LEGUMES A COSSE SECS
057	FRUIT,NUTS,FRESH,DRIED	W 6017	2.2	W 5786	1.7	W 5729	1.4	W 7996	1.8	FRUITS FRAIS OU SECS
0579	FRUIT FRESH OR DRIED NES	W 5344	1.9	W 5184	1.4	W 5360	1.3	W 6942	1.5	FRUITS FRAIS,SECS NDA
05795	PINEAPPLES,FRESH,DRIED	W 4017	1.4	W 4272	1.1	W 3	0.1			ANANAS FRAIS OU SECS
05797	OTH TROP FRUIT,FRESH,DRY					W 4910	1.2	W 5213	1.1	AVOCATS,MANGUES,GOYAVES
06	SUGAR AND PREPS,HONEY		16.4		34.4		16.5		17.5	SUCRES ET PRODUITS
061	SUGAR AND HONEY	W 228303	16.4	W 310015	34.4	W 198286	16.5	W 142668	17.5	SUCRES ET MIEL
0611	RAW BEET AND CANE SUGAR					W 17902	6.2	W 42000	11.0	SUCRES BRUTS
0612	REFINED SUGAR ETC	W 36500	9.0	W 100840	24.4					SUCRES RAFFINES
0615	MOLASSES	W 191651	7.4	W 209074	10.0	W 180382	10.3	W 100666	6.6	MELASSES
07	COFFEE,TEA,COCOA,SPICES		17.5		10.4		0.1		0.2	CAFE,THE,CACAO,EPICES
074	TEA AND MATE	W 16170	17.3	W 10862	10.2					THE ET MATE
0742	MATE	W 16170	17.3	W 10862	10.2					MATE
081	*FEEDING STUFF FOR ANIML	W 67393	7.1	W 88380	7.2	W 80822	9.0	W 53293	3.9	NOURRITURE POUR ANIMAUX
0813	OILCAKE AND OTH RESIDUES	W 61894	6.8	W 88335	7.2	W 54271	5.5	W 52788	3.8	TOURTEAUX
08132	— OF GROUNDNUTS					W 9224	0.8	W 43360	3.0	TOURTEAUX D'ARACHIDES
08133	— OF COTTON SEEDS					W 45047	4.7	W 4628	0.5	TOURTEAUX DE COTON
0819	FOOD WASTE AND FEED NES			W 45	0.1	W 26551	3.5	W 500	0.1	DECHETS,ALIMENTS NDA
08199	FODDER NES,INCL SWEETNED					W 26551	3.5	W 500	0.1	PREPARATIONS FOURRAGERES
2	CRUDE MATERLS,EXCL FUELS		119.5		225.3		397.9		138.9	MAT BRUTES NON COMESTIBLES
21	HIDES,SKINS,FURS UNDRSSD		2.5		0.9		2.6		0.7	CUIRS,PEAUX BRUTS
211	HIDES,SKINS,EXC FURS,RAW	W 2548	2.5	W 742	0.9	W 496	2.6	W 320	0.7	CUIRS ET PEAUX
2111	BOVINE,EQUINE HIDES,RAW	W 2197	1.6	W 413	0.3	W 6	0.1	W 24	0.1	PEAUX DE BOVINS
2117	SHEEP SKIN WITHOUT WOOL					W 452	2.2	W 139	0.5	PEAUX EPILEES D'OVINS
22	OIL SEEDS,OLEAGINOUS FRT		58.5		69.4		79.2		73.0	GRAINES,FRUITS OLEAGINEUX
222	SEEDS FOR'SOFT'FIXED OIL	W 151011	58.5	W 184183	69.4	W 125910	73.5	W 118338	61.4	GRAINES HUILES FIXES
2221	GROUNDNUTS,GREEN	W 14029	6.7	W 6700	3.1	W 41108	10.7	W 2160	0.8	ARACHIDES NON GRILLEES
2224	SUNFLOWER SEEDS	W 136982	51.9	W 177483	66.4			W 7700	1.2	GRAINES DE TOURNESOL
2225	SESAME SEEDS					W 84802	62.8	W 108478	59.5	GRAINES DE SESAME
223	SEEDS FOR OTH FIXED OILS					W 69856	5.8	W 76271	11.7	GRAINES AUTRES HUILES FIXES
2238	OIL SEEDS AND FRUITS NES					W 69856	5.8	W 76270	11.7	GRAINES D'OLEAGINEUX NDA
26	TEXTILE FIBRES AND WASTE		33.0		99.1		143.5		47.7	FIBRES TEXTILES
263	COTTON	W 58563	33.0	W 119607	99.1	W 83313	143.5	W 44795	47.7	COTON
2631	RAW COTTON,EXCL LINTERS	W 55789	32.5	W 119607	99.1	W 50541	87.3	W 42886	47.3	COTON EN MASSE
2634	COTTON,CARDED OR COMBED					W 32676	56.2	W 225	0.2	COTON CARDE OU PEIGNE
28	METALLIFEROUS ORES,SCRAP		0.4		0.9		2.6		0.7	MINERAIS METAL,DECHETS
287	BASE METAL ORES,CONC NES					W 22168	2.2			MINERAIS METAUX COMMUNS
2879	OTH NONFER ORE,CONCNTRTE					W 22168	2.2			MINERAIS D'AUTRES METAUX
28791	CHROMIUM ORE,CONCENTRATE					W 22168	2.2			MINERAIS DE CHROME
29	CRUDE ANIMAL,VEG MAT NES		25.1		54.8		170.2		16.8	MATIERES BRUTES ANIM,VEGET
292	CRUDE VEG MATERIALS NES	W 17373	25.1	W 30526	54.5	W 51558	170.1	W 22134	16.7	MAT BRUTES VEGETALES NDA
2922	NAT GUMS,RESINS,LACS,ETC	W 15394	24.1	W 27507	52.5	W 18629	141.1	W 11413	10.0	GOMME LAQUE
2924	VEG USED IN PHARMACY ETC	W 1382	0.6	W 1475	0.5	W 32927	29.1	W 10643	6.7	PLANTES MEDICINALES
2929	OTH CRUDE VEG MATERIALS	W 577	0.5	W 1544	1.7	W 2	0.1	W 56	0.1	MATIERES VEGETALES NDA
29298	OTH CRD VEG MATERIAL NES	W 577	0.5	W 1544	1.7	W 2	0.1	W 56	0.1	PRODUITS ORIGINE VEGET NDA
4	ANIMAL,VEGETABLE OIL,FAT		12.7		18.8		102.5		8.6	HUILES,GRAISSES ANIM,VEG
42	FIXED VEGETABLE OIL,FAT		12.7		18.8		102.5		8.6	HUILES VEGETALES FIXES
423	FIXED VEG OILS,SOFT	W 13365	12.7	W 33684	18.8	W 23282	102.5	W 14287	8.6	HUILES VEGET DOUCES FIXES
4234	GROUNDNUT(PEANUT) OIL	W 13365	12.7	W 33684	18.8	W 12489	13.0	W 14228	8.5	HUILE D'ARACHIDE
4239	OTH FIXED VEG OILS,SOFT					W 10793	89.6	W 59	0.1	AUTRES HUILES FIXES
42392	SESAME OIL					W 10793	89.6	W 59	0.1	HUILE DE SESAME
6	BASIC MANUFACTURES		5.7		8.5		42.1		18.5	ART MANUFACTURES
61	LEATHER,DRESSED FUR,ETC		3.6		5.6		41.3		4.1	CUIRS,PELLETERIES
611	LEATHER	W 1532	3.5	W 2846	5.6	W 18686	41.3	W 1934	4.1	CUIRS,PEAUX PREPARES
6113	CALF LEATHER	W 979	1.6	W 68	0.1			W 1	0.1	CUIRS,PEAUX DE VEAUX
6114	LEATHR BOVINE NES,EQUINE			W 1500	1.7	W 1993	2.0	W 1028	0.9	CUIRS DE BOVINS
6115	LEATHER FROM SHEEP,LAMBS	W 513	1.8	W 761	2.7	W 13921	34.7	W 553	2.1	PEAUX D'OVINS PREPAREES
6116	LEATHER OF OTH HIDE,SKIN	W 41	0.2	W 517	1.2	W 2773	4.8	W 351	1.1	PEAUX PREP D'AUTRES ANIMAUX
61169	LEATHER NES			W 9	0.2	W 2374	3.9	W 12	0.3	PEAUX PREPAREES NDA
65	TEXTILE YARN,FABRICS,ETC		1.7		0.9		0.8		13.8	FILS,TISSUS,ARTICLES TEXTILE
651	TEXTILE YARN	W 1082	1.6	W 569	0.7	W 455	0.8	W 4508	6.8	FILS TEXTILES
6512	WOOL,HAIR YARN,INCL TOPS							W 2927	4.6	FILS DE LAINE,DE POILS
65123	COMBED WOOL YARN IN BULK							W 2927	4.6	FILS CONT 85% LAINE PEIGNEE
6513	COTTON YARN	W 1082	1.6	W 529	0.7	W 455	0.8	W 1580	2.3	FILS DE COTON
653	WOVN MAN–MADE FIB FABRIC			L 1	0.1			W 1417	6.5	TISSUS FIBRES SYNTH,ARTIF
6534	DISC SYN BLEND FABRC NES							W 1400	6.4	TISSUS FIBRES SYNTH DISCONT
65341	DISC SYN FIB–COTTN FABRC							W 1400	6.4	TISSUS FIB SYNT DIS MEL COTO
69	METAL MANUFACTURES NES		0.4		2.0				0.1	ART MANUFACT EN METAL NDA
691	STRUCTURES AND PARTS NES	W 223	0.3	W 277	1.9					CONSTRUCT FER,ACIER,ALU
6911	STRUCTURES,PARTS IRN,STL	W 95	0.1	W 129	1.8					CONSTRUCT FER,ACIER,FONTE
7	MACHINES,TRANSPORT EQUIP		1.8		4.7		0.2		1.1	MACHINES MATERIEL TRANSPORT
72	MACHS FOR SPCL INDUSTRYS		0.4		1.8				0.1	MAC SPECIALES POUR INDUST
78	ROAD VEHICLES		0.7		2.1		0.1		0.2	VEHICULES ROUTIERS
784	MOTOR VEH PRTS,ACCES NES	W 4	0.1	W 125	1.4			W 195	0.1	PIECES 722,781,782,783
7849	OTHER MOTOR VEHCL PARTS	W 4	0.1	W 125	1.4			W 195	0.1	PIECES 722,781,782,783
9	GOODS NOT CLASSD BY KIND						26.1		30.2	ART TRANSACT NON CLASSES
941	*ZOO ANIMALS,PETS ETC					W 15996	7.5	W 56	0.1	ANIMAUX DE ZOO ETC
971	*GOLD,NON MONETARY NES					K 2643	18.6	K 2143	30.1	OR NON MONETAIRE
97101	NONMON GLD UNWRT,SEMIMFD					K 2643	18.6	K 2143	30.1	OR,ALLIAGES D'OR BRUTS

1. HISTORICAL SERIES, 1960–1995 GENERAL TRADE, IMPORTS C.I.F., EXPORTS F.O.B.
SERIES HISTORIQUES, 1960–1995 COMMERCE GENERAL, IMPORTATIONS C.A.F., EXPORTATIONS F.O.B

YEAR ANNEE	VALUE IN MILLION SURINAM.GUILDERS / VALEUR EN MILLION SURINAM.GUILDERS — MERCHANDISE – MARCHANDISE IMPORTS	EXPORTS	GOLD – OR IMPORTS	EXPORTS	CONVERSION FACTORS U.S. CENTS PER SURINAME GUILDER / FACTEURS DE CONVERSION CENTS E.U. PAR SURINAME GUILDER IMPORTS	EXPORTS	INDEX NUMBERS – INDICES: QUANTUM IMPORTS	QUANTUM EXPORTS	UNIT VALUE / VALEUR UNITAIRE IMPORTS	UNIT VALUE EXPORTS
1960	101.80	82.48			53.0264	53.0264				
1961	101.09	77.99			53.0264	53.0264				
1962	102.87	79.98			53.0264	53.0264				
1963	110.14	87.48			53.0264	53.0264				
1964	152.00	90.13			53.0264	53.0264				
1965	179.10	110.45			53.0264	53.0264				
1966	168.71	171.24			53.0264	53.0264				
1967	193.42	198.16			53.0264	53.0264				
1968	188.50	216.53			53.0264	53.0264				
1969	207.56	249.26			53.0264	53.0264				
1970	217.70	257.70			53.0264	53.0264				
1971	237.80	296.74			53.0432	53.0426				
1972	258.20	308.20			55.9039	55.9039				
1973	281.00	322.20			56.0221	56.0221				
1974	410.50	467.90			55.9620	55.9633				
1975	454.10	468.50			56.0220	56.0220				
1976	525.50	508.30			56.0220	56.0220				
1977	709.90	589.30			56.0223	56.0223				
1978	724.50	702.40			56.0224	56.0223				
1979	738.80	792.70			56.0224	56.0224				
1980	925.30	894.50			56.0224	56.0224				
1981	1010.60	815.20			56.0224	56.0224				
1982	936.40	735.70			56.0224	56.0224				
1983	785.90	623.50			56.0224	56.0224				
1984	698.90	650.50			56.0224	56.0224				
1985	603.60	587.00			56.0224	56.0224				
1986	584.40	597.77			56.0224	56.0224				
1987	525.37	546.26			56.0224	56.0224				
1988	626.36	730.63			56.0224	56.0224				
1989	790.60	966.50			56.0224	56.0224				
1990	842.50	843.30			56.0290	56.0290				
1991	909.00	648.10			56.0290	56.0290				
1992	1142.08	644.82			56.0290	56.0290				
1993	1798.44	2318.84			56.0290	56.0290				
1994	59609.51	60225.58			0.9103	0.8648				
1995	258916.70	214238.00			0.2251	0.2253				

2. IMPORTS BY BROAD ECONOMIC CATEGORY AND EXPORTS BY INDUSTRIAL ORIGIN. (PERCENTAGE OF TOTAL VALUE)
IMPORTATIONS PAR CATEGORIES ECONOMIQUES ET EXPORTATIONS PAR BRANCHE D'ACTIVITE.(EN POURCENTAGE DE LA VALEUR TOTALE)

IMPORTS – IMPORTATIONS

	1989	1990	1991	1992	1993	1994	1995
TOTAL IMPORTS–IMPORTATIONS TOTALES	100.	100.	100.	100.		100.	100.
1 FOOD BEV–ALIMENTATION BOISSONS	9.6	10.5	11.3	7.3		8.1	13.0
11 PRIMARY–PRODUITS DE BASE	4.0	4.0	3.5	1.9		3.3	3.2
111 FOR INDUSTRY–POUR L'INDUSTRIE	2.4	1.9	1.3	0.9		2.0	1.3
112 FOR HOUSEHOLDS–POUR LES MENAGES	1.6	2.1	2.2	1.0		1.4	1.9
12 PROCESSED–PRODUITS ELABORES	5.6	6.6	7.7	5.4		4.8	9.8
121 FOR INDUSTRY–POUR L'INDUSTRIE	1.0	1.8	2.4	1.4		1.8	2.3
122 FOR HOUSEHOLDS–POUR LES MENAGES	4.6	4.8	5.4	4.1		3.0	7.5
2 IND SUPPLIES–APPROV INDUSTRIELS	40.7	36.2	29.9	31.9		31.1	31.0
21 PRIMARY–PRODUITS DE BASE	2.5	2.1	2.0	1.7		2.1	1.2
22 PROCESSED–PRODUITS ELABORES	38.2	34.1	27.9	30.3		29.0	29.8
3 FUELS–COMBUSTIBLES	16.4	17.9	17.1	13.5		14.7	11.8
31 PRIMARY–PRODUITS DE BASE	2.9	3.4	2.9	2.4		3.7	1.9
32 PROCESSED–PRODUITS ELABORES	13.5	14.5	14.3	11.2		11.0	9.9
321 MOTOR SPIRIT–ESSENCE							
322 OTHER–AUTRES	13.5	14.5	14.3	11.2		11.0	9.9
4 MACHINERY–EQUIPEMENT	14.7	15.0	17.5	14.0		24.4	19.8
41 CAPITAL EQUIPMENT–MACHINES	12.8	13.0	15.7	12.6		21.5	17.5
42 PARTS–PIECES ACCESSOIRES	1.9	2.0	1.8	1.4		3.0	2.3
5 TRANSPORT–TRANSPORT	10.5	9.7	12.1	24.1		10.7	14.6
51 PASSENGER CARS–AUTOMOBILES	2.9	2.9	4.9	18.5		2.0	3.4
52 OTHER–AUTRES	4.3	3.1	3.6	2.8		5.3	5.8
521 INDUSTRIAL–INDUSTRIELS	3.9	2.7	3.3	2.3		5.1	5.4
522 NON INDUSTRIAL–NON INDUSTRIEL	0.4	0.5	0.3	0.5		0.2	0.4
53 PARTS–PIECES ACCESSOIRES	3.3	3.6	3.6	2.8		3.4	5.4
6 CONSUM GOODS–BIENS CONSOMMATION	7.8	10.2	11.3	8.9		10.6	9.6
61 DURABLE–DURABLES	1.8	2.6	2.6	2.4		2.1	2.1
62 SEMI DURABLE–SEMI DURABLES	4.0	5.1	5.2	3.9		5.7	5.3
63 NON DURABLE–NON DURABLES	2.0	2.5	3.5	2.6		2.8	2.2
7 GOODS NES–BIENS NDA	0.4	0.5	0.8	0.1		0.4	0.3

EXPORTS – EXPORTATIONS

	1989	1990	1991	1992	1993	1994	1995
TOTAL EXPORTS–EXPORTATIONS TOTALES	100.	100.	100.	100.		100.	100.
1 AGRICULTURE	15.0	15.5	17.9	16.9		12.5	12.1
2 MINING QUARRY–INDUS EXTRACTIVES	1.1	1.5	1.7	1.3		71.1	67.9
3 MANUFACTURING–IND MANUFACTUR	83.9	83.0	80.4	81.8		16.4	20.0
31 FOOD BEV TOBACCO–ALIM BOISS TAB	0.1	0.5	0.5	1.0		5.6	7.1
32 TEXTILES–INDUSTRIES TEXTILES	0.0	0.0	0.0	0.0		0.0	0.0
33 WOOD & PRODUCTS–BOIS & PRODUITS	0.3	0.1	0.2	0.3		0.4	0.5
34 PAPER & PRODUCTS–PAPIER & PRODT	0.0	0.0	0.0	0.0		0.0	0.0
35 CHEMICALS–INDUSTRIES CHIMIQUES	73.6	73.6	69.9	66.9		0.1	0.1
36 NON METAL MIN–MIN NON METAL	0.0	0.0	0.0	0.0		0.0	0.0
37 BASIC METAL–IND METAL BASE	9.5	8.2	8.9	12.2		8.7	10.8
38 METAL MANUF–MANUF METAL	0.3	0.5	1.0	1.3		1.6	1.5
39 OTH MANUF IND–AUTRES MANUF	0.0	0.0	0.0	0.0		0.0	0.0

3. TRADE BY PRINCIPAL COUNTRIES OF ORIGIN AND DESTINATION (VALUE IN MILLION U.S. DOLLARS)
ECHANGES SELON LES PRINCIPAUX PAYS D'ORIGINE ET DE DESTINATION (VALEUR EN MILLIONS DE DOLLARS EU)

COUNTRIES–PAYS	GENERAL IMPORTS C.I.F. IMPORTATIONS GENERALES C.A.F				
	1991	1992	1993	1994	1995
World	509.2	639.8	1007.6	542.6	582.8
Africa	0.0	0.0		0.0	3.5
Americas	313.2	379.3	793.9	360.9	387.9
– Northern America	198.5	255.4	447.8	260.7	250.0
– LAIA	22.6	23.5	127.2	27.7	59.4
– CACM	5.8	15.5	1.3	0.4	1.0
– Caribbean	82.1	78.3	208.2	63.4	62.6
– Rest of America	4.2	6.6	9.3	8.8	14.8
Asia excl fmr USSR	39.0	114.6		29.8	46.1
– Middle East	0.0	0.2		0.0	0.3
Asia former USSR					
Europe excl fmr USSR	157.0	145.8	151.0	151.9	145.4
– European Union	153.8	143.8	145.7	146.7	140.2
– Eastern Europe	0.1	0.1		0.5	0.1
– Rest of Europe	3.1	1.9	5.3	4.7	5.0
Europe former USSR					
Oceania	0.0	0.0			0.0
Other		0.0			
USA/Etats–Unis d'Amer	195.8	254.3	441.4	257.9	247.0
Netherlands/Pays–Bas	112.8	124.7	129.2	103.9	115.6
Trinidad and Tobago	57.1	62.7	187.0	56.3	42.9
Venezuela	3.2	5.9	115.6	16.4	17.4
Japan/Japon	19.0	99.8		15.3	12.4
Brazil/Brésil	15.4	13.3	8.0	6.6	36.5
Netherlands Antilles	17.8	8.9	12.9		14.8
United Kingdom	8.3	6.6	5.7	24.6	5.8
China, Hong Kong SAR	5.9	4.0		4.4	13.0
Belgium–Luxembourg	6.8	4.0	2.4	2.6	10.1
Germany/Allemagne	7.6	5.0	0.2	7.2	5.6
Panama	3.1	2.9	4.2	5.0	10.3
Italy/Italie	12.6	0.2	2.0	6.0	0.4
Guatemala	2.5	14.4	1.0		0.2
Canada	2.8	1.1	6.4	2.8	3.1
France, Monaco	4.0	1.9	5.4	1.9	2.4
Jamaica/Jamaïque	4.0	4.4	2.2	2.9	2.0
Other Asia n.e.s.	5.0	2.8		2.1	5.5
Guyana	0.7	3.0	4.4	3.2	4.0
Colombia/Colombie	2.1	2.4	2.0	3.2	3.3
Switzerland,Liechtenst.	1.7	0.8	3.2	1.5	2.6
China/Chine	1.6	3.0		1.3	3.8
Dominican Republic	3.2	1.6	4.0	0.1	0.5
Norway,Svalbard and JM	0.8	1.1	0.9	3.2	2.4
Korea, Republic of	4.3	1.3		2.5	0.1
Mexico/Mexique	1.2	1.8	1.2	1.0	2.0
Malaysia/Malaisie	0.0	0.0		0.2	6.4
Bahamas	0.0			4.1	1.6
India/Inde	0.5	0.4		2.2	1.5
Honduras	2.9	1.0			
So. African Customs Un				0.0	3.4
Indonesia/Indonésie	0.5	1.2		0.9	0.7
Thailand/Thaïlande	1.4	1.3		0.2	0.3
French Guiana	0.4	0.7	0.8	0.6	0.6
Singapore/Singapour	0.7	0.6		0.7	0.7
Caribbean n.e.s.			2.0		
Denmark/Danemark	0.4	0.3	0.5	0.3	0.1
Costa Rica	0.2	0.1		0.4	0.8
Korea Dem People's Rp		0.1			1.3
Barbados/Barbade	0.1	0.7	0.1	0.0	0.4

COUNTRIES–PAYS	EXPORTS EXPORTATIONS ES F.O.B.				
	1991	1992	1993	1994	1995
Monde	363.1	361.2	1299.2	536.8	482.7
Afrique			0.0	0.1	1.0
Amériques	87.5	95.2	588.0	140.5	172.5
– Amérique du Nord	46.4	40.9	343.5	95.6	108.8
– ALAI	29.4	38.1	205.2	32.6	24.7
– MCAC			0.0	0.1	0.0
– Caraïbes	11.1	15.8	36.5	11.2	37.2
– Autre Amérique	0.6	0.3	2.7	1.0	1.8
Asie anc. URSS exclus	28.0	18.9	30.0	36.3	30.1
– Moyen–Orient		0.0	0.0	0.0	
Asie ancienne URSS					
Europe anc. URSS exclus	245.6	247.1	681.2	356.6	273.2
– Union Européenne	122.8	170.7	395.7	204.6	154.7
– Europe de l'Est	0.0	0.0	0.0		
– Autre de l'Europe	122.8	76.5	285.5	152.1	118.5
Europe ancienne URSS	2.0			3.3	5.8
Océanie					
Autre		0.0			
Netherlands/Pays–Bas	94.5	104.2	349.9	145.5	132.8
Norway,Svalbard and JM	122.8	76.5	272.8	151.5	118.5
USA/Etats–Unis d'Amer	46.3	40.9	343.5	95.4	106.2
Brazil/Brésil	29.4	38.1	205.0	32.3	24.5
Japan/Japon	28.0	18.9	30.0	36.2	28.9
France, Monaco	8.4	50.1	14.3	7.4	8.2
Spain/Espagne	6.5	3.0	23.0	33.7	2.3
Netherlands Antilles	0.6	9.2	19.5		24.1
United Kingdom	6.4	9.6	7.7	16.0	10.6
Trinidad and Tobago	8.7	4.7	15.1	9.4	10.8
Other Europe n.e.s.			12.6		
Russian Federation				3.3	5.8
Martinique	1.7	1.7	1.4	1.2	1.1
Belgium–Luxembourg	1.5	0.0	0.6	1.4	0.7
Portugal	0.5	3.6	0.0		0.0
French Guiana	0.3	0.1	1.9	0.5	0.8
Germany/Allemagne	2.8	0.2	0.2	0.3	0.1
Canada	0.0	0.0	0.1	0.3	2.6
Guyana	0.3	0.2	0.8	0.5	1.0
Sweden/Suède	2.2				
Former USSR/Anc. URSS	2.0				
Guadeloupe	0.1	0.3	0.4	0.4	0.6
So. African Customs Un				0.1	1.0
Switzerland,Liechtenst.	0.0		0.2	0.5	0.0
China, Hong Kong SAR	0.0	0.0	0.0		0.5
Venezuela	0.0	0.1	0.1	0.3	0.0
China/Chine	0.0	0.0		0.0	0.5
Aruba					0.4
Barbados/Barbade		0.0	0.1	0.2	0.1
Macau/Macao					0.2
Italy/Italie	0.1	0.0		0.0	0.0
Colombia/Colombie		0.0	0.0	0.0	0.1
LAIA n.e.s.			0.1		
Philippines				0.1	
Jamaica/Jamaïque	0.0	0.0	0.0	0.0	0.0
Singapore/Singapour	0.0			0.0	0.0
El Salvador				0.0	0.0
Costa Rica				0.0	0.0
Dominican Republic				0.0	
Korea, Republic of	0.0	0.0	0.0	0.0	

(VALUE AS PERCENTAGE OF WORLD TOTAL)(VALEURS EN POURCENTAGE DU TOTAL MONDIAL)

	1986	1987	1988	1989	1990	1991	1992	1993	1994	1995
Africa					0.0	0.0	0.0		0.0	0.6
Americas	62.5	68.3	62.0	65.8	64.3	61.5	59.3	78.8	66.5	66.5
– Northern America	33.3	31.6	37.7	44.0	41.4	39.0	39.9	44.4	48.0	42.9
– LAIA	10.2	11.1	7.2	6.6	5.9	4.4	3.7	12.6	5.1	10.2
– CACM	0.1	0.1	0.1	0.0	0.1	1.1	2.4	0.1	0.1	0.2
– Caribbean	18.3	24.2	15.9	14.2	15.2	16.1	12.2	20.7	11.7	10.7
– Rest of America	0.7	1.3	1.1	1.0	1.7	0.8	1.0	0.9	1.6	2.5
Asia excl fmr USSR	7.9	3.8	5.4	7.7	6.0	7.7	17.9		5.5	7.9
– Middle East				0.0	0.0	0.0	0.0		0.0	0.0
Asia former USSR										
Europe excl fmr USSR	28.8	27.5	32.5	26.5	29.7	30.8	22.8	15.0	28.0	24.9
– European Union	28.5	27.3	31.3	26.3	29.3	30.2	22.5	14.5	27.0	24.1
– Eastern Europe			0.0	0.0	0.0	0.0	0.0		0.1	0.0
– Rest of Europe	0.4	0.2	1.2	0.2	0.4	0.6	0.3	0.5	0.9	0.9
Europe former USSR			0.0							
Oceania			0.0		0.0	0.0	0.0			0.0
Other							0.0			
USA/Etats–Unis d'Amer	32.8	31.4	37.3	43.9	41.3	38.4	39.7	43.8	47.5	42.4
Netherlands/Pays–Bas	19.1	19.7	23.6	20.1	23.5	22.2	19.5	12.8	19.1	19.8
Trinidad and Tobago	10.5	9.8	7.5	9.4	9.0	11.2	9.8	18.6	10.4	7.4
Venezuela	0.7	1.4	0.4	0.6	0.4	0.6	0.9	11.5	3.0	3.0
Japan/Japon	1.9	1.3	1.5	4.2	2.8	3.7	15.6		2.8	2.1
Brazil/Brésil	7.4	8.9	5.9	5.1	4.3	3.0	2.1	0.8	1.2	6.3
Netherlands Antilles			6.4	3.6	5.3	3.5	1.4	1.3		2.5
United Kingdom	2.0	2.3	2.9	1.5	1.2	1.6	1.0	0.6	4.5	1.0
China, Hong Kong SAR	1.8	0.9	1.5	1.6	1.1	1.2	0.6		0.8	2.2
Belgium–Luxembourg	0.8	1.0	0.5	0.8	1.9	1.3	0.6	0.2	0.5	1.7

	1986	1987	1988	1989	1990	1991	1992	1993	1994	1995
Afrique			0.5	1.3	0.0			0.0	0.0	0.2
Amériques	34.4	31.4	28.8	27.2	18.2	24.1	26.4	45.3	26.2	35.7
– Amérique du Nord	17.2	21.3	19.5	13.3	11.4	12.8	11.3	26.4	17.8	22.5
– ALAI	14.4	7.7	6.5	6.1	4.8	8.1	10.6	15.8	6.1	5.1
– MCAC			0.0					0.0	0.0	0.0
– Caraïbes	2.0	1.8	2.5	7.7	2.0	3.0	4.4	2.8	2.1	7.7
– Autre Amérique	0.8	0.7	0.2	0.1	0.1	0.2	0.1	0.2	0.2	0.4
Asie anc. URSS exclus	12.6	13.0	6.2	5.6	6.7	7.7	5.2	2.3	6.8	6.2
– Moyen–Orient				0.4			0.0	0.0	0.0	
Asie ancienne URSS										
Europe anc. URSS exclus	52.9	55.5	64.5	65.9	75.1	67.6	68.4	52.4	66.4	56.6
– Union Européenne	35.8	33.0	38.1	35.2	37.0	33.8	47.2	30.5	38.1	32.1
– Europe de l'Est				1.4		0.0	0.0	0.0		
– Autre de l'Europe	17.1	22.5	26.4	29.3	38.1	33.8	21.2	22.0	28.3	24.6
Europe ancienne URSS						0.6			0.6	1.2
Océanie					0.0					
Autre							0.0			
Netherlands/Pays–Bas	22.0	24.7	26.6	24.7	28.9	26.0	28.8	26.9	27.1	27.5
Norway,Svalbard and JM	16.1	21.8	26.4	29.0	35.4	33.8	21.2	21.0	28.2	24.5
USA/Etats–Unis d'Amer	16.9	20.1	19.5	13.3	11.4	12.8	11.3	26.4	17.8	22.0
Brazil/Brésil	8.8	6.9	6.5	6.1	4.8	8.1	10.5	15.8	6.0	5.1
Japan/Japon	12.6	13.0	6.2	5.2	6.7	7.7	5.2	2.3	6.7	6.0
France, Monaco	3.9	1.1	1.7	1.5	4.7	2.3	13.9	1.1	1.4	1.7
Spain/Espagne	0.1	0.1		0.5	0.7	1.8	0.8	1.8	6.3	0.5
Netherlands Antilles			0.2	0.1	0.1	0.2	2.5	1.5		5.0
United Kingdom	4.3	3.6	4.9	4.6	2.2	1.8	2.7	0.6	3.0	2.2
Trinidad and Tobago	0.0	0.3	0.9	7.0	1.5	2.4	1.3	1.2	1.7	2.2

4. General Imports C.I.F. by Commodities according to the S.I.T.C. (Rev. 2) in million U.S. Dollars
Importations Générales C.A.F. par Produits d'après la C.T.C.I. (Rév. 2) en millions de Dollars E.U.

SITC CTCI	COMMODITY	1992		1993		1994		1995		PRODUIT
		QUANTITY QUANTITE	VALUE VALEUR	QUANTITY QUANTITE	VALUE VALEUR	QUANTITY QUANTITE	VALUE VALEUR	QUANTITY QUANTITE	VALUE VALEUR	
	ALL COMMODITIES		639.9				542.6		582.9	TOUS PRODUITS
0	FOOD AND LIVE ANIMALS		36.8				40.3		67.9	ALIMENTS,ANIMAUX VIVANTS
01	MEAT AND PREPARATIONS		1.0				4.4		9.0	VIANDES ET PREPARATIONS
011	MEAT FRESH,CHILLD,FROZEN		0.2			W 2211	2.9	W 3922	5.3	VIANDES FRAICHES,REF,CONGE
0118	MEAT NES FRESH,CHLD,FRZN					W 2176	2.6	W 3806	5.1	AUTRES VIANDES,ABATS
01189	OTHER MEAT NES FRESH,ETC					W 2176	2.6	W 3806	5.1	VIANDE,ABATS COMESTIBLES
012	MEAT DRIED,SALTED,SMOKED		0.1			W 419	1.0	W 2243	2.8	VIANDE,ABATS SALES,SECHES
0121	PIG MEAT DRIED,SLTD,SMKD		0.1			W 191	0.5	W 1751	2.2	LARD,JAMBONS
02	DAIRY PRODCTS,BIRDS'EGGS		5.6				3.1		4.7	PRODUITS LAITIERS,OEUFS
022	MILK AND CREAM		2.9			W 1276	2.0	W 1205	3.2	LAIT ET CREME
0224	MILK,CREAM PRESERVED ETC		2.9			W 1212	1.9	W 1131	3.2	LAIT,CREME CONS,CONC
02242	MILK DRY,1.5% FAT OR LES		2.6			W 966	1.5	W 1003	3.1	LAIT POUDRE INF 1.5%
03	FISH AND PREPARATIONS		2.3				1.5		1.4	POISSONS ET PREPARATIONS
04	CEREALS AND PREPARATIONS		7.4				11.9		11.0	CEREALES ET PRODUITS
041	WHEAT ETC UNMILLED		5.6							FROMENT,EPEAUTRE
0412	OTHER WHEAT ETC UNMILLED		5.6							AUTRE FROMENT NON MOULU
045	CEREALS NES UNMILLED					W 60279	10.5	W 29933	7.2	AUTRES CEREALES NON MOULUES
0459	OTHER CEREALS UNMILLED					W 60279	10.5	W 29933	7.2	SARRASIN,MILLET,SORGHO
04599	OTH CEREALS UNMILLED NES					W 60279	10.5	W 29933	7.2	AUTRES CEREALES NDA
048	CEREAL ETC PREPARATIONS		1.5			W 714	1.3		2.8	PREPTNS A BASE CEREALES
05	VEGETABLES AND FRUIT		5.3				5.1		9.3	LEGUMES ET FRUITS
054	VEG ETC FRSH,SMPLY PRSVD		3.7			W 5884	3.2	W 7670	6.2	LEGUMES FRAIS,CONG,SECS
0546	VEGETABLES SIMPLY PRESVD					W 56	0.1	W 174	2.6	LEGUMES CONG,CONSER
05461	VEGETABLES FROZEN					W 56	0.1	W 170	2.6	LEGUMES CONGELES
06	SUGAR AND PREPS,HONEY		6.2				6.5		7.2	SUCRES ET PRODUITS
061	SUGAR AND HONEY		5.6			W 14757	5.6	W 22077	6.0	SUCRES ET MIEL
0611	RAW BEET AND CANE SUGAR		3.6			W 5765	3.2	W 6340	2.9	SUCRES BRUTS
0619	SUGARS AND SYRUPS NES		0.4			W 8978	2.3	W 15358	2.9	AUTRES SUCRES SIROPS
07	COFFEE,TEA,COCOA,SPICES		1.3				1.7		18.5	CAFE,THE,CACAO,EPICES
073	CHOCOLATE AND PRODUCTS		0.4			W 193	0.8	W 345	17.0	CHOCOLAT
081	*FEEDING STUFF FOR ANIML		1.0			W 1614	2.7		1.9	NOURRITURE POUR ANIMAUX
0819	FOOD WASTE AND FEED NES		0.3			W 171	2.5	W 8086	1.5	DECHETS,ALIMENTS NDA
08199	FODDER NES,INCL SWEETNED		0.3			W 171	2.5	W 8086	1.5	PREPARATIONS FOURRAGERES
09	MISC EDIBLE PRODUCTS		6.8				3.7		5.1	PREP ALIMENTAIRES DIVERSES
098	EDIBLE PRODCTS,PREPS NES		6.5			W 3447	3.6	W 7195	4.5	PREP ALIMENTAIRES NDA
09802	TEA,ETC EXTRACT,ESSENCE		2.5							EXTRAITS DE THE
09809	MISC FOOD PREPRTIONS NES		2.4			W 725	1.9	W 2025	2.7	PREP ALIMENTAIRES NDA
1	BEVERAGES AND TOBACCO		11.9				5.9		6.9	BOISSONS ET TABACS
11	BEVERAGES		7.6				3.4		4.9	BOISSONS
112	ALCOHOLIC BEVERAGES		6.6			W 1477	2.9	W 1953	3.6	BOISSONS ALCOOLIQUES
1123	BEER,ALE,STOUT,PORTER		2.1			W 688	0.5	W 983	0.8	BIERES
1124	DISTILLED ALCOHOLIC BEVS		4.1			W 661	2.0	W 753	2.5	ALCOOLS,EAUX–DE–VIE
11241	WHISKY		3.2			W 403	1.3	W 541	1.7	WHISKY
12	TOBACCO AND MANUFACTURES		4.3				2.5		2.0	TABACS BRUTS FABRIQUES
121	TOBACCO UNMNFCTRD,REFUSE		2.8			W 470	2.1	W 384	1.2	TABACS BRUTS,DECHETS
1211	TOBACCO,NOT STRIPPED		2.8			W 470	2.1	W 384	1.2	TABACS NON ECOTES
2	CRUDE MATERLS,EXCL FUELS		7.2				9.4		5.7	MAT BRUTES NON COMESTIBLES
27	CRUDE FERTLZR,MINRLS NES		6.7				8.7		5.0	ENGRAIS MINERAUX BRUTS
273	STONE,SAND AND GRAVEL		5.1			W 4729	0.6	W 2046	0.2	PIERRES,SABLES,GRAVIERS
2734	GRAVEL,CRUSHED STONE,ETC		5.0			W 2749	0.5	W 1570	0.1	PIERRES CONCASSEES
278	OTHER CRUDE MINERALS		1.6			W 118353	7.5		4.2	AUTRES MINERAUX BRUTS
2785	QUARTZ,MICA,FELSPAR,ETC					W 107802	4.9		2.6	QUARTZ,MICA,FELDSPATH
27851	NATURAL QUARTZ,QUARTZITE					W 107802	4.9		2.6	QUARTZ,QUARTZITES
2789	MINERALS CRUDE NES		1.2			W 3745	2.0	W 1995	1.2	MINERAUX BRUTS NDA
3	MINERAL FUELS ETC		86.6				79.5		68.7	COMBUSTIBLES MINERAUX LUB
32	COAL,COKE AND BRIQUETTES		7.4				14.3		5.9	HOUILLES,COKES,BRIQUETTES
322	COAL,LIGNITE AND PEAT		0.1			W 16638	14.3		5.7	HOUILLES,LIGNITES,TOURBE
3222	OTH COAL,NOT AGGLOMERATD		0.1			W 16621	14.3		5.7	AUTRES HOUILLES
323	BRIQUETS,COKE,SEMI–COKE		7.4			W 27	0.1	W 517	0.2	BRIQUETTES
33	PETROLEUM AND PRODUCTS		71.4				59.5		57.7	PETROLE ET DERIVES
334	PETROLEUM PRODUCTS,REFIN		69.7			W 269234	51.6		48.5	PRODUITS RAFFINES
3341	GASOLINE,OTH LIGHT OILS		16.3							ESSENCES POUR MOTEURS
33411	MOTOR,AVIATION SPIRIT		14.6							ESSENCES MOTEURS D'AVIONS
3344	FUEL OILS,NES		44.1							FUEL OILS
3345	LUBS,PETROLEUM OILS NES		8.9							HUILES LUBRIFIANTES
33452	LUBS (LOW PETRLM CONTNT)		8.2							PREPARATIONS LUBRIFIANTES
335	RESIDUAL PETRLM PROD NES		1.8			W 70530	7.9	W 49095	9.3	PRODUITS RESIDUELS NDA
3354	PETROLM BITUMEN,COKE ETC		1.7			W 70481	7.7	W 49052	9.2	BITUME,COKE DE PETROLE
33542	PETROLEUM COKE					W 69759	7.3	W 49004	9.1	COKE DE PETROLE
341	*GAS,NATURAL AND MANUFCT		7.9			W 33792	5.8	W 61497	5.2	GAZ NATUREL,GAZ MANUFACT
3414	PETROLEUM GASES, GASEOUS		7.9			W 23889	5.1	W 61489	5.2	GAZ DE PETROLE GAZEUX
4	ANIMAL,VEGETABLE OIL,FAT		5.4				4.4		6.6	HUILES,GRAISSES ANIM,VEG
42	FIXED VEGETABLE OIL,FAT		3.5				3.4		2.9	HUILES VEGETALES FIXES
423	FIXED VEG OILS,SOFT		3.4				2.5	W 1282	1.8	HUILES VEGET DOUCES FIXES
4232	SOYA BEAN OIL		3.4			W 2473	2.4	W 1065	1.6	HUILE DE SOJA
431	*PROCESD ANML VEG OIL,ET		0.2			W 306	0.7	W 373	3.7	HUILES,GRAISSES PREPAREES
4312	HYDROGENATED OIL,FAT		0.2			W 287	0.6	W 264	2.8	HUILES HYDROGENEES
5	CHEMCLS,RELATED PROD NES		81.8				80.7		86.4	PRODUITS CHIMIQUES
52	INORGANIC CHEMICALS		39.2				33.6		57.6	PROD CHIM INORGANIQUES
522	INORG ELEMNTS,OXIDES,ETC		39.2			W 233906	32.4	W 2309	56.9	ELEMENTS INORGANIQUES
5222	INORGANIC ACIDS ETC		0.8			W 233582	32.1	W 2304	56.7	ACIDES INORGANIQUES
52229	OTH INORGANIC ACIDS ETC		0.5			W 230522	30.9	W 2194	56.2	AUTRES ACIDES INORGANIQUES
5225	INORGANIC BASES ETC NES		38.3							AUTRES BASES OXYDES METAL
52253	SODIUM HYDROXIDE, OTHER		38.3							HYDROXYDE SODIUM AQUEUX
53	DYES,TANNING,COLOUR PROD		6.6				3.8		4.0	PROD TEINTURE,COLORANTS
533	PIGMENTS,PAINTS,ETC		6.6			W 1503	3.2	W 20395	3.6	PIGMENTS,PEINTURES,VERNIS
5331	COLOURING MATERIAL NES		0.9			W 1191	2.4	W 17209	2.5	AUT MATIERES COLORANTES
5334	VARNISHES,DISTEMPERS ETC		4.2			W 89	0.4	W 2206	0.6	PEINTURES A L'EAU
541	*MEDICINAL,PHARM PRODUCT		10.1			K 3215493	7.6	K 4285409	4.8	PROD MEDICINAUX PHARMACEUT
5411	PROVITAMINS AND VITAMINS		4.0							PROVITAMINES,VITAMINES
5417	MEDICAMENTS		5.6			K 188053	5.4	K 403095	2.9	MEDICAMENTS
54171	— CONTAINNG ANTIBIOTICS		0.1			K 188053	5.4	K 403095	2.9	MED CONTN ANTIBIOTIQUES
54179	— CONTNG OTH SUBSTANCES		5.5							MED CONT AUT SUBSTANCES
55	PERFUME,CLEANING ETC PRD		4.2				4.1		5.2	PROD POUR PARFUM,TOILETTE
553	PERFUMERY,COSMETICS,ETC		2.2			W 600	2.7	W 928	3.1	PRODUITS DE PARFUMERIE
554	SOAP,CLEANSING ETC PREPS		1.7			W 872	1.3	W 2054	2.0	SAVONS,PRODUITS DETERSIFS
562	*FERTILIZERS,MANUFACTURE		3.7			W 13626	9.8	W 6853	2.6	ENGRAIS MANUFACTURES
5621	CHEM NITROGENOUS FERTLZR		3.7			W 10530	9.5	W 5012	1.9	ENGRAIS AZOTES
56216	UREA		2.3			W 6160	1.7	W 3411	1.1	UREE
56219	CHEM NITROG FERTILZR NES		1.3			W 3959	7.4	W 1601	0.6	ENGRAIS AZOTES NDA
572	*EXPLOSIVES,PYROTECH PRO		0.6			W 492	2.8	W 188	0.5	EXPLOSIFS

4. General Imports C.I.F. by Commodities according to the S.I.T.C. (Rev. 2) in million U.S. Dollars
Importations Générales C.A.F. par Produits d'après la C.T.C.I. (Rév. 2) en millions de Dollars E.U.

SITC CTCI	COMMODITY	1992 QUANTITY QUANTITE	1992 VALUE VALEUR	1993 QUANTITY QUANTITE	1993 VALUE VALEUR	1994 QUANTITY QUANTITE	1994 VALUE VALEUR	1995 QUANTITY QUANTITE	1995 VALUE VALEUR	PRODUIT
5723	PYROTECHNIC ARTICLES		0.1			W 492	2.8	W 185	0.5	ARTICLES DE PYROTECHNIE
58	PLASTIC MATERIALS ETC		5.8				0.2		0.1	MAT PLAST ARTIFICIELLES
583	POLYMERIZATION ETC PRODS		4.2			W 55	0.2	W 31	0.1	PROD POLYMERISATION
5839	OTH POLYMRZTION ETC PROD		2.2			W 49	0.1	W 27	0.1	AUT PROD POLYMER COPOLYM
59	CHEMICAL MATERIALS NES		10.5				18.9		11.4	MAT PROD CHIMIQUES NDA
591	PESTICIDES,DISINFECTANTS		4.4			W 10655	3.1	W 929	4.0	DESINF,INSECT,FONG,HERB
5911	INSECTICIDES,FOR RETAIL		3.6			W 10364	1.6	W 228	0.9	INSECTICIDES VENTE DET
5914	DISINFECTANTS,ETC,FR RET					W 124	0.3	W 616	2.3	DESINFECTANTS VENTE DET
59149	RAT POISONS ETC FR RTAIL					W 124	0.3	W 616	2.3	ANTIPARASITES VENTE DET
598	MISCEL CHEM PRODUCTS NES		5.8			W 4414	15.4	W 710	7.1	PROD DIV INDUST CHIM NDA
5989	CHEM PRODUCTS,PREPS NES		5.1			W 3609	15.1	W 505	6.9	PROD PREP CHIMIQUES NDA
59899	OTH CHEM PRODS,PREPS,NES		4.5			W 3219	14.2	W 183	6.3	AUT PRODUITS CHIMIQUES NDA
6	BASIC MANUFACTURES		100.7				92.6		91.6	ART MANUFACTURES
62	RUBBER MANUFACTURES NES		6.6				11.2		7.5	CAOUTCHOUC MANUFACTURE
625	RUBBER TYRES, TUBES ETC		3.2			W 1694	5.2	W 7017	4.2	PNEUS CAOUTCHOUC VULCANISE
6251	TYRES NEW FOR MOTOR CARS		1.7			W 1132	1.7	W 6540	2.1	PNEUS POUR VOITURES
628	RUBBER ARTICLES NES		2.6			W 415	5.2	W 259	2.8	OUVRAGES CAOUTCHOUC NDA
6282	VULCANIZD RUBBER BELTING		0.9			W 152	2.1	W 131	0.8	COURROIES EN CAOUTCHOUC
6289	OTH RUBBER ARTICLES NES		1.7			W 258	3.1	W 120	1.9	AUT OUVR CAOUTCHOUC NDA
62898	UNHARD RUBBER PRODS NES		1.6			W 236	2.4	W 108	1.8	OUV CAOUT VULC NON DURCI
64	PAPER,PAPERBOARD AND MFR		8.6				13.9		11.3	PAPIERS,CARTONS & OUVRAGES
641	PAPER AND PAPERBOARD		2.5			W 2809	3.2		4.4	PAPIERS ET CARTONS
6418	COATED ETC PAPER NES BLK					W 516	1.1	W 663	1.8	PAP,CARTONS COUCHES,ENDUITS
64189	COATED PAPER ETC NES					W 516	1.1	W 663	1.8	PAPIERS,CARTONS COUCHES
642	PAPER,ETC,PRECUT,ARTS OF		6.1			W 4272	10.8	W 19929	7.0	PAP,CARTONS DECOUPES
6421	PAPER ETC CONTAINERS		2.5			W 2973	8.3	W 19090	4.5	BOITES,SACS EMBALLAGES
65	TEXTILE YARN,FABRICS,ETC		10.7				11.3		17.8	FILS,TISSUS,ARTICLES TEXTILE
651	TEXTILE YARN		2.9			W 15	0.1	W 90	0.2	FILS TEXTILES
6515	YARN OF 6514 FOR RETAIL		2.8							FILS CONT 85% FI SYNTHETIQ
652	COTTON FABRICS,WOVEN		3.2			W 344	1.3	W 204	1.4	TISSUS DE COTON
6521	GREY WOVEN COTTON FABRIC		3.2			W 344	1.3	W 204	1.4	TISSUS COT ECRUS NON MERCER
653	WOVN MAN-MADE FIB FABRIC		0.1			W 410	2.1	W 262	1.5	TISSUS FIBRES SYNTH,ARTIF
6534	DISC SYN BLEND FABRC NES		0.1			W 383	1.9	W 188	1.2	TISSUS FIBRES SYNTH DISCONT
65341	DISC SYN FIB-COTTN FABRC					W 383	1.9	W 188	1.2	TISSUS FIB SYNT DIS MEL COTO
657	SPECIAL TXTL FABRC,PRODS		1.5			W 377	2.5	W 414	9.0	TISSUS SPECIAUX
6577	TEXTILES FOR MACHINERY		0.5			W 43	0.4	W 68	7.6	OUATES,MECHES ART TEXT
65771	TEXTILE WADDING NES ETC		0.4			W 28	0.3	W 47	7.3	OUATES,ARTICLES EN OUATE
658	TEXTILE ARTICLES NES		2.4			W 869	1.8	W 516	2.1	ART FACONNES MAT TEXTILES
66	NONMETAL MINERAL MFS NES		34.5				13.1		16.9	ART MIN NON METALLIQUES
661	LIME,CEMENT,BLDG PRODS		6.3				7.1		11.3	CHAUX,CIMENTS MAT CONSTR
6611	LIME,QUICK,SLKD,HYDRAULC					W 1841	1.6		6.7	CHAUX ORDINAIRE,HYDRAUL
6612	CEMENT		5.5			W 54051	5.3	W 69844	4.3	CIMENTS HYDRAULIQUES
662	CLAY,REFRACTORY BLDG PRD		2.9			W 1802	1.8	W 3090	2.3	MAT CONST REFRACTAIRES
6624	BRICKS ETC NONREFRACTORY		2.0			W 1361	1.1	W 3040	1.8	BRIQUES ETC CERAM NON REFR
663	MINERAL MANUFCTURES NES		1.0			W 627	1.8		1.9	ART MIN MANUF NDA
665	GLASSWARE		23.1			W 1115	1.6	W 1039	1.0	OUVRAGES EN VERRE
6651	BOTTLES ETC OF GLASS		22.9							RECIPIENTS EN VERRE
66511	GLASS BOTTLES ETC NONVAC		22.9							BONBONNES,BOUTEILLES,ETC
67	IRON AND STEEL		18.6				17.9		16.9	FER ET ACIER
672	IRON,STEEL PRIMARY FORMS		2.2			W 4074	5.2	W 4806	5.4	LINGOTS FER,ACIER
6725	IRN,STL BLOOMS,SLABS,ETC		2.2			W 2228	3.4	W 3388	3.3	BLOOMS,BILLETTES FER ACIER
67251	IRN,SMPLE STL BLOOMS,ETC					W 2228	3.4	W 3388	3.3	BLOOMS ETC NON ACIER FIN
6727	IRN,STL COIL FR REROLLNG					W 1846	1.8	W 1418	2.1	EBAUCHES POUR TOLES FER
67271	IRON,SIMPLE STEEL COILS					W 1846	1.8	W 1418	2.1	EBAUCHES NON EN ACIER
673	IRON,STEEL SHAPES ETC		2.8			W 4570	3.3	W 7122	4.6	BARRES,PROFIL FER,ACIER
6732	IRON,STEEL BARS ETC		2.8			W 4570	3.3	W 7122	4.6	BARRES FER,ACIER
67325	OTH ALLOY STEEL BARS ETC					W 3750	2.5	W 6982	4.4	BARRES NON ACIERS ALLIES
674	IRN,STL UNIV,PLATE,SHEET		3.8							LARGES PLATS,TOLES
6749	OTH IRN,STL PLATES,SHEET		3.7							AUTRES TOLES FER,ACIER
678	IRON,STL TUBES,PIPES,ETC		9.5			W 4893	8.9	W 4464	6.4	TUBES,TUYAUX EN FONTE,FER
6781	CAST IRON TUBES,PIPES		8.5							TUBES,TUYAUX EN FONTE
6783	IRON,STL TUBES,PIPES NES		1.1			W 4893	8.9	W 4464	6.4	AUT TUBES,TUYAUX FER,ACIER
68	NON-FERROUS METALS		1.5				2.1		1.9	METAUX NON FERREUX
69	METAL MANUFACTURES NES		19.3				22.3		18.1	ART MANUFACT EN METAL NDA
691	STRUCTURES AND PARTS NES		2.0			W 834	3.7	W 980	2.7	CONSTRUCT FER,ACIER,ALU
6911	STRUCTURES,PARTS IRN,STL		1.1			W 732	3.2	W 927	2.2	CONSTRUCT FER,ACIER,FONTE
692	METAL TANKS,BOXES,ETC		0.7			W 569	1.9	W 1839	2.2	RECIPIENTS METALLIQUES
6924	MTL TRANSPORT BOXES ETC		0.6			W 569	1.9	W 1839	2.1	FUTS,TAMBOURS,BIDONS
69241	STL TRANSPORT BOXES ETC		0.6			W 569	1.9	W 1836	2.0	FUTS,TAMBOURS,BIDONS FER
693	WIRE PRODUCTS NON ELECTR		5.6			W 1001	1.7		1.1	OUVRAGES FILS METALLIQUES
6931	WIRE CABLES, ROPES ETC		5.1			W 778	1.3		0.7	CORDAGES EN FILS DE FER
69311	IRN,STEEL CABLE,ROPE ETC		4.2			W 754	1.2	W 313	0.6	CORDAGES FILS FER,ACIER
694	STL,COPPR NAILS,NUTS,ETC		1.7			W 1183	2.4	W 324	1.6	CLOUS,VIS,ECROUS
695	TOOLS		1.9			W 764	4.4	W 502	3.1	OUTILS A MAIN
6953	OTHER HAND TOOLS		1.7			W 591	2.9	W 159	1.5	AUTRES OUTILS A MAIN
69539	HAND TOOLS ETC NES		0.6			W 79	1.9	W 133	0.8	OUTILLAGE A MAIN NDA
697	BASE MTL HOUSEHOLD EQUIP		2.4			W 1022	2.3		1.2	ART MENAGE MET COMMUNS
699	BASE METAL MFRS NES		4.9				5.9		6.2	ART MANUFACTURES MET NDA
6997	IRON,STEEL ARTICLES NES		2.1			W 848	2.2	W 875	2.9	OUV FONTE,FER,ACIER NDA
69979	IRN,STL MANUFACTURES NES		2.1			W 848	2.2	W 875	2.9	AUT OUVRAGES EN FER NDA
7	MACHINES,TRANSPORT EQUIP		247.8				188.5		207.6	MACHINES MATERIEL TRANSPORT
71	POWER GENERATING EQUIPMT		11.0				10.6		26.2	MACHINES GENERATRICES
711	STEAM BOILERS & AUX PLNT		1.6			W 178	1.8		3.9	GENERATEURS VAPEUR EAU ETC
7111	STEAM BOILERS ETC		1.6			W 178	1.8		3.9	GENERATEURS VAPEUR EAU
713	INTRNL COMBUS PSTN ENGIN		6.2			W 724	8.0	W 549	21.8	MOTEURS EXPL COMB INT, PIECE
7133	MARINE PISTON ENGINES		2.3			W 691	7.1	W 532	21.3	MOTEURS EXPL POUR BATEAUX
71331	—— OUTBOARD					W 247	2.3	W 129	2.0	MOTEURS BATEAUX HORSBORD
71332	—— OTHER THAN OUTBOARD					W 445	4.9	W 402	19.3	MOT BATEAUX AUT HORSBORD
716	ROTATING ELECTRIC PLANT		3.2			W 54	0.8	W 78	0.5	APP ELECTR ROTATIFS,PIECES
72	MACHS FOR SPCL INDUSTRYS		33.7				10.7		13.2	MAC SPECIALES POUR INDUST
721	AGRIC MACHY,EXC TRACTORS		9.9				3.1	W 40240	3.0	MACHINES AGRICOLES
7211	CULTIVATING MACHINERY		9.6							MACH PREPARATION DU SOL
72118	OTH AGRIC,HORTIC MACHNRY		9.6							AUT MACHINES AGRICOLES
7212	HARVESTING ETC MACHINES					W 687	3.1	W 40189	2.7	ENGINS POUR LA RECOLTE
72121	LAWN MOWERS					W 687	3.1	W 40189	2.7	TONDEUSES A GAZON
722	TRACTORS NON-ROAD		6.0			W 1853	5.2		5.7	TRACTEURS
7224	WHEELED TRACTORS NES		5.8			W 1843	5.2	W 1365	4.7	TRACTEURS A ROUES
723	CIVIL ENGNEERG EQUIP ETC		16.5							APPAREILS DE GENIE CIVIL
7234	CONST,MINING MACHNRY NES		16.5							MACH POUR LA CONST, MINES
72342	SLFPRP SHOVELS,EXCAVATRS		6.6							PELLES MECANIQUES
72343	SLFPRP CONST ETC MCH NES		10.0							AUT MACH EXTR,TERRASSEM

4. General Imports C.I.F. by Commodities according to the S.I.T.C. (Rev. 2) in million U.S. Dollars
Importations Générales C.A.F. par Produits d'après la C.T.C.I. (Rév. 2) en millions de Dollars E.U.

SITC CTCI	COMMODITY	1992		1993		1994		1995		PRODUIT
		QUANTITY QUANTITE	VALUE VALEUR	QUANTITY QUANTITE	VALUE VALEUR	QUANTITY QUANTITE	VALUE VALEUR	QUANTITY QUANTITE	VALUE VALEUR	
728	OTH MACHY FOR SPCL INDUS		1.0			W 88	2.2	W 240	4.3	AUT MACH IND PARTICULIERES
7283	OTHR MINERAL WORKG MACHY		1.0			W 88	2.2	W 240	4.3	MACH TRIER,CRIBLER,BROYER
72834	MINRL MOULDING ETC MACHY					W 55	1.0	W 137	2.5	MACH AGGLO CIMENT ETC
74	GENRL INDUSTRL MACHY NES		24.1				66.5		61.1	MACH APP INDUSTRIE
741	HEATING,COOLING EQUIPMNT		4.3			W 227	2.1	W 359	2.3	MACH CHAUFFAGE,PIECES
7415	AIR-CONDITIONING MACHNRY		2.7			W 119	1.4	W 186	1.4	GROUPES CONDITION AIR
742	PUMPS FOR LIQUIDS ETC		5.9			W 422	17.7	W 580	7.7	POMPES MOTO-POMPES
7428	OTHER PUMPS FOR LIQUIDS		5.9			W 422	17.7	W 580	7.7	AUTRES POMPES POUR LIQ
74288	PUMPS FR LIQUIDS NES ETC		5.8			W 422	17.7	W 580	7.7	POMPES POUR LIQUIDES NDA
743	PUMPS NES,CENTRFUGES ETC					W 17108	5.6	W 301	4.5	POMPES COMPRES,VENT ETC
7435	CENTRIFUGES					W 17087	5.4	W 267	4.3	CENTRIF,ESSOREUSES
744	MECHANICAL HANDLING EQU		5.0			W 3113	23.5	W 4303	26.0	EQUIP MANUTENTION PIECES
7441	FORK LIFT TRCKS,ETC,PTS		5.0			W 77	1.4	W 31	1.1	CHARIOTS POUR USINES ETC
74411	FORK LIFT TRUCKS ETC		5.0							CHARIOTS POUR LES GARES
7442	LIFTING,LOADING MACH NES					W 3036	22.1	W 4272	25.0	APP LEVAGE,MANUTENTION
74421	PULLEY TACKLE,WINCHS ETC					W 3036	22.1	W 4272	25.0	PALANS,TREUILS
745	NONELEC MACHY,TOOLS NES		2.4			W 689	6.1	W 871	10.3	AUT MACH NON ELEC,PIECES
7451	POWER TOOLS NONELEC, PTS		1.9			W 598	5.2	W 786	9.6	OUT MACH PNEUM A MOTEUR
74511	POWER HAND TOOLS NONELEC		1.9			W 598	5.2	W 786	9.6	OUT MACH PNEUM A MOTEUR
749	NONELEC MACH PTS,ACC NES		6.6			W 53018	11.8	W 310	10.5	PIECES MACH NON ELEC NDA
7491	BALL,ROLLER,ETC BEARINGS		1.4			W 59	2.3	W 39	1.3	ROULEMENTS BILLES ETC
7492	COCKS,VALVES ETC NES		2.6			W 236	4.2	W 89	4.4	ART ROB,SIM POUR TUYAUX
7493	SHAFT,CRANK,PULLEY ETC		2.4			W 52709	5.2	W 169	4.6	ARBRES TRANS,VILEBREQUINS
75	OFFICE MACHNES,ADP EQUIP		4.3				6.6		9.8	MACH BUREAU TRAIT AUTOM
751	OFFICE MACHINES		4.3			W 27	0.5	W 65	0.7	MACH,APPAREILS DE BUREAU
7518	OFFICE MACHINES NES		4.1			W 17	0.4	W 51	0.5	MACH,APP DE BUREAU NDA
75188	OTHR OFFICE MACHINES NES		3.5							AUTRES MACH DE BUREAU
752	AUTOMTIC DATA PROC EQUIP					W 122	6.2	W 181	9.1	MACH TRAIT INFORMATION
7521	ANALOG,HYBRID COMPUTERS					W 122	6.2	W 181	9.1	MACH POUR TRAIT INFORMAT
76	TELECOMM,SOUND EQUIPMENT		7.7				6.5		7.5	EQUIPMENT DE TELECOM
764	TELECOM EQPT,PTS,ACC NES		3.8			W 134	4.7	W 124	4.4	EQUIP TELECOM,PIECES
7641	LINE TELEPHONE,ETC EQUIP		1.1			W 17	2.0	W 36	3.5	APP TELEPHON PAR FIL
7643	TV,RADIO TRANSMITTRS ETC		2.2			W 5	0.1		0.1	APP EMET TELE RADIO
7648	TELECOMM EQUIPMENT NES					W 52	2.4	W 23	0.6	APP TELECOM NDA
76481	RADIOTELEPHONE ETC RCVRS					W 52	2.4	W 23	0.6	RECEP RADIOTELEPHONIE
77	ELECTRIC MACHNRY NES ETC		25.1				45.3		31.8	MACH APP ELECT NDA
771	ELECTRIC POWER MACHY NES		0.1			W 261	8.4	W 422	5.6	MACH PROD,TRANS ELECTR
7712	OTH ELEC POWER MACHY NES					W 261	8.4	W 422	5.6	AUT APP PROD TRANSF ELEC
77122	INDUCTORS					W 261	8.4	W 422	5.6	BOBINES REACTANCE,SELFS
772	SWITCHGEAR ETC,PARTS NES		2.9			W 301	5.9	W 173	5.8	APP COUPURE,SECT ETC
7721	SWITCHGEAR ETC		2.7			W 301	5.9	W 173	5.8	APP COUPURE,SECTIONMNT
773	ELECTR DISTRIBUTNG EQUIP		2.7			W 396	4.3	W 887	11.3	EQUIPMT DISTRIBUTION ELECT
7731	INSULATED WIRE,CABLE ETC		2.5			W 321	3.9	W 850	10.6	FILS,CABLES ISOLES ELECT
775	HOUSEHOLD TYPE EQUIP NES		6.9				5.2	W 970	4.9	MACH,APP USAGE DOMESTQUE
7751	HOUSEHOLD LDRY EQUIP NES		1.3			W 164	2.0	W 167	0.8	MACH A LAVER ET SECHOIRS
77511	DOMESTIC WASHING MACHNES		1.3			W 164	2.0	W 167	0.8	MACH LAVER LINGE MOINS 6 KG
7752	DOM REFRIGERATRS,FREEZRS		2.2			W 237	2.1	W 505	2.3	REFRIG,CONGEL MENAGER
77521	DOMESTIC REFRIGERATORS		2.2			W 237	2.1	W 505	2.3	REFRIGERATEURS
778	ELECTRICAL MACHINERY NES		12.7			W 1283	20.2	W 1179	3.7	AUTRES MACH ELECT NDA
7781	BATTERIES,ACCUMULATORS		2.0			W 436	1.6	W 1004	1.8	PILES ET ACCUMULATEURS
7788	OTH ELEC MACHY,EQUIP NES		7.7			W 612	16.7	W 4	0.2	AUT MACH APP ELEC NDA
77881	ELECTRO-MAGNETS ETC		0.1			W 607	16.5		0.1	ELECTRO-AIMANTS
77886	OTH ELEC MACHINERY NES		7.7							AUT MACH APP ELECTRIQUES
78	ROAD VEHICLES		137.3				41.5		56.0	VEHICULES ROUTIERS
781	PASS MOTOR VEH EXC BUSES		118.7			W 2394	10.6	W 19486	19.7	AUTO TRANSPORT PERSONNES
782	LORRIES,SPCL MTR VEH NES		8.6			W 3697	26.4	W 6410	29.6	VEHICULES SPECIAUX,MARCH
7821	LORRIES,TRUCKS		7.9			W 3270	22.3	W 6164	26.7	VEHICULES TRANSP MARCHAND
7822	SPECIAL MOTOR VEHCLS NES		0.8			W 427	4.1	W 246	2.9	VEHICULES USAGES SPECIAUX
784	MOTOR VEH PRTS,ACCES NES		5.1				2.3	W 779	2.8	PIECES 722,781,782,783
7849	OTHER MOTOR VEHCL PARTS		4.8			W 389	2.2	W 728	2.7	PIECES 722,781,782,783
785	CYCLES,ETC MOTRZD OR NOT		3.4			W 235	1.2	W 657	2.6	MOTOCYCLES SCOOTERS
7852	CYCLES, ETC NON-MOTOR		2.4			W 124	0.7	W 435	1.5	VELOCIPEDES SANS MOTEUR
79	OTHR TRANSPORT EQUIPMENT		4.6				0.6		2.0	AUTRE MATERIEL TRANSPORT
793	SHIPS AND BOATS ETC		3.5			W 271	0.6	W 152	0.5	NAVIRES BATEAUX,ETC
7938	TUGS,SPECIAL VESSELS ETC		2.7			W 224	0.3	W 103	0.3	REMORQUEURS,BATEAUX SPEC
79381	TUGS		2.7				0.1	W 10	0.1	BATEAUX REMORQUEURS
8	MISC MANUFACTURED GOODS		61.7				41.5		41.7	ART MANUFACTURES DIVERS
821	*FURNITURE,PARTS THEREOF		2.1			W 618	1.6	W 1478	2.4	MEUBLES ET PIECES
8219	FURNITURE AND PARTS NES		1.6			W 563	1.4	W 1432	2.2	AUTRES MEUBLES ET PIECES
82199	OTHR FURN,FURN PARTS NES		1.4			W 531	1.2	W 1376	2.0	MEUBLES NDA AUTRES MATIERES
84	CLOTHING AND ACCESSORIES		8.4				8.1		7.9	VETEMENTS
842	MENS OUTERWEAR NOT KNIT		2.0							VET DESSUS POUR HOMMES
8429	— OTHER OUTER GARMENTS		2.0							AUT VET DES HOM MAT TEX
843	WOMENS OUTERWEAR NONKNIT		2.1							VET DESSUS FEMMES MAT TEX
8439	— OTHER OUTER GARMENTS		2.1							AUT VET DES FEM MAT TEXT
845	OUTERWEAR KNIT NONELASTC		2.2			W 473	5.1	W 413	3.8	VET DESSOUS,ACCES BONNET
8459	— OTHER,CLTHG ACCESRYS		2.2			W 393	3.6	W 339	3.3	AUT VET DESSUS DE BONNE
846	UNDER GARMENTS KNITTED		1.6			W 294	2.1	W 270	3.0	SOUS VETS DE BONNETERIE
8462	— OF COTTON NON ELASTIC					W 261	1.7	W 226	2.4	SOUS-VET BONNET COTON
84629	—— OTHER					W 261	1.7	W 226	2.4	AUT SOUS-VET BONNET COTON
851	*FOOTWEAR		3.6			W 561	5.9		5.5	CHAUSSURES
85101	FOOTWEAR RUBBER,PLASTIC		1.2			W 230	1.9	W 404	1.9	CHAUS SEMELLES CAOUTCH
85102	FOOTWEAR LEATHER		0.7			W 331	4.0	W 1449	3.6	CHAUS SEMELLES EN CUIR
87	PRECISION INSTRUMNTS NES		4.6				4.3		4.7	INSTRUM,APPAR SCIENT NDA
874	MEASURNG,CONTROLNG INSTR		3.3			W 45	4.0		4.1	INSTRUMENTS DE MESURE
88	PHOTO EQU,OPTICL GDS ETC		28.8				1.5		1.6	APP,FOURN PHOTO,OP,MONTR
882	PHOTO,CINEMA SUPPLIES		27.7			W 52	0.5	W 127	0.7	PRODUITS PHOTO,CINEMA
8822	PHOTO FILM EXC DEV CINMA		27.4			W 31	0.4	W 33	0.4	PLAQUES,PELLICULES,FILMS
88221	PHOTO FILM FLAT UNEXPOSD		27.3							PLAQUES PHOTO,FILMS SENS
89	MISC MANUFCTRD GOODS NES		13.1				19.4		19.1	ART MANUFACTURES DIVERS
892	PRINTED MATTER		3.4			W 170	3.4	W 603	3.2	IMPRIMES
8928	PRINTED MATTER NES		1.3			W 49	1.9	W 463	1.7	IMPRIMES NDA
893	ARTICLES OF PLASTIC NES		6.4			W 3660	10.1	W 4237	12.7	OUVRAGES EN MAT DIVIS 58
8932	PLSTC SANITRY,TOILET ART		0.1			W 1378	5.2	W 1757	5.5	OBJETS HYGIEN MAT DU 58
8939	MISC PLASTIC ARTICLES		6.0			W 2282	4.9	W 2480	7.2	ART DIVERS EN MAT DIV 58
89399	OTHR PLASTC ARTICLES NES					W 2178	4.7	W 2308	6.9	AUT OUV MAT DIV 58
897	GOLD,SILVER WARE,JEWELRY		0.2				1.7		0.3	BIJOUTERIE,ORFEVRERIE
899	OTHER MANUFACTURED GOODS		1.4				2.3		1.5	AUT ART MANUF DIVERS NDA

5. General Exports F.O.B. by Commodities according to the S.I.T.C. (Rev. 2) in million U.S. Dollars
Exportations Générales F.O.B. par Produits d'après la C.T.C.I. (Rév. 2) en millions de Dollars E.U.

SITC CTCI	COMMODITY	1992 QUANTITY QUANTITE	1992 VALUE VALEUR	1993 QUANTITY QUANTITE	1993 VALUE VALEUR	1994 QUANTITY QUANTITE	1994 VALUE VALEUR	1995 QUANTITY QUANTITE	1995 VALUE VALEUR	PRODUIT
	ALL COMMODITIES		361.3				536.8		482.7	TOUS PRODUITS
0	FOOD AND LIVE ANIMALS		64.0				92.2		86.2	ALIMENTS,ANIMAUX VIVANTS
03	FISH AND PREPARATIONS		25.6				49.8		40.4	POISSONS ET PREPARATIONS
034	FISH,FRESH,CHILLED,FROZN		2.4			W 3507	3.6	W 3356	2.4	POISSON FRAIS, REFRIG,CONG
0341	FISH FRSH,CHLLD,EX FILLT		2.2			W 3191	2.8	W 3207	2.1	POISSON FRAIS,REFRIGERE
036	SHELL FISH FRESH,FROZEN		23.2			W 3051	45.6	W 2468	37.1	CRUSTACES,MOLLUSQUES
04	CEREALS AND PREPARATIONS		26.6				29.5		33.0	CEREALES ET PRODUITS
042	RICE		26.5			W 82435	29.5	W 79316	33.0	RIZ
0421	RICE IN HUSK OR HUSKED		23.1							RIZ SANS AUTRE PREPARATION
04212	RICE HUSKED		23.1							RIZ CARGO
0422	RICE SEMI-MILLED,MILLED		3.5			W 82435	29.5	W 79316	33.0	RIZ POLI,GLACE INCL BRISURES
04221	RICE MILLED UNBROKEN		3.2			W 80375	29.1	W 74056	30.7	RIZ POLI,GLACE EXCL BRISURES
04222	RICE BROKEN		0.3			W 2060	0.4	W 5260	2.3	BRISURES DE RIZ
05	VEGETABLES AND FRUIT		11.7				12.9		12.7	LEGUMES ET FRUITS
054	VEG ETC FRSH,SMPLY PRSVD		1.6			W 3366	1.8	W 2088	1.2	LEGUMES FRAIS,CONG,SECS
0545	OTHER FRESH VEGETABLES		1.2			W 2373	1.0	W 1505	0.8	AUTRES LEGUMES FRAIS,REF
05459	FRESH VEGETABLES NES		1.2			W 2373	1.0	W 1503	0.8	LEGUMES FRAIS,REFRI NDA
057	FRUIT,NUTS,FRESH,DRIED		10.2			W 33447	11.2	W 36969	11.5	FRUITS FRAIS OU SECS
0573	BANANA,PLANTAIN,FRSH,DRY		0.1			W 33053	11.1	W 36554	11.3	BANANES FRAICHES,SECHEES
0579	FRUIT FRESH OR DRIED NES		9.9			W 224	0.1	W 369	0.2	FRUITS FRAIS,SECS NDA
05793	STONE FRUIT FRESH NES		9.7							FRUITS A NOYAU NDA FRAIS
2	CRUDE MATERLS,EXCL FUELS		242.4				367.5		308.6	MAT BRUTES NON COMESTIBLES
28	METALLIFEROUS ORES,SCRAP		241.5				367.3		307.0	MINERAIS METAL,DECHETS
287	BASE METAL ORES,CONC NES		241.5			W 1416235	366.4	W 1502224	306.9	MINERAIS METAUX COMMUNS
2873	ALUMINIUM ORES,ALUMINA		241.5			W 1416160	366.4	W 1502133	306.8	MINERAIS D'ALUMINIUM
28731	ALUMINIUM ORE,CONCNTRATE					W 1416160	366.4	W 1502133	306.8	MINERAIS D'ALUMINIUM
28732	ALUMINA(ALUMINIUM OXIDE)		241.5							ALUMINE (OXYDE ALUMINIUM)
3	MINERAL FUELS ETC		4.7				9.4		10.7	COMBUSTIBLES MINERAUX LUB
32	COAL,COKE AND BRIQUETTES		4.7							HOUILLES,COKES,BRIQUETTES
323	BRIQUETS,COKE,SEMI-COKE		4.7							BRIQUETTES
33	PETROLEUM AND PRODUCTS						9.4		10.7	PETROLE ET DERIVES
333	CRUDE PETROLEUM					W 138841	9.4	W 93546	10.7	HUILES BRUTES DE PETROLE
6	BASIC MANUFACTURES		45.5				49.7		53.3	ART MANUFACTURES
63	WOOD,CORK MANUFACTRS NES		0.9				2.2		2.0	OUVRAGES LIEGE ET BOIS
634	VENEERS,PLYWOOD,ETC		0.8			W 5314	2.1	W 23931	1.9	PLACAGES,CONTRE-PLAQUES
6342	PLYWOOD OF WOOD SHEETS		0.8			W 3841	1.8	W 2254	1.6	BOIS CONTRE-PLAQUES
68	NON-FERROUS METALS		43.7				45.7		50.1	METAUX NON FERREUX
684	ALUMINIUM		43.2			W 24656	45.7	W 29676	50.1	ALUMINIUM
6841	ALUMINIUM,ALLOYS,UNWRGHT		43.2					W 36	0.1	ALUMINIUM,ALLIAGES BRUTS
6842	ALUMINIUM,ALLOYS WORKED					W 24656	45.7	W 29641	50.1	ALUMINIUM,ALLIAGES OUVRE
68421	ALUMINIUM BARS,WIRE,ETC					W 24656	45.7	W 29641	50.1	BARRES,PROFILES FILS ALU
7	MACHINES,TRANSPORT EQUIP		3.6				5.2		5.2	MACHINES MATERIEL TRANSPORT
9	GOODS NOT CLASSD BY KIND		0.1				11.4		17.5	ART TRANSACT NON CLASSES
941	*ZOO ANIMALS,PETS ETC		0.1			W 49	3.1	W 242	2.2	ANIMAUX DE ZOO ETC
971	*GOLD,NON MONETARY NES		0.1			K 425	8.4	K 2563	15.4	OR NON MONETAIRE
97101	NONMON GLD UNWRT,SEMIMFD					K 425	8.4	K 2563	15.4	OR,ALLIAGES D'OR BRUTS

1. HISTORICAL SERIES, 1962–1997 GENERAL TRADE, IMPORTS C.I.F., EXPORTS F.O.B.
SERIES HISTORIQUES, 1962–1997 COMMERCE GENERAL, IMPORTATIONS C.A.F., EXPORTATIONS F.O.B

YEAR ANNEE	VALUE IN MILLION SWEDISH KRONOR / VALEUR EN MILLION SWEDISH KRONOR: MERCHANDISE – MARCHANDISE		GOLD – OR		CONVERSION FACTORS U.S. CENTS PER SWEDISH KRONA / FACTEURS DE CONVERSION CENTS E.U. PAR SWEDISH KRONA		INDEX NUMBERS – INDICES: QUANTUM		UNIT VALUE / VALEUR UNITAIRE	
	IMPORTS	EXPORTS	IMPORTS	EXPORTS	IMPORTS	EXPORTS	IMPORTS	EXPORTS	IMPORTS	EXPORTS
1962	16154.00	15129.00	71.50	12.00	19.3300	19.3300				
1963	17552.00	16568.00	33.30	12.40	19.3300	19.3300				
1964	19946.00	19014.00	36.70	14.10	19.3300	19.3300				
1965	22644.00	20541.00	53.60	13.50	19.3300	19.3300				
1966	23704.00	22071.00	42.20	12.90	19.3300	19.3300				
1967	24319.00	23422.00	37.40	15.20	19.3300	19.3300				
1968	26516.00	25553.00	24.00	11.90	19.3300	19.3300				
1969	30546.00	29445.00	25.30	13.70	19.3300	19.3300				
1970	36251.00	35150.00	15.80	12.80	19.3300	19.3300				
1971	36192.00	38224.00	10.70	49.00	19.5700	19.5600				
1972	38618.00	41749.00	13.50	9.00	21.0001	21.0045				
1973	46336.00	53153.00	25.00	17.00	22.9481	22.9562				
1974	72800.00	70514.00	42.00	29.00	22.6028	22.6017				
1975	74000.00	72012.00			24.1370	24.1378				
1976	84000.00	80195.00			23.0161	22.9878				
1977	90220.00	85680.00			22.3444	22.2837				
1978	92750.00	98210.00			22.2014	22.1916				
1979	122960.00	118210.00			23.3698	23.3525				
1980	141700.00	131010.00			23.6598	23.6390	70	69	64	57
1981	146040.00	144880.00			19.7517	19.7845	65	70	71	62
1982	173930.00	168130.00			15.8664	15.9504	68	72	80	70
1983	200368.00	210500.00			13.0361	13.0478	70	81	91	78
1984	218570.00	242810.50			12.0859	12.0993	73	87	94	83
1985	244654.20	260480.70			11.6830	11.7052	80	90	96	86
1986	232479.00	265104.00			14.0645	14.0577	83	93	88	86
1987	257386.00	281332.90			15.8164	15.8209	89	96	91	88
1988	280649.90	305040.10			16.3398	16.3552	94	99	94	92
1989	316590.00	332570.10			15.5189	15.5175	100	101	99	98
1990	320379.90	340039.90			16.9380	16.9221	100	100	100	100
1991	301260.00	332800.00			16.5973	16.5951	93	98	101	101
1992	290510.00	326040.00			17.2283	17.2230	95	99	99	98
1993	332489.90	388300.00			12.8385	12.8417	97	107	112	108
1994	397410.00	471600.10			13.0173	13.0093	108	114	117	113
1995	459800.00	567699.90			14.0610	14.0595	109	112	124	125
1996	448199.90	568900.10			14.9168	14.9164	102	106	120	120
1997	499600.10	631099.90			13.1087	13.1100		110	122	121

2. IMPORTS BY BROAD ECONOMIC CATEGORY AND EXPORTS BY INDUSTRIAL ORIGIN. (PERCENTAGE OF TOTAL VALUE)
IMPORTATIONS PAR CATEGORIES ECONOMIQUES ET EXPORTATIONS PAR BRANCHE D'ACTIVITE.(EN POURCENTAGE DE LA VALEUR TOTALE)

IMPORTS – IMPORTATIONS

	1991	1992	1993	1994	1995	1996	1997
TOTAL IMPORTS–IMPORTATIONS TOTALES	100.	100.	100.	100.	100.	100.	100.
1 FOOD BEV–ALIMENTATION BOISSONS	6.2	6.6	6.8	7.0	6.0	6.5	6.5
11 PRIMARY–PRODUITS DE BASE	2.9	2.9	2.8	2.9	2.9	3.0	3.1
111 FOR INDUSTRY–POUR L'INDUSTRIE	0.5	0.4	0.5	0.7	0.7	0.6	0.7
112 FOR HOUSEHOLDS–POUR LES MENAGES	2.4	2.5	2.3	2.2	2.2	2.4	2.3
12 PROCESSED–PRODUITS ELABORES	3.3	3.7	4.0	4.0	3.1	3.5	3.4
121 FOR INDUSTRY–POUR L'INDUSTRIE	0.4	0.4	0.4	0.5	0.4	0.4	0.4
122 FOR HOUSEHOLDS–POUR LES MENAGES	2.9	3.3	3.5	3.5	2.7	3.1	3.0
2 IND SUPPLIES–APPROV INDUSTRIELS	26.5	26.5	26.9	27.8	28.1	25.2	25.1
21 PRIMARY–PRODUITS DE BASE	2.6	2.9	2.7	2.8	2.9	2.3	2.4
22 PROCESSED–PRODUITS ELABORES	23.9	23.6	24.3	25.0	25.2	22.9	22.6
3 FUELS–COMBUSTIBLES	8.6	8.5	8.9	7.3	5.7	7.4	7.2
31 PRIMARY–PRODUITS DE BASE	5.5	5.3	5.8	4.6	4.0	5.4	5.6
32 PROCESSED–PRODUITS ELABORES	3.1	3.2	3.1	2.7	1.7	2.0	1.6
321 MOTOR SPIRIT–ESSENCE	1.2	1.1	1.0	0.6	0.5	0.5	0.5
322 OTHER–AUTRES	1.8	2.0	2.1	2.1	1.1	1.5	1.0
4 MACHINERY–EQUIPEMENT	24.3	24.3	25.6	26.6	29.8	29.4	29.8
41 CAPITAL EQUIPMENT–MACHINES	18.9	18.8	19.6	20.4	22.7	22.5	23.0
42 PARTS–PIECES ACCESSOIRES	5.4	5.6	6.0	6.2	7.0	6.9	6.8
5 TRANSPORT–TRANSPORT	13.5	12.7	11.5	12.2	13.4	13.9	14.2
51 PASSENGER CARS–AUTOMOBILES	3.5	3.6	2.8	3.3	3.0	3.6	4.5
52 OTHER–AUTRES	3.7	2.7	2.1	2.1	2.0	2.2	1.8
521 INDUSTRIAL–INDUSTRIELS	3.5	2.5	1.9	1.9	1.8	2.0	1.6
522 NON INDUSTRIAL–NON INDUSTRIEL	0.2	0.2	0.2	0.2	0.1	0.2	0.2
53 PARTS–PIECES ACCESSOIRES	6.3	6.4	6.6	6.8	8.4	8.1	8.0
6 CONSUM GOODS–BIENS CONSOMMATION	19.8	20.3	19.3	18.1	15.5	15.6	15.6
61 DURABLE–DURABLES	5.2	4.7	4.5	4.4	3.7	3.7	3.8
62 SEMI DURABLE–SEMI DURABLES	10.5	11.1	10.2	9.5	8.0	8.0	8.1
63 NON DURABLE–NON DURABLES	4.1	4.5	4.6	4.2	3.8	4.0	3.8
7 GOODS NES–BIENS NDA	0.9	1.0	0.7	1.0	1.5	2.0	1.7

EXPORTS – EXPORTATIONS

	1991	1992	1993	1994	1995	1996	1997
TOTAL EXPORTS–EXPORTATIONS TOTALES	100.	100.	100.	100.	100.	100.	100.
1 AGRICULTURE	0.8	0.7	0.5	0.6	0.7	0.8	0.9
2 MINING QUARRY–INDUS EXTRACTIVES	1.3	1.4	1.4	1.1	1.1	1.0	1.2
3 MANUFACTURING–IND MANUFACTUR	97.8	97.9	98.2	98.3	98.2	98.2	97.9
31 FOOD BEV TOBACCO–ALIM BOISS TAB	1.7	1.6	1.8	2.0	1.8	2.0	2.1
32 TEXTILES–INDUSTRIES TEXTILES	2.0	2.0	1.8	1.7	1.6	1.7	1.8
33 WOOD & PRODUCTS–BOIS & PRODUITS	4.0	4.3	4.7	5.1	4.6	4.2	4.3
34 PAPER & PRODUCTS–PAPIER & PRODT	14.7	14.2	12.9	12.2	12.9	11.4	10.7
35 CHEMICALS–INDUSTRIES CHIMIQUES	13.5	14.0	15.3	13.8	10.8	11.1	11.4
36 NON METAL MIN–MIN NON METAL	1.0	1.0	1.0	1.0	0.9	0.9	1.0
37 BASIC METAL–IND METAL BASE	7.7	7.5	7.5	8.0	7.3	6.8	6.6
38 METAL MANUF–MANUF METAL	52.0	52.1	52.1	53.5	50.1	52.4	52.8
39 OTH MANUF IND–AUTRES MANUF	1.4	1.0	0.9	1.0	8.1	7.7	7.2

3. TRADE BY PRINCIPAL COUNTRIES OF ORIGIN AND DESTINATION (VALUE IN MILLION U.S. DOLLARS)
ECHANGES SELON LES PRINCIPAUX PAYS D'ORIGINE ET DE DESTINATION (VALEUR EN MILLIONS DE DOLLARS EU)

COUNTRIES–PAYS	GENERAL IMPORTS C.I.F. IMPORTATIONS GENERALES C.A.F				
	1993	1994	1995	1996	1997
World	42652.2	51773.5	61646.7	64431.5	62864.6
Africa	203.0	379.2	324.3	436.0	544.0
Americas	4830.8	5629.7	4660.9	4876.7	4971.8
– Northern America	4129.1	4744.5	3854.6	4113.3	4186.4
– LAIA	499.3	720.9	650.4	578.0	609.0
– CACM	43.4	53.2	60.0	43.8	64.6
– Caribbean	97.7	56.6	47.0	44.2	35.7
– Rest of America	61.5	54.5	48.9	97.4	76.0
Asia excl fmr USSR	5685.0	6571.0	5427.4	5292.4	5554.9
– Middle East	693.2	601.5	582.3	526.6	459.8
Asia former USSR	4.2	13.6	2.8	2.3	3.6
Europe excl fmr USSR	30961.7	37432.7	49778.7	52237.9	50192.6
– European Union	26650.9	32202.0	42646.4	44590.0	42794.9
– Eastern Europe	577.9	829.4	1025.8	1062.2	1163.0
– Rest of Europe	3733.0	4401.3	6106.5	6585.6	6234.7
Europe former USSR	683.7	1140.1	1259.6	1344.5	1422.5
Oceania	176.1	157.8	192.9	241.6	175.3
Other	107.6	449.4			
Germany/Allemagne	7626.0	9433.9	12725.5	12566.3	12078.4
United Kingdom	4015.5	4954.9	6087.4	6833.0	6378.7
Denmark/Danemark	3037.8	3413.1	4597.4	5030.8	4720.9
Norway,Svalbard and JM	2752.6	3124.3	4620.6	5210.0	5034.6
USA/Etats–Unis d'Amer	3885.6	4413.4	3520.2	3871.2	3906.5
Netherlands/Pays–Bas	1981.4	2089.6	4671.3	5015.7	5003.2
Finland/Finlande	2646.5	3249.8	3821.6	3767.7	3440.4
France, Monaco	2280.1	2883.7	3414.8	3765.5	3735.3
Belgium–Luxembourg	1476.9	1789.0	2409.7	2430.6	2440.9
Japan/Japon	2132.8	2448.9	1872.8	1573.3	1701.2
Italy/Italie	1523.1	1988.7	1993.0	2152.6	1980.4
Switzerland,Liechtenst.	865.2	985.8	1364.3	1257.1	1077.7
Spain/Espagne	614.5	715.5	727.5	870.0	853.3
Austria/Autriche	554.8	637.2	742.5	746.3	853.2
China, Hong Kong SAR	328.7	341.6	863.4	915.6	978.0
China/Chine	827.5	1090.6	415.6	446.4	519.2
Ireland/Irlande	346.1	428.2	858.2	786.7	753.8
Poland/Pologne	319.3	462.8	591.2	594.3	624.1
Other Asia n.e.s.	501.2	550.6	456.7	482.9	504.3
Russian Federation	431.2	652.3	479.7	454.8	414.1
Portugal	458.7	509.7	494.5	477.6	444.2
Latvia/Lettonie	102.7	228.8	406.1	386.4	413.9
Korea, Republic of	301.3	384.7	273.1	273.1	284.7
Estonia/Estonie	94.4	166.8	293.8	398.1	491.1
Canada	237.0	321.0	267.9	241.6	279.3
Iran (Islamic Rep of)	188.5	192.7	265.6	242.9	230.3
Brazil/Brésil	179.6	298.0	210.4	174.1	222.1
Saudi Arabia	393.0	296.3	185.0	125.8	36.1
India/Inde	132.3	189.3	195.1	187.9	195.7
Thailand/Thaïlande	153.4	188.6	136.0	158.7	178.7
Czech Republic	95.7	129.6	163.3	185.6	233.3
Singapore/Singapour	152.5	185.3	162.7	152.5	145.3
Malaysia/Malaisie	157.3	223.0	120.1	105.5	149.7
Hungary/Hongrie	102.6	140.8	148.8	168.4	183.4
Australia/Australie	127.3	113.4	139.9	195.8	142.3
Egypt/Egypte	36.4	49.0	109.1	176.0	277.2
Venezuela	101.1	102.2	138.4	138.1	98.6
Turkey/Turquie	77.6	95.5	107.0	130.6	163.0
Greece/Grèce	89.5	108.7	102.9	147.2	112.2
Chile/Chili	80.7	89.3	115.3	96.7	97.0

COUNTRIES–PAYS	GENERAL EXPORTS F.O.B. EXPORTATIONS GENERALES F.O.B.				
	1993	1994	1995	1996	1997
Monde	49858.4	61299.7	77436.4	83408.2	81180.3
Afrique	1013.7	828.8	1243.1	1354.8	1286.8
Amériques	5790.3	6354.4	8752.2	9612.7	9905.2
– Amérique du Nord	4811.3	5249.8	7208.9	7853.7	7711.4
– ALAI	858.4	1039.3	1431.8	1652.2	2081.6
– MCAC	25.8	23.8	49.4	32.0	30.9
– Caraïbes	85.9	33.2	49.1	53.6	51.3
– Autre Amérique	8.9	8.2	13.0	21.1	30.1
Asie anc. URSS exclus	6081.8	6880.2	9641.5	11613.1	11441.7
– Moyen–Orient	1268.3	1046.7	1466.0	1715.0	2024.8
Asie ancienne URSS	25.5	23.7	24.3	46.6	49.2
Europe anc. URSS exclus	35466.0	41110.9	55184.0	58063.6	55402.4
– Union Européenne	29393.9	34018.7	45399.1	47047.0	44427.9
– Europe de l'Est	844.3	1111.2	1717.1	1914.2	2211.1
– Autre de l'Europe	5227.8	5981.0	8067.8	9102.5	8763.3
Europe ancienne URSS	571.8	802.3	1267.1	1427.3	1880.3
Océanie	757.3	849.6	1323.8	1290.0	1214.7
Autre	152.0	4449.8	0.3	0.1	0.0
Germany/Allemagne	7140.7	7648.1	10249.5	9910.1	9161.5
United Kingdom	5101.4	5744.9	7559.1	8085.1	7576.7
USA/Etats–Unis d'Amer	4192.9	4625.6	6302.5	7012.1	6870.0
Norway,Svalbard and JM	4050.4	4672.3	6102.6	7147.1	6894.4
Denmark/Danemark	3296.7	4016.6	5077.2	5329.4	5063.8
Netherlands/Pays–Bas	2524.0	3037.9	4365.8	4696.3	4605.4
Finland/Finlande	2274.4	2733.4	3966.9	4379.2	4379.5
France, Monaco	2671.7	2918.6	4118.6	3959.4	3801.4
Belgium–Luxembourg	2064.4	2878.1	3352.1	3745.2	3249.0
Italy/Italie	1848.0	2220.6	2857.0	2778.4	2623.3
Japan/Japon	1230.4	1542.9	2333.7	2710.2	2423.6
Spain/Espagne	937.7	1096.6	1631.9	1883.3	1788.6
Switzerland,Liechtenst.	935.7	1028.6	1586.0	1504.2	1361.1
China/Chine	624.7	971.1	1158.9	1391.6	1231.2
Australia/Australie	650.2	729.2	1135.3	1128.8	1068.8
Areas n.e.s.	1.0	4335.3	0.3	0.1	0.0
Poland/Pologne	422.3	562.1	928.1	1067.8	1326.4
Austria/Autriche	675.0	752.5	967.0	924.7	838.0
Canada	566.6	621.1	897.7	840.0	835.8
China, Hong Kong SAR	283.6	357.5	579.6	803.0	1022.7
Russian Federation	332.7	407.1	667.3	724.2	913.4
Singapore/Singapour	401.8	523.7	532.1	629.1	740.0
Korea, Republic of	372.2	453.0	640.2	652.6	671.9
Other Asia n.e.s.	434.7	449.1	623.5	584.7	613.0
Turkey/Turquie	347.7	189.2	435.0	661.6	825.2
Thailand/Thaïlande	328.8	367.6	557.3	643.5	532.5
Brazil/Brésil	212.3	311.7	538.3	641.2	707.1
Malaysia/Malaisie	253.1	377.9	527.9	564.1	546.4
Ireland/Irlande	314.4	392.7	472.0	551.3	517.5
Saudi Arabia	380.8	351.1	417.7	376.3	373.5
Greece/Grèce	275.6	338.1	372.4	368.4	425.0
Portugal	269.9	240.6	409.9	436.3	398.2
Indonesia/Indonésie	273.5	159.1	281.9	524.0	510.8
So. African Customs Un	72.7	198.4	394.3	467.3	437.0
India/Inde	145.5	247.5	288.0	512.3	298.7
Czech Republic	142.7	180.6	296.0	364.8	357.4
Hungary/Hongrie	179.7	279.3	319.0	289.1	265.4
Israel/Israël	257.2	170.6	351.9	307.6	242.3
Estonia/Estonie	104.4	190.8	237.1	262.9	407.3
Argentina/Argentine	130.2	190.5	222.5	283.2	368.1

(VALUE AS PERCENTAGE OF WORLD TOTAL)(VALEURS EN POURCENTAGE DU TOTAL MONDIAL)

	1988	1989	1990	1991	1992	1993	1994	1995	1996	1997
Africa	0.4	0.4	0.5	0.7	0.8	0.5	0.7	0.5	0.7	0.9
Americas	10.4	11.2	11.2	10.8	10.7	11.3	10.9	7.6	7.6	7.9
– Northern America	8.4	9.1	9.4	9.2	9.3	9.7	9.2	6.3	6.4	6.7
– LAIA	1.7	1.6	1.3	1.3	1.2	1.2	1.4	1.1	0.9	1.0
– CACM	0.2	0.2	0.1	0.1	0.1	0.1	0.1	0.1	0.1	0.1
– Caribbean	0.1	0.1	0.2	0.1	0.0	0.2	0.1	0.1	0.1	0.1
– Rest of America	0.1	0.3	0.1	0.1	0.1	0.1	0.1	0.1	0.2	0.1
Asia excl fmr USSR	12.2	12.0	11.4	12.4	12.5	13.3	12.7	8.8	8.2	8.8
– Middle East	0.9	1.1	1.1	1.3	1.3	1.6	1.2	0.9	0.8	0.7
Asia former USSR					0.0	0.0	0.0	0.0	0.0	0.0
Europe excl fmr USSR	74.9	74.1	75.0	74.4	73.8	72.6	72.3	80.7	81.1	79.8
– European Union	64.3	63.0	63.1	63.1	62.9	62.5	62.2	69.2	69.2	68.1
– Eastern Europe	2.1	1.9	1.7	1.4	1.5	1.4	1.6	1.7	1.6	1.9
– Rest of Europe	8.4	9.3	10.2	9.9	9.3	8.8	8.5	9.9	10.2	9.9
Europe former USSR	1.6	1.6	1.4	1.1	1.6	1.6	2.2	2.0	2.1	2.3
Oceania	0.4	0.5	0.3	0.4	0.4	0.4	0.3	0.3	0.4	0.3
Other	0.1	0.1	0.1	0.2	0.2	0.3	0.9			
Germany/Allemagne				18.8	18.5	17.9	18.2	20.6	19.5	19.2
United Kingdom	8.6	8.1	8.1	8.3	8.6	9.4	9.6	9.9	10.6	10.1
Denmark/Danemark	6.6	6.8	7.5	7.6	7.6	7.1	6.6	7.5	7.8	7.5
Norway,Svalbard and JM	6.1	7.0	7.9	7.7	6.9	6.5	6.0	7.5	8.1	8.0
USA/Etats–Unis d'Amer	7.5	8.2	8.7	8.5	8.8	9.1	8.5	5.7	6.0	6.2
Netherlands/Pays–Bas	4.1	4.2	4.1	4.3	4.3	4.6	4.0	7.6	7.8	8.0
Finland/Finlande	7.0	6.7	6.8	7.0	6.2	6.2	6.3	6.2	5.8	5.5
France, Monaco	5.0	5.3	5.0	4.9	5.1	5.3	5.6	5.5	5.8	5.9
Belgium–Luxembourg	3.2	3.1	3.0	3.2	3.5	3.5	3.5	3.9	3.8	3.9
Japan/Japon	6.4	6.1	5.1	5.1	5.1	5.0	4.7	3.0	2.4	2.7

	1988	1989	1990	1991	1992	1993	1994	1995	1996	1997
Afrique	1.9	1.8	1.6	1.5	1.3	2.0	1.4	1.6	1.6	1.6
Amériques	13.4	12.6	12.0	11.1	11.4	11.6	10.4	11.3	11.5	12.2
– Amérique du Nord	11.6	11.0	10.2	9.4	9.5	9.7	8.6	9.3	9.4	9.5
– ALAI	1.5	1.4	1.6	1.6	1.7	1.7	1.7	1.8	2.0	2.6
– MCAC	0.1	0.1	0.1	0.0	0.1	0.1	0.0	0.1	0.0	0.0
– Caraïbes	0.2	0.1	0.1	0.1	0.2	0.2	0.1	0.1	0.1	0.1
– Autre Amérique	0.0	0.0	0.0	0.0	0.0	0.0	0.0	0.0	0.0	0.0
Asie anc. URSS exclus	8.6	8.7	9.1	10.6	9.8	12.2	11.2	12.5	13.9	14.1
– Moyen–Orient	2.0	1.9	2.2	3.3	2.5	2.5	1.7	1.9	2.1	2.5
Asie ancienne URSS					0.0	0.1	0.0	0.0	0.1	0.1
Europe anc. URSS exclus	74.0	74.4	74.9	74.6	74.8	71.1	67.1	71.3	69.6	68.2
– Union Européenne	60.0	61.6	62.1	62.0	62.3	59.0	55.5	58.6	56.4	54.7
– Europe de l'Est	1.5	1.5	1.4	1.4	1.6	1.7	1.8	2.2	2.3	2.7
– Autre de l'Europe	12.5	11.3	11.4	11.2	11.0	10.5	9.8	10.4	10.9	10.8
Europe ancienne URSS	0.6	0.7	0.7	0.7	0.9	1.1	1.3	1.6	1.7	2.3
Océanie	1.3	1.5	1.5	1.2	1.4	1.5	1.4	1.7	1.5	1.5
Autre	0.2	0.3	0.2	0.3	0.3	0.3	7.3	0.0	0.0	0.0
Germany/Allemagne				15.1	14.9	14.3	12.5	13.2	11.9	11.3
United Kingdom	11.2	11.2	10.1	9.3	9.6	10.2	9.4	9.8	9.7	9.3
USA/Etats–Unis d'Amer	9.9	9.3	8.6	8.1	8.3	8.4	7.5	8.1	8.4	8.5
Norway,Svalbard and JM	9.3	8.2	8.3	8.4	8.4	8.1	7.6	7.9	8.6	8.5
Denmark/Danemark	6.9	6.6	6.8	7.0	7.1	6.6	6.6	6.6	6.4	6.2
Netherlands/Pays–Bas	4.8	5.0	5.3	5.4	5.6	5.1	5.0	5.6	5.6	5.7
Finland/Finlande	6.5	7.0	6.8	5.7	5.2	4.6	4.5	5.1	5.3	5.4
France, Monaco	5.3	5.3	5.4	5.5	5.8	5.4	4.8	5.3	4.7	4.7
Belgium–Luxembourg	4.1	3.8	3.8	3.8	4.2	4.1	4.7	4.3	4.5	4.0
Italy/Italie	4.0	4.4	4.7	4.5	4.4	3.7	3.6	3.7	3.3	3.2

4. General Imports C.I.F. by Commodities according to the S.I.T.C. (Rev. 2) in million U.S. Dollars
Importations Générales C.A.F. par Produits d'après la C.T.C.I. (Rév. 2) en millions de Dollars E.U.

SITC CTCI	COMMODITY	1994			1995			1996			1997			PRODUIT
		QUANTITY QUANTITE		VALUE VALEUR	QUANTITY QUANTITE		VALUE VALEUR	QUANTITY QUANTITE		VALUE VALEUR	QUANTITY QUANTITE		VALUE VALEUR	
	ALL COMMODITIES			51773.6			61646.8			64431.5			62864.7	TOUS PRODUITS
0	FOOD AND LIVE ANIMALS			3247.9			3496.4			3850.1			3798.7	ALIMENTS,ANIMAUX VIVANTS
01	MEAT AND PREPARATIONS			189.7			293.7			339.6			325.5	VIANDES ET PREPARATIONS
011	MEAT FRESH,CHILLD,FROZEN			134.4	W	40732	219.7	W	52988	260.9	W	51088	237.0	VIANDES FRAICHES,REF,CONGE
03	FISH AND PREPARATIONS			438.7			537.3			594.1			589.7	POISSONS ET PREPARATIONS
034	FISH,FRESH,CHILLED,FROZN			171.9	W	74398	272.4	W	83506	271.9	W	92789	293.5	POISSON FRAIS, REFRIG,CONG
04	CEREALS AND PREPARATIONS			256.1			256.9			305.2			292.3	CEREALES ET PRODUITS
048	CEREAL ETC PREPARATIONS			181.2	W	113940	208.7	W	139367	232.7	W	160635	233.7	PREPTNS A BASE CEREALES
05	VEGETABLES AND FRUIT			1054.2			1062.5			1192.1			1108.3	LEGUMES ET FRUITS
054	VEG ETC FRSH,SMPLY PRSVD			306.7	W	392870	371.2	W	397055	390.7	W	365906	340.2	LEGUMES FRAIS,CONG,SECS
0545	OTHER FRESH VEGETABLES			147.8	W	159034	169.9	W	165022	196.3	W	163175	176.5	AUTRES LEGUMES FRAIS,REF
057	FRUIT,NUTS,FRESH,DRIED	W	533203	452.6	W	464176	434.3	W	512877	529.1	W	535709	508.1	FRUITS FRAIS OU SECS
058	FRUIT PRESERVED,PREPARED	W	146153	213.6	W	99615	179.1			188.3	W	128658	181.5	CONSERVES DE FRUITS
07	COFFEE,TEA,COCOA,SPICES			546.1			573.6			533.2			633.0	CAFE,THE,CACAO,EPICES
071	COFFEE AND SUBSTITUTES			357.4	W	90781	371.2	W	101541	328.2			436.3	CAFE ET SUCCEDANES
0711	COFFEE GREEN,ROASTED,SUB			321.9	W	88738	336.4	W	98605	290.1			392.8	CAFE TORREFIE OU DECAFEINE
07111	COFFEE GREEN,HUSKS,SKINS			281.4	W	84265	307.7	W	91446	260.2	W	87745	361.1	CAFE NON TORREFIE
081	*FEEDING STUFF FOR ANIML	W	846568	258.2	W	830062	249.9			285.3			284.4	NOURRITURE POUR ANIMAUX
09	MISC EDIBLE PRODUCTS			242.5			255.5			287.3			254.8	PREP ALIMENTAIRES DIVERSES
098	EDIBLE PRODCTS,PREPS NES			232.0			243.4	W	73154	274.0	W	82683	242.7	PREP ALIMENTAIRES NDA
09809	MISC FOOD PREPRTIONS NES			156.3	W	29266	162.6	W	35340	187.0	W	45391	160.9	PREP ALIMENTAIRES NDA
1	BEVERAGES AND TOBACCO			622.0			388.9			567.2			503.4	BOISSONS ET TABACS
11	BEVERAGES			491.8			305.1			462.7			421.4	BOISSONS
112	ALCOHOLIC BEVERAGES	W	248022	473.4			287.9	W	220151	436.9	W	216783	375.5	BOISSONS ALCOOLIQUES
1121	WINE OF FRESH GRAPES ETC	W	160358	273.8			178.3	W	139289	284.1	W	130721	241.1	VINS DE RAISINS FRAIS
11212	WINE OF FRESH GRAPES	W	156001	263.5	W	91472	174.4	W	135190	273.6	W	126353	230.4	VINS DE MOUTS DE RAISINS
2	CRUDE MATERLS,EXCL FUELS			1857.8			2333.6			1967.2			1976.4	MAT BRUTES NON COMESTIBLES
24	CORK AND WOOD			460.0			624.6			422.7			516.2	LIEGE ET BOIS
247	OTH WOOD ROUGH,SQUARED	W	5684540	319.0	W	6864052	457.5	W	4540042	271.9	W	6784155	358.8	BOIS BRUTS EQUARRIS
2471	SAW-,VENEER-LOGS CONIFER	W	3086191	176.1	W	3279541	222.9	W	2178144	136.0	W	3417753	195.6	CONIFERES POUR SCIAGE,PLACAG
24711	— IN THE ROUGH	W	3086191	176.1	W	3279541	222.9	W	2178144	136.0	W	3417753	195.6	ECORCES OU DEGROSSIS
2472	SAW-,VENEER-LOGS NON-CON	W	2598349	142.9	W	3584511	234.6	W	2361897	135.9	W	3366402	163.2	NON CONIFERES SCIAGE,PLAC
24721	— IN THE ROUGH	W	2598349	142.9	W	3584511	234.6	W	2361897	135.9	W	3366402	163.2	BRUTS ECORCES DEGROSSIS
251	*PULP AND WASTE PAPER			157.9			305.5	W	772938	167.1	W	834240	167.8	PATES A PAPIER,DECHETS
27	CRUDE FERTLZR,MINRLS NES			234.5			275.8			263.2			259.7	ENGRAIS MINERAUX BRUTS
278	OTHER CRUDE MINERALS	W	2166792	174.1	W	2328971	200.9			191.6			208.8	AUTRES MINERAUX BRUTS
28	METALLIFEROUS ORES,SCRAP			503.1			624.8			579.2			587.6	MINERAIS METAL,DECHETS
282	IRON AND STEEL SCRAP	W	653370	186.9	W	338419	209.7	W	333221	172.0	W	536025	197.8	FERRAILLES
28202	— OF ALLOY STEEL	W	183693	128.4	W	195516	189.9	W	149032	148.0	W	184087	152.9	FERRAILLES D'ACIERS ALLIES
288	NONFERR METAL SCRAP NES	W	176403	143.2	W	175296	188.7	W	153538	191.3	W	155244	183.1	DECHETS NON FERREUX
29	CRUDE ANIMAL,VEG MAT NES			299.6			245.2			283.0			248.8	MATIERES BRUTES ANIM,VEGET
292	CRUDE VEG MATERIALS NES			265.3			222.1			260.1	W	53069	227.7	MAT BRUTES VEGETALES NDA
3	MINERAL FUELS ETC			3850.3			3620.7			4810.7			4540.3	COMBUSTIBLES MINERAUX LUB
32	COAL,COKE AND BRIQUETTES			217.3			266.5			244.5			244.9	HOUILLES,COKES,BRIQUETTES
322	COAL,LIGNITE AND PEAT	W	3116107	152.0	W	3607210	204.8	W	3391469	194.8	W	3431780	196.6	HOUILLES,LIGNITES,TOURBE
3222	OTH COAL,NOT AGGLOMERATD	W	3011646	145.8	W	3447685	194.2	W	3139894	179.8	W	3231236	185.3	AUTRES HOUILLES
33	PETROLEUM AND PRODUCTS			3417.2			3193.7			4313.2			4028.4	PETROLE ET DERIVES
333	CRUDE PETROLEUM	MW	17954	2113.3	MW	16411	2110.7	MW	19899	3034.2	MW	22700	3047.6	HUILES BRUTES DE PETROLE
334	PETROLEUM PRODUCTS,REFIN	W	7036367	1246.7	W	4987280	972.3			1231.1	W	4287509	934.9	PRODUITS RAFFINES
3341	GASOLINE,OTH LIGHT OILS	W	1567825	297.5	W	1665660	334.7			347.9	W	1546440	338.2	ESSENCES POUR MOTEURS
33411	MOTOR,AVIATION SPIRIT	W	1464905	275.2	W	1511931	306.0	W	1461139	317.7	W	1527315	333.3	ESSENCES MOTEURS D'AVIONS
3342	KEROSENE,OTH MEDIUM OILS	W	2030719	390.9	W	1028206	212.0	W	987948	229.6	W	1213850	256.9	PETR LAMPANTS,AUT HUIL
33421	KEROSENE INCL JET FUEL	W	2030719	390.9	W	1024005	210.5	W	983848	227.6	W	1210665	255.3	PETROLES LAMPANTS
3343	GAS OILS	W	976383	164.3				W	91	0.3	W	10165	1.6	GAS OILS
3344	FUEL OILS,NES	W	204603	19.8	W	1110374	121.4	W	1830344	251.0	W	1351862	218.6	FUEL OILS
3345	LUBS,PETROLEUM OILS NES	W	2256837	374.4	W	1183040	304.3	W	1450433	402.6	W	165193	119.6	HUILES LUBRIFIANTES
33451	LUBS(HIGH PETR CONT) ETC	W	2242940	348.6	W	1173229	272.4	W	1439928	373.3	W	154097	92.7	HUILES LUBRIF,H LOURDES
341	*GAS,NATURAL AND MANUFCT			125.1	W	2841172	160.6			253.1	W	1499699	267.1	GAZ NATUREL,GAZ MANUFACT
3413	PETROLM GASES,LIQUEFIED			124.9	W	2828826	158.2	W	1421623	252.9	W	1499637	266.9	GAZ DE PETROLE LIQUEFIE
4	ANIMAL,VEGETABLE OIL,FAT			134.4			171.6			134.8			191.7	HUILES,GRAISSES ANIM,VEG
5	CHEMCLS,RELATED PROD NES			5570.8			6405.6			6483.7			6120.9	PRODUITS CHIMIQUES
51	ORGANIC CHEMICALS			1057.1			1097.8			1141.2			1242.5	PROD CHIMIQ ORGANIQUES
511	HYDROCARBONS NES,DERIVS			195.5			143.1			115.0			155.6	HYDROCARBURES NDA
512	ALCOHOLS,PHENOLS ETC			174.2			57.1	W	77662	90.3	W	87373	134.2	PHENOLS,PHENOLS-ALCOOLS
514	NITROGEN-FNCTN COMPOUNDS			434.1			601.9	W	82434	655.1			694.6	COMPOSES FONCT AZOTEES
5148	OTH NITROGN-FNCTN CMPNDS			378.6			521.1	W	31260	574.4			618.0	AUTRES COMPOSES AZOTES
51482	IMIDE-,IMIDE-FNCT CMPNDS			346.8	W	10548	488.3	W	19214	538.1	W	12786	583.5	COMPOSES A FONCTION IMIDE
52	INORGANIC CHEMICALS			508.9			655.8			536.4			424.3	PROD CHIM INORGANIQUES
522	INORG ELEMNTS,OXIDES,ETC			234.2			257.2			236.5	W	856020	221.1	ELEMENTS INORGANIQUES
523	OTHR INORG CHEMICALS ETC			159.8			191.9			161.3			146.7	AUT PRODUITS CHIMIQUES INORG
524	RADIOACTIVE ETC MATERIAL			115.1			206.7			138.6			56.6	MATIERES RADIOACTIVES
5241	RADIOACTIVE ELEMENTS ETC			112.8			204.4			137.0			54.5	RADIOELEMENTS,ISOTOPES
53	DYES,TANNING,COLOUR PROD			389.5			472.0			481.1			438.2	PROD TEINTURE,COLORANTS
533	PIGMENTS,PAINTS,ETC	W	112233	294.2	W	120220	352.7	W	128189	361.6	W	123588	332.0	PIGMENTS,PEINTURES,VERNIS
541	*MEDICINAL,PHARM PRODUCT			1004.4			1167.1			1358.7			1232.1	PROD MEDICINAUX PHARMACEUT
5417	MEDICAMENTS			747.1	MK	24884	911.2	MK	36080	1044.1	MK	25164	955.6	MEDICAMENTS
54179	— CONTNG OTH SUBSTANCES	MK	23964	578.2	MK	18603	715.4	MK	31441	798.8	MK	20200	740.7	MED CONT AUT SUBSTANCES
55	PERFUME,CLEANING ETC PRD			509.9			527.5			542.6			489.2	PROD POUR PARFUM,TOILETTE
553	PERFUMERY,COSMETICS,ETC	W	34355	258.5	W	38840	248.3	W	38363	251.7	W	37209	238.0	PRODUITS DE PARFUMERIE
554	SOAP,CLEANSING ETC PREPS	W	178441	220.8	W	237129	245.6	W	179047	256.7	W	172059	219.1	SAVONS,PRODUITS DETERSIFS
5542	WASHING PREPARATIONS ETC	W	163297	188.7	W	223442	212.1	W	158532	213.3	W	155829	185.9	PROD ORG TENSIO-ACT NDA
58	PLASTIC MATERIALS ETC			1334.0			1649.6			1539.8			1471.7	MAT PLAST ARTIFICIELLES
582	PROD OF CONDENSATION ETC	W	209845	339.4	W	165376	437.8	W	165218	410.7	W	180867	386.0	PROD CONDENS,POLYCOND
5823	ALKYDS,OTHER POLYESTERS	W	59413	152.9	W	64946	206.7	W	66744	194.9	W	76584	183.8	ALKYDES ET AUT POLYESTERS
583	POLYMERIZATION ETC PRODS			963.7	W	711017	1178.2	W	746787	1098.3	W	780847	1057.9	PROD POLYMERISATION
5831	POLYETHYLENE	W	303040	288.4	W	262269	321.8	W	273192	284.7	W	273190	287.4	POLYETHYLENE
58311	— IN PRIMARY FORMS	W	268796	216.5	W	235463	261.4	W	242880	222.1	W	241263	230.5	POLYETHYLENE PRIMAIRES
5839	OTH POLYMRZTION ETC PROD	W	104497	243.7	W	136854	332.8	W	145636	324.5	W	170328	332.7	AUT PROD POLYMER COPOLYM
59	CHEMICAL MATERIALS NES			679.6			755.8			789.1			740.2	MAT PROD CHIMIQUES NDA
598	MISCEL CHEM PRODUCTS NES			466.6			519.5	W	486830	529.9	W	532586	518.6	PROD DIV INDUST CHIM NDA
5989	CHEM PRODUCTS,PREPS NES	W	387403	335.2	W	206921	385.0	W	215208	385.8	W	230802	371.0	PROD PREP CHIMIQUES NDA
59899	OTH CHEM PRODS,PREPS,NES	W	178820	240.4	W	126109	286.0	W	150947	275.1	W	125437	250.9	AUT PRODUITS CHIMIQUES NDA
6	BASIC MANUFACTURES			8511.9			10326.2			9905.4			9528.1	ART MANUFACTURES
62	RUBBER MANUFACTURES NES			665.2			862.4			887.4			838.3	CAOUTCHOUC MANUFACTURE
625	RUBBER TYRES, TUBES ETC	W	94892	353.3	W	110354	453.2	W	110524	493.6	W	121279	473.2	PNEUS CAOUTCHOUC VULCANISE
6251	TYRES NEW FOR MOTOR CARS	W	42839	184.3	W	43355	206.3	W	44428	237.7	W	48931	229.7	PNEUS POUR VOITURES
628	RUBBER ARTICLES NES	W	18482	189.4	W	29361	268.0	W	19526	254.7	W	19811	228.8	OUVRAGES CAOUTCHOUC NDA
6289	OTH RUBBER ARTICLES NES	W	14458	145.6	W	25568	213.7	W	15688	202.2	W	16480	182.4	AUT OUVR CAOUTCHOUC NDA
62898	UNHARD RUBBER PRODS NES	W	14344	145.0	W	17334	212.1	W	15395	201.0	W	16154	181.2	OUV CAOUT VULC NON DURCI
63	WOOD,CORK MANUFACTRS NES			275.0			345.0			343.8			343.9	OUVRAGES LIEGE ET BOIS
634	VENEERS,PLYWOOD,ETC	W	245791	162.1	W	264929	199.5	W	290227	207.8	W	312785	202.9	PLACAGES,CONTRE-PLAQUES

4. General Imports C.I.F. by Commodities according to the S.I.T.C. (Rev. 2) in million U.S. Dollars
Importations Générales C.A.F. par Produits d'après la C.T.C.I. (Rév. 2) en millions de Dollars E.U.

SITC CTCI	COMMODITY	1994 QUANTITY QUANTITE	1994 VALUE VALEUR	1995 QUANTITY QUANTITE	1995 VALUE VALEUR	1996 QUANTITY QUANTITE	1996 VALUE VALEUR	1997 QUANTITY QUANTITE	1997 VALUE VALEUR	PRODUIT
64	PAPER,PAPERBOARD AND MFR		831.5		1006.3		997.4		920.7	PAPIERS,CARTONS & OUVRAGES
641	PAPER AND PAPERBOARD	W 540582	474.9	W 491440	576.9	W 530470	595.9	W 589022	562.9	PAPIERS ET CARTONS
6418	COATED ETC PAPER NES BLK	W 96037	173.1	W 85885	183.8	W 88365	180.1	W 97934	177.5	PAP,CARTONS COUCHES,ENDUITS
642	PAPER,ETC,PRECUT,ARTS OF	W 163705	356.6		429.4	W 167454	401.6	W 159133	357.8	PAP,CARTONS DECOUPES
6428	PAPER ETC ARTICLES NES	W 89897	195.5		249.9	W 90540	211.0	W 82758	185.8	OUVRAGES EN PATE A PAPIER
65	TEXTILE YARN,FABRICS,ETC		1087.3		1157.8		1157.0		1104.2	FILS,TISSUS,ARTICLES TEXTILE
651	TEXTILE YARN		175.5		224.0		207.1		183.5	FILS TEXTILES
657	SPECIAL TXTL FABRC,PRODS		214.7		229.4		233.6		219.5	TISSUS SPECIAUX
658	TEXTILE ARTICLES NES		182.9		201.8		219.7		243.1	ART FACONNES MAT TEXTILES
66	NONMETAL MINERAL MFS NES		758.4		809.4		791.8		742.0	ART MIN NON METALLIQUES
663	MINERAL MANUFCTURES NES		179.0	W 250773	213.3	W 202552	203.3	W 202255	188.2	ART MIN MANUF NDA
664	GLASS		190.5		228.0		221.0		216.9	VERRE
67	IRON AND STEEL		2085.5		2796.0		2618.0		2560.1	FER ET ACIER
671	PIG IRON ETC		195.9	W 239315	269.9	W 218134	207.1		213.9	FONTE,SPIEGEL,POUDRES
6716	FERRO-ALLOYS	W 178372	179.9	W 186486	251.5	W 167936	190.9	W 187768	196.3	FERRO-ALLIAGES
67169	OTHER FERRO-ALLOYS	W 120677	143.9	W 134666	210.0	W 112427	144.3	W 128427	154.6	AUTRES FERRO-ALLIAGES
672	IRON,STEEL PRIMARY FORMS	W 385312	340.9	W 322122	314.0	W 410915	462.0	W 511717	528.7	LINGOTS FER,ACIER
6725	IRN,STL BLOOMS,SLABS,ETC	W 329903	305.9	W 245611	277.4	W 334184	420.7	W 419545	487.0	BLOOMS,BILLETTES FER ACIER
67254	STNLS STL ETC BLOOMS ETC	W 246890	263.7	W 122977	211.0	W 300508	383.3	W 370000	452.1	BLOOMS ETC ACIER INOXYD
673	IRON,STEEL SHAPES ETC	W 590015	336.8	W 703922	502.2	W 591368	398.5	W 664192	389.2	BARRES,PROFIL FER,ACIER
6732	IRON,STEEL BARS ETC	W 199937	149.0	W 268807	252.6	W 223011	194.8	W 252438	192.6	BARRES FER,ACIER
674	IRN,STL UNIV,PLATE,SHEET	W 1042119	700.4	W 1159278	1007.5	W 1110101	929.9	W 1270644	868.5	LARGES PLATS,TOLES
6746	IRN,STL THIN PLATE,ROLLD	W 255488	202.5	W 249283	274.0	W 230973	228.1	W 286081	222.5	TOLES LAM MOINS 3MM
6749	OTH IRN,STL PLATES,SHEET	W 450980	289.7	W 555396	439.0	W 532213	421.9	W 618857	400.7	AUTRES TOLES FER,ACIER
67491	— OF IRON OR SIMPLE STL	W 445338	276.2	W 549535	425.2	W 525466	409.8	W 588283	379.0	AUT TOLES AUTRES ACIER FIN
678	IRON,STL TUBES,PIPES,ETC	W 316395	348.4	W 364807	511.9	W 306745	446.9	W 338290	405.1	TUBES,TUYAUX EN FONTE,FER
6783	IRON,STL TUBES,PIPES NES	W 227528	181.6	W 253837	265.2	W 218050	230.6	W 236803	204.5	AUT TUBES,TUYAUX FER,ACIER
68	NON-FERROUS METALS		1189.5		1421.7		1197.8		1270.1	METAUX NON FERREUX
682	COPPER EXC CEMENT COPPER		319.3	W 120093	435.4	W 97418	312.1	W 106467	328.3	CUIVRE
6821	COPPER NES,ALLOYS,UNWRT		131.0	W 67773	206.0	W 50214	117.8	W 58573	136.5	CUIVRE BRUT
68212	COPPER REFINED,UNWROUGHT		130.0	W 67467	204.8	W 48517	113.1	W 56843	132.0	CUIVRE AFFINE BRUT
6822	COPPER,ALLOYS WORKED	W 50550	188.4	W 52320	229.5	W 47204	194.4	W 47894	191.9	CUIVRE,ALLIAGES OUVRES
684	ALUMINIUM	W 263471	582.8	W 206384	639.5	W 221300	579.3	W 260373	617.1	ALUMINIUM
6841	ALUMINIUM,ALLOYS,UNWRGHT	W 157387	260.9	W 89206	196.0	W 105523	182.2	W 126685	218.3	ALUMINIUM,ALLIAGES BRUTS
6842	ALUMINIUM,ALLOYS WORKED	W 106084	322.0	W 117178	443.5	W 115777	397.2	W 133688	398.9	ALUMINIUM,ALLIAGES OUVRE
68422	ALUMNM PLATE,SHEET,STRIP	W 66137	167.5	W 75811	245.0	W 77307	221.3	W 89544	228.5	TOLES, PLANCHES EN ALU
69	METAL MANUFACTURES NES		1533.8		1845.1		1831.2		1669.7	ART MANUFACT EN METAL NDA
694	STL,COPPR NAILS,NUTS,ETC	W 56357	216.7	W 70004	297.7	W 63305	267.0	W 62728	244.5	CLOUS,VIS,ECROUS
69402	IRN,STL NUTS,BOLTS,ETC	W 47779	195.1	W 59179	273.6	W 53320	244.9	W 52481	221.8	BOULONS,VIS,ECROUS FER,AC
695	TOOLS	W 21099	345.2	W 22624	428.9	W 23324	466.9	W 21972	410.3	OUTILS A MAIN
6954	BLADES,TIPS,ETC FR TOOLS	W 8794	209.5	W 8579	277.0	W 10846	308.0	W 9523	271.6	OUTILS POUR MACHINE-OUTIL
69541	PARTS TO INSERT IN TOOLS	W 7862	160.3	W 7210	191.7	W 9888	233.5	W 8505	201.7	OUTILS DE FORAGE
699	BASE METAL MFRS NES		612.2		723.6		690.0		633.5	ART MANUFACTURES MET NDA
6991	LOCKSMITHS WARES,ETC	W 28051	251.8	W 37416	316.1	W 30393	313.2	W 32217	279.1	ARTICLES DE SERRURERIE
69913	BASE MTL DOOR,ETC FITTNG	W 21480	174.5	W 27079	223.0	W 23700	214.0	W 25435	194.6	GARNITURES POUR MEUBLES
7	MACHINES,TRANSPORT EQUIP		19538.3		25719.4		26972.0		26965.8	MACHINES MATERIEL TRANSPORT
71	POWER GENERATING EQUIPMT		1303.5		2035.5		2039.6		1917.9	MACHINES GENERATRICES
713	INTRNL COMBUS PSTN ENGIN	W 56090	599.5	W 81473	823.0	W 73106	770.4	W 77830	764.1	MOTEURS EXPL COMB INT, PIECE
7139	PISTON ENGINE PARTS NES	W 44863	447.5	W 69568	654.0	W 63116	631.3	W 65258	606.8	PIECES POUR 713.2,3,8
714	ENGINES AND MOTORS NES	W 8121	235.4	W 6917	627.7	W 8073	744.7	W 7650	702.8	MOTEURS NON ELECTRIQUES
7149	ENGINE & MOTOR PARTS NES	W 8004	181.2	W 6369	345.3	W 7556	424.4	W 7165	431.1	PIECES 714 ET 718.88
71491	PARTS NES OF 7144,71481	W 447	126.4	W 668	262.9	W 987	348.9	W 1057	361.4	PIECES DES PROPULSEURS
716	ROTATING ELECTRIC PLANT	W 26231	282.8		344.7		346.9		296.1	APP ELECTR ROTATIFS,PIECES
7162	AC MTRS,GENRTRS,GEN SETS	W 15160	172.8	W 18058	226.3		219.7		190.2	MOTEURS ELECTRIQUES
71621	AC MTRS,INC UNIVRSL MTRS	W 14086	156.6	W 17012	207.3	W 14636	200.1	W 13734	172.7	MOT ELEC NON COUR CONTINU
72	MACHS FOR SPCL INDUSTRYS		1300.4		1776.6		2028.3		1893.5	MAC SPECIALES POUR INDUST
721	AGRIC MACHY,EXC TRACTORS		161.9		183.9		195.1		215.0	MACHINES AGRICOLES
725	PAPER ETC MILL MACHINERY	W 9026	148.1	W 15943	243.5	W 23361	347.5	W 12956	212.3	MACHINES FABR PATE PAPIER
7259	PTS NES OF MACHS OF 725	W 5944	81.8	W 11844	164.5	W 15621	218.4	W 9865	135.2	PIECES GROUPE 725
72591	PTS NES OF MACHS OF 7251	W 5283	64.8	W 10981	143.7	W 14605	193.5	W 9232	115.4	PIECES DU 725.1
726	PRINTG,BKBINDG MACHY,PTS	W 5497	164.6	W 5548	182.7	W 6724	210.7	W 5529	156.5	MACHINES POUR IMPRIMERIE
728	OTH MACHY FOR SPCL INDUS		496.2	W 37455	746.8		820.5	W 50486	877.0	AUT MACH IND PARTICULIERES
7284	MACHY FOR SPCL INDUS NES		370.7	W 22433	606.9		669.2	W 31688	722.7	MACH SPEC IND PARTICUL.
72848	OTH MCHY WITH INDIV FNCT	W 7548	171.9	W 12072	345.6	W 21178	390.3	W 18524	439.7	AUTRES MACHINES NDA
73	METALWORKING MACHINERY		439.7		527.8		599.3		597.3	MACH TRAVAIL DES METAUX
736	METALWORKING MACH-TOOLS		342.2		419.8	W 22575	477.7		409.8	MACH-OUTILS TRAVAIL METAUX
74	GENRL INDUSTRL MACHY NES		3012.8		3936.3		3855.5		3526.1	MACH APP INDUSTRIE
741	HEATING,COOLING EQUIPMNT	W 27723	386.2	W 32424	493.6	W 30940	513.0	W 36654	478.8	MACH CHAUFFAGE,PIECES
742	PUMPS FOR LIQUIDS ETC	W 18880	331.4	W 21930	455.2	W 22774	460.3	W 20471	413.2	POMPES MOTO-POMPES
743	PUMPS NES,CENTRFUGES ETC	W 39537	487.6	W 47816	637.8	W 43871	584.4	W 44808	552.0	POMPES COMPRES,VENT ETC
7431	PUMPS FOR GASES ETC	W 16395	184.1	W 19337	232.0	W 18814	237.4	W 19310	220.4	POMPES AIR A VIDE,COMPRES
744	MECHANICAL HANDLING EQU	W 71004	411.9	W 93256	522.4	W 92779	538.4	W 99207	506.8	EQUIP MANUTENTION PIECES
7442	LIFTING,LOADING MACH NES	W 18250	170.2	W 20047	187.7	W 22069	188.0	W 20146	173.2	APP LEVAGE,MANUTENTION
7449	PTS NES OF MACHY OF 7442	W 47438	205.7	W 66008	282.5	W 62382	288.9	W 70225	275.3	PIECES DU 744.2
745	NONELEC MACHY,TOOLS NES	W 14501	317.6	W 16131	349.8	W 18898	376.0	W 18043	328.1	AUT MACH NON ELEC,PIECES
7452	OTH NONELEC MCHS,PTS NES	W 11744	262.9	W 13281	282.7	W 16227	311.6	W 15511	268.7	AUT MACH NON ELEC,PIECES
749	NONELEC MACH PTS,ACC NES	W 92016	1078.3	W 116545	1477.9	W 109128	1383.7	W 112524	1247.3	PIECES MACH NON ELEC NDA
7491	BALL,ROLLER,ETC BEARINGS	W 29068	326.2	W 36265	503.0	W 29843	422.6	W 29098	370.1	ROULEMENTS BILLES ETC
7492	COCKS,VALVES ETC NES	W 13749	306.4	W 15008	383.9	W 14558	379.8	W 14142	334.5	ART ROB,SIM POUR TUYAUX
7493	SHAFT,CRANK,PULLEY ETC	W 41758	307.2	W 54583	407.4	W 54251	392.7	W 59660	366.0	ARBRES TRANS,VILEBREQUINS
75	OFFICE MACHNES,ADP EQUIP		2647.1		3549.1		3503.2		3353.9	MACH BUREAU TRAIT AUTOM
751	OFFICE MACHINES		178.2		165.2		154.8		169.3	MACH,APPAREILS DE BUREAU
752	AUTOMTIC DATA PROC EQUIP	W 20327	1715.3	W 29972	2370.1	W 29199	2361.0	W 31954	2306.4	MACH TRAIT INFORMATION
7522	DIGITAL COMPUTERS	W 1731	229.6	W 1524	272.2	W 1442	312.5	W 1554	349.3	MACH DIGITALES COMPLETES
7523	DIGITL CENTRL PROCESSORS	W 6278	656.3	W 8363	1007.2	W 7660	953.6	W 9312	907.7	UNITES CENTRALES
7524	DIGITL CENTRL STOR UNITS	W 966	198.7	W 1428	277.3	W 2109	291.3	W 2080	333.4	UNITES MEMOIRE CENTRALES
7525	ADP PERIPHERAL UNITS	W 10551	523.2	W 16772	625.1	W 15985	580.2	W 17408	567.2	UNITES PERIPHERIQUES
7528	OFF-LINE DATA PROC EQUIP	W 783	104.7	W 1869	184.6	W 1954	216.0	W 1577	145.8	MACH AUXIL TRAIT INFORM
759	OFFICE,ADP MCH PTS,ACCES	W 8200	753.8	W 8805	1013.9	W 9631	987.5	W 11175	878.2	PIECES DU 751 ET 752
7599	ACCTG,ETC,ADP MCH PTS,AC	W 6497	677.1	W 6348	879.5	W 7388	882.8	W 8861	776.7	PIECES DU 751 ET 752
76	TELECOMM,SOUND EQUIPMENT		2013.0		2874.5		2946.8		3366.5	EQUIPMENT DE TELECOM
761	TELEVISION RECEIVERS	W 19937	277.0		284.8	W 15736	256.7	W 18016	234.3	RECEPTEURS DE TELEVISION
7611	COLOUR TV RECEIVERS	W 19902	275.2	W 17470	282.8	W 15692	254.8	W 17972	232.7	RECEPTEURS COULEUR
762	RADIO BROADCAST RECEIVRS	W 7695	197.1	W 6920	210.9	W 5892	190.0	W 6986	198.0	RECEPTEURS RADIODIFFUSION
763	SOUND RECORDRS,PHONOGRPH		176.7	W 4448	194.4	W 3919	212.0	W 4348	176.4	PHONO,APP ENREGISTREMENT
7638	OTHR SOUND APPARATUS ETC	W 4176	175.8	W 4338	192.3	W 3887	211.4	W 4305	175.8	AUT APP D'ENREGIS,REPROD
764	TELECOM EQPT,PTS,ACC NES	W 17810	1362.3	W 22620	2184.6	W 21417	2288.3	W 26422	2757.9	EQUIP TELECOM,PIECES
7641	LINE TELEPHONE,ETC EQUIP	W 2958	250.4	W 3687	308.6	W 3540	322.6	W 4310	432.1	APP TELEPHON PAR FIL
7643	TV,RADIO TRANSMITTRS ETC	W 1185	320.0	W 1096	328.5	W 1237	373.7	W 1566	427.0	APP EMET TELE RADIO
7649	PTS NES OF EQUIPMT OF 76	W 8849	653.0	W 12653	1367.6	W 11914	1463.5	W 15147	1761.5	PIECES DE LA DIV 76
76491	PTS NES OF APPAR OF 7641	W 2210	243.2	W 2475	405.1	W 2357	383.4	W 2786	407.6	PIECES POUR 764.1

4. General Imports C.I.F. by Commodities according to the S.I.T.C. (Rev. 2) in million U.S. Dollars
Importations Générales C.A.F. par Produits d'après la C.T.C.I. (Rév. 2) en millions de Dollars E.U.

SITC CTCI	COMMODITY	1994 QUANTITY QUANTITE	1994 VALUE VALEUR	1995 QUANTITY QUANTITE	1995 VALUE VALEUR	1996 QUANTITY QUANTITE	1996 VALUE VALEUR	1997 QUANTITY QUANTITE	1997 VALUE VALEUR	PRODUIT
76493	TELECOMM EQUIPMT PTS NES	W 4738	388.3	W 8221	940.1	W 8083	1059.6	W 10675	1334.6	PIECES 761,762,764.3,8
77	ELECTRIC MACHNRY NES ETC		4030.7		5111.3		5430.8		5680.2	MACH APP ELECT NDA
771	ELECTRIC POWER MACHY NES	W 22739	278.6	W 24902	399.8	W 21377	395.1	W 22038	416.7	MACH PROD,TRANS ELECTR
7712	OTH ELEC POWER MACHY NES	W 9938	192.5	W 10154	286.4	W 10704	294.6	W 11628	307.8	AUT APP PROD TRANSF ELEC
77121	STATIC CONVERTERS ETC	W 3012	116.5	W 4101	168.4	W 4850	168.0	W 5994	192.6	CONVERTISSEURS STATIQUES
772	SWITCHGEAR ETC,PARTS NES	W 19566	864.5	W 22390	1115.1	W 23142	1153.4	W 24582	1152.7	APP COUPURE,SECT ETC
7721	SWITCHGEAR ETC	W 18199	703.2	W 20373	895.8	W 21001	912.5	W 21670	843.6	APP COUPURE,SECTIONMNT
7722	PRINTED CIRCUITS,PTS NES	W 892	109.4	W 1263	152.0	W 1292	173.0	W 2072	251.8	CIRCUITS ET PIECES
773	ELECTR DISTRIBUTNG EQUIP	W 38430	346.4	W 45132	467.9	W 40147	460.5	W 42329	422.9	EQUIPMT DISTRIBUTION ELECT
7731	INSULATED WIRE,CABLE ETC	W 32284	311.9	W 39013	423.0	W 31982	406.1	W 35742	382.4	FILS,CABLES ISOLES ELECT
775	HOUSEHOLD TYPE EQUIP NES	W 62144	448.6		453.4		532.1		600.3	MACH,APP USAGE DOMESTQUE
7758	ELECTRO–THERMIC APPL NES	W 20394	173.7		180.0		201.8		219.8	APP ELECTROTHERMIQ NDA
776	TRANSISTORS,VALVES,ETC		905.6		1236.5	W 3527	1362.2		1504.6	LAMPES,TUBES,VALVES
7764	ELECTRONIC MICROCIRCUITS	W 1017	683.2	W 1916	883.5	W 1259	1078.3	W 1396	1246.3	MICROSTRUCTURES ELECTRON
778	ELECTRICAL MACHINERY NES	W 91545	1070.3	W 96695	1315.3	W 122106	1398.5		1404.5	AUTRES MACH ELECT NDA
7781	BATTERIES,ACCUMULATORS	W 36799	218.1	W 37701	277.1	W 64634	286.1	W 76436	292.3	PILES ET ACCUMULATEURS
77812	ELECTRIC ACCUMULATORS	W 28341	154.2	W 29075	210.9	W 53818	200.9	W 65011	213.7	ACCUMULATEURS ELECTRIQ
7783	AUTOMOTIVE ELECTR EQUIP	W 15089	254.6	W 18208	335.6	W 16209	326.0	W 17737	294.5	EQUIP ELECT MOTEURS EXPL
7788	OTH ELEC MACHY,EQUIP NES	W 26128	381.8	W 28141	461.6	W 27157	529.8		570.5	AUT MACH APP ELEC NDA
77883	ELEC SIGNALLING EQU NES	W 863	72.2	W 1088	100.2	W 998	154.3	W 1248	205.1	APP ELECT SIGNAL ACOUS
78	ROAD VEHICLES		4028.6		5031.6		5581.7		5946.2	VEHICULES ROUTIERS
781	PASS MOTOR VEH EXC BUSES	W 158114	1724.3	W 155139	1837.7	W 194604	2320.6	W 261815	2809.3	AUTO TRANSPORT PERSONNES
782	LORRIES,SPCL MTR VEH NES	W 26499	267.3	W 37362	372.5	W 40108	418.9	W 44710	410.6	VEHICULES SPECIAUX,MARCH
7821	LORRIES,TRUCKS	W 24800	247.8	W 35505	354.0	W 36725	387.3	W 42187	387.7	VEHICULES TRANSP MARCHAND
784	MOTOR VEH PRTS,ACCES NES	W 275362	1716.6	W 356338	2506.7	W 320539	2469.5	W 338977	2328.7	PIECES 722,781,782,783
7849	OTHER MOTOR VEHCL PARTS	W 273911	1706.5	W 354767	2491.1	W 317842	2442.6	W 335674	2287.8	PIECES 722,781,782,783
79	OTHR TRANSPORT EQUIPMENT		762.8		877.0		987.2		684.8	AUTRE MATERIEL TRANSPORT
792	AIRCRAFT ETC		340.7		696.2		725.4		583.7	APP NAVIGATION AERIENNE
7923	AIRCRFT NES2000–15000KG	W 25	3.9	W 541	267.5	W 513	302.5	W 291	126.7	AERODYNES 2000 A 15000 KG
7924	AIRCRFT NES OVER 15000KG	W 199	115.9	W 619	157.5	W 185	137.6	W 249	188.7	AERODYNES PLUS 15000 KG
7929	AIRCRAFT PARTS NES	W 763	180.1	W 824	254.1	W 723	243.7	W 659	224.1	PIECES DU 792
793	SHIPS AND BOATS ETC		341.6		105.2	W 7609	145.3		45.6	NAVIRES BATEAUX,ETC
7932	SHIPS AND BOATS NES		328.7		94.3	W 5047	132.1	W 8377	36.3	NAVIRES ET BATEAUX
79323	OTHER CARGO VESSELS	V 354	271.8	V 1920	71.5	W 3071	107.5	W 5849	1.1	AUT BATEAUX TRANS MARCH
8	MISC MANUFACTURED GOODS		7946.5		8249.6		8492.0		8197.9	ART MANUFACTURES DIVERS
812	*PLUMBG,HEATNG,LGHTNG EQ	W 28427	217.8	W 27833	253.4	W 31681	258.8	W 32660	243.7	APPAR SANITAIRES CHAUFFAGE
8124	LIGHTING EQUIPMENT NES	W 19214	184.5	W 20321	218.4	W 22508	220.5	W 22764	208.0	APPAREILS ECLAIRAGE ETC
821	*FURNITURE,PARTS THEREOF	W 198089	763.7	W 176832	760.3	W 173322	756.1	W 194962	779.8	MEUBLES ET PIECES
8211	CHAIRS,SEATS AND PARTS	W 43711	263.5	W 39511	260.1	W 44010	288.1	W 49577	295.6	SIEGES ET PIECES
82111	CHAIRS AND OTHER SEATS	W 34768	186.9	W 30580	189.1	W 32778	195.0	W 37679	183.9	SIEGES
8219	FURNITURE AND PARTS NES	W 143134	379.5	W 126581	383.4	W 118869	354.5	W 133382	363.8	AUTRES MEUBLES ET PIECES
82192	WOOD FURNITURE NES	W 93710	245.9	W 82253	237.2	W 74582	219.2	W 86770	228.6	MEUBLES NDA EN BOIS
84	CLOTHING AND ACCESSORIES		2117.5		2129.5		2175.2		2118.6	VETEMENTS
842	MENS OUTERWEAR NOT KNIT		453.4	W 19417	504.9	W 16911	475.3	W 16437	423.2	VET DESSUS POUR HOMMES
8423	— TROUSERS,BREECHES ETC	W 9831	209.0	W 10218	246.0	W 9479	240.7	W 9051	206.7	PANTALONS HOMMES MAT TEX
843	WOMENS OUTERWEAR NONKNIT		530.6	W 19913	514.8	W 17002	518.9	W 17984	496.9	VET DESSUS FEMMES MAT TEX
8439	— OTHER OUTER GARMENTS		227.7	W 10090	214.3	W 9493	230.9	W 10560	244.0	AUT VET DES FEM MAT TEXT
845	OUTERWEAR KNIT NONELASTC		479.7	W 18713	412.3	W 18397	454.8	W 20825	483.9	VET DESSOUS,ACCES BONNET
8451	— JERSEYS,PULLOVERS ETC	W 13079	275.0	W 10519	227.4	W 10368	255.4	W 11468	261.6	CHANDAILS,PULL–OVERS ETC
8459	— OTHER,CLTHG ACCESRYS		165.4	W 6671	143.1	W 6862	163.4	W 8243	189.0	AUT VET DESSUS DE BONNE
846	UNDER GARMENTS KNITTED		270.2	W 15820	300.2	W 15657	337.9	W 16178	337.8	SOUS VETS DE BONNETERIE
8462	— OF COTTON NON ELASTIC		193.0	W 13210	220.0	W 12550	230.6	W 12929	235.4	SOUS–VET BONNET COTON
84629	—— OTHER		193.0	W 13210	220.0	W 12550	230.6	W 12929	235.4	AUT SOUS–VET BONNET COTON
848	HEADGEAR,NONTXTL CLOTHNG	W 14619	184.7		180.9	W 10441	175.4		170.0	VET ACCES MAT AUT QUE TEX
851	*FOOTWEAR	W 25351	433.9	W 21364	385.0	W 21677	404.9	W 23186	401.0	CHAUSSURES
85102	FOOTWEAR LEATHER	W 19036	369.1	W 15988	324.0	W 15207	326.3	W 15524	319.4	CHAUS SEMELLES EN CUIR
87	PRECISION INSTRUMNTS NES		1306.4		1539.9		1555.9		1443.8	INSTRUM,APPAR SCIENT NDA
872	MEDICAL INSTRUMENTS NES	W 5044	227.8	W 11881	303.5	W 5374	309.2	W 5231	300.6	INSTR,APP MEDIC–CHIR NDA
87202	OTH MEDICAL INSTRUMENTS	W 4540	207.2	W 11023	249.3	W 4550	260.8	W 4339	258.3	INSTRUM,APP MEDECINE
874	MEASURNG,CONTROLNG INSTR		891.7		1057.6		1081.0		976.5	INSTRUMENTS DE MESURE
8743	GAS,LIQUID CONTROL INSTR	W 2825	291.4	W 4243	370.1	W 3326	389.3	W 3084	307.9	APP,INSTR MESURE FLUIDES
8748	ELEC MEAS,CONTRL EQU NES	W 1326	187.2	W 1391	242.8	W 1229	235.0	W 1363	227.6	APP ELEC ELECTRO MESURE
87483	OTH ELCTRNC MEAS ETC EQU	W 1159	169.5	W 1247	225.7	W 1085	214.0	W 1166	200.9	AUT APP ELECTRO DE MESURE
88	PHOTO EQU,OPTICL GDS ETC		564.8		611.2		639.4		582.1	APP,FOURN PHOTO,OP,MONTR
882	PHOTO,CINEMA SUPPLIES		281.9		316.8		329.8		298.4	PRODUITS PHOTO,CINEMA
8822	PHOTO FILM EXC DEV CINMA		228.1		245.2		261.3		242.0	PLAQUES,PELLICULES,FILMS
89	MISC MANUFCTRD GOODS NES		2443.8		2467.6		2591.0		2524.0	ART MANUFACTURES DIVERS
892	PRINTED MATTER	W 111256	462.1		382.3		403.6		381.6	IMPRIMES
8921	PRINTED BOOKS,GLOBES,ETC	W 31719	170.8	W 23760	151.1	W 26693	162.4	W 23493	171.5	LIVRES,BROCHURES,CARTES
89211	PRINTED BOOKS,PAMPHLETS	W 30301	163.5	W 22318	143.9	W 25448	155.6	W 22585	167.1	LIVRES,BROCHURES
8928	PRINTED MATTER NES	W 53851	197.5		155.1		143.8		133.1	IMPRIMES NDA
893	ARTICLES OF PLASTIC NES		720.6		803.2		834.7		789.9	OUVRAGES EN MAT DIVIS 58
8931	PLSTC PACKG CONTNRS,LIDS	W 53418	194.3	W 51853	226.7	W 55818	221.0	W 60234	205.9	ART TRANSP EMBALLAGE ETC
8939	MISC PLASTIC ARTICLES	W 100339	511.4	W 90820	557.3	W 95572	593.7	W 101003	565.3	ART DIVERS EN MAT DIV 58
89399	OTHR PLASTC ARTICLES NES	W 81937	452.9	W 70711	485.9	W 71659	511.9	W 72328	480.8	AUT OUV MAT DIV 58
894	TOYS,SPORTING GOODS,ETC		370.2	W 38394	345.3	W 39998	383.2	W 42349	443.2	VOITURES ENFANTS,JOUETS
8942	TOYS,INDOOR GAMES ETC	W 28112	232.6	W 27186	209.6	W 27646	223.1	W 28780	276.0	JOUETS,JEUX ETC
898	MUSICAL INSTRUMENTS,PTS		412.9		452.7		471.3		427.8	INSTRUMENTS DE MUSIQUE
8983	SOUND RECRDNG TAPE,DISCS	W 13437	380.9	W 12686	421.9	W 12492	440.0	W 13444	397.1	SUPPORTS SON POUR 763
89832	RECORDED DISCS,TAPES ETC	W 6520	295.2	W 6404	346.2	W 6263	359.6	W 6851	326.5	DISQUES,PHONO,BANDES
899	OTHER MANUFACTURED GOODS		279.0		301.7		312.5		307.5	AUT ART MANUF DIVERS NDA
9	GOODS NOT CLASSD BY KIND		494.1		935.1		1249.0		1042.0	ART TRANSACT NON CLASSES
931	*SPECIAL TRANSACTIONS		325.9	W 2423335	883.4	W 2103377	1207.4	W 2295165	1010.9	TRANS.SPECIALES

5. General Exports F.O.B. by Commodities according to the S.I.T.C. (Rev. 2) in million U.S. Dollars
Exportations Générales F.O.B. par Produits d'après la C.T.C.I. (Rév. 2) en millions de Dollars E.U.

SITC CTCI	COMMODITY	1994		1995		1996		1997		PRODUIT
		QUANTITY QUANTITE	VALUE VALEUR	QUANTITY QUANTITE	VALUE VALEUR	QUANTITY QUANTITE	VALUE VALEUR	QUANTITY QUANTITE	VALUE VALEUR	
	ALL COMMODITIES		61299.8		77436.4		83408.3		81180.3	TOUS PRODUITS
0	FOOD AND LIVE ANIMALS		991.5		1416.7		1726.4		1869.4	ALIMENTS,ANIMAUX VIVANTS
03	FISH AND PREPARATIONS		120.4		244.8		287.5		328.2	POISSONS ET PREPARATIONS
04	CEREALS AND PREPARATIONS		228.0		259.3		400.8		441.2	CEREALES ET PRODUITS
07	COFFEE,TEA,COCOA,SPICES		192.1		236.3		242.7		212.7	CAFE,THE,CACAO,EPICES
09	MISC EDIBLE PRODUCTS		183.1		245.3		263.3		294.6	PREP ALIMENTAIRES DIVERSES
1	BEVERAGES AND TOBACCO		242.2		216.6		263.9		263.0	BOISSONS ET TABACS
11	BEVERAGES		217.5		193.0		235.5		233.9	BOISSONS
112	ALCOHOLIC BEVERAGES		205.5	W 72928	179.8	W 56427	218.6	W 53168	218.2	BOISSONS ALCOOLIQUES
1124	DISTILLED ALCOHOLIC BEVS		195.6	W 62319	173.1	W 43719	208.5	W 41427	207.8	ALCOOLS,EAUX–DE–VIE
11249	OTH ALCOHOLC BEVS,CMPNDS		195.4	W 62263	172.8	W 43143	206.3	W 40818	202.8	BOISSONS ALCOOLIQUES NDA
2	CRUDE MATERLS,EXCL FUELS		4812.2		6003.4		5240.6		5387.4	MAT BRUTES NON COMESTIBLES
24	CORK AND WOOD		2509.6		2807.4		2672.9		2694.9	LIEGE ET BOIS
248	WOOD SHAPED,SLEEPERS	W 5557911	2431.8	W 5385942	2640.9	W 5797146	2517.3	W 5682330	2569.9	BOIS SIMPLEMENT TRAVAILLES
2482	LUMBER SHAPED CONIFER	W 5527397	2417.5	W 5360885	2626.8	W 5768566	2499.4	W 5659096	2551.9	CONIFERES SCIES,RABOTES
24821	LUMBER SAWN ETC CONIFER	W 5462403	2367.0	W 5297569	2570.3	W 5711478	2453.0	W 5605321	2506.9	CONIFERES SCIES LONGITUD
251	*PULP AND WASTE PAPER		1345.1		2048.0	W 2856080	1444.4	W 3080543	1453.6	PATES A PAPIER,DECHETS
2517	SODA,SULPHATE WOOD PULP	W 2314120	1102.2	W 2056454	1659.1	W 2223711	1196.6	W 2348566	1182.6	PATES CHIMIQUES AU SULFATE
25172	— BLEACHED,NONDISSOLVNG	W 2206653	1062.1	W 1955922	1588.5	W 2099056	1142.8	W 2239306	1140.7	PATES BLANCHIES
28	METALLIFEROUS ORES,SCRAP		701.5		870.6		825.1		945.1	MINERAIS METAL,DECHETS
281	IRON ORE,CONCENTRATES	MW 15393	387.2	MW 16918	497.3	MW 15173	488.6		567.4	MINERAIS DE FER
2816	IRON ORE AGGLOMERATES	W 6912076	220.4	MW 9256	334.7	MW 9080	343.5	MW 10597	398.6	MINERAIS AGGLOMERES
3	MINERAL FUELS ETC		1557.1		1470.9		1835.3		1794.5	COMBUSTIBLES MINERAUX LUB
33	PETROLEUM AND PRODUCTS		1379.9		1434.2		1780.3		1734.7	PETROLE ET DERIVES
334	PETROLEUM PRODUCTS,REFIN		1292.1	W 8394185	1316.4	W 8451406	1641.7	MW 9499	1612.8	PRODUITS RAFFINES
3341	GASOLINE,OTH LIGHT OILS		306.3	W 2002566	366.7	W 1877769	386.6	W 2187986	452.6	ESSENCES POUR MOTEURS
33411	MOTOR,AVIATION SPIRIT	W 1681911	281.0	W 1796148	331.6	W 1627885	336.6	W 2003770	417.9	ESSENCES MOTEURS D'AVIONS
3343	GAS OILS	W 3598344	543.7			W 268836	126.9	W 102199	19.4	GAS OILS
3344	FUEL OILS,NES	W 3190	0.4	W 2709643	308.0	W 2536987	320.7	W 7009305	1022.8	FUEL OILS
3345	LUBS,PETROLEUM OILS NES	W 3395818	441.4	W 3670809	639.3	W 3670613	786.0	W 178275	113.1	HUILES LUBRIFIANTES
33451	LUBS(HIGH PETR CONT) ETC	W 3393392	432.2	W 3665399	620.5	W 3665051	765.6	W 173237	95.6	HUILES LUBRIF,H LOURDES
5	CHEMCLS,RELATED PROD NES		5565.8		4940.6		5466.7		5458.8	PRODUITS CHIMIQUES
51	ORGANIC CHEMICALS		621.9		369.9		388.8		334.4	PROD CHIMIQ ORGANIQUES
52	INORGANIC CHEMICALS		279.7		161.4		176.9		188.3	PROD CHIM INORGANIQUES
523	OTHR INORG CHEMICALS ETC		195.6		85.0		95.6		91.8	AUT PRODUITS CHIMIQUES INORG
53	DYES,TANNING,COLOUR PROD		285.1		370.0		410.1		385.0	PROD TEINTURE,COLORANTS
533	PIGMENTS,PAINTS,ETC		263.0		332.1	W 172211	376.8	W 194057	354.5	PIGMENTS,PEINTURES,VERNIS
541	*MEDICINAL,PHARM PRODUCT		2467.5		2546.2		2943.0		3012.9	PROD MEDICINAUX PHARMACEUT
5417	MEDICAMENTS		2323.7	MK 16683	2358.6	MK 27204	2755.8	MK 26488	2845.8	MEDICAMENTS
54172	— CONTAINING HORMONES		320.5	K 103914	259.5	K 151013	420.0	K 260887	431.2	MED CONTENANT HORMONES
54179	— CONTNG OTH SUBSTANCES	MK 16776	1946.5	MK 14629	2057.5	MK 23550	2240.1	MK 23077	2334.8	MED CONT AUT SUBSTANCES
55	PERFUME,CLEANING ETC PRD		234.4		287.1		328.3		313.0	PROD POUR PARFUM,TOILETTE
58	PLASTIC MATERIALS ETC		1096.7		628.5		630.1		645.8	MAT PLAST ARTIFICIELLES
583	POLYMERIZATION ETC PRODS		842.2		451.6		460.5	W 220902	478.7	PROD POLYMERISATION
5831	POLYETHYLENE		524.4	W 66497	157.3	W 72984	155.0	W 75941	147.3	POLYETHYLENE
58311	— IN PRIMARY FORMS		383.4							POLYETHYLENE PRIMAIRES
59	CHEMICAL MATERIALS NES		498.7		500.9		525.2		530.5	MAT PROD CHIMIQUES NDA
598	MISCEL CHEM PRODUCTS NES		341.4	W 451970	400.4	W 193257	412.9	W 187652	415.2	PROD DIV INDUST CHIM NDA
5989	CHEM PRODUCTS,PREPS NES		258.1	W 393914	347.5	W 89243	345.3	W 94328	344.2	PROD PREP CHIMIQUES NDA
59899	OTH CHEM PRODS,PREPS,NES		210.1	W 364842	282.9	W 59629	282.9	W 56537	291.1	AUT PRODUITS CHIMIQUES NDA
6	BASIC MANUFACTURES		15017.0		18477.7		18799.7		17600.1	ART MANUFACTURES
62	RUBBER MANUFACTURES NES		456.4		567.9		611.5		652.5	CAOUTCHOUC MANUFACTURE
625	RUBBER TYRES, TUBES ETC	W 37626	151.6	W 37342	178.0	W 53041	236.7		283.0	PNEUS CAOUTCHOUC VULCANISE
628	RUBBER ARTICLES NES		194.3	W 21248	252.2	W 28863	244.5	W 22636	244.6	OUVRAGES CAOUTCHOUC NDA
63	WOOD,CORK MANUFACTRS NES		695.7		910.8		954.0		908.0	OUVRAGES LIEGE ET BOIS
635	WOOD MANUFACTURES NES	W 297909	621.3	W 315105	814.6	W 321475	848.8	W 353954	792.0	ART MANUF EN BOIS NDA
6353	BUILDERS WOODWRK,PREFABS	W 214112	508.0	W 243104	691.7	W 248755	713.1	W 274699	663.4	OUVRAGES DE MENUISERIE
64	PAPER,PAPERBOARD AND MFR		5864.3		7674.5		7761.0		6960.9	PAPIERS,CARTONS & OUVRAGES
641	PAPER AND PAPERBOARD		5334.6	W 7771543	6964.3	W 7735648	6994.3	W 8563445	6270.8	PAPIERS ET CARTONS
6411	NEWSPRINT	W 2030184	931.2	W 1983414	1202.2	W 1958026	1365.0	W 2181614	1118.8	PAPIER JOURNAL
6412	PRINTG,WRITING PAPER NES	W 1127783	987.3	W 978745	1219.0	W 1071345	1230.4	W 1273847	1185.6	PAPIERS POUR L'IMPRESSION
64121	— UNCOATED	W 231544	185.6	W 174608	233.3	W 178802	198.6	W 195723	198.2	PAPIERS IMPRES NON COUCHES
64122	— COATED,IMPREGNATD ETC	W 896239	801.8	W 804137	985.8	W 892543	1031.8	W 1078124	987.4	PAPIERS IMPRESSION COUCHES
6413	KRAFT PAPER,PAPERBOARD	W 2380692	1270.5	W 2292075	1797.7	W 2192897	1626.6	W 2296867	1447.4	PAPIER ET CARTON KRAFT
64131	KRAFT LINER IN BULK	W 1366136	589.6	W 1343304	914.0	W 1324543	776.3	W 1346225	680.0	PAP KRAFT POUR COUVERTURES
64132	SACK KRAFT PAPER IN BULK	W 571864	352.0	W 476418	398.7	W 448821	406.2	W 478570	358.5	PAPIER KRAFT POUR SACS
64139	KRAFT PAPER PAPERBD,NES	W 442692	329.0	W 472353	485.1	W 419534	444.2	W 472073	409.0	PAPIER,CARTON KRAFT NDA
6415	PAPER,PAPERBRD,BULK,NES		885.6	W 1377627	1254.6	W 1381084	1261.1	W 1570577	1145.3	PAPIERS,CARTONS ROULEAUX
64159	OTHER PAPER ETC,BULK,NES	W 1083524	768.0	W 1104845	1074.0	W 1120908	1119.2	W 1289948	1015.2	AUT PAPIER ROULEAUX FEUILLES
6418	COATED ETC PAPER NES BLK	W 986824	1032.5	W 922835	1217.8	W 920643	1241.5	W 1030840	1140.8	PAP,CARTONS COUCHES,ENDUITS
64181	PLASTIC COATED PAPER ETC	W 396048	524.4	W 437908	721.5	W 405129	709.9	W 390297	581.4	PAP,CARTONS ENDUITS,RESINES
64189	COATED PAPER ETC NES	W 554230	472.7	W 440225	446.9	W 454738	475.3	W 576345	504.3	PAPIERS,CARTONS COUCHES
642	PAPER,ETC,PRECUT,ARTS OF	W 250579	529.7		710.3		766.7		690.2	PAP,CARTONS DECOUPES
6428	PAPER ETC ARTICLES NES	W 114476	274.6	W 129486	360.5	W 137817	387.4	W 144714	358.4	OUVRAGES EN PATE A PAPIER
65	TEXTILE YARN,FABRICS,ETC		623.6		766.3		825.8		785.7	FILS,TISSUS,ARTICLES TEXTILE
657	SPECIAL TXTL FABRC,PRODS		230.9		288.4		285.4		249.4	TISSUS SPECIAUX
66	NONMETAL MINERAL MFS NES		581.9		672.7		693.2		701.1	ART MIN NON METALLIQUES
664	GLASS		196.0		250.4		262.2		276.5	VERRE
67	IRON AND STEEL		3836.9		4282.7		4281.4		4059.4	FER ET ACIER
671	PIG IRON ETC		223.1	W 39148	27.0	W 87137	31.4	W 64436	26.9	FONTE,SPIEGEL,POUDRES
672	IRON,STEEL PRIMARY FORMS		591.4	W 532188	459.0		715.0		722.9	LINGOTS FER,ACIER
6725	IRN,STL BLOOMS,SLABS,ETC	W 153748	184.6	W 83587	164.0	W 103317	150.6	W 170161	163.4	BLOOMS,BILLETTES FER ACIER
6727	IRN,STL COIL FR REROLLNG		393.1	W 427382	273.1	W 727776	547.8	W 744288	543.3	EBAUCHES POUR TOLES FER
67274	STNLESS STEEL ETC COILS	W 173862	209.1	W 30548	82.4	W 248049	365.1	W 295818	392.9	EBAUCHES ACIER INOXYDBLE
673	IRON,STEEL SHAPES ETC		683.0	W 662391	869.2		768.8	W 781116	785.8	BARRES,PROFIL FER,ACIER
6732	IRON,STEEL BARS ETC	W 601070	449.3	W 470054	542.7	W 526243	531.7	W 646612	540.5	BARRES FER,ACIER
67325	OTH ALLOY STEEL BARS ETC	W 235255	227.1	W 196729	279.9	W 216456	278.6	W 277772	296.0	BARRES NON ACIERS ALLIES
674	IRN,STL UNIV,PLATE,SHEET		1557.5		1883.3	W 1696149	1728.7	W 1709310	1576.1	LARGES PLATS,TOLES
6744	IRN,STL HVY PLATE,ROLLED		486.6		457.3	W 414548	389.9	W 375253	319.7	TOLES LAMINEES PLUS 4.75 MM
67441	— OF IRON OR SIMPLE STL		193.5		228.8	W 351181	171.6	W 309467	132.0	TOLES NON ACIER FIN CARB
67443	— OF STAINLESS ETC STL	W 91602	211.9	W 46306	159.9	W 54217	153.4	W 53007	124.2	TOLES ACIER INOXYDABLE
6746	IRN,STL THIN PLATE,ROLLD		603.2		846.7	W 713486	786.8	W 726318	712.2	TOLES LAM MOINS 3MM
67461	— OF IRON OR SIMPLE STL		185.4		197.9	W 354619	230.5	W 345713	194.2	TOL NON AC FIN MOINS 3 MM
67463	— OF STAINLESS ETC STL	W 79805	240.4	W 98331	406.0	W 93088	320.7	W 108979	304.7	TOL ACIER INOX MOINS 3 MM
67464	— OF OTHER ALLOY STEEL	W 239951	177.4	W 267955	242.9	W 265780	235.7	W 271625	213.4	TOL NON AC ALL MOINS 3 MM
6749	OTH IRN,STL PLATES,SHEET		317.3		397.2	W 429511	386.5	W 449132	376.0	AUTRES TOLES FER,ACIER
67491	— OF IRON OR SIMPLE STL		282.5		349.8	W 415526	343.0	W 432792	335.6	AUT TOLES AUTRES ACIER FIN
677	IRN,STL WIRE(EXCL W ROD)	W 81487	187.5	W 90903	250.3	W 89236	239.1	W 99033	224.9	FILS EN FER,ACIER
678	IRON,STL TUBES,PIPES,ETC		570.8		772.6	W 245375	777.6	W 283077	701.9	TUBES,TUYAUX EN FONTE,FER
6782	IRON,STL SEAMLESS TUBES	W 134569	309.3	W 138887	421.6	W 127829	423.7	W 154286	392.0	TUBES,TUYAUX SANS SOUDURE
6783	IRON,STL TUBES,PIPES NES		177.1		244.6	W 103658	243.9	W 112029	199.0	AUT TUBES,TUYAUX FER,ACIER

5. General Exports F.O.B. by Commodities according to the S.I.T.C. (Rev. 2) in million U.S. Dollars
Exportations Générales F.O.B. par Produits d'après la C.T.C.I. (Rév. 2) en millions de Dollars E.U.

SITC CTCI	COMMODITY	1994		1995		1996		1997		PRODUIT
		QUANTITY QUANTITE	VALUE VALEUR	QUANTITY QUANTITE	VALUE VALEUR	QUANTITY QUANTITE	VALUE VALEUR	QUANTITY QUANTITE	VALUE VALEUR	
68	NON-FERROUS METALS		990.5		1280.5		1257.3		1261.4	METAUX NON FERREUX
682	COPPER EXC CEMENT COPPER		451.0	W 166389	607.9		576.9		532.0	CUIVRE
6822	COPPER,ALLOYS WORKED		407.8	W 145639	549.7	W 141015	503.1		459.5	CUIVRE,ALLIAGES OUVRES
68221	COPPER BARS,WIRE,ETC	W 70206	162.6	W 83927	247.4	W 78371	195.6	W 83082	194.6	BARRES,PROFILES ET FILS
684	ALUMINIUM	W 143614	398.6	W 148400	525.0	W 160605	510.5	W 179675	537.6	ALUMINIUM
6842	ALUMINIUM,ALLOYS WORKED	W 88366	315.6	W 91497	398.1	W 89941	383.4	W 107240	406.9	ALUMINIUM,ALLIAGES OUVRE
69	METAL MANUFACTURES NES		1901.1		2253.3		2344.7		2207.7	ART MANUFACT EN METAL NDA
691	STRUCTURES AND PARTS NES	W 73356	222.4	W 75819	288.7	W 81689	323.7	W 93782	323.0	CONSTRUCT FER,ACIER,ALU
695	TOOLS		755.8		820.3	W 20576	794.7	W 21219	724.3	OUTILS A MAIN
6953	OTHER HAND TOOLS		201.3		211.6	W 12265	196.9	W 12237	186.5	AUTRES OUTILS A MAIN
6954	BLADES,TIPS,ETC FR TOOLS		541.6	W 7277	590.6	W 7061	579.8	W 7758	524.2	OUTILS POUR MACHINE-OUTIL
69541	PARTS TO INSERT IN TOOLS	W 8456	242.0	W 3339	175.6	W 2818	182.3	W 3457	163.2	OUTILS DE FORAGE
69543	CARBIDE TOOL TIPS ETC	W 931	272.0	W 1140	385.3	W 1143	366.1	W 1176	330.3	PLAQUETTES,POINTES D'OUTILS
699	BASE METAL MFRS NES		535.0		665.6		701.6		671.7	ART MANUFACTURES MET NDA
7	MACHINES,TRANSPORT EQUIP		27591.6		32593.6		37119.8		36467.6	MACHINES MATERIEL TRANSPORT
71	POWER GENERATING EQUIPMT		2036.3		2810.2		3014.2		2778.5	MACHINES GENERATRICES
713	INTRNL COMBUS PSTN ENGIN	W 102348	1226.8		1434.7		1624.6	W 96583	1322.5	MOTEURS EXPL COMB INT, PIECE
7132	MOTOR VEHCL PISTN ENGINS	W 56849	692.7	W 77802	847.5	W 71316	1041.3	W 62053	827.9	MOTEURS EXPL POUR VEHICULES
7139	PISTON ENGINE PARTS NES	W 28314	300.0	W 18883	335.9	W 17421	317.1	W 16116	239.1	PIECES POUR 713.2,3,8
714	ENGINES AND MOTORS NES	W 1950	275.1	W 3028	642.2	W 2732	678.1	W 3034	821.6	MOTEURS NON ELECTRIQUES
7149	ENGINE & MOTOR PARTS NES	W 1702	235.3	W 2613	439.5	W 2264	497.8	W 2555	592.3	PIECES 714 ET 718.88
71491	PARTS NES OF 7144,71481	W 170	160.7	W 293	340.3	W 461	397.7	W 540	514.1	PIECES DES PROPULSEURS
716	ROTATING ELECTRIC PLANT	W 21716	301.2		450.9		395.1		380.6	APP ELECTR ROTATIFS,PIECES
718	OTH POWER GENERATG MACHY		181.3	W 7385	236.9	W 7335	261.2	W 7872	209.7	AUTRES MOTEURS PARTIES
72	MACHS FOR SPCL INDUSTRYS		2660.9		2667.6		2837.3		2532.7	MAC SPECIALES POUR INDUST
721	AGRIC MACHY,EXC TRACTORS		338.0		198.6		227.5		197.2	MACHINES AGRICOLES
723	CIVIL ENGNEERG EQUIP ETC		755.1	W 37104	329.5	W 36047	362.9	W 37420	323.4	APPAREILS DE GENIE CIVIL
7234	CONST,MINING MACHNRY NES	W 35486	543.2	W 15610	208.0	W 15162	232.6	W 13992	191.6	MACH POUR LA CONST, MINES
72342	SLFPRP SHOVELS,EXCAVATRS	W 21702	413.2	W 534	2.1	W 557	2.1	W 752	3.0	PELLES MECANIQUES
724	TEXTILE,LEATHER MACHNRY		192.2		228.5		225.8		230.6	MACH POUR INDUSTRIE TEXTILE
725	PAPER ETC MILL MACHINERY	W 26203	347.4	W 48326	634.7	W 38546	682.3	W 44287	549.3	MACHINES FABR PATE PAPIER
7251	PAPER,PULP MAKING MACHRY	W 13165	159.9	W 22127	284.1	W 15497	293.7	W 14969	244.9	MACHINES FABR PATE CARTON
7259	PTS NES OF MACHS OF 725	W 11093	153.9	W 22761	289.1	W 20149	316.8	W 25619	231.9	PIECES GROUPE 725
72591	PTS NES OF MACHS OF 7251	W 10266	140.6	W 20493	273.2	W 19101	299.8	W 24444	215.3	PIECES DU 725.1
728	OTH MACHY FOR SPCL INDUS	W 57659	818.4		1059.9		1097.7	W 56960	985.2	AUT MACH IND PARTICULIERES
7284	MACHY FOR SPCL INDUS NES	W 32520	622.2		798.2		821.4	W 29009	746.0	MACH SPEC IND PARTICUL.
72848	OTH MCHY WITH INDIV FNCT	W 17688	304.5	W 18678	366.8	W 14094	338.6	W 13760	313.0	AUTRES MACHINES NDA
72849	PTS OF MACHS OF 7284 ETC	W 7823	189.5	W 7212	205.0	W 8582	241.8	W 8020	230.0	PIECES DU 728.4 ETC
73	METALWORKING MACHINERY		582.4		743.8		931.8		779.6	MACH TRAVAIL DES METAUX
736	METALWORKING MACH-TOOLS		303.2		339.6		420.8		359.0	MACH-OUTILS TRAVAIL METAUX
737	METALWORKING MACHNRY NES		279.2		404.3	W 36235	511.1		420.6	MACH TRAV METAUX PIECES
7373	WELDING,BRAZING,ETC MCHS	W 9145	204.4	W 13497	314.8	W 16263	407.1		322.3	MACH SOUDAGE ETC PIECES
73732	ELECTRIC WELDERS,ETC	W 9086	203.0	W 13210	308.0	W 16101	403.5	W 14963	320.8	MACH ELECT POUR SOUDER
74	GENRL INDUSTRL MACHY NES		4834.3		4778.8		5202.2		4890.8	MACH APP INDUSTRIE
741	HEATING,COOLING EQUIPMNT	W 54180	733.7	W 52990	694.8	W 62705	801.4	W 58030	814.7	MACH CHAUFFAGE,PIECES
7416	HEATING,COOLING EQU NES	W 28739	409.8	W 25463	323.6	W 33533	386.7	W 21040	353.4	APP CHANGEMENT TEMP
742	PUMPS FOR LIQUIDS ETC	W 23733	391.9	W 26923	470.3	W 30425	505.5	W 25470	427.3	POMPES MOTO-POMPES
743	PUMPS NES,CENTRFUGES ETC	W 24878	436.5	W 27575	489.8	W 27627	479.2	W 28777	485.2	POMPES COMPRES,VENT ETC
744	MECHANICAL HANDLING EQU		1408.7		1221.1	W 150683	1395.7	W 148450	1250.5	EQUIP MANUTENTION PIECES
7441	FORK LIFT TRCKS,ETC,PTS	W 44693	278.7	W 48833	342.0	W 53866	418.7	W 53559	365.9	CHARIOTS POUR USINES ETC
74411	FORK LIFT TRUCKS ETC	W 44414	275.4	W 48536	339.0	W 53688	415.9	W 53366	363.2	CHARIOTS POUR LES GARES
7442	LIFTING,LOADING MACH NES		567.9		583.2	W 64244	630.9	W 61031	558.3	APP LEVAGE,MANUTENTION
74428	OTH HANDLING ETC MCH NES		501.0	W 71113	515.9	W 55595	547.7	W 53041	478.5	AUT APP LEVAGE ETC
7449	PTS NES OF MACHY OF 7442		562.2	W 28118	296.1	W 32573	346.2	W 33859	326.4	PIECES DU 744.2
745	NONELEC MACHY,TOOLS NES		912.4	W 34143	702.2	W 24388	753.9	W 26238	723.3	AUT MACH NON ELEC,PIECES
7451	POWER TOOLS NONELEC,PTS		416.6	W 4309	149.0	W 4703	192.1	W 5513	184.3	OUT MACH PNEUM A MOTEUR
74511	POWER HAND TOOLS NONELEC		334.5	W 1543	56.1	W 2504	99.6	W 2806	92.4	OUT MACH PNEUM A MOTEUR
7452	OTH NONELEC MCHS,PTS NES	W 19449	495.8	W 29834	553.3	W 19684	561.8	W 20725	539.1	AUT MACH NON ELEC NDA
74522	PACKAGNG,BOTTLNG,ETC MCH	W 7123	247.0	W 17204	313.3	W 6845	320.4	W 7286	299.0	MACH NETT BOUTEILLES,ETC
749	NONELEC MACH PTS,ACC NES	W 71782	951.5	W 84652	1200.8	W 85511	1266.8	W 90243	1189.9	PIECES MACH NON ELEC NDA
7491	BALL,ROLLER,ETC BEARINGS	W 31807	424.4	W 35787	541.6	W 36525	550.4	W 37734	528.4	ROULEMENTS BILLES ETC
7492	COCKS,VALVES ETC NES	W 10994	277.0	W 11090	316.6	W 12554	353.3	W 13280	326.7	ART ROB,SIM POUR TUYAUX
7493	SHAFT,CRANK,PULLEY ETC	W 22674	141.7	W 32873	235.9	W 31212	231.1	W 33943	218.8	ARBRES TRANS,VILEBREQUINS
75	OFFICE MACHNES,ADP EQUIP		832.2		962.2		1050.0		968.7	MACH BUREAU TRAIT AUTOM
752	AUTOMTIC DATA PROC EQUIP	W 3601	344.3	W 4001	395.4	W 4411	427.3		401.2	MACH TRAIT INFORMATION
759	OFFICE,ADP MCH PTS,ACCES	W 4113	363.0	W 4837	429.2	W 5265	467.8	W 5042	422.1	PIECES DU 751 ET 752
7599	ACCTG,ETC,ADP MCH PTS,AC	W 2839	303.0	W 2872	327.9	W 3201	366.9	W 2930	319.4	PIECES DU 751 ET 752
76	TELECOMM,SOUND EQUIPMENT		4344.2		6728.0		8812.0		10067.1	EQUIPMENT DE TELECOM
764	TELECOM EQPT,PTS,ACC NES		4192.7		6527.9		8589.0		9880.5	EQUIP TELECOM,PIECES
7641	LINE TELEPHONE,ETC EQUIP	W 2529	329.7	W 3178	435.1	W 3859	719.7	W 4133	774.8	APP TELEPHON PAR FIL
7643	TV,RADIO TRANSMITTRS ETC	W 3162	1323.0	W 5323	2488.8	W 7840	3357.8	W 11490	4371.2	APP EMET TELE RADIO
7649	PTS NES OF EQUIPMT OF 76		2475.9		3509.8		4421.0		4629.4	PIECES DE LA DIV 76
76491	PTS NES OF APPAR OF 7641	W 12242	1203.7	W 13325	1412.1	W 12767	1554.0	W 15511	1554.4	PIECES POUR 764.1
76493	TELECOMM EQUIPMT PTS NES	W 15272	1267.4	W 21711	2091.0	W 23932	2855.8	W 20479	3066.2	PIECES 761,762,764.3,8
77	ELECTRIC MACHNRY NES ETC		2976.6		3597.5		4701.3		4539.2	MACH APP ELECT NDA
771	ELECTRIC POWER MACHY NES	W 21791	329.3	W 22475	427.0	W 25084	811.4	W 20970	675.2	MACH PROD,TRANS ELECTR
7712	OTH ELEC POWER MACHY NES	W 5821	176.2	W 7094	264.0	W 9159	597.7	W 9936	523.5	AUT APP PROD TRANSF ELEC
77121	STATIC CONVERTERS ETC	W 2873	127.2	W 3717	196.2	W 5265	503.5	W 5958	442.4	CONVERTISSEURS STATIQUES
772	SWITCHGEAR ETC,PARTS NES	W 16655	650.7		755.9		1072.5		918.0	APP COUPURE,SECT ETC
7721	SWITCHGEAR ETC	W 16222	547.4	W 18400	631.4	W 21005	786.0	W 22518	758.6	APP COUPURE,SECTIONMNT
7722	PRINTED CIRCUITS,PTS NES	W 252	95.9	W 270	111.7	W 855	273.2	W 577	144.9	CIRCUITS ET PIECES
773	ELECTR DISTRIBUTNG EQUIP	W 73665	355.2		401.3	W 76539	504.6		563.4	EQUIPMT DISTRIBUTION ELECT
7731	INSULATED WIRE,CABLE ETC	W 71866	338.1	W 69583	375.3	W 74242	477.6	W 82561	539.8	FILS,CABLES ISOLES ELECT
774	ELECTRO-MEDCL,XRAY EQUIP	W 1841	204.6	W 3726	289.5	W 1846	243.7	W 1621	212.2	APPAREILS MEDICAUX
775	HOUSEHOLD TYPE EQUIP NES		610.6	W 115869	721.5		748.8		790.8	MACH,APP USAGE DOMESTQUE
7758	ELECTRO-THERMIC APPL NES		249.0	W 58642	289.8		295.0		294.5	APP ELECTROTHERMIQ NDA
77586	ELECTROTHERM DOM APP NES	W 22647	186.3	W 53148	211.9	W 34495	203.9	W 25342	192.8	APP ELECTRO THERMIQUES
776	TRANSISTORS,VALVES,ETC		269.6		309.2		496.1		569.0	LAMPES,TUBES,VALVES
7764	ELECTRONIC MICROCIRCUITS	W 529	217.6	W 559	234.7	W 972	418.2	W 711	492.3	MICROSTRUCTURES ELECTRON
778	ELECTRICAL MACHINERY NES		556.9		693.3		824.6		811.0	AUTRES MACH ELECT NDA
7781	BATTERIES,ACCUMULATORS		167.2	W 37061	192.6	W 43320	227.1	W 45175	255.0	PILES ET ACCUMULATEURS
7788	OTH ELEC MACHY,EQUIP NES		195.5	W 7003	255.6		320.2		290.2	AUT MACH APP ELEC NDA
78	ROAD VEHICLES		8074.4		8713.7		9004.7		8588.8	VEHICULES ROUTIERS
781	PASS MOTOR VEH EXC BUSES	W 252603	3403.8	W 282329	4261.4	W 266966	4163.0	W 260115	3949.9	AUTO TRANSPORT PERSONNES
782	LORRIES,SPCL MTR VEH NES		1428.6	W 40452	219.7	W 33122	193.9	W 35669	169.5	VEHICULES SPECIAUX,MARCH
7821	LORRIES,TRUCKS		1389.3	W 37256	198.3	W 29158	159.1	W 30724	137.8	VEHICULES TRANSP MARCHAND
783	ROAD MOTOR VEHICLES NES	W 11693	66.2	W 39127	400.6	W 54566	569.3	W 53018	482.2	VEHICULES ROUTIERS NDA
7832	TRACTORS FOR TR-TRAILERS	W 5594	37.0	W 32584	350.0	W 49981	556.7	W 48378	470.2	TRACTEURS ROUTIERS
784	MOTOR VEH PRTS,ACCES NES	W 392555	3050.1	W 490334	3688.0	W 437201	3916.3	W 482926	3809.6	PIECES 722,781,782,783
7841	MOTOR VEHICLE CHASSIS	W 28197	322.1	W 28488	349.3	W 29539	376.0	W 32879	371.1	CHASSIS 722,781,782,783
7842	MOTOR VEHICLE BODIES	W 20015	227.2	W 35413	390.2	W 35287	447.4	W 45653	518.0	CARROS 722,781,782,783

5. General Exports F.O.B. by Commodities according to the S.I.T.C. (Rev. 2) in million U.S. Dollars
Exportations Générales F.O.B. par Produits d'après la C.T.C.I. (Rév. 2) en millions de Dollars E.U.

SITC CTCI	COMMODITY	1994 QUANTITY QUANTITE	1994 VALUE VALEUR	1995 QUANTITY QUANTITE	1995 VALUE VALEUR	1996 QUANTITY QUANTITE	1996 VALUE VALEUR	1997 QUANTITY QUANTITE	1997 VALUE VALEUR	PRODUIT
7849	OTHER MOTOR VEHCL PARTS	W 344343	2500.9	W 426434	2948.5	W 372376	3093.1	W 404394	2920.6	PIECES 722,781,782,783
79	OTHR TRANSPORT EQUIPMENT		1250.7		1592.1		1566.7		1322.7	AUTRE MATERIEL TRANSPORT
792	AIRCRAFT ETC		431.6		1297.1		1259.8		940.0	APP NAVIGATION AERIENNE
7923	AIRCRFT NES2000–15000KG	W 248	205.6	W 811	632.4	W 1038	841.3	W 607	515.9	AERODYNES 2000 A 15000 KG
7924	AIRCRFT NES OVER 15000KG	W 108	73.7	W 389	369.0	W 192	53.4	W 134	69.7	AERODYNES PLUS 15000 KG
7929	AIRCRAFT PARTS NES	W 261	141.5	W 797	284.5	W 1408	356.7	W 543	345.9	PIECES DU 792
793	SHIPS AND BOATS ETC		720.8		129.0		108.8		143.8	NAVIRES BATEAUX,ETC
7932	SHIPS AND BOATS NES		535.1		98.2	W 5953	89.0	W 22442	125.1	NAVIRES ET BATEAUX
79323	OTHER CARGO VESSELS	V 843	442.7	V 2171	1.8	W 1417	4.7	W 18096	48.9	AUT BATEAUX TRANS MARCH
8	MISC MANUFACTURED GOODS		5044.6		6151.3		6692.8		6642.7	ART MANUFACTURES DIVERS
812	*PLUMBG,HEATNG,LGHTNG EQ		239.0		286.2	W 37326	318.0	W 42543	314.2	APPAR SANITAIRES CHAUFFAGE
821	*FURNITURE,PARTS THEREOF	W 306106	1013.0	W 323939	1274.1	W 435056	1445.2	W 359763	1332.3	MEUBLES ET PIECES
8211	CHAIRS,SEATS AND PARTS	W 31664	208.0	W 38614	295.8	W 45988	316.4	W 38588	267.4	SIEGES ET PIECES
82111	CHAIRS AND OTHER SEATS	W 25645	173.0	W 30375	236.6	W 36689	252.9	W 28181	202.1	SIEGES
8219	FURNITURE AND PARTS NES	W 256394	671.9	W 267562	814.9	W 371104	953.1	W 303706	902.9	AUTRES MEUBLES ET PIECES
82192	WOOD FURNITURE NES	W 156143	420.9	W 152879	491.6	W 169589	587.5	W 190243	546.8	MEUBLES NDA EN BOIS
84	CLOTHING AND ACCESSORIES		327.9		375.5		480.5		531.2	VETEMENTS
87	PRECISION INSTRUMNTS NES		1295.0		1597.0		1697.9		1744.3	INSTRUM,APPAR SCIENT NDA
872	MEDICAL INSTRUMENTS NES	W 6661	396.8	W 6673	493.0	W 7555	552.4	W 7557	609.0	INSTR,APP MEDIC–CHIR NDA
87202	OTH MEDICAL INSTRUMENTS	W 5801	299.6	W 5353	318.3	W 6288	395.0	W 6031	403.7	INSTRUM,APP MEDECINE
874	MEASURNG,CONTROLNG INSTR		851.0		1043.0		1080.2		1056.9	INSTRUMENTS DE MESURE
8748	ELEC MEAS,CONTRL EQU NES		296.0		364.4		356.3		318.2	APP ELEC ELECTRO MESURE
87483	OTH ELCTRNC MEAS ETC EQU		277.1	W 1013	314.5	W 1163	296.2	W 1167	259.8	AUT APP ELECTRO DE MESURE
88	PHOTO EQU,OPTICL GDS ETC		213.1		275.1		261.1		267.5	APP,FOURN PHOTO,OP,MONTR
89	MISC MANUFCTRD GOODS NES		1891.2		2266.2		2411.3		2374.8	ART MANUFACTURES DIVERS
892	PRINTED MATTER	W 42828	236.7		249.8		260.3		252.6	IMPRIMES
893	ARTICLES OF PLASTIC NES		846.5		1120.6		1200.5		1183.2	OUVRAGES EN MAT DIVIS 58
8931	PLSTC PACKG CONTNRS,LIDS	W 49735	165.6	W 64084	253.3	W 65974	255.5	W 76251	238.7	ART TRANSP EMBALLAGE ETC
8939	MISC PLASTIC ARTICLES	W 153373	647.1	W 200059	828.9	W 223417	901.8	W 249508	899.7	ART DIVERS EN MAT DIV 58
89391	PVC FLOORING TILES ETC	W 88076	230.8	W 128415	330.1	W 144617	365.0	W 164551	364.8	CHLORURE POLYVINYL PLAQ
89399	OTHR PLASTC ARTICLES NES	W 62482	400.0	W 68656	482.7	W 75188	515.1	W 79307	512.7	AUT OUV MAT DIV 58
899	OTHER MANUFACTURED GOODS		282.7		406.3		450.5		402.0	AUT ART MANUF DIVERS NDA
8996	HEARING,ORTHOPAEDIC AIDS		198.0		287.9		324.6		282.1	APPAREILS D'ORTHOPEDIE
89962	ORTHOPAEDIC ETC GOODS		195.5		284.5		322.0		280.5	APPAREILS D'ORTHOPEDIE
9	GOODS NOT CLASSD BY KIND		363.9		6093.6		6195.4		5614.2	ART TRANSACT NON CLASSES
931	*SPECIAL TRANSACTIONS		114.6	W 2638994	5924.9	W 2659468	5993.9	W 2701165	5472.5	TRANS.SPECIALES

1. HISTORICAL SERIES, 1962–1997 SPECIAL TRADE, IMPORTS C.I.F., EXPORTS F.O.B.
SERIES HISTORIQUES, 1962–1997 COMMERCE SPECIAL, IMPORTATIONS C.A.F., EXPORTATIONS F.O.B

YEAR ANNEE	VALUE IN MILLION SWISS FRANCS VALEUR EN MILLION SWISS FRANCS MERCHANDISE – MARCHANDISE		GOLD – OR		CONVERSION FACTORS U.S. CENTS PER SWISS FRANC FACTEURS DE CONVERSION CENTS E.U. PAR SWISS FRANC		INDEX NUMBERS – INDICES QUANTUM		UNIT VALUE VALEUR UNITAIRE	
	IMPORTS	EXPORTS	IMPORTS	EXPORTS	IMPORTS	EXPORTS	IMPORTS	EXPORTS	IMPORTS	EXPORTS
1962	12977.00	9524.00	8.00	56.00	23.2700	23.2700				
1963	13978.00	10378.00	11.00	64.00	23.2700	23.2700				
1964	15512.00	11367.00	28.00	89.00	23.2700	23.2700				
1965	15929.00	12861.00	42.00	143.00	23.2700	23.2700				
1966	17004.00	14204.00	55.00	135.00	23.2700	23.2700				
1967	17786.00	15165.00	43.00	139.00	23.2700	23.2700				
1968	19425.00	17349.00	29.00	304.00	23.2700	23.2700				
1969	22734.00	20009.00	19.00	131.00	23.2700	23.2700				
1970	27873.00	22140.00	25.00	104.00	23.2700	23.2700				
1971	29642.00	23617.00	20.00	103.00	24.1500	24.5200				
1972	32372.00	26188.00	30.00	124.00	26.1934	26.2005				
1973	36589.00	29948.00	29.00	170.00	31.7768	31.8118				
1974	42929.00	35353.00	61.00	456.00	33.6461	33.7418				
1975	34268.00	33430.00	104.00	180.00	38.8194	38.7588				
1976	36871.00	37045.00			40.0689	40.0737				
1977	43026.00	42159.00			41.7872	41.9408				
1978	42300.00	41779.00			56.2753	56.3936				
1979	48730.00	44024.00			60.2375	60.2100				
1980	60859.00	49608.00			59.7383	59.7366	68	71	100	84
1981	60094.10	52821.90			51.0799	51.1953	65	72	97	86
1982	58059.70	52658.70			49.3802	49.4196	64	69	96	90
1983	61064.50	53723.50			47.6858	47.6425	67	69	96	91
1984	69024.40	60654.10			42.6942	42.6404	72	77	101	92
1985	74750.30	66623.70			41.1001	41.2028	75	82	105	95
1986	73513.01	67004.00			55.8451	55.9428	82	86	94	92
1987	75171.01	67477.01			67.3161	67.3916	88	86	90	92
1988	82399.01	74064.00			68.4131	68.4703	93	91	93	93
1989	95209.01	84268.00			61.1358	61.1571	98	96	101	99
1990	96611.01	88257.01			72.1357	72.2812	100	100	100	100
1991	95032.00	87947.01			69.9788	69.9652	99	99	100	103
1992	86739.01	86148.00			71.2051	71.2762	94	103	102	103
1993	83767.01	86659.01			67.7145	67.7300	93	104	100	103
1994	87279.01	90213.01			73.4250	73.4244	102	109	95	102
1995	90775.01	92012.00			84.8318	84.8381	109	114	93	100
1996	91967.01	94174.00			80.9753	80.9196	110	115	94	101
1997	103088.00	105133.00			68.9459	68.9656	117	123	98	105

2. IMPORTS BY BROAD ECONOMIC CATEGORY AND EXPORTS BY INDUSTRIAL ORIGIN. (PERCENTAGE OF TOTAL VALUE)
IMPORTATIONS PAR CATEGORIES ECONOMIQUES ET EXPORTATIONS PAR BRANCHE D'ACTIVITE.(EN POURCENTAGE DE LA VALEUR TOTALE)

IMPORTS – IMPORTATIONS

	1991	1992	1993	1994	1995	1996	1997
TOTAL IMPORTS–IMPORTATIONS TOTALES	100.	100.	100.	100.	100.	100.	100.
1 FOOD BEV–ALIMENTATION BOISSONS	5.9	6.0	6.0	6.2	5.8	5.9	5.6
11 PRIMARY–PRODUITS DE BASE	2.8	2.8	2.8	2.9	2.6	2.6	2.5
111 FOR INDUSTRY–POUR L'INDUSTRIE	0.5	0.5	0.5	0.5	0.6	0.5	0.5
112 FOR HOUSEHOLDS–POUR LES MENAGES	2.3	2.3	2.3	2.4	2.1	2.1	2.0
12 PROCESSED–PRODUITS ELABORES	3.1	3.2	3.2	3.2	3.2	3.3	3.1
121 FOR INDUSTRY–POUR L'INDUSTRIE	0.3	0.3	0.3	0.3	0.3	0.3	0.3
122 FOR HOUSEHOLDS–POUR LES MENAGES	2.8	2.9	2.9	2.9	2.9	2.9	2.8
2 IND SUPPLIES–APPROV INDUSTRIELS	32.1	32.5	33.1	32.8	31.8	30.8	32.1
21 PRIMARY–PRODUITS DE BASE	5.8	5.9	6.3	5.4	3.8	4.6	4.8
22 PROCESSED–PRODUITS ELABORES	26.3	26.6	26.8	27.4	28.0	26.3	27.2
3 FUELS–COMBUSTIBLES	4.6	4.2	3.9	3.3	2.9	3.5	4.5
31 PRIMARY–PRODUITS DE BASE	1.7	1.5	1.6	1.4	1.3	1.7	1.5
32 PROCESSED–PRODUITS ELABORES	2.9	2.7	2.3	1.9	1.5	1.8	3.0
321 MOTOR SPIRIT–ESSENCE	1.2	1.1	0.9	0.7	0.6	0.7	1.1
322 OTHER–AUTRES	1.8	1.6	1.4	1.2	0.9	1.1	1.8
4 MACHINERY–EQUIPEMENT	20.3	20.5	20.5	21.0	22.6	22.2	21.4
41 CAPITAL EQUIPMENT–MACHINES	16.7	16.8	16.6	16.9	18.1	17.9	17.4
42 PARTS–PIECES ACCESSOIRES	3.6	3.6	3.8	4.2	4.5	4.3	4.1
5 TRANSPORT–TRANSPORT	12.4	11.6	10.2	10.8	12.0	12.5	11.4
51 PASSENGER CARS–AUTOMOBILES	6.4	6.5	5.7	6.3	6.2	6.2	5.5
52 OTHER–AUTRES	3.5	2.7	2.0	2.1	3.3	3.4	2.9
521 INDUSTRIAL–INDUSTRIELS	3.2	2.3	1.6	1.8	3.0	3.1	2.6
522 NON INDUSTRIAL–NON INDUSTRIEL	0.4	0.4	0.4	0.4	0.3	0.3	0.3
53 PARTS–PIECES ACCESSOIRES	2.4	2.5	2.5	2.4	2.5	2.9	3.0
6 CONSUM GOODS–BIENS CONSOMMATION	24.2	24.8	26.0	25.6	24.6	24.9	24.9
61 DURABLE–DURABLES	8.6	8.3	8.3	8.2	7.4	7.7	7.9
62 SEMI DURABLE–SEMI DURABLES	11.5	11.9	12.3	11.9	11.4	11.2	10.7
63 NON DURABLE–NON DURABLES	4.2	4.6	5.4	5.5	5.9	6.0	6.2
7 GOODS NES–BIENS NDA	0.4	0.4	0.4	0.3	0.3	0.2	0.2

EXPORTS – EXPORTATIONS

	1991	1992	1993	1994	1995	1996	1997
TOTAL EXPORTS–EXPORTATIONS TOTALES	100.	100.	100.	100.	100.	100.	100.
1 AGRICULTURE	0.5	0.5	0.4	0.4	0.4	0.4	0.4
2 MINING QUARRY–INDUS EXTRACTIVES	4.3	3.8	4.4	3.4	2.3	2.4	1.9
3 MANUFACTURING–IND MANUFACTUR	95.3	95.7	95.1	96.2	97.2	97.1	97.6
31 FOOD BEV TOBACCO–ALIM BOISS TAB	2.8	2.9	2.9	3.0	3.0	2.9	2.8
32 TEXTILES–INDUSTRIES TEXTILES	5.3	5.0	4.7	4.5	4.1	3.8	3.6
33 WOOD & PRODUCTS–BOIS & PRODUITS	0.4	0.4	0.4	0.4	0.4	0.4	0.4
34 PAPER & PRODUCTS–PAPIER & PRODT	2.5	2.5	2.3	2.5	2.7	2.5	2.6
35 CHEMICALS–INDUSTRIES CHIMIQUES	24.1	25.4	26.4	27.1	27.6	28.6	29.3
36 NON METAL MIN–MIN NON METAL	0.9	0.9	1.0	1.0	1.0	1.0	1.0
37 BASIC METAL–IND METAL BASE	3.7	3.6	3.2	3.5	3.4	3.2	3.9
38 METAL MANUF–MANUF METAL	50.2	49.5	48.1	48.7	50.4	50.5	49.4
39 OTH MANUF IND–AUTRES MANUF	5.2	5.4	6.1	5.5	4.6	4.3	4.6

3. TRADE BY PRINCIPAL COUNTRIES OF CONSIGNMENT AND DESTINATION (VALUE IN MILLION U.S. DOLLARS)
ECHANGES SELON LES PRINCIPAUX PAYS DE CONSIGNATION ET DE DESTINATION (VALEUR EN MILLIONS DE DOLLARS EU)

COUNTRIES–PAYS	SPECIAL IMPORTS C.I.F. IMPORTATIONS SPECIALES C.A.F				
	1993	1994	1995	1996	1997
World	60828.2	67997.4	80152.0	79264.4	75900.4
Africa	803.3	831.8	1035.2	1331.3	1126.3
Americas	4918.7	5458.3	6340.1	6881.7	7429.4
– Northern America	4314.0	4719.3	5456.2	6028.1	6657.2
– LAIA	386.3	504.2	674.3	574.3	521.3
– CACM	68.6	61.8	107.7	81.7	80.9
– Caribbean	33.9	61.4	53.2	91.4	127.3
– Rest of America	115.8	111.6	48.6	106.2	42.7
Asia excl fmr USSR	5990.3	6342.6	7043.6	6758.9	6798.2
– Middle East	495.6	605.0	654.8	724.5	818.8
Asia former USSR	10.4	15.1	11.3	14.2	12.7
Europe excl fmr USSR	48712.8	54701.7	65115.6	63765.9	59567.5
– European Union	47950.2	53876.7	63963.0	62640.8	58483.0
– Eastern Europe	376.4	466.1	707.0	718.9	724.1
– Rest of Europe	386.2	358.9	445.5	406.2	360.3
Europe former USSR	270.5	392.8	463.8	344.0	788.8
Oceania	122.1	137.8	142.4	168.5	177.5
Other	0.0	117.4	0.0	0.0	
Germany/Allemagne	19805.1	22273.6	27023.3	24886.7	22948.7
France, Monaco	6645.2	7466.5	9129.8	9155.8	8336.8
Italy/Italie	5948.5	6706.0	8121.1	8507.8	7455.3
USA/Etats–Unis d'Amer	3923.2	4498.0	5130.4	5686.9	6345.6
United Kingdom	4393.1	4501.3	4447.6	5090.6	4921.1
Netherlands/Pays–Bas	2743.6	3174.0	3680.3	3753.1	3949.2
Austria/Autriche	2473.5	2786.9	3388.9	3145.7	2862.8
Belgium–Luxembourg	2178.6	2564.8	2842.0	2797.0	2795.4
Japan/Japon	2349.4	2298.5	2532.2	2138.4	2121.8
Sweden/Suède	952.3	1155.1	1448.0	1279.9	1124.7
Spain/Espagne	837.6	963.9	1157.0	1307.0	1231.9
China/Chine	733.7	840.3	912.3	987.4	1077.1
Ireland/Irlande	527.1	651.4	725.8	895.1	1275.2
Denmark/Danemark	678.2	756.6	900.0	833.6	732.8
China, Hong Kong SAR	542.9	492.9	545.0	506.0	487.2
Other Asia n.e.s.	436.4	435.1	498.9	527.5	468.0
Finland/Finlande	370.3	445.6	550.5	475.6	427.6
Russian Federation	254.6	365.3	430.7	305.8	735.4
Thailand/Thaïlande	350.7	377.7	406.7	452.3	386.1
Portugal	313.1	342.1	441.8	420.0	340.9
Korea, Republic of	217.0	247.4	319.5	311.8	333.9
Canada	198.4	221.3	325.1	338.7	296.1
India/Inde	214.5	243.0	285.9	301.0	310.8
Libyan Arab Jamahiriya	200.7	243.0	298.0	332.4	205.2
Israel/Israël	201.4	263.8	290.6	223.5	216.3
So. African Customs Un	184.1	159.4	244.9	296.2	273.0
Saudi Arabia	186.3	185.5	235.5	217.0	326.4
Brazil/Brésil	182.6	232.2	249.8	232.3	236.6
Norway,Svalbard and JM	233.5	192.8	234.2	204.5	166.5
Turkey/Turquie	145.5	186.6	214.1	225.2	220.4
Nigeria/Nigéria	76.9	122.0	181.2	257.6	310.0
Czech Republic	107.4	143.9	212.0	219.6	229.4
Hungary/Hongrie	139.7	147.3	188.2	202.3	230.9
Singapore/Singapour	154.3	183.7	167.9	182.8	128.0
Malaysia/Malaisie	83.0	101.2	154.4	116.6	122.8
Poland/Pologne	72.0	90.4	142.5	128.6	128.1
Algeria/Algérie	112.2	80.8	54.9	165.4	143.5
Lebanon/Liban	58.6	98.9	80.0	155.8	121.1
Indonesia/Indonésie	66.6	83.4	98.7	106.5	123.9
Australia/Australie	79.7	90.1	83.5	99.7	107.0

COUNTRIES–PAYS	SPECIAL EXPORTS F.O.B. EXPORTATIONS SPECIALES F.O.B.				
	1993	1994	1995	1996	1997
Monde	63184.6	70360.1	81641.2	80842.8	76150.0
Afrique	1213.4	1258.9	1484.5	1439.0	1211.0
Amériques	7892.1	8693.5	9777.2	10446.2	10795.4
– Amérique du Nord	6139.1	6741.4	7722.7	8261.4	8561.8
– ALAI	1427.5	1638.0	1773.9	1899.2	1963.7
– MCAC	88.9	80.6	86.2	79.2	73.4
– Caraïbes	91.4	99.6	87.2	91.5	89.2
– Autre Amérique	145.3	133.9	107.2	114.9	107.4
Asie anc. URSS exclus	12068.6	13023.4	15703.1	15906.5	14730.3
– Moyen–Orient	2766.2	2234.1	2979.0	2971.2	3047.9
Asie ancienne URSS	41.5	69.2	57.3	60.7	45.8
Europe anc. URSS exclus	41056.9	44474.7	53256.9	51677.5	48022.9
– Union Européenne	39457.1	42662.4	50896.3	49146.0	45522.3
– Europe de l'Est	1011.7	1152.7	1576.3	1620.5	1644.1
– Autre de l'Europe	588.1	659.6	784.3	911.1	856.6
Europe ancienne URSS	311.4	414.4	459.0	497.8	585.1
Océanie	600.3	719.2	903.1	814.8	759.4
Autre	0.3	1706.9	0.0	0.1	
Germany/Allemagne	14494.7	16157.7	19437.6	18314.6	17031.7
USA/Etats–Unis d'Amer	5640.4	6265.3	7073.6	7593.2	7993.4
France, Monaco	5759.4	6192.7	7776.2	7577.6	6915.1
Italy/Italie	4914.0	5127.2	6192.6	6075.3	5684.6
United Kingdom	4341.1	4566.9	4972.1	5090.7	4415.2
Japan/Japon	2181.6	2657.2	3262.1	3369.4	3067.9
Austria/Autriche	2405.2	2484.4	2908.9	2481.6	2333.3
China, Hong Kong SAR	1980.7	2251.4	2411.7	2211.4	2205.4
Netherlands/Pays–Bas	1732.8	1838.0	2196.3	2113.3	1994.3
Belgium–Luxembourg	1589.7	1715.0	1828.2	1911.9	1802.8
Spain/Espagne	1269.2	1368.2	1729.2	1815.9	1874.0
Sweden/Suède	867.5	972.1	1130.6	1161.4	995.9
Singapore/Singapour	888.0	890.8	1077.5	1185.4	1049.6
Israel/Israël	797.7	846.3	822.1	1012.6	935.5
Saudi Arabia	1010.1	791.0	1008.3	738.8	742.3
Denmark/Danemark	665.1	717.3	963.5	824.5	706.4
Turkey/Turquie	583.9	405.7	803.4	939.0	1005.9
Korea, Republic of	417.4	657.6	826.9	951.9	808.8
Other Asia n.e.s.	646.1	707.3	795.5	763.0	748.3
China/Chine	638.4	627.7	715.4	728.0	646.7
Thailand/Thaïlande	536.7	652.1	743.3	734.1	621.3
Australia/Australie	503.0	605.5	762.6	684.4	621.0
Brazil/Brésil	369.8	493.5	682.2	744.9	745.2
Canada	469.0	468.5	644.4	664.0	558.7
Portugal	454.0	461.0	575.1	572.6	528.5
So. African Customs Un	424.7	485.1	600.7	581.7	395.6
Finland/Finlande	363.9	385.3	492.3	502.9	499.2
Greece/Grèce	396.5	403.6	475.0	465.6	475.4
Poland/Pologne	271.7	320.4	474.3	540.9	577.7
India/Inde	274.2	388.5	559.5	546.4	407.6
Malaysia/Malaisie	251.8	359.9	545.6	443.8	432.8
Norway,Svalbard and JM	343.7	349.0	419.8	456.0	371.7
Mexico/Mexique	365.9	395.6	328.3	368.1	437.2
United Arab Emirates	311.4	355.8	368.4	422.3	420.4
Czech Republic	269.6	298.7	408.4	447.5	424.9
Special Categories		1706.6			
Russian Federation	221.6	307.5	309.6	351.8	408.8
Indonesia/Indonésie	253.4	289.6	386.1	356.5	262.8
Hungary/Hongrie	278.3	298.5	319.4	301.1	312.9
Ireland/Irlande	203.8	272.9	218.9	238.1	265.8

(VALUE AS PERCENTAGE OF WORLD TOTAL)(VALEURS EN POURCENTAGE DU TOTAL MONDIAL)

	1988	1989	1990	1991	1992	1993	1994	1995	1996	1997
Africa	1.9	1.8	1.7	1.6	1.1	1.3	1.2	1.3	1.7	1.5
Americas	8.2	9.0	8.5	9.7	8.6	8.1	8.0	7.9	8.7	9.8
– Northern America	7.0	7.8	7.4	8.6	7.5	7.1	6.9	6.8	7.6	8.8
– LAIA	0.9	0.8	0.8	0.8	0.7	0.6	0.7	0.8	0.7	0.7
– CACM	0.1	0.1	0.1	0.1	0.1	0.1	0.1	0.1	0.1	0.1
– Caribbean	0.0	0.1	0.0	0.1	0.1	0.1	0.1	0.1	0.1	0.2
– Rest of America	0.2	0.2	0.2	0.1	0.2	0.2	0.2	0.1	0.1	0.1
Asia excl fmr USSR	9.9	9.5	9.5	9.8	9.8	9.8	9.3	8.8	8.5	9.0
– Middle East	0.9	0.7	1.1	1.1	0.7	0.8	0.9	0.8	0.9	1.1
Asia former USSR					0.0	0.0	0.0	0.0	0.0	0.0
Europe excl fmr USSR	79.5	79.1	79.6	77.9	79.8	80.1	80.4	81.2	80.4	78.5
– European Union	77.8	77.3	78.1	76.6	78.4	78.8	79.2	79.8	79.0	77.1
– Eastern Europe	0.8	0.8	0.7	0.6	0.6	0.6	0.7	0.9	0.9	1.0
– Rest of Europe	0.8	0.9	0.9	0.8	0.8	0.6	0.5	0.6	0.5	0.5
Europe former USSR	0.4	0.4	0.4	0.8	0.4	0.4	0.6	0.6	0.4	1.0
Oceania	0.2	0.2	0.2	0.2	0.2	0.2	0.2	0.2	0.2	0.2
Other	0.0			0.0	0.1	0.0	0.2	0.0	0.0	
Germany/Allemagne				32.8	33.4	32.6	32.8	33.7	31.4	30.2
France, Monaco	10.6	10.9	11.1	10.9	10.8	10.9	11.0	11.4	11.6	11.0
Italy/Italie	10.1	10.2	10.5	10.0	10.0	9.8	9.9	10.1	10.7	9.8
USA/Etats–Unis d'Amer	5.5	6.4	6.1	7.3	6.4	6.4	6.6	6.4	7.2	8.4
United Kingdom	5.7	5.6	5.3	5.5	5.8	7.2	6.6	5.5	6.4	6.5
Netherlands/Pays–Bas	4.2	4.1	4.1	4.1	4.4	4.5	4.7	4.6	4.7	5.2
Austria/Autriche	3.9	3.8	3.9	3.8	3.9	4.1	4.1	4.2	4.0	3.8
Belgium–Luxembourg	3.4	3.5	3.6	3.5	3.8	3.6	3.8	3.5	3.5	3.7
Japan/Japon	5.0	4.5	4.4	4.3	4.3	3.9	3.4	3.2	2.7	2.8
Sweden/Suède	2.1	2.0	1.9	1.8	1.7	1.6	1.7	1.8	1.6	1.5

	1988	1989	1990	1991	1992	1993	1994	1995	1996	1997
Afrique	2.4	2.1	2.1	2.1	1.8	1.9	1.8	1.8	1.8	1.6
Amériques	12.6	12.5	11.2	11.7	11.9	12.5	12.4	12.0	12.9	14.2
– Amérique du Nord	9.7	9.8	8.8	9.1	9.1	9.7	9.6	9.5	10.2	11.2
– ALAI	2.4	2.2	2.0	2.2	2.3	2.3	2.3	2.2	2.3	2.6
– MCAC	0.1	0.1	0.1	0.1	0.1	0.1	0.1	0.1	0.1	0.1
– Caraïbes	0.2	0.2	0.2	0.2	0.2	0.1	0.1	0.1	0.1	0.1
– Autre Amérique	0.2	0.2	0.2	0.2	0.2	0.2	0.2	0.1	0.1	0.1
Asie anc. URSS exclus	17.1	17.2	17.8	17.3	17.0	19.1	18.5	19.2	19.7	19.3
– Moyen–Orient	4.0	3.5	3.5	3.6	3.9	4.4	3.2	3.6	3.7	4.0
Asie ancienne URSS					0.0	0.1	0.1	0.1	0.1	0.1
Europe anc. URSS exclus	65.9	66.1	66.8	67.3	65.6	65.0	63.2	65.2	63.9	63.1
– Union Européenne	62.3	62.7	63.9	64.7	63.2	62.4	60.6	62.3	60.8	59.8
– Europe de l'Est	2.3	2.1	1.6	1.5	1.5	1.6	1.6	1.9	2.0	2.2
– Autre de l'Europe	1.4	1.3	1.2	1.1	0.9	0.9	0.9	1.0	1.1	1.1
Europe ancienne URSS	1.1	1.1	1.2	0.7	0.4	0.5	0.6	0.6	0.6	0.8
Océanie	0.9	1.0	1.0	0.9	0.9	1.0	1.0	1.1	1.0	1.0
Autre	0.0	0.0	0.0	0.0	2.3	0.0	2.4	0.0	0.0	
Germany/Allemagne				23.8	22.9	22.9	23.0	23.8	22.7	22.4
USA/Etats–Unis d'Amer	8.6	8.9	8.0	8.2	8.3	8.9	8.9	8.7	9.4	10.5
France, Monaco	9.4	9.8	9.9	9.6	9.2	9.1	8.8	9.5	9.4	9.1
Italy/Italie	8.3	8.5	8.9	8.7	8.6	7.8	7.3	7.6	7.5	7.5
United Kingdom	7.9	8.2	7.4	6.6	6.4	6.9	6.5	6.1	6.3	5.8
Japan/Japon	4.3	4.2	4.8	4.3	3.6	3.5	3.8	4.0	4.2	4.0
Austria/Autriche	3.6	3.5	3.7	3.8	3.6	3.8	3.5	3.6	3.1	3.1
China, Hong Kong SAR	2.3	2.6	2.6	2.6	2.7	3.1	3.2	3.0	2.7	2.9
Netherlands/Pays–Bas	2.8	2.7	2.7	2.7	2.7	2.7	2.6	2.7	2.6	2.6
Belgium–Luxembourg	2.2	2.3	2.3	2.4	2.7	2.5	2.4	2.2	2.4	2.4

4. Special Imports C.I.F. by Commodities according to the S.I.T.C. (Rev. 2) in million U.S. Dollars
Importations Spéciales C.A.F. par Produits d'après la C.T.C.I. (Rév. 2) en millions de Dollars E.U.

SITC CTCI	COMMODITY	1994		1995		1996		1997		PRODUIT
		QUANTITY QUANTITE	VALUE VALEUR	QUANTITY QUANTITE	VALUE VALEUR	QUANTITY QUANTITE	VALUE VALEUR	QUANTITY QUANTITE	VALUE VALEUR	
	ALL COMMODITIES		67997.4		80152.1		79264.5		75900.4	TOUS PRODUITS
0	FOOD AND LIVE ANIMALS		3674.7		3974.9		3961.4		3589.6	ALIMENTS,ANIMAUX VIVANTS
01	MEAT AND PREPARATIONS		408.4		425.6		478.4		436.1	VIANDES ET PREPARATIONS
011	MEAT FRESH,CHILLD,FROZEN	W 71240	326.5	W 67996	337.1	W 81270	384.2	W 80517	351.2	VIANDES FRAICHES,REF,CONGE
02	DAIRY PRODCTS,BIRDS'EGGS		270.0		306.9		320.6		278.6	PRODUITS LAITIERS,OEUFS
03	FISH AND PREPARATIONS		371.8		406.0		390.8		351.7	POISSONS ET PREPARATIONS
04	CEREALS AND PREPARATIONS		325.7		372.1		362.8		329.3	CEREALES ET PRODUITS
048	CEREAL ETC PREPARATIONS	W 142829	218.0	W 139648	229.6	W 154970	237.2	W 152857	214.8	PREPTNS A BASE CEREALES
05	VEGETABLES AND FRUIT		1291.4		1320.0		1286.5		1147.8	LEGUMES ET FRUITS
054	VEG ETC FRSH,SMPLY PRSVD	W 310593	406.6	W 338240	436.6	W 286068	418.5	W 286170	355.2	LEGUMES FRAIS,CONG,SECS
0545	OTHER FRESH VEGETABLES	W 159488	250.0	W 168145	269.1	W 155357	273.3	W 155359	233.3	AUTRES LEGUMES FRAIS,REF
05459	FRESH VEGETABLES NES	W 148146	234.7	W 152989	249.5	W 144427	256.4	W 145955	219.1	LEGUMES FRAIS,REFRI NDA
057	FRUIT,NUTS,FRESH,DRIED	W 457543	639.2	W 441354	617.6	W 427841	609.6	W 421048	568.8	FRUITS FRAIS OU SECS
0579	FRUIT FRESH OR DRIED NES	W 146657	225.4	W 142022	232.8	W 138962	213.8	W 135245	195.6	FRUITS FRAIS,SECS NDA
07	COFFEE,TEA,COCOA,SPICES		371.7		456.3		414.6		410.4	CAFE,THE,CACAO,EPICES
081	*FEEDING STUFF FOR ANIML	W 439413	242.4	W 415832	241.0	W 476498	251.7	W 519270	233.2	NOURRITURE POUR ANIMAUX
09	MISC EDIBLE PRODUCTS		233.7		265.6		280.5		254.7	PREP ALIMENTAIRES DIVERSES
098	EDIBLE PRODCTS,PREPS NES	W 53920	229.9	W 59195	260.6	W 64794	275.5	W 67232	249.1	PREP ALIMENTAIRES NDA
1	BEVERAGES AND TOBACCO		865.2		1007.4		1085.8		995.0	BOISSONS ET TABACS
11	BEVERAGES		663.0		817.0		854.1		789.7	BOISSONS
112	ALCOHOLIC BEVERAGES	W 254337	581.5	W 264844	712.5	W 265211	738.9	W 269352	699.2	BOISSONS ALCOOLIQUES
1121	WINE OF FRESH GRAPES ETC	W 176295	458.5	W 188695	573.1	W 185890	611.5	W 186631	585.1	VINS DE RAISINS FRAIS
11212	WINE OF FRESH GRAPES	W 174634	456.6	W 187372	571.0	W 184773	609.3	W 184624	583.0	VINS DE MOUTS DE RAISINS
2	CRUDE MATERLS,EXCL FUELS		1717.7		2016.3		1767.3		1632.9	MAT BRUTES NON COMESTIBLES
24	CORK AND WOOD		307.3		357.6		293.5		252.3	LIEGE ET BOIS
248	WOOD SHAPED,SLEEPERS	W 335943	243.6	W 346103	281.3	W 303962	231.3	W 283827	197.5	BOIS SIMPLEMENT TRAVAILLES
251	*PULP AND WASTE PAPER	W 599017	247.8	W 612448	393.4	W 598539	255.4	W 674773	237.5	PATES A PAPIER,DECHETS
2517	SODA,SULPHATE WOOD PULP	W 350198	186.7	W 348756	296.7	W 357478	202.2	W 375568	195.5	PATES CHIMIQUES AU SULFATE
25172	— BLEACHED,NONDISSOLVNG	W 325527	174.9	W 323288	277.3	W 337961	191.1	W 349785	182.8	PATES BLANCHIES
27	CRUDE FERTLZR,MINRLS NES		280.5		304.1		283.1		262.8	ENGRAIS MINERAUX BRUTS
29	CRUDE ANIMAL,VEG MAT NES		493.7		565.7		560.2		496.4	MATIERES BRUTES ANIM,VEGET
292	CRUDE VEG MATERIALS NES	W 99126	434.7	W 108024	501.6	W 109382	499.3	W 114178	442.8	MAT BRUTES VEGETALES NDA
3	MINERAL FUELS ETC		2310.9		2349.2		2837.6		3446.8	COMBUSTIBLES MINERAUX LUB
33	PETROLEUM AND PRODUCTS		1939.0		1909.6		2390.3		3021.2	PETROLE ET DERIVES
333	CRUDE PETROLEUM	W 4766577	607.6	W 4544005	641.2	W 5290311	886.1	W 4832714	736.1	HUILES BRUTES DE PETROLE
334	PETROLEUM PRODUCTS,REFIN	W 6941008	1279.3	W 6326300	1207.1	W 6320385	1446.3	MW 10119	2236.2	PRODUITS RAFFINES
3341	GASOLINE,OTH LIGHT OILS	W 2614010	494.7	W 2586671	503.2	W 2631092	586.8	W 4888860	1112.1	ESSENCES POUR MOTEURS
33411	MOTOR,AVIATION SPIRIT	W 2571023	483.9	W 2561187	495.3	W 2609086	579.3	W 3703150	843.1	ESSENCES MOTEURS D'AVIONS
33412	SPIRIT TYPE JET FUEL	W 26100	5.1	W 12602	2.6	W 10131	2.5	W 1173571	264.0	CARBUREACTEURS
3343	GAS OILS	W 4125787	684.3	W 3514166	591.2	W 3564432	763.5	W 4991723	1018.8	GAS OILS
341	*GAS,NATURAL AND MANUFCT	W 1853166	337.1	W 1959193	398.0	W 2176852	414.0	W 2094204	400.4	GAZ NATUREL,GAZ MANUFACT
3414	PETROLEUM GASES, GASEOUS	W 1821310	328.3	W 1925201	387.8	W 2146562	404.2	W 2062334	390.8	GAZ DE PETROLE GAZEUX
5	CHEMCLS,RELATED PROD NES		9513.2		11407.1		11418.9		11862.0	PRODUITS CHIMIQUES
51	ORGANIC CHEMICALS		2483.3		2938.4		3267.4		3383.2	PROD CHIMIQ ORGANIQUES
512	ALCOHOLS,PHENOLS ETC	W 199178	234.3	W 189445	278.1	W 196514	256.4	W 220275	258.9	PHENOLS,PHENOLS–ALCOOLS
513	CARBOXYLIC ACIDS ETC	W 211977	338.9	W 222696	473.8	W 206394	503.0	W 222271	383.4	ACIDES CARBOXYLIQUES
514	NITROGEN–FNCTN COMPOUNDS	W 161571	841.7	W 148162	928.7	W 155176	1147.2	W 179926	1370.4	COMPOSES FONCT AZOTEES
5145	AMINE–FUNCTION COMPOUNDS	W 96283	184.8	W 83863	197.5	W 85326	238.2	W 97009	211.2	COMPOSES FONCTION AMINE
5148	OTH NITROGN–FNCTN CMPNDS	W 34803	347.4	W 34810	493.7	W 36704	617.8	W 45516	798.9	AUTRES COMPOSES AZOTES
51482	IMIDE–,IMIDE–FNCT CMPNDS	W 18262	227.2	W 18858	345.0	W 19043	468.6	W 27410	648.4	COMPOSES A FONCTION IMIDE
515	ORG–INORG COMPOUNDS ETC	W 52185	548.1	W 53645	620.9	W 54634	734.6	W 62659	775.6	COMPOSES ORGANO–MINERAUX
5156	HETEROCYCLIC CMPDS ETC	W 43618	442.0	W 44681	502.5	W 44876	586.3	W 53218	664.8	COMPOSES HETEROCYCLIQUES
51569	OTH HETEROCYC CMPDS,ETC	W 10800	365.0	W 10966	392.0	W 12592	509.0	W 14718	571.8	AUT COMP HETEROCYCLIQUES
516	OTHER ORGANIC CHEMICALS	W 228736	424.3	W 217840	519.2	W 230766	529.8	W 258843	504.2	AUTRES PROD ORGANIQUES
5162	ALDEHYDE ETC FNCT CMPNDS	W 77666	194.8	W 87733	253.1	W 91027	244.4	W 104350	225.8	COMP FONCTION ALDEHYDE
52	INORGANIC CHEMICALS		293.4		346.3		387.7		359.8	PROD CHIM INORGANIQUES
53	DYES,TANNING,COLOUR PROD		965.3		1119.1		1036.8		1070.7	PROD TEINTURE,COLORANTS
531	SYNT DYE,NAT INDGO,LAKES	W 32708	593.4	W 30301	697.0	W 31673	641.0	W 42661	720.1	MAT COLOR ORGAN,LAQUES
5311	SYNTHIC ORGNIC DYESTUFFS	W 28611	567.0	W 27968	671.8	W 29356	611.3	W 39211	685.9	MAT COLOR ORGAN SYNTHET
533	PIGMENTS,PAINTS,ETC	W 308523	367.6	W 313116	418.3	W 266201	390.9	W 254918	344.7	PIGMENTS,PEINTURES,VERNIS
541	*MEDICINAL,PHARM PRODUCT	MK 26738	2415.0	MK 29077	2862.4	MK 31634	2877.2	MK 34480	3517.1	PROD MEDICINAUX PHARMACEUT
5415	HORMONES,NAT,SYN IN BULK	K 29879	118.8	K 92392	99.2	K 100647	125.5	K 129524	294.0	HORMONES
54159	OTHR HORMONES,DERIVS,ETC	K 22122	96.8	K 83336	72.6	K 92903	100.9	K 108942	267.0	AUTRES HORMONES
5416	GLYCOSIDES,GLANDS,SERA	K 1167308	606.7	K 1600653	499.4	K 1945872	374.4	K 1998872	519.1	HETEROSIDES
54164	ANTISERA,MICROB VACCINES	K 804109	570.6	K 1043656	455.5	K 1490758	343.5	K 1502551	489.0	SERUMS,VACCINS
5417	MEDICAMENTS	MK 18367	1386.3	MK 20284	1929.9	MK 22839	1996.1	MK 24559	2294.4	MEDICAMENTS
54171	— CONTAINNG ANTIBIOTICS	K 1464729	204.4	K 1470882	285.8	K 1381982	259.5	K 1254749	209.1	MED CONTN ANTIBIOTIQUES
54179	— CONTNG OTH SUBSTANCES	MK 15875	1100.3	MK 17863	1503.2	MK 20487	1592.4	MK 22256	1867.4	MED CONT AUT SUBSTANCES
55	PERFUME,CLEANING ETC PRD		814.9		948.7		905.7		813.3	PROD POUR PARFUM,TOILETTE
553	PERFUMERY,COSMETICS,ETC	W 30987	509.3	W 35456	593.3	W 37917	571.3	W 45429	488.8	PRODUITS DE PARFUMERIE
58	PLASTIC MATERIALS ETC		1684.2		2131.4		1858.8		1734.5	MAT PLAST ARTIFICIELLES
582	PROD OF CONDENSATION ETC	W 222523	512.9	W 237399	686.1	W 233736	602.4	W 265642	560.9	PROD CONDENS,POLYCOND
5823	ALKYDS,OTHER POLYESTERS	W 93188	246.6	W 101455	334.0	W 99332	279.0	W 123336	258.5	ALKYDES ET AUT POLYESTERS
583	POLYMERIZATION ETC PRODS	W 683736	1122.1	W 666914	1387.7	W 650699	1201.2	W 718494	1121.3	PROD POLYMERISATION
5831	POLYETHYLENE	W 247399	242.5	W 232029	310.7	W 212280	247.8	W 233807	254.6	POLYETHYLENE
5839	OTH POLYMRZTION ETC PROD	W 80595	309.4	W 89249	379.4	W 90769	350.9	W 101782	313.2	AUT PROD POLYMER COPOLYM
59	CHEMICAL MATERIALS NES		780.0		965.3		998.2		911.1	MAT PROD CHIMIQUES NDA
598	MISCEL CHEM PRODUCTS NES	W 703555	567.9	W 764573	705.5	W 725076	730.2	W 698499	636.8	PROD DIV INDUST CHIM NDA
5989	CHEM PRODUCTS,PREPS NES	W 669769	516.0	W 731521	644.4	W 692163	672.9	W 663311	583.1	PROD PREP CHIMIQUES NDA
59899	OTH CHEM PRODS,PREPS,NES	W 622375	404.2	W 686567	526.9	W 648638	561.1	W 615482	460.3	AUT PRODUITS CHIMIQUES NDA
6	BASIC MANUFACTURES		13658.4		15487.6		14710.6		14389.2	ART MANUFACTURES
62	RUBBER MANUFACTURES NES		543.3		641.7		608.1		524.1	CAOUTCHOUC MANUFACTURE
625	RUBBER TYRES, TUBES ETC	W 62638	331.1	W 66611	385.2	W 64793	375.0	W 64950	317.3	PNEUS CAOUTCHOUC VULCANISE
6251	TYRES NEW FOR MOTOR CARS	W 40634	235.9	W 42393	271.7	W 41731	264.4	W 43218	228.6	PNEUS POUR VOITURES
63	WOOD,CORK MANUFACTRS NES		609.1		750.3		703.5		614.2	OUVRAGES LIEGE ET BOIS
634	VENEERS,PLYWOOD,ETC	W 244232	228.6	W 264432	277.6	W 248237	238.1	W 256108	223.2	PLACAGES,CONTRE–PLAQUES
635	WOOD MANUFACTURES NES	W 156541	354.4	W 170797	442.1	W 166990	437.9	W 170751	366.4	ART MANUF EN BOIS NDA
6353	BUILDERS WOODWRK,PREFABS	W 90128	242.1	W 98765	308.3	W 95420	311.1	W 90857	248.7	OUVRAGES DE MENUISERIE
64	PAPER,PAPERBOARD AND MFR		1483.4		1829.2		1741.6		1553.8	PAPIERS,CARTONS & OUVRAGES
641	PAPER AND PAPERBOARD	W 916052	944.7	W 915102	1178.6	W 895364	1069.3	W 1018536	966.6	PAPIERS ET CARTONS
6412	PRINTG,WRITING PAPER NES	W 306636	315.6	W 289914	390.9	W 296245	352.5	W 372109	338.5	PAPIERS POUR L'IMPRESSION
64122	— COATED,IMPREGNATD ETC	W 258430	257.1	W 237757	308.0	W 238009	271.3	W 306272	266.3	PAPIERS IMPRESSION COUCHES
6418	COATED ETC PAPER NES BLK	W 110132	213.8	W 111355	249.0	W 110712	236.0	W 123467	223.4	PAP,CARTONS COUCHES,ENDUITS
642	PAPER,ETC,PRECUT,ARTS OF	W 212307	538.8	W 214347	650.6	W 229709	672.3	W 240316	587.3	PAP,CARTONS DECOUPES
6428	PAPER ETC ARTICLES NES	W 85340	218.6	W 85353	259.3	W 88993	260.8	W 93804	237.5	OUVRAGES EN PATE A PAPIER
65	TEXTILE YARN,FABRICS,ETC		1760.2		1938.0		1756.8		1547.5	FILS,TISSUS,ARTICLES TEXTILE
651	TEXTILE YARN	W 55360	366.8	W 56579	427.3	W 47314	355.6	W 49267	314.5	FILS TEXTILES
653	WOVN MAN–MADE FIB FABRIC	W 11483	205.5	W 10513	211.4	W 9617	182.3	W 10073	152.1	TISSUS FIBRES SYNTH,ARTIF
658	TEXTILE ARTICLES NES	W 16108	251.8	W 17280	296.4	W 17433	291.0	W 18220	269.7	ART FACONNES MAT TEXTILES
659	FLOOR COVERINGS,ETC	W 39027	303.3	W 37947	304.7	W 35962	280.1	W 34513	230.0	COUVRE–PARQUETS,TAPIS ETC
66	NONMETAL MINERAL MFS NES		3766.5		3294.6		3827.5		3772.4	ART MIN NON METALLIQUES

4. Special Imports C.I.F. by Commodities according to the S.I.T.C. (Rev. 2) in million U.S. Dollars
Importations Spéciales C.A.F. par Produits d'après la C.T.C.I. (Rév. 2) en millions de Dollars E.U.

SITC CTCI	COMMODITY	1994		1995		1996		1997		PRODUIT
		QUANTITY QUANTITE	VALUE VALEUR	QUANTITY QUANTITE	VALUE VALEUR	QUANTITY QUANTITE	VALUE VALEUR	QUANTITY QUANTITE	VALUE VALEUR	
663	MINERAL MANUFCTURES NES	W 513364	260.9	W 583963	324.3	W 626163	312.0	W 651594	285.8	ART MIN MANUF NDA
664	GLASS	W 156548	217.8	W 158879	268.3	W 163169	256.1	W 166300	231.5	VERRE
665	GLASSWARE	W 114682	279.6	W 106189	317.7	W 126623	318.5	W 149807	286.6	OUVRAGES EN VERRE
667	PEARL,PREC-,SEMI-P STONE		2538.9		1853.2		2436.6		2537.4	PERLES, PIERRES GEMMES
6672	DIAMONDS NONINDUST,UNSET		2070.2		1520.5		2051.5		2100.6	DIAMANTS BRUTS
66722	— SRTD,ROUGH,SIMPLY WKD		1362.8		912.0		1229.0		1223.8	DIAMANTS TRIES BRUTS
66729	— CUT ETC NOT SET		706.8		607.5		822.4		876.6	DIAMANTS TAILLES
6673	PREC-,SEMI-PR STONES NES		441.1		302.0		326.3		353.0	AUTRES PIERRES NON SERTIES
67	IRON AND STEEL		1755.3		2369.2		1790.2		1697.9	FER ET ACIER
673	IRON,STEEL SHAPES ETC	W 569721	378.4	W 646067	543.0	W 530046	414.1	W 600849	401.6	BARRES,PROFIL FER,ACIER
6732	IRON,STEEL BARS ETC	W 242340	178.4	W 311958	278.1	W 244515	214.4	W 269232	187.0	BARRES FER,ACIER
674	IRN,STL UNIV,PLATE,SHEET	W 936308	703.6	W 984352	977.9	W 765291	675.7	W 925303	659.2	LARGES PLATS,TOLES
6746	IRN,STL THIN PLATE,ROLLD	W 274178	243.2	W 301567	385.2	W 241553	258.0	W 279250	239.4	TOLES LAM MOINS 3MM
678	IRON,STL TUBES,PIPES,ETC	W 198662	360.0	W 188590	423.8	W 153854	350.1	W 178299	315.6	TUBES,TUYAUX EN FONTE,FER
68	NON-FERROUS METALS		1558.9		2014.2		1760.9		2404.2	METAUX NON FERREUX
681	SILVER,PLATINUM,ETC		451.6		548.3		536.0		1180.2	ARGENT ET PLATINE
6812	METALS OF PLATINUM GROUP		438.2		534.6		526.3		1170.4	PLATINE
68123	PLATINUM,ALLOYS UNWRGHT		279.2		382.4		345.7		696.4	PLATINE,ALLIAGES BRUTS
68124	OTH PLAT GRP METAL UNWRT		119.0		116.6		159.4		430.1	METAUX MINE PLAT ALL BRUTS
682	COPPER EXC CEMENT COPPER	W 109155	407.9	W 117313	551.4	W 107109	444.6	W 109251	421.8	CUIVRE
6822	COPPER,ALLOYS WORKED	W 101165	387.1	W 108830	522.8	W 99772	424.2	W 100163	397.7	CUIVRE,ALLIAGES OUVRES
68221	COPPER BARS,WIRE,ETC	W 61188	173.7	W 65391	245.2	W 61720	196.7	W 60177	179.0	BARRES,PROFILES ET FILS
684	ALUMINIUM	W 247713	579.9	W 249486	762.7	W 235111	650.9	W 270147	671.6	ALUMINIUM
6841	ALUMINIUM,ALLOYS,UNWRGHT	W 137164	211.4	W 130833	264.7	W 117406	203.6	W 143555	245.0	ALUMINIUM,ALLIAGES BRUTS
6842	ALUMINIUM,ALLOYS WORKED	W 110549	368.5	W 118652	498.0	W 117705	447.3	W 126592	426.7	ALUMINIUM,ALLIAGES OUVRE
69	METAL MANUFACTURES NES		2020.8		2494.6		2373.2		2140.3	ART MANUFACT EN METAL NDA
691	STRUCTURES AND PARTS NES	W 131303	389.0	W 143483	462.4	W 139921	447.8	W 137292	390.6	CONSTRUCT FER,ACIER,ALU
6911	STRUCTURES,PARTS IRN,STL	W 120568	284.2	W 132417	338.1	W 128146	327.3	W 125964	274.4	CONSTRUCT FER,ACIER,FONTE
694	STL,COPPR NAILS,NUTS,ETC	W 43451	202.5	W 52144	268.6	W 45653	235.3	W 47396	210.3	CLOUS,VIS,ECROUS
69402	IRN,STL NUTS,BOLTS,ETC	W 37954	180.9	W 46687	242.7	W 40692	211.6	W 42359	191.2	BOULONS,VIS,ECROUS FER,AC
695	TOOLS	W 14051	360.6	W 16407	499.2	W 16141	474.6	W 16190	424.0	OUTILS A MAIN
6954	BLADES,TIPS,ETC FR TOOLS	W 5659	223.0	W 6424	309.4	W 6603	294.1	W 7175	278.5	OUTILS POUR MACHINE-OUTIL
697	BASE MTL HOUSEHOLD EQUIP	W 32011	237.7	W 31288	266.8	W 31109	277.7	W 30783	245.2	ART MENAGE MET COMMUNS
699	BASE METAL MFRS NES	W 79094	612.0	W 82720	734.3	W 80039	693.9	W 82515	629.6	ART MANUFACTURES MET NDA
6991	LOCKSMITHS WARES,ETC	W 22775	215.5	W 24095	249.5	W 20802	214.2	W 22321	197.3	ARTICLES DE SERRURERIE
7	MACHINES,TRANSPORT EQUIP		20906.4		26770.2		26478.9		23912.3	MACHINES MATERIEL TRANSPORT
71	POWER GENERATING EQUIPMT		955.4		1099.0		1191.3		1222.6	MACHINES GENERATRICES
714	ENGINES AND MOTORS NES	W 2881	208.3	W 3379	233.2	W 5468	399.2	W 4558	495.4	MOTEURS NON ELECTRIQUES
7149	ENGINE & MOTOR PARTS NES	W 2718	166.3	W 2784	163.6	W 4934	212.2	W 4169	308.2	PIECES 714 ET 718.88
716	ROTATING ELECTRIC PLANT	W 22519	357.9	W 24204	434.4	W 22441	412.2	W 25500	386.2	APP ELECTR ROTATIFS,PIECES
7162	AC MTRS,GENRTRS,GEN SETS	W 14186	218.9	W 15700	274.7	W 14743	264.2	W 15781	251.0	MOTEURS ELECTRIQUES
71621	AC MTRS,INC UNIVRSL MTRS	W 12621	195.2	W 13820	245.1	W 12917	236.5	W 13772	223.7	MOT ELEC NON COUR CONTINU
72	MACHS FOR SPCL INDUSTRYS		1755.9		2342.0		2188.6		1881.1	MAC SPECIALES POUR INDUST
723	CIVIL ENGNEERG EQUIP ETC	W 21450	170.4	W 28230	241.0	W 23046	198.6	W 19089	137.5	APPAREILS DE GENIE CIVIL
724	TEXTILE,LEATHER MACHNRY	W 15866	243.7	W 21884	333.5	W 21219	307.9	W 25025	285.4	MACH POUR INDUSTRIE TEXTILE
726	PRINTG,BKBINDG MACHY,PTS	W 14063	229.6	W 17000	286.7	W 17479	319.4	W 18200	260.5	MACHINES POUR IMPRIMERIE
728	OTH MACHY FOR SPCL INDUS	W 39097	638.1	W 49711	910.7	W 44770	851.4	W 41497	713.4	AUT MACH IND PARTICULIERES
7284	MACHY FOR SPCL INDUS NES	W 21014	467.2	W 27124	674.5	W 25781	639.3	W 26274	565.3	MACH SPEC IND PARTICUL.
72848	OTH MCHY WITH INDIV FNCT	W 11477	262.4	W 13462	375.5	W 12399	339.8	W 12583	285.3	AUTRES MACHINES NDA
73	METALWORKING MACHINERY		471.4		777.1		768.2		626.5	MACH TRAVAIL DES METAUX
736	METALWORKING MACH-TOOLS	W 25363	395.7	W 35853	671.9	W 33728	650.7	W 33147	536.4	MACH-OUTILS TRAVAIL METAUX
74	GENRL INDUSTRL MACHY NES		2777.2		3626.8		3408.1		3021.8	MACH APP INDUSTRIE
741	HEATING,COOLING EQUIPMNT	W 33218	482.1	W 38752	627.4	W 37436	579.8	W 38775	521.2	MACH CHAUFFAGE,PIECES
7416	HEATING,COOLING EQU NES	W 15624	204.4	W 16544	262.2	W 15211	227.7	W 18097	231.1	APP CHANGEMENT TEMP
742	PUMPS FOR LIQUIDS ETC	W 9949	202.2	W 12848	269.9	W 10827	229.6	W 10013	189.9	POMPES MOTO-POMPES
743	PUMPS NES,CENTRFUGES ETC	W 23961	376.2	W 30210	514.5	W 28136	479.7	W 27283	414.2	POMPES COMPRES,VENT ETC
744	MECHANICAL HANDLING EQU	W 56420	474.9	W 65969	640.6	W 61470	581.5	W 59731	503.8	EQUIP MANUTENTION PIECES
7442	LIFTING,LOADING MACH NES	W 27045	235.4	W 32809	329.2	W 30119	297.0	W 30884	277.2	APP LEVAGE,MANUTENTION
745	NONELEC MACHY,TOOLS NES	W 17426	428.9	W 18963	513.2	W 18501	489.2	W 19322	455.2	AUT MACH NON ELEC,PIECES
7452	OTH NONELEC MCHS,PTS NES	W 16488	392.9	W 17896	470.1	W 17595	453.6	W 18393	423.0	AUT MACH NON ELEC,PIECES
749	NONELEC MACH PTS,ACC NES	W 46182	813.3	W 48805	1061.3	W 47450	1048.5	W 47124	937.7	PIECES MACH NON ELEC NDA
7492	COCKS,VALVES ETC NES	W 14999	345.4	W 15871	422.9	W 15294	402.7	W 16130	357.7	ART ROB,SIM POUR TUYAUX
7493	SHAFT,CRANK,PULLEY ETC	W 17016	194.5	W 18556	263.0	W 16910	251.3	W 17397	223.9	ARBRES TRANS,VILEBREQUINS
75	OFFICE MACHNES,ADP EQUIP		3309.8		3924.6		3885.7		3653.7	MACH BUREAU TRAIT AUTOM
751	OFFICE MACHINES	W 5118	212.6	W 5338	242.4	W 5441	226.8	W 5505	198.6	MACH,APPAREILS DE BUREAU
752	AUTOMTIC DATA PROC EQUIP	W 23177	2160.8	W 27404	2577.0	W 28213	2627.1	W 32426	2603.5	MACH TRAIT INFORMATION
7522	DIGITAL COMPUTERS	W 618	166.1	W 763	207.6	W 1032	291.0	W 936	288.8	MACH DIGITALES COMPLETES
7523	DIGITL CENTRL PROCESSORS	W 6562	976.0	W 7754	1127.7	W 7666	1094.3	W 10140	1148.9	UNITES CENTRALES
7524	DIGITL CENTRL STOR UNITS	W 1487	304.4	W 1573	385.7	W 1753	406.9	W 2003	401.5	UNITES MEMOIRE CENTRALES
7525	ADP PERIPHERAL UNITS	W 13840	590.6	W 16500	723.0	W 17110	688.1	W 18653	623.4	UNITES PERIPHERIQUES
759	OFFICE,ADP MCH PTS,ACCES	W 7653	936.5	W 8759	1105.3	W 9770	1032.0	W 10476	851.6	PIECES DU 751 ET 752
7599	ACCTG,ETC,ADP MCH PTS,AC	W 5649	832.0	W 6441	956.4	W 7430	919.0	W 7962	756.5	PIECES DU 751 ET 752
76	TELECOMM,SOUND EQUIPMENT		1510.8		1824.7		1896.1		1985.2	EQUIPMENT DE TELECOM
761	TELEVISION RECEIVERS	W 13393	237.0	W 13438	273.3	W 13298	266.8	W 13748	246.2	RECEPTEURS DE TELEVISION
7611	COLOUR TV RECEIVERS	W 13327	233.7	W 13380	270.3	W 13222	263.9	W 13700	244.2	RECEPTEURS COULEUR
764	TELECOM EQPT,PTS,ACC NES	W 10917	917.5	W 11740	1181.5	W 12525	1261.0	W 13116	1396.1	EQUIP TELECOM,PIECES
7641	LINE TELEPHONE,ETC EQUIP	W 1932	239.1	W 2854	417.6	W 3509	525.2	W 3648	543.2	APP TELEPHON PAR FIL
7643	TV,RADIO TRANSMITTRS ETC	W 838	177.2	W 655	195.6	W 714	223.5	W 1053	322.9	APP EMET TELE RADIO
7649	PTS NES OF EQUIPMT OF 76	W 3550	316.8	W 3478	331.8	W 3556	340.8	W 3767	383.1	PIECES DE LA DIV 76
76491	PTS NES OF APPAR OF 7641	W 652	132.5	W 887	186.3	W 859	203.1	W 1018	246.7	PIECES POUR 764.1
77	ELECTRIC MACHNRY NES ETC		3496.7		4332.3		4091.2		3833.7	MACH APP ELECT NDA
771	ELECTRIC POWER MACHY NES	W 12875	268.0	W 15727	370.1	W 16710	382.7	W 18643	375.3	MACH PROD,TRANS ELECTR
7712	OTH ELEC POWER MACHY NES	W 8577	206.6	W 10254	277.3	W 10878	286.7	W 11797	291.4	AUT APP PROD TRANSF ELEC
772	SWITCHGEAR ETC,PARTS NES	W 19784	908.2	W 22364	1144.9	W 22587	1102.1	W 25752	1074.7	APP COUPURE,SECT ETC
7721	SWITCHGEAR ETC	W 18798	808.9	W 21247	1020.9	W 21492	985.8	W 24390	957.3	APP COUPURE,SECTIONNMT
773	ELECTR DISTRIBUTNG EQUIP	W 26955	198.9	W 30862	261.4	W 30882	255.8	W 33182	245.7	EQUIPMT DISTRIBUTION ELECT
775	HOUSEHOLD TYPE EQUIP NES	W 57415	582.2	W 57658	656.1	W 57952	625.4	W 56454	544.4	MACH,APP USAGE DOMESTQUE
7758	ELECTRO-THERMIC APPL NES	W 22001	264.0	W 21718	294.1	W 21518	277.4	W 20890	240.2	APP ELECTROTHERMIQ NDA
776	TRANSISTORS,VALVES,ETC	W 1260	592.6	W 1504	771.4	W 1449	708.5	W 1463	680.6	LAMPES,TUBES,VALVES
7764	ELECTRONIC MICROCIRCUITS	W 488	429.5	W 599	571.9	W 615	533.4	W 709	535.3	MICROSTRUCTURES ELECTRON
778	ELECTRICAL MACHINERY NES	W 37061	780.6	W 38834	929.9	W 38559	824.5	W 39570	757.3	AUTRES MACH ELECT NDA
7788	OTH ELEC MACHY,EQUIP NES	W 7983	336.2	W 8500	422.9	W 7646	360.5	W 7787	337.7	AUT MACH APP ELEC NDA
78	ROAD VEHICLES		5846.8		6867.5		6630.6		5665.9	VEHICULES ROUTIERS
781	PASS MOTOR VEH EXC BUSES	W 332577	4276.3	W 331511	4974.7	W 345297	4923.8	W 338152	4142.2	AUTO TRANSPORT PERSONNES
782	LORRIES,SPCL MTR VEH NES	W 42122	492.0	W 50060	594.8	W 45243	518.0	W 45760	435.2	VEHICULES SPECIAUX,MARCH
7821	LORRIES,TRUCKS	W 39721	458.7	W 47314	557.5	W 42686	477.2	W 43892	407.0	VEHICULES TRANSP MARCHAND
784	MOTOR VEH PRTS,ACCES NES	W 43268	461.1	W 44785	547.2	W 44966	515.6	W 49951	489.2	PIECES 722,781,782,783
7849	OTHER MOTOR VEHCL PARTS	W 37437	436.7	W 38368	516.6	W 37820	485.3	W 42761	460.0	PIECES 722,781,782,783
785	CYCLES,ETC MOTRZD OR NOT	W 15504	328.5	W 15031	351.7	W 14782	348.2	W 14456	309.4	MOTOCYCLES SCOOTERS
79	OTHR TRANSPORT EQUIPMENT		782.8		1976.5		2419.3		2022.3	AUTRE MATERIEL TRANSPORT
791	RAILWAY VEHICLES	W 19841	101.7	W 18410	216.0	W 28276	335.2	W 21218	156.5	VEHIC MAT CHEMINS DE FER

4. Special Imports C.I.F. by Commodities according to the S.I.T.C. (Rev. 2) in million U.S. Dollars
Importations Spéciales C.A.F. par Produits d'après la C.T.C.I. (Rév. 2) en millions de Dollars E.U.

SITC CTCI	COMMODITY	1994 QUANTITY QUANTITE	1994 VALUE VALEUR	1995 QUANTITY QUANTITE	1995 VALUE VALEUR	1996 QUANTITY QUANTITE	1996 VALUE VALEUR	1997 QUANTITY QUANTITE	1997 VALUE VALEUR	PRODUIT
792	AIRCRAFT ETC	W 1575	614.3	W 2388	1694.7	W 2728	2018.0	W 3529	1814.7	APP NAVIGATION AERIENNE
7923	AIRCRFT NES2000–15000KG	W 263	162.2	W 322	235.0	W 321	349.0	W 218	155.8	AERODYNES 2000 A 15000 KG
7924	AIRCRFT NES OVER 15000KG	W 167	134.8	W 772	895.7	W 828	891.9	W 934	961.5	AERODYNES PLUS 15000 KG
7929	AIRCRAFT PARTS NES	W 1027	275.6	W 994	456.8	W 1313	714.7	W 2286	670.8	PIECES DU 792
8	MISC MANUFACTURED GOODS		14873.3		16688.7		16733.8		15718.6	ART MANUFACTURES DIVERS
812	*PLUMBG,HEATNG,LGHTNG EQ	W 33855	340.0	W 35920	410.1	W 36294	408.2	W 36486	358.7	APPAR SANITAIRES CHAUFFAGE
8124	LIGHTING EQUIPMENT NES	W 14737	233.7	W 16335	280.7	W 16386	282.9	W 16478	248.8	APPAREILS ECLAIRAGE ETC
821	*FURNITURE,PARTS THEREOF	W 289746	1575.6	W 308006	1875.7	W 305980	1825.7	W 320907	1573.2	MEUBLES ET PIECES
8211	CHAIRS,SEATS AND PARTS	W 53565	452.0	W 59268	537.6	W 56722	521.0	W 54926	442.8	SIEGES ET PIECES
82111	CHAIRS AND OTHER SEATS	W 48845	422.4	W 54470	501.2	W 52103	486.8	W 49991	410.7	SIEGES
8219	FURNITURE AND PARTS NES	W 224376	950.2	W 236592	1147.3	W 236577	1112.0	W 253137	963.3	AUTRES MEUBLES ET PIECES
82192	WOOD FURNITURE NES	W 152881	655.2	W 159852	781.5	W 155003	747.8	W 160326	630.2	MEUBLES NDA EN BOIS
831	*TRAVEL GOODS,HANDBAGS	W 12899	294.9	W 13696	332.1	W 12963	300.8	W 14297	277.0	ARTICLES DE VOYAGE ETC
84	CLOTHING AND ACCESSORIES		3470.6		3823.3		3733.2		3404.3	VETEMENTS
842	MENS OUTERWEAR NOT KNIT	W 16533	637.8	W 15524	668.4	W 16249	693.9	W 15639	618.1	VET DESSUS POUR HOMMES
8423	— TROUSERS,BREECHES ETC	W 9699	269.0	W 9111	286.3	W 9632	309.0	W 9208	272.7	PANTALONS HOMMES MAT TEX
843	WOMENS OUTERWEAR NONKNIT	W 15521	1060.1	W 15892	1203.8	W 16127	1117.4	W 16386	1000.9	VET DESSUS FEMMES MAT TEX
8431	— COATS AND JACKETS	W 2473	229.2	W 2581	263.2	W 2484	241.1	W 2585	215.7	MANT,VEST FEM MAT TEXTIL
8435	— BLOUSES	W 2789	213.6	W 2589	223.3	W 2532	191.7	W 2620	167.9	BLOUSES FEM MAT TEXTILES
8439	— OTHER OUTER GARMENTS	W 7600	396.6	W 7466	425.5	W 8019	423.5	W 8531	415.2	AUT VET DES FEM MAT TEXT
845	OUTERWEAR KNIT NONELASTC	W 23938	940.5	W 23158	1028.0	W 24209	1021.8	W 24817	951.0	VET DESSOUS,ACCES BONNET
8451	— JERSEYS,PULLOVERS ETC	W 15928	586.4	W 15026	622.3	W 16110	638.1	W 16479	607.7	CHANDAILS,PULL–OVERS ETC
8459	— OTHER,CLTHG ACCESRYS	W 6881	288.0	W 6842	320.8	W 6990	308.4	W 7271	280.2	AUT VET DESSUS DE BONNE
846	UNDER GARMENTS KNITTED	W 7028	300.2	W 7857	356.4	W 8025	354.9	W 8334	322.9	SOUS VETS DE BONNETERIE
848	HEADGEAR,NONTXTL CLOTHNG	W 6732	223.0	W 6617	224.5	W 6630	218.4	W 6782	206.0	VET ACCES MAT AUT QUE TEX
851	*FOOTWEAR	W 26182	669.2	W 26575	742.4	W 26273	721.8	W 26580	655.5	CHAUSSURES
85102	FOOTWEAR LEATHER	W 20579	591.1	W 20522	647.9	W 20060	630.0	W 20387	571.6	CHAUS SEMELLES EN CUIR
87	PRECISION INSTRUMNTS NES		1211.2		1451.7		1514.1		1371.4	INSTRUM,APPAR SCIENT NDA
872	MEDICAL INSTRUMENTS NES	W 3948	249.3	W 4086	294.0	W 4303	314.6	W 4461	297.0	INSTR,APP MEDIC–CHIR NDA
87202	OTH MEDICAL INSTRUMENTS	W 2988	215.5	W 3024	250.2	W 3142	267.3	W 3294	253.1	INSTRUM,APP MEDECINE
874	MEASURNG,CONTROLNG INSTR	W 8076	810.4	W 8895	983.3	W 8638	983.4	W 8697	862.6	INSTRUMENTS DE MESURE
88	PHOTO EQU,OPTICL GDS ETC		1139.2		1272.2		1228.5		1133.9	APP,FOURN PHOTO,OP,MONTR
882	PHOTO,CINEMA SUPPLIES	W 15877	259.0	W 15132	285.7	W 14973	267.2	W 15482	246.8	PRODUITS PHOTO,CINEMA
8822	PHOTO FILM EXC DEV CINMA	W 9262	216.4	W 8615	230.8	W 8703	219.8	W 9583	201.4	PLAQUES,PELLICULES,FILMS
885	WATCHES AND CLOCKS		578.0		630.9		607.9		552.1	HORLOGERIE
8851	WATCHES,MOVEMENTS,CASES		342.1		360.4		375.9		352.2	MONTRES,MOUVEMENTS,BOITES
8852	CLOCKS,CLOCK,WATCH PARTS		236.0		270.6		232.0		199.9	HORLOGES,MOUV,PARTIES
89	MISC MANUFCTRD GOODS NES		6172.9		6781.6		7002.0		6944.9	ART MANUFACTURES DIVERS
892	PRINTED MATTER	W 139980	1144.4	W 151039	1361.4	W 158103	1354.3	W 163376	1168.4	IMPRIMES
8921	PRINTED BOOKS,GLOBES,ETC	W 35849	449.8	W 34284	508.6	W 34621	496.9	W 33027	421.3	LIVRES,BROCHURES,CARTES
89211	PRINTED BOOKS,PAMPHLETS	W 34948	441.4	W 33386	498.9	W 33654	487.3	W 32151	413.4	LIVRES,BROCHURES
8922	NEWSPAPERS,PERIODICALS	W 48979	303.8	W 52982	377.4	W 49763	349.3	W 50811	299.8	JOURNAUX ET PERIODIQUES
8928	PRINTED MATTER NES	W 54000	365.6	W 62488	447.4	W 72591	480.7	W 78380	423.4	IMPRIMES NDA
89286	TRADE ADV MATRL,CATALOGS	W 44641	240.5	W 53285	311.3	W 62990	331.9	W 68231	293.4	IMPRIMES PUBLICITAIRES
893	ARTICLES OF PLASTIC NES		1078.6		1261.0		1176.0		1076.0	OUVRAGES EN MAT DIVIS 58
8931	PLSTC PACKG CONTNRS,LIDS	W 76953	313.4	W 74509	351.1	W 65607	297.9	W 74108	276.4	ART TRANSP EMBALLAGE ETC
8939	MISC PLASTIC ARTICLES	W 110040	731.3	W 113115	863.3	W 112952	831.5	W 119150	755.4	ART DIVERS EN MAT DIV 58
89399	OTHR PLASTC ARTICLES NES	W 99127	679.2	W 101770	802.4	W 101420	771.1	W 106769	702.5	AUT OUV MAT DIV 58
894	TOYS,SPORTING GOODS,ETC	W 38666	558.9	W 41278	667.9	W 41093	648.3	W 42419	613.8	VOITURES ENFANTS,JOUETS
8942	TOYS,INDOOR GAMES ETC	W 26218	356.3	W 27123	418.4	W 26294	379.5	W 28462	378.9	JOUETS,JEUX ETC
896	WORKS OF ART ETC		589.1		430.4		695.1		808.3	OBJETS D'ART
89601	HAND PAINTINGS ETC NES		342.7		270.3		508.6		603.6	TABLEAUX,PEINTURES
897	GOLD,SILVER WARE,JEWELRY		1598.2		1681.0		1694.2		1922.9	BIJOUTERIE,ORFEVRERIE
8973	PREC JEWLRY,GLD–SILVWARE		1522.6		1588.6		1616.5		1839.1	BIJOUX OR,ARGENT ORFEVRE
89731	PRECIOUS METAL JEWELLERY		1371.1		1412.7		1479.9		1735.1	ART BIJOUTERIE,JOAILLER
898	MUSICAL INSTRUMENTS,PTS	W 16224	721.4	W 16022	825.8	W 15708	873.2	W 16178	798.6	INSTRUMENTS DE MUSIQUE
8983	SOUND RECRDNG TAPE,DISCS	W 13742	633.1	W 13684	731.4	W 13535	786.1	W 14071	724.1	SUPPORTS SON POUR 763
89832	RECORDED DISCS,TAPES ETC	W 8577	544.0	W 9710	653.5	W 10039	708.5	W 10322	649.3	DISQUES,PHONO,BANDES
899	OTHER MANUFACTURED GOODS		357.4		406.3		421.7		428.8	AUT ART MANUF DIVERS NDA
8996	HEARING,ORTHOPAEDIC AIDS		170.1		197.8		211.1		240.5	APPAREILS D'ORTHOPEDIE
9	GOODS NOT CLASSD BY KIND		374.4		334.9		162.2		255.3	ART TRANSACT NON CLASSES
971	*GOLD,NON MONETARY NES	K 60499	221.5	K 69391	198.7	K 113737	72.6	K 138283	153.6	OR NON MONETAIRE

5. Special Exports F.O.B. by Commodities according to the S.I.T.C. (Rev. 2) in million U.S. Dollars
Exportations Spéciales F.O.B. par Produits d'après la C.T.C.I. (Rév. 2) en millions de Dollars E.U.

SITC CTCI	COMMODITY	1994		1995		1996		1997		PRODUIT
		QUANTITY QUANTITE	VALUE VALEUR	QUANTITY QUANTITE	VALUE VALEUR	QUANTITY QUANTITE	VALUE VALEUR	QUANTITY QUANTITE	VALUE VALEUR	
	ALL COMMODITIES		70360.1		81641.2		80842.8		76150.1	TOUS PRODUITS
0	FOOD AND LIVE ANIMALS		1618.3		1864.5		1799.6		1619.9	ALIMENTS,ANIMAUX VIVANTS
02	DAIRY PRODCTS,BIRDS'EGGS		409.9		488.0		428.1		379.9	PRODUITS LAITIERS,OEUFS
024	CHEESE AND CURD	W 59276	401.7	W 63965	460.6	W 57065	403.8	W 60703	362.4	FROMAGE ET CAILLEBOTTE
07	COFFEE,TEA,COCOA,SPICES		363.9		429.9		425.4		397.5	CAFE,THE,CACAO,EPICES
073	CHOCOLATE AND PRODUCTS	W 58576	273.2	W 61399	322.5	W 63197	322.1	W 66342	274.4	CHOCOLAT
09	MISC EDIBLE PRODUCTS		363.6		387.5		400.7		364.9	PREP ALIMENTAIRES DIVERSES
098	EDIBLE PRODCTS,PREPS NES	W 78532	362.6	W 74403	386.2	W 75669	399.4	W 79645	363.6	PREP ALIMENTAIRES NDA
09809	MISC FOOD PREPRTIONS NES	W 35339	239.3	W 33113	253.7	W 32744	272.6	W 33083	241.7	PREP ALIMENTAIRES NDA
1	BEVERAGES AND TOBACCO		513.9		545.1		541.5		482.6	BOISSONS ET TABACS
12	TOBACCO AND MANUFACTURES		396.9		431.6		426.2		349.7	TABACS BRUTS FABRIQUES
122	TOBACCO,MANUFACTURED	W 24730	353.5	W 27359	377.2	W 30200	379.5	W 26346	297.4	TABACS FABRIQUES
1222	CIGARETTES	W 23033	335.2	W 24822	356.8	W 26011	350.4	W 21579	264.4	CIGARETTES
2	CRUDE MATERLS,EXCL FUELS		791.5		983.1		824.2		846.7	MAT BRUTES NON COMESTIBLES
28	METALLIFEROUS ORES,SCRAP		191.9		279.0		243.6		291.4	MINERAIS METAL,DECHETS
5	CHEMCLS,RELATED PROD NES		17646.7		20837.2		21598.0		20756.2	PRODUITS CHIMIQUES
51	ORGANIC CHEMICALS		4648.8		5587.9		5844.8		5678.0	PROD CHIMIQ ORGANIQUES
513	CARBOXYLIC ACIDS ETC	W 43142	376.8	W 44613	399.7	W 49755	427.2	W 55999	366.5	ACIDES CARBOXYLIQUES
5139	OXY–FNCT ACIDS,DERIVATVS	W 29005	235.0	W 30100	293.8	W 32784	327.2	W 36988	274.4	ACIDES CARBOXYLIQUES
514	NITROGEN–FNCTN COMPOUNDS	W 77078	2370.9	W 81867	2925.7	W 82712	3018.2	W 58709	3023.9	COMPOSES FONCT AZOTEES
5145	AMINE–FUNCTION COMPOUNDS	W 7220	162.7	W 8703	255.5	W 6715	304.9	W 6297	204.1	COMPOSES FONCTION AMINE
5146	OXYGEN–FNCT AMINO–CMPNDS	W 7904	465.1	W 7174	507.1	W 8026	485.0	W 6640	536.1	COMP AMINES FONCT OXYGEN
5147	AMIDE–FNCT CMPD,EXC UREA	W 36922	472.2	W 44643	516.2	W 48695	521.5	W 21257	263.3	COMPOSES CARBOXYAMIDE
5148	OTH NITROGN–FNCTN CMPNDS	W 25032	1271.1	W 21347	1647.0	W 19276	1707.0	W 24516	2020.5	AUTRES COMPOSES AZOTES
51482	IMIDE–,IMIDE–FNCT CMPNDS	W 14657	1110.7	W 14963	1484.6	W 13183	1532.4	W 18301	1850.9	COMPOSES A FONCTION IMIDE
515	ORG–INORG COMPOUNDS ETC	W 26150	1424.1	W 25724	1699.8	W 27795	1841.0	W 27370	1740.3	COMPOSES ORGANO–MINERAUX
5156	HETEROCYCLIC CMPDS ETC	W 13999	1194.3	W 13582	1452.7	W 14929	1534.4	W 16298	1467.4	COMPOSES HETEROCYCLIQUES
51569	OTH HETEROCYC CMPDS,ETC	W 13736	1131.1	W 13242	1353.4	W 14577	1413.3	W 15984	1358.5	AUT COMP HETEROCYCLIQUES
516	OTHER ORGANIC CHEMICALS	W 28840	311.4	W 29112	367.0	W 30315	355.3	W 33751	369.4	AUTRES PROD ORGANIQUES
52	INORGANIC CHEMICALS		223.5		251.7		246.7		260.7	PROD CHIM INORGANIQUES
53	DYES,TANNING,COLOUR PROD		2191.8		2416.0		2234.4		2118.0	PROD TEINTURE,COLORANTS
531	SYNT DYE,NAT INDGO,LAKES	W 63160	1670.5	W 60743	1823.3	W 68144	1650.2	W 83029	1574.3	MAT COLOR ORGAN,LAQUES
5311	SYNTHIC ORGNIC DYESTUFFS	W 54422	1528.8	W 52463	1676.1	W 58488	1518.1	W 69025	1429.1	MAT COLOR ORGAN SYNTHET
533	PIGMENTS,PAINTS,ETC	W 72098	517.4	W 78175	587.4	W 87502	580.3	W 100829	539.2	PIGMENTS,PEINTURES,VERNIS
541	*MEDICINAL,PHARM PRODUCT		6325.0	MK 79981	7589.9	MK 79423	8411.3	MK 86184	8208.5	PROD MEDICINAUX PHARMACEUT
5411	PROVITAMINS AND VITAMINS	MK 32510	689.0	MK 31923	786.0	MK 31293	711.9	MK 33912	586.5	PROVITAMINES,VITAMINES
5413	ANTIBIOTICS IN BULK	K 433550	267.0	K 323563	291.4	K 300407	300.5	K 324105	268.8	ANTIBIOTIQUES NDA
54139	OTHER ANTIBIOTICS	K 368081	262.1	K 278299	287.2	K 243556	292.7	K 276257	262.4	AUTRES ANTIBIOTIQUES
5415	HORMONES,NAT,SYN IN BULK		126.4	K 116225	164.7	K 124011	237.4	K 137235	288.1	HORMONES
5416	GLYCOSIDES,GLANDS,SERA	K 1829399	535.7	K 1818036	889.9	K 1984818	920.1	K 1949698	859.2	HETEROSIDES
54164	ANTISERA,MICROB VACCINES	K 932904	438.8	K 1065306	794.4	K 1199269	812.9	K 1344288	765.7	SERUMS,VACCINS
5417	MEDICAMENTS	MK 37061	4067.4	MK 42455	4714.0	MK 42247	5483.3	MK 45884	5537.2	MEDICAMENTS
54171	— CONTAINNG ANTIBIOTICS	K 3390455	444.7	K 3220461	525.8	K 2549173	512.5	K 2564134	493.4	MED CONTN ANTIBIOTIQUES
54172	— CONTAINING HORMONES	K 630176	347.4	K 746606	506.4	K 745773	664.5	K 821061	711.1	MED CONTENANT HORMONES
54179	— CONTNG OTH SUBSTANCES	MK 32381	3139.3	MK 37830	3531.6	MK 38335	4144.8	MK 42005	4196.6	MED CONT AUT SUBSTANCES
5419	PHARMACEUTICAL GOODS NES	K 3013516	457.5	K 3146978	570.3	K 3267194	582.7	K 3751249	504.5	PREP,ART PHARMACEUTIQUES
54191	BANDAGES PREPARED ETC	K 2556768	359.5	K 2689808	436.9	K 2868817	461.9	K 3303748	378.8	OUATES,GAZES,BANDES
55	PERFUME,CLEANING ETC PRD		1412.6		1597.7		1493.7		1295.1	PROD POUR PARFUM,TOILETTE
551	ESSENTL OILS,PERFUME,ETC	W 24559	624.0	W 24224	707.9	W 24305	674.7	W 27320	636.9	HUILES ESSENTIELLES
5514	MIXED PERFUME SUBSTANCES	W 23684	597.6	W 23280	676.8	W 23426	642.9	W 26353	608.1	MELANGES SUBSTAN ODORIFER
553	PERFUMERY,COSMETICS,ETC	W 43299	607.7	W 28922	685.8	W 26449	618.7	W 26856	484.2	PRODUITS DE PARFUMERIE
58	PLASTIC MATERIALS ETC		1450.5		1736.8		1605.9		1563.5	MAT PLAST ARTIFICIELLES
582	PROD OF CONDENSATION ETC	W 163085	677.2	W 180177	828.5	W 197710	875.7	W 233197	893.0	PROD CONDENS,POLYCOND
5824	POLYAMIDES	W 34253	173.5	W 41083	222.3	W 50842	234.1	W 60926	239.6	POLYAMIDES
58241	— IN PRIMARY FORMS	W 34253	173.5	W 41083	222.3	W 50842	234.1	W 60926	239.6	POLYAMIDES PRIMAIRES
5826	EPOXIDE RESINS	W 55264	189.9	W 59105	221.9	W 70153	278.6	W 80653	304.9	RESINES EPOXYDES
58261	— IN PRIMARY FORMS	W 55264	189.9	W 59105	221.9	W 70153	278.6	W 80653	304.9	EPOXYDES PRIMAIRES
583	POLYMERIZATION ETC PRODS	W 282735	757.1	W 278180	887.1	W 223435	708.3	W 249347	650.4	PROD POLYMERISATION
5839	OTH POLYMRZTION ETC PROD	W 107269	410.0	W 105114	465.4	W 73931	345.3	W 83578	305.6	AUT PROD POLYMER COPOLYM
59	CHEMICAL MATERIALS NES		1375.1		1626.3		1729.2		1603.8	MAT PROD CHIMIQUES NDA
591	PESTICIDES,DISINFECTANTS	W 45737	555.4	W 48080	723.5	W 48222	764.6	W 51496	691.1	DESINF,INSECT,FONG,HERB
5912	FUNGICIDES,FOR RETAIL	W 11195	228.8	W 10796	256.4	W 13022	297.9	W 15617	283.4	FONGICIDES VENTE AU DET
5913	HERBICIDES,FOR RETAIL	W 19748	177.1	W 19059	261.4	W 18295	269.5	W 19767	251.1	HERBICIDES VENTE AU DET
598	MISCEL CHEM PRODUCTS NES	W 226297	710.4	W 197865	768.9	W 233215	805.0	W 264582	771.3	PROD DIV INDUST CHIM NDA
5989	CHEM PRODUCTS,PREPS NES	W 109321	651.2	W 104387	698.9	W 107085	737.1	W 122066	720.1	PROD PREP CHIMIQUES NDA
59899	OTH CHEM PRODS,PREPS,NES	W 73199	536.2	W 66298	568.3	W 61729	600.9	W 75194	596.5	AUT PRODUITS CHIMIQUES NDA
6	BASIC MANUFACTURES		11719.5		12885.5		12328.3		11713.0	ART MANUFACTURES
63	WOOD,CORK MANUFACTRS NES		251.3		302.2		287.8		273.4	OUVRAGES LIEGE ET BOIS
64	PAPER,PAPERBOARD AND MFR		1099.4		1465.6		1434.0		1436.8	PAPIERS,CARTONS & OUVRAGES
641	PAPER AND PAPERBOARD	W 847857	828.8	W 861390	1116.4	W 948661	1091.9	W 1124515	1099.1	PAPIERS ET CARTONS
6412	PRINTG,WRITING PAPER NES	W 196115	210.5	W 203483	311.4	W 217148	245.7	W 282795	265.9	PAPIERS POUR L'IMPRESSION
64122	— COATED,IMPREGNATD ETC	W 180913	190.8	W 187128	274.9	W 200169	220.3	W 244057	225.2	PAPIERS IMPRESSION COUCHES
6415	PAPER,PAPERBRD,BULK,NES	W 313494	211.3	W 329867	310.4	W 361713	274.3	W 363245	207.6	PAPIERS,CARTONS ROULEAUX
64159	OTHER PAPER ETC,BULK,NES	W 304432	186.2	W 321523	282.7	W 354487	241.1	W 356953	187.9	AUT PAPIER ROULEAUX FEUILLES
6418	COATED ETC PAPER NES BLK	W 158108	233.6	W 141172	268.7	W 166870	338.6	W 217179	390.6	PAP,CARTONS COUCHES,ENDUITS
642	PAPER,ETC,PRECUT,ARTS OF	W 102783	270.7	W 116946	349.2	W 122359	342.1	W 148448	337.7	PAP,CARTONS DECOUPES
65	TEXTILE YARN,FABRICS,ETC		2116.3		2266.8		2010.6		1793.5	FILS,TISSUS,ARTICLES TEXTILE
651	TEXTILE YARN	W 122871	658.9	W 117173	710.5	W 110892	600.4	W 112063	515.7	FILS TEXTILES
6514	SYN FIB YRN,BULK,MONOFIL	W 81004	332.8	W 82787	384.3	W 77248	316.7	W 80455	277.5	FILS CONT 85% FIB TEXT SYNTH
65142	— NONTXT ETC CONT PAMID	W 69729	252.5	W 73317	304.2	W 69555	253.7	W 73113	222.9	FILS NON TEX FI CON POLYAMID
652	COTTON FABRICS,WOVEN	W 19967	317.5	W 17417	325.3	W 10982	262.6	W 10518	234.5	TISSUS DE COTON
6522	WOVEN COTTON BLEACHD,ETC	W 15770	264.6	W 13448	271.4	W 8342	224.4	W 7790	198.7	TISSUS COTON BLANCHIS ETC
65224	BLCHED COTTON FABRIC NES	W 14593	221.7	W 12437	233.9	W 7459	195.3	W 6987	173.9	AUT TIS PLUS 85% COT BLANCHI
653	WOVN MAN–MADE FIB FABRIC	W 7695	218.3	W 6566	229.5	W 6542	202.2	W 6916	188.6	TISSUS FIBRES SYNTH,ARTIF
657	SPECIAL TXTL FABRC,PRODS	W 14136	303.5	W 12684	351.9	W 13660	331.1	W 17535	313.4	TISSUS SPECIAUX
66	NONMETAL MINERAL MFS NES		3004.9		2664.5		2735.0		2216.5	ART MIN NON METALLIQUES
663	MINERAL MANUFCTURES NES	W 51622	211.0	W 50553	257.8	W 57544	260.5	W 50929	238.0	ART MIN MANUF NDA
665	GLASSWARE	W 25970	202.2	W 30811	256.1	W 42578	251.9	W 40116	252.4	OUVRAGES EN VERRE
667	PEARL,PREC–,SEMI–P STONE		2404.9		1927.1		2022.3		1551.0	PERLES, PIERRES GEMMES
6672	DIAMONDS NONINDUST,UNSET		1956.1		1617.3		1691.7		1237.9	DIAMANTS BRUTS
66722	— SRTD,ROUGH,SIMPLY WKD		1353.4		1091.5		1080.6		736.4	DIAMANTS TRIES BRUTS
66729	— CUT ETC NOT SET		601.9		525.8		610.6		501.4	DIAMANTS TAILLES
6673	PREC–,SEMI–PR STONES NES		393.1		236.6		225.7		194.8	AUTRES PIERRES NON SERTIES
67	IRON AND STEEL		926.3		1095.6		892.8		904.8	FER ET ACIER
673	IRON,STEEL SHAPES ETC	W 549343	268.4	W 386949	289.0	W 332829	218.8	W 426614	245.3	BARRES,PROFIL FER,ACIER
678	IRON,STL TUBES,PIPES,ETC	W 253475	426.1	W 256084	518.3	W 232651	432.9	W 288815	429.2	TUBES,TUYAUX EN FONTE,FER
6783	IRON,STL TUBES,PIPES NES	W 226499	263.6	W 235216	345.1	W 216889	294.4	W 265073	297.1	AUT TUBES,TUYAUX FER,ACIER
68	NON–FERROUS METALS		1502.8		1677.2		1658.0		2066.5	METAUX NON FERREUX
681	SILVER,PLATINUM,ETC		688.8		639.5		680.8		1119.4	ARGENT ET PLATINE
6812	METALS OF PLATINUM GROUP		636.6		599.7		639.1		1076.7	PLATINE
68123	PLATINUM,ALLOYS UNWRGHT		331.8		351.6		405.6		511.2	PLATINE,ALLIAGES BRUTS

5. Special Exports F.O.B. by Commodities according to the S.I.T.C. (Rev. 2) in million U.S. Dollars
Exportations Spéciales F.O.B. par Produits d'après la C.T.C.I. (Rév. 2) en millions de Dollars E.U.

SITC CTCI	COMMODITY	1994 QUANTITY QUANTITE	1994 VALUE VALEUR	1995 QUANTITY QUANTITE	1995 VALUE VALEUR	1996 QUANTITY QUANTITE	1996 VALUE VALEUR	1997 QUANTITY QUANTITE	1997 VALUE VALEUR	PRODUIT
68124	OTH PLAT GRP METAL UNWRT		108.0		102.9		62.0		398.0	METAUX MINE PLAT ALL BRUTS
684	ALUMINIUM	W 143958	608.6	W 145926	781.8	W 147144	738.9	W 165306	712.2	ALUMINIUM
6842	ALUMINIUM,ALLOYS WORKED	W 136359	593.0	W 138465	760.9	W 138671	720.4	W 156361	694.4	ALUMINIUM,ALLIAGES OUVRE
68422	ALUMNM PLATE,SHEET,STRIP	W 57814	191.3	W 61371	266.4	W 61088	244.2	W 70273	242.7	TOLES, PLANCHES EN ALU
68423	ALUMINIUM FOIL	W 43867	260.2	W 45524	315.9	W 44970	293.9	W 47518	269.7	FEUILLES,BANDES MINCES AL
69	METAL MANUFACTURES NES		2559.3		3121.2		3046.1		2788.6	ART MANUFACT EN METAL NDA
691	STRUCTURES AND PARTS NES	W 67683	213.3	W 75462	255.3	W 71016	246.8	W 81977	227.3	CONSTRUCT FER,ACIER,ALU
694	STL,COPPR NAILS,NUTS,ETC	W 38326	495.5	W 40823	618.0	W 40821	591.3	W 46454	568.0	CLOUS,VIS,ECROUS
69402	IRN,STL NUTS,BOLTS,ETC	W 32558	372.8	W 35643	476.9	W 35540	455.3	W 40598	435.0	BOULONS,VIS,ECROUS FER,AC
695	TOOLS	W 14590	696.7	W 16533	891.2	W 17129	889.2	W 18556	817.8	OUTILS A MAIN
6953	OTHER HAND TOOLS	W 8673	286.8	W 9863	361.4	W 9962	360.8	W 11058	335.8	AUTRES OUTILS A MAIN
6954	BLADES,TIPS,ETC FR TOOLS	W 5688	396.6	W 6424	513.7	W 6883	512.3	W 7221	467.0	OUTILS POUR MACHINE–OUTIL
69541	PARTS TO INSERT IN TOOLS	W 4999	323.4	W 5642	418.2	W 5981	415.5	W 6358	388.4	OUTILS DE FORAGE
697	BASE MTL HOUSEHOLD EQUIP	W 15199	229.1	W 13490	236.4	W 13540	233.5	W 13792	200.9	ART MENAGE MET COMMUNS
699	BASE METAL MFRS NES	W 65925	664.7		809.2		771.0	W 73053	687.9	ART MANUFACTURES MET NDA
7	MACHINES,TRANSPORT EQUIP		20801.2		25624.5		25636.4		23706.5	MACHINES MATERIEL TRANSPORT
71	POWER GENERATING EQUIPMT		1430.5		1741.3		1887.6		1704.0	MACHINES GENERATRICES
714	ENGINES AND MOTORS NES	W 7302	426.5	W 4749	534.6	W 7474	652.1	W 9368	663.4	MOTEURS NON ELECTRIQUES
7149	ENGINE & MOTOR PARTS NES	W 7261	411.0	W 4724	523.3	W 7438	634.9	W 9270	620.5	PIECES 714 ET 718.88
71499	PARTS NES,OF 71488,71888	W 7187	386.9	W 4660	495.4	W 7381	610.3	W 8612	540.0	PIECES 714.88 ET 718.88
716	ROTATING ELECTRIC PLANT	W 26139	598.8	W 27774	768.4	W 28629	778.5	W 31236	680.3	APP ELECTR ROTATIFS,PIECES
7162	AC MTRS,GENRTRS,GEN SETS	W 6454	271.3	W 8002	354.7	W 8178	348.8	W 7780	318.9	MOTEURS ELECTRIQUES
71621	AC MTRS,INC UNIVRSL MTRS	W 5824	251.9	W 7198	326.7	W 7516	340.7	W 7498	313.6	MOT ELEC NON COUR CONTINU
72	MACHS FOR SPCL INDUSTRYS		5601.2		6925.0		6510.8		6294.8	MAC SPECIALES POUR INDUST
724	TEXTILE,LEATHER MACHNRY	W 63984	1809.6	W 78638	2285.6	W 70512	2008.6	W 80341	1904.3	MACH POUR INDUSTRIE TEXTILE
7244	SPINNING,EXTRDNG,ETC MCH	W 20294	494.5	W 30409	715.1	W 28237	663.9	W 33549	694.2	MACH POUR LE FILAGE
72442	FIBRE PROCESSNG MACH NES	W 9463	147.3	W 14001	250.9	W 11676	200.5	W 12922	205.0	MACH PREP MAT TEXTILES
72449	PTS NES OF MACHS OF 7244	W 3794	197.2	W 5422	238.4	W 6232	245.1	W 5758	251.1	PIECES DES MACH DU 724.4
7245	WEAVING,FELT MFG,ETC MCH	W 25627	579.6	W 29528	738.7	W 24416	579.2	W 26483	510.1	METIERS A TISSER,PIECES
72451	WEAVING MACHINES (LOOMS)	W 20661	455.8	W 22098	568.5	W 16266	397.1	W 17235	346.8	METIERS A TISSER
7246	AUXIL TXTL MCH,PARTS NES	W 7788	420.2	W 9095	499.1	W 7546	447.3	W 9563	397.7	MACH PR 724.51,52,53,61
72469	LOOM,KNT MCH ETC PTS NES	W 6066	345.0	W 6965	396.5	W 5626	354.6	W 7307	309.8	PIECES 724.51,52,53,61
725	PAPER ETC MILL MACHINERY	W 16525	466.0	W 18525	627.9	W 16998	550.5	W 18717	531.5	MACHINES FABR PATE PAPIER
7252	PAPER ETC PRODCT MFG MCH	W 10446	308.5	W 12254	415.8	W 11651	365.9	W 12996	351.9	AUT MACH TRAVAIL PAP,CAR
726	PRINTG,BKBINDG MACHY,PTS	W 30797	1025.8	W 33884	1177.5	W 31437	1048.3	W 36323	1022.0	MACHINES POUR IMPRIMERIE
7264	PRINTING PRESSES	W 9722	348.6	W 8475	283.4	W 8693	271.7	W 11293	323.0	MACHINES A IMPRIMER
72641	ROTARY PRINTING PRESSES	W 9722	348.6	W 8475	283.4	W 8693	271.7	W 11293	323.0	MACH IMPRIMER ROTATIVES
7267	OTH PRINTG & ANCILL MACH	W 6040	302.4	W 7246	394.6	W 5623	287.3	W 4920	211.5	AUT MACH IMPRIMERIE,PIEC
72672	MACH ANCILLARY TO PRINTG	W 4211	230.1	W 4777	275.9	W 4127	221.0	W 3768	164.4	APP AUXIL D'IMPRIMERIE
7268	BOOKBINDING MACHRY,PARTS	W 5235	196.2	W 5598	240.3	W 4938	222.8	W 5935	232.6	MACH BROCHAGE,RELIURE,PIEC
727	FOOD MACHRY NON–DOMESTIC	W 12286	354.2	W 12116	416.6	W 15205	440.2	W 16293	390.6	MACH INDUSTRIES ALIMENT
7272	OTH FOOD PROC MCHY,PARTS	W 6153	194.6	W 6849	260.0	W 8014	261.5	W 7597	218.1	AUT MACH IND ALIMENTAIRE
72722	INDUS FOOD PROC MACH NES	W 6150	194.4	W 6825	259.5	W 7982	260.8	W 7557	217.3	MACHINES BOULANGERIE
728	OTH MACHY FOR SPCL INDUS	W 55197	1814.9	W 61075	2258.5	W 61145	2307.3	W 69880	2290.0	AUT MACH IND PARTICULIERES
7281	MACH–TOOLS FR SPCL INDUS	W 9877	225.4	W 12216	284.6	W 11849	268.4	W 12119	266.2	MACH–OUTILS SPEC IND PART
7284	MACHY FOR SPCL INDUS NES	W 34222	1497.7	W 38794	1871.3	W 40812	1945.1	W 44385	1910.2	MACH SPEC IND PARTICUL.
72842	RUBBER,PLASTICS WRKG MCH	W 10267	365.9	W 10106	379.7	W 9828	368.9	W 12557	420.5	MACH IND CAOUT MAT PLAST
72848	OTH MCHY WITH INDIV FNCT	W 15735	754.6	W 17414	997.1	W 19733	1054.5	W 22073	1025.9	AUTRES MACHINES NDA
72849	PTS OF MACHS OF 7284 ETC	W 6678	306.7	W 7306	380.9	W 9270	423.0	W 8070	381.7	PIECES DU 728.4 ETC
73	METALWORKING MACHINERY		2239.9		2898.5		2760.2		2574.9	MACH TRAVAIL DES METAUX
736	METALWORKING MACH–TOOLS	W 51661	1860.8	W 55383	2325.2	W 52144	2230.7	W 55202	2050.8	MACH–OUTILS TRAVAIL METAUX
7361	METAL CUTTING MACH–TOOLS	W 24788	925.3	W 27901	1181.8	W 25688	1129.1	W 27595	1025.9	MACH–OUT ENLEVEMENT METAL
73611	ULTRASNC ETC MTLWKG MCHS	W 6982	310.2	W 7420	364.8	W 6773	319.4	W 6868	264.9	MACH–OUT ELECTRO–EROSION
73619	OTH MTL CUTTNG MCH–TOOLS	W 6505	254.1	W 6720	333.5	W 7426	376.1	W 8718	349.6	MACH A AFFUTER ETC METAL
7362	METAL FORMING MACH–TOOLS	W 13199	271.3	W 11852	317.1	W 10752	279.6	W 10671	239.4	MACH–OUTILS DEFORM METAL
7367	OTH METALWRKG MACH–TOOLS	W 5114	219.7	W 4623	229.5	W 4592	241.4	W 5983	240.8	AUT MACH–OUT POUR METAUX
7369	PTS NES OF TOOLS OF 736	W 7040	338.3	W 9268	443.5	W 9363	420.8	W 9254	398.4	PIECES GROUPE 736
737	METALWORKING MACHNRY NES	W 9396	379.2	W 12136	573.3	W 10763	529.6	W 17223	524.2	MACH TRAV METAUX PIECES
7373	WELDING,BRAZING,ETC MCHS	W 4019	285.5	W 4532	415.1	W 4408	413.3	W 5651	404.5	MACH SOUDAGE ETC PIECES
73732	ELECTRIC WELDERS,ETC	W 3878	281.7	W 4457	411.3	W 4338	410.0	W 5566	401.0	MACH ELECT POUR SOUDER
74	GENRL INDUSTRL MACHY NES		4285.6		5124.6		5141.1		4470.4	MACH APP INDUSTRIE
741	HEATING,COOLING EQUIPMNT	W 26216	707.0	W 27733	849.0	W 27613	816.3	W 28651	763.0	MACH CHAUFFAGE,PIECES
7416	HEATING,COOLING EQU NES	W 15442	478.4	W 17017	567.0	W 17454	554.8	W 17956	530.8	APP CHANGEMENT TEMP
742	PUMPS FOR LIQUIDS ETC	W 10206	257.7	W 12605	343.7	W 11647	335.6	W 11680	276.8	POMPES MOTO–POMPES
743	PUMPS NES,CENTRFUGES ETC	W 21918	723.9	W 24185	884.1	W 26493	969.3	W 25968	812.6	POMPES COMPRES,VENT ETC
7431	PUMPS FOR GASES ETC	W 9038	285.5	W 11351	361.3	W 12317	399.9	W 11346	331.9	POMPES AIR A VIDE,COMPRES
7439	PTS NES OF APP OF 7435,6	W 5389	248.1	W 5255	292.7	W 6260	322.8	W 7116	290.0	PIECES 743.5 ET 743.6
744	MECHANICAL HANDLING EQU	W 38670	583.9	W 39563	655.0	W 42955	660.2	W 46765	520.4	EQUIP MANUTENTION PIECES
7442	LIFTING,LOADING MACH NES	W 17259	278.9	W 16857	312.0	W 21326	370.9	W 25358	311.7	APP LEVAGE,MANUTENTION
74428	OTH HANDLING ETC MCH NES	W 10079	235.0	W 9780	250.0	W 8023	238.3	W 9353	174.2	AUT APP LEVAGE ETC
7449	PTS NES OF MACHY OF 7442	W 18914	286.9	W 20874	327.2	W 18867	268.2	W 17936	197.8	PIECES DU 744.2
745	NONELEC MACHY,TOOLS NES	W 19690	925.2	W 19520	1002.7	W 19517	968.2	W 21237	909.3	AUT MACH NON ELEC,PIECES
7452	OTH NONELEC MCHS,PTS NES	W 19381	900.6	W 19152	972.0	W 19123	939.8	W 20859	884.2	AUT MACH NON ELEC,PIECES
74522	PACKAGNG,BOTTLNG,ETC MCH	W 5210	365.1	W 5284	380.4	W 5586	378.2	W 6159	360.6	MACH NETT BOUTEILLES,ETC
74527	SPRAYING MACHINERY	W 7566	244.6	W 7460	272.8	W 6718	260.3	W 7446	250.2	APP PROJETER ETC LIQUID
749	NONELEC MACH PTS,ACC NES	W 54066	1088.2	W 57556	1390.5	W 55944	1391.7	W 56476	1188.5	PIECES MACH NON ELEC NDA
7492	COCKS,VALVES ETC NES	W 11973	507.7	W 13038	652.7	W 12654	629.5	W 12599	558.4	ART ROB,SIM POUR TUYAUX
7493	SHAFT,CRANK,PULLEY ETC	W 19743	249.5	W 22064	315.4	W 23033	322.9	W 24484	268.5	ARBRES TRANS,VILEBREQUINS
7499	OTH NONELEC MCHY PTS NES	W 20452	253.4	W 20109	315.8	W 18157	316.9	W 17945	272.3	PIECES NON ELECT NDA
75	OFFICE MACHNES,ADP EQUIP		714.5		1014.6		1087.5		1024.3	MACH BUREAU TRAIT AUTOM
752	AUTOMTIC DATA PROC EQUIP	W 2218	361.1	W 2679	519.0	W 2656	577.2	W 2446	509.6	MACH TRAIT INFORMATION
7523	DIGITL CENTRL PROCESSORS	W 1000	232.9	W 1300	363.8	W 1266	408.8	W 1090	369.4	UNITES CENTRALES
759	OFFICE,ADP MCH PTS,ACCES	W 2040	251.1	W 2005	324.7	W 1974	313.6	W 2036	329.4	PIECES DU 751 ET 752
7599	ACCTG,ETC,ADP MCH PTS,AC	W 1755	232.4	W 1718	299.7	W 1684	286.7	W 1729	298.0	PIECES DU 751 ET 752
76	TELECOMM,SOUND EQUIPMENT		698.8		803.4		816.6		842.1	EQUIPMENT DE TELECOM
764	TELECOM EQPT,PTS,ACC NES	W 5129	622.9	W 5125	719.0	W 5717	730.0	W 6992	770.9	EQUIP TELECOM,PIECES
7641	LINE TELEPHONE,ETC EQUIP	W 951	116.6	W 1464	247.3	W 1999	247.2	W 2345	230.4	APP TELEPHON PAR FIL
7649	PTS NES OF EQUIPMT OF 76	W 2774	262.4	W 2533	297.3	W 2931	332.2	W 3690	347.9	PIECES DE LA DIV 76
76491	PTS NES OF APPAR OF 7641	W 744	132.8	W 840	174.3	W 953	225.2	W 1493	245.4	PIECES POUR 764.1
77	ELECTRIC MACHNRY NES ETC		4583.5		5500.6		5443.9		5071.5	MACH APP ELECT NDA
771	ELECTRIC POWER MACHY NES	W 19760	351.9	W 23644	440.5	W 24343	441.4	W 26517	364.7	MACH PROD,TRANS ELECTR
7712	OTH ELEC POWER MACHY NES	W 13162	232.7	W 16402	303.0	W 17676	319.2	W 19492	262.5	AUT APP PROD TRANSF ELEC
772	SWITCHGEAR ETC,PARTS NES	W 24042	1734.8	W 26562	2153.3	W 26763	2157.0	W 31819	2022.5	APP COUPURE,SECT ETC
7721	SWITCHGEAR ETC	W 23329	1615.1	W 25679	1979.0	W 25935	1991.6	W 30830	1857.1	APP COUPURE,SECTIONMNT
773	ELECTR DISTRIBUTNG EQUIP	W 27894	296.8	W 31867	383.8	W 35128	416.1	W 36275	381.0	EQUIPMT DISTRIBUTION ELECT
7731	INSULATED WIRE,CABLE ETC	W 25141	235.4	W 29167	312.8	W 31776	329.5	W 32602	296.7	FILS,CABLES ISOLES ELECT
775	HOUSEHOLD TYPE EQUIP NES	W 16164	290.8	W 15072	286.2	W 13406	241.6	W 14788	231.6	MACH,APP USAGE DOMESTQUE
7758	ELECTRO–THERMIC APPL NES	W 11880	222.4	W 9164	199.4	W 7597	172.1	W 8503	168.2	APP ELECTROTHERMIQ NDA
776	TRANSISTORS,VALVES,ETC	W 717	327.5	W 904	439.7	W 934	461.1	W 858	426.1	LAMPES,TUBES,VALVES
7764	ELECTRONIC MICROCIRCUITS	W 385	211.2	W 410	286.2	W 332	313.1	W 290	295.8	MICROSTRUCTURES ELECTRON
778	ELECTRICAL MACHINERY NES		1444.2	W 48609	1635.9	W 53008	1576.3	W 58540	1507.4	AUTRES MACH ELECT NDA

5. Special Exports F.O.B. by Commodities according to the S.I.T.C. (Rev. 2) in million U.S. Dollars
Exportations Spéciales F.O.B. par Produits d'après la C.T.C.I. (Rév. 2) en millions de Dollars E.U.

SITC CTCI	COMMODITY	1994 QUANTITY QUANTITE	1994 VALUE VALEUR	1995 QUANTITY QUANTITE	1995 VALUE VALEUR	1996 QUANTITY QUANTITE	1996 VALUE VALEUR	1997 QUANTITY QUANTITE	1997 VALUE VALEUR	PRODUIT
7784	ELECTRO-MECH HAND TOOLS	W 27187	773.2	W 28352	856.2	W 26689	791.7	W 29961	767.5	OUTILS ELECTROMEC,PIECES
7788	OTH ELEC MACHY,EQUIP NES		462.3	W 9445	558.5	W 9373	569.0	W 9213	528.1	AUT MACH APP ELEC NDA
77886	OTH ELEC MACHINERY NES	W 2147	165.2	W 1979	194.8	W 1970	220.8	W 1999	229.2	AUT MACH APP ELECTRIQUES
78	ROAD VEHICLES		760.7		777.5		789.5		758.9	VEHICULES ROUTIERS
782	LORRIES,SPCL MTR VEH NES	W 23374	218.7	W 23654	195.4	W 29227	183.6	W 31376	154.2	VEHICULES SPECIAUX,MARCH
784	MOTOR VEH PRTS,ACCES NES	W 36342	291.3	W 37803	348.3	W 40414	363.4	W 47920	364.3	PIECES 722,781,782,783
7849	OTHER MOTOR VEHCL PARTS	W 33557	257.0	W 35381	315.9	W 38030	338.2	W 45496	342.0	PIECES 722,781,782,783
79	OTHR TRANSPORT EQUIPMENT		486.8		839.6		1199.5		966.0	AUTRE MATERIEL TRANSPORT
791	RAILWAY VEHICLES	W 13184	233.8	W 11310	240.3	W 14877	400.6	W 11729	233.3	VEHIC MAT CHEMINS DE FER
792	AIRCRAFT ETC	W 739	240.0	W 1776	588.0	W 1419	790.5	W 2023	725.3	APP NAVIGATION AERIENNE
7924	AIRCRFT NES OVER 15000KG	W 98	22.0	W 720	163.4	W 632	331.9	W 383	120.0	AERODYNES PLUS 15000 KG
7929	AIRCRAFT PARTS NES	W 255	88.2	W 521	128.1	W 453	179.7	W 1165	290.6	PIECES DU 792
8	MISC MANUFACTURED GOODS		16933.6		18402.5		17789.7		16531.9	ART MANUFACTURES DIVERS
812	*PLUMBG,HEATNG,LGHTNG EQ	W 31852	244.9	W 29314	262.0	W 30401	252.3	W 30268	217.6	APPAR SANITAIRES CHAUFFAGE
821	*FURNITURE,PARTS THEREOF	W 83514	660.2	W 88861	785.6	W 98447	766.3	W 110576	695.9	MEUBLES ET PIECES
8212	MED FURN,STUFFD FURNSHGS	W 6665	232.6	W 6892	267.1	W 6840	254.3	W 7564	244.5	MOB MEDICO-CHIRUR,PIECES
8219	FURNITURE AND PARTS NES	W 69292	311.4	W 73597	388.3	W 82992	392.0	W 94333	345.6	AUTRES MEUBLES ET PIECES
84	CLOTHING AND ACCESSORIES		668.2		715.1		698.1		669.7	VETEMENTS
842	MENS OUTERWEAR NOT KNIT	W 2286	190.8	W 2233	242.6	W 2469	250.1	W 2454	241.5	VET DESSUS POUR HOMMES
851	*FOOTWEAR	W 4967	226.2	W 4529	204.4	W 3576	169.5	W 3254	141.5	CHAUSSURES
87	PRECISION INSTRUMNTS NES		2686.2		3111.1		3072.0		2774.1	INSTRUM,APPAR SCIENT NDA
872	MEDICAL INSTRUMENTS NES	W 3835	452.8	W 3933	556.9	W 4277	594.5	W 4577	549.6	INSTR,APP MEDIC-CHIR NDA
87202	OTH MEDICAL INSTRUMENTS	W 3597	417.7	W 3742	518.6	W 4079	555.6	W 4393	531.9	INSTRUM,APP MEDECINE
874	MEASURNG,CONTROLNG INSTR	W 12352	1969.7	W 12205	2267.8	W 12292	2181.5	W 13477	1937.0	INSTRUMENTS DE MESURE
8742	MEASUR,DRAW ETC INST,PTS	W 2352	462.5	W 2355	544.4	W 2149	511.8	W 2289	420.4	INST DESSIN,TRACAGE,PCS
87421	MEASURNG,DRAWNG ETC INST	W 1984	354.0	W 1908	402.0	W 1764	374.6	W 1848	315.3	INSTRUM DESSIN,TRACAGE
8743	GAS,LIQUID CONTROL INSTR	W 3189	436.8	W 2859	473.6	W 2777	438.8	W 3058	380.1	APP,INSTR MESURE FLUIDES
8748	ELEC MEAS,CONTRL EQU NES	W 2201	438.7	W 2025	514.0	W 2147	526.1	W 2470	492.4	APP ELEC ELECTRO MESURE
87483	OTH ELCTRNC MEAS ETC EQU	W 2012	412.4	W 1838	481.9	W 1941	494.6	W 2319	463.5	AUT APP ELECTRO DE MESURE
8749	INSTR PTS NES,ACCESSORYS	W 2724	195.3	W 3275	244.4	W 3478	244.7	W 3766	214.3	PIECES 873,874.3,54,874.8
88	PHOTO EQU,OPTICL GDS ETC		6162.0		6861.6		6554.0		6096.7	APP,FOURN PHOTO,OP,MONTR
881	PHOTO APPARAT,EQUIPT NES	W 1208	152.6	W 1115	172.2	W 1449	223.8	W 1903	261.0	APP,EQUIP PHOTO NDA
885	WATCHES AND CLOCKS		5732.9		6368.9		6045.9		5597.9	HORLOGERIE
8851	WATCHES,MOVEMENTS,CASES		5288.5		5878.4		5646.5		5274.4	MONTRES,MOUVEMENTS,BOITES
88511	WATCHES		5099.0		5662.4		5465.0		5131.2	MONTRES POCHE,BRACELET
8852	CLOCKS,CLOCK,WATCH PARTS		444.4		490.5		399.5		323.6	HORLOGES,MOUV,PARTIES
88529	CLOCK,WATCH PARTS NES		370.4		396.5		310.2		250.6	FOURNIT D HORLOG NDA
89	MISC MANUFCTRD GOODS NES		6148.9		6326.8		6162.0		5834.7	ART MANUFACTURES DIVERS
892	PRINTED MATTER	W 96171	572.0	W 87845	584.4	W 81316	550.6	W 92990	468.4	IMPRIMES
8921	PRINTED BOOKS,GLOBES,ETC	W 16892	223.3	W 13632	188.4	W 12399	167.3	W 11248	127.2	LIVRES,BROCHURES,CARTES
89211	PRINTED BOOKS,PAMPHLETS	W 15936	211.4	W 12727	176.4	W 11715	154.8	W 10617	119.3	LIVRES,BROCHURES
8928	PRINTED MATTER NES	W 64417	250.8	W 59480	279.7	W 57176	275.6	W 71991	262.7	IMPRIMES NDA
893	ARTICLES OF PLASTIC NES		1033.7		1232.1		1210.0		1144.8	OUVRAGES EN MAT DIVIS 58
8931	PLSTC PACKG CONTNRS,LIDS	W 48021	245.5	W 51618	303.7	W 57372	296.0	W 72200	290.1	ART TRANSP EMBALLAGE ETC
8939	MISC PLASTIC ARTICLES	W 74360	677.3	W 76939	808.5	W 83569	809.1	W 98699	761.0	ART DIVERS EN MAT DIV 58
89399	OTHR PLASTC ARTICLES NES	W 60382	617.9	W 63198	739.7	W 69379	738.9	W 83575	700.4	AUT OUV MAT DIV 58
894	TOYS,SPORTING GOODS,ETC	W 21410	369.3	W 20433	375.0	W 22954	417.5	W 23941	347.2	VOITURES ENFANTS,JOUETS
8942	TOYS,INDOOR GAMES ETC	W 17965	271.4	W 16600	267.1	W 19561	283.7	W 20050	240.4	JOUETS,JEUX ETC
89423	TOYS NES	W 15840	241.4	W 14699	237.4	W 18003	258.8	W 18178	217.2	JOUETS,MODELES REDUITS
896	WORKS OF ART ETC		830.5		604.7		720.1		690.4	OBJETS D'ART
89601	HAND PAINTINGS ETC NES		505.4		352.8		452.8		436.0	TABLEAUX,PEINTURES
897	GOLD,SILVER WARE,JEWELRY		1997.4		2040.8		1735.7		1921.4	BIJOUTERIE,ORFEVRERIE
8973	PREC JEWLRY,GLD-SILVWARE		1968.2		2016.8		1702.9		1895.4	BIJOUX OR,ARGENT ORFEVRE
89731	PRECIOUS METAL JEWELLERY		1798.4		1829.6		1552.0		1727.6	ART BIJOUTERIE,JOAILLER
898	MUSICAL INSTRUMENTS,PTS	W 5566	411.3	W 5636	380.0	W 5694	406.2	W 4896	207.7	INSTRUMENTS DE MUSIQUE
8983	SOUND RECRDNG TAPE,DISCS	W 4933	379.0	W 4954	344.7	W 5040	371.9	W 4318	179.4	SUPPORTS SON POUR 763
89832	RECORDED DISCS,TAPES ETC	W 4581	369.1	W 4659	336.2	W 4644	360.5	W 3879	166.6	DISQUES,PHONO,BANDES
899	OTHER MANUFACTURED GOODS		794.2		927.4		939.6		914.8	AUT ART MANUF DIVERS NDA
8996	HEARING,ORTHOPAEDIC AIDS		674.5		795.2		812.4		808.6	APPAREILS D'ORTHOPEDIE
89962	ORTHOPAEDIC ETC GOODS		599.9		706.9		732.4		730.3	APPAREILS D'ORTHOPEDIE
9	GOODS NOT CLASSD BY KIND		192.4		355.8		171.6		257.9	ART TRANSACT NON CLASSES
971	*GOLD,NON MONETARY NES	K 18464	89.1	K 43001	301.4	K 60844	86.6	K 60271	150.9	OR NON MONETAIRE
97101	NONMON GLD UNWRT,SEMIMFD	K 9206	79.3	K 25479	287.4	K 7644	68.4	K 14357	135.1	OR,ALLIAGES D'OR BRUTS

1. HISTORICAL SERIES, 1962–1997 SPECIAL TRADE, IMPORTS C.I.F., EXPORTS F.O.B.
SERIES HISTORIQUES, 1962–1997 COMMERCE SPECIAL, IMPORTATIONS C.A.F., EXPORTATIONS F.O.B

YEAR ANNEE	VALUE IN MILLION SYRIAN POUNDS VALEUR EN MILLION SYRIAN POUNDS: MERCHANDISE – MARCHANDISE IMPORTS	MERCHANDISE – MARCHANDISE EXPORTS	GOLD – OR IMPORTS	GOLD – OR EXPORTS	CONVERSION FACTORS U.S. CENTS PER SYRIAN POUND FACTEURS DE CONVERSION CENTS E.U. PAR SYRIAN POUND IMPORTS	CONVERSION FACTORS EXPORTS	INDEX NUMBERS – INDICES: QUANTUM IMPORTS	QUANTUM EXPORTS	UNIT VALUE VALEUR UNITAIRE IMPORTS	UNIT VALUE VALEUR UNITAIRE EXPORTS
1962	862.20	616.90	0.03	0.27	27.0300	26.9600				
1963	896.20	720.60	0.01	0.35	26.1780	26.1780				
1964	896.40	672.40	2.03	0.16	26.1780	26.1780				
1965	810.10	640.80	2.09	2.92	26.1780	26.1780				
1966	1101.50	661.30	1.99	0.11	26.1780	26.1780				
1967	1008.60	581.40	0.49	0.04	26.1780	26.1780				
1968	1156.90	658.40	30.24		26.1780	26.1780				
1969	1405.40	789.90	5.92		26.1780	26.1780				
1970	1365.60	775.30	9.03		26.1780	26.1780				
1971	1677.30	743.50	2.67		26.1780	26.1780				
1972	2060.60	1097.60			26.1780	26.1780				
1973	2342.10	1341.30			26.1838	26.1732				
1974	4570.90	2914.00			26.9009	26.8951				
1975	6235.40	3440.90	62.79		27.0270	27.0270				
1976	9203.30	4141.30	150.90		25.7169	25.7175				
1977	10496.70	4199.00			25.3165	25.3165				
1978	9658.70	4159.80			25.4770	25.4770				
1979	13066.70	6453.30			25.4770	25.4770				
1980	16188.10	8272.70			25.4777	25.4777	133	55	62	105
1981	19781.00	8253.70			25.4777	25.4777	174	50	81	116
1982	15757.20	7953.60			25.4777	25.4777	150	53	76	102
1983	17829.00	7547.50			25.4777	25.4777	164	52	188	95
1984	16154.50	7274.80			25.4777	25.4777	153	49	82	97
1985	15570.50	6426.50			25.4777	25.4777	161	45	69	95
1986	10709.00	5198.90			25.4777	25.4777	152	44	82	70
1987	27915.01	15191.60			8.8889	8.8889	114	46	83	65
1988	25040.00	15092.70			8.9087	8.9087	98	51	102	62
1989	23543.81	33739.60			8.9087	8.9087	92	78	99	77
1990	26940.00	47280.00			8.9087	8.9087	100	100	100	100
1991	31070.00	38500.00			8.9087	8.9087	107	109	115	81
1992	39178.00	34720.00			8.9087	8.9087	143	105	98	68
1993	46467.70	35319.20			8.9087	8.9087	225	158	93	67
1994	61370.00	34200.00			8.9087	8.9087	276	171	105	72
1995	52860.00	40000.00			8.9087	8.9087	248	167	118	90
1996	60390.00	44890.00			8.9087	8.9087	250	164	125	95
1997	45210.74	43953.12			8.9087	8.9087				

2. IMPORTS BY BROAD ECONOMIC CATEGORY AND EXPORTS BY INDUSTRIAL ORIGIN. (PERCENTAGE OF TOTAL VALUE)
IMPORTATIONS PAR CATEGORIES ECONOMIQUES ET EXPORTATIONS PAR BRANCHE D'ACTIVITE.(EN POURCENTAGE DE LA VALEUR TOTALE)

IMPORTS – IMPORTATIONS

	1990	1991	1992	1993	1994	1995	1996
TOTAL IMPORTS–IMPORTATIONS TOTALES	100.		100.			100.	
1 FOOD BEV–ALIMENTATION BOISSONS	26.3		16.7			14.0	
11 PRIMARY–PRODUITS DE BASE	12.5		7.9			6.7	
111 FOR INDUSTRY–POUR L'INDUSTRIE	10.6		6.0			3.6	
112 FOR HOUSEHOLDS–POUR LES MENAGES	1.9		1.9			3.1	
12 PROCESSED–PRODUITS ELABORES	13.9		8.8			7.2	
121 FOR INDUSTRY–POUR L'INDUSTRIE	7.6		4.8			1.8	
122 FOR HOUSEHOLDS–POUR LES MENAGES	6.3		4.0			5.4	
2 IND SUPPLIES–APPROV INDUSTRIELS	45.0		41.2			46.4	
21 PRIMARY–PRODUITS DE BASE	3.4		1.8			1.7	
22 PROCESSED–PRODUITS ELABORES	41.6		39.4			44.7	
3 FUELS–COMBUSTIBLES	3.0		3.8			1.1	
31 PRIMARY–PRODUITS DE BASE	2.3		1.0			0.5	
32 PROCESSED–PRODUITS ELABORES	0.7		2.9			0.6	
321 MOTOR SPIRIT–ESSENCE	0.0		0.0			0.0	
322 OTHER–AUTRES	0.7		2.9			0.6	
4 MACHINERY–EQUIPEMENT	15.5		17.9			18.1	
41 CAPITAL EQUIPMENT–MACHINES	13.0		15.0			15.2	
42 PARTS–PIECES ACCESSOIRES	2.5		2.9			3.0	
5 TRANSPORT–TRANSPORT	5.6		16.2			13.7	
51 PASSENGER CARS–AUTOMOBILES	0.3		2.0			0.9	
52 OTHER–AUTRES	1.3		8.7			10.2	
521 INDUSTRIAL–INDUSTRIELS	1.3		8.7			10.1	
522 NON INDUSTRIAL–NON INDUSTRIEL	0.0		0.0			0.0	
53 PARTS–PIECES ACCESSOIRES	3.9		5.5			2.6	
6 CONSUM GOODS–BIENS CONSOMMATION	3.5		3.4			4.7	
61 DURABLE–DURABLES	0.9		1.4			1.2	
62 SEMI DURABLE–SEMI DURABLES	1.0		0.9			1.6	
63 NON DURABLE–NON DURABLES	1.6		1.1			1.9	
7 GOODS NES–BIENS NDA	1.1		0.7			2.0	

EXPORTS – EXPORTATIONS

	1990	1991	1992	1993	1994	1995	1996
TOTAL EXPORTS–EXPORTATIONS TOTALES	100.		100.			100.	
1 AGRICULTURE	14.7		18.1			16.4	
2 MINING QUARRY–INDUS EXTRACTIVES	35.8		61.3			56.1	
3 MANUFACTURING–IND MANUFACTUR	49.5		20.6			27.4	
31 FOOD BEV TOBACCO–ALIM BOISS TAB	3.2		1.4			2.5	
32 TEXTILES–INDUSTRIES TEXTILES	21.4		7.6			14.3	
33 WOOD & PRODUCTS–BOIS & PRODUITS	0.0		0.0			0.0	
34 PAPER & PRODUCTS–PAPIER & PRODT	0.2		0.1			0.3	
35 CHEMICALS–INDUSTRIES CHIMIQUES	23.6		10.1			7.9	
36 NON METAL MIN–MIN NON METAL	0.7		0.6			0.2	
37 BASIC METAL–IND METAL BASE	0.0		0.0			0.3	
38 METAL MANUF–MANUF METAL	0.3		0.7			1.6	
39 OTH MANUF IND–AUTRES MANUF	0.1		0.1			0.2	

3. TRADE BY PRINCIPAL COUNTRIES OF CONSIGNMENT AND CONSUMPTION (VALUE IN MILLION U.S. DOLLARS)
ECHANGES SELON LES PRINCIPAUX PAYS DE CONSIGNATION ET DE COMSOMMATION (VALEUR EN MILLIONS DE DOLLARS EU)

COUNTRIES–PAYS	SPECIAL IMPORTS C.I.F. IMPORTATIONS SPECIALES C.A.F				
	1992	1993	1994	1995	1996
World	3490.3	4139.8	5467.6	4708.8	5379.6
Africa	84.4	109.7	130.0	139.3	129.2
Americas	348.2	398.0	480.3	492.4	624.9
– Northern America	230.1	279.9	332.4	331.1	418.7
– LAIA	94.6	103.2	135.5	143.8	187.3
– CACM	1.1			10.7	
– Caribbean	22.4	14.9	12.4	4.9	18.9
– Rest of America	0.1			1.9	
Asia excl fmr USSR	1114.7	904.4	1335.7	1530.7	1773.4
– Middle East	358.5	397.1	512.0	530.2	599.8
Asia former USSR	0.1			0.6	
Europe excl fmr USSR	1834.8	2123.4	2462.5	2020.7	2096.4
– European Union	1365.3	1629.8	1931.8	1625.5	1739.4
– Eastern Europe	419.1	450.0	466.5	358.9	316.2
– Rest of Europe	50.5	43.6	64.2	36.3	40.8
Europe former USSR	73.9	145.7	114.2	423.6	408.7
Oceania	5.1			6.7	
Other	29.2	458.6		94.8	
Germany/Allemagne	352.1	421.4	465.8	490.6	432.9
Italy/Italie	285.6	340.1	474.3	355.7	360.2
Japan/Japon	346.9	338.4	552.9	205.6	263.9
USA/Etats–Unis d'Amer	217.1	266.6	314.8	318.7	389.7
Turkey/Turquie	216.6	224.4	259.9	263.7	311.0
France, Monaco	220.6	293.2	270.7	170.7	318.6
Romania/Roumanie	151.3	185.7	210.4	180.8	180.9
Korea, Republic of	85.3			287.7	370.0
China/Chine	88.6	94.0	200.2	180.5	160.9
Belgium–Luxembourg	108.6	140.1	153.3	145.0	145.9
United Kingdom	103.8	111.2	195.0	120.1	145.6
Ukraine	0.0			274.0	310.0
Russian Federation	73.7	145.7	114.2	148.7	98.7
Areas n.e.s.	26.5	458.6		93.0	
Bulgaria/Bulgarie	149.0	119.0	108.2	57.5	108.0
Netherlands/Pays–Bas	101.1	110.5	114.6	106.1	100.9
Brazil/Brésil	53.9	59.7	71.4	71.3	85.9
Saudi Arabia	43.7	47.3	75.0	78.6	91.1
Egypt/Egypte	42.9	54.4	69.4	69.6	82.7
Spain/Espagne	40.0	54.4	76.4	62.9	72.1
Jordan/Jordanie	22.5	20.9	60.3	74.0	108.0
Lebanon/Liban	46.6	65.3	55.1	56.8	56.6
Other Asia n.e.s.	64.4			84.1	117.8
Argentina/Argentine	31.6	43.5	64.1	40.0	83.7
Czech Republic		63.5	96.7	91.7	
Sweden/Suède	45.1	46.4	59.9	54.1	36.2
Austria/Autriche	42.8	43.2	48.7	42.4	54.9
India/Inde	24.1	37.7	32.0	36.4	53.7
Greece/Grèce	27.4	34.9	33.7	28.4	46.1
Switzerland,Liechtenst.	28.6	25.0	46.7	26.2	40.8
Sri Lanka	22.0	34.3	35.2	27.6	40.7
Hungary/Hongrie	32.4	45.7	27.4	19.6	27.3
Thailand/Thaïlande	28.0			61.9	57.0
Malaysia/Malaisie	45.7			46.5	39.6
Finland/Finlande	15.5	16.3	20.8	31.7	13.1
Poland/Pologne	27.6	36.1	23.7	9.1	
Iran (Islamic Rep of)	12.1	19.2	31.7	22.2	7.5
Tunisia/Tunisie	20.5	26.7	25.6	13.0	
Canada	13.0	13.3	17.6	12.4	29.1
Bangladesh	25.9			26.6	28.8

COUNTRIES–PAYS	SPECIAL EXPORTS F.O.B. EXPORTATIONS SPECIALES F.O.B.				
	1992	1993	1994	1995	1996
Monde	3093.1	3279.9	3547.3	3969.9	3998.8
Afrique	99.9	85.5	132.5	201.5	136.9
Amériques	53.1	96.3	50.7	73.0	22.3
– Amérique du Nord	24.9	89.3	46.8	62.0	15.4
– ALAI	7.1	6.9	3.9	10.7	6.9
– MCAC	0.0			0.1	
– Caraïbes	21.1		0.0	0.2	
– Autre Amérique				0.1	
Asie anc. URSS exclus	788.0	787.4	960.7	1102.3	1070.8
– Moyen–Orient	760.4	756.5	922.1	1032.8	998.0
Asie ancienne URSS	1.3			37.2	42.2
Europe anc. URSS exclus	2094.1	2010.1	2048.1	2370.8	2545.0
– Union Européenne	1953.7	1912.4	1979.1	2262.4	2478.5
– Europe de l'Est	123.3	70.2	67.6	85.9	36.9
– Autre de l'Europe	17.1	27.5	1.4	22.5	29.7
Europe ancienne URSS	54.1	87.7	245.2	184.3	157.8
Océanie	0.0			0.3	
Autre	2.5	79.5		0.6	
Italy/Italie	1083.6	967.6	956.1	927.6	1152.7
France, Monaco	574.3	481.1	440.4	578.6	623.2
Lebanon/Liban	401.5	331.2	389.9	308.9	221.6
Spain/Espagne	109.8	244.1	240.7	303.4	397.8
Saudi Arabia	133.5	154.0	195.9	194.8	193.9
Turkey/Turquie	42.9	67.9	87.5	230.0	286.9
Russian Federation	47.6	87.7	245.2	159.9	123.7
United Kingdom	64.7	102.0	189.1	164.9	91.6
Jordan/Jordanie	44.7	73.1	96.4	92.7	105.9
Germany/Allemagne	76.0	34.8	88.4	105.5	41.6
Kuwait/ Koweït	61.6	56.0	51.1	60.4	67.9
Greece/Grèce	12.4	7.6	22.0	125.9	100.5
Cyprus/Chypre	47.9	29.6	36.9	70.6	36.5
Libyan Arab Jamahiriya	18.2	25.7	50.5	60.6	28.3
USA/Etats–Unis d'Amer	24.3	60.1	42.6	35.7	15.4
United Arab Emirates	14.6	22.4	35.6	51.2	42.3
Netherlands/Pays–Bas	21.8	51.6	26.7	26.6	30.2
Romania/Roumanie	33.6	22.5	29.3	46.4	21.8
Tunisia/Tunisie	30.0	25.6	19.8	40.5	23.7
Bulgaria/Bulgarie	73.7	30.6	14.1	11.5	5.9
Algeria/Algérie	16.0	10.6	24.3	39.6	38.1
Egypt/Egypte	16.9	12.9	22.3	21.3	21.0
Portugal	0.5	20.0	11.4	13.7	38.5
Morocco/Maroc	9.6	7.5	11.7	32.0	21.3
Areas n.e.s.	0.6	79.5		0.2	
Poland/Pologne	12.4	13.8	16.9	15.9	6.6
India/Inde	0.0	11.3	16.9	4.7	28.7
Canada	0.6	29.2	4.1	26.3	
Qatar	8.6	8.1	12.4	10.8	14.5
Yugoslavia/Yougoslavie	0.2	10.3	0.4	19.6	23.1
Ukraine	5.9			21.5	18.6
Switzerland,Liechtenst.	16.9	17.3	0.9	2.9	6.6
Japan/Japon	9.2	9.5	11.2	8.3	4.5
Azerbaijan/Azerbaïdjan	0.0			17.0	23.2
Yemen/Yémen	2.2	6.4	9.9	5.3	7.2
Bahrain/Bahreïn	1.8	7.4	4.9	6.2	8.4
China, Hong Kong SAR	0.8	9.7	9.8	8.0	
Indonesia/Indonésie	0.8			14.3	11.4
Sudan/Soudan	8.3	3.0	3.9	4.8	4.5
Thailand/Thaïlande	3.4			12.3	7.2

(VALUE AS PERCENTAGE OF WORLD TOTAL)(VALEURS EN POURCENTAGE DU TOTAL MONDIAL)

	1987	1988	1989	1990	1991	1992	1993	1994	1995	1996
Africa	6.7	1.1	1.1	2.2	1.9	2.4	2.6	2.4	3.0	2.4
Americas	7.6	8.3	10.1	14.3	13.6	10.0	9.6	8.8	10.5	11.6
– Northern America	5.7	6.7	8.1	11.1	9.8	6.6	6.8	6.1	7.0	7.8
– LAIA	1.3	1.1	1.2	2.2	3.0	2.7	2.5	2.5	3.1	3.5
– CACM	0.0		0.0	0.1		0.0			0.2	
– Caribbean	0.6	0.5	0.7	0.9	0.8	0.6	0.4	0.2	0.1	0.4
– Rest of America						0.0			0.0	
Asia excl fmr USSR	24.7	30.7	29.2	26.6	21.0	31.9	21.8	24.4	32.5	33.0
– Middle East	15.6	12.9	16.7	13.4	12.8	10.3	9.6	9.4	11.3	11.2
Asia former USSR						0.0			0.0	
Europe excl fmr USSR	52.1	50.5	54.0	53.0	53.4	52.6	51.3	45.0	42.9	39.0
– European Union	39.2	39.9	45.2	44.3	41.4	39.1	39.4	35.3	34.5	32.3
– Eastern Europe	8.7	8.3	6.4	6.1	9.1	12.0	10.9	8.5	7.6	5.9
– Rest of Europe	4.2	2.3	2.3	2.5	2.9	1.4	1.1	1.2	0.8	0.8
Europe former USSR	8.3	8.6	4.4	2.8	1.3	2.1	3.5	2.1	9.0	7.6
Oceania	0.3	0.0	0.1	0.0		0.1			0.1	
Other	0.3	0.8	1.2	1.0	8.8	0.8	11.1		2.0	
Germany/Allemagne					10.1	10.1	10.2	8.5	10.4	8.0
Italy/Italie	6.8	6.2	7.0	6.4	7.3	8.2	8.2	8.7	7.6	6.7
Japan/Japon	3.0	11.2	4.2	3.3	4.5	9.9	8.2	10.1	4.4	4.9
USA/Etats–Unis d'Amer	5.3	6.4	7.9	10.7	9.4	6.2	6.4	5.8	6.8	7.2
Turkey/Turquie	2.9	6.0	7.7	7.7	9.5	6.2	5.4	4.8	5.6	5.8
France, Monaco	9.8	10.5	11.4	12.7	6.7	6.3	7.1	5.0	3.6	5.9
Romania/Roumanie	2.4	2.5	1.9	0.9	2.7	4.3	4.5	3.8	3.8	3.4
Korea, Republic of	0.2	0.3	0.4	0.9		2.4			6.1	6.9
China/Chine	1.2	1.3	1.4	1.7	2.0	2.5	2.3	3.7	3.8	3.0
Belgium–Luxembourg	1.6	2.7	4.0	3.3	3.4	3.1	3.4	2.8	3.1	2.7

	1987	1988	1989	1990	1991	1992	1993	1994	1995	1996
Afrique	1.0	2.2	2.0	2.9	3.5	3.2	2.6	3.7	5.1	3.4
Amériques	1.3	1.7	2.8	0.9	0.6	1.7	2.9	1.4	1.8	0.6
– Amérique du Nord	1.3	1.7	2.4	0.9	0.6	0.8	2.7	1.3	1.6	0.4
– ALAI	0.0	0.0	0.4	0.0	0.0	0.2	0.2	0.1	0.3	0.2
– MCAC				0.0		0.0			0.0	
– Caraïbes	0.0	0.0	0.0	0.0		0.7		0.0	0.0	
– Autre Amérique									0.0	
Asie anc. URSS exclus	12.8	19.8	20.8	19.5	22.6	25.5	24.0	27.1	27.8	26.8
– Moyen–Orient	12.0	18.8	19.9	19.1	22.4	24.6	23.1	26.0	26.0	25.0
Asie ancienne URSS						0.0			0.9	1.1
Europe anc. URSS exclus	64.1	47.0	38.4	43.6	53.8	67.7	61.3	57.7	59.7	63.6
– Union Européenne	47.4	33.9	31.3	41.7	48.1	63.2	58.3	55.8	57.0	62.0
– Europe de l'Est	15.4	11.9	6.2	1.4	5.0	4.0	2.1	1.9	2.2	0.9
– Autre de l'Europe	1.3	1.1	0.9	0.5	0.7	0.6	0.8	0.0	0.6	0.7
Europe ancienne URSS	20.8	29.1	35.7	32.7	18.9	1.7	2.7	6.9	4.6	3.9
Océanie			0.3	0.5		0.0			0.0	
Autre	0.0	0.3	0.0	0.0	0.6	0.1	2.4		0.0	
Italy/Italie	31.1	20.2	15.5	20.8	22.4	35.0	29.5	27.0	23.4	28.8
France, Monaco	9.9	7.0	9.6	12.8	17.7	18.6	14.7	12.4	14.6	15.6
Lebanon/Liban	0.8	3.8	4.5	6.3	9.6	13.0	10.1	11.0	7.8	5.5
Spain/Espagne	0.5	0.2	0.8	0.7	0.7	3.5	7.4	6.8	7.6	9.9
Saudi Arabia	1.7	3.8	6.0	6.4	5.8	4.3	4.7	5.5	4.9	4.8
Turkey/Turquie	0.4	0.3	0.9	2.7	2.7	1.4	2.1	2.5	5.8	7.2
Russian Federation						1.5	2.7	6.9	4.0	3.1
United Kingdom	1.1	0.6	0.9	2.0	1.9	2.1	3.1	5.3	4.2	2.3
Jordan/Jordanie	1.9	1.2	1.0	0.6	2.0	1.4	2.2	2.7	2.3	2.6
Germany/Allemagne					2.9	2.5	1.1	2.5	2.7	1.0

4. Special Imports C.I.F. by Commodities according to the S.I.T.C. (Rev. 2) in million U.S. Dollars
Importations Spéciales C.A.F. par Produits d'après la C.T.C.I. (Rév. 2) en millions de Dollars E.U.

SITC CTCI	COMMODITY	1993		1994		1995		1996		PRODUIT
		QUANTITY QUANTITE	VALUE VALEUR	QUANTITY QUANTITE	VALUE VALEUR	QUANTITY QUANTITE	VALUE VALEUR	QUANTITY QUANTITE	VALUE VALEUR	
	ALL COMMODITIES		4139.8		5467.7		4708.8			TOUS PRODUITS
0	FOOD AND LIVE ANIMALS		641.1		804.5		691.7			ALIMENTS,ANIMAUX VIVANTS
001	*LIVE ANIMALS FOR FOOD		122.7		95.5		55.1			ANIMAUX VIVANTS
0012	SHEEP AND GOATS,LIVE						53.0			ESPECES OVINE ET CAPRINE
00121	SHEEP,LIVE	W 2351	115.6	N 1350000	87.2	N 1087496	52.9			ESPECE OVINE
02	DAIRY PRODCTS,BIRDS'EGGS		33.7		31.6		30.2			PRODUITS LAITIERS,OEUFS
022	MILK AND CREAM					W 6870	17.7			LAIT ET CREME
0224	MILK,CREAM PRESERVED ETC					W 6865	17.6			LAIT,CREME CONS,CONC
02242	MILK DRY,1.5% FAT OR LES	W 7019	14.8	W 10976	17.4					LAIT POUDRE INF 1.5%
023	BUTTER	W 9930	17.9	W 6746	12.6	W 5501	12.1			BEURRE
03	FISH AND PREPARATIONS		0.8		10.8		60.3			POISSONS ET PREPARATIONS
037	FISH ETC PREPD,PRSVD NES					W 6877	59.8			POIS,CRUST,MOL PREPARES
0371	FISH PREPARD,PRESRVD NES					W 6877	59.8			CONSERVES DE POISSONS
04	CEREALS AND PREPARATIONS		199.4		145.5		121.5			CEREALES ET PRODUITS
042	RICE					W 142099	58.5			RIZ
0421	RICE IN HUSK OR HUSKED					W 142099	58.5			RIZ SANS AUTRE PREPARATION
04212	RICE HUSKED	W 143826	45.2	W 115861	42.4					RIZ CARGO
044	MAIZE UNMILLED	W 347585	45.0	W 399962	54.4	W 316645	45.7			MAIS NON MOULU
046	WHEAT ETC MEAL OR FLOUR					W 44164	15.2			SEMOULE FARINE,FROMENT
04601	FLOUR OF WHEAT OR MESLIN	W 404154	88.9	W 279487	48.7	W 44164	15.2			FARINE DE FROMENT
05	VEGETABLES AND FRUIT		31.7		210.5		98.9			LEGUMES ET FRUITS
054	VEG ETC FRSH,SMPLY PRSVD					W 19267	14.5			LEGUMES FRAIS,CONG,SECS
057	FRUIT,NUTS,FRESH,DRIED					W 65629	81.4			FRUITS FRAIS OU SECS
0573	BANANA,PLANTAIN,FRSH,DRY					W 52753	27.9			BANANES FRAICHES,SECHEES
0577	NUTS EDIBLE,FRESH,DRIED					W 6654	50.5			FRUITS A COQUES
05779	NUTS EDIBLE,FRSH,DRY,NES	W 3129	17.7	W 4323	32.1	W 3590	42.0			FRUITS A COQUES NDA
06	SUGAR AND PREPS,HONEY		113.4		142.4		116.0			SUCRES ET PRODUITS
061	SUGAR AND HONEY					W 319767	116.0			SUCRES ET MIEL
0611	RAW BEET AND CANE SUGAR	W 82559	23.5	W 84100	21.2	W 53500	20.0			SUCRES BRUTS
0612	REFINED SUGAR ETC	W 270978	83.7	W 345336	116.5	W 248315	90.4			SUCRES RAFFINES
07	COFFEE,TEA,COCOA,SPICES		72.0		89.0		99.5			CAFE,THE,CACAO,EPICES
071	COFFEE AND SUBSTITUTES					W 11759	38.7			CAFE ET SUCCEDANES
0711	COFFEE GREEN,ROASTED,SUB			W 10837	26.3	W 11607	34.2			CAFE TORREFIE OU DECAFEINE
07111	COFFEE GREEN,HUSKS,SKINS	W 13220	17.3			W 11606	34.2			CAFE NON TORREFIE
074	TEA AND MATE					W 26367	43.1			THE ET MATE
0741	TEA	W 20755	35.4	W 23518	36.3	W 16598	27.6			THE
0742	MATE	W 6937	7.7	W 8004	13.2	W 9769	15.6			MATE
081	*FEEDING STUFF FOR ANIML		54.8		59.6	W 143612	41.0			NOURRITURE POUR ANIMAUX
0813	OILCAKE AND OTH RESIDUES	W 112610	26.5	W 180065	42.3	W 93099	19.9			TOURTEAUX
08199	FODDER NES,INCL SWEETNED	W 35690	15.9	W 21281	9.4	W 28711	12.8			PREPARATIONS FOURRAGERES
09	MISC EDIBLE PRODUCTS		10.4		15.9		57.3			PREP ALIMENTAIRES DIVERSES
091	MARGARINE AND SHORTENING					W 59680	49.0			MARGARINE ET GRAISSES
0914	MARGARINE,EDIBLE FAT NES					W 59680	49.0			MARGARINES,SIMILI SAINDOUX
1	BEVERAGES AND TOBACCO		20.3		55.4		30.1			BOISSONS ET TABACS
12	TOBACCO AND MANUFACTURES		16.4		51.9		26.5			TABACS BRUTS FABRIQUES
122	TOBACCO,MANUFACTURED					W 1721	26.4			TABACS FABRIQUES
1222	CIGARETTES					W 1296	25.9			CIGARETTES
2	CRUDE MATERLS,EXCL FUELS		117.8		155.5		179.2			MAT BRUTES NON COMESTIBLES
22	OIL SEEDS,OLEAGINOUS FRT		10.3		9.3		16.8			GRAINES,FRUITS OLEAGINEUX
222	SEEDS FOR'SOFT'FIXED OIL					W 18899	16.1			GRAINES HUILES FIXES
2225	SESAME SEEDS	W 15846	10.1	W 10636	6.7	W 18809	15.8			GRAINES DE SESAME
24	CORK AND WOOD		57.9		92.1		121.8			LIEGE ET BOIS
248	WOOD SHAPED,SLEEPERS					W 197840	115.8			BOIS SIMPLEMENT TRAVAILLES
2482	LUMBER SHAPED CONIFER	W 141137	56.0							CONIFERES SCIES,RABOTES
24821	LUMBER SAWN ETC CONIFER			W 153640	90.0					CONIFERES SCIES LONGITUD
2483	LUMBER SHAPED NON–CONIFR					W 197840	115.8			NON CONIFERES SCIES,RABOTES
24831	LUMBER SAWN ETC NON–CON					W 197840	115.8			SCIES LONGITUDINALEMENT
3	MINERAL FUELS ETC		179.8		89.3		51.3			COMBUSTIBLES MINERAUX LUB
33	PETROLEUM AND PRODUCTS		161.8		64.6		28.6			PETROLE ET DERIVES
334	PETROLEUM PRODUCTS,REFIN					W 103874	27.5			PRODUITS RAFFINES
3343	GAS OILS					W 77475	14.3			GAS OILS
341	*GAS,NATURAL AND MANUFCT		17.3	W 109306	23.8	W 105027	21.6			GAZ NATUREL,GAZ MANUFACT
3413	PETROLM GASES,LIQUEFIED					W 105024	21.5			GAZ DE PETROLE LIQUEFIE
3414	PETROLEUM GASES, GASEOUS	W 74422	17.3			W 3	0.2			GAZ DE PETROLE GAZEUX
4	ANIMAL,VEGETABLE OIL,FAT		95.5		90.1		47.8			HUILES,GRAISSES ANIM,VEG
411	*ANIMAL OILS AND FATS		29.3		37.8	W 2216	1.6			HUILES,GRAISSES ANIMALES
41139	ANIMAL OILS,FATS NES	W 38143	28.9			W 1757	1.3			GRAISSES,HUILES ANIM NDA
42	FIXED VEGETABLE OIL,FAT		53.7		42.4		25.1			HUILES VEGETALES FIXES
423	FIXED VEG OILS,SOFT					W 30445	22.3			HUILES VEGET DOUCES FIXES
4232	SOYA BEAN OIL	W 31079	23.7	W 35854	28.2	W 30238	22.1			HUILE DE SOJA
4233	COTTON SEED OIL	W 45104	28.1	W 17238	11.0					HUILE DE COTON
431	*PROCESD ANML VEG OIL,ET		12.5		10.0	W 34938	21.2			HUILES,GRAISSES PREPAREES
5	CHEMCLS,RELATED PROD NES		453.2		462.4		479.1			PRODUITS CHIMIQUES
51	ORGANIC CHEMICALS		74.1		54.4		70.2			PROD CHIMIQ ORGANIQUES
514	NITROGEN–FNCTN COMPOUNDS					W 127601	35.5			COMPOSES FONCT AZOTEES
5147	AMIDE–FNCT CMPD,EXC UREA	W 304300	40.2	W 73759	13.5	W 122537	26.4			COMPOSES CARBOXYAMIDE
52	INORGANIC CHEMICALS		41.3		40.7		36.0			PROD CHIM INORGANIQUES
523	OTHR INORG CHEMICALS ETC					W 61464	23.6			AUT PRODUITS CHIMIQUES INORG
5232	OTH MTL CMPD OF INRG ACD					W 40985	17.0			SELS METALLIQUES
53	DYES,TANNING,COLOUR PROD		34.3		39.0		37.8			PROD TEINTURE,COLORANTS
531	SYNT DYE,NAT INDGO,LAKES					W 1685	14.5			MAT COLOR ORGAN,LAQUES
5312	SYNTH LUMIN,INDIGO,LAKES					W 1685	14.5			LUMINOPHORES ORGAN SYNTH
53121	SYN ORG LUMIN ETC,INDIGO	W 2206	16.7	W 2125	15.4	W 1650	14.5			PROD ORGANIQ SYNTH LUMIN
533	PIGMENTS,PAINTS,ETC					W 12020	21.7			PIGMENTS,PEINTURES,VERNIS
541	*MEDICINAL,PHARM PRODUCT		28.0		35.0	K 3356212	36.5			PROD MEDICINAUX PHARMACEUT
5417	MEDICAMENTS					K 2942659	16.6			MEDICAMENTS
55	PERFUME,CLEANING ETC PRD		16.4		18.3		16.4			PROD POUR PARFUM,TOILETTE
562	*FERTILIZERS,MANUFACTURE		69.2		65.2	W 402622	71.2			ENGRAIS MANUFACTURES
5621	CHEM NITROGENOUS FERTLZR	W 43207	5.2	W 130205	18.5	W 273831	39.7			ENGRAIS AZOTES
5622	CHEM PHOSPHATIC FERTILZR	W 394741	57.9	W 173964	43.1	W 118765	27.1			ENGRAIS PHOSPHATES
58	PLASTIC MATERIALS ETC		118.8		136.2		140.9			MAT PLAST ARTIFICIELLES
582	PROD OF CONDENSATION ETC			W 19291	20.4	W 19173	23.3			PROD CONDENS,POLYCOND
5829	OTH CONDNSATION,ETC PROD	W 19482	17.6							AUT PROD CONDENSATION
583	POLYMERIZATION ETC PRODS					W 97876	91.8			PROD POLYMERISATION
5831	POLYETHYLENE					W 46449	38.5			POLYETHYLENE
58311	— IN PRIMARY FORMS	W 50376	35.4	W 50625	33.9					POLYETHYLENE PRIMAIRES
5832	POLYPROPYLENE					W 19839	19.1			POLYPROPYLENE
58321	— IN PRIMARY FORMS	W 20490	15.2	W 22911	18.1					POLYPROPYLENE PRIMAIRES
58341	— IN PRIMARY FORMS	W 17570	13.1	W 18543	14.1					SOUS FORMES PRIMAIRES
58351	— IN PRIMARY FORMS	W 21738	25.7							SOUS FORMES PRIMAIRES
5839	OTH POLYMRZTION ETC PROD			W 29348	32.3					AUT PROD POLYMER COPOLYM

4. Special Imports C.I.F. by Commodities according to the S.I.T.C. (Rev. 2) in million U.S. Dollars
Importations Spéciales C.A.F. par Produits d'après la C.T.C.I. (Rév. 2) en millions de Dollars E.U.

SITC CTCI	COMMODITY	1993 QUANTITY QUANTITE	1993 VALUE VALEUR	1994 QUANTITY QUANTITE	1994 VALUE VALEUR	1995 QUANTITY QUANTITE	1995 VALUE VALEUR	1996 QUANTITY QUANTITE	1996 VALUE VALEUR	PRODUIT
584	CELLULOSE DERIVATIVS ETC	W 5252	8.2			W 13783	19.1			CEL REGEN NIT ACETATE
5849	OTH CELL DERIV,VULC FBRE					W 13080	17.9			AUT DERIV CHIM CELLUL
59	CHEMICAL MATERIALS NES		71.5		73.9		66.0			MAT PROD CHIMIQUES NDA
591	PESTICIDES,DISINFECTANTS					W 2873	25.6			DESINF,INSECT,FONG,HERB
5913	HERBICIDES,FOR RETAIL	W 4582	18.8	W 3394	28.0					HERBICIDES VENTE AU DET
598	MISCEL CHEM PRODUCTS NES					W 20162	34.6			PROD DIV INDUST CHIM NDA
5989	CHEM PRODUCTS,PREPS NES					W 19118	32.1			PROD PREP CHIMIQUES NDA
59899	OTH CHEM PRODS,PREPS,NES	W 21375	31.4	W 19526	31.5	W 17886	30.4			AUT PRODUITS CHIMIQUES NDA
6	BASIC MANUFACTURES		1084.3		1520.1		1500.8			ART MANUFACTURES
62	RUBBER MANUFACTURES NES		61.6		68.7		50.6			CAOUTCHOUC MANUFACTURE
625	RUBBER TYRES, TUBES ETC					W 14960	37.5			PNEUS CAOUTCHOUC VULCANISE
6252	TYRES,NEW,BUS OR LORRY	W 9669	21.9	W 9120	23.2	W 7587	20.8			PNEUS POUR AUTOBUS,CAMIONS
6259	OTH TYRES,TYRE CASES,ETC					W 7374	16.8			AUTRES PNEUS RECHAPES FLAPS
62599	TYRES NES,TYRE CASES,ETC					W 7366	16.7			PNEUS,FLAPS
64	PAPER,PAPERBOARD AND MFR		69.1		100.8		95.6			PAPIERS,CARTONS & OUVRAGES
641	PAPER AND PAPERBOARD					W 154910	82.1			PAPIERS ET CARTONS
6412	PRINTG,WRITING PAPER NES					W 19756	20.1			PAPIERS POUR L'IMPRESSION
64121	— UNCOATED	W 17123	10.9			W 19756	20.1			PAPIERS IMPRES NON COUCHES
64122	— COATED,IMPREGNATD ETC	W 32330	18.6	W 38299	21.4					PAPIERS IMPRESSION COUCHES
6413	KRAFT PAPER,PAPERBOARD					W 22392	15.2			PAPIER ET CARTON KRAFT
64159	OTHER PAPER ETC,BULK,NES			W 33353	24.2	W 6248	7.5			AUT PAPIER ROULEAUX FEUILLES
6418	COATED ETC PAPER NES BLK					W 39667	19.8			PAP,CARTONS COUCHES,ENDUITS
64189	COATED PAPER ETC NES					W 39081	19.3			PAPIERS,CARTONS COUCHES
65	TEXTILE YARN,FABRICS,ETC		343.4		378.6		328.1			FILS,TISSUS,ARTICLES TEXTILE
651	TEXTILE YARN					W 76965	157.7			FILS TEXTILES
6514	SYN FIB YRN,BULK,MONOFIL			W 77645	162.6	W 57830	119.2			FILS CONT 85% FIB TEXT SYNTH
65147	— OF OTH CONT SYN FIBRE	W 25038	80.8							FILS AUT FI TEXT SYNT CONT
65148	— OF DISCONT SYN FIBRES					W 15592	48.4			FILS CONT 85% FI TEXT SYNTH
6516	DISCON SYN FIB BLEND YRN					W 14363	26.5			FILS FIBR TEX SYNT DIS MOINS
65168	OTH DISC SYN BLEND YARN					W 12840	25.1			FILS TEXT SYNT MELANGE AUT F
653	WOVN MAN–MADE FIB FABRIC					W 9836	86.4			TISSUS FIBRES SYNTH,ARTIF
6531	CONT SYNT WEAVES NONPILE	W 2352	19.3	W 5093	57.2	W 5902	56.1			TISSUS FIBRES SYNTH CONTINUE
65315	CONT SYN TXTL FABRIC NES					W 5902	56.1			TIS PLUS 85% TEXT SYNT CONT
6532	DISC SYN TXTL FABRIC NES					W 2803	19.0			TIS DISC MOINS 85% FIBR TEXT
6534	DISC SYN BLEND FABRC NES	W 4154	42.1	W 3168	24.5					TISSUS FIBRES SYNTH DISCONT
6535	CONT REGN WEAVES NONPILE	W 2120	14.8	W 2537	36.5	W 255	2.8			TISSUS FIB TEXT ART CONTINU
657	SPECIAL TXTL FABRC,PRODS					W 12678	24.1			TISSUS SPECIAUX
6573	COATED ETC TEXTILES NES					W 10894	16.8			TISSUS,ART MATIERE TEXT NDA
65732	PLASTIC COATED TEXTILES	W 12853	14.6	W 11121	12.7	W 9361	11.2			TISSUS IMPREGNES
658	TEXTILE ARTICLES NES					W 101604	47.6			ART FACONNES MAT TEXTILES
6581	BAGS,SACKS OF TEXTILES	W 42596	19.7	W 25013	16.6	W 98415	26.6			SACS EMBALLAGE TEXTILES
6582	MADE–UP CANVAS GOODS					W 2502	16.7			BACHES,TENTES ETC
65821	MADE–UP COTTN CANVAS GDS					W 2502	16.7			BACHES,TENTES DE COTON
66	NONMETAL MINERAL MFS NES		47.5		96.5		112.4			ART MIN NON METALLIQUES
661	LIME,CEMENT,BLDG PRODS					W 549885	75.4			CHAUX,CIMENTS MAT CONSTR
6612	CEMENT					W 545602	72.3			CIMENTS HYDRAULIQUES
67	IRON AND STEEL		414.0		589.5		624.3			FER ET ACIER
672	IRON,STEEL PRIMARY FORMS	W 20317	5.2	W 7033	1.8	W 40977	18.3			LINGOTS FER,ACIER
673	IRON,STEEL SHAPES ETC	W 392738	129.3			W 524253	291.3			BARRES,PROFIL FER,ACIER
6732	IRON,STEEL BARS ETC			W 604404	286.2	W 459046	270.0			BARRES FER,ACIER
6733	IRON,STEEL PROFILES ETC					W 64993	21.0			PROFILES,PALPLAN FER,ACIER
674	IRN,STL UNIV,PLATE,SHEET	W 281362	126.1			W 240387	117.9			LARGES PLATS,TOLES
6744	IRN,STL HVY PLATE,ROLLED			W 158777	68.9					TOLES LAMINEES PLUS 4.75 MM
6746	IRN,STL THIN PLATE,ROLLD					W 163322	71.5			TOLES LAM MOINS 3MM
6749	OTH IRN,STL PLATES,SHEET					W 61017	34.7			AUTRES TOLES FER,ACIER
67491	— OF IRON OR SIMPLE STL			W 52474	30.4					AUT TOLES AUTRES ACIER FIN
677	IRN,STL WIRE(EXCL W ROD)					W 29960	20.1			FILS EN FER,ACIER
67701	IRON, SIMPLE STEEL WIRE	W 11709	11.3	W 10225	10.9	W 29960	20.1			FILS NON ACIER FIN CARBONE
67705	OTHER ALLOY STEEL WIRE	W 41946	13.8	W 35638	16.7					FILS ACIER AUT ACIERS ALLIES
678	IRON,STL TUBES,PIPES,ETC					W 100574	165.3			TUBES,TUYAUX EN FONTE,FER
6782	IRON,STL SEAMLESS TUBES					W 11840	18.5			TUBES,TUYAUX SANS SOUDURE
6783	IRON,STL TUBES,PIPES NES	W 70958	63.5	W 95297	87.0	W 72615	110.0			AUT TUBES,TUYAUX FER,ACIER
6785	IRON,STEEL TUBE FITTINGS	W 10574	24.9	W 9548	20.4	W 6441	23.7			ACCESSOIRES DE TUYAUTERIE
68	NON–FERROUS METALS		36.7		38.3		55.1			METAUX NON FERREUX
682	COPPER EXC CEMENT COPPER					W 6968	21.4			CUIVRE
6822	COPPER,ALLOYS WORKED					W 6935	21.4			CUIVRE,ALLIAGES OUVRES
68221	COPPER BARS,WIRE,ETC	W 4386	9.1	W 3264	7.6	W 5409	16.3			BARRES,PROFILES ET FILS
684	ALUMINIUM					W 11716	29.3			ALUMINIUM
6842	ALUMINIUM,ALLOYS WORKED					W 5478	15.4			ALUMINIUM,ALLIAGES OUVRE
69	METAL MANUFACTURES NES		102.7		233.0		224.9			ART MANUFACT EN METAL NDA
691	STRUCTURES AND PARTS NES					W 14219	64.2			CONSTRUCT FER,ACIER,ALU
6911	STRUCTURES,PARTS IRN,STL	W 4879	8.6	W 20904	103.2	W 14128	62.3			CONSTRUCT FER,ACIER,FONTE
69211	STEEL STORAGE TANKS ETC			W 7216	17.9	W 482	1.9			CUVES EN FONTE FER OU ACIER
694	STL,COPPR NAILS,NUTS,ETC					W 8748	17.7			CLOUS,VIS,ECROUS
69402	IRN,STL NUTS,BOLTS,ETC	W 1886	6.5	W 2424	9.7	W 7742	16.3			BOULONS,VIS,ECROUS FER,AC
695	TOOLS					W 11252	73.0			OUTILS A MAIN
6953	OTHER HAND TOOLS					W 10054	65.8			AUTRES OUTILS A MAIN
69539	HAND TOOLS ETC NES	W 1238	2.2	W 1138	2.1	W 9365	63.0			OUTILLAGE A MAIN NDA
699	BASE METAL MFRS NES					W 15332	34.5			ART MANUFACTURES MET NDA
6991	LOCKSMITHS WARES,ETC					W 4174	15.4			ARTICLES DE SERRURERIE
7	MACHINES,TRANSPORT EQUIP		1412.2		2034.0		1486.1			MACHINES MATERIEL TRANSPORT
71	POWER GENERATING EQUIPMT		100.9		264.8		82.4			MACHINES GENERATRICES
713	INTRNL COMBUS PSTN ENGIN					W 7847	30.5			MOTEURS EXPL COMB INT, PIECE
7132	MOTOR VEHCL PISTN ENGINS	W 18734	25.7	W 12451	32.9	W 4676	8.5			MOTEURS EXPL POUR VEHICULES
7139	PISTON ENGINE PARTS NES	W 3467	25.0	W 3586	31.9	W 1278	13.6			PIECES POUR 713.2,3,8
716	ROTATING ELECTRIC PLANT					W 4847	29.2			APP ELECTR ROTATIFS,PIECES
7161	DC MOTORS AND GENERATORS	W 2833	8.7	W 2280	9.7	W 1210	16.6			MOTEURS COURANT CONTINU
7162	AC MTRS,GENRTRS,GEN SETS	W 6204	33.4			W 1490	5.8			MOTEURS ELECTRIQUES
71622	AC GENERATORS			W 4937	61.7					GENER COURANT ALTERNATIF
718	OTH POWER GENERATG MACHY					W 1638	19.3			AUTRES MOTEURS PARTIES
7188	WIND,WATER,ETC ENGINES					W 1100	16.1			MOT MACHINES MOTRICES NDA
72	MACHS FOR SPCL INDUSTRYS		197.6		260.9		220.4			MAC SPECIALES POUR INDUST
722	TRACTORS NON–ROAD	W 20420	25.2	W 20791	23.1	W 12873	16.5			TRACTEURS
7223	TRACK–LAYING TRACTORS					W 12873	16.5			TRACTEURS A CHENILLES
723	CIVIL ENGNEERG EQUIP ETC					W 16656	54.9			APPAREILS DE GENIE CIVIL
7234	CONST,MINING MACHNRY NES					W 16108	54.2			MACH POUR LA CONST, MINES
724	TEXTILE,LEATHER MACHNRY					W 10889	84.9			MACH POUR INDUSTRIE TEXTILE
7244	SPINNING,EXTRDNG,ETC MCH	W 2614	5.8	W 6616	58.8	W 2889	51.2			MACH POUR LE FILAGE
72442	FIBRE PROCESSNG MACH NES					W 604	15.0			MACH PREP MAT TEXTILES
72443	SPINNING,REELING,ETC MCH					W 1981	33.9			MACH POUR LA FILATURE
72452	KNITTING MACHINES	W 1619	15.1	W 1736	10.4	W 675	3.7			METIERS A BONNETERIE

4. Special Imports C.I.F. by Commodities according to the S.I.T.C. (Rev. 2) in million U.S. Dollars
Importations Spéciales C.A.F. par Produits d'après la C.T.C.I. (Rév. 2) en millions de Dollars E.U.

SITC CTCI	COMMODITY	1993 QUANTITY QUANTITE	1993 VALUE VALEUR	1994 QUANTITY QUANTITE	1994 VALUE VALEUR	1995 QUANTITY QUANTITE	1995 VALUE VALEUR	1996 QUANTITY QUANTITE	1996 VALUE VALEUR	PRODUIT
7246	AUXIL TXTL MCH,PARTS NES	W 533	8.0	W 1012	16.7	W 228	6.5			MACH PR 724.51,52,53,61
728	OTH MACHY FOR SPCL INDUS					W 6536	36.5			AUT MACH IND PARTICULIERES
7284	MACHY FOR SPCL INDUS NES					W 4794	30.7			MACH SPEC IND PARTICUL.
72848	OTH MCHY WITH INDIV FNCT	W 3297	30.1	W 7171	54.9	W 4274	28.8			AUTRES MACHINES NDA
73	METALWORKING MACHINERY		16.0		12.5		9.9			MACH TRAVAIL DES METAUX
73732	ELECTRIC WELDERS,ETC	W 4185	14.3	W 4072	11.3	W 114	1.3			MACH ELECT POUR SOUDER
74	GENRL INDUSTRL MACHY NES		308.6		458.8		286.7			MACH APP INDUSTRIE
741	HEATING,COOLING EQUIPMNT					W 5751	42.4			MACH CHAUFFAGE,PIECES
742	PUMPS FOR LIQUIDS ETC					W 3571	34.9			POMPES MOTO–POMPES
7428	OTHER PUMPS FOR LIQUIDS					W 3212	32.2			AUTRES POMPES POUR LIQ
74288	PUMPS FR LIQUIDS NES ETC	W 2623	15.1	W 4007	17.0	W 3164	30.6			POMPES POUR LIQUIDES NDA
7429	PTS NES OF PUMPS OF 742	W 1349	13.0	W 4015	56.6					PIECES POUR GROUPE 742
743	PUMPS NES,CENTRFUGES ETC					W 6352	46.7			POMPES COMPRES,VENT ETC
7431	PUMPS FOR GASES ETC	W 4030	21.1	W 7060	90.5	W 142	1.1			POMPES AIR A VIDE,COMPRES
7434	FANS,BLOWERS,ETC,PARTS					W 4821	31.3			VENTILATEURS,SIMIL,PIECES
744	MECHANICAL HANDLING EQU					W 4114	23.0			EQUIP MANUTENTION PIECES
7442	LIFTING,LOADING MACH NES					W 3483	17.6			APP LEVAGE,MANUTENTION
74421	PULLEY TACKLE,WINCHS ETC	W 20746	79.3	W 19215	45.1					PALANS,TREUILS
74422	SHIP DERRICKS,CRANES ETC	W 4186	33.5	W 48	1.3					GRUES,PONTS ROULANTS
745	NONELEC MACHY,TOOLS NES					W 1639	26.0			AUT MACH NON ELEC,PIECES
7452	OTH NONELEC MCHS,PTS NES					W 1574	25.6			AUT MACH NON ELEC,PIECES
74522	PACKAGNG,BOTTLNG,ETC MCH	W 292	7.0	W 412	9.2	W 742	17.2			MACH NETT BOUTEILLES,ETC
749	NONELEC MACH PTS,ACC NES					W 13611	113.9			PIECES MACH NON ELEC NDA
7492	COCKS,VALVES ETC NES	W 4479	31.8	W 6243	66.9	W 8517	57.8			ART ROB,SIM POUR TUYAUX
7493	SHAFT,CRANK,PULLEY ETC	W 1263	10.5	W 983	9.7	W 3140	30.5			ARBRES TRANS,VILEBREQUINS
7499	OTH NONELEC MCHY PTS NES					W 845	16.3			PIECES NON ELECT NDA
75	OFFICE MACHNES,ADP EQUIP		19.4		20.1		26.8			MACH BUREAU TRAIT AUTOM
752	AUTOMTIC DATA PROC EQUIP					W 242	14.4			MACH TRAIT INFORMATION
76	TELECOMM,SOUND EQUIPMENT		150.5		89.6		76.3			EQUIPMENT DE TELECOM
762	RADIO BROADCAST RECEIVRS					W 1514	20.8			RECEPTEURS RADIODIFFUSION
764	TELECOM EQPT,PTS,ACC NES					W 972	47.5			EQUIP TELECOM,PIECES
7641	LINE TELEPHONE,ETC EQUIP					W 616	33.8			APP TELEPHON PAR FIL
76491	PTS NES OF APPAR OF 7641	W 3724	127.0	W 1515	45.6					PIECES POUR 764.1
77	ELECTRIC MACHNRY NES ETC		130.9		272.1		215.3			MACH APP ELECT NDA
7711	TRANSFORMERS,ELECTRICAL	W 2271	3.2	W 4964	42.9	W 4296	10.8			TRANSFO ELECTRIQUES
772	SWITCHGEAR ETC,PARTS NES					W 5608	72.9			APP COUPURE,SECT ETC
7721	SWITCHGEAR ETC	W 3076	26.3	W 6665	86.7	W 5572	72.7			APP COUPURE,SECTIONMNT
773	ELECTR DISTRIBUTNG EQUIP	W 13317	42.1			W 9915	53.5			EQUIPMT DISTRIBUTION ELECT
7731	INSULATED WIRE,CABLE ETC			W 8535	31.1	W 7391	47.1			FILS,CABLES ISOLES ELECT
778	ELECTRICAL MACHINERY NES					W 6094	64.2			AUTRES MACH ELECT NDA
7782	ELECTRIC LAMPS,BULBS					W 1935	22.9			LAMPES, TUBES ELECTRIQUES
7788	OTH ELEC MACHY,EQUIP NES					W 2195	27.6			AUT MACH APP ELEC NDA
77882	ELEC TRAFFIC CONTROL EQU	W 949	14.6			W 111	10.7			APP ELECT SIGNAL,SECURITE ET
77889	ELEC PARTS OF MACHY NES			W 1681	21.3	W 807	8.5			PIECES ELEC DE MACH NDA
78	ROAD VEHICLES		466.9		634.5		533.2			VEHICULES ROUTIERS
781	PASS MOTOR VEH EXC BUSES	W 12755	102.1	W 9499	67.5	W 4741	44.5			AUTO TRANSPORT PERSONNES
782	LORRIES,SPCL MTR VEH NES					W 43911	360.1			VEHICULES SPECIAUX,MARCH
7821	LORRIES,TRUCKS	W 40235	289.7	W 44232	422.3	W 42805	339.7			VEHICULES TRANSP MARCHAND
7822	SPECIAL MOTOR VEHCLS NES	W 1029	7.8	W 1140	16.5	W 1106	20.4			VEHICULES USAGES SPECIAUX
783	ROAD MOTOR VEHICLES NES					W 22857	70.0			VEHICULES ROUTIERS NDA
7831	BUSES	W 2463	2.6	W 650	11.9	W 6347	46.8			VOITURES TRANSPORT COMMUN
7832	TRACTORS FOR TR–TRAILERS					W 16509	23.3			TRACTEURS ROUTIERS
784	MOTOR VEH PRTS,ACCES NES					W 7235	29.6			PIECES 722,781,782,783
7849	OTHER MOTOR VEHCL PARTS	W 16457	42.7	W 14883	78.6	W 7026	28.7			PIECES 722,781,782,783
786	TRAILERS,NONMOTR VEH,NES					W 8053	20.5			REMORQUES,CADRES,CONTAIN
79	OTHR TRANSPORT EQUIPMENT		21.7		20.7		35.4			AUTRE MATERIEL TRANSPORT
793	SHIPS AND BOATS ETC					W 15157	22.5			NAVIRES BATEAUX,ETC
7932	SHIPS AND BOATS NES	W 20174	10.4			W 14823	19.8			NAVIRES ET BATEAUX
8	MISC MANUFACTURED GOODS		98.7		159.3		149.8			ART MANUFACTURES DIVERS
87	PRECISION INSTRUMNTS NES		42.2		78.4		59.7			INSTRUM,APPAR SCIENT NDA
872	MEDICAL INSTRUMENTS NES					W 556	23.5			INSTR,APP MEDIC–CHIR NDA
87201	DENTAL INSTRUMENTS					W 530	23.0			INSTRUM,APPAR DENTAIRE
874	MEASURNG,CONTROLNG INSTR					W 1848	33.4			INSTRUMENTS DE MESURE
8743	GAS,LIQUID CONTROL INSTR	W 473	11.2	W 1802	35.0	W 1082	11.4			APP,INSTR MESURE FLUIDES
8748	ELEC MEAS,CONTRL EQU NES					W 260	14.2			APP ELEC ELECTRO MESURE
87483	OTH ELCTRNC MEAS ETC EQU	W 254	11.9	W 815	31.5					AUT APP ELECTRO DE MESURE
88	PHOTO EQU,OPTICL GDS ETC		19.5		22.2		23.7			APP,FOURN PHOTO,OP,MONTR
89	MISC MANUFCTRD GOODS NES		30.3		46.5		44.3			ART MANUFACTURES DIVERS
9	GOODS NOT CLASSD BY KIND		37.3		97.6		93.3			ART TRANSACT NON CLASSES
931	*SPECIAL TRANSACTIONS				97.1		93.2			TRANS.SPECIALES

5. Special Exports F.O.B. by Commodities according to the S.I.T.C. (Rev. 2) in million U.S. Dollars
Exportations Spéciales F.O.B. par Produits d'après la C.T.C.I. (Rév. 2) en millions de Dollars E.U.

SITC CTCI	COMMODITY	1993 QUANTITY QUANTITE	1993 VALUE VALEUR	1994 QUANTITY QUANTITE	1994 VALUE VALEUR	1995 QUANTITY QUANTITE	1995 VALUE VALEUR	1996 QUANTITY QUANTITE	1996 VALUE VALEUR	PRODUIT
	ALL COMMODITIES		3279.9		3547.4		3969.9			TOUS PRODUITS
0	FOOD AND LIVE ANIMALS		456.0		567.8		462.1			ALIMENTS,ANIMAUX VIVANTS
001	*LIVE ANIMALS FOR FOOD		93.7		76.5		47.8			ANIMAUX VIVANTS
0012	SHEEP AND GOATS,LIVE						43.5			ESPECES OVINE ET CAPRINE
00121	SHEEP,LIVE	W 1045	82.6	N 806000	62.9	N 901036	40.8			ESPECE OVINE
02	DAIRY PRODCTS,BIRDS'EGGS		9.8		11.6		4.7			PRODUITS LAITIERS,OEUFS
04	CEREALS AND PREPARATIONS		22.1		40.0		78.1			CEREALES ET PRODUITS
041	WHEAT ETC UNMILLED	W 6639	1.8	W 10960	3.6	W 59082	19.9			FROMENT,EPEAUTRE
0411	DURUM WHEAT UNMILLED					W 59082	19.9			FROMENT DUR NON MOULU
043	BARLEY UNMILLED					W 594136	55.6			ORGE NON MONDEE
05	VEGETABLES AND FRUIT		293.6		381.4		284.8			LEGUMES ET FRUITS
054	VEG ETC FRSH,SMPLY PRSVD					W 213831	137.9			LEGUMES FRAIS,CONG,SECS
0541	POTATOES FRSH EXCL SWEET	W 67365	19.6	W 49928	18.8	W 44015	18.5			POMMES DE TERRE
0542	LEGUMINOUS VEGETBLES DRY	W 67049	24.1	W 126393	66.5	W 50322	35.7			LEGUMES A COSSE SECS
0544	TOMATOES FRESH	W 64255	24.8	W 93176	51.9	W 72906	42.3			TOMATES FRAICHES
0545	OTHER FRESH VEGETABLES					W 46045	40.6			AUTRES LEGUMES FRAIS,REF
05451	ALLIACEOUS VEGTBLS,FRESH	W 11982	7.0	W 16985	11.6	W 10182	5.9			OIGNONS,ECHALOTES,AUX
05459	FRESH VEGETABLES NES	W 83762	70.5	W 75587	61.6	W 35863	34.8			LEGUMES FRAIS,REFRI NDA
0548	EDIBLE VEG NES FRESH,DRY			W 6253	42.3	W 243	0.2			RACINES,TUBERCULES
056	VEGTBLES ETC PRSVD,PREPD					W 10998	17.3			CONSERVES DE LEGUMES
057	FRUIT,NUTS,FRESH,DRIED					W 91779	120.5			FRUITS FRAIS OU SECS
0575	GRAPES FRESH OR DRIED					W 21580	22.9			RAISINS FRAIS OU SECS
05751	GRAPES FRESH	W 11716	7.5	W 16928	14.4	W 21336	22.6			RAISINS FRAIS
0577	NUTS EDIBLE,FRESH,DRIED					W 9373	33.6			FRUITS A COQUES
05774	ALMONDS,FRESH OR DRIED					W 5413	16.0			AMANDES FRAICHES,SECHES
05779	NUTS EDIBLE,FRSH,DRY,NES	W 9828	34.6	W 6669	24.2	W 3877	17.6			FRUITS A COQUES NDA
0579	FRUIT FRESH OR DRIED NES					W 35623	42.8			FRUITS FRAIS,SECS NDA
05793	STONE FRUIT FRESH NES	W 24557	20.4	W 22854	23.9	W 17082	24.7			FRUITS A NOYAU NDA FRAIS
05798	OTHER FRESH FRUIT	W 41813	17.6	W 34828	14.4	W 13261	10.1			AUTRES FRUITS FRAIS
06	SUGAR AND PREPS,HONEY		10.8		11.3		10.3			SUCRES ET PRODUITS
07	COFFEE,TEA,COCOA,SPICES		24.8		46.3		35.7			CAFE,THE,CACAO,EPICES
075	SPICES					W 20391	24.6			EPICES
0752	SPICES,EX PEPPER,PIMENTO					W 20376	24.6			AUTRES EPICES
07525	SEEDS OF ANISE,CUMIN,ETC	W 15636	19.6	W 22508	36.6	W 19932	24.2			GRAINES ANIS,FENOUIL
2	CRUDE MATERLS,EXCL FUELS		227.9		271.0		303.9			MAT BRUTES NON COMESTIBLES
21	HIDES,SKINS,FURS UNDRSSD		6.3		7.9		34.5			CUIRS,PEAUX BRUTS
211	HIDES,SKINS,EXC FURS,RAW	W 2985	5.8			W 6330	34.3			CUIRS ET PEAUX
2116	SHEEP SKIN WITH WOOL					W 3023	25.0			PEAUX LAINEES D'OVINS
22	OIL SEEDS,OLEAGINOUS FRT		16.7		14.2		2.9			GRAINES,FRUITS OLEAGINEUX
2223	COTTON SEEDS	W 127892	15.5	W 107353	13.3	W 21	0.1			GRAINES DE COTON
26	TEXTILE FIBRES AND WASTE		182.8		206.1		227.8			FIBRES TEXTILES
263	COTTON					W 136445	224.6			COTON
2631	RAW COTTON,EXCL LINTERS	W 158923	174.3	W 150595	194.4	W 123660	213.0			COTON EN MASSE
27	CRUDE FERTLZR,MINRLS NES		16.6		19.1		23.4			ENGRAIS MINERAUX BRUTS
271	FERTILIZERS,CRUDE					W 1374236	22.4			ENGRAIS BRUTS
2713	NAT CALCM PHOSPHATES ETC	W 821423	15.4	W 881756	17.0	W 1374236	22.4			PHOSPHATES DE CALCIUM
29	CRUDE ANIMAL,VEG MAT NES		5.1		17.7		14.9			MATIERES BRUTES ANIM,VEGET
3	MINERAL FUELS ETC		2099.0		1994.8		2482.3			COMBUSTIBLES MINERAUX LUB
33	PETROLEUM AND PRODUCTS		2099.0		1994.8		2482.2			PETROLE ET DERIVES
333	CRUDE PETROLEUM					MW 18371	2205.2			HUILES BRUTES DE PETROLE
334	PETROLEUM PRODUCTS,REFIN					W 1475175	275.0			PRODUITS RAFFINES
3341	GASOLINE,OTH LIGHT OILS					W 384522	84.4			ESSENCES POUR MOTEURS
33411	MOTOR,AVIATION SPIRIT					W 338530	69.0			ESSENCES MOTEURS D'AVIONS
33412	SPIRIT TYPE JET FUEL					W 45992	15.5			CARBUREACTEURS
3343	GAS OILS					W 411953	72.1			GAS OILS
3344	FUEL OILS,NES					W 663219	113.3			FUEL OILS
4	ANIMAL,VEGETABLE OIL,FAT		0.4				13.7			HUILES,GRAISSES ANIM,VEG
42	FIXED VEGETABLE OIL,FAT		0.3		1.2		13.7			HUILES VEGETALES FIXES
423	FIXED VEG OILS,SOFT					W 5335	13.6			HUILES VEGET DOUCES FIXES
4235	OLIVE OIL					W 5260	13.5			HUILE D'OLIVE
5	CHEMCLS,RELATED PROD NES		13.8		15.5		24.1			PRODUITS CHIMIQUES
55	PERFUME,CLEANING ETC PRD		4.7		8.8		16.9			PROD POUR PARFUM,TOILETTE
6	BASIC MANUFACTURES		140.4		203.6		188.9			ART MANUFACTURES
61	LEATHER,DRESSED FUR,ETC		15.6		19.9		5.4			CUIRS,PELLETERIES
61161	LEATHER FROM GOAT,KID	W 2056	15.5	W 1756	19.3	W 95	0.9			PEAUX DE CAPRINS PREPAREES
65	TEXTILE YARN,FABRICS,ETC		94.0		148.6		136.9			FILS,TISSUS,ARTICLES TEXTILE
651	TEXTILE YARN					W 6064	14.2			FILS TEXTILES
6513	COTTON YARN	W 469	2.1	W 15662	10.1	W 5748	12.2			FILS DE COTON
653	WOVN MAN-MADE FIB FABRIC					W 3496	40.1			TISSUS FIBRES SYNTH,ARTIF
6531	CONT SYNT WEAVES NONPILE	W 952	7.5	W 893	11.0	W 1388	10.1			TISSUS FIBRES SYNTH CONTINUE
6532	DISC SYN TXTL FABRIC NES	W 503	3.9	W 919	16.9	W 159	1.1			TIS DISC MOINS 85% FIBR TEXT
6535	CONT REGN WEAVES NONPILE					W 1691	26.3			TISSUS FIB TEXT ART CONTINU
65355	CONT REGN TXTL FABRC NES					W 1691	26.3			TISSUS 85% TEXT ART CONT
655	KNITTED,ETC FABRICS	W 7293	43.7			W 5592	28.4			ETOF BONNETERIE PIECES ETC
6551	KNIT ETC SYNTH FAB NONEL					W 5544	27.5			ETOFFES BON NON ELAS TEXT
6552	OTHER KNIT ETC FAB NONEL			W 7781	57.0	W 45	0.9			ETOF BON NON ELAS NON SYNT
656	LACE,RIBBONS,TULLE,ETC					W 1109	17.1			TULLES,BRODERIE
658	TEXTILE ARTICLES NES					W 2490	21.8			ART FACONNES MAT TEXTILES
6584	LINENS ETC					W 1756	17.7			LINGE DE MAISON
65843	TABLE LINEN OF COTTON	W 964	6.7	W 811	12.1					LINGE DE TABLE DE COTON
69	METAL MANUFACTURES NES		12.8		17.1		19.0			ART MANUFACT EN METAL NDA
7	MACHINES,TRANSPORT EQUIP		86.8		22.5		33.0			MACHINES MATERIEL TRANSPORT
72	MACHS FOR SPCL INDUSTRYS		5.7		7.5		21.6			MAC SPECIALES POUR INDUST
723	CIVIL ENGNEERG EQUIP ETC					W 2598	13.2			APPAREILS DE GENIE CIVIL
7234	CONST,MINING MACHNRY NES					W 2598	13.2			MACH POUR LA CONST, MINES
74	GENRL INDUSTRL MACHY NES		23.9		7.9		4.9			MACH APP INDUSTRIE
78	ROAD VEHICLES		44.5		1.6		1.9			VEHICULES ROUTIERS
8	MISC MANUFACTURED GOODS		246.6		464.2		453.5			ART MANUFACTURES DIVERS
831	*TRAVEL GOODS,HANDBAGS		2.9	W 910	6.0	W 1876	13.4			ARTICLES DE VOYAGE ETC
84	CLOTHING AND ACCESSORIES		203.0		402.5		351.7			VETEMENTS
842	MENS OUTERWEAR NOT KNIT	W 2834	38.8			W 3764	37.7			VET DESSUS POUR HOMMES
843	WOMENS OUTERWEAR NONKNIT	W 2848	39.7			W 3259	32.5			VET DESSUS FEMMES MAT TEX
845	OUTERWEAR KNIT NONELASTC					W 7444	175.7			VET DESSOUS,ACCES BONNET
8459	— OTHER,CLTHG ACCESRYS	W 6112	64.7	W 1464	34.7					AUT VET DESSUS DE BONNE
846	UNDER GARMENTS KNITTED					W 5036	62.4			SOUS VETS DE BONNETERIE
8462	— OF COTTON NON ELASTIC					W 3588	20.6			SOUS-VET BONNET COTON
84621	—— MENS SHIRTS	W 2514	26.5							CHEMISES DE COTON
8463	— OF SYNTH FBR NONELAST					W 1291	39.1			SOUS-VET BONNET FIB SYNT
84632	—— MENS SHIRTS			W 2360	22.6					CHEMISES DE BON FIB SYNMT
847	TEXTILE CLTHNG ACCES NES					W 1537	29.7			ACCES VET MAT TEXT NDA
8472	CLTHNG ACCESRYS ETC KNIT					W 872	24.1			ACCES VET BONNE NDA

5. Special Exports F.O.B. by Commodities according to the S.I.T.C. (Rev. 2) in million U.S. Dollars
Exportations Spéciales F.O.B. par Produits d'après la C.T.C.I. (Rév. 2) en millions de Dollars E.U.

SITC CTCI	COMMODITY	1993 QUANTITY QUANTITE	1993 VALUE VALEUR	1994 QUANTITY QUANTITE	1994 VALUE VALEUR	1995 QUANTITY QUANTITE	1995 VALUE VALEUR	1996 QUANTITY QUANTITE	1996 VALUE VALEUR	PRODUIT
84721	KNIT GLOVES,ETC NONELAST	W 389	4.3	W 648	15.3	W 109	2.5			GANTERIE BONNET NON ELAS
84722	KNIT SOCKS,ETC NONELASTC					W 696	20.2			CHAUSSETTES BON. NON ELAS
84723	KNIT ARTICLES NES ELASTC			W 6704	153.8	W 66	1.5			ART NDA DE BONNET ELAST
851	*FOOTWEAR		12.8		34.5	W 8613	57.8			CHAUSSURES
85102	FOOTWEAR LEATHER	W 924	2.6	W 831	12.2	W 5232	47.3			CHAUS SEMELLES EN CUIR
85104	FOOTWEAR NES			W 2125	11.0	W 187	0.2			CHAUS SEMELLES AUT MAT
89	MISC MANUFCTRD GOODS NES		16.4		11.5		19.3			ART MANUFACTURES DIVERS

1. HISTORICAL SERIES, 1992–1997 GENERAL TRADE, IMPORTS F.O.B., EXPORTS F.O.B.
SERIES HISTORIQUES, 1992–1997 COMMERCE GENERAL, IMPORTATIONS F.O.B., EXPORTATIONS F.O.B

YEAR ANNEE	VALUE IN MILLION U.S. DOLLARS VALEUR EN MILLION U.S. DOLLARS MERCHANDISE – MARCHANDISE		GOLD – OR		CONVERSION FACTORS FACTEURS DE CONVERSION CENTS E.U. PAR		INDEX NUMBERS – INDICES QUANTUM		UNIT VALUE VALEUR UNITAIRE	
	IMPORTS	EXPORTS	IMPORTS	EXPORTS	IMPORTS	EXPORTS	IMPORTS	EXPORTS	IMPORTS	EXPORTS
1992	132.00	111.00								
1993	463.03	322.09								
1994	577.54	482.64								
1995	809.92	748.59								
1996	763.10	651.10								
1997	796.55	784.66								

2. IMPORTS BY BROAD ECONOMIC CATEGORY AND EXPORTS BY INDUSTRIAL ORIGIN. (PERCENTAGE OF TOTAL VALUE)
IMPORTATIONS PAR CATEGORIES ECONOMIQUES ET EXPORTATIONS PAR BRANCHE D'ACTIVITE.(EN POURCENTAGE DE LA VALEUR TOTALE)

IMPORTS – IMPORTATIONS

	1990	1991	1992	1993	1994	1995	1996
TOTAL IMPORTS–IMPORTATIONS TOTALES							
1 FOOD BEV–ALIMENTATION BOISSONS							
11 PRIMARY–PRODUITS DE BASE							
111 FOR INDUSTRY–POUR L'INDUSTRIE							
112 FOR HOUSEHOLDS–POUR LES MENAGES							
12 PROCESSED–PRODUITS ELABORES							
121 FOR INDUSTRY–POUR L'INDUSTRIE							
122 FOR HOUSEHOLDS–POUR LES MENAGES							
2 IND SUPPLIES–APPROV INDUSTRIELS							
21 PRIMARY–PRODUITS DE BASE							
22 PROCESSED–PRODUITS ELABORES							
3 FUELS–COMBUSTIBLES							
31 PRIMARY–PRODUITS DE BASE							
32 PROCESSED–PRODUITS ELABORES							
321 MOTOR SPIRIT–ESSENCE							
322 OTHER–AUTRES							
4 MACHINERY–EQUIPEMENT							
41 CAPITAL EQUIPMENT–MACHINES							
42 PARTS–PIECES ACCESSOIRES							
5 TRANSPORT–TRANSPORT							
51 PASSENGER CARS–AUTOMOBILES							
52 OTHER–AUTRES							
521 INDUSTRIAL–INDUSTRIELS							
522 NON INDUSTRIAL–NON INDUSTRIEL							
53 PARTS–PIECES ACCESSOIRES							
6 CONSUM GOODS–BIENS CONSOMMATION							
61 DURABLE–DURABLES							
62 SEMI DURABLE–SEMI DURABLES							
63 NON DURABLE–NON DURABLES							
7 GOODS NES–BIENS NDA							

EXPORTS – EXPORTATIONS

	1990	1991	1992	1993	1994	1995	1996
TOTAL EXPORTS–EXPORTATIONS TOTALES							
1 AGRICULTURE							
2 MINING QUARRY–INDUS EXTRACTIVES							
3 MANUFACTURING–IND MANUFACTUR							
31 FOOD BEV TOBACCO–ALIM BOISS TAB							
32 TEXTILES–INDUSTRIES TEXTILES							
33 WOOD & PRODUCTS–BOIS & PRODUITS							
34 PAPER & PRODUCTS–PAPIER & PRODT							
35 CHEMICALS–INDUSTRIES CHIMIQUES							
36 NON METAL MIN–MIN NON METAL							
37 BASIC METAL–IND METAL BASE							
38 METAL MANUF–MANUF METAL							
39 OTH MANUF IND–AUTRES MANUF							

3. TRADE BY PRINCIPAL COUNTRIES OF ORIGIN AND DESTINATION (VALUE IN MILLION U.S. DOLLARS)
ECHANGES SELON LES PRINCIPAUX PAYS D'ORIGINE ET DE DESTINATION (VALEUR EN MILLIONS DE DOLLARS EU)

COUNTRIES–PAYS	GENERAL IMPORTS F.O.B. IMPORTATIONS GENERALES F.O.B.				
	1992	1993	1994	1995	1996
World	160.7	532.1	547.0	809.9	668.1
Africa		0.3			
Americas		8.8	33.0	30.8	17.4
– Northern America		8.8	33.0	30.8	8.8
– LAIA		0.0			
– CACM					
– Caribbean					8.6
– Rest of America					
Asia excl fmr USSR		15.7	25.4	10.5	46.1
– Middle East		4.4	16.8	6.2	24.5
Asia former USSR		160.5	157.2	338.2	285.7
Europe excl fmr USSR		245.1	229.6	263.5	214.7
– European Union		227.0	126.3	210.1	107.7
– Eastern Europe		7.6	2.8	1.8	7.1
– Rest of Europe		10.5	100.5	51.6	99.9
Europe former USSR		101.0	91.2	149.0	104.0
Oceania		0.7			
Other					
Uzbekistan/Ouzbékistan	13.7	65.4	83.2	251.4	198.9
Russian Federation	57.9	83.8	60.7	136.0	74.4
United Kingdom		16.4	67.9	161.2	78.3
Switzerland,Liechtenst.		4.3	100.4	51.6	99.8
Kazakhstan	15.1	65.5	32.9	26.5	52.4
Turkmenistan/Turkménistn	18.0	26.0	39.4	57.4	26.3
Netherlands/Pays–Bas		115.6	16.4	3.8	5.3
USA/Etats–Unis d'Amer		8.7	31.9	25.3	7.4
Belgium–Luxembourg		21.0	22.8	25.1	0.3
Ukraine	9.0	4.4	13.6	2.2	19.2
Germany/Allemagne		9.4	5.4	14.2	9.1
France, Monaco		25.4	1.5	0.6	7.4
Turkey/Turquie		4.4	16.7	3.9	5.3
Austria/Autriche		9.9	9.6	1.4	0.6
Lithuania/Lituanie	0.8	4.3	13.6	0.7	1.9
Sweden/Suède		18.4			
China/Chine		10.5	4.8	0.4	1.3
Kyrgyzstan/Kirghizistan	2.5	2.1	1.0	2.7	7.2
Belarus/Bélarus	3.4	6.8	1.3	0.4	2.9
Pakistan			1.8	3.8	6.0
Iran (Islamic Rep of)			0.1	0.7	10.5
Estonia/Estonie	0.4	0.3	0.8	4.6	3.9
Latvia/Lettonie	0.7	1.1	1.1	5.1	1.5
British Virgin Islds					8.6
Canada		0.0	1.1	5.5	1.4
Korea, Republic of		0.1	0.6	0.1	7.1
Italy/Italie		5.4	0.8		1.4
Finland/Finlande		4.2			3.3
Ireland/Irlande			1.9	3.8	1.5
United Arab Emirates					6.6
Czech Republic		0.6	2.4	1.4	1.4
Norway,Svalbard and JM		5.3			
Bulgaria/Bulgarie		0.0	0.3		4.9
Poland/Pologne		4.0	0.1		0.1
Afghanistan		0.2	1.2		2.3
Cyprus/Chypre		0.0		1.6	2.0
Hungary/Hongrie		3.0		0.3	0.1
Korea Dem People's Rp		0.0	0.2		2.5
Azerbaijan/Azerbaïdjan	1.4	1.1			
Georgia/Géorgie	0.3	0.3	0.4		0.8

COUNTRIES–PAYS	GENERAL EXPORTS F.O.B. EXPORTATIONS GENERALES F.O.B.				
	1992	1993	1994	1995	1996
Monde	192.5	349.8	491.9	748.6	770.1
Afrique		0.0			0.1
Amériques		15.1	27.1	14.8	10.8
– Amérique du Nord		15.1	27.1	14.8	10.8
– ALAI					
– MCAC					
– Caraïbes					
– Autre Amérique					
Asie anc. URSS exclus		26.6	26.5	36.0	45.2
– Moyen–Orient		5.2	9.0	9.0	4.2
Asie ancienne URSS		45.2	36.7	144.7	236.9
Europe anc. URSS exclus		173.5	325.3	412.1	366.7
– Union Européenne		165.7	258.5	346.6	265.7
– Europe de l'Est		1.9	9.8	19.0	15.6
– Autre de l'Europe		5.8	57.0	46.5	85.4
Europe ancienne URSS		89.4	73.4	139.5	110.0
Océanie		0.0			
Autre					
Netherlands/Pays–Bas		1.1	147.6	255.1	218.1
Uzbekistan/Ouzbékistan	7.6	20.3	22.7	132.0	190.7
Russian Federation	40.6	62.5	46.2	95.3	78.9
United Kingdom		119.9	30.3	20.7	15.2
Switzerland,Liechtenst.		5.8	44.9	37.2	83.5
Belgium–Luxembourg		15.2	30.5	32.7	5.5
Kazakhstan	12.5	16.3	10.1	7.0	24.3
USA/Etats–Unis d'Amer		15.1	27.1	14.8	10.8
Finland/Finlande		7.8	18.1	20.1	8.9
Latvia/Lettonie	0.7	7.2	3.4	21.0	9.5
Austria/Autriche		10.8	16.7	9.7	3.5
Ukraine	10.0	4.9	5.1	9.3	10.8
Korea, Republic of		0.9	2.9	9.3	24.9
Japan/Japon		17.7	11.0	8.2	0.2
Lithuania/Lituanie	0.2	4.5	13.6	9.0	5.6
Hungary/Hongrie		0.0	3.4	13.5	10.4
Turkey/Turquie		5.2	7.6	8.1	1.9
Kyrgyzstan/Kirghizistan	2.0	4.1	2.0	2.6	10.5
Germany/Allemagne		0.7	12.9	4.7	2.6
Belarus/Bélarus	3.5	6.7	3.1	2.3	4.3
Turkmenistan/Turkménistn	3.7	3.5	1.7	2.2	8.5
Norway,Svalbard and JM			12.1	5.4	0.6
China/Chine		0.1	1.4	5.6	6.2
Italy/Italie		2.5	0.4	2.4	6.6
Korea Dem People's Rp		0.5		3.3	5.1
Azerbaijan/Azerbaïdjan	3.3	1.1	0.2	0.9	2.6
Slovakia/Slovaquie			3.4	0.7	3.8
Sweden/Suède		7.6			
Republic of Moldova	0.4	3.4	1.4		0.1
Slovenia/Slovénie				3.9	1.3
Romania/Roumanie			1.5	2.2	1.2
France, Monaco				0.2	4.4
Czech Republic		1.5	0.8	2.2	0.1
Estonia/Estonie	0.4	0.1	0.6	2.6	0.8
Iran (Islamic Rep of)			1.4	0.7	1.7
Afghanistan		0.8	0.8	0.3	1.5
Viet Nam			1.2	0.3	0.7
Pakistan		0.8			1.4
Greece/Grèce		0.1	1.6		0.1
Bulgaria/Bulgarie		0.5	0.7	0.4	0.1

(VALUE AS PERCENTAGE OF WORLD TOTAL)(VALEURS EN POURCENTAGE DU TOTAL MONDIAL)

	1987	1988	1989	1990	1991	1992	1993	1994	1995	1996
Africa							0.1			
Americas							1.7	6.0	3.8	2.6
– Northern America							1.6	6.0	3.8	1.3
– LAIA							0.0			
– CACM										
– Caribbean										1.3
– Rest of America										
Asia excl fmr USSR							2.9	4.6	1.3	6.9
– Middle East							0.8	3.1	0.8	3.7
Asia former USSR							30.2	28.7	41.8	42.8
Europe excl fmr USSR							46.1	42.0	32.5	32.1
– European Union							42.7	23.1	25.9	16.1
– Eastern Europe							1.4	0.5	0.2	1.1
– Rest of Europe							2.0	18.4	6.4	15.0
Europe former USSR							19.0	16.7	18.4	15.6
Oceania							0.1			
Other										
Uzbekistan/Ouzbékistan						8.5	12.3	15.2	31.0	29.8
Russian Federation						36.0	15.7	11.1	16.8	11.1
United Kingdom							3.1	12.4	19.9	11.7
Switzerland,Liechtenst.							0.8	18.4	6.4	14.9
Kazakhstan						9.4	12.3	6.0	3.3	7.8
Turkmenistan/Turkménistn						11.2	4.9	7.2	7.1	3.9
Netherlands/Pays–Bas							21.7	3.0	0.5	0.8
USA/Etats–Unis d'Amer							1.6	5.8	3.1	1.1
Belgium–Luxembourg							3.9	4.2	3.1	0.0
Ukraine						5.6	0.8	2.5	0.3	2.9

	1987	1988	1989	1990	1991	1992	1993	1994	1995	1996
Afrique							0.0			0.0
Amériques							4.3	5.5	2.0	1.4
– Amérique du Nord							4.3	5.5	2.0	1.4
– ALAI										
– MCAC										
– Caraïbes										
– Autre Amérique										
Asie anc. URSS exclus							7.6	5.4	4.8	5.9
– Moyen–Orient							1.5	1.8	1.2	0.5
Asie ancienne URSS							12.9	7.5	19.3	30.8
Europe anc. URSS exclus							49.6	66.1	55.0	47.6
– Union Européenne							47.4	52.6	46.3	34.5
– Europe de l'Est							0.6	2.0	2.5	2.0
– Autre de l'Europe							1.7	11.6	6.2	11.1
Europe ancienne URSS							25.5	14.9	18.6	14.3
Océanie							0.0			
Autre										
Netherlands/Pays–Bas							0.3	30.0	34.1	28.3
Uzbekistan/Ouzbékistan						4.0	5.8	4.6	17.6	24.8
Russian Federation						21.1	17.9	9.4	12.7	10.2
United Kingdom							34.3	6.2	2.8	2.0
Switzerland,Liechtenst.							1.7	9.1	5.0	10.8
Belgium–Luxembourg							4.4	6.2	4.4	0.7
Kazakhstan						6.5	4.6	2.1	0.9	3.2
USA/Etats–Unis d'Amer							4.3	5.5	2.0	1.4
Finland/Finlande							2.2	3.7	2.7	1.2
Latvia/Lettonie						0.4	2.1	0.7	2.8	1.2

4. General Imports F.O.B. by Commodities according to the S.I.T.C. (Rev. 2) in million U.S. Dollars
Importations Générales F.O.B. par Produits d'après la C.T.C.I. (Rév. 2) en millions de Dollars E.U.

SITC CTCI	COMMODITY	1993		1994		1995		1996		PRODUIT
		QUANTITY QUANTITE	VALUE VALEUR	QUANTITY QUANTITE	VALUE VALEUR	QUANTITY QUANTITE	VALUE VALEUR	QUANTITY QUANTITE	VALUE VALEUR	
	ALL COMMODITIES						809.9		668.1	TOUS PRODUITS
04	CEREALS AND PREPARATIONS						12.1		57.1	CEREALES ET PRODUITS
06	SUGAR AND PREPS,HONEY						4.1		2.1	SUCRES ET PRODUITS
11	BEVERAGES								7.1	BOISSONS
24	CORK AND WOOD						7.1		4.1	LIEGE ET BOIS
27	CRUDE FERTLZR,MINRLS NES						1.1		228.0	ENGRAIS MINERAUX BRUTS
3	MINERAL FUELS ETC						366.0		244.0	COMBUSTIBLES MINERAUX LUB
52	INORGANIC CHEMICALS						17.1		19.1	PROD CHIM INORGANIQUES
562	*FERTILIZERS,MANUFACTURE						2.1		6.1	ENGRAIS MANUFACTURES
62	RUBBER MANUFACTURES NES						4.1		2.1	CAOUTCHOUC MANUFACTURE
67	IRON AND STEEL						10.1		2.1	FER ET ACIER
69	METAL MANUFACTURES NES						2.1		16.1	ART MANUFACT EN METAL NDA
7	MACHINES,TRANSPORT EQUIP						93.1		89.1	MACHINES MATERIEL TRANSPORT
78	ROAD VEHICLES						12.1		7.1	VEHICULES ROUTIERS
821	*FURNITURE,PARTS THEREOF						13.1			MEUBLES ET PIECES
84	CLOTHING AND ACCESSORIES						4.1		3.1	VETEMENTS

5. General Exports F.O.B. by Commodities according to the S.I.T.C. (Rev. 2) in million U.S. Dollars
Exportations Générales F.O.B. par Produits d'après la C.T.C.I. (Rév. 2) en millions de Dollars E.U.

SITC CTCI	COMMODITY	1993		1994		1995		1996		PRODUIT
		QUANTITY QUANTITE	VALUE VALEUR	QUANTITY QUANTITE	VALUE VALEUR	QUANTITY QUANTITE	VALUE VALEUR	QUANTITY QUANTITE	VALUE VALEUR	
	ALL COMMODITIES						748.6		770.1	TOUS PRODUITS
11	BEVERAGES								5.1	BOISSONS
263	COTTON						214.0		181.0	COTON
27	CRUDE FERTLZR,MINRLS NES						1.1		116.0	ENGRAIS MINERAUX BRUTS
3	MINERAL FUELS ETC						123.0		175.0	COMBUSTIBLES MINERAUX LUB
52	INORGANIC CHEMICALS								3.1	PROD CHIM INORGANIQUES
67	IRON AND STEEL								4.1	FER ET ACIER
684	ALUMINIUM						390.0		263.0	ALUMINIUM
69	METAL MANUFACTURES NES						1.1		10.1	ART MANUFACT EN METAL NDA
7	MACHINES,TRANSPORT EQUIP						7.1		5.1	MACHINES MATERIEL TRANSPORT
78	ROAD VEHICLES						3.1		1.1	VEHICULES ROUTIERS

1. HISTORICAL SERIES, 1962–1997 GENERAL TRADE, IMPORTS C.I.F., EXPORTS F.O.B.
SERIES HISTORIQUES, 1962–1997 COMMERCE GENERAL, IMPORTATIONS C.A.F., EXPORTATIONS F.O.B

YEAR ANNEE	VALUE IN MILLION BAHT #1 / VALEUR EN MILLION BAHT #1 — MERCHANDISE –MARCHANDISE IMPORTS	EXPORTS	GOLD –OR IMPORTS	EXPORTS	CONVERSION FACTORS U.S. CENTS PER BAHT / FACTEURS DE CONVERSION CENTS E.U. PAR BAHT IMPORTS	EXPORTS	INDEX NUMBERS –INDICES QUANTUM IMPORTS	EXPORTS	UNIT VALUE / VALEUR UNITAIRE IMPORTS	EXPORTS
1962	11.50	9.53	0.16		4.7640	4.8460				
1963	12.80	9.68	0.15		4.8200	4.8200				
1964	14.25	12.34	0.10		4.8077	4.8077				
1965	16.18	12.94	0.14		4.8077	4.8077				
1966	25.35	14.31	0.12		4.8077	4.8077				
1967	22.19	14.17	0.15		4.8077	4.8077				
1968	24.10	13.68	0.18		4.8077	4.8077				
1969	26.89	14.72	0.14		4.8077	4.8077				
1970	27.01	14.77	0.11		4.8077	4.8077				
1971	26.79	17.28	0.03		4.8077	4.8077				
1972	30.88	22.49			4.8077	4.8077				
1973	42.18	32.23			4.8571	4.8516				
1974	64.04	50.25			4.9080	4.9080				
1975	66.84	48.44			4.9071	4.9070				
1976	72.88	60.80			4.9020	4.9020				
1977	94.18	71.20			4.9261	4.8899				
1978	108.90	83.07			4.9411	4.9056				
1979	146.16	108.18			4.9190	4.8878				
1980	188.69	133.20			4.8829	4.8839	38	41	81	79
1981	216.75	153.00			4.5911	4.5998	37	46	95	81
1982	196.62	159.73			4.3478	4.3478	32	52	98	76
1983	236.61	146.47			4.3478	4.3478	41	47	92	77
1984	245.15	175.24			4.2412	4.2302	43	57	93	77
1985	251.17	193.36			3.6803	3.6830	41	59	102	81
1986	241.36	233.38			3.8039	3.8044	40	48	76	82
1987	334.21	301.45			3.8880	3.8884	49	57	81	88
1988	513.11	403.57			3.9533	3.9529	68	72	89	95
1989	662.68	516.31			3.8888	3.8888	83	89	95	98
1990	844.45	589.81			3.9116	3.9116	100	100	100	100
1991	958.83	725.63			3.9192	3.9192	109	119	104	103
1992	1033.24	824.64			3.9371	3.9371	117	134	105	105
1993	1166.60	935.86			3.9496	3.9496	130	150	105	106
1994	1369.02	1137.60			3.9764	3.9764	151	177	107	109
1995	1829.40	1400.10			4.0137	4.0133	170	243	122	118
1996	1828.69	1407.20			3.9464	3.9459				
1997	1828.26	1806.93			3.2463	3.2255				

2. IMPORTS BY BROAD ECONOMIC CATEGORY AND EXPORTS BY INDUSTRIAL ORIGIN. (PERCENTAGE OF TOTAL VALUE)
IMPORTATIONS PAR CATEGORIES ECONOMIQUES ET EXPORTATIONS PAR BRANCHE D'ACTIVITE.(EN POURCENTAGE DE LA VALEUR TOTALE)

IMPORTS – IMPORTATIONS

	1991	1992	1993	1994	1995	1996	1997
TOTAL IMPORTS–IMPORTATIONS TOTALES	100.	100.	100.	100.	100.	100.	100.
1 FOOD BEV–ALIMENTATION BOISSONS	4.6	4.3	3.6	3.3	2.8	3.0	3.6
11 PRIMARY–PRODUITS DE BASE	3.2	2.9	2.2	2.0	1.6	1.7	2.2
111 FOR INDUSTRY–POUR L'INDUSTRIE	0.4	0.5	0.4	0.4	0.4	0.5	0.7
112 FOR HOUSEHOLDS–POUR LES MENAGES	2.8	2.4	1.8	1.5	1.2	1.2	1.5
12 PROCESSED–PRODUITS ELABORES	1.3	1.4	1.3	1.3	1.2	1.3	1.4
121 FOR INDUSTRY–POUR L'INDUSTRIE	0.2	0.2	0.2	0.2	0.2	0.2	0.2
122 FOR HOUSEHOLDS–POUR LES MENAGES	1.1	1.2	1.1	1.1	1.0	1.1	1.2
2 IND SUPPLIES–APPROV INDUSTRIELS	40.3	38.7	36.5	36.0	36.0	33.1	32.4
21 PRIMARY–PRODUITS DE BASE	9.1	5.7	5.4	4.9	4.7	4.3	3.7
22 PROCESSED–PRODUITS ELABORES	31.2	33.0	31.1	31.1	31.3	28.7	28.7
3 FUELS–COMBUSTIBLES	9.2	8.2	7.5	6.8	6.7	8.7	9.2
31 PRIMARY–PRODUITS DE BASE	4.1	4.4	4.0	4.1	4.2	6.4	7.7
32 PROCESSED–PRODUITS ELABORES	5.2	3.8	3.4	2.7	2.5	2.3	1.5
321 MOTOR SPIRIT–ESSENCE	0.4	0.5	0.4	0.2	0.1	0.1	0.0
322 OTHER–AUTRES	4.8	3.4	3.1	2.4	2.4	2.2	1.5
4 MACHINERY–EQUIPEMENT	31.9	31.1	33.5	36.0	36.6	37.3	39.3
41 CAPITAL EQUIPMENT–MACHINES	22.9	21.3	23.1	23.8	23.8	23.6	23.3
42 PARTS–PIECES ACCESSOIRES	8.9	9.9	10.4	12.2	12.8	13.7	16.0
5 TRANSPORT–TRANSPORT	7.6	10.3	11.3	11.1	11.1	10.2	7.9
51 PASSENGER CARS–AUTOMOBILES	1.3	2.3	3.3	2.8	2.2	1.6	0.9
52 OTHER–AUTRES	1.2	3.4	2.1	1.1	2.2	1.8	2.3
521 INDUSTRIAL–INDUSTRIELS	1.1	3.4	2.1	1.0	2.2	1.8	2.3
522 NON INDUSTRIAL–NON INDUSTRIEL	0.0	0.0	0.0	0.0	0.0	0.0	0.0
53 PARTS–PIECES ACCESSOIRES	5.2	4.5	6.0	7.1	6.7	6.8	4.7
6 CONSUM GOODS–BIENS CONSOMMATION	4.2	4.9	5.1	5.5	5.5	5.6	5.8
61 DURABLE–DURABLES	1.3	1.6	1.5	1.4	1.4	1.4	1.2
62 SEMI DURABLE–SEMI DURABLES	1.8	2.2	2.3	2.9	2.9	2.9	3.1
63 NON DURABLE–NON DURABLES	1.1	1.2	1.2	1.2	1.2	1.3	1.5
7 GOODS NES–BIENS NDA	2.3	2.4	2.6	1.5	1.3	2.1	1.8

EXPORTS – EXPORTATIONS

	1991	1992	1993	1994	1995	1996	1997
TOTAL EXPORTS–EXPORTATIONS TOTALES	100.	100.	100.	100.	100.		100.
1 AGRICULTURE	14.4	14.1	12.2	12.0	11.4		9.1
2 MINING QUARRY–INDUS EXTRACTIVES	4.2	3.2	3.1	2.9	2.6		2.3
3 MANUFACTURING–IND MANUFACTUR	81.4	82.7	84.7	85.1	86.0		88.6
31 FOOD BEV TOBACCO–ALIM BOISS TAB	16.7	16.2	13.2	13.2	12.8		13.1
32 TEXTILES–INDUSTRIES TEXTILES	21.3	19.8	18.5	17.2	15.0		12.8
33 WOOD & PRODUCTS–BOIS & PRODUITS	0.8	0.7	0.8	0.8	0.7		0.6
34 PAPER & PRODUCTS–PAPIER & PRODT	0.3	0.3	0.4	0.6	1.1		0.8
35 CHEMICALS–INDUSTRIES CHIMIQUES	5.5	5.7	8.3	7.3	10.1		8.6
36 NON METAL MIN–MIN NON METAL	1.0	1.2	1.5	1.4	1.3		1.4
37 BASIC METAL–IND METAL BASE	0.8	0.7	0.8	0.8	1.1		1.3
38 METAL MANUF–MANUF METAL	28.5	31.1	34.6	38.2	38.3		43.5
39 OTH MANUF IND–AUTRES MANUF	6.5	6.8	6.8	5.5	5.5		6.3

3. TRADE BY PRINCIPAL COUNTRIES OF ORIGIN AND DESTINATION (VALUE IN MILLION U.S. DOLLARS)
ECHANGES SELON LES PRINCIPAUX PAYS D'ORIGINE ET DE DESTINATION (VALEUR EN MILLIONS DE DOLLARS EU)

COUNTRIES–PAYS	GENERAL IMPORTS C.I.F. IMPORTATIONS GENERALES C.A.F				
	1993	1994	1995	1996	1997
World	46239.3	54437.2	70780.8	72316.2	62461.7
Africa	678.0	703.6	831.2	895.2	924.9
Americas	6443.8	7654.2	10126.9	10944.5	10245.9
– Northern America	5810.8	6839.3	8995.6	9703.5	9108.7
– LAIA	566.6	766.9	1079.4	1198.5	1105.0
– CACM	2.3	6.4	3.2	7.2	4.8
– Caribbean	13.3	10.2	16.5	11.7	4.2
– Rest of America	50.7	31.3	32.1	23.6	23.2
Asia excl fmr USSR	28048.8	33389.9	43275.5	43746.8	37540.1
– Middle East	1436.7	1816.3	2523.1	3939.7	4475.5
Asia former USSR	1.6	1.4	12.5	30.0	102.0
Europe excl fmr USSR	8787.7	9490.9	12841.2	12407.2	10018.1
– European Union	7694.2	8186.7	11291.4	10885.6	8711.9
– Eastern Europe	381.2	383.9	308.3	371.3	295.4
– Rest of Europe	712.4	920.3	1241.5	1150.3	1010.8
Europe former USSR	626.7	945.6	1296.3	1030.3	700.8
Oceania	1137.7	1307.0	1597.9	1724.5	1605.1
Other	514.9	944.5	799.4	1537.8	1324.9
Japan/Japon	13962.0	16435.1	21622.2	20444.8	15974.4
USA/Etats–Unis d'Amer	5381.5	6448.1	8509.8	9039.7	8685.3
Singapore/Singapour	2969.6	3437.3	4161.4	4002.0	3146.2
Germany/Allemagne	2482.2	3182.2	3749.1	3654.5	2956.4
Other Asia n.e.s.	2335.3	2758.2	3420.5	3144.6	2860.9
Malaysia/Malaisie	1674.0	2647.9	3234.3	3606.3	2973.0
Korea, Republic of	1947.8	1978.0	2474.1	2683.2	2230.8
China/Chine	1090.5	1387.7	2094.6	1953.4	2255.1
United Kingdom	1055.3	1150.6	1455.5	1591.3	1288.1
Australia/Australie	951.1	1074.5	1321.0	1400.9	1277.5
France, Monaco	917.3	751.2	1946.6	1142.0	843.3
Areas n.e.s.	514.9	944.5	799.4	1537.8	1324.9
Italy/Italie	906.9	838.7	1086.8	1304.5	859.9
Russian Federation	620.7	930.3	1264.6	895.0	572.0
Switzerland,Liechtenst.	575.3	754.9	979.2	954.3	783.6
Oman	300.5	396.0	682.6	1052.9	1408.0
China, Hong Kong SAR	536.2	689.8	745.8	854.0	824.7
Indonesia/Indonésie	512.2	451.5	672.7	939.6	884.6
United Arab Emirates	447.0	569.8	678.3	779.1	854.4
Saudi Arabia	484.4	527.1	572.2	619.3	846.8
India/Inde	522.6	528.1	629.2	639.8	580.2
Netherlands/Pays–Bas	403.0	501.3	698.2	595.8	660.7
Belgium–Luxembourg	544.0	478.6	652.0	631.7	470.8
Sweden/Suède	416.3	456.6	585.4	597.7	503.0
Brazil/Brésil	341.7	456.6	501.9	570.0	464.4
Canada	427.6	389.1	479.3	545.0	418.3
Philippines	180.6	353.3	579.4	575.5	553.5
Finland/Finlande	309.5	236.8	375.7	445.3	416.1
Iran (Islamic Rep of)	67.4	91.1	223.1	621.7	425.2
Spain/Espagne	175.0	201.4	255.6	338.6	271.8
Denmark/Danemark	231.3	198.6	257.0	220.4	181.1
Israel/Israël	124.6	229.4	219.9	260.6	204.8
Brunei Darussalam	214.1	182.7	289.4	215.1	85.3
So. African Customs Un	151.0	126.9	219.5	237.1	244.5
New Zealand	139.2	155.9	203.8	218.0	218.1
Yemen/Yémen	15.1	0.6	90.7	296.7	479.8
Norway,Svalbard and JM	113.7	142.3	228.6	166.3	185.2
Chile/Chili	82.1	148.8	179.0	174.1	175.8
Myanmar	155.0	157.2	221.2	129.9	82.3
Poland/Pologne	115.0	133.5	138.5	211.1	144.8

COUNTRIES–PAYS	EXPORTS EXPORTATIONS ES F.O.B.				
	1993	1994	1995	1996	1997
Monde	37166.9	45235.5	56439.4		58282.5
Afrique	969.2	994.9	1196.8		1003.8
Amériques	8928.9	10620.6	11273.4		12779.8
– Amérique du Nord	8526.1	10088.5	10692.0		12091.2
– ALAI	216.0	330.1	363.7		527.6
– MCAC	9.1	9.0	13.8		21.1
– Caraïbes	37.8	43.9	68.9		36.2
– Autre Amérique	139.9	149.2	135.0		103.8
Asie anc. URSS exclus	18619.2	23891.0	32070.5		32018.4
– Moyen–Orient	1531.7	1463.6	2327.0		1721.7
Asie ancienne URSS	1.4	3.0	29.8		11.7
Europe anc. URSS exclus	7415.7	8012.3	9833.0		10302.1
– Union Européenne	6467.9	7070.1	8517.2		9394.3
– Europe de l'Est	530.5	481.9	743.5		312.7
– Autre de l'Europe	417.3	460.3	572.3		595.1
Europe ancienne URSS	256.8	334.4	454.1		147.0
Océanie	625.6	767.0	931.2		1120.8
Autre	350.3	612.3	650.6		898.8
USA/Etats–Unis d'Amer	8006.5	9519.6	10078.3		11448.7
Japan/Japon	6299.9	7725.2	9475.4		8733.9
Singapore/Singapour	4457.7	6165.4	7919.1		6433.2
China, Hong Kong SAR	1958.7	2385.4	2920.8		3468.9
United Kingdom	1188.4	1344.7	1618.9		2143.1
Malaysia/Malaisie	1039.9	1098.7	1554.1		2505.6
Germany/Allemagne	1479.7	1591.8	1638.1		1439.9
Netherlands/Pays–Bas	1156.9	1257.7	1801.2		1876.8
China/Chine	538.7	927.9	1640.1		1790.2
Other Asia n.e.s.	738.4	981.8	1353.1		1592.5
France, Monaco	773.5	810.3	977.9		960.6
Australia/Australie	511.9	642.2	777.6		958.2
Belgium–Luxembourg	582.9	661.0	744.9		874.2
Korea, Republic of	461.5	571.5	800.1		994.0
Indonesia/Indonésie	202.3	440.2	811.3		1243.5
United Arab Emirates	476.5	578.4	1008.6		573.9
Areas n.e.s.	350.3	612.3	650.6		898.8
Canada	518.2	568.2	613.0		641.2
Italy/Italie	463.7	471.3	572.3		617.9
Saudi Arabia	501.9	434.7	567.5		393.3
Switzerland,Liechtenst.	355.5	384.6	491.6		502.2
Poland/Pologne	436.8	389.2	599.1		163.8
Philippines	197.8	223.2	414.5		695.8
Spain/Espagne	271.8	307.9	450.7		419.6
Viet Nam	115.8	253.7	467.7		549.7
Lao People's Dem Rep	175.0	291.3	354.4		384.2
Myanmar	151.6	238.8	347.5		405.6
Cambodia/Cambodge	179.3	260.2	334.1		310.3
Russian Federation	251.6	303.9	403.3		115.3
India/Inde	73.9	192.7	290.2		302.8
So. African Customs Un	133.7	180.3	217.9		275.4
Israel/Israël	125.1	136.5	182.2		287.1
Denmark/Danemark	112.2	135.5	170.1		229.0
Sweden/Suède	136.7	153.8	147.2		171.8
Pakistan	76.4	143.0	204.9		156.9
Sri Lanka	88.5	120.3	217.0		148.8
Iran (Islamic Rep of)	135.0	68.7	190.2		166.3
Panama	136.9	143.4	126.9		95.7
Brazil/Brésil	40.8	98.1	160.7		187.4
Bangladesh	72.1	83.5	192.2		136.5

(VALUE AS PERCENTAGE OF WORLD TOTAL)(VALEURS EN POURCENTAGE DU TOTAL MONDIAL)

	1988	1989	1990	1991	1992	1993	1994	1995	1996	1997
Africa	1.5	1.2	1.0	1.4	1.5	1.5	1.3	1.2	1.2	1.5
Americas	16.8	14.9	13.9	13.3	14.4	13.9	14.1	14.3	15.1	16.4
– Northern America	14.9	12.6	11.9	11.6	12.7	12.6	12.6	12.7	13.4	14.6
– LAIA	1.9	2.2	2.0	1.7	1.5	1.2	1.4	1.5	1.7	1.8
– CACM	0.0	0.0	0.0	0.0	0.0	0.0	0.0	0.0	0.0	0.0
– Caribbean	0.0	0.0	0.0	0.0	0.0	0.0	0.0	0.0	0.0	0.0
– Rest of America	0.0	0.0	0.0	0.0	0.1	0.1	0.1	0.0	0.0	0.0
Asia excl fmr USSR	58.7	62.2	62.7	63.2	61.9	60.7	61.3	61.1	60.5	60.1
– Middle East	3.5	4.2	3.9	3.0	3.2	3.1	3.3	3.6	5.4	7.2
Asia former USSR						0.0	0.0	0.0	0.0	0.2
Europe excl fmr USSR	20.1	18.3	19.2	18.8	18.2	19.0	17.4	18.1	17.2	16.0
– European Union	16.6	15.1	15.9	15.7	15.9	16.6	15.0	16.0	15.1	13.9
– Eastern Europe	1.4	1.2	1.1	0.9	0.8	0.8	0.7	0.4	0.5	0.5
– Rest of Europe	2.1	2.0	2.2	2.1	1.6	1.5	1.7	1.8	1.6	1.6
Europe former USSR	0.3	0.3	0.5	0.7	0.8	1.4	1.7	1.8	1.4	1.1
Oceania	2.1	2.4	2.0	2.1	2.7	2.5	2.4	2.3	2.4	2.6
Other	0.6	0.7	0.6	0.6	0.5	1.1	1.7	1.1	2.1	2.1
Japan/Japon	29.0	30.3	30.4	29.4	29.3	30.2	30.2	30.5	28.3	25.6
USA/Etats–Unis d'Amer	13.6	11.3	10.8	10.6	11.7	11.6	11.8	12.0	12.5	13.9
Singapore/Singapour	7.4	7.7	7.4	8.0	7.3	6.4	6.3	5.9	5.5	5.0
Germany/Allemagne				5.6	5.3	5.4	5.8	5.3	5.1	4.7
Other Asia n.e.s.	4.2	5.0	5.2	4.8	5.5	5.1	5.1	4.8	4.3	4.6
Malaysia/Malaisie	2.1	2.6	3.4	3.2	3.9	3.6	4.9	4.6	5.0	4.8
Korea, Republic of	2.8	2.9	3.1	4.2	4.4	4.2	3.6	3.5	3.7	3.6
China/Chine	3.4	2.9	3.3	3.1	3.0	2.4	2.5	3.0	2.7	3.6
United Kingdom	3.0	2.6	2.7	2.3	2.3	2.3	2.1	2.1	2.2	2.1
Australia/Australie	1.7	2.0	1.7	1.7	2.2	2.1	2.0	1.9	1.9	2.0

	1988	1989	1990	1991	1992	1993	1994	1995	1996	1997
Afrique	3.5	3.0	2.5	2.8	2.5	2.6	2.2	2.1		1.7
Amériques	22.7	24.4	25.5	24.1	25.1	24.0	23.5	20.0		21.9
– Amérique du Nord	21.9	23.2	24.0	22.7	23.9	22.9	22.3	18.9		20.7
– ALAI	0.1	0.3	0.5	0.6	0.7	0.6	0.7	0.6		0.9
– MCAC	0.0	0.0	0.0	0.0	0.0	0.0	0.0	0.0		0.0
– Caraïbes	0.3	0.3	0.2	0.1	0.1	0.1	0.1	0.1		0.1
– Autre Amérique	0.4	0.6	0.7	0.6	0.5	0.4	0.3	0.2		0.2
Asie anc. URSS exclus	47.6	46.8	44.5	45.7	46.4	50.1	52.8	56.8		54.9
– Moyen–Orient	5.7	5.7	4.8	4.6	4.4	4.1	3.2	4.1		3.0
Asie ancienne URSS						0.0	0.0	0.1		0.0
Europe anc. URSS exclus	23.4	21.9	24.9	24.7	23.0	20.0	17.7	17.4		17.7
– Union Européenne	21.8	20.2	22.6	21.7	20.5	17.4	15.6	15.1		16.1
– Europe de l'Est	0.2	0.3	0.7	1.7	1.3	1.4	1.1	1.3		0.5
– Autre de l'Europe	1.4	1.4	1.5	1.3	1.2	1.1	1.0	1.0		1.0
Europe ancienne URSS	0.4	1.3	0.4	0.3	0.6	0.7	0.7	0.8		0.3
Océanie	2.1	2.2	1.9	1.9	2.0	1.7	1.7	1.6		1.9
Autre	0.3	0.4	0.4	0.5	0.4	0.9	1.4	1.2		1.5
USA/Etats–Unis d'Amer	20.1	21.7	22.7	21.3	22.5	21.5	21.0	17.9		19.6
Japan/Japon	16.0	17.0	17.2	18.1	17.5	17.0	17.1	16.8		15.0
Singapore/Singapour	7.7	7.1	7.3	8.2	8.7	12.0	13.6	14.0		11.0
China, Hong Kong SAR	4.5	4.0	4.5	4.7	4.6	5.3	5.3	5.2		6.0
United Kingdom	3.7	3.7	4.1	3.6	3.6	3.2	3.0	2.9		3.7
Malaysia/Malaisie	3.0	2.9	2.5	2.4	2.6	2.8	2.4	2.8		4.3
Germany/Allemagne				5.2	4.4	4.0	3.5	2.9		2.5
Netherlands/Pays–Bas	5.5	4.9	4.8	4.4	4.3	3.1	2.8	3.2		3.2
China/Chine	3.0	2.7	1.2	1.2	1.2	1.4	2.1	2.9		3.1
Other Asia n.e.s.	1.8	1.6	1.6	1.7	1.9	2.0	2.2	2.4		2.7

4. General Imports C.I.F. by Commodities according to the S.I.T.C. (Rev. 2) in million U.S. Dollars
Importations Générales C.A.F. par Produits d'après la C.T.C.I. (Rév. 2) en millions de Dollars E.U.

SITC CTCI	COMMODITY	1994 QUANTITY QUANTITE	1994 VALUE VALEUR	1995 QUANTITY QUANTITE	1995 VALUE VALEUR	1996 QUANTITY QUANTITE	1996 VALUE VALEUR	1997 QUANTITY QUANTITE	1997 VALUE VALEUR	PRODUIT
	ALL COMMODITIES		54437.2		70780.8		72316.2		62461.8	TOUS PRODUITS
0	FOOD AND LIVE ANIMALS		2017.0		2243.4		2482.1		2443.1	ALIMENTS,ANIMAUX VIVANTS
02	DAIRY PRODCTS,BIRDS'EGGS		247.5		332.7		371.1		373.4	PRODUITS LAITIERS,OEUFS
022	MILK AND CREAM	W 123095	209.5	W 140676	285.8	W 141720	320.9	W 175742	337.6	LAIT ET CREME
0224	MILK,CREAM PRESERVED ETC	W 117596	201.7	W 134386	275.1	W 135851	308.6	W 170043	327.9	LAIT,CREME CONS,CONC
03	FISH AND PREPARATIONS		689.1		697.2		686.0		793.6	POISSONS ET PREPARATIONS
034	FISH,FRESH,CHILLED,FROZN	W 1238801	556.0	W 611929	500.4	W 510466	500.9	W 537466	595.9	POISSON FRAIS, REFRIG,CONG
0342	FISH FROZEN,EXCL FILLETS	W 1189643	529.2	W 547954	460.8	W 501877	481.5	W 527745	577.6	POISSONS CONGELES
04	CEREALS AND PREPARATIONS		271.5		348.9		424.8		346.7	CEREALES ET PRODUITS
05	VEGETABLES AND FRUIT		178.2		194.1		180.2		145.6	LEGUMES ET FRUITS
081	*FEEDING STUFF FOR ANIML	W 1612181	483.6	W 1487461	496.1	W 1724279	630.8	W 2166045	617.8	NOURRITURE POUR ANIMAUX
0813	OILCAKE AND OTH RESIDUES	W 1230757	256.9	W 1065875	231.7	W 1238436	329.4	W 1854116	427.3	TOURTEAUX
08131	— OF SOYA BEANS	W 902708	201.4	W 688516	166.0	W 790148	235.5	W 1502125	348.3	TOURTEAUX DE SOJA
1	BEVERAGES AND TOBACCO		240.9		262.3		279.6		209.1	BOISSONS ET TABACS
2	CRUDE MATERLS,EXCL FUELS		2790.4		3475.6		3257.6		2674.8	MAT BRUTES NON COMESTIBLES
22	OIL SEEDS,OLEAGINOUS FRT		35.1		71.7		143.6		286.5	GRAINES,FRUITS OLEAGINEUX
222	SEEDS FOR'SOFT'FIXED OIL	W 99401	29.1	W 207629	63.2	W 425763	138.1	W 875246	282.2	GRAINES HUILES FIXES
2222	SOYA BEANS	W 97998	28.0	W 203157	60.5	W 418811	135.1	W 869397	279.7	FEVES DE SOJA
24	CORK AND WOOD		945.8		1086.8		931.1		606.6	LIEGE ET BOIS
247	OTH WOOD ROUGH,SQUARED	W 1380602	294.6	W 1075884	402.5	W 699216	249.1	W 687878	176.5	BOIS BRUTS EQUARRIS
2472	SAW–,VENEER–LOGS NON–CON	W 1352967	287.3	W 1045151	394.8	W 668358	241.7	W 632276	166.8	NON CONIFERES SCIAGE,PLAC
24721	— IN THE ROUGH	W 1352967	287.3	W 1045151	394.8	W 668358	241.7	W 632276	166.8	BRUTS ECORCES DEGROSSIS
248	WOOD SHAPED,SLEEPERS	W 2185672	649.1	W 1535141	682.0	W 1613154	679.2	W 1747995	428.5	BOIS SIMPLEMENT TRAVAILLES
2483	LUMBER SHAPED NON–CONIFR	W 2111256	627.9	W 1457187	647.8	W 1537853	644.2	W 1671424	399.5	NON CONIFERES SCIES,RABOTES
24831	LUMBER SAWN ETC NON–CON	W 2103486	624.9	W 1444654	643.0	W 1521129	636.9	W 1661432	395.3	SCIES LONGITUDINALEMENT
251	*PULP AND WASTE PAPER	W 850048	290.9	W 1025542	525.3	W 997791	372.6	W 1035844	295.7	PATES A PAPIER,DECHETS
2517	SODA,SULPHATE WOOD PULP	W 206915	106.7	W 252520	216.1	W 300175	186.5	W 326010	156.3	PATES CHIMIQUES AU SULFATE
26	TEXTILE FIBRES AND WASTE		714.9		868.2		885.2		658.1	FIBRES TEXTILES
263	COTTON	W 347561	568.5	W 346831	680.0	W 367343	693.5	W 288837	477.3	COTON
2631	RAW COTTON,EXCL LINTERS	W 321608	548.8	W 326750	661.0	W 353870	680.0	W 280938	470.7	COTON EN MASSE
27	CRUDE FERTLZR,MINRLS NES		164.4		179.5		191.8		161.5	ENGRAIS MINERAUX BRUTS
28	METALLIFEROUS ORES,SCRAP		309.2		312.2		303.3		279.6	MINERAIS METAL,DECHETS
282	IRON AND STEEL SCRAP	W 1158764	257.3	W 1035683	229.1	W 899238	199.6	W 728217	141.5	FERRAILLES
28209	— OF OTHR IRON OR STEEL	W 1155884	256.9	W 1012022	224.8	W 893145	198.2	W 720504	140.3	FERRAILLES DE FER
3	MINERAL FUELS ETC		3738.2		4844.6		6397.0		5839.0	COMBUSTIBLES MINERAUX LUB
33	PETROLEUM AND PRODUCTS		3656.3		4745.0		6221.3		5714.1	PETROLE ET DERIVES
333	CRUDE PETROLEUM	MW 14820	2145.6	MW 21273	2851.6	MW 27647	4445.0	MW 31190	4694.3	HUILES BRUTES DE PETROLE
334	PETROLEUM PRODUCTS,REFIN	MW 9539	1428.1	MW 10458	1758.6	W 8580992	1638.6	W 4389062	915.2	PRODUITS RAFFINES
3343	GAS OILS	W 4289028	648.1	W 4935468	811.1	W 4426338	843.9	W 1746639	296.0	GAS OILS
3344	FUEL OILS,NES	W 3176092	330.3	W 3393567	404.2	W 2746381	323.2	W 525221	68.9	FUEL OILS
3345	LUBS,PETROLEUM OILS NES	W 627145	255.7	W 1285451	421.0	W 1072164	397.3	W 2112322	539.3	HUILES LUBRIFIANTES
33451	LUBS(HIGH PETR CONT) ETC	W 606878	197.5	W 1262774	351.5	W 1047285	323.9	W 2087772	481.6	HUILES LUBRIF,H LOURDES
5	CHEMCLS,RELATED PROD NES		5516.5		7191.8		6759.0		5994.0	PRODUITS CHIMIQUES
51	ORGANIC CHEMICALS		1657.8		2512.7		2035.8		1680.5	PROD CHIMIQ ORGANIQUES
511	HYDROCARBONS NES,DERIVS	W 922097	511.8	W 1004125	754.4	W 1092592	592.4	W 744127	369.0	HYDROCARBURES NDA
5111	ACYCLIC HYDROCARBONS	W 379592	178.7	W 366626	200.2	W 243753	108.7	W 109834	56.5	HYDROCARBURES ACYCLIQUES
5112	CYCLIC HYDROCARBONS	W 256317	139.2	W 328094	300.3	W 560116	306.5	W 289434	126.1	HYDROCARBURES CYCLIQUES
5113	HALOG DERIV OF HYDROCARB	W 285111	192.2	W 308480	251.9	W 287719	175.2	W 341426	183.8	DERIVES HALOGENES HYDROCAR
512	ALCOHOLS,PHENOLS ETC		186.3		291.6	W 334216	216.0		242.8	PHENOLS,PHENOLS–ALCOOLS
5121	ACYCLIC ALCOHOLS,DERIVS		153.4		250.4	W 319231	179.4		207.0	ALCOOLS ACYCLIQUES
513	CARBOXYLIC ACIDS ETC	W 533344	435.1	W 597520	725.1	W 496776	490.8	W 491448	387.4	ACIDES CARBOXYLIQUES
5138	POLYACIDS AND DERIVATIVS	W 398955	307.0	W 459015	528.9	W 338030	312.6	W 329664	213.4	ACIDES POLYCARBOXYLIQUES
51389	OTH POLYACIDS ETC,DERIVS	W 317376	250.1	W 364128	419.9	W 269934	258.7	W 271733	180.3	ACIDES POLYCARBOXYLIQUES
514	NITROGEN–FNCTN COMPOUNDS	W 94202	201.6	W 120448	305.8	W 130625	295.7	W 136339	283.4	COMPOSES FONCT AZOTEES
515	ORG–INORG COMPOUNDS ETC	W 77526	189.6	W 81975	268.2	W 90231	273.2	W 80746	232.5	COMPOSES ORGANO–MINERAUX
52	INORGANIC CHEMICALS		287.6		358.2		368.9		356.2	PROD CHIM INORGANIQUES
53	DYES,TANNING,COLOUR PROD		488.9		585.5		549.8		487.1	PROD TEINTURE,COLORANTS
531	SYNT DYE,NAT INDGO,LAKES	W 16119	165.1	W 18625	200.8	W 17386	171.8	W 17864	152.4	MAT COLOR ORGAN,LAQUES
533	PIGMENTS,PAINTS,ETC	W 116497	312.7	W 123542	370.4	W 123243	364.5	W 130714	323.3	PIGMENTS,PEINTURES,VERNIS
541	*MEDICINAL,PHARM PRODUCT	MK 14424	383.9	MK 16814	469.2	MK 16635	505.2	MK 17852	511.8	PROD MEDICINAUX PHARMACEUT
5417	MEDICAMENTS	K 7885584	173.9	MK 9732	220.9	MK 10073	256.8	MK 10610	278.6	MEDICAMENTS
54179	— CONTNG OTH SUBSTANCES	K 6202432	136.7	K 7802919	176.0	K 8460901	200.7	K 8505088	225.3	MED CONT AUT SUBSTANCES
55	PERFUME,CLEANING ETC PRD		254.0		302.6		302.5		335.2	PROD POUR PARFUM,TOILETTE
562	*FERTILIZERS,MANUFACTURE	W 3015364	537.9	W 3152555	633.4	W 3435269	718.3	W 2988266	548.5	ENGRAIS MANUFACTURES
5629	FERTILIZERS NES	W 1923398	385.4	W 1851682	418.7	W 2050378	469.7	W 1495413	323.9	ENGRAIS NDA
56291	NIT–PHOS–POT FERTLZR NES	W 1062550	221.4	W 1111800	247.2	W 907388	220.1	W 816496	188.4	ENGRAIS CONT N P K
56292	NITROG–PHOS FERTLZR NES	W 849287	161.5	W 731586	169.3	W 1121964	244.7	W 662049	131.7	ENGRAIS NDA CONT N P
58	PLASTIC MATERIALS ETC		1253.4		1505.7		1411.0		1261.7	MAT PLAST ARTIFICIELLES
582	PROD OF CONDENSATION ETC	W 124578	320.3	W 169151	453.7	W 208892	436.3	W 172292	396.6	PROD CONDENS,POLYCOND
583	POLYMERIZATION ETC PRODS	W 606407	893.1		1004.7	W 551223	935.3		823.0	PROD POLYMERISATION
5833	POLYSTYRENE,ITS COPOLYMR	W 118876	156.0	W 134064	240.1	W 110608	178.8		154.6	POLYPROPYLENE COPOLYMERES
58331	— IN PRIMARY FORMS	W 117761	152.7	W 132271	234.6	W 109224	175.7		151.9	SOUS FORMES PRIMAIRES
5839	OTH POLYMRZTION ETC PROD	W 133076	362.3	W 139861	408.7	W 141248	395.7	W 104202	385.5	AUT PROD POLYMER COPOLYM
59	CHEMICAL MATERIALS NES		646.6		802.0		847.5	W 144991	803.9	MAT PROD CHIMIQUES NDA
598	MISCEL CHEM PRODUCTS NES	W 286429	437.7	W 330095	558.5	W 337794	581.9	W 325011	555.8	PROD DIV INDUST CHIM NDA
5989	CHEM PRODUCTS,PREPS NES	W 214258	312.4	W 247972	407.3	W 258038	436.8	W 247370	419.2	PROD PREP CHIMIQUES NDA
59899	OTH CHEM PRODS,PREPS,NES	W 173580	249.0	W 197112	328.8	W 205061	334.7	W 194816	330.6	AUT PRODUITS CHIMIQUES NDA
6	BASIC MANUFACTURES		10331.9		13811.8		12872.7		10684.5	ART MANUFACTURES
61	LEATHER,DRESSED FUR,ETC		328.4		319.7		289.8		277.6	CUIRS,PELLETERIES
611	LEATHER	W 22481	273.5	W 19632	260.1	W 20705	250.9	W 18561	231.2	CUIRS,PEAUX PREPARES
6114	LEATHR BOVINE NES,EQUINE	W 19598	201.4	W 16876	183.2	W 18102	160.6	W 16768	167.1	CUIRS DE BOVINS
62	RUBBER MANUFACTURES NES		263.7		332.0		335.0		302.9	CAOUTCHOUC MANUFACTURE
628	RUBBER ARTICLES NES	W 13709	166.8	W 19846	212.8	W 14191	217.5	W 14764	203.0	OUVRAGES CAOUTCHOUC NDA
64	PAPER,PAPERBOARD AND MFR		567.0		761.1		667.9		546.8	PAPIERS,CARTONS & OUVRAGES
641	PAPER AND PAPERBOARD	W 534949	452.9	W 483040	617.2	W 431697	517.7	W 364046	408.2	PAPIERS ET CARTONS
6418	COATED ETC PAPER NES BLK	W 68827	159.7	W 78677	221.8	W 73846	203.3	W 82278	208.2	PAP,CARTONS COUCHES,ENDUITS
64189	COATED PAPER ETC NES	W 63531	146.7	W 71467	203.0	W 67631	187.5	W 74485	191.5	PAPIERS,CARTONS COUCHES
65	TEXTILE YARN,FABRICS,ETC		1359.3		1533.6		1411.9		1249.0	FILS,TISSUS,ARTICLES TEXTILE
651	TEXTILE YARN	W 48196	209.4	W 74749	272.3	W 51272	242.4	W 53491	218.5	FILS TEXTILES
652	COTTON FABRICS,WOVEN		210.6	W 20268	197.5		180.1	W 16402	165.7	TISSUS DE COTON
6522	WOVEN COTTON BLEACHD,ETC		196.6	W 17925	184.0		167.0	W 14315	155.0	TISSUS COTON BLANCHIS ETC
653	WOVN MAN–MADE FIB FABRIC		419.6	W 66830	465.6	W 53087	408.4	W 48960	325.0	TISSUS FIBRES SYNTH,ARTIF
6531	CONT SYNT WEAVES NONPILE		200.5	W 26042	209.9	W 18537	199.9	W 18374	173.9	TISSUS FIBRES SYNTH CONTINUE
65315	CONT SYN TXTL FABRIC NES		196.3	W 25666	203.8	W 18171	194.1	W 17448	164.4	TIS PLUS 85% TEXT SYNT CONT
655	KNITTED,ETC FABRICS	W 18325	186.8	W 19226	216.0	W 17279	192.2	W 79982	195.0	ETOF BONNETERIE PIECES ETC
6552	OTHER KNIT ETC FAB NONEL	W 18325	186.8	W 19226	216.0	W 17279	192.2	W 79982	195.0	ETOF BON NON ELAS NON SYNT
657	SPECIAL TXTL FABRC,PRODS	W 31986	199.5	W 31723	219.1	W 30640	211.7	W 31506	198.5	TISSUS SPECIAUX
66	NONMETAL MINERAL MFS NES		1299.4		1663.7		1748.5		1154.7	ART MIN NON METALLIQUES
664	GLASS		167.2		243.4		341.8		185.7	VERRE
667	PEARL,PREC–,SEMI–P STONE		884.8		1074.5		1083.0		681.9	PERLES, PIERRES GEMMES
6672	DIAMONDS NONINDUST,UNSET		736.4		894.9		899.1		560.0	DIAMANTS BRUTS

4. General Imports C.I.F. by Commodities according to the S.I.T.C. (Rev. 2) in million U.S. Dollars
Importations Générales C.A.F. par Produits d'après la C.T.C.I. (Rév. 2) en millions de Dollars E.U.

SITC CTCI	COMMODITY	1994 QUANTITY QUANTITE	1994 VALUE VALEUR	1995 QUANTITY QUANTITE	1995 VALUE VALEUR	1996 QUANTITY QUANTITE	1996 VALUE VALEUR	1997 QUANTITY QUANTITE	1997 VALUE VALEUR	PRODUIT
66721	— ROUGH,UNSORTED		158.8		197.4		222.2		197.4	DIAMANTS BRUTS NON TRIES
66722	— SRTD,ROUGH,SIMPLY WKD		189.4		178.7		183.3		130.7	DIAMANTS TRIES BRUTS
66729	— CUT ETC NOT SET		388.3		518.9		493.6		232.0	DIAMANTS TAILLES
67	IRON AND STEEL		3753.2		5223.4		4600.7		3635.8	FER ET ACIER
672	IRON,STEEL PRIMARY FORMS	W 4765723	1166.5	W 5339195	1748.0	W 5479744	1654.1	W 4267258	1242.8	LINGOTS FER,ACIER
6725	IRN,STL BLOOMS,SLABS,ETC	W 3209330	580.1	W 3428055	908.8	W 3995590	1021.8	W 3256455	789.5	BLOOMS,BILLETTES FER ACIER
67251	IRN,SMPLE STL BLOOMS,ETC	W 3208612	578.9	W 3427278	907.3	W 3994143	1018.9	W 3255593	787.7	BLOOMS ETC NON ACIER FIN
6727	IRN,STL COIL FR REROLLNG	W 1556371	586.4	W 1911073	839.1	W 1484076	631.8	W 1010759	453.3	EBAUCHES POUR TOLES FER
67271	IRON,SIMPLE STEEL COILS	W 1472962	508.5	W 1811457	726.7	W 1402282	524.1	W 916043	321.2	EBAUCHES NON EN ACIER
673	IRON,STEEL SHAPES ETC	W 1929636	791.8	W 1703677	831.8	W 1424328	696.9	W 1026162	463.3	BARRES,PROFIL FER,ACIER
6731	IRON,STEEL WIRE ROD	W 693262	288.7	W 774818	360.1	W 611019	289.1	W 490809	208.5	FIL MACHINE FER,ACIER
6732	IRON,STEEL BARS ETC	W 645011	286.4	W 322509	232.4	W 237642	195.6	W 171021	131.0	BARRES FER,ACIER
67326	IRN,OTH STL BARS HOTROLD	W 548764	174.9	W 189249	74.6	W 114371	52.5	W 87029	37.1	BARRES PLEINES FER,ACIER
6733	IRON,STEEL PROFILES ETC	W 591364	216.7	W 606349	239.3	W 575667	212.3	W 364332	123.9	PROFILES,PALPLAN FER,ACIER
674	IRN,STL UNIV,PLATE,SHEET	W 2440486	1380.2	W 3252352	2076.9	W 2747416	1733.6	W 2492239	1477.5	LARGES PLATS,TOLES
6744	IRN,STL HVY PLATE,ROLLED	W 558955	205.6	W 704328	311.9	W 535878	232.6	W 358625	152.1	TOLES LAMINEES PLUS 4.75 MM
67441	— OF IRON OR SIMPLE STL	W 541108	182.3	W 678615	266.5	W 505077	190.6	W 330091	122.1	TOLES NON ACIER FIN CARB
6746	IRN,STL THIN PLATE,ROLLD	W 1322035	783.0	W 1827452	1199.6	W 1572398	971.2	W 1463554	846.4	TOLES LAM MOINS 3MM
67461	— OF IRON OR SIMPLE STL	W 1242646	639.1	W 1737030	1002.7	W 1497282	821.8	W 1400837	735.7	TOL NON AC FIN MOINS 3 MM
6749	OTH IRN,STL PLATES,SHEET	W 369399	265.9	W 440883	374.3	W 430125	367.6	W 441283	337.5	AUTRES TOLES FER,ACIER
67491	— OF IRON OR SIMPLE STL	W 367212	258.5	W 430805	357.2	W 422702	348.1	W 434566	320.7	AUT TOLES AUTRES ACIER FIN
678	IRON,STL TUBES,PIPES,ETC	W 180811	249.9	W 276363	353.4	W 263507	318.4	W 239909	288.3	TUBES,TUYAUX EN FONTE,FER
68	NON-FERROUS METALS		1183.2		1801.5		1617.3		1404.7	METAUX NON FERREUX
682	COPPER EXC CEMENT COPPER	W 233166	579.8	W 221583	793.2	W 218826	705.2	W 213498	629.3	CUIVRE
6821	COPPER NES,ALLOYS,UNWRT	W 177013	368.3	W 154091	461.7	W 161159	435.2	W 157364	384.3	CUIVRE BRUT
68212	COPPER REFINED,UNWROUGHT	W 176954	368.1	W 153976	461.1	W 160789	433.8	W 157227	383.6	CUIVRE AFFINE BRUT
6822	COPPER,ALLOYS WORKED	W 56153	211.5	W 67492	331.6	W 57667	270.1	W 56135	245.1	CUIVRE,ALLIAGES OUVRES
684	ALUMINIUM	W 234418	462.6	W 316096	780.7	W 284463	673.6	W 304868	594.7	ALUMINIUM
6841	ALUMINIUM,ALLOYS,UNWRGHT	W 184547	283.0	W 254158	511.4	W 220807	405.1	W 238099	349.5	ALUMINIUM,ALLIAGES BRUTS
6842	ALUMINIUM,ALLOYS WORKED	W 49871	179.7	W 61938	269.4	W 63656	268.6	W 66769	245.3	ALUMINIUM,ALLIAGES OUVRE
69	METAL MANUFACTURES NES		1527.9		2097.0		2123.8		2045.9	ART MANUFACT EN METAL NDA
694	STL,COPPR NAILS,NUTS,ETC	W 38828	306.2	W 40112	357.9	W 47581	372.1	W 35208	272.2	CLOUS,VIS,ECROUS
69402	IRN,STL NUTS,BOLTS,ETC	W 36406	298.2	W 37768	345.5	W 45107	363.7	W 33130	265.2	BOULONS,VIS,ECROUS FER,AC
695	TOOLS	W 25440	272.1	W 30369	409.9	W 29436	393.4	W 27227	361.8	OUTILS A MAIN
6954	BLADES,TIPS,ETC FR TOOLS	W 5938	191.0	W 7453	303.8	W 7021	290.7	W 8930	286.1	OUTILS POUR MACHINE-OUTIL
69541	PARTS TO INSERT IN TOOLS	W 4778	151.1	W 6037	251.1	W 5626	237.4	W 6938	243.3	OUTILS DE FORAGE
699	BASE METAL MFRS NES	W 123328	743.2	W 124301	1022.3	W 119543	1098.8	W 137887	1219.0	ART MANUFACTURES MET NDA
6997	IRON,STEEL ARTICLES NES	W 57842	383.7	W 58535	608.8	W 61394	668.4	W 82677	746.8	OUV FONTE,FER,ACIER NDA
69979	IRN,STL MANUFACTURES NES	W 57734	383.3	W 58443	608.7	W 61266	668.1	W 82667	746.8	AUT OUVRAGES EN FER NDA
6998	MFRS NES OF CPR,NIKL,ETC	W 8902	80.7	W 8556	94.7	W 8397	139.2	W 12312	207.6	OUVRAGES EN CU,NI,AL,PB,ZN
7	MACHINES,TRANSPORT EQUIP		25495.4		33551.8		34054.3		29319.6	MACHINES MATERIEL TRANSPORT
71	POWER GENERATING EQUIPMT		1456.7		1690.5		1559.6		1410.2	MACHINES GENERATRICES
713	INTRNL COMBUS PSTN ENGIN		583.2		619.5		682.3		531.5	MOTEURS EXPL COMB INT, PIECE
7139	PISTON ENGINE PARTS NES	W 87146	411.0	W 39768	431.2	W 39660	484.1	W 31178	364.7	PIECES POUR 713.2,3,8
716	ROTATING ELECTRIC PLANT		751.5		847.3		712.3		697.6	APP ELECTR ROTATIFS,PIECES
7161	DC MOTORS AND GENERATORS	N 5227213	257.8	N 1488868	198.4	N 1304315	172.9		169.9	MOTEURS COURANT CONTINU
7162	AC MTRS,GENRTRS,GEN SETS		276.7		363.7	MN 81701	346.4	MN 104197	304.3	MOTEURS ELECTRIQUES
71621	AC MTRS,INC UNIVRSL MTRS	MN 84494	236.6	MN 92643	315.6	MN 81425	321.1	MN 102524	278.1	MOT ELEC NON COUR CONTINU
7169	PTS NES OF ROT ELEC PLNT	W 10023	216.8	W 11560	284.8	W 10253	192.7	W 21260	223.4	PIECES MAC APP ROTATIFS
72	MACHS FOR SPCL INDUSTRYS		3124.1		4186.3		4252.9		2794.4	MAC SPECIALES POUR INDUST
722	TRACTORS NON-ROAD	N 55519	212.1	N 85455	244.9	N 45222	265.4	N 13718	191.8	TRACTEURS
7224	WHEELED TRACTORS NES	N 53982	142.0	N 84059	191.4	N 43634	221.0	N 12957	153.2	TRACTEURS A ROUES
723	CIVIL ENGNEERG EQUIP ETC		602.5		725.4		833.6		420.0	APPAREILS DE GENIE CIVIL
7234	CONST,MINING MACHNRY NES		431.5	N 14270	523.2	N 17037	568.6	N 84839	266.6	MACH POUR LA CONST, MINES
72342	SLFPRP SHOVELS,EXCAVATRS	N 11411	301.6	N 6507	395.7	N 9524	365.2	N 3474	132.5	PELLES MECANIQUES
724	TEXTILE,LEATHER MACHNRY		545.3		642.0		480.6		409.4	MACH POUR INDUSTRIE TEXTILE
7244	SPINNING,EXTRDNG,ETC MCH		220.7		258.5		161.6		178.3	MACH POUR LE FILAGE
725	PAPER ETC MILL MACHINERY		75.9		177.0		272.7		123.5	MACHINES FABR PATE PAPIER
726	PRINTG,BKBINDG MACHY,PTS		168.3		235.8		195.0		125.0	MACHINES POUR IMPRIMERIE
728	OTH MACHY FOR SPCL INDUS		1395.0		1930.4		1980.7		1388.1	AUT MACH IND PARTICULIERES
7281	MACH-TOOLS FR SPCL INDUS		171.7		230.9		160.9		74.2	MACH-OUTILS SPEC IND PART
7283	OTHR MINERAL WORKG MACHY		185.5		239.4		276.8		125.9	MACH TRIER,CRIBLER,BROYER
7284	MACHY FOR SPCL INDUS NES		1038.0		1460.3		1543.2		1188.1	MACH SPEC IND PARTICUL.
72842	RUBBER,PLASTICS WRKG MCH		291.9	N 27529	396.2	N 33203	368.8	N 53722	252.2	MACH IND CAOUT MAT PLAST
72848	OTH MCHY WITH INDIV FNCT	N 946399	567.8	N 1047118	848.1	N 711543	817.0	N 486019	723.8	AUTRES MACHINES NDA
73	METALWORKING MACHINERY		856.2		1141.0		1543.3		1522.9	MACH TRAVAIL DES METAUX
736	METALWORKING MACH-TOOLS		549.5		829.2		964.5		966.4	MACH-OUTILS TRAVAIL METAUX
7361	METAL CUTTING MACH-TOOLS		281.1	N 123188	398.0	N 250314	412.1	N 137501	314.8	MACH-OUT ENLEVEMENT METAL
7362	METAL FORMING MACH-TOOLS	N 18969	148.0	N 33646	245.6	N 46563	259.0		249.3	MACH-OUTILS DEFORM METAL
737	METALWORKING MACHNRY NES		306.7		311.8		578.8		556.6	MACH TRAV METAUX PIECES
7372	ROLLING MILLS AND ROLLS		169.3		125.2		395.5		342.0	LAMINOIRS CYLINDRES PIEC
73721	ROLLING MILLS		133.1	N 6559	75.2	N 4754	209.6		242.1	LAMINOIRS ET TRAINS
74	GENRL INDUSTRL MACHY NES		3463.6		4753.9		4917.0		3775.2	MACH APP INDUSTRIE
741	HEATING,COOLING EQUIPMNT		864.0		1309.4		1409.4		1002.3	MACH CHAUFFAGE,PIECES
7416	HEATING,COOLING EQU NES		485.1		841.7		997.8		639.7	APP CHANGEMENT TEMP
742	PUMPS FOR LIQUIDS ETC		340.0		396.6		388.2		235.8	POMPES MOTO-POMPES
7428	OTHER PUMPS FOR LIQUIDS	N 2252284	184.4	N 2199063	242.0	N 8158854	237.4	MN 11057	138.7	AUTRES POMPES POUR LIQ
74288	PUMPS FR LIQUIDS NES ETC	N 1953879	153.2	N 2005134	214.1	N 8123235	208.0	MN 11050	124.8	POMPES POUR LIQUIDES NDA
743	PUMPS NES,CENTRFUGES ETC		550.5		766.2		683.4		592.6	POMPES COMPRES,VENT ETC
7431	PUMPS FOR GASES ETC	N 8104986	311.9	N 7064492	410.0	N 7345346	383.3	N 6712413	301.1	POMPES AIR A VIDE,COMPRES
744	MECHANICAL HANDLING EQU		545.2		684.5		770.1		586.4	EQUIP MANUTENTION PIECES
7442	LIFTING,LOADING MACH NES		382.8		416.5	N 725406	420.7		375.5	APP LEVAGE,MANUTENTION
74428	OTH HANDLING ETC MCH NES		169.2		202.4	N 575606	187.5	N 476505	185.9	AUT APP LEVAGE ETC
745	NONELEC MACHY,TOOLS NES		269.5		384.5		361.5		281.5	AUT MACH NON ELEC,PIECES
7452	OTH NONELEC MCHS,PTS NES		248.3		355.0		330.5		257.7	AUT MACH NON ELEC,PIECES
749	NONELEC MACH PTS,ACC NES		894.7		1212.9		1304.5		1076.9	PIECES MACH NON ELEC NDA
7491	BALL,ROLLER,ETC BEARINGS	MN 273791	210.2	MN 288197	276.9	MN 339729	322.2	MN 378305	256.5	ROULEMENTS BILLES ETC
7492	COCKS,VALVES ETC NES	W 32152	228.7	W 17767	290.2	W 21825	286.4	W 15504	217.2	ART ROB,SIM POUR TUYAUX
7493	SHAFT,CRANK,PULLEY ETC	MN 227322	203.6	MN 356106	271.0	MN 573765	304.4	MN 691489	233.9	ARBRES TRANS,VILEBREQUINS
7499	OTH NONELEC MCHY PTS NES	W 17456	252.4	W 11880	374.9	W 14333	391.7	W 13992	369.5	PIECES NON ELECT NDA
74991	FOUNDRY MOULDS ETC NES	W 15129	199.8	W 9345	288.3	W 11300	296.5	W 9570	270.7	MOULES POUR METAUX
75	OFFICE MACHNES,ADP EQUIP		2389.8		2979.0		3132.3		3307.9	MACH BUREAU TRAIT AUTOM
752	AUTOMTIC DATA PROC EQUIP		510.0		631.1	N 2185742	643.7	N 2392383	544.4	MACH TRAIT INFORMATION
7525	ADP PERIPHERAL UNITS	N 1192196	207.7	N 977038	252.0	N 887951	237.4	N 820598	196.3	UNITES PERIPHERIQUES
7528	OFF-LINE DATA PROC EQUIP		65.2		137.8	N 676262	194.0	N 1100825	196.1	MACH AUXIL TRAIT INFORM
759	OFFICE,ADP MCH PTS,ACCES	W 12742	1734.0	W 17382	2170.4	W 11291	2315.4	W 13691	2649.2	PIECES DU 751 ET 752
7599	ACCTG,ETC,ADP MCH PTS,AC	W 10397	1680.0	W 11072	2090.5	W 9481	2251.0	W 11848	2580.9	PIECES DU 751 ET 752
76	TELECOMM,SOUND EQUIPMENT		2118.8		2295.5		2113.7		2102.6	EQUIPMENT DE TELECOM
764	TELECOM EQPT,PTS,ACC NES		1799.4		1978.9		1759.0		1871.4	EQUIP TELECOM,PIECES
7641	LINE TELEPHONE,ETC EQUIP	MN 15434	372.7	MN 13798	329.9	N 4675314	318.1		409.0	APP TELEPHON PAR FIL
7643	TV,RADIO TRANSMITTRS ETC	N 1345162	474.9	N 1901622	507.7	N 1239408	398.9	N 1232860	370.2	APP EMET TELE RADIO

4. General Imports C.I.F. by Commodities according to the S.I.T.C. (Rev. 2) in million U.S. Dollars
Importations Générales C.A.F. par Produits d'après la C.T.C.I. (Rév. 2) en millions de Dollars E.U.

SITC CTCI	COMMODITY	1994 QUANTITY QUANTITE	1994 VALUE VALEUR	1995 QUANTITY QUANTITE	1995 VALUE VALEUR	1996 QUANTITY QUANTITE	1996 VALUE VALEUR	1997 QUANTITY QUANTITE	1997 VALUE VALEUR	PRODUIT
7649	PTS NES OF EQUIPMT OF 76	W 24851	809.3	W 24766	950.0	W 28248	859.0	W 27539	943.3	PIECES DE LA DIV 76
76491	PTS NES OF APPAR OF 7641	W 6097	153.4	W 2063	150.3	W 2336	197.5	W 3456	285.2	PIECES POUR 764.1
76493	TELECOMM EQUIPMT PTS NES	W 9527	350.0	W 11713	476.0	W 13304	417.2	W 14833	408.1	PIECES 761,762,764.3,8
76499	PARTS ETC OF SOUND EQUIP	W 3913	273.8	W 6067	291.4	W 7280	211.4	W 4566	228.5	PIECES NDA POUR 763
77	ELECTRIC MACHNRY NES ETC		6885.5		9499.8		10006.8		10032.8	MACH APP ELECT NDA
771	ELECTRIC POWER MACHY NES		373.7		517.8		541.9		565.4	MACH PROD,TRANS ELECTR
7711	TRANSFORMERS,ELECTRICAL	MN 68895	160.7	MN 85796	179.9	MN 97915	179.3	MN 122461	208.9	TRANSFO ELECTRIQUES
7712	OTH ELEC POWER MACHY NES		213.1		338.0		362.7		356.5	AUT APP PROD TRANSF ELEC
772	SWITCHGEAR ETC,PARTS NES	W 74153	1277.3	W 52123	1755.8	W 51617	1667.5	W 47352	1786.4	APP COUPURE,SECT ETC
7721	SWITCHGEAR ETC	W 54512	960.1	W 40423	1192.0	W 38510	1126.4	W 37385	1281.2	APP COUPURE,SECTIONMNT
7722	PRINTED CIRCUITS,PTS NES	W 6808	195.7	W 6122	395.5	W 9629	395.5	W 7009	366.4	CIRCUITS ET PIECES
773	ELECTR DISTRIBUTNG EQUIP	W 45972	372.4	W 61407	481.4	W 59356	587.8	W 57131	699.3	EQUIPMT DISTRIBUTION ELECT
7731	INSULATED WIRE,CABLE ETC	W 33330	291.0	W 47506	383.9	W 41259	473.5	W 44810	601.4	FILS,CABLES ISOLES ELECT
776	TRANSISTORS,VALVES,ETC		3493.3		4993.7		5558.4		5451.8	LAMPES,TUBES,VALVES
7761	TV PICTURE TUBES	MN 16878	336.1	MN 19238	608.5	N 8689215	810.7	MN 11590	832.4	TUBES CATHODIQUES
7763	DIODES,TRANSISTORS,ETC	MN 4447089	277.2	MN 7373259	420.7	MN 7027417	509.8	MN 8756993	437.5	DIODES,TRANSISTORS
7764	ELECTRONIC MICROCIRCUITS	MN 1968549	1427.6	MN 2315878	1870.6	MN 3632359	1973.6	MN 3775550	1756.4	MICROSTRUCTURES ELECTRON
7768	ELCTRNC COMP PTS,CRYSTLS		1377.9		2045.8		2224.0		2391.1	CRIST PIEZO–ELEC,PCS 776
77689	ELECTRNIC COMPON PTS NES	W 5539	1345.7	W 13509	2007.2	W 9808	2190.2	W 11624	2361.4	PIECES DU GROUPE 776
778	ELECTRICAL MACHINERY NES		1141.8		1455.0		1345.9		1270.6	AUTRES MACH ELECT NDA
7783	AUTOMOTIVE ELECTR EQUIP		177.3		229.8		167.0		105.0	EQUIP ELECT MOTEURS EXPL
7788	OTH ELEC MACHY,EQUIP NES		778.8		983.2		928.2		941.9	AUT MACH APP ELEC NDA
77884	ELECTRICAL CONDENSERS	W 9235	290.2	W 8946	426.4	W 8364	381.0	W 17293	384.9	CONDENSATEURS ELECTRIQUES
77886	OTH ELEC MACHINERY NES		226.9		316.8		289.3		304.6	AUT MACH APP ELECTRIQUES
78	ROAD VEHICLES		4042.2		5237.3		4845.9		2306.9	VEHICULES ROUTIERS
781	PASS MOTOR VEH EXC BUSES	N 394648	1537.9	N 437203	1549.6	N 162860	1118.4		538.3	AUTO TRANSPORT PERSONNES
782	LORRIES,SPCL MTR VEH NES	N 17056	159.3	N 13322	196.9	N 14697	272.9	N 6980	136.3	VEHICULES SPECIAUX,MARCH
7821	LORRIES,TRUCKS	N 16400	119.1	N 13060	159.7	N 14347	223.0	N 6457	73.0	VEHICULES TRANSP MARCHAND
784	MOTOR VEH PRTS,ACCES NES		1977.1		3021.6		3062.8		1412.8	PIECES 722,781,782,783
7841	MOTOR VEHICLE CHASSIS	N 370180	867.1		1318.1	N 95807	1083.5	N 26235	431.5	CHASSIS 722,781,782,783
7849	OTHER MOTOR VEHCL PARTS	W 228644	1103.2	W 197155	1692.7	W 1265801	1964.6	W 140778	971.1	PIECES 722,781,782,783
785	CYCLES,ETC MOTRZD OR NOT		289.9		379.7		254.2		120.0	MOTOCYCLES SCOOTERS
7853	INVAL CARR, PTS OF 785		286.7		375.6		250.0		116.2	FAUTEUILS INVALIDES,PIECES
78539	PARTS,ACCES NES OF 785	W 35578	286.4	W 65382	375.3	W 28183	249.4	W 12786	115.7	PIECES DU 785
79	OTHR TRANSPORT EQUIPMENT		1158.9		1668.9		1683.1		2067.1	AUTRE MATERIEL TRANSPORT
792	AIRCRAFT ETC		905.8		1327.1		1180.6		1687.6	APP NAVIGATION AERIENNE
7924	AIRCRFT NES OVER 15000KG	N 1	149.8	N 8	941.2	N 4	490.7	N 6	885.2	AERODYNES PLUS 15000 KG
7929	AIRCRAFT PARTS NES	W 973	746.5	W 720	331.6	W 11081	586.0	W 999	642.6	PIECES DU 792
793	SHIPS AND BOATS ETC		243.1		306.8	N 28587	365.7	N 284779	344.2	NAVIRES BATEAUX,ETC
7932	SHIPS AND BOATS NES		158.1		231.3	N 1477	190.4	N 7232	138.8	NAVIRES ET BATEAUX
7938	TUGS,SPECIAL VESSELS ETC		79.5	N 19380	75.4	N 19526	173.8	N 210345	204.4	REMORQUEURS,BATEAUX SPEC
79382	SPECL PURPOSE VESSLS ETC	N 33	73.4	N 24	55.3	N 18109	160.0	N 116	199.5	BAT–PHARES,–POMPES,DRAGUES
8	MISC MANUFACTURED GOODS		3078.2		3938.8		4165.0		3716.2	ART MANUFACTURES DIVERS
87	PRECISION INSTRUMNTS NES		696.1		940.2		973.5		912.5	INSTRUM,APPAR SCIENT NDA
874	MEASURNG,CONTROLNG INSTR		524.1		703.1		722.1		710.1	INSTRUMENTS DE MESURE
8742	MEASUR,DRAW ETC INST,PTS		202.4		260.3		254.7		255.2	INST DESSIN,TRACAGE,PCS
87421	MEASURNG,DRAWNG ETC INST	N 5680400	195.3	N 6199589	248.6	N 6889276	242.4	N 7128669	238.9	INSTRUM DESSIN,TRACAGE
88	PHOTO EQU,OPTICL GDS ETC		535.7		612.8		672.0		543.2	APP,FOURN PHOTO,OP,MONTR
885	WATCHES AND CLOCKS		256.2		284.6		298.2		238.7	HORLOGERIE
89	MISC MANUFCTRD GOODS NES		1672.7		2154.5		2254.0		1935.4	ART MANUFACTURES DIVERS
893	ARTICLES OF PLASTIC NES		744.7		904.9		897.4		886.3	OUVRAGES EN MAT DIVIS 58
8939	MISC PLASTIC ARTICLES	W 56941	672.1	W 69410	820.2	W 71702	800.8	W 79215	783.6	ART DIVERS EN MAT DIV 58
89399	OTHR PLASTC ARTICLES NES	W 54431	665.5	W 67411	814.7	W 69068	794.8	W 76885	778.3	AUT OUV MAT DIV 58
898	MUSICAL INSTRUMENTS,PTS		503.5		717.5		747.6		556.9	INSTRUMENTS DE MUSIQUE
8983	SOUND RECRDNG TAPE,DISCS	MN 1747253	478.8	MN 2493075	686.9	MN 912066	716.4	MN 1201011	537.3	SUPPORTS SON POUR 763
89831	PREPD SND RECORDNG MEDIA	MN 1682729	405.1	MN 2449330	510.9	MN 872470	536.2	MN 1155147	391.8	SUPPORTS PREPARES
9	GOODS NOT CLASSD BY KIND		1173.6		1380.2		1969.5		1511.9	ART TRANSACT NON CLASSES
931	*SPECIAL TRANSACTIONS	W 175686	751.7		851.9	W 202952	1385.9	W 136515	1043.2	TRANS.SPECIALES
971	*GOLD,NON MONETARY NES	K 18423	391.7	K 247984	472.4	K 46683	473.2	K 203500	377.5	OR NON MONETAIRE
97101	NONMON GLD UNWRT,SEMIMFD	K 18406	391.7	K 247848	472.3	K 46607	473.1	K 202984	377.5	OR,ALLIAGES D'OR BRUTS

5. General Exports F.O.B. by Commodities according to the S.I.T.C. (Rev. 2) in million U.S. Dollars
Exportations Générales F.O.B. par Produits d'après la C.T.C.I. (Rév. 2) en millions de Dollars E.U.

SITC CTCI	COMMODITY	1994 QUANTITY QUANTITE	1994 VALUE VALEUR	1995 QUANTITY QUANTITE	1995 VALUE VALEUR	1996 QUANTITY QUANTITE	1996 VALUE VALEUR	1997 QUANTITY QUANTITE	1997 VALUE VALEUR	PRODUIT
	ALL COMMODITIES		45235.6		56439.4				58282.6	TOUS PRODUITS
0	FOOD AND LIVE ANIMALS		9305.5		10689.4				10390.1	ALIMENTS,ANIMAUX VIVANTS
01	MEAT AND PREPARATIONS		499.3		550.5				547.3	VIANDES ET PREPARATIONS
011	MEAT FRESH,CHILLD,FROZEN	W 159393	409.4	W 157644	411.7			W 157237	373.0	VIANDES FRAICHES,REF,CONGE
0114	POULTRY FRESH CHLLD,FRZN	W 158941	408.3	W 156943	409.5			W 156038	369.5	VOLAILLES MORTES
03	FISH AND PREPARATIONS		4188.0		4447.2				4211.1	POISSONS ET PREPARATIONS
034	FISH,FRESH,CHILLED,FROZN	W 300967	349.2	W 314827	410.1			W 335570	416.0	POISSON FRAIS, REFRIG,CONG
0342	FISH FROZEN,EXCL FILLETS	W 144548	206.9	W 169350	249.9			W 170706	256.2	POISSONS CONGELES
036	SHELL FISH FRESH,FROZEN	W 267616	2326.1	W 246511	2411.7			W 222572	1885.4	CRUSTACES,MOLLUSQUES
037	FISH ETC PREPD,PRSVD NES	W 474864	1489.1	W 437239	1590.7			W 430972	1882.0	POIS,CRUST,MOL PREPARES
0371	FISH PREPARD,PRESRVD NES	W 401282	854.0	W 354126	820.7			W 331788	853.6	CONSERVES DE POISSONS
0372	SHELL FISH PREPRD,PRESVD	W 73582	635.1	W 83113	770.0			W 99184	1028.4	CRUSTACES,COQUIL PREPARES
04	CEREALS AND PREPARATIONS		1777.8		2163.5				2331.8	CEREALES ET PRODUITS
042	RICE	W 4858638	1558.3	W 6197991	1951.6			W 5567570	2099.7	RIZ
0422	RICE SEMI–MILLED, MILLED	W 4735397	1524.1	W 6103303	1922.7			W 5418999	2039.2	RIZ POLI,GLACE INCL BRISURES
04221	RICE MILLED UNBROKEN	W 4266909	1428.3	W 5533482	1783.6			W 4713083	1869.1	RIZ POLI,GLACE EXCL BRISURES
05	VEGETABLES AND FRUIT		1491.6		1491.6				1467.2	LEGUMES ET FRUITS
054	VEG ETC FRSH,SMPLY PRSVD	W 4905802	612.6	W 3379050	545.1			W 4422547	504.9	LEGUMES FRAIS,CONG,SECS
0548	EDIBLE VEG NES FRESH,DRY	W 4730773	485.5	W 3226212	415.8			W 4287582	394.6	RACINES,TUBERCULES
05481	ROOTS,TUBERS FRESH,DRY	W 4730184	484.4	W 3225613	413.2			W 4286266	393.5	RACINES DE MANIOC ETC
056	VEGTBLES ETC PRSVD,PREPD	W 493113	222.2	W 383653	240.3			W 393362	212.0	CONSERVES DE LEGUMES
0565	VEGTBLES PRSVD,PREPD NES	W 191732	142.7	W 184516	167.8			W 177423	161.6	LEGUMES PREPARES CONSERVE
057	FRUIT,NUTS,FRESH,DRIED	W 154766	110.8	W 173609	139.6			W 297961	242.4	FRUITS FRAIS OU SECS
0579	FRUIT FRESH OR DRIED NES	W 128844	94.3	W 141471	120.6			W 265814	226.3	FRUITS FRAIS,SECS NDA
058	FRUIT PRESERVED,PREPARED	W 1001004	546.1	W 700915	566.7			W 581132	508.0	CONSERVES DE FRUITS
0589	FRUIT PREPRD,PRESRVD,NES	W 837713	376.0	W 524030	369.9			W 434559	328.6	FRUITS PREPARES CONSERV
05899	FRUIT,NUTS NES,PRESERVED	W 831517	369.6	W 519713	365.5			W 430334	323.3	FRUITS PREP CONSERV NDA
06	SUGAR AND PREPS,HONEY		765.6		1269.3				1105.6	SUCRES ET PRODUITS
061	SUGAR AND HONEY	W 3459455	732.7	W 4962412	1229.1			W 4925674	1070.3	SUCRES ET MIEL
0611	RAW BEET AND CANE SUGAR	W 1902062	487.7	W 2800616	832.4			W 2449852	563.2	SUCRES BRUTS
0612	REFINED SUGAR ETC	W 708762	196.4	W 958614	322.2			W 1582388	452.7	SUCRES RAFFINES
07	COFFEE,TEA,COCOA,SPICES		106.9		216.0				110.5	CAFE,THE,CACAO,EPICES
071	COFFEE AND SUBSTITUTES	W 68598	88.7	W 76769	190.0			W 72238	73.1	CAFE ET SUCCEDANES
0711	COFFEE GREEN,ROASTED,SUB	W 68150	85.6	W 76144	185.3			W 71296	67.2	CAFE TORREFIE OU DECAFEINE
07111	COFFEE GREEN,HUSKS,SKINS	W 68089	85.4	W 76104	185.1			W 71249	67.0	CAFE NON TORREFIE
081	*FEEDING STUFF FOR ANIML	W 272329	204.9	W 281383	235.7			W 251203	263.6	NOURRITURE POUR ANIMAUX
0819	FOOD WASTE AND FEED NES	W 177051	191.3	W 167394	221.1			W 171138	251.5	DECHETS,ALIMENTS NDA
08199	FODDER NES,INCL SWEETNED	W 175454	191.0	W 165014	220.7			W 168994	251.1	PREPARATIONS FOURRAGERES
09	MISC EDIBLE PRODUCTS		228.3		269.9				302.1	PREP ALIMENTAIRES DIVERSES
098	EDIBLE PRODCTS,PREPS NES	W 26	0.1	W 32	0.1			W 101	0.2	PREP ALIMENTAIRES NDA
09809	MISC FOOD PREPRTIONS NES	W 119396	143.4	W 114964	171.7			W 158973	190.9	PREP ALIMENTAIRES NDA
1	BEVERAGES AND TOBACCO		164.7		143.8				210.2	BOISSONS ET TABACS
2	CRUDE MATERLS,EXCL FUELS		2207.7		3232.9				2612.1	MAT BRUTES NON COMESTIBLES
23	RUBBER, CRUDE		1669.1		2462.1				1861.7	CAOUTCHOUC BRUT
232	NATURAL RUBBER,GUMS	W 1735557	1663.1	W 1747396	2458.8			W 1920179	1854.7	LATEX CAOUTCHOUC NATUREL
23201	NATURAL RUBBER LATEX	W 246359	169.0	W 287128	288.5			W 368772	274.9	LATEX NATUREL
23202	OTHER NATURAL RUBBER	W 1102983	1142.7	W 1089677	1628.7			W 1057548	1090.9	CAOUTCHOUC NATUREL
23203	BALATA,GUTTA–PERCHA, ETC	W 386215	351.5	W 370591	541.7			W 493860	489.0	BALATA,GUTTA–PERCHA
26	TEXTILE FIBRES AND WASTE		123.1		214.0				168.7	FIBRES TEXTILES
3	MINERAL FUELS ETC		352.3		409.6				1374.2	COMBUSTIBLES MINERAUX LUB
33	PETROLEUM AND PRODUCTS		223.2		257.3				1164.1	PETROLE ET DERIVES
334	PETROLEUM PRODUCTS,REFIN	W 829693	221.9	W 1322195	252.3			W 3026302	1001.3	PRODUITS RAFFINES
3341	GASOLINE,OTH LIGHT OILS	W 440786	116.1	W 497730	80.0			W 193931	400.9	ESSENCES POUR MOTEURS
33411	MOTOR,AVIATION SPIRIT	W 440693	116.1	W 497493	79.9			W 193931	400.9	ESSENCES MOTEURS D'AVIONS
3343	GAS OILS	W 87635	16.8	W 115849	23.8			W 1776339	368.2	GAS OILS
341	*GAS,NATURAL AND MANUFCT	W 830029	129.1	W 924251	152.4			W 1114646	210.2	GAZ NATUREL,GAZ MANUFACT
3413	PETROLM GASES,LIQUEFIED	W 801151	124.3	W 924195	152.4			W 1114646	210.2	GAZ DE PETROLE LIQUEFIE
34139	OTH HYDROCARBON GAS LQFD	W 801063	124.3	W 923919	152.1			W 1112979	209.6	HYDROCARBURES GAZEUX NDA
5	CHEMCLS,RELATED PROD NES		1256.2		2126.7				2441.7	PRODUITS CHIMIQUES
51	ORGANIC CHEMICALS		131.1		238.8				454.9	PROD CHIMIQ ORGANIQUES
53	DYES,TANNING,COLOUR PROD		189.1		462.0				104.5	PROD TEINTURE,COLORANTS
533	PIGMENTS,PAINTS,ETC	W 30152	147.2	W 39105	414.7			W 25484	47.4	PIGMENTS,PEINTURES,VERNIS
5335	GLAZES,DRIERS,PUTTY ETC	W 4967	104.1	W 8737	330.8			W 4939	8.5	PREPTNS COLOR UTILISES CERAM
53352	ARTISTS COLOURS	W 661	92.4	W 2633	314.6			W 248	1.8	COULEURS PEINT ARTISTIQUE
55	PERFUME,CLEANING ETC PRD		109.6		147.2				193.2	PROD POUR PARFUM,TOILETTE
58	PLASTIC MATERIALS ETC		417.5		713.3				1025.6	MAT PLAST ARTIFICIELLES
583	POLYMERIZATION ETC PRODS	W 277404	328.7	W 484563	564.3			W 980079	877.4	PROD POLYMERISATION
5831	POLYETHYLENE	W 26201	21.2	W 134592	109.3			W 227842	186.2	POLYETHYLENE
58311	— IN PRIMARY FORMS	W 25777	20.4	W 133504	108.1			W 225380	182.9	POLYETHYLENE PRIMAIRES
5832	POLYPROPYLENE	W 56907	52.5	W 110137	122.3			W 225949	182.8	POLYPROPYLENE
5839	OTH POLYMRZTION ETC PROD	W 87849	144.6	W 74507	153.7			W 96985	152.0	AUT PROD POLYMER COPOLYM
59	CHEMICAL MATERIALS NES		269.3		370.1				428.4	MAT PROD CHIMIQUES NDA
592	STARCH,INULIN,GLUTEN,ETC	W 162	0.3	W 668749	272.0			W 951669	305.5	AMIDONS,INUL,GLUT FROM
6	BASIC MANUFACTURES		5514.5		6741.4				6919.0	ART MANUFACTURES
61	LEATHER,DRESSED FUR,ETC		417.3		473.0				537.9	CUIRS,PELLETERIES
611	LEATHER	W 15462	228.0	W 17564	269.7			W 21758	311.3	CUIRS,PEAUX PREPARES
6114	LEATHR BOVINE NES,EQUINE	W 8202	138.0	W 9605	158.9			W 11386	160.9	CUIRS DE BOVINS
612	LEATHER ETC MANUFACTURES	W 41598	189.0	W 43767	202.8			W 39556	225.7	OUVRAGES EN CUIRS NDA
62	RUBBER MANUFACTURES NES		354.1		436.1				524.4	CAOUTCHOUC MANUFACTURE
625	RUBBER TYRES, TUBES ETC	MN 95038	192.6	MN 102842	232.4			MN 96963	283.8	PNEUS CAOUTCHOUC VULCANISE
63	WOOD,CORK MANUFACTRS NES		260.0		296.9				278.0	OUVRAGES LIEGE ET BOIS
635	WOOD MANUFACTURES NES	W 68755	225.5	W 80668	262.6			W 72712	245.3	ART MANUF EN BOIS NDA
6354	WOOD MFRS DOMESTIC ETC	W 39486	153.0	W 44443	177.5			W 47432	179.8	ART MANUF USAGE DOMESTIQUE
64	PAPER,PAPERBOARD AND MFR		168.0		342.4				396.4	PAPIERS,CARTONS & OUVRAGES
641	PAPER AND PAPERBOARD	W 191229	75.2	W 251612	145.8			W 600669	294.9	PAPIERS ET CARTONS
6415	PAPER,PAPERBRD,BULK,NES	W 107190	39.5	W 116643	61.2			W 363873	190.6	PAPIERS,CARTONS ROULEAUX
642	PAPER,ETC,PRECUT,ARTS OF	W 29452	92.9	W 38637	196.7			W 37704	101.6	PAP,CARTONS DECOUPES
65	TEXTILE YARN,FABRICS,ETC		1690.3		1987.3				2060.0	FILS,TISSUS,ARTICLES TEXTILE
651	TEXTILE YARN	W 201096	508.7	W 171319	565.7			W 207255	619.4	FILS TEXTILES
6514	SYN FIB YRN,BULK,MONOFIL	W 62831	164.5	W 53384	164.0			W 84787	195.5	FILS CONT 85% FIB TEXT SYNTH
6516	DISCON SYN FIB BLEND YRN	W 47550	145.4	W 38283	126.0			W 43017	125.3	FILS FIBR TEX SYN DIS MOINS
652	COTTON FABRICS,WOVEN		229.6	W 36374	269.0			W 45721	317.5	TISSUS DE COTON
6522	WOVEN COTTON BLEACHD,ETC		107.0	W 15724	160.1			W 20616	188.2	TISSUS COTON BLANCHIS ETC
653	WOVN MAN–MADE FIB FABRIC		502.3	W 224	1.5			W 727	4.0	TISSUS FIBRES SYNTH,ARTIF
6531	CONT SYNT WEAVES NONPILE		123.7	W 25316	172.7			W 27532	208.7	TISSUS FIBRES SYNTH CONTINUE
65315	CONT SYN TXTL FABRIC NES		101.9	W 22200	149.0			W 23628	182.5	TIS PLUS 85% TEXT SYNT CONT
6534	DISC SYN BLEND FABRC NES		193.0	W 33708	232.2			W 37993	235.7	TISSUS FIBRES SYNTH DISCONT
65341	DISC SYN FIB–COTTN FABRC		134.0	W 24672	172.7			W 27805	167.9	TISSUS FIB SYNT DIS MEL COTO
657	SPECIAL TXTL FABRC,PRODS	W 73	0.5	W 38871	174.7			W 46280	179.0	TISSUS SPECIAUX
658	TEXTILE ARTICLES NES	W 46986	171.2	W 44998	183.7			W 38165	178.8	ART FACONNES MAT TEXTILES
66	NONMETAL MINERAL MFS NES		1639.8		1861.1				1576.3	ART MIN NON METALLIQUES

5. General Exports F.O.B. by Commodities according to the S.I.T.C. (Rev. 2) in million U.S. Dollars
Exportations Générales F.O.B. par Produits d'après la C.T.C.I. (Rév. 2) en millions de Dollars E.U.

SITC CTCI	COMMODITY	1994 QUANTITY QUANTITE	1994 VALUE VALEUR	1995 QUANTITY QUANTITE	1995 VALUE VALEUR	1996 QUANTITY QUANTITE	1996 VALUE VALEUR	1997 QUANTITY QUANTITE	1997 VALUE VALEUR	PRODUIT
661	LIME,CEMENT,BLDG PRODS	W 2952792	117.7	W 3657132	160.1			W 6463460	255.5	CHAUX,CIMENTS MAT CONSTR
6612	CEMENT	W 2934452	112.6	W 3621696	150.6			W 6415962	245.9	CIMENTS HYDRAULIQUES
666	POTTERY	W 62258	172.5	W 59225	173.1			W 59367	178.1	POTERIE
667	PEARL,PREC–,SEMI–P STONE		1061.6		1201.1				828.5	PERLES, PIERRES GEMMES
6672	DIAMONDS NONINDUST,UNSET		587.5		754.1				500.6	DIAMANTS BRUTS
66729	— CUT ETC NOT SET		558.7		703.7				474.0	DIAMANTS TAILLES
6673	PREC–,SEMI–PR STONES NES		450.4		423.4				305.4	AUTRES PIERRES NON SERTIES
67	IRON AND STEEL		278.6		485.1				516.2	FER ET ACIER
678	IRON,STL TUBES,PIPES,ETC	W 276140	207.3	W 324729	251.3			W 262774	221.1	TUBES,TUYAUX EN FONTE,FER
68	NON–FERROUS METALS		75.5		112.9				243.5	METAUX NON FERREUX
69	METAL MANUFACTURES NES		631.4		747.1				786.8	ART MANUFACT EN METAL NDA
697	BASE MTL HOUSEHOLD EQUIP		133.5	W 6	0.1				220.3	ART MENAGE MET COMMUNS
6974	BASE MTL DMSTC ARTIC NES	W 16897	101.3	W 18943	119.9			W 27778	179.3	ARTICLES NDA FONTE,FER,ETC
699	BASE METAL MFRS NES	W 69009	189.3	W 79871	237.6			W 81264	240.0	ART MANUFACTURES MET NDA
7	MACHINES,TRANSPORT EQUIP		15062.5		18989.6				22335.6	MACHINES MATERIEL TRANSPORT
71	POWER GENERATING EQUIPMT		384.6		536.8				908.0	MACHINES GENERATRICES
716	ROTATING ELECTRIC PLANT		306.9		427.5				745.6	APP ELECTR ROTATIFS,PIECES
7162	AC MTRS,GENRTRS,GEN SETS	N 22810	0.5	N 5758	0.7			MN 190492	595.9	MOTEURS ELECTRIQUES
71621	AC MTRS,INC UNIVRSL MTRS	MN 84923	264.4	MN 110224	320.9			MN 190348	592.0	MOT ELEC NON COUR CONTINU
72	MACHS FOR SPCL INDUSTRYS		159.1		169.9				237.8	MAC SPECIALES POUR INDUST
74	GENRL INDUSTRL MACHY NES		1245.5		1715.4				1710.2	MACH APP INDUSTRIE
741	HEATING,COOLING EQUIPMNT		596.5		888.4				981.3	MACH CHAUFFAGE,PIECES
7415	AIR–CONDITIONING MACHNRY	N 2442228	536.5	N 3754873	809.8			N 3899743	884.3	GROUPES CONDITION AIR
743	PUMPS NES,CENTRFUGES ETC		169.5		236.1				158.4	POMPES COMPRES,VENT ETC
749	NONELEC MACH PTS,ACC NES		371.0		437.3				375.2	PIECES MACH NON ELEC NDA
7491	BALL,ROLLER,ETC BEARINGS	MN 656400	215.6	MN 769325	262.1			MN 731893	250.3	ROULEMENTS BILLES ETC
75	OFFICE MACHNES,ADP EQUIP		4130.0		5692.6				7443.5	MACH BUREAU TRAIT AUTOM
751	OFFICE MACHINES	N 1863	0.3	N 1752	0.3			MN 19448	314.3	MACH,APPAREILS DE BUREAU
7512	CALCULATNG,ACCTG,ETC MCH	MN 47473	245.8	N 1512	0.1			MN 18284	127.8	MACHINE A CALCULER ETC
75121	CALCULATING MACHINES	MN 47469	245.6	MN 44402	312.4			MN 18270	127.4	MACHINES A CALCULER
7518	OFFICE MACHINES NES	N 1164366	169.7	N 1395651	165.7			N 1128704	179.2	MACH,APP DE BUREAU NDA
75182	PHOTO,THERMOCOPY APPARAT	N 412403	164.2	N 411614	157.9			N 496377	172.8	APPAREILS DE PHOTOCOPIE
752	AUTOMTIC DATA PROC EQUIP	N 8015	1.7		2869.5			MN 28881	2776.2	MACH TRAIT INFORMATION
7524	DIGITL CENTRL STOR UNITS	MN 23863	1683.1	MN 26387	1965.6			MN 16042	1073.3	UNITES MEMOIRE CENTRALES
7525	ADP PERIPHERAL UNITS	N 2153691	343.0	N 3972132	628.2			N 8656114	1346.8	UNITES PERIPHERIQUES
7528	OFF–LINE DATA PROC EQUIP	N 2029493	83.4	N 2873425	253.8			N 3585685	344.4	MACH AUXIL TRAIT INFORM
759	OFFICE,ADP MCH PTS,ACCES	W 44444	1596.6	W 62652	2343.7			W 85322	4353.2	PIECES DU 751 ET 752
7599	ACCTG,ETC,ADP MCH PTS,AC	W 41887	1563.0	W 55574	2294.4			W 81355	4260.7	PIECES DU 751 ET 752
76	TELECOMM,SOUND EQUIPMENT		2717.2		3032.4				3327.3	EQUIPMENT DE TELECOM
761	TELEVISION RECEIVERS	N 5653821	882.9	N 6027983	955.3			N 6692416	1047.9	RECEPTEURS DE TELEVISION
7611	COLOUR TV RECEIVERS	N 5616027	881.0	N 5669492	946.1			N 6690223	1047.6	RECEPTEURS COULEUR
763	SOUND RECORDRS,PHONOGRPH	MN 9000	594.1	N 4832	0.8			MN 10374	665.9	PHONO,APP ENREGISTREMENT
7631	ELECTRIC GRAMOPHONES ETC	N 855279	46.7	N 440	0.1			N 3353222	238.5	ELECTROPHON,TOURNE–DISQ
76318	OTH ELEC GRAMOPHONES ETC	N 855075	46.6	N 1348786	74.6			N 3275779	238.4	AUT ELECTRO,TOURNE–DISQ
7638	OTHR SOUND APPARATUS ETC	N 8144867	547.4	N 5425120	446.3			N 7020340	427.5	AUT APP D'ENREGIS,REPROD
76381	TV IMAGE,SND RECRDRS ETC	N 5545404	503.8	N 3869803	416.4			N 5493317	343.8	APP ENREG,REPRO IMAG,SON
764	TELECOM EQPT,PTS,ACC NES		1233.7		1539.9				1515.5	EQUIP TELECOM,PIECES
7641	LINE TELEPHONE,ETC EQUIP	MN 19657	355.9	MN 50758	438.7			MN 16577	526.9	APP TELEPHON PAR FIL
7649	PTS NES OF EQUIPMT OF 76	W 39522	684.1	W 43553	902.7			W 33264	744.4	PIECES DE LA DIV 76
76493	TELECOMM EQUIPMT PTS NES	W 12757	265.1	W 16315	345.5			W 14024	285.8	PIECES 761,762,764.3,8
76499	PARTS ETC OF SOUND EQUIP	W 24185	368.2	W 24828	495.8			W 14704	341.5	PIECES NDA POUR 763
77	ELECTRIC MACHNRY NES ETC		4921.2		6370.2				6906.7	MACH APP ELECT NDA
771	ELECTRIC POWER MACHY NES		336.9		564.4				708.3	MACH PROD,TRANS ELECTR
7711	TRANSFORMERS,ELECTRICAL	MN 96405	142.8	MN 146070	269.7			MN 129481	309.6	TRANSFO ELECTRIQUES
77118	OTHER ELEC TRANSFORMERS	MN 72641	130.3	MN 99964	216.6			MN 124235	230.3	AUTRES TRANSFO ELECTRIQ
7712	OTH ELEC POWER MACHY NES		194.2		294.7				398.7	AUT APP PROD TRANSF ELEC
77121	STATIC CONVERTERS ETC	MN 31139	94.5	MN 37835	162.1			MN 37742	211.8	CONVERTISSEURS STATIQUES
772	SWITCHGEAR ETC,PARTS NES	W 13038	631.8	W 16973	972.1			W 20356	1095.6	APP COUPURE,SECT ETC
7721	SWITCHGEAR ETC	W 6274	180.9	W 8510	378.8			W 10712	405.0	APP COUPURE,SECTIONMNT
7722	PRINTED CIRCUITS,PTS NES	W 4489	401.9	W 6672	557.4			W 7169	642.9	CIRCUITS ET PIECES
773	ELECTR DISTRIBUTNG EQUIP	W 43336	478.6	W 40065	519.3			W 46482	538.2	EQUIPMT DISTRIBUTION ELECT
7731	INSULATED WIRE,CABLE ETC	W 40757	451.4	W 36611	478.8			W 43324	501.8	FILS,CABLES ISOLES ELECT
775	HOUSEHOLD TYPE EQUIP NES		521.7		628.5				615.2	MACH,APP USAGE DOMESTQUE
7752	DOM REFRIGERATRS,FREEZRS	N 744959	161.3	N 1251751	251.4			N 863888	194.2	REFRIG,CONGEL MENAGER
77521	DOMESTIC REFRIGERATORS	N 720797	155.3	N 1232447	245.8			N 820549	187.8	REFRIGERATEURS
7758	ELECTRO–THERMIC APPL NES		231.8		277.5				278.9	APP ELECTROTHERMIQ NDA
77586	ELECTROTHERM DOM APP NES	N 3822980	190.2	N 4201714	224.8			N 4875725	231.7	APP ELECTRO THERMIQUES
776	TRANSISTORS,VALVES,ETC		2244.1		2935.1				3380.6	LAMPES,TUBES,VALVES
7761	TV PICTURE TUBES	N 2250767	135.8	N 2815839	174.3			N 2609007	166.9	TUBES CATHODIQUES
7763	DIODES,TRANSISTORS,ETC	MN 5387006	230.4	MN 7689469	312.4			MN 11728572	618.1	DIODES,TRANSISTORS
7764	ELECTRONIC MICROCIRCUITS	MN 3008615	1456.4	MN 4000114	1939.4			MN 4941505	1978.7	MICROSTRUCTURES ELECTRON
7768	ELCTRNC COMP PTS,CRYSTLS	W 2	0.1	W 2	0.4			W 8	0.2	CRIST PIEZO–ELEC,PCS 776
77689	ELECTRNIC COMPON PTS NES	W 2961	360.6	W 3434	417.9			W 4833	519.8	PIECES DU GROUPE 776
778	ELECTRICAL MACHINERY NES		706.9		748.1				564.2	AUTRES MACH ELECT NDA
7783	AUTOMOTIVE ELECTR EQUIP		353.0	MN 42653	208.7			MN 25936	54.3	EQUIP ELECT MOTEURS EXPL
77831	IGNITION,STARTING EQUIP	N 50385	0.3	MN 9436	58.9			N 7218648	28.0	APP ELEC ALLUM,DEMARRAGE
7788	OTH ELEC MACHY,EQUIP NES		254.1		411.8				342.9	AUT MACH APP ELEC NDA
78	ROAD VEHICLES		858.6		724.4				1126.2	VEHICULES ROUTIERS
782	LORRIES,SPCL MTR VEH NES	N 7326	78.9	N 7266	83.6			N 79818	533.8	VEHICULES SPECIAUX,MARCH
7821	LORRIES,TRUCKS	N 7252	74.1	N 7196	81.3			N 41731	529.5	VEHICULES TRANSP MARCHAND
784	MOTOR VEH PRTS,ACCES NES	W 47	0.5		140.1				164.6	PIECES 722,781,782,783
7849	OTHER MOTOR VEHCL PARTS	W 46006	383.0	W 17931	139.0			W 33330	163.7	PIECES 722,781,782,783
785	CYCLES,ETC MOTRZD OR NOT	W 56	0.9		393.5				340.5	MOTOCYCLES SCOOTERS
7853	INVAL CARR, PTS OF 785	W 56	0.9	W 44	0.2			W 71	0.7	FAUTEUILS INVALIDES,PIECES
78539	PARTS,ACCES NES OF 785	W 15614	127.9	W 21560	217.5			W 20314	172.1	PIECES DU 785
79	OTHR TRANSPORT EQUIPMENT		567.0		633.0				567.2	AUTRE MATERIEL TRANSPORT
792	AIRCRAFT ETC		489.3		0.2				547.5	APP NAVIGATION AERIENNE
7929	AIRCRAFT PARTS NES	W 1184	470.1	W 4235	557.2			W 502	546.1	PIECES DU 792
8	MISC MANUFACTURED GOODS		10997.4		13529.7				9818.2	ART MANUFACTURES DIVERS
821	*FURNITURE,PARTS THEREOF		707.8		752.8				717.8	MEUBLES ET PIECES
8211	CHAIRS,SEATS AND PARTS		296.9		294.4			N 107	0.1	SIEGES ET PIECES
82111	CHAIRS AND OTHER SEATS	MN 31736	266.7	MN 25867	268.4			MN 16594	244.5	SIEGES
8219	FURNITURE AND PARTS NES		349.7		403.4				402.5	AUTRES MEUBLES ET PIECES
82192	WOOD FURNITURE NES	MN 13220	231.6	MN 16365	266.0			MN 14061	269.5	MEUBLES NDA EN BOIS
831	*TRAVEL GOODS,HANDBAGS		419.5	N 27624	0.2				395.8	ARTICLES DE VOYAGE ETC
83102	TRAVEL GDS,TOILET–CASES	MN 28014	216.2	MN 27404	245.2			MN 20103	235.9	ARTICLES DE VOYAGE
84	CLOTHING AND ACCESSORIES		4540.0		5043.2				3721.7	VETEMENTS
842	MENS OUTERWEAR NOT KNIT	MN 227967	1055.1	MN 158078	882.5			MN 121924	676.8	VET DESSUS POUR HOMMES
8423	— TROUSERS,BREECHES ETC	MN 129267	539.3	MN 96156	433.3			MN 83731	303.3	PANTALONS HOMMES MAT TEX
8424	— JACKETS,BLAZERS ETC	MN 16371	137.4	MN 9613	135.0			MN 11334	177.1	VESTES HOMMES MAT TEXTIL
8429	— OTHER OUTER GARMENTS	MN 76212	331.1	MW 1	0.1			MN 25317	175.3	AUT VET DES HOM MAT TEX

5. General Exports F.O.B. by Commodities according to the S.I.T.C. (Rev. 2) in million U.S. Dollars
Exportations Générales F.O.B. par Produits d'après la C.T.C.I. (Rév. 2) en millions de Dollars E.U.

SITC CTCI	COMMODITY	1994 QUANTITY QUANTITE	1994 VALUE VALEUR	1995 QUANTITY QUANTITE	1995 VALUE VALEUR	1996 QUANTITY QUANTITE	1996 VALUE VALEUR	1997 QUANTITY QUANTITE	1997 VALUE VALEUR	PRODUIT
843	WOMENS OUTERWEAR NONKNIT	MN 193836	1149.2	MN 167131	1132.7				644.2	VET DESSUS FEMMES MAT TEX
8433	— DRESSES	MN 49927	268.7	MN 46917	264.9			MN 25317	111.7	ROBES EN MAT–TEXTILES
8435	— BLOUSES	MN 35398	176.7	MN 24789	141.3			MN 14243	72.4	BLOUSES FEM MAT TEXTILES
8439	— OTHER OUTER GARMENTS	MN 87887	506.6	MN 74330	503.8			W 20	0.3	AUT VET DES FEM MAT TEXT
844	UNDER GARMENTS NOT KNIT	MN 142383	517.2	MN 95468	418.2			MN 48209	208.5	VETEMENT DESSOUS MAT TEX
8441	— MENS SHIRTS	MN 101091	446.1	MN 69940	348.6			MN 32982	173.9	CHEMISES HOMMES MAT TEXT
84411	—— OF COTTON	MN 68641	317.4	MN 40811	221.9			MN 22971	129.5	CHEMISES HOMMES DE COTON
845	OUTERWEAR KNIT NONELASTC	N 54458	1.1		963.3				978.0	VET DESSOUS,ACCES BONNET
8451	— JERSEYS,PULLOVERS ETC	MN 34785	234.4	MN 36307	247.2			MN 38784	333.8	CHANDAILS,PULL–OVERS ETC
8459	— OTHER,CLTHG ACCESRYS	N 5761	0.8		660.1				603.4	AUT VET DESSUS DE BONNE
846	UNDER GARMENTS KNITTED		683.4		828.6				720.0	SOUS VETS DE BONNETERIE
8462	— OF COTTON NON ELASTIC	MN 173665	332.6	MN 188361	462.4			MN 180931	337.0	SOUS–VET BONNET COTON
84629	—— OTHER	MN 173665	332.6	MN 188361	462.4			MN 180931	337.0	AUT SOUS–VET BONNET COTON
8463	— OF SYNTH FBR NONELAST		0.1		243.5			N 21461	0.1	SOUS–VET BONNET FIB SYNT
84632	—— MENS SHIRTS	MN 43675	221.4	MN 39758	234.6			MN 46730	287.8	CHEMISES DE BON FIB SYNMT
848	HEADGEAR,NONTXTL CLOTHNG		306.8		708.3				398.9	VET ACCES MAT AUT QUE TEX
8482	PLASTC,RUBBR CLTHG,ACCES		201.7		593.5				300.8	VET ACCES MAT PLAS ARTIF
84821	PLASTIC CLTHG,INC GLOVES	W 3824	43.0	W 7649	199.7			W 4047	18.5	VET ACCES MAT PLAS ARTIF
84822	RUBBER CLOTHING,ACCESRYS	MP 2717864	158.8	P 2048	0.1			MP 3848597	282.4	VET ACCES CAOUT VULCAN
851	*FOOTWEAR	MP 267899	1485.9	MP 287407	2088.8			MP 156806	1047.3	CHAUSSURES
85101	FOOTWEAR RUBBER,PLASTIC	MP 185586	703.9	MP 218874	1342.7			MP 96109	316.4	CHAUS SEMELLES CAOUTCH
85102	FOOTWEAR LEATHER	MP 79821	764.1	MP 66738	731.3			MP 60145	728.2	CHAUS SEMELLES EN CUIR
87	PRECISION INSTRUMNTS NES		258.3		311.4				405.3	INSTRUM,APPAR SCIENT NDA
88	PHOTO EQU,OPTICL GDS ETC		545.8		685.6				678.0	APP,FOURN PHOTO,OP,MONTR
881	PHOTO APPARAT,EQUIPT NES		100.2		153.5				215.8	APP,EQUIP PHOTO NDA
8811	CAMERAS STILL,FLASH APP		97.1	N 7892	0.2				210.9	APPAREILS PHOTO,PIECES
885	WATCHES AND CLOCKS		376.1		446.3				390.5	HORLOGERIE
8852	CLOCKS,CLOCK,WATCH PARTS		278.2		320.7				306.4	HORLOGES,MOUV,PARTIES
88529	CLOCK,WATCH PARTS NES		237.2		260.4				245.5	FOURNIT D HORLOG NDA
89	MISC MANUFCTRD GOODS NES		2916.4		4065.0				2738.6	ART MANUFACTURES DIVERS
892	PRINTED MATTER	W 9489	89.4	W 18388	181.8			W 10744	37.1	IMPRIMES
893	ARTICLES OF PLASTIC NES		750.0	W 237	1.5			W 277	2.4	OUVRAGES EN MAT DIVIS 58
8931	PLSTC PACKG CONTNRS,LIDS	W 155440	246.2	W 145642	322.8			W 144786	276.5	ART TRANSP EMBALLAGE ETC
8939	MISC PLASTIC ARTICLES	W 68360	497.9	W 465422	1191.2			W 91059	284.4	ART DIVERS EN MAT DIV 58
89399	OTHR PLASTC ARTICLES NES	W 64024	481.2	W 454088	1022.5			W 70457	251.1	AUT OUV MAT DIV 58
894	TOYS,SPORTING GOODS,ETC		680.8		744.2				567.2	VOITURES ENFANTS,JOUETS
8942	TOYS,INDOOR GAMES ETC		440.4		482.7				344.4	JOUETS,JEUX ETC
89423	TOYS NES	MN 611074	290.0	MN 314565	321.3			MN 174591	246.6	JOUETS,MODELES REDUITS
8947	OTH SPORT GDS,FAIR AMUSM		222.4		247.8				220.9	AUT ART DE SPORT
89472	OTH OUTDOOR SPORT GOODS		191.2		217.9				193.7	ART POUR JEUX PLEIN AIR
897	GOLD,SILVER WARE,JEWELRY		830.0		928.9				998.0	BIJOUTERIE,ORFEVRERIE
8973	PREC JEWLRY,GLD–SILVWARE		760.2		853.4				936.2	BIJOUX OR,ARGENT ORFEVRE
89731	PRECIOUS METAL JEWELLERY		738.3		837.2				899.2	ART BIJOUTERIE,JOAILLER
898	MUSICAL INSTRUMENTS,PTS		215.0		223.0			N 37174	2.3	INSTRUMENTS DE MUSIQUE
8983	SOUND RECRDNG TAPE,DISCS	MN 242777	175.6	MN 321456	180.2			MN 342833	246.5	SUPPORTS SON POUR 763
89831	PREPD SND RECORDNG MEDIA	MN 223948	166.6	MN 289670	170.7			MN 313969	218.0	SUPPORTS PREPARES
899	OTHER MANUFACTURED GOODS		302.9		308.1				238.9	AUT ART MANUF DIVERS NDA
8999	OTHER MANUF GOODS NES	W 14541	136.0	W 8498	134.7			W 5824	95.5	OUVRAGES DIVERS NDA
9	GOODS NOT CLASSD BY KIND		349.9		553.0				2109.5	ART TRANSACT NON CLASSES
931	*SPECIAL TRANSACTIONS	W 23950	311.1		480.8			W 64392	1549.4	TRANS.SPECIALES
971	*GOLD,NON MONETARY NES	K 108458	34.3	K 43451	62.3			K 49174	523.7	OR NON MONETAIRE
97101	NONMON GLD UNWRT,SEMIMFD	K 8551	26.4	K 6583	50.9			K 43244	504.6	OR,ALLIAGES D'OR BRUTS

FOOT NOTES – NOTES

TABLE 1 –
1 Values are in thousand million baht.
TABLEAU 1 –
1 Les valeurs sont exprimées en milliards de baht.

1. HISTORICAL SERIES, 1993–1996 GENERAL TRADE, IMPORTS F.O.B., EXPORTS F.O.B.
SERIES HISTORIQUES, 1993–1996 COMMERCE GENERAL, IMPORTATIONS F.O.B., EXPORTATIONS F.O.B

YEAR ANNEE	VALUE IN MILLION U.S. DOLLARS VALEUR EN MILLION U.S. DOLLARS MERCHANDISE –MARCHANDISE IMPORTS	EXPORTS	GOLD –OR IMPORTS	EXPORTS	CONVERSION FACTORS FACTEURS DE CONVERSION CENTS E.U. PAR IMPORTS	EXPORTS	INDEX NUMBERS –INDICES QUANTUM IMPORTS	EXPORTS	UNIT VALUE VALEUR UNITAIRE IMPORTS	EXPORTS
1993	1199.35	1055.30								
1994	1484.09	1086.34								
1995	1718.90	1204.05								
1996	1626.92	1147.44								

2. IMPORTS BY BROAD ECONOMIC CATEGORY AND EXPORTS BY INDUSTRIAL ORIGIN. (PERCENTAGE OF TOTAL VALUE)
IMPORTATIONS PAR CATEGORIES ECONOMIQUES ET EXPORTATIONS PAR BRANCHE D'ACTIVITE.(EN POURCENTAGE DE LA VALEUR TOTALE)

IMPORTS – IMPORTATIONS

	1989	1990	1991	1992	1993	1994	1995
TOTAL IMPORTS–IMPORTATIONS TOTALES							
1 FOOD BEV–ALIMENTATION BOISSONS							
11 PRIMARY–PRODUITS DE BASE							
111 FOR INDUSTRY–POUR L'INDUSTRIE							
112 FOR HOUSEHOLDS–POUR LES MENAGES							
12 PROCESSED–PRODUITS ELABORES							
121 FOR INDUSTRY–POUR L'INDUSTRIE							
122 FOR HOUSEHOLDS–POUR LES MENAGES							
2 IND SUPPLIES–APPROV INDUSTRIELS							
21 PRIMARY–PRODUITS DE BASE							
22 PROCESSED–PRODUITS ELABORES							
3 FUELS–COMBUSTIBLES							
31 PRIMARY–PRODUITS DE BASE							
32 PROCESSED–PRODUITS ELABORES							
321 MOTOR SPIRIT–ESSENCE							
322 OTHER–AUTRES							
4 MACHINERY–EQUIPEMENT							
41 CAPITAL EQUIPMENT–MACHINES							
42 PARTS–PIECES ACCESSOIRES							
5 TRANSPORT–TRANSPORT							
51 PASSENGER CARS–AUTOMOBILES							
52 OTHER–AUTRES							
521 INDUSTRIAL–INDUSTRIELS							
522 NON INDUSTRIAL–NON INDUSTRIEL							
53 PARTS–PIECES ACCESSOIRES							
6 CONSUM GOODS–BIENS CONSOMMATION							
61 DURABLE–DURABLES							
62 SEMI DURABLE–SEMI DURABLES							
63 NON DURABLE–NON DURABLES							
7 GOODS NES–BIENS NDA							

EXPORTS – EXPORTATIONS

	1989	1990	1991	1992	1993	1994	1995
TOTAL EXPORTS–EXPORTATIONS TOTALES							
1 AGRICULTURE							
2 MINING QUARRY–INDUS EXTRACTIVES							
3 MANUFACTURING–IND MANUFACTUR							
31 FOOD BEV TOBACCO–ALIM BOISS TAB							
32 TEXTILES–INDUSTRIES TEXTILES							
33 WOOD & PRODUCTS–BOIS & PRODUITS							
34 PAPER & PRODUCTS–PAPIER & PRODT							
35 CHEMICALS–INDUSTRIES CHIMIQUES							
36 NON METAL MIN–MIN NON METAL							
37 BASIC METAL–IND METAL BASE							
38 METAL MANUF–MANUF METAL							
39 OTH MANUF IND–AUTRES MANUF							

3. TRADE BY PRINCIPAL COUNTRIES OF ORIGIN AND DESTINATION (VALUE IN MILLION U.S. DOLLARS)
ECHANGES SELON LES PRINCIPAUX PAYS D'ORIGINE ET DE DESTINATION (VALEUR EN MILLIONS DE DOLLARS EU)

COUNTRIES–PAYS	GENERAL IMPORTS F.O.B. IMPORTATIONS GENERALES F.O.B.				
	1991	1992	1993	1994	1995
World		1206.1	1199.4	1484.1	1718.9
Africa		26.0	27.1	7.4	6.7
Americas		41.0	35.3	64.0	83.3
– Northern America		30.3	28.5	52.3	63.9
– LAIA		10.0	6.6	11.7	19.1
– CACM		0.7	0.2	0.0	0.3
– Caribbean			0.0		0.0
– Rest of America					
Asia excl fmr USSR		78.6	78.3	122.9	112.4
– Middle East		56.4	51.5	75.4	70.3
Asia former USSR					
Europe excl fmr USSR		869.5	838.8	1114.9	1372.6
– European Union		465.6	412.5	550.6	689.5
– Eastern Europe		243.7	186.5	317.9	329.2
– Rest of Europe		160.2	239.8	246.3	353.9
Europe former USSR		163.4	138.1	46.4	62.8
Oceania		8.1	8.7	5.1	12.2
Other					
Germany/Allemagne		171.4	160.3	254.4	283.0
Bulgaria/Bulgarie		173.0	130.9	241.7	255.9
Slovenia/Slovénie		97.6	173.7	162.2	116.5
Italy/Italie		122.7	77.8	109.9	179.3
Russian Federation		163.4	138.1	46.4	62.8
Croatia/Croatie		47.9	45.4	59.5	56.3
Turkey/Turquie		32.5	34.3	47.7	55.2
USA/Etats–Unis d'Amer		28.0	26.4	49.5	57.8
Yugoslavia/Yougoslavie					161.1
Greece/Grèce		49.0	52.2	23.5	28.9
Netherlands/Pays–Bas		36.2	15.5	40.0	43.4
Austria/Autriche		21.4	23.3	42.5	45.0
France, Monaco		10.4	19.0	35.2	36.1
Switzerland,Liechtenst.		14.5	20.3	24.4	19.7
Belgium–Luxembourg		19.6	24.6	16.6	15.4
Romania/Roumanie		12.1	12.6	17.4	16.8
Hungary/Hongrie		18.4	8.0	12.2	14.9
United Kingdom		14.9	12.4	2.4	20.2
Poland/Pologne		16.4	12.4	9.4	9.3
Slovakia/Slovaquie				24.7	21.3
Japan/Japon		7.1	9.6	12.7	14.6
Spain/Espagne		10.0	7.7	7.5	18.0
Iran (Islamic Rep of)		18.5	12.6	2.9	6.4
Sweden/Suède		5.7	8.3	12.3	11.3
Korea, Republic of		2.7	1.4	11.5	20.4
Other Asia n.e.s.		9.4	12.1	13.8	
Libyan Arab Jamahiriya		11.2	20.0	1.3	1.2
Australia/Australie		8.1	8.2	4.9	11.7
Albania/Albanie		3.9	7.3	8.2	8.2
Brazil/Brésil		5.6	1.9	7.6	9.4
Denmark/Danemark		3.2	9.7	4.8	6.6
Czech Republic			15.3	4.5	2.7
Jordan/Jordanie		4.6	3.7	6.1	7.7
Former Czechoslovakia		20.0			
Cyprus/Chypre				18.5	
China/Chine		2.4	3.2	5.4	4.7
Egypt/Egypte		3.2	4.9	3.7	3.3
Canada		2.3	2.1	2.8	6.1
Other Africa n.e.s.		8.9	0.7	1.6	
Ecuador/Equateur		1.1	1.2	1.9	4.2

COUNTRIES–PAYS	GENERAL EXPORTS F.O.B. EXPORTATIONS GENERALES F.O.B.				
	1991	1992	1993	1994	1995
Monde		1198.6	1055.3	1086.3	1204.0
Afrique		15.2	9.3	14.1	11.8
Amériques		81.1	63.2	41.1	36.3
– Amérique du Nord		75.9	62.8	41.0	36.2
– ALAI		5.2	0.2	0.1	0.1
– MCAC			0.0		
– Caraïbes		0.0	0.1		
– Autre Amérique					
Asie anc. URSS exclus		70.3	100.4	91.2	67.5
– Moyen–Orient		37.4	52.2	49.7	41.2
Asie ancienne URSS					
Europe anc. URSS exclus		799.1	689.9	800.6	958.6
– Union Européenne		503.6	372.5	361.1	407.8
– Europe de l'Est		125.2	159.9	304.0	324.4
– Autre de l'Europe		170.3	157.5	135.5	226.4
Europe ancienne URSS		98.1	114.9	76.4	87.2
Océanie		2.4	1.4	1.1	0.8
Autre					
Germany/Allemagne		239.3	148.3	146.0	153.1
Bulgaria/Bulgarie		63.5	82.8	239.7	256.0
Italy/Italie		89.4	93.8	125.8	118.4
Russian Federation		98.1	114.9	76.4	87.2
Slovenia/Slovénie		82.8	89.3	71.4	72.4
USA/Etats–Unis d'Amer		72.8	61.7	39.5	35.6
Croatia/Croatie		54.5	38.3	29.9	32.1
Turkey/Turquie		17.5	43.8	35.4	38.3
Switzerland,Liechtenst.		32.9	29.0	34.0	36.9
Greece/Grèce		38.7	49.6	12.7	14.2
Albania/Albanie		21.2	35.7	28.0	24.7
Netherlands/Pays–Bas		39.9	13.9	14.6	29.7
France, Monaco		18.7	21.3	23.6	23.5
Austria/Autriche		20.8	15.8	19.2	30.3
Yugoslavia/Yougoslavie					84.8
Korea, Republic of		6.6	13.7	31.0	25.0
United Kingdom		21.6	13.0	5.9	21.1
Belgium–Luxembourg		23.0	6.9	5.4	10.0
Romania/Roumanie		9.1	9.6	11.2	13.4
Hungary/Hongrie		4.1	9.1	11.7	10.8
Egypt/Egypte		8.9	8.2	7.2	8.5
Japan/Japon		18.0	10.7	1.2	1.1
Other Asia n.e.s.		6.7	15.4	8.8	
Czech Republic			17.2	3.4	4.3
Iran (Islamic Rep of)		17.5	2.7	1.0	1.1
Former Czechoslovakia		21.2			
Poland/Pologne		6.0	5.6	3.4	4.4
Slovakia/Slovaquie				6.6	10.8
Sweden/Suède		6.0	2.2	2.1	2.2
Spain/Espagne		1.4	4.1	3.4	2.3
Denmark/Danemark		3.6	2.2	2.2	2.8
Cyprus/Chypre				9.3	
Other Africa n.e.s.		2.7	0.2	6.1	
Canada		3.1	1.1	1.5	0.7
China/Chine			5.7	0.0	0.0
Australia/Australie		2.4	1.4	1.0	0.8
Jordan/Jordanie		0.5	3.2	1.1	0.8
Argentina/Argentine		5.1			
India/Inde		0.8	2.7	0.5	0.0
Syrian Arab Republic		0.0	1.4	1.9	0.3

(VALUE AS PERCENTAGE OF WORLD TOTAL)(VALEURS EN POURCENTAGE DU TOTAL MONDIAL)

	1986	1987	1988	1989	1990	1991	1992	1993	1994	1995
Africa							2.2	2.3	0.5	0.4
Americas							3.4	2.9	4.3	4.8
– Northern America							2.5	2.4	3.5	3.7
– LAIA							0.8	0.6	0.8	1.1
– CACM							0.1	0.0	0.0	0.0
– Caribbean								0.0		0.0
– Rest of America										
Asia excl fmr USSR							6.5	6.5	8.3	6.5
– Middle East							4.7	4.3	5.1	4.1
Asia former USSR										
Europe excl fmr USSR							72.1	69.9	75.1	79.9
– European Union							38.6	34.4	37.1	40.1
– Eastern Europe							20.2	15.5	21.4	19.2
– Rest of Europe							13.3	20.0	16.6	20.6
Europe former USSR							13.5	11.5	3.1	3.7
Oceania							0.7	0.7	0.3	0.7
Other										
Germany/Allemagne							14.2	13.4	17.1	16.5
Bulgaria/Bulgarie							14.3	10.9	16.3	14.9
Slovenia/Slovénie							8.1	14.5	10.9	6.8
Italy/Italie							10.2	6.5	7.4	10.4
Russian Federation							13.5	11.5	3.1	3.7
Croatia/Croatie							4.0	3.8	4.0	3.3
Turkey/Turquie							2.7	2.9	3.2	3.2
USA/Etats–Unis d'Amer							2.3	2.2	3.3	3.4
Yugoslavia/Yougoslavie										9.4
Greece/Grèce							4.1	4.4	1.6	1.7

	1986	1987	1988	1989	1990	1991	1992	1993	1994	1995
Afrique							1.3	0.9	1.3	1.0
Amériques							6.8	6.0	3.8	3.0
– Amérique du Nord							6.3	6.0	3.8	3.0
– ALAI							0.4	0.0	0.0	0.0
– MCAC								0.0		
– Caraïbes							0.0	0.0		
– Autre Amérique										
Asie anc. URSS exclus							5.9	9.5	8.4	5.6
– Moyen–Orient							3.1	4.9	4.6	3.4
Asie ancienne URSS										
Europe anc. URSS exclus							66.7	65.4	73.7	79.6
– Union Européenne							42.0	35.3	33.2	33.9
– Europe de l'Est							10.4	15.2	28.0	26.9
– Autre de l'Europe							14.2	14.9	12.5	18.8
Europe ancienne URSS							8.2	10.9	7.0	7.2
Océanie							0.2	0.1	0.1	0.1
Autre										
Germany/Allemagne							20.0	14.1	13.4	12.7
Bulgaria/Bulgarie							5.3	7.8	22.1	21.3
Italy/Italie							7.5	8.9	11.6	9.8
Russian Federation							8.2	10.9	7.0	7.2
Slovenia/Slovénie							6.9	8.5	6.6	6.0
USA/Etats–Unis d'Amer							6.1	5.8	3.6	3.0
Croatia/Croatie							4.6	3.6	2.8	2.7
Turkey/Turquie							1.5	4.1	3.3	3.2
Switzerland,Liechtenst.							2.7	2.7	3.1	3.1
Greece/Grèce							3.2	4.7	1.2	1.2

4. General Imports F.O.B. by Commodities according to the S.I.T.C. (Rev. 2) in million U.S. Dollars
Importations Générales F.O.B. par Produits d'après la C.T.C.I. (Rév. 2) en millions de Dollars E.U.

SITC CTCI	COMMODITY	1992 QUANTITY QUANTITE	1992 VALUE VALEUR	1993 QUANTITY QUANTITE	1993 VALUE VALEUR	1994 QUANTITY QUANTITE	1994 VALUE VALEUR	1995 QUANTITY QUANTITE	1995 VALUE VALEUR	PRODUIT
	ALL COMMODITIES				1199.4		1484.1		1719.0	TOUS PRODUITS
0	FOOD AND LIVE ANIMALS				206.3		282.3		280.8	ALIMENTS,ANIMAUX VIVANTS
001	*LIVE ANIMALS FOR FOOD				12.0		3.4		6.1	ANIMAUX VIVANTS
00119	— OTHR THAN FR BREEDING			W 6973	4.9					BOVINS NON REPRODUCTEURS
01	MEAT AND PREPARATIONS				48.2		66.3		64.6	VIANDES ET PREPARATIONS
01112	BOVINE MEAT BONELESS			W 300	9.1					VIANDES BOVIN DESOSSEES
0114	POULTRY FRESH CHLLD,FRZN			W 9588	11.6			W 13500	11.6	VOLAILLES MORTES
0142	SAUSAGES INCLDING TINNED			W 3482	8.4			W 8938	21.2	SAUCISSES,SAUCISSONS
02	DAIRY PRODCTS,BIRDS'EGGS				17.5		23.3		20.9	PRODUITS LAITIERS,OEUFS
022	MILK AND CREAM							W 13447	7.4	LAIT ET CREME
024	CHEESE AND CURD			W 6365	10.1			W 1853	3.8	FROMAGE ET CAILLEBOTTE
03	FISH AND PREPARATIONS				9.2		5.5		6.9	POISSONS ET PREPARATIONS
04	CEREALS AND PREPARATIONS				27.4		47.9		30.8	CEREALES ET PRODUITS
041	WHEAT ETC UNMILLED							W 45398	5.4	FROMENT,EPEAUTRE
0411	DURUM WHEAT UNMILLED			W 27327	6.8					FROMENT DUR NON MOULU
04601	FLOUR OF WHEAT OR MESLIN			W 31761	7.5					FARINE DE FROMENT
05	VEGETABLES AND FRUIT				30.9		61.1		71.7	LEGUMES ET FRUITS
0561	VEG DRIED EXC LEGUMINOUS							W 784	7.2	LEGUM DESSECH,DESHYDRAT
05659	OTH VEG PRESVD,PREPD NES							W 5728	5.4	LEGUM PREPAP,CONSERV NDA
0573	BANANA,PLANTAIN,FRSH,DRY							W 18493	5.9	BANANES FRAICHES,SECHEES
0585	FRUIT OR VEGETABLE JUICE							W 6054	6.2	JUS DE FRUITS
06	SUGAR AND PREPS,HONEY				15.1		27.3		28.3	SUCRES ET PRODUITS
061	SUGAR AND HONEY			W 29737	10.4					SUCRES ET MIEL
0612	REFINED SUGAR ETC							W 50853	21.9	SUCRES RAFFINES
07	COFFEE,TEA,COCOA,SPICES				20.7		20.2		24.2	CAFE,THE,CACAO,EPICES
07111	COFFEE GREEN,HUSKS,SKINS							W 3810	7.2	CAFE NON TORREFIE
07112	COFFEE ROASTED			W 598	8.0					CAFE TORREFIE
073	CHOCOLATE AND PRODUCTS			W 2025	5.9			W 2238	6.8	CHOCOLAT
081	*FEEDING STUFF FOR ANIML				9.3		12.1		11.4	NOURRITURE POUR ANIMAUX
08131	— OF SOYA BEANS			W 13017	4.8					TOURTEAUX DE SOJA
09	MISC EDIBLE PRODUCTS				16.6		15.8		16.4	PREP ALIMENTAIRES DIVERSES
09806	YEASTS,BAKING POWDERS			W 148	5.8					LEVURES
09809	MISC FOOD PREPRTIONS NES			W 1019	4.6			W 1703	6.9	PREP ALIMENTAIRES NDA
1	BEVERAGES AND TOBACCO				31.6		24.5		17.4	BOISSONS ET TABACS
12	TOBACCO AND MANUFACTURES				28.9		21.6		14.3	TABACS BRUTS FABRIQUES
1211	TOBACCO,NOT STRIPPED			W 7417	20.4			W 5807	10.0	TABACS NON ECOTES
2	CRUDE MATERLS,EXCL FUELS				66.7		75.3		78.8	MAT BRUTES NON COMESTIBLES
21	HIDES,SKINS,FURS UNDRSSD				6.1		7.1		11.6	CUIRS,PEAUX BRUTS
24	CORK AND WOOD				6.0		7.7		7.2	LIEGE ET BOIS
26	TEXTILE FIBRES AND WASTE				25.6		26.2		25.2	FIBRES TEXTILES
2631	RAW COTTON,EXCL LINTERS			W 4669	6.1			W 3965	9.8	COTON EN MASSE
26659	— OTHER							W 10157	10.5	FIBRES AUTRES
27	CRUDE FERTLZR,MINRLS NES				13.8		21.0		16.5	ENGRAIS MINERAUX BRUTS
27131	— UNGROUND			W 89182	7.1			W 105002	8.4	PHOSPHATES NON MOULUS
28	METALLIFEROUS ORES,SCRAP				7.6		0.9		2.8	MINERAIS METAL,DECHETS
2815	IRON ORE,CONC,NOT AGGLOM			W 43808	4.9					MINERAIS NON AGGLOMERES
29	CRUDE ANIMAL,VEG MAT NES				1.6		4.4		7.4	MATIERES BRUTES ANIM,VEGET
3	MINERAL FUELS ETC				191.2		161.0		199.0	COMBUSTIBLES MINERAUX LUB
32	COAL,COKE AND BRIQUETTES				13.8		13.6		13.4	HOUILLES,COKES,BRIQUETTES
3221	ANTHRACITE,NOT AGGLOMRTD			W 63086	6.9					ANTHRACITE
3232	COKE,SEMI–COKE,RTRT CRBN			W 45485	5.9			W 53902	8.8	COKES ET SEMI–COKES
33	PETROLEUM AND PRODUCTS				176.2		144.9		181.4	PETROLE ET DERIVES
333	CRUDE PETROLEUM			W 933301	123.1			W 159190	22.5	HUILES BRUTES DE PETROLE
3341	GASOLINE,OTH LIGHT OILS			W 74687	18.6			W 192405	44.6	ESSENCES POUR MOTEURS
3343	GAS OILS			W 94696	16.6			W 574290	90.2	GAS OILS
3345	LUBS,PETROLEUM OILS NES			W 8595	9.1			W 9946	11.6	HUILES LUBRIFIANTES
5	CHEMCLS,RELATED PROD NES				186.2		196.9		205.1	PRODUITS CHIMIQUES
51	ORGANIC CHEMICALS				32.8		42.2		50.9	PROD CHIMIQ ORGANIQUES
51215	ETHYLENE GLYCOL							W 5534	5.4	ETHYLENE–GLYCOL
51384	TEREPHTHALIC ACID ESTERS							W 11724	13.2	ESTERS DE L'ACIDE TEREPHTALI
51483	ACRYLONITRILE			W 12603	8.2			W 9962	10.7	ACRYLONITRILE
52	INORGANIC CHEMICALS				17.0		15.4		12.7	PROD CHIM INORGANIQUES
53	DYES,TANNING,COLOUR PROD				22.7		18.5		14.5	PROD TEINTURE,COLORANTS
541	*MEDICINAL,PHARM PRODUCT				27.1		31.4		35.0	PROD MEDICINAUX PHARMACEUT
5417	MEDICAMENTS							K 1106000	14.5	MEDICAMENTS
55	PERFUME,CLEANING ETC PRD				24.9		20.2		18.3	PROD POUR PARFUM,TOILETTE
562	*FERTILIZERS,MANUFACTURE				9.6		10.8		7.4	ENGRAIS MANUFACTURES
572	*EXPLOSIVES,PYROTECH PRO				23.0		26.2		34.1	EXPLOSIFS
58	PLASTIC MATERIALS ETC				6.8		8.0		9.2	MAT PLAST ARTIFICIELLES
59	CHEMICAL MATERIALS NES				22.7		24.7		23.3	MAT PROD CHIMIQUES NDA
6	BASIC MANUFACTURES				203.9		204.1		269.3	ART MANUFACTURES
61	LEATHER,DRESSED FUR,ETC				6.6		3.9		5.5	CUIRS,PELLETERIES
62	RUBBER MANUFACTURES NES				15.8		12.5		15.2	CAOUTCHOUC MANUFACTURE
6252	TYRES,NEW,BUS OR LORRY			W 3685	8.4			W 1908	6.3	PNEUS POUR AUTOBUS,CAMIONS
63	WOOD,CORK MANUFACTRS NES				10.2		9.8		8.8	OUVRAGES LIEGE ET BOIS
64	PAPER,PAPERBOARD AND MFR				27.1		36.1		41.0	PAPIERS,CARTONS & OUVRAGES
65	TEXTILE YARN,FABRICS,ETC				50.4		38.0		41.5	FILS,TISSUS,ARTICLES TEXTILE
6513	COTTON YARN			W 3525	7.8			W 1827	5.7	FILS DE COTON
65316	CONT SYN BLEND FABRC NES			W 18	6.3					TIS SYNTH MOINS 85% MAT TEX
65751	CORDAGE,CABLE,ROPE,TWINE			W 2118	7.9					CORDAGES TRESSES OU NON
66	NONMETAL MINERAL MFS NES				13.1		17.0		23.1	ART MIN NON METALLIQUES
67	IRON AND STEEL				45.3		38.2		75.9	FER ET ACIER
67326	IRN,OTH STL BARS HOTROLD			W 28891	8.2			W 22840	6.2	BARRES PLEINES FER,ACIER
6745	IRN,STL MED PLATE,ROLLED							W 24554	6.7	TOLES 3 A 4.75 MM
68	NON–FERROUS METALS				15.7		22.2		32.0	METAUX NON FERREUX
686	ZINC							W 66458	15.6	ZINC
69	METAL MANUFACTURES NES				20.3		26.8		26.7	ART MANUFACT EN METAL NDA
691	STRUCTURES AND PARTS NES			W 2030	5.7					CONSTRUCT FER,ACIER,ALU
6997	IRON,STEEL ARTICLES NES			W 282	5.5					OUV FONTE,FER,ACIER NDA
7	MACHINES,TRANSPORT EQUIP				199.6		292.2		334.7	MACHINES MATERIEL TRANSPORT
71	POWER GENERATING EQUIPMT				10.8		18.6		7.2	MACHINES GENERATRICES
7132	MOTOR VEHCL PISTN ENGINS			W 339	6.2					MOTEURS EXPL POUR VEHICULES
72	MACHS FOR SPCL INDUSTRYS				33.4		34.6		43.8	MAC SPECIALES POUR INDUST
72842	RUBBER,PLASTICS WRKG MCH							W 387	5.8	MACH IND CAOUT MAT PLAST
72843	TOBACCO WORKING MACH NES			W 81	7.1					MACH POUR IND DU TABAC
74	GENRL INDUSTRL MACHY NES				51.3		41.4		51.4	MACH APP INDUSTRIE
74132	INDUST FURNACES NONELECT			W 2	6.2					FOURS NON ELECTRIQUES
74522	PACKAGNG,BOTTLNG,ETC MCH			W 81	9.3			W 208	6.1	MACH NETT BOUTEILLES,ETC
75	OFFICE MACHNES,ADP EQUIP				11.2		16.1		18.7	MACH BUREAU TRAIT AUTOM
752	AUTOMTIC DATA PROC EQUIP							W 74	6.9	MACH TRAIT INFORMATION
76	TELECOMM,SOUND EQUIPMENT				10.8		20.8		18.3	EQUIPMENT DE TELECOM

4. General Imports F.O.B. by Commodities according to the S.I.T.C. (Rev. 2) in million U.S. Dollars
Importations Générales F.O.B. par Produits d'après la C.T.C.I. (Rév. 2) en millions de Dollars E.U.

SITC CTCI	COMMODITY	1992		1993		1994		1995		PRODUIT
		QUANTITY QUANTITE	VALUE VALEUR	QUANTITY QUANTITE	VALUE VALEUR	QUANTITY QUANTITE	VALUE VALEUR	QUANTITY QUANTITE	VALUE VALEUR	
77	ELECTRIC MACHNRY NES ETC				27.3		32.1		34.3	MACH APP ELECT NDA
78	ROAD VEHICLES				52.2		125.4		156.0	VEHICULES ROUTIERS
781	PASS MOTOR VEH EXC BUSES			W 1583	13.2			W 11453	96.3	AUTO TRANSPORT PERSONNES
7821	LORRIES,TRUCKS			W 1766	4.7			W 3617	18.7	VEHICULES TRANSP MARCHAND
7822	SPECIAL MOTOR VEHCLS NES							W 715	5.6	VEHICULES USAGES SPECIAUX
7832	TRACTORS FOR TR–TRAILERS			W 2058	10.2			W 2293	11.9	TRACTEURS ROUTIERS
8	MISC MANUFACTURED GOODS				79.1		144.2		154.3	ART MANUFACTURES DIVERS
821	*FURNITURE,PARTS THEREOF				11.3		9.2		9.4	MEUBLES ET PIECES
84	CLOTHING AND ACCESSORIES				30.6		76.2		74.8	VETEMENTS
8424	— JACKETS,BLAZERS ETC							W 480	8.3	VESTES HOMMES MAT TEXTIL
8439	— OTHER OUTER GARMENTS							W 1464	18.7	AUT VET DES FEM MAT TEXT
84411	—— OF COTTON			W 1064	5.4			W 907	11.7	CHEMISES HOMMES DE COTON
851	*FOOTWEAR				8.1		23.1		24.1	CHAUSSURES
85102	FOOTWEAR LEATHER							W 1265	14.0	CHAUS SEMELLES EN CUIR
87	PRECISION INSTRUMNTS NES				8.7		11.2		15.0	INSTRUM,APPAR SCIENT NDA
88	PHOTO EQU,OPTICL GDS ETC				2.7		4.6		4.8	APP,FOURN PHOTO,OP,MONTR
89	MISC MANUFCTRD GOODS NES				15.8		17.3		23.3	ART MANUFACTURES DIVERS
8931	PLSTC PACKG CONTNRS,LIDS							W 2207	5.3	ART TRANSP EMBALLAGE ETC
9	GOODS NOT CLASSD BY KIND				33.3		102.4		176.0	ART TRANSACT NON CLASSES

5. General Exports F.O.B. by Commodities according to the S.I.T.C. (Rev. 2) in million U.S. Dollars
Exportations Générales F.O.B. par Produits d'après la C.T.C.I. (Rév. 2) en millions de Dollars E.U.

SITC CTCI	COMMODITY	1992 QUANTITY QUANTITE	1992 VALUE VALEUR	1993 QUANTITY QUANTITE	1993 VALUE VALEUR	1994 QUANTITY QUANTITE	1994 VALUE VALEUR	1995 QUANTITY QUANTITE	1995 VALUE VALEUR	PRODUIT
	ALL COMMODITIES				1055.3		1086.4		1204.1	TOUS PRODUITS
0	FOOD AND LIVE ANIMALS				116.3		110.4		131.9	ALIMENTS,ANIMAUX VIVANTS
001	*LIVE ANIMALS FOR FOOD				5.4		0.9		0.4	ANIMAUX VIVANTS
01	MEAT AND PREPARATIONS				9.7		7.9		10.3	VIANDES ET PREPARATIONS
0111	BOVINE MEAT FRESH,FROZEN			W 1582	5.7					VIANDES BOVIN FRAI,REF
0112	MUTTON ETC FRSH,CHLD,FRN			W 1152	3.4			W 1810	7.9	VIANDE DE MOUTON
02	DAIRY PRODCTS,BIRDS'EGGS				4.5		4.0		3.4	PRODUITS LAITIERS,OEUFS
04	CEREALS AND PREPARATIONS				12.7		5.2		11.3	CEREALES ET PRODUITS
04221	RICE MILLED UNBROKEN			W 9001	6.3					RIZ POLI,GLACE EXCL BRISURES
05	VEGETABLES AND FRUIT				54.9		70.8		88.5	LEGUMES ET FRUITS
0544	TOMATOES FRESH							W 17902	7.2	TOMATES FRAICHES
05459	FRESH VEGETABLES NES							W 1221	6.1	LEGUMES FRAIS,REFRI NDA
0561	VEG DRIED EXC LEGUMINOUS							W 1023	10.9	LEGUM DESSECH,DESHYDRAT
0574	APPLES FRESH							W 25736	9.4	POMMES FRAICHES
0585	FRUIT OR VEGETABLE JUICE							W 4707	5.2	JUS DE FRUITS
06	SUGAR AND PREPS,HONEY				4.1		3.6		4.0	SUCRES ET PRODUITS
07	COFFEE,TEA,COCOA,SPICES				15.5		11.9		10.3	CAFE,THE,CACAO,EPICES
073	CHOCOLATE AND PRODUCTS							W 2151	6.9	CHOCOLAT
09	MISC EDIBLE PRODUCTS				6.9		5.9		3.6	PREP ALIMENTAIRES DIVERSES
1	BEVERAGES AND TOBACCO				100.5		62.1		88.1	BOISSONS ET TABACS
11	BEVERAGES				29.7		19.0		31.0	BOISSONS
1121	WINE OF FRESH GRAPES ETC			W 45416	17.6			W 69372	28.1	VINS DE RAISINS FRAIS
12	TOBACCO AND MANUFACTURES				70.8		43.1		57.1	TABACS BRUTS FABRIQUES
1211	TOBACCO,NOT STRIPPED			W 41219	43.7			W 12065	41.6	TABACS NON ECOTES
1222	CIGARETTES			W 4308	26.9			W 1483	15.3	CIGARETTES
2	CRUDE MATERLS,EXCL FUELS				64.7		77.2		93.0	MAT BRUTES NON COMESTIBLES
21	HIDES,SKINS,FURS UNDRSSD				5.5		6.1		7.7	CUIRS,PEAUX BRUTS
2116	SHEEP SKIN WITH WOOL							W 1363	5.1	PEAUX LAINEES D'OVINS
24	CORK AND WOOD				16.7		21.4		20.8	LIEGE ET BOIS
24831	LUMBER SAWN ETC NON–CON			W 49165	14.6			W 55111	15.7	SCIES LONGITUDINALEMENT
26	TEXTILE FIBRES AND WASTE				18.4		23.3		28.0	FIBRES TEXTILES
26652	— POLYESTER							W 3737	6.7	FIBRES EN POLYESTERS
27	CRUDE FERTLZR,MINRLS NES				6.8		6.5		9.4	ENGRAIS MINERAUX BRUTS
27312	MARBLE,ETC BLDG STONE			W 13484	4.3			W 13049	7.5	MARBRES,TRAVERTINS
28	METALLIFEROUS ORES,SCRAP				12.8		14.5		20.1	MINERAIS METAL,DECHETS
2871	CPR ORE ETC,CEMENT COPPR							W 16480	6.6	MINERAIS DE CUIVRE,MATTES
2874	LEAD ORES,CONCENTRATES			W 24094	8.1			W 26548	8.1	MINERAIS DE PLOMB
29	CRUDE ANIMAL,VEG MAT NES				3.3		4.3		6.5	MATIERES BRUTES ANIM,VEGET
3	MINERAL FUELS ETC				1.9		1.5		4.9	COMBUSTIBLES MINERAUX LUB
33	PETROLEUM AND PRODUCTS				1.7		1.4		4.8	PETROLE ET DERIVES
5	CHEMCLS,RELATED PROD NES				47.5		47.5		66.8	PRODUITS CHIMIQUES
51	ORGANIC CHEMICALS				2.2		3.8		4.9	PROD CHIMIQ ORGANIQUES
52	INORGANIC CHEMICALS				10.5		9.5		17.2	PROD CHIM INORGANIQUES
52229	OTH INORGANIC ACIDS ETC			W 8286	8.7					AUTRES ACIDES INORGANIQUES
541	*MEDICINAL,PHARM PRODUCT				21.4		22.9		25.4	PROD MEDICINAUX PHARMACEUT
5417	MEDICAMENTS							K 751000	21.1	MEDICAMENTS
55	PERFUME,CLEANING ETC PRD				1.8		2.3		4.7	PROD POUR PARFUM,TOILETTE
572	*EXPLOSIVES,PYROTECH PRO				3.3		3.3		4.3	EXPLOSIFS
58	PLASTIC MATERIALS ETC				2.8		1.7		4.7	MAT PLAST ARTIFICIELLES
59	CHEMICAL MATERIALS NES				1.7		2.4		4.0	MAT PROD CHIMIQUES NDA
6	BASIC MANUFACTURES				362.6		409.4		441.2	ART MANUFACTURES
61	LEATHER,DRESSED FUR,ETC				5.7		8.2		7.6	CUIRS,PELLETERIES
62	RUBBER MANUFACTURES NES				9.1		12.4		15.4	CAOUTCHOUC MANUFACTURE
63	WOOD,CORK MANUFACTRS NES				3.4		3.4		6.0	OUVRAGES LIEGE ET BOIS
65	TEXTILE YARN,FABRICS,ETC				76.1		72.7		71.4	FILS,TISSUS,ARTICLES TEXTILE
6513	COTTON YARN			W 3026	7.6			W 897	8.5	FILS DE COTON
65152	— OF DISCONTIN FIBRES			W 1229	4.1					FILS CONT 85% FI TEXT SYNT
65214	GREY WOVEN COTTON NES			W 2233	5.8					AUT TISSUS 85% COTON ECRUS
65499	PILE,CHENILLE FABRIC NES			W 593	5.6					VELOURS NDA
655	KNITTED,ETC FABRICS			W 1451	8.4			W 1769	6.2	ETOF BONNETERIE PIECES ETC
65751	CORDAGE,CABLE,ROPE,TWINE			W 5853	11.3			W 5926	11.9	CORDAGES TRESSES OU NON
65841	BED LINEN OF COTTON			W 2019	6.6			W 1377	4.4	LINGE DE LIT DE COTON
66	NONMETAL MINERAL MFS NES				21.9		18.1		20.4	ART MIN NON METALLIQUES
67	IRON AND STEEL				114.2		79.2		104.1	FER ET ACIER
67162	FERRO–SILICON			W 46941	22.7			W 55181	30.9	FERRO–SILICIUM
67169	OTHER FERRO–ALLOYS			W 18789	30.7			W 17505	48.1	AUTRES FERRO–ALLIAGES
6744	IRN,STL HVY PLATE,ROLLED			W 13520	25.0					TOLES LAMINEES PLUS 4.75 MM
678	IRON,STL TUBES,PIPES,ETC			W 3340	3.7			W 7324	5.2	TUBES,TUYAUX EN FONTE,FER
68	NON–FERROUS METALS				105.2		186.0		184.0	METAUX NON FERREUX
68212	COPPER REFINED,UNWROUGHT			W 21359	35.7			W 39609	96.8	CUIVRE AFFINE BRUT
6841	ALUMINIUM,ALLOYS,UNWRGHT							W 3620	6.0	ALUMINIUM,ALLIAGES BRUTS
68512	REF LEAD(EXC ALLOY)UNWRT			W 25329	13.0			W 20416	12.4	PLOMB AFFINE BRUT
6863	ZINC,ALLOYS WKD,INC DUST			W 57509	32.9			W 39639	21.2	ZINC ET ALLIAGES OUVRES
68915	MAGNESIUM UNWROUGHT			W 12237	5.3					MAGNESIUM BRUT
69	METAL MANUFACTURES NES				26.3		28.4		29.6	ART MANUFACT EN METAL NDA
69741	— OF IRON OR STEEL			W 2820	7.8					ART NDA EN FONTE,FER
7	MACHINES,TRANSPORT EQUIP				171.0		133.5		155.8	MACHINES MATERIEL TRANSPORT
71	POWER GENERATING EQUIPMT				5.1		5.4		18.4	MACHINES GENERATRICES
72	MACHS FOR SPCL INDUSTRYS				5.0		4.1		6.3	MAC SPECIALES POUR INDUST
73	METALWORKING MACHINERY				6.1		3.6		7.3	MACH TRAVAIL DES METAUX
74	GENRL INDUSTRL MACHY NES				9.7		11.4		19.3	MACH APP INDUSTRIE
77	ELECTRIC MACHNRY NES ETC				95.8		72.8		77.5	MACH APP ELECT NDA
7711	TRANSFORMERS,ELECTRICAL			W 21676	52.9					TRANSFO ELECTRIQUES
7712	OTH ELEC POWER MACHY NES							W 16147	43.5	AUT APP PROD TRANSF ELEC
77521	DOMESTIC REFRIGERATORS			W 4073	13.4			W 1358	4.3	REFRIGERATEURS
77812	ELECTRIC ACCUMULATORS			W 4714	8.3					ACCUMULATEURS ELECTRIQ
78	ROAD VEHICLES				48.0		34.7		21.6	VEHICULES ROUTIERS
7831	BUSES			W 3740	35.7			W 369	3.4	VOITURES TRANSPORT COMMUN
7849	OTHER MOTOR VEHCL PARTS			W 1751	9.4			W 2145	9.9	PIECES 722,781,782,783
79	OTHR TRANSPORT EQUIPMENT				1.3		1.3		4.6	AUTRE MATERIEL TRANSPORT
8	MISC MANUFACTURED GOODS				190.6		242.4		220.8	ART MANUFACTURES DIVERS
812	*PLUMBG,HEATNG,LGHTNG EQ				8.1		4.6		4.9	APPAR SANITAIRES CHAUFFAGE
821	*FURNITURE,PARTS THEREOF				23.8		50.2		41.5	MEUBLES ET PIECES
82192	WOOD FURNITURE NES			W 5128	13.9			W 2831	7.2	MEUBLES NDA EN BOIS
84	CLOTHING AND ACCESSORIES				129.9		115.4		112.8	VETEMENTS
8423	— TROUSERS,BREECHES ETC			W 1231	9.9			W 992	5.8	PANTALONS HOMMES MAT TEX
8424	— JACKETS,BLAZERS ETC			W 867	8.1			W 693	8.6	VESTES HOMMES MAT TEXTIL
8431	— COATS AND JACKETS							W 737	8.4	MANT,VEST FEM MAT TEXTIL
8439	— OTHER OUTER GARMENTS							W 1952	18.4	AUT VET DES FEM MAT TEXT
84411	—— OF COTTON			W 1801	16.1			W 2524	19.5	CHEMISES HOMMES DE COTON
84419	—— OF OTHER FIBRES			W 855	11.0			W 679	5.4	CHEMISES HOMMES AUT FIBR

5. General Exports F.O.B. by Commodities according to the S.I.T.C. (Rev. 2) in million U.S. Dollars
Exportations Générales F.O.B. par Produits d'après la C.T.C.I. (Rév. 2) en millions de Dollars E.U.

SITC CTCI	COMMODITY	1992		1993		1994		1995		PRODUIT
		QUANTITY QUANTITE	VALUE VALEUR	QUANTITY QUANTITE	VALUE VALEUR	QUANTITY QUANTITE	VALUE VALEUR	QUANTITY QUANTITE	VALUE VALEUR	
8451	— JERSEYS,PULLOVERS ETC			W 464	6.1					CHANDAILS,PULL–OVERS ETC
8483	FUR ETC,CLOTHES,PRODUCTS			W 385	6.3			W 247	4.6	VETEMENTS DE FOURRURE
851	*FOOTWEAR				22.1		66.1		53.9	CHAUSSURES
85102	FOOTWEAR LEATHER			W 1359	17.2			W 3073	44.9	CHAUS SEMELLES EN CUIR
89	MISC MANUFCTRD GOODS NES				5.0		4.3		6.6	ART MANUFACTURES DIVERS

1. HISTORICAL SERIES, 1962–1997 SPECIAL TRADE, IMPORTS C.I.F., EXPORTS F.O.B.
SERIES HISTORIQUES, 1962–1997 COMMERCE SPECIAL, IMPORTATIONS C.A.F., EXPORTATIONS F.O.B

YEAR ANNEE	VALUE IN MILLION C.F.A. FRANCS / VALEUR EN MILLION C.F.A. FRANCS — MERCHANDISE –MARCHANDISE		GOLD –OR		CONVERSION FACTORS U.S. CENTS PER C.F.A. FRANC FACTEURS DE CONVERSION CENTS E.U. PAR C.F.A. FRANC		INDEX NUMBERS –INDICES — QUANTUM		UNIT VALUE VALEUR UNITAIRE	
	IMPORTS	EXPORTS	IMPORTS	EXPORTS	IMPORTS	EXPORTS	IMPORTS	EXPORTS	IMPORTS	EXPORTS
1962	6724.00	4239.00			0.4051	0.4051				
1963	7167.00	4509.00			0.4051	0.4051				
1964	10286.00	7448.00			0.4051	0.4051				
1965	11100.00	6679.00			0.4051	0.4051				
1966	11668.00	8872.00			0.4051	0.4051				
1967	11133.00	7894.00			0.4051	0.4051				
1968	11623.00	9549.00			0.4051	0.4051				
1969	14572.00	11477.00			0.3870	0.3895				
1970	17928.00	15176.00			0.3601	0.3601				
1971	19455.00	13626.00			0.3601	0.3601				
1972	21381.00	12659.00			0.3967	0.3960				
1973	22388.00	13755.00			0.4492	0.4465				
1974	28612.00	45174.00			0.4163	0.4183				
1975	37270.00	26922.00			0.4666	0.4698				
1976	44419.00	24914.00			0.4180	0.4222				
1977	69834.00	39115.00			0.4072	0.4075				
1978	100898.00	54238.00			0.4462	0.4434				
1979	110208.00	46432.00			0.4704	0.4704				
1980	116357.00	71285.00			0.4731	0.4698				
1981	117763.30	57438.40			0.3680	0.3680				
1982	128354.00	58173.00			0.3043	0.3043				
1983	108140.80	61921.10			0.2624	0.2624				
1984	118460.10	83588.00			0.2289	0.2289				
1985	129406.00	85380.00			0.2226	0.2226				
1986	107983.00	70551.01			0.2888	0.2888				
1987	127308.00	73212.00			0.3327	0.3327				
1988	145170.00	72209.01			0.3357	0.3357				
1989	150533.00	78188.00			0.3135	0.3135				
1990	158287.00	72942.00			0.3673	0.3673				
1991	125220.00	71433.01			0.3545	0.3545				
1992	104461.00	72779.01			0.3778	0.3778				
1993	50810.00	38512.00			0.3532	0.3532				
1994	123265.00	90053.01			0.1801	0.1801				
1995	191812.00	104218.00			0.2008	0.2009				
1996	278000.10	188300.00			0.1955	0.1955				
1997	292000.00	201400.00			0.1715	0.1720				

2. IMPORTS BY BROAD ECONOMIC CATEGORY AND EXPORTS BY INDUSTRIAL ORIGIN. (PERCENTAGE OF TOTAL VALUE)
IMPORTATIONS PAR CATEGORIES ECONOMIQUES ET EXPORTATIONS PAR BRANCHE D'ACTIVITE.(EN POURCENTAGE DE LA VALEUR TOTALE)

IMPORTS – IMPORTATIONS

	1988	1989	1990	1991	1992	1993	1994
TOTAL IMPORTS–IMPORTATIONS TOTALES	100.	100.	100.	100.			
1 FOOD BEV–ALIMENTATION BOISSONS	20.6	20.5	17.0	18.5			
11 PRIMARY–PRODUITS DE BASE	8.8	8.7	6.7	7.0			
111 FOR INDUSTRY–POUR L'INDUSTRIE	3.8	3.9	3.8	2.9			
112 FOR HOUSEHOLDS–POUR LES MENAGES	5.0	4.8	2.9	4.0			
12 PROCESSED–PRODUITS ELABORES	11.8	11.8	10.3	11.6			
121 FOR INDUSTRY–POUR L'INDUSTRIE	1.4	1.5	1.1	2.2			
122 FOR HOUSEHOLDS–POUR LES MENAGES	10.4	10.3	9.1	9.4			
2 IND SUPPLIES–APPROV INDUSTRIELS	33.4	32.1	33.8	26.3			
21 PRIMARY–PRODUITS DE BASE	1.1	1.6	1.6	1.8			
22 PROCESSED–PRODUITS ELABORES	32.2	30.5	32.3	24.5			
3 FUELS–COMBUSTIBLES	5.4	6.1	8.0	9.7			
31 PRIMARY–PRODUITS DE BASE	0.0	0.1	0.1	0.1			
32 PROCESSED–PRODUITS ELABORES	5.3	6.0	7.9	9.6			
321 MOTOR SPIRIT–ESSENCE	1.6	2.5	3.3	9.6			
322 OTHER–AUTRES	3.7	3.5	4.6	0.0			
4 MACHINERY–EQUIPEMENT	11.7	12.9	10.0	15.5			
41 CAPITAL EQUIPMENT–MACHINES	10.4	11.3	8.5	13.7			
42 PARTS–PIECES ACCESSOIRES	1.3	1.7	1.4	1.8			
5 TRANSPORT–TRANSPORT	10.9	10.8	11.2	11.6			
51 PASSENGER CARS–AUTOMOBILES	3.0	3.0	3.3	3.3			
52 OTHER–AUTRES	4.5	4.7	4.1	5.0			
521 INDUSTRIAL–INDUSTRIELS	4.2	4.3	3.6	4.4			
522 NON INDUSTRIAL–NON INDUSTRIEL	0.3	0.4	0.5	0.7			
53 PARTS–PIECES ACCESSOIRES	3.3	3.1	3.7	3.3			
6 CONSUM GOODS–BIENS CONSOMMATION	17.7	17.1	19.5	17.6			
61 DURABLE–DURABLES	2.2	2.7	2.7	1.8			
62 SEMI DURABLE–SEMI DURABLES	5.3	4.5	5.1	4.6			
63 NON DURABLE–NON DURABLES	10.2	9.8	11.7	11.2			
7 GOODS NES–BIENS NDA	0.4	0.5	0.6	0.9			

EXPORTS – EXPORTATIONS

	1988	1989	1990	1991	1992	1993	1994
TOTAL EXPORTS–EXPORTATIONS TOTALES	100.	100.	100.	100.			
1 AGRICULTURE	37.3	31.8	35.5	31.8			
2 MINING QUARRY–INDUS EXTRACTIVES	50.1	53.3	44.6	49.3			
3 MANUFACTURING–IND MANUFACTUR	12.6	14.9	19.8	18.9			
31 FOOD BEV TOBACCO–ALIM BOISS TAB	4.0	6.2	8.9	8.1			
32 TEXTILES–INDUSTRIES TEXTILES	0.5	0.7	2.8	0.7			
33 WOOD & PRODUCTS–BOIS & PRODUITS	0.0	0.0	0.1	0.0			
34 PAPER & PRODUCTS–PAPIER & PRODT	0.6	0.5	0.6	0.5			
35 CHEMICALS–INDUSTRIES CHIMIQUES	0.6	0.6	0.6	5.3			
36 NON METAL MIN–MIN NON METAL	1.1	2.1	2.6	1.2			
37 BASIC METAL–IND METAL BASE	1.0	2.0	1.3	0.3			
38 METAL MANUF–MANUF METAL	3.7	1.5	1.0	1.8			
39 OTH MANUF IND–AUTRES MANUF	1.0	1.4	1.9	0.9			

3. TRADE BY PRINCIPAL COUNTRIES OF ORIGIN AND DESTINATION (VALUE IN MILLION U.S. DOLLARS)
ECHANGES SELON LES PRINCIPAUX PAYS D'ORIGINE ET DE DESTINATION (VALEUR EN MILLIONS DE DOLLARS EU)

COUNTRIES–PAYS	SPECIAL IMPORTS C.I.F. IMPORTATIONS SPECIALES C.A.F				
	1990	1991	1992	1993	1994
World	581.4	443.9	394.7	179.5	222.0
Africa	101.3	69.0	53.0	38.1	46.5
Americas	44.7	36.8	9.5	12.5	16.7
– Northern America	37.5	29.1	3.8	11.2	12.7
– LAIA	6.7	2.8	5.2	0.8	3.0
– CACM	0.0	0.0	0.0	0.0	0.1
– Caribbean	0.5	4.3	0.4	0.4	0.5
– Rest of America	0.0	0.6	0.1	0.1	0.4
Asia excl fmr USSR	86.0	78.3	62.8	34.9	32.3
– Middle East	1.5	1.3	1.8	0.4	2.2
Asia former USSR					
Europe excl fmr USSR	346.1	258.5	236.4	93.0	125.4
– European Union	332.7	248.8	230.2	87.8	119.9
– Eastern Europe	2.5	0.7	1.6	2.8	1.4
– Rest of Europe	10.9	9.1	4.6	2.4	4.2
Europe former USSR	1.2	0.1	0.3	0.0	0.1
Oceania	0.8	0.3	1.3	0.9	1.0
Other	1.3	0.8	0.0	0.0	0.0
France, Monaco	177.2	146.9	134.9	50.1	53.3
Netherlands/Pays–Bas	52.7	33.5	23.8	9.4	11.5
Cote d'Ivoire	46.9	16.8	11.9	7.5	13.9
Japan/Japon	25.0	29.7	20.5	8.0	7.8
USA/Etats–Unis d'Amer	30.8	28.5	3.5	11.0	12.2
Germany/Allemagne		18.5	23.1	10.6	21.9
United Kingdom	21.8	16.3	9.1	3.2	7.5
China, Hong Kong SAR	14.9	10.9	11.0	8.0	7.4
Nigeria/Nigéria	13.1	12.8	9.9	9.9	5.7
Italy/Italie	13.3	14.0	10.7	5.2	6.6
Belgium–Luxembourg	10.4	9.1	9.5	3.2	6.8
China/Chine	8.9	6.0	9.5	6.7	5.9
Former Fed Rep Germany	35.0				
Spain/Espagne	9.6	4.9	7.9	2.8	5.9
Other Asia n.e.s.	10.6	10.3	4.2	2.3	2.2
Mauritania/Mauritanie	3.0	3.1	5.2	4.1	11.4
Benin/Bénin	5.7	4.0	4.7	5.4	3.3
Ghana	7.7	5.3	4.3	1.8	2.0
Singapore/Singapour	7.4	5.6	3.1	0.9	0.7
Norway,Svalbard and JM	7.7	3.6	1.3	1.3	3.3
Thailand/Thaïlande	4.4	4.6	4.4	1.9	0.8
Korea, Republic of	5.1	3.6	3.1	1.6	2.1
Cameroon/Cameroun	0.5	12.5	2.2	0.0	0.1
Gabon	5.8	3.4	1.7	1.5	1.5
Denmark/Danemark	5.7	1.9	2.1	1.1	2.8
Switzerland,Liechtenst.	3.1	5.3	3.0	1.1	0.7
Pakistan	3.2	2.3	3.2	2.0	2.0
So. African Customs Un	0.1	0.6	3.6	4.8	3.5
Senegal/Sénégal	5.5	1.6	1.3	1.5	1.6
Brazil/Brésil	1.7	1.9	3.3	0.7	1.6
Greece/Grèce	1.5	0.6	4.5	0.7	1.1
Canada	6.6	0.6	0.2	0.2	0.5
Burkina Faso	2.1	1.6	1.3	0.5	0.6
Austria/Autriche	2.2	1.1	1.6	0.8	0.5
Angola	3.8	1.2	0.4	0.0	0.8
Argentina/Argentine	3.1	0.8	0.8	0.1	0.6
Mauritius/Maurice	0.0	2.6	2.6	0.0	
Finland/Finlande	1.2	0.3	1.9	0.4	1.3
Turkey/Turquie	1.3	0.6	0.6	0.3	2.1
Tunisia/Tunisie	2.5	0.7	0.8	0.0	0.9

COUNTRIES–PAYS	SPECIAL EXPORTS F.O.B. EXPORTATIONS SPECIALES F.O.B.				
	1990	1991	1992	1993	1994
Monde	267.9	253.2	275.0	136.0	162.2
Afrique	46.2	48.2	68.7	25.7	26.7
Amériques	42.4	47.7	58.0	31.5	44.0
– Amérique du Nord	36.4	28.9	57.0	18.1	27.7
– ALAI	6.0	18.7	1.0	13.4	16.3
– MCAC		0.0			
– Caraïbes	0.1	0.1			0.0
– Autre Amérique			0.1		
Asie anc. URSS exclus	47.0	58.2	63.5	47.8	49.4
– Moyen–Orient	1.5	0.0	0.1	0.1	0.0
Asie ancienne URSS					
Europe anc. URSS exclus	118.4	82.3	80.8	30.3	37.0
– Union Européenne	109.6	74.6	63.4	28.2	32.1
– Europe de l'Est	3.1	3.8	15.5	1.8	4.0
– Autre de l'Europe	5.7	3.9	1.8	0.3	0.9
Europe ancienne URSS	12.6	10.4			0.0
Océanie	1.2	0.0	4.0	0.7	5.0
Autre	0.1	6.4			
Canada	33.4	28.7	56.2	17.9	27.5
Other Asia n.e.s.	6.9	14.9	23.5	19.9	21.7
France, Monaco	26.3	17.0	14.1	6.7	8.1
Nigeria/Nigéria	8.8	19.4	25.6	8.7	6.2
Spain/Espagne	17.1	17.2	11.8	0.7	1.6
Philippines	11.5	12.5	5.4	9.8	8.8
India/Inde	14.1	6.5	15.6	3.7	2.9
Netherlands/Pays–Bas	8.8	2.2	10.1	8.9	5.8
Thailand/Thaïlande	1.7	9.3	12.9	6.6	5.2
Italy/Italie	14.2	10.4	6.4	2.0	2.5
Poland/Pologne	3.1	3.6	15.5	1.8	4.0
Benin/Bénin	5.7	5.1	6.2	4.4	4.3
Mexico/Mexique	4.3	17.9		1.2	1.6
Br. Indian Ocean Terr	3.2	4.6	14.3	2.6	
Burkina Faso	8.8	5.7	4.9	1.4	3.8
Portugal	14.6	4.0	1.5	1.5	2.9
Former USSR/Anc. URSS	12.6	10.4			
Indonesia/Indonésie	2.2	4.1	1.4	4.0	9.2
Greece/Grèce	3.8	8.0	3.5	1.5	2.1
Germany/Allemagne		7.1	6.2	2.6	2.6
Belgium–Luxembourg	5.9	2.1	4.2	2.7	3.3
Ghana	4.1	2.9	4.2	2.3	3.5
Bolivia/Bolivie				4.2	12.4
Morocco/Maroc	2.5	1.7	3.2	2.4	2.8
Niger	3.6	3.3	3.5	1.1	0.6
United Kingdom	3.9	3.9	1.5	0.9	1.2
Former Fed Rep Germany	10.0				
Denmark/Danemark	3.8	2.3	1.7	0.4	1.2
Switzerland,Liechtenst.	3.4	3.0	1.8	0.3	0.8
Brazil/Brésil		0.0	0.0	7.0	1.6
Singapore/Singapour	0.8	3.6	2.3	0.4	
Malaysia/Malaisie	1.5	1.8	1.3	1.0	1.4
Areas n.e.s.	0.1	6.4			
Bangladesh	5.7	0.5		0.4	
China/Chine	0.2	4.6		1.6	0.0
Australia/Australie	1.2		1.2		3.3
Guinea/Guinée	3.7	0.2	1.2	0.1	0.1
Palau			2.8	0.7	1.7
Uruguay	1.7	0.8	0.9	1.0	0.8
USA/Etats–Unis d'Amer	3.0	0.2	0.8	0.2	0.2

(VALUE AS PERCENTAGE OF WORLD TOTAL)(VALEURS EN POURCENTAGE DU TOTAL MONDIAL)

	1985	1986	1987	1988	1989	1990	1991	1992	1993	1994
Africa	10.2	5.4	12.0	10.3	12.5	17.4	15.5	13.4	21.3	20.9
Americas	6.0	4.9	5.1	8.1	8.0	7.7	8.3	2.4	7.0	7.5
– Northern America	5.1	4.2	4.8	7.2	7.0	6.4	6.6	1.0	6.2	5.7
– LAIA	0.5	0.2	0.2	0.8	0.8	1.1	0.6	1.3	0.5	1.3
– CACM		0.0	0.0	0.0	0.0	0.0	0.0	0.0	0.0	0.0
– Caribbean	0.0	0.3	0.0	0.0	0.1	0.1	1.0	0.1	0.2	0.2
– Rest of America	0.4	0.3	0.0	0.0	0.0	0.0	0.1	0.0	0.1	0.2
Asia excl fmr USSR	14.5	15.4	13.7	15.1	15.0	14.8	17.6	15.9	19.5	14.5
– Middle East	0.0	0.0	0.6	0.9	0.4	0.3	0.3	0.5	0.2	1.0
Asia former USSR										
Europe excl fmr USSR	68.4	73.5	68.6	66.0	64.3	59.5	58.2	59.9	51.8	56.5
– European Union	67.2	69.5	66.8	64.6	62.3	57.2	56.0	58.3	48.9	54.0
– Eastern Europe	0.3	1.2	0.5	0.4	0.9	0.4	0.2	0.4	1.6	0.6
– Rest of Europe	1.0	2.9	1.3	0.9	1.1	1.9	2.0	1.2	1.3	1.9
Europe former USSR	0.9	0.6	0.4	0.4	0.0	0.2	0.0	0.1	0.0	0.0
Oceania	0.0	0.1	0.0	0.0	0.0	0.1	0.1	0.3	0.5	0.5
Other		0.1	0.2	0.2	0.2	0.2	0.2	0.0	0.0	0.0
France, Monaco	31.9	32.0	32.7	31.0	29.6	30.5	33.1	34.2	27.9	24.0
Netherlands/Pays–Bas	10.2	11.2	9.3	10.6	11.8	9.1	7.5	6.0	5.3	5.2
Cote d'Ivoire	5.4	2.3	5.5	2.4	2.6	8.1	3.8	3.0	4.2	6.3
Japan/Japon	6.6	5.4	5.0	3.9	4.2	4.3	6.7	5.2	4.5	3.5
USA/Etats–Unis d'Amer	3.9	2.3	3.6	5.8	5.9	5.3	6.4	0.9	6.1	5.5
Germany/Allemagne							4.2	5.8	5.9	9.9
United Kingdom	6.3	6.7	7.1	6.3	4.2	3.8	3.7	2.3	1.8	3.4
China, Hong Kong SAR	0.3	0.9	1.6	1.9	2.1	2.6	2.5	2.8	4.4	3.3
Nigeria/Nigéria	0.8	0.2	0.8	2.0	1.7	2.3	2.9	2.5	5.5	2.5
Italy/Italie	2.3	2.3	2.5	2.6	3.0	2.3	3.2	2.7	2.9	3.0

	1985	1986	1987	1988	1989	1990	1991	1992	1993	1994
Afrique	9.1	8.6	11.1	11.5	14.0	17.3	19.0	25.0	18.9	16.4
Amériques	3.1	13.8	13.5	13.6	14.5	15.8	18.8	21.1	23.1	27.2
– Amérique du Nord	2.7	13.0	13.0	12.9	12.6	13.6	11.4	20.7	13.3	17.1
– ALAI	0.4	0.8	0.4	0.7	1.9	2.2	7.4	0.3	9.8	10.1
– MCAC							0.0			
– Caraïbes		0.0	0.0			0.0	0.0			0.0
– Autre Amérique	0.0			0.0				0.0		
Asie anc. URSS exclus	4.0	8.1	10.5	9.8	15.3	17.5	23.0	23.1	35.1	30.5
– Moyen–Orient	0.4	0.4	2.1	1.8	0.3	0.6	0.0	0.0	0.1	0.0
Asie ancienne URSS										
Europe anc. URSS exclus	80.6	65.1	57.6	58.8	49.8	44.2	32.5	29.4	22.3	22.8
– Union Européenne	69.1	56.1	52.0	51.8	43.8	40.9	29.5	23.1	20.7	19.8
– Europe de l'Est	3.8	3.0	3.9	4.9	4.4	1.2	1.5	5.6	1.4	2.5
– Autre de l'Europe	7.8	5.9	1.7	2.0	1.6	2.1	1.5	0.7	0.2	0.6
Europe ancienne URSS	2.8	3.9	6.6	4.0	2.0	4.7	4.1			0.0
Océanie	0.3		0.0	2.1	4.4	0.4	0.0	1.5	0.5	3.1
Autre		0.6	0.8	0.2	0.0	0.1	2.5			
Canada	1.1	1.0	5.7	12.7	12.5	12.5	11.3	20.4	13.1	17.0
Other Asia n.e.s.	0.4	2.4	2.6	1.6	3.3	2.6	5.9	8.5	14.7	13.4
France, Monaco	23.1	11.8	7.7	8.1	8.7	9.8	6.7	5.1	4.9	5.0
Nigeria/Nigéria	0.4	1.0	1.0	0.8	2.5	3.3	7.7	9.3	6.4	3.8
Spain/Espagne	1.4	2.4	7.4	7.3	7.7	6.4	6.8	4.3	0.5	1.0
Philippines			1.6	3.3	5.0	4.3	4.9	2.0	7.2	5.4
India/Inde	1.0	1.5	1.6	2.2	3.2	5.3	2.6	5.7	2.7	1.8
Netherlands/Pays–Bas	21.9	20.5	14.8	11.7	6.3	3.3	0.9	3.7	6.5	3.6
Thailand/Thaïlande	0.4	0.1	0.3	0.5	1.2	0.6	3.7	4.7	4.8	3.2
Italy/Italie	6.6	6.1	7.0	5.2	7.5	5.3	4.1	2.3	1.5	1.5

4. Special Imports C.I.F. by Commodities according to the S.I.T.C. (Rev. 2) in million U.S. Dollars
Importations Spéciales C.A.F. par Produits d'après la C.T.C.I. (Rév. 2) en millions de Dollars E.U.

SITC CTCI	COMMODITY	1991 QUANTITY QUANTITE	1991 VALUE VALEUR	1992 QUANTITY QUANTITE	1992 VALUE VALEUR	1993 QUANTITY QUANTITE	1993 VALUE VALEUR	1994 QUANTITY QUANTITE	1994 VALUE VALEUR	PRODUIT
	ALL COMMODITIES		444.0		394.7		179.5			TOUS PRODUITS
0	FOOD AND LIVE ANIMALS		72.4		83.8		41.9			ALIMENTS,ANIMAUX VIVANTS
001	*LIVE ANIMALS FOR FOOD	W 1919	1.6		1.1		0.5			ANIMAUX VIVANTS
01	MEAT AND PREPARATIONS		0.8		3.1		1.6			VIANDES ET PREPARATIONS
011	MEAT FRESH,CHILLD,FROZEN	W 42	0.2		1.7		1.4			VIANDES FRAICHES,REF,CONGE
0114	POULTRY FRESH CHLLD,FRZN		0.1		1.2	W 1608	1.2			VOLAILLES MORTES
02	DAIRY PRODCTS,BIRDS'EGGS		5.6		5.8		2.6			PRODUITS LAITIERS,OEUFS
022	MILK AND CREAM	W 3654	4.9	W 3968	5.1	W 2124	2.3			LAIT ET CREME
0223	MILK AND CREAM FRESH	W 1074	1.0	W 959	1.0	W 691	0.7			LAIT,CREME FRAIS
0224	MILK,CREAM PRESERVED ETC	W 2579	4.0	W 3009	4.1	W 1433	1.7			LAIT,CREME CONS,CONC
02243	MILK DRY,OVER 1.5% FAT	W 339	0.7	W 1361	2.1	W 461	0.8			LAIT POUDRE SUP 1.5%
02249	MILK(EX DRY) PRSVD,SWEET	W 1706	2.3	W 1648	2.1	W 936	0.9			LAIT CONS,CONC SUCRE
03	FISH AND PREPARATIONS		16.7		15.8		9.2			POISSONS ET PREPARATIONS
034	FISH,FRESH,CHILLED,FROZN	W 26495	14.7		14.6		8.8			POISSON FRAIS, REFRIG,CONG
0341	FISH FRSH,CHLLD,EX FILLT	W 1282	0.6		0.2	W 2879	1.2			POISSON FRAIS,REFRIGERE
0342	FISH FROZEN,EXCL FILLETS	W 25213	14.1	W 26029	14.5		7.6			POISSONS CONGELES
037	FISH ETC PREPD,PRSVD NES	W 934	1.4		0.7		0.3			POIS,CRUST,MOL PREPARES
0371	FISH PREPARD,PRESRVD NES	W 933	1.4		0.7		0.3			CONSERVES DE POISSONS
04	CEREALS AND PREPARATIONS		21.6		35.1		14.8			CEREALES ET PRODUITS
041	WHEAT ETC UNMILLED	W 56693	11.3	W 116926	25.8	W 131247	6.8			FROMENT,EPEAUTRE
0411	DURUM WHEAT UNMILLED	W 52793	10.4	W 114247	24.9	W 127498	5.6			FROMENT DUR NON MOULU
0412	OTHER WHEAT ETC UNMILLED	W 3900	1.0	W 2679	0.9	W 3749	1.2			AUTRE FROMENT NON MOULU
042	RICE	W 25811	6.4	W 24017	6.1	W 30219	6.7			RIZ
0422	RICE SEMI–MILLED,MILLED	W 25736	6.4	W 23201	5.9	W 29836	6.6			RIZ POLI,GLACE INCL BRISURES
04221	RICE MILLED UNBROKEN	W 14556	3.5	W 13794	3.8	W 16529	3.9			RIZ POLI,GLACE EXCL BRISURES
04222	RICE BROKEN	W 11180	3.0	W 9407	2.1	W 13307	2.8			BRISURES DE RIZ
046	WHEAT ETC MEAL OR FLOUR	W 1542	0.6	W 2566	1.3	W 803	0.4			SEMOULE FARINE,FROMENT
048	CEREAL ETC PREPARATIONS	W 4205	2.8		1.3		0.8			PREPTNS A BASE CEREALES
0483	MACARONI,SPAGHETTI ETC	W 2484	2.0	W 542	0.6	W 355	0.4			PATES ALIMENTAIRES
05	VEGETABLES AND FRUIT		6.2		5.2		3.7			LEGUMES ET FRUITS
054	VEG ETC FRSH,SMPLY PRSVD	W 7593	5.1		1.0		0.7			LEGUMES FRAIS,CONG,SECS
0546	VEGETABLES SIMPLY PRESVD	W 3900	4.5	W 70	0.1		0.1			LEGUMES CONG,CONSER
05461	VEGETABLES FROZEN	W 3756	4.5	W 38	0.1	W 1	0.1			LEGUMES CONGELES
056	VEGTBLES ETC PRSVD,PREPD	W 410	0.4		3.8		2.9			CONSERVES DE LEGUMES
0565	VEGTBLES PRSVD,PREPD NES	W 344	0.4		3.6		2.9			LEGUMES PREPARES CONSERVE
05659	OTH VEG PRESVD,PREPD NES	W 295	0.3		3.6		2.9			LEGUM PREPAP,CONSERV NDA
06	SUGAR AND PREPS,HONEY		7.8		7.1		3.5			SUCRES ET PRODUITS
061	SUGAR AND HONEY	W 15286	7.2		6.6		3.3			SUCRES ET MIEL
0611	RAW BEET AND CANE SUGAR	W 8965	4.7	W 4591	2.6	W 2696	1.3			SUCRES BRUTS
0612	REFINED SUGAR ETC	W 6124	2.4	W 8877	4.1	W 4838	2.0			SUCRES RAFFINES
07	COFFEE,TEA,COCOA,SPICES		1.0		0.7		0.8			CAFE,THE,CACAO,EPICES
09	MISC EDIBLE PRODUCTS		11.1		9.5		5.2			PREP ALIMENTAIRES DIVERSES
098	EDIBLE PRODCTS,PREPS NES	W 6592	10.2		8.5		4.9			PREP ALIMENTAIRES NDA
09805	SOUPS AND BROTHS	W 6018	9.2	W 3759	6.6	W 2499	3.2			SOUPES,POTAGES,BOUILLONS
09809	MISC FOOD PREPRTIONS NES	W 133	0.4	W 1189	1.4		1.4			PREP ALIMENTAIRES NDA
1	BEVERAGES AND TOBACCO		25.2		19.5		10.3			BOISSONS ET TABACS
11	BEVERAGES		7.2		5.7		3.1			BOISSONS
112	ALCOHOLIC BEVERAGES	W 3777	6.8	W 2497	5.4	W 2201	3.0			BOISSONS ALCOOLIQUES
1121	WINE OF FRESH GRAPES ETC	W 2491	2.7	W 1399	1.5	W 1527	1.3			VINS DE RAISINS FRAIS
11212	WINE OF FRESH GRAPES	W 1411	1.7	W 504	0.7	W 828	0.8			VINS DE MOUTS DE RAISINS
1124	DISTILLED ALCOHOLIC BEVS	W 1257	4.1	W 1053	3.9	W 673	1.8			ALCOOLS,EAUX–DE–VIE
11241	WHISKY	W 339	1.7	W 191	1.2	W 186	0.8			WHISKY
11249	OTH ALCOHOLC BEVS,CMPNDS	W 912	2.4	W 859	2.7	W 486	1.0			BOISSONS ALCOOLIQUES NDA
12	TOBACCO AND MANUFACTURES		18.1		13.8		7.2			TABACS BRUTS FABRIQUES
122	TOBACCO,MANUFACTURED	W 1130	18.0		13.8		7.2			TABACS FABRIQUES
1222	CIGARETTES	W 1096	17.8	W 800	13.8	W 496	7.2			CIGARETTES
2	CRUDE MATERLS,EXCL FUELS		9.1		8.0		1.4			MAT BRUTES NON COMESTIBLES
24	CORK AND WOOD		2.3		1.5		0.5			LIEGE ET BOIS
26	TEXTILE FIBRES AND WASTE		3.6		4.2		0.1			FIBRES TEXTILES
269	WASTE OF TEXTILE FABRICS	W 5413	3.3	W 6519	4.1	W 8	0.1			FRIPERIE DRILLES,CHIFFONS
26901	BULK TEXT WSTE,OLD CLTHG	W 5348	3.3	W 6366	4.0	W 2	0.1			ART ET ACCESS D'HABILLEMENT
27	CRUDE FERTLZR,MINRLS NES		3.2		2.0		0.8			ENGRAIS MINERAUX BRUTS
278	OTHER CRUDE MINERALS	W 41710	2.5		1.2		0.6			AUTRES MINERAUX BRUTS
2783	COMMON SALT,ETC	W 17442	1.6	W 8784	0.9	W 939	0.3			SEL
3	MINERAL FUELS ETC		43.6		25.2		14.3			COMBUSTIBLES MINERAUX LUB
33	PETROLEUM AND PRODUCTS		43.4		24.8		14.2			PETROLE ET DERIVES
334	PETROLEUM PRODUCTS,REFIN	W 173521	42.7		24.5		14.0			PRODUITS RAFFINES
3341	GASOLINE,OTH LIGHT OILS	W 173518	42.7							ESSENCES POUR MOTEURS
33419	OTH LIGHT PETROLEUM OILS	W 173518	42.7							AUTRES HUILES LEGERES
4	ANIMAL,VEGETABLE OIL,FAT		4.8		4.7		1.5			HUILES,GRAISSES ANIM,VEG
42	FIXED VEGETABLE OIL,FAT		4.8		4.6		1.5			HUILES VEGETALES FIXES
423	FIXED VEG OILS,SOFT	W 3924	3.0		2.8		1.0			HUILES VEGET DOUCES FIXES
4232	SOYA BEAN OIL	W 1238	1.0	W 1235	1.3	W 548	0.5			HUILE DE SOJA
4234	GROUNDNUT(PEANUT) OIL	W 2445	1.8	W 633	0.6	W 319	0.3			HUILE D'ARACHIDE
424	FIXED VEG OIL NONSOFT	W 2657	1.9		1.9		0.5			AUTRES HUILES VEG FIXES
4249	FIXED VEGETABLE OILS NES	W 1726	1.3	W 1263	1.3	W 55	0.1			HUILES VEGET FIXES NDA
5	CHEMCLS,RELATED PROD NES		52.7		47.7		29.3			PRODUITS CHIMIQUES
52	INORGANIC CHEMICALS		1.5		1.3		0.5			PROD CHIM INORGANIQUES
53	DYES,TANNING,COLOUR PROD		1.2		1.3		0.6			PROD TEINTURE,COLORANTS
541	*MEDICINAL,PHARM PRODUCT	K 1212167	21.1		26.1		10.2			PROD MEDICINAUX PHARMACEUT
5416	GLYCOSIDES,GLANDS,SERA	K 22307	0.7		1.3		0.9			HETEROSIDES
54164	ANTISERA,MICROB VACCINES	K 22012	0.7		1.1		0.7			SERUMS,VACCINS
5417	MEDICAMENTS	K 1145939	19.8		24.4		9.1			MEDICAMENTS
54171	— CONTAINNG ANTIBIOTICS	K 898826	16.5		18.8		0.5			MED CONTN ANTIBIOTIQUES
54172	— CONTAINING HORMONES	K 86008	1.5	K 36000	0.6		0.5			MED CONTENANT HORMONES
54179	— CONTNG OTH SUBSTANCES	K 158981	1.7	K 335000	5.1	K 541000	8.2			MED CONT AUT SUBSTANCES
55	PERFUME,CLEANING ETC PRD		4.6		3.9		2.7			PROD POUR PARFUM,TOILETTE
553	PERFUMERY,COSMETICS,ETC	W 2260	1.7		1.8		1.0			PRODUITS DE PARFUMERIE
554	SOAP,CLEANSING ETC PREPS	W 3540	2.5		1.8	W 1306	1.6			SAVONS,PRODUITS DETERSIFS
5541	SOAPS	W 3061	1.7	W 1699	1.2	W 948	1.0			SAVONS,PROD TENSIO–ACTIFS
562	*FERTILIZERS,MANUFACTURE	W 17266	4.9		4.7		7.9			ENGRAIS MANUFACTURES
5621	CHEM NITROGENOUS FERTLZR	W 14008	3.9	W 6831	1.6		2.4			ENGRAIS AZOTES
56216	UREA	W 14008	3.9	W 6810	1.5	W 8169	2.4			UREE
5629	FERTILIZERS NES	W 3256	1.1		3.2	W 23954	5.5			ENGRAIS NDA
56291	NIT–PHOS–POT FERTLZR NES	W 3250	1.1	W 23	3.2	W 3232	0.8			ENGRAIS CONT N P K
56292	NITROG–PHOS FERTILZR NES			W 98	0.1	W 17722	4.1			ENGRAIS NDA CONT N P
56299	OTHER FERTILIZERS NES	W 6	0.1		0.1	W 3000	0.8			AUTRES ENGRAIS NDA
58	PLASTIC MATERIALS ETC		4.3		3.9		1.7			MAT PLAST ARTIFICIELLES
582	PROD OF CONDENSATION ETC	W 2675	2.0		1.4		0.8			PROD CONDENS,POLYCOND
5826	EPOXIDE RESINS	W 2650	2.0	W 1932	1.4	W 963	0.8			RESINES EPOXYDES
58261	— IN PRIMARY FORMS	W 2650	2.0	W 1932	1.4	W 963	0.8			EPOXYDES PRIMAIRES

4. Special Imports C.I.F. by Commodities according to the S.I.T.C. (Rev. 2) in million U.S. Dollars
Importations Spéciales C.A.F. par Produits d'après la C.T.C.I. (Rév. 2) en millions de Dollars E.U.

SITC CTCI	COMMODITY	1991		1992		1993		1994		PRODUIT
		QUANTITY QUANTITE	VALUE VALEUR	QUANTITY QUANTITE	VALUE VALEUR	QUANTITY QUANTITE	VALUE VALEUR	QUANTITY QUANTITE	VALUE VALEUR	
583	POLYMERIZATION ETC PRODS	W 966	2.3		2.3		0.9			PROD POLYMERISATION
5839	OTH POLYMRZTION ETC PROD	W 885	2.0	W 740	1.9		0.9			AUT PROD POLYMER COPOLYM
59	CHEMICAL MATERIALS NES		14.6		6.1		5.8			MAT PROD CHIMIQUES NDA
591	PESTICIDES,DISINFECTANTS	W 2597	13.2	W 1559	5.1	W 1625	5.0			DESINF,INSECT,FONG,HERB
5911	INSECTICIDES,FOR RETAIL	W 1728	9.7	W 812	3.2	W 1075	4.0			INSECTICIDES VENTE DET
5914	DISINFECTANTS,ETC,FR RET	W 844	3.3	W 709	1.8	W 508	0.6			DESINFECTANTS VENTE DET
59149	RAT POISONS ETC FR RTAIL	W 835	3.2	W 698	1.8	W 484	0.5			ANTIPARASITES VENTE DET
6	BASIC MANUFACTURES		78.5		79.0		23.9			ART MANUFACTURES
62	RUBBER MANUFACTURES NES		5.5		7.9		1.3			CAOUTCHOUC MANUFACTURE
625	RUBBER TYRES, TUBES ETC	W 984	3.0	W 836	2.4		1.0			PNEUS CAOUTCHOUC VULCANISE
6252	TYRES,NEW,BUS OR LORRY	W 466	2.0	W 417	1.7	W 21	0.6			PNEUS POUR AUTOBUS,CAMIONS
628	RUBBER ARTICLES NES	W 383	2.1		4.9		0.3			OUVRAGES CAOUTCHOUC NDA
6282	VULCANIZD RUBBER BELTING	W 318	1.6	W 915	4.4	W 505	0.2			COURROIES EN CAOUTCHOUC
64	PAPER,PAPERBOARD AND MFR		8.0		8.7		3.3			PAPIERS,CARTONS & OUVRAGES
641	PAPER AND PAPERBOARD	W 1929	2.0		2.5		0.8			PAPIERS ET CARTONS
642	PAPER,ETC,PRECUT,ARTS OF	W 3464	6.0		6.3		2.5			PAP,CARTONS DECOUPES
6421	PAPER ETC CONTAINERS	W 1909	2.9	W 1927	4.1		1.6			BOITES,SACS EMBALLAGES
65	TEXTILE YARN,FABRICS,ETC		30.0		22.4		8.6			FILS,TISSUS,ARTICLES TEXTILE
652	COTTON FABRICS,WOVEN	W 2999	23.2		14.1		3.7			TISSUS DE COTON
6522	WOVEN COTTON BLEACHD,ETC	W 2314	22.6		13.6		3.1			TISSUS COTON BLANCHIS ETC
65224	BLCHED COTTON FABRIC NES	W 2247	22.5		13.4		3.0			AUT TIS PLUS 85% COT BLANCHI
653	WOVN MAN–MADE FIB FABRIC	W 1523	2.6		2.5		2.1			TISSUS FIBRES SYNTH,ARTIF
6534	DISC SYN BLEND FABRC NES	W 1204	2.0		1.9	W 1232	1.8			TISSUS FIBRES SYNTH DISCONT
65341	DISC SYN FIB–COTTN FABRC	W 752	1.2		1.0	W 919	1.3			TISSUS FIB SYNT DIS MEL COTO
657	SPECIAL TXTL FABRC,PRODS	W 562	2.2		2.0		1.4			TISSUS SPECIAUX
6575	CORDAGE AND MANUFACTURES	W 368	1.8		1.7		1.0			FICELLES,CORDES,CORDAGES
65752	NETTING OF ROPE,TWINE	W 181	1.4	W 191	1.4		0.8			FILETS MAT DU 657.51
658	TEXTILE ARTICLES NES	W 597	1.4		3.2		1.3			ART FACONNES MAT TEXTILES
6581	BAGS,SACKS OF TEXTILES	W 281	0.6		2.2		0.6			SACS EMBALLAGE TEXTILES
6584	LINENS ETC	W 252	0.6		0.9	W 395	0.7			LINGE DE MAISON
66	NONMETAL MINERAL MFS NES		12.9		18.4		5.4			ART MIN NON METALLIQUES
661	LIME,CEMENT,BLDG PRODS	W 168236	8.7		15.9	W 391255	4.4			CHAUX,CIMENTS MAT CONSTR
6612	CEMENT	W 163607	7.1		14.0	W 389490	3.8			CIMENTS HYDRAULIQUES
6618	MNRL BLDG PRD UNFIRD NES	W 4002	1.4	W 4905	1.6	W 1390	0.5			MAT CONST AMIANTE–CIMENT
66183	ASBESTOS–,FIBRE–CMNT PRD	W 3590	1.1	W 4687	1.4	W 1340	0.4			OUVRAGES AMIANTE–CIMENT
662	CLAY,REFRACTORY BLDG PRD	W 2613	1.5	W 2086	1.2	W 898	0.4			MAT CONST REFRACTAIRES
6624	BRICKS ETC NONREFRACTORY	W 2580	1.4	W 1990	1.0	W 816	0.4			BRIQUES ETC CERAM NON REFR
67	IRON AND STEEL		8.7		10.7		2.5			FER ET ACIER
673	IRON,STEEL SHAPES ETC	W 6087	2.2		2.7		0.9			BARRES,PROFIL FER,ACIER
6732	IRON,STEEL BARS ETC	W 5212	1.8		2.2		0.8			BARRES FER,ACIER
67326	IRN,OTH STL BARS HOTROLD	W 103	0.1	W 3104	1.3	W 2865	0.7			BARRES PLEINES FER,ACIER
67327	IRN, OTH STL BARS FORGED	W 4322	1.4		0.9		0.1			BARRES FORGEES CREUSES
674	IRN,STL UNIV,PLATE,SHEET	W 4509	3.4		5.2		0.8			LARGES PLATS,TOLES
6747	TINNED PLATES,SHEETS	W 209	0.4	W 2825	2.5	W 87	0.2			TOLES ETAMEES EN ACIER
6749	OTH IRN,STL PLATES,SHEET	W 1882	1.5		2.2					AUTRES TOLES FER,ACIER
67491	— OF IRON OR SIMPLE STL	W 1867	1.5	W 3314	2.2					AUT TOLES AUTRES ACIER FIN
678	IRON,STL TUBES,PIPES,ETC	W 1769	2.0		1.0		0.4			TUBES,TUYAUX EN FONTE,FER
68	NON–FERROUS METALS		2.5		1.1		0.2			METAUX NON FERREUX
69	METAL MANUFACTURES NES		10.2		9.5		2.7			ART MANUFACT EN METAL NDA
691	STRUCTURES AND PARTS NES	W 1218	1.9	W 1443	1.3	W 48	0.2			CONSTRUCT FER,ACIER,ALU
6911	STRUCTURES,PARTS IRN,STL	W 1083	1.5	W 1389	1.1	W 19	0.1			CONSTRUCT FER,ACIER,FONTE
694	STL,COPPR NAILS,NUTS,ETC	W 307	1.3		1.4		0.4			CLOUS,VIS,ECROUS
697	BASE MTL HOUSEHOLD EQUIP	W 4063	1.7		1.7		0.9			ART MENAGE MET COMMUNS
6974	BASE MTL DMSTC ARTIC NES	W 3929	1.4		1.5		0.9			ARTICLES NDA FONTE,FER,ETC
69741	— OF IRON OR STEEL	W 3873	1.3	W 1356	1.4		0.8			ART NDA EN FONTE,FER
699	BASE METAL MFRS NES	W 631	2.2		3.2		0.6			ART MANUFACTURES MET NDA
7	MACHINES,TRANSPORT EQUIP		125.6		98.6		39.1			MACHINES MATERIEL TRANSPORT
71	POWER GENERATING EQUIPMT		9.3		3.4		1.2			MACHINES GENERATRICES
713	INTRNL COMBUS PSTN ENGIN	W 231	1.6		1.6		0.3			MOTEURS EXPL COMB INT, PIECE
716	ROTATING ELECTRIC PLANT	W 439	7.6		1.6		0.8			APP ELECTR ROTATIFS,PIECES
7162	AC MTRS,GENRTRS,GEN SETS	W 363	6.6		0.5		0.5			MOTEURS ELECTRIQUES
71623	GEN SETS WITH PISTN ENGN	W 336	6.2		0.2	W 82	0.3			GROUPES MOTEUR EXPLOSION
72	MACHS FOR SPCL INDUSTRYS		14.5		11.4		3.0			MAC SPECIALES POUR INDUST
722	TRACTORS NON–ROAD	W 660	3.3		1.0	W 85	0.3			TRACTEURS
7223	TRACK–LAYING TRACTORS	W 546	2.9	W 49	0.2	W 3	0.1			TRACTEURS A CHENILLES
723	CIVIL ENGNEERG EQUIP ETC	W 389	2.2		4.2		0.2			APPAREILS DE GENIE CIVIL
7234	CONST,MINING MACHNRY NES	W 352	1.8		2.8	W 3	0.1			MACH POUR LA CONST, MINES
7239	CONSTR ETC MACHY PTS NES	W 37	0.5	W 120	1.3		0.1			PIECES 723.41–723.46
724	TEXTILE,LEATHER MACHNRY	W 392	2.1		2.0		0.9			MACH POUR INDUSTRIE TEXTILE
7244	SPINNING,EXTRDNG,ETC MCH	W 55	1.0		1.3		0.7			MACH POUR LE FILAGE
72449	PTS NES OF MACHS OF 7244	W 52	1.0		1.3		0.7			PIECES DES MACH DU 724.4
727	FOOD MACHRY NON–DOMESTIC	W 582	3.8		0.8		0.5			MACH INDUSTRIES ALIMENT
7271	GRAIN WORKING MCHY,PARTS	W 386	3.6	W 298	0.8	W 283	0.4			MACH POUR MINOTERIE,PIEC
72711	GRAIN MILLING ETC MACHRY	W 379	3.5	W 268	0.7	W 260	0.3			MACHINES POUR MINOTERIE
728	OTH MACHY FOR SPCL INDUS	W 185	2.5		2.7		0.8			AUT MACH IND PARTICULIERES
7283	OTHR MINERAL WORKG MACHY	W 72	1.6		1.9	W 37	0.3			MACH TRIER,CRIBLER,BROYER
73	METALWORKING MACHINERY		0.7		0.4		0.6			MACH TRAVAIL DES METAUX
74	GENRL INDUSTRL MACHY NES		17.7		13.6		4.4			MACH APP INDUSTRIE
741	HEATING,COOLING EQUIPMNT	W 210	2.0		1.3		0.8			MACH CHAUFFAGE,PIECES
742	PUMPS FOR LIQUIDS ETC	W 130	1.7		1.4		1.1			POMPES MOTO–POMPES
7428	OTHER PUMPS FOR LIQUIDS	W 71	1.3		1.0	W 66	1.0			AUTRES POMPES POUR LIQ
74288	PUMPS FR LIQUIDS NES ETC	W 60	1.0		0.7	W 61	0.8			POMPES POUR LIQUIDES NDA
743	PUMPS NES,CENTRFUGES ETC	W 133	2.1		2.0		0.7			POMPES COMPRES,VENT ETC
744	MECHANICAL HANDLING EQU	W 843	4.8		2.6		0.4			EQUIP MANUTENTION PIECES
7442	LIFTING,LOADING MACH NES	W 348	1.9		0.8		0.3			APP LEVAGE,MANUTENTION
74428	OTH HANDLING ETC MCH NES	W 274	1.5		0.7		0.2			AUT APP LEVAGE ETC
7449	PTS NES OF MACHY OF 7442	W 331	2.0	W 172	1.7		0.1			PIECES DU 744.2
745	NONELEC MACHY,TOOLS NES	W 108	2.5		1.4		1.2			AUT MACH NON ELEC,PIECES
7452	OTH NONELEC MCHS,PTS NES	W 106	2.4		1.3		1.2			AUT MACH NON ELEC,PIECES
74522	PACKAGNG,BOTTLNG,ETC MCH	W 71	1.4		0.8	W 5	0.5			MACH NETT BOUTEILLES,ETC
749	NONELEC MACH PTS,ACC NES	W 285	4.9		5.1		0.5			PIECES MACH NON ELEC NDA
7491	BALL,ROLLER,ETC BEARINGS	W 89	1.3		1.4		0.2			ROULEMENTS BILLES ETC
7493	SHAFT,CRANK,PULLEY ETC	W 109	2.4		2.8		0.2			ARBRES TRANS,VILEBREQUINS
75	OFFICE MACHNES,ADP EQUIP		4.9		4.5		2.0			MACH BUREAU TRAIT AUTOM
752	AUTOMTIC DATA PROC EQUIP	W 29	2.5		2.5		1.3			MACH TRAIT INFORMATION
7528	OFF–LINE DATA PROC EQUIP	W 12	1.1	W 26	1.2	W 13	0.9			MACH AUXIL TRAIT INFORM
76	TELECOMM,SOUND EQUIPMENT		16.7		5.7		4.4			EQUIPMENT DE TELECOM
761	TELEVISION RECEIVERS	W 309	2.2	W 288	1.8	W 146	0.8			RECEPTEURS DE TELEVISION
7611	COLOUR TV RECEIVERS	W 187	1.7	W 176	1.4	W 81	0.6			RECEPTEURS COULEUR
763	SOUND RECORDRS,PHONOGRPH	W 52	0.6		0.4		1.4			PHONO,APP ENREGISTREMENT
7638	OTHR SOUND APPARATUS ETC	W 51	0.6		0.4		1.4			AUT APP D'ENREGIS,REPROD

4. Special Imports C.I.F. by Commodities according to the S.I.T.C. (Rev. 2) in million U.S. Dollars
Importations Spéciales C.A.F. par Produits d'après la C.T.C.I. (Rév. 2) en millions de Dollars E.U.

SITC CTCI	COMMODITY	1991		1992		1993		1994		PRODUIT
		QUANTITY QUANTITE	VALUE VALEUR	QUANTITY QUANTITE	VALUE VALEUR	QUANTITY QUANTITE	VALUE VALEUR	QUANTITY QUANTITE	VALUE VALEUR	
76388	DICTATING MACHINES ETC	W 30	0.2		0.2		1.3			MACHINES A DICTER
764	TELECOM EQPT,PTS,ACC NES	W 265	13.4		3.2		2.2			EQUIP TELECOM,PIECES
7641	LINE TELEPHONE,ETC EQUIP	W 199	11.9		1.7		0.7			APP TELEPHON PAR FIL
7643	TV,RADIO TRANSMITTRS ETC	W 9	0.5		0.3		1.0			APP EMET TELE RADIO
77	ELECTRIC MACHNRY NES ETC		16.9		12.5		5.9			MACH APP ELECT NDA
772	SWITCHGEAR ETC,PARTS NES	W 175	2.7		2.3		0.7			APP COUPURE,SECT ETC
7721	SWITCHGEAR ETC	W 173	2.6		2.2		0.7			APP COUPURE,SECTIONMNT
773	ELECTR DISTRIBUTNG EQUIP	W 867	5.0		2.7		1.0			EQUIPMT DISTRIBUTION ELECT
7731	INSULATED WIRE,CABLE ETC	W 851	5.0		2.7		0.5			FILS,CABLES ISOLES ELECT
775	HOUSEHOLD TYPE EQUIP NES	W 329	1.5		1.2		0.6			MACH,APP USAGE DOMESTQUE
778	ELECTRICAL MACHINERY NES	W 3816	6.0		5.5		3.3			AUTRES MACH ELECT NDA
7781	BATTERIES,ACCUMULATORS	W 3675	4.8		4.5		2.8			PILES ET ACCUMULATEURS
77811	PRIMARY BATTERIES,CELLS	W 3436	3.8		3.4		2.4			PILES ELECTRIQUES,PIECES
78	ROAD VEHICLES		41.4		45.1		16.5			VEHICULES ROUTIERS
781	PASS MOTOR VEH EXC BUSES	W 3684	14.5	W 4568	15.6	W 2522	6.2			AUTO TRANSPORT PERSONNES
782	LORRIES,SPCL MTR VEH NES	W 1226	4.1	W 1530	4.2		1.6			VEHICULES SPECIAUX,MARCH
7821	LORRIES,TRUCKS	W 893	2.3	W 1517	4.1		0.5			VEHICULES TRANSP MARCHAND
7822	SPECIAL MOTOR VEHCLS NES	W 332	1.8	W 13	0.1	W 89	1.2			VEHICULES USAGES SPECIAUX
783	ROAD MOTOR VEHICLES NES	W 2071	6.3	W 1720	5.8	W 969	2.7			VEHICULES ROUTIERS NDA
7831	BUSES	W 1648	5.0	W 1197	4.6	W 704	2.4			VOITURES TRANSPORT COMMUN
7832	TRACTORS FOR TR–TRAILERS	W 423	1.4	W 523	1.3	W 265	0.4			TRACTEURS ROUTIERS
784	MOTOR VEH PRTS,ACCES NES	W 343	4.1	W 631	5.1		0.9			PIECES 722,781,782,783
7849	OTHER MOTOR VEHCL PARTS	W 322	3.8	W 605	5.1		0.9			PIECES 722,781,782,783
785	CYCLES,ETC MOTRZD OR NOT	W 970	3.7		3.9		1.3			MOTOCYCLES SCOOTERS
7851	MOTORCYCLES ETC	W 747	2.7	W 987	3.4	W 242	1.0			MOTO VELO MOTEUR AUXIL
786	TRAILERS,NONMOTR VEH,NES	W 4517	8.9	W 10226	10.7	W 5836	4.1			REMORQUES,CADRES,CONTAIN
7861	TRAILERS,TRANSP CONTAINR	W 3918	8.4	W 9863	10.3	W 5665	4.0			REMORQUES TOUS VEHICULES
78613	CONTAINERS INC ROAD–RAIL	W 3821	8.2	W 9645	9.5	W 5577	3.9			CADRES ET CONTAINERS
79	OTHR TRANSPORT EQUIPMENT		3.9		2.5		1.5			AUTRE MATERIEL TRANSPORT
792	AIRCRAFT ETC	W 18	3.3		1.8		1.5			APP NAVIGATION AERIENNE
7929	AIRCRAFT PARTS NES	W 17	3.3	W 6	1.8		1.5			PIECES DU 792
8	MISC MANUFACTURED GOODS		28.6		24.6		17.8			ART MANUFACTURES DIVERS
821	*FURNITURE,PARTS THEREOF	W 404	1.6		1.3		0.5			MEUBLES ET PIECES
831	*TRAVEL GOODS,HANDBAGS	W 557	1.0		1.0		0.6			ARTICLES DE VOYAGE ETC
84	CLOTHING AND ACCESSORIES		7.3		7.2		6.1			VETEMENTS
845	OUTERWEAR KNIT NONELASTC	W 265	1.0		1.6		1.6			VET DESSOUS,ACCES BONNET
8459	— OTHER,CLTHG ACCESRYS	W 245	0.9		1.1		1.6			AUT VET DESSUS DE BONNE
84594	—— OF REGENERTD FIBRES				0.1	W 7	0.7			AUT VET DESSUS FIB ARTIF
846	UNDER GARMENTS KNITTED	W 1810	4.0		3.0		2.9			SOUS VETS DE BONNETERIE
8462	— OF COTTON NON ELASTIC	W 1697	3.7		1.6	W 836	1.8			SOUS–VET BONNET COTON
84629	—— OTHER	W 1642	3.5		1.3	W 763	1.6			AUT SOUS–VET BONNET COTON
8463	— OF SYNTH FBR NONELAST	W 102	0.3		0.9	W 269	0.8			SOUS–VET BONNET FIB SYNT
84633	—— MENS NES			W 228	0.8	W 238	0.7			SOUS–VET BON FIB SYN
847	TEXTILE CLTHNG ACCES NES	W 137	0.9		1.2		0.4			ACCES VET MAT TEXT NDA
851	*FOOTWEAR	W 2065	3.4		3.5		5.2			CHAUSSURES
85101	FOOTWEAR RUBBER,PLASTIC	W 1497	2.4		2.3		3.5			CHAUS SEMELLES CAOUTCH
85102	FOOTWEAR LEATHER	W 518	1.1		0.9		1.6			CHAUS SEMELLES EN CUIR
87	PRECISION INSTRUMNTS NES		3.2		2.9		1.6			INSTRUM,APPAR SCIENT NDA
872	MEDICAL INSTRUMENTS NES	W 254	1.4		0.8		0.8			INSTR,APP MEDIC–CHIR NDA
87202	OTH MEDICAL INSTRUMENTS	W 246	0.9	W 22	0.3		0.8			INSTRUM,APP MEDECINE
874	MEASURNG,CONTROLNG INSTR	W 51	1.4		1.5		0.5			INSTRUMENTS DE MESURE
89	MISC MANUFCTRD GOODS NES		10.4		7.5		3.8			ART MANUFACTURES DIVERS
892	PRINTED MATTER	W 6559	3.5		3.1		1.3			IMPRIMES
8921	PRINTED BOOKS,GLOBES,ETC	W 6402	2.0		2.0		0.6			LIVRES,BROCHURES,CARTES
89211	PRINTED BOOKS,PAMPHLETS	W 6399	1.9	W 254	2.0		0.6			LIVRES,BROCHURES
893	ARTICLES OF PLASTIC NES		3.1		2.3		1.1			OUVRAGES EN MAT DIVIS 58
8931	PLSTC PACKG CONTNRS,LIDS	W 448	1.2	W 1768	1.2		0.5			ART TRANSP EMBALLAGE ETC
8939	MISC PLASTIC ARTICLES	W 493	1.9		1.1		0.6			ART DIVERS EN MAT DIV 58
89399	OTHR PLASTC ARTICLES NES	W 420	1.7		1.0		0.6			AUT OUV MAT DIV 58
894	TOYS,SPORTING GOODS,ETC	W 152	1.5		0.3		0.8			VOITURES ENFANTS,JOUETS
8946	NON–MILITARY ARMS,AMMO	W 30	0.9		0.1		0.7			ARMES NON MILITAIRES
89463	HUNTNG,SPORTNG AMMUNTION	W 23	0.3			W 55	0.7			MUNITIONS
9	GOODS NOT CLASSD BY KIND		3.8		4.0		0.5			ART TRANSACT NON CLASSES
951	*WAR FIREARMS,AMMUNITION	W 115	3.8		0.1		0.4			VEHIC BLINDES ARMES
95101	ARMORED FIGHTNG VEHICLES	W 82	2.0	W 1	0.1	W 6	0.3			CHARS DE COMBAT
95104	SIDEARMS AND PARTS NES	W 32	1.6							ARMES BLANCHES

5. Special Exports F.O.B. by Commodities according to the S.I.T.C. (Rev. 2) in million U.S. Dollars
Exportations Spéciales F.O.B. par Produits d'après la C.T.C.I. (Rév. 2) en millions de Dollars E.U.

SITC CTCI	COMMODITY	1991		1992		1993		1994		PRODUIT
		QUANTITY QUANTITE	VALUE VALEUR	QUANTITY QUANTITE	VALUE VALEUR	QUANTITY QUANTITE	VALUE VALEUR	QUANTITY QUANTITE	VALUE VALEUR	
	ALL COMMODITIES		253.3		275.0		136.1			TOUS PRODUITS
0	FOOD AND LIVE ANIMALS		43.7		63.6		26.2			ALIMENTS,ANIMAUX VIVANTS
001	*LIVE ANIMALS FOR FOOD			W 5	0.1	W 3290	0.7			ANIMAUX VIVANTS
0011	BOVINE SPECIES,LIVE					W 3290	0.7			ESPECE BOVINE
03	FISH AND PREPARATIONS		0.6		0.5		0.7			POISSONS ET PREPARATIONS
036	SHELL FISH FRESH,FROZEN	W 94	0.6	W 113	0.5		0.5			CRUSTACES,MOLLUSQUES
04	CEREALS AND PREPARATIONS		9.3		19.1		2.5			CEREALES ET PRODUITS
041	WHEAT ETC UNMILLED	W 9693	2.3	W 42505	11.6					FROMENT,EPEAUTRE
0411	DURUM WHEAT UNMILLED	W 9693	2.3	W 42505	11.6					FROMENT DUR NON MOULU
046	WHEAT ETC MEAL OR FLOUR	W 16094	6.9	W 18018	7.5	W 1677	2.2			SEMOULE FARINE,FROMENT
04601	FLOUR OF WHEAT OR MESLIN	W 16094	6.9	W 18018	7.5	W 1677	2.2			FARINE DE FROMENT
07	COFFEE,TEA,COCOA,SPICES		20.7		29.1		16.1			CAFE,THE,CACAO,EPICES
071	COFFEE AND SUBSTITUTES	W 9290	9.1		18.0		10.6			CAFE ET SUCCEDANES
0711	COFFEE GREEN,ROASTED,SUB	W 9290	9.1	W 19	18.0	W 13100	10.6			CAFE TORREFIE OU DECAFEINE
07111	COFFEE GREEN,HUSKS,SKINS	W 9290	9.1	W 19	18.0	W 13099	10.6			CAFE NON TORREFIE
072	COCOA	W 6279	11.0	W 6142	10.2	W 5446	5.2			CACAO
0721	COCOA BEANS,RAW,ROASTED	W 6279	11.0	W 6142	10.2	W 5446	5.2			CACAO EN FEVES
075	SPICES	W 200	0.6	W 254	0.9		0.4			EPICES
0752	SPICES,EX PEPPER,PIMENTO	W 155	0.5	W 250	0.9	W 118	0.4			AUTRES EPICES
081	*FEEDING STUFF FOR ANIML	W 28119	2.4		2.9	W 16539	1.8			NOURRITURE POUR ANIMAUX
0813	OILCAKE AND OTH RESIDUES	W 15116	1.8		2.6	W 13019	1.6			TOURTEAUX
08133	— OF COTTON SEEDS	W 15116	1.8	W 4516	2.6	W 13019	1.6			TOURTEAUX DE COTON
09	MISC EDIBLE PRODUCTS		10.0		10.9		4.2			PREP ALIMENTAIRES DIVERSES
091	MARGARINE AND SHORTENING	W 653	0.8	W 708	1.0	W 591	0.5			MARGARINE ET GRAISSES
0914	MARGARINE,EDIBLE FAT NES	W 653	0.8	W 708	1.0	W 591	0.5			MARGARINES,SIMILI SAINDOUX
09149	OTH PREPARED EDIBLE FATS	W 653	0.8	W 708	1.0	W 591	0.5			SIMILI–SAINDOUX
098	EDIBLE PRODCTS,PREPS NES	W 5476	9.3		10.0		3.8			PREP ALIMENTAIRES NDA
09805	SOUPS AND BROTHS	W 5385	9.1	W 4938	9.7	W 2145	3.6			SOUPES,POTAGES,BOUILLONS
1	BEVERAGES AND TOBACCO		0.2		0.9		0.3			BOISSONS ET TABACS
2	CRUDE MATERLS,EXCL FUELS		186.7		185.3		96.6			MAT BRUTES NON COMESTIBLES
223	SEEDS FOR OTH FIXED OILS	W 1241	0.4	W 4441	1.1	W 1112	0.2			GRAINES AUTRES HUILES FIXES
26	TEXTILE FIBRES AND WASTE		60.5		57.6		50.8			FIBRES TEXTILES
263	COTTON	W 35832	55.5	W 38577	55.8		47.1			COTON
2631	RAW COTTON,EXCL LINTERS	W 35643	55.3	W 38577	55.8	W 42342	47.1			COTON EN MASSE
266	SYNTHETIC FIBRES TO SPIN	W 1781	3.0			W 2181	3.2			FIBRES SYNTHETIQUES
2666	CONTIN FILAMNT TOW SYNTH	W 1781	3.0			W 2181	3.2			CABLES POUR DISCONTINUS
26662	— OF POLYESTER FIBRES	W 1781	3.0			W 2181	3.2			DE FIBRES EN POLYESTERS
269	WASTE OF TEXTILE FABRICS	W 228	2.0	W 205	1.8	W 53	0.5			FRIPERIE DRILLES,CHIFFONS
26901	BULK TEXT WSTE,OLD CLTHG	W 228	2.0	W 205	1.8	W 53	0.5			ART ET ACCESS D'HABILLEMENT
27	CRUDE FERTLZR,MINRLS NES		124.7		126.4		44.6			ENGRAIS MINERAUX BRUTS
271	FERTILIZERS,CRUDE	W 3114911	122.8	W 2835000	125.7	W 1435000	44.6			ENGRAIS BRUTS
2713	NAT CALCM PHOSPHATES ETC	W 3114911	122.8	W 2835000	125.7	W 1435000	44.6			PHOSPHATES DE CALCIUM
27131	— UNGROUND	W 3114911	122.8	W 2835000	125.7	W 1435000	44.6			PHOSPHATES NON MOULUS
278	OTHER CRUDE MINERALS	W 58297	1.8		0.6	W 732	0.1			AUTRES MINERAUX BRUTS
2785	QUARTZ,MICA,FELSPAR,ETC	W 52223	1.6							QUARTZ,MICA,FELDSPATH
27852	MICA,MICA WASTE	W 52223	1.6							MICA
29	CRUDE ANIMAL,VEG MAT NES		1.1		0.3		1.1			MATIERES BRUTES ANIM,VEGET
291	CRUDE ANIMAL MTRIALS NES					W 566	1.1			MATIERES BRUTES ANIMALES
2919	OTH ANIMAL MATERIALS NES					W 566	1.1			MAT ORIGINE ANIMALE NDA
29192	BRUSH–MAKING HAIR,ETC					W 266	0.7			SOIES DE PORC
292	CRUDE VEG MATERIALS NES	W 455	1.1		0.3					MAT BRUTES VEGETALES NDA
2925	SEEDS,ETC FOR PLANTING	W 349	0.9							SEMENCES NDA
3	MINERAL FUELS ETC		6.0		0.5		0.4			COMBUSTIBLES MINERAUX LUB
33	PETROLEUM AND PRODUCTS		5.9		0.5		0.4			PETROLE ET DERIVES
334	PETROLEUM PRODUCTS,REFIN	W 21013	5.9	W 2089	0.5	W 1950	0.4			PRODUITS RAFFINES
3341	GASOLINE,OTH LIGHT OILS	W 21013	5.9							ESSENCES POUR MOTEURS
33419	OTH LIGHT PETROLEUM OILS	W 21013	5.9							AUTRES HUILES LEGERES
4	ANIMAL,VEGETABLE OIL,FAT		0.7		2.9		0.3			HUILES,GRAISSES ANIM,VEG
42	FIXED VEGETABLE OIL,FAT		0.7		2.9		0.2			HUILES VEGETALES FIXES
424	FIXED VEG OIL NONSOFT	W 271	0.2		2.9	W 190	0.2			AUTRES HUILES VEG FIXES
4249	FIXED VEGETABLE OILS NES	W 20	0.1	W 213	2.3	W 1	0.1			HUILES VEGET FIXES NDA
5	CHEMCLS,RELATED PROD NES		2.8		5.9		1.7			PRODUITS CHIMIQUES
58	PLASTIC MATERIALS ETC		2.2		5.0		1.6			MAT PLAST ARTIFICIELLES
582	PROD OF CONDENSATION ETC	W 1086	0.9	W 1300	0.9		0.2			PROD CONDENS,POLYCOND
5826	EPOXIDE RESINS	W 1076	0.9	W 1221	0.9	W 272	0.2			RESINES EPOXYDES
58261	— IN PRIMARY FORMS	W 1076	0.9	W 1221	0.9	W 272	0.2			EPOXYDES PRIMAIRES
583	POLYMERIZATION ETC PRODS	W 633	1.3		1.5	W 527	1.3			PROD POLYMERISATION
5839	OTH POLYMRZTION ETC PROD	W 554	1.2	W 276	1.0	W 369	1.2			AUT PROD POLYMER COPOLYM
6	BASIC MANUFACTURES		7.8		6.9		2.6			ART MANUFACTURES
64	PAPER,PAPERBOARD AND MFR		1.3		1.4		1.0			PAPIERS,CARTONS & OUVRAGES
642	PAPER,ETC,PRECUT,ARTS OF	W 1291	1.3		1.4		1.0			PAP,CARTONS DECOUPES
6421	PAPER ETC CONTAINERS	W 1186	1.2	W 694	1.1	W 504	0.8			BOITES,SACS EMBALLAGES
65	TEXTILE YARN,FABRICS,ETC		1.1		0.7		0.9			FILS,TISSUS,ARTICLES TEXTILE
658	TEXTILE ARTICLES NES	W 560	0.6		0.1		0.5			ART FACONNES MAT TEXTILES
66	NONMETAL MINERAL MFS NES		3.1		4.1		0.5			ART MIN NON METALLIQUES
661	LIME,CEMENT,BLDG PRODS	W 68949	3.1	W 86129	4.1	W 8372	0.4			CHAUX,CIMENTS MAT CONSTR
6612	CEMENT	W 68926	3.1	W 86107	4.1	W 8372	0.4			CIMENTS HYDRAULIQUES
67	IRON AND STEEL		0.8		0.2		0.1			FER ET ACIER
69	METAL MANUFACTURES NES		1.4		0.5		0.2			ART MANUFACT EN METAL NDA
693	WIRE PRODUCTS NON ELECTR	W 930	1.0	W 14	0.1	W 155	0.2			OUVRAGES FILS METALLIQUES
6935	METAL FENCING,GAUZE,ETC	W 926	1.0	W 14	0.1	W 155	0.2			TOILES EN FER,ACIER,CUIVRE
69351	IRN,STL FENCNG,GAUZE ETC	W 926	1.0	W 14	0.1	W 155	0.2			TOILES EN FER,ACIER
7	MACHINES,TRANSPORT EQUIP		2.6		5.6		4.6			MACHINES MATERIEL TRANSPORT
72	MACHS FOR SPCL INDUSTRYS		0.3		0.4		2.5			MAC SPECIALES POUR INDUST
723	CIVIL ENGNEERG EQUIP ETC	W 18	0.2		0.4	W 154	0.8			APPAREILS DE GENIE CIVIL
7234	CONST,MINING MACHNRY NES	W 15	0.2		0.3	W 133	0.7			MACH POUR LA CONST, MINES
728	OTH MACHY FOR SPCL INDUS	W 5	0.1	W 2	0.1	W 251	1.5			AUT MACH IND PARTICULIERES
7283	OTHR MINERAL WORKG MACHY	W 4	0.1			W 234	1.4			MACH TRIER,CRIBLER,BROYER
72834	MINRL MOULDING ETC MACHY					W 70	0.6			MACH AGGLO CIMENT ETC
72839	PTS NES OF MACHY OF 7283					W 163	0.7			PIECES MACH DU 728.3
76	TELECOMM,SOUND EQUIPMENT		0.4		2.2		0.2			EQUIPMENT DE TELECOM
761	TELEVISION RECEIVERS	W 27	0.3	W 46	1.1	W 15	0.2			RECEPTEURS DE TELEVISION
763	SOUND RECORDRS,PHONOGRPH	W 4	0.1		0.9					PHONO,APP ENREGISTREMENT
7638	OTHR SOUND APPARATUS ETC	W 4	0.1		0.9					AUT APP D'ENREGIS,REPROD
76388	DICTATING MACHINES ETC	W 4	0.1		0.9					MACHINES A DICTER
78	ROAD VEHICLES		1.3		1.4		1.3			VEHICULES ROUTIERS
782	LORRIES,SPCL MTR VEH NES	W 60	0.2	W 54	0.5	W 98	0.5			VEHICULES SPECIAUX,MARCH
8	MISC MANUFACTURED GOODS		3.2		3.7		3.7			ART MANUFACTURES DIVERS
821	*FURNITURE,PARTS THEREOF	W 82	0.5		1.2		1.3			MEUBLES ET PIECES
8212	MED FURN,STUFFD FURNSHGS	W 6	0.1		0.1	W 75	0.9			MOB MEDICO–CHIRUR,PIECES
82121	MEDICAL FURNITURE,PARTS	W 6	0.1	W 3	0.1	W 68	0.9			MOBILIER MED,TABLE OPER ETC

5. Special Exports F.O.B. by Commodities according to the S.I.T.C. (Rev. 2) in million U.S. Dollars
Exportations Spéciales F.O.B. par Produits d'après la C.T.C.I. (Rév. 2) en millions de Dollars E.U.

SITC CTCI	COMMODITY	1991		1992		1993		1994		PRODUIT
		QUANTITY QUANTITE	VALUE VALEUR	QUANTITY QUANTITE	VALUE VALEUR	QUANTITY QUANTITE	VALUE VALEUR	QUANTITY QUANTITE	VALUE VALEUR	
8219	FURNITURE AND PARTS NES	W 70	0.5	W 147	1.2		0.4			AUTRES MEUBLES ET PIECES
82192	WOOD FURNITURE NES	W 67	0.4	W 137	1.1		0.3			MEUBLES NDA EN BOIS
84	CLOTHING AND ACCESSORIES		0.5		0.4		1.3			VETEMENTS
843	WOMENS OUTERWEAR NONKNIT	W 2	0.1		0.1	W 126	1.2			VET DESSUS FEMMES MAT TEX
8439	— OTHER OUTER GARMENTS	W 2	0.1	W 5	0.1	W 126	1.2			AUT VET DES FEM MAT TEXT
84399	—— OF OTHER FIBRES			W 3	0.1	W 120	1.1			VET DES FEM NDA AUT FIBR
89	MISC MANUFCTRD GOODS NES		2.2		1.6		1.2			ART MANUFACTURES DIVERS
893	ARTICLES OF PLASTIC NES	W 1145	1.8		1.0		1.1			OUVRAGES EN MAT DIVIS 58
8939	MISC PLASTIC ARTICLES	W 1142	1.8	W 195	0.9		0.9			ART DIVERS EN MAT DIV 58
89399	OTHR PLASTC ARTICLES NES	W 1142	1.8	W 195	0.9		0.9			AUT OUV MAT DIV 58

1. HISTORICAL SERIES, 1961–1996 GENERAL TRADE, IMPORTS C.I.F., EXPORTS F.O.B.
SERIES HISTORIQUES, 1961–1996 COMMERCE GENERAL, IMPORTATIONS C.A.F., EXPORTATIONS F.O.B

YEAR ANNEE	VALUE IN MILLION PA'ANGA / VALEUR EN MILLION PA'ANGA MERCHANDISE – MARCHANDISE IMPORTS	EXPORTS	GOLD – OR IMPORTS	EXPORTS	CONVERSION FACTORS U.S. CENTS PER PA'ANGA FACTEURS DE CONVERSION CENTS E.U. PAR PA'ANGA IMPORTS	EXPORTS	INDEX NUMBERS – INDICES QUANTUM IMPORTS	EXPORTS	UNIT VALUE / VALEUR UNITAIRE IMPORTS	EXPORTS
1961	2.80	2.80			112.0000	112.0000				
1962	2.50	1.70			112.0000	112.0000				
1963	2.40	1.90			112.0000	112.0000				
1964	3.90	2.30			112.0000	112.0000				
1965	3.40	2.50			112.0000	112.0000				
1966	4.10	3.60			112.0000	112.0000				
1967	5.70	3.60			112.0000	112.0000				
1968	5.20	3.80			112.0000	112.0000				
1969	5.10	3.40			112.0000	112.0000				
1970	5.50	2.70			112.0000	112.0000				
1971	6.30	2.20			112.0000	112.0000				
1972	7.50	2.10			119.1000	119.1000				
1973	8.00	3.20			142.2690	142.2690				
1974	11.80	4.60			143.5400	144.4000				
1975	13.00	4.60			131.4840	131.4970				
1976	11.70	3.20			122.4950	122.2410				
1977	17.70	6.30			111.0240	110.8930				
1978	22.30	5.10			114.5410	114.7780				
1979	26.20	6.90			111.7600	111.4260				
1980	30.10	6.90			114.2140	114.0920				
1981	35.10	6.30			114.1400	114.1400				
1982	41.20	4.30			100.8997	101.1425				
1983	41.70	6.60			90.1371	89.8909				
1984	46.60	10.40			87.9600	87.9600				
1985	58.90	7.80			69.9997	70.1367				
1986	60.82	8.71			66.7995	66.6049				
1987	68.46	8.80			70.2228	69.7457				
1988	70.69	9.50			78.9162	79.5745				
1989	68.34	11.63			78.7337	78.7810				
1990	78.99	14.46			78.1020	77.7020				
1991	76.82	17.99			77.0898	76.7370				
1992	84.29	17.40			74.2620	73.4164				
1993	84.93	23.43			72.2432	71.9736				
1994	91.21	18.37			75.9378	76.9754				
1995	98.03	18.44			78.7142	78.8349				
1996	91.81	13.57			81.2079	81.7550				

2. IMPORTS BY BROAD ECONOMIC CATEGORY AND EXPORTS BY INDUSTRIAL ORIGIN. (PERCENTAGE OF TOTAL VALUE)
IMPORTATIONS PAR CATEGORIES ECONOMIQUES ET EXPORTATIONS PAR BRANCHE D'ACTIVITE.(EN POURCENTAGE DE LA VALEUR TOTALE)

IMPORTS – IMPORTATIONS

	1990	1991	1992	1993	1994	1995	1996
TOTAL IMPORTS–IMPORTATIONS TOTALES	100.	100.	100.	100.	100.	100.	
1 FOOD BEV–ALIMENTATION BOISSONS	24.9	23.2	23.3	25.2	26.5	25.0	
11 PRIMARY–PRODUITS DE BASE	6.8	6.4	6.8	7.8	7.2	8.1	
111 FOR INDUSTRY–POUR L'INDUSTRIE	0.3	0.4	0.3	0.4	0.5	0.5	
112 FOR HOUSEHOLDS–POUR LES MENAGES	6.5	6.0	6.5	7.3	6.7	7.7	
12 PROCESSED–PRODUITS ELABORES	18.1	16.8	16.5	17.4	19.3	16.9	
121 FOR INDUSTRY–POUR L'INDUSTRIE	4.1	3.9	3.9	3.6	3.8	3.4	
122 FOR HOUSEHOLDS–POUR LES MENAGES	14.0	12.9	12.6	13.9	15.5	13.5	
2 IND SUPPLIES–APPROV INDUSTRIELS	26.3	25.6	31.5	30.4	33.4	30.2	
21 PRIMARY–PRODUITS DE BASE	3.1	2.8	3.0	3.5	3.9	2.8	
22 PROCESSED–PRODUITS ELABORES	23.1	22.8	28.5	26.9	29.4	27.4	
3 FUELS–COMBUSTIBLES	13.2	15.8	12.7	13.6	12.0	12.3	
31 PRIMARY–PRODUITS DE BASE	0.6	0.7	0.8	0.8	0.8	0.9	
32 PROCESSED–PRODUITS ELABORES	12.6	15.1	11.9	12.8	11.2	11.5	
321 MOTOR SPIRIT–ESSENCE	3.6	4.6	3.3	4.6	4.4	4.2	
322 OTHER–AUTRES	9.0	10.4	8.6	8.2	6.8	7.2	
4 MACHINERY–EQUIPEMENT	8.9	8.3	10.6	10.9	7.3	11.7	
41 CAPITAL EQUIPMENT–MACHINES	7.3	7.5	9.0	8.4	6.1	10.2	
42 PARTS–PIECES ACCESSOIRES	1.5	0.8	1.6	2.5	1.3	1.4	
5 TRANSPORT–TRANSPORT	7.7	9.4	7.4	6.9	6.9	6.6	
51 PASSENGER CARS–AUTOMOBILES	2.1	2.0	1.1	1.1	1.2	1.3	
52 OTHER–AUTRES	3.4	4.8	4.3	2.9	3.5	3.2	
521 INDUSTRIAL–INDUSTRIELS	3.3	4.8	4.1	2.8	3.4	3.1	
522 NON INDUSTRIAL–NON INDUSTRIEL	0.1	0.1	0.1	0.1	0.1	0.2	
53 PARTS–PIECES ACCESSOIRES	2.2	2.6	2.0	2.9	2.2	2.0	
6 CONSUM GOODS–BIENS CONSOMMATION	17.6	17.1	14.1	12.7	13.4	13.8	
61 DURABLE–DURABLES	3.4	2.5	2.7	2.4	3.1	3.2	
62 SEMI DURABLE–SEMI DURABLES	7.5	8.0	5.9	5.6	5.3	5.9	
63 NON DURABLE–NON DURABLES	6.7	6.5	5.5	4.7	5.0	4.6	
7 GOODS NES–BIENS NDA	1.4	0.6	0.4	0.3	0.4	0.3	

EXPORTS – EXPORTATIONS

	1990	1991	1992	1993	1994	1995	1996
TOTAL EXPORTS–EXPORTATIONS TOTALES	100.	100.	100.	100.	100.	100.	
1 AGRICULTURE	70.9	81.9	76.8	82.5	83.6	83.0	
2 MINING QUARRY–INDUS EXTRACTIVES			0.0	0.1	0.4	0.2	
3 MANUFACTURING–IND MANUFACTUR	29.1	18.1	23.1	17.4	16.0	16.7	
31 FOOD BEV TOBACCO–ALIM BOISS TAB	3.2	2.6	6.1	4.7	9.4	8.9	
32 TEXTILES–INDUSTRIES TEXTILES	16.1	9.5	10.4	5.4	1.9	1.3	
33 WOOD & PRODUCTS–BOIS & PRODUITS			0.0		0.1	0.0	
34 PAPER & PRODUCTS–PAPIER & PRODT		0.0	0.0	0.0	0.0	0.0	
35 CHEMICALS–INDUSTRIES CHIMIQUES		0.6	0.2	0.2	0.4	0.4	
36 NON METAL MIN–MIN NON METAL	0.4	0.0				0.0	
37 BASIC METAL–IND METAL BASE							
38 METAL MANUF–MANUF METAL	3.5	1.9	4.1	5.1	2.2	2.0	
39 OTH MANUF IND–AUTRES MANUF	5.9	3.5	2.2	1.9	2.0	4.1	

3. TRADE BY PRINCIPAL COUNTRIES OF ORIGIN AND DESTINATION (VALUE IN MILLION U.S. DOLLARS)
ECHANGES SELON LES PRINCIPAUX PAYS D'ORIGINE ET DE DESTINATION (VALEUR EN MILLIONS DE DOLLARS EU)

COUNTRIES–PAYS	GENERAL IMPORTS C.I.F. IMPORTATIONS GENERALES C.A.F				
	1992	1993	1994	1995	1996
World	62.6	61.6	69.1	77.1	74.6
Africa		0.0	0.0	0.0	
Americas	5.8	5.9	6.0	8.5	8.9
– Northern America	5.2	5.5	5.7	8.1	8.5
– LAIA	0.6	0.4	0.3	0.4	0.4
– CACM					
– Caribbean	0.0	0.0	0.0	0.0	
– Rest of America					
Asia excl fmr USSR	13.8	7.6	8.9	8.9	8.4
– Middle East		0.0	0.0	0.0	0.0
Asia former USSR					
Europe excl fmr USSR	1.7	2.2	0.8	2.8	1.7
– European Union	1.7	2.2	0.7	2.8	1.7
– Eastern Europe	0.0	0.0	0.0	0.0	
– Rest of Europe	0.0	0.0	0.0	0.0	0.0
Europe former USSR	0.0				
Oceania	41.2	45.9	53.4	56.5	55.5
Other				0.5	
New Zealand	18.7	24.2	30.9	29.1	28.0
Australia/Australie	14.9	13.9	16.9	21.5	22.1
USA/Etats–Unis d'Amer	5.2	5.5	5.7	8.0	8.5
Fiji/Fidji	7.5	7.3	5.3	5.8	5.3
Japan/Japon	7.8	4.3	4.6	4.3	5.1
China/Chine	3.3	0.7	1.1	1.1	0.9
United Kingdom	0.9	1.1	0.3	2.3	1.0
Singapore/Singapour	0.3	0.6	0.8	1.3	0.3
China, Hong Kong SAR	0.9	0.5	0.6	0.3	0.3
Other Asia n.e.s.	0.5	0.4	0.4	0.5	0.4
Chile/Chili	0.5	0.3	0.3	0.4	0.4
Germany/Allemagne	0.3	0.7	0.2	0.2	0.4
Indonesia/Indonésie	0.3	0.3	0.4	0.3	0.4
Thailand/Thaïlande	0.2	0.2	0.4	0.3	0.4
Korea, Republic of	0.3	0.3	0.3	0.3	0.2
Samoa	0.2	0.5	0.1	0.1	0.0
Malaysia/Malaisie	0.1	0.2	0.2	0.2	0.1
Italy/Italie	0.0	0.2	0.1	0.1	0.1
India/Inde	0.0	0.1	0.1	0.1	0.2
Areas n.e.s.				0.5	
Sweden/Suède	0.1	0.0	0.1	0.0	0.1
France, Monaco	0.2	0.0	0.0	0.1	0.0
Canada	0.0	0.0	0.0	0.1	0.0
Pakistan	0.1	0.0	0.0	0.0	0.0
Denmark/Danemark	0.0	0.0	0.0	0.0	0.0
Kiribati			0.0		
US Misc Pacific Islands		0.0			

COUNTRIES–PAYS	GENERAL EXPORTS F.O.B. EXPORTATIONS GENERALES F.O.B.				
	1992	1993	1994	1995	1996
Monde	12.8	16.9	14.0	14.7	12.3
Afrique			0.0	0.0	
Amériques	2.3	2.9	3.4	3.3	2.8
– Amérique du Nord	2.3	2.9	3.4	3.3	2.8
– ALAI					
– MCAC					
– Caraïbes					
– Autre Amérique					
Asie anc. URSS exclus	6.6	9.8	8.2	8.2	6.0
– Moyen–Orient					
Asie ancienne URSS					
Europe anc. URSS exclus	0.0	0.1	0.1	0.4	0.3
– Union Européenne	0.0	0.1	0.1	0.4	0.3
– Europe de l'Est					
– Autre de l'Europe	0.0				
Europe ancienne URSS					
Océanie	3.8	4.1	2.4	2.8	3.3
Autre					
Japan/Japon	6.5	9.4	7.1	7.0	5.6
USA/Etats–Unis d'Amer	2.3	2.9	3.3	3.3	2.7
New Zealand	1.4	2.0	0.8	1.3	1.9
Australia/Australie	1.4	1.2	0.6	0.7	0.7
Samoa	0.7	0.7	0.5	0.5	0.1
China, Hong Kong SAR	0.1	0.4	0.6	0.6	0.1
Fiji/Fidji	0.3	0.1	0.3	0.2	0.5
Singapore/Singapour		0.0	0.3	0.4	0.2
Other Asia n.e.s.	0.0	0.0	0.2	0.1	0.0
France, Monaco		0.1		0.2	0.0
Germany/Allemagne			0.0	0.0	0.2
United Kingdom	0.0	0.0	0.0	0.1	0.0
Denmark/Danemark				0.0	0.1
Korea, Republic of		0.0	0.0	0.0	0.0
Canada		0.0	0.0	0.0	0.0
Kiribati		0.0	0.0		
Italy/Italie	0.0				
India/Inde		0.0		0.0	
Malaysia/Malaisie		0.0			0.0
Sweden/Suède	0.0		0.0		

(VALUE AS PERCENTAGE OF WORLD TOTAL)(VALEURS EN POURCENTAGE DU TOTAL MONDIAL)

	1987	1988	1989	1990	1991	1992	1993	1994	1995	1996
Africa		0.0					0.0	0.0	0.0	
Americas	5.1	7.8	11.6	11.1	10.6	9.2	9.6	8.8	11.0	12.0
– Northern America	4.8	7.6	11.5	11.0	10.0	8.3	9.0	8.3	10.5	11.4
– LAIA	0.2	0.2	0.1	0.1	0.5	0.9	0.6	0.5	0.5	0.6
– CACM										
– Caribbean	0.0			0.0	0.0	0.0	0.0	0.0	0.0	
– Rest of America					0.1					
Asia excl fmr USSR	17.3	20.3	23.2	20.9	16.4	22.1	12.4	12.9	11.5	11.3
– Middle East					0.0		0.0	0.0	0.0	0.0
Asia former USSR										
Europe excl fmr USSR	6.5	2.2	2.7	1.9	2.2	2.8	3.5	1.1	3.6	2.3
– European Union	6.4	2.2	2.6	1.6	2.2	2.7	3.5	1.0	3.6	2.3
– Eastern Europe	0.0	0.0	0.0	0.3	0.0	0.0	0.0	0.0	0.0	
– Rest of Europe	0.1	0.0	0.0	0.0	0.0	0.0	0.0	0.1	0.0	0.0
Europe former USSR	0.0		0.1	0.0	0.0	0.0				
Oceania	71.1	69.7	62.4	66.0	70.8	65.9	74.5	77.2	73.2	74.4
Other									0.6	
New Zealand	35.9	30.2	30.5	32.5	29.6	29.9	39.3	44.8	37.7	37.5
Australia/Australie	25.7	28.6	22.3	21.7	25.5	23.8	22.6	24.5	27.9	29.7
USA/Etats–Unis d'Amer	4.8	7.6	11.5	11.0	9.9	8.3	8.9	8.2	10.4	11.4
Fiji/Fidji	8.7	10.2	9.2	11.4	15.5	11.9	11.8	7.7	7.6	7.1
Japan/Japon	8.8	7.6	7.2	6.5	9.0	12.5	6.9	6.7	5.6	6.9
China/Chine	1.6	2.9	1.3	1.5	1.8	5.2	1.1	1.7	1.4	1.2
United Kingdom	4.3	1.1	1.4	1.1	1.0	1.5	1.9	0.4	3.0	1.4
Singapore/Singapour	4.0	4.9	8.7	8.5	1.5	0.5	0.9	1.2	1.7	0.5
China, Hong Kong SAR	1.0	1.6	1.9	1.7	1.5	1.4	0.9	0.9	0.4	0.4
Other Asia n.e.s.	1.0	1.1	1.5	0.8	1.1	0.8	0.7	0.5	0.6	0.5

	1987	1988	1989	1990	1991	1992	1993	1994	1995	1996
Afrique								0.0	0.1	
Amériques	16.2	29.2	22.8	23.5	16.0	18.0	16.9	23.9	22.6	22.4
– Amérique du Nord	16.2	29.2	22.8	23.5	16.0	18.0	16.9	23.9	22.6	22.4
– ALAI										
– MCAC										
– Caraïbes										
– Autre Amérique										
Asie anc. URSS exclus	5.4	4.9	16.7	31.9	58.5	51.7	58.1	58.6	55.9	48.5
– Moyen–Orient			0.0							
Asie ancienne URSS										
Europe anc. URSS exclus	0.2	0.5	0.2	1.8	1.6	0.4	0.8	0.4	2.5	2.5
– Union Européenne	0.2	0.5	0.2	1.8	1.6	0.4	0.8	0.4	2.5	2.5
– Europe de l'Est				0.0						
– Autre de l'Europe						0.0				
Europe ancienne URSS										
Océanie	77.0	65.4	60.4	42.9	24.0	30.0	24.2	17.1	18.9	26.5
Autre	1.2	0.0								
Japan/Japon	1.6	4.4	16.4	31.9	58.0	51.2	55.9	50.8	47.9	45.6
USA/Etats–Unis d'Amer	14.7	29.0	22.7	23.5	16.0	18.0	16.9	23.7	22.6	22.3
New Zealand	40.1	33.0	31.9	21.0	8.6	10.9	12.0	6.0	8.8	15.5
Australia/Australie	26.2	18.2	21.9	16.0	8.9	11.2	7.1	4.4	4.8	6.1
Samoa	0.3	0.8	0.4	4.0	3.7	5.2	4.2	3.9	3.7	0.6
China, Hong Kong SAR	0.0	0.0	0.0	0.0	0.0	0.5	2.1	4.0	4.3	1.2
Fiji/Fidji	0.5	5.2	1.5	1.6	2.6	2.3	0.7	2.0	1.4	4.1
Singapore/Singapour			0.0				0.0	2.0	2.6	1.6
Other Asia n.e.s.	1.4	0.3	0.1		0.3	0.0	0.0	1.6	0.8	0.0
France, Monaco		0.0		1.7	1.4		0.5		1.6	0.2

4. General Imports C.I.F. by Commodities according to the S.I.T.C. (Rev. 2) in million U.S. Dollars
Importations Générales C.A.F. par Produits d'après la C.T.C.I. (Rév. 2) en millions de Dollars E.U.

SITC CTCI	COMMODITY	1993 QUANTITY QUANTITE	1993 VALUE VALEUR	1994 QUANTITY QUANTITE	1994 VALUE VALEUR	1995 QUANTITY QUANTITE	1995 VALUE VALEUR	1996 QUANTITY QUANTITE	1996 VALUE VALEUR	PRODUIT
	ALL COMMODITIES		61.6		69.1		77.1		74.6	TOUS PRODUITS
0	FOOD AND LIVE ANIMALS		14.2		17.1		17.6		19.7	ALIMENTS,ANIMAUX VIVANTS
01	MEAT AND PREPARATIONS		6.0		6.7		7.5			VIANDES ET PREPARATIONS
011	MEAT FRESH,CHILLD,FROZEN	W 4742	4.1	W 5181	4.1	W 5406	5.4			VIANDES FRAICHES,REF,CONGE
0111	BOVINE MEAT FRESH,FROZEN	W 192	0.3	W 138	0.3	W 430	0.8			VIANDES BOVIN FRAI,REF
0112	MUTTON ETC FRSH,CHLD,FRN	W 3376	2.8	W 3950	2.7	W 3581	3.2			VIANDE DE MOUTON
0114	POULTRY FRESH CHLLD,FRZN	W 1131	1.1	W 1039	1.2	W 1316	1.4			VOLAILLES MORTES
014	MEAT PREPD,PRSVD,NES ETC	W 648	1.9	W 804	2.6	W 701	2.0			CONSERVES DE VIANDES
0142	SAUSAGES INCLDING TINNED	W 49	0.1	W 106	0.2	W 257	0.4			SAUCISSES,SAUCISSONS
0149	OTH PREPARD,PRESRVD MEAT	W 599	1.9	W 697	2.4	W 444	1.6			AUTRES PREP DE VIANDES
02	DAIRY PRODCTS,BIRDS'EGGS		1.4		1.8		1.9			PRODUITS LAITIERS,OEUFS
022	MILK AND CREAM	W 625	0.8	W 766	1.0	W 766	1.0			LAIT ET CREME
0224	MILK,CREAM PRESERVED ETC	W 536	0.7	W 696	0.9	W 686	0.9			LAIT,CREME CONS,CONC
02241	WHEY	W 344	0.3	W 546	0.5	W 501	0.5			LACTOSERUM (PETIT LAIT)
02242	MILK DRY,1.5% FAT OR LES	W 192	0.4	W 150	0.5	W 184	0.5			LAIT POUDRE INF 1.5%
023	BUTTER	W 247	0.5	W 310	0.7	W 322	0.8			BEURRE
03	FISH AND PREPARATIONS		0.5		0.6		0.7			POISSONS ET PREPARATIONS
037	FISH ETC PREPD,PRSVD NES	W 273	0.4	W 399	0.5	W 471	0.6			POIS,CRUST,MOL PREPARES
0371	FISH PREPARD,PRESRVD NES	W 273	0.4	W 397	0.5	W 470	0.6			CONSERVES DE POISSONS
04	CEREALS AND PREPARATIONS		2.6		3.4		3.3			CEREALES ET PRODUITS
046	WHEAT ETC MEAL OR FLOUR	W 4387	1.6	W 5265	2.0	W 4576	1.9			SEMOULE FARINE,FROMENT
04601	FLOUR OF WHEAT OR MESLIN	W 4386	1.6	W 5264	2.0	W 4573	1.9			FARINE DE FROMENT
048	CEREAL ETC PREPARATIONS		1.0		1.3	W 625	1.3			PREPTNS A BASE CEREALES
0483	MACARONI,SPAGHETTI ETC	W 161	0.3	W 200	0.4	W 249	0.4			PATES ALMENTAIRES
0484	BAKERY PRODUCTS		0.3		0.4	W 149	0.4			PRODUITS DE BOULANGERIE
0488	OTH CEREAL PREPS,MALT EX	W 130	0.4	W 123	0.4	W 95	0.4			EXTRAITS DE MALT
05	VEGETABLES AND FRUIT		0.8		1.1		1.2			LEGUMES ET FRUITS
057	FRUIT,NUTS,FRESH,DRIED	W 148	0.2	W 234	0.3	W 216	0.3			FRUITS FRAIS OU SECS
058	FRUIT PRESERVED,PREPARED	W 281	0.4	W 408	0.6	W 403	0.6			CONSERVES DE FRUITS
0585	FRUIT OR VEGETABLE JUICE	W 178	0.2	W 294	0.4	W 308	0.4			JUS DE FRUITS
06	SUGAR AND PREPS,HONEY		1.1		1.2		1.3			SUCRES ET PRODUITS
061	SUGAR AND HONEY		0.7	W 2415	0.9	W 2263	0.9			SUCRES ET MIEL
0612	REFINED SUGAR ETC	W 2142	0.7	W 2396	0.9	W 2253	0.8			SUCRES RAFFINES
062	SUGAR CANDY NON–CHOCLATE	W 200	0.4	W 183	0.4	W 194	0.5			SUCRERIES
07	COFFEE,TEA,COCOA,SPICES		0.4		0.6		0.5			CAFE,THE,CACAO,EPICES
081	*FEEDING STUFF FOR ANIML		0.3		0.5		0.5			NOURRITURE POUR ANIMAUX
0819	FOOD WASTE AND FEED NES	W 571	0.2	W 672	0.3	W 807	0.4			DECHETS,ALIMENTS NDA
08193	BEET–PULP,BAGASSE,ETC	W 570	0.2	W 672	0.3	W 807	0.4			PULPES,AUTRES DECHETS
09	MISC EDIBLE PRODUCTS		1.5		1.5		1.3			PREP ALIMENTAIRES DIVERSES
091	MARGARINE AND SHORTENING	W 240	0.3	W 144	0.2	W 128	0.2			MARGARINE ET GRAISSES
0914	MARGARINE,EDIBLE FAT NES	W 237	0.3	W 143	0.2	W 128	0.2			MARGARINES,SIMILI SAINDOUX
098	EDIBLE PRODCTS,PREPS NES		1.2		1.4		1.1			PREP ALIMENTAIRES NDA
09806	YEASTS,BAKING POWDERS	W 94	0.2	W 103	0.3	W 107	0.3			LEVURES
09809	MISC FOOD PREPRTIONS NES		0.9		0.9		0.7			PREP ALIMENTAIRES NDA
1	BEVERAGES AND TOBACCO		2.8		3.1		3.6		3.8	BOISSONS ET TABACS
11	BEVERAGES		1.5		1.7		2.1			BOISSONS
111	NON–ALCOHL BEVERAGES NES	W 1156	0.8	W 1181	0.8	W 1854	1.2			BOISSONS NON ALCOOLIQUES
11101	WATERS,ICE AND SNOW	W 1098	0.8	W 1140	0.8	W 1752	1.2			EAU,EAUX MINERALES
112	ALCOHOLIC BEVERAGES	W 656	0.8	W 776	0.9	W 709	0.9			BOISSONS ALCOOLIQUES
1123	BEER,ALE,STOUT,PORTER	W 607	0.7	W 739	0.8	W 660	0.8			BIERES
12	TOBACCO AND MANUFACTURES		1.4		1.5		1.6			TABACS BRUTS FABRIQUES
122	TOBACCO,MANUFACTURED	W 99	1.4	W 97	1.5	W 102	1.6			TABACS FABRIQUES
1222	CIGARETTES	W 68	0.9	W 64	1.0	W 70	1.0			CIGARETTES
1223	OTH MANUFACTURED TOBACCO	W 30	0.5	W 34	0.6	W 32	0.6			TABACS FUMER,CHIQUER,PRISER
2	CRUDE MATERLS,EXCL FUELS		2.8		3.8		3.8		3.3	MAT BRUTES NON COMESTIBLES
24	CORK AND WOOD		1.5		2.0		2.2			LIEGE ET BOIS
248	WOOD SHAPED,SLEEPERS	W 3222	1.3	W 4401	1.9	W 4624	2.1			BOIS SIMPLEMENT TRAVAILLES
26	TEXTILE FIBRES AND WASTE		0.3		0.3		0.4			FIBRES TEXTILES
269	WASTE OF TEXTILE FABRICS	W 183	0.3	W 187	0.3	W 206	0.4			FRIPERIE DRILLES,CHIFFONS
26902	RAGS,WASTE CORDAGE ETC	W 183	0.3			W 206	0.4			DRILLES ET CHIFFONS
27	CRUDE FERTLZR,MINRLS NES		0.4		0.4		0.6			ENGRAIS MINERAUX BRUTS
278	OTHER CRUDE MINERALS	W 780	0.3		0.4		0.6			AUTRES MINERAUX BRUTS
2789	MINERALS CRUDE NES	W 525	0.3		0.3		0.5			MINERAUX BRUTS NDA
27896	NATURAL ASPHALT,BITUMEN	W 525	0.3	W 494	0.3	W 1222	0.5			BITUMES,ASPHALTES NATURELS
29	CRUDE ANIMAL,VEG MAT NES		0.7		1.1		0.8			MATIERES BRUTES ANIM,VEGET
292	CRUDE VEG MATERIALS NES		0.7		1.1		0.8			MAT BRUTES VEGETALES NDA
2925	SEEDS,ETC FOR PLANTING			W 118	1.1					SEMENCES NDA
2929	OTH CRUDE VEG MATERIALS		0.6				0.8			MATIERES VEGETALES NDA
29298	OTH CRD VEG MATERIAL NES		0.6			W 74	0.7			PRODUITS ORIGINE VEGET NDA
3	MINERAL FUELS ETC		8.4		8.4		9.6		9.4	COMBUSTIBLES MINERAUX LUB
33	PETROLEUM AND PRODUCTS		8.0		7.9		8.9			PETROLE ET DERIVES
334	PETROLEUM PRODUCTS,REFIN	W 1758776	7.9	W 29818	7.8		8.9			PRODUITS RAFFINES
3341	GASOLINE,OTH LIGHT OILS	W 13334	3.9	W 14479	3.9	W 14730	4.4			ESSENCES POUR MOTEURS
33411	MOTOR,AVIATION SPIRIT	W 9710	2.9	W 11367	3.1	W 10930	3.3			ESSENCES MOTEURS D'AVIONS
33412	SPIRIT TYPE JET FUEL	W 3624	1.1	W 3112	0.9	W 3800	1.1			CARBUREACTEURS
3343	GAS OILS	W 12338	3.3	W 15012	3.6	W 16327	4.2			GAS OILS
3344	FUEL OILS,NES	W 1732682	0.5							FUEL OILS
3345	LUBS,PETROLEUM OILS NES	W 421	0.4	W 326	0.4		0.5			HUILES LUBRIFIANTES
33451	LUBS(HIGH PETR CONT) ETC	W 414	0.4	W 321	0.3	W 426	0.5			HUILES LUBRIF,H LOURDES
341	*GAS,NATURAL AND MANUFCT	W 742	0.5	W 861	0.6	W 1042	0.7			GAZ NATUREL,GAZ MANUFACT
3413	PETROLM GASES,LIQUEFIED	W 742	0.5	W 861	0.6	W 1042	0.7			GAZ DE PETROLE LIQUEFIE
4	ANIMAL,VEGETABLE OIL,FAT		0.2		0.3		0.3		0.3	HUILES,GRAISSES ANIM,VEG
5	CHEMCLS,RELATED PROD NES		4.4		5.8		5.4		5.6	PRODUITS CHIMIQUES
53	DYES,TANNING,COLOUR PROD		0.4		0.5		0.5			PROD TEINTURE,COLORANTS
533	PIGMENTS,PAINTS,ETC		0.3		0.5		0.5			PIGMENTS,PEINTURES,VERNIS
5335	GLAZES,DRIERS,PUTTY ETC		0.3		0.3		0.5			PREPTNS COLOR UTILISES CERAM
53351	PREPRD PIGMENT,GLAZE ETC		0.3				0.5			PIGMENTS OPACIFIANTS
541	*MEDICINAL,PHARM PRODUCT		1.3		1.6		1.6			PROD MEDICINAUX PHARMACEUT
5419	PHARMACEUTICAL GOODS NES		1.3		1.6		1.6			PREP,ART PHARMACEUTIQUES
54199	OTH PHARMACEUTICAL GOODS		1.3				1.6			AUT PREP PHARMACEUTIQUES
55	PERFUME,CLEANING ETC PRD		1.3		1.5		1.4			PROD POUR PARFUM,TOILETTE
553	PERFUMERY,COSMETICS,ETC		0.5		0.5		0.5			PRODUITS DE PARFUMERIE
554	SOAP,CLEANSING ETC PREPS		0.9		1.0		1.0			SAVONS,PRODUITS DETERSIFS
5542	WASHING PREPARATIONS ETC	W 325	0.6	W 408	0.8	W 445	0.7			PROD ORG TENSIO–ACT NDA
562	*FERTILIZERS,MANUFACTURE	W 2685	0.7	W 3905	1.3	W 2266	0.9			ENGRAIS MANUFACTURES
5629	FERTILIZERS NES	W 2685	0.7	W 3905	1.3	W 2266	0.9			ENGRAIS NDA
58	PLASTIC MATERIALS ETC		0.3		0.3		0.3			MAT PLAST ARTIFICIELLES
585	PLASTIC MATERIAL NES		0.2		0.3	W 139	0.3			RESINES ARTIFICIELLES
5852	OTH ART PLASTIC MTLS NES		0.2			W 139	0.3			AUT MAT PLAST ARTIFICIEL
58529	OTH HIGH POLYMRS ETC,NES		0.2			W 139	0.3			AUT HAUTS POLYMERES
59	CHEMICAL MATERIALS NES		0.6		0.7		0.8			MAT PROD CHIMIQUES NDA

4. General Imports C.I.F. by Commodities according to the S.I.T.C. (Rev. 2) in million U.S. Dollars
Importations Générales C.A.F. par Produits d'après la C.T.C.I. (Rév. 2) en millions de Dollars E.U.

SITC CTCI	COMMODITY	1993 QUANTITY QUANTITE	1993 VALUE VALEUR	1994 QUANTITY QUANTITE	1994 VALUE VALEUR	1995 QUANTITY QUANTITE	1995 VALUE VALEUR	1996 QUANTITY QUANTITE	1996 VALUE VALEUR	PRODUIT
591	PESTICIDES,DISINFECTANTS				0.5					DESINF,INSECT,FONG,HERB
598	MISCEL CHEM PRODUCTS NES		0.4		0.1		0.7			PROD DIV INDUST CHIM NDA
5989	CHEM PRODUCTS,PREPS NES		0.4				0.6			PROD PREP CHIMIQUES NDA
59899	OTH CHEM PRODS,PREPS,NES		0.4				0.6			AUT PRODUITS CHIMIQUES NDA
6	BASIC MANUFACTURES		12.1		13.7		15.0		11.7	ART MANUFACTURES
61	LEATHER,DRESSED FUR,ETC		0.3		0.2		0.1			CUIRS,PELLETERIES
611	LEATHER		0.3		0.2		0.1			CUIRS,PEAUX PREPARES
6118	LEATHER SPECIALLY FINSHD		0.2				0.1			CUIRS,PEAUX TANNES
61181	CHAMOIS–DRESSED LEATHER		0.2				0.1			CUIRS,PEAUX CHAMOISES
62	RUBBER MANUFACTURES NES		0.4		0.4		0.5			CAOUTCHOUC MANUFACTURE
625	RUBBER TYRES, TUBES ETC	N 22918	0.3	N 18356	0.3	N 27402	0.4			PNEUS CAOUTCHOUC VULCANISE
63	WOOD,CORK MANUFACTRS NES		1.2		1.6		1.5			OUVRAGES LIEGE ET BOIS
634	VENEERS,PLYWOOD,ETC	V 1670	0.8	V 1600	0.9	V 1694	0.9			PLACAGES,CONTRE–PLAQUES
6341	VENEER SHEETS ETC			V 1600	0.9					BOIS SIMPLEMENT SCIES
6344	WOOD–BASED PANELS NES	V 1670	0.8			V 1694	0.9			PANNEAUX SUPPORT BOIS NDA
63443	CELLULAR WOOD PANELS	V 1670	0.8			V 1694	0.9			PANNEAUX CELLULAIRES
635	WOOD MANUFACTURES NES		0.4		0.8		0.6			ART MANUF EN BOIS NDA
6353	BUILDERS WOODWRK,PREFABS		0.2		0.5		0.1			OUVRAGES DE MENUISERIE
6354	WOOD MFRS DOMESTIC ETC		0.1		0.2		0.4			ART MANUF USAGE DOMESTIQUE
63549	WOOD MFRS,DOMESTIC NES		0.1				0.4			OUVRAGES DE TABLETTERIE
64	PAPER,PAPERBOARD AND MFR		2.4		2.9		2.6			PAPIERS,CARTONS & OUVRAGES
641	PAPER AND PAPERBOARD		0.4		0.4		0.5			PAPIERS ET CARTONS
6412	PRINTG,WRITING PAPER NES		0.3		0.2		0.4			PAPIERS POUR L'IMPRESSION
642	PAPER,ETC,PRECUT,ARTS OF		2.0		2.6		2.1			PAP,CARTONS DECOUPES
6421	PAPER ETC CONTAINERS		1.3		1.6		1.0			BOITES,SACS EMBALLAGES
6424	PAPER ETC CT TO SIZE NES				0.8					PAP,CARTONS DECOUPES
6428	PAPER ETC ARTICLES NES		0.8				1.2			OUVRAGES EN PATE A PAPIER
64282	PUNCHED CARD MACH CARDS		0.8				1.2			CARTES POUR MACHINES
65	TEXTILE YARN,FABRICS,ETC		1.0		1.0		1.1			FILS,TISSUS,ARTICLES TEXTILE
652	COTTON FABRICS,WOVEN	A 205	0.3	A 180	0.3	A 151	0.2			TISSUS DE COTON
6521	GREY WOVEN COTTON FABRIC			A 177	0.3					TISSUS COT ECRUS NON MERCER
6522	WOVEN COTTON BLEACHD,ETC	A 205	0.3	A 3	0.1	A 151	0.2			TISSUS COTON BLANCHIS ETC
65221	COTTON GAUZE BLEACHD,ETC	A 204	0.3			A 148	0.2			TISSUS COTON POINT DE GAZE
654	OTH WOVEN TEXTILE FABRIC		0.3		0.3	A 219	0.3			TISSUS AUT COTON SYNT,ARTIF
6549	WOVEN FABRICS NES		0.3	A 2	0.1	A 219	0.3			TISSUS NDA
65499	PILE,CHENILLE FABRIC NES		0.3			A 219	0.3			VELOURS NDA
659	FLOOR COVERINGS,ETC		0.2		0.2		0.4			COUVRE–PARQUETS,TAPIS ETC
6591	LINOLEUM ETC	A 37	0.2	A 40	0.2	A 41	0.3			LINO COUVRE–PARQUETS
66	NONMETAL MINERAL MFS NES		1.3		2.1		2.7			ART MIN NON METALLIQUES
661	LIME,CEMENT,BLDG PRODS		0.8		1.3		1.5			CHAUX,CIMENTS MAT CONSTR
6612	CEMENT	W 8471	0.8	W 9699	1.2	W 10094	1.4			CIMENTS HYDRAULIQUES
664	GLASS		0.3		0.3		0.5			VERRE
6649	GLASS NES		0.2				0.5			VERRE NDA
66494	GLASS FIBRE AND PROD NES		0.2				0.5			LAINE DE VERRE,FIBRES
666	POTTERY		0.1		0.2		0.3			POTERIE
6664	PORCELN,CHINA HOUSE WARE		0.1		0.2		0.3			VAISSELLE,ARTS MEN PORC
67	IRON AND STEEL		1.0		1.1		1.6			FER ET ACIER
672	IRON,STEEL PRIMARY FORMS	W 319	0.3	W 574	0.4	W 586	0.4			LINGOTS FER,ACIER
6724	IRN,STL INGOTS,LUMPS,ETC	W 319	0.3	W 574	0.4	W 586	0.4			FER,ACIER LINGOTS,MASSES
673	IRON,STEEL SHAPES ETC		0.4		0.4		0.6			BARRES,PROFIL FER,ACIER
678	IRON,STL TUBES,PIPES,ETC	W 561	0.5	W 465	0.4	W 768	0.7			TUBES,TUYAUX EN FONTE,FER
6785	IRON,STEEL TUBE FITTINGS	W 561	0.5	W 465	0.4	W 768	0.7			ACCESSOIRES DE TUYAUTERIE
69	METAL MANUFACTURES NES		4.7		4.6		5.0			ART MANUFACT EN METAL NDA
691	STRUCTURES AND PARTS NES	W 1457	1.9	W 1450	1.8	W 1250	1.9			CONSTRUCT FER,ACIER,ALU
6911	STRUCTURES,PARTS IRN,STL	W 539	0.9	W 794	1.1	W 497	1.1			CONSTRUCT FER,ACIER,FONTE
6912	STRUCTURES,PARTS ALUMNM	W 918	1.0	W 656	0.7	W 753	0.8			CONSTRUCT ALUMINIUM
692	METAL TANKS,BOXES,ETC		0.5		0.2		0.3			RECIPIENTS METALLIQUES
6924	MTL TRANSPORT BOXES ETC		0.4		0.1		0.2			FUTS,TAMBOURS,BIDONS
69241	STL TRANSPORT BOXES ETC		0.4		0.1		0.2			FUTS,TAMBOURS,BIDONS FER
693	WIRE PRODUCTS NON ELECTR		0.4		0.5		0.6			OUVRAGES FILS METALLIQUES
6932	IRON,STEEL FENCING WIRE	W 425	0.3	W 528	0.4	W 593	0.4			RONCES DE FER OU ACIER
694	STL,COPPR NAILS,NUTS,ETC		0.8		0.4		0.6			CLOUS,VIS,ECROUS
69401	IRON,STEEL NAILS ETC		0.5		0.3		0.4			CLOUS,POINTES FER,ACIER
69402	IRN,STL NUTS,BOLTS,ETC		0.4		0.1		0.3			BOULONS,VIS,ECROUS FER,AC
695	TOOLS		0.5		0.6		0.6			OUTILS A MAIN
6951	HAND TOOLS,AGRIC,FOREST		0.3		0.3		0.2			BECHES,PELLES,PIOCHES
6953	OTHER HAND TOOLS		0.2		0.4		0.5			AUTRES OUTILS A MAIN
697	BASE MTL HOUSEHOLD EQUIP		0.2		0.4		0.4			ART MENAGE MET COMMUNS
6978	BASE MTL HOUSE EQUIP NES		0.2		0.4		0.4			ART MENAGE MET COMMUNS
69782	BASE MTL DECOR ARTICLES		0.2		0.3		0.4			AUT OBJETS ORNEM INTERIEUR
699	BASE METAL MFRS NES		0.5		0.9		0.7			ART MANUFACTURES MET NDA
6998	MFRS NES OF CPR,NIKL,ETC		0.3		0.6		0.5			OUVRAGES EN CU,NI,AL,PB,ZN
69985	ZINC MANUFACTURES NES		0.2		0.5		0.4			OUVRAGES EN ZINC
7	MACHINES,TRANSPORT EQUIP		11.7		11.7		15.9		15.1	MACHINES MATERIEL TRANSPORT
71	POWER GENERATING EQUIPMT		0.4		0.3		0.2			MACHINES GENERATRICES
713	INTRNL COMBUS PSTN ENGIN		0.3		0.3	N 100	0.2			MOTEURS EXPL COMB INT, PIECE
72	MACHS FOR SPCL INDUSTRYS		0.5		0.7		0.5			MAC SPECIALES POUR INDUST
721	AGRIC MACHY,EXC TRACTORS		0.3		0.3		0.2			MACHINES AGRICOLES
722	TRACTORS NON–ROAD		0.3		0.4	N 42	0.3			TRACTEURS
74	GENRL INDUSTRL MACHY NES		1.9		1.1		1.4			MACH APP INDUSTRIE
741	HEATING,COOLING EQUIPMNT		0.3		0.3		0.2			MACH CHAUFFAGE,PIECES
743	PUMPS NES,CENTRFUGES ETC		0.2		0.3		0.4			POMPES COMPRES,VENT ETC
749	NONELEC MACH PTS,ACC NES		1.5		0.7		0.9			PIECES MACH NON ELEC NDA
7499	OTH NONELEC MCHY PTS NES		1.5		0.7		0.9			PIECES NON ELECT NDA
74999	MACH PARTS NONELEC NES		1.5				0.9			PIECES MACHINES NDA
75	OFFICE MACHNES,ADP EQUIP		0.6		0.8		0.9			MACH BUREAU TRAIT AUTOM
751	OFFICE MACHINES		0.6		0.8		0.9			MACH,APPAREILS DE BUREAU
7512	CALCULATNG,ACCTG,ETC MCH		0.5		0.7		0.9			MACHINE A CALCULER ETC
76	TELECOMM,SOUND EQUIPMENT		1.7		0.8		1.5			EQUIPMENT DE TELECOM
762	RADIO BROADCAST RECEIVRS		0.4		0.3		0.3			RECEPTEURS RADIODIFFUSION
764	TELECOM EQPT,PTS,ACC NES		1.4		0.6		1.1			EQUIP TELECOM,PIECES
77	ELECTRIC MACHNRY NES ETC		2.5		3.2		7.0			MACH APP ELECT NDA
772	SWITCHGEAR ETC,PARTS NES		0.6		0.7		3.7			APP COUPURE,SECT ETC
773	ELECTR DISTRIBUTNG EQUIP		0.5		0.7		1.0			EQUIPMT DISTRIBUTION ELECT
7732	ELECTRC INSULATING EQUIP		0.5		0.7		1.0			EQUIP ISOL ELECTRIQUE
774	ELECTRO–MEDCL,XRAY EQUIP	N 17	0.1	N 11	0.1	N 3	0.4			APPAREILS MEDICAUX
7741	ELECTRO–MEDICAL EQUIPMNT	N 17	0.1	N 11	0.1	N 3	0.4			APP ELECTRICITE MEDICALE
775	HOUSEHOLD TYPE EQUIP NES		0.5		0.7		1.1			MACH,APP USAGE DOMESTQUE
7752	DOM REFRIGERATRS,FREEZRS	N 978	0.3	N 1437	0.5	N 1406	0.6			REFRIG,CONGEL MENAGER
7757	DOMESTIC ELECTRC EQU NES		0.2		0.2		0.4			APP ELECTR DOMEST NDA
778	ELECTRICAL MACHINERY NES		1.1		1.2		1.1			AUTRES MACH ELECT NDA

4. General Imports C.I.F. by Commodities according to the S.I.T.C. (Rev. 2) in million U.S. Dollars
Importations Générales C.A.F. par Produits d'après la C.T.C.I. (Rév. 2) en millions de Dollars E.U.

SITC CTCI	COMMODITY	1993 QUANTITY QUANTITE	1993 VALUE VALEUR	1994 QUANTITY QUANTITE	1994 VALUE VALEUR	1995 QUANTITY QUANTITE	1995 VALUE VALEUR	1996 QUANTITY QUANTITE	1996 VALUE VALEUR	PRODUIT
7781	BATTERIES,ACCUMULATORS		0.4		0.5		0.4			PILES ET ACCUMULATEURS
77811	PRIMARY BATTERIES,CELLS		0.3		0.5		0.3			PILES ELECTRIQUES,PIECES
7782	ELECTRIC LAMPS,BULBS		0.2		0.5		0.5			LAMPES, TUBES ELECTRIQUES
7788	OTH ELEC MACHY,EQUIP NES		0.6		0.3		0.3			AUT MACH APP ELEC NDA
77886	OTH ELEC MACHINERY NES		0.5		0.3		0.2			AUT MACH APP ELECTRIQUES
78	ROAD VEHICLES		3.2		4.0		4.0			VEHICULES ROUTIERS
781	PASS MOTOR VEH EXC BUSES	N 390	0.7	N 494	0.9	N 593	1.1			AUTO TRANSPORT PERSONNES
782	LORRIES,SPCL MTR VEH NES	N 367	1.5	N 475	2.2	N 428	2.1			VEHICULES SPECIAUX,MARCH
7821	LORRIES,TRUCKS	N 56	0.3	N 213	1.1	N 67	0.3			VEHICULES TRANSP MARCHAND
7822	SPECIAL MOTOR VEHCLS NES	N 311	1.3	N 262	1.2	N 361	1.8			VEHICULES USAGES SPECIAUX
783	ROAD MOTOR VEHICLES NES	N 24	0.3	N 11	0.2	N 46	0.3			VEHICULES ROUTIERS NDA
784	MOTOR VEH PRTS,ACCES NES		0.7		0.7		0.4			PIECES 722,781,782,783
7849	OTHER MOTOR VEHCL PARTS		0.6		0.7		0.4			PIECES 722,781,782,783
79	OTHR TRANSPORT EQUIPMENT		1.1		1.1		0.8			AUTRE MATERIEL TRANSPORT
792	AIRCRAFT ETC		0.6		0.3		0.6			APP NAVIGATION AERIENNE
7928	AIRCRAFT NES,ASSOC EQUIP		0.6		0.3		0.6			APP NAVIG AERIENNE NDA
79282	BALLOONS AND AIRSHIPS		0.6		0.3		0.6			AEROSTATS
793	SHIPS AND BOATS ETC		0.6		0.8		0.3			NAVIRES BATEAUX,ETC
7933	VESSELS FOR BREAKING UP	N 53	0.5		0.5	N 47	0.1			BATEAUX A DEPECER
7938	TUGS,SPECIAL VESSELS ETC		0.2		0.3		0.2			REMORQUEURS,BATEAUX SPEC
8	MISC MANUFACTURED GOODS		5.2		5.3		5.9		5.8	ART MANUFACTURES DIVERS
812	*PLUMBG,HEATNG,LGHTNG EQ		0.4		0.4		0.4			APPAR SANITAIRES CHAUFFAGE
8122	CERAMIC PLUMBNG FIXTURES		0.2		0.2		0.3			EVIERS,LAVABOS,CUVETTES
821	*FURNITURE,PARTS THEREOF		0.6		0.8		1.2			MEUBLES ET PIECES
8212	MED FURN,STUFFD FURNSHGS		0.2				0.6			MOB MEDICO–CHIRUR,PIECES
82122	MATTRESSES ETC		0.2				0.6			SOMMIERS,ARTICLES DE LITERIE
8219	FURNITURE AND PARTS NES		0.3				0.5			AUTRES MEUBLES ET PIECES
84	CLOTHING AND ACCESSORIES		0.8		0.7		0.8			VETEMENTS
842	MENS OUTERWEAR NOT KNIT		0.3		0.2		0.2			VET DESSUS POUR HOMMES
848	HEADGEAR,NONTXTL CLOTHNG		0.4		0.4		0.5			VET ACCES MAT AUT QUE TEX
8482	PLASTC,RUBBR CLTHG,ACCES		0.4		0.4		0.5			VET ACCES MAT PLAS ARTIF
84822	RUBBER CLOTHING,ACCESRYS		0.4		0.4		0.5			VET ACCES CAOUT VULCAN
851	*FOOTWEAR	P 140755	0.4		0.4	P 171156	0.4			CHAUSSURES
87	PRECISION INSTRUMNTS NES		0.7		0.4		0.4			INSTRUM,APPAR SCIENT NDA
874	MEASURNG,CONTROLNG INSTR		0.7		0.3		0.2			INSTRUMENTS DE MESURE
88	PHOTO EQU,OPTICL GDS ETC		0.3		0.4		0.3			APP,FOURN PHOTO,OP,MONTR
881	PHOTO APPARAT,EQUIPT NES		0.1		0.3	N 326	0.2			APP,EQUIP PHOTO NDA
89	MISC MANUFCTRD GOODS NES		2.3		2.3		2.6			ART MANUFACTURES DIVERS
892	PRINTED MATTER		0.4		0.4		0.5			IMPRIMES
8921	PRINTED BOOKS,GLOBES,ETC		0.4		0.3		0.4			LIVRES,BROCHURES,CARTES
893	ARTICLES OF PLASTIC NES		0.7		0.8		0.9			OUVRAGES EN MAT DIVIS 58
894	TOYS,SPORTING GOODS,ETC		0.4		0.4		0.4			VOITURES ENFANTS,JOUETS
8947	OTH SPORT GDS,FAIR AMUSM		0.2		0.3		0.3			AUT ART DE SPORT
895	OFFICE SUPPLIES NES		0.6		0.6		0.5			ART PAPET NDA
8951	BASE MTL OFFICE SUPPLIES		0.2		0.1		0.2			MAT BUREAU METAUX COMMUNS
8959	OTHER OFFICE SUPPLIES		0.3		0.4		0.3			AUT ART DE PAPETERIE
89592	SLATES FOR WRITING		0.3		0.4		0.3			ARDOISES
899	OTHER MANUFACTURED GOODS		0.3		0.3		0.4			AUT ART MANUF DIVERS NDA
9	GOODS NOT CLASSD BY KIND		0.2		0.3		0.3		0.2	ART TRANSACT NON CLASSES
931	*SPECIAL TRANSACTIONS		0.2		0.3		0.3			TRANS.SPECIALES

5. General Exports F.O.B. by Commodities according to the S.I.T.C. (Rev. 2) in million U.S. Dollars
Exportations Générales F.O.B. par Produits d'après la C.T.C.I. (Rév. 2) en millions de Dollars E.U.

SITC CTCI	COMMODITY	1993		1994		1995		1996		PRODUIT
		QUANTITY QUANTITE	VALUE VALEUR	QUANTITY QUANTITE	VALUE VALEUR	QUANTITY QUANTITE	VALUE VALEUR	QUANTITY QUANTITE	VALUE VALEUR	
	ALL COMMODITIES		16.9		14.1		14.7		12.3	TOUS PRODUITS
0	FOOD AND LIVE ANIMALS		14.6		12.6		13.2		9.8	ALIMENTS,ANIMAUX VIVANTS
03	FISH AND PREPARATIONS		2.5		3.1		3.5			POISSONS ET PREPARATIONS
034	FISH,FRESH,CHILLED,FROZN	W 391	1.8	W 384	1.7	W 432	2.1			POISSON FRAIS, REFRIG,CONG
036	SHELL FISH FRESH,FROZEN			W 17	0.1	W 13	0.1			CRUSTACES,MOLLUSQUES
037	FISH ETC PREPD,PRSVD NES	W 58	0.7	W 107	1.4	W 151	1.3			POIS,CRUST,MOL PREPARES
0371	FISH PREPARD,PRESRVD NES		0.1	W 1	0.1	W 4	0.1			CONSERVES DE POISSONS
0372	SHELL FISH PREPRD,PRESVD	W 57	0.7	W 106	1.4	W 148	1.3			CRUSTACES,COQUIL PREPARES
05	VEGETABLES AND FRUIT		10.2		7.5		7.5			LEGUMES ET FRUITS
054	VEG ETC FRSH,SMPLY PRSVD	W 19900	10.0	W 18489	7.4	W 10116	7.4			LEGUMES FRAIS,CONG,SECS
0545	OTHER FRESH VEGETABLES			W 17266	6.9					AUTRES LEGUMES FRAIS,REF
05451	ALLIACEOUS VEGTBLS,FRESH			W 17266	6.9					OIGNONS,ECHALOTES,AULX
0548	EDIBLE VEG NES FRESH,DRY	W 19900	10.0	W 1223	0.6	W 10116	7.4			RACINES,TUBERCULES
05488	VEG PRODTS NES FRESH,DRY	W 19900	10.0			W 10115	7.4			PROD VEGET ALIM HUMAINE
057	FRUIT,NUTS,FRESH,DRIED		0.2	W 443	0.1	W 588	0.2			FRUITS FRAIS OU SECS
0577	NUTS EDIBLE,FRESH,DRIED	W 856	0.2	W 401	0.1	W 438	0.1			FRUITS A COQUES
05771	COCONUTS FRESH OR DRIED	W 856	0.2	W 401	0.1	W 438	0.1			NOIX DE COCO
0579	FRUIT FRESH OR DRIED NES	W 48	0.1	W 42	0.1	W 149	0.1			FRUITS FRAIS,SECS NDA
05798	OTHER FRESH FRUIT	W 48	0.1	W 21	0.1	W 149	0.1			AUTRES FRUITS FRAIS
07	COFFEE,TEA,COCOA,SPICES		2.0		2.1		2.3			CAFE,THE,CACAO,EPICES
075	SPICES	W 36	2.0	W 37	2.1	W 52	2.3			EPICES
0752	SPICES,EX PEPPER,PIMENTO	W 36	2.0	W 37	2.1	W 52	2.3			AUTRES EPICES
07521	VANILLA	W 36	2.0			W 52	2.3			VANILLE
1	BEVERAGES AND TOBACCO						0.1		0.2	BOISSONS ET TABACS
2	CRUDE MATERLS,EXCL FUELS		0.1		0.6		0.4		0.8	MAT BRUTES NON COMESTIBLES
27	CRUDE FERTLZR,MINRLS NES		0.1		0.1		0.1			ENGRAIS MINERAUX BRUTS
277	NATURAL ABRASIVES NES		0.1		0.1		0.1			ABRASIFS NATURELS NDA
2772	OTHER NATURAL ABRASIVES		0.1		0.1		0.1			AUTR ABRASIFS NATURELS NDA
29	CRUDE ANIMAL,VEG MAT NES		0.1		0.6		0.4			MATIERES BRUTES ANIM,VEGET
292	CRUDE VEG MATERIALS NES	W 53	0.1		0.6	W 96	0.4			MAT BRUTES VEGETALES NDA
2924	VEG USED IN PHARMACY ETC			W 235	0.6					PLANTES MEDICINALES
2926	LIVE PLANTS,BULBS,ETC	W 53	0.1			W 96	0.4			BULBES,TUBERCULES
29269	LIVE PLANTS NES	W 53	0.1			W 96	0.4			AUTRES PLANTES VIVANTES
4	ANIMAL,VEGETABLE OIL,FAT		0.1							HUILES,GRAISSES ANIM,VEG
42	FIXED VEGETABLE OIL,FAT		0.1							HUILES VEGETALES FIXES
424	FIXED VEG OIL NONSOFT	V 320	0.1							AUTRES HUILES VEG FIXES
4243	COCONUT (COPRA) OIL	V 320	0.1							HJUILE DE COPRAH
5	CHEMCLS,RELATED PROD NES		0.1		0.1		0.1		0.1	PRODUITS CHIMIQUES
53	DYES,TANNING,COLOUR PROD		0.1		0.1		0.1			PROD TEINTURE,COLORANTS
533	PIGMENTS,PAINTS,ETC		0.1		0.1		0.1			PIGMENTS,PEINTURES,VERNIS
5335	GLAZES,DRIERS,PUTTY ETC		0.1		0.1		0.1			PREPTNS COLOR UTILISES CERAM
53351	PREPRD PIGMENT,GLAZE ETC		0.1				0.1			PIGMENTS OPACIFIANTS
6	BASIC MANUFACTURES		0.6		0.4		0.3		0.3	ART MANUFACTURES
61	LEATHER,DRESSED FUR,ETC		0.5		0.3		0.2			CUIRS,PELLETERIES
612	LEATHER ETC MANUFACTURES		0.5		0.3		0.2			OUVRAGES EN CUIRS NDA
6121	LEATHER BELTING ETC		0.4		0.3		0.2			ARTICLES EN CUIR ETC
6122	HARNESS–MAKERS GOODS	N 9906	0.1							ART SELLERIE,BOURRELLERIE
6129	LEATHER MANUFACTURES NES		0.1		0.1		0.1			AUT OUV CUIR NAT,ARTIF
69	METAL MANUFACTURES NES		0.1		0.1		0.1			ART MANUFACT EN METAL NDA
7	MACHINES,TRANSPORT EQUIP		0.8		0.3		0.3		0.6	MACHINES MATERIEL TRANSPORT
71	POWER GENERATING EQUIPMT		0.5		0.1		0.1			MACHINES GENERATRICES
711	STEAM BOILERS & AUX PLNT		0.5		0.1		0.1			GENERATEURS VAPEUR EAU ETC
7111	STEAM BOILERS ETC		0.5		0.1		0.1			GENERATEURS VAPEUR EAU
716	ROTATING ELECTRIC PLANT		0.1		0.1		0.1			APP ELECTR ROTATIFS,PIECES
78	ROAD VEHICLES		0.1		0.1		0.2			VEHICULES ROUTIERS
781	PASS MOTOR VEH EXC BUSES	N 3	0.1	N 6	0.1	N 13	0.2			AUTO TRANSPORT PERSONNES
79	OTHR TRANSPORT EQUIPMENT		0.3		0.2		0.1			AUTRE MATERIEL TRANSPORT
792	AIRCRAFT ETC		0.1		0.1		0.1			APP NAVIGATION AERIENNE
7928	AIRCRAFT NES,ASSOC EQUIP		0.1		0.1		0.1			APP NAVIG AERIENNE NDA
79282	BALLOONS AND AIRSHIPS		0.1		0.1		0.1			AEROSTATS
793	SHIPS AND BOATS ETC		0.2	N 8	0.1	N 2	0.1			NAVIRES BATEAUX,ETC
7932	SHIPS AND BOATS NES		0.2	N 8	0.1	N 2	0.1			NAVIRES ET BATEAUX
8	MISC MANUFACTURED GOODS		0.6		0.2		0.4		0.6	ART MANUFACTURES DIVERS
84	CLOTHING AND ACCESSORIES		0.5				0.1			VETEMENTS
842	MENS OUTERWEAR NOT KNIT		0.2							VET DESSUS POUR HOMMES
847	TEXTILE CLTHNG ACCES NES		0.3				0.1			ACCES VET MAT TEXT NDA
8471	— NOT KNITTED		0.3							ACCES VET MAT TEX NON BON
8472	CLTHNG ACCESRYS ETC KNIT		0.1				0.1			ACCES VET BONNE NDA
89	MISC MANUFCTRD GOODS NES		0.1		0.2		0.4			ART MANUFACTURES DIVERS
899	OTHER MANUFACTURED GOODS		0.1		0.2		0.4			AUT ART MANUF DIVERS NDA
8991	CARVED,MOULDED GOODS		0.1		0.1		0.2			MAT A TAILLER,A MOULER
8997	BASKETWORK,BROOMS ETC		0.1		0.1		0.2			OUVRAGES VANNERIE NDA
89971	BASKETWORK,WICKERWRK,ETC		0.1			N 1325	0.1			OUVRAGES DE VANNERIE
8999	OTHER MANUF GOODS NES		0.1		0.1		0.1			OUVRAGES DIVERS NDA
9	GOODS NOT CLASSD BY KIND		0.3		0.2		0.3		0.3	ART TRANSACT NON CLASSES
931	*SPECIAL TRANSACTIONS		0.3		0.2		0.3			TRANS.SPECIALES

1. HISTORICAL SERIES, 1962–1997 SPECIAL TRADE, IMPORTS C.I.F., EXPORTS F.O.B.
SERIES HISTORIQUES, 1962–1997 COMMERCE SPECIAL, IMPORTATIONS C.A.F., EXPORTATIONS F.O.B

YEAR ANNEE	VALUE IN MILLION T.T. DOLLARS VALEUR EN MILLION T.T. DOLLARS MERCHANDISE –MARCHANDISE IMPORTS	EXPORTS	GOLD –OR IMPORTS	EXPORTS	CONVERSION FACTORS U.S. CENTS PER T.T. DOLLAR FACTEURS DE CONVERSION CENTS E.U. PAR T.T. DOLLAR IMPORTS	EXPORTS	INDEX NUMBERS –INDICES QUANTUM IMPORTS	EXPORTS	UNIT VALUE VALEUR UNITAIRE IMPORTS	EXPORTS
1962	605.60	592.00			58.3300	58.3300				
1963	646.40	640.70			58.3300	58.3300				
1964	730.60	699.00			58.3300	58.3300				
1965	817.00	690.50			58.3300	58.3300				
1966	777.70	735.10			58.3300	58.3300				
1967	723.90	763.40			57.5600	57.6200				
1968	854.50	943.30			50.0000	50.0000				
1969	966.40	947.70			50.0000	50.0000				
1970	1084.90	960.60			50.0000	50.0000				
1971	1326.70	1038.70			50.0000	50.0000				
1972	1467.60	1068.40			52.2057	52.2335				
1973	1536.30	1368.30			50.6524	50.6026				
1974	3777.60	4165.90			48.9015	48.9279				
1975	3243.90	3878.50			45.3567	45.2311				
1976	4826.90	5393.50			40.9433	41.0367				
1977	4340.40	5231.50			41.6670	41.6670				
1978	4752.00	4902.00			41.6670	41.6670				
1979	5067.00	6265.00			41.6670	41.6670				
1980	7664.90	9804.10			41.6670	41.6670	106	86	30	66
1981	7462.00	9033.50			41.6670	41.6670	99	76	34	73
1982	8878.40	7372.40			41.6670	41.6670	97	78	39	70
1983	6190.90	5632.10			41.6668	41.6668	110	76	39	69
1984	4605.90	5216.20			41.6667	41.6667	124	88	39	69
1985	3731.00	5236.00			41.0083	40.7656	109	93	39	65
1986	4860.20	4988.60			27.7780	27.7780	112	91	52	64
1987	4387.50	5264.60			27.7780	27.7780	88	90	60	67
1988	4310.30	5424.20			26.1589	26.0473	87	95	86	66
1989	5190.40	6706.90			23.5290	23.5290	106	94	99	84
1990	4712.30	8330.70			23.5290	23.5290	100	100	100	100
1991	5993.90	7541.80			23.5290	23.5290				
1992	4963.50	7188.30			23.5294	23.5294				
1993	7495.30	8800.90			19.5173	18.8856				
1994	6700.90	11055.20			16.8689	16.8830				
1995	10191.10	14608.60			16.8153	16.8092				
1996	12866.80	15014.40			16.6649	16.6511				
1997	18705.90	15887.60			15.9884	16.0054				

2. IMPORTS BY BROAD ECONOMIC CATEGORY AND EXPORTS BY INDUSTRIAL ORIGIN. (PERCENTAGE OF TOTAL VALUE)
IMPORTATIONS PAR CATEGORIES ECONOMIQUES ET EXPORTATIONS PAR BRANCHE D'ACTIVITE.(EN POURCENTAGE DE LA VALEUR TOTALE)

IMPORTS – IMPORTATIONS

	1990	1991	1992	1993	1994	1995	1996
TOTAL IMPORTS–IMPORTATIONS TOTALES	100.	100.	100.	100.	100.	100.	100.
1 FOOD BEV–ALIMENTATION BOISSONS	16.3	13.3	15.1	13.4	13.9	11.3	11.8
11 PRIMARY–PRODUITS DE BASE	8.5	6.4	7.2	6.4	7.3	5.3	4.8
111 FOR INDUSTRY–POUR L'INDUSTRIE	4.6	3.2	3.7	3.6	4.5	3.4	2.8
112 FOR HOUSEHOLDS–POUR LES MENAGES	3.9	3.2	3.5	2.9	2.8	1.9	2.0
12 PROCESSED–PRODUITS ELABORES	7.9	6.9	7.9	7.0	6.6	6.0	7.0
121 FOR INDUSTRY–POUR L'INDUSTRIE	1.3	1.4	1.3	1.0	1.1	1.1	1.6
122 FOR HOUSEHOLDS–POUR LES MENAGES	6.6	5.6	6.6	6.0	5.5	4.9	5.4
2 IND SUPPLIES–APPROV INDUSTRIELS	36.8	33.9	34.4	27.8	24.8	22.5	28.7
21 PRIMARY–PRODUITS DE BASE	6.1	4.4	4.7	2.8	6.5	5.3	4.5
22 PROCESSED–PRODUITS ELABORES	30.6	29.6	29.7	25.0	18.3	17.2	24.3
3 FUELS–COMBUSTIBLES	11.3	14.6	9.0	15.9	0.6	0.5	19.1
31 PRIMARY–PRODUITS DE BASE	9.5	13.1	8.2	15.5	0.0	0.0	18.4
32 PROCESSED–PRODUITS ELABORES	1.8	1.5	0.8	0.4	0.5	0.4	0.7
321 MOTOR SPIRIT–ESSENCE		0.0	0.0	0.0	0.0	0.0	0.0
322 OTHER–AUTRES	1.8	1.5	0.8	0.4	0.5	0.4	0.7
4 MACHINERY–EQUIPEMENT	20.6	19.4	22.2	27.3	20.1	27.1	21.4
41 CAPITAL EQUIPMENT–MACHINES	16.6	15.6	18.6	24.2	18.4	25.6	18.3
42 PARTS–PIECES ACCESSOIRES	4.0	3.7	3.7	3.1	1.6	1.5	3.1
5 TRANSPORT–TRANSPORT	4.1	8.5	8.0	6.6	6.6	6.4	10.2
51 PASSENGER CARS–AUTOMOBILES	0.7	2.5	3.2	2.0	2.3	2.5	3.2
52 OTHER–AUTRES	0.8	2.3	1.8	2.1	1.6	1.7	4.4
521 INDUSTRIAL–INDUSTRIELS	0.7	2.2	1.7	2.0	1.5	1.6	4.3
522 NON INDUSTRIAL–NON INDUSTRIEL	0.0	0.1	0.0	0.1	0.0	0.1	0.0
53 PARTS–PIECES ACCESSOIRES	2.6	3.7	3.1	2.6	2.8	2.2	2.6
6 CONSUM GOODS–BIENS CONSOMMATION	10.4	9.5	10.4	8.6	10.1	9.8	8.2
61 DURABLE–DURABLES	1.5	2.0	2.5	1.9	1.9	2.2	2.0
62 SEMI DURABLE–SEMI DURABLES	3.7	3.4	3.1	2.9	3.6	3.4	3.1
63 NON DURABLE–NON DURABLES	5.2	4.1	4.8	3.8	4.5	4.2	3.1
7 GOODS NES–BIENS NDA	0.5	0.7	0.8	0.4	23.9	22.6	0.5

EXPORTS – EXPORTATIONS

	1990	1991	1992	1993	1994	1995	1996
TOTAL EXPORTS–EXPORTATIONS TOTALES	100.	100.	100.	100.	100.	100.	100.
1 AGRICULTURE	0.6	0.5	0.6	1.0	0.8	0.7	0.9
2 MINING QUARRY–INDUS EXTRACTIVES	37.0	31.7	25.9	24.0	19.8	18.4	19.2
3 MANUFACTURING–IND MANUFACTUR	62.4	67.7	73.5	75.0	79.4	80.9	79.8
31 FOOD BEV TOBACCO–ALIM BOISS TAB	5.0	5.4	5.7	6.9	6.1	6.5	7.3
32 TEXTILES–INDUSTRIES TEXTILES	0.5	0.5	0.6	0.9	0.8	0.8	0.8
33 WOOD & PRODUCTS–BOIS & PRODUITS	0.2	0.2	0.2	0.3	0.3	0.4	0.4
34 PAPER & PRODUCTS–PAPIER & PRODT	0.7	0.9	1.2	1.7	1.4	1.4	1.7
35 CHEMICALS–INDUSTRIES CHIMIQUES	45.1	50.8	54.0	51.0	46.1	45.7	54.4
36 NON METAL MIN–MIN NON METAL	1.0	1.2	1.4	1.7	1.5	1.3	1.3
37 BASIC METAL–IND METAL BASE	6.9	6.5	7.9	8.6	1.5	2.3	8.5
38 METAL MANUF–MANUF METAL	2.8	2.0	2.3	3.8	2.4	3.4	5.2
39 OTH MANUF IND–AUTRES MANUF	0.2	0.3	0.2	0.2	19.3	19.2	0.1

3. TRADE BY PRINCIPAL COUNTRIES OF ORIGIN AND DESTINATION (VALUE IN MILLION U.S. DOLLARS)
ECHANGES SELON LES PRINCIPAUX PAYS D'ORIGINE ET DE DESTINATION (VALEUR EN MILLIONS DE DOLLARS EU)

COUNTRIES–PAYS	SPECIAL IMPORTS C.I.F. IMPORTATIONS SPECIALES C.A.F				
	1992	1993	1994	1995	1996
World	1435.6	1462.9	1133.7	1723.7	2204.5
Africa	2.2	0.7	2.0	7.2	17.8
Americas	984.8	1013.3	787.4	1178.5	1555.1
– Northern America	678.8	650.9	612.7	960.3	919.8
– LAIA	211.6	292.8	113.4	146.6	534.8
– CACM	4.8	5.2	5.9	8.4	8.1
– Caribbean	73.0	50.1	45.3	48.7	50.7
– Rest of America	16.6	14.2	10.1	14.4	41.6
Asia excl fmr USSR	167.5	126.5	127.4	159.1	206.1
– Middle East	2.2	1.9	2.5	4.3	2.5
Asia former USSR					
Europe excl fmr USSR	260.3	303.5	199.7	358.3	406.4
– European Union	238.1	292.5	183.5	330.0	378.6
– Eastern Europe	4.4	1.3	3.5	7.6	11.5
– Rest of Europe	17.8	9.7	12.7	20.7	16.4
Europe former USSR	0.1	0.2	0.3	1.5	0.8
Oceania	18.6	16.0	14.2	13.0	15.6
Other	2.2	2.7	2.8	6.0	2.7
USA/Etats–Unis d'Amer	605.0	578.6	547.4	872.1	840.1
Venezuela	139.1	246.3	32.9	49.9	268.3
United Kingdom	112.2	118.7	94.2	124.7	131.8
Canada	73.8	72.3	65.3	88.2	79.7
Germany/Allemagne	37.1	96.3	23.5	101.6	110.4
Japan/Japon	96.7	56.1	52.2	55.7	89.0
Brazil/Brésil	49.5	32.1	59.7	70.0	73.3
Colombia/Colombie	4.5	3.9	3.1	6.7	153.9
Netherlands/Pays–Bas	20.6	16.1	15.5	24.4	41.4
Korea, Republic of	15.4	15.7	16.9	33.3	35.3
Jamaica/Jamaïque	31.0	20.7	20.8	20.4	19.3
China/Chine	14.8	15.8	17.8	22.4	32.0
Barbados/Barbade	20.5	19.1	17.8	15.7	16.8
France, Monaco	17.1	20.3	10.6	15.8	20.7
Other Asia n.e.s.	17.9	15.9	12.9	14.3	16.8
Ireland/Irlande	14.3	13.8	10.2	11.1	16.2
Italy/Italie	11.8	7.7	8.5	17.1	18.1
Switzerland,Liechtenst.	15.2	7.0	11.2	14.1	11.7
Mexico/Mexique	6.7	5.0	9.3	14.5	20.0
New Zealand	11.4	10.0	9.3	7.7	11.6
Guyana	7.0	6.7	7.1	10.0	12.5
Belgium–Luxembourg	7.5	6.5	6.0	8.9	8.7
Suriname/Surinam	4.0	4.3	0.2	0.1	25.2
Spain/Espagne	3.4	2.8	3.2	7.4	11.8
Argentina/Argentine	8.6	3.4	4.3	3.3	7.3
Australia/Australie	6.3	6.0	4.9	5.3	4.0
China, Hong Kong SAR	5.1	4.7	4.9	5.0	5.1
India/Inde	3.0	3.6	3.9	6.3	7.2
Sweden/Suède	3.7	2.2	3.1	7.9	6.4
Denmark/Danemark	4.5	3.4	2.5	4.2	4.9
Austria/Autriche	4.1	2.5	3.6	4.0	4.4
Norway,Svalbard and JM	2.4	2.6	1.5	6.3	4.6
Netherlands Antilles	6.3	1.8	1.1	3.1	3.9
Malaysia/Malaisie	2.4	3.0	2.6	3.9	3.8
Singapore/Singapour	4.9	3.3	1.9	2.7	2.7
Thailand/Thaïlande	1.4	1.3	4.4	4.0	4.3
Areas n.e.s.	2.2	2.7	2.8	6.0	1.0
Belize/Bélize	5.2	2.1	1.9	2.1	2.7
Indonesia/Indonésie	2.5	2.3	2.5	2.4	3.2
Nigeria/Nigéria	0.3	0.0	0.0	0.0	12.5

COUNTRIES–PAYS	EXPORTS EXPORTATIONS ES F.O.B.				
	1992	1993	1994	1995	1996
Monde	1868.9	1662.1	1954.3	2467.0	2569.3
Afrique	33.0	28.8	17.2	15.4	8.6
Amériques	1646.7	1471.9	1709.3	2122.0	2278.0
– Amérique du Nord	942.7	826.1	983.6	1110.1	1311.5
– ALAI	127.5	87.1	167.7	212.5	190.6
– MCAC	18.9	18.3	18.1	18.4	20.1
– Caraïbes	408.2	387.8	381.1	586.8	585.8
– Autre Amérique	149.4	152.7	158.8	194.3	170.0
Asie anc. URSS exclus	43.0	52.0	52.8	42.6	10.1
– Moyen–Orient	0.1	0.3	24.2	24.9	0.5
Asie ancienne URSS					
Europe anc. URSS exclus	110.3	84.5	156.0	261.7	247.6
– Union Européenne	109.3	80.5	150.4	249.9	247.1
– Europe de l'Est	0.0	0.0	0.0	0.3	0.2
– Autre de l'Europe	1.0	4.0	5.6	11.5	0.4
Europe ancienne URSS	0.1	0.3	0.0	0.0	0.1
Océanie	5.3	2.5	0.6	1.7	1.4
Autre	30.5	22.2	18.4	23.6	23.5
USA/Etats–Unis d'Amer	908.2	792.3	907.1	1058.5	1254.0
Jamaica/Jamaïque	30.9	71.8	119.3	207.9	220.7
Barbados/Barbade	64.1	72.8	70.5	85.4	89.6
Guyana	42.3	59.7	59.8	80.6	90.2
France, Monaco	34.8	25.0	54.3	70.6	136.2
Netherlands Antilles	120.7	53.0	29.1	38.2	33.9
Canada	34.5	33.7	74.4	46.5	57.5
Suriname/Surinam	41.7	37.0	37.6	49.6	68.9
United Kingdom	32.0	33.6	36.6	61.6	48.0
Colombia/Colombie	33.7	31.2	52.7	58.7	33.8
Dominican Republic	33.8	31.1	23.3	55.0	46.0
French Guiana	48.2	38.4	37.9	47.0	
Saint Lucia/Ste–Lucie	29.6	30.9	33.0	35.9	40.8
Mexico/Mexique	26.3	19.0	29.8	44.7	39.5
Venezuela	31.5	14.3	32.2	30.0	48.6
Grenada/Grenade	21.2	28.9	25.1	31.7	36.1
Bunkers, ship stores	29.5	22.0	18.3	23.6	23.5
Brazil/Brésil	19.0	2.7	16.1	38.6	24.8
Netherlands/Pays–Bas	9.9	1.5	28.8	42.2	18.3
Antigua and Barbuda	15.5	14.7	21.3	17.4	16.2
Cuba	12.0	8.9	6.7	20.4	26.3
Saint Kitts and Nevis	14.3	15.5	10.7	14.3	15.3
Chile/Chili	6.4	8.6	17.0	18.2	17.2
Panama	12.9	13.8	19.4	12.4	7.2
St Vincent & Grenadines	18.1	21.0			26.3
Dominica/Dominique	10.5	10.1	11.1	13.7	16.0
Martinique	6.1	8.6	11.9	28.1	
Italy/Italie	2.5	0.4	15.7	26.6	8.1
Guadeloupe	9.6	9.5	10.4	20.5	
Japan/Japon	19.3	18.4	4.6	0.7	6.4
Germany/Allemagne	6.5	9.1	5.4	18.9	9.4
Middle East n.e.s.			22.4	24.8	
Cote d'Ivoire	26.6	11.8	7.6		
Korea, Republic of	5.5	16.2	17.4	6.5	0.0
Ecuador/Equateur	10.0	7.9	7.2	8.4	7.5
Spain/Espagne	4.1	2.7	3.4	12.9	11.4
Belgium–Luxembourg	13.0	5.2	0.2	7.2	8.5
Costa Rica	7.4	5.7	6.8	4.3	4.0
Peru/Pérou	0.5	2.6	7.6	11.0	3.4
Aruba	11.9	5.7	1.9	2.9	2.3

(VALUE AS PERCENTAGE OF WORLD TOTAL)(VALEURS EN POURCENTAGE DU TOTAL MONDIAL)

	1987	1988	1989	1990	1991	1992	1993	1994	1995	1996
Africa	0.1	4.4	2.9	4.6	1.2	0.2	0.1	0.2	0.4	0.8
Americas	63.0	60.9	72.2	68.5	69.8	68.6	69.3	69.4	68.4	70.5
– Northern America	48.7	43.3	55.1	46.4	44.5	47.3	44.5	54.0	55.7	41.7
– LAIA	7.9	9.2	7.7	14.5	19.1	14.7	20.0	10.0	8.5	24.3
– CACM	0.8	0.9	0.6	0.3	0.5	0.3	0.4	0.5	0.5	0.4
– Caribbean	4.7	6.4	7.7	6.2	4.8	5.1	3.4	4.0	2.8	2.3
– Rest of America	0.8	1.1	1.1	1.2	0.9	1.2	1.0	0.9	0.8	1.9
Asia excl fmr USSR	10.6	10.1	5.2	7.9	10.2	11.7	8.6	11.2	9.2	9.3
– Middle East	0.6	1.1	0.1	0.2	0.2	0.2	0.1	0.2	0.2	0.1
Asia former USSR										
Europe excl fmr USSR	23.9	21.9	18.0	17.2	16.7	18.1	20.7	17.6	20.8	18.4
– European Union	22.9	20.7	17.1	16.5	15.7	16.6	20.0	16.2	19.1	17.2
– Eastern Europe	0.1	0.1	0.2	0.2	0.2	0.3	0.1	0.3	0.4	0.5
– Rest of Europe	1.0	1.1	0.7	0.6	0.8	1.2	0.7	1.1	1.2	0.7
Europe former USSR	0.0	0.5	0.0	0.0	0.3	0.0	0.0	0.0	0.1	0.0
Oceania	2.1	1.6	1.5	1.6	1.3	1.3	1.1	1.2	0.8	0.7
Other	0.2	0.5	0.3	0.2	0.5	0.2	0.2	0.3	0.3	0.1
USA/Etats–Unis d'Amer	42.1	38.0	50.1	40.5	39.6	42.1	39.6	48.3	50.6	38.1
Venezuela	1.4	2.6	3.0	7.5	13.9	9.7	16.8	2.9	2.9	12.2
United Kingdom	9.2	9.9	7.6	7.5	7.4	7.8	8.1	8.3	7.2	6.0
Canada	6.7	5.3	5.0	5.8	4.9	5.1	4.9	5.8	5.1	3.6
Germany/Allemagne					1.9	2.6	6.6	2.1	5.9	5.0
Japan/Japon	5.3	5.2	2.1	3.5	5.6	6.7	3.8	4.6	3.2	4.0
Brazil/Brésil	3.4	2.8	3.2	4.1	3.8	3.4	2.2	5.3	4.1	3.3
Colombia/Colombie	2.2	1.5	0.2	1.3	0.3	0.3	0.3	0.3	0.4	7.0
Netherlands/Pays–Bas	2.2	3.1	2.3	1.7	1.8	1.4	1.1	1.4	1.4	1.9
Korea, Republic of	1.0	0.7	0.6	0.6	0.7	1.1	1.1	1.5	1.9	1.6

	1987	1988	1989	1990	1991	1992	1993	1994	1995	1996
Afrique	0.2	0.7	0.7	0.6	1.0	1.8	1.7	0.9	0.6	0.3
Amériques	82.4	86.1	86.5	86.5	84.8	88.1	88.6	87.5	86.0	88.7
– Amérique du Nord	60.3	60.1	57.1	58.3	51.7	50.4	49.7	50.3	45.0	51.0
– ALAI	3.3	3.3	2.7	3.1	7.7	6.8	5.2	8.6	8.6	7.4
– MCAC	0.6	0.6	0.4	0.2	0.3	1.0	1.1	0.9	0.7	0.8
– Caraïbes	13.6	17.1	20.2	19.2	18.4	21.8	23.3	19.5	23.8	22.8
– Autre Amérique	4.7	5.0	6.1	5.7	6.7	8.0	9.2	8.1	7.9	6.6
Asie anc. URSS exclus	3.4	2.9	2.2	1.8	3.2	2.3	3.1	2.7	1.7	0.4
– Moyen–Orient	0.0	0.0	0.2	0.2	0.1	0.0	0.0	1.2	1.0	0.0
Asie ancienne URSS										
Europe anc. URSS exclus	12.7	8.9	9.6	9.7	9.6	5.9	5.1	8.0	10.6	9.6
– Union Européenne	12.6	8.8	9.1	8.5	9.5	5.8	4.8	7.7	10.1	9.6
– Europe de l'Est	0.0	0.0	0.0	0.0	0.0	0.0	0.0	0.0	0.0	0.0
– Autre de l'Europe	0.0	0.0	0.4	1.3	0.0	0.1	0.2	0.3	0.5	0.0
Europe ancienne URSS	0.0	0.1	0.0			0.0	0.0	0.0	0.0	0.0
Océanie	0.0	0.0	0.0	0.2	0.0	0.3	0.1	0.0	0.1	0.1
Autre	1.2	1.2	1.1	1.2	1.4	1.6	1.3	0.9	1.0	0.9
USA/Etats–Unis d'Amer	58.4	57.6	56.1	56.9	50.0	48.6	47.7	46.4	42.9	48.8
Jamaica/Jamaïque	2.5	2.5	3.7	2.7	2.1	1.7	4.3	6.1	8.4	8.6
Barbados/Barbade	3.1	3.4	3.9	3.5	3.3	3.4	4.4	3.6	3.5	3.5
Guyana	0.5	0.7	1.5	1.3	1.5	2.3	3.6	3.1	3.3	3.5
France, Monaco	1.4	1.8	2.2	1.1	1.4	1.9	1.5	2.8	2.9	5.3
Netherlands Antilles		1.8	2.1	3.0	4.2	6.5	3.2	1.5	1.5	1.3
Canada	1.9	2.2	1.0	1.4	1.8	1.8	2.0	3.8	1.9	2.2
Suriname/Surinam	2.3	2.0	2.1	2.1	1.9	2.2	2.2	1.9	2.0	2.7
United Kingdom	3.1	2.7	2.5	2.8	2.2	1.7	2.0	1.9	2.5	1.9
Colombia/Colombie	0.2	0.7	0.2	0.2	1.6	1.8	1.9	2.7	2.4	1.3

4. Special Imports C.I.F. by Commodities according to the S.I.T.C. (Rev. 2) in million U.S. Dollars
Importations Spéciales C.A.F. par Produits d'après la C.T.C.I. (Rév. 2) en millions de Dollars E.U.

SITC CTCI	COMMODITY	1993 QUANTITY QUANTITE	1993 VALUE VALEUR	1994 QUANTITY QUANTITE	1994 VALUE VALEUR	1995 QUANTITY QUANTITE	1995 VALUE VALEUR	1996 QUANTITY QUANTITE	1996 VALUE VALEUR	PRODUIT
	ALL COMMODITIES		1462.9		1133.8		1723.7		2204.5	TOUS PRODUITS
0	FOOD AND LIVE ANIMALS		183.3		136.9		184.8		242.1	ALIMENTS,ANIMAUX VIVANTS
01	MEAT AND PREPARATIONS		20.0		15.7		15.8		18.1	VIANDES ET PREPARATIONS
011	MEAT FRESH,CHILLD,FROZEN	W 9189	15.2	W 6912	11.9	W 10630	10.3	W 7047	12.1	VIANDES FRAICHES,REF,CONGE
0111	BOVINE MEAT FRESH,FROZEN	W 3998	8.0	W 2896	6.2	W 2097	4.1	W 2124	4.7	VIANDES BOVIN FRAI,REF
01112	BOVINE MEAT BONELESS	W 3485	7.3	W 2684	5.7	W 1910	3.8	W 2042	4.4	VIANDES BOVIN DESOSSEES
02	DAIRY PRODCTS,BIRDS'EGGS		39.9		25.7		35.3		46.3	PRODUITS LAITIERS,OEUFS
022	MILK AND CREAM	W 13183	28.1	W 12657	21.3	W 13203	29.6	W 11127	27.9	LAIT ET CREME
0224	MILK,CREAM PRESERVED ETC	W 12979	27.7	W 12529	21.1	W 13055	29.3	W 11021	27.6	LAIT,CREME CONS,CONC
02242	MILK DRY,1.5% FAT OR LES	W 2768	6.2	W 3515	6.0	W 4305	9.7	W 3480	8.2	LAIT POUDRE INF 1.5%
02243	MILK DRY,OVER 1.5% FAT	W 8986	20.2	W 7133	13.4	W 7101	17.8	W 6146	17.9	LAIT POUDRE SUP 1.5%
024	CHEESE AND CURD	W 3430	7.1				0.4	W 4104	12.1	FROMAGE ET CAILLEBOTTE
03	FISH AND PREPARATIONS		4.4		5.0		5.2		6.0	POISSONS ET PREPARATIONS
04	CEREALS AND PREPARATIONS		57.7		45.4		66.6		78.3	CEREALES ET PRODUITS
041	WHEAT ETC UNMILLED	W 120210	20.3	W 85120	16.1	W 130877	27.4	W 105549	24.9	FROMENT,EPEAUTRE
0412	OTHER WHEAT ETC UNMILLED	W 120210	20.3	W 74413	14.4	W 130877	27.4	W 105549	24.9	AUTRE FROMENT NON MOULU
042	RICE	W 59786	12.7	W 16612	11.3	W 41109	16.1	W 59963	15.6	RIZ
0422	RICE SEMI-MILLED,MILLED	W 58974	12.5	W 11584	9.7	W 37964	15.2	W 55419	13.6	RIZ POLI,GLACE INCL BRISURES
04221	RICE MILLED UNBROKEN	W 58674	12.4	W 11027	9.6	W 36890	15.0	W 48876	12.5	RIZ POLI,GLACE EXCL BRISURES
044	MAIZE UNMILLED	W 88597	13.4	W 41875	9.9	W 86008	14.0	W 88903	18.3	MAIS NON MOULU
048	CEREAL ETC PREPARATIONS	W 8348	8.0	W 2628	5.4	W 3268	6.1	W 12360	15.8	PREPTNS A BASE CEREALES
0488	OTH CEREAL PREPS,MALT EX	W 1116	3.1	W 2030	4.4	W 1869	4.4	W 2419	6.0	EXTRAITS DE MALT
05	VEGETABLES AND FRUIT		29.5		21.6		25.2		36.3	LEGUMES ET FRUITS
054	VEG ETC FRSH,SMPLY PRSVD	W 47753	22.6	W 35490	15.5	W 49505	16.9	W 55182	25.2	LEGUMES FRAIS,CONG,SECS
0541	POTATOES FRSH EXCL SWEET	W 19046	5.7	W 23969	6.8	W 31984	6.3	W 24592	5.8	POMMES DE TERRE
0542	LEGUMINOUS VEGETBLES DRY	W 10624	5.5					W 14527	8.1	LEGUMES A COSSE SECS
0545	OTHER FRESH VEGETABLES	W 13269	7.0	W 7370	4.6	W 8485	5.6	W 10571	6.2	AUTRES LEGUMES FRAIS,REF
05451	ALLIACEOUS VEGTBLS,FRESH	W 8185	4.7	W 7325	4.6	W 8482	5.6	W 7607	4.7	OIGNONS,ECHALOTES,AULX
0546	VEGETABLES SIMPLY PRESVD	W 3601	3.9	W 4095	4.0	W 8908	5.0	W 4808	4.7	LEGUMES CONG,CONSER
05461	VEGETABLES FROZEN	W 3554	3.8	W 4087	4.0	W 8894	5.0	W 4804	4.6	LEGUMES CONGELES
06	SUGAR AND PREPS,HONEY		3.3		0.8		9.1		17.7	SUCRES ET PRODUITS
061	SUGAR AND HONEY	W 6574	2.6	W 7	0.1	W 24641	8.3	W 35079	16.6	SUCRES ET MIEL
0611	RAW BEET AND CANE SUGAR	W 4983	1.6	W 1	0.1	W 24609	8.3	W 30958	13.2	SUCRES BRUTS
07	COFFEE,TEA,COCOA,SPICES		5.9		2.9		3.8		6.8	CAFE,THE,CACAO,EPICES
081	*FEEDING STUFF FOR ANIML	W 41799	9.9	W 51940	13.0	W 41062	14.2	W 39395	12.1	NOURRITURE POUR ANIMAUX
0819	FOOD WASTE AND FEED NES	W 27829	9.2	W 43624	12.1	W 32716	12.6	W 26863	9.5	DECHETS,ALIMENTS NDA
08199	FODDER NES,INCL SWEETNED	W 27824	9.2	W 43624	12.1	W 32716	12.6	W 26863	9.5	PREPARATIONS FOURRAGERES
09	MISC EDIBLE PRODUCTS		12.6		6.6		9.1		20.3	PREP ALIMENTAIRES DIVERSES
098	EDIBLE PRODCTS,PREPS NES	W 3059	9.7	W 1734	3.5	W 3047	4.9	W 4918	16.7	PREP ALIMENTAIRES NDA
09809	MISC FOOD PREPRTIONS NES	W 1252	6.6	W 233	0.4	W 559	0.8	W 3102	12.4	PREP ALIMENTAIRES NDA
1	BEVERAGES AND TOBACCO		6.0		6.9		7.5		11.8	BOISSONS ET TABACS
11	BEVERAGES		3.2		3.9		4.8		7.6	BOISSONS
2	CRUDE MATERLS,EXCL FUELS		65.9		96.9		107.2		124.1	MAT BRUTES NON COMESTIBLES
22	OIL SEEDS,OLEAGINOUS FRT		30.2		32.9		29.0		32.9	GRAINES,FRUITS OLEAGINEUX
222	SEEDS FOR'SOFT'FIXED OIL	W 95555	30.0	W 78525	32.6	W 94737	28.5	W 85434	32.3	GRAINES HUILES FIXES
2222	SOYA BEANS	W 92781	27.3	W 75531	29.7	W 91527	25.3	W 79889	28.5	FEVES DE SOJA
24	CORK AND WOOD		8.2		0.8		1.1		14.2	LIEGE ET BOIS
248	WOOD SHAPED,SLEEPERS	W 13089	7.0	W 1277	0.8	W 1540	1.1	W 19767	12.8	BOIS SIMPLEMENT TRAVAILLES
2482	LUMBER SHAPED CONIFER	W 12780	6.8	W 1205	0.7	W 1372	0.9	W 19020	12.4	CONIFERES SCIES,RABOTES
24821	LUMBER SAWN ETC CONIFER	W 12650	6.8					W 17870	11.6	CONIFERES SCIES LONGITUD
27	CRUDE FERTLZR,MINRLS NES		5.5		4.5		7.6		10.2	ENGRAIS MINERAUX BRUTS
28	METALLIFEROUS ORES,SCRAP		16.3		55.8		65.6		60.7	MINERAIS METAL,DECHETS
281	IRON ORE,CONCENTRATES	W 199417	15.3	W 1450539	55.0	W 1531650	65.1	W 1183178	59.5	MINERAIS DE FER
2816	IRON ORE AGGLOMERATES	W 89719	12.2	W 1450539	55.0	W 1531650	65.1	W 1183178	59.5	MINERAIS AGGLOMERES
3	MINERAL FUELS ETC		233.3		7.7		9.4		423.5	COMBUSTIBLES MINERAUX LUB
33	PETROLEUM AND PRODUCTS		232.5		6.5		7.8		421.8	PETROLE ET DERIVES
333	CRUDE PETROLEUM	W 2345857	226.1	W 4	0.1	W 11	0.1	W 2905392	406.0	HUILES BRUTES DE PETROLE
334	PETROLEUM PRODUCTS,REFIN	W 6463	5.6	W 11557	5.5	W 16797	6.8	W 48831	14.7	PRODUITS RAFFINES
3345	LUBS,PETROLEUM OILS NES	W 6285	5.4	W 6904	4.4	W 9463	5.3	W 12019	7.3	HUILES LUBRIFIANTES
33451	LUBS(HIGH PETR CONT) ETC	W 5831	4.2	W 6766	3.8	W 9315	4.5	W 11836	6.6	HUILES LUBRIF,H LOURDES
4	ANIMAL,VEGETABLE OIL,FAT		5.9		7.9		5.8		11.7	HUILES,GRAISSES ANIM,VEG
42	FIXED VEGETABLE OIL,FAT		1.7		5.5		2.5		6.8	HUILES VEGETALES FIXES
423	FIXED VEG OILS,SOFT	W 506	0.9	W 3940	4.9	W 733	1.2	W 4258	5.4	HUILES VEGET DOUCES FIXES
4232	SOYA BEAN OIL			W 3302	4.0	W 46	0.1	W 3317	4.1	HUILE DE SOJA
5	CHEMCLS,RELATED PROD NES		157.9		75.2		108.1		216.5	PRODUITS CHIMIQUES
51	ORGANIC CHEMICALS		10.8		1.8		2.4		14.8	PROD CHIMIQ ORGANIQUES
511	HYDROCARBONS NES,DERIVS	W 4153	4.6	W 691	1.0	W 927	1.5	W 4713	5.5	HYDROCARBURES NDA
52	INORGANIC CHEMICALS		17.1		8.0		11.4		21.9	PROD CHIM INORGANIQUES
522	INORG ELEMNTS,OXIDES,ETC	W 9381	5.2	W 7289	4.2	W 10898	6.5	W 10003	7.5	ELEMENTS INORGANIQUES
523	OTHR INORG CHEMICALS ETC	W 22998	11.8	W 12037	3.8	W 14697	4.9	W 47547	14.3	AUT PRODUITS CHIMIQUES INORG
5232	OTH MTL CMPD OF INRG ACD	W 13903	5.4	W 11441	2.9	W 14174	4.2	W 12715	6.5	SELS METALLIQUES
53	DYES,TANNING,COLOUR PROD		8.0		6.3		7.8		11.5	PROD TEINTURE,COLORANTS
533	PIGMENTS,PAINTS,ETC	W 1790	6.4	W 2201	4.5	W 2631	6.3	W 9189	10.2	PIGMENTS,PEINTURES,VERNIS
541	*MEDICINAL,PHARM PRODUCT	K 2000398	31.7		29.0		29.6	K 2439310	36.1	PROD MEDICINAUX PHARMACEUT
5417	MEDICAMENTS	K 1605552	27.5	K 1700377	26.3	K 1309709	26.3	K 2054126	31.0	MEDICAMENTS
54179	— CONTNG OTH SUBSTANCES	K 1459977	22.0	K 1526489	20.0	K 1211005	20.8	K 1925642	24.0	MED CONT AUT SUBSTANCES
55	PERFUME,CLEANING ETC PRD		17.3		14.2		34.6		21.3	PROD POUR PARFUM,TOILETTE
553	PERFUMERY,COSMETICS,ETC	W 1899	7.0	W 1959	6.4	W 2362	25.1	W 2497	9.5	PRODUITS DE PARFUMERIE
554	SOAP,CLEANSING ETC PREPS	W 4330	7.1	W 4539	7.3	W 5197	8.8	W 5626	8.2	SAVONS,PRODUITS DETERSIFS
5542	WASHING PREPARATIONS ETC	W 3173	5.0	W 2902	4.6	W 3244	5.0	W 3441	4.3	PROD ORG TENSIO-ACT NDA
58	PLASTIC MATERIALS ETC		33.9		0.7		3.5		50.3	MAT PLAST ARTIFICIELLES
582	PROD OF CONDENSATION ETC	W 10297	14.1	W 185	0.4	W 1453	3.2	W 11390	16.2	PROD CONDENS,POLYCOND
5823	ALKYDS,OTHER POLYESTERS							W 7513	12.1	ALKYDES ET AUT POLYESTERS
58231	— IN PRIMARY FORMS							W 7513	12.1	SOUS FORMES PRIMAIRES
5829	OTH CONDNSATION,ETC PROD	W 7701	10.3							AUT PROD CONDENSATION
583	POLYMERIZATION ETC PRODS	W 12379	19.3	W 42	0.2	W 70	0.3	W 21778	33.7	PROD POLYMERISATION
5831	POLYETHYLENE	W 3763	6.4							POLYETHYLENE
5839	OTH POLYMRZTION ETC PROD	W 4159	8.5					W 19217	31.6	AUT PROD POLYMER COPOLYM
59	CHEMICAL MATERIALS NES		36.6		13.1		15.8		56.7	MAT PROD CHIMIQUES NDA
591	PESTICIDES,DISINFECTANTS	W 1822	8.0	W 1892	7.4	W 1768	8.3	W 2009	10.0	DESINF,INSECT,FONG,HERB
5911	INSECTICIDES,FOR RETAIL	W 945	4.1	W 1011	3.9	W 849	5.1	W 1125	6.5	INSECTICIDES VENTE DET
598	MISCEL CHEM PRODUCTS NES	W 8440	25.6	W 1457	2.5	W 1671	3.7	W 13057	43.0	PROD DIV INDUST CHIM NDA
5982	ANTI-KNOCK PREPARTNS ETC	W 2510	9.2					W 2916	10.7	PREPARAT ANTIDETONANTES
5989	CHEM PRODUCTS,PREPS NES	W 5683	16.0	W 1212	2.3	W 1332	3.3	W 9747	31.9	PROD PREP CHIMIQUES NDA
59898	COMPOUND CATALYSTS	W 644	2.4					W 1377	7.7	CATALYSEURS COMPOSITES
59899	OTH CHEM PRODS,PREPS,NES	W 4374	12.4	W 156	1.1	W 135	1.3	W 7146	22.2	AUT PRODUITS CHIMIQUES NDA
6	BASIC MANUFACTURES		243.3		171.7		247.0		358.8	ART MANUFACTURES
62	RUBBER MANUFACTURES NES		15.6		13.8		15.5		20.2	CAOUTCHOUC MANUFACTURE
625	RUBBER TYRES, TUBES ETC	W 5416	8.2	W 4551	10.4	W 7486	11.8	W 6297	11.1	PNEUS CAOUTCHOUC VULCANISE
6251	TYRES NEW FOR MOTOR CARS	W 1326	3.1	W 1112	4.0	W 2429	4.5	W 1392	3.9	PNEUS POUR VOITURES
6259	OTH TYRES,TYRE CASES,ETC	W 3582	3.7	W 2983	4.6	W 3686	4.2	W 4114	4.1	AUTRES PNEUS RECHAPES FLAPS

4. Special Imports C.I.F. by Commodities according to the S.I.T.C. (Rev. 2) in million U.S. Dollars
Importations Spéciales C.A.F. par Produits d'après la C.T.C.I. (Rév. 2) en millions de Dollars E.U.

SITC CTCI	COMMODITY	1993 QUANTITY QUANTITE	1993 VALUE VALEUR	1994 QUANTITY QUANTITE	1994 VALUE VALEUR	1995 QUANTITY QUANTITE	1995 VALUE VALEUR	1996 QUANTITY QUANTITE	1996 VALUE VALEUR	PRODUIT
62599	TYRES NES,TYRE CASES,ETC	W 3468	3.4	W 2868	4.3	W 3534	3.8	W 3239	3.7	PNEUS,FLAPS
63	WOOD,CORK MANUFACTRS NES		9.3		10.3		3.2		13.8	OUVRAGES LIEGE ET BOIS
634	VENEERS,PLYWOOD,ETC	W 11331	8.2	W 956	0.6	W 1488	1.4	W 12939	10.6	PLACAGES,CONTRE–PLAQUES
6342	PLYWOOD OF WOOD SHEETS	W 10957	7.9					W 11890	9.8	BOIS CONTRE–PLAQUES
635	WOOD MANUFACTURES NES	W 583	1.0	W 1101	9.7	W 1198	1.9	W 1084	3.2	ART MANUF EN BOIS NDA
6353	BUILDERS WOODWRK,PREFABS	W 227	0.5	W 803	9.2	W 73	1.0	W 219	2.1	OUVRAGES DE MENUISERIE
64	PAPER,PAPERBOARD AND MFR		48.5		28.6		41.5		68.8	PAPIERS,CARTONS & OUVRAGES
641	PAPER AND PAPERBOARD	W 40203	36.3	W 13839	14.9	W 18291	23.2	W 48269	52.5	PAPIERS ET CARTONS
6411	NEWSPRINT	W 4451	4.1	W 4384	3.7	W 8993	7.8	W 6289	6.7	PAPIER JOURNAL
6413	KRAFT PAPER,PAPERBOARD	W 14815	9.6					W 15789	12.9	PAPIER ET CARTON KRAFT
64139	KRAFT PAPER PAPERBD,NES							W 15789	12.9	PAPIER,CARTON KRAFT NDA
6415	PAPER,PAPERBRD,BULK,NES	W 7137	6.9	W 33	0.2	W 26	0.2	W 12451	12.4	PAPIERS,CARTONS ROULEAUX
64159	OTHER PAPER ETC,BULK,NES	W 6956	6.5	W 33	0.2	W 26	0.2	W 10297	9.7	AUT PAPIER ROULEAUX FEUILLES
6417	CORRUGATED PAPER ETC,BLK	W 6726	8.0	W 8240	8.6	W 7627	10.7	W 6545	9.5	PAPIERS,CARTONS ONDULES
64172	CREPED HSHOLD PAPER ETC	W 5694	7.2	W 7920	8.2	W 7358	10.3	W 6139	9.2	PAPIER NON KRAFT CREPE
6418	COATED ETC PAPER NES BLK	W 4838	5.3	W 1076	2.3	W 1244	3.8	W 5574	9.2	PAP,CARTONS COUCHES,ENDUITS
64189	COATED PAPER ETC NES	W 787	1.8	W 984	2.1	W 1141	3.5	W 5477	8.9	PAPIERS,CARTONS COUCHES
642	PAPER,ETC,PRECUT,ARTS OF	W 24221	12.2	W 8801	13.8	W 9696	18.4	W 7575	16.4	PAP,CARTONS DECOUPES
6421	PAPER ETC CONTAINERS	W 22754	8.3	W 6614	8.5	W 7816	12.2	W 5785	10.2	BOITES,SACS EMBALLAGES
65	TEXTILE YARN,FABRICS,ETC		45.8		28.0		31.9		52.9	FILS,TISSUS,ARTICLES TEXTILE
652	COTTON FABRICS,WOVEN	W 1184	5.9	W 1330	6.2	W 904	5.1	W 1079	6.0	TISSUS DE COTON
6522	WOVEN COTTON BLEACHD,ETC	W 1153	5.7	W 1242	5.8	W 878	4.9	W 1060	5.9	TISSUS COTON BLANCHIS ETC
65224	BLCHED COTTON FABRIC NES	W 1040	5.1	W 1130	5.0	W 761	4.1	W 851	4.5	AUT TIS PLUS 85% COT BLANCHI
653	WOVN MAN–MADE FIB FABRIC	W 2811	17.4	W 1762	11.0	W 2224	14.4	W 3128	21.6	TISSUS FIBRES SYNTH,ARTIF
6532	DISC SYN TXTL FABRIC NES	W 995	6.7	W 905	5.7	W 1082	7.4	W 1427	10.5	TIS DISC MOINS 85% FIBR TEXT
6534	DISC SYN BLEND FABRC NES	W 820	4.8					W 1072	6.6	TISSUS FIBRES SYNTH DISCONT
655	KNITTED,ETC FABRICS	W 808	5.4					W 934	6.3	ETOF BONNETERIE PIECES ETC
6552	OTHER KNIT ETC FAB NONEL	W 808	5.4					W 934	6.3	ETOF BON NON ELAS NON SYNT
657	SPECIAL TXTL FABRC,PRODS	W 1531	7.7	W 768	4.6	W 824	5.1	W 1401	7.5	TISSUS SPECIAUX
66	NONMETAL MINERAL MFS NES		17.1		14.0		18.6		37.1	ART MIN NON METALLIQUES
662	CLAY,REFRACTORY BLDG PRD	W 8621	5.2	W 3672	2.5	W 9847	5.1	W 28296	18.3	MAT CONST REFRACTAIRES
6623	REFRACTORY BUILDING PROD	W 5031	3.3	W 3566	2.4	W 9839	5.1	W 18929	13.3	BRIQUES REFRACTAIRES
66232	REFRACTRY BRICKS ETC NES	W 3498	2.4					W 7899	7.7	BRIQUES ETC REFRACTAIRES
664	GLASS	W 9531	4.1	W 4861	5.3	W 4137	5.3	W 6812	5.6	VERRE
67	IRON AND STEEL		49.6		31.9		80.1		83.2	FER ET ACIER
671	PIG IRON ETC	W 3964	1.7	W 6062	3.5	W 8355	4.7	W 8072	7.2	FONTE,SPIEGEL,POUDRES
6716	FERRO–ALLOYS	W 3931	1.7	W 5963	3.4	W 8348	4.6	W 8031	7.1	FERRO–ALLIAGES
672	IRON,STEEL PRIMARY FORMS		1.1	W 1567	1.2	W 5811	2.7	W 21428	8.0	LINGOTS FER,ACIER
673	IRON,STEEL SHAPES ETC	W 9499	4.3	W 1040	0.9	W 6681	4.1	W 16173	9.8	BARRES,PROFIL FER,ACIER
6733	IRON,STEEL PROFILES ETC	W 9205	3.9	W 643	0.6	W 5575	3.3	W 14707	8.7	PROFILES,PALPLAN FER,ACIER
674	IRN,STL UNIV,PLATE,SHEET	W 16944	12.8	W 16155	13.0	W 29252	26.6	W 25832	21.6	LARGES PLATS,TOLES
6744	IRN,STL HVY PLATE,ROLLED	W 4456	2.8	W 4062	2.8	W 9242	8.2	W 5897	3.5	TOLES LAMINEES PLUS 4.75 MM
67441	— OF IRON OR SIMPLE STL	W 4454	2.8	W 4047	2.7	W 8460	7.7	W 5391	3.1	TOLES NON ACIER FIN CARB
6749	OTH IRN,STL PLATES,SHEET	W 9411	7.8	W 9857	8.5	W 16921	15.5	W 13701	12.4	AUTRES TOLES FER,ACIER
67491	— OF IRON OR SIMPLE STL	W 7290	6.2	W 8912	7.7	W 15469	14.1	W 12126	11.0	AUT TOLES AUTRES ACIER FIN
678	IRON,STL TUBES,PIPES,ETC	W 22535	28.4	W 4693	13.1	W 136079	41.6	W 21656	34.9	TUBES,TUYAUX EN FONTE,FER
6782	IRON,STL SEAMLESS TUBES	W 13709	5.8	W 9	0.1	W 10	0.1	W 5841	7.0	TUBES,TUYAUX SANS SOUDURE
6783	IRON,STL TUBES,PIPES NES	W 7711	17.3	W 4161	10.0	W 135127	36.5	W 14231	21.2	AUT TUBES,TUYAUX FER,ACIER
6785	IRON,STEEL TUBE FITTINGS	W 1108	5.4	W 523	3.1	W 941	5.1	W 1583	6.8	ACCESSOIRES DE TUYAUTERIE
68	NON–FERROUS METALS		12.7		3.0		5.9		20.4	METAUX NON FERREUX
684	ALUMINIUM	W 1847	8.1	W 6	0.1	W 9	0.2	W 2823	13.4	ALUMINIUM
6842	ALUMINIUM,ALLOYS WORKED	W 1626	7.6	W 6	0.1	W 9	0.2	W 2528	12.7	ALUMINIUM,ALLIAGES OUVRE
68423	ALUMINIUM FOIL	W 1329	6.5					W 1510	9.2	FEUILLES,BANDES MINCES AL
69	METAL MANUFACTURES NES		44.3		41.8		50.3		61.9	ART MANUFACT EN METAL NDA
691	STRUCTURES AND PARTS NES	W 1683	5.1	W 2350	5.2	W 6988	4.6	W 4880	6.5	CONSTRUCT FER,ACIER,ALU
6911	STRUCTURES,PARTS IRN,STL	W 979	2.3	W 1984	3.5	W 6713	3.6	W 4734	6.0	CONSTRUCT FER,ACIER,FONTE
692	METAL TANKS,BOXES,ETC	W 4281	9.4	W 5445	8.8	W 4292	7.8	W 4159	11.5	RECIPIENTS METALLIQUES
6924	MTL TRANSPORT BOXES ETC	W 4071	9.2	W 5405	8.6	W 4080	7.3	W 4109	11.2	FUTS,TAMBOURS,BIDONS
69241	STL TRANSPORT BOXES ETC	W 2795	5.1	W 4962	7.5	W 3740	6.4	W 2956	6.3	FUTS,TAMBOURS,BIDONS FER
694	STL,COPPR NAILS,NUTS,ETC	W 830	3.6	W 954	3.7	W 1167	4.6	W 1156	5.4	CLOUS,VIS,ECROUS
695	TOOLS	W 560	5.7	W 565	6.5	W 620	10.1	W 774	8.6	OUTILS A MAIN
6954	BLADES,TIPS,ETC FR TOOLS	W 233	3.1	W 134	3.8	W 101	5.3	W 101	4.4	OUTILS POUR MACHINE–OUTIL
697	BASE MTL HOUSEHOLD EQUIP	W 1211	5.0	W 1156	4.1	W 1085	4.8	W 2025	6.3	ART MENAGE MET COMMUNS
699	BASE METAL MFRS NES	W 3143	13.0	W 2568	10.2	W 4923	12.9	W 5286	18.1	ART MANUFACTURES MET NDA
6991	LOCKSMITHS WARES,ETC	W 933	4.5	W 280	1.7	W 307	2.0	W 953	5.4	ARTICLES DE SERRURERIE
7	MACHINES,TRANSPORT EQUIP		480.3		288.7		562.0		675.1	MACHINES MATERIEL TRANSPORT
71	POWER GENERATING EQUIPMT		21.3		34.3		37.0		46.9	MACHINES GENERATRICES
712	STEAM ENGINES,TURBINES	W 11	1.2	W 40	5.7	W 25	1.4	W 45	1.7	MACHINES A VAPEUR D'EAU PIEC
7129	STM ENGINE ETC PARTS NES	W 9	1.2	W 33	5.0	W 24	1.3	W 27	1.1	PARTIES,PIECES DU 712.6
713	INTRNL COMBUS PSTN ENGIN	W 2201	7.1	W 2182	9.4	W 2826	9.6	W 2850	13.3	MOTEURS EXPL COMB INT, PIECE
714	ENGINES AND MOTORS NES	W 48	8.9	W 58	14.2	W 116	18.6	W 180	21.1	MOTEURS NON ELECTRIQUES
7149	ENGINE & MOTOR PARTS NES	W 41	7.7	W 42	10.0	W 77	13.9	W 151	16.1	PIECES 714 ET 718.88
71499	PARTS NES,OF 71488,71888	W 35	5.7	W 33	7.9	W 62	9.6	W 138	14.6	PIECES 714.88 ET 718.88
716	ROTATING ELECTRIC PLANT	W 276	3.1	W 339	4.4	W 543	7.5	W 5114	8.1	APP ELECTR ROTATIFS,PIECES
7162	AC MTRS,GENRTRS,GEN SETS	W 180	2.0	W 250	3.0	W 397	5.4	W 4199	5.9	MOTEURS ELECTRIQUES
72	MACHS FOR SPCL INDUSTRYS		48.6		21.9		38.7		49.7	MAC SPECIALES POUR INDUST
723	CIVIL ENGNEERG EQUIP ETC	W 1168	13.2	W 610	2.4	W 633	4.7	W 1601	7.8	APPAREILS DE GENIE CIVIL
7234	CONST,MINING MACHNRY NES	W 1022	11.1	W 524	1.8	W 582	3.8	W 1387	4.8	MACH POUR LA CONST, MINES
72346	OTH CONST,MINING MCH NES	W 899	10.5	W 14	0.1	W 35	0.2	W 4	0.1	AUT MACH EXTRACTION,EXCAV ET
728	OTH MACHY FOR SPCL INDUS	W 2324	26.8	W 655	10.9	W 4106	20.0	W 2056	28.2	AUT MACH IND PARTICULIERES
7283	OTHR MINERAL WORKG MACHY	W 178	2.6	W 343	3.6	W 3243	4.1	W 803	7.2	MACH TRIER,CRIBLER,BROYER
7284	MACHY FOR SPCL INDUS NES	W 1817	20.6	W 313	7.3	W 862	15.9	W 1152	19.8	MACH SPEC IND PARTICUL.
72848	OTH MCHY WITH INDIV FNCT	W 308	14.5	W 187	3.9	W 537	8.6	W 654	8.5	AUTRES MACHINES NDA
72849	PTS OF MACHS OF 7284 ETC	W 1300	3.5	W 119	3.4	W 260	6.9	W 283	7.8	PIECES DU 728.4 ETC
73	METALWORKING MACHINERY		3.1		3.7		5.0		11.2	MACH TRAVAIL DES METAUX
737	METALWORKING MACHNRY NES	W 244	1.5	W 392	3.5	W 1458	4.6	W 1199	9.2	MACH TRAV METAUX PIECES
74	GENRL INDUSTRL MACHY NES		196.2		86.0		241.3		198.7	MACH APP INDUSTRIE
741	HEATING,COOLING EQUIPMNT	W 14013	105.4	W 9725	42.8	W 22781	179.6	W 12330	92.8	MACH CHAUFFAGE,PIECES
7413	INDUS FURNACES ETC,PARTS	W 4527	16.5	W 5261	18.7	W 3826	23.9	W 730	10.2	FOURS IND,LABOR,PIECES
74132	INDUST FURNACES NONELECT	W 4433	16.0	W 5235	18.5	W 3807	23.7	W 700	9.6	FOURS NON ELECTRIQUES
7416	HEATING,COOLING EQU NES	W 9055	86.2	W 3087	19.8	W 18120	150.3	W 9975	75.0	APP CHANGEMENT TEMP
742	PUMPS FOR LIQUIDS ETC	W 1510	27.4	W 1066	9.7	W 1686	11.6	W 1375	12.4	POMPES MOTO–POMPES
7428	OTHER PUMPS FOR LIQUIDS	W 831	21.4	W 672	3.5	W 906	5.5	W 845	4.9	AUTRES POMPES POUR LIQ
74288	PUMPS FR LIQUIDS NES ETC	W 811	20.9	W 662	3.2	W 896	5.2	W 838	4.7	POMPES POUR LIQUIDES NDA
7429	PTS NES OF PUMPS OF 742	W 315	5.0	W 228	4.9	W 496	4.4	W 341	5.8	PIECES POUR GROUPE 742
743	PUMPS NES,CENTRFUGES ETC	W 732	9.3	W 1028	12.2	W 1145	13.1	W 2745	19.4	POMPES COMPRES,VENT ETC
7431	PUMPS FOR GASES ETC	W 230	2.6	W 425	3.7	W 511	4.7	W 1545	6.8	POMPES AIR A VIDE,COMPRES
7439	PTS NES OF APP OF 7435,6	W 98	3.2	W 182	4.8	W 137	3.5	W 317	4.8	PIECES 743.5 ET 743.6
744	MECHANICAL HANDLING EQU		12.9	W 3082	14.6	W 3001	23.0	W 4219	27.0	EQUIP MANUTENTION PIECES
7441	FORK LIFT TRCKS,ETC,PTS	W 213	0.7	W 268	1.1	W 965	2.4	W 1145	7.0	CHARIOTS POUR USINES ETC
74411	FORK LIFT TRUCKS ETC	W 212	0.6	W 266	1.1	W 964	2.4	W 1143	7.0	CHARIOTS POUR LES GARES

4. Special Imports C.I.F. by Commodities according to the S.I.T.C. (Rev. 2) in million U.S. Dollars
Importations Spéciales C.A.F. par Produits d'après la C.T.C.I. (Rév. 2) en millions de Dollars E.U.

SITC CTCI	COMMODITY	1993 QUANTITY QUANTITE	1993 VALUE VALEUR	1994 QUANTITY QUANTITE	1994 VALUE VALEUR	1995 QUANTITY QUANTITE	1995 VALUE VALEUR	1996 QUANTITY QUANTITE	1996 VALUE VALEUR	PRODUIT
7442	LIFTING,LOADING MACH NES	W 705	3.9	W 1060	3.3	W 1121	5.4	W 2158	6.5	APP LEVAGE,MANUTENTION
7449	PTS NES OF MACHY OF 7442		8.4	W 1754	10.3	W 915	15.3	W 916	13.5	PIECES DU 744.2
745	NONELEC MACHY,TOOLS NES	W 1500	8.9	W 462	5.4	W 1114	12.1	W 560	9.4	AUT MACH NON ELEC,PIECES
7452	OTH NONELEC MCHS,PTS NES	W 1482	8.4	W 413	4.8	W 830	10.7	W 464	7.8	AUT MACH NON ELEC,PIECES
74522	PACKAGNG,BOTTLNG,ETC MCH	W 350	5.4	W 78	2.2	W 327	6.5	W 156	3.1	MACH NETT BOUTEILLES,ETC
749	NONELEC MACH PTS,ACC NES		32.5	W 132	1.7	W 76	2.2	W 3255	37.9	PIECES MACH NON ELEC NDA
7492	COCKS,VALVES ETC NES	W 4982	12.5					W 1298	17.8	ART ROB,SIM POUR TUYAUX
7493	SHAFT,CRANK,PULLEY ETC	W 273	7.6					W 544	8.9	ARBRES TRANS,VILEBREQUINS
7499	OTH NONELEC MCHY PTS NES		9.4	W 132	1.7	W 76	2.2	W 736	5.9	PIECES NON ELECT NDA
74992	METAL–PLASTIC GASKETS		6.6					W 265	2.2	JOINTS METALLOPLASTIQUES
75	OFFICE MACHNES,ADP EQUIP		19.1		23.4		35.6		42.2	MACH BUREAU TRAIT AUTOM
751	OFFICE MACHINES	W 101	2.6	W 112	3.6	W 168	4.7	W 179	4.5	MACH,APPAREILS DE BUREAU
752	AUTOMTIC DATA PROC EQUIP	W 190	11.5	W 366	14.3	W 388	21.5	W 1127	26.7	MACH TRAIT INFORMATION
7522	DIGITAL COMPUTERS	W 79	5.8	W 87	9.0	W 166	12.1	W 240	13.5	MACH DIGITALES COMPLETES
7525	ADP PERIPHERAL UNITS	W 73	3.1	W 237	3.1	W 136	5.0	W 216	9.4	UNITES PERIPHERIQUES
759	OFFICE,ADP MCH PTS,ACCES	W 122	5.1	W 234	5.7	W 147	9.5	W 497	11.1	PIECES DU 751 ET 752
7599	ACCTG,ETC,ADP MCH PTS,AC	W 61	4.1	W 210	4.8	W 113	8.0	W 448	9.3	PIECES DU 751 ET 752
76	TELECOMM,SOUND EQUIPMENT		28.0		24.2		41.7		33.8	EQUIPMENT DE TELECOM
761	TELEVISION RECEIVERS	W 412	4.0	W 403	2.4	W 669	6.6	W 712	6.8	RECEPTEURS DE TELEVISION
7611	COLOUR TV RECEIVERS	W 400	3.9	W 397	2.4	W 661	6.5	W 701	6.7	RECEPTEURS COULEUR
764	TELECOM EQPT,PTS,ACC NES	W 349	21.6	W 490	20.5	W 698	32.1	W 550	22.7	EQUIP TELECOM,PIECES
7641	LINE TELEPHONE,ETC EQUIP	W 186	15.9	W 212	11.5	W 424	22.8	W 250	12.0	APP TELEPHON PAR FIL
7643	TV,RADIO TRANSMITTRS ETC	W 41	2.0	W 63	4.2	W 76	3.7	W 41	3.2	APP EMET TELE RADIO
77	ELECTRIC MACHNRY NES ETC		39.3		44.4		53.8		67.6	MACH APP ELECT NDA
771	ELECTRIC POWER MACHY NES	W 389	2.8	W 1117	6.3	W 931	5.9	W 946	6.8	MACH PROD,TRANS ELECTR
7711	TRANSFORMERS,ELECTRICAL	W 173	1.2	W 840	4.2	W 626	3.5	W 642	3.5	TRANSFO ELECTRIQUES
77118	OTHER ELEC TRANSFORMERS	W 173	1.2	W 833	4.2	W 616	3.5	W 638	3.4	AUTRES TRANSFO ELECTRIQ
772	SWITCHGEAR ETC,PARTS NES	W 383	8.0	W 374	8.7	W 563	9.5	W 1076	13.4	APP COUPURE,SECT ETC
7721	SWITCHGEAR ETC	W 377	7.6	W 366	8.3	W 553	8.7	W 1068	12.6	APP COUPURE,SECTIONMNT
773	ELECTR DISTRIBUTNG EQUIP	W 1000	5.2		8.7	W 1661	9.2	W 4675	10.6	EQUIPMT DISTRIBUTION ELECT
7731	INSULATED WIRE,CABLE ETC	W 864	4.3	W 2729	7.0	W 1517	7.4	W 1913	9.4	FILS,CABLES ISOLES ELECT
775	HOUSEHOLD TYPE EQUIP NES	W 2080	10.2	W 2895	9.7		15.0	W 4394	17.0	MACH,APP USAGE DOMESTQUE
7752	DOM REFRIGERATRS,FREEZRS	W 936	4.5	W 1078	3.7	W 1547	6.5	W 1586	7.4	REFRIG,CONGEL MENAGER
778	ELECTRICAL MACHINERY NES	W 2532	11.9	W 2390	11.2	W 4118	14.2	W 5369	18.3	AUTRES MACH ELECT NDA
7788	OTH ELEC MACHY,EQUIP NES	W 1428	4.5	W 1909	6.5	W 2612	7.8	W 3825	7.8	AUT MACH APP ELEC NDA
77887	ELECTRICAL CARBONS	W 1378	3.1	W 1882	5.9	W 2498	7.0	W 3667	4.2	PIECES CHARBON,GRAPHITE
78	ROAD VEHICLES		48.4		41.8		64.9		113.3	VEHICULES ROUTIERS
781	PASS MOTOR VEH EXC BUSES	W 3673	28.6	W 2432	26.1	W 4736	43.3	W 7239	70.5	AUTO TRANSPORT PERSONNES
782	LORRIES,SPCL MTR VEH NES	W 984	7.1	W 1878	11.6	W 2498	17.6	W 2741	18.7	VEHICULES SPECIAUX,MARCH
7821	LORRIES,TRUCKS	W 728	4.8	W 1761	11.1	W 2148	15.8	W 2498	16.4	VEHICULES TRANSP MARCHAND
784	MOTOR VEH PRTS,ACCES NES	W 2304	8.9	W 1	0.1	W 1	0.1	W 7957	18.5	PIECES 722,781,782,783
7842	MOTOR VEHICLE BODIES	W 1	0.1					W 2742	7.2	CARROS 722,781,782,783
7849	OTHER MOTOR VEHCL PARTS	W 2302	8.9					W 5100	11.2	PIECES 722,781,782,783
79	OTHR TRANSPORT EQUIPMENT		76.8		9.3		44.4		112.0	AUTRE MATERIEL TRANSPORT
792	AIRCRAFT ETC	W 108	24.3	W 128	7.6	W 138	7.6	W 151	74.5	APP NAVIGATION AERIENNE
7921	HELICOPTERS	W 10	5.3	W 2	1.1	W 2	1.0	W 4	0.6	HELICOPTERES
7924	AIRCRFT NES OVER 15000KG	W 69	13.6	W 100	0.9	W 100	0.8	W 110	69.6	AERODYNES PLUS 15000 KG
7929	AIRCRAFT PARTS NES	W 29	5.5	W 26	5.7	W 31	5.8	W 37	4.4	PIECES DU 792
793	SHIPS AND BOATS ETC	W 7464	52.6	W 964	1.8		36.8	W 9050	37.4	NAVIRES BATEAUX,ETC
7932	SHIPS AND BOATS NES	W 277	0.8	W 6	0.1		6.0	W 280	2.3	NAVIRES ET BATEAUX
79323	OTHER CARGO VESSELS	W 65	0.3			W 82	5.7	W 139	2.0	AUT BATEAUX TRANS MARCH
7938	TUGS,SPECIAL VESSELS ETC	W 7161	51.6	W 958	1.7	W 7117	30.9	W 8770	35.1	REMORQUEURS,BATEAUX SPEC
79382	SPECL PURPOSE VESSLS ETC	W 7111	50.6	W 918	1.4	W 6996	30.1	W 8725	34.6	BAT–PHARES,–POMPES,DRAGUES
8	MISC MANUFACTURED GOODS		83.5		72.8		105.2		133.2	ART MANUFACTURES DIVERS
821	*FURNITURE,PARTS THEREOF	W 1369	4.4	W 944	3.6	W 1615	6.1	W 1882	6.9	MEUBLES ET PIECES
84	CLOTHING AND ACCESSORIES		3.2		2.8		6.3		8.1	VETEMENTS
851	*FOOTWEAR	W 586	5.3	W 795	6.4	W 1238	9.0	W 1202	11.2	CHAUSSURES
85102	FOOTWEAR LEATHER	W 370	3.9	W 447	4.5	W 757	6.3	W 803	8.9	CHAUS SEMELLES EN CUIR
87	PRECISION INSTRUMNTS NES		17.0		14.6		25.3		32.3	INSTRUM,APPAR SCIENT NDA
874	MEASURNG,CONTROLNG INSTR		15.1	W 546	12.4	W 950	21.9	W 636	28.3	INSTRUMENTS DE MESURE
8741	SURVEYING INSTRUMENTS	W 26	2.6	W 33	3.3	W 51	5.3	W 50	2.8	INST GEODESIE,TOPO ETC
8743	GAS,LIQUID CONTROL INSTR		2.7	W 31	1.1	W 69	1.4	W 279	7.2	APP,INSTR MESURE FLUIDES
8748	ELEC MEAS,CONTRL EQU NES	W 164	5.9	W 132	3.4	W 126	9.1	W 62	6.8	APP ELEC ELECTRO MESURE
87483	OTH ELCTRNC MEAS ETC EQU	W 164	5.9	W 130	3.3	W 125	9.0	W 61	6.7	AUT APP ELECTRO DE MESURE
88	PHOTO EQU,OPTICL GDS ETC		4.8		3.4		4.4		7.9	APP,FOURN PHOTO,OP,MONTR
89	MISC MANUFCTRD GOODS NES		45.6		39.3		51.4		62.2	ART MANUFACTURES DIVERS
892	PRINTED MATTER	W 1808	14.4	W 1173	11.5	W 1186	12.2	W 2149	16.9	IMPRIMES
8921	PRINTED BOOKS,GLOBES,ETC	W 1140	9.9	W 1112	9.0	W 1082	8.7	W 1377	9.7	LIVRES,BROCHURES,CARTES
89211	PRINTED BOOKS,PAMPHLETS	W 1097	9.6	W 1068	8.8	W 1034	8.4	W 1334	9.4	LIVRES,BROCHURES
893	ARTICLES OF PLASTIC NES	W 5548	18.6		18.2		26.1		27.6	OUVRAGES EN MAT DIVIS 58
8931	PLSTC PACKG CONTNRS,LIDS	W 2618	9.9	W 4910	10.0	W 5445	13.7	W 3650	13.9	ART TRANSP EMBALLAGE ETC
8939	MISC PLASTIC ARTICLES	W 2753	8.5	W 2991	8.0	W 4496	12.0	W 4309	13.1	ART DIVERS EN MAT DIV 58
89399	OTHR PLASTC ARTICLES NES	W 1819	7.3	W 1910	6.7	W 2652	10.1	W 2825	11.3	AUT OUV MAT DIV 58
9	GOODS NOT CLASSD BY KIND		4.1		269.5		387.0		8.2	ART TRANSACT NON CLASSES
931	*SPECIAL TRANSACTIONS	W 2319	3.8		268.9		386.0	W 3345	7.9	TRANS.SPECIALES

5. Special Exports F.O.B. by Commodities according to the S.I.T.C. (Rev. 2) in million U.S. Dollars
Exportations Spéciales F.O.B. par Produits d'après la C.T.C.I. (Rév. 2) en millions de Dollars E.U.

SITC CTCI	COMMODITY	1993 QUANTITY QUANTITE	1993 VALUE VALEUR	1994 QUANTITY QUANTITE	1994 VALUE VALEUR	1995 QUANTITY QUANTITE	1995 VALUE VALEUR	1996 QUANTITY QUANTITE	1996 VALUE VALEUR	PRODUIT
	ALL COMMODITIES		1662.2		1954.3		2467.0		2569.3	TOUS PRODUITS
0	FOOD AND LIVE ANIMALS		94.8		87.9		116.2		140.9	ALIMENTS,ANIMAUX VIVANTS
02	DAIRY PRODCTS,BIRDS'EGGS		4.3		5.7		9.8		7.9	PRODUITS LAITIERS,OEUFS
022	MILK AND CREAM	W 3125	4.1	W 3352	5.6	W 7554	9.5	W 4663	7.8	LAIT ET CREME
0224	MILK,CREAM PRESERVED ETC	W 1695	3.1	W 3297	5.5	W 7535	9.4	W 2785	6.2	LAIT,CREME CONS,CONC
03	FISH AND PREPARATIONS		6.3		6.0		6.5		12.4	POISSONS ET PREPARATIONS
034	FISH,FRESH,CHILLED,FROZN	W 2601	3.9	W 3784	5.6	W 4097	6.2	W 5077	9.6	POISSON FRAIS, REFRIG,CONG
04	CEREALS AND PREPARATIONS		14.3		8.7		11.9		32.0	CEREALES ET PRODUITS
048	CEREAL ETC PREPARATIONS	W 7762	13.9	W 75847	8.6	W 57069	10.2	W 11975	29.6	PREPTNS A BASE CEREALES
0481	PREPD BREAKFAST FOOD ETC	W 1831	4.6	W 75044	5.7	W 56362	7.5	W 2964	9.6	CEREALES TRAVAILLEES
0484	BAKERY PRODUCTS	W 4032	7.1					W 6500	14.1	PRODUITS DE BOULANGERIE
04841	BREAD,BISCUIT,COM WAFERS							W 3111	7.8	PAINS,BISCUITS DE MER
05	VEGETABLES AND FRUIT		7.9		7.1		8.4		13.5	LEGUMES ET FRUITS
06	SUGAR AND PREPS,HONEY		30.5		34.3		51.6		34.1	SUCRES ET PRODUITS
061	SUGAR AND HONEY	W 51592	27.6	W 57277	30.7	W 86065	45.5	W 49436	28.2	SUCRES ET MIEL
0611	RAW BEET AND CANE SUGAR	W 51074	27.3	W 52109	28.1	W 67119	41.8	W 44990	27.6	SUCRES BRUTS
07	COFFEE,TEA,COCOA,SPICES		10.3		6.1		6.5		10.1	CAFE,THE,CACAO,EPICES
081	*FEEDING STUFF FOR ANIML	W 49363	11.8	W 59313	12.6	W 54430	12.1	W 60272	16.9	NOURRITURE POUR ANIMAUX
0813	OILCAKE AND OTH RESIDUES	W 42520	10.8	W 49065	10.7	W 37350	8.0	W 45193	13.1	TOURTEAUX
08131	— OF SOYA BEANS	W 42520	10.8	W 49065	10.7	W 37350	8.0	W 45193	13.1	TOURTEAUX DE SOJA
09	MISC EDIBLE PRODUCTS		8.1		6.0		7.5		11.1	PREP ALIMENTAIRES DIVERSES
098	EDIBLE PRODCTS,PREPS NES	W 4576	6.4	W 3506	4.2	W 41080	5.4	W 6819	8.4	PREP ALIMENTAIRES NDA
1	BEVERAGES AND TOBACCO		32.2		39.8		53.1		61.7	BOISSONS ET TABACS
11	BEVERAGES		31.8		39.5		52.0		59.9	BOISSONS
111	NON–ALCOHL BEVERAGES NES	W 17824	12.3	W 25737	14.8	W 68477	35.5	W 67821	33.9	BOISSONS NON ALCOOLIQUES
11102	FLAVORED WATERS NON–ALCO	W 17736	12.2	W 25518	14.7	W 68156	35.4	W 65853	33.7	LIMONADES,EAUX GAZEUSES
112	ALCOHOLIC BEVERAGES	W 21875	19.5	W 31360	24.7	W 21411	16.5	W 30782	26.0	BOISSONS ALCOOLIQUES
1123	BEER,ALE,STOUT,PORTER	W 10283	9.4	W 21280	13.5	W 15093	8.8	W 13421	9.3	BIERES
1124	DISTILLED ALCOHOLIC BEVS	W 11590	10.2	W 10052	11.2	W 6272	7.8	W 17008	16.6	ALCOOLS,EAUX–DE–VIE
11249	OTH ALCOHOLC BEVS,CMPNDS	W 11574	10.2	W 10052	11.2	W 6271	7.8	W 17007	16.6	BOISSONS ALCOOLIQUES NDA
2	CRUDE MATERLS,EXCL FUELS		4.1		2.7		4.9		9.5	MAT BRUTES NON COMESTIBLES
3	MINERAL FUELS ETC		957.6		960.8		1180.9		1291.5	COMBUSTIBLES MINERAUX LUB
33	PETROLEUM AND PRODUCTS		920.9		926.6		1118.1		1238.8	PETROLE ET DERIVES
333	CRUDE PETROLEUM	W 2760088	361.9	W 2788688	352.8	W 2986937	391.4	W 2657375	439.6	HUILES BRUTES DE PETROLE
334	PETROLEUM PRODUCTS,REFIN	W 4772378	553.8	W 4811338	569.8	W 5075580	722.3	W 5091425	794.8	PRODUITS RAFFINES
3341	GASOLINE,OTH LIGHT OILS	W 604323	112.3	W 648379	110.0	W 808367	134.4	W 527430	117.8	ESSENCES POUR MOTEURS
33411	MOTOR,AVIATION SPIRIT	W 604323	112.3	W 648379	110.0	W 808367	134.4	W 525721	117.4	ESSENCES MOTEURS D'AVIONS
3342	KEROSENE,OTH MEDIUM OILS	W 359593	66.1	W 455312	78.7	W 493795	84.1	W 409288	87.0	PETR LAMPANTS,AUT HUIL
33421	KEROSENE INCL JET FUEL	W 358917	65.9	W 454640	78.4	W 493790	84.1	W 398089	84.6	PETROLES LAMPANTS
3343	GAS OILS	W 775117	130.6	W 23131	4.4	W 26103	4.8	W 1287527	236.6	GAS OILS
3344	FUEL OILS,NES	W 2997493	230.2	W 3602692	342.6	W 3715033	479.0	W 2781745	322.0	FUEL OILS
3345	LUBS,PETROLEUM OILS NES	W 35852	14.8	W 81824	34.4	W 32283	20.2	W 85433	31.6	HUILES LUBRIFIANTES
33451	LUBS(HIGH PETR CONT) ETC	W 35843	14.8	W 81824	34.4	W 32268	20.2	W 85426	31.6	HUILES LUBRIF,H LOURDES
335	RESIDUAL PETRLM PROD NES	W 31856	5.3	W 23329	4.0	W 25832	4.5	W 24989	4.5	PRODUITS RESIDUELS NDA
341	*GAS,NATURAL AND MANUFCT	W 196086	36.7	W 207833	34.2	W 195364	62.8	W 31544	52.8	GAZ NATUREL,GAZ MANUFACT
3413	PETROLM GASES,LIQUEFIED	W 196085	36.7	W 207833	34.2	W 195364	62.8	W 31544	52.8	GAZ DE PETROLE LIQUEFIE
34131	LIQUEFIED PROPANE,BUTANE	W 179779	33.2	W 160208	27.0	W 95272	41.6	W 20101	31.2	PROPANE,BUTANE LIQUEFIES
34139	OTH HYDROCARBON GAS LQFD	W 16306	3.6	W 47624	7.3	W 100092	21.2	W 11443	21.6	HYDROCARBURES GAZEUX NDA
5	CHEMCLS,RELATED PROD NES		278.6		315.6		386.1		583.5	PRODUITS CHIMIQUES
51	ORGANIC CHEMICALS		40.6		0.2		0.4		123.8	PROD CHIMIQ ORGANIQUES
512	ALCOHOLS,PHENOLS ETC	W 391852	39.7	W 98	0.2	W 277	0.3	W 697393	123.2	PHENOLS,PHENOLS–ALCOOLS
5121	ACYCLIC ALCOHOLS,DERIVS	W 391852	39.7	W 98	0.2	W 277	0.3	W 697390	123.2	ALCOOLS ACYCLIQUES
51211	METHYL ALCOHOL(METHANOL)	W 391822	39.7					W 697106	122.7	ALCOOLS METHYLIQUES
52	INORGANIC CHEMICALS		149.1		231.0		261.8		301.8	PROD CHIM INORGANIQUES
522	INORG ELEMNTS,OXIDES,ETC	W 1399213	149.1	W 1588193	231.0	W 1465591	261.7	W 1749252	301.6	ELEMENTS INORGANIQUES
5225	INORGANIC BASES ETC NES	W 1397729	148.5	W 1587467	230.4	W 1443946	261.0	W 1748138	300.9	AUTRES BASES OXYDES METAL
52251	AMMONIA,ANHYDROUS ETC	W 1397724	148.5	W 1587465	230.4	W 1443942	261.0	W 1748120	300.9	AMMONIAC LIQUEFIE
55	PERFUME,CLEANING ETC PRD		18.3		18.2		18.6		21.9	PROD POUR PARFUM,TOILETTE
553	PERFUMERY,COSMETICS,ETC	W 1310	5.6	W 1049	4.3	W 706	5.3	W 1220	5.6	PRODUITS DE PARFUMERIE
554	SOAP,CLEANSING ETC PREPS	W 9661	12.8	W 14061	14.0	W 12570	13.3	W 13678	16.4	SAVONS,PRODUITS DETERSIFS
5542	WASHING PREPARATIONS ETC	W 7474	8.7	W 11978	10.0	W 11058	10.6	W 11950	12.7	PROD ORG TENSIO–ACT NDA
562	*FERTILIZERS,MANUFACTURE	W 513830	59.3	W 341833	58.8	W 512230	96.3	W 606801	115.7	ENGRAIS MANUFACTURES
5621	CHEM NITROGENOUS FERTLZR	W 511367	59.0	W 340298	58.4	W 502171	94.0	W 603844	114.9	ENGRAIS AZOTES
56216	UREA	W 511315	59.0	W 340296	58.4	W 502152	94.0	W 603026	114.3	UREE
6	BASIC MANUFACTURES		209.6		105.9		151.4		325.0	ART MANUFACTURES
63	WOOD,CORK MANUFACTRS NES		5.1		5.9		9.0		9.6	OUVRAGES LIEGE ET BOIS
635	WOOD MANUFACTURES NES	W 1308	5.0	W 1613	5.8	W 2647	9.0	W 2619	8.2	ART MANUF EN BOIS NDA
6353	BUILDERS WOODWRK,PREFABS	W 1164	4.7	W 1317	5.4	W 2529	8.6	W 2431	7.6	OUVRAGES DE MENUISERIE
64	PAPER,PAPERBOARD AND MFR		20.1		26.1		33.3		35.8	PAPIERS,CARTONS & OUVRAGES
642	PAPER,ETC,PRECUT,ARTS OF	W 9165	18.8	W 14285	24.9	W 13943	31.0	W 15570	33.7	PAP,CARTONS DECOUPES
6421	PAPER ETC CONTAINERS	W 4794	3.6	W 5473	5.3	W 7045	9.7	W 8392	11.2	BOITES,SACS EMBALLAGES
6428	PAPER ETC ARTICLES NES	W 2769	10.9	W 5698	13.2	W 3638	13.9	W 3694	14.8	OUVRAGES EN PATE A PAPIER
64285	PAPER ETC DIAPERS ETC	W 2526	10.2	W 5235	12.0	W 3165	12.4	W 3133	13.6	SERVIETTES HYGIENIQUES
65	TEXTILE YARN,FABRICS,ETC		5.5		6.1		7.0		9.0	FILS,TISSUS,ARTICLES TEXTILE
66	NONMETAL MINERAL MFS NES		26.7		28.8		32.5		33.6	ART MIN NON METALLIQUES
661	LIME,CEMENT,BLDG PRODS	W 329239	16.6	W 461447	16.1	W 305720	17.4	W 358992	20.5	CHAUX,CIMENTS MAT CONSTR
6612	CEMENT	W 329210	16.5	W 461412	16.1	W 305715	17.4	W 358941	20.3	CIMENTS HYDRAULIQUES
665	GLASSWARE	W 19281	8.9	W 24877	11.4	W 27318	12.8	W 18658	9.4	OUVRAGES EN VERRE
6651	BOTTLES ETC OF GLASS	W 19226	8.9	W 24854	11.4	W 27276	12.8	W 18637	9.4	RECIPIENTS EN VERRE
66511	GLASS BOTTLES ETC NONVAC	W 19226	8.9	W 24854	11.4	W 27276	12.8	W 18637	9.4	BONBONNES,BOUTEILLES,ETC
67	IRON AND STEEL		142.2		28.3		53.5		212.6	FER ET ACIER
671	PIG IRON ETC	W 155533	15.1	W 232400	22.7	W 325211	40.6	W 163508	25.9	FONTE,SPIEGEL,POUDRES
6713	IRON,STL POWDER,SHOT,ETC	W 155533	15.1	W 232400	22.7	W 325211	40.6	W 163508	25.9	POUDRES,GREN FER,ACIER
67133	SPONGE IRON OR STEEL	W 155533	15.1	W 232395	22.7	W 325163	40.5	W 163508	25.9	FER,ACIER SPONGIEUX AUT POUD
673	IRON,STEEL SHAPES ETC	W 401755	122.4	W 10892	4.0	W 18734	6.1	W 620457	181.1	BARRES,PROFIL FER,ACIER
6731	IRON,STEEL WIRE ROD	W 372852	111.3	W 2	0.1	W 4	0.1	W 582742	166.9	FIL MACHINE FER,ACIER
67311	IRON,SIMPLE STL WIRE ROD							W 582740	166.9	FIL MACH AUT ACIER FIN
67314	STNLESS STL ETC WIRE ROD	W 372849	111.3							FIL MACH ACIER INOXYDABLE
6732	IRON,STEEL BARS ETC	W 28530	10.9	W 10793	3.9	W 18545	5.9	W 35708	13.5	BARRES FER,ACIER
67322	HIGH CARBON STL BARS ETC	W 32	0.1					W 21824	8.1	BARRES ACIER FIN CARBONE
67324	STNLESS STL ETC BARS ETC	W 21919	8.2						0.1	BARRES ACIER INOXYDABLE
69	METAL MANUFACTURES NES		8.5		9.7		13.8		18.3	ART MANUFACT EN METAL NDA
7	MACHINES,TRANSPORT EQUIP		46.1		28.1		48.8		96.9	MACHINES MATERIEL TRANSPORT
74	GENRL INDUSTRL MACHY NES		4.9		7.6		13.4		23.0	MACH APP INDUSTRIE
741	HEATING,COOLING EQUIPMNT	W 478	3.6	W 732	6.5	W 3912	9.3	W 1372	12.0	MACH CHAUFFAGE,PIECES
76	TELECOMM,SOUND EQUIPMENT		8.0		2.8		2.9		3.2	EQUIPMENT DE TELECOM
764	TELECOM EQPT,PTS,ACC NES	W 77	6.0		1.5	W 109	1.7	W 29	1.5	EQUIP TELECOM,PIECES
77	ELECTRIC MACHNRY NES ETC		9.6		3.5		5.5		10.5	MACH APP ELECT NDA
79	OTHR TRANSPORT EQUIPMENT		17.3		6.4		20.0		51.8	AUTRE MATERIEL TRANSPORT
792	AIRCRAFT ETC	W 45	14.3	W 100	4.8	W 117	18.7	W 82	11.6	APP NAVIGATION AERIENNE
7921	HELICOPTERS			W 4	0.2	W 99	18.4			HELICOPTERES

5. Special Exports F.O.B. by Commodities according to the S.I.T.C. (Rev. 2) in million U.S. Dollars
Exportations Spéciales F.O.B. par Produits d'après la C.T.C.I. (Rév. 2) en millions de Dollars E.U.

SITC CTCI	COMMODITY	1993		1994		1995		1996		PRODUIT
		QUANTITY QUANTITE	VALUE VALEUR	QUANTITY QUANTITE	VALUE VALEUR	QUANTITY QUANTITE	VALUE VALEUR	QUANTITY QUANTITE	VALUE VALEUR	
7924	AIRCRFT NES OVER 15000KG	W 17	12.9	W 74	4.3			W 75	11.4	AERODYNES PLUS 15000 KG
793	SHIPS AND BOATS ETC	W 2703	3.0	W 230	1.7	W 132	1.4	W 7328	40.2	NAVIRES BATEAUX,ETC
7938	TUGS,SPECIAL VESSELS ETC	W 2530	2.3	W 100	0.9	W 22	0.1	W 6813	38.5	REMORQUEURS,BATEAUX SPEC
79382	SPECL PURPOSE VESSLS ETC	W 2500	2.2	W 97	0.8			W 6370	37.4	BAT–PHARES,–POMPES,DRAGUES
8	MISC MANUFACTURED GOODS		35.4		34.6		48.6		53.5	ART MANUFACTURES DIVERS
84	CLOTHING AND ACCESSORIES		8.6		9.6		11.5		11.5	VETEMENTS
87	PRECISION INSTRUMNTS NES		2.0		1.9		10.8		8.6	INSTRUM,APPAR SCIENT NDA
874	MEASURNG,CONTROLNG INSTR	W 26	1.9	W 37	1.9	W 152	10.8	W 190	8.6	INSTRUMENTS DE MESURE
89	MISC MANUFCTRD GOODS NES		19.6		17.4		19.7		25.4	ART MANUFACTURES DIVERS
892	PRINTED MATTER		7.7	W 216	2.2	W 179	2.5	W 883	6.3	IMPRIMES
8928	PRINTED MATTER NES		5.8	W 36	0.2	W 29	0.3	W 465	3.5	IMPRIMES NDA
893	ARTICLES OF PLASTIC NES	W 3429	7.6	W 5359	10.8		12.1	W 235	0.5	OUVRAGES EN MAT DIVIS 58
8939	MISC PLASTIC ARTICLES	W 1667	3.1	W 3191	6.6	W 3705	6.7	W 2958	6.6	ART DIVERS EN MAT DIV 58
89399	OTHR PLASTC ARTICLES NES	W 1655	3.1	W 3185	6.6	W 3638	6.6	W 2793	6.3	AUT OUV MAT DIV 58
9	GOODS NOT CLASSD BY KIND		1.6		375.1		471.8		0.6	ART TRANSACT NON CLASSES
931	*SPECIAL TRANSACTIONS	W 451	1.6		375.1		471.8	W 113	0.6	TRANS.SPECIALES

1. HISTORICAL SERIES, 1962–1997 GENERAL TRADE, IMPORTS C.I.F., EXPORTS F.O.B. #1
SERIES HISTORIQUES, 1962–1997 COMMERCE GENERAL, IMPORTATIONS C.A.F., EXPORTATIONS F.O.B

YEAR ANNEE	VALUE IN MILLION TUNISIAN DINARS VALEUR EN MILLION TUNISIAN DINARS MERCHANDISE –MARCHANDISE		GOLD –OR		CONVERSION FACTORS U.S. CENTS PER TUNISIAN DINAR FACTEURS DE CONVERSION CENTS E.U. PAR TUNISIAN DINAR		INDEX NUMBERS –INDICES QUANTUM		UNIT VALUE VALEUR UNITAIRE	
	IMPORTS	EXPORTS	IMPORTS	EXPORTS	IMPORTS	EXPORTS	IMPORTS	EXPORTS	IMPORTS	EXPORTS
1962	90.89	48.69			238.1000	238.1000				
1963	93.66	52.92			238.1000	238.1000				
1964	110.85	57.30			219.9400	221.6100				
1965	129.06	62.92			190.5000	190.5000				
1966	131.22	76.39			190.5000	190.5000				
1967	137.09	78.36			190.5000	190.5000				
1968	114.50	82.83			190.5000	190.5000				
1969	139.78	86.96			190.5000	190.5000				
1970	160.40	95.80			190.4750	190.4750				
1971	179.96	113.30			192.5840	193.1270				
1972	222.22	150.33			209.5850	209.5090				
1973	286.10	178.80			238.8350	235.5800				
1974	488.66	397.70			230.8460	231.6810				
1975	572.82	345.58			248.5570	247.5730				
1976	656.72	338.26			232.8750	232.9480				
1977	782.47	398.25			233.1700	233.0380				
1978	899.73	468.42			240.2780	240.4260				
1979	1156.70	726.70			246.2620	246.4110				
1980	1428.40	904.80			246.9210	246.9610	92	102	48	53
1981	1866.00	1234.00			203.1444	202.8433	94	100	54	61
1982	2001.90	1169.40			169.9572	169.8244	98	100	59	67
1983	2106.40	1280.50			147.2836	146.1933	93	92	61	69
1984	2508.90	1399.10			128.2434	128.4135	100	91	66	76
1985	2287.00	1443.00			113.5613	112.7762	77	82	71	76
1986	2295.10	1403.70			125.9538	125.3746	93	92	70	68
1987	2509.10	1770.70			121.1012	120.7976	68	95	77	78
1988	3167.00	2055.40			116.4737	116.5065	85	96	81	83
1989	4163.60	2782.00			105.3758	105.3051	101	110	89	95
1990	4826.40	3087.40			114.2170	114.2412	100	100	100	100
1991	4789.00	3417.10			108.3609	108.2603	107	110	99	98
1992	5688.80	3549.70			113.0507	113.2195	104	111	94	95
1993	6237.20	3818.10			99.6265	99.5838	116	121	94	96
1994	6647.30	4696.60			98.9991	99.1623	120	137		101
1995	7464.10	5172.90			105.8798	105.8455				
1996	7498.80	5372.00			102.6863	102.6930				
1997	8756.00	6147.90			90.3855	90.4285				

2. IMPORTS BY BROAD ECONOMIC CATEGORY AND EXPORTS BY INDUSTRIAL ORIGIN. (PERCENTAGE OF TOTAL VALUE)
IMPORTATIONS PAR CATEGORIES ECONOMIQUES ET EXPORTATIONS PAR BRANCHE D'ACTIVITE.(EN POURCENTAGE DE LA VALEUR TOTALE)

IMPORTS – IMPORTATIONS

	1991	1992	1993	1994	1995	1996	1997
TOTAL IMPORTS–IMPORTATIONS TOTALES	100.	100.	100.	100.	100.	100.	100.
1 FOOD BEV–ALIMENTATION BOISSONS	6.0	6.2	6.3	7.8	10.5	7.4	8.1
11 PRIMARY–PRODUITS DE BASE	2.9	2.8	3.0	3.8	6.5	3.7	4.7
111 FOR INDUSTRY–POUR L'INDUSTRIE	1.7	1.8	1.8	2.6	5.4	2.9	3.7
112 FOR HOUSEHOLDS–POUR LES MENAGES	1.2	1.0	1.2	1.2	1.1	0.8	1.0
12 PROCESSED–PRODUITS ELABORES	3.1	3.4	3.3	4.0	4.0	3.7	3.4
121 FOR INDUSTRY–POUR L'INDUSTRIE	1.6	1.3	1.4	1.9	1.8	1.9	1.5
122 FOR HOUSEHOLDS–POUR LES MENAGES	1.5	2.0	1.9	2.0	2.1	1.8	1.9
2 IND SUPPLIES–APPROV INDUSTRIELS	44.6	45.4	42.8	43.4	44.4	44.2	42.1
21 PRIMARY–PRODUITS DE BASE	5.7	4.7	3.9	4.5	4.8	4.6	4.2
22 PROCESSED–PRODUITS ELABORES	39.0	40.6	38.9	38.9	39.6	39.6	37.8
3 FUELS–COMBUSTIBLES	8.1	7.4	7.7	7.5	7.2	8.3	7.8
31 PRIMARY–PRODUITS DE BASE	2.5	3.0	2.8	3.4	4.1	3.6	3.1
32 PROCESSED–PRODUITS ELABORES	5.6	4.4	5.0	4.2	3.1	4.6	4.7
321 MOTOR SPIRIT–ESSENCE	0.6	0.7	0.8	0.7	0.6	0.8	0.9
322 OTHER–AUTRES	5.0	3.7	4.2	3.5	2.5	3.8	3.8
4 MACHINERY–EQUIPEMENT	22.3	20.8	22.0	19.8	17.8	19.3	19.0
41 CAPITAL EQUIPMENT–MACHINES	19.2	17.7	18.8	16.9	15.2	16.6	16.4
42 PARTS–PIECES ACCESSOIRES	3.1	3.1	3.2	2.9	2.6	2.7	2.6
5 TRANSPORT–TRANSPORT	7.7	9.5	10.3	9.6	8.1	7.9	10.2
51 PASSENGER CARS–AUTOMOBILES	0.6	1.3	2.6	3.2	3.0	3.2	3.6
52 OTHER–AUTRES	3.2	4.3	3.2	3.2	2.3	1.6	3.6
521 INDUSTRIAL–INDUSTRIELS	3.1	4.3	3.2	3.1	2.2	1.6	3.6
522 NON INDUSTRIAL–NON INDUSTRIEL	0.1	0.0	0.0	0.0	0.0	0.0	0.0
53 PARTS–PIECES ACCESSOIRES	3.9	3.9	4.5	3.2	2.8	3.1	3.0
6 CONSUM GOODS–BIENS CONSOMMATION	11.2	10.7	10.6	11.8	12.0	12.8	12.8
61 DURABLE–DURABLES	1.9	1.5	1.4	1.4	1.4	1.4	1.3
62 SEMI DURABLE–SEMI DURABLES	5.6	5.7	6.1	7.0	7.4	8.2	8.2
63 NON DURABLE–NON DURABLES	3.7	3.5	3.1	3.4	3.1	3.2	3.2
7 GOODS NES–BIENS NDA	0.1	0.0	0.2	0.1	0.1	0.0	0.0

EXPORTS – EXPORTATIONS

	1991	1992	1993	1994	1995	1996	1997
TOTAL EXPORTS–EXPORTATIONS TOTALES	100.	100.	100.	100.	100.	100.	100.
1 AGRICULTURE	4.8	4.1	4.7	4.0	3.6	3.1	3.0
2 MINING QUARRY–INDUS EXTRACTIVES	13.1	14.0	10.9	8.8	8.3	9.8	7.9
3 MANUFACTURING–IND MANUFACTUR	82.1	81.9	84.4	87.2	88.2	87.1	89.2
31 FOOD BEV TOBACCO–ALIM BOISS TAB	10.5	6.2	6.8	9.0	6.4	4.4	8.2
32 TEXTILES–INDUSTRIES TEXTILES	38.8	43.4	46.4	47.5	49.8	50.9	48.5
33 WOOD & PRODUCTS–BOIS & PRODUITS	0.1	0.1	0.3	0.1	0.1	0.2	0.2
34 PAPER & PRODUCTS–PAPIER & PRODT	0.9	0.8	0.9	0.6	0.8	0.6	0.7
35 CHEMICALS–INDUSTRIES CHIMIQUES	16.8	15.9	13.6	14.2	14.4	16.0	15.6
36 NON METAL MIN–MIN NON METAL	2.1	2.5	2.0	1.6	2.1	1.5	1.6
37 BASIC METAL–IND METAL BASE	1.4	1.4	0.9	2.2	1.3	1.2	1.2
38 METAL MANUF–MANUF METAL	11.0	11.0	12.9	11.4	12.6	11.5	12.6
39 OTH MANUF IND–AUTRES MANUF	0.5	0.5	0.6	0.6	0.5	0.7	0.6

3. TRADE BY PRINCIPAL COUNTRIES OF ORIGIN AND DESTINATION (VALUE IN MILLION U.S. DOLLARS)
ECHANGES SELON LES PRINCIPAUX PAYS D'ORIGINE ET DE DESTINATION (VALEUR EN MILLIONS DE DOLLARS EU)

COUNTRIES–PAYS	GENERAL IMPORTS C.I.F. IMPORTATIONS GENERALES C.A.F				
	1993	1994	1995	1996	1997
World	6214.0	6483.9	7903.0	7698.2	7947.0
Africa	273.5	372.6	540.2	515.0	471.3
Americas	487.8	597.0	588.4	541.2	622.1
– Northern America	387.3	462.5	474.8	357.9	401.2
– LAIA	90.4	125.2	99.0	168.9	206.0
– CACM	0.1	0.6	2.0	0.3	1.8
– Caribbean	10.0	8.5	12.2	13.8	12.4
– Rest of America	0.0	0.3	0.5	0.1	0.7
Asia excl fmr USSR	444.4	495.1	573.4	632.3	667.5
– Middle East	132.5	159.5	226.2	220.8	182.6
Asia former USSR				0.0	6.6
Europe excl fmr USSR	4787.5	4858.5	5916.1	5846.3	5979.0
– European Union	4602.3	4665.0	5642.0	5569.8	5796.8
– Eastern Europe	88.6	76.5	121.9	153.8	71.2
– Rest of Europe	96.7	117.0	152.3	122.7	111.0
Europe former USSR	98.9	104.1	230.6	98.5	125.4
Oceania	4.0	8.9	11.1	6.9	7.4
Other	117.9	47.6	43.2	57.9	67.7
France, Monaco	1668.2	1779.6	2024.6	1878.5	1890.0
Italy/Italie	1134.4	999.8	1209.0	1451.8	1534.9
Germany/Allemagne	807.7	791.9	993.7	976.6	1073.5
USA/Etats–Unis d'Amer	358.4	426.9	400.0	320.5	341.1
Belgium–Luxembourg	268.5	283.2	354.3	348.0	317.9
Spain/Espagne	201.4	233.3	329.4	303.5	330.8
Libyan Arab Jamahiriya	52.1	120.8	203.9	234.7	242.7
Netherlands/Pays–Bas	136.3	137.5	206.2	179.7	161.3
United Kingdom	140.5	144.3	159.2	144.4	208.0
Japan/Japon	143.2	151.8	140.9	163.6	194.3
Russian Federation	98.9	104.1	228.5	82.9	116.8
Algeria/Algérie	99.0	124.9	179.8	127.1	76.4
Switzerland,Liechtenst.	77.8	96.0	114.4	103.7	93.5
Turkey/Turquie	57.1	84.6	105.9	100.4	86.4
Sweden/Suède	80.6	69.5	82.7	84.2	78.7
Areas n.e.s.	115.3	45.4	41.5	57.5	67.1
Argentina/Argentine	37.1	44.2	23.6	84.7	127.4
China/Chine	49.1	49.0	54.7	61.0	66.9
Greece/Grèce	52.2	45.1	72.0	66.0	41.2
Brazil/Brésil	43.4	63.8	43.9	59.1	63.2
Morocco/Maroc	48.6	46.7	59.7	58.6	48.5
Finland/Finlande	48.0	52.5	64.9	44.6	49.7
Canada	28.9	35.5	74.8	37.4	60.1
Portugal	7.3	54.9	60.9	29.3	33.2
Poland/Pologne	44.3	39.7	32.3	38.1	20.3
Korea, Republic of	26.9	24.7	34.0	35.7	51.8
Saudi Arabia	19.7	28.3	44.9	34.6	42.9
Other Asia n.e.s.	23.5	28.8	30.5	35.7	38.2
Egypt/Egypte	24.1	25.4	30.2	30.7	40.2
Austria/Autriche	22.6	37.8	29.4	25.9	32.9
Denmark/Danemark	22.4	27.1	41.6	25.6	30.5
Syrian Arab Republic	26.2	24.2	45.6	32.5	8.6
Romania/Roumanie	2.4	4.7	28.4	68.9	31.4
Cote d'Ivoire	26.7	24.6	26.6	23.3	17.3
India/Inde	12.2	11.2	13.1	23.2	35.1
Czech Republic	21.5	15.2	28.9	19.8	5.4
Malaysia/Malaisie	9.6	12.7	18.7	24.1	15.6
China, Hong Kong SAR	12.4	11.1	13.4	21.1	15.6
Bulgaria/Bulgarie	9.0	11.2	24.3	18.6	5.2
Ireland/Irlande	12.2	8.4	14.2	11.8	14.2

COUNTRIES–PAYS	GENERAL EXPORTS F.O.B. EXPORTATIONS GENERALES F.O.B.				
	1993	1994	1995	1996	1997
Monde	3804.5	4584.5	5474.6	5517.4	5559.4
Afrique	322.5	331.9	463.0	394.9	387.8
Amériques	54.8	83.6	117.4	121.2	91.4
– Amérique du Nord	32.5	50.0	71.2	76.5	40.5
– ALAI	11.6	24.8	24.2	27.4	34.6
– MCAC	0.1	0.9	0.0	0.0	3.0
– Caraïbes	10.6	7.6	21.6	16.3	12.9
– Autre Amérique	0.0	0.2	0.4	0.9	0.3
Asie anc. URSS exclus	246.1	266.9	310.1	343.3	390.9
– Moyen–Orient	141.3	115.7	117.4	141.5	157.3
Asie ancienne URSS				6.9	0.3
Europe anc. URSS exclus	3077.3	3747.6	4411.8	4483.3	4446.9
– Union Européenne	3022.1	3666.4	4324.1	4419.2	4358.4
– Europe de l'Est	30.5	20.1	28.0	24.8	20.7
– Autre de l'Europe	24.7	61.0	59.7	39.4	67.8
Europe ancienne URSS	8.4	2.8	1.5	2.8	4.3
Océanie	0.5	1.4	2.8	6.7	1.9
Autre	94.9	150.4	168.0	158.3	236.0
France, Monaco	1142.8	1232.2	1536.4	1419.8	1417.0
Italy/Italie	620.7	885.9	1021.4	1143.4	1186.7
Germany/Allemagne	660.8	712.8	861.0	862.3	807.9
Belgium–Luxembourg	276.5	297.7	357.1	395.5	339.7
Libyan Arab Jamahiriya	188.5	156.5	192.4	195.9	257.1
Spain/Espagne	96.0	216.8	221.5	199.4	200.1
Netherlands/Pays–Bas	117.3	141.1	156.1	171.5	156.8
Areas n.e.s.	71.8	114.8	137.0	140.1	168.9
India/Inde	49.3	81.2	98.3	119.3	153.0
Algeria/Algérie	66.6	106.1	185.5	96.1	37.8
United Kingdom	50.4	68.8	81.6	106.4	161.7
USA/Etats–Unis d'Amer	31.7	48.0	69.1	75.4	37.5
Turkey/Turquie	51.2	42.1	33.7	49.4	59.3
Switzerland,Liechtenst.	20.4	49.4	48.2	27.2	51.2
Bunkers, ship stores	23.1	35.6	31.1	18.3	67.0
Morocco/Maroc	35.1	27.8	26.8	37.5	33.0
Greece/Grèce	2.8	54.3	31.4	37.7	20.5
China/Chine	11.3	24.8	31.1	18.6	25.0
Egypt/Egypte	6.6	16.2	24.5	26.8	24.0
Saudi Arabia	20.0	16.2	15.6	23.1	21.4
Indonesia/Indonésie	27.8	10.5	18.9	14.9	16.1
Poland/Pologne	21.7	14.4	17.0	15.5	16.8
Iran (Islamic Rep of)	7.3	6.6	15.8	26.3	28.8
Portugal	4.9	7.2	11.2	32.3	26.9
Brazil/Brésil	7.0	16.4	15.7	18.6	21.6
Ireland/Irlande	22.1	10.8	10.9	16.1	13.6
Syrian Arab Republic	24.9	15.9	25.2	3.1	2.7
Denmark/Danemark	15.1	14.2	14.0	14.0	9.9
Japan/Japon	6.9	15.6	16.2	17.3	9.0
Cuba	8.9	5.8	19.5	15.9	11.3
Lebanon/Liban	4.4	6.4	12.4	8.5	11.5
Sweden/Suède	7.2	7.9	10.8	9.5	7.7
Pakistan	0.0	0.0	20.3	18.1	3.5
Bahrain/Bahreïn	10.4	6.9	5.8	10.4	7.8
Jordan/Jordanie	8.2	14.0	1.6	1.3	9.2
Cameroon/Cameroun	7.8	7.0	7.9	5.3	5.6
Austria/Autriche	3.4	5.4	6.6	8.8	9.0
United Arab Emirates	3.6	4.3	4.5	8.9	8.1
Cote d'Ivoire	4.3	3.2	5.7	7.1	5.9
Argentina/Argentine	0.0	2.6	0.4	7.6	12.3

(VALUE AS PERCENTAGE OF WORLD TOTAL)(VALEURS EN POURCENTAGE DU TOTAL MONDIAL)

	1988	1989	1990	1991	1992	1993	1994	1995	1996	1997
Africa	5.6	5.9	4.9	4.8	5.5	4.4	5.7	6.8	6.7	5.9
Americas	12.2	9.5	8.1	8.0	7.9	7.8	9.2	7.4	7.0	7.8
– Northern America	9.4	6.3	6.1	6.4	5.9	6.2	7.1	6.0	4.6	5.0
– LAIA	2.6	2.7	1.5	1.4	1.7	1.5	1.9	1.3	2.2	2.6
– CACM	0.0	0.0	0.1	0.0	0.0	0.0	0.0	0.0	0.0	0.0
– Caribbean	0.2	0.5	0.3	0.2	0.2	0.2	0.1	0.2	0.2	0.2
– Rest of America	0.0	0.0	0.0	0.0	0.0	0.0	0.0	0.0	0.0	0.0
Asia excl fmr USSR	7.4	8.8	7.7	7.1	6.8	7.2	7.6	7.3	8.2	8.4
– Middle East	3.8	5.5	4.0	2.5	2.0	2.1	2.5	2.9	2.9	2.3
Asia former USSR									0.0	0.1
Europe excl fmr USSR	73.1	73.6	77.0	78.1	77.2	77.0	74.9	74.9	75.9	75.2
– European Union	68.5	68.9	72.4	74.1	73.3	74.1	71.9	71.4	72.4	72.9
– Eastern Europe	2.8	3.2	2.5	2.0	2.2	1.4	1.2	1.5	2.0	0.9
– Rest of Europe	1.8	1.5	2.1	2.0	1.8	1.6	1.8	1.9	1.6	1.4
Europe former USSR	1.1	1.7	1.7	1.4	1.3	1.6	1.6	2.9	1.3	1.6
Oceania	0.2	0.2	0.0	0.1	0.1	0.1	0.1	0.1	0.1	0.1
Other	0.3	0.3	0.6	0.5	1.1	1.9	0.7	0.5	0.8	0.9
France, Monaco	24.8	26.3	27.9	26.1	25.5	26.8	27.4	25.6	24.4	23.8
Italy/Italie	13.3	13.7	15.9	17.5	18.2	18.3	15.4	15.3	18.9	19.3
Germany/Allemagne				14.3	14.0	13.0	12.2	12.6	12.7	13.5
USA/Etats–Unis d'Amer	7.1	5.1	5.2	4.8	5.0	5.8	6.6	5.1	4.2	4.3
Belgium–Luxembourg	4.8	4.7	4.8	5.4	4.7	4.3	4.4	4.5	4.5	4.0
Spain/Espagne	4.6	3.8	3.1	3.1	3.3	3.2	3.6	4.2	3.9	4.2
Libyan Arab Jamahiriya	0.2	0.4	0.5	0.6	0.8	0.8	1.9	2.6	3.0	3.1
Netherlands/Pays–Bas	2.4	2.4	2.6	2.2	2.2	2.2	2.1	2.6	2.3	2.0
United Kingdom	1.7	1.5	1.7	1.8	1.8	2.3	2.2	2.0	1.9	2.6
Japan/Japon	1.3	1.4	1.8	2.3	2.3	2.3	2.3	1.8	2.1	2.4

	1988	1989	1990	1991	1992	1993	1994	1995	1996	1997
Afrique	5.7	8.2	8.8	9.4	9.0	8.5	7.2	8.5	7.2	7.0
Amériques	1.6	3.2	1.8	1.5	1.7	1.4	1.8	2.1	2.2	1.6
– Amérique du Nord	1.1	2.4	0.9	0.8	0.9	0.9	1.1	1.3	1.4	0.7
– ALAI	0.3	0.4	0.7	0.5	0.6	0.3	0.5	0.4	0.5	0.6
– MCAC	0.0	0.1	0.0	0.1	0.0	0.0	0.0	0.0	0.0	0.1
– Caraïbes	0.0	0.3	0.2	0.1	0.1	0.3	0.2	0.4	0.3	0.2
– Autre Amérique	0.1	0.0	0.0	0.0	0.1	0.0	0.0	0.0	0.0	0.0
Asie anc. URSS exclus	11.5	10.8	7.6	6.8	7.2	6.5	5.8	5.7	6.2	7.0
– Moyen–Orient	4.6	5.0	4.2	2.8	3.2	3.7	2.5	2.1	2.6	2.8
Asie ancienne URSS									0.1	0.0
Europe anc. URSS exclus	77.7	75.7	79.1	78.9	80.0	80.9	81.7	80.6	81.3	80.0
– Union Européenne	75.0	74.0	78.1	76.9	78.3	79.4	80.0	79.0	80.1	78.4
– Europe de l'Est	1.6	0.9	0.3	1.1	1.0	0.8	0.4	0.5	0.4	0.4
– Autre de l'Europe	1.1	0.7	0.6	0.9	0.6	0.6	1.3	1.1	0.7	1.2
Europe ancienne URSS	1.1	0.7	1.2	1.1	0.3	0.2	0.1	0.0	0.1	0.1
Océanie	0.0	0.0	0.0	0.0	0.0	0.0	0.0	0.1	0.1	0.0
Autre	2.4	1.4	1.5	2.2	1.8	2.5	3.3	3.1	2.9	4.2
France, Monaco	25.8	24.6	26.6	25.3	27.1	30.0	26.9	28.1	25.7	25.5
Italy/Italie	18.9	18.7	21.2	19.7	17.1	16.3	19.3	18.7	20.7	21.3
Germany/Allemagne				16.4	17.0	17.4	15.5	15.7	15.6	14.5
Belgium–Luxembourg	5.9	6.1	7.0	6.2	6.9	7.3	6.5	6.5	7.2	6.1
Libyan Arab Jamahiriya	1.6	4.1	4.6	5.5	4.4	5.0	3.4	3.5	3.6	4.6
Spain/Espagne	3.4	2.7	2.6	3.7	2.7	2.5	4.7	4.0	3.6	3.6
Netherlands/Pays–Bas	2.9	2.5	2.5	2.7	2.6	3.1	3.1	2.9	3.1	2.8
Areas n.e.s.	2.0	1.2	1.0	0.9	1.1	1.9	2.5	2.5	2.5	3.0
India/Inde	3.4	2.8	1.2	1.8	1.9	1.3	1.8	1.8	2.2	2.8
Algeria/Algérie	2.5	2.2	2.3	2.1	2.4	1.8	2.3	3.4	1.7	0.7

4. General Imports C.I.F. by Commodities according to the S.I.T.C. (Rev. 2) in million U.S. Dollars
Importations Générales C.A.F. par Produits d'après la C.T.C.I. (Rév. 2) en millions de Dollars E.U.

SITC CTCI	COMMODITY	1994 QUANTITY QUANTITE	1994 VALUE VALEUR	1995 QUANTITY QUANTITE	1995 VALUE VALEUR	1996 QUANTITY QUANTITE	1996 VALUE VALEUR	1997 QUANTITY QUANTITE	1997 VALUE VALEUR	PRODUIT
	ALL COMMODITIES		6483.9		7903.1		7698.2		7947.1	TOUS PRODUITS
0	FOOD AND LIVE ANIMALS		478.3		787.6		541.8		672.8	ALIMENTS,ANIMAUX VIVANTS
02	DAIRY PRODCTS,BIRDS'EGGS		45.3		57.7		30.9		41.4	PRODUITS LAITIERS,OEUFS
022	MILK AND CREAM	W 28332	29.8	W 19135	38.1	W 12346	21.1	W 26477	28.9	LAIT ET CREME
0224	MILK,CREAM PRESERVED ETC	W 16516	25.0	W 19113	38.1	W 10197	20.0	W 13752	23.1	LAIT,CREME CONS,CONC
04	CEREALS AND PREPARATIONS		183.4		442.5		265.2		324.1	CEREALES ET PRODUITS
041	WHEAT ETC UNMILLED	W 851996	98.7	W 1652381	301.6	W 860299	184.5	W 1205319	205.3	FROMENT,EPEAUTRE
0411	DURUM WHEAT UNMILLED	W 49492	11.4	W 687345	146.0	W 205003	54.2	W 238503	49.4	FROMENT DUR NON MOULU
0412	OTHER WHEAT ETC UNMILLED	W 802503	87.4	W 965035	155.6	W 655296	130.3	W 966817	155.9	AUTRE FROMENT NON MOULU
043	BARLEY UNMILLED	W 454239	36.9	W 687203	79.7	W 31757	4.4	W 303711	43.1	ORGE NON MONDEE
044	MAIZE UNMILLED	W 254076	32.3	W 328896	45.5	W 314762	59.8	W 445707	62.6	MAIS NON MOULU
05	VEGETABLES AND FRUIT		34.2		75.7		35.1		37.3	LEGUMES ET FRUITS
054	VEG ETC FRSH,SMPLY PRSVD	W 49654	17.4	W 100872	49.8	W 55645	19.6	W 55187	20.3	LEGUMES FRAIS,CONG,SECS
0541	POTATOES FRSH EXCL SWEET	W 37084	12.4	W 64022	26.4	W 31263	13.1	W 26166	12.4	POMMES DE TERRE
06	SUGAR AND PREPS,HONEY		91.5		72.8		89.9		83.4	SUCRES ET PRODUITS
061	SUGAR AND HONEY	W 283534	90.3	W 186794	70.4	W 241700	88.4	W 246477	82.1	SUCRES ET MIEL
0611	RAW BEET AND CANE SUGAR	W 85161	25.1	W 55522	17.2	W 69300	20.7	W 83309	22.8	SUCRES BRUTS
0612	REFINED SUGAR ETC	W 192803	62.7	W 125900	50.3	W 165213	63.8	W 154909	55.6	SUCRES RAFFINES
07	COFFEE,TEA,COCOA,SPICES		44.2		50.4		45.4		51.4	CAFE,THE,CACAO,EPICES
071	COFFEE AND SUBSTITUTES	W 9141	17.3	W 8401	30.1	W 7484	20.8	W 10937	24.2	CAFE ET SUCCEDANES
0711	COFFEE GREEN,ROASTED,SUB	W 8861	14.9	W 8045	25.9	W 7096	16.6	W 10513	20.6	CAFE TORREFIE OU DECAFEINE
07111	COFFEE GREEN,HUSKS,SKINS	W 8857	14.8	W 8040	25.8	W 6997	16.4	W 9994	20.0	CAFE NON TORREFIE
081	*FEEDING STUFF FOR ANIML	W 213470	44.8	W 227008	45.9	W 157821	43.7	W 239271	71.7	NOURRITURE POUR ANIMAUX
0813	OILCAKE AND OTH RESIDUES	W 148864	33.4	W 139075	30.5	W 153599	41.4	W 211880	65.6	TOURTEAUX
08131	— OF SOYA BEANS	W 148851	33.4	W 139075	30.5	W 153599	41.4	W 211880	65.6	TOURTEAUX DE SOJA
1	BEVERAGES AND TOBACCO		54.8		65.4		64.4		78.6	BOISSONS ET TABACS
12	TOBACCO AND MANUFACTURES		46.9		58.5		58.2		70.7	TABACS BRUTS FABRIQUES
122	TOBACCO,MANUFACTURED	W 3768	33.3	W 4308	41.5	W 4273	39.8	W 5802	48.3	TABACS FABRIQUES
1222	CIGARETTES	W 3482	31.6	W 3988	39.8	W 3662	36.5	W 4768	43.9	CIGARETTES
2	CRUDE MATERLS,EXCL FUELS		372.3		486.1		402.9		400.8	MAT BRUTES NON COMESTIBLES
24	CORK AND WOOD		104.4		111.9		84.6		109.5	LIEGE ET BOIS
248	WOOD SHAPED,SLEEPERS	W 215517	90.7	W 191130	96.3	W 169401	73.7	W 232876	97.8	BOIS SIMPLEMENT TRAVAILLES
2482	LUMBER SHAPED CONIFER	W 190343	76.2	W 166303	81.3	W 152595	65.0	W 204083	83.4	CONIFERES SCIES,RABOTES
24821	LUMBER SAWN ETC CONIFER	W 190341	76.1	W 166300	81.3	W 152591	65.0	W 204068	83.4	CONIFERES SCIES LONGITUD
251	*PULP AND WASTE PAPER	W 46013	19.5	W 67715	48.3	W 56492	25.0	W 56135	24.4	PATES A PAPIER,DECHETS
2517	SODA,SULPHATE WOOD PULP	W 28228	12.8	W 46886	37.6	W 38819	18.9	W 41679	17.8	PATES CHIMIQUES AU SULFATE
25172	— BLEACHED,NONDISSOLVNG	W 12077	5.9	W 24291	24.8	W 22869	13.4	W 23689	12.2	PATES BLANCHIES
26	TEXTILE FIBRES AND WASTE		104.5		140.3		125.1		105.2	FIBRES TEXTILES
263	COTTON	W 29431	45.0	W 33230	68.8	W 28262	53.7	W 24207	42.4	COTON
2631	RAW COTTON,EXCL LINTERS	W 29412	44.9	W 33225	68.8	W 28218	53.6	W 24180	42.3	COTON EN MASSE
269	WASTE OF TEXTILE FABRICS	W 44079	30.2	W 43624	38.0	W 50004	47.2	W 44613	36.6	FRIPERIE DRILLES,CHIFFONS
26901	BULK TEXT WSTE,OLD CLTHG	W 43920	30.0	W 43497	37.7	W 49763	47.0	W 44492	36.4	ART ET ACCESS D'HABILLEMENT
27	CRUDE FERTLZR,MINRLS NES		112.9		140.2		120.9		118.8	ENGRAIS MINERAUX BRUTS
274	SULPHUR,UNRSTD IRN PYRTE	W 1454797	81.4	W 1419179	100.7	W 1443472	80.6	W 1692993	84.0	SOUFRE ET PYRITES
2741	SULPHUR,EX SULP IN 52215	W 1454787	81.4	W 1419169	100.7	W 1443453	80.6	W 1692993	84.0	SOUFRE
278	OTHER CRUDE MINERALS	W 135966	20.5	W 134027	23.3	W 163800	26.5	W 154994	23.1	AUTRES MINERAUX BRUTS
3	MINERAL FUELS ETC		496.3		575.2		647.9		634.9	COMBUSTIBLES MINERAUX LUB
33	PETROLEUM AND PRODUCTS		340.8		358.8		473.0		512.3	PETROLE ET DERIVES
333	CRUDE PETROLEUM	W 608253	74.4	W 917883	121.3	W 757987	118.9	W 935168	138.4	HUILES BRUTES DE PETROLE
334	PETROLEUM PRODUCTS,REFIN	W 2011645	257.7	W 1512456	228.3	W 1947358	341.9	W 2245440	361.6	PRODUITS RAFFINES
3341	GASOLINE,OTH LIGHT OILS	W 346805	57.2	W 310376	54.9	W 336042	73.8	W 527761	105.5	ESSENCES POUR MOTEURS
33411	MOTOR,AVIATION SPIRIT	W 247963	40.7	W 228667	39.1	W 246161	53.0	W 285537	54.7	ESSENCES MOTEURS D'AVIONS
33412	SPIRIT TYPE JET FUEL	W 64720	10.7	W 44381	9.4	W 50662	12.3	W 153137	33.3	CARBUREACTEURS
3344	FUEL OILS,NES	W 1588083	173.1	W 1142202	149.0	W 1552325	239.8	W 1657538	230.7	FUEL OILS
3345	LUBS,PETROLEUM OILS NES	W 76691	27.3	W 59854	24.4	W 58980	28.4	W 60122	25.5	HUILES LUBRIFIANTES
33451	LUBS(HIGH PETR CONT) ETC	W 75287	24.4	W 58562	21.1	W 57615	24.5	W 58892	22.3	HUILES LUBRIF,H LOURDES
341	*GAS,NATURAL AND MANUFCT	W 2219295	142.5	W 2950647	198.5	W 2064548	159.7	W 980243	109.9	GAZ NATUREL,GAZ MANUFACT
3413	PETROLM GASES,LIQUEFIED	W 160214	27.1	W 169649	39.3	W 193241	50.1	W 216421	57.4	GAZ DE PETROLE LIQUEFIE
34139	OTH HYDROCARBON GAS LQFD	W 160214	27.1	W 169638	39.2	W 193241	50.1	W 216368	57.3	HYDROCARBURES GAZEUX NDA
3414	PETROLEUM GASES, GASEOUS	W 2059080	115.5	W 2780998	159.3	W 1871307	109.6	W 763822	52.6	GAZ DE PETROLE GAZEUX
4	ANIMAL,VEGETABLE OIL,FAT		98.8		127.9		128.7		97.1	HUILES,GRAISSES ANIM,VEG
42	FIXED VEGETABLE OIL,FAT		89.4		117.6		115.7		90.1	HUILES VEGETALES FIXES
423	FIXED VEG OILS,SOFT	W 144571	83.8	W 168322	111.1	W 183682	106.8	W 141622	77.4	HUILES VEGET DOUCES FIXES
4232	SOYA BEAN OIL	W 141418	81.9	W 134679	90.1	W 116946	67.7	W 109710	60.1	HUILE DE SOJA
4239	OTH FIXED VEG OILS,SOFT	W 3150	1.9	W 33641	21.0	W 66736	39.1	W 31861	17.3	AUTRES HUILES FIXES
42391	RAPE,COLZA,MUSTARD OILS	W 3150	1.9	W 33641	21.0	W 66736	39.1	W 31860	17.3	H NAVETTE COLZA MOUTARDE
5	CHEMCLS,RELATED PROD NES		549.8		700.3		686.5		663.8	PRODUITS CHIMIQUES
51	ORGANIC CHEMICALS		50.8		73.2		68.7		67.5	PROD CHIMIQ ORGANIQUES
513	CARBOXYLIC ACIDS ETC	W 11884	15.0	W 12517	24.4	W 13338	19.5	W 12339	16.9	ACIDES CARBOXYLIQUES
52	INORGANIC CHEMICALS		76.4		102.5		110.4		91.6	PROD CHIM INORGANIQUES
522	INORG ELEMNTS,OXIDES,ETC	W 335963	57.4	W 356346	80.1	W 402966	87.4	W 406243	72.4	ELEMENTS INORGANIQUES
5225	INORGANIC BASES ETC NES	W 308738	46.8	W 341253	68.0	W 380833	74.6	W 372827	59.9	AUTRES BASES OXYDES METAL
52251	AMMONIA,ANHYDROUS ETC	W 228710	36.9	W 266044	54.6	W 298299	58.6	W 270098	44.2	AMMONIAC LIQUEFIE
53	DYES,TANNING,COLOUR PROD		41.3		52.2		48.1		47.8	PROD TEINTURE,COLORANTS
533	PIGMENTS,PAINTS,ETC	W 16508	29.4	W 16171	36.9	W 14728	33.3	W 18648	32.5	PIGMENTS,PEINTURES,VERNIS
541	*MEDICINAL,PHARM PRODUCT	K 6923140	144.2	K 7541878	161.5	K 5415518	160.5	K 6339152	168.4	PROD MEDICINAUX PHARMACEUT
5417	MEDICAMENTS	K 6197105	122.3	K 6812524	131.3	K 4604180	131.3	K 5432087	135.9	MEDICAMENTS
54179	— CONTNG OTH SUBSTANCES	K 5807243	105.8	K 6318346	112.1	K 4203942	111.8	K 5047600	113.1	MED CONT AUT SUBSTANCES
55	PERFUME,CLEANING ETC PRD		25.4		33.5		29.5		29.7	PROD POUR PARFUM,TOILETTE
58	PLASTIC MATERIALS ETC		137.9		193.0		175.7		178.0	MAT PLAST ARTIFICIELLES
582	PROD OF CONDENSATION ETC	W 15293	25.8	W 15987	32.7	W 15018	29.8	W 20762	34.9	PROD CONDENS,POLYCOND
583	POLYMERIZATION ETC PRODS	W 107376	105.8	W 108803	152.5	W 126587	137.5	W 128945	135.7	PROD POLYMERISATION
5831	POLYETHYLENE	W 45371	36.6	W 47658	57.1	W 54428	51.8	W 59510	56.9	POLYETHYLENE
58311	— IN PRIMARY FORMS	W 43962	33.9	W 45988	52.7	W 53319	49.0	W 57830	53.4	POLYETHYLENE PRIMAIRES
5834	POLYVINYL CHLORIDE	W 28782	29.8	W 27440	36.4	W 32355	32.5	W 30654	29.6	CHLORURE DE POLYVINYLE
58341	— IN PRIMARY FORMS	W 26989	24.1	W 25394	28.9	W 30182	24.5	W 28455	22.5	SOUS FORMES PRIMAIRES
59	CHEMICAL MATERIALS NES		65.6		75.0		86.3		73.9	MAT PROD CHIMIQUES NDA
591	PESTICIDES,DISINFECTANTS	W 2086	14.3	W 1812	11.4	W 3127	23.9	W 2824	17.9	DESINF,INSECT,FONG,HERB
598	MISCEL CHEM PRODUCTS NES	W 21760	42.2	W 24081	51.3	W 26945	50.5	W 25326	44.6	PROD DIV INDUST CHIM NDA
5989	CHEM PRODUCTS,PREPS NES	W 16749	31.3	W 17031	35.4	W 20482	36.0	W 19533	33.0	PROD PREP CHIMIQUES NDA
59899	OTH CHEM PRODS,PREPS,NES	W 11686	18.9	W 11072	22.8	W 13580	23.9	W 13239	22.0	AUT PRODUITS CHIMIQUES NDA
6	BASIC MANUFACTURES		1845.1		2268.5		2236.2		2152.9	ART MANUFACTURES
61	LEATHER,DRESSED FUR,ETC		98.8		131.0		151.5		163.9	CUIRS,PELLETERIES
611	LEATHER	W 5461	73.8	W 6674	99.2	W 7089	110.4	W 8361	116.2	CUIRS,PEAUX PREPARES
6114	LEATHR BOVINE NES,EQUINE	W 3264	48.0	W 3966	61.0	W 4276	68.9	W 4552	69.6	CUIRS DE BOVINS
612	LEATHER ETC MANUFACTURES	W 2750	24.6	W 3716	31.7	W 4758	40.6	W 5513	47.6	OUVRAGES EN CUIRS NDA
6123	PREPRD PARTS OF FOOTWEAR	W 2702	21.5	W 3670	30.4	W 4703	39.0	W 5395	45.5	PARTIES DE CHAUSSURES
62	RUBBER MANUFACTURES NES		40.7		65.0		71.5		51.1	CAOUTCHOUC MANUFACTURE
621	MATERIALS OF RUBBER	W 2222	10.0	W 3671	25.0	W 2901	12.7	W 2944	11.7	PRODUITS EN CAOUTCHOUC
625	RUBBER TYRES, TUBES ETC	W 2953	12.1	W 4184	17.8	W 9247	34.1	W 5438	18.9	PNEUS CAOUTCHOUC VULCANISE
628	RUBBER ARTICLES NES	W 2197	18.8	W 2118	22.3	W 2687	24.8	W 2186	20.6	OUVRAGES CAOUTCHOUC NDA

4. General Imports C.I.F. by Commodities according to the S.I.T.C. (Rev. 2) in million U.S. Dollars
Importations Générales C.A.F. par Produits d'après la C.T.C.I. (Rév. 2) en millions de Dollars E.U.

SITC CTCI	COMMODITY	1994 QUANTITY QUANTITE	1994 VALUE VALEUR	1995 QUANTITY QUANTITE	1995 VALUE VALEUR	1996 QUANTITY QUANTITE	1996 VALUE VALEUR	1997 QUANTITY QUANTITE	1997 VALUE VALEUR	PRODUIT
63	WOOD,CORK MANUFACTRS NES		60.5		22.8		18.6		14.2	OUVRAGES LIEGE ET BOIS
635	WOOD MANUFACTURES NES	W 9517	47.7	W 3545	10.8	W 3281	5.5	W 2676	5.2	ART MANUF EN BOIS NDA
6353	BUILDERS WOODWRK,PREFABS	W 7650	44.0	W 1126	7.1	W 551	1.8	W 782	2.5	OUVRAGES DE MENUISERIE
64	PAPER,PAPERBOARD AND MFR		84.4		127.0		99.3		100.4	PAPIERS,CARTONS & OUVRAGES
641	PAPER AND PAPERBOARD	W 80887	63.2	W 91101	99.7	W 178387	77.4	W 99791	76.7	PAPIERS ET CARTONS
6413	KRAFT PAPER,PAPERBOARD	W 24692	11.0	W 31307	25.1	W 21027	13.1	W 25033	12.2	PAPIER ET CARTON KRAFT
6418	COATED ETC PAPER NES BLK	W 15213	22.2	W 14282	26.5	W 28970	23.9	W 19438	24.2	PAP,CARTONS COUCHES,ENDUITS
64189	COATED PAPER ETC NES	W 14075	20.0	W 12394	23.0	W 27676	21.6	W 17697	21.7	PAPIERS,CARTONS COUCHES
642	PAPER,ETC,PRECUT,ARTS OF	W 8779	21.2	W 9658	27.3	W 8690	22.0	W 10932	23.8	PAP,CARTONS DECOUPES
65	TEXTILE YARN,FABRICS,ETC		1063.4		1288.6		1295.2		1245.3	FILS,TISSUS,ARTICLES TEXTILE
651	TEXTILE YARN	W 19101	107.8	W 19357	123.9	W 18402	117.0	W 19519	113.2	FILS TEXTILES
6514	SYN FIB YRN,BULK,MONOFIL	W 9261	55.1	W 9950	65.1	W 9895	62.7	W 9212	54.7	FILS CONT 85% FIB TEXT SYNTH
65141	— TEXTRD,CONT POLYAMIDE	W 1400	20.0	W 1452	23.8	W 1746	23.9	W 1734	20.7	FILS TEXT FIB CONT POLYAMID
6516	DISCON SYN FIB BLEND YRN	W 4351	21.1	W 4110	21.8	W 2665	14.9	W 2710	14.2	FILS FIBR TEX SYNT DIS MOINS
652	COTTON FABRICS,WOVEN	W 52761	478.1	W 54447	587.2	W 56904	605.2	W 60336	575.5	TISSUS DE COTON
6521	GREY WOVEN COTTON FABRIC	W 3014	30.2	W 2915	38.7	W 4453	48.2	W 3403	36.1	TISSUS COT ECRUS NON MERCER
65214	GREY WOVEN COTTON NES	W 2640	26.3	W 2489	32.5	W 3291	38.1	W 2472	27.1	AUT TISSUS 85% COTON ECRUS
6522	WOVEN COTTON BLEACHD,ETC	W 49746	448.0	W 51532	548.6	W 52451	557.0	W 56933	539.4	TISSUS COTON BLANCHIS ETC
65224	BLCHED COTTON FABRIC NES	W 44589	390.2	W 46651	485.4	W 46943	494.1	W 49898	463.0	AUT TIS PLUS 85% COT BLANCHI
65225	BLCHD COTN BLEND FAB NES	W 4327	47.5	W 4034	50.8	W 4748	51.8	W 5445	57.4	AUT TIS MOINS 85% COT BLANCH
653	WOVN MAN-MADE FIB FABRIC	W 20823	284.7	W 23218	364.0	W 24061	349.3	W 26946	339.2	TISSUS FIBRES SYNTH,ARTIF
6531	CONT SYNT WEAVES NONPILE	W 3938	47.8	W 4308	63.9	W 4175	57.5	W 5062	55.8	TISSUS FIBRES SYNTH CONTINUE
65315	CONT SYN TXTL FABRIC NES	W 3367	41.9	W 3934	55.9	W 3799	49.3	W 4634	49.4	TIS PLUS 85% TEXT SYNT CONT
6532	DISC SYN TXTL FABRIC NES	W 4097	55.9	W 4811	71.8	W 5641	79.7	W 6041	77.1	TIS DISC MOINS 85% FIBR TEXT
6534	DISC SYN BLEND FABRC NES	W 8515	112.9	W 9293	137.5	W 9537	131.7	W 10783	129.8	TISSUS FIBRES SYNTH DISCONT
65341	DISC SYN FIB-COTTN FABRC	W 5356	61.3	W 5739	71.6	W 5602	65.0	W 5986	60.4	TISSUS FIB SYNT DIS MEL COTO
65349	OTH DISC SYN BLEND FABRC	W 2108	32.7	W 2497	45.0	W 2613	41.8	W 3068	40.9	TISSUS FIB SYNT MEL MAT AUT
6536	DISC REGN TXTL FABRC NES	W 838	18.8	W 1190	27.0	W 1276	24.0	W 1122	17.5	TISSUS 85% TEXT ART DISC
6538	DISC REG BLEND FABRC NES	W 2058	30.5	W 2275	41.5	W 2419	42.4	W 2868	45.0	TIS MOINS 85% TEXT ART DISC
65383	DISC REG-CONT MAN-MD FAB	W 1586	23.9	W 1824	33.9	W 1359	22.6	W 1636	26.7	TISSUS TEX ART CONT MEL SYNT
654	OTH WOVEN TEXTILE FABRIC	W 2989	40.4	W 1696	39.5	W 2068	44.5	W 3359	43.8	TISSUS AUT COTON SYNT,ARTIF
6543	WOVEN WOOL ETC FABRC NES	W 981	17.5	W 981	21.1	W 1264	28.5	W 1401	27.5	TISSUS LAINE,POILS FINS NDA
655	KNITTED,ETC FABRICS	W 2664	37.9	W 2908	44.1	W 3346	46.7	W 3731	47.2	ETOF BONNETERIE PIECES ETC
6552	OTHER KNIT ETC FAB NONEL	W 2664	37.9	W 2908	44.1	W 3346	46.7	W 3731	47.2	ETOF BON NON ELAS NON SYNT
656	LACE,RIBBONS,TULLE,ETC	W 2043	45.4	W 2352	54.0	W 2204	53.5	W 3492	55.9	TULLES,BRODERIE
65601	NARROW FABRICS NES	W 893	18.9	W 1148	24.4	W 1122	22.7	W 1926	21.8	RUBANS SANS TRAME EN FILS
657	SPECIAL TXTL FABRC,PRODS	W 6947	61.9	W 7116	68.4	W 6765	64.2	W 7738	60.5	TISSUS SPECIAUX
6572	BONDED FIBRE TEXTLS NES	W 3440	30.6	W 3312	31.7	W 2991	26.1	W 3313	22.4	TISSUS NON TISSES
6573	COATED ETC TEXTILES NES	W 2217	19.1	W 2427	23.8	W 2398	25.7	W 2873	26.1	TISSUS,ART MATIERE TEXT NDA
66	NONMETAL MINERAL MFS NES		59.5		75.2		68.7		69.2	ART MIN NON METALLIQUES
67	IRON AND STEEL		230.2		294.5		267.2		258.3	FER ET ACIER
672	IRON,STEEL PRIMARY FORMS	W 101680	26.1	W 72167	27.0	W 101941	29.2	W 143443	38.2	LINGOTS FER,ACIER
6725	IRN,STL BLOOMS,SLABS,ETC	W 80282	18.9	W 29417	7.6	W 68313	17.4	W 108967	26.6	BLOOMS,BILLETTES FER ACIER
67251	IRN,SMPLE STL BLOOMS,ETC	W 80282	18.9	W 29417	7.6	W 68313	17.4	W 108966	26.6	BLOOMS ETC NON ACIER FIN
673	IRON,STEEL SHAPES ETC	W 110834	38.0	W 291749	94.7	W 232084	79.0	W 223308	69.0	BARRES,PROFIL FER,ACIER
6732	IRON,STEEL BARS ETC	W 28952	11.7	W 207873	62.7	W 134753	43.8	W 138171	39.8	BARRES FER,ACIER
67326	IRN,OTH STL BARS HOTROLD	W 20343	6.0	W 197644	54.6	W 123812	35.4	W 126872	33.3	BARRES PLEINES FER,ACIER
674	IRN,STL UNIV,PLATE,SHEET	W 162468	78.2	W 201142	113.2	W 165861	94.0	W 194027	94.1	LARGES PLATS,TOLES
6746	IRN,STL THIN PLATE,ROLLD	W 97311	37.5	W 130102	57.3	W 97404	40.2	W 123344	47.6	TOLES LAM MOINS 3MM
67461	— OF IRON OR SIMPLE STL	W 95546	34.2	W 128391	52.5	W 95530	35.2	W 120788	43.0	TOL NON AC FIN MOINS 3 MM
678	IRON,STL TUBES,PIPES,ETC	W 58813	72.8	W 24037	41.3	W 28550	48.9	W 34897	48.2	TUBES,TUYAUX EN FONTE,FER
6782	IRON,STL SEAMLESS TUBES	W 39514	43.4	W 17984	24.2	W 18679	29.2	W 24943	30.2	TUBES,TUYAUX SANS SOUDURE
68	NON-FERROUS METALS		69.9		91.2		97.1		87.9	METAUX NON FERREUX
682	COPPER EXC CEMENT COPPER	W 11640	31.8	W 12752	45.5	W 18086	55.1	W 17294	48.7	CUIVRE
6822	COPPER,ALLOYS WORKED	W 10095	27.9	W 10697	38.5	W 14991	46.3	W 15030	43.3	CUIVRE,ALLIAGES OUVRES
68221	COPPER BARS,WIRE,ETC	W 8661	22.0	W 9444	31.5	W 13325	38.0	W 13712	36.9	BARRES,PROFILES ET FILS
684	ALUMINIUM	W 6554	19.0	W 10333	32.7	W 8988	26.1	W 7440	21.5	ALUMINIUM
69	METAL MANUFACTURES NES		138.1		173.5		167.6		162.9	ART MANUFACT EN METAL NDA
699	BASE METAL MFRS NES	W 9975	64.8	W 10891	74.5	W 11812	76.7	W 11322	70.3	ART MANUFACTURES MET NDA
7	MACHINES,TRANSPORT EQUIP		1893.7		2043.3		2095.3		2349.2	MACHINES MATERIEL TRANSPORT
71	POWER GENERATING EQUIPMT		135.4		106.7		131.8		176.8	MACHINES GENERATRICES
711	STEAM BOILERS & AUX PLNT	W 2185	20.0	W 719	6.4	W 1878	14.9	W 2270	15.5	GENERATEURS VAPEUR EAU ETC
713	INTRNL COMBUS PSTN ENGIN	W 5588	56.3	W 13370	61.2	W 4791	59.5	W 6298	64.6	MOTEURS EXPL COMB INT, PIECE
7132	MOTOR VEHCL PISTN ENGINS	W 3724	21.4	W 2636	18.5	W 2488	16.7	W 3774	24.5	MOTEURS EXPL POUR VEHICULES
7139	PISTON ENGINE PARTS NES	W 1616	30.7	W 10271	36.3	W 1955	37.1	W 2195	35.1	PIECES POUR 713.2,3,8
714	ENGINES AND MOTORS NES	W 238	16.6	W 252	13.4	W 1127	31.7	W 2389	45.1	MOTEURS NON ELECTRIQUES
7148	GAS TURBINES NES	W 21	0.9	W 144	2.0	W 173	8.4	W 1971	26.4	TURBINES A GAZ
71488	OTHER GAS TURBINES NES	W 21	0.9	W 144	2.0	W 173	8.4	W 1971	26.4	AUTRES TURBINES A GAZ
7149	ENGINE & MOTOR PARTS NES	W 217	15.7	W 103	11.4	W 953	23.3	W 418	18.8	PIECES 714 ET 718.88
716	ROTATING ELECTRIC PLANT	W 1983	23.4	W 1921	20.3	W 1996	20.3	W 3087	37.2	APP ELECTR ROTATIFS,PIECES
7162	AC MTRS,GENRTRS,GEN SETS	W 1574	20.0	W 1355	16.4	W 1448	15.2	W 1913	22.6	MOTEURS ELECTRIQUES
72	MACHS FOR SPCL INDUSTRYS		288.9		351.9		400.1		368.4	MAC SPECIALES POUR INDUST
722	TRACTORS NON-ROAD	W 4839	27.0	W 5278	30.1	W 6046	37.6	W 4814	25.9	TRACTEURS
7224	WHEELED TRACTORS NES	W 4818	27.0	W 5261	30.0	W 5934	37.3	W 4804	25.9	TRACTEURS A ROUES
723	CIVIL ENGNEERG EQUIP ETC	W 9053	48.2	W 11559	68.0	W 11625	72.6	W 11846	70.7	APPAREILS DE GENIE CIVIL
7234	CONST,MINING MACHNRY NES	W 7973	38.3	W 10391	52.8	W 10046	58.1	W 10397	57.8	MACH POUR LA CONST, MINES
72342	SLFPRP SHOVELS,EXCAVATRS	W 5169	24.6	W 6053	29.2	W 7829	44.0	W 6901	33.7	PELLES MECANIQUES
724	TEXTILE,LEATHER MACHNRY	W 5780	87.9	W 6651	100.7	W 7114	110.5	W 8139	109.0	MACH POUR INDUSTRIE TEXTILE
7243	SEWING MACHS,NEEDLES ETC	W 1975	45.1	W 1845	48.7	W 1953	50.4	W 2264	48.5	MACHINES A COUDRE,PIECES
72431	SEWING MACHINES	W 1717	37.0	W 1576	38.4	W 1573	38.2	W 1877	38.9	MACHINES A COUDRE
7247	TEXTILE MACHINERY NES	W 1535	15.9	W 1902	21.9	W 2564	25.1	W 2486	24.8	MACH LAVAGE,TEINTURE TEX
726	PRINTG,BKBINDG MACHY,PTS	W 1036	20.4	W 711	14.3	W 787	16.4	W 754	13.4	MACHINES POUR IMPRIMERIE
727	FOOD MACHRY NON-DOMESTIC	W 1050	15.1	W 1286	24.3	W 2224	33.1	W 1800	25.3	MACH INDUSTRIES ALIMENT
7272	OTH FOOD PROC MCHY,PARTS	W 965	13.6	W 998	22.3	W 1925	30.2	W 1052	18.0	AUT MACH IND ALIMENTAIRE
728	OTH MACHY FOR SPCL INDUS	W 8476	66.6	W 12509	93.6	W 11562	102.5	W 11823	97.5	AUT MACH IND PARTICULIERES
7283	OTHR MINERAL WORKG MACHY	W 3064	21.0	W 4911	23.0	W 5746	32.7	W 6092	22.2	MACH TRIER,CRIBLER,BROYER
7284	MACHY FOR SPCL INDUS NES	W 4666	41.0	W 5565	57.4	W 4383	58.2	W 3743	62.0	MACH SPEC IND PARTICUL.
72848	OTH MCHY WITH INDIV FNCT	W 2957	23.0	W 4126	32.4	W 2317	23.9	W 1930	26.6	AUTRES MACHINES NDA
73	METALWORKING MACHINERY		26.5		28.6		28.3		30.9	MACH TRAVAIL DES METAUX
74	GENRL INDUSTRL MACHY NES		338.3		394.0		395.7		388.4	MACH APP INDUSTRIE
741	HEATING,COOLING EQUIPMNT	W 8976	77.8	W 11849	108.1	W 10720	96.3	W 9615	86.3	MACH CHAUFFAGE,PIECES
7414	NONDOM REFRIG EQUIPT,PTS	W 4587	29.2	W 6139	40.5	W 5470	37.5	W 4861	33.2	MAT PRODUCTION DU FROID
74141	REFRIG EQUIP NONDOMESTIC	W 1304	15.2	W 1582	20.4	W 1989	23.2	W 1504	19.5	REFIG INDUSTRIELS
7416	HEATING,COOLING EQU NES	W 1610	23.7	W 2179	34.5	W 2332	31.6	W 1774	27.0	APP CHANGEMENT TEMP
742	PUMPS FOR LIQUIDS ETC	W 2187	45.8	W 4642	38.3	W 2325	40.4	W 2754	47.9	POMPES MOTO-POMPES
743	PUMPS NES,CENTRFUGES ETC	W 5606	60.3	W 6287	71.9	W 5270	67.6	W 5908	63.4	POMPES COMPRES,VENT ETC
7431	PUMPS FOR GASES ETC	W 3428	23.9	W 3456	28.2	W 2556	22.1	W 2796	22.2	POMPES AIR A VIDE,COMPRES
7436	GAS,LIQUID FILTERS ETC	W 1430	20.3	W 2101	27.8	W 1790	27.9	W 1979	26.2	APP POUR FILT DES LIQUIDES
744	MECHANICAL HANDLING EQU	W 4915	31.6	W 6785	41.8	W 6262	42.1	W 6893	46.2	EQUIP MANUTENTION PIECES
7442	LIFTING,LOADING MACH NES	W 2666	18.6	W 3854	23.6	W 3540	23.9	W 3521	24.5	APP LEVAGE,MANUTENTION
745	NONELEC MACHY,TOOLS NES	W 1662	30.9	W 2007	34.3	W 1790	38.4	W 2484	37.9	AUT MACH NON ELEC,PIECES

4. General Imports C.I.F. by Commodities according to the S.I.T.C. (Rev. 2) in million U.S. Dollars
Importations Générales C.A.F. par Produits d'après la C.T.C.I. (Rév. 2) en millions de Dollars E.U.

SITC CTCI	COMMODITY	1994 QUANTITY QUANTITE	1994 VALUE VALEUR	1995 QUANTITY QUANTITE	1995 VALUE VALEUR	1996 QUANTITY QUANTITE	1996 VALUE VALEUR	1997 QUANTITY QUANTITE	1997 VALUE VALEUR	PRODUIT
7452	OTH NONELEC MCHS,PTS NES	W 1587	29.4	W 1938	32.7	W 1678	36.2	W 2349	35.7	AUT MACH NON ELEC,PIECES
74522	PACKAGNG,BOTTLNG,ETC MCH	W 648	17.9	W 632	21.5	W 711	25.7	W 717	22.9	MACH NETT BOUTEILLES,ETC
749	NONELEC MACH PTS,ACC NES	W 7606	92.2	W 13152	100.0	W 11060	111.2	W 10244	107.0	PIECES MACH NON ELEC NDA
7492	COCKS,VALVES ETC NES	W 2290	36.6	W 2319	37.4	W 2717	38.9	W 3068	40.0	ART ROB,SIM POUR TUYAUX
7493	SHAFT,CRANK,PULLEY ETC	W 4018	29.8	W 9376	34.0	W 6681	38.5	W 5459	35.2	ARBRES TRANS,VILEBREQUINS
75	OFFICE MACHNES,ADP EQUIP		76.8		94.4		93.2		94.7	MACH BUREAU TRAIT AUTOM
752	AUTOMTIC DATA PROC EQUIP	W 800	52.6	W 888	61.4	W 990	66.3	W 1351	70.2	MACH TRAIT INFORMATION
76	TELECOMM,SOUND EQUIPMENT		98.1		118.3		127.5		96.0	EQUIPMENT DE TELECOM
764	TELECOM EQPT,PTS,ACC NES	W 2705	86.6	W 3634	102.9	W 3754	114.7	W 5280	83.4	EQUIP TELECOM,PIECES
7641	LINE TELEPHONE,ETC EQUIP	W 420	32.4	W 839	44.8	W 633	54.0	W 282	15.3	APP TELEPHON PAR FIL
7643	TV,RADIO TRANSMITTRS ETC	W 174	20.1	W 153	12.4	W 264	20.2	W 69	7.7	APP EMET TELE RADIO
7649	PTS NES OF EQUIPMT OF 76	W 1914	27.0	W 2319	32.1	W 2611	34.7	W 4550	53.7	PIECES DE LA DIV 76
77	ELECTRIC MACHNRY NES ETC		365.0		415.8		433.9		502.7	MACH APP ELECT NDA
771	ELECTRIC POWER MACHY NES	W 2332	37.0	W 3671	43.3	W 3279	41.4	W 6398	61.7	MACH PROD,TRANS ELECTR
7712	OTH ELEC POWER MACHY NES	W 1645	26.1	W 2518	34.4	W 2396	31.5	W 4000	41.5	AUT APP PROD TRANSF ELEC
772	SWITCHGEAR ETC,PARTS NES	W 5642	115.4	W 5034	120.1	W 5263	128.3	W 7112	148.4	APP COUPURE,SECT ETC
7721	SWITCHGEAR ETC	W 4908	100.4	W 4289	106.4	W 4580	111.3	W 6431	137.4	APP COUPURE,SECTIONMNT
773	ELECTR DISTRIBUTNG EQUIP	W 8558	66.3	W 9255	87.1	W 11266	111.7	W 20048	118.3	EQUIPMT DISTRIBUTION ELECT
7731	INSULATED WIRE,CABLE ETC	W 7243	54.9	W 8504	76.0	W 10115	99.3	W 18350	103.6	FILS,CABLES ISOLES ELECT
776	TRANSISTORS,VALVES,ETC	W 2815	47.4	W 2562	43.9	W 2130	42.0	W 3003	47.8	LAMPES,TUBES,VALVES
7761	TV PICTURE TUBES	W 2221	21.4	W 2050	23.2	W 1705	19.7	W 2298	23.1	TUBES CATHODIQUES
778	ELECTRICAL MACHINERY NES	W 5700	76.7	W 6014	83.2	W 5661	82.5	W 7825	95.7	AUTRES MACH ELECT NDA
7783	AUTOMOTIVE ELECTR EQUIP	W 1891	21.6	W 1827	22.4	W 2049	22.6	W 2932	26.2	EQUIP ELECT MOTEURS EXPL
7788	OTH ELEC MACHY,EQUIP NES	W 988	35.6	W 1441	39.9	W 1066	38.5	W 1727	45.7	AUT MACH APP ELEC NDA
77886	OTH ELEC MACHINERY NES	W 255	23.1	W 290	23.9	W 372	26.0	W 450	29.0	AUT MACH APP ELECTRIQUES
78	ROAD VEHICLES		395.8		441.7		469.8		526.5	VEHICULES ROUTIERS
781	PASS MOTOR VEH EXC BUSES	W 28323	209.6	W 24481	238.9	W 20764	244.3	W 30304	284.2	AUTO TRANSPORT PERSONNES
782	LORRIES,SPCL MTR VEH NES	W 16701	67.5	W 17461	80.1	W 13487	97.8	W 13492	110.3	VEHICULES SPECIAUX,MARCH
7821	LORRIES,TRUCKS	W 15369	55.6	W 15609	63.9	W 11868	85.1	W 11370	87.9	VEHICULES TRANSP MARCHAND
784	MOTOR VEH PRTS,ACCES NES	W 9270	94.4	W 21190	96.4	W 9272	100.8	W 11935	104.1	PIECES 722,781,782,783
7849	OTHER MOTOR VEHCL PARTS	W 7106	74.8	W 18584	74.0	W 7025	78.1	W 9501	82.0	PIECES 722,781,782,783
79	OTHR TRANSPORT EQUIPMENT		169.2		92.2		15.4		165.2	AUTRE MATERIEL TRANSPORT
791	RAILWAY VEHICLES	W 888	3.0	W 1512	6.5	W 828	3.8	W 1696	27.8	VEHIC MAT CHEMINS DE FER
7913	MECHAN–PROPELLED RY CARS							W 415	23.9	AUTOMOTRICES,DRAISINES
792	AIRCRAFT ETC	W 162	116.6	W 115	78.5	W 12	3.2	W 15	3.6	APP NAVIGATION AERIENNE
7924	AIRCRFT NES OVER 15000KG	W 153	114.6	W 95	75.7					AERODYNES PLUS 15000 KG
793	SHIPS AND BOATS ETC	W 17608	49.7	W 2772	7.3	W 5408	8.5	W 15513	133.9	NAVIRES BATEAUX,ETC
7932	SHIPS AND BOATS NES	W 7125	6.6	W 1643	3.2	W 5103	7.9	W 15339	132.7	NAVIRES ET BATEAUX
79323	OTHER CARGO VESSELS	W 7001	4.9			W 534	4.0	W 13000	124.3	AUT BATEAUX TRANS MARCH
7938	TUGS,SPECIAL VESSELS ETC	W 10461	43.1	W 1124	4.0	W 288	0.6	W 169	1.2	REMORQUEURS,BATEAUX SPEC
79382	SPECL PURPOSE VESSLS ETC	W 10362	42.7	W 1030	3.5			W 87	0.1	BAT–PHARES,–POMPES,DRAGUES
8	MISC MANUFACTURED GOODS		671.4		828.4		875.7		879.5	ART MANUFACTURES DIVERS
812	*PLUMBG,HEATNG,LGHTNG EQ	W 6009	20.2	W 6646	24.5	W 6754	24.5	W 6852	21.8	APPAR SANITAIRES CHAUFFAGE
84	CLOTHING AND ACCESSORIES		335.7		434.9		475.5		492.6	VETEMENTS
842	MENS OUTERWEAR NOT KNIT	W 5544	75.5	W 5954	91.6	W 6720	107.7	W 7763	111.9	VET DESSUS POUR HOMMES
8423	— TROUSERS,BREECHES ETC	W 2204	32.3	W 2278	36.1	W 3384	54.9	W 3324	47.2	PANTALONS HOMMES MAT TEX
8429	— OTHER OUTER GARMENTS	W 2839	30.9	W 2979	37.1	W 2850	36.1	W 3924	48.0	AUT VET DES HOM MAT TEX
843	WOMENS OUTERWEAR NONKNIT	W 2684	39.0	W 2792	47.7	W 3421	61.1	W 3607	60.6	VET DESSUS FEMMES MAT TEX
8439	— OTHER OUTER GARMENTS	W 1424	25.7	W 1323	30.1	W 1960	41.8	W 1844	44.0	AUT VET DES FEM MAT TEXT
844	UNDER GARMENTS NOT KNIT	W 3771	70.7	W 4713	98.9	W 5202	110.7	W 7005	127.7	VETEMENT DESSOUS MAT TEX
8441	— MENS SHIRTS	W 3258	60.9	W 4187	88.6	W 4504	97.9	W 6366	117.4	CHEMISES HOMMES MAT TEXT
84412	—— OF SYNTHETIC FIBRES	W 3037	55.4	W 3893	79.9	W 4205	88.3	W 6013	107.4	CHEMISES HOMMES FIB SYNT
845	OUTERWEAR KNIT NONELASTC	W 3191	50.6	W 4012	60.5	W 3946	57.7	W 4632	61.4	VET DESSOUS,ACCES BONNET
8451	— JERSEYS,PULLOVERS ETC	W 2275	28.7	W 3136	37.6	W 3090	38.3	W 3461	39.4	CHANDAILS,PULL–OVERS ETC
846	UNDER GARMENTS KNITTED	W 3295	67.7	W 4604	98.4	W 5678	103.6	W 6108	108.6	SOUS VETS DE BONNETERIE
8462	— OF COTTON NON ELASTIC	W 2655	30.1	W 3837	50.0	W 4773	61.1	W 5354	67.6	SOUS–VET BONNET COTON
84629	—— OTHER	W 2655	30.1	W 3837	50.0	W 4773	61.1	W 5354	67.6	AUT SOUS–VET BONNET COTON
8465	CORSETS,GARTERS,ETC	W 626	37.3	W 751	48.2	W 736	42.1	W 735	40.7	CORSETS,GAINES ART SIM
84651	BRASSIERES	W 547	34.2	W 635	43.5	W 645	38.8	W 637	37.3	SOUTIENS–GORGE,BUSTIERS
847	TEXTILE CLTHNG ACCES NES	W 1223	21.0	W 1261	24.0	W 1358	24.6	W 869	14.3	ACCES VET MAT TEXT NDA
87	PRECISION INSTRUMNTS NES		86.4		105.4		108.4		99.7	INSTRUM,APPAR SCIENT NDA
874	MEASURNG,CONTROLNG INSTR	W 1476	60.6	W 1577	77.0	W 1449	78.8	W 1649	75.4	INSTRUMENTS DE MESURE
88	PHOTO EQU,OPTICL GDS ETC		35.7		36.5		39.3		34.8	APP,FOURN PHOTO,OP,MONTR
89	MISC MANUFCTRD GOODS NES		182.2		212.1		212.6		214.0	ART MANUFACTURES DIVERS
892	PRINTED MATTER	W 3593	31.6	W 3818	34.5	W 4102	35.7	W 4298	35.8	IMPRIMES
893	ARTICLES OF PLASTIC NES		63.7	W 12232	85.9		84.8	W 17622	86.8	OUVRAGES EN MAT DIVIS 58
8939	MISC PLASTIC ARTICLES	W 6643	46.0	W 8334	61.1	W 9136	61.0	W 12290	63.2	ART DIVERS EN MAT DIV 58
89399	OTHR PLASTC ARTICLES NES	W 6191	45.0	W 7800	59.3	W 8582	59.5	W 11423	61.1	AUT OUV MAT DIV 58
899	OTHER MANUFACTURED GOODS		51.4		57.9		58.8		52.0	AUT ART MANUF DIVERS NDA
8998	SMALLWARES,TOILETRYS ETC	W 2369	43.2	W 2400	47.3	W 2238	47.6	W 2688	41.5	ART MERCERIE,TOILETTE
89983	BUTTONS,STUDS,ETC	W 1171	27.6	W 1175	29.3	W 1075	29.1	W 1155	24.7	BOUTONS,BOUTONS–PRESSION
9	GOODS NOT CLASSD BY KIND		23.8		20.7		19.2		17.8	ART TRANSACT NON CLASSES

5. General Exports F.O.B. by Commodities according to the S.I.T.C. (Rev. 2) in million U.S. Dollars
Exportations Générales F.O.B. par Produits d'après la C.T.C.I. (Rév. 2) en millions de Dollars E.U.

SITC CTCI	COMMODITY	1994 QUANTITY QUANTITE	1994 VALUE VALEUR	1995 QUANTITY QUANTITE	1995 VALUE VALEUR	1996 QUANTITY QUANTITE	1996 VALUE VALEUR	1997 QUANTITY QUANTITE	1997 VALUE VALEUR	PRODUIT
	ALL COMMODITIES		4584.5		5474.7		5517.4		5559.4	TOUS PRODUITS
0	FOOD AND LIVE ANIMALS		224.6		247.1		235.0		253.0	ALIMENTS,ANIMAUX VIVANTS
03	FISH AND PREPARATIONS		79.1		76.7		89.0		95.8	POISSONS ET PREPARATIONS
034	FISH,FRESH,CHILLED,FROZN	W 2445	24.3	W 1528	18.8	W 2125	21.5	W 1633	14.3	POISSON FRAIS, REFRIG,CONG
0341	FISH FRSH,CHLLD,EX FILLT	W 2289	23.1	W 1344	18.0	W 1984	20.8	W 1551	13.9	POISSON FRAIS,REFRIGERE
036	SHELL FISH FRESH,FROZEN	W 10661	54.1	W 8035	57.0	W 10310	66.2	W 13127	79.2	CRUSTACES,MOLLUSQUES
04	CEREALS AND PREPARATIONS		34.2		42.9		36.3		59.7	CEREALES ET PRODUITS
046	WHEAT ETC MEAL OR FLOUR	W 53071	11.0	W 62260	15.6	W 32564	10.0	W 68456	20.3	SEMOULE FARINE,FROMENT
04601	FLOUR OF WHEAT OR MESLIN	W 53071	11.0	W 62260	15.6	W 32564	10.0	W 68456	20.3	FARINE DE FROMENT
048	CEREAL ETC PREPARATIONS	W 11603	15.7	W 6240	14.9	W 6441	17.1	W 13003	25.3	PREPTNS A BASE CEREALES
05	VEGETABLES AND FRUIT		72.7		85.3		74.7		71.4	LEGUMES ET FRUITS
057	FRUIT,NUTS,FRESH,DRIED	W 44263	66.8	W 48196	76.2	W 42220	60.1	W 37744	54.5	FRUITS FRAIS OU SECS
0579	FRUIT FRESH OR DRIED NES	W 22284	56.9	W 22336	63.2	W 19825	49.1	W 22310	48.0	FRUITS FRAIS,SECS NDA
05796	DATES,FRESH OR DRIED	W 20782	55.5	W 20872	61.7	W 18216	48.0	W 21310	47.2	DATTES FRAICHES OU SECHES
1	BEVERAGES AND TOBACCO		58.9		57.0		46.9		90.2	BOISSONS ET TABACS
11	BEVERAGES		24.2		19.2		17.4		29.0	BOISSONS
112	ALCOHOLIC BEVERAGES	W 15037	22.2	W 11689	16.8	W 9696	14.5	W 8486	25.0	BOISSONS ALCOOLIQUES
1124	DISTILLED ALCOHOLIC BEVS	W 1305	13.3	W 1042	9.9	W 560	7.5	W 2033	18.8	ALCOOLS,EAUX-DE-VIE
12	TOBACCO AND MANUFACTURES		34.8		37.8		29.5		61.2	TABACS BRUTS FABRIQUES
122	TOBACCO,MANUFACTURED	W 2776	32.0	W 1857	31.1	W 3063	28.6	W 3968	59.8	TABACS FABRIQUES
1222	CIGARETTES	W 1918	26.8	W 1042	26.7	W 2244	24.7	W 2872	49.3	CIGARETTES
2	CRUDE MATERLS,EXCL FUELS		80.6		115.9		116.3		101.4	MAT BRUTES NON COMESTIBLES
26	TEXTILE FIBRES AND WASTE		9.8		16.3		19.0		18.4	FIBRES TEXTILES
269	WASTE OF TEXTILE FABRICS	W 9875	5.5	W 16532	11.4	W 21580	16.9	W 25349	16.0	FRIPERIE DRILLES,CHIFFONS
27	CRUDE FERTLZR,MINRLS NES		41.3		45.0		50.2		51.0	ENGRAIS MINERAUX BRUTS
271	FERTILIZERS,CRUDE	W 1296052	32.2	W 1308203	33.9	W 1205749	36.7	W 1247043	41.3	ENGRAIS BRUTS
2713	NAT CALCM PHOSPHATES ETC	W 1296052	32.2	W 1308203	33.9	W 1205749	36.7	W 1247043	41.3	PHOSPHATES DE CALCIUM
27131	— UNGROUND	W 1296052	32.2	W 1308203	33.9	W 1205749	36.7	W 1247043	41.3	PHOSPHATES NON MOULUS
28	METALLIFEROUS ORES,SCRAP		12.2		35.2		25.5		11.7	MINERAIS METAL,DECHETS
287	BASE METAL ORES,CONC NES	W 19926	3.8	W 97609	22.8	W 82613	19.0	W 12831	2.7	MINERAIS METAUX COMMUNS
2875	ZINC ORES,CONCENTRATES	W 17856	3.4	W 87636	20.8	W 73938	16.6	W 6914	1.7	MINERAIS DE ZINC
3	MINERAL FUELS ETC		434.6		463.7		579.9		504.6	COMBUSTIBLES MINERAUX LUB
33	PETROLEUM AND PRODUCTS		434.2		462.6		578.9		503.8	PETROLE ET DERIVES
333	CRUDE PETROLEUM	W 3233453	352.2	W 3123982	377.9	W 3147701	462.0	W 2795499	376.2	HUILES BRUTES DE PETROLE
334	PETROLEUM PRODUCTS,REFIN	W 666168	82.0	W 620148	84.7	W 802287	117.0	W 879873	127.6	PRODUITS RAFFINES
3341	GASOLINE,OTH LIGHT OILS	W 101816	23.5	W 101041	23.4	W 116995	31.6	W 104418	27.4	ESSENCES POUR MOTEURS
33411	MOTOR,AVIATION SPIRIT	W 101816	23.5	W 101041	23.4	W 116995	31.6	W 104418	27.4	ESSENCES MOTEURS D'AVIONS
3344	FUEL OILS,NES	W 473681	43.1	W 417425	44.6	W 601536	68.5	W 541583	60.9	FUEL OILS
3345	LUBS,PETROLEUM OILS NES	W 90443	15.3	W 73706	13.4	W 83757	16.9	W 233629	39.4	HUILES LUBRIFIANTES
33451	LUBS(HIGH PETR CONT) ETC	W 90427	15.3	W 73650	13.3	W 83683	16.8	W 233547	39.1	HUILES LUBRIF,H LOURDES
4	ANIMAL,VEGETABLE OIL,FAT		302.2		230.5		123.6		268.2	HUILES,GRAISSES ANIM,VEG
42	FIXED VEGETABLE OIL,FAT		301.9		230.2		123.4		267.9	HUILES VEGETALES FIXES
423	FIXED VEG OILS,SOFT	W 197786	301.8	W 90825	230.2	W 30529	123.4	W 129573	263.7	HUILES VEGET DOUCES FIXES
4235	OLIVE OIL	W 197783	301.8	W 90825	230.2	W 30529	123.4	W 129573	263.7	HUILE D'OLIVE
5	CHEMCLS,RELATED PROD NES		527.6		651.3		700.9		694.6	PRODUITS CHIMIQUES
52	INORGANIC CHEMICALS		223.1		271.6		306.9		334.1	PROD CHIM INORGANIQUES
522	INORG ELEMNTS,OXIDES,ETC	W 1143453	167.2	W 1166124	204.6	W 1202359	225.0	W 1347573	256.2	ELEMENTS INORGANIQUES
5222	INORGANIC ACIDS ETC	W 1143090	166.7	W 1165790	204.2	W 1202128	224.4	W 1346794	255.1	ACIDES INORGANIQUES
52224	PHOSPHORIC ACIDS ETC	W 1141989	166.2	W 1128388	202.0	W 1198458	224.2	W 1345267	254.4	ACIDES PHOSPHORIQUES
523	OTHR INORG CHEMICALS ETC	W 166843	55.9	W 149761	67.0	W 164872	81.8	W 183735	78.0	AUT PRODUITS CHIMIQUES INORG
5231	METAL CMPD OF INORG ACID	W 48341	16.6	W 35962	21.5	W 32176	25.8	W 28843	21.9	SELS METALLIQUES
52311	FLUORIDES ETC	W 26170	15.4	W 32330	20.5	W 29601	24.9	W 27107	21.3	FLUORURES
5232	OTH MTL CMPD OF INRG ACD	W 118500	39.4	W 113743	45.5	W 132659	56.1	W 154859	56.1	SELS METALLIQUES
52322	PHOSPHITES,PHOSPHATES	W 114364	38.5	W 111762	44.9	W 130906	55.5	W 151968	55.3	PHOSPHITES,PHOSPHATES
541	*MEDICINAL,PHARM PRODUCT	K 258229	23.5	K 145453	12.8	K 229713	6.4	K 620170	14.6	PROD MEDICINAUX PHARMACEUT
5417	MEDICAMENTS	K 203415	22.7	K 75263	11.9	K 180672	5.4	K 546839	14.1	MEDICAMENTS
54179	— CONTNG OTH SUBSTANCES	K 181764	19.4	K 71756	11.6	K 177045	5.2	K 518973	13.1	MED CONT AUT SUBSTANCES
55	PERFUME,CLEANING ETC PRD		26.1		26.8		29.1		40.7	PROD POUR PARFUM,TOILETTE
553	PERFUMERY,COSMETICS,ETC	W 2288	14.8	W 1662	13.4	W 1718	16.7	W 1847	24.3	PRODUITS DE PARFUMERIE
562	*FERTILIZERS,MANUFACTURE	W 1534987	229.8	W 1619119	298.2	W 1628099	327.4	W 1487792	279.7	ENGRAIS MANUFACTURES
5622	CHEM PHOSPHATIC FERTILZR	W 869455	112.1	W 801150	123.8	W 751346	128.1	W 713039	114.7	ENGRAIS PHOSPHATES
56222	SUPERPHOSPHATES	W 776498	100.6	W 743728	117.0	W 704737	122.9	W 672779	110.5	SUPERPHOSPHATES
5629	FERTILIZERS NES	W 646138	115.4	W 748044	163.9	W 844709	193.7	W 766700	163.4	ENGRAIS NDA
56292	NITROG-PHOS FERTILZR NES	W 646138	115.4	W 748044	163.9	W 844709	193.7	W 766684	163.1	ENGRAIS NDA CONT N P
6	BASIC MANUFACTURES		557.9		660.6		549.5		517.6	ART MANUFACTURES
61	LEATHER,DRESSED FUR,ETC		94.6		110.9		126.4		135.7	CUIRS,PELLETERIES
612	LEATHER ETC MANUFACTURES	W 3273	82.0	W 3053	101.8	W 3308	114.5	W 3976	125.4	OUVRAGES EN CUIRS NDA
6123	PREPRD PARTS OF FOOTWEAR	W 3215	79.3	W 2999	98.6	W 3212	109.9	W 3781	118.5	PARTIES DE CHAUSSURES
62	RUBBER MANUFACTURES NES		27.2		35.2		42.2		21.8	CAOUTCHOUC MANUFACTURE
625	RUBBER TYRES, TUBES ETC	W 7453	21.9	W 8224	28.6	W 10158	35.7	W 5316	16.4	PNEUS CAOUTCHOUC VULCANISE
6252	TYRES,NEW,BUS OR LORRY	W 2174	7.9	W 2682	10.6	W 6106	21.2	W 2223	7.1	PNEUS POUR AUTOBUS,CAMIONS
64	PAPER,PAPERBOARD AND MFR		19.6		28.8		23.6		24.7	PAPIERS,CARTONS & OUVRAGES
642	PAPER,ETC,PRECUT,ARTS OF	W 9707	13.9	W 13518	21.4	W 11620	18.7	W 14795	19.6	PAP,CARTONS DECOUPES
65	TEXTILE YARN,FABRICS,ETC		153.7		165.5		151.1		126.7	FILS,TISSUS,ARTICLES TEXTILE
651	TEXTILE YARN	W 5787	29.1	W 5054	29.0	W 4146	22.4	W 4860	25.7	FILS TEXTILES
652	COTTON FABRICS,WOVEN	W 13094	52.6	W 13922	62.5	W 11955	58.8	W 10528	45.3	TISSUS DE COTON
6522	WOVEN COTTON BLEACHD,ETC	W 11632	46.3	W 12742	55.7	W 10406	49.7	W 9352	40.4	TISSUS COTON BLANCHIS ETC
65224	BLCHED COTTON FABRIC NES	W 11559	45.5	W 12684	55.1	W 10373	49.3	W 9259	39.7	AUT TIS PLUS 85% COT BLANCHI
653	WOVN MAN-MADE FIB FABRIC	W 4812	26.4	W 5089	30.1	W 4145	24.0	W 2569	13.3	TISSUS FIBRES SYNTH,ARTIF
6534	DISC SYN BLEND FABRC NES	W 3305	20.0	W 3890	23.5	W 2274	12.1	W 1763	7.1	TISSUS FIBRES SYNTH DISCONT
658	TEXTILE ARTICLES NES	W 2893	21.1	W 2433	24.0	W 2356	30.0	W 2357	27.1	ART FACONNES MAT TEXTILES
6589	OTH TEXTILE ARTICLES NES	W 1162	11.7	W 1188	15.9	W 1064	21.7	W 1421	19.0	AUT ART EN TEXTILES NDA
66	NONMETAL MINERAL MFS NES		75.8		118.7		85.2		92.5	ART MIN NON METALLIQUES
661	LIME,CEMENT,BLDG PRODS	W 988518	39.6	W 1727857	75.9	W 1053334	46.5	W 1259621	45.0	CHAUX,CIMENTS MAT CONSTR
6612	CEMENT	W 986069	38.7	W 1723426	74.2	W 1047972	44.2	W 1253125	42.7	CIMENTS HYDRAULIQUES
662	CLAY,REFRACTORY BLDG PRD	W 27393	11.5	W 23820	12.7	W 29083	12.4	W 48925	17.0	MAT CONST REFRACTAIRES
6624	BRICKS ETC NONREFRACTORY	W 27046	11.4	W 23513	12.5	W 28876	12.3	W 48420	16.8	BRIQUES ETC CERAM NON REFR
67	IRON AND STEEL		92.0		57.5		54.1		58.7	FER ET ACIER
674	IRN,STL UNIV,PLATE,SHEET	W 60675	23.0	W 83542	36.3	W 83100	36.3	W 91930	42.7	LARGES PLATS,TOLES
6749	OTH IRN,STL PLATES,SHEET	W 60479	22.9	W 82864	36.0	W 83065	36.2	W 91924	42.7	AUTRES TOLES FER,ACIER
67491	— OF IRON OR SIMPLE STL	W 60479	22.9	W 82863	35.9	W 83065	36.2	W 91924	42.7	AUT TOLES AUTRES ACIER FIN
678	IRON,STL TUBES,PIPES,ETC	W 102815	62.3	W 18166	14.0	W 14224	14.0	W 14701	10.6	TUBES,TUYAUX EN FONTE,FER
6783	IRON,STL TUBES,PIPES NES	W 99010	56.6	W 11928	9.7	W 12243	9.1	W 12604	7.6	AUT TUBES,TUYAUX FER,ACIER
69	METAL MANUFACTURES NES		81.8		122.8		44.6		39.2	ART MANUFACT EN METAL NDA
699	BASE METAL MFRS NES	W 12633	67.0	W 13704	107.4	W 9534	27.6	W 11016	23.3	ART MANUFACTURES MET NDA
6997	IRON,STEEL ARTICLES NES	W 1123	51.0	W 1495	72.8	W 1272	6.3	W 1463	5.7	OUV FONTE,FER,ACIER NDA
69979	IRN,STL MANUFACTURES NES	W 1121	51.0	W 1495	72.8	W 1272	6.3	W 1463	5.7	AUT OUVRAGES EN FER NDA
7	MACHINES,TRANSPORT EQUIP		392.5		515.2		538.8		602.4	MACHINES MATERIEL TRANSPORT
71	POWER GENERATING EQUIPMT		12.1		17.4		16.0		18.0	MACHINES GENERATRICES
72	MACHS FOR SPCL INDUSTRYS		13.3		18.8		22.4		25.5	MAC SPECIALES POUR INDUST
74	GENRL INDUSTRL MACHY NES		27.9		41.0		44.4		38.5	MACH APP INDUSTRIE

5. General Exports F.O.B. by Commodities according to the S.I.T.C. (Rev. 2) in million U.S. Dollars
Exportations Générales F.O.B. par Produits d'après la C.T.C.I. (Rév. 2) en millions de Dollars E.U.

SITC CTCI	COMMODITY	1994			1995			1996			1997			PRODUIT
		QUANTITY QUANTITE		VALUE VALEUR	QUANTITY QUANTITE		VALUE VALEUR	QUANTITY QUANTITE		VALUE VALEUR	QUANTITY QUANTITE		VALUE VALEUR	
749	NONELEC MACH PTS,ACC NES	W	6620	18.4	W	5666	22.1	W	5508	21.6	W	6000	18.5	PIECES MACH NON ELEC NDA
7493	SHAFT,CRANK,PULLEY ETC	W	6129	14.5	W	5063	15.4	W	4885	15.7	W	5371	12.9	ARBRES TRANS,VILEBREQUINS
76	TELECOMM,SOUND EQUIPMENT			38.7			36.7			37.5			53.0	EQUIPMENT DE TELECOM
764	TELECOM EQPT,PTS,ACC NES	W	1292	33.3	W	1355	30.4	W	1657	33.1	W	2783	52.3	EQUIP TELECOM,PIECES
7642	MICROPH,LOUDSPKR,AMPLIFR	W	713	8.2	W	926	11.5	W	1162	12.7	W	2071	17.2	MICRO,HAUT–PARLEUR,AMPLI
7649	PTS NES OF EQUIPMT OF 76	W	566	24.0	W	421	18.3	W	490	20.0	W	706	34.9	PIECES DE LA DIV 76
76493	TELECOMM EQUIPMT PTS NES	W	538	22.3	W	404	16.5	W	462	18.9	W	678	34.4	PIECES 761,762,764.3,8
77	ELECTRIC MACHNRY NES ETC			268.0			355.1			383.7			422.9	MACH APP ELECT NDA
771	ELECTRIC POWER MACHY NES	W	3417	32.7	W	4294	55.7	W	3941	47.5	W	5042	50.7	MACH PROD,TRANS ELECTR
7712	OTH ELEC POWER MACHY NES	W	1427	24.6	W	2155	43.8	W	2233	38.6	W	2361	37.6	AUT APP PROD TRANSF ELEC
77122	INDUCTORS	W	1417	22.5	W	2140	39.5	W	2150	34.9	W	2216	33.3	BOBINES REACTANCE,SELFS
772	SWITCHGEAR ETC,PARTS NES	W	2864	70.1	W	2633	90.7	W	2875	99.6	W	3476	95.2	APP COUPURE,SECT ETC
7721	SWITCHGEAR ETC	W	2652	60.3	W	2150	71.5	W	2376	78.0	W	2865	76.3	APP COUPURE,SECTIONMNT
773	ELECTR DISTRIBUTNG EQUIP	W	8084	120.0	W	9073	149.9	W	13346	181.6	W	16060	215.4	EQUIPMT DISTRIBUTION ELECT
7731	INSULATED WIRE,CABLE ETC	W	7917	118.2	W	9036	149.3	W	13334	181.6	W	16024	215.2	FILS,CABLES ISOLES ELECT
778	ELECTRICAL MACHINERY NES	W	3793	32.2	W	3883	45.5	W	4247	47.5	W	4769	47.5	AUTRES MACH ELECT NDA
7788	OTH ELEC MACHY,EQUIP NES	W	378	23.0	W	510	36.2	W	481	36.3	W	561	35.4	AUT MACH APP ELEC NDA
77886	OTH ELEC MACHINERY NES	W	162	19.8	W	188	26.0	W	195	26.6	W	217	24.4	AUT MACH APP ELECTRIQUES
78	ROAD VEHICLES			25.2			37.2			28.6			32.7	VEHICULES ROUTIERS
784	MOTOR VEH PRTS,ACCES NES	W	2907	15.3	W	2575	17.4	W	2142	19.7	W	2291	20.2	PIECES 722,781,782,783
7849	OTHER MOTOR VEHCL PARTS	W	2896	15.2	W	2567	17.4	W	2084	19.5	W	2291	20.2	PIECES 722,781,782,783
8	MISC MANUFACTURED GOODS			2006.0			2533.8			2627.0			2527.9	ART MANUFACTURES DIVERS
831	*TRAVEL GOODS,HANDBAGS	W	793	11.8	W	829	24.6	W	716	19.2	W	672	17.1	ARTICLES DE VOYAGE ETC
84	CLOTHING AND ACCESSORIES			1839.6			2322.1			2396.5			2298.7	VETEMENTS
842	MENS OUTERWEAR NOT KNIT	W	52716	870.3	W	54178	1068.8	W	57690	1127.2	W	60159	1056.4	VET DESSUS POUR HOMMES
8423	— TROUSERS,BREECHES ETC	W	36738	585.1	W	37058	711.3	W	40595	778.5	W	41251	709.4	PANTALONS HOMMES MAT TEX
8424	— JACKETS,BLAZERS ETC	W	803	27.3	W	969	40.0	W	934	39.3	W	1258	46.9	VESTES HOMMES MAT TEXTIL
8429	— OTHER OUTER GARMENTS	W	14920	250.4	W	15928	308.3	W	15988	301.8	W	17360	290.9	AUT VET DES HOM MAT TEX
843	WOMENS OUTERWEAR NONKNIT	W	17892	441.9	W	20828	580.6	W	22300	609.5	W	24966	609.3	VET DESSUS FEMMES MAT TEX
8431	— COATS AND JACKETS	W	3415	85.0	W	3257	93.4	W	3129	92.5	W	3086	80.9	MANT,VEST FEM MAT TEXTIL
8433	— DRESSES	W	1139	29.9	W	2199	61.8	W	2141	59.4	W	1914	45.1	ROBES EN MAT–TEXTILES
8434	— SKIRTS	W	3050	74.6	W	3392	91.4	W	3082	76.1	W	2740	60.4	JUPES EN MAT TEXTILES
8435	— BLOUSES	W	2016	57.1	W	2179	76.2	W	2156	70.9	W	2300	62.8	BLOUSES FEM MAT TEXTILES
8439	— OTHER OUTER GARMENTS	W	8071	188.1	W	9620	250.7	W	11539	300.0	W	14667	350.8	AUT VET DES FEM MAT TEXT
844	UNDER GARMENTS NOT KNIT	W	5328	131.0	W	5454	155.3	W	5252	149.1	W	5557	139.2	VETEMENT DESSOUS MAT TEX
8441	— MENS SHIRTS	W	3897	101.9	W	4081	119.8	W	3953	114.8	W	4271	110.6	CHEMISES HOMMES MAT TEXT
84411	—— OF COTTON	W	2655	69.8	W	3048	90.3	W	3168	93.5	W	2993	81.2	CHEMISES HOMMES DE COTON
84412	—— OF SYNTHETIC FIBRES	W	1242	32.1	W	1034	29.5	W	785	21.3	W	1278	29.5	CHEMISES HOMMES FIB SYNT
8442	— MENS,OTHR THAN SHIRTS	W	999	19.1	W	935	22.2	W	861	22.5	W	726	18.7	SOUS–VET HOMMES MAT TEXT
845	OUTERWEAR KNIT NONELASTC	W	7216	165.5	W	8811	209.6	W	8520	212.8	W	10284	211.0	VET DESSOUS,ACCES BONNET
8451	— JERSEYS,PULLOVERS ETC	W	3510	60.8	W	4596	83.1	W	4891	102.8	W	5770	105.6	CHANDAILS,PULL–OVERS ETC
8452	— WOMENS DRESSES ETC	W	733	18.0	W	784	21.7	W	623	17.6	W	422	11.1	ROBES,JUPES BONNETERIE
8459	— OTHER,CLTHG ACCESRYS	W	2973	86.7	W	3431	104.9	W	3006	92.5	W	4092	94.5	AUT VET DESSUS DE BONNE
846	UNDER GARMENTS KNITTED	W	6023	190.1	W	7391	262.3	W	8327	255.4	W	9160	241.4	SOUS VETS DE BONNETERIE
8462	— OF COTTON NON ELASTIC	W	4455	79.9	W	5420	111.1	W	6498	124.9	W	7171	120.1	SOUS–VET BONNET COTON
84629	—— OTHER	W	4455	79.9	W	5420	111.1	W	6498	124.9	W	7171	120.1	AUT SOUS–VET BONNET COTON
8463	— OF SYNTH FBR NONELAST	W	486	15.7	W	583	21.1	W	523	14.8	W	407	10.4	SOUS–VET BONNET FIB SYNT
8465	CORSETS,GARTERS,ETC	W	1083	94.7	W	1389	130.2	W	1306	115.9	W	1582	111.0	CORSETS,GAINES ART SIM
84651	BRASSIERES	W	927	87.7	W	1255	123.0	W	1166	108.8	W	1395	103.3	SOUTIENS–GORGE,BUSTIERS
847	TEXTILE CLTHNG ACCES NES	W	1235	23.7	W	1215	25.1	W	1416	25.1	W	1264	21.0	ACCES VET MAT TEXT NDA
8472	CLTHNG ACCESRYS ETC KNIT	W	874	18.7	W	830	20.1	W	934	18.6	W	792	14.1	ACCES VET BONNE NDA
84722	KNIT SOCKS,ETC NONELASTC	W	815	18.4	W	754	19.4	W	884	18.0	W	780	14.0	CHAUSSETTES BON. NON ELAS
848	HEADGEAR,NONTXTL CLOTHNG	W	446	17.4	W	504	20.7	W	446	17.6	W	478	20.7	VET ACCES MAT AUT QUE TEX
851	*FOOTWEAR	W	6126	73.9	W	6976	99.2	W	7270	110.5	W	8487	113.8	CHAUSSURES
85102	FOOTWEAR LEATHER	W	5348	68.9	W	6673	93.8	W	6881	101.7	W	7900	102.3	CHAUS SEMELLES EN CUIR
88	PHOTO EQU,OPTICL GDS ETC			22.2			20.8			24.0			15.7	APP,FOURN PHOTO,OP,MONTR
89	MISC MANUFCTRD GOODS NES			34.9			37.3			45.3			43.0	ART MANUFACTURES DIVERS
893	ARTICLES OF PLASTIC NES	W	2039	9.3	W	3677	12.0	W	3249	17.6	W	3581	18.8	OUVRAGES EN MAT DIVIS 58

FOOT NOTES – NOTES

TABLE 1 –
1 Prior to 1974, special trade.
TABLEAU 1 –
1 Avant 1974, commerce spécial.

1. HISTORICAL SERIES, 1962–1997 SPECIAL TRADE, IMPORTS C.I.F., EXPORTS F.O.B.
SERIES HISTORIQUES, 1962–1997 COMMERCE SPECIAL, IMPORTATIONS C.A.F., EXPORTATIONS F.O.B

YEAR ANNEE	VALUE IN MILLION U.S. DOLLARS / VALEUR EN MILLION U.S. DOLLARS — MERCHANDISE–MARCHANDISE IMPORTS	MERCHANDISE–MARCHANDISE EXPORTS	GOLD–OR IMPORTS	GOLD–OR EXPORTS	CONVERSION FACTORS FACTEURS DE CONVERSION CENTS E.U. PAR — IMPORTS	CONVERSION FACTORS EXPORTS	INDEX NUMBERS–INDICES — QUANTUM IMPORTS	QUANTUM EXPORTS	UNIT VALUE / VALEUR UNITAIRE IMPORTS	UNIT VALUE / VALEUR UNITAIRE EXPORTS
1962	622.20	381.20								
1963	690.70	368.10								
1964	542.00	410.80								
1965	577.00	458.92								
1966	724.60	490.50								
1967	690.70	522.30								
1968	770.40	496.40								
1969	753.90	536.80								
1970	893.94	588.47								
1971	1087.40	676.59								
1972	1507.87	884.97								
1973	2036.66	1317.08								
1974	3719.72	1532.18								
1975	4738.58	1401.08								
1976	5128.64	1960.21								
1977	5796.28	1753.01								
1978	4599.01	2288.16								
1979	5069.37	2291.44								
1980	7910.00	2910.00					34	20	118	119
1981	8933.00	4703.00					41	31	115	106
1982	8843.00	5746.00					42	38	90	75
1983	9235.00	5728.00					49	40	105	95
1984	10757.00	7134.00					60	50	101	88
1985	11343.00	7958.00					68	65	102	84
1986	11105.00	7457.00					76	71	86	82
1987	14158.00	10190.00					86	88	92	94
1988	14335.00	11662.00					87	101	92	90
1989	15792.00	11625.00					87	95	95	91
1990	22302.00	12959.00					100	100	100	100
1991	21047.01	13594.00					96	107	97	99
1992	22872.00	14716.00					98	110	95	100
1993	29174.00	15343.00					134	117	89	98
1994	23270.00	18106.00					105	134	90	94
1995	35710.00	21639.01					135	140	105	107
1996	42931.01	23075.01					162	142	105	101
1997	48585.10	26244.70								

2. IMPORTS BY BROAD ECONOMIC CATEGORY AND EXPORTS BY INDUSTRIAL ORIGIN. (PERCENTAGE OF TOTAL VALUE)
IMPORTATIONS PAR CATEGORIES ECONOMIQUES ET EXPORTATIONS PAR BRANCHE D'ACTIVITE.(EN POURCENTAGE DE LA VALEUR TOTALE)

IMPORTS – IMPORTATIONS

	1991	1992	1993	1994	1995	1996	1997
TOTAL IMPORTS–IMPORTATIONS TOTALES	100.	100.	100.	100.	100.	100.	100.
1 FOOD BEV–ALIMENTATION BOISSONS	3.6	3.7	3.7	3.6	5.6	4.8	3.7
11 PRIMARY–PRODUITS DE BASE	1.5	1.5	2.1	1.3	3.0	2.6	2.1
111 FOR INDUSTRY–POUR L'INDUSTRIE	1.1	1.1	1.6	1.0	2.4	2.3	1.7
112 FOR HOUSEHOLDS–POUR LES MENAGES	0.4	0.4	0.4	0.3	0.5	0.3	0.4
12 PROCESSED–PRODUITS ELABORES	2.1	2.2	1.6	2.3	2.6	2.1	1.6
121 FOR INDUSTRY–POUR L'INDUSTRIE	0.9	0.8	0.8	1.0	0.9	0.7	0.7
122 FOR HOUSEHOLDS–POUR LES MENAGES	1.2	1.4	0.8	1.3	1.7	1.4	0.9
2 IND SUPPLIES–APPROV INDUSTRIELS	37.3	38.3	37.9	41.2	43.4	38.2	37.8
21 PRIMARY–PRODUITS DE BASE	6.5	7.0	7.1	8.3	8.1	7.3	7.3
22 PROCESSED–PRODUITS ELABORES	30.8	31.3	30.8	32.8	35.3	30.8	30.6
3 FUELS–COMBUSTIBLES	17.7	16.2	13.3	16.2	12.8	13.7	10.2
31 PRIMARY–PRODUITS DE BASE	15.8	15.0	11.7	14.8	11.8	12.3	8.9
32 PROCESSED–PRODUITS ELABORES	1.9	1.2	1.5	1.4	1.0	1.4	1.3
321 MOTOR SPIRIT–ESSENCE	0.3	0.3	0.4	0.4	0.3	0.4	0.4
322 OTHER–AUTRES	1.6	0.9	1.2	1.0	0.7	1.0	1.0
4 MACHINERY–EQUIPEMENT	26.7	24.9	24.2	24.0	21.8	25.2	25.1
41 CAPITAL EQUIPMENT–MACHINES	21.8	20.2	20.1	19.9	18.6	21.8	21.3
42 PARTS–PIECES ACCESSOIRES	4.9	4.8	4.2	4.0	3.2	3.4	3.8
5 TRANSPORT–TRANSPORT	8.5	11.3	15.1	10.2	11.4	10.9	13.5
51 PASSENGER CARS–AUTOMOBILES	1.2	1.6	2.5	1.0	0.9	2.4	3.4
52 OTHER–AUTRES	3.3	4.7	7.9	5.6	6.3	4.6	4.7
521 INDUSTRIAL–INDUSTRIELS	3.1	4.6	7.8	5.5	6.3	4.5	4.6
522 NON INDUSTRIAL–NON INDUSTRIEL	0.2	0.1	0.2	0.1	0.0	0.1	0.1
53 PARTS–PIECES ACCESSOIRES	4.0	5.0	4.7	3.7	4.2	4.0	5.4
6 CONSUM GOODS–BIENS CONSOMMATION	5.7	5.2	5.3	4.4	4.8	6.4	6.9
61 DURABLE–DURABLES	1.4	1.5	1.5	1.2	1.4	2.2	2.4
62 SEMI DURABLE–SEMI DURABLES	1.6	1.7	1.6	1.5	1.8	2.5	2.6
63 NON DURABLE–NON DURABLES	2.6	2.0	2.2	1.7	1.5	1.7	1.9
7 GOODS NES–BIENS NDA	0.6	0.4	0.5	0.4	0.3	0.9	2.8

EXPORTS – EXPORTATIONS

	1991	1992	1993	1994	1995	1996	1997
TOTAL EXPORTS–EXPORTATIONS TOTALES	100.	100.	100.	100.	100.	100.	100.
1 AGRICULTURE	19.5	14.9	15.4	13.1	10.2	11.0	10.6
2 MINING QUARRY–INDUS EXTRACTIVES	2.2	1.9	1.6	1.5	1.9	1.0	1.1
3 MANUFACTURING–IND MANUFACTUR	78.4	83.2	83.1	85.4	88.0	88.0	88.3
31 FOOD BEV TOBACCO–ALIM BOISS TAB	8.4	8.7	8.6	9.5	9.9	9.7	9.6
32 TEXTILES–INDUSTRIES TEXTILES	36.6	39.8	39.2	38.4	40.6	38.9	39.3
33 WOOD & PRODUCTS–BOIS & PRODUITS	0.3	0.3	0.3	0.4	0.4	0.3	0.3
34 PAPER & PRODUCTS–PAPIER & PRODT	0.5	0.5	0.5	0.7	0.7	0.7	0.7
35 CHEMICALS–INDUSTRIES CHIMIQUES	8.7	8.3	7.4	7.9	8.3	7.6	7.4
36 NON METAL MIN–MIN NON METAL	3.4	3.5	3.0	3.2	3.2	3.4	3.5
37 BASIC METAL–IND METAL BASE	10.9	10.4	12.9	12.9	10.6	9.8	10.0
38 METAL MANUF–MANUF METAL	9.4	11.4	11.0	11.9	13.8	15.8	15.9
39 OTH MANUF IND–AUTRES MANUF	0.3	0.2	0.3	0.4	0.4	1.8	1.8

3. TRADE BY PRINCIPAL COUNTRIES OF ORIGIN AND SALE (VALUE IN MILLION U.S. DOLLARS)
ECHANGES SELON LES PRINCIPAUX PAYS D'ORIGINE ET DE VENTE (VALEUR EN MILLIONS DE DOLLARS EU)

COUNTRIES–PAYS	SPECIAL IMPORTS C.I.F. IMPORTATIONS SPECIALES C.A.F				
	1993	1994	1995	1996	1997
World	29429.3	23268.0	35707.5	42930.3	48585.1
Africa	715.9	860.7	1384.5	2028.0	2197.3
Americas	4036.1	2923.0	4723.2	4395.1	5452.7
– Northern America	3491.5	2566.4	4016.7	3622.5	4652.5
– LAIA	523.3	329.2	658.1	662.4	751.7
– CACM	4.3	2.0	3.1	13.2	14.2
– Caribbean	5.8	5.8	2.3	33.8	5.4
– Rest of America	11.3	19.6	43.0	63.3	28.9
Asia excl fmr USSR	6390.0	4798.2	6647.1	7593.5	8406.6
– Middle East	2689.2	2414.2	2533.2	3069.1	2500.5
Asia former USSR	219.0	218.2	343.8	329.1	468.7
Europe excl fmr USSR	15659.7	12221.5	18932.5	25146.9	27405.0
– European Union	13874.1	10914.9	16862.5	22704.8	24869.8
– Eastern Europe	968.5	671.5	1054.2	1105.5	1125.7
– Rest of Europe	817.1	635.0	1015.9	1336.6	1409.5
Europe former USSR	2065.5	1616.0	3018.0	2745.1	3218.1
Oceaniu	261.3	301.3	344.8	410.4	546.5
Other	81.9	329.1	313.6	282.3	890.1
Germany/Allemagne	4533.0	3645.6	5547.6	7583.0	8021.2
USA/Etats–Unis d'Amer	3350.7	2429.4	3724.0	3287.6	4329.6
Italy/Italie	2558.3	2008.5	3193.1	4245.1	4463.1
France, Monaco	1952.4	1458.2	1995.8	2739.5	2967.3
United Kingdom	1546.0	1169.7	1829.8	2486.3	2763.2
Russian Federation	1542.3	1044.9	2082.4	1900.2	2174.3
Japan/Japon	1620.8	967.5	1400.0	1414.5	2040.1
Saudi Arabia	1499.7	1228.8	1383.0	1706.3	1017.6
Netherlands/Pays–Bas	869.9	740.0	1084.3	1416.7	1484.9
Belgium–Luxembourg	683.0	531.7	911.9	1114.9	1216.7
Switzerland,Liechtenst.	650.5	471.7	816.3	1126.3	1104.0
Spain/Espagne	430.7	380.2	592.6	989.0	1275.8
Ukraine	472.7	535.1	856.3	744.5	917.8
Iran (Islamic Rep of)	667.0	692.4	689.5	805.3	646.4
Korea, Republic of	621.2	285.3	566.1	714.6	1085.5
Sweden/Suède	427.6	283.2	517.8	655.4	896.6
China/Chine	255.2	257.9	539.0	551.3	787.5
Algeria/Algérie	23.0	94.7	448.0	727.9	768.0
Austria/Autriche	318.8	210.7	294.0	540.3	502.6
Libyan Arab Jamahiriya	131.0	319.6	385.2	476.3	533.1
Other Asia n.e.s.	287.6	188.9	350.6	450.4	510.7
Romania/Roumanie	300.8	228.9	367.9	437.4	394.1
Bulgaria/Bulgarie	243.2	195.4	402.0	358.0	408.9
Australia/Australie	206.5	226.3	235.4	304.1	444.5
Brazil/Brésil	250.8	206.0	267.9	290.5	330.1
Areas n.e.s.	81.9	329.1	313.6	0.4	529.5
Canada	140.8	137.0	292.7	334.4	311.1
Finland/Finlande	178.0	142.5	240.9	253.1	341.4
Greece/Grèce	120.5	105.1	200.7	283.4	430.8
Syrian Arab Republic	68.5	43.9	258.1	309.9	456.3
Malaysia/Malaisie	159.7	170.5	272.3	233.6	283.2
Egypt/Egypte	105.1	124.2	210.6	270.8	398.9
India/Inde	151.9	110.8	222.9	254.9	300.9
So. African Customs Un	208.4	160.6	132.2	256.1	183.8
Israel/Israël	121.8	125.9	166.6	192.0	233.7
Argentina/Argentine	146.2	49.8	208.6	152.3	248.0
Denmark/Danemark	135.9	96.3	188.8	170.0	200.9
United Arab Emirates	314.5	338.8	42.0	23.0	25.5
Ireland/Irlande	71.5	101.1	193.0	144.3	207.0
China, Hong Kong SAR	86.4	73.9	138.6	199.7	162.9

COUNTRIES–PAYS	SPECIAL EXPORTS F.O.B. EXPORTATIONS SPECIALES F.O.B.				
	1993	1994	1995	1996	1997
Monde	15348.9	18106.0	21598.7	23047.7	26244.7
Afrique	706.3	842.7	1063.9	1154.7	1232.4
Amériques	1127.6	1733.8	1752.1	1872.8	2370.8
– Amérique du Nord	1036.2	1600.1	1608.3	1717.1	2143.9
– ALAI	83.0	99.3	92.8	102.8	146.0
– MCAC	0.8	3.8	3.0	4.3	13.4
– Caraïbes	4.2	19.0	44.4	30.0	45.1
– Autre Amérique	3.4	11.6	3.6	18.6	22.5
Asie anc. URSS exclus	3685.9	3871.6	3567.4	3844.4	3971.3
– Moyen–Orient	2062.3	2060.6	2077.5	2183.0	2218.5
Asie ancienne URSS	494.0	511.2	616.8	859.4	1088.5
Europe anc. URSS exclus	8608.1	9795.7	12628.7	12986.1	14014.0
– Union Européenne	7602.8	8637.1	11076.8	11467.4	12248.3
– Europe de l'Est	622.2	751.1	1065.6	987.8	1073.1
– Autre de l'Europe	383.1	407.5	486.3	530.9	692.7
Europe ancienne URSS	554.0	912.2	1477.7	1807.2	2487.9
Océanie	27.1	42.3	53.3	64.4	75.5
Autre	146.0	396.6	438.8	458.9	1004.2
Germany/Allemagne	3654.3	3934.3	5033.6	5152.2	5253.5
USA/Etats–Unis d'Amer	986.5	1520.7	1512.6	1616.8	2027.1
Russian Federation	505.3	820.3	1232.1	1494.5	2056.5
Italy/Italie	750.3	1033.6	1455.8	1438.4	1387.2
United Kingdom	835.1	888.9	1134.5	1246.7	1511.3
France, Monaco	771.3	851.2	1032.6	1041.9	1163.4
Netherlands/Pays–Bas	517.0	621.0	736.4	764.4	779.2
Saudi Arabia	652.4	609.4	467.3	430.1	535.0
Belgium–Luxembourg	295.4	371.0	451.4	487.7	563.6
Spain/Espagne	198.9	233.6	360.3	366.1	439.2
Iran (Islamic Rep of)	289.7	249.8	265.6	296.4	307.0
Areas n.e.s.	146.0	396.6	438.8	17.7	393.3
Syrian Arab Republic	238.9	253.9	270.7	308.7	268.8
Austria/Autriche	226.6	249.0	275.1	287.7	300.2
Romania/Roumanie	151.7	175.3	301.6	312.7	358.8
Switzerland,Liechtenst.	215.9	238.9	237.8	274.8	318.2
Poland/Pologne	234.8	249.5	272.4	252.9	255.3
Egypt/Egypte	191.4	194.5	245.2	314.4	304.5
Algeria/Algérie	82.2	237.6	269.0	278.0	316.0
Israel/Israël	80.2	178.1	239.6	254.0	391.5
Libyan Arab Jamahiriya	246.3	179.4	238.2	243.6	186.7
Singapore/Singapour	121.0	184.6	142.7	247.9	365.7
Free zones/Zone franches				441.1	610.9
China/Chine	511.9	354.8	67.0	65.1	44.4
Greece/Grèce	118.2	168.9	209.7	235.6	298.2
China, Hong Kong SAR	117.7	236.5	216.6	219.4	238.3
United Arab Emirates	129.5	184.6	188.6	210.6	264.7
Azerbaijan/Azerbaïdjan	68.2	132.1	160.7	239.2	319.7
Ukraine	39.5	76.3	198.1	267.0	337.1
Cyprus/Chypre	153.7	130.2	197.1	200.9	228.2
Uzbekistan/Ouzbékistan	213.5	64.5	138.1	229.9	210.6
Japan/Japon	158.5	186.5	179.9	166.6	143.8
Lebanon/Liban	99.6	160.6	159.3	182.9	199.6
Bulgaria/Bulgarie	86.2	133.7	183.0	153.0	175.9
Kazakhstan	67.9	131.8	149.9	163.3	210.6
Other Asia n.e.s.	310.7	180.9	107.8	39.3	49.3
Iraq	160.1	141.0	119.2	188.0	53.9
Jordan/Jordanie	105.0	111.7	169.4	147.8	106.9
Denmark/Danemark	84.4	91.6	133.3	147.4	172.1
Kuwait/ Koweït	103.7	128.3	118.7	106.9	125.7

(VALUE AS PERCENTAGE OF WORLD TOTAL)(VALEURS EN POURCENTAGE DU TOTAL MONDIAL)

	1988	1989	1990	1991	1992	1993	1994	1995	1996	1997
Africa	4.7	6.7	6.0	3.6	3.5	2.4	3.7	3.9	4.7	4.5
Americas	14.6	17.2	13.5	13.5	13.6	13.7	12.6	13.2	10.2	11.2
– Northern America	12.3	14.4	11.1	11.5	11.8	11.9	11.0	11.2	8.4	9.6
– LAIA	2.3	2.7	2.4	2.0	1.7	1.8	1.4	1.8	1.5	1.5
– CACM	0.0	0.0	0.0	0.0	0.0	0.0	0.0	0.0	0.0	0.0
– Caribbean	0.0	0.0	0.0	0.0	0.0	0.0	0.0	0.0	0.1	0.0
– Rest of America	0.0	0.1	0.1	0.0	0.0	0.0	0.1	0.1	0.1	0.1
Asia excl fmr USSR	24.7	21.0	22.7	23.1	22.3	21.7	20.6	18.6	17.7	17.3
– Middle East	17.2	14.3	11.9	11.5	11.2	9.1	10.4	7.1	7.1	5.1
Asia former USSR					0.5	0.7	0.9	1.0	0.8	1.0
Europe excl fmr USSR	51.4	49.8	51.5	54.0	54.3	53.2	52.5	53.0	58.6	56.4
– European Union	44.1	41.0	44.4	47.0	46.6	47.1	46.9	47.2	52.9	51.2
– Eastern Europe	3.0	3.3	3.3	3.7	3.7	3.3	2.9	3.0	2.6	2.3
– Rest of Europe	4.3	5.5	3.8	3.3	4.0	2.8	2.7	2.8	3.1	2.9
Europe former USSR	3.1	3.8	5.6	5.2	5.0	7.0	6.9	8.5	6.4	6.6
Oceania	1.6	1.0	0.7	0.6	0.7	0.9	1.3	1.0	1.0	1.1
Other		0.5	0.0	0.0	0.1	0.3	1.4	0.9	0.7	1.8
Germany/Allemagne				15.4	16.4	15.4	15.7	15.5	17.7	16.5
USA/Etats–Unis d'Amer	10.6	13.3	10.2	10.7	11.4	11.4	10.4	10.4	7.7	8.9
Italy/Italie	7.0	6.8	7.7	8.8	8.4	8.7	8.6	8.9	9.9	9.2
France, Monaco	5.8	4.7	6.0	5.8	5.9	6.6	6.3	5.6	6.4	6.1
United Kingdom	5.2	4.6	4.5	5.5	5.2	5.3	5.0	5.1	5.8	5.7
Russian Federation					4.6	5.2	4.5	5.8	4.4	4.5
Japan/Japon	3.9	3.4	5.0	5.2	4.9	5.5	4.2	3.9	3.3	4.2
Saudi Arabia	1.6	1.3	3.2	8.7	7.3	5.1	5.3	3.9	4.0	2.1
Netherlands/Pays–Bas	2.7	2.8	2.6	3.0	3.1	3.0	3.2	3.0	3.3	3.1
Belgium–Luxembourg	3.3	2.8	2.3	2.6	2.4	2.3	2.3	2.6	2.6	2.5

	1988	1989	1990	1991	1992	1993	1994	1995	1996	1997
Afrique	6.7	6.6	5.8	6.0	5.3	4.6	4.7	4.9	5.0	4.7
Amériques	7.4	9.3	8.3	7.6	6.7	7.3	9.6	8.1	8.1	9.0
– Amérique du Nord	7.0	8.9	8.0	7.1	6.2	6.8	8.8	7.4	7.5	8.2
– ALAI	0.3	0.2	0.2	0.4	0.3	0.5	0.5	0.4	0.4	0.6
– MCAC	0.0	0.0	0.0	0.0	0.0	0.0	0.0	0.0	0.0	0.1
– Caraïbes	0.0	0.1	0.0	0.1	0.1	0.0	0.1	0.2	0.1	0.2
– Autre Amérique	0.0	0.0	0.1	0.1	0.1	0.0	0.1	0.0	0.1	0.1
Asie anc. URSS exclus	31.9	22.7	19.8	21.4	22.2	24.0	21.4	16.5	16.7	15.1
– Moyen–Orient	23.0	17.8	13.4	14.0	13.8	13.4	11.4	9.6	9.5	8.5
Asie ancienne URSS					1.4	3.2	2.8	2.9	3.7	4.1
Europe anc. URSS exclus	51.4	53.3	61.6	60.1	60.3	56.1	54.1	58.5	56.3	53.4
– Union Européenne	46.1	48.7	55.4	54.0	53.9	49.5	47.7	51.3	49.8	46.7
– Europe de l'Est	2.4	2.1	2.4	3.3	3.6	4.1	4.1	4.9	4.3	4.1
– Autre de l'Europe	2.9	2.6	3.8	2.8	2.8	2.5	2.3	2.3	2.3	2.6
Europe ancienne URSS	2.3	6.1	4.1	4.5	3.3	3.6	5.0	6.8	7.8	9.5
Océanie	0.2	0.4	0.2	0.2	0.2	0.2	0.2	0.2	0.3	0.3
Autre	0.0	1.6	0.2	0.2	0.6	1.0	2.2	2.0	2.0	3.8
Germany/Allemagne				25.1	24.9	23.8	21.7	23.3	22.4	20.0
USA/Etats–Unis d'Amer	6.5	8.4	7.5	6.7	5.9	6.4	8.4	7.0	7.0	7.7
Russian Federation					3.0	3.3	4.5	5.7	6.5	7.8
Italy/Italie	8.2	8.4	8.5	7.1	6.4	4.9	5.7	6.7	6.2	5.3
United Kingdom	4.9	5.3	5.7	5.0	5.4	5.4	4.9	5.3	5.4	5.8
France, Monaco	4.3	5.1	5.7	5.1	5.5	5.0	4.7	4.8	4.5	4.4
Netherlands/Pays–Bas	3.0	3.5	3.4	3.5	3.4	3.4	3.4	3.4	3.3	3.0
Saudi Arabia	3.1	3.1	2.6	3.6	3.3	4.3	3.4	2.2	1.9	2.0
Belgium–Luxembourg	2.3	2.2	2.4	2.1	2.0	1.9	2.0	2.1	2.1	2.1
Spain/Espagne	0.9	1.2	1.5	1.8	2.0	1.3	1.3	1.7	1.6	1.7

4. Special Imports C.I.F. by Commodities according to the S.I.T.C. (Rev. 2) in million U.S. Dollars
Importations Spéciales C.A.F. par Produits d'après la C.T.C.I. (Rév. 2) en millions de Dollars E.U.

SITC CTCI	COMMODITY	1994		1995		1996		1997		PRODUIT
		QUANTITY QUANTITE	VALUE VALEUR	QUANTITY QUANTITE	VALUE VALEUR	QUANTITY QUANTITE	VALUE VALEUR	QUANTITY QUANTITE	VALUE VALEUR	
	ALL COMMODITIES		23268.0		35707.5		42930.4		48585.1	TOUS PRODUITS
0	FOOD AND LIVE ANIMALS		465.2		1480.2		1748.9		1423.8	ALIMENTS,ANIMAUX VIVANTS
001	*LIVE ANIMALS FOR FOOD	W 9483	22.8	W 178306	341.9	W 74547	165.2	W 947	17.1	ANIMAUX VIVANTS
0011	BOVINE SPECIES,LIVE	W 9190	14.5	W 176530	330.3	W 73303	152.3	W 29	0.3	ESPECE BOVINE
00111	— PURE BRED FR BREEDING	W 3528	7.5	W 36304	107.4	W 26374	77.2	W 29	0.3	BOVINS REPRODUCTEURS
00119	— OTHR THAN FR BREEDING	W 5662	7.0	W 140226	222.9	W 46929	75.1			BOVINS NON REPRODUCTEURS
04	CEREALS AND PREPARATIONS		165.0		470.6		785.5		730.1	CEREALES ET PRODUITS
041	WHEAT ETC UNMILLED	W 495905	76.0	W 1253331	243.7	W 2146930	485.1	W 2551789	457.4	FROMENT,EPEAUTRE
0412	OTHER WHEAT ETC UNMILLED	W 336288	40.5	W 1128724	213.1	W 1997962	445.0	W 2438694	430.1	AUTRE FROMENT NON MOULU
042	RICE	W 197993	56.3	W 307846	109.5	W 211482	82.1	W 286327	94.8	RIZ
044	MAIZE UNMILLED	W 14878	3.8	W 623975	92.5	W 897440	175.7	W 853809	130.4	MAIS NON MOULU
05	VEGETABLES AND FRUIT		47.7		87.6		93.6		175.5	LEGUMES ET FRUITS
06	SUGAR AND PREPS,HONEY		10.4		202.8		293.1		43.5	SUCRES ET PRODUITS
061	SUGAR AND HONEY	W 113907	8.8	W 432591	199.7	W 772302	286.8	W 116811	36.2	SUCRES ET MIEL
0612	REFINED SUGAR ETC	W 569	0.3	W 402159	189.1	W 581219	242.5	W 62059	24.7	SUCRES RAFFINES
081	*FEEDING STUFF FOR ANIML	W 314925	85.1	W 436439	101.1	W 428409	149.8	W 489309	184.1	NOURRITURE POUR ANIMAUX
1	BEVERAGES AND TOBACCO		152.6		173.4		290.6		393.2	BOISSONS ET TABACS
12	TOBACCO AND MANUFACTURES		139.9		160.0		272.1		383.0	TABACS BRUTS FABRIQUES
121	TOBACCO UNMNFCTRD,REFUSE	W 16693	86.5	W 21639	134.4	W 42962	240.1	W 54397	341.2	TABACS BRUTS,DECHETS
1212	TOBACCO STRIPPED OR PART	W 13676	85.4	W 18602	131.7	W 33953	223.3	W 49631	333.5	TABACS PART ECOTES
2	CRUDE MATERLS,EXCL FUELS		2272.5		3512.2		3538.2		3888.9	MAT BRUTES NON COMESTIBLES
21	HIDES,SKINS,FURS UNDRSSD		281.6		464.4		675.6		589.3	CUIRS,PEAUX BRUTS
211	HIDES,SKINS,EXC FURS,RAW	W 122805	281.3	W 171702	462.8	W 253079	672.2	W 236585	585.2	CUIRS ET PEAUX
2116	SHEEP SKIN WITH WOOL	W 80593	131.0	W 92647	213.4	W 151689	387.9	W 145711	364.0	PEAUX LAINEES D'OVINS
2117	SHEEP SKIN WITHOUT WOOL	W 25372	128.0	W 27703	164.4	W 33053	181.5	W 24301	136.0	PEAUX EPILEES D'OVINS
22	OIL SEEDS,OLEAGINOUS FRT		75.5		204.5		249.9		259.6	GRAINES,FRUITS OLEAGINEUX
222	SEEDS FOR'SOFT'FIXED OIL	W 265343	75.1	W 612309	203.7	W 823917	249.4	W 911959	258.8	GRAINES HUILES FIXES
2224	SUNFLOWER SEEDS	W 94664	30.2	W 357035	120.5	W 640373	183.1	W 564609	141.5	GRAINES DE TOURNESOL
23	RUBBER, CRUDE		130.8		241.5		239.6		205.4	CAOUTCHOUC BRUT
232	NATURAL RUBBER,GUMS	W 64654	69.0	W 83759	135.6	W 86379	127.3	W 92976	106.9	LATEX CAOUTCHOUC NATUREL
23202	OTHER NATURAL RUBBER	W 52832	58.0	W 71008	118.2	W 72976	109.2	W 77590	90.7	CAOUTCHOUC NATUREL
24	CORK AND WOOD		160.8		145.3		182.6		167.2	LIEGE ET BOIS
247	OTH WOOD ROUGH,SQUARED	W 933915	148.1	W 622345	118.2	W 788904	138.1	W 652830	123.9	BOIS BRUTS EQUARRIS
2471	SAW–,VENEER–LOGS CONIFER	W 599554	88.2	W 465038	70.3	W 502755	68.1	W 399148	64.7	CONIFERES POUR SCIAGE,PLACAG
24711	— IN THE ROUGH	W 599554	88.2	W 465038	70.3	W 502755	68.1	W 399148	64.7	ECORCES OU DEGROSSIS
251	*PULP AND WASTE PAPER	W 240226	102.3	W 315838	246.1	W 228908	126.6	W 324916	143.6	PATES A PAPIER,DECHETS
2517	SODA,SULPHATE WOOD PULP	W 185992	89.3	W 235691	214.5	W 189973	110.6	W 247070	124.2	PATES CHIMIQUES AU SULFATE
25172	— BLEACHED,NONDISSOLVNG	W 178493	87.0	W 231771	212.0	W 187945	109.3	W 246573	124.0	PATES BLANCHIES
26	TEXTILE FIBRES AND WASTE		489.8		808.7		695.4		1052.4	FIBRES TEXTILES
263	COTTON	W 149063	240.1	W 187303	383.3	W 169168	302.3	W 362973	632.6	COTON
2631	RAW COTTON,EXCL LINTERS	W 147059	239.0	W 182561	381.1	W 166747	299.8	W 356813	628.6	COTON EN MASSE
266	SYNTHETIC FIBRES TO SPIN	W 60593	84.7	W 62220	118.8	W 72926	114.1	W 90828	136.9	FIBRES SYNTHETIQUES
267	OTHER MAN–MADE FIBRES	W 55087	85.6	W 77671	159.1	W 69571	169.0	W 82727	167.3	AUTR FIBR TEXT ARTIF SYNTH
2671	REGENERATD FIBRE TO SPIN	W 49786	82.7	W 67275	151.8	W 63226	164.3	W 74858	161.9	FIBRES TEXT ARTIFIC
268	WOOL(EXC TOPS),ANML HAIR	W 27376	65.1	W 43315	133.1	W 40238	99.6	W 42284	107.8	LAINES ET POILS
27	CRUDE FERTLZR,MINRLS NES		81.1		118.0		125.6		186.5	ENGRAIS MINERAUX BRUTS
28	METALLIFEROUS ORES,SCRAP		908.3		1218.6		1171.1		1201.8	MINERAIS METAL,DECHETS
281	IRON ORE,CONCENTRATES	W 1951330	46.7	W 3221358	107.5	W 2991253	116.0	W 2950732	106.5	MINERAIS DE FER
282	IRON AND STEEL SCRAP	W 5917325	848.9	W 6851971	1081.3	W 7042138	991.4	W 7734735	987.4	FERRAILLES
28209	— OF OTHR IRON OR STEEL	W 5916852	848.8	W 6848247	1079.2	W 7027321	987.8	W 7721211	984.7	FERRAILLES DE FER
3	MINERAL FUELS ETC		3838.0		4657.8		5941.0		5043.9	COMBUSTIBLES MINERAUX LUB
32	COAL,COKE AND BRIQUETTES		401.9		321.3		623.5		626.4	HOUILLES,COKES,BRIQUETTES
322	COAL,LIGNITE AND PEAT	W 7339517	377.9	W 5159675	287.8	W 8821653	580.7	MW 9686	560.8	HOUILLES,LIGNITES,TOURBE
3222	OTH COAL,NOT AGGLOMERATD	W 6582088	344.7	W 4330834	238.1	W 7842637	519.6	MW 9445	539.6	AUTRES HOUILLES
33	PETROLEUM AND PRODUCTS		2807.5		3329.5		4042.9		3767.1	PETROLE ET DERIVES
333	CRUDE PETROLEUM	MW 21181	2432.2	MW 23605	2917.2	MW 22767	3416.0	MW 23324	3194.2	HUILES BRUTES DE PETROLE
334	PETROLEUM PRODUCTS,REFIN	W 1884316	302.2	W 1756626	330.3	W 2426066	534.6	W 2310562	495.5	PRODUITS RAFFINES
3341	GASOLINE,OTH LIGHT OILS	W 545853	88.3	W 627746	111.5	W 803315	170.0	W 839919	177.2	ESSENCES POUR MOTEURS
33411	MOTOR,AVIATION SPIRIT	W 301706	51.2	W 349967	62.2	W 767892	162.6	W 782787	163.8	ESSENCES MOTEURS D'AVIONS
3343	GAS OILS	W 665190	97.9	W 560199	86.7				0.1	GAS OILS
3344	FUEL OILS,NES	W 571078	55.9	W 457656	53.1	W 1533653	280.6	W 445746	57.0	FUEL OILS
3345	LUBS,PETROLEUM OILS NES	W 66558	50.5	W 54335	61.3	W 87954	83.7	W 1024478	261.0	HUILES LUBRIFIANTES
33451	LUBS(HIGH PETR CONT) ETC	W 55232	24.0	W 39944	22.4	W 69657	36.9	W 1002112	210.1	HUILES LUBRIF,H LOURDES
335	RESIDUAL PETRLM PROD NES	W 1544099	73.3	W 1504274	82.1	W 1710893	92.4	W 1341167	77.5	PRODUITS RESIDUELS NDA
341	*GAS,NATURAL AND MANUFCT		628.6		1007.1	MW 11995	1262.8	W 2117995	566.5	GAZ NATUREL,GAZ MANUFACT
3413	PETROLM GASES,LIQUEFIED	W 1842077	256.9	W 3139134	484.8	W 6369723	741.7	W 2117899	566.4	GAZ DE PETROLE LIQUEFIE
34139	OTH HYDROCARBON GAS LQFD	W 1842077	256.9	W 3138231	484.6	W 6367693	741.0	W 2112668	565.1	HYDROCARBURES GAZEUX NDA
3414	PETROLEUM GASES, GASEOUS	MV 5048399	371.7	MV 5660032	522.3	W 5625323	521.2	W 96	0.1	GAZ DE PETROLE GAZEUX
4	ANIMAL,VEGETABLE OIL,FAT		459.0		638.1		490.4		569.8	HUILES,GRAISSES ANIM,VEG
42	FIXED VEGETABLE OIL,FAT		404.1		537.2		383.1		461.7	HUILES VEGETALES FIXES
423	FIXED VEG OILS,SOFT	W 426714	254.0	W 462889	311.2	W 309251	181.7	W 399295	227.8	HUILES VEGET DOUCES FIXES
4232	SOYA BEAN OIL	W 137756	80.9	W 141153	93.4	W 105766	61.4	W 164428	94.0	HUILE DE SOJA
4236	SUNFLOWER SEED OIL	W 287624	171.3	W 305594	206.5	W 191724	112.6	W 229878	128.6	HUILE DE TOURNESOL
424	FIXED VEG OIL NONSOFT	W 281660	150.2	W 321295	226.0	W 310373	201.5	W 374281	233.9	AUTRES HUILES VEG FIXES
4242	PALM OIL	W 201239	96.9	W 200473	135.3	W 174776	101.9	W 231817	131.6	HUILE DE PALME
5	CHEMCLS,RELATED PROD NES		3145.2		5236.3		5599.9		6317.6	PRODUITS CHIMIQUES
51	ORGANIC CHEMICALS		890.2		1521.1		1386.4		1489.1	PROD CHIMIQ ORGANIQUES
511	HYDROCARBONS NES,DERIVS	W 321756	155.8	W 379141	244.8	W 386356	182.7	W 399069	202.8	HYDROCARBURES NDA
5112	CYCLIC HYDROCARBONS	W 161752	85.4	W 176833	128.7	W 165903	74.4	W 187758	83.4	HYDROCARBURES CYCLIQUES
512	ALCOHOLS,PHENOLS ETC		99.1		166.5	W 303859	166.8	W 315912	161.8	PHENOLS,PHENOLS–ALCOOLS
5121	ACYCLIC ALCOHOLS,DERIVS		91.2		154.2	W 295711	155.0	W 306047	147.7	ALCOOLS ACYCLIQUES
513	CARBOXYLIC ACIDS ETC	W 180399	178.2	W 234607	344.5	W 274923	320.3	W 347574	324.7	ACIDES CARBOXYLIQUES
5137	MONOACIDS AND DERIVATIVS	W 116072	101.9	W 127544	176.8	W 141697	151.6	W 163320	157.7	ACIDES MONOCARBOXYLIQUES
5138	POLYACIDS AND DERIVATIVS	W 56257	49.6	W 94528	116.3	W 120399	118.0	W 176145	133.3	ACIDES POLYCARBOXYLIQUES
514	NITROGEN–FNCTN COMPOUNDS	W 144770	242.1	W 183760	424.3	W 167037	384.5	W 226032	440.3	COMPOSES FONCT AZOTEES
5148	OTH NITROGN–FNCTN CMPNDS	W 117238	156.3	W 155021	311.6	W 137381	268.6	W 190648	313.9	AUTRES COMPOSES AZOTES
51483	ACRYLONITRILE	W 82137	54.8	W 111339	146.6	W 89633	74.4	W 132710	111.7	ACRYLONITRILE
515	ORG–INORG COMPOUNDS ETC	W 26280	163.2	W 33583	253.8	W 28663	248.7	W 34487	268.3	COMPOSES ORGANO–MINERAUX
5156	HETEROCYCLIC CMPDS ETC	W 18376	113.8	W 22796	178.3	W 17526	168.9	W 21371	182.2	COMPOSES HETEROCYCLIQUES
51569	OTH HETEROCYC CMPDS,ETC	W 2794	93.0	W 4338	136.9	W 4652	142.2	W 5521	153.3	AUT COMP HETEROCYCLIQUES
52	INORGANIC CHEMICALS		282.9		441.6		477.0		442.5	PROD CHIM INORGANIQUES
522	INORG ELEMNTS,OXIDES,ETC		173.9		287.9	W 1038159	290.1	W 1022398	254.5	ELEMENTS INORGANIQUES
5225	INORGANIC BASES ETC NES	W 484971	82.9	W 616534	150.8	W 557022	128.7	W 563823	114.7	AUTRES BASES OXYDES METAL
52251	AMMONIA,ANHYDROUS ETC	W 378634	60.2	W 504819	113.4	W 414180	86.0	W 413252	78.2	AMMONIAC LIQUEFIE
523	OTHR INORG CHEMICALS ETC	W 152369	102.7	W 196269	146.6	W 262478	178.8	W 336159	180.7	AUT PRODUITS CHIMIQUES INORG
53	DYES,TANNING,COLOUR PROD		392.9		561.0		640.1		698.7	PROD TEINTURE,COLORANTS
531	SYNT DYE,NAT INDGO,LAKES	W 20613	228.1	W 25064	299.6	W 33494	344.9	W 42718	376.2	MAT COLOR ORGAN,LAQUES
5311	SYNTHIC ORGNIC DYESTUFFS	W 19481	217.3	W 23557	284.9	W 31507	327.4	W 40224	357.9	MAT COLOR ORGAN SYNTHET
533	PIGMENTS,PAINTS,ETC	W 57697	157.6	W 77557	249.1	W 90713	274.6	W 121995	300.1	PIGMENTS,PEINTURES,VERNIS
541	*MEDICINAL,PHARM PRODUCT	K 4917751	357.1	K 5769920	550.9	K 5026284	635.0	K 7828371	811.1	PROD MEDICINAUX PHARMACEUT
5413	ANTIBIOTICS IN BULK	K 545938	100.6	K 731139	138.5	K 685414	148.0	K 691086	180.2	ANTIBIOTIQUES NDA

4. Special Imports C.I.F. by Commodities according to the S.I.T.C. (Rev. 2) in million U.S. Dollars
Importations Spéciales C.A.F. par Produits d'après la C.T.C.I. (Rév. 2) en millions de Dollars E.U.

SITC CTCI	COMMODITY	1994 QUANTITY QUANTITE	1994 VALUE VALEUR	1995 QUANTITY QUANTITE	1995 VALUE VALEUR	1996 QUANTITY QUANTITE	1996 VALUE VALEUR	1997 QUANTITY QUANTITE	1997 VALUE VALEUR	PRODUIT
5417	MEDICAMENTS	K 2143112	134.0	K 2419026	227.7	K 1760347	282.2	K 4038229	381.4	MEDICAMENTS
54179	— CONTNG OTH SUBSTANCES	K 1562147	88.1	K 1960728	146.8	K 1358266	186.5	K 2227966	260.3	MED CONT AUT SUBSTANCES
55	PERFUME,CLEANING ETC PRD		134.4		219.9		306.3		405.9	PROD POUR PARFUM,TOILETTE
551	ESSENTL OILS,PERFUME,ETC	W 3715	58.6	W 4990	89.6	W 6887	136.3	W 8159	153.0	HUILES ESSENTIELLES
5514	MIXED PERFUME SUBSTANCES	W 3497	56.6	W 4711	85.6	W 6508	132.1	W 7706	148.9	MELANGES SUBSTAN ODORIFER
562	*FERTILIZERS,MANUFACTURE	W 1402353	168.7	W 2489070	362.3	W 2003364	330.8	W 2048140	317.7	ENGRAIS MANUFACTURES
5621	CHEM NITROGENOUS FERTLZR	W 793128	67.6	W 1700703	199.0	W 1431325	201.0	W 1369424	166.4	ENGRAIS AZOTES
5629	FERTILIZERS NES	W 451772	83.0	W 636342	143.2	W 430451	110.0	W 559079	134.7	ENGRAIS NDA
56292	NITROG–PHOS FERTILZR NES	W 435337	77.8	W 624931	136.4	W 416898	101.1	W 545911	125.2	ENGRAIS NDA CONT N P
58	PLASTIC MATERIALS ETC		626.1		1130.0		1277.0		1548.5	MAT PLAST ARTIFICIELLES
582	PROD OF CONDENSATION ETC	W 79011	162.3	W 112147	290.1	W 123875	326.6	W 166785	360.9	PROD CONDENS,POLYCOND
583	POLYMERIZATION ETC PRODS	W 404445	435.9	W 539447	796.3	W 735010	901.6	W 1039113	1136.7	PROD POLYMERISATION
5831	POLYETHYLENE	W 92881	77.6	W 103617	131.2	W 169939	176.0	W 220801	225.9	POLYETHYLENE
58311	— IN PRIMARY FORMS	W 88242	66.7	W 97284	112.8	W 162471	155.6	W 210867	201.2	POLYETHYLENE PRIMAIRES
5832	POLYPROPYLENE	W 118118	100.7	W 184642	220.4	W 247670	238.4	W 337578	294.0	POLYPROPYLENE
58321	— IN PRIMARY FORMS	W 110864	83.8	W 175491	190.4	W 238822	209.8	W 328047	268.5	POLYPROPYLENE PRIMAIRES
5833	POLYSTYRENE,ITS COPOLYMR	W 66785	71.4	W 86609	139.1	W 110005	132.7	W 143181	142.5	POLYPROPYLENE COPOLYMERES
58331	— IN PRIMARY FORMS	W 66308	70.3	W 85948	137.2	W 109402	130.8	W 141893	139.6	SOUS FORMES PRIMAIRES
5834	POLYVINYL CHLORIDE	W 67238	63.7	W 77799	91.9	W 103553	102.8	W 190025	174.3	CHLORURE DE POLYVINYLE
58341	— IN PRIMARY FORMS	W 65151	56.6	W 74357	78.0	W 99364	85.6	W 184092	153.8	SOUS FORMES PRIMAIRES
5839	OTH POLYMRZTION ETC PROD	W 43205	85.8	W 63611	152.6	W 72831	174.3	W 107739	213.1	AUT PROD POLYMER COPOLYM
59	CHEMICAL MATERIALS NES		287.0		441.8		537.8		592.9	MAT PROD CHIMIQUES NDA
598	MISCEL CHEM PRODUCTS NES	W 204804	202.9	W 192819	301.2	W 188978	368.2	W 227362	406.0	PROD DIV INDUST CHIM NDA
5989	CHEM PRODUCTS,PREPS NES	W 82117	129.6	W 123777	218.4	W 138679	277.7	W 168409	309.0	PROD PREP CHIMIQUES NDA
59899	OTH CHEM PRODS,PREPS,NES	W 62469	91.2	W 100677	147.8	W 110815	196.1	W 133464	227.1	AUT PRODUITS CHIMIQUES NDA
6	BASIC MANUFACTURES		4063.2		6732.3		7186.7		8233.1	ART MANUFACTURES
61	LEATHER,DRESSED FUR,ETC		182.7		235.9		290.3		308.2	CUIRS,PELLETERIES
611	LEATHER	W 11493	157.2	W 12892	195.7	W 14882	222.1	W 12973	199.9	CUIRS,PEAUX PREPARES
6115	LEATHER FROM SHEEP,LAMBS	W 6500	94.4	W 5619	95.2	W 6955	127.9	W 6233	108.5	PEAUX D'OVINS PREPAREES
62	RUBBER MANUFACTURES NES		115.2		170.6		255.7		277.3	CAOUTCHOUC MANUFACTURE
64	PAPER,PAPERBOARD AND MFR		309.4		706.9		726.2		722.5	PAPIERS,CARTONS & OUVRAGES
641	PAPER AND PAPERBOARD		246.9		604.9	W 741087	611.0	W 874724	589.1	PAPIERS ET CARTONS
6411	NEWSPRINT	W 124703	54.9	W 218286	173.7	W 254980	169.7	W 315032	146.1	PAPIER JOURNAL
6413	KRAFT PAPER,PAPERBOARD	W 54418	29.6	W 134195	111.0	W 129423	86.1	W 125260	69.5	PAPIER ET CARTON KRAFT
6415	PAPER,PAPERBRD,BULK,NES	W 83642	66.2	W 89194	110.7	W 117969	111.7	W 157325	99.4	PAPIERS,CARTONS ROULEAUX
65	TEXTILE YARN,FABRICS,ETC		1121.7		1834.4		1966.4		2362.6	FILS,TISSUS,ARTICLES TEXTILE
651	TEXTILE YARN	W 153521	464.5	W 216382	771.7	W 214051	737.5	W 272777	817.1	FILS TEXTILES
6513	COTTON YARN	W 53289	167.3	W 58795	221.7	W 41058	142.7	W 41165	137.2	FILS DE COTON
6514	SYN FIB YRN,BULK,MONOFIL	W 44326	137.3	W 67244	250.8	W 70478	258.2	W 106727	329.6	FILS CONT 85% FIB TEXT SYNTH
65142	— NONTXT ETC CONT PAMID	W 28954	98.0	W 42679	173.6	W 45041	179.6	W 61232	216.7	FILS NON TEX FI CON POLYAMID
6517	REGEN FIBRE YARN,MONOFIL	W 22053	68.2	W 32470	118.5	W 30690	112.6	W 34340	114.9	FILS TEXT ART NON VENTE DT
652	COTTON FABRICS,WOVEN	W 35586	185.9	W 55511	346.9	W 41590	303.1	W 49814	380.9	TISSUS DE COTON
6521	GREY WOVEN COTTON FABRIC	W 21458	81.1	W 28616	134.4	W 17487	86.4	W 15961	84.7	TISSUS COT ECRUS NON MERCER
65214	GREY WOVEN COTTON NES	W 17915	59.6	W 26104	117.8	W 15671	73.8	W 13535	69.5	AUT TISSUS 85% COTON ECRUS
6522	WOVEN COTTON BLEACHD,ETC	W 14128	104.8	W 26895	212.6	W 24102	216.8	W 33853	296.3	TISSUS COTON BLANCHIS ETC
65224	BLCHED COTTON FABRIC NES	W 12543	92.6	W 23781	186.0	W 21305	189.2	W 26086	232.9	AUT TIS PLUS 85% COT BLANCHI
653	WOVN MAN–MADE FIB FABRIC	W 42989	223.4	W 74776	421.1	W 70564	462.6	W 75455	560.7	TISSUS FIBRES SYNTH,ARTIF
6531	CONT SYNT WEAVES NONPILE	W 13500	66.1	W 23602	108.9	W 22475	139.2	W 29363	225.2	TISSUS FIBRES SYNTH CONTINUE
65315	CONT SYN TXTL FABRIC NES	W 13134	64.1	W 22767	103.1	W 21682	132.4	W 27639	205.8	TIS PLUS 85% TEXT SYNT CONT
6536	DISC REGN TXTL FABRC NES	W 17779	72.5	W 27685	128.7	W 23575	104.3	W 14632	63.3	TISSUS 85% TEXT ART DISC
654	OTH WOVEN TEXTILE FABRIC	W 10700	46.1	W 15506	63.3	W 18076	114.7	W 15258	160.4	TISSUS AUT COTON SYNT,ARTIF
655	KNITTED,ETC FABRICS	W 15435	90.6	W 8334	64.3	W 10555	90.3	W 12624	108.5	ETOF BONNETERIE PIECES ETC
6552	OTHER KNIT ETC FAB NONEL	W 15435	90.6	W 8334	64.3	W 10555	90.3	W 12624	108.5	ETOF BON NON ELAS NON SYNT
657	SPECIAL TXTL FABRC,PRODS		87.2		125.1	W 25339	163.3	W 35286	212.0	TISSUS SPECIAUX
66	NONMETAL MINERAL MFS NES		199.4		343.1		431.9		419.6	ART MIN NON METALLIQUES
67	IRON AND STEEL		1315.9		2115.4		1940.7		2346.7	FER ET ACIER
671	PIG IRON ETC	W 729103	154.8	W 758425	196.4	W 576953	183.0	W 435532	154.3	FONTE,SPIEGEL,POUDRES
6712	PIG IRN,SPIEGELEISEN ETC	W 563513	76.9	W 585407	100.0	W 395423	68.0	W 244447	43.0	FONTES BRUTES
6716	FERRO–ALLOYS	W 163537	76.1	W 169226	93.0	W 177360	110.9	W 183196	105.8	FERRO–ALLIAGES
672	IRON,STEEL PRIMARY FORMS	W 2007134	424.7	W 2103465	613.0	W 1858132	488.8	W 2631111	659.6	LINGOTS FER,ACIER
6725	IRN,STL BLOOMS,SLABS,ETC	W 1620415	313.5	W 1009621	240.1	W 838039	197.7	W 1390012	321.2	BLOOMS,BILLETTES FER ACIER
67251	IRN,SMPLE STL BLOOMS,ETC	W 1615472	308.6	W 880100	206.1	W 819497	185.8	W 1386318	315.3	BLOOMS ETC NON ACIER FIN
6727	IRN,STL COIL FR REROLLNG	W 386700	111.2	W 1093278	372.5	W 1020061	291.1	W 1228057	336.9	EBAUCHES POUR TOLES FER
67271	IRON,SIMPLE STEEL COILS	W 353183	97.0	W 1040631	346.0	W 984986	274.6	W 1186689	316.9	EBAUCHES NON EN ACIER
673	IRON,STEEL SHAPES ETC	W 262806	104.1	W 277786	155.0	W 277202	159.5	W 412359	185.4	BARRES,PROFIL FER,ACIER
674	IRN,STL UNIV,PLATE,SHEET	W 808367	434.8	W 1543394	959.7	W 1293450	836.6	W 1847976	946.4	LARGES PLATS,TOLES
6744	IRN,STL HVY PLATE,ROLLED	W 137927	48.9	W 358362	140.7	W 213984	98.7	W 370724	130.1	TOLES LAMINEES PLUS 4.75 MM
67441	— OF IRON OR SIMPLE STL	W 131761	38.4	W 352572	124.5	W 203885	75.0	W 357545	108.9	TOLES NON ACIER FIN CARB
6745	IRN,STL MED PLATE,ROLLED	W 148451	68.3	W 202661	117.2	W 212222	113.6	W 392997	156.8	TOLES 3 A 4.75 MM
6746	IRN,STL THIN PLATE,ROLLD	W 415253	240.1	W 771742	523.8	W 559817	386.0	W 774203	438.7	TOLES LAM MOINS 3MM
67461	— OF IRON OR SIMPLE STL	W 361669	140.0	W 708593	344.4	W 480354	211.2	W 678593	260.9	TOL NON AC FIN MOINS 3 MM
67463	— OF STAINLESS ETC STL	W 51052	96.1	W 60507	173.2	W 74537	168.0	W 88560	169.1	TOL ACIER INOX MOINS 3 MM
6749	OTH IRN,STL PLATES,SHEET	W 54497	43.9	W 73447	72.8	W 190696	146.1	W 190037	140.2	AUTRES TOLES FER,ACIER
67491	— OF IRON OR SIMPLE STL	W 51817	36.9	W 71668	66.9	W 188912	141.4	W 187402	132.6	AUT TOLES AUTRES ACIER FIN
678	IRON,STL TUBES,PIPES,ETC	W 114573	132.9	W 90000	141.9	W 161602	230.2	W 204186	325.1	TUBES,TUYAUX EN FONTE,FER
68	NON–FERROUS METALS		399.2		752.3		768.8		965.2	METAUX NON FERREUX
682	COPPER EXC CEMENT COPPER	W 83087	166.5	W 94330	295.6	W 121355	306.6	W 151571	376.8	CUIVRE
6821	COPPER NES,ALLOYS,UNWRT	W 58899	104.2	W 63690	179.7	W 84072	185.6	W 115855	264.1	CUIVRE BRUT
68212	COPPER REFINED,UNWROUGHT	W 26248	56.0	W 42054	114.6	W 51956	113.6	W 85711	191.2	CUIVRE AFFINE BRUT
6822	COPPER,ALLOYS WORKED	W 24188	62.4	W 30640	116.0	W 37283	121.0	W 35716	112.7	CUIVRE,ALLIAGES OUVRES
684	ALUMINIUM	W 93875	169.3	W 142913	343.6	W 151509	328.2	W 199819	425.9	ALUMINIUM
6841	ALUMINIUM,ALLOYS,UNWRGHT	W 67462	102.5	W 101577	219.5	W 99312	173.5	W 139034	247.0	ALUMINIUM,ALLIAGES BRUTS
6842	ALUMINIUM,ALLOYS WORKED	W 26413	66.9	W 41336	124.2	W 52197	154.8	W 60785	179.0	ALUMINIUM,ALLIAGES OUVRE
69	METAL MANUFACTURES NES		391.7		531.1		749.1		770.2	ART MANUFACT EN METAL NDA
699	BASE METAL MFRS NES	W 35636	174.1	W 36845	225.9	W 44109	302.7	W 54637	301.8	ART MANUFACTURES MET NDA
7	MACHINES,TRANSPORT EQUIP		7657.1		11470.4		15169.6		18574.5	MACHINES MATERIEL TRANSPORT
71	POWER GENERATING EQUIPMT		444.7		594.5		890.8		1533.6	MACHINES GENERATRICES
713	INTRNL COMBUS PSTN ENGIN	W 16939	207.3	W 27448	368.2	W 34248	479.5	W 48030	586.7	MOTEURS EXPL COMB INT, PIECE
7132	MOTOR VEHCL PISTN ENGINS	W 7495	82.4	W 15981	190.2	W 19389	240.0	W 26711	298.5	MOTEURS EXPL POUR VEHICULES
7139	PISTON ENGINE PARTS NES	W 6649	87.8	W 6855	110.7	W 6891	127.9	W 11774	166.5	PIECES POUR 713.2,3,8
714	ENGINES AND MOTORS NES	W 582	76.2	W 1674	60.5	W 1276	87.2	W 8160	425.3	MOTEURS NON ELECTRIQUES
7149	ENGINE & MOTOR PARTS NES	W 251	25.7	W 345	26.9	W 366	34.2	W 2159	239.1	PIECES 714 ET 718.88
716	ROTATING ELECTRIC PLANT	W 8475	124.3	W 8366	114.3	W 16794	183.6	W 23706	290.0	APP ELECTR ROTATIFS,PIECES
7162	AC MTRS,GENRTRS,GEN SETS	W 6183	59.4	W 6501	71.7	W 13714	133.4	W 17164	162.3	MOTEURS ELECTRIQUES
72	MACHS FOR SPCL INDUSTRYS		1457.0		2583.1		4195.4		3873.3	MAC SPECIALES POUR INDUST
723	CIVIL ENGNEERG EQUIP ETC	W 12915	81.9	W 23302	156.0	W 49608	313.9	W 64527	418.2	APPAREILS DE GENIE CIVIL
7234	CONST,MINING MACHNRY NES	W 11639	69.7	W 21635	142.5	W 46342	289.9	W 60415	386.6	MACH POUR LA CONST, MINES
72342	SLFPRP SHOVELS,EXCAVATRS	W 8181	45.7	W 17225	98.1	W 37867	216.2	W 50631	292.2	PELLES MECANIQUES
724	TEXTILE,LEATHER MACHNRY	W 50144	685.2	W 91040	1541.2	W 148793	2410.8	W 125930	2009.7	MACH POUR INDUSTRIE TEXTILE
7243	SEWING MACHS,NEEDLES ETC	W 3105	57.6	W 6912	148.7	W 7119	170.5	W 5148	152.4	MACHINES A COUDRE,PIECES
72431	SEWING MACHINES	W 2925	48.7	W 6674	133.8	W 6734	153.7	W 4892	134.5	MACHINES A COUDRE

4. Special Imports C.I.F. by Commodities according to the S.I.T.C. (Rev. 2) in million U.S. Dollars
Importations Spéciales C.A.F. par Produits d'après la C.T.C.I. (Rév. 2) en millions de Dollars E.U.

SITC CTCI	COMMODITY	1994 QUANTITY QUANTITE	1994 VALUE VALEUR	1995 QUANTITY QUANTITE	1995 VALUE VALEUR	1996 QUANTITY QUANTITE	1996 VALUE VALEUR	1997 QUANTITY QUANTITE	1997 VALUE VALEUR	PRODUIT
7244	SPINNING,EXTRDNG,ETC MCH	W 21970	274.9	W 33849	593.3	W 52045	842.5	W 50371	748.4	MACH POUR LE FILAGE
72442	FIBRE PROCESSNG MACH NES	W 4599	56.9	W 10754	166.0	W 17665	227.8	W 18434	215.9	MACH PREP MAT TEXTILES
72443	SPINNING,REELING,ETC MCH	W 12195	133.4	W 20594	345.5	W 30102	494.9	W 28393	418.6	MACH POUR LA FILATURE
7245	WEAVING,FELT MFG,ETC MCH	W 14032	183.4	W 36833	515.5	W 61365	845.8	W 42037	591.3	METIERS A TISSER,PIECES
72451	WEAVING MACHINES (LOOMS)	W 6773	58.8	W 23977	257.0	W 37541	363.7	W 23294	215.2	METIERS A TISSER
72452	KNITTING MACHINES	W 4633	85.4	W 7263	169.0	W 10883	281.0	W 8255	212.5	METIERS A BONNETERIE
72453	GIMPING,WARPING ETC MCHS	W 2551	37.8	W 5369	87.6	W 12620	198.1	W 10117	158.9	METIERS A TULLE ETC
7247	TEXTILE MACHINERY NES	W 8516	118.6	W 9683	189.6	W 21660	398.4	W 21449	362.4	MACH LAVAGE,TEINTURE TEX
72474	OTH TEXTILE MACHNERY NES	W 6286	99.1	W 7988	165.9	W 18064	345.0	W 16777	295.4	MACH LAVAGE ETC MAT TEXT
726	PRINTG,BKBINDG MACHY,PTS	W 4906	80.5	W 6446	134.0	W 12067	266.8	W 11462	208.5	MACHINES POUR IMPRIMERIE
727	FOOD MACHRY NON-DOMESTIC	W 3033	53.3	W 2758	57.7	W 5630	154.9	W 4161	99.5	MACH INDUSTRIES ALIMENT
7272	OTH FOOD PROC MCHY,PARTS	W 2530	50.5	W 2719	57.3	W 5440	151.3	W 3917	94.4	AUT MACH IND ALIMENTAIRE
728	OTH MACHY FOR SPCL INDUS	W 32479	507.6	W 30292	564.0	W 52315	847.3	W 61823	914.3	AUT MACH IND PARTICULIERES
7283	OTHR MINERAL WORKG MACHY	W 8606	83.0	W 6531	60.9	W 13899	137.1	W 15818	130.0	MACH TRIER,CRIBLER,BROYER
7284	MACHY FOR SPCL INDUS NES	W 20876	380.2	W 20528	453.8	W 33430	635.6	W 39745	690.0	MACH SPEC IND PARTICUL.
72842	RUBBER,PLASTICS WRKG MCH	W 7606	113.6	W 7841	122.5	W 12359	207.8	W 13767	222.3	MACH IND CAOUT MAT PLAST
72848	OTH MCHY WITH INDIV FNCT	W 8873	166.5	W 8445	206.5	W 11079	224.8	W 16231	321.8	AUTRES MACHINES NDA
73	METALWORKING MACHINERY		317.4		373.7		378.6		478.4	MACH TRAVAIL DES METAUX
736	METALWORKING MACH-TOOLS	W 13247	160.3	W 17954	223.5	W 28605	306.3	W 46258	367.3	MACH-OUTILS TRAVAIL METAUX
7361	METAL CUTTING MACH-TOOLS	W 5543	71.1	W 7865	87.6	W 15480	127.6	W 24393	160.8	MACH-OUT ENLEVEMENT METAL
737	METALWORKING MACHNRY NES	W 8384	157.1	W 5952	150.2	W 6063	72.3	W 9623	111.1	MACH TRAV METAUX PIECES
7372	ROLLING MILLS AND ROLLS	W 5969	104.4	W 4191	110.2	W 3574	20.7	W 5442	33.2	LAMINOIRS CYLINDRES PIEC
73721	ROLLING MILLS	W 4080	80.2	W 2437	84.4	W 488	7.8	W 623	13.1	LAMINOIRS ET TRAINS
74	GENRL INDUSTRL MACHY NES		1271.7		1584.6		2137.2		2499.7	MACH APP INDUSTRIE
741	HEATING,COOLING EQUIPMNT	W 20707	265.7	W 31256	354.1	W 37882	515.8	W 44712	500.8	MACH CHAUFFAGE,PIECES
7413	INDUS FURNACES ETC,PARTS	W 5666	88.2	W 6761	71.0	W 8637	139.4	W 7677	75.8	FOURS IND,LABOR,PIECES
74132	INDUST FURNACES NONELECT	W 4832	74.8	W 5075	48.9	W 6830	111.7	W 5538	40.3	FOURS NON ELECTRIQUES
7415	AIR-CONDITIONING MACHNRY	W 3025	42.4	W 6150	84.9	W 10379	131.5	W 13223	164.4	GROUPES CONDITION AIR
7416	HEATING,COOLING EQU NES	W 5632	76.1	W 6782	95.2	W 7909	108.8	W 8600	114.4	APP CHANGEMENT TEMP
742	PUMPS FOR LIQUIDS ETC	W 5595	102.1	W 6989	143.5	W 8856	189.3	W 11893	265.6	POMPES MOTO-POMPES
7428	OTHER PUMPS FOR LIQUIDS	W 2289	44.4	W 2817	69.7	W 4095	94.5	W 5324	151.2	AUTRES POMPES POUR LIQ
743	PUMPS NES,CENTRFUGES ETC	W 14456	188.1	W 19780	309.3	W 25507	371.2	W 32413	374.6	POMPES COMPRES,VENT ETC
7436	GAS,LIQUID FILTERS ETC	W 4345	83.1	W 4074	75.0	W 8453	167.6	W 9629	136.4	APP POUR FILT DES LIQUIDES
7439	PTS NES OF APP OF 7435,6	W 1099	25.1	W 3740	113.7	W 2243	55.0	W 3046	61.8	PIECES 743.5 ET 743.6
744	MECHANICAL HANDLING EQU	W 17980	164.7	W 16965	166.1	W 33006	258.3	W 52141	359.2	EQUIP MANUTENTION PIECES
7442	LIFTING,LOADING MACH NES	W 11707	119.9	W 8692	107.8	W 15677	137.0	W 25320	192.5	APP LEVAGE,MANUTENTION
74428	OTH HANDLING ETC MCH NES	W 7599	83.6	W 4941	62.2	W 7216	85.9	W 13504	119.7	AUT APP LEVAGE ETC
745	NONELEC MACHY,TOOLS NES	W 6602	180.4	W 5864	165.9	W 8043	262.3	W 10618	293.2	AUT MACH NON ELEC,PIECES
7452	OTH NONELEC MCHS,PTS NES	W 6204	172.7	W 5207	149.3	W 7089	233.5	W 9463	261.7	AUT MACH NON ELEC,PIECES
74522	PACKAGNG,BOTTLNG,ETC MCH	W 2961	103.5	W 2627	100.7	W 3930	152.8	W 4321	150.9	MACH NETT BOUTEILLES,ETC
749	NONELEC MACH PTS,ACC NES	W 21494	370.9	W 22226	446.1	W 30058	540.6	W 41521	706.6	PIECES MACH NON ELEC NDA
7491	BALL,ROLLER,ETC BEARINGS	W 4898	72.6	W 6254	109.0	W 8246	130.5	W 10697	147.6	ROULEMENTS BILLES ETC
7492	COCKS,VALVES ETC NES	W 4630	86.4	W 5530	119.6	W 7335	151.5	W 11428	214.4	ART ROB,SIM POUR TUYAUX
7493	SHAFT,CRANK,PULLEY ETC	W 7564	108.3	W 7583	124.6	W 8043	130.7	W 12212	161.7	ARBRES TRANS,VILEBREQUINS
7499	OTH NONELEC MCHY PTS NES	W 4402	103.8	W 2858	93.0	W 6433	128.0	W 7184	183.0	PIECES NON ELECT NDA
74991	FOUNDRY MOULDS ETC NES	W 2638	75.0	W 1471	58.2	W 4917	88.2	W 5617	143.8	MOULES POUR METAUX
75	OFFICE MACHNES,ADP EQUIP		398.4		687.0		770.5		913.2	MACH BUREAU TRAIT AUTOM
752	AUTOMTIC DATA PROC EQUIP	W 4319	276.3	W 9263	481.6	W 9694	531.0	W 12110	613.9	MACH TRAIT INFORMATION
7523	DIGITL CENTRL PROCESSORS	W 641	75.0	W 1891	128.5	W 963	120.6	W 1287	132.2	UNITES CENTRALES
7525	ADP PERIPHERAL UNITS	W 2279	95.8	W 5254	189.6	W 6471	217.5	W 8367	230.3	UNITES PERIPHERIQUES
759	OFFICE,ADP MCH PTS,ACCES	W 1024	79.2	W 1441	130.4	W 2589	140.6	W 3329	173.6	PIECES DU 751 ET 752
7599	ACCTG,ETC,ADP MCH PTS,AC	W 828	71.8	W 1217	119.5	W 2317	127.1	W 3016	157.7	PIECES DU 751 ET 752
76	TELECOMM,SOUND EQUIPMENT		537.4		633.8		834.4		1162.7	EQUIPMENT DE TELECOM
764	TELECOM EQPT,PTS,ACC NES	W 9851	513.6	W 12003	590.8	W 15059	673.1	W 18341	937.2	EQUIP TELECOM,PIECES
7643	TV,RADIO TRANSMITTRS ETC	W 1026	135.0	W 849	256.5	W 905	267.8	W 1587	444.2	APP EMET TELE RADIO
7648	TELECOMM EQUIPMENT NES	W 1009	183.6	W 1025	61.6	W 1492	60.3	W 1984	60.4	APP TELECOM NDA
76483	RADAR APPARATUS ETC	W 647	136.7	W 267	23.1	W 608	27.4	W 609	25.5	APP DE RADIOGUIDAGE ETC
7649	PTS NES OF EQUIPMT OF 76	W 5546	125.7	W 6591	159.6	W 7494	215.2	W 7127	255.5	PIECES DE LA DIV 76
76493	TELECOMM EQUIPMT PTS NES	W 4361	97.2	W 5553	117.9	W 6670	132.0	W 5871	137.5	PIECES 761,762,764.3,8
77	ELECTRIC MACHNRY NES ETC		1173.1		1469.4		2030.4		2565.4	MACH APP ELECT NDA
771	ELECTRIC POWER MACHY NES	W 3044	69.9	W 4153	69.1	W 7302	100.5	W 9651	132.3	MACH PROD,TRANS ELECTR
772	SWITCHGEAR ETC,PARTS NES	W 8515	267.2	W 7672	311.4	W 9513	394.9	W 13797	471.2	APP COUPURE,SECT ETC
7721	SWITCHGEAR ETC	W 7820	242.6	W 7133	284.6	W 8786	360.5	W 12609	425.8	APP COUPURE,SECTIONMNT
773	ELECTR DISTRIBUTNG EQUIP	W 9236	99.0	W 10095	118.2	W 11528	127.1	W 16089	148.6	EQUIPMT DISTRIBUTION ELECT
774	ELECTRO-MEDCL,XRAY EQUIP	W 954	55.1	W 816	68.4	W 1427	137.6	W 1767	135.5	APPAREILS MEDICAUX
775	HOUSEHOLD TYPE EQUIP NES	W 14911	88.0	W 20807	135.6	W 45329	287.9	W 75127	409.7	MACH,APP USAGE DOMESTQUE
776	TRANSISTORS,VALVES,ETC	W 22445	258.3	W 31732	356.1	W 42676	483.4	W 71305	698.9	LAMPES,TUBES,VALVES
7761	TV PICTURE TUBES	W 21172	114.4	W 30526	181.1	W 41376	254.1	W 68745	359.5	TUBES CATHODIQUES
7764	ELECTRONIC MICROCIRCUITS	W 796	93.5	W 567	117.5	W 550	160.5	W 768	248.1	MICROSTRUCTURES ELECTRON
778	ELECTRICAL MACHINERY NES	W 39654	336.0	W 46997	410.9	W 54665	499.4	W 61934	569.5	AUTRES MACH ELECT NDA
7788	OTH ELEC MACHY,EQUIP NES	W 28634	215.5	W 29696	222.6	W 26761	254.6	W 28461	276.5	AUT MACH APP ELEC NDA
77887	ELECTRICAL CARBONS	W 24898	71.4	W 25904	85.9	W 23117	81.6	W 23912	78.1	PIECES CHARBON,GRAPHITE
78	ROAD VEHICLES		871.1		1521.8		2623.6		4056.8	VEHICULES ROUTIERS
781	PASS MOTOR VEH EXC BUSES	W 24781	222.1	W 43026	327.2	W 77390	1018.0	W 161480	1672.9	AUTO TRANSPORT PERSONNES
782	LORRIES,SPCL MTR VEH NES	W 20007	141.0	W 26380	178.1	W 59499	397.8	W 111632	708.9	VEHICULES SPECIAUX,MARCH
7821	LORRIES,TRUCKS	W 14227	84.7	W 21464	127.6	W 53331	325.9	W 97874	596.0	VEHICULES TRANSP MARCHAND
783	ROAD MOTOR VEHICLES NES	W 3349	39.1	W 15924	191.8	W 27901	302.5	W 58896	408.7	VEHICULES ROUTIERS NDA
7831	BUSES	W 1203	12.4	W 4059	31.9	W 9081	69.1	W 32620	145.8	VOITURES TRANSPORT COMMUN
7832	TRACTORS FOR TR-TRAILERS	W 2146	26.7	W 11865	160.0	W 18820	233.5	W 26276	262.9	TRACTEURS ROUTIERS
784	MOTOR VEH PRTS,ACCES NES	W 46098	425.7	W 84531	767.8	W 87949	798.5	W 137838	1149.7	PIECES 722,781,782,783
7849	OTHER MOTOR VEHCL PARTS	W 45137	413.7	W 77482	742.5	W 82617	772.0	W 130568	1114.7	PIECES 722,781,782,783
79	OTHR TRANSPORT EQUIPMENT		1186.7		2022.8		1309.2		1491.8	AUTRE MATERIEL TRANSPORT
791	RAILWAY VEHICLES	W 3665	104.9	W 4482	109.8	W 7148	189.1	W 10221	126.2	VEHIC MAT CHEMINS DE FER
7913	MECHAN-PROPELLED RY CARS	W 2255	93.3	W 1426	95.6	W 2577	163.6	W 826	57.3	AUTOMOTRICES,DRAISINES
792	AIRCRAFT ETC		802.4		1377.6	W 1834	763.2	W 1865	977.1	APP NAVIGATION AERIENNE
7923	AIRCRFT NES2000-15000KG	N 18	25.9	N 65	450.5	W 124	155.8	W 169	106.2	AERODYNES 2000 A 15000 KG
7924	AIRCRFT NES OVER 15000KG	N 21	691.5	N 26	706.5	W 1347	502.4	W 887	518.5	AERODYNES PLUS 15000 KG
7929	AIRCRAFT PARTS NES	W 197	59.9	W 162	121.8	W 303	90.9	W 555	317.5	PIECES DU 792
793	SHIPS AND BOATS ETC		279.5		535.5		357.0	W 4570	388.7	NAVIRES BATEAUX,ETC
7932	SHIPS AND BOATS NES		255.8		483.4		329.5	W 1388	339.4	NAVIRES ET BATEAUX
79323	OTHER CARGO VESSELS		237.2		451.5		241.4	W 379	317.8	AUT BATEAUX TRANS MARCH
8	MISC MANUFACTURED GOODS		1130.8		1727.2		2376.2		2813.1	ART MANUFACTURES DIVERS
812	*PLUMBG,HEATNG,LGHTNG EQ	W 10805	43.4	W 21520	104.5	W 19591	138.7	W 19691	148.1	APPAR SANITAIRES CHAUFFAGE
821	*FURNITURE,PARTS THEREOF	W 8698	43.0	W 12552	78.0	W 19293	139.6	W 27140	179.7	MEUBLES ET PIECES
84	CLOTHING AND ACCESSORIES		35.3		49.1		152.5		233.1	VETEMENTS
87	PRECISION INSTRUMNTS NES		417.2		566.2		647.7		735.2	INSTRUM,APPAR SCIENT NDA
872	MEDICAL INSTRUMENTS NES	W 2526	127.1	W 3639	176.7	W 3460	182.4	W 4092	216.1	INSTR,APP MEDIC-CHIR NDA
87202	OTH MEDICAL INSTRUMENTS	W 2256	119.1	W 3225	163.9	W 2982	167.0	W 3565	197.9	INSTRUM,APP MEDECINE
874	MEASURNG,CONTROLNG INSTR	W 4156	243.3	W 6369	341.3	W 6518	396.6	W 7070	441.6	INSTRUMENTS DE MESURE
88	PHOTO EQU,OPTICL GDS ETC		159.8		246.7		322.1		354.8	APP,FOURN PHOTO,OP,MONTR
882	PHOTO,CINEMA SUPPLIES	W 8431	79.8	W 11594	113.8	W 12869	131.0	W 14215	138.6	PRODUITS PHOTO,CINEMA

4. Special Imports C.I.F. by Commodities according to the S.I.T.C. (Rev. 2) in million U.S. Dollars
Importations Spéciales C.A.F. par Produits d'après la C.T.C.I. (Rév. 2) en millions de Dollars E.U.

SITC CTCI	COMMODITY	1994 QUANTITY QUANTITE	1994 VALUE VALEUR	1995 QUANTITY QUANTITE	1995 VALUE VALEUR	1996 QUANTITY QUANTITE	1996 VALUE VALEUR	1997 QUANTITY QUANTITE	1997 VALUE VALEUR	PRODUIT
89	MISC MANUFCTRD GOODS NES		409.6		642.6		878.9		1030.4	ART MANUFACTURES DIVERS
892	PRINTED MATTER	W 24787	81.8	W 11779	76.3	W 9008	86.4	W 10464	95.1	IMPRIMES
893	ARTICLES OF PLASTIC NES		134.2		243.6		345.5		376.7	OUVRAGES EN MAT DIVIS 58
8939	MISC PLASTIC ARTICLES	W 17850	110.5	W 28648	194.7	W 38440	286.9	W 52235	310.2	ART DIVERS EN MAT DIV 58
89399	OTHR PLASTC ARTICLES NES	W 15527	104.8	W 24612	185.0	W 31727	268.9	W 45207	288.0	AUT OUV MAT DIV 58
899	OTHER MANUFACTURED GOODS		80.5		103.6		142.5		178.8	AUT ART MANUF DIVERS NDA
9	GOODS NOT CLASSD BY KIND		84.9		80.2		589.2		1327.8	ART TRANSACT NON CLASSES
931	*SPECIAL TRANSACTIONS				0.1		354.2		1154.3	TRANS.SPECIALES
951	*WAR FIREARMS,AMMUNITION		84.1		79.0	W 2205	36.8	W 7957	171.5	VEHIC BLINDES ARMES
95101	ARMORED FIGHTNG VEHICLES	W 4413	70.2	W 2031	43.0			W 559	12.7	CHARS DE COMBAT
971	*GOLD,NON MONETARY NES	K 900	0.2	K 109	0.2	K 16097	197.7	K 13155	0.2	OR NON MONETAIRE
97101	NONMON GLD UNWRT,SEMIMFD	K 171	0.2	K 60	0.2	K 16097	197.7	K 9	0.1	OR,ALLIAGES D'OR BRUTS

5. Special Exports F.O.B. by Commodities according to the S.I.T.C. (Rev. 2) in million U.S. Dollars
Exportations Spéciales F.O.B. par Produits d'après la C.T.C.I. (Rév. 2) en millions de Dollars E.U.

SITC CTCI	COMMODITY	1994		1995		1996		1997		PRODUIT
		QUANTITY QUANTITE	VALUE VALEUR	QUANTITY QUANTITE	VALUE VALEUR	QUANTITY QUANTITE	VALUE VALEUR	QUANTITY QUANTITE	VALUE VALEUR	
	ALL COMMODITIES		18106.1		21598.7		23047.8		26244.8	TOUS PRODUITS
0	FOOD AND LIVE ANIMALS		3298.3		3414.9		3552.4		4077.3	ALIMENTS,ANIMAUX VIVANTS
001	*LIVE ANIMALS FOR FOOD	W 85554	221.8	W 40612	130.3	W 24107	83.3	W 23302	81.3	ANIMAUX VIVANTS
0012	SHEEP AND GOATS,LIVE	W 85526	221.4	W 40602	130.1	W 24093	83.1	W 23252	81.1	ESPECES OVINE ET CAPRINE
00121	SHEEP,LIVE	W 83239	216.6	W 40246	129.1	W 24058	83.0	W 23244	81.1	ESPECE OVINE
03	FISH AND PREPARATIONS		70.2		84.8		101.5		124.7	POISSONS ET PREPARATIONS
04	CEREALS AND PREPARATIONS		383.1		450.3		515.4		645.0	CEREALES ET PRODUITS
041	WHEAT ETC UNMILLED	W 980029	88.5	W 232587	22.7	W 7494	2.0	W 15424	3.8	FROMENT,EPEAUTRE
0412	OTHER WHEAT ETC UNMILLED	W 892181	79.7	W 232165	22.5	W 7140	1.8	W 11531	2.5	AUTRE FROMENT NON MOULU
046	WHEAT ETC MEAL OR FLOUR	W 564750	107.7	W 629146	143.8	W 570576	175.4	W 864918	262.7	SEMOULE FARINE,FROMENT
04601	FLOUR OF WHEAT OR MESLIN	W 538712	99.1	W 610268	135.9	W 551355	166.9	W 844111	253.7	FARINE DE FROMENT
048	CEREAL ETC PREPARATIONS	W 163544	123.9	W 241524	232.8	W 306386	309.3	W 346856	303.6	PREPTNS A BASE CEREALES
0484	BAKERY PRODUCTS	W 65795	81.5	W 122341	171.9	W 172289	237.8	W 192961	221.9	PRODUITS DE BOULANGERIE
04842	PASTRY, CAKES ETC	W 53167	67.1	W 108080	152.3	W 139516	192.8	W 148118	169.8	PATISSERIE ETC.
05	VEGETABLES AND FRUIT		2003.4		2176.8		2216.0		2467.8	LEGUMES ET FRUITS
054	VEG ETC FRSH,SMPLY PRSVD	W 1096199	452.7	W 833241	470.5	W 1379638	608.4	W 1290731	620.6	LEGUMES FRAIS,CONG,SECS
0542	LEGUMINOUS VEGETBLES DRY	W 411667	166.7	W 282624	198.4	W 502249	269.1	W 489748	255.0	LEGUMES A COSSE SECS
0545	OTHER FRESH VEGETABLES	W 131125	50.8	W 178464	65.2	W 281241	77.7	W 210620	77.1	AUTRES LEGUMES FRAIS,REF
0546	VEGETABLES SIMPLY PRESVD	W 194180	145.8	W 158748	135.0	W 225622	176.8	W 221788	173.2	LEGUMES CONG,CONSER
05461	VEGETABLES FROZEN	W 189670	140.4	W 153576	126.7	W 218462	164.3	W 212894	158.7	LEGUMES CONGELES
056	VEGTBLES ETC PRSVD,PREPD	W 173896	187.1	W 159860	194.2	W 162120	184.0	W 169032	191.3	CONSERVES DE LEGUMES
0565	VEGTBLES PRSVD,PREPD NES	W 149638	128.4	W 140572	142.5	W 140211	131.3	W 152478	132.8	LEGUMES PREPARES CONSERVE
05651	VEGTBLS,FRUIT IN VINEGAR	W 121435	94.8	W 107323	93.4	W 112099	90.7	W 119350	89.3	LEGUM CONSERV AU VINAIGRE
057	FRUIT,NUTS,FRESH,DRIED	W 941518	1079.9	W 986293	1211.2	W 944058	1103.5	W 839831	1267.5	FRUITS FRAIS OU SECS
0571	ORANGES, MANDARINS ETC	W 196444	76.6	W 206074	73.5	W 210033	82.2	W 161005	67.4	ORANGES,MAND,CLEMENTINES
0572	LEMONS,GRAPEFRUIT ETC	W 192963	80.0	W 186712	79.8	W 158990	77.0	W 109161	46.7	AUTRES AGRUMES FRAIS,SECS
05721	LEMONS,LIMES,FRESH,DRIED	W 153462	64.7	W 140663	63.9	W 110440	59.7	W 62321	29.5	CITRONS ET LIMES
0575	GRAPES FRESH OR DRIED	W 199504	188.9	W 194930	204.6	W 200278	206.0	W 214261	224.5	RAISINS FRAIS OU SECS
05752	GRAPES DRIED(RAISINS)	W 173246	176.2	W 169701	190.0	W 171868	188.4	W 180858	206.3	RAISINS SECS
0576	FIGS,FRESH OR DRIED	W 40218	66.6	W 40703	77.9	W 40704	75.1	W 39451	68.9	FIGUES FRAICHES,SECHES
0577	NUTS EDIBLE,FRESH,DRIED	W 141138	523.9	W 196380	610.4	W 154228	469.7	W 151173	664.5	FRUITS A COQUES
05775	HAZELNUTS,FRESH OR DRIED	W 134251	510.0	W 185712	590.8	W 144018	444.4	W 138559	622.3	NOISETTES FRAICHES,SECHES
0579	FRUIT FRESH OR DRIED NES	W 138673	130.3	W 133668	153.1	W 123350	159.6	W 116840	168.3	FRUITS FRAIS,SECS NDA
05799	OTHER DRIED FRUIT	W 47671	91.8	W 53395	102.8	W 47371	111.4	W 44796	117.9	AUTRES FRUITS SECHES
058	FRUIT PRESERVED,PREPARED	W 150324	283.8	W 151474	301.1	W 188440	320.2	W 196294	388.6	CONSERVES DE FRUITS
0585	FRUIT OR VEGETABLE JUICE	W 45135	36.6	W 52535	66.8	W 75730	84.5	W 61577	54.7	JUS DE FRUITS
05857	JUICE OF OTHER FRUIT,VEG	W 42929	35.1	W 48795	64.5	W 70323	80.5	W 57251	51.9	JUS AUTRES FRUITS,LEGUMES
0589	FRUIT PREPRD,PRESRVD,NES	W 65229	178.7	W 70249	182.0	W 77100	178.4	W 88732	248.4	FRUITS PREPARES CONSERV
05891	NUTS ROASTD(INCL PEANUT)	W 47384	154.8	W 50627	154.7	W 49142	141.2	W 51832	202.8	FRUITS A COQUE GRILLES
06	SUGAR AND PREPS,HONEY		314.9		196.0		210.2		268.5	SUCRES ET PRODUITS
061	SUGAR AND HONEY	W 486084	171.5	W 20827	10.3	W 11069	15.4	W 186207	81.3	SUCRES ET MIEL
0612	REFINED SUGAR ETC	W 456971	162.5	W 4090	1.8	W 3955	2.8	W 169021	61.1	SUCRES RAFFINES
062	SUGAR CANDY NON–CHOCLATE	W 60143	143.5	W 74132	185.8	W 74074	194.9	W 109373	187.2	SUCRERIES
07	COFFEE,TEA,COCOA,SPICES		96.1		125.4		144.4		172.2	CAFE,THE,CACAO,EPICES
073	CHOCOLATE AND PRODUCTS	W 23133	48.6	W 37684	80.1	W 39860	87.6	W 43804	93.1	CHOCOLAT
09	MISC EDIBLE PRODUCTS		140.7		197.6		206.5		235.8	PREP ALIMENTAIRES DIVERSES
091	MARGARINE AND SHORTENING	W 110112	89.7	W 140921	140.4	W 131824	124.5	W 151819	129.9	MARGARINE ET GRAISSES
0914	MARGARINE,EDIBLE FAT NES	W 110112	89.7	W 140921	140.4	W 131803	124.5	W 151816	129.9	MARGARINES,SIMILI SAINDOUX
09141	MARGARINE	W 106874	87.0	W 140765	140.3	W 130598	123.0	W 146895	125.6	MARGARINE
098	EDIBLE PRODCTS,PREPS NES		51.1		57.2	W 56824	82.1	W 68063	106.0	PREP ALIMENTAIRES NDA
09806	YEASTS,BAKING POWDERS	W 39596	42.3	W 45367	44.1	W 49255	69.7	W 57644	89.8	LEVURES
1	BEVERAGES AND TOBACCO		471.2		467.4		738.2		753.7	BOISSONS ET TABACS
11	BEVERAGES		47.6		86.0		104.7		70.9	BOISSONS
12	TOBACCO AND MANUFACTURES		423.7		381.5		633.6		682.8	TABACS BRUTS FABRIQUES
121	TOBACCO UNMNFCTRD,REFUSE	W 103712	395.2	W 82590	244.6	W 162027	538.6	W 162516	564.6	TABACS BRUTS,DECHETS
1211	TOBACCO,NOT STRIPPED	W 86471	384.8	W 72967	240.1	W 151449	529.3	W 151255	554.5	TABACS NON ECOTES
122	TOBACCO,MANUFACTURED		28.5	W 61008	136.9	W 12746	95.0	W 17216	118.3	TABACS FABRIQUES
1222	CIGARETTES	W 2510	12.6	W 8525	37.5	W 10529	89.0	W 12270	100.4	CIGARETTES
1223	OTH MANUFACTURED TOBACCO	W 9294	15.9	W 52483	99.4	W 2121	4.8	W 4942	17.9	TABACS FUMER,CHIQUER,PRISER
2	CRUDE MATERLS,EXCL FUELS		604.9		774.2		680.8		689.9	MAT BRUTES NON COMESTIBLES
26	TEXTILE FIBRES AND WASTE		153.0		167.4		278.0		209.9	FIBRES TEXTILES
263	COTTON	W 79147	56.6	W 59861	47.9	W 146850	171.4	W 110112	100.7	COTON
2631	RAW COTTON,EXCL LINTERS	W 27149	31.4	W 2911	6.1	W 76035	124.1	W 37040	57.2	COTON EN MASSE
266	SYNTHETIC FIBRES TO SPIN	W 54336	78.5	W 52003	99.9	W 53047	83.0	W 47606	77.0	FIBRES SYNTHETIQUES
27	CRUDE FERTLZR,MINRLS NES		215.1		248.9		112.3		124.9	ENGRAIS MINERAUX BRUTS
278	OTHER CRUDE MINERALS	W 1846801	189.9	W 2442963	220.1	W 1694440	80.7	W 1856173	88.9	AUTRES MINERAUX BRUTS
2789	MINERALS CRUDE NES	W 850717	131.3	W 1020239	147.6	W 350517	18.0	W 361878	17.7	MINERAUX BRUTS NDA
27894	CRUDE NATURAL BORATES	W 622346	120.9	W 683584	133.8	W 1	0.1	W 9	0.1	BORATES NATURELS BRUTS
28	METALLIFEROUS ORES,SCRAP		92.7		193.7		154.3		200.9	MINERAIS METAL,DECHETS
287	BASE METAL ORES,CONC NES	W 740026	54.2	W 1261794	161.3	W 836434	119.7	W 990470	158.3	MINERAIS METAUX COMMUNS
2879	OTH NONFER ORE,CONCNTRTE	W 604541	34.3	W 1022291	94.7	W 541195	63.1	W 639373	64.2	MINERAIS D'AUTRES METAUX
28791	CHROMIUM ORE,CONCENTRATE	W 602100	33.6	W 1013303	93.3	W 527697	60.1	W 623914	61.0	MINERAIS DE CHROME
29	CRUDE ANIMAL,VEG MAT NES		73.9		99.5		77.4		81.7	MATIERES BRUTES ANIM,VEGET
3	MINERAL FUELS ETC		245.7		290.7		269.5		195.6	COMBUSTIBLES MINERAUX LUB
33	PETROLEUM AND PRODUCTS		233.9		279.8		243.8		171.9	PETROLE ET DERIVES
334	PETROLEUM PRODUCTS,REFIN	W 2310558	226.3	W 2537823	264.6	W 2121273	237.3	W 1449444	166.3	PRODUITS RAFFINES
3344	FUEL OILS,NES	W 2060290	177.0	W 2096508	187.2	W 1646920	156.1	W 1008049	85.8	FUEL OILS
4	ANIMAL,VEGETABLE OIL,FAT		182.1		324.6		231.1		271.5	HUILES,GRAISSES ANIM,VEG
42	FIXED VEGETABLE OIL,FAT		97.5		204.4		127.0		170.5	HUILES VEGETALES FIXES
423	FIXED VEG OILS,SOFT	W 60236	63.3	W 107024	170.6	W 44767	93.5	W 124343	147.6	HUILES VEGET DOUCES FIXES
4235	OLIVE OIL	W 14472	21.0	W 58203	120.7	W 23277	74.4	W 48122	87.2	HUILE D'OLIVE
431	*PROCESD ANML VEG OIL,ET	W 82987	82.5	W 102738	113.4	W 103438	96.0	W 113456	100.3	HUILES,GRAISSES PREPAREES
4312	HYDROGENATED OIL,FAT	W 78481	79.8	W 98120	109.7	W 91836	90.3	W 101974	95.4	HUILES HYDROGENEES
5	CHEMCLS,RELATED PROD NES		724.6		874.5		868.3		1039.7	PRODUITS CHIMIQUES
51	ORGANIC CHEMICALS		113.4		121.4		102.7		92.2	PROD CHIMIQ ORGANIQUES
52	INORGANIC CHEMICALS		145.8		150.9		25.1		71.9	PROD CHIM INORGANIQUES
523	OTHR INORG CHEMICALS ETC	W 442252	106.5	W 468838	115.3	W 70464	16.0	W 143338	34.4	AUT PRODUITS CHIMIQUES INORG
5232	OTH MTL CMPD OF INRG ACD	W 358147	85.3	W 367525	89.1	W 6113	2.2	W 43577	13.7	SELS METALLIQUES
52328	BORATES AND PERBORATES	W 202535	63.1	W 204934	64.8	W 3443	1.3	W 38635	11.6	BORATES ET PERBORATES
53	DYES,TANNING,COLOUR PROD		34.4		52.1		74.8		95.3	PROD TEINTURE,COLORANTS
541	*MEDICINAL,PHARM PRODUCT	K 6951046	78.1	K 5577256	63.3	K 4751668	97.0	K 6656354	113.6	PROD MEDICINAUX PHARMACEUT
5417	MEDICAMENTS	K 3431469	66.6	K 1935473	45.5	K 1489270	60.2	K 2727924	75.8	MEDICAMENTS
55	PERFUME,CLEANING ETC PRD		118.3		223.2		315.9		389.6	PROD POUR PARFUM,TOILETTE
554	SOAP,CLEANSING ETC PREPS	W 119833	101.7	W 212129	195.4	W 296736	271.0	W 376344	326.4	SAVONS,PRODUITS DETERSIFS
5541	SOAPS	W 78269	69.9	W 104934	109.5	W 140383	148.3	W 165705	175.1	SAVONS,PROD TENSIO–ACTIFS
5542	WASHING PREPARATIONS ETC	W 41073	30.8	W 105934	83.4	W 153722	117.0	W 205528	140.9	PROD ORG TENSIO–ACT NDA
58	PLASTIC MATERIALS ETC		163.8		194.9		182.9		210.7	MAT PLAST ARTIFICIELLES
583	POLYMERIZATION ETC PRODS	W 141334	118.9	W 75792	128.8	W 73591	118.9	W 72085	135.7	PROD POLYMERISATION
6	BASIC MANUFACTURES		5707.4		6262.9		6573.9		7836.9	ART MANUFACTURES
62	RUBBER MANUFACTURES NES		231.1		276.9		252.0		278.0	CAOUTCHOUC MANUFACTURE
625	RUBBER TYRES, TUBES ETC	W 73506	200.9	W 82041	227.5	W 71135	203.8	W 81955	224.9	PNEUS CAOUTCHOUC VULCANISE

5. Special Exports F.O.B. by Commodities according to the S.I.T.C. (Rev. 2) in million U.S. Dollars
Exportations Spéciales F.O.B. par Produits d'après la C.T.C.I. (Rév. 2) en millions de Dollars E.U.

SITC CTCI	COMMODITY	1994 QUANTITY QUANTITE	1994 VALUE VALEUR	1995 QUANTITY QUANTITE	1995 VALUE VALEUR	1996 QUANTITY QUANTITE	1996 VALUE VALEUR	1997 QUANTITY QUANTITE	1997 VALUE VALEUR	PRODUIT
6251	TYRES NEW FOR MOTOR CARS	W 30367	83.6	W 38147	109.2	W 34705	102.3	W 40295	115.8	PNEUS POUR VOITURES
6252	TYRES,NEW,BUS OR LORRY	W 25538	71.8	W 24554	68.6	W 19335	55.6	W 24910	67.1	PNEUS POUR AUTOBUS,CAMIONS
64	PAPER,PAPERBOARD AND MFR		109.1		128.3		129.5		158.3	PAPIERS,CARTONS & OUVRAGES
641	PAPER AND PAPERBOARD		81.9		81.4	W 55525	65.2	W 67895	74.0	PAPIERS ET CARTONS
642	PAPER,ETC,PRECUT,ARTS OF	W 19828	27.3	W 23323	46.9	W 48493	64.3	W 60724	84.4	PAP,CARTONS DECOUPES
65	TEXTILE YARN,FABRICS,ETC		2194.7		2526.7		2722.7		3354.6	FILS,TISSUS,ARTICLES TEXTILE
651	TEXTILE YARN	W 218751	597.7	W 154317	505.8	W 169380	512.5	W 220049	652.1	FILS TEXTILES
6513	COTTON YARN	W 86807	250.5	W 39733	137.9	W 44534	139.3	W 70026	224.4	FILS DE COTON
6514	SYN FIB YRN,BULK,MONOFIL	W 75763	155.7	W 65611	174.1	W 74894	174.8	W 86579	196.3	FILS CONT 85% FIB TEXT SYNTH
65142	— NONTXT ETC CONT PAMID	W 52985	100.1	W 53432	128.1	W 57008	118.3	W 61035	116.8	FILS NON TEX FI CON POLYAMID
6516	DISCON SYN FIB BLEND YRN	W 35547	134.0	W 32309	140.1	W 34743	149.0	W 42046	173.7	FILS FIBR TEX SYNT DIS MOINS
65168	OTH DISC SYN BLEND YARN	W 26904	97.1	W 24192	97.4	W 28207	112.2	W 34832	135.6	FILS TEXT SYNT MELANGE AUT F
652	COTTON FABRICS,WOVEN	W 68599	341.1	W 56328	372.9	W 59693	392.5	W 69921	434.6	TISSUS DE COTON
6521	GREY WOVEN COTTON FABRIC	W 35243	137.4	W 20211	105.1	W 17270	84.7	W 19104	90.8	TISSUS COT ECRUS NON MERCER
65214	GREY WOVEN COTTON NES	W 31372	116.6	W 17581	89.0	W 15281	71.3	W 16616	76.0	AUT TISSUS 85% COTON ECRUS
6522	WOVEN COTTON BLEACHD,ETC	W 33356	203.7	W 36117	267.8	W 42423	307.8	W 50816	343.9	TISSUS COTON BLANCHIS ETC
65224	BLCHED COTTON FABRIC NES	W 30434	173.0	W 32385	234.4	W 38579	270.7	W 42858	276.1	AUT TIS PLUS 85% COT BLANCHI
653	WOVN MAN–MADE FIB FABRIC	W 34810	326.6	W 40877	547.5	W 41533	478.4	W 61316	565.5	TISSUS FIBRES SYNTH,ARTIF
6531	CONT SYNT WEAVES NONPILE	W 7464	64.1	W 7549	150.5	W 6267	71.6	W 13363	84.6	TISSUS FIBRES SYNTH CONTINUE
65315	CONT SYN TXTL FABRIC NES	W 7205	62.0	W 6896	144.6	W 5897	68.5	W 12352	76.7	TIS PLUS 85% TEXT SYNT CONT
6534	DISC SYN BLEND FABRC NES	W 7635	75.5	W 8290	101.5	W 9563	130.6	W 19745	194.5	TISSUS FIBRES SYNTH DISCONT
65343	DISC SYN–CONT MAN–MD FAB	W 1438	10.5	W 1204	15.8	W 3316	49.9	W 11511	94.4	TISSUS FIB SYNT MEL TEXT SY
65349	OTH DISC SYN BLEND FABRC	W 5299	56.0	W 6369	77.1	W 5519	71.5	W 7307	89.2	TISSUS FIB SYNT MEL MAT AUT
6536	DISC REGN TXTL FABRC NES	W 8983	85.9	W 9214	107.1	W 10533	117.0	W 9027	97.3	TISSUS 85% TEXT ART DISC
6538	DISC REG BLEND FABRC NES	W 3489	37.1	W 7940	99.4	W 7536	86.0	W 8788	97.0	TIS MOINS 85% TEXT ART DISC
65383	DISC REG–CONT MAN–MD FAB	W 2859	30.8	W 6975	90.5	W 5983	75.5	W 6190	79.4	TISSUS TEX ART CONT MEL SYNT
654	OTH WOVEN TEXTILE FABRIC	W 2156	42.6	W 3019	68.0	W 8215	82.4	W 4453	83.8	TISSUS AUT COTON SYNT,ARTIF
655	KNITTED,ETC FABRICS	W 25839	140.6	W 13127	84.4	W 19399	123.5	W 31036	183.3	ETOF BONNETERIE PIECES ETC
6552	OTHER KNIT ETC FAB NONEL	W 25839	140.6	W 13127	84.4	W 19399	123.5	W 31036	183.3	ETOF BON NON ELAS NON SYNT
656	LACE,RIBBONS,TULLE,ETC	W 3349	43.4	W 4146	58.1	W 5864	73.2	W 8541	94.3	TULLES,BRODERIE
657	SPECIAL TXTL FABRC,PRODS		77.1		115.6	W 23625	150.2	W 40384	207.0	TISSUS SPECIAUX
6573	COATED ETC TEXTILES NES	W 13801	68.2	W 18896	103.2	W 18510	97.9	W 26069	131.1	TISSUS,ART MATIERE TEXT NDA
65733	RUBBERIZED TEXT NOT KNIT	W 12889	65.2	W 17450	96.8	W 15282	84.4	W 20151	100.3	TISSUS CAOUTCHOUTES
658	TEXTILE ARTICLES NES	W 65834	372.5	W 78681	523.3	W 98186	603.1	W 140601	783.9	ART FACONNES MAT TEXTILES
6581	BAGS,SACKS OF TEXTILES	W 27037	67.6	W 33960	106.0	W 41843	124.8	W 60168	148.3	SACS EMBALLAGE TEXTILES
6584	LINENS ETC	W 24862	205.0	W 28478	275.5	W 34100	310.9	W 51090	431.7	LINGE DE MAISON
65841	BED LINEN OF COTTON	W 7938	64.2	W 8023	80.4	W 10138	92.2	W 15813	128.5	LINGE DE LIT DE COTON
65845	OTHER LINEN OF COTTON	W 8323	67.5	W 10913	103.4	W 13734	120.6	W 20926	168.1	LINGE DE TOILETTE COTON
65849	OTH FURN ART OF OTH FIBR	W 6870	54.8	W 7290	62.3	W 6897	63.0	W 10059	93.1	AUT ART AMEUBLEMENT AUT FIBR
6589	OTH TEXTILE ARTICLES NES	W 8488	81.8	W 10488	122.3	W 14133	138.1	W 19987	172.2	AUT ART EN TEXTILES NDA
65898	KNITTED ETC ARTICLES NES	W 8302	81.0	W 10330	120.2	W 13957	136.7	W 19844	170.6	ART BONNET NON ELASTIQUE
659	FLOOR COVERINGS,ETC	W 27819	253.4	W 30169	251.4	W 41524	307.4	W 62209	350.4	COUVRE–PARQUETS,TAPIS ETC
6592	CARPETS ETC KNOTTED	W 3391	126.8	W 2769	108.7	W 3255	139.0	W 3402	150.8	TAPIS POINTS NOUES,ENROULES
65921	— OF WOOL OR FINE HAIR	W 3235	93.9	W 2654	89.7	W 2819	104.7	W 2901	110.2	TAP NOUES,ENROULES LAINE
6595	MAN–MADE TXTL CARPTS NES	W 18754	85.9	W 23373	111.0	W 33892	135.1	W 53753	164.2	TAPIS MAT TEXT SYNT ARTIF
65952	— WOVEN	W 16017	77.3	W 21845	106.1	W 27080	118.9	W 24575	105.9	TAPIS MAT TEXT SYNT TISSES
66	NONMETAL MINERAL MFS NES		529.7		632.5		713.0		850.3	ART MIN NON METALLIQUES
661	LIME,CEMENT,BLDG PRODS	W 4711980	202.6	W 4339744	211.6	W 3414517	220.6	W 4334218	279.0	CHAUX,CIMENTS MAT CONSTR
6612	CEMENT	W 4569740	145.2	W 4173593	141.2	W 3216286	135.2	W 4081141	170.9	CIMENTS HYDRAULIQUES
6613	BUILDING STONE ETC WORKD	W 105330	50.8	W 130546	63.7	W 170322	79.2	W 206404	94.6	PIERRES A BATIR
66132	BUILDING STONE WORKED	W 105190	50.8	W 129585	63.6	W 169927	79.2	W 206183	94.4	OUVR EN PIERRES DE TAILLE
662	CLAY,REFRACTORY BLDG PRD	W 267989	100.0	W 409974	142.5	W 525501	175.6	W 562101	184.2	MAT CONST REFRACTAIRES
6624	BRICKS ETC NONREFRACTORY	W 248360	90.7	W 350167	129.6	W 473820	160.8	W 523228	168.4	BRIQUES ETC CERAM NON REFR
66245	GLAZED CERAMIC SETTS ETC	W 238656	88.4	W 335055	126.6	W 437797	153.2	W 484212	159.9	AUT CARREAUX CERAMIQUE
664	GLASS	W 178342	88.8	W 168385	100.8	W 178940	103.6	W 227449	114.5	VERRE
665	GLASSWARE	W 108671	118.0	W 103524	143.5	W 121405	170.6	W 214686	220.7	OUVRAGES EN VERRE
6652	HOUSEHLD,HOTEL ETC GLASS	W 62278	99.3	W 76190	129.2	W 94698	153.9	W 155915	193.7	OBJETS VERRE TABLE,CUISINE
67	IRON AND STEEL		2160.2		1997.6		1954.2		2263.6	FER ET ACIER
671	PIG IRON ETC	W 195519	60.7	W 70750	73.6	W 184941	77.5	W 244242	81.2	FONTE,SPIEGEL,POUDRES
6716	FERRO–ALLOYS	W 102729	48.7	W 69924	73.2	W 93427	61.8	W 94828	59.4	FERRO–ALLIAGES
67169	OTHER FERRO–ALLOYS	W 102692	48.7	W 68507	72.2	W 92953	61.3	W 94546	59.1	AUTRES FERRO–ALLIAGES
672	IRON,STEEL PRIMARY FORMS	W 2659809	599.8	W 1887884	483.5	W 1362837	344.4	W 1796853	452.4	LINGOTS FER,ACIER
6725	IRN,STL BLOOMS,SLABS,ETC	W 2128551	452.2	W 1747468	430.8	W 1045218	254.5	W 1381821	328.2	BLOOMS,BILLETTES FER ACIER
67251	IRN,SMPLE STL BLOOMS,ETC	W 2100357	437.6	W 1725406	417.0	W 1023483	241.1	W 1321424	305.2	BLOOMS ETC NON ACIER FIN
6727	IRN,STL COIL FR REROLLNG	W 515218	145.9	W 140291	52.6	W 317617	89.9	W 414468	124.0	EBAUCHES POUR TOLES FER
67271	IRON,SIMPLE STEEL COILS	W 515159	145.8	W 140149	52.3	W 317592	89.9	W 414464	124.0	EBAUCHES NON EN ACIER
673	IRON,STEEL SHAPES ETC	W 4961988	1284.6	W 3848104	1094.7	W 4320701	1198.4	W 4569114	1236.0	BARRES,PROFIL FER,ACIER
6731	IRON,STEEL WIRE ROD	W 788545	201.8	W 637613	182.1	W 822883	230.4	W 857928	230.0	FIL MACHINE FER,ACIER
67311	IRON,SIMPLE STL WIRE ROD	W 788528	201.8	W 636701	181.8	W 819643	229.3	W 857718	229.8	FIL MACH AUT ACIER FIN
6732	IRON,STEEL BARS ETC	W 4009081	1036.2	W 2909950	811.4	W 3332539	913.6	W 3495279	938.2	BARRES FER,ACIER
67326	IRN,OTH STL BARS HOTROLD	W 3959657	1015.8	W 2820918	770.8	W 3255837	882.1	W 3416719	905.0	BARRES PLEINES FER,ACIER
6733	IRON,STEEL PROFILES ETC	W 164361	46.7	W 300541	101.2	W 165279	54.5	W 215907	67.8	PROFILES,PALPLAN FER,ACIER
67331	SMALL U,I,H SECTIONS ETC	W 154441	43.0	W 253674	84.7	W 150428	47.8	W 202339	62.0	PROFILES MOINS 80MM
674	IRN,STL UNIV,PLATE,SHEET	W 105840	42.1	W 127554	57.9	W 221446	95.3	W 434615	186.6	LARGES PLATS,TOLES
6746	IRN,STL THIN PLATE,ROLLD	W 58181	21.2	W 32893	16.5	W 159033	62.6	W 366346	148.9	TOLES LAM MOINS 3MM
67461	— OF IRON OR SIMPLE STL	W 56171	20.4	W 32723	16.0	W 158879	62.4	W 365387	147.8	TOL NON AC FIN MOINS 3 MM
678	IRON,STL TUBES,PIPES,ETC	W 315153	153.7	W 448009	245.8	W 351262	190.3	W 515571	257.7	TUBES,TUYAUX EN FONTE,FER
6783	IRON,STL TUBES,PIPES NES	W 310239	139.9	W 439371	231.0	W 341324	171.5	W 502511	234.3	AUT TUBES,TUYAUX FER,ACIER
68	NON–FERROUS METALS		167.5		271.4		297.9		337.6	METAUX NON FERREUX
682	COPPER EXC CEMENT COPPER	W 35971	88.1	W 48118	149.0	W 62836	165.8	W 67865	174.2	CUIVRE
6822	COPPER,ALLOYS WORKED	W 30865	77.5	W 44301	139.9	W 52716	142.8	W 60659	159.8	CUIVRE,ALLIAGES OUVRES
68221	COPPER BARS,WIRE,ETC	W 30325	76.0	W 44149	139.1	W 51960	140.1	W 59907	157.3	BARRES,PROFILES ET FILS
684	ALUMINIUM	W 34640	77.4	W 41003	118.5	W 50753	126.9	W 51451	141.5	ALUMINIUM
6842	ALUMINIUM,ALLOYS WORKED	W 27453	67.4	W 29541	97.4	W 35338	103.3	W 50019	139.1	ALUMINIUM,ALLIAGES OUVRE
69	METAL MANUFACTURES NES		237.3		333.7		402.3		470.9	ART MANUFACT EN METAL NDA
691	STRUCTURES AND PARTS NES	W 25973	43.2	W 46836	69.5	W 67345	101.0	W 59056	103.7	CONSTRUCT FER,ACIER,ALU
6911	STRUCTURES,PARTS IRN,STL	W 22612	29.4	W 43598	48.4	W 61949	71.0	W 51865	69.0	CONSTRUCT FER,ACIER,FONTE
697	BASE MTL HOUSEHOLD EQUIP	W 24721	73.7	W 25857	86.4	W 32252	95.2	W 43091	117.6	ART MENAGE MET COMMUNS
699	BASE METAL MFRS NES	W 18008	42.0	W 29509	69.0	W 34126	82.0	W 44803	96.1	ART MANUFACTURES MET NDA
7	MACHINES,TRANSPORT EQUIP		1696.4		2374.0		2890.2		3344.1	MACHINES MATERIEL TRANSPORT
71	POWER GENERATING EQUIPMT		131.3		171.2		198.1		245.6	MACHINES GENERATRICES
713	INTRNL COMBUS PSTN ENGIN	W 5243	84.0	W 7111	113.1	W 11686	117.1	W 13433	135.1	MOTEURS EXPL COMB INT, PIECE
7139	PISTON ENGINE PARTS NES	W 4898	81.9	W 6690	110.1	W 10673	108.8	W 11576	122.5	PIECES POUR 713.2,3,8
72	MACHS FOR SPCL INDUSTRYS		117.5		122.4		157.8		223.4	MAC SPECIALES POUR INDUST
74	GENRL INDUSTRL MACHY NES		195.9		246.7		299.1		333.6	MACH APP INDUSTRIE
741	HEATING,COOLING EQUIPMNT	W 7999	57.6	W 11952	78.0	W 10915	73.7	W 14536	84.2	MACH CHAUFFAGE,PIECES
744	MECHANICAL HANDLING EQU	W 15055	29.4	W 24797	46.2	W 32702	70.3	W 44715	75.2	EQUIP MANUTENTION PIECES
749	NONELEC MACH PTS,ACC NES	W 5195	46.0	W 6884	55.1	W 11086	74.2	W 12430	81.7	PIECES MACH NON ELEC NDA
76	TELECOMM,SOUND EQUIPMENT		199.4		243.1		300.7		458.5	EQUIPMENT DE TELECOM
761	TELEVISION RECEIVERS	W 16761	153.0	W 19850	201.6	W 21018	216.6	W 45072	388.5	RECEPTEURS DE TELEVISION
7611	COLOUR TV RECEIVERS	W 16761	153.0	W 19844	201.6	W 21018	216.6	W 45067	388.4	RECEPTEURS COULEUR

5. Special Exports F.O.B. by Commodities according to the S.I.T.C. (Rev. 2) in million U.S. Dollars
Exportations Spéciales F.O.B. par Produits d'après la C.T.C.I. (Rév. 2) en millions de Dollars E.U.

SITC CTCI	COMMODITY	1994		1995		1996		1997		PRODUIT
		QUANTITY QUANTITE	VALUE VALEUR	QUANTITY QUANTITE	VALUE VALEUR	QUANTITY QUANTITE	VALUE VALEUR	QUANTITY QUANTITE	VALUE VALEUR	
764	TELECOM EQPT,PTS,ACC NES	W 1700	43.0	W 1498	40.6	W 2618	83.3	W 2855	68.9	EQUIP TELECOM,PIECES
77	ELECTRIC MACHNRY NES ETC		527.0		748.1		965.7		995.3	MACH APP ELECT NDA
771	ELECTRIC POWER MACHY NES	W 12545	70.8	W 15649	82.0	W 24814	127.8	W 29290	139.7	MACH PROD,TRANS ELECTR
7711	TRANSFORMERS,ELECTRICAL	W 11969	65.1	W 14939	73.5	W 23785	117.2	W 28429	131.5	TRANSFO ELECTRIQUES
77111	LIQUID DIELEC TRANSFRMRS	W 9993	48.4	W 12252	49.0	W 18696	78.7	W 22837	94.7	TRANSFO DIELEC LIQUIDE
772	SWITCHGEAR ETC,PARTS NES	W 3421	44.2	W 4241	57.7	W 5622	86.7	W 5452	78.0	APP COUPURE,SECT ETC
7721	SWITCHGEAR ETC	W 3356	32.6	W 4176	49.9	W 5532	76.6	W 5010	70.0	APP COUPURE,SECTIONMNT
773	ELECTR DISTRIBUTNG EQUIP	W 39070	218.5	W 51269	308.3	W 65182	402.5	W 86410	356.0	EQUIPMT DISTRIBUTION ELECT
7731	INSULATED WIRE,CABLE ETC	W 38784	216.4	W 50352	305.3	W 64723	399.6	W 85932	352.3	FILS,CABLES ISOLES ELECT
775	HOUSEHOLD TYPE EQUIP NES	W 49482	152.6	W 74670	237.4	W 80778	259.9	W 100906	315.6	MACH,APP USAGE DOMESTQUE
7752	DOM REFRIGERATRS,FREEZRS	W 29975	87.3	W 46001	132.1	W 37984	115.5	W 39858	125.2	REFRIG,CONGEL MENAGER
77521	DOMESTIC REFRIGERATORS	W 29416	85.4	W 43897	125.4	W 34295	103.4	W 36161	112.7	REFRIGERATEURS
7758	ELECTRO-THERMIC APPL NES	W 17091	55.3	W 23546	84.9	W 36943	118.7	W 47559	135.1	APP ELECTROTHERMIQ NDA
77586	ELECTROTHERM DOM APP NES	W 13263	41.2	W 17288	63.3	W 22935	82.3	W 27663	86.9	APP ELECTRO THERMIQUES
778	ELECTRICAL MACHINERY NES	W 12376	37.1	W 19110	59.8	W 24591	81.2	W 27846	97.1	AUTRES MACH ELECT NDA
78	ROAD VEHICLES		413.8		725.9		843.8		730.4	VEHICULES ROUTIERS
781	PASS MOTOR VEH EXC BUSES	W 10923	70.9	W 30990	251.2	W 32123	269.6	W 18020	118.4	AUTO TRANSPORT PERSONNES
783	ROAD MOTOR VEHICLES NES	W 20100	119.1	W 11203	142.7	W 757765	244.3	W 20190	191.6	VEHICULES ROUTIERS NDA
7831	BUSES	W 20082	119.0	W 11162	142.4	W 757719	244.2	W 20141	191.4	VOITURES TRANSPORT COMMUN
784	MOTOR VEH PRTS,ACCES NES	W 41097	117.1	W 60774	181.9	W 61104	193.7	W 81529	276.7	PIECES 722,781,782,783
7849	OTHER MOTOR VEHCL PARTS	W 40025	114.4	W 59728	177.4	W 59150	186.2	W 78247	264.4	PIECES 722,781,782,783
786	TRAILERS,NONMOTR VEH,NES	W 83072	84.4	W 82796	91.1	W 72358	85.9	W 71475	77.1	REMORQUES,CADRES,CONTAIN
7861	TRAILERS,TRANSP CONTAINR	W 82335	82.4	W 82284	89.1	W 71395	83.2	W 69048	68.2	REMORQUES TOUS VEHICULES
78613	CONTAINERS INC ROAD-RAIL	W 81787	81.5	W 81562	87.6	W 70444	80.5	W 68036	65.1	CADRES ET CONTAINERS
79	OTHR TRANSPORT EQUIPMENT		79.0		74.7		68.3		280.6	AUTRE MATERIEL TRANSPORT
792	AIRCRAFT ETC		22.4		3.9	W 112	10.7	W 640	147.1	APP NAVIGATION AERIENNE
793	SHIPS AND BOATS ETC		53.8		67.4		57.3	W 11463	132.3	NAVIRES BATEAUX,ETC
7932	SHIPS AND BOATS NES		53.7		58.3		48.8	W 2895	125.0	NAVIRES ET BATEAUX
79323	OTHER CARGO VESSELS		51.0		47.2		39.1	W 2117	99.8	AUT BATEAUX TRANS MARCH
8	MISC MANUFACTURED GOODS		5165.6		6801.2		6963.0		7770.8	ART MANUFACTURES DIVERS
812	*PLUMBG,HEATNG,LGHTNG EQ	W 46457	84.7	W 59241	105.6	W 73238	122.2	W 87945	128.4	APPAR SANITAIRES CHAUFFAGE
821	*FURNITURE,PARTS THEREOF	W 20360	55.7	W 25127	75.6	W 26146	80.2	W 35879	93.7	MEUBLES ET PIECES
84	CLOTHING AND ACCESSORIES		4581.8		6118.8		6070.9		6699.0	VETEMENTS
842	MENS OUTERWEAR NOT KNIT	W 21902	366.8	W 25527	525.5	W 24879	500.1	W 31810	588.2	VET DESSUS POUR HOMMES
8423	— TROUSERS,BREECHES ETC	W 12383	162.7	W 16301	261.4	W 16823	281.6	W 22642	366.8	PANTALONS HOMMES MAT TEX
8429	— OTHER OUTER GARMENTS	W 5274	103.8	W 5362	142.6	W 3595	85.8	W 3584	75.9	AUT VET DES HOM MAT TEX
843	WOMENS OUTERWEAR NONKNIT	W 42891	846.6	W 52073	1220.8	W 60169	1255.4	W 64588	1313.7	VET DESSUS FEMMES MAT TEX
8431	— COATS AND JACKETS	W 3947	103.2	W 5243	155.0	W 6236	170.0	W 7404	183.9	MANT,VEST FEM MAT TEXTIL
8433	— DRESSES	W 1626	39.1	W 3894	122.8	W 3778	113.8	W 3374	88.8	ROBES EN MAT-TEXTILES
8434	— SKIRTS	W 2271	51.9	W 3468	96.7	W 3475	82.6	W 3818	90.6	JUPES EN MAT TEXTILES
8435	— BLOUSES	W 6267	172.2	W 6978	229.6	W 7433	217.4	W 9208	242.6	BLOUSES FEM MAT TEXTILES
8439	— OTHER OUTER GARMENTS	W 28115	467.6	W 31696	591.2	W 38526	654.7	W 40212	693.1	AUT VET DES FEM MAT TEXT
844	UNDER GARMENTS NOT KNIT	W 13947	260.1	W 16974	382.8	W 14747	323.5	W 16874	338.8	VETEMENT DESSOUS MAT TEX
8441	— MENS SHIRTS	W 9869	207.5	W 12311	315.3	W 10216	263.0	W 10499	261.1	CHEMISES HOMMES MAT TEXT
84411	—— OF COTTON	W 8125	172.4	W 10563	273.8	W 8691	232.6	W 7935	211.3	CHEMISES HOMMES DE COTON
845	OUTERWEAR KNIT NONELASTC	W 82240	1520.5	W 84185	1991.0	W 98472	2014.3	W 113203	2097.8	VET DESSOUS,ACCES BONNET
8451	— JERSEYS,PULLOVERS ETC	W 36957	705.4	W 35476	860.3	W 50467	1036.7	W 56016	1021.6	CHANDAILS,PULL-OVERS ETC
8452	— WOMENS DRESSES ETC	W 6258	125.6	W 8001	216.8	W 5585	136.6	W 5677	127.4	ROBES,JUPES BONNETERIE
8459	— OTHER,CLTHG ACCESRYS	W 39026	689.6	W 40708	914.0	W 42420	841.0	W 51510	948.8	AUT VET DESSUS DE BONNE
846	UNDER GARMENTS KNITTED	W 53488	946.7	W 61965	1308.9	W 70231	1384.5	W 88518	1680.6	SOUS VETS DE BONNETERIE
8462	— OF COTTON NON ELASTIC	W 45424	805.1	W 51042	1086.2	W 59044	1170.0	W 76139	1457.3	SOUS-VET BONNET COTON
84629	—— OTHER	W 45424	805.1	W 51042	1086.2	W 59044	1170.0	W 76139	1457.3	AUT SOUS-VET BONNET COTON
8463	— OF SYNTH FBR NONELAST	W 7722	131.5	W 10281	199.6	W 10554	195.1	W 11549	197.1	SOUS-VET BONNET FIB SYNT
84632	—— MENS SHIRTS	W 5444	104.5	W 7833	164.8	W 7436	150.8	W 7952	149.9	CHEMISES DE BON FIB SYNMT
847	TEXTILE CLTHNG ACCES NES	W 14201	167.5	W 15794	218.4	W 17283	237.2	W 19436	264.2	ACCES VET MAT TEXT NDA
8472	CLTHNG ACCESRYS ETC KNIT	W 10439	119.8	W 12286	163.6	W 13681	182.1	W 15267	201.6	ACCES VET BONNE NDA
84722	KNIT SOCKS,ETC NONELASTC	W 10405	119.5	W 12227	162.2	W 13632	180.8	W 15153	199.5	CHAUSSETTES BON. NON ELAS
848	HEADGEAR,NONTXTL CLOTHNG		474.0		471.7	W 5478	356.1	W 11854	416.0	VET ACCES MAT AUT QUE TEX
8481	LEATHER CLOTHES,ACCESSOR	W 6758	410.4	W 5862	406.6	W 4477	308.7	W 9624	283.9	VET ACCES MAT CUIR ARTIF
8483	FUR ETC,CLOTHES,PRODUCTS	W 794	61.2	W 630	60.3	W 361	41.4	W 1040	125.4	VETEMENTS DE FOURRURE
84831	ARTICLES OF FURSKIN,NES	W 793	61.2	W 625	60.0	W 360	41.4	W 1034	124.8	PELLETERIES OUVREES NDA
851	*FOOTWEAR	W 13283	158.8	W 12331	112.6	W 16197	148.8	W 29525	198.6	CHAUSSURES
85102	FOOTWEAR LEATHER	W 6780	121.4	W 5311	70.6	W 7147	91.1	W 12863	135.5	CHAUS SEMELLES EN CUIR
89	MISC MANUFCTRD GOODS NES		233.2		328.5		463.3		560.4	ART MANUFACTURES DIVERS
893	ARTICLES OF PLASTIC NES		73.4		123.6		159.7		218.7	OUVRAGES EN MAT DIVIS 58
8931	PLSTC PACKG CONTNRS,LIDS	W 16704	35.1	W 31184	68.3	W 44066	90.9	W 59385	115.3	ART TRANSP EMBALLAGE ETC
8939	MISC PLASTIC ARTICLES	W 14907	35.4	W 14703	50.4	W 20764	62.3	W 46726	96.2	ART DIVERS EN MAT DIV 58
89399	OTHR PLASTC ARTICLES NES	W 13141	33.1	W 13838	48.6	W 19831	60.1	W 45010	92.7	AUT OUV MAT DIV 58
897	GOLD,SILVER WARE,JEWELRY		49.3		65.8		116.2		168.2	BIJOUTERIE,ORFEVRERIE
8973	PREC JEWLRY,GLD-SILVWARE		48.0		64.5		114.8		167.4	BIJOUX OR,ARGENT ORFEVRE
89731	PRECIOUS METAL JEWELLERY		46.0		62.1		111.6		163.4	ART BIJOUTERIE,JOAILLER
898	MUSICAL INSTRUMENTS,PTS		67.4		83.9	W 19633	115.0	W 17430	91.3	INSTRUMENTS DE MUSIQUE
8983	SOUND RECRDNG TAPE,DISCS	W 9767	66.7	W 17067	83.1	W 19532	114.1	W 17285	89.9	SUPPORTS SON POUR 763
89831	PREPD SND RECORDNG MEDIA	W 8919	41.2	W 16241	73.5	W 18199	91.3	W 16532	81.0	SUPPORTS PREPARES
9	GOODS NOT CLASSD BY KIND		10.3		14.8		280.8		265.6	ART TRANSACT NON CLASSES
931	*SPECIAL TRANSACTIONS	W 5	0.1		0.1		259.0		239.6	TRANS.SPECIALES

1. HISTORICAL SERIES, 1992–1996 GENERAL TRADE, IMPORTS C.I.F., EXPORTS F.O.B.
SERIES HISTORIQUES, 1992–1996 COMMERCE GENERAL, IMPORTATIONS C.A.F., EXPORTATIONS F.O.B

YEAR ANNEE	VALUE IN MILLION U.S. DOLLARS VALEUR EN MILLION U.S. DOLLARS MERCHANDISE – MARCHANDISE		GOLD – OR		CONVERSION FACTORS FACTEURS DE CONVERSION CENTS E.U. PAR		INDEX NUMBERS – INDICES QUANTUM		UNIT VALUE VALEUR UNITAIRE	
	IMPORTS	EXPORTS	IMPORTS	EXPORTS	IMPORTS	EXPORTS	IMPORTS	EXPORTS	IMPORTS	EXPORTS
1992	30.00	908.00								
1993	501.20	1049.00								
1994	894.00	2010.00								
1995	777.00	1939.00								
1996	1313.50	1692.60								

2. IMPORTS BY BROAD ECONOMIC CATEGORY AND EXPORTS BY INDUSTRIAL ORIGIN. (PERCENTAGE OF TOTAL VALUE)
IMPORTATIONS PAR CATEGORIES ECONOMIQUES ET EXPORTATIONS PAR BRANCHE D'ACTIVITE. (EN POURCENTAGE DE LA VALEUR TOTALE)

IMPORTS – IMPORTATIONS

	1990	1991	1992	1993	1994	1995	1996
TOTAL IMPORTS–IMPORTATIONS TOTALES							
1 FOOD BEV–ALIMENTATION BOISSONS							
11 PRIMARY–PRODUITS DE BASE							
111 FOR INDUSTRY–POUR L'INDUSTRIE							
112 FOR HOUSEHOLDS–POUR LES MENAGES							
12 PROCESSED–PRODUITS ELABORES							
121 FOR INDUSTRY–POUR L'INDUSTRIE							
122 FOR HOUSEHOLDS–POUR LES MENAGES							
2 IND SUPPLIES–APPROV INDUSTRIELS							
21 PRIMARY–PRODUITS DE BASE							
22 PROCESSED–PRODUITS ELABORES							
3 FUELS–COMBUSTIBLES							
31 PRIMARY–PRODUITS DE BASE							
32 PROCESSED–PRODUITS ELABORES							
321 MOTOR SPIRIT–ESSENCE							
322 OTHER–AUTRES							
4 MACHINERY–EQUIPEMENT							
41 CAPITAL EQUIPMENT–MACHINES							
42 PARTS–PIECES ACCESSOIRES							
5 TRANSPORT–TRANSPORT							
51 PASSENGER CARS–AUTOMOBILES							
52 OTHER–AUTRES							
521 INDUSTRIAL–INDUSTRIELS							
522 NON INDUSTRIAL–NON INDUSTRIEL							
53 PARTS–PIECES ACCESSOIRES							
6 CONSUM GOODS–BIENS CONSOMMATION							
61 DURABLE–DURABLES							
62 SEMI DURABLE–SEMI DURABLES							
63 NON DURABLE–NON DURABLES							
7 GOODS NES–BIENS NDA							

EXPORTS – EXPORTATIONS

	1990	1991	1992	1993	1994	1995	1996
TOTAL EXPORTS–EXPORTATIONS TOTALES							
1 AGRICULTURE							
2 MINING QUARRY–INDUS EXTRACTIVES							
3 MANUFACTURING–IND MANUFACTUR							
31 FOOD BEV TOBACCO–ALIM BOISS TAB							
32 TEXTILES–INDUSTRIES TEXTILES							
33 WOOD & PRODUCTS–BOIS & PRODUITS							
34 PAPER & PRODUCTS–PAPIER & PRODT							
35 CHEMICALS–INDUSTRIES CHIMIQUES							
36 NON METAL MIN–MIN NON METAL							
37 BASIC METAL–IND METAL BASE							
38 METAL MANUF–MANUF METAL							
39 OTH MANUF IND–AUTRES MANUF							

3. TRADE BY PRINCIPAL COUNTRIES OF PURCHASE AND SALE (VALUE IN MILLION U.S. DOLLARS)
ECHANGES SELON LES PRINCIPAUX PAYS D'ACHAT ET DE VENTE (VALEUR EN MILLIONS DE DOLLARS EU)

COUNTRIES–PAYS	GENERAL IMPORTS C.I.F. IMPORTATIONS GENERALES C.A.F 1992	1993	1994	1995	1996
World			1467.8	1364.0	1313.5
Africa				0.4	0.2
Americas			56.6	53.5	395.2
– Northern America			56.6	53.5	395.2
– LAIA					
– CACM					
– Caribbean					
– Rest of America					
Asia excl fmr USSR			373.1	356.9	307.3
– Middle East			305.4	316.4	236.3
Asia former USSR			258.1	224.0	102.9
Europe excl fmr USSR			299.0	174.0	183.3
– European Union			206.3	150.1	143.3
– Eastern Europe			47.6	11.9	21.1
– Rest of Europe			45.1	12.0	18.9
Europe former USSR			453.5	529.9	306.3
Oceania					
Other					
Ukraine			256.9	416.4	127.5
USA/Etats–Unis d'Amer			56.6	53.5	395.2
Turkey/Turquie			181.8	160.4	120.3
Russian Federation			154.4	95.8	154.6
Azerbaijan/Azerbaïdjan			72.1	73.2	34.9
Cyprus/Chypre			17.1	102.1	59.3
Germany/Allemagne			61.3	52.1	51.3
Iran (Islamic Rep of)			75.1	36.4	45.2
Armenia/Arménie			46.6	62.5	23.1
Kazakhstan			42.5	31.4	22.2
France, Monaco			6.8	16.3	49.4
Georgia/Géorgie			35.5	22.7	13.9
Italy/Italie			57.8	7.3	5.2
Austria/Autriche			29.7	31.2	4.4
United Kingdom			19.1	19.2	18.7
China, Hong Kong SAR			11.6	13.2	29.3
Uzbekistan/Ouzbékistan			19.5	28.5	5.5
United Arab Emirates			21.8	13.2	10.7
Switzerland,Liechtenst.			17.8	9.0	18.5
Afghanistan			24.2	6.6	4.1
Lithuania/Lituanie			12.9	4.0	15.7
Czech Republic			18.3	2.6	7.9
Tajikistan/Tadjikistan			24.0	1.9	2.1
Yugoslavia/Yougoslavie			22.3	1.8	
China/Chine			4.6	7.7	11.3
Japan/Japon			7.4	7.5	8.3
Kyrgyzstan/Kirghizistan			17.9	3.8	1.2
Pakistan			10.6	1.8	10.4
Ireland/Irlande			4.3	13.9	2.0
Belarus/Bélarus			13.3	6.0	0.9
Netherlands/Pays–Bas			11.4	6.8	1.3
Sweden/Suède			9.5	1.1	7.4
Bulgaria/Bulgarie			6.2	4.5	5.4
India/Inde			6.1	3.1	6.9
Latvia/Lettonie			11.1	1.7	1.4
Hungary/Hongrie			10.6	0.5	1.5
Lebanon/Liban			5.9	4.1	0.8
Slovakia/Slovaquie			6.1	3.4	0.9
Republic of Moldova			3.0	3.1	3.5
Estonia/Estonie			1.9	2.9	2.7

COUNTRIES–PAYS	GENERAL EXPORTS F.O.B. EXPORTATIONS GENERALES F.O.B. 1992	1993	1994	1995	1996
Monde			2145.1	1880.7	1692.6
Afrique				0.2	
Amériques			42.3	35.2	45.1
– Amérique du Nord			35.0	33.5	43.4
– ALAI					
– MCAC					
– Caraïbes			6.8	0.4	1.7
– Autre Amérique			0.5	1.3	
Asie anc. URSS exclus			178.6	623.1	251.2
– Moyen–Orient			130.2	521.4	119.1
Asie ancienne URSS			926.0	397.1	292.4
Europe anc. URSS exclus			215.9	282.6	229.8
– Union Européenne			136.8	142.1	101.0
– Europe de l'Est			24.2	17.6	10.6
– Autre de l'Europe			54.9	122.9	118.2
Europe ancienne URSS			740.4	541.8	855.1
Océanie					
Autre					
Ukraine			603.7	460.3	700.2
Kazakhstan			283.2	127.4	179.8
Cyprus/Chypre			20.3	344.1	1.8
Russian Federation			113.7	66.8	144.3
Turkey/Turquie			78.4	149.6	79.3
Armenia/Arménie			69.8	132.9	86.5
Switzerland,Liechtenst.			49.1	116.8	114.9
Georgia/Géorgie			208.5	53.3	0.2
Azerbaijan/Azerbaïdjan			192.1	49.9	11.2
Uzbekistan/Ouzbékistan			144.3	21.3	3.8
China, Hong Kong SAR			18.1	36.0	104.1
United Kingdom			31.8	43.5	40.5
USA/Etats–Unis d'Amer			35.0	31.9	43.4
Germany/Allemagne			34.0	32.6	17.8
Pakistan			0.1	40.9	12.7
Italy/Italie			36.2	13.0	1.2
Iran (Islamic Rep of)			21.6	11.4	16.9
United Arab Emirates			9.9	16.3	21.1
Afghanistan			19.3	9.1	12.9
Sweden/Suède			7.6	17.2	12.9
Austria/Autriche			9.9	13.0	12.7
Ireland/Irlande			12.1	8.3	14.4
Tajikistan/Tadjikistan			15.6	5.4	10.0
Czech Republic			17.2	3.5	1.9
Kyrgyzstan/Kirghizistan			12.5	6.9	0.9
Bulgaria/Bulgarie			0.6	10.8	7.9
Gibraltar			5.8	6.1	3.3
Spain/Espagne			2.6	10.7	
Latvia/Lettonie			10.6	0.7	0.1
Lithuania/Lituanie			3.1	5.6	1.8
China/Chine			1.5	7.1	1.8
Republic of Moldova			1.3	3.0	4.7
Slovakia/Slovaquie			5.7	3.1	0.1
British Virgin Islds			6.8	0.4	1.7
Belarus/Bélarus			6.0	2.3	0.5
Estonia/Estonie			2.0	3.1	3.5
Indonesia/Indonésie			7.0	0.3	
India/Inde			2.3	2.2	
Korea, Republic of			0.1	3.5	
Portugal				3.0	

(VALUE AS PERCENTAGE OF WORLD TOTAL)(VALEURS EN POURCENTAGE DU TOTAL MONDIAL)

	1987	1988	1989	1990	1991	1992	1993	1994	1995	1996
Africa									0.0	0.0
Americas								3.9	3.9	30.1
– Northern America								3.9	3.9	30.1
– LAIA										
– CACM										
– Caribbean										
– Rest of America										
Asia excl fmr USSR								25.4	26.2	23.4
– Middle East								20.8	23.2	18.0
Asia former USSR								17.6	16.4	7.8
Europe excl fmr USSR								20.4	12.8	14.0
– European Union								14.1	11.0	10.9
– Eastern Europe								3.2	0.9	1.6
– Rest of Europe								3.1	0.9	1.4
Europe former USSR								30.9	38.8	23.3
Oceania										
Other										
Ukraine								17.5	30.5	9.7
USA/Etats–Unis d'Amer								3.9	3.9	30.1
Turkey/Turquie								12.4	11.8	9.2
Russian Federation								10.5	7.0	11.8
Azerbaijan/Azerbaïdjan								4.9	5.4	2.7
Cyprus/Chypre								1.2	7.5	4.5
Germany/Allemagne								4.2	3.8	3.9
Iran (Islamic Rep of)								5.1	2.7	3.4
Armenia/Arménie								3.2	4.6	1.8
Kazakhstan								2.9	2.3	1.7

	1987	1988	1989	1990	1991	1992	1993	1994	1995	1996
Afrique									0.0	
Amériques								2.0	1.9	2.7
– Amérique du Nord								1.6	1.8	2.6
– ALAI										
– MCAC										
– Caraïbes								0.3	0.0	0.1
– Autre Amérique								0.0	0.1	
Asie anc. URSS exclus								8.3	33.1	14.8
– Moyen–Orient								6.1	27.7	7.0
Asie ancienne URSS								43.2	21.1	17.3
Europe anc. URSS exclus								10.1	15.0	13.6
– Union Européenne								6.4	7.6	6.0
– Europe de l'Est								1.1	0.9	0.6
– Autre de l'Europe								2.6	6.5	7.0
Europe ancienne URSS								34.5	28.8	50.5
Océanie										
Autre										
Ukraine								28.1	24.5	41.4
Kazakhstan								13.2	6.8	10.6
Cyprus/Chypre								0.9	18.3	0.1
Russian Federation								5.3	3.6	8.5
Turkey/Turquie								3.7	8.0	4.7
Armenia/Arménie								3.3	7.1	5.1
Switzerland,Liechtenst.								2.3	6.2	6.8
Georgia/Géorgie								9.7	2.8	0.0
Azerbaijan/Azerbaïdjan								9.0	2.7	0.7
Uzbekistan/Ouzbékistan								6.7	1.1	0.2

4. General Imports C.I.F. by Commodities according to the S.I.T.C. (Rev. 2) in million U.S. Dollars
Importations Générales C.A.F. par Produits d'après la C.T.C.I. (Rév. 2) en millions de Dollars E.U.

SITC CTCI	COMMODITY	1993		1994		1995		1996		PRODUIT
		QUANTITY QUANTITE	VALUE VALEUR	QUANTITY QUANTITE	VALUE VALEUR	QUANTITY QUANTITE	VALUE VALEUR	QUANTITY QUANTITE	VALUE VALEUR	
	ALL COMMODITIES						1364.0		1313.5	TOUS PRODUITS
01	MEAT AND PREPARATIONS						38.1		54.1	VIANDES ET PREPARATIONS
02	DAIRY PRODCTS,BIRDS'EGGS						34.1		34.1	PRODUITS LAITIERS,OEUFS
04	CEREALS AND PREPARATIONS						62.1		122.0	CEREALES ET PRODUITS
054	VEG ETC FRSH,SMPLY PRSVD						5.1		8.1	LEGUMES FRAIS,CONG,SECS
057	FRUIT,NUTS,FRESH,DRIED						9.1		3.1	FRUITS FRAIS OU SECS
06	SUGAR AND PREPS,HONEY						34.1		42.1	SUCRES ET PRODUITS
11	BEVERAGES						44.1		17.1	BOISSONS
24	CORK AND WOOD						10.1		10.1	LIEGE ET BOIS
263	COTTON						10.1		11.1	COTON
3	MINERAL FUELS ETC						75.1		35.1	COMBUSTIBLES MINERAUX LUB
52	INORGANIC CHEMICALS						13.1		9.1	PROD CHIM INORGANIQUES
53	DYES,TANNING,COLOUR PROD						11.1		13.1	PROD TEINTURE,COLORANTS
541	*MEDICINAL,PHARM PRODUCT						21.1		30.1	PROD MEDICINAUX PHARMACEUT
55	PERFUME,CLEANING ETC PRD						11.1		10.1	PROD POUR PARFUM,TOILETTE
562	*FERTILIZERS,MANUFACTURE						28.1		8.1	ENGRAIS MANUFACTURES
572	*EXPLOSIVES,PYROTECH PRO						18.1		12.1	EXPLOSIFS
62	RUBBER MANUFACTURES NES						29.1		34.1	CAOUTCHOUC MANUFACTURE
64	PAPER,PAPERBOARD AND MFR						7.1		19.1	PAPIERS,CARTONS & OUVRAGES
65	TEXTILE YARN,FABRICS,ETC						13.1		18.1	FILS,TISSUS,ARTICLES TEXTILE
66	NONMETAL MINERAL MFS NES						11.1		13.1	ART MIN NON METALLIQUES
67	IRON AND STEEL						26.1		27.1	FER ET ACIER
684	ALUMINIUM						9.1		15.1	ALUMINIUM
69	METAL MANUFACTURES NES						118.0		103.1	ART MANUFACT EN METAL NDA
7	MACHINES,TRANSPORT EQUIP						413.0		442.0	MACHINES MATERIEL TRANSPORT
78	ROAD VEHICLES						50.1		34.1	VEHICULES ROUTIERS
792	AIRCRAFT ETC								4.1	APP NAVIGATION AERIENNE
793	SHIPS AND BOATS ETC						7.1			NAVIRES BATEAUX,ETC
821	*FURNITURE,PARTS THEREOF						13.1		8.1	MEUBLES ET PIECES
84	CLOTHING AND ACCESSORIES						41.1		33.1	VETEMENTS
851	*FOOTWEAR						29.1		19.1	CHAUSSURES

5. General Exports F.O.B. by Commodities according to the S.I.T.C. (Rev. 2) in million U.S. Dollars
Exportations Générales F.O.B. par Produits d'après la C.T.C.I. (Rév. 2) en millions de Dollars E.U.

SITC CTCI	COMMODITY	1993 QUANTITY QUANTITE	1993 VALUE VALEUR	1994 QUANTITY QUANTITE	1994 VALUE VALEUR	1995 QUANTITY QUANTITE	1995 VALUE VALEUR	1996 QUANTITY QUANTITE	1996 VALUE VALEUR	PRODUIT
	ALL COMMODITIES						1880.7		1692.6	TOUS PRODUITS
263	COTTON						450.0		350.0	COTON
3	MINERAL FUELS ETC						1358.0		1288.0	COMBUSTIBLES MINERAUX LUB
52	INORGANIC CHEMICALS						8.1		5.1	PROD CHIM INORGANIQUES

1. HISTORICAL SERIES, 1962–1997 GENERAL TRADE, IMPORTS C.I.F., EXPORTS F.O.B.
SERIES HISTORIQUES, 1962–1997 COMMERCE GENERAL, IMPORTATIONS C.A.F., EXPORTATIONS F.O.B

YEAR ANNEE	VALUE IN MILLION UGANDA SHILLINGS VALEUR EN MILLION UGANDA SHILLINGS MERCHANDISE – MARCHANDISE		GOLD – OR		CONVERSION FACTORS U.S. CENTS PER UGANDA SHILLING FACTEURS DE CONVERSION CENTS E.U. PAR UGANDA SHILLING		INDEX NUMBERS – INDICES QUANTUM		UNIT VALUE VALEUR UNITAIRE	
	IMPORTS	EXPORTS	IMPORTS	EXPORTS	IMPORTS	EXPORTS	IMPORTS	EXPORTS	IMPORTS	EXPORTS
1962	6.79	0.96		0.24	1400.0000	1400.0000				
1963	8.17	1.25	0.24		1400.0000	1400.0000				
1964	9.28	1.52	0.64		1400.0000	1400.0000				
1965	11.51	1.47	0.44		1400.0000	1400.0000				
1966	11.88	1.55	1.04		1400.0000	1400.0000				
1967	11.37	1.56	0.84		1400.0000	1400.0000				
1968	11.76	1.54	0.44		1400.0000	1400.0000				
1969	12.47	1.66	0.84		1400.0000	1400.0000				
1970	12.29	2.01			1400.0000	1400.0000				
1971	17.83	1.86			1400.0000	1400.0000				
1972	11.58	2.02			1400.0000	1400.0000				
1973	11.38	2.04			1428.8500	1421.3100				
1974	15.22	2.25			1399.8000	1399.8000				
1975	15.27	1.90			1360.1200	1353.1400				
1976	14.24	3.01			1195.2000	1194.8700				
1977	19.92	4.86			1209.1400	1209.1500				
1978	19.63	2.68			1301.2400	1303.9800				
1979	14.72	32.46			1339.0900	1341.7400				
1980	22.00	26.00			1348.2500	1348.2500				
1981	172.50	122.00			200.0000	200.0000				
1982	354.38	328.00			106.3800	106.3800				
1983	580.00	593.00			64.9773	64.9773				
1984	1238.40	1388.00			27.7778	27.7778				
1985	2002.56	2600.00			14.8810	14.8810				
1986	4300.00	6100.00			7.1429	7.1429				
1987	36336.00	13684.00			2.3343	2.3343				
1988	94112.00	29070.00			0.9422	0.9422				
1989	87851.00	55674.00			0.4494	0.4482				
1990	125059.00	64653.00			0.2331	0.2350				
1991	137250.00	146661.00			0.1428	0.1360				
1992	580685.00	159387.00			0.0886	0.0897				
1993		213846.00				0.0836				
1994	850411.10	393960.00			0.1034	0.1040				
1995	1024317.00	446086.00			0.1032	0.1032				
1996	1247000.00	614000.10			0.0954	0.0956				
1997	1426000.00	595000.00			0.0923	0.0933				

2. IMPORTS BY BROAD ECONOMIC CATEGORY AND EXPORTS BY INDUSTRIAL ORIGIN. (PERCENTAGE OF TOTAL VALUE)
IMPORTATIONS PAR CATEGORIES ECONOMIQUES ET EXPORTATIONS PAR BRANCHE D'ACTIVITE. (EN POURCENTAGE DE LA VALEUR TOTALE)

IMPORTS – IMPORTATIONS

	1990	1991	1992	1993	1994	1995	1996
TOTAL IMPORTS–IMPORTATIONS TOTALES							
1 FOOD BEV–ALIMENTATION BOISSONS							
11 PRIMARY–PRODUITS DE BASE							
111 FOR INDUSTRY–POUR L'INDUSTRIE							
112 FOR HOUSEHOLDS–POUR LES MENAGES							
12 PROCESSED–PRODUITS ELABORES							
121 FOR INDUSTRY–POUR L'INDUSTRIE							
122 FOR HOUSEHOLDS–POUR LES MENAGES							
2 IND SUPPLIES–APPROV INDUSTRIELS							
21 PRIMARY–PRODUITS DE BASE							
22 PROCESSED–PRODUITS ELABORES							
3 FUELS–COMBUSTIBLES							
31 PRIMARY–PRODUITS DE BASE							
32 PROCESSED–PRODUITS ELABORES							
321 MOTOR SPIRIT–ESSENCE							
322 OTHER–AUTRES							
4 MACHINERY–EQUIPEMENT							
41 CAPITAL EQUIPMENT–MACHINES							
42 PARTS–PIECES ACCESSOIRES							
5 TRANSPORT–TRANSPORT							
51 PASSENGER CARS–AUTOMOBILES							
52 OTHER–AUTRES							
521 INDUSTRIAL–INDUSTRIELS							
522 NON INDUSTRIAL–NON INDUSTRIEL							
53 PARTS–PIECES ACCESSOIRES							
6 CONSUM GOODS–BIENS CONSOMMATION							
61 DURABLE–DURABLES							
62 SEMI DURABLE–SEMI DURABLES							
63 NON DURABLE–NON DURABLES							
7 GOODS NES–BIENS NDA							

EXPORTS – EXPORTATIONS

	1990	1991	1992	1993	1994	1995	1996
TOTAL EXPORTS–EXPORTATIONS TOTALES							
1 AGRICULTURE							
2 MINING QUARRY–INDUS EXTRACTIVES							
3 MANUFACTURING–IND MANUFACTUR							
31 FOOD BEV TOBACCO–ALIM BOISS TAB							
32 TEXTILES–INDUSTRIES TEXTILES							
33 WOOD & PRODUCTS–BOIS & PRODUITS							
34 PAPER & PRODUCTS–PAPIER & PRODT							
35 CHEMICALS–INDUSTRIES CHIMIQUES							
36 NON METAL MIN–MIN NON METAL							
37 BASIC METAL–IND METAL BASE							
38 METAL MANUF–MANUF METAL							
39 OTH MANUF IND–AUTRES MANUF							

3. TRADE BY PRINCIPAL COUNTRIES OF ORIGIN AND DESTINATION (VALUE IN MILLION U.S. DOLLARS)
ECHANGES SELON LES PRINCIPAUX PAYS D'ORIGINE ET DE DESTINATION (VALEUR EN MILLIONS DE DOLLARS EU)

COUNTRIES–PAYS	GENERAL IMPORTS C.I.F. IMPORTATIONS GENERALES C.A.F				
	1992	1993	1994	1995	1996
World	524.4			1047.6	816.0
Africa	140.4			305.0	263.5
Americas	37.0			43.5	33.5
– Northern America	36.6			43.5	33.5
– LAIA					
– CACM					
– Caribbean	0.4				
– Rest of America					
Asia excl fmr USSR	178.0			330.4	235.4
– Middle East	48.2			65.0	46.6
Asia former USSR					
Europe excl fmr USSR	165.2			323.8	240.7
– European Union	155.8			314.3	225.8
– Eastern Europe	0.8				
– Rest of Europe	8.6			9.5	14.9
Europe former USSR					
Oceania					
Other	0.1				
Kenya	118.4			280.7	245.5
United Kingdom	52.2			126.9	103.5
Japan/Japon	51.7			99.4	66.3
India/Inde	23.9			61.4	47.2
United Arab Emirates	14.8			61.7	44.4
Germany/Allemagne	26.8			37.3	30.7
Italy/Italie	15.0			46.8	22.7
USA/Etats–Unis d'Amer	25.3			31.5	22.3
China, Hong Kong SAR	7.7			30.1	21.8
France, Monaco	13.7			25.4	19.0
United Rep of Tanzania	17.0			23.1	15.6
Belgium–Luxembourg	11.2			27.5	15.2
China/Chine	20.5			20.1	10.0
Singapore/Singapour	16.0			17.3	10.8
Denmark/Danemark	5.3			19.3	16.8
Netherlands/Pays–Bas	8.8			19.8	10.5
Malaysia/Malaisie	2.5			17.0	18.5
Canada	11.3			12.1	11.2
Switzerland,Liechtenst.	7.9			7.6	9.3
Korea, Republic of	3.3			12.5	6.4
Spain/Espagne	13.0			4.4	3.9
Middle East n.e.s.	19.1				
Pakistan	2.2			7.5	5.9
Bahrain/Bahreïn	12.8				
Sweden/Suède	3.3			5.2	3.5
Norway,Svalbard and JM	0.5			0.9	5.6
Saudi Arabia	1.5			3.3	2.1
Zimbabwe	1.4			1.2	2.3
Other Asia n.e.s.	2.1				2.0
Other Africa n.e.s.	3.7				
Finland/Finlande	1.5			1.6	
Austria/Autriche	2.6				
European Union n.e.s.	2.5				
Yugoslavia/Yougoslavie	0.2			0.9	
Eastern Europe n.e.s.	0.8				
Cuba	0.4				
Areas n.e.s.	0.1				

COUNTRIES–PAYS	GENERAL EXPORTS F.O.B. EXPORTATIONS GENERALES F.O.B.				
	1992	1993	1994	1995	1996
Monde	171.4				
Afrique	22.4				
Amériques	15.7				
– Amérique du Nord	15.7				
– ALAI					
– MCAC					
– Caraïbes					
– Autre Amérique					
Asie anc. URSS exclus	5.2				
– Moyen–Orient	0.8				
Asie ancienne URSS					
Europe anc. URSS exclus	109.4				
– Union Européenne	109.4				
– Europe de l'Est					
– Autre de l'Europe					
Europe ancienne URSS					
Océanie					
Autre					
United Kingdom	35.6				
Belgium–Luxembourg	21.1				
Kenya	19.0				
Spain/Espagne	15.9				
USA/Etats–Unis d'Amer	14.0				
France, Monaco	10.9				
Netherlands/Pays–Bas	8.9				
Germany/Allemagne	7.4				
Italy/Italie	7.3				
Other Africa n.e.s.	3.4				
Korea, Republic of	2.2				
Canada	1.7				
Greece/Grèce	1.0				
Japan/Japon	1.0				
Portugal	0.9				
China, Hong Kong SAR	0.7				
European Union n.e.s.	0.4				
Saudi Arabia	0.4				
Other Asia n.e.s.	0.3				
Middle East n.e.s.	0.2				
United Arab Emirates	0.2				
Singapore/Singapour	0.1				

(VALUE AS PERCENTAGE OF WORLD TOTAL)(VALEURS EN POURCENTAGE DU TOTAL MONDIAL)

	1987	1988	1989	1990	1991	1992	1993	1994	1995	1996
Africa	16.7	20.5	17.7	15.9	19.3	26.8			29.1	32.3
Americas	4.5	7.5	9.0	7.2	3.7	7.0			4.2	4.1
– Northern America	4.0	4.0	5.8	6.2	3.4	7.0			4.2	4.1
– LAIA										
– CACM										
– Caribbean	0.5	3.6	3.3	1.0	0.3	0.1				
– Rest of America										
Asia excl fmr USSR	30.0	31.4	30.8	30.4	34.5	33.9			31.5	28.9
– Middle East	8.0	7.3	12.2	15.3	10.4	9.2			6.2	5.7
Asia former USSR										
Europe excl fmr USSR	47.2	38.7	40.8	45.2	41.5	31.5			30.9	29.5
– European Union	39.5	35.2	39.0	43.0	38.7	29.7			30.0	27.7
– Eastern Europe	0.1	0.2	0.7	1.0	1.3	0.2				
– Rest of Europe	7.6	3.2	1.1	1.3	1.5	1.6			0.9	1.8
Europe former USSR										
Oceania										
Other			0.1	0.0	0.0	0.0				
Kenya	15.8	19.3	16.1	12.9	15.8	22.6			26.8	30.1
United Kingdom	12.5	12.9	12.7	14.8	13.9	10.0			12.1	12.7
Japan/Japon	6.7	5.7	5.8	5.3	9.0	9.9			9.5	8.1
India/Inde	3.6	2.3	3.2	2.5	2.8	4.5			5.9	5.8
United Arab Emirates	0.7	0.8	0.8	1.1	1.0	2.8			5.9	5.4
Germany/Allemagne					6.4	5.1			3.6	3.8
Italy/Italie	11.7	6.9	4.1	9.2	5.4	2.9			4.5	2.8
USA/Etats–Unis d'Amer	3.8	3.6	4.8	5.6	2.9	4.8			3.0	2.7
China, Hong Kong SAR	0.6	1.0	1.5	1.5	1.8	1.5			2.9	2.7
France, Monaco	1.5	1.1	1.9	2.5	3.2	2.6			2.4	2.3

	1987	1988	1989	1990	1991	1992	1993	1994	1995	1996
Afrique	0.6	0.6	1.4	7.1	10.8	13.1				
Amériques	21.3	12.6	12.2	10.7	10.9	9.1				
– Amérique du Nord	21.3	12.6	12.2	10.7	10.9	9.1				
– ALAI			0.0							
– MCAC										
– Caraïbes										
– Autre Amérique										
Asie anc. URSS exclus	4.4	3.3	3.9	4.1	5.9	3.0				
– Moyen–Orient	0.2		0.0	0.8	0.6	0.4				
Asie ancienne URSS										
Europe anc. URSS exclus	68.8	75.1	66.2	71.2	66.0	63.8				
– Union Européenne	68.8	75.1	66.2	71.2	66.0	63.8				
– Europe de l'Est										
– Autre de l'Europe										
Europe ancienne URSS										
Océanie										
Autre										
United Kingdom	13.6	14.7	7.5	7.7	15.7	20.8				
Belgium–Luxembourg	7.3	8.4	7.9	8.9	5.8	12.3				
Kenya	0.5	0.6	1.3	4.3	7.8	11.1				
Spain/Espagne	11.7	12.7	13.6	14.3	8.9	9.3				
USA/Etats–Unis d'Amer	21.1	12.4	12.2	10.2	10.1	8.1				
France, Monaco	7.5	8.9	7.9	12.2	12.6	6.4				
Netherlands/Pays–Bas	17.6	12.3	8.9	7.9	4.7	5.2				
Germany/Allemagne					4.5	4.3				
Italy/Italie	4.6	7.2	7.5	13.3	11.0	4.3				
Other Africa n.e.s.	0.0	0.0	0.1	2.8	3.0	2.0				

4. General Imports C.I.F. by Commodities according to the S.I.T.C. (Rev. 2) in million U.S. Dollars
Importations Générales C.A.F. par Produits d'après la C.T.C.I. (Rév. 2) en millions de Dollars E.U.

SITC CTCI	COMMODITY	1993		1994		1995		1996		PRODUIT
		QUANTITY QUANTITE	VALUE VALEUR	QUANTITY QUANTITE	VALUE VALEUR	QUANTITY QUANTITE	VALUE VALEUR	QUANTITY QUANTITE	VALUE VALEUR	
	ALL COMMODITIES						1047.7		816.1	TOUS PRODUITS
0	FOOD AND LIVE ANIMALS						90.3		54.0	ALIMENTS,ANIMAUX VIVANTS
04	CEREALS AND PREPARATIONS						39.8		31.7	CEREALES ET PRODUITS
05	VEGETABLES AND FRUIT						12.8		5.2	LEGUMES ET FRUITS
06	SUGAR AND PREPS,HONEY						26.7		7.6	SUCRES ET PRODUITS
09	MISC EDIBLE PRODUCTS						6.9		5.6	PREP ALIMENTAIRES DIVERSES
2	CRUDE MATERLS,EXCL FUELS						37.1		38.5	MAT BRUTES NON COMESTIBLES
22	OIL SEEDS,OLEAGINOUS FRT						2.9		4.0	GRAINES,FRUITS OLEAGINEUX
26	TEXTILE FIBRES AND WASTE						23.5		22.5	FIBRES TEXTILES
27	CRUDE FERTLZR,MINRLS NES						9.5		11.2	ENGRAIS MINERAUX BRUTS
3	MINERAL FUELS ETC						78.2		91.8	COMBUSTIBLES MINERAUX LUB
33	PETROLEUM AND PRODUCTS						77.8		91.5	PETROLE ET DERIVES
4	ANIMAL,VEGETABLE OIL,FAT						47.1		31.8	HUILES,GRAISSES ANIM,VEG
411	*ANIMAL OILS AND FATS						5.0		0.4	HUILES,GRAISSES ANIMALES
42	FIXED VEGETABLE OIL,FAT						27.4		21.9	HUILES VEGETALES FIXES
431	*PROCESD ANML VEG OIL,ET						14.8		9.6	HUILES,GRAISSES PREPAREES
5	CHEMCLS,RELATED PROD NES						105.5		116.9	PRODUITS CHIMIQUES
51	ORGANIC CHEMICALS						5.4		4.3	PROD CHIMIQ ORGANIQUES
52	INORGANIC CHEMICALS						6.7		4.9	PROD CHIM INORGANIQUES
53	DYES,TANNING,COLOUR PROD						4.4		4.5	PROD TEINTURE,COLORANTS
541	*MEDICINAL,PHARM PRODUCT						40.4		46.4	PROD MEDICINAUX PHARMACEUT
55	PERFUME,CLEANING ETC PRD						9.0		11.6	PROD POUR PARFUM,TOILETTE
562	*FERTILIZERS,MANUFACTURE						3.5		3.9	ENGRAIS MANUFACTURES
572	*EXPLOSIVES,PYROTECH PRO						12.3		14.6	EXPLOSIFS
58	PLASTIC MATERIALS ETC						7.9		3.7	MAT PLAST ARTIFICIELLES
59	CHEMICAL MATERIALS NES						16.3		23.6	MAT PROD CHIMIQUES NDA
6	BASIC MANUFACTURES						205.7		162.0	ART MANUFACTURES
62	RUBBER MANUFACTURES NES						16.9		17.1	CAOUTCHOUC MANUFACTURE
64	PAPER,PAPERBOARD AND MFR						20.8		17.6	PAPIERS,CARTONS & OUVRAGES
65	TEXTILE YARN,FABRICS,ETC						37.6		25.3	FILS,TISSUS,ARTICLES TEXTILE
66	NONMETAL MINERAL MFS NES						41.9		33.3	ART MIN NON METALLIQUES
67	IRON AND STEEL						49.5		35.1	FER ET ACIER
68	NON-FERROUS METALS						8.4		11.3	METAUX NON FERREUX
69	METAL MANUFACTURES NES						29.1		21.4	ART MANUFACT EN METAL NDA
7	MACHINES,TRANSPORT EQUIP						327.4		248.6	MACHINES MATERIEL TRANSPORT
71	POWER GENERATING EQUIPMT						10.5		9.5	MACHINES GENERATRICES
72	MACHS FOR SPCL INDUSTRYS						53.1		30.5	MAC SPECIALES POUR INDUST
73	METALWORKING MACHINERY						4.6		3.3	MACH TRAVAIL DES METAUX
74	GENRL INDUSTRL MACHY NES						29.7		26.9	MACH APP INDUSTRIE
75	OFFICE MACHNES,ADP EQUIP						11.9		10.5	MACH BUREAU TRAIT AUTOM
76	TELECOMM,SOUND EQUIPMENT						26.3		16.5	EQUIPEMENT DE TELECOM
77	ELECTRIC MACHNRY NES ETC						39.6		32.7	MACH APP ELECT NDA
78	ROAD VEHICLES						149.1		115.6	VEHICULES ROUTIERS
79	OTHR TRANSPORT EQUIPMENT						3.1		3.6	AUTRE MATERIEL TRANSPORT
8	MISC MANUFACTURED GOODS						78.9		41.1	ART MANUFACTURES DIVERS
812	*PLUMBG,HEATNG,LGHTNG EQ						4.1		3.5	APPAR SANITAIRES CHAUFFAGE
821	*FURNITURE,PARTS THEREOF						9.1		4.0	MEUBLES ET PIECES
831	*TRAVEL GOODS,HANDBAGS						3.0		2.8	ARTICLES DE VOYAGE ETC
84	CLOTHING AND ACCESSORIES						14.8		12.9	VETEMENTS
851	*FOOTWEAR						5.9		4.8	CHAUSSURES
87	PRECISION INSTRUMNTS NES						7.8		10.4	INSTRUM,APPAR SCIENT NDA
89	MISC MANUFCTRD GOODS NES						31.7		3.0	ART MANUFACTURES DIVERS

5. General Exports F.O.B. by Commodities according to the S.I.T.C. (Rev. 2) in million U.S. Dollars
Exportations Générales F.O.B. par Produits d'après la C.T.C.I. (Rév. 2) en millions de Dollars E.U.

SITC CTCI	COMMODITY	1993 QUANTITY QUANTITE	1993 VALUE VALEUR	1994 QUANTITY QUANTITE	1994 VALUE VALEUR	1995 QUANTITY QUANTITE	1995 VALUE VALEUR	1996 QUANTITY QUANTITE	1996 VALUE VALEUR	PRODUIT
	ALL COMMODITIES		201.2		464.0		575.9		665.3	TOUS PRODUITS
0	FOOD AND LIVE ANIMALS						473.1		478.5	ALIMENTS,ANIMAUX VIVANTS
03	FISH AND PREPARATIONS		9.0		12.3		32.8		25.1	POISSONS ET PREPARATIONS
04	CEREALS AND PREPARATIONS						26.7		19.2	CEREALES ET PRODUITS
044	MAIZE UNMILLED	W 160438	23.4	W 95453	30.2	W 86149	23.1	W 86552	17.9	MAIS NON MOULU
05	VEGETABLES AND FRUIT						19.0		17.1	LEGUMES ET FRUITS
054	VEG ETC FRSH,SMPLY PRSVD							W 40308	16.2	LEGUMES FRAIS,CONG,SECS
0542	LEGUMINOUS VEGETBLES DRY	W 47532	12.6	W 35329	12.0	W 38758	16.2	W 40308	16.2	LEGUMES A COSSE SECS
07	COFFEE,TEA,COCOA,SPICES						392.3		415.3	CAFE,THE,CACAO,EPICES
071	COFFEE AND SUBSTITUTES	W 114169	106.8	W 194360	342.8	W 168860	383.0	W 278711	396.3	CAFE ET SUCCEDANES
0711	COFFEE GREEN,ROASTED,SUB	W 114169	106.8	W 194360	342.8	W 168860	383.0			CAFE TORREFIE OU DECAFEINE
072	COCOA	W 1313	0.8	W 680	0.7	W 552	0.5	W 1414	1.1	CACAO
0721	COCOA BEANS,RAW,ROASTED	W 1313	0.8	W 680	0.7	W 552	0.5			CACAO EN FEVES
074	TEA AND MATE			W 10972	11.9	W 10681	8.8	W 14610	17.1	THE ET MATE
0741	TEA	W 10175	11.2	W 10972	11.9	W 10681	8.8			THE
1	BEVERAGES AND TOBACCO						10.9		8.3	BOISSONS ET TABACS
12	TOBACCO AND MANUFACTURES		7.0				9.7		7.4	TABACS BRUTS FABRIQUES
121	TOBACCO UNMNFCTRD,REFUSE	W 3854	7.0	W 4082	8.1	W 3525	7.4	W 3118	7.4	TABACS BRUTS,DECHETS
2	CRUDE MATERLS,EXCL FUELS						35.7		43.3	MAT BRUTES NON COMESTIBLES
21	HIDES,SKINS,FURS UNDRSSD						10.2		7.9	CUIRS,PEAUX BRUTS
211	HIDES,SKINS,EXC FURS,RAW					W 5106	10.2	W 5017	7.9	CUIRS ET PEAUX
2111	BOVINE,EQUINE HIDES,RAW	W 5259	5.3	W 7697	12.9	W 5106	10.2	W 5017	7.9	PEAUX DE BOVINS
2114	GOAT AND KID SKINS,RAW	W 486	0.7							PEAUX DE CAPRINS
22	OIL SEEDS,OLEAGINOUS FRT						8.9		10.5	GRAINES,FRUITS OLEAGINEUX
222	SEEDS FOR'SOFT'FIXED OIL					W 13677	8.2	W 20030	10.3	GRAINES HUILES FIXES
2222	SOYA BEANS	W 7076	2.1	W 1802	0.8	W 3972	1.9	W 8493	2.9	FEVES DE SOJA
2225	SESAME SEEDS	W 8372	2.8	W 4245	1.6	W 9314	5.9	W 11462	7.4	GRAINES DE SESAME
26	TEXTILE FIBRES AND WASTE						11.5		22.2	FIBRES TEXTILES
263	COTTON	W 7961	5.6	W 3841	3.6	W 5580	9.7	W 9756	15.4	COTON
2631	RAW COTTON,EXCL LINTERS	W 7961	5.6	W 3841	3.6	W 5580	9.7			COTON EN MASSE
29	CRUDE ANIMAL,VEG MAT NES						3.3		2.2	MATIERES BRUTES ANIM,VEGET
292	CRUDE VEG MATERIALS NES					K 241292	0.4	K 379504	2.2	MAT BRUTES VEGETALES NDA
2924	VEG USED IN PHARMACY ETC			W 232	0.6	K 241292	0.4	K 379504	2.2	PLANTES MEDICINALES
3	MINERAL FUELS ETC						2.9		4.3	COMBUSTIBLES MINERAUX LUB
351	*ELECTRIC CURRENT	W 256182	0.8	H 245651	2.3	H 195500	2.5			ENERGIE ELECTRIQUE
4	ANIMAL,VEGETABLE OIL,FAT						1.5		17.8	HUILES,GRAISSES ANIM,VEG
42	FIXED VEGETABLE OIL,FAT						1.5		17.2	HUILES VEGETALES FIXES
5	CHEMCLS,RELATED PROD NES						5.7		36.3	PRODUITS CHIMIQUES
52	INORGANIC CHEMICALS						1.1		32.1	PROD CHIM INORGANIQUES
55	PERFUME,CLEANING ETC PRD						3.1		2.5	PROD POUR PARFUM,TOILETTE
554	SOAP,CLEANSING ETC PREPS					W 4420	3.0	W 3657	2.4	SAVONS,PRODUITS DETERSIFS
5541	SOAPS	W 2597	1.4	W 2452	1.8	W 4420	3.0	W 3657	2.4	SAVONS,PROD TENSIO–ACTIFS
6	BASIC MANUFACTURES						10.6		20.9	ART MANUFACTURES
65	TEXTILE YARN,FABRICS,ETC						2.1		3.2	FILS,TISSUS,ARTICLES TEXTILE
67	IRON AND STEEL						2.5		14.3	FER ET ACIER
68	NON–FERROUS METALS						1.8		0.1	METAUX NON FERREUX
69	METAL MANUFACTURES NES						3.3		2.1	ART MANUFACT EN METAL NDA
695	TOOLS					W 793	1.9	W 267	0.6	OUTILS A MAIN
6951	HAND TOOLS,AGRIC,FOREST		0.4		1.1	W 793	1.9	W 267	0.6	BECHES,PELLES,PIOCHES
7	MACHINES,TRANSPORT EQUIP						6.6		9.7	MACHINES MATERIEL TRANSPORT
78	ROAD VEHICLES						4.3		6.7	VEHICULES ROUTIERS
8	MISC MANUFACTURED GOODS						2.6		2.6	ART MANUFACTURES DIVERS
9	GOODS NOT CLASSD BY KIND						26.6		18.5	ART TRANSACT NON CLASSES
931	*SPECIAL TRANSACTIONS									TRANS.SPECIALES
971	*GOLD,NON MONETARY NES	K 11	0.1	K 1	0.3		26.6		18.5	OR NON MONETAIRE

1. HISTORICAL SERIES, 1992–1997 GENERAL TRADE, IMPORTS C.I.F., EXPORTS F.O.B.
SERIES HISTORIQUES, 1992–1997 COMMERCE GENERAL, IMPORTATIONS C.A.F., EXPORTATIONS F.O.B

YEAR ANNEE	VALUE IN MILLION U.S. DOLLARS / VALEUR EN MILLION U.S. DOLLARS: MERCHANDISE – MARCHANDISE		GOLD – OR		CONVERSION FACTORS FACTEURS DE CONVERSION CENTS E.U. PAR		INDEX NUMBERS – INDICES: QUANTUM		UNIT VALUE VALEUR UNITAIRE	
	IMPORTS	EXPORTS	IMPORTS	EXPORTS	IMPORTS	EXPORTS	IMPORTS	EXPORTS	IMPORTS	EXPORTS
1992	2219.00	3774.00								
1993	2651.00	3222.00								
1994	10748.00	10305.00								
1995	16052.00	13317.00								
1996	18639.01	14441.00								
1997	17261.60	14231.90								

2. IMPORTS BY BROAD ECONOMIC CATEGORY AND EXPORTS BY INDUSTRIAL ORIGIN. (PERCENTAGE OF TOTAL VALUE)
IMPORTATIONS PAR CATEGORIES ECONOMIQUES ET EXPORTATIONS PAR BRANCHE D'ACTIVITE.(EN POURCENTAGE DE LA VALEUR TOTALE)

IMPORTS – IMPORTATIONS

	1991	1992	1993	1994	1995	1996	1997
TOTAL IMPORTS–IMPORTATIONS TOTALES							
1 FOOD BEV–ALIMENTATION BOISSONS							
11 PRIMARY–PRODUITS DE BASE							
111 FOR INDUSTRY–POUR L'INDUSTRIE							
112 FOR HOUSEHOLDS–POUR LES MENAGES							
12 PROCESSED–PRODUITS ELABORES							
121 FOR INDUSTRY–POUR L'INDUSTRIE							
122 FOR HOUSEHOLDS–POUR LES MENAGES							
2 IND SUPPLIES–APPROV INDUSTRIELS							
21 PRIMARY–PRODUITS DE BASE							
22 PROCESSED–PRODUITS ELABORES							
3 FUELS–COMBUSTIBLES							
31 PRIMARY–PRODUITS DE BASE							
32 PROCESSED–PRODUITS ELABORES							
321 MOTOR SPIRIT–ESSENCE							
322 OTHER–AUTRES							
4 MACHINERY–EQUIPEMENT							
41 CAPITAL EQUIPMENT–MACHINES							
42 PARTS–PIECES ACCESSOIRES							
5 TRANSPORT–TRANSPORT							
51 PASSENGER CARS–AUTOMOBILES							
52 OTHER–AUTRES							
521 INDUSTRIAL–INDUSTRIELS							
522 NON INDUSTRIAL–NON INDUSTRIEL							
53 PARTS–PIECES ACCESSOIRES							
6 CONSUM GOODS–BIENS CONSOMMATION							
61 DURABLE–DURABLES							
62 SEMI DURABLE–SEMI DURABLES							
63 NON DURABLE–NON DURABLES							
7 GOODS NES–BIENS NDA							

EXPORTS – EXPORTATIONS

	1991	1992	1993	1994	1995	1996	1997
TOTAL EXPORTS–EXPORTATIONS TOTALES							
1 AGRICULTURE							
2 MINING QUARRY–INDUS EXTRACTIVES							
3 MANUFACTURING–IND MANUFACTUR							
31 FOOD BEV TOBACCO–ALIM BOISS TAB							
32 TEXTILES–INDUSTRIES TEXTILES							
33 WOOD & PRODUCTS–BOIS & PRODUITS							
34 PAPER & PRODUCTS–PAPIER & PRODT							
35 CHEMICALS–INDUSTRIES CHIMIQUES							
36 NON METAL MIN–MIN NON METAL							
37 BASIC METAL–IND METAL BASE							
38 METAL MANUF–MANUF METAL							
39 OTH MANUF IND–AUTRES MANUF							

3. TRADE BY PRINCIPAL COUNTRIES OF ORIGIN AND DESTINATION (VALUE IN MILLION U.S. DOLLARS)
ECHANGES SELON LES PRINCIPAUX PAYS D'ORIGINE ET DE DESTINATION (VALEUR EN MILLIONS DE DOLLARS EU)

COUNTRIES–PAYS	GENERAL IMPORTS C.I.F. IMPORTATIONS GENERALES C.A.F				
	1993	1994	1995	1996	1997
World	9533.0	10748.0	15484.0	17623.9	17261.6
Africa	78.0	26.7	51.9	71.6	273.7
Americas	343.7	253.4	649.1	886.0	797.9
– Northern America	231.0	243.5	448.3	608.2	693.3
– LAIA	76.7	9.9	146.2	143.5	83.8
– CACM			10.4	17.2	2.0
– Caribbean	36.0		44.2	117.1	14.6
– Rest of America					4.1
Asia excl fmr USSR	215.3	143.9	457.3	587.0	837.2
– Middle East	47.0	8.9	67.6	109.5	199.3
Asia former USSR	1559.7	948.5	1130.4	1939.4	1576.3
Europe excl fmr USSR	1786.3	2085.4	3742.9	4311.8	5053.4
– European Union	1099.0	1198.5	2311.1	2800.9	3378.6
– Eastern Europe	436.0	520.4	1236.1	1333.7	1403.0
– Rest of Europe	251.3	366.5	195.7	177.2	271.8
Europe former USSR	5540.0	7026.9	9074.5	9425.6	8701.2
Oceania	2.0	12.9	19.3	23.0	21.9
Other					
Russian Federation	4999.0	6349.4	8249.1	8686.1	7837.9
Turkmenistan/Turkménistn	1339.0	687.9	680.5	1604.9	972.3
Germany/Allemagne	462.0	655.0	958.3	1155.2	1308.9
USA/Etats–Unis d'Amer	224.0	220.2	419.3	562.1	650.9
Belarus/Bélarus	288.0	339.9	526.4	382.4	391.4
Poland/Pologne	77.0	123.2	476.7	505.9	549.9
Italy/Italie	96.0	126.8	271.8	341.6	400.4
Kazakhstan	82.0	164.9	323.3	242.7	403.7
France, Monaco	157.0	84.9	195.9	244.3	308.1
Switzerland,Liechtenst.	225.0	334.3	131.8	93.1	154.6
Hungary/Hongrie	115.0	99.9	169.6	233.9	197.4
Lithuania/Lituanie	167.0	68.0	129.5	155.4	242.4
Czech Republic	46.0	127.5	157.1	206.6	219.7
Austria/Autriche	121.0	99.1	132.6	169.0	224.7
Slovakia/Slovaquie	68.0	75.3	152.8	182.1	204.5
United Kingdom	53.0	59.1	142.8	189.0	232.4
Netherlands/Pays–Bas	88.0	62.6	149.2	179.3	192.9
Bulgaria/Bulgarie	93.0	68.8	128.4	124.8	142.9
Japan/Japon	44.0	30.3	106.9	114.9	150.0
Belgium–Luxembourg	15.0	21.3	111.3	124.7	154.0
Republic of Moldova	33.0	171.9	61.1	71.7	73.8
China/Chine	53.0	33.0	83.7	89.7	125.6
Romania/Roumanie	37.0	25.7	151.5	80.4	86.9
Brazil/Brésil	74.0	9.2	137.5	111.7	49.0
Uzbekistan/Ouzbékistan	53.0	55.0	73.4	61.1	126.4
Turkey/Turquie	12.0	8.9	67.6	109.5	162.0
Latvia/Lettonie	31.0	70.3	81.8	91.6	82.9
Finland/Finlande	22.0	24.6	88.4	95.7	120.5
India/Inde	15.0	24.3	74.3	93.2	82.4
Sweden/Suède	10.0	12.6	46.9	66.7	136.7
Guinea/Guinée	69.0	26.7	51.9	71.6	50.6
Greece/Grèce	24.0	7.7	84.5	59.9	64.8
Denmark/Danemark	8.0	17.0	49.0	67.4	98.1
Azerbaijan/Azerbaïdjan	55.7	40.7	53.2	30.7	47.0
Spain/Espagne	4.0	5.5	46.5	58.7	85.0
Korea, Republic of	4.0	4.7	27.5	47.9	113.2
Cuba	35.0		44.2	117.1	0.7
Estonia/Estonie	22.0	27.4	26.6	38.4	72.8
Israel/Israël	5.0	27.9	39.9	49.6	51.3
Ireland/Irlande	13.0	22.3	33.9	49.4	48.1

COUNTRIES–PAYS	GENERAL EXPORTS F.O.B. EXPORTATIONS GENERALES F.O.B.				
	1993	1994	1995	1996	1997
Monde	7817.0	10305.0	13128.2	14331.0	14231.9
Afrique	131.5	58.2	106.3	96.9	472.4
Amériques	231.0	363.5	330.0	494.5	652.5
– Amérique du Nord	178.0	358.7	273.1	364.1	316.3
– ALAI	30.0	2.6	20.1	38.1	152.5
– MCAC	3.0				4.1
– Caraïbes	3.0	2.2	36.8	92.3	171.0
– Autre Amérique	17.0				8.6
Asie anc. URSS exclus	931.9	1322.3	2355.8	2579.2	3829.2
– Moyen–Orient	302.0	319.5	804.8	983.6	1382.6
Asie ancienne URSS	624.2	502.3	538.2	811.6	742.8
Europe anc. URSS exclus	1805.9	2143.8	2677.2	3068.7	3447.5
– Union Européenne	840.0	978.8	1356.9	1537.0	1760.1
– Europe de l'Est	647.0	773.1	1253.6	1405.2	1456.8
– Autre de l'Europe	318.9	391.9	66.7	126.5	230.6
Europe ancienne URSS	4076.8	5402.8	6622.9	6759.1	5067.4
Océanie	10.0				16.8
Autre					
Russian Federation	3544.8	4065.4	5697.9	5527.7	3723.0
China/Chine	271.0	506.1	755.4	769.2	1100.9
Belarus/Bélarus	350.0	542.3	545.9	732.7	825.5
Turkey/Turquie	142.0	116.3	453.0	410.8	670.8
Germany/Allemagne	172.0	282.6	338.7	418.7	568.6
Italy/Italie	141.0	200.2	424.6	344.7	395.0
USA/Etats–Unis d'Amer	164.0	358.7	273.1	364.1	300.4
Hungary/Hongrie	181.0	170.4	298.1	373.8	318.8
Poland/Pologne	123.0	150.0	274.5	362.5	380.3
Republic of Moldova	76.0	489.3	151.9	236.4	294.4
Turkmenistan/Turkménistn	195.0	222.0	270.2	271.6	176.7
Slovakia/Slovaquie	45.0	125.4	216.4	231.5	279.3
Switzerland,Liechtenst.	225.0	391.9	66.7	126.5	75.9
Bulgaria/Bulgarie	144.0	129.8	179.2	138.6	154.8
Thailand/Thaïlande	52.0	113.2	124.8	325.2	99.6
Uzbekistan/Ouzbékistan	93.0	73.3	114.1	176.7	236.0
Austria/Autriche	201.0	170.8	77.3	101.8	107.7
India/Inde	65.0	54.2	231.4	82.0	225.3
Czech Republic	80.0	125.7	118.1	142.1	173.9
Romania/Roumanie	74.0	71.8	167.3	156.7	149.0
Lithuania/Lituanie	62.0	193.1	127.3	130.4	102.3
Other Asia n.e.s.	56.0	87.1	80.2	79.9	303.7
Syrian Arab Republic	4.0	17.4	83.8	196.0	260.9
Egypt/Egypte	69.0	58.2	106.3	96.9	184.7
Kazakhstan	114.0	119.2	94.4	89.7	93.7
United Kingdom	36.0	77.0	176.0	134.4	87.4
Netherlands/Pays–Bas	121.0	35.5	113.3	100.0	121.4
Azerbaijan/Azerbaïdjan	185.2	79.0	41.6	88.6	87.6
Lebanon/Liban	6.0	7.7	141.6	154.4	153.1
Cyprus/Chypre	118.0	156.7	35.0	39.5	37.3
Iran (Islamic Rep of)	7.0	17.9	34.9	116.2	189.6
Latvia/Lettonie	33.0	94.0	63.9	78.4	78.9
France, Monaco	30.0	38.8	45.2	112.8	101.5
Greece/Grèce	41.0	46.7	39.7	96.9	80.4
Belgium–Luxembourg	21.0	46.0	68.7	79.3	84.8
Spain/Espagne	12.0	17.6	64.1	84.0	117.5
Korea, Republic of	28.0	67.4	79.3	59.5	51.9
Japan/Japon	19.0	26.2	65.6	81.3	92.8
British Virgin Islds		2.2	36.8	92.3	150.6
Philippines	12.9	58.4	86.0	55.1	68.1

(VALUE AS PERCENTAGE OF WORLD TOTAL)(VALEURS EN POURCENTAGE DU TOTAL MONDIAL)

	1988	1989	1990	1991	1992	1993	1994	1995	1996	1997
Africa						0.8	0.2	0.3	0.4	1.6
Americas						3.6	2.4	4.2	5.0	4.6
– Northern America						2.4	2.3	2.9	3.5	4.0
– LAIA						0.8	0.1	0.9	0.8	0.5
– CACM								0.1	0.1	0.0
– Caribbean						0.4		0.3	0.7	0.1
– Rest of America										0.0
Asia excl fmr USSR						2.3	1.3	3.0	3.3	4.8
– Middle East						0.5	0.1	0.4	0.6	1.2
Asia former USSR						16.4	8.8	7.3	11.0	9.1
Europe excl fmr USSR						18.7	19.4	24.2	24.5	29.3
– European Union						11.5	11.2	14.9	15.9	19.6
– Eastern Europe						4.6	4.8	8.0	7.6	8.1
– Rest of Europe						2.6	3.4	1.3	1.0	1.6
Europe former USSR						58.1	65.4	58.6	53.5	50.4
Oceania						0.0	0.1	0.1	0.1	0.1
Other										
Russian Federation						52.4	59.1	53.3	49.3	45.4
Turkmenistan/Turkménistn						14.0	6.4	4.4	9.1	5.6
Germany/Allemagne						4.8	6.1	6.2	6.6	7.6
USA/Etats–Unis d'Amer						2.3	2.0	2.7	3.2	3.8
Belarus/Bélarus						3.0	3.2	3.4	2.2	2.3
Poland/Pologne						0.8	1.1	3.1	2.9	3.2
Italy/Italie						1.0	1.2	1.8	1.9	2.3
Kazakhstan						0.9	1.5	2.1	1.4	2.3
France, Monaco						1.6	0.8	1.3	1.4	1.8
Switzerland,Liechtenst.						2.4	3.1	0.9	0.5	0.9

	1988	1989	1990	1991	1992	1993	1994	1995	1996	1997
Afrique						1.7	0.6	0.8	0.7	3.3
Amériques						3.0	3.5	2.5	3.5	4.6
– Amérique du Nord						2.3	3.5	2.1	2.5	2.2
– ALAI						0.4	0.0	0.2	0.3	1.1
– MCAC						0.0				0.0
– Caraïbes						0.0	0.0	0.3	0.6	1.2
– Autre Amérique						0.2				0.1
Asie anc. URSS exclus						11.9	12.8	17.9	18.0	26.9
– Moyen–Orient						3.9	3.1	6.1	6.9	9.7
Asie ancienne URSS						8.0	4.9	4.1	5.7	5.2
Europe anc. URSS exclus						23.1	20.8	20.4	21.4	24.2
– Union Européenne						10.7	9.5	10.3	10.7	12.4
– Europe de l'Est						8.3	7.5	9.5	9.8	10.2
– Autre de l'Europe						4.1	3.8	0.5	0.9	1.6
Europe ancienne URSS						52.2	52.4	50.4	47.2	35.6
Océanie						0.1				0.1
Autre										
Russian Federation						45.3	39.5	43.4	38.6	26.2
China/Chine						3.5	4.9	5.8	5.4	7.7
Belarus/Bélarus						4.5	5.3	4.2	5.1	5.8
Turkey/Turquie						1.8	1.1	3.5	2.9	4.7
Germany/Allemagne						2.2	2.7	2.6	2.9	4.0
Italy/Italie						1.8	1.9	3.2	2.4	2.8
USA/Etats–Unis d'Amer						2.1	3.5	2.1	2.5	2.1
Hungary/Hongrie						2.3	1.7	2.3	2.6	2.2
Poland/Pologne						1.6	1.5	2.1	2.5	2.7
Republic of Moldova						1.0	4.7	1.2	1.6	2.1

4. General Imports C.I.F. by Commodities according to the S.I.T.C. (Rev. 2) in million U.S. Dollars
Importations Générales C.A.F. par Produits d'après la C.T.C.I. (Rév. 2) en millions de Dollars E.U.

SITC CTCI	COMMODITY	1994		1995		1996		1997		PRODUIT
		QUANTITY QUANTITE	VALUE VALEUR	QUANTITY QUANTITE	VALUE VALEUR	QUANTITY QUANTITE	VALUE VALEUR	QUANTITY QUANTITE	VALUE VALEUR	
	ALL COMMODITIES		10748.0				17623.9		17261.6	TOUS PRODUITS
0	FOOD AND LIVE ANIMALS		156.0							ALIMENTS,ANIMAUX VIVANTS
01	MEAT AND PREPARATIONS						151.0			VIANDES ET PREPARATIONS
06	SUGAR AND PREPS,HONEY						307.0			SUCRES ET PRODUITS
11	BEVERAGES						90.1			BOISSONS
12	TOBACCO AND MANUFACTURES						150.0			TABACS BRUTS FABRIQUES
22	OIL SEEDS,OLEAGINOUS FRT						63.1			GRAINES,FRUITS OLEAGINEUX
24	CORK AND WOOD						123.0			LIEGE ET BOIS
263	COTTON						97.1			COTON
28	METALLIFEROUS ORES,SCRAP						212.0			MINERAIS METAL,DECHETS
3	MINERAL FUELS ETC		5495.8				8376.0			COMBUSTIBLES MINERAUX LUB
5	CHEMCLS,RELATED PROD NES		555.4							PRODUITS CHIMIQUES
51	ORGANIC CHEMICALS						160.0			PROD CHIMIQ ORGANIQUES
52	INORGANIC CHEMICALS						120.0			PROD CHIM INORGANIQUES
541	*MEDICINAL,PHARM PRODUCT						255.0			PROD MEDICINAUX PHARMACEUT
572	*EXPLOSIVES,PYROTECH PRO						289.0			EXPLOSIFS
6	BASIC MANUFACTURES		476.4							ART MANUFACTURES
62	RUBBER MANUFACTURES NES						473.0			CAOUTCHOUC MANUFACTURE
64	PAPER,PAPERBOARD AND MFR						306.0			PAPIERS,CARTONS & OUVRAGES
65	TEXTILE YARN,FABRICS,ETC						137.0			FILS,TISSUS,ARTICLES TEXTILE
67	IRON AND STEEL						281.0			FER ET ACIER
682	COPPER EXC CEMENT COPPER						73.1			CUIVRE
684	ALUMINIUM						93.1			ALUMINIUM
69	METAL MANUFACTURES NES						164.0			ART MANUFACT EN METAL NDA
7	MACHINES,TRANSPORT EQUIP		1828.6				2953.0			MACHINES MATERIEL TRANSPORT
78	ROAD VEHICLES						450.0			VEHICULES ROUTIERS
8	MISC MANUFACTURED GOODS		123.0							ART MANUFACTURES DIVERS
821	*FURNITURE,PARTS THEREOF						101.1			MEUBLES ET PIECES
851	*FOOTWEAR						68.1			CHAUSSURES

5. General Exports F.O.B. by Commodities according to the S.I.T.C. (Rev. 2) in million U.S. Dollars
Exportations Générales F.O.B. par Produits d'après la C.T.C.I. (Rév. 2) en millions de Dollars E.U.

SITC CTCI	COMMODITY	1994		1995		1996		1997		PRODUIT
		QUANTITY QUANTITE	VALUE VALEUR	QUANTITY QUANTITE	VALUE VALEUR	QUANTITY QUANTITE	VALUE VALEUR	QUANTITY QUANTITE	VALUE VALEUR	
	ALL COMMODITIES		10305.0				14331.0		14232.0	TOUS PRODUITS
0	FOOD AND LIVE ANIMALS		422.0							ALIMENTS,ANIMAUX VIVANTS
01	MEAT AND PREPARATIONS						304.0			VIANDES ET PREPARATIONS
02	DAIRY PRODCTS,BIRDS'EGGS						194.0			PRODUITS LAITIERS,OEUFS
04	CEREALS AND PREPARATIONS						594.0			CEREALES ET PRODUITS
06	SUGAR AND PREPS,HONEY						675.0			SUCRES ET PRODUITS
11	BEVERAGES						453.0			BOISSONS
22	OIL SEEDS,OLEAGINOUS FRT						244.0			GRAINES,FRUITS OLEAGINEUX
24	CORK AND WOOD						55.1			LIEGE ET BOIS
28	METALLIFEROUS ORES,SCRAP						495.0			MINERAIS METAL,DECHETS
3	MINERAL FUELS ETC		1015.0				627.0			COMBUSTIBLES MINERAUX LUB
4	ANIMAL,VEGETABLE OIL,FAT		55.7				185.0			HUILES,GRAISSES ANIM,VEG
5	CHEMCLS,RELATED PROD NES		1024.0							PRODUITS CHIMIQUES
51	ORGANIC CHEMICALS						169.0			PROD CHIMIQ ORGANIQUES
52	INORGANIC CHEMICALS						604.0			PROD CHIM INORGANIQUES
541	*MEDICINAL,PHARM PRODUCT						74.1			PROD MEDICINAUX PHARMACEUT
562	*FERTILIZERS,MANUFACTURE						573.0			ENGRAIS MANUFACTURES
572	*EXPLOSIVES,PYROTECH PRO						92.1			EXPLOSIFS
6	BASIC MANUFACTURES		3684.1							ART MANUFACTURES
611	LEATHER						108.1			CUIRS,PEAUX PREPARES
62	RUBBER MANUFACTURES NES						300.0			CAOUTCHOUC MANUFACTURE
64	PAPER,PAPERBOARD AND MFR						101.1			PAPIERS,CARTONS & OUVRAGES
67	IRON AND STEEL						3387.0			FER ET ACIER
682	COPPER EXC CEMENT COPPER						69.1			CUIVRE
684	ALUMINIUM						161.0			ALUMINIUM
69	METAL MANUFACTURES NES						947.0			ART MANUFACT EN METAL NDA
7	MACHINES,TRANSPORT EQUIP		2077.5				1783.0			MACHINES MATERIEL TRANSPORT
78	ROAD VEHICLES						234.0			VEHICULES ROUTIERS
793	SHIPS AND BOATS ETC						139.0			NAVIRES BATEAUX,ETC
8	MISC MANUFACTURED GOODS		155.3							ART MANUFACTURES DIVERS
821	*FURNITURE,PARTS THEREOF						44.1			MEUBLES ET PIECES
84	CLOTHING AND ACCESSORIES						262.0			VETEMENTS
851	*FOOTWEAR						69.1			CHAUSSURES

1. HISTORICAL SERIES, 1959–1996 GENERAL TRADE, IMPORTS C.I.F., EXPORTS F.O.B. # 1
SERIES HISTORIQUES, 1959–1996 COMMERCE GENERAL, IMPORTATIONS C.A.F., EXPORTATIONS F.O.B

YEAR ANNEE	VALUE IN MILLION U.S. DOLLARS / VALEUR EN MILLION U.S. DOLLARS: MERCHANDISE –MARCHANDISE		GOLD –OR		CONVERSION FACTORS FACTEURS DE CONVERSION CENTS E.U. PAR		INDEX NUMBERS –INDICES: QUANTUM		UNIT VALUE VALEUR UNITAIRE	
	IMPORTS	EXPORTS	IMPORTS	EXPORTS	IMPORTS	EXPORTS	IMPORTS	EXPORTS	IMPORTS	EXPORTS
1959	7.00									
1961	15.00									
1962	22.00	10.00								
1963	34.00	32.00								
1964	50.00	120.00								
1966	70.00	243.00								
1967	130.00	260.00								
1968	220.00	338.00								
1969	307.00	428.00								
1970	267.21	550.00								
1971	308.56	971.00								
1972	481.79	1082.00								
1973	823.35	1801.00								
1974	1704.94	6391.61								
1975	2668.56	6969.67								
1976	3326.50	8683.82								
1977	5047.77	9707.15								
1978	5368.40	9154.34								
1979	6960.46	13595.42								
1980	8752.23	20678.13								
1981	9645.68	20239.84								
1982	9439.75	17328.45								
1983	8293.76	15084.96								
1984	6936.39	13826.74								
1985	6548.50	13124.23								
1986	6421.83	15837.06								
1987	7225.68	10341.04								
1988	8521.21	2783.91								
1989	10009.60	15718.59								
1990	11198.63	3945.08								
1991	13745.84	4936.99								
1992	17409.61									
1993	19520.15	20423.00								
1994	23883.00	20906.00								
1995	26967.00	24332.00								
1996	27114.00	21237.00								

2. IMPORTS BY BROAD ECONOMIC CATEGORY AND EXPORTS BY INDUSTRIAL ORIGIN. (PERCENTAGE OF TOTAL VALUE)
IMPORTATIONS PAR CATEGORIES ECONOMIQUES ET EXPORTATIONS PAR BRANCHE D'ACTIVITE.(EN POURCENTAGE DE LA VALEUR TOTALE)

IMPORTS – IMPORTATIONS

	1990	1991	1992	1993	1994	1995	1996
TOTAL IMPORTS–IMPORTATIONS TOTALES							
1 FOOD BEV–ALIMENTATION BOISSONS							
11 PRIMARY–PRODUITS DE BASE							
111 FOR INDUSTRY–POUR L'INDUSTRIE							
112 FOR HOUSEHOLDS–POUR LES MENAGES							
12 PROCESSED–PRODUITS ELABORES							
121 FOR INDUSTRY–POUR L'INDUSTRIE							
122 FOR HOUSEHOLDS–POUR LES MENAGES							
2 IND SUPPLIES–APPROV INDUSTRIELS							
21 PRIMARY–PRODUITS DE BASE							
22 PROCESSED–PRODUITS ELABORES							
3 FUELS–COMBUSTIBLES							
31 PRIMARY–PRODUITS DE BASE							
32 PROCESSED–PRODUITS ELABORES							
321 MOTOR SPIRIT–ESSENCE							
322 OTHER–AUTRES							
4 MACHINERY–EQUIPEMENT							
41 CAPITAL EQUIPMENT–MACHINES							
42 PARTS–PIECES ACCESSOIRES							
5 TRANSPORT–TRANSPORT							
51 PASSENGER CARS–AUTOMOBILES							
52 OTHER–AUTRES							
521 INDUSTRIAL–INDUSTRIELS							
522 NON INDUSTRIAL–NON INDUSTRIEL							
53 PARTS–PIECES ACCESSOIRES							
6 CONSUM GOODS–BIENS CONSOMMATION							
61 DURABLE–DURABLES							
62 SEMI DURABLE–SEMI DURABLES							
63 NON DURABLE–NON DURABLES							
7 GOODS NES–BIENS NDA							

EXPORTS – EXPORTATIONS

	1990	1991	1992	1993	1994	1995	1996
TOTAL EXPORTS–EXPORTATIONS TOTALES							
1 AGRICULTURE							
2 MINING QUARRY–INDUS EXTRACTIVES							
3 MANUFACTURING–IND MANUFACTUR							
31 FOOD BEV TOBACCO–ALIM BOISS TAB							
32 TEXTILES–INDUSTRIES TEXTILES							
33 WOOD & PRODUCTS–BOIS & PRODUITS							
34 PAPER & PRODUCTS–PAPIER & PRODT							
35 CHEMICALS–INDUSTRIES CHIMIQUES							
36 NON METAL MIN–MIN NON METAL							
37 BASIC METAL–IND METAL BASE							
38 METAL MANUF–MANUF METAL							
39 OTH MANUF IND–AUTRES MANUF							

3. TRADE BY PRINCIPAL COUNTRIES OF ORIGIN AND DESTINATION (VALUE IN MILLION U.S. DOLLARS)
ECHANGES SELON LES PRINCIPAUX PAYS D'ORIGINE ET DE DESTINATION (VALEUR EN MILLIONS DE DOLLARS EU)

COUNTRIES–PAYS	GENERAL IMPORTS C.I.F. IMPORTATIONS GENERALES C.A.F				
	1992	1993	1994	1995	1996
World		19250.0	23883.0	26967.0	
Africa					
Americas					
– Northern America					
– LAIA					
– CACM					
– Caribbean					
– Rest of America					
Asia excl fmr USSR					
– Middle East					
Asia former USSR					
Europe excl fmr USSR					
– European Union					
– Eastern Europe					
– Rest of Europe					
Europe former USSR					
Oceania					
Other					
Malaysia/Malaisie		400.0	557.0	756.0	
Saudi Arabia		490.0	476.0	592.0	
Indonesia/Indonésie		390.0	379.0	477.0	
Pakistan		227.0	437.0	390.0	
Iran (Islamic Rep of)		248.0	241.0	286.0	
Turkey/Turquie		150.0	199.0	211.0	
Bahrain/Bahreïn		130.0	140.0	122.0	
Qatar		123.0	119.0	135.0	
Lebanon/Liban		84.0	90.0	76.0	
Jordan/Jordanie		62.0	67.0	69.0	
Egypt/Egypte		58.0	62.0	51.0	
Syrian Arab Republic		35.0	38.0	32.0	
Kuwait/ Koweït		58.0			
Yemen/Yémen		6.0	6.0	21.0	
Somalia/Somalie		8.0	9.0	16.0	
Bangladesh		8.0	12.0	11.0	
Tunisia/Tunisie			5.0	5.0	
Oman		3.0	3.0	1.0	
Morocco/Maroc		2.0	2.0	3.0	
Libyan Arab Jamahiriya		2.0	2.0	2.0	
Azerbaijan/Azerbaïdjan			1.0	2.0	
Mozambique		1.0	1.0		
Sudan/Soudan				2.0	
Kyrgyzstan/Kirghizistan			1.0		
Uganda/Ouganda				1.0	

COUNTRIES–PAYS	GENERAL EXPORTS F.O.B. EXPORTATIONS GENERALES F.O.B.				
	1992	1993	1994	1995	1996
Monde		20423.0	20906.0	24332.0	
Afrique					
Amériques					
– Amérique du Nord					
– ALAI					
– MCAC					
– Caraïbes					
– Autre Amérique					
Asie anc. URSS exclus					
– Moyen–Orient					
Asie ancienne URSS					
Europe anc. URSS exclus					
– Union Européenne					
– Europe de l'Est					
– Autre de l'Europe					
Europe ancienne URSS					
Océanie					
Autre					
Oman		1049.0	1018.0	1088.0	
Iran (Islamic Rep of)		1001.0	972.0	883.0	
Pakistan		296.0	269.0	496.0	
Saudi Arabia		256.0	271.0	332.0	
Yemen/Yémen		29.0	30.0	204.0	
Turkey/Turquie			220.0	38.0	
Qatar		65.0	63.0	109.0	
Morocco/Maroc		104.0	107.0	15.0	
Bahrain/Bahreïn		58.0	59.0	75.0	
Bangladesh		38.0	39.0	72.0	
Kuwait/ Koweït			123.0		
Malaysia/Malaisie		27.0	20.0	33.0	
Mozambique		24.0	25.0	28.0	
Azerbaijan/Azerbaïdjan			8.0	62.0	
Indonesia/Indonésie		8.0	8.0	39.0	
Maldives		10.0	12.0	18.0	
Jordan/Jordanie		8.0	8.0	15.0	
Uganda/Ouganda		8.0	8.0	10.0	
Sudan/Soudan		8.0	8.0	9.0	
Somalia/Somalie		7.0	7.0	8.0	
Syrian Arab Republic		4.0	4.0	14.0	
Egypt/Egypte		4.0	4.0	13.0	
Djibouti		5.0	5.0	6.0	
Tunisia/Tunisie		1.0	1.0	2.0	
Algeria/Algérie		1.0	1.0	1.0	
Brunei Darussalam		1.0	1.0	1.0	
Afghanistan		1.0	1.0	1.0	

(VALUE AS PERCENTAGE OF WORLD TOTAL)(VALEURS EN POURCENTAGE DU TOTAL MONDIAL)

	1987	1988	1989	1990	1991	1992	1993	1994	1995	1996
Africa	0.7	0.8		0.7						
Americas	9.4	11.1		10.5						
– Northern America	8.3	9.7		9.4						
– LAIA	1.0	1.2		1.1						
– CACM	0.1	0.1		0.1						
– Caribbean	0.0	0.0		0.0						
– Rest of America	0.0	0.0		0.0						
Asia excl fmr USSR	49.7	50.9		50.7						
– Middle East	10.0	9.0		10.2						
Asia former USSR										
Europe excl fmr USSR	37.2	34.7		35.4						
– European Union	34.6	32.2		32.3						
– Eastern Europe	0.6	0.8		0.8						
– Rest of Europe	1.9	1.8		2.3						
Europe former USSR	0.0	0.1		0.1						
Oceania	2.9	2.5		2.2						
Other				0.3						
Malaysia/Malaisie	0.8	1.2		1.6			2.1	2.3	2.8	
Saudi Arabia	2.5	2.5		3.6			2.5	2.0	2.2	
Indonesia/Indonésie	0.6	1.1		1.2			2.0	1.6	1.8	
Pakistan	1.1	1.4		1.2			1.2	1.8	1.4	
Iran (Islamic Rep of)	2.0	1.5		1.5			1.3	1.0	1.1	
Turkey/Turquie	0.8	1.0		0.8			0.8	0.8	0.8	
Bahrain/Bahreïn	1.6	0.9		1.1			0.7	0.6	0.5	
Qatar	0.7	0.5		1.1			0.6	0.5	0.5	
Lebanon/Liban	0.8	0.8		0.5			0.4	0.4	0.3	
Areas n.e.s.				0.3						

	1987	1988	1989	1990	1991	1992	1993	1994	1995	1996
Afrique										
Amériques										
– Amérique du Nord										
– ALAI										
– MCAC										
– Caraïbes										
– Autre Amérique										
Asie anc. URSS exclus										
– Moyen–Orient										
Asie ancienne URSS										
Europe anc. URSS exclus										
– Union Européenne										
– Europe de l'Est										
– Autre de l'Europe										
Europe ancienne URSS										
Océanie										
Autre										
Oman							5.1	4.9	4.5	
Iran (Islamic Rep of)							4.9	4.6	3.6	
Pakistan							1.4	1.3	2.0	
Saudi Arabia							1.3	1.3	1.4	
Yemen/Yémen							0.1	0.1	0.8	
Turkey/Turquie								1.1	0.2	
Qatar							0.3	0.3	0.4	
Morocco/Maroc							0.5	0.5	0.1	
Bahrain/Bahreïn							0.3	0.3	0.3	
Areas n.e.s.										

4. General Imports C.I.F. by Commodities according to the S.I.T.C. (Rev. 2) in million U.S. Dollars
Importations Générales C.A.F. par Produits d'après la C.T.C.I. (Rév. 2) en millions de Dollars E.U.

SITC CTCI	COMMODITY	1993		1994		1995		1996		PRODUIT
		QUANTITY QUANTITE	VALUE VALEUR	QUANTITY QUANTITE	VALUE VALEUR	QUANTITY QUANTITE	VALUE VALEUR	QUANTITY QUANTITE	VALUE VALEUR	
	ALL COMMODITIES									TOUS PRODUITS

5. General Exports F.O.B. by Commodities according to the S.I.T.C. (Rev. 2) in million U.S. Dollars
Exportations Générales F.O.B. par Produits d'après la C.T.C.I. (Rév. 2) en millions de Dollars E.U.

SITC CTCI	COMMODITY	1993 QUANTITY QUANTITE	1993 VALUE VALEUR	1994 QUANTITY QUANTITE	1994 VALUE VALEUR	1995 QUANTITY QUANTITE	1995 VALUE VALEUR	1996 QUANTITY QUANTITE	1996 VALUE VALEUR	PRODUIT
	ALL COMMODITIES		20423.0		20906.0		24332.0		21237.0	TOUS PRODUITS
333	CRUDE PETROLEUM	M	10735.5	M	10518.1	M	11312.3	M	13176.9	HUILES BRUTES DE PETROLE
334	PETROLEUM PRODUCTS,REFIN		1590.9		1541.2		2809.2		2838.4	PRODUITS RAFFINES
341	*GAS,NATURAL AND MANUFCT		597.9		679.0		1262.5	M	1549.2	GAZ NATUREL,GAZ MANUFACT

FOOT NOTES – NOTES

TABLE 1 –
1 Excludes exports of most crude petroleum in 1988, 1990 an d 1991.
TABLEAU 1 –
1 Les exportations des huiles brutes de pétrole son t exclus pour les années 1988, 1990 et 1991.

1. HISTORICAL SERIES, 1962–1997 GENERAL TRADE, IMPORTS C.I.F., EXPORTS F.O.B.
SERIES HISTORIQUES, 1962–1997 COMMERCE GENERAL, IMPORTATIONS C.A.F., EXPORTATIONS F.O.B

YEAR ANNEE	VALUE IN MILLION POUNDS STERLING VALEUR EN MILLION POUNDS STERLING MERCHANDISE –MARCHANDISE IMPORTS	EXPORTS	GOLD –OR IMPORTS	EXPORTS	CONVERSION FACTORS U.S. CENTS PER POUND STERLING FACTEURS DE CONVERSION CENTS E.U. PAR POUND STERLING IMPORTS	EXPORTS	INDEX NUMBERS –INDICES QUANTUM IMPORTS	EXPORTS	UNIT VALUE VALEUR UNITAIRE IMPORTS	EXPORTS
1962	4628.00	4062.00	434.60	372.50	280.0000	280.0000				
1963	4983.00	4365.00	436.30	251.20	280.0000	280.0000				
1964	5659.00	4565.00	520.30	256.90	280.0000	280.0000				
1965	5751.00	4901.00	504.90	993.50	280.0000	280.0000				
1966	5947.00	5241.00	337.50	485.40	280.0000	280.0000				
1967	6434.00	5214.00	444.50	821.80	275.0000	275.8000				
1968	7890.00	6402.00	672.20	836.90	240.0000	240.0000				
1969	8315.00	7298.00	222.00	196.00	240.0000	240.0000				
1970	9040.00	8076.00	448.30	288.20	240.0000	240.0000				
1971	9821.00	9187.00	485.70	341.00	243.4790	243.6190				
1972	11143.00	9759.00	317.50	321.00	249.7390	249.7950				
1973	15852.00	12505.00	482.40	673.00	245.0120	245.1590				
1974	23234.00	16600.00	645.40	1558.00	234.2090	234.2540				
1975	24046.00	19607.00			221.6850	221.4390				
1976	31084.00	25277.00			179.3690	179.5010				
1977	36219.00	31990.00			174.4810	174.6370				
1978	39533.00	35380.00			191.8700	191.9490				
1979	46925.00	40637.00			212.4490	212.6690				
1980	49773.00	47357.00			232.1860	232.5720	55	67	64	65
1981	51168.60	50998.10			200.7584	201.6149	53	66	69	71
1982	56978.20	55557.80			174.9931	174.7287	56	68	75	76
1983	66101.10	60684.30			151.6394	151.5036	61	70	82	82
1984	78967.40	70488.30			134.1827	134.0828	68	75	89	88
1985	84789.60	85027.00			128.8708	129.3632	70	80	93	93
1986	86176.00	72988.00			146.6377	146.5649	75	83	89	86
1987	94026.00	79849.01			164.2177	164.3225	80	87	91	89
1988	106571.00	81655.01			178.0212	178.1671	92	88	94	93
1989	121699.00	93771.01			163.6989	163.4824	100	94	98	97
1990	126086.00	103692.00			178.0931	178.7275	100	100	100	100
1991	118786.00	104877.00			176.6736	176.6890	95	101	101	101
1992	125867.00	108508.00			176.0892	175.6021	101	103	102	103
1993	137404.00	120936.00			150.1562	150.1285	101	103	112	116
1994	147564.00	133030.00			153.2705	153.3559	108	116	115	118
1995	168055.00	153353.00			157.8776	157.8292	112	125	127	126
1996	184113.00	167764.00			156.1388	156.2493	124	136	127	128
1997	187135.00	171594.00			163.8195	163.8048	133	145	120	121

2. IMPORTS BY BROAD ECONOMIC CATEGORY AND EXPORTS BY INDUSTRIAL ORIGIN. (PERCENTAGE OF TOTAL VALUE)
IMPORTATIONS PAR CATEGORIES ECONOMIQUES ET EXPORTATIONS PAR BRANCHE D'ACTIVITE.(EN POURCENTAGE DE LA VALEUR TOTALE)

IMPORTS – IMPORTATIONS

	1991	1992	1993	1994	1995	1996	1997
TOTAL IMPORTS–IMPORTATIONS TOTALES	100.	100.	100.	100.	100.	100.	100.
1 FOOD BEV–ALIMENTATION BOISSONS	9.6	9.9	9.5	9.2	9.0	8.9	8.4
11 PRIMARY–PRODUITS DE BASE	3.7	3.8	3.7	3.6	3.5	3.4	3.3
111 FOR INDUSTRY–POUR L'INDUSTRIE	0.6	0.7	0.7	0.7	0.6	0.6	0.6
112 FOR HOUSEHOLDS–POUR LES MENAGES	3.1	3.1	2.9	2.8	2.8	2.8	2.7
12 PROCESSED–PRODUITS ELABORES	5.9	6.1	5.9	5.6	5.5	5.5	5.2
121 FOR INDUSTRY–POUR L'INDUSTRIE	0.9	0.9	0.9	0.9	0.9	0.9	0.8
122 FOR HOUSEHOLDS–POUR LES MENAGES	5.0	5.2	4.9	4.7	4.6	4.6	4.4
2 IND SUPPLIES–APPROV INDUSTRIELS	28.9	27.8	26.5	27.8	29.0	27.3	25.8
21 PRIMARY–PRODUITS DE BASE	4.2	3.8	4.3	4.0	4.0	4.0	3.8
22 PROCESSED–PRODUITS ELABORES	24.7	23.9	22.2	23.8	25.0	23.3	22.0
3 FUELS–COMBUSTIBLES	6.3	5.5	5.3	4.0	3.5	3.8	3.5
31 PRIMARY–PRODUITS DE BASE	4.4	4.0	3.9	2.7	2.4	2.7	2.4
32 PROCESSED–PRODUITS ELABORES	1.9	1.5	1.4	1.3	1.1	1.1	1.1
321 MOTOR SPIRIT–ESSENCE	0.5	0.3	0.3	0.3	0.2	0.2	0.2
322 OTHER–AUTRES	1.4	1.2	1.1	1.1	0.9	0.9	0.9
4 MACHINERY–EQUIPEMENT	22.6	23.2	24.5	24.7	26.1	26.6	26.8
41 CAPITAL EQUIPMENT–MACHINES	16.4	16.8	18.0	17.9	18.8	18.6	19.5
42 PARTS–PIECES ACCESSOIRES	6.2	6.4	6.5	6.8	7.3	8.0	7.3
5 TRANSPORT–TRANSPORT	13.8	15.0	16.0	16.6	15.6	16.3	17.8
51 PASSENGER CARS–AUTOMOBILES	4.6	5.3	6.2	6.2	5.9	6.2	7.3
52 OTHER–AUTRES	2.1	1.9	2.3	2.9	2.0	2.1	4.2
521 INDUSTRIAL–INDUSTRIELS	1.9	1.8	2.1	2.8	1.8	1.9	4.0
522 NON INDUSTRIAL–NON INDUSTRIEL	0.2	0.2	0.2	0.2	0.2	0.2	0.2
53 PARTS–PIECES ACCESSOIRES	7.1	7.8	7.6	7.5	7.6	8.0	6.3
6 CONSUM GOODS–BIENS CONSOMMATION	16.6	17.2	17.1	16.9	15.9	15.9	16.7
61 DURABLE–DURABLES	5.2	5.2	5.0	5.2	4.5	4.5	4.7
62 SEMI DURABLE–SEMI DURABLES	8.4	8.9	8.9	8.4	8.0	8.2	8.6
63 NON DURABLE–NON DURABLES	3.0	3.1	3.2	3.3	3.4	3.2	3.4
7 GOODS NES–BIENS NDA	1.6	1.5	1.0	0.8	1.0	1.1	1.0

EXPORTS – EXPORTATIONS

	1991	1992	1993	1994	1995	1996	1997
TOTAL EXPORTS–EXPORTATIONS TOTALES	100.	100.	100.	100.	100.	100.	100.
1 AGRICULTURE	1.9	2.1	1.6	1.5	1.5	1.4	1.2
2 MINING QUARRY–INDUS EXTRACTIVES	6.7	6.3	6.1	7.3	6.8	7.2	6.3
3 MANUFACTURING–IND MANUFACTUR	91.2	91.6	92.4	91.3	91.7	91.4	92.4
31 FOOD BEV TOBACCO–ALIM BOISS TAB	5.9	6.5	6.4	6.4	6.3	5.8	5.7
32 TEXTILES–INDUSTRIES TEXTILES	4.8	4.9	4.9	4.9	4.7	4.8	4.5
33 WOOD & PRODUCTS–BOIS & PRODUITS	0.2	0.2	0.1	0.2	0.2	0.2	0.3
34 PAPER & PRODUCTS–PAPIER & PRODT	2.8	2.9	3.0	2.9	2.9	2.7	2.6
35 CHEMICALS–INDUSTRIES CHIMIQUES	18.1	18.6	19.7	18.7	18.0	17.7	17.3
36 NON METAL MIN–MIN NON METAL	1.3	1.3	1.3	1.2	1.3	1.2	1.2
37 BASIC METAL–IND METAL BASE	5.0	4.6	4.5	4.6	4.9	4.3	3.9
38 METAL MANUF–MANUF METAL	49.1	48.4	49.0	48.9	50.3	51.8	53.9
39 OTH MANUF IND–AUTRES MANUF	4.1	4.3	3.4	3.5	3.1	2.9	3.1

3. TRADE BY PRINCIPAL COUNTRIES OF CONSIGNMENT AND DESTINATION (VALUE IN MILLION U.S. DOLLARS)
ECHANGES SELON LES PRINCIPAUX PAYS DE CONSIGNATION ET DE DESTINATION (VALEUR EN MILLIONS DE DOLLARS EU)

COUNTRIES–PAYS	GENERAL IMPORTS C.I.F. IMPORTATIONS GENERALES C.A.F				
	1993	1994	1995	1996	1997
World	211726.2	224551.9	262572.1	283851.0	305135.4
Africa	4692.1	4733.4	5516.5	6084.5	6292.3
Americas	33841.8	34349.4	40832.3	45447.8	51003.1
– Northern America	29651.2	30200.1	35906.2	39993.0	45443.1
– LAIA	3185.3	3153.9	3850.2	4175.1	4297.1
– CACM	131.1	188.6	194.5	211.7	244.1
– Caribbean	641.5	585.7	643.4	801.2	768.3
– Rest of America	232.8	221.1	237.9	266.9	250.5
Asia excl fmr USSR	41978.8	40822.4	47533.4	53259.1	58685.8
– Middle East	4828.8	3581.8	3907.6	4335.0	5167.4
Asia former USSR	96.8	121.6	94.2	84.4	74.3
Europe excl fmr USSR	126037.5	139233.1	162673.8	171935.8	181256.9
– European Union	109202.9	123305.8	144117.7	151892.9	160922.9
– Eastern Europe	1648.9	2048.4	2671.4	2747.4	3184.4
– Rest of Europe	15185.7	13878.9	15884.7	17295.5	17149.6
Europe former USSR	1733.8	1950.1	2313.8	3042.6	3573.2
Oceania	2655.5	2696.0	2979.5	3348.9	3471.5
Other	690.0	645.8	628.6	648.0	778.2
Germany/Allemagne	28972.9	32773.4	40247.3	40827.6	41151.0
USA/Etats–Unis d'Amer	26638.9	27290.2	32129.4	36088.8	41156.5
France, Monaco	19626.9	22612.1	25038.9	26533.2	28331.0
Netherlands/Pays–Bas	12712.4	14981.4	17628.9	18744.7	19932.4
Japan/Japon	13810.3	13551.5	15178.0	14041.6	15415.3
Italy/Italie	9798.7	11012.2	12982.7	14606.5	15622.3
Belgium–Luxembourg	9508.1	10592.2	12338.2	12906.2	14565.9
Ireland/Irlande	7955.8	8677.1	10800.8	10962.1	11885.4
Switzerland,Liechtenst.	7639.4	7383.3	8142.5	8488.3	8061.0
Norway,Svalbard and JM	6746.9	5685.8	6828.9	7781.5	8071.9
Sweden/Suède	5860.9	6375.9	6780.5	7151.5	7615.5
Spain/Espagne	4758.9	5582.0	6858.3	7771.3	8199.4
China, Hong Kong SAR	4850.0	4720.1	5587.0	6358.6	7124.3
Finland/Finlande	3081.5	3453.6	3717.7	3890.4	4065.0
Canada	3000.0	2882.9	3756.9	3878.0	4183.8
Singapore/Singapour	2613.2	2907.4	3482.4	4016.3	4445.5
Denmark/Danemark	3083.5	3230.7	3398.9	3620.1	3803.8
China/Chine	2147.1	2516.4	3059.4	3437.8	4087.3
Other Asia n.e.s.	2616.8	2423.0	2726.2	3260.5	3836.3
Malaysia/Malaisie	2259.2	1845.4	2349.0	3715.8	3318.1
Korea, Republic of	1743.6	1680.2	2465.6	3182.3	3667.3
Portugal	1792.4	1921.5	2269.2	2531.6	2861.3
India/Inde	1761.6	1975.6	2266.3	2515.0	2657.7
So. African Customs Un	1767.8	1625.7	1900.0	2083.6	2554.6
Australia/Australie	1611.6	1629.7	1753.1	2023.3	2246.4
Austria/Autriche	1571.1	1560.1	1397.1	1749.6	2252.7
Russian Federation	1330.1	1233.5	1524.9	1990.2	2419.2
Thailand/Thaïlande	1246.8	1399.6	1641.7	1854.5	2002.1
Brazil/Brésil	1461.8	1409.1	1557.5	1534.7	1564.4
Saudi Arabia	2061.9	1133.6	1137.9	1174.9	1633.1
Indonesia/Indonésie	1133.4	1199.4	1427.0	1531.0	1685.6
Turkey/Turquie	860.7	962.7	1254.9	1456.4	1709.3
Israel/Israël	890.1	877.3	1092.8	1298.7	1441.5
Poland/Pologne	726.9	835.2	1007.4	936.5	1017.6
New Zealand	803.0	826.8	910.2	986.6	946.4
Philippines	447.9	374.5	556.4	1398.0	1247.0
Areas n.e.s.	690.0	645.8	628.6	648.0	778.2
Greece/Grèce	479.9	533.8	659.4	598.3	637.1
Pakistan	524.7	550.1	573.2	610.3	621.1
Czech Republic	396.8	426.6	507.6	582.0	762.5

COUNTRIES–PAYS	GENERAL EXPORTS F.O.B. EXPORTATIONS GENERALES F.O.B.				
	1993	1994	1995	1996	1997
Monde	171699.8	202857.9	239948.0	259277.0	278906.9
Afrique	5909.7	6214.0	7478.1	7841.7	8110.6
Amériques	29454.4	33432.4	36360.0	39237.3	44456.9
– Amérique du Nord	26150.1	29464.0	31962.9	34594.0	38632.1
– ALAI	2363.2	2976.7	3047.0	3525.4	4614.8
– MCAC	117.2	123.7	157.8	157.7	183.1
– Caraïbes	635.2	694.2	966.5	736.5	782.2
– Autre Amérique	188.7	173.8	225.9	223.7	244.7
Asie anc. URSS exclus	29927.0	32535.7	38796.3	43579.7	49040.9
– Moyen–Orient	9427.3	8231.8	10059.3	12463.8	16207.4
Asie ancienne URSS	123.9	137.9	113.7	192.2	385.0
Europe anc. URSS exclus	101605.7	124729.6	150423.6	160664.0	168389.3
– Union Européenne	92845.7	114388.9	138047.5	146654.8	152893.5
– Europe de l'Est	2109.6	2453.4	3430.9	4418.9	4800.5
– Autre de l'Europe	6650.5	7887.3	8945.3	9590.3	10695.3
Europe ancienne URSS	1013.9	1344.5	1776.3	2187.1	2774.6
Océanie	2982.3	3635.1	4123.2	4675.3	4824.7
Autre	682.9	828.6	876.8	899.7	925.0
USA/Etats–Unis d'Amer	23342.0	26486.3	29071.8	31472.7	35007.6
Germany/Allemagne	21944.7	25810.7	31141.1	31573.9	32585.7
France, Monaco	16540.9	20139.7	23390.2	25904.4	26285.8
Netherlands/Pays–Bas	11377.2	14296.9	18867.5	20308.6	22000.2
Ireland/Irlande	8692.0	10660.8	12564.0	13974.9	15607.0
Belgium–Luxembourg	7139.7	10909.0	12744.8	12916.5	13342.6
Italy/Italie	8306.3	10160.4	12009.9	12240.5	13037.6
Spain/Espagne	6164.5	7708.8	9636.3	10470.3	10700.1
Sweden/Suède	4341.9	5134.4	6148.2	6738.0	7059.2
Japan/Japon	3983.8	4587.1	5970.6	6661.0	6843.1
Switzerland,Liechtenst.	3413.1	3766.2	4355.0	5029.7	4945.8
China, Hong Kong SAR	3258.0	3523.4	4192.9	4567.2	5259.5
Saudi Arabia	2741.5	2323.7	2595.3	3879.1	6225.3
Australia/Australie	2399.6	2935.9	3348.1	3852.0	4021.4
Norway,Svalbard and JM	2281.2	3099.1	3154.8	3228.9	4350.6
Canada	2768.1	2939.3	2859.8	3084.8	3531.6
Denmark/Danemark	2196.7	2716.5	3324.2	3437.7	3400.9
Singapore/Singapour	2146.3	2712.2	3264.8	3350.6	3346.5
So. African Customs Un	1734.0	2211.1	2946.0	2991.9	2730.5
India/Inde	1696.4	2011.3	2655.8	2666.2	2580.6
Finland/Finlande	1696.0	1989.4	2574.1	2761.6	2503.3
Portugal	1831.5	1881.4	2294.8	2576.4	2812.1
United Arab Emirates	1973.6	1707.7	1868.9	2178.0	2533.6
Turkey/Turquie	1571.1	1247.6	1827.3	2446.4	2894.4
Malaysia/Malaisie	1448.7	2001.6	1877.5	1812.3	1974.5
Israel/Israël	1315.6	1582.1	1749.5	1977.5	1930.7
Korea, Republic of	1195.6	1489.1	1820.0	2036.5	2003.8
Austria/Autriche	1368.7	1587.1	1686.1	1937.5	1820.2
Poland/Pologne	1077.6	1077.6	1491.0	2110.6	2218.6
Greece/Grèce	1245.4	1393.8	1666.2	1814.5	1738.7
Russian Federation	828.5	1085.1	1373.7	1576.7	2019.0
Other Asia n.e.s.	1002.5	1127.6	1518.2	1470.5	1693.2
Thailand/Thaïlande	989.9	1143.4	1320.4	1521.8	1411.6
China/Chine	1110.2	1295.6	1301.2	1153.8	1507.4
Brazil/Brésil	623.1	805.5	1064.6	1322.5	1683.9
Indonesia/Indonésie	497.1	561.3	829.4	1294.0	1149.1
Areas n.e.s.	682.9	828.6	876.8	899.7	925.0
Czech Republic	431.7	574.2	896.4	1116.4	1162.6
Nigeria/Nigéria	952.8	702.2	681.1	676.4	698.2
Kuwait/ Koweït	467.9	478.5	869.4	904.7	824.8

(VALUE AS PERCENTAGE OF WORLD TOTAL)(VALEURS EN POURCENTAGE DU TOTAL MONDIAL)

	1988	1989	1990	1991	1992	1993	1994	1995	1996	1997
Africa	2.2	2.1	2.4	2.3	2.1	2.2	2.1	2.1	2.1	2.1
Americas	13.9	14.9	15.0	15.1	14.4	16.0	15.3	15.6	16.0	16.7
– Northern America	12.1	13.1	13.3	13.3	12.5	14.0	13.4	13.7	14.1	14.9
– LAIA	1.3	1.4	1.3	1.3	1.4	1.5	1.4	1.5	1.5	1.4
– CACM	0.0	0.0	0.1	0.0	0.0	0.1	0.1	0.1	0.1	0.1
– Caribbean	0.3	0.3	0.4	0.3	0.3	0.3	0.3	0.2	0.3	0.3
– Rest of America	0.1	0.1	0.1	0.1	0.1	0.1	0.1	0.1	0.1	0.1
Asia excl fmr USSR	15.4	15.2	14.8	16.1	16.9	19.8	18.2	18.1	18.8	19.2
– Middle East	1.8	1.7	1.9	1.8	2.0	2.3	1.6	1.5	1.5	1.7
Asia former USSR						0.0	0.1	0.0	0.0	0.0
Europe excl fmr USSR	65.9	65.3	65.1	64.0	64.1	59.5	62.0	62.0	60.6	59.4
– European Union	58.1	57.8	57.4	56.4	56.9	51.6	54.9	54.9	53.5	52.7
– Eastern Europe	0.8	0.8	0.6	0.5	0.6	0.8	0.9	1.0	1.0	1.0
– Rest of Europe	7.0	6.8	7.1	7.1	6.6	7.2	6.2	6.0	6.1	5.6
Europe former USSR	0.7	0.7	0.7	0.8	0.6	0.8	0.9	0.9	1.1	1.2
Oceania	1.2	1.2	1.3	1.2	1.3	1.3	1.2	1.1	1.2	1.1
Other	0.6	0.6	0.6	0.6	0.6	0.3	0.3	0.2	0.2	0.3
Germany/Allemagne				14.9	15.1	13.7	14.6	15.3	14.4	13.5
USA/Etats–Unis d'Amer	10.2	11.2	11.5	11.6	11.0	12.6	12.2	12.2	12.7	13.5
France, Monaco	8.8	8.9	9.4	9.3	9.7	9.3	10.1	9.5	9.3	9.3
Netherlands/Pays–Bas	7.8	7.9	8.3	8.4	7.9	6.0	6.7	6.7	6.6	6.5
Japan/Japon	6.1	5.8	5.4	5.7	5.9	6.5	6.0	5.8	4.9	5.1
Italy/Italie	5.5	5.5	5.3	5.4	5.4	4.6	4.9	4.9	5.1	5.1
Belgium–Luxembourg	4.7	4.7	4.5	4.6	4.6	4.5	4.7	4.7	4.5	4.8
Ireland/Irlande	3.6	3.5	3.6	3.7	4.0	3.8	3.9	4.1	3.9	3.9
Switzerland,Liechtenst.	3.7	3.4	3.4	3.2	3.1	3.6	3.3	3.1	3.0	2.6
Norway,Svalbard and JM	2.9	3.0	3.3	3.6	3.1	3.2	2.5	2.6	2.7	2.6

	1988	1989	1990	1991	1992	1993	1994	1995	1996	1997
Afrique	4.1	3.6	3.6	3.5	3.3	3.4	3.1	3.1	3.0	2.9
Amériques	17.4	17.1	16.1	14.2	14.5	17.2	16.5	15.2	15.1	15.9
– Amérique du Nord	15.7	15.5	14.5	12.5	12.9	15.2	14.5	13.3	13.3	13.9
– ALAI	1.2	1.0	1.1	1.1	1.1	1.4	1.5	1.3	1.4	1.7
– MCAC	0.1	0.1	0.1	0.1	0.1	0.1	0.1	0.1	0.1	0.1
– Caraïbes	0.4	0.4	0.4	0.4	0.3	0.4	0.3	0.4	0.3	0.3
– Autre Amérique	0.1	0.1	0.1	0.1	0.1	0.1	0.1	0.1	0.1	0.1
Asie anc. URSS exclus	15.2	15.6	14.8	14.6	14.8	17.4	16.0	16.2	16.8	17.6
– Moyen–Orient	5.6	5.7	4.9	5.2	5.1	5.5	4.1	4.2	4.8	5.8
Asie ancienne URSS						0.1	0.1	0.0	0.1	0.1
Europe anc. URSS exclus	59.6	59.7	62.1	65.1	64.4	59.2	61.5	62.7	62.0	60.4
– Union Européenne	54.6	54.9	57.3	60.6	60.0	54.1	56.4	57.5	56.6	54.8
– Europe de l'Est	0.8	0.7	0.6	0.7	1.0	1.2	1.2	1.4	1.7	1.7
– Autre de l'Europe	4.2	4.1	4.1	3.8	3.5	3.9	3.9	3.7	3.7	3.8
Europe ancienne URSS	0.6	0.7	0.6	0.3	0.4	0.6	0.7	0.7	0.8	1.0
Océanie	2.1	2.3	2.0	1.6	1.6	1.7	1.8	1.7	1.8	1.7
Autre	0.9	1.0	0.8	0.7	0.9	0.4	0.4	0.4	0.3	0.3
USA/Etats–Unis d'Amer	13.2	13.1	12.6	10.9	11.4	13.6	13.1	12.1	12.1	12.6
Germany/Allemagne				14.0	14.0	12.8	12.7	13.0	12.2	11.7
France, Monaco	10.1	10.2	10.5	11.1	10.6	9.6	9.9	9.7	10.0	9.4
Netherlands/Pays–Bas	6.8	7.1	7.3	7.9	7.8	6.6	7.0	7.9	7.8	7.9
Ireland/Irlande	5.0	5.0	5.1	5.1	5.3	5.1	5.3	5.2	5.4	5.6
Belgium–Luxembourg	5.2	5.2	5.5	5.6	5.3	4.2	5.4	5.3	5.0	4.8
Italy/Italie	5.0	4.9	5.4	5.9	5.7	4.8	5.0	5.0	4.7	4.7
Spain/Espagne	3.4	3.4	3.6	4.2	4.2	3.6	3.8	4.0	4.0	3.8
Sweden/Suède	2.7	2.6	2.6	2.4	2.2	2.5	2.5	2.6	2.6	2.5
Japan/Japon	2.1	2.5	2.5	2.2	2.1	2.3	2.3	2.5	2.6	2.5

4. General Imports C.I.F. by Commodities according to the S.I.T.C. (Rev. 2) in million U.S. Dollars
Importations Générales C.A.F. par Produits d'après la C.T.C.I. (Rév. 2) en millions de Dollars E.U.

SITC CTCI	COMMODITY	1994 QUANTITY QUANTITE	1994 VALUE VALEUR	1995 QUANTITY QUANTITE	1995 VALUE VALEUR	1996 QUANTITY QUANTITE	1996 VALUE VALEUR	1997 QUANTITY QUANTITE	1997 VALUE VALEUR	PRODUIT
	ALL COMMODITIES		224552.0		262572.1		283851.3		305135.5	TOUS PRODUITS
0	FOOD AND LIVE ANIMALS		18381.0		20975.7		22321.2		22308.6	ALIMENTS,ANIMAUX VIVANTS
01	MEAT AND PREPARATIONS		2889.3		3618.9		3939.1		3680.1	VIANDES ET PREPARATIONS
011	MEAT FRESH,CHILLD,FROZEN	W 571132	1551.9	W 665635	1889.6	W 691035	2110.8	W 692247	2069.4	VIANDES FRAICHES,REF,CONGE
012	MEAT DRIED,SALTED,SMOKED		631.0	W 229378	851.5	W 262780	1062.2	W 236013	834.8	VIANDE,ABATS SALES,SECHES
0121	PIG MEAT DRIED,SLTD,SMKD		625.9	W 228694	847.9	W 262417	1060.2	W 235847	833.5	LARD,JAMBONS
014	MEAT PREPD,PRSVD,NES ETC	W 224409	706.4	W 258610	877.8	W 229868	766.1	W 238845	776.0	CONSERVES DE VIANDES
02	DAIRY PRODCTS,BIRDS'EGGS		1514.7		1588.7		1710.4		1675.1	PRODUITS LAITIERS,OEUFS
024	CHEESE AND CURD	W 210361	812.2	W 209655	841.8	W 310656	983.4	W 231921	936.5	FROMAGE ET CAILLEBOTTE
03	FISH AND PREPARATIONS		1550.7		1775.2		1901.1		1915.5	POISSONS ET PREPARATIONS
037	FISH ETC PREPD,PRSVD NES	W 151833	629.8	W 178488	793.6	W 193871	851.3	W 196102	837.6	POIS,CRUST,MOL PREPARES
04	CEREALS AND PREPARATIONS		1751.9		1849.7		2025.1		2103.8	CEREALES ET PRODUITS
048	CEREAL ETC PREPARATIONS	W 460610	865.4	W 508465	978.0	W 531962	1125.5	W 639231	1184.5	PREPTNS A BASE CEREALES
05	VEGETABLES AND FRUIT		5086.0		6083.0		6489.5		6482.5	LEGUMES ET FRUITS
054	VEG ETC FRSH,SMPLY PRSVD	W 2371968	1771.6	W 2973950	2214.5	W 2511957	2218.8	W 2494215	2315.0	LEGUMES FRAIS,CONG,SECS
0545	OTHER FRESH VEGETABLES	W 746942	760.7	W 840778	927.8	W 871629	986.4	W 905636	1131.2	AUTRES LEGUMES FRAIS,REF
05459	FRESH VEGETABLES NES	W 514297	659.2	W 577267	800.1	W 653648	894.8	W 690502	1012.1	LEGUMES FRAIS,REFRI NDA
057	FRUIT,NUTS,FRESH,DRIED	W 2556733	2260.0	W 2641393	2515.1	W 2773690	2812.6	W 2802230	2871.8	FRUITS FRAIS OU SECS
058	FRUIT PRESERVED,PREPARED	W 651892	772.4	W 707696	933.8	W 750074	1017.7	W 719737	906.4	CONSERVES DE FRUITS
06	SUGAR AND PREPS,HONEY		1214.2		1309.1		1355.1		1287.6	SUCRES ET PRODUITS
061	SUGAR AND HONEY		1060.7		1158.6	W 2340911	1202.7	W 2228988	1107.2	SUCRES ET MIEL
0611	RAW BEET AND CANE SUGAR	W 1232162	777.1	W 1203783	840.7	W 1232829	856.2	W 1243954	791.9	SUCRES BRUTS
07	COFFEE,TEA,COCOA,SPICES		1858.8		1986.4		1976.8		2043.9	CAFE,THE,CACAO,EPICES
081	*FEEDING STUFF FOR ANIML		1180.2	W 5293894	1255.2	W 4956126	1335.2	W 4274473	1331.6	NOURRITURE POUR ANIMAUX
09	MISC EDIBLE PRODUCTS		1141.2		1268.9		1280.3		1448.1	PREP ALIMENTAIRES DIVERSES
098	EDIBLE PRODCTS,PREPS NES	W 345808	1052.5	W 412157	1173.7	W 337559	1179.2	W 397068	1348.3	PREP ALIMENTAIRES NDA
09809	MISC FOOD PREPRTIONS NES	W 217394	777.1	W 294960	899.9	W 218492	927.3	W 233223	1005.3	PREP ALIMENTAIRES NDA
1	BEVERAGES AND TOBACCO		3357.0		3854.2		4455.2		4849.4	BOISSONS ET TABACS
11	BEVERAGES		2776.0		3097.0		3482.5		3913.1	BOISSONS
112	ALCOHOLIC BEVERAGES	W 1598057	2598.3	W 1545404	2860.7	W 1683598	3264.2	W 1775798	3680.5	BOISSONS ALCOOLIQUES
1121	WINE OF FRESH GRAPES ETC	W 905530	1773.4	W 873062	1970.0	W 950170	2296.2	W 1011774	2659.2	VINS DE RAISINS FRAIS
11212	WINE OF FRESH GRAPES	W 849998	1718.6	W 798757	1887.9	W 879619	2201.3	W 961816	2581.8	VINS DE MOUTS DE RAISINS
12	TOBACCO AND MANUFACTURES		581.1		757.2		972.8		936.3	TABACS BRUTS FABRIQUES
2	CRUDE MATERLS,EXCL FUELS		8398.8		9799.1		9611.7		9948.7	MAT BRUTES NON COMESTIBLES
24	CORK AND WOOD		2136.0		1864.6		1897.7		2152.4	LIEGE ET BOIS
248	WOOD SHAPED,SLEEPERS	W 4415847	2011.8	W 3116420	1691.3	W 3358647	1707.6	W 4011121	1992.3	BOIS SIMPLEMENT TRAVAILLES
2482	LUMBER SHAPED CONIFER	W 3992707	1617.1	W 2752534	1307.4	W 2935929	1325.0	W 3566665	1571.2	CONIFERES SCIES,RABOTES
24821	LUMBER SAWN ETC CONIFER	W 3942351	1576.0	W 2726268	1275.3	W 2907986	1284.1	W 3525041	1508.0	CONIFERES SCIES LONGITUD
251	*PULP AND WASTE PAPER		978.4		1655.2		1091.9	W 1967023	1020.5	PATES A PAPIER,DECHETS
2517	SODA,SULPHATE WOOD PULP	W 1503144	728.0	W 1536836	1243.7	W 1460455	817.2	W 1513147	776.0	PATES CHIMIQUES AU SULFATE
25172	— BLEACHED,NONDISSOLVNG	W 1442695	696.8	W 1453236	1175.4	W 1363098	766.0	W 1427603	732.5	PATES BLANCHIES
26	TEXTILE FIBRES AND WASTE		917.0		1016.0		1012.9		989.6	FIBRES TEXTILES
28	METALLIFEROUS ORES,SCRAP		1779.5		2352.0		2517.4		2646.0	MINERAIS METAL,DECHETS
29	CRUDE ANIMAL,VEG MAT NES		967.5		1085.9		1137.4		1255.0	MATIERES BRUTES ANIM,VEGET
292	CRUDE VEG MATERIALS NES	W 251595	804.2	W 242477	930.4	W 267309	977.2	W 297832	1092.0	MAT BRUTES VEGETALES NDA
3	MINERAL FUELS ETC		9145.0		9323.4		11011.7		10790.5	COMBUSTIBLES MINERAUX LUB
32	COAL,COKE AND BRIQUETTES		938.2		984.4		1112.4		1186.0	HOUILLES,COKES,BRIQUETTES
322	COAL,LIGNITE AND PEAT		880.0		916.3		1016.4	MW 19849	1092.0	HOUILLES,LIGNITES,TOURBE
3222	OTH COAL,NOT AGGLOMERATD	MW 13379	708.6	MW 13955	724.4	MW 16472	880.5	MW 10072	583.9	AUTRES HOUILLES
33	PETROLEUM AND PRODUCTS		7146.9		7431.2		8981.1		8652.4	PETROLE ET DERIVES
333	CRUDE PETROLEUM	MW 39838	4637.8	MW 40349	5109.7	MW 40996	6296.6	MW 41417	5971.0	HUILES BRUTES DE PETROLE
334	PETROLEUM PRODUCTS,REFIN	MW 17495	2347.6	MW 14507	2170.5	MW 14461	2518.8	MW 14554	2510.6	PRODUITS RAFFINES
3344	FUEL OILS,NES	MW 9697	929.7	W 8657147	961.0	W 8119906	1029.9	MW 9432	1226.2	FUEL OILS
4	ANIMAL,VEGETABLE OIL,FAT		807.2		959.6		1072.1		1028.6	HUILES,GRAISSES ANIM,VEG
5	CHEMCLS,RELATED PROD NES		21318.5		27161.3		27847.8		28478.4	PRODUITS CHIMIQUES
51	ORGANIC CHEMICALS		5300.6		7492.9		7542.4		7529.3	PROD CHIMIQ ORGANIQUES
511	HYDROCARBONS NES,DERIVS		645.5		1041.2		793.0	W 1342812	763.6	HYDROCARBURES NDA
512	ALCOHOLS,PHENOLS ETC		679.5		941.6		888.6	W 1469435	910.5	PHENOLS,PHENOLS–ALCOOLS
513	CARBOXYLIC ACIDS ETC		879.7		1176.7		1116.9	W 713745	1078.5	ACIDES CARBOXYLIQUES
514	NITROGEN–FNCTN COMPOUNDS		1703.6		2046.5		2304.6	W 606093	2227.6	COMPOSES FONCT AZOTEES
5148	OTH NITROGN–FNCTN CMPNDS	W 80591	609.8	W 114993	829.3	W 401639	1000.6	W 111362	787.2	AUTRES COMPOSES AZOTES
515	ORG–INORG COMPOUNDS ETC		829.4		1611.8		1758.2	W 90645	1882.9	COMPOSES ORGANO–MINERAUX
5156	HETEROCYCLIC CMPDS ETC	W 29507	352.5	W 43606	1214.1	W 41396	1140.2	W 42787	1224.5	COMPOSES HETEROCYCLIQUES
51569	OTH HETEROCYC CMPDS,ETC	W 25331	325.7	W 37685	775.3	W 35287	977.1	W 36769	1198.0	AUT COMP HETEROCYCLIQUES
52	INORGANIC CHEMICALS		1660.0		1773.3		1995.3		1886.5	PROD CHIM INORGANIQUES
522	INORG ELEMNTS,OXIDES,ETC		676.5		852.8		905.0	W 2658233	925.1	ELEMENTS INORGANIQUES
53	DYES,TANNING,COLOUR PROD		1206.9		1461.2		1550.7		1615.5	PROD TEINTURE,COLORANTS
533	PIGMENTS,PAINTS,ETC		715.3		895.9	W 387669	965.4	W 540147	1030.4	PIGMENTS,PEINTURES,VERNIS
541	*MEDICINAL,PHARM PRODUCT		3467.5		4325.7		4719.4		5194.6	PROD MEDICINAUX PHARMACEUT
5417	MEDICAMENTS	MK 40219	2367.9	MK 47994	2990.3	MK 62078	3217.1		3767.4	MEDICAMENTS
54179	— CONTNG OTH SUBSTANCES	MK 32244	1864.9	MK 35251	2249.4	MK 39743	2284.2	MK 65382	2679.7	MED CONT AUT SUBSTANCES
55	PERFUME,CLEANING ETC PRD		1795.8		2142.1		2265.4		2492.0	PROD POUR PARFUM,TOILETTE
553	PERFUMERY,COSMETICS,ETC	W 130167	935.9	W 135208	1141.2	W 195418	1208.3	W 184189	1304.2	PRODUITS DE PARFUMERIE
58	PLASTIC MATERIALS ETC		5172.6		6746.6		6214.4		6343.8	MAT PLAST ARTIFICIELLES
582	PROD OF CONDENSATION ETC	W 500266	1320.2	W 603195	1745.3	W 573644	1630.6	W 671305	1693.4	PROD CONDENS,POLYCOND
5823	ALKYDS,OTHER POLYESTERS	W 198133	522.1	W 269860	789.6	W 240146	669.7	W 289190	701.3	ALKYDES ET AUT POLYESTERS
583	POLYMERIZATION ETC PRODS		3709.6		4837.4	W 3225230	4405.8	W 3427921	4464.4	PROD POLYMERISATION
5831	POLYETHYLENE	W 1036339	874.2	W 953672	1201.2	W 982045	1037.1	W 1019144	981.2	POLYETHYLENE
58311	— IN PRIMARY FORMS	W 952150	726.5	W 885367	1017.7	W 911875	855.7	W 943615	802.6	POLYETHYLENE PRIMAIRES
5834	POLYVINYL CHLORIDE	W 698596	730.2	W 550060	878.0	W 530214	726.1	W 548471	722.9	CHLORURE DE POLYVINYLE
5839	OTH POLYMRZTION ETC PROD	W 719363	938.2	W 577441	1249.6	W 597350	1222.6	W 833770	1380.9	AUT PROD POLYMER COPOLYM
59	CHEMICAL MATERIALS NES		2182.6		2554.8		2777.1		2855.0	MAT PROD CHIMIQUES NDA
598	MISCEL CHEM PRODUCTS NES		1361.2		1575.5	W 830125	1725.9	W 982630	1809.5	PROD DIV INDUST CHIM NDA
5989	CHEM PRODUCTS,PREPS NES		1017.6	W 554003	1207.6	W 532442	1353.6	W 701663	1432.1	PROD PREP CHIMIQUES NDA
59899	OTH CHEM PRODS,PREPS,NES	W 396440	737.6	W 427747	886.6	W 399048	1031.4	W 472566	1091.8	AUT PRODUITS CHIMIQUES NDA
6	BASIC MANUFACTURES		36808.4		44106.7		45107.4		46696.7	ART MANUFACTURES
62	RUBBER MANUFACTURES NES		1879.4		2237.3		2361.8		2304.6	CAOUTCHOUC MANUFACTURE
625	RUBBER TYRES, TUBES ETC	W 311112	1166.4	W 367765	1394.2	W 408790	1501.4	W 406758	1399.5	PNEUS CAOUTCHOUC VULCANISE
6251	TYRES NEW FOR MOTOR CARS	W 150447	654.9	W 180491	799.3	W 194076	879.9	W 191623	829.2	PNEUS POUR VOITURES
63	WOOD,CORK MANUFACTRS NES		1431.7		1504.0		1628.3		1724.9	OUVRAGES LIEGE ET BOIS
634	VENEERS,PLYWOOD,ETC		842.8		857.8		839.2		838.1	PLACAGES,CONTRE–PLAQUES
64	PAPER,PAPERBOARD AND MFR		6544.1		8246.1		7903.2		7782.5	PAPIERS,CARTONS & OUVRAGES
641	PAPER AND PAPERBOARD	W 7335217	5491.4	W 6913201	6958.1	W 7181277	6643.7	W 7898983	6519.3	PAPIERS ET CARTONS
6411	NEWSPRINT	W 1696477	805.0	W 1553070	1022.2	W 1525272	1134.9	W 1628373	974.2	PAPIER JOURNAL
6412	PRINTG,WRITING PAPER NES	W 1736343	1499.6	W 1586319	1952.1	W 1582113	1663.9	W 1964540	1820.0	PAPIERS POUR L'IMPRESSION
64122	— COATED,IMPREGNATD ETC	W 1496848	1284.0	W 1396493	1706.7	W 1420032	1485.8	W 1748963	1604.0	PAPIERS IMPRESSION COUCHES
6415	PAPER,PAPERBRD,BULK,NES	W 1610816	1211.5	W 1622654	1616.1	W 1819274	1567.8	W 1817565	1436.7	PAPIERS,CARTONS ROULEAUX
64159	OTHER PAPER ETC,BULK,NES	W 1470860	1087.0	W 1521479	1488.9	W 1712193	1454.6	W 1687146	1305.4	AUT PAPIER ROULEAUX FEUILLES
6418	COATED ETC PAPER NES BLK	W 866524	1021.6	W 758909	1134.4	W 799433	1115.2	W 838731	1121.9	PAP,CARTONS COUCHES,ENDUITS
64189	COATED PAPER ETC NES	W 650614	737.0	W 529421	746.1	W 593762	765.4	W 614412	764.6	PAPIERS,CARTONS COUCHES
642	PAPER,ETC,PRECUT,ARTS OF	W 357494	1052.8	W 380828	1288.1	W 419207	1259.6	W 449797	1263.2	PAP,CARTONS DECOUPES

4. General Imports C.I.F. by Commodities according to the S.I.T.C. (Rev. 2) in million U.S. Dollars
Importations Générales C.A.F. par Produits d'après la C.T.C.I. (Rév. 2) en millions de Dollars E.U.

SITC CTCI	COMMODITY	1994 QUANTITY QUANTITE	1994 VALUE VALEUR	1995 QUANTITY QUANTITE	1995 VALUE VALEUR	1996 QUANTITY QUANTITE	1996 VALUE VALEUR	1997 QUANTITY QUANTITE	1997 VALUE VALEUR	PRODUIT
65	TEXTILE YARN,FABRICS,ETC		6783.9		7581.5		7946.9		8358.0	FILS,TISSUS,ARTICLES TEXTILE
651	TEXTILE YARN		1653.2	W 385045	1819.8	W 396564	1848.7	W 443263	1928.8	FILS TEXTILES
6514	SYN FIB YRN,BULK,MONOFIL	W 173604	724.6	W 190930	840.8	W 202813	858.3	W 250164	945.8	FILS CONT 85% FIB TEXT SYNTH
652	COTTON FABRICS,WOVEN	W 142288	897.0	W 140677	989.4	W 145395	1043.4	W 150204	1092.3	TISSUS DE COTON
653	WOVN MAN–MADE FIB FABRIC	W 172058	1521.8	W 180153	1738.2	W 186441	1706.3	W 183147	1634.2	TISSUS FIBRES SYNTH,ARTIF
657	SPECIAL TXTL FABRC,PRODS	W 130272	687.5	W 128088	799.2	W 139865	869.1	W 179400	877.5	TISSUS SPECIAUX
659	FLOOR COVERINGS,ETC	W 215377	712.9	W 217375	747.6	W 267710	838.0	W 268517	960.4	COUVRE–PARQUETS,TAPIS ETC
66	NONMETAL MINERAL MFS NES		6317.5		7055.3		7740.2		8422.5	ART MIN NON METALLIQUES
664	GLASS		654.9		788.9	W 545803	748.8	W 577949	708.8	VERRE
667	PEARL,PREC–,SEMI–P STONE		4038.1		4517.9		5170.1		5706.1	PERLES, PIERRES GEMMES
6672	DIAMONDS NONINDUST,UNSET		3961.6		4434.9		5074.3		5532.3	DIAMANTS BRUTS
66721	— ROUGH,UNSORTED		821.8		764.5		778.9		1157.2	DIAMANTS BRUTS NON TRIES
66722	— SRTD,ROUGH,SIMPLY WKD		2726.8		3223.7		3686.5		3512.8	DIAMANTS TRIES BRUTS
67	IRON AND STEEL		4513.2		5829.6		5663.9		5554.3	FER ET ACIER
672	IRON,STEEL PRIMARY FORMS	W 1223016	576.1	W 1807826	1050.6	W 1301312	909.3	W 1330812	798.7	LINGOTS FER,ACIER
673	IRON,STEEL SHAPES ETC	W 1347028	743.9	W 1459955	983.4	W 1241558	823.7	W 1534487	940.4	BARRES,PROFIL FER,ACIER
674	IRN,STL UNIV,PLATE,SHEET	W 2717364	1839.0	W 2621157	2097.9	W 2752633	2056.2	W 2856868	2035.0	LARGES PLATS,TOLES
678	IRON,STL TUBES,PIPES,ETC	W 616781	746.8	W 667263	905.1		1079.1	W 792248	1052.8	TUBES,TUYAUX EN FONTE,FER
68	NON–FERROUS METALS		4552.8		6021.5		5924.1		6064.7	METAUX NON FERREUX
681	SILVER,PLATINUM,ETC		706.7		1208.5		822.8		983.5	ARGENT ET PLATINE
6811	SILVER UNWKD,PARTLY WRKD		309.6		804.6		524.0		654.3	ARGENT BRUT MI–OUVRE
682	COPPER EXC CEMENT COPPER	W 448084	1206.4	W 459492	1598.1	W 515754	1556.0	W 579549	1682.3	CUIVRE
6821	COPPER NES,ALLOYS,UNWRT	W 270685	615.0	W 280187	814.9	W 338052	816.7	W 371276	879.0	CUIVRE BRUT
68212	COPPER REFINED,UNWROUGHT	W 260808	589.1	W 277507	802.3	W 330629	795.6	W 368361	872.2	CUIVRE AFFINE BRUT
684	ALUMINIUM		1744.4		2133.6	W 1062963	2453.8	W 839634	2103.0	ALUMINIUM
6841	ALUMINIUM,ALLOYS,UNWRGHT	W 477326	662.5	W 388089	751.9	W 653109	1108.6	W 437065	764.5	ALUMINIUM,ALLIAGES BRUTS
6842	ALUMINIUM,ALLOYS WORKED	W 385040	1082.0	W 388062	1381.8	W 409854	1345.2	W 402569	1338.5	ALUMINIUM,ALLIAGES OUVRE
68422	ALUMNM PLATE,SHEET,STRIP	W 275374	685.5	W 270339	855.4	W 273667	813.7	W 260079	787.3	TOLES, PLANCHES EN ALU
69	METAL MANUFACTURES NES		4254.9		5068.8		5321.0		5821.8	ART MANUFACT EN METAL NDA
695	TOOLS	W 58061	758.6	W 65939	953.7	W 61948	896.8	W 76647	1055.9	OUTILS A MAIN
699	BASE METAL MFRS NES	W 342974	1583.9	W 340642	1860.0	W 337991	2047.8	W 371389	2199.2	ART MANUFACTURES MET NDA
7	MACHINES,TRANSPORT EQUIP		91512.8		107873.9		120046.4		133847.0	MACHINES MATERIEL TRANSPORT
71	POWER GENERATING EQUIPMT		5975.5		7097.5		8146.6		8884.4	MACHINES GENERATRICES
713	INTRNL COMBUS PSTN ENGIN	W 275204	2101.5	W 336370	2664.5	W 325378	2692.5	W 348745	2276.4	MOTEURS EXPL COMB INT, PIECE
7132	MOTOR VEHCL PISTN ENGINS	W 65460	713.0	W 69233	870.9	W 83076	958.7	W 49607	536.7	MOTEURS EXPL POUR VEHICULES
7139	PISTON ENGINE PARTS NES	W 177354	1017.0	W 236682	1363.1	W 208956	1295.3	W 207997	1248.4	PIECES POUR 713.2,3,8
714	ENGINES AND MOTORS NES	W 12549	2949.2	W 10355	3211.6	W 16333	4188.0	W 17083	5325.1	MOTEURS NON ELECTRIQUES
7144	REACTION ENGINES	W 1370	803.7	W 1433	804.2	W 2315	1152.1	W 2450	1431.5	PROPULSEURS A REACTION
7149	ENGINE & MOTOR PARTS NES	W 8278	1614.0	W 6983	1898.6	W 11878	2442.2	W 11803	3097.1	PIECES 714 ET 718.88
71491	PARTS NES OF 7144,71481	W 1555	1028.5	W 1822	1223.9	W 2662	1579.5	W 3813	2258.1	PIECES DES PROPULSEURS
71499	PARTS NES,OF 71488,71888	W 6723	585.5	W 5161	674.8	W 9216	862.8	W 7990	839.0	PIECES 714.88 ET 718.88
716	ROTATING ELECTRIC PLANT	W 57244	675.7	W 61118	846.4	W 62616	894.3	W 73376	947.7	APP ELECTR ROTATIFS,PIECES
72	MACHS FOR SPCL INDUSTRYS		5104.2		6260.9		6198.6		6779.0	MAC SPECIALES POUR INDUST
723	CIVIL ENGNEERG EQUIP ETC	W 117476	741.1	W 124552	900.0	W 113962	789.4	W 126258	901.5	APPAREILS DE GENIE CIVIL
726	PRINTG,BKBINDG MACHY,PTS	W 27573	813.2	W 35861	1069.1	W 35401	1059.7	W 47849	1106.8	MACHINES POUR IMPRIMERIE
728	OTH MACHY FOR SPCL INDUS	W 93404	1535.4	W 97086	1876.9	W 100889	2045.9	W 114333	2358.4	AUT MACH IND PARTICULIERES
7284	MACHY FOR SPCL INDUS NES	W 60309	1235.8	W 58824	1522.0	W 65412	1678.3	W 71223	1898.5	MACH SPEC IND PARTICUL.
73	METALWORKING MACHINERY		1086.6		1523.8		1619.2		1912.8	MACH TRAVAIL DES METAUX
736	METALWORKING MACH–TOOLS		812.9	W 70425	1204.4	W 72764	1327.3	W 91611	1495.8	MACH–OUTILS TRAVAIL METAUX
74	GENRL INDUSTRL MACHY NES		8226.7		9735.5		10430.9		11387.9	MACH APP INDUSTRIE
741	HEATING,COOLING EQUIPMNT	W 96032	1152.1	W 99607	1406.2	W 108664	1556.1	W 373276	1726.8	MACH CHAUFFAGE,PIECES
742	PUMPS FOR LIQUIDS ETC	W 46508	984.0	W 50051	1164.6	W 50724	1176.6	W 77012	1219.4	POMPES MOTO–POMPES
743	PUMPS NES,CENTRFUGES ETC	W 99906	1255.4	W 129510	1501.5	W 143523	1743.6	W 303658	1869.7	POMPES COMPRES,VENT ETC
744	MECHANICAL HANDLING EQU	W 206556	1404.9	W 296812	1829.8	W 326509	1899.9	W 318102	2187.5	EQUIP MANUTENTION PIECES
7449	PTS NES OF MACHY OF 7442	W 110439	690.4	W 173516	913.5	W 145275	925.1	W 163305	1011.0	PIECES DU 744.2
745	NONELEC MACHY,TOOLS NES	W 48548	1037.0	W 53121	1089.2	W 55791	1208.1	W 69928	1351.8	AUT MACH NON ELEC,PIECES
7452	OTH NONELEC MCHS,PTS NES	W 42835	877.1	W 46902	933.8	W 50962	1052.7	W 63128	1181.8	AUT MACH NON ELEC,PIECES
749	NONELEC MACH PTS,ACC NES	W 203933	2393.6	W 226755	2744.4	W 344854	2846.9	W 302508	3032.9	PIECES MACH NON ELEC NDA
7492	COCKS,VALVES ETC NES	W 63628	974.1	W 62359	1044.4	W 96123	1153.2	W 100712	1246.5	ART ROB,SIM POUR TUYAUX
75	OFFICE MACHINES,ADP EQUIP		16235.5		19334.4		19924.2		22778.9	MACH BUREAU TRAIT AUTOM
751	OFFICE MACHINES	W 31502	780.9	W 31629	911.3	W 33669	822.8	W 32751	855.6	MACH,APPAREILS DE BUREAU
752	AUTOMTIC DATA PROC EQUIP	W 146063	9919.4	W 158339	11945.5	W 163849	11988.6	W 297927	13808.5	MACH TRAIT INFORMATION
7522	DIGITAL COMPUTERS	W 8805	930.0	W 9365	1421.3	W 15330	1903.5	W 17704	1998.8	MACH DIGITALES COMPLETES
7523	DIGITL CENTRL PROCESSORS	W 18591	2581.9	W 23119	3042.1	W 25272	2682.1	W 24081	2622.1	UNITES CENTRALES
7524	DIGITL CENTRL STOR UNITS	W 14935	2336.7	W 17773	3397.5	W 17826	3429.3	W 123756	4601.9	UNITES MEMOIRE CENTRALES
7525	ADP PERIPHERAL UNITS	W 81059	2449.6	W 77062	2477.9	W 86427	2584.6	W 107577	2953.5	UNITES PERIPHERIQUES
7528	OFF–LINE DATA PROC EQUIP	W 22375	1546.4	W 30727	1509.0	W 17974	1232.3	W 23231	1472.6	MACH AUXIL TRAIT INFORM
759	OFFICE,ADP MCH PTS,ACCES	W 102474	5535.3	W 83544	6477.7	W 92494	7112.9	W 143005	8115.0	PIECES DU 751 ET 752
7599	ACCTG,ETC,ADP MCH PTS,AC	W 62911	4953.8	W 46380	5815.2	W 60469	6407.5	W 114699	7342.2	PIECES DU 751 ET 752
76	TELECOMM,SOUND EQUIPMENT		7663.8		9887.4		11745.6		13184.9	EQUIPMENT DE TELECOM
762	RADIO BROADCAST RECEIVRS	W 52863	890.5	W 43870	965.5	W 43393	860.1	W 43777	776.1	RECEPTEURS RADIODIFFUSION
763	SOUND RECORDRS,PHONOGRPH	W 22781	1011.1	W 22810	1095.5	W 29774	1454.6	W 25279	1344.4	PHONO,APP ENREGISTREMENT
7638	OTHR SOUND APPARATUS ETC	W 20560	988.7	W 21046	1067.7	W 28152	1425.6	W 23702	1313.9	AUT APP D'ENREGIS,REPROD
76381	TV IMAGE,SND RECRDRS ETC	W 12054	666.1	W 11205	668.4	W 15346	1077.0	W 14011	946.2	APP ENREG,REPRO IMAG,SON
764	TELECOM EQPT,PTS,ACC NES		5234.5		7176.3		8672.0	W 234643	10221.3	EQUIP TELECOM,PIECES
7641	LINE TELEPHONE,ETC EQUIP	W 19315	1214.2	W 23080	2136.0	W 28137	3197.8	W 32783	3681.7	APP TELEPHON PAR FIL
7643	TV,RADIO TRANSMITTRS ETC		1019.4		1521.0		2003.8	W 869	125.9	APP EMET TELE RADIO
7649	PTS NES OF EQUIPMT OF 76	W 308776	2051.7	W 83046	2456.8	W 59538	2539.3	W 67177	2996.2	PIECES DE LA DIV 76
76491	PTS NES OF APPAR OF 7641	W 9870	661.7	W 7037	786.8	W 9641	917.3	W 13083	1275.6	PIECES POUR 764.1
76493	TELECOMM EQUIPMT PTS NES	W 19499	911.5	W 26741	1147.3	W 25969	1063.1	W 24755	1184.4	PIECES 761,762,764.3,8
77	ELECTRIC MACHNRY NES ETC		16065.2		20577.9		24046.6		23520.4	MACH APP ELECT NDA
771	ELECTRIC POWER MACHY NES	W 45258	803.3	W 48727	1025.3	W 75074	1344.2	W 100954	1530.3	MACH PROD,TRANS ELECTR
7712	OTH ELEC POWER MACHY NES	W 34077	620.9	W 35600	821.3	W 55283	1104.2	W 73794	1233.2	AUT APP PROD TRANSF ELEC
772	SWITCHGEAR ETC,PARTS NES	W 79610	2587.1	W 87977	3124.4	W 92992	3286.4	W 121882	3572.2	APP COUPURE,SECT ETC
7721	SWITCHGEAR ETC	W 68939	1961.4	W 73800	2368.2	W 76934	2491.4	W 102678	2662.3	APP COUPURE,SECTIONMNT
773	ELECTR DISTRIBUTNG EQUIP		1054.2	W 540133	1352.3	W 244630	1524.2	W 246668	1541.1	EQUIPMT DISTRIBUTION ELECT
7731	INSULATED WIRE,CABLE ETC	W 168289	965.3	W 533644	1252.4	W 235732	1423.0	W 234323	1434.7	FILS,CABLES ISOLES ELECT
775	HOUSEHOLD TYPE EQUIP NES		1593.8	W 305587	1818.9	W 279006	1764.3	W 304143	1932.3	MACH,APP USAGE DOMESTQUE
776	TRANSISTORS,VALVES,ETC	W 139373	5626.1	W 113579	7918.8	W 124762	10888.4	W 134551	9105.5	LAMPES,TUBES,VALVES
7763	DIODES,TRANSISTORS,ETC	W 3876	621.7	W 6044	811.8	W 5440	770.8	W 7416	773.5	DIODES,TRANSISTORS
7764	ELECTRONIC MICROCIRCUITS	W 8406	4035.6	W 11569	5894.2	W 20196	8722.7	W 16886	6929.5	MICROSTRUCTURES ELECTRON
778	ELECTRICAL MACHINERY NES		4076.3		4951.6	W 312870	4789.1	W 313491	5433.6	AUTRES MACH ELECT NDA
7788	OTH ELEC MACHY,EQUIP NES	W 46643	2304.5	W 95715	2720.2	W 71535	2632.5	W 69809	3012.0	AUT MACH APP ELEC NDA
77886	OTH ELEC MACHINERY NES	W 1287	662.9	W 12810	862.5	W 13386	908.0	W 9370	962.6	AUT MACH APP ELECTRIQUES
78	ROAD VEHICLES		24666.0		28489.4		32177.7		36240.5	VEHICULES ROUTIERS
781	PASS MOTOR VEH EXC BUSES	W 1311667	13957.4	W 1361527	15580.8	W 1544335	17727.7	W 1837957	22267.9	AUTO TRANSPORT PERSONNES
782	LORRIES,SPCL MTR VEH NES		1793.5		2247.4	W 224875	2091.8	W 309561	2464.0	VEHICULES SPECIAUX,MARCH
7821	LORRIES,TRUCKS	W 171974	1489.6	W 233542	2151.3	W 215000	2002.0	W 292115	2325.0	VEHICULES TRANSP MARCHAND
784	MOTOR VEH PRTS,ACCES NES	W 1201019	7655.2	W 1456205	9272.3	W 1457193	10861.9	W 1358873	9746.4	PIECES 722,781,782,783
7849	OTHER MOTOR VEHCL PARTS	W 1177444	7446.2	W 1438442	9116.5	W 1439889	10731.0	W 1323913	9408.4	PIECES 722,781,782,783
785	CYCLES,ETC MOTRZD OR NOT	W 58935	604.4	W 73821	685.0	W 76897	766.0	W 79835	962.0	MOTOCYCLES SCOOTERS

4. General Imports C.I.F. by Commodities according to the S.I.T.C. (Rev. 2) in million U.S. Dollars
Importations Générales C.A.F. par Produits d'après la C.T.C.I. (Rév. 2) en millions de Dollars E.U.

SITC CTCI	COMMODITY	1994		1995		1996		1997		PRODUIT
		QUANTITY QUANTITE	VALUE VALEUR	QUANTITY QUANTITE	VALUE VALEUR	QUANTITY QUANTITE	VALUE VALEUR	QUANTITY QUANTITE	VALUE VALEUR	
79	OTHR TRANSPORT EQUIPMENT		6489.7		4967.6		5757.4		9158.6	AUTRE MATERIEL TRANSPORT
791	RAILWAY VEHICLES	W 47041	1117.1	W 22667	346.9	W 12284	133.6	W 14206	186.6	VEHIC MAT CHEMINS DE FER
792	AIRCRAFT ETC		5280.1		4128.1		5398.1	W 19109	8700.0	APP NAVIGATION AERIENNE
7924	AIRCRFT NES OVER 15000KG	W 2	2695.9		1047.6		1919.1			AERODYNES PLUS 15000 KG
7929	AIRCRAFT PARTS NES		2356.9		2756.4		3124.8			PIECES DU 792
8	MISC MANUFACTURED GOODS		33022.7		36093.8		39734.3		44517.9	ART MANUFACTURES DIVERS
812	*PLUMBG,HEATNG,LGHTNG EQ	W 116757	655.4	W 147257	716.5	W 141485	826.8	W 162766	938.6	APPAR SANITAIRES CHAUFFAGE
821	*FURNITURE,PARTS THEREOF	W 440269	1745.6	W 427511	1915.2	W 476445	2209.5	W 563937	2504.6	MEUBLES ET PIECES
8219	FURNITURE AND PARTS NES	W 317342	1115.7	W 314347	1209.3	W 350039	1370.6	W 404577	1552.6	AUTRES MEUBLES ET PIECES
84	CLOTHING AND ACCESSORIES		7359.6		8273.6		9617.0		11044.6	VETEMENTS
842	MENS OUTERWEAR NOT KNIT	W 64607	1203.9	W 61791	1308.0	W 66401	1500.9	W 71780	1724.4	VET DESSUS POUR HOMMES
843	WOMENS OUTERWEAR NONKNIT	W 87746	1763.7	W 77572	2042.0	W 87701	2370.4	W 96630	2680.0	VET DESSUS FEMMES MAT TEX
8439	— OTHER OUTER GARMENTS	W 34484	637.6	W 32928	713.9	W 39341	876.7	W 43025	1031.9	AUT VET DES FEM MAT TEXT
844	UNDER GARMENTS NOT KNIT	W 39572	659.0	W 48800	827.5	W 48712	846.9	W 42770	833.0	VETEMENT DESSOUS MAT TEX
845	OUTERWEAR KNIT NONELASTC	W 107051	1791.9	W 94029	1834.7	W 108534	2222.8	W 125322	2779.3	VET DESSOUS,ACCES BONNET
8451	— JERSEYS,PULLOVERS ETC	W 59008	996.5	W 52113	1065.8	W 59305	1236.5	W 69189	1551.6	CHANDAILS,PULL–OVERS ETC
8459	— OTHER,CLTHG ACCESRYS	W 41624	674.7	W 37302	656.6	W 44631	861.8	W 51090	1075.4	AUT VET DESSUS DE BONNE
846	UNDER GARMENTS KNITTED	W 70650	1112.9	W 80386	1336.4	W 91002	1636.6	W 91427	1845.0	SOUS VETS DE BONNETERIE
8462	— OF COTTON NON ELASTIC	W 50846	705.1	W 55949	852.6	W 63983	1044.8	W 63123	1170.5	SOUS–VET BONNET COTON
84629	—— OTHER	W 50846	705.1	W 55949	852.6	W 63983	1044.8	W 63123	1170.5	AUT SOUS–VET BONNET COTON
851	*FOOTWEAR	W 142804	2002.8	W 140994	2188.6	W 155223	2522.3	W 165669	2896.4	CHAUSSURES
85102	FOOTWEAR LEATHER	W 81881	1320.7	W 109382	1876.8	W 115554	2105.8	W 120645	2444.5	CHAUS SEMELLES EN CUIR
87	PRECISION INSTRUMNTS NES		4550.4		5358.5		5956.0		6448.8	INSTRUM,APPAR SCIENT NDA
872	MEDICAL INSTRUMENTS NES	W 25346	772.4	W 24716	900.4	W 27409	990.3	W 30325	1135.5	INSTR,APP MEDIC–CHIR NDA
87202	OTH MEDICAL INSTRUMENTS	W 19192	692.0	W 21006	799.5	W 23370	871.3	W 24211	968.0	INSTRUM,APP MEDECINE
874	MEASURNG,CONTROLNG INSTR	W 38183	3301.3	W 53082	3848.0	W 47940	4319.4	W 60502	4548.7	INSTRUMENTS DE MESURE
8741	SURVEYING INSTRUMENTS	W 3778	664.0	W 3844	783.8	W 3987	958.6	W 5092	990.1	INST GEODESIE,TOPO ETC
8748	ELEC MEAS,CONTRL EQU NES	W 3813	620.7	W 5753	749.9	W 5083	852.6	W 5085	903.2	APP ELEC ELECTRO MESURE
8749	INSTR PTS NES,ACCESSORYS	W 9989	675.7	W 10577	721.9	W 12418	778.1	W 15513	785.1	PIECES 873,874.3,54,874.8
88	PHOTO EQU,OPTICL GDS ETC		2908.3		3253.4		3480.4		3664.5	APP,FOURN PHOTO,OP,MONTR
882	PHOTO,CINEMA SUPPLIES	W 91267	1273.5	W 95081	1442.4	W 100989	1461.0	W 101283	1566.8	PRODUITS PHOTO,CINEMA
8822	PHOTO FILM EXC DEV CINMA	W 57692	991.0	W 60389	1093.0	W 63524	1130.6	W 63144	1251.3	PLAQUES,PELLICULES,FILMS
885	WATCHES AND CLOCKS		709.2		782.6		849.8		921.6	HORLOGERIE
89	MISC MANUFCTRD GOODS NES		13205.0		13699.8		14293.7		16180.3	ART MANUFACTURES DIVERS
892	PRINTED MATTER		1578.2		1774.9	W 318696	2094.2	W 436954	1950.6	IMPRIMES
8921	PRINTED BOOKS,GLOBES,ETC	W 168218	870.5	W 175005	1043.8	W 152664	1004.7	W 171694	1050.7	LIVRES,BROCHURES,CARTES
89211	PRINTED BOOKS,PAMPHLETS	W 155305	826.1	W 163108	995.5	W 140626	954.9	W 156367	999.0	LIVRES,BROCHURES
893	ARTICLES OF PLASTIC NES		2490.0		2834.4		2881.3		3110.9	OUVRAGES EN MAT DIVIS 58
8931	PLSTC PACKG CONTNRS,LIDS	W 284346	826.4	W 351964	981.2	W 466520	983.7	W 486161	1021.1	ART TRANSP EMBALLAGE ETC
8939	MISC PLASTIC ARTICLES	W 356282	1614.3	W 353751	1795.6	W 381081	1839.4	W 528031	2009.4	ART DIVERS EN MAT DIV 58
89399	OTHR PLASTC ARTICLES NES	W 302411	1452.4	W 298750	1622.0	W 319736	1665.5	W 462420	1815.4	AUT OUV MAT DIV 58
894	TOYS,SPORTING GOODS,ETC		2046.0	W 279995	2303.6	W 301666	2491.0	W 322966	2912.8	VOITURES ENFANTS,JOUETS
8942	TOYS,INDOOR GAMES ETC	W 209982	1641.2	W 223330	1792.5	W 239903	1911.7	W 258396	2283.3	JOUETS,JEUX ETC
89423	TOYS NES	W 111127	799.9	W 113285	851.4	W 118566	902.7	W 130987	954.1	JOUETS,MODELES REDUITS
89424	INDOOR GAME EQUIPMENT	W 54277	543.8	W 53149	559.2	W 67691	658.2	W 73189	975.6	ART,JEUX DE SOCIETE
896	WORKS OF ART ETC		1966.9		1619.9		1235.4		1631.3	OBJETS D'ART
89601	HAND PAINTINGS ETC NES		1165.6		1016.5		673.5		935.5	TABLEAUX,PEINTURES
897	GOLD,SILVER WARE,JEWELRY		1858.5		1624.4		1887.8		2455.7	BIJOUTERIE,ORFEVRERIE
8973	PREC JEWLRY,GLD–SILVWARE		1728.8		1476.9		1738.6		2310.9	BIJOUX OR,ARGENT ORFEVRE
89731	PRECIOUS METAL JEWELLERY		1653.3		1416.6		1663.5		2218.4	ART BIJOUTERIE,JOAILLER
898	MUSICAL INSTRUMENTS,PTS	W 109980	2085.6	W 103700	2141.8	W 127099	2205.0	W 114307	2447.9	INSTRUMENTS DE MUSIQUE
8983	SOUND RECRDNG TAPE,DISCS	W 92370	1897.5	W 92267	1951.5	W 116867	1997.3	W 102949	2213.3	SUPPORTS SON POUR 763
89831	PREPD SND RECORDNG MEDIA	W 62264	688.0	W 67528	699.6	W 88671	659.3	W 62692	643.7	SUPPORTS PREPARES
89832	RECORDED DISCS,TAPES ETC	W 30106	1209.6	W 24740	1252.0	W 28196	1338.0	W 40257	1569.6	DISQUES,PHONO,BANDES
899	OTHER MANUFACTURED GOODS		763.3		885.2		972.8		1043.5	AUT ART MANUF DIVERS NDA
9	GOODS NOT CLASSD BY KIND		1801.0		2424.9		2643.9		2670.2	ART TRANSACT NON CLASSES
931	*SPECIAL TRANSACTIONS		1037.4	W 132860	1593.3		1835.0		2010.9	TRANS.SPECIALES

5. General Exports F.O.B. by Commodities according to the S.I.T.C. (Rev. 2) in million U.S. Dollars
Exportations Générales F.O.B. par Produits d'après la C.T.C.I. (Rév. 2) en millions de Dollars E.U.

SITC CTCI	COMMODITY	1994		1995		1996		1997		PRODUIT
		QUANTITY QUANTITE	VALUE VALEUR	QUANTITY QUANTITE	VALUE VALEUR	QUANTITY QUANTITE	VALUE VALEUR	QUANTITY QUANTITE	VALUE VALEUR	
	ALL COMMODITIES		202858.0		239948.1		259277.1		278907.0	TOUS PRODUITS
0	FOOD AND LIVE ANIMALS		9329.7		10939.5		10652.3		10533.3	ALIMENTS,ANIMAUX VIVANTS
01	MEAT AND PREPARATIONS		1744.9		2259.6		1620.3		1445.6	VIANDES ET PREPARATIONS
011	MEAT FRESH,CHILLD,FROZEN	W 605905	1580.0	W 767218	2108.7	W 545445	1444.6	W 578840	1250.1	VIANDES FRAICHES,REF,CONGE
0111	BOVINE MEAT FRESH,FROZEN	W 231141	737.0	W 271824	937.7	W 63061	219.3	W 6043	24.7	VIANDES BOVIN FRAI,REF
02	DAIRY PRODCTS,BIRDS'EGGS		994.4		1192.9		1055.4		1137.1	PRODUITS LAITIERS,OEUFS
03	FISH AND PREPARATIONS		992.8		1091.1		1110.8		1079.2	POISSONS ET PREPARATIONS
04	CEREALS AND PREPARATIONS		1882.6		2232.6		2638.1		2424.8	CEREALES ET PRODUITS
048	CEREAL ETC PREPARATIONS	W 859058	1085.6	W 886499	1230.7	W 1028865	1515.5	W 973278	1475.4	PREPTNS A BASE CEREALES
07	COFFEE,TEA,COCOA,SPICES		989.2		1061.6		1052.7		1095.5	CAFE,THE,CACAO,EPICES
1	BEVERAGES AND TOBACCO		5697.2		6524.4		6810.6		7396.7	BOISSONS ET TABACS
11	BEVERAGES		4340.7		4728.9		4913.5		5388.2	BOISSONS
112	ALCOHOLIC BEVERAGES	W 1012986	4153.7	W 1089406	4492.7	W 1200874	4652.1	W 1200740	5151.0	BOISSONS ALCOOLIQUES
1124	DISTILLED ALCOHOLIC BEVS	W 655318	3803.3	W 723842	4096.3	W 731398	4084.0	W 787517	4530.2	ALCOOLS,EAUX–DE–VIE
11241	WHISKY	W 550769	3388.9	W 601509	3647.4	W 604066	3609.1	W 657109	3976.9	WHISKY
12	TOBACCO AND MANUFACTURES		1356.6		1795.6		1897.1		2008.6	TABACS BRUTS FABRIQUES
122	TOBACCO,MANUFACTURED	W 77892	1336.3	W 99626	1775.7	W 105629	1870.8	W 116275	1971.2	TABACS FABRIQUES
1222	CIGARETTES	W 63209	1209.7	W 83215	1620.5	W 87566	1685.2	W 94835	1763.8	CIGARETTES
2	CRUDE MATERLS,EXCL FUELS		3528.8		4211.7		3930.0		3927.3	MAT BRUTES NON COMESTIBLES
26	TEXTILE FIBRES AND WASTE		777.4		886.3		862.5		824.8	FIBRES TEXTILES
27	CRUDE FERTLZR,MINRLS NES		657.3		765.6		776.5		803.4	ENGRAIS MINERAUX BRUTS
28	METALLIFEROUS ORES,SCRAP		1008.5		1192.5		1029.2		1035.8	MINERAIS METAL,DECHETS
3	MINERAL FUELS ETC		13629.0		14621.6		17170.3		16948.5	COMBUSTIBLES MINERAUX LUB
33	PETROLEUM AND PRODUCTS		13029.6		13780.7		16161.5		15684.5	PETROLE ET DERIVES
333	CRUDE PETROLEUM	MW 77612	9193.2	MW 79065	10144.5	MW 76484	11683.5	MW 69851	10332.5	HUILES BRUTES DE PETROLE
334	PETROLEUM PRODUCTS,REFIN		3611.6		3348.8		4139.1	MW 26292	5022.7	PRODUITS RAFFINES
3341	GASOLINE,OTH LIGHT OILS	W 8059224	1379.2	W 7879863	1426.9	W 8867788	1805.6	MW 11649	2408.2	ESSENCES POUR MOTEURS
33411	MOTOR,AVIATION SPIRIT	W 6341127	1081.1	W 5864814	1049.9	W 7319638	1478.5	MW 9583	1938.5	ESSENCES MOTEURS D'AVIONS
3343	GAS OILS	W 6233450	919.5	W 5553256	858.7	W 5016593	943.5	W 90595	29.9	GAS OILS
3345	LUBS,PETROLEUM OILS NES	W 1399233	470.9	W 912899	446.6	W 1408788	618.3	W 3700737	1072.7	HUILES LUBRIFIANTES
33451	LUBS(HIGH PETR CONT) ETC	W 1361460	391.2	W 871857	346.6	W 1364422	494.6	W 3652698	940.3	HUILES LUBRIF,H LOURDES
341	*GAS,NATURAL AND MANUFCT	W 3329823	484.7	W 4068154	719.8	W 4492706	866.2	W 5496416	1110.2	GAZ NATUREL,GAZ MANUFACT
3413	PETROLM GASES,LIQUEFIED	W 2642206	423.8	W 3442570	648.1	W 3518857	770.5	W 4157343	978.4	GAZ DE PETROLE LIQUEFIE
34131	LIQUEFIED PROPANE,BUTANE	W 2435252	386.1	W 3244395	603.0	W 3374698	743.1	W 3981288	935.6	PROPANE,BUTANE LIQUEFIES
5	CHEMCLS,RELATED PROD NES		27912.3		32282.0		33905.5		34972.8	PRODUITS CHIMIQUES
51	ORGANIC CHEMICALS		7140.2		7751.3		8094.3		8255.1	PROD CHIMIQ ORGANIQUES
511	HYDROCARBONS NES,DERIVS		1148.8		1408.4		1176.4	W 2540853	1216.6	HYDROCARBURES NDA
5111	ACYCLIC HYDROCARBONS	W 1547724	554.5	W 1646631	791.1	W 1544506	642.1	W 1640808	719.9	HYDROCARBURES ACYCLIQUES
513	CARBOXYLIC ACIDS ETC		1159.8		1617.7		1308.4	W 1163193	1290.2	ACIDES CARBOXYLIQUES
514	NITROGEN–FNCTN COMPOUNDS		2167.9		2108.8		2622.9	W 517723	2420.1	COMPOSES FONCT AZOTEES
5148	OTH NITROGN–FNCTN CMPNDS	W 147192	869.4	W 128779	818.8	W 148587	1066.3	W 105891	952.4	AUTRES COMPOSES AZOTES
51482	IMIDE–,IMIDE–FNCT CMPNDS	W 10117	695.9	W 11351	582.3	W 10500	776.8	W 12155	674.8	COMPOSES A FONCTION IMIDE
515	ORG–INORG COMPOUNDS ETC		1671.1		1509.2	W 107874	1804.8	W 116006	2010.6	COMPOSES ORGANO–MINERAUX
5156	HETEROCYCLIC CMPDS ETC	W 61521	1413.4	W 72879	1190.7	W 56481	1403.4	W 61110	1499.4	COMPOSES HETEROCYCLIQUES
51569	OTH HETEROCYC CMPDS,ETC	W 61300	1405.7	W 72563	1180.2	W 56135	1381.8	W 60954	1490.6	AUT COMP HETEROCYCLIQUES
52	INORGANIC CHEMICALS		1716.9		1940.0		1870.3		1954.8	PROD CHIM INORGANIQUES
523	OTHR INORG CHEMICALS ETC		664.2		789.6		761.9	W 634461	742.1	AUT PRODUITS CHIMIQUES INORG
53	DYES,TANNING,COLOUR PROD		2247.2		2548.7		2557.4		2468.0	PROD TEINTURE,COLORANTS
531	SYNT DYE,NAT INDGO,LAKES		785.3		881.1	W 98182	889.9	W 106949	843.7	MAT COLOR ORGAN,LAQUES
5311	SYNTHIC ORGNIC DYESTUFFS	W 41485	371.5	W 8438	79.3	W 85679	827.0	W 11177	87.0	MAT COLOR ORGAN SYNTHET
533	PIGMENTS,PAINTS,ETC		1418.9		1620.3		1615.8	W 511575	1569.6	PIGMENTS,PEINTURES,VERNIS
541	*MEDICINAL,PHARM PRODUCT		6080.0		7720.1		8320.2		8940.3	PROD MEDICINAUX PHARMACEUT
5417	MEDICAMENTS	MK 101954	4732.1	MK 96231	6135.3	MK 111653	6752.8	MK 124670	7393.7	MEDICAMENTS
54171	— CONTAINNG ANTIBIOTICS	MK 11735	854.2	MK 12344	1009.0	MK 15760	1071.9	MK 17256	1156.7	MED CONTN ANTIBIOTIQUES
54179	— CONTNG OTH SUBSTANCES	MK 87364	3437.0	MK 80348	4599.6	MK 91354	4924.1	MK 101036	5553.9	MED CONT AUT SUBSTANCES
55	PERFUME,CLEANING ETC PRD		3015.2		3325.3		3766.4		4099.1	PROD POUR PARFUM,TOILETTE
553	PERFUMERY,COSMETICS,ETC	W 295908	1787.3	W 339041	1873.5	W 427461	2269.9	W 640763	2612.1	PRODUITS DE PARFUMERIE
554	SOAP,CLEANSING ETC PREPS	W 542531	781.7	W 636594	927.9	W 609085	896.7	W 564820	864.6	SAVONS,PRODUITS DETERSIFS
58	PLASTIC MATERIALS ETC		3774.1		4546.9		4492.5		4410.5	MAT PLAST ARTIFICIELLES
582	PROD OF CONDENSATION ETC	W 471315	979.1	W 503862	1214.8	W 508269	1185.3	W 526760	1081.7	PROD CONDENS,POLYCOND
5823	ALKYDS,OTHER POLYESTERS	W 266457	555.3	W 291863	729.7	W 293759	679.9	W 318717	592.8	ALKYDES ET AUT POLYESTERS
583	POLYMERIZATION ETC PRODS		2746.7		3278.1		3253.9	W 1775595	3161.7	PROD POLYMERISATION
5839	OTH POLYMRZTION ETC PROD	W 143359	516.4	W 143665	603.2	W 172065	680.6	W 510307	1075.9	AUT PROD POLYMER COPOLYM
59	CHEMICAL MATERIALS NES		3742.7		4233.1		4528.7		4586.1	MAT PROD CHIMIQUES NDA
591	PESTICIDES,DISINFECTANTS	W 145976	981.7	W 152415	1130.6	W 159150	1259.7	W 173796	1210.6	DESINF,INSECT,FONG,HERB
598	MISCEL CHEM PRODUCTS NES		2543.2		2861.0		3008.0	W 1169555	3071.1	PROD DIV INDUST CHIM NDA
5982	ANTI–KNOCK PREPARTNS ETC	W 339755	875.7	W 333111	919.8	W 337437	989.5	W 333205	881.9	PREPARAT ANTIDETONANTES
5989	CHEM PRODUCTS,PREPS NES	W 681049	1567.7	W 792929	1941.3	W 785092	1908.3	W 764595	2067.7	PROD PREP CHIMIQUES NDA
59899	OTH CHEM PRODS,PREPS,NES	W 554544	1147.8	W 559362	1388.9	W 647076	1468.0	W 503514	1518.1	AUT PRODUITS CHIMIQUES NDA
6	BASIC MANUFACTURES		29852.3		35676.4		36423.4		37363.7	ART MANUFACTURES
62	RUBBER MANUFACTURES NES		1794.5		2079.6		2235.4		2229.4	CAOUTCHOUC MANUFACTURE
625	RUBBER TYRES, TUBES ETC	W 292241	1125.8	W 308066	1273.3	W 325505	1326.1	W 317623	1213.9	PNEUS CAOUTCHOUC VULCANISE
64	PAPER,PAPERBOARD AND MFR		3042.9		3656.9		3652.7		3818.7	PAPIERS,CARTONS & OUVRAGES
641	PAPER AND PAPERBOARD	W 1742670	2242.1	W 1664343	2635.6	W 1708399	2548.1	W 2073816	2659.0	PAPIERS ET CARTONS
6415	PAPER,PAPERBRD,BULK,NES	W 556747	654.2	W 544461	766.4	W 567783	725.1	W 710629	739.7	PAPIERS,CARTONS ROULEAUX
6418	COATED ETC PAPER NES BLK	W 332360	599.0	W 346290	741.0	W 340189	711.6	W 366583	753.2	PAP,CARTONS COUCHES,ENDUITS
642	PAPER,ETC,PRECUT,ARTS OF	W 1333561	800.9	W 421216	1021.4	W 363267	1104.7	W 373365	1159.7	PAP,CARTONS DECOUPES
65	TEXTILE YARN,FABRICS,ETC		4498.8		5173.6		5403.8		5644.8	FILS,TISSUS,ARTICLES TEXTILE
651	TEXTILE YARN		1262.9		1480.8		1497.3	W 299446	1577.0	FILS TEXTILES
657	SPECIAL TXTL FABRC,PRODS	W 89934	699.6	W 89343	836.4	W 94716	881.8	W 103593	949.8	TISSUS SPECIAUX
66	NONMETAL MINERAL MFS NES		6746.9		7510.2		8087.4		8343.7	ART MIN NON METALLIQUES
663	MINERAL MANUFCTURES NES	W 512427	692.3	W 739745	882.2	W 877803	861.0	W 981962	881.4	ART MIN MANUF NDA
667	PEARL,PREC–,SEMI–P STONE		4322.2		4585.2		5141.2		5294.4	PERLES, PIERRES GEMMES
6672	DIAMONDS NONINDUST,UNSET		4273.5		4527.0		5088.6		5190.6	DIAMANTS BRUTS
66721	— ROUGH,UNSORTED		463.9		380.5		858.7		620.8	DIAMANTS BRUTS NON TRIES
66722	— SRTD,ROUGH,SIMPLY WKD		3569.7		3804.1		3880.0		4038.0	DIAMANTS TRIES BRUTS
67	IRON AND STEEL		5670.8		7107.5		6628.3		6178.5	FER ET ACIER
672	IRON,STEEL PRIMARY FORMS	W 2013208	914.2	W 1789482	1187.0	W 2041681	1125.6	W 1912038	956.2	LINGOTS FER,ACIER
6725	IRN,STL BLOOMS,SLABS,ETC	W 1164983	616.1	W 1103884	862.2	W 1150227	807.5	W 916804	656.1	BLOOMS,BILLETTES FER ACIER
673	IRON,STEEL SHAPES ETC	W 3554070	1599.9	W 3663998	1921.5	W 3565632	1577.7	W 3410162	1373.9	BARRES,PROFIL FER,ACIER
6733	IRON,STEEL PROFILES ETC	W 1710687	739.1	W 1688781	818.9	W 1684485	760.3	W 1435725	615.9	PROFILES,PALPLAN FER,ACIER
674	IRN,STL UNIV,PLATE,SHEET	W 2457798	1764.3	W 2468447	2244.8	W 2589362	2046.0	W 2847351	1929.5	LARGES PLATS,TOLES
6749	OTH IRN,STL PLATES,SHEET	W 858372	573.6	W 870605	720.7	W 891434	712.2	W 1015968	713.7	AUTRES TOLES FER,ACIER
678	IRON,STL TUBES,PIPES,ETC		817.5		1025.9		1148.2	W 975469	1175.8	TUBES,TUYAUX EN FONTE,FER
68	NON–FERROUS METALS		3402.6		4491.8		4189.3		4536.4	METAUX NON FERREUX
681	SILVER,PLATINUM,ETC		849.3		875.2		1042.3		1047.1	ARGENT ET PLATINE
682	COPPER EXC CEMENT COPPER		771.4		1009.7	W 252580	889.3	W 255059	850.8	CUIVRE
6822	COPPER,ALLOYS WORKED	W 201326	665.8	W 227349	917.9	W 220537	808.5	W 225196	778.6	CUIVRE,ALLIAGES OUVRES
684	ALUMINIUM		1164.9		1773.6	W 507566	1399.5	W 687759	1727.8	ALUMINIUM
6842	ALUMINIUM,ALLOYS WORKED	W 281643	798.4	W 312204	1086.9	W 302286	1033.4	W 314896	1062.9	ALUMINIUM,ALLIAGES OUVRE
69	METAL MANUFACTURES NES		3841.7		4638.9		4965.5		5234.6	ART MANUFACT EN METAL NDA

5. General Exports F.O.B. by Commodities according to the S.I.T.C. (Rev. 2) in million U.S. Dollars
Exportations Générales F.O.B. par Produits d'après la C.T.C.I. (Rév. 2) en millions de Dollars E.U.

SITC CTCI	COMMODITY	1994 QUANTITY QUANTITE	1994 VALUE VALEUR	1995 QUANTITY QUANTITE	1995 VALUE VALEUR	1996 QUANTITY QUANTITE	1996 VALUE VALEUR	1997 QUANTITY QUANTITE	1997 VALUE VALEUR	PRODUIT
695	TOOLS	W 48259	670.6	W 53753	800.6	W 54323	907.5	W 59387	934.4	OUTILS A MAIN
699	BASE METAL MFRS NES	W 259907	1354.9	W 284630	1658.8	W 298004	1830.7		1946.4	ART MANUFACTURES MET NDA
7	MACHINES,TRANSPORT EQUIP		83824.5		102470.3		114371.2		128645.3	MACHINES MATERIEL TRANSPORT
71	POWER GENERATING EQUIPMT		9359.6		10195.5		11225.7		14384.6	MACHINES GENERATRICES
713	INTRNL COMBUS PSTN ENGIN	W 284841	3068.9	W 331162	3611.9	W 323878	3728.3	W 357237	4002.9	MOTEURS EXPL COMB INT, PIECE
7132	MOTOR VEHCL PISTN ENGINS	W 141834	1526.9	W 159628	1730.9	W 151825	1701.3	W 153636	1787.4	MOTEURS EXPL POUR VEHICULES
7139	PISTON ENGINE PARTS NES	W 79777	909.4	W 95586	1046.2	W 97132	1173.4	W 129488	1324.1	PIECES POUR 713.2,3,8
714	ENGINES AND MOTORS NES	W 23465	4634.8	W 23692	4861.3	W 26454	5604.2	W 28659	8227.6	MOTEURS NON ELECTRIQUES
7144	REACTION ENGINES	W 2517	2228.9	W 4086	2194.9	W 5551	2316.6	W 6390	3873.9	PROPULSEURS A REACTION
7149	ENGINE & MOTOR PARTS NES	W 14188	1848.8	W 15406	2143.7	W 18318	2751.6	W 18455	3643.8	PIECES 714 ET 718.88
71491	PARTS NES OF 7144,71481	W 2136	1094.2	W 1986	1196.4	W 2740	1756.6	W 3324	2465.1	PIECES DES PROPULSEURS
71499	PARTS NES,OF 71488,71888	W 12052	754.6	W 13419	947.4	W 15578	995.0	W 15131	1178.7	PIECES 714.88 ET 718.88
716	ROTATING ELECTRIC PLANT	W 117174	1115.7	W 125631	1217.1	W 128096	1311.7	W 145732	1376.2	APP ELECTR ROTATIFS,PIECES
7162	AC MTRS,GENRTRS,GEN SETS	W 84185	768.5	W 88579	838.2	W 95120	952.4	W 109635	1031.1	MOTEURS ELECTRIQUES
72	MACHS FOR SPCL INDUSTRYS		6771.0		8083.4		8591.6		9381.6	MAC SPECIALES POUR INDUST
722	TRACTORS NON-ROAD	W 225192	1178.8	W 244665	1438.9	W 269059	1728.8	W 276404	1863.4	TRACTEURS
7224	WHEELED TRACTORS NES	W 225019	1178.6	W 244434	1438.2	W 268914	1727.7	W 274440	1848.7	TRACTEURS A ROUES
723	CIVIL ENGNEERG EQUIP ETC		1548.2		1928.1		1870.5	W 522132	2142.9	APPAREILS DE GENIE CIVIL
7234	CONST,MINING MACHNRY NES	W 216212	1157.5		1493.2	W 236783	1372.2	W 442015	1558.1	MACH POUR LA CONST, MINES
72342	SLFPRP SHOVELS,EXCAVATRS	W 190393	960.1	W 233476	1249.7	W 202014	1108.1	W 416232	1324.0	PELLES MECANIQUES
724	TEXTILE,LEATHER MACHNRY	W 45512	664.9	W 40820	713.7	W 35867	624.4	W 36724	661.0	MACH POUR INDUSTRIE TEXTILE
726	PRINTG,BKBINDG MACHY,PTS	W 52078	873.8	W 54498	915.9	W 33293	889.7	W 65023	956.9	MACHINES POUR IMPRIMERIE
728	OTH MACHY FOR SPCL INDUS	W 141429	1653.6	W 152780	2053.6	W 165345	2303.4	W 173422	2558.8	AUT MACH IND PARTICULIERES
7284	MACHY FOR SPCL INDUS NES	W 69888	1189.3	W 74728	1487.3	W 83638	1683.0	W 95007	1884.9	MACH SPEC IND PARTICUL.
73	METALWORKING MACHINERY		1181.2		1435.7		1650.0		1644.5	MACH TRAVAIL DES METAUX
736	METALWORKING MACH-TOOLS	W 71486	834.0	W 77359	1067.7	W 74511	1230.8	W 63004	1130.6	MACH-OUTILS TRAVAIL METAUX
74	GENRL INDUSTRL MACHY NES		8576.0		10524.6		11682.3		12665.4	MACH APP INDUSTRIE
741	HEATING,COOLING EQUIPMNT	W 83938	1168.1	W 101910	1503.5	W 126525	1705.9	W 108100	1768.6	MACH CHAUFFAGE,PIECES
742	PUMPS FOR LIQUIDS ETC	W 41429	855.3	W 49850	976.9	W 58386	1103.3	W 57642	1249.1	POMPES MOTO-POMPES
743	PUMPS NES,CENTRFUGES ETC	W 111828	1651.6	W 129679	2094.9	W 139865	2275.7	W 146917	2487.7	POMPES COMPRES,VENT ETC
7436	GAS,LIQUID FILTERS ETC	W 49495	576.2	W 52568	799.7	W 59345	856.0	W 56506	900.6	APP POUR FILT DES LIQUIDES
744	MECHANICAL HANDLING EQU	W 251701	1573.4	W 300466	2010.3	W 317090	2307.7	W 306701	2390.4	EQUIP MANUTENTION PIECES
7441	FORK LIFT TRCKS,ETC,PTS	W 126472	583.4	W 156758	825.1	W 162478	961.4	W 157630	902.1	CHARIOTS POUR USINES ETC
74411	FORK LIFT TRUCKS ETC	W 124281	571.3	W 154812	809.7	W 160359	944.6	W 155155	880.4	CHARIOTS POUR LES GARES
745	NONELEC MACHY,TOOLS NES	W 38558	895.3	W 40065	1003.8	W 44028	1127.6	W 45159	1227.2	AUT MACH NON ELEC,PIECES
7452	OTH NONELEC MCHS,PTS NES	W 34817	775.2	W 36664	890.1	W 40950	1014.3	W 42191	1116.3	AUT MACH NON ELEC,PIECES
749	NONELEC MACH PTS,ACC NES	W 168143	2432.6	W 271667	2935.4	W 190158	3162.3	W 200944	3542.7	PIECES MACH NON ELEC NDA
7492	COCKS,VALVES ETC NES	W 50343	986.0	W 55812	1159.6	W 59822	1263.1	W 59056	1410.0	ART ROB,SIM POUR TUYAUX
75	OFFICE MACHNES,ADP EQUIP		14420.0		18317.6		18951.2		21407.6	MACH BUREAU TRAIT AUTOM
751	OFFICE MACHINES	W 43531	1067.2	W 39144	1060.9	W 47004	1100.2	W 45280	1330.8	MACH,APPAREILS DE BUREAU
7518	OFFICE MACHINES NES	W 37998	892.8	W 33942	867.0	W 40195	903.6	W 40882	1072.7	MACH,APP DE BUREAU NDA
752	AUTOMTIC DATA PROC EQUIP	W 107990	8663.1	W 116497	11531.3	W 139246	11932.0	W 192863	13748.0	MACH TRAIT INFORMATION
7522	DIGITAL COMPUTERS	W 3108	588.8	W 3993	1012.4	W 8923	1979.7	W 12356	1829.7	MACH DIGITALES COMPLETES
7523	DIGITL CENTRL PROCESSORS	W 33801	4075.8	W 38953	5402.5	W 44976	4895.2	W 58230	5523.3	UNITES CENTRALES
7524	DIGITL CENTRL STOR UNITS	W 8794	1520.5	W 11185	2418.5	W 8771	1853.3	W 9489	2157.2	UNITES MEMOIRE CENTRALES
7525	ADP PERIPHERAL UNITS	W 55767	1813.2	W 56700	1958.2	W 66160	2054.4	W 90315	2182.4	UNITES PERIPHERIQUES
7528	OFF-LINE DATA PROC EQUIP	W 5420	584.7	W 5044	652.0	W 9257	921.8	W 20231	1716.0	MACH AUXIL TRAIT INFORM
759	OFFICE,ADP MCH PTS,ACCES	W 40204	4689.8	W 61719	5725.5	W 45467	5919.2	W 48926	6328.9	PIECES DU 751 ET 752
7599	ACCTG,ETC,ADP MCH PTS,AC	W 28926	4223.3	W 36479	5271.1	W 32056	5402.0	W 33596	5705.2	PIECES DU 751 ET 752
76	TELECOMM,SOUND EQUIPMENT		7284.2		9978.4		11826.4		13700.9	EQUIPMENT DE TELECOM
761	TELEVISION RECEIVERS	W 88613	1231.4	W 88416	1342.9	W 119706	1864.3	W 138862	1886.9	RECEPTEURS DE TELEVISION
7611	COLOUR TV RECEIVERS	W 88339	1219.6	W 88093	1330.0	W 118697	1854.4	W 138655	1877.9	RECEPTEURS COULEUR
763	SOUND RECORDRS,PHONOGRPH	W 13702	712.7	W 14733	788.0	W 17555	1005.3	W 16540	890.8	PHONO,APP ENREGISTREMENT
7638	OTHR SOUND APPARATUS ETC	W 13443	705.3	W 14333	776.1	W 17072	989.9	W 16182	880.7	AUT APP D'ENREGIS,REPROD
76381	TV IMAGE,SND RECRDRS ETC	W 10590	526.7	W 11383	581.7	W 14417	811.7	W 13521	715.8	APP ENREG,REPRO IMAG,SON
764	TELECOM EQPT,PTS,ACC NES		5020.5		7432.1		8552.1	W 225185	10586.5	EQUIP TELECOM,PIECES
7641	LINE TELEPHONE,ETC EQUIP	W 9837	1010.6	W 13705	2040.3	W 22214	2834.4	W 121231	3846.7	APP TELEPHON PAR FIL
7643	TV,RADIO TRANSMITTRS ETC		1711.6		2488.4		2649.9	W 1062	225.1	APP EMET TELE RADIO
7649	PTS NES OF EQUIPMT OF 76	W 112847	1489.3	W 42319	1925.2	W 37981	2167.8	W 43490	2489.8	PIECES DE LA DIV 76
76491	PTS NES OF APPAR OF 7641	W 5239	442.0	W 4407	463.3	W 5934	797.3	W 8322	987.9	PIECES POUR 764.1
76493	TELECOMM EQUIPMT PTS NES	W 15425	917.2	W 17040	1276.6	W 25026	1211.9	W 27398	1351.2	PIECES 761,762,764.3,8
77	ELECTRIC MACHNRY NES ETC		14808.3		18381.7		19466.3		19196.9	MACH APP ELECT NDA
771	ELECTRIC POWER MACHY NES	W 31438	522.9	W 37589	787.4	W 65684	955.7	W 42684	1042.9	MACH PROD,TRANS ELECTR
772	SWITCHGEAR ETC,PARTS NES	W 62188	2117.9	W 74486	2600.7	W 81745	2941.7	W 86263	3386.7	APP COUPURE,SECT ETC
7721	SWITCHGEAR ETC	W 56932	1694.9	W 68186	1993.5	W 61972	2258.5	W 75381	2554.4	APP COUPURE,SECTIONMNT
773	ELECTR DISTRIBUTNG EQUIP	W 127445	764.2	W 153368	952.5	W 158903	1023.1	W 154213	1081.3	EQUIPMT DISTRIBUTION ELECT
7731	INSULATED WIRE,CABLE ETC	W 118115	641.7	W 138766	789.8	W 143090	871.6	W 142778	937.4	FILS,CABLES ISOLES ELECT
775	HOUSEHOLD TYPE EQUIP NES	W 114967	963.1	W 146308	1188.6	W 152311	1278.6	W 174812	1279.9	MACH,APP USAGE DOMESTQUE
7758	ELECTRO-THERMIC APPL NES	W 49526	509.2	W 70927	668.1	W 83029	800.1	W 99596	745.3	APP ELECTROTHERMIQ NDA
776	TRANSISTORS,VALVES,ETC		6345.6		8055.0		7828.5	W 88119	6506.2	LAMPES,TUBES,VALVES
7763	DIODES,TRANSISTORS,ETC	W 2053	628.1	W 2882	795.2	W 4765	774.1	W 3627	706.2	DIODES,TRANSISTORS
7764	ELECTRONIC MICROCIRCUITS	W 4734	5139.8	W 8334	6535.5	W 9495	6321.5	W 7254	5019.2	MICROSTRUCTURES ELECTRON
778	ELECTRICAL MACHINERY NES		3739.2		4362.1	W 236051	5003.9	W 246159	5490.6	AUTRES MACH ELECT NDA
7788	OTH ELEC MACHY,EQUIP NES		2244.0	W 46828	2758.1	W 48702	3027.9	W 41794	3250.8	AUT MACH APP ELEC NDA
77886	OTH ELEC MACHINERY NES		862.7	W 14529	1094.5	W 12509	1300.4	W 9977	1410.6	AUT MACH APP ELECTRIQUES
78	ROAD VEHICLES		14293.3		18487.0		22524.7		24400.4	VEHICULES ROUTIERS
781	PASS MOTOR VEH EXC BUSES	W 711467	7765.1	W 953226	11008.5	W 1137975	13428.4	W 1264573	14513.7	AUTO TRANSPORT PERSONNES
782	LORRIES,SPCL MTR VEH NES		1167.5		1290.2	W 237049	1704.0	W 221076	1584.4	VEHICULES SPECIAUX,MARCH
7821	LORRIES,TRUCKS	W 107005	754.9	W 161149	1076.1	W 213839	1494.6	W 205447	1466.5	VEHICULES TRANSP MARCHAND
784	MOTOR VEH PRTS,ACCES NES	W 675628	4600.3	W 782618	5240.5	W 917300	6280.7	W 980737	7188.1	PIECES 722,781,782,783
7849	OTHER MOTOR VEHCL PARTS	W 644844	4392.6	W 747790	4967.8	W 867211	5902.0	W 936535	6810.0	PIECES 722,781,782,783
79	OTHR TRANSPORT EQUIPMENT		7131.1		7066.8		8453.4		11863.5	AUTRE MATERIEL TRANSPORT
791	RAILWAY VEHICLES	W 31960	650.7	W 15114	163.2	W 18342	197.2	W 12179	155.5	VEHIC MAT CHEMINS DE FER
792	AIRCRAFT ETC		5713.0		6209.6		7359.6	W 20599	9558.3	APP NAVIGATION AERIENNE
7923	AIRCRFT NES2000-15000KG		865.6		799.5		1099.5			AERODYNES 2000 A 15000 KG
7924	AIRCRFT NES OVER 15000KG		738.6		998.8		819.3	W 2	114.7	AERODYNES PLUS 15000 KG
7929	AIRCRAFT PARTS NES		3866.5		4210.9		5083.7			PIECES DU 792
793	SHIPS AND BOATS ETC		767.4		694.1	W 32261	896.7	W 81266	2149.8	NAVIRES BATEAUX,ETC
7931	WARSHIPS		66.2	W 8805	288.8	W 7346	452.8	W 19681	1000.9	NAVIRES DE GUERRE
8	MISC MANUFACTURED GOODS		26403.5		29743.2		32465.6		35449.9	ART MANUFACTURES DIVERS
821	*FURNITURE,PARTS THEREOF	W 416107	1108.6	W 318758	1337.5	W 822267	1552.2	W 367368	1636.2	MEUBLES ET PIECES
8219	FURNITURE AND PARTS NES	W 265473	713.3	W 265872	852.6	W 732436	993.4	W 314405	1058.4	AUTRES MEUBLES ET PIECES
84	CLOTHING AND ACCESSORIES		3966.7		4454.7		4940.7		5047.3	VETEMENTS
842	MENS OUTERWEAR NOT KNIT	W 40510	642.6	W 23859	666.3	W 22667	684.3	W 22674	657.7	VET DESSUS POUR HOMMES
843	WOMENS OUTERWEAR NONKNIT	W 24607	970.0	W 28572	1081.9	W 31786	1229.2	W 29212	1207.4	VET DESSUS FEMMES MAT TEX
845	OUTERWEAR KNIT NONELASTC	W 30760	1058.0	W 32918	1107.4	W 34940	1255.0	W 34234	1328.0	VET DESSOUS,ACCES BONNET
8451	— JERSEYS,PULLOVERS ETC	W 17043	626.0	W 18114	640.4	W 19291	718.7	W 18813	760.2	CHANDAILS,PULL-OVERS ETC
851	*FOOTWEAR	W 28922	672.0	W 28862	748.8	W 33050	886.7	W 32572	921.9	CHAUSSURES
85102	FOOTWEAR LEATHER	W 16897	424.5	W 23963	673.4	W 27940	807.0	W 27394	838.2	CHAUS SEMELLES EN CUIR
87	PRECISION INSTRUMNTS NES		5587.1		6485.4		7179.2		8389.8	INSTRUM,APPAR SCIENT NDA
872	MEDICAL INSTRUMENTS NES	W 23550	875.6	W 26739	1021.6	W 32496	1188.0	W 34910	1286.1	INSTR,APP MEDIC-CHIR NDA

5. General Exports F.O.B. by Commodities according to the S.I.T.C. (Rev. 2) in million U.S. Dollars
Exportations Générales F.O.B. par Produits d'après la C.T.C.I. (Rév. 2) en millions de Dollars E.U.

SITC CTCI	COMMODITY	1994		1995		1996		1997		PRODUIT
		QUANTITY QUANTITE	VALUE VALEUR	QUANTITY QUANTITE	VALUE VALEUR	QUANTITY QUANTITE	VALUE VALEUR	QUANTITY QUANTITE	VALUE VALEUR	
87202	OTH MEDICAL INSTRUMENTS	W 20349	715.0	W 22747	820.7	W 27186	942.1	W 30328	1050.0	INSTRUM,APP MEDECINE
874	MEASURNG,CONTROLNG INSTR	W 56527	4083.3	W 54021	4792.6	W 65489	5273.6	W 56646	6243.1	INSTRUMENTS DE MESURE
8741	SURVEYING INSTRUMENTS	W 2787	695.0	W 2970	783.5	W 3365	946.9	W 5054	1142.6	INST GEODESIE,TOPO ETC
87411	NAVIG INSTR NONELEC ETC	W 846	556.6	W 1036	625.9	W 920	750.4	W 1028	887.6	INSTR NAVIGATION
8743	GAS,LIQUID CONTROL INSTR	W 20158	569.3	W 15495	671.7	W 25811	784.0	W 12186	872.3	APP,INSTR MESURE FLUIDES
8748	ELEC MEAS,CONTRL EQU NES	W 6946	981.6	W 6550	1179.6	W 6640	1328.8	W 6737	1750.3	APP ELEC ELECTRO MESURE
87483	OTH ELCTRNC MEAS ETC EQU	W 6193	866.1	W 5562	1029.1	W 5133	1031.8	W 5756	1187.0	AUT APP ELECTRO DE MESURE
8749	INSTR PTS NES,ACCESSORYS	W 11637	788.2	W 13345	977.8	W 13301	987.8	W 14548	1032.6	PIECES 873,874.3,54,874.8
88	PHOTO EQU,OPTICL GDS ETC		2537.5		2795.3		2995.8		3006.7	APP,FOURN PHOTO,OP,MONTR
882	PHOTO,CINEMA SUPPLIES	W 164619	1610.2	W 165651	1822.3	W 162717	1889.0	W 209824	1808.5	PRODUITS PHOTO,CINEMA
8822	PHOTO FILM EXC DEV CINMA	W 125519	1457.8	W 122395	1601.5	W 117728	1651.7	W 138113	1550.2	PLAQUES,PELLICULES,FILMS
89	MISC MANUFCTRD GOODS NES		11999.4		13311.9		14155.8		15561.9	ART MANUFACTURES DIVERS
892	PRINTED MATTER		2795.8		3149.4	W 332870	3439.2	W 364913	3434.1	IMPRIMES
8921	PRINTED BOOKS,GLOBES,ETC	W 160508	1508.1	W 152145	1710.3	W 161973	1837.5	W 156840	1905.7	LIVRES,BROCHURES,CARTES
89211	PRINTED BOOKS,PAMPHLETS	W 156605	1466.0	W 148638	1665.7	W 157411	1786.3	W 152137	1854.7	LIVRES,BROCHURES
8928	PRINTED MATTER NES	W 62408	609.4	W 68263	701.0	W 78450	840.0	W 109259	715.5	IMPRIMES NDA
893	ARTICLES OF PLASTIC NES		2008.7		2451.0		2650.7		2927.8	OUVRAGES EN MAT DIVIS 58
8939	MISC PLASTIC ARTICLES	W 262396	1317.9	W 325149	1632.7	W 318092	1766.0	W 359942	2056.9	ART DIVERS EN MAT DIV 58
89399	OTHR PLASTC ARTICLES NES	W 188185	1116.8	W 242784	1397.3	W 238973	1515.3	W 279346	1781.5	AUT OUV MAT DIV 58
894	TOYS,SPORTING GOODS,ETC		1109.4	W 118438	1344.7	W 113695	1423.9	W 94440	1392.3	VOITURES ENFANTS,JOUETS
8942	TOYS,INDOOR GAMES ETC	W 93252	842.2	W 92720	1036.3	W 79100	1064.1	W 69832	1038.5	JOUETS,JEUX ETC
896	WORKS OF ART ETC		1964.4		2039.0		1834.3		2305.8	OBJETS D'ART
89601	HAND PAINTINGS ETC NES		1015.7		1067.9		868.2		1200.0	TABLEAUX,PEINTURES
89606	ANTIQUES NES		618.9		695.5		654.6		764.0	OBJETS D'ANTIQUITE
897	GOLD,SILVER WARE,JEWELRY		1545.5		1449.2		1623.6		1973.4	BIJOUTERIE,ORFEVRERIE
8973	PREC JEWLRY,GLD–SILVWARE		1355.1		1269.6		1454.0		1801.4	BIJOUX OR,ARGENT ORFEVRE
89731	PRECIOUS METAL JEWELLERY		1257.3		1104.9		1305.0		1674.0	ART BIJOUTERIE,JOAILLER
898	MUSICAL INSTRUMENTS,PTS	W 63799	1594.3	W 118561	1751.7	W 76622	1928.6	W 118640	2151.8	INSTRUMENTS DE MUSIQUE
8983	SOUND RECRDNG TAPE,DISCS	W 59347	1507.4	W 114805	1648.7	W 73030	1839.8	W 115100	2055.2	SUPPORTS SON POUR 763
89832	RECORDED DISCS,TAPES ETC	W 31027	1148.7	W 81981	1240.3	W 42132	1434.0	W 55666	1612.2	DISQUES,PHONO,BANDES
899	OTHER MANUFACTURED GOODS		653.2		743.9		847.1		912.8	AUT ART MANUF DIVERS NDA
9	GOODS NOT CLASSD BY KIND		2400.2		3090.9		3231.9		3246.9	ART TRANSACT NON CLASSES
931	*SPECIAL TRANSACTIONS		1268.7	W 92426	1319.8		1443.3		1559.4	TRANS.SPECIALES
951	*WAR FIREARMS,AMMUNITION		668.0		1156.2		1230.9	W 11146	1267.1	VEHIC BLINDES ARMES
95101	ARMORED FIGHTNG VEHICLES		154.5	W 7812	723.2	W 6962	624.8	W 4855	332.8	CHARS DE COMBAT
95109	PARTS OF ARMS NES		57.4		41.1		80.4	W 5519	898.1	PIECES POUR ARMES

1. HISTORICAL SERIES, 1962–1997 GENERAL TRADE, IMPORTS C.I.F., EXPORTS F.O.B.
SERIES HISTORIQUES, 1962–1997 COMMERCE GENERAL, IMPORTATIONS C.A.F., EXPORTATIONS F.O.B

YEAR ANNEE	VALUE IN MILLION TANZ.SHILLINGS VALEUR EN MILLION TANZ.SHILLINGS MERCHANDISE –MARCHANDISE		GOLD # 1 –OR		CONVERSION FACTORS U.S. CENTS PER TANZ.SHILLING FACTEURS DE CONVERSION CENTS E.U. PAR TANZ.SHILLING		INDEX NUMBERS –INDICES QUANTUM		UNIT VALUE VALEUR UNITAIRE	
	IMPORTS	EXPORTS	IMPORTS	EXPORTS	IMPORTS	EXPORTS	IMPORTS	EXPORTS	IMPORTS	EXPORTS
1962	1030.00	1116.20		25.40	14.0000	14.0000				
1963	1055.20	1371.20	0.40	25.60	14.0000	14.0000				
1964	1193.20	1530.70	0.40	23.40	14.0000	14.0000				
1965	1333.80	1399.80	0.80	22.80	14.0000	14.0000				
1966	1612.10	1785.20	1.00	14.20	14.0000	14.0000				
1967	1576.70	1667.60	0.20	4.60	14.0000	14.0000				
1968	1833.80	1717.80		4.80	14.0000	14.0000				
1969	1710.00	1792.40		4.80	14.0000	14.0000				
1970	2274.20	1851.90		2.00	14.0000	14.0000				
1971	2725.60	1988.80	0.20		14.0000	14.0000				
1972	2956.10	2276.60			14.0000	14.0000				
1973	3478.90	2586.80			14.2860	14.2160				
1974	5257.90	2860.60			14.0000	14.0000				
1975	5694.20	2763.80			13.5806	13.4653				
1976	4752.00	3846.00			11.9235	11.9387				
1977	6161.00	4198.00			12.1397	12.1391				
1978	8798.00	3669.00			12.9859	13.0059				
1979	8885.00	4216.00			12.1221	12.1239				
1980	10046.40	4160.50			12.2029	12.2028				
1981	10047.00	5087.00			12.0673	12.0572				
1982	10519.00	4230.00			10.7530	10.7520				
1983	9207.00	4130.00			8.9309	8.8700				
1984	13373.00	6135.00			6.8618	6.5676				
1985	16966.00	6173.00			5.7418	5.7274				
1986	30576.99	11285.00			2.9180	2.9190				
1987	59340.00	18512.00			1.5240	1.5230				
1988	80828.00	27040.99			0.9960	0.9960				
1989	146705.20	52777.01			0.6800	0.7075				
1990	265984.00	64571.01			0.5129	0.5128				
1991	338990.00	74708.00			0.4561	0.4573				
1992	449479.90	123966.00			0.3232	0.3324				
1993	615990.00	181147.00			0.2431	0.2485				
1994	765756.90	265177.00			0.1965	0.1958				
1995	968910.00	390377.90			0.1733	0.1754				
1996	804948.90	441344.00			0.1721	0.1718				
1997	818703.10	438798.00			0.1632	0.1637				

2. IMPORTS BY BROAD ECONOMIC CATEGORY AND EXPORTS BY INDUSTRIAL ORIGIN. (PERCENTAGE OF TOTAL VALUE)
IMPORTATIONS PAR CATEGORIES ECONOMIQUES ET EXPORTATIONS PAR BRANCHE D'ACTIVITE.(EN POURCENTAGE DE LA VALEUR TOTALE)

IMPORTS – IMPORTATIONS

	1988	1989	1990	1991	1992	1993	1994
TOTAL IMPORTS–IMPORTATIONS TOTALES							
1 FOOD BEV–ALIMENTATION BOISSONS							
11 PRIMARY–PRODUITS DE BASE							
111 FOR INDUSTRY–POUR L'INDUSTRIE							
112 FOR HOUSEHOLDS–POUR LES MENAGES							
12 PROCESSED–PRODUITS ELABORES							
121 FOR INDUSTRY–POUR L'INDUSTRIE							
122 FOR HOUSEHOLDS–POUR LES MENAGES							
2 IND SUPPLIES–APPROV INDUSTRIELS							
21 PRIMARY–PRODUITS DE BASE							
22 PROCESSED–PRODUITS ELABORES							
3 FUELS–COMBUSTIBLES							
31 PRIMARY–PRODUITS DE BASE							
32 PROCESSED–PRODUITS ELABORES							
321 MOTOR SPIRIT–ESSENCE							
322 OTHER–AUTRES							
4 MACHINERY–EQUIPEMENT							
41 CAPITAL EQUIPMENT–MACHINES							
42 PARTS–PIECES ACCESSOIRES							
5 TRANSPORT–TRANSPORT							
51 PASSENGER CARS–AUTOMOBILES							
52 OTHER–AUTRES							
521 INDUSTRIAL–INDUSTRIELS							
522 NON INDUSTRIAL–NON INDUSTRIEL							
53 PARTS–PIECES ACCESSOIRES							
6 CONSUM GOODS–BIENS CONSOMMATION							
61 DURABLE–DURABLES							
62 SEMI DURABLE–SEMI DURABLES							
63 NON DURABLE–NON DURABLES							
7 GOODS NES–BIENS NDA							

EXPORTS – EXPORTATIONS

	1988	1989	1990	1991	1992	1993	1994
TOTAL EXPORTS–EXPORTATIONS TOTALES							
1 AGRICULTURE							
2 MINING QUARRY–INDUS EXTRACTIVES							
3 MANUFACTURING–IND MANUFACTUR							
31 FOOD BEV TOBACCO–ALIM BOISS TAB							
32 TEXTILES–INDUSTRIES TEXTILES							
33 WOOD & PRODUCTS–BOIS & PRODUITS							
34 PAPER & PRODUCTS–PAPIER & PRODT							
35 CHEMICALS–INDUSTRIES CHIMIQUES							
36 NON METAL MIN–MIN NON METAL							
37 BASIC METAL–IND METAL BASE							
38 METAL MANUF–MANUF METAL							
39 OTH MANUF IND–AUTRES MANUF							

3. TRADE BY PRINCIPAL COUNTRIES OF ORIGIN AND DESTINATION (VALUE IN MILLION U.S. DOLLARS)
ECHANGES SELON LES PRINCIPAUX PAYS D'ORIGINE ET DE DESTINATION (VALEUR EN MILLIONS DE DOLLARS EU)

COUNTRIES–PAYS	GENERAL IMPORTS C.I.F. IMPORTATIONS GENERALES C.A.F 1990	1991	1992	1993	1994
World	1021.4				
Africa	44.2				
Americas	46.9				
– Northern America	36.1				
– LAIA	8.3				
– CACM					
– Caribbean	1.3				
– Rest of America	1.2				
Asia excl fmr USSR	266.0				
– Middle East	123.4				
Asia former USSR					
Europe excl fmr USSR	629.6				
– European Union	576.3				
– Eastern Europe	23.7				
– Rest of Europe	29.6				
Europe former USSR	2.1				
Oceania	7.8				
Other	24.8				
Areas n.e.s.	24.8				
United Kingdom	174.8				
Former Fed Rep Germany	102.8				
Japan/Japon	79.1				
Italy/Italie	68.6				
United Arab Emirates	45.4				
Netherlands/Pays–Bas	44.7				
Iran (Islamic Rep of)	44.1				
France, Monaco	43.9				
Belgium–Luxembourg	32.8				
Sweden/Suède	31.3				
Denmark/Danemark	28.8				
Ireland/Irlande	27.2				
Qatar	25.0				
Canada	20.1				
China/Chine	18.8				
Kenya	18.1				
Former German Dem Rep	17.7				
India/Inde	17.6				
USA/Etats–Unis d'Amer	16.0				
Norway,Svalbard and JM	12.7				
Switzerland,Liechtenst.	11.5				
Finland/Finlande	11.0				
Singapore/Singapour	9.0				
Australia/Australie	7.6				
Other Africa n.e.s.	7.1				
Spain/Espagne	5.8				
Argentina/Argentine	5.5				
Former SFR Yugoslavia	5.3				
China, Hong Kong SAR	5.3				
Zambia/Zambie	5.2				
Saudi Arabia	5.1				
Former Czechoslovakia	5.0				
Zimbabwe	4.7				
Bangladesh	3.0				
So. African Customs Un	3.0				
Austria/Autriche	3.0				
Pakistan	2.9				
Brazil/Brésil	2.7				
Former USSR/Anc. URSS	2.1				

COUNTRIES–PAYS	GENERAL EXPORTS F.O.B. EXPORTATIONS GENERALES F.O.B. 1990	1991	1992	1993	1994
Monde	416.0				
Afrique	36.3				
Amériques	29.2				
– Amérique du Nord	29.1				
– ALAI	0.0				
– MCAC					
– Caraïbes	0.0				
– Autre Amérique	0.0				
Asie anc. URSS exclus	157.9				
– Moyen–Orient	8.2				
Asie ancienne URSS					
Europe anc. URSS exclus	179.7				
– Union Européenne	167.5				
– Europe de l'Est	2.7				
– Autre de l'Europe	9.5				
Europe ancienne URSS	1.0				
Océanie	1.1				
Autre	10.8				
Areas n.e.s.	10.8				
India/Inde	69.3				
Former Fed Rep Germany	51.5				
United Kingdom	44.0				
USA/Etats–Unis d'Amer	28.2				
Netherlands/Pays–Bas	22.3				
Other Asia n.e.s.	17.1				
Japan/Japon	16.1				
Portugal	15.7				
Singapore/Singapour	13.1				
Pakistan	12.8				
Kenya	12.1				
Italy/Italie	12.0				
China, Hong Kong SAR	11.2				
Switzerland,Liechtenst.	7.4				
Belgium–Luxembourg	7.0				
Spain/Espagne	5.0				
Finland/Finlande	4.6				
Indonesia/Indonésie	4.1				
Uganda/Ouganda	4.0				
Turkey/Turquie	3.9				
Zimbabwe	3.4				
France, Monaco	3.1				
Malaysia/Malaisie	2.7				
Thailand/Thaïlande	2.4				
Sudan/Soudan	2.3				
United Arab Emirates	2.0				
Zambia/Zambie	2.0				
Former SFR Yugoslavia	1.8				
Egypt/Egypte	1.7				
Dem Rep of the Congo	1.6				
Other Africa n.e.s.	1.5				
Burundi	1.2				
Somalia/Somalie	1.1				
Former USSR/Anc. URSS	1.0				
Saudi Arabia	1.0				
Canada	1.0				
Hungary/Hongrie	0.9				
Mozambique	0.9				
Malawi	0.9				

(VALUE AS PERCENTAGE OF WORLD TOTAL)(VALEURS EN POURCENTAGE DU TOTAL MONDIAL)

	1985	1986	1987	1988	1989	1990	1991	1992	1993	1994
Africa	5.3	6.4	5.4	4.2	4.5	4.3				
Americas	6.9	5.7	4.9	4.3	4.0	4.6				
– Northern America	6.3	4.3	4.8	3.9	3.7	3.5				
– LAIA	0.6	0.3	0.1	0.2	0.1	0.8				
– CACM										
– Caribbean	0.0	1.0	0.0	0.3	0.2	0.1				
– Rest of America					0.0	0.1				
Asia excl fmr USSR	38.2	34.5	30.4	31.3	33.1	26.0				
– Middle East	20.0	13.8	11.9	10.7	16.7	12.1				
Asia former USSR										
Europe excl fmr USSR	48.1	52.3	57.4	58.8	54.6	61.6				
– European Union	44.0	47.3	53.8	54.5	50.9	56.4				
– Eastern Europe	0.6	0.2	0.2	0.6	0.7	2.3				
– Rest of Europe	3.5	4.8	3.4	3.7	3.0	2.9				
Europe former USSR	0.8	0.8	0.2	0.2	0.5	0.2				
Oceania	0.4	0.4	0.5	0.3	0.2	0.8				
Other	0.4		1.2	0.9	3.1	2.4				
Areas n.e.s.	0.4		1.2	0.9	3.1	2.4				
United Kingdom	11.1	12.1	14.5	17.3	16.3	17.1				
Former Fed Rep Germany	8.9	10.7	12.4	11.8	9.7	10.1				
Japan/Japon	8.9	11.6	11.2	12.5	9.7	7.7				
Italy/Italie	8.4	6.7	9.3	7.8	9.1	6.7				
United Arab Emirates	2.2	5.5	4.5	3.5	5.2	4.4				
Netherlands/Pays–Bas	3.9	4.0	5.1	5.1	4.0	4.4				
Iran (Islamic Rep of)	8.7	2.5	0.0	2.5	3.0	4.3				
France, Monaco	1.0	1.6	1.1	1.3	2.1	4.3				
Belgium–Luxembourg	2.9	3.3	1.7	1.9	3.1	3.2				

	1985	1986	1987	1988	1989	1990	1991	1992	1993	1994
Afrique	7.0	6.3	11.5	11.1	14.1	8.7				
Amériques	2.1	2.5	2.5	3.0	3.6	7.0				
– Amérique du Nord	2.1	2.3	2.5	3.0	3.6	7.0				
– ALAI	0.0	0.1			0.0	0.0				
– MCAC										
– Caraïbes		0.0	0.0	0.0	0.0	0.0				
– Autre Amérique					0.0	0.0				
Asie anc. URSS exclus	26.1	19.7	26.2	27.6	29.3	38.0				
– Moyen–Orient	2.6	0.4	1.4	1.2	1.4	2.0				
Asie ancienne URSS										
Europe anc. URSS exclus	57.8	67.8	56.5	51.6	47.6	43.2				
– Union Européenne	55.4	66.5	53.4	50.4	46.4	40.3				
– Europe de l'Est	1.2	0.2	1.3	0.3	0.3	0.7				
– Autre de l'Europe	1.2	1.1	1.8	0.9	0.9	2.3				
Europe ancienne URSS	0.4	0.2	0.7	0.2	0.2	0.2				
Océanie	0.4	0.3	0.5	0.4	0.3	0.3				
Autre	6.3	3.2	2.1	6.1	4.9	2.6				
Areas n.e.s.	6.3	3.2	2.1	6.1	4.9	2.6				
India/Inde	3.3	4.5	7.5	6.4	2.5	16.7				
Former Fed Rep Germany	19.4	24.2	13.1	14.2	14.1	12.4				
United Kingdom	15.4	12.4	10.4	10.1	11.9	10.6				
USA/Etats–Unis d'Amer	1.7	2.0	2.2	2.6	3.1	6.8				
Netherlands/Pays–Bas	5.7	7.0	8.2	5.8	5.7	5.4				
Other Asia n.e.s.	1.2	1.9	2.8	4.2	5.2	4.1				
Japan/Japon	3.1	4.4	3.8	4.6	4.6	3.9				
Portugal	1.8	2.5	2.9	4.0	3.2	3.8				
Singapore/Singapour	7.5	4.0	3.5	2.7	5.1	3.2				

4. General Imports C.I.F. by Commodities according to the S.I.T.C. (Rev. 2) in million U.S. Dollars
Importations Générales C.A.F. par Produits d'après la C.T.C.I. (Rév. 2) en millions de Dollars E.U.

SITC CTCI	COMMODITY	1991 QUANTITY QUANTITE	1991 VALUE VALEUR	1992 QUANTITY QUANTITE	1992 VALUE VALEUR	1993 QUANTITY QUANTITE	1993 VALUE VALEUR	1994 QUANTITY QUANTITE	1994 VALUE VALEUR	PRODUIT
	ALL COMMODITIES		1546.9		1452.8		1497.5		1504.8	TOUS PRODUITS
0	FOOD AND LIVE ANIMALS		55.2		48.0		93.8		127.3	ALIMENTS,ANIMAUX VIVANTS
3	MINERAL FUELS ETC		164.1		146.2		169.3		148.9	COMBUSTIBLES MINERAUX LUB
65	TEXTILE YARN,FABRICS,ETC		305.0		330.1		216.3		232.0	FILS,TISSUS,ARTICLES TEXTILE
69	METAL MANUFACTURES NES		125.8		112.1		110.2		107.4	ART MANUFACT EN METAL NDA
7	MACHINES,TRANSPORT EQUIP		712.5		525.0		530.0		546.3	MACHINES MATERIEL TRANSPORT
781	PASS MOTOR VEH EXC BUSES		280.7		223.1		171.0		163.9	AUTO TRANSPORT PERSONNES
9	GOODS NOT CLASSD BY KIND		170.9		291.5		378.1			ART TRANSACT NON CLASSES

5. General Exports F.O.B. by Commodities according to the S.I.T.C. (Rev. 2) in million U.S. Dollars
Exportations Générales F.O.B. par Produits d'après la C.T.C.I. (Rév. 2) en millions de Dollars E.U.

SITC CTCI	COMMODITY	1991		1992		1993		1994		PRODUIT
		QUANTITY QUANTITE	VALUE VALEUR	QUANTITY QUANTITE	VALUE VALEUR	QUANTITY QUANTITE	VALUE VALEUR	QUANTITY QUANTITE	VALUE VALEUR	
	ALL COMMODITIES		340.9		412.1		450.2		519.3	TOUS PRODUITS
05773	CASHEW NUTS,FRESH,DRIED		16.1		21.6		22.7		52.0	NOIX DE CAJOU
071	COFFEE AND SUBSTITUTES		75.6		57.6		98.0		115.1	CAFE ET SUCCEDANES
0711	COFFEE GREEN,ROASTED,SUB		75.6		57.6		98.0		115.1	CAFE TORREFIE OU DECAFEINE
07523	CLOVES		3.3		5.3		4.7			GIROFLES
263	COTTON		62.2		94.3		78.8		104.7	COTON
2631	RAW COTTON,EXCL LINTERS		62.2		94.3		78.8		104.7	COTON EN MASSE
265	VEG FIBRE,EXCL COTN,JUTE				1.4		3.6		5.2	FIBRES VEGETALES
2654	SISAL,AGAVE FIBRES,WASTE		2.2		1.4		3.6		5.2	SISAL,AUTRES AGAVES
27	CRUDE FERTLZR,MINRLS NES		38.7							ENGRAIS MINERAUX BRUTS
33	PETROLEUM AND PRODUCTS				8.3		14.0		5.5	PETROLE ET DERIVES
334	PETROLEUM PRODUCTS,REFIN		6.3		8.3		14.0		5.5	PRODUITS RAFFINES
6	BASIC MANUFACTURES		56.7							ART MANUFACTURES
8	MISC MANUFACTURED GOODS		80.1							ART MANUFACTURES DIVERS

FOOT NOTES – NOTES

TABLE 1 –

1 The gold trade includes refined and unrefined or partly–worked gold and excludes gold specie.

TABLEAU 1 –

1 Le commerce de l'or comprend l'or raffiné ou non et l'o r partiellement travaillé mais exclut les pièces d e monnaie.

1. HISTORICAL SERIES, 1962–1997 GENERAL TRADE, IMPORTS C.I.F., EXPORTS F.O.B. # 1
SERIES HISTORIQUES, 1962–1997 COMMERCE GENERAL, IMPORTATIONS C.A.F., EXPORTATIONS F.O.B

YEAR ANNEE	VALUE IN MILLION U.S. DOLLARS / VALEUR EN MILLION U.S. DOLLARS — MERCHANDISE –MARCHANDISE IMPORTS	EXPORTS	GOLD –OR IMPORTS	EXPORTS	CONVERSION FACTORS FACTEURS DE CONVERSION CENTS E.U. PAR — IMPORTS	EXPORTS	INDEX NUMBERS –INDICES — QUANTUM IMPORTS	EXPORTS	UNIT VALUE VALEUR UNITAIRE IMPORTS	EXPORTS
1962	16457.00	21715.00	151.00	381.00						
1963	17211.00	23389.00	44.00	204.00						
1964	18750.00	26652.00	41.00	423.00						
1965	21431.00	27532.00	102.00	1285.00						
1966	25620.00	30434.00	42.00	457.00						
1967	26892.00	31627.00	33.00	1005.00						
1968	33226.00	34636.00	226.00	839.00						
1969	36043.00	38006.00	237.00	12.00						
1970	39756.00	42590.00	237.00	38.00						
1971	45516.00	43498.00	284.00	51.00						
1972	55282.00	48959.00	358.00	63.00						
1973	68656.00	70246.00	356.00	146.00						
1974	107112.00	97144.00	397.00	228.00						
1975	105880.00	108113.00	434.00	569.00						
1976	132498.00	115413.00	331.00	342.00						
1977	160411.00	121293.00	532.00	1043.00						
1978	186044.00	143766.00	862.00	1123.00						
1979	222228.00	182025.00	1468.00	4929.00						
1980	256984.00	220786.00	2717.00	3705.00			54	74	88	78
1981	273352.20	233666.10	2126.00	3111.00			56	72	92	85
1982	254884.50	212277.20	1830.00	1115.60			53	64	91	86
1983	269878.30	200537.60	1897.10	1349.00			58	60	87	87
1984	341176.80	223999.00					72	64	89	89
1985	361626.40	218828.00					79	63	87	88
1986	382295.00	227158.00					87	63	84	88
1987	424442.10	254122.00					90	71	89	90
1988	459542.00	322426.80					93	84	94	97
1989	492922.10	363812.10					98	93	97	99
1990	516986.80	393592.00					100	100	100	100
1991	508363.00	421730.00					98	106	100	101
1992	553923.00	448163.00					106	113	101	101
1993	603438.00	464773.10					117	116	100	101
1994	689214.90	512626.90					131	126	102	104
1995	770852.10	584742.90					140	137	106	109
1996	822024.90	625072.90					148	145	107	109
1997	899019.00	688697.00					166	162	105	108

2. IMPORTS BY BROAD ECONOMIC CATEGORY AND EXPORTS BY INDUSTRIAL ORIGIN. (PERCENTAGE OF TOTAL VALUE)
IMPORTATIONS PAR CATEGORIES ECONOMIQUES ET EXPORTATIONS PAR BRANCHE D'ACTIVITE.(EN POURCENTAGE DE LA VALEUR TOTALE)

IMPORTS – IMPORTATIONS

	1991	1992	1993	1994	1995	1996	1997
TOTAL IMPORTS–IMPORTATIONS TOTALES	100.	100.	100.	100.	100.	100.	100.
1 FOOD BEV–ALIMENTATION BOISSONS	5.5	5.3	4.9	4.8	4.5	4.6	4.6
11 PRIMARY–PRODUITS DE BASE	3.1	2.9	2.7	2.6	2.5	2.4	2.5
111 FOR INDUSTRY–POUR L'INDUSTRIE	0.8	0.7	0.7	0.7	0.8	0.7	0.8
112 FOR HOUSEHOLDS–POUR LES MENAGES	2.3	2.1	2.0	1.9	1.7	1.7	1.7
12 PROCESSED–PRODUITS ELABORES	2.5	2.5	2.2	2.1	2.0	2.2	2.1
121 FOR INDUSTRY–POUR L'INDUSTRIE	0.4	0.4	0.4	0.3	0.3	0.4	0.4
122 FOR HOUSEHOLDS–POUR LES MENAGES	2.1	2.1	1.8	1.8	1.7	1.8	1.8
2 IND SUPPLIES–APPROV INDUSTRIELS	18.6	18.3	18.3	18.9	19.4	19.2	19.0
21 PRIMARY–PRODUITS DE BASE	2.4	2.3	2.2	2.2	2.2	2.2	2.2
22 PROCESSED–PRODUITS ELABORES	16.2	16.1	16.0	16.8	17.2	16.9	16.8
3 FUELS–COMBUSTIBLES	11.4	10.6	9.8	8.7	8.1	9.4	9.1
31 PRIMARY–PRODUITS DE BASE	8.6	8.2	7.7	6.8	6.6	7.4	7.3
32 PROCESSED–PRODUITS ELABORES	2.8	2.4	2.1	1.8	1.5	2.0	1.8
321 MOTOR SPIRIT–ESSENCE	0.9	1.0	0.8	0.6	0.5	0.8	0.7
322 OTHER–AUTRES	1.9	1.4	1.3	1.2	1.0	1.2	1.1
4 MACHINERY–EQUIPEMENT	21.9	22.5	24.0	25.6	27.8	26.9	26.7
41 CAPITAL EQUIPMENT–MACHINES	15.9	16.2	17.0	17.4	17.8	17.8	18.1
42 PARTS–PIECES ACCESSOIRES	6.0	6.3	7.0	8.2	10.0	9.0	8.6
5 TRANSPORT–TRANSPORT	19.2	18.7	18.6	18.6	17.4	17.1	17.1
51 PASSENGER CARS–AUTOMOBILES	9.3	8.7	8.9	9.1	8.6	8.4	8.3
52 OTHER–AUTRES	2.8	3.0	2.9	2.7	2.6	2.6	2.7
521 INDUSTRIAL–INDUSTRIELS	2.6	2.8	2.6	2.5	2.4	2.4	2.5
522 NON INDUSTRIAL–NON INDUSTRIEL	0.2	0.2	0.2	0.2	0.2	0.2	0.2
53 PARTS–PIECES ACCESSOIRES	7.0	7.0	6.8	6.7	6.2	6.2	6.2
6 CONSUM GOODS–BIENS CONSOMMATION	20.2	21.3	21.2	20.3	19.6	19.5	20.0
61 DURABLE–DURABLES	6.0	6.2	6.1	6.0	5.7	5.6	5.7
62 SEMI DURABLE–SEMI DURABLES	12.5	13.3	13.3	12.5	12.1	12.0	12.4
63 NON DURABLE–NON DURABLES	1.7	1.9	1.9	1.7	1.8	1.9	2.0
7 GOODS NES–BIENS NDA	3.2	3.3	3.1	3.2	3.2	3.3	3.4

EXPORTS – EXPORTATIONS

	1991	1992	1993	1994	1995	1996	1997
TOTAL EXPORTS–EXPORTATIONS TOTALES	100.	100.	100.	100.	100.	100.	100.
1 AGRICULTURE	7.0	7.0	6.6	6.1	6.6	6.7	5.2
2 MINING QUARRY–INDUS EXTRACTIVES	3.0	2.1	1.7	1.6	1.7	1.7	1.6
3 MANUFACTURING–IND MANUFACTUR	90.0	90.9	91.7	92.3	91.6	91.6	93.2
31 FOOD BEV TOBACCO–ALIM BOISS TAB	5.0	5.2	5.2	5.4	5.1	5.0	4.6
32 TEXTILES–INDUSTRIES TEXTILES	2.5	2.7	2.8	2.8	2.8	2.9	2.9
33 WOOD & PRODUCTS–BOIS & PRODUITS	1.0	1.0	1.1	1.0	0.9	0.9	0.8
34 PAPER & PRODUCTS–PAPIER & PRODT	3.2	3.2	3.0	3.1	3.5	3.0	2.8
35 CHEMICALS–INDUSTRIES CHIMIQUES	13.5	13.7	13.6	13.7	14.0	13.7	13.9
36 NON METAL MIN–MIN NON METAL	0.8	0.8	0.9	0.9	0.8	0.9	0.9
37 BASIC METAL–IND METAL BASE	2.6	2.2	2.0	2.0	2.5	2.2	2.2
38 METAL MANUF–MANUF METAL	56.3	57.1	58.2	58.7	57.4	58.6	60.5
39 OTH MANUF IND–AUTRES MANUF	5.0	5.0	5.0	4.9	4.6	4.6	4.5

3. TRADE BY PRINCIPAL COUNTRIES OF ORIGIN AND DESTINATION (VALUE IN MILLION U.S. DOLLARS)
ECHANGES SELON LES PRINCIPAUX PAYS D'ORIGINE ET DE DESTINATION (VALEUR EN MILLIONS DE DOLLARS EU)

COUNTRIES–PAYS	GENERAL IMPORTS C.I.F. IMPORTATIONS GENERALES C.A.F				
	1993	1994	1995	1996	1997
World	603153.4	689029.9	770821.4	817627.1	898025.5
Africa	15729.9	15099.3	16241.7	19457.0	21084.7
Americas	191362.2	223549.8	256319.2	285821.2	315578.6
– Northern America	113609.0	131935.9	148299.8	159709.6	171371.2
– LAIA	66586.2	79291.3	94430.9	110692.3	126344.2
– CACM	4607.4	5150.2	6266.5	7285.6	8877.4
– Caribbean	6022.6	6595.7	6690.1	7441.9	8270.2
– Rest of America	536.9	576.7	631.8	692.0	715.8
Asia excl fmr USSR	268858.6	304986.9	336422.7	338417.2	369310.0
– Middle East	13296.3	13174.6	13533.3	14515.6	16386.4
Asia former USSR	94.5	142.7	232.6	339.8	192.9
Europe excl fmr USSR	119849.3	135995.6	151101.8	162942.3	179441.8
– European Union	109253.5	123883.2	136815.1	147426.7	162538.1
– Eastern Europe	1532.5	2139.0	2263.1	2424.4	3294.3
– Rest of Europe	9063.3	9973.4	12023.5	13091.3	13609.4
Europe former USSR	2151.6	3979.9	5013.1	4617.3	5456.4
Oceania	5107.5	5275.5	5490.2	6031.7	6960.9
Other	0.0		0.1	0.3	
Canada	113580.4	131916.2	148277.9	159691.2	171330.6
Japan/Japon	110417.7	122468.0	127195.3	117962.9	124265.7
Mexico/Mexique	40720.7	50333.5	62745.6	74108.1	87119.8
China/Chine	33673.2	41345.8	48505.6	54396.4	65811.6
Germany/Allemagne	29461.1	32688.4	38041.6	39989.2	44191.2
Other Asia n.e.s.	26300.4	27942.0	30157.6	31022.4	33718.3
United Kingdom	22361.8	25817.7	27663.8	29669.2	33475.5
Korea, Republic of	17779.0	20374.3	24890.5	23297.4	23797.6
France, Monaco	15689.8	17316.0	17768.1	19202.8	21345.4
Singapore/Singapour	13049.2	15656.3	18897.2	20648.2	20368.1
Italy/Italie	13829.3	15442.0	17304.7	19001.0	20182.3
Malaysia/Malaisie	10922.5	14418.6	17980.8	18330.7	18522.8
Thailand/Thaïlande	8982.3	10799.2	11854.4	11798.4	13055.7
Venezuela	8707.3	8989.4	10427.9	13718.9	14389.4
China, Hong Kong SAR	10000.1	10141.4	10744.7	10262.0	10675.2
Brazil/Brésil	8021.3	9307.3	9428.3	9296.2	10149.5
Saudi Arabia	8431.5	8306.8	8897.8	9442.7	10135.1
Indonesia/Indonésie	5886.9	7020.2	7954.8	8742.6	9736.6
Philippines	5175.5	6025.1	7364.3	8496.4	10797.3
Switzerland,Liechtenst.	6184.1	6604.4	7878.3	8023.4	8644.9
Belgium–Luxembourg	5598.1	6861.7	6478.7	7185.3	8371.2
Netherlands/Pays–Bas	5722.8	6358.4	6769.0	7011.8	7683.1
Sweden/Suède	4690.0	5243.1	6467.3	7375.4	7532.5
India/Inde	4883.0	5663.2	6090.5	6528.5	7711.8
Israel/Israël	4526.9	5336.6	5840.4	6545.8	7459.3
Nigeria/Nigéria	5609.2	4705.9	5055.0	6171.3	6704.5
Spain/Espagne	3204.3	3809.6	4160.2	4563.1	4910.7
Ireland/Irlande	2574.4	2952.7	4149.5	4870.4	5958.8
Colombia/Colombie	3270.3	3406.6	3992.0	4525.0	5033.8
Australia/Australie	3513.8	3423.5	3560.5	4117.7	4895.5
Russian Federation	1844.6	3432.7	4269.2	3744.6	4523.1
Dominican Republic	2757.5	3187.8	3511.1	3676.9	4444.7
Norway,Svalbard and JM	2035.9	2499.3	3251.1	4058.0	3924.6
Angola	2237.5	2209.2	2390.2	2855.1	2935.8
So. African Customs Un	1994.7	2279.3	2443.6	2588.2	2814.7
Chile/Chili	1692.6	2072.4	2197.0	2580.5	2626.9
Finland/Finlande	1720.5	1928.0	2391.2	2464.2	2527.9
Denmark/Danemark	1740.8	2211.5	2032.8	2222.9	2225.0
Algeria/Algérie	1710.8	1664.3	1807.2	2270.4	2645.6
Ecuador/Equateur	1562.9	1937.0	2157.9	2121.3	2280.3

COUNTRIES–PAYS	EXPORTS EXPORTATIONS ES F.O.B.				
	1993	1994	1995	1996	1997
Monde	464757.2	512336.9	582964.7	622784.3	687532.5
Afrique	9285.9	9204.0	9908.1	10595.7	11400.1
Amériques	178630.9	206843.8	222341.7	241457.6	283930.1
– Amérique du Nord	100456.9	114556.5	126323.2	132867.3	150465.2
– ALAI	65007.9	78199.0	79739.8	92229.0	114494.1
– MCAC	4774.0	5350.6	6026.9	6353.4	7452.1
– Caraïbes	6502.2	6919.0	7987.8	8164.2	9540.4
– Autre Amérique	1889.9	1818.7	2264.0	1843.8	1978.4
Asie anc. URSS exclus	150416.1	163906.6	199889.0	210153.6	217514.4
– Moyen–Orient	15991.9	14002.6	14787.4	17067.3	18712.2
Asie ancienne URSS	378.1	559.0	422.1	948.4	922.2
Europe anc. URSS exclus	112165.9	116877.9	133655.8	140813.4	154893.7
– Union Européenne	101472.2	107745.1	123604.7	127915.2	141399.3
– Europe de l'Est	2123.5	1737.1	1896.9	2186.4	2691.7
– Autre de l'Europe	8570.1	7395.7	8154.2	10711.7	10802.7
Europe ancienne URSS	3602.1	3005.1	3387.7	4120.0	4107.6
Océanie	9934.8	11686.6	12795.3	14066.4	14424.1
Autre	343.5	254.0	565.2	629.2	340.2
Canada	100188.9	114253.0	126021.7	132579.6	150120.4
Japan/Japon	47932.8	53453.4	64259.7	67514.6	65657.9
Mexico/Mexique	41602.7	50834.2	46309.3	56758.6	71354.8
United Kingdom	26369.8	26831.6	28826.4	30914.9	36433.8
Korea, Republic of	14775.5	18028.3	25413.1	26582.9	25066.6
Germany/Allemagne	18946.1	19226.2	22370.0	23468.8	24459.6
Other Asia n.e.s.	16249.5	17077.5	19294.9	18412.7	20387.7
Netherlands/Pays–Bas	12839.2	13590.4	16557.3	16614.0	19821.2
Singapore/Singapour	11675.1	13021.6	15318.1	16685.3	17727.4
France, Monaco	13272.5	13627.7	14250.0	14836.4	16581.7
China, Hong Kong SAR	9870.8	11444.7	14218.9	13955.0	15111.1
Belgium–Luxembourg	9436.9	11172.5	12832.4	12760.4	14139.3
China/Chine	8767.1	9286.7	11748.1	11977.7	12804.9
Brazil/Brésil	6045.4	8118.4	11443.6	12699.2	15912.3
Australia/Australie	8271.6	9779.9	10788.4	11991.6	12040.8
Malaysia/Malaisie	6064.5	6964.6	8818.4	8521.2	10827.8
Italy/Italie	6460.3	7195.6	8867.7	8791.2	8982.0
Switzerland,Liechtenst.	6793.5	5601.5	6245.8	8377.1	8313.9
Saudi Arabia	6665.6	6010.5	6085.0	7295.2	8450.8
Thailand/Thaïlande	3768.5	4861.0	6401.9	7211.3	7357.2
Israel/Israël	4420.2	5006.0	5593.2	6009.0	5993.8
Philippines	3529.1	3888.3	5294.1	6124.7	7427.4
Spain/Espagne	4180.9	4624.8	5529.3	5485.8	5543.7
Venezuela	4597.9	4041.7	4641.2	4740.8	6607.5
Argentina/Argentine	3770.0	4466.3	4189.3	4515.6	5807.8
Colombia/Colombie	3229.1	4070.3	4628.2	4708.7	5198.6
Ireland/Irlande	2730.6	3415.5	4094.8	3659.5	4641.0
Chile/Chili	2605.3	2775.9	3613.1	4131.5	4374.9
Indonesia/Indonésie	2770.0	2811.0	3356.0	3965.0	4531.7
Egypt/Egypte	2762.6	2843.8	2985.3	3146.1	3840.0
Turkey/Turquie	3433.6	2753.5	2727.2	2886.1	3539.4
India/Inde	2761.1	2296.3	3295.7	3318.1	3615.6
Dominican Republic	2349.5	2799.5	3016.6	3183.2	3928.2
Russian Federation	2967.0	2578.8	2826.2	3340.1	3288.7
Sweden/Suède	2353.5	2519.8	3076.6	3428.6	3315.7
So. African Customs Un	2247.6	2220.5	2818.2	3162.0	3076.2
United Arab Emirates	1811.3	1593.0	1993.7	2526.9	2605.6
Costa Rica	1547.3	1866.6	1739.1	1813.6	2023.5
Austria/Autriche	1324.7	1372.1	2016.7	2008.2	2073.1
New Zealand	1247.3	1508.3	1692.8	1726.9	1956.7

(VALUE AS PERCENTAGE OF WORLD TOTAL)(VALEURS EN POURCENTAGE DU TOTAL MONDIAL)

	1988	1989	1990	1991	1992	1993	1994	1995	1996	1997
Africa	2.5	3.0	3.3	2.9	2.7	2.6	2.2	2.1	2.4	2.3
Americas	29.4	30.3	31.1	31.3	31.3	31.7	32.4	33.3	35.0	35.1
– Northern America	17.7	18.1	18.1	18.4	18.3	18.8	19.1	19.2	19.5	19.1
– LAIA	10.2	10.6	11.4	11.1	11.1	11.0	11.5	12.3	13.5	14.1
– CACM	0.5	0.5	0.5	0.6	0.7	0.8	0.7	0.8	0.9	1.0
– Caribbean	0.9	0.9	1.0	1.1	1.0	1.0	1.0	0.9	0.9	0.9
– Rest of America	0.1	0.1	0.1	0.1	0.1	0.1	0.1	0.1	0.1	0.1
Asia excl fmr USSR	43.8	43.8	42.4	43.7	44.2	44.6	44.3	43.6	41.4	41.1
– Middle East	2.3	2.9	3.4	2.9	2.6	2.2	1.9	1.8	1.8	1.8
Asia former USSR					0.0	0.0	0.0	0.0	0.0	0.0
Europe excl fmr USSR	23.0	21.5	21.9	20.8	20.7	19.9	19.7	19.6	19.9	20.0
– European Union	21.0	19.6	20.0	18.9	18.9	18.1	18.0	17.7	18.0	18.1
– Eastern Europe	0.4	0.3	0.3	0.2	0.2	0.3	0.3	0.3	0.3	0.4
– Rest of Europe	1.6	1.6	1.7	1.7	1.6	1.5	1.4	1.6	1.6	1.5
Europe former USSR	0.1	0.2	0.2	0.2	0.2	0.4	0.6	0.7	0.6	0.6
Oceania	1.2	1.2	1.2	1.1	1.0	0.8	0.8	0.7	0.7	0.8
Other				0.0	0.0	0.0		0.0	0.0	
Canada	17.7	18.1	18.1	18.4	18.3	18.8	19.1	19.2	19.5	19.1
Japan/Japon	20.2	19.7	18.1	18.8	18.1	18.3	17.8	16.5	14.4	13.8
Mexico/Mexique	5.1	5.6	5.9	6.2	6.5	6.8	7.3	8.1	9.1	9.7
China/Chine	2.0	2.6	3.1	4.0	5.0	5.6	6.0	6.3	6.7	7.3
Germany/Allemagne				5.3	5.3	4.9	4.7	4.9	4.9	4.9
Other Asia n.e.s.	5.7	5.2	4.6	4.8	4.7	4.4	4.1	3.9	3.8	3.8
United Kingdom	4.1	3.8	4.0	3.7	3.7	3.7	3.7	3.6	3.6	3.7
Korea, Republic of	4.6	4.2	3.7	3.5	3.1	2.9	3.0	3.2	2.8	2.6
France, Monaco	2.8	2.7	2.6	2.7	2.8	2.6	2.5	2.3	2.3	2.4
Singapore/Singapour	1.8	1.9	2.0	2.0	2.1	2.2	2.3	2.5	2.5	2.3

	1988	1989	1990	1991	1992	1993	1994	1995	1996	1997
Afrique	2.2	2.1	2.0	2.1	2.2	2.0	1.8	1.7	1.7	1.7
Amériques	35.4	35.0	34.9	35.2	37.1	38.4	40.4	38.1	38.8	41.3
– Amérique du Nord	21.9	21.6	21.2	20.2	20.2	21.6	22.4	21.7	21.3	21.9
– ALAI	10.9	10.7	11.1	12.4	14.2	14.0	15.3	13.7	14.8	16.7
– MCAC	0.7	0.7	0.7	0.8	1.0	1.0	1.0	1.0	1.0	1.1
– Caraïbes	1.5	1.6	1.5	1.4	1.4	1.4	1.4	1.4	1.3	1.4
– Autre Amérique	0.4	0.4	0.4	0.3	0.3	0.4	0.4	0.4	0.3	0.3
Asie anc. URSS exclus	30.7	31.6	31.2	31.6	31.5	32.4	32.0	34.3	33.7	31.6
– Moyen–Orient	2.8	2.9	2.6	3.3	3.5	3.4	2.7	2.5	2.7	2.7
Asie ancienne URSS					0.0	0.1	0.1	0.1	0.2	0.1
Europe anc. URSS exclus	26.6	27.3	28.4	27.8	25.9	24.1	22.8	22.9	22.6	22.5
– Union Européenne	24.5	25.2	26.3	25.7	24.1	21.8	21.0	21.2	20.5	20.6
– Europe de l'Est	0.3	0.3	0.3	0.3	0.4	0.5	0.3	0.3	0.4	0.4
– Autre de l'Europe	1.8	1.8	1.8	1.8	1.4	1.8	1.4	1.4	1.7	1.6
Europe ancienne URSS	0.9	1.2	0.8	0.8	0.8	0.8	0.6	0.6	0.7	0.6
Océanie	2.5	2.7	2.5	2.3	2.4	2.1	2.3	2.2	2.3	2.1
Autre	1.7	0.1	0.1	0.1	0.1	0.1	0.0	0.1	0.1	0.0
Canada	21.8	21.5	21.1	20.2	20.2	21.6	22.3	21.6	21.3	21.8
Japan/Japon	11.6	12.3	12.4	11.4	10.7	10.3	10.4	11.0	10.8	9.5
Mexico/Mexique	6.4	6.9	7.2	7.9	9.1	9.0	9.9	7.9	9.1	10.4
United Kingdom	5.7	5.7	6.0	5.2	5.1	5.7	5.2	4.9	5.0	5.3
Korea, Republic of	3.3	3.7	3.7	3.7	3.3	3.2	3.5	4.4	4.3	3.6
Germany/Allemagne				5.0	4.7	4.1	3.8	3.8	3.8	3.6
Other Asia n.e.s.	3.7	3.1	2.9	3.1	3.4	3.5	3.3	3.3	3.0	3.0
Netherlands/Pays–Bas	3.1	3.1	3.3	3.2	3.1	2.8	2.7	2.8	2.7	2.9
Singapore/Singapour	1.8	2.0	2.0	2.1	2.2	2.5	2.5	2.6	2.7	2.6
France, Monaco	3.1	3.2	3.5	3.6	3.3	2.9	2.7	2.4	2.4	2.4

4. General Imports C.I.F. by Commodities according to the S.I.T.C. (Rev. 2) in million U.S. Dollars
Importations Générales C.A.F. par Produits d'après la C.T.C.I. (Rév. 2) en millions de Dollars E.U.

SITC CTCI	COMMODITY	1994		1995		1996		1997		PRODUIT
		QUANTITY QUANTITE	VALUE VALEUR	QUANTITY QUANTITE	VALUE VALEUR	QUANTITY QUANTITE	VALUE VALEUR	QUANTITY QUANTITE	VALUE VALEUR	
	ALL COMMODITIES		689030.0		770821.6		817627.3		898025.6	TOUS PRODUITS
0	FOOD AND LIVE ANIMALS		27500.2		29317.9		31114.1		34543.4	ALIMENTS,ANIMAUX VIVANTS
01	MEAT AND PREPARATIONS		2812.7		2487.0		2469.1		2819.7	VIANDES ET PREPARATIONS
011	MEAT FRESH,CHILLD,FROZEN	W 961089	2240.4	W 898160	1936.8	W 897442	1940.5	W 1014467	2294.2	VIANDES FRAICHES,REF,CONGE
03	FISH AND PREPARATIONS		6939.3		7100.8		7026.9		8078.4	POISSONS ET PREPARATIONS
034	FISH,FRESH,CHILLED,FROZN	W 659413	2250.7	W 716359	2457.8	W 743169	2510.7	W 755610	2765.9	POISSON FRAIS, REFRIG,CONG
036	SHELL FISH FRESH,FROZEN	W 395027	3613.1	W 378944	3535.4	W 382459	3309.4	W 431465	3939.5	CRUSTACES,MOLLUSQUES
05	VEGETABLES AND FRUIT		7020.1		7576.2		8600.0		8875.6	LEGUMES ET FRUITS
054	VEG ETC FRSH,SMPLY PRSVD	W 2561506	1861.6	W 3094520	2159.3	W 3554145	2488.0	W 3712717	2611.2	LEGUMES FRAIS,CONG,SECS
057	FRUIT,NUTS,FRESH,DRIED	W 5721292	3044.0	W 5881258	3263.5	W 6248328	3570.2	W 6491610	3714.8	FRUITS FRAIS OU SECS
07	COFFEE,TEA,COCOA,SPICES		4145.1		5013.0		4899.4		6131.5	CAFE,THE,CACAO,EPICES
071	COFFEE AND SUBSTITUTES	W 934100	2571.9	W 991945	3356.9	W 1125113	2884.1	W 1182889	3988.4	CAFE ET SUCCEDANES
0711	COFFEE GREEN,ROASTED,SUB	W 910097	2433.0	W 968163	3169.2	W 1097855	2692.5	W 1158276	3819.9	CAFE TORREFIE OU DECAFEINE
07111	COFFEE GREEN,HUSKS,SKINS	W 892346	2347.4	W 953158	3067.2	W 1076140	2573.6	W 1130882	3662.7	CAFE NON TORREFIE
1	BEVERAGES AND TOBACCO		5518.1		5673.8		7031.4		8054.9	BOISSONS ET TABACS
11	BEVERAGES		4611.0		4902.6		5647.2		6376.0	BOISSONS
112	ALCOHOLIC BEVERAGES	W 1859097	4211.0	W 1947724	4498.2	W 2175470	5164.7	W 2485174	5790.8	BOISSONS ALCOOLIQUES
2	CRUDE MATERLS,EXCL FUELS		19140.7		22311.4		22871.4		23658.3	MAT BRUTES NON COMESTIBLES
23	RUBBER, CRUDE		1664.3		2399.1		2198.7		1992.0	CAOUTCHOUC BRUT
24	CORK AND WOOD		7070.1		6552.1		7927.4		8600.1	LIEGE ET BOIS
248	WOOD SHAPED,SLEEPERS		6878.6		6302.4		7689.4		8371.3	BOIS SIMPLEMENT TRAVAILLES
2482	LUMBER SHAPED CONIFER		6433.4		5856.0		7246.1		7833.2	CONIFERES SCIES,RABOTES
24821	LUMBER SAWN ETC CONIFER	MW 22972	6106.8	MW 24357	5543.2	MW 25518	6862.5	MW 25239	7345.1	CONIFERES SCIES LONGITUD
251	*PULP AND WASTE PAPER	W 5370499	2453.2	W 5886600	3983.9	W 5618410	2791.6	W 6482807	2776.1	PATES A PAPIER,DECHETS
2517	SODA,SULPHATE WOOD PULP	W 4389972	2079.4	W 4716589	3479.7	W 4478109	2382.8	W 5080809	2361.7	PATES CHIMIQUES AU SULFATE
25172	—BLEACHED,NONDISSOLVNG	W 4232617	2000.8	W 4589770	3398.0	W 4342095	2315.3	W 4874660	2274.6	PATES BLANCHIES
28	METALLIFEROUS ORES,SCRAP		3514.8		4314.7		4377.2		4468.1	MINERAIS METAL,DECHETS
29	CRUDE ANIMAL,VEG MAT NES		1786.8		2206.7		2427.7		2697.4	MATIERES BRUTES ANIM,VEGET
3	MINERAL FUELS ETC		60150.8		63051.8		77126.3		82620.4	COMBUSTIBLES MINERAUX LUB
33	PETROLEUM AND PRODUCTS		52765.4		56113.5		69065.9		73427.3	PETROLE ET DERIVES
333	CRUDE PETROLEUM	MW 369773	40930.2	MW 369781	45481.9	MW 364442	53331.1	MW 418616	57427.1	HUILES BRUTES DE PETROLE
334	PETROLEUM PRODUCTS,REFIN	MW 86842	11408.8	MW 69606	10191.1	MW 86603	15152.5	MW 89356	15275.5	PRODUITS RAFFINES
3341	GASOLINE,OTH LIGHT OILS	MW 26473	4448.8	MW 22396	4036.8	MW 31737	6841.2	MW 31109	6688.2	ESSENCES POUR MOTEURS
33411	MOTOR,AVIATION SPIRIT	MW 13847	2479.9	MW 9420	1882.1	MW 17188	3855.0	MW 17044	3817.1	ESSENCES MOTEURS D'AVIONS
33419	OTH LIGHT PETROLEUM OILS	MW 12577	1958.8	MW 12698	2102.9	MW 14514	2977.8	MW 14045	2866.7	AUTRES HUILES LEGERES
3344	FUEL OILS,NES	MW 41559	4168.7	MW 29736	3370.8	MW 35798	4761.5	MW 36165	4572.9	FUEL OILS
341	*GAS,NATURAL AND MANUFCT		5677.9		5266.8		6455.1		7458.9	GAZ NATUREL,GAZ MANUFACT
3413	PETROLM GASES,LIQUEFIED		1734.3		2000.6		2507.5		2342.2	GAZ DE PETROLE LIQUEFIE
3414	PETROLEUM GASES, GASEOUS	MV 72561264	3943.6	MV 81301227	3266.3	MV 82812782	3947.6	MV 84772792	5116.8	GAZ DE PETROLE GAZEUX
5	CHEMCLS,RELATED PROD NES		34812.1		41345.7		45799.5		51223.4	PRODUITS CHIMIQUES
51	ORGANIC CHEMICALS		11236.9		13866.8		15383.2		17405.0	PROD CHIMIQ ORGANIQUES
514	NITROGEN–FNCTN COMPOUNDS	W 376847	3234.5	W 370172	3715.4	W 410263	4377.2	W 461239	4804.3	COMPOSES FONCT AZOTEES
515	ORG–INORG COMPOUNDS ETC	W 210797	2555.2	W 203065	3408.4	W 223039	4231.6	W 279837	5582.3	COMPOSES ORGANO–MINERAUX
5156	HETEROCYCLIC CMPDS ETC	W 94092	1862.3	W 88948	2367.3	W 106323	2916.3	W 157923	4093.9	COMPOSES HETEROCYCLIQUES
51569	OTH HETEROCYC CMPDS,ETC	W 67550	1793.9	W 67304	2292.5	W 76174	2831.1	W 81624	3970.5	AUT COMP HETEROCYCLIQUES
52	INORGANIC CHEMICALS		4400.1		4995.2		5272.8		5456.2	PROD CHIM INORGANIQUES
522	INORG ELEMNTS,OXIDES,ETC		2119.0		2574.3		2548.3		2702.8	ELEMENTS INORGANIQUES
541	*MEDICINAL,PHARM PRODUCT		4755.1		5605.4	MK 92203	7150.4	MK 120432	8819.1	PROD MEDICINAUX PHARMACEUT
5417	MEDICAMENTS	K 4667786	2224.6		2830.8	MK 32882	3686.7	MK 42242	5291.0	MEDICAMENTS
54179	— CONTNG OTH SUBSTANCES	K 2785525	1138.1	MK 18984	1353.5	MK 23837	2037.2	MK 33945	3460.1	MED CONT AUT SUBSTANCES
55	PERFUME,CLEANING ETC PRD		2063.5		2391.3		2511.4		2751.8	PROD POUR PARFUM,TOILETTE
58	PLASTIC MATERIALS ETC		5608.7		6730.1		6989.8		7757.7	MAT PLAST ARTIFICIELLES
583	POLYMERIZATION ETC PRODS	W 2663691	3977.2	W 2849803	4785.7	W 3106082	4858.4	W 3365758	5446.9	PROD POLYMERISATION
59	CHEMICAL MATERIALS NES		3149.8		3876.5		4492.4		4702.3	MAT PROD CHIMIQUES NDA
598	MISCEL CHEM PRODUCTS NES		2009.4		2563.4		2980.2		3196.2	PROD DIV INDUST CHIM NDA
5989	CHEM PRODUCTS,PREPS NES	W 432252	1688.4	W 493331	2190.6	W 620703	2593.3	W 522748	2764.2	PROD PREP CHIMIQUES NDA
6	BASIC MANUFACTURES		83922.0		94767.0		96861.3		106596.4	ART MANUFACTURES
62	RUBBER MANUFACTURES NES		5036.7		5418.5		5423.6		5917.7	CAOUTCHOUC MANUFACTURE
625	RUBBER TYRES, TUBES ETC	MN 157236	3218.1	MN 164460	3328.5	MN 156539	3242.9	MN 175778	3595.5	PNEUS CAOUTCHOUC VULCANISE
63	WOOD,CORK MANUFACTRS NES		3638.4		4004.6		4352.4		4979.9	OUVRAGES LIEGE ET BOIS
64	PAPER,PAPERBOARD AND MFR		9727.7		13174.1		12353.7		12533.1	PAPIERS,CARTONS & OUVRAGES
641	PAPER AND PAPERBOARD		8466.4		11512.5		10454.3		10504.1	PAPIERS ET CARTONS
6411	NEWSPRINT	W 7149976	3517.6	W 7082891	4597.7	W 6305744	4221.2	W 6503265	3743.8	PAPIER JOURNAL
6415	PAPER,PAPERBRD,BULK,NES		2065.5	W 3592713	3042.3	W 3308408	2629.1	W 3751995	2695.8	PAPIERS,CARTONS ROULEAUX
64159	OTHER PAPER ETC,BULK,NES		1924.3	W 3291886	2855.8	W 3033121	2491.2	W 3447069	2561.4	AUT PAPIER ROULEAUX FEUILLES
65	TEXTILE YARN,FABRICS,ETC		9688.4		10475.0		10731.5		12482.3	FILS,TISSUS,ARTICLES TEXTILE
658	TEXTILE ARTICLES NES	W 296628	2127.0	W 342917	2534.5	W 347398	2497.5	W 428313	2997.8	ART FACONNES MAT TEXTILES
66	NONMETAL MINERAL MFS NES		13975.9		15128.8		16394.1		18664.1	ART MIN NON METALLIQUES
667	PEARL,PREC–,SEMI–P STONE		6448.9		6687.0		7431.0		8583.2	PERLES, PIERRES GEMMES
6672	DIAMONDS NONINDUST,UNSET		5754.9		5984.4		6600.7		7610.6	DIAMANTS BRUTS
66729	— CUT ETC NOT SET		4957.7		5335.0		5840.1		6956.9	DIAMANTS TAILLES
67	IRON AND STEEL		15664.4		15634.5		16693.3		17594.3	FER ET ACIER
672	IRON,STEEL PRIMARY FORMS	MW 12072	3962.9	W 8358858	3361.3	MW 11709	3994.4	MW 11707	3983.3	LINGOTS FER,ACIER
673	IRON,STEEL SHAPES ETC	W 4097774	2168.7	W 4535061	2509.7	W 4915140	2666.9	W 5517510	2912.1	BARRES,PROFIL FER,ACIER
674	IRN,STL UNIV,PLATE,SHEET	W 8398575	5061.3	W 6748360	4528.3	W 7238574	4575.4	W 7952970	4934.7	LARGES PLATS,TOLES
68	NON–FERROUS METALS		11818.8		14823.0		13881.3		15475.3	METAUX NON FERREUX
682	COPPER EXC CEMENT COPPER	W 877127	2360.9	W 904608	3057.2	W 1052085	3021.6	W 1177248	3324.1	CUIVRE
684	ALUMINIUM	W 3132715	5067.5		5947.8		4946.0		5685.6	ALUMINIUM
6841	ALUMINIUM,ALLOYS,UNWRGHT	W 2495871	3571.4	W 1979827	3838.1	W 1950993	3150.3	W 2097194	3605.5	ALUMINIUM,ALLIAGES BRUTS
69	METAL MANUFACTURES NES		12637.9		14327.0		15245.6		17074.2	ART MANUFACT EN METAL NDA
694	STL,COPPR NAILS,NUTS,ETC	W 1154978	2080.5	W 1230124	2336.2	W 1219709	2302.4	W 1305436	2386.5	CLOUS,VIS,ECROUS
695	TOOLS		2150.8		2463.9		2513.3		2966.0	OUTILS A MAIN
699	BASE METAL MFRS NES		4705.1		5206.7		5860.5		6576.1	ART MANUFACTURES MET NDA
7	MACHINES,TRANSPORT EQUIP		314381.3		357625.5		368994.4		402540.1	MACHINES MATERIEL TRANSPORT
71	POWER GENERATING EQUIPMT		19945.7		20923.0		22870.6		24905.7	MACHINES GENERATRICES
713	INTRNL COMBUS PSTN ENGIN		10392.4		11436.9		12280.6		12069.1	MOTEURS EXPL COMB INT, PIECE
7132	MOTOR VEHCL PISTN ENGINS	N 4584948	5991.7	N 4299247	6334.7	N 4370053	7093.1	N 4336028	6782.7	MOTEURS EXPL POUR VEHICULES
7139	PISTON ENGINE PARTS NES	W 565141	2952.7	W 660039	3337.6	W 513514	3479.3	W 556767	3537.2	PIECES POUR 713.2,3,8
714	ENGINES AND MOTORS NES		5809.2		5354.0		6274.6		8379.7	MOTEURS NON ELECTRIQUES
7144	REACTION ENGINES	N 967	2411.7	N 1225	1477.8	N 2499	1584.1	N 2583	2680.9	PROPULSEURS A REACTION
7149	ENGINE & MOTOR PARTS NES		3078.1		3520.0		4231.9		5215.3	PIECES 714 ET 718.88
71491	PARTS NES OF 7144,71481		2381.8		2653.7		3335.0		4287.2	PIECES DES PROPULSEURS
716	ROTATING ELECTRIC PLANT		3103.4		3401.8		3431.3		3720.9	APP ELECTR ROTATIFS,PIECES
72	MACHS FOR SPCL INDUSTRYS		16384.9		18616.3		18095.8		20668.5	MAC SPECIALES POUR INDUST
723	CIVIL ENGNEERG EQUIP ETC	N 668074	2649.7		2740.9		2667.2		3342.9	APPAREILS DE GENIE CIVIL
7234	CONST,MINING MACHNRY NES	N 153063	2356.9	N 139894	2389.1	N 126700	2242.7	N 112159	2769.1	MACH POUR LA CONST, MINES
724	TEXTILE,LEATHER MACHNRY		2763.7		2715.5		2329.5		2553.0	MACH POUR INDUSTRIE TEXTILE
728	OTH MACHY FOR SPCL INDUS		5418.5		6704.0		6938.1		7911.9	AUT MACH IND PARTICULIERES
7284	MACHY FOR SPCL INDUS NES		4329.8		5346.7		5344.4		6089.9	MACH SPEC IND PARTICUL.
72848	OTH MCHY WITH INDIV FNCT	N 115658	1759.9	MN 22882	2249.3	MN 15595	2331.6	MN 18285	2711.9	AUTRES MACHINES NDA
73	METALWORKING MACHINERY		4653.9		5985.9		6844.0		7371.1	MACH TRAVAIL DES METAUX

4. General Imports C.I.F. by Commodities according to the S.I.T.C. (Rev. 2) in million U.S. Dollars
Importations Générales C.A.F. par Produits d'après la C.T.C.I. (Rév. 2) en millions de Dollars E.U.

SITC CTCI	COMMODITY	1994 QUANTITY QUANTITE	1994 VALUE VALEUR	1995 QUANTITY QUANTITE	1995 VALUE VALEUR	1996 QUANTITY QUANTITE	1996 VALUE VALEUR	1997 QUANTITY QUANTITE	1997 VALUE VALEUR	PRODUIT
736	METALWORKING MACH–TOOLS		3744.6		4801.1		5285.9		5925.5	MACH–OUTILS TRAVAIL METAUX
74	GENRL INDUSTRL MACHY NES		21983.9		24951.2		26096.1		27350.7	MACH APP INDUSTRIE
741	HEATING,COOLING EQUIPMNT		2485.5		2754.6		3298.8		3247.3	MACH CHAUFFAGE,PIECES
743	PUMPS NES,CENTRFUGES ETC		3704.7		4202.4		4436.4		4280.2	POMPES COMPRES,VENT ETC
744	MECHANICAL HANDLING EQU		3607.3		4242.7		4358.1		5084.7	EQUIP MANUTENTION PIECES
745	NONELEC MACHY,TOOLS NES		2257.2		2478.7		2736.2		2900.9	AUT MACH NON ELEC,PIECES
749	NONELEC MACH PTS,ACC NES		8071.5		9224.8		9129.8		9536.4	PIECES MACH NON ELEC NDA
7492	COCKS,VALVES ETC NES	W 95118	2737.9		3108.1		3291.4		3730.8	ART ROB,SIM POUR TUYAUX
7493	SHAFT,CRANK,PULLEY ETC		2289.2		2699.9		2718.1		2604.8	ARBRES TRANS,VILEBREQUINS
75	OFFICE MACHNES,ADP EQUIP		53004.8		63962.7		67549.7		76158.2	MACH BUREAU TRAIT AUTOM
751	OFFICE MACHINES	MN 124081	3939.4	MN 144411	4586.0	MN 130670	4500.6	MN 147779	4659.0	MACH,APPAREILS DE BUREAU
7518	OFFICE MACHINES NES	MN 30016	2766.2	MN 35201	3492.9	MN 39111	3419.5	MN 43602	3478.7	MACH,APP DE BUREAU NDA
75182	PHOTO,THERMOCOPY APPARAT	N 1279580	2078.1	N 1576128	2492.7	N 1530372	2358.1	N 1569093	2429.7	APPAREILS DE PHOTOCOPIE
752	AUTOMTIC DATA PROC EQUIP	MN 209594	30614.6	MN 259645	35423.0	MN 270210	39934.7	MN 340206	45703.6	MACH TRAIT INFORMATION
7522	DIGITAL COMPUTERS	N 1947987	2355.2	N 1446058	2244.5	N 2340974	3451.7	N 3398673	4444.2	MACH DIGITALES COMPLETES
7523	DIGITL CENTRL PROCESSORS	N 2903653	2984.9	N 2501373	2759.9	MN 15356	4125.4	MN 11258	3342.3	UNITES CENTRALES
7524	DIGITL CENTRL STOR UNITS	MN 77397	11116.8	MN 97602	14451.1	MN 112633	16621.5	MN 145662	19735.9	UNITES MEMOIRE CENTRALES
7525	ADP PERIPHERAL UNITS	MN 88191	11727.9	MN 107017	12936.3	MN 113519	13071.4	MN 147504	15166.2	UNITES PERIPHERIQUES
7528	OFF–LINE DATA PROC EQUIP	MN 39144	2418.7	MN 51065	3020.9	MN 26328	2638.5	MN 32363	2992.2	MACH AUXIL TRAIT INFORM
759	OFFICE,ADP MCH PTS,ACCES		18451.0		23953.9		23114.5		25795.7	PIECES DU 751 ET 752
7599	ACCTG,ETC,ADP MCH PTS,AC		16585.0		22157.0		21324.5		23860.9	PIECES DU 751 ET 752
76	TELECOMM,SOUND EQUIPMENT		33068.6		35007.8		34700.9		37249.1	EQUIPMENT DE TELECOM
761	TELEVISION RECEIVERS	MN 20248	3632.5	MN 20277	3820.5	MN 20831	4025.6	MN 23292	4426.0	RECEPTEURS DE TELEVISION
7611	COLOUR TV RECEIVERS	MN 18146	3503.8	MN 18681	3711.0	MN 19395	3917.2	MN 21860	4321.0	RECEPTEURS COULEUR
762	RADIO BROADCAST RECEIVRS	MN 125716	6053.3	MN 119991	6142.5	MN 126081	5457.7	MN 124889	5865.4	RECEPTEURS RADIODIFFUSION
7621	MTR VEHC RADIO RECEIVERS	MN 23395	2284.9	MN 21879	2366.4	MN 23127	2339.9	MN 24869	2686.2	RECEPTEURS RADIO AUTO
763	SOUND RECORDRS,PHONOGRPH	MN 77637	6352.4	MN 77672	6397.5	MN 74601	7404.7	MN 79992	7568.4	PHONO,APP ENREGISTREMENT
7638	OTHR SOUND APPARATUS ETC	MN 76380	6271.0	MN 77109	6351.1	MN 74240	7358.8	MN 79459	7529.5	AUT APP D'ENREGIS,REPROD
76381	TV IMAGE,SND RECRDRS ETC	MN 19342	3575.5	MN 20209	3531.0	MN 22009	4814.6	MN 25584	4967.2	APP ENREG,REPRO IMAG,SON
76388	DICTATING MACHINES ETC	MN 57038	2695.5	MN 56901	2820.2	MN 52231	2544.3	MN 53875	2562.4	MACHINES A DICTER
764	TELECOM EQPT,PTS,ACC NES		17030.5		18647.4		17813.0		19389.5	EQUIP TELECOM,PIECES
7641	LINE TELEPHONE,ETC EQUIP	MN 116309	3618.4	MN 147884	3695.1		5197.3		5950.7	APP TELEPHON PAR FIL
7643	TV,RADIO TRANSMITTRS ETC		4543.9		5023.9		4019.2		4349.6	APP EMET TELE RADIO
7648	TELECOMM EQUIPMENT NES		2511.3		2844.1		1150.4		1172.5	APP TELECOM NDA
7649	PTS NES OF EQUIPMT OF 76		4812.4		5425.0		5701.6		6137.2	PIECES DE LA DIV 76
76493	TELECOMM EQUIPMT PTS NES		2544.6		2747.2		2663.2		2875.1	PIECES 761,762,764.3,8
77	ELECTRIC MACHNRY NES ETC		59444.7		77109.1		77394.4		82228.4	MACH APP ELECT NDA
771	ELECTRIC POWER MACHY NES		2814.9		3653.7		5037.4		6121.2	MACH PROD,TRANS ELECTR
7712	OTH ELEC POWER MACHY NES		2218.4		2942.7		4287.1		5230.7	AUT APP PROD TRANSF ELEC
77121	STATIC CONVERTERS ETC		1340.5		1727.2	MN 179521	2997.0	MN 186031	3754.5	CONVERTISSEURS STATIQUES
772	SWITCHGEAR ETC,PARTS NES	MN 47422621	8475.0		9698.7		9860.4		11083.1	APP COUPURE,SECT ETC
7721	SWITCHGEAR ETC	MN 2953185	6329.0		7073.9		7309.0		8234.1	APP COUPURE,SECTIONMNT
773	ELECTR DISTRIBUTNG EQUIP		4970.5		5568.0		6109.2		7016.0	EQUIPMT DISTRIBUTION ELECT
7731	INSULATED WIRE,CABLE ETC	W 99738	4848.6		5430.6		5967.9		6845.1	FILS,CABLES ISOLES ELECT
775	HOUSEHOLD TYPE EQUIP NES		4380.7		4618.3		4917.0		5273.7	MACH,APP USAGE DOMESTQUE
7758	ELECTRO–THERMIC APPL NES		2244.4		2349.8		2411.5		2562.8	APP ELECTROTHERMIQ NDA
776	TRANSISTORS,VALVES,ETC		27631.8		40956.6		38410.6		38327.7	LAMPES,TUBES,VALVES
7763	DIODES,TRANSISTORS,ETC	MN 17114917	1987.7	MN 21779001	2553.6	MN 20945979	2657.1	MN 26849168	3049.0	DIODES,TRANSISTORS
7764	ELECTRONIC MICROCIRCUITS	MN 10684578	23383.0	MN 12970935	35487.1	MN 13420557	33010.5	MN 16275891	32666.3	MICROSTRUCTURES ELECTRON
778	ELECTRICAL MACHINERY NES		9255.1		10542.2		10902.2		12070.9	AUTRES MACH ELECT NDA
7788	OTH ELEC MACHY,EQUIP NES		4530.2		5417.6		5364.8		5982.0	AUT MACH APP ELEC NDA
78	ROAD VEHICLES		97209.8		102639.9		105477.6		114623.9	VEHICULES ROUTIERS
781	PASS MOTOR VEH EXC BUSES	N 4103564	62648.7	N 4121023	66127.0	N 4070205	68088.0	N 4365669	74140.5	AUTO TRANSPORT PERSONNES
782	LORRIES,SPCL MTR VEH NES	N 733937	9673.2	N 675477	10192.9	N 706649	10964.7	N 764786	12568.5	VEHICULES SPECIAUX,MARCH
7821	LORRIES,TRUCKS	N 732940	9593.0	N 674533	10076.0	N 705708	10807.7	N 763856	12431.2	VEHICULES TRANSP MARCHAND
783	ROAD MOTOR VEHICLES NES	N 43627	1771.2	N 40848	2238.7	N 46519	2281.2	N 50369	2736.4	VEHICULES ROUTIERS NDA
784	MOTOR VEH PRTS,ACCES NES		20707.6		21156.0		21382.1		22249.5	PIECES 722,781,782,783
7849	OTHER MOTOR VEHCL PARTS		20271.6		20713.4	W 3948065	20874.2	W 5765685	21707.4	PIECES 722,781,782,783
785	CYCLES,ETC MOTRZD OR NOT	MN 13338	1937.8		2340.9		2213.6		2304.2	MOTOCYCLES SCOOTERS
79	OTHR TRANSPORT EQUIPMENT		8685.4		8429.8		9965.7		11984.9	AUTRE MATERIEL TRANSPORT
792	AIRCRAFT ETC		6818.3		6387.3		7709.5		9855.1	APP NAVIGATION AERIENNE
7923	AIRCRFT NES2000–15000KG	N 327	1910.8	N 275	1692.3	N 306	2326.8	N 342	2770.4	AERODYNES 2000 A 15000 KG
7929	AIRCRAFT PARTS NES		2626.1		2592.3	W 27612	3441.6	W 30733	4881.9	PIECES DU 792
8	MISC MANUFACTURED GOODS		118656.8		129077.4		136597.9		154253.2	ART MANUFACTURES DIVERS
812	*PLUMBG,HEATNG,LGHTNG EQ	MN 400528	2103.3		2359.2		2625.9		2958.1	APPAR SANITAIRES CHAUFFAGE
821	*FURNITURE,PARTS THEREOF		8290.3		9128.2		10200.2		11989.2	MEUBLES ET PIECES
8211	CHAIRS,SEATS AND PARTS		3726.7		4042.2		4579.2		5389.1	SIEGES ET PIECES
82111	CHAIRS AND OTHER SEATS	MN 84376	2241.7	MN 79066	2286.1	MN 82677	2530.8	MN 98597	2951.4	SIEGES
8219	FURNITURE AND PARTS NES		4023.7		4559.0		5080.8		5995.7	AUTRES MEUBLES ET PIECES
82192	WOOD FURNITURE NES		2429.2		2702.9		3042.1		3566.0	MEUBLES NDA EN BOIS
831	*TRAVEL GOODS,HANDBAGS		3290.8		3629.7		3790.9		4057.7	ARTICLES DE VOYAGE ETC
84	CLOTHING AND ACCESSORIES		38860.0		41582.3		43506.3		50489.1	VETEMENTS
842	MENS OUTERWEAR NOT KNIT	W 331496	6049.2	W 354384	6577.8	W 362582	6966.8	W 436601	8356.6	VET DESSUS POUR HOMMES
8423	— TROUSERS,BREECHES ETC	W 203775	3025.8	W 236627	3589.9	W 246805	3840.6	W 299948	4656.9	PANTALONS HOMMES MAT TEX
8429	— OTHER OUTER GARMENTS	W 104996	2083.6	W 95784	1964.8	W 94219	2045.2	W 111316	2457.0	AUT VET DES HOM MAT TEX
843	WOMENS OUTERWEAR NONKNIT	W 493822	11210.2	W 490288	11345.8	W 508275	11913.3	W 586656	13405.5	VET DESSUS FEMMES MAT TEX
8435	— BLOUSES	W 89060	2480.5	W 76421	2078.7	W 73338	2008.4	W 77269	2219.7	BLOUSES FEM MAT TEXTILES
8439	— OTHER OUTER GARMENTS	W 309310	5451.1	W 308969	5630.3	W 319514	5939.6	W 393677	7174.8	AUT VET DES FEM MAT TEXT
844	UNDER GARMENTS NOT KNIT	W 178379	3623.0	W 189810	3863.7	W 175812	3559.4	W 179231	3685.2	VETEMENT DESSOUS MAT TEX
8441	— MENS SHIRTS	W 144776	2958.5	W 154038	3168.4	W 137912	2829.2	W 139868	2927.8	CHEMISES HOMMES MAT TEXT
84411	—— OF COTTON	W 112073	2231.5	W 121444	2480.0	W 107388	2241.7	W 110863	2349.7	CHEMISES HOMMES DE COTON
845	OUTERWEAR KNIT NONELASTC	W 482142	9128.6	W 485808	9619.3	W 489583	9996.6	W 596320	12259.7	VET DESSOUS,ACCES BONNET
8451	— JERSEYS,PULLOVERS ETC	W 301309	5612.1	W 294738	5750.8	W 291526	5982.1	W 358811	7478.6	CHANDAILS,PULL–OVERS ETC
8459	— OTHER,CLTHG ACCESRYS	W 165927	3144.5	W 174661	3440.0	W 179903	3552.6	W 218439	4261.2	AUT VET DESSUS DE BONNE
846	UNDER GARMENTS KNITTED	W 230152	4049.8	W 309814	5384.4	W 369249	6049.8	W 475479	7399.9	SOUS VETS DE BONNETERIE
8462	— OF COTTON NON ELASTIC	W 149224	1982.4	W 197232	2632.8	W 247297	3153.3	W 334167	4050.5	SOUS–VET BONNET COTON
84629	—— OTHER	W 149224	1982.4	W 197232	2632.8	W 247297	3153.3	W 334167	4050.5	AUT SOUS–VET BONNET COTON
848	HEADGEAR,NONTXTL CLOTHNG		3876.7		3792.5		3969.0		4101.5	VET ACCES MAT AUT QUE TEX
851	*FOOTWEAR		11697.4	MP 1416870	12177.0	MP 1385068	12761.0	MP 1497951	13996.2	CHAUSSURES
85101	FOOTWEAR RUBBER,PLASTIC	MP 469447	2604.3	MP 474513	2749.3	MP 489280	2850.8	MP 541816	2987.4	CHAUS SEMELLES CAOUTCH
85102	FOOTWEAR LEATHER	MP 920628	8993.3	MP 907684	9341.7	MP 862635	9822.7	MP 919097	10905.3	CHAUS SEMELLES EN CUIR
87	PRECISION INSTRUMNTS NES		10265.1		11948.3		12814.1		14450.6	INSTRUM,APPAR SCIENT NDA
872	MEDICAL INSTRUMENTS NES		2200.0		2496.8		2735.6		2992.5	INSTR,APP MEDIC–CHIR NDA
874	MEASURNG,CONTROLNG INSTR		6237.4		7345.3		7896.1		8960.3	INSTRUMENTS DE MESURE
88	PHOTO EQU,OPTICL GDS ETC		9062.3		9926.8		10230.9		10818.0	APP,FOURN PHOTO,OP,MONTR
881	PHOTO APPARAT,EQUIPT NES		2389.4		2690.6		2911.8		3289.2	APP,EQUIP PHOTO NDA
882	PHOTO,CINEMA SUPPLIES		2400.7		2578.7		2485.9		2583.3	PRODUITS PHOTO,CINEMA
885	WATCHES AND CLOCKS		2645.7		2749.2		2798.8		2837.8	HORLOGERIE
8851	WATCHES,MOVEMENTS,CASES		2202.1		2299.8		2345.3		2382.2	MONTRES,MOUVEMENTS,BOITES
88511	WATCHES		2134.8		2221.7		2262.9		2308.5	MONTRES POCHE,BRACELET
89	MISC MANUFCTRD GOODS NES		35087.9		38326.2		40669.0		45494.6	ART MANUFACTURES DIVERS

4. General Imports C.I.F. by Commodities according to the S.I.T.C. (Rev. 2) in million U.S. Dollars
Importations Générales C.A.F. par Produits d'après la C.T.C.I. (Rév. 2) en millions de Dollars E.U.

SITC CTCI	COMMODITY	1994 QUANTITY QUANTITE	1994 VALUE VALEUR	1995 QUANTITY QUANTITE	1995 VALUE VALEUR	1996 QUANTITY QUANTITE	1996 VALUE VALEUR	1997 QUANTITY QUANTITE	1997 VALUE VALEUR	PRODUIT
892	PRINTED MATTER		2329.1		2702.0		2811.7		2990.1	IMPRIMES
893	ARTICLES OF PLASTIC NES		5453.3		6195.7		6436.0		6884.9	OUVRAGES EN MAT DIVIS 58
8939	MISC PLASTIC ARTICLES		4350.8		4834.6		4991.7		5209.0	ART DIVERS EN MAT DIV 58
89399	OTHR PLASTC ARTICLES NES	W 123172	4118.6		4559.8		4687.3		4867.7	AUT OUV MAT DIV 58
894	TOYS,SPORTING GOODS,ETC		12631.9		13900.5		15531.7		18220.6	VOITURES ENFANTS,JOUETS
8942	TOYS,INDOOR GAMES ETC		9805.9		10880.5		12606.6		15194.2	JOUETS,JEUX ETC
89423	TOYS NES		4173.2		4681.4		5580.5		6878.6	JOUETS,MODELES REDUITS
89424	INDOOR GAME EQUIPMENT		3159.2		3066.7		3668.2		4718.4	ART,JEUX DE SOCIETE
8947	OTH SPORT GDS,FAIR AMUSM		2343.7		2607.4		2514.1		2619.8	AUT ART DE SPORT
896	WORKS OF ART ETC		2437.5		2684.2		2793.2		3584.2	OBJETS D'ART
897	GOLD,SILVER WARE,JEWELRY		4596.0		4470.3		4502.0		4725.9	BIJOUTERIE,ORFEVRERIE
8973	PREC JEWLRY,GLD–SILVWARE		3693.9		3846.7		3952.0		4153.6	BIJOUX OR,ARGENT ORFEVRE
89731	PRECIOUS METAL JEWELLERY		3426.2		3552.3		3742.5		3931.1	ART BIJOUTERIE,JOAILLER
898	MUSICAL INSTRUMENTS,PTS	MN 1884935	3696.4		3989.2		4170.9		4237.1	INSTRUMENTS DE MUSIQUE
8983	SOUND RECRDNG TAPE,DISCS	MN 1810243	2768.5		2922.4		3128.3		3117.8	SUPPORTS SON POUR 763
899	OTHER MANUFACTURED GOODS		2781.0		3150.9		3195.1		3538.5	AUT ART MANUF DIVERS NDA
9	GOODS NOT CLASSD BY KIND		23663.7		26203.6		29580.3		32896.7	ART TRANSACT NON CLASSES
931	*SPECIAL TRANSACTIONS		21115.4		23492.2		26293.8		29313.0	TRANS.SPECIALES
971	*GOLD,NON MONETARY NES	K 174199	1933.9	K 185364	2154.3	K 245935	2739.0	K 295399	3030.4	OR NON MONETAIRE
97101	NONMON GLD UNWRT,SEMIMFD	K 151306	1819.0	K 170260	2030.1	K 232591	2635.3	K 280479	2944.6	OR,ALLIAGES D'OR BRUTS

5. General Exports F.O.B. by Commodities according to the S.I.T.C. (Rev. 2) in million U.S. Dollars
Exportations Générales F.O.B. par Produits d'après la C.T.C.I. (Rév. 2) en millions de Dollars E.U.

SITC CTCI	COMMODITY	1994 QUANTITY QUANTITE	1994 VALUE VALEUR	1995 QUANTITY QUANTITE	1995 VALUE VALEUR	1996 QUANTITY QUANTITE	1996 VALUE VALEUR	1997 QUANTITY QUANTITE	1997 VALUE VALEUR	PRODUIT
	ALL COMMODITIES		512337.0		582964.9		622784.3		687532.7	TOUS PRODUITS
0	FOOD AND LIVE ANIMALS		35454.0		42223.2		45773.7		41236.7	ALIMENTS,ANIMAUX VIVANTS
01	MEAT AND PREPARATIONS		5211.9		6481.9		7007.3		6946.2	VIANDES ET PREPARATIONS
011	MEAT FRESH,CHILLD,FROZEN	W 2543236	4795.1	W 3241497	5995.3	W 3685414	6426.7	W 3920114	6273.3	VIANDES FRAICHES,REF,CONGE
0111	BOVINE MEAT FRESH,FROZEN	W 518943	2255.2	W 583442	2596.6	W 598430	2381.8	W 679043	2440.3	VIANDES BOVIN FRAI,REF
01112	BOVINE MEAT BONELESS	W 456579	2034.1	W 515822	2316.5	W 520785	2099.6	W 597462	2171.2	VIANDES BOVIN DESOSSEES
0114	POULTRY FRESH CHLLD,FRZN	W 1463908	1425.1	W 1940278	1843.4	W 2306203	2311.2	W 2482581	2200.5	VOLAILLES MORTES
03	FISH AND PREPARATIONS		3153.2		3298.1		3058.6		2739.5	POISSONS ET PREPARATIONS
034	FISH,FRESH,CHILLED,FROZN	W 653821	1842.6	W 692340	2078.2	W 717911	1902.5	W 683011	1686.0	POISSON FRAIS, REFRIG,CONG
04	CEREALS AND PREPARATIONS		11570.1		16285.9		18437.4		13013.9	CEREALES ET PRODUITS
041	WHEAT ETC UNMILLED	MW 30572	4061.2	MW 32417	5457.8	MW 31154	6307.0	MW 25768	4181.8	FROMENT,EPEAUTRE
0412	OTHER WHEAT ETC UNMILLED	MW 29360	3825.4	MW 31289	5226.4	MW 30144	6092.4	MW 24314	3896.3	AUTRE FROMENT NON MOULU
044	MAIZE UNMILLED	MW 35877	4187.2	MW 60238	7535.0	MW 52407	8626.1	MW 41792	5419.0	MAIS NON MOULU
05	VEGETABLES AND FRUIT		7138.8		7537.9		7781.7		7916.8	LEGUMES ET FRUITS
054	VEG ETC FRSH,SMPLY PRSVD	W 3056975	1872.3	W 3087824	1996.9	W 3102536	1941.6	W 3322010	2085.5	LEGUMES FRAIS,CONG,SECS
057	FRUIT,NUTS,FRESH,DRIED	W 3855408	3549.9	W 3842471	3871.1	W 3829554	4047.8	W 4010349	3987.9	FRUITS FRAIS OU SECS
081	*FEEDING STUFF FOR ANIML	MW 17710	3458.7	MW 20200	3798.7	MW 18437	4387.1	MW 20124	4867.7	NOURRITURE POUR ANIMAUX
0819	FOOD WASTE AND FEED NES	MW 9052	1929.3	MW 10349	2123.2	W 8714425	2235.5	MW 9246	2291.6	DECHETS,ALIMENTS NDA
09	MISC EDIBLE PRODUCTS		2283.3		2167.7		2512.4		2724.1	PREP ALIMENTAIRES DIVERSES
098	EDIBLE PRODCTS,PREPS NES		2136.0		1989.8		2362.0		2585.1	PREP ALIMENTAIRES NDA
09809	MISC FOOD PREPRTIONS NES	W 288851	1649.3	W 593089	1507.2	W 664687	1830.6	W 709186	1977.6	PREP ALIMENTAIRES NDA
1	BEVERAGES AND TOBACCO		8015.5		8086.1		8024.9		8063.0	BOISSONS ET TABACS
12	TOBACCO AND MANUFACTURES		6740.7		6668.2		6663.7		6587.5	TABACS BRUTS FABRIQUES
122	TOBACCO,MANUFACTURED		5423.7		5263.9		5267.9		5004.8	TABACS FABRIQUES
1222	CIGARETTES		5011.4	W 235289	4812.1	W 246172	4764.8	W 220722	4455.6	CIGARETTES
2	CRUDE MATERLS,EXCL FUELS		27256.9		34758.6		32252.9		32177.0	MAT BRUTES NON COMESTIBLES
21	HIDES,SKINS,FURS UNDRSSD		1551.2		1776.7		1711.2		1687.1	CUIRS,PEAUX BRUTS
22	OIL SEEDS,OLEAGINOUS FRT		4724.8		5921.0		7855.1		7984.1	GRAINES,FRUITS OLEAGINEUX
222	SEEDS FOR'SOFT'FIXED OIL	MW 18777	4669.1	MW 23692	5869.4	MW 26467	7797.0	MW 26965	7889.1	GRAINES HUILES FIXES
2222	SOYA BEANS	MW 18126	4354.8	MW 22842	5427.7	MW 25961	7457.8	MW 26368	7502.8	FEVES DE SOJA
24	CORK AND WOOD		5580.8		5666.2		5542.7		5179.1	LIEGE ET BOIS
247	OTH WOOD ROUGH,SQUARED	W 13502	4.4	MW 11141	2450.7	MW 10508	2286.6	MW 9878	1846.5	BOIS BRUTS EQUARRIS
2471	SAW–,VENEER–LOGS CONIFER	W 11034	3.7	MW 9926	2150.7	MW 9484	2026.7	W 8555010	1526.9	CONIFERES POUR SCIAGE,PLACAG
24711	— IN THE ROUGH	W 11034	3.7	MW 9926	2150.7	MW 9484	2026.7	W 8555010	1526.9	ECORCES OU DEGROSSIS
248	WOOD SHAPED,SLEEPERS		2656.0		2638.3		2672.0		2800.6	BOIS SIMPLEMENT TRAVAILLES
251	*PULP AND WASTE PAPER	MW 13302	3838.9	MW 17189	6279.5	MW 13246	4079.1	MW 13408	3899.4	PATES A PAPIER,DECHETS
2517	SODA,SULPHATE WOOD PULP	W 4971183	2175.4	W 6004967	3642.0	W 5201087	2391.2	W 5179826	2295.0	PATES CHIMIQUES AU SULFATE
25172	— BLEACHED,NONDISSOLVNG	W 4819432	2122.4	W 5679394	3530.0	W 5010693	2331.6	W 4995372	2238.8	PATES BLANCHIES
26	TEXTILE FIBRES AND WASTE		3953.4		5359.3		4372.8		4253.2	FIBRES TEXTILES
263	COTTON	W 1885712	2724.0	W 2173018	3765.4	W 1612194	2801.4	W 1707246	2765.4	COTON
2631	RAW COTTON,EXCL LINTERS	W 1747443	2655.6	W 2043758	3686.8	W 1498497	2717.7	W 1567989	2682.1	COTON EN MASSE
27	CRUDE FERTLZR,MINRLS NES		1553.4		1577.1		1581.1		1697.1	ENGRAIS MINERAUX BRUTS
28	METALLIFEROUS ORES,SCRAP		3771.7		5592.4		4381.3		4739.1	MINERAIS METAL,DECHETS
3	MINERAL FUELS ETC		9210.7		10720.6		12512.5		12957.2	COMBUSTIBLES MINERAUX LUB
32	COAL,COKE AND BRIQUETTES		2963.8		3714.3		3852.7		3566.8	HOUILLES,COKES,BRIQUETTES
322	COAL,LIGNITE AND PEAT	MW 64972	2861.7	W 63584	1.8	W 36758	3.2		3410.0	HOUILLES,LIGNITES,TOURBE
3222	OTH COAL,NOT AGGLOMERATD	MW 64480	2825.3	W 62269	1.6	W 33945	3.1		3341.6	AUTRES HOUILLES
33	PETROLEUM AND PRODUCTS		5669.4		6212.7		7833.7		8472.6	PETROLE ET DERIVES
334	PETROLEUM PRODUCTS,REFIN	MW 24512	4265.5		4528.1	W 811808	147.9	W 1040020	200.7	PRODUITS RAFFINES
3341	GASOLINE,OTH LIGHT OILS	MW 10250	1715.4	MW 9218	1668.0	MW 9997	2126.9	MW 11218	2335.2	ESSENCES POUR MOTEURS
335	RESIDUAL PETRLM PROD NES	MW 20124	1350.7	MW 21406	1679.5	MW 22183	1914.1	MW 23802	2070.9	PRODUITS RESIDUELS NDA
4	ANIMAL,VEGETABLE OIL,FAT		1780.3		2428.4		1743.1		2096.4	HUILES,GRAISSES ANIM,VEG
5	CHEMCLS,RELATED PROD NES		51138.2		60220.1		61202.1		68864.8	PRODUITS CHIMIQUES
51	ORGANIC CHEMICALS		13078.7		16411.1		15067.5		16837.6	PROD CHIMIQ ORGANIQUES
511	HYDROCARBONS NES,DERIVS	W 5757015	2887.7	W 6132476	3726.7		3024.1		3072.1	HYDROCARBURES NDA
5112	CYCLIC HYDROCARBONS	W 2648130	1215.3	W 3026972	1773.9		1269.6		1118.6	HYDROCARBURES CYCLIQUES
512	ALCOHOLS,PHENOLS ETC	W 2189761	1461.6		2096.8		1846.6		2076.7	PHENOLS,PHENOLS–ALCOOLS
513	CARBOXYLIC ACIDS ETC	W 2055878	2042.1	W 2094054	2721.3	W 1877659	2097.2	W 2357786	2503.8	ACIDES CARBOXYLIQUES
514	NITROGEN–FNCTN COMPOUNDS	W 1734181	3401.0	W 1754582	3819.7	W 1815746	3585.2	W 1926485	3984.8	COMPOSES FONCT AZOTEES
5148	OTH NITROGN–FNCTN CMPNDS	W 1126532	1933.7	W 1114678	2338.6	W 1105536	1985.9	W 1206773	2178.1	AUTRES COMPOSES AZOTES
515	ORG–INORG COMPOUNDS ETC	W 410450	1911.4	W 467150	2301.7	W 505905	2623.7	W 530297	3214.8	COMPOSES ORGANO–MINERAUX
52	INORGANIC CHEMICALS		4147.8		4573.7		4728.7		5420.9	PROD CHIM INORGANIQUES
523	OTHR INORG CHEMICALS ETC		1535.1		1817.5		1878.5		2053.3	AUT PRODUITS CHIMIQUES INORG
53	DYES,TANNING,COLOUR PROD		2305.1		2568.7		2720.3		3289.9	PROD TEINTURE,COLORANTS
533	PIGMENTS,PAINTS,ETC		1760.0		1999.8		2086.6		2527.3	PIGMENTS,PEINTURES,VERNIS
541	*MEDICINAL,PHARM PRODUCT		6184.5		6554.0	MK 207384	7330.1	MK 208894	8230.6	PROD MEDICINAUX PHARMACEUT
5416	GLYCOSIDES,GLANDS,SERA	MK 9547	1600.1		1762.7	MK 26624	2077.5	MK 22034	2266.3	HETEROSIDES
5417	MEDICAMENTS		2333.7		2295.2	MK 99026	2802.6	MK 110635	3412.1	MEDICAMENTS
54179	— CONTNG OTH SUBSTANCES		1447.1		1280.2	MK 78339	1662.8	MK 90650	2212.7	MED CONT AUT SUBSTANCES
55	PERFUME,CLEANING ETC PRD		3644.3		3943.1		4436.7		5015.1	PROD POUR PARFUM,TOILETTE
553	PERFUMERY,COSMETICS,ETC	W 116370	1808.4		1970.2		2275.1		2715.5	PRODUITS DE PARFUMERIE
562	*FERTILIZERS,MANUFACTURE		2706.4		3226.4		3076.5		3074.4	ENGRAIS MANUFACTURES
5629	FERTILIZERS NES		2706.4		3226.4		3076.5		3074.4	ENGRAIS NDA
56299	OTHER FERTILIZERS NES		2706.4		3226.4		3076.5		3074.4	AUTRES ENGRAIS NDA
58	PLASTIC MATERIALS ETC		11486.4		13854.3		14185.5		15871.8	MAT PLAST ARTIFICIELLES
582	PROD OF CONDENSATION ETC	W 1536676	3561.0	W 1721958	4206.3	W 1760961	4386.4	W 2152519	4856.0	PROD CONDENS,POLYCOND
583	POLYMERIZATION ETC PRODS		7118.3	W 5559545	8691.7	W 6170625	8841.4	W 6934282	10083.8	PROD POLYMERISATION
5831	POLYETHYLENE	W 1592690	1542.3	W 1699576	2041.3	W 2056586	2113.0	W 2174689	2427.1	POLYETHYLENE
5839	OTH POLYMRZTION ETC PROD		2601.5	W 1423102	3048.9	W 1493332	3118.9	W 1747322	3598.3	AUT PROD POLYMER COPOLYM
59	CHEMICAL MATERIALS NES		7344.9		8853.7		9344.4		10847.2	MAT PROD CHIMIQUES NDA
598	MISCEL CHEM PRODUCTS NES	W 2091887	5506.5	W 2366314	6717.1	W 2496082	6867.2	W 29549	168.9	PROD DIV INDUST CHIM NDA
5989	CHEM PRODUCTS,PREPS NES	W 1022343	4009.3	W 1223924	4991.0	W 1331570	5351.2	W 1418965	6071.7	PROD PREP CHIMIQUES NDA
59899	OTH CHEM PRODS,PREPS,NES	W 703440	2740.4	W 832673	3438.3	W 884644	3735.5	W 925062	4208.2	AUT PRODUITS CHIMIQUES NDA
6	BASIC MANUFACTURES		44913.2		54444.2		57025.2		63598.6	ART MANUFACTURES
62	RUBBER MANUFACTURES NES		3111.5		3570.5		3875.4		4730.7	CAOUTCHOUC MANUFACTURE
625	RUBBER TYRES, TUBES ETC	MN 41972	1646.3	MN 43877	1901.1	MN 45404	2009.1	MN 52216	2467.2	PNEUS CAOUTCHOUC VULCANISE
63	WOOD,CORK MANUFACTRS NES		1826.9		1916.9		2056.0		2305.0	OUVRAGES LIEGE ET BOIS
64	PAPER,PAPERBOARD AND MFR		7721.4		9888.2		10191.3		10654.7	PAPIERS,CARTONS & OUVRAGES
641	PAPER AND PAPERBOARD		5444.0		7221.5		7206.4		7486.6	PAPIERS ET CARTONS
6413	KRAFT PAPER,PAPERBOARD	W 3584804	1469.6	W 3931265	2186.0	W 4407608	2032.6	W 4965038	2148.2	PAPIER ET CARTON KRAFT
6418	COATED ETC PAPER NES BLK	W 1547238	1496.0	W 1909036	1959.4	W 1994045	2007.4	W 2154712	2194.2	PAP,CARTONS COUCHES,ENDUITS
642	PAPER,ETC,PRECUT,ARTS OF		2277.4		2666.7		2985.0		3168.2	PAP,CARTONS DECOUPES
65	TEXTILE YARN,FABRICS,ETC		6617.5		7404.8		8023.0		9202.1	FILS,TISSUS,ARTICLES TEXTILE
657	SPECIAL TXTL FABRC,PRODS	W 244388	1563.5	W 242734	1722.1	W 259644	1763.2	W 318930	2143.0	TISSUS SPECIAUX
66	NONMETAL MINERAL MFS NES		6159.6		6928.3		7556.0		8410.5	ART MIN NON METALLIQUES
664	GLASS		1717.4		1934.1		2233.1		2572.2	VERRE
667	PEARL,PREC–,SEMI–P STONE		2189.3		2471.1		2659.8		2754.8	PERLES, PIERRES GEMMES
6672	DIAMONDS NONINDUST,UNSET		1939.6		2181.7		2398.6		2471.5	DIAMANTS BRUTS
66729	— CUT ETC NOT SET		1738.4		2010.1		2179.1		2258.9	DIAMANTS TAILLES
67	IRON AND STEEL		4234.0		6151.5		5716.3		6695.2	FER ET ACIER
678	IRON,STL TUBES,PIPES,ETC	W 926193	1419.6	W 1076608	1765.9	W 1077863	1872.4	W 1476579	2319.6	TUBES,TUYAUX EN FONTE,FER

5. General Exports F.O.B. by Commodities according to the S.I.T.C. (Rev. 2) in million U.S. Dollars
Exportations Générales F.O.B. par Produits d'après la C.T.C.I. (Rév. 2) en millions de Dollars E.U.

SITC CTCI	COMMODITY	1994		1995		1996		1997		PRODUIT
		QUANTITY QUANTITE	VALUE VALEUR	QUANTITY QUANTITE	VALUE VALEUR	QUANTITY QUANTITE	VALUE VALEUR	QUANTITY QUANTITE	VALUE VALEUR	
68	NON–FERROUS METALS		5387.7		7521.8		7194.8		7774.8	METAUX NON FERREUX
684	ALUMINIUM	W 1257869	2797.2	W 1407199	3814.2	W 1360463	3534.7	W 1414493	3833.8	ALUMINIUM
6842	ALUMINIUM,ALLOYS WORKED	W 870577	2193.1	W 958982	3000.2	W 913873	2810.3	W 1040537	3195.2	ALUMINIUM,ALLIAGES OUVRE
68422	ALUMNM PLATE,SHEET,STRIP	W 638613	1527.2	W 709080	2174.7	W 646831	1911.4	W 766366	2214.7	TOLES, PLANCHES EN ALU
69	METAL MANUFACTURES NES		8831.9		10019.2		11252.0		12478.0	ART MANUFACT EN METAL NDA
695	TOOLS		1601.9		1806.7		1904.9		2379.0	OUTILS A MAIN
699	BASE METAL MFRS NES		3939.5		4520.8		5136.5		5623.3	ART MANUFACTURES MET NDA
7	MACHINES,TRANSPORT EQUIP		252062.8		281184.4		305748.7		352175.6	MACHINES MATERIEL TRANSPORT
71	POWER GENERATING EQUIPMT		20870.2		22429.9		23169.1		28135.1	MACHINES GENERATRICES
713	INTRNL COMBUS PSTN ENGIN		8263.9		8833.4		9028.8		10486.3	MOTEURS EXPL COMB INT, PIECE
7132	MOTOR VEHCL PISTN ENGINS	N 1511953	3326.1	N 1733053	3734.8	N 1637695	3629.8	N 1897305	4464.4	MOTEURS EXPL POUR VEHICULES
7139	PISTON ENGINE PARTS NES	W 337690	3318.8	W 262520	3436.5	W 304754	3742.6	W 415905	4062.7	PIECES POUR 713.2,3,8
714	ENGINES AND MOTORS NES		8517.5		8757.0		9277.8		11911.5	MOTEURS NON ELECTRIQUES
7144	REACTION ENGINES	N 5955	2379.9	N 13460	1659.0	N 9004	2068.6	N 12130	2199.7	PROPULSEURS A REACTION
7149	ENGINE & MOTOR PARTS NES		5095.8		5594.6		6118.6		8156.8	PIECES 714 ET 718.88
71491	PARTS NES OF 7144,71481		3495.2		3839.6		4204.4		5371.1	PIECES DES PROPULSEURS
71499	PARTS NES,OF 71488,71888		1600.7		1755.0		1914.2		2785.8	PIECES 714.88 ET 718.88
716	ROTATING ELECTRIC PLANT		2677.8		3077.1		3052.7		3572.7	APP ELECTR ROTATIFS,PIECES
72	MACHS FOR SPCL INDUSTRYS		19713.0		23339.4		25605.6		29366.5	MAC SPECIALES POUR INDUST
721	AGRIC MACHY,EXC TRACTORS		2048.9		2125.3		2453.1		2870.9	MACHINES AGRICOLES
723	CIVIL ENGNEERG EQUIP ETC	N 827751	5953.9		6274.8		7060.3		8383.3	APPAREILS DE GENIE CIVIL
7234	CONST,MINING MACHNRY NES	N 117607	2533.8	N 110322	2157.6	N 116043	2257.4	N 170016	3056.0	MACH POUR LA CONST, MINES
7239	CONSTR ETC MACHY PTS NES	N 706345	3311.7		3766.0		4511.3		5189.4	PIECES 723.41–723.46
728	OTH MACHY FOR SPCL INDUS		6883.0		9392.2		10298.0		11580.6	AUT MACH IND PARTICULIERES
7284	MACHY FOR SPCL INDUS NES		5847.8		8194.7		9098.5		10006.7	MACH SPEC IND PARTICUL.
72848	OTH MCHY WITH INDIV FNCT	N 54116	2948.0	N 938433	4788.8	N 1004705	5297.5	N 1092502	5709.1	AUTRES MACHINES NDA
72849	PTS OF MACHS OF 7284 ETC		2002.9		2376.0		2715.6		3078.2	PIECES DU 728.4 ETC
73	METALWORKING MACHINERY		3922.1		4601.6		5216.8		5651.6	MACH TRAVAIL DES METAUX
736	METALWORKING MACH–TOOLS		2987.1		3682.2		4261.8		4371.3	MACH–OUTILS TRAVAIL METAUX
74	GENRL INDUSTRL MACHY NES		23579.7		26141.3		28549.4		32687.2	MACH APP INDUSTRIE
741	HEATING,COOLING EQUIPMNT		4970.5		5656.1		6033.4		6891.0	MACH CHAUFFAGE,PIECES
7415	AIR–CONDITIONING MACHNRY	N 3162572	1792.1		1945.7		2101.8		2284.9	GROUPES CONDITION AIR
742	PUMPS FOR LIQUIDS ETC		2267.3		2418.8		2563.1		3043.9	POMPES MOTO–POMPES
743	PUMPS NES,CENTRFUGES ETC		4655.4		5205.2		5827.0		6891.5	POMPES COMPRES,VENT ETC
7431	PUMPS FOR GASES ETC	N 5247501	1628.6	N 5870285	1747.9	N 8618395	1958.3	MN 9620	2296.8	POMPES AIR A VIDE,COMPRES
7436	GAS,LIQUID FILTERS ETC	N 245093	1648.8		1767.8		2031.3		2404.2	APP POUR FILT DES LIQUIDES
744	MECHANICAL HANDLING EQU		4049.0		4667.3		5213.2		5783.2	EQUIP MANUTENTION PIECES
7449	PTS NES OF MACHY OF 7442		2527.4		2758.8		3054.9		3166.1	PIECES DU 744.2
745	NONELEC MACHY,TOOLS NES		2671.7		2790.8		3052.2		3384.4	AUT MACH NON ELEC,PIECES
7452	OTH NONELEC MCHS,PTS NES		2210.2		2307.9		2553.8		2773.1	AUT MACH NON ELEC,PIECES
749	NONELEC MACH PTS,ACC NES		4966.1		5403.3		5860.9		6693.4	PIECES MACH NON ELEC NDA
7492	COCKS,VALVES ETC NES		1964.8		2238.5		2500.3		2868.3	ART ROB,SIM POUR TUYAUX
75	OFFICE MACHNES,ADP EQUIP		35396.2		41947.1		45751.3		51641.2	MACH BUREAU TRAIT AUTOM
752	AUTOMTIC DATA PROC EQUIP	MN 31145	20427.3	MN 33660	23077.6	MN 36792	25220.1	MN 43015	28107.9	MACH TRAIT INFORMATION
7522	DIGITAL COMPUTERS	N 1016623	1893.4	N 1085680	2022.4	N 1459484	2551.6	N 1481863	2450.1	MACH DIGITALES COMPLETES
7523	DIGITL CENTRL PROCESSORS	N 3000386	6821.4	N 3114544	7274.0	MN 9853	10346.7	N 7751062	9605.7	UNITES CENTRALES
7524	DIGITL CENTRL STOR UNITS	MN 9131	4537.5	MN 10383	5150.4	MN 9255	3559.3	MN 13134	5190.2	UNITES MEMOIRE CENTRALES
7525	ADP PERIPHERAL UNITS	MN 12856	4314.8	MN 13144	4747.6	N 8428398	2613.6	MN 10572	3332.3	UNITES PERIPHERIQUES
7528	OFF–LINE DATA PROC EQUIP	N 5027040	2358.5	N 5821162	3401.3	N 7564980	5363.0	MN 9745	6552.2	MACH AUXIL TRAIT INFORM
759	OFFICE,ADP MCH PTS,ACCES		14018.0		17768.0		19350.7		22321.5	PIECES DU 751 ET 752
7599	ACCTG,ETC,ADP MCH PTS,AC		13120.7		16811.6		18238.9		20970.8	PIECES DU 751 ET 752
76	TELECOMM,SOUND EQUIPMENT		17128.6		20331.6		21414.4		26055.6	EQUIPMENT DE TELECOM
764	TELECOM EQPT,PTS,ACC NES		14810.3		17842.4		18735.0		22703.2	EQUIP TELECOM,PIECES
7641	LINE TELEPHONE,ETC EQUIP	N 3724156	2548.8		3247.9		3887.7		4766.6	APP TELEPHON PAR FIL
7643	TV,RADIO TRANSMITTRS ETC		4153.2		5275.4		5215.4	MN 15459	6364.8	APP EMET TELE RADIO
7649	PTS NES OF EQUIPMT OF 76		5947.2		7072.6		7186.7		8430.8	PIECES DE LA DIV 76
76491	PTS NES OF APPAR OF 7641		2189.7		2494.5		2710.9		2991.7	PIECES POUR 764.1
76493	TELECOMM EQUIPMT PTS NES		3448.5		4188.7		3954.9		4963.0	PIECES 761,762,764.3,8
77	ELECTRIC MACHNRY NES ETC		52771.3		65452.3		69983.7		77997.7	MACH APP ELECT NDA
771	ELECTRIC POWER MACHY NES		1873.9		2153.2		2510.3		3253.3	MACH PROD,TRANS ELECTR
7712	OTH ELEC POWER MACHY NES		1589.7		1816.4		2078.9		2770.1	AUT APP PROD TRANSF ELEC
772	SWITCHGEAR ETC,PARTS NES	MN 8650843	7235.9		8319.1		9168.7		10494.6	APP COUPURE,SECT ETC
7721	SWITCHGEAR ETC	MN 4370226	5365.7		6175.1		6893.2		7733.4	APP COUPURE,SECTIONMNT
7722	PRINTED CIRCUITS,PTS NES	MN 181290	1528.0	MN 333852	1744.2	MN 369450	1810.0	MN 464789	2168.1	CIRCUITS ET PIECES
773	ELECTR DISTRIBUTNG EQUIP		3643.1		4102.5		4545.9		5217.4	EQUIPMT DISTRIBUTION ELECT
7731	INSULATED WIRE,CABLE ETC	W 234664	3263.9		3679.5		4121.1		4763.2	FILS,CABLES ISOLES ELECT
774	ELECTRO–MEDCL,XRAY EQUIP		2958.2		3349.2		3803.1		3904.7	APPAREILS MEDICAUX
7741	ELECTRO–MEDICAL EQUIPMNT		1808.8		2012.6		2437.3		2430.0	APP ELECTRICITE MEDICALE
775	HOUSEHOLD TYPE EQUIP NES		2384.8		2465.0		2633.9		2800.6	MACH,APP USAGE DOMESTQUE
776	TRANSISTORS,VALVES,ETC		26452.2		35711.3		37451.2		41188.3	LAMPES,TUBES,VALVES
7763	DIODES,TRANSISTORS,ETC	MN 3896721	1685.4	MN 5346029	2332.1	MN 5576293	2505.6	MN 5848483	2880.6	DIODES,TRANSISTORS
7764	ELECTRONIC MICROCIRCUITS	MN 12625404	22589.4	MN 14553772	30589.0	MN 14051114	31889.1	MN 17236568	34346.0	MICROSTRUCTURES ELECTRON
778	ELECTRICAL MACHINERY NES		8223.4		9352.2		9870.8		11139.1	AUTRES MACH ELECT NDA
7783	AUTOMOTIVE ELECTR EQUIP	MN 54884	1697.5		1529.0		1640.2		1812.8	EQUIP ELECT MOTEURS EXPL
7788	OTH ELEC MACHY,EQUIP NES		4456.2		5586.8		5878.7		6485.2	AUT MACH APP ELEC NDA
78	ROAD VEHICLES		46304.9		49221.8		51702.8		57429.2	VEHICULES ROUTIERS
781	PASS MOTOR VEH EXC BUSES	N 1224954	16662.0	N 1232604	16799.3	N 1239379	17176.0	N 1297106	17116.4	AUTO TRANSPORT PERSONNES
782	LORRIES,SPCL MTR VEH NES	N 353207	4599.0	N 327799	5318.4	N 396251	6763.0	N 502557	8261.3	VEHICULES SPECIAUX,MARCH
7821	LORRIES,TRUCKS	N 347721	4176.5	N 319633	4839.9	N 388582	6274.2	N 492876	7689.9	VEHICULES TRANSP MARCHAND
784	MOTOR VEH PRTS,ACCES NES		22106.2		23816.7		24628.2		28396.7	PIECES 722,781,782,783
7849	OTHER MOTOR VEHCL PARTS	W 74258	21674.9	W 3293723	23373.1	W 3260132	24110.7		27768.7	PIECES 722,781,782,783
79	OTHR TRANSPORT EQUIPMENT		32377.2		27719.7		34355.8		43211.7	AUTRE MATERIEL TRANSPORT
792	AIRCRAFT ETC		30431.3		25612.7		32456.7		40607.8	APP NAVIGATION AERIENNE
7923	AIRCRFT NES2000–15000KG	N 438	1382.7	N 63218	1147.7	N 558	3510.9	N 560	3325.5	AERODYNES 2000 A 15000 KG
7924	AIRCRFT NES OVER 15000KG	N 314	18068.3	N 192	12656.7	N 285	15843.0	N 352	22517.4	AERODYNES PLUS 15000 KG
7929	AIRCRAFT PARTS NES		9872.5		10568.0	W 53372	11953.1	W 57804	13550.5	PIECES DU 792
8	MISC MANUFACTURED GOODS		56496.7		62106.2		67819.6		76649.6	ART MANUFACTURES DIVERS
821	*FURNITURE,PARTS THEREOF		3728.8		3806.4		4085.9		4762.4	MEUBLES ET PIECES
8211	CHAIRS,SEATS AND PARTS		1644.3		1793.7		1867.5		2260.7	SIEGES ET PIECES
84	CLOTHING AND ACCESSORIES		5620.7		6657.3		7520.1		8678.0	VETEMENTS
846	UNDER GARMENTS KNITTED	W 94929	1355.5	W 133385	1707.6	W 157957	1946.9	W 192098	2363.0	SOUS VETS DE BONNETERIE
87	PRECISION INSTRUMNTS NES		17177.5		19358.9		21463.1		25312.3	INSTRUM,APPAR SCIENT NDA
872	MEDICAL INSTRUMENTS NES		3860.6		4294.6		4914.6		5688.5	INSTR,APP MEDIC–CHIR NDA
87202	OTH MEDICAL INSTRUMENTS		3405.2		3791.2		4397.9		5081.2	INSTRUM,APP MEDECINE
874	MEASURNG,CONTROLNG INSTR		11848.5		13484.9		14673.7		17178.5	INSTRUMENTS DE MESURE
8742	MEASUR,DRAW ETC INST,PTS		1379.7		1699.9		2284.9		2711.5	INST DESSIN,TRACAGE,PCS
87421	MEASURNG,DRAWNG ETC INST		1128.1		1370.5		1918.8		2295.4	INSTRUM DESSIN,TRACAGE
8743	GAS,LIQUID CONTROL INSTR	MN 35113	2450.5		2623.5		2554.7		3220.1	APP,INSTR MESURE FLUIDES
8748	ELEC MEAS,CONTRL EQU NES	MN 12278	4276.1		4887.8		5388.5		6103.4	APP ELEC ELECTRO MESURE
87483	OTH ELCTRNC MEAS ETC EQU	MN 9779	3944.1		4560.7		5008.5		5691.8	AUT APP ELECTRO DE MESURE
8749	INSTR PTS NES,ACCESSORYS		1759.0		2196.3		2266.7		2622.1	PIECES 873,874.3,54,874.8

5. General Exports F.O.B. by Commodities according to the S.I.T.C. (Rev. 2) in million U.S. Dollars
Exportations Générales F.O.B. par Produits d'après la C.T.C.I. (Rév. 2) en millions de Dollars E.U.

SITC CTCI	COMMODITY	1994 QUANTITY QUANTITE	1994 VALUE VALEUR	1995 QUANTITY QUANTITE	1995 VALUE VALEUR	1996 QUANTITY QUANTITE	1996 VALUE VALEUR	1997 QUANTITY QUANTITE	1997 VALUE VALEUR	PRODUIT
88	PHOTO EQU,OPTICL GDS ETC		4229.2		4690.9		5315.4		5653.7	APP,FOURN PHOTO,OP,MONTR
882	PHOTO,CINEMA SUPPLIES		2115.9		2420.5		2789.8		2970.9	PRODUITS PHOTO,CINEMA
8822	PHOTO FILM EXC DEV CINMA		1689.1		1833.1		2240.4		2422.7	PLAQUES,PELLICULES,FILMS
89	MISC MANUFCTRD GOODS NES		24043.9		25828.9		27608.1		30200.2	ART MANUFACTURES DIVERS
892	PRINTED MATTER		4089.3		4406.6		4428.2		4710.3	IMPRIMES
8921	PRINTED BOOKS,GLOBES,ETC	MN 951721	1894.8		2017.4		2051.4		2161.4	LIVRES,BROCHURES,CARTES
89211	PRINTED BOOKS,PAMPHLETS	MN 919493	1861.6	MN 1035132	1988.2	MN 1001831	2022.4	MN 1048937	2125.7	LIVRES,BROCHURES
893	ARTICLES OF PLASTIC NES		4963.4		5393.9		6221.2		7115.9	OUVRAGES EN MAT DIVIS 58
8939	MISC PLASTIC ARTICLES		3636.5		3851.2		4535.7		5198.5	ART DIVERS EN MAT DIV 58
89399	OTHR PLASTC ARTICLES NES	W 149232	3381.4		3599.4		4252.0		4889.1	AUT OUV MAT DIV 58
894	TOYS,SPORTING GOODS,ETC		3689.6		4230.6		4287.6		4497.2	VOITURES ENFANTS,JOUETS
8942	TOYS,INDOOR GAMES ETC		2176.3		2269.8		2313.1		2486.6	JOUETS,JEUX ETC
896	WORKS OF ART ETC		1693.5		1487.2		1508.1		1864.6	OBJETS D'ART
898	MUSICAL INSTRUMENTS,PTS		6266.4		6584.6		6874.4		7139.9	INSTRUMENTS DE MUSIQUE
8983	SOUND RECRDNG TAPE,DISCS		5846.7		6139.2	MN 709754	6123.1	MN 726799	6388.4	SUPPORTS SON POUR 763
89831	PREPD SND RECORDNG MEDIA		2046.0		2250.2	MN 463074	2670.1	MN 557040	2603.2	SUPPORTS PREPARES
89832	RECORDED DISCS,TAPES ETC	MN 15278	3800.8		3889.0	MN 254178	3547.3	MN 174145	3867.9	DISQUES,PHONO,BANDES
899	OTHER MANUFACTURED GOODS		1853.1		2034.1		2287.5		2552.7	AUT ART MANUF DIVERS NDA
9	GOODS NOT CLASSD BY KIND		26009.2		26793.4		30682.1		29714.3	ART TRANSACT NON CLASSES
931	*SPECIAL TRANSACTIONS		16675.4		17700.0		19342.5		20630.8	TRANS.SPECIALES
951	*WAR FIREARMS,AMMUNITION		3625.9		3953.5		4612.6		3327.1	VEHIC BLINDES ARMES
95101	ARMORED FIGHTNG VEHICLES		1677.4		1619.1		2222.0		1158.7	CHARS DE COMBAT
95106	AMMUNITION NES	MN 14568995	1295.3		1848.7		1509.9		1536.4	PROJECTILES,MUNITIONS
971	*GOLD,NON MONETARY NES	K 501752	5676.6	K 461805	5098.5	K 585745	6671.3	K 562951	5694.0	OR NON MONETAIRE
97101	NONMON GLD UNWRT,SEMIMFD	K 404682	4898.6	K 358861	4307.4	K 483771	5795.4	K 490451	5136.6	OR,ALLIAGES D'OR BRUTS

FOOT NOTES – NOTES

TABLE 1 –
1 Prior to 1974, imports f.o.b.
TABLEAU 1 –
1 Avant 1974, les importations sont f.a.b.

Uruguay

1. HISTORICAL SERIES, 1962–1997 SPECIAL TRADE, IMPORTS C.I.F., EXPORTS F.O.B.
SERIES HISTORIQUES, 1962–1997 COMMERCE SPECIAL, IMPORTATIONS C.A.F., EXPORTATIONS F.O.B

YEAR ANNEE	VALUE IN MILLION U.S. DOLLARS VALEUR EN MILLION U.S. DOLLARS MERCHANDISE –MARCHANDISE		GOLD –OR		CONVERSION FACTORS FACTEURS DE CONVERSION CENTS E.U. PAR		INDEX NUMBERS –INDICES QUANTUM		UNIT VALUE VALEUR UNITAIRE	
	IMPORTS	EXPORTS	IMPORTS	EXPORTS	IMPORTS	EXPORTS	IMPORTS	EXPORTS	IMPORTS	EXPORTS
1962	230.50	153.40								
1963	176.90	165.20								
1964	198.40	178.90								
1965	150.40	191.20								
1966	164.00	185.80								
1967	171.40	158.70								
1968	157.40	179.20								
1969	197.30	200.30								
1970	230.90	232.70								
1971	228.90	205.70								
1972	211.60	214.10								
1973	284.80	321.50								
1974	486.70	382.10								
1975	556.40	383.80								
1976	587.20	546.50								
1977	729.90	607.50								
1978	774.30	686.10								
1979	1206.30	788.10								
1980	1680.30	1058.50								
1981	1641.10	1215.40								99
1982	1110.00	1022.90								100
1983	787.50	1045.10								89
1984	775.70	924.60								83
1985	707.80	853.60								85
1986	870.00	1087.80								79
1987	1141.90	1189.20								78
1988	1157.20	1404.50								88
1989	1202.80	1598.80								100
1990	1342.90	1692.90								105
1991	1636.50	1604.70								100
1992	2045.10	1702.50								100
1993	2325.70	1645.30								99
1994	2786.10	1913.40								93
1995	2866.90	2106.00								95
1996	3322.80	2397.20								105
1997	3716.00	2729.50								102

2. IMPORTS BY BROAD ECONOMIC CATEGORY AND EXPORTS BY INDUSTRIAL ORIGIN. (PERCENTAGE OF TOTAL VALUE)
IMPORTATIONS PAR CATEGORIES ECONOMIQUES ET EXPORTATIONS PAR BRANCHE D'ACTIVITE.(EN POURCENTAGE DE LA VALEUR TOTALE)

IMPORTS – IMPORTATIONS

	1991	1992	1993	1994	1995	1996	1997
TOTAL IMPORTS–IMPORTATIONS TOTALES	100.	100.	100.	100.	100.	100.	100.
1 FOOD BEV–ALIMENTATION BOISSONS	6.5	8.1	7.1	9.4	9.4	9.5	9.1
11 PRIMARY–PRODUITS DE BASE	3.5	4.5	3.2	3.7	3.1	3.3	2.9
111 FOR INDUSTRY–POUR L'INDUSTRIE	0.8	2.1	0.7	1.1	0.5	0.8	0.6
112 FOR HOUSEHOLDS–POUR LES MENAGES	2.7	2.4	2.5	2.5	2.6	2.4	2.3
12 PROCESSED–PRODUITS ELABORES	3.0	3.6	3.9	5.7	6.3	6.2	6.2
121 FOR INDUSTRY–POUR L'INDUSTRIE	1.1	1.1	1.0	1.4	1.4	1.4	1.2
122 FOR HOUSEHOLDS–POUR LES MENAGES	1.9	2.5	2.9	4.3	4.9	4.8	5.0
2 IND SUPPLIES–APPROV INDUSTRIELS	36.9	30.9	29.6	31.9	31.9	33.3	31.5
21 PRIMARY–PRODUITS DE BASE	3.7	2.7	2.2	3.1	3.4	3.1	2.5
22 PROCESSED–PRODUITS ELABORES	33.2	28.2	27.4	28.8	28.5	30.2	29.0
3 FUELS–COMBUSTIBLES	15.6	10.4	8.5	8.1	10.1	10.8	9.1
31 PRIMARY–PRODUITS DE BASE	13.5	7.5	1.7	0.6	6.6	7.2	5.8
32 PROCESSED–PRODUITS ELABORES	2.1	2.8	6.7	7.6	3.5	3.6	3.3
321 MOTOR SPIRIT–ESSENCE	1.9	0.2	1.5	4.0		1.7	0.5
322 OTHER–AUTRES	0.2	2.6	5.2	3.6	3.5	1.8	2.8
4 MACHINERY–EQUIPEMENT	17.3	16.1	17.9	16.8	18.0	19.4	19.7
41 CAPITAL EQUIPMENT–MACHINES	15.7	14.6	16.2	15.3	16.5	17.9	17.9
42 PARTS–PIECES ACCESSOIRES	1.7	1.6	1.7	1.5	1.5	1.6	1.8
5 TRANSPORT–TRANSPORT	12.2	15.8	17.9	16.4	14.2	11.6	14.2
51 PASSENGER CARS–AUTOMOBILES	7.2	7.9	10.6	10.1	7.1	4.6	4.7
52 OTHER–AUTRES	2.1	4.6	4.0	3.2	4.3	4.3	4.7
521 INDUSTRIAL–INDUSTRIELS	1.6	3.9	3.1	2.2	3.5	3.6	4.0
522 NON INDUSTRIAL–NON INDUSTRIEL	0.4	0.7	0.9	1.0	0.8	0.7	0.7
53 PARTS–PIECES ACCESSOIRES	2.9	3.2	3.2	3.2	2.7	2.6	4.8
6 CONSUM GOODS–BIENS CONSOMMATION	11.5	18.7	19.1	17.4	16.4	15.4	16.4
61 DURABLE–DURABLES	3.9	10.3	8.8	6.5	5.3	4.6	4.9
62 SEMI DURABLE–SEMI DURABLES	4.5	5.4	7.1	7.3	7.1	6.8	7.1
63 NON DURABLE–NON DURABLES	3.0	3.0	3.2	3.5	4.0	4.1	4.4
7 GOODS NES–BIENS NDA	0.0	0.0	0.1	0.0	0.0	0.0	0.0

EXPORTS – EXPORTATIONS

	1991	1992	1993	1994	1995	1996	1997
TOTAL EXPORTS–EXPORTATIONS TOTALES	100.	100.	100.	100.	100.	100.	100.
1 AGRICULTURE	16.4	14.5	14.9	13.7	17.2	14.7	16.1
2 MINING QUARRY–INDUS EXTRACTIVES	0.2	0.3	0.2	0.2	0.2	0.2	0.2
3 MANUFACTURING–IND MANUFACTUR	83.4	85.2	84.9	86.1	82.6	85.1	83.7
31 FOOD BEV TOBACCO–ALIM BOISS TAB	30.1	28.3	29.6	31.2	30.7	35.4	35.7
32 TEXTILES–INDUSTRIES TEXTILES	37.7	40.0	33.9	30.1	30.9	30.4	27.3
33 WOOD & PRODUCTS–BOIS & PRODUITS	0.0	0.1	0.1	0.2	0.3	0.3	0.3
34 PAPER & PRODUCTS–PAPIER & PRODT	1.7	1.5	1.6	1.4	1.5	1.9	2.2
35 CHEMICALS–INDUSTRIES CHIMIQUES	8.2	8.1	7.9	7.5	8.9	8.6	8.3
36 NON METAL MIN–MIN NON METAL	1.4	1.7	2.0	1.6	1.3	1.4	1.5
37 BASIC METAL–IND METAL BASE	0.8	0.6	0.6	0.6	0.9	1.1	1.2
38 METAL MANUF–MANUF METAL	2.8	4.2	8.7	12.6	7.3	5.6	6.8
39 OTH MANUF IND–AUTRES MANUF	0.7	0.6	0.6	0.9	0.7	0.3	0.2

3. TRADE BY PRINCIPAL COUNTRIES OF CONSIGNMENT AND SALE (VALUE IN MILLION U.S. DOLLARS)
ECHANGES SELON LES PRINCIPAUX PAYS DE CONSIGNATION ET DE VENTE (VALEUR EN MILLIONS DE DOLLARS EU)

COUNTRIES–PAYS	SPECIAL IMPORTS C.I.F. IMPORTATIONS SPECIALES C.A.F				
	1993	1994	1995	1996	1997
World	2332.9	2707.2	2865.7	3322.4	3715.6
Africa	22.3	17.0	41.6	86.0	53.0
Americas	1416.9	1786.8	1799.9	2096.2	2321.2
– Northern America	249.3	285.4	303.3	431.1	462.1
– LAIA	1142.8	1465.7	1469.2	1641.8	1833.2
– CACM	0.3	1.0	0.8	1.4	2.0
– Caribbean	6.3	6.1	6.0	6.7	9.7
– Rest of America	18.3	28.6	20.6	15.2	14.3
Asia excl fmr USSR	305.1	296.6	343.1	381.8	474.7
– Middle East	22.1	6.5	60.1	67.4	75.9
Asia former USSR	0.0	0.1	0.0	0.0	
Europe excl fmr USSR	562.0	564.0	640.8	691.4	781.1
– European Union	522.7	514.5	597.5	644.9	717.7
– Eastern Europe	12.6	20.0	13.9	12.7	25.7
– Rest of Europe	26.7	29.6	29.4	33.7	37.7
Europe former USSR	14.1	23.5	1.0	19.7	33.6
Oceania	3.4	11.1	3.5	7.9	16.9
Other	9.2	7.9	35.9	39.4	35.1
Brazil/Brésil	608.1	745.7	698.5	745.5	801.8
Argentina/Argentine	432.1	608.9	608.6	690.7	790.8
USA/Etats–Unis d'Amer	210.6	262.5	283.9	405.7	433.1
Italy/Italie	234.9	137.8	147.8	171.4	170.6
Germany/Allemagne	79.5	93.7	104.1	100.4	117.6
France, Monaco	71.3	79.0	100.3	117.9	119.9
Spain/Espagne	51.9	83.1	106.3	103.3	116.5
Japan/Japon	125.0	78.6	73.3	72.1	97.1
Korea, Republic of	43.7	50.5	49.9	61.7	78.4
Chile/Chili	36.5	45.5	49.3	55.4	62.9
United Kingdom	37.3	41.7	41.1	52.4	65.7
Mexico/Mexique	46.4	39.2	41.5	48.9	52.4
China, Hong Kong SAR	39.0	45.8	37.7	38.5	44.2
Venezuela	3.8	11.3	25.2	63.7	88.5
China/Chine	15.6	28.1	34.6	49.5	63.9
Iran (Islamic Rep of)	18.5	0.0	33.4	62.7	57.3
Other Asia n.e.s.	25.9	30.8	30.7	34.9	42.5
Switzerland,Liechtenst.	25.3	28.2	28.1	27.9	34.3
Canada	38.6	22.7	18.3	25.3	29.0
Netherlands/Pays–Bas	16.2	20.8	24.5	22.3	31.7
Sweden/Suède	3.5	18.6	24.1	28.8	38.1
Panama	18.3	28.6	20.6	15.2	14.1
Nigeria/Nigéria		0.0	30.4	61.7	0.0
Russian Federation	13.7	22.4		17.7	33.2
India/Inde	6.7	16.0	16.4	18.6	23.8
Areas n.e.s.	9.2	5.6	28.8	15.8	20.6
Paraguay	6.5	8.6	13.6	25.3	23.7
Belgium–Luxembourg	9.0	13.6	16.5	14.8	20.5
So. African Customs Un	5.9	12.0	7.7	8.8	28.1
Denmark/Danemark	6.8	6.1	12.2	13.9	14.0
Israel/Israël	5.4	9.0	10.7	12.5	14.3
Singapore/Singapour	11.1	12.6	11.8	7.3	8.3
Saudi Arabia	0.0	3.5	23.6	0.1	14.0
Free zones/Zone franches		2.4		23.6	14.5
Australia/Australie	1.8	6.9	3.5	4.1	12.4
Egypt/Egypte	10.6	0.4	0.2	0.1	17.0
Malaysia/Malaisie	2.5	6.2	6.1	4.7	6.2
Finland/Finlande	2.6	6.1	3.7	6.2	6.7
Colombia/Colombie	1.7	3.0	9.0	5.4	5.9
Austria/Autriche	4.6	4.8	5.5	3.3	5.5

COUNTRIES–PAYS	SPECIAL EXPORTS F.O.B. EXPORTATIONS SPECIALES F.O.B.				
	1993	1994	1995	1996	1997
Monde	1606.5	1914.5	2106.2	2397.4	2729.5
Afrique	4.6	4.6	15.8	20.0	27.7
Amériques	981.2	1186.3	1268.0	1604.1	1716.6
– Amérique du Nord	157.7	147.1	142.6	159.8	191.5
– ALAI	813.3	1027.1	1115.1	1435.3	1509.8
– MCAC	2.3	1.1	5.5	3.2	1.7
– Caraïbes	7.5	10.5	4.3	3.2	12.6
– Autre Amérique	0.3	0.4	0.6	2.6	0.9
Asie anc. URSS exclus	237.4	280.5	334.9	313.4	393.1
– Moyen–Orient	26.8	28.1	39.0	39.4	52.4
Asie ancienne URSS	0.0				0.0
Europe anc. URSS exclus	360.6	411.8	460.2	426.5	546.8
– Union Européenne	344.7	398.1	438.2	407.0	515.8
– Europe de l'Est	8.8	2.7	6.0	6.7	5.8
– Autre de l'Europe	7.1	11.0	16.0	12.8	25.2
Europe ancienne URSS	3.6	10.7	7.4	14.9	17.3
Océanie	1.7	1.0	3.7	4.1	2.5
Autre	17.5	19.5	16.2	14.4	25.5
Brazil/Brésil	366.2	493.5	700.1	908.4	940.2
Argentina/Argentine	279.1	382.3	267.1	267.9	354.3
USA/Etats–Unis d'Amer	146.9	132.4	126.3	144.1	162.7
China/Chine	88.0	115.0	123.5	116.2	123.2
Germany/Allemagne	104.4	121.3	118.0	93.8	120.4
United Kingdom	64.6	71.9	87.1	53.9	116.5
Italy/Italie	49.1	60.3	65.4	73.7	91.1
Chile/Chili	52.3	41.3	39.9	115.7	56.7
China, Hong Kong SAR	41.1	33.2	48.8	86.2	60.5
Netherlands/Pays–Bas	47.2	48.2	54.8	39.6	58.2
Israel/Israël	45.6	55.4	48.5	5.7	66.4
Spain/Espagne	19.0	33.2	53.3	37.8	58.7
Paraguay	16.1	24.1	24.9	49.5	60.7
Peru/Pérou	37.1	22.5	36.8	36.5	31.9
Mexico/Mexique	40.3	46.6	14.9	26.9	32.4
France, Monaco	28.9	25.0	24.2	18.9	24.7
Japan/Japon	13.7	20.8	18.6	24.8	28.7
Sweden/Suède	6.6	12.6	10.3	62.1	8.9
Canada	10.7	14.7	16.2	14.0	28.8
Areas n.e.s.	17.5	18.0	14.9	13.4	19.8
Colombia/Colombie	14.9	12.5	18.3	15.1	15.8
Iran (Islamic Rep of)	10.5	2.5	15.1	19.5	24.5
Belgium–Luxembourg	12.0	14.1	7.4	15.4	16.7
Saudi Arabia	11.8	18.7	10.9	9.3	9.3
Malaysia/Malaisie	0.4	0.1	17.2	12.6	24.1
Other Asia n.e.s.	10.0	9.9	11.9	6.8	8.1
Russian Federation	3.5	9.2	7.0	14.1	12.7
Venezuela	3.7	2.3	11.0	12.9	15.1
Korea, Republic of	4.5	7.8	9.7	11.2	10.2
Turkey/Turquie	2.8	4.3	9.9	6.6	10.6
Norway,Svalbard and JM	2.4	3.2	6.1	8.4	13.5
Switzerland,Liechtenst.	4.2	7.5	9.3	3.1	6.0
Senegal/Sénégal		2.1	8.5	7.9	11.5
Portugal	6.1	3.1	3.7	5.5	9.0
Singapore/Singapour	3.9	3.5	7.4	2.6	2.6
Finland/Finlande	1.2	1.6	6.2	2.4	4.8
India/Inde	1.1	2.3	5.8	2.2	4.3
So. African Customs Un	0.9	1.0	3.8	4.0	4.6
Poland/Pologne	5.0	0.8	2.1	3.6	2.8
Denmark/Danemark	2.7	3.5	3.5	1.8	2.2

(VALUE AS PERCENTAGE OF WORLD TOTAL)(VALEURS EN POURCENTAGE DU TOTAL MONDIAL)

	1988	1989	1990	1991	1992	1993	1994	1995	1996	1997
Africa	2.1	3.3	1.0	5.7	2.0	1.0	0.6	1.5	2.6	1.4
Americas	59.7	63.5	60.1	59.7	57.2	60.7	66.0	62.8	63.1	62.5
– Northern America	8.4	13.0	10.8	10.5	9.9	10.7	10.5	10.6	13.0	12.4
– LAIA	50.4	49.6	48.7	48.4	46.4	49.0	54.1	51.3	49.4	49.3
– CACM	0.0		0.0	0.0	0.0	0.0	0.0	0.0	0.0	0.1
– Caribbean	0.6	0.5	0.1	0.0	0.1	0.3	0.2	0.2	0.2	0.3
– Rest of America	0.3	0.5	0.5	0.7	0.8	0.8	1.1	0.7	0.5	0.4
Asia excl fmr USSR	9.7	9.1	12.3	13.7	20.3	13.1	11.0	12.0	11.5	12.8
– Middle East	3.2	2.3	5.0	5.1	4.7	0.9	0.2	2.1	2.0	2.0
Asia former USSR						0.0	0.0	0.0	0.0	
Europe excl fmr USSR	26.6	23.5	23.4	20.5	18.2	24.1	20.8	22.4	20.8	21.0
– European Union	23.3	20.5	20.2	18.3	16.4	22.4	19.0	20.9	19.4	19.3
– Eastern Europe	1.3	1.2	0.8	0.5	0.4	0.5	0.7	0.5	0.4	0.7
– Rest of Europe	2.0	1.8	2.4	1.8	1.4	1.1	1.1	1.0	1.0	1.0
Europe former USSR	1.7	0.3	3.0	0.2	0.0	0.6	0.9	0.0	0.6	0.9
Oceania	0.1	0.3	0.1	0.1	1.6	0.1	0.4	0.1	0.2	0.5
Other	0.0	0.0	0.0	0.1	0.6	0.4	0.3	1.3	1.2	0.9
Brazil/Brésil	26.1	26.5	23.3	24.0	23.6	26.1	27.5	24.4	22.4	21.6
Argentina/Argentine	15.2	15.4	15.5	17.5	17.2	18.5	22.5	21.2	20.8	21.3
USA/Etats–Unis d'Amer	7.9	12.1	9.9	9.9	9.3	9.0	9.7	9.9	12.2	11.7
Italy/Italie	2.5	2.8	3.5	2.9	3.4	10.1	5.1	5.2	5.2	4.6
Germany/Allemagne				4.9	4.5	3.4	3.5	3.6	3.0	3.2
France, Monaco	4.4	3.1	2.9	3.3	3.0	3.1	2.9	3.5	3.5	3.2
Spain/Espagne	2.1	1.7	1.7	1.9	1.6	2.2	3.1	3.7	3.1	3.1
Japan/Japon	3.0	2.9	3.2	3.8	5.0	5.4	2.9	2.6	2.2	2.6
Korea, Republic of	0.7	0.8	0.9	1.2	6.1	1.9	1.9	1.7	1.9	2.1
Chile/Chili	1.9	1.7	1.4	1.7	1.7	1.6	1.7	1.7	1.7	1.7

	1988	1989	1990	1991	1992	1993	1994	1995	1996	1997
Afrique	2.2	1.2	1.6	0.6	0.4	0.3	0.2	0.7	0.8	1.0
Amériques	40.1	50.1	51.2	52.5	53.4	61.1	62.0	60.2	66.9	62.9
– Amérique du Nord	12.0	12.0	10.9	11.1	11.5	9.8	7.7	6.8	6.7	7.0
– ALAI	27.1	36.9	39.2	40.3	41.5	50.6	53.7	52.9	59.9	55.3
– MCAC	0.0	0.1	0.1	0.1	0.1	0.1	0.1	0.3	0.1	0.1
– Caraïbes	0.9	1.1	1.0	1.0	0.3	0.5	0.6	0.2	0.1	0.5
– Autre Amérique	0.0	0.0	0.0	0.0	0.0	0.0	0.0	0.0	0.1	0.0
Asie anc. URSS exclus	21.0	16.1	13.2	15.6	15.7	14.8	14.7	15.9	13.1	14.4
– Moyen–Orient	5.0	6.2	4.4	2.1	1.9	1.7	1.5	1.9	1.6	1.9
Asie ancienne URSS						0.0				0.0
Europe anc. URSS exclus	30.5	27.4	27.3	26.9	28.6	22.4	21.5	21.9	17.8	20.0
– Union Européenne	26.9	24.2	25.1	25.4	26.7	21.5	20.8	20.8	17.0	18.9
– Europe de l'Est	2.7	2.5	1.6	0.9	1.4	0.5	0.1	0.3	0.3	0.2
– Autre de l'Europe	0.9	0.7	0.6	0.6	0.5	0.4	0.6	0.8	0.5	0.9
Europe ancienne URSS	5.7	4.1	5.2	3.2	0.2	0.2	0.6	0.4	0.6	0.6
Océanie	0.3	0.1	0.1	0.3	0.2	0.1	0.1	0.2	0.2	0.1
Autre	0.3	0.9	1.4	0.9	1.5	1.1	1.0	0.8	0.6	0.9
Brazil/Brésil	16.4	27.6	29.6	24.4	17.5	22.8	25.8	33.2	37.9	34.4
Argentina/Argentine	7.3	4.9	4.8	10.4	15.4	17.4	20.0	12.7	11.2	13.0
USA/Etats–Unis d'Amer	11.2	11.1	9.4	10.1	10.7	9.1	6.9	6.0	6.0	6.0
China/Chine	9.8	4.7	3.9	6.4	5.6	5.5	6.0	5.9	4.8	4.5
Germany/Allemagne				8.7	8.1	6.5	6.3	5.6	3.9	4.4
United Kingdom	4.0	4.0	4.1	3.8	4.1	4.0	3.8	4.1	2.3	4.3
Italy/Italie	3.8	3.5	4.4	3.9	4.6	3.1	3.1	3.1	3.1	3.3
Chile/Chili	0.8	1.0	1.0	1.4	3.1	3.3	2.2	1.9	4.8	2.1
China, Hong Kong SAR	1.5	1.5	1.0	1.9	2.9	2.6	1.7	2.3	3.6	2.2
Netherlands/Pays–Bas	4.3	3.3	3.2	3.0	3.3	2.9	2.5	2.6	1.7	2.1

4. Special Imports C.I.F. by Commodities according to the S.I.T.C. (Rev. 2) in million U.S. Dollars
Importations Spéciales C.A.F. par Produits d'après la C.T.C.I. (Rév. 2) en millions de Dollars E.U.

SITC CTCI	COMMODITY	1994		1995		1996		1997		PRODUIT
		QUANTITY QUANTITE	VALUE VALEUR	QUANTITY QUANTITE	VALUE VALEUR	QUANTITY QUANTITE	VALUE VALEUR	QUANTITY QUANTITE	VALUE VALEUR	
	ALL COMMODITIES		2707.2		2865.8		3322.4		3715.6	TOUS PRODUITS
0	FOOD AND LIVE ANIMALS		239.0		247.0		293.0		312.2	ALIMENTS,ANIMAUX VIVANTS
01	MEAT AND PREPARATIONS		8.8		8.2		10.7		12.9	VIANDES ET PREPARATIONS
04	CEREALS AND PREPARATIONS		53.8		32.8		49.5		45.2	CEREALES ET PRODUITS
041	WHEAT ETC UNMILLED	W 66819	10.0	W 477	0.2	W 37714	8.4	W 9134	1.9	FROMENT,EPEAUTRE
0411	DURUM WHEAT UNMILLED	W 62292	9.3	W 340	0.1	W 494	0.3	W 541	0.2	FROMENT DUR NON MOULU
044	MAIZE UNMILLED	W 139446	18.8	W 66441	11.9	W 54097	12.3	W 43306	9.2	MAIS NON MOULU
048	CEREAL ETC PREPARATIONS	W 6853	11.2	W 15913	14.5	W 14412	18.8	W 16585	22.8	PREPTNS A BASE CEREALES
0484	BAKERY PRODUCTS	W 3318	5.7	W 8642	8.8	W 8297	11.5	W 8603	14.1	PRODUITS DE BOULANGERIE
05	VEGETABLES AND FRUIT		51.3		51.8		54.5		61.4	LEGUMES ET FRUITS
054	VEG ETC FRSH,SMPLY PRSVD	W 61710	16.9	W 28098	14.8	W 46514	16.2	W 50179	19.0	LEGUMES FRAIS,CONG,SECS
057	FRUIT,NUTS,FRESH,DRIED	W 60284	19.6		20.3	W 56033	23.3	W 55646	25.3	FRUITS FRAIS OU SECS
0573	BANANA,PLANTAIN,FRSH,DRY	W 47760	11.6	W 35470	14.0	W 47285	16.1	W 45900	17.0	BANANES FRAICHES,SECHEES
058	FRUIT PRESERVED,PREPARED	W 9959	8.5	W 11075	10.3	W 8835	8.0	W 8970	9.5	CONSERVES DE FRUITS
06	SUGAR AND PREPS,HONEY		34.6		35.7		41.0		40.9	SUCRES ET PRODUITS
061	SUGAR AND HONEY	W 88712	28.4	W 88456	29.1	W 107816	33.4	W 108429	32.7	SUCRES ET MIEL
0611	RAW BEET AND CANE SUGAR	W 75222	26.3	W 81845	27.8	W 93724	29.7	W 96142	28.7	SUCRES BRUTS
07	COFFEE,TEA,COCOA,SPICES		46.3		55.5		56.8		57.2	CAFE,THE,CACAO,EPICES
073	CHOCOLATE AND PRODUCTS	W 2276	7.8	W 3672	9.1	W 3687	11.1	W 3745	12.3	CHOCOLAT
074	TEA AND MATE	W 23657	30.0	W 24515	35.5	W 25986	35.9	W 25861	33.3	THE ET MATE
0742	MATE	W 22995	28.5	W 23747	33.9	W 25304	34.3	W 25221	31.7	MATE
081	*FEEDING STUFF FOR ANIML	W 39180	9.1	W 24397	7.6	W 55125	15.1	W 41965	15.7	NOURRITURE POUR ANIMAUX
09	MISC EDIBLE PRODUCTS		26.9		45.8		53.9		63.4	PREP ALIMENTAIRES DIVERSES
098	EDIBLE PRODCTS,PREPS NES	W 6964	25.3		43.3	W 14293	51.0	W 16349	59.8	PREP ALIMENTAIRES NDA
09809	MISC FOOD PREPRTIONS NES	W 4097	21.3	W 33944	38.4	W 9148	44.2	W 9046	49.0	PREP ALIMENTAIRES NDA
1	BEVERAGES AND TOBACCO		33.9		29.0		42.6		49.5	BOISSONS ET TABACS
11	BEVERAGES		24.6		23.7		26.1		30.3	BOISSONS
112	ALCOHOLIC BEVERAGES	W 10933	18.0		18.3	W 17360	21.7	W 15877	24.2	BOISSONS ALCOOLIQUES
1124	DISTILLED ALCOHOLIC BEVS	W 2320	10.7	W 1850	9.8	W 4290	12.7	W 3211	13.6	ALCOOLS,EAUX–DE–VIE
11241	WHISKY	W 2042	10.1	W 1678	8.1	W 3931	12.1	W 2862	12.8	WHISKY
12	TOBACCO AND MANUFACTURES		9.3		5.4		16.6		19.2	TABACS BRUTS FABRIQUES
121	TOBACCO UNMNFCTRD,REFUSE	W 4233	9.1	W 1855	4.8	W 5836	15.8	W 6308	17.3	TABACS BRUTS,DECHETS
1211	TOBACCO,NOT STRIPPED	W 3714	7.6	W 1684	4.3	W 5157	14.1	W 5883	15.7	TABACS NON ECOTES
2	CRUDE MATERLS,EXCL FUELS		94.4		126.5		125.1		125.0	MAT BRUTES NON COMESTIBLES
23	RUBBER, CRUDE		17.6		24.6		23.1		23.3	CAOUTCHOUC BRUT
233	RUBBER,SYNTHTIC,RECLAIMD	W 10554	13.9		19.9	W 13043	19.1	W 15267	19.6	LATEX CAOUTCH SYNTH REGEN
2331	SYNTHETIC RUBBER ETC	W 10519	13.9		19.9	W 13023	19.1	W 15192	19.5	LATEX CAOUTCH SYNTHETIQUE
23312	OTH SYNTHTC RUBBER LATEX	W 1941	2.3		9.0	W 6817	9.8	W 4017	5.0	AUTRES LATEX CAOUT SYNTH
24	CORK AND WOOD		9.8		9.9		11.8		15.8	LIEGE ET BOIS
248	WOOD SHAPED,SLEEPERS	W 28661	9.5		9.6	W 25761	11.3	W 35559	15.5	BOIS SIMPLEMENT TRAVAILLES
26	TEXTILE FIBRES AND WASTE		37.2		57.8		47.3		37.8	FIBRES TEXTILES
263	COTTON	W 7876	11.3	W 4906	9.0	W 4928	8.2	W 4230	7.3	COTON
2631	RAW COTTON,EXCL LINTERS	W 6746	10.6	W 4508	8.5	W 4323	7.7	W 3809	6.9	COTON EN MASSE
268	WOOL(EXC TOPS),ANML HAIR	W 9957	19.0	W 16731	42.9	W 14841	30.9	W 9982	21.8	LAINES ET POILS
2681	WOOL GREASY,FLEECE–WSHED	W 9895	18.7	W 16457	42.0	W 14813	30.6	W 9899	21.5	LAINE EN SUINT
27	CRUDE FERTLZR,MINRLS NES		10.8		8.1		12.1		14.8	ENGRAIS MINERAUX BRUTS
29	CRUDE ANIMAL,VEG MAT NES		7.1		8.5		10.7		11.9	MATIERES BRUTES ANIM,VEGET
3	MINERAL FUELS ETC		226.1		291.3		362.4		340.7	COMBUSTIBLES MINERAUX LUB
33	PETROLEUM AND PRODUCTS		210.8		280.6		346.8		328.6	PETROLE ET DERIVES
333	CRUDE PETROLEUM				177.3	W 1505118	225.3	W 703634	203.1	HUILES BRUTES DE PETROLE
334	PETROLEUM PRODUCTS,REFIN	W 747314	204.5	W 539687	101.4	W 541457	118.2	W 611832	123.2	PRODUITS RAFFINES
3341	GASOLINE,OTH LIGHT OILS	W 581863	156.6			W 389020	82.0	W 79645	18.5	ESSENCES POUR MOTEURS
33411	MOTOR,AVIATION SPIRIT	W 18455	2.8			W 3326	1.5	W 79645	18.5	ESSENCES MOTEURS D'AVIONS
33412	SPIRIT TYPE JET FUEL	W 277847	48.4			W 103822	24.5			CARBUREACTEURS
33419	OTH LIGHT PETROLEUM OILS	W 285561	105.5			W 281872	56.2			AUTRES HUILES LEGERES
3342	KEROSENE,OTH MEDIUM OILS	W 75638	13.2					W 2819	1.3	PETR LAMPANTS,AUT HUIL
33421	KEROSENE INCL JET FUEL	W 75638	13.2					W 2819	1.3	PETROLES LAMPANTS
3344	FUEL OILS,NES	W 84195	28.5			W 143663	28.6	W 522205	95.9	FUEL OILS
341	*GAS,NATURAL AND MANUFCT		15.3		10.5	W 55595	15.4	W 42629	11.8	GAZ NATUREL,GAZ MANUFACT
3413	PETROLM GASES,LIQUEFIED	W 78909	15.3	W 44020	10.5	W 55513	15.3	W 42509	11.7	GAZ DE PETROLE LIQUEFIE
34139	OTH HYDROCARBON GAS LQFD	W 53278	9.7	W 44020	10.5	W 55513	15.3	W 42509	11.7	HYDROCARBURES GAZEUX NDA
4	ANIMAL,VEGETABLE OIL,FAT		19.2		18.0		19.4		20.7	HUILES,GRAISSES ANIM,VEG
42	FIXED VEGETABLE OIL,FAT		16.0		13.8		13.6		13.9	HUILES VEGETALES FIXES
423	FIXED VEG OILS,SOFT	W 16094	12.8		10.4	W 11186	10.1	W 9894	10.0	HUILES VEGET DOUCES FIXES
4236	SUNFLOWER SEED OIL	W 15011	11.5	W 9648	9.2	W 10739	8.8	W 9394	8.3	HUILE DE TOURNESOL
5	CHEMCLS,RELATED PROD NES		395.3		426.0		543.9		599.5	PRODUITS CHIMIQUES
51	ORGANIC CHEMICALS		61.5		73.0		68.0		71.7	PROD CHIMIQ ORGANIQUES
513	CARBOXYLIC ACIDS ETC	W 12984	12.2	W 11442	17.8	W 12712	14.5	W 15560	16.7	ACIDES CARBOXYLIQUES
5137	MONOACIDS AND DERIVATIVS	W 8405	7.4	W 6669	10.0	W 8309	9.5	W 10722	11.0	ACIDES MONOCARBOXYLIQUES
514	NITROGEN–FNCTN COMPOUNDS	W 2668	17.9		19.7	W 1864	17.7	W 2075	17.2	COMPOSES FONCT AZOTEES
5148	OTH NITROGN–FNCTN CMPNDS	W 1276	13.3	W 1179	15.0	W 1121	12.4	W 1238	11.8	AUTRES COMPOSES AZOTES
51482	IMIDE–,IMIDE–FNCT CMPNDS	W 108	8.1	W 103	10.0	W 131	7.7	W 164	6.8	COMPOSES A FONCTION IMIDE
515	ORG–INORG COMPOUNDS ETC	W 822	12.7	W 826	13.5	W 886	15.2	W 1039	17.7	COMPOSES ORGANO–MINERAUX
5156	HETEROCYCLIC CMPDS ETC	W 411	9.0	W 335	9.5	W 299	10.7	W 310	10.5	COMPOSES HETEROCYCLIQUES
51569	OTH HETEROCYC CMPDS,ETC	W 405	8.6	W 332	9.4	W 295	10.5	W 306	10.2	AUT COMP HETEROCYCLIQUES
52	INORGANIC CHEMICALS		19.8		20.2		21.2		25.9	PROD CHIM INORGANIQUES
523	OTHR INORG CHEMICALS ETC	W 42009	15.1		15.0	W 29893	15.2		17.4	AUT PRODUITS CHIMIQUES INORG
53	DYES,TANNING,COLOUR PROD		33.6		30.7		32.6		36.3	PROD TEINTURE,COLORANTS
531	SYNT DYE,NAT INDGO,LAKES	W 1139	14.4	W 933	12.0	W 1343	12.9	W 1254	12.3	MAT COLOR ORGAN,LAQUES
5311	SYNTHIC ORGNIC DYESTUFFS	W 1030	13.6	W 798	11.2	W 1053	12.0	W 996	11.5	MAT COLOR ORGAN SYNTHET
533	PIGMENTS,PAINTS,ETC	W 6106	15.4		16.5	W 6331	16.6	W 8205	19.8	PIGMENTS,PEINTURES,VERNIS
541	*MEDICINAL,PHARM PRODUCT		64.6		81.1		97.5		112.0	PROD MEDICINAUX PHARMACEUT
5413	ANTIBIOTICS IN BULK	K 40049	6.1	K 86957	11.0	K 112743	14.0	K 70270	10.6	ANTIBIOTIQUES NDA
5417	MEDICAMENTS	K 1913763	45.4		55.2	K 2721582	63.9	K 2881396	78.4	MEDICAMENTS
54171	— CONTAINNG ANTIBIOTICS	K 105021	6.8		9.0	K 222536	9.9	K 190321	12.4	MED CONTN ANTIBIOTIQUES
54179	— CONTNG OTH SUBSTANCES	K 1595552	30.8	K 4699858	36.0	K 2326128	43.4	K 2551829	54.2	MED CONT AUT SUBSTANCES
55	PERFUME,CLEANING ETC PRD		36.6		44.9		58.7		69.2	PROD POUR PARFUM,TOILETTE
551	ESSENTL OILS,PERFUME,ETC	W 332	7.1	W 333	8.7	W 401	9.0	W 416	9.6	HUILES ESSENTIELLES
553	PERFUMERY,COSMETICS,ETC	W 3844	17.2		21.8	W 7613	27.8	W 7666	33.6	PRODUITS DE PARFUMERIE
554	SOAP,CLEANSING ETC PREPS	W 7770	12.4	W 9588	14.4	W 19241	22.0	W 21295	26.1	SAVONS,PRODUITS DETERSIFS
5542	WASHING PREPARATIONS ETC	W 5613	8.9	W 5442	9.7	W 14154	15.4	W 16313	19.3	PROD ORG TENSIO–ACT NDA
562	*FERTILIZERS,MANUFACTURE	W 195351	38.1		20.0	W 362889	80.8	W 354289	67.7	ENGRAIS MANUFACTURES
5621	CHEM NITROGENOUS FERTLZR	W 68508	10.9		8.9	W 85117	18.0	W 112723	16.6	ENGRAIS AZOTES
56216	UREA	W 66655	10.6	W 37896	8.4	W 82581	17.3	W 108348	15.7	UREE
5629	FERTILIZERS NES	W 100234	23.2	W 32389	7.8	W 214661	51.5	W 192290	42.8	ENGRAIS NDA
56292	NITROG–PHOS FERTILZR NES	W 60785	15.3	W 20929	4.9	W 204210	48.8	W 186937	41.4	ENGRAIS NDA CONT N P
58	PLASTIC MATERIALS ETC		82.3		98.6		105.7		123.4	MAT PLAST ARTIFICIELLES
582	PROD OF CONDENSATION ETC	W 8562	14.1		20.2	W 9900	17.5	W 14958	21.8	PROD CONDENS,POLYCOND
5823	ALKYDS,OTHER POLYESTERS	W 5105	6.8		13.5	W 7084	10.2	W 11813	13.5	ALKYDES ET AUT POLYESTERS
58231	— IN PRIMARY FORMS	W 4997	6.0	W 5590	12.1	W 6899	8.9	W 11646	12.4	SOUS FORMES PRIMAIRES
583	POLYMERIZATION ETC PRODS	W 67239	62.9		72.4	W 72292	80.6	W 82144	95.3	PROD POLYMERISATION

4. Special Imports C.I.F. by Commodities according to the S.I.T.C. (Rev. 2) in million U.S. Dollars
Importations Spéciales C.A.F. par Produits d'après la C.T.C.I. (Rév. 2) en millions de Dollars E.U.

SITC CTCI	COMMODITY	1994 QUANTITY QUANTITE	1994 VALUE VALEUR	1995 QUANTITY QUANTITE	1995 VALUE VALEUR	1996 QUANTITY QUANTITE	1996 VALUE VALEUR	1997 QUANTITY QUANTITE	1997 VALUE VALEUR	PRODUIT
5831	POLYETHYLENE	W 33297	25.0	W 26574	28.3	W 30404	31.7	W 34000	38.3	POLYETHYLENE
58311	— IN PRIMARY FORMS	W 32446	22.8	W 24196	26.0	W 29431	29.2	W 32225	33.9	POLYETHYLENE PRIMAIRES
5832	POLYPROPYLENE	W 7012	8.3	W 7104	11.2	W 9863	13.1	W 13825	15.6	POLYPROPYLENE
5834	POLYVINYL CHLORIDE	W 14256	12.2		14.8	W 18525	15.0	W 18307	17.9	CHLORURE DE POLYVINYLE
58341	— IN PRIMARY FORMS	W 13823	11.0	W 13386	12.9	W 17802	12.8	W 17360	14.9	SOUS FORMES PRIMAIRES
5839	OTH POLYMRZTION ETC PROD	W 5910	8.6	W 5393	8.4	W 5756	9.7	W 7334	11.6	AUT PROD POLYMER COPOLYM
59	CHEMICAL MATERIALS NES		58.9		57.5		79.4		93.3	MAT PROD CHIMIQUES NDA
591	PESTICIDES,DISINFECTANTS	W 5439	23.3	W 4052	24.6	W 8735	36.3	W 10630	46.0	DESINF,INSECT,FONG,HERB
5913	HERBICIDES,FOR RETAIL	W 1756	9.1	W 623	11.9	W 3811	18.3	W 4832	23.4	HERBICIDES VENTE AU DET
598	MISCEL CHEM PRODUCTS NES	W 17888	29.9		26.8	W 16365	34.5	W 18050	37.2	PROD DIV INDUST CHIM NDA
5989	CHEM PRODUCTS,PREPS NES	W 14671	22.3		20.2	W 12366	24.6	W 14929	29.3	PROD PREP CHIMIQUES NDA
59899	OTH CHEM PRODS,PREPS,NES	W 12107	16.9	W 9950	14.9	W 8813	18.2	W 9916	20.6	AUT PRODUITS CHIMIQUES NDA
6	BASIC MANUFACTURES		428.3		468.5		551.9		591.0	ART MANUFACTURES
61	LEATHER,DRESSED FUR,ETC		31.0		32.6		50.0		37.3	CUIRS,PELLETERIES
611	LEATHER	W 2417	28.3		29.8	W 5010	45.3	W 2977	33.6	CUIRS,PEAUX PREPARES
6114	LEATHR BOVINE NES,EQUINE	W 2046	24.5		27.4	W 4814	42.8	W 2855	31.4	CUIRS DE BOVINS
62	RUBBER MANUFACTURES NES		26.9		29.0		32.1		39.9	CAOUTCHOUC MANUFACTURE
625	RUBBER TYRES, TUBES ETC	W 4748	17.1		18.8	W 6080	20.9	W 7865	26.5	PNEUS CAOUTCHOUC VULCANISE
63	WOOD,CORK MANUFACTRS NES		15.9		14.3		13.0		14.1	OUVRAGES LIEGE ET BOIS
635	WOOD MANUFACTURES NES	W 14487	11.5		9.3	W 10532	7.8	W 8219	7.0	ART MANUF EN BOIS NDA
6353	BUILDERS WOODWRK,PREFABS	W 13357	10.1		7.8	W 8740	6.1	W 6175	4.6	OUVRAGES DE MENUISERIE
64	PAPER,PAPERBOARD AND MFR		67.6		86.3		101.9		113.8	PAPIERS,CARTONS & OUVRAGES
641	PAPER AND PAPERBOARD	W 56320	39.6		50.7	W 69520	60.0	W 76541	65.7	PAPIERS ET CARTONS
6411	NEWSPRINT	W 15093	8.5	W 10026	7.0	W 13063	10.6	W 9982	6.1	PAPIER JOURNAL
6415	PAPER,PAPERBRD,BULK,NES	W 11975	8.1		13.4	W 19762	14.7	W 22623	15.1	PAPIERS,CARTONS ROULEAUX
64159	OTHER PAPER ETC,BULK,NES	W 8402	6.8	W 8635	10.0	W 11088	10.9	W 13477	11.1	AUT PAPIER ROULEAUX FEUILLES
6418	COATED ETC PAPER NES BLK	W 7370	10.0		14.1	W 10773	17.6	W 12472	23.7	PAP,CARTONS COUCHES,ENDUITS
64181	PLASTIC COATED PAPER ETC	W 1017	2.9		5.6	W 2423	7.9	W 3830	13.5	PAP,CARTONS ENDUITS,RESINES
642	PAPER,ETC,PRECUT,ARTS OF	W 17763	28.1		35.7	W 22395	42.0	W 25273	48.1	PAP,CARTONS DECOUPES
6421	PAPER ETC CONTAINERS	W 10184	9.9		12.4	W 10699	13.8	W 13023	16.1	BOITES,SACS EMBALLAGES
6428	PAPER ETC ARTICLES NES	W 4458	12.0		16.5	W 7947	19.3	W 8195	22.0	OUVRAGES EN PATE A PAPIER
64285	PAPER ETC DIAPERS ETC	W 3118	8.9	W 3904	12.1	W 5626	14.7	W 5538	16.1	SERVIETTES HYGIENIQUES
65	TEXTILE YARN,FABRICS,ETC		83.1		94.8		103.0		125.4	FILS,TISSUS,ARTICLES TEXTILE
651	TEXTILE YARN	W 2742	14.3		17.4	W 3505	19.0	W 3405	20.9	FILS TEXTILES
652	COTTON FABRICS,WOVEN	W 2074	13.8		14.6	W 2389	16.1	W 2393	17.7	TISSUS DE COTON
6522	WOVEN COTTON BLEACHD,ETC	W 1929	13.2		13.7	W 2259	15.3	W 2184	16.5	TISSUS COTON BLANCHIS ETC
65224	BLCHED COTTON FABRIC NES	W 1493	9.8		9.6	W 1869	11.9	W 1805	12.8	AUT TIS PLUS 85% COT BLANCHI
653	WOVN MAN-MADE FIB FABRIC	W 1460	14.9		18.0	W 1906	18.5	W 3007	27.6	TISSUS FIBRES SYNTH,ARTIF
6531	CONT SYNT WEAVES NONPILE	W 620	5.5		7.3	W 965	8.6	W 1527	13.6	TISSUS FIBRES SYNTH CONTINUE
65315	CONT SYN TXTL FABRIC NES	W 513	4.4		6.5	W 890	7.9	W 1406	12.3	TIS PLUS 85% TEXT SYNT CONT
654	OTH WOVEN TEXTILE FABRIC	W 2284	8.3		6.9	W 1545	6.0	W 1654	7.1	TISSUS AUT COTON SYNT,ARTIF
657	SPECIAL TXTL FABRC,PRODS	W 2562	10.1		10.9	W 2448	12.3	W 3429	15.5	TISSUS SPECIAUX
658	TEXTILE ARTICLES NES	W 2330	11.6		16.1	W 4273	19.2	W 5088	23.1	ART FACONNES MAT TEXTILES
6584	LINENS ETC	W 867	6.7		8.9	W 1118	9.3	W 1186	10.9	LINGE DE MAISON
66	NONMETAL MINERAL MFS NES		55.5		59.1		60.7		67.1	ART MIN NON METALLIQUES
661	LIME,CEMENT,BLDG PRODS	W 82988	16.0		16.3	W 243433	17.3	W 129105	13.4	CHAUX,CIMENTS MAT CONSTR
6612	CEMENT	W 68540	10.3	W 137072	9.9	W 226831	10.6	W 105382	5.5	CIMENTS HYDRAULIQUES
662	CLAY,REFRACTORY BLDG PRD	W 51738	10.5		11.2	W 55748	11.9	W 64469	15.5	MAT CONST REFRACTAIRES
6624	BRICKS ETC NONREFRACTORY	W 50274	9.5		10.3	W 54204	10.8	W 62552	13.8	BRIQUES ETC CERAM NON REFR
664	GLASS		12.1		12.0	W 14241	12.1	W 16009	15.3	VERRE
665	GLASSWARE	W 12531	9.9		12.1	W 18322	11.2	W 18713	12.8	OUVRAGES EN VERRE
67	IRON AND STEEL		63.7		68.7		89.9		84.0	FER ET ACIER
673	IRON,STEEL SHAPES ETC	W 48418	18.0		15.2	W 31111	12.8	W 35427	14.9	BARRES,PROFIL FER,ACIER
674	IRN,STL UNIV,PLATE,SHEET	W 63182	34.5		39.0	W 62621	39.8	W 78501	51.8	LARGES PLATS,TOLES
6746	IRN,STL THIN PLATE,ROLLD	W 32341	16.6	W 28618	20.4	W 32512	20.9	W 37822	25.7	TOLES LAM MOINS 3MM
67461	— OF IRON OR SIMPLE STL	W 30975	13.7	W 25761	13.5	W 27540	13.3	W 30732	15.8	TOL NON AC FIN MOINS 3 MM
6749	OTH IRN,STL PLATES,SHEET	W 11449	7.9		7.3	W 10042	7.5	W 16874	12.6	AUTRES TOLES FER,ACIER
67491	— OF IRON OR SIMPLE STL	W 11428	7.8	W 9584	7.3	W 10009	7.4	W 16865	12.6	AUT TOLES AUTRES ACIER FIN
678	IRON,STL TUBES,PIPES,ETC	W 3807	5.3		6.8	W 22127	29.3	W 5808	7.7	TUBES,TUYAUX EN FONTE,FER
6781	CAST IRON TUBES,PIPES	W 446	0.4		2.6	W 16323	20.6	W 598	0.9	TUBES,TUYAUX EN FONTE
68	NON-FERROUS METALS		21.0		25.1		25.6		29.5	METAUX NON FERREUX
682	COPPER EXC CEMENT COPPER	W 3225	9.4		10.6	W 3227	10.7	W 3652	11.4	CUIVRE
6822	COPPER,ALLOYS WORKED	W 3219	9.4		10.5	W 3205	10.7	W 3618	11.4	CUIVRE,ALLIAGES OUVRES
684	ALUMINIUM	W 4252	9.1		12.0	W 5229	12.2	W 6640	15.6	ALUMINIUM
69	METAL MANUFACTURES NES		64.0		59.0		76.1		80.2	ART MANUFACT EN METAL NDA
695	TOOLS	W 1609	9.8		9.2	W 1766	8.9	W 1424	10.0	OUTILS A MAIN
697	BASE MTL HOUSEHOLD EQUIP	W 3401	13.3		11.7	W 3594	14.2	W 3705	16.7	ART MENAGE MET COMMUNS
699	BASE METAL MFRS NES	W 2971	15.5		14.6	W 4208	19.6	W 4377	20.7	ART MANUFACTURES MET NDA
7	MACHINES,TRANSPORT EQUIP		1002.6		988.0		1075.4		1312.6	MACHINES MATERIEL TRANSPORT
71	POWER GENERATING EQUIPMT		17.8		23.3		23.8		23.8	MACHINES GENERATRICES
713	INTRNL COMBUS PSTN ENGIN	W 1389	7.9		8.7	W 2026	9.7	W 2269	13.3	MOTEURS EXPL COMB INT, PIECE
72	MACHS FOR SPCL INDUSTRYS		102.8		131.2		172.3		193.7	MAC SPECIALES POUR INDUST
721	AGRIC MACHY,EXC TRACTORS	W 5175	19.4		26.1	W 10086	41.8	W 10806	53.3	MACHINES AGRICOLES
7211	CULTIVATING MACHINERY	W 2941	6.4		9.5	W 5972	15.7	W 5355	16.5	MACH PREPARATION DU SOL
7212	HARVESTING ETC MACHINES	W 1996	11.0		12.8	W 3763	21.3	W 4561	27.9	ENGINS POUR LA RECOLTE
72123	OTH HARVSTER,MOWRS,BALER	W 507	2.3		4.7	W 1369	8.7	W 2337	14.7	AUT MACH POUR LA RECOLTE
722	TRACTORS NON-ROAD	W 3863	16.3		20.8	W 6903	33.9	W 5803	30.8	TRACTEURS
7224	WHEELED TRACTORS NES	W 3847	16.2		20.8	W 6848	33.7	W 5759	30.7	TRACTEURS A ROUES
723	CIVIL ENGNEERG EQUIP ETC	W 3183	9.0		8.2	W 3186	12.8	W 4361	17.2	APPAREILS DE GENIE CIVIL
7234	CONST,MINING MACHNRY NES	W 3010	8.0		7.1	W 2850	11.3	W 3774	14.6	MACH POUR LA CONST, MINES
724	TEXTILE,LEATHER MACHNRY	W 1146	15.5		18.8	W 1134	18.2	W 1102	16.4	MACH POUR INDUSTRIE TEXTILE
725	PAPER ETC MILL MACHINERY	W 206	3.3		12.3	W 846	10.4	W 158	3.2	MACHINES FABR PATE PAPIER
726	PRINTG,BKBINDG MACHY,PTS	W 337	7.0		9.0	W 473	7.5	W 232	5.5	MACHINES POUR IMPRIMERIE
727	FOOD MACHRY NON-DOMESTIC	W 611	9.4		8.3	W 1009	12.7	W 806	11.9	MACH INDUSTRIES ALIMENT
7272	OTH FOOD PROC MCHY,PARTS	W 589	9.0		6.3	W 750	11.2	W 571	9.6	AUT MACH IND ALIMENTAIRE
72722	INDUS FOOD PROC MACH NES	W 574	8.5		5.8	W 714	10.8	W 544	9.1	MACHINES BOULANGERIE
728	OTH MACHY FOR SPCL INDUS	W 3060	23.4		28.0	W 5980	35.4	W 8470	55.7	AUT MACH IND PARTICULIERES
7284	MACHY FOR SPCL INDUS NES	W 2214	19.1		19.4	W 4381	26.8	W 5977	42.8	MACH SPEC IND PARTICUL.
72848	OTH MCHY WITH INDIV FNCT	W 1408	9.0		12.3	W 3441	17.3	W 5186	29.4	AUTRES MACHINES NDA
74	GENRL INDUSTRL MACHY NES		110.8		129.8		152.4		162.8	MACH APP INDUSTRIE
741	HEATING,COOLING EQUIPMNT	W 3965	29.9		43.4	W 7674	51.9	W 6158	46.2	MACH CHAUFFAGE,PIECES
7413	INDUS FURNACES ETC,PARTS	W 430	3.2		9.7	W 1732	7.2	W 323	3.3	FOURS IND,LABOR,PIECES
74132	INDUST FURNACES NONELECT	W 216	1.6		8.9	W 1669	6.5	W 259	2.2	FOURS NON ELECTRIQUES
7414	NONDOM REFRIG EQUIPT,PTS	W 2052	13.3		16.8	W 3168	19.5	W 3231	20.5	MAT PRODUCTION DU FROID
74141	REFRIG EQUIP NONDOMESTIC	W 1735	11.7		15.6	W 2705	17.4	W 2895	18.3	REFIG INDUSTRIELS
7415	AIR-CONDITIONING MACHNRY	W 675	7.1		8.3	W 943	9.7	W 1315	12.9	GROUPES CONDITION AIR
7416	HEATING,COOLING EQU NES	W 765	5.9		8.4	W 1748	14.9	W 1243	9.0	APP CHANGEMENT TEMP
742	PUMPS FOR LIQUIDS ETC	W 558	7.5		10.0	W 909	10.6	W 885	12.1	POMPES MOTO-POMPES
743	PUMPS NES,CENTRFUGES ETC	W 1817	14.2		13.5	W 2155	16.3	W 2152	21.9	POMPES COMPRES,VENT ETC
744	MECHANICAL HANDLING EQU	W 4717	12.1		12.1	W 4356	19.5	W 3876	17.5	EQUIP MANUTENTION PIECES
745	NONELEC MACHY,TOOLS NES	W 2274	22.2		28.0	W 2068	27.6	W 2190	36.1	AUT MACH NON ELEC,PIECES

4. Special Imports C.I.F. by Commodities according to the S.I.T.C. (Rev. 2) in million U.S. Dollars
Importations Spéciales C.A.F. par Produits d'après la C.T.C.I. (Rév. 2) en millions de Dollars E.U.

SITC CTCI	COMMODITY	1994 QUANTITY QUANTITE	1994 VALUE VALEUR	1995 QUANTITY QUANTITE	1995 VALUE VALEUR	1996 QUANTITY QUANTITE	1996 VALUE VALEUR	1997 QUANTITY QUANTITE	1997 VALUE VALEUR	PRODUIT
7452	OTH NONELEC MCHS,PTS NES	W 1384	20.0		24.5	W 1863	23.7	W 1976	32.0	AUT MACH NON ELEC,PIECES
74522	PACKAGNG,BOTTLNG,ETC MCH	W 313	10.1		14.8	W 365	12.3	W 525	17.8	MACH NETT BOUTEILLES,ETC
749	NONELEC MACH PTS,ACC NES	W 1808	25.1		23.1	W 2895	26.8	W 2000	29.2	PIECES MACH NON ELEC NDA
7492	COCKS,VALVES ETC NES	W 637	9.4	W 4307	9.6	W 1249	12.5	W 955	12.5	ART ROB,SIM POUR TUYAUX
75	OFFICE MACHNES,ADP EQUIP		43.9		59.8		75.3		97.9	MACH BUREAU TRAIT AUTOM
752	AUTOMTIC DATA PROC EQUIP	W 558	29.3		43.1	W 1420	52.6	W 1700	65.7	MACH TRAIT INFORMATION
7523	DIGITL CENTRL PROCESSORS	W 255	13.0		16.2	W 353	16.8	W 313	16.9	UNITES CENTRALES
7525	ADP PERIPHERAL UNITS	W 216	8.8	W 166	12.9	W 731	19.2	W 1096	27.8	UNITES PERIPHERIQUES
759	OFFICE,ADP MCH PTS,ACCES	W 129	6.7		9.6	W 400	12.9	W 646	21.3	PIECES DU 751 ET 752
7599	ACCTG,ETC,ADP MCH PTS,AC	W 103	5.5		7.8	W 340	10.9	W 600	19.1	PIECES DU 751 ET 752
76	TELECOMM,SOUND EQUIPMENT		136.1		114.3		150.9		168.4	EQUIPMENT DE TELECOM
761	TELEVISION RECEIVERS	W 2792	35.2		27.5	W 2339	25.3	W 2518	29.7	RECEPTEURS DE TELEVISION
7611	COLOUR TV RECEIVERS	W 2619	32.8		26.7	W 2256	24.6	W 2466	29.3	RECEPTEURS COULEUR
762	RADIO BROADCAST RECEIVRS	W 1375	19.5		16.5	W 1040	13.4	W 1129	16.3	RECEPTEURS RADIODIFFUSION
7628	OTHER RADIO RECEIVERS	W 899	12.8		9.6	W 519	7.0	W 602	8.6	AUTRES RECEPT RADIO
763	SOUND RECORDRS,PHONOGRPH	W 307	10.9		7.7	W 173	5.2	W 203	7.2	PHONO,APP ENREGISTREMENT
7638	OTHR SOUND APPARATUS ETC	W 294	10.7		7.6	W 168	5.2	W 200	7.2	AUT APP D'ENREGIS,REPROD
76381	TV IMAGE,SND RECRDRS ETC	W 237	9.1		6.1	W 115	3.7	W 141	5.6	APP ENREG,REPRO IMAG,SON
764	TELECOM EQPT,PTS,ACC NES	W 1309	70.6		62.8	W 1914	107.1	W 1936	115.3	EQUIP TELECOM,PIECES
7641	LINE TELEPHONE,ETC EQUIP	W 293	11.1		10.2	W 607	31.1	W 552	29.2	APP TELEPHON PAR FIL
7643	TV,RADIO TRANSMITTRS ETC	W 64	9.3	W 186	22.6	W 379	39.9	W 325	35.4	APP EMET TELE RADIO
7649	PTS NES OF EQUIPMT OF 76	W 645	44.7		25.1	W 580	31.4	W 661	45.1	PIECES DE LA DIV 76
76491	PTS NES OF APPAR OF 7641	W 503	41.5	W 1346	22.0	W 294	22.7	W 320	27.2	PIECES POUR 764.1
76493	TELECOMM EQUIPMT PTS NES	W 133	3.0		2.9	W 262	8.4	W 320	17.1	PIECES 761,762,764.3,8
77	ELECTRIC MACHNRY NES ETC		184.1		158.8		154.9		218.5	MACH APP ELECT NDA
771	ELECTRIC POWER MACHY NES	W 1168	9.1		15.5	W 1612	10.5	W 2006	16.4	MACH PROD,TRANS ELECTR
7711	TRANSFORMERS,ELECTRICAL	W 691	4.4		10.8	W 824	4.7	W 1143	8.0	TRANSFO ELECTRIQUES
77111	LIQUID DIELEC TRANSFRMRS	W 434	1.8	W 700	9.6	W 668	3.1	W 897	5.3	TRANSFO DIELEC LIQUIDE
772	SWITCHGEAR ETC,PARTS NES	W 1772	33.8		25.3	W 1941	28.0	W 2015	35.5	APP COUPURE,SECT ETC
7721	SWITCHGEAR ETC	W 1761	33.1		24.0	W 1843	26.5	W 1969	34.2	APP COUPURE,SECTIONMNT
773	ELECTR DISTRIBUTNG EQUIP	W 6943	26.7		12.9	W 3647	12.7	W 3984	17.2	EQUIPMT DISTRIBUTION ELECT
7731	INSULATED WIRE,CABLE ETC	W 6505	25.4	W 4250	12.4	W 3259	11.9	W 3578	15.8	FILS,CABLES ISOLES ELECT
775	HOUSEHOLD TYPE EQUIP NES	W 13554	60.7		55.2	W 13131	57.1	W 13182	60.8	MACH,APP USAGE DOMESTQUE
7751	HOUSEHOLD LDRY EQUIP NES	W 4933	14.3		12.2	W 4085	12.1	W 4244	12.1	MACH A LAVER ET SECHOIRS
77511	DOMESTIC WASHING MACHNES	W 4831	13.8		11.7	W 4012	11.8	W 4171	11.8	MACH LAVER LINGE MOINS 6 KG
7752	DOM REFRIGERATRS,FREEZRS	W 4444	21.1		17.7	W 4531	19.6	W 4955	23.2	REFRIG,CONGEL MENAGER
77521	DOMESTIC REFRIGERATORS	W 3338	16.1		13.5	W 3452	15.3	W 3877	18.4	REFRIGERATEURS
7757	DOMESTIC ELECTRC EQU NES	W 2247	11.4		10.9	W 2239	10.1	W 1774	9.7	APP ELECTR DOMEST NDA
7758	ELECTRO–THERMIC APPL NES	W 1822	12.8		12.9	W 2137	14.0	W 1999	13.8	APP ELECTROTHERMIQ NDA
77586	ELECTROTHERM DOM APP NES	W 1042	8.3		8.3	W 1496	10.1	W 1356	9.7	APP ELECTRO THERMIQUES
778	ELECTRICAL MACHINERY NES	W 6824	46.1		40.4	W 6975	41.7	W 10082	76.4	AUTRES MACH ELECT NDA
7781	BATTERIES,ACCUMULATORS	W 3204	9.1		10.8	W 3965	11.5	W 4410	14.2	PILES ET ACCUMULATEURS
7783	AUTOMOTIVE ELECTR EQUIP	W 1403	14.1		8.0	W 1016	9.4	W 3832	39.4	EQUIP ELECT MOTEURS EXPL
77831	IGNITION,STARTING EQUIP	W 1035	10.3		4.8	W 562	5.7	W 3430	35.2	APP ELEC ALLUM,DEMARRAGE
7788	OTH ELEC MACHY,EQUIP NES	W 417	10.9		10.9	W 493	8.7	W 396	9.3	AUT MACH APP ELEC NDA
78	ROAD VEHICLES		398.7		361.2		333.5		435.4	VEHICULES ROUTIERS
781	PASS MOTOR VEH EXC BUSES	W 35561	272.6		203.8	W 22546	154.0	W 23670	175.3	AUTO TRANSPORT PERSONNES
782	LORRIES,SPCL MTR VEH NES	W 8774	47.5		76.9	W 14914	95.6	W 18155	116.7	VEHICULES SPECIAUX,MARCH
7821	LORRIES,TRUCKS	W 8006	45.3		72.8	W 14311	92.3	W 17349	111.8	VEHICULES TRANSP MARCHAND
783	ROAD MOTOR VEHICLES NES	W 832	6.4		15.3	W 1703	13.9	W 1950	18.0	VEHICULES ROUTIERS NDA
7832	TRACTORS FOR TR–TRAILERS	W 408	3.1		9.4	W 956	8.3	W 1229	10.8	TRACTEURS ROUTIERS
784	MOTOR VEH PRTS,ACCES NES	W 5583	37.8		33.3	W 5805	37.0	W 13114	82.8	PIECES 722,781,782,783
7849	OTHER MOTOR VEHCL PARTS	W 5533	37.4		32.7	W 5661	36.2	W 13034	82.3	PIECES 722,781,782,783
785	CYCLES,ETC MOTRZD OR NOT	W 4886	31.1		27.1	W 4878	26.1	W 5213	33.3	MOTOCYCLES SCOOTERS
7851	MOTORCYCLES ETC	W 2665	24.0		20.8	W 2774	20.8	W 2759	24.5	MOTO VELO MOTEUR AUXIL
8	MISC MANUFACTURED GOODS		268.1		271.1		308.2		364.1	ART MANUFACTURES DIVERS
812	*PLUMBG,HEATNG,LGHTNG EQ	W 1751	7.4		8.1	W 1976	9.0	W 2325	12.5	APPAR SANITAIRES CHAUFFAGE
821	*FURNITURE,PARTS THEREOF	W 13774	26.2		24.2	W 11678	25.5	W 14970	38.4	MEUBLES ET PIECES
8211	CHAIRS,SEATS AND PARTS	W 3136	8.0		6.3	W 2223	6.7	W 2985	11.4	SIEGES ET PIECES
8219	FURNITURE AND PARTS NES	W 10314	15.3		14.2	W 8793	14.9	W 11067	21.0	AUTRES MEUBLES ET PIECES
82192	WOOD FURNITURE NES	W 8533	10.1		10.0	W 6955	9.7	W 8527	13.3	MEUBLES NDA EN BOIS
84	CLOTHING AND ACCESSORIES		52.0		45.8		47.5		58.0	VETEMENTS
842	MENS OUTERWEAR NOT KNIT	W 929	11.8		7.5	W 331	5.9	W 342	7.6	VET DESSUS POUR HOMMES
843	WOMENS OUTERWEAR NONKNIT	W 425	8.5		9.1	W 377	7.5	W 376	9.3	VET DESSUS FEMMES MAT TEX
845	OUTERWEAR KNIT NONELASTC	W 531	11.5		11.5	W 571	12.6	W 565	14.6	VET DESSOUS,ACCES BONNET
846	UNDER GARMENTS KNITTED	W 417	7.9		7.5	W 562	10.5	W 614	13.2	SOUS VETS DE BONNETERIE
851	*FOOTWEAR	W 2886	23.8		24.9	W 4360	32.1	W 4391	35.3	CHAUSSURES
85102	FOOTWEAR LEATHER	W 1743	16.4		17.3	W 2607	20.9	W 2462	21.8	CHAUS SEMELLES EN CUIR
87	PRECISION INSTRUMNTS NES		31.2		34.7		44.3		45.9	INSTRUM,APPAR SCIENT NDA
872	MEDICAL INSTRUMENTS NES	W 344	10.9		14.6	W 472	13.0	W 429	15.8	INSTR,APP MEDIC–CHIR NDA
87202	OTH MEDICAL INSTRUMENTS	W 294	9.7	W 13816	13.0	W 396	11.8	W 367	13.8	INSTRUM,APP MEDECINE
874	MEASURNG,CONTROLNG INSTR		16.2		16.6	W 673	26.2	W 676	23.5	INSTRUMENTS DE MESURE
88	PHOTO EQU,OPTICL GDS ETC		22.6		21.7		24.4		26.7	APP,FOURN PHOTO,OP,MONTR
882	PHOTO,CINEMA SUPPLIES		10.1		10.8	W 1137	12.4		13.9	PRODUITS PHOTO,CINEMA
89	MISC MANUFCTRD GOODS NES		100.9		107.7		120.5		142.0	ART MANUFACTURES DIVERS
893	ARTICLES OF PLASTIC NES		39.8		47.6	W 15832	54.3		65.0	OUVRAGES EN MAT DIVIS 58
8931	PLSTC PACKG CONTNRS,LIDS	W 5536	17.3		21.6	W 8542	25.4	W 11557	32.9	ART TRANSP EMBALLAGE ETC
8939	MISC PLASTIC ARTICLES	W 6206	22.0		25.2	W 7145	28.2	W 7374	31.4	ART DIVERS EN MAT DIV 58
89399	OTHR PLASTC ARTICLES NES	W 5567	20.3		23.5	W 6126	26.2	W 6297	29.0	AUT OUV MAT DIV 58
894	TOYS,SPORTING GOODS,ETC	W 4161	24.5		23.6	W 5510	24.1	W 5237	28.2	VOITURES ENFANTS,JOUETS
8942	TOYS,INDOOR GAMES ETC	W 3249	18.6		16.2	W 4078	17.4	W 3854	21.1	JOUETS,JEUX ETC
89423	TOYS NES	W 1959	10.4		9.2	W 2297	9.8	W 2056	9.0	JOUETS,MODELES REDUITS
898	MUSICAL INSTRUMENTS,PTS	W 676	10.2		10.3	W 712	11.2	W 746	12.3	INSTRUMENTS DE MUSIQUE
8983	SOUND RECRDNG TAPE,DISCS	W 584	8.9		8.8	W 618	9.8	W 649	10.7	SUPPORTS SON POUR 763
899	OTHER MANUFACTURED GOODS		15.1		13.6		16.3		19.1	AUT ART MANUF DIVERS NDA

5. Special Exports F.O.B. by Commodities according to the S.I.T.C. (Rev. 2) in million U.S. Dollars
Exportations Spéciales F.O.B. par Produits d'après la C.T.C.I. (Rév. 2) en millions de Dollars E.U.

SITC CTCI	COMMODITY	1994 QUANTITY QUANTITE	1994 VALUE VALEUR	1995 QUANTITY QUANTITE	1995 VALUE VALEUR	1996 QUANTITY QUANTITE	1996 VALUE VALEUR	1997 QUANTITY QUANTITE	1997 VALUE VALEUR	PRODUIT
	ALL COMMODITIES		1914.5		2106.2		2397.5		2729.6	TOUS PRODUITS
0	FOOD AND LIVE ANIMALS		766.6		902.4		1070.3		1243.7	ALIMENTS,ANIMAUX VIVANTS
001	*LIVE ANIMALS FOR FOOD	W 59591	46.4	W 103866	95.3	W 31832	33.1	W 38944	37.6	ANIMAUX VIVANTS
0011	BOVINE SPECIES,LIVE	W 40535	35.0	W 97284	90.7	W 20369	25.5	W 18783	26.3	ESPECE BOVINE
00119	— OTHR THAN FR BREEDING	W 40403	34.7	W 96549	88.7	W 20335	25.4	W 18464	24.9	BOVINS NON REPRODUCTEURS
0012	SHEEP AND GOATS,LIVE	W 17183	10.5	W 5357	4.0	W 10381	7.0	W 19100	10.7	ESPECES OVINE ET CAPRINE
00121	SHEEP,LIVE	W 17183	10.5	W 5357	4.0	W 10381	7.0	W 19089	10.7	ESPECE OVINE
01	MEAT AND PREPARATIONS		267.1		275.8		356.9		443.1	VIANDES ET PREPARATIONS
011	MEAT FRESH,CHILLD,FROZEN	W 110526	242.2	W 101602	249.6	W 157868	334.1	W 205791	419.7	VIANDES FRAICHES,REF,CONGE
0111	BOVINE MEAT FRESH,FROZEN	W 88753	203.7	W 83687	213.8	W 131769	280.2	W 176291	363.9	VIANDES BOVIN FRAI,REF
01111	BOVINE MEAT WITH BONE IN	W 17674	20.0	W 19196	23.8	W 40965	48.6	W 62257	79.5	VIANDES BOVIN NON DESOSS
01112	BOVINE MEAT BONELESS	W 71078	183.7	W 64492	190.1	W 90804	231.7	W 114034	284.4	VIANDES BOVIN DESOSSEES
0112	MUTTON ETC FRSH,CHLD,FRN	W 11238	19.3	W 7756	16.8	W 13532	30.2	W 16047	32.7	VIANDE DE MOUTON
0115	HORSE MEAT FRSH,CHLD,FRN	W 4602	9.6	W 4191	9.4	W 4568	10.4	W 5192	11.2	VIANDES DE CHEVAL
0116	EDIBLE OFFAL FRESH,CH,FR	W 4332	7.7	W 3955	7.7	W 4789	10.2	W 6376	9.8	ABATS COMESTIBLES
014	MEAT PREPD,PRSVD,NES ETC	W 7160	20.8	W 7700	23.8	W 9589	21.4	W 8517	21.8	CONSERVES DE VIANDES
0149	OTH PREPARD,PRESRVD MEAT	W 7020	19.9	W 7439	22.3	W 9392	20.6	W 8295	20.9	AUTRES PREP DE VIANDES
02	DAIRY PRODCTS,BIRDS'EGGS		102.0		104.0		143.7		138.1	PRODUITS LAITIERS,OEUFS
022	MILK AND CREAM	W 79018	51.2	W 62721	54.5	W 95307	72.3	W 114426	73.6	LAIT ET CREME
0223	MILK AND CREAM FRESH	W 60979	16.6	W 47129	18.2	W 76587	28.1	W 97508	36.8	LAIT,CREME FRAIS
0224	MILK,CREAM PRESERVED ETC	W 18039	34.7	W 15593	36.4	W 18721	44.2	W 16918	36.9	LAIT,CREME CONS,CONC
02242	MILK DRY,1.5% FAT OR LES	W 10643	20.2	W 10888	25.6	W 9539	21.7	W 9315	20.0	LAIT POUDRE INF 1.5%
02243	MILK DRY,OVER 1.5% FAT	W 7397	14.6	W 4348	10.5	W 8534	21.1	W 7580	16.9	LAIT POUDRE SUP 1.5%
023	BUTTER	W 9614	16.9	W 5944	13.0	W 9583	20.2	W 16171	25.4	BEURRE
024	CHEESE AND CURD	W 11285	33.4	W 11041	36.0	W 16289	50.7	W 11959	38.6	FROMAGE ET CAILLEBOTTE
03	FISH AND PREPARATIONS		81.2		94.3		95.7		109.4	POISSONS ET PREPARATIONS
034	FISH,FRESH,CHILLED,FROZN	W 70401	72.8	W 77723	81.5	W 86027	80.3	W 75315	84.7	POISSON FRAIS, REFRIG,CONG
0341	FISH FRSH,CHLLD,EX FILLT	W 10322	4.9	W 21666	10.2	W 30576	14.8	W 21440	14.3	POISSON FRAIS,REFRIGERE
0342	FISH FROZEN,EXCL FILLETS	W 46771	41.5	W 39428	36.2	W 36282	29.7	W 41055	39.8	POISSONS CONGELES
0344	FISH FILLETS,FROZEN	W 13308	26.5	W 16625	35.1	W 19170	35.8	W 12811	30.6	FILETS CONGELES
036	SHELL FISH FRESH,FROZEN	W 1423	2.9	W 2890	5.5	W 5480	8.9	W 4639	14.6	CRUSTACES,MOLLUSQUES
037	FISH ETC PREPD,PRSVD NES	W 2135	5.5	W 2343	7.3	W 2074	6.0	W 2542	9.1	POIS,CRUST,MOL PREPARES
04	CEREALS AND PREPARATIONS		196.8		252.3		351.5		416.9	CEREALES ET PRODUITS
041	WHEAT ETC UNMILLED			W 58820	13.2	W 69883	10.0	W 159672	35.3	FROMENT,EPEAUTRE
0412	OTHER WHEAT ETC UNMILLED			W 58817	13.2	W 69883	10.0	W 149918	34.0	AUTRE FROMENT NON MOULU
042	RICE	W 417375	151.4	W 482919	163.0	W 642521	228.6	W 684545	255.3	RIZ
0421	RICE IN HUSK OR HUSKED	W 98633	29.2	W 133144	35.4	W 223276	62.8	W 229523	69.5	RIZ SANS AUTRE PREPARATION
04211	RICE IN THE HUSK	W 34589	7.7	W 67068	14.0	W 112181	24.9	W 101910	24.5	RIZ PADDY
04212	RICE HUSKED	W 64043	21.5	W 66076	21.5	W 111095	38.0	W 127614	45.1	RIZ CARGO
0422	RICE SEMI–MILLED,MILLED	W 318742	122.3	W 349776	127.7	W 419245	165.8	W 455022	185.9	RIZ POLI,GLACE INCL BRISURES
04221	RICE MILLED UNBROKEN	W 284317	116.1	W 298606	117.3	W 363999	153.4	W 406900	171.7	RIZ POLI,GLACE EXCL BRISURES
04222	RICE BROKEN	W 34425	6.2	W 51170	10.4	W 55246	12.5	W 48122	14.3	BRISURES DE RIZ
043	BARLEY UNMILLED	W 3026	0.6	W 375	0.1	W 78043	19.0	W 146331	32.1	ORGE NON MONDEE
046	WHEAT ETC MEAL OR FLOUR	W 108	0.1	W 7017	2.3	W 19346	7.3	W 19231	4.9	SEMOULE FARINE,FROMENT
04601	FLOUR OF WHEAT OR MESLIN	W 108	0.1	W 7016	2.3	W 19346	7.3	W 19231	4.9	FARINE DE FROMENT
048	CEREAL ETC PREPARATIONS	W 124973	44.9	W 158320	72.8	W 165293	85.9	W 174419	88.8	PREPTNS A BASE CEREALES
0482	MALT INCLUDING FLOUR	W 119919	33.2	W 150073	54.5	W 154534	65.1	W 161106	64.5	MALT MEME TORREFIE
0484	BAKERY PRODUCTS	W 1996	4.4	W 5421	11.6	W 6275	11.4	W 6629	14.7	PRODUITS DE BOULANGERIE
04841	BREAD,BISCUIT,COM WAFERS	W 1751	3.9	W 3891	8.0	W 4838	8.3	W 5387	11.8	PAINS,BISCUITS DE MER
0488	OTH CEREAL PREPS,MALT EX	W 2401	6.8	W 1654	5.5	W 2688	7.8	W 4820	7.8	EXTRAITS DE MALT
05	VEGETABLES AND FRUIT		57.7		61.9		65.4		66.2	LEGUMES ET FRUITS
057	FRUIT,NUTS,FRESH,DRIED	W 139055	53.4	W 128200	55.5	W 137383	58.5	W 132923	60.4	FRUITS FRAIS OU SECS
0571	ORANGES, MANDARINS ETC	W 109379	42.1	W 94507	40.5	W 108406	45.5	W 104232	46.6	ORANGES,MAND,CLEMENTINES
05711	ORANGES,FRESH OR DRIED	W 87294	29.7	W 76521	29.1	W 77030	27.8	W 75815	28.7	ORANGES FRAICHES,SECHEES
05712	MANDARINS ETC FRESH, DRY	W 22085	12.5	W 17986	11.4	W 31376	17.7	W 28417	17.9	MANDARINES,CLEMENTINES
0572	LEMONS,GRAPEFRUIT ETC	W 27717	10.5	W 30023	13.1	W 21502	9.1	W 23354	10.8	AUTRES AGRUMES FRAIS,SECS
05721	LEMONS,LIMES,FRESH,DRIED	W 21029	8.0	W 25050	11.0	W 16627	7.2	W 19906	9.4	CITRONS ET LIMES
06	SUGAR AND PREPS,HONEY		8.2		11.0		13.9		16.5	SUCRES ET PRODUITS
061	SUGAR AND HONEY	W 13346	7.6	W 14536	10.7	W 13505	13.1	W 14736	15.1	SUCRES ET MIEL
0616	NATURAL HONEY	W 4833	4.0	W 7147	7.5	W 6466	10.2	W 7714	12.2	MIEL NATUREL
081	*FEEDING STUFF FOR ANIML	W 41822	5.9	W 23345	5.2	W 26362	7.2	W 39186	10.4	NOURRITURE POUR ANIMAUX
1	BEVERAGES AND TOBACCO		6.5		9.7		25.6		34.6	BOISSONS ET TABACS
11	BEVERAGES		5.6		8.0		6.6		8.0	BOISSONS
112	ALCOHOLIC BEVERAGES	W 10782	5.6	W 16835	7.6	W 26863	6.6	W 15119	7.8	BOISSONS ALCOOLIQUES
1123	BEER,ALE,STOUT,PORTER	W 10626	5.2	W 16502	7.1	W 25893	5.4	W 13941	5.3	BIERES
12	TOBACCO AND MANUFACTURES		0.9		1.7		19.0		26.7	TABACS BRUTS FABRIQUES
122	TOBACCO,MANUFACTURED	W 107	0.9	W 185	1.7	W 3688	19.0	W 7886	26.6	TABACS FABRIQUES
1222	CIGARETTES	W 107	0.9	W 185	1.7	W 3688	19.0	W 7885	26.6	CIGARETTES
2	CRUDE MATERLS,EXCL FUELS		121.8		129.2		140.2		163.7	MAT BRUTES NON COMESTIBLES
21	HIDES,SKINS,FURS UNDRSSD		11.6		6.5		10.0		5.4	CUIRS,PEAUX BRUTS
211	HIDES,SKINS,EXC FURS,RAW	W 6044	11.3	W 2870	6.3	W 4615	9.4	W 2992	4.7	CUIRS ET PEAUX
22	OIL SEEDS,OLEAGINOUS FRT		4.8		9.9		11.9		22.5	GRAINES,FRUITS OLEAGINEUX
222	SEEDS FOR'SOFT'FIXED OIL	W 6044	4.7	W 12005	9.6	W 47810	11.5	W 65716	22.4	GRAINES HUILES FIXES
2224	SUNFLOWER SEEDS	W 2132	3.8	W 12005	9.6	W 47810	11.5	W 65109	22.2	GRAINES DE TOURNESOL
24	CORK AND WOOD		11.8		30.5		35.4		42.7	LIEGE ET BOIS
247	OTH WOOD ROUGH,SQUARED	W 89189	8.0	W 245218	25.0	W 389480	27.6	W 267185	34.8	BOIS BRUTS EQUARRIS
2472	SAW–,VENEER–LOGS NON–CON	W 82269	6.7	W 237401	24.0	W 384911	26.9	W 264916	34.4	NON CONIFERES SCIAGE,PLAC
24721	— IN THE ROUGH	W 82269	6.7	W 237401	24.0	W 384911	26.9	W 264916	34.4	BRUTS ECORCES DEGROSSIS
248	WOOD SHAPED,SLEEPERS	W 22216	3.9	W 29519	5.6	W 36412	7.9	W 29360	7.9	BOIS SIMPLEMENT TRAVAILLES
26	TEXTILE FIBRES AND WASTE		68.5		55.9		55.6		62.8	FIBRES TEXTILES
268	WOOL(EXC TOPS),ANML HAIR	W 32495	63.9	W 18028	48.9	W 20919	49.3	W 22063	55.7	LAINES ET POILS
2681	WOOL GREASY,FLEECE–WSHED	W 16288	34.3	W 7759	25.8	W 8003	21.1	W 9782	24.3	LAINE EN SUINT
2682	WOOL DEGREASED,UNCOMBED	W 8753	20.2	W 4642	14.5	W 6617	18.4	W 6146	19.3	LAINE DEGRAISSEE
2686	WASTE OF WOOL,HAIR NES	W 7112	9.1	W 5382	8.2	W 6019	9.6	W 5878	11.9	DECHETS LAINE ET POILS
26861	— NOT PULLD OR GARNETTD	W 6993	8.9	W 5311	8.1	W 5930	9.5	W 5693	11.6	DECHETS LAINE ET POILS
29	CRUDE ANIMAL,VEG MAT NES		18.3		17.6		20.7		22.6	MATIERES BRUTES ANIM,VEGET
291	CRUDE ANIMAL MTRIALS NES	W 16388	15.5	W 18050	15.7	W 20808	18.2	W 24425	19.4	MATIERES BRUTES ANIMALES
2919	OTH ANIMAL MATERIALS NES	W 15739	15.3	W 17771	15.6	W 20554	18.2	W 22884	19.0	MAT ORIGINE ANIMALE NDA
29193	GUT,BLADDERS,ETC NONFISH	W 6621	12.1	W 6291	12.9	W 7961	15.2	W 8965	14.8	BOYAUX,VESSIES
3	MINERAL FUELS ETC		8.2		22.6		27.4		19.0	COMBUSTIBLES MINERAUX LUB
33	PETROLEUM AND PRODUCTS		0.7		18.9		24.4		17.8	PETROLE ET DERIVES
334	PETROLEUM PRODUCTS,REFIN	W 550	0.7	W 109681	18.8	W 155028	24.3	W 51497	17.8	PRODUITS RAFFINES
3341	GASOLINE,OTH LIGHT OILS			W 44928	7.3	W 45365	8.1	W 29916	8.0	ESSENCES POUR MOTEURS
3344	FUEL OILS,NES	W 154	0.2	W 63892	11.0	W 102139	13.2	W 19274	7.9	FUEL OILS
351	*ELECTRIC CURRENT		7.5		3.8		3.1		1.2	ENERGIE ELECTRIQUE
4	ANIMAL,VEGETABLE OIL,FAT		8.5		9.2		12.1		17.9	HUILES,GRAISSES ANIM,VEG
411	*ANIMAL OILS AND FATS	W 19361	7.0	W 19247	7.7	W 24084	9.0	W 35124	11.8	HUILES,GRAISSES ANIMALES
4113	ANIML OIL,FAT,GREASE NES	W 19323	7.0	W 19178	7.6	W 24030	9.0	W 35052	11.8	HUILES,GRAISSES ANIMALES NDA
41132	FATS OF BOVINE,SHEEP,ETC	W 19044	6.8	W 18659	7.3	W 23254	8.5	W 34150	11.1	SUIFS BRUTS FONDUS
5	CHEMCLS,RELATED PROD NES		101.4		116.7		129.4		143.4	PRODUITS CHIMIQUES
52	INORGANIC CHEMICALS		9.1		7.9		8.2		9.9	PROD CHIM INORGANIQUES

5. Special Exports F.O.B. by Commodities according to the S.I.T.C. (Rev. 2) in million U.S. Dollars
Exportations Spéciales F.O.B. par Produits d'après la C.T.C.I. (Rév. 2) en millions de Dollars E.U.

SITC CTCI	COMMODITY	1994 QUANTITY QUANTITE	1994 VALUE VALEUR	1995 QUANTITY QUANTITE	1995 VALUE VALEUR	1996 QUANTITY QUANTITE	1996 VALUE VALEUR	1997 QUANTITY QUANTITE	1997 VALUE VALEUR	PRODUIT
523	OTHR INORG CHEMICALS ETC	W 10080	6.7	W 7708	5.2	W 8310	5.9	W 9337	6.6	AUT PRODUITS CHIMIQUES INORG
5231	METAL CMPD OF INORG ACID	W 9343	6.4	W 7190	5.1	W 8286	5.9	W 9272	6.6	SELS METALLIQUES
52319	OTH SULPHATES,PERSLPHTES	W 9227	6.4	W 6881	5.0	W 7512	5.8	W 7861	6.3	AUTRE SULFATES,ALUNS
53	DYES,TANNING,COLOUR PROD		14.5		16.2		15.4		33.3	PROD TEINTURE,COLORANTS
533	PIGMENTS,PAINTS,ETC	W 5504	9.6	W 4386	10.5	W 5209	11.1	W 5315	28.9	PIGMENTS,PEINTURES,VERNIS
5334	VARNISHES,DISTEMPERS ETC	W 5205	9.3	W 4066	9.4	W 5052	10.6	W 5198	28.6	PEINTURES A L'EAU
53342	OTH PAINTS,VARNISHES ETC	W 2175	5.0	W 1747	5.6	W 2456	6.8	W 2186	24.7	AUTRES PEINTURES,VERNIS
541	*MEDICINAL,PHARM PRODUCT		14.0		24.0	K 1213282	22.4		22.6	PROD MEDICINAUX PHARMACEUT
5417	MEDICAMENTS	K 292735	9.6	K 547648	18.8	K 1008981	16.3	K 998792	15.6	MEDICAMENTS
54171	— CONTAINNG ANTIBIOTICS	K 32081	3.3	K 73006	7.8	K 128920	8.4	K 54871	6.8	MED CONTN ANTIBIOTIQUES
54179	— CONTNG OTH SUBSTANCES	K 260266	6.2	K 468229	10.9	K 872852	7.7	K 936460	8.5	MED CONT AUT SUBSTANCES
55	PERFUME,CLEANING ETC PRD		12.0		9.6		6.6		5.0	PROD POUR PARFUM,TOILETTE
554	SOAP,CLEANSING ETC PREPS	W 10553	9.5	W 7874	7.3	W 5661	4.5	W 2990	2.8	SAVONS,PRODUITS DETERSIFS
5542	WASHING PREPARATIONS ETC	W 7337	6.0	W 6681	5.9	W 4881	3.5	W 2289	1.9	PROD ORG TENSIO–ACT NDA
562	*FERTILIZERS,MANUFACTURE	W 34902	5.5	W 32970	6.5	W 64283	14.3	W 68552	16.0	ENGRAIS MANUFACTURES
5629	FERTILIZERS NES	W 19904	4.1	W 16985	4.3	W 48034	12.0	W 62931	15.0	ENGRAIS NDA
56291	NIT–PHOS–POT FERTLZR NES	W 8899	1.8	W 10287	2.5	W 38235	9.2	W 45278	10.6	ENGRAIS CONT N P K
58	PLASTIC MATERIALS ETC		26.2		31.2		39.4		33.7	MAT PLAST ARTIFICIELLES
582	PROD OF CONDENSATION ETC	W 6008	9.1	W 5453	11.5	W 7845	11.7	W 4921	7.7	PROD CONDENS,POLYCOND
5823	ALKYDS,OTHER POLYESTERS	W 5048	7.1	W 4980	10.3	W 7447	10.3	W 4433	5.8	ALKYDES ET AUT POLYESTERS
58231	— IN PRIMARY FORMS	W 5048	7.1	W 4980	10.3	W 7447	10.3	W 4433	5.8	SOUS FORMES PRIMAIRES
583	POLYMERIZATION ETC PRODS	W 12746	17.1	W 12259	19.6	W 20569	27.7	W 21478	25.4	PROD POLYMERISATION
5834	POLYVINYL CHLORIDE	W 4953	7.1	W 2928	5.5	W 9273	11.3	W 7458	9.6	CHLORURE DE POLYVINYLE
58341	— IN PRIMARY FORMS	W 4426	5.7	W 2286	3.6	W 8551	9.5	W 7039	8.7	SOUS FORMES PRIMAIRES
59	CHEMICAL MATERIALS NES		14.9		16.3		17.1		15.5	MAT PROD CHIMIQUES NDA
592	STARCH,INULIN,GLUTEN,ETC	W 1354	5.8	W 1336	6.8	W 1332	6.7	W 1032	4.6	AMIDONS,INUL,GLUT FROM
5922	ALBUMINOID SUBSTAN,GLUES	W 1354	5.8	W 1331	6.8	W 1332	6.7	W 1032	4.6	MAT ALBUMIN,COLLES
6	BASIC MANUFACTURES		487.1		589.3		669.7		713.0	ART MANUFACTURES
61	LEATHER,DRESSED FUR,ETC		138.2		187.2		210.8		225.4	CUIRS,PELLETERIES
611	LEATHER	W 16662	121.8	W 19263	159.4	W 24541	177.1	W 26588	188.6	CUIRS,PEAUX PREPARES
6114	LEATHR BOVINE NES,EQUINE	W 15789	118.4	W 18635	156.2	W 24425	176.2	W 26161	186.1	CUIRS DE BOVINS
612	LEATHER ETC MANUFACTURES	W 420	3.3	W 823	4.2	W 1448	8.4	W 965	6.8	OUVRAGES EN CUIRS NDA
613	FUR SKINS TANNED,DRESSED	W 731	13.2	W 1019	23.7	W 959	25.4	W 1333	30.1	PELLETERIES
62	RUBBER MANUFACTURES NES		31.8		35.1		37.4		44.5	CAOUTCHOUC MANUFACTURE
621	MATERIALS OF RUBBER	W 11157	20.1	W 9494	22.0	W 11476	24.0	W 17599	31.0	PRODUITS EN CAOUTCHOUC
62104	UNHARD VULC RUBBER,BASIC	W 11141	20.1	W 9483	22.0	W 11406	23.8	W 13166	25.6	PLAQUES,FEUILLES CAOUT
625	RUBBER TYRES, TUBES ETC	W 3763	11.7	W 4220	13.2	W 3868	13.5	W 3954	13.5	PNEUS CAOUTCHOUC VULCANISE
6252	TYRES,NEW,BUS OR LORRY	W 2912	9.1	W 2824	9.7	W 2647	9.2	W 2421	8.3	PNEUS POUR AUTOBUS,CAMIONS
64	PAPER,PAPERBOARD AND MFR		21.5		26.7		34.2		51.1	PAPIERS,CARTONS & OUVRAGES
641	PAPER AND PAPERBOARD	W 19778	14.9	W 14939	15.7	W 21626	22.0	W 32915	33.8	PAPIERS ET CARTONS
6412	PRINTG,WRITING PAPER NES	W 808	1.1	W 1013	1.5	W 6452	7.6	W 19615	22.9	PAPIERS POUR L'IMPRESSION
64122	— COATED,IMPREGNATD ETC	W 808	1.1	W 912	1.4	W 5469	6.7	W 18406	21.8	PAPIERS IMPRESSION COUCHES
6415	PAPER,PAPERBRD,BULK,NES	W 10414	8.6	W 7862	9.8	W 12178	12.5	W 8130	7.5	PAPIERS,CARTONS ROULEAUX
64159	OTHER PAPER ETC,BULK,NES	W 10190	8.4	W 7786	9.7	W 11803	12.0	W 7906	7.2	AUT PAPIER ROULEAUX FEUILLES
642	PAPER,ETC,PRECUT,ARTS OF	W 7280	6.7	W 9985	11.0	W 11673	12.3	W 15434	17.4	PAP,CARTONS DECOUPES
6421	PAPER ETC CONTAINERS	W 6102	5.0	W 9011	9.4	W 8101	8.9	W 8016	8.1	BOITES,SACS EMBALLAGES
65	TEXTILE YARN,FABRICS,ETC		250.4		290.6		327.2		313.9	FILS,TISSUS,ARTICLES TEXTILE
651	TEXTILE YARN	W 44060	181.8	W 37896	210.6	W 51486	253.5	W 46591	229.6	FILS TEXTILES
6512	WOOL,HAIR YARN,INCL TOPS	W 42895	176.0	W 36143	201.4	W 49228	242.5	W 45191	222.2	FILS DE LAINE,DE POILS
65121	WOOL TOPS	W 42826	175.3	W 36107	200.8	W 49191	242.0	W 45139	221.4	RUBANS LAINE PEIGN,TOPS
6517	REGEN FIBRE YARN,MONOFIL	W 863	4.5	W 1305	6.7	W 1876	8.7	W 910	4.9	FILS TEXT ART NON VENTE DT
65171	CONT VISCOSE RAYON YARN	W 666	3.5	W 1180	6.1	W 1768	8.3	W 739	4.2	FILS RAY,VIS NON VENTE DET
653	WOVN MAN–MADE FIB FABRIC	W 645	7.1	W 709	8.7	W 914	10.4	W 1037	11.9	TISSUS FIBRES SYNTH,ARTIF
654	OTH WOVEN TEXTILE FABRIC	W 2408	51.5	W 2453	57.2	W 2151	48.7	W 2672	58.2	TISSUS AUT COTON SYNT,ARTIF
6542	WOVEN WOOL,HAIR NONPILE	W 2080	47.2	W 2199	52.5	W 1899	42.8	W 2226	50.2	TIS PLUS 85% LAINE,POILS
65422	WOVN COMB WOOL,FINE HAIR	W 1927	45.1	W 2069	50.7	W 1682	39.9	W 1854	43.7	TISSUS 85% LAINE,PLS PEIG
66	NONMETAL MINERAL MFS NES		28.2		24.6		28.4		37.4	ART MIN NON METALLIQUES
661	LIME,CEMENT,BLDG PRODS	W 42393	3.6	W 45599	3.5	W 67005	4.8	W 173385	12.7	CHAUX,CIMENTS MAT CONSTR
6612	CEMENT	W 40811	2.7	W 44189	2.8	W 64402	3.8	W 167472	10.9	CIMENTS HYDRAULIQUES
662	CLAY,REFRACTORY BLDG PRD	W 23537	10.4	W 18507	8.7	W 25582	9.9	W 23125	9.0	MAT CONST REFRACTAIRES
6624	BRICKS ETC NONREFRACTORY	W 23392	10.3	W 18348	8.7	W 25355	9.8	W 22869	8.9	BRIQUES ETC CERAM NON REFR
66245	GLAZED CERAMIC SETTS ETC	W 22018	9.9	W 17942	8.5	W 24619	9.6	W 22641	8.8	AUT CARREAUX CERAMIQUE
665	GLASSWARE	W 13375	7.6	W 11651	7.1	W 13939	8.1	W 18882	9.6	OUVRAGES EN VERRE
6651	BOTTLES ETC OF GLASS	W 13332	6.8	W 11603	6.6	W 13876	7.7	W 18872	9.4	RECIPIENTS EN VERRE
66511	GLASS BOTTLES ETC NONVAC	W 13329	6.8	W 11603	6.6	W 13876	7.7	W 18864	9.4	BONBONNES,BOUTEILLES,ETC
67	IRON AND STEEL		8.4		10.8		17.1		22.7	FER ET ACIER
678	IRON,STL TUBES,PIPES,ETC	W 6070	5.8	W 4859	7.9	W 7964	13.0	W 11358	18.3	TUBES,TUYAUX EN FONTE,FER
6783	IRON,STL TUBES,PIPES NES	W 6062	5.8	W 4835	7.8	W 7909	12.9	W 11323	18.2	AUT TUBES,TUYAUX FER,ACIER
68	NON–FERROUS METALS		4.1		7.1		9.2		11.3	METAUX NON FERREUX
684	ALUMINIUM	W 928	4.0	W 1860	6.8	W 1777	6.8	W 2105	7.9	ALUMINIUM
6842	ALUMINIUM,ALLOYS WORKED	W 928	4.0	W 1860	6.8	W 1776	6.8	W 2097	7.9	ALUMINIUM,ALLIAGES OUVRE
69	METAL MANUFACTURES NES		4.7		7.4		5.5		6.4	ART MANUFACT EN METAL NDA
7	MACHINES,TRANSPORT EQUIP		222.9		125.8		106.9		153.7	MACHINES MATERIEL TRANSPORT
72	MACHS FOR SPCL INDUSTRYS		4.3		8.2		7.4		13.7	MAC SPECIALES POUR INDUST
728	OTH MACHY FOR SPCL INDUS	W 249	3.5	W 390	6.3	W 455	6.3	W 474	10.8	AUT MACH IND PARTICULIERES
7284	MACHY FOR SPCL INDUS NES	W 194	3.5	W 353	6.1	W 297	6.1	W 442	10.7	MACH SPEC IND PARTICUL.
72848	OTH MCHY WITH INDIV FNCT	W 140	3.1	W 207	5.5	W 224	5.2	W 416	10.2	AUTRES MACHINES NDA
74	GENRL INDUSTRL MACHY NES		2.9		3.6		6.3		9.3	MACH APP INDUSTRIE
77	ELECTRIC MACHNRY NES ETC		16.2		15.9		13.6		44.8	MACH APP ELECT NDA
775	HOUSEHOLD TYPE EQUIP NES	W 610	4.4	W 931	7.0	W 1315	9.1	W 990	7.8	MACH,APP USAGE DOMESTQUE
778	ELECTRICAL MACHINERY NES	W 867	9.7	W 381	4.3	W 245	0.7		30.9	AUTRES MACH ELECT NDA
7783	AUTOMOTIVE ELECTR EQUIP	W 660	9.4	W 267	3.9	W 2	0.1	W 2674	30.1	EQUIP ELECT MOTEURS EXPL
77831	IGNITION,STARTING EQUIP	W 659	9.4	W 266	3.9	W 2	0.1	W 2674	30.1	APP ELEC ALLUM,DEMARRAGE
78	ROAD VEHICLES		197.1		92.2		71.1		77.7	VEHICULES ROUTIERS
781	PASS MOTOR VEH EXC BUSES	W 13735	166.0	W 5388	66.8	W 3767	42.5	W 2258	25.4	AUTO TRANSPORT PERSONNES
782	LORRIES,SPCL MTR VEH NES	W 171	2.2			W 10	0.1	W 2390	24.2	VEHICULES SPECIAUX,MARCH
7821	LORRIES,TRUCKS	W 171	2.2			W 10	0.1	W 2387	24.2	VEHICULES TRANSP MARCHAND
784	MOTOR VEH PRTS,ACCES NES	W 2384	27.5	W 2089	21.8	W 2837	25.1	W 3130	23.3	PIECES 722,781,782,783
7849	OTHER MOTOR VEHCL PARTS	W 2383	27.5	W 2055	21.5	W 2835	25.0	W 3130	23.3	PIECES 722,781,782,783
8	MISC MANUFACTURED GOODS		186.2		191.1		209.7		224.6	ART MANUFACTURES DIVERS
821	*FURNITURE,PARTS THEREOF	W 2906	5.8	W 6419	13.1	W 7131	12.8	W 9704	15.2	MEUBLES ET PIECES
8211	CHAIRS,SEATS AND PARTS	W 2264	3.8	W 4770	8.4	W 4874	7.8	W 7852	11.3	SIEGES ET PIECES
82111	CHAIRS AND OTHER SEATS	W 2264	3.8	W 4770	8.4	W 4874	7.8	W 7848	11.3	SIEGES
84	CLOTHING AND ACCESSORIES		135.2		131.4		141.4		152.8	VETEMENTS
842	MENS OUTERWEAR NOT KNIT	W 783	28.2	W 672	24.6	W 780	27.3	W 731	30.4	VET DESSUS POUR HOMMES
8421	— OVERCOATS,OTHER COATS	W 187	6.7	W 191	6.3	W 160	5.0	W 143	5.5	MANTEAUX HOMMES MAT TEXT
84211	—— OF WOOL,FINE HAIR	W 168	5.8	W 176	5.5	W 150	4.5	W 127	4.8	MANTEAUX HOMMES DE LAINE
8423	— TROUSERS,BREECHES ETC	W 291	6.6	W 228	6.0	W 301	6.9	W 278	7.4	PANTALONS HOMMES MAT TEX
8424	— JACKETS,BLAZERS ETC	W 174	9.2	W 155	7.9	W 205	10.1	W 182	10.4	VESTES HOMMES MAT TEXTIL
843	WOMENS OUTERWEAR NONKNIT	W 526	20.3	W 525	25.7	W 646	31.2	W 713	41.1	VET DESSUS FEMMES MAT TEX
8431	— COATS AND JACKETS	W 366	13.7	W 331	15.0	W 407	18.3	W 479	26.2	MANT,VEST FEM MAT TEXTIL

Uruguay

5. Special Exports F.O.B. by Commodities according to the S.I.T.C. (Rev. 2) in million U.S. Dollars
Exportations Spéciales F.O.B. par Produits d'après la C.T.C.I. (Rév. 2) en millions de Dollars E.U.

SITC CTCI	COMMODITY	1994		1995		1996		1997		PRODUIT
		QUANTITY QUANTITE	VALUE VALEUR	QUANTITY QUANTITE	VALUE VALEUR	QUANTITY QUANTITE	VALUE VALEUR	QUANTITY QUANTITE	VALUE VALEUR	
8439	— OTHER OUTER GARMENTS	W 108	3.9	W 119	6.1	W 140	6.8	W 144	8.5	AUT VET DES FEM MAT TEXT
845	OUTERWEAR KNIT NONELASTC	W 349	17.4	W 1111	17.2	W 469	17.6	W 390	22.8	VET DESSOUS,ACCES BONNET
8451	— JERSEYS,PULLOVERS ETC	W 317	15.1	W 1090	15.4	W 435	15.8	W 343	18.7	CHANDAILS,PULL–OVERS ETC
848	HEADGEAR,NONTXTL CLOTHNG	W 1224	61.3	W 1243	56.1	W 939	57.3	W 640	49.5	VET ACCES MAT AUT QUE TEX
8481	LEATHER CLOTHES,ACCESSOR	W 413	21.3	W 618	18.9	W 321	16.3	W 133	9.3	VET ACCES MAT CUIR ARTIF
8483	FUR ETC,CLOTHES,PRODUCTS	W 781	39.6	W 597	36.7	W 583	40.2	W 477	39.6	VETEMENTS DE FOURRURE
84831	ARTICLES OF FURSKIN,NES	W 781	39.6	W 597	36.7	W 583	40.2	W 477	39.6	PELLETERIES OUVREES NDA
851	*FOOTWEAR	W 1810	20.8	W 1406	17.1	W 1593	20.0	W 1333	18.1	CHAUSSURES
85102	FOOTWEAR LEATHER	W 725	16.3	W 524	11.9	W 834	15.1	W 643	13.8	CHAUS SEMELLES EN CUIR
89	MISC MANUFCTRD GOODS NES		15.1		19.5		22.5		26.7	ART MANUFACTURES DIVERS
892	PRINTED MATTER	W 2170	4.1	W 1925	4.2	W 4371	9.9	W 4800	9.3	IMPRIMES
8928	PRINTED MATTER NES	W 1798	3.0	W 1909	4.1	W 4360	9.8	W 4795	9.3	IMPRIMES NDA
89286	TRADE ADV MATRL,CATALOGS	W 1795	2.9	W 1856	3.6	W 4293	9.3	W 4657	8.1	IMPRIMES PUBLICITAIRES
893	ARTICLES OF PLASTIC NES		4.9	W 1796	8.6	W 1886	7.6	W 3470	12.2	OUVRAGES EN MAT DIVIS 58
8939	MISC PLASTIC ARTICLES	W 857	3.1	W 1389	7.0	W 997	4.7	W 1870	6.5	ART DIVERS EN MAT DIV 58
9	GOODS NOT CLASSD BY KIND		5.8		10.7		6.6		16.5	ART TRANSACT NON CLASSES
971	*GOLD,NON MONETARY NES	K 10	0.2	K 527	5.1	K 550	6.2	K 2441	16.2	OR NON MONETAIRE
97101	NONMON GLD UNWRT,SEMIMFD	K 10	0.2	K 527	5.1	K 550	6.2	K 2441	16.2	OR,ALLIAGES D'OR BRUTS

1. HISTORICAL SERIES, 1992–1997 GENERAL TRADE, IMPORTS C.I.F., EXPORTS F.O.B.
SERIES HISTORIQUES, 1992–1997 COMMERCE GENERAL, IMPORTATIONS C.A.F., EXPORTATIONS F.O.B

YEAR ANNEE	VALUE IN MILLION U.S. DOLLARS VALEUR EN MILLION U.S. DOLLARS MERCHANDISE – MARCHANDISE		GOLD – OR		CONVERSION FACTORS FACTEURS DE CONVERSION CENTS E.U. PAR		INDEX NUMBERS – INDICES QUANTUM		UNIT VALUE VALEUR UNITAIRE	
	IMPORTS	EXPORTS	IMPORTS	EXPORTS	IMPORTS	EXPORTS	IMPORTS	EXPORTS	IMPORTS	EXPORTS
1992	929.30	869.30								
1993	958.00	721.00								
1994	2479.00	3044.00								
1995	2900.00	3100.00								
1996	4721.10	4590.20								
1997	4523.00	4387.50								

2. IMPORTS BY BROAD ECONOMIC CATEGORY AND EXPORTS BY INDUSTRIAL ORIGIN. (PERCENTAGE OF TOTAL VALUE)
IMPORTATIONS PAR CATEGORIES ECONOMIQUES ET EXPORTATIONS PAR BRANCHE D'ACTIVITE.(EN POURCENTAGE DE LA VALEUR TOTALE)

IMPORTS – IMPORTATIONS

	1990	1991	1992	1993	1994	1995	1996
TOTAL IMPORTS–IMPORTATIONS TOTALES							
1 FOOD BEV–ALIMENTATION BOISSONS							
11 PRIMARY–PRODUITS DE BASE							
111 FOR INDUSTRY–POUR L'INDUSTRIE							
112 FOR HOUSEHOLDS–POUR LES MENAGES							
12 PROCESSED–PRODUITS ELABORES							
121 FOR INDUSTRY–POUR L'INDUSTRIE							
122 FOR HOUSEHOLDS–POUR LES MENAGES							
2 IND SUPPLIES–APPROV INDUSTRIELS							
21 PRIMARY–PRODUITS DE BASE							
22 PROCESSED–PRODUITS ELABORES							
3 FUELS–COMBUSTIBLES							
31 PRIMARY–PRODUITS DE BASE							
32 PROCESSED–PRODUITS ELABORES							
321 MOTOR SPIRIT–ESSENCE							
322 OTHER–AUTRES							
4 MACHINERY–EQUIPEMENT							
41 CAPITAL EQUIPMENT–MACHINES							
42 PARTS–PIECES ACCESSOIRES							
5 TRANSPORT–TRANSPORT							
51 PASSENGER CARS–AUTOMOBILES							
52 OTHER–AUTRES							
521 INDUSTRIAL–INDUSTRIELS							
522 NON INDUSTRIAL–NON INDUSTRIEL							
53 PARTS–PIECES ACCESSOIRES							
6 CONSUM GOODS–BIENS CONSOMMATION							
61 DURABLE–DURABLES							
62 SEMI DURABLE–SEMI DURABLES							
63 NON DURABLE–NON DURABLES							
7 GOODS NES–BIENS NDA							

EXPORTS – EXPORTATIONS

	1990	1991	1992	1993	1994	1995	1996
TOTAL EXPORTS–EXPORTATIONS TOTALES							
1 AGRICULTURE							
2 MINING QUARRY–INDUS EXTRACTIVES							
3 MANUFACTURING–IND MANUFACTUR							
31 FOOD BEV TOBACCO–ALIM BOISS TAB							
32 TEXTILES–INDUSTRIES TEXTILES							
33 WOOD & PRODUCTS–BOIS & PRODUITS							
34 PAPER & PRODUCTS–PAPIER & PRODT							
35 CHEMICALS–INDUSTRIES CHIMIQUES							
36 NON METAL MIN–MIN NON METAL							
37 BASIC METAL–IND METAL BASE							
38 METAL MANUF–MANUF METAL							
39 OTH MANUF IND–AUTRES MANUF							

3. TRADE BY PRINCIPAL COUNTRIES OF PURCHASE AND DESTINATION (VALUE IN MILLION U.S. DOLLARS)
ECHANGES SELON LES PRINCIPAUX PAYS D'ACHAT ET DE DESTINATION (VALEUR EN MILLIONS DE DOLLARS EU)

COUNTRIES–PAYS	GENERAL IMPORTS C.I.F. IMPORTATIONS GENERALES C.A.F				
	1992	1993	1994	1995	1996
World			2609.5	2747.9	4711.7
Africa				2.4	4.1
Americas			99.8	33.1	439.1
– Northern America			99.8	33.1	439.1
– LAIA					
– CACM					
– Caribbean					
– Rest of America					
Asia excl fmr USSR			271.8	728.6	1187.4
– Middle East			72.1	188.0	631.1
Asia former USSR			599.5	284.7	424.6
Europe excl fmr USSR			787.1	824.8	1241.1
– European Union			337.8	501.1	925.3
– Eastern Europe			128.4	201.5	121.5
– Rest of Europe			320.9	122.2	194.3
Europe former USSR			815.9	864.9	1147.3
Oceania			24.4	3.1	5.3
Other					
Russian Federation			739.7	719.5	884.5
Germany/Allemagne			176.7	371.9	578.3
Korea, Republic of			26.4	429.1	325.9
Switzerland,Liechtenst.			320.9	118.6	188.1
USA/Etats–Unis d'Amer			93.0	30.4	434.5
Tajikistan/Tadjikistan			319.2	43.9	154.7
Turkey/Turquie			67.2	85.6	357.8
Kazakhstan			154.0	173.1	165.3
Hungary/Hongrie			87.5	145.6	47.9
United Arab Emirates			4.4	70.1	182.1
Ukraine			49.0	61.4	142.6
Kyrgyzstan/Kirghizistan			26.3	34.1	94.0
Netherlands/Pays–Bas			51.8	35.3	67.1
United Kingdom			17.3	27.8	105.4
China/Chine			88.1	23.4	32.1
Turkmenistan/Turkménistn			99.3	31.9	3.0
Belarus/Bélarus			12.3	50.0	62.2
Japan/Japon			23.6	44.6	54.3
Lithuania/Lituanie			7.7	28.4	48.7
France, Monaco			11.1	15.4	54.3
Italy/Italie			23.6	22.1	32.0
Czech Republic			16.1	33.4	25.6
Austria/Autriche			27.0	10.1	22.4
Syrian Arab Republic				25.2	32.1
Iran (Islamic Rep of)			0.5	2.7	51.1
India/Inde			4.1	13.9	31.9
Pakistan			1.2	9.2	38.3
Indonesia/Indonésie			33.0	5.2	8.9
Belgium–Luxembourg			15.2	4.3	25.7
Romania/Roumanie			4.4	10.0	25.6
Singapore/Singapour			1.6	4.3	31.8
Denmark/Danemark			1.7	9.9	25.6
Australia/Australie			24.4	3.1	5.3
Poland/Pologne			17.2	4.5	9.8
Israel/Israël			2.9	7.2	19.2
China, Hong Kong SAR			18.4	2.3	4.3
Sweden/Suède			12.3	2.8	4.9
Bulgaria/Bulgarie			2.9	6.3	9.6
Latvia/Lettonie			6.5	3.7	6.3
Canada			6.8	2.7	4.6

COUNTRIES–PAYS	GENERAL EXPORTS F.O.B. EXPORTATIONS GENERALES F.O.B.				
	1992	1993	1994	1995	1996
Monde			2548.8	2821.3	4210.8
Afrique				0.3	
Amériques			23.6	14.7	
– Amérique du Nord			19.9	11.1	
– ALAI					
– MCAC					
– Caraïbes					
– Autre Amérique			3.7	3.6	
Asie anc. URSS exclus			233.9	324.6	
– Moyen–Orient			42.0	109.8	
Asie ancienne URSS			730.2	481.9	
Europe anc. URSS exclus			677.7	973.8	
– Union Européenne			423.4	502.5	
– Europe de l'Est			35.2	49.2	
– Autre de l'Europe			219.1	422.1	
Europe ancienne URSS			875.5	662.1	
Océanie					
Autre					
Russian Federation			680.4	549.1	490.5
Switzerland,Liechtenst.			219.1	422.1	352.0
United Kingdom			168.5	222.8	345.3
Tajikistan/Tadjikistan			313.3	155.8	148.6
Kazakhstan			281.4	227.3	66.8
Korea, Republic of			39.9	143.7	252.4
Netherlands/Pays–Bas			152.9	142.3	126.2
USA/Etats–Unis d'Amer			19.9	11.1	265.6
Ukraine			142.4	43.6	45.4
China/Chine			76.3	33.8	119.5
Kyrgyzstan/Kirghizistan			58.4	67.3	98.8
Italy/Italie			26.4	71.4	102.9
Turkey/Turquie			40.5	105.9	39.8
Germany/Allemagne			24.7	22.4	89.7
Austria/Autriche			41.6	41.1	39.8
Turkmenistan/Turkménistn			75.9	26.6	4.5
Belarus/Bélarus			28.4	31.7	27.6
Belgium–Luxembourg			7.5	0.2	63.1
Poland/Pologne			21.2	27.1	10.0
Indonesia/Indonésie			36.8	5.0	7.5
Latvia/Lettonie			6.6	15.0	22.4
Lithuania/Lituanie			16.1	10.3	15.4
Afghanistan			3.9	16.5	19.9
France, Monaco			1.0	0.2	36.5
China, Hong Kong SAR			18.2	5.2	7.8
Ireland/Irlande				0.8	23.2
Bulgaria/Bulgarie			7.9	12.7	3.3
Estonia/Estonie			0.5	9.3	13.9
Iran (Islamic Rep of)				0.7	19.9
Czech Republic			3.0	1.8	13.3
Israel/Israël			8.4	1.1	6.6
Hungary/Hongrie			1.5	0.8	13.2
India/Inde			0.5	4.2	10.0
Japan/Japon			5.1	1.5	6.6
Panama			3.7	3.6	5.3
United Arab Emirates			0.9	0.1	10.0
Azerbaijan/Azerbaïdjan			1.1	4.0	5.3
Cyprus/Chypre			0.6	3.1	4.6
Romania/Roumanie			0.3	4.6	3.0
Pakistan			0.2	0.1	6.6

(VALUE AS PERCENTAGE OF WORLD TOTAL)(VALEURS EN POURCENTAGE DU TOTAL MONDIAL)

	1987	1988	1989	1990	1991	1992	1993	1994	1995	1996
Africa									0.1	0.1
Americas								3.8	1.2	9.3
– Northern America								3.8	1.2	9.3
– LAIA										
– CACM										
– Caribbean										
– Rest of America										
Asia excl fmr USSR								10.4	26.5	25.2
– Middle East								2.8	6.8	13.4
Asia former USSR								23.0	10.4	9.0
Europe excl fmr USSR								30.2	30.0	26.3
– European Union								12.9	18.2	19.6
– Eastern Europe								4.9	7.3	2.6
– Rest of Europe								12.3	4.4	4.1
Europe former USSR								31.3	31.5	24.4
Oceania								0.9	0.1	0.1
Other										
Russian Federation								28.3	26.2	18.8
Germany/Allemagne								6.8	13.5	12.3
Korea, Republic of								1.0	15.6	6.9
Switzerland,Liechtenst.								12.3	4.3	4.0
USA/Etats–Unis d'Amer								3.6	1.1	9.2
Tajikistan/Tadjikistan								12.2	1.6	3.3
Turkey/Turquie								2.6	3.1	7.6
Kazakhstan								5.9	6.3	3.5
Hungary/Hongrie								3.4	5.3	1.0
United Arab Emirates								0.2	2.6	3.9

	1987	1988	1989	1990	1991	1992	1993	1994	1995	1996
Afrique									0.0	
Amériques								0.9	0.5	
– Amérique du Nord								0.8	0.4	
– ALAI										
– MCAC										
– Caraïbes										
– Autre Amérique								0.1	0.1	
Asie anc. URSS exclus								9.2	11.5	
– Moyen–Orient								1.6	3.9	
Asie ancienne URSS								28.6	17.1	
Europe anc. URSS exclus								26.6	34.5	
– Union Européenne								16.6	17.8	
– Europe de l'Est								1.4	1.7	
– Autre de l'Europe								8.6	15.0	
Europe ancienne URSS								34.3	23.5	
Océanie										
Autre										
Russian Federation								26.7	19.5	11.6
Switzerland,Liechtenst.								8.6	15.0	8.4
United Kingdom								6.6	7.9	8.2
Tajikistan/Tadjikistan								12.3	5.5	3.5
Kazakhstan								11.0	8.1	1.6
Korea, Republic of								1.6	5.1	6.0
Netherlands/Pays–Bas								6.0	5.0	3.0
USA/Etats–Unis d'Amer								0.8	0.4	6.3
Ukraine								5.6	1.5	1.1
China/Chine								3.0	1.2	2.8

4. General Imports C.I.F. by Commodities according to the S.I.T.C. (Rev. 2) in million U.S. Dollars
Importations Générales C.A.F. par Produits d'après la C.T.C.I. (Rév. 2) en millions de Dollars E.U.

SITC CTCI	COMMODITY	1993 QUANTITY QUANTITE	1993 VALUE VALEUR	1994 QUANTITY QUANTITE	1994 VALUE VALEUR	1995 QUANTITY QUANTITE	1995 VALUE VALEUR	1996 QUANTITY QUANTITE	1996 VALUE VALEUR	PRODUIT
	ALL COMMODITIES				2609.5		2747.9			TOUS PRODUITS
0	FOOD AND LIVE ANIMALS				766.9					ALIMENTS,ANIMAUX VIVANTS
01	MEAT AND PREPARATIONS						53.1			VIANDES ET PREPARATIONS
02	DAIRY PRODCTS,BIRDS'EGGS						15.1			PRODUITS LAITIERS,OEUFS
04	CEREALS AND PREPARATIONS						245.0			CEREALES ET PRODUITS
06	SUGAR AND PREPS,HONEY						102.1			SUCRES ET PRODUITS
24	CORK AND WOOD						31.1			LIEGE ET BOIS
3	MINERAL FUELS ETC				651.9		38.1			COMBUSTIBLES MINERAUX LUB
5	CHEMCLS,RELATED PROD NES				125.6					PRODUITS CHIMIQUES
51	ORGANIC CHEMICALS						22.1			PROD CHIMIQ ORGANIQUES
52	INORGANIC CHEMICALS						41.1			PROD CHIM INORGANIQUES
541	*MEDICINAL,PHARM PRODUCT						57.1			PROD MEDICINAUX PHARMACEUT
562	*FERTILIZERS,MANUFACTURE						14.1			ENGRAIS MANUFACTURES
572	*EXPLOSIVES,PYROTECH PRO						30.1			EXPLOSIFS
6	BASIC MANUFACTURES				247.5					ART MANUFACTURES
62	RUBBER MANUFACTURES NES						34.1			CAOUTCHOUC MANUFACTURE
64	PAPER,PAPERBOARD AND MFR						12.1			PAPIERS,CARTONS & OUVRAGES
65	TEXTILE YARN,FABRICS,ETC						35.1			FILS,TISSUS,ARTICLES TEXTILE
66	NONMETAL MINERAL MFS NES						19.1			ART MIN NON METALLIQUES
67	IRON AND STEEL						76.1			FER ET ACIER
69	METAL MANUFACTURES NES						80.1			ART MANUFACT EN METAL NDA
7	MACHINES,TRANSPORT EQUIP				411.7		1235.0			MACHINES MATERIEL TRANSPORT
78	ROAD VEHICLES						191.0			VEHICULES ROUTIERS
792	AIRCRAFT ETC						16.1			APP NAVIGATION AERIENNE
8	MISC MANUFACTURED GOODS				19.2					ART MANUFACTURES DIVERS
821	*FURNITURE,PARTS THEREOF						60.1			MEUBLES ET PIECES
84	CLOTHING AND ACCESSORIES						19.1			VETEMENTS
851	*FOOTWEAR						12.1			CHAUSSURES

5. General Exports F.O.B. by Commodities according to the S.I.T.C. (Rev. 2) in million U.S. Dollars
Exportations Générales F.O.B. par Produits d'après la C.T.C.I. (Rév. 2) en millions de Dollars E.U.

SITC CTCI	COMMODITY	1993 QUANTITY QUANTITE	1993 VALUE VALEUR	1994 QUANTITY QUANTITE	1994 VALUE VALEUR	1995 QUANTITY QUANTITE	1995 VALUE VALEUR	1996 QUANTITY QUANTITE	1996 VALUE VALEUR	PRODUIT
	ALL COMMODITIES				2548.8		2821.3			TOUS PRODUITS
0	FOOD AND LIVE ANIMALS				50.9					ALIMENTS,ANIMAUX VIVANTS
263	COTTON						1890.0			COTON
3	MINERAL FUELS ETC				399.0		333.0			COMBUSTIBLES MINERAUX LUB
4	ANIMAL,VEGETABLE OIL,FAT				17.4					HUILES,GRAISSES ANIM,VEG
5	CHEMCLS,RELATED PROD NES				61.9					PRODUITS CHIMIQUES
51	ORGANIC CHEMICALS						9.1			PROD CHIMIQ ORGANIQUES
52	INORGANIC CHEMICALS						9.1			PROD CHIM INORGANIQUES
562	*FERTILIZERS,MANUFACTURE						56.1			ENGRAIS MANUFACTURES
6	BASIC MANUFACTURES				118.8					ART MANUFACTURES
66	NONMETAL MINERAL MFS NES						11.1			ART MIN NON METALLIQUES
67	IRON AND STEEL						21.1			FER ET ACIER
682	COPPER EXC CEMENT COPPER						120.0			CUIVRE
69	METAL MANUFACTURES NES						10.1			ART MANUFACT EN METAL NDA
7	MACHINES,TRANSPORT EQUIP				218.2		75.1			MACHINES MATERIEL TRANSPORT
792	AIRCRAFT ETC						27.1			APP NAVIGATION AERIENNE
84	CLOTHING AND ACCESSORIES						10.1			VETEMENTS

1. HISTORICAL SERIES, 1962–1997 SPECIAL TRADE, IMPORTS C.I.F., EXPORTS F.O.B. # 1
SERIES HISTORIQUES, 1962–1997 COMMERCE SPECIAL, IMPORTATIONS C.A.F., EXPORTATIONS F.O.B

YEAR ANNEE	VALUE IN MILLION VATU / VALEUR EN MILLION VATU: MERCHANDISE – MARCHANDISE		GOLD – OR		CONVERSION FACTORS U.S. CENTS PER VATU / FACTEURS DE CONVERSION CENTS E.U. PAR VATU		INDEX NUMBERS – INDICES: QUANTUM		UNIT VALUE / VALEUR UNITAIRE	
	IMPORTS	EXPORTS	IMPORTS	EXPORTS	IMPORTS	EXPORTS	IMPORTS	EXPORTS	IMPORTS	EXPORTS
1962	559.80	495.60			1.1140	1.1140				
1963	543.60	579.40			1.1140	1.1140				
1964	605.50	810.80			1.1140	1.1140				
1965	647.20	819.50			1.1140	1.1140				
1966	735.20	931.80			1.1140	1.1140				
1967	864.60	1063.00			1.1140	1.1140				
1968	908.10	1043.20			1.1140	1.1140				
1969	1057.20	1002.20			1.0730	1.0730				
1970	1310.70	1161.50			0.9902	0.9902				
1971	1814.20	1284.90			0.9902	0.9902				
1972	2372.50	1206.20			1.0905	1.0905				
1973	2489.80	1498.10			1.2391	1.2391				
1974	3857.40	2370.50			1.1462	1.1473				
1975	2622.10	789.70			1.2837	1.2828				
1976	2628.10	1291.80			1.1465	1.1305				
1977	4155.00	2914.00			1.2505	1.2505				
1978	4614.00	3082.00			1.3538	1.3538				
1979	5020.00	3240.00			1.4463	1.4463				
1980	4922.00	2449.00			1.4426	1.4445				
1981	5116.00	2832.00			1.1407	1.1450				
1982	5663.00	2201.00			1.0479	1.0464				
1983	6292.00	2940.00			1.0049	1.0027				
1984	6811.00	4395.00			1.0083	1.0117				
1985	7378.00	3263.00			0.9459	0.9430				
1986	6105.00	1841.00			0.9327	0.9337				
1987	7638.00	1943.00			0.9121	0.9141				
1988	7361.00	2066.00			0.9579	0.9582				
1989	8250.00	2560.00			0.8575	0.8469				
1990	11211.00	2202.00			0.8549	0.8538				
1991	9216.00	2035.00			0.8968	0.8954				
1992	9276.00	2677.00			0.8819	0.8835				
1993	9581.00	2758.00			0.8226	0.8224				
1994	10404.00	2911.00			0.8402	0.8632				
1995	10659.00	3173.00			0.8917	0.8908				
1996	10888.00	3368.00			0.8953	0.8968				
1997		4089.00				0.8642				

2. IMPORTS BY BROAD ECONOMIC CATEGORY AND EXPORTS BY INDUSTRIAL ORIGIN. (PERCENTAGE OF TOTAL VALUE)
IMPORTATIONS PAR CATEGORIES ECONOMIQUES ET EXPORTATIONS PAR BRANCHE D'ACTIVITE.(EN POURCENTAGE DE LA VALEUR TOTALE)

IMPORTS – IMPORTATIONS

	1990	1991	1992	1993	1994	1995	1996
TOTAL IMPORTS–IMPORTATIONS TOTALES				100.	100.		
1 FOOD BEV–ALIMENTATION BOISSONS				19.4	18.6		
11 PRIMARY–PRODUITS DE BASE				7.3	6.9		
111 FOR INDUSTRY–POUR L'INDUSTRIE				4.7	4.5		
112 FOR HOUSEHOLDS–POUR LES MENAGES				2.6	2.4		
12 PROCESSED–PRODUITS ELABORES				12.2	11.7		
121 FOR INDUSTRY–POUR L'INDUSTRIE				3.0	2.4		
122 FOR HOUSEHOLDS–POUR LES MENAGES				9.2	9.3		
2 IND SUPPLIES–APPROV INDUSTRIELS				20.5	21.3		
21 PRIMARY–PRODUITS DE BASE				0.7	0.7		
22 PROCESSED–PRODUITS ELABORES				19.9	20.7		
3 FUELS–COMBUSTIBLES				9.1	6.7		
31 PRIMARY–PRODUITS DE BASE				0.8	0.5		
32 PROCESSED–PRODUITS ELABORES				8.4	6.1		
321 MOTOR SPIRIT–ESSENCE				8.4	6.1		
322 OTHER–AUTRES				0.0	0.0		
4 MACHINERY–EQUIPEMENT				15.0	19.7		
41 CAPITAL EQUIPMENT–MACHINES				14.0	18.8		
42 PARTS–PIECES ACCESSOIRES				1.0	0.9		
5 TRANSPORT–TRANSPORT				13.0	11.0		
51 PASSENGER CARS–AUTOMOBILES							
52 OTHER–AUTRES				7.7	7.1		
521 INDUSTRIAL–INDUSTRIELS				7.6	7.0		
522 NON INDUSTRIAL–NON INDUSTRIEL				0.1	0.1		
53 PARTS–PIECES ACCESSOIRES				5.4	3.9		
6 CONSUM GOODS–BIENS CONSOMMATION				20.2	20.0		
61 DURABLE–DURABLES				4.6	5.1		
62 SEMI DURABLE–SEMI DURABLES				9.3	9.0		
63 NON DURABLE–NON DURABLES				6.3	6.0		
7 GOODS NES–BIENS NDA				2.6	2.6		

EXPORTS – EXPORTATIONS

	1990	1991	1992	1993	1994	1995	1996
TOTAL EXPORTS–EXPORTATIONS TOTALES	100.	100.		100.	100.		
1 AGRICULTURE	54.7	51.7		53.1	55.9		
2 MINING QUARRY–INDUS EXTRACTIVES							
3 MANUFACTURING–IND MANUFACTUR	45.3	48.3		46.9	44.1		
31 FOOD BEV TOBACCO–ALIM BOISS TAB	27.4	24.7		24.9	22.8		
32 TEXTILES–INDUSTRIES TEXTILES	1.8	8.5		0.1	0.1		
33 WOOD & PRODUCTS–BOIS & PRODUITS	5.7	5.6		8.0	12.7		
34 PAPER & PRODUCTS–PAPIER & PRODT	0.0			0.0	0.5		
35 CHEMICALS–INDUSTRIES CHIMIQUES	1.8	0.1		0.0	0.0		
36 NON METAL MIN–MIN NON METAL		0.0			0.0		
37 BASIC METAL–IND METAL BASE				0.7			
38 METAL MANUF–MANUF METAL	2.7	1.8		2.1	0.6		
39 OTH MANUF IND–AUTRES MANUF	5.9	7.7		11.1	7.4		

3. TRADE BY PRINCIPAL COUNTRIES OF ORIGIN AND DESTINATION (VALUE IN MILLION U.S. DOLLARS)
ECHANGES SELON LES PRINCIPAUX PAYS D'ORIGINE ET DE DESTINATION (VALEUR EN MILLIONS DE DOLLARS EU)

COUNTRIES–PAYS	SPECIAL IMPORTS C.I.F. IMPORTATIONS SPECIALES C.A.F				
	1992	1993	1994	1995	1996
World	81.1	73.5	83.3	92.6	94.1
Africa		0.0	0.0		
Americas		0.9	1.6		
– Northern America		0.8	1.4		
– LAIA		0.1	0.2		
– CACM					
– Caribbean		0.0			
– Rest of America					
Asia excl fmr USSR	12.4	14.7	20.9	14.6	10.5
– Middle East					
Asia former USSR					
Europe excl fmr USSR	6.4	6.3	8.0	5.0	5.9
– European Union	6.4	6.2	7.9	5.0	5.9
– Eastern Europe					
– Rest of Europe		0.1	0.1		
Europe former USSR					
Oceania	47.2	51.6	52.8	61.6	66.4
Other	13.3	0.0			
Australia/Australie	29.7	31.1	31.2	37.1	40.7
New Zealand	8.2	10.1	10.7	11.2	10.9
Japan/Japon	7.4	6.0	7.9	7.1	5.1
New Caledonia	5.1	4.8	5.1	7.5	7.9
France, Monaco	6.4	4.6	5.9	5.0	5.9
Fiji/Fidji	4.2	4.2	3.7	5.8	6.9
China, Hong Kong SAR	2.8	2.6	5.0	2.8	2.9
Singapore/Singapour	2.3	2.0	2.7	4.7	2.6
Areas n.e.s.	13.3	0.0			
Papua New Guinea		1.1	1.8		
China/Chine		1.1	1.0		
USA/Etats–Unis d'Amer		0.8	1.2		
Malaysia/Malaisie		0.1	1.6		
Korea, Republic of		0.8	0.8		
Thailand/Thaïlande		0.7	0.7		
United Kingdom		0.6	0.8		
Italy/Italie		0.4	0.7		
India/Inde		0.4	0.4		
Other Asia n.e.s.		0.5	0.3		
Indonesia/Indonésie		0.4	0.3		
Germany/Allemagne		0.3	0.2		
Solomon Islands		0.2	0.3		
Chile/Chili		0.1	0.2		
Netherlands/Pays–Bas		0.1	0.1		
Sweden/Suède		0.1	0.1		
Philippines		0.1	0.0		
Denmark/Danemark		0.1	0.0		
Canada		0.0	0.1		
Bangladesh			0.1		
Belgium–Luxembourg		0.1	0.0		
Wallis and Futuna Is		0.0	0.0		

COUNTRIES–PAYS	SPECIAL EXPORTS F.O.B. EXPORTATIONS SPECIALES F.O.B.				
	1992	1993	1994	1995	1996
Monde	22.4	17.6	20.7	28.6	30.2
Afrique		0.1	0.0		
Amériques		0.1	0.3		
– Amérique du Nord		0.0	0.0		
– ALAI					
– MCAC					
– Caraïbes			0.3		
– Autre Amérique		0.0			
Asie anc. URSS exclus	4.2	8.2	9.7		
– Moyen–Orient			0.0		
Asie ancienne URSS					
Europe anc. URSS exclus	8.3	5.6	6.8		
– Union Européenne	8.3	5.6	6.7		
– Europe de l'Est		0.0	0.0		
– Autre de l'Europe			0.0		
Europe ancienne URSS					
Océanie	2.9	3.7	3.8		
Autre	7.0		0.2		
Japan/Japon	3.3	5.1	4.9	5.5	3.9
European Union n.e.s.	8.3			8.6	
Bangladesh		1.7	3.2	2.3	7.5
Australia/Australie	1.8	1.9	1.6	2.4	0.9
Netherlands/Pays–Bas		3.2	4.2		
Areas n.e.s.	7.0		0.2		
New Caledonia	1.0	1.2	1.2	1.4	0.4
Korea, Republic of	0.9	0.7	0.7	0.7	1.5
United Kingdom		1.9	1.5		
Germany/Allemagne		0.1	0.9		
Other Asia n.e.s.		0.5	0.4		
Solomon Islands		0.3	0.5		
New Zealand	0.1	0.2	0.1	0.1	
France, Monaco		0.4	0.1		
Wallis and Futuna Is		0.1	0.2		
China, Hong Kong SAR		0.1	0.2		
Netherlands Antilles			0.3		
Fiji/Fidji		0.0	0.1		
Singapore/Singapour			0.1		
China/Chine			0.1		
Papua New Guinea		0.0	0.0		
USA/Etats–Unis d'Amer		0.0	0.0		
Canada		0.0	0.0		
Belgium–Luxembourg			0.0		
Philippines		0.0			
Malaysia/Malaisie		0.0	0.0		
Thailand/Thaïlande		0.0			
Italy/Italie		0.0			
India/Inde		0.0			

(VALUE AS PERCENTAGE OF WORLD TOTAL)(VALEURS EN POURCENTAGE DU TOTAL MONDIAL)

	1987	1988	1989	1990	1991	1992	1993	1994	1995	1996
Africa							0.0	0.0		
Americas							1.2	1.9		
– Northern America							1.1	1.7		
– LAIA							0.1	0.3		
– CACM										
– Caribbean							0.0			
– Rest of America										
Asia excl fmr USSR	16.7	17.1	11.6		15.6	15.3	19.9	25.1	15.8	11.2
– Middle East										
Asia former USSR										
Europe excl fmr USSR	8.0	4.9	5.4		7.5	7.9	8.6	9.6	5.5	6.2
– European Union	8.0	4.9	5.4		7.5	7.9	8.5	9.5	5.5	6.2
– Eastern Europe										
– Rest of Europe							0.1	0.1		
Europe former USSR										
Oceania	64.4	64.9	64.4		60.1	58.2	70.2	63.4	66.6	70.5
Other	10.9	13.1			16.8	16.4	0.0			
Australia/Australie	38.4	43.4	39.1	37.1	35.9	36.6	42.4	37.5	40.1	43.3
New Zealand	11.9	10.5	13.0	10.3	11.1	10.0	13.7	12.9	12.1	11.5
Japan/Japon	8.7	9.4	11.6	12.2	8.1	9.1	8.1	9.5	7.7	5.4
New Caledonia	5.4	4.1	3.0	2.7	5.0	6.3	6.5	6.1	8.1	8.3
France, Monaco	8.0	4.9	5.4	7.6	7.5	7.9	6.2	7.1	5.5	6.2
Fiji/Fidji	8.7	6.9	9.3	9.2	8.1	5.2	5.7	4.5	6.2	7.4
China, Hong Kong SAR	4.2	3.9			3.9	3.5	3.5	6.0	3.0	3.1
Singapore/Singapour	3.9	3.8			3.6	2.8	2.7	3.2	5.1	2.7
Areas n.e.s.	10.9	13.1			16.8	16.4	0.0			
Papua New Guinea							1.5	2.1		

	1987	1988	1989	1990	1991	1992	1993	1994	1995	1996
Afrique							0.3	0.1		
Amériques				0.0	0.0		0.3	1.6		
– Amérique du Nord				0.0	0.0		0.3	0.0		
– ALAI										
– MCAC										
– Caraïbes								1.6		
– Autre Amérique							0.1			
Asie anc. URSS exclus	29.6	17.1	18.7	23.3	29.8	18.9	46.7	46.6		
– Moyen–Orient								0.0		
Asie ancienne URSS										
Europe anc. URSS exclus	48.8	61.9	55.0	52.5	48.9	37.0	31.6	32.6		
– Union Européenne	48.8	61.9	55.0	52.5	48.9	37.0	31.6	32.5		
– Europe de l'Est							0.0	0.0		
– Autre de l'Europe								0.1		
Europe ancienne URSS										
Océanie	18.7	7.7	17.8	24.1	21.2	12.9	21.0	18.2		
Autre	3.0	13.3	8.6	0.1	0.2	31.2		1.0		
Japan/Japon	22.1	15.3	18.5	18.2	22.0	14.8	29.1	23.8	19.4	13.0
European Union n.e.s.	48.8					37.0			30.1	
Bangladesh							9.6	15.6	8.2	24.8
Australia/Australie	13.3	4.2	10.1	12.3	13.3	8.1	10.6	7.6	8.4	2.9
Netherlands/Pays–Bas		51.7	28.6	25.7	38.5		18.3	20.0		
Areas n.e.s.	3.0	13.3	8.6	0.1	0.2	31.2		1.0		
New Caledonia	5.2	3.5	7.7	7.7	5.2	4.4	6.7	5.6	4.8	1.4
Korea, Republic of	7.5			3.7	7.5	4.1	4.2	3.3	2.5	4.8
United Kingdom				0.9	1.0		11.0	7.3		
Germany/Allemagne					2.1		0.3	4.4		

4. Special Imports C.I.F. by Commodities according to the S.I.T.C. (Rev. 2) in million U.S. Dollars
Importations Spéciales C.A.F. par Produits d'après la C.T.C.I. (Rév. 2) en millions de Dollars E.U.

SITC CTCI	COMMODITY	1993		1994		1995		1996		PRODUIT
		QUANTITY QUANTITE	VALUE VALEUR	QUANTITY QUANTITE	VALUE VALEUR	QUANTITY QUANTITE	VALUE VALEUR	QUANTITY QUANTITE	VALUE VALEUR	
	ALL COMMODITIES		73.6		83.3		92.6		94.2	TOUS PRODUITS
0	FOOD AND LIVE ANIMALS		12.5		13.2		14.6		19.2	ALIMENTS,ANIMAUX VIVANTS
01	MEAT AND PREPARATIONS		1.2		1.2					VIANDES ET PREPARATIONS
011	MEAT FRESH,CHILLD,FROZEN	W 333	0.7	W 348	0.8					VIANDES FRAICHES,REF,CONGE
0114	POULTRY FRESH CHLLD,FRZN	W 316	0.6	W 329	0.7					VOLAILLES MORTES
012	MEAT DRIED,SALTED,SMOKED	W 56	0.3	W 29	0.2					VIANDE,ABATS SALES,SECHES
0121	PIG MEAT DRIED,SLTD,SMKD	W 56	0.3	W 29	0.2					LARD,JAMBONS
014	MEAT PREPD,PRSVD,NES ETC	W 141	0.3	W 203	0.4					CONSERVES DE VIANDES
0149	OTH PREPARD,PRESRVD MEAT	W 127	0.3							AUTRES PREP DE VIANDES
02	DAIRY PRODCTS,BIRDS'EGGS		0.9		1.2					PRODUITS LAITIERS,OEUFS
022	MILK AND CREAM	W 398	0.6	W 525	0.9					LAIT ET CREME
0223	MILK AND CREAM FRESH	W 283	0.3	W 369	0.4					LAIT,CREME FRAIS
0224	MILK,CREAM PRESERVED ETC	W 116	0.3	W 156	0.5					LAIT,CREME CONS,CONC
02242	MILK DRY,1.5% FAT OR LES	W 113	0.3							LAIT POUDRE INF 1.5%
03	FISH AND PREPARATIONS		0.8		0.9					POISSONS ET PREPARATIONS
037	FISH ETC PREPD,PRSVD NES	W 626	0.7	W 616	0.7					POIS,CRUST,MOL PREPARES
0371	FISH PREPARD,PRESRVD NES	W 624	0.7	W 610	0.7					CONSERVES DE POISSONS
04	CEREALS AND PREPARATIONS		5.3		5.4					CEREALES ET PRODUITS
042	RICE	W 7713	3.4	W 7937	3.6					RIZ
0421	RICE IN HUSK OR HUSKED	W 7713	3.4	W 7937	3.6					RIZ SANS AUTRE PREPARATION
04211	RICE IN THE HUSK	W 7713	3.4	W 7937	3.6					RIZ PADDY
046	WHEAT ETC MEAL OR FLOUR	W 2398	0.9	W 1661	0.6					SEMOULE FARINE,FROMENT
04601	FLOUR OF WHEAT OR MESLIN	W 2398	0.9	W 1658	0.6					FARINE DE FROMENT
048	CEREAL ETC PREPARATIONS	W 1367	1.1	W 2305	1.2					PREPTNS A BASE CEREALES
0481	PREPD BREAKFAST FOOD ETC	W 215	0.3	W 527	0.5					CEREALES TRAVAILLEES
04812	CEREAL ROASTED, PUFFED	W 212	0.3							PRODTS BASE CEREALES
0484	BAKERY PRODUCTS	W 207	0.5	W 205	0.4					PRODUITS DE BOULANGERIE
04841	BREAD,BISCUIT,COM WAFERS	W 207	0.5							PAINS,BISCUITS DE MER
05	VEGETABLES AND FRUIT		1.5		1.6					LEGUMES ET FRUITS
054	VEG ETC FRSH,SMPLY PRSVD	W 850	0.6	W 488	0.5					LEGUMES FRAIS,CONG,SECS
0545	OTHER FRESH VEGETABLES	W 555	0.3	W 260	0.3					AUTRES LEGUMES FRAIS,REF
056	VEGTBLES ETC PRSVD,PREPD	W 816	0.4	W 1290	0.6					CONSERVES DE LEGUMES
0564	FLOUR ETC OF FRUIT,VEGET	W 771	0.3	W 1243	0.5					FARINES,SEMOULES,FLOCONS
05643	POTATO FLOUR,MEAL,FLAKES	W 770	0.3							FLOCONS DE POMMES DE TERRE
057	FRUIT,NUTS,FRESH,DRIED	W 231	0.3	W 180	0.3					FRUITS FRAIS OU SECS
058	FRUIT PRESERVED,PREPARED	W 1107	0.4	W 685	0.4					CONSERVES DE FRUITS
06	SUGAR AND PREPS,HONEY		0.9		0.9					SUCRES ET PRODUITS
061	SUGAR AND HONEY	W 1375	0.7	W 1296	0.6					SUCRES ET MIEL
0611	RAW BEET AND CANE SUGAR	W 1371	0.7	W 1268	0.6					SUCRES BRUTS
062	SUGAR CANDY NON–CHOCLATE	W 80	0.3	W 84	0.3					SUCRERIES
07	COFFEE,TEA,COCOA,SPICES		0.6		0.6					CAFE,THE,CACAO,EPICES
073	CHOCOLATE AND PRODUCTS	W 83	0.4	W 69	0.4					CHOCOLAT
081	*FEEDING STUFF FOR ANIML	W 1347	0.6	W 1250	0.6					NOURRITURE POUR ANIMAUX
0819	FOOD WASTE AND FEED NES	W 1347	0.6	W 1250	0.6					DECHETS,ALIMENTS NDA
08199	FODDER NES,INCL SWEETNED	W 1347	0.6	W 1250	0.6					PREPARATIONS FOURRAGERES
09	MISC EDIBLE PRODUCTS		1.0		1.1					PREP ALIMENTAIRES DIVERSES
091	MARGARINE AND SHORTENING	W 160	0.3	W 187	0.4					MARGARINE ET GRAISSES
0914	MARGARINE,EDIBLE FAT NES	W 159	0.3	W 186	0.4					MARGARINES,SIMILI SAINDOUX
09141	MARGARINE	W 159	0.3							MARGARINE
098	EDIBLE PRODCTS,PREPS NES	W 492	0.7	W 442	0.8					PREP ALIMENTAIRES NDA
09809	MISC FOOD PREPRTIONS NES	W 224	0.4	W 201	0.4					PREP ALIMENTAIRES NDA
1	BEVERAGES AND TOBACCO		3.0		3.6		3.4		3.6	BOISSONS ET TABACS
11	BEVERAGES		2.2		2.8					BOISSONS
111	NON–ALCOHL BEVERAGES NES	W 633	0.5	W 657	0.7					BOISSONS NON ALCOOLIQUES
11102	FLAVORED WATERS NON–ALCO	W 540	0.4	W 553	0.6					LIMONADES,EAUX GAZEUSES
112	ALCOHOLIC BEVERAGES	W 1200	1.7	W 1499	2.1					BOISSONS ALCOOLIQUES
1121	WINE OF FRESH GRAPES ETC	W 317	0.8	W 669	1.0					VINS DE RAISINS FRAIS
11212	WINE OF FRESH GRAPES	W 315	0.8							VINS DE MOUTS DE RAISINS
1123	BEER,ALE,STOUT,PORTER	W 757	0.6	W 553	0.5					BIERES
1124	DISTILLED ALCOHOLIC BEVS	W 125	0.4	W 270	0.7					ALCOOLS,EAUX–DE–VIE
11249	OTH ALCOHOLC BEVS,CMPNDS	W 125	0.4							BOISSONS ALCOOLIQUES NDA
12	TOBACCO AND MANUFACTURES		0.9		0.9					TABACS BRUTS FABRIQUES
122	TOBACCO,MANUFACTURED		0.9	W 36	0.9					TABACS FABRIQUES
1221	CIGARS,CHEROOTS,ETC	W 19	0.7							CIGARES
2	CRUDE MATERLS,EXCL FUELS		0.8		0.6		1.0		1.3	MAT BRUTES NON COMESTIBLES
3	MINERAL FUELS ETC		6.9		5.7		7.8		8.8	COMBUSTIBLES MINERAUX LUB
33	PETROLEUM AND PRODUCTS		6.3		5.3					PETROLE ET DERIVES
334	PETROLEUM PRODUCTS,REFIN		6.2	W 20919	5.2					PRODUITS RAFFINES
341	*GAS,NATURAL AND MANUFCT	W 938	0.6	W 886	0.5					GAZ NATUREL,GAZ MANUFACT
3413	PETROLM GASES,LIQUEFIED	W 938	0.6	W 886	0.5					GAZ DE PETROLE LIQUEFIE
34139	OTH HYDROCARBON GAS LQFD	W 938	0.6	W 886	0.5					HYDROCARBURES GAZEUX NDA
4	ANIMAL,VEGETABLE OIL,FAT		0.4		0.4		0.4		0.6	HUILES,GRAISSES ANIM,VEG
42	FIXED VEGETABLE OIL,FAT		0.3		0.3					HUILES VEGETALES FIXES
5	CHEMCLS,RELATED PROD NES		4.5		5.1		6.4		6.5	PRODUITS CHIMIQUES
53	DYES,TANNING,COLOUR PROD		0.8		0.5					PROD TEINTURE,COLORANTS
533	PIGMENTS,PAINTS,ETC	W 418	0.8	W 165	0.5					PIGMENTS,PEINTURES,VERNIS
5334	VARNISHES,DISTEMPERS ETC	W 350	0.7	W 110	0.4					PEINTURES A L'EAU
53341	WATER–THINNED PAINTS	W 144	0.4	W 75	0.3					PEINTURES DILUEES
541	*MEDICINAL,PHARM PRODUCT		1.3		1.1					PROD MEDICINAUX PHARMACEUT
5417	MEDICAMENTS		1.2	W 55	1.0					MEDICAMENTS
54171	— CONTAINNG ANTIBIOTICS		1.2	W 55	1.0					MED CONTN ANTIBIOTIQUES
55	PERFUME,CLEANING ETC PRD		1.3		2.0					PROD POUR PARFUM,TOILETTE
553	PERFUMERY,COSMETICS,ETC	W 82	0.7	W 956	1.4					PRODUITS DE PARFUMERIE
554	SOAP,CLEANSING ETC PREPS	W 623	0.6	W 627	0.6					SAVONS,PRODUITS DETERSIFS
5541	SOAPS	W 349	0.3	W 401	0.3					SAVONS,PROD TENSIO–ACTIFS
5542	WASHING PREPARATIONS ETC	W 268	0.4	W 216	0.3					PROD ORG TENSIO–ACT NDA
58	PLASTIC MATERIALS ETC		0.2		0.3					MAT PLAST ARTIFICIELLES
59	CHEMICAL MATERIALS NES		0.7		0.9					MAT PROD CHIMIQUES NDA
591	PESTICIDES,DISINFECTANTS	W 169	0.4	W 286	0.6					DESINF,INSECT,FONG,HERB
5911	INSECTICIDES,FOR RETAIL	W 169	0.4							INSECTICIDES VENTE DET
6	BASIC MANUFACTURES		13.2		16.4		18.9		16.0	ART MANUFACTURES
62	RUBBER MANUFACTURES NES		1.2		1.2					CAOUTCHOUC MANUFACTURE
621	MATERIALS OF RUBBER	W 42	0.4	W 62	0.4					PRODUITS EN CAOUTCHOUC
62104	UNHARD VULC RUBBER,BASIC	W 37	0.3							PLAQUES,FEUILLES CAOUT
625	RUBBER TYRES, TUBES ETC	W 177	0.8	W 192	0.7					PNEUS CAOUTCHOUC VULCANISE
6251	TYRES NEW FOR MOTOR CARS	W 158	0.7	W 181	0.7					PNEUS POUR VOITURES
63	WOOD,CORK MANUFACTRS NES		0.9		1.5					OUVRAGES LIEGE ET BOIS
634	VENEERS,PLYWOOD,ETC		0.3		0.9					PLACAGES,CONTRE–PLAQUES
6349	WOOD SIMPLY SHAPED NES				0.5					BOIS SIMPL TRAVAILLES NDA
63491	HOOPWOOD,SPLIT POLES ETC			V 17444	0.5					BOIS ETC
635	WOOD MANUFACTURES NES	W 214	0.7		0.6					ART MANUF EN BOIS NDA

4. Special Imports C.I.F. by Commodities according to the S.I.T.C. (Rev. 2) in million U.S. Dollars
Importations Spéciales C.A.F. par Produits d'après la C.T.C.I. (Rév. 2) en millions de Dollars E.U.

SITC CTCI	COMMODITY	1993 QUANTITY QUANTITE	1993 VALUE VALEUR	1994 QUANTITY QUANTITE	1994 VALUE VALEUR	1995 QUANTITY QUANTITE	1995 VALUE VALEUR	1996 QUANTITY QUANTITE	1996 VALUE VALEUR	PRODUIT
6353	BUILDERS WOODWRK,PREFABS	W 34	0.5		0.4					OUVRAGES DE MENUISERIE
64	PAPER,PAPERBOARD AND MFR		1.6		1.7					PAPIERS,CARTONS & OUVRAGES
641	PAPER AND PAPERBOARD	W 432	0.8		0.8					PAPIERS ET CARTONS
6412	PRINTG,WRITING PAPER NES	W 210	0.4	W 136	0.3					PAPIERS POUR L'IMPRESSION
64121	— UNCOATED	W 208	0.4	W 136	0.3					PAPIERS IMPRES NON COUCHES
642	PAPER,ETC,PRECUT,ARTS OF	W 353	0.9	W 319	1.0					PAP,CARTONS DECOUPES
6423	EXERCISE BOOKS ETC	W 93	0.4	W 81	0.4					REGISTRES,CAHIERS,CARNETS
6424	PAPER ETC CT TO SIZE NES	W 174	0.3	W 147	0.3					PAP,CARTONS DECOUPES
65	TEXTILE YARN,FABRICS,ETC		1.8		1.7					FILS,TISSUS,ARTICLES TEXTILE
652	COTTON FABRICS,WOVEN	W 79	0.6	W 58	0.3					TISSUS DE COTON
6521	GREY WOVEN COTTON FABRIC	W 68	0.5	W 48	0.3					TISSUS COT ECRUS NON MERCER
65215	GREY WOVN COTN BLEND NES	W 51	0.4	W 39	0.2					AUT TIS MOINS 85% COT ECRUS
653	WOVN MAN-MADE FIB FABRIC	W 70	0.3	W 133	0.4					TISSUS FIBRES SYNTH,ARTIF
658	TEXTILE ARTICLES NES	W 90	0.6		0.8					ART FACONNES MAT TEXTILES
6589	OTH TEXTILE ARTICLES NES	W 79	0.5		0.6					AUT ART EN TEXTILES NDA
65898	KNITTED ETC ARTICLES NES	W 78	0.5	W 111	0.6					ART BONNET NON ELASTIQUE
66	NONMETAL MINERAL MFS NES		2.3		2.6					ART MIN NON METALLIQUES
661	LIME,CEMENT,BLDG PRODS	W 11055	1.4	W 17250	1.6					CHAUX,CIMENTS MAT CONSTR
6612	CEMENT	W 10918	1.2	W 17157	1.5					CIMENTS HYDRAULIQUES
662	CLAY,REFRACTORY BLDG PRD	W 450	0.4	W 663	0.5					MAT CONST REFRACTAIRES
6624	BRICKS ETC NONREFRACTORY	W 418	0.4	W 585	0.4					BRIQUES ETC CERAM NON REFR
66245	GLAZED CERAMIC SETTS ETC	W 341	0.3	W 415	0.3					AUT CARREAUX CERAMIQUE
67	IRON AND STEEL		1.9		3.8					FER ET ACIER
673	IRON,STEEL SHAPES ETC	W 999	0.7	W 2397	0.8					BARRES,PROFIL FER,ACIER
6731	IRON,STEEL WIRE ROD	W 183	0.1	W 519	0.3					FIL MACHINE FER,ACIER
6732	IRON,STEEL BARS ETC	W 665	0.5	W 1606	0.4					BARRES FER,ACIER
674	IRN,STL UNIV,PLATE,SHEET	W 744	0.6	W 354	0.4					LARGES PLATS,TOLES
6745	IRN,STL MED PLATE,ROLLED	W 534	0.5	W 282	0.3					TOLES 3 A 4.75 MM
67454	— OF OTHER ALLOY STEEL	W 532	0.5	W 282	0.3					TOLES NON ACIERS ALLIES
678	IRON,STL TUBES,PIPES,ETC	W 415	0.2	W 3001	2.6					TUBES,TUYAUX EN FONTE,FER
6781	CAST IRON TUBES,PIPES	W 247	0.1	W 2853	2.4					TUBES,TUYAUX EN FONTE
68	NON-FERROUS METALS		0.4		0.4					METAUX NON FERREUX
69	METAL MANUFACTURES NES		3.5		4.0					ART MANUFACT EN METAL NDA
691	STRUCTURES AND PARTS NES	W 800	1.0	W 438	0.8					CONSTRUCT FER,ACIER,ALU
6911	STRUCTURES,PARTS IRN,STL	W 764	0.8	W 400	0.7					CONSTRUCT FER,ACIER,FONTE
692	METAL TANKS,BOXES,ETC	W 242	0.4	W 379	0.5					RECIPIENTS METALLIQUES
6924	MTL TRANSPORT BOXES ETC	W 227	0.4	W 310	0.4					FUTS,TAMBOURS,BIDONS
693	WIRE PRODUCTS NON ELECTR	W 308	0.4	W 334	0.6					OUVRAGES FILS METALLIQUES
6935	METAL FENCING,GAUZE,ETC	W 237	0.3	W 204	0.3					TOILES EN FER,ACIER,CUIVRE
69351	IRN,STL FENCNG,GAUZE ETC	W 234	0.3	W 204	0.3					TOILES EN FER,ACIER
694	STL,COPPR NAILS,NUTS,ETC	W 162	0.4	W 185	0.4					CLOUS,VIS,ECROUS
69402	IRN,STL NUTS,BOLTS,ETC	W 53	0.2	W 67	0.3					BOULONS,VIS,ECROUS FER,AC
695	TOOLS	W 60	0.5	W 65	0.5					OUTILS A MAIN
6953	OTHER HAND TOOLS	W 33	0.3	W 33	0.3					AUTRES OUTILS A MAIN
697	BASE MTL HOUSEHOLD EQUIP	W 90	0.4	W 115	0.5					ART MENAGE MET COMMUNS
699	BASE METAL MFRS NES		0.5	W 207	0.7					ART MANUFACTURES MET NDA
7	MACHINES,TRANSPORT EQUIP		22.0		26.5		27.3		22.1	MACHINES MATERIEL TRANSPORT
71	POWER GENERATING EQUIPMT		1.1		1.2					MACHINES GENERATRICES
713	INTRNL COMBUS PSTN ENGIN		0.5		0.4					MOTEURS EXPL COMB INT, PIECE
7131	AIRCRAFT PSTN ENGINS,PTS		0.4		0.3					MOTEURS EXPL P.AVIATION, PIE
716	ROTATING ELECTRIC PLANT		0.5		0.6					APP ELECTR ROTATIFS,PIECES
7162	AC MTRS,GENRTRS,GEN SETS		0.3		0.4					MOTEURS ELECTRIQUES
7169	PTS NES OF ROT ELEC PLNT		0.3		0.3					PIECES MAC APP ROTATIFS
72	MACHS FOR SPCL INDUSTRYS		2.3		5.3					MAC SPECIALES POUR INDUST
721	AGRIC MACHY,EXC TRACTORS		0.4		0.4					MACHINES AGRICOLES
722	TRACTORS NON-ROAD		0.1		1.0					TRACTEURS
7224	WHEELED TRACTORS NES		0.1		1.0					TRACTEURS A ROUES
723	CIVIL ENGNEERG EQUIP ETC		1.4		3.2					APPAREILS DE GENIE CIVIL
7234	CONST,MINING MACHNRY NES		1.4		3.2					MACH POUR LA CONST, MINES
72341	SELF-PROPELLD DOZERS,ETC		1.1		2.9					BULLDOZERS
72345	PILE DRIVERS,ETC		0.2		0.3					CHASSE-NEIGE
727	FOOD MACHRY NON-DOMESTIC		0.1		0.3					MACH INDUSTRIES ALIMENT
7272	OTH FOOD PROC MCHY,PARTS		0.1		0.3					AUT MACH IND ALIMENTAIRE
72722	INDUS FOOD PROC MACH NES		0.1		0.3					MACHINES BOULANGERIE
74	GENRL INDUSTRL MACHY NES		2.2		2.9					MACH APP INDUSTRIE
741	HEATING,COOLING EQUIPMNT		0.5		0.3					MACH CHAUFFAGE,PIECES
7415	AIR-CONDITIONING MACHNRY		0.4		0.1					GROUPES CONDITION AIR
742	PUMPS FOR LIQUIDS ETC		0.4		0.8					POMPES MOTO-POMPES
7428	OTHER PUMPS FOR LIQUIDS		0.4		0.8					AUTRES POMPES POUR LIQ
74281	GARAGE-TYPE FUEL PUMPS		0.4							POMPES DISTRIB CARBURNTS
743	PUMPS NES,CENTRFUGES ETC		0.3		0.4					POMPES COMPRES,VENT ETC
7431	PUMPS FOR GASES ETC		0.2		0.3					POMPES AIR A VIDE,COMPRES
744	MECHANICAL HANDLING EQU		0.6		0.8					EQUIP MANUTENTION PIECES
7449	PTS NES OF MACHY OF 7442		0.4		0.5					PIECES DU 744.2
745	NONELEC MACHY,TOOLS NES		0.3		0.4					AUT MACH NON ELEC,PIECES
749	NONELEC MACH PTS,ACC NES		0.3		0.4					PIECES MACH NON ELEC NDA
75	OFFICE MACHNES,ADP EQUIP		1.5		1.5					MACH BUREAU TRAIT AUTOM
751	OFFICE MACHINES		0.4		0.4					MACH,APPAREILS DE BUREAU
7518	OFFICE MACHINES NES		0.3		0.3					MACH,APP DE BUREAU NDA
75182	PHOTO,THERMOCOPY APPARAT		0.3		0.3					APPAREILS DE PHOTOCOPIE
752	AUTOMTIC DATA PROC EQUIP		1.0		0.9					MACH TRAIT INFORMATION
7521	ANALOG,HYBRID COMPUTERS		1.0		0.9					MACH POUR TRAIT INFORMAT
76	TELECOMM,SOUND EQUIPMENT		2.9		4.7					EQUIPMENT DE TELECOM
762	RADIO BROADCAST RECEIVRS		0.9		1.3					RECEPTEURS RADIODIFFUSION
7622	PORTABLE RADIO RECEIVERS		0.9		1.3					RECEPT PORTATIFS RADIO
764	TELECOM EQPT,PTS,ACC NES		1.7		3.0					EQUIP TELECOM,PIECES
7641	LINE TELEPHONE,ETC EQUIP		0.5		2.0					APP TELEPHON PAR FIL
7643	TV,RADIO TRANSMITTRS ETC		0.7		0.4					APP EMET TELE RADIO
7649	PTS NES OF EQUIPMT OF 76		0.5		0.5					PIECES DE LA DIV 76
76493	TELECOMM EQUIPMT PTS NES		0.5		0.5					PIECES 761,762,764.3,8
77	ELECTRIC MACHNRY NES ETC		3.9		3.8					MACH APP ELECT NDA
772	SWITCHGEAR ETC,PARTS NES		0.8		0.8					APP COUPURE,SECT ETC
7721	SWITCHGEAR ETC		0.8		0.8					APP COUPURE,SECTIONMNT
773	ELECTR DISTRIBUTNG EQUIP		0.6		0.6					EQUIPMT DISTRIBUTION ELECT
7731	INSULATED WIRE,CABLE ETC		0.6		0.6					FILS,CABLES ISOLES ELECT
774	ELECTRO-MEDCL,XRAY EQUIP		0.6		0.3					APPAREILS MEDICAUX
7741	ELECTRO-MEDICAL EQUIPMNT		0.5		0.3					APP ELECTRICITE MEDICALE
775	HOUSEHOLD TYPE EQUIP NES		1.0		0.9					MACH,APP USAGE DOMESTQUE
7752	DOM REFRIGERATRS,FREEZRS		0.7		0.5					REFRIG,CONGEL MENAGER
77521	DOMESTIC REFRIGERATORS		0.7		0.5					REFRIGERATEURS
778	ELECTRICAL MACHINERY NES		1.0		1.2					AUTRES MACH ELECT NDA

4. Special Imports C.I.F. by Commodities according to the S.I.T.C. (Rev. 2) in million U.S. Dollars
Importations Spéciales C.A.F. par Produits d'après la C.T.C.I. (Rév. 2) en millions de Dollars E.U.

SITC CTCI	COMMODITY	1993		1994		1995		1996		PRODUIT
		QUANTITY QUANTITE	VALUE VALEUR	QUANTITY QUANTITE	VALUE VALEUR	QUANTITY QUANTITE	VALUE VALEUR	QUANTITY QUANTITE	VALUE VALEUR	
7781	BATTERIES,ACCUMULATORS		0.6		0.6					PILES ET ACCUMULATEURS
77811	PRIMARY BATTERIES,CELLS		0.4							PILES ELECTRIQUES,PIECES
78	ROAD VEHICLES		5.7		5.9					VEHICULES ROUTIERS
782	LORRIES,SPCL MTR VEH NES		4.4		4.6					VEHICULES SPECIAUX,MARCH
7821	LORRIES,TRUCKS		4.3		4.3					VEHICULES TRANSP MARCHAND
7822	SPECIAL MOTOR VEHCLS NES		0.2		0.4					VEHICULES USAGES SPECIAUX
783	ROAD MOTOR VEHICLES NES		0.4		0.4					VEHICULES ROUTIERS NDA
7831	BUSES		0.4		0.4					VOITURES TRANSPORT COMMUN
784	MOTOR VEH PRTS,ACCES NES		0.8		0.9					PIECES 722,781,782,783
7849	OTHER MOTOR VEHCL PARTS		0.8		0.9					PIECES 722,781,782,783
79	OTHR TRANSPORT EQUIPMENT		2.4		1.4					AUTRE MATERIEL TRANSPORT
792	AIRCRAFT ETC		1.7		0.6					APP NAVIGATION AERIENNE
7929	AIRCRAFT PARTS NES		1.6		0.5					PIECES DU 792
793	SHIPS AND BOATS ETC		0.7		0.8					NAVIRES BATEAUX,ETC
7932	SHIPS AND BOATS NES		0.7		0.7					NAVIRES ET BATEAUX
79321	YACHTS,SPORTS VESSLS ETC		0.3		0.3					BATEAUX DE PLAISANCE
79322	TANKERS OF ALL KINDS				0.5					BATEAUX–CITERNES
79323	OTHER CARGO VESSELS		0.4							AUT BATEAUX TRANS MARCH
8	MISC MANUFACTURED GOODS		8.9		10.1		11.2		14.3	ART MANUFACTURES DIVERS
812	*PLUMBG,HEATNG,LGHTNG EQ		0.4		0.4					APPAR SANITAIRES CHAUFFAGE
8124	LIGHTING EQUIPMENT NES		0.3		0.3					APPAREILS ECLAIRAGE ETC
821	*FURNITURE,PARTS THEREOF		0.7		0.8					MEUBLES ET PIECES
8212	MED FURN,STUFFD FURNSHGS		0.2		0.3					MOB MEDICO–CHIRUR,PIECES
82122	MATTRESSES ETC		0.2		0.3					SOMMIERS,ARTICLES DE LITERIE
8219	FURNITURE AND PARTS NES		0.5		0.4					AUTRES MEUBLES ET PIECES
82191	METAL FURNITURE NES		0.5		0.4					MEUBLES NDA EN METAL
831	*TRAVEL GOODS,HANDBAGS	W 36	0.3	W 29	0.3					ARTICLES DE VOYAGE ETC
83102	TRAVEL GDS,TOILET–CASES	W 36	0.3	W 29	0.3					ARTICLES DE VOYAGE
84	CLOTHING AND ACCESSORIES		1.7		1.5					VETEMENTS
842	MENS OUTERWEAR NOT KNIT	W 41	0.4	W 38	0.3					VET DESSUS POUR HOMMES
8422	— SUITS	W 37	0.4	W 36	0.3					COMPLETS HOMMES MAT TEXT
84221	—— OF WOOL,FINE HAIR	W 37	0.4							COMPLETS HOMMES LAINE
845	OUTERWEAR KNIT NONELASTC	W 35	0.4	W 38	0.3					VET DESSOUS,ACCES BONNET
846	UNDER GARMENTS KNITTED	W 68	0.6	W 53	0.5					SOUS VETS DE BONNETERIE
8462	— OF COTTON NON ELASTIC	W 55	0.5	W 49	0.5					SOUS–VET BONNET COTON
84629	—— OTHER	W 55	0.5	W 40	0.4					AUT SOUS–VET BONNET COTON
851	*FOOTWEAR	W 78	0.4	W 60	0.4					CHAUSSURES
87	PRECISION INSTRUMNTS NES		0.6		0.8					INSTRUM,APPAR SCIENT NDA
874	MEASURNG,CONTROLNG INSTR		0.5		0.7					INSTRUMENTS DE MESURE
8741	SURVEYING INSTRUMENTS		0.2		0.4					INST GEODESIE,TOPO ETC
88	PHOTO EQU,OPTICL GDS ETC		0.6		1.0					APP,FOURN PHOTO,OP,MONTR
882	PHOTO,CINEMA SUPPLIES	W 20	0.3	W 14	0.2					PRODUITS PHOTO,CINEMA
885	WATCHES AND CLOCKS		0.2		0.5					HORLOGERIE
8851	WATCHES,MOVEMENTS,CASES		0.2		0.5					MONTRES,MOUVEMENTS,BOITES
88511	WATCHES		0.2		0.5					MONTRES POCHE,BRACELET
89	MISC MANUFCTRD GOODS NES		4.5		5.3					ART MANUFACTURES DIVERS
892	PRINTED MATTER		1.0	W 736	1.0					IMPRIMES
8921	PRINTED BOOKS,GLOBES,ETC	W 72	0.6	W 669	0.7					LIVRES,BROCHURES,CARTES
89211	PRINTED BOOKS,PAMPHLETS	W 64	0.5							LIVRES,BROCHURES
893	ARTICLES OF PLASTIC NES	W 509	1.3	W 515	1.6					OUVRAGES EN MAT DIVIS 58
8931	PLSTC PACKG CONTNRS,LIDS	W 170	0.4	W 180	0.6					ART TRANSP EMBALLAGE ETC
8939	MISC PLASTIC ARTICLES	W 324	0.9	W 326	1.0					ART DIVERS EN MAT DIV 58
89399	OTHR PLASTC ARTICLES NES	W 226	0.6	W 228	0.8					AUT OUV MAT DIV 58
894	TOYS,SPORTING GOODS,ETC		1.0		1.1					VOITURES ENFANTS,JOUETS
8942	TOYS,INDOOR GAMES ETC		0.6		0.6					JOUETS,JEUX ETC
89423	TOYS NES		0.4							JOUETS,MODELES REDUITS
89424	INDOOR GAME EQUIPMENT		0.3		0.4					ART,JEUX DE SOCIETE
8947	OTH SPORT GDS,FAIR AMUSM		0.4		0.5					AUT ART DE SPORT
89471	FISHNG,HUNTNG EQUIP NES		0.1		0.5					HAMECONS ET EPUISETTES
89472	OTH OUTDOOR SPORT GOODS		0.3							ART POUR JEUX PLEIN AIR
895	OFFICE SUPPLIES NES		0.4		0.4					ART PAPET NDA
897	GOLD,SILVER WARE,JEWELRY		0.2	W 51	0.3					BIJOUTERIE,ORFEVRERIE
898	MUSICAL INSTRUMENTS,PTS		0.6		0.7					INSTRUMENTS DE MUSIQUE
8983	SOUND RECRDNG TAPE,DISCS		0.4		0.6					SUPPORTS SON POUR 763
89832	RECORDED DISCS,TAPES ETC		0.3		0.5					DISQUES,PHONO,BANDES
899	OTHER MANUFACTURED GOODS		0.3		0.4					AUT ART MANUF DIVERS NDA
9	GOODS NOT CLASSD BY KIND		1.9		2.2		2.0		2.3	ART TRANSACT NON CLASSES
931	*SPECIAL TRANSACTIONS		1.9		2.1					TRANS.SPECIALES

5. Special Exports F.O.B. by Commodities according to the S.I.T.C. (Rev. 2) in million U.S. Dollars
Exportations Spéciales F.O.B. par Produits d'après la C.T.C.I. (Rév. 2) en millions de Dollars E.U.

SITC CTCI	COMMODITY	1993 QUANTITY QUANTITE	1993 VALUE VALEUR	1994 QUANTITY QUANTITE	1994 VALUE VALEUR	1995 QUANTITY QUANTITE	1995 VALUE VALEUR	1996 QUANTITY QUANTITE	1996 VALUE VALEUR	PRODUIT
	ALL COMMODITIES		17.7		20.8		28.7		30.2	TOUS PRODUITS
0	FOOD AND LIVE ANIMALS		6.7		7.9					ALIMENTS,ANIMAUX VIVANTS
01	MEAT AND PREPARATIONS		3.9		4.0					VIANDES ET PREPARATIONS
011	MEAT FRESH,CHILLD,FROZEN	W 1634	3.9	W 1628	3.9					VIANDES FRAICHES,REF,CONGE
0111	BOVINE MEAT FRESH,FROZEN	W 1620	3.9	W 1599	3.9		3.9	W 1247	3.9	VIANDES BOVIN FRAI,REF
01111	BOVINE MEAT WITH BONE IN	W 209	0.6	W 443	1.2					VIANDES BOVIN NON DESOSS
01112	BOVINE MEAT BONELESS	W 1411	3.4	W 1156	2.8					VIANDES BOVIN DESOSSEES
02	DAIRY PRODCTS,BIRDS'EGGS		0.1		0.1					PRODUITS LAITIERS,OEUFS
024	CHEESE AND CURD	W 1	0.1	W 16	0.1					FROMAGE ET CAILLEBOTTE
03	FISH AND PREPARATIONS		0.2		0.3					POISSONS ET PREPARATIONS
036	SHELL FISH FRESH,FROZEN	W 25	0.2	W 61	0.3					CRUSTACES,MOLLUSQUES
05	VEGETABLES AND FRUIT		1.3		1.5					LEGUMES ET FRUITS
054	VEG ETC FRSH,SMPLY PRSVD	W 1503	1.3	W 2177	1.5					LEGUMES FRAIS,CONG,SECS
0545	OTHER FRESH VEGETABLES	W 1456	1.1	W 2088	1.0					AUTRES LEGUMES FRAIS,REF
05459	FRESH VEGETABLES NES	W 1456	1.1	W 2088	1.0					LEGUMES FRAIS,REFRI NDA
0548	EDIBLE VEG NES FRESH,DRY	W 47	0.2	W 89	0.5					RACINES,TUBERCULES
05482	SUGAR BEET FRSH DRY,CANE	W 44	0.2							BETTERAVES,CANNES A SUCRE
05488	VEG PRODTS NES FRESH,DRY			W 89	0.5					PROD VEGET ALIM HUMAINE
07	COFFEE,TEA,COCOA,SPICES		1.3		2.2					CAFE,THE,CACAO,EPICES
072	COCOA	W 1401	1.3	W 1706	2.0		1.2	W 1584	1.5	CACAO
0721	COCOA BEANS,RAW,ROASTED	W 1401	1.3	W 1686	2.0			W 1584	1.5	CACAO EN FEVES
075	SPICES	W 1	0.1	W 100	0.2					EPICES
0751	PEPPER AND PIMENTO	W 1	0.1	W 100	0.2					POIVRE,PIMENTS
09	MISC EDIBLE PRODUCTS		0.1		0.1					PREP ALIMENTAIRES DIVERSES
098	EDIBLE PRODCTS,PREPS NES	W 27	0.1	W 20	0.1					PREP ALIMENTAIRES NDA
09809	MISC FOOD PREPRTIONS NES	W 27	0.1	W 20	0.1					PREP ALIMENTAIRES NDA
2	CRUDE MATERLS,EXCL FUELS		8.1		10.2					MAT BRUTES NON COMESTIBLES
21	HIDES,SKINS,FURS UNDRSSD		0.3		0.4					CUIRS,PEAUX BRUTS
211	HIDES,SKINS,EXC FURS,RAW	W 356	0.3	W 387	0.4					CUIRS ET PEAUX
2111	BOVINE,EQUINE HIDES,RAW						0.6	W 73	0.5	PEAUX DE BOVINS
2112	CALF AND KIP SKINS,RAW	W 356	0.3	W 387	0.4					PEAUX DE VEAUX
22	OIL SEEDS,OLEAGINOUS FRT		5.9		7.7					GRAINES,FRUITS OLEAGINEUX
223	SEEDS FOR OTH FIXED OILS	W 28140	5.9	W 26441	7.7			W 30026	11.2	GRAINES AUTRES HUILES FIXES
2231	COPRA	W 28140	5.9	W 26441	7.7		10.0	W 30026	11.2	COPRAH
24	CORK AND WOOD		1.8		1.9					LIEGE ET BOIS
245	FUEL WOOD NES, CHARCOAL	W 543	0.3							BOIS DE CHAUFFAGE
24502	WOOD CHARCOAL	W 543	0.3							CHARBON DE BOIS
246	PULPWOOD,CHIPS,WOODWASTE			W 999	0.5					BOIS DE TRITURATION
24602	PULPWOOD CHIPS,PARTICLES			W 999	0.5					EN FORME DE PLAQUETTES
247	OTH WOOD ROUGH,SQUARED	W 4126	0.7	W 237	0.1					BOIS BRUTS EQUARRIS
2471	SAW–,VENEER–LOGS CONIFER	W 4126	0.7	W 237	0.1			W 337	3.2	CONIFERES POUR SCIAGE,PLACAG
24711	— IN THE ROUGH	W 4126	0.7	W 237	0.1			W 337	3.2	ECORCES OU DEGROSSIS
248	WOOD SHAPED,SLEEPERS	W 1205	1.0	W 2295	1.3		2.3			BOIS SIMPLEMENT TRAVAILLES
2482	LUMBER SHAPED CONIFER	W 356	0.2	W 2227	1.2					CONIFERES SCIES,RABOTES
24821	LUMBER SAWN ETC CONIFER	W 356	0.2	W 2206	1.1					CONIFERES SCIES LONGITUD
24822	LUMBER PLANED ETC CONIFR			W 21	0.1					CONIFER RABOTES,RAINES
2483	LUMBER SHAPED NON–CONIFR	W 849	0.8	W 68	0.2					NON CONIFERES SCIES,RABOTES
24831	LUMBER SAWN ETC NON–CON	W 738	0.6							SCIES LONGITUDINALEMENT
24832	LUMBER PLANED ETC NONCON	W 111	0.3	W 68	0.2					RABOTES,RAINES,LANGUETES
29	CRUDE ANIMAL,VEG MAT NES		0.2		0.3					MATIERES BRUTES ANIM,VEGET
291	CRUDE ANIMAL MTRIALS NES	W 200	0.2	W 114	0.3					MATIERES BRUTES ANIMALES
2911	BONES,IVORY,HORNS,ETC	W 19	0.2	W 54	0.2			W 7259	0.9	OS,CORNES,SABOTS
29115	CORAL, SHELLS, AND WASTE	W 19	0.2	W 54	0.2		1.0	W 7259	0.9	CORAIL & SIMILAIRES
2919	OTH ANIMAL MATERIALS NES	W 180	0.1	W 60	0.1					MAT ORIGINE ANIMALE NDA
29199	ANIMAL PRODUCTS,NES	W 180	0.1	W 60	0.1					PROD ORIGINE ANIMALE NDA
2924	VEG USED IN PHARMACY ETC						0.5	W 64	0.7	PLANTES MEDICINALES
6	BASIC MANUFACTURES		0.7		1.0					ART MANUFACTURES
63	WOOD,CORK MANUFACTRS NES		0.5		0.9					OUVRAGES LIEGE ET BOIS
634	VENEERS,PLYWOOD,ETC	W 937	0.5	W 2084	0.7					PLACAGES,CONTRE–PLAQUES
6341	VENEER SHEETS ETC	W 354	0.2	W 57	0.1					BOIS SIMPLEMENT SCIES
6342	PLYWOOD OF WOOD SHEETS	W 221	0.2	W 163	0.2					BOIS CONTRE–PLAQUES
6349	WOOD SIMPLY SHAPED NES	W 293	0.2	W 1864	0.5					BOIS SIMPL TRAVAILLES NDA
63491	HOOPWOOD,SPLIT POLES ETC	W 293	0.2	W 1864	0.5					BOIS ETC
635	WOOD MANUFACTURES NES	W 14	0.1	W 74	0.3					ART MANUF EN BOIS NDA
6353	BUILDERS WOODWRK,PREFABS	W 10	0.1	W 52	0.3					OUVRAGES DE MENUISERIE
64	PAPER,PAPERBOARD AND MFR				0.2					PAPIERS,CARTONS & OUVRAGES
642	PAPER,ETC,PRECUT,ARTS OF			W 191	0.2					PAP,CARTONS DECOUPES
6421	PAPER ETC CONTAINERS			W 191	0.1					BOITES,SACS EMBALLAGES
68	NON–FERROUS METALS		0.2							METAUX NON FERREUX
682	COPPER EXC CEMENT COPPER	W 218	0.2							CUIVRE
6822	COPPER,ALLOYS WORKED	W 218	0.2							CUIVRE,ALLIAGES OUVRES
68221	COPPER BARS,WIRE,ETC	W 218	0.2							BARRES,PROFILES ET FILS
7	MACHINES,TRANSPORT EQUIP		0.4		0.2					MACHINES MATERIEL TRANSPORT
77	ELECTRIC MACHNRY NES ETC		0.4		0.1					MACH APP ELECT NDA
776	TRANSISTORS,VALVES,ETC	W 6	0.4	W 2	0.1					LAMPES,TUBES,VALVES
7764	ELECTRONIC MICROCIRCUITS	W 6	0.4	W 2	0.1					MICROSTRUCTURES ELECTRON
8	MISC MANUFACTURED GOODS		0.7		0.7					ART MANUFACTURES DIVERS
89	MISC MANUFCTRD GOODS NES		0.6		0.7					ART MANUFACTURES DIVERS
899	OTHER MANUFACTURED GOODS	W 55	0.6	W 215	0.7					AUT ART MANUF DIVERS NDA
8991	CARVED,MOULDED GOODS	W 22	0.2	W 4	0.1					MAT A TAILLER,A MOULER
89911	GOODS OF ANML CARVNG MTL	W 22	0.2	W 4	0.1					ECAILLE,NACRE,IVOIRE ETC
8998	SMALLWARES,TOILETRYS ETC	W 34	0.4	W 211	0.6					ART MERCERIE,TOILETTE
89983	BUTTONS,STUDS,ETC	W 34	0.4	W 211	0.6					BOUTONS,BOUTONS–PRESSION
9	GOODS NOT CLASSD BY KIND		1.4		1.0					ART TRANSACT NON CLASSES
931	*SPECIAL TRANSACTIONS	W 182	1.4	W 81	1.0		4.0			TRANS.SPECIALES

FOOT NOTES – NOTES

TABLE 1 –
1 Prior to 1980, general trade.
TABLEAU 1 –
1 Avant 1980, commerce général.

1. HISTORICAL SERIES, 1962–1997 GENERAL TRADE, IMPORTS F.O.B., EXPORTS F.O.B.
SERIES HISTORIQUES, 1962–1997 COMMERCE GENERAL, IMPORTATIONS F.O.B., EXPORTATIONS F.O.B

YEAR ANNEE	VALUE IN MILLION BOLIVARES VALEUR EN MILLION BOLIVARES MERCHANDISE –MARCHANDISE		GOLD –OR		CONVERSION FACTORS U.S. CENTS PER BOLIVAR FACTEURS DE CONVERSION CENTS E.U. PAR BOLIVAR		INDEX NUMBERS –INDICES QUANTUM		UNIT VALUE VALEUR UNITAIRE	
	IMPORTS	EXPORTS	IMPORTS	EXPORTS	IMPORTS	EXPORTS	IMPORTS	EXPORTS	IMPORTS	EXPORTS
1962	3871.00	8689.00	21.16	0.07	25.2900	29.8500				
1963	3703.00	8807.00	19.24	0.03	29.8500	29.8500				
1964	4886.00	9241.00	30.17		23.1900	29.2500				
1965	5590.00	12076.00	36.93	0.10	23.2100	22.7300				
1966	5120.00	11941.00	34.03		23.2100	22.7300				
1967	5632.00	11238.00	39.78		22.2207	22.7300				
1968	6532.00	11175.00	33.26		22.2242	22.2192				
1969	6748.00	11104.00	23.29		22.2247	22.2262				
1970	7382.00	14379.00	27.68	7.30	22.2247	22.2307				
1971	8252.00	13996.00	28.92	0.30	22.2187	22.2198				
1972	9471.00	12993.00	30.41	0.20	22.7272	22.7279				
1973	10856.00	20431.00			23.2331	23.2731				
1974	16249.00	47435.00			23.3383	23.3370				
1975	22834.00	39876.00			23.3383	23.3370				
1976	25841.00	41057.00			23.3083	23.3094				
1977	41971.00	43506.00			23.2962	23.2962				
1978	45599.00	41957.00			23.2964	23.2964				
1979	41323.00	64024.00			23.2964	23.2964				
1980	45804.00	85501.00			23.2964	23.2964			11	12
1981	50706.00	86388.00			23.2964	23.2964			12	13
1982	50093.00	70583.00			23.2964	23.2964			13	12
1983	33739.00	64470.00			23.2704	23.2694			14	11
1984	47566.00	99934.00			14.4527	14.3466			17	16
1985	55637.00	94034.00			13.3333	13.3333			19	16
1986	67427.10	77842.99			12.7547	11.1250			23	10
1987	115135.50	123353.00			7.5658	8.5746			38	19
1988	213008.00	154703.00			5.3877	6.5370			44	20
1989	239964.90	448466.90			2.9295	2.8691			83	60
1990	347899.90	831200.00			2.1394	2.1394			100	100
1991	637700.10	863000.00			1.7651	1.7651			119	94
1992	961900.00	975399.90			1.4705	1.4705			140	109
1993	1107200.00	1311800.00			1.1081	1.1081			189	127
1994	1324000.00	2409799.00			0.7018	0.7018			341	
1995	2202099.00	3332600.00			0.5731	0.5623			514	
1996	4179899.00	9803100.00			0.2348	0.2352			1098	
1997		11297800.00				0.2047			1339	

2. IMPORTS BY BROAD ECONOMIC CATEGORY AND EXPORTS BY INDUSTRIAL ORIGIN. (PERCENTAGE OF TOTAL VALUE)
IMPORTATIONS PAR CATEGORIES ECONOMIQUES ET EXPORTATIONS PAR BRANCHE D'ACTIVITE.(EN POURCENTAGE DE LA VALEUR TOTALE)

IMPORTS – IMPORTATIONS

	1991	1992	1993	1994	1995	1996	1997
TOTAL IMPORTS–IMPORTATIONS TOTALES	100.	100.	100.	100.	100.	100.	
1 FOOD BEV–ALIMENTATION BOISSONS	8.5	7.8	8.4	10.5	11.2	10.8	
11 PRIMARY–PRODUITS DE BASE	3.2	2.9	3.2	4.1	4.4	4.2	
111 FOR INDUSTRY–POUR L'INDUSTRIE	2.1	1.9	2.0	2.8	2.8	3.0	
112 FOR HOUSEHOLDS–POUR LES MENAGES	1.0	1.0	1.2	1.4	1.7	1.2	
12 PROCESSED–PRODUITS ELABORES	5.3	4.8	5.2	6.4	6.8	6.7	
121 FOR INDUSTRY–POUR L'INDUSTRIE	1.6	1.5	1.5	2.5	2.8	2.3	
122 FOR HOUSEHOLDS–POUR LES MENAGES	3.7	3.4	3.7	3.9	4.0	4.4	
2 IND SUPPLIES–APPROV INDUSTRIELS	37.9	30.6	30.6	33.7	39.6	38.6	
21 PRIMARY–PRODUITS DE BASE	3.5	3.0	3.6	3.9	4.7	5.5	
22 PROCESSED–PRODUITS ELABORES	34.3	27.6	27.0	29.8	34.9	33.1	
3 FUELS–COMBUSTIBLES	1.7	0.8	0.6	1.1	0.5	0.8	
31 PRIMARY–PRODUITS DE BASE	0.2	0.3	0.1	0.0	0.0	0.0	
32 PROCESSED–PRODUITS ELABORES	1.4	0.5	0.5	1.1	0.5	0.7	
321 MOTOR SPIRIT–ESSENCE	0.5	0.0	0.0	0.2	0.0	0.0	
322 OTHER–AUTRES	0.9	0.4	0.5	0.9	0.5	0.7	
4 MACHINERY–EQUIPEMENT	32.3	33.2	32.8	31.8	24.7	27.4	
41 CAPITAL EQUIPMENT–MACHINES	26.4	28.9	28.5	27.0	19.9	22.1	
42 PARTS–PIECES ACCESSOIRES	5.9	4.3	4.3	4.7	4.8	5.3	
5 TRANSPORT–TRANSPORT	12.4	19.0	17.9	13.2	12.4	11.6	
51 PASSENGER CARS–AUTOMOBILES	4.5	8.8	8.6	6.4	5.9	5.0	
52 OTHER–AUTRES	3.1	4.8	4.7	3.6	2.9	3.1	
521 INDUSTRIAL–INDUSTRIELS	3.0	4.7	4.5	3.6	2.8	3.0	
522 NON INDUSTRIAL–NON INDUSTRIEL	0.1	0.1	0.2	0.1	0.1	0.1	
53 PARTS–PIECES ACCESSOIRES	4.8	5.4	4.5	3.2	3.6	3.5	
6 CONSUM GOODS–BIENS CONSOMMATION	7.0	8.4	9.6	9.6	11.6	10.6	
61 DURABLE–DURABLES	1.8	2.2	2.5	2.1	2.7	2.4	
62 SEMI DURABLE–SEMI DURABLES	3.4	4.4	4.8	4.5	5.9	5.0	
63 NON DURABLE–NON DURABLES	1.7	1.8	2.3	2.9	3.0	3.2	
7 GOODS NES–BIENS NDA	0.3	0.2	0.1	0.1	0.1	0.2	

EXPORTS – EXPORTATIONS

	1991	1992	1993	1994	1995	1996	1997
TOTAL EXPORTS–EXPORTATIONS TOTALES	100.	100.	100.	100.	100.	100.	100.
1 AGRICULTURE	1.1	1.2	1.4	1.3	1.0	1.0	1.2
2 MINING QUARRY–INDUS EXTRACTIVES	53.4	52.9	49.8	50.6	46.3	56.2	56.9
3 MANUFACTURING–IND MANUFACTUR	45.6	45.9	48.8	48.1	52.7	42.8	42.0
31 FOOD BEV TOBACCO–ALIM BOISS TAB	1.2	1.5	1.5	1.7	1.9	1.4	1.3
32 TEXTILES–INDUSTRIES TEXTILES	0.4	0.5	0.6	0.6	0.6	0.3	0.3
33 WOOD & PRODUCTS–BOIS & PRODUITS	0.0	0.0	0.0	0.0	0.0	0.0	0.0
34 PAPER & PRODUCTS–PAPIER & PRODT	0.4	0.4	0.4	0.5	0.7	0.5	0.5
35 CHEMICALS–INDUSTRIES CHIMIQUES	32.7	32.1	33.4	31.5	36.2	29.8	30.4
36 NON METAL MIN–MIN NON METAL	0.8	0.8	0.9	1.1	1.1	1.0	1.1
37 BASIC METAL–IND METAL BASE	8.0	8.0	7.7	8.5	8.2	6.5	5.3
38 METAL MANUF–MANUF METAL	2.0	2.6	4.0	4.2	3.9	3.2	2.9
39 OTH MANUF IND–AUTRES MANUF	0.0	0.1	0.2	0.1	0.1	0.1	0.1

3. TRADE BY PRINCIPAL COUNTRIES OF ORIGIN AND DESTINATION (VALUE IN MILLION U.S. DOLLARS)
ECHANGES SELON LES PRINCIPAUX PAYS D'ORIGINE ET DE DESTINATION (VALEUR EN MILLIONS DE DOLLARS EU)

COUNTRIES–PAYS	GENERAL IMPORTS F.O.B. IMPORTATIONS GENERALES F.O.B.				
	1993	1994	1995	1996	1997
World	11266.6	8036.7	10791.3	8902.2	
Africa	26.7	60.5	29.8	40.4	
Americas	7275.9	5394.8	7706.7	6526.6	
– Northern America	5567.7	3998.4	5052.0	4297.1	
– LAIA	1474.9	1208.5	2291.0	2005.6	
– CACM	20.8	33.6	77.1	29.0	
– Caribbean	87.8	60.4	83.4	75.0	
– Rest of America	124.8	93.9	203.1	119.9	
Asia excl fmr USSR	1305.0	738.2	912.4	584.5	
– Middle East	9.2	17.0	22.9	12.3	
Asia former USSR					
Europe excl fmr USSR	2599.3	1794.2	2067.0	1686.7	
– European Union	2475.4	1694.9	1935.8	1596.8	
– Eastern Europe	10.6	8.4	19.6	13.9	
– Rest of Europe	113.3	90.9	111.6	76.0	
Europe former USSR	18.4	2.6	13.6	4.2	
Oceania	41.3	46.4	61.7	59.9	
Other	0.0	0.1	0.0	0.0	
USA/Etats–Unis d'Amer	5201.4	3704.5	4594.5	4001.7	
Colombia/Colombie	469.6	401.2	818.8	682.1	
Japan/Japon	860.8	450.0	473.7	300.2	
Germany/Allemagne	625.8	445.0	521.3	401.3	
Italy/Italie	533.5	299.1	323.8	331.0	
Brazil/Brésil	398.2	254.0	415.5	362.0	
Canada	366.1	293.6	457.3	294.5	
Mexico/Mexique	219.3	181.6	351.6	356.8	
Argentina/Argentine	213.1	190.8	292.9	291.7	
France, Monaco	328.4	217.8	249.7	179.1	
United Kingdom	286.9	207.6	217.1	184.2	
Spain/Espagne	235.0	138.3	250.0	184.9	
Netherlands/Pays–Bas	167.2	154.3	135.3	106.9	
Panama	116.8	93.1	201.0	118.3	
Other Asia n.e.s.	123.3	78.0	142.7	90.7	
Belgium–Luxembourg	137.3	105.3	111.8	78.7	
Peru/Pérou	83.0	77.1	154.9	98.6	
Chile/Chili	74.6	64.7	119.7	116.8	
Switzerland,Liechtenst.	97.4	82.2	93.8	65.6	
Korea, Republic of	99.5	63.1	102.5	63.5	
China, Hong Kong SAR	114.3	40.6	62.0	54.9	
New Zealand	30.8	42.2	53.7	55.0	
Sweden/Suède	66.5	38.7	30.5	34.6	
Paraguay	2.9	22.0	82.9	45.7	
Netherlands Antilles	37.1	24.2	45.5	28.2	
Denmark/Danemark	30.1	32.1	29.5	24.6	
So. African Customs Un	19.9	26.7	27.0	33.2	
Finland/Finlande	28.4	23.3	29.3	21.6	
Singapore/Singapour	26.9	24.3	26.0	16.8	
Guatemala	2.6	19.7	53.6	15.9	
Trinidad and Tobago	16.0	21.0	22.3	28.3	
Ecuador/Equateur	7.9	7.9	29.6	32.7	
Austria/Autriche	17.3	18.2	17.2	18.4	
Israel/Israël	15.9	19.6	19.6	7.0	
Malaysia/Malaisie	18.6	9.0	18.6	12.8	
Ireland/Irlande	7.5	7.7	11.5	23.1	
Norway,Svalbard and JM	13.9	8.1	16.9	9.6	
India/Inde	13.1	10.8	15.0	9.5	
Indonesia/Indonésie	11.3	11.7	16.4	6.4	
Turkey/Turquie	4.7	10.1	18.5	9.5	

COUNTRIES–PAYS	GENERAL EXPORTS F.O.B. EXPORTATIONS GENERALES F.O.B.				
	1993	1994	1995	1996	1997
Monde	15208.1	16649.7	18914.2	22674.4	21657.7
Afrique	51.1	15.4	35.7	144.0	16.8
Amériques	13236.6	14488.4	16493.8	20155.2	19511.9
– Amérique du Nord	8596.4	8863.1	9892.3	14237.4	13346.4
– ALAI	1823.0	2390.3	3941.0	2876.8	3361.5
– MCAC	376.0	406.6	377.4	442.1	507.3
– Caraïbes	2130.0	1868.3	1802.1	2405.5	2114.0
– Autre Amérique	311.2	960.1	481.1	193.3	182.7
Asie anc. URSS exclus	391.4	366.6	375.0	233.8	169.3
– Moyen–Orient	14.3	8.1	8.0	22.4	8.7
Asie ancienne URSS					0.0
Europe anc. URSS exclus	1326.5	1519.6	1742.3	1914.1	1299.8
– Union Européenne	1281.2	1490.7	1722.3	1877.5	1267.9
– Europe de l'Est	0.3	7.4	0.8	0.1	20.4
– Autre de l'Europe	45.0	21.4	19.3	36.5	11.6
Europe ancienne URSS	3.8	10.5	43.9	15.7	17.6
Océanie	8.5	1.4	0.4	0.6	1.5
Autre	190.2	247.8	223.1	211.1	640.7
USA/Etats–Unis d'Amer	8472.1	8648.7	9645.7	13862.5	12824.7
Colombia/Colombie	910.1	1174.9	1423.2	1221.4	1104.5
Netherlands Antilles	1358.6	1051.2	927.3	1344.5	1084.6
Brazil/Brésil	377.0	568.2	1683.9	737.9	937.4
Germany/Allemagne	342.5	342.2	345.1	474.1	251.3
Netherlands/Pays–Bas	335.5	244.2	317.5	475.7	283.1
Suriname/Surinam	249.4	888.4	389.0	2.6	4.3
United Kingdom	262.5	437.2	531.8	203.8	25.5
Dominican Republic	195.4	315.3	242.6	344.4	329.7
Canada	123.5	211.1	215.8	292.7	520.6
Areas n.e.s.	190.2	247.8	223.1	8.9	640.7
Peru/Pérou	89.4	97.2	239.4	304.9	434.1
Mexico/Mexique	224.4	251.9	177.6	143.5	336.7
Japan/Japon	223.7	283.1	292.8	144.8	74.1
Ecuador/Equateur	44.5	146.1	215.2	177.1	269.7
Chile/Chili	128.4	106.1	138.7	195.2	144.8
Guatemala	110.4	108.6	143.0	154.0	172.2
Trinidad and Tobago	183.8	154.8	75.9	144.1	106.0
Costa Rica	60.2	87.3	129.5	163.8	203.9
Italy/Italie	64.6	128.8	158.1	158.2	113.4
Sweden/Suède	54.6	75.5	104.2	136.9	247.4
Spain/Espagne	47.6	103.6	78.2	195.6	179.3
Aruba				316.8	254.0
Anguilla	102.8	125.5	305.4	3.2	0.1
Panama	48.6	61.8	61.8	149.0	170.2
Cuba	120.3	89.6	111.7	119.2	21.1
Belgium–Luxembourg	84.9	100.9	61.4	112.5	32.3
El Salvador	108.8	118.3	63.8	45.6	51.3
France, Monaco	59.2	41.7	81.7	79.7	72.0
Jamaica/Jamaïque	70.4	67.7	49.0	42.5	66.9
Nicaragua	86.5	81.2	18.7	29.9	45.3
Bunkers, ship stores				202.2	
Bahamas	57.8	30.3	46.4	51.3	13.4
British Virgin Islds	0.7	0.7	0.7	0.5	195.3
Argentina/Argentine	31.2	35.0	36.0	60.2	34.5
Uruguay	9.5	7.9	16.9	30.9	90.1
Portugal	12.0	13.3	33.9	39.4	55.3
Honduras	10.1	11.2	22.5	48.8	34.6
Korea, Republic of	21.9	22.3	36.1	22.9	17.9
Bermuda/Bermudes	0.8	3.3	30.8	82.3	1.0

(VALUE AS PERCENTAGE OF WORLD TOTAL)(VALEURS EN POURCENTAGE DU TOTAL MONDIAL)

	1988	1989	1990	1991	1992	1993	1994	1995	1996	1997
Africa	0.6	0.5	0.4	0.5	0.4	0.2	0.8	0.3	0.5	
Americas	58.5	59.1	63.4	65.9	64.9	64.6	67.1	71.4	73.3	
– Northern America	45.8	46.5	49.6	50.5	48.8	49.4	49.8	46.8	48.3	
– LAIA	10.0	9.3	11.1	12.7	13.1	13.1	15.0	21.2	22.5	
– CACM	0.1	0.1	0.0	0.1	0.2	0.2	0.4	0.7	0.3	
– Caribbean	1.2	1.7	1.4	1.2	1.1	0.8	0.8	0.8	0.8	
– Rest of America	1.4	1.4	1.3	1.4	1.6	1.1	1.2	1.9	1.3	
Asia excl fmr USSR	7.9	6.5	6.5	7.5	10.6	11.6	9.2	8.5	6.6	
– Middle East	0.0	0.1	0.1	0.1	0.1	0.1	0.2	0.2	0.1	
Asia former USSR										
Europe excl fmr USSR	32.1	32.9	28.8	25.2	23.4	23.1	22.3	19.2	18.9	
– European Union	29.5	30.5	27.0	23.6	22.3	22.0	21.1	17.9	17.9	
– Eastern Europe	0.5	0.5	0.2	0.4	0.1	0.1	0.1	0.2	0.2	
– Rest of Europe	2.2	2.0	1.6	1.1	0.9	1.0	1.1	1.0	0.9	
Europe former USSR	0.0	0.4	0.1	0.2	0.4	0.2	0.0	0.1	0.0	
Oceania	0.8	0.6	0.9	0.8	0.4	0.4	0.6	0.6	0.7	
Other	0.0	0.0	0.0	0.0	0.0	0.0	0.0	0.0	0.0	
USA/Etats–Unis d'Amer	42.6	44.3	46.7	47.8	46.6	46.2	46.1	42.6	45.0	
Colombia/Colombie	1.4	1.4	2.2	2.9	3.8	4.2	5.0	7.6	7.7	
Japan/Japon	5.4	4.1	3.9	5.0	7.5	7.6	5.6	4.4	3.4	
Germany/Allemagne				7.0	6.5	5.6	5.5	4.8	4.5	
Italy/Italie	6.1	7.3	4.8	4.7	4.8	4.7	3.7	3.0	3.7	
Brazil/Brésil	4.8	4.0	4.0	4.5	3.9	3.5	3.2	3.9	4.1	
Canada	3.2	2.2	2.9	2.8	2.2	3.2	3.7	4.2	3.3	
Mexico/Mexique	1.2	0.9	1.5	1.5	2.0	1.9	2.3	3.3	4.0	
Argentina/Argentine	1.0	1.5	1.9	2.2	1.8	1.9	2.4	2.7	3.3	
France, Monaco	3.3	3.0	3.5	2.3	1.9	2.9	2.7	2.3	2.0	

	1988	1989	1990	1991	1992	1993	1994	1995	1996	1997
Afrique	0.2	0.3	0.1	0.2	0.3	0.3	0.1	0.2	0.6	0.1
Amériques	60.4	75.3	69.5	75.7	83.3	87.0	87.0	87.2	88.9	90.1
– Amérique du Nord	50.3	59.2	54.2	55.9	55.3	56.5	53.2	52.3	62.8	61.6
– ALAI	5.7	5.5	6.7	7.6	9.0	12.0	14.4	20.8	12.7	15.5
– MCAC	2.0	1.9	2.0	1.6	2.4	2.5	2.4	2.0	1.9	2.3
– Caraïbes	2.2	8.4	6.3	10.3	14.7	14.0	11.2	9.5	10.6	9.8
– Autre Amérique	0.3	0.3	0.3	0.2	1.9	2.0	5.8	2.5	0.9	0.8
Asie anc. URSS exclus	5.1	4.6	4.4	3.6	3.8	2.6	2.2	2.0	1.0	0.8
– Moyen–Orient	0.2	0.1	0.1	0.2	0.2	0.1	0.0	0.0	0.1	0.0
Asie ancienne URSS										0.0
Europe anc. URSS exclus	16.5	16.8	14.2	12.9	10.9	8.7	9.1	9.2	8.4	6.0
– Union Européenne	13.9	15.0	14.0	12.5	10.7	8.4	9.0	9.1	8.3	5.9
– Europe de l'Est	0.2	0.2	0.1	0.1	0.0	0.0	0.0	0.0	0.0	0.1
– Autre de l'Europe	2.5	1.6	0.2	0.3	0.2	0.3	0.1	0.1	0.2	0.1
Europe ancienne URSS	0.1	0.0	0.0	0.1	0.0	0.0	0.1	0.2	0.1	0.1
Océanie	0.0	0.1	0.1	0.0	0.0	0.1	0.0	0.0	0.0	0.0
Autre	17.6	2.9	11.5	7.5	1.7	1.3	1.5	1.2	0.9	3.0
USA/Etats–Unis d'Amer	47.0	55.3	51.6	52.0	54.2	55.7	51.9	51.0	61.1	59.2
Colombia/Colombie	1.6	1.9	2.1	2.0	3.5	6.0	7.1	7.5	5.4	5.1
Netherlands Antilles	0.4	6.3	0.3	6.1	9.4	8.9	6.3	4.9	5.9	5.0
Brazil/Brésil	1.8	1.6	1.9	2.2	1.8	2.5	3.4	8.9	3.3	4.3
Germany/Allemagne				4.3	2.4	2.3	2.1	1.8	2.1	1.2
Netherlands/Pays–Bas	3.6	3.8	3.9	2.6	4.0	2.2	1.5	1.7	2.1	1.3
Suriname/Surinam	0.0	0.0	0.1	0.0	1.4	1.6	5.3	2.1	0.0	0.0
United Kingdom	1.2	1.4	0.9	1.2	0.7	1.7	2.6	2.8	0.9	0.1
Dominican Republic	0.8	0.4	1.5	0.8	0.9	1.3	1.9	1.3	1.5	1.5
Canada	3.3	3.9	2.6	3.9	1.1	0.8	1.3	1.1	1.3	2.4

4. General Imports F.O.B. by Commodities according to the S.I.T.C. (Rev. 2) in million U.S. Dollars
Importations Générales F.O.B. par Produits d'après la C.T.C.I. (Rév. 2) en millions de Dollars E.U.

SITC CTCI	COMMODITY	1994 QUANTITY QUANTITE	1994 VALUE VALEUR	1995 QUANTITY QUANTITE	1995 VALUE VALEUR	1996 QUANTITY QUANTITE	1996 VALUE VALEUR	1997 QUANTITY QUANTITE	1997 VALUE VALEUR	PRODUIT
	ALL COMMODITIES		8036.8	.	10791.3		8902.3			TOUS PRODUITS
0	FOOD AND LIVE ANIMALS		800.7		1165.0		1123.0			ALIMENTS,ANIMAUX VIVANTS
02	DAIRY PRODCTS,BIRDS'EGGS		125.0		177.7		182.4			PRODUITS LAITIERS,OEUFS
022	MILK AND CREAM	W 60128	114.8	W 71130	152.6	W 72865	169.1			LAIT ET CREME
0224	MILK,CREAM PRESERVED ETC	W 58055	111.1	W 68684	148.9	W 71162	166.9			LAIT,CREME CONS,CONC
02243	MILK DRY,OVER 1.5% FAT	W 40926	78.7	W 64934	142.8	W 66321	158.5			LAIT POUDRE SUP 1.5%
04	CEREALS AND PREPARATIONS		350.1		428.2		529.5			CEREALES ET PRODUITS
041	WHEAT ETC UNMILLED	W 1063447	183.1	W 1036179	193.8	W 939444	201.1			FROMENT,EPEAUTRE
0411	DURUM WHEAT UNMILLED	W 437731	80.6	W 305432	64.5	W 309233	66.4			FROMENT DUR NON MOULU
0412	OTHER WHEAT ETC UNMILLED	W 625715	102.5	W 730748	129.4	W 630210	134.7			AUTRE FROMENT NON MOULU
044	MAIZE UNMILLED	W 791594	106.9	W 1055210	144.6	W 1075459	222.0			MAIS NON MOULU
048	CEREAL ETC PREPARATIONS	W 191735	47.1	W 166563	63.9	W 195574	89.7			PREPTNS A BASE CEREALES
0482	MALT INCLUDING FLOUR	W 174501	34.0	W 146098	43.4	W 172366	65.6			MALT MEME TORREFIE
05	VEGETABLES AND FRUIT		123.0		179.3		124.3			LEGUMES ET FRUITS
054	VEG ETC FRSH,SMPLY PRSVD	W 188035	80.8	W 245234	125.8	W 166303	84.0			LEGUMES FRAIS,CONG,SECS
0542	LEGUMINOUS VEGETBLES DRY	W 66869	38.8	W 111111	73.9	W 81433	48.5			LEGUMES A COSSE SECS
057	FRUIT,NUTS,FRESH,DRIED	W 34796	31.6	W 38787	37.0	W 26603	24.9			FRUITS FRAIS OU SECS
06	SUGAR AND PREPS,HONEY		88.5		171.3		82.3			SUCRES ET PRODUITS
061	SUGAR AND HONEY	W 251633	81.1	W 440350	156.3	W 227862	71.0			SUCRES ET MIEL
0611	RAW BEET AND CANE SUGAR	W 203358	63.0	W 346581	123.9	W 195830	57.5			SUCRES BRUTS
081	*FEEDING STUFF FOR ANIML	W 319521	82.3	W 501939	126.1	W 441572	141.0			NOURRITURE POUR ANIMAUX
0813	OILCAKE AND OTH RESIDUES	W 291006	68.6	W 480388	111.1	W 408322	118.4			TOURTEAUX
08131	— OF SOYA BEANS	W 291004	68.6	W 480381	111.1	W 408310	118.4			TOURTEAUX DE SOJA
09	MISC EDIBLE PRODUCTS		13.3		28.7		38.4			PREP ALIMENTAIRES DIVERSES
098	EDIBLE PRODCTS,PREPS NES	W 4621	13.1	W 7643	23.9	W 7926	33.1			PREP ALIMENTAIRES NDA
09809	MISC FOOD PREPRTIONS NES	W 2683	7.5	W 4412	16.0	W 4026	27.2			PREP ALIMENTAIRES NDA
1	BEVERAGES AND TOBACCO		99.0		105.2		95.1			BOISSONS ET TABACS
11	BEVERAGES		90.2		88.6		70.6			BOISSONS
112	ALCOHOLIC BEVERAGES	W 21699	89.9	W 20646	88.3	W 27791	70.0			BOISSONS ALCOOLIQUES
1124	DISTILLED ALCOHOLIC BEVS	W 16269	80.6	W 14945	78.5	W 18663	56.7			ALCOOLS,EAUX-DE-VIE
11241	WHISKY	W 13539	71.4	W 11368	67.0	W 14773	50.1			WHISKY
2	CRUDE MATERLS,EXCL FUELS		374.3		671.1		440.5			MAT BRUTES NON COMESTIBLES
22	OIL SEEDS,OLEAGINOUS FRT		32.1		66.7		46.0			GRAINES,FRUITS OLEAGINEUX
222	SEEDS FOR'SOFT'FIXED OIL	W 123572	31.3	W 234035	66.0	W 147159	45.7			GRAINES HUILES FIXES
2222	SOYA BEANS	W 122101	29.5	W 230827	62.8	W 145331	44.4			FEVES DE SOJA
23	RUBBER, CRUDE		54.6		100.5		68.7			CAOUTCHOUC BRUT
232	NATURAL RUBBER,GUMS	W 19204	22.5	W 24242	40.3	W 18005	27.1			LATEX CAOUTCHOUC NATUREL
233	RUBBER,SYNTHTIC,RECLAIMD	W 31979	32.2	W 43560	60.2	W 35520	41.6			LATEX CAOUTCH SYNTH REGEN
2331	SYNTHETIC RUBBER ETC	W 31436	31.9	W 42449	59.6	W 35095	41.3			LATEX CAOUTCH SYNTHETIQUE
23315	POLYBUTADIENE–STYRN(SBR)	W 19322	16.0	W 26198	33.1	W 19605	20.4			POLYBUTADIENE–STYRENE
251	*PULP AND WASTE PAPER	W 362136	129.5	W 440830	254.8	W 291450	113.0			PATES A PAPIER,DECHETS
2511	WASTE PAPER,PPRBOARD ETC	W 184417	34.2	W 238540	79.4	W 132144	26.5			DECHETS DE PAPIER
2517	SODA,SULPHATE WOOD PULP	W 168015	90.8	W 198091	171.8	W 155685	84.1			PATES CHIMIQUES AU SULFATE
25172	— BLEACHED,NONDISSOLVNG	W 138484	77.0	W 166796	147.3	W 133231	73.9			PATES BLANCHIES
26	TEXTILE FIBRES AND WASTE		41.5		93.4		70.2			FIBRES TEXTILES
263	COTTON	W 20835	28.6	W 34316	74.5	W 30779	53.1			COTON
2631	RAW COTTON,EXCL LINTERS	W 20755	28.6	W 34008	73.9	W 30568	52.9			COTON EN MASSE
27	CRUDE FERTLZR,MINRLS NES		55.9		74.6		65.9			ENGRAIS MINERAUX BRUTS
278	OTHER CRUDE MINERALS	W 372878	42.9	W 492280	58.1	W 454431	49.3			AUTRES MINERAUX BRUTS
2782	REFRACTORY MINERALS NES	W 134611	22.9	W 236284	34.4	W 140740	25.7			ARGILE MINERAUX REFRACTAIRES
28	METALLIFEROUS ORES,SCRAP		38.0		49.2		51.7			MINERAIS METAL,DECHETS
282	IRON AND STEEL SCRAP	W 140705	19.7	W 173107	25.1	W 250111	35.0			FERRAILLES
3	MINERAL FUELS ETC		123.7		125.1		131.7			COMBUSTIBLES MINERAUX LUB
33	PETROLEUM AND PRODUCTS		113.6		105.7		114.8			PETROLE ET DERIVES
334	PETROLEUM PRODUCTS,REFIN	W 381963	79.3	W 46298	36.0	W 213472	50.1			PRODUITS RAFFINES
3345	LUBS,PETROLEUM OILS NES	W 88127	36.4	W 45434	35.2	W 143578	45.0			HUILES LUBRIFIANTES
33451	LUBS(HIGH PETR CONT) ETC	W 86687	32.7	W 43532	30.1	W 140894	39.0			HUILES LUBRIF,H LOURDES
335	RESIDUAL PETRLM PROD NES	W 213920	34.3	W 379799	69.7	W 348592	64.7			PRODUITS RESIDUELS NDA
3354	PETROLM BITUMEN,COKE ETC	W 178635	22.2	W 283448	37.4	W 270996	45.4			BITUME,COKE DE PETROLE
33542	PETROLEUM COKE	W 151823	18.0	W 282570	36.4	W 270424	44.4			COKE DE PETROLE
4	ANIMAL,VEGETABLE OIL,FAT		139.2		205.3		122.6			HUILES,GRAISSES ANIM,VEG
411	*ANIMAL OILS AND FATS	W 53428	21.4	W 79678	36.0	W 59702	27.0			HUILES,GRAISSES ANIMALES
4113	ANIML OIL,FAT,GREASE NES	W 53359	21.1	W 79514	35.6	W 59624	26.7			HUILES,GRAISSES ANIMALES NDA
41132	FATS OF BOVINE,SHEEP,ETC	W 53299	20.9	W 79400	35.1	W 59509	26.5			SUIFS BRUTS FONDUS
42	FIXED VEGETABLE OIL,FAT		114.1		161.5		90.7			HUILES VEGETALES FIXES
423	FIXED VEG OILS,SOFT	W 180438	108.2	W 214813	149.2	W 125609	83.2			HUILES VEGET DOUCES FIXES
4232	SOYA BEAN OIL	W 137941	81.2	W 155042	104.3	W 94642	62.7			HUILE DE SOJA
4236	SUNFLOWER SEED OIL	W 38762	23.6	W 54296	37.7	W 30160	18.0			HUILE DE TOURNESOL
5	CHEMCLS,RELATED PROD NES		1085.3		1735.1		1320.4			PRODUITS CHIMIQUES
51	ORGANIC CHEMICALS		311.4		507.1		357.5			PROD CHIMIQ ORGANIQUES
511	HYDROCARBONS NES,DERIVS	W 105199	43.8	W 88201	64.1	W 70823	40.9			HYDROCARBURES NDA
5112	CYCLIC HYDROCARBONS	W 71518	28.1	W 55222	43.8	W 46925	23.0			HYDROCARBURES CYCLIQUES
512	ALCOHOLS,PHENOLS ETC	W 83021	36.0	W 40423	50.3	W 42370	46.2			PHENOLS,PHENOLS–ALCOOLS
5121	ACYCLIC ALCOHOLS,DERIVS	W 77716	28.2	W 30759	36.2	W 29906	33.1			ALCOOLS ACYCLIQUES
513	CARBOXYLIC ACIDS ETC	W 56012	63.6	W 84821	122.1	W 49219	62.5			ACIDES CARBOXYLIQUES
5137	MONOACIDS AND DERIVATIVS	W 21349	27.5	W 30234	50.4	W 19427	27.2			ACIDES MONOCARBOXYLIQUES
5138	POLYACIDS AND DERIVATIVS	W 29903	24.3	W 48273	55.0	W 25223	23.9			ACIDES POLYCARBOXYLIQUES
51389	OTH POLYACIDS ETC,DERIVS	W 27233	21.5	W 40269	45.0	W 20706	20.1			ACIDES POLYCARBOXYLIQUES
514	NITROGEN–FNCTN COMPOUNDS	W 19334	65.1	W 24819	97.8	W 23440	74.9			COMPOSES FONCT AZOTEES
5148	OTH NITROGN–FNCTN CMPNDS	W 9968	34.2	W 12287	52.1	W 12403	43.4			AUTRES COMPOSES AZOTES
515	ORG–INORG COMPOUNDS ETC	W 10593	70.8	W 13713	89.1	W 11860	73.7			COMPOSES ORGANO–MINERAUX
5156	HETEROCYCLIC CMPDS ETC	W 3438	36.4	W 5650	51.1	W 4223	35.7			COMPOSES HETEROCYCLIQUES
51569	OTH HETEROCYC CMPDS,ETC	W 1662	34.1	W 2656	46.2	W 2609	32.6			AUT COMP HETEROCYCLIQUES
516	OTHER ORGANIC CHEMICALS	W 26817	32.3	W 121781	84.1	W 132618	59.5			AUTRES PROD ORGANIQUES
5161	ETHERS,EPOXIDES,ACETALS	W 16178	15.1	W 108242	56.5	W 122364	42.4			ETHERS–OXYDES,ALCOOLS
51611	ETHERS,ETHER–ALCOHOL,ETC	W 7366	7.4	W 97432	44.9	W 112347	32.1			ETHERS–OXYDES
52	INORGANIC CHEMICALS		103.7		204.6		165.0			PROD CHIM INORGANIQUES
522	INORG ELEMNTS,OXIDES,ETC	W 151699	39.1	W 416557	98.0	W 333316	64.3			ELEMENTS INORGANIQUES
5225	INORGANIC BASES ETC NES	W 26687	6.7	W 306850	55.0	W 236938	28.0			AUTRES BASES OXYDES METAL
52252	SODIUM HYDROXIDE, SOLID	W 2409	0.9	W 286942	44.9	W 128605	9.8			HYDROXYDE DE SODIUM
523	OTHR INORG CHEMICALS ETC	W 171207	63.9	W 336454	105.9	W 298014	99.9			AUT PRODUITS CHIMIQUES INORG
5231	METAL CMPD OF INORG ACID	W 44710	24.8	W 92461	46.2	W 98615	46.9			SELS METALLIQUES
5232	OTH MTL CMPD OF INRG ACD	W 123409	35.4	W 237851	53.0	W 194945	47.0			SELS METALLIQUES
52323	NEUTRAL SODIUM CARBONATE	W 87011	14.5	W 208996	33.9	W 161125	27.8			CARBONATE NEUTRE SODIUM
53	DYES,TANNING,COLOUR PROD		59.7		99.1		75.5			PROD TEINTURE,COLORANTS
533	PIGMENTS,PAINTS,ETC	W 12375	31.1	W 22378	61.5	W 18081	46.0			PIGMENTS,PEINTURES,VERNIS
541	*MEDICINAL,PHARM PRODUCT	K 8511513	144.1	MK 11155	206.2	MK 13514	182.1			PROD MEDICINAUX PHARMACEUT
5413	ANTIBIOTICS IN BULK	K 282425	26.6	K 539764	45.7	K 537291	31.1			ANTIBIOTIQUES NDA
54139	OTHER ANTIBIOTICS	K 187957	19.3	K 354410	36.5	K 367354	24.3			AUTRES ANTIBIOTIQUES
5417	MEDICAMENTS	K 6204359	68.4	K 7874380	94.6	MK 9903	96.6			MEDICAMENTS
54179	— CONTNG OTH SUBSTANCES	K 5933876	43.0	K 7327202	56.1	K 8963049	57.3			MED CONT AUT SUBSTANCES

4. General Imports F.O.B. by Commodities according to the S.I.T.C. (Rev. 2) in million U.S. Dollars
Importations Générales F.O.B. par Produits d'après la C.T.C.I. (Rév. 2) en millions de Dollars E.U.

SITC CTCI	COMMODITY	1994 QUANTITY QUANTITE	1994 VALUE VALEUR	1995 QUANTITY QUANTITE	1995 VALUE VALEUR	1996 QUANTITY QUANTITE	1996 VALUE VALEUR	1997 QUANTITY QUANTITE	1997 VALUE VALEUR	PRODUIT
55	PERFUME,CLEANING ETC PRD		72.1		120.8		98.5			PROD POUR PARFUM,TOILETTE
551	ESSENTL OILS,PERFUME,ETC	W 1891	31.5	W 2256	38.6	W 2209	33.5			HUILES ESSENTIELLES
5514	MIXED PERFUME SUBSTANCES	W 1630	28.3	W 1970	33.1	W 1958	26.3			MELANGES SUBSTAN ODORIFER
553	PERFUMERY,COSMETICS,ETC	W 4651	23.1	W 10105	40.8	W 8291	31.8			PRODUITS DE PARFUMERIE
554	SOAP,CLEANSING ETC PREPS	W 11573	17.7	W 28272	41.4	W 25768	33.3			SAVONS,PRODUITS DETERSIFS
58	PLASTIC MATERIALS ETC		162.8		276.9		200.8			MAT PLAST ARTIFICIELLES
582	PROD OF CONDENSATION ETC	W 14985	37.1	W 21113	58.8	W 17487	44.4			PROD CONDENS,POLYCOND
583	POLYMERIZATION ETC PRODS	W 76836	97.5	W 121162	181.5	W 97138	122.4			PROD POLYMERISATION
5834	POLYVINYL CHLORIDE	W 23396	21.0	W 43120	48.3	W 45652	31.1			CHLORURE DE POLYVINYLE
58341	— IN PRIMARY FORMS	W 22734	18.9	W 41563	42.7	W 44274	28.5			SOUS FORMES PRIMAIRES
5839	OTH POLYMRZTION ETC PROD	W 12736	28.0	W 16715	44.4	W 15908	37.5			AUT PROD POLYMER COPOLYM
584	CELLULOSE DERIVATIVS ETC	W 10105	26.6	W 10990	32.8	W 11118	30.1			CEL REGEN NIT ACETATE
59	CHEMICAL MATERIALS NES		213.9		285.1		213.3			MAT PROD CHIMIQUES NDA
591	PESTICIDES,DISINFECTANTS	W 3613	17.7	W 6937	37.9	W 7041	35.2			DESINF,INSECT,FONG,HERB
598	MISCEL CHEM PRODUCTS NES	W 91801	178.7	W 73411	225.6	W 62796	159.7			PROD DIV INDUST CHIM NDA
5982	ANTI-KNOCK PREPARTNS ETC	W 51410	68.9	W 21987	89.7	W 17372	59.3			PREPARAT ANTIDETONANTES
5989	CHEM PRODUCTS,PREPS NES	W 32919	100.0	W 41324	121.1	W 37145	89.7			PROD PREP CHIMIQUES NDA
59898	COMPOUND CATALYSTS	W 8943	43.4	W 8119	43.0	W 5625	26.0			CATALYSEURS COMPOSITES
59899	OTH CHEM PRODS,PREPS,NES	W 16095	45.3	W 24368	64.3	W 24081	51.1			AUT PRODUITS CHIMIQUES NDA
6	BASIC MANUFACTURES		1174.9		1808.8		1523.9			ART MANUFACTURES
61	LEATHER,DRESSED FUR,ETC		16.8		35.2		18.0			CUIRS,PELLETERIES
62	RUBBER MANUFACTURES NES		65.1		105.1		110.1			CAOUTCHOUC MANUFACTURE
625	RUBBER TYRES, TUBES ETC	W 10334	30.5	W 16384	55.3	W 20978	65.2			PNEUS CAOUTCHOUC VULCANISE
628	RUBBER ARTICLES NES	W 2593	25.7	W 3387	36.8	W 4025	32.8			OUVRAGES CAOUTCHOUC NDA
64	PAPER,PAPERBOARD AND MFR		159.2		245.6		166.0			PAPIERS,CARTONS & OUVRAGES
641	PAPER AND PAPERBOARD	W 163233	123.8	W 169632	168.7	W 120308	116.9			PAPIERS ET CARTONS
6411	NEWSPRINT	W 107219	59.2	W 106298	76.9	W 68456	52.3			PAPIER JOURNAL
6418	COATED ETC PAPER NES BLK	W 20569	29.4	W 23814	36.6	W 19954	28.7			PAP,CARTONS COUCHES,ENDUITS
642	PAPER,ETC,PRECUT,ARTS OF	W 19809	35.4	W 28847	77.0	W 23931	49.2			PAP,CARTONS DECOUPES
6421	PAPER ETC CONTAINERS	W 6558	8.1	W 10443	34.2	W 10700	19.6			BOITES,SACS EMBALLAGES
65	TEXTILE YARN,FABRICS,ETC		173.8		276.2		205.3			FILS,TISSUS,ARTICLES TEXTILE
651	TEXTILE YARN	W 5258	22.1	W 8534	40.6	W 8017	30.4			FILS TEXTILES
652	COTTON FABRICS,WOVEN	W 5866	27.4	W 10016	60.5	W 11222	49.6			TISSUS DE COTON
6522	WOVEN COTTON BLEACHD,ETC	W 5316	24.9	W 9513	58.1	W 10845	48.2			TISSUS COTON BLANCHIS ETC
65224	BLCHED COTTON FABRIC NES	W 3712	19.3	W 7104	45.9	W 8591	41.0			AUT TIS PLUS 85% COT BLANCHI
653	WOVN MAN-MADE FIB FABRIC	W 7188	45.0	W 9224	66.6	W 7980	43.8			TISSUS FIBRES SYNTH,ARTIF
6531	CONT SYNT WEAVES NONPILE	W 3609	22.8	W 4858	34.1	W 3461	21.3			TISSUS FIBRES SYNTH CONTINUE
657	SPECIAL TXTL FABRC,PRODS	W 7159	46.5	W 9485	57.9	W 7462	44.4			TISSUS SPECIAUX
6573	COATED ETC TEXTILES NES	W 3713	26.0	W 5770	32.5	W 4305	23.3			TISSUS,ART MATIERE TEXT NDA
65733	RUBBERIZED TEXT NOT KNIT	W 3337	24.2	W 5394	30.2	W 4048	21.6			TISSUS CAOUTCHOUTES
66	NONMETAL MINERAL MFS NES		108.1		120.8		114.5			ART MIN NON METALLIQUES
662	CLAY,REFRACTORY BLDG PRD	W 58753	38.0		40.2	W 48942	34.9			MAT CONST REFRACTAIRES
6623	REFRACTORY BUILDING PROD	W 21912	24.8	W 20290	29.6	W 21695	27.6			BRIQUES REFRACTAIRES
67	IRON AND STEEL		305.0		463.4		492.4			FER ET ACIER
672	IRON,STEEL PRIMARY FORMS	W 22623	8.1	W 128596	43.1	W 114633	42.4			LINGOTS FER,ACIER
6727	IRN,STL COIL FR REROLLNG	W 20273	7.1	W 59669	23.1	W 109962	39.4			EBAUCHES POUR TOLES FER
67271	IRON,SIMPLE STEEL COILS	W 19992	6.5	W 59557	22.8	W 109296	38.6			EBAUCHES NON EN ACIER
673	IRON,STEEL SHAPES ETC	W 65151	33.2	W 101009	56.7	W 93290	51.2			BARRES,PROFIL FER,ACIER
674	IRN,STL UNIV,PLATE,SHEET	W 122598	68.4	W 172866	119.1	W 121563	87.8			LARGES PLATS,TOLES
6744	IRN,STL HVY PLATE,ROLLED	W 25191	12.4	W 111224	59.2	W 36815	20.4			TOLES LAMINEES PLUS 4.75 MM
67441	— OF IRON OR SIMPLE STL	W 24382	10.6	W 110520	57.0	W 35933	17.5			TOLES NON ACIER FIN CARB
6746	IRN,STL THIN PLATE,ROLLD	W 81647	41.5	W 31815	30.6	W 12148	15.9			TOLES LAM MOINS 3MM
67461	— OF IRON OR SIMPLE STL	W 76484	31.6	W 26426	15.6	W 6668	4.9			TOL NON AC FIN MOINS 3 MM
678	IRON,STL TUBES,PIPES,ETC	W 171347	165.5	W 189473	206.2	W 243578	276.4			TUBES,TUYAUX EN FONTE,FER
6782	IRON,STL SEAMLESS TUBES	W 153560	131.1	W 164784	157.4	W 200228	204.3			TUBES,TUYAUX SANS SOUDURE
6783	IRON,STL TUBES,PIPES NES	W 11564	13.1	W 15895	18.6	W 32395	32.0			AUT TUBES,TUYAUX FER,ACIER
6785	IRON,STEEL TUBE FITTINGS	W 6129	20.9	W 8746	30.0	W 10752	39.8			ACCESSOIRES DE TUYAUTERIE
68	NON-FERROUS METALS		144.8		270.5		165.6			METAUX NON FERREUX
682	COPPER EXC CEMENT COPPER	W 21757	54.1	W 33480	111.0	W 25598	71.2			CUIVRE
6821	COPPER NES,ALLOYS,UNWRT	W 14275	30.7	W 22968	71.1	W 17232	42.8			CUIVRE BRUT
68212	COPPER REFINED,UNWROUGHT	W 14203	30.4	W 22883	70.7	W 17175	42.5			CUIVRE AFFINE BRUT
6822	COPPER,ALLOYS WORKED	W 7481	23.5	W 10513	40.0	W 8367	28.5			CUIVRE,ALLIAGES OUVRES
684	ALUMINIUM	W 25378	60.7	W 31025	102.9	W 18339	60.3			ALUMINIUM
6842	ALUMINIUM,ALLOYS WORKED	W 24921	59.3	W 30470	100.8	W 18055	59.7			ALUMINIUM,ALLIAGES OUVRE
68422	ALUMNM PLATE,SHEET,STRIP	W 21899	48.3	W 25974	77.1	W 13906	40.6			TOLES, PLANCHES EN ALU
686	ZINC	W 16077	17.9	W 32646	35.2	W 15887	19.1			ZINC
6861	ZINC,ALLOYS UNWROUGHT	W 15034	16.1	W 32092	33.9	W 15358	17.9			ZINC ET ALLIAGES BRUTS
69	METAL MANUFACTURES NES		183.6		263.3		232.6			ART MANUFACT EN METAL NDA
695	TOOLS	W 4117	47.2	W 5762	72.5	W 4434	56.8			OUTILS A MAIN
6954	BLADES,TIPS,ETC FR TOOLS	W 1305	29.0	W 1494	40.4	W 1328	36.6			OUTILS POUR MACHINE-OUTIL
69541	PARTS TO INSERT IN TOOLS	W 763	23.0	W 919	32.5	W 831	28.7			OUTILS DE FORAGE
699	BASE METAL MFRS NES	W 12105	69.2	W 21624	96.5	W 19064	88.5			ART MANUFACTURES MET NDA
6997	IRON,STEEL ARTICLES NES	W 3785	22.4	W 5450	28.0	W 5479	30.6			OUV FONTE,FER,ACIER NDA
69979	IRN,STL MANUFACTURES NES	W 3542	21.9	W 5217	27.6	W 5222	30.1			AUT OUVRAGES EN FER NDA
7	MACHINES,TRANSPORT EQUIP		3583.5		3983.3		3380.4			MACHINES MATERIEL TRANSPORT
71	POWER GENERATING EQUIPMT		345.3		297.7		233.3			MACHINES GENERATRICES
713	INTRNL COMBUS PSTN ENGIN	W 24962	80.1	W 27677	117.2	W 28431	95.2			MOTEURS EXPL COMB INT, PIECE
7139	PISTON ENGINE PARTS NES	W 4232	51.8	W 5640	75.3	W 5168	61.3			PIECES POUR 713.2,3,8
714	ENGINES AND MOTORS NES	W 457	44.2	W 558	55.6	W 954	45.5			MOTEURS NON ELECTRIQUES
7149	ENGINE & MOTOR PARTS NES	W 318	28.1	W 366	33.3	W 643	30.7			PIECES 714 ET 718.88
71499	PARTS NES,OF 71488,71888	W 311	27.7	W 362	32.2	W 638	30.1			PIECES 714.88 ET 718.88
716	ROTATING ELECTRIC PLANT	W 15236	160.2	W 9966	84.2	W 8819	68.9			APP ELECTR ROTATIFS,PIECES
7161	DC MOTORS AND GENERATORS	W 4675	75.8	W 697	7.9	W 974	11.1			MOTEURS COURANT CONTINU
7162	AC MTRS,GENRTRS,GEN SETS	W 8969	73.2	W 8173	63.3	W 6977	48.3			MOTEURS ELECTRIQUES
71621	AC MTRS,INC UNIVRSL MTRS	W 3776	32.6	W 4687	34.4	W 3970	29.9			MOT ELEC NON COUR CONTINU
71622	AC GENERATORS	W 4525	33.4	W 2852	21.8	W 1717	11.5			GENER COURANT ALTERNATIF
718	OTH POWER GENERATG MACHY	W 2442	38.3	W 1337	25.0	W 1220	15.3			AUTRES MOTEURS PARTIES
7188	WIND,WATER,ETC ENGINES	W 2336	36.5	W 1316	24.9	W 663	14.7			MOT MACHINES MOTRICES NDA
71882	OTH HYDRAULIC ENGNS,MTRS	W 2185	33.0	W 1137	19.5	W 415	7.1			MACH MOTRICES HYDRAULQUES
72	MACHS FOR SPCL INDUSTRYS		279.0		356.8		339.5			MAC SPECIALES POUR INDUST
723	CIVIL ENGNEERG EQUIP ETC	W 10079	54.0	W 14103	88.1	W 16256	87.8			APPAREILS DE GENIE CIVIL
7234	CONST,MINING MACHNRY NES	W 7474	26.1	W 11357	45.4	W 11624	37.9			MACH POUR LA CONST, MINES
7239	CONSTR ETC MACHY PTS NES	W 2525	27.7	W 2616	42.1	W 4534	49.8			PIECES 723.41-723.46
724	TEXTILE,LEATHER MACHNRY	W 3600	28.6	W 3837	39.8	W 3379	27.9			MACH POUR INDUSTRIE TEXTILE
725	PAPER ETC MILL MACHINERY	W 2172	24.6	W 663	11.9	W 836	9.3			MACHINES FABR PATE PAPIER
727	FOOD MACHRY NON-DOMESTIC	W 3147	37.0	W 2222	39.3	W 3245	43.9			MACH INDUSTRIES ALIMENT
7272	OTH FOOD PROC MCHY,PARTS	W 2738	32.6	W 1884	33.6	W 2637	38.2			AUT MACH IND ALIMENTAIRE
72722	INDUS FOOD PROC MACH NES	W 1844	29.9	W 1492	30.1	W 2101	33.3			MACHINES BOULANGERIE
728	OTH MACHY FOR SPCL INDUS	W 9073	103.5	W 17565	138.1	W 14384	128.0			AUT MACH IND PARTICULIERES
7284	MACHY FOR SPCL INDUS NES	W 6094	82.9	W 14186	107.3	W 11275	103.2			MACH SPEC IND PARTICUL.
72848	OTH MCHY WITH INDIV FNCT	W 2806	39.2	W 10639	53.0	W 5973	53.2			AUTRES MACHINES NDA

4. General Imports F.O.B. by Commodities according to the S.I.T.C. (Rev. 2) in million U.S. Dollars
Importations Générales F.O.B. par Produits d'après la C.T.C.I. (Rév. 2) en millions de Dollars E.U.

SITC CTCI	COMMODITY	1994 QUANTITY QUANTITE	1994 VALUE VALEUR	1995 QUANTITY QUANTITE	1995 VALUE VALEUR	1996 QUANTITY QUANTITE	1996 VALUE VALEUR	1997 QUANTITY QUANTITE	1997 VALUE VALEUR	PRODUIT
73	METALWORKING MACHINERY		48.8		79.7		46.2			MACH TRAVAIL DES METAUX
736	METALWORKING MACH–TOOLS	W 4896	28.2	W 4224	32.6	W 4124	22.5			MACH–OUTILS TRAVAIL METAUX
737	METALWORKING MACHNRY NES	W 4791	20.7	W 6827	47.2	W 5868	23.8			MACH TRAV METAUX PIECES
74	GENRL INDUSTRL MACHY NES		897.1		914.2		917.1			MACH APP INDUSTRIE
741	HEATING,COOLING EQUIPMNT	W 56272	398.2	W 23654	184.4	W 23579	157.3			MACH CHAUFFAGE,PIECES
7413	INDUS FURNACES ETC,PARTS	W 2698	28.8	W 1865	11.6	W 1707	16.2			FOURS IND,LABOR,PIECES
7415	AIR–CONDITIONING MACHNRY	W 3991	18.7	W 6391	34.6	W 9038	36.6			GROUPES CONDITION AIR
7416	HEATING,COOLING EQU NES	W 48440	341.1	W 13167	117.3	W 9080	81.5			APP CHANGEMENT TEMP
742	PUMPS FOR LIQUIDS ETC	W 7430	83.6	W 9684	119.3	W 10781	126.0			POMPES MOTO–POMPES
7428	OTHER PUMPS FOR LIQUIDS	W 2220	23.6	W 3053	34.3	W 3418	44.4			AUTRES POMPES POUR LIQ
74288	PUMPS FR LIQUIDS NES ETC	W 2187	23.4	W 2944	32.6	W 3324	38.4			POMPES POUR LIQUIDES NDA
7429	PTS NES OF PUMPS OF 742	W 3083	32.0	W 3505	42.4	W 4248	40.1			PIECES POUR GROUPE 742
743	PUMPS NES,CENTRFUGES ETC	W 9689	94.0	W 15744	160.7	W 18968	193.0			POMPES COMPRES,VENT ETC
7431	PUMPS FOR GASES ETC	W 4766	28.4	W 10042	85.1	W 10510	109.6			POMPES AIR A VIDE,COMPRES
7436	GAS,LIQUID FILTERS ETC	W 2235	21.9	W 2890	27.3	W 3776	30.3			APP POUR FILT DES LIQUIDES
7439	PTS NES OF APP OF 7435,6	W 1850	33.7	W 2095	37.8	W 3470	40.6			PIECES 743.5 ET 743.6
744	MECHANICAL HANDLING EQU	W 10082	60.1	W 16692	116.0	W 15306	83.8			EQUIP MANUTENTION PIECES
7442	LIFTING,LOADING MACH NES	W 4473	25.1	W 9881	70.0	W 6970	42.9			APP LEVAGE,MANUTENTION
74428	OTH HANDLING ETC MCH NES	W 1387	10.0	W 6633	57.4	W 2711	14.7			AUT APP LEVAGE ETC
745	NONELEC MACHY,TOOLS NES	W 2571	45.6	W 3325	65.7	W 4660	79.3			AUT MACH NON ELEC,PIECES
7452	OTH NONELEC MCHS,PTS NES	W 2306	40.6	W 2999	58.0	W 4142	71.3			AUT MACH NON ELEC,PIECES
74522	PACKAGNG,BOTTLNG,ETC MCH	W 766	22.7	W 1055	30.0	W 1966	43.8			MACH NETT BOUTEILLES,ETC
749	NONELEC MACH PTS,ACC NES	W 13100	215.9	W 15607	268.3	W 19611	278.0			PIECES MACH NON ELEC NDA
7491	BALL,ROLLER,ETC BEARINGS	W 2454	33.9	W 3004	48.3	W 3168	42.9			ROULEMENTS BILLES ETC
7492	COCKS,VALVES ETC NES	W 4421	76.2	W 5311	93.9	W 9025	120.2			ART ROB,SIM POUR TUYAUX
7493	SHAFT,CRANK,PULLEY ETC	W 4390	62.6	W 5071	75.6	W 5182	67.1			ARBRES TRANS,VILEBREQUINS
7499	OTH NONELEC MCHY PTS NES	W 1835	43.4	W 2221	50.8	W 2237	47.8			PIECES NON ELECT NDA
75	OFFICE MACHINES,ADP EQUIP		195.2		341.3		292.4			MACH BUREAU TRAIT AUTOM
751	OFFICE MACHINES	W 2181	36.9	W 2238	47.0	W 2230	33.2			MACH,APPAREILS DE BUREAU
7518	OFFICE MACHINES NES	W 969	24.6	W 1221	31.6	W 1062	21.8			MACH,APP DE BUREAU NDA
752	AUTOMTIC DATA PROC EQUIP	W 2900	123.3	W 4299	218.9	W 5151	205.0			MACH TRAIT INFORMATION
7522	DIGITAL COMPUTERS	W 871	52.8	W 1361	86.6	W 465	28.7			MACH DIGITALES COMPLETES
7523	DIGITL CENTRL PROCESSORS	W 171	11.0	W 384	24.3	W 700	47.4			UNITES CENTRALES
7525	ADP PERIPHERAL UNITS	W 1313	39.0	W 1737	62.9	W 2042	37.7			UNITES PERIPHERIQUES
7528	OFF–LINE DATA PROC EQUIP	W 428	11.2	W 586	25.9	W 1675	75.6			MACH AUXIL TRAIT INFORM
759	OFFICE,ADP MCH PTS,ACCES	W 1467	35.0	W 1793	75.6	W 2105	54.3			PIECES DU 751 ET 752
7599	ACCTG,ETC,ADP MCH PTS,AC	W 1165	26.7	W 1559	64.8	W 1804	45.4			PIECES DU 751 ET 752
76	TELECOMM,SOUND EQUIPMENT		284.0		305.5		270.3			EQUIPMENT DE TELECOM
761	TELEVISION RECEIVERS	W 4424	24.9	W 5900	49.2	W 6294	36.9			RECEPTEURS DE TELEVISION
7611	COLOUR TV RECEIVERS	W 3726	22.9	W 5413	47.0	W 5652	35.2			RECEPTEURS COULEUR
764	TELECOM EQPT,PTS,ACC NES	W 4463	226.8	W 4304	196.0	W 4669	193.9			EQUIP TELECOM,PIECES
7641	LINE TELEPHONE,ETC EQUIP	W 1105	48.7	W 981	47.0	W 1008	43.3			APP TELEPHON PAR FIL
7643	TV,RADIO TRANSMITTRS ETC	W 1054	93.7	W 1140	97.8	W 1432	112.1			APP EMET TELE RADIO
7649	PTS NES OF EQUIPMT OF 76	W 1362	65.0	W 1182	36.4	W 1375	29.7			PIECES DE LA DIV 76
76493	TELECOMM EQUIPMT PTS NES	W 734	37.1	W 643	21.7	W 828	17.7			PIECES 761,762,764.3,8
77	ELECTRIC MACHNRY NES ETC		426.1		514.1		427.9			MACH APP ELECT NDA
771	ELECTRIC POWER MACHY NES	W 4991	47.8	W 5598	50.5	W 5149	38.6			MACH PROD,TRANS ELECTR
7711	TRANSFORMERS,ELECTRICAL	W 3132	33.4	W 3731	32.6	W 3068	17.4			TRANSFO ELECTRIQUES
772	SWITCHGEAR ETC,PARTS NES	W 5134	110.5	W 4711	98.9	W 5317	95.0			APP COUPURE,SECT ETC
7721	SWITCHGEAR ETC	W 4985	102.4	W 4580	92.3	W 5159	88.4			APP COUPURE,SECTIONMNT
773	ELECTR DISTRIBUTNG EQUIP	W 9968	58.6	W 6610	47.7	W 7541	48.7			EQUIPMT DISTRIBUTION ELECT
7731	INSULATED WIRE,CABLE ETC	W 8168	50.4	W 5105	41.6	W 5487	40.2			FILS,CABLES ISOLES ELECT
775	HOUSEHOLD TYPE EQUIP NES	W 13231	46.1	W 23099	95.7	W 23074	73.3			MACH,APP USAGE DOMESTQUE
7752	DOM REFRIGERATRS,FREEZRS	W 5488	15.3	W 11731	42.0	W 12464	32.5			REFRIG,CONGEL MENAGER
77521	DOMESTIC REFRIGERATORS	W 5192	13.5	W 10968	37.4	W 11444	27.2			REFRIGERATEURS
776	TRANSISTORS,VALVES,ETC	W 616	28.5	W 609	35.2	W 531	28.2			LAMPES,TUBES,VALVES
778	ELECTRICAL MACHINERY NES	W 29049	127.1	W 36094	171.0	W 33569	136.1			AUTRES MACH ELECT NDA
7788	OTH ELEC MACHY,EQUIP NES	W 15433	59.3	W 18605	73.2	W 13003	64.5			AUT MACH APP ELEC NDA
77887	ELECTRICAL CARBONS	W 14016	36.1	W 17326	46.0	W 11247	33.9			PIECES CHARBON,GRAPHITE
78	ROAD VEHICLES		807.9		1061.8		803.2			VEHICULES ROUTIERS
781	PASS MOTOR VEH EXC BUSES	W 70695	512.3	W 92027	637.4	W 73904	444.2			AUTO TRANSPORT PERSONNES
782	LORRIES,SPCL MTR VEH NES	W 31768	168.1	W 48190	249.8	W 35835	208.6			VEHICULES SPECIAUX,MARCH
7821	LORRIES,TRUCKS	W 30290	158.1	W 45561	231.4	W 33176	190.2			VEHICULES TRANSP MARCHAND
784	MOTOR VEH PRTS,ACCES NES	W 24207	90.7	W 31469	136.9	W 28348	107.2			PIECES 722,781,782,783
7849	OTHER MOTOR VEHCL PARTS	W 21747	76.8	W 28790	120.8	W 25480	92.2			PIECES 722,781,782,783
79	OTHR TRANSPORT EQUIPMENT		300.4		112.6		50.9			AUTRE MATERIEL TRANSPORT
791	RAILWAY VEHICLES	W 4933	68.5	W 4210	10.2	W 932	5.9			VEHIC MAT CHEMINS DE FER
7914	RY COACHES NES NOT POWRD	W 1002	49.8		0.1					VOITURES A VOYAGEURS
793	SHIPS AND BOATS ETC	W 58598	212.6	W 22019	80.5	W 18287	33.1			NAVIRES BATEAUX,ETC
7938	TUGS,SPECIAL VESSELS ETC	W 42925	190.4	W 15745	65.4	W 4145	18.1			REMORQUEURS,BATEAUX SPEC
79382	SPECL PURPOSE VESSLS ETC	W 37889	181.5	W 13845	62.2	W 1776	12.8			BAT–PHARES,–POMPES,DRAGUES
8	MISC MANUFACTURED GOODS		653.5		988.8		758.8			ART MANUFACTURES DIVERS
821	*FURNITURE,PARTS THEREOF	W 8092	31.4	W 8278	31.7	W 8863	32.9			MEUBLES ET PIECES
84	CLOTHING AND ACCESSORIES		135.2		275.4		147.9			VETEMENTS
842	MENS OUTERWEAR NOT KNIT	W 3241	22.8	W 5244	51.3	W 3315	25.4			VET DESSUS POUR HOMMES
8423	— TROUSERS,BREECHES ETC	W 2629	18.0	W 4661	43.4	W 2849	21.7			PANTALONS HOMMES MAT TEX
843	WOMENS OUTERWEAR NONKNIT	W 2896	29.5	W 3938	50.3	W 2596	28.9			VET DESSUS FEMMES MAT TEX
844	UNDER GARMENTS NOT KNIT	W 2127	18.2	W 3198	35.8	W 1812	17.1			VETEMENT DESSOUS MAT TEX
846	UNDER GARMENTS KNITTED	W 3188	35.1	W 4842	85.4	W 3052	47.0			SOUS VETS DE BONNETERIE
8462	— OF COTTON NON ELASTIC	W 2358	25.6	W 3763	60.2	W 2403	35.8			SOUS–VET BONNET COTON
84629	—— OTHER	W 2260	24.7	W 3615	58.5	W 2248	34.8			AUT SOUS–VET BONNET COTON
851	*FOOTWEAR	W 3251	19.9	W 5145	39.4	W 4423	29.4			CHAUSSURES
87	PRECISION INSTRUMNTS NES		152.7		189.1		175.8			INSTRUM,APPAR SCIENT NDA
872	MEDICAL INSTRUMENTS NES	W 1576	26.1	W 2333	35.4	W 1632	22.4			INSTR,APP MEDIC–CHIR NDA
874	MEASURNG,CONTROLNG INSTR	W 3336	118.9	W 3931	142.1	W 3872	145.0			INSTRUMENTS DE MESURE
8743	GAS,LIQUID CONTROL INSTR	W 1000	28.9	W 1052	34.4	W 979	31.1			APP,INSTR MESURE FLUIDES
8748	ELEC MEAS,CONTRL EQU NES	W 513	33.0	W 555	40.6	W 579	41.6			APP ELEC ELECTRO MESURE
87483	OTH ELCTRNC MEAS ETC EQU	W 355	25.3	W 327	31.7	W 382	31.2			AUT APP ELECTRO DE MESURE
88	PHOTO EQU,OPTICL GDS ETC		67.3		93.6		55.7			APP,FOURN PHOTO,OP,MONTR
882	PHOTO,CINEMA SUPPLIES	W 3547	36.7	W 4191	49.3	W 3450	32.5			PRODUITS PHOTO,CINEMA
8822	PHOTO FILM EXC DEV CINMA	W 1946	26.5	W 2576	33.8	W 2210	22.1			PLAQUES,PELLICULES,FILMS
89	MISC MANUFCTRD GOODS NES		225.3		326.3		293.6			ART MANUFACTURES DIVERS
892	PRINTED MATTER	W 9529	56.8	W 9348	67.1	W 10115	70.5			IMPRIMES
8921	PRINTED BOOKS,GLOBES,ETC	W 4548	32.7	W 4714	39.7	W 4329	33.8			LIVRES,BROCHURES,CARTES
89211	PRINTED BOOKS,PAMPHLETS	W 4396	32.2	W 4552	38.7	W 4136	33.1			LIVRES,BROCHURES
893	ARTICLES OF PLASTIC NES		62.2		90.4		90.0			OUVRAGES EN MAT DIVIS 58
8939	MISC PLASTIC ARTICLES	W 8365	45.9	W 11975	68.3	W 13459	63.2			ART DIVERS EN MAT DIV 58
89399	OTHR PLASTC ARTICLES NES	W 7884	44.5	W 11143	64.8	W 12805	61.3			AUT OUV MAT DIV 58
894	TOYS,SPORTING GOODS,ETC	W 9294	40.3	W 12384	67.7	W 12833	57.6			VOITURES ENFANTS,JOUETS
8942	TOYS,INDOOR GAMES ETC	W 7512	32.3	W 8625	48.7	W 9300	42.2			JOUETS,JEUX ETC
898	MUSICAL INSTRUMENTS,PTS	W 3082	28.9	W 2470	44.8	W 2472	37.5			INSTRUMENTS DE MUSIQUE

4. General Imports F.O.B. by Commodities according to the S.I.T.C. (Rev. 2) in million U.S. Dollars
Importations Générales F.O.B. par Produits d'après la C.T.C.I. (Rév. 2) en millions de Dollars E.U.

SITC CTCI	COMMODITY	1994			1995			1996			1997		PRODUIT
		QUANTITY QUANTITE		VALUE VALEUR	QUANTITY QUANTITE		VALUE VALEUR	QUANTITY QUANTITE		VALUE VALEUR	QUANTITY QUANTITE	VALUE VALEUR	
8983	SOUND RECRDNG TAPE,DISCS	W	2410	25.3	W	2129	41.7	W	2264	35.7			SUPPORTS SON POUR 763
89832	RECORDED DISCS,TAPES ETC	W	445	16.5	W	401	27.6	W	596	26.9			DISQUES,PHONO,BANDES

5. General Exports F.O.B. by Commodities according to the S.I.T.C. (Rev. 2) in million U.S. Dollars
Exportations Générales F.O.B. par Produits d'après la C.T.C.I. (Rév. 2) en millions de Dollars E.U.

SITC CTCI	COMMODITY	1994 QUANTITY QUANTITE	1994 VALUE VALEUR	1995 QUANTITY QUANTITE	1995 VALUE VALEUR	1996 QUANTITY QUANTITE	1996 VALUE VALEUR	1997 QUANTITY QUANTITE	1997 VALUE VALEUR	PRODUIT
	ALL COMMODITIES		16649.7		18914.3		22674.5		21657.7	TOUS PRODUITS
0	FOOD AND LIVE ANIMALS		334.5		347.8		337.0		374.1	ALIMENTS,ANIMAUX VIVANTS
03	FISH AND PREPARATIONS		88.6		75.7		83.3		112.7	POISSONS ET PREPARATIONS
036	SHELL FISH FRESH,FROZEN	W 5368	42.2	W 5789	31.3	W 28180	39.9	W 11227	76.5	CRUSTACES,MOLLUSQUES
04	CEREALS AND PREPARATIONS		64.5		95.2		65.2		90.2	CEREALES ET PRODUITS
1	BEVERAGES AND TOBACCO		104.7		162.4		157.0		103.5	BOISSONS ET TABACS
11	BEVERAGES		48.4		86.2		70.0		62.0	BOISSONS
112	ALCOHOLIC BEVERAGES	W 46621	37.8	W 102261	66.2	W 117024	47.4	W 94607	43.7	BOISSONS ALCOOLIQUES
12	TOBACCO AND MANUFACTURES		56.4		76.2		87.0		41.5	TABACS BRUTS FABRIQUES
122	TOBACCO,MANUFACTURED	W 9135	56.3	W 12888	75.6	W 17849	86.9	W 5695	36.8	TABACS FABRIQUES
1222	CIGARETTES	W 8287	54.7	W 11897	70.9	W 16668	84.9	W 4713	33.0	CIGARETTES
2	CRUDE MATERLS,EXCL FUELS		286.9		189.2		165.6		172.8	MAT BRUTES NON COMESTIBLES
28	METALLIFEROUS ORES,SCRAP		227.9		134.6		94.8		95.2	MINERAIS METAL,DECHETS
281	IRON ORE,CONCENTRATES		139.1	W 984	0.1			W 801513	15.5	MINERAIS DE FER
2815	IRON ORE,CONC,NOT AGGLOM		139.1	W 984	0.1			W 562878	7.7	MINERAIS NON AGGLOMERES
287	BASE METAL ORES,CONC NES	W 260731	43.4	W 391064	70.1	W 166526	25.5	W 252217	22.0	MINERAIS METAUX COMMUNS
2873	ALUMINIUM ORES,ALUMINA	W 260243	43.2	W 389620	69.0	W 165731	25.1	W 251582	21.8	MINERAIS D'ALUMINIUM
28732	ALUMINA(ALUMINIUM OXIDE)	W 260243	43.2	W 351140	68.1	W 165731	25.1	W 89395	19.0	ALUMINE (OXYDE ALUMINIUM)
3	MINERAL FUELS ETC		12644.5		14559.3		18628.2		18064.5	COMBUSTIBLES MINERAUX LUB
32	COAL,COKE AND BRIQUETTES		116.4		117.5		85.6		107.3	HOUILLES,COKES,BRIQUETTES
322	COAL,LIGNITE AND PEAT	W 3591169	116.4	W 3648845	117.5	W 2502475	85.6	W 3084220	107.3	HOUILLES,LIGNITES,TOURBE
3222	OTH COAL,NOT AGGLOMERATD	W 3591169	116.4	W 3648845	117.5	W 2502249	85.6	W 3084220	107.3	AUTRES HOUILLES
33	PETROLEUM AND PRODUCTS		12528.2		14441.9		18542.6		17957.3	PETROLE ET DERIVES
333	CRUDE PETROLEUM		8004.4		8576.4		12615.5		12176.8	HUILES BRUTES DE PETROLE
334	PETROLEUM PRODUCTS,REFIN		4523.7		5863.0		5923.7		5773.3	PRODUITS RAFFINES
5	CHEMCLS,RELATED PROD NES		504.2		788.9		704.0		679.5	PRODUITS CHIMIQUES
51	ORGANIC CHEMICALS		222.2		336.9		285.8		353.1	PROD CHIMIQ ORGANIQUES
512	ALCOHOLS,PHENOLS ETC	W 348493	95.2	W 604589	156.9	W 1038106	131.0	W 1078937	186.6	PHENOLS,PHENOLS–ALCOOLS
5121	ACYCLIC ALCOHOLS,DERIVS	W 339955	92.8	W 604339	156.5	W 1037840	130.6	W 1078857	186.5	ALCOOLS ACYCLIQUES
51211	METHYL ALCOHOL(METHANOL)	W 301567	76.1	W 574989	138.0	W 991912	109.6	W 1037028	161.7	ALCOOLS METHYLIQUES
516	OTHER ORGANIC CHEMICALS	W 449608	104.8	W 332209	99.1	W 484402	121.8	W 518761	135.6	AUTRES PROD ORGANIQUES
5161	ETHERS,EPOXIDES,ACETALS	W 449100	104.3	W 332033	98.9	W 484137	121.4	W 518509	134.9	ETHERS–OXYDES,ALCOOLS
51611	ETHERS,ETHER–ALCOHOL,ETC	W 449062	104.2	W 332033	98.9	W 484137	121.4	W 518509	134.9	ETHERS–OXYDES
52	INORGANIC CHEMICALS		53.3		83.8		68.0		50.8	PROD CHIM INORGANIQUES
522	INORG ELEMNTS,OXIDES,ETC	W 80931	27.4	W 220316	57.0	W 111561	40.3	W 140922	36.5	ELEMENTS INORGANIQUES
562	*FERTILIZERS,MANUFACTURE	W 17810	3.0	W 400753	75.8	W 125795	25.7	W 150511	20.4	ENGRAIS MANUFACTURES
5621	CHEM NITROGENOUS FERTLZR	W 715	0.2	W 390502	74.5	W 102587	21.1	W 121066	15.5	ENGRAIS AZOTES
56216	UREA	W 713	0.2	W 390336	74.4	W 102513	21.1	W 121066	15.5	UREE
58	PLASTIC MATERIALS ETC		102.9		154.5		177.4		112.0	MAT PLAST ARTIFICIELLES
583	POLYMERIZATION ETC PRODS	W 98641	83.1	W 127862	114.5	W 215463	151.1	W 130124	88.5	PROD POLYMERISATION
5831	POLYETHYLENE	W 46582	36.9	W 59503	51.5	W 140772	91.1	W 39354	36.3	POLYETHYLENE
58311	— IN PRIMARY FORMS	W 46013	36.1	W 57771	50.1	W 139858	90.5	W 37700	35.4	POLYETHYLENE PRIMAIRES
59	CHEMICAL MATERIALS NES		61.7		58.5		64.9		64.7	MAT PROD CHIMIQUES NDA
6	BASIC MANUFACTURES		1893.3		2135.3		2072.0		1764.8	ART MANUFACTURES
64	PAPER,PAPERBOARD AND MFR		75.4		119.2		103.1		113.5	PAPIERS,CARTONS & OUVRAGES
641	PAPER AND PAPERBOARD	W 93078	53.3	W 101458	80.2	W 102403	65.9	W 144218	83.7	PAPIERS ET CARTONS
65	TEXTILE YARN,FABRICS,ETC		59.2		62.0		60.7		31.8	FILS,TISSUS,ARTICLES TEXTILE
66	NONMETAL MINERAL MFS NES		187.2		204.0		222.9		242.0	ART MIN NON METALLIQUES
661	LIME,CEMENT,BLDG PRODS	W 1893584	69.4	W 3139651	96.4	W 2900424	120.3	W 3223424	124.9	CHAUX,CIMENTS MAT CONSTR
6612	CEMENT	W 1885563	66.1	W 3130970	92.6	W 2889865	116.8	W 3214202	120.9	CIMENTS HYDRAULIQUES
67	IRON AND STEEL		639.1		621.8		725.1		777.3	FER ET ACIER
671	PIG IRON ETC	W 1074697	114.7	W 1180099	143.8	W 1113916	150.2	W 1237039	150.9	FONTE,SPIEGEL,POUDRES
6713	IRON,STL POWDER,SHOT,ETC	W 1016868	91.1	W 1105516	104.2	W 1054013	114.2	W 1158621	115.4	POUDRES,GREN FER,ACIER
67133	SPONGE IRON OR STEEL	W 1016832	91.1	W 1105458	104.2	W 1024399	113.4	W 1136676	113.2	FER,ACIER SPONGIEUX AUT POUD
672	IRON,STEEL PRIMARY FORMS	W 1260367	252.9	W 803679	167.9	W 1316823	286.8	W 1235664	262.2	LINGOTS FER,ACIER
6724	IRN,STL INGOTS,LUMPS,ETC	W 506089	59.5	W 342033	44.2	W 260205	34.8	W 505942	64.0	FER,ACIER LINGOTS,MASSES
67245	IRN,STL BLOCKS,LUMPS,ETC	W 505991	59.5	W 341864	44.2	W 260154	34.8	W 505821	64.0	FER,ACIER EN MASSES
6725	IRN,STL BLOOMS,SLABS,ETC	W 449354	101.8	W 356638	87.3	W 807705	184.5	W 451671	121.8	BLOOMS,BILLETTES FER ACIER
67251	IRN,SMPLE STL BLOOMS,ETC	W 449353	101.8	W 356573	87.3	W 807679	184.5	W 451432	121.7	BLOOMS ETC NON ACIER FIN
6727	IRN,STL COIL FR REROLLNG	W 304924	91.6	W 105009	36.5	W 248914	67.6	W 278051	76.4	EBAUCHES POUR TOLES FER
67271	IRON,SIMPLE STEEL COILS	W 302680	90.5	W 104468	36.2	W 248536	67.4	W 278003	76.4	EBAUCHES NON EN ACIER
673	IRON,STEEL SHAPES ETC	W 311522	97.1	W 284082	89.4	W 405967	115.9	W 423231	119.8	BARRES,PROFIL FER,ACIER
6731	IRON,STEEL WIRE ROD	W 173111	52.2	W 148435	45.8	W 265155	72.9	W 278049	79.7	FIL MACHINE FER,ACIER
67311	IRON,SIMPLE STL WIRE ROD	W 172143	51.9	W 147804	45.6	W 265044	72.8	W 278007	79.7	FIL MACH AUT ACIER FIN
674	IRN,STL UNIV,PLATE,SHEET	W 344038	142.7	W 368469	183.2	W 282944	126.9	W 495619	193.8	LARGES PLATS,TOLES
6746	IRN,STL THIN PLATE,ROLLD	W 225738	87.6	W 256479	121.7	W 162488	66.5	W 362109	144.8	TOLES LAM MOINS 3MM
67461	— OF IRON OR SIMPLE STL	W 225710	87.5	W 256262	121.6	W 162439	66.4	W 362087	144.7	TOL NON AC FIN MOINS 3 MM
68	NON–FERROUS METALS		749.0		929.4		751.8		372.9	METAUX NON FERREUX
684	ALUMINIUM	W 556872	734.4	W 500282	913.7	W 444088	734.1	W 213214	360.8	ALUMINIUM
6841	ALUMINIUM,ALLOYS,UNWRGHT	W 459870	582.0	W 407724	728.4	W 352223	544.0	W 118642	191.2	ALUMINIUM,ALLIAGES BRUTS
6842	ALUMINIUM,ALLOYS WORKED	W 97003	152.5	W 92558	185.4	W 91864	190.2	W 94571	169.7	ALUMINIUM,ALLIAGES OUVRE
68421	ALUMINIUM BARS,WIRE,ETC	W 57186	85.4	W 52669	91.6	W 54269	118.4	W 46444	83.2	BARRES,PROFILES FILS ALU
68422	ALUMNM PLATE,SHEET,STRIP	W 35700	58.7	W 33945	78.3	W 25759	48.6	W 18873	38.5	TOLES, PLANCHES EN ALU
69	METAL MANUFACTURES NES		112.9		114.4		148.1		153.3	ART MANUFACT EN METAL NDA
693	WIRE PRODUCTS NON ELECTR	W 27306	30.6	W 25848	39.3	W 142551	69.5	W 33368	56.5	OUVRAGES FILS METALLIQUES
7	MACHINES,TRANSPORT EQUIP		516.6		537.0		475.6		397.8	MACHINES MATERIEL TRANSPORT
78	ROAD VEHICLES		416.5		440.3		367.2		290.8	VEHICULES ROUTIERS
781	PASS MOTOR VEH EXC BUSES	W 20884	205.1	W 19288	228.9	W 21261	212.1	W 14726	175.4	AUTO TRANSPORT PERSONNES
782	LORRIES,SPCL MTR VEH NES	W 15426	96.3	W 14848	105.2	W 9529	46.4	W 4181	33.7	VEHICULES SPECIAUX,MARCH
7821	LORRIES,TRUCKS	W 15153	95.4	W 14513	104.2	W 9407	45.7	W 4115	32.9	VEHICULES TRANSP MARCHAND
784	MOTOR VEH PRTS,ACCES NES	W 50335	85.5	W 53605	96.6	W 55312	104.4	W 49529	79.9	PIECES 722,781,782,783
7849	OTHER MOTOR VEHCL PARTS	W 49991	83.7	W 53420	95.4	W 54695	100.7	W 48897	78.5	PIECES 722,781,782,783
8	MISC MANUFACTURED GOODS		89.8		89.3		86.8		97.3	ART MANUFACTURES DIVERS
89	MISC MANUFCTRD GOODS NES		52.7		54.4		48.8		62.7	ART MANUFACTURES DIVERS
9	GOODS NOT CLASSD BY KIND		272.8		100.1		44.0		0.3	ART TRANSACT NON CLASSES
971	*GOLD,NON MONETARY NES	K 37233	272.5	K 8013	100.1	K 3230	41.3			OR NON MONETAIRE
97101	NONMON GLD UNWRT,SEMIMFD	K 22233	272.5	K 8013	100.1	K 3230	41.3			OR,ALLIAGES D'OR BRUTS

1. HISTORICAL SERIES, 1975–1996 GENERAL TRADE, IMPORTS C.I.F., EXPORTS F.O.B.
SERIES HISTORIQUES, 1975–1996 COMMERCE GENERAL, IMPORTATIONS C.A.F., EXPORTATIONS F.O.B

YEAR ANNEE	VALUE IN MILLION U.S. DOLLARS / VALEUR EN MILLION U.S. DOLLARS — MERCHANDISE –MARCHANDISE		GOLD –OR		CONVERSION FACTORS FACTEURS DE CONVERSION CENTS E.U. PAR		INDEX NUMBERS –INDICES — QUANTUM		UNIT VALUE VALEUR UNITAIRE	
	IMPORTS	EXPORTS	IMPORTS	EXPORTS	IMPORTS	EXPORTS	IMPORTS	EXPORTS	IMPORTS	EXPORTS
1975	1040.06	202.85								
1976	799.90	230.11								
1977	1141.84	456.08								
1978	1160.00	482.00								
1979	1225.00	535.00								
1986	2155.00	823.00								
1987	2455.00	854.00								
1988	2757.00	1038.00								
1989	2566.00	1946.00								
1990	2752.00	2404.00								
1991	2338.00	2087.00								
1992	2540.00	2580.00								
1993	3924.00	2985.00								
1994	5825.00	4054.00								
1995	8155.00	5448.00								
1996	11144.00	7255.00								

2. IMPORTS BY BROAD ECONOMIC CATEGORY AND EXPORTS BY INDUSTRIAL ORIGIN. (PERCENTAGE OF TOTAL VALUE)
IMPORTATIONS PAR CATEGORIES ECONOMIQUES ET EXPORTATIONS PAR BRANCHE D'ACTIVITE.(EN POURCENTAGE DE LA VALEUR TOTALE)

IMPORTS – IMPORTATIONS

	1989	1990	1991	1992	1993	1994	1995
TOTAL IMPORTS–IMPORTATIONS TOTALES							
1 FOOD BEV–ALIMENTATION BOISSONS							
11 PRIMARY–PRODUITS DE BASE							
111 FOR INDUSTRY–POUR L'INDUSTRIE							
112 FOR HOUSEHOLDS–POUR LES MENAGES							
12 PROCESSED–PRODUITS ELABORES							
121 FOR INDUSTRY–POUR L'INDUSTRIE							
122 FOR HOUSEHOLDS–POUR LES MENAGES							
2 IND SUPPLIES–APPROV INDUSTRIELS							
21 PRIMARY–PRODUITS DE BASE							
22 PROCESSED–PRODUITS ELABORES							
3 FUELS–COMBUSTIBLES							
31 PRIMARY–PRODUITS DE BASE							
32 PROCESSED–PRODUITS ELABORES							
321 MOTOR SPIRIT–ESSENCE							
322 OTHER–AUTRES							
4 MACHINERY–EQUIPEMENT							
41 CAPITAL EQUIPMENT–MACHINES							
42 PARTS–PIECES ACCESSOIRES							
5 TRANSPORT–TRANSPORT							
51 PASSENGER CARS–AUTOMOBILES							
52 OTHER–AUTRES							
521 INDUSTRIAL–INDUSTRIELS							
522 NON INDUSTRIAL–NON INDUSTRIEL							
53 PARTS–PIECES ACCESSOIRES							
6 CONSUM GOODS–BIENS CONSOMMATION							
61 DURABLE–DURABLES							
62 SEMI DURABLE–SEMI DURABLES							
63 NON DURABLE–NON DURABLES							
7 GOODS NES–BIENS NDA							

EXPORTS – EXPORTATIONS

	1989	1990	1991	1992	1993	1994	1995
TOTAL EXPORTS–EXPORTATIONS TOTALES							
1 AGRICULTURE							
2 MINING QUARRY–INDUS EXTRACTIVES							
3 MANUFACTURING–IND MANUFACTUR							
31 FOOD BEV TOBACCO–ALIM BOISS TAB							
32 TEXTILES–INDUSTRIES TEXTILES							
33 WOOD & PRODUCTS–BOIS & PRODUITS							
34 PAPER & PRODUCTS–PAPIER & PRODT							
35 CHEMICALS–INDUSTRIES CHIMIQUES							
36 NON METAL MIN–MIN NON METAL							
37 BASIC METAL–IND METAL BASE							
38 METAL MANUF–MANUF METAL							
39 OTH MANUF IND–AUTRES MANUF							

Viet Nam

3. TRADE BY PRINCIPAL COUNTRIES OF PURCHASE AND SALE (VALUE IN MILLION U.S. DOLLARS)
ECHANGES SELON LES PRINCIPAUX PAYS D'ACHAT ET DE VENTE (VALEUR EN MILLIONS DE DOLLARS EU)

COUNTRIES–PAYS	GENERAL IMPORTS C.I.F. IMPORTATIONS GENERALES C.A.F				
	1991	1992	1993	1994	1995
World	2338.1	2540.8	3924.0	5825.8	8155.4
Africa	2.2	4.9			14.9
Americas	10.4	24.8	27.0	71.6	157.0
– Northern America	6.9	16.0	22.5	71.0	155.3
– LAIA					
– CACM					
– Caribbean	3.5	8.8	4.5	0.6	1.7
– Rest of America					
Asia excl fmr USSR	1418.5	1662.5	2713.7	3896.8	6277.6
– Middle East					
Asia former USSR					
Europe excl fmr USSR	351.1	308.7	504.9	593.5	792.0
– European Union	301.2	253.6	456.9	504.4	664.0
– Eastern Europe	44.5	14.9	24.6	36.5	52.3
– Rest of Europe	5.4	40.2	23.4	52.6	75.7
Europe former USSR	358.1	100.3	167.6	314.8	150.7
Oceania	11.0	19.8	33.0	69.3	103.9
Other	181.3	408.2	451.0	749.9	452.2
Singapore/Singapour	722.2	821.6	1058.3	1145.9	1425.2
Korea, Republic of	152.1	211.2	481.5	720.5	1253.5
Japan/Japon	157.7	239.4	452.3	585.7	915.7
Areas n.e.s.	144.8	385.3	420.1	727.3	430.6
Other Asia n.e.s.	59.3	72.7	217.9	396.1	901.3
China, Hong Kong SAR	194.8	142.9	145.4	318.6	418.9
France, Monaco	147.9	159.9	267.4	239.6	276.6
Thailand/Thaïlande	14.2	41.2	99.5	225.7	439.7
Russian Federation		100.1	144.3	288.7	144.8
China/Chine	18.4	31.8	85.5	144.2	329.7
Germany/Allemagne	101.2	40.6	72.0	149.1	175.5
Indonesia/Indonésie	49.4	39.8	84.5	116.3	190.0
Former USSR/Anc. URSS	358.1				
Malaysia/Malaisie	6.2	35.9	24.8	66.1	190.5
Lao People's Dem Rep	3.3	7.7	41.9	102.9	84.0
Australia/Australie	9.6	15.8	30.3	63.9	100.6
USA/Etats–Unis d'Amer	1.1	2.0	3.8	44.3	130.4
Switzerland,Liechtenst.	5.0	39.5	13.4	26.3	74.6
Special Categories	36.5	22.9	30.9	22.6	21.6
India/Inde	24.0	9.0	8.1	28.2	61.5
Italy/Italie	1.2	6.0	34.8	34.2	53.6
Netherlands/Pays–Bas	8.4	16.2	25.8	25.1	36.3
United Kingdom	9.0	3.7	11.4	19.3	50.7
Canada	5.8	14.0	18.7	26.7	24.9
Sweden/Suède	14.2	12.8	18.5	18.6	22.6
Poland/Pologne	8.4	6.7	15.2	23.8	21.9
Cambodia/Cambodge	5.2	6.7	7.6	17.7	23.5
Ukraine		0.2	22.2	26.1	5.9
Philippines	10.6	0.5	1.9	15.0	24.7
Belgium–Luxembourg	6.8	5.0	8.1	9.3	21.7
Hungary/Hongrie	13.6	3.2	4.7	7.8	19.3
Korea Dem People's Rp	1.1	2.1	4.5	13.9	19.4
Austria/Autriche	2.5	3.9	13.6	5.4	15.3
Norway,Svalbard and JM	0.0		10.0	26.3	1.1
Finland/Finlande	10.0	5.5	5.3	3.8	11.7
Former Czechoslovakia	18.9	4.3			
Cuba	3.5	8.8	4.5	0.6	1.7
Egypt/Egypte	2.2				14.9
New Zealand	1.4	4.0	2.7	5.4	3.3
Czech Republic			4.7	3.1	4.0

COUNTRIES–PAYS	GENERAL EXPORTS F.O.B. EXPORTATIONS GENERALES F.O.B.				
	1991	1992	1993	1994	1995
Monde	2087.1	2580.7	2985.2	4054.3	5448.9
Afrique	13.3	23.0	6.3	19.6	27.8
Amériques	6.0	21.4	37.6	131.6	232.3
– Amérique du Nord	1.3	2.7	6.0	100.7	187.5
– ALAI					
– MCAC					
– Caraïbes	4.7	18.7	31.6	30.9	44.8
– Autre Amérique					
Asie anc. URSS exclus	1602.4	1901.6	2157.4	2907.3	3914.1
– Moyen–Orient	0.7	14.2	12.5	21.3	35.7
Asie ancienne URSS					
Europe anc. URSS exclus	138.9	262.4	265.1	452.5	758.2
– Union Européenne	119.3	239.8	229.8	393.7	647.1
– Europe de l'Est	16.5	15.8	24.6	29.0	47.2
– Autre de l'Europe	3.1	6.8	10.7	29.8	63.9
Europe ancienne URSS	214.5	105.7	136.7	94.9	87.4
Océanie	5.2	21.4	54.7	49.7	56.7
Autre	101.8		289.6		
Japan/Japon	719.3	833.9	936.9	1179.3	1461.0
Singapore/Singapour	425.0	401.7	380.3	593.5	689.8
China, Hong Kong SAR	223.3	201.7	169.0	196.8	256.7
Other Asia n.e.s.	58.3	67.3	141.9	220.0	439.4
China/Chine	19.3	95.6	135.8	295.7	361.9
France, Monaco	83.1	132.3	95.0	116.8	169.1
Korea, Republic of	51.3	93.5	99.4	86.4	235.3
Germany/Allemagne	6.7	34.4	50.1	115.2	218.0
Russian Federation		104.8	135.4	90.2	80.8
Thailand/Thaïlande	57.7	71.5	71.8	97.6	101.3
Areas n.e.s.	101.8		289.6		
Malaysia/Malaisie	14.5	68.4	55.8	64.8	110.5
Cambodia/Cambodge	6.3	6.4	96.2	77.3	94.6
USA/Etats–Unis d'Amer	0.9	0.1	0.1	94.9	169.7
Former USSR/Anc. URSS	214.5				
Netherlands/Pays–Bas	16.1	20.1	28.1	60.6	79.7
United Kingdom	2.4	27.5	23.0	55.7	74.6
Australia/Australie	5.2	21.4	54.7	46.0	55.3
Indonesia/Indonésie	16.5	10.9	22.9	35.3	53.8
Cuba	4.7	18.7	31.6	30.9	44.8
Switzerland,Liechtenst.	0.8	5.7	10.6	28.3	61.8
Italy/Italie	3.8	7.2	8.1	20.4	57.1
Iraq	0.7	14.2	12.5	21.3	35.7
Lao People's Dem Rep	3.6	16.0	14.4	20.9	20.6
India/Inde	5.5	19.4	18.9	14.1	10.4
Belgium–Luxembourg	0.1	6.4	11.8	15.1	34.6
Hungary/Hongrie	5.0	6.2	8.7	12.3	20.9
Algeria/Algérie	13.3	10.0	6.1	10.6	11.1
Philippines	0.7	1.0	1.6	3.6	41.5
Poland/Pologne	4.2	6.1	9.7	10.4	16.6
Austria/Autriche	5.9	10.7	10.0	7.5	9.3
Libyan Arab Jamahiriya		13.0	0.2	9.0	16.7
Canada	0.4	2.6	5.9	5.8	17.8
Bulgaria/Bulgarie	3.1	1.2	3.3	4.3	2.0
Sweden/Suède	1.2	1.2	3.7	2.4	4.7
Czech Republic			2.9	2.0	7.7
Ukraine		0.8	0.9	4.3	6.5
Former Czechoslovakia	4.2	2.1			
New Zealand				3.7	1.4
Norway,Svalbard and JM	0.0	0.7	0.1	1.4	2.1

(VALUE AS PERCENTAGE OF WORLD TOTAL)(VALEURS EN POURCENTAGE DU TOTAL MONDIAL)

	1986	1987	1988	1989	1990	1991	1992	1993	1994	1995
Africa					0.1	0.1	0.2			0.2
Americas		0.4	0.3	0.4	0.4	0.4	1.0	0.7	1.2	1.9
– Northern America		0.0		0.1	0.2	0.3	0.6	0.6	1.2	1.9
– LAIA										
– CACM										
– Caribbean		0.4	0.3	0.3	0.3	0.1	0.3	0.1	0.0	0.0
– Rest of America										
Asia excl fmr USSR		8.4	8.8	11.1	36.7	60.7	65.4	69.2	66.9	77.0
– Middle East										
Asia former USSR										
Europe excl fmr USSR		10.3	11.2	9.3	14.3	15.0	12.1	12.9	10.2	9.7
– European Union		1.9	3.6	2.4	9.7	12.9	10.0	11.6	8.7	8.1
– Eastern Europe		8.3	7.6	6.9	4.1	1.9	0.6	0.6	0.6	0.6
– Rest of Europe					0.5	0.2	1.6	0.6	0.9	0.9
Europe former USSR		70.4	65.3	59.7	44.0	15.3	3.9	4.3	5.4	1.8
Oceania		0.4	0.1	0.4	0.4	0.5	0.8	0.8	1.2	1.3
Other					4.1	7.8	16.1	11.5	12.9	5.5
Singapore/Singapour		1.0	1.3	1.6	18.1	30.9	32.3	27.0	19.7	17.5
Korea, Republic of		0.3	0.2	0.6	1.9	6.5	8.3	12.3	12.4	15.4
Japan/Japon		4.2	5.0	4.1	6.1	6.7	9.4	11.5	10.1	11.2
Areas n.e.s.					3.3	6.2	15.2	10.7	12.5	5.3
Other Asia n.e.s.					1.5	2.5	2.9	5.6	6.8	11.1
China, Hong Kong SAR		1.4	1.1	4.0	7.2	8.3	5.6	3.7	5.5	5.1
France, Monaco		1.5	3.3	2.0	4.5	6.3	6.3	6.8	4.1	3.4
Thailand/Thaïlande		0.0	0.1	0.1	0.6	0.6	1.6	2.5	3.9	5.4
Russian Federation							3.9	3.7	5.0	1.8
China/Chine					0.2	0.8	1.3	2.2	2.5	4.0

	1986	1987	1988	1989	1990	1991	1992	1993	1994	1995
Afrique					0.2	0.6	0.9	0.2	0.5	0.5
Amériques		1.4			0.6	0.3	0.8	1.3	3.2	4.3
– Amérique du Nord		0.1			0.1	0.1	0.1	0.2	2.5	3.4
– ALAI										
– MCAC										
– Caraïbes		1.3			0.5	0.2	0.7	1.1	0.8	0.8
– Autre Amérique										
Asie anc. URSS exclus		20.5			42.5	76.8	73.7	72.3	71.7	71.8
– Moyen–Orient		0.4			0.2	0.0	0.6	0.4	0.5	0.7
Asie ancienne URSS										
Europe anc. URSS exclus		22.6			12.1	6.7	10.2	8.9	11.2	13.9
– Union Européenne		3.6			5.4	5.7	9.3	7.7	9.7	11.9
– Europe de l'Est		18.9			6.5	0.8	0.6	0.8	0.7	0.9
– Autre de l'Europe					0.2	0.1	0.3	0.4	0.7	1.2
Europe ancienne URSS		39.2			38.3	10.3	4.1	4.6	2.3	1.6
Océanie		0.6			0.3	0.2	0.8	1.8	1.2	1.0
Autre						4.9		9.7		
Japan/Japon		6.0	5.8	13.4	14.2	34.5	32.3	31.4	29.1	26.8
Singapore/Singapour		6.7	5.9	3.6	8.1	20.4	15.6	12.7	14.6	12.7
China, Hong Kong SAR		5.8	6.3	4.1	10.1	10.7	7.8	5.7	4.9	4.7
Other Asia n.e.s.					1.2	2.8	2.6	4.8	5.4	8.1
China/Chine				0.0	0.3	0.9	3.7	4.5	7.3	6.6
France, Monaco		3.3	2.9	4.1	4.8	4.0	5.1	3.2	2.9	3.1
Korea, Republic of		0.5	0.7	1.3	1.1	2.5	3.6	3.3	2.1	4.3
Germany/Allemagne						0.3	1.3	1.7	2.8	4.0
Russian Federation							4.1	4.5	2.2	1.5
Thailand/Thaïlande		0.0	0.1	0.8	2.2	2.8	2.8	2.4	2.4	1.9

4. General Imports C.I.F. by Commodities according to the S.I.T.C. (Rev. 2) in million U.S. Dollars
Importations Générales C.A.F. par Produits d'après la C.T.C.I. (Rév. 2) en millions de Dollars E.U.

SITC CTCI	COMMODITY	1992 QUANTITY QUANTITE	1992 VALUE VALEUR	1993 QUANTITY QUANTITE	1993 VALUE VALEUR	1994 QUANTITY QUANTITE	1994 VALUE VALEUR	1995 QUANTITY QUANTITE	1995 VALUE VALEUR	PRODUIT
	ALL COMMODITIES				3924.0		5825.8		8155.4	TOUS PRODUITS
022	MILK AND CREAM				16.7		39.4		64.1	LAIT ET CREME
046	WHEAT ETC MEAL OR FLOUR				68.1		73.2		82.7	SEMOULE FARINE,FROMENT
062	SUGAR CANDY NON-CHOCLATE				120.6		337.6		446.7	SUCRERIES
122	TOBACCO,MANUFACTURED				59.1		79.1		97.1	TABACS FABRIQUES
263	COTTON				20.7		29.6		121.1	COTON
334	PETROLEUM PRODUCTS,REFIN				638.8		657.1		630.4	PRODUITS RAFFINES
5417	MEDICAMENTS				86.1		121.7		69.2	MEDICAMENTS
562	*FERTILIZERS,MANUFACTURE				389.4		575.5		649.0	ENGRAIS MANUFACTURES
56216	UREA				163.8		229.9		271.2	UREE
5911	INSECTICIDES,FOR RETAIL				33.5		59.0		100.5	INSECTICIDES VENTE DET
651	TEXTILE YARN				131.3		234.1		370.5	FILS TEXTILES
6612	CEMENT				7.1		31.0		72.1	CIMENTS HYDRAULIQUES
6613	BUILDING STONE ETC WORKD				89.7		373.3		542.0	PIERRES A BATIR

5. General Exports F.O.B. by Commodities according to the S.I.T.C. (Rev. 2) in million U.S. Dollars
Exportations Générales F.O.B. par Produits d'après la C.T.C.I. (Rév. 2) en millions de Dollars E.U.

SITC CTCI	COMMODITY	1992		1993		1994		1995		PRODUIT
		QUANTITY QUANTITE	VALUE VALEUR	QUANTITY QUANTITE	VALUE VALEUR	QUANTITY QUANTITE	VALUE VALEUR	QUANTITY QUANTITE	VALUE VALEUR	
	ALL COMMODITIES				2985.2		4054.3		5448.9	TOUS PRODUITS
03	FISH AND PREPARATIONS				427.2		551.2		621.4	POISSONS ET PREPARATIONS
0342	FISH FROZEN,EXCL FILLETS				24.7		27.7		51.7	POISSONS CONGELES
036	SHELL FISH FRESH,FROZEN				231.6		330.8		278.2	CRUSTACES,MOLLUSQUES
042	RICE				310.0		476.0		429.5	RIZ
05773	CASHEW NUTS,FRESH,DRIED				189.8		223.8		470.8	NOIX DE CAJOU
071	COFFEE AND SUBSTITUTES				195.2		489.7		928.9	CAFE ET SUCCEDANES
0741	TEA				44.0		49.3		43.2	THE
0751	PEPPER AND PIMENTO				21.6		28.3		43.1	POIVRE,PIMENTS
232	NATURAL RUBBER,GUMS				83.5		138.8		217.9	LATEX CAOUTCHOUC NATUREL
248	WOOD SHAPED,SLEEPERS				86.2		2.7			BOIS SIMPLEMENT TRAVAILLES
322	COAL,LIGNITE AND PEAT				65.9		84.9		112.8	HOUILLES,LIGNITES,TOURBE
333	CRUDE PETROLEUM				732.2		792.2		964.2	HUILES BRUTES DE PETROLE
656	LACE,RIBBONS,TULLE,ETC				22.2		18.3		20.5	TULLES,BRODERIE
687	TIN				15.0		15.9		18.9	ETAIN
84	CLOTHING AND ACCESSORIES				238.8		475.6		765.5	VETEMENTS
851	*FOOTWEAR				68.1		122.1		296.4	CHAUSSURES
896	WORKS OF ART ETC				20.6		20.8		18.8	OBJETS D'ART

1. HISTORICAL SERIES, 1991–1995 GENERAL TRADE, IMPORTS C.I.F., EXPORTS F.O.B.
SERIES HISTORIQUES, 1991–1995 COMMERCE GENERAL, IMPORTATIONS C.A.F., EXPORTATIONS F.O.B

YEAR ANNEE	VALUE IN MILLION YEMENI RIALS VALEUR EN MILLION YEMENI RIALS MERCHANDISE –MARCHANDISE IMPORTS	EXPORTS	GOLD –OR IMPORTS	EXPORTS	CONVERSION FACTORS U.S. CENTS PER YEMENI RIAL FACTEURS DE CONVERSION CENTS E.U. PAR YEMENI RIAL IMPORTS	EXPORTS	INDEX NUMBERS –INDICES QUANTUM IMPORTS	EXPORTS	UNIT VALUE VALEUR UNITAIRE IMPORTS	EXPORTS
1991	23509.52	7684.78			8.3263	8.3263				
1992	31075.62	5693.35			8.3263	8.3263				
1993	33883.23	4494.60			8.3263	8.3263				
1994	25070.22	11215.60			8.3263	8.3263				
1995	64590.68	74785.12			1.9984	1.9984				

2. IMPORTS BY BROAD ECONOMIC CATEGORY AND EXPORTS BY INDUSTRIAL ORIGIN. (PERCENTAGE OF TOTAL VALUE)
IMPORTATIONS PAR CATEGORIES ECONOMIQUES ET EXPORTATIONS PAR BRANCHE D'ACTIVITE.(EN POURCENTAGE DE LA VALEUR TOTALE)

IMPORTS – IMPORTATIONS

	1989	1990	1991	1992	1993	1994	1995
TOTAL IMPORTS–IMPORTATIONS TOTALES			100.				100.
1 FOOD BEV–ALIMENTATION BOISSONS			25.8				24.1
11 PRIMARY–PRODUITS DE BASE			11.1				8.6
111 FOR INDUSTRY–POUR L'INDUSTRIE			6.7				4.7
112 FOR HOUSEHOLDS–POUR LES MENAGES			4.4				3.9
12 PROCESSED–PRODUITS ELABORES			14.7				15.5
121 FOR INDUSTRY–POUR L'INDUSTRIE			3.7				6.0
122 FOR HOUSEHOLDS–POUR LES MENAGES			10.9				9.4
2 IND SUPPLIES–APPROV INDUSTRIELS			16.8				34.5
21 PRIMARY–PRODUITS DE BASE			1.2				3.1
22 PROCESSED–PRODUITS ELABORES			15.6				31.4
3 FUELS–COMBUSTIBLES			40.5				7.8
31 PRIMARY–PRODUITS DE BASE							0.0
32 PROCESSED–PRODUITS ELABORES			40.5				7.8
321 MOTOR SPIRIT–ESSENCE			12.5				1.6
322 OTHER–AUTRES			28.0				6.2
4 MACHINERY–EQUIPEMENT			5.0				13.1
41 CAPITAL EQUIPMENT–MACHINES			4.7				11.0
42 PARTS–PIECES ACCESSOIRES			0.3				2.1
5 TRANSPORT–TRANSPORT			6.4				10.0
51 PASSENGER CARS–AUTOMOBILES			1.8				2.4
52 OTHER–AUTRES			0.7				2.7
521 INDUSTRIAL–INDUSTRIELS			0.7				2.7
522 NON INDUSTRIAL–NON INDUSTRIEL			0.0				0.0
53 PARTS–PIECES ACCESSOIRES			3.9				4.9
6 CONSUM GOODS–BIENS CONSOMMATION			5.5				10.3
61 DURABLE–DURABLES			1.4				2.4
62 SEMI DURABLE–SEMI DURABLES			1.2				4.4
63 NON DURABLE–NON DURABLES			2.9				3.5
7 GOODS NES–BIENS NDA			0.0				0.0

EXPORTS – EXPORTATIONS

	1989	1990	1991	1992	1993	1994	1995
TOTAL EXPORTS–EXPORTATIONS TOTALES			100.				100.
1 AGRICULTURE			8.0				2.2
2 MINING QUARRY–INDUS EXTRACTIVES			0.4				89.8
3 MANUFACTURING–IND MANUFACTUR			91.6				8.0
31 FOOD BEV TOBACCO–ALIM BOISS TAB			1.0				1.1
32 TEXTILES–INDUSTRIES TEXTILES			0.4				0.3
33 WOOD & PRODUCTS–BOIS & PRODUITS							0.0
34 PAPER & PRODUCTS–PAPIER & PRODT			0.0				0.1
35 CHEMICALS–INDUSTRIES CHIMIQUES			89.4				4.8
36 NON METAL MIN–MIN NON METAL							0.0
37 BASIC METAL–IND METAL BASE			0.1				0.1
38 METAL MANUF–MANUF METAL			0.6				1.6
39 OTH MANUF IND–AUTRES MANUF							0.0

3. TRADE BY PRINCIPAL COUNTRIES OF ORIGIN AND DESTINATION (VALUE IN MILLION U.S. DOLLARS)
ECHANGES SELON LES PRINCIPAUX PAYS D'ORIGINE ET DE DESTINATION (VALEUR EN MILLIONS DE DOLLARS EU)

COUNTRIES–PAYS	GENERAL IMPORTS C.I.F. IMPORTATIONS GENERALES C.A.F 1991	1992	1993	1994	1995
World	770.3	2587.9	2821.3	2087.4	2844.1
Africa	28.2	117.1	143.2	127.9	130.8
Americas	23.5	309.6	343.9	217.9	330.8
– Northern America	7.6	250.7	275.0	197.8	226.7
– LAIA	15.9	58.9	68.8	20.1	99.8
– CACM			0.0		0.1
– Caribbean			0.1		0.0
– Rest of America					4.2
Asia excl fmr USSR	477.1	1304.9	1310.7	1020.8	1635.3
– Middle East	290.4	558.7	669.3	576.8	937.8
Asia former USSR					
Europe excl fmr USSR	166.1	781.3	962.9	661.7	721.7
– European Union	144.0	746.0	910.6	632.7	679.8
– Eastern Europe	21.3	25.9	43.9	23.1	27.5
– Rest of Europe	0.9	9.4	8.4	5.9	14.4
Europe former USSR	47.2	21.0	8.1	6.2	12.3
Oceania	25.9	51.2	50.0	51.5	12.0
Other	2.3	2.7	2.5	1.4	1.3
United Arab Emirates	84.2	213.2	272.0	219.0	403.5
USA/Etats–Unis d'Amer	6.7	238.0	270.8	188.6	217.9
Saudi Arabia	23.9	192.5	196.4	215.6	275.4
United Kingdom	37.1	142.7	147.4	116.4	136.6
Malaysia/Malaisie	39.8	109.4	141.7	99.1	183.0
France, Monaco	21.9	91.6	199.9	123.1	120.0
Japan/Japon	21.8	180.9	131.5	93.2	112.8
Turkey/Turquie	4.7	100.4	142.0	95.3	101.7
Singapore/Singapour	31.2	127.7	111.3	74.6	99.0
Italy/Italie	7.2	132.9	95.1	85.7	96.4
Netherlands/Pays–Bas	12.2	111.6	125.2	85.5	57.0
Belgium–Luxembourg	19.1	97.5	103.1	92.5	61.4
Germany/Allemagne	20.8	88.2	108.9	62.0	93.2
China/Chine	34.5	76.0	92.4	44.2	100.5
Brazil/Brésil	15.9	54.4	63.6	17.4	96.9
Kuwait/ Koweït	106.4	1.5	10.3	5.8	105.5
India/Inde	17.8	46.3	47.8	29.9	45.5
Thailand/Thaïlande	23.5	92.6	30.3	17.6	19.0
Australia/Australie	24.6	51.2	43.1	51.5	11.0
Somalia/Somalie	10.0	49.2	43.8	28.8	41.6
Korea, Republic of	7.3	44.2	43.0	29.6	41.9
Djibouti	6.1	21.1	49.0	48.4	16.2
Egypt/Egypte	3.4	25.0	34.4	27.0	37.6
Jordan/Jordanie	2.9	22.1	25.2	13.5	37.3
Greece/Grèce	0.3	14.6	23.0	25.5	27.9
European Union n.e.s.		23.8	41.1	6.1	18.0
Denmark/Danemark	20.4	17.7	18.1	11.7	20.4
Romania/Roumanie	10.6	13.8	28.0	17.5	10.3
Indonesia/Indonésie	0.5	11.5	12.9	9.0	37.3
Other Asia n.e.s.	1.5	21.6	10.5	24.1	8.0
China, Hong Kong SAR	2.3	16.9	7.3	11.0	23.3
Bahrain/Bahreïn	9.1	20.5	11.4	15.8	1.0
Iraq	57.5	0.0			
Sweden/Suède	2.4	5.3	16.5	8.6	20.8
Former USSR/Anc. URSS	47.2				
Russian Federation		21.0	8.1	6.2	10.6
Sri Lanka	5.9	13.4	6.3	6.7	9.3
Austria/Autriche	1.1	10.5	14.1	7.7	7.9
Sudan/Soudan	6.4	2.8	7.1	16.6	4.3
Canada	0.9	12.5	4.2	9.2	8.9

COUNTRIES–PAYS	EXPORTS EXPORTATIONS ES F.O.B. 1991	1992	1993	1994	1995
Monde	202.3	329.0	374.2	933.9	3431.5
Afrique	19.2	27.3	23.7	96.7	357.4
Amériques	18.2	116.6	3.8	130.0	307.1
– Amérique du Nord	18.2	116.2	3.7	113.4	10.8
– ALAI		0.4	0.1	16.5	296.2
– MCAC					
– Caraïbes					0.0
– Autre Amérique				0.2	0.1
Asie anc. URSS exclus	82.5	104.0	297.2	616.5	2703.6
– Moyen–Orient	14.3	34.7	45.2	94.1	164.8
Asie ancienne URSS					
Europe anc. URSS exclus	79.3	58.1	45.8	83.6	37.7
– Union Européenne	78.5	57.6	45.7	63.4	37.3
– Europe de l'Est			0.0	11.6	0.4
– Autre de l'Europe	0.8	0.5		8.6	0.0
Europe ancienne URSS					0.1
Océanie				0.0	0.2
Autre	3.0		3.7	5.1	25.4
China/Chine			52.9	22.9	800.8
Korea, Republic of	0.1	0.5	21.5	195.0	656.6
Japan/Japon	17.8	55.5	98.0	124.0	420.4
Singapore/Singapour	9.1	7.2	53.6	133.6	347.3
Brazil/Brésil		0.4	0.1	16.5	296.2
Egypt/Egypte	6.2	0.2	0.1	64.0	223.3
USA/Etats–Unis d'Amer	10.0	116.2	3.4	113.4	8.5
Thailand/Thaïlande				0.1	233.9
Saudi Arabia	0.0	22.4	28.7	37.7	59.1
Malaysia/Malaisie		4.3	1.1	25.9	73.4
So. African Customs Un					101.4
Bahrain/Bahreïn		5.9	3.9	29.9	48.5
India/Inde	28.7	0.5	22.5	19.1	4.6
France, Monaco	6.1	4.9	17.0	29.0	17.3
Somalia/Somalie	1.2	11.7	14.0	21.7	18.6
Netherlands/Pays–Bas	46.8	3.3	0.0	10.5	5.3
United Arab Emirates	4.0	4.1	7.1	14.0	33.7
Italy/Italie	12.0	8.3	5.9	22.3	9.4
Germany/Allemagne	0.1	39.2	1.0	0.0	0.7
Areas n.e.s.				2.5	24.8
Austria/Autriche			19.9		
Kuwait/ Koweït	0.2	0.0		8.3	9.8
Djibouti	4.9	4.7	6.3	0.5	1.8
Sudan/Soudan	4.1	8.6	0.4	1.0	1.7
Greece/Grèce	13.4				
Pakistan	8.9	0.7	0.8	0.9	0.9
Bulgaria/Bulgarie				11.6	
Ethiopia/Ethiopie			2.4	6.3	2.6
Bunkers, ship stores	3.0		3.7	2.6	0.6
Iraq	9.8				
Jordan/Jordanie		1.7	2.7	2.8	2.6
Switzerland,Liechtenst.	0.8			8.6	0.0
Turkey/Turquie	0.3		1.4	0.3	6.5
Bermuda/Bermudes	8.2				
Eritrea/Erythrée				2.3	4.6
United Kingdom	0.1	1.3	0.9	0.7	2.4
Ethiopia, incl Eritrea	2.5	1.8			
Syrian Arab Republic		0.6	0.8	0.8	1.8
Sri Lanka	3.6				0.0
China, Hong Kong SAR		0.7	1.5	0.8	0.5

(VALUE AS PERCENTAGE OF WORLD TOTAL)(VALEURS EN POURCENTAGE DU TOTAL MONDIAL)

	1986	1987	1988	1989	1990	1991	1992	1993	1994	1995
Africa					5.6	3.7	4.5	5.1	6.1	4.6
Americas					6.9	3.1	12.0	12.2	10.4	11.6
– Northern America					6.0	1.0	9.7	9.7	9.5	8.0
– LAIA					0.8	2.1	2.3	2.4	1.0	3.5
– CACM								0.0		0.0
– Caribbean								0.0		0.0
– Rest of America										0.1
Asia excl fmr USSR					42.0	61.9	50.4	46.5	48.9	57.5
– Middle East					18.6	37.7	21.6	23.7	27.6	33.0
Asia former USSR										
Europe excl fmr USSR					35.6	21.6	30.2	34.1	31.7	25.4
– European Union					33.7	18.7	28.8	32.3	30.3	23.9
– Eastern Europe					1.3	2.8	1.0	1.6	1.1	1.0
– Rest of Europe					0.6	0.1	0.4	0.3	0.3	0.5
Europe former USSR					3.8	6.1	0.8	0.3	0.3	0.4
Oceania					5.6	3.4	2.0	1.8	2.5	0.4
Other					0.5	0.3	0.1	0.1	0.1	0.0
United Arab Emirates					3.7	10.9	8.2	9.6	10.5	14.2
USA/Etats–Unis d'Amer					5.5	0.9	9.2	9.6	9.0	7.7
Saudi Arabia					8.0	3.1	7.4	7.0	10.3	9.7
United Kingdom					5.8	4.8	5.5	5.2	5.6	4.8
Malaysia/Malaisie					3.0	5.2	4.2	5.0	4.7	6.4
France, Monaco					6.9	2.8	3.5	7.1	5.9	4.2
Japan/Japon					4.1	2.8	7.0	4.7	4.5	4.0
Turkey/Turquie					0.8	0.6	3.9	5.0	4.6	3.6
Singapore/Singapour					3.2	4.0	4.9	3.9	3.6	3.5
Italy/Italie					2.3	0.9	5.1	3.4	4.1	3.4

	1986	1987	1988	1989	1990	1991	1992	1993	1994	1995
Afrique					4.5	9.5	8.3	6.3	10.4	10.4
Amériques					41.2	9.0	35.5	1.0	13.9	9.0
– Amérique du Nord					41.2	9.0	35.3	1.0	12.1	0.3
– ALAI							0.1	0.0	1.8	8.6
– MCAC										
– Caraïbes					0.0					0.0
– Autre Amérique									0.0	0.0
Asie anc. URSS exclus					14.2	40.8	31.6	79.4	66.0	78.8
– Moyen–Orient					7.0	7.1	10.5	12.1	10.1	4.8
Asie ancienne URSS										
Europe anc. URSS exclus					37.3	39.2	17.7	12.2	9.0	1.1
– Union Européenne					36.6	38.8	17.5	12.2	6.8	1.1
– Europe de l'Est					0.6			0.0	1.2	0.0
– Autre de l'Europe					0.1	0.4	0.1		0.9	0.0
Europe ancienne URSS					0.4					0.0
Océanie									0.0	0.0
Autre					2.3	1.5		1.0	0.5	0.7
China/Chine								14.1	2.5	23.3
Korea, Republic of					0.0	0.0	0.1	5.7	20.9	19.1
Japan/Japon					1.7	8.8	16.9	26.2	13.3	12.3
Singapore/Singapour					2.0	4.5	2.2	14.3	14.3	10.1
Brazil/Brésil							0.1	0.0	1.8	8.6
Egypt/Egypte					0.0	3.1	0.1	0.0	6.9	6.5
USA/Etats–Unis d'Amer					37.2	4.9	35.3	0.9	12.1	0.2
Thailand/Thaïlande									0.0	6.8
Saudi Arabia					2.9	0.0	6.8	7.7	4.0	1.7
Malaysia/Malaisie					0.2		1.3	0.3	2.8	2.1

4. General Imports C.I.F. by Commodities according to the S.I.T.C. (Rev. 2) in million U.S. Dollars
Importations Générales C.A.F. par Produits d'après la C.T.C.I. (Rév. 2) en millions de Dollars E.U.

SITC CTCI	COMMODITY	1992 QUANTITY QUANTITE	1992 VALUE VALEUR	1993 QUANTITY QUANTITE	1993 VALUE VALEUR	1994 QUANTITY QUANTITE	1994 VALUE VALEUR	1995 QUANTITY QUANTITE	1995 VALUE VALEUR	PRODUIT
	ALL COMMODITIES		2587.9		2821.3		2087.5		1290.8	TOUS PRODUITS
0	FOOD AND LIVE ANIMALS		728.0		737.5		675.0		285.2	ALIMENTS,ANIMAUX VIVANTS
001	*LIVE ANIMALS FOR FOOD		56.5		49.9		47.2	W 13956	20.3	ANIMAUX VIVANTS
0011	BOVINE SPECIES,LIVE							W 8675	12.0	ESPECE BOVINE
0012	SHEEP AND GOATS,LIVE							W 5224	7.5	ESPECES OVINE ET CAPRINE
01	MEAT AND PREPARATIONS		30.7		55.7		59.2		20.7	VIANDES ET PREPARATIONS
011	MEAT FRESH,CHILLD,FROZEN							W 22343	20.6	VIANDES FRAICHES,REF,CONGE
0114	POULTRY FRESH CHLLD,FRZN							W 17787	17.0	VOLAILLES MORTES
02	DAIRY PRODCTS,BIRDS'EGGS		85.6		134.5		75.4		30.5	PRODUITS LAITIERS,OEUFS
022	MILK AND CREAM							W 16347	20.3	LAIT ET CREME
0224	MILK,CREAM PRESERVED ETC							W 16332	20.3	LAIT,CREME CONS,CONC
02242	MILK DRY,1.5% FAT OR LES							W 14670	18.9	LAIT POUDRE INF 1.5%
024	CHEESE AND CURD							W 2682	4.0	FROMAGE ET CAILLEBOTTE
025	EGGS,BIRDS,FRESH,PRSRVD							W 2692	5.6	OEUFS
0251	— IN SHELL							W 2681	5.6	OEUFS EN COQUILLE
04	CEREALS AND PREPARATIONS		310.9		257.1		297.6		94.2	CEREALES ET PRODUITS
041	WHEAT ETC UNMILLED							W 754461	36.5	FROMENT,EPEAUTRE
042	RICE							W 124937	15.5	RIZ
0422	RICE SEMI-MILLED,MILLED							W 124937	15.5	RIZ POLI,GLACE INCL BRISURES
044	MAIZE UNMILLED							W 58893	5.8	MAIS NON MOULU
046	WHEAT ETC MEAL OR FLOUR							W 523257	32.0	SEMOULE FARINE,FROMENT
04601	FLOUR OF WHEAT OR MESLIN							W 523237	32.0	FARINE DE FROMENT
05	VEGETABLES AND FRUIT		42.7		43.8		44.1		22.6	LEGUMES ET FRUITS
054	VEG ETC FRSH,SMPLY PRSVD							W 20287	6.4	LEGUMES FRAIS,CONG,SECS
0542	LEGUMINOUS VEGETBLES DRY							W 19052	6.0	LEGUMES A COSSE SECS
056	VEGTBLES ETC PRSVD,PREPD							W 13397	8.6	CONSERVES DE LEGUMES
0565	VEGTBLES PRSVD,PREPD NES							W 11799	8.2	LEGUMES PREPARES CONSERVE
05659	OTH VEG PRESVD,PREPD NES							W 11473	7.9	LEGUM PREPAP,CONSERV NDA
058	FRUIT PRESERVED,PREPARED							W 8053	4.4	CONSERVES DE FRUITS
06	SUGAR AND PREPS,HONEY		138.5		134.5		88.6		67.2	SUCRES ET PRODUITS
061	SUGAR AND HONEY							W 187205	64.9	SUCRES ET MIEL
0611	RAW BEET AND CANE SUGAR							W 11025	4.5	SUCRES BRUTS
0612	REFINED SUGAR ETC							W 163621	57.0	SUCRES RAFFINES
07	COFFEE,TEA,COCOA,SPICES		34.0		21.8		31.1		17.2	CAFE,THE,CACAO,EPICES
074	TEA AND MATE							W 8265	10.4	THE ET MATE
0741	TEA							W 8265	10.4	THE
075	SPICES							W 5607	6.1	EPICES
0752	SPICES,EX PEPPER,PIMENTO							W 4477	4.8	AUTRES EPICES
081	*FEEDING STUFF FOR ANIML		10.5		18.1		9.1	W 12751	4.3	NOURRITURE POUR ANIMAUX
09	MISC EDIBLE PRODUCTS		15.4		18.5		17.0		6.6	PREP ALIMENTAIRES DIVERSES
098	EDIBLE PRODCTS,PREPS NES							W 4212	6.6	PREP ALIMENTAIRES NDA
1	BEVERAGES AND TOBACCO		49.3		50.2		49.1		27.2	BOISSONS ET TABACS
12	TOBACCO AND MANUFACTURES		47.5		43.7		48.0		26.5	TABACS BRUTS FABRIQUES
121	TOBACCO UNMNFCTRD,REFUSE							W 9232	25.7	TABACS BRUTS,DECHETS
1213	TOBACCO REFUSE							W 9232	25.7	DECHETS DE TABACS
2	CRUDE MATERLS,EXCL FUELS		93.4		90.6		62.1		36.8	MAT BRUTES NON COMESTIBLES
22	OIL SEEDS,OLEAGINOUS FRT		8.0		14.8		10.7		3.6	GRAINES,FRUITS OLEAGINEUX
24	CORK AND WOOD		64.2		63.5		40.1		25.5	LIEGE ET BOIS
248	WOOD SHAPED,SLEEPERS							W 102956	23.9	BOIS SIMPLEMENT TRAVAILLES
2482	LUMBER SHAPED CONIFER							W 73375	19.3	CONIFERES SCIES,RABOTES
2483	LUMBER SHAPED NON-CONIFR							W 29581	4.6	NON CONIFERES SCIES,RABOTES
27	CRUDE FERTLZR,MINRLS NES		14.8		5.8		5.5		2.3	ENGRAIS MINERAUX BRUTS
3	MINERAL FUELS ETC		157.0		188.1		108.4		101.9	COMBUSTIBLES MINERAUX LUB
33	PETROLEUM AND PRODUCTS		156.6		187.7		108.3		101.4	PETROLE ET DERIVES
334	PETROLEUM PRODUCTS,REFIN							W 835643	100.8	PRODUITS RAFFINES
3341	GASOLINE,OTH LIGHT OILS							W 174735	20.7	ESSENCES POUR MOTEURS
33411	MOTOR,AVIATION SPIRIT							W 174536	20.6	ESSENCES MOTEURS D'AVIONS
3343	GAS OILS							W 262751	22.6	GAS OILS
3344	FUEL OILS,NES							W 359486	35.2	FUEL OILS
3345	LUBS,PETROLEUM OILS NES							W 38191	22.3	HUILES LUBRIFIANTES
33451	LUBS(HIGH PETR CONT) ETC							W 37385	22.0	HUILES LUBRIF,H LOURDES
4	ANIMAL,VEGETABLE OIL,FAT		55.6		62.5		39.6		57.7	HUILES,GRAISSES ANIM,VEG
42	FIXED VEGETABLE OIL,FAT		51.8		55.2		39.4		57.4	HUILES VEGETALES FIXES
423	FIXED VEG OILS,SOFT							W 40117	20.8	HUILES VEGET DOUCES FIXES
4232	SOYA BEAN OIL							W 29968	15.0	HUILE DE SOJA
4234	GROUNDNUT(PEANUT) OIL							W 8006	5.2	HUILE D'ARACHIDE
424	FIXED VEG OIL NONSOFT							W 70501	36.7	AUTRES HUILES VEG FIXES
4242	PALM OIL							W 23667	10.2	HUILE DE PALME
4249	FIXED VEGETABLE OILS NES							W 46291	26.2	HUILES VEGET FIXES NDA
5	CHEMCLS,RELATED PROD NES		172.0		211.7		161.6		106.0	PRODUITS CHIMIQUES
51	ORGANIC CHEMICALS		6.1		9.3		2.8		3.7	PROD CHIMIQ ORGANIQUES
52	INORGANIC CHEMICALS		11.2		16.8		7.9		9.7	PROD CHIM INORGANIQUES
522	INORG ELEMNTS,OXIDES,ETC							W 10794	3.9	ELEMENTS INORGANIQUES
523	OTHR INORG CHEMICALS ETC							W 29725	5.8	AUT PRODUITS CHIMIQUES INORG
53	DYES,TANNING,COLOUR PROD		7.8		11.4		8.6		6.4	PROD TEINTURE,COLORANTS
533	PIGMENTS,PAINTS,ETC							W 3789	6.1	PIGMENTS,PEINTURES,VERNIS
541	*MEDICINAL,PHARM PRODUCT		53.4		69.5		63.0	K 3367773	29.3	PROD MEDICINAUX PHARMACEUT
5417	MEDICAMENTS							K 3202602	28.0	MEDICAMENTS
55	PERFUME,CLEANING ETC PRD		11.2		12.9		13.9		12.1	PROD POUR PARFUM,TOILETTE
554	SOAP,CLEANSING ETC PREPS							W 9790	6.5	SAVONS,PRODUITS DETERSIFS
5542	WASHING PREPARATIONS ETC							W 9384	5.9	PROD ORG TENSIO-ACT NDA
562	*FERTILIZERS,MANUFACTURE		6.3		4.2		1.2	W 25487	6.4	ENGRAIS MANUFACTURES
58	PLASTIC MATERIALS ETC		45.5		44.5		43.4		22.3	MAT PLAST ARTIFICIELLES
583	POLYMERIZATION ETC PRODS							W 24985	19.7	PROD POLYMERISATION
59	CHEMICAL MATERIALS NES		27.5		36.9		19.1		15.9	MAT PROD CHIMIQUES NDA
591	PESTICIDES,DISINFECTANTS							W 2121	5.6	DESINF,INSECT,FONG,HERB
598	MISCEL CHEM PRODUCTS NES							W 9068	8.1	PROD DIV INDUST CHIM NDA
5989	CHEM PRODUCTS,PREPS NES							W 7889	7.4	PROD PREP CHIMIQUES NDA
59899	OTH CHEM PRODS,PREPS,NES							W 6813	6.3	AUT PRODUITS CHIMIQUES NDA
6	BASIC MANUFACTURES		626.5		671.9		444.2		296.6	ART MANUFACTURES
62	RUBBER MANUFACTURES NES		49.6		61.7		43.4		27.7	CAOUTCHOUC MANUFACTURE
625	RUBBER TYRES, TUBES ETC							W 13320	23.4	PNEUS CAOUTCHOUC VULCANISE
6251	TYRES NEW FOR MOTOR CARS							W 11898	20.5	PNEUS POUR VOITURES
63	WOOD,CORK MANUFACTRS NES		37.4		36.6		21.0		9.7	OUVRAGES LIEGE ET BOIS
634	VENEERS,PLYWOOD,ETC							W 84172	9.0	PLACAGES,CONTRE-PLAQUES
6342	PLYWOOD OF WOOD SHEETS							W 84090	8.9	BOIS CONTRE-PLAQUES
64	PAPER,PAPERBOARD AND MFR		57.4		57.2		41.4		35.6	PAPIERS,CARTONS & OUVRAGES
641	PAPER AND PAPERBOARD							W 38176	26.1	PAPIERS ET CARTONS
6411	NEWSPRINT							W 15782	12.1	PAPIER JOURNAL
6412	PRINTG,WRITING PAPER NES							W 9334	5.2	PAPIERS POUR L'IMPRESSION
6415	PAPER,PAPERBRD,BULK,NES							W 9692	5.2	PAPIERS,CARTONS ROULEAUX

4. General Imports C.I.F. by Commodities according to the S.I.T.C. (Rev. 2) in million U.S. Dollars
Importations Générales C.A.F. par Produits d'après la C.T.C.I. (Rév. 2) en millions de Dollars E.U.

SITC CTCI	COMMODITY	1992 QUANTITY QUANTITE	1992 VALUE VALEUR	1993 QUANTITY QUANTITE	1993 VALUE VALEUR	1994 QUANTITY QUANTITE	1994 VALUE VALEUR	1995 QUANTITY QUANTITE	1995 VALUE VALEUR	PRODUIT
642	PAPER,ETC,PRECUT,ARTS OF							W 7386	9.5	PAP,CARTONS DECOUPES
6421	PAPER ETC CONTAINERS							W 5359	4.5	BOITES,SACS EMBALLAGES
65	TEXTILE YARN,FABRICS,ETC		53.1		66.6		50.5		31.3	FILS,TISSUS,ARTICLES TEXTILE
653	WOVN MAN–MADE FIB FABRIC							W 3244	10.3	TISSUS FIBRES SYNTH,ARTIF
657	SPECIAL TXTL FABRC,PRODS							W 4021	4.6	TISSUS SPECIAUX
658	TEXTILE ARTICLES NES							W 6185	6.9	ART FACONNES MAT TEXTILES
659	FLOOR COVERINGS,ETC							W 7108	5.8	COUVRE–PARQUETS,TAPIS ETC
66	NONMETAL MINERAL MFS NES		99.5		82.4		58.5		33.4	ART MIN NON METALLIQUES
661	LIME,CEMENT,BLDG PRODS							W 345123	18.7	CHAUX,CIMENTS MAT CONSTR
6612	CEMENT							W 343125	17.8	CIMENTS HYDRAULIQUES
662	CLAY,REFRACTORY BLDG PRD							W 22243	6.6	MAT CONST REFRACTAIRES
6624	BRICKS ETC NONREFRACTORY							W 22144	6.5	BRIQUES ETC CERAM NON REFR
665	GLASSWARE							W 7106	4.4	OUVRAGES EN VERRE
67	IRON AND STEEL		225.5		256.9		145.0		98.3	FER ET ACIER
673	IRON,STEEL SHAPES ETC							W 206278	39.2	BARRES,PROFIL FER,ACIER
6731	IRON,STEEL WIRE ROD							W 151403	29.0	FIL MACHINE FER,ACIER
6732	IRON,STEEL BARS ETC							W 32235	6.1	BARRES FER,ACIER
6733	IRON,STEEL PROFILES ETC							W 22641	4.2	PROFILES,PALPLAN FER,ACIER
674	IRN,STL UNIV,PLATE,SHEET							W 42342	20.9	LARGES PLATS,TOLES
678	IRON,STL TUBES,PIPES,ETC							W 40667	34.9	TUBES,TUYAUX EN FONTE,FER
6781	CAST IRON TUBES,PIPES							W 20195	21.2	TUBES,TUYAUX EN FONTE
6782	IRON,STL SEAMLESS TUBES							W 12562	7.1	TUBES,TUYAUX SANS SOUDURE
68	NON–FERROUS METALS		37.8		34.2		32.2		15.5	METAUX NON FERREUX
684	ALUMINIUM							W 7583	14.9	ALUMINIUM
6842	ALUMINIUM,ALLOYS WORKED							W 6483	14.9	ALUMINIUM,ALLIAGES OUVRE
68421	ALUMINIUM BARS,WIRE,ETC							W 2303	5.9	BARRES,PROFILES FILS ALU
68423	ALUMINIUM FOIL							W 2703	7.4	FEUILLES,BANDES MINCES AL
69	METAL MANUFACTURES NES		64.6		74.6		50.9		44.0	ART MANUFACT EN METAL NDA
691	STRUCTURES AND PARTS NES							W 9815	14.1	CONSTRUCT FER,ACIER,ALU
6911	STRUCTURES,PARTS IRN,STL							W 9762	14.0	CONSTRUCT FER,ACIER,FONTE
692	METAL TANKS,BOXES,ETC							W 5516	6.9	RECIPIENTS METALLIQUES
6924	MTL TRANSPORT BOXES ETC							W 5056	5.6	FUTS,TAMBOURS,BIDONS
69243	IRN,STL COMP GAS CYLINDR							W 4265	4.4	RECIP FER,ACIER GAZ COMP
695	TOOLS							W 1278	4.9	OUTILS A MAIN
697	BASE MTL HOUSEHOLD EQUIP							W 2579	4.4	ART MENAGE MET COMMUNS
699	BASE METAL MFRS NES							W 8785	8.7	ART MANUFACTURES MET NDA
7	MACHINES,TRANSPORT EQUIP		564.6		638.1		427.9		298.2	MACHINES MATERIEL TRANSPORT
71	POWER GENERATING EQUIPMT		28.5		39.4		32.9		16.9	MACHINES GENERATRICES
713	INTRNL COMBUS PSTN ENGIN							W 1743	7.4	MOTEURS EXPL COMB INT, PIECE
7139	PISTON ENGINE PARTS NES							W 460	4.3	PIECES POUR 713.2,3,8
716	ROTATING ELECTRIC PLANT							W 1213	9.2	APP ELECTR ROTATIFS,PIECES
7162	AC MTRS,GENRTRS,GEN SETS							W 1163	7.2	MOTEURS ELECTRIQUES
72	MACHS FOR SPCL INDUSTRYS		81.8		140.5		74.9		32.2	MAC SPECIALES POUR INDUST
723	CIVIL ENGNEERG EQUIP ETC							W 4282	21.7	APPAREILS DE GENIE CIVIL
7234	CONST,MINING MACHNRY NES							W 2449	7.6	MACH POUR LA CONST, MINES
7239	CONSTR ETC MACHY PTS NES							W 1789	14.0	PIECES 723.41–723.46
728	OTH MACHY FOR SPCL INDUS							W 1198	6.2	AUT MACH IND PARTICULIERES
7284	MACHY FOR SPCL INDUS NES							W 608	4.1	MACH SPEC IND PARTICUL.
74	GENRL INDUSTRL MACHY NES		113.4		128.8		58.5		57.1	MACH APP INDUSTRIE
741	HEATING,COOLING EQUIPMNT							W 1319	6.4	MACH CHAUFFAGE,PIECES
742	PUMPS FOR LIQUIDS ETC							W 2705	9.8	POMPES MOTO–POMPES
7428	OTHER PUMPS FOR LIQUIDS							W 1674	6.5	AUTRES POMPES POUR LIQ
743	PUMPS NES,CENTRFUGES ETC							W 981	4.5	POMPES COMPRES,VENT ETC
744	MECHANICAL HANDLING EQU							W 1221	7.3	EQUIP MANUTENTION PIECES
7442	LIFTING,LOADING MACH NES							W 781	6.2	APP LEVAGE,MANUTENTION
74422	SHIP DERRICKS,CRANES ETC							W 163	4.6	GRUES,PONTS ROULANTS
745	NONELEC MACHY,TOOLS NES							W 940	6.7	AUT MACH NON ELEC,PIECES
7452	OTH NONELEC MCHS,PTS NES							W 848	5.9	AUT MACH NON ELEC,PIECES
74522	PACKAGNG,BOTTLNG,ETC MCH							W 284	3.9	MACH NETT BOUTEILLES,ETC
749	NONELEC MACH PTS,ACC NES							W 2969	22.6	PIECES MACH NON ELEC NDA
7492	COCKS,VALVES ETC NES							W 2333	14.1	ART ROB,SIM POUR TUYAUX
7499	OTH NONELEC MCHY PTS NES							W 481	6.8	PIECES NON ELECT NDA
74992	METAL–PLASTIC GASKETS							W 69	4.3	JOINTS METALLOPLASTIQUES
75	OFFICE MACHNES,ADP EQUIP		14.8		16.1		11.0		13.5	MACH BUREAU TRAIT AUTOM
751	OFFICE MACHINES							W 249	8.4	MACH,APPAREILS DE BUREAU
7518	OFFICE MACHINES NES							W 170	7.6	MACH,APP DE BUREAU NDA
75182	PHOTO,THERMOCOPY APPARAT							W 82	7.2	APPAREILS DE PHOTOCOPIE
76	TELECOMM,SOUND EQUIPMENT		31.1		50.7		23.6		16.2	EQUIPMENT DE TELECOM
761	TELEVISION RECEIVERS							W 472	4.0	RECEPTEURS DE TELEVISION
764	TELECOM EQPT,PTS,ACC NES							W 830	10.4	EQUIP TELECOM,PIECES
7641	LINE TELEPHONE,ETC EQUIP							W 172	4.0	APP TELEPHON PAR FIL
7649	PTS NES OF EQUIPMT OF 76							W 146	4.3	PIECES DE LA DIV 76
77	ELECTRIC MACHNRY NES ETC		76.7		88.2		85.9		67.4	MACH APP ELECT NDA
772	SWITCHGEAR ETC,PARTS NES							W 1940	15.1	APP COUPURE,SECT ETC
773	ELECTR DISTRIBUTNG EQUIP							W 6358	16.0	EQUIPMT DISTRIBUTION ELECT
7731	INSULATED WIRE,CABLE ETC							W 6106	15.2	FILS,CABLES ISOLES ELECT
774	ELECTRO–MEDCL,XRAY EQUIP							W 244	6.2	APPAREILS MEDICAUX
7741	ELECTRO–MEDICAL EQUIPMNT							W 198	5.0	APP ELECTRICITE MEDICALE
775	HOUSEHOLD TYPE EQUIP NES							W 3779	9.4	MACH,APP USAGE DOMESTQUE
778	ELECTRICAL MACHINERY NES							W 11219	18.1	AUTRES MACH ELECT NDA
7781	BATTERIES,ACCUMULATORS							W 9179	10.8	PILES ET ACCUMULATEURS
77811	PRIMARY BATTERIES,CELLS							W 6931	4.8	PILES ELECTRIQUES,PIECES
77812	ELECTRIC ACCUMULATORS							W 2202	5.8	ACCUMULATEURS ELECTRIQ
78	ROAD VEHICLES		182.9		157.3		130.7		85.5	VEHICULES ROUTIERS
781	PASS MOTOR VEH EXC BUSES							W 12418	31.2	AUTO TRANSPORT PERSONNES
782	LORRIES,SPCL MTR VEH NES							W 9668	26.4	VEHICULES SPECIAUX,MARCH
7821	LORRIES,TRUCKS							W 9162	22.1	VEHICULES TRANSP MARCHAND
7822	SPECIAL MOTOR VEHCLS NES							W 506	4.3	VEHICULES USAGES SPECIAUX
783	ROAD MOTOR VEHICLES NES							W 2319	5.4	VEHICULES ROUTIERS NDA
7831	BUSES							W 2256	4.9	VOITURES TRANSPORT COMMUN
784	MOTOR VEH PRTS,ACCES NES							W 4373	18.9	PIECES 722,781,782,783
7849	OTHER MOTOR VEHCL PARTS							W 4311	18.8	PIECES 722,781,782,783
79	OTHR TRANSPORT EQUIPMENT		32.8		13.1		8.2		6.9	AUTRE MATERIEL TRANSPORT
792	AIRCRAFT ETC							W 36	6.7	APP NAVIGATION AERIENNE
7929	AIRCRAFT PARTS NES							W 35	6.7	PIECES DU 792
8	MISC MANUFACTURED GOODS		140.6		170.4		120.0		81.2	ART MANUFACTURES DIVERS
812	*PLUMBG,HEATNG,LGHTNG EQ		9.5		8.6		8.3	W 5780	7.0	APPAR SANITAIRES CHAUFFAGE
8124	LIGHTING EQUIPMENT NES							W 2371	4.0	APPAREILS ECLAIRAGE ETC
821	*FURNITURE,PARTS THEREOF		12.5		20.9		5.6	W 3238	6.2	MEUBLES ET PIECES
8219	FURNITURE AND PARTS NES							W 2783	5.5	AUTRES MEUBLES ET PIECES
82192	WOOD FURNITURE NES							W 2356	4.3	MEUBLES NDA EN BOIS

4. General Imports C.I.F. by Commodities according to the S.I.T.C. (Rev. 2) in million U.S. Dollars
Importations Générales C.A.F. par Produits d'après la C.T.C.I. (Rév. 2) en millions de Dollars E.U.

SITC CTCI	COMMODITY	1992		1993		1994		1995		PRODUIT
		QUANTITY QUANTITE	VALUE VALEUR	QUANTITY QUANTITE	VALUE VALEUR	QUANTITY QUANTITE	VALUE VALEUR	QUANTITY QUANTITE	VALUE VALEUR	
84	CLOTHING AND ACCESSORIES		31.0		37.1		40.7		18.9	VETEMENTS
842	MENS OUTERWEAR NOT KNIT							W 3721	10.1	VET DESSUS POUR HOMMES
8429	— OTHER OUTER GARMENTS							W 3721	10.1	AUT VET DES HOM MAT TEX
843	WOMENS OUTERWEAR NONKNIT							W 191	5.8	VET DESSUS FEMMES MAT TEX
8439	— OTHER OUTER GARMENTS							W 191	5.8	AUT VET DES FEM MAT TEXT
851	*FOOTWEAR		13.0		12.9		13.7	W 4206	8.3	CHAUSSURES
85102	FOOTWEAR LEATHER							W 1622	4.2	CHAUS SEMELLES EN CUIR
87	PRECISION INSTRUMNTS NES		33.6		29.4		14.1		6.9	INSTRUM,APPAR SCIENT NDA
874	MEASURNG,CONTROLNG INSTR							W 170	4.1	INSTRUMENTS DE MESURE
88	PHOTO EQU,OPTICL GDS ETC		4.4		10.8		2.9		2.9	APP,FOURN PHOTO,OP,MONTR
89	MISC MANUFCTRD GOODS NES		35.6		48.9		33.5		30.3	ART MANUFACTURES DIVERS
893	ARTICLES OF PLASTIC NES							W 7814	16.0	OUVRAGES EN MAT DIVIS 58
8939	MISC PLASTIC ARTICLES							W 5063	11.5	ART DIVERS EN MAT DIV 58
89391	PVC FLOORING TILES ETC							W 3719	9.3	CHLORURE POLYVINYL PLAQ
899	OTHER MANUFACTURED GOODS								6.3	AUT ART MANUF DIVERS NDA

5. General Exports F.O.B. by Commodities according to the S.I.T.C. (Rev. 2) in million U.S. Dollars
Exportations Générales F.O.B. par Produits d'après la C.T.C.I. (Rév. 2) en millions de Dollars E.U.

SITC CTCI	COMMODITY	1992 QUANTITY QUANTITE	1992 VALUE VALEUR	1993 QUANTITY QUANTITE	1993 VALUE VALEUR	1994 QUANTITY QUANTITE	1994 VALUE VALEUR	1995 QUANTITY QUANTITE	1995 VALUE VALEUR	PRODUIT
	ALL COMMODITIES		329.0		374.3		933.9		1587.5	TOUS PRODUITS
0	FOOD AND LIVE ANIMALS		36.4		47.3		61.6		37.9	ALIMENTS,ANIMAUX VIVANTS
02	DAIRY PRODCTS,BIRDS'EGGS		0.8		2.9		3.3		0.7	PRODUITS LAITIERS,OEUFS
03	FISH AND PREPARATIONS		6.2		8.6		8.6		9.5	POISSONS ET PREPARATIONS
04	CEREALS AND PREPARATIONS		5.3		5.6		6.9		1.9	CEREALES ET PRODUITS
05	VEGETABLES AND FRUIT		1.7		2.9		1.9		2.6	LEGUMES ET FRUITS
07	COFFEE,TEA,COCOA,SPICES		21.5		26.2		37.7		22.0	CAFE,THE,CACAO,EPICES
071	COFFEE AND SUBSTITUTES							W 3876	21.8	CAFE ET SUCCEDANES
0711	COFFEE GREEN,ROASTED,SUB							W 3876	21.8	CAFE TORREFIE OU DECAFEINE
07111	COFFEE GREEN,HUSKS,SKINS							W 3548	20.6	CAFE NON TORREFIE
1	BEVERAGES AND TOBACCO		3.6		3.4		3.3		3.1	BOISSONS ET TABACS
11	BEVERAGES		1.3		1.9		1.3		0.8	BOISSONS
12	TOBACCO AND MANUFACTURES		2.3		1.5		2.0		2.4	TABACS BRUTS FABRIQUES
2	CRUDE MATERLS,EXCL FUELS		33.3		25.0		24.2		17.7	MAT BRUTES NON COMESTIBLES
21	HIDES,SKINS,FURS UNDRSSD		16.1		8.1		9.4		3.3	CUIRS,PEAUX BRUTS
27	CRUDE FERTLZR,MINRLS NES		1.4		2.8				1.8	ENGRAIS MINERAUX BRUTS
28	METALLIFEROUS ORES,SCRAP		7.5		5.4		2.3		6.2	MINERAIS METAL,DECHETS
29	CRUDE ANIMAL,VEG MAT NES		7.9		8.3		12.2		6.2	MATIERES BRUTES ANIM,VEGET
291	CRUDE ANIMAL MTRIALS NES							W 346	5.8	MATIERES BRUTES ANIMALES
3	MINERAL FUELS ETC		244.8		285.1		830.9		1497.1	COMBUSTIBLES MINERAUX LUB
33	PETROLEUM AND PRODUCTS		241.7		285.1		830.4		1497.0	PETROLE ET DERIVES
333	CRUDE PETROLEUM							MW 13724	1423.9	HUILES BRUTES DE PETROLE
334	PETROLEUM PRODUCTS,REFIN							W 452995	34.2	PRODUITS RAFFINES
3342	KEROSENE,OTH MEDIUM OILS							W 50084	5.7	PETR LAMPANTS,AUT HUIL
33421	KEROSENE INCL JET FUEL							W 50084	5.7	PETROLES LAMPANTS
3344	FUEL OILS,NES							W 377234	25.4	FUEL OILS
335	RESIDUAL PETRLM PROD NES							W 422536	39.0	PRODUITS RESIDUELS NDA
3352	MINERAL TARS AND PRODCTS							W 422536	39.0	GOUDRONS MINERAUX
341	*GAS,NATURAL AND MANUFCT		3.1		0.1		0.5	W 1281	0.1	GAZ NATUREL,GAZ MANUFACT
4	ANIMAL,VEGETABLE OIL,FAT		3.1		2.0		2.6		1.7	HUILES,GRAISSES ANIM,VEG
42	FIXED VEGETABLE OIL,FAT		3.0		2.0		2.6		1.1	HUILES VEGETALES FIXES
5	CHEMCLS,RELATED PROD NES		5.1		4.7		5.0		2.0	PRODUITS CHIMIQUES
55	PERFUME,CLEANING ETC PRD		5.0		4.4		5.0		1.7	PROD POUR PARFUM,TOILETTE
6	BASIC MANUFACTURES		1.1		3.3		2.2		7.6	ART MANUFACTURES
7	MACHINES,TRANSPORT EQUIP		0.4		0.2		0.5		14.4	MACHINES MATERIEL TRANSPORT
8	MISC MANUFACTURED GOODS		1.3		3.7		3.9		6.5	ART MANUFACTURES DIVERS
851	*FOOTWEAR		0.5		1.7		1.5	W 373	0.7	CHAUSSURES
89	MISC MANUFCTRD GOODS NES		0.4		1.7		1.8		1.1	ART MANUFACTURES DIVERS

1. HISTORICAL SERIES, 1992–1997 SPECIAL TRADE, IMPORTS C.I.F., EXPORTS F.O.B.
SERIES HISTORIQUES, 1992–1997 COMMERCE SPECIAL, IMPORTATIONS C.A.F., EXPORTATIONS F.O.B

YEAR ANNEE	VALUE IN MILLION U.S. DOLLARS VALEUR EN MILLION U.S. DOLLARS MERCHANDISE –MARCHANDISE		GOLD –OR		CONVERSION FACTORS FACTEURS DE CONVERSION CENTS E.U. PAR		INDEX NUMBERS –INDICES QUANTUM		UNIT VALUE VALEUR UNITAIRE	
	IMPORTS	EXPORTS	IMPORTS	EXPORTS	IMPORTS	EXPORTS	IMPORTS	EXPORTS	IMPORTS	EXPORTS
1992	3630.00	2480.00								
1993	3748.00	2320.00								
1994	3866.00	2160.00								
1995	3984.00	2000.00								
1996	4102.00	1842.00								
1997	4798.70	2367.80								

2. IMPORTS BY BROAD ECONOMIC CATEGORY AND EXPORTS BY INDUSTRIAL ORIGIN. (PERCENTAGE OF TOTAL VALUE)
IMPORTATIONS PAR CATEGORIES ECONOMIQUES ET EXPORTATIONS PAR BRANCHE D'ACTIVITE.(EN POURCENTAGE DE LA VALEUR TOTALE)

IMPORTS – IMPORTATIONS

	1991	1992	1993	1994	1995	1996	1997
TOTAL IMPORTS–IMPORTATIONS TOTALES		100.				100.	100.
1 FOOD BEV–ALIMENTATION BOISSONS		7.2				12.2	12.6
11 PRIMARY–PRODUITS DE BASE		4.9				6.2	7.2
111 FOR INDUSTRY–POUR L'INDUSTRIE		2.3				2.1	2.7
112 FOR HOUSEHOLDS–POUR LES MENAGES		2.6				4.1	4.5
12 PROCESSED–PRODUITS ELABORES		2.3				6.0	5.3
121 FOR INDUSTRY–POUR L'INDUSTRIE		0.5				1.7	0.6
122 FOR HOUSEHOLDS–POUR LES MENAGES		1.8				4.4	4.7
2 IND SUPPLIES–APPROV INDUSTRIELS		40.8				43.0	36.8
21 PRIMARY–PRODUITS DE BASE		4.4				7.3	5.9
22 PROCESSED–PRODUITS ELABORES		36.4				35.8	30.8
3 FUELS–COMBUSTIBLES		22.8				14.0	16.0
31 PRIMARY–PRODUITS DE BASE		11.7				6.0	10.5
32 PROCESSED–PRODUITS ELABORES		11.1				8.0	5.5
321 MOTOR SPIRIT–ESSENCE							
322 OTHER–AUTRES		11.1				8.0	5.5
4 MACHINERY–EQUIPEMENT		14.6				14.3	13.5
41 CAPITAL EQUIPMENT–MACHINES		12.5				12.3	11.3
42 PARTS–PIECES ACCESSOIRES		2.1				2.1	2.2
5 TRANSPORT–TRANSPORT		5.4				6.2	5.3
51 PASSENGER CARS–AUTOMOBILES		1.8				2.3	1.6
52 OTHER–AUTRES		1.2				1.7	1.7
521 INDUSTRIAL–INDUSTRIELS		1.1				1.6	1.6
522 NON INDUSTRIAL–NON INDUSTRIEL		0.0				0.0	0.0
53 PARTS–PIECES ACCESSOIRES		2.5				2.2	2.0
6 CONSUM GOODS–BIENS CONSOMMATION		9.0				9.3	9.3
61 DURABLE–DURABLES		1.9				2.6	1.9
62 SEMI DURABLE–SEMI DURABLES		5.1				5.0	5.1
63 NON DURABLE–NON DURABLES		2.0				1.8	2.4
7 GOODS NES–BIENS NDA		0.2				0.9	6.5

EXPORTS – EXPORTATIONS

	1991	1992	1993	1994	1995	1996	1997
TOTAL EXPORTS–EXPORTATIONS TOTALES		100.				100.	100.
1 AGRICULTURE		10.2				9.7	3.8
2 MINING QUARRY–INDUS EXTRACTIVES		2.4				1.0	0.8
3 MANUFACTURING–IND MANUFACTUR		87.4				89.3	95.4
31 FOOD BEV TOBACCO–ALIM BOISS TAB		9.6				19.7	13.3
32 TEXTILES–INDUSTRIES TEXTILES		17.7				7.6	6.7
33 WOOD & PRODUCTS–BOIS & PRODUITS		2.1				3.0	10.8
34 PAPER & PRODUCTS–PAPIER & PRODT		1.3				0.9	1.3
35 CHEMICALS–INDUSTRIES CHIMIQUES		12.5				14.2	19.5
36 NON METAL MIN–MIN NON METAL		1.6				3.0	2.1
37 BASIC METAL–IND METAL BASE		15.6				19.5	23.4
38 METAL MANUF–MANUF METAL		23.2				18.7	14.3
39 OTH MANUF IND–AUTRES MANUF		3.8				2.5	4.0

3. TRADE BY PRINCIPAL COUNTRIES OF ORIGIN AND DESTINATION (VALUE IN MILLION U.S. DOLLARS)
ECHANGES SELON LES PRINCIPAUX PAYS D'ORIGINE ET DE DESTINATION (VALEUR EN MILLIONS DE DOLLARS EU)

COUNTRIES–PAYS	SPECIAL IMPORTS C.I.F. IMPORTATIONS SPECIALES C.A.F					COUNTRIES–PAYS	SPECIAL EXPORTS F.O.B. EXPORTATIONS SPECIALES F.O.B.				
	1993	1994	1995	1996	1997		1993	1994	1995	1996	1997
World			3859.2	4101.9	4798.7	Monde			2538.5	1841.7	2367.8
Africa			55.9	106.0	175.8	Afrique			100.2	38.6	57.3
Americas			343.4	348.3	343.4	Amériques			109.0	43.6	27.5
– Northern America			200.2	126.0	140.9	– Amérique du Nord			105.0	36.9	18.8
– LAIA			119.4	181.2	187.5	– ALAI			2.3	2.4	6.2
– CACM			6.3	5.4	5.9	– MCAC			0.0	0.3	0.1
– Caribbean			10.9	34.9	8.3	– Caraïbes			0.8	2.2	2.4
– Rest of America			6.7	0.8	0.9	– Autre Amérique			0.9	1.8	0.1
Asia excl fmr USSR			355.9	327.8	412.4	Asie anc. URSS exclus			245.9	91.0	98.9
– Middle East			125.9	125.3	141.0	– Moyen–Orient			203.9	58.3	62.8
Asia former USSR				6.7	13.0	Asie ancienne URSS				1.0	2.9
Europe excl fmr USSR			2491.1	3011.9	3321.6	Europe anc. URSS exclus			1531.4	1489.9	1977.6
– European Union			1689.5	1724.9	1979.1	– Union Européenne			1113.5	586.4	838.7
– Eastern Europe			710.3	657.6	554.2	– Europe de l'Est			363.1	188.8	201.4
– Rest of Europe			91.3	629.4	788.3	– Autre de l'Europe			54.8	714.7	937.5
Europe former USSR			601.0	289.5	525.3	Europe ancienne URSS			547.2	176.4	200.6
Oceania			11.9	11.6	7.2	Océanie			4.9	1.3	3.0
Other				0.1	0.0	Autre					
Germany/Allemagne			578.8	523.8	644.5	Russian Federation			538.2	156.4	176.5
Italy/Italie			370.3	434.6	482.1	Bosnia and Herzegovina				380.5	447.4
Russian Federation			580.8	224.6	453.6	Germany/Allemagne			417.0	146.4	218.0
Bulgaria/Bulgarie			187.4	219.0	123.4	Italy/Italie			302.0	180.6	272.4
Bosnia and Herzegovina				230.0	283.1	TFYR Macedonia				211.8	221.2
TFYR Macedonia				212.7	289.4	Greece/Grèce			103.8	94.9	115.8
Greece/Grèce			140.0	147.7	180.3	Romania/Roumanie			194.0	62.5	47.0
Austria/Autriche			164.5	123.5	156.2	Switzerland,Liechtenst.			38.9	83.8	166.9
Romania/Roumanie			197.1	123.0	100.9	France, Monaco			60.4	55.3	52.0
USA/Etats–Unis d'Amer			145.5	119.4	133.6	Bulgaria/Bulgarie			65.0	62.9	38.0
France, Monaco			125.8	134.4	135.5	USA/Etats–Unis d'Amer			100.2	33.1	15.6
Hungary/Hongrie			114.6	128.5	126.3	United Kingdom			49.7	27.5	71.8
United Kingdom			106.5	98.0	92.0	Hungary/Hongrie			45.1	29.7	60.0
Switzerland,Liechtenst.			88.8	112.3	89.4	Austria/Autriche			68.9	26.7	37.7
Slovakia/Slovaquie			122.8	46.4	63.0	Netherlands/Pays–Bas			53.3	21.4	32.6
Libyan Arab Jamahiriya			40.3	68.3	120.7	Cyprus/Chypre			46.8	36.8	20.6
Netherlands/Pays–Bas			58.2	76.0	92.8	Egypt/Egypte			36.5	20.6	37.5
Poland/Pologne			86.7	58.1	60.7	Turkey/Turquie			45.2	12.0	26.8
China/Chine			81.8	48.0	67.1	Slovenia/Slovénie				28.7	37.1
Sweden/Suède			32.8	86.0	59.9	Croatia/Croatie				1.1	58.5
Japan/Japon			58.3	57.6	59.3	Belgium–Luxembourg			16.9	20.2	14.0
Belgium–Luxembourg			58.4	51.3	61.3	Poland/Pologne			23.5	6.2	20.0
Brazil/Brésil			56.4	57.7	55.4	Slovakia/Slovaquie			24.7	6.5	15.1
Czech Republic				79.7	79.5	Ukraine			6.0	14.9	18.0
Turkey/Turquie			37.0	40.2	67.2	Iran (Islamic Rep of)			31.0	1.4	5.2
Ukraine			17.6	55.0	60.0	Kuwait/ Koweït			35.3	0.2	0.1
Slovenia/Slovénie				55.7	74.7	Czech Republic				14.4	19.3
Iran (Islamic Rep of)			42.4	35.7	33.1	China/Chine			9.5	10.8	8.0
Ecuador/Equateur			7.1	42.0	56.7	India/Inde			9.6	7.3	7.9
Cyprus/Chypre			21.6	42.3	31.3	Norway,Svalbard and JM			11.5	8.7	4.2
Peru/Pérou			23.8	35.8	26.5	Libyan Arab Jamahiriya			22.2	1.2	0.2
Canada			54.6	6.6	7.3	Israel/Israël			6.3	7.6	9.5
Denmark/Danemark			16.8	13.9	26.1	Sweden/Suède			15.0	3.6	3.6
Korea, Republic of			16.0	17.5	22.6	Syrian Arab Republic			16.2	2.4	2.4
Argentina/Argentine			11.0	18.1	24.0	Spain/Espagne			8.2	1.1	10.3
Indonesia/Indonésie			3.3	12.1	36.9	Albania/Albanie			10.9	6.7	2.0
Spain/Espagne			12.6	17.7	22.0	Denmark/Danemark			10.1	2.6	4.6
Cuba			10.7	33.7	1.2	Nigeria/Nigéria			13.2	0.7	1.0
India/Inde			9.7	10.5	23.4	Lebanon/Liban			9.6	2.3	2.7
Israel/Israël			13.6	13.2	11.3	Saudi Arabia			12.6	0.3	0.9

(VALUE AS PERCENTAGE OF WORLD TOTAL)(VALEURS EN POURCENTAGE DU TOTAL MONDIAL)

	1988	1989	1990	1991	1992	1993	1994	1995	1996	1997		1988	1989	1990	1991	1992	1993	1994	1995	1996	1997
Africa					1.4			1.4	2.6	3.7	Afrique					3.9			3.9	2.1	2.4
Americas					8.9			8.9	8.5	7.2	Amériques					4.3			4.3	2.4	1.2
– Northern America					5.2			5.2	3.1	2.9	– Amérique du Nord					4.1			4.1	2.0	0.8
– LAIA					3.1			3.1	4.4	3.9	– ALAI					0.1			0.1	0.1	0.3
– CACM					0.2			0.2	0.1	0.1	– MCAC					0.0			0.0	0.0	0.0
– Caribbean					0.3			0.3	0.8	0.2	– Caraïbes					0.0			0.0	0.1	0.1
– Rest of America					0.2			0.2	0.0	0.0	– Autre Amérique					0.0			0.0	0.1	0.0
Asia excl fmr USSR					9.2			9.2	8.0	8.6	Asie anc. URSS exclus					9.7			9.7	4.9	4.2
– Middle East					3.3			3.3	3.1	2.9	– Moyen–Orient					8.0			8.0	3.2	2.7
Asia former USSR									0.2	0.3	Asie ancienne URSS									0.1	0.1
Europe excl fmr USSR					64.5			64.6	73.4	69.2	Europe anc. URSS exclus					60.3			60.3	80.9	83.5
– European Union					43.8			43.8	42.1	41.2	– Union Européenne					43.9			43.9	31.8	35.4
– Eastern Europe					18.4			18.4	16.0	11.5	– Europe de l'Est					14.3			14.3	10.3	8.5
– Rest of Europe					2.4			2.4	15.3	16.4	– Autre de l'Europe					2.2			2.2	38.8	39.6
Europe former USSR					15.6			15.6	7.1	10.9	Europe ancienne URSS					21.6			21.6	9.6	8.5
Oceania					0.3			0.3	0.3	0.2	Océanie					0.2			0.2	0.1	0.1
Other					0.0				0.0	0.0	Autre					0.0					
Germany/Allemagne					15.0			15.0	12.8	13.4	Russian Federation					21.2			21.2	8.5	7.5
Italy/Italie					9.6			9.6	10.6	10.0	Bosnia and Herzegovina									20.7	18.9
Russian Federation					15.1			15.1	5.5	9.5	Germany/Allemagne					16.4			16.4	8.0	9.2
Bulgaria/Bulgarie					4.9			4.9	5.3	2.6	Italy/Italie					11.9			11.9	9.8	11.5
Bosnia and Herzegovina									5.6	5.9	TFYR Macedonia									11.5	9.3
TFYR Macedonia									5.2	6.0	Greece/Grèce					4.1			4.1	5.2	4.9
Greece/Grèce					3.6			3.6	3.6	3.8	Romania/Roumanie					7.6			7.6	3.4	2.0
Austria/Autriche					4.3			4.3	3.0	3.3	Switzerland,Liechtenst.					1.5			1.5	4.6	7.0
Romania/Roumanie					5.1			5.1	3.0	2.1	France, Monaco					2.4			2.4	3.0	2.2
USA/Etats–Unis d'Amer					3.8			3.8	2.9	2.8	Bulgaria/Bulgarie					2.6			2.6	3.4	1.6

4. Special Imports C.I.F. by Commodities according to the S.I.T.C. (Rev. 2) in million U.S. Dollars
Importations Spéciales C.A.F. par Produits d'après la C.T.C.I. (Rév. 2) en millions de Dollars E.U.

SITC CTCI	COMMODITY	1994 QUANTITY QUANTITE	1994 VALUE VALEUR	1995 QUANTITY QUANTITE	1995 VALUE VALEUR	1996 QUANTITY QUANTITE	1996 VALUE VALEUR	1997 QUANTITY QUANTITE	1997 VALUE VALEUR	PRODUIT
	ALL COMMODITIES						4101.9		4798.8	TOUS PRODUITS
0	FOOD AND LIVE ANIMALS						501.4		583.0	ALIMENTS,ANIMAUX VIVANTS
01	MEAT AND PREPARATIONS						34.2		28.9	VIANDES ET PREPARATIONS
011	MEAT FRESH,CHILLD,FROZEN					W 19715	29.2	W 19845	24.5	VIANDES FRAICHES,REF,CONGE
0111	BOVINE MEAT FRESH,FROZEN					W 7013	12.9	W 5866	10.0	VIANDES BOVIN FRAI,REF
02	DAIRY PRODCTS,BIRDS'EGGS						21.2		15.9	PRODUITS LAITIERS,OEUFS
03	FISH AND PREPARATIONS						19.0		24.9	POISSONS ET PREPARATIONS
034	FISH,FRESH,CHILLED,FROZN						13.2	W 14375	16.5	POISSON FRAIS, REFRIG,CONG
04	CEREALS AND PREPARATIONS						34.0		94.4	CEREALES ET PRODUITS
041	WHEAT ETC UNMILLED					W 21293	2.8	W 295231	57.1	FROMENT,EPEAUTRE
0412	OTHER WHEAT ETC UNMILLED					W 17841	2.2	W 259156	50.1	AUTRE FROMENT NON MOULU
048	CEREAL ETC PREPARATIONS					W 11166	12.5	W 28526	22.9	PREPTNS A BASE CEREALES
05	VEGETABLES AND FRUIT						134.3		188.0	LEGUMES ET FRUITS
054	VEG ETC FRSH,SMPLY PRSVD					W 104908	26.4	W 129550	42.7	LEGUMES FRAIS,CONG,SECS
0545	OTHER FRESH VEGETABLES					W 39020	10.7	W 63590	21.1	AUTRES LEGUMES FRAIS,REF
05459	FRESH VEGETABLES NES					W 33149	9.8	W 45462	17.5	LEGUMES FRAIS,REFRI NDA
057	FRUIT,NUTS,FRESH,DRIED						94.0	W 218189	127.0	FRUITS FRAIS OU SECS
0571	ORANGES, MANDARINS ETC					W 33355	13.8	W 53670	19.7	ORANGES,MAND,CLEMENTINES
0573	BANANA,PLANTAIN,FRSH,DRY					W 66244	59.3	W 96814	78.1	BANANES FRAICHES,SECHEES
06	SUGAR AND PREPS,HONEY						81.8		20.8	SUCRES ET PRODUITS
061	SUGAR AND HONEY					W 166997	72.7	W 16312	6.6	SUCRES ET MIEL
0611	RAW BEET AND CANE SUGAR					W 120484	47.2	W 6984	2.5	SUCRES BRUTS
0612	REFINED SUGAR ETC					W 45931	24.8	W 8715	3.5	SUCRES RAFFINES
07	COFFEE,TEA,COCOA,SPICES						80.0		114.3	CAFE,THE,CACAO,EPICES
071	COFFEE AND SUBSTITUTES					W 10666	33.9	W 18135	50.6	CAFE ET SUCCEDANES
0711	COFFEE GREEN,ROASTED,SUB					W 10589	33.2	W 17944	49.1	CAFE TORREFIE OU DECAFEINE
07111	COFFEE GREEN,HUSKS,SKINS					W 10550	32.9	W 17856	48.7	CAFE NON TORREFIE
073	CHOCOLATE AND PRODUCTS					W 8758	30.0	W 12572	44.5	CHOCOLAT
081	*FEEDING STUFF FOR ANIML					W 119969	65.5		46.1	NOURRITURE POUR ANIMAUX
0813	OILCAKE AND OTH RESIDUES					W 62791	20.6	W 35850	12.0	TOURTEAUX
08131	— OF SOYA BEANS					W 60358	20.3	W 35734	12.0	TOURTEAUX DE SOJA
0814	MEAT OR FISH MEAL FODDER					W 47499	38.5	W 36533	27.9	FARINES DE VIANDES,POISSONS
08142	FISH MEAL FODDER					W 47475	38.5	W 36532	27.9	FARINES DE POISSONS
09	MISC EDIBLE PRODUCTS						27.0		45.3	PREP ALIMENTAIRES DIVERSES
098	EDIBLE PRODCTS,PREPS NES						25.2		42.7	PREP ALIMENTAIRES NDA
09809	MISC FOOD PREPRTIONS NES					W 2967	21.4	W 6626	36.2	PREP ALIMENTAIRES NDA
1	BEVERAGES AND TOBACCO						36.5		82.7	BOISSONS ET TABACS
11	BEVERAGES						25.9		57.2	BOISSONS
111	NON-ALCOHL BEVERAGES NES					W 16149	10.8	W 52340	33.3	BOISSONS NON ALCOOLIQUES
11102	FLAVORED WATERS NON-ALCO					W 16069	10.7	W 52207	33.2	LIMONADES,EAUX GAZEUSES
112	ALCOHOLIC BEVERAGES						15.2	W 22500	23.9	BOISSONS ALCOOLIQUES
12	TOBACCO AND MANUFACTURES						10.7		25.6	TABACS BRUTS FABRIQUES
121	TOBACCO UNMNFCTRD,REFUSE					W 3355	10.2	W 7582	22.0	TABACS BRUTS,DECHETS
1212	TOBACCO STRIPPED OR PART					W 1568	6.5	W 3181	14.8	TABACS PART ECOTES
2	CRUDE MATERLS,EXCL FUELS						425.7		397.2	MAT BRUTES NON COMESTIBLES
22	OIL SEEDS,OLEAGINOUS FRT						34.5		5.9	GRAINES,FRUITS OLEAGINEUX
222	SEEDS FOR'SOFT'FIXED OIL					W 101357	34.1	W 8664	5.5	GRAINES HUILES FIXES
2222	SOYA BEANS					W 67654	22.7	W 4741	1.4	FEVES DE SOJA
23	RUBBER, CRUDE						26.8		25.7	CAOUTCHOUC BRUT
233	RUBBER,SYNTHTIC,RECLAIMD					W 11745	18.1	W 12196	16.9	LATEX CAOUTCH SYNTH REGEN
2331	SYNTHETIC RUBBER ETC					W 11423	17.9	W 11832	16.6	LATEX CAOUTCH SYNTHETIQUE
24	CORK AND WOOD						66.2		87.4	LIEGE ET BOIS
248	WOOD SHAPED,SLEEPERS					W 191540	53.7	W 423487	82.6	BOIS SIMPLEMENT TRAVAILLES
2482	LUMBER SHAPED CONIFER					W 150258	39.3	W 397347	74.1	CONIFERES SCIES,RABOTES
24821	LUMBER SAWN ETC CONIFER					W 149346	38.9	W 396970	74.0	CONIFERES SCIES LONGITUD
2483	LUMBER SHAPED NON-CONIFR					W 40579	14.2	W 25637	8.4	NON CONIFERES SCIES,RABOTES
251	*PULP AND WASTE PAPER						15.4		11.8	PATES A PAPIER,DECHETS
26	TEXTILE FIBRES AND WASTE						47.0		42.7	FIBRES TEXTILES
263	COTTON					W 8807	16.5	W 8414	16.0	COTON
2631	RAW COTTON,EXCL LINTERS					W 8075	15.6	W 7608	15.0	COTON EN MASSE
266	SYNTHETIC FIBRES TO SPIN						13.9	W 6440	11.1	FIBRES SYNTHETIQUES
27	CRUDE FERTLZR,MINRLS NES						41.6		41.5	ENGRAIS MINERAUX BRUTS
278	OTHER CRUDE MINERALS					W 310133	23.6	W 330455	22.1	AUTRES MINERAUX BRUTS
2783	COMMON SALT,ETC					W 200191	12.7	W 268697	12.6	SEL
28	METALLIFEROUS ORES,SCRAP						182.4		166.9	MINERAIS METAL,DECHETS
281	IRON ORE,CONCENTRATES					W 987662	33.1	W 1067248	40.1	MINERAIS DE FER
2815	IRON ORE,CONC,NOT AGGLOM					W 798294	25.2	W 783600	28.7	MINERAIS NON AGGLOMERES
287	BASE METAL ORES,CONC NES						136.1	W 261481	114.7	MINERAIS METAUX COMMUNS
2871	CPR ORE ETC,CEMENT COPPR					W 189580	115.4	W 164401	85.0	MINERAIS DE CUIVRE,MATTES
28711	COPPER ORES,EXCL MATTE					W 189580	115.4	W 164401	85.0	MINERAIS DE CUIVRE
2874	LEAD ORES,CONCENTRATES					W 28212	10.8	W 36606	15.3	MINERAIS DE PLOMB
3	MINERAL FUELS ETC						575.1		771.9	COMBUSTIBLES MINERAUX LUB
32	COAL,COKE AND BRIQUETTES						56.7		69.1	HOUILLES,COKES,BRIQUETTES
323	BRIQUETS,COKE,SEMI-COKE					W 431958	51.2	W 568199	64.2	BRIQUETTES
3232	COKE,SEMI-COKE,RTRT CRBN					W 409154	50.4	W 552640	63.6	COKES ET SEMI-COKES
33	PETROLEUM AND PRODUCTS						478.2		564.6	PETROLE ET DERIVES
333	CRUDE PETROLEUM					W 1321098	228.9	W 2292220	368.3	HUILES BRUTES DE PETROLE
334	PETROLEUM PRODUCTS,REFIN					W 1045557	236.4	W 696292	182.5	PRODUITS RAFFINES
335	RESIDUAL PETRLM PROD NES						13.0	W 52356	13.9	PRODUITS RESIDUELS NDA
341	*GAS,NATURAL AND MANUFCT					W 169398	9.3	W 978774	132.0	GAZ NATUREL,GAZ MANUFACT
3414	PETROLEUM GASES, GASEOUS					W 160812	6.2	W 969959	130.2	GAZ DE PETROLE GAZEUX
351	*ELECTRIC CURRENT						31.0		6.3	ENERGIE ELECTRIQUE
5	CHEMCLS,RELATED PROD NES						564.0		613.5	PRODUITS CHIMIQUES
51	ORGANIC CHEMICALS						84.6		89.3	PROD CHIMIQ ORGANIQUES
513	CARBOXYLIC ACIDS ETC					W 10602	17.2		15.1	ACIDES CARBOXYLIQUES
514	NITROGEN-FNCTN COMPOUNDS					W 5954	24.0		28.4	COMPOSES FONCT AZOTEES
5148	OTH NITROGN-FNCTN CMPNDS					W 2724	13.5	W 3285	14.3	AUTRES COMPOSES AZOTES
515	ORG-INORG COMPOUNDS ETC						13.5		17.3	COMPOSES ORGANO-MINERAUX
52	INORGANIC CHEMICALS						63.9		64.4	PROD CHIM INORGANIQUES
522	INORG ELEMNTS,OXIDES,ETC						25.2		28.1	ELEMENTS INORGANIQUES
523	OTHR INORG CHEMICALS ETC						38.2		35.7	AUT PRODUITS CHIMIQUES INORG
5231	METAL CMPD OF INORG ACID					W 22875	14.6	W 23636	13.6	SELS METALLIQUES
5232	OTH MTL CMPD OF INRG ACD						20.3	W 77162	18.4	SELS METALLIQUES
53	DYES,TANNING,COLOUR PROD						50.8		49.7	PROD TEINTURE,COLORANTS
531	SYNT DYE,NAT INDGO,LAKES					W 1194	13.2	W 1584	12.7	MAT COLOR ORGAN,LAQUES
533	PIGMENTS,PAINTS,ETC					W 13242	35.6	W 16953	35.6	PIGMENTS,PEINTURES,VERNIS
5334	VARNISHES,DISTEMPERS ETC					W 6107	18.7	W 6908	16.0	PEINTURES A L'EAU
53342	OTH PAINTS,VARNISHES ETC					W 4717	14.7	W 5041	12.3	AUTRES PEINTURES,VERNIS
541	*MEDICINAL,PHARM PRODUCT						61.1		78.4	PROD MEDICINAUX PHARMACEUT
5417	MEDICAMENTS						32.8	K 900743	43.4	MEDICAMENTS
54179	— CONTNG OTH SUBSTANCES					K 361695	16.8	K 498363	26.8	MED CONT AUT SUBSTANCES

4. Special Imports C.I.F. by Commodities according to the S.I.T.C. (Rev. 2) in million U.S. Dollars
Importations Spéciales C.A.F. par Produits d'après la C.T.C.I. (Rév. 2) en millions de Dollars E.U.

SITC CTCI	COMMODITY	1994		1995		1996		1997		PRODUIT
		QUANTITY QUANTITE	VALUE VALEUR	QUANTITY QUANTITE	VALUE VALEUR	QUANTITY QUANTITE	VALUE VALEUR	QUANTITY QUANTITE	VALUE VALEUR	
55	PERFUME,CLEANING ETC PRD						50.4		70.3	PROD POUR PARFUM,TOILETTE
553	PERFUMERY,COSMETICS,ETC					W 3390	10.0	W 6172	22.6	PRODUITS DE PARFUMERIE
554	SOAP,CLEANSING ETC PREPS					W 30470	31.6	W 31796	37.0	SAVONS,PRODUITS DETERSIFS
5542	WASHING PREPARATIONS ETC					W 27316	26.5	W 27950	30.5	PROD ORG TENSIO–ACT NDA
562	*FERTILIZERS,MANUFACTURE						31.6		34.5	ENGRAIS MANUFACTURES
5621	CHEM NITROGENOUS FERTLZR					W 47644	7.7	W 123174	17.5	ENGRAIS AZOTES
5623	CHEM POTASSIC FERTILIZER						13.0		7.0	ENGRAIS POTASSIQUES
56231	POTASSIUM CHLORIDE					W 101419	13.0	W 54747	7.0	CHLORURE DE POTASSIUM
58	PLASTIC MATERIALS ETC						127.4		118.7	MAT PLAST ARTIFICIELLES
582	PROD OF CONDENSATION ETC					W 9307	23.0	W 15176	26.7	PROD CONDENS,POLYCOND
583	POLYMERIZATION ETC PRODS						99.3	W 74012	86.3	PROD POLYMERISATION
5831	POLYETHYLENE						29.1	W 24654	22.9	POLYETHYLENE
58311	— IN PRIMARY FORMS					W 30781	27.9	W 21964	20.3	POLYETHYLENE PRIMAIRES
5832	POLYPROPYLENE					W 15424	17.1	W 8380	9.7	POLYPROPYLENE
58321	— IN PRIMARY FORMS					W 14314	12.9	W 7017	5.6	POLYPROPYLENE PRIMAIRES
5834	POLYVINYL CHLORIDE					W 19232	20.3	W 18941	20.7	CHLORURE DE POLYVINYLE
58341	— IN PRIMARY FORMS					W 16879	15.3	W 16218	14.8	SOUS FORMES PRIMAIRES
5839	OTH POLYMRZTION ETC PROD					W 5758	14.3	W 7844	14.7	AUT PROD POLYMER COPOLYM
59	CHEMICAL MATERIALS NES						94.6		108.2	MAT PROD CHIMIQUES NDA
591	PESTICIDES,DISINFECTANTS					W 1743	23.4	W 3073	36.2	DESINF,INSECT,FONG,HERB
5913	HERBICIDES,FOR RETAIL					W 781	12.0	W 1296	17.0	HERBICIDES VENTE AU DET
598	MISCEL CHEM PRODUCTS NES					W 27147	63.8		62.9	PROD DIV INDUST CHIM NDA
5982	ANTI–KNOCK PREPARTNS ETC					W 3336	14.0	W 2824	12.5	PREPARAT ANTIDETONANTES
5989	CHEM PRODUCTS,PREPS NES					W 20120	45.0		44.7	PROD PREP CHIMIQUES NDA
59899	OTH CHEM PRODS,PREPS,NES					W 15038	32.7	W 25906	34.5	AUT PRODUITS CHIMIQUES NDA
6	BASIC MANUFACTURES						829.1		809.0	ART MANUFACTURES
61	LEATHER,DRESSED FUR,ETC						19.2		26.3	CUIRS,PELLETERIES
612	LEATHER ETC MANUFACTURES						14.6		18.6	OUVRAGES EN CUIRS NDA
6123	PREPRD PARTS OF FOOTWEAR					W 1337	14.5	W 1990	18.5	PARTIES DE CHAUSSURES
62	RUBBER MANUFACTURES NES						36.4		29.6	CAOUTCHOUC MANUFACTURE
625	RUBBER TYRES, TUBES ETC					W 14940	24.6		17.5	PNEUS CAOUTCHOUC VULCANISE
6252	TYRES,NEW,BUS OR LORRY					W 4242	15.5	W 3713	12.1	PNEUS POUR AUTOBUS,CAMIONS
63	WOOD,CORK MANUFACTRS NES						20.1		83.6	OUVRAGES LIEGE ET BOIS
635	WOOD MANUFACTURES NES					W 5685	8.5	W 133952	72.5	ART MANUF EN BOIS NDA
6359	OTHER WOOD MANUFACTURES					W 532	0.9	W 129503	65.7	OUVRAGES EN BOIS NDA
63599	OTHER WOOD ARTICLES NES					W 392	0.8	W 129443	65.7	AUTRES OUVRAGES EN BOIS NDA
64	PAPER,PAPERBOARD AND MFR						157.5		157.5	PAPIERS,CARTONS & OUVRAGES
641	PAPER AND PAPERBOARD					W 128236	117.2		115.5	PAPIERS ET CARTONS
6411	NEWSPRINT					W 18070	13.1	W 27258	14.8	PAPIER JOURNAL
6412	PRINTG,WRITING PAPER NES					W 17592	20.6	W 21048	21.9	PAPIERS POUR L'IMPRESSION
64122	— COATED,IMPREGNATD ETC					W 14604	16.9	W 15945	16.9	PAPIERS IMPRESSION COUCHES
6413	KRAFT PAPER,PAPERBOARD					W 36275	25.4	W 35403	22.8	PAPIER ET CARTON KRAFT
64132	SACK KRAFT PAPER IN BULK					W 23757	17.3	W 19575	13.6	PAPIER KRAFT POUR SACS
6415	PAPER,PAPERBRD,BULK,NES					W 29992	30.4	W 28209	26.6	PAPIERS,CARTONS ROULEAUX
64159	OTHER PAPER ETC,BULK,NES					W 25299	26.6	W 25004	24.3	AUT PAPIER ROULEAUX FEUILLES
6418	COATED ETC PAPER NES BLK					W 8136	15.1	W 12031	18.1	PAP,CARTONS COUCHES,ENDUITS
642	PAPER,ETC,PRECUT,ARTS OF					W 23445	40.3	W 18704	42.1	PAP,CARTONS DECOUPES
6421	PAPER ETC CONTAINERS					W 12884	15.8	W 7385	12.9	BOITES,SACS EMBALLAGES
6428	PAPER ETC ARTICLES NES					W 4116	11.9	W 6774	20.9	OUVRAGES EN PATE A PAPIER
64285	PAPER ETC DIAPERS ETC					W 2638	8.5	W 4903	16.2	SERVIETTES HYGIENIQUES
65	TEXTILE YARN,FABRICS,ETC						234.5		127.2	FILS,TISSUS,ARTICLES TEXTILE
651	TEXTILE YARN						23.6		28.5	FILS TEXTILES
652	COTTON FABRICS,WOVEN					W 102992	151.7	W 11018	27.9	TISSUS DE COTON
6521	GREY WOVEN COTTON FABRIC					W 95953	127.1	W 694	1.8	TISSUS COT ECRUS NON MERCER
65215	GREY WOVN COTN BLEND NES					W 95456	125.7	W 46	0.3	AUT TIS MOINS 85% COT ECRUS
6522	WOVEN COTTON BLEACHD,ETC					W 7038	24.7	W 10324	26.2	TISSUS COTON BLANCHIS ETC
65224	BLCHED COTTON FABRIC NES					W 6398	20.1	W 9619	22.7	AUT TIS PLUS 85% COT BLANCHI
653	WOVN MAN–MADE FIB FABRIC					W 1959	13.3		17.2	TISSUS FIBRES SYNTH,ARTIF
657	SPECIAL TXTL FABRC,PRODS						23.6		24.0	TISSUS SPECIAUX
66	NONMETAL MINERAL MFS NES						64.5		87.2	ART MIN NON METALLIQUES
661	LIME,CEMENT,BLDG PRODS					W 87581	11.4	W 315054	25.2	CHAUX,CIMENTS MAT CONSTR
6612	CEMENT					W 54585	3.0	W 283444	17.3	CIMENTS HYDRAULIQUES
662	CLAY,REFRACTORY BLDG PRD					W 73926	14.3	W 80584	18.6	MAT CONST REFRACTAIRES
663	MINERAL MANUFCTURES NES						12.6		13.9	ART MIN MANUF NDA
664	GLASS					W 20496	18.0	W 26723	17.0	VERRE
67	IRON AND STEEL						171.4		150.1	FER ET ACIER
671	PIG IRON ETC					W 15468	13.0		12.2	FONTE,SPIEGEL,POUDRES
672	IRON,STEEL PRIMARY FORMS					W 99577	23.6	W 127980	32.4	LINGOTS FER,ACIER
6725	IRN,STL BLOOMS,SLABS,ETC					W 91410	21.1	W 124081	30.7	BLOOMS,BILLETTES FER ACIER
67251	IRN,SMPLE STL BLOOMS,ETC					W 90546	19.9	W 122642	29.5	BLOOMS ETC NON ACIER FIN
673	IRON,STEEL SHAPES ETC						43.5	W 117181	43.0	BARRES,PROFIL FER,ACIER
6731	IRON,STEEL WIRE ROD						22.4	W 71099	21.8	FIL MACHINE FER,ACIER
67311	IRON,SIMPLE STL WIRE ROD					W 76097	22.1	W 33091	10.3	FIL MACH AUT ACIER FIN
6732	IRON,STEEL BARS ETC					W 31917	15.8	W 31194	15.1	BARRES FER,ACIER
674	IRN,STL UNIV,PLATE,SHEET					W 56657	43.5	W 34217	27.9	LARGES PLATS,TOLES
678	IRON,STL TUBES,PIPES,ETC					W 30349	32.1	W 28598	25.6	TUBES,TUYAUX EN FONTE,FER
6782	IRON,STL SEAMLESS TUBES					W 16629	19.7	W 17341	16.0	TUBES,TUYAUX SANS SOUDURE
68	NON–FERROUS METALS						64.7		69.2	METAUX NON FERREUX
682	COPPER EXC CEMENT COPPER					W 11349	28.9		22.2	CUIVRE
6821	COPPER NES,ALLOYS,UNWRT					W 10248	25.7	W 6491	16.0	CUIVRE BRUT
68211	COPPER UNREF,EXC CEMENT					W 8035	20.7	W 4321	10.9	CUIVRE POUR AFFINAGE
684	ALUMINIUM					W 6811	23.1	W 11428	31.1	ALUMINIUM
6842	ALUMINIUM,ALLOYS WORKED					W 5467	21.0	W 7257	23.7	ALUMINIUM,ALLIAGES OUVRE
69	METAL MANUFACTURES NES						61.4		78.7	ART MANUFACT EN METAL NDA
699	BASE-METAL MFRS NES						19.0		22.5	ART MANUFACTURES MET NDA
7	MACHINES,TRANSPORT EQUIP						795.7		854.8	MACHINES MATERIEL TRANSPORT
71	POWER GENERATING EQUIPMT						25.8		28.2	MACHINES GENERATRICES
713	INTRNL COMBUS PSTN ENGIN						17.1		19.3	MOTEURS EXPL COMB INT, PIECE
72	MACHS FOR SPCL INDUSTRYS						102.1		140.3	MAC SPECIALES POUR INDUST
722	TRACTORS NON–ROAD					W 2324	4.6	W 3852	17.6	TRACTEURS
7224	WHEELED TRACTORS NES					W 2316	4.6	W 3834	17.5	TRACTEURS A ROUES
723	CIVIL ENGNEERG EQUIP ETC						9.7		16.0	APPAREILS DE GENIE CIVIL
724	TEXTILE,LEATHER MACHNRY						11.8		17.7	MACH POUR INDUSTRIE TEXTILE
726	PRINTG,BKBINDG MACHY,PTS						10.6		15.7	MACHINES POUR IMPRIMERIE
727	FOOD MACHRY NON–DOMESTIC						15.6	W 2436	20.5	MACH INDUSTRIES ALIMENT
7272	OTH FOOD PROC MCHY,PARTS					W 936	14.1	W 1406	19.5	AUT MACH IND ALIMENTAIRE
72722	INDUS FOOD PROC MACH NES					W 925	13.6	W 1395	19.2	MACHINES BOULANGERIE
728	OTH MACHY FOR SPCL INDUS						39.2		39.4	AUT MACH IND PARTICULIERES
7284	MACHY FOR SPCL INDUS NES						25.6		26.3	MACH SPEC IND PARTICUL.
72842	RUBBER,PLASTICS WRKG MCH					W 2326	13.4	W 1796	12.7	MACH IND CAOUT MAT PLAST
73	METALWORKING MACHINERY						14.4		15.6	MACH TRAVAIL DES METAUX

4. Special Imports C.I.F. by Commodities according to the S.I.T.C. (Rev. 2) in million U.S. Dollars
Importations Spéciales C.A.F. par Produits d'après la C.T.C.I. (Rév. 2) en millions de Dollars E.U.

SITC CTCI	COMMODITY	1994 QUANTITY QUANTITE	1994 VALUE VALEUR	1995 QUANTITY QUANTITE	1995 VALUE VALEUR	1996 QUANTITY QUANTITE	1996 VALUE VALEUR	1997 QUANTITY QUANTITE	1997 VALUE VALEUR	PRODUIT
74	GENRL INDUSTRL MACHY NES						115.4		141.1	MACH APP INDUSTRIE
741	HEATING,COOLING EQUIPMNT					W 2970	24.8		31.9	MACH CHAUFFAGE,PIECES
743	PUMPS NES,CENTRFUGES ETC					W 2168	18.5	W 2701	20.0	POMPES COMPRES,VENT ETC
744	MECHANICAL HANDLING EQU						13.6	W 3857	13.8	EQUIP MANUTENTION PIECES
745	NONELEC MACHY,TOOLS NES						27.1		35.0	AUT MACH NON ELEC,PIECES
7452	OTH NONELEC MCHS,PTS NES						24.4		30.9	AUT MACH NON ELEC,PIECES
74522	PACKAGNG,BOTTLNG,ETC MCH					W 768	19.6	W 924	24.5	MACH NETT BOUTEILLES,ETC
749	NONELEC MACH PTS,ACC NES						23.1		28.0	PIECES MACH NON ELEC NDA
75	OFFICE MACHNES,ADP EQUIP						73.9		100.9	MACH BUREAU TRAIT AUTOM
752	AUTOMTIC DATA PROC EQUIP						46.7	W 1542	72.0	MACH TRAIT INFORMATION
7523	DIGITL CENTRL PROCESSORS					W 65	8.4	W 102	24.2	UNITES CENTRALES
7524	DIGITL CENTRL STOR UNITS					W 96	10.3	W 161	16.3	UNITES MEMOIRE CENTRALES
7525	ADP PERIPHERAL UNITS					W 1061	21.5	W 1172	24.4	UNITES PERIPHERIQUES
759	OFFICE,ADP MCH PTS,ACCES						20.1		21.9	PIECES DU 751 ET 752
7599	ACCTG,ETC,ADP MCH PTS,AC					W 635	18.9	W 640	20.8	PIECES DU 751 ET 752
76	TELECOMM,SOUND EQUIPMENT						160.5		86.2	EQUIPMENT DE TELECOM
762	RADIO BROADCAST RECEIVRS						36.2	W 447	11.4	RECEPTEURS RADIODIFFUSION
7622	PORTABLE RADIO RECEIVERS					W 251	34.1	W 94	7.9	RECEPT PORTATIFS RADIO
764	TELECOM EQPT,PTS,ACC NES						115.6		64.9	EQUIP TELECOM,PIECES
7641	LINE TELEPHONE,ETC EQUIP					W 587	82.7	W 463	37.0	APP TELEPHON PAR FIL
7649	PTS NES OF EQUIPMT OF 76						18.3	W 597	21.3	PIECES DE LA DIV 76
76491	PTS NES OF APPAR OF 7641					W 144	13.4	W 189	16.9	PIECES POUR 764.1
77	ELECTRIC MACHNRY NES ETC						102.0		137.0	MACH APP ELECT NDA
772	SWITCHGEAR ETC,PARTS NES						22.0		20.9	APP COUPURE,SECT ETC
7721	SWITCHGEAR ETC					W 748	19.9	W 952	19.3	APP COUPURE,SECTIONMNT
774	ELECTRO–MEDCL,XRAY EQUIP					W 90	12.1	W 147	19.1	APPAREILS MEDICAUX
775	HOUSEHOLD TYPE EQUIP NES						11.5		23.2	MACH,APP USAGE DOMESTQUE
776	TRANSISTORS,VALVES,ETC						16.3		13.8	LAMPES,TUBES,VALVES
778	ELECTRICAL MACHINERY NES						33.4		46.4	AUTRES MACH ELECT NDA
7788	OTH ELEC MACHY,EQUIP NES						15.2		26.8	AUT MACH APP ELEC NDA
77887	ELECTRICAL CARBONS					W 5384	6.3	W 29796	19.3	PIECES CHARBON,GRAPHITE
78	ROAD VEHICLES						184.3		164.6	VEHICULES ROUTIERS
781	PASS MOTOR VEH EXC BUSES					W 21689	95.6	W 13423	78.0	AUTO TRANSPORT PERSONNES
782	LORRIES,SPCL MTR VEH NES					W 10044	25.4	W 4080	22.6	VEHICULES SPECIAUX,MARCH
7821	LORRIES,TRUCKS					W 9661	23.0	W 3798	20.0	VEHICULES TRANSP MARCHAND
783	ROAD MOTOR VEHICLES NES					W 4758	24.9	W 1732	19.7	VEHICULES ROUTIERS NDA
7832	TRACTORS FOR TR–TRAILERS					W 3071	19.4	W 1072	12.5	TRACTEURS ROUTIERS
784	MOTOR VEH PRTS,ACCES NES					W 3254	23.9	W 6072	34.7	PIECES 722,781,782,783
7849	OTHER MOTOR VEHCL PARTS					W 2862	20.5	W 5707	32.8	PIECES 722,781,782,783
79	OTHR TRANSPORT EQUIPMENT						17.6		41.2	AUTRE MATERIEL TRANSPORT
793	SHIPS AND BOATS ETC					W 6789	4.0	W 10506	19.8	NAVIRES BATEAUX,ETC
7932	SHIPS AND BOATS NES					W 6564	3.9	W 9525	19.7	NAVIRES ET BATEAUX
79323	OTHER CARGO VESSELS					W 6511	3.6	W 9431	19.4	AUT BATEAUX TRANS MARCH
8	MISC MANUFACTURED GOODS						327.3		366.5	ART MANUFACTURES DIVERS
821	*FURNITURE,PARTS THEREOF					W 12498	33.6	W 12816	29.4	MEUBLES ET PIECES
8219	FURNITURE AND PARTS NES					W 9808	23.7	W 9936	20.1	AUTRES MEUBLES ET PIECES
82192	WOOD FURNITURE NES					W 6900	15.0	W 6071	12.1	MEUBLES NDA EN BOIS
84	CLOTHING AND ACCESSORIES						75.1		81.0	VETEMENTS
842	MENS OUTERWEAR NOT KNIT					W 570	11.1	W 1562	18.2	VET DESSUS POUR HOMMES
843	WOMENS OUTERWEAR NONKNIT					W 1843	40.8	W 1905	31.3	VET DESSUS FEMMES MAT TEX
8431	— COATS AND JACKETS					W 937	27.2	W 955	16.6	MANT,VEST FEM MAT TEXTIL
851	*FOOTWEAR					W 4792	48.4	W 5712	47.1	CHAUSSURES
85102	FOOTWEAR LEATHER					W 4223	43.6	W 4850	42.0	CHAUS SEMELLES EN CUIR
87	PRECISION INSTRUMNTS NES						64.3		65.6	INSTRUM,APPAR SCIENT NDA
872	MEDICAL INSTRUMENTS NES						37.5		32.4	INSTR,APP MEDIC–CHIR NDA
87202	OTH MEDICAL INSTRUMENTS					W 776	33.7	W 947	27.9	INSTRUM,APP MEDECINE
874	MEASURNG,CONTROLNG INSTR						22.3		29.9	INSTRUMENTS DE MESURE
88	PHOTO EQU,OPTICL GDS ETC						17.2		19.5	APP,FOURN PHOTO,OP,MONTR
89	MISC MANUFCTRD GOODS NES						81.2		110.1	ART MANUFACTURES DIVERS
892	PRINTED MATTER						7.0		17.7	IMPRIMES
893	ARTICLES OF PLASTIC NES						37.4		45.9	OUVRAGES EN MAT DIVIS 58
8931	PLSTC PACKG CONTNRS,LIDS					W 4360	10.5	W 7861	15.1	ART TRANSP EMBALLAGE ETC
8939	MISC PLASTIC ARTICLES					W 4525	26.1	W 6679	30.1	ART DIVERS EN MAT DIV 58
89399	OTHR PLASTC ARTICLES NES					W 3749	24.1	W 6010	28.5	AUT OUV MAT DIV 58
899	OTHER MANUFACTURED GOODS						15.9		13.7	AUT ART MANUF DIVERS NDA
9	GOODS NOT CLASSD BY KIND						36.7		312.5	ART TRANSACT NON CLASSES
931	*SPECIAL TRANSACTIONS					W 5870	35.0	W 1325495	311.3	TRANS.SPECIALES

5. Special Exports F.O.B. by Commodities according to the S.I.T.C. (Rev. 2) in million U.S. Dollars
Exportations Spéciales F.O.B. par Produits d'après la C.T.C.I. (Rév. 2) en millions de Dollars E.U.

SITC CTCI	COMMODITY	1994 QUANTITY QUANTITE	1994 VALUE VALEUR	1995 QUANTITY QUANTITE	1995 VALUE VALEUR	1996 QUANTITY QUANTITE	1996 VALUE VALEUR	1997 QUANTITY QUANTITE	1997 VALUE VALEUR	PRODUIT
	ALL COMMODITIES						1841.8		2367.8	TOUS PRODUITS
0	FOOD AND LIVE ANIMALS						406.4		279.4	ALIMENTS,ANIMAUX VIVANTS
001	*LIVE ANIMALS FOR FOOD					W 1906	3.6	W 6869	9.4	ANIMAUX VIVANTS
01	MEAT AND PREPARATIONS						30.8		19.4	VIANDES ET PREPARATIONS
011	MEAT FRESH,CHILLD,FROZEN					W 2353	5.8	W 1666	3.6	VIANDES FRAICHES,REF,CONGE
014	MEAT PREPD,PRSVD,NES ETC					W 8324	24.0	W 5045	15.0	CONSERVES DE VIANDES
0142	SAUSAGES INCLDING TINNED					W 6439	15.0	W 3486	9.4	SAUCISSES,SAUCISSONS
0149	OTH PREPARD,PRESRVD MEAT					W 1885	9.1	W 1559	5.7	AUTRES PREP DE VIANDES
04	CEREALS AND PREPARATIONS						147.0		51.4	CEREALES ET PRODUITS
041	WHEAT ETC UNMILLED					W 446008	70.8	W 15106	3.6	FROMENT,EPEAUTRE
0411	DURUM WHEAT UNMILLED					W 335126	55.2	W 45	0.1	FROMENT DUR NON MOULU
0412	OTHER WHEAT ETC UNMILLED					W 110882	15.6	W 15061	3.6	AUTRE FROMENT NON MOULU
044	MAIZE UNMILLED					W 255155	44.4	W 118927	28.6	MAIS NON MOULU
046	WHEAT ETC MEAL OR FLOUR					W 55408	13.8	W 19584	6.3	SEMOULE FARINE,FROMENT
04601	FLOUR OF WHEAT OR MESLIN					W 55099	13.7	W 19490	6.2	FARINE DE FROMENT
048	CEREAL ETC PREPARATIONS					W 12722	16.1	W 6415	11.2	PREPTNS A BASE CEREALES
0484	BAKERY PRODUCTS					W 4150	11.1	W 4264	9.6	PRODUITS DE BOULANGERIE
04842	PASTRY, CAKES ETC					W 2808	8.0	W 2178	5.0	PATISSERIE ETC.
05	VEGETABLES AND FRUIT						158.0		141.2	LEGUMES ET FRUITS
054	VEG ETC FRSH,SMPLY PRSVD					W 31813	28.5	W 22193	22.0	LEGUMES FRAIS,CONG,SECS
0545	OTHER FRESH VEGETABLES					W 8109	12.7	W 4270	8.9	AUTRES LEGUMES FRAIS,REF
05459	FRESH VEGETABLES NES					W 6045	12.3	W 3374	8.5	LEGUMES FRAIS,REFRI NDA
0546	VEGETABLES SIMPLY PRESVD					W 9725	12.0	W 7469	11.1	LEGUMES CONG,CONSER
05461	VEGETABLES FROZEN					W 8456	6.5	W 5934	5.6	LEGUMES CONGELES
056	VEGTBLES ETC PRSVD,PREPD					W 4513	16.5	W 14079	23.6	CONSERVES DE LEGUMES
0561	VEG DRIED EXC LEGUMINOUS					W 1164	12.0	W 1370	14.7	LEGUM DESSECH,DESHYDRAT
0565	VEGTBLES PRSVD,PREPD NES					W 3302	4.4	W 12664	8.8	LEGUMES PREPARES CONSERVE
058	FRUIT PRESERVED,PREPARED					W 96346	107.8		89.9	CONSERVES DE FRUITS
0585	FRUIT OR VEGETABLE JUICE					W 9127	18.3	W 8773	7.5	JUS DE FRUITS
05857	JUICE OF OTHER FRUIT,VEG					W 7515	16.8	W 6546	6.0	JUS AUTRES FRUITS,LEGUMES
0586	FRUIT TEMPORARILY PRESVD					W 83165	85.2	W 79811	79.0	FRUITS CONSERV TEMPORAIRE
05861	FRUIT,FRZN WITHOUT SUGAR					W 80262	83.3	W 77096	77.8	FRUITS CONG SANS SUCRE
06	SUGAR AND PREPS,HONEY						6.4		5.8	SUCRES ET PRODUITS
07	COFFEE,TEA,COCOA,SPICES						16.0		14.9	CAFE,THE,CACAO,EPICES
073	CHOCOLATE AND PRODUCTS					W 2997	11.2	W 3190	11.6	CHOCOLAT
081	*FEEDING STUFF FOR ANIML					W 145815	22.9	W 97918	16.4	NOURRITURE POUR ANIMAUX
0819	FOOD WASTE AND FEED NES					W 105568	15.6	W 50524	8.0	DECHETS,ALIMENTS NDA
08193	BEET-PULP,BAGASSE,ETC					W 79972	7.4	W 36603	3.6	PULPES,AUTRES DECHETS
08199	FODDER NES,INCL SWEETNED					W 25549	8.2	W 13901	4.4	PREPARATIONS FOURRAGERES
09	MISC EDIBLE PRODUCTS						15.7		16.3	PREP ALIMENTAIRES DIVERSES
098	EDIBLE PRODCTS,PREPS NES					W 8844	13.3	W 15677	15.4	PREP ALIMENTAIRES NDA
09809	MISC FOOD PREPRTIONS NES					W 6086	7.9	W 13002	10.7	PREP ALIMENTAIRES NDA
1	BEVERAGES AND TOBACCO						101.0		77.7	BOISSONS ET TABACS
11	BEVERAGES						30.1		28.0	BOISSONS
112	ALCOHOLIC BEVERAGES						25.5	W 44818	23.9	BOISSONS ALCOOLIQUES
1123	BEER,ALE,STOUT,PORTER					W 39636	14.8	W 37347	14.5	BIERES
1124	DISTILLED ALCOHOLIC BEVS						6.1	W 1702	5.5	ALCOOLS,EAUX-DE-VIE
12	TOBACCO AND MANUFACTURES						71.0		49.8	TABACS BRUTS FABRIQUES
121	TOBACCO UNMNFCTRD,REFUSE					W 3283	7.8	W 1088	2.9	TABACS BRUTS,DECHETS
122	TOBACCO,MANUFACTURED					W 5594	63.2	W 4459	47.0	TABACS FABRIQUES
1222	CIGARETTES					W 5545	63.1	W 4200	46.4	CIGARETTES
2	CRUDE MATERLS,EXCL FUELS						86.7		128.1	MAT BRUTES NON COMESTIBLES
21	HIDES,SKINS,FURS UNDRSSD						7.7		8.2	CUIRS,PEAUX BRUTS
211	HIDES,SKINS,EXC FURS,RAW					W 6010	7.7	W 6821	8.2	CUIRS ET PEAUX
2111	BOVINE,EQUINE HIDES,RAW					W 4159	5.6	W 3915	4.8	PEAUX DE BOVINS
23	RUBBER, CRUDE						4.5		17.8	CAOUTCHOUC BRUT
233	RUBBER,SYNTHTIC,RECLAIMD					W 5366	4.3	W 28251	17.8	LATEX CAOUTCH SYNTH REGEN
2331	SYNTHETIC RUBBER ETC					W 5233	4.3	W 28114	17.8	LATEX CAOUTCH SYNTHETIQUE
23315	POLYBUTADIENE-STYRN(SBR)					W 5039	4.1	W 28017	17.7	POLYBUTADIENE-STYRENE
24	CORK AND WOOD						46.0		68.1	LIEGE ET BOIS
247	OTH WOOD ROUGH,SQUARED					W 15821	4.0	W 61942	7.2	BOIS BRUTS EQUARRIS
248	WOOD SHAPED,SLEEPERS					W 105022	41.9	W 166175	60.7	BOIS SIMPLEMENT TRAVAILLES
2483	LUMBER SHAPED NON-CONIFR					W 96139	39.1	W 150977	56.8	NON CONIFERES SCIES,RABOTES
24831	LUMBER SAWN ETC NON-CON					W 91674	36.2	W 144316	53.3	SCIES LONGITUDINALEMENT
26	TEXTILE FIBRES AND WASTE						6.2		10.6	FIBRES TEXTILES
267	OTHER MAN-MADE FIBRES					W 3506	5.1	W 7711	10.1	AUTR FIBR TEXT ARTIF SYNTH
2671	REGENERATD FIBRE TO SPIN					W 3109	4.7	W 7376	9.9	FIBRES TEXT ARTIFIC
26711	DISCN REGEN FIBRE UNCMBD					W 2928	4.5	W 7293	9.7	FIBRES TEX ARTIF DISCONT
28	METALLIFEROUS ORES,SCRAP						6.0		5.4	MINERAIS METAL,DECHETS
29	CRUDE ANIMAL,VEG MAT NES						8.5		8.4	MATIERES BRUTES ANIM,VEGET
292	CRUDE VEG MATERIALS NES						7.3	W 4335	7.4	MAT BRUTES VEGETALES NDA
3	MINERAL FUELS ETC						39.9		47.1	COMBUSTIBLES MINERAUX LUB
33	PETROLEUM AND PRODUCTS						29.0		32.7	PETROLE ET DERIVES
334	PETROLEUM PRODUCTS,REFIN					W 134954	23.8	W 193465	32.1	PRODUITS RAFFINES
341	*GAS,NATURAL AND MANUFCT						2.8	W 33367	7.4	GAZ NATUREL,GAZ MANUFACT
3413	PETROLM GASES,LIQUEFIED					W 8829	2.8	W 33357	7.4	GAZ DE PETROLE LIQUEFIE
4	ANIMAL,VEGETABLE OIL,FAT						8.0		20.4	HUILES,GRAISSES ANIM,VEG
42	FIXED VEGETABLE OIL,FAT						4.1		16.6	HUILES VEGETALES FIXES
423	FIXED VEG OILS,SOFT					W 4591	4.1		16.6	HUILES VEGET DOUCES FIXES
4236	SUNFLOWER SEED OIL					W 3866	3.5	W 8483	9.7	HUILE DE TOURNESOL
5	CHEMCLS,RELATED PROD NES						162.4		308.5	PRODUITS CHIMIQUES
51	ORGANIC CHEMICALS						20.0		78.3	PROD CHIMIQ ORGANIQUES
511	HYDROCARBONS NES,DERIVS						7.3		34.3	HYDROCARBURES NDA
5111	ACYCLIC HYDROCARBONS					W 13388	5.0	W 63645	20.1	HYDROCARBURES ACYCLIQUES
51112	PROPYLENE					W 12204	4.1	W 52957	15.3	PROPYLENE
5113	HALOG DERIV OF HYDROCARB						2.0	W 32173	13.5	DERIVES HALOGENES HYDROCAR
51131	VINYL CHLORIDE					W 4993	1.9	W 28378	12.4	CHLORURE DE VINYLE
512	ALCOHOLS,PHENOLS ETC						2.5		11.5	PHENOLS,PHENOLS-ALCOOLS
5121	ACYCLIC ALCOHOLS,DERIVS						2.5		11.5	ALCOOLS ACYCLIQUES
51211	METHYL ALCOHOL(METHANOL)					W 14625	2.2	W 66149	10.9	ALCOOLS METHYLIQUES
513	CARBOXYLIC ACIDS ETC						7.7		27.6	ACIDES CARBOXYLIQUES
5137	MONOACIDS AND DERIVATIVS					W 6216	7.6	W 58683	27.1	ACIDES MONOCARBOXYLIQUES
51371	ACETIC ACID,ITS SALTS					W 6095	7.4	W 58559	26.9	ACIDE ACETIQUE,SELS
52	INORGANIC CHEMICALS						13.1		19.9	PROD CHIM INORGANIQUES
522	INORG ELEMNTS,OXIDES,ETC						6.3		10.1	ELEMENTS INORGANIQUES
523	OTHR INORG CHEMICALS ETC						6.9		9.9	AUT PRODUITS CHIMIQUES INORG
53	DYES,TANNING,COLOUR PROD						10.3		7.1	PROD TEINTURE,COLORANTS
533	PIGMENTS,PAINTS,ETC						8.8		6.7	PIGMENTS,PEINTURES,VERNIS
5334	VARNISHES,DISTEMPERS ETC					W 2606	6.9	W 1906	6.0	PEINTURES A L'EAU
53342	OTH PAINTS,VARNISHES ETC					W 1693	5.7	W 1231	5.2	AUTRES PEINTURES,VERNIS
541	*MEDICINAL,PHARM PRODUCT						46.3		65.5	PROD MEDICINAUX PHARMACEUT

5. Special Exports F.O.B. by Commodities according to the S.I.T.C. (Rev. 2) in million U.S. Dollars
Exportations Spéciales F.O.B. par Produits d'après la C.T.C.I. (Rév. 2) en millions de Dollars E.U.

SITC CTCI	COMMODITY	1994 QUANTITY QUANTITE	1994 VALUE VALEUR	1995 QUANTITY QUANTITE	1995 VALUE VALEUR	1996 QUANTITY QUANTITE	1996 VALUE VALEUR	1997 QUANTITY QUANTITE	1997 VALUE VALEUR	PRODUIT
5416	GLYCOSIDES,GLANDS,SERA					K 54379	6.1	K 43997	6.5	HETEROSIDES
5417	MEDICAMENTS					K 1763605	38.4	MK 305969	58.3	MEDICAMENTS
54171	— CONTAINNG ANTIBIOTICS					K 263110	6.8	MK 302938	12.4	MED CONTN ANTIBIOTIQUES
54172	— CONTAINING HORMONES					K 138389	6.1	K 60154	1.3	MED CONTENANT HORMONES
54179	— CONTNG OTH SUBSTANCES					K 1348105	25.2	K 2959102	44.0	MED CONT AUT SUBSTANCES
55	PERFUME,CLEANING ETC PRD						9.1		7.4	PROD POUR PARFUM,TOILETTE
562	*FERTILIZERS,MANUFACTURE						13.7		16.4	ENGRAIS MANUFACTURES
5621	CHEM NITROGENOUS FERTLZR					W 45029	6.4	W 43973	5.1	ENGRAIS AZOTES
5629	FERTILIZERS NES					W 27651	5.8	W 61852	10.3	ENGRAIS NDA
56291	NIT-PHOS-POT FERTLZR NES					W 25167	5.6	W 56621	9.8	ENGRAIS CONT N P K
58	PLASTIC MATERIALS ETC						40.1		93.8	MAT PLAST ARTIFICIELLES
583	POLYMERIZATION ETC PRODS						36.0		90.9	PROD POLYMERISATION
5831	POLYETHYLENE						26.4		58.8	POLYETHYLENE
58311	— IN PRIMARY FORMS					W 37067	26.0	W 85645	58.3	POLYETHYLENE PRIMAIRES
5832	POLYPROPYLENE					W 9308	6.4	W 21181	13.4	POLYPROPYLENE
58321	— IN PRIMARY FORMS					W 9271	6.2	W 20930	13.0	POLYPROPYLENE PRIMAIRES
5834	POLYVINYL CHLORIDE					W 2452	1.0	W 32091	17.4	CHLORURE DE POLYVINYLE
58341	— IN PRIMARY FORMS					W 2339	0.7	W 32024	17.2	SOUS FORMES PRIMAIRES
59	CHEMICAL MATERIALS NES						9.9		20.4	MAT PROD CHIMIQUES NDA
598	MISCEL CHEM PRODUCTS NES						4.7		15.7	PROD DIV INDUST CHIM NDA
5989	CHEM PRODUCTS,PREPS NES						4.6	W 26172	15.6	PROD PREP CHIMIQUES NDA
59899	OTH CHEM PRODS,PREPS,NES					W 1829	2.2	W 23517	13.8	AUT PRODUITS CHIMIQUES NDA
6	BASIC MANUFACTURES						618.2		994.1	ART MANUFACTURES
61	LEATHER,DRESSED FUR,ETC						17.9		18.5	CUIRS,PELLETERIES
611	LEATHER						11.1		12.3	CUIRS,PEAUX PREPARES
6114	LEATHR BOVINE NES,EQUINE					W 2275	8.6	W 2639	9.8	CUIRS DE BOVINS
62	RUBBER MANUFACTURES NES						52.4		70.2	CAOUTCHOUC MANUFACTURE
621	MATERIALS OF RUBBER						8.1		7.8	PRODUITS EN CAOUTCHOUC
625	RUBBER TYRES, TUBES ETC						38.0	W 23047	54.6	PNEUS CAOUTCHOUC VULCANISE
6251	TYRES NEW FOR MOTOR CARS					W 8065	23.4	W 13827	34.7	PNEUS POUR VOITURES
6259	OTH TYRES,TYRE CASES,ETC					W 4502	10.9	W 8463	17.8	AUTRES PNEUS RECHAPES FLAPS
62599	TYRES NES,TYRE CASES,ETC					W 3678	8.7	W 7084	14.9	PNEUS,FLAPS
628	RUBBER ARTICLES NES					W 1692	6.4	W 2493	7.9	OUVRAGES CAOUTCHOUC NDA
63	WOOD,CORK MANUFACTRS NES						13.8		194.8	OUVRAGES LIEGE ET BOIS
634	VENEERS,PLYWOOD,ETC					W 11832	7.6	W 11869	7.2	PLACAGES,CONTRE-PLAQUES
635	WOOD MANUFACTURES NES					W 5242	6.2		187.7	ART MANUF EN BOIS NDA
6359	OTHER WOOD MANUFACTURES					W 1002	1.7	W 481901	183.1	OUVRAGES EN BOIS NDA
63599	OTHER WOOD ARTICLES NES					W 955	1.7	W 481847	183.1	AUTRES OUVRAGES EN BOIS NDA
64	PAPER,PAPERBOARD AND MFR						12.2		12.6	PAPIERS,CARTONS & OUVRAGES
641	PAPER AND PAPERBOARD					W 5859	6.1		7.6	PAPIERS ET CARTONS
642	PAPER,ETC,PRECUT,ARTS OF						6.1		5.0	PAP,CARTONS DECOUPES
65	TEXTILE YARN,FABRICS,ETC						46.1		43.3	FILS,TISSUS,ARTICLES TEXTILE
651	TEXTILE YARN						11.5		11.1	FILS TEXTILES
653	WOVN MAN-MADE FIB FABRIC						6.4		5.7	TISSUS FIBRES SYNTH,ARTIF
658	TEXTILE ARTICLES NES						8.0		3.8	ART FACONNES MAT TEXTILES
659	FLOOR COVERINGS,ETC						9.6	W 7714	13.6	COUVRE-PARQUETS,TAPIS ETC
6591	LINOLEUM ETC					W 2409	3.6	W 5369	8.0	LINO COUVRE-PARQUETS
65912	LINOLEUM ETC TXTLE BASED					W 2409	3.6	W 5369	8.0	LINOLEUMS TOUS USAGES
66	NONMETAL MINERAL MFS NES						53.8		49.4	ART MIN NON METALLIQUES
661	LIME,CEMENT,BLDG PRODS					W 117918	10.3	W 53245	4.8	CHAUX,CIMENTS MAT CONSTR
6612	CEMENT					W 102162	7.4	W 40186	2.7	CIMENTS HYDRAULIQUES
662	CLAY,REFRACTORY BLDG PRD					W 128884	25.6	W 152787	25.1	MAT CONST REFRACTAIRES
6623	REFRACTORY BUILDING PROD					W 27756	15.5	W 34577	14.3	BRIQUES REFRACTAIRES
66232	REFRACTRY BRICKS ETC NES					W 23176	13.5	W 28675	13.6	BRIQUES ETC REFRACTAIRES
6624	BRICKS ETC NONREFRACTORY					W 101128	10.2	W 118210	10.9	BRIQUES ETC CERAM NON REFR
66242	ROOFNG TILES ETC,CERAMIC					W 67177	6.6	W 62008	6.3	TUILES,ORNEMENTS ARCH
665	GLASSWARE						6.5		8.3	OUVRAGES EN VERRE
67	IRON AND STEEL						95.9		224.4	FER ET ACIER
671	PIG IRON ETC					W 7662	17.5	W 10527	17.1	FONTE,SPIEGEL,POUDRES
6716	FERRO-ALLOYS					W 6499	17.4	W 7183	16.5	FERRO-ALLIAGES
67169	OTHER FERRO-ALLOYS					W 6487	17.4	W 7183	16.5	AUTRES FERRO-ALLIAGES
672	IRON,STEEL PRIMARY FORMS						37.9	W 270117	69.3	LINGOTS FER,ACIER
6727	IRN,STL COIL FR REROLLNG					W 145268	37.8	W 269984	69.3	EBAUCHES POUR TOLES FER
67271	IRON,SIMPLE STEEL COILS					W 145019	37.7	W 269324	68.1	EBAUCHES NON EN ACIER
674	IRN,STL UNIV,PLATE,SHEET						24.5	W 366355	117.1	LARGES PLATS,TOLES
6745	IRN,STL MED PLATE,ROLLED						2.0	W 158204	40.9	TOLES 3 A 4.75 MM
67451	— OF IRON OR SIMPLE STL					W 6362	2.0	W 158185	40.9	TOLES AUT NON ACIER FIN
6746	IRN,STL THIN PLATE,ROLLD					W 40506	14.2	W 132497	46.5	TOLES LAM MOINS 3MM
67461	— OF IRON OR SIMPLE STL					W 40124	13.9	W 132156	46.3	TOL NON AC FIN MOINS 3 MM
6749	OTH IRN,STL PLATES,SHEET					W 11249	5.7	W 53973	23.6	AUTRES TOLES FER,ACIER
67491	— OF IRON OR SIMPLE STL					W 11052	5.3	W 53751	23.5	AUT TOLES AUTRES ACIER FIN
678	IRON,STL TUBES,PIPES,ETC					W 8802	9.7	W 20304	13.4	TUBES,TUYAUX EN FONTE,FER
6785	IRON,STEEL TUBE FITTINGS					W 2785	6.5	W 3344	7.2	ACCESSOIRES DE TUYAUTERIE
68	NON-FERROUS METALS						263.4		329.4	METAUX NON FERREUX
681	SILVER,PLATINUM,ETC						7.1		4.4	ARGENT ET PLATINE
6811	SILVER UNWKD,PARTLY WRKD						7.1		3.4	ARGENT BRUT MI-OUVRE
68113	SILVER UNWROUGHT						7.1		3.2	ARGENT ET ALLIAGES BRUTS
682	COPPER EXC CEMENT COPPER						151.7		176.2	CUIVRE
6821	COPPER NES,ALLOYS,UNWRT						103.9		114.5	CUIVRE BRUT
68212	COPPER REFINED,UNWROUGHT					W 74352	103.8	W 80269	114.1	CUIVRE AFFINE BRUT
6822	COPPER,ALLOYS WORKED					W 21229	47.9		61.8	CUIVRE,ALLIAGES OUVRES
68221	COPPER BARS,WIRE,ETC					W 12176	23.5	W 15050	30.0	BARRES,PROFILES ET FILS
68222	COPPER PLATE,SHEET,STRIP					W 4725	11.1	W 5196	13.2	TOLES DE PLUS 0.15 MM
68225	COPPER TUBES,PIPES,ETC					W 3928	12.1	W 6880	17.6	TUBES,TUYAUX EN CUIVRE
684	ALUMINIUM						62.8		107.6	ALUMINIUM
6841	ALUMINIUM,ALLOYS,UNWRGHT					W 39140	54.2	W 62524	97.0	ALUMINIUM,ALLIAGES BRUTS
6842	ALUMINIUM,ALLOYS WORKED						8.7		10.6	ALUMINIUM,ALLIAGES OUVRE
68422	ALUMNM PLATE,SHEET,STRIP					W 1805	5.0	W 3784	8.3	TOLES, PLANCHES EN ALU
685	LEAD					W 25794	15.0		13.4	PLOMB
6851	LEAD,ALLOYS UNWROUGHT					W 25612	14.9	W 19659	13.1	PLOMB,ALLIAGES BRUTS
68512	REF LEAD(EXC ALLOY)UNWRT					W 25140	14.5	W 17604	11.7	PLOMB AFFINE BRUT
686	ZINC					W 23967	19.5	W 22648	20.0	ZINC
6861	ZINC,ALLOYS UNWROUGHT					W 22308	18.9	W 22538	19.7	ZINC ET ALLIAGES BRUTS
689	NON-FER BASE METALS NES						7.3		8.2	AUT METAUX NON FERREUX
6891	TUNGST,MOLYB,TANTAL,MAGN						7.2		8.0	TUNG,MOLYB,TANT,MAG BRUTS
68915	MAGNESIUM UNWROUGHT					W 2926	7.2	W 3711	7.9	MAGNESIUM BRUT
69	METAL MANUFACTURES NES						63.2		51.9	ART MANUFACT EN METAL NDA
691	STRUCTURES AND PARTS NES					W 5794	9.4	W 2156	4.3	CONSTRUCT FER,ACIER,ALU
6911	STRUCTURES,PARTS IRN,STL					W 5476	7.4	W 1789	2.0	CONSTRUCT FER,ACIER,FONTE
695	TOOLS						14.1		16.4	OUTILS A MAIN
6954	BLADES,TIPS,ETC FR TOOLS						12.7		14.6	OUTILS POUR MACHINE-OUTIL

5. Special Exports F.O.B. by Commodities according to the S.I.T.C. (Rev. 2) in million U.S. Dollars
Exportations Spéciales F.O.B. par Produits d'après la C.T.C.I. (Rév. 2) en millions de Dollars E.U.

SITC CTCI	COMMODITY	1994		1995		1996		1997		PRODUIT
		QUANTITY QUANTITE	VALUE VALEUR	QUANTITY QUANTITE	VALUE VALEUR	QUANTITY QUANTITE	VALUE VALEUR	QUANTITY QUANTITE	VALUE VALEUR	
69541	PARTS TO INSERT IN TOOLS					W 443	11.6	W 564	13.6	OUTILS DE FORAGE
697	BASE MTL HOUSEHOLD EQUIP						8.5		9.8	ART MENAGE MET COMMUNS
6973	DMSTC HEATG,COOKG APPARA					W 4352	6.4	W 4497	6.0	APPS CHAUF NON ELECTRIQ
699	BASE METAL MFRS NES						20.8		12.8	ART MANUFACTURES MET NDA
6991	LOCKSMITHS WARES,ETC					W 913	14.0	W 1209	5.4	ARTICLES DE SERRURERIE
69913	BASE MTL DOOR,ETC FITTNG					W 743	12.6	W 832	4.2	GARNITURES POUR MEUBLES
7	MACHINES,TRANSPORT EQUIP						220.5		226.1	MACHINES MATERIEL TRANSPORT
71	POWER GENERATING EQUIPMT						15.5		21.6	MACHINES GENERATRICES
713	INTRNL COMBUS PSTN ENGIN						6.4		10.8	MOTEURS EXPL COMB INT, PIECE
7139	PISTON ENGINE PARTS NES					W 553	5.2	W 1355	10.0	PIECES POUR 713.2,3,8
716	ROTATING ELECTRIC PLANT						7.7	W 2674	8.7	APP ELECTR ROTATIFS,PIECES
7162	AC MTRS,GENRTRS,GEN SETS					W 1938	6.7	W 2448	8.1	MOTEURS ELECTRIQUES
71621	AC MTRS,INC UNIVRSL MTRS					W 1917	6.6	W 2423	8.0	MOT ELEC NON COUR CONTINU
72	MACHS FOR SPCL INDUSTRYS						18.3		22.7	MAC SPECIALES POUR INDUST
73	METALWORKING MACHINERY						10.5		13.4	MACH TRAVAIL DES METAUX
736	METALWORKING MACH–TOOLS						8.9		9.3	MACH–OUTILS TRAVAIL METAUX
7361	METAL CUTTING MACH–TOOLS						5.6		5.5	MACH–OUT ENLEVEMENT METAL
74	GENRL INDUSTRL MACHY NES						41.1		39.1	MACH APP INDUSTRIE
744	MECHANICAL HANDLING EQU						5.6	W 2508	5.6	EQUIP MANUTENTION PIECES
749	NONELEC MACH PTS,ACC NES						24.3		20.4	PIECES MACH NON ELEC NDA
7491	BALL,ROLLER,ETC BEARINGS					W 1034	9.2	W 995	6.2	ROULEMENTS BILLES ETC
7492	COCKS,VALVES ETC NES					W 2042	12.1	W 1952	11.0	ART ROB,SIM POUR TUYAUX
77	ELECTRIC MACHNRY NES ETC						73.8		62.9	MACH APP ELECT NDA
772	SWITCHGEAR ETC,PARTS NES						6.3		4.5	APP COUPURE,SECT ETC
7721	SWITCHGEAR ETC					W 355	6.3	W 320	4.5	APP COUPURE,SECTIONMNT
773	ELECTR DISTRIBUTNG EQUIP					W 14844	43.9		29.4	EQUIPMT DISTRIBUTION ELECT
7731	INSULATED WIRE,CABLE ETC					W 14271	41.9	W 11793	27.5	FILS,CABLES ISOLES ELECT
775	HOUSEHOLD TYPE EQUIP NES						9.3		8.8	MACH,APP USAGE DOMESTQUE
7758	ELECTRO–THERMIC APPL NES						7.6		5.8	APP ELECTROTHERMIQ NDA
778	ELECTRICAL MACHINERY NES						10.0		11.2	AUTRES MACH ELECT NDA
7781	BATTERIES,ACCUMULATORS					W 2945	7.3		9.3	PILES ET ACCUMULATEURS
77812	ELECTRIC ACCUMULATORS					W 2901	7.1	W 4930	9.1	ACCUMULATEURS ELECTRIQ
78	ROAD VEHICLES						31.7		50.6	VEHICULES ROUTIERS
781	PASS MOTOR VEH EXC BUSES					W 1630	8.5	W 2487	11.5	AUTO TRANSPORT PERSONNES
784	MOTOR VEH PRTS,ACCES NES					W 3528	18.2	W 9622	31.5	PIECES 722,781,782,783
7849	OTHER MOTOR VEHCL PARTS					W 3503	18.1	W 9547	31.3	PIECES 722,781,782,783
79	OTHR TRANSPORT EQUIPMENT						25.9		9.0	AUTRE MATERIEL TRANSPORT
792	AIRCRAFT ETC						12.5	W 57	0.7	APP NAVIGATION AERIENNE
7924	AIRCRFT NES OVER 15000KG					W 84	12.1	W 46	0.4	AERODYNES PLUS 15000 KG
793	SHIPS AND BOATS ETC					W 6375	11.2		6.9	NAVIRES BATEAUX,ETC
7932	SHIPS AND BOATS NES					W 6173	10.9		6.0	NAVIRES ET BATEAUX
79323	OTHER CARGO VESSELS					W 6097	10.8	W 7366	6.0	AUT BATEAUX TRANS MARCH
8	MISC MANUFACTURED GOODS						163.9		197.9	ART MANUFACTURES DIVERS
812	*PLUMBG,HEATNG,LGHTNG EQ					W 3581	6.9	W 5053	7.8	APPAR SANITAIRES CHAUFFAGE
821	*FURNITURE,PARTS THEREOF					W 18580	46.0		43.6	MEUBLES ET PIECES
8211	CHAIRS,SEATS AND PARTS					W 10024	21.8	W 11224	23.4	SIEGES ET PIECES
82111	CHAIRS AND OTHER SEATS					W 9945	21.7	W 11220	23.4	SIEGES
8219	FURNITURE AND PARTS NES					W 6892	20.5	W 7067	18.1	AUTRES MEUBLES ET PIECES
82192	WOOD FURNITURE NES					W 5303	16.8	W 5030	14.4	MEUBLES NDA EN BOIS
84	CLOTHING AND ACCESSORIES						57.4		79.2	VETEMENTS
842	MENS OUTERWEAR NOT KNIT					W 1335	13.0	W 2554	21.5	VET DESSUS POUR HOMMES
8424	— JACKETS,BLAZERS ETC					W 336	3.7	W 843	7.9	VESTES HOMMES MAT TEXTIL
843	WOMENS OUTERWEAR NONKNIT					W 3579	25.4	W 4600	28.1	VET DESSUS FEMMES MAT TEX
8431	— COATS AND JACKETS					W 1670	10.3	W 2023	11.3	MANT,VEST FEM MAT TEXTIL
8439	— OTHER OUTER GARMENTS					W 983	8.1	W 1286	8.7	AUT VET DES FEM MAT TEXT
844	UNDER GARMENTS NOT KNIT						4.6		9.9	VETEMENT DESSOUS MAT TEX
8441	— MENS SHIRTS					W 543	4.3	W 811	9.4	CHEMISES HOMMES MAT TEXT
845	OUTERWEAR KNIT NONELASTC						5.6	W 646	5.8	VET DESSOUS,ACCES BONNET
846	UNDER GARMENTS KNITTED						5.2	W 1460	9.8	SOUS VETS DE BONNETERIE
851	*FOOTWEAR					W 3550	22.0	W 4031	20.8	CHAUSSURES
85102	FOOTWEAR LEATHER					W 2318	16.1	W 2389	15.5	CHAUS SEMELLES EN CUIR
89	MISC MANUFCTRD GOODS NES						26.6		40.8	ART MANUFACTURES DIVERS
892	PRINTED MATTER						4.8		14.2	IMPRIMES
8924	PICTURE POSTCARDS ETC					W 16	0.4		9.8	CARTES POSTALES,DECALCOM
89242	PICTRE PST–,GREETNG–CRDS					W 5	0.2	W 3141	9.6	CARTES POSTALES
893	ARTICLES OF PLASTIC NES						9.6		16.1	OUVRAGES EN MAT DIVIS 58
8939	MISC PLASTIC ARTICLES					W 2334	6.4	W 7226	13.8	ART DIVERS EN MAT DIV 58
89391	PVC FLOORING TILES ETC					W 1301	1.9	W 6095	10.4	CHLORURE POLYVINYL PLAQ
899	OTHER MANUFACTURED GOODS						6.0		4.4	AUT ART MANUF DIVERS NDA
9	GOODS NOT CLASSD BY KIND						35.4		88.9	ART TRANSACT NON CLASSES
931	*SPECIAL TRANSACTIONS					W 12805	33.8	W 271291	86.9	TRANS.SPECIALES

1. HISTORICAL SERIES, 1962–1997 GENERAL TRADE, IMPORTS F.O.B., EXPORTS F.O.B.
SERIES HISTORIQUES, 1962–1997 COMMERCE GENERAL, IMPORTATIONS F.O.B., EXPORTATIONS F.O.B

YEAR ANNEE	VALUE IN MILLION ZAMBIAN KWACHAS / VALEUR EN MILLION ZAMBIAN KWACHAS: MERCHANDISE –MARCHANDISE		GOLD –OR		CONVERSION FACTORS U.S. CENTS PER ZAMBIAN KWACHA / FACTEURS DE CONVERSION CENTS E.U. PAR ZAMBIAN KWACHA		INDEX NUMBERS –INDICES: QUANTUM		UNIT VALUE / VALEUR UNITAIRE	
	IMPORTS	EXPORTS	IMPORTS	EXPORTS	IMPORTS	EXPORTS	IMPORTS	EXPORTS	IMPORTS	EXPORTS
1962		239.21				140.0000				
1963		257.97				140.0000				
1964	156.44	335.52			140.0000	140.0000				
1965	210.74	380.29			140.0000	140.0000				
1966	246.11	493.46			140.0000	140.0000				
1967	306.26	470.01			140.0000	140.0000				
1968	325.17	544.42			140.0000	140.0000				
1969	311.77	766.49			140.0000	140.0000				
1970	340.71	714.96			140.0000	140.0000				
1971	399.28	485.18			140.0000	140.0000				
1972	402.47	541.56			140.0000	140.0000				
1973	346.87	741.96			154.2040	154.6520				
1974	506.64	905.09			155.4090	155.4090				
1975	597.60	521.05			155.4090	155.4090				
1976	468.70	751.90			139.7610	138.3850				
1977	529.30	708.00			126.6550	126.7530				
1978	492.60	686.80			127.5140	126.5610				
1979	593.70	593.60			126.3180	126.2210				
1980	876.70	1023.30			126.7030	126.9670				
1981	924.40	936.50			114.8568	114.6455				
1982	930.00	950.50			107.5856	107.5536				
1983	893.20	1047.50			78.7534	78.7268				
1984	1107.90	1188.10			54.8574	55.1157				
1985	2133.00	1508.00			33.4604	36.2879				
1986	4447.69	5366.58			13.5540	13.1141				
1987	6627.47	8058.70			11.1551	10.8293				
1988	6898.13	9786.20			12.1651	12.0411				
1989	10901.80	18434.00			7.1433	7.2921				
1990	37627.60	39143.30			3.3475	3.3505				
1991	60000.00	69600.00			1.6018	1.5468				
1992	172900.00	193600.00			0.5620	0.6083				
1993	553400.00	448199.90			0.2264	0.2234				
1994	805299.90	713799.90			0.1332	0.1312				
1995	1284600.00	1185900.00			0.1185	0.1183				
1996		993400.00				0.0839				
1997		1119099.00				0.0756				

2. IMPORTS BY BROAD ECONOMIC CATEGORY AND EXPORTS BY INDUSTRIAL ORIGIN. (PERCENTAGE OF TOTAL VALUE)
IMPORTATIONS PAR CATEGORIES ECONOMIQUES ET EXPORTATIONS PAR BRANCHE D'ACTIVITE.(EN POURCENTAGE DE LA VALEUR TOTALE)

IMPORTS – IMPORTATIONS

	1987	1988	1989	1990	1991	1992	1993
TOTAL IMPORTS–IMPORTATIONS TOTALES							
1 FOOD BEV–ALIMENTATION BOISSONS							
11 PRIMARY–PRODUITS DE BASE							
111 FOR INDUSTRY–POUR L'INDUSTRIE							
112 FOR HOUSEHOLDS–POUR LES MENAGES							
12 PROCESSED–PRODUITS ELABORES							
121 FOR INDUSTRY–POUR L'INDUSTRIE							
122 FOR HOUSEHOLDS–POUR LES MENAGES							
2 IND SUPPLIES–APPROV INDUSTRIELS							
21 PRIMARY–PRODUITS DE BASE							
22 PROCESSED–PRODUITS ELABORES							
3 FUELS–COMBUSTIBLES							
31 PRIMARY–PRODUITS DE BASE							
32 PROCESSED–PRODUITS ELABORES							
321 MOTOR SPIRIT–ESSENCE							
322 OTHER–AUTRES							
4 MACHINERY–EQUIPEMENT							
41 CAPITAL EQUIPMENT–MACHINES							
42 PARTS–PIECES ACCESSOIRES							
5 TRANSPORT–TRANSPORT							
51 PASSENGER CARS–AUTOMOBILES							
52 OTHER–AUTRES							
521 INDUSTRIAL–INDUSTRIELS							
522 NON INDUSTRIAL–NON INDUSTRIEL							
53 PARTS–PIECES ACCESSOIRES							
6 CONSUM GOODS–BIENS CONSOMMATION							
61 DURABLE–DURABLES							
62 SEMI DURABLE–SEMI DURABLES							
63 NON DURABLE–NON DURABLES							
7 GOODS NES–BIENS NDA							

EXPORTS – EXPORTATIONS

	1987	1988	1989	1990	1991	1992	1993
TOTAL EXPORTS–EXPORTATIONS TOTALES							100.
1 AGRICULTURE							2.1
2 MINING QUARRY–INDUS EXTRACTIVES							0.8
3 MANUFACTURING–IND MANUFACTUR							97.1
31 FOOD BEV TOBACCO–ALIM BOISS TAB							2.2
32 TEXTILES–INDUSTRIES TEXTILES							1.3
33 WOOD & PRODUCTS–BOIS & PRODUITS							0.1
34 PAPER & PRODUCTS–PAPIER & PRODT							0.1
35 CHEMICALS–INDUSTRIES CHIMIQUES							0.9
36 NON METAL MIN–MIN NON METAL							1.4
37 BASIC METAL–IND METAL BASE							88.8
38 METAL MANUF–MANUF METAL							1.0
39 OTH MANUF IND–AUTRES MANUF							1.5

3. TRADE BY PRINCIPAL COUNTRIES OF ORIGIN AND DESTINATION (VALUE IN MILLION U.S. DOLLARS)
ECHANGES SELON LES PRINCIPAUX PAYS D'ORIGINE ET DE DESTINATION (VALEUR EN MILLIONS DE DOLLARS EU)

COUNTRIES–PAYS	GENERAL IMPORTS F.O.B. IMPORTATIONS GENERALES F.O.B.				
	1989	1990	1991	1992	1993
World	1258.3	1237.7			
Africa	386.5	390.2			
Americas	78.3	136.9			
– Northern America	77.5	134.2			
– LAIA	0.9	2.6			
– CACM		0.1			
– Caribbean		0.0			
– Rest of America		0.1			
Asia excl fmr USSR	156.6	212.2			
– Middle East	6.0	73.9			
Asia former USSR					
Europe excl fmr USSR	636.4	497.7			
– European Union	612.8	479.5			
– Eastern Europe	1.1	2.9			
– Rest of Europe	22.5	15.3			
Europe former USSR	0.2	0.2			
Oceania	0.3	0.3			
Other					
So. African Customs Un	286.5	224.2			
United Kingdom	256.0	200.4			
Former Fed Rep Germany	184.0	144.0			
USA/Etats–Unis d'Amer	67.1	125.5			
Japan/Japon	105.6	82.6			
Zimbabwe	73.9	57.9			
Italy/Italie	38.7	30.3			
Madagascar	0.1	66.7			
Finland/Finlande	29.6	23.2			
India/Inde	29.3	22.9			
Sweden/Suède	24.6	19.2			
Netherlands/Pays–Bas	19.8	15.5			
Iran (Islamic Rep of)		35.1			
Kuwait/ Koweït		33.7			
Belgium–Luxembourg	17.5	13.7			
France, Monaco	15.9	12.5			
Switzerland,Liechtenst.	14.4	11.3			
Denmark/Danemark	14.3	11.2			
Algeria/Algérie		20.5			
Dem Rep of the Congo	11.5	9.0			
Canada	10.3	8.6			
Bangladesh	0.0	11.1			
Kenya	5.8	4.5			
Malawi	5.5	4.3			
Saudi Arabia	5.0	3.9			
China/Chine	4.4	3.4			
Ireland/Irlande	4.2	3.3			
Norway,Svalbard and JM	4.0	3.1			
Israel/Israël	3.8	3.0			
Other Asia n.e.s.	2.9	3.4			
Greece/Grèce	3.5	2.7			
United Rep of Tanzania	2.9	2.2			
Austria/Autriche	2.5	1.9			
Thailand/Thaïlande		4.3			
Spain/Espagne	1.9	1.5			
Former SFR Yugoslavia	3.3	0.2			
Brazil/Brésil	0.9	2.4			
China, Hong Kong SAR	1.8	1.4			
Singapore/Singapour	0.5	2.1			
Korea, Republic of	0.9	1.6			

COUNTRIES–PAYS	GENERAL EXPORTS F.O.B. EXPORTATIONS GENERALES F.O.B.				
	1989	1990	1991	1992	1993
Monde	667.8	594.8			920.5
Afrique	56.0	46.2			73.5
Amériques	13.9	9.8			3.3
– Amérique du Nord	13.8	9.8			3.3
– ALAI	0.1	0.1			
– MCAC		0.0			
– Caraïbes					
– Autre Amérique					
Asie anc. URSS exclus	363.1	351.3			566.4
– Moyen–Orient	38.7	32.0			66.2
Asie ancienne URSS					
Europe anc. URSS exclus	231.9	187.3			276.8
– Union Européenne	227.2	181.9			274.0
– Europe de l'Est	0.2				0.4
– Autre de l'Europe	4.4	5.5			2.4
Europe ancienne URSS					
Océanie	0.1	0.1			0.5
Autre					
Japan/Japon	223.2	184.3			122.0
France, Monaco	98.1	81.0			94.9
Belgium–Luxembourg	48.6	34.4			99.4
Saudi Arabia	38.7	32.0			64.0
India/Inde	44.1	36.4			52.4
Malaysia/Malaisie	27.7	22.9			74.1
Thailand/Thaïlande		40.7			61.5
Pakistan	0.4	0.5			83.3
Indonesia/Indonésie	24.1	19.9			28.6
Zimbabwe	21.8	18.0			27.4
Italy/Italie	32.2	26.6			7.6
Greece/Grèce	19.6	16.2			29.4
Singapore/Singapour	0.2	11.0			51.5
United Kingdom	14.7	12.1			14.1
Netherlands/Pays–Bas	7.9	6.5			24.4
Dem Rep of the Congo	10.1	8.3			11.7
USA/Etats–Unis d'Amer	13.8	9.8			3.3
So. African Customs Un	3.0	2.5			17.8
Kenya	9.4	7.7			5.3
Other Asia n.e.s.		0.0			16.2
Malawi	5.2	4.3			5.6
Switzerland,Liechtenst.	3.5	5.3			2.4
China, Hong Kong SAR	1.4	1.1			8.6
Former Fed Rep Germany	4.7	3.9			
United Rep of Tanzania	3.8	3.1			1.1
Korea, Republic of	3.2	2.5			
Burundi	1.5	1.2			2.2
Spain/Espagne	0.4	0.4			2.0
United Arab Emirates		0.0			2.1
Angola	1.1	0.9			0.1
Mozambique	0.1	0.1			1.9
Israel/Israël	0.0	0.0			2.0
Germany/Allemagne					2.0
Australia/Australie	0.1	0.1			0.5
Ireland/Irlande	0.3	0.3			0.1
Former SFR Yugoslavia	0.7				
Portugal	0.2	0.2			0.0
Norway,Svalbard and JM	0.2	0.2			0.0
Finland/Finlande	0.2	0.1			0.0
Albania/Albanie					0.3

(VALUE AS PERCENTAGE OF WORLD TOTAL)(VALEURS EN POURCENTAGE DU TOTAL MONDIAL)

	1984	1985	1986	1987	1988	1989	1990	1991	1992	1993
Africa	29.1	25.2	22.6	28.5	24.5	30.7	31.5			
Americas	8.0	11.5	12.0	10.9	25.0	6.2	11.1			
– Northern America	7.4	11.3	11.5	10.6	24.9	6.2	10.8			
– LAIA	0.6	0.2	0.5	0.3	0.1	0.1	0.2			
– CACM	0.0	0.0		0.0	0.0		0.0			
– Caribbean	0.0	0.0	0.0		0.0		0.0			
– Rest of America	0.0	0.0					0.0			
Asia excl fmr USSR	30.7	28.8	29.5	20.9	25.3	12.4	17.1			
– Middle East	23.0	20.0	17.8	12.2	10.2	0.5	6.0			
Asia former USSR										
Europe excl fmr USSR	31.5	33.8	35.9	39.6	24.9	50.6	40.2			
– European Union	28.0	30.3	32.6	37.7	22.7	48.7	38.7			
– Eastern Europe	0.3	0.3	0.3	0.0	0.9	0.1	0.2			
– Rest of Europe	3.3	3.2	3.0	1.9	1.3	1.8	1.2			
Europe former USSR	0.1	0.3	0.0	0.0	0.1	0.0	0.0			
Oceania	0.5	0.3	0.1	0.1	0.1	0.0	0.0			
Other										
So. African Customs Un	22.1	20.2	18.6	18.7	19.2	22.8	18.1			
United Kingdom	13.8	16.0	16.4	10.4	2.2	20.3	16.2			
Former Fed Rep Germany	5.8	4.8	6.3	10.8	6.0	14.6	11.6			
USA/Etats–Unis d'Amer	6.8	10.5	10.3	9.4	24.0	5.3	10.1			
Japan/Japon	3.9	5.9	8.6	6.4	9.5	8.4	6.7			
Zimbabwe	5.3	3.5	3.0	8.7	4.0	5.9	4.7			
Italy/Italie	1.6	1.1	2.3	1.4	4.4	3.1	2.4			
Madagascar			0.0	0.0	0.0	0.0	5.4			
Finland/Finlande	0.3	0.3	0.4	1.3	0.8	2.4	1.9			
India/Inde	1.4	0.7	0.7	0.7	3.9	2.3	1.9			

	1984	1985	1986	1987	1988	1989	1990	1991	1992	1993
Afrique	6.2	8.3	8.1	5.8	6.2	8.4	7.8			8.0
Amériques	10.0	3.1	6.2	4.9	23.8	2.1	1.7			0.4
– Amérique du Nord	9.6	2.9	6.1	4.8	23.8	2.1	1.6			0.4
– ALAI	0.3	0.2	0.1	0.0	0.0	0.0	0.0			
– MCAC	0.0		0.0				0.0			
– Caraïbes										
– Autre Amérique										
Asie anc. URSS exclus	46.3	46.0	45.5	49.5	43.0	54.4	59.1			61.5
– Moyen–Orient	0.0	1.1	8.3	7.7	5.5	5.8	5.4			7.2
Asie ancienne URSS										
Europe anc. URSS exclus	37.5	42.3	40.1	39.8	26.9	34.7	31.5			30.1
– Union Européenne	33.8	40.8	38.7	37.5	25.4	34.0	30.6			29.8
– Europe de l'Est	0.7	0.7	0.4	0.1		0.0				0.0
– Autre de l'Europe	3.0	0.8	1.0	2.3	1.5	0.7	0.9			0.3
Europe ancienne URSS	0.0	0.1	0.1							
Océanie	0.1	0.1	0.0		0.0	0.0	0.0			0.1
Autre										
Japan/Japon	23.2	22.9	12.9	15.4	22.3	33.4	31.0			13.3
France, Monaco	5.7	6.9	9.4	10.3	5.8	14.7	13.6			10.3
Belgium–Luxembourg	5.3	3.3	6.7	8.3	3.7	7.3	5.8			10.8
Saudi Arabia		1.1	8.3	7.7	5.5	5.8	5.4			7.0
India/Inde	5.9	8.5	11.6	11.5	6.4	6.6	6.1			5.7
Malaysia/Malaisie	2.8		0.5	2.0	2.6	4.1	3.8			8.0
Thailand/Thaïlande	1.3	2.0	6.3	10.7	3.2		6.8			6.7
Pakistan	0.0	0.0	0.1	0.1	0.1	0.1	0.1			9.1
Indonesia/Indonésie	1.5	1.6	1.2	1.0	2.1	3.6	3.3			3.1
Zimbabwe	2.2	2.7	0.6	1.0	2.3	3.3	3.0			3.0

4. General Imports F.O.B. by Commodities according to the S.I.T.C. (Rev. 2) in million U.S. Dollars
Importations Générales F.O.B. par Produits d'après la C.T.C.I. (Rév. 2) en millions de Dollars E.U.

SITC CTCI	COMMODITY	1990		1991		1992		1993		PRODUIT
		QUANTITY QUANTITE	VALUE VALEUR	QUANTITY QUANTITE	VALUE VALEUR	QUANTITY QUANTITE	VALUE VALEUR	QUANTITY QUANTITE	VALUE VALEUR	
	ALL COMMODITIES									TOUS PRODUITS

5. General Exports F.O.B. by Commodities according to the S.I.T.C. (Rev. 2) in million U.S. Dollars
Exportations Générales F.O.B. par Produits d'après la C.T.C.I. (Rév. 2) en millions de Dollars E.U.

SITC CTCI	COMMODITY	1990		1991		1992		1993		PRODUIT
		QUANTITY QUANTITE	VALUE VALEUR	QUANTITY QUANTITE	VALUE VALEUR	QUANTITY QUANTITE	VALUE VALEUR	QUANTITY QUANTITE	VALUE VALEUR	
	ALL COMMODITIES								920.6	TOUS PRODUITS
0	FOOD AND LIVE ANIMALS								24.4	ALIMENTS,ANIMAUX VIVANTS
04	CEREALS AND PREPARATIONS								4.4	CEREALES ET PRODUITS
044	MAIZE UNMILLED							W 7031	4.0	MAIS NON MOULU
05	VEGETABLES AND FRUIT								3.3	LEGUMES ET FRUITS
054	VEG ETC FRSH,SMPLY PRSVD							W 3201	3.0	LEGUMES FRAIS,CONG,SECS
06	SUGAR AND PREPS,HONEY								13.6	SUCRES ET PRODUITS
061	SUGAR AND HONEY							W 8983	13.6	SUCRES ET MIEL
0611	RAW BEET AND CANE SUGAR							W 8235	13.3	SUCRES BRUTS
1	BEVERAGES AND TOBACCO								7.8	BOISSONS ET TABACS
12	TOBACCO AND MANUFACTURES								7.2	TABACS BRUTS FABRIQUES
121	TOBACCO UNMNFCTRD,REFUSE							W 5831	7.1	TABACS BRUTS,DECHETS
1211	TOBACCO,NOT STRIPPED							W 1378	2.8	TABACS NON ECOTES
1212	TOBACCO STRIPPED OR PART							W 3707	3.7	TABACS PART ECOTES
2	CRUDE MATERLS,EXCL FUELS								12.0	MAT BRUTES NON COMESTIBLES
26	TEXTILE FIBRES AND WASTE								6.3	FIBRES TEXTILES
266	SYNTHETIC FIBRES TO SPIN							W 1051	4.7	FIBRES SYNTHETIQUES
2666	CONTIN FILAMNT TOW SYNTH							W 998	4.6	CABLES POUR DISCONTINUS
26661	— OF POLYAMIDE FIBRES							W 721	3.6	DE FIBRES EN POLYAMIDES
3	MINERAL FUELS ETC								15.8	COMBUSTIBLES MINERAUX LUB
351	*ELECTRIC CURRENT							H 17927	13.5	ENERGIE ELECTRIQUE
5	CHEMCLS,RELATED PROD NES								3.7	PRODUITS CHIMIQUES
6	BASIC MANUFACTURES								845.9	ART MANUFACTURES
65	TEXTILE YARN,FABRICS,ETC								10.7	FILS,TISSUS,ARTICLES TEXTILE
651	TEXTILE YARN							W 5735	9.9	FILS TEXTILES
6513	COTTON YARN							W 4498	8.6	FILS DE COTON
66	NONMETAL MINERAL MFS NES								17.5	ART MIN NON METALLIQUES
661	LIME,CEMENT,BLDG PRODS							W 167848	6.7	CHAUX,CIMENTS MAT CONSTR
6611	LIME,QUICK,SLKD,HYDRAULC							W 121459	3.7	CHAUX ORDINAIRE,HYDRAUL
6612	CEMENT							W 46386	3.1	CIMENTS HYDRAULIQUES
664	GLASS								5.8	VERRE
6645	CAST,ROLLED GLASS UNWRKD							A 3	5.8	VERRE COULE NON TRAVAILLE
667	PEARL,PREC–,SEMI–P STONE								4.9	PERLES, PIERRES GEMMES
6673	PREC–,SEMI–PR STONES NES								3.1	AUTRES PIERRES NON SERTIES
68	NON–FERROUS METALS								810.4	METAUX NON FERREUX
682	COPPER EXC CEMENT COPPER							W 411173	787.9	CUIVRE
6821	COPPER NES,ALLOYS,UNWRT							W 407578	766.1	CUIVRE BRUT
68212	COPPER REFINED,UNWROUGHT							W 407578	766.1	CUIVRE AFFINE BRUT
6822	COPPER,ALLOYS WORKED							W 3595	21.9	CUIVRE,ALLIAGES OUVRES
68221	COPPER BARS,WIRE,ETC							W 2199	20.5	BARRES,PROFILES ET FILS
686	ZINC							W 4156	5.4	ZINC
6861	ZINC,ALLOYS UNWROUGHT							W 4156	5.4	ZINC ET ALLIAGES BRUTS
689	NON–FER BASE METALS NES							W 876	14.7	AUT METAUX NON FERREUX
6899	BASE METALS NES,CERMETS							W 876	14.7	METAUX COMMUNS NDA
68999	BASE MTL NES UNWRT,WASTE							W 876	14.7	AUT METAUX COM BRUTS NDA
69	METAL MANUFACTURES NES								6.1	ART MANUFACT EN METAL NDA
699	BASE METAL MFRS NES								6.0	ART MANUFACTURES MET NDA
6999	OTHR BASE METAL MFRS ETC							W 1	5.8	OUVRAGES EN TUNGST,MOLYB
69999	BASE MTLS NES WRGHT,MFRS							W 1	5.8	MET COMMUNS OUVRES NDA
7	MACHINES,TRANSPORT EQUIP								7.1	MACHINES MATERIEL TRANSPORT
77	ELECTRIC MACHNRY NES ETC								4.0	MACH APP ELECT NDA
773	ELECTR DISTRIBUTNG EQUIP							W 601	3.7	EQUIPMT DISTRIBUTION ELECT
7731	INSULATED WIRE,CABLE ETC							W 601	3.7	FILS,CABLES ISOLES ELECT

1. HISTORICAL SERIES, 1962–1997 GENERAL TRADE, IMPORTS C.I.F., EXPORTS F.O.B.
SERIES HISTORIQUES, 1962–1997 COMMERCE GENERAL, IMPORTATIONS C.A.F., EXPORTATIONS F.O.B

YEAR ANNEE	VALUE IN MILLION ZIMB. DOLLARS VALEUR EN MILLION ZIMB. DOLLARS MERCHANDISE –MARCHANDISE IMPORTS	EXPORTS	GOLD –OR IMPORTS	EXPORTS	CONVERSION FACTORS U.S. CENTS PER ZIMB. DOLLAR FACTEURS DE CONVERSION CENTS E.U. PAR ZIMB. DOLLAR IMPORTS	EXPORTS	INDEX NUMBERS –INDICES QUANTUM IMPORTS	EXPORTS	UNIT VALUE VALEUR UNITAIRE IMPORTS	EXPORTS
1962	286.00	145.64			140.0000	140.0000				
1963	269.60	150.18			140.0000	140.0000				
1964	216.47	274.85			140.0000	140.0000				
1965	239.58	322.82			140.0000	140.0000				
1966	169.41	200.80			140.0000	140.0000				
1967	187.05	194.37			140.0000	140.0000				
1968	207.05	187.77			140.0000	140.0000				
1969	199.43	231.86			140.0000	140.0000				
1970	234.88	262.23			140.0000	140.0000				
1971	282.38	284.02			140.0000	140.0000				
1972	274.59	341.33			151.9950	151.9950				
1973	308.60	389.10			178.0000	178.0000				
1974	438.30	531.20			177.5990	177.5990				
1975	461.90	531.30			173.7000	173.7000				
1976	382.70	557.40			162.0000	162.0000				
1977	388.10	550.80			160.2500	160.2500				
1978	403.70	609.30			146.6430	146.2120				
1979	549.30	715.70			170.5940	170.0230				
1980	809.40	909.20			159.4310	156.5030				34
1981	1017.70	971.70			144.6500	144.6500				38
1982	1081.80	968.40			132.1764	131.4394				37
1983	1061.60	1150.20			99.0609	98.0913				41
1984	1200.70	1453.00			79.9061	79.0148				54
1985	1446.50	1795.50			62.0425	61.7810				64
1986	1886.50	2170.30			60.0580	59.9465				66
1987	2003.00	2371.40			60.1372	60.0821				
1988	2349.70	2966.40			55.5000	55.5000				
1989	3438.10	3267.30			47.3200	47.3200				
1990	4528.20	4231.40			40.8500	40.8500				
1991	7443.10	5546.50			27.3624	27.5909				
1992	11232.30	7365.70			19.6003	19.5754				
1993	11798.40	10164.20			15.4029	15.3949				
1994	18270.61	15364.70			12.2667	12.2414				
1995	23049.41	18359.10			11.5465	11.5140				
1996	28095.10	24209.30			10.0270	9.9029				
1997	36555.72	25631.82			8.4591	8.3015				

2. IMPORTS BY BROAD ECONOMIC CATEGORY AND EXPORTS BY INDUSTRIAL ORIGIN. (PERCENTAGE OF TOTAL VALUE)
IMPORTATIONS PAR CATEGORIES ECONOMIQUES ET EXPORTATIONS PAR BRANCHE D'ACTIVITE.(EN POURCENTAGE DE LA VALEUR TOTALE)

IMPORTS – IMPORTATIONS

	1991	1992	1993	1994	1995	1996	1997
TOTAL IMPORTS–IMPORTATIONS TOTALES	100.	100.	100.	100.	100.	100.	
1 FOOD BEV–ALIMENTATION BOISSONS	1.1	6.2	6.0	3.8	4.8	7.9	
11 PRIMARY–PRODUITS DE BASE	0.5	2.2	2.7	1.6	2.3	4.3	
111 FOR INDUSTRY–POUR L'INDUSTRIE	0.4	2.0	1.9	0.9	1.5	3.0	
112 FOR HOUSEHOLDS–POUR LES MENAGES	0.1	0.3	0.7	0.7	0.8	1.3	
12 PROCESSED–PRODUITS ELABORES	0.6	4.0	3.3	2.2	2.4	3.6	
121 FOR INDUSTRY–POUR L'INDUSTRIE	0.3	2.3	2.0	1.1	1.0	1.8	
122 FOR HOUSEHOLDS–POUR LES MENAGES	0.3	1.7	1.3	1.1	1.4	1.8	
2 IND SUPPLIES–APPROV INDUSTRIELS	37.2	38.7	36.9	35.3	33.5	32.4	
21 PRIMARY–PRODUITS DE BASE	2.9	12.7	7.6	1.9	2.4	3.4	
22 PROCESSED–PRODUITS ELABORES	34.2	26.0	29.4	33.4	31.0	29.0	
3 FUELS–COMBUSTIBLES	12.2	11.7	14.3	9.7	8.9	10.2	
31 PRIMARY–PRODUITS DE BASE	0.3	0.3	0.1	0.2	0.1	0.6	
32 PROCESSED–PRODUITS ELABORES	11.9	11.4	14.2	9.5	8.7	9.6	
321 MOTOR SPIRIT–ESSENCE	3.1	2.6	4.3	2.2	2.6	2.5	
322 OTHER–AUTRES	8.8	8.8	9.9	7.3	6.1	7.1	
4 MACHINERY–EQUIPEMENT	24.9	24.3	22.5	27.7	27.9	26.1	
41 CAPITAL EQUIPMENT–MACHINES	21.7	21.6	19.5	24.1	25.0	23.4	
42 PARTS–PIECES ACCESSOIRES	3.2	2.7	3.0	3.6	2.9	2.6	
5 TRANSPORT–TRANSPORT	17.4	12.5	14.2	14.6	15.0	13.5	
51 PASSENGER CARS–AUTOMOBILES	2.4	1.7	2.7	3.4	2.9	3.1	
52 OTHER–AUTRES	9.8	6.6	6.8	7.5	8.6	7.1	
521 INDUSTRIAL–INDUSTRIELS	9.7	6.5	6.6	7.4	8.5	7.0	
522 NON INDUSTRIAL–NON INDUSTRIEL	0.1	0.1	0.2	0.2	0.1	0.2	
53 PARTS–PIECES ACCESSOIRES	5.1	4.2	4.7	3.7	3.6	3.2	
6 CONSUM GOODS–BIENS CONSOMMATION	4.2	4.0	4.3	6.6	6.5	7.4	
61 DURABLE–DURABLES	1.2	1.7	1.2	2.2	1.9	2.4	
62 SEMI DURABLE–SEMI DURABLES	1.0	0.8	1.3	1.9	2.4	2.7	
63 NON DURABLE–NON DURABLES	1.9	1.5	1.7	2.5	2.2	2.3	
7 GOODS NES–BIENS NDA	3.1	2.5	1.7	2.3	3.4	2.5	

EXPORTS – EXPORTATIONS

	1991	1992	1993	1994	1995	1996	1997
TOTAL EXPORTS–EXPORTATIONS TOTALES	100.	100.	100.	100.	100.	100.	
1 AGRICULTURE	47.5	42.0	39.4	49.6	38.0	46.8	
2 MINING QUARRY–INDUS EXTRACTIVES	5.6	7.7	6.3	4.6	6.3	5.7	
3 MANUFACTURING–IND MANUFACTUR	46.9	50.3	54.4	45.8	55.7	47.5	
31 FOOD BEV TOBACCO–ALIM BOISS TAB	6.8	5.1	8.4	10.3	10.4	10.7	
32 TEXTILES–INDUSTRIES TEXTILES	7.9	10.6	10.3	8.6	9.2	6.0	
33 WOOD & PRODUCTS–BOIS & PRODUITS	0.6	1.0	1.3	1.6	2.0	2.3	
34 PAPER & PRODUCTS–PAPIER & PRODT	0.5	0.6	1.9	1.3	1.0	0.9	
35 CHEMICALS–INDUSTRIES CHIMIQUES	2.3	3.5	4.0	2.4	3.8	4.3	
36 NON METAL MIN–MIN NON METAL	0.9	0.9	1.0	0.8	0.9	0.8	
37 BASIC METAL–IND METAL BASE	22.2	21.4	17.6	12.6	18.7	14.4	
38 METAL MANUF–MANUF METAL	4.3	5.4	8.0	6.5	7.1	5.4	
39 OTH MANUF IND–AUTRES MANUF	1.4	1.6	2.0	1.7	2.6	2.5	

3. TRADE BY PRINCIPAL COUNTRIES OF ORIGIN AND DESTINATION (VALUE IN MILLION U.S. DOLLARS)
ECHANGES SELON LES PRINCIPAUX PAYS D'ORIGINE ET DE DESTINATION (VALEUR EN MILLIONS DE DOLLARS EU)

COUNTRIES–PAYS	GENERAL IMPORTS C.I.F. IMPORTATIONS GENERALES C.A.F				
	1993	1994	1995	1996	1997
World	1817.3	2241.3	2658.9	2813.5	3092.2
Africa	582.8	814.1	1139.8	1228.9	1320.9
Americas	213.1	165.3	209.0	207.8	232.0
– Northern America	174.6	129.6	145.8	154.6	184.8
– LAIA	37.5	33.5	61.6	52.4	45.9
– CACM	0.0	0.0	0.0	0.0	0.1
– Caribbean	0.9	2.2	1.3	0.6	1.2
– Rest of America	0.0	0.0	0.2	0.1	0.0
Asia excl fmr USSR	222.7	312.8	391.6	401.4	488.9
– Middle East	3.4	18.0	22.2	14.4	29.4
Asia former USSR	0.1	0.2	0.1	1.0	0.3
Europe excl fmr USSR	570.7	693.4	720.6	749.2	775.2
– European Union	518.9	609.0	664.3	692.9	707.0
– Eastern Europe	11.9	8.5	7.5	8.1	17.6
– Rest of Europe	40.0	75.8	48.8	48.2	50.6
Europe former USSR	0.4	70.4	2.6	0.6	2.6
Oceania	19.5	20.4	23.1	54.8	60.7
Other	208.1	164.7	172.0	169.9	
So. African Customs Un	553.1	782.4	1092.2	1141.0	1203.4
United Kingdom	183.7	230.4	210.3	223.2	227.5
Japan/Japon	125.0	144.1	195.5	144.5	171.9
Areas n.e.s.	207.8	164.7	172.0	169.9	
USA/Etats–Unis d'Amer	162.0	118.9	119.9	140.9	171.4
Germany/Allemagne	88.6	131.6	135.1	136.7	142.3
France, Monaco	44.8	45.9	99.9	87.0	80.1
Italy/Italie	27.5	43.5	49.2	69.3	57.0
Netherlands/Pays–Bas	46.8	43.5	46.0	49.3	54.3
Switzerland,Liechtenst.	35.0	67.1	39.3	42.0	34.6
Sweden/Suède	37.6	31.2	33.0	28.1	29.8
Korea, Republic of	6.6	24.3	27.2	39.7	55.6
Belgium–Luxembourg	24.6	27.1	33.2	28.1	37.4
Australia/Australie	15.6	15.5	16.0	45.7	51.4
Other Asia n.e.s.	14.9	29.7	26.2	28.7	37.9
China/Chine	32.1	20.6	27.8	21.5	32.7
China, Hong Kong SAR	12.4	24.3	32.8	30.2	33.4
Argentina/Argentine	22.5	10.7	39.8	20.6	23.8
India/Inde	7.0	13.4	17.0	40.1	33.1
Brazil/Brésil	13.5	19.7	19.8	30.1	17.6
Denmark/Danemark	12.6	15.8	16.3	15.6	23.4
Zambia/Zambie	14.1	6.6	15.4	14.9	27.0
Canada	12.7	10.6	25.7	13.7	13.3
Finland/Finlande	17.1	12.0	9.1	24.0	11.7
Russian Federation	0.4	70.3	0.1	0.5	2.2
Israel/Israël				30.0	37.8
Malaysia/Malaisie	7.9	15.6	10.1	21.5	11.9
Spain/Espagne	17.1	9.2	9.2	9.0	13.1
Austria/Autriche	13.3	11.4	12.3	10.5	9.8
Mauritius/Maurice	5.0	6.7	12.9	16.0	15.3
Malawi	2.1	4.0	5.5	23.8	16.0
Singapore/Singapour	2.0	6.2	9.4	16.5	15.3
Mozambique	0.7	5.3	4.6	12.3	22.9
Norway,Svalbard and JM	4.9	7.0	8.8	5.0	15.9
Kenya	4.0	4.1	3.6	12.4	15.9
Saudi Arabia	2.2	10.7	11.8	2.9	9.9
New Zealand	3.7	4.9	6.2	8.7	9.2
Portugal	3.0	3.4	6.6	4.3	7.0
Ireland/Irlande	1.9	2.8	3.3	7.1	8.7
Pakistan	0.8	7.5	7.7	2.6	4.2

COUNTRIES–PAYS	GENERAL EXPORTS F.O.B. EXPORTATIONS GENERALES F.O.B.				
	1993	1994	1995	1996	1997
Monde	1318.9	1967.5	1845.9	2121.9	2127.7
Afrique	498.5	653.1	601.1	595.7	707.2
Amériques	113.7	150.4	109.7	184.5	142.8
– Amérique du Nord	97.5	144.2	91.4	145.0	128.6
– ALAI	15.8	5.9	17.2	39.1	13.6
– MCAC	0.1	0.0	0.0	0.0	0.0
– Caraïbes	0.3	0.2	1.0	0.4	0.6
– Autre Amérique	0.0	0.1	0.1	0.0	
Asie anc. URSS exclus	193.9	304.6	303.3	406.9	340.5
– Moyen–Orient	15.8	29.1	8.2	28.8	24.9
Asie ancienne URSS	0.0	0.1	0.2	0.0	0.0
Europe anc. URSS exclus	502.0	833.9	807.2	910.9	879.8
– Union Européenne	439.8	724.5	743.4	750.3	773.5
– Europe de l'Est	8.5	49.9	29.5	87.8	37.5
– Autre de l'Europe	53.7	59.5	34.3	72.8	68.8
Europe ancienne URSS	1.8	1.8	1.0	6.0	19.4
Océanie	8.8	23.0	15.5	17.7	16.8
Autre	0.3	0.6	7.9	0.3	
So. African Customs Un	268.1	357.0	340.8	312.3	354.4
United Kingdom	145.7	254.4	237.2	222.2	235.5
Germany/Allemagne	78.9	140.3	151.9	166.8	165.2
Japan/Japon	95.5	125.0	145.5	106.6	130.1
USA/Etats–Unis d'Amer	94.2	124.4	87.6	139.8	122.9
Zambia/Zambie	66.9	65.7	92.9	91.1	116.9
Italy/Italie	48.8	58.4	87.6	90.6	85.4
Netherlands/Pays–Bas	46.3	88.9	65.2	78.7	71.8
Mozambique	54.0	60.8	51.6	77.9	71.1
Malawi	42.7	78.3	49.9	60.8	79.1
Belgium–Luxembourg	32.7	48.1	54.1	36.9	57.6
China/Chine	22.8	47.1	56.4	71.2	17.8
Switzerland,Liechtenst.	44.4	43.5	20.8	58.9	46.4
Portugal	10.9	28.6	36.4	38.0	46.4
Spain/Espagne	17.2	26.3	31.0	35.2	41.9
France, Monaco	19.8	32.0	31.6	20.0	21.7
Indonesia/Indonésie	12.5	26.6	22.6	37.5	24.8
Poland/Pologne	7.5	25.5	18.2	25.1	20.5
China, Hong Kong SAR	9.9	5.8	13.4	40.3	21.7
Philippines	10.9	30.4	10.7	13.0	13.3
Czech Republic	0.5	7.3	1.7	51.8	11.9
Australia/Australie	7.7	18.9	12.0	14.5	13.2
Kenya	12.2	14.4	3.4	10.3	20.2
India/Inde	9.0	8.4	13.2	12.9	15.1
United Rep of Tanzania	5.0	25.2	9.7	5.1	13.4
Sweden/Suède	10.0	10.2	11.8	13.1	12.0
Norway,Svalbard and JM	7.1	13.2	6.6	10.8	17.6
Thailand/Thaïlande	1.9	9.8	7.6	11.8	24.1
Greece/Grèce	10.6	8.3	6.4	20.0	7.0
Denmark/Danemark	2.9	13.0	11.0	7.9	14.8
Dem Rep of the Congo	3.9	18.3	8.5	6.3	9.8
Brazil/Brésil	3.5	2.7	10.0	20.4	6.3
Turkey/Turquie	1.6	0.3	5.1	19.5	15.9
Israel/Israël				27.6	14.1
Austria/Autriche	11.9	6.3	7.7	8.8	6.8
Other Asia n.e.s.	0.7	1.2	3.2	23.7	11.4
Angola	3.2	10.7	11.7	7.0	7.4
Singapore/Singapour	5.4	6.6	7.6	8.3	11.7
Canada	3.3	19.7	3.8	5.1	5.6
Egypt/Egypte	20.8	0.3	9.1	2.2	4.8

(VALUE AS PERCENTAGE OF WORLD TOTAL)(VALEURS EN POURCENTAGE DU TOTAL MONDIAL)

	1988	1989	1990	1991	1992	1993	1994	1995	1996	1997
Africa			26.3	30.7	28.4	32.1	36.3	42.9	43.7	42.7
Americas			13.8	7.3	19.9	11.7	7.4	7.9	7.4	7.5
– Northern America			12.5	6.4	9.6	9.6	5.8	5.5	5.5	6.0
– LAIA			1.2	0.9	10.3	2.1	1.5	2.3	1.9	1.5
– CACM			0.0	0.0	0.0	0.0	0.0	0.0	0.0	0.0
– Caribbean			0.0	0.0	0.0	0.0	0.1	0.0	0.0	0.0
– Rest of America			0.0	0.0	0.0	0.0	0.0	0.0	0.0	0.0
Asia excl fmr USSR			10.5	11.0	9.6	12.3	14.0	14.7	14.3	15.8
– Middle East			0.1	0.3	0.1	0.2	0.8	0.8	0.5	1.0
Asia former USSR						0.0	0.0	0.0	0.0	0.0
Europe excl fmr USSR			33.3	39.6	31.5	31.4	30.9	27.1	26.6	25.1
– European Union			30.0	36.9	29.0	28.6	27.2	25.0	24.6	22.9
– Eastern Europe			0.9	0.3	0.2	0.7	0.4	0.3	0.3	0.6
– Rest of Europe			2.5	2.4	2.3	2.2	3.4	1.8	1.7	1.6
Europe former USSR			0.1	0.0	0.1	0.0	3.1	0.1	0.0	0.1
Oceania			2.8	1.2	0.9	1.1	0.9	0.9	1.9	2.0
Other			13.2	10.2	9.6	11.4	7.4	6.5	6.0	
So. African Customs Un			24.1	28.8	26.4	30.4	34.9	41.1	40.6	38.9
United Kingdom			11.5	15.3	12.0	10.1	10.3	7.9	7.9	7.4
Japan/Japon			4.6	6.0	5.9	6.9	6.4	7.4	5.1	5.6
Areas n.e.s.			13.2	9.9	9.4	11.4	7.4	6.5	6.0	
USA/Etats–Unis d'Amer			11.4	5.5	9.0	8.9	5.3	4.5	5.0	5.5
Germany/Allemagne				9.4	6.4	4.9	5.9	5.1	4.9	4.6
France, Monaco			2.1	3.0	1.7	2.5	2.0	3.8	3.1	2.6
Italy/Italie			2.2	2.4	2.1	1.5	1.9	1.9	2.5	1.8
Netherlands/Pays–Bas			2.0	1.7	1.5	2.6	1.9	1.7	1.8	1.8
Switzerland,Liechtenst.			2.0	2.2	1.8	1.9	3.0	1.5	1.5	1.1

	1988	1989	1990	1991	1992	1993	1994	1995	1996	1997
Afrique			32.3	30.9	33.4	37.8	33.2	32.6	28.1	33.2
Amériques			8.0	6.6	7.6	8.6	7.6	5.9	8.7	6.7
– Amérique du Nord			7.3	6.1	6.7	7.4	7.3	5.0	6.8	6.0
– ALAI			0.7	0.4	0.7	1.2	0.3	0.9	1.8	0.6
– MCAC			0.0	0.0	0.0	0.0	0.0	0.0	0.0	0.0
– Caraïbes			0.0	0.0	0.3	0.0	0.0	0.1	0.0	0.0
– Autre Amérique			0.0	0.0	0.0	0.0	0.0	0.0	0.0	
Asie anc. URSS exclus			12.5	14.6	15.9	14.7	15.5	16.4	19.2	16.0
– Moyen–Orient			0.4	0.7	0.7	1.2	1.5	0.4	1.4	1.2
Asie ancienne URSS						0.0	0.0	0.0	0.0	0.0
Europe anc. URSS exclus			45.8	46.9	41.9	38.1	42.4	43.7	42.9	41.3
– Union Européenne			42.2	42.6	34.7	33.3	36.8	40.3	35.4	36.4
– Europe de l'Est			0.6	0.6	1.2	0.6	2.5	1.6	4.1	1.8
– Autre de l'Europe			3.0	3.7	6.0	4.1	3.0	1.9	3.4	3.2
Europe ancienne URSS			0.0	0.0	0.1	0.1	0.1	0.1	0.3	0.9
Océanie			1.2	1.0	0.9	0.7	1.2	0.8	0.8	0.8
Autre			0.3	0.0	0.1	0.0	0.0	0.4	0.0	
So. African Customs Un			15.1	17.0	19.1	20.3	18.1	18.5	14.7	16.7
United Kingdom			10.9	13.8	11.4	11.0	12.9	12.8	10.5	11.1
Germany/Allemagne				10.6	6.9	6.0	7.1	8.2	7.9	7.8
Japan/Japon			5.5	7.2	6.6	7.2	6.4	7.9	5.0	6.1
USA/Etats–Unis d'Amer			6.5	5.8	6.4	7.1	6.3	4.7	6.6	5.8
Zambia/Zambie			3.5	3.6	3.8	5.1	3.3	5.0	4.3	5.5
Italy/Italie			4.6	3.6	3.7	3.7	3.0	4.7	4.3	4.0
Netherlands/Pays–Bas			4.3	3.0	3.2	3.5	4.5	3.5	3.7	3.4
Mozambique			3.7	2.7	3.4	4.1	3.1	2.8	3.7	3.3
Malawi			4.8	3.3	3.2	3.2	4.0	2.7	2.9	3.7

4. General Imports C.I.F. by Commodities according to the S.I.T.C. (Rev. 2) in million U.S. Dollars
Importations Générales C.A.F. par Produits d'après la C.T.C.I. (Rév. 2) en millions de Dollars E.U.

SITC CTCI	COMMODITY	1994 QUANTITY QUANTITE	1994 VALUE VALEUR	1995 QUANTITY QUANTITE	1995 VALUE VALEUR	1996 QUANTITY QUANTITE	1996 VALUE VALEUR	1997 QUANTITY QUANTITE	1997 VALUE VALEUR	PRODUIT
	ALL COMMODITIES		2241.3		2658.9		2813.6			TOUS PRODUITS
0	FOOD AND LIVE ANIMALS		54.0		97.9		199.4			ALIMENTS,ANIMAUX VIVANTS
03	FISH AND PREPARATIONS		10.1		13.4		26.5			POISSONS ET PREPARATIONS
034	FISH,FRESH,CHILLED,FROZN	W 13363	7.6	W 14421	8.6	W 13749	18.5			POISSON FRAIS, REFRIG,CONG
0342	FISH FROZEN,EXCL FILLETS	W 13117	7.1	W 14168	7.8	W 13170	17.0			POISSONS CONGELES
04	CEREALS AND PREPARATIONS		23.1		45.2		115.3			CEREALES ET PRODUITS
041	WHEAT ETC UNMILLED		13.1	W 80890	29.5	W 248439	68.0			FROMENT,EPEAUTRE
0412	OTHER WHEAT ETC UNMILLED	W 16665	13.1	W 80890	29.5	W 248010	67.9			AUTRE FROMENT NON MOULU
042	RICE	W 25721	7.1	W 29080	9.9	W 16948	9.0			RIZ
0422	RICE SEMI–MILLED,MILLED	W 25525	7.0	W 28950	9.9	W 16945	9.0			RIZ POLI,GLACE INCL BRISURES
04221	RICE MILLED UNBROKEN	W 23584	6.5	W 27293	9.3	W 15763	8.5			RIZ POLI,GLACE EXCL BRISURES
044	MAIZE UNMILLED	W 1289	0.9	W 2266	0.7	W 126867	25.6			MAIS NON MOULU
05	VEGETABLES AND FRUIT		10.5		15.0		25.0			LEGUMES ET FRUITS
054	VEG ETC FRSH,SMPLY PRSVD	W 8452	7.1		9.8	W 11701	7.0			LEGUMES FRAIS,CONG,SECS
058	FRUIT PRESERVED,PREPARED	W 531	0.9	W 928	1.9	W 12254	11.9			CONSERVES DE FRUITS
0585	FRUIT OR VEGETABLE JUICE	W 449	0.6	W 626	1.3	W 11917	11.3			JUS DE FRUITS
05857	JUICE OF OTHER FRUIT,VEG	W 302	0.4	W 437	1.0	W 11152	10.1			JUS AUTRES FRUITS,LEGUMES
06	SUGAR AND PREPS,HONEY		0.9		1.9		12.0			SUCRES ET PRODUITS
061	SUGAR AND HONEY		0.4	W 12533	1.1	W 26463	10.8			SUCRES ET MIEL
0611	RAW BEET AND CANE SUGAR			W 785	0.3	W 23926	10.0			SUCRES BRUTS
081	*FEEDING STUFF FOR ANIML	W 6723	2.5	W 54650	13.0	W 26462	7.9			NOURRITURE POUR ANIMAUX
0813	OILCAKE AND OTH RESIDUES	W 636	0.2	W 46591	9.3	W 17482	3.7			TOURTEAUX
1	BEVERAGES AND TOBACCO		8.4		10.8		28.1			BOISSONS ET TABACS
11	BEVERAGES		7.5		9.2		10.3			BOISSONS
12	TOBACCO AND MANUFACTURES		1.0		1.7		17.9			TABACS BRUTS FABRIQUES
121	TOBACCO UNMNFCTRD,REFUSE	W 346	0.4	W 1019	1.4	W 11005	17.5			TABACS BRUTS,DECHETS
1212	TOBACCO STRIPPED OR PART	W 20	0.1	W 294	0.6	W 5003	8.9			TABACS PART ECOTES
2	CRUDE MATERLS,EXCL FUELS		73.2		92.4		84.8			MAT BRUTES NON COMESTIBLES
22	OIL SEEDS,OLEAGINOUS FRT		3.7		5.9		9.1			GRAINES,FRUITS OLEAGINEUX
222	SEEDS FOR'SOFT'FIXED OIL	W 5520	3.7	W 12916	5.8	W 25344	8.9			GRAINES HUILES FIXES
23	RUBBER, CRUDE		13.6		16.8		16.0			CAOUTCHOUC BRUT
232	NATURAL RUBBER,GUMS	W 6221	7.9	W 5319	10.0	W 5382	9.4			LATEX CAOUTCHOUC NATUREL
251	*PULP AND WASTE PAPER	W 30165	10.4	W 20991	9.9	W 21017	8.6			PATES A PAPIER,DECHETS
26	TEXTILE FIBRES AND WASTE		13.9		15.9		23.7			FIBRES TEXTILES
263	COTTON	W 451	0.1	W 3047	6.4	W 8641	15.1			COTON
2631	RAW COTTON,EXCL LINTERS	W 3	0.1	W 3015	6.3	W 8612	15.0			COTON EN MASSE
27	CRUDE FERTLZR,MINRLS NES		13.9		13.5		13.1			ENGRAIS MINERAUX BRUTS
278	OTHER CRUDE MINERALS		8.5		8.2		8.4			AUTRES MINERAUX BRUTS
28	METALLIFEROUS ORES,SCRAP		10.3		23.0		6.3			MINERAIS METAL,DECHETS
287	BASE METAL ORES,CONC NES		10.2		22.9		6.3			MINERAIS METAUX COMMUNS
2871	CPR ORE ETC,CEMENT COPPR	W 4388	7.6		21.7		5.5			MINERAIS DE CUIVRE,MATTES
28712	COPPER MATTE,CEMENT COPR	W 3988	7.6	W 3530	21.7	W 1973	5.5			MATTES DE CUIVRE
3	MINERAL FUELS ETC		222.4		240.1		292.7			COMBUSTIBLES MINERAUX LUB
33	PETROLEUM AND PRODUCTS		215.7		234.1		275.0			PETROLE ET DERIVES
334	PETROLEUM PRODUCTS,REFIN	MW 11912	210.2	W 5527377	228.9	W 3205166	269.8			PRODUITS RAFFINES
3341	GASOLINE,OTH LIGHT OILS	W 1708650	50.2	W 358642	68.5	W 570320	71.5			ESSENCES POUR MOTEURS
33411	MOTOR,AVIATION SPIRIT	W 1705217	48.8	W 356921	67.5	W 567547	70.0			ESSENCES MOTEURS D'AVIONS
3342	KEROSENE,OTH MEDIUM OILS	W 335168	32.6	W 155085	28.6	W 203263	45.5			PETR LAMPANTS,AUT HUIL
33421	KEROSENE INCL JET FUEL	W 335070	32.6	W 155078	28.6	W 203257	45.5			PETROLES LAMPANTS
3343	GAS OILS	W 8090418	109.1	W 4916213	114.6	W 671551	127.8			GAS OILS
3345	LUBS,PETROLEUM OILS NES	W 1156922	18.2	W 97188	17.3	W 1759995	25.1			HUILES LUBRIFIANTES
33451	LUBS(HIGH PETR CONT) ETC	W 1156045	16.7	W 96799	16.5	W 1759666	24.4			HUILES LUBRIF,H LOURDES
341	*GAS,NATURAL AND MANUFCT		3.3		1.8		15.9			GAZ NATUREL,GAZ MANUFACT
3413	PETROLM GASES,LIQUEFIED	W 6507	2.2	W 9082	1.7	W 133169	15.6			GAZ DE PETROLE LIQUEFIE
34139	OTH HYDROCARBON GAS LQFD	W 6369	2.1	W 8968	1.7	W 132987	15.5			HYDROCARBURES GAZEUX NDA
4	ANIMAL,VEGETABLE OIL,FAT		42.2		44.4		54.4			HUILES,GRAISSES ANIM,VEG
411	*ANIMAL OILS AND FATS	W 40946	18.7	W 24353	16.0	W 25989	16.6			HUILES,GRAISSES ANIMALES
4113	ANIML OIL,FAT,GREASE NES	W 40919	18.7	W 24311	16.0	W 25976	16.5			HUILES,GRAISSES ANIMALES NDA
41132	FATS OF BOVINE,SHEEP,ETC	W 40868	18.6	W 24274	15.9	W 25927	16.5			SUIFS BRUTS FONDUS
42	FIXED VEGETABLE OIL,FAT		22.6		26.2		36.5			HUILES VEGETALES FIXES
423	FIXED VEG OILS,SOFT	W 18856	12.9	W 26512	21.4	W 33053	23.5			HUILES VEGET DOUCES FIXES
4232	SOYA BEAN OIL	W 18821	12.8	W 21005	16.7	W 28284	19.8			HUILE DE SOJA
424	FIXED VEG OIL NONSOFT	W 16792	9.7	W 7143	4.9	W 17957	13.0			AUTRES HUILES VEG FIXES
4242	PALM OIL	W 14541	8.0	W 6355	4.1	W 17429	12.4			HUILE DE PALME
5	CHEMCLS,RELATED PROD NES		360.6		358.5		367.1			PRODUITS CHIMIQUES
51	ORGANIC CHEMICALS		40.4		32.3		32.4			PROD CHIMIQ ORGANIQUES
513	CARBOXYLIC ACIDS ETC	W 5760	7.1	W 3657	6.7	W 4837	6.9			ACIDES CARBOXYLIQUES
514	NITROGEN–FNCTN COMPOUNDS	W 1540	7.7	W 1782	8.0	W 1910	8.5			COMPOSES FONCT AZOTEES
515	ORG–INORG COMPOUNDS ETC	W 4017	12.4	W 21591	4.7	W 1260	4.2			COMPOSES ORGANO–MINERAUX
5154	ORGANO–SULPHUR CMPNDS	W 3606	10.2	W 21297	2.9	W 1036	2.6			THIOCOMPOSES ORGANIQUES
52	INORGANIC CHEMICALS		54.2		56.5		51.4			PROD CHIM INORGANIQUES
522	INORG ELEMNTS,OXIDES,ETC		26.4		30.5		23.2			ELEMENTS INORGANIQUES
5225	INORGANIC BASES ETC NES		15.1		20.9		13.7			AUTRES BASES OXYDES METAL
52251	AMMONIA,ANHYDROUS ETC		9.9		13.2	W 34031	7.7			AMMONIAC LIQUEFIE
523	OTHR INORG CHEMICALS ETC		27.7		25.9		28.2			AUT PRODUITS CHIMIQUES INORG
5231	METAL CMPD OF INORG ACID	W 15324	8.3	W 14577	7.9	W 13383	7.2			SELS METALLIQUES
5232	OTH MTL CMPD OF INRG ACD	W 130533	16.6	W 31279	15.3	W 34735	18.5			SELS METALLIQUES
52325	CYANIDES,COMPLEX CYANIDE	W 6913	7.0	W 5151	6.7	W 6531	9.2			CYANURES SIMPLES,COMPLEXES
53	DYES,TANNING,COLOUR PROD		46.0		21.3		19.3			PROD TEINTURE,COLORANTS
531	SYNT DYE,NAT INDGO,LAKES	W 2283	35.9	W 916	9.3	W 834	8.5			MAT COLOR ORGAN,LAQUES
5311	SYNTHIC ORGNIC DYESTUFFS	W 2165	34.7	W 857	8.5	W 770	7.9			MAT COLOR ORGAN SYNTHET
533	PIGMENTS,PAINTS,ETC		9.4		11.1		10.0			PIGMENTS,PEINTURES,VERNIS
541	*MEDICINAL,PHARM PRODUCT		34.0		34.9		35.9			PROD MEDICINAUX PHARMACEUT
5417	MEDICAMENTS		13.3		17.1		19.5			MEDICAMENTS
54173	— CONTAINING ALKALOIDS		5.5		8.4		9.6			MED CONTEN ALCALOIDES
55	PERFUME,CLEANING ETC PRD		14.1		20.2		22.6			PROD POUR PARFUM,TOILETTE
551	ESSENTL OILS,PERFUME,ETC	W 753	6.8	W 1481	11.8	W 1213	12.7			HUILES ESSENTIELLES
5514	MIXED PERFUME SUBSTANCES	W 686	6.0	W 1416	11.0	W 1171	12.0			MELANGES SUBSTAN ODORIFER
562	*FERTILIZERS,MANUFACTURE	W 142778	27.4	W 99859	23.0	W 177705	32.5			ENGRAIS MANUFACTURES
5621	CHEM NITROGENOUS FERTLZR	W 74467	10.7	W 50703	11.9	W 34821	7.5			ENGRAIS AZOTES
5623	CHEM POTASSIC FERTILIZER	W 55142	14.0	W 34820	7.8	W 54277	14.9			ENGRAIS POTASSIQUES
56231	POTASSIUM CHLORIDE	W 41541	8.0	W 12281	2.6	W 35690	6.7			CHLORURE DE POTASSIUM
5629	FERTILIZERS NES	W 12043	2.6	W 14326	3.4	W 87294	9.9			ENGRAIS NDA
572	*EXPLOSIVES,PYROTECH PRO		13.1		14.9		14.8			EXPLOSIFS
5722	FUSES,PRIMERS,DETONATORS	W 558	6.4	W 655	8.0	W 750	9.3			MECHES,CORDEAUX,AMORCES
58	PLASTIC MATERIALS ETC		72.3		89.6		77.7			MAT PLAST ARTIFICIELLES
582	PROD OF CONDENSATION ETC	W 8815	12.3	W 9248	13.9	W 8480	11.5			PROD CONDENS,POLYCOND
583	POLYMERIZATION ETC PRODS	W 62027	58.0	W 57867	73.6	W 57739	64.3			PROD POLYMERISATION
5831	POLYETHYLENE	W 22390	18.2	W 24565	27.3	W 21750	21.9			POLYETHYLENE
58311	— IN PRIMARY FORMS	W 22277	17.8	W 24190	26.8	W 21310	21.1			POLYETHYLENE PRIMAIRES
5832	POLYPROPYLENE	W 14570	12.8	W 14496	17.5	W 13096	14.1			POLYPROPYLENE

4. General Imports C.I.F. by Commodities according to the S.I.T.C. (Rev. 2) in million U.S. Dollars
Importations Générales C.A.F. par Produits d'après la C.T.C.I. (Rév. 2) en millions de Dollars E.U.

SITC CTCI	COMMODITY	1994 QUANTITY QUANTITE	1994 VALUE VALEUR	1995 QUANTITY QUANTITE	1995 VALUE VALEUR	1996 QUANTITY QUANTITE	1996 VALUE VALEUR	1997 QUANTITY QUANTITE	1997 VALUE VALEUR	PRODUIT
58321	— IN PRIMARY FORMS	W 13882	11.3	W 13690	15.4	W 12305	11.9			POLYPROPYLENE PRIMAIRES
5834	POLYVINYL CHLORIDE	W 15890	12.6	W 9768	11.4	W 13866	11.6			CHLORURE DE POLYVINYLE
58341	— IN PRIMARY FORMS	W 15756	12.3	W 9581	10.8	W 13748	11.3			SOUS FORMES PRIMAIRES
5839	OTH POLYMRZTION ETC PROD	W 4573	8.3	W 3718	9.3	W 4227	9.8			AUT PROD POLYMER COPOLYM
59	CHEMICAL MATERIALS NES		59.3		66.4		80.9			MAT PROD CHIMIQUES NDA
591	PESTICIDES,DISINFECTANTS	W 5358	27.7	W 39098	29.4	W 9954	44.2			DESINF,INSECT,FONG,HERB
5911	INSECTICIDES,FOR RETAIL	W 1943	12.0	W 27419	15.9	W 6264	25.6			INSECTICIDES VENTE DET
5913	HERBICIDES,FOR RETAIL	W 2086	10.3	W 1834	9.2	W 1682	9.0			HERBICIDES VENTE AU DET
598	MISCEL CHEM PRODUCTS NES		28.1		33.9		33.5			PROD DIV INDUST CHIM NDA
5982	ANTI-KNOCK PREPARTNS ETC	W 4281	7.8	W 2784	6.6	W 3414	8.6			PREPARAT ANTIDETONANTES
5989	CHEM PRODUCTS,PREPS NES		17.6		20.0		19.8			PROD PREP CHIMIQUES NDA
59899	OTH CHEM PRODS,PREPS,NES		10.6		11.8		11.3			AUT PRODUITS CHIMIQUES NDA
6	BASIC MANUFACTURES		369.5		458.3		456.8			ART MANUFACTURES
62	RUBBER MANUFACTURES NES		29.6		34.6		44.0			CAOUTCHOUC MANUFACTURE
625	RUBBER TYRES, TUBES ETC	W 3685	14.6	W 5181	18.8	W 7314	26.1			PNEUS CAOUTCHOUC VULCANISE
6252	TYRES,NEW,BUS OR LORRY	W 1152	4.9	W 2331	7.9	W 3133	11.3			PNEUS POUR AUTOBUS,CAMIONS
628	RUBBER ARTICLES NES		11.2		11.8		13.2			OUVRAGES CAOUTCHOUC NDA
6289	OTH RUBBER ARTICLES NES	W 460	7.2	W 326	6.8	W 421	5.9			AUT OUVR CAOUTCHOUC NDA
62898	UNHARD RUBBER PRODS NES	W 446	7.2	W 322	6.7	W 411	5.9			OUV CAOUT VULC NON DURCI
64	PAPER,PAPERBOARD AND MFR		48.2		52.3		50.6			PAPIERS,CARTONS & OUVRAGES
641	PAPER AND PAPERBOARD	W 42604	38.6	W 36629	41.9	W 40481	38.8			PAPIERS ET CARTONS
6413	KRAFT PAPER,PAPERBOARD	W 16241	10.3	W 16226	14.3	W 15881	10.3			PAPIER ET CARTON KRAFT
64139	KRAFT PAPER PAPERBD,NES	W 5311	3.6	W 12289	11.2	W 10535	7.3			PAPIER,CARTON KRAFT NDA
6415	PAPER,PAPERBRD,BULK,NES	W 7095	10.5	W 5889	10.5	W 7174	9.2			PAPIERS,CARTONS ROULEAUX
64159	OTHER PAPER ETC,BULK,NES	W 6835	10.0	W 5494	9.7	W 7099	9.0			AUT PAPIER ROULEAUX FEUILLES
6418	COATED ETC PAPER NES BLK	W 7773	8.8	W 5183	7.6	W 4613	7.1			PAP,CARTONS COUCHES,ENDUITS
64189	COATED PAPER ETC NES	W 7241	7.4	W 4361	5.6	W 3185	4.8			PAPIERS,CARTONS COUCHES
642	PAPER,ETC,PRECUT,ARTS OF		9.6		10.5	W 8755	11.8			PAP,CARTONS DECOUPES
65	TEXTILE YARN,FABRICS,ETC		96.4		115.7		121.7			FILS,TISSUS,ARTICLES TEXTILE
651	TEXTILE YARN	W 3672	13.4	W 3494	13.7	W 2950	10.4			FILS TEXTILES
6514	SYN FIB YRN,BULK,MONOFIL	W 2509	7.7	W 1755	6.5	W 1879	6.6			FILS CONT 85% FIB TEXT SYNTH
652	COTTON FABRICS,WOVEN	A 9745	18.2	A 12185	27.2	A 12460	22.0			TISSUS DE COTON
6522	WOVEN COTTON BLEACHD,ETC	A 8725	16.5	A 11424	25.9	A 10823	19.5			TISSUS COTON BLANCHIS ETC
65224	BLCHED COTTON FABRIC NES	A 6842	12.5	A 9367	22.1	A 8542	16.2			AUT TIS PLUS 85% COT BLANCHI
653	WOVN MAN-MADE FIB FABRIC	A 13899	30.8	A 14293	30.6	A 35209	42.4			TISSUS FIBRES SYNTH,ARTIF
6531	CONT SYNT WEAVES NONPILE	A 4403	8.4	A 4800	10.7	A 9233	13.4			TISSUS FIBRES SYNTH CONTINUE
65315	CONT SYN TXTL FABRIC NES	A 3773	7.5	A 4055	9.4	A 8280	12.0			TIS PLUS 85% TEXT SYNT CONT
6532	DISC SYN TXTL FABRIC NES	A 1543	3.2	A 1935	4.3	A 7022	8.9			TIS DISC MOINS 85% FIBR TEXT
6534	DISC SYN BLEND FABRC NES	A 5648	13.1	A 4519	9.6	A 8964	13.3			TISSUS FIBRES SYNTH DISCONT
65349	OTH DISC SYN BLEND FABRC	A 3263	8.8	A 2390	6.1	A 4866	8.3			TISSUS FIB SYNT MEL MAT AUT
657	SPECIAL TXTL FABRC,PRODS		18.0		20.4		16.8			TISSUS SPECIAUX
6573	COATED ETC TEXTILES NES		12.5		10.4		10.7			TISSUS,ART MATIERE TEXT NDA
658	TEXTILE ARTICLES NES		3.1		6.4		13.5			ART FACONNES MAT TEXTILES
6583	BLANKETS ETC NON ELECTRC	W 4	0.1	W 14	0.1	W 1603	9.6			COUVERTURES
65833	SYN FIB BLANKETS ETC NES	W 1	0.1	W 2	0.1	W 1537	9.1			COUVERTURES FIBRES SYNTHET
66	NONMETAL MINERAL MFS NES		32.9		35.5		45.8			ART MIN NON METALLIQUES
661	LIME,CEMENT,BLDG PRODS	W 34190	6.7	W 45539	7.3	W 945202	10.3			CHAUX,CIMENTS MAT CONSTR
662	CLAY,REFRACTORY BLDG PRD		9.6		10.0		16.2			MAT CONST REFRACTAIRES
6623	REFRACTORY BUILDING PROD	W 7668	6.9	W 8115	7.1	W 12157	11.7			BRIQUES REFRACTAIRES
664	GLASS		7.0		6.8		7.9			VERRE
67	IRON AND STEEL		84.1		102.5		96.0			FER ET ACIER
672	IRON,STEEL PRIMARY FORMS		9.0		12.3		8.5			LINGOTS FER,ACIER
6727	IRN,STL COIL FR REROLLNG	W 20167	8.6	W 23142	11.7	W 80973	8.5			EBAUCHES POUR TOLES FER
67271	IRON,SIMPLE STEEL COILS	W 19821	8.1	W 22511	10.6	W 31961	7.6			EBAUCHES NON EN ACIER
673	IRON,STEEL SHAPES ETC	W 43639	16.7	W 49148	23.7	W 201280	20.7			BARRES,PROFIL FER,ACIER
6732	IRON,STEEL BARS ETC	W 7019	6.8	W 15536	7.8	W 55134	9.0			BARRES FER,ACIER
6733	IRON,STEEL PROFILES ETC	W 23041	6.5	W 14253	8.1	W 133003	7.5			PROFILES,PALPLAN FER,ACIER
674	IRN,STL UNIV,PLATE,SHEET	W 42039	40.2	W 78424	48.2	W 749248	42.5			LARGES PLATS,TOLES
6744	IRN,STL HVY PLATE,ROLLED	W 686	8.2	W 22520	12.1	W 29757	10.5			TOLES LAMINEES PLUS 4.75 MM
67441	— OF IRON OR SIMPLE STL	W 11	7.6	W 22092	11.6	W 29288	10.1			TOLES NON ACIER FIN CARB
6746	IRN,STL THIN PLATE,ROLLD	W 22953	13.1	W 27715	16.9	W 133710	13.1			TOLES LAM MOINS 3MM
67461	— OF IRON OR SIMPLE STL	W 22183	12.4	W 27516	16.6	W 133084	12.8			TOL NON AC FIN MOINS 3 MM
6749	OTH IRN,STL PLATES,SHEET	W 258	7.6	W 12105	8.6	W 184313	9.4			AUTRES TOLES FER,ACIER
67491	— OF IRON OR SIMPLE STL	W 115	7.3	W 11619	8.1	W 182967	8.8			AUT TOLES AUTRES ACIER FIN
678	IRON,STL TUBES,PIPES,ETC	W 7151	12.3	W 7637	11.8	W 11432	16.4			TUBES,TUYAUX EN FONTE,FER
6783	IRON,STL TUBES,PIPES NES	W 3001	3.5	W 4062	4.1	W 6289	8.7			AUT TUBES,TUYAUX FER,ACIER
68	NON-FERROUS METALS		17.7		20.3		18.0			METAUX NON FERREUX
684	ALUMINIUM	W 10811	9.3	W 2944	7.9	W 63998	10.0			ALUMINIUM
6842	ALUMINIUM,ALLOYS WORKED	W 9291	7.0	W 2319	6.7	W 32913	8.0			ALUMINIUM,ALLIAGES OUVRE
69	METAL MANUFACTURES NES		52.2		86.2		72.0			ART MANUFACT EN METAL NDA
691	STRUCTURES AND PARTS NES	W 1187	1.8	W 6644	12.4	W 5767	15.2			CONSTRUCT FER,ACIER,ALU
6911	STRUCTURES,PARTS IRN,STL	W 1111	1.4	W 6488	11.8	W 5617	14.4			CONSTRUCT FER,ACIER,FONTE
692	METAL TANKS,BOXES,ETC		2.5		7.3		8.9			RECIPIENTS METALLIQUES
693	WIRE PRODUCTS NON ELECTR	W 2433	5.1	W 4196	10.4	W 2628	6.7			OUVRAGES FILS METALLIQUES
695	TOOLS		20.1		22.5		14.5			OUTILS A MAIN
6953	OTHER HAND TOOLS	W 827	9.5	W 2108	13.2	W 1101	8.0			AUTRES OUTILS A MAIN
6954	BLADES,TIPS,ETC FR TOOLS	W 692	10.4	W 524	9.2	W 380	6.3			OUTILS POUR MACHINE-OUTIL
69541	PARTS TO INSERT IN TOOLS	W 602	7.9	W 427	6.9	W 291	4.5			OUTILS DE FORAGE
699	BASE METAL MFRS NES		14.3		19.9	W 3021	16.7			ART MANUFACTURES MET NDA
7	MACHINES,TRANSPORT EQUIP		934.7		1107.8		1081.5			MACHINES MATERIEL TRANSPORT
71	POWER GENERATING EQUIPMT		60.5		64.0		39.5			MACHINES GENERATRICES
713	INTRNL COMBUS PSTN ENGIN		27.4		27.0		22.8			MOTEURS EXPL COMB INT, PIECE
7139	PISTON ENGINE PARTS NES	W 579	11.9	W 498	13.0	W 403	9.4			PIECES POUR 713.2,3,8
716	ROTATING ELECTRIC PLANT		22.6		23.9		10.6			APP ELECTR ROTATIFS,PIECES
7162	AC MTRS,GENRTRS,GEN SETS		19.5		16.4		6.2			MOTEURS ELECTRIQUES
71621	AC MTRS,INC UNIVRSL MTRS	N 75536	2.5	N 71791	14.5	N 57169	3.3			MOT ELEC NON COUR CONTINU
71623	GEN SETS WITH PISTN ENGN	W 448	16.7	W 141	1.7	W 212	2.6			GROUPES MOTEUR EXPLOSION
72	MACHS FOR SPCL INDUSTRYS		183.5		247.3		224.0			MAC SPECIALES POUR INDUST
721	AGRIC MACHY,EXC TRACTORS		13.8		13.8		15.1			MACHINES AGRICOLES
7212	HARVESTING ETC MACHINES		8.4		7.4		7.4			ENGINS POUR LA RECOLTE
722	TRACTORS NON-ROAD	N 12467	38.6	N 1475	25.4	N 2663	43.3			TRACTEURS
7224	WHEELED TRACTORS NES	N 12464	38.5	N 1474	25.4	N 2663	43.3			TRACTEURS A ROUES
723	CIVIL ENGNEERG EQUIP ETC		41.0		64.9		53.2			APPAREILS DE GENIE CIVIL
7234	CONST,MINING MACHNRY NES		37.2		60.3		49.5			MACH POUR LA CONST, MINES
72341	SELF-PROPELLD DOZERS,ETC	N 12220	12.1	N 433955	14.4		8.3			BULLDOZERS
72342	SLFPRP SHOVELS,EXCAVATRS	N 151	20.2	N 446610	30.8	N 253249	24.2			PELLES MECANIQUES
72343	SLFPRP CONST ETC MCH NES	W 198	2.3	W 690	12.3	W 1096	13.7			AUT MACH EXTR,TERRASSEM
724	TEXTILE,LEATHER MACHNRY		26.3		21.9		25.8			MACH POUR INDUSTRIE TEXTILE
7245	WEAVING,FELT MFG,ETC MCH		8.7		2.8		6.2			METIERS A TISSER,PIECES
726	PRINTG,BKBINDG MACHY,PTS	W 349	6.3	W 423	8.7	W 600	13.5			MACHINES POUR IMPRIMERIE
727	FOOD MACHRY NON-DOMESTIC	W 716	8.6	W 1369	19.4	W 1772	18.0			MACH INDUSTRIES ALIMENT

4. General Imports C.I.F. by Commodities according to the S.I.T.C. (Rev. 2) in million U.S. Dollars
Importations Générales C.A.F. par Produits d'après la C.T.C.I. (Rév. 2) en millions de Dollars E.U.

SITC CTCI	COMMODITY	1994 QUANTITY QUANTITE	1994 VALUE VALEUR	1995 QUANTITY QUANTITE	1995 VALUE VALEUR	1996 QUANTITY QUANTITE	1996 VALUE VALEUR	1997 QUANTITY QUANTITE	1997 VALUE VALEUR	PRODUIT
7272	OTH FOOD PROC MCHY,PARTS	W 526	5.3	W 1073	14.2	W 993	12.2			AUT MACH IND ALIMENTAIRE
72722	INDUS FOOD PROC MACH NES	W 513	5.2	W 1073	14.2	W 963	12.1			MACHINES BOULANGERIE
728	OTH MACHY FOR SPCL INDUS	W 6087	46.5	W 11549	87.1	W 5720	51.6			AUT MACH IND PARTICULIERES
7281	MACH–TOOLS FR SPCL INDUS	W 611	4.5	W 1658	14.7	W 500	4.7			MACH–OUTILS SPEC IND PART
72812	MACH–TOOLS TO WORK WOOD	W 406	3.5	W 1553	13.5	W 375	3.1			MACH–OUT POUR TRAVAIL BOIS
7283	OTHR MINERAL WORKG MACHY	W 1729	23.0	W 7634	43.5	W 1994	14.8			MACH TRIER,CRIBLER,BROYER
72831	MINRAL SORTING ETC MACHY	W 509	11.6	W 820	6.7	W 255	2.1			MACH TRIER MAT MINERALES
72832	MINRL CRUSHING ETC MACHY	W 668	6.2	W 4122	21.4	W 765	5.4			MACH CONCASSER MAT MINER
72839	PTS NES OF MACHY OF 7283	W 230	2.7	W 1873	10.6	W 397	3.4			PIECES MACH DU 728.3
7284	MACHY FOR SPCL INDUS NES	W 3746	19.1	W 2257	29.0	W 3226	32.2			MACH SPEC IND PARTICUL.
72842	RUBBER,PLASTICS WRKG MCH	W 2666	9.6	W 820	9.3	W 1336	13.5			MACH IND CAOUT MAT PLAST
72848	OTH MCHY WITH INDIV FNCT	W 834	5.2	W 1036	14.0	W 1001	13.5			AUTRES MACHINES NDA
73	METALWORKING MACHINERY		15.5		11.4		12.1			MACH TRAVAIL DES METAUX
736	METALWORKING MACH–TOOLS	W 1091	8.4	W 1355	8.9	W 1427	7.5			MACH–OUTILS TRAVAIL METAUX
737	METALWORKING MACHNRY NES	W 699	7.1	W 341	2.6	W 436	4.7			MACH TRAV METAUX PIECES
74	GENRL INDUSTRL MACHY NES		163.0		171.1		188.0			MACH APP INDUSTRIE
741	HEATING,COOLING EQUIPMNT		19.0		25.7		30.9			MACH CHAUFFAGE,PIECES
7415	AIR–CONDITIONING MACHNRY	W 590	5.0	W 823	5.5	W 898	10.2			GROUPES CONDITION AIR
7416	HEATING,COOLING EQU NES	W 503	6.3	W 2010	8.6	W 2520	10.9			APP CHANGEMENT TEMP
742	PUMPS FOR LIQUIDS ETC	W 1031	18.2	W 1568	20.5	W 1509	20.2			POMPES MOTO–POMPES
7428	OTHER PUMPS FOR LIQUIDS	W 633	10.2	W 1097	13.3	W 840	11.2			AUTRES POMPES POUR LIQ
74288	PUMPS FR LIQUIDS NES ETC	W 535	8.5	W 927	10.3	W 695	9.4			POMPES POUR LIQUIDES NDA
743	PUMPS NES,CENTRFUGES ETC		25.4		30.9		31.4			POMPES COMPRES,VENT ETC
7431	PUMPS FOR GASES ETC	W 1210	10.5	W 1363	11.6	W 1851	14.1			POMPES AIR A VIDE,COMPRES
7436	GAS,LIQUID FILTERS ETC		7.6	W 1436	9.1	W 1697	9.7			APP POUR FILT DES LIQUIDES
744	MECHANICAL HANDLING EQU	W 3384	28.1	W 4993	31.1	W 6935	35.9			EQUIP MANUTENTION PIECES
7442	LIFTING,LOADING MACH NES	W 1705	15.8	W 2590	14.2	W 4773	21.4			APP LEVAGE,MANUTENTION
74428	OTH HANDLING ETC MCH NES	W 605	7.0	W 1625	7.8	W 2891	10.9			AUT APP LEVAGE ETC
7449	PTS NES OF MACHY OF 7442	W 665	6.4	W 1431	11.4	W 1198	9.4			PIECES DU 744.2
745	NONELEC MACHY,TOOLS NES		20.6		17.8		26.7			AUT MACH NON ELEC,PIECES
7452	OTH NONELEC MCHS,PTS NES		19.6		16.4		25.4			AUT MACH NON ELEC,PIECES
74522	PACKAGNG,BOTTLNG,ETC MCH	W 527	11.8	W 214	5.7	W 573	8.7			MACH NETT BOUTEILLES,ETC
74527	SPRAYING MACHINERY	W 758	5.5	W 1018	6.6	W 2665	12.1			APP PROJETER ETC LIQUID
749	NONELEC MACH PTS,ACC NES	W 2047	52.0	W 2815	45.3	W 3118	43.1			PIECES MACH NON ELEC NDA
7491	BALL,ROLLER,ETC BEARINGS	W 737	13.2	W 583	11.1	W 586	10.0			ROULEMENTS BILLES ETC
7492	COCKS,VALVES ETC NES	W 702	14.8	W 737	10.6	W 914	11.7			ART ROB,SIM POUR TUYAUX
7493	SHAFT,CRANK,PULLEY ETC	W 1	16.2	W 1144	18.6	W 1076	16.1			ARBRES TRANS,VILEBREQUINS
7499	OTH NONELEC MCHY PTS NES	W 606	7.9	W 351	5.2	W 543	5.4			PIECES NON ELECT NDA
75	OFFICE MACHNES,ADP EQUIP		38.4		48.9		51.2			MACH BUREAU TRAIT AUTOM
751	OFFICE MACHINES	N 27154	8.2	N 83467	8.7	N 115360	7.4			MACH,APPAREILS DE BUREAU
752	AUTOMTIC DATA PROC EQUIP	N 21740	22.9	N 46131	30.4	N 161310	32.7			MACH TRAIT INFORMATION
7522	DIGITAL COMPUTERS	N 4497	8.6	N 10830	11.8	N 20913	10.5			MACH DIGITALES COMPLETES
7525	ADP PERIPHERAL UNITS	N 6074	6.6	N 21937	8.4	N 94758	11.7			UNITES PERIPHERIQUES
759	OFFICE,ADP MCH PTS,ACCES		7.5		9.9	W 224	11.2			PIECES DU 751 ET 752
7599	ACCTG,ETC,ADP MCH PTS,AC		5.6		8.3	W 190	9.6			PIECES DU 751 ET 752
76	TELECOMM,SOUND EQUIPMENT		66.5		79.4		109.0			EQUIPMENT DE TELECOM
761	TELEVISION RECEIVERS	N 35086	5.8	N 28927	5.0	N 149991	9.1			RECEPTEURS DE TELEVISION
7611	COLOUR TV RECEIVERS	N 27158	5.4	N 20030	4.5	N 97516	8.5			RECEPTEURS COULEUR
764	TELECOM EQPT,PTS,ACC NES		52.0		64.8		86.6			EQUIP TELECOM,PIECES
7641	LINE TELEPHONE,ETC EQUIP		15.6		25.0	N 251823	45.6			APP TELEPHON PAR FIL
7643	TV,RADIO TRANSMITTRS ETC	N 9342	9.1	N 32095	18.6	N 62730	17.2			APP EMET TELE RADIO
7648	TELECOMM EQUIPMENT NES		17.5		12.2		1.6			APP TELECOM NDA
76483	RADAR APPARATUS ETC		15.8		10.6	W 461	1.2			APP DE RADIOGUIDAGE ETC
7649	PTS NES OF EQUIPMT OF 76		9.3		8.0		21.0			PIECES DE LA DIV 76
76493	TELECOMM EQUIPMT PTS NES		7.4		4.9	W 802	18.7			PIECES 761,762,764.3,8
77	ELECTRIC MACHNRY NES ETC		131.7		144.8		139.1			MACH APP ELECT NDA
771	ELECTRIC POWER MACHY NES		10.8		35.0		18.3			MACH PROD,TRANS ELECTR
7711	TRANSFORMERS,ELECTRICAL	N 89346	4.4	N 490892	28.6	N 149682	11.8			TRANSFO ELECTRIQUES
77111	LIQUID DIELEC TRANSFRMRS	N 55799	2.1	N 42596	11.2	N 59312	3.0			TRANSFO DIELEC LIQUIDE
77118	OTHER ELEC TRANSFORMERS	N 33547	2.3	N 448296	17.4	N 90370	8.8			AUTRES TRANSFO ELECTRIQ
772	SWITCHGEAR ETC,PARTS NES		45.0		37.4		38.5			APP COUPURE,SECT ETC
7721	SWITCHGEAR ETC	W 1301	42.1	W 1763	35.5	W 3667	37.5			APP COUPURE,SECTIONMNT
773	ELECTR DISTRIBUTNG EQUIP		19.4		23.7	W 7114	28.9			EQUIPMT DISTRIBUTION ELECT
7731	INSULATED WIRE,CABLE ETC	W 8372	17.5	W 6478	19.6	W 6773	27.3			FILS,CABLES ISOLES ELECT
774	ELECTRO–MEDCL,XRAY EQUIP		13.7		8.1		8.7			APPAREILS MEDICAUX
7742	X–RAY APPARATUS ETC		12.9		7.0		6.8			APPAREILS A RAYONS X
775	HOUSEHOLD TYPE EQUIP NES		18.4		13.1		17.6			MACH,APP USAGE DOMESTQUE
7752	DOM REFRIGERATRS,FREEZRS	N 7046	12.3	N 16895	4.3	N 665007	7.6			REFRIG,CONGEL MENAGER
77521	DOMESTIC REFRIGERATORS	N 6089	11.8	N 13465	3.2	N 417656	5.3			REFRIGERATEURS
778	ELECTRICAL MACHINERY NES		22.2		24.8		24.3			AUTRES MACH ELECT NDA
78	ROAD VEHICLES		257.0		316.9		306.8			VEHICULES ROUTIERS
781	PASS MOTOR VEH EXC BUSES		76.7		75.6	N 9364	87.7			AUTO TRANSPORT PERSONNES
782	LORRIES,SPCL MTR VEH NES	N 48743	108.3	N 64087	153.8	N 10890	133.1			VEHICULES SPECIAUX,MARCH
7821	LORRIES,TRUCKS	N 48645	101.4	N 63987	140.6	N 10778	128.1			VEHICULES TRANSP MARCHAND
7822	SPECIAL MOTOR VEHCLS NES	N 98	6.9	N 100	13.2	N 112	5.1			VEHICULES USAGES SPECIAUX
783	ROAD MOTOR VEHICLES NES	N 3504	46.5	N 72706	49.6	N 3521	54.2			VEHICULES ROUTIERS NDA
7831	BUSES	N 2724	24.4	N 31667	31.1	N 1997	26.8			VOITURES TRANSPORT COMMUN
7832	TRACTORS FOR TR–TRAILERS	N 780	22.1	N 41039	18.6	N 1524	27.5			TRACTEURS ROUTIERS
784	MOTOR VEH PRTS,ACCES NES		19.1		27.8		24.3			PIECES 722,781,782,783
7849	OTHER MOTOR VEHCL PARTS		18.8		25.5	W 2604	22.2			PIECES 722,781,782,783
79	OTHR TRANSPORT EQUIPMENT		18.8		24.3		12.1			AUTRE MATERIEL TRANSPORT
792	AIRCRAFT ETC		16.0		22.2		9.8			APP NAVIGATION AERIENNE
7923	AIRCRFT NES2000–15000KG	N 5	2.6	N 2549	8.8		2.9			AERODYNES 2000 A 15000 KG
7929	AIRCRAFT PARTS NES	W 26	7.9	W 40	8.1	W 14	5.0			PIECES DU 792
8	MISC MANUFACTURED GOODS		120.9		146.2		174.6			ART MANUFACTURES DIVERS
821	*FURNITURE,PARTS THEREOF		4.9		5.5		11.3			MEUBLES ET PIECES
851	*FOOTWEAR	P 808857	6.6	P 1509280	7.8	P 3630466	10.8			CHAUSSURES
87	PRECISION INSTRUMNTS NES		41.7		47.0		54.4			INSTRUM,APPAR SCIENT NDA
872	MEDICAL INSTRUMENTS NES		14.2		15.1		30.2			INSTR,APP MEDIC–CHIR NDA
87202	OTH MEDICAL INSTRUMENTS		13.8		14.2		29.0			INSTRUM,APP MEDECINE
874	MEASURNG,CONTROLNG INSTR		24.7		28.3		20.9			INSTRUMENTS DE MESURE
8748	ELEC MEAS,CONTRL EQU NES		5.5		12.5		6.1			APP ELEC ELECTRO MESURE
87483	OTH ELCTRNC MEAS ETC EQU		4.4		11.7		5.4			AUT APP ELECTRO DE MESURE
88	PHOTO EQU,OPTICL GDS ETC		9.8		12.2		12.5			APP,FOURN PHOTO,OP,MONTR
89	MISC MANUFCTRD GOODS NES		48.5		60.4		73.2			ART MANUFACTURES DIVERS
892	PRINTED MATTER		19.5		17.2		18.0			IMPRIMES
8921	PRINTED BOOKS,GLOBES,ETC		15.2		11.9		10.8			LIVRES,BROCHURES,CARTES
89211	PRINTED BOOKS,PAMPHLETS		15.1		11.3		10.7			LIVRES,BROCHURES
893	ARTICLES OF PLASTIC NES		9.8		17.9		19.5			OUVRAGES EN MAT DIVIS 58
8939	MISC PLASTIC ARTICLES		6.4		12.7		11.3			ART DIVERS EN MAT DIV 58
89399	OTHR PLASTC ARTICLES NES		5.7		12.0		10.4			AUT OUV MAT DIV 58

4. General Imports C.I.F. by Commodities according to the S.I.T.C. (Rev. 2) in million U.S. Dollars
Importations Générales C.A.F. par Produits d'après la C.T.C.I. (Rév. 2) en millions de Dollars E.U.

SITC CTCI	COMMODITY	1994		1995		1996		1997		PRODUIT
		QUANTITY QUANTITE	VALUE VALEUR	QUANTITY QUANTITE	VALUE VALEUR	QUANTITY QUANTITE	VALUE VALEUR	QUANTITY QUANTITE	VALUE VALEUR	
898	MUSICAL INSTRUMENTS,PTS		5.4		7.4		10.4			INSTRUMENTS DE MUSIQUE
8983	SOUND RECRDNG TAPE,DISCS		5.3		7.2		10.2			SUPPORTS SON POUR 763
9	GOODS NOT CLASSD BY KIND		56.0		102.9		74.4			ART TRANSACT NON CLASSES
931	*SPECIAL TRANSACTIONS		39.7		78.0		60.2			TRANS.SPECIALES
971	*GOLD,NON MONETARY NES	K 4638	5.3	K 19647	13.2	K 32665	5.3			OR NON MONETAIRE
97101	NONMON GLD UNWRT,SEMIMFD	K 4638	5.3	K 19647	13.2	K 32665	5.3			OR,ALLIAGES D'OR BRUTS

5. General Exports F.O.B. by Commodities according to the S.I.T.C. (Rev. 2) in million U.S. Dollars
Exportations Générales F.O.B. par Produits d'après la C.T.C.I. (Rév. 2) en millions de Dollars E.U.

SITC CTCI	COMMODITY	1994 QUANTITY QUANTITE	1994 VALUE VALEUR	1995 QUANTITY QUANTITE	1995 VALUE VALEUR	1996 QUANTITY QUANTITE	1996 VALUE VALEUR	1997 QUANTITY QUANTITE	1997 VALUE VALEUR	PRODUIT
	ALL COMMODITIES		1967.5		1846.0		2122.0			TOUS PRODUITS
0	FOOD AND LIVE ANIMALS		389.2		306.2		329.6			ALIMENTS,ANIMAUX VIVANTS
001	*LIVE ANIMALS FOR FOOD	N 7517960	11.1	N 8216425	11.0	N 6419813	6.8			ANIMAUX VIVANTS
0014	LIVE POULTRY	N 7492638	6.3	N 8194631	5.7	N 6411929	5.2			VOLAILLES VIVANTES
01	MEAT AND PREPARATIONS		20.2		24.6		19.3			VIANDES ET PREPARATIONS
011	MEAT FRESH,CHILLD,FROZEN	W 11207	8.0	W 15016	12.5	W 9512	11.7			VIANDES FRAICHES,REF,CONGE
0111	BOVINE MEAT FRESH,FROZEN	W 9002	5.1	W 12247	7.0	W 6735	6.1			VIANDES BOVIN FRAI,REF
01112	BOVINE MEAT BONELESS	W 8950	5.1	W 12224	7.0	W 6724	6.0			VIANDES BOVIN DESOSSEES
014	MEAT PREPD,PRSVD,NES ETC	W 4245	12.3	W 3929	12.0	W 2689	7.6			CONSERVES DE VIANDES
0149	OTH PREPARD,PRESRVD MEAT	W 4232	12.2	W 3915	12.0	W 2684	7.6			AUTRES PREP DE VIANDES
02	DAIRY PRODCTS,BIRDS'EGGS		14.0		14.2		13.8			PRODUITS LAITIERS,OEUFS
022	MILK AND CREAM	W 13351	9.6	W 13501	11.3	W 14925	11.0			LAIT ET CREME
0224	MILK,CREAM PRESERVED ETC	W 9203	7.6	W 13243	11.1	W 12842	9.8			LAIT,CREME CONS,CONC
02243	MILK DRY,OVER 1.5% FAT	W 8327	5.7	W 11362	7.7	W 11698	7.7			LAIT POUDRE SUP 1.5%
04	CEREALS AND PREPARATIONS		171.8		65.5		59.4			CEREALES ET PRODUITS
041	WHEAT ETC UNMILLED	W 1577	0.6	W 86379	8.4	W 54883	6.0			FROMENT,EPEAUTRE
0412	OTHER WHEAT ETC UNMILLED	W 1500	0.5	W 70614	7.0	W 26922	3.7			AUTRE FROMENT NON MOULU
044	MAIZE UNMILLED	W 1279928	146.3	W 287818	33.5	W 234920	35.2			MAIS NON MOULU
045	CEREALS NES UNMILLED	W 19916	8.2	W 1954	0.6	W 7744	1.5			AUTRES CEREALES NON MOULUES
0459	OTHER CEREALS UNMILLED	W 19916	8.2	W 1954	0.6	W 7744	1.5			SARRASIN,MILLET,SORGHO
04599	OTH CEREALS UNMILLED NES	W 13695	6.7	W 255	0.1	W 28	0.1			AUTRES CEREALES NDA
046	WHEAT ETC MEAL OR FLOUR	W 16331	2.9	W 31753	9.6	W 14626	5.8			SEMOULE FARINE,FROMENT
04601	FLOUR OF WHEAT OR MESLIN	W 16331	2.9	W 31751	9.6	W 14626	5.8			FARINE DE FROMENT
047	OTHER CEREAL MEALS,FLOUR	W 40977	7.4	W 19848	4.1	W 443	0.2			AUTRES SEMOULES,FARINES
04702	MEAL OR GROATS NON–WHEAT	W 37572	6.9	W 18774	3.9	W 227	0.1			GRUAUX,SEMOULES DE CEREALES
048	CEREAL ETC PREPARATIONS	W 13223	6.7	W 22946	9.5	W 22985	11.1			PREPTNS A BASE CEREALES
0482	MALT INCLUDING FLOUR	W 10710	4.7	W 21265	7.5	W 20719	8.0			MALT MEME TORREFIE
05	VEGETABLES AND FRUIT		24.7		41.0		33.6			LEGUMES ET FRUITS
054	VEG ETC FRSH,SMPLY PRSVD	W 17483	14.9	W 9996	24.6	W 9353	15.7			LEGUMES FRAIS,CONG,SECS
0545	OTHER FRESH VEGETABLES	W 6097	8.6	W 4699	19.5	W 6014	13.7			AUTRES LEGUMES FRAIS,REF
05459	FRESH VEGETABLES NES	W 5297	8.3	W 4552	19.4	W 5554	13.2			LEGUMES FRAIS,REFRI NDA
057	FRUIT,NUTS,FRESH,DRIED	W 16851	5.1	W 28096	12.3	W 29551	14.0			FRUITS FRAIS OU SECS
0571	ORANGES, MANDARINS ETC	W 12535	2.6	W 19263	6.0	W 22332	5.4			ORANGES,MAND,CLEMENTINES
05711	ORANGES,FRESH OR DRIED	W 12496	2.6	W 19228	6.0	W 21727	5.2			ORANGES FRAICHES,SECHEES
0579	FRUIT FRESH OR DRIED NES	W 1281	1.8	W 1983	4.8	W 1389	6.5			FRUITS FRAIS,SECS NDA
06	SUGAR AND PREPS,HONEY		101.9		83.4		118.8			SUCRES ET PRODUITS
061	SUGAR AND HONEY	W 243548	96.8	W 1780498	76.3	W 198613	111.3			SUCRES ET MIEL
0611	RAW BEET AND CANE SUGAR	W 182059	88.6	W 129407	62.1	W 143985	94.5			SUCRES BRUTS
0612	REFINED SUGAR ETC	W 16475	5.0	W 1645771	13.9	W 44102	16.0			SUCRES RAFFINES
062	SUGAR CANDY NON–CHOCLATE	W 3827	5.2	W 4126	7.2	W 4434	7.6			SUCRERIES
07	COFFEE,TEA,COCOA,SPICES		29.0		41.7		44.8			CAFE,THE,CACAO,EPICES
071	COFFEE AND SUBSTITUTES	W 4321	12.5	W 10209	26.5	W 10656	26.4			CAFE ET SUCCEDANES
0711	COFFEE GREEN,ROASTED,SUB	W 4313	12.5	W 10202	26.5	W 10540	26.1			CAFE TORREFIE OU DECAFEINE
07111	COFFEE GREEN,HUSKS,SKINS	W 4303	12.4	W 10062	26.1	W 10526	26.0			CAFE NON TORREFIE
074	TEA AND MATE	W 9688	11.4	W 9156	11.0	W 11540	12.8			THE ET MATE
0741	TEA	W 9688	11.4	W 9156	11.0	W 11540	12.8			THE
081	*FEEDING STUFF FOR ANIML	W 57905	10.0	W 77757	17.0	W 83697	22.7			NOURRITURE POUR ANIMAUX
0812	BRAN,POLLARD,SHARPS,ETC	W 8016	2.0	W 27739	6.8	W 2827	1.1			SONS
08122	BRAN,ETC OF OTHR CEREALS	W 7931	2.0	W 22855	5.9	W 2757	1.1			SONS D'AUTRES CEREALES
0813	OILCAKE AND OTH RESIDUES	W 22187	3.7	W 5933	1.5	W 36775	11.9			TOURTEAUX
08131	— OF SOYA BEANS	W 10222	2.1	W 5065	1.4	W 20225	10.0			TOURTEAUX DE SOJA
0819	FOOD WASTE AND FEED NES	W 26223	4.1	W 43711	8.7	W 43983	9.7			DECHETS,ALIMENTS NDA
08199	FODDER NES,INCL SWEETNED	W 26195	4.1	W 43171	8.7	W 43903	9.6			PREPARATIONS FOURRAGERES
09	MISC EDIBLE PRODUCTS		6.8		7.5		10.0			PREP ALIMENTAIRES DIVERSES
091	MARGARINE AND SHORTENING	W 5729	5.1	W 3844	5.0	W 6415	7.3			MARGARINE ET GRAISSES
0914	MARGARINE,EDIBLE FAT NES	W 5729	5.1	W 3844	5.0	W 6415	7.3			MARGARINES,SIMILI SAINDOUX
1	BEVERAGES AND TOBACCO		669.0		485.1		740.3			BOISSONS ET TABACS
12	TOBACCO AND MANUFACTURES		665.6		481.7		737.4			TABACS BRUTS FABRIQUES
121	TOBACCO UNMNFCTRD,REFUSE	W 298896	649.1	W 175966	470.9	W 5647726	724.0			TABACS BRUTS,DECHETS
1211	TOBACCO,NOT STRIPPED	W 54187	133.6	W 14258	47.7	W 26726	115.4			TABACS NON ECOTES
1212	TOBACCO STRIPPED OR PART	W 227087	509.2	W 155063	420.6	W 5613590	604.3			TABACS PART ECOTES
1213	TOBACCO REFUSE	W 17622	6.3	W 6646	2.7	W 7409	4.4			DECHETS DE TABACS
122	TOBACCO,MANUFACTURED	W 7880	16.6	W 2085	10.9	W 4062	13.5			TABACS FABRIQUES
1222	CIGARETTES	W 6458	13.3	W 818	8.5	W 1753	8.7			CIGARETTES
2	CRUDE MATERLS,EXCL FUELS		218.0		232.9		264.0			MAT BRUTES NON COMESTIBLES
21	HIDES,SKINS,FURS UNDRSSD		8.3		5.4		6.6			CUIRS,PEAUX BRUTS
211	HIDES,SKINS,EXC FURS,RAW	W 3458	8.3	W 1499	5.4	W 1743	6.6			CUIRS ET PEAUX
22	OIL SEEDS,OLEAGINOUS FRT		13.0		4.5		2.3			GRAINES,FRUITS OLEAGINEUX
222	SEEDS FOR'SOFT'FIXED OIL	W 34653	13.0	W 8045	3.8	W 6529	2.1			GRAINES HUILES FIXES
2222	SOYA BEANS	W 23377	7.0	W 1404	0.7	W 1643	0.8			FEVES DE SOJA
24	CORK AND WOOD		22.1		27.5		26.9			LIEGE ET BOIS
248	WOOD SHAPED,SLEEPERS	W 811998	20.4	W 186038	24.4	W 111732	22.7			BOIS SIMPLEMENT TRAVAILLES
2482	LUMBER SHAPED CONIFER	W 785749	19.2	W 129785	22.1	W 100773	19.3			CONIFERES SCIES,RABOTES
24821	LUMBER SAWN ETC CONIFER	W 636625	18.1	W 120479	21.5	W 92715	17.0			CONIFERES SCIES LONGITUD
26	TEXTILE FIBRES AND WASTE		64.3		54.0		86.3			FIBRES TEXTILES
263	COTTON	W 48118	60.5	W 28259	50.5	W 44615	80.8			COTON
2631	RAW COTTON,EXCL LINTERS	W 47102	59.0	W 26755	45.3	W 43833	79.3			COTON EN MASSE
27	CRUDE FERTLZR,MINRLS NES		73.0		96.3		90.3			ENGRAIS MINERAUX BRUTS
273	STONE,SAND AND GRAVEL	W 147187	10.6	W 242720	11.6	W 170438	17.0			PIERRES,SABLES,GRAVIERS
2731	BLDG,DIMENSION STONE	W 108154	10.5	W 104581	11.4	W 157892	16.8			PIERRES DE TAILLE
27313	GRANITE,SANDSTONE,ETC	W 107458	10.2	W 103660	11.1	W 156320	16.5			GYPSE,BASALTE,GRES
278	OTHER CRUDE MINERALS	W 160288	62.0		84.7	W 234201	73.3			AUTRES MINERAUX BRUTS
2784	ASBESTOS CRDE,SMPLY WRKD	W 129289	56.5	W 174558	70.0	W 152091	63.8			AMIANTE (ASBESTE)
2789	MINERALS CRUDE NES	W 17578	1.9	W 32482	9.6	W 48239	5.4			MINERAUX BRUTS NDA
27893	TALC,NATURAL STEATITE	W 82	0.1	W 674	6.1	W 952	0.2			STEATITE NATURELLE
28	METALLIFEROUS ORES,SCRAP		12.1		7.5		11.9			MINERAIS METAL,DECHETS
282	IRON AND STEEL SCRAP	W 77912	10.3	W 61716	4.4	W 53013	3.4			FERRAILLES
28209	— OF OTHR IRON OR STEEL	W 66219	9.1	W 38250	2.9	W 37150	2.3			FERRAILLES DE FER
29	CRUDE ANIMAL,VEG MAT NES		25.5		37.9		39.9			MATIERES BRUTES ANIM,VEGET
292	CRUDE VEG MATERIALS NES		25.0		37.2		39.3			MAT BRUTES VEGETALES NDA
2927	CUT FLOWERS AND FOLIAGE		19.4		32.6		33.5			FLEURS,FEUILLAGES COUPES
29271	CUT FLOWERS		19.3		32.6		33.5			FLEURS ET BOUTONS
3	MINERAL FUELS ETC		14.1		23.7		31.9			COMBUSTIBLES MINERAUX LUB
32	COAL,COKE AND BRIQUETTES		10.3		11.2		10.0			HOUILLES,COKES,BRIQUETTES
323	BRIQUETS,COKE,SEMI–COKE	W 280061	8.5	W 406928	9.6	W 360291	9.3			BRIQUETTES
3232	COKE,SEMI–COKE,RTRT CRBN	W 280061	8.5	W 406928	9.6	W 360291	9.3			COKES ET SEMI–COKES
33	PETROLEUM AND PRODUCTS		3.8		12.4		21.6			PETROLE ET DERIVES
334	PETROLEUM PRODUCTS,REFIN	W 27464	2.8	W 83721	6.9	W 119521	20.2			PRODUITS RAFFINES
3345	LUBS,PETROLEUM OILS NES	W 2496	2.5	W 78926	6.7	W 106248	18.9			HUILES LUBRIFIANTES
33451	LUBS(HIGH PETR CONT) ETC	W 2258	2.1	W 78752	6.6	W 106248	18.9			HUILES LUBRIF,H LOURDES
335	RESIDUAL PETRLM PROD NES		1.1		5.6	W 7141	1.5			PRODUITS RESIDUELS NDA

5. General Exports F.O.B. by Commodities according to the S.I.T.C. (Rev. 2) in million U.S. Dollars
Exportations Générales F.O.B. par Produits d'après la C.T.C.I. (Rév. 2) en millions de Dollars E.U.

SITC CTCI	COMMODITY	1994		1995		1996		1997		PRODUIT
		QUANTITY QUANTITE	VALUE VALEUR	QUANTITY QUANTITE	VALUE VALEUR	QUANTITY QUANTITE	VALUE VALEUR	QUANTITY QUANTITE	VALUE VALEUR	
5	CHEMCLS,RELATED PROD NES		36.2		46.7		56.0			PRODUITS CHIMIQUES
51	ORGANIC CHEMICALS		2.2		6.6		5.3			PROD CHIMIQ ORGANIQUES
512	ALCOHOLS,PHENOLS ETC		1.3		6.0		5.0			PHENOLS,PHENOLS-ALCOOLS
53	DYES,TANNING,COLOUR PROD		9.1		8.6		12.4			PROD TEINTURE,COLORANTS
532	DYES NES,TANNING PROD	W 8934	7.6	W 8743	7.2	W 11746	11.3			EXTRAITS TEINTURE,TANNAGE
5322	DYE,TANN EXTRCTS,TANNINS	W 8933	7.6	W 8742	7.2	W 11738	11.3			EXT TAN ORIG VEG,TANNINS
53222	DYEING EXTRCTS VEG,ANMAL	W 4006	4.2	W 3997	4.1	W 4856	7.1			MATI COLOR VEGET ANIMALE
541	*MEDICINAL,PHARM PRODUCT		5.0		5.9		6.2			PROD MEDICINAUX PHARMACEUT
55	PERFUME,CLEANING ETC PRD		8.2		9.4		11.5			PROD POUR PARFUM,TOILETTE
554	SOAP,CLEANSING ETC PREPS	W 6791	6.9	W 6283	7.8	W 7866	8.9			SAVONS,PRODUITS DETERSIFS
5541	SOAPS	W 6121	6.0	W 5648	6.8	W 7213	7.6			SAVONS,PROD TENSIO-ACTIFS
562	*FERTILIZERS,MANUFACTURE		4.1	W 27811	7.1	W 46853	11.9			ENGRAIS MANUFACTURES
5629	FERTILIZERS NES	W 6448	1.2	W 19959	5.2	W 35515	9.7			ENGRAIS NDA
6	BASIC MANUFACTURES		412.0		531.5		465.1			ART MANUFACTURES
61	LEATHER,DRESSED FUR,ETC		12.5		21.9		15.8			CUIRS,PELLETERIES
611	LEATHER	W 3014	11.0	W 8466	20.6	W 6403	14.0			CUIRS,PEAUX PREPARES
6114	LEATHR BOVINE NES,EQUINE	W 2984	11.0	W 8463	19.9	W 6327	13.3			CUIRS DE BOVINS
62	RUBBER MANUFACTURES NES		3.4		5.1		6.4			CAOUTCHOUC MANUFACTURE
63	WOOD,CORK MANUFACTRS NES		10.7		12.2		25.4			OUVRAGES LIEGE ET BOIS
634	VENEERS,PLYWOOD,ETC		4.9		6.6		10.5			PLACAGES,CONTRE-PLAQUES
6342	PLYWOOD OF WOOD SHEETS	W 2210	2.0	W 3571	3.0	W 7036	8.8			BOIS CONTRE-PLAQUES
635	WOOD MANUFACTURES NES		5.8		5.6		14.9			ART MANUF EN BOIS NDA
6353	BUILDERS WOODWRK,PREFABS	W 7824	5.2	W 5429	5.0	W 10951	14.4			OUVRAGES DE MENUISERIE
64	PAPER,PAPERBOARD AND MFR		9.6		15.2		17.3			PAPIERS,CARTONS & OUVRAGES
641	PAPER AND PAPERBOARD	W 9221	5.1	W 18746	10.2	W 26522	11.0			PAPIERS ET CARTONS
6415	PAPER,PAPERBRD,BULK,NES	W 5691	2.8	W 8821	5.7	W 7015	4.5			PAPIERS,CARTONS ROULEAUX
65	TEXTILE YARN,FABRICS,ETC		76.2		62.8		48.1			FILS,TISSUS,ARTICLES TEXTILE
651	TEXTILE YARN	W 10052	24.6	W 4135	26.7	W 4543	16.2			FILS TEXTILES
6513	COTTON YARN	W 9740	23.5	W 3879	25.5	W 4243	14.7			FILS DE COTON
652	COTTON FABRICS,WOVEN	A 32804	33.6	A 21615	20.6	A 25789	18.1			TISSUS DE COTON
6521	GREY WOVEN COTTON FABRIC	A 27963	26.8	A 18348	13.6	A 21406	12.0			TISSUS COT ECRUS NON MERCER
65214	GREY WOVEN COTTON FABRIC	A 14623	13.6	A 17673	13.0	A 21400	12.0			AUT TISSUS 85% COTON ECRUS
65215	GREY WOVN COTN BLEND NES	A 13339	13.3	A 674	0.6	A 6	0.1			AUT TIS MOINS 85% COT ECRUS
6522	WOVEN COTTON BLEACHD,ETC	A 4841	6.8	A 3267	7.1	A 4383	6.1			TISSUS COTON BLANCHIS ETC
65224	BLCHED COTTON FABRIC NES	A 4477	6.4	A 3078	6.8	A 2783	3.7			AUT TIS PLUS 85% COT BLANCHI
658	TEXTILE ARTICLES NES		11.2		6.5		7.6			ART FACONNES MAT TEXTILES
66	NONMETAL MINERAL MFS NES		21.7		26.0		28.5			ART MIN NON METALLIQUES
661	LIME,CEMENT,BLDG PRODS	W 156937	10.8	W 177424	12.5	W 148674	10.8			CHAUX,CIMENTS MAT CONSTR
6612	CEMENT	W 149530	8.1	W 167180	9.3	W 135658	8.1			CIMENTS HYDRAULIQUES
667	PEARL,PREC-,SEMI-P STONE		6.3		9.1		12.3			PERLES, PIERRES GEMMES
6672	DIAMONDS NONINDUST,UNSET		3.9		6.9		9.4			DIAMANTS BRUTS
66721	— ROUGH,UNSORTED		3.9		6.9		9.4			DIAMANTS BRUTS NON TRIES
67	IRON AND STEEL		137.5		234.2		199.8			FER ET ACIER
671	PIG IRON ETC		115.2		214.1		168.9			FONTE,SPIEGEL,POUDRES
6716	FERRO-ALLOYS	W 209904	115.2		214.1	W 272680	168.9			FERRO-ALLIAGES
67169	OTHER FERRO-ALLOYS	W 209901	115.2	W 279343	214.1	W 272680	168.9			AUTRES FERRO-ALLIAGES
672	IRON,STEEL PRIMARY FORMS		5.0	W 43298	6.1	W 65404	13.4			LINGOTS FER,ACIER
6727	IRN,STL COIL FR REROLLNG	W 8462	1.4	W 20499	3.0	W 39330	8.7			EBAUCHES POUR TOLES FER
67271	IRON,SIMPLE STEEL COILS	W 8431	1.4	W 20401	3.0	W 39330	8.7			EBAUCHES NON EN ACIER
673	IRON,STEEL SHAPES ETC		7.1	W 11079	5.2	W 26627	9.2			BARRES,PROFIL FER,ACIER
68	NON-FERROUS METALS		109.4		110.3		102.9			METAUX NON FERREUX
682	COPPER EXC CEMENT COPPER		19.6	W 8447	16.9	W 11954	20.0			CUIVRE
6821	COPPER NES,ALLOYS,UNWRT	W 7896	14.3	W 7499	14.7	W 10541	18.4			CUIVRE BRUT
68212	COPPER REFINED,UNWROUGHT	W 7867	14.2	W 7474	14.6	W 10491	18.2			CUIVRE AFFINE BRUT
683	NICKEL	W. 17100	80.6		87.8	W 11950	77.1			NICKEL
6831	NICKEL,ALLOYS UNWROUGHT	W 17100	80.6	W 12859	87.8	W 11950	77.1			NICKEL ET ALLIAGES BRUTS
689	NON-FER BASE METALS NES	W 1093	7.1	W 361	4.4	W 350	4.1			AUT METAUX NON FERREUX
6899	BASE METALS NES,CERMETS	W 978	6.3	W 361	4.4	W 330	4.0			METAUX COMMUNS NDA
68999	BASE MTL NES UNWRT,WASTE	W 978	6.3	W 361	4.4	W 330	4.0			AUT METAUX COM BRUTS NDA
69	METAL MANUFACTURES NES		31.7		44.3		21.4			ART MANUFACT EN METAL NDA
691	STRUCTURES AND PARTS NES	W 4852	3.5	W 4142	5.9	W 4018	3.1			CONSTRUCT FER,ACIER,ALU
6911	STRUCTURES,PARTS IRN,STL	W 4837	3.5	W 4119	5.9	W 3988	3.0			CONSTRUCT FER,ACIER,FONTE
693	WIRE PRODUCTS NON ELECTR	W 7384	4.5	W 8434	5.9	W 6871	4.4			OUVRAGES FILS METALLIQUES
694	STL,COPPR NAILS,NUTS,ETC	W 1430	1.2	W 2705	8.6	W 1711	1.4			CLOUS,VIS,ECROUS
69401	IRON,STEEL NAILS ETC	W 742	0.4	W 2218	7.8	W 1269	0.7			CLOUS,POINTES FER,ACIER
697	BASE MTL HOUSEHOLD EQUIP		16.5		14.9		6.9			ART MENAGE MET COMMUNS
6974	BASE MTL DMSTC ARTIC NES	W 2320	15.8	W 1784	14.1	W 1887	5.9			ARTICLES NDA FONTE,FER,ETC
69743	— OF ALUMINIUM	W 518	11.8	W 602	11.8	W 501	2.4			ARTICLES NDA EN ALUMINIUM
699	BASE METAL MFRS NES		3.7		6.8		3.8			ART MANUFACTURES MET NDA
7	MACHINES,TRANSPORT EQUIP		49.3		49.2		59.3			MACHINES MATERIEL TRANSPORT
71	POWER GENERATING EQUIPMT		5.1		8.1		7.0			MACHINES GENERATRICES
713	INTRNL COMBUS PSTN ENGIN		4.7		6.2		6.4			MOTEURS EXPL COMB INT, PIECE
7131	AIRCRAFT PSTN ENGINS,PTS		4.6		6.0	N 2450	6.2			MOTEURS EXPL P.AVIATION, PIE
72	MACHS FOR SPCL INDUSTRYS		8.6		9.6		11.9			MAC SPECIALES POUR INDUST
74	GENRL INDUSTRL MACHY NES		2.9		6.9		5.3			MACH APP INDUSTRIE
77	ELECTRIC MACHNRY NES ETC		9.6		7.4		9.1			MACH APP ELECT NDA
78	ROAD VEHICLES		12.9		10.0		11.9			VEHICULES ROUTIERS
79	OTHR TRANSPORT EQUIPMENT		8.3		5.0		12.6			AUTRE MATERIEL TRANSPORT
791	RAILWAY VEHICLES		6.5		2.6		1.0			VEHIC MAT CHEMINS DE FER
792	AIRCRAFT ETC		1.6		1.7		8.7			APP NAVIGATION AERIENNE
7923	AIRCRFT NES2000-15000KG	N 3	0.2	N 5	0.9	N 8	7.8			AERODYNES 2000 A 15000 KG
8	MISC MANUFACTURED GOODS		159.8		161.9		141.4			ART MANUFACTURES DIVERS
812	*PLUMBG,HEATNG,LGHTNG EQ		0.5		7.7	W 184	1.0			APPAR SANITAIRES CHAUFFAGE
8124	LIGHTING EQUIPMENT NES		0.4		7.6	W 61	0.9			APPAREILS ECLAIRAGE ETC
81242	LAMPS,FITTINGS BASE METL		0.2		7.4	W 52	0.7			APPAREILS D'ECLAIRAGE
821	*FURNITURE,PARTS THEREOF		31.2		21.3		21.7			MEUBLES ET PIECES
8219	FURNITURE AND PARTS NES	W 10529	29.2	W 8700	19.7	W 8397	20.2			AUTRES MEUBLES ET PIECES
82191	METAL FURNITURE NES	W 2128	12.4	W 1449	2.2	W 917	1.3			MEUBLES NDA EN METAL
82192	WOOD FURNITURE NES	W 7850	15.0	W 6729	15.7	W 7141	17.9			MEUBLES NDA EN BOIS
84	CLOTHING AND ACCESSORIES		63.9		61.2		50.5			VETEMENTS
842	MENS OUTERWEAR NOT KNIT	N 4637553	27.2	N 3307289	23.8	N 3075549	23.3			VET DESSUS POUR HOMMES
8423	— TROUSERS,BREECHES ETC	N 4325098	25.4	N 3053702	21.4	N 2622821	19.9			PANTALONS HOMMES MAT TEX
843	WOMENS OUTERWEAR NONKNIT	N 1143787	14.5	N 1469590	8.6	N 1082481	4.4			VET DESSUS FEMMES MAT TEX
8433	— DRESSES	N 751360	7.6	N 211479	1.6	N 139583	0.7			ROBES EN MAT-TEXTILES
844	UNDER GARMENTS NOT KNIT	N 750266	3.5	N 1125445	6.4	N 834310	3.4			VETEMENT DESSOUS MAT TEX
8441	— MENS SHIRTS	N 703656	3.4	N 1111429	6.4	N 824732	3.3			CHEMISES HOMMES MAT TEXT
845	OUTERWEAR KNIT NONELASTC	N 524452	8.5	N 1225198	8.3	N 1257970	7.7			VET DESSOUS,ACCES BONNET
846	UNDER GARMENTS KNITTED		10.0		13.8		11.4			SOUS VETS DE BONNETERIE
8462	— OF COTTON NON ELASTIC	N 3554687	6.8	N 3746020	8.5	N 4111832	7.9			SOUS-VET BONNET COTON
84629	—— OTHER	N 3554687	6.8	N 3746020	8.5	N 4111832	7.9			AUT SOUS-VET BONNET COTON
851	*FOOTWEAR	P 1041533	10.5	P 1675782	13.7	P 1012422	6.4			CHAUSSURES

5. General Exports F.O.B. by Commodities according to the S.I.T.C. (Rev. 2) in million U.S. Dollars
Exportations Générales F.O.B. par Produits d'après la C.T.C.I. (Rév. 2) en millions de Dollars E.U.

SITC CTCI	COMMODITY	1994 QUANTITY QUANTITE	1994 VALUE VALEUR	1995 QUANTITY QUANTITE	1995 VALUE VALEUR	1996 QUANTITY QUANTITE	1996 VALUE VALEUR	1997 QUANTITY QUANTITE	1997 VALUE VALEUR	PRODUIT
85103	SHOES WOOD–,CORK–SOLED	P 1003644	4.8	P 700528	8.3	P 233829	2.6			CHAUS SEMELLES BOIS,LIEGE
89	MISC MANUFCTRD GOODS NES		49.9		53.0		57.5			ART MANUFACTURES DIVERS
892	PRINTED MATTER		15.7		3.0		2.1			IMPRIMES
8928	PRINTED MATTER NES		14.5		1.5		0.7			IMPRIMES NDA
89283	UNISSUED BANKNOTES ETC		14.3		1.4		0.4			TIMBRES–POSTE FISCAUX
893	ARTICLES OF PLASTIC NES		3.7		4.7		7.0			OUVRAGES EN MAT DIVIS 58
896	WORKS OF ART ETC		11.9		14.6		9.0			OBJETS D'ART
89603	ORIGINAL SCULPTURE ETC		4.4		7.2		4.6			PROD ORIG STATUAIRE
89605	COINS,NATURE COLLECTIONS		7.0		7.4		4.3			COLLECTIONS ZOOLOG,BOTAN
897	GOLD,SILVER WARE,JEWELRY		16.3		27.8		30.7			BIJOUTERIE,ORFEVRERIE
8973	PREC JEWLRY,GLD–SILVWARE		16.3		27.7		30.7			BIJOUX OR,ARGENT ORFEVRE
89731	PRECIOUS METAL JEWELLERY		16.3		27.7		30.7			ART BIJOUTERIE,JOAILLER
9	GOODS NOT CLASSD BY KIND		15.4		6.8		33.6			ART TRANSACT NON CLASSES
971	*GOLD,NON MONETARY NES	K 44986	8.6	K 2648	0.5	K 143386	27.6			OR NON MONETAIRE
97101	NONMON GLD UNWRT,SEMIMFD	K 454	5.4			K 720	22.4			OR,ALLIAGES D'OR BRUTS

كيفية الحصول على منشورات الأمم المتحدة

يمكن الحصول على منشورات الأمم المتحدة من المكتبات ودور التوزيع في جميع أنحاء العالم . استعلم عنها من المكتبة التي تتعامل معها أو اكتب إلى : الأمم المتحدة ، قسم البيع في نيويورك أو في جنيف .

如何购取联合国出版物

联合国出版物在全世界各地的书店和经售处均有发售。请向书店询问或写信到纽约或日内瓦的联合国销售组。

HOW TO OBTAIN UNITED NATIONS PUBLICATIONS

United Nations publications may be obtained from bookstores and distributors throughout the world. Consult your bookstore or write to: United Nations, Sales Section, New York or Geneva.

COMMENT SE PROCURER LES PUBLICATIONS DES NATIONS UNIES

Les publications des Nations Unies sont en vente dans les librairies et les agences dépositaires du monde entier. Informez-vous auprès de votre libraire ou adressez-vous à : Nations Unies, Section des ventes, New York ou Genève.

КАК ПОЛУЧИТЬ ИЗДАНИЯ ОРГАНИЗАЦИИ ОБЪЕДИНЕННЫХ НАЦИЙ

Издания Организации Объединенных Наций можно купить в книжных магазинах и агентствах во всех районах мира. Наводите справки об изданиях в вашем книжном магазине или пишите по адресу: Организация Объединенных Наций, Секция по продаже изданий, Нью-Йорк или Женева.

COMO CONSEGUIR PUBLICACIONES DE LAS NACIONES UNIDAS

Las publicaciones de las Naciones Unidas están en venta en librerías y casas distribuidoras en todas partes del mundo. Consulte a su librero o diríjase a: Naciones Unidas, Sección de Ventas, Nueva York o Ginebra.

Litho in United Nations, New York
98-93415—April 1999—3,420
ISBN 92-1-061177-2

United Nations publication
Sales No. E/F.99.XVII.2, vol. I
ST/ESA/STAT/SER.G/46